TABLE OF CONTENTS

D0944178

This edition of the MOTOR Auto Repair Manual, Mechanical Repair, Volume 1, covers specifications [...] 2004-2008 Chrysler LLC, Ford Motor Company and General Motors Corporation models available at ti[...] Repair, Volume 2 covers Dash Gauges, Speed Controls, Wiper Systems, Passive Restraints, Dash Panel Service, Anti-Lock Brakes and Active Suspension Systems. The remaining vehicle information is located in Volume 1.

This manual is divided into four sections using three tabs. The section before Tab 1 covers Vehicle Identification, Air Bag System Precautions, Computer Relearn Procedures, Service Reminder & Warning Lamp Reset Procedures, Vehicle Lift Points, Non-Standard Tire & Wheel Size Adjustment To Ride Height Specifications & Tire Size Adjustment Charts, Electrical Symbol & Wire Color Code Identification and Vehicle Maintenance Schedules. Tab 1 covers Chrysler LLC vehicles. Tab 2 covers Ford Motor Company vehicles. Tab 3 covers General Motors Corporation vehicles. Each tabbed section starts on page 1-1. Data reported in this manual is subject to change.

MANUAL INFORMATION LOCATOR, Inside Rear Cover

SPECIAL SERVICE TOOLS, Inside Rear Cover

VEHICLE IDENTIFICATION 0-1

AIR BAG SYSTEM PRECAUTIONS 0-8

COMPUTER RELEARN PROCEDURES 0-31

SERVICE REMINDER & WARNING LAMP RESET PROCEDURES 0-34

VEHICLE LIFT POINTS 0-51

NON-STANDARD TIRE & WHEEL SIZE ADJUSTMENT TO RIDE HEIGHT SPECIFICATIONS & TIRE SIZE ADJUSTMENT CHARTS 0-61

ELECTRICAL SYMBOL & WIRE COLOR CODE IDENTIFICATION 0-63

VEHICLE MAINTENANCE SCHEDULES 0-73

CHRYSLER LLC—TAB 1

Page No.

CHRYSLER

Concorde, 300M 3-1
Crossfire 4-1
Sebring Convertible & Sedan 2-1
Sebring Coupe 1-1
300 6-1

DODGE

Avenger 2-1
Caliber 7-1
Charger 6-1
Intrepid 3-1
Magnum 6-1
Neon 5-1
Stratus Coupe 1-1
Stratus Sedan 2-1

GENERAL SERVICE

Air Bag Systems (Volume 2) 4-1
Air Conditioning 8-1
Alternators 11-1

Page No.

Anti-Lock Brakes (Volume 2) 6-1
Cooling Fans 9-1
Cruise Control (Volume 2) 2-1
Dash Gauges (Volume 2) 1-1
Dash Panel Service (Volume 2) 5-1
Disc Brakes 14-1
Drum Brakes 15-1
Engine Rebuilding Specifications 21-1
Front Drive Axles 18-1
Gauges, Dash (Volume 2) 1-1
Hydraulic Brake Systems 16-1
Machine Shop Specifications 21-1
Passive Restraint Systems (Volume 2) 4-1
Power Brake Units 17-1
Power Steering 13-1
Rear Drive Axles 19-1
Speed Controls (Volume 2) 2-1
Starter Motors 10-1
Steering Columns 12-1
Supplemental Restraint Systems (Volume 2) 4-1
Tire Pressure Monitoring System 20-1
Wiper Systems (Volume 2) 3-1

FORD MOTOR COMPANY—TAB 2

FORD

Crown Victoria 2-1
Focus 6-1
Freestyle 7-1
Fusion 1-1
Mustang 4-1
Taurus (2004-07) 5-1
Taurus & Taurus X (2008) 7-1
Thunderbird 3-1
500 7-1

LINCOLN

LS 3-1
MKZ 1-1
Town Car 2-1
Zephyr 1-1

MERCURY

Grand Marquis 2-1
Marauder 2-1
Milan 1-1

TABLE OF CONTENTS-Continued

Page No.

MERCURY CONTINUED

Montego 7-1
Sable (2004-07) 5-1
Sable (2008) 7-1

GENERAL SERVICE

Active Suspension Systems (Volume 2) 7-1
Air Bag Systems (Volume 2) 4-1
Air Conditioning 8-1
Alternators 11-1
Anti-Lock Brakes (Volume 2) 6-1
Cooling Fans 9-1
Cruise Control (Volume 2) 2-1
Dash Gauges (Volume 2) 1-1
Dash Panel Service (Volume 2) 5-1
Disc Brakes 14-1

Page No.

Drum Brakes 15-1
Engine Rebuilding Specifications 21-1
Front Drive Axles 18-1
Gauges, Dash (Volume 2) 1-1
Hydraulic Brake Systems 16-1
Machine Shop Specifications 21-1
Passive Restraint Systems (Volume 2) 4-1
Power Brake Units 17-1
Power Steering 13-1
Rear Drive Axles 19-1
Speed Controls (Volume 2) 2-1
Starter Motors 10-1
Steering Columns 12-1
Supplemental Restraint Systems (Volume 2) 4-1
Tire Pressure Monitoring Systems 20-1
Wiper Systems (Volume 2) 3-1

GENERAL MOTORS CORP.—TAB 3

Page No.

BUICK

Century, Regal 6-1
LaCrosse 6-1
LeSabre, Park Avenue 2-1
Lucerne 10-1

CADILLAC

CTS 8-1
DeVille, DTS, Seville & STS 9-1
XLR 13-1

CHEVROLET

Aveo 15-1
Cavalier 5-1
Cobalt 5-1
Corvette 7-1
Impala, Monte Carlo 6-1
Malibu (2004-05) 1-1
Malibu (2006-08) 14-1
Malibu Maxx 14-1

OLDSMOBILE

Alero 1-1

PONTIAC

Bonneville 2-1
Grand Am 1-1
Grand Prix 6-1
GTO 3-1
G5 5-1
G6 14-1
Solstice 4-1
Sunfire 5-1
Vibe 11-1

Page No.

SATURN 12-1

GENERAL SERVICE

Active Suspension Systems (Volume 2) 7-1
Air Bag Systems (Volume 2) 4-1
Air Conditioning 16-1
Alternators 19-1
Anti-Lock Brakes (Volume 2) 6-1
Cooling Fans 17-1
Cruise Control (Volume 2) 2-1
Dash Gauges (Volume 2) 1-1
Dash Panel Service (Volume 2) 5-1
Disc Brakes 22-1
Drum Brakes 23-1
Engine Rebuilding Specifications 29-1
Front Drive Axles 26-1
Gauges, Dash (Volume 2) 1-1
Hydraulic Brake Systems 24-1
Machine Shop Specifications 29-1
Passive Restraint Systems (Volume 2) 4-1
Power Brake Units 25-1
Power Steering 21-1
Rear Drive Axles 27-1
Speed Controls (Volume 2) 2-1
Starter Motors 18-1
Steering Columns 20-1
Supplemental Restraint Systems (Volume 2) 4-1
Tire Pressure Monitoring System 28-1
Wiper Systems (Volume 2) 3-1

VEHICLE IDENTIFICATION
INDEX

	PAGE NO.	FIG. NO.
Buick	0-1	1
Cadillac	0-3	2
Chevrolet	0-4	3
Chrysler	0-5	4
Dodge	0-6	5
Eagle	0-8	6
Ford	0-9	7
Geo	0-11	8
Lincoln	0-11	9
Mercury	0-12	10
Oldsmobile	0-13	11
Plymouth	0-14	12
Pontiac	0-15	13
Saturn	0-17	14

DIGIT 1   Country Of Origin
1	USA
2	Canada
3	Mexico
4	USA

DIGIT 2   Manufacturer
G	General Motors

DIGIT 3   Make
4	Buick

DIGIT 4   Restraint System
A	Manual Belts
B	Automatic Belts
C	Passive/Inflatable

DIGIT 4-5   Model/Series

AG	Century Special & Wagon
AG	Century
AG	Century T-Type
AG	Century Special
AG	Century Special
AG	Century Special & Wagon
AG	Century T-Type
AG	Century
AH	Century Custom
AH	Century Custom
AL	Century Limited
AL	Century Estate Wagon
AL	Century Estate Wagon
AL	Century Limited
BN	Roadmaster
BN	Roadmaster
BN	LeSabre Custom
BN	LeSabre Custom
BP	LeSabre Limited
BP	LeSabre Limited
BR	Roadmaster Estate Wagon
BR	LeSabre Estate Wagon
BR	LeSabre Estate Wagon
BR	Roadmaster Estate Wagon
BT	Roadmaster Limited
BT	Roadmaster Limited
BV	Electra Estate Wagon
BV	Electra Estate Wagon
CF	Electra T-Type
CF	Electra T-Type
CU	Park Avenue Ultra
CU	Electra Park Avenue Ultra
CU	Electra Park Avenue Ultra
CU	Park Avenue Ultra
CW	Electra Park Avenue
CW	Park Avenue
CW	Electra Park Avenue
CW	Park Avenue
CX	Electra Limited
CX	Electra
CX	Electra Limited
CX	Electra
EC	Reatta
EC	Reatta
EY	Riviera T-Type
EY	Riviera T-Type
EZ	Riviera
EZ	Riviera
GD	Riviera
GD	Riviera
GJ	Regal
GJ	Regal
GK	Regal T-Type
GK	Regal T-Type
GM	Regal Limited
GM	Regal Limited

DIGIT 4-5   Model/Series

HD	Lucerne CXL
HD	Lucerne CXL
HE	Lucerne CXS
HE	Lucerne CXS
HH	LeSabre
HH	LeSabre
HP	Lucerne CX
HP	LeSabre Custom
HP	Lucerne CX
HP	LeSabre Custom
HR	Lucerne CXL, Special
HR	Lucerne CXL
HR	LeSabre Limited
HR	Lucerne CXL, Special
HR	LeSabre Limited
HR	Lucerne CXL
JE	Skyhawk T-Type
JE	Skyhawk T-Type
JS	Skyhawk Custom
JS	Skyhawk
JS	Skyhawk Custom
JS	Skyhawk
JT	Skyhawk Limited
JT	Skyhawk Limited
NC	Skylark 4D Custom
NC	Skylark 4D Custom
ND	Skylark 4D Luxury
ND	Skylark Limited
ND	Skylark Limited
ND	Skylark 4D Luxury
NJ	Somerset
NJ	Skylark Limited
NJ	Skylark Custom
NJ	Somerset
NJ	Skylark
NJ	Skylark 2D Custom
NJ	Skylark Custom
NJ	Skylark Limited
NJ	Skylark 2D Custom
NJ	Skylark
NK	Somerset T-Type
NK	Somerset T-Type
NM	Skylark Gran Sport
NM	Skylark Gran Sport
NM	Skylark 2D Limited
NM	Skylark Limited
NM	Skylark 2D Limited
NM	Somerset Limited
NM	Skylark Limited
NM	Somerset Limited
NV	Skylark
NV	Skylark Custom
NV	Skylark
NV	Skylark Custom
WB	Regal 2D Gran Sport
WB	Regal Custom
WB	Regal LS
WB	Regal Custom
WB	Regal 2D Gran Sport
WB	Regal LS
WC	LaCrosse CX
WC	LaCrosse CX
WD	LaCrosse CXL
WD	Regal Limited
WD	LaCrosse CXL
WD	Regal Limited
WE	LaCrosse CXS
WE	LaCrosse CXS
WF	Regal 4D Gran Sport
WF	Regal Gran Sport
WF	Regal GS
WF	Regal GS

ARM0700000000186

Fig. 1   VIN Identification (Part 1 of 3). Buick

Part 1 of 3 — Buick

DIGIT 4-5 Model/Series

Code	Model/Series
WF	Regal Gran Sport
WF	Regal 4D Gran Sport
WS	Century Custom
WY	Century Custom
WY	Century Limited
WY	Century Limited
XB	Somerset
XB	Skylark Custom
XB	Somerset
XC	Skylark Custom
XC	Skylark Limited
XC	Skylark Limited

DIGIT 5 Carline/Series

Code	Carline/Series
B	Skylark Custom
B	Skylark
C	Skylark Limited
D	Skylark Sport
D	Skylark T-Type
E	Skyhawk T-Type
E	Century Wagon
G	Century T-Type
H	Century
H	Century
J	Century Custom
J	Century Limited
K	Regal
K	Regal T-Type
K	Regal Sport
L	Regal Limited
M	Century Limited
M	Regal Limited
N	LeSabre Custom
N	LeSabre
P	LeSabre
P	LeSabre Limited
R	LeSabre Estate Wagon
R	Electra Limited
S	Electra Estate Wagon
S	Skyhawk
T	Skyhawk
T	Skyhawk Limited
U	Electra Park Avenue
V	Electra Estate Wagon
W	Electra Park Avenue
X	Electra Limited
Y	Riviera T-Type
Z	Riviera

DIGIT 6 Body Type

Code	Body Type
11	2D Coupe
11	2D Hatchback
19	2D Coupe
27	2D Coupe
35	4D Sedan
37	4D Wagon
47	2D Coupe
57	2D Coupe
67	2D Convertible
69	4D Sedan
77	2D Hatchback

DIGIT 6-7 Body Type

Code	Body Type
11	2D Coupe
19	4D Sedan
27	2D Coupe
35	4D Wagon
37	2D Coupe
47	2D Coupe
57	2D Convertible
67	4D Sedan
69	2D Hatchback

DIGIT 7 Restraint System

Code	Restraint System
1	Dual Front Airbags w/Manual Belts
1	Manual Belts
2	Dual Front Airbag w/Manual Belts
3	Driverside Airbag w/Manual Belts
3	Dual Front Airbags w/Manual Belts & Passenger Sensor
3	Dual Front, Side & Roof Airbags w/Manual Belts

Part 2 of 3 — Buick

DIGIT 7 Restraint System

Code	Restraint System
4	Dual Front & Side Airbags w/Manual Belts
4	2nd Generation Dual Front & Side Airbags w/Manual Belts
4	Dual Front & Roof Airbags w/Manual Belts
5	Automatic Belts
5	Driverside Airbag w/Automatic Belts
5	Dual Front & Driver's Side Airbags w/Manual Belts
5	Dual Front Airbags w/Manual Belts
6	Dual Front Airbags w/Manual Belts & Passenger Sensor
7	Dual Front, Side Airbags w/Manual Belts & Occupar
8	Dual Front, Side & Roof Airbags w/Manual Belts & Passenger Sei

DIGIT 8 Engine

Code	Engine
0	1.8L I-4 EFI
1	3.8L V6 SFI S/C
1	2.0L I-4 EFI
2	3.8L V6 MPI S/C
2	3.8L V6 SFI
3	3.8L V6 SFI
3	3.8L V6 FI TBO
3	3.8L V8 4BBL T/C
3	3.8L V8 2BBL
3	2.3L I-4 EFI OHC
4	2.2L I-4 MPI
4	4.1L V6 4BBL
5	2.5L I-4 2BBL
7	3.6L V6 SFI
7	3.8L V6 SFI
7	5.7L V8 TBI
8	3.8L V6 2BBL
9	3.8L V6 SFI
A	3.8L V6 2BBL
B	2.0L I-4 2BBL
B	3.8L V6 SFI
C	5.7L V8 Dsl
D	2.3L I-4 EFI Quad
E	5.0L V8 TBI
G	1.8L I-4 2BBL
H	5.0L V8 4BBL
J	3.1L V6 SFI
J	1.8L I-4 MPI
K	3.8L V6 SFI
K	2.0L I-4 EFI
L	3.0L V6 MPI
L	3.8L V6 MPI
M	2.0L I-4 EFI
M	3.1L V6 MPI
N	3.3L V6 MPI
N	5.7L V8 Dsl
P	2.0L I-4 EFI
R	5.7L V8 4BBL Dsl
R	5.7L V8 MPI
S	2.5L I-4 TBI
T	4.3L V8 2BBL
T	3.1L V6 MPI
T	4.3L V6 Dsl
U	2.4L I-4 SFI DOHC
U	2.5L I-4 TBI
W	4.3L V6 Dsl
W	2.8L V6 2BBL
X	2.8L V6 MPI
X	4.6L V8 SFI DOHC
Y	5.0L V8 4BBL
Z	2.8L V6 2BBL HO

DIGIT 10 Model Year

Code	Model Year
1	2001
2	2002

Fig. 1 VIN Identification (Part 2 of 3). Buick

Part 3 of 3 — Buick

DIGIT 10 Model Year

Code	Model Year
3	2003
4	2004
5	2005
6	2006
7	2007
8	2008
B	1981
C	1982
D	1983
E	1984
F	1985
G	1986
H	1987
J	1988
K	1989
L	1990
M	1991
N	1992
P	1993
R	1994
S	1995
T	1996
V	1997
W	1998
X	1999
Y	2000

DIGIT 11 Assembly Plant

Code	Assembly Plant
1	Oshawa #2, ON, Canada
1	Wentzville, MO, USA
2	Ste. Therese, PQ, Canada
4	Orion, MI, USA
6	Oklahoma City, OK, USA
A	Lakewood, GA, USA
B	Lansing, MI, USA
B	Lansing, MI, USA
C	Doraville, GA, USA
D	Doraville, GA, USA
E	Linden, NJ, USA
G	Framingham, MA, USA
H	Flint, MI, USA
J	Janesville, WI, USA
K	Leeds, MO, USA
K	Linden, NJ, USA
M	Lansing, MI, USA
P	Pontiac, MI, USA
R	Arlington, TX, USA
S	Ramos Arizpe, Mexico
T	Tarrytown, NY, USA
U	Hamtramck, MI, USA
W	Willow Run, MI, USA
X	Fairfax, KS, USA
Z	Fremont, CA, USA

Fig. 1 VIN Identification (Part 3 of 3). Buick

ARM070000000190

Fig. 2 VIN Identification (Part 2 of 2). Cadillac

DIGIT 10 — Model Year

Code	Year
J	1988
K	1989
L	1990
M	1991
N	1992
P	1993
R	1994
S	1995
T	1996
V	1997
W	1998
X	1999
Y	2000

DIGIT 11 — Assembly Plant

Code	Plant
0	Lansing, MI, USA
4	Orion, MI, USA
5	Bowling Green, KY, USA
9	Detroit, MI, USA
C	Southgate, CA, USA
E	Pontiac East, MI, USA
E	Linden, NJ, USA
J	Janesville, WI, USA
K	Leeds, MO, USA
R	Russelsheim, Germany
R	Arlington, TX, USA
U	Hamtramck, MI, USA

ARM070000000189

Fig. 2 VIN Identification (Part 1 of 2). Cadillac

DIGIT 1 — Country Of Origin

Code	Description
1	USA
W	Germany

DIGIT 2 — Manufacturer

Code	Description
0	Opel
G	General Motors

DIGIT 3 — Make

Code	Description
6	Cadillac

DIGIT 4 — Restraint System

Code	Description
A	Manual Belts

DIGIT 4-5 — Carline/Series

Code	Description
CB	DeVille Sixty Special
CB	Fleetwood
CD	DeVille
CG	Fleetwood Sixty Special
CS	Fleetwood Sixty Special
CT	DeVille Touring
DC	STS-V8
DG	STS
DM	CTS
DN	CTS-V
DP	CTS High Feature
DP	CTS High Feature V6
DW	STS
DW	Brougham RWD
DW	Fleetwood RWD
DW	Fleetwood Brougham RWD
DX	STS-V
EC	Eldorado ETC Collector's Edition
EL	Eldorado ESC
EL	Eldorado
ET	Eldorado Touring
ET	Eldorado ETC
JG	Cimarron
KD	DTS
KD	DeVille
KE	DeVille D'Elegance
KE	DeVille DHS
KF	DeVille DTS
KF	DeVille Concours
KS	Seville
KS	Seville SLS
KY	Seville STS
KY	Seville Touring
VR	Allante
VR	Allante Convertible w/Hardtop
VS	Catera
YV	XLR

DIGIT 5 — Carline/Series

Code	Description
B	Fleetwood, Brougham
B	Fleetwood
D	DeVille
F	Fleetwood Limousine
G	Cimarron
L	Eldorado
M	DeVille RWD
S	Seville

DIGIT 6 — Body Type

Code	Description
1	2D Coupe
3	2D Convertible
5	2D Coupe/Convertible
6	4D Sedan

DIGIT 6-7 — Body Type

Code	Description
23	4D Sedan Limousine
33	4D Sedan Limousine
47	2D Coupe
57	2D Coupe
67	2D Convertible
69	4D Sedan

DIGIT 7 — Restraint System

Code	Description
1	Manual Belts
2	Dual Front & Side Airbags w/Manual Belts
2	Dual Front Airbags w/Manual Belts
3	Driverside Airbag w/Manual Belts
4	Automatic Belts
4	Dual Front & Side Airbags w/Manual Belts
5	Dual Front & Side Airbags w/Manual Belts
6	Dual Front & Side Airbags w/Auto Passenger Sensor
6	Dual Front & Side Airbags w/Manual Belts & Occupant Sens
7	Dual Front, Front & Side Airbags, Front-to-Rear Head Curtai
7	Dual Front, Front & Rear Side Airbags & Manual Belts
8	Dual Front, Side & Roof Airbags w/Manual Belts & Occupar

DIGIT 8 — Engine

Code	Description
1	2.0L I-4 EFI
3	4.5L V8 EFI
4	4.1L V6 4BBL
5	4.5L V8 DFI
5	6.0L V8 4BBL
7	3.6L V6 SFI
7	4.1L V8 SFI
7	5.7L V8 MPI
8	5.7L V8 TBI
8	4.1L V8 DFI
8	4.1L V8 TBI
8	4.5L V8 MPI
9	6.0L V8 MPI
9	4.6L V8 MPI
9	5.0L V8 4BBL
A	4.6L V8 SFI DOHC
A	4.6L V8 SFI
B	4.9L V8 MPI
D	4.4L V8 MFI S/C
D	4.4L V8 MFI S/C DOHC
E	5.0L V8 TBI
G	1.8L L4 2BBL
N	3.2L V6 SFI DOHC
N	5.7L V8 Dsl
P	2.0L I-4 EFI
P	5.7L V8 MPI
R	3.0L V6 MPI
S	5.7L V8 SFI HO
T	2.8L V6 MPI
T	4.3L V6 Dsl
U	6.0L V8 SFI HO
V	3.6L V6 SFI
W	2.8L V8 MPI
Y	5.0L V8 4BBL
Y	4.6L V8 SFI DOHC
Y	4.6L V8 MPI DOHC

DIGIT 10 — Model Year

Code	Year
1	2001
2	2002
3	2003
4	2004
5	2005
6	2006
7	2007
8	2008
B	1981
C	1982
D	1983
E	1984
F	1985
G	1986
H	1987

Fig. 3 VIN Identification (Part 1 of 3). Chevrolet

DIGIT 1	Country Of Origin
1	USA
2	Canada
3	Mexico
4	USA
J	Japan
K	Korea

DIGIT 2	Manufacturer
8	Isuzu
C	Cami
G	General Motors
L	General Motors
Y	Nummi

DIGIT 3	Make
1	Chevrolet

DIGIT 4	Restraint System
A	Manual Belts

DIGIT 4-5	Carline/Series
AJ	Cobalt Base
AK	Cobalt LEV 1
AK	Cobalt LS
AL	Cobalt LEV 2
AL	Cobalt LT
AM	Cobalt SS
AM	Cobalt LEV 3
AN	Cobalt Sport Sedan
AP	Cobalt SS Supercharged
AP	Cobalt Sport Coupe
AW	Celebrity
AZ	Cobalt LT Sedan
AZ	Cobalt LTZ Sedan
BL	Caprice
BL	Caprice Classic
BL	Impala SS
BL	Impala SS
BN	Caprice Classic
BN	Caprice Classic LS
BN	Impala SS
BU	Caprice Brougham
FP	Camaro
FS	Camaro Berlinetta
GZ	Monte Carlo
JC	Cavalier RS
JC	Cavalier VL
JC	Cavalier CS
JD	Cavalier RS
JE	Cavalier CS
JE	Cavalier Type 10 & Conv
JF	Cavalier RS
JF	Cavalier Z24
JF	Cavalier LS Sedan
JF	Cavalier LS
JH	Cavalier LS Sport
JS	Cavalier LS Coupe
LD	Corsica
LT	Corsica
LT	Corsica LT
LV	Beretta
LW	Beretta GT
LW	Beretta Z26
LZ	Beretta GTZ
LZ	Corsica LTZ
MR	Sprint
MR	Metro
MS	Sprint ER
ND	Malibu
ND	Malibu Classic
NE	Malibu LS
RF	Spectrum
RF	Spectrum Coupe

DIGIT 5	Carline/Series
B	Chevette
B	Chevette CS
C	Cavalier
D	Cavalier
D	Cavalier RS
E	Cavalier Type 10
H	Citation Coupe
J	Chevette Coupe
J	Chevette Scooter
L	Impala
N	Caprice Classic
P	Camaro Sport Coupe
S	Camaro Berlinetta
W	Malibu
W	Celebrity
W	Malibu
W	Malibu Classic
X	Citation
Y	Corvette
Z	Monte Carlo

DIGIT 6	Body Type
1	2D Coupe/Sedan
1	2D Coupe

Fig. 3 VIN Identification (Part 2 of 3). Chevrolet

DIGIT 4-5	Carline/Series
RG	Spectrum Sedan
SK	Nova
SK	Prizm
TB	Chevette CS
TD	Aveo Base & LS
TD	Aveo Base
TG	Aveo LT
TJ	Aveo LS & LT
WB	Impala LS
WC	Impala 2LT
WC	Impala 3LT
WD	Impala SS
WF	Impala
WH	Impala LS
WJ	Monte Carlo LS
WK	Monte Carlo LT
WK	Monte Carlo LT 3.9L
WL	Monte Carlo SS SC
WL	Lumina
WL	Lumina LS
WM	Lumina LS 3.5L
WN	Monte Carlo LTZ
WN	Lumina LTZ
WN	Lumina LS
WP	Lumina Euro
WP	Impala SS
WS	Lumina Z34
WS	Impala Police
WT	Impala LT 3.5
WU	Impala LTZ
WW	Monte Carlo LS
WX	Monte Carlo SS
WX	Monte Carlo Z34
WX	Monte Carlo LT
WZ	Monte Carlo SS S/C
XX	Citation II
YY	Corvette
YZ	Corvette ZR1
ZL	Lumina LS
ZS	Malibu
ZS	Malibu LS
ZT	Malibu LT
ZT	Malibu LS
ZU	Malibu LS
ZU	Malibu LT
ZU	Malibu LTZ
ZW	Malibu SS

DIGIT 6	Body Type
2	2D Coupe Liftback
2	2D Hatchback
2	2D Hatchback/Liftback
3	2D Liftback
5	2D Convertible
6	4D Sedan
6	4D Sedan Maxx
8	4D Hatchback
8	4D Hatchback, Sedan
8	4D Station Wagon

DIGIT 6-7	Body Type
07	2D Coupe
08	2D Hatchback
11	4D Sedan/Hatchback
19	2D Coupe
27	2D Coupe/Hatchback
35	4D 2-Seat Wagon
37	2D Coupe/Hatchback
47	2D Hatchback Sport
67	2D Convertible
68	4D Hatchback
68	4D Sedan/Hatchback
69	4D Sedan
69	4D Sedan/Hatchback
77	2D Coupe/Hatchback
87	2D Hatchback
87	2D Sedan/Hatchback

DIGIT 7	Restraint System
1	Active Seat Belt Restraints
1	Dual Front Airbags w/Active Seat Belt Restraints
1	Dual Front Airbags w/Active Seat Belt Restraints
1	Manual Belts
2	Dual Front & Side Airbags w/Manual Belts
2	Dual Front & Side Airbags w/Manual Belts
2	Dual Front Airbags w/Active Seat Belt Restraints
3	Driverside Airbag w/Manual Belts
3	Dual Front, Side & Head Curtain Airbags w/Manual Belts
4	Automatic Belts
4	Dual Front & Head Curtain Airbags w/Manual Belts
4	Dual Front & Roof Airbags w/Manual Belts
4	Dual Front & Side Airbags w/Active Seat Belt Restraints
4	Dual Front & Side Airbags w/Manual Belts
4	Passive Automatic Belts
5	Dual Front Airbags w/Active Seat Belt Restraints & Occupa...
5	Driverside Airbag w/Automatic Belts
5	Dual Front Airbags w/Manual Belts & Occupant Sensor
5	Dual Front & Driver's Side Airbags w/Manual Belts
6	Dual Front, Side & Head Curtain Airbags w/Active Seat Belt Restraints & C...
7	Dual Front, Side & Head Curtain Airbags w/Manual Belts
7	Dual Front, Side & Head Curtain Airbags w/Manual Belts, O...
8	Dual Front & Head Curtain Airbags w/Manual Belts
8	Dual Front & Roof Airbags w/Manual Belts & Passenger Se...
9	Dual Front Airbags w/Active Seat Belt Restraints & Occupa...

DIGIT 8	Engine
1	3.8L V6 SFI S/C
1	3.9L V6 SFI
1	2.8L V6 2BBL
1	2.0L I4 EFI
2	1.3L I4 EFI SOHC
2	2.5L I4 TBI
2	2.5L I4 EFI
2	1.0L I-3 Turbo
3	3.8L V6 2BBL
3	3.9L V6 SFI
4	1.6L I4 2BBL
4	2.2L I4 MPI
5	1.0L I-3 2V

DIGIT 8	Engine
5	1.6L I4 MPI
5	5.7L V8 SFI DOHC
5	2.5L I4 2BBL
6	1.6L I4 MPI DOHC Flex Fuel
6	2.2L I4 MPI DOHC
6	5.7L V8 4BBL
6	1.0L I-3 EFI SOHC
7	1.5L I4 2BBL
7	5.0L V8 EFI
7	5.7L V8 CPI
7	5.7L V8 EFI
8	5.7L V8 TBI
8	5.7L V8 TPI
8	3.5L V6 SFI
9	1.5L I4 FI Tbo
9	1.6L I4 2BBL
9	3.8L V6 2BBL
9	1.3L I4 EFI
A	2.3L I4 MPI
A	3.8L V6 2BBL
B	2.4L I4 MPI DOHC
C	5.3L V8 SFI S/C
C	1.6L I4 2BBL
C	5.3L V8 SFI Cylinder Deactivation
D	1.6L I4 MPI DOHC
D	2.3L I4 MFI
D	1.8L I4 Dsl
E	7.0L V8 SFI
E	3.4L V6 SFI
E	5.0L V8 TBI
F	5.0L V8 MPI
F	2.5L I4 2BBL
F	2.2L I4 MPI DOHC
F	2.2L I4 MPI DOHC
G	2.2L I4 TBI
G	5.7L V8 SFI
G	5.0L V8 4BBL
G	1.8L I4 2BBL
G	5.7L V8 MPI
H	5.0L V8 4BBL
J	4.4L V8 2BBL
J	5.7L V8 SFI
J	3.1L V6 SFI
J	5.7L V8 MPI
K	1.5L I4 2BBL
K	3.8L V6 SFI (Flex Fuel)
K	3.8L V6 2BBL
K	3.5L V6 SFI Flex Fuel
K	3.5L V6 SFI (Flex Fuel)
L	2.8L V6 2BBL
L	5.7L V8 4BBL
M	1.0L I-3 2BBL
M	3.1L V6 SFI
N	3.5L V6 SFI
N	3.8L V6 SFI
N	5.7L V8 Dsl
P	5.7L V8 FI Dsl
P	5.7L V8 SFI
P	2.0L I4 MPI DOHC SC
P	5.7L V8 SFI Flex Fuel
R	2.5L I4 TBI
R	3.9L V6 SFI
S	2.8L V6 EFI
S	3.4L V6 SFI
S	5.0L V8 TBI
S	5.7L V8 SFI HO
T	2.4L I4 SFI DOHC
T	3.1L V6 SFI
T	4.3L V6 DSL

Fig. 3 VIN Identification (Part 3 of 3). Chevrolet

DIGIT 8 — Engine

Code	Engine
T	4.3L V6 EFI
U	6.0L V8 SFI OHV
V	4.3L V8 FI Dsl
V	4.3L V8 SFI
W	4.3L V8 SFI
W	3.1L V6 MPI
W	2.8L V6 MPI
W	6.2L V8 SFI OHV
X	2.8L V6 2BBL
X	3.4L V6 SFI DOHC
Y	5.0L V8 4BBL
Y	7.0L V8 SFI
Z	2.8L V6 2BBL HO
Z	4.3L V6 EFI

DIGIT 10 — Model Year

Code	Model Year
1	2001
2	2002
3	2003
4	2004
5	2005
6	2006
7	2007
8	2008
B	1981
C	1982
D	1983
E	1984
F	1985
G	1986
H	1987
J	1988
K	1989
L	1990
M	1991
N	1992
P	1993
R	1994
S	1995
T	1996
V	1997
W	1998
X	1999
Y	2000

DIGIT 11 — Assembly Plant

Code	Assembly Plant
1	Oshawa, ON, Canada
2	Oshawa #2, ON, Canada
2	Ste. Therese, PQ, Canada
3	Kawasaki, Japan
5	Bowling Green, KY, USA
6	Oklahoma City, OK, USA
6	Ingersoll, ON, Canada
7	Lordstown, OH, USA
8	Fujisawa, Japan
8	Fujisawa, Japan
9	Oshawa #1, ON, Canada
9	Detroit, MI, USA
A	Lakewood, GA, USA
B	Lansing, MI, USA
B	Baltimore, MD, USA
B	Bupyung S. Korea
B	Lansing, MI, USA - Craft Center
C	South Gate, CA, USA
C	Lansing, MI, USA - South Plant
D	Doraville, GA, USA
D	Linden, NJ, USA
E	Fairfax, KS, USA
F	Framingham, MA, USA
G	Flint, MI, USA
H	Janesville, WI, USA
K	Kosai, Japan

ARM0700000000193

Fig. 4 VIN Identification (Part 1 of 2). Chrysler

DIGIT 1 — Country Of Origin

Code	Country Of Origin
1	USA
2	Canada
3	Mexico
4	USA - MMMA
J	Japan
W	Germany

DIGIT 2 — Manufacturer

Code	Manufacturer
A	Imperial
C	Chrysler
C	Chrysler
J	Chrysler

DIGIT 3 — Vehicle Type

Code	Vehicle Type
3	Passenger Car
4	Multipurpose Passenger Vehicle
8	Multipurpose Passenger Vehicle w/Side Airbags
A	PT Cruiser w/Side Airbags

DIGIT 4 — Restraint System

Code	Restraint System
A	Dual Front Airbags w/Manual Belts
A	Dual Airbags w/Manual Belts
A	Active Front & Side Airbags
B	Driverside Airbag w/Motorized Passenger Belt
B	Manual Seat Belts
C	Automatic Seat Belts
E	Dual Airbags w/Manual Belts
E	Dual Front Airbags w/Manual Belts
E	Dual Front Airbags w/Manual Belts & w/o Side Airbags
H	Dual Airbags w/Manual Belts
H	Dual Front Airbags w/Manual Belts
H	Front, Next Generation, Multi Stage w/Side Airbags
J	Hybrid Airbags
J	Front, Next Generation, MultiStage
J	Dual Front Airbags w/Manual Belts
K	Front, Next Generation, Multi Stage w/o Side Side Airbags
K	Front, Advanced Multi Stage Airbags w/o Side Airbags
L	Front, Advanced Multi Stage Airbags w/Side Airbags
L	Front, Advanced , Multi Stage Airbags w/Side Side Airbags
X	Advanced Front Multi-Stage Airbags w/Front & Rear Side A
Y	Driverside Airbag w/Manual Belts
Y	Driverside Airbag w/Automatic Passenger Belt

DIGIT 4* — GVWR

Code	GVWR
E	3001-4000 Lbs
F	4001-5000 Lbs

DIGIT 5 — Carline

Code	Carline
A	300
A	300 RWD
A	Laser
C	Lebaron 4D
C	Sebring
C	New Yorker
C	Lebaron 4D
C	Conquest
D	LHS
D	Concorde
D	LHS
E	New Yorker
F	Fifth Avenue
F	New Yorker
G	Sebring Coupe
H	Lebaron GTS
J	Lebaron 2D
J	Cirrus
J	Cordoba
K	300 AWD
L	Concorde
L	Sebring
L	Sebring Convertible
L	Lebaron
M	Fifth Avenue
M	Crossfire
N	New Yorker
N	Newport
R	Cordoba
R	New Yorker
S	E Class
T	New Yorker Turbo
T	Lebaron 2D
U	New Yorker
U	Sebring
V	Imperial
V	Fifth Avenue
W	Prowler
Y	Fifth Avenue
Y	Imperial
Y	PT Cruiser

DIGIT 6 — Series

Code	Series
3	Concorde LXi
3	Medium
3	Sebring TSi
4	High
4	High Line
4	Sebring Base
4	Sebring LX
4	Base
5	Concorde LX
5	Concorde Limited
5	Touring
5	Sebring Touring
5	Sebring Lxi
5	Sebring Coupe Limited
5	Premium
5	Base/Touring/Limited
5	Base/LTD
5	Base
6	Premium Line
6	Special
6	C
6	Sebring Limited
6	Limited
6	Fifth Avenue
6	Crossfire
6	300C
7	Base
7	Performance
7	X Series
7	Special
7	SRT-6
7	Sebring GTC
7	GT
7	SRT8
B	Base

DIGIT 7 — Body Type

Code	Body Type
1	2D Sedan
1	2D Coupe
2	2D Specialty Hardtop
2	2D Pillared Hardtop
2	2D Hardtop
3	2D Specialty Hardtop
3	4D Sedan
3	2D Hatchback
5	2D Convertible
5	2D Convertible/Open Body
5	2D Roadster
6	4D Sedan
7	2D Pillared Hardtop
8	Hatchback
8	4D Hatchback

ARM0700000000170

Fig. 5 VIN Identification (Part 1 of 3). Dodge

DIGIT 1 — Country Of Origin

Code	Country Of Origin
1	USA
2	Canada
3	Mexico
4	USA - MMMA
J	Japan

DIGIT 2 — Make

Code	Make
B	Dodge
D	Dodge

DIGIT 3 — Vehicle Type

Code	Vehicle Type
3	Passenger Car
4	Multi-Purpose Passenger Vehicle
8	Multi-Purpose Passenger Vehicle w/Side Airbags

DIGIT 4 — Restraint

Code	Restraint
A	Dual Front Airbags w/Manual Belts
A	Dual Airbags w/Manual Belts
A	Driverside Airbag w/Motorized Passenger Belt
A	Active Front & Side Airbags
B	Manual Seat Belts
B	Automatic Belts
C	Automatic Seat Belt
C	Automatic Seat Belts
E	Driverside Airbag
E	Active Driver & Passenger Airbags
E	Dual Front Airbags w/Manual Belts
H	Dual Front Airbags w/Manual Belts
H	Front, Next Generation, Multi Stage w/Side Airbags
H	Dual Airbags, Passenger Hybrid w/Manual Belts
J	Dual Front Airbags Next Generation Multi Stage
J	Dual Front Next Generation Multi Stage w/Side Airbags
J	Front, Next Generation, Multi Stage w/o Side Side Airbags
X	Driverside Airbag w/Manual Seat Belts
X	Driverside Airbag w/Manual Passenger Belt
Y	Driverside Airbag w/Automatic Passenger Belt

DIGIT 4* — Restraint System

Code	Restraint System
C	Automatic Seat Belts
K	Dual Front MultiStage Airbags w/o side Airbags
L	Dual Front MultiStage Airbags w/side Airbags

DIGIT 4+ — GVWR/Brake System

Code	GVWR/Brake System
F	4001-5000 Lbs, Hydraulic
G	5001-6000 Lbs, Hydraulic

DIGIT 5 — Carline

Code	Carline
A	Colt
A	Daytona
A	Spirit
A	Charger RWD
B	Caliber FWD
B	Charger
B	Monaco
B	Conquest
C	Dynasty
C	Daytona
C	Avenger FWD Sedan
C	Avenger AWD Sedan
D	Challenger
D	Stratus Coupe
D	Intrepid
D	Stealth
D	Pacifica
E	Aries
E	600
E	Stealth
E	Caliber AWD
E	Colt
G	Colt Wagon
G	Daytona
G	Diplomat
G	Colt Wagon AWD
H	Stratus
H	Lancer
J	Mirada
J	Stratus

DIGIT 5 — Carline

Code	Carline
J	Stratus Sedan
K	Charger AWD
K	Aries
L	Stratus Sedan
L	024 Omni
L	Omni
M	Diplomat
M	Stealth
N	Stealth FWD
N	Stealth Turbo
P	Stealth AWD
R	Shadow
R	Viper
S	St. Regis
S	Neon
U	Shadow
U	Dynasty
U	Avenger
V	Colt
V	600 2D Coupe/Convertible
V	Colt Wagon
V	400
W	Colt Wagon AWD
X	Lancer
X	Mirada
Z	Omni
Z	Viper

DIGIT 5* — Line

Code	Line
V	Magnum RWD
Z	Magnum AWD

DIGIT 6 — Series

Code	Series
1	Base, S
2	Economy
2	Base
2	Low
2	SE
3	Medium
3	SE
3	High
3	SXT
4	Avenger SE
4	Base
4	High
4	Magnum SE
4	SE
4	Magnum SXT
5	Avenger SXT
5	ES/SXT
5	ES
5	Magnum R/T
5	Premium
5	R/T
5	R/T Coupe
5	SXT
6	Pacifica
6	R/T
6	Turbo Z
6	Turbo
6	SRT-4
6	SRT-10
6	Shelby Z
6	IROC R/T
6	ES Turbo
6	ACR
7	Special
7	Performance
7	IROC
7	Avenger R/T

ARM0700000000172

Fig. 5 VIN Identification (Part 1 of 3). Dodge

Fig. 4 VIN Identification (Part 2 of 2). Chrysler

DIGIT 7 — Body Type

Code	Body Type
9	2D Coupe
9	4D Wagon
B	Hatchback

DIGIT 8 — Engine

Code	Engine
3	3.0L V6 MPI
3	3.0L V8 TBI
8	2.4L I-4 DOHC TURBO
8	2.4L I-4 EFI DOHC Turbo
B	2.2L I-4 Turbo
B	2.4L I-4 SFI DOHC
B	2.4L I-4 2BBL
B	2.4L I-4 DOHC SMPI
B	2.4L I-4 MPI
C	2.0L I-4 SFI SOHC
C	2.2L I-4 2BBL
C	2.2L I-4 EFI Turbo
C	2.2L I-4
D	2.2L I-4 EFI
D	2.2L I-4 TBI
D	2.6L I-4 2BBL
E	2.6L I-4 2BBL
E	3.7L I-6 1BBL
E	2.2L I-4 FI Turbo
E	2.2L I-4 Turbo
E	2.4L I-4 SFI DOHC Turbo
F	3.5L V6 MPI
F	3.7L I-6 1BBL
G	3.5L V6 SFI SOHC
G	3.0L V6 MPI SOHC
G	3.5L V6 MPI SOHC HO
G	3.5L V6 EFI HO SOHC
G	3.5L V6 MPI SOHC
H	2.4L I-4 EFI DOHC
H	2.5L V6 EFI DOHC Turbo
H	2.5L I-4 TBI
J	5.7L V8 SFI SOHC
J	3.0L V6 MPI SOHC
J	3.8L V6 EFI
J	5.7L V8 HEMI MAGNUM
K	3.7L L-6 1BBL
K	5.7L V8 EFI
L	5.2L V8 EFI
L	3.2L V6 EFI SOHC
L	3.5L V6 MPI HO
L	2.4L I-4 VVT EFI DOHC
L	3.8L V6 MPI
M	3.8L V6 2BBL
M	5.2L V8 2BBL
M	5.2L V8 2BBL HD
M	5.2L V8 EFI
M	5.2L V8 4BBL
M	3.5L V6 MPI High Output
M	3.5L V6 MPI SOHC
N	5.2L V8 2BBL
N	2.6L I-4 T/C I/C
N	3.2L V6 SFI SOHC
P	5.2L V8 2BBL
P	5.2L V8 4BBL HD
R	2.5L V6 SFI SOHC
R	2.7L L-6 MPI DOHC
R	2.7L L-6 SFI DOHC
R	3.3L V6 EFI
S	2.4L I-4 SFI DOHC HO Turbo
T	2.7L V6 MPI FFV
U	3.0L V6 MPI
U	3.0L V6 MPI
U	2.7L V6 SFI DOHC
U	2.7L V6 MPI DOHC

DIGIT 8 — Engine

Code	Engine
V	3.5L V6 EFI SOHC
V	3.5L V6 EFI HO SOHC
W	6.1L V8 SRT HEMI
X	2.4L I-4 EFI DOHC
Y	2.0L I-4 SFI DOHC

DIGIT 10 — Model Year

Code	Model Year
1	2001
2	2002
3	2003
4	2004
5	2005
6	2006
7	2007
8	2008
B	1981
C	1982
D	1983
E	1984
F	1985
G	1986
H	1987
J	1988
K	1989
L	1990
M	1991
N	1992
P	1993
R	1994
S	1995
T	1996
V	1997
W	1998
X	1999
Y	2000

DIGIT 11 — Assembly Plant

Code	Assembly Plant
A	Auburn Hills, MI, USA
A	Lynch RD, USA
C	Jefferson, MI, USA
D	Belvidere, IL, USA
E	Normal, IL, USA
F	Newark, DE, USA
G	St. Louis #1, MO, USA
H	Brampton, ON, Canada
H	Bramalea, ON, Canada
N	Sterling Heights, MI, USA
R	Windsor, Canada
T	Toluca, Mexico
U	Mizushima, Japan
V	Conner Ave, Detroit, MI, USA
W	Kenosha #1, USA
X	Osnabrueck, Germany
X	St. Louis #2, MO, USA
Y	Kenosha #2, USA
Y	Nagoya 1, Japan
Z	Okazaki, Japan

ARM0700000000171

Fig. 4 VIN Identification (Part 2 of 2). Chrysler

ARM070000000174

Fig. 5 VIN Identification (Part 3 of 3). Dodge

DIGIT 10	Model Year
8	2008
B	1981
C	1982
D	1983
E	1984
F	1985
G	1986
H	1987
J	1988
K	1989
L	1990
M	1991
N	1992
P	1993
R	1994
S	1995
T	1996
V	1997
W	1998
X	1999
Y	2000

DIGIT 11	Assembly Plant
A	Mizushima 2, Japan
B	St. Louis South, MO, USA
C	Jefferson North Assembly, Detroit, MI, USA
D	Belvidere, IL, USA
E	Normal, IL, USA
F	Newark, NJ, USA
G	St. Louis #1, MO, USA
H	Bramalea, ON, Canada
H	Brampton, ON, Canada
J	Nagoya 3, Japan
N	Sterling Heights, MI, USA
P	Nagoya 2, Japan
R	Windsor, On, Canada
T	Toluca, Mexico
U	Mizushima 1, Japan
U	Mizushima, Japan
V	Detroit, MI, USA
W	Kenosha #1, WI, USA
X	St. Louis #2, MO, USA
Y	Kenosha #2, WI, USA
Y	Nagoya 1, Japan
Z	Okazaki, Japan

ARM070000000173

Fig. 5 VIN Identification (Part 2 of 3). Dodge

DIGIT 8	Engine
G	3.5L V8 MPI SOHC HO
G	2.4L I-4 MPI
G	2.4L I-4 MPI SOHC
G	2.6L I-4
H	5.7L V8 HEMI
H	3.0L V6 MPI SOHC
H	2.5L V6 EFI
H	2.5L V6 SFI
H	2.5L V6 SFI SOHC
H	2.6L I-4 Tbo
H	3.7L I-6
J	3.2L V6 SFI SOHC
J	2.5L I-4 MPI Turbo
J	3.0L V6 MPI DOHC
J	2.4L I-4 MPI PZEV
J	2.5L I-4 FI Turbo
K	5.2L V8 2BBL
K	3.0L V6 MPI Tbo DOHC
K	2.5L I-4 TBI
K	2.4L I-4 SFI DOHC
K	1.5L I-4
M	3.5L V6 MPI SOHC
M	3.5L V6 MPI
M	5.2L V8
N	3.5L H/O V6 MPI
N	2.5L V6 SFI SOHC
N	5.2L V8 HD
P	5.2L V8 2BBL
P	5.2L V8
R	2.7L V6 MPI DOHC
R	2.7L V6 MPI
R	2.7L V6 SFI DOHC
R	3.3L V6 MPI
R	5.2L V8 4BBL
S	2.4L 4 SFI DOHC TURBO
S	2.4L I-4 SFI DOHC HOT
S	2.4L I-4 SFI DOHC TURBO
T	3.0L V6 MPI
T	2.7L V6 MPI FFV
T	2.7L V6 MPI
U	3.3L I-4 MPI
U	2.7L V6 SFI DOHC
U	3.0L V6 MPI
V	3.3L V6 SFI Flex
V	3.5L V6 MPI SOHC
V	2.0L I-4 MPI
V	2.5L I-4 TBI Flex Fuel
V	3.5L V6 EFI SOHC HO
V	3.5L V6 EFI SOHC Magnum
W	3.5L V6 SOHC
W	6.1L V8 SMPI SRT HEMI
X	2.4L I-4 SFI DOHC HOT
X	2.4L I-4 SFI DOHC
Y	1.5L I-4 MPI
Y	2.0L I-4 SFI DOHC
Z	8.3L V10 SFI
Z	1.6L I-4 Turbo
Z	1.5L I-4 MPI

DIGIT 10	Model Year
1	2001
2	2002
3	2003
4	2004
5	2005
6	2006
7	2007

Fig. 5 VIN Identification (Part 2 of 3). Dodge

DIGIT 6	Series
7	Shelby
7	SRT-8
7	R/T
8	R/T Turbo

DIGIT 7	Body Type
1	4D Wagon AWD
1	4D Wagon
1	4D Sedan
2	2D Coupe
2	2D Pillared Hardtop
2	2D Coupe
3	4D Sedan
3	2D Hatchback
4	2D Convertible/Open Body
5	2D Convertible / Open Body
5	2D Convertible
6	4D Sedan
7	Hatchback Tall
7	4D Pillared Hardtop
8	Hatchback Tall
8	4D Hatchback
8	4D Wagon
9	2D Specialty Coupe
9	4D Wagon

DIGIT 8	Engine
2	5.7L V8 SFI Hemi
2	1.4L I-4 2BBL
3	1.6L I-4 2BBL
3	3.0L V6 MPI
3	6.1L V8 SMPI HEMI
4	5.2L V8 2BBL
4	2.6L I-4
A	1.7L I-4 2BBL
A	1.6L I-4 2BBL
A	2.2L I-4 Turbo
A	2.2L I-4 FI Turbo
A	1.4L I-4 2BBL
A	1.5L I-4 MPI
B	2.2L I-4 MPI Turbo
B	2.0L I-4 SFI SOHC
B	3.0L V6 MPI
B	1.7L I-4 2BBL
B	1.6L I-4 2BBL
C	1.8L I-4 MPI
C	3.0L V6 MPI Turbo
C	2.2L I-4 EFI Turbo
C	2.2L I-4 2BBL
C	2.2L I-4
D	2.0L I-4 SFI DOHC
D	1.8L I-4 SFI SOHC
D	1.8L I-4 MPI
D	2.2L I-4 Turbo
D	2.2L I-4 EFI
D	2.0L I-4 EFI
E	2.6L I-4
E	2.2L I-4 Turbo
E	3.7L I-6
E	8.0L V10 SFI
E	3.7L I-6 HD
F	3.7L I-6
F	3.5L V6 MPI
F	2.2L I-4 2BBL HO
F	2.0L I-4 SFI SOHC HP
F	1.6L I-4 Turbo
F	2.0L I-4 SFI SOHC
F	3.5L V6 SFI SOHC HO
G	3.5L V6 HO MPI

DIGIT 1 Country Of Origin
1 = USA
2 = Canada
4 = USA - MMMA
J = Japan
V = France

DIGIT 2 Make
E = Eagle
F = Eagle (Renault)
X = Eagle

DIGIT 3 Vehicle Type
1 = Passenger Car
3 = Passenger Car
M = Passenger Car

DIGIT 4 Engine
F = 2.2L I-4 EFI
J = 3.0L V6 MPI
Z = 2.5L I-4 TBI

DIGIT 4* Restraint System
A = Dual Airbags w/Manual Belts
B = Manual Seat Belts
C = Automatic Seat Belts
E = Driverside Airbag
H = Dual Airbags w/Manual Belts

DIGIT 5 Transmission
F = Automatic
H = Manual
P = 4 Spd Automatic/Column 2F
T = 4 Spd Automatic/Column AR4

DIGIT 5-6 Line/Series
A1 = Summit DL FWD
A1 = Summit DL 2D
A2 = Summit ES FWD
A2 = Summit ES 2D
A2 = Summit ES FWD
A2 = Summit DL FWD
A2 = Summit DL 4D w/1.5L
A3 = Summit LX FWD
A3 = Summit DL 4D w/1.8L
A3 = Summit ESi FWD
A3 = Summit ES 2D w/Sport Appearance Pkg
A4 = Summit ESi FWD
A4 = Summit ESi FWD
A4 = Summit ES FWD
A4 = Summit ES 4D w/1.8L
B2 = Summit DL Wagon FWD
B3 = Summit DL Wagon FWD
B4 = Summit LX Wagon FWD
B5 = Premier LX
B5 = Summit ES Wagon FWD
B6 = Premier ES Limited
B6 = Premier ES
C3 = Summit Wagon AWD
C4 = Summit Wagon AWD
C5 = Summit Wagon AWD
C5 = Summit Wagon AWD w/Custom Pkg
D5 = Vision ESi
D6 = Vision TSi
F3 = Talon DL FWD
F4 = Talon ES FWD
F5 = Talon TSi FWD
G5 = Talon TSi AWD
G6 = Talon TSi AWD
K2 = Talon FWD
K4 = Talon ESi FWD
K5 = Talon TSi Turbo FWD
L5 = Talon TSi Turbo AWD

DIGIT 5-6 Line/Series
S4 = Talon
S5 = Talon TSi 2WD
T6 = Talon TSi 4WD
U1 = Summit
U2 = Summit
U2 = Summit ES
U3 = Summit
U3 = Summit DL
U4 = Summit LX
U5 = Summit ES
U5 = Summit LX
V2 = Summit DL
V5 = Summit LX
W4 = Summit AWD
W5 = Summit AWD w/Custom Pkg

DIGIT 6-7 Carline/Body Type
45 = Medallion 4D Sedan
48 = Medallion 4D Wagon
55 = Premier 4D Sedan

DIGIT 7 Body Type
0 = 4D Wagon
1 = 2D Sedan
4 = 2D Hatchback
6 = 4D Sedan

DIGIT 8* Trim Level/Restraint
7 = ES/Manual Seat Belts
9 = LX/Manual Seat Belts
B = Deluxe Pkg/Manual Seat Belts
C = Luxury Pkg/Manual Seat Belts
E = Deluxe 7-Passenger Pkg/Manual Seat Belts
G = Deluxe Pkg/Automatic Seat Belts
H = Luxury Pkg/Automatic Seat Belts
J = Deluxe 7-Passenger Pkg/Automatic Seat Belts
K = Luxury 7-Passenger Pkg/Automatic Seat Belts

DIGIT 8* Engine
A = 1.5L I-4 MPI
B = 1.8L I-4 MPI
C = 1.8L I-4 MPI
D = 1.8L I-4 MPI
E = 2.0L I-4 MPI DOHC
F = 2.0L I-4 MPI DOHC T/C I/C
F = 3.5L V6 MPI 24V
G = 2.4L I-4 MPI SOHC
H = 2.5L I-4 FI
R = 2.0L I-4 MPI DOHC
T = 3.3L V6 MPI
U = 3.0L V6 MPI
U = 2.0L I-4 EFI Turbo
W = 2.4L I-4 MPI
X = 1.5L I-4 MPI
X = 2.0L I-4 SFI DOHC
Y = 1.6L I-4 MPI

DIGIT 9 CHECK DIGIT
0-9 or X

DIGIT 10 Model Year
J = 1988
K = 1989
L = 1990
M = 1991
N = 1992
P = 1993
R = 1994
S = 1995
T = 1996
V = 1997
W = 1998

DIGIT 11 Assembly Plant
2 = Maubeuge, France
5 = Haren, France
A = Bramalea, ON, Canada
E = Bloomington - Normal, IL, USA
F = Newark, DE, USA
H = Bramalea, ON, Canada
J = Nagoya 3, Japan
P = Nagoya 2, Japan
U = Mizushima, Japan
Y = Nagoya 1, Japan
Z = Okazaki, Japan

ARM0600000000019

Fig. 6 VIN Identification (Part 2 of 2). Eagle

ARM0600000000018

Fig. 6 VIN Identification (Part 1 of 2). Eagle

DIGIT 1-3 World Manufacturer Identifier

Code	Description
1F7	MSX International, USA
1FA	Ford Motor Company, USA
1ZV	AutoAlliance International
12V	Automotive Alliance International (USA)
2FA	Ford Motor Company of Canada
2FD	Ford Motor Co., Canada, Truck (Incomplete Vehicle)
3FA	Ford Motor Company, Mexico
3FA	Ford Motor Company of Mexico
KNJ	Kia Motors Inc., Korea

DIGIT 4 Restraint System

Code	Description
A	Driverside Airbag w/Driver & Rear Manual Belts & Front Pas
B	Manual Belts
C	Driverside Airbag w/Manual Belts
F	2nd Generation Dual Airbags w/Manual Belts
F	Active Belts, Dual Front Airbags
H	2nd Generation Dual Airbags & Side Airbags, Curtains or C
H	2nd Generation Front & Side Airbags w/Manual Belts
H	Dual Front & Front Side Airbags w/Manual Belts
K	2nd Generation Dual Front & Side Airbags w/Manual Belts
L	Dual Front Airbags w/Manual Belts
P	Front Automatic Belts & Rear Manual Belts
R	Driverside Airbag w/Front Automatic Belts & Rear Manual E
S	Dual Airbags w/Front Automatic Belts & Rear Manual Belts

DIGIT 5 Designation

Code	Description
P	Passenger Car - Ford Make
T	Passenger Car
T	Passenger Car - Ford Make

DIGIT 6-7 Carline/Series/Body Style

Code	Description
01	Fusion SE AWD 4D Sedan
01	EXP 2D Hatchback
02	Fusion SEL AWD 4D Sedan
04	Escort L 2D Hatchback
04	Escort Base 2D Hatchback
05	Festiva L 2D Hatchback
05	Fusion SE FWD 4D Sedan
05	Aspire SE 2D Hatchback
06	Escort GT 2D Hatchback
06	Aspire 2D Hatchback
06	Festiva L Plus 2D Hatchback
06	Festiva GL 2D Hatchback
06	Festiva L 2D Hatchback
06	Fusion SEL FWD 4D Sedan
06	Aspire 4D Hatchback
06	Escort GLX 4D Hatchback
07	Fusion SE FWD 4D Sedan
07	Aspire SE 2D Hatchback
07	Escort GT 2D Hatchback
07	Fusion SE 4D Sedan
07	Festiva SE 4D Sedan
08	Festiva GL 2D Hatchback
08	Fusion SEL 4D Sedan
08	Fusion SEL FWD 4D Sedan
09	Escort 4D Wagon
10	Escort L 4D Wagon
10	Mustang L 2D Coupe
10	Mustang 2D Coupe
10	Escort Pony 2D Hatchback
10	Escort LX 4D Sedan
10	Escort GL 4D Wagon
10	Escort Base 4D Sedan
11	Escort Base 2D Hatchback
11	Escort ZX2 2D Hatchback
11	Escort LX 4D Wagon
11	Escort GLX 4D Wagon
11	Escort LX 2D Hatchback
12	Mustang Ghia 2D Coupe
12	Mustang GLX 2D Coupe
12	Escort Ghia 2D Hatchback
12	Escort GT 2D Hatchback
13	Escort SE 4D Sedan
13	Escort L 4D Sedan
13	Escort L 4D Hatchback
13	Mustang GLX 2D Hatchback
13	Escort Base 4D Hatchback
13	Escort LX 4D Sedan
14	Mustang Ghia 2D Coupe
14	Escort LX 4D Hatchback
15	Escort L 2D Hatchback
15	Escort GL 2D Hatchback
15	Mustang 2D Hatchback
15	Escort SE 4D Wagon
16	Escort LX 4D Sedan
16	Mustang GLX 2D Hatchback
16	Mustang GL 2D Hatchback
16	Escort LX-E 4D Sedan
17	Escort Exp Luxury 2D Coupe
18	Tempo L 2D Coupe
18	Escort Exp Sport 2D Coupe
19	Tempo GL 2D Coupe
20	Fairmont Futura 2D Sedan
20	LTD Crown Victoria 2D Sedan
20	Tempo GLX 2D Coupe
20	Probe SE 2D Hatchback
20	Probe Base 2D Hatchback
20	Fairmont 2D Sedan
20	Escort Pony 2D Hatchback
21	Probe GL 2D Hatchback
21	Tempo L 4D Sedan
21	Escort GL 2D Hatchback
21	Escort LX 2D Hatchback
21	Fairmont 4D Sedan
21	Fairmont Futura 4D Sedan
22	Probe LX 2D Hatchback
22	Fairmont Futura 2D Coupe
22	Probe GT 2D Hatchback
23	Tempo GL 4D Sedan
23	Tempo GLX 4D Sedan
23	Five Hundred 4D Sedan SE FWD
23	Fairmont 4D Wagon
23	Escort GT 2D Hatchback
24	Tempo LX 4D Sedan
24	Taurus SEL FWD 4D Sedan
25	Escort LX 4D Sedan
25	Five Hundred 4D Sedan Limited FWD
25	Escort GLX 4D Hatchback
25	Taurus Limited FWD 4D Sedan
26	Granada 4D Sedan
26	Five Hundred 4D Sedan SE AWD
26	Granada 4D Wagon
26	Mustang 2D Coupe
27	Escort Pony 2D Hatchback
27	Mustang L 2D Coupe
27	Five Hundred 4D Sedan Limited AWD
27	Mustang LX 2D Convertible
27	Taurus SEL AWD 4D Sedan
27	Mustang GT 2D Convertible
27	Mustang 2D Convertible
28	Granada 2D Sedan
28	Five Hundred 4D Sedan SEL AWD
28	Mustang 2D Hatchback
28	Mustang L 2D Hatchback
28	Mustang LX 2D Hatchback
28	Mustang SVO 2D Hatchback
28	Taurus Limited AWD 4D Sedan
28	Escort GLX 4D Wagon
28	Escort LX 2D Hatchback
29	Taurus 4D Sedan
30	Tempo L 2D Coupe
30	Focus SVT 4D Hatchback
30	Taurus 4D Wagon
31	Tempo GL 2D Coupe
31	Focus ZX3 2D Hatchback
31	Escort Pony 2D Hatchback
31	Escort Base 2D Hatchback
31	Escort L 2D Hatchback
32	Escort GL 2D Hatchback
32	Mustang 2D Hatchback
32	LTD 2D Sedan
32	Escort LX 4D Sedan
32	Tempo LX 2D Coupe
33	Escort GT 2D Hatchback
33	Mustang GLX 2D Hatchback
33	Tempo Sport GL 2D Coupe
33	Focus LX 4D Sedan
33	LTD 4D Sedan
33	Tempo GLS 2D Coupe
34	Escort L 4D Wagon
34	Focus SE 4D Sedan
34	Focus ZX4 4D Sedan
34	LTD Crown Victoria 2D Sedan
35	Tempo AWD 2D Coupe
35	Fairmont Futura 2D Sedan
35	Focus ZTW 4D Wagon
35	Escort LX 4D Wagon
35	Escort GL 4D Wagon
36	LTD Crown Victoria 4D Sedan
36	Escort Base 4D Hatchback
36	Escort L 4D Hatchback
36	Escort L 4D Wagon
36	Fairmont Futura 4D Sedan
36	Tempo GL 4D Sedan
36	Focus ZTW 4D Wagon
36	Focus SE 4D Sedan
37	Focus GL 4D Wagon
37	Escort GL 4D Hatchback
37	Escort LX 4D Hatchback
37	Fairmont Futura 2D Coupe
37	Focus ZX5 4D Hatchback
37	LTD S 4D Sedan
37	LTD S 4D Wagon
38	Tempo LX 4D Sedan
38	LTD 4D Wagon
38	Focus ZTS 4D Sedan
38	Tempo GLS 4D Sedan
38	Escort ST 4D Sedan
39	Focus SVT 2D Hatchback
39	LTD 4D Sedan
39	LTD 4D Squire Wagon
39	Tempo AWD 4D Sedan
40	LTD 4D Wagon
40	Mustang Base 2D Coupe
40	Mustang L 2D Coupe
41	Mustang LX 2D Coupe
42	Thunderbird 2D Coupe
42	Mustang GTS 2D Coupe
42	Mustang GT 2D Coupe
42	Mustang Cobra 2D Hatchback
42	Mustang GT 2D Hatchback
43	LTD Crown Victoria 2D Sedan
44	LTD Crown Victoria 4D Sedan
44	Mustang 2D Hatchback
44	Mustang GT 2D Hatchback
44	Mustang LX Limited Edition 2D Convertible
44	LTD Crown Victoria Country Squire 4D Wagon
45	Mustang Cobra 2D Hatchback
45	Mustang GT 2D Coupe
46	Thunderbird 2D Coupe
46	Mustang Cobra 2D Convertible
47	Mustang Cobra 2D Coupe
48	Mustang Cobra 2D Coupe
49	Mustang Cobra 2D Convertible
50	Taurus L 4D Sedan
51	Taurus MT5 4D Sedan
51	Taurus G 4D Sedan
52	Taurus LX 4D Sedan
52	Taurus GL 2D Sedan
52	Taurus GL 4D Sedan
53	Taurus SE 4D Sedan
53	Taurus SE Comfort 4D Sedan
53	Taurus GT 4D Sedan
54	Taurus SE 4D Sedan - 2V
54	Taurus SE 4D Sedan - 4V
55	Taurus SHO 4D Sedan
55	Taurus L 4D Wagon
55	Taurus SES 4D Sedan
56	Taurus SEL 4D Sedan
56	Taurus MT5 Wagon
57	Taurus GL 4D Wagon
57	Taurus SE 4D Wagon
58	Taurus LX 4D Wagon
58	Taurus SE 4D Wagon
58	Taurus SE Comfort 4D Wagon
59	Taurus SEL 4D Wagon
60	Thunderbird 2D Convertible
60	Thunderbird 2D Coupe
60	Thunderbird 2D Sport Coupe
60	Thunderbird Base 2D Coupe
61	Thunderbird Sport 2D Coupe
62	Thunderbird 2D Convertible
62	Thunderbird LX 2D Coupe
63	Thunderbird Pacific Coast Roadster
64	Thunderbird 2D Convertible Neiman Marcus
64	Thunderbird 2D Coupe
64	Thunderbird Super Coupe
64	Thunderbird Turbo 2D Coupe
65	Contour Base 4D Sedan
65	Contour Base 4D Sedan - Early Production
65	Contour GL 4D Sedan
65	Contour GL 4D Sedan - Early Production
65	Contour LX 4D Sedan
66	Contour SE 4D Sedan
66	Contour Sport 4D Sedan
66	Contour LX 4D Sedan
66	Contour LX 4D Sedan - Early Production
67	Contour SE V6 4D Sedan - Early Production
67	Contour SE 4D Sedan
68	Contour SVT 4D Sedan
69	50th Anniversary Feature Car
70	Crown Victoria 4D Sedan LWB - Fleet
70	LTD Crown Victoria 2D Coupe
71	Crown Victoria 4D Sedan
71	LTD Crown Victoria LX 2D Coupe
72	Crown Victoria 4D Sedan w/Police Interceptor Package
72	Crown Victoria 4D Sedan - Fleet
72	LTD Crown Victoria Base 4D Sedan
73	Crown Victoria S 4D Sedan
73	LTD Crown Victoria Base 4D Sedan
74	LTD Crown Victoria LX 4D Sedan
74	Crown Victoria 4D Sedan
75	Crown Victoria Touring 4D Sedan
76	LTD Crown Victoria Base 4D Wagon
77	LTD Crown Victoria LX 4D Wagon
78	LTD Crown Victoria Country Squire 4D Wagon
79	LTD Crown Victoria Country Squire LX 4D Wagon
80	Mustang GT 2D Coupe
82	Mustang Base 2D Coupe
84	Mustang Cobra 2D Convertible
85	Mustang GT 2D Coupe
88	Mustang Shelby GT500 2D Coupe

Fig. 7   VIN Identification (Part 1 of 4). Ford

ARM070000000175

Fig. 7   VIN Identification (Part 2 of 4). Ford

ARM070000000176

Fig. 7 VIN Identification (Part 4 of 4). Ford

DIGIT 8	Engine
R	3.8L V8 EFI S/C
R	4.6L V8 EFI DOHC Ram Air
S	2.3L I-4 CFI HSC+
S	2.3L I-4 EFI HSO
S	3.0L V6 EFI DOHC
S	5.4L V8 DOHC S/C 4-Valve
T	5.4L V8 SC DOHC
T	5.0L V8 EFI HO
T	2.3L I-4 EFI T/C I/C
U	3.0L V6 EFI
V	4.6L V8 EFI FFV SOHC
V	4.6L V8 EFI DOHC
W	2.3L I-4 EFI SOHC T/C
W	2.3L I-4 EFI SOHC Turbo
W	3.5L V6 DOHC SFI
W	4.6L V8 EFI SOHC
X	2.3L I-4 EFI SOHC
X	4.6L V6 EFI SOHC
X	2.3L I-4 EFI HSC
Y	3.3L I-4 1BBL
Y	3.0L V6 EFI DOHC SHO
Y	4.6L V8 EFI DOHC SC
Z	2.0L I-4 EFI DOHC GFP
Z	2.3L I-4 DOHC
Z	2.3L I-4 EFI DOHC
Z	2.3L I-4 DOHC PZEV

DIGIT 11	Assembly Plant
R	Hermosillo, Mexico
R	San Jose, CA, USA
T	AAI: Flat Rock, MI
T	Edison, NJ, USA
U	Louisville, KY, USA
W	Wayne, MI, USA
X	St. Thomas, ON, Canada
Y	Wixom, MI, USA
Z	St. Louis, MO, USA

Fig. 7 VIN Identification (Part 4 of 4). Ford

ARM07000000178

Fig. 7 VIN Identification (Part 3 of 4). Ford

DIGIT 6-7	Carline/Series/Body Style
89	Mustang Shelby GT500 2D Convertible
90	GT
90	Escort Pony 2D Hatchback
91	Escort LX 2D Hatchback
93	Escort GT 2D Hatchback
95	Escort LX 4D Hatchback
98	Escort LX 4D Wagon

DIGIT 8	Engine
1	3.0L V6 EFI DOHC
1	3.0L V6 Duratec
2	3.0L V6 SFI FFV - Methanol
2	3.0L V6 SFI FFV - Ethanol
2	3.0L V6 EFI Flex Fuel
2	1.6L I-4 2BBL
2	3.0L V6 EFI FFV
3	3.8L V6 CFI
3	3.8L V6 2BBL
3	2.0L I-4 SFI DOHC
3	2.0L I-4 SFI HO
4	3.8L V6 EFI
4	1.6L I-4 2BBL HO
5	2.0L I-4 SFI HO
5	1.6L I-4 EFI
5	3.9L V6 EFI
6	4.6L V8 EFI SOHC
6	1.6L I-4 1BBL OHC LPG
8	1.6L I-4 EFI Tbo
8	1.6L I-4 EFI Turbo
9	1.8L I-4 EFI DOHC
9	4.6L V8 EFI SOHC CNG
9	1.9L I-4 CFI
A	1.9L I-4 2BBL
A	3.9L V8 EFI DOHC
A	2.0L I-4 EFI DOHC
A	2.3L I-4 1BBL
A	2.3L I-4 1BBL OHC
A	2.3L I-4 2BBL
B	2.5L V6 EFI DOHC
B	3.3L I-6 1BBL
B	3.3L I-6 1BBL
C	2.2L I-4 EFI
C	3.8L V6 EFI S/C
C	2.5L I-4 CFI HSC
D	5.0L V8 EFI SHP
D	4.2L V8 2BBL
E	5.0L V8 EFI
F	5.0L V8 EFI HO
F	5.0L V8 2BBL
F	5.0L V8 4BBL
G	2.5L V6 EFI DOHC HO
G	5.8L V8 EFI 2BBL HO
H	1.3L I-4 EFI
H	1.3L I-4 EFI SOHC
H	2.0L I-4 FI Dsl
H	4.6L V8 SOHC 3-Valve
J	1.9L I-4 EFI
J	1.9L I-4 EFI HO
K	1.3L I-4 2BBL
L	2.2L I-4 EFI T/C I/C
L	2.5L V6 EFI DOHC
M	5.0L V8 EFI HO
M	2.3L I-4 EFI
N	2.0L I-4 DOHC
N	2.5L I-4 EFI
N	3.4L V8 EFI DOHC SHO
N	4.0L V6 SOHC 2-Valve
N	2.0L I-4 DOHC PZEV
P	2.0L I-4 SPI
R	3.2L V6 EFI DOHC SHO
R	2.3L I-4 1BBL HSC

DIGIT 10	Model Year
1	2001
2	2002
3	2003
4	2004
5	2005
6	2006
7	2007
8	2008
B	1981
C	1982
D	1983
E	1984
F	1985
G	1986
H	1987
J	1988
K	1989
L	1990
M	1991
N	1992
P	1993
R	1994
S	1995
T	1996
V	1997
W	1998
X	1999
Y	2000

DIGIT 11	Assembly Plant
5	AAI - Flat Rock, MI, USA
5	AAI: Flat Rock, MI
6	Mazda-Kia, Korea
A	Atlanta, GA, USA
B	Oakville, ON, Canada
F	Dearborn, MI, USA
G	Chicago, IL, USA
G	Chicago, Illinois
G	Chicago, Illinois, USA
H	Lorain, OH, USA
K	Kansas City, MO, USA
M	Cuautitlan, Mexico
O	Detroit Empowerment Zone; Detroit, MI, USA

Fig. 7 VIN Identification (Part 3 of 4). Ford

ARM07000000177

Fig. 8 VIN Identification. Geo

DIGIT 1 — Country Of Origin
1 = United States
J = Japan

DIGIT 1-3 — World Manufacturer Identifier
2C1 = CAMI - GM of Canada, Suzuki J.V.
JG1 = Chevrolet Passenger Car - Built by Suzuki

DIGIT 2 — Manufacturer
8 = Isuzu
Y = Nummi

DIGIT 3 — Make
1 = Chevrolet

DIGIT 4-5 — Carline/Series
MR = Metro Base
MR = Metro LSi
MS = Metro Base
MS = Metro XFi
RF = Storm
RT = Storm GSi
SK = Prizm Base
SK = Prizm Base & LSi
SL = Prizm GSi

DIGIT 6 — Body Type
2 = 2D Hatchback/Liftback
3 = 2D Convertible
4 = 2D Station Wagon
5 = 4D Sedan
6 = 4D Hatchback/Liftback
7 = 4D Liftback

DIGIT 7 — Restraint System
1 = Manual Belts
2 = Dual Front Airbags w/Manual Belts
3 = Driverside Airbag w/Manual Belts
4 = Passive Automatic Belts

DIGIT 8 — Engine
5 = 1.6L I-4 MPI
6 = 1.6L I-4 MPI
6 = 1.6L I-4 EFI DOHC
6 = 1.0L I-3 EFI SOHC
8 = 1.8L I-4 EFI DOHC
8 = 1.8L I-4 MPI
9 = 1.3L I-4 EFI SOHC

DIGIT 9 — CHECK DIGIT
0-9 or X

DIGIT 10 — Model Year
K = 1989
L = 1990
M = 1991
N = 1992
P = 1993
R = 1994
S = 1995
T = 1996
V = 1997

DIGIT 11 — Assembly Plant
6 = Ingersoll, ON, Canada
7 = Fujisawa, Japan
K = Kosai, Japan
W = Iwata, Japan
Z = Fremont, USA

ARM060000000023

Fig. 9 VIN Identification. Lincoln

DIGIT 1-3 — World Manufacturer Identifier
1L1 = Ford Motor Company, USA - Lincoln, Limousine
1LJ = Ford Motor Company, USA - Lincoln, Hearse
1LN = Ford Motor Company, USA - Lincoln
1MR = Ford Motor Company, USA - Continental
3LN = Ford Motor Company, Mexico - Lincoln

DIGIT 4 — Restraint System
B = Manual Belts
C = Driverside Airbag w/Manual Belts
F = 2nd Generation Dual Airbags w/Manual Belts
F = 2nd Generation Dual Front Airbags w/Manual Belts
H = 2nd Generation Front & Side Airbags w/Manual Belts
L = Dual Front Airbags w/Manual Belts

DIGIT 5 — Designation
L = Passenger Car - Lincoln Make
M = Passenger Car - Lincoln Make
P = Passenger Car

DIGIT 6-7 — Carline/Body Style
26 = MKZ 4D Sedan FWD
26 = Zephyr 4D Sedan
28 = MKZ 4D Sedan AWD
81 = Town Car Signature 4D Sedan
81 = Town Car Executive 4D Sedan
81 = Town Car 4D Sedan
82 = Town Car Signature 4D Sedan
82 = Town Car Signature Limited 4D Sedan
83 = Town Car Cartier 4D Sedan
83 = Town Car Designer Series 4D Sedan
83 = Town Car Ultimate 4D Sedan
84 = Town Car Executive L 4D Sedan
84 = Town Car Signature Special Edition 4D Sedan
85 = Town Car Signature Ultimate L 4D Sedan
85 = Town Car Cartier L 4D Sedan
85 = Town Car Signature L 4D Sedan
86 = LS V6
87 = LS V8
88 = Town Car Executive 4D Sedan
91 = Mark VII Base 2D Coupe
91 = Mark VIII Base 2D Coupe
92 = Mark VIII Bill Blass Designer 2D Coupe
92 = Mark VIII LSC 2D Coupe
93 = Town Car 2D Coupe
93 = Mark VII LSC 2D Coupe
94 = Town Car LSC 2D Sedan
95 = Mark VI 4D Sedan
96 = Mark VI 2D Coupe
96 = Town Car 4D Sedan
97 = Continental 4D Sedan
98 = Continental Givenchy Designer 4D Sedan
98 = Mark VI 2D Coupe
98 = Mark VII 2D Coupe
98 = Continental Signature 4D Sedan
99 = Mark VI 4D Sedan

DIGIT 8 — Engine
1 = 3.0L V6 SFI DOHC
3 = 3.8L V6 EFI
4 = 3.8L V6 EFI
A = 3.9L V8 EFI DOHC
E = 5.0L V8 EFI HO
F = 5.0L V8 EFI
L = 2.4L I-6 FI TDsl
M = 5.0L V8 SFI HO
S = 3.0L V6 EFI DOHC
T = 3.5L V6 SFI DOHC
V = 4.6L V8 EFI FFV
V = 4.6L V8 EFI DOHC
W = 4.6L V8 EFI SOHC

DIGIT 10 — Model Year
1 = 2001
2 = 2002
3 = 2003
4 = 2004
5 = 2005
6 = 2006
7 = 2007
B = 1981
C = 1982
D = 1983
E = 1984
F = 1985
G = 1986
H = 1987
J = 1988
K = 1989
L = 1990
M = 1991
N = 1992
P = 1993
R = 1994
S = 1995
T = 1996
V = 1997
W = 1998
X = 1999
Y = 2000

DIGIT 11 — Assembly Plant
R = Hermosillo, Mexico
Y = Wixom, MI, USA

ARM070000000179

DIGIT 1-3 World Manufacturer Identifier

1ME	Ford Motor Company, USA - Mercury
1ZW	Auto Alliance International, Inc
2ME	Ford Motor Company of Canada - Mercury
3MA	Ford Motor Company of Mexico - Mercury
3ME	Ford Motor Company of Mexico - Mercury
6MP	Ford Motor Company of Australia, Ltd.
WF1	Merkur

DIGIT 4 Restraint System

A	Driverside Airbag w/Manual Driver & Rear Belts & Automati
B	Manual Belts
C	Driverside Airbag w/Manual Belts
F	2nd Generation Dual Front Airbags w/Manual Belts
H	2nd Generation Dual Front & Front Side Airbags w/Manual Belts
H	2nd Generation Dual Front Airbags & Side Airbags, Curtains or C
L	Dual Front Airbags w/Manual Belts
P	Automatic Front Belts & Manual Rear Belts
R	Driverside Airbag w/Automatic Front Belts & Manual Rear E
S	Dual Front Airbags w/Automatic Front Belts and Manual Re

DIGIT 5 Designation

M	Passenger Car - Mercury Make
P	Ford Make
P	Passenger Car
T	Ford Import

DIGIT 6-7 Carline/Body Style

01	Milan Base AWD 4D Sedan
01	Capri Base 2D Convertible
02	Milan Premier AWD 4D Sedan
03	Capri XR2 2D Convertible
07	Milan Base 4D Sedan
07	Milan Base FWD 4D Sedan
08	Milan Premier 4D Sedan
08	Milan Premier FWD 4D Sedan
10	Tracer Base 4D Sedan
10	Tracer GS 4D Sedan
11	Tracer Base 2D Hatchback
12	Tracer Base 4D Hatchback
13	Tracer Base 4D Wagon
13	Tracer GS 4D Wagon
14	Tracer LS 4D Sedan
15	Tracer LS 4D Wagon
15	Tracer LTS 4D Sedan
20	Lynx L 2D Hatchback
21	Lynx GS 2D Hatchback
23	Lynx XR3 2D Hatchback
25	Lynx GS 4D Sedan
28	Lynx GS 4D Wagon
31	Topaz GS 2D Coupe
33	Topaz GS Sport 2D Coupe
33	Topaz XR5 2D Coupe
36	Topaz GS 4D Sedan
37	Topaz LS 4D Sedan
38	Topaz LTS 4D Sedan
38	Topaz GS Sport 4D Sedan
40	Montego 4D Sedan Luxury FWD
40	Sable Base FWD 4D Sedan
41	Sable Base AWD 4D Sedan
41	Montego 4D Sedan Luxury AWD
42	Montego 4D Sedan Premier FWD
42	Sable Premier FWD 4D Sedan
43	Montego 4D Sedan Premier AWD
43	Sable Premier AWD 4D Sedan
50	Sable LS 4D Sedan
51	Sable GS 4D Sedan
51	Lynx L 2D Hatchback
51	LN7 2D Hatchback
52	Lynx GS 2D Hatchback
53	Lynx XR3 2D Hatchback
53	Sable LS Premium 4D Sedan
53	Sable LS 4D Sedan
54	Lynx L 2D Hatchback
54	Lynx Base 2D Hatchback
55	Lynx GS 2D Hatchback
55	Sable LS Premium 4D Sedan
55	Sable GS 4D Wagon
55	Sable LS 4D Sedan
57	Lynx RS 2D Hatchback
58	Sable LS Premium 4D Wagon
58	Sable LS 4D Wagon
58	Sable GS 4D Wagon
58	Lynx LS 2D Hatchback
58	Lynx L 4D Wagon
59	Lynx GS 4D Wagon
59	Sable LS 4D Wagon
59	Sable LS Premium 4D Wagon
60	Lynx L 4D Wagon
60	Cougar LS 2D Coupe
60	Cougar I-4 2D Coupe
61	Lynx GS 4D Wagon
61	LN7 2D Hatchback
62	Cougar V6 2D Coupe
62	Cougar S 2D Coupe
62	Cougar XR-7 2D Coupe
63	Cougar V6 2D Coupe
63	Lynx L 4D Hatchback
63	Lynx LS 4D Sedan
64	Lynx GS 4D Sedan
64	Lynx 4D Hatchback
65	Lynx 4D Wagon
65	Lynx Base 4D Hatchback
65	Mystique Base 4D Sedan
65	Mystique GS 4D Sedan
65	Lynx L 4D Hatchback
66	Mystique LS 4D Sedan
66	Lynx L 4D Liftgate
66	Lynx GS 4D Hatchback
67	Capri 2D Hatchback
68	Lynx LTS 4D Hatchback
68	Capri GS 2D Hatchback
70	Zephyr 2D Sedan
71	Zephyr 4D Sedan
72	Topaz GS 2D Coupe
72	Grand Marquis LS 2D Sedan
72	Zephyr Z-7 2D Sedan
73	Zephyr 4D Wagon
73	Topaz LS 2D Coupe
74	Grand Marquis GS 4D Sedan
75	Topaz XRS 2D Coupe
75	Grand Marquis LSE 4D Sedan
75	Grand Marquis LS 4D Sedan
75	Grand Marquis Marauder 4D Sedan
76	Cougar GS 2D Coupe
76	Topaz LS 4D Sedan
77	Cougar 4D Sedan
78	Grand Marquis Colony Park GS 4D Wagon
78	Cougar GS 4D Wagon
79	Capri 2D Hatchback
79	Grand Marquis Colony Park LS 4D Wagon
81	Marquis 4D Sedan
82	Marquis Brougham 2D Sedan
83	Grand Marquis Brougham 4D Sedan
84	Grand Marquis 2D Sedan
85	Grand Marquis 4D Sedan
86	Zephyr 4D Sedan
87	Sable 4D Sedan
87	Zephyr Z 2D Coupe
87	Marquis 4D Wagon
87	Lynx GS 2D Hatchback
87	Zephyr Z-7 2D Sedan

Fig. 10 VIN Identification (Part 1 of 2). Mercury

DIGIT 6-7 Carline/Body Style

88	Sable 4D Wagon
88	Marquis Colony Park 4D Wagon
89	Marquis 4D Sedan
90	Marquis 4D Wagon
90	Cougar XR-7 2D Coupe
92	Cougar 2D Coupe
93	Grand Marquis 2D Sedan
94	Grand Marquis Colony Park 4D Wagon
95	Grand Marquis 4D Sedan

DIGIT 8 Engine

1	3.0L V6 EFI DOHC
1	3.0L V6 Duratec
2	3.0L V6 Duratec
2	3.0L V6 EFI FFV
2	1.6L I-4 2BBL
2	3.8L V6 2BBL
3	2.0L I-4 EFI DOHC
3	3.8L V6 EFI
4	1.6L I-4 2BBL HO
4	3.8L V6 EFI
5	1.6L I-4 EFI
6	1.6L I-4 EFI Turbo
6	4.6L V8 EFI SOHC
8	2.3L I-4 1BBL LPG
8	1.8L I-4 EFI DOHC
9	1.9L I-4 EFI
9	1.9L I-4 2BBL
A	2.3L I-4 2BBL
A	3.3L I-4 1BBL SOHC
B	3.3L I-6 1BBL
D	2.5L I-4 EFI HSC
D	4.2L V8 1BBL
D	4.2L V8 2BBL
F	5.0L V8 EFI
F	5.0L V8 4BBL HO
F	5.0L V8 2BBL
G	5.8L V8 2BBL HO
G	2.5L V6 EFI DOHC HO
H	2.0L I-4 Dsl
J	1.9L I-4 EFI HO
L	1.9L I-4 EFI
L	2.5L V6 EFI DOHC
M	4.2L V8 EFI HO
M	5.0L V8 EFI HO
P	2.0L I-4 SPI
R	3.8L V6 EFI S/C
R	2.3L I-4 1BBL HSC
S	2.3L I-4 EFI HSO
S	3.0L V6 EFI DOHC
T	5.0L V8 EFI HO
U	3.0L V6 EFI
V	2.9L V6 EFI
V	4.6L V8 EFI DOHC
V	4.6L V8 FFV SOHC
W	2.3L I-4 EFI T/C I/C
W	2.3L I-4 EFI Turbo
W	3.5L V6 EFI
W	4.6L V8 EFI
W	4.6L V8 EFI SOHC
X	3.3L I-6 1BBL
X	2.3L I-4 EFI HSC
Z	1.6L I-4 EFI DOHC
Z	2.3L I4 EFI DOHC

DIGIT 10 Model Year

1	2001
2	2002
3	2003
4	2004
5	2005
6	2006
7	2007
8	2008
B	1981
C	1982
D	1983
E	1984
F	1985
G	1986
H	1987
J	1988
K	1989
L	1990
M	1991
N	1992
P	1993
R	1994
S	1995
T	1996
V	1997
W	1998
X	1999
Y	2000

DIGIT 11 Assembly Plant

5	AAI: Flat Rock, MI, USA
8	Broadmeadows: Campbellfield, Australia
A	Atlanta, GA, USA
B	Oakville, ON, Canada
F	Dearborn, MI, USA
G	Chicago, IL, USA
G	Chicago, Illinois
H	Lorain, OH, USA
K	Kansas City, MO, USA
M	Cuautitlan, Mexico
M	Rheine, Germany
R	Hermosillo, Mexico
R	San Jose, CA, USA
T	Edison, NJ, USA
T	Metuchen, NJ, USA
W	Wayne, MI, USA
X	St. Thomas, ON, Canada
Z	St. Louis, MO, USA

Fig. 10 VIN Identification (Part 2 of 2). Mercury

ARM070000000180

ARM070000000181

DIGIT 10 — Model Year

Code	Year
T	1996
V	1997
W	1998
X	1999
Y	2000

DIGIT 11 — Assembly Plant

Code	Plant
1	Wentzville, MO, USA
2	Ste. Therese, PQ, Canada
4	Orion, MI, USA
6	Oklahoma City, OK, USA
9	Oshawa #1, ON, Canada
B	Detroit, MI, USA
B	Lansing, MI, USA
C	Doraville, GA, USA
D	Linden, NJ, USA
E	Linden, NJ, USA
F	Fairfax II, KS, USA
G	Framingham, MA, USA
H	Flint, MI, USA
K	Leeds, MO, USA
K	Linden, NJ, USA
M	Lansing, MI, USA
P	Pontiac, MI, USA
R	Arlington, TX, USA
S	Ramos Arizpe, Mexico
U	Hamtramck, MI, USA
W	Willow Run, MI, USA
X	Fairfax, KS, USA
Y	Wilmington, DE, USA

DIGIT 8 — Engine

Code	Engine
0	1.8L I-4 TBI
1	2.0L I-4 EFI
1	3.8L V6 MPI
3	2.3L I-4 MPI
3	3.8L V6 MPI
4	2.2L I-4 MPI
4	4.1L V6 4BBL
5	2.5L I-4 2BBL
7	5.7L V8 TBI
8	4.3L V8 2BBL
9	5.0L V8 4BBL
9	3.8L V6 2BBL
A	2.3L I-4 HO Quad 4
B	2.0L I-4 EFI
B	3.8L V6 SFI
C	3.8L V6 MPI
C	4.0L V8 SFI
D	2.3L I-4 Quad 4
D	3.0L V6 2BBL
E	3.4L V6 SFI
E	5.0L V8 TBI
F	4.3L V8 2BBL
F	2.0L I-4 MPI DOHC
G	1.8L I-4 2BBL
H	3.5L V6 MPI
H	5.0L V8 4BBL
J	3.1L V6 MPI
K	2.0L I-4 EFI
K	3.8L V6 MPI S/C
L	3.0L V6 MPI
L	3.8L V6 MPI
M	3.1L V6 MPI
M	2.0L I-4 EFI
N	3.3L V6 MPI
N	5.7L V8 Dsl
P	2.0L I-4 EFI
R	2.5L I-4 TBI
T	4.3L V6 Dsl
T	3.1L V6 MPI
T	2.4L I-4 MPI
U	2.5L I-4 TBI
W	4.3L V6 Dsl
W	2.8L V6 MPI
X	3.4L V6 MPI
X	2.8L V6 2BBL
Y	5.0L V8 4BBL
Z	2.8L V6 2BBL HO

DIGIT 9 — CHECK DIGIT

= 0-9 or X

DIGIT 10 — Model Year

Code	Year
1	2001
2	2002
3	2003
4	2004
B	1981
C	1982
D	1983
E	1984
F	1985
G	1986
H	1987
J	1988
K	1989
L	1990
M	1991
N	1992
P	1993
R	1994
S	1995

Fig. 11 VIN Identification (Part 2 of 2). Oldsmobile

ARM060000000028

DIGIT 1 — Country Of Origin

Code	Country
1	USA
2	Canada
3	Mexico

DIGIT 2 — Manufacturer

Code	Manufacturer
G	General Motors

DIGIT 3 — Make

Code	Make
3	Oldsmobile

DIGIT 4 — Restraint System

Code	System
A	Manual Belts

DIGIT 4-5 — Carline/Series

Code	Carline/Series
6K	Cutlass Salon 442
AG	Cutlass Ciera S
AJ	Cutlass Ciera SL
AJ	Cutlass Ciera Base
AJ	Cutlass Ciera LS
AJ	Cutlass Ciera S
AJ	Cutlass Ciera S Cruiser Wagon
AL	Cutlass Ciera Base
AL	Cutlass Ciera S
AM	Cutlass Ciera SL
AM	Cutlass Ciera Brougham
AS	Cutlass Ciera International
BN	Eighty Eight Royale
BP	Eighty Eight Custom Cruiser
BY	Eighty Eight Brougham
CV	Ninety Eight Regency Sedan
CW	Ninety Eight Touring Sedan
CW	Ninety Eight Regency Elite
CX	Ninety Eight Regency
CX	Ninety Eight Regency Elite
EV	Toronado Trofeo
EZ	Toronado
GK	Cutlass Salon Coupe
GM	Cutlass Supreme Brougham RWD
GR	Cutlass Supreme RWD
GR	Aurora
GS	Aurora
HC	Eighty Eight Anniversary Edition
HC	Regency
HN	Eighty Eight Base
HN	Eighty Eight LS
HY	Eighty Eight Royale
HY	Eighty Eight Royale LSS
HY	Eighty Eight LSS
HY	Eighty Eight Royale Brougham
HY	Eighty Eight Royale LS
JC	Firenza Base
JC	Firenza S
JD	Firenza GT
JD	Firenza LC
JD	Firenza LX
JD	Firenza SX
JD	Firenza GL
NB	Cutlass GL
NB	Calais
NF	Cutlass Calais S
NF	Calais
NF	Alero GLS
NF	Achieva SL
NG	Achieva GLS
NK	Alero GX
NK	Cutlass Calais International
NL	Achieva
NL	Achieva S
NL	Alero GL
NT	Cutlass Calais Supreme
NT	Cutlass Calais SL

DIGIT 4-5 — Carline/Series

Code	Carline/Series
NT	Calais Supreme
WH	Cutlass Supreme Base
WH	Cutlass Supreme S
WH	Cutlass Supreme SL
WH	Intrigue
WR	Intrigue GX
WR	Cutlass Supreme International
WS	Cutlass Supreme SL
WS	Intrigue GL
WT	Cutlass Supreme Convertible
WX	Intrigue GLS

DIGIT 5 — Carline

Code	Carline
B	Omega
C	Firenza
D	Firenza LX
D	Firenza SX
D	Firenza Brougham
E	Omega Brougham
G	Ninety Eight Regency
G	Cutlass Ciera
G	Cutlass
H	Ninety Eight Brougham
H	Cutlass Cruiser
J	Cutlass Ciera LS
K	Cutlass Calais
L	Delta Eighty Eight
L	Cutlass Ciera Brougham
M	Ninety Eight Brougham
M	Cutlass Supreme Brougham
N	Delta Eighty Eight Royale
P	Delta Eighty Eight Custom Cruiser
R	Eighty Eight Royale
R	Cutlass LS
V	Ninety Eight Luxury
V	Delta Eighty Eight Royale Brougham LS
W	Ninety Eight Regency Brougham
X	Ninety Eight Regency
Y	Delta Eighty Eight Royale
Z	Toronado Brougham

DIGIT 6-7 — Body Type

Code	Body Type
11	2D Notchback Sedan
19	4D Sedan
27	2D Coupe
35	4D 2-Seat Wagon
37	2D Notchback Special Coupe
47	2D Notchback Special Coupe
47	2D Coupe
57	2D Notchback Sedan
69	4D Sedan
69	4D Notchback Sedan
77	2D Coupe

DIGIT 6 — Body Type

Code	Body Type
1	2D Sedan
1	2D Coupe/Sedan
2	2D Coupe
3	2D Hatchback
5	2D Convertible
6	4D Sedan
8	4D Station Wagon

DIGIT 7 — Restraint System

Code	System
1	Manual Belts
2	Dual Front Airbags w/Manual Belts
3	Driverside Airbag w/Manual Belts
4	Automatic Belts
5	Dual Front & Side Airbags w/Manual Belts
5	Driverside Airbag w/Automatic Belts
6	Dual Front & Side Airbags, Auto Passenger Sensor w/Manu

Fig. 11 VIN Identification (Part 1 of 2). Oldsmobile

ARM060000000027

ARM0600000000030

DIGIT 1 — Country Of Origin
- 1 = USA
- 2 = Canada
- 3 = Mexico
- 4 = USA - MMMA
- J = Japan

DIGIT 2 — Manufacturer
- P = Plymouth

DIGIT 3 — Vehicle Type
- 3 = Passenger Car
- 4 = Multi-Purpose Passenger Vehicle

DIGIT 4 — Restraint
- A = Driverside Airbag w/Automatic Passenger Belt
- A = Dual Front & Side Airbags w/Manual Belts
- B = Driverside Airbag w/Manual Belts
- B = Manual Belts
- B = Manual Seat Belts
- C = Automatic Belts
- C = Automatic Seat Belts
- E = Driverside Airbag
- H = Dual Airbags w/Manual Belts
- H = Dual Airbags w/Manual Belts
- P = Manual Seat Belts
- X = Driverside Airbag w/Manual Belts
- Y = Driverside Airbag w/Automatic Passenger Belt

DIGIT 4* — GVWR/Brake System
- E = 3001-4000 Lbs. Hydraulic
- F = 4001-5000 Lbs. Hydraulic Brakes

DIGIT 5 — Carline
- A = Colt
- B = Gran Fury Salon
- C = Conquest
- D = Sapporo
- E = Champ
- G = Colt
- G = Colt Vista
- J = Caravelle
- K = Reliant
- L = Horizon
- M = Horizon
- P = Reliant

DIGIT 5-6 — Carline
- A4 = Acclaim
- A5 = Acclaim LE
- A7 = Acclaim LX
- B1 = Gran Fury Salon
- B2 = Gran Fury Salon
- F3 = Laser
- F4 = Laser RS & RS Turbo FWD
- G4 = Laser RS Turbo AWD
- J3 = Caravelle
- J4 = Caravelle
- J4 = Breeze
- K4 = Caravelle SE
- K4 = Reliant
- L1 = Horizon
- M1 = Horizon
- M2 = Gran Fury Salon
- M3 = Gran Fury Special
- M4 = Horizon Turismo
- P2 = Sundance America
- P2 = Sundance
- P4 = Sundance
- P4 = Sundance Highline
- P6 = Sundance Duster
- P6 = Sundance RS
- S2 = Neon Base
- S2 = Neon Competition
- S3 = Laser
- S4 = Sundance
- S4 = Neon Highline
- S4 = Laser RS 2WD
- S6 = Neon Sport
- T4 = Laser RS AWD
- W6 = Prowler

DIGIT 6 — Series
- 1 = Base
- 1 = Miser
- 2 = Low
- 2 = Base
- 3 = Medium
- 3 = DLX
- 3 = High
- 4 = Custom
- 4 = Turismo
- 4 = SE
- 4 = DLX
- 4 = Base
- 5 = High
- 5 = Euro
- 5 = Premium
- 5 = Turismo
- 5 = Custom
- 5 = Turismo 2.2

DIGIT 7 — Body Type
- 0 = Wagon
- 1 = 2D Sedan
- 1 = Wagon
- 2 = 2D Pillared Hardtop
- 3 = 2D Hardtop
- 4 = 2D Hatchback
- 5 = 2D Convertible
- 6 = 4D Sedan
- 7 = 4D Pillared Hardtop
- 7 = 4D Sedan
- 8 = 4D Hatchback
- 9 = 4D Wagon
- 9 = Wagon

DIGIT 8 — Engine
- 2 = 1.4L I-4 2BBL
- 3 = 1.6L I-4 2BBL
- 3 = 3.0L V6 2BBL
- 4 = 5.2L V8 2BBL
- 7 = 2.6L I-4 2BBL
- A = 1.7L I-4 2BBL
- A = 1.5L I-4 MPI
- A = 1.6L I-4 2BBL
- A = 1.6L I-4 2BBL
- B = 1.6L I-4 2BBL
- B = 1.8L I-4 MPI
- B = 2.2L I-4 2BBL
- B = 1.7L I-4 2BBL
- C = 2.0L I-4 SFI SOHC
- C = 2.2L I-4 Turbo
- C = 1.8L I-4 MPI
- D = 2.6L I-4 2BBL
- D = 1.8L I-4 MPI
- D = 2.0L I-4
- D = 2.0L I-4 2BBL
- D = 2.2L I-4 TBI
- E = 3.7L 6 Cyl 1BBL
- E = 2.0L I-4 MPI DOHC
- E = 2.2L I-4 Turbo
- F = 1.6L I-4 Turbo
- F = 2.0L I-4 DOHC T/C I/C
- F = 3.5L V6 MPI
- F = 3.7L 6 Cyl 1BBL

Fig. 12 VIN Identification (Part 1 of 2). Plymouth

ARM0600000000029

DIGIT 8 — Engine
- G = 3.5L V6 MPI SOHC HO
- G = 2.4L I-4 MPI
- G = 2.4L I-4 MPI SOHC
- G = 2.6L I-4 2BBL
- H = 2.5L I-4 EFI
- H = 2.6L I-4 Tbo
- J = 2.5L I-4 Turbo
- K = 1.5L I-4
- K = 2.5L I-4 TBI
- L = 5.2L V8 2BBL
- M = 5.2L V8 2BBL
- N = 2.6L I-4 Tbo
- N = 5.2L V8 4BBL
- P = 5.2L V8 2BBL
- R = 2.0L I-4 MPI DOHC
- R = 5.2L V8 4BBL
- S = 5.2L V8 4BBL
- T = 1.8L I-4 MPI
- U = 2.0L I-4 MPI DOHC Turbo
- V = 2.5L I-4 TBI Flex Fuel
- V = 2.0L I-4 MPI
- W = 2.4L I-4 MPI
- X = 2.4L I-4 SFI
- X = 1.5L I-4 MPI
- Y = 2.0L I-4 SFI DOHC
- Z = 2.0L I-4 MPI
- Z = 1.6L I-4 Turbo

DIGIT 9 — CHECK DIGIT
- = 0-9 or X

DIGIT 10 — Model Year
- 1 = 2001
- B = 1981
- C = 1982
- D = 1983
- E = 1984
- F = 1985
- G = 1986
- H = 1987
- J = 1988
- K = 1989
- L = 1990
- M = 1991
- N = 1992
- P = 1993
- R = 1994
- S = 1995
- T = 1996
- V = 1997
- W = 1998
- X = 1999
- Y = 2000

DIGIT 11 — Assembly Plant
- A = Mizushima 2, Japan
- A = Lynch Road, USA
- C = Jefferson North Assembly, Detroit, MI, USA
- D = Belvidere Assembly
- D = Belvidere, IL, USA
- E = Bloomington - Normal, IL USA
- F = Newark, NJ, USA
- G = St. Louis #1, USA
- J = Nagoya 3, Japan
- N = Sterling Heights, MI, USA
- P = Nagoya 2, Japan
- R = Windsor, Canada
- T = Toluca, Mexico
- T = Toluca Assembly
- U = Mizushima, Japan
- U = Mizushima 1, Japan
- V = Detroit, MI, USA
- W = Kenosha #1, WI, USA
- X = St. Louis #2, USA
- Y = Kenosha #2, WI, USA
- Y = Nagoya 1, Japan
- Y = Nagoya, Japan
- Z = Okazaki, Japan

DIGIT 12 — Transmission
- 4 = 5-Speed Manual - Federal
- 5 = 5-Speed Manual - California
- 7 = Automatic - Federal
- 8 = Automatic - California

Fig. 12 VIN Identification (Part 2 of 2). Plymouth

Fig. 13 VIN Identification (Part 1 of 3). Pontiac

DIGIT 1	Country Of Origin
1	USA
2	Canada
3	Mexico
4	USA
K	Korea

DIGIT 1-3	Manufacturer Identification
5Y2	Pontiac, Nummi
6G2	Pontiac, Australia

DIGIT 2	Manufacturer
G	General Motors
L	Daewoo

DIGIT 3	Make
2	Pontiac

DIGIT 4	Restraint System
A	Manual Belts

DIGIT 4-5	Carline/Series
AE	6000 SE
AF	6000
AF	6000 LE
AG	6000 LE
AH	6000 STE
AJ	6000 SE
AL	G5 Base
AN	G5 GT
BL	Parisienne
BT	Parisienne Brougham
FS	Firebird
FV	Formula
FV	Trans AM
FW	Trans AM
FW	Trans AM GTA
FX	Firebird SE
GJ	Grand Prix
GK	Grand Prix LE
GN	Grand Prix SE
GP	Grand Prix Brougham
GR	Bonneville Brougham
GS	Bonneville LE
HX	Bonneville
HX	Bonneville LE
HX	Bonneville SE
HY	Bonneville SLE
HY	Bonneville SSE
HY	Bonneville SSEi
HZ	Bonneville GXP
HZ	Bonneville LE
HZ	Bonneville SE
HZ	Bonneville SSE
HZ	Bonneville SSEi
JB	Sunfire GT Coupe
JB	Sunfire LE & Convertible
JB	Sunfire SE & Convertible
JB	Sunfire SE
JB	Sunfire SE Convertible
JB	Sunfire GT Convertible
JC	Sunbird LE
JC	Sunbird SE
JD	Sunbird LE
JD	Sunbird GT
JD	Sunbird GT
JD	Sunbird SE
JL	Sunbird SE
JU	Sunbird GT
MB	Solstice Base Roadster
MB	Solstice Convertible
MG	Solstice GXP Roadster
NE	Grand AM

DIGIT 4-5	Carline/Series
NE	Grand AM LE
NE	Grand AM SE
NF	Grand AM SE1
NG	Grand AM SE2
NG	Grand AM
NV	Grand AM GT1
NV	Grand AM LE
NW	Grand AM GT
NW	Grand AM SE
PE	Fiero Coupe
PE	Fiero Formula
PF	Fiero SE Coupe
PG	Fiero GT Coupe
PM	Fiero Sport Coupe
SL	Vibe FWD
SL	Vibe AWD
SM	Vibe GT
SN	1000
TL	1000
TN	Lemans SE
TN	Lemans LE
TN	Lemans SE
TR	Lemans GSE
TS	Lemans GSE
TX	Lemans Aerocoupe
TX	Lemans Coupe
VX	GTO
WC	Grand Prix GXP
WH	Grand Prix LE
WJ	Grand Prix SE
WJ	Grand Prix
WJ	Grand Prix LE
WK	Grand Prix SE1
WP	Grand Prix Base
WP	Grand Prix GT
WP	Grand Prix SE
WR	Grand Prix GT
WR	Grand Prix GTP
WS	Grand Prix GTP
WS	Grand Prix GT2
WT	Grand Prix STE
ZF	G6 Base I4 Sedan
ZG	G6 Base
ZG	G6 Base V6 Sedan
ZH	G6 GT
ZM	G6 GTP

DIGIT 5	Carline
B	J2000
B	Sunbird 2000
C	J2000 LE
C	Sunbird 2000 LE
D	J2000 SE
D	Sunbird 2000 SE
D	Lemans
D	Grand Lemans
E	J2000 S
F	Fiero SE Coupe
F	6000
F	6000 LE
G	6000 STE
H	6000
J	6000 LE
J	Grand Prix
K	Grand Prix LE
K	Grand Prix LJ
L	1000
L	Catalina
L	Parisienne
M	1000
M	Fiero Sport Coupe
N	Bonneville
NE	Grand AM

Fig. 13 VIN Identification (Part 2 of 3). Pontiac

DIGIT 8	Engine
0	1.8L I-4 TBI
1	3.8L V6 SFI S/C
1	3.9L V6 SFI
1	2.8L V6 2BBL
2	2.5L I-4 TBI
2	3.8L V6 SFI
3	2.3L I-4 MPI
3	3.8L V6 SFI
4	2.2L I-4 MPI SOHC
4	4.1L V6 4BBL
4	3.8L V6 SFI S/C
5	2.5L I-4 2BBL
6	1.6L I-4 TBI
6	3.6L V6 SFI
7	5.0L V8 CPI
8	2.5L I-4 EFI
8	3.5L V6 SFI
8	1.8L I-4 MPI
8	5.7L V8 MPI
9	2.8L V6 MPI
A	2.3L I-4 MPI Quad HO
A	3.8L V6 2BBL
B	2.4L I4 MFI
B	2.4L I4 SFI
C	3.8L V6 MPI
C	5.3L V8 SFI
C	1.6L I-4 2BBL
C	2.3L I-4 EFI Quad 4
D	2.3L I-4 MPI DOHC
D	2.3L I-4 MPI Quad 4
E	3.4L V6 SFI
E	5.0L V8 TBI
F	2.5L I-4 2BBL
F	5.0L V8 MPI
F	2.2L I-4 MPI DOHC
F	2.2L I4 MFI SOHC
G	2.5L I-4 EFI
G	5.0L V8 4BBL
G	5.7L SFI V8
G	5.7L V8 MPI
G	1.8L I-4 2BBL
H	2.0L V8 4BBL
H	5.0L V8 4BBL
J	1.8L I-4 FI Turbo
J	1.8L I-4 F1 Turbo
J	3.1L V6 SFI
J	2.0L I-4 TBI
J	1.8L I-4 Turbo
K	2.0L I-4 Turbo
K	3.8L V6 2BBL
K	3.8L V6 MPI
K	3.8L V6 SFI
L	3.0L V6 EFI
L	2.8L V6 2BBL
L	1.8L I-4 SFI DOHC
M	2.0L-I4 Turbo
M	2.0L I-4 Turbo
M	3.1L V6 SFI
N	3.3L V6 MPI
N	3.5L V6 SFI
P	5.7L V8 EFI
P	5.7L V8 MPI
P	2.0L I-4 EFI
P	2.8L V6 MPI
P	2.0L I-4 MPI
R	2.5L I-4 TBI
S	2.8L V6 MPI
S	3.4L V6 SFI HO
S	4.3L V8 2BBL
T	2.4L I-4 EFI DOHC

DIGIT 5	Carline
P	Grand Prix Brougham
R	Bonneville Brougham
S	Firebird
S	Bonneville LE
T	Firebird Esprit
T	Phoenix SE
T	Parisienne Brougham
V	Phoenix SJ
V	Formula
W	Trans AM
X	Firebird SE
X	Trans AM Turbo Special
Y	Phoenix
Z	Phoenix LE
Z	Phoenix LJ

DIGIT 6	Body Type
1	2D Coupe/Sedan
1	2D Coupe
1	2D Coupe, Notchback
1	2D Coupe, Notchback Special
2	2D Hatchback
2	2D Hatchback/Liftback
3	2D Convertible
5	Coupe Convertible
5	4D Sedan
6	4D All Purpose w/Liftgate
6	4D Hatchback
8	Station Wagon

DIGIT 6-7	Body Type
08	2D Hatchback
19	4D Notchback Sedan
27	2D Notchback Coupe
35	4D Wagon
37	2D Notchback Special Coupe
67	2D Convertible
68	4D Hatchback
69	4D Notchback Sedan
77	2D Hatchback
87	2D Coupe
97	2D Notchback Sport Coupe

DIGIT 7	Restraint System
1	Manual Belts
1	Active Belts
2	Dual Front Airbags w/Manual Belts
2	Dual Front & Side Airbags w/Manual Belts
3	Driverside Airbag w/Manual Belts
3	Dual Front Airbags w/Manual Belts
3	Dual Front & Side Airbags w/Manual Belts & Auto Passenger Sens
4	Automatic Belts
4	Dual Front Airbags w/Manual Belts & Occupant Sensor
4	Dual Front & Side Airbags & Roof Airbags w/Manual Belts
4	Dual Front & Front Side Airbags & Manual Belts w/Oc
5	Driverside Airbag w/Manual Belts
5	Dual Front Airbags w/Manual Belts & Auto Pas
5	Dual Front & Front Side Airbags w/Manual Belts & C
6	Dual Front, Front & Rear Side Airbags w/Automatic Belts
6	Dual Front & Roof Airbags w/Manual Belts
6	Dual Front Airbags w/Manual Belts & Occupant Sen
6	Dual Front, Front Side Airbags & Roof Airbags w/Manual Bt
7	Dual Front, Front & Rear Side Airbags & Manual Belts
7	Dual Front & Front Side Airbags & Manual Belts & C
7	Dual Front, Side-Impact & Roof Airbags w/Manual Belts w/Occupar
7	Dual Front, Side & Roof Airbags w/Manual Belts & Occupar
8	Dual Front, Side-impact & Roof Airbags w/Manual Belts & C
8	Dual Front, Side & Roof Airbags w/Manual Belts & Occupant Sen

DIGIT 8   Engine

T	4.9L V8 4BBL
T	4.3L V6 Dsl
T	2.4L I-4 MPI DOHC
T	3.1L V6 MPI
U	2.5L I-4 TBI
U	6.0L SFI V8
V	3.1L V6 EFI
V	3.0L V6 TBI
W	4.9L V8 4BBL
W	2.8L V6 MPI
X	2.8L V6 2BBL
X	3.4L V6 EFI DOHC
X	2.0L I4 T/C
Y	4.6L V8 MPI
Y	5.0L V8 4BBL
Z	4.3L V6 EFI
Z	2.8L V6 2BBL

DIGIT 10   Model Year

1	2001
2	2002
3	2003
4	2004
5	2005
6	2006
7	2007
8	2008
B	1981
C	1982
D	1983
E	1984
F	1985
G	1986
H	1987
J	1988
K	1989
L	1990
M	1991
N	1992
P	1993
R	1994
S	1995
T	1996
V	1997
W	1998
X	1999
Y	2000

DIGIT 11   Assembly Plant

1	Oshawa # 2, ON, Canada
1	Wentzville, MO, USA
1	Oshawa #2, ON, Canada
1	Oshawa, ON, Canada
2	Ste. Therese, PQ, Canada
4	Orion, MI, USA
6	Oklahoma City, OK, USA
7	Lordstown, OH, USA
9	Oshawa # 1, ON, Canada
9	Oshawa #1, ON, Canada
A	Lakewood, GA, USA
B	Lansing, MI, USA
B	Pupyong, Korea
B	Baltimore, MD, USA
C	Lansing, MI, USA
F	Fairfax II, KS, USA
G	Framingham, MA, USA
H	Flint, MI, USA
J	Janesville, WI, USA
K	Leeds, MO, USA
L	Elizabeth, Australia
L	Van Nuys, CA, USA
M	Lansing, MI, USA

DIGIT 11   Assembly Plant

N	Norwood, OH, USA
P	Pontiac, MI, USA
S	Ramos Arizpe, Mexico
T	Tarrytown, NY, USA
U	Hamtramck, MI, USA
W	Willow Run, MI, USA
X	Fairfax, KS, USA
X	Fairfax I, KS, USA
Y	Wilmington DE, USA
Y	Wilmington, DE, USA
Z	Fremont, CA, USA

ARM0700000000184

Fig. 13   VIN Identification (Part 3 of 3). Pontiac

DIGIT 1	Country Of Origin
1	USA

DIGIT 2	Manufacturer
G	General Motors

DIGIT 3	Make
8	Saturn

DIGIT 4-5	Carline/Series
AF	Level 1 Sedan 5sp
AG	Level 1 Sedan at
AH	Level I Base
AJ	Level 2 Sedan at
AK	Level 3 Sedan 5sp
AL	Level 3 Sedan at
AM	Level 2 Quad Coupe 5sp
AN	Level 2 Quad Coupe at
AT	Level 3 Quad Coupe Red Line
AU	Level II Base
AV	Level 3 Quad Coupe 5sp
AW	Level 3 Quad Coupe at
AX	Level III Base
AY	Level 3 Quad Coupe Red Line
AZ	Level 2 Sedan 5sp
JC	L300 Base
JD	L300 Mid-level
JL	L300 Up-level
JR	L100 5sp
JR	LS 5sp
JS	L100 at
JS	LS at
JT	L200 5sp
JT	LS1 5sp
JT	LW200 5sp
JU	LS1 at
JU	LW200 at
JU	L200 at
JU	LW1 at
JW	L300 at
JW	LW300 at
JW	LS2 at
JW	LW2 at
MB	Sky Convertible
MG	Sky Convertible RedLine
ZE	SC1 5sp
ZF	SC1 at
ZF	SL 5sp
ZG	SC 5sp
ZG	SC2 5sp
ZG	SL1 5sp
ZG	SW1 5sp
ZH	SL1 at
ZH	SC2 at
ZH	SW1 at
ZH	SC at
ZJ	SL2 5sp
ZJ	SW2 5sp
ZK	SL2 at
ZK	SW2 at
ZM	SW2 5sp
ZN	SC1 5sp
ZN	SW2 at
ZP	SC1 at
ZR	Aura Hybrid
ZR	SC2 5sp
ZS	Aura XE
ZS	SL 5sp Spring Special
ZV	Aura XR
ZY	SC2 at

DIGIT 6	Body Type
1	4D Quad Coupe
1	2D Coupe

DIGIT 6	Body Type
3	2D Convertible
5	4D Sedan
8	4D Wagon

DIGIT 7	Restraint System
1	Dual Front Airbags w/Manual Belts
2	Dual Front Airbags w/Manual Belts
3	Dual Front Airbags, Roof Curtain Airbags w/Manual Belts & Automatic Belts
4	Dual Front & Roof Airbags w/Manual Belts
4	Dual Front & Side Airbags w/Manual Belts
5	Driverside Airbag w/Automatic Belts
5	Dual Front Airbags w/Manual Belts & Occupant Sensor
7	Dual Front, Side & Roof Airbags w/Manual Belts & Occupar
8	Dual Front & Roof Airbags w/Manual Belts w/Occupant Sen

DIGIT 8	Engine
5	2.4L I4 SFI DOHC Hybrid Ecotec
7	1.9L I-4 MPI DOHC
7	3.6L V6 SFI DOHC
8	1.9L I-4 TBI
9	1.9L I-4 TBI
B	2.4L I-4 MPI DOHC
F	2.2L I-4 SFI DOHC
N	3.5L V6 SFI DOHC
P	2.0L I-4 SFI DOHC S/C
R	3.0L V6 SFI DOHC
X	2.0L I4 T/C

DIGIT 10	Model Year
1	2001
2	2002
3	2003
4	2004
5	2005
6	2006
7	2007
8	2008
M	1991
N	1992
P	1993
R	1994
S	1995
T	1996
V	1997
W	1998
X	1999
Y	2000

DIGIT 11	Assembly Plant
F	Fairfax, KS, USA
S	Spring Hill, TN, USA
Y	Wilmington, DE, USA
Y	Wilmington DE, USA
Z	Spring Hill, TN, USA

ARM0700000000185

Fig. 14   VIN Identification. Saturn

AIR BAG SYSTEM PRECAUTIONS

INDEX

	Page No.
Chrysler	0-18
Arming	0-18
Disarming	0-18
Ford Motor Co.	0-18
Arming	0-24
Crown Victoria & Grand Marquis	0-24
Five-Hundred, Freestyle & Montego	0-24
Focus	0-25
Fusion, Milan & Zephyr	0-25
LS	0-25

	Page No.
Mustang	0-26
Sable, Taurus & Taurus X	0-27
Thunderbird	0-28
Town Car	0-29
Disarming	0-18
Crown Victoria & Grand Marquis	0-18
Five-Hundred, Freestyle & Montego	0-19
Focus	0-19
Fusion, Milan & Zephyr	0-19
LS	0-20

	Page No.
Mustang	0-21
Sable, Taurus & Taurus X	0-21
Thunderbird	0-22
Town Car	0-23
General Motors	0-29
Arming	0-29
Disarming	0-29
Saturn	0-30
Arming	0-30
Disarming	0-30

CHRYSLER

Disarming

It may be required to access and record Diagnostic Trouble Codes (DTCs) prior to disarming the air bag system.
1. Place ignition switch in Lock position.
2. Disconnect and isolate battery ground cable and or cable remote terminal at remote battery post as required.
3. **Wait at least two minutes after disconnection before doing any further work on vehicle.** The air bag system is designed to retain enough voltage to deploy air bags for short time even after battery has been disconnected.

Arming

After any air bag component testing or service, do not connect the battery ground cable, personal injury or death may result if the "System Test" is not performed first using a suitably programmed scan tool.

If flash is incorrect or fault detected, refer to **MOTOR's "Air Bag Quick Reference Guide."**
1. **Ensure no one is inside vehicle and ignition switch is in Lock position.**
2. Connect battery ground or negative remote cable or terminal.
3. **From safe location at sides or below air bag modules,** turn ignition switch to On position.
4. SRS lamp should light for 7–10 seconds and remain off for at least 45 seconds to indicate SRS is functioning properly.

FORD MOTOR CO.

Disarming

CROWN VICTORIA & GRAND MARQUIS

2004
1. Disconnect battery ground cable.

2. Wait at least one minute for backup power supply in Restraints Control Module (RCM) to deplete its' stored energy.
3. Remove two steering wheel back cover plugs and two air bag module bolts.
4. Release two air bag retaining tabs. Label driver air bag squib number on air bag module connector before disconnecting.
5. Remove wire harness from holder.
6. Disconnect horn switch electrical connector.
7. Remove air bag module.
8. Attach restraint system diagnostic tools 418-F395, or equivalent, to clockspring side of driver air bag module electrical connectors.
9. Disconnect rear window defroster switch, clock and air bag deactivation lamp electrical connectors, then remove trim panel.
10. Open glove compartment and disconnect glove compartment isolator.
11. While pushing in on two glove compartment door tabs, lower glove compartment door.
12. Remove air bag module bolts through glove compartment opening.
13. Place one hand in glove compartment opening and push air bag module out from instrument panel. **Do not handle passenger air bag module by grabbing edges of deployment doors.**
14. Attach restraint system diagnostic tools 418-F395, or equivalent, to vehicle harness side of passenger air bag module electrical connectors.
15. Remove front seats.
16. Access passenger safety belt retractor and pretensioner located behind passenger side B-pillar.
17. Disconnect passenger safety belt retractor and pretensioner electrical connector.
18. Attach restraint system diagnostic tool 418-F088, or equivalent, to passenger safety belt retractor and pretensioner electrical connector.
19. Access driver safety belt retractor and pretensioner located behind driver side B-pillar.
20. Disconnect driver safety belt retractor

and pretensioner electrical connector.
21. Attach restraint system diagnostic tool 418-F088, or equivalent, to driver safety belt retractor and pretensioner electrical connector.
22. Connect battery ground cable.

2005
1. Turn all vehicle accessories OFF.
2. Turn ignition switch to OFF position.
3. Remove Restraints Control Module (RCM) fuse F2.22 (10A) from Central Junction Box (CJB).
4. Turn ignition ON and visually monitor air bag indicator for 30 seconds. The air bag indicator will remain lit continuously if correct RCM is removed.
5. Turn ignition switch to OFF position.
6. Disconnect battery ground cable and wait at least 60 seconds for power to deplete.
7. Remove driver's side air bag module from steering wheel.
8. Disconnect driver's side air bag module electrical connectors from module.
9. Attach restraint system diagnostic tool to clockspring electrical connectors the top of steering column.
10. Separate trim panel pulling out to release retaining clips.
11. Slide trim panel to the righthand side aligning the keyway and pullout trim panel from instrument panel.
12. Disconnect rear window defrost switch, clock connector, passenger's side air bag deactivation (PAD) indicator then remove trim panel.
13. Open glove compartment and disconnect glove compartment isolator.
14. Pushing in glove compartment tabs, lower door.
15. Separate passenger's side air bag module electrical connector and pin-type retainer from bracket, disconnect passenger's side air bag electrical connector.
16. Remove passenger's side air bag module bolts, then the passenger's side air bag module.
17. Separate locking insert from passenger's side air bag module jumper harness electrical connector.
18. Disconnect passenger's side air bag module electrical connector tabs.

19. Attach two restraint system diagnostic tools to two passenger's side air bag module jumper harness electrical connectors and align and install locking inserts to electrical connectors.
20. Connect passenger's side air bag module jumper harness to passenger's side air bag module electrical connector on vehicle wiring harness.
21. **On models less side impact air bag modules,** if side air bag bridge resistor is removed, an open circuit fault will be generated by the restraints control module.
22. **On models less side impact air bag modules,** if a restraint system diagnostic tool is installed at the side air bag floor electrical connector, a low resistance fault will be generated by RCM.
23. **On models equipped with side impact air bag modules,** proceed as follows:
    a. Disconnect passenger's seat side air bag module electrical connector.
    b. Attach restraint system diagnostic tool to seat harness side of passenger's seat side air bag module electrical connector.
    c. Disconnect driver's seat side air bag module electrical connector.
    d. Attach restraint system diagnostic tool to seat harness side of driver's seat side air bag module electrical connector.
24. **On all models,** install RCM fuse F2.22 (10A) to CJB.
25. Connect battery ground cable as required.

2006-07

1. Turn all vehicle accessories Off.
2. Turn ignition switch to Off position.
3. Open kick panel cover located on left-hand end of instrument panel and remove Restraints Control Module (RCM) fuse from Central Junction Box (CJB).
4. Turn ignition On and visually monitor air bag indicator for at least 30 seconds. Air bag indicator will remain lit continuously if correct RCM fuse has been removed. If air bag indicator does not remain lit continuously, remove correct RCM fuse before proceeding.
5. Turn ignition switch to OFF position.
6. Disconnect battery ground cable and isolate as required. **Wait at least 60 seconds for power supply to deplete.**

FIVE-HUNDRED, FREESTYLE & MONTEGO

1. Turn all vehicle accessories to OFF position.
2. Turn ignition switch to OFF position.
3. Remove Restraints Control Module (RCM) fuse from Smart Junction Box (SJB), SJB is located below lefthand side of instrument panel.
4. Turn ignition switch ON and visually monitor air bag indicator for 30 seconds. Air bag indicator will remain on if correct fuse has been removed. If indicator lamp does not remain on, re-

move correct fuse from SJB.
5. Turn ignition switch to OFF position.
6. Disconnect battery ground cable and isolate as required. **Wait at least 60 seconds for power supply to deplete.**

FOCUS
2004

1. Disconnect and isolate battery ground cable.
2. **On models equipped with auxiliary batteries and power supplies,** disconnect and isolate these items also.
3. **On all models,** wait one minute for backup power supply to deplete.
4. Remove two air bag module mounting bolts, then disconnect air bag and horn electrical connectors.
5. Remove driver's air bag module from steering wheel. **When carrying live air bag module, ensure bag and trim cover are pointed away from your body. Place module on bench with trim cover facing upward.**
6. Connect air bag simulator tool No. 418-037, or equivalent, to air bag wiring harness at top steering column.
7. Remove mounting screws and glove compartment.
8. Disconnect passenger's air bag module electrical connector.
9. Connect Rotunda air bag simulator tool 418-138, or equivalent, to wiring harness in place of passenger's air bag module.
10. From beneath driver's seat, disconnect side impact air bag module electrical connector. Connect Rotunda air bag simulator tool 418-139, or equivalent, to connector on wiring harness side of side impact air bag harness.
11. From beneath passenger's seat, disconnect side impact air bag module electrical connector. Connect Rotunda air bag simulator tool 418-139, or equivalent, to connector on wiring harness side of side impact air bag harness.
12. Disconnect driver's seat belt pretensioner electrical connector. Connect Rotunda air bag simulator tool 418-139, or equivalent, to connector on wiring harness side of seat belt pretensioner harness.
13. Disconnect passenger's seat belt pretensioner electrical connector. Connect Rotunda air bag simulator tool 418-139, or equivalent, to connector on wiring harness side of seat belt pretensioner harness.
14. Connect battery ground cable.

2005

1. Turn all vehicle accessories to OFF position.
2. Turn ignition switch to OFF position.
3. Remove restraints control module (RCM) fuse F2.60 (7.5A) from central junction box (CJB).
4. Turn ignition ON and visually monitor air bag indicator for 30 seconds. Air bag indicator will remain lit continuously if correct RCM fuse removed.
5. Turn ignition switch to OFF position.

6. Disconnect battery ground cable and wait at least 60 seconds for power to deplete.
7. Remove driver's side air bag module bolts and retaining clips then the air bag module.
8. Disconnect driver's side air bag module electrical connector.
9. Connect restraint system diagnostic tool to driver's air bag module electrical connector on clockspring.
10. Open glove compartment.
11. Remove ventilation pipe and detach defroster pipe from heater housing and defrost vent.
12. Remove passenger's air bag module trim cover retaining bolts, detach passenger's air bag module trim cover from instrument panel.
13. Remove passenger's side air bag module trim cover.
14. Remove passenger's air bag module and reinforcement bracket from instrument panel.
15. Remove passenger's side air bag module, disconnecting electrical connectors.
16. Connect restraint system diagnostic tools to vehicle harness side of passenger's side air bag module electrical connectors.
17. **On models equipped with side impact air bag modules,** proceed as follows:
    a. Disconnect passenger's seat electrical connector from under seat.
    b. Connect restraint system diagnostic tool to vehicle harness side of passenger's seat side air bag module electrical connector.
    c. Disconnect driver's seat electrical connector from under seat.
    d. Connect restraint system diagnostic tool to vehicle harness side of driver's seat side air bag module electrical connector.
18. **On all models,** install RCM fuse F2.60 (7.5A) to CJB.
19. Connect battery ground cable.

2006-07

1. Turn all vehicle accessories Off.
2. Turn ignition switch to Off position.
3. Open kick panel cover located on left-hand side end of instrument panel and remove Restraints Control Module (RCM) fuse from Central Junction Box (CJB).
4. Turn ignition On and visually monitor air bag indicator for at least 30 seconds. If air bag indicator remains lit, correct RCM fuse has been removed. If air bag indicator does not remain lit, remove correct RCM fuse.
5. Turn ignition switch to Off position.
6. Disconnect battery ground cable and isolate as required. **Wait at least 60 seconds for power supply to deplete.**

FUSION, MILAN & ZEPHYR

1. Turn all vehicle accessories Off.
2. Turn ignition switch to Off position.
3. Remove cover from Smart Junction Box (SJB) which is located below left-hand side of instrument panel, remove

AIR BAG SYSTEM PRECAUTIONS

Restraints Control Module (RCM) fuse from SJB.

4. Turn ignition On and visually monitor air bag indicator for at least 30 seconds. Air bag indicator will remain lit continuously if correct RCM fuse has been removed. If air bag indicator does not remain lit continuously, remove correct RCM fuse.
5. Turn ignition switch to Off position.
6. Disconnect battery ground cable and isolate as required. **Wait at least 60 seconds for power supply to deplete.**

LS

2004

1. Disconnect and isolate battery ground cable.
2. **On models equipped with auxiliary batteries and power supplies,** disconnect and isolate these items.
3. **On all models,** wait one minute for backup power supply to deplete.
4. Remove two rear cover plugs from steering wheel in order to access air bag module screws.
5. Remove driver's air bag module mounting bolts and disconnect electrical connector.
6. Remove air bag module. **When carrying live air bag module, ensure bag and trim cover are pointed away from your body. Place module on bench with trim cover facing upward.**
7. Connect Rotunda air bag simulator tool No. 418-F395, or equivalent, to air bag wiring harness at top steering column.
8. Remove glove compartment.
9. Reaching over cross-car beam, slide passenger's air bag connector lock downward. Squeeze connector lock tabs and pull connector from air bag.
10. Connect Rotunda air bag simulator tool No. 418-F395, or equivalent, to vehicle side of passenger's air bag wiring harness connector.
11. From beneath driver's seat, disconnect side impact air bag module electrical connector. Connect Rotunda air bag simulator tool 418–133, or equivalent, to connector on wiring harness side of side impact air bag harness.
12. From beneath passenger's seat, disconnect side impact air bag module electrical connector. Connect Rotunda air bag simulator tool 418–133, or equivalent, to connector on wiring harness side of side impact air bag harness.
13. Remove driver's side B-pillar pillar trim.
14. Access and disconnect driver's side seat belt pretensioner electrical connector. Connect Rotunda seat belt pretensioner simulator tool 105-R0012, or equivalent, to seat belt pretensioner electrical connector.
15. Remove passenger's side B-pillar pillar trim.
16. Access and disconnect passenger's side seat belt pretensioner electrical connector. Connect Rotunda seat belt

pretensioner simulator tool 105-R0012, or equivalent, to seat belt pretensioner electrical connector.
17. Connect battery ground cable.

2005

Less Roof Panel Air Bag Modules

1. Turn all vehicle accessories to OFF position.
2. Turn ignition switch to OFF position.
3. Remove restraints control module (RCM) fuse F2.05 (10A) from central junction box (CJB).
4. Turn ignition switch to ON position and visually monitor air bag indicator for 30 seconds. Air bag indicator will remain lit continuously if correct RCM fuse has been removed.
5. Turn ignition switch to OFF position.
6. Disconnect battery ground cable and wait 60 seconds for power to deplete.
7. Remove two steering wheel plugs, then the driver's side air bag module bolts.
8. Disconnect and remove driver's side air bag module.
9. Attach restraint system diagnostic tools to clockspring electrical connectors at top of steering column.
10. Remove glove compartment.
11. Locate passenger's side air bag module electrical connector, then disconnect passenger's air bag module electrical connector.
12. Attach restraint system diagnostic tool to vehicle harness side of passenger's side air bag module electrical connector.
13. **On models equipped with side impact air bag modules,** remove A-pillar trim panel.
14. **On all models,** release tab and disconnect passenger's seat side impact air bag or passenger's seat side impact thorax air bag electrical connector.
15. Attach restraint system diagnostic tool to vehicle harness side of passenger's seat side impact air bag electrical connector.
16. From under driver's seat, release tab and disconnect driver's seat side impact air bag or driver's seat side thorax air bag electrical connectors.
17. Attach restraint system diagnostic tool to vehicle harness side of driver's seat side impact air bag electrical connector.
18. Install RCM fuse F2.05 to CJB and connect battery ground cable.

With Roof Panel Air Bag Modules

1. Turn all vehicle accessories to OFF position.
2. Turn ignition switch to OFF position.
3. Remove restraints control module (RCM) fuse F2.05 (10A) from central junction box (CJB).
4. Turn ignition switch to ON position and visually monitor air bag indicator for 30 seconds. Air bag indicator will remain lit continuously if correct RCM fuse has

been removed.
5. Turn ignition switch to OFF position.
6. Disconnect battery ground cable and wait 60 seconds for power to deplete.
7. Remove two steering wheel plugs, then the driver's side air bag module bolts.
8. Disconnect and remove driver's side air bag module.
9. Attach restraint system diagnostic tools to clockspring electrical connectors at top of steering column.
10. Remove A-pillar trim panel and disconnect driver's side roof panel air bag module electrical connectors.
11. Attach restraint system diagnostic tool to vehicle harness side of driver's side roof panel air bag module electrical connector.
12. Remove glove compartment.
13. Locate passenger's side air bag module electrical connector, then disconnect passenger's air bag module electrical connector.
14. Attach restraint system diagnostic tool to vehicle harness side of passenger's side air bag module electrical connector.
15. **On models equipped with side impact air bag modules,** remove A-pillar trim panel.
16. **On all models,** disconnect passenger's side roof panel air bag module electrical connector.
17. Attach restraint system diagnostic tool to vehicle harness side of passenger's side roof panel air bag module electrical connector.
18. Release tab and disconnect passenger's seat side impact air bag or passenger's seat side impact thorax air bag electrical connector.
19. Attach restraint system diagnostic tool to vehicle harness side of passenger's seat side thorax air bag electrical connector.
20. From under driver's seat, release tab and disconnect driver's seat side impact air bag or driver's seat side thorax air bag electrical connectors.
21. Attach restraint system diagnostic tool to vehicle harness side of driver seat side thorax air bag electrical connector.
22. Install RCM fuse F2.05 to CJB and connect battery ground cable.

2006

1. Turn all vehicle accessories Off.
2. Turn ignition switch to Off position.
3. Open kick panel cover on Central Junction Box (CJB), then remove Restraints Control Module (RCM) fuse from CJB. CJB is located on righthand end of instrument panel.
4. Turn ignition On and visually monitor air bag indicator for at least 30 seconds. Air bag indicator will remain lit continuously if correct RCM fuse has been removed. If air bag indicator does not remain lit continuously, remove correct RCM fuse.
5. Turn ignition switch to Off position.
6. Disconnect battery ground cable and isolate as required. **Wait at least 60**

seconds for power supply to deplete.

MUSTANG

2004-05

1. Turn all vehicle accessories to OFF position.
2. Turn ignition switch to OFF position.
3. Remove restraints control module (RCM) fuse F2.17 (10A) from smart junction box (SJB).
4. Turn ignition ON and visually monitor air bag indicator for 30 seconds. Air bag indicator will remain lit continuously if correct RCM fuse is removed.
5. Turn ignition switch to OFF position.
6. Disconnect battery ground cable.
7. Allow at least one minute for back-up power supply to deplete.
8. **On models equipped with auxiliary batteries and power supplies,** disconnect and isolate these items also.
9. **On all models,** remove two rear cover plugs from steering wheel in order to access air bag module screws.
10. Remove driver's air bag module mounting screws and washers, then disconnect electrical connector.
11. Remove air bag module. **Place module on bench with trim cover facing upward.**
12. Connect Rotunda air bag simulator tool, or equivalent, to air bag wiring at top of steering column.
13. Open glove compartment, press sides inward to release it from instrument panel and lower glove compartment to floor.
14. Remove righthand air conditioning duct and passenger's air bag mounting bolts from instrument panel steel reinforcement.
15. Disconnect electrical connector at lower lefthand corner of passenger's air bag module and remove connector from instrument panel reinforcement.
16. Gently pull upon each corner of air bag cover to disconnect from instrument panel and push air bag module out from behind instrument panel. **Place module on bench with trim cover facing upward.**
17. Install second air bag simulator Rotunda air bag simulator tool, or equivalent, on passenger's air bag harness.
18. **On models equipped with side impact air bag module,** proceed as follows:
    a. Release red locking tab and disconnect passenger's side impact air bag module electrical connector.
    b. Attach restraint system diagnostic tool to vehicle harness side of passenger's side impact air bag module electrical connector.
    c. Release red locking tab and disconnect driver's side impact air bag module electrical connector.
    d. Attach restraint system diagnostic tool to vehicle harness side of driver's side impact air bag module electrical connector.
19. **On all models,** install RCM fuse 2.17 (10A) to SJB.
20. Connect battery ground cable.

2006-08

1. Turn all vehicle accessories Off.
2. Turn ignition switch to Off position.
3. Remove cover from Smart Junction Box (SJB) located on righthand side kick panel.
4. Remove Restraints Control Module (RCM) fuse from SJB.
5. Turn ignition On and visually monitor air bag indicator for at least 30 seconds. I If air bag indicator remains lit continuously correct RCM fuse has been removed. If air bag indicator does not remain lit continuously, remove correct RCM fuse.
6. Turn ignition switch to Off position.
7. Disconnect battery ground cable and isolate as required. **Wait at least 60 seconds for power supply to deplete.**

SABLE, TAURUS & TAURUS X

2004

1. Move front seat to full rear and highest position.
2. Disconnect and isolate battery ground cable.
3. **On models equipped with auxiliary batteries and power supplies,** disconnect and isolate these items also.
4. **On all models,** wait one minute for back-up power supply to deplete.
5. Remove mounting screws and pull out release clips, then remove lower steering column cover with reinforcement.
6. Disconnect driver's air bag sliding contact electrical connect at base of steering column.
7. Connect driver's air bag restraint system diagnostic tool 418-F403, or equivalent, to vehicle side of driver's air bag sliding contact four-pin electrical connector.
8. Open glove compartment, push in on tabs and release glove compartment.
9. Through glove compartment opening, remove two passenger's air bag module mounting bolts.
10. Pull lefthand corner of passenger's air bag trim cover away from instrument panel.
11. From left to right, slide across seam between instrument panel and trim cover to release trim cover retaining clips.
12. Pull passenger's air bag module and trim cover away from instrument panel.
13. Disconnect passenger's air bag module electrical connector and remove harness retainer from air bag module.
14. Remove passenger's air bag module. **When carrying live air bag module, ensure bag and trim cover are pointed away from your body. Place module on bench with trim cover facing upward.**
15. Connect passenger's air bag restraint system diagnostic tool 418-F403, or equivalent, to vehicle side of passenger's air bag electrical connector.
16. **On models equipped with side impact air bags,** disconnect passenger's seat air bag electrical connector

and attach side impact air bag restraint system diagnostic tool 418-133, or equivalent, to side impact air bag floor electrical connector on passenger's side.
17. **On all models,** disconnect passenger's seat belt pretensioner electrical connector.
18. Attach passenger's seat belt pretensioner restraint system diagnostic tool 418-F407, or equivalent, to floor electrical connector.
19. **On models equipped with side impact air bags,** disconnect driver's seat air bag electrical connector and attach side impact air bag restraint system diagnostic tool 418-133, or equivalent, to side impact air bag floor electrical connector on driver's side.
20. **On all models,** disconnect driver's seat belt pretensioner electrical connector.
21. Attach driver's seat belt pretensioner restraint system diagnostic tool 418-F405, or equivalent, to floor electrical connector.
22. Connect battery ground cable.

2005

1. Turn all vehicle accessories to OFF position.
2. Turn ignition switch to OFF position.
3. Remove restraints control module (RCM) fuse F2.20 (10A) from smart junction box (SJB).
4. Turn ignition ON and visually monitor air bag indicator for 30 seconds. Air bag indicator will remain lit continuously if correct RCM fuse has been removed.
5. Turn ignition switch to OFF position.
6. Disconnect battery ground cable and wait 60 seconds for power to deplete.
7. Remove driver's side air bag module cover plugs, then the bolts and air bag module.
8. Release two retaining tabs and disconnect driver's side air bag module electrical connector. **Label squib number on module electrical connector before disconnecting for installation.**
9. Attach restraint system diagnostic tools to clockspring electrical connectors at top of steering column.
10. Open and release glove compartment to lowest position.
11. Remove passenger's side air bag module retaining bolts.
12. Separate passenger's side air bag module and trim cover from instrument panel.
13. Remove passenger's side air bag module and trim cover, disconnecting electrical connectors as required.
14. Attach restraint system diagnostic tool to vehicle harness side of passenger's side air bag module electrical connector.
15. **On models equipped with side impact air bag modules,** proceed as follows:
    a. Disconnect passenger's seat side impact air bag module electrical connector.
    b. Attach restraint system diagnostic

tool to vehicle harness side of passenger's seat side impact air bag module electrical connector.

c. Disconnect driver's seat side impact air bag module electrical connector.

d. Attach restraint system diagnostic tool to vehicle harness side of driver's seat side impact air bag module electrical connector.

16. **On all models,** install RCM fuse F2.20 (10A) to SJB.

17. Connect battery ground cable.

2006

1. Turn all vehicle accessories Off.
2. Turn ignition switch to Off position.
3. At smart junction box (SJB) located on lefthand side of instrument panel, remove cover and restraints control module (RCM) fuse F2.20 (10A) from SJB.
4. Turn ignition On and visually monitor air bag indicator for at least 30 seconds. Air bag indicator will remain lit continuously if correct RCM fuse has been removed. If air bag indicator does not remain lit continuously, remove correct RCM fuse before proceeding.
5. Turn ignition switch to Off position.
6. Disconnect battery ground cable and isolate as required. **Wait at least 60 seconds for power supply to deplete.**

2008

1. Turn all vehicle accessories to OFF position.
2. Turn ignition switch to OFF position.
3. Remove Restraints Control Module (RCM) fuse from Smart Junction Box (SJB), SJB is located below lefthand side of instrument panel.
4. Turn ignition switch ON and visually monitor air bag indicator for 30 seconds. Air bag indicator will remain on if correct fuse has been removed. If indicator lamp does not remain on, remove correct fuse from SJB.
5. Turn ignition switch to OFF position.
6. Disconnect battery ground cable and isolate as required. **Wait at least 60 seconds for power supply to deplete.**

THUNDERBIRD

2004

1. Disconnect battery ground cable and wait at least one minute for back-up power supply to deplete.
2. Remove two pin-type retainers from lower steering column opening finish panel, pull out on finish panel far enough to access and disconnect electrical connectors.
3. Remove lower steering column finish panel.
4. Remove two pin-type retainers from driver side lower insulator panel.
5. Remove light socket from insulator panel and panel from instrument panel.
6. Remove mounting screws and disconnect hood latch from steering column reinforcement.

7. Remove mounting screw and heater duct.
8. Position carpet aside and loosen two driver side instrument panel tunnel brace bolts.
9. Remove mounting screws and lower steering column reinforcement from instrument panel.
10. Disconnect clockspring electrical connector located at base of steering column.
11. Attach restraint system diagnostic tool No. 418-F088, or equivalent, to clockspring electrical connector.
12. Remove glove compartment and door.
13. Locate passenger air bag module electrical connector by reaching through glove compartment opening towards center of instrument panel and above cross-car beam. **Passenger air bag module connector is not visible because of its mounting position in instrument panel.**
14. Disconnect passenger air bag module electrical connector.
15. Attach restraint system diagnostic tool No. 418-F395, or equivalent, to vehicle harness side of passenger air bag electrical connector.
16. Connect battery ground cable and move front seats to highest and most forward positions.
17. Disconnect battery ground cable and wait at least one minute for back-up power supply to deplete.
18. Disconnect passenger seat side impact air bag electrical connector located under passenger seat.
19. Attach restraint system diagnostic tool No. 418-F133, or equivalent, to passenger seat side impact air bag electrical connector.
20. Remove passenger side door scuff plate and weather stripping.
21. Remove safety belt from passenger seat guide.
22. Remove speaker grille from passenger side rear trim panel.
23. Remove snap screws and passenger side rear trim panel.
24. Disconnect passenger safety belt retractor pretensioner electrical connector.
25. Attach restraint system diagnostic tool No. 418-F395, or equivalent, to passenger safety belt retractor pretensioner electrical connector.
26. Disconnect driver seat side impact air bag electrical connector located under driver seat.
27. Attach restraint system diagnostic tool No. 418-F133, or equivalent, to driver seat side impact air bag electrical connector.
28. Remove driver side door scuff plate and weather stripping.
29. Remove safety belt from driver seat guide.
30. Remove speaker grille from driver side rear trim panel.
31. Remove snap screws and driver side rear trim panel.
32. Disconnect driver safety belt retractor pretensioner electrical connector.
33. Attach restraint system diagnostic tool No. 418-F395, or equivalent, to driver

safety belt retractor pretensioner electrical connector.
34. Connect battery ground cable.

2005

1. Disconnect battery ground cable and isolate as required. **Wait at least 60 seconds for power supply to deplete.**
2. Remove two steering wheel back cover plugs and two driver's side air bag module bolts.
3. Remove driver's side air bag module, disconnecting electrical connectors as required.
4. Attach a restraint system diagnostic tool to clockspring electrical connector at top of steering wheel.
5. Remove glove compartment and door as required.
6. Disconnect passenger's side air bag module electrical connector locking clip. **This is a blind operation due to electrical connector mounting location.**
7. Attach a restraint system diagnostic tool to vehicle harness side of passenger's side air bag module electrical connector.
8. Connect battery ground cable.
9. Place front seats to highest and most forward position.
10. Disconnect battery ground cable and isolate as required. **Wait at least 60 seconds for power supply to deplete.**
11. Disconnect passenger's seat side impact air bag module electrical connector from under seat.
12. Attach a restraint system diagnostic tool to side impact air bag module electrical connector.
13. Remove passenger's side door scuff plate and weather-stripping.
14. Remove safety belt from passenger's seat guide.
15. Separate passenger's side rear trim panel.
16. Disconnect passenger's side safety belt retractor pretensioner electrical connector.
17. Attach a restraint system diagnostic tool to passenger's side safety belt retractor pretensioner electrical connector.
18. Disconnect driver's seat side impact air bag module electrical connector from under seat.
19. Attach a restraint system diagnostic tool to side impact air bag module electrical connector.
20. Remove driver's side door scuff plate and weather-stripping.
21. Remove safety belt from driver's seat guide.
22. Remove driver's side rear trim panel.
23. Disconnect driver's side safety belt retractor pretensioner electrical connector.
24. Attach a restraint system diagnostic tool to driver's side safety belt retractor pretensioner electrical connector.
25. Connect battery ground cable.
26. With restraint system diagnostic tools connected at all devices, prove out system as required.

27. Disconnect battery ground cable and isolate as required. **Wait at least 60 seconds for power supply to deplete.**

TOWN CAR

2004

1. Disconnect and isolate battery ground cable.
2. **On models equipped with auxiliary batteries and power supplies,** disconnect and isolate these items.
3. **On all models,** wait one minute for back-up power supply to deplete.
4. Remove steering column opening lower finish panel by removing parking brake release then pulling out at top of panel to release retaining clips.
5. Remove mounting bolts and steering column lower reinforcement.
6. Remove lefthand lower instrument panel insulator.
7. Pushing in on release tab, disconnect clockspring electrical connector at base of steering column.
8. Attach restraint system diagnostic tool No. 418-F403, or equivalent to vehicle harness side of clockspring electrical connector.
9. Remove audio unit.
10. Remove instrument panel cluster finish panel from instrument panel.
11. Open glove compartment and disconnect glove compartment isolator.
12. While pushing in on two glove compartment door tabs, position glove compartment downward.
13. Through glove compartment opening, remove passenger air bag module wire harness pin type fasteners from instrument panel.
14. Through glove box opening, remove passenger air bag module bolts.
15. Placing one hand in glove compartment opening, push passenger air bag module out from instrument panel. **Do not handle air bag module by grabbing edges of deployment doors.**
16. Disconnect passenger air bag module electrical connector and remove air bag module.
17. Attach restraint system diagnostic tool No. 418-F403, or equivalent, to vehicle harness side of passenger side impact air bag module electrical connector.
18. Connect battery ground cable.
19. Move and tilt front seats to highest and most forward position.
20. Disconnect battery ground cable and wait at least one minute for back-up power supply to deplete.
21. **On models equipped less side impact air bags,** proceed as follows:
    a. **Do not deactivate side impact air bags module circuit by removing side impact air bag bridge resistor from side impact air bag floor electrical connector.**
    b. If side impact air bag bridge resistor is removed, an open circuit fault will be generated by restraints control module (RCM).
    c. If restraint system diagnostic tool is installed at side impact air bag floor electrical connector, low resistance

fault will be generated by RCM.
22. **On models equipped with side impact air bags,** proceed as follows:
    a. From under front passenger seat, release tab and disconnect passenger seat side impact air bag electrical connector.
    b. Attach restraint system diagnostic tool No. 418-FO88, or equivalent, to vehicle harness side of passenger seat side impact air bag electrical connector.
23. **On all models,** remove passenger side B-pillar lower trim panel.
24. Push in on release tab and disconnect passenger safety belt retractor pretensioner electrical connector.
25. Attach restraint system diagnostic tool No. 418-FO88, or equivalent, to vehicle harness side of passenger safety belt retractor pretensioner electrical connector.
26. **On models equipped with side impact air bags,** proceed as follows:
    a. From under driver seat, release tab and disconnect driver seat side impact air bag electrical connector.
    b. Attach restraint system diagnostic tool No. 418-FO88, or equivalent, to vehicle harness side of driver seat side impact air bag electrical connector.
27. **On all models,** remove driver side B-pillar lower trim panel.
28. Push in on release tab and disconnect driver safety belt retractor pretensioner electrical connector.
29. Attach restraint system diagnostic tool to vehicle harness side of driver side safety belt retractor pretensioner electrical connector.
30. Connect battery ground cable.
31. With restraint system diagnostic tools installed on all deployable devices, prove out supplemental restraint system.
32. Turn ignition switch from Off to Run position and visually monitor air bag indicator with air bag modules and pretensioners or restraint system diagnostic tools installed.
33. Air bag lamp will illuminate for approximately six seconds and turn off.
34. If air bag supplemental restraint system fault is present, air bag indicator will either fail to illuminate, remain illuminate continuously or flash.
35. Disconnect battery ground cable and wait for at least one minute for back-up power supply to deplete.

2005

1. Turn all vehicle accessories to OFF position.
2. Turn ignition switch to OFF position.
3. Remove restraints control module (RCM) fuse F2.2 (10A) from central junction box (CJB).
4. Turn ignition ON and visually monitor air bag indicator for 30 seconds. Air bag indicator will remain lit continuously if correct fuse has been removed.
5. Turn ignition switch to OFF position.
6. Disconnect battery ground cable and isolate as required. **Wait at least 60 seconds for power supply to deplete.**

7. Remove driver's side air bag module using a suitable flatbladed screwdriver placed through one of four holes to disengage spring clips and locking pins.
8. Disconnect and remove driver's side air bag module, disconnecting electrical connectors as required.
9. Attach a restraint system diagnostic tool to clockspring electrical connectors at top of steering wheel.
10. Open glove compartment, disconnect glove compartment isolator.
11. Position glove compartment door downward while pushing inward on door tabs.
12. Disconnect passenger's side air bag module electrical connector.
13. Remove passenger's side air bag module bolts, pushing air bag module out from instrument panel.
14. Disconnect electrical connectors from passenger's side air bag module jumper harness.
15. Depress two locking tabs on side of passenger's side air bag module jumper harness electrical connector and disconnect.
16. Attach two restraint system diagnostic tools to two passenger's side air bag module jumper harness electrical connectors, install locking inserts to connectors.
17. Connect passenger's side air bag module jumper harness to passenger's side air bag module electrical connector at vehicle wiring harness.
18. Connect battery ground cable.
19. Place front seats to their highest and most forward position.
20. Disconnect battery ground cable and isolate as required. **Wait at least 60 seconds for power supply to deplete.**
21. Disconnect passenger's seat side impact air bag module electrical connector.
22. Attach a restraint system diagnostic tool to seat harness side of passenger's seat side impact air bag module electrical connector.
23. Disconnect driver's seat side impact air bag module electrical connector.
24. Attach a restraint system diagnostic tool to seat harness side of driver's seat side impact air bag module electrical connector.
25. Install RCM fuse F2.2 (10A) to CJB.
26. Connect battery ground cable.

2006–07

1. Turn all vehicle accessories Off.
2. Turn ignition switch to Off position.
3. Open kick panel cover located on lefthand end of instrument panel and remove Restraints Control Module (RCM) fuse from Central Junction Box (CJB).
4. Turn ignition On and visually monitor air bag indicator for at least 30 seconds. Air bag indicator will remain lit continuously if correct RCM fuse has been removed. If air bag indicator does not remain lit continuously, remove correct RCM fuse before proceeding.
5. Turn ignition switch to Off position.
6. Disconnect battery ground cable and

isolate as required. **Wait at least 60 seconds for power supply to deplete.**

Arming

If flash is incorrect or fault detected, refer to **MOTOR's "Air Bag Quick Reference Guide."**

CROWN VICTORIA & GRAND MARQUIS

2004

1. Disconnect battery ground cable.
2. Wait at least one minute for back-up power supply to deplete.
3. Remove restraint system diagnostic tool from driver safety belt retractor and pretensioner electrical connector.
4. Connect driver safety belt retractor and pretensioner electrical connectors.
5. Remove restraint system diagnostic tool from passenger safety belt retractor and pretensioner electrical connectors.
6. Connect passenger safety belt retractor and pretensioner electrical connectors.
7. Install front seats.
8. Remove restraint system diagnostic tools from passenger air bag module electrical connectors.
9. Install passenger air bag module electrical connector.
10. Remove restraint system diagnostic tools from driver air bag module electrical connectors.
11. Install driver air bag module electrical connector.
12. Connect battery ground cable.
13. Turn ignition switch from OFF to RUN position and visually monitor air bag indicator with air bag modules and safety belt pretensioners or restraint system diagnostic tools installed.
14. Air bag indicator will light continuously for approximately six seconds and then turn off.
15. If air bag supplemental restraint system (SRS) fault is present, air bag indicator will either fail to light, remain lit continuously, or flash.
16. Flashing might not occur until approximately 30 seconds after ignition switch has been turned from OFF to RUN position. This is time required for restraints control module (RCM) to complete testing of SRS.
17. If air bag indicator is inoperative and SRS fault exists, chime will sound in pattern of five sets of five beeps. If this occurs, air bag indicator will need to be repaired before diagnosis can continue.

2005

1. Remove RCM fuse F2.22 (10A) from CJB.
2. Disconnect battery ground cable and isolate as required. **Wait at least 60 seconds for power supply to deplete.**
3. **On models equipped with side impact air bag modules,** proceed as follows:
   a. Remove restraint system diagnostic tool from driver's seat side impact air bag module electrical connector.
   b. Connect driver's seat side impact air bag module electrical connector at lower rear of seat cushion pan.
   c. Remove restraint diagnostic tool from passenger's seat side impact air bag module electrical connector.
   d. Connect passenger's seat side impact air bag module electrical connector at lower rear of seat cushion pan.
4. **On all models,** disconnect passenger's side air bag module electrical connector on vehicle wiring harness.
5. Separate locking inserts and disconnect two restraint diagnostic tools from passenger's side air bag module jumper harness electrical connectors.
6. Align and connect passenger's side air bag module jumper harness electrical connectors to passenger's side air bag module and install locking inserts.
7. Ensure J-nuts on passenger's side air bag module are fully attached into slots as required.
8. Install passenger's side air bag module into instrument panel, then the bolts.
9. Connect passenger's side air bag module electrical connector and attach retainer to bracket.
10. Install trim panel and connect glove compartment isolator.
11. Remove restraint system diagnostic tools from clockspring electrical connectors from steering column.
12. **There are two steering wheels for these models, if installing a new steering wheel, Ensure correct wheel is being installed.**
13. Identify and install correct driver's side air bag module, connect horn electrical connector and air bag module electrical connectors.
14. Align driver's side air bag module locking pins to openings in steering wheel and position driver's side air bag module on steering wheel.
15. With locking pins aligned, push inward seating four locking pins to spring clips.
16. **Ensure all restraint system diagnostic tools from vehicle and all SRS components are connected.**
17. Turn ignition switch to ON position.
18. Install RCM fuse F2.22 (10A) to CJB and replace cover.
19. Connect battery ground cable.
20. Prove out system as follows:
   a. Turn ignition key to OFF position.
   b. Wait 10 seconds, then turn key to ON position and visually monitor air bag indicator.
   c. Air bag indicator will be lit continuously for 6 seconds then turn Off.
   d. If air bag system fault is present, air bag indicator will fail to light, remain lit continuously or flash.
   e. Flashing will occur up to 30 seconds after ignition switch has been turned from the OFF to ON position.
   f. If fault occurs, a chime will sound.

2006–07

1. Ensure all restraint system diagnostic tool(s) have been removed and all SRS components are connected.
2. Turn ignition switch to On position.
3. Install Restraints Control Module (RCM) fuse into Central Junction Block (CJB) and close cover.
4. **Ensure nobody is in vehicle and that there is nothing blocking or set in front of any air bag module when battery ground cable is connected.** Connect battery ground cable.
5. Prove out SRS as follows:
   a. Turn ignition key from On to Off position. Wait 10 seconds, then turn key back to On and visually monitor air bag indicator with air bag modules installed. Air bag indicator will light continuously for approximately 6 seconds and then turn Off. If an air bag SRS fault is present, air bag indicator will fail to light, remain lit continuously or flash.
   b. Flashing might not occur until approximately 30 seconds after ignition switch has been turned from Off to On position. This is time required for RCM to complete testing of SRS. If air bag indicator is inoperative and a SRS fault exists, a chime will sound in a pattern of 5 sets of 5 beeps. If this occurs, air bag indicator and any SRS fault discovered must be diagnosed and repaired.
   c. Clear all continuous DTC's from RCM using a suitable scan tool.

FIVE-HUNDRED, FREESTYLE & MONTEGO

1. Ensure all restraint system diagnostic tool(s) have been removed and all SRS components are connected.
2. Turn ignition switch from Off to On position.
3. Install Restraints Control Module (RCM) fuse into Smart Junction Box (SJB) and close cover.
4. **Ensure nobody is in vehicle and that there is nothing blocking or set in front of any air bag module when battery ground cable is connected.** Connect battery ground cable.
5. Prove out SRS as follows:
   a. Turn ignition key from On to Off position. Wait 10 seconds, then turn key back to On and visually monitor air bag indicator with air bag modules installed. Air bag indicator will light continuously for approximately 6 seconds and then turn Off. If an air bag SRS fault is present, air bag indicator will fail to light, remain lit continuously or flash.
   b. Flashing might not occur until approximately 30 seconds after ignition switch has been turned from Off to On position. This is time required for RCM to complete testing of SRS. If air bag indicator is inoperative and a SRS fault exists, a chime will sound in a pattern of 5

sets of 5 beeps. If this occurs, air bag indicator and any SRS fault discovered must be diagnosed and repaired.

c. Clear all continuous DTC's from RCM using a suitable scan tool.

FOCUS

2004

1. Disconnect and isolate battery ground cable.
2. **On models equipped with auxiliary batteries and power supplies,** disconnect and isolate these items.
3. **On all models,** wait one minute for back-up power supply to deplete.
4. Remove air bag simulator from harness on top of steering column.
5. Connect driver's air bag connector.
6. Position driver's air bag on steering wheel and secure with two bolts. **When carrying live air bag module, ensure bag and trim cover are pointed away from your body. Place module on bench with trim cover facing upward.**
7. **Torque** mounting screws to 44 inch lbs.
8. Remove air bag simulator from passenger's air bag harness connector.
9. Connect passenger's air bag module electrical connector.
10. Remove air bag simulator from driver's side seat belt pretensioner connector.
11. Connect driver's side seat belt pretensioner electrical connector.
12. Remove air bag simulator from driver's side impact air bag connector.
13. Connect driver's side impact air bag electrical connector.
14. Remove air bag simulator from passenger's side seat belt pretensioner connector.
15. Connect passenger's side seat belt pretensioner electrical connector.
16. Remove air bag simulator from passenger's side impact air bag connector.
17. Connect passenger's side impact air bag electrical connector.
18. Install glove compartment.
19. Connect battery ground cable.
20. **From safe location at sides or below air bag modules,** place ignition switch in Run position and observe air bag warning lamp operating. Indicator lamp should light for approximately six seconds and turn off.
21. Reset radio stations and clock.

2005

1. Remove RCM fuse F2.60 (7.5A) from CJB.
2. Disconnect battery ground cable and isolate as required. **Wait at least 60 seconds for power supply to deplete.**
3. **On models equipped with side impact air bag modules,** remove restraint system diagnostic tool from vehicle harness side of driver's seat side impact air bag modules electrical connectors, then install driver's seat electrical connector.
4. **On models equipped with side im-**

pact air bag modules, remove restraint system diagnostic tool from vehicle harness side of passenger's seat side impact air bag modules electrical connectors, then install passenger's seat electrical connector.

5. **On all models,** loosen passenger's side air bag module floating bracket nuts, remove restraint system diagnostic tools, then install passenger's side air bag module and connect electrical connectors.
6. Attach passenger's side air bag module and reinforcement bracket to instrument panel.
7. Install passenger's side air bag module trim cover.
8. Install passenger's side air bag module trim cover bolts, do not tighten bolts at this time.
9. **Torque** passenger's side air bag module floating bracket bolts to 104 inch lbs.
10. **Torque** passenger's side air bag module trim cover bolts to 104 inch lbs.
11. Install defroster pipe to heater housing and defroster vent.
12. Install ventilation pipe and retaining clip.
13. Close glove compartment door.
14. Remove restraint system diagnostic tool from driver's side air bag module electrical connector at clockspring.
15. Install driver's side air bag module electrical connector, then the air bag module to steering wheel connecting clips and bolts.
16. Ensure all restraint system diagnostic tools from SRS system and all SRS components are connected.
17. Turn ignition switch from OFF to ON position.
18. Instal RCM fuse F2.60 (7.5A) to CJB.
19. Connect battery ground cable.
20. Prove out system as follows:
    a. Turn ignition key to OFF position.
    b. Wait 10 seconds, then turn key to ON position and visually monitor air bag indicator.
    c. Air bag indicator will be lit continuously for 6 seconds then turn Off.
    d. If air bag system fault is present, air bag indicator will fail to light, remain lit continuously or flash.
    e. Flashing will occur up to 30 seconds after ignition switch has been turned from the OFF to ON position.
    f. If fault occurs, a chime will sound.

2006-07

1. Ensure all restraint system diagnostic tool(s) have been removed and all SRS components are connected.
2. Turn ignition switch from Off to On position.
3. Install Restraints Control Module (RCM) fuse into Central Junction Block (CJB) and close cover.
4. **Ensure nobody is in vehicle and that there is nothing blocking or set in front of any air bag module when battery ground cable is connected.** Connect battery ground cable.
5. Prove out SRS as follows:
    a. Turn ignition key from On to Off position. Wait 10 seconds, then turn

key back to On and visually monitor air bag indicator with air bag modules installed. Air bag indicator will light continuously for approximately 6 seconds and then turn Off. If an air bag SRS fault is present, air bag indicator will fail to light, remain lit continuously or flash at a 5 Hz rate (RCM not configured).

b. Flashing might not occur until approximately 30 seconds after ignition switch has been turned from Off to On position. This is time required for RCM to complete testing of SRS. If air bag indicator is inoperative and a SRS fault exists, a chime will sound in a pattern of 5 sets of 5 beeps. If this occurs, air bag indicator and any SRS fault discovered must be diagnosed and repaired.

c. Clear all continuous DTC's from RCM using a suitable scan tool.

FUSION, MILAN & ZEPHYR

1. Ensure all restraint system diagnostic tool(s) have been removed and all SRS components are connected.
2. Turn ignition switch from Off to On position.
3. Install Restraints Control Module (RCM) fuse into Smart Junction Box (SJB) and close cover.
4. **Ensure nobody is in vehicle and that there is nothing blocking or set in front of any air bag module when battery ground cable is connected.** Connect battery ground cable.
5. Prove out SRS as follows:
    a. Turn ignition key from On to Off position. Wait 10 seconds, then turn key back to On and visually monitor air bag indicator with air bag modules installed. Air bag indicator will light continuously for approximately six seconds and then turn Off. If an air bag SRS fault is present, air bag indicator will fail to light, remain lit continuously or flash at a 5 Hz rate (RCM not configured).
    b. Flashing might not occur until approximately 30 seconds after ignition switch has been turned from Off to On position. This is time required for RCM to complete testing of SRS. If air bag indicator is inoperative and a SRS fault exists, a chime will sound in a pattern of 5 sets of 5 beeps. If this occurs, air bag indicator and any SRS fault discovered must be diagnosed and repaired.
    c. Clear all continuous DTC's from RCM using a suitable scan tool.

LS

2004

1. Disconnect and isolate battery ground cable.
2. **On models equipped with auxiliary batteries and power supplies,** disconnect and isolate these items.
3. **On all models,** wait one minute for back-up power supply to deplete.

4. Remove seat belt pretensioner simulator tool from passenger's seat belt pretensioner harness connector.
5. Connect passenger's seat belt pretensioner electrical connector.
6. Install passenger side B-pillar pillar trim.
7. Remove seat belt pretensioner simulator tool from driver's seat belt pretensioner harness connector.
8. Connect driver's seat belt pretensioner electrical connector.
9. Install driver side B-pillar pillar trim.
10. Remove air bag simulator tool from harness connector at top of steering column.
11. Connect driver's air bag electrical connector.
12. Position driver's air bag on steering wheel and secure with its bolts. **When carrying live air bag module, ensure bag and trim cover are pointed away from your body. Place module on bench with trim cover facing upward.**
13. **Torque** mounting bolts to 108 inch lbs.
14. Remove air bag simulator from passenger's air bag harness connector.
15. Connect passenger's air bag module electrical connector.
16. Install glove compartment.
17. Remove air bag simulator from passenger's side impact air bag connector.
18. Connect passenger's side impact air bag electrical connector.
19. Remove air bag simulator from driver's side impact air bag connector.
20. Connect driver's side impact air bag electrical connector.
21. Connect battery ground cable.
22. **From safe location at sides or below air bag modules,** place ignition switch in Run position and observe air bag warning lamp operating. Indicator lamp should light for approximately six seconds and turn off.
23. Reset radio stations and clock.

2005

1. Remove RCM fuse F2.05 (10A) from CJB.
2. Disconnect battery ground cable and isolate as required. **Wait at least 60 seconds for power supply to deplete.**
3. **On models less side impact air bag modules,** remove restraint system diagnostic tool from vehicle harness side of driver's seat side impact air bag electrical connectors.
4. **On models equipped with side impact air bag modules,** remove restraint system diagnostic tool from vehicle harness side of driver's seat side thorax impact air bag module electrical connector.
5. **On all models,** connect driver's seat side impact air bag module or driver's seat side thorax impact air bag module electrical connector.
6. **On models less roof panel air bag modules,** remove restraint system diagnostic tool from vehicle side harness side of passenger's seat side impact air bag module electrical connector.

7. **On models equipped with side impact air bag modules,** remove restraint system diagnostic tool from vehicle harness side of passenger's seat side thorax air bag electrical connector.
8. **On all models,** connect passenger's seat side thorax or passenger's seat side impact air bag module electrical connectors.
9. **On models equipped with roof panel air bag modules,** remove restraint system diagnostic tool from vehicle harness side of passenger's side roof panel air bag module electrical connector.
10. **On models equipped with roof panel air bag modules,** connect passenger's side roof panel air bag module electrical connector, then install A-pillar trim panel.
11. **On all models,** remove restraint system diagnostic tool from vehicle harness side of passenger's side air bag module electrical connector, then connect passenger's side air bag module electrical connectors.
12. Install glove compartment.
13. **On models equipped with roof panel air bag modules,** remove restraint system diagnostic tool from vehicle harness side of driver's side roof panel air bag module electrical connector, then connect module electrical connectors and install A-pillar trim panel.
14. **On all models,** remove restraint system diagnostic tool from clockspring electrical connectors at steering column.
15. Install driver's side air bag module electrical connectors, then the module to steering wheel.
16. Install driver's side air bag module bolts and plugs and **torque** to 108 inch lbs.
17. Turn ignition switch from OFF to ON position.
18. Install RCM fuse F2.05 (10A) to CJB and replace cover.
19. Prove out system as follows:
    a. Turn ignition key to OFF position.
    b. Wait 10 seconds, then turn key to ON position and visually monitor air bag indicator.
    c. Air bag indicator will be lit continuously for 6 seconds then turn Off.
    d. If air bag system fault is present, air bag indicator will fail to light, remain lit continuously or flash.
    e. Flashing will occur up to 30 seconds after ignition switch has been turned from the OFF to ON position.
    f. If fault occurs, a chime will sound.

2006

1. Ensure all restraint system diagnostic tool(s) have been removed and all SRS components are connected.
2. Turn ignition switch from Off to On position.
3. Install Restraints Control Module (RCM) fuse into Central Junction Block (CJB) and close cover.
4. **Ensure nobody is in vehicle and that there is nothing blocking or set**

in front of any air bag module when battery ground cable is connected. Connect battery ground cable.
5. Prove out SRS as follows:
    a. Turn ignition key from On to Off position. Wait 10 seconds, then turn key back to On and visually monitor air bag indicator with air bag modules installed. Air bag indicator will light continuously for approximately 6 seconds and then turn Off. If an air bag SRS fault is present, air bag indicator will fail to light, remain lit continuously or flash.
    b. Flashing might not occur until approximately 30 seconds after ignition switch has been turned from Off to On position. This is time required for RCM to complete testing of SRS. If air bag indicator is inoperative and a SRS fault exists, a chime will sound in a pattern of 5 sets of 5 beeps. If this occurs, air bag indicator and any SRS fault discovered must be diagnosed and repaired.
    c. Clear all continuous DTC's from RCM using a suitable scan tool.

MUSTANG

2004-05

1. Disconnect battery ground cable.
2. **On models equipped with auxiliary batteries and power supplies,** disconnect and isolate these items.
3. **On all models,** allow at least one minute for back-up power supply to deplete.
4. **On models equipped with side impact air bag modules,** proceed as follows:
    a. Remove restraint system diagnostic tool from vehicle harness side of driver's side impact air bag module electrical connector.
    b. Connect driver's side air bag module electrical connector and reset red locking tab.
    c. remove restraint system diagnostic tool from vehicle harness side of passenger's side air bag module electrical connector.
    d. Connect passenger's side air bag module electrical connector and reset red locking tab.
5. **On all models,** remove air bag simulator tool from harness connector at top of steering column.
6. Connect driver's air bag connector.
7. Position driver's air bag on steering wheel and secure with four nut and bolt assemblies.
8. **Torque** driver's air bag module mounting bolts/nuts to 80 inch lbs.
9. Remove air bag simulator tool from passenger's air bag module harness then position module in instrument panel.
10. Attach connector to instrument panel reinforcement and wiring harness.
11. Install passenger's air bag mounting bolt.
12. **Torque** passenger's air bag module mounting bolts to 80 inch lbs.

13. Press gently on air bag module corners to engage with instrument panel trim and install righthand side air conditioning duct.
14. Press sides of glove compartment together and lift into position in instrument panel. Close glove compartment door.
15. Turn ignition switch from OFF to ON position.
16. Install RCM fuse F2.17 (10A) to SJB and replace cover.
17. Connect battery ground cable.
18. Prove out system as follows:
    a. Turn ignition key to OFF position.
    b. Wait 10 seconds, then turn key to ON position and visually monitor air bag indicator.
    c. Air bag indicator will be lit continuously for 6 seconds then turn Off.
    d. If air bag system fault is present, air bag indicator will fail to light, remain lit continuously or flash.
    e. Flashing will occur up to 30 seconds after ignition switch has been turned from the OFF to ON position.
    f. If fault occurs, a chime will sound.

2006-08

1. Ensure all restraint system diagnostic tool(s) have been removed and all SRS components are connected.
2. Turn ignition switch from Off to On position.
3. Install RCM fuse 17 (10A) to SJB and close cover.
4. **Ensure nobody is in vehicle and that there is nothing blocking or set in front of any air bag module when battery ground cable is connected.** Connect battery ground cable.
5. Prove out SRS as follows:
    a. Turn ignition key from On to Off position. Wait 10 seconds, then turn key back to On and visually monitor air bag indicator with air bag modules installed. Air bag indicator will light continuously for approximately 6 seconds and then turn Off. If an air bag SRS fault is present, air bag indicator will fail to light, remain lit continuously or flash.
    b. Flashing might not occur until approximately 30 seconds after ignition switch has been turned from Off to On position. This is time required for RCM to complete testing of SRS. If air bag indicator is inoperative and a SRS fault exists, a chime will sound in a pattern of 5 sets of 5 beeps. If this occurs, air bag indicator and any SRS fault discovered must be diagnosed and repaired.
    c. Clear all continuous DTC's from RCM using a suitable scan tool.

SABLE, TAURUS & TAURUS X

2004

1. Disconnect and isolate battery ground cable.
2. **On models equipped with auxiliary batteries and power supplies,** disconnect and isolate these items also.

3. **On all models,** wait one minute for back-up power supply to deplete.
4. Disconnect driver's air bag restraint system diagnostic tool from vehicle side of driver's air bag sliding contact electrical connector.
5. Connect driver's air bag sliding contact electrical connector.
6. Install steering column lower cover and reinforcement.
7. Disconnect passenger's air bag restraint system diagnostic tool from vehicle side of passenger's air bag electrical connector.
8. Inspect position of passenger's air bag module J-nuts.
9. Position air bag module and trim cover to instrument panel. **When carrying live air bag module, ensure bag and trim cover are pointed away from your body. Place module on bench with trim cover facing upward.**
10. Install wiring harness pin retaining to air bag module.
11. Connect passenger's air bag module electrical connector.
12. Align air bag module channels with instrument panel rails.
13. Starting at lefthand side of air bag module trim cover, install upper and lower alignment pins into instrument panel.
14. Working from left to right, install trim cover alignment pins and retainers into instrument panel. When all channels and rails are aligned, gap around perimeter of air bag module trim cover will be even.
15. Through glove compartment opening, install passengers air bag module mounting bolts.
16. **Torque** mounting bolts to 71 inch lbs.
17. Close glove compartment.
18. Disconnect passenger's seat belt pretensioner restraint system diagnostic tool from 10 pin floor electrical connector.
19. Connect passenger's seat belt pretensioner electrical connector.
20. **On models equipped with side impact air bags,** disconnect side impact air bag restraint system diagnostic tool from side impact air bag floor electrical connector on passenger's side. Connect side impact air bag electrical connector on passenger's side.
21. **On all models,** disconnect driver's seat belt pretensioner restraint system diagnostic tool from 10 pin floor electrical connector.
22. Connect driver's seat belt pretensioner electrical connector.
23. **On models equipped with side impact air bags,** disconnect side impact air bag restraint system diagnostic tool from side impact air bag floor electrical connector on driver's side.
24. **On models equipped with side impact air bags,** connect side impact air bag electrical connector on driver's side.
25. **On all models,** connect battery ground cable.
26. **From safe location at sides or below air bag modules,** place ignition switch in Run position and observe air bag

warning lamp operating. Indicator lamp should light for approximately six seconds and turn off.

2005

1. Remove RCM fuse F2.20 (10A) from SJB.
2. Disconnect battery ground cable and isolate as required. **Wait at least 60 seconds for power supply to deplete.**
3. **On models equipped with side impact air bag modules,** proceed as follows:
    a. Remove restraint system diagnostic tool from vehicle harness side of driver seat side impact air bag module electrical connector.
    b. Connect driver's seat side impact air bag module electrical connector.
    c. Remove restraint system diagnostic tool from vehicle harness side of passenger's seat side impact air bag module electrical connector.
    d. Connect passenger's seat side impact air bag module electrical connector.
4. **On all models,** remove restraint system diagnostic tool from vehicle harness side of passenger's seat side air bag module electrical connector.
5. Install passenger's side air bag module electrical connector, position air bag module in alignment channels and install module and trim cover to instrument panel.
6. Install trim cover tabs and alignment pins into instrument panel moving from lefthand to righthand side.
7. Install passenger's side air bag module bolts, **torque** to 80 inch lbs.
8. Close glove compartment.
9. Remove restraint system diagnostic tools from clockspring electrical connectors at steering column.
10. Connect driver's side air bag module electrical connectors and place module to steering wheel.
11. Install two driver's side air bag module bolts, **torque** to 80 inch lbs.
12. Install two driver's side air bag module back cover nuts.
13. Turn ignition switch from OFF to ON position.
14. Install RCM fuse F2.20 (10A) to SJB and install cover.
15. Connect battery ground cable.
16. Prove out system as follows:
    a. Turn ignition key to OFF position.
    b. Wait 10 seconds, then turn key to ON position and visually monitor air bag indicator.
    c. Air bag indicator will be lit continuously for 6 seconds then turn Off.
    d. If air bag system fault is present, air bag indicator will fail to light, remain lit continuously or flash.
    e. Flashing will occur up to 30 seconds after ignition switch has been turned from the OFF to ON position.
    f. If fault occurs, a chime will sound.

2006

1. Ensure all restraint system diagnostic tool(s) have been removed and all SRS components are connected.

2. Turn ignition switch from Off to On position.
3. Install RCM fuse F2.20 (10A) to SJB and close cover.
4. **Ensure nobody is in vehicle and that there is nothing blocking or set in front of any air bag module when battery ground cable is connected.** Connect battery ground cable.
5. Prove out SRS as follows:
   a. Turn ignition key from On to Off position. Wait 10 seconds, then turn key back to On and visually monitor air bag indicator with air bag modules installed. Air bag indicator will light continuously for approximately 6 seconds and then turn Off. If an air bag SRS fault is present, air bag indicator will fail to light, remain lit continuously or flash.
   b. Flashing might not occur until approximately 30 seconds after ignition switch has been turned from Off to On position. This is time required for RCM to complete testing of SRS. If air bag indicator is inoperative and a SRS fault exists, a chime will sound in a pattern of 5 sets of 5 beeps. If this occurs, air bag indicator and any SRS fault discovered must be diagnosed and repaired.
   c. Clear all continuous DTC's from RCM using a suitable scan tool.

2008

1. Ensure all restraint system diagnostic tool(s) have been removed and all SRS components are connected.
2. Turn ignition switch from Off to On position.
3. Install Restraints Control Module (RCM) fuse into Smart Junction Box (SJB) and close cover.
4. **Ensure nobody is in vehicle and that there is nothing blocking or set in front of any air bag module when battery ground cable is connected.** Connect battery ground cable.
5. Prove out SRS as follows:
   a. Turn ignition key from On to Off position. Wait 10 seconds, then turn key back to On and visually monitor air bag indicator with air bag modules installed. Air bag indicator will light continuously for approximately 6 seconds and then turn Off. If an air bag SRS fault is present, air bag indicator will fail to light, remain lit continuously or flash.
   b. Flashing might not occur until approximately 30 seconds after ignition switch has been turned from Off to On position. This is time required for RCM to complete testing of SRS. If air bag indicator is inoperative and a SRS fault exists, a chime will sound in a pattern of 5 sets of 5 beeps. If this occurs, air bag indicator and any SRS fault discovered must be diagnosed and repaired.
   c. Clear all continuous DTC's from RCM using a suitable scan tool.

THUNDERBIRD

2004

1. Disconnect battery ground cable and wait at least one minute for back-up power supply to deplete.
2. Remove diagnostic tool No. 418-F395, or equivalent, from driver side safety belt retractor pretensioner electrical connector.
3. Connect driver side safety belt retractor pretensioner electrical connector.
4. Install driver side rear trim panel and speaker grille.
5. Position safety belt back into driver seat guide, then install driver side door weather stripping and scuff plate.
6. Remove diagnostic tool No. 418-F133, or equivalent, from driver seat side impact air bag module electrical connector located under driver seat.
7. Connect driver seat side impact air bag module electrical connector.
8. Remove diagnostic tool No. 418-F395, or equivalent, from passenger side safety belt retractor pretensioner electrical connector.
9. Connect passenger side safety belt retractor pretensioner electrical connector.
10. Install passenger side rear trim panel and speaker grille.
11. Position safety belt back into passenger seat guide, then install passenger side door weather-stripping and scuff plate.
12. Remove diagnostic tool No. 418-F133, or equivalent, from passenger seat side impact air bag module electrical connector located under passenger seat.
13. Connect passenger seat side impact air bag module electrical connector.
14. Connect battery ground cable and move seats as far rearward as possible.
15. Disconnect battery ground cable and wait at least one minute for back-up power supply to deplete.
16. Reach through glove compartment opening and remove diagnostic tool No. 418-F395, or equivalent, from passenger air bag module electrical connector located behind center of instrument panel, above cross-car brace.
17. Connect passenger air bag module electrical connector, then install glove compartment and door.
18. Remove diagnostic tool No. 418-F088, or equivalent, from clockspring electrical connector located at base of steering column.
19. Connect clockspring electrical connector and install steering column reinforcement.
20. Tighten two driver side instrument panel tunnel brace bolts and position carpet back in place.
21. Install heater duct and hood latch.
22. Install driver side insulator panel and light socket.
23. Connect electrical connectors and in-

stall lower steering column opening finish panel.
24. Connect battery ground cable.
25. **From safe location at sides or below air bag modules,** place ignition switch in RUN position and observe air bag warning lamp operating. Indicator lamp should light for approximately six seconds and turn off.

2005

1. Disconnect battery ground cable and isolate as required. **Wait at least 60 seconds for power supply to deplete.**
2. Remove restraint system diagnostic tool from driver's side safety belt retractor pretensioner electrical connector.
3. Install driver's side safety belt retractor pretensioner electrical connector.
4. Install driver's side rear trim panel and speaker grille.
5. Place safety belt into driver's seat guide.
6. Install driver's side door weatherstripping and scuff plate.
7. Remove restraint system diagnostic tool from under driver's seat side impact air bag module floor electrical connector.
8. Connect driver's seat side impact air bag module electrical connector.
9. Remove restraint system diagnostic tool from passenger's side safety belt retractor pretensioner electrical connector.
10. Install passenger's side safety belt retractor pretensioner electrical connector.
11. Install passenger's side rear trim panel and speaker grille.
12. Place safety belt into passenger's seat guide.
13. Install passenger's side door weatherstripping and scuff plate.
14. Remove restraint system diagnostic tool from under passenger's seat side impact air bag module floor electrical connector.
15. Connect passenger's seat side impact air bag module electrical connector.
16. Connect battery ground cable.
17. Place front seats in rearward position.
18. Disconnect battery ground cable and isolate as required. **Wait at least 60 seconds for power supply to deplete.**
19. Remove restraint system diagnostic tool from vehicle harness side of passenger's side air bag module electrical connector.
20. Connect passenger's side air bag module electrical connector.
21. Install glove compartment and door.
22. Remove restraint system diagnostic tool from top of steering column.
23. Install driver's side air bag module to steering wheel, connecting electrical connectors as required.
24. Install two module bolts, **torque** to 108 inch lbs.
25. Install two back cover plugs.
26. Connect battery ground cable.
27. Prove out system as follows:

a. Turn ignition key to OFF position.
b. Wait 10 seconds, then turn key to ON position and visually monitor air bag indicator.
c. Air bag indicator will be lit continuously for 6 seconds then turn Off.
d. If air bag system fault is present, air bag indicator will fail to light, remain lit continuously or flash.
e. Flashing will occur up to 30 seconds after ignition switch has been turned from the OFF to ON position.
f. If fault occurs, a chime will sound.

TOWN CAR

2004

1. Disconnect and isolate battery ground cable.
2. **On models equipped with auxiliary batteries and power supplies,** disconnect and isolate these items also.
3. **On all models,** wait one minute for back-up power supply to deplete.
4. Remove air bag simulator from harness connector at top of steering column.
5. Connect driver's air bag module and horn to clockspring electrical connectors. **When carrying live air bag module, ensure bag and trim cover are pointed away from your body. Place module on bench with trim cover facing upward.**
6. Position driver's air bag module to steering wheel.
7. Install two driver's air bag module to steering wheel mounting bolts, **torque** to 108 inch lbs.
8. Install two steering wheel spoke bolt covers, if equipped.
9. Remove air bag simulator at passenger's air bag connector.
10. Connect passenger's air bag electrical connector and close glove compartment.
11. Remove air bag simulator from side impact air bag connector located beneath driver's seat and connect side impact air bag electrical connector.
12. Remove air bag simulator from side impact air bag connector located beneath passenger's seat and connect side impact air bag electrical connector.
13. If front seats were removed, install as follows:
    a. Position front seat in vehicle.
    b. Move front seat all way forward, then install seat track rear bolts and covers.
    c. Move front seat all way rearward, then install seat track front bolts and covers.
    d. Disconnect side air simulator tools from side impact air bag module floor connectors at driver's and passenger's sides.
    e. Connect driver's and passenger's front seat electrical connectors.
14. Connect battery ground cable.
15. **From safe location at sides or below air bag modules,** place ignition switch in Run position and observe air bag warning lamp operating. Indicator lamp should light for approximately six

seconds and turn off.

2005

1. Remove RCM fuse F2.2 (10A) from CJB.
2. Disconnect battery ground cable and isolate as required. **Wait at least 60 seconds for power supply to deplete.**
3. Remove restraint system diagnostic tool from driver's seat side impact air bag electrical connector.
4. Connect driver's seat side impact air bag module electrical connector from under rear of seat cushion pan.
5. Remove restraint system diagnostic tool from passenger's seat side impact air bag module electrical connector.
6. Connect passenger's seat side impact air bag module electrical connector from under rear of seat cushion.
7. Disconnect passenger's side air bag module jumper harness from passenger's side air bag electrical connector on vehicle wiring harness.
8. Separate locking inserts and disconnect two restraint system diagnostic tools from passenger's side air bag module jumper harness electrical connectors.
9. Align and connect passenger's air bag module jumper harness electrical connectors to module, install locking inserts and attach passenger's air bag module electrical connector pin-type retainer to passenger's air bag module.
10. Ensure J-clips on back of passenger's air bag module are locked into slots.
11. Ensure retaining clips on back of passenger's air bag module are locked onto ears.
12. Install passenger's side air bag module into instrument panel.
13. Install passenger's side air bag module bolts, **torque** to 80 inch lbs.
14. Connect passenger's side air bag module electrical connector.
15. Connect glove compartment isolator, close glove compartment.
16. Remove restraint system diagnostic tools from clockspring electrical connectors at top of steering column.
17. Ensure if new steering wheel is being installed, it is the same OEM that came off. **On early build models, tower is on lefthand side, on later built models, tower is on righthand side.**
18. Install driver's side air bag module, connect electrical connectors and align locking pins to openings in steering wheel and position air bag module in place.
19. Ensure all restraint system diagnostic tools have been removed and all SRS components connected.
20. Turn ignition switch from OFF to ON position.
21. Install RCM fuse F2.2 (10A) to CJB and replace cover.
22. Connect battery ground cable.
23. Prove out system as follows:
    a. Turn ignition key to OFF position.
    b. Wait 10 seconds, then turn key to ON position and visually monitor air bag indicator.

c. Air bag indicator will be lit continuously for 6 seconds then turn Off.
d. If air bag system fault is present, air bag indicator will fail to light, remain lit continuously or flash.
e. Flashing will occur up to 30 seconds after ignition switch has been turned from the OFF to ON position.
f. If fault occurs, a chime will sound.

2006-07

1. Ensure all restraint system diagnostic tool(s) have been removed and all SRS components are connected.
2. Turn ignition switch to On position.
3. Install Restraints Control Module (RCM) fuse into Central Junction Block (CJB) and close cover.
4. **Ensure nobody is in vehicle and that there is nothing blocking or set in front of any air bag module when battery ground cable is connected.** Connect battery ground cable.
5. Prove out SRS as follows:
    a. Turn ignition key from On to Off position. Wait 10 seconds, then turn key back to On and visually monitor air bag indicator with air bag modules installed. Air bag indicator will light continuously for approximately 6 seconds and then turn Off. If an air bag SRS fault is present, air bag indicator will fail to light, remain lit continuously or flash.
    b. Flashing might not occur until approximately 30 seconds after ignition switch has been turned from Off to On position. This is time required for RCM to complete testing of SRS. If air bag indicator is inoperative and a SRS fault exists, a chime will sound in a pattern of 5 sets of 5 beeps. If this occurs, air bag indicator and any SRS fault discovered must be diagnosed and repaired.
    c. Clear all continuous DTC's from RCM using a suitable scan tool.

GENERAL MOTORS

The inflatable restraint Sensing and Diagnostic Module (SDM) maintains a reserved energy supply. The reserved energy supply provides deployment power for the air bags if the SDM loses battery power during a collision. Deployment power is available for as much as one minute after disconnecting the vehicle power. Waiting one minute before working on the system after disabling the SIR system prevents deployment of the air bags from the reserved energy supply.

Disarming

The Sensing and Diagnostic Module (SDM) may have more than one fused power input. To ensure there is no unwanted SIR deployment, personal injury, or unnecessary SIR system repairs, remove all fuses supplying power to SDM. With all SDM fuses removed and the ignition switch in the ON position,

AIR BAG SYSTEM PRECAUTIONS

the AIR BAG warning indicator illuminates. This is normal operation, and does not indicate a SIR system malfunction.

1. Turn steering wheel so wheels are pointing straight ahead.
2. Place ignition in OFF position.
3. Locate and remove fuse(s) supplying power to SDM.
4. Wait at least one minute before working on system.

Arming

1. Place ignition in OFF position.
2. Install fuse(s) supplying power to SDM.
3. Turn ignition switch to ON position.
4. AIR BAG indicator will flash then turn OFF.
5. If AIR BAG indicator does not operate as described. Refer to **MOTOR's "Air Bag Quick Reference Guide."**

SATURN

The inflatable restraint Sensing and Diagnostic Module (SDM) maintains a reserved energy supply. The reserved energy supply provides deployment power for the air bags if the SDM loses battery power during a collision. Deployment power is available for as much as one minute after disconnecting the vehicle power. Waiting one minute before working on the system after disabling the SIR system prevents deployment of the air bags from the reserved energy supply.

Disarming

The Sensing and Diagnostic Module (SDM) may have more than one fused power input. To ensure there is no unwanted SIR deployment, personal injury, or unnecessary SIR system repairs, remove all fuses supplying power to SDM. With all SDM fuses removed and the ignition switch in the ON position, the AIR BAG warning indicator illuminates. This is normal operation, and does not indicate a SIR system malfunction.

1. Turn steering wheel so wheels are pointing straight ahead.
2. Place ignition in OFF position.
3. Locate and remove fuse(s) supplying power to SDM.
4. Wait at least one minute before working on system.

Arming

1. Place ignition in OFF position.
2. Install fuse(s) supplying power to SDM.
3. Turn ignition switch to ON position.
4. AIR BAG indicator will flash then turn OFF.
5. If AIR BAG indicator does not operate as described. Refer to **MOTOR's "Air Bag Quick Reference Guide."**

COMPUTER RELEARN PROCEDURE

INDEX

	Page No.
Chrysler	0-31
Body Control Module (BCM)	0-31
PCM/SKREEM Programming	0-31
Powertrain Control Module (PCM)	0-32
Powertrain Control Module/ SKIM Programming	0-31
Programming Ignition Keys To The Skim	0-31
Programming PCM	0-31
Programming SKIM	0-31
Programming Ignition Keys To SKREEM/WCM	0-32
Sentry Key Immobilizer System (SKIS)	0-32

	Page No.
Transmission Control Module (TCM)	0-32
Ford Motor Co.	0-32
Powertrain Control Module (PCM)	0-32
Automatic Data Transfer	0-32
Manual Data Entry	0-32
General Motors	0-32
Body Control Module (BCM)	0-32
Dash Integration Module (DIM)	0-32
Electronic Brake Control Module (EBCM)	0-32
Instrument Panel Integration Module (IPM)	0-32
Powertrain Control Module	

	Page No.
(PCM)	0-32
Rear Integration Module	0-33
Theft Deterrent System Programming	0-33
Saturn	0-33
PCM/ECM Learning Procedure	0-33
Passlock Theft Deterrent Relearn Procedure	0-33
Auto Learn Method	0-33
Seed & Key Method	0-33
Remote Keyless Entry Synchronization	0-33

CHRYSLER

Body Control Module (BCM)

Before replacing a BCM, use a diagnostic scan tool or access using the customer programmable access mode (refer to the vehicle owners manual) to retrieve the current settings for the BCM programmable features, mainly the Country Code. These settings must be programmed to the replacement BCM before returning the vehicle to service.

PCM/SKREEM Programming

The SKIS Secret Key is an ID code that is unique to each SKREEM/WCM. This code is programmed and stored in the SKREEM/WCM, the PCM, and each ignition key transponder chip. When the PCM or SKREEM/WCM is replaced, it is required to program the Secret Key into the new module using a diagnostic scan tool. Follow the programming steps outlined in the diagnostic scan tool for "PCM Replaced" or "WCM Replaced" under "Miscellaneous Functions" for the "WCM/Wireless Control Module" menu item as appropriate.

Powertrain Control Module/SKIM Programming

Before replacing the PCM for a failed driver, control circuit or ground circuit, be sure to inspect the related component/circuit integrity for failures not detected due to a double fault in the circuit. Most PCM driver/control circuit failures are caused by internal component failures, relay and solenoids and shorted circuits, pull-ups, drivers and switched circuits. These failures are

difficult to detect when a double fault has occurred and only one DTC has set.

When a PCM and the SKIM are replaced at the same time perform the following steps in order: 1. Program the new PCM. 2. Program the new SKIM. 3. Replace all ignition keys and program them to the new SKIM.

PROGRAMMING PCM

The SKIS Secret Key is an ID code that is unique to each SKIM. This code is programmed and stored in the SKIM, PCM and transponder chip (ignition keys). When replacing the PCM it is required to program the secret key into the new PCM using the scan tool. Perform the following steps to program the secret key into the PCM.

1. Turn ignition switch on and place transmission in park/neutral.
2. Use scan tool and select THEFT ALARM, SKIM then MISCELLANEOUS.
3. Select PCM REPLACED (GAS ENGINE).
4. Enter secured access mode by entering vehicle four-digit PIN.
5. Select ENTER to update PCM VIN.
6. **If three attempts are made to enter secure access mode using an incorrect PIN, secured access mode will be locked out for one hour. To exit this lockout mode, turn ignition to RUN position for one hour then enter correct PIN. Ensure all accessories are turned off. Also monitor battery state and connect a battery charger if required.**
7. Press ENTER to transfer secret key SKIM will send secret key to the PCM.
8. Press Page Back to get to Select System menu and select ENGINE, MISCELLANEOUS, and SRI MEMORY CHECK.
9. The scan tool will ask, Is odometer reading between XX and XX? Select the YES or NO button on scan tool. If NO is selected, scan tool will read, Enter odometer Reading. Enter odometer reading from Instrument Panel and press ENTER.

PROGRAMMING SKIM

If the PCM and the SKIM are replaced at the same time, all vehicle keys will need to be replaced and programmed to the new SKIM.

1. Turn ignition switch on and place transmission in park/neutral.
2. Use scan tool and select THEFT ALARM, SKIM then MISCELLANEOUS.
3. Select PCM REPLACED (GAS ENGINE).
4. Program vehicle four-digit PIN into SKIM.
5. Select COUNTRY CODE and enter correct country.
6. Be sure to enter correct country code. If incorrect country code is programmed into SKIM, SKIM must be replaced.
7. Select YES to update VIN (the SKIM will learn the VIN from the PCM).
8. Press ENTER to transfer secret key (PCM will send secret key to SKIM).
9. Program ignition keys to SKIM.

PROGRAMMING IGNITION KEYS TO THE SKIM

A maximum of eight keys can be learned to each SKIM. Once a key is learned to a SKIM it (the key) cannot be transferred to another vehicle.

1. Turn ignition switch on and place transmission in park/neutral.
2. Use scan tool and select THEFT ALARM, SKIM then MISCELLANEOUS.
3. Select PROGRAM IGNITION KEY'S.
4. Enter secured access mode by entering vehicle four-digit PIN.
5. If ignition key programming is unsuccessful, scan tool will display one of following messages:
   a. Programming Not Attempted — The scan tool attempts to read the programmed key status and there are no keys programmed into SKIM memory.
   b. Programming Key Failed (Possible

Used Key From Wrong Vehicle) — SKIM is unable to program key due to one of following, faulty ignition key transponder ignition key is programmed to another vehicle.

c. Eight Keys Already Learned, Programming Not Done — SKIM transponder ID memory is full.

6. Obtain ignition keys to be programmed from customer (8 keys maximum).
7. Erase all ignition keys by selecting MISCELLANEOUS and ERASE ALL CURRENT IGN. KEYS using scan tool.
8. Program all ignition keys. Learned Key In Ignition — Ignition key transponder ID is currently programmed in SKIM memory.

Powertrain Control Module (PCM)

Anytime the PCM is replaced the VIN and vehicle mileage must be programmed into the new PCM. If the PCM is not programmed, Diagnostic Trouble Codes (DTCs) will set. To program the PCM, connect a DRB or suitably programmed scan tool to the Data Link Connector (DLC) and follow scan tool manufacturers instructions. On models equipped with the Sentry Key Immobilizer System (SKIS), refer to "Sentry Key Immobilizer System (SKIS)" to program secret key into the PCM.

Programming Ignition Keys To SKREEM/WCM

Each ignition key transponder also has a unique ID code that is assigned at the time the key is manufactured. When a key is programmed into the SKREEM/WCM, the transponder ID code is learned by the module and the transponder acquires the unique Secret Key ID code from the SKREEM/WCM. To program ignition keys into the SKREEM/WCM, follow the programming steps outlined in the diagnostic scan tool for "Program Ignition Keys or Key FOBs" under "Miscellaneous Functions" for the "WCM/Wireless Control Module" menu item.

A maximum of eight keys can be learned to each SKREEM/WCM. Once a key is learned to a SKREEM/WCM, that key has acquired the Secret Key for that SKREEM/WCM and cannot be used on any other vehicle at the same time.

If ignition key programming is unsuccessful, the scan tool will display one of the following error messages:

1. Programming Not Attempted — The scan tool attempts to read the programmed key status and there are no keys programmed into SKREEM memory.
2. Programming Key Failed (Possible Used Key From Wrong Vehicle) — SKREEM/WCM is unable to program an ignition key transponder due to one of the following:
   a. The ignition key transponder is faulty.

b. The ignition key transponder is or has been already programmed to another vehicle.

3. 8 Keys Already Learned, Programming Not Done — The SKREEM/FCM transponder ID memory is full.
4. Learned Key In Ignition — The ID for the ignition key transponder currently in the ignition lock cylinder is already programmed into SKREEM/WCM memory.

Sentry Key Immobilizer System (SKIS)

When replacing the PCM on these models, it will be required to program the SKIS I.D. code into the new PCM. The new PCM will not allow the engine to operate unless it receives the correct I.D. code from the Sentry Key Immobilizer Module (SKIM). Use the following procedure to program the secret key into the PCM.

1. Obtain vehicle's four-digit PIN number.
2. Ensure transmission or transaxle is in Park or Neutral and turn ignition to ON position.
3. Connect DRB or suitably programmed scan tool to Data Link Connector (DLC).
4. Select THEFT ALARM, SKIM, MISCELLANEOUS and PCM REPLACED from scan tool menu.
5. Enter secured access mode by entering vehicle's four-digit PIN number.
6. Press ENTER to transfer secret key code to PCM.
7. **If incorrect code is entered three times, secured access mode will be locked out for one hour. To exit lockout mode, turn ignition key to RUN position for one hour and enter correct PIN (ensure accessories are turned off and monitor state of battery charge, connect battery charger).**

Transmission Control Module (TCM)

The adaptation procedure requires the use of the appropriate scan tool. This program allows the electronic transmission system to calibrate itself. This will provide the proper baseline transmission operation.

FORD MOTOR CO.

Powertrain Control Module (PCM)

AUTOMATIC DATA TRANSFER

1. Prior to removing old PCM, connect suitably programmed scan tool to Data Link Connector (DLC).
2. Follow scan tool manufacturers' instructions to download data from old PCM.

3. Install new PCM and connect scan tool to DLC.
4. Follow scan tool manufacturers' instructions to download data from scan tool to replacement PCM.

MANUAL DATA ENTRY

1. Install new PCM.
2. Connect suitably programmed scan tool to Data Link Connector (DLC).
3. Follow scan tool manufacturers' instructions to manually program VID block data to PCM. If instructed by scan tool to contact "AS BUILT" data center, proceed as follows.
   a. Contact Fed World website at "fedworld.gov."
   b. Select auto service information and search for "Calibrations" or "Vehicle Calibrations."
   c. Specify vehicle manufacturer, model name and model year as required.

GENERAL MOTORS

Body Control Module (BCM)

Connect a Tech 2 or suitably programmed scan tool to Data Link Connector (DLC) and follow manufacturer's instructions.

Dash Integration Module (DIM)

Connect a Tech 2 or suitably programmed scan tool to Data Link Connector (DLC) and follow manufacturer's instructions.

Electronic Brake Control Module (EBCM)

Connect a Tech 2 or suitably programmed scan tool to Data Link Connector (DLC) and follow manufacturer's instructions.

Instrument Panel Integration Module (IPM)

Connect a Tech 2 or suitably programmed scan tool to Data Link Connector (DLC) and follow manufacturer's instructions.

Powertrain Control Module (PCM)

Connect a Tech 2 or suitably programmed scan tool to Data Link Connector (DLC) and follow manufacturer's instructions.

Rear Integration Module

Connect a Tech 2 or suitably programmed scan tool to Data Link Connector (DLC) and follow manufacturer's instructions.

Theft Deterrent System Programming

Connect a Tech 2 or suitably programmed scan tool to Data Link Connector (DLC) and follow manufacturer's instructions.

SATURN

PCM/ECM Learning Procedure

If the battery is disconnected or if the PCM is replaced, the PCM must go through the learning process. To allow the PCM to relearn, proceed as follows:

1. Start vehicle and run until engine reaches normal operating temperature.
2. Drive vehicle at part throttle, with moderate acceleration and idle conditions until normal performance returns.
3. Park vehicle and engage parking brake with engine running.

4. **On models equipped with automatic transaxle,** place transaxle in Drive position.
5. **On models equipped with manual transaxle,** place transaxle in Neutral position.
6. **On all models,** allow vehicle to idle for approximately two minutes until engine idle stabilizes. Ensure engine is at normal operating temperature.

Passlock Theft Deterrent Relearn Procedure

There are two methods used to reprogram the Passlock security system, the Seed and Key method and the Auto Learn method. If no components were replaced or the Passlock sensor was the only component replaced, the Auto Learn technique may be used to program the security system. If the BCM or PCM were replaced then the "Seed & Key" method must be used.

SEED & KEY METHOD

1. Turn ignition On.
2. Inspect for body control module (BCM) or powertrain control module (PCM) diagnostic trouble codes (DTCs) using suitably programmed scan tool.
3. Record and repair DTCs.
4. Turn ignition Off.
5. Select "Passlock Relearn" option using suitably programmed scan tool.
6. Wait for 10 minutes and observe security telltale changing from Flashing to On to Off.
7. If ignition is turned Off before telltale changes state, relearn procedure must be performed again.
8. Turn ignition Off.
9. Vehicle should start on next ignition switch cycle.

AUTO LEARN METHOD

1. Turn ignition On.
2. Momentarily turn ignition to Crank position, but do not start vehicle.
3. Wait for 10 minutes.
4. Observe SECURITY telltale changing from Flashing to On to Off.
5. If ignition is turned Off before telltale changes state, procedure will have to be performed again.
6. Turn Ignition Off.
7. Repeat procedure two more times.
8. If vehicle does not start on next ignition switch cycle, repeat procedure.

Remote Keyless Entry Synchronization

The remote keyless entry system does not send the same signal twice. The body control module (BCM) will not execute a signal if it has been sent previously. To synchronize a transmitter with the BCM, simultaneously press and hold the Lock and Unlock buttons on the transmitter for approximately ten seconds near the vehicle. The doors locks will cycle to confirm synchronization.

TABLE OF CONTENTS

	Page No.		Page No.
CHRYSLER	0-34	GENERAL MOTORS CORP.	0-41
FORD MOTOR CO.	0-37		

Chrysler

INDEX

	Page No.		Page No.		Page No.
Air Bag Warning Lamp	0-34	Concorde, Intrepid, LHS, Vision, 300M & 1994–96 New Yorker	0-35	Concorde, Intrepid, LHS, Vision, 300M & 1994–96 New Yorker	0-35
Anti-Lock Brake System Warning Lamp	0-34	Sebring Convertible	0-35	Compass Calibration	0-36
Check Engine Lamp	0-34	Electronic Vehicle Information Center	0-35	Power Loss/Limit Lamp	0-36
Check Engine Or Malfunction Indicator Lamp	0-34	1992–93 Dynasty, Fifth Avenue, Imperial & New Yorker	0-35	Vehicle Maintenance Monitor (VMM) System	0-36
Colt & Summit	0-34	Low Coolant Warning Lamp	0-36	Self Diagnosis	0-36
Except Colt & Summit	0-34	Overhead Travel Information System (OTIS)	0-35	Troubleshooting	0-36
Compass & Temperature Mini Trip Computer	0-35				

AIR BAG WARNING LAMP

If the Air Bag warning lamp lights and stays on, diagnosis and repair of the air bag system will be required to reset the lamp.

ANTI-LOCK BRAKE SYSTEM WARNING LAMP

This lamp should light when the ignition is turned On. The lamp may light for as long as 30 seconds as a bulb and system inspection. If the lamp remains lit or lights while operating the vehicle, a fault condition in the anti-lock brake system is indicated. When the lamp is lit, turn ignition Off and start the engine again. If the lamp still remains lit, the anti-lock brake system should be serviced. The brake system will remain functional, but without the anti-lock function. After servicing the anti-lock brake system, the lamp will automatically reset. On some models, it may be required to operate the vehicle at a speed over 18 mph and make several hard brake applications from 40 mph to reset the lamp.

CHECK ENGINE LAMP

The Check Engine lamp should light for approximately 3 seconds after the ignition has been turned On as a bulb inspection. If improper or no signals are received by the Single Board Engine Controller (SBEC) from various sensors or if the PCM enters its Limp-In mode, the SBEC will light the Check Engine lamp. After diagnosing and servicing the fuel injection system or emission related systems, the SBEC memory will be cleared after approximately 40–100 ignition key On-Off cycles.

The Check Engine lamp may light if the fuel filler cap has not been completely tightened. The lamp should turn off after the cap has been properly tightened and the vehicle has successfully completed a predetermined number of trip cycles.

On Monaco and Premier models, this lamp should light during engine starting as a bulb inspection. Once the engine has started, the lamp should go off. If the lamp remains lit, the fuel injection and emission control system diagnosis should be performed using tester DRB II. During the diagnosis and repair procedure with tester DRB II, the Check Engine lamp will be reset.

CHECK ENGINE OR MALFUNCTION INDICATOR LAMP

Except Colt & Summit

The powertrain control module monitors a variety of sensors in the fuel injection, ignition, emission and engines systems. Each time the ignition is turned On, the instrument panel MIL should light for approximately two seconds and then go out. If the PCM senses a fault condition with a monitored circuit often enough to indicate an actual fault condition or if it enters its Limp-In mode, it stores a Diagnostic Trouble Code (DTC) in the PCM's memory. If the code applies to a non-emissions related components or system and the fault condition is repaired or ceases to exist, the PCM cancels the code after 40 warm-up cycles. DTCs that affect vehicle emissions light the MIL. Use a suitably programmed scan tool to retrieve and erase DTC's and to reset the MIL.

On 1998 and newer models, the Check Engine lamp may light if the fuel filler cap has not been completely tightened. The lamp should turn off after the cap has been properly tightened and the vehicle has successfully completed a predetermined number of trip cycles.

Colt & Summit

This lamp is used to monitor fuel injection and emission control system components for faults. When the ignition is turned On, the lamp will light for 2–3 seconds as a bulb inspection. If the lamp remains on, a fault in the fuel injection or emission control system is indicated. If fault is intermittent, the lamp will go off when the Electronic Control Unit (ECU) receives a normal signal from the faulting component. If the ECU receives an improper signal from a faulting component for a time longer than that programmed into the ECU, a code will be stored in the ECU memory and the Malfunction Indicator Lamp should light. After

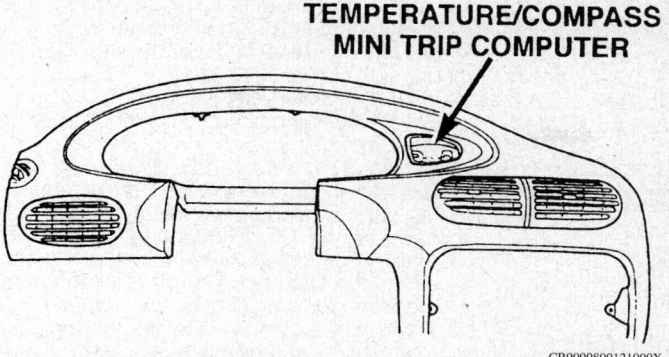

TEMPERATURE/COMPASS MINI TRIP COMPUTER

CR9099800121000X

Fig. 1 Compass/temperature mini trip computer. Concorde, Intrepid, LHS, Vision, 300M & 1994–96 New Yorker

servicing the indicated component, the Malfunction Indicator Lamp can be reset by clearing the ECU memory. The ECU memory is cleared by using a suitable scan tool or disconnecting the battery ground cable for approximately 10 seconds.

COMPASS & TEMPERATURE MINI TRIP COMPUTER

Concorde, Intrepid, LHS, Vision, 300M & 1994–96 New Yorker

1. Set mini trip computer to Compass/Temperature mode, **Fig. 1.**
2. Press US/M and STEP buttons simultaneously until VAR and current variance zone number is displayed.
3. Press STEP until proper variance zone number is displayed, **Fig. 2.**
4. After 5 seconds of inactivity, displayed zone will be set automatically. Ensure accuracy of compass by pointing vehicle in N, S, E and W directions.

Sebring Convertible

If the CAL indicator lights, the compass will need to be calibrated. This should be done on a level surface free of large metal objects such as other vehicles, bridges, buildings, railroads and underground cables. Proceed as follows:

1. Drive in complete circles, keeping steering wheel in fixed position, at speeds of 7–10 mph until CAL indicator turns Off. This may require two to six turns.
2. When CAL indicator turns Off, compass has been calibrated and should now display proper headings.
3. Inspect for proper calibrations by selecting North, South, East and West.
4. If compass does not appear to be reading accurately, calibration procedure should be repeated in another area.

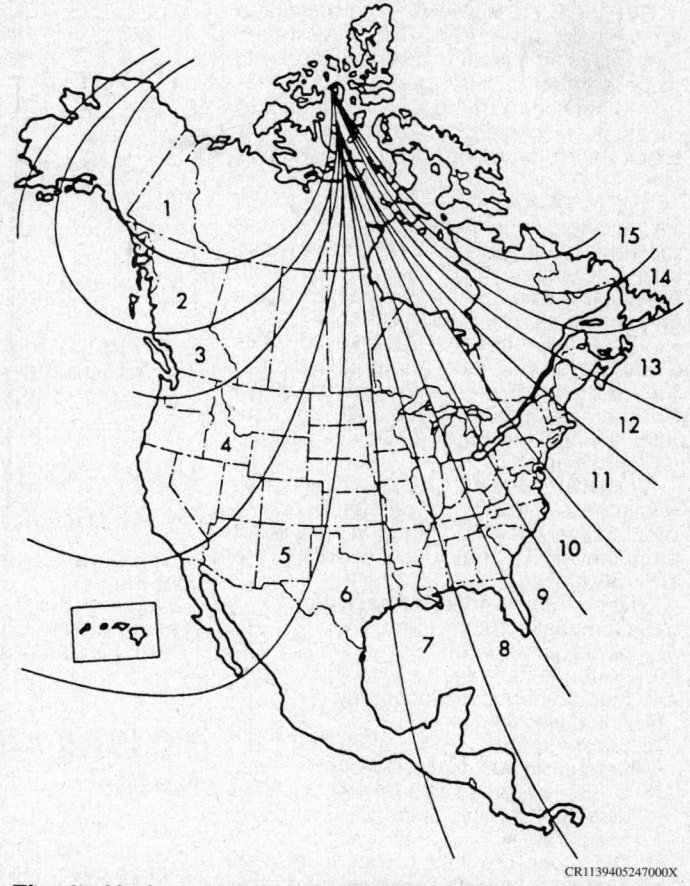

CR1139405247000X

Fig. 2 Variance zone map. Concorde, Intrepid, LHS, Vision, 300M & 1994–96 New Yorker

ELECTRONIC VEHICLE INFORMATION CENTER

1992–93 Dynasty, Fifth Avenue, Imperial & New Yorker

The Electronic Vehicle Information Center is a computer controlled warning system which monitors various sensors used on the vehicle. The system supplements the warning indicators in the instrument cluster. When a warning message has been activated, a tone will sound to attract the driver's attention. The warning message will then be displayed on the overhead console until the condition has been corrected or a new display function is called up, **Fig. 3.** A tone will announce each new warning condition. The "Service Reminder" warning message will be indicated at 7,500 mile or 12 month intervals to indicate that required service is to be performed. After performing the required service, the Service Reminder message can be reset by using a DRB II diagnostic readout tool.

OVERHEAD TRAVEL INFORMATION SYSTEM (OTIS)

Concorde, Intrepid, LHS, Vision, 300M & 1994–96 New Yorker

Overhead Travel Information System (OTIS) is a module with six informational displays and four buttons. When the ignition is turned ON, OTIS blanks the display for one second and returns to the display active when the vehicle was last turned OFF.

LOW OIL PRESSURE—This message will be displayed when a low engine oil pressure condition exists. If message is encountered with vehicle operating at idle speed, increase engine RPM. If message remains or if message is encountered while operating vehicle, the engine lubricating system should be inspected and serviced immediately. After engine lubricating system has been serviced, the message will be automatically cancelled.

SERVICE REMINDER—This message will be indicated at 7,500 mile or 12 month intervals to indicate that required service is to be performed. After performing the required service, with the Service Reminder message displayed, depress the Vehicle Electronic Information Center Reset button.

TURN SIGNAL ON—This message will be indicated when the turn signal is on and the vehicle has traveled a distance over ½ mile at a speed more than 15 mph. The message will be reset when the turn signal lever has been returned to Off.

VOLTAGE IMPROPER—When this message is displayed, a fault condition in the charging or electrical system exists. After servicing, the message will be reset after the ignition has been cycled to the OFF position.

WASHER FLUID LOW—When this message is displayed, bring washer fluid to proper level. This message will be reset after the ignition has been cycled to the OFF position.

The six informational displays are:
1. Compass/temperature.
2. Average fuel economy.
3. Distance to empty.
4. Instantaneous fuel economy.
5. Trip odometer.
6. Elapsed time.

The four buttons on the OTIS are:
1. STEP—Depress this button to select display modes except Compass/temperature.
2. C/T—Depress this button to display compass (vehicle direction) and temperature.
3. U/SM—Switches display information between English and Metric readings.
4. RESET—Depress this button to reset current display (for displays that can be reset.)

COMPASS CALIBRATION

Do not attempt to set compass calibration near large metal objects, such as other vehicles, buildings or bridges.
1. Remove magnetic devices from roof panel.
2. Turn ignition On.
3. Press C/T button to select Compass/temperature display.
4. Depress and hold RESET button for approximately five seconds. VAR symbol will light during this time.
5. Continue to hold RESET button for approximately 10 seconds until CAL symbol lights.
6. Drive vehicle through three complete 360° turns in no less than 48 seconds. Compass will be calibrated when CAL symbol is extinguished.
7. Press and hold RESET button for approximately five seconds until VAR symbol is lit.
8. OTIS will display variance zone and VAR.
9. Press STEP button to display variance zone, **Fig. 2**.
10. Press RESET button to set new variance zone and resume normal operation.

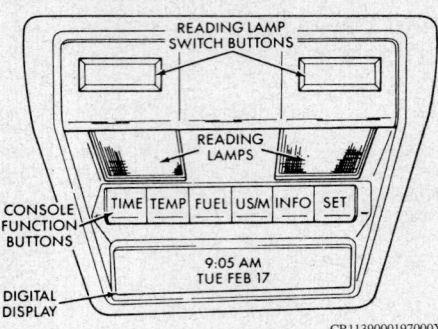

Fig. 3 Electronic Vehicle Information Center display console. 1992–93 Dynasty, Fifth Avenue, Imperial & New Yorker

LOW COOLANT WARNING LAMP

The Low Coolant warning lamp should light whenever coolant level in the coolant reservoir is below a predetermined level. Add coolant to bring reservoir to proper level to turn lamp off.

POWER LOSS/LIMIT LAMP

The Power Loss/Limit lamp should light for approximately 3 seconds after the ignition has been turned On as a bulb inspection. If improper or no signals are received by the logic module from various sensors, the logic module will light the Power Loss/Limit lamp. After diagnosing and servicing the fuel injection system or EGR system (California models with EGR sensor), the logic module memory can be cleared by disconnecting and connecting the battery quick-disconnect.

VEHICLE MAINTENANCE MONITOR (VMM) SYSTEM

This system monitors regular service and maintenance intervals, engine oil level, engine coolant level, windshield washer fluid level, brake and tail lamps, door ajar and oil, coolant and washer sensors.

When the vehicle is started and no faults are present, the display will indicate "MONITOR." If the monitor detects a fault, it will be noted on the display. If more than one fault is noted, the fault of the highest priority will be displayed first. The display will then note all existing faults and return to the fault of highest priority. The VMM fault messages are as follows:

DOOR—Door Ajar—Close door indicated on vehicle outline display to reset monitor.

LAMP—Brake or Tail Lamp Outage—The display should light when brake is ap-

plied or headlamp switch is in the On position and a burned out lamp bulb is present. To reset monitor, replace burned out bulb.

COOLANT—Low Engine Coolant Level—Bringing coolant to proper level will reset monitor.

OIL—Low Engine Oil Level—The system will inspect engine oil level approximately 12 minutes after the ignition has been turned Off. A low oil level condition must be indicated three consecutive times before the monitor will display "Oil." To reset monitor, add oil to bring to proper level. Then, while display is indicating the "Oil" message, depress RESET select switch until a beep is noted. Even if RESET select switch is not depressed, the system will automatically reset monitor after three proper oil level readings have been obtained.

WASHER—Low Washer Fluid Level—Bringing washer fluid to proper level will reset monitor.

SERVICE—Perform Required Service and Maintenance—This message will be indicated at 7,500 mile intervals to indicate that required service is to be performed. After performing required service, depress the Reset select switch until a beep is noted.

SENSOR—This message will be indicated when a defect in the oil, coolant or washer sensor circuit is noted. Refer to "Self Diagnosis."

MILES (KMS)—Mile to next scheduled service interval.

Self Diagnosis

To diagnose, depress and hold the Check and List select switches, then turn ignition On. With the instrument cluster switch in the English mode, all diagnosis will be performed automatically in sequence. With the instrument cluster in the Metric mode, the Check select switch will have to be depressed to proceed to the next test. The display will indicate which components are faulty or satisfactory. After completing diagnosis, depress Check and List select switches to exit diagnosis mode.

Troubleshooting

1. If a condition of no display or improper information exists, start engine and inspect the following:
   a. **On models less passive restraint,** inspect fuses 8 and 19 in fuse panel. **On models equipped with passive restraint,** inspect fuses 2 and 8 in fuse panel. Replace any blown fuses.
   b. **On all models,** inspect terminal Nos. 1 and 5 of connector A using a suitable voltmeter. Voltmeter should indicate battery voltage. If not, inspect for open circuit to fuse panel.
   c. Connect a suitable ohmmeter between terminal Nos. 15 and 18 of connector A. Ohmmeter should indicate zero ohms. If a no display condition is present, replace monitor. If an improper information condition is present, refer to "Self

Diagnosis." If reading is other than zero ohms, inspect for open circuit.

d. With all doors closed, connect an ohmmeter between terminal Nos. 6, 7, 8 and 9 of connector A. Ohmmeter should indicate an infinite reading. If reading is other than infinite, inspect for short circuit to ground.

2. If monitor fails to change modes, disconnect electrical connector B and proceed as follows:

a. With Check select switch depressed, connect ohmmeter between terminal Nos. 2 and 4 of connector B. If ohmmeter reading is zero ohms, proceed to step b. If ohmmeter reading is other than zero ohms, replace mode select switches.

b. With List select switch depressed, connect ohmmeter between terminal Nos. 2 and 3 of connector B. If ohmmeter reading is zero ohms,

proceed to step c. If ohmmeter reading is other than zero ohms, replace mode select switches.

c. With Reset select switch depressed, connect ohmmeter between terminal Nos. 2 and 5 of connector B. Ohmmeter reading should be zero ohms. If ohmmeter reading is other than zero ohms, replace mode select switches.

Ford Motor Co.

INDEX

	Page No.
Air Bag Warning Lamp	0-37
Anti-Lock Brake Warning Lamp	0-37
Check Engine Lamp	0-37
EEC-IV	0-37
1992–93	0-37
1995–97	0-38
EEC-V	0-38
Check Fuel Cap Lamp	0-38
Electronic Compass	0-38
Continental	0-38
Mark VIII	0-38
Town Car	0-38
Low Coolant Warning System	0-38
Low Oil Level Warning Indicator	0-38
Malfunction Indicator Lamp (MIL)	0-39

	Page No.
Message Center	0-39
Crown Victoria, Grand Marquis & Town Car	0-39
Mark VIII	0-39
Air Ride Switch Off	0-39
Change Oil Soon Or Oil Change Required	0-39
Check Air Ride System	0-39
Check Charging System	0-39
Check Engine Temp	0-39
Check Exterior Lamps	0-39
Low Engine Coolant	0-39
Service Interval Reminder	0-39
Continental	0-39
Cougar	0-39
1992–93	0-39
1999	0-39

	Page No.
2000–02	0-40
LS	0-40
Change Oil Soon Or Oil Change Required	0-40
Mark VIII	0-40
Change Oil Soon Or Oil Change Required	0-40
Probe	0-40
Electronic Instrument Cluster	0-40
Vehicle Maintenance Monitor	0-40
Thunderbird	0-40
1992–93	0-40

AIR BAG WARNING LAMP

If the Air Bag warning lamp lights and stays on, diagnosis and repair of the air bag system will be required to reset the lamp.

ANTI-LOCK BRAKE WARNING LAMP

This lamp should light when the ignition is turned On. It may light for as long as 30 seconds as a bulb and system inspect. If the lamp remains lit or lights while operating the vehicle, a fault condition in the anti-lock brake system is indicated. When the lamp is lit, turn ignition Off and start engine again. If the lamp still remains lit, the anti-lock brake system should be serviced. The brake system will remain functional, but without the anti-lock function. After servicing the anti-lock brake system, the lamp will automatically reset when the vehicle is operated at a speed over 25 mph.

CHECK ENGINE LAMP

EEC-IV

1992-93

EXCEPT FESTIVA, PROBE w/2.2L ENGINE & ESCORT & TRACER w/1.8L ENGINE

This lamp should light when the ignition is turned On. After the engine is started, the lamp should go off, unless a fault condition is detected by the EEC-IV system. Following diagnosis and repair, the Check Engine/MIL lamp will automatically reset when the stored codes are cleared from the EEC-IV system memory. After diagnosis and repair, the EEC-IV memory may be cleared of stored codes as follows:

1. With ignition turned Off, connect a jumper wire between Self Test and Self Test Input (STI) connectors, **Fig. 1. On Crown Victoria, Grand Marquis and Town Car models,** the Self Test and STI connectors are gray in color and are located on the front of the lefthand

fender apron, near the Electronic Engine Control (EEC) relay. **On Mustang models,** the Self Test and STI connectors are gray in color and are located on the lefthand fender apron. **On Tempo and Topaz models,** the Self Test connector is gray in color and the STI connector is black in color and they are both located on the righthand fender apron, near the front of the strut tower. **On Taurus and Sable models,** the Self Test and STI connectors are gray in color and are located on the righthand fender apron, near the front of the engine in the area of the AIR pump and alternator. **On 1992–93 Thunderbird and Cougar models,** the Self Test and STI connectors are gray in color and are located on the righthand fender apron, near the strut tower.

2. **On all models,** turn ignition On, then disconnect jumper wire from test connector terminals. Disconnect jumper as soon as Check Engine lamp starts flashing.

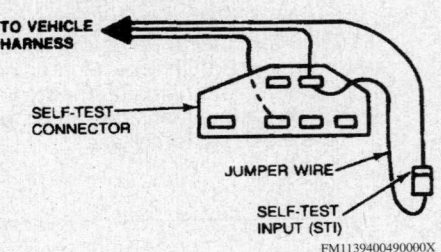

MESSAGE CENTER (CONTINENTAL ONLY)

MALFUNCTION INDICATOR
LIGHT (WITH JUMPER WIRE)

TO VEHICLE
HARNESS

SELF-TEST
CONNECTOR

JUMPER WIRE

SELF-TEST
INPUT (STI)

FM11394004900000X

Fig. 1 Jumper wire connections for resetting Check Engine lamp. EEC-IV Except Festiva, Probe w/2.2L Engine & Escort & Tracer w/1.8L engine

FESTIVA

The Check Engine Indicator lamp should light when the ignition is in the RUN position with the engine not operating. When the engine is started, the Check Engine lamp should go off. If the lamp remains on, a service code has been stored in the EEC-IV self test system memory. After diagnosis and repair, the self test memory may be cleared of stored codes as follows:

1. With ignition turned Off, connect a jumper wire between Self Test Input (STI) connector terminal and ground. The STI connector is located in rear lefthand side of engine compartment, **Fig. 2.**
2. Turn ignition On, then disconnect and reconnect jumper wire connected between STI connector and ground.
3. Disconnect jumper from STI connector as soon as Check Engine lamp stops flashing.
4. Disconnect battery ground cable and depress brake pedal for approximately 5–10 seconds.
5. Connect battery ground cable.

ESCORT, PROBE & TRACER w/1.8L & 2.2L ENGINES

This lamp should light when the ignition is turned On. After engine is started, the lamp should go off, unless a fault condition is detected by the system. After diagnosis and repair, the Check Engine lamp will automatically reset when stored codes are cleared from the system memory. After diagnosis and repair, memory may be cleared of stored codes as follows:

1. Disconnect battery ground cable, then depress brake pedal for approximately 5–10 seconds.
2. Connect battery ground cable again.

1995–97

This lamp should light when the ignition is turned On. After engine starts, the lamp should go off, unless a fault condition is detected by the EEC-IV system. A diagnostic trouble code is stored in the PCM. Following diagnosis and repair, the Check Engine/MIL lamp will automatically reset when stored diagnostic trouble codes are cleared from PCM memory. The PCM reset proce-

dure allows the scan tool to command the PCM to clear all diagnostic trouble codes.

PCM RESET USING STAR TESTER

1. Turn ignition Off.
2. Perform required vehicle preparation and visual inspection.
3. Connect Star tester, then select vehicle model and year.
4. Follow operating instructions on tester screen. Select Generic OBD II Functions.
5. Press CONT button if all OBD II monitors are not complete.
6. Turn ignition On.
7. Select Clear Diagnostic Codes and press Start key.

PCM RESET USING GENERIC SCAN TOOL

1. Turn ignition Off.
2. Connect scan tool to DLC.
3. Turn ignition On.
4. Perform scan tool reset, then turn ignition Off.

KEEP ALIVE MEMORY (KAM) RESET & PCM RESET LESS ELECTRONIC TESTER

To clear KAM, disconnect battery ground cable for at least 5 minutes. This will also result in PCM reset.

EEC-V

1. Turn ignition Off.
2. Connect scan tool to DLC.
3. Turn ignition On.
4. Perform scan tool reset and turn ignition Off.
5. **On 1998 and newer models,** Check Engine lamp may light if fuel filler cap has not been completely tightened. Lamp should turn off after cap has been properly tightened and vehicle has successfully completed predetermined number of trip cycles.

CHECK FUEL CAP LAMP

The Check Fuel Cap Lamp will illuminate momentarily when the ignition switch is placed in ON position as a bulb check. If the lamp remains On, inspect fuel cap for proper installation. After properly installing the fuel cap the lamp should go off after a normal period of driving.

ELECTRONIC COMPASS

Continental

1. Determine magnetic zone, **Fig. 3.**
2. Insert suitable rod into compass module, **Fig. 4,** and press internal switch until ZONE and current zone setting are displayed.
3. Turn ignition On and release switch.
4. Press internal switch until proper zone number is displayed, release to exit zone setting mode and lock in zone.

Mark VIII

1. Press and hold COMPASS button,

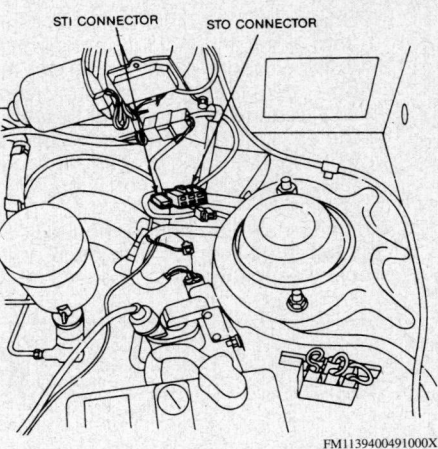

STI CONNECTOR   STO CONNECTOR

FM11394004910000X

Fig. 2 STI connector location. Festiva

then the RESET button until ECO-ZONE and RSETCAL is displayed.
2. Press FUEL ECONOMY button to enter the zone set mode.
3. Refer to **Fig. 3** for proper compass zone selection.
4. Press RESET until correct zone is selected.
5. Press COMPASS button to end zone adjustment.

Town Car

The compass module is located at the back of the rearview mirror.
1. Select compass magnetic zone, **Fig. 3.**
2. Press and hold reset button on top of compass module until message center display reads current magnetic zone setting.
3. Press calibration button on compass module to select proper zone setting.
4. To exit zone setting mode, do not press any buttons for 10 seconds.

LOW COOLANT WARNING SYSTEM

The low coolant warning lamp should light whenever the coolant level in the coolant recovery bottle is ¼ to ¾ inch or more below the cold full mark. Raise coolant level in recovery bottle to the cold full mark to turn lamp off.

On models equipped with GEM module and low coolant level warning system, the low coolant level indicator lights for two seconds during engine startup or when ignition is turned to RUN. If coolant level falls below specification for more than 15 seconds, the GEM module generates a single one second tone. Raise coolant level in recovery bottle to specified level to turn lamp off.

LOW OIL LEVEL WARNING INDICATOR

This system is used to indicate when the engine oil level is 1½ quarts or more below the specified level. The lamp should light

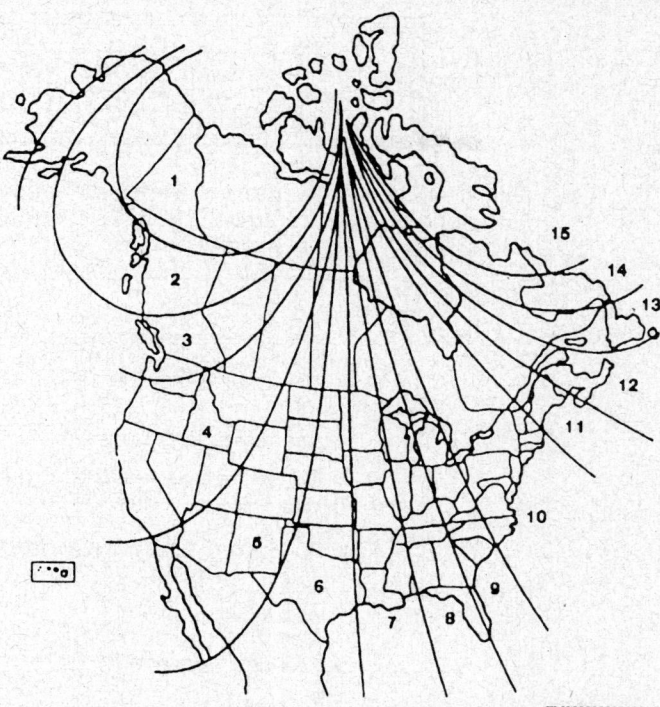

Fig. 3 Magnetic zone map. Continental, Mark VIII & Town Car

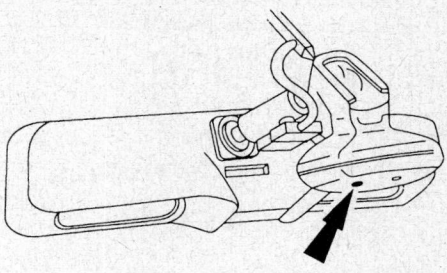

Fig. 4 Compass module location. Continental

during engine starting. If the oil level is sufficient, the lamp will go off when the engine is operating. If the oil level is low, the lamp will remain on until engine oil is added and the ignition is turned Off. The module will take approximately 5 minutes to reset. If the engine is started during this period, the last recorded reading will be displayed.

MALFUNCTION INDICATOR LAMP (MIL)

Refer to "Check Engine Lamp" for lamp reset procedure.

MESSAGE CENTER

Crown Victoria, Grand Marquis & Town Car

The message center may be located to the right of the instrument cluster, or it may be a part of the cluster itself. It consists of three buttons: Select, E/M and Reset. The E/M button switches the display between English and Metric. The Reset button set data to zero of instantaneous information. The Select button cycles the message display through the following selections:
1. Average speed.
2. Fuel remaining.
3. Average fuel economy and instantaneous fuel economy.
4. Distance to empty.
5. Trip distance.

Mark VIII

AIR RIDE SWITCH OFF

This warning message is displayed when the air suspension service switch, located in the luggage compartment, is turned Off.

CHECK AIR RIDE SYSTEM

This warning message is displayed when an air suspension system diagnostic trouble code is detected by the air suspension/EVO control module.

CHECK CHARGING SYSTEM

This warning message is displayed when the electrical system is not maintaining a proper voltage at the message center.

CHECK ENGINE TEMP

This warning message is displayed when the coolant is overheating.

LOW ENGINE COOLANT

This warning message is displayed when the engine coolant level is below the cold line of the coolant recovery reservoir.

CHECK EXTERIOR LAMPS

This warning message is displayed when one of the following lamps is turned on and at least one is burned out: stop lamp, rear parking lamp or low beam headlamp.

CHANGE OIL SOON OR OIL CHANGE REQUIRED

The oil life functions include oil life, change oil soon and oil change required. The oil life is determined by three functions: Smart Tach pulses, miles driven and time elapsed.

When the oil life drops down to the range of 1–5%, the "Change Oil Soon" message will appear. When oil life is 0%, the "Oil Change Required" message will appear.

Depressing the oil change reset button will reset the oil life to 100%.

SERVICE INTERVAL REMINDER

Continental

After performing the required interval service, the service interval reminder mileage display on the instrument cluster can be reset as follows:
1. Depress System Check button on instrument panel. Service interval reminder mileage should be displayed on fuel computer display, **Fig. 5.**
2. Depress Reset button. Service interval reminder mileage should start flashing.
3. Depress Reset and System Check buttons at same time to reset mileage.

Cougar

1992-93

At approximately 7,500 miles, for models less super charged engine, the engine oil change indicator on the Vehicle Maintenance Monitor will indicate an oil change is needed. On models with super charged engine, the need for engine oil change will be indicated at 5,000 miles. After completing the required service, the oil change indicate can be reset by depressing the reset switch, **Fig. 6.**

1999

Some of these models are equipped with an optional overhead warning lamp system which includes a Service Interval reminder. This will light after approximately 358 days or 4800 miles to indicate that routine service is needed.

After service has been performed, the lamp can be reset by holding the trip computer SELECT and UNITS buttons for 5 seconds. The Service Interval lamp will light, then turn off after approximately four seconds.

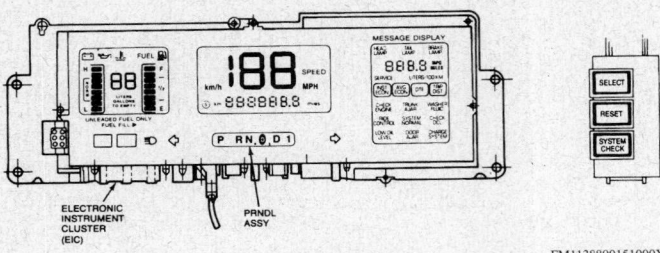

Fig. 5 Instrument cluster & message center.
Continental

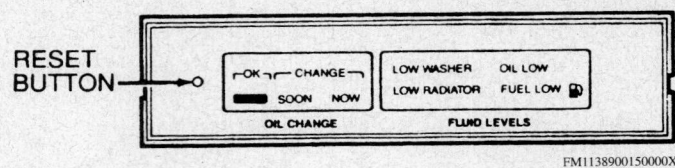

Fig. 6 Oil change interval indicator reset switch
access hole location. 1992–93 Cougar &
Thunderbird

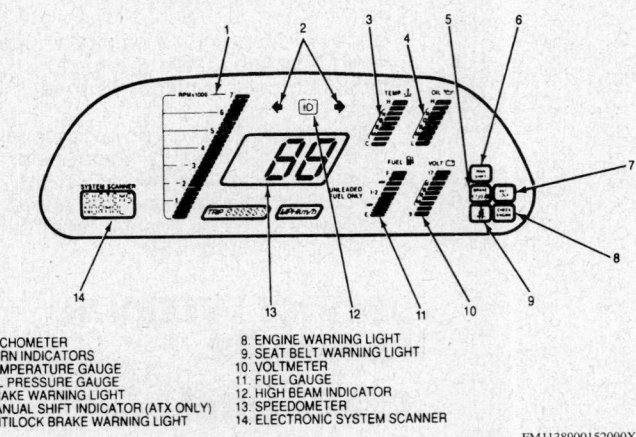

1. TACHOMETER
2. TURN INDICATORS
3. TEMPERATURE GAUGE
4. OIL PRESSURE GAUGE
5. BRAKE WARNING LIGHT
6. MANUAL SHIFT INDICATOR (ATX ONLY)
7. ANTILOCK BRAKE WARNING LIGHT
8. ENGINE WARNING LIGHT
9. SEAT BELT WARNING LIGHT
10. VOLTMETER
11. FUEL GAUGE
12. HIGH BEAM INDICATOR
13. SPEEDOMETER
14. ELECTRONIC SYSTEM SCANNER

Fig. 7 Electronic instrument cluster. Probe

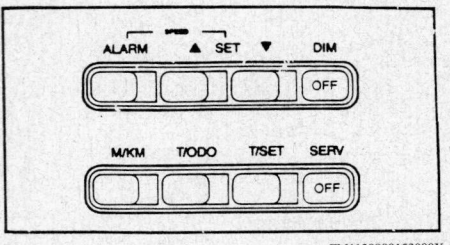

Fig. 8 Speed alarm keyboard.
Probe

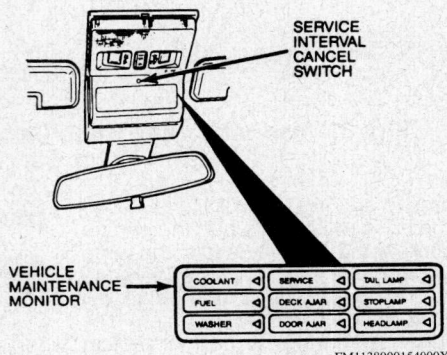

Fig. 9 Vehicle maintenance
monitor. Probe

2000-02

The maintenance interval warning indicator is controlled by the HEC. The HEC illuminates the indicator advising a scheduled maintenance (which is dependant on time of distance). The indicator is reset by placing the ignition switch in position II and depressing SELECT & UNITS buttons simultaneously for five seconds until maintenance light extinguishes.

LS

CHANGE OIL SOON OR OIL CHANGE REQUIRED

The oil life functions include "Oil Life OK, Change Oil Soon" and "Oil Change Required." The oil life is determined by the engine oil level and temperature sensors, ABS control module, odometer data and PCM RPM data.

When the oil life reaches the range of 1–5%, the "Change Oil Soon" message will appear. When the oil life is 0%, the "Oil Change Required" message will appear.

Depressing the oil change RESET button will reset the oil life to 100%.

Mark VIII

CHANGE OIL SOON OR OIL CHANGE REQUIRED

The oil life functions include "Oil Life OK, Change Oil Soon" and "Oil Change Required." The oil life is determined by the en-

gine oil level and temperature sensors, ABS control module, odometer data and PCM RPM data.

When the oil life reaches the range of 1–5%, the "Change Oil Soon" message will appear. When oil life is 0%, the "Oil Change Required" message will appear.

Depressing the oil change RESET button will reset the oil life to 100%.

Probe

ELECTRONIC INSTRUMENT CLUSTER

At 7,500 mile intervals, a Service Check message will be displayed under the System Scanner nomenclature on the instrument cluster for 3 minutes after engine starts, **Fig. 7.** After performing the required interval service, reset the service interval by depressing and holding the Service reset button, located on the speed alarm keyboard, until three tones have sounded, **Fig. 8.**

VEHICLE MAINTENANCE MONITOR

At 7,500 mile intervals a Service lamp,

located on the overhead map lamp console, should light for 3 minutes after engine start, **Fig. 9.** After performing the required interval service, reset the service interval. **On models equipped with speed alarm keypad,** depress and hold the Service reset button, until three tones have sounded. **On models less speed alarm keypad,** locate reset hole in overhead console, then use a suitable tool to depress the reset button located behind the hole.

Thunderbird

1992-93

At approximately 7,500 miles, for models less super charged engine, the engine oil change indicator on the Vehicle Maintenance Monitor will indicate an oil change is needed. On models with super charged engine, the need for engine oil change will be indicated at 5,000 miles. After completing the required service, the oil change indicate can be reset by depressing the reset switch, **Fig. 6.**

General Motors Corp.

INDEX

	Page No.		Page No.		Page No.
Air Bag Warning Lamp	0-41	Malibu Maxx & 2006-08		Metro	0-47
Anti-Lock Warning Lamp	0-41	Malibu	0-44	Prizm	0-47
Change Automatic		Oldsmobile	0-44	Storm	0-47
Transmission/Transaxle Fluid		Alero	0-44	**Check Gauge Warning Lamp**	0-47
Indicator	0-41	Aurora	0-45	**Check Info Center Warning**	
DeVille & Seville	0-41	Eighty Eight, LSS,		**Lamp**	0-47
Eldorado	0-41	Ninety-Eight & Regency	0-45	Eldorado & Seville	0-47
2000	0-41	Except Alero, Aurora, Eighty		1992	0-47
2001-02	0-41	Eight, Intrigue, LSS,		**Driver Information Center**	0-47
Change Engine Oil Message	0-41	Ninety-Eight & Toronado	0-45	Aurora	0-47
Buick	0-41	Intrigue	0-45	1995-99	0-47
Century & Regal	0-41	Toronado	0-45	Bonneville	0-48
LaCrosse	0-42	Pontiac	0-45	Eighty-Eight, LSS &	
LeSabre & Park Avenue	0-42	Bonneville	0-45	Ninety-Eight	0-49
Lucerne	0-42	Firebird	0-46	1992-93	0-49
Riviera	0-42	G5	0-46	1994-96	0-49
Roadmaster	0-42	G6	0-46	Eldorado & Seville	0-48
Cadillac	0-42	GTO	0-46	1992	0-48
Allante	0-42	Grand Am	0-46	**Engine Coolant Temperature**	
CTS	0-42	Grand Prix	0-46	**Telltale Lamp**	0-50
DTS	0-43	Solstice	0-46	**Low Coolant Lamp**	0-50
DeVille	0-43	Saturn	0-46	**Low Oil Dipstick**	0-50
Eldorado & Seville	0-43	Aura	0-46	**Low Oil Pressure Telltale Lamp**	0-50
Fleetwood (RWD)	0-43	ION	0-46	**Low Washer Fluid Indicator**	0-50
STS & XLR	0-43	L Series	0-47	**Malfunction Indicator Lamp**	
Sixty Special	0-43	S Series	0-47	**(MIL)**	0-50
Chevrolet	0-43	Sky	0-47	**Passlock Telltale Lamp**	0-50
Camaro	0-43	**Check Engine Or Service**		**Service Air Cond Lamp**	0-50
Caprice & Impala SS	0-44	**Now/Soon Engine Indicator**		**Service Electrical System**	
Cobalt	0-43	**Lamps**	0-47	**Lamp**	0-50
Corvette	0-43	Except LeMans, Metro, Prizm &		**Service Telltale Lamp**	0-50
Impala & Monte Carlo	0-44	Storm	0-47		
Lumina	0-44	LeMans	0-47		

AIR BAG WARNING LAMP

If the air bag warning lamp lights and stays on, diagnosis and repair of the air bag system will be required to reset the lamp.

ANTI-LOCK WARNING LAMP

This lamp should light when the ignition is turned On. The lamp may light for as long as 30 seconds as a bulb and system inspection. If lamp remains lit or lights while operating the vehicle, a fault condition in the anti-lock brake system is indicated. When lamp is lit, turn ignition Off and restart engine. If lamp still remains lit, the anti-lock brake system should be serviced. The brake system will remain functional, but without the anti-lock function. After servicing the anti-lock brake system the lamp will automatically reset. **On some models,** it may be required to operate vehicle at a speed over 18 mph to reset lamp.

CHANGE AUTOMATIC TRANSMISSION/ TRANSAXLE FLUID INDICATOR

DeVille & Seville

1. Turn ignition switch to ON position.
2. Press INFO button on Driver Information Center (DIC) button to display "Trans Fluid Life."
3. Press and hold Info RESET button on DIC until display reads "100% Trans Fluid Life."
4. Place ignition switch in Off position.

Eldorado

2000

1. Turn ignition switch to ON position.
2. Press INFO button on Driver Information Center (DIC) button to display "Trans Fluid Life."
3. Press and hold Info RESET button on DIC until display reads "100% Trans Fluid Life."
4. Place ignition switch in Off position.

2001-02

1. Turn ignition switch to ON position.
2. Press and hold OFF and REAR DEFOG buttons on climate control until "Trans Fluid Life Reset" appears on DIC
3. Place ignition switch in Off position.

CHANGE ENGINE OIL MESSAGE

Buick

CENTURY & REGAL

1997

The Driver Information Center (DIC) engine oil life monitor indicates when to change oil. The "Change Oil" or "Change Oil Soon" messages might appear before 2,000 miles when operating under severe conditions.

To reset the oil change indicator after an oil change, proceed as follows:
1. Turn ignition On.
2. Fully depress and release accelerator pedal three times in 5 seconds.
3. If "Change Oil" or "Change Oil Soon" message flashes twice, indicator has properly reset.

4. If "Change Oil" or "Change Oil Soon" message stays on for 5 seconds, indicator has not properly reset and must be reset again.
5. **On models equipped with Oil Life Monitor,** press and hold RESET button for more than 5 seconds while oil monitor is being displayed or until oil life percentage reaches 100%.

1999

The Engine Oil Life monitor indicates when an oil and filter change are needed, usually from 3000–10,000 miles since the last change. The CHANGE OIL SOON indicator may light even before 3000 miles if the vehicle has been operated under severe service.

The monitor will not detect dust in the oil. If operating in dusty conditions be sure to change the oil and filter every 3000 miles or sooner if the CHANGE OIL SOON lamp lights.

To reset the Engine Oil Life monitor proceed as follows:
1. Turn ignition On, but do not start engine.
2. Fully depress and release accelerator pedal three times within 5 seconds.
3. If CHANGE OIL SOON lamp flashes twice, this means system is properly reset.
4. If CHANGE OIL SOON lamp lights and stays lit for 5 seconds, system did not reset. Repeat reset procedure.

2000-05

To reset the Engine Oil Life monitor proceed as follows:
1. Turn ignition On, but do not start engine.
2. Fully depress and release accelerator pedal three times within 5 seconds. The oil life indicator will begin to flash indicating the system is resetting.
3. Place ignition switch in Off position, then start engine.
4. The engine oil change light should illuminate as a bulb check and then go Off.
5. If oil change light remains On, repeat reset procedure.

LACROSSE

WITH DRIVER INFORMATION CENTER (DIC)

To reset the Engine Oil Life monitor proceed as follows:
1. Press option button on DIC until ENGINE OIL MONITOR appears on DIC screen.
2. Press set/reset button to reset system.
3. Next screen indicates that CHANGE OIL SOON message has been reset.
4. If vehicle has uplevel DIC, when gages button is pressed and OIL LIFE REMAINING mode appears, it should read 100 percent OIL LIFE REMAINING.
5. Turn key to OFF.

LESS DRIVER INFORMATION CENTER (DIC)

To reset the Engine Oil Life monitor proceed as follows:

1. With engine off, turn ignition key to RUN.
2. Fully press and release accelerator pedal slowly three times within five seconds.
3. Turn key to OFF, then start vehicle.

LESABRE & PARK AVENUE

1992-95

After the engine oil has been changed, the "Change Oil Soon" lamp must be reset. With ignition On, use a pencil to depress the RESET button, located under the right-hand side of the instrument panel, for 5 seconds. The lamp should flash four times to indicate the Oil Life Monitor System has been reset.

1996-97

After the engine oil has been changed, display the oil life index on the DIC, then hold the RESET button for 5 seconds. When a DIC message of RESET is displayed and the oil life index equals 100%, the reset is complete.

1998

1. Turn ignition to Run.
2. Press TRIP button on driver information center until OIL LIFE REMAINING is displayed.
3. Press and hold RESET for 6 seconds, then turn ignition off.

1999

1. Turn ignition On, then press TRIP button on driver information center (DIC) switch to view various menu choices and stop on OIL LIFE REMAINING. A message will display percentage of oil life remaining.
2. Press and hold RESET button on DIC switch for at least two seconds. A message will display the percentage of oil life remaining as 99%. The engine oil life monitor is now reset.
3. Turn ignition Off.

LUCERNE

1. Display "OIL LIFE REMAINING" on DIC.
2. **On models with button equipped DIC,** press and hold SET/RESET button on DIC for more than five seconds.
3. **On models with DIC less buttons,** press and hold trip odometer reset stem for more than five seconds.
4. **On all models,** oil life will change to 100%.
5. If "CHANGE ENGINE OIL SOON" message comes back on when you start vehicle, engine oil life system has not reset. Repeat procedure.

ROADMASTER

1994

After engine oil has been changed, the Change Oil lamp must be reset. Remove the instrument panel fuse box cover. With ignition On, depress the OIL RESET button for 5 seconds. The Change Oil lamp should go off.

1995-96

1. Turn ignition On, without starting engine.
2. Within 5 seconds, depress accelerator pedal to wide open position and release three times.
3. When lamp goes out, engine oil life monitor is reset. PCM will acknowledge if reset was successful by flashing Change Oil lamp twice, then will turn lamp off. If lamp does not reset, turn ignition Off and repeat procedure.

RIVIERA

1997-98

1. Turn ignition to Run.
2. Press TRIP button on driver information center until OIL LIFE REMAINING is displayed.
3. Press and hold RESET for 6 seconds, then turn ignition off.

1999

1. Turn ignition to On, then press TRIP button on driver information center (DIC) switch to view various menu choices and stop on OIL LIFE REMAINING. A message will display percentage of oil life remaining.
2. Press and hold RESET button on DIC switch for at least two seconds. A message will display percentage of oil life remaining as 99%. The engine oil life monitor is now reset.
3. Turn ignition Off.

Cadillac

ALLANTE

Press RANGE button until oil index appears, then simultaneously press and hold the AVG SPD and RANGE buttons for a minimum of 5 seconds.

CTS

LESS DRIVER INFORMATION CENTER (DIC)

1. With engine OFF, turn ignition key to RUN.
2. Fully press and release accelerator pedal slowly three times within five seconds.
3. Turn key to OFF, then start vehicle.
4. If light or message comes back on when you start vehicle, "OIL LIFE SYSTEM" has not reset. Repeat the procedure.

WITH DRIVER INFORMATION CENTER (DIC)

Less Navigation System

1. Access Driver Information Center (DIC) menu by pressing arrow key on INFO button located on righthand side of DIC.
2. When "100% ENGINE OIL LIFE" is highlighted, press and hold CLR button.
3. Percentage will return to 100 and oil life indicator will be reset.
4. If percentage will not return to 100, repeat procedure.

With Navigation System

1. Turn system on by pressing PWR/VOL knob once. PWR/VOL knob is located on lefthand side of Driver Information Center (DIC).
2. Access vehicle information menu by pressing INFO button on lefthand side DIC.
3. Turn TUNE/SEL knob on righthand side of DIC until "Engine Oil Life" is highlighted and press knob to select it.
4. When "100% Engine Oil Life" is displayed, press multi-function button next to "Reset" prompt in upper right-hand corner of display.
5. Percentage will return to 100 and oil life indicator will reset.
6. If percentage does not return to 100, repeat procedure.

DEVILLE

1992

Press RANGE and FUEL USED buttons simultaneously to display oil life index, then press the RANGE and RESET buttons until "Change Oil Soon" light flashes (approximately 5 seconds). The oil life index will not remain displayed.

1993

Reset the Engine Oil Life Index (EOLI) after each oil change by pressing the RANGE and RESET keys on the Fuel Data Center for 5–50 seconds. The "Change Oil Soon" lamp will flash four times to indicate that the index has been reset.

1994–98

Press the INFORMATION button until Oil Life Index is displayed, then press and hold RESET button until Oil Life Index resets to 100 (approximately 5 seconds).

1999

1. Turn ignition On, then press TRIP button on driver information center (DIC) switch to view various menu choices and stop on OIL LIFE REMAINING. A message will display percentage of oil life remaining.
2. Press and hold RESET button on DIC switch for at least two seconds. A message will display the percentage of oil life remaining as 99%. The engine oil life monitor is now reset.
3. Turn ignition Off.

2000–05

1. Turn ignition On, press Gauge Info button on Driver Information Center (DIC) switch to view various menu choices and stop on OIL LIFE REMAINING. Message will display percentage of oil life remaining.
2. Press and hold RESET button on DIC switch until display reads Oil Life Index 100% Normal.
3. Turn ignition Off.

DTS

The Engine Oil Life System calculates when to change the engine oil and filter based on vehicle use. Anytime the oil is changed, reset the system so it can calculate when the next oil change is required. If a situation occurs where you change the oil prior to a CHANGE ENGINE OIL SOON message in the Driver Information Center (DIC) being turned on, reset the system.

1. Turn key to ON position without starting engine.
2. Press INFO button on Driver Information Center (DIC) until OIL LIFE REMAINING is displayed.
3. Press and hold INFO RESET button until 100% is displayed. This resets oil life indicator.
4. Turn key to OFF.

ELDORADO & SEVILLE

1992

Press and hold the ENG DATA and RANGE buttons for a minimum of 5 seconds.

1993

Press the INFORMATION button until oil life index is displayed, then press STORE/RECALL until oil life index resets to 100 (approximately 5 seconds).

1994–98

Press the INFORMATION button until Oil Life Index is displayed, then press and hold RESET button until Oil Life Index resets to 100 (approximately 5 seconds).

1999

1. Turn ignition On, then press TRIP button on driver information center (DIC) switch to view various menu choices and stop on OIL LIFE REMAINING. A message will display percentage of oil life remaining.
2. Press and hold RESET button on DIC switch for at least two seconds. A message will display the percentage of oil life remaining as 99%. The engine oil life monitor is now reset.
3. Turn ignition Off.

2000–04

1. Turn ignition On, press Gauge Info button on Driver Information Center (DIC) switch to view various menu choices and stop on OIL LIFE REMAINING. Message will display percentage of oil life remaining.
2. Press and hold RESET button on DIC switch until display reads Oil Life Index 100% Normal.
3. Turn ignition Off.

FLEETWOOD (RWD)

REAR WHEEL DRIVE

1. Turn ignition On, without starting engine.
2. Press accelerator pedal to wide open throttle (WOT) position and release three times within 5 seconds.
3. If "Change Oil" warning indicator goes out, system has been reset.
4. If "Change Oil" warning indicator does not reset, turn ignition Off and repeat procedure.

1992 FRONT WHEEL DRIVE

Press RANGE and FUEL USED buttons simultaneously to display oil life index, then press the RANGE and RESET buttons until "Change Oil Soon" light flashes (approximately 5 seconds). The oil life index will not remain displayed.

SIXTY SPECIAL

1993

Reset the Engine Oil Life Index (EOLI) after each oil change by pressing the RANGE and RESET keys on the Fuel Data Center for 5–50 seconds. The "Change Oil Soon" lamp will flash four times to indicate that the index has been reset.

STS & XLR

The Engine Oil Life System calculates when to change your engine oil and filter based on vehicle use. Anytime your oil is changed, reset the system so it can calculate when the next oil change is required. If a situation occurs where you change your oil prior to a CHANGE ENGINE OIL SOON message in the DIC being turned on, reset the system.

1. Press up or down arrow to scroll DIC to show OIL LIFE.
2. Once XXX% ENGINE OIL LIFE menu item is highlighted, press and hold RESET button until percentage shows 100%.
3. If percentage does not return to 100% or if CHANGE ENGINE OIL SOON message comes back on when you start your vehicle, engine oil life system has not reset. Repeat procedure.

Chevrolet

CAMARO

1. Turn ignition to Run, engine Off.
2. Press TRIP/OIL RESET button on instrument panel for 12 seconds. OIL CHANGE lamp will start to flash to confirm system is reset. When reset is complete lamp will go out.
3. Turn ignition Off.

COBALT

1. Turn ignition to RUN, with engine off.
2. Press information and reset buttons on DIC at same time to enter personalization menu.
3. Press information button to scroll through available personalization menu modes until DIC display shows OIL-LIFE RESET.
4. Press and hold reset button until the DIC display shows ACKNOWLEDGED.
5. This will tell you system has been reset.
6. Turn key to LOCK.

CORVETTE

1992–96

1. Turn ignition key to On position, without starting engine.
2. Press ENG MET button on the trip monitor and release, then press and release again within 5 seconds.
3. Within 5 seconds of previous step, press and hold GAUGES button on trip

monitor. "Change Oil" lamp will flash.
4. Hold GAUGES button until "Change Oil" lamp stops flashing and goes out.
5. When lamp goes out, engine oil life monitor is reset. If it does not reset, turn ignition Off and repeat procedure.

1997

1. Turn ignition to Run.
2. Press TRIP button on the Driver Information Center (DIC) switch to view menu. Stop at OIL LIFE REMAINING. A message will display percentage of oil life remaining.
3. Press and hold the DIC switch RESET button for at least two seconds. A message will display the percentage of oil life remaining as 100%. Oil life monitor has been reset.
4. Turn ignition Off.

1998-2000

The Driver Information Center (DIC) engine oil life monitor indicates when to change oil, usually 3000–7500 miles, although the "Change Oil" message might appear before 3000 miles when operating under severe conditions.

To reset the oil life monitor after an oil change, proceed as follows:
1. Turn ignition On.
2. Press TRIP button on DIC to view menu choices and stop on "Oil Life Remaining."
3. Press and hold RESET button for more than two seconds. When remaining oil life percentage changes to 99%, monitor has been properly reset.
4. Turn ignition Off.

2001-08

1. Turn ignition switch On with engine off.
2. Press TRIP button until "OIL LIFE" percentage is displayed.
3. Press RESET button and hold for two seconds, "OIL LIFE REMAIN" percent will appear.

IMPALA & MONTE CARLO

2002-05

Less DE Series Radio

The Engine Oil Life monitor indicates when an oil and filter change are needed, usually 3000–10,000 miles since the last change. The CHANGE OIL SOON indicator may light even before 3000 miles if the vehicle has been operated under severe service.

The monitor will not detect dust in the oil. If operating in dusty conditions, change the oil and filter every 3000 miles, or less, if the CHANGE OIL SOON lamp lights.

To reset the Engine Oil Life monitor proceed as follows:
1. Turn ignition On, but do not start engine.
2. Fully depress and release accelerator pedal three times within five seconds.
3. If CHANGE OIL SOON lamp flashes twice, this means system is properly reset.
4. If CHANGE OIL SOON lamp lights and stays lit for five seconds, system did not reset. Repeat reset procedure.

With DE Series Radio

1. Place ignition switch in On position with radio Off.
2. Press and hold Disp button on radio for at least five seconds until Settings is displayed.
3. Press Seek up or down arrow to scroll though main menu.
4. Scroll until Oil Life appears on display.
5. Press Rev or Next button to enter submenu. Reset will be displayed.
6. Press Disp button to reset. A chime will be heard to ensure new setting and Done will be displayed for one second.
7. Once message has been reset, scroll until Exit appears on display.
8. Press Disp button to exit programming. A chime will be heard to ensure exit.

2006-08

1. Display OIL LIFE REMAINING on DIC.
2. Press and hold SET/RESET button on DIC for more than five seconds. The oil life will change to 100%.
3. If "CHANGE ENGINE OIL SOON" message comes back on when you start vehicle, engine oil life system has not reset. Repeat procedure.

CAPRICE & IMPALA SS

1994

After engine oil has been changed, the "Change Oil" lamp must be reset. Remove the instrument panel fuse box cover. With ignition On, depress the OIL RESET button for 5 seconds. The lamp should go off.

1995-96

1. Turn ignition On, without starting engine.
2. Within 5 seconds, depress accelerator pedal to wide open position and release three times.
3. When lamp goes out, engine oil life monitor is reset. PCM will acknowledge if reset was successful by flashing "Change Oil" lamp twice, then will turn lamp off. If lamp does not reset, turn ignition Off and repeat procedure.

LUMINA

1998-2001

The Engine Oil Life monitor indicates when an oil and filter change are needed, usually 3000–10,000 miles since the last change. The CHANGE OIL SOON indicator may light even before 3000 miles if the vehicle has been operated under severe service.

The monitor will not detect dust in the oil. If operating in dusty conditions, change the oil and filter every 3000 miles, or less, if the CHANGE OIL SOON lamp lights.

To reset the Engine Oil Life monitor proceed as follows:
1. Turn ignition On, but do not start engine.
2. Fully depress and release accelerator pedal three times within five seconds.
3. If CHANGE OIL SOON lamp flashes twice, this means system is properly reset.
4. If CHANGE OIL SOON lamp lights and

stays lit for five seconds, system did not reset. Repeat reset procedure.

MALIBU MAXX & 2006-08 MALIBU

1. Display OIL LIFE RESET on DIC.
2. Press and hold ENTER button for at least one second.
3. An ACKNOWLEDGED display message will appear for three seconds or until next button is pressed. This will tell you system has been reset.
4. Turn key to OFF.
5. If "CHANGE ENGINE OIL" light comes back on when you start vehicle, engine oil life system has not reset. Repeat procedure.

Oldsmobile

ALERO

1999-2003

The Engine Oil Life monitor indicates when an oil and filter change are needed, usually 3000–7500 miles since the last change. The indicator may light even before 3000 miles if the vehicle has been operated under severe service.

The monitor will not detect dust in the oil. If operating in dusty conditions, change the oil and filter every 3000 miles, or less, if the CHANGE OIL SOON lamp lights.

To reset the Engine Oil Life monitor proceed as follows:
1. Turn ignition On, but do not start engine.
2. Press and release RESET button. RESET button is located in driver's side instrument panel fuse block. CHANGE OIL indicator will begin flashing.
3. Press and release RESET button again.
4. Reset is complete when light goes out and chime sounds.

2004

When the system has calculated that oil life has been diminished, it will indicate that an oil change is necessary. A "CHANGE ENGINE OIL SOON" message will come on. Change the engine oil as soon as possible within the next 600 miles. It is possible that, if driving under the best conditions, the oil life may not indicate that an oil change is necessary for over a year. However, the engine oil and filter must be changed at least once a year and at this time the system must be reset. If the system is ever reset accidentally, change the engine oil at 3000 miles since last oil change. Use the following procedure to reset engine oil life
1. Turn the ignition to ON, with engine off.
2. Slowly fully press and release accelerator pedal three times within five seconds.
3. Reset is complete when chimes sound and CHANGE OIL lamp goes out.
4. If lamp stays on and no chime is heard, repeat reset procedure.
5. If the CHANGE OIL lamp comes back on when the vehicle is started, the engine oil life system has not reset. Repeat procedure.

AURORA

1995

When the engine oil life index has reached 10 or less, the Driver Information System display will indicate distance to oil change and sound a beep when the ignition is placed in the RUN or ACC position for the first time each day. When the engine oil life index has reached zero, the Driver Information System display will indicate "Change Oil Now" and sound a beep, when ignition is turned to RUN or ACC for the first time each day. After engine oil change has been performed, the oil life index may be reset as follows:

1. Depress TEST button and release, then depress OIL button and release.
2. Depress and hold the RESET button for 5–7 seconds.

1996-99

After the engine oil has been changed, display the oil life index on the DIC, then hold the RESET button for 5 seconds. When a DIC message of RESET is displayed and the oil life index equals 100%, the reset is complete.

2001-03

1. Place ignition switch in On position.
2. Press the Select right arrow button on the driver information center until the Oil Life % is displayed.
3. Press and hold the RESET button until the display indicates Oil Life 100%.
4. Engine oil life monitor is reset.

INTRIGUE

The "Change Oil" lamp will light when the engine oil's useful life is close to its expiration. This lighting may appear earlier than outlined in the owner's manual, depending on driving patterns.

To reset the oil life monitor after an oil change, proceed as follows:
1. Turn ignition On.
2. Fully depress and release accelerator pedal three times in five seconds.
3. If "Change Oil" message flashes, monitor has properly reset.
4. If "Change Oil" message stays on for five seconds, monitor has not properly reset and must be reset again.
5. **On models equipped with U20 option,** reset oil life low indicator as follows:
   a. Press and hold MODE button until light appears next to OIL LIFE.
   b. Press and hold trip RESET button until oil life percentage changes to 99%.

EIGHTY EIGHT, LSS, NINETY-EIGHT & REGENCY

1992-95

When the engine oil life index has reached 10 or less, the Driver Information System display will indicate distance to oil change and sound a beep when the ignition

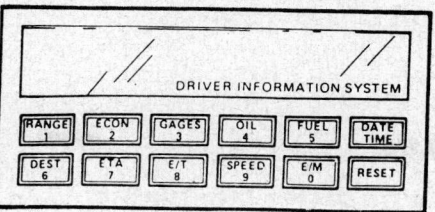

Fig. 1 Driver Information Center. Oldsmobile except Alero, Aurora, Eighty Eight, Intrigue, LSS, Ninety-Eight & Toronado

is placed in the RUN or ACC position for the first time each day. When the engine oil life index has reached zero, the Driver Information System display will indicate "Change Oil Now" and sound a beep, when ignition is turned to RUN or ACC for the first time each day. After engine oil change has been performed, the oil life index may be reset as follows:

1. **On 1992–93 models,** depress TEST button and release, then depress OIL button and release.
2. **On 1994–95 models,** select OIL menu by depressing MODE button.
3. **On all models,** depress and hold the RESET button for 5–7 seconds.

1996-97

After the engine oil has been changed, display the oil life index on the DIC, then hold the RESET button for 5 seconds. When a DIC message of RESET is displayed and the oil life index equals 100%, the reset is complete.

1998-99

The Driver Information Center (DIC) engine oil life monitor indicates when to change oil, usually between 3000–7500 miles, although the "Change Oil" message might appear before 3000 miles when operating under severe conditions.

To reset the oil life monitor after an oil change, proceed as follows:
1. Turn ignition On.
2. Press TRIP button on DIC to view menu choices, then stop on "Oil Life Remaining."
3. Press and hold RESET button for more than 5 seconds. Monitor has been properly reset when remaining oil life percentage changes to 100%.
4. Turn ignition Off.

EXCEPT ALERO, AURORA, EIGHTY EIGHT, INTRIGUE, LSS, NINETY-EIGHT & TORONADO

When the engine oil life index has reached 10 or less, the Driver Information System display will indicate distance to oil change and sound a beep when ignition is turned to Run or Accessory for the first time each day. When the engine oil life index has reached 0, the Driver Information System

display will indicate Change Oil Now and sound a beep when ignition is turned to Run or Accessory for the first time each day. After engine oil change has been performed, the oil life index may be reset by depressing and holding the Oil and Reset buttons for approximately 5 seconds, **Fig. 1.**

TORONADO

1992

Less CRT Driver Information Display

Oil life is displayed by pressing the ENG DATA button on the Driver Information System (DIS) keypad several times. To reset the oil life index, press and hold the RESET/ENTER key for 5 seconds while the oil life is displayed.

With Driver Information Display

Oil life may be displayed by pressing the INFO button and then selecting the OIL LIFE option. Oil life is reset is reset by pressing RESET on the oil life display and then pressing YES on the confirmation screen. This will reset the oil life index and OIL LIFE INDEX 100. The Change Oil message will remain off until the next oil change is needed.

Pontiac

BONNEVILLE

1992-95

After changing engine oil and filter, if required, reset service interval indicator by depressing and releasing the service reminder button until the desired item is displayed. When the desired item is displayed, do not release service reminder button. After button has been depressed for approximately 10 seconds, the service interval mileage display will begin to count down in 500 mile intervals. When desired service interval mileage is reached, release button. The service interval reminder indicates miles to service, not miles from last service.

1996-97

After the engine oil has been changed, display the oil life index on the DIC, then hold the RESET button for 5 seconds. When a DIC message of RESET is displayed and the oil life index equals 99% or 100%, the reset is complete.

1998

1. Turn ignition switch to RUN position.
2. Press TRIP button on driver information center (DIC) switch to view menu choices.
3. Select OIL LIFE REMAINING.
4. Press and hold RESET button on DIC for more than 5 seconds until oil life changes to 100%.
5. Turn ignition switch to OFF position.

1999

1. Turn ignition switch to RUN position.
2. Press and hold reset button in glove compartment for at least 5 seconds but not more than 60 seconds.
3. After 5 seconds, observe the CHANGE OIL SOON light flash four times before light turns OFF.
4. Engine oil life monitor has been reset.

2000-05

1. Display "OIL LIFE" on Driver Information Center (DIC).
2. Press and hold RESET button on DIC until display reads OIL LIFE 100%.
3. Engine oil life monitor is now reset.

FIREBIRD

1. Turn ignition to Run, engine Off.
2. Press TRIP/OIL RESET button on instrument panel for 12 seconds. OIL CHANGE lamp will start to flash to confirm system is reset. When reset is complete lamp will go out.
3. Turn ignition Off.

GRAND AM

When the system has calculated that oil life has been diminished, it will indicate that an oil change is necessary. A "CHANGE ENGINE OIL SOON" message will come on. Change the engine oil as soon as possible within the next 600 miles. It is possible that, if driving under the best conditions, the oil life may not indicate that an oil change is necessary for over a year. However, the engine oil and filter must be changed at least once a year and at this time the system must be reset. If the system is ever reset accidentally, change the engine oil at 3000 miles since last oil change. Use the following procedure to reset engine oil life

1. Turn the ignition to ON, with engine off.
2. Slowly fully press and release accelerator pedal three times within five seconds.
3. Reset is complete when chimes sound and CHANGE OIL lamp goes out.
4. If lamp stays on and no chime is heard, repeat reset procedure.
5. If CHANGE OIL lamp comes back on when vehicle is started, engine oil life system has not reset. Repeat procedure.

GRAND PRIX

1992-96

Ensure oil life indicator is displayed by pressing Driver Information System SYSTEMS CHECK button. Press and hold the RESET button until oil life display is returned to 100%.

1997-99

Change Oil Soon Indicator

1. Turn ignition On, but do not start engine.
2. Fully depress and release accelerator three times within 5 seconds.
3. If "Change Oil Soon" lamp flashes this means system is resetting.
4. Turn ignition Off, then start engine.
5. If "Change Oil Soon" lamp lights, repeat procedure.

Oil Life Monitor

Press trip calculator MODE button until light appears next to "Oil Life," then press and hold RESET button until oil life percentage reaches 100%.

2000-03

With Driver Information Center (DIC)

1. Turn ignition On, but do not start engine.
2. Fully depress and release accelerator pedal three times within five seconds. Oil life indicator will begin to flash indicating system is resetting.
3. Place ignition switch in Off position and start engine.
4. Engine oil change light should illuminate as a bulb check and then go Off.
5. If oil change light remains On, repeat reset procedure.

Less Driver Information Center (DIC)

1. Press trip MODE button until light appears next to OIL LIFE.
2. Press and hold trip RESET button until oil life percentage changes to 99 percent.

2004-08

1. Press options button on Driver Information Center (DIC) until "ENGINE OIL MONITOR" appears on DIC screen.
2. Press set/reset button to reset system.
3. Next screen indicates engine oil monitor system has been reset.
4. If vehicle is equipped with trip computer DIC, when gage button is pressed and OIL LIFE REMAINING mode appears, it should read 100 percent OIL LIFE REMAINING.
5. Turn key to OFF.
6. If "CHANGE ENGINE OIL SOON" message comes back on when you start vehicle, engine oil life system has not reset. Repeat procedure.

GTO

1. With engine off, turn ignition key to ON.
2. Fully press and release accelerator pedal slowly two times within five seconds.
3. Turn key to LOCK.
4. If Service Engine Oil message comes back on when you start your vehicle, engine oil life system has not reset. Repeat the procedure.

G5

1. Turn ignition to RUN with engine OFF.
2. Press INFO and RESET buttons on Driver Information Center (DIC) at same time to enter personalization menu.
3. Press INFO button to scroll through available personalization menu modes until DIC display shows OIL-LIFE RESET.
4. Press and hold RESET button until DIC display shows ACKNOWLEDGED, this will tell you system has been reset.

5. Turn the key to LOCK.
6. If "CHANGE ENGINE OIL SOON" message comes back on when you start vehicle, engine oil life system has not reset. Repeat procedure.

G6

1. With CHANGE OIL SOON message displayed, press any of three DIC buttons to clear CHANGE OIL SOON message.
2. Display OIL LIFE RESET on DIC.
3. Press and hold ENTER button for at least one second.
4. An ACKNOWLEDGED display message will appear for three seconds or until next button is pressed.
5. This will tell you system has been reset.
6. Turn ignition to OFF.
7. If "CHANGE ENGINE OIL" message comes back on when you start vehicle, engine oil life system has not reset. Repeat procedure.

SOLSTICE

1. Turn ignition to RUN, with engine off.
2. Press INFO and RESET buttons on DIC at same time to enter personalization menu.
3. Press INFO button to scroll through available personalization menu modes until DIC display shows OIL-LIFE RESET.
4. Press and hold RESET button until DIC display shows ACKNOWLEDGED. This will tell you system has been reset.
5. Turn key to LOCK.
6. If "CHANGE ENGINE OIL SOON" message comes back on when you start vehicle, engine oil life system has not reset. Repeat procedure.

Saturn

AURA

1. With "CHANGE OIL SOON" message displayed on Driver Information Center (DIC), press either of the DIC buttons to clear "CHANGE OIL SOON" message.
2. Display "OIL LIFE RESET" on DIC.
3. Press and hold ENTER button for at least one second. An "ACKNOWLEDGED" display message will appear for three seconds or until next button is pressed. This will indicate system has been reset.
4. Turn the ignition to OFF.
5. If "CHANGE OIL SOON" message comes back on when vehicle is started, engine oil life system has not reset. Repeat procedure.

ION

1. Turn ignition key to RUN position.
2. Press trip odometer reset stem once or twice until "OIL LIFE" message is flashing on message center.
3. Press and hold instrument panel trip odometer button for few seconds until chime sounds five times and "RESET" is displayed on message center.
4. When reset is complete, odometer will

again be displayed in message center.

5. Turn ignition key to LOCK.
6. If "CHG OIL" message comes back on when you start vehicle, engine oil life system has not reset. Repeat procedure.

L SERIES

2000-02

1. Turn ignition switch to RUN position.
2. Remove underhood fuse block cover, press red OIL RESET button and hold for five seconds.
3. Turn ignition switch off.
4. Turn ignition switch to RUN position and ensure "SERVICE OIL SOON" lamp turns off after 30 seconds.
5. If lamp does not turn off, repeat procedure.

2003-05

1. Turn ignition to RUN, with engine OFF.
2. Fully press and release accelerator pedal three times within five seconds.
3. If "Change Oil" light flashes, system has been reset. Light will flash for up to 30 seconds or until ignition is turned OFF.
4. If "Change Oil" light comes on again and stays on for 30 seconds at next ignition cycle, system did not reset. Repeat reset procedure.

S SERIES

The PCM has the ability to calculate when the engine oil needs to be changed based on vehicle mileage, engine revolutions and engine coolant temperature. The PCM bases the engine oil change interval within a window of 3000–6000 miles regardless of engine revolutions and engine coolant temperature. To reset the PCM oil life monitor, proceed as follows:

1. Remove cover from underhood fuse relay center.
2. Place ignition switch in On position.
3. Press red Oil Reset Button and hold for five seconds.
4. If "Change Engine Oil Soon" lamp is flashing, system is reset. Lamp will flash for 30 seconds or until ignition switch is placed in Off position.
5. If lamp comes On and remains On for 30 seconds at next ignition On cycle, lamp did not reset. Reset procedure must be performed again.

SKY

1. Turn ignition to RUN, with engine off.
2. Press INFO and RESET buttons on DIC at same time to enter personalization menu.
3. Press INFO button to scroll through available personalization menu modes until DIC display shows OIL-LIFE RESET.
4. Press and hold RESET button until DIC display shows ACKNOWLEDGED. This will tell you system has been reset.
5. Turn key to LOCK.
6. If "CHANGE ENGINE OIL SOON" message comes back on when you start vehicle, engine oil life system has not reset. Repeat procedure.

CHECK ENGINE OR SERVICE NOw/SOON ENGINE INDICATOR LAMPS

The Check Engine lamp may light if the fuel filler cap has not been completely tightened. This lamp should turn off after the cap has been properly tightened and the vehicle has successfully completed a predetermined number of trip cycles.

Except LeMans, Metro, Prizm & Storm

The Check Engine lamp should light when the ignition is turned On. When the engine is started, the lamp should go off. If the lamp remains On for 10 seconds or constantly after the engine is started, the self diagnosis system has detected a fault condition and has stored a code in the system Electronic Control Module (ECM) or Powertrain Control Module (PCM). After diagnosis and repair, the ECM memory can be cleared of codes as follows:

1. **On models except Cadillac with DEFI,** proceed as follows:
   a. Remove ECM/PCM fuse or disconnect battery ground cable for approximately 30 seconds, with ignition turned Off.
   b. If battery ground cable is disconnected to clear codes, components such as clocks, electronically tuned radios etc., will have to be reset.
2. **On Cadillac models equipped with DEFI,** the ECM/PCM power feed is connected by a pigtail, inline fuse holder, at the positive battery terminal. To clear codes within ECM/PCM system and protect components that need resetting, disconnect inline fuse.
3. **On Eldorado and Seville models,** stored codes are cleared during self-diagnostic procedure.

LeMans

The Check Engine lamp should light when the ignition is turned On. When the engine is started, them should go off. If the lamp remains On for 10 seconds or constantly after the engine is started, the self diagnosis system has detected a fault condition and has stored a code in the system Electronic Control Module (ECM). After diagnosis and repair, the ECM memory can be cleared of codes, by disconnecting battery ground cable for 10 seconds, with ignition turned Off.

Metro

The Check Engine lamp should light when the ignition is turned On with engine not operating. When engine is started, the Check Engine lamp should go off. If lamp remains on, a code has been stored by the Electronic Control Module (ECM) memory. After diagnosis and repair, turn ignition Off and clear codes stored in the ECM memory by disconnecting the battery ground cable, for approximately 20 seconds.

The Check Engine lamp may light if the fuel filler cap has not been completely tightened. This lamp should turn off after the cap has been properly tightened and the vehicle has successfully completed a predetermined number of trip cycles.

Prizm

The Check Engine lamp should light when the ignition is in ON position with engine not operating. When engine is started, the Check Engine lamp should go off. If lamp remains on, a code has been stored by the Electronic Control Unit (ECU) memory. After diagnosis and repair, turn ignition Off and clear codes stored in the ECU memory by removing the Stop Fuse. The Stop fuse is located in a fuse panel, in the passenger compartment, on driver's side, behind kick panel. The fuse must be removed for 10 seconds or longer, depending on ambient temperature. The lower the ambient temperature, the longer the fuse will have to be removed.

Storm

The Check Engine lamp should light when the ignition is in the On position with engine not operating. When engine is started, the Check Engine lamp should go off. If lamp remains on, a code has been stored by the Electronic Control Module (ECM) memory. After diagnosis and repair, turn ignition Off, then clear codes stored in the ECM memory by disconnecting the battery ground cable for approximately 30 seconds.

CHECK GAUGE WARNING LAMP

The Check Gauge warning lamp will light to warn the driver to inspect the oil pressure gauge, engine coolant temperature gauge and the voltmeter. When lit, the "Check Gauge" lamp indicates that one of these gauges is operating in an abnormal range.

CHECK INFO CENTER WARNING LAMP

Eldorado & Seville

1992

This lamp will light for a few seconds when the ignition is turned On as a bulb inspection. If lamp remains lit, a message is stored in the Driver Information Center. Refer to "Driver Information Center."

DRIVER INFORMATION CENTER

Aurora

1995-99

The Driver Information Center Display is

located on the instrument panel (Eighty-Eight and Ninety-Eight models with digital cluster or touring sedan gauge cluster). It provides traveling and performance information on the following:

1. Date and Time—This information is displayed for 5 seconds when the ignition is turned On. The DT/TM button may be depressed at any time to display current date and time.
2. Fuel Economy—The ECON button displays average fuel economy.
3. Remaining Fuel/Fuel Used—Depressing FUEL button displays amount of fuel used since reset button was last pressed. Depressing FUEL button a second time displays amount of fuel remaining.
4. Fuel Range—Depress RANGE to display distance that may be driven before refueling. To display amount of fuel used from a specific starting point, depress FUEL then RESET.
5. Average Speed—Depress SPEED to display average speed. To reset average speed, depress SPEED then RESET.
6. Remaining Oil Life and Oil Change Information—The OIL button displays information on oil life. Refer to "Change Oil Or Change Oil Now Message" for reset procedure.
7. Engine Coolant Temperature, Oil Pressure, Battery Voltage and Tachometer—Depressing GAGES once displays coolant temperature. Pressing GAGES a second time displays oil pressure. Pressing GAGES a third time displays battery voltage. Pressing GAGES a fourth time displays tachometer RPM.
8. Distance To Destination—Depress DEST then RESET and enter length of trip. Display will then count backwards to zero distance remaining. When the display reaches zero, "TRIP COMPLETE" is displayed. This message will clear when the TEST button is depressed or the ignition is turned Off.
9. Estimated Time of Arrival—After entering distance to destination, Press ETA button to display time remaining to destination (based on average speed).
10. Elapsed Time—Depressing the E/T button activates a stopwatch that records up to 100 hours.

Bonneville

The Driver Information Center Display is located on the instrument panel. When the ignition is turned On, the display will go through a bulb inspection in which the vehicle graph and message title will be displayed in sequence. After the sequence has been completed, all messages and vehicle graph will remain lit for approximately two seconds. After approximately two seconds, if all monitored systems are functioning properly, the message titles should go off and only the vehicle outline should be lit. If a fault condition in any of the monitored systems is present, the particular title for the monitored system should light and its

approximate location on the vehicle graphic display should light. The following messages will be displayed:

1. **Function Monitor**—The coolant level, fuel level and windshield washer levels are monitored when ignition is turned On.
   a. Coolant Level—This message will be indicated when engine coolant level in the radiator drops below a predetermined level. To cancel message, inspect cooling system, then add coolant to bring system to proper level.
   b. Fuel Level—This message will be indicated when fuel level is 5 gallons or less. To cancel message add fuel to fuel tank.
   c. Washer Fluid—This message will be indicated when windshield washer fluid is at about 40% of capacity. To cancel message, add washer fluid to reservoir.
2. **Lamp Check**—The headlamps, tail lamps, brake lamps and turn signal lamps will be inspected whenever the lamp system is activated. To cancel this message, replace bulb or inspect and repair electrical system as required for lamp system indicated.
3. **Security**—Door, Hood Or Trunk Ajar are monitored. This message will appear when the indicated component is open or improperly closed. To cancel message, properly close indicated component.
4. **Service Reminder**—Oil change, oil filter change, engine tune-up and tire rotation intervals are monitored.
   a. After the bulb inspection sequence has been completed, the service interval can be inspected by depressing the service reminder button. Depressing the button once will display the Change Oil indication and mileage remaining to service interval. Depressing the button a second time, will display the Change Oil Filter indication and mileage remaining to service interval. Depressing the button a third time will display the Rotate Tires and mileage to service interval. Depressing the button a fourth time will display Tune-Up indication and mileage to service interval.
   b. After completing the required service, reset service interval indicator by depressing and releasing the service reminder button until the desired item is displayed. When the desired item is displayed, do not release service reminder button. After button has been depressed for approximately 10 seconds, the service interval mileage display will begin to count down in 500 mile intervals. When desired service interval mileage is reached, release button. The service interval reminder indicates miles to service, not miles from last service.

Eldorado & Seville

1992

This system incorporates a warning lamp, located on the instrument cluster, that is lit when the ignition is in the On position. After a few seconds the lamp should go off, unless a message in The Driver Information System is present. The driver information center will display the following messages:

A/C Overheated—A/C Compressor Off—This message is displayed when excessive pressure in the refrigerant system is encountered. When this condition is encountered, the A/C Compressor clutch will be de-energized and cool air will not be delivered to the vehicle interior. The message will continue to appear and the A/C compressor clutch will continue to be de-energized until the system pressure returns to normal range. If this message frequently appears, the A/C system should be serviced.

A/C Sensor Fault—This message will be displayed when the sensor controlling A/C compressor clutch cycling has failed. When this sensor has failed, the A/C compressor will not operate and the A/C system will emit warmer air. After servicing system and replacing sensor, the display message will be cancelled.

Battery Volts High—This message will appear when the charging system is overcharging the battery. After completing charging system diagnosis and repair, the message will be cancelled when battery voltage returns to 11.5–15.5 volts with engine operating. Battery voltage can be displayed on the Drive Information Center Display by depressing the Eng-Data button three times.

Battery Volts Low—If this message is displayed while driving the vehicle or after vehicle has been started, a fault condition in the charging system is present or battery has been drained. After diagnosing charging system or electrical system for cause of battery drain, the message will be cancelled when engine is operating and battery voltage is between 11.5–15.5 volts. Battery voltage can be displayed on the Drive Information Center Display by depressing the Eng-Data button three times.

Change Engine Oil—When the engine oil life index has reached 0, the Change Engine Oil message will be indicated. After performing the engine oil change, the engine Oil Life Index may be reset by depressing and holding the Engine Data and Range buttons for at least 5 seconds.

Cooling Fan Fault—This message will appear when the engine cooling fan system inoperative. After repairing cooling fan system the message will be automatically cancelled.

Engine Hot—A/C Compressor Off—This message will appear when A/C system is Auto or Defrost and engine coolant temperature is excessive. The A/C compressor clutch will be automatically de-energized when excessive engine coolant temperatures are encountered. When engine coolant temperature returns to normal, the A/C compressor clutch will be energized and the message on the display will be cancelled.

Front Or Rear Door Ajar—This message will appear when the transmission selector lever is moved out of the Park position and a door is not properly closed. The message can be cancelled by properly closing the indicated door.

Fuel Level Very Low—When low fuel level conditions are encountered this message will appear. To cancel message, add fuel.

Gear Select Problem—This message will appear if a fault condition in the transaxle gear select system is encountered while operating vehicle. After performing required service, the message will automatically be cancelled.

Headlamps Or Parking Lamps On—This message will be displayed when the headlamp switch is On, vehicle is moving and the sensed level of outside light indicates that headlamps should not be lit. This message may be cancelled by turning the headlamp switch Off.

Headlamps Suggested—This message will be displayed when the Twilight Sentinel is in the Off position, vehicle is moving and the sensed level of outside light indicates that headlamps should be lit. This message may be cancelled by activating the Twilight Sentinel System.

Low A/C Refrigerant—A/C Compressor Off—This message will be displayed when the A/C system detects a refrigerant charge low enough to cause compressor damage. When this condition is encountered, the A/C compressor clutch is de-energized and the A/C system is switched from AUTO to ECON. The system will remain in ECON until required repairs are made and system is recharged. After completing required repairs and recharging the system, A/C system operation will return to normal and the message on the display will be cancelled.

Low A/C Refrigerant—Service A/C Soon—This message will be displayed when the A/C system detects that refrigerant charge is low enough to cause a reduction in cooling capacity. This message will be displayed until system has been recharged.

Low Washer Fluid—This message will appear when windshield washer fluid level is low. To cancel message, refill windshield washer fluid reservoir.

Oil Life Index—The oil life index is a series of numerals ranging from 0–100. The 100 is indicated when engine oil has been drained and replacement engine oil has been installed. The 0 is an indication that the engine oil should be changed. The oil life index is accessed by depressing the Engine Data button four times.

Service Electrical System—This message will appear when a fault condition in the charging system is present. After repairing charging system, the message will be automatically cancelled.

Set Timing Mode—This message will appear if ignition timing is improperly set. After performing required service, the message will automatically be cancelled.

Starting Disabled/Due to Theft

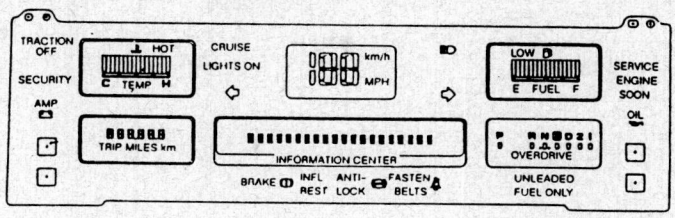

Fig. 2 Driver information center. 1992–93 Eighty-Eight & Ninety-Eight

System/Remove Ignition Key—This message is an indication of a fault condition in the vehicle security system that may prohibit the vehicle from being restarted after the ignition has been turned Off. After servicing the vehicle security system the message will be automatically cancelled.

System Satisfactory—This message will be displayed for approximately 5 seconds after ignition has been turned On, unless a fault condition in the system has been detected. After approximately 5 seconds the display will return to the last display function selected.

System Problem—Service Car Soon—This message will be displayed when one or more of the vehicle computers supplying information to the Driver Information Center become faulty. After diagnosis and repair of the faulty computer, the message will be automatically cancelled.

Theft System Problem/Car May Not Start—This message will appear when the vehicle security system senses an improper ignition key has been placed in the ignition. After removing key from ignition, the Driver Information Center display will indicate "Wait 3 Minutes," "Wait 2 Minutes," Wait 1 Minute and then "Start Car." When the "Start Car" message appears, insert ignition key and attempt to start vehicle. If message appears again, inspect ignition key for damage and replace as required. If key appears to be satisfactory, clean pellet contacts with a soft cloth and attempt to restart vehicle.

Trunk Open—This message will appear when the ignition is the Run position and the trunk is not properly closed. The message can be cancelled by properly closing the trunk.

Eighty-Eight, LSS & Ninety-Eight

1992-93

The Driver Information Center Display, **Fig. 2,** is located on the instrument panel (Eighty-Eight and Ninety-Eight models with digital cluster or touring sedan gauge cluster). It provides traveling and performance information on the following:

1. Date and Time—This information is displayed for 5 seconds when the ignition is turned On. The DT/TM button may be depressed at any time to display current date and time.
2. Fuel Economy—The ECON button displays average fuel economy.
3. Remaining Fuel/Fuel Used—Depressing FUEL button displays

amount of fuel used since reset button was last pressed. Depressing FUEL button a second time displays amount of fuel remaining.
4. Fuel Range—Depress RANGE to display distance that may be driven before refueling. To display amount of fuel used from a specific starting point, depress FUEL then RESET.
5. Average Speed—Depress SPEED to display average speed. To reset average speed, depress SPEED then RESET.
6. Remaining Oil Life and Oil Change Information—The OIL button displays information on oil life. Refer to "Change Oil Or Change Oil Now Message" for reset procedure.
7. Engine Coolant Temperature, Oil Pressure, Battery Voltage and Tachometer—Depressing GAGES once displays coolant temperature. Pressing GAGES a second time displays oil pressure. Pressing GAGES a third time displays battery voltage. Pressing GAGES a fourth time displays tachometer RPM.
8. Distance To Destination—Depress DEST then RESET and enter length of trip. Display will then count backwards to zero distance remaining. When the display reaches zero, "TRIP COMPLETE" is displayed. This message will clear when the TEST button is depressed or the ignition is turned Off.
9. Estimated Time of Arrival—After entering distance to destination, Press ETA button to display time remaining to destination (based on average speed).
10. Elapsed Time—Depressing the E/T button activates a stopwatch that records up to 100 hours.

1994-96

The Driver Information Center Display, **Fig. 3,** is located on the instrument panel. When the ignition is turned On, the display will go through a system inspection while the message "Monitored Systems OK" is displayed. If no fault conditions are detected, the screen returns to the mode displayed before the ignition was turned Off.

There are four buttons that control the functions of the driver information center:

1. The MODE button, when pressed, cycles through a series of displays in the following order:
   a. ECON—Average fuel economy and instantaneous fuel economy.
   b. FUEL—Amount of fuel used since last fuel-used reset, and fuel remaining.

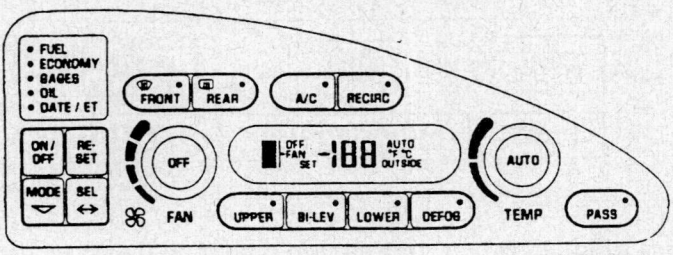

Fig. 3 Driver information center. LSS, 1994–96 Eighty Eight & Ninety Eight

c. RANGE—Fuel range and low fuel range.
d. OIL—Oil life index and next required oil change.
e. GAGES—Oil pressure, tachometer and battery voltage information.
f. ET—Elapsed time since last reset.
g. DT/TM—Date and time.
2. The ON/OFF button is used to input numbers and to blank out the display.
3. The RESET button is used with other buttons to reset the system. Depressing this button once enters the reset mode. Pressing this button again aborts the reset.
4. The SEL button is used to select different displays within a specific mode. For example, when the SEL button is depressed while in the GAGES mode, the display will cycle from oil pressure to battery voltage to tachometer.

ENGINE COOLANT TEMPERATURE TELLTALE LAMP

If the engine coolant temperature if more than 244°F, or if the transaxle fluid temperature if more than 284°F, the coolant temperature telltale lamp will light. The PCM will turn the cooling fan on if an ECT DTC is active.

LOW COOLANT LAMP

This lamp should light when engine coolant level in the radiator drops below a predetermined level. To turn lamp off, inspect cooling system and add coolant to bring system to proper level.

LOW OIL DIPSTICK

The Low Oil indicator ground is controlled by the PCM. To inspect for a low oil condition, the PCM inspects the low oil level sensor after the ignition has been turned to the Off or Lock position. The PCM inspects for a low oil condition 32 minutes after the ignition is turned Off if the previous ignition cycle was less than 12 minutes. The PCM inspects for a low oil condition 3 minutes after the ignition is turned off if the previous ignition cycle was less than 12 minutes.

LOW OIL PRESSURE TELLTALE LAMP

The engine oil pressure switch is normally closed and open when engine oil pressure is 1.4–5.8 psi. If the lamp is lit with engine running, inspect wiring for oil pressure switch circuit and the engine lubrication system for proper oil pump output pressure.

LOW WASHER FLUID INDICATOR

The windshield washer solvent tank has a switch that closes when the washer solvent level becomes low, illuminating the "Low Washer Fluid" indicator.

MALFUNCTION INDICATOR LAMP (MIL)

As a bulb and system check, the lamp will light with the ignition On and the engine not running. When the engine is started, the lamp will turn off. If the lamp remains On, the self diagnostic system has detected a fault. If the fault is intermittent or the system is repaired, the lamp will go Off after three trips but a diagnostic trouble code (DTC) will be stored in the PCM. Use a suitably programmed scan tool to retrieve and erase any DTCs using the "Clear DTC Information" option. If the lamp remains lit while the engine is running or when a fault is suspected because of a driveability problem, perform an OBD system inspection. Scan the serial data stream using a suitably programmed scan tool.

PASSLOCK TELLTALE LAMP

The instrument panel cluster contains the security telltale lamp. The security telltale has three modes of operation: Off, Flashing & On. The security telltale will be off if ignition is in the Off position or if the ignition is in the Run, Start or ACC position and the security system diagnostics have all passed. The security telltale will be on if the body control module (BCM) is performing a bulb test at vehicle start up, the security system diagnostics have not yet completed at vehicle start up or if a security system diagnostic trouble code (DTC) is set in the BCM or PCM. The security telltale will be flashing if the tamper hall effect has been triggered, there was improper Passlock sensor data to the BCM for more than five seconds during vehicle start, there was no Passlock sensor data to the BCM for more than five seconds during vehicle start or there was improper password from the BCM to the PCM after five seconds during vehicle start. Repair or replace components. Retrieve and clear any associated DTCs to reset the telltale lamp.

SERVICE AIR COND LAMP

This lamp should light when the air conditioning system detects a low refrigerant charge. The lamp should light for approximately two seconds after ignition has been turned On as a bulb inspection.

If while operating vehicle, the lamp lights for approximately 60 seconds and then goes off, the refrigerant level is low enough to cause reduced cooling capacity. At this point the blower motor will increase speed to try to offset the loss in cooling capacity. The lamp will be automatically reset after system has been inspected and refrigerant charge has been brought to proper level.

If lamp is lit for approximately 60 seconds after engine start up, the refrigerant charge may be low enough to cause air conditioning compressor damage. When this condition is encountered, the air conditioning compressor clutch is de-energized and the air conditioning system is switched from Auto to Econ. The system will remain in ECON until required repairs are made and system is recharged. After completing required repairs and recharging the system, air conditioning system operation will return to normal and the lamp will be automatically reset.

SERVICE ELECTRICAL SYSTEM LAMP

This lamp should light when a fault condition in the charging system is present. The lamp should light during engine starting as a bulb inspection. If lamp is lit while engine is operating, the charging system should be inspected. After repairing charging system, the lamp will be automatically reset.

SERVICE TELLTALE LAMP

The service telltale lamp is used for non-emissions related failures which without being serviced could lead to component damage to other sub systems. As a bulb check, the lamp will light for 2–3 seconds and then turn off. If the lamp remains lit, the system has detected a fault condition. If the condition is intermittent or the system is repaired, the lamp will turn off 3 seconds after the PCM diagnostic test passes. Any DTCs will be stored in the freeze frame/failure records. Use a suitably programmed scan tool to retrieve and erase any DTCs using the "Clear DTC Information" option.

VEHICLE LIFT POINTS

TABLE OF CONTENTS

	Page No.		Page No.
CHRYSLER	0-51	**GENERAL MOTORS CORP.**	0-55
FORD MOTOR CO.	0-53	**SATURN**	0-59

Chrysler

INDEX

	PAGE NO.	FIG. NO.
Avenger	0-52	6
Caliber	0-51	1
Charger	0-51	2
Concorde	0-52	3
Crossfire	0-52	4
Intrepid	0-52	3
Magnum	0-51	2
Neon	0-51	1

	PAGE NO.	FIG. NO.
Sebring:		
Convertible	0-52	6
Coupe	0-52	5
Sedan	0-52	6
Stratus:		
Coupe	0-52	5
Sedan	0-52	6
300	0-51	2
300M	0-52	3

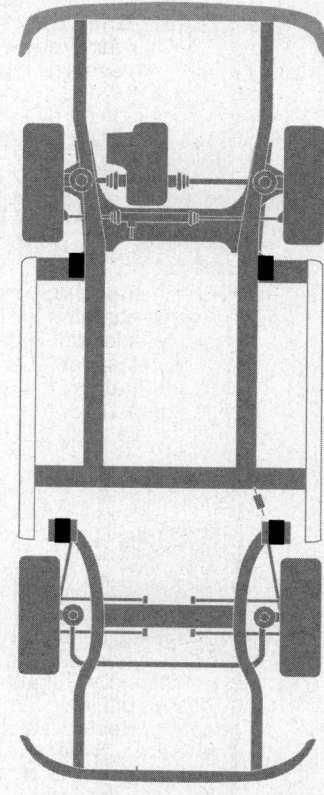

ALCR00006

Fig. 1   Vehicle Lift Points. Caliber & Neon

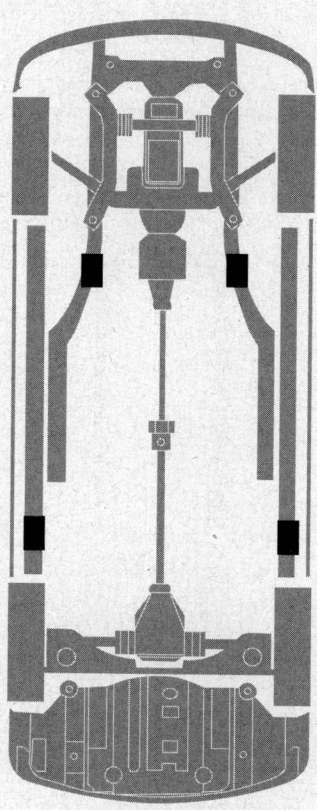

ALCR040009

Fig. 2   Vehicle Lift Points. Charger, Magnum & 300

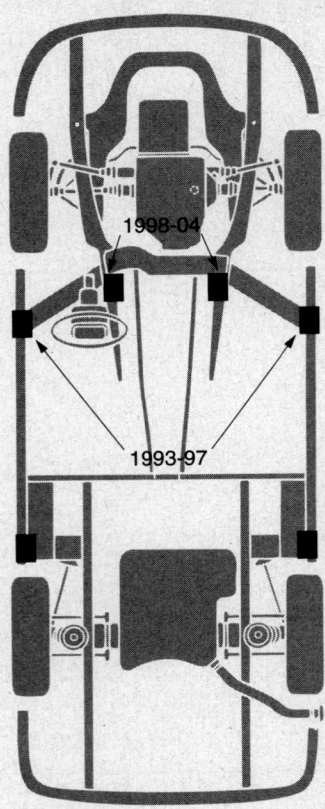

ALCR00005

Fig. 3   Vehicle Lift Points. Concorde, Intrepid & 300M

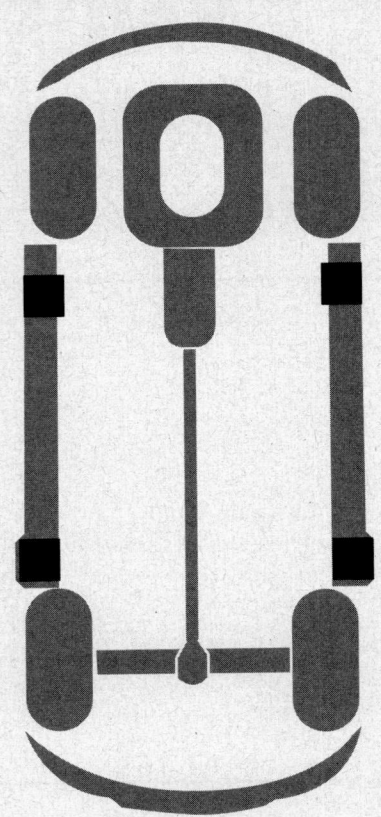

ALCR040006

Fig. 4   Vehicle Lift Points. Crossfire

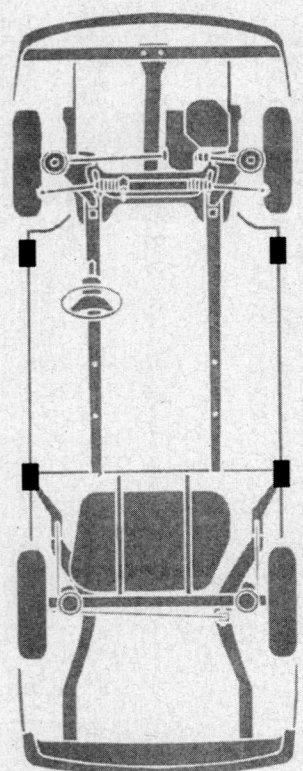

ALCR00008

Fig. 5   Vehicle Lift Points. Sebring Coupe & Stratus Coupe

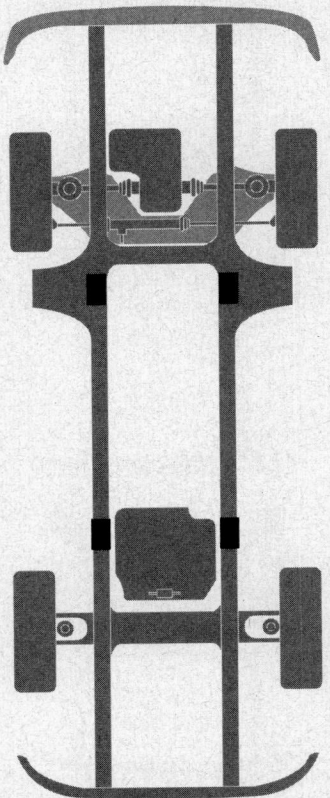

ALCR00007

Fig. 6   Vehicle Lift Points. Avenger, Sebring Sedan, Sebring Convertible & Stratus Sedan

Ford Motor Co.

INDEX

	PAGE NO.	FIG. NO.
Crown Victoria	0-54	4
Five-Hundred	0-54	3
Focus	0-54	5
Freestyle	0-54	3
Fusion	0-53	1
Grand Marquis	0-54	4
LS	0-55	8
Marauder	0-54	4
Milan	0-53	1
Montego	0-54	3

	PAGE NO.	FIG. NO.
Mustang:		
2004	0-54	6
2005–08	0-55	7
Sable	0-53	2
Taurus & Taurus X:		
2004–06	0-53	2
2008	0-54	3
Thunderbird	0-55	8
Town Car	0-54	4
Zephyr	0-53	1

Jacking Points — Front

Jacking Points — Rear

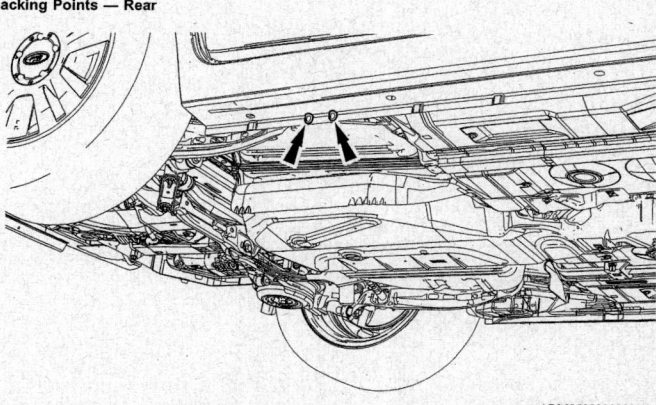

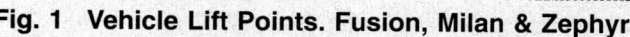

ARM0500000000267

Fig. 1   Vehicle Lift Points. Fusion, Milan & Zephyr

AIR SUSPENSION
Turn air suspension off
(switch located in trunk on right side or
jack storage area)
before jacking or hoisting vehicle.
On 1996-99 Sable/Taurus models
use a cushioned pad on rear
contact pad to prevent paint damage.

ALFD00007

Fig. 2   Vehicle Lift Points. 2004–06 Sable & Taurus

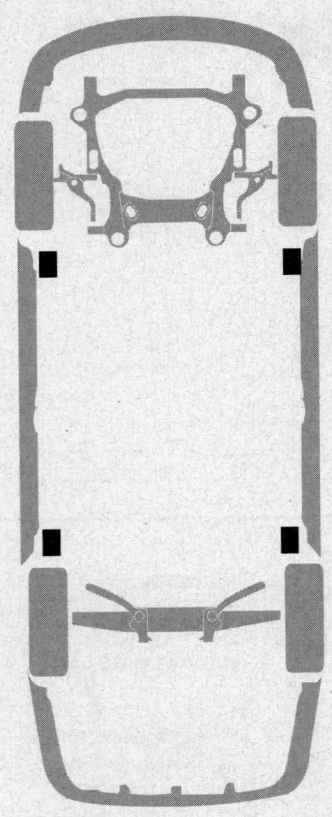

ALFD040001

Fig. 3   Vehicle Lift Points. Five-Hundred, Freestyle, Montego & 2008 Taurus & Taurus X

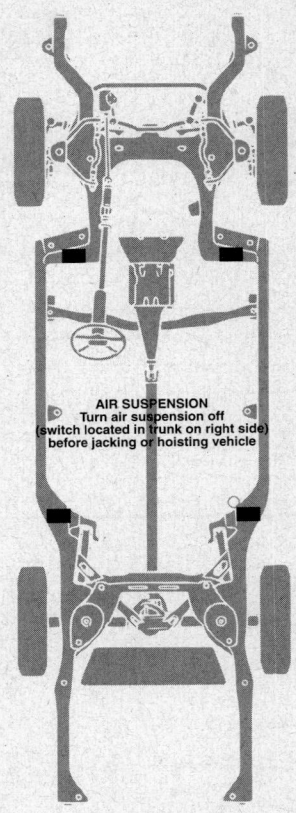

AIR SUSPENSION
Turn air suspension off
(switch located in trunk on right side)
before jacking or hoisting vehicle

ALFD00005

Fig. 4   Vehicle Lift Points. Crown Victoria, Grand Marquis, Marauder & Town Car

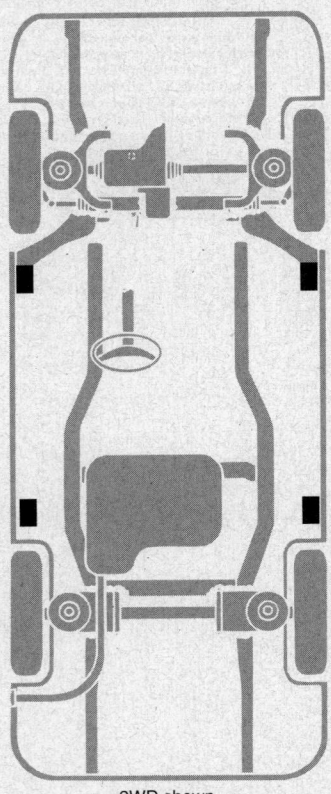

2WD shown

ALMA00002

Fig. 5   Vehicle Lift Points. Focus

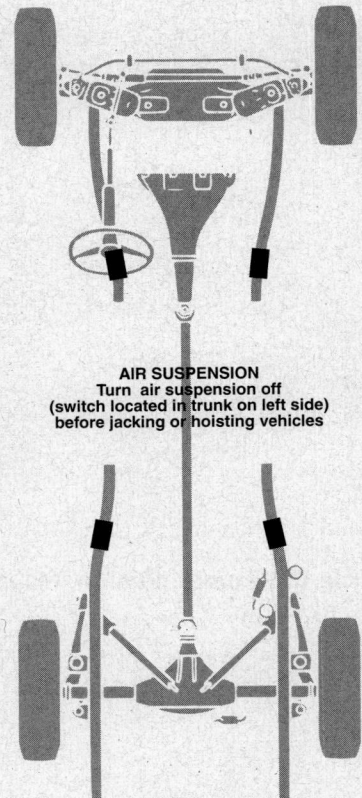

AIR SUSPENSION
Turn air suspension off
(switch located in trunk on left side)
before jacking or hoisting vehicles

ALFD00004

Fig. 6   Vehicle Lift Points. 2004 Mustang

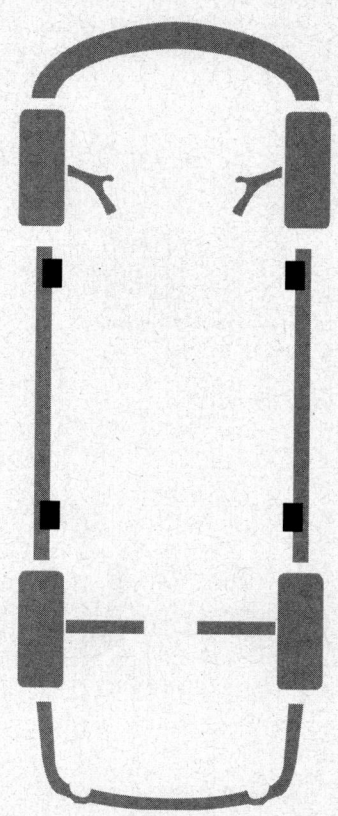

Fig. 7   Vehicle Lift Points. 2005–07 Mustang

ALFD040002

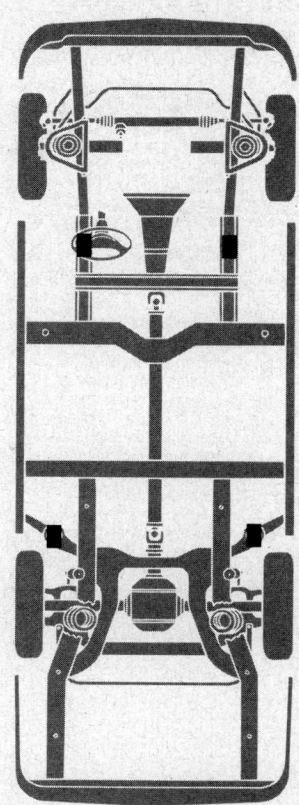

Fig. 8   Vehicle Lift Points. LS & Thunderbird

ALFD00012

General Motors Corp.

INDEX

	PAGE NO.	FIG. NO.
Alero	0-56	1
Aveo	0-56	2
Bonneville	0-56	3
Cavalier	0-57	5
Century	0-57	6
Cobalt	0-56	1
Corvette	0-57	7
CTS	0-57	8
Deville	0-56	4
DTS	0-57	8
Grand Am	0-56	1
Grand Prix	0-57	6
GTO	0-58	9
G5	0-56	1
G6	0-56	1

	PAGE NO.	FIG. NO.
Impala	0-57	6
LaCrosse	0-58	10
LeSabre	0-56	3
Lucerne	0-57	8
Malibu	0-56	1
Malibu Maxx	0-56	1
Monte Carlo	0-57	6
Park Avenue	0-56	4
Regal	0-57	6
Seville	0-56	4
Solstice	0-59	13
STS	0-57	8
Sunfire	0-57	5
Vibe	0-58	11
XLR	0-58	12

VEHICLE LIFT POINTS

Frame contact hoist pads must not contact fenders, floor pan or rocker panels. Position front hoist pads under front frame rail shipping slot reinforcement with long side of pad parallel to frame rails. Position rear hoist pads under rear frame shipping slot reinforcement with long side parallel to frame rails. Outer edge of rear hoist pad must be aligned with outer edge of frame rail shipping slot reinforcement outer edge.

ALGM00030

Fig. 1   Vehicle Lift Points. Alero, Cobalt, Grand Am, G5, G6, Malibu & Malibu Maxx

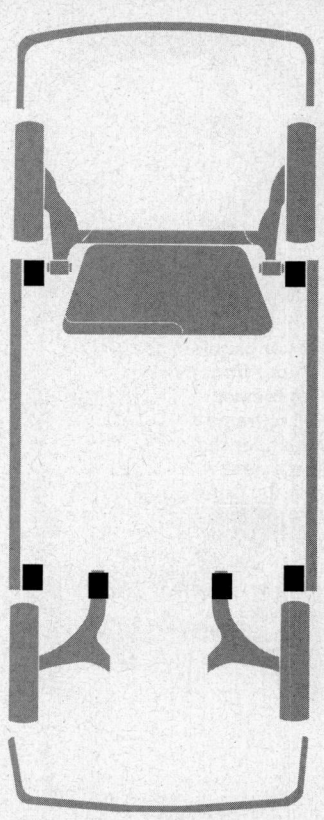

ALGM00037

Fig. 2   Vehicle Lift Points. Aveo

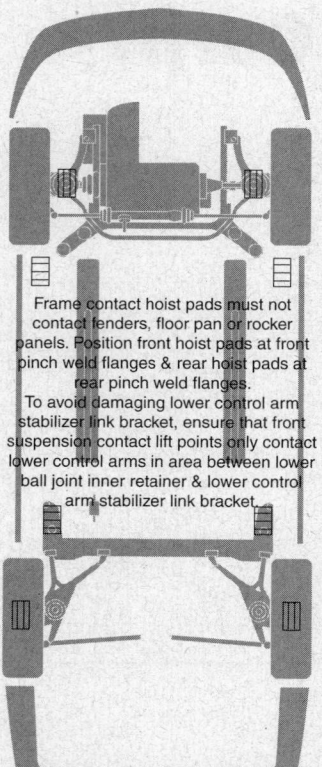

Frame contact hoist pads must not contact fenders, floor pan or rocker panels. Position front hoist pads at front pinch weld flanges & rear hoist pads at rear pinch weld flanges. To avoid damaging lower control arm stabilizer link bracket, ensure that front suspension contact lift points only contact lower control arms in area between lower ball joint inner retainer & lower control arm stabilizer link bracket.

ALGM00029

Fig. 3   Vehicle Lift Points. Bonneville & LeSabre

Frame contact hoist pads must not contact fenders, floor pan or rocker panels. Position front hoist pads under front frame rail shipping slot reinforcement with long side of pad parallel to frame rails. Position rear hoist pads under rear frame shipping slot reinforcement with long side parallel to frame rails. Outer edge of rear hoist pad must be aligned with outer edge of frame rail shipping slot reinforcement outer edge.

To avoid damaging lower control arm stabilizer link bracket, ensure that front suspension contact lift points only contact lower control arms in area between lower ball joint inner retainer & lower control arm stabilizer link bracket.

ALGM00012

Fig. 4   Vehicle Lift Points. Deville, Park Avenue & Seville

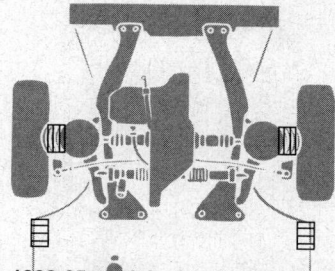

On 1998-05 models, frame contact hoist pads must not contact fenders, floor pan or rocker panels. Position front hoist pads under front frame rail shipping slot reinforcement with long side of pad parallel to frame rails. Position rear hoist pads under rear frame shipping slot reinforcement with long side parallel to frame rails. Outer edge of rear hoist pad must be aligned with outer edge of frame rail shipping slot reinforcement outer edge.

ALGM00002

Fig. 5   Vehicle Lift Points. Cavalier & Sunfire

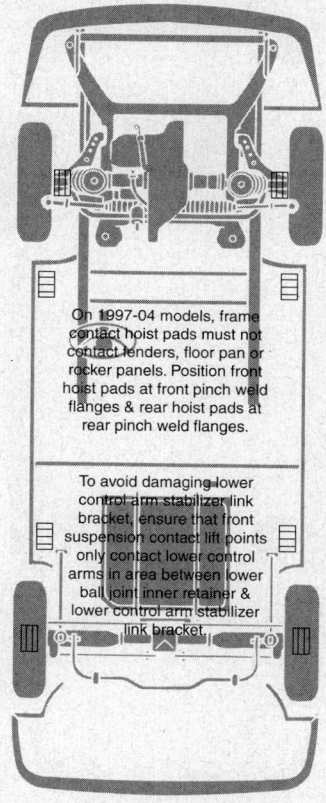

On 1997-04 models, frame contact hoist pads must not contact fenders, floor pan or rocker panels. Position front hoist pads at front pinch weld flanges & rear hoist pads at rear pinch weld flanges.

To avoid damaging lower control arm stabilizer link bracket, ensure that front suspension contact lift points only contact lower control arms in area between lower ball joint inner retainer & lower control arm stabilizer link bracket.

ALGM00018

Fig. 6   Vehicle Lift Points. Century, Grand Prix, Impala, Monte Carlo & Regal

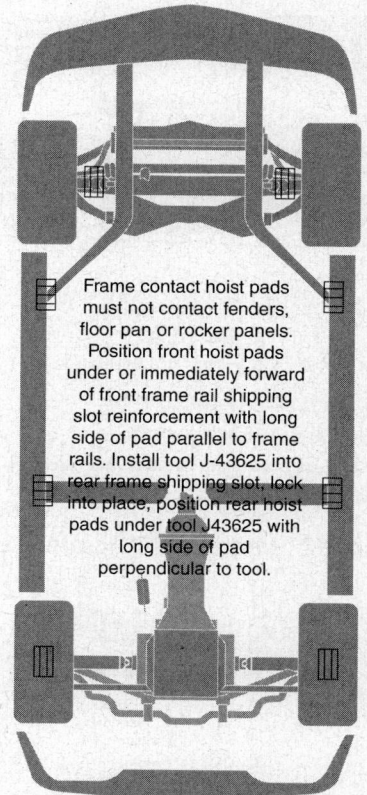

Frame contact hoist pads must not contact fenders, floor pan or rocker panels. Position front hoist pads under or immediately forward of front frame rail shipping slot reinforcement with long side of pad parallel to frame rails. Install tool J-43625 into rear frame shipping slot, lock into place, position rear hoist pads under tool J43625 with long side of pad perpendicular to tool.

ALGM00033

Fig. 7   Vehicle Lift Points. Corvette

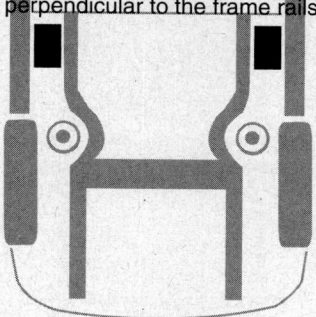

Position the frame contact front hoist pads as follows:
Under the Front frame rail reinforcement.
The long sides of the pads, if applicable parallel to the frame rails.
Under the rear Frame rail at the rear axle cradle mount flange.
The long sides of the pads, if applicable perpendicular to the frame rails.

ALGM00035

Fig. 8   Vehicle Lift Points. CTS, DTS, Lucerne & STS

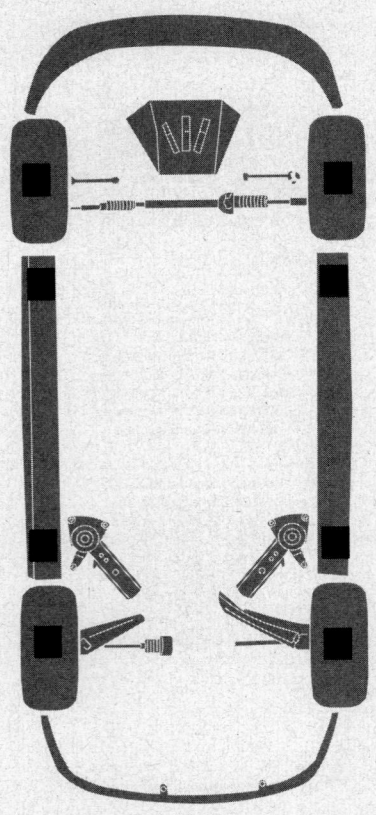

ALGM04038

Fig. 9   Vehicle Lift Points. GTO

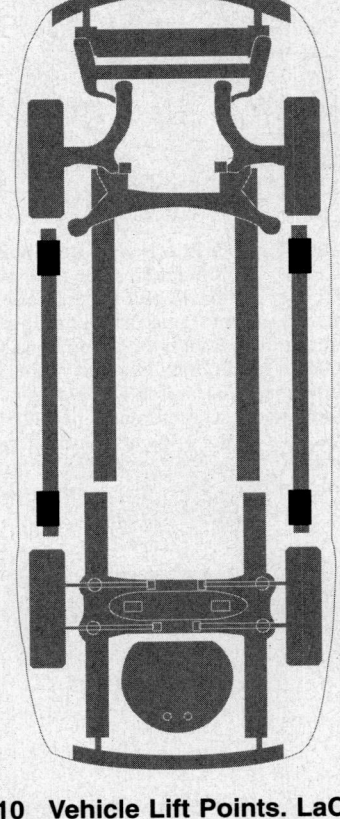

ALGM04039

Fig. 10   Vehicle Lift Points. LaCrosse

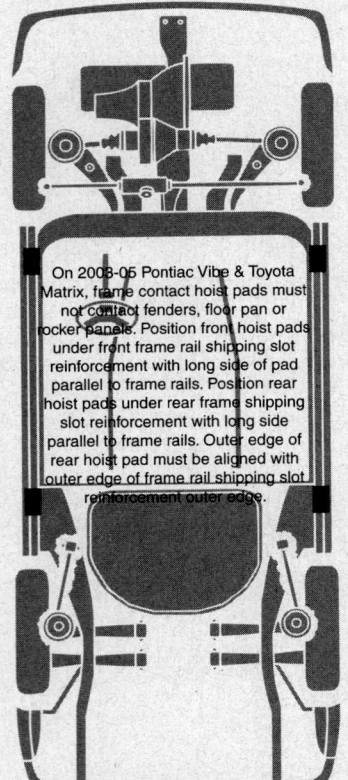

On 2003-05 Pontiac Vibe & Toyota Matrix, frame contact hoist pads must not contact fenders, floor pan or rocker panels. Position front hoist pads under front frame rail shipping slot reinforcement with long side of pad parallel to frame rails. Position rear hoist pads under rear frame shipping slot reinforcement with long side parallel to frame rails. Outer edge of rear hoist pad must be aligned with outer edge of frame rail shipping slot reinforcement outer edge.

ALTA00003

Fig. 11   Vehicle Lift Points. Vibe

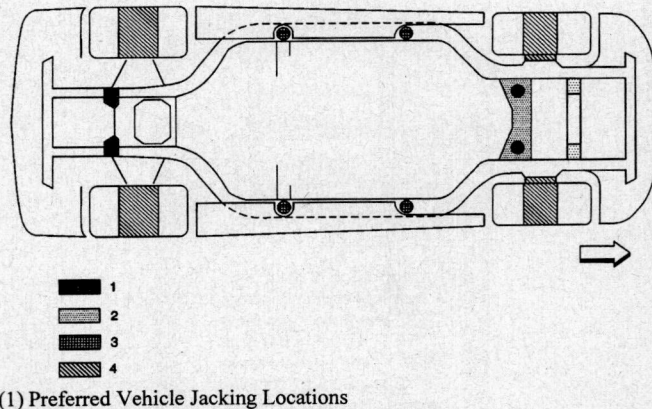

(1) Preferred Vehicle Jacking Locations
(2) Optional Vehicle Jacking Locations
(3) Frame Contact Hoist Locations, Optional Vehicle Jacking Locations
(4) Suspension Contact Hoist Locations

ARM0300000000689

Fig. 12   Vehicle Lift Points. XLR

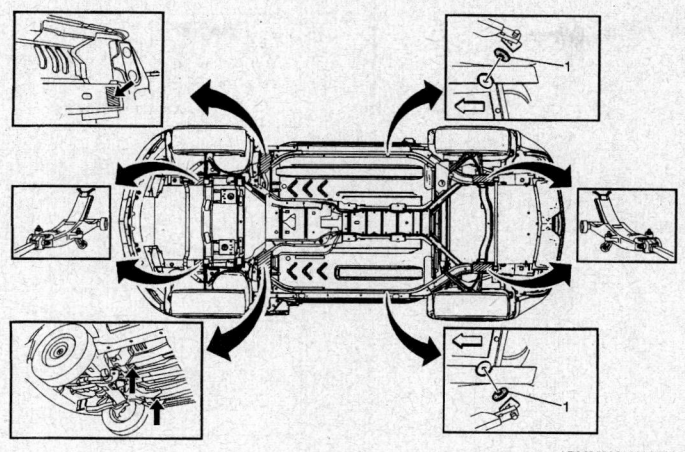

Fig. 13 Vehicle Lift Points. Solstice

ARM0500000000266

Saturn

INDEX

	PAGE NO.	FIG. NO.		PAGE NO.	FIG. NO.
Aura	0-59	1	L-Series	0-60	3
ION	0-59	2	Sky	0-60	4

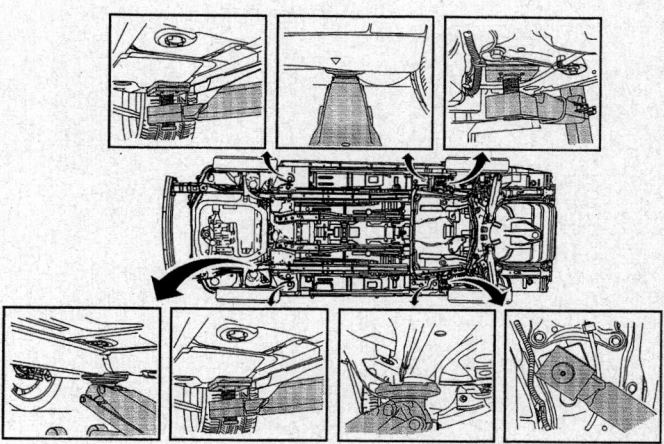

Fig. 1 Vehicle Lift Points. Aura

ARM0600000000004

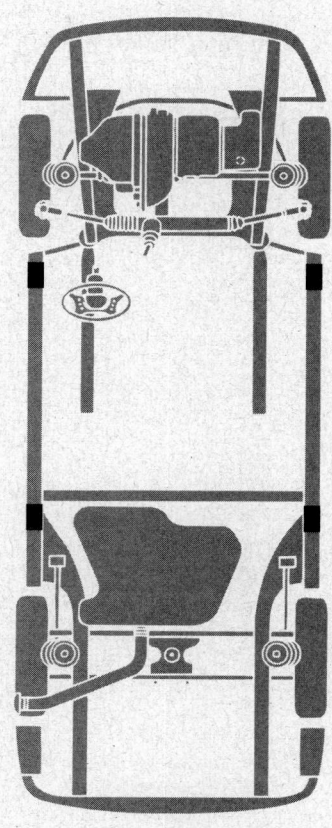

ALSN00001

Fig. 2 Vehicle Lift Points. ION

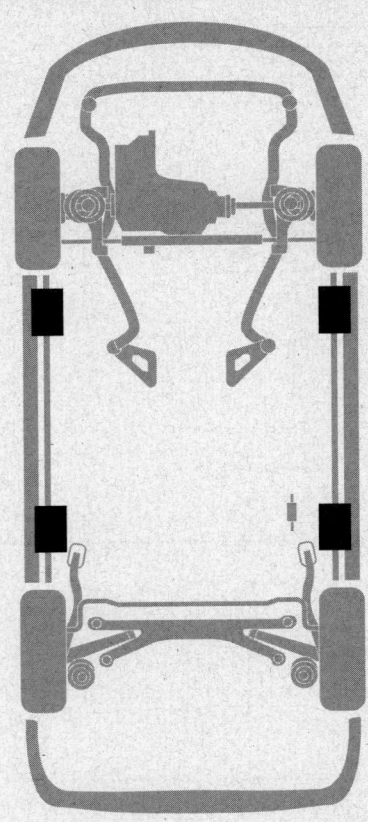

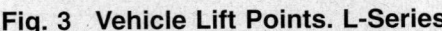

ALSN00002

Fig. 3   Vehicle Lift Points. L-Series

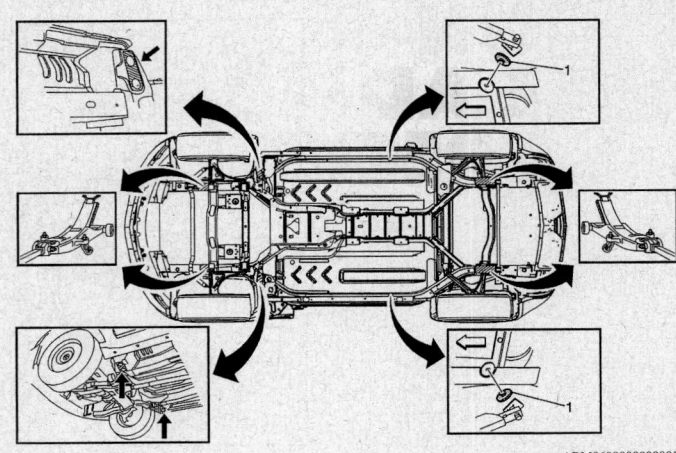

ARM0600000000005

Fig. 4   Vehicle Lift Points. Sky

NON-STANDARD TIRE & WHEEL SIZE ADJUSTMENT TO RIDE HEIGHT SPECIFICATIONS & TIRE SIZE ADJUSTMENT CHARTS

INDEX

	Page No.		Page No.		Page No.
Aspect Ratio Adjustment For Alpha-Numeric Radial Ply Tires	0-62	Aspect Ratio Adjustment For P225–275 Metric Radial & Bias Ply Tires	0-62	Section Width Adjustment For Alpha-Numeric Radial Ply Tires	0-62
Aspect Ratio Adjustment For P145–215 Metric Radial & Bias Ply Tires	0-61	Section Width Adjustment For Alpha-Numeric Bias Ply Tires	0-62	Section Width Adjustment for Metric Radial & Bias Ply Tires	0-61

SECTION WIDTH ADJUSTMENT FOR METRIC RADIAL & BIAS PLY TIRES

These specifications are approximate and are only intended for use in making approximate ride height inspections and adjustments on models with non-standard tires. These specifications should not be used in place of those recommended by the vehicle manufacturer.

Standard Tire	Optional Tire, Tire Section Width Change Adjustment To Ride Height Specification, Inch													
	P145	P155	P165	P175	P185	P195	P205	P215	P225	P235	P245	P255	P265	P275
P145	0	+.25	+.50	—	—	—	—	—	—	—	—	—	—	—
P155	–.25	0	+.25	+.50	—	—	—	—	—	—	—	—	—	—
P165	–.50	–.25	0	+.25	+.50	—	—	—	—	—	—	—	—	—
P175	—	–.50	–.25	0	+.25	+.50	—	—	—	—	—	—	—	—
P185	—	—	–.50	–.25	0	+.25	+.50	—	—	—	—	—	—	—
P195	—	—	—	–.50	–.25	0	+.25	+.50	—	—	—	—	—	—
P205	—	—	—	—	–.50	–.25	0	+.25	+.50	—	—	—	—	—
P215	—	—	—	—	—	–.50	–.25	0	+.25	+.50	—	—	—	—
P225	—	—	—	—	—	—	–.50	–.25	0	+.25	+.50	—	—	—
P235	—	—	—	—	—	—	—	–.50	–.25	0	+.25	+.50	—	—
P245	—	—	—	—	—	—	—	—	–.50	–.25	0	+.25	+.50	—
P255	—	—	—	—	—	—	—	—	—	–.50	–.25	0	+.25	+.50
P265	—	—	—	—	—	—	—	—	—	—	–.50	–.25	0	+.25
P275	—	—	—	—	—	—	—	—	—	—	—	–.50	–.25	0

ASPECT RATIO ADJUSTMENT FOR P145-215 METRIC RADIAL & BIAS PLY TIRES

These specifications are approximate and are only intended for use in making approximate ride height inspections and adjustments on models with non-standard tires. These specifications should not be used in place of those recommended by the vehicle manufacturer.

Standard Tire	Optional Tire, Tire Aspect Ratio Change to Ride Height Specification, Inch				
	60	65	70	75	80
60	0	+.38	+.75	—	—
65	–.38	0	+.38	+.75	—
70	–.75	–.38	0	+.38	+.75
75	—	–.75	–.38	0	+.38
80	—	—	–.75	–.38	0

ASPECT RATIO ADJUSTMENT FOR P225-275 METRIC RADIAL & BIAS PLY TIRES

These specifications are approximate and are only intended for use in making approximate ride height inspections and adjustments on models with non-standard tires. These specifications should not be used in place of those recommended by the vehicle manufacturer.

Standard Tire	Optional Tire, Tire Aspect Ratio Change to Ride Height Specification, Inch				
	60	65	70	75	80
60	0	+.50	+1.00	—	—
65	−.50	0	+.50	+1.00	—
70	−1.00	−.50	0	+.50	+1.00
75	—	−.75	−.50	0	+.50
80	—	—	−1.00	−.50	0

SECTION WIDTH ADJUSTMENT FOR ALPHA-NUMERIC RADIAL PLY TIRES

These specifications are approximate and are only intended for use in making approximate ride height inspections and adjustments on models with non-standard tires. These specifications should not be used in place of those recommended by the vehicle manufacturer.

Standard Tire	Optional Tire, Tire Section Width Change Adjustment To Ride Height Specification, Inch						
	DR	ER	FR	GR	HR	JR	LR
DR	0	+.19	+.44	—	—	—	—
ER	−.19	0	+.25	+.50	—	—	—
FR	−.44	−.25	0	+.25	+.63	—	—
GR	—	−.50	−.25	0	+.31	+.50	—
HR	—	—	−.63	−.31	0	+.19	+.44
JR	—	—	—	−.50	−.19	0	+.25
LR	—	—	—	—	−.44	−.25	0

ASPECT RATIO ADJUSTMENT FOR ALPHA-NUMERIC RADIAL PLY TIRES

These specifications are approximate and are only intended for use in making approximate ride height inspections and adjustments on models with non-standard tires. These specifications should not be used in place of those recommended by the vehicle manufacturer.

Standard Tire	Optional Tire, Change Adjustment to Ride Height Specification, Inch		
	60	70	78
60	0	+.50	+.62
70	−.50	0	+.13
78	−.62	−.13	0

SECTION WIDTH ADJUSTMENT FOR ALPHA-NUMERIC BIAS PLY TIRES

These specifications are approximate and are only intended for use in making approximate ride height inspections and adjustments on models with non-standard tires. These specifications should not be used in place of those recommended by the vehicle manufacturer.

Standard Tire	Optional Tire, Change Adjustment To Ride Height Specifications, Inch							
	A	B	C	D	E	F	G	H
A	0	+.25	+.50	—	—	—	—	—
B	−.25	0	+.25	+.38	—	—	—	—
C	−.50	−.25	0	+.13	+.37	—	—	—
D	—	−.37	−.13	0	+.25	+.50	—	—
E	—	—	−.38	−.25	0	+.25	+.50	—
F	—	—	—	−.50	−.25	0	+.25	+.56
G	—	—	—	—	−.50	−.25	0	+.31
H	—	—	—	—	—	−.56	−.31	0

ELECTRICAL SYMBOL & WIRE COLOR CODE IDENTIFICATION

TABLE OF CONTENTS

Page No.

ELECTRICAL SYMBOL IDENTIFICATION 0-63

Page No.

WIRE COLOR CODE IDENTIFICATION 0-71

Electrical Symbol Identification

INDEX

	PAGE NO.	FIG. NO.
Chrysler	0-63	1
Ford Motor Co.:		
New Style Wiring	0-64	2

	PAGE NO.	FIG. NO.
Old Style Wiring	0-66	3
General Motors Corp.	0-67	4
Saturn	0-70	5

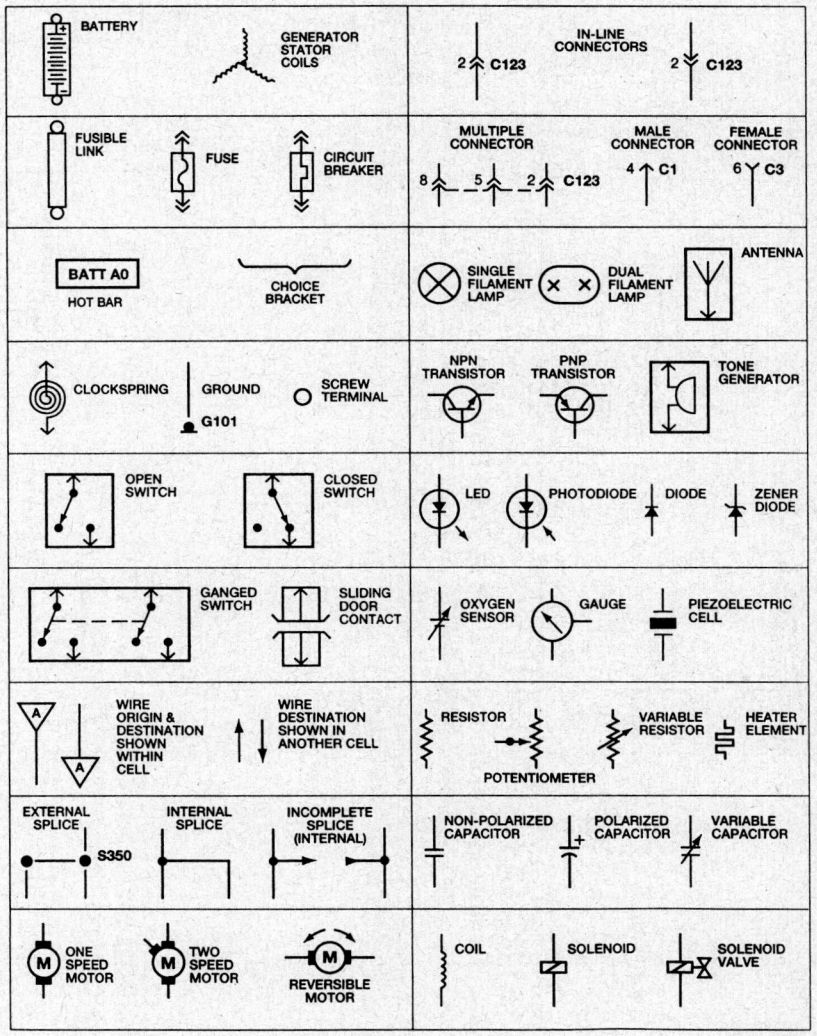

CR9049800087000X

Fig. 1   Symbol Identification. Chrysler

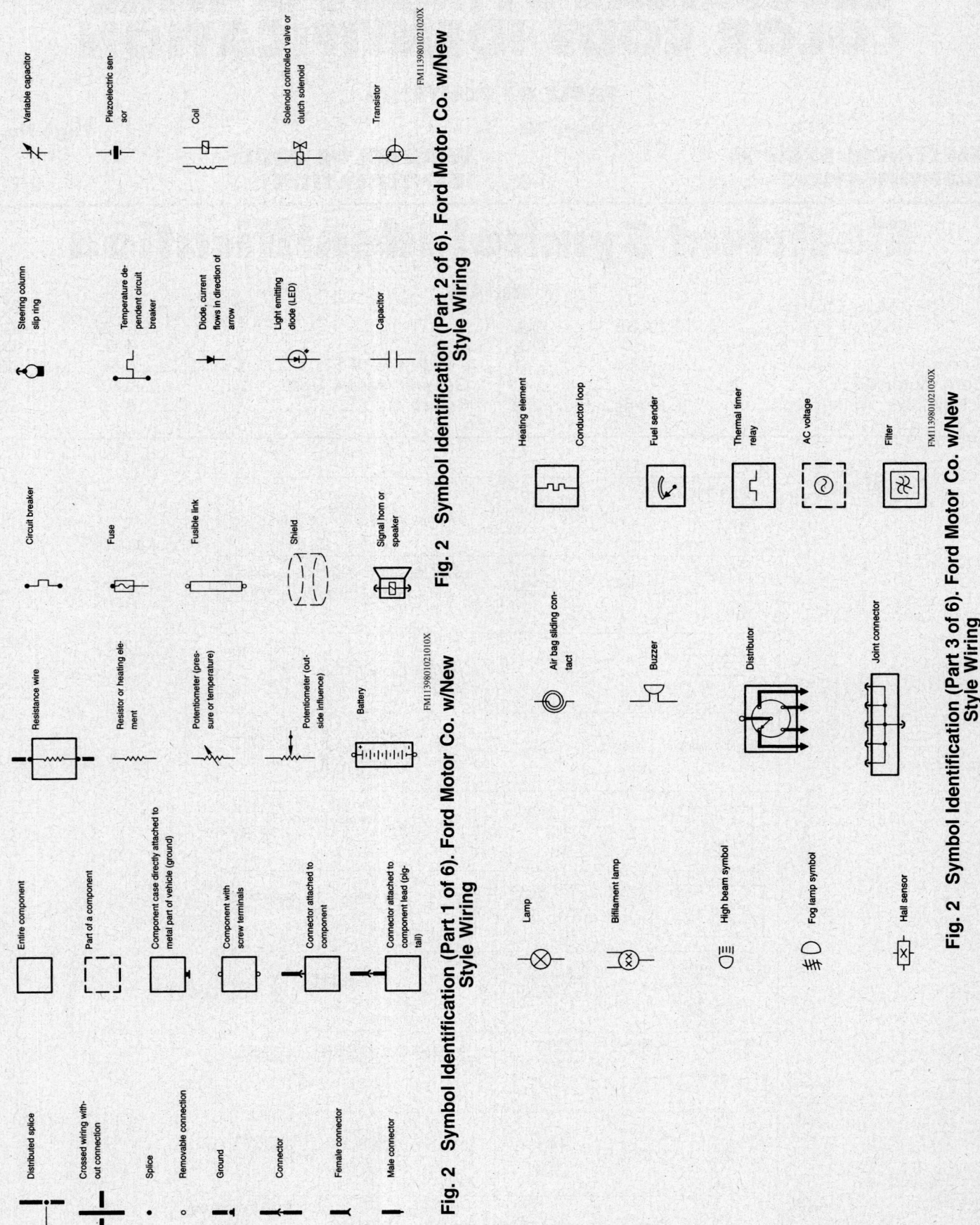

Fig. 2 Symbol Identification (Part 1 of 6). Ford Motor Co. w/New Style Wiring

Fig. 2 Symbol Identification (Part 2 of 6). Ford Motor Co. w/New Style Wiring

Fig. 2 Symbol Identification (Part 3 of 6). Ford Motor Co. w/New Style Wiring

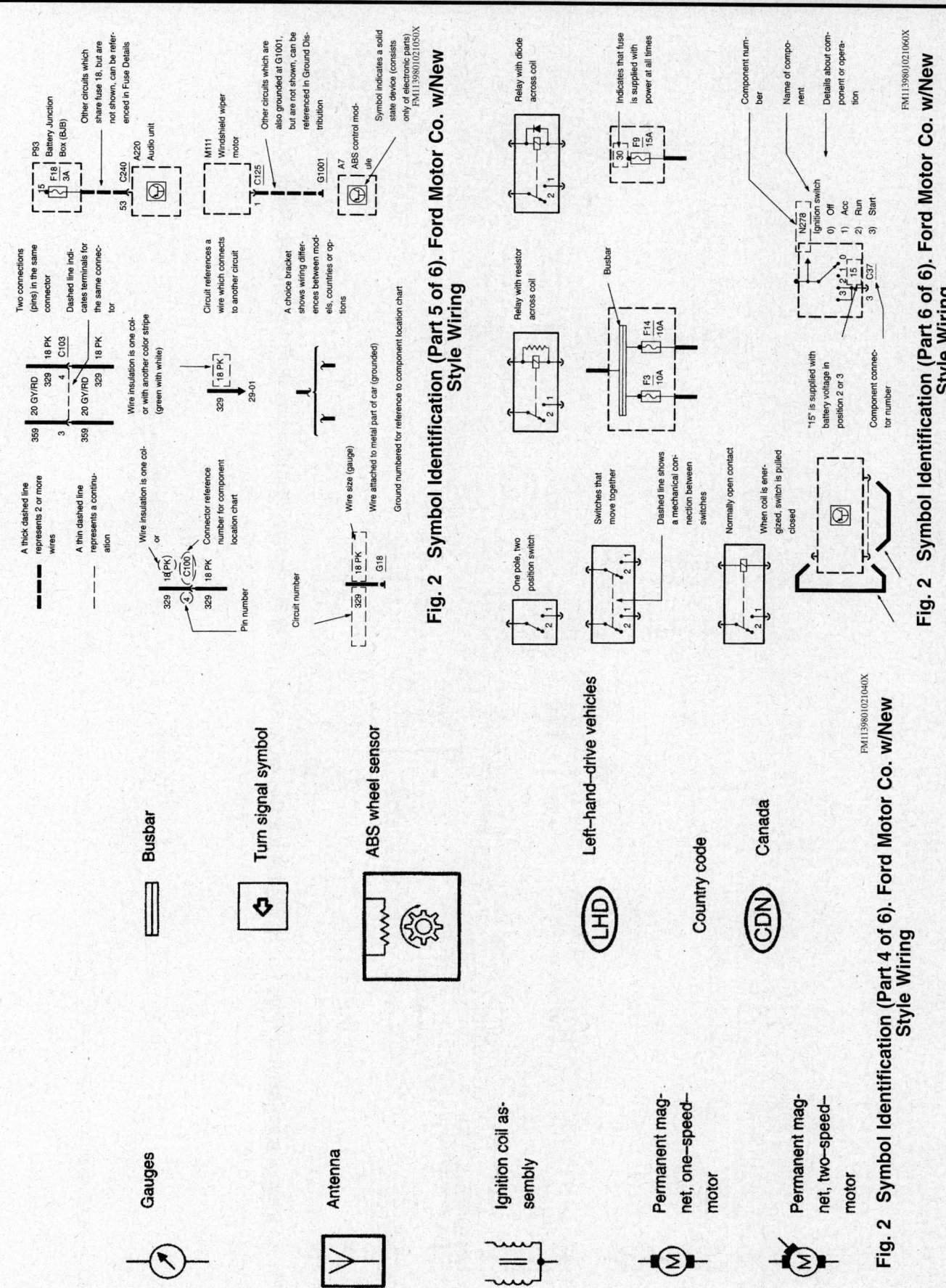

Fig. 2   Symbol Identification (Part 5 of 6). Ford Motor Co. w/New Style Wiring

Fig. 2   Symbol Identification (Part 6 of 6). Ford Motor Co. w/New Style Wiring

Fig. 2   Symbol Identification (Part 4 of 6). Ford Motor Co. w/New Style Wiring

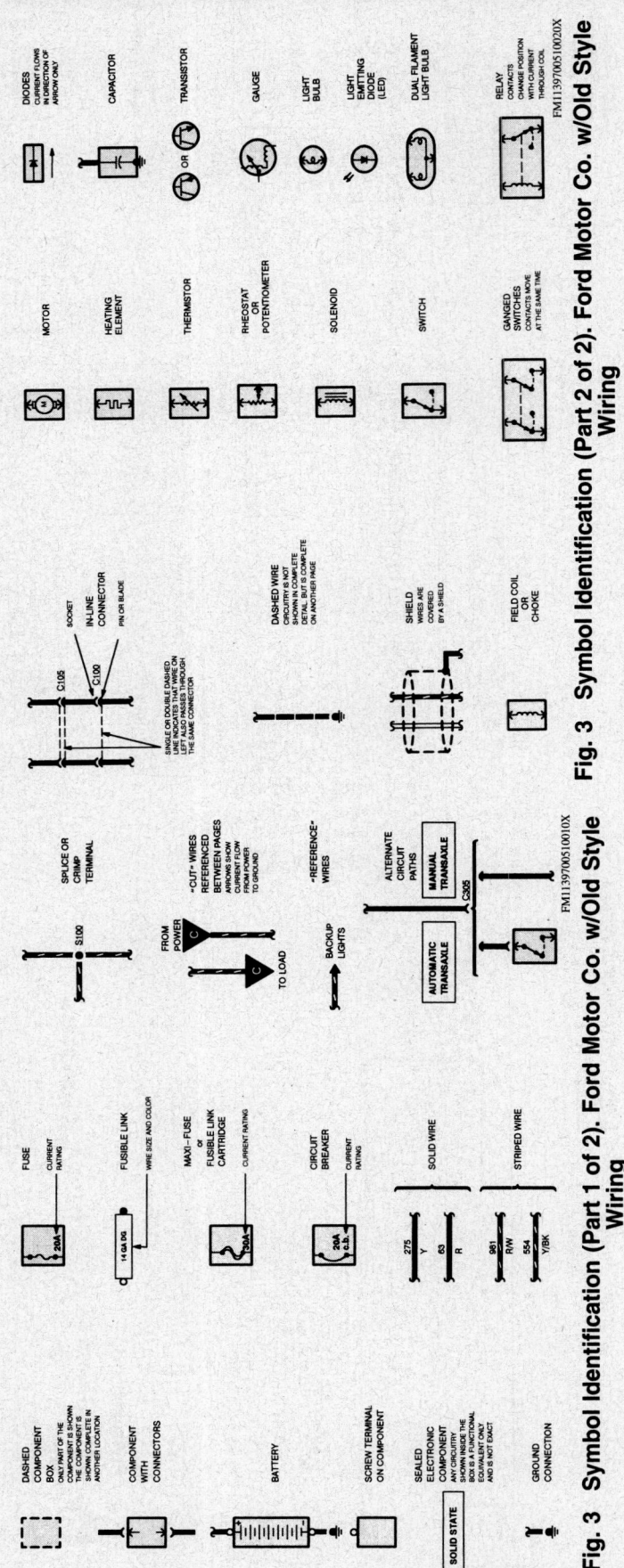

Fig. 3   Symbol Identification (Part 2 of 2). Ford Motor Co. w/Old Style Wiring

Fig. 3   Symbol Identification (Part 1 of 2). Ford Motor Co. w/Old Style Wiring

Symbol	Description
⚠ (SIR/SRS icon)	Supplemental Inflatable Restraint (SIR) or Supplemental Restraint System (SRS) Icon This icon is used to alert the technician that the system contains SIR/SRS components that require certain precautions before servicing.
⚠ OBD II icon	On-Board Diagnostic (OBD II) Icon This icon is used to alert the technician that the circuit is essential for proper OBD II emission controls circuit operation. Any circuit which, if it fails, causes the malfunction indicator lamp (MIL) to turn on, is identified as an OBD II circuit.
⚠ Important icon	Important Icon This icon is used to alert the technician that there is additional information that will aid in servicing a system.
Hot At All Times Hot In Run Hot In Start Hot In Acc And Run Hot In Run And Start Hot In Run, Bulb Test And Start Hot With Headlamp Switch In Park Or Head Hot In Retained Accessory Power (RAP)	Voltage Indicator Boxes These boxes are used on schematics to indicate when voltage is present at a fuse.
⌐ ¬ (dashed box)	Partial Component When a component is represented in a dashed box, the component or its wiring is not shown in its entirety.

Fig. 4 Symbol Identification (Part 1 of 4). General Motors Corp.

Symbol	Description
▢	Entire Component When a component is represented in a solid box the component or its wiring is shown in its entirety.
⌁	Fuse
⌒	Circuit Breaker
▬	Fusible Link
12 ▢	Connector Attached to Component

Symbol	Description
12 ⟨ ▢	Pigtail Connector
⟶○ ▢	Bolt On or Screw On Eyelet Terminal
12 ⟨ C100	Inline Harness Connector
● S100	Splice
⬤ P100	Pass Through the Grommet

Fig. 4 Symbol Identification (Part 2 of 4). General Motors Corp.

Symbol	Description
⊥ G100	Chassis Ground
▢●	Case Ground
⊖	Single Filament Light Bulbs
⊘	Double Filament Light Bulb
⊕	Light Emitting Diodes

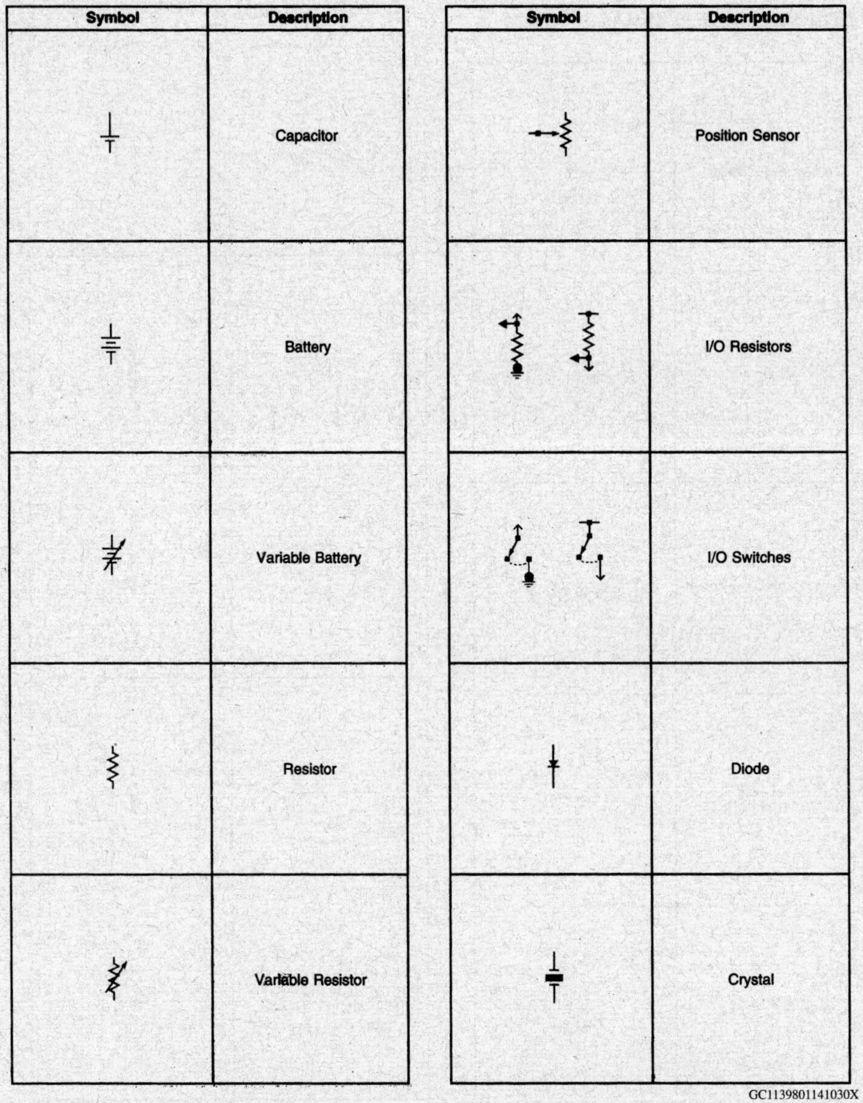

Symbol	Description		Symbol	Description
	Position Sensor			Capacitor
	I/O Resistors			Battery
	I/O Switches			Variable Battery
	Diode			Resistor
	Crystal			Variable Resistor

GC11398011410J0X

Fig. 4 Symbol Identification (Part 3 of 4). General Motors Corp.

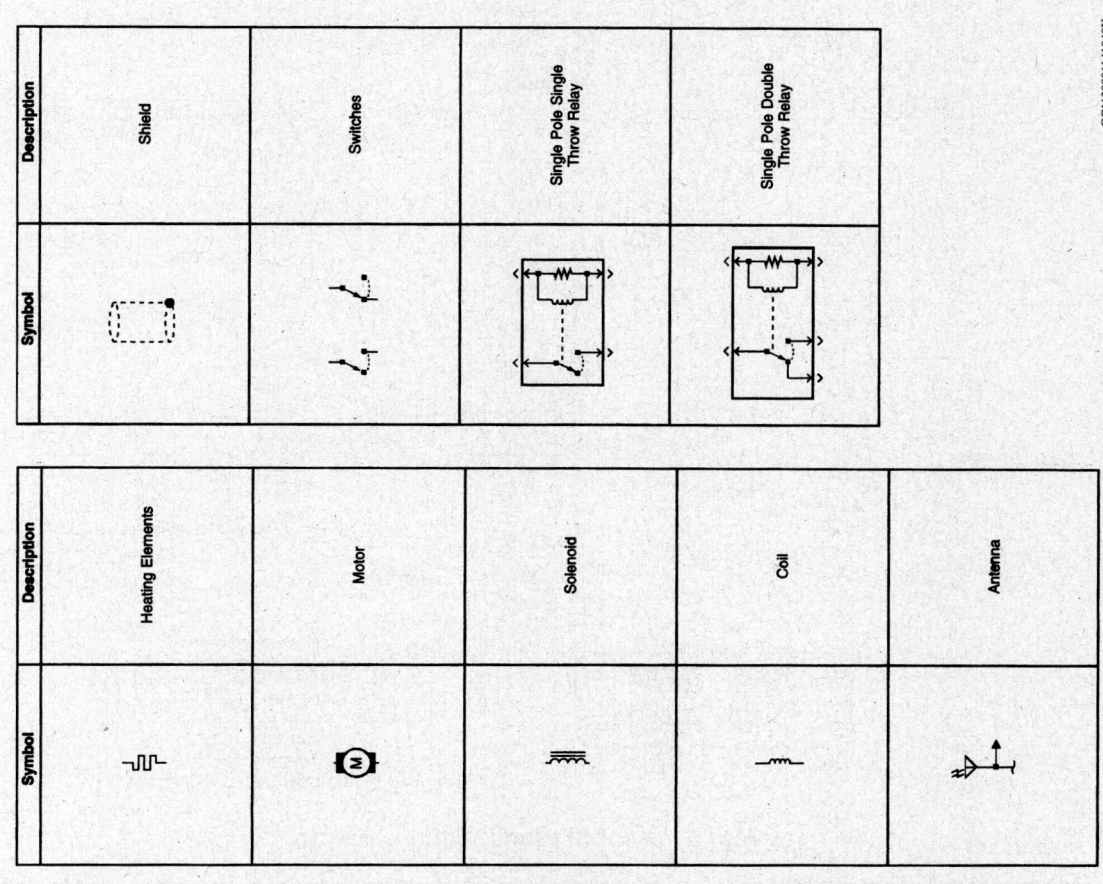

Fig. 4 Symbol Identification (Part 4 of 4). General Motors Corp.

GC113980114104OX

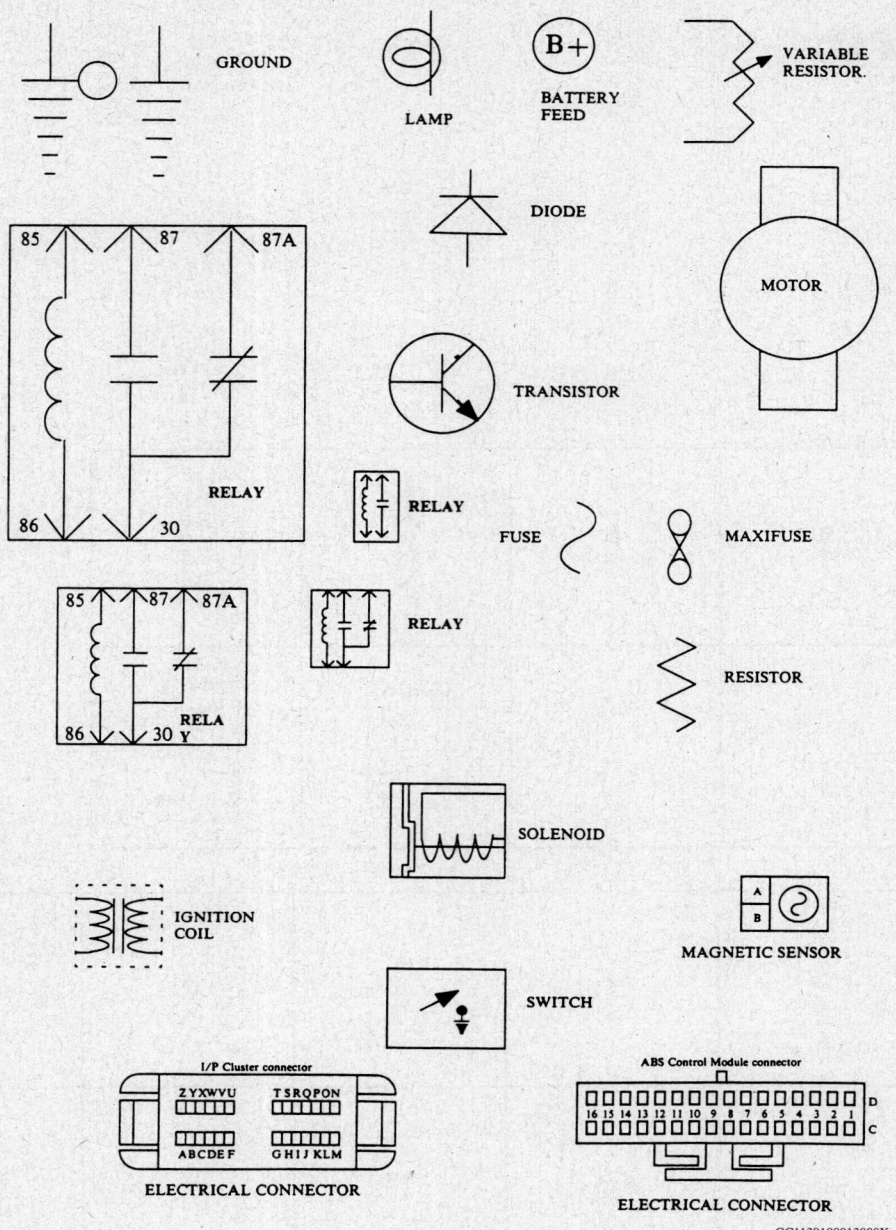

Fig. 5 Symbol Identification. Saturn

GC1139100013000X

Wire Color Code Identification

Abbreviation	Wire Color
CHRYSLER DOMESTIC	
BK	Black
BL	Blue
BR	Brown
DB	Dark Blue
DG	Dark Green
GY	Gray
LB	Light Blue
LG	Light Green
OR	Orange
PK	Pink
RD	Red
TN	Tan
VT	Violet
WT	White
YL	Yellow
CHRYSLER IMPORTS	
B	Black
BR	Brown
GR	Gray
GY	Green
L	Blue
LG	Light Green
O	Orange
P	Pink
R	Red
SB	Sky Blue
V	Violet
W	White
Y	Yellow
FORD MOTOR CO. w/NEW STYLE WIRING	
BK	Black
BN	Brown
BR	Brown
BU	Blue
GN	Green
GY	Gray
LG	Light Green
NA	Natural
OG	Orange
P	Purple
PK	Pink
RD	Red
SR	Silver
VT	Violet
WH	White
YE	Yellow

Continued

ELECTRICAL SYMBOL & WIRE COLOR CODE IDENTIFICATION

Abbreviation	Wire Color
FORD MOTOR CO. w/OLD STYLE WIRING	
BK	Black
BL	Blue
BN	Brown
BR	Brown
DB	Dark Blue
DG	Dark Green
GN	Green
GY	Gray
LB	Light Blue
LG	Light Green
N	Natural
O	Orange
P	Purple
PK	Pink
R	Red
T	Tan
W	White
Y	Yellow
GENERAL MOTORS & SATURN	
Black	BLK
Blue	BLU
Brown	BRN
DK BLU	Dark Blue
DK GRN	Dark Green
GRN	Green
GRY	Gray
LT BLU	Light Blue
LT GRN	Light Green
LT GRY	Light Gray
ORN	Orange
PNK	Pink
PPL	Purple
RED	Red
TAN	Tan
VIO	Violet
WHT	White
YEL	Yellow

VEHICLE MAINTENANCE SCHEDULES

TABLE OF CONTENTS

	Page No.
ALERO, GRAND AM & MALIBU	0-93
AVENGER, CALIBER, NEON, NEON SRT-4, SEBRING CONVERTIBLE, SEBRING SEDAN & STRATUS SEDAN	0-74
AVEO	0-95
BONNEVILLE, LESABRE, LUCERNE & PARK AVENUE	0-97
CAVALIER & SUNFIRE	0-99
CENTURY, GRAND PRIX, IMPALA, LACROSSE, REGAL & MONTE CARLO	0-101
CHARGER, MAGNUM & 300	0-76
COBALT & G5	0-103
CONCORDE, INTREPID & 300M	0-77
CORVETTE	0-105
CROSSFIRE	0-79
CROWN VICTORIA, GRAND MARQUIS & MARAUDER	0-82

	Page No.
CTS, DTS, STS & XLR	0-107
DEVILLE & SEVILLE	0-109
FIVE HUNDRED, FUSION, MILAN, MONTEGO, SABLE, TAURUS & ZEPHYR	0-84
FOCUS	0-85
FREESTYLE & TAURUS X	0-86
G6 & MALIBU MAXX	0-113
GTO	0-111
LS & TOWN CAR	0-88
MUSTANG	0-90
SATURN	0-119
SEBRING COUPE & STRATUS COUPE	0-80
SOLSTICE	0-115
THUNDERBIRD	0-91
VIBE	0-117

Avenger, Caliber, Neon, Neon SRT-4, Sebring Convertible, Sebring Sedan & Stratus Sedan

Service Interval In Miles①

Recommended Service & Intervals (Months)

Note: Across the top of the schedule, service intervals are listed in miles (e.g. 7500, 15,000, 24,000, 30,000 … up to ~105,000) with the corresponding interval in months. Symbols used in the grid: X = perform service, S = severe service, N = normal service.

Service Item	Service Interval / Notes
BODY	
Inspect Supplemental Restraint System	X (at scheduled grid intervals)
BRAKES	
Inspect Brake Connections, Hoses & Lines	Normal Service Every 6 Months Or 7500 Miles, Severe Service Every 3000 Miles
Inspect Brake Drums & Rotors (Normal Service Every 18 Mos.)	Normal (N) / Severe (S) service at scheduled grid intervals
Inspect Brake Pads, Linings & Wheel Bearings	Normal Service Every 18,000 Miles; Severe Every 12,000 Miles
CLUTCH & TRANSMISSION	
Change Automatic Transaxle Filter, Fluid & Adjust Bands	Severe Service Every 60,000 Miles
Replace Manual Transaxle Fluid, Neon SRT-4	Severe Service Every 48,000 Miles
DRIVESHAFT	
Inspect CV Joints	S / X at scheduled grid intervals
ENGINE	
Change Engine Coolant	At 60 Months Or 100,000 Miles, Whichever Comes First
Change Engine Oil, Neon SRT-4	Normal Service Every 6 Months Or 5000 Miles; Severe Service Every 3 Months Or 3000 Miles
Change Engine Oil (Normal Service Every 6 Mos.), Except Neon SRT-4	Normal Service Every 6000 Miles; Severe Service Every 3000 Miles
Change Engine Oil Filter, Except Neon SRT-4	Normal Service Every 6000 Miles; Severe Service Every 3000 Miles
Change Engine Oil Filter Neon SRT-4	Normal Service Every 6 Months Or 5000 Miles; Severe Service Every 3 Months Or 3000 Miles
Change Flex Fuel Oil, 2.7L	Every 5 Months Or 5000 Miles
Inspect Air Filter②	Normal Service Every 6000 Miles; Severe Service Every 3000 Miles
Inspect Coolant Level	At Every Engine Oil Change
Inspect EVAP & Fuel Systems Filler Pipe, Hoses, Lines, Tank & Cap	X (at scheduled grid interval)

Service Interval In Miles ①

Recommended Service & Intervals (Months) — Mileage table (mileage milestones read across the top, from 3,600 up through 97,500 miles)

ENGINE — Service Item	Service Interval / Marking
Inspect Exhaust System	Marked S / N / X across the mileage schedule
Inspect PCV Valve ②	Normal Service Every 48 Months Or 60,000 Miles; Severe Service Every 30,000 Miles
Inspect & Adjust Drive Belts,	Marked X at scheduled mileage intervals
Replace Drive Belts, 2.7L Except Sebring Convertible	Every 60,000 Miles
Replace Drive Belts, 2004–05 Sebring Convertible 2.7L	Normal Service Inspect & Adjust At 60,000 Miles, Replace At 105,000 Miles; Severe Service Every 60,000 Miles
Replace Drive Belts, 2006–08 Sebring Convertible 2.7L	Normal Service Inspect & Adjust At 60,000 Miles, Replace At 102,000 Miles; Severe Service Every 60,000 Miles
Replace Air Filter	Every 30,000 Miles
Replace Ignition Cables, 2.4L	Every 60,000 Miles
Replace Spark Plugs, 2.0L & 2.4L	Marked X at scheduled mileage intervals (≈30,000 / 60,000 Miles)
Replace Spark Plugs, 2.7L	Every 100,000 Miles
Replace Timing Belt, 2004–05 2.0L	Normal Service At 105,000 Miles; Severe Service At 102,000 Miles
Replace Timing Belt, 2004–05 2.4L Except Neon SRT-4	Normal Service At 102,000 Miles; Severe Service At 90,000 Miles
Replace Timing Belt, 2006–08 2.4L	Normal Service At 120,000 Miles; Severe Service At 90,000 Miles
Replace Timing Belt, 2.4L Neon SRT-4	Normal Service Every 102,000 Miles; Severe Service Every 105,000 Miles

STEERING, SUSPENSION & TIRES — Service Item	Service Interval / Marking
Inspect Ball Joints	Marked X at scheduled mileage intervals
Lubricate Suspension & Steering Linkage	Marked X at scheduled mileage intervals
Rotate Tires & Adjust Pressure, Except Neon SRT-4	Inspect And Rotate Tires Every 6000 Miles
Rotate Tires & Adjust Pressure, Neon SRT-4	Normal Service Every 5000 Miles; Severe Service Every 6000 Miles

Mos. — Months
N — Normal Service
S — Severe Service
X — Normal Or Severe Service
① — After vehicles passes 99,000 mile mark return to beginning of mileage table & start cycle over again.
② — This maintenance is recommended by DaimlerChrysler Corporation to the owner but is not required to maintain the emissions warranty.

VEHICLE MAINTENANCE SCHEDULES, AVENGER, CALIBER, NEON, NEON SRT-4, SEBRING CONVERTIBLE, SEBRING SEDAN & STRATUS SEDAN

Charger, Magnum & 300

Service Interval In Miles ①

Recommended Service & Intervals (Months)

Service	Recommended Interval
BODY	
Replace A/C Filter	Normal Service Every 12 Months Or 12,000 Miles; Severe Service Every 15,000 Miles
BRAKES	
Inspect Brake Connections, Hoses & Lines	Normal Service Every 6 Months Or 7500 Miles; Severe Service Every 3 Months Or 3000 Miles
Inspect Brake Drums & Rotors	Normal Service Every 18,000 Miles; Severe Service Every 9000 Miles
Inspect Brake Pads & Linings, 2005	Normal Service Every 18,000 Miles; Severe Service Every 9000 Miles
Inspect Brake Pads & Linings, 2006–07	Normal Service Every 18,000 Miles; Severe Service Every 12,000 Miles
CLUTCH & TRANSMISSION	
Change Automatic Transmission Fluid & Filter	Severe Service Replace Every 60,000 Miles
Change Transfer Case Fluid AWD	Severe Service Every 48,000 Miles
Check Transfer Case Fluid	Severe Service Every 48,000 Miles
Check Transmission Lubricant & Level Condition	Severe Service At Every Oil Change
DRIVE AXLE & DRIVESHAFT	
Inspect CV & Driveshaft Joint Boots	X (at scheduled intervals)
Replace Front Differential Fluid, AWD	Severe Service Every 48,000 Miles
Replace Rear Differential Fluid, AWD	Severe Service Every 48,000 Miles
Replace Rear Axle Fluid	Severe Service Every 48,000 Miles
ENGINE	
Change Engine Coolant	Every 60 Months Or 102,000 Miles
Change Engine Oil & Filter	Normal Service Every 6 Months Or 6000 Miles; Severe Service Every 3000 Miles
Inspect Coolant Level, Hoses & Clamps	At Every Oil Change
Inspect Drive Belts	Every 72,000 Miles
Inspect Exhaust System	At Every Oil Change (S)
Inspect PCV Valve ②	S (at scheduled intervals)
Replace Air Filter	Normal Service At 30,000 Miles; Severe Service Inspect Every 15,000 Miles & Replace Every 30,000 Miles
Replace PCV Filter	Normal Service Inspect at 60,000 Miles, Severe Service Inspect At 30,000 Miles Thereafter. Replace If Necessary

Concorde, Intrepid & 300M

Service Interval In Miles ①

Recommended Service & Intervals (Months)	7500	15000	22500	30000	37500	45000	52500	60000	67500	75000	82500	90000	97500	99000

ENGINE

Service	Interval
Replace Spark Plugs, 2.7L & 3.5L, Charger & 6.1L 300C SRT8	Normal Service Every 96,000 Miles; Severe Service Every 99,000 Miles
Replace Spark Plugs, 2.7L & 3.5L, 300C & Magnum	Every 100,000 Miles
Replace Spark Plugs, 5.7L	X
Replace Timing Belt, 3.5L	Normal Service Every 102,000 Miles; Severe Service Every 105,000 Miles — X

STEERING, SUSPENSION & TIRES

Service	Interval / Marks
Change Power Steering Fluid, 300C SRT8	Severe Service Every 60,000 Miles
Inspect Bushings, Arms, CV Joints, Seals, Springs & Jounce Bumpers	S X S X S X S X S X S X S X S (S = Severe Service, X = Normal Or Severe Service)
Lubricate Ball Joints (Every 18 Mos.)	X
Lubricate Steering Linkage (Every 12 Mos.)	X
Replace Power Steering Fluid	Severe Service Every 60,000 Miles
Rotate Tires & Adjust Pressure	Every 6000 Miles

N — Normal Service
S — Severe Service
X — Normal Or Severe Service
① — After vehicle passes 99,000 mile mark return to beginning of mileage table & start cycle over again.
② — This maintenance is recommended by DaimlerChrysler Corporation to the owner, but not required to maintain the warranty of the PCV Valve.

Service Interval In Miles ①

Recommended Service & Intervals (Months)	7500	15000	22500	30000	37500	45000	52500	60000	67500	75000	82500	90000	97500	99000

BODY

Service	Marks
Inspect Supplemental Restraint System	X … X

Service Interval In Miles ①

Recommended Service & Intervals (Months)

Service Item	3000	6000	7500	9000	12000	15000	18000	21000	24000	27000	30000	36000	39000	45000	48000	51000	57000	60000	63000	67500	72000	75000	81000	84000	87000	90000	93000	99000	Interval / Notes
BRAKES																													
Inspect Brake Connections, Hoses & Lines																													Normal Service Every 12,000 Miles; Severe Service Every 9000 Miles
Inspect Brake Drums & Rotors						S					N			S				N				S				N			
Inspect Brake Pads, Linings						S					N			S				N				S				N			
CLUTCH & TRANSMISSION																													
Change Automatic Transaxle Fluid & Filter																													Severe Service Every 60,000 Miles
DRIVESHAFT & CV JOINTS																													
Inspect CV Joints	S	S	S	X	S	S	N	S	S	S	X	S	S	N	S	S	S	X	S	S	N	S	S	S	X	S	S	N	
ENGINE																													
Change Engine Coolant																													Every 60 Months Or 100,000 Miles
Change Engine Oil (Normal Service Every 6 Mos.)																													Normal Service Every 6000 Miles; Severe Service Every 3000 Miles
Change Engine Oil Filter (Normal Service Every 6 Mos.)																													Normal Service Every 6000 Miles; Severe Service Every 3000 Miles
Inspect Air Filter																													At Every Oil Change
Inspect EVAP & Fuel Systems Filler Pipe, Hoses, Lines, Tank & Cap											X															X			
Inspect Exhaust System	S	S	S	X	S	S	N	S	S	S	X	S	S	N	S	S	S	X	S	S	N	S	S	S	X	S	S	N	
Inspect PCV Valve																													Normal Service Replace at 60,000 Miles & Inspect Every 30,000 Miles & Inspect Every 30,000 Thereafter; Severe Service Replace Every 30,000 Miles
Inspect & Adjust Drive Belts											X							X								X			
Replace Air Filter											X							X								X			
Replace Drive Belts																													Normal Service Every 102,000 Miles; Severe Service Every 102,000 Miles
Replace Spark Plugs																													Normal Service Every 100,000 Miles; Severe Service Every 100,000 Miles
Replace Timing Belt, 3.2L & 3.5L																													Normal Service Every 102,000 Miles; Severe Service Federal Emissions Every 100,000 Miles; California Emissions Every 105,000 Miles
STEERING, SUSPENSION & TIRES																													
Inspect Ball Joints																													At Every Oil Change
Lubricate Suspension & Steering Linkage											S							S								S			
Rotate Tires & Adjust Pressure																													Every 6000 Miles

Mos. — Months
N — Normal Service
S — Severe Service
X — Normal Or Severe Service
① — After vehicles passes 99,000 mile mark return to beginning of mileage table & start cycle over again.

Crossfire

Service Interval In Miles ①④

Miles (×1,000): 93000 · 90000 · 87000 · 84000 · 81000 · 78000 · 75000 · 72000 · 69000 · 66000 · 63000 · 60000 · 57000 · 54000 · 51000 · 48000 · 45000 · 42000 · 39000 · 36000 · 33000 · 30000 · 27000 · 24000 · 21000 · 18000 · 15000 · 12000 · 9000 · 6000 · 3000

Recommended Service & Intervals (Months)

Service	Interval
BODY	
Inspect Body And Paint For Damage And Corrosion	Every 24 Months
Inspect Headlamp Aiming②	Schedule B
Inspect Seat Belts②	Schedule B
Lubricate Hood Hinges And Latches ②	Schedules A And B
Replace Cabin Air Filter	Every 18,500 Miles
BRAKES	
Inspect Brake Connections, Hoses & Lines②	Schedule B
Inspect Brake Drums & Rotors	Schedule B
Inspect Brake Pads & Linings②	Schedules A And B
Inspect Parking Brake②	Schedule B
CLUTCH & TRANSMISSION	
Change Automatic Transmission Fluid & Filter	Replace At 80,000 Miles, After This Change, Automatic Transmission Fluid Is Changed For Life
Check Transmission Lubricant & Level Condition②	Schedules A And B
DRIVE AXLE & DRIVESHAFT	
Inspect Driveshaft Flex Discs	Every 48 Months Or 50,000 Miles
ENGINE	
Change Engine Coolant	Every 60 Months Or 100,000 Miles
Change Engine Oil & Filter②③	Schedules A And B
Inspect Coolant Level, Hoses & Clamps②	Schedules A And B
Inspect Drive Belts②	Schedule B
Inspect Exhaust System②	Schedule B
Replace Air Filter	Every 48 Months Or 60,000 Miles
Replace Fuel Filter	Every 48 Months Or 60,000 Miles
Replace Spark Plugs	Every 60 Months Or 100,000 Miles
STEERING, SUSPENSION & TIRES	
Inspect Chassis Components For Damage And Corrision	Every 48 Months

Service Interval In Miles①④

Recommended Service & Intervals (Months)	Service Interval In Miles
Inspect Front Ball Joints And Boots②	Schedule B
Inspect Steering Components And Boots②	Schedule B
Inspect Tires	Schedules A And B
Retighten Locking Bolts For Steering	Every 48 Months Or 50,000 Miles
Rotate Tires②	Schedule B

N — Normal Service
S — Severe Service
X — Normal Or Severe Service

① — After vehicle passes 99,000 mile mark return to beginning of mileage table & start cycle over again.
② — There are two FSS symbols that will appear in the main odometer display next to suggested service. Service Schedule A is represented by one wrench symbol. Service Schedule B is represented by two wrench symbols. Follow Schedule A for first service interval, Schedule B for second service interval and so on.
③ — The initial oil change interval is set at 7000 miles. For very light driving cycles the interval can extend beyond the 7000 miles. For severe driving conditions the oil change interval can be significantly less than 7000 miles. Engine and oil filter should be changed at schedule A and B.
④ — This Vehicle Is Equipped With The Flexible Service System (FSS)

Sebring Coupe & Stratus Coupe

Service Interval In Miles①

Recommended Service & Intervals (Months)	Service Interval In Miles
BODY	
Inspect Supplemental Restraint System Components	Every 10 Years From Vehicle Build Date
BRAKES	
Inspect Brake Connections, Hoses & Lines	Every 12 Months Or 15,000 Miles
Inspect Disc Brake Pads (Every 12 Mos.), 2004	Normal Service Check for Wear Every 15,000 Miles; Severe Service Every 6000 Miles
Inspect Disc Brake Pads (Every 12 Mos.), 2005	Normal Service Check for Wear Every 18,000 Miles; Severe Service Every 12,000 Miles
Inspect Drum Brake Shoes (Every 24 Mos.), 2004	Normal Service Check For Wear Every 30,000 Miles; Severe Service Every 15,000 Miles

Service Interval In Miles①

Recommended Service & Intervals (Months)	Service Interval / Notes
BRAKES	
Inspect Drum Brake Shoes (Every 24 Mos.), 2005	Normal Service Check For Wear Every 18,000 Miles; Severe Service Every 12,000 Miles
CLUTCH & TRANSMISSION	
Change Or Inspect Automatic Transaxle Fluid & Filter	Normal Service, Inspect Every 15,000 Miles; Severe Service, Inspect Every 15,000 Miles, Change Fluid & Filter Every 30,000 Miles
Change Manual Transaxle Lubricant	(S markings at intervals)
DRIVESHAFT & CV JOINTS	
Inspect CV Joint Boots (Every 12 Mos.)	(X markings at intervals)
ENGINE	
Change Engine Coolant, 2004	At 48 Months Or 60,000 Miles Then Every 24 Months Or 30,000 Miles
Change Engine Coolant, 2005	At 48 Months Or 60,000 Miles
Change Engine Oil (Normal Service Every 6 Mos./Severe Service Every 3 Mos.)	(S / N / X markings at intervals)
Change Engine Oil & Filter	Normal Service Every 6 Months Or 6000 Miles; Severe Service Every 3 Months Or 3000 Miles
Change Flex Fuel Oil, 2.7Liter	Every 5 Months Or 5000 Miles
Inspect Air Filter	(S / X markings at intervals)
Inspect Coolant Level	At Every Engine Oil Change
Inspect Distributor Cap & Rotor	(X markings at intervals)
Inspect EVAP System	(X markings at intervals)
Inspect Exhaust System & Heat Shields	(S / N / X markings at intervals)
Inspect Fuel Filler Cap	(X markings at intervals)
Inspect Fuel Hoses, Lines & Connections	(X markings at intervals)
Inspect Fuel Tank	(X markings at intervals)
Inspect & Adjust Drive Belts	(X markings at intervals)
Replace Air Filter	Normal Service Every 30,000 Miles; Severe Service Every 15,000 Miles
Replace Spark Plugs, DOHC	(S markings at intervals)
Replace Spark Plugs, Standard Tip	Normal Service Every 30,000 Miles; Severe Service Every 15,000 Miles
Replace Spark Plugs, Iridium Tip	Every 102,000 Miles
Replace Timing Belt	(X marking at interval)

STEERING, SUSPENSION & TIRES

Recommended Service & Intervals (Months) — Service Interval In Miles①

Mileage columns: 3000, 6000, 9000, 12,000, 15,000, 18,000, 21,000, 24,000, 27,000, 30,000, 33,000, 36,000, 39,000, 42,000, 45,000, 48,000, 51,000, 54,000, 57,000, 60,000, 63,000, 66,000, 69,000, 72,000, 75,000, 78,000, 81,000, 84,000, 87,000, 90,000, 93,000, 96,000, 99,000

Recommended Service	Service Interval
Inspect Ball Joints & Steering Linkage Grease Seals (Every 24 Mos.)	X at 27,000 and 57,000 miles
Lubricate Suspension & Steering Linkage (Every 24 Mos.)	X at 24,000 and 54,000 miles
Rotate Tires & Adjust Pressure	Normal Service Every 6 Months Or 6000 Miles; Severe Service Every 3 Months Or 3000 Miles

Mos. — Months
N — Normal Service
S — Severe Service
X — Normal Or Severe Service
① — After vehicles passes 99,000 mile mark return to beginning of mileage table & start cycle over again.

Crown Victoria, Grand Marquis & Marauder

Recommended Service — Service Interval In Miles①

Mileage columns: 3000, 6000, 9000, 12,000, 15,000, 18,000, 21,000, 24,000, 27,000, 30,000, 33,000, 36,000, 39,000, 42,000, 45,000, 48,000, 51,000, 54,000, 57,000, 60,000

BODY

Recommended Service	Service Interval
Inspect A/C Refrigerant Charge & System Operation	Every 12 Months Or 15,000 Miles
Inspect Instrument Panel Warning Lamps & Gauges	At Every Engine Oil Change
Lubricate Body Hardware & Hinges	X at 15,000, 45,000, 60,000 miles
Lubricate Hood Latch Pivot Points & All Contact Areas	X at 15,000, 30,000, 45,000, 60,000 miles
Replace Cabin Air Filter	Every 15,000 Miles If Equipped

BRAKES

Recommended Service	Service Interval
Inspect Brake Drums, Linings, Pads, Rotors, Lubricate Caliper Slide Rails	Normal Service Every 15,000 Miles; Severe Service Every 5000 Miles
Inspect Parking Brake System Operation	X at 15,000, 30,000, 45,000, 60,000 miles

CLUTCH & TRANSMISSION

Recommended Service	Service Interval
Change Automatic Transmission Fluid & Filter, 2004	Normal Service Inspect Every 15,000 Miles; Change Every 30,000 Miles
Change Automatic Transmission Fluid & Filter, 2005–07	Normal Service Inspect Every 15,000 Miles Change At 150,000 Miles; Severe Service Change Every 30,000 Miles
Lubricate Transmission Control Linkage	X at 30,000 and 60,000 miles

Vehicle Maintenance Schedules

Service Interval In Miles ①

Mileage columns are in thousands of miles: 3, 6, 9, 12, 15, 18, 21, 24, 27, 30, 33, 36, 39, 42, 45, 48, 51, 54, 57, 60.

Recommended Service	3	6	9	12	15	18	21	24	27	30	33	36	39	42	45	48	51	54	57	60	Interval / Notes
DRIVE AXLE & DRIVESHAFT																					
Change Differential Lubricant										②											
Lubricate Driveshaft					X										X						
ENGINE																					
Change Engine Coolant																					Replace Premium Gold Coolant, Every 5 Years Or 100,000 Miles Thereafter Replace Every 36 Months Or 50,000 Miles
Change Engine Oil & Filter																					Normal Service Every 5000 Miles; Severe Service Every 3000 Miles
Inspect Cooling System & Protection Level																					Annually Or Every 15,000 Miles
Inspect Drive Belts																					
Inspect Exhaust System					X																Every 100,000 Miles
Inspect Fluid & Lubricant Levels																					At Every Engine Oil Change
Inspect Fuel System Connections, Hoses & Lines					X										X						
Inspect & Clean Choke Linkage, 5.8L					X										X						
Inspect & Replace Engine Air Filter					S										S						
Replace Engine Air Filter																					
Replace Fuel Filter																					Every 30,000 Miles
Replace Fuel Filter Element & Housing O-Ring Seal, Drain Coalescent Filter Bowl, 2004–05 NGV																					Every 15 Years From Date On Tank From Manufacturer
Replace PCV Valve																					Normal Service Every 30,000 Miles; Severe Service Every 15,000 Miles
Replace Spark Plugs, Except NGV																					Every 100,000 Miles
Replace Spark Plugs, NGV																				X	Normal Service Every 100,000 Miles; Severe Service Every 60,000 Miles
STEERING, SUSPENSION & TIRES																					
Inspect & Repack Front Wheel Bearings																				X	
Lubricate Steering & Suspension Components										X										X	
Rotate Tires																					Normal Service Inspect For Wear & Rotate Every 5000 Miles

N — Normal Service
NGV — Natural Gas Vehicle
S — Severe Service
X — Normal Or Severe Service
① — After vehicle has passed 60,000 mile mark return to beginning of mileage table & start cycle over again.
② — Normal Vehicle Axle Maintenance: Rear axle units containing synthetic lubricant are lubricated for life. These lubricants are not to be checked or changed unless a leak is suspected, service is required or the axle assembly has been submerged in water. The axle lubricant should be changed anytime the axle has been submerged in water. Non-synthetic rear axle lubricants should be replaced every 100,000 miles under normal operating conditions. Non-synthetic rear axle lubricants should be replaced every 3000 miles or 3 months, whichever occurs first, during extended trailer tow operation above (70°F) ambient and wide open throttle for extended periods above 45 mph. The 3000 mile lube change interval may be waived if the axle was filled with 75W140 synthetic gear lubricant meeting Ford specification WSL-M2C192–A. Add four ounces of additive friction modifier C8AZ-19B546–A or equivalent for complete refill of Traction-Lok rear axles. The rear axle lubricant should be changed anytime the axle has been submerged in water. Police and Taxi Vehicle Axle Maintenance: Replace rear axle lubricant every 160,000 km (100,000 miles). Rear axle lubricant change may be waived if the axle was filled with 75W140 synthetic gear lubricant meeting Ford specification WSL-M2C192–A. Add four ounces of additive friction modifier C8AZ-19B546–A or equivalent for complete refill of Traction-Lok rear axles. The rear axle lubricant should be changed anytime the axle has been submerged in water.

Five Hundred, Fusion, Milan, Montego, Sable, Taurus & Zephyr

Service Interval In Miles ①

Recommended Service	Service Interval / Notes
BODY	
Inspect A/C Refrigerant Charge & System Operation	Every 12 Months Or 15,000 Miles, Before Warm Season Arrives
Inspect Instrument Panel Warning Lamps & Gauges	At Every Engine Oil Change
Lubricate Body Hardware & Hinges	✗ (15,000 / 30,000 / 45,000 / 60,000)
Lubricate Hood Latch Pivot Points & All Contact Areas	✗ (15,000 / 30,000 / 45,000 / 60,000)
Replace Passenger Compartment Pollen Filter	✗ (15,000 / 30,000 / 45,000 / 60,000)
BRAKES	
Inspect Brake Drums, Linings, Pads, Rotors, Lubricate Caliper Slide Rails	Normal Service Every 15,000 Miles; Severe Service Every 5000 Miles
Inspect Brake Lines & Hoses	S / N / S / N (15,000 / 30,000 / 45,000 / 60,000)
Inspect Parking Brake System Operation	✗ (15,000 / 30,000 / 45,000 / 60,000)
CLUTCH & TRANSMISSION	
Change Automatic Transmission Fluid & Filter, Sable & Taurus	Inspect Every 15,000 Miles; Replace Every 30,000 Miles
Change Continuous Variable Transmission (CVT) Fluid & Filter, Five Hundred & Montego	Every 60,000 Miles
Lubricate Transmission Control Linkage	✗ (30,000 / 60,000)
DRIVESHAFT	
Inspect CV Joint Boots	✗ (30,000 / 60,000)
ENGINE	
Change Engine Coolant	Replace Premium Gold Coolant, Every 5 Years Or 100,000 Miles Thereafter Replace Every 50,000 Miles
Change Engine Oil & Filter	S / N (alternating)
Inspect Cooling System & Protection Level	Annually Or Every 15,000 Miles
Inspect Drive Belts	Inspect Accessory Drive Belts Every 100,000 Miles.
Inspect Engine Air Filter	✗ (30,000 / 60,000)
Inspect Exhaust System	✗ (30,000 / 60,000)
Inspect Fluid & Lubricant Levels	At Every Engine Oil Change
Inspect Fuel System Connections, Hoses & Lines	✗ (30,000 / 60,000)
Replace Crankcase Emission Filter Or PCV Filter Element, 2.5L	Normal Service Every 30,000 Miles; More Frequently In Severe Service
Replace Fuel Filter ②	Normal Service Every 30,000 Miles; Severe Service Every 15,000 Miles
Replace PCV Valve	Every 100,000 Miles
Replace Spark Plugs	Normal Service Every 100,000 Miles; Severe Service Every 60,000 Miles

Recommended Service — Service Interval In Miles①

STEERING, SUSPENSION & TIRES

Recommended Service	Service Interval
Lubricate Steering & Suspension Components	X (every 15,000 miles: 15000, 30000, 45000, 60000)
Rotate Tires	Normal Service Inspect For Wear And Rotate Every 5000 Miles

N — Normal Service
S — Severe Service
X — Normal Or Severe Service
① — After vehicle has passed 60,000 mile mark return to beginning of mileage table & start cycle over again.
② — On vehicles equipped with California emissions.

Focus

Recommended Service — Service Interval In Miles①

BODY

Recommended Service	Service Interval
Inspect A/C Refrigerant Charge & System Operation	Every 12 Months Or 15,000 Miles
Inspect Instrument Panel Warning Lamps & Gauges	At Every Engine Oil Change
Lubricate Body Hardware & Hinges	X
Lubricate Hood Latch Pivot Points & All Contact Areas	X
Tighten Body Fasteners	S
Replace Cabin Air Filter	Every 15,000 Miles

BRAKES

Recommended Service	Service Interval
Inspect Brake Drums, Linings, Pads, Rotors, Lubricate Caliper Slide Rails	Normal Service Every 15,000 Miles; Severe Service Every 5000 Miles
Inspect Parking Brake System Operation	X

CLUTCH & TRANSMISSION

Recommended Service	Service Interval
Change Automatic Transmission Fluid & Filter	Inspect Every 15,000 Miles; Replace Every 30,000 Miles
Inspect Clutch Pedal Operation	X
Lubricate Transmission Control Linkage	X

DRIVESHAFT

Recommended Service	Service Interval
Inspect CV Joint Boots	X

Recommended Service — Service Interval In Miles①

Recommended Service	3000	5000	6000	7500	9000	10500	12000	13500	15000	18000	21000	22500	24000	25500	27000	30000	33000	36000	37500	39000	42000	45000	48000	50000	51000	52500	54000	55000	57000	60000
ENGINE																														
Change Engine Coolant — Replace Premium Gold Coolant, Every 5 Years Or 100,000 Miles Thereafter Replace Every 36 Months Or 50,000 Miles																														
Change Engine Oil & Filter — Normal Service Every 5000 Miles; Severe Service Every 3000 Miles																														
Inspect Cooling System & Protection Level — Annually Or Every 15,000 Miles																														
Inspect Drive Belts — Every 100,000 Miles																														
Inspect Engine Air Filter②																														X
Inspect Exhaust System																														X
Inspect Fuel System Connections, Hoses & Lines									X													X								
Replace Fuel Filter — Normal Service Every 30,000 Miles; Severe Service Every 15,000 Miles																														
Replace PCV Valve — Every 100,000 Miles																														
Replace Spark Plugs — Normal Service Every 100,000 Miles; Severe Service Every 60,000 Miles																														
Replace Timing Belt, 2.0L — Every 120,000 Miles																														
STEERING, SUSPENSION & TIRES																														
Inspect & Repack Rear Wheel Bearings																X														X
Lubricate Steering & Suspension Components									X												X									X
Rotate Tires — Normal Service Inspect For Wear And Rotate Every 5000 Miles																														
Tighten Chassis Fasteners									S																					S

FFV — Flexible Fuel Vehicle
N — Normal Service
NGV — Natural Gas Vehicle
S — Severe Service
X — Normal Or Severe Service
① — After vehicle has passed 60,000 mile mark return to beginning of mileage table & start cycle over again.
② — Not required on 2.3L engine.

Freestyle & Taurus X

Recommended Service — Service Interval In Miles①

Recommended Service	3000	5000	6000	7500	9000	10500	12000	13500	15000	18000	21000	22500	24000	25500	27000	30000	33000	36000	37500	39000	42000	45000	48000	50000	51000	52500	54000	55000	57000	60000
BRAKES																														
Inspect Brake Hoses & Lines									X							X						X								X
Inspect Disc & Drum Brake System, Lubricate Caliper Slide Rails — Normal Service Every 15,000 Miles; Severe Service Every 5000 Miles																														

Service Interval In Miles①

Interval columns (left to right): 60000, 57500, 55000, 52500, 50000, 47500, 45000, 42500, 40000, 37500, 35000, 32500, 30000, 27500, 25000, 22500, 20000, 17500, 15000, 12500, 10000, 7500, 5000, 2500

Recommended Service	Service Interval / Notes
BRAKES	
Inspect Parking Brake Operation	X
Replace Cabin Air Filter, If Equipped	Every 15,000 Miles
CLUTCH & TRANSMISSION	
Change CVT Fluid & High Pressure Filter	X
Change Manual Transmission Lubricant	Every 60,000 Miles
Change Transfer Case Fluid	X
Inspect & Lubricate Automatic Transmission Cable Linkage	Normal Service Every 150,000 Miles; Severe Service Every 60,000 Miles (N/S)
Lubricate Transfer Case Shift Lever Pivot Bolt & Control Rod Connecting Pins	S / X
DRIVE AXLE & DRIVESHAFT⑤	
Change Differential Lubricant	②
Lubricate Driveshaft Grease Fittings, Double Cardan Joint Centering Ball & Slip Yoke	N / S
Lubricate RH Front Drive Axle Shaft Slip Yoke, 4WD Models	X
ENGINE	
Change Engine Coolant	Replace Premium Gold Coolant, Every 5 Years Or 100,000 Miles Thereafter Replace Every 36 Months Or 50,000 Miles
Change Engine Oil & Filter	S N S N S N S X (N/S at intervals)
Inspect Cooling System & Protection Level	S N S X S N S N (N/S/X at intervals)
Inspect Drive Belts	Every 100,000 Miles
Inspect Exhaust System	N S N S (N/S at intervals)
Inspect Spark Plug Wires	S / X
Replace Engine Air Filter & Crankcase Emission Filter Elements	X
Replace Fuel Filter③	
Replace NGV Tanks④	Every 15 Years From Date Of Tank Manufacture
Replace PCV Valve	4 Cylinder Every 60,000 Miles; Except 4 Cylinder Every 100,000 Miles
Replace Spark Plugs	Normal Service Every 100,000 Miles; Severe Service Every 60,000 Miles
STEERING, SUSPENSION & TIRES	
Inspect Power Steering Fluid Level	At Every Engine Oil Change
Inspect Spindle Needle Bearing Thrust Bearing & Hub Lock Lubrication	X
Lubricate Steering Linkage	S
Repack Front Wheel Bearings	S N S (N/S at intervals)
Rotate Tires & Inspect Wheel Lug Nut Security	Normal Service Inspect For Wear And Rotate Every 5000 Miles; X

N — Normal Service
S — Severe Service
X — Normal Or Severe Service
① — After vehicle has passed 60,000 mile mark return to beginning of mileage table & start cycle over again.

② — Normal Vehicle Axle Maintenance: Rear axle and power take off (PTO) units containing synthetic lubricant and light duty trucks equipped with Ford-design axles are lubricated for life. These lubricants are not to be checked or changed unless a leak is suspected, service is required or the axle assembly has been submerged in water. The axle lubricant and PTO lubricant should be changed anytime the axle and PTO has been submerged in water. Non-synthetic rear axle lubricants should be replaced every 3000 miles or 3 months, whichever occurs first, during extended trailer tow operation above (70°F) ambient and wide open throttle for extended periods above 45 mph. The 3000 mile lube change interval may be waived if the axle was filled with 75W140 synthetic gear lubricant meeting Ford specification WSL-M2C192–A, part number F1TZ-19580–B or equivalent. Add four ounces of additive friction modifier C8AZ-19B546–A (EST-M2C118–A) or equivalent for complete refill of Traction-Lok rear axles. The rear axle lubricant should be changed anytime the axle has been submerged in water.

③ — On models equipped with California emissions.

④ — On natural gas equipped models.

⑤ — Police and Taxi Vehicle Axle Maintenance: Replace rear axle lubricant every 160,000km (100,000 miles). Rear axle lubricant change may be waived if the axle was filled with 75W140 synthetic gear lubricant meeting Ford specification WSL-M2C192–A. Add four ounces of additive friction modifier C8AZ-19B546–A(EST-M2C118–A) or equivalent for complete refill of Traction-Lok rear axles. The rear axle lubricant should be changed anytime the axle has been submerged in water.

LS & Town Car

Recommended Service	Service Interval In Miles ①
BODY	
Inspect A/C Refrigerant Charge & System Operation	Every 12 Months Or 15,000 Miles, Before Warm Season Arrives
Inspect Instrument Panel Warning Lamps & Gauges	At Every Engine Oil Change
Lubricate Body Hardware & Hinges	X at 45,000 & 60,000
Lubricate Hood Latch Pivot Points & All Contact Areas	X at 7,500 / 15,000 / 22,500 / 30,000 / 37,500 / 45,000 / 52,500 / 60,000
Replace Passenger Compartment Pollen Filter	Normal Service Every 15,000 Miles
BRAKES	
Inspect Brake Drums, Linings, Pads, Rotors, Lubricate Caliper Slide Rails	Normal Service Every 15,000 Miles; Severe Service Every 5000 Miles
Inspect Brake Lines & Hoses	Normal Service Every 30,000 Miles; Severe Service Every 12,000 Miles
Inspect Parking Brake System Operation	X at 30,000 & 60,000
CLUTCH & TRANSMISSION	
Change Automatic Transmission Fluid & Filter, Continental & Town Car	Inspect Every 15,000 Miles; Change Every 30,000 Miles
Change Automatic Transmission Fluid & Filter, LS	Normal Service Inspect Every 15,000 Miles, Change Every 150,000 Miles; Severe Service Change Every 30,000 Miles
Change Manual Transmission Fluid, Lincoln LS	Every 60,000 Miles
Lubricate Transmission Control Linkage	X at 15,000
DRIVE AXLE & DRIVESHAFT	
Change Differential Lubricant	②
Inspect CV Joint Boots	X at 45,000 & 60,000
Lubricate Driveshaft	X at 15,000 & 45,000

Service Interval In Miles columns: 3750, 7500, 11250, 15000, 18750, 22500, 26250, 30000, 33750, 37500, 41250, 45000, 48750, 52500, 56250, 60000

Recommended Service

Service Interval In Miles ①

Mileage interval columns (approx., left to right):
3000, 5000, 6000, 7500, 9000, 10500, 12000, 15000, 18000, 21000, 24000, 25000, 27000, 30000, 33000, 36000, 39000, 42000, 45000, 48000, 51000, 54000, 57000, 60000

ENGINE

Recommended Service	Service Interval / Notes
Change Engine Coolant	Replace Premium Gold Coolant, Every 5 Years Or 100,000 Miles Thereafter Replace Every 36 Months Or 50,000 Miles
Change Engine Oil & Filter	S N S N S N S X S N S N S X S N S N S X S N S N S (N = Normal, S = Severe)
Inspect Cooling System & Protection Level	Annually Or Every 15,000 Miles
Inspect Drive Belts	Every 100,000 Miles
Inspect Engine Air Filter	X (every 30,000 Miles)
Inspect Exhaust System	X (every 15,000 Miles)
Inspect Fuel System Connections, Hoses & Lines	X
Replace Fuel Filter	Normal Service Every 30,000 Miles; Severe Service Every 15,000 Miles
Replace PCV Valve	Every 100,000 Miles
Replace Spark Plugs	Normal Service Every 100,000 Miles; Severe Service Every 60,000 Miles

STEERING, SUSPENSION & TIRES

Recommended Service	Service Interval / Notes
Inspect & Repack Front Wheel Bearings, Town Car	X (every 30,000 Miles)
Lubricate Steering & Suspension Components	X
Rotate Tires	Normal Service Inspect for Wear And Rotate Every 5000 Miles

N — Normal Service
S — Severe Service
X — Normal Or Severe Service

① — After vehicle has passed 60,000 mile mark return to beginning of mileage table & start cycle over again.

② — Normal Vehicle Axle Maintenance: Rear axle units containing synthetic lubricant are lubricated for life. These lubricants are not to be checked or changed unless a leak is suspected, service is required or the axle assembly has been submerged in water. The axle lubricant should be changed anytime the axle has been submerged in water. Non-synthetic rear axle lubricants should be replaced every 100,000 miles under normal operating conditions. Non-synthetic rear axle lubricants should be replaced every 3000 miles or 3 months, whichever occurs first, during extended trailer tow operation above (70°F) ambient and wide open throttle for extended periods above 45 mph. The 3000 mile lube change interval may be waived if the axle was filled with 75W140 synthetic gear lubricant meeting Ford specification WSL-M2C192-A. Add four ounces of additive friction modifier C8AZ-19B546-A or equivalent for complete refill of Traction-Lok rear axles. The rear axle lubricant should be changed anytime the axle has been submerged in water.

Mustang

Service Interval In Miles ①

Recommended Service	Service Interval In Miles
BODY	
Inspect A/C Refrigerant Charge & System Operation	Every 12 Months Or 15,000 Miles
Inspect Instrument Panel Warning Lamps & Gauges	At Every Engine Oil Change
Lubricate Body Hardware & Hinges	X
Lubricate Hood Latch Pivot Points & All Contact Areas	X
Replace Cabin Air Filter	Every 15,000 Miles, If Equipped
BRAKES	
Inspect Brake Drums, Linings, Pads, Rotors, Lubricate Caliper Slide Rails	Normal Service Every 15,000 Miles; Severe Service Every 5,000 Miles
Inspect Parking Brake System Operation	X
CLUTCH & TRANSMISSION	
Change Automatic Transmission Fluid & Filter, 2004	Inspect Every 15,000 Miles; Change Every 30,000 Miles.
Change Automatic Transmission Fluid & Filter, 2005–08	Inspect Every 15,000 Miles Change At 150,000 Miles; Severe Service Change Every 30,000 Miles.
Lubricate Transmission Control Linkage	X
DRIVE AXLE & DRIVESHAFT	
Change Differential Lubricant	③ X
Lubricate Driveshaft	X
ENGINE	
Change Engine Coolant	Replace Premium Gold Coolant, Every 5 Years Or 100,000 Miles Thereafter Replace Every 36 Months Or 50,000 Miles — S N S X S N S S S N S N S X S N S
Change Engine Oil & Filter	Annually Or Every 15,000 Miles
Inspect Cooling System & Protection Level	
Inspect Drive Belts	Every 100,000 Miles
Inspect Engine Air Filter	S
Inspect Exhaust System	X
Inspect Fluid & Lubricant Levels	At Every Engine Oil Change
Inspect Fuel System Connections, Hoses & Lines	X
Inspect Timing Belt, 2.3L SOHC	
Replace Engine Air Filter	Every 30,000 Miles
Replace Fuel Filter, ②	
Replace PCV Valve	Normal Service Every 30,000 Miles; Severe Service Every 15,000 Miles
Replace Spark Plugs	Every 100,000 Miles / Normal Service Every 100,000 Miles; Severe Service Every 60,000 Miles
STEERING, SUSPENSION & TIRES	
Inspect & Repack Front Wheel Bearings	X X
Lubricate Steering & Suspension Components	X
Rotate Tires	Normal Service Inspect For Wear And Rotate Every 5000 Miles.

N — Normal Service
NGV — Natural Gas Vehicle
S — Severe Service
X — Normal Or Severe Service
① — After vehicle has passed 60,000 mile mark return to beginning of mileage table & start cycle over again.
② — On All vehicles equipped with California emissions.
③ — Normal Vehicle Axle Maintenance: Rear axle units containing synthetic lubricant are lubricated for life. These lubricants are not to be checked or changed unless a leak is suspected, service is required or the axle assembly has been submerged in water. The axle lubricant should be changed anytime the axle has been submerged in water. Non-synthetic rear axle lubricants should be replaced every 100,000 miles under normal operating conditions. Non-synthetic rear axle lubricants should be replaced every 3000 miles or 3 months, whichever occurs first, during extended trailer tow operation above (70°F) ambient and wide open throttle for extended periods above 45 mph. The 3000 mile lube change interval may be waived if the axle was filled with 75W140 synthetic gear lubricant meeting Ford specification WSL-M2C192–A. Add four ounces of additive friction modifier C8AZ-19B546–A or equivalent for complete refill of Traction-Lok rear axles. The rear axle lubricant should be changed anytime the axle has been submerged in water.

Thunderbird

Service Interval In Miles①

Recommended Service	3000	5000	6000	7500	9000	10500	12000	13500	15000	16500	18000	19500	21000	22500	24000	25500	27000	28500	30000	31500	33000	34500	36000	37500	39000	40500	42000	43500	45000	46500	48000	49500	51000	52500	54000	55500	57000	58500	60000
BODY																																							
Inspect A/C Refrigerant Charge & System Operation	Every 12 Months Or 15,000 Miles																																						
Inspect Instrument Panel Warning Lamps & Gauges	At Every Engine Oil Change																																						
Lubricate Body Hardware & Hinges									X										X										X										X
Lubricate Hood Latch Pivot Points & All Contact Areas									X										X										X										X
BRAKES																																							
Inspect Brake Drums, Linings, Pads, Rotors, Lubricate Caliper Slide Rails	Normal Service Every 15,000 Miles; Severe Service Every 5000 Miles																																						
Inspect Parking Brake System Operation																			X																				X
CLUTCH & TRANSMISSION																																							
Change Automatic Transmission Fluid & Filter	Normal Service Inspect Every 15,000 Miles, Change Every 150,000 Miles; Severe Service Every 30,000 Miles																																						
Lubricate Transmission Control Linkage									X										X										X										X
DRIVE AXLE & DRIVESHAFT																																							
Lubricate Driveshaft									X										X										X										X
ENGINE																																							
Change Engine Coolant	Green Coolant, Every 45,000 Miles, Then Every 30,000 Miles Thereafter. Replace Orange Coolant, Every 150,000 Miles, Replace Yellow Coolant Every 5 Years Or 100,000 Miles																																						
Change Engine Oil & Filter	S		S	N	S		S		X		S		S	N	S		S		X		S		S	N	S		S		X		S		S	N	S		S		X
Inspect Cooling System & Protection Level	Annually Or Every 15,000 Miles																																						
Inspect Drive Belts	Every 100,000 Miles																																						
Inspect Exhaust System									X										X										X										X
Inspect Fluid & Lubricant Levels	At Every Engine Oil Change																																						
Inspect Fuel System Connections, Hoses & Lines									X										X										X										X

Service Interval In Miles①

Recommended Service	35000	37500	40000	42500	45000	47500	50000	52500	55000	57500	60000
ENGINE											
Inspect & Replace Engine Air Filter		S			X			S			X
Replace Engine Air Filter	Every 30,000 Miles										
Replace Fuel Filter	Normal Service Every 30,000 Miles; Severe Service Every 15,000 Miles										
Replace PCV Valve	4 Cylinder Every 60,000 Miles; V6 Every 100,000 Miles										
Replace Spark Plugs	Normal Service Every 100,000 Miles; Severe Service Every 60,000 Miles										
STEERING, SUSPENSION & TIRES											
Lubricate Steering & Suspension Components	X				X						X
Rotate Tires	Normal Service Inspect For Wear And Rotate Every 5000 Miles										

N — Normal Service
NGV — Natural Gas Vehicle
S — Severe Service
X — Normal Or Severe Service
① — After vehicle has passed 60,000 mile mark return to beginning of mileage table & start cycle over again.

Alero, Grand Am & Malibu

Service Interval In Miles①

Recommended Service	Interval / Notes
BODY	
Clean Power Antenna Mast	(per mileage schedule)
Inspect Lamps, Seat Belts & Warning Devices	At Least Once Every 6 Months
Lubricate Hinges, Latches, Lock Cylinders & Strikers	At Engine Oil Changes Or At Least Every 12 Months
Replace Cabin Air Filter If Equipped	Every 12 Months Or When DIC Light Comes On
BRAKES	
Inspect Brake System	At Oil And Filter Change Intervals
Inspect Parking Brake Operation	At Least Once Every 12 Months
Lubricate Parking Brake Cable Guides	(per mileage schedule)
CLUTCH & TRANSAXLE	
Change Automatic Transmission Fluid & Filter	No Normal Service Required; Severe Service Every 50,000 Miles
Inspect Neutral Safety & BTSI Operation & Lubricate Shift Linkage	(per mileage schedule)
DRIVESHAFT	
Inspect CV Joint Boots	At Engine Oil Changes & Tire Rotations
ENGINE	
Change Engine Coolant	Every 150,000 Miles
Change Engine Oil & Filter, w/Turbo②	(per mileage schedule)
Change Engine Oil & Filter	As Indicated By Oil Life System. Do Not Exceed 12 Months Between Oil And Filter Change Intervals
Inspect Accessory Drive Belts	Every 150,000 Miles
Inspect Exhaust System	Every 25,000 Miles
Inspect Fuel System	Every 25,000 Miles
Inspect Spark Plug Wires	At Spark Plug Changes
Inspect Thermostatically Controlled Air Cleaner	(per mileage schedule)
Operation & Fuel & PCV System	(per mileage schedule)
Inspect Throttle Linkage Operation	At Air Cleaner Element Changes

VEHICLE MAINTENANCE SCHEDULES, ALERO, GRAND AM & MALIBU

Service Interval In Miles[1]

Recommended Service	3000	6000	9000	12000	15000	18000	21000	24000	27000	30000	33000	36000	39000	42000	45000	48000	51000	54000	57000	60000	63000	66000	69000	72000	75000	78000	81000	84000	87000	90000	93000	96000	99000
ENGINE																																	
Replace Air Filter & PCV Filter, 2004 [3]								Every 25,000 Miles																									
Replace Air Filter & PCV Filter, 2005 [3]										Every 50,000 Miles																							
Replace Spark Plugs [3]																				Every 100,000 Miles													
Replace Timing Belt																				X													
STEERING, SUSPENSION & TIRES																																	
Inspect Steering & Suspension System										At Tire Rotations																							
Lubricate Chassis & Suspension	S	N	S	N	S	N	S	X	S	N	S	N	S	N	S	N	S	X	S	N	S	N	S	N	S	N	S	X	S	N	S	N	N
Rotate Tires										At Every Oil And Filter Change Intervals																							

N — Normal Service
S — Severe Service
X — Normal Or Severe Service
BTSI — Brake Transmission Shift Interlock
IAC — Idle Air Control
ISC — Idle Speed Control System

[1] — After vehicle passes 99,000 mile mark return to beginning of mileage table & start cycle over again.

[2] — If equipped, the engine oil life monitor will indicate when to change engine oil, usually 3000–10,000 miles. Under severe driving conditions, engine oil may need to be changed before 3000 miles. If vehicle is driven in a dusty area, change engine oil every 3000 miles.

[3] — The U.S. Environmental Protection Agency or the California Air Resources Board has determined the the failure to perform this maintenance item will not nullify the emission warranty or limit recall liabability prior to the completion of the vehicle's useful life. The vehicle manufacturer, however, urge that all recommended maintenance services be performed at the indicated intervals & the maintenance be recorded.

Aveo

Service Interval In Miles ①

Recommended Service	3000	6000	7500	9000	12000	15000	21000	24000	27000	30000	33000	36000	42000	45000	48000	51000	54000	57000	60000	63000	66000	72000	75000	78000	81000	84000	87000	90000	93000	96000
BODY																														
Inspect Body Fastener Security	— Severe Service Every 5000 Miles																													
Inspect Lamps & Warning Devices	S	S	N	S	S	X	S	S	N	S	S	X	S	S	N	S	S	X	S	S	N	S	S	X	S	S	N	S	S	X
Inspect Seat Belts & Related Components	— At Least Once Every 12 Months																													
Inspect Supplemental Restraint System	colspan — 10 Years From Vehicle Build Date, Then Every 24 Months Thereafter																													
Lubricate Lock Cylinders	— At Least Once Every 12 Months																													
Replace Cabin Air Filter	— Every 15,000 Miles; In Dusty Areas Replace More Often																													
BRAKES																														
Change Brake Fluid, Aveo	— Every 24 Months Or 30,000 Miles																													
Inspect Brake System Hoses, Lines & Connections	— Normal Service Every 15,000 Miles; Severe Service Every 5000 Miles																													
CLUTCH & TRANSAXLE																														
Change Automatic Transmission Fluid & Filter						S								S									S							
Change Clutch Fluid	— Every 24 Months Or 30,000 Miles																													
Change Differential & Manual Transaxle Lubricant						S								S									S							
Inspect Neutral Safety & Shift Interlock Switch Operation	— At Least Once Every 12 Months																													
Inspect Transaxle Lubricant Level	— At Every Engine Oil Change																													
DRIVESHAFT																														
Inspect CV Joint Boots & Tighten Driveshaft Flange	— Normal Service Every 15,000 Miles; Severe Service Every 5000 Miles																													
ENGINE																														
Change Engine Coolant	— Every 24 Months Or 30,000 Miles																													
Change Engine Oil & Filter	— Normal Service Every 7500 Miles; Severe Service Every 3000 Miles																													
Inspect Cooling System & Drive Belts				X								X		X														X		
Inspect Engine Valve Clearance														X					X									X		
Inspect EVAP Charcoal Canister	— Every 72 Months Or 60,000 Miles																													

Recommended Service — Service Interval In Miles ①

ENGINE

Recommended Service	Interval / Notes
Inspect EVAP & Fuel System Prizm	X (Every 30,000 Miles)
Inspect EVAP System	Every 30,000 Miles
Inspect Exhaust System	X (Every 30,000 Miles)
Inspect PVC System	Every 30,000 Miles
Inspect Thermostatic Air Cleaner System Operation	X (Every 30,000 Miles)
Inspect Timing Belt	Every 30,000 Miles
Replace Air Filter Element	Normal Service Every 30,000 Miles; More Frequently In Severe Service Or Dusty Conditions
Replace Fuel Filter	Every 90,000 Miles
Replace Spark Plugs	Every 30,000 Miles
Replace Spark Plug Wires	Every 60,000 Miles
Replace Timing Belt	Every 60,000 Miles

STEERING, SUSPENSION & TIRES

Recommended Service	Interval / Notes
Inspect Chassis Fastener Security	Severe Service Every 5000 Miles
Inspect Steering & Suspension	S — Severe Service Every 5000 Miles; X at 90,000 Miles
Lubricate Chassis & Suspension	At Every Engine Oil Change
Rotate Tires	Normal Service Every 7500 Miles; Severe Service Every 6000 Miles

N — Normal Service
S — Severe Service
X — Normal Or Severe Service
① — After vehicle passes 99,000 mile mark return to beginning of mileage table & start cycle over again.

Bonneville, LeSabre, Lucerne & Park Avenue

Recommended Service — Service Interval In Miles ①

Service interval columns (miles): 3000, 6000, 7500, 9000, 12000, 18000, 21000, 24000, 27000, 30000, 33000, 36000, 42000, 45000, 51000, 57000, 63000, 66000, 69000, 72000, 75000, 81000, 84000, 87000, 90000, 93000, 96000 (S = Severe Service, N = Normal Service)

BODY

Recommended Service	Interval / Marking
Clean Power Antenna Mast	S N S N S N ... (X marks at intervals)
Flush Vehicle Underside, Inspect Drain Holes	At Least Every 12 Months
Inspect Lamps & Seat Belts & Warning Devices	At Least Once Every 6 Months
Lubricate Hinges, Latches, Lock Cylinders & Strikers	At Engine Oil Changes Or At Least Every 12 Months
Replace Passenger Compartment Air Filter	Every 15,000 Miles

BRAKES

Recommended Service	Interval / Marking
Inspect Brake Fluid Level	Every 6 Months
Inspect Brake System	Normal Service Every 7500 Miles; Severe Service Every 6000 Miles
Inspect Parking Brake Operation	At Least Once Every 12 Months
Lubricate Parking Brake Cable Guides	S N S N S N ...

CLUTCH & TRANSAXLE

Recommended Service	Interval / Marking
Change Automatic Transmission Fluid & Filter ③	Normal Service Every 100,000 Miles; Severe Service Every 50,000 Miles
Inspect Neutral Safety & BTSI & Lubricate Shift Linkage	S N S N S N ...

DRIVESHAFT

Recommended Service	Interval / Marking
Inspect CV Joint Boots	At Engine Oil Changes & Tire Rotations

ENGINE

Recommended Service	Interval / Marking
Change Engine Coolant ④	Every 60 Months Or 150,000 Miles
Change Engine Oil & Filter ②	S S S X S S S ... (At Engine Oil Changes)
Inspect Drive Belts	At 150,000 Miles
Inspect Exhaust System	At Engine Oil Changes
Inspect Fuel System & PCV Valve & Supercharger Lubricant Level ④	X (at intervals)
Inspect Spark Plug Wires	At Spark Plug Changes
Inspect TBI Unit Mounting Fastener Security	S N

Service Interval In Miles①

Recommended Service	3000	6000	7500	9000	12000	15000	18000	21000	24000	27000	30000	33000	36000	39000	42000	45000	48000	51000	54000	57000	60000	63000	66000	69000	72000	75000	78000	81000	84000	87000	90000	93000	96000	99000
ENGINE																																		
Inspect Thermostatically Controlled Air Cleaner Operation											X										X										X			
Inspect Throttle Linkage Operation	At Engine Oil Or Air Cleaner Element Changes																																	
Replace Air Filter & PCV Filter ④	Every 30,000 Miles																																	
Replace Spark Plugs ④	Every 100,000 Miles																																	
STEERING, SUSPENSION & TIRES																																		
Inspect Power Steering Fluid Level & Suspension System	At Engine Oil Changes & Tire Rotations																																	
Lubricate Chassis & Suspension	S	S	N	S	S	X	S	S	S	S	X	S	S	S	S	X	S	S	S	S	X	S	S	S	S	X	S	S	S	S	X	S	S	S
Rotate Tires	Normal Service Inspect For Wear & Rotate Every 7500 Miles; Severe Service Every 6000 Miles																																	

N — Normal Service
S — Severe Service
X — Normal Or Severe Service
BTSI — Brake Transmission Shift Interlock
IAC — Idle Air Control
ISC — Idle Speed Control System

① — After vehicle passes 99,000 mile mark return to beginning of mileage table & start cycle over again.

② — If equipped, the engine oil life monitor will indicate when to change engine oil, usually 3000–10,000 miles. Under severe driving conditions, engine oil may need to be changed before 3000 miles. If vehicle is driven in a dusty area, change engine oil every 3000 miles.

③ — If vehicle is used in hilly or mountainous terrain, heavy city traffic where outside temperature reaches 90° F or higher or uses such as high performance operation.

④ — The U.S. Environmental Protection Agency or the California Air Resources Board has determined the failure to perform this maintenance item will not nullify the emission warranty or limit recall liability prior to the completion of the vehicle's useful life. We, however, urge that all recommended maintenance services be performed at the indicated intervals and the maintenance be recorded.

Cavalier & Sunfire

Service Interval In Miles①

Interval columns (miles, left → right):
3000, 6000, 7500, 9000, 12000, 15000, 18000, 21000, 22500, 24000, 27000, 30000, 33000, 36000, 37500, 39000, 42000, 45000, 48000, 51000, 52500, 54000, 57000, 60000, 63000, 66000, 67500, 69000, 72000, 75000, 78000, 81000, 82500, 84000, 87000, 90000, 93000, 96000, 97500, 99000

Recommended Service	Service Interval / Marks
BODY	
Inspect Lamps, Seat Belt & Warning Devices	At Least Once Every 6 Months
Lubricate Hinges, Latches, Lock Cylinders & Strikers	At Engine Oil Changes Or At Least Every 12 Months
Replace Passenger Compartment Air Filter	X — at 15000, 30000, 45000, 60000, 75000, 90000
BRAKES	
Inspect Brake System	Normal Service At 7500 Miles; Severe Service Every 6000 Miles (S / N)
Inspect Parking Brake Operation	At Least Once Every 12 Months
Lubricate Parking Brake Cable Guides	S / N (severe every 6000 / normal every 7500)
CLUTCH & TRANSAXLE	
Change Automatic Transmission Fluid & Filter	No Normal Service Required; Severe Service Every 50,000 Miles
Inspect Neutral Safety & BTSI Operation & Lubricate Shift Linkage	S / N (severe every 6000 / normal every 7500)
DRIVESHAFT	
Inspect CV Joint Boots	At Tire Rotations
ENGINE	
Change Engine Coolant	Every 60 Months Or 150,000 Miles (S)
Change Engine Oil & Filter, Less Turbo	S S X pattern (S severe every 3000 / X normal every 7500)
Change Engine Oil & Filter, w/Turbo	X — at every interval
Inspect Drive Belt	Every 150,000 Miles (X)
Inspect EGR System & Fuel & PCV System	X — at 30000, 60000, 90000
Inspect Exhaust System	X — at 30000, 60000, 90000
Inspect Spark Plug Wires	At Spark Plug Changes
Inspect Thermostatically Controlled Air Cleaner Operation	X — at 30000, 60000, 90000
Inspect Throttle Linkage Operation	At Engine Oil Or Air Cleaner Element Changes

Service Interval In Miles[1]

Recommended Service	3000	6000	9000	12000	15000	18000	21000	24000	27000	30000	33000	36000	39000	42000	45000	48000	51000	54000	57000	60000	63000	66000	69000	72000	75000	78000	81000	84000	87000	90000	93000	96000	99000
ENGINE																																	
Replace Air Filter										X										X									X				
Replace Spark Plugs, Except CNG														Every 100,000 Miles																			
STEERING, SUSPENSION & TIRES																																	
Inspect Steering & Suspension System												At Tire Rotations																					
Lubricate Chassis & Suspension		S	N	S	N	S	N	S	N	S	N	S	N	S	N	S	N	S	N	S	N	S	N	S	N	S	N	S	X	S	N	S	N
Rotate Tires											Normal Service Inspect For Wear & Rotate Every 7500 Miles; Severe Service Every 6000 Miles																						

CNG — Compressed Natural Gas
N — Normal Service
S — Severe Service
X — Normal Or Severe Service
BTSI — Brake Transmission Shift Interlock
IAC — Idle Air Control
ISC — Idle Speed Control System
[1] — After vehicle passes 99,000 mile mark return to beginning of mileage table & start cycle over again.

Century, Grand Prix, Impala, LaCrosse, Regal & Monte Carlo

Service Interval In Miles ①

Recommended Service	7,500	15,000	22,500	30,000	37,500	45,000	52,500	60,000	67,500	75,000	82,500	90,000	97,500	105,000	112,500	120,000	127,500	135,000	142,500	150,000
BODY																				
Inspect Lamps, Seat Belts & Warning Devices	At Least Once Every 6 Months																			
Lubricate Hinges, Latches, Lock Cylinders & Strikers	At Engine Oil Changes Or At Least Every 12 Months																			
Replace Passenger Compartment Air Filter					X					X					X					X
BRAKES																				
Inspect Brake System	Every 6 Months																			
Inspect Disc Brake Pads, Rotors, Shoes & Drums	At Engine Oil And Filter Change Intervals																			
Inspect Parking Brake Operation	At Least Once Every 12 Months																			
Lubricate Parking Brake Cable Guides	S	S	N	S	X	S	S	N	S	X	S	S	N	S	X	S	S	N	S	X
CLUTCH & TRANSAXLE																				
Change Automatic Transmission Fluid & Filter	Normal Service Every 100,000 Miles; Severe Service Every 50,000 Miles																			
Inspect Neutral Safety & BTSI & Lubricate Shift Linkage	S	S	N	S	X	S	S	N	S	X	S	S	N	S	X	S	S	N	S	X
DRIVE AXLE & DRIVESHAFT																				
Inspect CV Joint Boots	At Tire Rotations																			
ENGINE																				
Change Engine Coolant	Every 150,000 Miles																			X
Change Engine Oil & Filter, Less Turbo ②	S	S	N	S	X	S	S	N	S	X	S	S	N	S	X	S	S	N	S	X
Change Engine Oil & Filter, w/Turbo ②	X	X	X	X	X	X	X	X	X	X	X	X	X	X	X	X	X	X	X	X
Inspect Drive Belts & EGR System	Inspect Every 150,000 Miles																			
Inspect Exhaust System	At Engine Oil Changes																			
Inspect Fuel Filter & PCV System													X							
Inspect Spark Plug Wires	At Spark Plug Changes																			

Service Interval In Miles ①

Recommended Service	3000	6000	7500	9000	12000	15000	18000	21000	24000	27000	30000	33000	36000	39000	42000	45000	48000	51000	54000	57000	60000	63000	66000	69000	72000	75000	78000	81000	84000	87000	90000	93000	96000	99000
ENGINE																																		
Inspect Supercharger Oil Level	→ Every 25,000 Miles Or 36 Months If Equipped																																	
Inspect TBI Unit Mounting Fastener Security		S	N																															
Inspect Throttle Linkage Operation	→ At Air Cleaner Element Changes																																	
Replace Air Filter & PCV Filter, 2004–05						S					X									S										X				
Replace Air Filter, 2006–08	→ Every 50,000 Miles																																	
Replace Spark Plugs	→ Every 100,000 Miles																																	
STEERING, SUSPENSION & TIRES																																		
Inspect Steering & Suspension System	→ At Tire Rotations																																	
Lubricate Chassis & Suspension	→ At Engine Oil Changes																																	
Rotate Tires ③	→ Engine Oil And Filter Change Intervals																																	

CNG — Compressed Natural Gas
N — Normal Service
S — Severe Service
X — Normal Or Severe Service
BTSI — Brake Transmission Shift Interlock
IAC — Idle Air Control
ISC — Idle Speed Control System

① — After vehicle passes 99,000 mile mark return to beginning of mileage table & start cycle over again.

② — If equipped, the engine oil life monitor will indicate when to change engine oil, ususally 3000–10,000 miles. Engine oil and filter must be changed at least once every 12 months. Under severe driving conditions, engine oil may need to be changed before 3000 miles. If vehicle is driven in a dusty area, change engine oil every 3000 miles.

③ — Tire Inflation Monitor System, if equipped, must be reset when tires are rotated.

Cobalt & G5

Service Interval In Miles [1]

Recommended Service	Interval / Miles
BODY	
Inspect Lamps, Seat Belt & Warning Devices	At Least Once Every 6 Months
Lubricate Hinges, Latches, Lock Cylinders & Strikers	At Engine Oil Changes Or At Least Every 12 Months
Replace Passenger Compartment Air Filter	X at 15,000; 30,000; 45,000; 60,000; 75,000; 90,000
BRAKES	
Inspect Brake System	At Engine Oil Changes Or At Least Every 12 Months
Inspect Parking Brake Operation	At Least Once Every 12 Months
CLUTCH & TRANSAXLE	
Change Automatic Transmission Fluid & Filter	No Normal Service Required; Severe Service Every 50,000 Miles
DRIVESHAFT	
Inspect CV Joint Boots	At Tire Rotations
ENGINE	
Change Engine Coolant	Every 60 Months Or 150,000 Miles
Change Engine Oil & Filter	[2]
Inspect Drive Belt	Every 150,000 Miles
Inspect Exhaust System	Every 25,000 Miles
Inspect Fuel System	Every 25,000 Miles
Inspect Spark Plug Wires	At Spark Plug Changes
Replace Air Filter	Every 50,000 Miles
Replace Spark Plugs	Every 100,000 Miles

Mileage column headings (in thousands): 3000, 6000, 9000, 12000, 15000, 18000, 21000, 24000, 27000, 30000, 33000, 36000, 39000, 42000, 45000, 48000, 51000, 54000, 57000, 60000, 63000, 66000, 69000, 72000, 75000, 78000, 81000, 84000, 87000, 90000

Service Interval In Miles①

Recommended Service	3,000	6,000	9,000	12,000	15,000	18,000	21,000	24,000	27,000	30,000	33,000	36,000	39,000	42,000	45,000	48,000	51,000	54,000	57,000	60,000	63,000	66,000	69,000	72,000	75,000	78,000	81,000	84,000	87,000	90,000	93,000	96,000	99,000

STEERING, SUSPENSION & TIRES

Recommended Service	Interval
Inspect Steering & Suspension System	At Tire Rotations
Rotate Tires	At Oil Change Intervals

CNG-Compressed Natural Gas
N — Normal Service
S — Severe Service
X — Normal Or Severe Service
BTSI — Brake Transmission Shift Interlock
IAC — Idle Air Control
ISC — Idle Speed Control System
① — After vehicle passes 99,000 mile mark return to beginning of mileage table & start cycle over again.
② — On models equipped with Engine Oil Life Moniter, change engine oil when message appears in message display center. Do not exceed 12 months between oil and filter change intervals.

Corvette

Service Interval In Miles ①

Note: the chart columns represent mileage intervals (7,500-mile increments up to approximately 97,500 miles), each subdivided into S (Severe) and N (Normal) service. "X" indicates service required. Several services are defined by the descriptive interval text shown in the right-hand column. The grid mark positions are reproduced to the best reading of the page.

BODY

Recommended Service	Interval / Notes
Clean Power Antenna Mast	marked at periodic intervals (S/N + X)
Inspect Lamps, Seat Belts & Warning Devices	At Least Once Every 6 Months
Lubricate Hinges, Latches, Lock Cylinders & Strikers	At Engine Oil Changes Or At Least Every 12 Months
Replace Passenger Compartment Air Filter	marked at periodic intervals (X)

BRAKES

Recommended Service	Interval / Notes
Inspect Brake System	Normal Service At 7500 Miles, Then Every 10,000 Miles Thereafter; Severe Service Every 7500 Miles
Inspect Parking Brake Operation	At Least Once Every 12 Months
Lubricate Parking Brake Cable Guides	marked at periodic intervals (S/N + X)

CLUTCH & TRANSAXLE

Recommended Service	Interval / Notes
Change Automatic Transmission Fluid & Filter	Normal Service Every 100,000 Miles; Severe Service Every 50,000 Miles
Inspect Neutral Safety & BTSI Operation & Lubricate Shift Linkage	marked at periodic intervals (S/N + X)

ENGINE

Recommended Service	Interval / Notes
Change Engine Coolant	Every 150,000 Miles
Change Engine Oil & Filter ②	Every 12 Months Or As Indicated By Oil Life Monitor
Inspect Air Cleaner Element	Every 15,000 Miles
Inspect Drive Belts	Every 150,000 Miles
Inspect Exhaust System	Every 25,000 Miles
Inspect Fuel System	Every 25,000 Miles
Inspect Spark Plug Wires	At Spark Plug Changes
Inspect TBI Unit Mounting Fastener Security	(S/N marked)
Inspect Thermostatically Controlled Air Cleaner Operation	marked at periodic intervals (X)
Inspect Throttle Linkage Operation	At Air Cleaner Element Changes
Replace Air Filter	Every 50,000 Miles
Replace Spark Plugs	Every 100,000 Miles

Recommended Service

Service Interval In Miles ①

Recommended Service	3000	6000	7500	9000	12000	15000	18000	21000	22500	24000	27000	30000	33000	36000	37500	39000	42000	45000	48000	51000	52500	54000	57000	60000	63000	66000	67500	69000	72000	75000	78000	81000	82500	84000	87000	90000	93000	96000	97500	99000

STEERING, SUSPENSION & TIRES

Service	3000	6000	7500	9000	12000	15000	18000	21000	22500	24000	27000	30000	33000	36000	37500	39000	42000	45000	48000	51000	52500	54000	57000	60000	63000	66000	67500	69000	72000	75000	78000	81000	82500	84000	87000	90000	93000	96000	97500	99000
Inspect Steering & Suspension System	At Tire Rotations																																							
Lubricate Chassis & Suspension	S	S	N	S	S	X	S	S	N	S	S	X	S	S	N	S	S	X	S	S	N	S	S	X	S	S	N	S	S	X	S	S	N	S	S	X	S	S	N	S
Rotate Tires		S	N	S	S	N	S	S	N	S	S	N	S	S	N	S	S	N	S	S	N	S	S	N	S	S	N	S	S	N	S	S	N	S	S	N	S	S	N	S

N — Normal Service
S — Severe Service
X — Normal Or Severe Service
BTSI — Brake Transmission Shift Interlock
IAC — Idle Air Control
ISC — Idle Speed Control System
① — After vehicle passes 99,000 mile mark return to beginning of mileage table & start cycle over again.
② — If equipped, the engine oil life monitor will indicate when to change engine oil, ususally 3000—10,000 miles. Under severe driving conditions, engine oil may need to be changed before 3000 miles. If vehicle is driven in a dusty area, change engine oil every 3000 miles.

CTS, DTS, STS & XLR

Recommended Service — Service Interval In Miles①

BODY

Recommended Service	Interval / Notes
Flush Vehicle Underside, Inspect Drain Holes	At Least Every 12 Months, Especially In Winter & Springtime
Inspect Lamps, Seat Belts & Warning Devices	At Least Once Every 6 Months
Lubricate Hinges, Latches, Lock Cylinders & Strikers	At Engine Oil Changes Or At Least Every 12 Months
Replace Passenger Compartment Air Filter	X (at indicated mileage intervals)

BRAKES

Recommended Service	Interval / Notes
Change Brake Fluid, CTS-V	Severe Service Every 25,000 Miles
Inspect Brake System	At Engine Oil Changes Or At Least Every 12 Months
Inspect Parking Brake Operation	At Least Once Every 12 Months
Lubricate Parking Brake Cable Guides	S N (at indicated mileage intervals)

CLUTCH & TRANSAXLE/TRANSMISSION

Recommended Service	Interval / Notes
Change Automatic Transmission Fluid & Filter, 2004–05	No Normal Service; Severe Service Every 50,000 Miles
Change Automatic Transmission Fluid & Filter, 2006–08	Normal Service Every 100,000 Miles; Severe Service Every 50,000 Miles
Change Hydraulic Clutch Fluid	High Performance Operation Only Every 25,000 Miles
Change Rear Axle Fluid	Every 50,000 Miles See ③
Change Transfer Case Fluid	Trailer Tow Operation Only Every 50,000 Miles
Change 6 Speed Manual Transmission Fluid	Severe Service Every 50,000 Miles
Inspect Neutral Safety & BTSI Operation	S N (at indicated mileage intervals)
Lubricate Transmission Shift Linkage	S N (at indicated mileage intervals)

DRIVE AXLE

Recommended Service	Interval / Notes
Change Rear Axle Fluid, CTS-V	Severe Service Every 50,000 Miles

ENGINE

Recommended Service	Interval / Notes
Change Engine Coolant	Every 60 Months Or 150,000 Miles

Service Interval In Miles ①

Service interval columns (miles): 3000, 7500, 9000, 12500, 18000, 21000, 24500, 27000, 30000, 33000, 36000, 37500, 39000, 42500, 45000, 48000, 51000, 54000, 57000, 60000, 63000, 67500, 69000, 72500, 75000, 78000, 81000, 82500, 84000, 87000, 90000, 93000, 96000, 99000

ENGINE

Recommended Service	Service Interval / Marks
Change Engine Oil & Filter ②	As Indicated By Oil Life System. Do Not Exceed 12 Months Between Oil And Filter Change Intervals
Inspect Air Cleaner Element	X (at multiple intervals)
Inspect Drive Belts	At 150,000 Miles
Inspect EGR System	X (at multiple intervals)
Inspect Exhaust System	Every 25,000 Miles
Inspect Fuel Filler Cap	X (at multiple intervals)
Inspect Fuel System Hoses, Lines & Connections	Every 25,000 Miles
Inspect Spark Plug Wires	At Spark Plug Changes
Inspect Throttle Body Bore & Valve Plates For Deposits, DTS & STS	Every 25,000 Miles
Replace Air Filter	Every 50,000 Miles
Replace Fuel Filter, CTS	Every 100,000 Miles
Replace Spark Plugs	Every 100,000 Miles

STEERING, SUSPENSION & TIRES

Recommended Service	Service Interval / Marks
Inspect Steering & Suspension System	At Tire Rotations
Lubricate Chassis & Suspension	S N S N S N S N S N S N S N S N S N S N
Rotate Tires	Initial Service At 5000 Miles, Then Every 10,000 Miles Thereafter

N — Normal Service
S — Severe Service
X — Normal Or Severe Service
BTSI — Brake Transmission Shift Interlock
IAC — Idle Air Control
ISC — Idle Speed Control System

① — After vehicle passes 99,000 mile mark return to beginning of mileage table & start cycle over again.
② — If equipped, the engine oil life monitor will indicate when to change engine oil, usually 3000–10,000 miles. Under severe driving conditions, engine oil may need to be changed before 3000 miles. If vehicle is driven in a dusty area, change engine oil every 3000 miles.
③ — Change fluid if used for high performance operation or if vehicle has been driven for 3000 miles with a transmission fluid temperature at 290 degrees F or higher without an auxiliary fluid cooler.

DeVille & Seville

Recommended Service — Service Interval In Miles ①

Service Interval columns (in miles): 7500, 15000, 22500, 30000, 37500, 45000, 52500, 60000, 67500, 75000, 82500, 90000, 97500, 105000, 112500, 120000, 127500, 135000, 142500, 150000

Recommended Service	Service Interval In Miles ①
BODY	
Flush Vehicle Underside, Inspect Drain Holes	At Least Every 12 Months
Inspect Lamps, Seat Belts & Warning Devices	At Least Once Every 6 Months
Replace Passenger Compartment Air Filter	X (per chart intervals)
Replace Seat Cushion Filter	Every 24 Months Or 25,000 Miles
Replace Seat Back Filter	Every 60 Months Or 50,000 Miles
BRAKES	
Inspect Brake System, Inspect Parking Brake Operation	Every 7500 Miles / At Least Once Every 12 Months
Lubricate Parking Brake Cable Guides	S / N — X (per chart intervals)
CLUTCH & TRANSAXLE	
Change Automatic Transmission Fluid & Filter	No Normal Service Required; Severe Service Every 50,000 Miles
Inspect Neutral Safety & BTSI Operation	S / N — X (per chart intervals)
Lubricate Transmission Shift Linkage	S / N — X (per chart intervals)
DRIVESHAFT	
Inspect CV Joint Boots	At Engine Oil Changes & Tire Rotations
ENGINE	
Change Engine Coolant	Every 150,000 Miles
Change Engine Oil & Filter	As Indicated By Oil Life System. Do Not Exceed 12 Months Between Oil And Filter Change Intervals
Inspect Drive Belts & EGR System	Every 150,000 Miles
Inspect Exhaust System	Every 25,000 Miles
Inspect Fuel System	Every 25,000 Miles
Inspect Spark Plug Wires	At Spark Plug Changes
Inspect Thermostatically Controlled Air Cleaner Operation	Every 25,000 Miles
Inspect Throttle Body	Every 25,000 Miles

Service Interval In Miles ①

Recommended Service	Service Interval In Miles ①
ENGINE	
Inspect Throttle Linkage Operation	At Engine Oil Or Air Cleaner Element Changes
Replace Air Filter, 2004	Every 25,000 Miles
Replace Air Filter, 2005	Every 50,000 Miles
Replace Spark Plugs	Every 100,000 Miles
STEERING, SUSPENSION & TIRES	
Inspect Steering & Suspension System	At Tire Rotations
Lubricate Chassis & Suspension	S N S N S N X S N S N S N X S N S N S N X S N S N
Rotate Tires	Inspect For Wear & Rotate Every 7500 Miles

Mileage interval columns (in thousands): 3750, 7500, 11250, 15000, 18750, 22500, 26250, 30000, 33750, 37500, 41250, 45000, 48750, 52500, 56250, 60000, 63750, 67500, 71250, 75000, 78750, 82500, 86250, 90000, 93750, 97500

N — Normal Service
S — Severe Service
X — Normal Or Severe Service
BTSI — Brake Transmission Shift Interlock
IAC — Idle Air Control
ISC — Idle Speed Control System
① — After vehicle passes 99,000 mile mark return to beginning of mileage table & start cycle over again.

GTO

Service Interval In Miles①

The following schedule lists recommended services across service intervals in miles (ranging from 3,000 through 99,000 miles). For each item the interval note or service indicator (X = perform service; S = Severe service schedule; N = Normal service schedule) is shown.

Recommended Service	Service Interval / Note
BODY	
Flush Vehicle Underside, Inspect Drain Holes	At Least Every 12 Months, Especially In Winter & Springtime
Inspect Lamps, Seat Belts & Warning Devices	At Least Once Every 6 Months
Lubricate Hinges, Latches, Lock Cylinders & Strikers	At Engine Oil Changes Or At Least Every 12 Months
Replace Passenger Compartment Air Filter	X (at indicated intervals — 15,000 / 30,000 / 45,000 / 60,000 / 75,000 / 90,000 miles)
BRAKES	
Inspect Brake System	Every 5000 Miles
Inspect Parking Brake Operation	At Least Once Every 12 Months
Lubricate Parking Brake Cable Guides	S / N (at indicated intervals)
CLUTCH & TRANSAXLE	
Change Automatic Transmission Fluid & Filter	Normal Service Every 50,000 Miles; Severe Service Every 25,000 Miles
Inspect Neutral Safety & BTSI Operation	S / N (at indicated intervals)
Lubricate Transmission Shift Linkage	S / N (at indicated intervals)
ENGINE	
Change Engine Coolant	Every 60 Months Or 150,000 Miles
Change Engine Oil & Filter	As Indicated By Oil Life System. Do Not Exceed 12 Months Between Oil And Filter Change Intervals
Inspect Air Cleaner Element	X (at indicated intervals)
Inspect Drive Belts	Every 150,000 Miles
Inspect Exhaust System	Every 25,000 Miles
Inspect Fuel Filler Cap	X (at indicated intervals)
Inspect Fuel System Hoses, Lines & Connections	Every 25,000 Miles
Replace Spark Plug Wires	At Spark Plug Changes
Replace Engine Air Filter	Every 25,000 Miles
Replace Spark Plugs	Every 100,000 Miles
STEERING, SUSPENSION & TIRES	
Inspect Steering & Suspension System	At Tire Rotations

Service Interval In Miles ①

Recommended Service	3000	6000	7500	9000	12000	15000	18000	21000	22500	24000	27000	30000	33000	36000	37500	39000	42000	45000	48000	51000	52500	54000	57000	60000	63000	66000	67500	69000	72000	75000	78000	81000	82500	84000	87000	90000	93000	96000	97500	99000
STEERING, SUSPENSION & TIRES																																								
Lubricate Chassis & Suspension	S	S	N	S	S	X	S	S	N	S	S	X	S	S	N	S	S	X	S	S	N	S	S	X	S	S	N	S	S	X	S	S	N	S	S	X	S	S	N	S
Rotate Tires	Inspect For Wear At Each Oil Change																																							

N — Normal Service
S — Severe Service
X — Normal Or Severe Service
BTSI — Brake Transmission Shift Interlock
IAC — Idle Air Control
ISC — Idle Speed Control System
① — After vehicle passes 99,000 mile mark return to beginning of mileage table & start cycle over again.

G6 & Malibu Maxx

Service Interval In Miles①

Recommended Service	Service Interval
BODY	
Inspect Lamps, Seat Belts & Warning Devices	At Least Once Every 6 Months
Lubricate Hinges, Latches, Lock Cylinders & Strikers	At Engine Oil Changes Or At Least Every 12 Months
BRAKES	
Inspect Brake System	At Oil And Filter Change Intervals
Inspect Parking Brake Operation	At Least Once Every 12 Months
CLUTCH & TRANSAXLE	
Change Automatic Transmission Fluid & Filter	No Normal Service Required; Severe Service Every 50,000 Miles
Inspect Neutral Safety & BTSI Operation & Lubricate Shift Linkage	See mileage chart below (S = Severe, N = Normal)
DRIVESHAFT	
Inspect CV Joint Boots	At Engine Oil Changes & Tire Rotations
ENGINE	
Change Engine Coolant	Every 60 Months Or 150,000 Miles
Change Engine Oil & Filter②	As Indicated By Oil Life System. Do Not Exceed 12 Months Between Oil And Filter Change Intervals
Inspect Accessory Drive Belts	Every 150,000 Miles
Inspect Exhaust System	Every 25,000 Miles
Inspect Fuel System	Every 25,000 Miles
Inspect Spark Plug Wires	At Spark Plug Changes
Inspect Throttle Linkage Operation	At Air Cleaner Element Changes
Replace Air Filter③	Every 50,000 Miles
Replace Spark Plugs③	Every 100,000 Miles

Inspect Neutral Safety & BTSI Operation & Lubricate Shift Linkage — marks across Service Interval In Miles:

Miles	Mark
22,500	S
30,000	N
37,500	S
45,000	N
52,500	S
60,000	X
67,500	S
75,000	N
82,500	S
90,000	X
97,500	S

Service Interval In Miles①

Recommended Service	3000	6000	9000	12000	15000	18000	21000	24000	27000	30000	33000	36000	39000	42000	45000	48000	51000	54000	57000	60000	63000	66000	69000	72000	75000	78000	81000	84000	87000	90000	93000	96000	99000

STEERING, SUSPENSION & TIRES

Recommended Service	Interval
Inspect Steering & Suspension System	At Tire Rotations
Rotate Tires	At Every Oil And Filter Change Intervals

N — Normal Service
S — Severe Service
X — Normal Or Severe Service
BTSI — Brake Transmission Shift Interlock
IAC — Idle Air Control
ISC — Idle Speed Control System

① — After vehicle passes 99,000 mile mark return to beginning of mileage table & start cycle over again.

② — If equipped, the engine oil life monitor will indicate when to change engine oil, usually 3000–10,000 miles. Under severe driving conditions, engine oil may need to be changed before 3000 miles. If vehicle is driven in a dusty area, change engine oil every 3000 miles.

③ — The U.S. Environmental Protection Agency or the California air Resources Board has determined the the failure to perform this maintenance item will not nullify the emission warranty or limit recall liability prior to the completion of the vehicle's useful life. The vehicle manufacturer, however, urge that all recommended mainte-nance services be performed at the indicated intervals & the maintenance be recorded.

Solstice

Recommended Service — Service Interval In Miles①

Service Interval In Miles①:	3600	7500	9000	12000	15000	18000	21000	24000	27000	30000	33000	36000	39000	42000	45000	48000	51000	54000	57000	60000	63000	66000	69000	72000	75000	78000	81000	84000	87000	90000	93000	96000	99000

BODY

- Inspect Lamps, Seat Belts & Warning Devices — At Least Once Every 6 Months
- Lubricate Hinges, Latches, Lock Cylinders & Strikers — At Engine Oil Changes Or At Least Every 12 Months

BRAKES

- Inspect Brake System — At Oil And Filter Change Intervals
- Inspect Parking Brake Operation — At Least Once Every 12 Months

CLUTCH & TRANSAXLE

- Change Automatic Transmission Fluid & Filter — No Normal Service Required; Severe Service Every 50,000 Miles
- Inspect Neutral Safety & BTSI Operation & Lubricate Shift Linkage — S N S N X S N S N S N X S N S N S N

DRIVESHAFT

- Inspect CV Joint Boots — At Engine Oil Changes & Tire Rotations

ENGINE

- Change Engine Coolant — Every 60 Months Or 150,000 Miles
- Change Engine Oil & Filter② — As Indicated By Oil Life System. Do Not Exceed 12 Months Between Oil And Filter Change Intervals
- Inspect Accessory Drive Belts — Every 150,000 Miles
- Inspect Exhaust System — Every 25,000 Miles
- Inspect Fuel System — Every 25,000 Miles
- Inspect Spark Plug Wires — At Spark Plug Changes
- Inspect Throttle Linkage Operation — At Air Cleaner Element Changes
- Replace Air Filter③ — Inspect And Replace If Necessary Every 30,000 Miles
- Replace Spark Plugs③ — Every 100,000 Miles

Service Interval In Miles ①

Recommended Service	3000	6000	7500	9000	12000	15000	18000	21000	22500	24000	27000	30000	33000	36000	37500	39000	42000	45000	48000	51000	52500	54000	57000	60000	67500	75000	82500	90000	93000	96000	97500	99000

STEERING, SUSPENSION & TIRES

Recommended Service	Marks
Inspect Steering & Suspension System	At Tire Rotations
Lubricate Chassis & Suspension	S N S N S N X S N S N S N X S N
Rotate Tires	At Every Oil And Filter Change Intervals

N — Normal Service
S — Severe Service
X — Normal Or Severe Service
BTSI — Brake Transmission Shift Interlock
IAC — Idle Air Control
ISC — Idle Speed Control System

① — After vehicle passes 99,000 mile mark return to beginning of mileage table & start cycle over again.

② — If equipped, the engine oil life monitor will indicate when to change engine oil. Under severe driving conditions, engine oil may need to be changed before 3000 miles. If vehicle is driven in a dusty area, change engine oil every 3000 miles.

③ — The U.S. Environmental Protection Agency or the California air Resources Board has determined the the failure to perform this maintenance item will not nullify the emission warranty or limit recall libability prior to the completion of the vehicle's useful life. The vehicle manufacturer, however, urge that all recommended maintenance services be performed at the indicated intervals & the maintenance be recorded.

Vibe

Service Interval In Miles①

Recommended Service	3750	7500	11250	15000	18750	22500	26250	30000	33750	37500	41250	45000	48750	52500	56250	60000	63750	67500	71250	75000	78750	82500	86250	90000	93750	97500
BODY																										
Inspect Lamps, Seat Belts & Warning Devices	At Least Once Every 6 Months →																									
Lubricate Hinges, Latches, Lock Cylinders & Strikers	At Engine Oil Changes Or At Least Every 12 Months →																									
Replace Passenger Compartment Air Filter				X				X				X				X				X				X		
BRAKES																										
Inspect Brake System, 2004		X		X		X		X		X		X		X		X		X		X		X		X		X
Inspect Brake System, 2005–08	Every 5000 Miles →																									
CLUTCH & TRANSMISSION																										
Change Automatic Transmission Fluid & Filter																S										
Change Manual Transmission Fluid & Filter								S								S								S		
Change Transfer Case Fluid				S				S				S				S				S				S		
DRIVE AXLE																										
Change Differential Lubricant				S				S				S				S				S				S		
Lubricate Driveshaft	S	S	N	S	S	S	X	S	S	S	N	S	S	S	X	S	S	S	N	S	S	S	X	S	S	N
ENGINE																										
Change Engine Coolant 2004 (Every 24 Months)																X										
Change Engine Coolant, 2005–08 (Every 60 Months)	Every 100,000 Miles →																									
Change Engine Oil & Filter, 2004 (Normal Service Every 12 Months; Severe Service Every 3 Months)	S	S	S	X	S	S	S	X	S	S	S	X	S	S	S	X	S	S	S	X	S	S	S	X	S	S
Change Engine Oil & Filter, 2005–08 (Every 3 Months)		X		X		X		X		X		X		X		X		X		X		X		X		X
Inspect Accessory Drive Belt (48 Months)																X										
Inspect Engine Air Filter				S				S				S				S				S				S		
Inspect Engine Valve Clearance (48 Months)																X										
Inspect Exhaust System	At Engine Oil Changes →																									

Service Interval In Miles [1]

Recommended Service	3,750	7,500	11,250	15,000	18,750	22,500	26,250	30,000	33,750	37,500	41,250	45,000	48,750	52,500	56,250	60,000	63,750	67,500	71,250	75,000	78,750	82,500	86,250	90,000	93,750	97,500
ENGINE																										
Inspect Fuel & Emission System								X								X								X		
Replace Engine Air Filter (Every 24 Months)								X								X								X		
Replace Spark Plugs	Every 120,000 Miles																									
STEERING, SUSPENSION & TIRES																										
Rotate Tires, 2004	S	N	S	N	S	N	S	N	S	N	S	N	S	N	S	N	S	N	S	N	S	N	S	N	S	N
Rotate Tires, 2005–08	N	S	N	S	N	S	N	S	N	S	N	S	N	S	N	S	N	S	N	S	N	S	N	S	N	S

Every 5000 Miles

N — Normal Service
S — Severe Service
X — Normal Or Severe Service
[1] — After vehicle passes 99,000 mile mark return to beginning of mileage table & start cycle over again.

Saturn

Service Interval In Miles①

Recommended Service	3000	6000	7500	9000	12000	15000	18000	21000	24000	27000	30000	33000	36000	39000	42000	45000	48000	51000	54000	57000	60000	63000	66000	69000	72000	75000	78000	81000	84000	87000	90000	93000	96000	99000
BODY																																		
Inspect Seat Belts & Restraint Systems	At Least Once Every 6 Months																																	
Inspect Wiper Blades & Inserts	At Least Once Every 6 Months																																	
Lubricate Door Check Straps & Hinges						X		X		X		X		X		X		X		X		X		X		X		X		X		X		X
Lubricate Headlamp Doors					X		X		X		X		X		X		X		X		X		X		X		X		X		X		X	
Lubricate Hood Latch					X		X		X		X		X		X		X		X		X		X		X		X		X		X		X	
Lubricate Sunroof					X		X		X		X		X		X		X		X		X		X		X		X		X		X		X	
Replace Cabin Air Filter	Every 24 Months Or 18,000 Miles; In Dusty Areas Change More Often																																	
BRAKES																																		
Inspect Brake Drums & Shoes	At Oil Change Intervals																																	
Inspect Brake Hoses, Lines & Connections	At Oil Change Intervals																																	
Inspect Disc Brake Calipers For Freedom Of Movement (Lubricate If Required)	At Oil Change Intervals																																	
Inspect Disc Brake Pads & Rotors	At Oil Change Intervals																																	
CLUTCH & TRANSAXLE																																		
Add DEX-CVT Additive to VTi Variable Transmission	Every 50,000 Miles																																	
Change Automatic Transaxle Fluid & Filter, L-Series	No Normal Service; Severe Service Every 50,000 Miles																																	
Change VTi Transaxle Fluid & Filter	Normal Service Every 100,000 Miles; Severe Service Every 50,000 Miles																																	
DRIVESHAFT																																		
Inspect CV Joint Boots	X	X	X	X	X	X	X	X	X	X	X	X	X	X	X	X	X	X	X	X	X	X	X	X	X	X	X	X	X	X	X	X	X	X
ENGINE																																		
Change Engine Coolant & Inspect Pressure Cap	Every 60 Months Or 150,000 Miles																																	
Change Engine Oil & Filter②	S	X	S	X	S	X	S	X	S	X	S	X	S	X	S	X	S	X	S	X	S	X	S	X	S	X	S	X	S	X	S	X	S	X
Inspect Air Filter	Severe Service Every 15,000 Miles										X										X										X			
Inspect Cooling System & Protection Level																		X																
Inspect Drive Belts & Coolant Hoses, 2004–05	Every 25,000 Miles																																	

Service Interval In Miles①

The interval columns run in miles (in thousands): 30,000 · 36,000 · 67,500 · 90,000 … continuing across the chart (12,000; 15,000; 18,000; 21,000; 24,000; 27,000; 30,000; 33,000; 36,000; 39,000; 42,000; 45,000; 48,000; 51,000; 54,000; 57,000; 60,000; 63,000; 67,500; 72,000; 75,000; 78,000; 81,000; 82,500; 84,000; 87,000; 90,000; 93,000; 96,000; 99,000).

Recommended Service	Service Interval
ENGINE	
Inspect Drive Belts & Coolant Hoses, 2006–08 Except 2.0L L4 Supercharged	Every 150,000 Miles
Inspect Drive Belts & Coolant Hoses, 2006–08 2.0L L4 Supercharged	Every 50,000 Miles
Inspect Exhaust System	Every 25,000 Miles
Inspect Fuel System	Every 25,000 Miles
Inspect Fuel Tank Filler Cap	X (24,000 Miles; 75,000 Miles)
Replace Air Filter, 2004	Every 25,000 Miles
Replace Air Filter, 2005–08	Every 50,000 Miles
Replace Drive Belt, Ion Red Line	Every 50,000 Miles
Replace Fuel Filter	Every 100,000 Miles
Replace Spark Plugs	Every 100,000 Miles
Replace Timing Belt	Every 100,000 Miles
STEERING, SUSPENSION & TIRES	
Inspect Ball Joint Seals	X (at each listed service interval)
Inspect Suspension	X (at each listed service interval)
Rotate Tires	Every 6000 Miles

N — Normal Service
S — Severe Service
X — Normal Or Severe Service
BTSI — Brake Transaxle Shift Interlock
① — After vehicle passes 100,000 mile mark return to beginning of mileage table & start cycle over again.
② — On models equipped with Engine Oil Life Moniter, change engine oil when message appears in message display center. Do not exceed 12 months between oil and filter change intervals.

CHRYSLER LLC

Page No.

CHRYSLER

Concorde, 300M 3-1
Crossfire 4-1
Sebring Convertible & Sedan 2-1
Sebring Coupe 1-1
300 6-1

DODGE

Avenger 2-1
Caliber 7-1
Charger 6-1
Intrepid 3-1
Magnum 6-1
Neon 5-1
Stratus Coupe. 1-1
Stratus Sedan 2-1

GENERAL SERVICE

Air Bag Systems (Volume 2) 4-1
Air Conditioning 8-1
Alternators 11-1

Page No.

Anti-Lock Brakes (Volume 2) 6-1
Cooling Fans. 9-1
Cruise Control (Volume 2) 2-1
Dash Gauges (Volume 2) 1-1
Dash Panel Service (Volume 2) 5-1
Disc Brakes. 14-1
Drum Brakes. 15-1
Engine Rebuilding Specifications. 21-1
Front Drive Axles 18-1
Gauges, Dash (Volume 2) 1-1
Hydraulic Brake Systems 16-1
Machine Shop Specifications 21-1
Passive Restraint Systems (Volume 2) 4-1
Power Brake Units 17-1
Power Steering 13-1
Rear Drive Axles. 19-1
Speed Controls (Volume 2). 2-1
Starter Motors 10-1
Steering Columns. 12-1
Supplemental Restraint Systems (Volume 2) 4-1
Tire Pressure Monitoring System. 20-1
Wiper Systems (Volume 2) 3-1

CHRYSLER LLC

Page No.

CHRYSLER

Concorde, 300M 3-1
Crossfire . . . ., ... 4-1
Sebring Convertible & Sedan 2-1
Sebring Coupe 1-1
300 6-1

DODGE

Avenger 2-1
Caliber 7-1
Charger 6-1
Intrepid 3-1
Magnum 6-1
Neon 5-1
Stratus Coupe. 1-1
Stratus Sedan 2-1

GENERAL SERVICE

Air Bag Systems (Volume 2) 4-1
Air Conditioning 8-1
Alternators 11-1

Page No.

Anti-Lock Brakes (Volume 2) 6-1
Cooling Fans. 9-1
Cruise Control (Volume 2) 2-1
Dash Gauges (Volume 2) 1-1
Dash Panel Service (Volume 2) 5-1
Disc Brakes. 14-1
Drum Brakes. 15-1
Engine Rebuilding Specifications 21-1
Front Drive Axles 18-1
Gauges, Dash (Volume 2) 1-1
Hydraulic Brake Systems 16-1
Machine Shop Specifications 21-1
Passive Restraint Systems (Volume 2) 4-1
Power Brake Units 17-1
Power Steering 13-1
Rear Drive Axles. 19-1
Speed Controls (Volume 2). 2-1
Starter Motors 10-1
Steering Columns. 12-1
Supplemental Restraint Systems (Volume 2) 4-1
Tire Pressure Monitoring System 20-1
Wiper Systems (Volume 2) 3-1

SEBRING COUPE & STRATUS COUPE

NOTE: Refer To The Rear Of This Manual For Vehicle Manufacturers Special Service Tool Suppliers.

INDEX OF SERVICE OPERATIONS

Page No.

AIR BAG SYSTEM
PRECAUTIONS 0-18
BRAKES
Anti-Lock Brakes (Volume 2).. 6-1
Disc Brakes.................. 14-1
Drum Brakes................. 15-1
Hydraulic Brake Systems 16-1
Power Brake Units........... 17-1
COMPUTER RELEARN
PROCEDURE 0-31
ELECTRICAL
Air Bag System (Volume 2) ... 4-1
Air Conditioning.............. 8-1
Alternator, Replace 1-4
Alternators.................. 11-1
Blower Motor, Replace........ 1-5
Coil Pack, Replace 1-4
Cooling Fans 9-1
Cruise Control (Volume 2) 2-1
Dash Gauges (Volume 2) 1-1
Dash Panel Service
(Volume 2)................... 5-1
Distributor, Replace 1-4
Evaporator Case, Replace 1-5
Evaporator Core, Replace 1-5
Fuel Pump Relay Location.... 1-4
Fuse Panel & Flasher
Location 1-4
Heater Core, Replace......... 1-5
Ignition Lock, Replace 1-4
Ignition Switch, Replace 1-4
Instrument Cluster, Replace... 1-5
Multi-Function Switch,
Replace 1-5
Neutral Safety Switch,
Replace 1-5
Passive Restraint Systems
(Volume 2).................. 4-1
Precautions.................. 1-4
Radio, Replace 1-5
Speed Controls (Volume 2) ... 2-1
Starter Motors 10-1
Starter, Replace 1-4
Steering Columns............ 12-1
Steering Wheel, Replace...... 1-5
Wiper Motor, Replace......... 1-5
Wiper Systems (Volume 2).... 3-1
ELECTRICAL SYMBOL
IDENTIFICATION 0-63
FRONT DRIVE AXLES 18-1
FRONT SUSPENSION &
STEERING
Ball Joint Inspection 1-22
Coil Spring, Replace 1-22
Control Arm, Replace 1-22
Crossmember, Replace 1-23
Driveshaft, Replace........... 1-22
Hub & Bearing, Replace 1-22
Power Steering 13-1
Power Steering Gear,
Replace 1-23

Page No.

Power Steering Pump,
Replace 1-23
Power Steering System
Bleed....................... 1-23
Precautions.................. 1-22
Shock Absorber, Replace 1-22
Stabilizer Bar, Replace 1-23
Steering Columns............ 12-1
Steering Knuckle, Replace.... 1-22
Tightening Specifications...... 1-25
NON-STANDARD TIRE &
WHEEL SIZE
ADJUSTMENT TO RIDE
HEIGHT SPECIFICATIONS
& TIRE SIZE CHART 0-61
REAR SUSPENSION
Coil Spring, Replace.......... 1-19
Control Arm, Replace 1-19
Description 1-19
Hub & Bearing, Replace 1-19
Knuckle, Replace 1-19
Shock Absorber, Replace 1-19
Stabilizer Bar, Replace........ 1-19
Tightening Specifications...... 1-21
Trailing Arm, Replace 1-19
SERVICE REMINDER &
WARNING LAMP RESET
PROCEDURES 0-34
SPECIFICATIONS
Fluid Capacities & Cooling
System Data................. 1-3
Front Wheel Alignment
Specifications................ 1-2
General Engine
Specifications................ 1-2
Lubricant Data............... 1-3
Rear Wheel Alignment
Specifications................ 1-2
Tune Up Specifications 1-2
Vehicle Ride Height
Specifications................ 1-3
VEHICLE
IDENTIFICATION 0-1
VEHICLE LIFT POINTS 0-51
VEHICLE MAINTENANCE
SCHEDULES 0-73
WHEEL ALIGNMENT
Description 1-26
Front Wheel Alignment........ 1-26
Preliminary Inspection 1-26
Rear Wheel Alignment 1-26
Wheel Alignment
Specifications................ 1-2
WIRE COLOR CODE
IDENTIFICATION 0-63
2.4L ENGINE
Belt Tension Data............ 1-10
Camshaft, Replace 1-9
Compression Pressure........ 1-7
Cooling System Bleed 1-10

Page No.

Crankshaft Rear Oil Seal,
Replace 1-10
Crankshaft Seal, Replace 1-10
Cylinder Head, Replace....... 1-8
Engine Rebuilding
Specifications................ 21-1
Engine, Replace 1-7
Engine Mount, Replace 1-7
Exhaust Manifold, Replace.... 1-8
Front Cover, Replace 1-8
Fuel Filter, Replace 1-11
Fuel Pump, Replace 1-11
Intake Manifold, Replace...... 1-7
Main & Rod Bearings 1-10
Oil Pan, Replace............. 1-10
Oil Pump, Replace........... 1-10
Oil Pump Service 1-10
Piston & Rod Assembly 1-9
Precautions.................. 1-7
Radiator, Replace 1-11
Rocker Arms, Replace 1-8
Thermostat, Replace......... 1-10
Tightening Specifications...... 1-12
Timing Belt, Replace......... 1-8
Water Pump, Replace 1-11
3.0L ENGINE
Belt Tension Data............ 1-16
Camshaft, Replace 1-15
Compression Pressure........ 1-13
Cooling System Bleed 1-16
Crankshaft Rear Oil Seal,
Replace 1-15
Crankshaft Seal, Replace 1-15
Cylinder Head, Replace....... 1-14
Engine Rebuilding
Specifications................ 21-1
Engine, Replace 1-13
Engine Mount, Replace 1-13
Exhaust Manifold, Replace.... 1-14
Front Cover, Replace 1-14
Fuel Filter, Replace 1-16
Fuel Pump, Replace 1-16
Intake Manifold, Replace...... 1-13
Intake Manifold Plenum,
Replace 1-13
Main & Rod Bearings 1-15
Oil Pan, Replace............. 1-15
Oil Pump, Replace........... 1-16
Oil Pump Service 1-16
Precautions.................. 1-13
Radiator, Replace 1-16
Rocker Arms, Replace 1-14
Serpentine Drive Belt 1-16
Thermostat, Replace......... 1-16
Tightening Specifications...... 1-18
Timing Belt, Replace......... 1-14
Water Pump, Replace 1-16

Specifications

GENERAL ENGINE SPECIFICATIONS

Year	Engine		Fuel System	Bore x Stroke, Inches	Comp. Ratio	Net HP @ RPM	Maximum Torque, Ft. Lbs. @ RPM	Normal Oil Pressure @ Idle, psi
	Liter	VIN Code①						
2004–05	2.4L	G	MFI	3.41 x 3.94	9.0	147 @ 5500	158 @ 4000	11.4
	3.0L	H	MFI	3.59 x 2.99	9.0	200 @ 5500	205 @ 4500	11.6

MFI — Multi-Port Fuel Injection
SMFI — Sequential Multi-Port Fuel
    Injection

① — Eighth digit of Vehicle Identification Number (VIN) denotes engine code.

TUNE UP SPECIFICATIONS

Engine Liter	Spark Plug Gap, Inch	Firing Order④	Ignition Timing °BTDC			Curb Idle Speed		Fuel Pump Pressure, psi③	Valve Lash, Inch
			Man. Trans.	Auto. Trans.	Mark.	Man. Trans.	Auto. Trans.		
2.4L	.039–.043	1-3-4-2	10	10	⑤	700②	700②	47–50	①
3.0L	.039–.043	1-2-3-4-5-6	15	15	⑤	700②	700②	47–50	①

BTDC — Before Top Dead Center
① — Equipped w/hydraulic lash adjusters.
② — Non-adjustable.
③ — Remove rear seat cushion, then the protector. Disconnect fuel pump connector. Start engine & let run until it stops naturally, then turn ignition to Off. Connect fuel pump connector, install protector & rear seat cushion. Remove cover from service valve on fuel rail. Connect suitable fuel pressure test gauge to service valve. Switch ignition in Run position, then use scan tool to activate fuel pump & pressurize system.
④ — Before disconnecting wires from coil unit, determine location of ignition wires in coil towers, as position may have been altered from that outlined.
⑤ — Equipped w/crankshaft position sensor.

FRONT WHEEL ALIGNMENT SPECIFICATIONS

Year	Camber Angle, Degrees ①		Toe, Inch③		Caster, Degrees		Ball Joint Wear
	Limits	Desired	Limits	Desired	Limits	Desired	
2004–05	-.50 to +.05	0	-.12 to +.12	0	+2.50 to +3.50	+3.00	②

① — Not adjustable.

② — Refer to "Ball Joint Inspection" in "Front Suspension & Steering."

③ — Toe in (+); toe out (-).

REAR WHEEL ALIGNMENT SPECIFICATIONS

Year	Camber, Degrees			Total Toe, Inch①	
	Limits	Desired	Max. LH/RH Deviation	Limits	Desired
2004–05	-1.83 to -.83	-1.33	.50	0 to +.24	+.12

① — Toe in (+); toe out (-).

VEHICLE RIDE HEIGHT SPECIFICATIONS

Model	Year	Body Style	Manufacturer's Original Tire Size	Measurement Points & Specifications[2]					
				Front			Rear		
				Dim., [3]	Specification		Dim., [3]	Specification	
					Inches	mm		Inches	mm
Sebring Coupe	2004–05	2.4L	[1]	G	6.20	157	H	6.20	157
		3.0L	[1]	G	5.90	150	H	5.90	150
Stratus Coupe	2004–05	2.4L	[1]	G	6.20	157	H	6.20	157
		3.0L	[1]	G	5.90	150	H	5.90	150

G Dim — Ground to Front Rocker Panel

H Dim — Ground to Rear Rocker Panel

[1] — See door sticker or inside of glove box for manufacturer's original tire size specifications.

[2] — Measurement is w/fuel, radiator coolant & engine oil full, spare tire, jack, hand tools & mats in designated positions & tires properly inflated.

[3] — Refer to **Fig. A**.

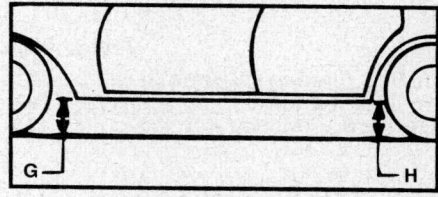

CRQ121

Fig. A   Dimensions G & H

FLUID CAPACITIES & COOLING SYSTEM DATA

Year	Engine	Coolant Capacity, Qts.	Coolant Type	Radiator Cap Relief Pressure, Lbs.	Thermo. Opening Temp. °F	Fuel Tank Capacity, Gals.	Engine Oil Refill, Qts.[1]	Transaxle Oil, Qts.	
								Manual	Auto.
2004	2.4L	7.4	Ethylene Glycol	11–15	190	16.4	4.2	2.3	8.1
	3.0L	8.5	Ethylene Glycol	11–15	190	16.4	4.2	3.0	8.5
2005	2.4L	8.4	Long Life	14–18	190	16.3	4.2	2.3	8.1
	3.0L	9.6	Long Life	14–18	190	16.3	4.2	3.0	8.9

[1] — Capacity without oil filter. Add additional 1/2 quart when changing filter.

LUBRICANT DATA

Year	Lubricant Type			
	Transaxle		Power Steering	Brake System
	Manual	Automatic		
2004–05	API GL-4	Diamond ATF SP-III or SP-IIM	ATF 59602	DOT 3 or 4

Electrical

NOTE: On Air Bag Equipped Models, Refer To "Air Bag System Precautions" Located In The Front Of This Manual For System Disarming & Arming Procedures.

NOTE: Refer To "Computer Relearn Procedures" Located In The Front Of This Manual When Battery Power To The Computer Has Been Interrupted.

INDEX

	Page No.		Page No.		Page No.
Air Bag System (Volume 2)	4-1	Distributor, Replace	1-4	Precautions	1-4
Air Conditioning	8-1	3.0L Engine	1-4	Air Bag Systems	1-4
Alternator, Replace	1-4	Evaporator Case, Replace	1-5	Battery Ground Cable	1-4
2.4L Engine	1-4	Evaporator Core, Replace	1-5	Radio, Replace	1-5
3.0L Engine	1-4	Fuel Pump Relay Location	1-4	Speed Controls (Volume 2)	2-1
Alternators	11-1	Fuse Panel & Flasher Location	1-4	Starter Motors	10-1
Blower Motor, Replace	1-5	Heater Core, Replace	1-5	Starter, Replace	1-4
Coil Pack, Replace	1-4	Ignition Lock, Replace	1-4	Steering Columns	12-1
2.4L Engine	1-4	Ignition Switch, Replace	1-4	Steering Wheel, Replace	1-5
Cooling Fans	9-1	Instrument Cluster, Replace	1-5	Wiper Motor, Replace	1-5
Cruise Control (Volume 2)	2-1	Multi-Function Switch, Replace	1-5	Wiper Systems (Volume 2)	3-1
Dash Gauges (Volume 2)	1-1	Neutral Safety Switch, Replace	1-5		
Dash Panel Service (Volume 2)	5-1	Passive Restraint Systems (Volume 2)	4-1		

PRECAUTIONS

Air Bag Systems

Refer to "Air Bag System Precautions" in the front of this manual for system disarming and arming procedures.

Battery Ground Cable

Prior to service, disconnect battery ground cable and isolate as required.

FUSE PANEL & FLASHER LOCATION

The engine compartment fuse panel is located on the lefthand side of the engine compartment. The interior fuse panel is located behind the lefthand side of the instrument panel. The turn signal and hazard flashers are incorporated into the ETACS-ECU.

FUEL PUMP RELAY LOCATION

The fuel pump relay is located behind the lefthand side of the instrument panel, lefthand of the steering column, **Fig. 1.**

STARTER

REPLACE

1. Remove air cleaner assembly.
2. **On models equipped with 2.4L engines,** remove cover from starter.
3. **On all engines,** disconnect starter electrical connectors.

4. Remove starter mounting bolts, then starter.
5. Reverse procedure to install, noting the following:
   a. **Torque** starter mounting bolts to 21–25 ft. lbs.
   b. **Torque** battery cable to solenoid retaining bolt to 36–52 inch lbs.

ALTERNATOR

REPLACE

2.4L Engine

1. Remove oil pressure hose and tube assembly clamp bolts, **Fig. 2.**
2. Remove oil return tube assembly clamp bolt.
3. Remove drive belts, then water pump pulley.
4. Remove oil level gauge unit.
5. Disconnect alternator electrical connector.
6. Remove alternator brace, then alternator.
7. Reverse procedure to install. **Torque** alternator mounting bolts to 26–40 ft. lbs.

3.0L Engine

1. Remove drive belt, then oil level gauge unit, **Fig. 3.**
2. Disconnect alternator electrical connector.
3. Remove alternator.
4. Reverse procedure to install. **Torque** alternator mounting bolt to 26–40 ft. lbs.

DISTRIBUTOR

REPLACE

3.0L Engine

1. Disconnect distributor electrical connector, then spark plug wires.
2. Remove intake manifold plenum as outlined in "Intake Manifold, Replace" in the "3.0L Engine" section.
3. Remove distributor assembly.
4. Reverse procedure to install, aligning mating marks on distributor housing and coupling.

COIL PACK

REPLACE

2.4L Engine

1. Remove spark plug wires.
2. Remove coil pack mounting bolts, then coil pack.
3. Reverse procedure to install. **Torque** mounting bolts to 70–104 inch lbs.

IGNITION LOCK

REPLACE

Refer to "Ignition Switch, Replace" for ignition lock replacement.

IGNITION SWITCH

REPLACE

1. Remove steering column upper and lower covers, **Fig. 4.**
2. Remove key ring antenna and key reminder switch.

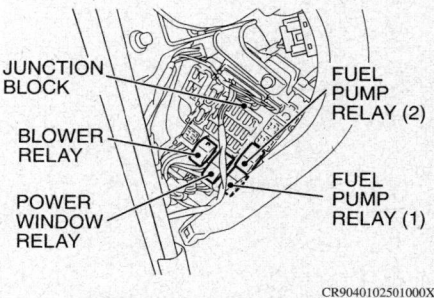

Fig. 1 Fuel pump relay location

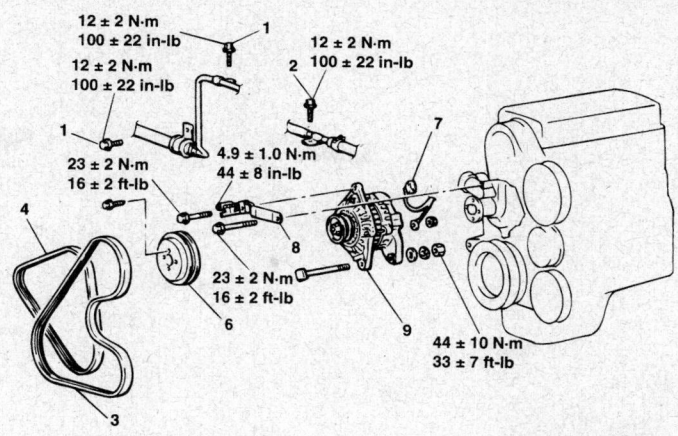

Fig. 2 Alternator replacement. 2.4L engine

3. Insert key into cylinder lock and turn to ACC position, then cylinder, using a suitable Phillips head screwdriver.
4. Remove ignition switch.
5. Reverse procedure to install, noting the following:
   a. If a new ignition key is used it must be registered using scan tool No. MB9911502, or equivalent.
   b. Follow scan tool manufactures instructions for key registration.

NEUTRAL SAFETY SWITCH
REPLACE

The neutral safety switch is located at the lower lefthand side of the transaxle housing, under the air cleaner assembly, **Fig. 5.**
1. Disconnect neutral safety switch electrical connector.
2. Remove switch from transaxle case.
3. Reverse procedure to install.

MULTI-FUNCTION SWITCH
REPLACE

1. Remove steering wheel as outlined in "Steering Wheel, Replace."
2. Remove instrument panel lower cover.
3. Remove upper and lower steering column cover.
4. Remove multi-function switch.
5. Reverse procedure to install.

STEERING WHEEL
REPLACE

1. Remove air bag module.
2. Remove steering wheel using suitable puller.
3. Reverse procedure to install. **Torque** steering wheel nut to 26–36 ft. lbs.

INSTRUMENT CLUSTER
REPLACE

1. Remove steering wheel as outlined in "Steering Wheel, Replace."

2. Remove meter hood from instrument panel.
3. Remove instrument cluster, disconnect electrical connectors and vehicle speed sensor.
4. Reverse procedure to install.

RADIO
REPLACE

1. Remove center panel assembly.
2. Remove radio, tape and/or CD player.
3. Remove radio bracket.
4. Reverse procedure to install.

WIPER MOTOR
REPLACE

1. Remove wiper arm and blade assembly.
2. Remove front deck garnish/cowl screen.
3. Remove wiper motor and link assembly, then disconnect motor electrical connector.
4. Reverse procedure to install.

BLOWER MOTOR
REPLACE

1. Remove glove compartment.
2. Remove air purifier assembly.
3. Remove joint duct, then resistor.
4. Remove blower motor assembly.
5. Reverse procedure to install.

HEATER CORE
REPLACE

1. Remove driver's side front undercover panel, center panel assembly, glove compartment and passenger's side undercover panel using suitable flat-bladed tool.
2. Remove joint duct assembly.

3. **On models equipped with A/C,** proceed as follows:
   a. Remove automatic compressor controller.
   b. Recover refrigerant as outlined in "Air Conditioning."
   c. Remove A/C pipe, expansion valve, then the evaporator core.
   d. Remove drain hose.
4. **On all models,** drain coolant into suitable container.
5. Remove heater hoses.
6. Remove radio as outlined in "Radio, Replace."
7. Remove heater control assembly.
8. Remove steering wheel as outlined in "Steering Wheel, Replace."
9. Remove floor console in numbered sequence, **Fig. 6.**
10. Remove instrument panel as outlined in "Dash Panel Service."
11. Remove front deck crossmember, then foot duct.
12. Remove heater/cooler unit, then heater core.
13. Reverse procedure to install.

EVAPORATOR CASE
REPLACE

Refer to "Heater Core, Replace" for evaporator case replacement.

EVAPORATOR CORE
REPLACE

Refer to "Heater Core, Replace" for evaporator core replacement.

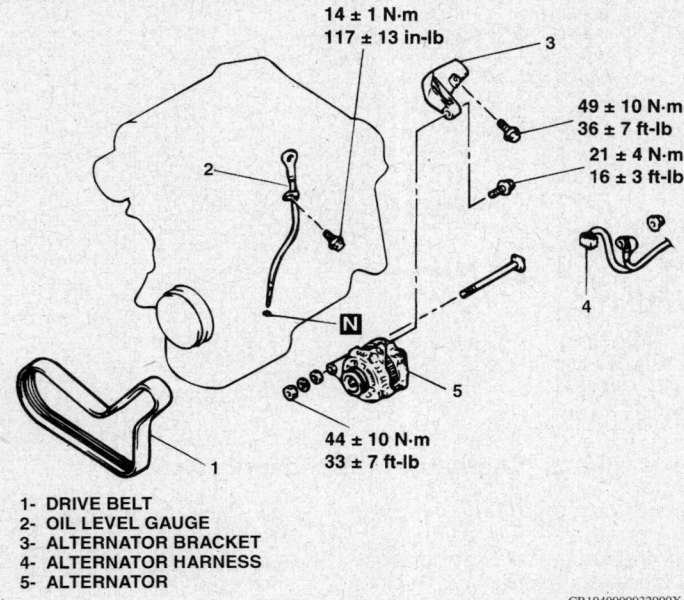

14 ± 1 N·m
117 ± 13 in-lb

49 ± 10 N·m
36 ± 7 ft-lb

21 ± 4 N·m
16 ± 3 ft-lb

44 ± 10 N·m
33 ± 7 ft-lb

1- DRIVE BELT
2- OIL LEVEL GAUGE
3- ALTERNATOR BRACKET
4- ALTERNATOR HARNESS
5- ALTERNATOR

CR1040000032000X

Fig. 3   Alternator replacement. 3.0L engine

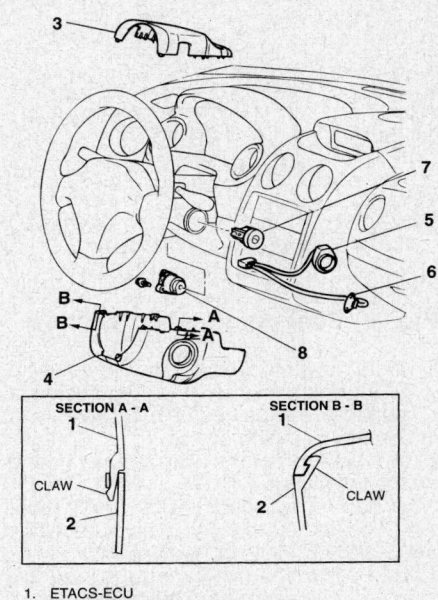

SECTION A - A

SECTION B - B

CLAW

CLAW

1. ETACS-ECU
2. IMMOBILIZER-ECU
3. COLUMN COVER UPPER
4. COLUMN COVER LOWER
5. KEY RING ANTENNA
6. KEY REMINDER SWITCH
7. STEERING LOCK CYLINDER
8. IGNITION SWITCH

CR1040100034000X

Fig. 4   Ignition switch replacement

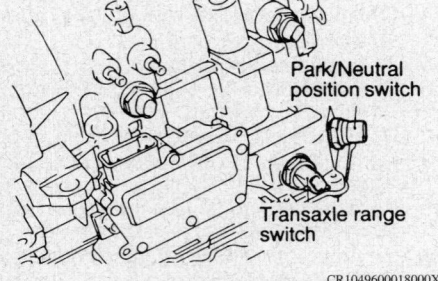

Park/Neutral
position switch

Transaxle range
switch

CR1049600018000X

Fig. 5   Neutral safety switch

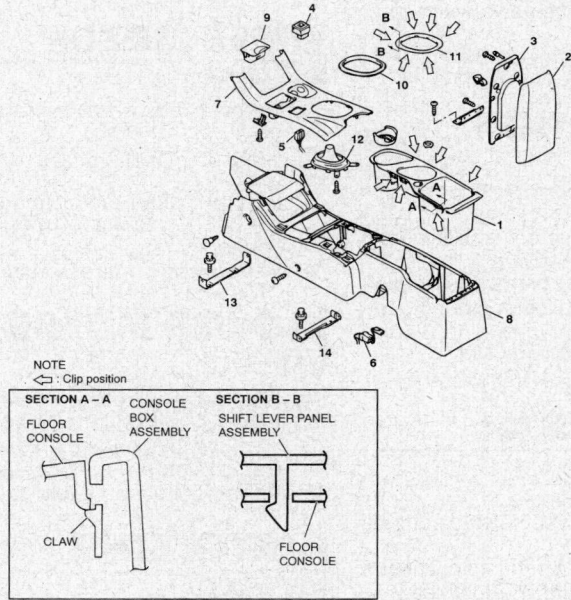

NOTE
⟵ : Clip position

SECTION A – A

CONSOLE
BOX
ASSEMBLY

FLOOR
CONSOLE

CLAW

SECTION B – B

SHIFT LEVER PANEL
ASSEMBLY

FLOOR
CONSOLE

1. CONSOLE BOX ASSEMBLY
2. CONSOLE LID
3. CONSOLE LID COVER
4. DOOR MIRROR CONTROL SWITCH
5. DOOR MIRROR CONTROL SWITCH HARNESS
6. ACCCESSARY SOCKET HARNESS
7. FLOOR CONSOLE INDICATOR PANEL
8. FLOOR CONSOLE
9. ASHTRAY
10. SHIFT LEVER PANEL ASSEMBLY <M/T>
11. GARNISH <A/T>
12. SHIFT LEVER BOOT <M/T>
13. FLOOR CONSOLE BRACKET A
14. FLOOR CONSOLE BRACKET B

CR9140000071000X

Fig. 6   Floor console removal

2.4L Engine

NOTE: On Air Bag Equipped Models, Refer To "Air Bag System Precautions" Located In The Front Of This Manual For System Disarming & Arming Procedures.

NOTE: Refer To "Computer Relearn Procedures" Located In The Front Of This Manual When Battery Power To The Computer Has Been Interrupted.

INDEX

	Page No.
Belt Tension Data	1-10
Camshaft, Replace	1-9
Compression Pressure	1-7
Cooling System Bleed	1-10
Crankshaft Rear Oil Seal, Replace	1-10
Crankshaft Seal, Replace	1-10
Cylinder Head, Replace	1-8
Engine Rebuilding Specifications	21-1
Engine, Replace	1-7
Engine Mount, Replace	1-7
Exhaust Manifold, Replace	1-8

	Page No.
Front Cover, Replace	1-8
Fuel Filter, Replace	1-11
Fuel Pump, Replace	1-11
Intake Manifold, Replace	1-7
Main & Rod Bearings	1-10
Oil Pan, Replace	1-10
Oil Pump, Replace	1-10
Oil Pump Service	1-10
Piston & Rod Assembly	1-9
Precautions	1-7
Air Bag Systems	1-7
Battery Ground Cable	1-7
Fuel System Pressure Relief	1-7

	Page No.
Radiator, Replace	1-11
Rocker Arms, Replace	1-8
Thermostat, Replace	1-10
Tightening Specifications	1-12
Timing Belt, Replace	1-8
Front	1-8
Installation	1-8
Removal	1-8
Rear	1-9
Installation	1-9
Removal	1-9
Water Pump, Replace	1-11

PRECAUTIONS

Air Bag Systems

Refer to "Air Bag System Precautions" in the front of this manual for system disarming and arming procedures.

Battery Ground Cable

Prior to service, disconnect battery ground cable and isolate as required.

Fuel System Pressure Relief

1. Remove fuel pump relay.
2. Start engine and let it run until it stops, then turn ignition switch off.
3. Reconnect fuel pump relay.

COMPRESSION PRESSURE

Perform compression test with engine at normal operating temperature, spark plugs removed, crankshaft position sensor disconnected and throttle wide open. Standard compression pressure at cranking speed is 185 psi. The minimum compression pressure is 139 psi with a maximum variation between cylinders of 14 psi.

ENGINE MOUNT

REPLACE

1. Hold engine with a chain block or similar tool.
2. Remove reserve tank.
3. Raise and support engine to remove weight from engine mount bracket using a suitable floor jack.
4. Remove engine mount insulator mounting bolt, mount bracket then stopper.
5. Reverse procedure to install, tightening to specifications.

ENGINE

REPLACE

1. Release fuel pressure as outlined in "Precautions."
2. Mark and remove hood.
3. Remove strut tower bar.
4. Drain engine oil into suitable container.
5. Remove radiator as outlined in "Radiator, Replace."
6. Remove air cleaner, then front exhaust pipe.
7. Disconnect accelerator cable, then purge hose.
8. Disconnect required vacuum hose connections.
9. Disconnect the following electrical connections:
   a. Ignition coil.
   b. Fuel injectors.
   c. Ignition failure sensor.
   d. Manifold differential pressure sensor.
   e. Throttle position sensor.
   f. Heated oxygen sensor.
   g. Capacitor.
   h. Engine coolant temperature sensor.
   i. Camshaft position sensor.
   j. Knock sensor.
   k. Engine coolant temperature gauge unit.
   l. Idle air control motor.
   m. Evaporative emission purge solenoid valve.
   n. EGR solenoid valve.
   o. Alternator.
   p. Fuel high pressure hose.
   q. Fuel return hose.
   r. Oil pressure switch.
   s. Crankshaft position sensor.
   t. Power steering pressure switch.
10. Disconnect high pressure fuel hose, then fuel return hose.
11. Remove oil dipstick and guide.
12. Remove pressure hose, then heater hose.
13. Remove drive belts.
14. Remove power steering pump with hoses attached and position aside.
15. Remove A/C compressor with lines attached and position aside.
16. Remove transaxle as in **MOTOR's "Domestic Transmission, In-Vehicle Service" manual** or **"Transmission Service DVD."**
17. Support engine with jack and hold engine with chain block or similar support tool.
18. Place jack under engine oil pan with piece of wood in between, then raise engine so that weight of engine is no longer on engine mount bracket.
19. Remove engine mount stopper, then engine.
20. Reverse procedure to install. Tighten all fasteners to specifications.

INTAKE MANIFOLD

REPLACE

1. Release fuel pressure as outlined in "Precautions."
2. Drain engine coolant into suitable container, then remove air cleaner assembly.

TIMING BELT SIDE

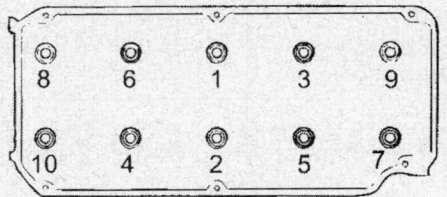

Fig. 1   Cylinder head bolt removal

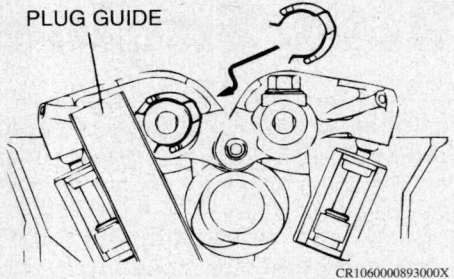

Fig. 2   Rocker arm shaft spring installation

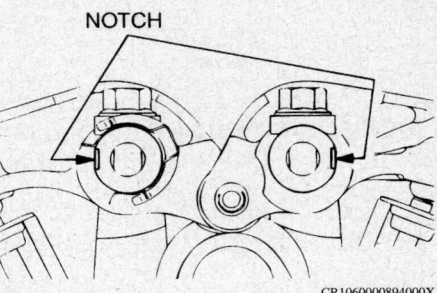

Fig. 3   Rocker arm shaft notch direction

3. Disconnect accelerator cable.
4. Disconnect throttle position sensor and idle air control motor electrical connectors.
5. Remove throttle body assembly.
6. Disconnect purge hose, then brake booster vacuum hose.
7. Disconnect ignition coil, fuel injectors, ignition failure sensor and manifold differential pressure sensor electrical connectors.
8. Disconnect evaporative emission purge solenoid valve and EGR solenoid valve connectors.
9. Disconnect high pressure and return fuel hoses.
10. Remove oil dipstick and guide.
11. Remove PCV hose and fuel hose.
12. Remove fuel rail, injector and fuel pressure regulator.
13. Remove insulator, then vacuum pipe.
14. Remove EGR valve.
15. Remove intake manifold.
16. Reverse procedure to install.

EXHAUST MANIFOLD
REPLACE

1. Remove front heated oxygen sensor.
2. Remove heat protector, then engine hanger.
3. Remove exhaust manifold and bracket.
4. Reverse procedure to install.

CYLINDER HEAD
REPLACE

1. Release fuel pressure as outlined in "Precautions," then drain cooling system.
2. Remove strut tower brace, then air cleaner assembly.
3. Remove thermostat case assembly.
4. Remove front exhaust pipe.
5. Disconnect accelerator cable.
6. Disconnect purge hose, then brake booster vacuum hose connections.
7. Disconnect the following electrical connectors:
   a. Ignition coil and injectors.
   b. Manifold differential pressure sensor.
   c. Throttle position sensor.
   d. Heated oxygen sensor.
   e. Capacitor.
   f. Engine coolant temperature sensor.
   g. Camshaft position sensor.
   h. Idle air control motor.

i. Evaporative emission purge solenoid valve.
j. EGR solenoid.
8. Disconnect fuel pressure and return hoses.
9. Remove oil dipstick and guide.
10. Remove spark plug wires, then ignition coil.
11. Remove upper radiator hose.
12. Disconnect PCV hose.
13. Remove rocker cover, then spark plug guide oil seal.
14. Remove timing belt as outlined in "Timing Belt, Replace."
15. Remove power steering pressure switch.
16. Remove power steering pump with hose attached and position aside.
17. Remove exhaust manifold bracket.
18. Loosen bolts in two or three steps using cylinder head bolt removal tool No. MB991654, or equivalent, in numbered sequence, **Fig. 1**.
19. Remove cylinder head, do not damage plug guides when removing bolts.
20. Reverse procedure to install, noting the following:
   a. Measure cylinder head bolts, if length below head of bolt is more than 3.91 inches, replace bolt.
   b. Tighten cylinder head bolts in five steps using reverse order of cylinder head bolt removal outlined in **Fig. 1**. First step, **torque** bolts to 55–61 ft. lbs. Second step; fully loosen bolts in sequence. Third step, **torque** bolts to 14–16 ft. lbs. Fourth step, tighten an additional 90.° Fifth step, tighten an additional 90.°

ROCKER ARMS
REPLACE

1. Remove breather hose, then PCV hose and valve.
2. Remove valve cover.
3. Hold lash adjuster in place using lash adjuster holding tool No. MD998443, or equivalent, to remove rocker arm shafts.
4. Remove rocker arm shaft springs, then rocker arms.
5. Remove lash adjusters.
6. Reverse procedure to install, noting the following:
   a. Install rocker arm shaft spring to intake side rocker arm shaft, **Fig. 2**.
   b. Ensure notch in end of rocker arm

shaft is positioned as outlined, **Fig. 3**.

FRONT COVER
REPLACE

1. Remove drive belts.
2. Remove water pump pulley, then crankshaft pulley.
3. Remove timing belt upper cover, then lower cover.
4. Reverse procedure to install.

TIMING BELT
REPLACE
Front
REMOVAL

1. Remove front cover as outlined in "Front Cover, Replace."
2. Turn crankshaft clockwise to align camshaft sprocket timing marks, **Fig. 4**.
3. Loosen timing belt tensioner bolt.
4. If old timing belt is to be used, mark flat side of belt with an arrow to indicate clockwise rotating direction.
5. Move tensioner pulley toward water pump side, then remove timing belt.

INSTALLATION

1. Align timing marks on camshaft sprocket, crankshaft sprocket and oil pump sprocket, **Fig. 5**.
2. Remove cylinder block plug and insert a suitable .3 inch Phillips head screw driver, **Fig. 6**.
3. Ensure screwdriver goes in 2.4 inches or more. If screwdriver will only go in 1.0 inch, turn sprocket one revolution and insert screw driver again. **Do not remove screw driver until timing belt is installed.**
4. To eliminate belt tension slack, install timing belt in following order; over crankshaft sprocket, oil pump sprocket, then camshaft sprocket.
5. Set tension pulley so pin holes are at bottom, then press lightly against timing belt. Temporarily tighten bolt.
6. Adjust timing belt tension as follows:
   a. Remove rubber plug from rear of timing belt cover, then tighten adjusting screw tool No. MD998738,

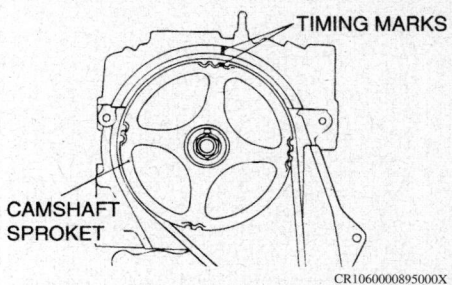

Fig. 4 Camshaft sprocket timing marks

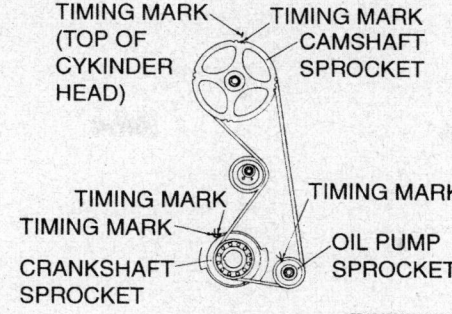

Fig. 5 Timing marks

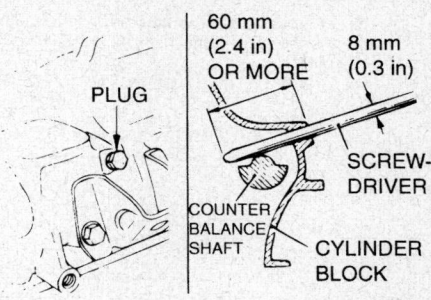

Fig. 6 Cylinder block plug location

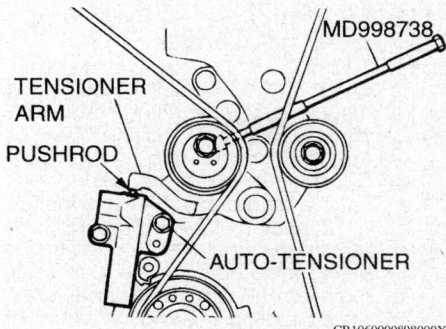

Fig. 7 Adjusting screw tool installation

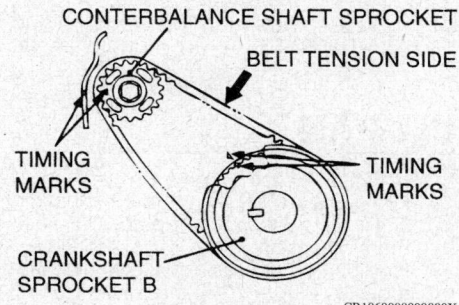

Fig. 8 Counterbalance shaft sprocket & crankshaft sprocket timing marks

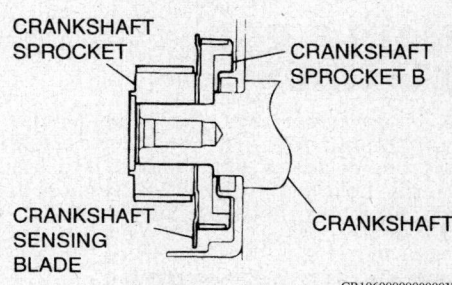

Fig. 9 Crankshaft sensing blade installation

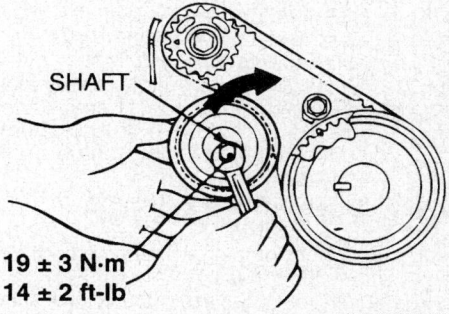

Fig. 10 Timing belt tensioner adjustment

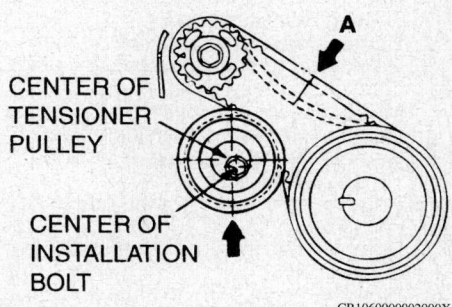

Fig. 11 Timing belt deflection

or equivalent, by hand until tensioner arm is touching auto-tensioner pushrod, **Fig. 7.**

b. Turn crankshaft ¼ turn counterclockwise, then turn clockwise until timing marks are aligned.

c. Loosen tensioner pulley bolt, then use tensioner pulley socket tool No. MD998767, or equivalent, to **torque** bolt to 32–40 ft. lbs., while applying 31 inch lbs., of tension to belt.

d. Turn crankshaft two revolutions clockwise to align timing marks.

e. After 15 minutes, measure protrusion of auto tensioner pushrod. Protrusion should be .15–.18 inch. If protrusion is not as specified, repeat steps A through D.

7. Ensure timing marks on each sprocket are aligned.

8. Install front cover.

Rear
REMOVAL

1. Remove front timing belt as outlined in "Timing Belt, Replace."
2. Remove crankshaft sprocket using crankshaft holding tool No. MB991367, or equivalent.
3. Remove crankshaft sensing blade.
4. Remove rear timing belt tensioner, then rear timing belt.

INSTALLATION

1. Install rear timing belt crankshaft sprocket, ensure timing marks are aligned, **Fig. 8.**
2. Install rear timing belt, ensure there is no slack in belt.
3. Install crankshaft sensing as outlined, **Fig. 9.**
4. Adjust timing belt tension as follows:
   a. Temporarily fix timing belt tensioner so center of pulley is to lefthand and above center of mounting bolt.
   b. Holding timing belt tensioner up in direction of arrow, **Fig. 10,** apply pressure on timing belt so belt is taut. **Torque** bolt to 12–16 ft. lbs.
   c. Ensure timing belt deflection at point (A) is .2–.3 inch, **Fig. 11.**

CAMSHAFT
REPLACE

1. Remove air cleaner assembly.
2. Remove rocker arms as outlined in "Rocker Arms, Replace."

3. Remove camshaft position sensor support.
4. Remove camshaft position sensing cylinder, then camshaft sprocket.
5. Remove spark plug guide oil seal.
6. Remove camshaft sprocket using end yoke holder tool No. MB990767 and crankshaft pulley holding tool No. MD998719, or equivalents.
7. Remove camshaft oil seal, then camshaft.
8. Reverse procedure to install, noting the following:
   a. Install camshaft oil seal using oil seal installer tool No. MD998713, or equivalent.

PISTON & ROD ASSEMBLY

The front mark on piston must face timing belt side of engine. Connecting rods and caps must be installed in original positions. **Torque** bolts to 13–15 ft. lbs., then an additional 90–94°.

CRANKSHAFT JOURNAL OUT-SIDE DIAMETER		CYLINDER BLOCK BEARING BORE	CRANKSHAFT BEARING	CRANKSHAFT BEARING FOR NO.3
IDENTIFICA-TION COLOR	SIZE mm (in)	IDENTIFICATION MARK	IDENTIFICATION MARK OR COLOR	IDENTIFICATION MARK OR COLOR
Yellow	56.994 - 57.000 (2.2439 - 2.2441)	0	1 or Green	0 or Black
		1	2 or Yellow	1 or Green
		2	3 or None	2 or Yellow
None	56.988 - 56.994 (2.2436 - 2.2439)	0	2 or Yellow	1 or Green
		1	3 or None	2 or Yellow
		2	4 or Blue	3 or None
White	56.982 - 56.988 (2.2438 - 2.2436)	0	3 or None	2 or Yellow
		1	4 or Blue	3 or None
		2	5 or Red	4 or Blue

CR1060000905000X

Fig. 12 Main bearing selection chart

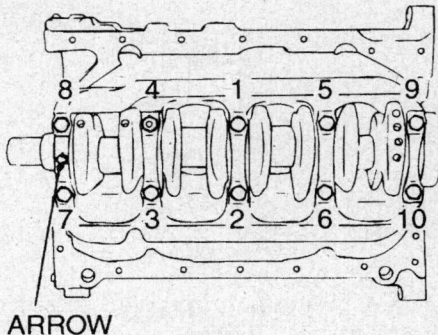

ARROW

CR1060000906000X

Fig. 13 Main bearing tightening sequence

MAIN & ROD BEARINGS

If bearing replacement is required, measure crankshaft journal diameter and select appropriate bearing from the chart, **Fig. 12**. **Torque** bolts to 17–19 ft. lbs., in sequence, **Fig. 13**, then an additional 90°.

CRANKSHAFT SEAL
REPLACE

1. Remove front timing belt as outlined in "Timing Belt, Replace."
2. Remove crankshaft position sensor.
3. Remove crankshaft sprocket using crankshaft spanner tool No. MB991367, or equivalent.
4. Remove crankshaft sensing blade.
5. Remove rear timing belt as outlined in "Timing Belt, Replace."
6. Remove rear timing belt crankshaft sprocket.
7. Remove key, then the crankshaft front oil seal.
8. Reverse procedure to install, noting the following:
   a. Apply engine oil to entire inside diameter of oil seal lip.
   b. Press in oil seal using crankshaft oil seal installer tool No. MD998375, or equivalent, until it is flush with front case.
   c. Install crankshaft sensing blade, **Fig. 9**.

CRANKSHAFT REAR OIL SEAL
REPLACE

1. Remove oil pan as outlined under "Oil Pan, Replace."
2. Remove transaxle as outlined in **MO-TOR's "Domestic Transmission, In-Vehicle Service" manual or "Transmission Service DVD."**
3. Remove flywheel, then crankshaft bushing.
4. Remove crankshaft rear oil seal.
5. Reverse procedure to install, noting the following:
   a. Apply a small amount of engine oil to entire inside diameter of oil seal lip.
   b. Tap in oil seal using oil seal installer

tool Nos. MB990938 and MD998776, or equivalents, **Fig. 14**.

OIL PAN
REPLACE

1. Drain engine oil, then remove dipstick.
2. Remove front exhaust pipe, then bell housing cover.
3. Remove oil pan using oil pan removal tool No. MD998727, or equivalent.
4. Reverse procedure to install, noting the following:
   a. Apply sealant part No. MD970389, or equivalent, around gasket surface of oil pan.
   b. Install oil pan within 15 minutes of applying sealant.
   c. Allow sealant to dry at least one hour before starting engine.

OIL PUMP
REPLACE

1. Remove oil filter, then oil pressure switch.
2. Remove oil pan as outlined in "Oil Pan, Replace."
3. Remove oil screen, then oil screen gasket.
4. Remove plug on front case using plug wrench tool No. MD998162 and plug wrench retainer tool No. MD998783, or equivalents.
5. Remove plug on side of cylinder block.
6. Insert a suitable screw driver to lock counterbalance shaft, then remove flange bolt.
7. Remove relief plug, gasket, relief spring and plunger.
8. Remove oil filter bracket, then gasket.
9. Remove oil pump front case assembly.
10. Remove oil pump cover.
11. Remove oil pump driven gear, then drive gear and crankshaft front oil seal.
12. Remove oil pump oil seal and counterbalance shaft oil seal, then front case.
13. Remove righthand and lefthand counterbalance shafts.
14. Remove counterbalance shaft front bearing using bearing puller tool No. MD998371, or equivalent.
15. Remove righthand and lefthand rear counterbalance shaft bearings.
16. Reverse procedure to install, noting the following:
   a. Install righthand rear counterbal-

ance shaft bearing ensuring oil holes are aligned, using bearing installer tool No. MD998705, or equivalent.
   b. Install lefthand rear counterbalance shaft bearing using bearing installer stopper tool No. MB991603, or equivalent installed on cylinder block.
   c. Install front counterbalance shaft bearing using bearing installer tool No. MD998705, or equivalent, ensuring oil holes are aligned.
   d. Install crankshaft front oil seal using oil seal installer tool No. MD998375, or equivalent.
   e. Ensure oil pump gear marks are aligned, **Fig. 15**.
   f. Install oil pump case assembly using crankshaft front oil seal guide tool No. MD998285, or equivalent set on front end of crankshaft.

OIL PUMP SERVICE

1. Ensure oil pump gears rotate smoothly with no looseness.
2. Inspect for ridge wear on contact surface between front case and gear surface of oil pump cover.
3. Inspect gear side clearance. Clearance should be .004–.006 inch for drive gear and .003–.004 inch for driven gear.

BELT TENSION DATA

Apply 22 lbs., of force to middle of belt between alternator pulley and water pump pulley. Deflection should be .26–.35 inch.

COOLING SYSTEM BLEED

Start and run engine until it reaches operating temperature. Accelerate engine repeatedly to 3000 RPM. After engine has cooled down remove radiator cap and fill to top.

THERMOSTAT
REPLACE

1. Drain coolant into suitable container.
2. Remove air cleaner assembly.

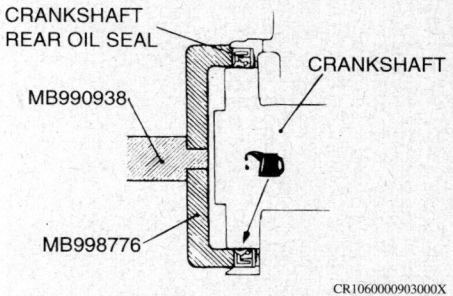

Fig. 14 Crankshaft rear oil seal installation

3. Disconnect lower radiator hose, then water inlet fitting.
4. Remove thermostat.
5. Reverse procedure to install. Install thermostat with jiggle valve facing straight up.

WATER PUMP
REPLACE

1. Drain coolant into suitable container.
2. Remove timing belt tensioner as outlined in "Timing Belt, Replace."
3. Remove alternator brace as outlined in "Alternator, Replace" in "Electrical" section.
4. Remove water pump assembly.
5. Reverse procedure to install.

RADIATOR
REPLACE

1. Drain coolant into suitable container,

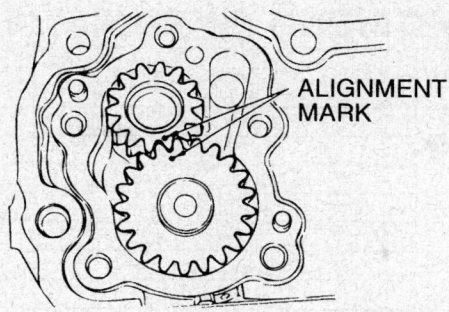

Fig. 15 Oil pump gear alignment marks

then disconnect radiator hoses.
2. Remove reserve tank assembly.
3. **On models equipped with automatic transaxles,** disconnect transaxle cooler lines.
4. **On all models,** remove radiator supports, then radiator.
5. Remove radiator fan motor assembly.
6. Reverse procedure to install.

FUEL PUMP
REPLACE

1. Remove rear seat cushion, then access plate.
2. Relieve fuel pressure as outlined in "Precautions."
3. Disconnect fuel hose and electrical connector.
4. Remove fuel pump module using tank cap wrench tool No. MB991480, or equivalent.

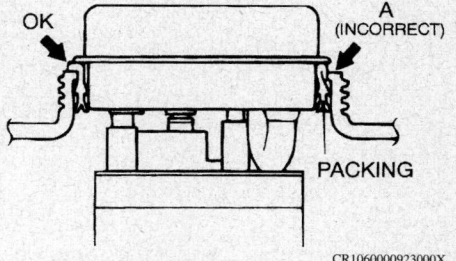

Fig. 16 Fuel pump packing installation

5. Reverse procedure to install, noting the following:
   a. Install packing to fuel tank **Fig. 16,** then install fuel pump module.
   b. Align mating mark on fuel pump module with mark on fuel tank.
   c. Tighten to specifications.

FUEL FILTER
REPLACE

1. Remove fuel pump as outlined in "Fuel Pump, Replace."
2. Remove thermistor case, then fuel gage unit.
3. Remove packing, then reservoir cup.
4. Remove pump support assembly.
5. Remove electrical harness, then lock bracket.
6. Remove fuel pump, then fuel filter.
7. Reverse procedure to install.

TIGHTENING SPECIFICATIONS

Year	Component	Torque Ft. Lbs.
2004–05	Auto-Tensioner Attaching Bolt	14–20
	Camshaft Position Sensor	10–11
	Camshaft Sprocket	58–72
	Connecting Rod Bearing Cap	③
	Crankshaft Pulley	14–22
	Crankshaft Sprocket	⑤
	Cylinder Head	②
	Drive Plate	94–102
	Engine Mount (M12x74)	56–74
	Engine Mount (M12x108)	51–69
	Engine Mount Bracket	56–72
	Exhaust Manifold	20–24
	Exhaust Manifold Bracket	22–30
	Flywheel (Manual Trans.)	95–101
	Front Case	15–19
	Ignition Coil Bolt	70–104①
	Intake Manifold Bolt	44–52①
	Intake Manifold Nut	12–16
	Intake Manifold Stay	21–23
	Main Bearing Cap	④
	Oil Filter Bracket	12–16
	Oil Pan	53–69①
	Oil Pan Drain Plug	25–33
	Oil Pump Cover	11–13
	Power Steering Pump	29–43
	Rocker Arm Shaft	21–25
	Rocker Cover	27–35
	Timing Belt Lower Cover	88–104①
	Timing Belt Tensioner	12–16
	Timing Belt Upper Cover	114–120①
	Water Pump Pulley	69–77

① — Inch lbs.
② — Refer to "Cylinder Head, Replace" for tightening procedures & specifications.
③ — Refer to "Piston & Rod Assembly" for tightening procedure & specifications.
④ — Refer to "Main & Rod Bearings" for tightening procedure & specifications.
⑤ — 2004 80–94 ft. lbs.; 2005 123 ft. lbs.

3.0L Engine

NOTE: On Air Bag Equipped Models, Refer To "Air Bag System Precautions" Located In The Front Of This Manual For System Disarming & Arming Procedures.

NOTE: Refer To "Computer Relearn Procedures" Located In The Front Of This Manual When Battery Power To The Computer Has Been Interrupted.

INDEX

	Page No.		Page No.		Page No.
Belt Tension Data	1-16	Engine Mount, Replace	1-13	Inspection	1-16
Camshaft, Replace	1-15	Exhaust Manifold, Replace	1-14	Precautions	1-13
Lefthand Bank	1-15	Front Cover, Replace	1-14	Air Bag Systems	1-13
Righthand Bank	1-15	Fuel Filter, Replace	1-16	Battery Ground Cable	1-13
Compression Pressure	1-13	Fuel Pump, Replace	1-16	Fuel System Pressure Relief	1-13
Cooling System Bleed	1-16	Intake Manifold, Replace	1-13	Radiator, Replace	1-16
Crankshaft Rear Oil Seal,		Intake Manifold Plenum,		Rocker Arms, Replace	1-14
Replace	1-15	Replace	1-13	Serpentine Drive Belt	1-16
Crankshaft Seal, Replace	1-15	Main & Rod Bearings	1-15	Thermostat, Replace	1-16
Front	1-15	Oil Pan, Replace	1-15	Tightening Specifications	1-18
Cylinder Head, Replace	1-14	Oil Pump, Replace	1-16	Timing Belt, Replace	1-14
Engine Rebuilding		Oil Pump Service	1-16	Installation	1-14
Specifications	21-1	Assemble	1-16	Removal	1-14
Engine, Replace	1-13	Disassemble	1-16	Water Pump, Replace	1-16

PRECAUTIONS

Air Bag Systems

Refer to "Air Bag System Precautions" in front of this manual for system disarming and arming procedures.

Battery Ground Cable

Prior to service, disconnect battery ground cable and isolate as required.

Fuel System Pressure Relief

1. Remove fuel pump relay.
2. Start engine and let it run until it stops naturally, then turn ignition to off position.
3. Reconnect fuel pump relay.

COMPRESSION PRESSURE

Perform compression pressure inspection with throttle valve wide open and crankshaft position sensor disconnected. Standard compression pressure is 119 psi at cranking speed. The minimum pressure is 83 psi with a maximum variance between cylinders of 14 psi.

ENGINE MOUNT

REPLACE

1. Place a suitable jack under engine, then raise jack enough to remove weight from engine mount.
2. Remove coolant reserve tank, then suction hose, **Fig. 1.**
3. Remove insulator mounting bolt, then mount bracket, **Fig. 1.**
4. Remove engine mount stopper, then dynamic damper, **Fig. 2.**
5. Reverse procedure to install.

ENGINE

REPLACE

1. Remove hood, then drain coolant into suitable container.
2. Release fuel pressure as outlined in "Precautions."
3. Remove strut tower brace, then air cleaner assembly.
4. Remove radiator reserve tank, then front exhaust pipe.
5. Disconnect accelerator cable.
6. Disconnect engine wiring harness electrical connections.
7. Disconnect high-pressure fuel hose, then return hose.
8. Disconnect heater hoses.
9. Remove drive belts.
10. Remove A/C compressor with lines attached, then position aside.
11. Remove power steering pump with hose attached, then position aside.
12. Remove engine mount stay.
13. Remove transaxle as outlined in **MOTOR's "Domestic Transmission, In-Vehicle Service" manual or "Transmission Service DVD."**
14. Remove engine mount bracket, then stopper.
15. Remove engine assembly.
16. Reverse procedure to install.

INTAKE MANIFOLD

REPLACE

1. Release fuel pressure as outlined in "Precautions."
2. Drain engine coolant into suitable container.
3. Remove air cleaner assembly, then throttle body.
4. Remove strut tower brace.
5. Disconnect engine wiring harness electrical connections.
6. Disconnect brake booster vacuum hose connection.
7. Remove EGR valve, then the pipe connection.
8. Remove power steering pump drive belt.
9. Remove power steering pump bracket stay.
10. Remove intake manifold plenum as outlined under "Intake Manifold Plenum, Replace."
11. Disconnect high-pressure fuel hose, then return hose.
12. Remove fuel rail, then fuel pressure regulator.
13. Remove timing belt lefthand and righthand and upper covers.
14. Remove intake manifold.
15. Reverse procedure to install, noting the following:
    a. Install intake gasket, **Fig. 3.**
    b. Tighten intake bolts to specification using sequence, **Fig. 4.**

INTAKE MANIFOLD PLENUM

REPLACE

1. Disconnect engine wiring harness

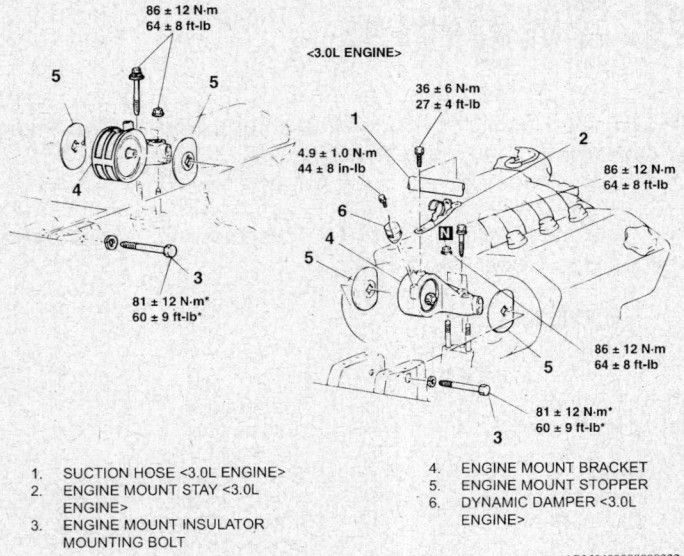

<3.0L ENGINE>

86 ± 12 N·m
64 ± 8 ft-lb

36 ± 6 N·m
27 ± 4 ft-lb

4.9 ± 1.0 N·m
44 ± 8 in-lb

86 ± 12 N·m
64 ± 8 ft-lb

81 ± 12 N·m*
60 ± 9 ft-lb*

86 ± 12 N·m
64 ± 8 ft-lb

81 ± 12 N·m*
60 ± 9 ft-lb*

1. SUCTION HOSE <3.0L ENGINE>
2. ENGINE MOUNT STAY <3.0L ENGINE>
3. ENGINE MOUNT INSULATOR MOUNTING BOLT
4. ENGINE MOUNT BRACKET
5. ENGINE MOUNT STOPPER
6. DYNAMIC DAMPER <3.0L ENGINE>

ARM0400000000322

Fig. 1   Engine mount replacement

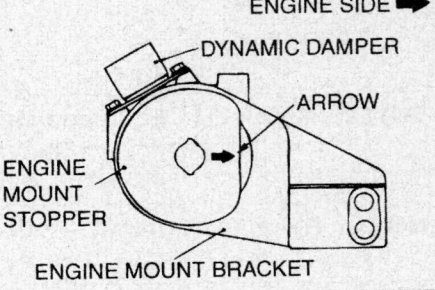

CR1060000907000X

Fig. 2   Engine mount stopper replacement

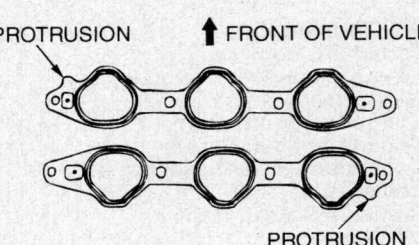

CR1060000908000X

Fig. 3   Intake manifold gasket installation

electrical connectors.
2. Disconnect engine vacuum connectors.
3. Remove EGR Valve, then EGR pipe connection.
4. Remove drive belts, then power steering bracket.
5. Remove front and rear intake manifold plenum stays.
6. Remove engine mount stay, then intake manifold plenum.
7. Reverse procedure to install noting the following:
   a. Install intake plenum gasket as outlined, **Fig. 5**.
   b. Tighten all nuts and bolts to specifications.

EXHAUST MANIFOLD
REPLACE

1. Remove front exhaust pipe.
2. Remove air cleaner assembly, then battery and battery tray.
3. Remove engine oil dipstick guide, then strut tower brace.
4. Remove lefthand bank manifold upper and lower heat shields.
5. Remove lefthand exhaust manifold, then EGR pipe.
6. Remove righthand bank manifold upper and lower heat shields.
7. Remove righthand exhaust manifold.
8. Reverse procedure to install.

CYLINDER HEAD
REPLACE

1. Drain engine coolant into suitable container.
2. Remove timing belt as outlined in "Timing Belt, Replace."
3. Remove alternator, then intake manifold as outlined in "Intake Manifold, Replace."
4. Remove exhaust manifold as outlined in "Exhaust Manifold, Replace."
5. Remove water inlet pipe.

6. Remove valve cover blow by hose, then breather hose.
7. Remove PCV hose, then spark plug wires.
8. Remove valve covers, then timing belt rear cover.
9. Loosen cylinder head bolts using cylinder head bolt wrench tool No. MD998051, or equivalent, in two or three steps in sequence, **Fig. 6**.
10. Reverse procedure to install, noting the following:
   a. Install cylinder head bolt washers with rounded shoulder facing up.
   b. **Torque** cylinder head bolts in two or three steps to 77– 83 ft. lbs., using sequence, **Fig. 7**.
   c. Loosen bolts in sequence, **Fig. 6**.
   d. **Torque** cylinder head bolts in two or three steps to 77– 83 ft. lbs., using sequence, **Fig. 7**.

ROCKER ARMS
REPLACE

1. Remove intake manifold as outlined in "Intake Manifold, Replace."
2. Remove breather hose, then PCV valve from valve cover.
3. Remove valve cover.
4. Remove rocker arm shaft cap.
5. Install lash adjuster holder tool No. MD998713, or equivalent, to prevent lash adjuster from coming free.
6. Remove rocker arms and shaft.
7. Reverse procedure to install, noting the following:
   a. Rotate camshaft until dowel pin on front end is located as outlined, **Fig. 8**.
   b. Ensure notch in end of rocker arm shaft is facing in direction outlined, **Fig. 9**.

FRONT COVER
REPLACE

1. Remove power steering pump drive belt.

2. Remove crankshaft pulley using end yoke holder tool No. MB990767 and crankshaft pulley holder pin tool No. MD998715, or equivalents.
3. Remove power steering pump tensioner pulley.
4. Remove righthand and lefthand timing belt upper covers.
5. Remove timing belt lower cover.
6. Reverse procedure to install.

TIMING BELT
REPLACE
Removal

1. Remove alternator, then engine mount as outlined in "Engine Mount, Replace."
2. Remove timing belt cover as outlined in "Front Cover, Replace."
3. Remove righthand side engine support bracket.
4. Turn crankshaft clockwise to align each timing mark, then set No. 1 cylinder at TDC on compression stroke, **Fig. 10**.
5. Chalk an arrow on flat side of belt to indicate clockwise direction, if using old timing belt.
6. Loosen center bolt of tensioner pulley, then remove timing belt.
7. Remove auto tensioner.

Installation

1. Align timing marks on camshaft sprockets with marks on rocker covers, then timing mark on crankshaft with mark on engine block, **Fig. 10**.
2. Install timing belt in the following order:
   a. Crankshaft sprocket.
   b. Idler pulley.

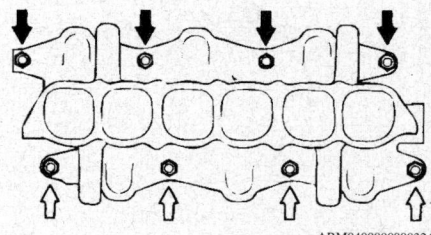

RIGHT BANK
LEFT BANK

Fig. 4 Intake manifold bolt tightening sequence (Part 1 of 2)

ARM0400000000324

ORDER	MOUNTING NUTS	TIGHTENING TORQUE
1st	Right-bank nuts	6.4 ± 1.4 N·m (56 ± 13 in-lb)
2nd	Left-bank nuts	22 ± 1 N·m (16 ± 1 ft-lb)
3rd	Right-bank nuts	22 ± 1 N·m (16 ± 1 ft-lb)
4th	Left-bank nuts	22 ± 1 N·m (16 ± 1 ft-lb)
5th	Right-bank nuts	22 ± 1 N·m (16 ± 1 ft-lb)

CR1060000909000X

Fig. 4 Intake manifold bolt tightening sequence (Part 2 of 2)

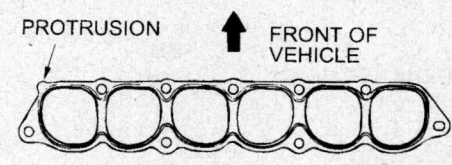

PROTRUSION   FRONT OF VEHICLE

ARM0400000000326

Fig. 5 Intake manifold plenum gasket installation

c. Lefthand bank camshaft sprocket.
d. Water pump pulley.
e. Righthand bank camshaft sprocket.
f. Tensioner pulley.
3. Turn righthand bank camshaft sprocket counterclockwise until tension side of timing belt is firmly stretched, then inspect timing marks.
4. Push tensioner pulley into timing belt and temporarily tighten center bolt using tensioner wrench tool No. MD998767, or equivalent.
5. Turn crankshaft ¼ turn counterclockwise, then turn clockwise until timing marks are aligned using crankshaft pulley spacer tool No. MD998769, or equivalent.
6. Loosen center bolt of tensioner pulley.
7. Apply 39 inch lbs., of tension torque to timing belt using tensioner wrench tool No. MD998767, or equivalent and suitable torque wrench, **Fig. 11.** Tighten center bolt to specifications.
8. Place two wooden blocks in a suitable vise, then place auto-tensioner perpendicular between blocks. If there is a plug at base of tensioner, insert a washer to protect plug.
9. Slowly compress pushrod of auto-tensioner until pin hole (A) in pushrod is aligned with pin hole (B) in cylinder, then insert a suitable pin into holes, **Fig. 12.**
10. Install auto-tensioner on engine, then remove pin.
11. Turn crankshaft clockwise twice to align timing marks.
12. Wait at least five minutes, then inspect that auto-tensioner push rod extends .15–.20 inch. If not repeat steps 5 through 11.
13. Install engine support bracket, tighten bolts in sequence, **Fig. 13,** to specifications.
14. Install timing belt cover as outlined in "Front Cover, Replace."

CAMSHAFT
REPLACE
Lefthand Bank

1. Remove timing belt as outlined in "Timing Belt, Replace."

2. Remove thermostat housing assembly.
3. Disconnect blow by hose, then PCV hose from valve cover.
4. Remove spark plug wires, then valve cover.
5. Remove rocker arm and shaft assembly as outlined in "Rocker Arms, Replace."
6. Remove camshaft sprocket using end yoke holder tool No. MB990767 and crankshaft pulley holder pin tool No. MD998715, or equivalents.
7. Remove thrust plate, then camshaft.
8. Reverse procedure to install.

Righthand Bank

1. Remove timing belt as outlined in "Timing Belt, Replace."
2. Remove intake plenum as outlined in "Intake Manifold, Replace."
3. Disconnect breather hose, then blow by hose from valve cover.
4. Remove spark plug wires, then valve cover.
5. Remove rocker arms and shaft assembly as outlined in "Rocker Arms, Replace."
6. Remove distributor assembly.
7. Remove camshaft sprocket using end yoke holder tool No. MB990767 and crankshaft pulley holder pin tool No. MD998715, or equivalents.
8. Remove camshaft.
9. Reverse procedure to install, noting the following:
   a. Align timing mark on camshaft sprocket with mark on cylinder head.
   b. Align mating marks on distributor housing and coupling.

MAIN & ROD BEARINGS

If bearing replacement is required, measure crankshaft journal diameter and select correct bearing from chart, **Fig. 14.**

Cylinder block bearing bore diameter identification marks are stamped on block, **Fig. 15.**

Install bearing cap with arrow facing timing belt side, then **torque** bolts is sequence **Fig. 16,** to 65–73 ft. lbs.

CRANKSHAFT SEAL
REPLACE
Front

1. Remove timing belt as outlined in "Timing Belt, Replace."
2. Remove crankshaft position sensor, then sensing blade.
3. Remove crankshaft spacer and key.
4. Remove crankshaft front oil seal.
5. Reverse procedure to install, noting the following:
   a. Apply a small amount of engine oil to seal lip before installing.
   b. Tap oil seal into front case using crankshaft front oil seal installer tool No. MD998717, or equivalent.

CRANKSHAFT REAR OIL SEAL
REPLACE

1. Remove transaxle as outlined in **MOTOR's "Domestic Transmission, In-Vehicle Service" manual or "Transmission Service DVD."**
2. Remove flywheel or drive plate.
3. Remove rear oil seal.
4. Reverse procedure to install, noting the following:
   a. Apply a small amount of engine oil to seal lip before installing.
   b. Tap in rear oil seal using crankshaft rear seal installer tool No. MD998718, or equivalent.

OIL PAN
REPLACE

1. Drain engine oil into suitable container, then remove front exhaust pipe.
2. Remove lower oil pan bolts, then lower oil pan.
3. Disconnect starter motor connector, then remove starter motor.
4. Remove oil dipstick, then dipstick guide.
5. Remove upper oil pan bolts, then insert two M10 bolts into bolt holes and separate upper oil pan from cylinder block, **Fig. 17.**
6. Reverse procedure to install, noting the following:
   a. Tighten upper oil pan bolts to specifications using sequence, **Fig. 18.**
   b. Tighten upper oil pan bolts to specifications using sequence, **Fig. 19.**

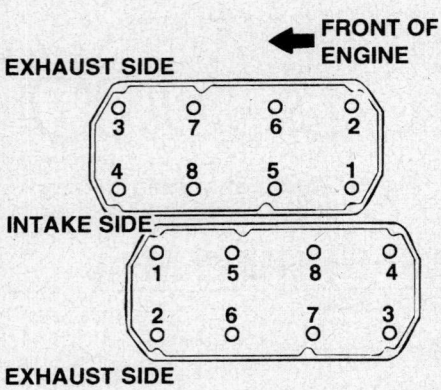

Fig. 6 Cylinder head bolt loosening sequence

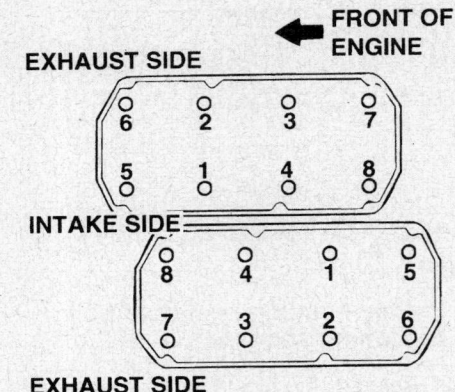

Fig. 7 Cylinder head bolt tightening sequence

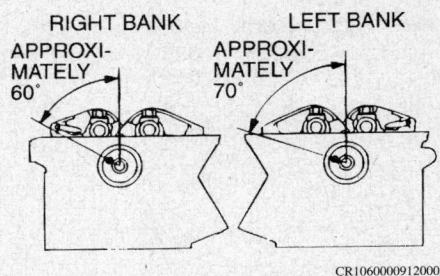

Fig. 8 Camshaft alignment

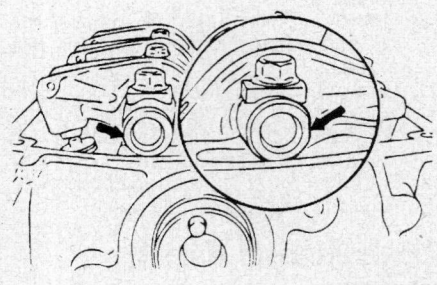

Fig. 9 Rocker arm shaft notch position

OIL PUMP

REPLACE

1. Remove oil pressure switch.
2. Remove oil filter, then oil filter bracket.
3. Remove oil pan as outlined in "Oil Pan, Replace."
4. Remove lower baffle plate, then oil screen.
5. Remove upper baffle plate, then plug.
6. Remove relief spring, then relief plunger.
7. Remove crankshaft front oil seal as outlined in "Crankshaft Oil Seal, Replace."
8. Remove oil pump case assembly.
9. Reverse procedure to install.

OIL PUMP SERVICE

Disassemble

1. Remove oil pump cover.
2. Scribe alignment marks on outer and inner rotors for assembly reference.
3. Remove outer and inner rotors.

Inspection

Refer to "Engine Rebuilding Specifications."

Assemble

1. Apply engine oil to rotors.
2. Align marks, then install rotors.

BELT TENSION DATA

Refer **Figs. 20 and 21** to for belt tension data.

SERPENTINE DRIVE BELT

1. Loosen tensioner pulley fixing nut, then remove belt.

2. Install belt and **torque** fixing bolt temporarily to 11 ft. lbs., then adjust belt tension using adjusting bolt.

COOLING SYSTEM BLEED

Start engine and bring to operating temperature. Rev engine repeatedly to 3000 RPM. After engine has cooled down remove radiator cap and fill to top of radiator.

THERMOSTAT

REPLACE

1. Drain engine coolant into suitable container.
2. Remove air cleaner assembly, then lower radiator hose.
3. Remove thermostat housing, then thermostat.
4. Reverse procedure to install. Ensure jiggle valve on thermostat is facing up.

WATER PUMP

REPLACE

1. Drain engine coolant into suitable container.
2. Remove timing belt as outlined in "Timing Belt, Replace."

3. Remove thermostat as outlined in "Thermostat, Replace."
4. Remove water pump assembly.
5. Reverse procedure to install.

RADIATOR

REPLACE

1. Drain engine coolant into suitable container.
2. Disconnect reserve tank hose, then remove reserve tank.
3. Remove upper and lower radiator hoses.
4. **On models equipped with automatic transaxle,** disconnect oil cooler lines.
5. **On all models,** remove radiator supports.
6. Remove radiator, then fan motor assembly.
7. Reverse procedure to install.

FUEL PUMP

REPLACE

1. Remove rear seat cushion, then access plate.
2. Relieve fuel pressure as outlined in "Precautions."
3. Disconnect fuel hose and electrical connector.
4. Remove fuel pump module using tank cap wrench tool No. MB991480, or equivalent.
5. Reverse procedure to install, noting the following:
   a. Install packing to fuel tank and fuel pump module, **Fig. 22.**
   b. Align mating mark on fuel pump module with mark on fuel tank.

FUEL FILTER

REPLACE

1. Remove fuel pump as outlined in "Fuel Pump, Replace."
2. Remove thermistor case, then fuel gage unit.
3. Remove packing, then reservoir cup.
4. Remove pump support assembly.
5. Remove electrical harness, then lock bracket.
6. Remove fuel pump, then fuel filter.
7. Reverse procedure to install.

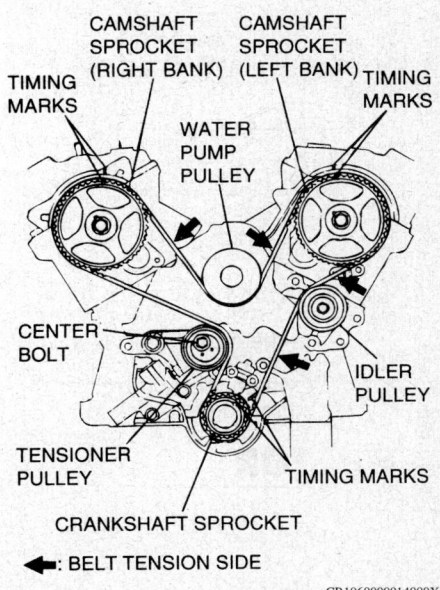

Fig. 10　Timing belt alignment marks

← : BELT TENSION SIDE

CR1060000914000X

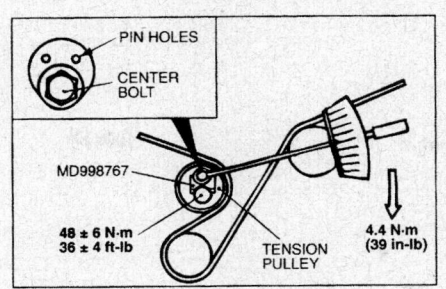

Fig. 11　Timing belt tension torque

CR1060000915000X

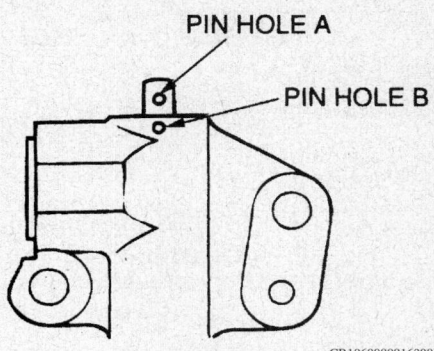

Fig. 12　Auto-tensioner pin hole alignment

CR1060000916000X

CRANKSHAFT JOURNAL OUTSIDE DIAMETER		CYLINDER BLOCK BEARING BORE	CRANK-SHAFT BEARING
ID COLOR	SIZE mm (inch)	ID MARK	ID COLOR
Yellow	59.990 - 59.996 (2.3618 - 2.3620)	I	Pink
		II	Red
		III	Green
None	59.984 - 59.990 (2.3616 - 2.3618)	I	Red
		II	Green
		III	Black
White	59.978 - 59.984 (2.3613 - 2.3616)	I	Green
		II	Black
		III	Brown

CR1060000925000X

Fig. 14　Crankshaft bearing selection chart

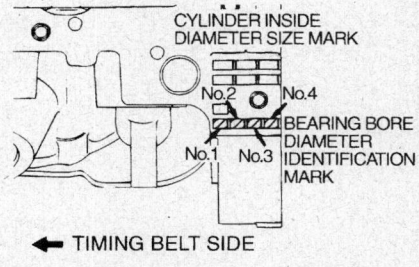

Fig. 15　Block bearing bore identification location

CR1060000926000X

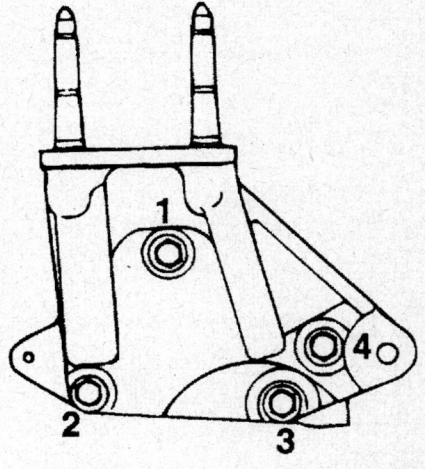

Fig. 13　Engine support bracket tightening sequence

CR1060000917000X

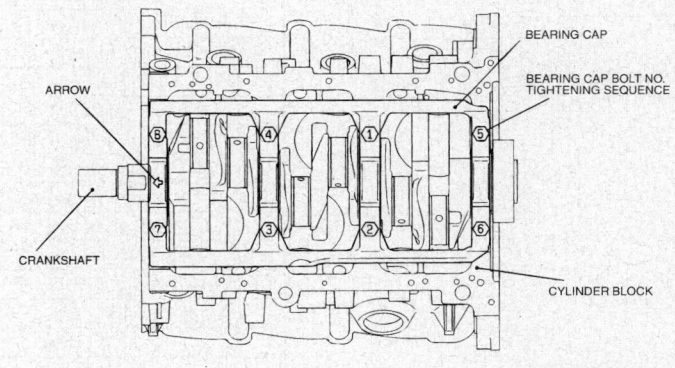

Fig. 16　Bearing cap bolt tightening sequence

CR1060000927000X

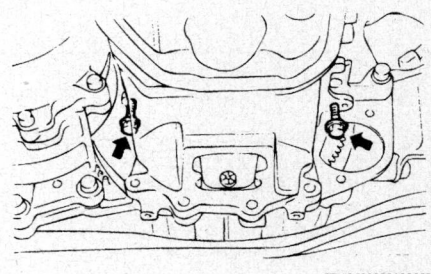

Fig. 17　Upper oil pan removal

CR1060000918000X

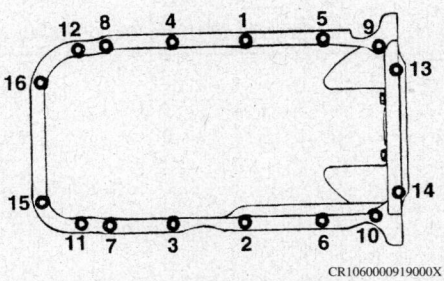

Fig. 18　Upper oil pan tightening sequence

CR1060000919000X

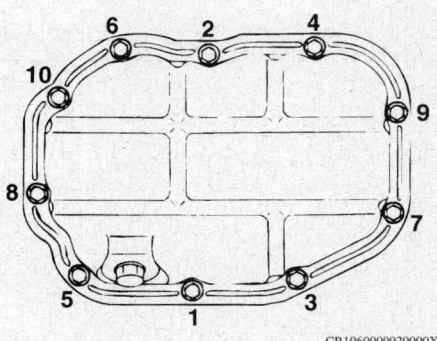

Fig. 19　Lower oil pan tightening sequence

CR1060000920000X

ITEMS	DURING ADJUSTMENT	DURING REPLACEMENT
Vibration frequency Hz	141 - 153	170 - 190
Tension N (lb)	539 - 637 (121 - 143)	785 - 981 (176 - 221)
Deflection (Reference value) mm (in)	9.0 - 10.1 (0.35 - 0.40)	6.2 - 7.6 (0.24 - 0.30)

CR1060000921000X

Fig. 20 Alternator & A/C compressor belt tension chart

ITEMS	WHEN CHECKED	DURING ADJUSTMENT	DURING REPLACEMENT
Vibration frequency Hz	125 - 154	133 - 148	160 - 183
Tension N (lb)	373 - 569 (84 - 128)	422 - 520 (95 - 117)	608 - 804 (137 - 181)
Deflection (Reference value) mm (in)	11.0 - 14.2 (0.43 - 0.56)	11.7 - 13.4 (0.46 - 0.53)	8.4 - 9.3 (0.33 - 0.37)

CR1060000922000X

Fig. 21 Power steering pump belt tension chart

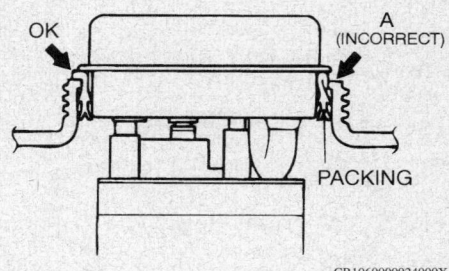

CR1060000924000X

Fig. 22 Fuel pump packing installation

TIGHTENING SPECIFICATIONS

Year	Component	Torque Ft. Lbs.
2004–05	Alternator & A/C Compressor Belt Tensioner	29–43
	Camshaft Sprocket	58–73
	Connecting Rod Bearing Cap	37–39
	Crankshaft Bearing Cap	③
	Crankshaft Pulley	131–137
	Cylinder Head	②
	EGR Valve Bolt	12–14
	Engine Mount	51–69
	Engine Mount Bracket	58–72
	Engine Support Bracket	30–36
	Exhaust Manifold	30–36
	Intake Manifold Nuts	15–17
	Intake Manifold Plenum Nut & Bolts	12–14
	Intake Manifold Plenum Stay Bolts	④
	Oil Pan (Lower)	88–104①
	Oil Pan (Upper)	43–51①
	Oil Pump Case (M8 Bolt)	113–130①
	Oil Pump Case (M10 Bolt)	24–36
	Power Steering Pump Belt Tensioner	26–40
	Rocker Arm Shaft	21–25
	Thermostat Housing	100–130①
	Timing Belt Cover	88–104①
	Timing Belt Tensioner Pulley	32–40
	Valve Cover	27–35①
	Water Pump	14–20

① — Inch Lbs.
② — Refer to "Cylinder Head, Replace" for tightening procedures & specifications.
③ — Refer to "Main & Rod Bearings" for tightening procedures & specifications.
④ — M8 bolts, 12–14 ft. lbs.; M10 bolts, 22–30 ft. lbs.

3.0L ENGINE

Rear Suspension

NOTE: On Air Bag Equipped Models, Refer To "Air Bag System Precautions" Located In The Front Of This Manual For System Disarming & Arming Procedures.

NOTE: Refer To "Computer Relearn Procedures" Located In The Front Of This Manual When Battery Power To The Computer Has Been Interrupted.

NOTE: Prior To Performing Any Service Operations, Consult The "Technical Service Bulletins" Section For Related Information.

INDEX

	Page No.		Page No.		Page No.
Coil Spring, Replace	1-19	Description	1-19	Stabilizer Bar, Replace	1-19
Control Arm, Replace	1-19	Hub & Bearing, Replace	1-19	Tightening Specifications	1-21
Lower	1-19	Knuckle, Replace	1-19	Trailing Arm, Replace	1-19
Upper	1-19	Shock Absorber, Replace	1-19		

DESCRIPTION

The rear suspension is a modified double-wishbone design with coil springs and direct acting shock absorbers, **Fig. 1.** The rear axle consists of a knuckle, rear hub, unit bearing and axle shaft. The unit bearing is press-fitted to the rear axle shaft and bolted to the knuckle. On models equipped with Anti-Lock Brakes ABS, a rotor for detecting vehicle speed is located on the axle shaft and a speed sensor is located on the knuckle.

HUB & BEARING
REPLACE

1. Raise and support vehicle, then remove wheel and tire assembly.
2. **On models equipped with anti-lock brakes,** remove rear speed sensor.
3. **On models equipped with rear disc brakes,** remove brake caliper assembly and the disc, suspend brake caliper aside, **Fig. 2.**
4. **On models equipped with drum brakes,** remove brake drum and shoe.
5. **On all models,** remove rear hub and anti-lock brake rotor.
6. Reverse procedure to install.

SHOCK ABSORBER
REPLACE

1. Remove shock absorber cap.
2. Remove flange nuts under cap.
3. Remove shock absorber lower bolt and shock absorber.
4. Reverse procedure to install.

COIL SPRING
REPLACE

Disassemble as outlined, **Fig. 3.** Compress coil spring using compressor tool Nos. MB991237 and MB991239, or equivalents.

CONTROL ARM
REPLACE

Upper

1. Raise and support vehicle.
2. Remove upper arm to knuckle attaching bolt, **Fig. 4.**
3. Remove upper arm mounting bolt, then upper arm assembly and bracket.
4. Reverse procedure to install.

Lower

1. Raise and support vehicle.
2. Remove stabilizer link, **Fig. 5.**
3. **On models equipped with anti-lock brakes,** remove wheel speed sensor clamp bolts.
4. **On all models,** remove lower arm assembly and knuckle connecting bolt.
5. Remove lower arm mounting bolt.
6. Disconnect toe control arm ball joint from knuckle.
7. Remove toe control arm mounting bolt.
8. Remove toe control arm assembly.
9. Reverse procedure to install.

KNUCKLE
REPLACE

1. Raise and support vehicle.
2. Remove rear hub as outlined in "Hub & Bearing, Replace."
3. Remove trailing arm, **Fig. 6.**
4. Remove lower arm and toe control arm. Loosen nut but do not remove.
5. Remove shock absorber and upper arm.
6. Remove knuckle.
7. **On models less anti-lock brakes,** remove hub cap.
8. **On all models,** reverse procedure to install.

TRAILING ARM
REPLACE

1. Raise and support vehicle.
2. Remove knuckle and trailing arm assembly attaching bolt.
3. Remove grommet.
4. Remove trailing arm assembly mounting bolt, then stopper and trailing arm.
5. Reverse procedure to install.

STABILIZER BAR
REPLACE

1. Raise and support vehicle.
2. Remove stabilizer link mounting nuts.
3. Remove stabilizer link.
4. Remove stabilizer bar brackets and bushings.
5. Remove stabilizer bar.
6. Reverse procedure to install.

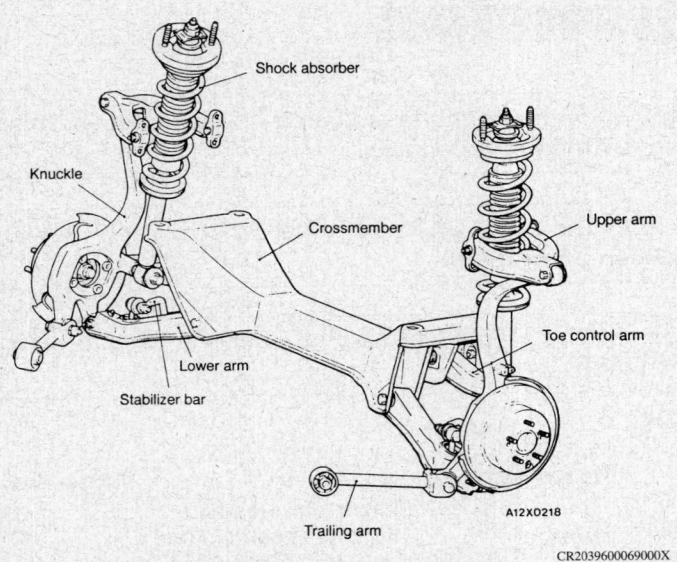

Fig. 1 Rear suspension

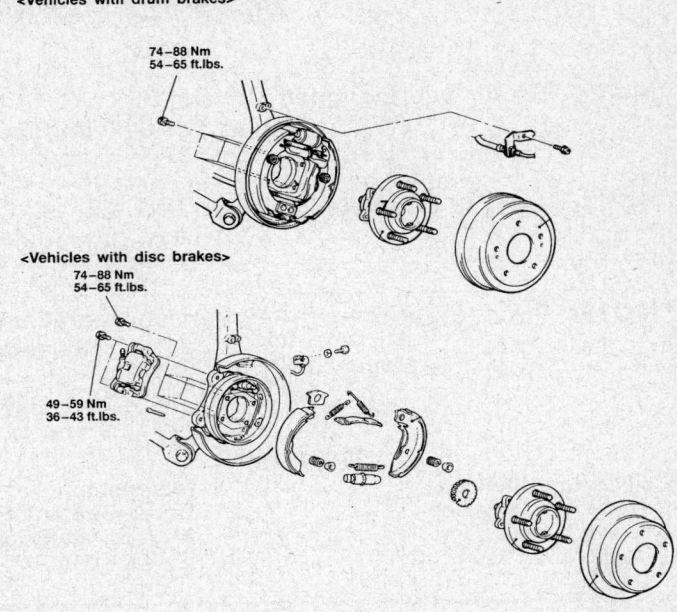

<Vehicles with drum brakes>

74–88 Nm
54–65 ft.lbs.

<Vehicles with disc brakes>

74–88 Nm
54–65 ft.lbs.

49–59 Nm
36–43 ft.lbs.

Fig. 2 Rear hub removal

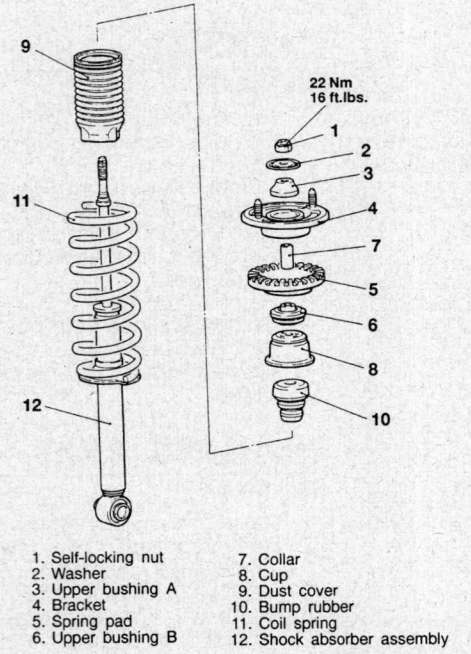

22 Nm
16 ft.lbs.

1. Self-locking nut
2. Washer
3. Upper bushing A
4. Bracket
5. Spring pad
6. Upper bushing B
7. Collar
8. Cup
9. Dust cover
10. Bump rubber
11. Coil spring
12. Shock absorber assembly

Fig. 3 Coil spring replacement

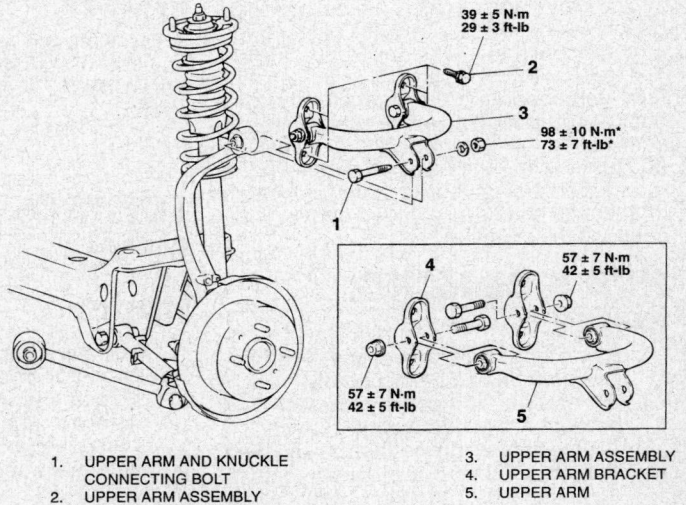

39 ± 5 N·m
29 ± 3 ft-lb

98 ± 10 N·m*
73 ± 7 ft-lb*

57 ± 7 N·m
42 ± 5 ft-lb

57 ± 7 N·m
42 ± 5 ft-lb

1. UPPER ARM AND KNUCKLE CONNECTING BOLT
2. UPPER ARM ASSEMBLY MOUNTING BOLTS
3. UPPER ARM ASSEMBLY
4. UPPER ARM BRACKET
5. UPPER ARM

Fig. 4 Upper control arm replacement

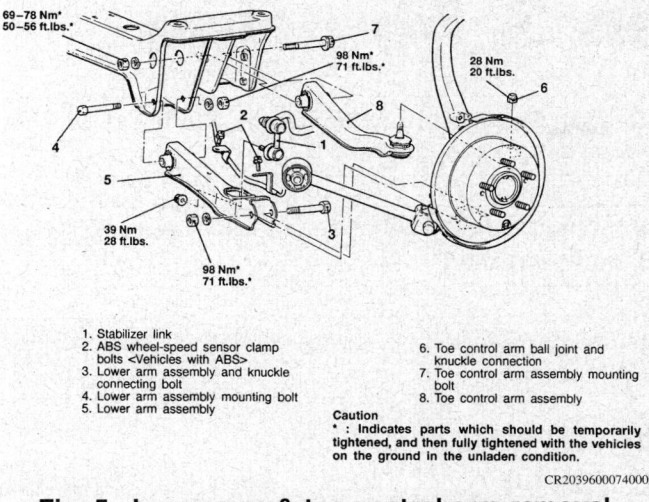

Fig. 5 Lower arm & toe control arm removal

1. Stabilizer link
2. ABS wheel-speed sensor clamp bolts <Vehicles with ABS>
3. Lower arm assembly and knuckle connecting bolt
4. Lower arm assembly mounting bolt
5. Lower arm assembly
6. Toe control arm ball joint and knuckle connection
7. Toe control arm assembly mounting bolt
8. Toe control arm assembly

Caution
* : Indicates parts which should be temporarily tightened, and then fully tightened with the vehicles on the ground in the unladen condition.

CR2039600074000X

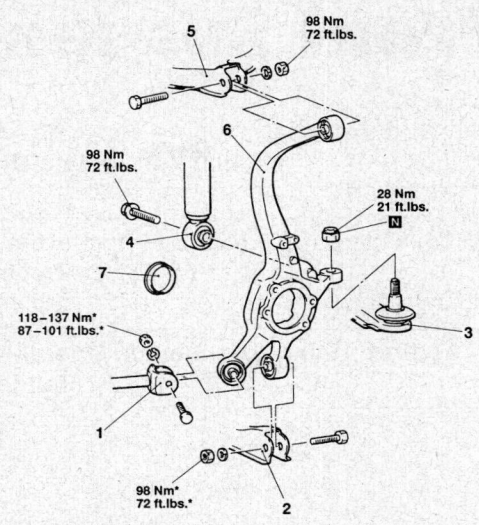

1. Trailing arm connection
2. Lower arm connection
3. Toe control arm connection
4. Shock absorber connection
5. Upper arm connection
6. Knuckle
7. Hub cap <Vehicles without ABS>

Caution
*: Indicates parts which should be temporarily tightened, and then fully tightened with the vehicle on the ground in the unladen condition.

CR2039600072000X

Fig. 6 Knuckle replacement

TIGHTENING SPECIFICATIONS

Year	Component	Torque/Ft. Lbs.
2004–05	Brake Hose Connection	11
	Caliper Mounting Bolts	36–43
	Crossmember Mounting Self-Locking Nuts	64
	Lower Arm & Knuckle Connecting Nut	71
	Lower Arm Mounting Nuts	71
	Shock Absorber Lower Bolt	72
	Shock Absorber Upper Flange Bolts	32
	Shock Tower Self-Locking Nut	16
	Stabilizer Bar Bracket Bolts	7–10
	Stabilizer Link Mounting Nuts	28
	Toe Control Arm Ball Joint & Knuckle Attaching Nut	20
	Trailing Arm Attaching Nut	87–101
	Trailing Arm Mounting Bolt	99–114
	Upper Arm Assembly Mounting Bolt	28
	Upper Arm Bracket Nuts	41
	Upper Arm & Knuckle Attaching Bolt	72
	Wheel Lug Nuts	87–101

Front Suspension & Steering

NOTE: On Air Bag Equipped Models, Refer To "Air Bag System Precautions" Located In The Front Of This Manual For System Disarming & Arming Procedures.

NOTE: Refer To "Computer Relearn Procedures" Located In The Front Of This Manual When Battery Power To The Computer Has Been Interrupted.

NOTE: Prior To Performing Any Service Operations, Consult The "Technical Service Bulletins" Section For Related Information.

INDEX

	Page No.		Page No.		Page No.
Ball Joint Inspection	1-22	Hub & Bearing, Replace	1-22	Battery Ground Cable	1-22
Coil Spring, Replace	1-22	Power Steering	13-1	Shock Absorber, Replace	1-22
Control Arm, Replace	1-22	Power Steering Gear, Replace	1-23	Stabilizer Bar, Replace	1-23
Lower	1-22	Power Steering Pump, Replace	1-23	Steering Columns	12-1
Upper	1-22	Power Steering System Bleed	1-23	Steering Knuckle, Replace	1-22
Crossmember, Replace	1-23	Precautions	1-22	Tightening Specifications	1-25
Driveshaft, Replace	1-22	Air Bag Systems	1-22		

PRECAUTIONS

Air Bag Systems

Refer to "Air Bag System Precautions" in the front of this manual for system disarming and arming procedures.

Battery Ground Cable

Prior to service, disconnect battery ground cable and isolate as required.

HUB & BEARING
REPLACE

1. Raise and support vehicle, then remove tire.
2. **On models equipped with anti-lock brakes,** remove front speed sensor.
3. **On all models,** remove brake caliper assembly and suspend with wire.
4. Remove brake disc.
5. Remove driveshaft nut cotter pin.
6. Remove driveshaft end nut.
7. Remove tie rod and stabilizer link.
8. Disconnect lower arm from steering knuckle.
9. Remove hub assembly.
10. Reverse procedure to install.

DRIVESHAFT
REPLACE

1. **On models equipped with anti-lock brakes,** disconnect front speed sensor.
2. **On all models,** remove brake hose clip and cotter pin.
3. Remove drive shaft nut, **Fig. 1.**
4. Loosen but do not remove ball joint nut using steering linkage puller tool No. MB991113, or equivalent.
5. Loosen but do not remove tie rod end using steering linkage puller tool No. MB991113, or equivalent.
6. Disconnect stabilizer link.
7. Push driveshaft out from hub using puller body tool No. MB991354, puller bar tool No. MB990242 and yoke holder tool No. MB990767, or equivalents.
8. Insert a suitable pry bar between transaxle case and driveshaft, then remove driveshaft.
9. Reverse procedure to install.

BALL JOINT INSPECTION

Use torque wrench tool No. MB990326, or equivalent, to measure ball joint breakaway torque. Breakaway torque should be as specified in **Fig. 2.**

COIL SPRING
REPLACE

Remove shock absorber as outlined in "Shock Absorber, Replace" then disassemble shock/coil spring unit, **Fig. 3.**

SHOCK ABSORBER
REPLACE

1. Remove stabilizer link mounting nut.
2. Remove shock absorber upper mounting nuts.
3. Raise and support vehicle.
4. Remove shock absorber lower mounting bolt.
5. Remove damper fork mounting bolt and damper fork.
6. Remove shock absorber from vehicle.
7. Reverse procedure to install.

CONTROL ARM
REPLACE
Upper

1. Raise and support vehicle.
2. Disconnect upper arm ball joint from knuckle, **Fig. 4.**
3. Remove self-locking nut, then upper arm assembly.
4. Remove dust cover.
5. Reverse procedure to install. Install upper arm shaft at angle, **Fig. 5.**

Lower

1. Raise and support vehicle.
2. Disconnect lower ball joint from steering knuckle using ball joint remover/installer tool No. MB990799, or equivalent, **Fig. 6.**
3. Remove lower arm mounting bolt.
4. **On models equipped with 2.4L engine,** remove lower arm clamp, **Fig. 6.**
5. **On all models,** remove lower arm.
6. Reverse procedure to install.

STEERING KNUCKLE
REPLACE

1. Raise and support vehicle.
2. Remove front wheel and tire assembly.
3. **On models equipped with anti-lock brakes,** remove front wheel speed sensor.
4. **On all models,** remove hub assembly as outlined in "Hub & Bearing, Replace."
5. Refer to **Fig. 7** for steering knuckle removal.
6. Reverse procedure to install.

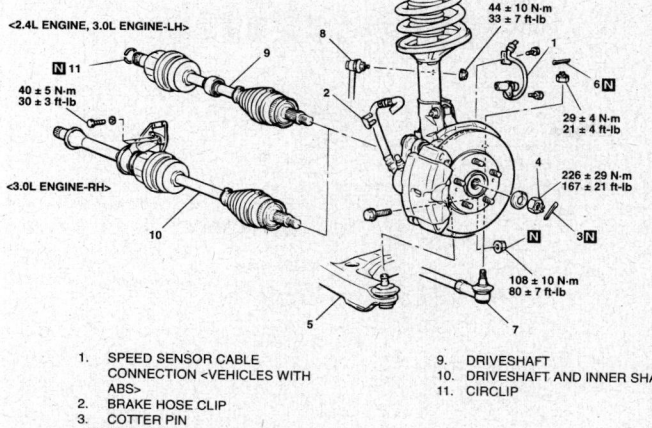

Fig. 1 Driveshaft replacement

1. SPEED SENSOR CABLE CONNECTION <VEHICLES WITH ABS>
2. BRAKE HOSE CLIP
3. COTTER PIN
4. DRIVESHAFT NUT
5. LOWER ARM BALL JOINT CONNECTION
6. COTTER PIN
7. TIE ROD END CONNECTION
8. STABILIZER LINK CONNECTION
9. DRIVESHAFT
10. DRIVESHAFT AND INNER SHAFT
11. CIRCLIP

CR2020000173000X

Ball Joint	Breakaway Torque, Inch Lbs.
Lower Ball Joint	22–54
Stabilizer Link	30–80

Fig. 2 Ball joint specifications

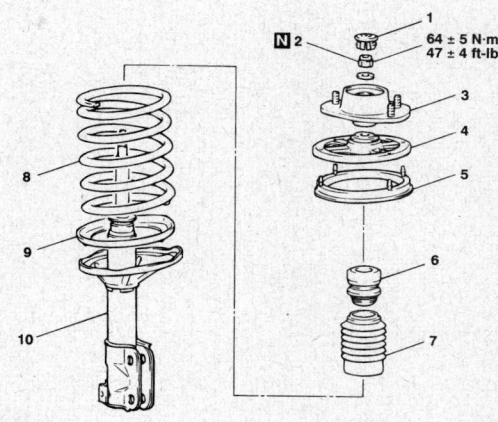

1. DUST COVER
2. JAM NUT
3. STRUT INSULATOR
4. SPRING SEAT, UPPER
5. SPRING PAD, UPPER
6. BUMP RUBBER
7. DUST COVER
8. COIL SPRING
9. SPRING PAD, LOWER
10. STRUT ASSEMBLY

CR2020000174000X

Fig. 3 Coil spring replacement

STABILIZER BAR

REPLACE

1. Raise and support vehicle.
2. Remove stabilizer link mounting nut.
3. Remove stabilizer link.
4. Remove stabilizer bar bracket and bushing.
5. Remove stabilizer bar.
6. Reverse procedure to install.

CROSSMEMBER

REPLACE

1. Drain power steering fluid, then remove center member.
2. Remove front exhaust pipe.
3. Remove stabilizer bar as outlined in "Stabilizer Bar, Replace."
4. Remove lower arm, then clamp.
5. Remove crossmember mounting nuts, then crossmember.
6. Reverse procedure to install.

POWER STEERING GEAR

REPLACE

1. Drain power steering fluid.
2. Remove transaxle and front roll stopper bolt, then center member.
3. Remove front exhaust pipe.
4. Remove stabilizer bar as outlined in "Stabilizer Bar, Replace."
5. Remove steering shaft assembly connecting bolt.

6. Disconnect tie rod ends using steering linkage puller tool No. MB991113, or equivalent.
7. Disconnect return hose, then pressure tube.
8. Remove cylinder clamp, then steering gear.
9. Reverse procedure to install. Add power steering fluid and bleed as outlined in "Power Steering System Bleed."

POWER STEERING PUMP

REPLACE

1. Drain power steering fluid into a suitable container.
2. Remove power steering pump drive belt.
3. Disconnect suction hose.
4. Disconnect pressure hose from pump.
5. Remove gasket or O-ring.
6. Disconnect pressure switch electrical connector.

7. Remove oil pump and bracket.
8. Reverse procedure to install. Add power steering fluid and bleed system as outlined in "Power Steering System Bleed."

POWER STEERING SYSTEM BLEED

1. Raise and support front wheels.
2. Disconnect high tension ignition cable, then while operating starter motor intermittently, turn steering wheel full lefthand and full righthand five or six times.
3. Connect ignition cable, then start engine and run at idle.
4. Turn steering wheel to lefthand and righthand until there are no bubbles in reservoir.
5. Confirm fluid is not milky and that fluid level is up to specified position on dipstick.
6. Confirm there is very little change in fluid level when steering wheel is turned to lefthand or righthand.

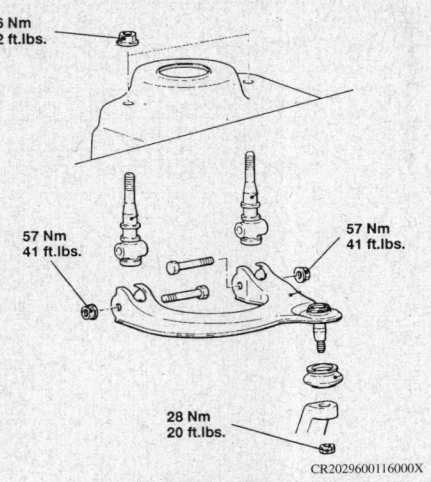

Fig. 4 Upper arm removal

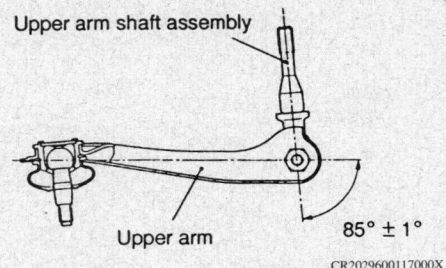

Fig. 5 Upper arm shaft installation

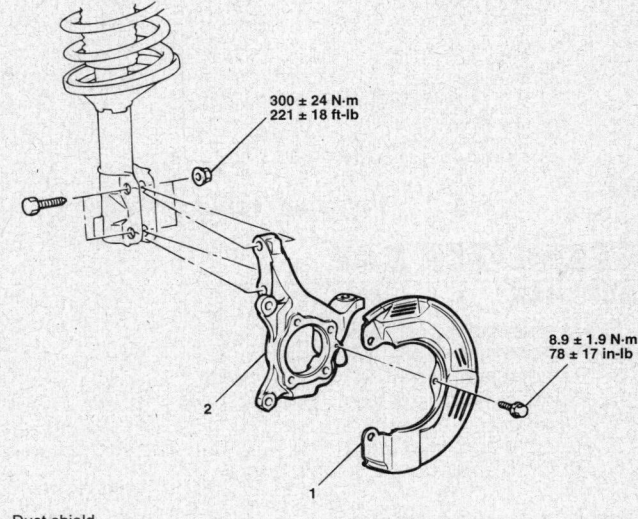

1. Dust shield
2. Knuckle

Fig. 7 Steering knuckle replacement

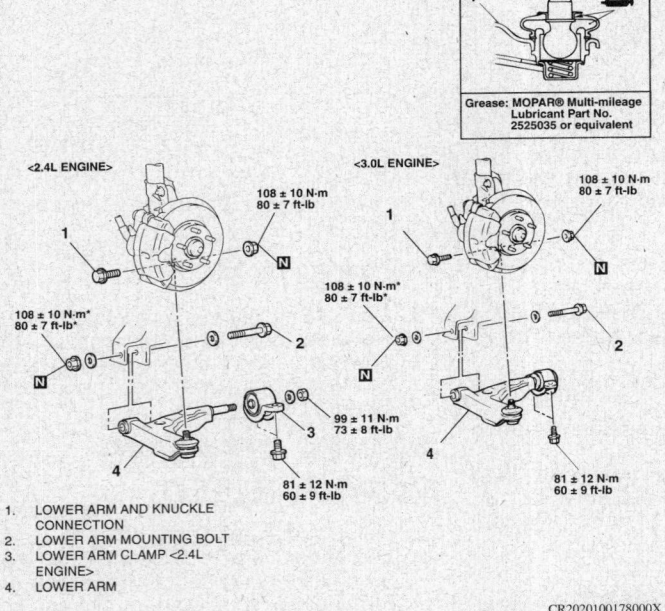

1. LOWER ARM AND KNUCKLE CONNECTION
2. LOWER ARM MOUNTING BOLT
3. LOWER ARM CLAMP <2.4L ENGINE>
4. LOWER ARM

CR2020100178000X

Fig. 6 Lower control arm replacement

TIGHTENING SPECIFICATIONS

Year	Component	Torque/Ft. Lbs.
2004–05	Axle Nut	145–188
	Centermember Rear Assembly Bolts	64
	Centermember To Bracket Bolts	32
	Centermember To Crossmember Bolts	51–58
	Compression Lower Arm Ball Joint To Knuckle	43–51
	Compression Lower Arm Mounting Bolt	60
	Crossmember Lower Plate Bolts	71–85
	Crossmember To Rear Roll Bracket Bolts	32
	Damper Fork Mounting Bolt	75
	Damper Fork To Lateral Lower Arm Through Bolt	65
	Driveshaft Nut	145–188
	Driveshaft To Transaxle Bolt	30
	Hub Nut	145–188
	Joint Assembly & Steering Gear Connection	13
	Lateral Lower Arm Mounting Bolt & Nut	71–85
	Lateral Lower Arm To Knuckle Nuts	43–52
	Power Steering Gear Clamp Bolts	51
	Power Steering Pipe Connection	11
	Power Steering Pump Bracket Bolt (2.4L - M8)	18–24
	Power Steering Pump Bracket Bolt (2.4L - M10)	29–43
	Power Steering Pump Bracket Bolts (3.0L - M8)	14–20
	Power Steering Pump Bracket Bolts (3.0L - M10)	26–40
	Shock Absorber Lower Mounting Bolt	64
	Shock Absorber Upper Mounting Nut	32
	Stabilizer Bar Bracket	28
	Stabilizer Link Mounting Nut	28
	Tie Rod End To Steering Knuckle	18–25
	Upper Arm Self-Locking Nut	62
	Upper Arm Shaft To Control Arm	41

Wheel Alignment

INDEX

	Page No.		Page No.		Page No.
Description	1-26	Caster	1-26	Rear Wheel Alignment	1-26
Front Wheel Alignment	1-26	Toe-In	1-26	Wheel Alignment	
Camber	1-26	Preliminary Inspection	1-26	Specifications	1-2

DESCRIPTION

Caster and camber are preset at the factory and cannot be adjusted. If camber is not within specifications, inspect and replace bent or damaged components.

PRELIMINARY INSPECTION

Wheel alignment should be measured with alignment equipment on a level surface. The suspension, steering system and wheels should be serviced to normal condition prior to measurement of wheel alignment. Inspect wheel runout as follows:

1. Raise and support vehicle.
2. While slowly turning wheel, measure runout with dial indicator.
3. Radial and lateral runout should be .05 inch or less for steel wheel, and .04 inch or less for aluminum wheel.
4. If wheel runout exceeds limit, replace wheel.

FRONT WHEEL ALIGNMENT

Caster

Caster is preset from the factory and cannot be adjusted.

Camber

1. Measure camber, use table, **Fig. 1,** to select proper camber adjusting bolt.
2. Replace upper and lower knuckle to strut attaching bolt with new bolts, **Fig. 2.**
3. Loosely tighten bolts, push or pull on front axle to adjust camber, **Fig. 3.**
4. **Torque** upper and lower knuckle to strut attaching bolt to 203–240 ft. lbs.

Toe-In

If toe measurement is not within specifications, adjust as follows:

BOLT DIAMETER mm (in)	CAMBER ADJUSTING VALUE					
	0°15'	0°30'	0°45'	1°00'	1°15'	1°30'
Upper bolt 16.0 (0.63)	•	•				
14.9 (0.59)			•	•		
14.1 (0.56)					•	
13.6 (0.54)						•
Lower bolt 16.0 (0.63)	•					
14.9 (0.59)		•	•			
14.1 (0.56)				•	•	
13.6 (0.54)						•

CR2040100062000X

Fig. 1   Camber adjusting bolt selection table

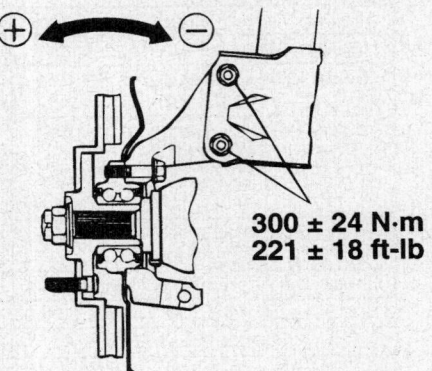

300 ± 24 N·m
221 ± 18 ft-lb

CR2040100064000X

Fig. 3   Camber adjustment

1. Undo clips and turn lefthand and righthand tie rod turnbuckles by same amount in opposite directions, **Fig. 4.**
2. Toe will move out as lefthand turnbuckle is turned toward front of vehicle and righthand turnbuckle is turned toward rear of vehicle.

REAR WHEEL ALIGNMENT

Toe is adjusted by turning the toe control arm mounting bolt to the lefthand or righthand in equal amounts, **Fig. 5.** Turning the lefthand bolt clockwise adjusts in the toe-

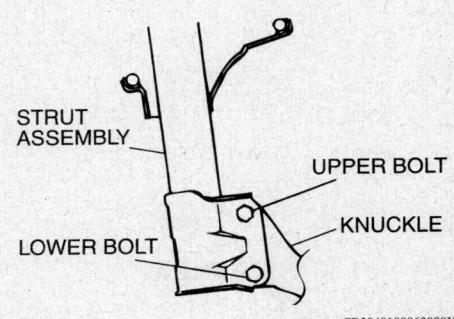

STRUT ASSEMBLY
UPPER BOLT
LOWER BOLT
KNUCKLE

CR2040100063000X

Fig. 2   Camber adjusting bolts

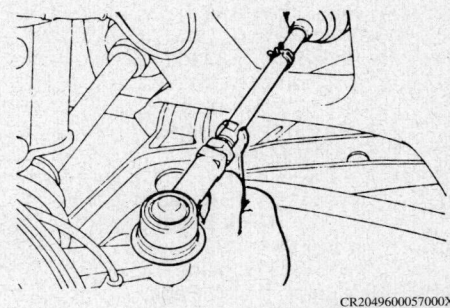

CR2049600057000X

Fig. 4   Front toe adjustment

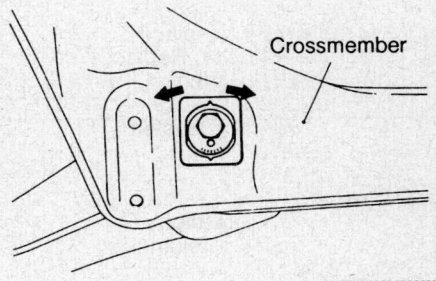

Crossmember

CR2049600058000X

Fig. 5   Rear toe adjustment

out direction. Turning the righthand bolt clockwise adjusts in the toe-in direction. Toe adjustments are made in graduations of .05 inch.

AVENGER, SEBRING CONVERTIBLE, SEBRING SEDAN & STRATUS SEDAN

NOTE: Refer To The Rear Of This Manual For Manufacturer's Special Service Tool Supplies.

INDEX OF SERVICE OPERATIONS

Page No.

AIR BAG SYSTEM
PRECAUTIONS 0-18
BRAKES
  Anti-Lock Brakes (Volume 2).. 6-1
  Disc Brakes.................. 14-1
  Drum Brakes 15-1
  Hydraulic Brake Systems 16-1
  Power Brake Units 17-1
COMPUTER RELEARN
PROCEDURE 0-31
ELECTRICAL
  Air Bag System (Volume 2) ... 4-1
  Air Conditioning.............. 8-1
  Alternator, Replace 2-5
  Alternators.................. 2-1
  Blower Motor, Replace 2-7
  Cooling Fans 9-1
  Cruise Control (Volume 2) 2-1
  Dash Gauges (Volume 2) 1-1
  Dash Panel Service
  (Volume 2).................. 5-1
  Evaporator Core, Replace 2-7
  Fuel Pump Relay Location.... 2-5
  Fuse Panel Location.......... 2-5
  Heater Core, Replace 2-7
  Ignition Coil & Coil Pack,
  Replace 2-5
  Ignition Coil Capacitor,
  Replace 2-6
  Ignition Lock, Replace 2-6
  Ignition Switch, Replace 2-6
  Instrument Cluster, Replace... 2-7
  Multi-function Switch,
  Replace 2-6
  Passive Restraint Systems
  (Volume 2).................. 4-1
  Precautions................. 2-5
  Radio, Replace 2-7
  Relay Center Location 2-5
  Speed Controls (Volume 2) ... 2-1
  Starter Motors 10-1
  Starter, Replace 2-5
  Steering Columns............ 12-1
  Steering Wheel, Replace...... 2-6
  Wiper Motor, Replace......... 2-7
  Wiper Systems (Volume 2).... 3-1
ELECTRICAL SYMBOL
IDENTIFICATION 0-63
FRONT DRIVE AXLES 18-1
FRONT SUSPENSION &
STEERING
  Ball Joint, Replace 2-32
  Ball Joint Inspection 2-32
  Coil Spring & Strut Service.... 2-32
  Control Arm, Replace 2-33
  Driveshaft, Replace 2-31
  Hub & Bearing, Replace 2-31
  Power Steering 13-1

Page No.

  Power Steering Gear,
  Replace 2-34
  Power Steering Pump,
  Replace 2-35
  Shock Absorber, Replace 2-33
  Stabilizer Bar, Replace........ 2-34
  Steering Columns............ 12-1
  Steering Knuckle, Replace 2-34
  Strut, Replace 2-32
  Technical Service Bulletins.... 2-36
  Tie Rod, Replace 2-34
  Tightening Specifications...... 2-37
  Wheel Bearing, Adjust 2-31
NON-STANDARD TIRE &
WHEEL SIZE
ADJUSTMENT TO RIDE
HEIGHT SPECIFICATIONS
& TIRE SIZE CHART 0-61
REAR SUSPENSION
  Coil Spring, Replace.......... 2-27
  Control Arm, Replace 2-28
  Description 2-27
  Hub & Bearing, Replace 2-27
  Knuckle, Replace 2-28
  Lateral Link, Replace 2-29
  Shock Absorber, Replace 2-27
  Stabilizer Bar, Replace 2-28
  Tightening Specifications...... 2-30
SERVICE REMINDER &
WARNING LAMP RESET
PROCEDURES 0-34
SPECIFICATIONS
  Fluid Capacities & Cooling
  System Data................. 2-4
  Front Wheel Alignment
  Specifications............... 2-3
  General Engine
  Specifications............... 2-2
  Lubricant Data.............. 2-4
  Rear Wheel Alignment
  Specifications............... 2-3
  Tune Up Specifications....... 2-2
  Vehicle Ride Height
  Specifications............... 2-3
TIRE PRESSURE
MONITORING SYSTEM 20-1
VEHICLE
IDENTIFICATION 0-1
VEHICLE LIFT POINTS 0-51
VEHICLE MAINTENANCE
SCHEDULES 0-73
WHEEL ALIGNMENT
  Description 2-38
  Front Wheel Alignment 2-38
  Precautions 2-38
  Preliminary Inspection 2-38
  Rear Wheel Alignment 2-38
  Thrust Angle 2-38

Page No.

  Wheel Alignment
  Specifications............... 2-3
WIRE COLOR CODE
IDENTIFICATION 0-63
2.4L ENGINE
  Balance Shaft, Replace....... 2-11
  Belt Tension Data............ 2-13
  Camshaft, Replace 2-11
  Camshaft Lobe Lift
  Specifications............... 2-10
  Compression Pressure....... 2-8
  Cooling System Bleed 2-13
  Crankshaft Rear Oil Seal,
  Replace 2-12
  Crankshaft Seal, Replace..... 2-12
  Cylinder Head, Replace....... 2-10
  Engine Rebuilding
  Specifications............... 21-1
  Engine, Replace 2-9
  Engine Mount, Replace 2-9
  Exhaust Manifold, Replace.... 2-9
  Front Cover, Replace 2-11
  Fuel Filter, Replace 2-14
  Fuel Pump, Replace 2-14
  Intake Manifold, Replace..... 2-9
  Main & Rod Bearings 2-11
  Oil Pan, Replace............ 2-12
  Oil Pump, Replace........... 2-12
  Oil Pump Service............ 2-12
  Piston & Rod Assembly....... 2-11
  Precautions................. 2-8
  Radiator, Replace........... 2-13
  Rocker Arms, Replace 2-10
  Serpentine Drive Belt 2-13
  Technical Service Bulletins.... 2-14
  Thermostat, Replace......... 2-13
  Tightening Specifications...... 2-17
  Timing Belt, Replace......... 2-11
  Valve Arrangement........... 2-10
  Valve Clearance
  Specifications............... 2-10
  Valve Cover, Replace 2-10
  Water Pump, Replace 2-13
2.7L ENGINE
  Belt Tension Data............ 2-19
  Compression Pressure........ 2-18
  Cooling System Bleed 2-19
  Engine Rebuilding
  Specifications............... 21-1
  Engine, Replace 2-18
  Engine Mount, Replace 2-18
  Fuel Filter, Replace 2-20
  Fuel Pump, Replace 2-20
  Precautions................. 2-18
  Radiator, Replace........... 2-20
  Serpentine Drive Belt 2-19
  Technical Service Bulletins.... 2-20
  Thermostat, Replace......... 2-20
  Tightening Specifications...... 2-21

	Page No.		Page No.		Page No.
Water Pump, Replace	2-20	Specifications	21-1	Piston & Rod Assembly	2-24
3.5L ENGINE		Engine, Replace	2-22	Precautions	2-22
Camshaft, Replace	2-24	Engine Mount, Replace	2-22	Radiator, Replace	2-25
Compression Pressure	2-22	Exhaust Manifold, Replace	2-23	Rocker Arms, Replace	2-24
Cooling System Bleed	2-25	Fuel Filter, Replace	2-25	Thermostat, Replace	2-25
Crankshaft Rear Oil Seal,		Fuel Pump, Replace	2-25	Tightening Specifications	2-26
Replace	2-24	Intake Manifold, Replace	2-22	Timing Belt, Replace	2-24
Crankshaft Seal, Replace	2-24	Main & Rod Bearings	2-24	Valve Clearance	
Cylinder Head, Replace	2-23	Oil Pan, Replace	2-24	Specifications	2-24
Engine Rebuilding		Oil Pump, Replace	2-25	Valve Cover, Replace	2-24
		Oil Pump Service	2-25	Water Pump, Replace	2-25

Specifications

GENERAL ENGINE SPECIFICATIONS

Year	Engine		Fuel System	Bore & Stroke, Inches	Comp-ression. Ratio	Net HP @ RPM	Maximum Torque, Ft. Lbs. @ RPM	Normal Oil Pressure, psi @ 3000 RPM
	Liter	VIN Code①						
2004–06	2.4L	G/X	SMPI	3.440 x 3.980	9.5	150 @ 5200	167 @ 4000	25–80
	2.7L	U	SMPI	3.386 x 3.091	9.7	200 @ 5800	190 @ 4850	45–105
2007–08	2.4L②	K	SMPI	3.46 x 3.82	10.5	173 @ 6000	166 @ 4400	25–80
	2.7L②	R	SMPI	3.38 x 3.09	9.9	189 @ 6400	191 @ 4000	45–105
	3.5L②	M	SMPI	3.78 x 3.19	10.0	235 @ 6400	232 @ 4000	45–105

SMPI — Sequential Multi-Port Injection

① — Eighth digit of Vehicle Identification Number (VIN) denotes engine code.

② — Avenger & Sebring sedan models.

TUNE UP SPECIFICATIONS

Year & Engine	Spark Plug Gap, Inch	Ignition Timing			Minimum Air Flow Idle Speed, RPM②	Fuel Pump Pressure, psi	Valve Clearance
		Firing Order	Firing Order Fig.	°BTDC			
2.4L	.048	1-3-4-2	A	②	600–1300	58	①
2.7L	.048	1-2-3-4-5-6	B	②	350–700	58	①

BTDC — Before Top Dead Center

① — Equipped w/hydraulic valve adjusters. No adjustment is required.

② — Controlled by PCM; not adjustable.

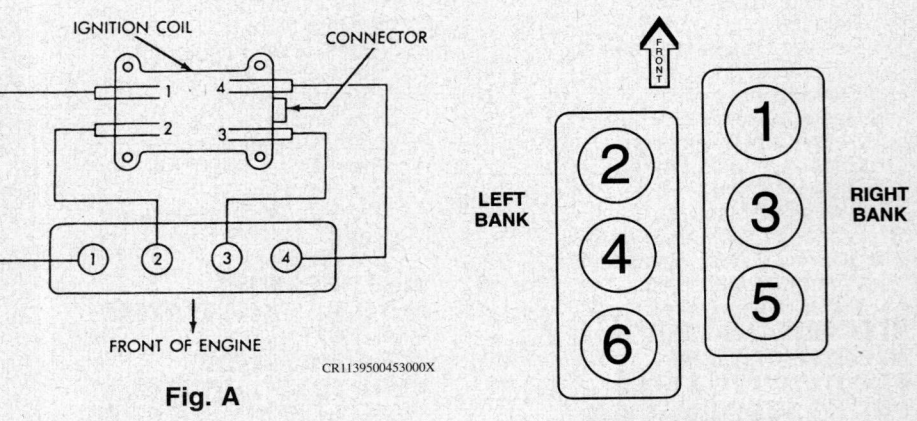

FRONT OF ENGINE

Fig. A

FIRING ORDER 1-2-3-4-5-6

Fig. B

FRONT WHEEL ALIGNMENT SPECIFICATIONS

Year	Model	Camber Angle, Degrees		Toe, Degrees③		Caster, Degrees①	Ball Joint Wear
		Limits	Desired	Individual	Total		
2004–06	All	-.90 to +.30	-.30	+.12	+.24	+3.30	②
2007–08	④	-.50 to +.30	-.10	+.05	+.10	+3.0	②

① — Not adjustable.
② — Refer to Ball Joint Inspection in Front Suspension & Steering section.
③ — Toe in (+); toe out (-).
④ — Avenger & Sebring sedan modesl.

REAR WHEEL ALIGNMENT SPECIFICATIONS

Year	Model	Camber Angle, Degrees		Toe, Degrees①		Thrust Angle, Degrees	
		Limits	Desired	Individual	Total	Limits	Desired
2004–06	All	-1.10 to +.10	-.50	+.05	+.10	-.15 to +.15	0
2007–08	②	-1.10 to -.10	-.60	+.10	+.20	-.15 to +.15	0

① — Toe in (+); toe out (-).
② — Avenger & Sebring sedan models.

VEHICLE RIDE HEIGHT SPECIFICATIONS

Year	Body Style	Manufacturer's Original Tire Size	Measurement Points & Specifications②					
			Front			Rear		
			Dim.	Specification		Dim.	Specification	
				Inches	mm		Inches	mm
2004–06	All	①	A	27.75	705	B	28.00	710
2007–08③	2.4L	16	A	6.69	170	B	8.07	205
	2.4L	17	A	6.81	173	B	8.15	207
	2.7L	17	A	6.77	172	B	8.15	207
	2.7L– 3.5L	18	A	6.89	175	B	8.27	210

A Dim — 2004–06 models, ground to lower edge of front wheelwell.

B Dim — 2004–06 models, ground to lower edge of rear wheelwell.

A Dim — 2007–08 models, ground to behind PLP hole.

B Dim — 2007–08 models, ground to rear toe adjustment cam bolt.

① — See door sticker or inside of glove box for manufacturers original tire size specifications. If tires on vehicle do not match manufacturers original tire size & measurement is not within limits, it will be required to refer to the Non-Standard Tire & Wheel Size Adjustment To Ride Height Specification & Tire Size Adjustment Charts in the front of this manual for approximate changes in ride height specifications.

② — Measurement is w/fuel, radiator coolant, engine oil full, jack, hand tools & mats in designated positions and tires properly inflated.

③ — Avenger & Sebring sedan modesl.

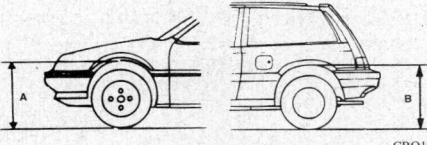

Fig. A   Dimensions A & B

FLUID CAPACITIES & COOLING SYSTEM DATA

Year	Engine	Coolant Capacity, Qts.	Coolant Type	Radiator Cap Relief Pressure, Lbs.	Thermostat Opening Temperature, °F	Fuel Tank Capacity, Gals.	Engine Oil Refill, Qts.①	Transaxle Oil, Qts.	
								Manual Trans.	Auto. Trans.
2004–06	2.4L	8.0	Ethylene Glycol	10–18	192–199	16	5.0	③	②
	2.7L	9.5	Ethylene Glycol	10–18	192–199	16	5.0	③	②
2007–08	2.4L④	7.2	Ethylene Glyco	14–18	179–203	16.9	5.0	—	⑤
	2.7L④	9.5	Ethylene Glyco	14–18	179–203	16.9	6.0	—	⑤
	3.5L④	10.3	Ethylene Glyco	14–18	179–203	16.9	6.0	—	⑥

① — Includes filter change.

② — Service fill, 4.0 qts.; overhaul fill w/torque converter, 9.1 qts.

③ — T350 transaxle; 2.5 qts, T850 transaxle; 2.8 qts.

④ — Sebring sedan model.

⑤ — 41TE and 41AE, service fill, 4.0 qts.; overhaul fill w/torque converter, 9.2 qts.

⑥ — 62TE, service fill, 5.5 qts.: overhaul fill w/torque converter, 9.0 qts.

LUBRICANT DATA

Year	Lubricant Type			
	Transaxle		Power Steering	Brake System
	Manual	Automatic		
2004–08	Mopar ATF+4 Type 9602	Mopar ATF+4 Type 9602	Mopar ATF+4 Type 9602	DOT 3

Electrical

NOTE: On Air Bag Equipped Models, Refer To "Air Bag System Precautions" Located In The Front Of This Manual For System Disarming & Arming Procedures.

NOTE: Refer To "Computer Relearn Procedures" Located In The Front Of This Manual When Battery Power To The Computer Has Been Interrupted.

NOTE: Prior To Performing Any Service Operations Listed In This Section, Consult The "Technical Service Bulletins" Section For Related Information.

INDEX

	Page No.
Air Bag System (Volume 2)	4-1
Air Conditioning	8-1
Alternator, Replace	2-5
2.4L Engine	2-5
2.7L Engine	2-5
3.5L Engine	2-5
Alternators	11-1
Blower Motor, Replace	2-7
Cooling Fans	9-1
Cruise Control (Volume 2)	2-1
Dash Gauges (Volume 2)	1-1
Dash Panel Service (Volume 2)	5-1
Evaporator Core, Replace	2-7
2007–08 Avenger & Sebring Sedan	2-8

	Page No.
Except 2007–08 Avenger & Sebring Sedan	2-7
Fuel Pump Relay Location	2-5
Fuse Panel Location	2-5
Heater Core, Replace	2-7
2007–08 Avenger & Sebring Sedan	2-7
Except 2007–08 Avenger & Sebring Sedan	2-7
Ignition Coil & Coil Pack, Replace	2-5
2.4L Engine	2-5
2.7L Engine	2-5
2004–05	2-5
2006–08	2-5
3.5L Engine	2-6

	Page No.
Ignition Coil Capacitor, Replace	2-6
Ignition Lock, Replace	2-6
2007–08 Avenger & Sebring Sedan	2-6
Except 2007–08 Avenger & Sebring Sedan	2-6
Ignition Switch, Replace	2-6
2007–08 Avenger & Sebring Sedan	2-6
Except 2007–08 Avenger & Sebring Sedan	2-6
Instrument Cluster, Replace	2-7
2007–08 Avenger & Sebring Sedan	2-7
Except 2007–08 Avenger & Sebring Sedan	2-7

	Page No.		Page No.		Page No.
Multi-Function Switch, Replace	2-6	Air Bag Systems	2-5	2.7L Engine	2-5
2007–08 Avenger & Sebring Sedan	2-6	Battery Ground Cable	2-5	3.5L Engine	2-5
Except 2007–08 Avenger & Sebring Sedan	2-6	Radio, Replace	2-7	Steering Columns	12-1
Passive Restraint Systems (Volume 2)	4-1	Relay Center Location	2-5	Steering Wheel, Replace	2-6
Precautions	2-5	Speed Controls (Volume 2)	2-1	Wiper Motor, Replace	2-7
		Starter Motors	10-1	Wiper Systems (Volume 2)	3-1
		Starter, Replace	2-5		
		2.4L Engine	2-5		

PRECAUTIONS
Air Bag Systems

Refer to Air Bag System Precautions in the front of this manual for system disarming and arming procedures.

Battery Ground Cable

Prior to service, disconnect battery ground cable and isolate as required.

FUSE PANEL LOCATION

The interior accessory fuse panel is located between the instrument panel and the driver's side door. The door must be open to access the fuse panel. The fuse panel contains the headland relay, horn relay, rear window defogger relay, circuit breakers, and several fuses.

FUEL PUMP RELAY LOCATION

The fuel pump relay is located in the Power Distribution Center (PDC), which is near the battery on the lefthand side of the engine compartment.

RELAY CENTER LOCATION

The engine compartment relays are located in the Power Distribution Center (PDC) next to the battery. The PDC contains the starter relay, radiator fan relay, air conditioning compressor clutch relay, auto shutdown relay, wiper relay, back-up lamp relay, transaxle control relay, fuel pump relay and several fuses.

STARTER
REPLACE
2.4L Engine

1. Remove air cleaner box.
2. Remove lower and upper bolt, then ground wire.
3. Remove starter and wires from starter.
4. Reverse procedure to install. **Torque** mounting bolts to 40 ft. lbs.

2.7L Engine

1. Raise and support vehicle.
2. Disconnect electrical connector and remove O2 sensor.

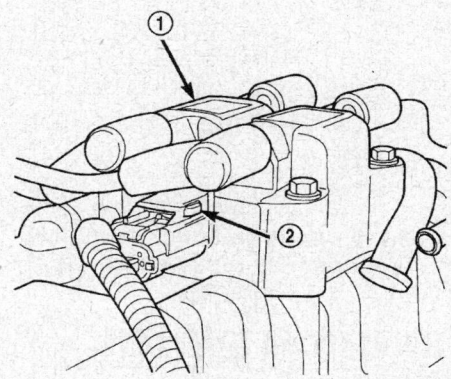

1 - COIL
2 - LOCKING TAB

Fig. 1   Ignition coil pack replacement. 2.4L engine

3. Remove front mount bracket from engine block.
4. Disconnect battery cable from starter.
5. Remove lower mounting bolt and starter.
6. Reverse procedure to install noting the following:
   a. **Torque** upper and lower mounting bolts to 40 ft. lbs.
   b. **Torque** front mount through bolt to 45 ft. lbs.

3.5L Engine

1. Raise and support vehicle.
2. Remove lower engine cover.
3. Remove front engine mount through bolt.
4. Remove transmission crossmember.
5. Remove front engine mount bracket and bolts as outlined under "Front Engine Mount, Replace."
6. Remove starter motor mounting bolts, then starter.
7. Reverse procedure to install. **Torque** starter mounting bolts to 40 ft. lbs.

ALTERNATOR
REPLACE
2.4L Engine

1. Remove drive belt cover.
2. Unplug field circuit from alternator.
3. Remove B+ terminal cover by spreading cover using suitable small flat blade tool.
4. Remove B+ terminal nut and wire.

5. Raise and support vehicle.
6. Remove serpentine drive belt.
7. Lower vehicle and remove MAP sensor from intake manifold.
8. Remove mounting bolts and alternator.
9. Reverse procedure to install.

2.7L Engine

1. Raise and support vehicle.
2. Remove splash shield and loosen serpentine drive belt.
3. Remove lower mounting bolt, then lower vehicle.
4. Disconnect air conditioning pressure switch and clutch electrical connectors.
5. Remove engine oil dip stick.
6. Remove two upper mounting bolts and alternator.
7. Reverse procedure to install.

3.5L Engine

1. Remove engine cover.
2. Disconnect battery cable and electrical connection from alternator.
3. Remove drive belt.
4. Remove alternator mounting bolts, then alternator.
5. Reverse procedure to install. **Torque** mounting bolts to 19 ft. lbs.

IGNITION COIL & COIL PACK
REPLACE
2.4L Engine

1. Disconnect coil pack electrical connector, **Fig. 1**.
2. Remove spark plug cables from coil pack by twisting cable and boot assembly, then pulling outward.
3. Remove mounting bolts and coil pack.
4. Reverse procedure to install.

2.7L Engine
2004–05

1. Disconnect ignition coil electrical connector, **Fig. 2**.
2. Remove mounting bolts and coil.
3. Reverse procedure to install. **Torque** mounting bolts to 55 inch lbs.

2006–08

1. Remove air cleaner box.

2. Place suitable floor jack under engine for support.
3. Loosen transmission mount bolts, but do not remove.
4. Lower engine and transmission.
5. Remove 1 fastener from each ignition coil assembly.
6. Disconnect lefthand and righthand ignition coil electrical connectors.
7. The center ignition coils will have to be rotated to remove electrical connector.
8. Twist, pull up and toward rear of vehicle to remove drivers side ignition coil.
9. Twist, pull straight up, then tip toward drivers side of vehicle to remove center ignition coil.
10. Twist, then pull straight up to remove passenger side ignition coil.
11. Reverse procedure to install tightening ignition coil mounting bolts to 65 inch lbs.

3.5L Engine

1. Remove engine cover.
2. Remove intake manifold as outlined under "Intake Manifold, Replace."
3. Disconnect electrical connector from ignition coils.
4. Remove mounting bolt and engine cover studs.
5. Reverse procedure to install.

IGNITION COIL CAPACITOR, REPLACE

1. Disconnect capacitor electrical connector, **Fig. 2.**
2. Remove mounting nut and capacitor.
3. Reverse procedure to install.

IGNITION LOCK
REPLACE

Except 2007-08 Avenger & Sebring Sedan

1. Remove upper steering column shroud.
2. Pull lower shroud down far enough to access lock cylinder retaining tab.
3. Place ignition key cylinder in RUN position.
4. Depress retaining tab and remove ignition lock.
5. Reverse procedure to install.

2007-08 Avenger & Sebring Sedan

1. Remove instrument cluster bezel.
2. Insert key into ignition and rotate to vertical position.
3. Depress locking pin for key cylinder, using a suitable thin flat blade screw driver.
4. Reverse procedure to install.

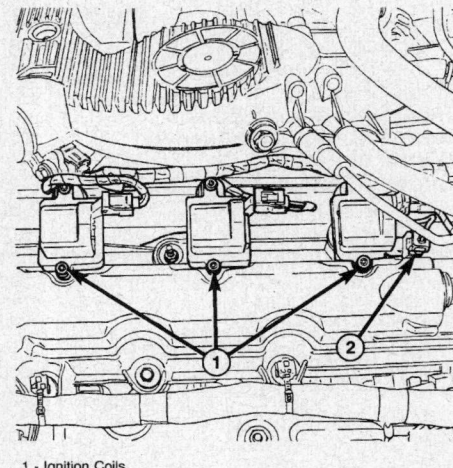

1 - Ignition Coils
2 - Ignition Capacitor

CR1110200290000X

Fig. 2   Ignition coils & ignition coil capacitor replacement. 2.7L engine

IGNITION SWITCH
REPLACE

Except 2007-08 Avenger & Sebring Sedan

1. Remove fuse panel cover from lefthand end of instrument panel.
2. Remove instrument panel top cover end mounting screw.
3. Pull center bezel off.
4. Remove top cover to center of instrument panel mounting screws.
5. Pull instrument panel top cover up enough to gain access to knee bolster screws.
6. Remove lower mounting screws and knee bolster.
7. Remove lower steering column shroud mounting screws.
8. Pull lower shroud to clear ignition cylinder and key release.
9. Hold tilt wheel lever down and remove lower shroud by sliding it forward.
10. Tilt wheel to full down position and remove upper steering column shroud.
11. Remove multiplication switch to lock housing mounting screws.
12. Place ignition key cylinder in RUN position.
13. Depress lock cylinder retaining tab and remove key cylinder.
14. Disconnect ignition switch electrical connectors.
15. Remove ignition switch mounting screw .
16. Depress retaining tabs and pull ignition switch from steering column.
17. Reverse procedure to install.

2007-08 Avenger & Sebring Sedan

1. Remove radio bezel.

2. Remove instrument cluster bezel.
3. Remove knee bolster.
4. Disconnect electrical connectors from back of instrument cluster.
5. Position instrument cluster to the left.
6. Remove ignition switch front mounting screws.
7. Remove rear mounting screw and washer.
8. Unclip ignition switch from mounting using a thin flat blade screw driver, then push switch back to remove.
9. Push switch back and down to opening from knee bolster area.
10. Disconnect shift interlock cable.
11. Remove ignition switch.
12. Reverse procedure to install.

MULTI-FUNCTION SWITCH
REPLACE

Except 2007-08 Avenger & Sebring Sedan

1. Remove upper steering column cover.
2. Remove multiplication switch mounting screws.
3. Disconnect wire connectors. Lift switch straight up to remove.
4. Reverse procedure to install.

2007-08 Avenger & Sebring Sedan

1. Remove upper and lower steering column shrouds.
2. Remove mounting screw on righthand multi-function switch, **Fig. 3.**
3. Slide switch away from clockspring far enough to disengage tab on bottom of switch housing.
4. Disconnect jumper harness.
5. Remove switch from clockspring.
6. Reverse procedure to install.

STEERING WHEEL
REPLACE

1. Place front wheels in straight ahead position.
2. Remove and disconnect speed control switches.
3. Disarm air bag system as outlined under "Precautions."
4. Remove speed control switch or covers from steering wheel, then disconnect electrical connectors.
5. Remove air bag module mounting bolts from steering wheel.
6. Lift module and disconnect wire connector by lifting secondary latch and using finger grips. **Do not use metallic tool to pry connector off.**
7. Disconnect horn wire.
8. Remove speed control wires from under brackets and from wire guides.
9. Remove driver's air bag module.
10. Disconnect horn wire from air bag

mounting bracket and remove speed control wires from under bracket.

11. Loosen mounting bolt and steering wheel using suitable wheel puller tool.
12. Remove mounting bolt and steering wheel.
13. Reverse procedure to install, noting the following:
    a. **Torque** steering wheel bolt to 40 ft. lbs.
    b. **Torque** air bag module bolts to 75–95 inch lbs. Tighten lefthand side bolt first.

INSTRUMENT CLUSTER
REPLACE

Except 2007–08 Avenger & Sebring Sedan

1. Remove lefthand end cap.
2. Pry power mirror switch upward using trim stick tool No. C-4755, or equivalent.
3. Gently pry up on instrument panel center trim bezel.
4. Disconnect HVAC control connector.
5. Remove mounting screw and passenger side trim bezel by unsnapping retaining clips.
6. Remove lefthand lower instrument panel trim mounting screws.
7. Remove cluster bezel mounting screws.
8. **On models equipped with Mini-Trip Computer (CMTC/Traveler),** disconnect module.
9. **On all models,** pry cluster bezel from instrument panel.
10. Tilt steering column to its lowest position and depress hazard switch.
11. Remove cluster mounting screws.
12. Pull cluster rearward and disconnect 26-way electrical connector.
13. Remove cluster by tilting downward slightly and sliding sideways.
14. Reverse procedure to install.

2007–08 Avenger & Sebring Sedan

1. Remove upper instrument panel.
2. Remove four instrument cluster retaining screws.
3. Pull instrument cluster rearward to access electrical connectors.
4. Disconnect electrical connectors, then remove cluster.
5. Reverse procedure to install.

RADIO
REPLACE

REQ and RET radios must be in "Transportation Mode" before removal. With ignition in RUN or ACC position, press SET and SCAN at same time until radio displays "Transportation."

1. Remove center bezel and two radio mounting screws.
2. Pull radio straight out, then disconnect

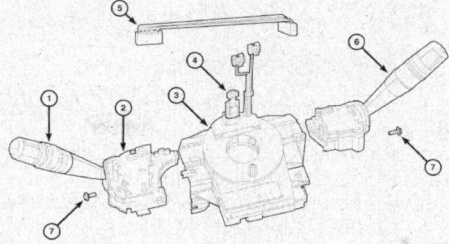

1-LEFTHAND MULTI-FUNCTION SWITCH
2-STEERING CONTROL MODULE
3-CLOCKSPRING
4-LOCKING TAB
5-JUMPER HARNESS
6-RIGHTHAND MULTI-FICTION SWITCH
7-MOUNTING SCREW

ARM0600000000322

Fig. 3   Multi-function switch. 2007–08 Avenger & Sebring Sedan

both electrical connectors, antenna cable and radio ground strap.
3. Remove radio.
4. Reverse procedure to install.

WIPER MOTOR
REPLACE

1. Remove wiper arms and blades.
2. Remove cowl screen.
3. Remove mounting screws and lift wiper motor to access harness clip.
4. Disconnect harness clip at forward mounting leg.
5. Disconnect motor electrical connector.
6. Disconnect drive linkage at motor output crank, then separate ball cap from ball using suitable ball joint separator tool.
7. Remove motor.
8. Reverse procedure to install. **Torque** mounting screws to 96–108 inch. lbs.

BLOWER MOTOR
REPLACE

1. Remove lower righthand silencer panel.
2. Remove righthand sill plate and kick panel.
3. Fold back righthand upper corner of carpet and disconnect blower motor electrical connector.
4. Remove three mounting screws and blower motor.
5. Reverse procedure to install.

HEATER CORE
REPLACE

Except 2007–08 Avenger & Sebring Sedan

1. Recover air conditioning system as outlined in "Air Conditioning" chapter.
2. Drain engine coolant into suitable container, then disconnect heater hoses from heater core.
3. Remove quick connect clips from air conditioning lines at expansion valve.
4. Remove air conditioning lines from ex-

pansion valve using quick connectors tool kit No. 7193, or equivalent. Cap air conditioning lines.
5. Remove expansion valve.
6. Remove shifter boot.
7. Remove console to shifter bracket front mounting screws.
8. Remove console to floor bracket rear mounting screws.
9. Engage parking brake and pull console off of floor bracket.
10. Disconnect electrical connectors and remove floor console.
11. Remove rear heat ducts.
12. Remove HVAC housing to dash panel mounting nuts in engine compartment.
13. Remove instrument panel as outlined in "Dash Panel Service" chapter.
14. Disconnect electrical connector from lefthand side of HVAC housing.
15. Remove HVAC housing.
16. Disconnect recirculation motor electrical connector.
17. Remove wiring harness connector from top of housing.
18. Remove seal around evaporator core inlet/outlet.
19. Remove housing top mounting screw.
20. Separate upper from lower housing and remove heater core.
21. Reverse procedure to install.

2007–08 Avenger & Sebring Sedan

1. Recover air conditioning system as outlined in "Air Conditioning" chapter.
2. Partially drain cooling system into suitable container.
3. Remove heat shield located next to fire wall in engine compartment.
4. Disconnect A/C liquid and suction lines from evaporator.
5. Disconnect heater hoses from heater core tubes.
6. Remove instrument panel as outlined in "Dash Panel Service" chapter.
7. Remove rear floor ducts.
8. Remove condensation drain tube.
9. Remove righthand HVAC housing to dash panel retaining nut.
10. Pull HVAC housing rearward to remove housing assembly from passenger compartment.
11. Remove foam seal from flange located on front of HVAC housing.
12. Remove flange to front of HVAC housing retaining screw, then remove flange.
13. Carefully pull heater core out of driver side of air distribution housing.
14. Reverse procedure to install.

EVAPORATOR CORE
REPLACE

Except 2007–08 Avenger & Sebring Sedan

1. Remove HVAC housing as outlined under "Heater Case, Replace."

2. Remove HVAC to instrument panel mounting bolts and separate HVAC housing from instrument panel.
3. Disconnect recirculation motor electrical connector.
4. Remove wiring harness connector from top of housing.
5. Remove seal around evaporator core inlet/outlet.
6. Remove housing to mounting screw.
7. Separate upper housing from lower.
8. Remove evaporator temperature sensor.
9. Remove evaporator and Styrofoam seal around evaporator.
10. Reverse procedure to install.

2007–08 Avenger & Sebring Sedan

1. Remove heater core as outlined under "Heater Core, Replace."
2. Remove air distribution housing to HVAC housing retaining clips.
3. Remove air distribution housing to rear of HVAC housing attaching screws.
4. Remove air distribution housing from rear of HVAC housing.
5. Remove wire lead bracket and blower motor from bottom of HVAC housing.
6. Remove blower motor resistor.
7. Disengage evaporator temperature sensor retaining tabs using suitable needle nose pliers, then remove sensor.
8. Remove foam seal from front halves of HVAC housing. Replace seal if deformed or damaged.
9. Remove attaching screws and retaining clips that secure HVAC halves together.
10. Disengage nine plastic retaining tabs that secure HVAC halves together.
11. Carefully remove evaporator from HVAC housing.
12. Reverse procedure to install.

2.4L Engine

NOTE: On Air Bag Equipped Models, Refer To "Air Bag System Precautions" Located In The Front Of This Manual For System Disarming & Arming Procedures.

NOTE: Refer To "Computer Relearn Procedures" Located In The Front Of This Manual When Battery Power To The Computer Has Been Interrupted.

NOTE: Prior To Performing Any Service Operations Listed In This Section, Consult The "Technical Service Bulletins" Section For Related Information.

INDEX

	Page No.
Balance Shaft, Replace	2-11
Belt Tension Data	2-13
Camshaft, Replace	2-11
Camshaft Lobe Lift Specifications	2-10
Compression Pressure	2-8
Cooling System Bleed	2-13
Crankshaft Rear Oil Seal, Replace	2-12
Crankshaft Seal, Replace	2-12
Cylinder Head, Replace	2-10
Engine Rebuilding Specifications	21-1
Engine, Replace	2-9
Engine Mount, Replace	2-9
Front	2-9
Lefthand	2-9
Rear Mount	2-9
Righthand	2-9

	Page No.
Exhaust Manifold, Replace	2-9
Front Cover, Replace	2-11
Fuel Filter, Replace	2-14
Fuel Pump, Replace	2-14
Intake Manifold, Replace	2-9
Main & Rod Bearings	2-11
Oil Pan, Replace	2-12
Oil Pump, Replace	2-12
Oil Pump Service	2-12
Assemble	2-13
Disassemble	2-12
Inspection	2-12
Piston & Rod Assembly	2-11
Precautions	2-8
Air Bag Systems	2-8
Battery Ground Cable	2-8
Fuel System Pressure Relief	2-8
Radiator, Replace	2-13
Rocker Arms, Replace	2-10

	Page No.
Serpentine Drive Belt	2-13
Air Conditioning Compressor & Alternator Belt	2-13
Installation	2-13
Removal	2-13
Technical Service Bulletins	2-14
Incorrect Oil Filter	2-14
Irregular Engine Snapping Sound	2-14
Low Or No Cabin Heat	2-14
Thermostat, Replace	2-13
Tightening Specifications	2-17
Timing Belt, Replace	2-11
Installation	2-11
Removal	2-11
Valve Arrangement	2-10
Valve Clearance Specifications	2-10
Valve Cover, Replace	2-10
Water Pump, Replace	2-13

PRECAUTIONS
Air Bag Systems

Refer to "Air Bag System Precautions" in the front of this manual for system disarming and arming procedures.

Battery Ground Cable

Prior to service, disconnect battery ground cable and isolate as required.

Fuel System Pressure Relief

1. Remove fuel pump relay from power distribution center.
2. Start and run engine until it stalls.
3. Attempt to restart engine until it will no longer run, then turn ignition key to OFF position.
4. Install fuel pump relay, then erase any DTC's that may have been stored because of removing fuel pump relay.

COMPRESSION PRESSURE

Compression pressure should be 170–225 psi with no more than a 25% variation in pressure between cylinders.

ENGINE MOUNT
REPLACE

Front

1. Raise and support vehicle.
2. Remove front mount to bracket horizontal through bolt, **Fig. 1.**
3. Remove AIR pump.
4. Remove vertical bolts and front mount.
5. Reverse procedure to install.

Lefthand

1. Support transaxle with suitable jack.
2. Remove air cleaner assembly.
3. Disconnect speed control servo bracket and position aside.
4. Remove three engine mount to transaxle mounting bolts, **Fig. 2.**
5. Remove mounting bolts and lefthand mount.
6. Reverse procedure to install.

Righthand

1. Remove coolant overflow bottle.
2. Raise and support vehicle, then remove inner wheel splash guard.
3. Remove righthand engine support assembly mounting bolts from frame rail, **Fig. 3.**
4. Lower vehicle and support engine with suitable floor jack.
5. Remove three engine support to engine bracket mounting bolts.
6. Reverse procedure to install.

Rear Mount

1. Raise and support vehicle, then remove lefthand front wheel.
2. Support transaxle with suitable transaxle jack.
3. Remove mount and rear suspension crossover insulator mounting bolt, **Fig. 4.**
4. Remove four mounting bolts and transaxle mount.
5. Reverse procedure to install.

ENGINE
REPLACE

1. Relieve fuel system pressure as outlined in "Precautions."
2. Drain coolant into suitable container.
3. Recover refrigerant as outlined in "Air Conditioning" chapter.
4. Remove throttle body air inlet hose and air cleaner assembly.
5. Remove upper radiator crossmember, then upper and lower radiator hoses.
6. Disconnect transaxle oil cooler lines at transaxle. Plug lines and fittings.
7. Disconnect air conditioning lines from condenser and remove cooling module.
8. Disconnect electrical harness from transaxle and shift cable.
9. Disconnect engine electrical harness from PCM and bulkhead connector.
10. Raise and support vehicle, then remove front tire and wheel assemblies.

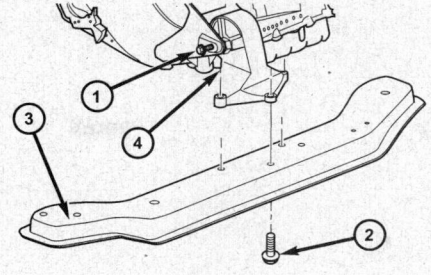

1 - HORIZONTAL THROUGH BOLT
2 - VERTICAL BOLT(S)
3 - LOWER RADIATOR CROSSMEMBER
4 - FRONT ENGINE MOUNT

CR1060100964000X

Fig. 1   Front engine mount replacement

11. Remove both splash shields.
12. Remove both drive axles as outlined in "Front Wheel Drive Axles" chapter.
13. Drain engine oil into suitable container and remove accessory drive belts.
14. Remove power steering pump from bracket and position aside.
15. Disconnect heater return hose from pipe connection.
16. Disconnect air conditioning compressor electrical connector.
17. Disconnect oxygen sensor electrical connector.
18. Remove exhaust pipe to manifold mounting nuts and catalytic convertor pipe band clamp.
19. Remove catalytic convertor pipe from resonator pipe.
20. Disconnect from hanger and remove catalytic convertor pipe.
21. Remove front and rear engine mount through bolts.
22. Remove rear mount bracket from transmission.
23. Remove structural collar and torque reaction bracket, **Fig. 5.**
24. Mark flex plate to torque converter position for installation alignment, then remove torque converter bolts.
25. Lower vehicle, then disconnect battery positive cable from Power Distribution Center (PDC).
26. Disconnect throttle and speed control cables, then coolant recovery overflow hose.
27. Remove heater hose from thermostat housing and disconnect all engine ground straps.
28. Disconnect brake booster and vapor purge hoses, then fuel line from fuel rail.
29. Remove intake manifold as outlined under "Intake Manifold, Replace."
30. Remove alternator.
31. Remove air conditioning suction line at compressor.
32. Remove compressor. Plug ports and lines.
33. Raise and support vehicle.
34. Support engine using dolly and cradle tool Nos. 6135 and 6710, or equivalents.
35. Install post tool No. 6848, or equivalent.

36. Loosen engine cradle mounts to position engine locating holes in bedplate.
37. Lower vehicle until engine rests on cradle mounts. Tighten mounts to cradle frame.
38. Lower vehicle so weight of engine and transaxle is only on cradle.
39. Remove left and righthand vertical mount mounting bolts.
40. Slowly raise and support vehicle.
41. Remove engine and transaxle on cradle around body flanges.
42. Reverse procedure to install, noting the following:
    a. Place structural collar into position between transaxle and oil pan, install transaxle bolt 1 hand tight, **Fig. 5.**
    b. Install collar to oil pan bolts 4 and 5 hand tight.
    c. Position torque reaction bracket in place, then install bolts 2 and 3 hand tight.
    d. **Torque** bolts 1–3 to 75 ft. lbs.
    e. Install bolts 6 and 7 through torque reduction bracket into block hand tight.
    f. **Torque** bolts 4 and 5 to 35 ft. lbs.
    g. **Torque** bolts 6 and 7 to 45 ft. lbs.
    h. **Torque** front engine mount through bolt to 45 ft. lbs.

INTAKE MANIFOLD
REPLACE

1. Relieve fuel system pressure as outlined in "Precautions."
2. Drain engine coolant into suitable container.
3. Remove throttle body air inlet hose and air cleaner housing assembly.
4. Remove throttle and speed control cables from throttle lever and bracket.
5. Remove EGR and oil dipstick tubes.
6. Disconnect vacuum hoses from intake manifold.
7. Disconnect fuel supply line at fuel rail.
8. Remove fastener holding fuel rail bracket to side of cylinder head.
9. Disconnect fuel injectors, then knock and ECT sensors' electrical connectors.
10. Disconnect IAC, then throttle position and MAP sensors' electrical connectors.
11. Disconnect air conditioning pressure switch and compressor clutch, then alternator electrical connectors.
12. Position wiring harness aside and remove fuel rail.
13. Remove coolant outlet connector.
14. Remove mounting bolts and intake manifold.
15. Reverse procedure to install, noting the following:
    a. Install new gasket.
    b. Tighten intake manifold bolts gradually in sequence, **Fig. 6.**

EXHAUST MANIFOLD
REPLACE

1. Raise and support vehicle.
2. Remove exhaust system, **Fig. 7.**

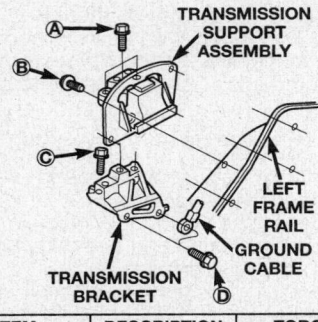

ITEM	DESCRIPTION	TORQUE
A	Bolt	61 N·m (45 ft. lbs.)
B	Bolt	33 N·m (24 ft. lbs.)
C	Bolt	61 N·m (45 ft. lbs.)
D	Bolt	61 N·m (45 ft. lbs.)

CR1069500598000X

Fig. 2 Lefthand engine mount replacement

3. Remove lefthand front tire and wheel assembly.
4. Support transaxle with suitable transaxle jack.
5. Remove mount and rear suspension crossover insulator mounting bolt, **Fig. 4.**
6. Remove four mounting bolts and transaxle mount.
7. Remove exhaust manifold heat shield.
8. Disconnect oxygen sensor electrical connector.
9. Remove mounting bolts and exhaust manifold.
10. Reverse procedure to install noting the following:
    a. Install new gasket.
    b. Tighten bolts in sequence, **Fig. 8.**

CYLINDER HEAD
REPLACE

1. Relieve fuel system pressure as outlined in "Precautions."
2. Remove throttle body air inlet hose and air cleaner housing assembly.
3. Drain coolant into suitable container.
4. Remove intake manifold as outlined under "Intake Manifold, Replace."
5. Disconnect heater hose from thermostat housing.
6. Remove heater tube support bracket from cylinder head.
7. Disconnect Camshaft Position (CMP) sensor and EGR solenoid electrical connectors.
8. Raise and support vehicle, then disconnect exhaust pipe from exhaust manifold.
9. Remove accessory drive belts and crankshaft damper.
10. Remove timing belt as outlined under "Timing Belt, Replace."
11. Remove camshaft sprockets.
12. Remove timing belt idler pulley and rear timing belt cover.
13. Remove air cleaner inlet duct.

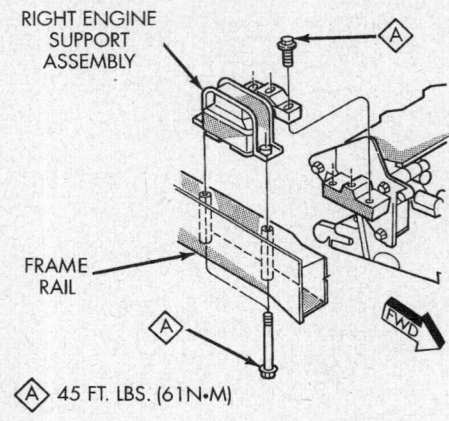

Ⓐ 45 FT. LBS. (61N·M)

CR1069500593000X

Fig. 3 Righthand engine mount replacement

14. Disconnect coil pack electrical connector.
15. Remove spark plug cables from coil pack by twisting cable and boot assembly, then pulling outward.
16. Remove mounting bolts and coil pack.
17. Remove mounting bolts and valve cover.
18. Remove valve cover as outlined under "Valve Cover, Replace."
19. Remove camshafts and rocker arms.
20. Remove mounting bolts and cylinder head.
21. Reverse procedure to install, noting the following:
    a. Apply oil to cylinder head bolts.
    b. **Torque** cylinder head bolts to 25 ft. lbs., in sequence, **Fig. 9.**
    c. **Torque** head bolts to 50 ft. lbs., in sequence.
    d. **Torque** bolts to 50 ft. lbs., in sequence.
    e. Tighten bolts an additional 90° in sequence.

VALVE COVER
REPLACE

1. Disconnect engine ground strap.
2. Disconnect coil pack electrical connector.
3. Remove spark plug cables from coil pack by twisting cable and boot assembly, then pulling outward.
4. Remove mounting bolts and coil pack.
5. Remove mounting bolts and valve cover.
6. Reverse procedure to install, noting the following:
    a. Install new valve cover gaskets and spark plug seals. **Do not allow oil or solvents to contact timing belt.**
    b. Apply silicone rubber adhesive sealant to camshaft cap corners and at top edge of half-round seal.
    c. **Torque** valve cover mounting bolts to 40 inch lbs.
    d. **Torque** mounting bolts to 80 inch lbs.
    e. **Torque** bolts to 105 inch lbs.

Fig. 4 Rear engine mount replacement

TORQUE	
A	61 N·m (45 ft. lbs.)
B	110 N·m (80 ft. lbs.)

CR1069500600000X

VALVE ARRANGEMENT

Intake valves are located on intake manifold side of engine and exhaust valves are located on exhaust manifold side of engine.

CAMSHAFT LOBE LIFT SPECIFICATIONS

Engine	Lift, Inch	
	Intake	Exhaust
2.4L	.324	①

① — 2002–03, .256 inch; .2004–07, .259 inch.

VALVE CLEARANCE SPECIFICATIONS

These engines are equipped with hydraulic lash adjusters designed to maintain zero lash at all times.

ROCKER ARMS
REPLACE

1. Disconnect engine ground strap.
2. Disconnect coil pack electrical connector.
3. Remove spark plug cables from coil pack by twisting cable and boot assembly, then pulling outward.
4. Remove mounting bolts and coil pack.
5. Remove mounting bolts and valve cover.
6. Remove spark plugs.
7. Rotate engine until camshaft lobe on rocker being removed is positioned on its base circle. Piston should be a minimum of .25 inch below TDC.
8. Depress valve assembly until rocker arms can be removed using valve spring compressor tool Nos. 8215-A and 8436 or equivalents.
9. Reverse procedure to install, noting the following:
    a. Install new valve cover gaskets and spark plug seals. **Do not allow oil or solvents to contact timing belt.**
    b. Apply silicone rubber adhesive sealant to camshaft cap corners and at top edge of half-round seal.

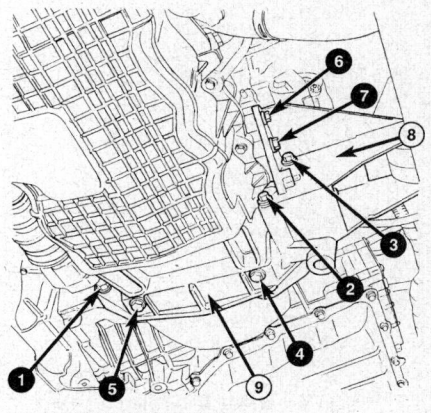

1-7 - BOLT TIGHTENING SEQUENCE
8 - TORQUE REACTION BRACKET
9 - STRUCTURAL COLLAR

CR1060100965000X

Fig. 5 Structural collar & torque reaction bracket replacement

c. **Torque** valve cover mounting bolts to 40 inch lbs.
d. **Torque** mounting bolts to 80 inch lbs.
e. **Torque** bolts to 105 inch lbs.

FRONT COVER
REPLACE

1. Remove mounting bolts and upper cover, **Fig. 10.**
2. Raise and support vehicle, then remove righthand front tire and wheel assembly.
3. Remove belt splash shield and accessory drive belts.
4. Remove mounting bolt and crankshaft damper using puller tool No. 1026 and insert tool No. 6827, or equivalents.
5. Remove air conditioning alternator belt tensioner, then lower vehicle.
6. Remove drive belt cover.
7. Unplug field circuit from alternator.
8. Remove B+ terminal cover by spreading cover using suitable small flat blade tool.
9. Remove B+ terminal nut and wire.
10. Lower vehicle and remove MAP sensor from intake manifold.
11. Remove mounting bolts and alternator.
12. Remove alternator mounting bracket.
13. Raise and support vehicle.
14. Remove mounting bolts and lower cover, **Fig. 10.**
15. Reverse procedure to install.

TIMING BELT
REPLACE
REMOVAL

1. Remove timing belt front covers as outlined under "Front Cover, Replace."
2. Align crankshaft and camshaft sprocket timing marks, **Fig. 11.**
3. Position 6 mm hex head wrench to timing belt tensioner pulley and insert 3 mm hex head wrench into tensioner pulley pin hole, **Fig. 12.**
4. Rotate tensioner pulley counterclock-

wise until 3 mm hex head wrench can be inserted into cylinder block. locking hole.
5. Remove timing belt.

INSTALLATION

1. Ensure crankshaft sprocket timing mark is aligned.
2. Position camshaft sprockets so exhaust sprocket is ½ notch below intake sprocket, **Fig. 13.**
3. Install timing belt over crankshaft sprocket, then around water pump sprocket, idler pulley, camshaft sprockets and tensioner pulley.
4. Remove slack from belt by moving exhaust camshaft sprocket counterclockwise and align timing marks.
5. Remove 3 mm hex head wrench from cylinder block and tensioner.
6. Rotate crankshaft sprocket two revolutions in normal engine rotation direction.
7. Ensure all timing marks are aligned and install front covers as outlined under "Front Cover, Replace."

CAMSHAFT
REPLACE

1. Remove valve cover as outlined under "Valve Cover, Replace."
2. Remove timing belt, sprockets and covers as outlined under "Timing Belt, Replace."
3. Remove outside bearing caps L1, R1, L6 and R6.
4. Loosen camshaft bearing cap mounting bolts one camshaft at a time in sequence, **Fig. 14.**
5. Identify camshafts before removing from head. **Camshafts are not interchangeable.**
6. Reverse procedure to install, noting the following:
   a. Install left and righthand inside camshaft bearing caps, and R6 outside camshaft bearing cap.
   b. **Tighten** caps in sequence one camshaft at a time, **Fig. 15.**
   c. **Outside camshaft bearing cap R6, is to be tightened as an inside bearing cap.**
   d. Install outside camshaft bearing caps L1, R1 and L6, tighten.

BALANCE SHAFT
REPLACE

1. Remove timing belt front cover as outlined under "Front Cover, Replace."
2. Remove gear cover double ended retaining stud, chain covers and gears, **Fig. 16.**
3. Remove balance shaft gear and chain sprocket mounting bolts.
4. Remove crankshaft chain sprocket and chain using two pry bars to work sprocket back and forth.
5. Remove carrier rear cover and balance shafts.
6. Remove four carrier to crankcase mounting bolts.
7. Reverse procedure to install, noting the following:

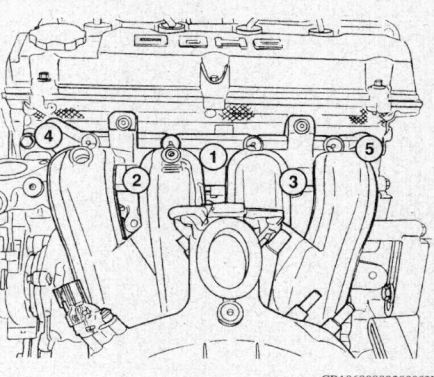

CR1060000928000X

Fig. 6 Intake manifold tightening sequence

a. Align balance shaft gears dot marks and ensure keys face upward, **Fig. 17.**
b. Align balance shaft timing chain and gear timing marks, **Fig. 18.**
c. Position .039 inch thick and 2.75 inches long shim between tensioner and chain.
d. Push tensioner and shim against timing chain with 5.5–6.6 lbs force, **Fig. 19.**
e. Tighten top bottom tensioner bolts with force applied to timing chain.

PISTON & ROD ASSEMBLY

1. L or H stamping on front portion of piston must face toward front of engine.
2. Connecting rod and cap are stamped on side with cylinder number identification.
3. Numbered side of connecting rod cap must be installed on same side as numbered side of rod.
4. **Torque** cap bolts to 20 ft. lbs.
5. Tighten bolts an additional 90°.

MAIN & ROD BEARINGS

All upper and lower bearing shells in the crankcase have oil grooves.

Upper and lower bearing No. 3 halves are flanged to carry the crankshaft thrust loads and are not interchangeable with any other bearing halves.

All bearing cap bolts removed during service procedures are to be cleaned and oiled before installation.

Bearing shells are available in standard and .001 and .010 inch undersized: **Never install an undersize bearing that will reduce clearance below specifications.**

Torque main bearing M8 cap bolts to 20–21 ft. lbs., and M11 bolts to 30 ft. lbs., plus an additional ¼ turn, in sequence

1. Install main bearing shells with lubrication groove in cylinder block. Ensure oil holes in block line up with oil holes in bearings. Bearing tabs must seat in block tab slots.

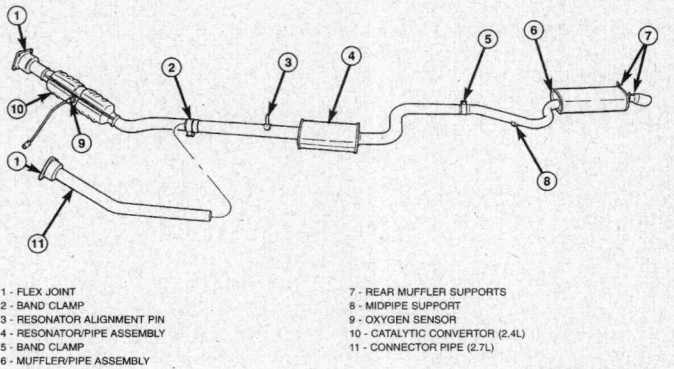

1 - FLEX JOINT
2 - BAND CLAMP
3 - RESONATOR ALIGNMENT PIN
4 - RESONATOR/PIPE ASSEMBLY
5 - BAND CLAMP
6 - MUFFLER/PIPE ASSEMBLY
7 - REAR MUFFLER SUPPORTS
8 - MIDPIPE SUPPORT
9 - OXYGEN SENSOR
10 - CATALYTIC CONVERTOR (2.4L)
11 - CONNECTOR PIPE (2.7L)

CR1070200020000X

Fig. 7 Exhaust system replacement

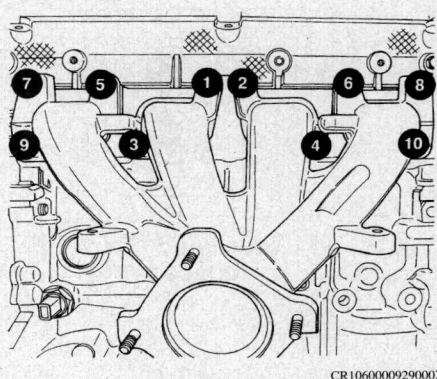

CR1060000929000X

Fig. 8 Exhaust manifold tightening sequence

2. Oil the bearings and journals, then install crankshaft. **Do not get oil on bedplate mating surface.**
3. Ensure both cylinder block and bedplate surfaces are clean.
4. Apply .059–.078 inch bead of anaerobic sealer Mopar Bed Plate Sealant, or equivalent, to cylinder block, **Fig. 20.**
5. Install lower main bearings into main bearing cap/bedplate. Ensure bearing tabs are seated into bedplate slots.
6. Position main bearing/bedplate onto engine block.
7. Lubricate bolt threads with suitable, clean engine oil. Wipe off any excess oil.
8. Install main bearing bedplate to engine block bolts 11, 17 and 20 hand tight, **Fig. 21.**
9. Tighten bolts down together until bedplate contacts cylinder block.
10. Rotate crankshaft until piston No. 4 is at TDC.
11. Move crankshaft rearward to limits of travel
12. Move crankshaft forward to limits of travel.
13. Hold crankshaft in it's furthest forward position by wedging an appropriate tool between rear of cylinder block (not bed plate) and rear crankshaft counterweight.
14. **Torque** mounting bolts 1–10 to 30 ft. lbs., in sequence, **Fig. 21.**
15. Remove wedge tool.
16. **Torque** bolts 1–10 to 30 ft. lbs., in sequence.
17. Tighten bolts and additional 90° in sequence.
18. Install main bearing bedplate engine block bolts 11–20.
19. **Torque** mounting bolts to 20 ft. lbs., in sequence.
20. After main bearing bedplate is installed, ensure crankshaft turning torque does not exceed 50 in. lbs.

CRANKSHAFT SEAL
REPLACE

1. Remove components to access crankshaft sprocket as outlined under "Timing Belt, Replace."
2. Remove crankshaft sprocket using sprocket remover tool No. 6793 and insert tool No. C-4685-C2, or equivalents, **Fig. 22.**
3. Remove front crankshaft seal using oil seal remover tool No. 6771, or equivalent, **Fig. 23.**
4. Reverse procedure to install, noting the following:
   a. Install new seal using seal installation tool No. 6780-1, or equivalent.
   b. Install crankshaft sprocket using installed tool No. 6792, or equivalent.

CRANKSHAFT REAR OIL SEAL
REPLACE

1. Remove transaxle as outlined in **MOTOR's "Domestic Transmission Manual, In-Vehicle Service" manual or "Transmission Service DVD."**
2. remove flex plate.
3. Insert suitable 3/16 screwdriver between dust lip and metal case of seal seat. Pry out seal.
4. Reverse procedure to install, noting the following:
   a. Seal should be installed dry with THIS SIDE OUT mark facing away from block.
   b. Install seal flush with block surface using pilot tool No. 6926-1, seal installation tool No. 6926-2 and handle tool No. C-4171, or equivalents.

OIL PAN
REPLACE

1. Drain engine oil into suitable container.
2. Remove front engine torque bracket from bending strut and insulator mount.
3. Remove mounting bolts, then the collar and bending strut from engine, oil pan and transaxle.
4. Remove mounting bolts and oil pan.
5. Reverse procedure to install. Apply Molar silicone rubber adhesive sealant, or equivalent, at oil pump to engine block parting line and on oil pan gasket to hold gasket in place.

OIL PUMP
REPLACE

1. Remove components to access oil pump as outlined under "Timing Belt, Replace."
2. Remove oil pick-up tube.
3. Remove mounting bolts and oil pump.
4. Reverse procedure to install.

OIL PUMP SERVICE
Disassemble

1. Remove relief valve plug and gasket, then spring and relief valve.
2. Remove mounting bolts and cover.
3. Remove pump rotors.

Inspection

1. Clean all components thoroughly in suitable solvent. Mating surface of oil pump should be smooth. Replace pump cover if scratched or grooved.
2. Measure clearance between suitable straightedge and pump cover. If measurement is more than . 001 inch, replace cover.
3. Measure thickness and diameter of outer rotor. If outer rotor thickness is .301 inch or less, or if diameter is 3.148 inches or less, replace outer rotor.
4. If inner rotor measures .301 inch or less, replace inner rotor.
5. Place outer rotor into pump housing and press to one side. Measure clearance between rotor and housing. If measurement is .015 inch or more, replace housing.
6. Install inner rotor into pump housing. If clearance between inner and outer rotors is .008 inch or more, replace rotors.
7. Measure clearance between straightedge and pump housing face between bolt holes. If measurement is .004 inch, or more, replace pump.
8. Inspect oil pressure relief valve plunger for scoring and for free operation within its bore. Small marks may be removed with 400 grit wet/dry sandpaper.
9. Oil pump relief valve spring should be approximately 2.39 inches long, Spring should have 18–19 lbs. of resistance when compressed to 1.6 inches. Replace spring if it is not within specifications.

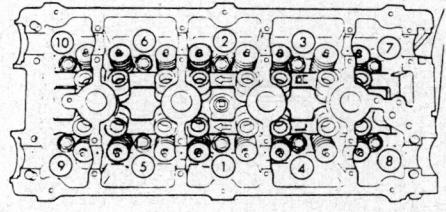

Fig. 9   Cylinder head tightening sequence

CR1069500565000X

Assemble

1. Install inner rotor with chamfer facing cast iron oil pump cover.
2. Apply Molar gasket maker lightly to cover mounting surface on pump body.
3. Install cover and tighten.
4. Install relief valve, spring, gasket and cap, then tighten.
5. Prime oil pump by filling rotor cavity with suitable, clean engine oil.
6. Apply Molar gasket maker to oil pump.
7. Install oil-ring into counter bore on oil pump body discharge passage.
8. Install oil pump slowly onto crankshaft until seated to engine block.

BELT TENSION DATA

Refer to **Fig. 24** for belt tension data.

SERPENTINE DRIVE BELT

Air Conditioning Compressor & Alternator Belt

REMOVAL

1. Raise and support vehicle.
2. Remove righthand front tire and wheel assembly.
3. Remove drive belt splash shield.
4. Insert suitable ⅜ inch drive breaker bar into square opening of belt tensioner pivot plate.
5. Rotate belt tensioner clockwise until tensioner bottoms out, then remove belt from pulleys.

INSTALLATION

1. Insert suitable ⅜ inch drive breaker bar into square opening of belt tensioner pivot plate.
2. Install belt over all pulleys except air conditioning compressor drive pulley, **Fig. 25**.
3. Rotate belt tensioner clockwise until tensioner bottoms out and belt can be installed over air conditioning compressor pulley.
4. Gently release tensioner.
5. Install drive belt splash shield, then the tire and wheel assembly.

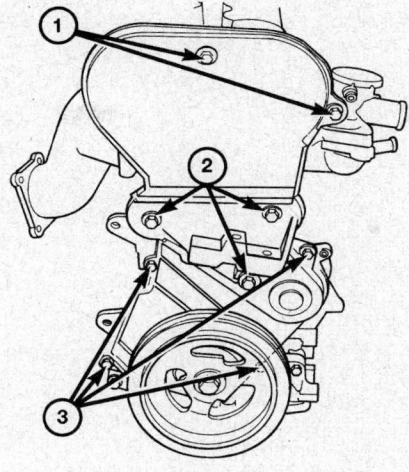

1 - UPPER TIMING BELT COVER FASTENERS
2 - ENGINE SUPPORT BRACKET FASTENERS
3 - LOWER TIMING BELT COVER FASTENERS

CR1060100966000X

Fig. 10   Front cover replacement

COOLING SYSTEM BLEED

This procedure has been revised by a Technical Service Bulletin.

1. Install cooling system filling aid tool No. 8195, or equivalent that looks like funnel that attaches to filler neck in place of pressure cap along with attached hose clip.
2. Pinch off overflow hose attach to fill neck.
3. Attach 5–6.5 foot length of clear ¼ inch I.D. clear hose to bleed valve. Pit other end of hose in suitable container.
4. Open cooling system bleed valve located on water outlet connector near front of engine.
5. Pour suitable coolant mixture into large side of filling aid tool.
6. Slowly fill cooling system, using large side of cooling aid.
7. When steady stream of coolant comes out of clear hose, close bleed valve. Continue filling to top of filling aid tool.
8. Remove overflow hose clip. Excess fluid will drain into coolant bottle overflow.
9. Remove filling aid.
10. Ensure pressure cap bottom seal and filler neck are clean and free of debris.
11. Install coolant bottle pressure cap.

THERMOSTAT
REPLACE

1. Drain coolant to below thermostat into suitable container.
2. Loosen clamp, then disconnect hoses at coolant outlet connector and thermostat housing.
3. Remove coolant outlet connector to thermostat housing mounting bolts.
4. Remove coolant outlet connector.
5. Remove thermostat and gasket.

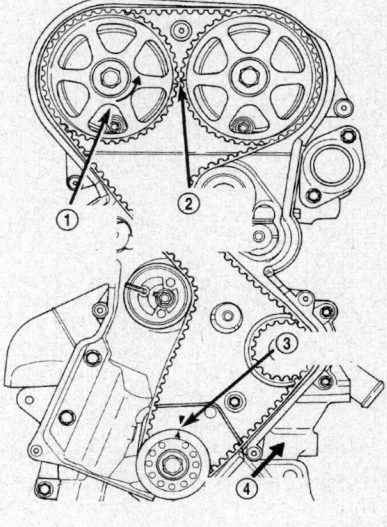

1 - ROTATE CAMSHAFT SPROCKET TO TAKE UP BELT SLACK
2 - CAMSHAFT TIMING MARKS 1/2 NOTCH LOCATION
3 - CRANKSHAFT AT TDC
4 - INSTALL BELT IN THIS DIRECTION

CR1069500624000A

Fig. 11   Crankshaft & camshaft sprocket timing mark alignment

6. Reverse procedure to install, noting the following:
   a. Install new gasket.
   b. Align air bleed with notch in coolant outlet connector.

WATER PUMP
REPLACE

1. Raise and support vehicle, then remove righthand inner splash shield.
2. Remove accessory drive belts.
3. Drain coolant into suitable container.
4. Support engine from bottom and remove righthand engine mount.
5. Remove mounting bolts, then position power steering pump and bracket aside. Power steering lines do not need to be disconnected.
6. Remove timing belt as outlined under "Timing Belt, Replace."
7. Remove mounting bolts water pump.
8. Reverse procedure to install. Install new O-ring gasket in water pump body O-ring groove.

RADIATOR
REPLACE

1. Drain coolant into suitable container, then remove upper radiator crossmember.
2. Disconnect electrical connector and remove radiator fan.
3. Disconnect hoses from radiator.
4. Remove screw holding support bracket for transmission cooler tubes to lefthand side of radiator.
5. Remove air conditioning lines support bracket.
6. Carefully lift out radiator.
7. Reverse procedure to install.

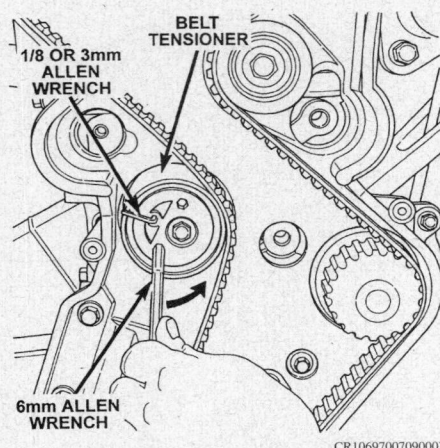

Fig. 12 Locking timing belt tensioner in release position

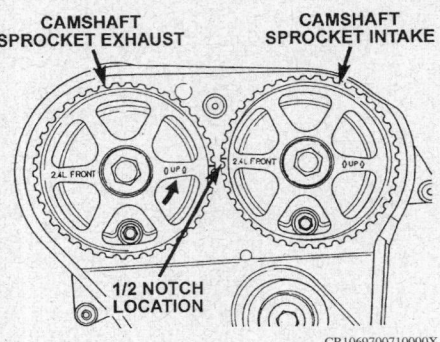

Fig. 13 Camshaft sprocket alignment

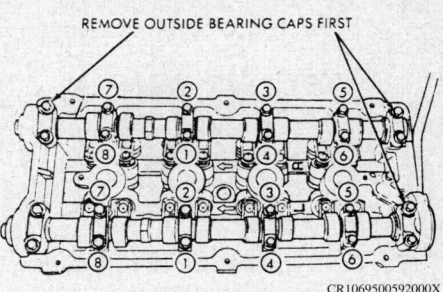

Fig. 14 Camshaft bearing cap removal sequence

FUEL PUMP

REPLACE

The electric fuel pump is not serviceable. If the fuel pump requires service, the entire fuel pump module must be replaced.

1. Relieve fuel system pressure as outlined in "Precautions."
2. Drain and remove fuel tank.
3. Disconnect fuel filter lines at fuel pump module.
4. Clean top of tank to remove dirt and debris.
5. Remove lockout securing pump module with fuel pump module ring spanner tool No. 6856, or equivalent, **Fig. 26.**
6. Remove fuel pump module and O-ring from tank. Discard O-ring.
7. Reverse procedure to install. Install new pump module O-ring.

FUEL FILTER

REPLACE

The fuel filter is part of the fuel pressure regulator and is located on top of the fuel pump module.

1. Relieve fuel system pressure as outlined in "Precautions."
2. Drain fuel tank into suitable container.
3. Raise and support vehicle on hoist.
4. Support fuel tank with suitable transmission jack.
5. Remove strap bolts lower tank slightly.
6. Disconnect fuel filler vent tube, fuel line and vapor line.
7. Disconnect vacuum line from LDP.
8. Loosen clamp and remove fuel filler tube.
9. Unlock and disconnect fuel pump module electrical connector.
10. Lower fuel tank.
11. Disconnect fuel supply line at filter/regulator nipple.
12. Depress locking spring tab on side of

fuel regulator, rotate 90° counterclockwise and remove.
13. Reverse procedure to install.

TECHNICAL SERVICE BULLETINS

Irregular Engine Snapping Sound

On some of these models there may be an irregular engine snapping sound. The sound is irregular, not periodic or harmonious. The sound is more higher pitch snapping, not low metallic knock. The sound may be noticed when the engine is idling in PARK between idle and 1400 RPM at normal operating temperature. The sound is on the upper end (cylinder head) toward the front (passenger side).

This condition may be caused the cam bearing caps L2–L5 and R2–R5.

To correct this condition, proceed as follows:

1. Remove valve cover as outlined under "Valve Cover, Replace."
2. Remove L2 cam bearing cap, **Fig. 27.**
3. **Do not remove L1/R1 or L6 cam bearing caps. Do not loosen L1/R1 or L6 cam bearing caps mounting bolts.**
4. **Remove one cam bearing cap at a time.**
5. Lightly chamfer two bores radius edges using suitable, small hand file, **Fig. 28.**
6. Create a 45° chamfer, .039–.059 inch wide along edge of each bore radios.
7. **Do not scratch bore surface.**
8. Clean part of aluminum filings.
9. Install L2 cam bearing cap and loosely install mounting bolts.
10. Twist cam bearing cap clockwise (as viewed from top of engine) by hand.
11. **Torque** bolts to 105 inch lbs while maintaining clockwise twisting force on cam bearing cap.
12. Repeat procedure on cam bearing caps L3, L4, L5, R2, R3, R4, R5 and R6.

Low Or No Cabin Heat

On some of these models there may be low or no cabin heat, engine overheating and/or coolant bottle damage after servicing the cooling system.

This condition may be caused by not filling cooling system completely.

To correct this condition, proceed as follows:

1. Install cooling system filling aid tool No. 8195, or equivalent that looks like funnel that attaches to filler neck in place of pressure cap along with attached hose clip.
2. Pinch off overflow hose attach to fill neck.
3. Attach 5–6.5 foot length of clear ¼ inch I.D. clear hose to bleed valve. Pit other end of hose in suitable container.
4. Open cooling system bleed valve located on water outlet connector near front of engine.
5. Pour suitable coolant mixture into large side of filling aid tool.
6. Slowly fill cooling system, using large side of cooling aid.
7. When steady stream of coolant comes out of clear hose, close bleed valve. Continue filling to top of filling aid tool.
8. Remove overflow hose clip. Excess fluid will drain into coolant bottle overflow.
9. Remove filling aid.
10. Ensure pressure cap bottom seal and filler neck are clean and free of debris.
11. Install coolant bottle pressure cap.

Incorrect Oil Filter

On some of these models there may be oil loss and engine damage.

This condition may be caused by installing oil filter (part No. MD360935) for 2.4L SOHC Mitsubishi Motors Corp (MCC) used in Sebring Coupe and Stratus Coupe models on 2.4L DOHC DaimlerChrysler engine used in Sebring Convertible, Sebring Sedan and Stratus Sedan.

To correct this condition, install correct filter (part No. 04105409) on 2.4L DOHC engine.

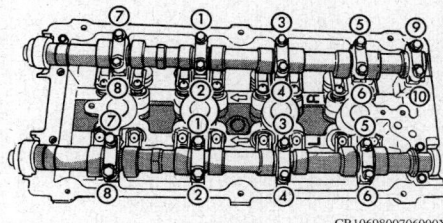

Fig. 15 Camshaft bearing cap tightening sequence

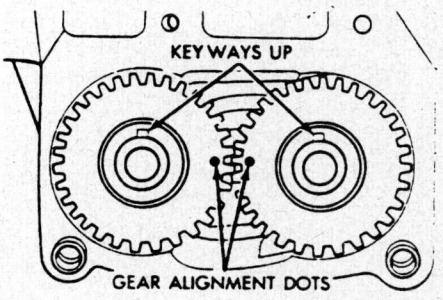

Fig. 17 Balance shaft gear alignment

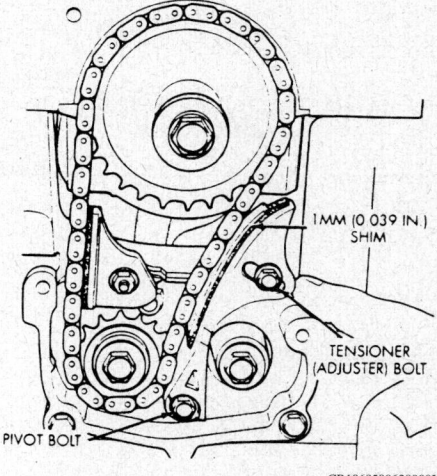

Fig. 18 Balance shaft timing chain & gears alignment

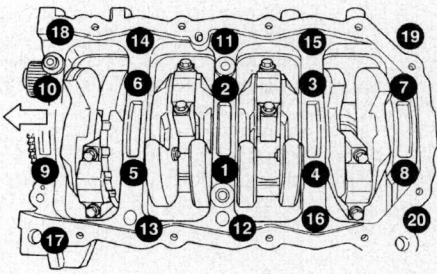

Fig. 21 Main bearing bolt tightening sequence

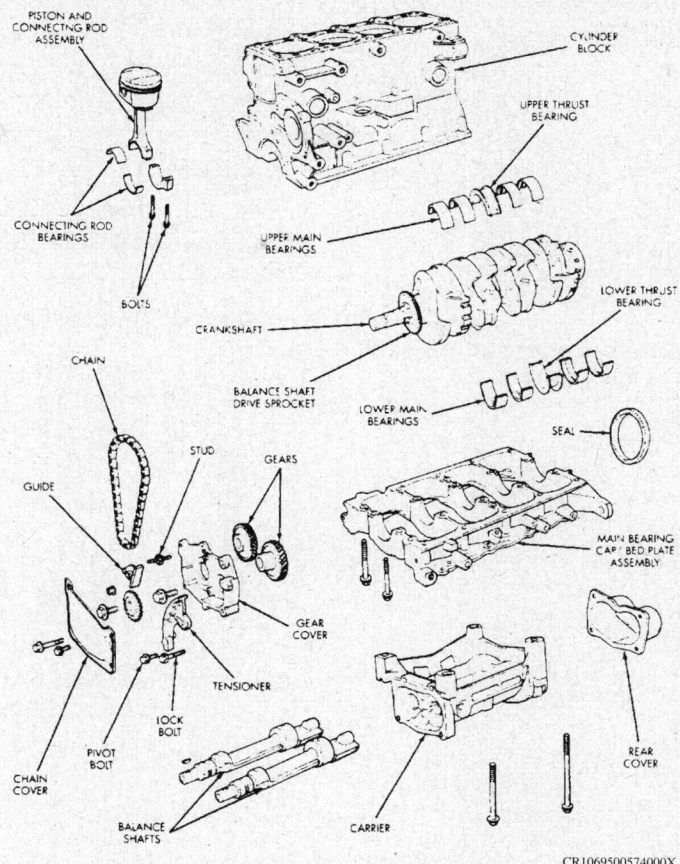

Fig. 16 Exploded view of cylinder block

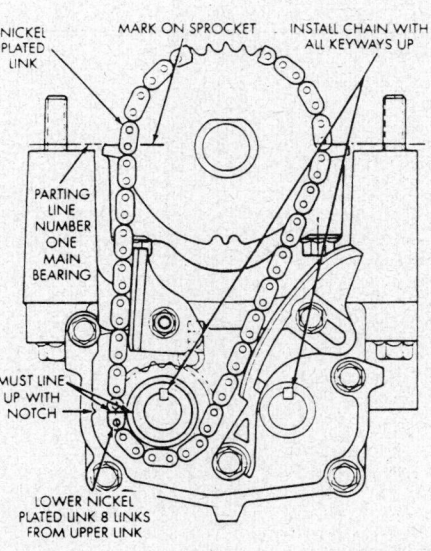

Fig. 19 Balance shaft timing chain tension adjustment

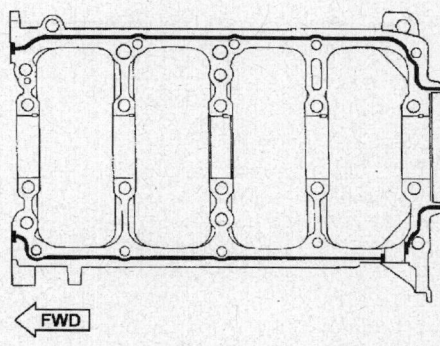

Fig. 20 Sealer application

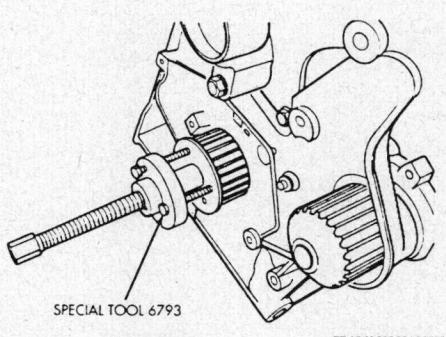

Fig. 22 Crankshaft sprocket replacement

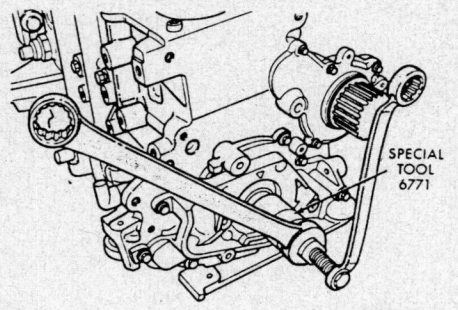

Fig. 23 Front crankshaft oil seal replacement

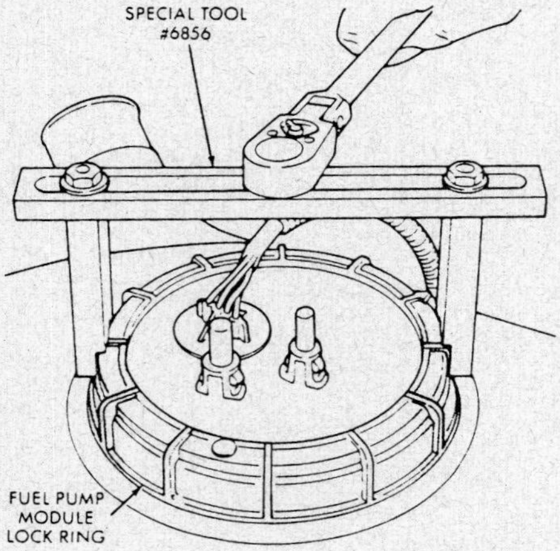

SPECIAL TOOL 6771

CR1069500577000X

Accessory Drive Belt	Belt Tension		
Air Conditioning Compressor/ Generator	Dynamic Tensioned		
Power Steering Pump	New	120 - 180 lbs.	160 - 223 Hz
	Used*	70 - 115 lbs.	114 - 179 Hz

*A belt is considered used after 15 minutes of run-in time.

CR1060200978000X

Fig. 24 Belt tension chart

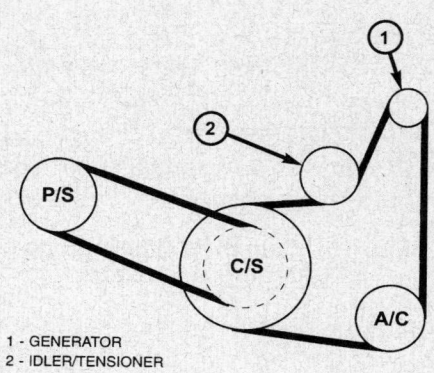

1 - GENERATOR
2 - IDLER/TENSIONER

CR1060100968000X

Fig. 25 Serpentine drive belt routing

SPECIAL TOOL #6856

FUEL PUMP MODULE LOCK RING

CR1029503770000X

Fig. 26 Fuel pump module lockout

FRONT

R1 R2 R3 R4 R5 R6

L1 L2 L3 L4 L5 L6

ARM0400000000983

Fig. 27 Camshaft bearing cap identification

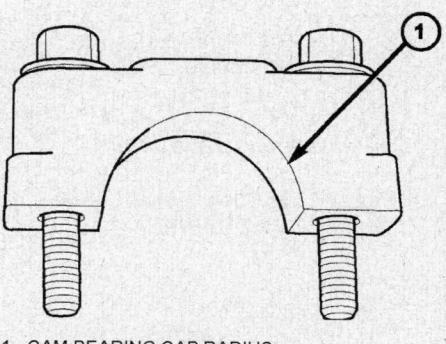

1- CAM BEARING CAP RADIUS

ARM0400000000984

Fig. 28 Camshaft bearing cap chamfer area

2.4L ENGINE

TIGHTENING SPECIFICATIONS

Year	Component	Torque/Ft. Lbs.
2004–08	Balance Shaft Carrier	40
	Balance Shaft Cover	105①
	Balance Shaft Sprocket	20
	Balance Shaft Timing Chain Tensioner	105①
	Camshaft Sprocket	85
	Connecting Rod Cap	②
	Crankshaft Damper	100
	Cylinder Head	⑤
	Engine Mount	③
	Exhaust Manifold	17
	Exhaust Manifold Heat Shield	105①
	Flex Plate	70
	Fuel Pump Module Lock Ring	40
	Fuel Rail To Intake Manifold	16–17
	Fuel Tank Drain Plug	32①
	Intake Manifold	20
	Oil Filter	97①
	Oil Pan	105①
	Oil Pan Drain Plug	20
	Oil Pump	20
	Oil Pump Cover	105①
	Oil Pump Pickup Tube	17
	Oil Pump Relief Valve Retaining Cap	40
	Rocker Arm & Shaft	21
	Spark Plugs	13
	Thermostat Housing	16–17
	Throttle Body Support Bracket	96–108①
	Throttle Body To Intake	16
	Timing Belt Cover (M6)	105①
	Timing Belt Cover (M8)	20
	Timing Belt Cover, Screws	50①
	Timing Belt Tensioner	45
	Valve Cover	④
	Water Pump	105①

① — Inch lbs.
② — Refer to "Piston & Rod Assembly" for tightening procedure & specifications.
③ — Refer to "Engine Mount, Replace" illustrations for tightening specifications.
④ — Refer to "Valve Cover, Replace" for tightening procedure & specifications.
⑤ — Refer to "Cylinder Head, Replace" for tightening procedure & specifications.

2.7L Engine

NOTE: Refer to "2.7L Engine" in "Concorde, Intrepid & 300M" Chapter For Procedures Not Covered In This Section.

NOTE: On Air Bag Equipped Models, Refer To "Air Bag System Precautions" Located In The Front Of This Manual For System Disarming & Arming Procedures.

NOTE: Refer To "Computer Relearn Procedures" Located In The Front Of This Manual When Battery Power To The Computer Has Been Interrupted.

NOTE: Prior To Performing Any Service Operations Listed In This Section, Consult The "Technical Service Bulletins" Section For Related Information.

INDEX

	Page No.		Page No.		Page No.
Belt Tension Data	2-19	Fuel Filter, Replace	2-20	Power Steering Pump Belt	2-19
Compression Pressure	2-18	Fuel Pump, Replace	2-20	Technical Service Bulletins	2-20
Cooling System Bleed	2-19	Precautions	2-18	Low Or No Cabin Heat	2-20
Engine Rebuilding		Air Bag Systems	2-18	Thermostat, Replace	2-20
Specifications	21-1	Battery Ground Cable	2-18	Tightening Specifications	2-21
Engine, Replace	2-18	Fuel System Pressure Relief	2-18	Water Pump, Replace	2-20
Engine Mount, Replace	2-18	Radiator, Replace	2-20		
Front	2-18	Serpentine Drive Belt	2-19		
Lefthand	2-18	Air Conditioning Compressor/			
Rear	2-18	Alternator Belt	2-19		
Righthand	2-18				

PRECAUTIONS

Air Bag Systems

Refer to "Air Bag System Precautions" in the front of this manual for system disarming and arming procedures.

Battery Ground Cable

Prior to service, disconnect battery ground cable and isolate as required.

Fuel System Pressure Relief

1. Remove fuel pump relay from power distribution center.
2. Start and run engine until it stalls.
3. Attempt to restart engine until it will no longer run, then turn ignition key to OFF position.
4. Install fuel pump relay, then erase any DTC's that may have been stored because of removing fuel pump relay.

COMPRESSION PRESSURE

The minimum compression pressure should be no less than 100 psi and the maximum variation between cylinders should be no more than 25%.

ENGINE MOUNT

REPLACE

Front

1. Raise and support vehicle, then remove front mount to bracket horizontal through bolt, **Fig. 1**.
2. Remove vertical bolts and front mount.
3. Reverse procedure to install.

Lefthand

1. Remove throttle body air inlet hose and air cleaner housing assembly.
2. Remove two mounting nuts and position speed control servo bracket aside.
3. Support transaxle with suitable floor jack and wooden block.
4. Remove three vertical bolts from mount to transaxle bracket, **Fig. 2**.
5. Slightly lower transaxle.
6. Remove frame rail bolts and mount.
7. Reverse procedure to install.

Rear

1. Remove throttle body air inlet hose and air cleaner housing assembly.
2. Remove three rear mount bracket to transaxle case vertical bolts, **Fig. 3**.
3. Raise and support vehicle, then remove rear mount bracket through bolt.
4. Remove rear mount bracket to tran-

saxle case horizontal bolt.
5. Remove mount bracket.
6. Remove rear mount to suspension crossmember mounting bolts and rear mount.
7. Reverse procedure to install.

Righthand

1. Remove engine coolant overflow container, then heater tube mounting screw.
2. Raise and support vehicle, then remove inner splash shield.
3. Remove heater tube rear mounting screw.
4. Remove righthand engine support assembly vertical bolts from frame rail, **Fig. 4**.
5. Lower vehicle, then support engine using suitable floor jack and block of wood placed under oil pan.
6. Remove mounting bolts and righthand engine mount.
7. Reverse procedure to install.

ENGINE

REPLACE

1. Relieve fuel system pressure as outlined in "Precautions."
2. Drain coolant into suitable container.
3. Recover air conditioning refrigerant as outlined in "Air Conditioning" chapter.

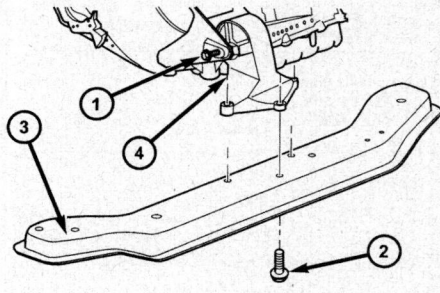

1 - HORIZONTAL THROUGH BOLT
2 - VERTICAL BOLT(S)
3 - LOWER RADIATOR CROSSMEMBER
4 - FRONT ENGINE MOUNT

CR1060000933000X

Fig. 1 Front engine mount replacement

4. Remove throttle body air inlet hose and air cleaner housing assembly.
5. Raise and support vehicle, then remove both front tire and wheel assemblies.
6. Remove left and righthand splash shields.
7. Remove front fascia to and lower air shield to crossmember mounting bolts.
8. Remove front bumper fascia. Lower vehicle.
9. Remove upper radiator crossmember, then disconnect upper and lower radiator hoses at radiator.
10. Disconnect transaxle oil cooler lines at transaxle. Plug openings.
11. Disconnect air conditioning lines at condenser and remove cooling fan module.
12. Disconnect transaxle electrical connectors and shift cable.
13. Disconnect engine electrical harness from PCM and bulkhead connectors.
14. Remove ABS brake module and position aside.
15. Disconnect brake line from retaining clips, then raise and support vehicle.
16. Remove both axle shafts as outlined in "Front Drive Axle" chapter.
17. Remove through bolt and front engine mount from lower radiator crossmember.
18. Remove lower radiator crossmember and accessory drive belts.
19. Remove, then position power steering pump and bracket with lines attached aside.
20. Disconnect heater return from pipe connection at righthand front frame rail area.
21. Disconnect electrical connector, remove and position air conditioning compressor aside.
22. Remove structural collar and exhaust cross-under pipe.
23. Remove rear engine mount and transaxle bracket, then drain engine oil into suitable container.
24. Remove transaxle torque converter housing cover.
25. Mark flex plate to torque converter position for installation alignment, then remove torque converter bolts.

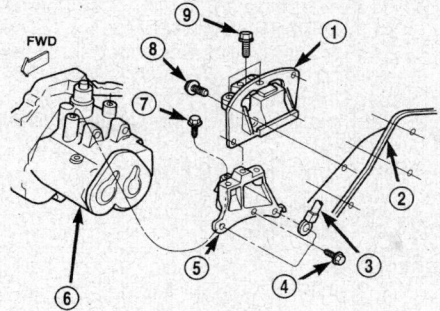

1 - TRANSMISSION SUPPORT ASSEMBLY
2 - LEFT FRAME RAIL
3 - GROUND CABLE
4 - BOLT (D)
5 - TRANSMISSION BRACKET
6 - TRANSMISSION
7 - BOLT (C)
8 - BOLT (B)
9 - BOLT (A)

CR1060000930000X

Fig. 2 Lefthand side engine mount replacement

26. Lower vehicle, then disconnect positive cable from battery and PDC.
27. Disconnect ground cable from lefthand side transaxle mount bracket.
28. Disconnect throttle and speed control cables.
29. Disconnect coolant pressure bottle hose from engine outlet connector.
30. Disconnect heater hose from engine outlet connector.
31. Disconnect ground strap at righthand shock tower, then fuel line.
32. Disconnect brake booster and vapor purge vacuum hoses.
33. Disconnect all engine ground straps.
34. Lower vehicle enough to install engine dolly tool No. 6135 and cradle tool No. 6710 with posts tool No. 6848, or equivalents.
35. Loosen cradle engine mounts to allow movement for positioning onto engine locating holes on engine block, compressor mount bracket and oil pan rail.
36. Lower vehicle and position cradle until engine is resting on posts. Tighten post mounts to cradle frame.
37. Lower vehicle so only weight of engine is on cradle.
38. Remove left and righthand engine mount bolts.
39. Slowly raise vehicle and remove engine.
40. Reverse procedure to install.

BELT TENSION DATA

Refer to **Fig. 5** for belt tension data.

SERPENTINE DRIVE BELT

Air Conditioning Compressor/ Alternator Belt

1. Raise and support vehicle, then re-

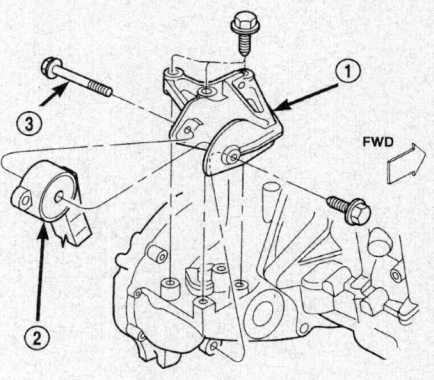

1 - REAR TORQUE BRACKET
2 - REAR MOUNT
3 - THROUGH BOLT

CR1060000931000X

Fig. 3 Rear engine mount replacement

move righthand front tire and wheel assembly.
2. Remove splash shield.
3. Loosen tensioner locking bolt and pivot bolt.
4. Rotate tensioner clockwise and remove belt.
5. Reverse procedure to install.

Power Steering Pump Belt

1. Raise and support vehicle, then remove righthand front tire and wheel assembly.
2. Remove splash shield.
3. Loosen tensioner locking bolt and pivot bolt.
4. Rotate tensioner clockwise and remove air conditioning compressor/ alternator belt.
5. Loosen adjusting bolt, then pivot power steering pump and remove belt.
6. Reverse procedure to install.

COOLING SYSTEM BLEED

This procedure has been revised by a Technical Service Bulletin.
1. Install cooling system filling aid tool No. 8195, or equivalent that looks like funnel that attaches to filler neck in place of pressure cap along with attached hose clip.
2. Pinch off overflow hose attach to fill neck.
3. Attach 5–6.5 foot length of clear ¼ inch I.D. clear hose to bleed valve. Pit other end of hose in suitable container.
4. Open cooling system bleed valve located on water outlet connector near front of engine.
5. Pour suitable coolant mixture into large side of filling aid tool.
6. Slowly fill cooling system, using large side of cooling aid.
7. When steady stream of coolant comes

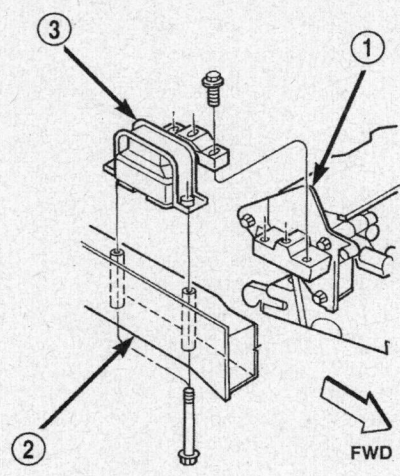

1 - ENGINE SUPPORT BRACKET
2 - FRAME RAIL
3 - RIGHT ENGINE MOUNT

CR1060000932000X

Fig. 4   Righthand side mount replacement

out of clear hose, close bleed valve. Continue filling to top of filling aid tool.
8. Remove overflow hose clip. Excess fluid will drain into coolant bottle overflow.
9. Remove filling aid.
10. Ensure pressure cap bottom seal and filler neck are clean and free of debris.
11. Install coolant bottle pressure cap.

THERMOSTAT

REPLACE

1. Drain cooling system into suitable container.
2. Raise and support vehicle.
3. Remove righthand front tire and wheel assembly.
4. Remove belt splash shield.
5. Remove accessory drive belts and lower alternator mounting bolt.
6. Lower vehicle and disconnect alternator electrical connectors.
7. Disconnect air conditioning clutch and pressure sensor electrical connectors.
8. Remove oil dipstick and tube, Plug hole.
9. Remove alternator and disconnect hoses at thermostat housing.
10. Remove mounting bolts and thermostat housing.
11. Reverse procedure to install. Install thermostat with bleed valve located at 12 o'clock position.

WATER PUMP

REPLACE

1. Drain cooling system into suitable container.

2. Remove timing chain cover as outlined under "Front Cover, Replace."
3. Remove timing chain and guides as outlined under "Timing Chain, Replace."
4. Remove mounting bolts and water pump.
5. Reverse procedure to install.

RADIATOR

REPLACE

1. Drain cooling system into suitable container.
2. Remove upper radiator crossmember.
3. Disconnect electrical connector, and remove radiator fan.
4. Disconnect radiator hoses.
5. Remove screw holding support bracket for transaxle cooler tubes at lefthand side of radiator.
6. Remove air conditioning lines support bracket from righthand side of radiator.
7. Remove mounting screws and air conditioning condenser.
8. Remove radiator.
9. Reverse procedure to install.

FUEL PUMP

REPLACE

1. Relieve fuel system pressure as outlined in "Precautions."
2. Drain fuel tank into suitable container.
3. Raise vehicle and support on hoist.
4. Support fuel tank with suitable transmission jack.
5. Remove strap bolts and lower tank slightly.
6. Disconnect fuel filler vent tube, fuel line and vapor line.
7. Disconnect vacuum line from LDP.
8. Loosen clamp and remove fuel filler tube.
9. Unlock and disconnect fuel pump module electrical connector.
10. Lower fuel tank.
11. Disconnect fuel line from fuel pump module by depressing quick connect retainers.
12. Disconnect fuel pump electrical connector by pushing down on retainer and pulling connector off.
13. Remove fuel pump module lock nut using spanner wrench tool No. 6856, or equivalent.
14. Remove fuel pump and O-ring seal from tank. Discard old seal.
15. Reverse procedure to install.

FUEL FILTER

REPLACE

The fuel filter is part of the fuel pressure regulator and is located on top of the fuel pump module.
1. Relieve fuel system pressure as outlined in "Precautions."

Accessory Drive Belt		Belt Tension	
Air Conditioning Compressor/ Generator	New	185 - 235 lbs.	204 - 230 Hz
	Used*	110 - 160 lbs.	157 - 190 Hz
Power Steering Pump	New	120 - 180 lbs.	122 - 170 Hz
	Used*	70 - 115 lbs.	94 - 136 Hz
*A belt is considered used after 15 minutes of run-in time.			

CR1060200977000X

Fig. 5   Belt tension data

2. Remove fuel tank as outlined under "Fuel Pump, Replace."
3. Disconnect fuel supply line at filter/ regulator nipple.
4. Depress locking spring tab on side of fuel regulator, rotate 90° counterclockwise and remove.
5. Slide tank forward allowing fill neck to clear suspension crossmember, then lower tank to remove.
6. Reverse procedure to install.

TECHNICAL SERVICE BULLETINS

Low Or No Cabin Heat

On some of these models there may be low or no cabin heat, engine overheating and/or coolant bottle damage after servicing the cooling system.

This condition may be caused by not filling cooling system completely.

To correct this condition, proceed as follows:
1. Install cooling system filling aid tool No. 8195, or equivalent that looks like funnel that attaches to filler neck in place of pressure cap along with attached hose clip.
2. Pinch off overflow hose attach to fill neck.
3. Attach 5–6.5 foot length of clear ¼ inch I.D. clear hose to bleed valve. Pit other end of hose in suitable container.
4. Open cooling system bleed valve located on water outlet connector near front of engine.
5. Pour suitable coolant mixture into large side of filling aid tool.
6. Slowly fill cooling system, using large side of cooling aid.
7. When steady stream of coolant comes out of clear hose, close bleed valve. Continue filling to top of filling aid tool.
8. Remove overflow hose clip. Excess fluid will drain into coolant bottle overflow.
9. Remove filling aid.
10. Ensure pressure cap bottom seal and filler neck are clean and free of debris.
11. Install coolant bottle pressure cap.

TIGHTENING SPECIFICATIONS

Year	Component	Torque Ft. Lbs.
2004–08	Air Conditioning Compressor	21
	Alternator Bracket	30
	Engine Mount To Bracket, Rear	45
	Engine Mount To Crossmember, Rear	45
	Engine Mount To Frame Rail, Lefthand	24
	Engine Mount To Frame Rail, Righthand	45
	Engine Mount To Support Bracket, Righthand	45
	Engine Mount To Transaxle Bracket, Lefthand	45
	Engine Mount Bracket To Transaxle, Rear	80
	Front Engine Mount, Front	45
	Thermostat Housing	105①
	Water Pump	105①

① — Inch lbs.

3.5L Engine

NOTE: On Air Bag Equipped Models, Refer To "Air Bag System Precautions" Located In The Front Of This Manual For System Disarming & Arming Procedures.

NOTE: Refer To "Computer Relearn Procedures" Located In The Front Of This Manual When Battery Power To The Computer Has Been Interrupted.

NOTE: Prior To Performing Any Service Operations Listed In This Section, Consult The "Technical Service Bulletins" Section For Related Information.

INDEX

	Page No.
Camshaft, Replace	2-24
Compression Pressure	2-22
Cooling System Bleed	2-25
Crankshaft Rear Oil Seal, Replace	2-24
Crankshaft Seal, Replace	2-24
Cylinder Head, Replace	2-23
Lefthand	2-23
Righthand	2-23
Engine Rebuilding Specifications	21-1
Engine, Replace	2-22
Engine Mount, Replace	2-22
Front Engine Mount	2-22
Lefthand Engine Mount	2-22

	Page No.
Rear Engine Mount	2-22
Righthand Engine Mount	2-22
Exhaust Manifold, Replace	2-23
Front	2-23
Rear	2-23
Fuel Filter, Replace	2-25
Fuel Pump, Replace	2-25
Intake Manifold, Replace	2-22
Lower	2-22
Upper	2-22
Main & Rod Bearings	2-24
Oil Pan, Replace	2-24
Oil Pump, Replace	2-25
Oil Pump Service	2-25
Assemble	2-25

	Page No.
Disassemble	2-25
Inspection	2-25
Piston & Rod Assembly	2-24
Precautions	2-22
Air Bag Systems	2-22
Battery Ground Cable	2-22
Fuel System Pressure Relief	2-22
Radiator, Replace	2-25
Rocker Arms, Replace	2-24
Thermostat, Replace	2-25
Tightening Specifications	2-26
Timing Belt, Replace	2-24
Valve Clearance Specifications	2-24
Valve Cover, Replace	2-24
Water Pump, Replace	2-25

PRECAUTIONS

Air Bag Systems

Refer to "Air Bag System Precautions" in the front of this manual for system disarming and arming procedures.

Battery Ground Cable

Prior to service, disconnect battery ground cable and isolate as required.

Fuel System Pressure Relief

1. Remove fuel pump relay from power distribution center.
2. Start and run engine until it stalls.
3. Attempt to restart engine until it will no longer run, then turn ignition key to OFF position.
4. Install fuel pump relay, then erase any DTC's that may have been stored because of removing fuel pump relay.

COMPRESSION PRESSURE

The minimum compression pressure should be no less than 100 psi and the maximum variation between cylinders should be no more than 25%.

ENGINE MOUNT
REPLACE

Lefthand Engine Mount

1. Disconnect battery ground cable.
2. Remove air cleaner housing assembly.
3. Support transmission with suitable floor jack and block of wood.
4. Remove mounting bolts then mount.
5. Reverse procedure to install.

Righthand Engine Mount

1. Remove power steering fluid reservoir.
2. Disconnect ground strap.
3. Support engine with suitable jack and block of wood.
4. Remove engine mount bracket bolts, then bracket.
5. Remove engine mount bolts, then engine mount.
6. Reverse procedure to install.

Front Engine Mount

1. Raise and support vehicle.
2. Remove fore aft member to mount bolts.
3. Remove through bolt.
4. Remove fore aft member mounting bolts, then member.
5. Remove front engine mount.
6. Reverse procedure to install.

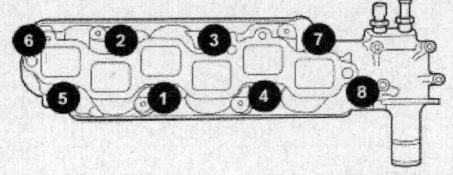

ARM0600000000323

Fig. 1 Lower intake manifold tightening sequence

Rear Engine Mount

1. Remove three top mount bracket bolts.
2. Raise and support vehicle.
3. Remove four lower mount to cradle bolts.
4. Remove rear engine mount.
5. Reverse procedure to install.

ENGINE
REPLACE

1. Remove engine cover.
2. Drain coolant into suitable container.
3. Recover air conditioning refrigerant as outlined in "Air Conditioning" chapter.
4. Relieve fuel system pressure as outlined in "Precautions."
5. Disconnect fuel line from fuel rail inlet and position aside.
6. Remove air cleaner assembly.
7. Remove intake manifold as outlined under "Intake Manifold, Replace."
8. Raise and support vehicle.
9. Remove lower engine protection shield.
10. Disconnect exhaust extension pipe and gasket from cross-under pipe.
11. Remove center brace.
12. Remove cross under pipe.
13. Remove righthand front half shaft assembly as outlined in "Front Drive Axle" chapter.
14. Remove rear exhaust manifold as outlined under "Exhaust Manifold, Replace," then PTU.
15. Remove lefthand, righthand and front splash shields.
16. Remove front engine mount bracket.
17. Remove starter as outlined under "Starter Motor, Replace."
18. Disconnect electrical connector from solenoid/pressure switch at transmission and position harness aside.
19. Disconnect both output speed sensor electrical connections and position harness aside.
20. Disconnect lower radiator hose from return tube.
21. Lower vehicle.
22. Remove lefthand front half shaft as outlined in "Front Drive Axle" chapter, then inner wheel well.
23. Disconnect crankshaft electrical connector.
24. Remove crankshaft sensor mounting bolt, then sensor.
25. Disconnect gearshift cable from transmission and position aside.
26. Disconnect battery cables from lefthand shock tower and position aside.
27. Disconnect both PCM harness connectors and position aside.

28. Disconnect heater core supply hose from intake manifold outlet.
29. Disconnect coolant reservoir hose from bottle and position aside.
30. Disconnect upper radiator hose from thermostat housing.
31. Disconnect both A/C lines from A/C compressor.
32. Disconnect A/C pressure transducer electrical connector.
33. Remove A/C discharge line from condenser.
34. Remove front exhaust manifold as outlined under "Exhaust Manifold, Replace."
35. Remove cooling fan assembly.
36. Disconnect power steering pressure and supply hoses from pump.
37. Remove transmission as outlined in MOTOR'S "Domestic Transmission, In-Vehicle Service" manual or "Transmission Service DVD."
38. Install engine lift bracket tool No. 8334, or equivalent to front of engine.
39. Attach engine lift chains.
40. Remove three right hand engine mount bolts.
41. Remove ground strap from hood and position hood back.
42. Remove engine.
43. Reverse position to install.

INTAKE MANIFOLD
REPLACE

Lower

1. Relieve fuel system pressure as outlined in "Precautions."
2. Drain cooling system into suitable container.
3. Disconnect upper radiator hose from thermostat housing.
4. Remove upper intake manifold as outlined under "Upper Intake Manifold, Replace."
5. Disconnect fuel injector and coolant temperature sensor electrical connections.
6. Disconnect heater supply and return hoses from intake manifold.
7. Disconnect fuel supply hose from fuel rail.
8. Remove fuel rail attaching bolts.
9. Remove fuel rail and injectors as an assembly.
10. Remove lower intake manifold attaching bolts, then position ignition coil capacitor aside.
11. Remove intake manifold.
12. Reverse procedure to install, noting the following:
   a. **Torque** bolts in sequence, **Fig. 1**, to 21 ft. lbs.

Upper

1. Remove engine cover.
2. Remove air cleaner housing and inlet hose.
3. Disconnect EGR tube.
4. Disconnect PCV, EVAP purge solenoid, EGR tube and power brake booster vacuum hoses.
5. Disconnect manifold tuning valve,

short runner valve, TPS and MAP sensor electrical connectors.

6. Remove rear manifold retaining brackets.
7. Remove intake manifold mounting bolts, then manifold.
8. Reverse procedure to install, noting the following:
   a. **Torque** mount bolts to 105 inch lbs. working from center outward.

EXHAUST MANIFOLD
REPLACE
Front

1. Raise and support vehicle.
2. Remove lower engine cover.
3. Remove front cross-under pipe mounting bolts.
4. Remove upper O2 sensor.
5. Loosen oil level indicator tube retaining bolt, then position dipstick out of the way.
6. Remove lower O2 sensor.
7. Remove mounting bolts, then exhaust manifold.
8. Reverse procedure to install, noting the following:
   a. **Torque** mounting bolts to 17 ft. lbs. starting from the center working outward.

Rear

1. Raise and support vehicle.
2. Remove lower engine cover.
3. Remove righthand front halfshaft assembly as outlined in "Front Drive Axle" chapter.
4. Remove extension pipe retaining nuts.
5. Remove bracket to bell housing retainer.
6. Remove center crossmember.
7. Remove exhaust manifold cross-under pipe.
8. Remove front extension pipe.
9. Remove rear lower O2 sensor.
10. Remove lower heat shield retainers.
11. Remove upper heat shield nuts.
12. Remove rear upper O2 sensor and heat shields.
13. Remove mounting bolts, then exhaust manifold.
14. Reverse procedure to install, noting the following:
   a. **Torque** mounting bolts to 17 ft. lbs. starting from the center working outward.

CYLINDER HEAD
REPLACE
Lefthand

1. Relieve fuel system pressure as outlined in "Precautions."
2. Drain cooling system into suitable container.
3. Remove engine cover.
4. Remove air cleaner housing.
5. Remove radiator fan assembly.
6. Remove coolant recovery bottle.

ARM0600000000324

Fig. 2   Cylinder head tightening sequence

7. Remove alternator as outlined under "Alternator, Replace."
8. Disconnect fuel line at fuel rail.
9. Remove upper and lower intake manifolds as outlined under "Intake Manifold, Replace."
10. Raise and support vehicle.
11. Remove front exhaust manifold as outlined under "Front Exhaust Manifold, Replace."
12. Remove righthand front tire and inner splash shield.
13. Remove accessory drive belt.
14. Remove righthand engine mount as outlined under "Engine Mount, Replace."
15. Support engine with suitable jack.
16. Remove lower crossmember, then lower engine.
17. Remove vibration damper mounting bolt.
18. Remove damper using puller tool Nos. 1023 and 9020–R or equivalent.
19. Remove lower accessory drive belt idler pulley.
20. Remove power steering reservoir mounting bolts, then position reservoir aside.
21. Remove lower outer timing belt cover bolts.
22. Lower vehicle.
23. Remove upper drive belt idler pulley.
24. Remove belt tensioner.
25. Support engine with suitable floor jack and block of wood.
26. Remove upper engine mount as outlined under "Engine Mount, Replace."
27. Remove remaining timing cover bolts, then timing cover.
28. Remove timing belt as outlined under "Timing Belt, Replace."
29. Remove lefthand valve cover to cylinder head ground strap.
30. Remove lefthand valve cover.
31. Remove camshaft as outlined under "Camshaft, Replace."
32. Counterhold left cam gear and loosen cam gear retaining bolt.
33. Remove front timing belt housing to cylinder head bolts.
34. Remove left camshaft thrust plate.
35. Carefully push camshaft out of back of cylinder head approximately 3.5 inches, then remove camshaft sprocket bolt.
36. Remove cylinder head bolts in reverse order of tightening sequence, **Fig. 2**.
37. Remove cylinder head.
38. Reverse procedure to install, noting the following:
   a. First pass **torque** cylinder head

bolts in sequence, **Fig. 2,** to 45 ft. lbs.
   b. Second pass **torque** to 65 ft. lbs.
   c. Third pass **torque** to 65 ft. lbs.
   d. Final pass turn an additional 90°.
   e. Bolt torque after 90° turn should be over 90 ft. lbs., if not replace bolt.

Righthand

1. Relieve fuel system pressure as outlined in "Precautions."
2. Drain cooling system into suitable container.
3. Remove engine cover.
4. Remove air cleaner housing.
5. Remove coolant recovery bottle.
6. Remove alternator as outlined under "Alternator, Replace."
7. Disconnect fuel line at fuel rail.
8. Remove upper and lower intake manifolds as outlined under "Intake Manifold, Replace."
9. Raise and support vehicle.
10. Remove rear exhaust manifold as outlined under "Rear Exhaust Manifold, Replace."
11. Remove right front tire and inner splash shield.
12. Remove accessory drive belt.
13. Remove righthand engine mount as outlined under "Engine Mount, Replace."
14. Support engine with suitable jack.
15. Remove lower crossmember, then lower engine.
16. Remove vibration damper mounting bolt.
17. Remove damper using puller tool Nos. 1023 and 9020–R or equivalent.
18. Remove lower accessory drive belt idler pulley.
19. Remove lower outer timing belt cover bolts.
20. Lower vehicle.
21. Remove upper accessory drive belt idler pulley.
22. Remove belt tensioner.
23. Support engine with suitable floor jack and block of wood.
24. Remove upper engine mount as outlined under "Engine Mount, Replace."
25. Remove power steering reservoir mounting bolts, then position reservoir aside.
26. Remove remaining timing belt cover bolts, then cover.
27. Remove timing belt as outlined under "Timing Belt, Replace."
28. Remove righthand valve cover to cylinder head ground strap.
29. Remove EGR valve and tube assembly.
30. Remove righthand valve cover.
31. Remove right camshaft as outlined under "Camshaft, Replace."
32. Counterhold cam gear, then loosen right cam gear retaining bolt.
33. Remove inner timing cover to righthand cylinder head retaining bolts.
34. Remove right rear camshaft thrust plate.
35. Carefully push camshaft out of back of cylinder head approximately 3.5 inches, then remove camshaft sprocket bolt.

36. Remove cylinder head bolts in reverse order of tightening sequence, **Fig. 2.**
37. Remove cylinder head.
38. Reverse procedure to install, noting the following:
    a. First pass **torque** cylinder head bolts in sequence, **Fig. 2,** to 45 ft. lbs.
    b. Second pass **torque** to 65 ft. lbs.
    c. Third pass **torque** to 65 ft. lbs.
    d. Final pass turn an additional 90°.
    e. Bolt torque after 90° turn should be over 90 ft. lbs., if not replace bolt.

VALVE COVER
REPLACE

1. Remove upper intake manifold as outlined under "Intake Manifold, Replace."
2. Cover lower intake manifold with suitable cover during service.
3. Remove three ignition coils.
4. Remove upper intake manifold support bracket from engine.
5. Lift wire harness, then remove MVA from valve cover as required.
6. Loosen valve cover mounting bolts, then remove valve cover.
7. Reverse procedure to install.

VALVE CLEARANCE SPECIFICATIONS

These engines are equipped with hydraulic lash adjusters designed to maintain zero lash at all times.

ROCKER ARMS
REPLACE

1. Remove valve covers as outlined under "Valve Cover, Replace."
2. Identify rocker arm assembly and rocker arms before disassembly.
3. Remove rocker arm mounting bolts.
4. Remove rocker arm assembly.
5. Reverse procedure to install.

TIMING BELT
REPLACE

The 3.5L engine is **NOT** a freewheeling engine. Therefore, loosen valve train rocker assemblies before servicing timing drive.
1. Relieve fuel system pressure as outlined in "Precautions."
2. Remove valve covers as outlined under "Valve Cover, Replace."
3. Remove front timing belt cover.
4. Mark timing belt running direction.
5. Rotate engine clockwise until crankshaft mark aligns with TDC mark on oil pump housing and camshaft sprocket timing marks are aligned with marks on rear cover, **Fig. 3.**
6. Remove timing belt tensioner, then timing belt.
7. Reverse procedure to install, noting the following:
    a. When tensioner is removed from engine it is necessary to compress plunger into tensioner body.
    b. Place tensioner into a vise and

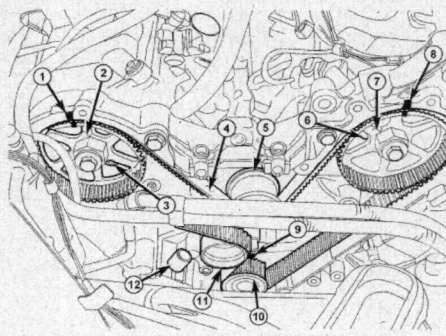

1- CAMSHAFT REFERENCE MARK
2- CAMSHAFT SPROCKET
3- CAMSHAFT SENSOR
4- TIMING BELT
5- IDLER PULLEY
6- CAMSHAFT SENSOR
7- CAMSHAFT SPROCKET
8- CAMSHAFT REFERENCE MARK
9- TDC MARK
10- CARNKSHAFT SPROCKET
11- TENSIONER PULLEY
12- CRANKSHAFT SENSOR

ARM0600000000325

Fig. 3   Timing belt alignment marks

SLOWLY compress plunger. Total bleed down of tensioner should take about five minutes.
    c. When plunger is compressed into tensioner body install a pin through body and plunger to retain plunger in place until tensioner is installed.

CAMSHAFT
REPLACE

1. Relieve fuel system pressure as outlined in "Precautions."
2. Remove front timing belt cover.
3. Position crankshaft sprocket to TDC mark on oil pump housing by turning crankshaft in clockwise direction.
4. Install a dial indicator in number 1 cylinder to check TDC of piston. Rotate crankshaft until piston is at exactly TDC.
5. Remove camshaft retainer/thrust plate from rear of righthand cylinder head.
6. Remove rocker arm assemblies as outlined under "Rocker Arm, Replace."
7. Remove timing belt and tensioner as outlined under "Timing Belt, Replace."
8. Remove left camshaft gear retaining bolt and washer.
9. Hold the left camshaft sprocket with suitable 7/16 wrench or equivalent, then remove sprocket.
10. Repeat steps above to remove righthand sprocket gear, then raise right side of engine enough to allow clearance for removal of bolt.
11. To remove righthand camshaft, remove EGR assembly.
12. Remove camshaft thrust plate.
13. Remove camshaft from rear of cylinder head.
14. Reverse procedure to install.

PISTON & ROD ASSEMBLY

1. Arrow on top of piston must be pointing toward front of engine.
2. Arrow on top of piston must point to front of engine and oil squirt hole on connecting rod faces right side of cylinder bore.
3. Torque connecting rod bolts to 20 ft. lbs., plus ¼ turn.

MAIN & ROD BEARINGS

1. For main bearing selection, block and crankshaft have grade identification marks.
2. Marks for cylinder block main bore grade are located on left side pan rail. These grade marks 1, 2, or 3 are read left to right, corresponding to main bore 1, 2, 3, 4. **Fig. 4.**
3. Grade marks for crankshaft are located on rearmost crankshaft counter weight. Crankshaft journal grade marks A, B, or C are read left to right, corresponding with journal number 1, 2, 3, 4. **Fig. 5.**

CRANKSHAFT SEAL
REPLACE

1. Remove timing belt as outlined under "Timing Belt, Replace."
2. Remove crankshaft sprocket using tool No. L-4407-A, or equivalent.
3. Tap dowel pin out of crankshaft.
4. Remove crankshaft seal using tool No. 6341A, or equivalent.
5. Reverse procedure to install, noting the following:
    a. Install seal using installer tool No. 6342, or equivalent.
    b. Install dowel pin to .047 inch protrusion.

CRANKSHAFT REAR OIL SEAL
REPLACE

1. Remove transmission as outlined in **MOTOR's "Domestic Transmission Manual, In-Vehicle Service" manual or "Transmission Service DVD."**
2. Remove flex plate.
3. Remove seven rear main seal carrier to engine block upper bolts.
4. Remove rear main seal carrier from engine block and oil pan.
5. Clean sealant residue from engine block and oil pan.
6. Reverse procedure to install.

OIL PAN
REPLACE

1. Remove engine oil dipstick and tube.
2. Raise and support vehicle.
3. Remove front crossmember.
4. Remove crossover pipe.
5. Loosen front exhaust manifold.
6. Remove oil pan bell housing bolts.
7. Drain oil into suitable container, then remove oil filter.
8. Remove oil pan mounting bolts, then oil pan and gasket.
9. Reverse procedure to install.

OIL PUMP
REPLACE

1. Drain cooling system into suitable container.
2. Remove timing belt as outlined under "Timing Belt, Replace."
3. Remove crankshaft sprocket.
4. Remove oil pan as outlined under "Oil Pan, Replace."
5. Remove oil pickup tube.
6. Remove oil pump retaining bolts, then oil pump.
7. Reverse procedure to install.

OIL PUMP SERVICE
Disassemble

1. Drill a 1/8 inch hole into relief valve retainer cap and insert a self-threading sheet metal screw into cap.
2. Clamp screw into a vise and while supporting oil pump body, remove cap by tapping oil pump body using a soft hammer.
3. Remove spring and relief valve.
4. Remove oil pump cover retaining screws, then cover.
5. Remove pump rotors, then inspect for damage or wear.
6. Reverse procedure to install.

Inspection

1. Lay a straightedge across pump cover surface. If a .001 inch feeler gauge can be inserted between cover and straight edge, cover should be replaced.
2. Measure thickness and diameter of outer rotor. If outer rotor thickness measures .563 inch or less, or if diameter 3.141 inches or less, replace outer rotor.
3. If inner rotor measures .563 inch or less replace inner rotor.
4. Slide outer rotor into body, press to one side with fingers and measure clearance between rotor and body. If measurement is .015 inch or more, replace body only if outer rotor is in specifications.
5. Install inner rotor into body. If clearance between inner and outer rotors is .008 inch or more, replace both rotors.
6. Place a straightedge across face of the body, between bolt holes. If a feeler gauge of .003 inch or more can be inserted between rotors and straightedge, replace pump assembly **ONLY** if rotors are in specs.
7. Inspect oil pressure relief valve plunger for scoring and free operation in its bore. Small marks may be removed with 400-grit wet or dry sandpaper.
8. Relief valve spring has a free length of approximately 1.95 inch, it should test between 23-25 lbs. when compressed to 1-1¹/₃₂ inch. Replace spring that fails to meet specifications.

Main Bearing Bore Grade Marks		
1	2	3
A	(3) Standard	(2) +.003 mm (+0.0002 in.)	(1) +0.006 mm (+0.0003 in.)
B	(4) -0.003 mm (-0.0002 in.)	(3) Standard	(2) +.003 mm (+0.0002 in.)
C	(5) -0.006 mm (-0.0003 in.)	(4) -0.003 mm (-0.0001 in.)	(3) Standard

ARM0600000000327

Fig. 4   Main bearing selection chart

Assemble

1. Assemble oil pump using new parts as required.
2. Torque oil pump cover screws to 105 inch lbs.
3. Prime oil pump before installation by filling rotor cavity with engine oil.
4. If oil pressure is low and pump is within specifications, inspect for worn engine bearings or other reasons for oil pressure loss.

COOLING SYSTEM BLEED

1. Install cooling system filling aid tool No. 8195, or equivalent that looks like funnel that attaches to filler neck in place of pressure cap along with attached hose clip.
2. Pinch off overflow hose attach to fill neck.
3. Attach 5–6.5 foot length of clear ¼ inch I.D. clear hose to bleed valve. Put other end of hose in suitable container.
4. Open cooling system bleed valve located on water outlet connector near front of engine.
5. Pour suitable coolant mixture into large side of filling aid tool.
6. Slowly fill cooling system, using large side of cooling aid.
7. When steady stream of coolant comes out of clear hose, close bleed valve. Continue filling to top of filling aid tool.
8. Remove overflow hose clip. Excess fluid will drain into coolant bottle overflow.
9. Remove filling aid.
10. Ensure pressure cap bottom seal and filler neck are clean and free of debris.
11. Install coolant bottle pressure cap.

THERMOSTAT
REPLACE

1. Drain cooling system into suitable container.

2. Disconnect upper radiator hose from thermostat housing.
3. Remove thermostat housing bolts.
4. Remove thermostat housing, then thermostat and gasket.
5. Reverse procedure to install.

RADIATOR
REPLACE

1. Remove engine cover, then air cleaner housing.
2. Recover air conditioning refrigerant as outlined in "Air Conditioning" chapter.
3. Drain cooling system into suitable container.
4. Remove lower engine and front splash shields.
5. Remove upper and lower radiator hoses at radiator.
6. Disconnect radiator fan electrical connector.
7. Disconnect A/C line at condenser.
8. Remove screw that holds support bracket for transmission cooler tubes at left side of radiator.
9. Remove upper radiator supports.
10. Remove radiator/condenser assembly.
11. Separate A/C condenser from radiator.
12. Separate radiator cooling fans from radiator.
13. Reverse procedure to install.

WATER PUMP
REPLACE

1. Drain cooling system into suitable container.
2. Remove timing belt as outlined under "Timing Belt, Replace."
3. Remove water pump mounting bolts. **Note** position of longer bolt for installation.
4. Remove water pump.
5. Reverse procedure to install.

FUEL PUMP
REPLACE

1. Relieve fuel system pressure as outlined in "Precautions."
2. Raise and support vehicle.
3. Drain and remove fuel tank.
4. Disconnect fuel line from fuel pump module.
5. Disconnect fuel pump module electrical connector.
6. Mark fuel pump location.
7. Remove lock ring using tool No. 9340, or equivalent.
8. Remove fuel pump and o-ring. Discard oil seal.
9. Reverse procedure to install.

FUEL FILTER
REPLACE

Fuel filter is contained with fuel pump module. Refer to "Fuel Pump, Replace" for removal procedure.

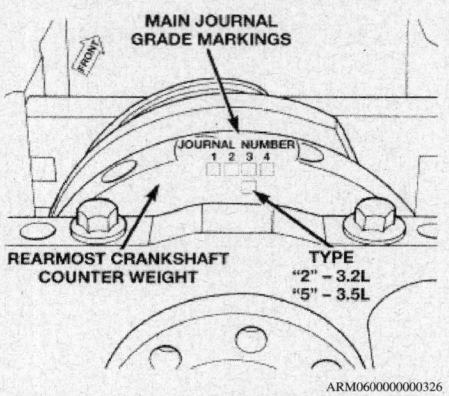

Fig. 5 Crankshaft markings

TIGHTENING SPECIFICATIONS

Year	Component	Torque Ft. Lbs.
2007–08	Camshaft Sprocket Bolt, Lefthand	75②
	Camshaft Sprocket Bolt, Righthand	75②
	Camshaft Thrust Plate Bolts	21
	Connecting Rod Cap Bolts	
	Crankshaft Main Cap Bolts-Inner	15③
	Crankshaft Main Cap Bolts-Outer	20③
	Exhaust Manifold To Cylinder Head Bolts	17
	Flex Plate to Crankshaft	70
	Flex Plate To Torque Converter	55
	Intake Manifold-Lower	21
	Intake Manifold-Upper	105①
	Left Engine Mount To Cradle	55
	Oil Pan Drain Plug	20
	Oil Pan M6 Bolts	105①
	Oil Pan M8 Bolts	21
	Oil Pump To Block M8 Bolts	21
	Oil Pump To Block M10 Bolts	40
	Oil Pump Cover Bolts	105①
	Oil Pump Pickup Tube	21
	Right Engine Mount To Cradle	55
	Timing Belt Cover M6 Bolts	105①
	Timing Belt Cover M8 Bolts	21
	Timing Belt Cover M10 Bolts	40
	Timing Belt Tensioner	21
	Timing Belt Tensioner Pulley	45
	Upper Engine Mount To Frame Rail	50
	Upper Engine Mount To Timing Cover	40
	Valve Cover Bolts	90①

① — Inch lbs.
② — Plus 90°.
③ — Plus ¼ turn.

Rear Suspension

NOTE: On Air Bag Equipped Models, Refer To "Air Bag System Precautions" Located In The Front Of This Manual For System Disarming & Arming Procedures.

NOTE: Refer To "Computer Relearn Procedures" Located In The Front Of This Manual When Battery Power To The Computer Has Been Interrupted.

NOTE: Prior To Performing Any Service Operations Listed In This Section, Consult The "Technical Service Bulletins" Section For Related Information.

INDEX

	Page No.		Page No.		Page No.
Coil Spring, Replace	2-27	2007–08 Avenger & Sebring		Forward	2-29
Control Arm, Replace	2-28	Sedan	2-28	Rear	2-29
2007–08 Avenger & Sebring		Except 2007–08 Avenger &		Shock Absorber, Replace	2-27
Sedan	2-28	Sebring Sedan	2-28	2007–08 Avenger & Sebring	
Lower	2-28	Lateral Link, Replace	2-29	Sedan	2-27
Upper	2-28	2007–08 Avenger & Sebring		Sebring Sedan	2-27
Except 2007–08 Avenger &		Sedan	2-29	Except 2007–08 Avenger &	
Sebring Sedan	2-28	Forward	2-29	Sebring Sedan	2-27
Description	2-27	Rear	2-29	Stabilizer Bar, Replace	2-28
Hub & Bearing, Replace	2-27	Except 2007–08 Avenger &		Tightening Specifications	2-30
Knuckle, Replace	2-28	Sebring Sedan	2-29		

DESCRIPTION

The rear suspension is a fully independent short and long arm style suspension, **Figs. 1, and 2.** An upper control arm bolts to the top of each rear cast knuckle to the rear suspension crossmember. The movement of the rear knuckle is controlled laterally by two lower lateral links going from the front and rear of the knuckle to the rear crossmember and upper control arm. Fore and aft movement of the knuckle is controlled by a trailing arm.

HUB & BEARING
REPLACE

All models are equipped with permanently lubricated, sealed-for-life wheel bearings. There is no periodic lubrication or maintenance recommended for these units. If servicing is required, proceed as follows:
1. Raise and support vehicle, then remove rear tire and wheel assembly.
2. Remove disc or drum brakes.
3. **On ABS equipped models,** remove wheel speed sensor mounting screw from hub/bearing.
4. **On all models,** remove hub/bearing to knuckle mounting bolts.
5. Remove hub and bearing.
6. Reverse procedure to install.

SHOCK ABSORBER
REPLACE

Except 2007–08 Avenger & Sebring Sedan

1. Roll back carpeting and remove shock tower cover.
2. Remove two mounting nuts.
3. Raise and support vehicle, then remove tire and wheel assembly.
4. Remove shock clevis bracket to knuckle mounting bolt, **Fig. 3.**
5. Remove shock absorber clevis bracket from knuckle by pushing down on suspension.
6. Move shock absorber downward and tilt top of shock outward.
7. Remove shock through top of wheelwell opening.
8. Reverse procedure to install.

2007–08 Avenger & Sebring Sedan
SEBRING SEDAN

1. Roll back carpeting to access upper mounting nuts.
2. Remove two mounting nuts.
3. Raise and support vehicle.
4. Remove rear tire and wheel assembly.
5. Remove trim cover from bottom of lower control arm.
6. Remove lower shock mounting bolt and nut.
7. Remove shock.
8. Reverse procedure to install.

COIL SPRING
REPLACE

1. Position shock in suitable vise, **Fig. 4.**
2. Mark assembly right or lefthand.
3. Compress coil spring using coil spring compressor tool No. GP-2020-S2.5, or equivalent.
4. Keep shock shaft rod from turning using suitable tool and remove shock shaft nut.
5. Remove washer, shock mounting bracket, washer and dust shield.
6. Remove coil spring and spring compressor.
7. Reverse procedure to install.

CONTROL ARM
REPLACE

Except 2007-08 Avenger & Sebring Sedan

1. Raise and support vehicle, then remove both rear tire and wheel assemblies.
2. Roll back carpeting and remove shock tower cover.
3. Remove two mounting nuts.
4. Raise and support vehicle, then remove tire and wheel assembly.
5. Remove shock clevis bracket to knuckle mounting bolt, **Fig. 3.**
6. Remove shock absorber clevis bracket from knuckle by pushing down on suspension.
7. Move shock absorber downward and tilt top of shock outward.
8. Remove shock through top of wheelwell opening.
9. Remove muffler support bracket from rear frame, **Fig. 5.**
10. Remove hanger bracket from rear suspension crossmember and move exhaust down far as possible.
11. Remove cotter pin and castle nut from ball joint.
12. **On models equipped with ABS,** remove speed sensor heads from knuckle.
13. **On all models,** separate control arm ball joint from rear knuckle using puller tool No. CT-1106, or equivalent. **Install castle nut on ball joint stud to protect threads.**
14. Support crossmember by positioning suitable floor jack and block of wood under center of crossmember.
15. Remove routing clips for wheel speed sensor cable from brackets on both upper control arms.
16. Remove four rear suspension crossmember to rear frame rails mounting bolts.
17. Lower rear suspension crossmember far enough to access upper control arm pivot bar to crossmember mounting bolts.
18. Remove two mounting bolts and upper control arm, **Fig. 6.**
19. Reverse procedure to install, noting the following:
    a. Align upper control arm pivot bar with mounting holes in rear suspension crossmember.
    b. Position appropriate size drift into position hole in each side of rear suspension crossmember and crossmember locating holes in frame rails, then tighten frame rail mounting bolts.

2007-08 Avenger & Sebring Sedan

LOWER

1. Raise and support vehicle.

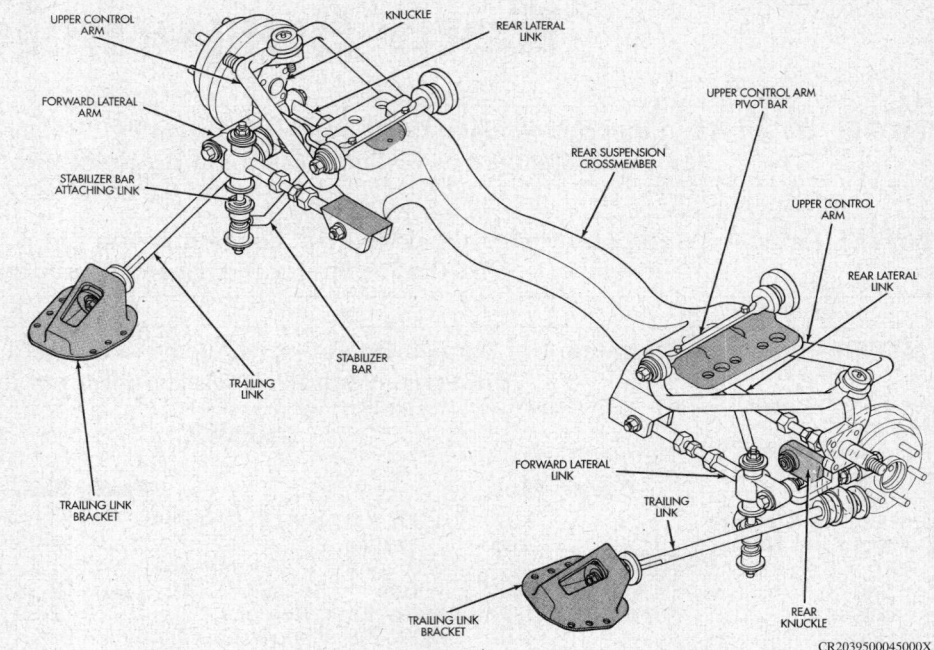

Fig. 1 Rear suspension components

2. Holding lower stabilizer link stud stationary, remove trailing link to lower control arm nut.
3. Remove lower shock bolt as outlined under "Shock Absorber, Replace."
4. Remove lower control arm to knuckle bolt and nut.
5. Remove lower control arm to rear crossmember bolt and nut.
6. Remove lower control arm.
7. Reverse procedure to install.

UPPER

1. Raise and support vehicle.
2. Remove wheel and tire assembly.
3. Remove upper control arm to knuckle bolt and nut.
4. Remove upper control arm to crossmember bolt and nut.
5. Remove upper control arm.
6. Reverse procedure to install.

KNUCKLE
REPLACE

Except 2007-08 Avenger & Sebring Sedan

1. Raise and support vehicle, then remove rear tire and wheel assembly.
2. Remove brake drum or disc brake.
3. Remove rear wheel speed sensor.
4. Remove parking brake cable from brake actuator lever.
5. Position a 1/2 inch box end wrench over parking brake cable retainer and collapse retaining tabs, **Fig. 7.**
6. Pull brake cable from brake support plate.
7. Remove mounting nut, washer, then the hub and bearing assembly from knuckle.

8. Remove four rear support plate to knuckle mounting bolts.
9. Remove brake support plate, brake shoes and wheel cylinder.
10. Remove forward and rear lateral links to knuckle mounting nuts and bolts.
11. Separate from rear knuckle using puller tool No. CT-1106, or equivalent. **Install castle nut on ball joint stud to protect threads.**
12. Remove knuckle.
13. Reverse procedure to install.

2007-08 Avenger & Sebring Sedan

1. Raise and support vehicle.
2. Remove wheel and tire assembly.
3. Remove brake tube bracket to knuckle mounting bolt.
4. Remove hub & bearing as outlined under "Hub & Bearing, Replace."
5. Remove knuckle to trailing link mounting bolts.
6. Remove toe link to knuckle mounting bolt.
7. Remove lower control arm to knuckle mounting bolt.
8. Remove upper control arm to knuckle mounting bolt.
9. Remove knuckle.
10. Reverse procedure to install.

STABILIZER BAR
REPLACE

1. Raise and support vehicle, then remove both rear tire and wheel assemblies.
2. Remove nuts attaching stabilizer link isolator bushings to stabilizer links using suitable wrench to prevent stabilizer links from rotating.
3. Remove stabilizer bar bushing clamp

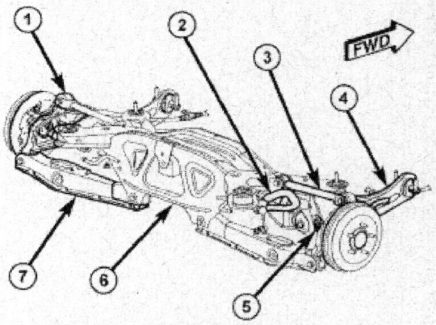

1- Knuckle
2- Stabilizer Bar
3- Upper Control Arm
4- Trailing Arm
5- Toe Link
6- Rear Crossmember
7- Lower Control Arm

ARM0600000000328

Fig. 2   Rear suspension components. 2007–08 Avenger & Sebring Sedan

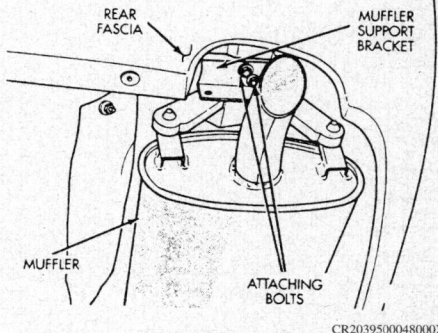

CR2039500048000X

Fig. 5   Muffler support bracket replacement

to rear suspension crossmember mounting bolts, **Fig. 8.**
4. Remove rear stabilizer bar to crossmember bushing clamps and bushings from stabilizer bar.
5. Remove stabilizer bar.
6. Reverse procedure to install.

LATERAL LINK
REPLACE

Except 2007–08 Avenger & Sebring Sedan
FORWARD

1. Raise and support vehicle, then remove rear tire and wheel assembly.
2. Remove rear stabilizer bar attaching link from forward lateral link to knuckle, **Fig. 9.**

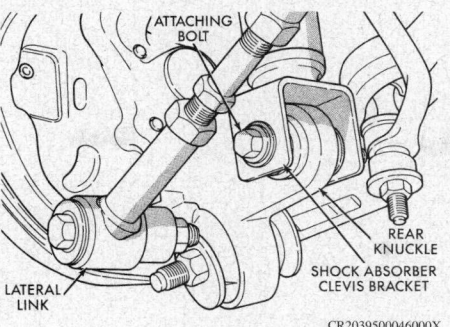

CR2039500046000X

Fig. 3   Shock & knuckle replacement

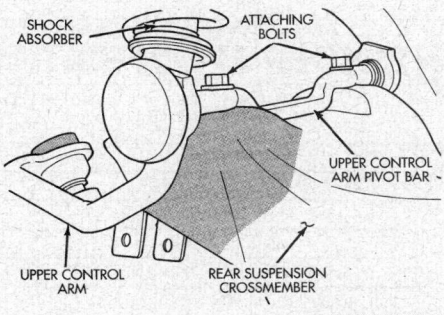

CR2039500049000X

Fig. 6   Upper control arm & crossmember replacement

3. Remove lateral link to knuckle mounting nut and bolt.
4. Remove mounting bolt and lateral link.
5. Reverse procedure to install.

REAR

1. Raise and support vehicle, then remove rear tire and wheel assembly.
2. Remove lateral link to knuckle mounting nut and bolt, **Fig. 10.**
3. Remove mounting nut and bolt, then the lateral link.
4. Reverse procedure to install.

2007–08 Avenger & Sebring Sedan
FORWARD

1. Raise and support vehicle.
2. Remove forward link to knuckle mounting bolt.
3. Mark position of cam bolt on crossmember using suitable marker.
4. While holding cam bolt head stationary, loosen and remove forward link mounting cam bolt nut and washer.
5. Remove cam bolt, then forward link.
6. Reverse procedure to install.

REAR

1. Raise and support vehicle.
2. Remove rear tire and wheel assembly.
3. Remove brake flex hose and tube

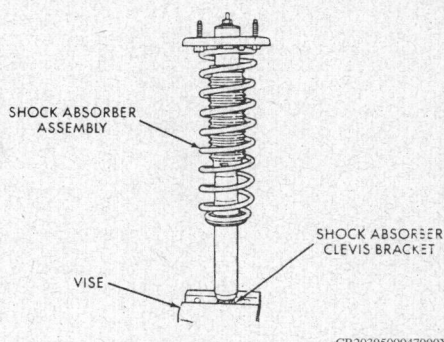

CR2039500047000X

Fig. 4   Coil spring removal

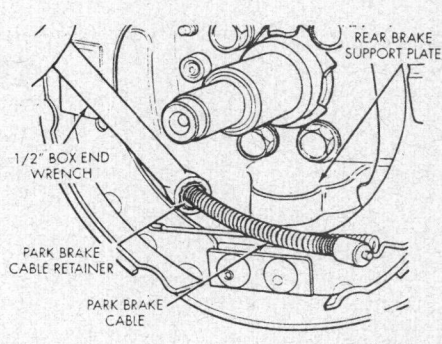

CR2039500050000X

Fig. 7   Parking brake cable replacement

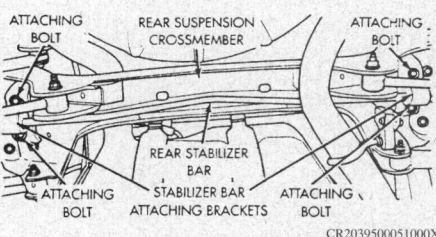

CR2039500051000X

Fig. 8   Rear stabilizer bar replacement

bracket to rear link retaining screw.
4. Remove brake tube from routing clip on rear link.
5. Remove wheel speed sensor to rear link routing clips.
6. Remove hub & bearing as outlined under "Hub & Bearing, Replace."
7. Remove parking brake cable from lever on brake shoe.
8. Remove parking brake cable to brake support plate retaining pin.
9. Slide brake support plate with brake shoes off end of parking brake cable.
10. Pull parking brake cable from rear link.
11. Remove knuckle to rear link mounting bolts.
12. Remove rear link to body mounting bolts.
13. Remove rear link.
14. Reverse procedure to install.

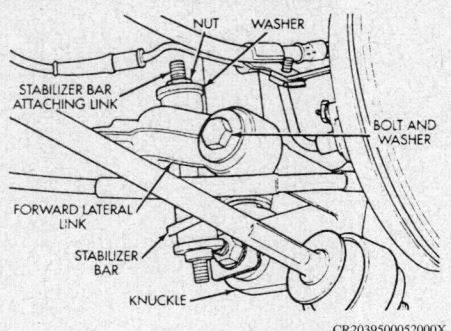

Fig. 9 Forward lateral link replacement

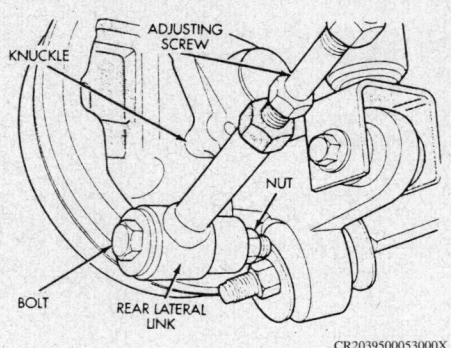

Fig. 10 Rear lateral link replacement

TIGHTENING SPECIFICATIONS

Year	Component	Torque Ft. Lbs.
2004–06	Ball Joint	80
	Brake Support Plate To Knuckle	45
	Hub & Bearing	185
	Lateral Link	70
	Lateral Link To Knuckle	90
	Lateral Link To Suspension Crossmember	65
	Shock Assembly Clevis Bracket To Knuckle	70
	Shock Assembly Shaft	40
	Shock Assembly To Body	40
	Stabilizer Bar Bracket	24
	Stabilizer Bar Isolator Bushing	24
	Stabilizer Bar To Lateral Link	23
	Trailing Link Bracket	21
	Trailing Link Shaft	85
	Upper Ball Joint To Knuckle Castle Nut	63
	Upper Control Arm Pivot Bar To Crossmember	70
	Wheel Lug Nuts	100
2007–08	Brake Tube Bracket Knuckle Mounting Screw	11
	Brake Flex Hose Rear Link Mounting Screw	17
	Forward Link Knuckle Nut	77
	Forward Link Cam Bolt Nut	26
	Hub & Bearing Mounting Bolts	77
	Hub Nut	181
	Lower Control Arm Nut	77
	Lower Control Arm Crossmember Nut	73
	Lower Shock Absorber Nut	73
	Rear Link Body Bolts	81
	Rear Link Knuckle Bolts	44
	Shock Rod Nut	18
	Stabilizer Link Nuts	35
	Upper Control Arm Knuckle Nut	77
	Upper Control Arm Crossmember Nut	77
	Upper Shock Absorber Nut	35
	Wheel Lug Nuts	100

Front Suspension & Steering

NOTE: On Air Bag Equipped Models, Refer To "Air Bag System Precautions" Located In The Front Of This Manual For System Disarming & Arming Procedures.

NOTE: Refer To "Computer Relearn Procedures" Located In The Front Of This Manual When Battery Power To The Computer Has Been Interrupted.

NOTE: Prior To Performing Any Service Operations Listed In This Section, Consult The "Technical Service Bulletins" Section For Related Information.

INDEX

	Page No.
Ball Joint, Replace	2-32
2007–08 Avenger & Sebring Sedan	2-32
Except 2007–08 Avenger & Sebring Sedan	2-32
Ball Joint Inspection	2-32
Lower	2-32
Upper	2-32
Coil Spring & Strut Service	2-32
Control Arm, Replace	2-33
2007–08 Avenger & Sebring Sedan	2-33
Lower	2-33
Except 2007–08 Avenger & Sebring Sedan	2-33
Lower	2-33
Upper	2-33
Driveshaft, Replace	2-31

	Page No.
2007–08 Avenger & Sebring Sedan	2-32
Except 2007–08 Avenger & Sebring Sedan	2-31
Hub & Bearing, Replace	2-31
2007–08 Avenger & Sebring Sedan	2-31
Except 2007–08 Avenger & Sebring Sedan	2-31
Power Steering	13-1
Power Steering Gear, Replace	2-34
2007–08 Avenger & Sebring Sedan	2-34
Except 2007–08 Avenger & Sebring Sedan	2-34
Power Steering Pump, Replace	2-35
2.4L Engines	2-35
2.7L Engine	2-35

	Page No.
3.5L Engine	2-35
Shock Absorber, Replace	2-33
Stabilizer Bar, Replace	2-34
2007–08 Avenger & Sebring Sedan	2-34
Except 2007–08 Avenger & Sebring Sedan	2-34
Steering Columns	12-1
Steering Knuckle, Replace	2-34
Strut, Replace	2-32
2007–08 Avenger & Sebring Sedan	2-32
Technical Service Bulletins	2-36
Pop Or Clunk From Front Of Vehicle	2-36
Tie Rod, Replace	2-34
Tightening Specifications	2-37
Wheel Bearing, Adjust	2-31

WHEEL BEARING

ADJUST

These models are equipped with permanently-sealed front wheel bearings. There is no periodic lubrication or maintenance recommended.

HUB & BEARING

REPLACE

Except 2007–08 Avenger & Sebring Sedan

1. Raise and support vehicle.
2. Remove front stub axle cotter pin, lock nut and spring washer.
3. Lower vehicle, then loosen hub nut while vehicle is on ground and brakes are applied.
4. Raise and support vehicle, then remove from tire and wheel assembly.
5. Remove front disc brake caliper and brake disc assembly, then support aside from steering knuckle.
6. Remove outer tie rod end to steering knuckle.

7. Remove steering knuckle tie rod end using remover tool No. MB-991113, or equivalent.
8. Remove speed sensor cable routing bracket, **Fig. 1.**
9. Remove cotter pin and castle nut from stud of lower ball joint at steering knuckle.
10. Turn steering knuckle so front of steering knuckle is facing as far outboard in wheelwell as possible.
11. Separate steering knuckle from stud of lower ball joint by lightly tap boss. **Do not hit lower control arm or ball joint grease seal.**
12. Separate from ball joint stud by lifting up on steering knuckle. **Support driveshaft so it does not hang by inner Constant Velocity (CV) joint.**
13. Separate steering knuckle from outer CV joint by pulling away, **Fig. 2.**
14. Remove upper ball joint to steering knuckle cotter pin and nut.
15. Remove upper ball joint stud using puller tool No. C3894-A, or equivalent.
16. Remove steering knuckle.
17. Mount steering knuckle securely in suitable vise and remove three hub/bearing assembly to steering knuckle bolts.
18. Remove hub/bearing from steering knuckle. **If bearing does not come out, tap lightly using rubber mallet.**

19. Reverse remaining procedure to install.

2007–08 Avenger & Sebring Sedan

1. Raise and support vehicle.
2. Remove wheel and tire assembly.
3. Loosen hub nut from half shaft with brakes applied, then remove hub nut.
4. Remove brake rotor.
5. Remove hub and bearing to knuckle mounting bolts.
6. Slide hub and bearing off half shaft and out of knuckle.
7. Reverse procedure to install.

DRIVESHAFT

REPLACE

Except 2007–08 Avenger & Sebring Sedan

1. Loosen, but do not remove, stub axle to hub/bearing mounting nut while vehicle is on ground and brakes applied.
2. Raise and support vehicle, then remove front tire and wheel assembly.

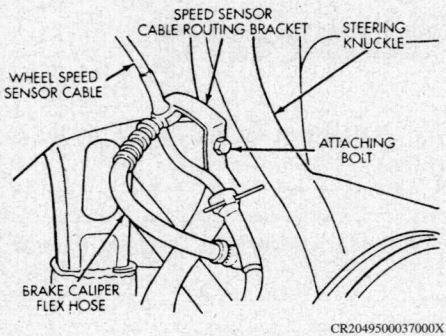

Fig. 1 Speed sensor cable routing bracket replacement

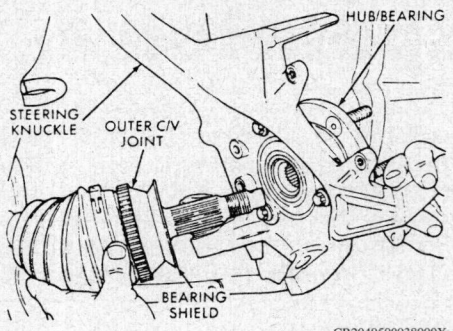

Fig. 2 Steering knuckle & outer CV joint replacement

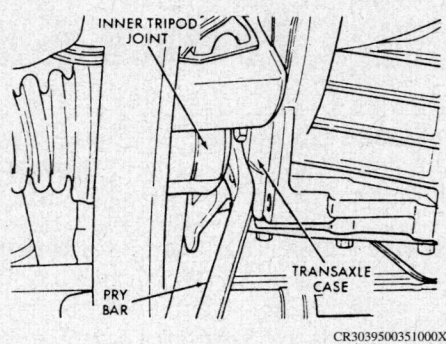

Fig. 3 Inner tripod joint replacement

3. Remove brake caliper and support aside. Remove brake disc.
4. Remove tie rod end mounting nut and tie rod end stud from steering knuckle using remover tool No. MB-991113, or equivalent.
5. Remove vehicle speed sensor cable routing bracket.
6. Remove lower ball joint at steering knuckle, cotter pin and castle nut.
7. Turn steering knuckle so front of knuckle is facing as far outboard in wheelwell as possible.
8. Separate from stud of lower ball joint by lightly tap boss on steering knuckle.
9. Pull steering knuckle out and away from outer CV joint.
10. Support outer end of driveshaft, insert suitable pry bar between tripod joint and transaxle case side gear as far as possible by hand, **Fig. 3.**
11. Hold inner tripod joint and interconnecting shaft of driveshaft.
12. Remove inner tripod joint from transaxle by pulling it straight out of transaxle side gear.
13. Reverse procedure to install.

2007–08 Avenger & Sebring Sedan

1. Raise and support vehicle.
2. Remove wheel and tire assembly.
3. Loosen halfshaft nut with brakes applied, then remove nut.
4. Remove caliper adapter to steering knuckle mounting bolts.
5. Remove disc brake caliper assembly from steering knuckle.
6. Remove brake rotor from hub and bearing.
7. Remove steering knuckle to strut mounting bolts.
8. Pull steering knuckle from strut clevis bracket.
9. Pull steering knuckle down and away from outer C/V joint, while pulling joint out of hub bearing.
10. Support outer end of halfshaft, then pry inner tripod joint away from transaxle case using suitable pry bar.
11. Remove steering knuckle from clevis bracket.
12. Pull steering knuckle down and away from outer C/V joint, while pulling joint out of intermediate shaft.
13. Remove mid-shaft bearing to support

bracket bolts, then intermediate shaft.
14. Reverse procedure to install.

BALL JOINT INSPECTION

Lower

1. Raise and support vehicle.
2. Install dial indicator so it contacts top surface of steering knuckle near lower ball joint stud castle nut.
3. Grasp tire and wheel assembly, then push it up and down firmly.
4. Record amount of up and down movement of steering knuckle from dial indicator.
5. Replace lower control arm if movement exceeds .059 inch.

Upper

With the weight of the vehicle resting on its wheels, attempt to move the grease fitting with no mechanical assistance. If any movement of the grease fitting is detected, the ball joint is worn.

BALL JOINT

REPLACE

Except 2007–08 Avenger & Sebring Sedan

The ball joints are not replaceable component of the control arms. If determined to be faulty, the entire control arm will have to be replaced.

2007–08 Avenger & Sebring Sedan

1. Raise and support vehicle.
2. Remove wheel and tire assembly.
3. Loosen hub nut with brakes applied, then remove nut.
4. Remove brake rotor.
5. Remove wheel speed sensor to knuckle routing clip.
6. Remove wheel speed sensor from knuckle.

7. Remove lower ball joint to control arm retaining nut.
8. Remove ball joint from control arm using tool No. 9360, or suitable equivalent.
9. Lift knuckle out of lower control arm, **Fig. 4.**
10. Pull knuckle off axle half shaft outer C/V joint splines.
11. Tap ends of snap-ring with a drift punch and remove it from ball joint, through access hole in knuckle.
12. Remove ball joint from knuckle using remover tool No.s 9964-3, 9964-4 and 8441-1, or equivalent.
13. Reverse procedure to install.

STRUT

REPLACE

2007–08 Avenger & Sebring Sedan

1. Raise and support vehicle.
2. Remove wheel and tire assembly.
3. Remove flex hose routing bracket to strut attaching screw.
4. Remove stabilizer link to strut retaining nut.
5. Remove strut to knuckle mounting bolts using suitable punch. **Note: Strut to knuckle attaching bolts are serrated and must not be turned during removal. Hold bolts stationary in knuckle while removing nuts.**
6. Lower vehicle enough to open hood without tires touching floor.
7. Remove upper strut mount to strut tower retaining nuts, then remove strut.
8. Reverse procedure to install.

COIL SPRING & STRUT SERVICE

1. Place strut assembly in suitable coil spring compressor.
2. Compress spring until tension is relieved from upper mount and bearing.
3. Remove strut retaining nut using strut nut wrench tool No. 9362, or equivalent.
4. Remove clamp from bottom of coil spring and remove strut out through

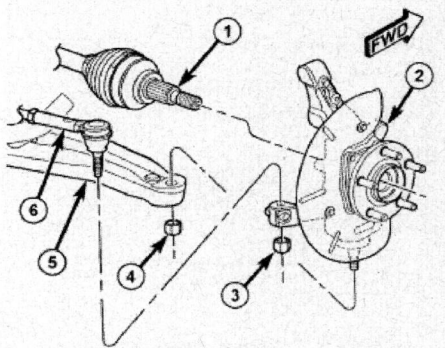
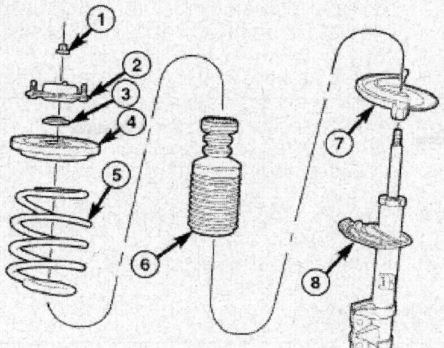
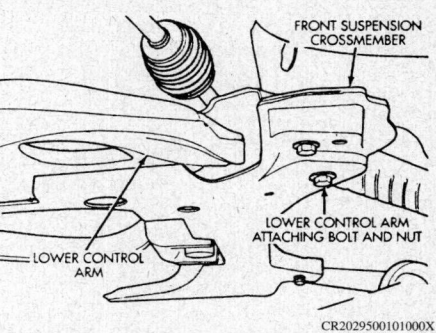

Fig. 6 Lower control arm replacement

1- Halfshaft
2- Knuckle
3- Nut
4- Nut
5- Lower Control Arm
6- Tie Rod

ARM0600000000330

Fig. 4 Ball joint replacement. 2007–08 Avenger & Sebring Sedan

1 – Strut Nut
2 – Upper Mount
3 – Bearing
4 – Spring Seat
5 – Spring
6 – Jounce Bumper
7 – Lower Spring Isolator
8 – Strut

ARM0600000000331

Fig. 5 Strut & spring service

bottom of coil spring. The dust shield and jounce bumper will come out with strut, **Fig. 5.**
5. Remove lower spring isolator from strut seat.
6. Slide dust shield and jounce bumper from strut rod.
7. Remove upper mount and bearing from top of upper spring seat and isolator.
8. Reverse procedure to assemble.

SHOCK ABSORBER
REPLACE

1. Raise and support vehicle, then remove front tire and wheel assembly.
2. Remove vehicle speed sensor cable routing bracket.
3. Remove upper ball joint stud to steering knuckle cotter pin and castle nut.
4. Remove upper ball joint stud from steering knuckle using pull tool No. C-3894-A, or equivalent.
5. Position steering outward toward rear of wheelwell.
6. Remove shock clevis to shock pinch bolt.
7. Remove shock to lower control arm through bolt.
8. Remove clevis from shock by carefully tapping it off shock fluid reservoir with suitable soft brass drift,
9. Remove four shock/upper control arm mounting bracket to shock tower mounting bolts.
10. Remove shock and upper control arm mounting bracket through front area of wheelwell.
11. Reverse procedure to install.

CONTROL ARM
REPLACE

Except 2007–08 Avenger & Sebring Sedan

LOWER

1. Raise and support vehicle, then remove front tire and wheel assembly.
2. Remove lower ball joint heat shield.
3. Remove disc brake caliper and support aside, then brake disc.
4. Disconnect ball joint from steering knuckle, then turn steering knuckle so front of knuckle is facing as far outboard as possible.
5. Separate steering knuckle from lower ball joint by lightly tapping with suitable rubber mallet.
6. Remove shock absorber clevis from lower control.
7. Remove nut attaching stabilizer bar link assembly to lower control arm using an Allen wrench to prevent stabilizer bar link from rotating.
8. Remove stabilizer bar bushing to front suspension crossmember and body mounting bolts.
9. Lower one side of stabilizer bar away from lower control arm.
10. Remove nut and bolt attaching rear isolator bushing of lower control arm, then nut and bolt attaching front isolator bushing of lower control arm, **Fig. 6.**
11. Remove front isolator bushing of lower

control arm to front suspension crossmember.
12. Remove front of lower control arm from front suspension crossmember.
13. Remove rear of lower control arm from between top and bottom half of front suspension crossmember, keeping lower control arm as level as possible.
14. Reverse procedure to install.

UPPER

1. Raise and support vehicle, then remove front tire and wheel assembly.
2. Remove vehicle speed sensor cable routing bracket.
3. Remove upper ball joint stud to steering knuckle cotter pin and castle nut.
4. Remove upper ball joint stud from steering knuckle using puller tool No. C-3894-A, or equivalent, then position steering outward toward rear of wheelwell.
5. Remove shock clevis to shock pinch bolt.
6. Remove shock to lower control arm through bolt.
7. Remove clevis from shock by carefully tapping clevis with suitable, soft brass drift off shock fluid reservoir.
8. Remove four upper control arm/shock absorber mounting bracket to shock tower mounting bolts.
9. Remove shock absorber and upper control arm mounting bracket.
10. Reverse procedure to install.

2007–08 Avenger & Sebring Sedan

LOWER

1. Raise and support vehicle.
2. Remove tire and wheel assembly.
3. Remove lower ball joint to control arm retaining nut.
4. Remove lower ball joint from lower control arm using remove tool No. 9360, or equivalent.
5. Remove both stabilizer link to stabilizer bar retaining nuts.
6. Rotate ends of stabilizer bar upward

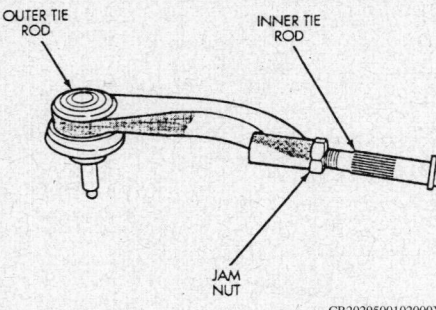

Fig. 7 Tie rod replacement

away from lower control arm.
7. Remove lower control arm to crossmember mounting bolt.
8. Remove control arm.
9. Reverse procedure to install.

STEERING KNUCKLE
REPLACE

Refer to "Hub & Bearing, Replace" for knuckle replacement procedures.

STABILIZER BAR
REPLACE

Except 2007-08 Avenger & Sebring Sedan

1. Raise and support vehicle.
2. Remove stabilizer bar link to lower control arm nut using suitable hex wrench to prevent stabilizer bar link from rotating.
3. Remove stabilizer bar bushing to front suspension crossmember mounting bolts.
4. Remove bushings, bushing retainers, links and stabilizer bar.
5. Reverse procedure to install.

2007-08 Avenger & Sebring Sedan

1. Raise and support vehicle.
2. Remove rear engine mount as outlined under "Engine Mount, Replace."
3. Remove front engine mount through bolt.
4. Remove both stabilizer link to stabilizer bar retaining nuts.
5. Remove power steering hose routing clamps to crossmember retaining screws.
6. Remove four screws mounting heat shield over steering gear.
7. Remove steering gear to crossmember mounting bolts.
8. Mark location of front crossmember on body near each mounting bolt.
9. Support crossmember with suitable transmission jack.
10. Support steering gear in place when lowering crossmember.
11. Remove crossmember to body mounting bolts.

12. Remove crossmember reinforcement bracket mounting screws, then brackets.
13. Lower crossmember using jack until there is enough space present to remove stabilizer bar.
14. Remove stabilizer bushing retainers to crossmember attaching screws, then retainers.
15. Remove stabilizer bushings, then stabilizer bar.
16. Reverse procedure to install.

TIE ROD
REPLACE

1. Raise and support vehicle, then remove front tire and wheel assembly.
2. Remove tie rod end to steering knuckle mounting nuts.
3. Remove both tie rod end studs from steering knuckles using removal tool No. MB-991113, or equivalent.
4. Loosen inner to outer tie rod jam nut, then remove outer tie rod from inner tie rod, **Fig. 7.**
5. Remove jam nut.
6. Expand tie rod boot to inner tie rod clamp using suitable pliers, then remove inner tie rod from steering gear.
7. Reverse procedure to install.

POWER STEERING GEAR
REPLACE

Except 2007-08 Avenger & Sebring Sedan

1. Siphon power steering fluid from remote power steering reservoir.
2. Remove intermediate shaft coupler pinch bolt retaining pin from inside vehicle.
3. Remove pinch bolt from intermediate shaft coupler.
4. Separate intermediate shaft coupler from gear shaft.
5. Raise and support vehicle, then remove both front tire and wheel assemblies.
6. Remove both outer tie rod ends to steering knuckle mounting nuts.
7. Separate both tie rod end studs from steering knuckles using remover tool No. MB-991113, or equivalent.
8. Mark front suspension crossmember on body for installation alignment, **Fig. 8.**
9. Mark installed position (side to side) of front suspension crossmember, **Fig. 9.**
10. Remove stabilizer bar bushing clamp to body mounting bolts.
11. Remove three ABS control unit bolts, then secure unit to body for suspension crossmember removal. **Do not let unit hang by brake tubes.**
12. Remove shock absorber clevis to left and righthand lower control arms mounting bolts.

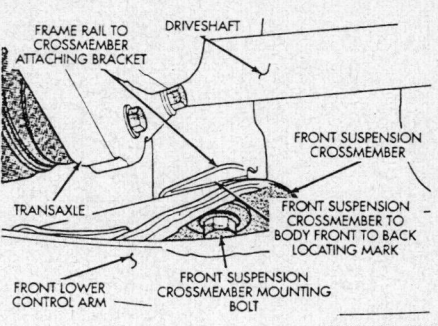

Fig. 8 Front suspension crossmember front to back locating mark (Part 1 of 2)

13. Remove two engine support bracket to front suspension crossmember mounting bolts.
14. Support front suspension crossmember using suitable jackstand.
15. Remove front suspension crossmember to frame rail mounting bolts from both sides of vehicle, then the rear mounting bolts.
16. Lower front suspension crossmember enough to allow steering gear to be removed from crossmember. **Ensure crossmember is supported by jackstand.**
17. Drain power steering gear fluid, pressure and return hoses into suitable container.
18. Disconnect power steering harness connector from fluid reservoir switch.
19. Remove steering gear mounting bolts, **Figs. 10 through 12.**
20. Remove steering gear.
21. Reverse procedure to install.

2007-08 Avenger & Sebring Sedan

1. Siphon power steering fluid from remote power steering reservoir.
2. Turn steering wheel right until intermediate shaft coupling bolt can be accessed.
3. Remove intermediate shaft coupling bolt. Do not separate intermediate shaft from pitman shaft at this time.
4. Position wheel in straight ahead position.
5. Raise and support vehicle.
6. Remove wheel and tire assemblies.
7. Remove outer tie rod end to knuckle retaining nuts.
8. Separate outer tie rod ends from knuckles using remover tool No. 9360, or equivalent.
9. Remove rear engine mount as outlined under "Engine Mount, Replace."
10. Remove front engine mount through bolt.
11. Remove fore/aft crossmember to core support mounting bolts.
12. Remove fore/aft crossmember to crossmember mounting bolts, then fore/aft crossmember.
13. Remove power steering routing hose clamps to crossmember attaching screws.

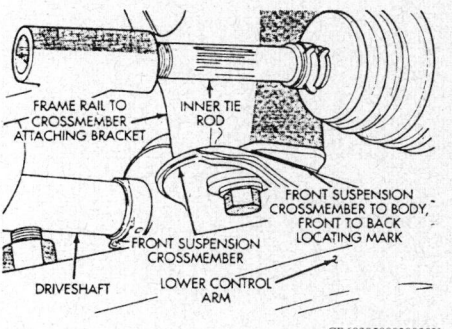

Fig. 8 Front suspension crossmember front to back locating mark (Part 2 of 2)

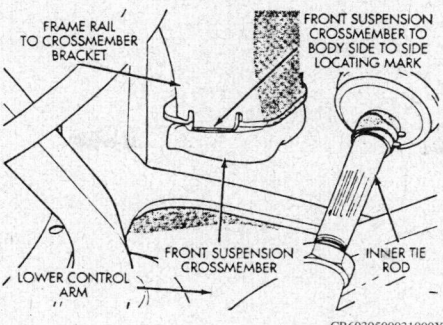

Fig. 9 Front suspension crossmember side to side locating mark

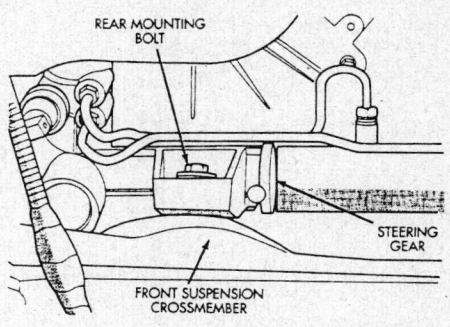

Fig. 10 Steering gear mounting isolator bolts. Rear

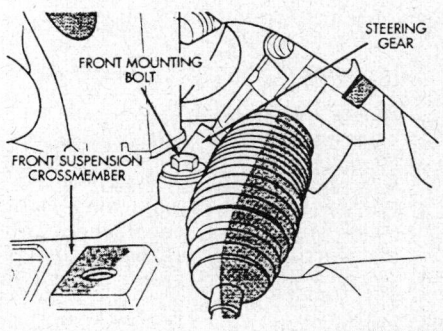

Fig. 11 Steering gear mounting isolator bolts. Front

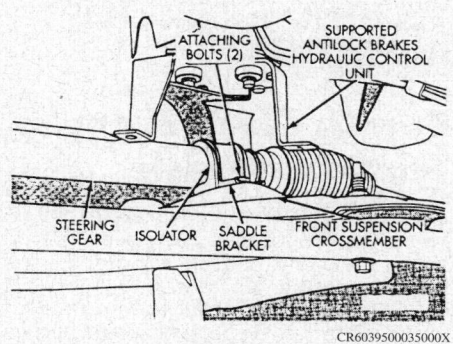

Fig. 12 Steering gear saddle bracket mounting bolts

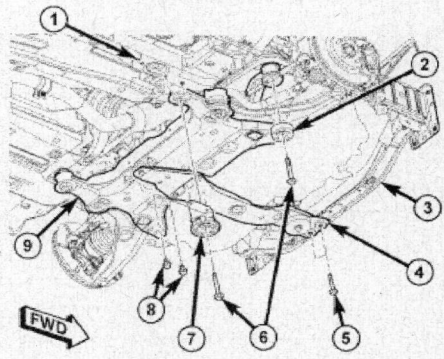

1 – Body
2 – Mount
3 – Core Support
4 – Fore/Aft Crossmember
5 – Bolt
6 – Bolt
7 – Reinforcement Bracket
8 – Screw
9 – Crossmember

Fig. 13 Steering gear removal. 2007–08 Avenger & Sebring Sedan

14. Remove pressure and return hoses from steering gear.
15. Remove heat shield from righthand side of steering gear.
16. Mark location of crossmember on body near mounting bolts, **Fig. 13.**
17. Support crossmember with suitable transmission jack.
18. Remove crossmember to body mounting bolts.
19. Remove crossmember reinforcement brackets.
20. Lower crossmember enough to access intermediate shaft coupling, then slide coupling off pinion shaft.
21. Remove dash seals as needed.
22. Remove steering gear to crossmember mounting bolts, then remove steering gear.
23. Reverse procedure to install.

POWER STEERING PUMP
REPLACE
2.4L Engines

1. Siphon power steering fluid from remote power steering fluid reservoir.
2. Raise and support vehicle, then remove righthand tire and wheel assembly.
3. Remove splash shield from righthand front wheelwell.
4. Disconnect power steering fluid pressure hose from pressure fitting on

power steering pump and drain remaining fluid into suitable container.
5. Remove hose clamp and power steering supply hose.
6. Remove power steering pump adjusting nut and pump to aluminum mounting bracket mounting bolt.
7. Remove ABS hydraulic control unit heat shield.
8. Remove speed sensor cable sealing grommet from inner fender, disconnect wheel speed sensor cable from wiring harness and secure aside.
9. Pull harness through hole in inner fender and unclip wiring harness through from frame rail.
10. Remove ABS sealing plug from hole in firewall.
11. Remove power steering pump front bracket to mounting bracket top mounting bolt, **Fig. 14.**
12. Remove power steering pump drive belt.
13. Remove power steering pump and bracket.
14. Reverse procedure to install.

2.7L Engine

1. Siphon power steering fluid out of remote power steering fluid reservoir.
2. Remove power steering pump supply fitting hose.
3. Raise and support vehicle, then remove drive belt splash shield.
4. Remove power steering fluid pressure hose from pump.
5. Remove oxygen sensor harness and clip from edge of pump heat shield.

6. Remove stamped pump adjuster bracket slot bolt and drive belt.
7. Pivot pump out past full-adjust position and remove three steering pump bracket mounting bolts.
8. Remove power steering pump through opening between frame rail and right-hand driveshaft.
9. Reverse procedure to install.

3.5L Engine

1. Siphon power steering fluid out of remote power steering fluid reservoir.
2. Remove engine cover.
3. Disconnect pressure hose at pump.
4. Remove pressure hose routing clamp bolt at engine cylinder head.
5. Remove supply hose from supply fitting.
6. Raise and support vehicle.
7. Remove wheel and tire assembly.
8. Remove drive belt splash shield, then drive belt.
9. Lower vehicle.
10. Remove right engine mount bracket to mount retaining nuts.

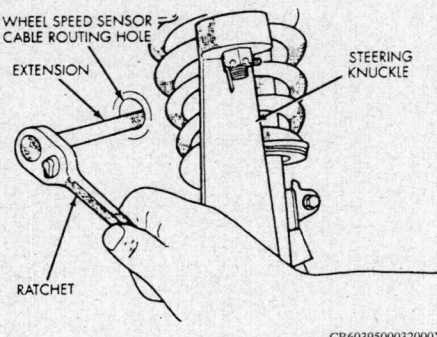

Fig. 14   Power steering pump mounting bracket replacement. 2.4L engines

11. Position floor jack and suitable block of wood on engine oil pan.
12. Raise engine enough to access power steering pump mounting bolts.
13. Remove power steering pump mounting bolts through pulley openings.
14. Remove power steering pump.
15. Reverse procedure to install.

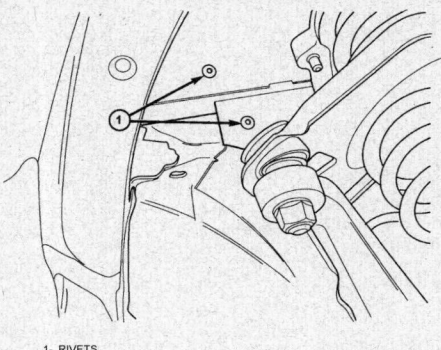

1- RIVETS

Fig. 15   Rivet location. Righthand

TECHNICAL SERVICE BULLETINS

Pop Or Clunk From Front Of Vehicle

On some of these models there may be intermittent front end popping or clunk-type sound while driving over road that causes body to come under a twisting load. This sound may also be produced when parked and idling by turning steering wheel quickly 90° left, than right.

This condition may be caused by front shock tower/wheel well area.

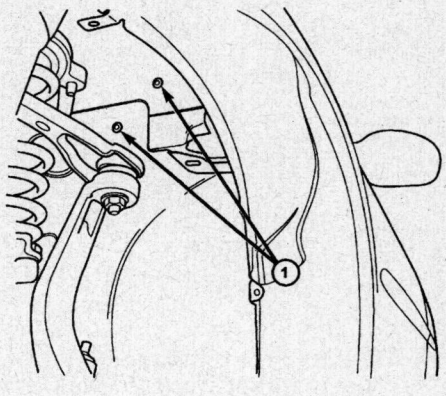

1- RIVETS

Fig. 16   Rivet location. Lefthand

To correct this condition, proceed as follows:

1. Raise and support vehicle, then remove both front tire and wheel assemblies.
2. Remove wheel splash shield.
3. Drill two $17/64$ inch diameter holes from inside shock tower/wheel wheel area into wet plenum, **Figs. 15 and 16.**
4. Apply suitable corrosion inhibitor to bare metal surfaces.
5. Install rivets (part No. 06033864) in holes using suitable riveter.
6. Install wheel well splash shield.
7. Repeat procedure on opposite side.

TIGHTENING SPECIFICATIONS

Year	Component	Torque/Ft. Lbs.
2004–06	Ball Joint Stud To Shock Tower	23
	Ball Joint Stud To Steering Gear	70
	Disc Brake Caliper	16
	Front Cross-Member	120
	Front Stub Axle	180
	Lower Control Arm	120
	Outer Tie Rod To Inner Tie Rod Lock Nut	55
	Power Steering Bracket	40
	Power Steering Pump	40
	Power Steering & Return Hose	21–23
	Pressure Hose To Return Hose	84①
	Shock Absorber Shaft	40
	Shock Assembly Clevis Bracket	68
	Stabilizer Bar	75
	Stabilizer Bar Bushing	45
	Steering Gear	50
	Tie Rod End To Steering Knuckle	45
	Wheel Lug Nuts	100
2007–08	Crossmember Mounting Bolts	100
	Crossmember Reinforcement Bracket Mounting Screws	37
	Hub and Bearing Bolts	60
	Hub Nut	97
	Intermediate Shaft Coupling Bolt	35
	Lower Ball Joint Stud Nut	70
	Lower Control Arm Pivot Bolt	107
	Lower Control Arm Pivot Nut	107
	Power Steering Pump Mounting Bolts	19
	Power Steering Pump Pressure Fitting	65
	Pressure Hose Tube Nut	24
	Return Hose Tube Nut	15
	Stabilizer Bar Link Nuts	43
	Strut Clevis To Knuckle Nuts	103
	Strut Rod Nut	44
	Strut To Tower Nuts	35
	Suspension Crossmember Mounting Bolts	140
	Tie Rod End Knuckle Nut	97
	Tie Rod Jam Nut	55
	Wheel Lug Nuts	100

① — Inch lbs.

Wheel Alignment

INDEX

	Page No.		Page No.		Page No.
Description	2-38	Precautions	2-38	Wheel Alignment	
Front Wheel Alignment	2-38	Preliminary Inspection	2-38	Specifications	2-3
Camber	2-38	Rear Wheel Alignment	2-38		
Toe	2-38	Thrust Angle	2-38		

PRECAUTIONS

When hoisting vehicle a frame contact type hoist must be used. Any equipment designed to lift vehicles by the rear axle cannot be used, as damage to rear suspension components will occur. Do not attempt to modify any suspension or steering components by heating or bending of the component.

DESCRIPTION

This vehicle is equipped with a non-adjustable front caster and camber suspension. Front caster and camber settings are determined at the time of design and require no adjustment during alignment. Though not adjustable, front caster and camber must be inspected and components replaced when outside of vehicle specification. Inspect all components for damage or signs of bending and replace as required.

PRELIMINARY INSPECTION

1. Ensure gas tank is full.
2. Inspect tire pressure and inflate specification. Ensure tires are of same size and tread.
3. Inspect front tire and wheel radial runout.
4. Ensure all suspension fasteners are tightened properly.
5. Inspect ball joints and steering linkage for wear, looseness or damage.
6. Inspect all suspension component rubber bushings for wear or deterioration.

FRONT WHEEL ALIGNMENT

Camber

Camber adjustment is not normally re-

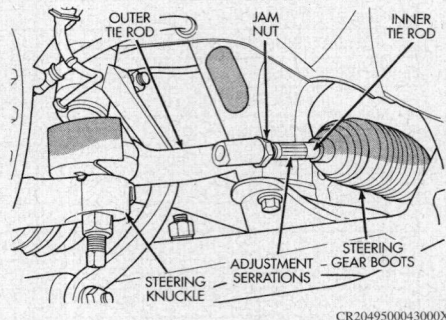

Fig. 1 Inner & outer tie rod adjustment

quired. Inspect all front suspension components for damage or wear, then inspect rear alignment setting prior to adjusting camber setting.

1. Mark position of all shock assembly mounting bolts on shock tower of side to be adjusted.
2. Raise and support vehicle by frame until front tires and suspension are not supporting vehicle.
3. Loosen shock mounting bolts on side to be adjusted. Only loosen far enough to allow removal of plastic locating pins that align upper mounting bracket with shock tower.
4. Remove both plastic retaining pins using suitable punch or pliers.
5. Position shock assembly inboard or outboard as required to adjust camber. Ensure fore and aft position is same as marked and that rearward and forward bolts are moved an equal length.
6. **Do not enlarge any existing holes to increase adjustment range.**
7. **Torque** upper shock assembly mounting bolts to 68 ft. lbs.
8. Lower vehicle, then bounce front and rear of vehicle an equal amount of times.

9. Inspect camber setting and adjust as required.

Toe

1. Perform rear wheel alignment as outlined under "Rear Wheel Alignment."
2. Loosen front inner and outer tie rod jam nuts.
3. Rotate inner tie rod end at steering gear to set toe, **Fig. 1.**

REAR WHEEL ALIGNMENT

The following procedures have been revised by a Technical Service Bulletin.

To verify whether rear camber is adjustable on a particular vehicle, look for the presence of an adjusting screw on the forward lateral links as well as the rearward lateral links of the rear suspension (Lateral link adjusting screws). Rear camber can be adjusted using the adjusting screws located in both the forward and rearward lateral links.

Vehicles without an adjusting screw on the rearward lateral link do not have camber adjustment capabilities, but still allow for toe adjustment using the adjusting screw in the forward lateral link.

If rear camber is outside of specifications on a vehicle without an adjustment screw on the rearward link, a service link with an adjustment screw is available to provide that adjustment.

THRUST ANGLE

The thrust angle is the average of the toe settings on each rear wheel. If measurement is not within specifications, adjust rear wheel toe to provide each wheel with ½ of the total toe measurement. When adjusting, do not exceed the total toe specification.

CONCORDE, INTREPID & 300M

NOTE: Refer To Rear Of This Manual For Vehicle Manufacturer's Special Service Tool Suppliers.

INDEX OF SERVICE OPERATIONS

Page No.

AIR BAG SYSTEM PRECAUTIONS 0-18
BRAKES
  Anti-Lock Brakes (Volume 2).. 6-1
  Disc Brakes................... 14-1
  Drum Brakes 15-1
  Hydraulic Brake Systems 16-1
  Power Brake Units........... 17-1
COMPUTER RELEARN PROCEDURE 0-31
ELECTRICAL
  Air Bag System (Volume 2).... 4-1
  Air Conditioning............... 8-1
  Alternator, Replace 3-4
  Alternators................... 11-1
  Blower Motor, Replace........ 3-6
  Coil Pack, Replace 3-5
  Cooling Fans 9-1
  Cruise Control (Volume 2) 2-1
  Dash Gauges (Volume 2) 1-1
  Dash Panel Service (Volume 2).................. 5-1
  Dimmer Switch, Replace 3-5
  Evaporator Core, Replace 3-6
  Fuel Pump Relay Location 3-4
  Fuse Panel & Flasher Location 3-4
  Headlamp Switch, Replace ... 3-5
  Heater Core, Replace......... 3-6
  Ignition Lock, Replace 3-5
  Ignition Switch, Replace 3-5
  Instrument Cluster, Replace... 3-6
  Multi-Function Switch, Replace 3-5
  Passive Restraint Systems (Volume 2).................. 4-1
  Precautions.................. 3-4
  Radio, Replace............... 3-6
  Speed Controls (Volume 2) ... 2-1
  Starter Motors 10-1
  Starter, Replace 3-4
  Steering Columns............ 12-1
  Steering Wheel, Replace...... 3-6
  Stop Light Switch, Replace ... 3-5
  Technical Service Bulletins.... 3-7
  Turn Signal Switch, Replace .. 3-5
  Wiper Motor, Replace......... 3-6
  Wiper Switch, Replace........ 3-6
  Wiper Systems (Volume 2).... 3-1
ELECTRICAL SYMBOL IDENTIFICATION 0-63
FRONT DRIVE AXLES 18-1
FRONT SUSPENSION & STEERING
  Ball Joint Inspection 3-29
  Control Arm, Replace 3-29
  Hub & Bearing, Replace 3-29
  Power Steering 13-1
  Power Steering Gear, Replace 3-30
  Power Steering Pump, Replace 3-31
  Power Steering System Bleed 3-31

Page No.

Precautions.................... 3-29
Stabilizer Bar, Replace........ 3-29
Steering Columns............. 12-1
Steering Knuckle, Replace.... 3-29
Strut Dampner, Replace 3-30
Tension Strut, Replace 3-30
Tie Rod End, Replace 3-30
Tightening Specifications...... 3-35
NON-STANDARD TIRE & WHEEL SIZE ADJUSTMENT TO RIDE HEIGHT SPECIFICATIONS & TIRE SIZE CHART 0-61
REAR AXLE & SUSPENSION
  Lateral Link, Replace 3-26
  Rear Crossmember, Replace . 3-25
  Rear Wheel Spindle, Replace. 3-25
  Stabilizer Bar, Replace........ 3-26
  Strut, Replace 3-25
  Strut Service................. 3-25
  Technical Service Bulletins.... 3-27
  Tightening Specifications...... 3-28
SERVICE REMINDER & WARNING LAMP RESET PROCEDURES 0-34
SPECIFICATIONS
  Fluid Capacities & Cooling System Data................ 3-3
  Front Wheel Alignment Specifications................ 3-3
  General Engine Specifications................ 3-2
  Lubricant Data............... 3-3
  Rear Wheel Alignment Specifications................ 3-3
  Tune Up Specifications 3-2
VEHICLE IDENTIFICATION 0-1
VEHICLE LIFT POINTS 0-51
VEHICLE MAINTENANCE SCHEDULES 0-73
WHEEL ALIGNMENT
  Front Wheel Alignment........ 3-36
  Preliminary Inspection 3-36
  Rear Wheel Alignment 3-36
  Wheel Alignment Specifications................ 3-3
WIRE COLOR CODE IDENTIFICATION 0-63
2.7L ENGINE
  Belt Tension Data........... 3-14
  Camshaft, Replace 3-12
  Compression Pressure........ 3-8
  Cooling System Bleed 3-15
  Crankshaft Damper, Replace.. 3-11
  Crankshaft Rear Oil Seal, Replace 3-13
  Crankshaft Seal, Replace 3-13
  Crankshaft Sprocket, Replace 3-13
  Crankshaft, Replace 3-12
  Cylinder Head, Replace....... 3-9

Page No.

Engine Rebuilding Specifications................ 21-1
Engine, Replace 3-8
Engine Mount, Replace 3-8
Exhaust Manifold, Replace.... 3-9
Front Cover, Replace 3-11
Fuel Filter, Replace 3-15
Fuel Pump, Replace 3-15
Hydraulic Lifters, Replace..... 3-11
Intake Manifold, Replace..... 3-8
Main & Rod Bearings 3-13
Oil Pan, Replace............. 3-13
Oil Pump, Replace........... 3-14
Oil Pump Service............ 3-14
Piston & Rod Assembly 3-12
Precautions.................. 3-8
Radiator, Replace............ 3-15
Rocker Arms, Replace........ 3-10
Separated Accessory Drive System 3-14
Serpentine Drive Belt 3-14
Structural Collar, Replace 3-8
Thermostat, Replace......... 3-15
Tightening Specifications...... 3-16
Timing Chain, Replace........ 3-11
Timing Chain Tensioner, Replace 3-12
Timing Chain Tensioner Bleed...................... 3-12
Valve Adjustment 3-10
Valve Cover, Replace......... 3-10
Valve Springs, Replace 3-10
Water Pump, Replace 3-15
3.5L ENGINE
  Belt Tension Data........... 3-22
  Camshaft, Replace 3-20
  Camshaft Oil Seal, Replace... 3-20
  Camshaft Timing, Adjust 3-21
  Compression Pressure........ 3-17
  Cooling System Bleed 3-22
  Crankshaft Damper, Replace.. 3-20
  Crankshaft Rear Oil Seal, Replace 3-22
  Crankshaft Seal, Replace 3-22
  Crankshaft, Replace 3-21
  Cylinder Head, Replace....... 3-19
  Engine Rebuilding Specifications................ 21-1
  Engine, Replace 3-17
  Engine Mount, Replace 3-17
  Exhaust Manifold, Replace.... 3-18
  Front Cover, Replace 3-20
  Fuel Filter, Replace 3-23
  Fuel Pump, Replace 3-23
  Intake Manifold, Replace..... 3-18
  Main & Rod Bearings 3-21
  Oil Pan, Replace............. 3-22
  Oil Pump, Replace........... 3-22
  Oil Pump Service............ 3-22
  Piston & Rod Assembly 3-21
  Precautions.................. 3-17
  Radiator, Replace............ 3-23
  Rocker Arms, Replace........ 3-19
  Separated Accessory Drive System 3-22

	Page No.		Page No.		Page No.
Serpentine Drive Belt	3-22	Tightening Specifications	3-24	Valve Cover, Replace	3-19
Spark Plug Tubes, Replace	3-19	Timing Belt, Replace	3-20	Valve Springs, Replace	3-19
Structural Collar, Replace	3-17	Timing Belt Tensioner Bleed	3-21	Water Pump, Replace	3-23
Thermostat, Replace	3-23	Valve Adjustment	3-19		

Specifications

GENERAL ENGINE SPECIFICATIONS

Engine	Engine Code①	Fuel System	Bore & Stroke, Inch	Comp. Ratio	Brake HP @ RPM	Maximum Torque, Ft. Lbs. @ RPM	Normal Oil Pressure, psi	
							Idle	3000 RPM
2.7L	R	SMPI	3.386 x 3.091	9.7	200 @ 5800	190 @ 4850	5	45–105
3.5L	G/V	SMPI	3.780 x 3.189	9.9	250 @ 6400	250 @ 3900	5	45–105

SMPI — Sequential Multi-Port Fuel Injection

① — Eighth digit of VIN denotes engine code.

TUNE UP SPECIFICATIONS

Engine	Spark Plug Gap, Inch	Firing Order Fig.④	Ignition Timing		Idle Speed, RPM	Fuel Pump Pressure, psi⑥	Valve Clearance, Inch
			°BTDC	Mark			
2.7L	.048–.058	A	②	⑤	①	58	③
3.5L	.048–.053	A	②	⑤	①	58	③

BTDC — Before Top Dead Center
N — Neutral
① — Controlled by PCM.
② — Direct (Distributorless) Ignition System (DIS). Not adjustable.
③ — Equipped w/hydraulic lash adjusters. No adjustment is required.

④ — Before disconnecting wires from coil unit, determine location of No. 1 wire, as position may have been altered from that in **Fig. A.**

⑤ — Equipped w/crankshaft position sensor.

⑥ — Remove cover from service valve on fuel rail. Connect suitable fuel pressure test gauge to service valve. With ignition switch in Run position, use Diagnostic Read-Out Box to activate fuel pump & pressurize system.

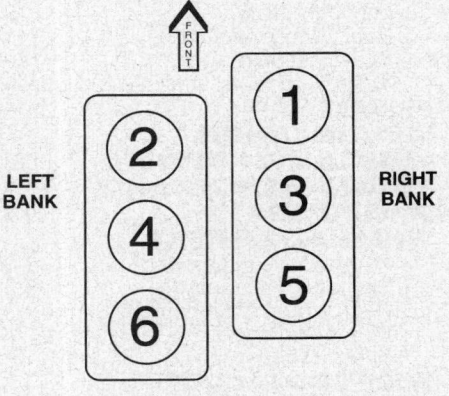

FIRING ORDER 1-2-3-4-5-6
CRI139800545000X

Fig. A

FRONT WHEEL ALIGNMENT SPECIFICATIONS

Year	Camber Angle, Degrees①		Caster Angle, Degrees①		Toe In, Degrees		Ball Joint Wear
	Limits	Desired	Limits	Desired	Limits	Desired	
2004	−.6 to +.6②	0	+2 to +4③	+3	+.2 to −.2	0	④

① — Reference angle only. Not adjustable.

② — Side to side differential not to exceed .7°.

③ — Side to side differential not to exceed 1°.

④ — Refer to "Ball Joint Inspection" in "Front Suspension & Steering."

REAR WHEEL ALIGNMENT SPECIFICATIONS

Year	Camber Angle, Degrees①		Toe In, Degrees		Thrust Angle①
	Limits	Desired	Limits	Desired	
2004	−.70 to +.30	−.20	−.20 to +.40	+.10	−.15 to +.15

① — Reference angle only; not adjustable.

FLUID CAPACITIES & COOLING SYSTEM DATA

Engine	Coolant Capacity, Qts.	Recommended Engine Coolant Type	Radiator Cap Relief Pressure, Lbs.	Thermostat. Opening Temp., °F	Fuel Tank, Gals.	Engine Oil Refill, Qts.①	Transmission Oil, Qts.②	Differential Oil, Qts.
2.7L	9.4	Ethylene Glycol	16	203–220	17	5.0	9.3	.78
3.5L	9.4	Ethylene Glycol	16	203–220	17	5.0	9.3	.78

① — Includes oil filter.

② — Approximate; make final inspection w/dipstick. Includes torque converter sump.

LUBRICANT DATA

This chart has been revised by a Technical Service Bulletin.

Year	Lubricant Type			
	Transmission	Differential	Power Steering	Brake System
2004	Mopar ATF+ 4 Type 9602	Mopar 75W-90 Hypoid Gear Lubricant	ATF+4 (MS9602)	DOT 3

Electrical

NOTE: On Air Bag Equipped Models, Refer To "Air Bag System Precautions" Located In The Front Of This Manual For System Disarming & Arming Procedures.

NOTE: Refer To "Computer Relearn Procedures" Located In The Front Of This Manual When Battery Power To The Computer Has Been Interrupted.

NOTE: Prior To Performing Any Service Operations Listed In This Section, Consult The "Technical Service Bulletins" Section For Related Information.

INDEX

	Page No.		Page No.		Page No.
Air Bag System (Volume 2)	4-1	Fuse Panel & Flasher Location	3-4	Starter Motors	10-1
Air Conditioning	8-1	Headlamp Switch, Replace	3-5	Starter, Replace	3-4
Alternator, Replace	3-4	Heater Core, Replace	3-6	Steering Columns	12-1
2.7L Engine	3-4	Ignition Lock, Replace	3-5	Steering Wheel, Replace	3-6
3.5L Engine	3-4	Cylinder	3-5	Installation	3-6
Alternators	11-1	Housing	3-5	Removal	3-6
Blower Motor, Replace	3-6	Ignition Switch, Replace	3-5	Stop Light Switch, Replace	3-5
Coil Pack, Replace	3-5	Instrument Cluster, Replace	3-6	Installation	3-5
Cooling Fans	9-1	Multi-Function Switch, Replace	3-5	Removal	3-5
Cruise Control (Volume 2)	2-1	Passive Restraint Systems		Technical Service Bulletins	3-7
Dash Gauges (Volume 2)	1-1	(Volume 2)	4-1	Instrument Cluster Changes	
Dash Panel Service		Precautions	3-4	Brightness	3-7
(Volume 2)	5-1	Air Bag Systems	3-4	Turn Signal Switch, Replace	3-5
Dimmer Switch, Replace	3-5	Battery Ground Cable	3-4	Wiper Motor, Replace	3-6
Evaporator Core, Replace	3-6	Radio, Replace	3-6	Wiper Switch, Replace	3-6
Fuel Pump Relay Location	3-4	Speed Controls (Volume 2)	2-1	Wiper Systems (Volume 2)	3-1

PRECAUTIONS

Air Bag Systems

Refer to "Air Bag System Precautions" in the front of this manual for system disarming and arming procedures.

Battery Ground Cable

Prior to service, disconnect battery ground cable and isolate as required.

FUSE PANEL & FLASHER LOCATION

The fuse panel/junction block is located under the lefthand side of the instrument panel. The hazard flasher unit is located under the lefthand side of the instrument panel between the junction block and the brake pedal.

FUEL PUMP RELAY LOCATION

The fuel pump relay is located in the power distribution center. The power distribution center is located in the engine compartment in front coolant reservoir bottle.

STARTER
REPLACE

1. Raise and support vehicle using suitable lift.
2. Remove bolts mounting starter to transmission.
3. Remove battery feed wire from starter.
4. Remove starter solenoid assembly from transmission housing, then position starter to access Connector Positive Assurance (CPA) wiring connector.
5. Slightly lift engine to relieve lefthand engine mount pressure using suitable jack stand beneath engine.
6. Remove lefthand engine mount mounting bolts.
7. Raise engine slightly to allow for clearance for starter removal.
8. Slide starter motor out between catalyst and engine mount, disconnect posi-lock starter solenoid connector and remove starter.
9. Reverse procedure install. **Torque** starter mounting bolts to 40 ft. lbs., and solenoid battery nut to 90 inch lbs.

ALTERNATOR
REPLACE

2.7L Engine

1. Raise and support vehicle.

2. Remove lower plastic splash shield from under engine compartment.
3. Remove transmission cooler and position aside. **Do not disconnect cooler hydraulic lines.**
4. Remove lower radiator crossmember support, then support radiator with suitable jack stand.
5. Loosen alternator adjusting T-bolt, then the pivot bolt. Do not remove bolts.
6. Remove alternator drive belt.
7. Disconnect alternator field circuit plug.
8. Remove battery terminal retaining nut, then battery terminal wire.
9. Remove pivot bolt, then the alternator. Do not lose spacer.
10. Reverse procedure to install, noting the following:
    a. **Torque** battery terminal nut to 90 inch lbs.
    b. **Torque** pivot bolt to 40 ft. lbs.

3.5L Engine

1. Remove upper radiator support and position aside.
2. Loosen lower alternator mounting bolt. Do not remove bolt.
3. Loosen pivot bolt and drive belt adjustment bolts, then remove drive belt.
4. Remove lower mounting bolt and disconnect alternator field circuit plug.
5. Remove battery terminal wire retaining nut and terminal wire.

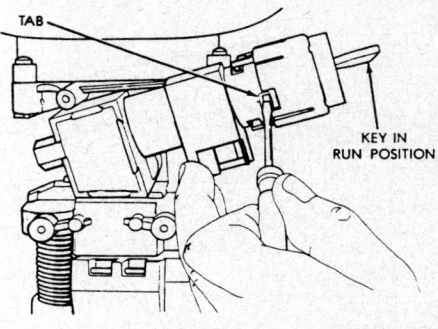

Fig. 1   Lock cylinder replacement

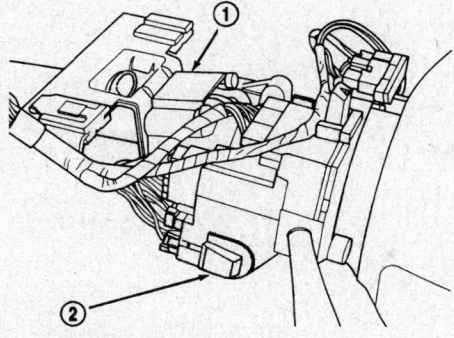

1 – STEERING COLUMN
2 – IGNITION SWITCH

Fig. 2   Ignition switch replacement

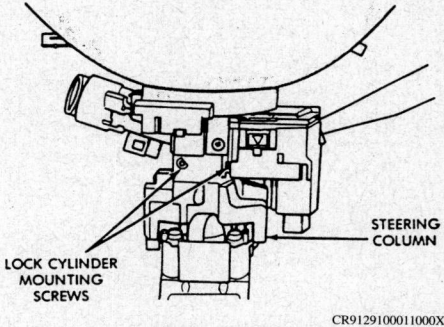

Fig. 3   Lock cylinder housing replacement

---

6. Remove pivot bolt, then alternator.
7. Reverse procedure to install, noting the following:
   a. **Torque** battery terminal wire retaining nut to 85 inch lbs.
   b. **Torque** lower mounting bolt and pivot bolt to 40 ft. lbs.

COIL PACK
REPLACE

These engines are equipped with a coil on plug ignition system. Each cylinder has a dedicated coil sitting atop each plug. No secondary wires are required and connection from the coil to plug is made with a boot that is attached to the coil.
1. Clean area around coil and spark plug with compressed air spray.
2. Disconnect electrical connector from ignition coil.
3. **On models equipped with 3.5L engines,** alternately loosen coil retaining screws back and forth. **Do not lose spacers under coil.**
4. **On all models,** remove fasteners and ignition coil.
5. Reverse procedure to install, noting following:
   a. **On models equipped with 2.7L engines, torque** mounting screws to 55 inch lbs.
   b. **On models equipped with 3.5L engine, torque** mounting screws to 60 inch lbs.

IGNITION LOCK
REPLACE

Cylinder

1. Remove tilt lever.
2. Remove upper and lower column covers.
3. Turn ignition key to Run position, then depress lock cylinder mounting tab and slide cylinder out of housing, **Fig. 1.**
4. Reverse procedure to install.

Housing

1. Remove upper and lower column covers.
2. Remove tilt lever.
3. Remove tilt lever, then upper and lower column covers.

---

4. Remove Sentry Key Immobilizer Module (SKIM), if equipped.
5. Remove multi-function switch.
6. Disconnect electrical connector from ignition switch.
7. Remove ignition switch mounting screws and ignition switch, **Fig. 2.**
8. Center punch tamper proof screws, **Fig. 3.**
9. Drill out screw heads using a ¼ inch drill bit.
10. Remove lock cylinder housing from steering column.
11. Remove bolts from steering column.
12. Reverse procedure to install. Tighten new tamper proof screws until heads twist off.

IGNITION SWITCH
REPLACE

1. Remove tilt lever, then upper and lower column covers.
2. Remove Sentry Key Immobilizer Module (SKIM), if equipped.
3. Remove multi-function switch.
4. Disconnect electrical connector from ignition switch.
5. Remove ignition switch mounting screws and ignition switch, **Fig. 2.**
6. Reverse procedure to install. Align tab on ignition switch with slot on lock housing.

HEADLAMP SWITCH
REPLACE

1. Open front door and remove lefthand end cover.
2. Remove screw from lefthand end of instrument panel and pull headlight bezel rearward to disengage clips.
3. Remove headlight switch screws and pull switch out to disconnect electrical connectors.
4. Remove headlight switch.
5. Reverse procedure to install.

STOP LIGHT SWITCH
REPLACE

Removal

1. Press and hold brake pedal.

---

2. Rotate switch 30° counterclockwise, pull rearward and remove from bracket.
3. Disconnect wiring harness connector.

Installation

1. Hold stop lamp switch firmly in one hand, then using other hand, pull plunger outward until it ratchets to its fully extended position.
2. Connect wiring harness connector.
3. Press brake pedal as far down as possible, then install switch in bracket by aligning switch index key with mounting bracket square hole slot.
4. When fully installed, rotate switch 30° clockwise to lock.
5. Gently pull brake pedal back until pedal stops moving and switch plunger ratchets to correct position.

MULTI-FUNCTION SWITCH
REPLACE

1. Remove tilt lever, then the upper and lower steering column covers.
2. Remove multi-function switch to column mounting screws.
3. Disconnect multi-function switch electrical connections.
4. Reverse procedure to install. **Torque** multi-function switch to column screws to 17 inch lbs.

TURN SIGNAL SWITCH
REPLACE

1. Remove tilt lever, then the upper and lower steering column covers.
2. Remove multi-function switch to column mounting screws.
3. Disconnect multi-function switch electrical connections.
4. Reverse procedure to install. **Torque** multi-function switch to column screws to 17 inch lbs.

DIMMER SWITCH
REPLACE

1. Remove tilt lever, then the upper and lower steering column covers.
2. Remove multi-function switch to column mounting screws.

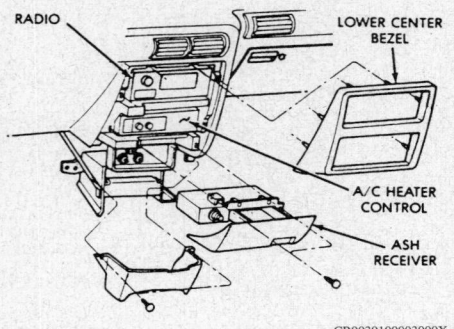

Fig. 4   Radio replacement

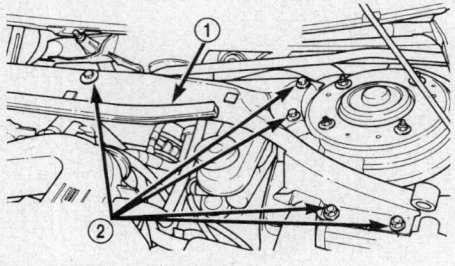

1 – TOWER TO TOWER SUPPORT
2 – RETAINING BOLTS

CR9020000443000X

Fig. 5   Tower to tower support removal

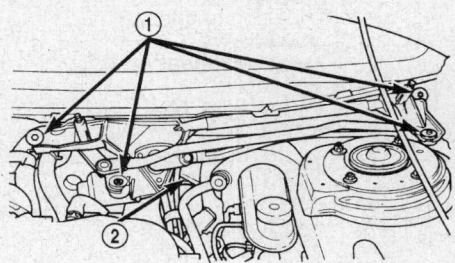

1 – RETAINING BOLTS
2 – WIPER MOTOR CONNECTOR

CR9020000444000X

Fig. 6   Wiper module retaining bolt removal

3. Disconnect multi-function switch electrical connections.
4. Reverse procedure to install. **Torque** multi-function switch to column screws to 17 inch lbs.

STEERING WHEEL
REPLACE
Removal

1. Lock steering column by turning steering wheel ½ turn (180°) clockwise from straight ahead position.
2. Place ignition in Off/Lock position and remove ignition key. This will ensure no damage occurs to clockspring.
3. Remove driver's air bag module as outlined in "Passive Restraint Systems" chapter.
4. Remove steering wheel mounting nut from steering column shaft.
5. Remove steering wheel using steering wheel puller tool No. C-3428B, or equivalent.

Installation

1. Ensure steering wheel is positioned ½ turn (180°) to right.
2. Lock column into position with ignition cylinder lock.
3. Ensure turn signal stalk is in neutral, then pull all wires through larger opening of hub area on wheel.
4. Install steering wheel, ensure flats on hub align with clockspring.
5. Install steering wheel mounting nut and tighten nut to draw steering wheel onto column. **Torque** steering column shaft nut to 45 ft. lbs.
6. Connect wiring harness on air bag module.
7. Install drivers air bag module into steering wheel as outlined in "Passive Restraint Systems" chapter.

INSTRUMENT CLUSTER
REPLACE

1. Remove instrument panel lefthand end cap.
2. Remove steering column shroud cover, then tilt steering wheel down.
3. **On 300M models,** remove one screw from cluster bezel.
4. **On all models,** remove all items to expose bezel mounting screws.

5. Remove two screws over upper cluster bezel in instrument panel brow and all remaining screws.
6. Remove instrument panel cluster bezel using a trim stick tool No. C-4755, or equivalent.
7. Remove instrument cluster screws and disengage upper latch.
8. Remove instrument cluster from panel. **Instrument panel wiring harness connectors are mounted directly to rear panel. A force of approximately 20–30 lbs. will be required to disengage cluster from connectors.**
9. Reverse procedure to install.

RADIO
REPLACE

1. Remove lower center bezel, radio mounting screws, then remove radio, **Fig. 4.**
2. Pull radio straight out and disconnect electrical and antenna connections.
3. Remove radio ground strap, then radio.
4. Reverse procedure to install.

WIPER MOTOR
REPLACE

1. Remove wiper arms.
2. Remove cowl screen panel.
3. Remove wiper module mounting bolt from top of tower to tower beam.
4. Remove tower to tower support bolts, **Fig. 5.**
5. Remove wiper module retaining bolts, **Fig. 6.**
6. Remove wiper module and disconnect electrical connector.
7. Disconnect wiper module master link from motor crank with ball and socket wedge. Do not damage ball, socket or seal when removing.
8. Remove nut to crank arm, **Fig. 7.**
9. Remove wiper motor from wiper module.
10. Reverse procedure to install.

WIPER SWITCH
REPLACE

1. Remove tilt lever, then the upper and lower steering column covers.
2. Remove multi-function switch to column mounting screws.

3. Disconnect multi-function switch electrical connections.
4. Reverse procedure to install. **Torque** multi-function switch to column screws to 17 inch lbs.

BLOWER MOTOR
REPLACE

1. Remove lower righthand under panel duct.
2. Disconnect blower motor connector from resistor block/power module.
3. Squeeze blower motor wiring grommet, push grommet through blower motor housing cover.
4. Remove blower motor housing cover.
5. Remove blower motor mounting screws, lower blower motor from housing.
6. Reverse procedure to install.

HEATER CORE
REPLACE

1. Remove heater and air conditioning housing as outlined under "Evaporator Core, Replace."
2. Remove heater core attaching screws, then heater core.
3. Reverse procedure to install.

EVAPORATOR CORE
REPLACE

1. Recover refrigerant as outlined in "Air Conditioning" chapter.
2. Drain engine coolant into suitable container.
3. Remove instrument panel as outlined in "Dash Panel Service" chapter.
4. Remove air cleaner hose and distribution duct from engine.
5. Remove fasteners from heater hoses at dash panel and remove hoses from heater core.
6. Plug heater core inlet and outlet tubes to block coolant from entering interior.
7. Remove one nut at expansion valve retaining both air conditioning lines to expansion valve.
8. Cap expansion valve and air conditioning openings.
9. Remove three housing to dash panel retaining nuts from engine compartment side of dash panel.
10. Remove defrost duct retaining screws and duct.

11. Remove housing to dash panel retaining nuts and screws.
12. Remove rear seat heat duct retaining screws and duct.
13. Remove rear seat heat duct elbow push pin fastener.
14. Disconnect harness connector.
15. Gently pull housing rearward from dash panel.
16. Remove recirculation door actuator.
17. Remove recirculation door and housing.
18. Remove upper housing mounting screws, then upper half of heater housing.
19. Lift evaporator out of lower housing.
20. Transfer expansion valve onto new evaporator using new gaskets.
21. Reverse procedure to install.

TECHNICAL SERVICE BULLETINS

Instrument Cluster Changes Brightness

On some of these models the instrument cluster illumination changes brightness. Models equipped with auto-lamp may also have headlamps or fog lamps come on at unexpected times.

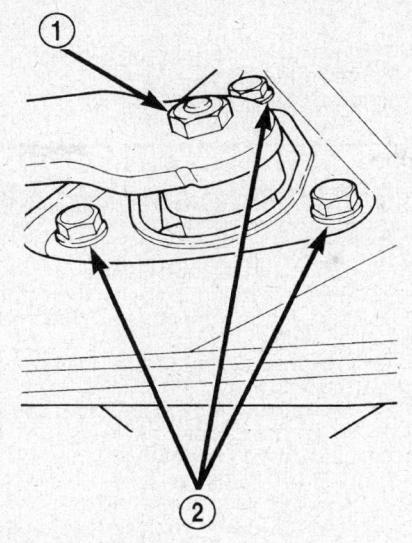

1 – CRANK ARM NUT
2 – WIPER MOTOR RETAINING BOLTS

CR9020000445000X

Fig. 7 Wiper motor crank arm removal

This condition may be caused by the headlamp switch wiring connector.

To correct this condition, apply dielectric grease to headlamp switch wiring connector as follows:

1. Disconnect and isolate battery ground cable.
2. Remove instrument panel lefthand end cap.
3. Remove steering column shroud cover.
4. Tilt steering column down to lowest position.
5. **On Limited and 300M models,** remove cluster bezel mounting screw.
6. **On all models,** remove two mounting screws over upper cluster bezel in panel brow area.
7. **On Intrepid, Limited and 300M models,** remove four cluster mounting screws.
8. **On Concorde models,** remove five cluster mounting screws.
9. **On all models,** pry out instrument cluster pane; bezel using suit trim stick.
10. Clean contacts by disconnecting and connecting headlamp switch wire harness connector three times.
11. Disconnect connector and apply suitable dielectric grease to terminals.
12. Connect connector and assembly instrument panel.

2.7L Engine

NOTE: On Air Bag Equipped Models, Refer To "Air Bag System Precautions" Located In The Front Of This Manual For System Disarming & Arming Procedures.

NOTE: Refer To "Computer Relearn Procedures" Located In The Front Of This Manual When Battery Power To The Computer Has Been Interrupted.

INDEX

	Page No.		Page No.		Page No.
Belt Tension Data	3-14	Engine, Replace	3-8	Installation	3-12
Camshaft, Replace	3-12	Engine Mount, Replace	3-8	Removal	3-12
Installation	3-12	Lefthand & Righthand	3-8	**Precautions**	3-8
Removal	3-12	Rear	3-8	Air Bag Systems	3-8
Compression Pressure	3-8	Exhaust Manifold, Replace	3-9	Battery Ground Cable	3-8
Cooling System Bleed	3-15	Lefthand	3-9	Fuel System Pressure Relief	3-8
Crankshaft Damper, Replace	3-11	Righthand	3-9	**Radiator, Replace**	3-15
Crankshaft Rear Oil Seal, Replace	3-13	Front Cover, Replace	3-11	**Rocker Arms, Replace**	3-10
		Fuel Filter, Replace	3-15	Installation	3-10
Installation	3-13	Fuel Pump, Replace	3-15	Removal	3-10
Removal	3-13	Hydraulic Lifters, Replace	3-11	**Separated Accessory Drive**	
Crankshaft, Replace	3-12	Intake Manifold, Replace	3-8	**System**	3-14
Installation	3-13	Lower	3-9	Air Conditioning	3-14
Removal	3-12	Upper	3-8	Installation	3-14
Crankshaft Seal, Replace	3-13	Main & Rod Bearings	3-13	Removal	3-14
Crankshaft Sprocket, Replace	3-13	Oil Pan, Replace	3-13	**Serpentine Drive Belt**	3-14
Installation	3-13	Installation	3-14	**Structural Collar, Replace**	3-8
Removal	3-13	Removal	3-13	**Thermostat, Replace**	3-15
Cylinder Head, Replace	3-9	Oil Pump, Replace	3-14	**Tightening Specifications**	3-16
Engine Rebuilding		Oil Pump Service	3-14	**Timing Chain, Replace**	3-11
Specifications	21-1	Piston & Rod Assembly	3-12	Installation	3-11

	Page No.		Page No.		Page No.
Removal	3-11	Timing Chain Tensioner Bleed	3-12	Valve Springs, Replace	3-10
Timing Chain Tensioner, Replace	3-12	Valve Adjustment	3-10	Water Pump, Replace	3-15
		Valve Cover, Replace	3-10		

PRECAUTIONS

Air Bag Systems

Refer to "Air Bag System Precautions" in the front of this manual for system disarming and arming procedures.

Battery Ground Cable

Prior to service, disconnect battery ground cable and isolate as required.

Fuel System Pressure Relief

1. Remove fuel pump relay for power distribution center.
2. Start and run engine until it stalls.
3. Attempt to start engine until it no longer runs.
4. Turn ignition switch to Off position.
5. Place rag or towel under fuel line quick-connector fitting at fuel rail.
6. Install fuel pump relay.
7. One or more Diagnostic Trouble Codes (DTCs) may have been stored because of removing fuel pump relay. Clear these DTCs with suitably programmed scan tool.

COMPRESSION PRESSURE

The minimum compression pressure should be no less than 100 psi and the maximum variation between cylinders should be no more than 25%.

ENGINE MOUNT
REPLACE

Lefthand & Righthand

1. Raise and support vehicle.
2. Remove isolator mounting nuts from top of mounting bracket.
3. Support engine with suitable jack, place suitable wood block between oil pan and jack.
4. Remove lower mounting nuts from frame.
5. Raise engine carefully, then remove isolator with heat shield.
6. Reverse procedure to install.

Rear

1. Raise and support vehicle.
2. Support transmission with suitable jack.
3. Remove mounting nuts, then crossmember bolts and mount.
4. Reverse procedure to install.

STRUCTURAL COLLAR
REPLACE

1. Raise and support vehicle.
2. Remove mounting bolts, then structural collar from oil pan and transmission housing.
3. Reverse procedure to install, noting the following;
   a. **Torque** vertical collar oil pan bolts to 10 inch lbs.
   b. **Torque** collar to transmission bolts to 40 ft. lbs.
   c. Start with center vertical bolt and work outward, **torque** mounting bolts to 40 ft. lbs.

ENGINE
REPLACE

1. Remove fuel pump relay for power distribution center.
2. Start and run engine until it stalls.
3. Attempt to start engine until it no longer runs.
4. Turn ignition switch to Off position.
5. Place rag or towel under fuel line quick-connector fitting at fuel rail.
6. Install fuel pump relay.
7. Mark hood position at hinges and remove, then drain cooling system into suitable container.
8. Remove wiper arms, left and righthand cowl screens (covers), then cowl support.
9. Remove air cleaner assembly and air inlet hose, then upper radiator crossmember.
10. Disconnect hood release cable from latch, then remove cooling fan module.
11. Disconnect upper radiator hose from engine and lower hose from radiator, then transmission cooler lines from radiator.
12. Remove air conditioning condenser to radiator attaching bolts, then transmission cooler line support bracket.
13. Remove mounting screw from lefthand side of radiator, then radiator from engine compartment.
14. Remove accessory drive belts.
15. Remove power steering pump mounting bolts, then position pump aside.
16. Disconnect air conditioning compressor electrical connector, then remove compressor mounting bolts and position aside.
17. Remove exhaust manifold V-band clamps, then disconnect throttle and speed control cables.
18. Disconnect coolant pressure bottle and heater hoses.
19. Disconnect fuel line, vacuum lines, electrical connectors and engine ground straps.
20. Raise and support vehicle, then drain engine oil into suitable container.
21. Remove catalytic converter down pipe front and rear attaching bolts.
22. Remove structural collar mounting bolts and structural collar.
23. Mark flexplate to torque converter position for installation alignment, then remove converter mounting bolts.
24. Disconnect transmission cooler line brackets from engine, then remove starter.
25. Remove crankshaft position sensor.
26. Remove lower transmission to cylinder block attaching bolts.
27. Lower vehicle and remove fuel line from throttle body.
28. Remove electrical harness bracket and to throttle body retaining screws.
29. Remove electrical harness and transmission shift cable retaining bracket.
30. Remove throttle body support bracket attaching bolts.
31. Remove transmission to cylinder block double-ended bolts.
32. Remove upper transmission to cylinder block bolts.
33. Remove left and righthand engine mount insulator to engine mount bracket mounting bolts.
34. Remove cam sensor from lefthand cylinder head.
35. Attach suitable lifting device to engine and support transmission with suitable floor jack, then remove engine.
36. Reverse procedure to install.

INTAKE MANIFOLD
REPLACE

Upper

1. Remove air inlet resonator and inlet tube.
2. Remove throttle and speed control cables from throttle arm and bracket, then bracket.
3. Disconnect Manifold Absolute Pressure (MAP), Intake Air Temperature (IAT), Throttle Position (TPS) sensors, Manifold Tune Valve (MTV) and Idle Air Control (IAC) motor electrical connectors.
4. Disconnect vapor purge, brake booster, speed control servo and Positive Crankcase Ventilation (PCV) hoses.
5. Remove Exhaust Gas Recirculation (EGR) tube.
6. Loosen throttle body support bracket upper attaching bolt, then lefthand and righthand support bracket attaching bolts.
7. Release retaining clip and engine cover.
8. Remove upper manifold mounting bolts and upper manifold.
9. Reverse procedure to install, noting the following:

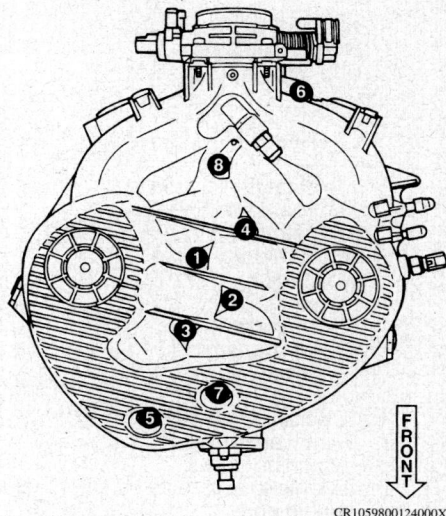

CR1059800124000X

Fig. 1 Upper intake manifold tightening sequence

a. Ensure fuel injectors and wiring harnesses are positioned aside.
b. Tighten manifold in sequence, **Fig. 1**.

Lower

1. Remove fuel pump relay for power distribution center.
2. Start and run engine until it stalls.
3. Attempt to start engine until it no longer runs.
4. Turn ignition switch to Off position.
5. Place rag or towel under fuel line quick-connector fitting at fuel rail.
6. Install fuel pump relay.
7. Remove air inlet resonator and inlet tube.
8. Remove throttle and speed control cables from throttle arm and bracket, then bracket.
9. Disconnect Manifold Absolute Pressure (MAP), Intake Air Temperature (IAT), Throttle Position (TPS) sensors, Manifold Tune Valve (MTV) and Idle Air Control (IAC) motor electrical connectors.
10. Disconnect vapor purge, brake booster, speed control servo and Positive Crankcase Ventilation (PCV) hoses.
11. Remove Exhaust Gas Recirculation (EGR) tube.
12. Loosen throttle body support bracket upper attaching bolt, then lefthand and righthand support bracket attaching bolts.
13. Release retaining clip and engine cover.
14. Remove upper manifold mounting bolts and upper manifold.
15. Remove fuel rail fuel supply hose, then the fuel rail support bracket to throttle body support bracket mounting screw.
16. Remove mounting bolts, then the fuel rail and injectors as an assembly.
17. Remove mounting bolts and the lower intake manifold.
18. Reverse procedure to install, noting the following:
    a. To properly position manifold, in-

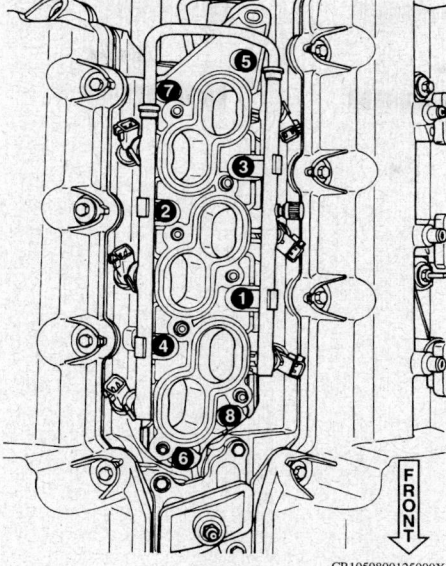

CR1059800125000X

Fig. 2 Lower intake manifold tightening sequence

stall rearmost bolt and tighten 2–3 turns.
b. Tighten bolts in sequence, **Fig. 2**.

EXHAUST MANIFOLD
REPLACE
Lefthand

1. Raise and support vehicle.
2. Remove exhaust system and lefthand catalytic converter.
3. Remove transmission dipstick tube mounting bolt and rotate housing away from engine.
4. Lower vehicle.
5. Disconnect electrical connectors and remove harness mounting screws from support bracket, then engine wiring harness support bracket from cylinder head.
6. Disconnect connector and remove exhaust manifold oxygen sensor.
7. Remove engine oil dipstick tube.
8. Remove mounting screws and heat shield.
9. Remove mounting bolts and exhaust manifold.
10. Reverse procedure to install.

Righthand

1. Remove air intake plenum and air filter housing.
2. Remove battery cable housing tube to transmission housing mounting bolt.
3. Remove EGR tube to exhaust manifold and EGR valve mounting bolts.
4. Disconnect electrical connector and exhaust manifold oxygen sensor.
5. Remove manifold to catalytic converter V-band clamp.
6. Remove mounting screws and heat shields.
7. Remove mounting bolts and exhaust manifold.

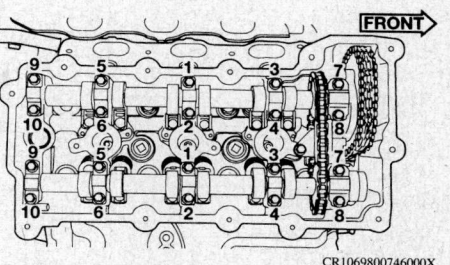

CR1069800746000X

Fig. 3 Camshaft bearing cap tightening sequence

8. Reverse procedure to install.

CYLINDER HEAD
REPLACE

1. Remove fuel pump relay for power distribution center.
2. Start and run engine until it stalls.
3. Attempt to start engine until it no longer runs.
4. Turn ignition switch to Off position.
5. Place rag or towel under fuel line quick-connector fitting at fuel rail.
6. Install fuel pump relay.
7. Drain cooling system into suitable container and remove accessory drive belts.
8. Remove upper radiator crossmember and fan module.
9. Remove accessory and air conditioning belts.
10. Remove damper using crankshaft damper holder tool No. 8191, or equivalent, and three-jaw puller tool No. 1023, or equivalent.
11. Remove upper and lower intake manifolds as outlined under "Intake Manifold, Replace."
12. Remove cylinder head cover as outlined under "Valve Cover, Replace."
13. Remove upper radiator support crossmember, then fan module and accessory drive belts.
14. Remove power steering pump from mounting bracket, then accessory drive belt tensioner pulley and bracket.
15. Remove mounting bolts and timing chain cover.
16. Remove water outlet connector.
17. Rotate crankshaft until crankshaft sprocket timing mark aligns with oil pump housing timing mark, then remove timing chain.
18. Remove primary timing chain as outlined under "Timing Chain, Replace" then the secondary chain tensioner mounting bolts.
19. Loosen camshaft bearing cap bolts in reverse order of tightening sequence, **Fig. 3**.
20. Remove bearing caps, then the camshafts, secondary chain and tensioner as an assembly. **Mark bearing cap position for installation alignment.**
21. Remove catalytic converter pipe V-band clamps at exhaust manifold.
22. Remove cylinder head mounting bolts in reverse order of tightening sequence, **Fig. 4**.
23. Remove cylinder head.

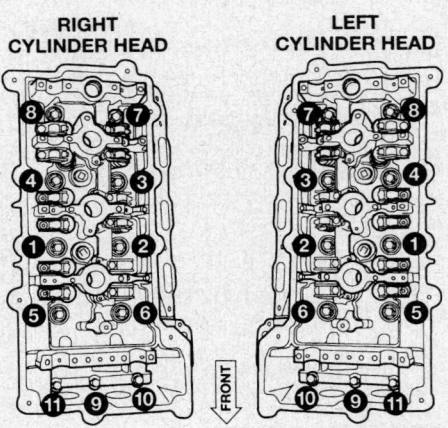

RIGHT CYLINDER HEAD LEFT CYLINDER HEAD

CR1069800748000X

Fig. 4 Cylinder head bolt tightening sequence

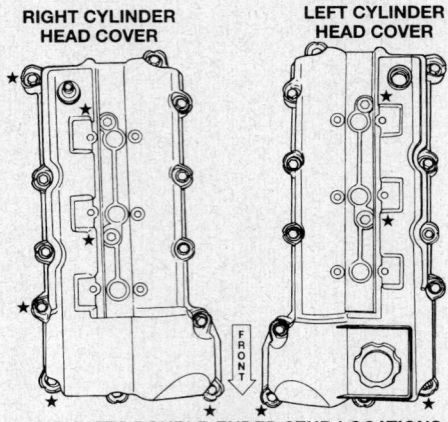

RIGHT CYLINDER HEAD COVER LEFT CYLINDER HEAD COVER

★ INDICATES DOUBLE-ENDED STUD LOCATIONS

CR1069800745000X

Fig. 5 Valve cover replacement

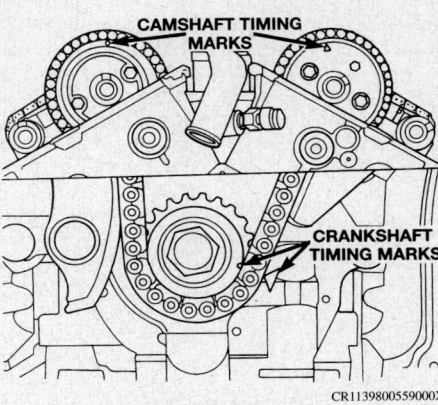

CAMSHAFT TIMING MARKS

CRANKSHAFT TIMING MARKS

CR1139800559000X

Fig. 6 Timing chain mark alignment

24. Reverse procedure to install, noting the following:
   a. Cylinder head bolts are tightened using a torque plus angle procedure, bolts with stretched threads must be replaced.
   b. Lubricate bolt threads with suitable, clean engine oil.
   c. **Torque** cylinder head bolt Nos. 1–8 in sequence to 35 ft. lbs, **Fig. 4.**
   d. **Torque** head bolt bolts in sequence to 55 ft. lbs.
   e. Tighten bolts an additional 90° in sequence.
   f. **Torque** cylinder head bolt Nos. 9–11 in sequence to 21 ft. lbs.

VALVE COVER

REPLACE

1. Remove air inlet resonator and inlet tube.
2. Remove throttle and speed control cables from throttle arm and bracket, then bracket.
3. Disconnect Manifold Absolute Pressure (MAP), Intake Air Temperature (IAT), Throttle Position (TPS) sensors, Manifold Tune Valve (MTV) and Idle Air Control (IAC) motor electrical connectors.
4. Disconnect vapor purge, brake booster, speed control servo and Positive Crankcase Ventilation (PCV) hoses.
5. Remove Exhaust Gas Recirculation (EGR) tube.
6. Loosen throttle body support bracket upper attaching bolt, then lefthand and righthand support bracket attaching bolts.
7. Release retaining clip and engine cover.
8. Remove upper manifold mounting bolts and upper manifold.
9. Disconnect ignition coil electrical connectors.
10. Remove ground strap from righthand cylinder head, then disconnect electrical and vacuum harness retaining clips from studs.
11. Remove ignition coil capacitor fasteners, then lefthand and righthand upper intake manifold support brackets.

12. Loosen mounting bolts and remove cylinder head covers. Mounting bolts will remain in cover.
13. Reverse procedure to install. Ensure double-ended studs are in correct locations, **Fig. 5.**

VALVE ADJUSTMENT

Equipped with hydraulic lash adjusters. No adjustment is required.

ROCKER ARMS

REPLACE

Removal

1. Remove valve covers as outlined under "Valve Cover, Replace."
2. Turn crankshaft to rotate engine until cam lobe is on base circle (heel) of rocker arm being removed.
3. Depress valve spring enough to release tension and remove rocker arm using valve spring compressor tool No. 8215 and Adapter tool No. 8216, or equivalent.
4. Identify rocker arm position.

Installation

1. Lubricate rocker arm with suitable, clean engine oil.
2. Turn crankshaft until cam lobe is on base circle (heel) of rocker arm being removed.
3. Depress valve spring enough to release tension using valve spring compressor tool No. 8215 and adapter tool No. 8216, or equivalents.
4. Install rocker arm in original position and release valve spring tension.
5. Install valve cover as outlined under "Valve Cover, Replace."

VALVE SPRINGS

REPLACE

Ensure piston is at TDC on cylinder from which valve spring(s) is being removed.

1. Remove fuel pump relay for power distribution center.
2. Start and run engine until it stalls.
3. Attempt to start engine until it no longer runs.
4. Turn ignition switch to Off position.
5. Place rag or towel under fuel line quick-connector fitting at fuel rail.
6. Install fuel pump relay.
7. Remove air cleaner housing cover and inlet hose.
8. Remove air inlet resonator and inlet tube.
9. Remove throttle and speed control cables from throttle arm and bracket, then bracket.
10. Disconnect Manifold Absolute Pressure (MAP), Intake Air Temperature (IAT), Throttle Position (TPS) sensors, Manifold Tune Valve (MTV) and Idle Air Control (IAC) motor electrical connectors.
11. Disconnect vapor purge, brake booster, speed control servo and Positive Crankcase Ventilation (PCV) hoses.
12. Remove Exhaust Gas Recirculation (EGR) tube.
13. Loosen throttle body support bracket upper attaching bolt, then lefthand and righthand support bracket attaching bolts.
14. Release retaining clip and engine cover
15. Remove upper manifold mounting bolts and upper manifold.
16. Remove valve covers as outlined under "Valve Cover, Replace."
17. Remove upper radiator crossmember and fan module.
18. Remove accessory and air conditioning belts.
19. Remove damper using crankshaft damper holder tool No. 8191, or equivalent, and three-jaw puller tool No. 1023, or equivalent.
20. Remove timing chain as outlined under "Timing Chain, Replace."
21. Remove primary timing chain as outlined under "Timing Chain, Replace" then the secondary chain tensioner mounting bolts.
22. Loosen camshaft bearing cap bolts in reverse order of tightening sequence, **Fig. 3.**

23. Remove bearing caps, then the camshafts, secondary chain and tensioner as an assembly. **Mark bearing cap position for installation alignment.**
24. Install suitable spark plug adapter into cylinder being serviced, then apply 90–100 psi air pressure to hold valves in place.
25. Compress valve spring using valve spring compressor tool No. MD-998772A with adapter tool No. 6779, or equivalent, then remove valve locks, retainer and spring.
26. Remove valve stem seals using suitable valve seal tool.
27. Reverse procedure to install, noting the following:
    a. Push valve steam seal/seat firmly and squarely over valve guide with stem as guide.
    b. Do not force seal against guide top.
    c. When install retainer locks, compress spring only enough to install locks.

HYDRAULIC LIFTERS
REPLACE

1. Remove rocker arm as outlined under "Rocker Arm, Replace."
2. Mark position of hydraulic lash adjuster installation alignment.
3. Remove hydraulic lash adjuster.
4. Reverse procedure to install. Ensure adjuster is partially full of oil.

CRANKSHAFT DAMPER
REPLACE

1. Remove upper radiator crossmember and fan module.
2. Remove accessory and air conditioning belts.
3. Remove damper using crankshaft damper holder tool No. 8191, or equivalent, and three-jaw puller tool No. 1023, or equivalent.
4. Reverse procedure to install.

FRONT COVER
REPLACE

1. Remove upper radiator support crossmember, then fan module and accessory drive belts.
2. Remove upper radiator crossmember and fan module.
3. Remove accessory and air conditioning belts.
4. Remove damper using crankshaft damper holder tool No. 8191, or equivalent, and three-jaw puller tool No. 1023, or equivalent.
5. Remove power steering pump from mounting bracket, then accessory drive belt tensioner pulley and bracket.
6. Remove mounting bolts and timing chain cover.
7. Reverse procedure to install, noting the following:
    a. Apply 1/8 inch bead of suitable silicone rubber adhesive sealant to parting lines between oil pan and cylinder block.
    b. Use crankshaft seal Installer and

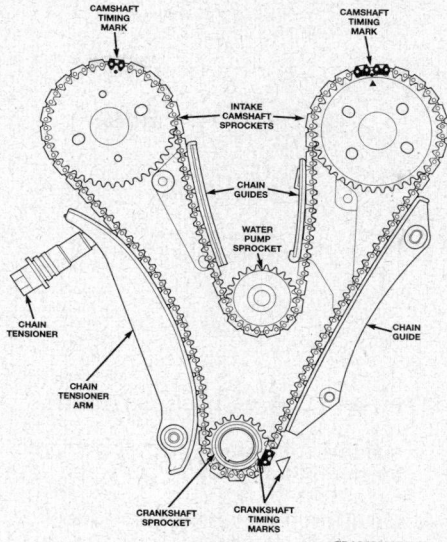

Fig. 7   Primary timing chain alignment marks

sleeve tool No. 6780-2, or equivalent, to install crankshaft seal.

TIMING CHAIN
REPLACE

With the timing chain removed, avoid turning the camshaft or crankshaft. If movement is required, exercise caution to avoid valve damage caused by piston contact.

Removal

1. Remove air inlet resonator and inlet tube.
2. Remove throttle and speed control cables from throttle arm and bracket, then bracket.
3. Disconnect Manifold Absolute Pressure (MAP), Intake Air Temperature (IAT), Throttle Position (TPS) sensors, Manifold Tune Valve (MTV) and Idle Air Control (IAC) motor electrical connectors.
4. Disconnect vapor purge, brake booster, speed control servo and Positive Crankcase Ventilation (PCV) hoses.
5. Remove Exhaust Gas Recirculation (EGR) tube.
6. Loosen throttle body support bracket upper attaching bolt, then lefthand and righthand support bracket attaching bolts.
7. Release retaining clip and engine cover.
8. Remove upper manifold mounting bolts and upper manifold.
9. Remove valve covers as outlined under "Valve Cover, Replace."
10. Remove upper radiator crossmember and fan module.
11. Remove accessory and air conditioning belts.
12. Remove damper using crankshaft damper holder tool No. 8191, or equivalent, and three-jaw puller tool No. 1023, or equivalent.

13. Remove upper radiator crossmember and fan module.
14. Remove damper using crankshaft damper holder tool No. 8191, or equivalent, and three-jaw puller tool No. 1023, or equivalent.
15. Remove power steering pump from mounting bracket, then accessory drive belt tensioner pulley and bracket.
16. Remove mounting bolts and timing chain cover.
17. Rotate crankshaft to align crankshaft sprocket timing marks and oil pump housing marks. Cylinder No. 1 should be at 60° ATDC.
18. Remove primary timing chain tensioner from righthand cylinder head.
19. Remove camshaft position sensor from lefthand cylinder head, then chain guide access plug.
20. Remove righthand camshaft sprocket mounting bolts, then damper and sprocket.
21. Remove mounting bolts and lefthand camshaft sprocket.
22. Remove lower chain guide, then tensioner arm and primary timing chain.

Installation

1. Align crankshaft sprocket and oil pump housing timing marks, **Fig. 6.**
2. Place lefthand side primary chain sprocket on chain so timing mark is between two plated links.
3. Lower primary chain with lefthand side sprocket through lefthand cylinder head opening.
4. Loosely position lefthand side camshaft sprocket over camshaft hub.
5. Align plated link to crankshaft sprocket timing mark, **Fig. 7.**
6. Position primary chain onto water pump drive sprocket.
7. Align righthand camshaft sprocket timing mark to timing chain plated link and loosely position over camshaft hub.
8. Ensure all plated links are properly aligned to sprocket timing marks.
9. Install lefthand lower chain guide and tensioner arm.
10. Install chain guide access plug to lefthand cylinder head.
11. Remove tensioner from housing and place check ball end into shallow end of timing chain tensioner resetting gauge tool No. 8186, or equivalent.
12. Slowly depress tensioner until oil is purged from cylinder, then install into housing.
13. Position cylinder plunger into deeper end of timing chain tensioner resetting gauge tool No. 8186, or equivalent, then apply downward force until tensioner bottoms against top edge of tool.
14. Install chain tensioner into righthand cylinder head.
15. Insert suitable 3/8 inch square drive extension with breaker bar into righthand cylinder bank intake camshaft drive hub, then rotate until camshaft hub aligns with camshaft sprocket and damper bolt holes.
16. Install sprocket mounting bolts.

17. Insert suitable ⅜ inch square drive extension with breaker bar into lefthand cylinder bank intake camshaft drive hub, then rotate until camshaft hub aligns with camshaft sprocket and damper bolt holes.
18. Install sprocket mounting bolts.
19. Rotate engine slightly clockwise to remove timing chain slack.
20. Gently pry tensioner arm toward tensioner slightly, then release tensioner arm and ensure tensioner extends.
21. Install front cover, crankshaft damper, cylinder heads, camshaft position sensor and upper intake manifold.

TIMING CHAIN TENSIONER
REPLACE

Refer to "Timing Chain, Replace" for tensioner replacement.

TIMING CHAIN TENSIONER BLEED

Refer to "Timing Chain, Replace" for tensioner bleed.

CAMSHAFT
REPLACE

With the timing chain removed, avoid turning the camshaft or crankshaft. If movement is required, exercise caution to avoid valve damage caused by piston contact.

Removal

1. Remove primary timing chain as outlined under "Timing Chain, Replace" then the secondary chain tensioner mounting bolts.
2. Loosen camshaft bearing cap bolts in reverse order of tightening sequence, **Fig. 3.**
3. Remove bearing caps, then the camshafts, secondary chain and tensioner as an assembly. **Mark bearing cap position for installation alignment.**
4. Remove tensioner and chain from camshaft.

Installation

1. Assemble camshaft chain on cams with plated links facing front and aligned with camshaft sprocket dots, **Fig. 8.**
2. **On models equipped with early build tensioners that separate into subcomponents,** proceed as follows:
   a. Separate cylinder from tensioner housing.
   b. Carefully drain housing oil without removing internal components.
   c. Assemble plunger to housing.
   d. Compress tensioner with hand pressure and lock with fabricated lock pin.
3. **On models equipped with late build tensioners that do not separate into subcomponents,** place tensioner into

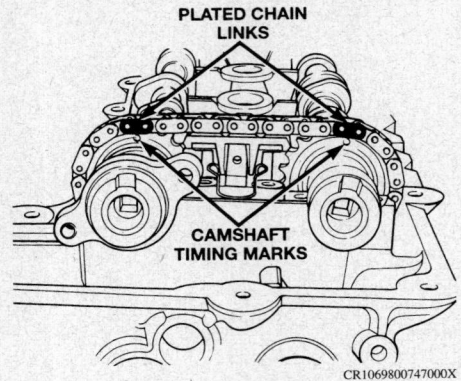

Fig. 8   Camshaft chain timing

suitable soft jaw vise, slowly compress tensioner and install fabricated lock pin.
4. **On all models,** remove tensioner from vise and install between camshafts and chain.
5. Rotate cams so plated links and sprocket dots are at 12 o'clock position, then install to cylinder head. Ensure rocker arms are correctly seated and in proper positions.
6. Install bearing caps into their original positions.
7. **Torque** bearing cap retaining bolts gradually in sequence to 108 inch lbs., **Fig. 3.**
8. Install secondary chain tensioner mounting bolts.
9. Measure camshaft endplay.
10. Install primary timing chain as outlined under "Timing Chain, Replace."

PISTON & ROD ASSEMBLY
Removal

1. Remove cylinder bores top ridge with suitable ridge reamer before removing pistons.
2. Rotate crankshaft so connecting rod is centered in cylinder bore.
3. Mark connecting rod and bearing caps with permanent ink marker or suitable scribe tool for assembly. Do not use stamp or punch to mark connecting rods.
4. Remove connecting rod cap.
5. Remove piston and rod assembly from top of cylinder block. using connecting rod guide tools No. 8189, or equivalent.
6. Install bearing cap on mating rod.

Installation

1. Install oil ring expander.
2. Place one end of upper side rail between piston ring groove and expander, then hold end firmly and press down portion to be installed until side rail is in position. **Do not use piston ring expander.**
3. Place one end of lower side rail between piston ring groove and expander, then hold end firmly and press down

portion to be installed until side rail is in position. **Do not use piston ring expander.**
4. Install No. 2 intermediate piston ring. Ensure manufacturers I.D. dot mark faces up, towards top of piston, **Fig. 9.**
5. Install piston ring No. 1.
6. Position piston ring end gaps, **Fig. 10.**
7. Ensure compression ring gaps are staggered so neither is in line with oil ring rail gap.
8. Ensure oil ring expander ends are butted and rail gaps properly located before installing ring compressor.
9. Immerse piston head and rings in clean engine oil, slide ring compressor over piston and tighten. Ensure ring position does not change.
10. Position bearing onto connecting rod. Ensure bearing half hole aligns with connecting rod hole.
11. Lubricate bearing surface with engine oil.
12. Install connecting rod guide tools No. 8189, or equivalent.
13. Pistons are marked on top with arrow and F above pin boss. These marks must point toward front of engine in both cylinder banks.
14. Connecting rod oil squirt hole faces major thrust (righthand) side of block.
15. Rotate crankshaft so connecting rod journal is centered in cylinder bore, then insert rod and piston into bore and guide rod over crankshaft journal.
16. Tap piston down cylinder bore and guide connecting rod onto connecting rod journal using suitable hammer handle.
17. Lubricate rod bolts and bearing surfaces with engine oil.
18. Install connecting rod cap and bearing.

CRANKSHAFT
REPLACE

Removal

1. Remove engine as outlined under "Engine, Replace."
2. Drain engine oil into suitable container and remove oil filter.
3. Remove mounting bolts, then the structural collar from oil pan and transmission housing.
4. Remove mounting bolts, oil pan and gasket. Ensure timing cover to oil pan bolts are removed, before removing pan.
5. Remove accessory drive idler pulley bracket.
6. Remove air inlet resonator and inlet tube.
7. Remove throttle and speed control cables from throttle arm and bracket, then bracket.
8. Disconnect Manifold Absolute Pressure (MAP), Intake Air Temperature (IAT), Throttle Position (TPS) sensors, Manifold Tune Valve (MTV) and Idle Air Control (IAC) motor electrical connectors.
9. Disconnect vapor purge, brake booster, speed control servo and Positive Crankcase Ventilation (PCV) hoses.

10. Remove Exhaust Gas Recirculation (EGR) tube.
11. Loosen throttle body support bracket upper attaching bolt, then lefthand and righthand support bracket attaching bolts.
12. Release retaining clip and engine cover.
13. Remove upper manifold mounting bolts and upper manifold.
14. Remove valve covers as outlined under "Valve Cover, Replace."
15. Remove upper radiator support crossmember, then the fan module and accessory drive belts.
16. Remove upper radiator crossmember and fan module.
17. Remove accessory and air conditioning belts.
18. Remove damper using crankshaft damper holder tool No. 8191, or equivalent, and three-jaw puller tool No. 1023, or equivalent.
19. Remove power steering pump from mounting bracket, then accessory drive belt tensioner pulley and bracket.
20. Remove mounting bolts and timing chain cover.
21. Remove timing chain as outlined under "Timing Chain, Replace."
22. Remove sprocket using crankshaft damper bolt and suitable puller.
23. Remove oil pump as outlined under "Oil Pump, Replace."
24. Remove transmission and drive plate.
25. Insert suitable 3/16 inch wide flat bladed screwdriver between lip and seal metal case.
26. Angle screwdriver through dust lip against metal case and pry out seal. **Do not allow screwdriver blade to contact seal surface.**
27. Remove structural windage tray.
28. Mark connecting rod cap position for assembly using permanent ink marker or suitable scribe tool. Do not use punch or stamp to mark connecting rods.
29. Remove connecting rod bearing caps.
30. Remove main bearing cap and tie bolts, then main bearing caps.
31. Remove crankshaft.

Installation

Upper and lower bearing halves are not interchangeable.
1. Lubricate upper main bearing halves with engine oil.
2. Push crankshaft forward.
3. Roll lubricate front thrust washer onto machined shelf between No. 3 upper main bulk head and crankshaft thrust surface. Ensure crankshaft thrust washer coated and oil groove side faces crankshaft thrust surface.
4. Move crankshaft rearward.
5. Roll lubricate rear thrust washer onto machined shelf between No. 3 upper main bulk head and crankshaft thrust surface. Ensure crankshaft thrust washer coated and oil groove side faces crankshaft thrust surface.
6. Lubricate lower main bearings with engine oil, then install main bearings and caps.

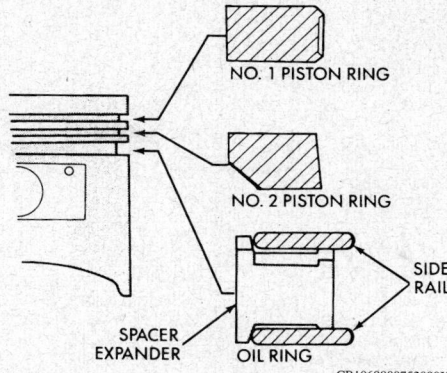

Fig. 9 Piston ring installation

7. **Torque** inside main bearing cap bolts to 15 ft. lbs., then tighten an addition 1/4 turn.
8. Measure crankshaft endplay.
9. Install connecting rods and measure side clearance.
10. Install windage tray.
11. Lubricate windage tray mounting bolts with engine oil, **torque** to 20 ft. lbs., then tighten an addition 1/4 turn.
12. Install main cap tie bolts.
13. Install rear crankshaft oil seal retainer and oil seal.
14. Install oil pump, crankshaft sprocket, timing chain, front cover and valve covers.
15. Install accessory drive idler pulley bracket, then oil pickup tube and O-ring.
16. Install oil pan and filter, then oil dipstick tube.
17. Install engine and fill crankcase with suitable oil.

CRANKSHAFT SPROCKET
REPLACE

With the timing chain removed, avoid turning the camshaft or crankshaft. If movement is required, exercise caution to avoid valve damage caused by piston contact.

Removal

1. Remove timing chain as outlined under "Timing Chain, Replace."
2. Remove sprocket using crankshaft damper bolt and suitable puller.

Installation

1. Install sprocket until it bottoms against crankshaft step flange using crankshaft seal and sprocket installer tool No. 6780-1 and Crankshaft Damper Installer Screw tool No. 8179, or equivalent.
2. Measure from sprocket outer face to end of crankshaft. Ensure measurement is 1.5174–1.5574 inches.
3. Install primary timing chain.

MAIN & ROD BEARINGS

Refer to "Crankshaft, Replace" for main and rod bearings service.

CRANKSHAFT SEAL
REPLACE

1. Remove upper radiator crossmember and fan module.
2. Remove accessory and air conditioning belts.
3. Remove damper using crankshaft damper holder tool No. 8191, or equivalent, and three-jaw puller tool No. 1023, or equivalent.
4. Insert crankshaft damper remover insert tool No. 8194, or equivalent, into crankshaft nose.
5. Remove seal using crankshaft seal remover tool No. 6771, or equivalent.
6. Reverse procedure to install. Using crankshaft seal protector tool No. 6780-2, crankshaft seal and sprocket installer tool 6780-1 and crankshaft damper installer screw tool No. 8179, or equivalents.

CRANKSHAFT REAR OIL SEAL
REPLACE

Removal

1. Remove transmission and drive plate.
2. Insert suitable 3/16 inch wide flat bladed screwdriver between lip and seal metal case.
3. Angle screwdriver through dust lip against metal case and pry out seal. **Do not allow screwdriver blade to contact seal surface.**

Installation

1. Place magnetic base of crankshaft rear seal pilot guide tool No. 6926-1, or equivalent, on crankshaft.
2. Place seal over pilot tool, ensure seal lip faces towards crankshaft.
3. Drive seal into retainer housing until seal is flush with surface using crankshaft rear seal installer tool No. 6926-2 and handle tool No. C-4171, or equivalents.
4. Install drive plate and transmission.

OIL PAN
REPLACE

Removal

1. Remove dipstick and tube, then raise and support vehicle.
2. Drain engine oil into suitable container, then remove oil filter.
3. Disconnect suspension stabilizer bar and position aside.
4. Remove mounting bolts, then the structural collar from oil pan and transmission housing.

5. Remove mounting bolts, oil pan and gasket. Ensure timing cover to oil pan bolts are removed, before removing pan.

Installation

1. Apply ⅛ inch bead of suitable silicone rubber adhesive sealant to front T-joints, **Fig. 11.**
2. Install gasket to block.
3. Install oil pan, then finger tighten bolts and nuts until gasket's rubber seal is compressed.
4. Install timing chain cover and **torque** mounting bolts (4) to 105 inch lbs.
5. **Torque** front mounting bolts to 21 ft. lbs.
6. **Torque** mounting nuts to 105 inch lbs.
7. **Torque** vertical collar oil pan bolts to 10 inch lbs.
8. **Torque** collar to transmission bolts to 40 ft. lbs.
9. Start with center vertical bolt and work outward, **torque** mounting bolts to 40 ft. lbs.
10. Install oil filter and drain plug, then lower vehicle and install dipstick and tube.
11. Connect stabilizer bar.
12. Fill crankcase with suitable oil.

OIL PUMP
REPLACE

1. Remove crankshaft damper as outlined under "Crankshaft, Replace."
2. Remove upper radiator support crossmember, then fan module and accessory drive belts.
3. Remove upper radiator crossmember and fan module.
4. Remove accessory and air conditioning belts.
5. Remove damper using crankshaft damper holder tool No. 8191, or equivalent, and three-jaw puller tool No. 1023, or equivalent.
6. Remove power steering pump from mounting bracket, then accessory drive belt tensioner pulley and bracket.
7. Remove mounting bolts and timing chain cover.
8. Remove timing chain as outlined under "Timing Chain, Replace."
9. Remove crankshaft sprocket as outlined under "Crankshaft, Replace."
10. Remove dipstick and tube, then raise and support vehicle.
11. Drain engine oil into suitable container, then remove oil filter.
12. Disconnect suspension stabilizer bar and position aside.
13. Remove mounting bolts, then the structural collar from oil pan and transmission housing.
14. Remove mounting bolts, oil pan and gasket. Ensure timing cover to oil pan bolts are removed, before removing pan.

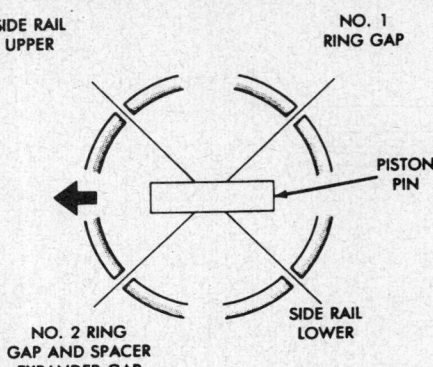

Fig. 10 Piston ring end gap positions

CR1069800753000X

15. Remove oil pickup tube and O-ring.
16. With cylinder No. 1 at 60° ATDC, ensure crankshaft sprocket timing marks and oil pump marks are aligned.
17. Remove mounting bolts, then oil pump.
18. Reverse procedure to install, noting the following:
    a. Prime pump with suitable, clean engine oil before installation.
    b. Ensure crankshaft sprocket and oil pump marks align, with crankshaft positioned at cylinder No. 1 at 60° ATDC.

OIL PUMP SERVICE

1. Remove retaining cap, spring and pressure relief valve.
2. Remove mounting screws and lift cover plate off.
3. Remove pump rotors.
4. Wash components in suitable solvent, then inspect for damage or wear.
5. Lay straightedge across pump cover surface. If .001 inch feeler gauge can be inserted between cover and straight edge, replace cover.
6. Measure thickness and diameter of rotors.
7. If outer rotor thickness is less than .373 inch or rotor diameter is less than 3.5108 inches, replace rotor.
8. If inner rotor thickness is less than .373 inch, replace rotor.
9. Slide outer rotor into body, press to one side with fingers and measure clearance between rotor and body. If clearance is more than .015 inch, replace body.
10. Install inner rotor and measure clearance between rotors. If clearance is more than .003 inch, replace pump assembly.
11. Inspect oil pressure relief valve plunger for scoring and free operation in bore. Small marks may be removed with 400-grit wet or dry sandpaper.
12. Relief valve spring free length should be approximately 1.95 inches. Com-

press spring with 23–25 lbs. If length is not 1.34 inches, replace spring.
13. Reverse procedure to assemble.

BELT TENSION DATA

Belt	Belt Tension, Lbs.	
	New	**Used**
Accessory①	180–200	120
Air Conditioning②	150–170	120

① — Poly-V Belt.
② — V-Belt.

SERPENTINE DRIVE BELT

1. Loosen tensioner pulley locking nut.
2. Loosen belt adjusting bolt.
3. Remove accessory drive belt.
4. Reverse procedure to install.

SEPARATED ACCESSORY DRIVE SYSTEM

Air Conditioning

REMOVAL

1. Remove alternator/power steering serpentine drive belt.
2. Loosen tensioner locking and pivot bolts. Do not remove.
3. Insert suitable ½ inch drive breaker bar into belt tensioner square opening, rotate tensioner counterclockwise until belt can be removed from pulleys.
4. Slowly rotate tensioner clockwise to relieve spring load.

INSTALLATION

1. Insert suitable ½ inch drive breaker bar into tensioner square opening, then hold counterclockwise pressure on tensioner while removing locking bolt.
2. Carefully release tensioner torsion spring load.
3. Remove pivot bolt, tensioner and spring from front timing cover.
4. Insert spring arm into appropriate New or Used tensioner belt position.
5. Install torsion spring, tensioner and pivot bolt.
6. Apply counterclockwise pressure on tensioner until locking bolt can be installed using ½ inch drive breaker bar.
7. Rotate tensioner counterclockwise until belt can be installed on pulleys.
8. Release tensioner and remove socket wrench.
9. Install accessory drive belt.

COOLING SYSTEM BLEED

1. Close radiator drain hand tight.
2. Attach approximately 48 inches of ¼ inch I.D. clear hose to bleed valve.
3. Route hose away from accessory drive belt, drive pulleys and electrical cooling fan and into a clean container.
4. Open cooling system bleed valve, then attach filling aid funnel tool No. 8195, or equivalent, to pressure bottle filler neck.
5. Pinch overflow hose between coolant bottle chambers.
6. Pour 50/50 mix of suitable coolant and distilled water into large section of filling funnel.
7. Slowly fill until steady stream of coolant flows from bleed valve hose.
8. Close bleed valve and continue filling system to top of funnel.
9. Remove overflow hose clip and allow funnel to drain into overflow chamber.
10. Remove funnel and install coolant pressure bottle cap.
11. Remove bleed valve hose, then start and run engine until operating temperature is reached.
12. Shut off engine and allow to cool.
13. With engine cold, ensure pressure chamber level is between MIN and MAX marks.

THERMOSTAT
REPLACE

1. Drain cooling system into suitable container.
2. Remove oil dipstick tube, cover tube opening to prevent coolant from entering engine.
3. Raise and support vehicle.
4. Remove lefthand isolator mounting nuts from top of mounting bracket.
5. Support engine with suitable jack, place suitable wood block between oil pan and jack.
6. Remove lower mounting nuts from frame.
7. Raise engine carefully, then remove lefthand isolator with heat shield.
8. Remove alternator support strut, then disconnect electrical connector.
9. Remove transmission dipstick tube bracket mounting bolt.
10. Remove lower heater and radiator hoses from thermostat housing.
11. Remove thermostat housing mounting bolts, then thermostat and housing.
12. Reverse procedure to install. Ensure thermostat is installed with bleed valve at 12 o'clock position.

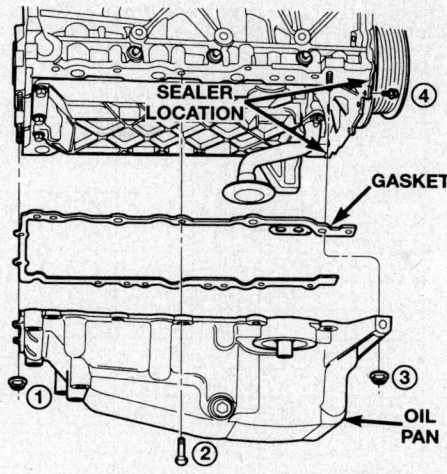

Fig. 11 Oil pan replacement

CR1069800750000X

WATER PUMP
REPLACE

1. Drain cooling system into suitable container.
2. Remove upper radiator crossmember.
3. Remove radiator fan assembly.
4. Remove accessory and air conditioning drive belts.
5. Remove timing chain and all chain guides as outlined under "Timing Chain, Replace."
6. Remove water pump mounting bolts, then water pump and gasket.
7. Reverse procedure to install.

RADIATOR
REPLACE

1. Drain cooling system into suitable container.
2. Remove upper radiator crossmember, then clamps and hoses from radiator.
3. Disconnect transmission hoses from cooler. Plug hose to prevent contamination.
4. Disconnect engine oil cooler lines.
5. Disconnect radiator fan electrical connector, then remove mounting bolts and fan module.
6. Remove air conditioning condenser mounting bolts and transmission cooler line bracket.
7. Lift condenser up enough to clear upper mounting clips, then rest condenser on lower radiator crossmember.
8. Remove radiator.
9. Reverse procedure to install.

FUEL PUMP
REPLACE

1. Remove fuel pump relay for power distribution center.
2. Start and run engine until it stalls.
3. Attempt to start engine until it no longer runs.
4. Turn ignition switch to Off position.
5. Place rag or towel under fuel line quick-connector fitting at fuel rail.
6. Install fuel pump relay.
7. Remove rear seat, then disconnect fuel pump electrical connector.
8. Raise and support vehicle, then drain fuel tank into suitable container.
9. Loosen brackets from body and swing rear stabilizer bar toward rear.
10. Remove fuel filler tube from tank, then disconnect fuel and EVAP lines.
11. Position suitable transmission jack under fuel tank, then remove fuel tank strap bolts, passenger side first.
12. Lower fuel tank, then remove purge and vent lines.
13. Depress quick connector retainers, then fuel line from pump.
14. Slide fuel pump module electrical connector lock to unlock, then push connector retainer down and pull off module.
15. Remove fuel pump module locknut using fuel pump removal/installation tool No. 6856, or equivalent.
16. Remove fuel pump and O-ring seal.
17. Reverse procedure to install.

FUEL FILTER
REPLACE

A combination fuel filter/pressure regulator is located on top of fuel pump module. A separate frame mount filter is not used.
1. Remove fuel pump relay for power distribution center.
2. Start and run engine until it stalls.
3. Attempt to start engine until it no longer runs.
4. Turn ignition switch to Off position.
5. Place rag or towel under fuel line quick-connector fitting at fuel rail.
6. Install fuel pump relay.
7. Lower fuel tank as outlined under "Fuel Pump, Replace."
8. Remove fuel tank purge and vent lines.
9. Disconnect pressure regulator fuel line, then push locking tab in from locking slot and turn pressure regulator to unlock.
10. Pull regulator straight up and remove.
11. Reverse procedure to install.

TIGHTENING SPECIFICATIONS

Year	Component	Torque Ft. Lbs.
2004	Fuel Pump Module	40
	Fuel Rail	16
	Fuel Tank Straps	44
	Intake Manifold	105①②
	Oil Pan	④
	Oil Pan Drain Plug	25
	Oil Pan Filter	15
	Oil Pump	21
	Oil Pump Cover	105①
	Oil Pump Pickup Tube	21
	Oil Pump Pressure Relief Valve Cap	105①
	PCV Valve	60①
	Rear Crankshaft Seal Retainer	108①
	Spark Plug	15
	Starter	30
	Structural Collar	③
	Thermostat Housing	105①
	Throttle Body	105①
	Throttle Body Support Bracket, Lower	50①
	Throttle Body Support Bracket, Upper	105①
	Timing Chain Cover, M6	105①
	Timing Chain Cover, M10	40
	Timing Chain Guide	21
	Timing Chain Guide Access Plug	15
	Timing Chain Tensioner	40
	Water Outlet Housing	105①
	Water Outlet Housing Bleed	105①
	Water Pump	105①

① — Inch lbs.

② — Refer to "Intake Manifold, Replace" for tightening specifications and sequence.

③ — Refer to "Structural Collar, Replace" for tightening specifications and sequence.

④ — Refer to "Oil Pan, Replace" for tightening specifications and sequence.

NOTE: On Air Bag Equipped Models, Refer To "Air Bag System Precautions" Located In The Front Of This Manual For System Disarming & Arming Procedures.

NOTE: Refer To "Computer Relearn Procedures" Located In The Front Of This Manual When Battery Power To The Computer Has Been Interrupted.

NOTE: Prior To Performing Any Service Operations Listed In This Section, Consult The "Technical Service Bulletins" Section For Related Information.

INDEX

	Page No.		Page No.		Page No.
Belt Tension Data	3-22	Exhaust Manifold, Replace	3-18	Radiator, Replace	3-23
Camshaft, Replace	3-20	Lefthand	3-18	Rocker Arms, Replace	3-19
Camshaft Oil Seal, Replace	3-20	Righthand	3-18	Installation	3-19
Camshaft Timing, Adjust	3-21	Front Cover, Replace	3-20	Removal	3-19
Compression Pressure	3-17	Fuel Filter, Replace	3-23	Separated Accessory Drive	
Cooling System Bleed	3-22	Fuel Pump, Replace	3-23	System	3-22
Crankshaft Damper, Replace	3-20	Intake Manifold, Replace	3-18	Air Conditioning	3-22
Crankshaft Rear Oil Seal,		Lower	3-18	Serpentine Drive Belt	3-22
Replace	3-22	Upper	3-18	Spark Plug Tubes, Replace	3-19
Crankshaft, Replace	3-21	Main & Rod Bearings	3-21	Structural Collar, Replace	3-17
Installation	3-21	Installation	3-21	Thermostat, Replace	3-23
Removal	3-21	Removal	3-21	Tightening Specifications	3-24
Crankshaft Seal, Replace	3-22	Oil Pan, Replace	3-22	Timing Belt, Replace	3-20
Installation	3-22	Oil Pump, Replace	3-22	Installation	3-20
Removal	3-22	Oil Pump Service	3-22	Removal	3-20
Cylinder Head, Replace	3-19	Piston & Rod Assembly	3-21	Timing Belt Tensioner Bleed	3-21
Engine Rebuilding		Precautions	3-17	Valve Adjustment	3-19
Specifications	21-1	Air Bag Systems	3-17	Valve Cover, Replace	3-19
Engine, Replace	3-17	Battery Ground Cable	3-17	Valve Springs, Replace	3-19
Engine Mount, Replace	3-17	Fuel System Pressure Relief	3-17	Water Pump, Replace	3-23

PRECAUTIONS

Air Bag Systems

Refer to "Air Bag System Precautions" in the front of this manual for system disarming and arming procedures.

Battery Ground Cable

Prior to service, disconnect battery ground cable and isolate as required.

Fuel System Pressure Relief

1. Remove fuel pump relay for power distribution center.
2. Start and run engine until it stalls.
3. Attempt to start engine until it no longer runs.
4. Turn ignition switch to Off position.
5. Place rag or towel under fuel line quick-connector fitting at fuel rail.
6. Install fuel pump relay.

7. One or more Diagnostic Trouble Codes (DTCs) may have been stored because of removing fuel pump relay. Clear these DTCs with suitably programmed scan tool.

COMPRESSION PRESSURE

The minimum compression pressure should be no less than 100 psi and the maximum variation between cylinders should be no more than 25%.

ENGINE MOUNT
REPLACE

Refer to "2.7L Engine" for engine mount replacement.

STRUCTURAL COLLAR
REPLACE

Refer to "2.7L Engine" for structural collar replacement.

ENGINE
REPLACE

1. Remove fuel pump relay for power distribution center.
2. Start and run engine until it stalls.
3. Attempt to start engine until it no longer runs.
4. Turn ignition switch to Off position.
5. Place rag or towel under fuel line quick-connector fitting at fuel rail.
6. Install fuel pump relay.
7. Mark hood position at hinges and remove, then drain cooling system into suitable container.
8. Remove wiper arms, left and righthand cowl covers, then cowl support.
9. remove wiper arms, left and righthand cowl screens, then strut tower brace.
10. Remove air cleaner assembly and air inlet hose, then upper radiator crossmember.
11. Disconnect hood release cable from latch, then remove radiator fan assembly and accessory drive belts.
12. Drain coolant into suitable container.
13. Disconnect upper radiator hose at engine and lower hose at radiator, then engine oil and transmission cooler lines from radiator.

14. Remove power steering line bracket at lefthand side of radiator, then air conditioning condenser to radiator attaching bolts.
15. Remove radiator, then accessory drive belts.
16. Remove alternator, then the power steering pump mounting bolts. Position pump aside.
17. Remove air conditioning compressor mounting bolts. Position compressor aside.
18. Remove righthand exhaust manifold V-band clamps, then righthand catalytic converter down pipe front and rear support bracket attaching bolts.
19. Remove fuel pump relay for power distribution center.
20. Start and run engine until it stalls.
21. Attempt to start engine until it no longer runs.
22. Turn ignition switch to Off position.
23. Place rag or towel under fuel line quick-connector fitting at fuel rail.
24. Install fuel pump relay.
25. Disconnect fuel line.
26. Disconnect throttle and speed control cables, then coolant bottle hoses.
27. Disconnect vacuum lines and engine ground straps from both cylinder heads.
28. Remove air cleaner housing and inlet hose.
29. Remove throttle and speed control cables from throttle arm and bracket.
30. Disconnect Secondary Runner Valve (SRV), Manifold Tuning Valve (MTV), Throttle Position Sensor (TPS), Idle Air Control (IAC) and Intake Air Temperature/Manifold Absolute Pressure (TMAP) electrical connectors.
31. Disconnect SRV reservoir, speed control reservoir and Positive Crankcase Ventilation (PCV) vacuum hoses.
32. Remove left and righthand side intake manifold supports, then support brackets at intake manifold front corners and MTV.
33. Remove EGR tubes mounting clips.
34. Remove mounting bolts and upper manifold.
35. Disconnect heater hoses, then remove rear throttle body support bracket.
36. Remove water piper fastener at transmission to block bolt, then four upper transmission to cylinder block bolts.
37. Disconnect all remaining electrical connections, then raise and support vehicle.
38. Drain engine oil into suitable container, then remove structural collar mounting bolts.
39. Mark flexplate to torque converter position, then remove converter attaching bolts.
40. Disconnect transmission cooler line brackets from engine.
41. Remove lefthand exhaust manifold V-band clamp, then starter.
42. Remove left and righthand engine mount bolts.
43. Remove crankshaft position sensor and lower transmission to cylinder block bolts.
44. Lower vehicle, then attach suitable lifting device to engine.

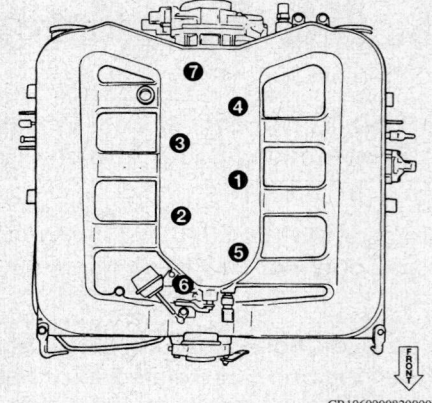

Fig. 1 Upper intake manifold bolt tightening sequence

45. Support transmission with suitable floor jack, place suitable block of wood between transmission and jack.
46. Remove engine from vehicle.
47. Reverse procedure to install.

INTAKE MANIFOLD
REPLACE

Upper

1. Remove air cleaner housing and inlet hose.
2. Remove throttle and speed control cables from throttle arm and bracket.
3. Disconnect Secondary Runner Valve (SRV), Manifold Tuning Valve (MTV), Throttle Position Sensor (TPS), Idle Air Control (IAC) and Intake Air Temperature/Manifold Absolute Pressure (TMAP) electrical connectors.
4. Disconnect SRV reservoir, speed control reservoir and Positive Crankcase Ventilation (PCV) vacuum hoses.
5. Remove left and righthand side intake manifold supports, then support brackets at intake manifold front corners and MTV.
6. Remove EGR tubes mounting clips.
7. Remove mounting bolts and upper manifold.
8. Reverse procedure to install, noting the following:
   a. Hand start all intake manifold mounting bolts.
   b. Tighten bolts in sequence, **Fig. 1**.

Lower

1. Remove fuel pump relay for power distribution center.
2. Start and run engine until it stalls.
3. Attempt to start engine until it no longer runs.
4. Turn ignition switch to Off position.
5. Place rag or towel under fuel line quick-connector fitting at fuel rail.
6. Install fuel pump relay.
7. Drain cooling system into suitable container.
8. Remove air cleaner housing and inlet hose.

9. Remove throttle and speed control cables from throttle arm and bracket.
10. Disconnect Secondary Runner Valve (SRV), Manifold Tuning Valve (MTV), Throttle Position Sensor (TPS), Idle Air Control (IAC) and Intake Air Temperature/Manifold Absolute Pressure (TMAP) electrical connectors.
11. Disconnect SRV reservoir, speed control reservoir and Positive Crankcase Ventilation (PCV) vacuum hoses.
12. Remove left and righthand side intake manifold supports, then support brackets at intake manifold front corners and MTV.
13. Remove EGR tubes mounting clips.
14. Remove mounting bolts and upper manifold.
15. Disconnect fuel injectors and coolant temperature sensor electrical connectors, then heater hose quick connect tee from heater tube.
16. Disconnect fuel rail fuel supply hose from fuel rail, then remove fuel rail support bracket to throttle body support bracket mounting screw.
17. Remove fuel rail and injector assembly mounting bolts, then fuel rail and injectors.
18. Remove lower intake manifold mounting bolts and manifold.
19. Reverse procedure to install. Gradually **torque** mounting bolts in sequence to 21 ft. lbs., **Fig. 2**.

EXHAUST MANIFOLD
REPLACE

Lefthand

1. Raise and support vehicle using suitable lift.
2. Remove exhaust system, then loosen converter pipe support mounting bolt at transmission.
3. Lower vehicle and remove exhaust manifold connector V-band clamp.
4. Disconnect connector and remove exhaust manifold oxygen sensor.
5. Remove mounting screws and heat shield.
6. Remove mounting bolts and exhaust manifold.
7. Reverse procedure to install.

Righthand

1. Raise and support vehicle, then remove exhaust system.
2. Loosen converter pipe support mounting bolt at transmission mount.
3. Loosen air conditioning drive belt, then lower vehicle.
4. Remove air cleaner housing and air inlet tube.
5. Remove manifold V-band clamp.
6. Remove air conditioning compressor mounting bolts, position compressor aside.
7. Remove engine oil dipstick tube, then air conditioning compressor bracket.

8. Remove oxygen sensor and heat shields.
9. Remove exhaust manifold mounting bolts and manifold.
10. Reverse procedure to install.

CYLINDER HEAD
REPLACE

1. Remove upper radiator crossmember, then fan module and accessory drive belts.
2. Remove upper radiator crossmember and fan module.
3. Remove damper using crankshaft damper holder tool No. 8191, or equivalent, and three-jaw puller tool No. 1023, or equivalent.
4. Remove damper using crankshaft damper holder tool No. 8191, or equivalent, and three-jaw puller tool No. 1023, or equivalent.
5. Remove lower belt cover, stamped steel cover and lefthand cast cover.
6. Remove camshaft sprockets as outlined under "Camshaft Sprocket, Replace."
7. Remove upper and lower intake manifolds as outlined under "Intake Manifold, Replace."
8. Remove exhaust manifold to catalytic converter pipe connection V-band clamps.
9. Remove rear timing belt cover to cylinder head attaching bolts, then rear covers.
10. Remove mounting bolts and cylinder heads.
11. Reverse procedure to install, noting the following:
    a. **Cylinder head bolts with stretched threads must be replaced.**
    b. Lubricate bolt threads with suitable, clean engine oil.
    c. **Torque** cylinder head bolts in sequence to 45 ft. lbs., **Fig. 3.**
    d. **Torque** head bolts in sequence to 65 ft. lbs.
    e. **Torque** bolts in sequence to 65 ft. lbs.
    f. Tighten bolts an additional 90° in sequence.
    g. If final cylinder head bolt **torque** is not 90 ft. lbs, replace bolts.
    h. Install new O-ring seal in righthand rear timing belt cover.

VALVE COVER
REPLACE

1. Remove air cleaner housing and inlet hose.
2. Remove throttle and speed control cables from throttle arm and bracket.
3. Disconnect Secondary Runner Valve (SRV), Manifold Tuning Valve (MTV), Throttle Position Sensor (TPS), Idle Air Control (IAC) and Intake Air Temperature/Manifold Absolute Pressure (TMAP) electrical connectors.
4. Disconnect SRV reservoir, speed control reservoir and Positive Crankcase Ventilation (PCV) vacuum hoses.
5. Remove left and righthand side intake

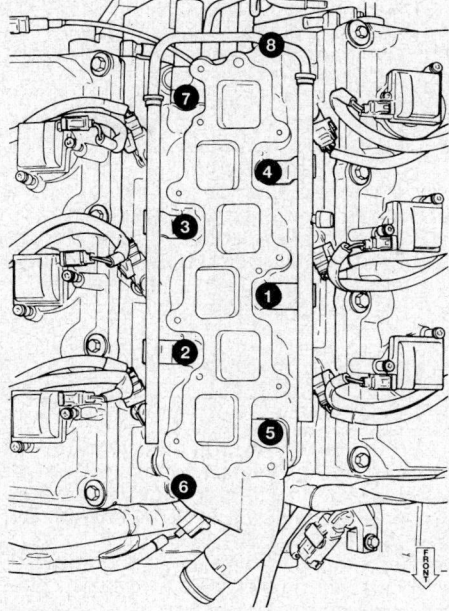

CR1059800127000X

Fig. 2 Lower intake manifold bolt tightening sequence

manifold supports, then support brackets at intake manifold front corners and MTV.
6. Remove EGR tubes mounting clips.
7. Remove mounting bolts and upper manifold.
8. Cover lower intake manifold.
9. Disconnect electrical connectors and remove ignition coils.
10. Remove mounting bolts and cylinder head cover.
11. Reverse procedure to install, noting the following:
    a. Remove spark plug tube seals.
    b. Position new seal with part number facing cylinder head cover and install with Installer tool No. MB-998306, or equivalent.

SPARK PLUG TUBES
REPLACE

1. Remove cylinder head cover as outlined under "Valve Cover, Replace."
2. Remove tube from cylinder head using suitable locking pliers.
3. Apply suitable lubricant to new tube approximately .039 inch from tube end, in a .118 inch wide area.
4. Install seater end of tube into cylinder head, then carefully install tube using suitable hardwood block and mallet until seated into bore bottom.
5. Install cylinder head cover.

VALVE ADJUSTMENT

Rocker arms are equipped with hydraulic lash adjusters. No adjustment is required.

ROCKER ARMS
REPLACE
Removal

1. Remove cylinder head covers as outlined under "Valve Cover, Replace."
2. Identify rocker arm assembly and rocker arm for installation alignment.
3. Remove mounting bolts and rocker arm assembly. **To prevent air ingestion into lash adjusters, avoid turning rocker arm assembly upside down. Do not rest rocker arm assembly on lash adjusters.**
4. Install screw, nut, spacer and washer into pin, then tighten screw into pin, loosen nut and pull out shaft support dowel, **Fig. 4.**
5. Remove rocker arms and pedestals in order.

Installation

1. Install rocker arms and pedestals into shaft. Rocker shaft notches face up. Righthand cylinder bank notches face toward rear and lefthand notches face toward front.
2. Press new dowel pins until they bottom against shaft in pedestal. Pins pass through pedestal into exhaust rocker shafts.
3. Rotate camshafts until lobes are in neutral position, **Fig. 5.**
4. Install rocker arm and shaft assembly. Ensure identification marks face front of engine on lefthand head and toward rear of engine on righthand head.
5. Tighten mounting bolts in sequence, **Fig. 6.**

VALVE SPRINGS
REPLACE

Ensure piston is at TDC on cylinder from which valve spring(s) is being removed.

1. Remove fuel pump relay for power distribution center.
2. Start and run engine until it stalls.
3. Attempt to start engine until it no longer runs.
4. Turn ignition switch to Off position.
5. Place rag or towel under fuel line quick-connector fitting at fuel rail.
6. Install fuel pump relay.
7. Remove air cleaner housing and hose.
8. Remove air cleaner housing and inlet hose.
9. Remove throttle and speed control cables from throttle arm and bracket.
10. Disconnect Secondary Runner Valve (SRV), Manifold Tuning Valve (MTV), Throttle Position Sensor (TPS), Idle Air Control (IAC) and Intake Air Temperature/Manifold Absolute Pressure (TMAP) electrical connectors.
11. Disconnect SRV reservoir, speed control reservoir and Positive Crankcase Ventilation (PCV) vacuum hoses.
12. Remove left and righthand side intake manifold supports, then support brackets at intake manifold front corners and MTV.

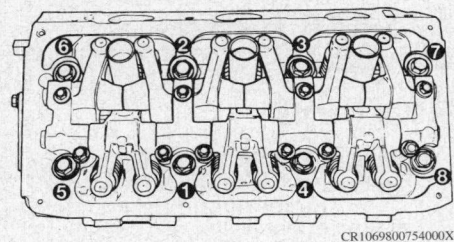

Fig. 3 Cylinder head bolt tightening sequence

13. Remove EGR tubes mounting clips.
14. Remove mounting bolts and upper manifold.
15. Remove valve cover as outlined under "Valve Cover, Replace."
16. Turn crankshaft to rotate engine until cam lobe is on base circle (heel) of rocker arm being removed.
17. Depress valve spring enough to release tension and remove rocker arm using valve spring compressor tool No. 8215 and adapter tool No. 8216, or equivalent.
18. Rotate crankshaft clockwise until No. 1 piston is at TDC.
19. Install suitable spark plug adapter into cylinder being serviced, then apply 90–100 psi air pressure to hold valves in place.
20. Compress valve spring using valve spring compressor tool No. MD-998772-A with adapter tool No. 6527, or equivalent, then remove valve locks, retainer and spring.
21. Remove valve stem seals using suitable valve seal tool.
22. Repeat procedure in firing sequence 1-2-3-4-5-6. **Ensure piston is at TDC on cylinder from which valve spring(s) is being removed.**
23. Reverse procedure to install, noting the following:
    a. Push valve steam seal/seat firmly and squarely over valve guide with stem as guide.
    b. Do not force seal against guide top.
    c. When installer retainer locks, compress spring only enough to install locks.

CRANKSHAFT DAMPER
REPLACE

1. Remove upper radiator crossmember and fan module.
2. Remove accessory drive belts.
3. Hold crankshaft damper with holder tool No. 8191, or equivalent, then remove center bolt.
4. Remove damper using three-jaw puller tool No. 1023 and crankshaft damper remover insert tool No. C-4685-C2, or equivalents.
5. Reverse procedure to install.

FRONT COVER
REPLACE

1. Remove upper radiator support crossmember, then fan module and accessory drive belts.

2. Remove upper radiator crossmember and fan module.
3. Remove accessory and air conditioning belts.
4. Remove damper using crankshaft damper holder tool No. 8191, or equivalent, and three-jaw puller tool No. 1023, or equivalent.
5. Remove lower belt cover, stamped steel cover and lefthand cast cover.
6. **Do not remove cover sealer.** If some sealer is missing, replace with suitable silicone rubber adhesive sealant.
7. Reverse procedure to install.

TIMING BELT
REPLACE

With the timing belt removed, avoid turning the camshaft or crankshaft. If movement is required, exercise caution to avoid valve damage caused by piston contact.

This procedure can only be used when camshaft sprockets have not been loosened or removed. If camshaft sprockets have been loosened or removed, refer to "Camshaft Timing, Adjust" for proper procedure.

Removal

1. Remove upper radiator crossmember and disconnect radiator fan electrical connector.
2. Remove fan module and accessory drive belts, then fan module.
3. Remove damper using crankshaft damper holder tool No. 8191, or equivalent, and three-jaw puller tool No. 1023, or equivalent.
4. Remove lower belt cover, stamped steel cover and lefthand cast cover.
5. If reusing timing belt, mark rotational direction on belt.
6. Turn crankshaft clockwise until crankshaft mark aligns with oil pump housing TDC mark and camshaft sprocket timing marks are between rear cover marks, **Fig. 7.**
7. Mark camshaft sprocket timing mark position to two rear timing cover timing marks.
8. Remove timing belt tensioner and store with plunger facing up.
9. Remove timing belt.

Installation

1. Align crankshaft sprocket timing mark with oil pump housing TDC mark, **Fig. 7.**
2. Align camshaft sprocket marks between reference marks on rear cover.
3. Slowly preload tensioner with suitable vise, then install locking pin. Store pin with plunger facing up until ready to install.
4. Install timing belt in a counterclockwise direction starting at crankshaft sprocket.
5. Ensure camshaft sprocket marks are still between rear cover marks.
6. Hold tensioner pulley against belt, then install tensioner.

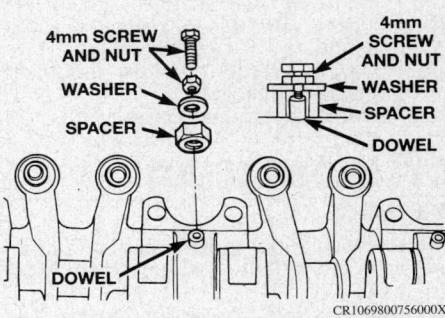

Fig. 4 Rocker arm dowel removal

7. Pull retaining pin and allow tensioner to extend to pulley bracket.
8. Ensure camshaft sprocket marks are still aligned.
9. Rotate crankshaft sprocket two revolutions and ensure timing marks align.
10. Install front cover, crankshaft damper, accessory drive belts and cooling fan module.
11. Install upper radiator crossmember.

CAMSHAFT
REPLACE

With the timing belt removed, avoid turning the camshaft or crankshaft. If movement is required, exercise caution to avoid valve damage caused by piston contact.

1. Remove timing belt as outlined under "Timing Belt, Replace."
2. Hold camshaft sprocket with suitable box wrench, then remove bolt and washer. If engine is in vehicle, it may be required to lift engine side.
3. Remove camshaft sprocket.
4. Camshaft sprockets are not interchangeable. Lefthand sprocket has DIS pickup slots, righthand sprocket does not.
5. Remove cylinder head as outlined under "Cylinder Head, Replace."
6. Remove rear camshaft cover and O-ring.
7. Carefully remove camshaft from rear of cylinder head.
8. Reverse procedure to install. Lubricate camshaft journals and cam with suitable, clean engine oil before installation.

CAMSHAFT OIL SEAL
REPLACE

1. Remove camshaft sprocket(s) as outlined under "Camshaft, Replace."
2. Remove oil seal using camshaft seal remover tool No. C-3981B, or equivalent.
3. Reverse procedure to install, noting the following:
   a. Lightly coat oil seal lip with suitable, clean engine oil.
   b. Install oil seal with seal protector sleeve tool No. 6788 and seal installer tool No. 6052, or equivalent.

CAMSHAFT TIMING
ADJUST

With the timing belt removed, avoid turning the camshaft or crankshaft. If movement is required, exercise caution to avoid valve damage caused by piston contact.

1. Align crankshaft sprocket timing mark with oil pump housing TDC mark, **Fig. 7**.
2. Install dial indicator into cylinder No. 1, then rotate crankshaft until piston is exactly at TDC.
3. Install camshaft alignment tools No. 6642, or equivalent, on rear of each cylinder head.
4. Slowly preload tensioner with suitable vise and install locking pin. Store pin with plunger facing up until ready to install.
5. Install camshaft sprockets, align timing marks between rear cover timing marks.
6. Install new mounting bolts. Lefthand mounting bolt is 10 inches long, righthand 8⅜ inches. Do not tighten at this time.
7. Install timing belt starting at crankshaft sprocket and going in counterclockwise direction. Maintain tension on belt when installing belt around tensioner pulley.
8. Ensure camshaft sprocket timing marks are still fall between rear cover marks.
9. Hold tensioner pulley against belt, install tensioner.
10. Pull retaining pin and allow tensioner to extend to pulley bracket.
11. Ensure No. 1 piston is at TDC, then hold camshaft sprocket hex with suitable wrench and tighten camshaft bolts.
12. Remove dial indicator and install spark plug.

TIMING BELT TENSIONER BLEED

Operate engine at 1600–2000 RPM for 10–15 minutes. This will purge air from tensioner and noise will dissipate.

PISTON & ROD ASSEMBLY

Refer to "2.7L Engine" for piston and rod assembly service.

CRANKSHAFT
REPLACE
Removal

1. Remove engine as outlined under "Engine, Replace."
2. Drain engine oil into suitable container.
3. Remove mounting bolts, then structural collar from oil pan and transmission housing.
4. Remove engine oil cooler line, then transmission oil cooler line clips.

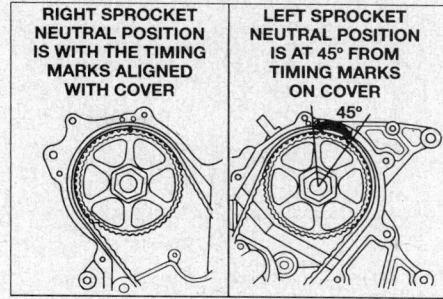

Fig. 5 Camshaft sprockets neutral position

5. Remove mounting bolts, oil pan and gasket.
6. Remove upper radiator crossmember and fan module.
7. Remove accessory and air conditioning belts.
8. Remove damper using crankshaft damper holder tool No. 8191, or equivalent, and three-jaw puller tool No. 1023, or equivalent.
9. Remove accessory drive belt idler pulley.
10. Remove lower belt cover, stamped steel cover and lefthand cast cover.
11. Remove timing belt and tensioner as outlined under "Timing Chain, Replace."
12. Remove damper using crankshaft damper holder tool No. 8191, or equivalent, and three-jaw puller tool No. 1023, or equivalent.
13. Insert crankshaft damper remover insert tool No. 8194, or equivalent, into crankshaft nose.
14. Remove seal using crankshaft seal remover tool No. 6771, or equivalent.
15. Tap crankshaft dowel pin out, then remove oil pump assembly.
16. Remove rear oil seal retainer.
17. Mark connecting rod bearing caps for assembly, then remove.
18. Mark main bearing caps for assembly, then remove.
19. Remove crankshaft.

Installation

Upper and lower bearing halves are not interchangeable.

1. Lubricate upper main bearing halves with engine oil.
2. Push crankshaft forward.
3. Roll lubricate front thrust washer onto machined shelf between No. 2 upper main bulk head and crankshaft thrust surface.
4. Move crankshaft rearward.
5. Roll lubricate rear thrust washer onto machined shelf between No. 2 upper main bulk head and crankshaft thrust surface.
6. Lubricate lower main bearings with engine oil, then install main bearings and caps.
7. **Torque** inside main bearing cap bolts to 15 ft. lbs., then tighten an additional ¼ turn.
8. Measure crankshaft end play.

9. Install connecting rods and measure side clearance.
10. Install windage tray.
11. Lubricate windage tray mounting bolts with engine oil, **torque** to 20 ft. lbs., then tighten an additional ¼ turn.
12. Install main cap tie bolts.
13. Install rear crankshaft oil seal retainer and oil seal.
14. Install oil pump, crankshaft dowel pin, crankshaft sprocket, timing belt, covers and crankshaft damper.
15. Install accessory drive idler pulley, then oil pickup tube and pan.
16. Install engine and fill crankcase with suitable oil.

MAIN & ROD BEARINGS
Removal

1. Remove dipstick and tube, then raise and support vehicle.
2. Drain engine oil into suitable container.
3. Remove mounting bolts, then structural collar from oil pan and transmission housing.
4. Remove engine oil cooler line, then transmission oil cooler line clips.
5. Remove mounting bolts, oil pan and gasket.
6. Mark bearing caps for assembly.
7. Remove bearing caps one at a time.
8. Insert main bearing tool No. C-3059, or equivalent, into crankshaft oil hole, rotate crankshaft clockwise and force bearing shell upper half out.

Installation

When installing new upper bearing shells, slightly chamfer sharp edges from plain side.

1. Lubricate main bearing with suitable, clean engine oil.
2. Start bearing in place and insert main bearing tool No. C-3059, or equivalent, into crankshaft oil hole.
3. Slowly rotate crankshaft counterclockwise, sliding bearing into place, then remove tool.
4. Lubricate and install lower bearing half.
5. Lubricate main bearing cap bolts and finger tighten.
6. Move crankshaft to forward travel limit.
7. Roll lubricate front thrust washer onto machined shelf between No. 2 upper main bulk head and crankshaft thrust surface.
8. Move crankshaft rearward.
9. Roll lubricate rear thrust washer onto machined shelf between No. 2 upper main bulk head and crankshaft thrust surface.
10. Install main bearing cap and tighten inner bolts finger tight.
11. **Torque** inside main bearing cap bolts to 15 ft. lbs., then tighten an additional ¼ turn.
12. Measure crankshaft end play.
13. Install windage tray.

14. Lubricate windage tray mounting bolts with engine oil, **torque** bolts to 20 ft. lbs., then tighten an additional ¼ turn.
15. Install main cap tie bolts.
16. Install oil pump, pickup tube and oil pan.
17. Install engine and fill crankcase with suitable oil.

CRANKSHAFT SEAL
REPLACE
Removal

1. Remove timing belt as outlined under "Timing Belt, Replace."
2. Remove crankshaft sprocket using crankshaft sprocket puller tool No. L-4407-A, or equivalent.
3. Tape dowel pin out of crankshaft.
4. Remove seal using crankshaft seal remover tool No. 6341A, or equivalent.

Installation

1. Install crankshaft seal using crankshaft seal installer tool No. 6342, or equivalent.
2. Install crankshaft dowel pin to .047 inch protrusion.
3. Install crankshaft sprocket using crankshaft sprocket installer tool No. 6641, or equivalent.
4. Install timing belt.

CRANKSHAFT REAR OIL SEAL
REPLACE

Refer to "2.7L Engine" for crankshaft rear oil seal replacement.

OIL PAN
REPLACE

1. Remove dipstick and tube, then raise and support vehicle.
2. Drain engine oil into suitable container.
3. Remove mounting bolts, then structural collar from oil pan and transmission housing.
4. Remove engine oil cooler line, then transmission oil cooler line clips.
5. Remove mounting bolts, oil pan and gasket.
6. Reverse procedure to install. Apply ⅛ inch bead of suitable silicone rubber adhesive sealant to parting line of oil pump housing and rear seal retainer.

OIL PUMP
REPLACE

1. Drain cooling system into suitable container, then remove fan module and accessory drive belts.
2. Remove upper radiator crossmember and fan module.
3. Remove accessory and air conditioning belts.
4. Remove damper using crankshaft damper holder tool No. 8191, or equiv-

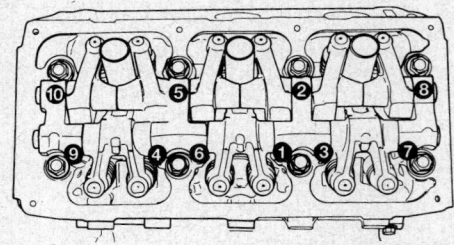

CR1069800758000X

Fig. 6   Rocker arm & shaft assembly bolt tightening sequence

alent, and three-jaw puller tool No. 1023, or equivalent.
5. Remove lower belt cover, stamped steel cover and lefthand cast cover.
6. Insert crankshaft damper remover insert tool No. 8194, or equivalent, into crankshaft nose.
7. Remove seal using crankshaft seal remover tool No. 6771, or equivalent.
8. Remove dipstick and tube, then raise and support vehicle.
9. Drain engine oil into suitable container.
10. Remove mounting bolts, then structural collar from oil pan and transmission housing.
11. Remove engine oil cooler line, then transmission oil cooler line clips.
12. Remove mounting bolts, oil pan and gasket.
13. Remove mounting bolts, then oil pump and gasket.
14. Reverse procedure to install, noting the following:
    a. Prime oil pump before installing.
    b. Install new O-ring with oil pickup tube.

OIL PUMP SERVICE

1. Remove cotter pin and drill ⅛ inch hole into relief valve retainer cap, then insert self-threading sheet metal screw into cap.
2. Clamp screw into suitable vise, support oil pump body and remove cap by tapping on body with suitable soft hammer.
3. Discard cap, then remove spring and pressure relief valve.
4. Remove mounting screws and lift cover plate off.
5. Remove pump rotors.
6. Wash components in suitable solvent, then inspect for damage or wear.
7. Lay straightedge across pump cover surface. If .001 inch feeler gauge can be inserted between cover and straight edge, replace cover.
8. Measure thickness and diameter of rotors.
9. If outer rotor thickness is less than .563 inch, or rotor diameter is less than 3.141 inches, replace rotor.
10. If inner rotor thickness is less than .563 inch, replace rotor.
11. Slide outer rotor into body, press to one side with fingers and measure clearance between rotor and body. If clearance is more than .015 inch, replace body.

12. Install inner rotor and measure clearance between rotors. If clearance is more than .008 inch, replace pump assembly.
13. Place straightedge across body face between bolt holes. If clearance between rotors and straightedge is more than .003 inch replace pump assembly.
14. Inspect oil pressure relief valve plunger for scoring and free operation in bore. Small marks may be removed with 400-grit wet or dry sandpaper.
15. Relief valve spring free length should be approximately 1.95 inches. Compress spring with 23–25 lbs. If length is not 1.34 inches, replace spring.
16. Reverse procedure to assemble.

BELT TENSION DATA

Belt	Tension, Lbs.	
	New	Used
Accessory①	180–200	120
Air Conditioning②	150–170	120

① — Poly-V Belt.
② — V-Belt.

SERPENTINE DRIVE BELT

1. Remove tensioner pulley locking nut.
2. Raise and support vehicle.
3. Remove push clips attaching lower air shield to engine cradle, then air shield from under vehicle.
4. Loosen tensioner adjusting bolt until belt can be removed.
5. Reverse procedure to install.

SEPARATED ACCESSORY DRIVE SYSTEM
Air Conditioning

1. Loosen tensioner pulley locking nut.
2. Loosen belt adjusting bolt.
3. Remove accessory drive belt.
4. Loosen tensioner pulley locknut, then tensioner pulley adjusting bolt until belt can be removed.
5. Reverse procedure to install.

COOLING SYSTEM BLEED

1. Close radiator drain hand tight.
2. Attach approximately 48 inches of ¼ inch I.D. clear hose to bleed valve.
3. Route hose away from accessory drive belt, drive pulleys and electrical cooling fan and into a clean container.
4. Open cooling system bleed valve, then attach filling aid funnel tool No. 8195, or equivalent, to pressure bottle filler neck.
5. Pinch overflow hose between coolant bottle chambers.

6. Pour 50/50 mix of suitable coolant and distilled water into large section of filling funnel.
7. Slowly fill until steady stream of coolant flows from bleed valve hose.
8. Close bleed valve and continue filling system to top of funnel.
9. Remove overflow hose clip and allow funnel to drain into overflow chamber.
10. Remove funnel and install coolant pressure bottle cap.
11. Remove bleed valve hose, then start and run engine until operating temperature is reached.
12. Shut off engine and allow to cool.
13. With engine cold, ensure pressure chamber level is between MIN and MAX marks.

THERMOSTAT
REPLACE

1. Drain cooling system into suitable container, then raise and support vehicle.
2. Disconnect engine oil pressure and power steering pressure switch electrical connectors.
3. Disconnect radiator and heater hoses from thermostat.
4. Remove mounting bolts, housing, thermostat and gasket.
5. Reverse procedure to install.

WATER PUMP
REPLACE

1. Drain cooling system into suitable container.

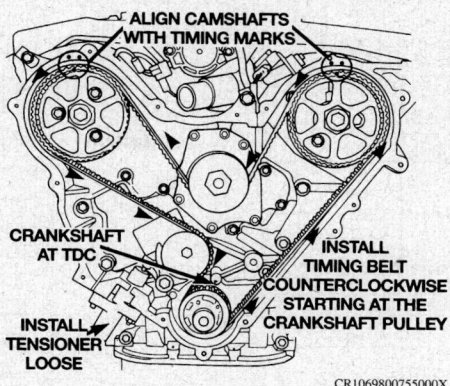

Fig. 7 Camshaft sprocket timing mark alignment

2. Remove accessory drive belts.
3. Remove timing belt components required to access water pump as outlined under "Timing Belt, Replace."
4. Remove mount bolt and water pump.
5. Reverse procedure to install. Apply suitable dielectric grease to O-ring.

RADIATOR
REPLACE

1. Drain cooling system into suitable container.
2. Remove upper radiator crossmember, then clamps and hoses from radiator.
3. Disconnect transmission hoses from cooler. Plug hose to prevent contamination.

4. Disconnect engine oil cooler lines.
5. Disconnect radiator fan electrical connector, then remove mounting bolts and fan module.
6. Remove air conditioning condenser mounting bolts and transmission cooler line bracket.
7. Lift condenser up enough to clear upper mounting clips, then rest condenser on lower radiator crossmember.
8. Remove radiator.
9. Reverse procedure to install.

FUEL PUMP
REPLACE

Refer to "2.7L Engine" for fuel pump replacement.

FUEL FILTER
REPLACE

Refer to "2.7L Engine" for fuel filter replacement.

TIGHTENING SPECIFICATIONS

Year	Component	Torque Ft. Lbs.
2004	Air Conditioning Belt Tensioner	40
	Air Conditioning Compressor To Bracket	21
	Air Conditioning Compressor To Engine Block	40
	Air Conditioning Condenser	45①
	Air Conditioning Condenser Inlet Tube Bracket	45①
	Alternator	40
	Camshaft Sprocket	②
	Camshaft Thrust Plate	21
	Cooling System Bleed	72①
	Connecting Rod Cap	③
	Crankshaft Damper	70
	Crankshaft Main Bearing Cap	③
	Crankshaft Main Bearing Cap, Tie Bolts	21
	Cylinder Head	⑥
	Cylinder Head Cover	105①
	Engine Mount Bracket	45
	Engine Mount Isolator	40
	Exhaust Manifold Heat Shield	105①
	Exhaust Manifold To Cylinder Head	17
	Exhaust Pipe Flange	25
	Fan Blade	45①
	Fan Module	45①
	Fan Motor	25①
	Fuel Pump Module	40
	Fuel Rail	96①
	Fuel Tank Straps	40
	Intake Manifold, Lower	21④
	Intake Manifold, Upper	105④
	Oil Pan	105①
	Oil Pan Drain Plug	20

TIGHTENING SPECIFICATIONS—Continued

Year	Component	Torque Ft. Lbs.
2004	Oil Pan Filter	15
	Oil Pump Cover	105①
	Oil Pump Pick-Up Tube	21
	PCV Valve	60①
	Rear Crankshaft Seal Retainer	105①
	Rocker Arm & Shaft	23
	Spark Plug	20
	Spark Plug Tube	45
	Structural Collar	⑤
	Thermostat Housing	105①
	Throttle Body	105①
	Timing Belt Cover, M6	105①
	Timing Belt Cover, M8	21
	Timing Belt Cover, M10	40
	Timing Belt Tensioner	21
	Timing Belt Tensioner Pulley	45
	Water Outlet Housing	72①
	Water Pump	105①

① — Inch lbs.

② — Righthand side, 75 ft. lbs., then an additional ¼ turn; lefthand side, 85 ft. lbs., then an additional ¼.

③ — Refer to Crankshaft, Replace for tightening specifications and sequence.

④ — Refer to Intake Manifold, Replace for tightening procedure.

⑤ — Refer to Structural Collar, Replace for tightening specifications and sequence.

⑥ — Refer to Cylinder Head, Replace for tightening specifications and sequence.

Rear Axle & Suspension

NOTE: On Air Bag Equipped Models, Refer To "Air Bag System Precautions" Located In The Front Of This Manual For System Disarming & Arming Procedures.

NOTE: Refer To "Computer Relearn Procedures" Located In The Front Of This Manual When Battery Power To The Computer Has Been Interrupted.

NOTE: Prior To Performing Any Service Operations Listed In This Section, Consult The "Technical Service Bulletins" Section For Related Information.

INDEX

	Page No.		Page No.		Page No.
Lateral Link, Replace	3-26	Rear Crossmember, Replace	3-25	Strut, Replace	3-25
Lefthand	3-26	Installation	3-26	Strut Service	3-25
Front	3-26	Removal	3-25	Technical Service Bulletins	3-27
Rear	3-27	Rear Wheel Spindle, Replace	3-25	Rear Strut Squeak	3-27
Righthand	3-27	Stabilizer Bar, Replace	3-26	Tightening Specifications	3-28

REAR WHEEL SPINDLE
REPLACE

1. Raise and support vehicle, then remove rear tire and wheel assemblies.
2. Remove rear caliper assembly and suspend from frame using suitable wire.
3. Remove rear disc brake rotor.
4. Remove rear hub and bearing assembly.
5. Remove speed sensor head from rear disc brake adapter, **Fig. 1.**
6. Remove speed sensor cable routing tube from trailing arm.
7. Remove disc brake adapter, disc shield, park brake shoes and park brake cable as an assembly, **Fig. 2.**
8. Disconnect trailing arm from trailing arm bracket, **Fig. 3.**
9. Disconnect lateral rod from spindle, **Fig. 4.**
10. Loosen and remove rear spindle to strut assembly pinch bolt.
11. Tap suitable center punch into hole on spindle until punch is jammed into hole, **Fig. 5. Do not punch hole in strut with center punch.**
12. Tap on top surface of spindle using suitable hammer, driving it down and off strut assembly, **Fig. 6.**
13. Remove spindle from vehicle.
14. Reverse procedure to install. Push or tap spindle assembly onto strut until notch in spindle is tightly seated against locating tab on strut assembly.

STRUT
REPLACE

1. Remove rear seat cushion and back assembly.
2. Remove upper and lower quarter trim panels.
3. Remove rear parcel shelf trim panel.

4. Remove rear speakers and mounting plates, then disconnect speaker wiring.
5. Raise and support vehicle, then remove rear wheel and tire assembly.
6. Remove rear caliper assembly and suspend from frame using suitable wire.
7. Remove rear disc brake rotor.
8. Remove speed sensor cable routing tube on trailing arm bracket to spindle.
9. Remove bolt attaching lateral link to rear spindle assembly, **Fig. 7.**
10. Remove rear strut assembly to stabilizer bar attaching link at stabilizer bar.
11. Loosen and remove rear spindle to strut assembly pinch bolt.
12. Tap suitable center punch into hole on spindle until punch is jammed into hole, **Fig. 5. Do not punch hole in strut with center punch.**
13. Tap on top surface of spindle using suitable hammer, driving it down and off strut assembly, **Fig. 6.**
14. Let rear spindle and assembled components hang from trailing arm while strut is out of vehicle.
15. Lower vehicle.
16. Remove rear upper strut mount retaining nuts through luggage compartment.
17. Remove strut from vehicle.
18. Reverse procedure to install. Push or tap spindle assembly onto strut until notch in spindle is tightly seated against locating tab on strut assembly.

STRUT SERVICE

1. Position strut assembly in suitable vise.
2. Mark strut assembly lower spring isolator, spring and upper strut mount for assembly reference.
3. Position spring compressor tool No. 7520, or equivalent, on strut assembly

spring and compress coil spring until all load is removed from upper strut mount assembly.
4. Install strut rod ratchet socket tool No. 6864, or equivalent, on strut nut.
5. Insert an 8 mm Allen wrench into end of strut shaft and remove shaft nut from shaft.
6. Remove upper strut mount assembly from strut shaft.
7. Remove coil spring, plate, spring compressor, dust shield, jounce bumper and lower spring isolator.
8. Inspect all components for signs of abnormal wear or failure, replace as required.
9. Reverse procedure to install. Align marks made during disassembly.

REAR CROSSMEMBER
REPLACE

Removal

1. Open fuel filler door and remove filler neck mounting screws and cap.
2. Raise and support vehicle, then remove rear tire and wheel assemblies.
3. Remove lateral links mounting bolts and nuts. Lefthand front lateral link bolt cannot be removed until crossmember is lowered.
4. Remove brake tubes mounting screws from lefthand stabilizer bar isolator bushing retainer.
5. Remove stabilizer bar isolation bushing retaining frame rail mounting bolts and allow bar to hang down.
6. Remove tensioner from intermediate parking brake cable, then from lefthand rear parking brake cable.
7. Remove righthand rear parking brake cable from intermediate parking brake cable.

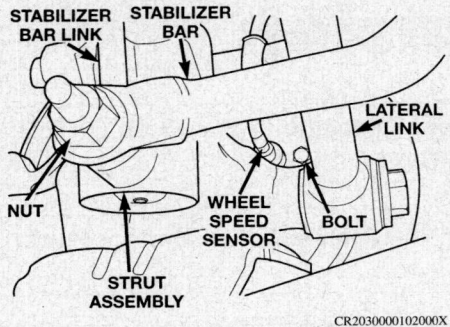

Fig. 1   Speed sensor head

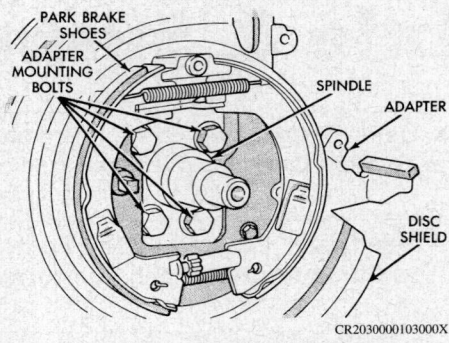

Fig. 2   Disc brake adapter mounting

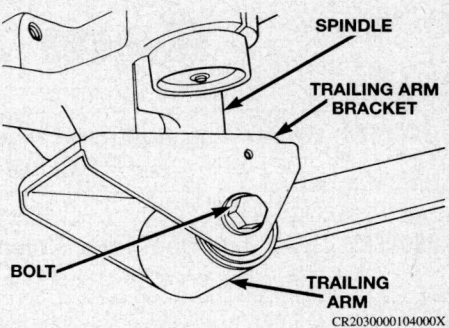

Fig. 3   Trailing arm to bracket bolt

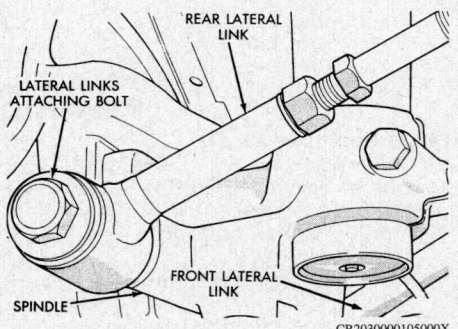

Fig. 4   Lateral links to spindle attaching bolts

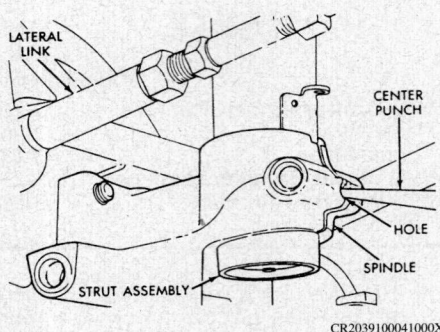

Fig. 5   Center punch installed in spindle

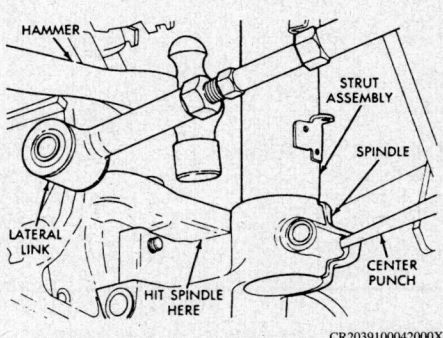

Fig. 6   Spindle removal

8. Remove retainer clips and rear parking brake cables from crossmember.
9. Remove brake proportioning valve mounting nuts.
10. Position suitable transmission jack under muffler.
11. Disconnect exhaust resonator hanger from rear frame rail, then muffler hangers on each side of muffler.
12. Lower jack and muffler enough to access crossmember.
13. Remove fuel filler neck lefthand frame rail mounting screw.
14. Remove crossmember rear corner mounting bolts, then lower crossmember as low as possible to access lateral link mounting bolt at lefthand front corner.
15. Remove mounting bolt and link, then the crossmember.

Installation

1. Install rear suspension crossmember above muffler. Ensure brake tubes are properly routed as crossmember is installed.
2. Install rear proportioning valve mounting brackets and nuts, then intermediate parking brake cable routing clip.
3. Attach lefthand front lateral link to crossmember, then install mounting bolt through front of crossmember. Do not install nut at this time.
4. Raise crossmember against frame rails and install, but do not tighten two rear mounting bolts at this time.
5. Raise exhaust into place, then install hangers.
6. Install mounting screw and attach fuel filler neck to lefthand frame rail.

7. Position rear parking brake cables into crossmember alignment holes, then install retaining clips.
8. Connect righthand rear parking brake cable to intermediate parking brake cable, then install parking brake cable tensioner.
9. Install stabilizer bar isolator bushing retainer mounting bolts.
10. Tighten rear suspension crossmember rear mounting bolts.
11. Install brake tubes mounting screws.
12. Install remaining lateral links and mounting bolts. Forward mounting bolts must point towards rear and rear mounting bolts should point towards front.
13. Install lateral link mounting nuts but do not tighten now. **Tighten mounting bolts when vehicle is at curb riding height.**
14. Install tire and wheel assemblies. Tighten wheel mounting stud nuts to half, then fill specifications.
15. Lower vehicle, then install filler neck mounting screws and fuel filler cap.
16. Tighten lateral arm to crossmember mounting bolts.
17. Inspect and set rear wheel toe.

STABILIZER BAR
REPLACE

1. Raise and support vehicle using suitable lift.
2. Remove stabilizer bar to strut attaching link stud nuts using suitable thin wrench to keep attaching link stud from turning.
3. Remove links from stabilizer bar.

4. Remove stabilizer bar isolator bushing retainers mounting bolts, then stabilizer bar.
5. Mount bar in suitable soft jawed vise, then carefully pry back upper bushing retainer wider end tabs from lower half.
6. Tap bushing retainer upper half forward using suitable hammer and brass drift punch.
7. Remove lower half of bushing retainer, then bushing.
8. Remove bar from vise, then repeat procedure to remove other bushing.
9. Reverse procedure to install. Bushing slit points toward front of vehicle.

LATERAL LINK
REPLACE
Lefthand
FRONT

1. Raise and support vehicle, then remove lefthand rear tire and wheel assembly.
2. Remove lateral link to spindle mounting nut and bolt.
3. Remove link to rear crossmember mounting nut. Bolt cannot be removed now.
4. Remove brake tubes to lefthand stabilizer bar isolator bushing retainer mounting screws.
5. Remove stabilizer bar isolator bushing retainers mounting bolts.
6. Remove fuel filler neck to frame rail mounting screw, then position suitable transmission jack under fuel tank.
7. Remove righthand, then lefthand fuel tank mounting strap mounting bolts, allow straps to hang.

8. Lower fuel tank enough to remove lateral link to crossmember mounting bolt, then lefthand front lateral link.
9. Reverse procedure to install, noting the following:
   a. Do not tighten lateral link mounting bolt until vehicle is at curb riding height.
   b. Inspect and correct rear wheel toe.

REAR

1. Raise and support vehicle, then remove tire and wheel assemblies.
2. Remove lateral link to rear crossmember mounting nuts and bolts.
3. Remove lateral links.
4. Reverse procedure to install, noting the following:
   a. Do not tighten lateral link mounting bolt until vehicle is at curb riding height.
   b. Inspect and correct rear wheel toe.

Righthand

1. Raise and support vehicle, then remove tire and wheel assemblies.
2. Remove lateral link to rear crossmember mounting nuts and bolts.
3. Remove lateral links.
4. Reverse procedure to install, noting the following:
   a. Do not tighten lateral link mounting bolt until vehicle is at curb riding height.
   b. Inspect and correct rear wheel toe.

TECHNICAL SERVICE BULLETINS

Rear Strut Squeak

On some of these models there may be a rear strut squeaking during suspension jounce.

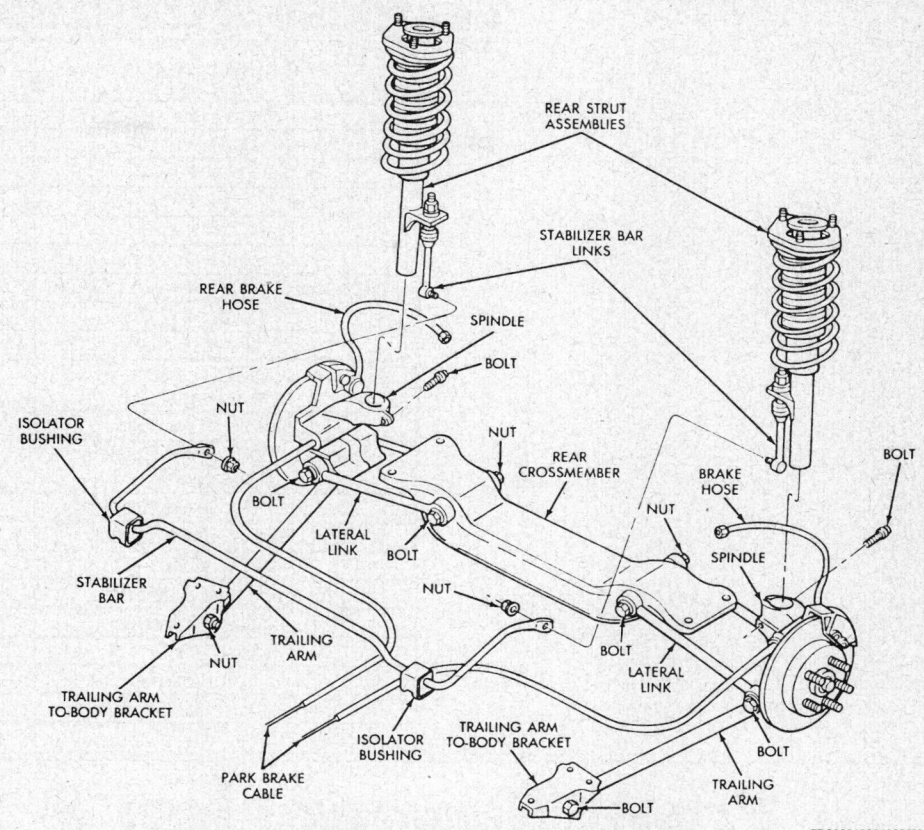

Fig. 7 Exploded view of rear suspension

This condition may be caused by rear strut striker cap.

To correct this condition, replace rear strut striker as follows:
1. Remove and disassemble the rear struts as outlined in "Strut, Replace" and "Strut Service."
2. Remove strut striker cap.
3. Install revised strut striker cap (part No. 05194743AA).
4. Install strut.

TIGHTENING SPECIFICATIONS

Year	Component	Torque Ft. Lbs.
2004	Brake Hose	35
	Brake Hose Bracket	17
	Brake Support Plate	80
	Caliper Adapter To Spindle	85
	Caliper To Adapter	16
	Crossmember To Body	75
	Hub & Bearing Assembly To Spindle	124
	Lateral Link Jam Nut	65
	Lateral Link To Spindle	100
	Lateral Link To Suspension Crossmember	70
	Spindle Mounting Bolts	80
	Stabilizer Bar Isolator Bushing Retainer	30
	Stabilizer Bar To Strut Link	70
	Strut Shaft To Upper Mount	55
	Strut To Body	19
	Strut To Spindle Pinch Bolt	40
	Strut To Stabilizer Bar Link	17
	Trailing Arm	75
	Trailing Arm Bracket	80
	Trailing Arm Bracket To Body	45
	Wheel Lug Nut	100

Front Suspension & Steering

NOTE: On Air Bag Equipped Models, Refer To "Air Bag System Precautions" Located In The Front Of This Manual For System Disarming & Arming Procedures.

NOTE: Refer To "Computer Relearn Procedures" Located In The Front Of This Manual When Battery Power To The Computer Has Been Interrupted.

NOTE: Prior To Performing Any Service Operations Listed In This Section, Consult The "Technical Service Bulletins" Section For Related Information.

INDEX

	Page No.
Ball Joint Inspection	3-29
Control Arm, Replace	3-29
Lower	3-29
Hub & Bearing, Replace	3-29
Power Steering	13-1
Power Steering Gear, Replace	3-30
Power Steering Pump, Replace	3-31
Power Steering System Bleed	3-31
Precautions	3-29
Air Bag Systems	3-29
Battery Ground Cable	3-29
Stabilizer Bar, Replace	3-29
Steering Columns	12-1
Steering Knuckle, Replace	3-29
Strut Dampner, Replace	3-30
Tension Strut, Replace	3-30
Tie Rod End, Replace	3-30
Inner	3-30
Outer	3-30
Tightening Specifications	3-35

PRECAUTIONS

Air Bag Systems

Refer to "Air Bag System Precautions" in the front of this manual for system disarming and arming procedures.

Battery Ground Cable

Prior to service, disconnect battery ground cable and isolate as required.

HUB & BEARING

REPLACE

1. Raise and support vehicle, then remove tire and wheel.
2. Remove front caliper assembly and rotor from steering knuckle as outlined in "Disc Brakes" chapter.
3. Remove hub and bearing retaining nut.
4. Remove hub bolts, then the hub and bearing assembly from steering knuckle by sliding it straight off end of hub axle. **CAUTION: When removing hub and bearing assembly from steering knuckle, be careful not to damage flinger disc on hub and bearing assembly. If flinger disc is damaged, hub and bearing assembly must be replaced, Fig. 1.**
5. If hub and bearing will not slide out of knuckle, insert suitable pry bar between hub and steering knuckle, **Fig. 2.**
6. Reverse procedure to install, noting the following:
   a. Install new hub and bearing retaining nut.
   b. Install tire and wheel assembly tightening mounting nuts in sequence until all nuts are tightened to half specification, **Fig. 3.**
   c. Repeat tightening sequence to full specification.
   d. Lower vehicle, with brakes applied, tighten hub and braining retaining nut.

BALL JOINT INSPECTION

The lower ball joint is serviced with the lower control arm.
1. Raise and support front of vehicle.
2. Grasp tire at top and bottom, then apply in and out force on wheel and tire assembly.
3. While applying force to tire, look for movement between lower ball joint and lower control arm.
4. If there is any movement, replace lower control arm.

CONTROL ARM

REPLACE

LOWER

1. Raise and support vehicle, then remove tire and wheel assembly.

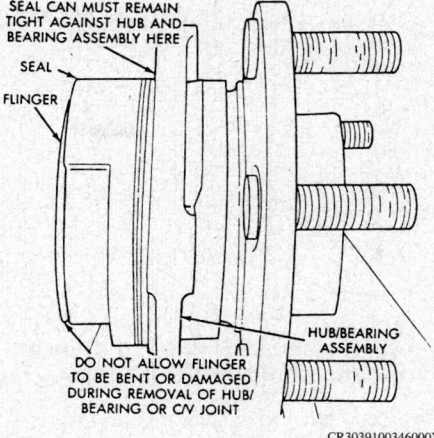

CR3039100346000X

Fig. 1   Hub & bearing assembly

2. Remove ball joint stud to steering knuckle clamp nut and bolt, **Fig. 4.**
3. Insert suitable pry bar between lower control arm and steering knuckle to separate ball joint stud from steering knuckle, **Fig. 5. Do not pull steering knuckle away from vehicle after separating ball joint, this may allow the inner tripod joint to separate.**
4. Remove and discard tension strut to cradle nut and washer from end of tension strut, **Fig. 6. Never reuse tension strut nut.**
5. Loosen and remove lower control arm pivot bushing bolt.
6. Separate lower control arm and tension strut from cradle as an assembly by first removing pivot bushing from cradle and then sliding tension strut out of isolator bushing, **Fig. 7.**
7. Reverse procedure to install. Tighten lower control arm pivot bushing to cradle bracket attaching bolt with full weight of vehicle on suspension.

STEERING KNUCKLE

REPLACE

1. Raise and support vehicle, then remove tire and wheel assembly.
2. Remove brake caliper and rotor as outlined under "Caliper, Replace" in "Disc Brakes" chapter.
3. Remove ABS speed sensor screw.
4. Carefully remove speed sensor head from knuckle. If sensor has seized due to corrosion use a hammer and a punch to tap edge of sensor ear, rocking sensor until free, **Fig. 8. Do not use pliers on sensor head.**
5. Remove hub and bearing retaining nut.
6. Remove hub bolts, then the hub and bearing assembly from steering knuckle by sliding it straight off end of hub axle. **CAUTION: When removing hub and bearing assembly from steering knuckle, be careful not to damage flinger disc on hub and bearing assembly. If flinger disc is damaged, hub and bearing assembly must be replaced, Fig. 1.**
7. If hub and bearing will not slide out of

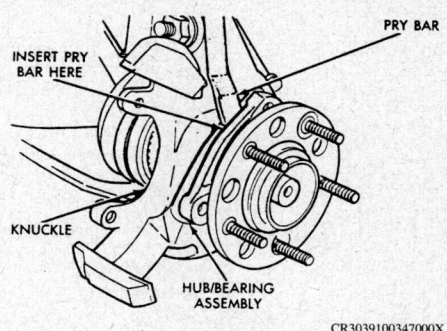

CR3039100347000X

Fig. 2   Hub & bearing removal

knuckle, insert suitable pry bar between hub and steering knuckle, **Fig. 2.**
8. Remove ball joint stud to steering knuckle clamp nut and bolt, **Fig. 4.**
9. Insert suitable pry bar between lower control arm and steering knuckle to separate ball joint stud from steering knuckle, **Fig. 5. Do not pull steering knuckle away from vehicle after separating ball joint, this may allow the inner tripod joint to separate.**
10. Remove strut assembly to steering knuckle attaching bolts. **Strut bolts have a serrated shaft for a tight fit into steering knuckle. Turn nut on bolts only, do not turn bolts.**
11. Remove steering knuckle from vehicle.
12. Reverse procedure to install, noting the following:
    a. **Strut bolts have a serrated shaft so do not turn bolts in steering knuckle. Turn nut on bolts do not turn bolts.**
    b. Coat speed sensor head with high temperature multi-purpose EP grease before installing.
    c. Lower vehicle and with brake applied, tighten new hub and bearing retaining nut.

STABILIZER BAR

REPLACE

1. Remove righthand upper mount to strut tower mounting nut and washer.
2. Raise and support vehicle, then remove righthand front tire and wheel assembly.
3. Remove mounting nut and righthand stabilizer bar attaching link at strut.
4. Remove mounting nut and lefthand stabilizer bar attaching link at strut.
5. Loosen but do not remove righthand outer tie rod end to strut arm mounting nut.
6. Release righthand outer tie rod end from strut steering arm using puller tool No. C-3894A, or equivalent, then remove nut and tie rod.
7. **On models equipped with anti-lock brakes,** remove speed sensor cable routing bracket.
8. **On all models,** remove strut to steering knuckle mounting bolts, then the righthand front strut.
9. Remove structural collar to engine oil pan mounting bolts, then stabilizer

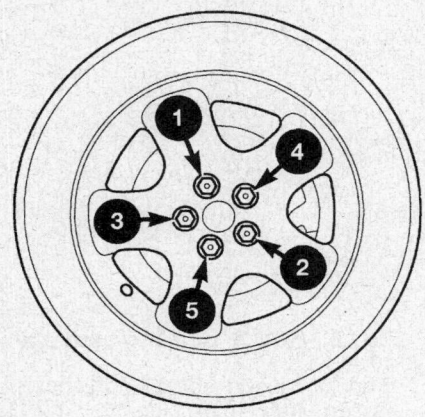

Fig. 3   Tire & wheel nut tightening sequence

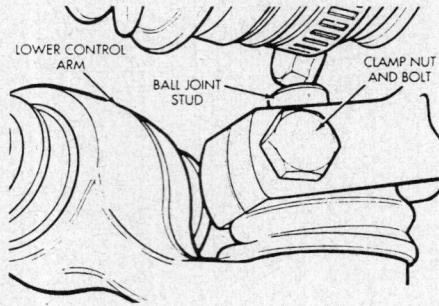

Fig. 4   Ball joint stud to steering knuckle clamp nut & bolt removal

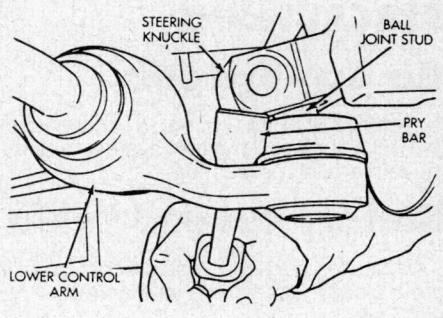

Fig. 5   Ball joint separation

bushing retainers to cradle mounting bolts.

10. Remove stabilizer bar isolator bushing retainers and bushings.
11. Position suitable transmission jack under engine oil pan, place suitable wood block between jack and oil pan.
12. Carefully raise jack until motor mounts clear cradle.
13. Rotate stabilizer bar and remove through righthand wheel opening. **Be careful to not pull knuckle outward.**
14. Reverse procedure to install.

STRUT DAMPNER
REPLACE

1. Raise and support vehicle, then remove tire and wheel assembly.
2. Remove stabilizer bar link at strut assembly, **Fig. 9.**
3. Loosen, but do not remove, outer tie rod end nut, then remove outer tie rod end using suspension component puller tool No. C-3894A, or equivalent.
4. Remove speed sensor cable routing bracket from strut assembly.
5. Remove brake caliper and brake rotor as outlined in "Disc Brakes" chapter. Suspend caliper from frame using suitable wire.
6. Disconnect lower strut from steering knuckle. **Strut bolts have a serrated shaft for a tight fit into steering knuckle. Turn nut on bolts only, do not turn bolts.**
7. Disconnect upper strut from shock tower and remove strut assembly from vehicle.
8. To service damper, proceed as follows:
   a. Position strut assembly in suitable vise.
   b. Mark strut unit, lower spring isolator, spring and upper strut mount for assembly reference.
   c. Install spring compressor tool No. 7520, or equivalent, **Fig. 10,** on coil spring and compress coil spring to release load from upper strut mount assembly.
   d. Install strut rod socket tool No.

6864, or equivalent, on strut shaft nut; then remove strut shaft nut, **Fig. 11.**
   e. Remove upper strut mount, jounce bumper, seat/bearing, dust shield, coil spring and lower spring mount from strut, **Fig. 12.**
   f. Reverse procedure to assemble, align marks made during disassembly.
9. Reverse procedure to install. **Strut bolts have a serrated shaft; do not turn bolts in steering knuckle. Turn nut on bolts instead of turning bolts.**

TENSION STRUT
REPLACE

1. Raise and support vehicle, then remove tire and wheel assembly.
2. Remove ball joint stud to steering knuckle clamp nut and bolt, **Fig. 4.**
3. Insert suitable pry bar between lower control arm and steering knuckle to separate ball joint stud from steering knuckle, **Fig. 5. Do not pull steering knuckle away from vehicle after separating ball joint, this may allow the inner tripod joint to separate.**
4. Remove and discard tension strut to cradle nut and washer from end of tension strut, **Fig. 6. Never reuse tension strut nut.**
5. Loosen and remove lower control arm pivot bushing bolt.
6. Separate lower control arm and tension strut from cradle as an assembly by first removing pivot bushing from cradle and then sliding tension strut out of isolator bushing, **Fig. 7.**
7. Separate tension strut from lower control arm.
8. Install replacement tension strut into lower control arm. Position tension strut with word "Front" positioned away from control arm, **Fig. 13.**
9. Install lower control arm and tension strut into vehicle.
10. Install washer and new nut on tension strut.
11. Install tire and wheel assembly.
12. Tighten lower control arm pivot bushing to cradle bracket attaching bolt with full weight of vehicle on suspension.

TIE ROD END
REPLACE
Outer

1. Raise and support vehicle.
2. Remove tire and wheel assembly.
3. Loosen pinch bolt on tie rod sleeve, then remove tie rod to steering arm mounting nut.
4. Remove tie rod from steering arm using suspension component puller tool No. C-3894A, or equivalent.
5. Remove tie rod from sleeve.
6. Reverse procedure to install, noting the following:

Inner

1. Position wheels straight ahead.
2. Remove caps, mounting nuts and wiper arms, then wiper module and cowl covers.
3. Remove mounting bolts, then reinforcement.
4. Remove inline resonator and inlet hose from throttle body, then air inlet hose from air cleaner housing.
5. Raise and support vehicle until wheels are just off the ground.
6. Remove wheel assembly.
7. Turn steering wheel to full righthand position.
8. Remove tie rod end to steering arm mounting nut, then remove tie rod using suspension component puller tool No. C-3894A, or equivalent.
9. Bend back tie rod to steering gear mounting bolt mounting plate retaining tabs.
10. Remove mounting bolts, mounting plate and washers.
11. Rotate loose end of mounting plate for clearance.
12. Remove tie rod assembly through wheel opening.
13. Loosen pinch bolt at inner to outer tie rod adjusting sleeve.
14. Remove tie rod from inner adjuster sleeve.
15. Reverse procedure to install.

POWER STEERING GEAR
REPLACE

1. Position wheels straight ahead.

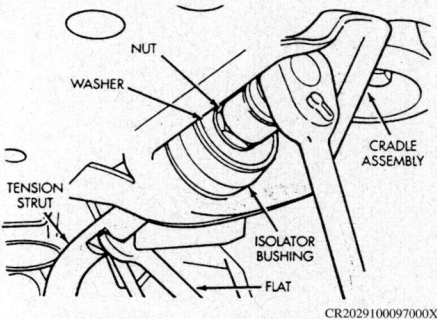

Fig. 6 Tension strut to cradle mounting

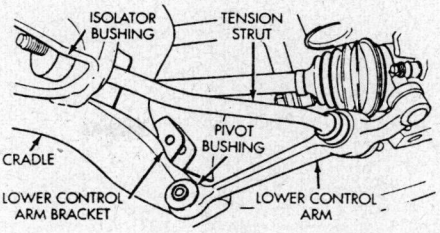

Fig. 7 Lower control arm removal

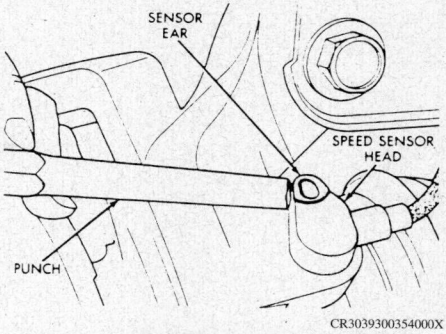

Fig. 8 Speed sensor removal

2. Remove caps, mounting nuts and wiper arms, then wiper module and cowl covers.
3. Remove mounting bolts, then reinforcement.
4. Remove inline resonator and inlet hose from throttle body, then air inlet hose from air cleaner housing.
5. Raise and support vehicle until wheels are just off the ground.
6. Lock steering wheel from rotating, **to avoid damaging clock spring.**
7. Remove steering column coupler retaining pin and bolt, then separate intermediate steering shaft from column coupler.
8. Bend back tie rod to steering gear mounting bolt mounting plate retaining tabs.
9. Remove mounting bolts, mounting plate and washers, then lay tie rods on top of transmission bell housing, **Fig. 14.**
10. Drain as much power steering fluid as possible from reservoir.
11. Remove power steering fluid pressure and return hoses from steering gear.
12. **On models equipped with speed proportional steering gear,** remove solenoid wiring harness connector.
13. **On all models,** remove mounting nuts, then the master cylinder with brake tubes connected from vacuum booster. Carefully position master cylinder upright on lefthand side valve cover.
14. Remove steering gear to crossmember lefthand, then righthand side mounting bolts.
15. Slide steering gear and intermediate shaft into engine compartment to access intermediate shaft flex coupler roll pin, **Fig. 15.**
16. Remove roll pin and separate inter-mediate steering shaft from steering gear, using roll pin remover tool No. 6831-A, or equivalent.
17. Raise and support vehicle, then remove righthand front tire and wheel assembly.
18. Remove tie rod end to steering arm mounting nut, using suspension puller tool No. C-3894-A, or equivalent, then the tie rod.
19. **On models equipped with 2.7L engine,** turn front of lefthand front tire and wheel assembly as far outward as possible.
20. **On all models,** slide steering gear end through righthand side inner fender tie rod hole until approximately half gear is through hole.
21. Lift lefthand end of gear up between engine and cowl, then pull gear out.

POWER STEERING PUMP
REPLACE

1. Drain as much power steering fluid as possible from power steering reservoir.
2. Remove power steering fluid return hose from reservoir, then let fluid drain from reservoir and pump into suitable container.
3. Cap power steering fluid reservoir fitting.
4. Remove pressure hose from power steering pump and let remaining fluid drain from pump into container.
5. **On models equipped with 3.5L engines,** remove power steering pressure switch wiring harness connector.
6. **On all models,** loosen serpentine drive belt tensioner locknut, then remove power steering pump drive belt from power steering pump pulley.
7. Remove pump mounting bolts through pulley face holes.
8. Insert suitable screwdriver between pump and tensioner bracket sleeve, then push sleeve forward in tensioner bracket until it is flush with tensioner bracket back.
9. Remove pump and pulley as an assembly.
10. Reverse procedure to install, noting the following:
    a. Long mounting bolt is install in tensioner bracket sleeve.
    b. Ensure return hose clamp is installed past nipple upset bead.

POWER STEERING SYSTEM BLEED

During bleeding procedure, keep fluid in reservoir at correct level.
1. Raise and support front of vehicle.
2. Manually turn oil pump pulley a few times.
3. Turn steering wheel from stop to stop five or six times.
4. Disconnect high tension cable, then operate starter motor intermittently while turning steering wheel from stop to stop five or six times.
5. Connect high tension cable and start engine.
6. Turn steering wheel from stop to stop until no bubbles appear in reservoir.
7. Ensure fluid is not milky and that at proper level.
8. Confirm there is little or no change in fluid level when steering wheel is turned from stop to stop.
9. Ensure difference in fluid level is no more than .2 inch with engine running and when it is stopped.
10. If fluid level is not as specified, system is not completely bled. Repeat procedure.

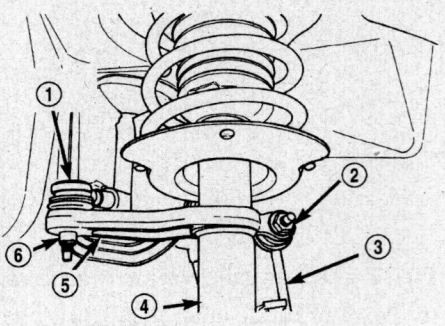

1 - OUTER TIE ROD
2 - NUT
3 - STABILIZER BAR ATTACHING LINK
4 - STRUT ASSEMBLY
5 - STEERING ARM
6 - NUT

CR2020100179000X

Fig. 9   Stabilizer bar link at strut

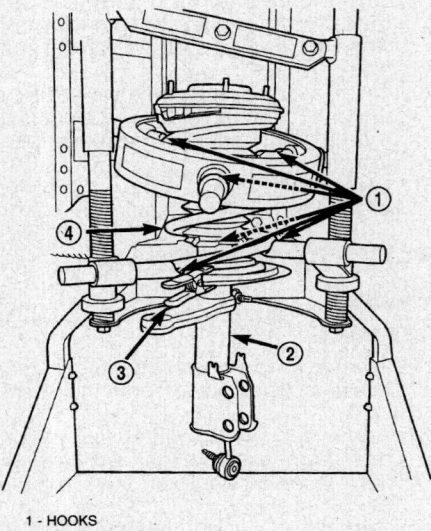

1 - HOOKS
2 - STRUT ASSEMBLY
3 - CLAMP
4 - COIL SPRING

CR2020100181000X

**Fig. 10   Strut assembly in
compressor**

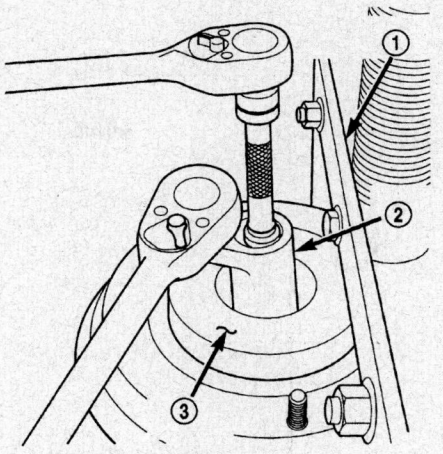

1 - SPRING COMPRESSOR
2 - SPECIAL TOOL 6864
3 - UPPER MOUNT

CR2020100182000X

Fig. 11 Strut shaft removal

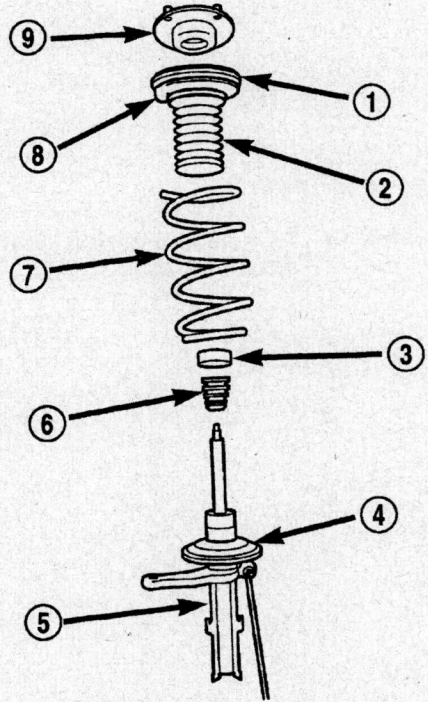

1 - SEAT AND BEARING
2 - DUST SHIELD
3 - CUP
4 - LOWER SPRING ISOLATOR
5 - STRUT
6 - JOUNCE BUMPER
7 - COIL SPRING
8 - UPPER SPRING ISOLATOR
9 - UPPER MOUNT

CR2020100180000X

**Fig. 12 Exploded view of strut
assembly**

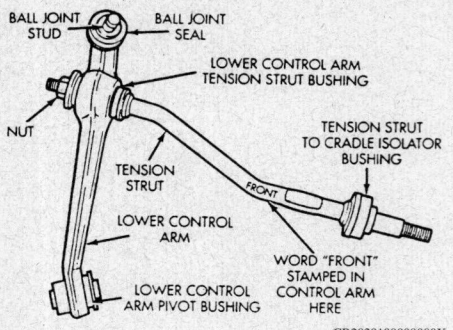

Fig. 13 Tension strut removal from control arm

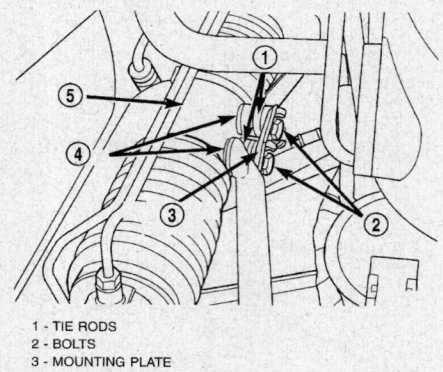

1 - TIE RODS
2 - BOLTS
3 - MOUNTING PLATE
4 - WASHERS
5 - STEERING GEAR

CR6030100231000X

Fig. 14 Tie rod to steering gear attaching bolts

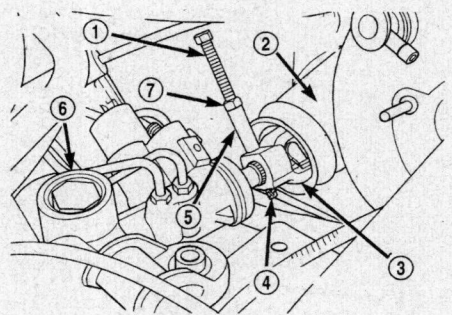

1 - SPECIAL TOOL 6831–A
2 - DASH PANEL SEAL & BOOT
3 - FLEX JOINT
4 - KNURLED NUT
5 - SLEEVE
6 - STEERING GEAR
7 - NUT

CR6030100232000X

Fig. 15 Steering gear roll pin removal

TIGHTENING SPECIFICATIONS

Year	Component	Torque Ft. Lbs.
2004	Ball Joint Stud To Steering Knuckle	40
	Disc Brake Caliper	16
	Front Cradle Assembly To Body	120
	Hub & Bearing Assembly To Steering Knuckle	80
	Hub & Bearing Axle Nut	105
	Inner Tie Rod To Steering Gear	74
	Lower Control Arm To Cradle Pivot	105
	Master Cylinder Mounting Nuts	21
	Outer Tie Rod Adjuster Pinch Bolt	28
	Outer Tie Rod To Steering Arm Nut	27
	Power Steering Fluid Pressure Hose To Discharge Fitting	62
	Power Steering Pressure Hose Tube	35
	Power Steering Pressure Switch	15
	Power Steering Pump To Bracket Bolts	21
	Power Steering Return Tube	23
	Reservoir Mounting Bolts, Pulley Side (2.7L)	10
	Reservoir Mounting Bolts, Rear (2.7L)	18
	Reservoir Mounting Bolts (3.5L)	①105
	Stabilizer Bar Attaching Link To Strut	17
	Stabilizer Bar Bushing Retainer To Cradle	45
	Stabilizer Bar Link Lower Nut	65
	Stabilizer Bar Link Upper Nut	70
	Steering Gear To Crossmember	43
	Strut Assembly Shaft	70
	Strut Assembly To Shock Tower	28
	Strut Assembly To Steering Knuckle	150②
	Sway Bar To Strut Link	70
	Tension Strut	95
	Wheel Lug Nut	100③

① — Inch lbs.
② — Strut bolts have a serrated shaft. Do not turn bolts in steering knuckle. Turn nuts on bolts. Do not turn bolts.
③ — Refer to Hub & Bearing, Replace for tightening sequence.

Wheel Alignment

INDEX

	Page No.		Page No.		Page No.
Front Wheel Alignment	3-36	Preliminary Inspection	3-36	Wheel Alignment	
Camber	3-36	Rear Wheel Alignment	3-36	Specifications	3-3
Toe	3-36	Toe	3-36		

PRELIMINARY INSPECTION

Before any attempt is made to change or correct front wheel alignment, the following inspections and required corrections must be made.

1. Ensure tire pressure is at recommended pressure, all tires should be same size and in good condition and have approximately same wear.
2. Inspect front wheels and tire assembly for radial runout.
3. Inspect lower ball joint and steering linkage for looseness.
4. Inspect for broken or damaged front and rear springs.
5. **Just prior to each alignment reading, the vehicle should be jounced (rear first, then front) by grasping bumper at center and jouncing each end of vehicle an equal number of times. Always release bumpers at bottom of down cycle.**

FRONT WHEEL ALIGNMENT

Camber

If front camber is not within specifications, strut and steering knuckles are not bent or damaged there are special undersize camber adjustment bolts and nuts are available to allow adjustment. This involves replacing the original clevis to knuckle bolts using the following procedure.

1. Raise and support front of vehicle, then remove tire and wheel assemblies.
2. Remove strut assembly to steering knuckle attaching bolts. **Strut bolts have a serrated shaft for a tight fit into steering knuckle. Turn nut on bolts only, do not turn bolts.**
3. Loosely install special undersize cam-

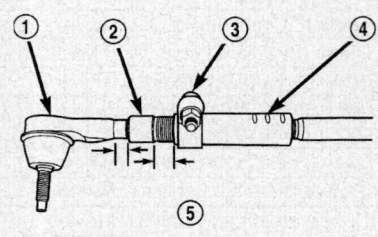

1 - OUTER TIE ROD
2 - ADJUSTER
3 - PINCH BOLT
4 - INNER TIE ROD
5 - ALLOWABLE THREADS EXPOSED ON OUTER TIE ROD AND ADJUSTER IS A MAXIMUM OF 20 MILLIMETERS. REFER TO AREA INDICATED ABOVE ON THE OUTER TIE ROD AND ADJUSTER.

CR2040100067000X

Fig. 1   Front tie rod adjustment dimensions

ber bolts so nuts are toward front of vehicle.
4. Install wheels lower vehicle, then jounce front and rear of vehicle.
5. Adjust front camber to specifications by pulling in or pushing outward on top of wheel assembly.
6. Inspect and correct toe as required.

Toe

1. Center steering wheel and hold with steering wheel clamp.
2. Loosen tie rod adjustment sleeve jam nuts.
3. Rotate adjustment sleeve to align toe. **When setting toe, maximum threads exposed on inner and outer tie rod can not exceed 20 mm, Fig. 1.**
4. Tighten adjustment pinch bolt as follows.
   a. Install a tie rod adjustment tool on neck area of outer tie rod to maintain correct perpendicular orientation of tie rod stud within tie rod end, **Fig. 2.**
   b. **Torque** tie rod adjustment pinch nut to 28 ft. lbs.
   c. Remove steering wheel clamp.

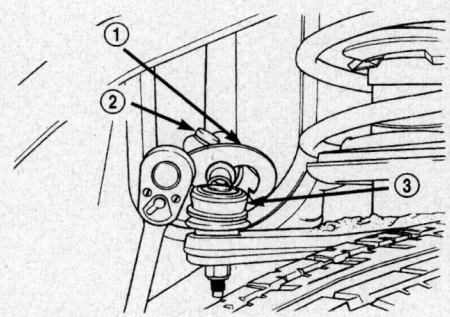

1 - ADJUSTMENT TOOL
2 - ADJUSTMENT PINCH BOLT
3 - TIE ROD END

CR2040100068000X

Fig. 2   Front wheel toe adjustment location

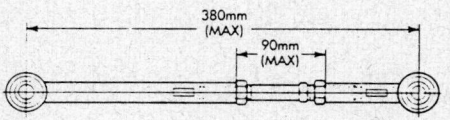

CR2049100035000X

Fig. 3   Rear tie rod adjustment dimensions

REAR WHEEL ALIGNMENT

Toe

1. Loosen lateral link adjustment link jam nuts.
2. Rotate adjustment link as required to set rear wheel toe.
3. **Do not exceed maximum length dimension of lateral links, Fig. 3. Both dimensions must be inspected.**
4. **Torque** lateral links locknuts to 65 ft. lbs.

CROSSFIRE

NOTE: Refer To Rear Of This Manual For Vehicle Manufacturer's Special Service Tool Suppliers.

INDEX OF SERVICE OPERATIONS

Page No.

AIR BAG SYSTEM PRECAUTIONS 0-18
BRAKES
Anti-Lock Brakes (Volume 2).. 6-1
Disc Brakes................... 14-1
Drum Brakes 15-1
Hydraulic Brake Systems 16-1
Power Brake Units............ 17-1
COMPUTER RELEARN PROCEDURE 0-31
ELECTRICAL
Air Bag System (Volume 2) ... 4-1
Air Conditioning............... 8-1
Alternator, Replace 4-3
Alternators................... 11-1
Blower Motor, Replace........ 4-5
Coil Pack, Replace 4-3
Cooling Fans 9-1
Cruise Control (Volume 2) 2-1
Dash Gauges (Volume 2) 1-1
Dash Panel Service (Volume 2).................. 4-1
Dimmer Switch, Replace...... 4-4
Evaporator Core, Replace 4-6
Fuel Pump Relay Location.... 4-3
Fuse Panel & Flasher Location 4-3
Headlamp Switch, Replace.... 4-4
Heater Core, Replace......... 4-5
Ignition Lock, Replace 4-3
Ignition Switch, Replace 4-4
Instrument Cluster, Replace... 4-4
Multi-Function Switch, Replace 4-4
Passive Restraint Systems (Volume 2)................... 4-1
Precautions................... 4-3
Radio, Replace 4-4
Speed Controls (Volume 2) ... 2-1
Starter Motors 10-1
Starter, Replace 4-3
Steering Columns............. 12-1
Steering Wheel, Replace...... 4-4
Stop Light Switch, Replace ... 4-4
Turn Signal Switch, Replace .. 4-4
Wiper Motor, Replace......... 4-5
Wiper Systems (Volume 2).... 3-1
Wiper Switch, Replace........ 4-5
ELECTRICAL SYMBOL IDENTIFICATION 0-63
FRONT DRIVE AXLES 26-1
FRONT SUSPENSION & STEERING
Ball Joint, Replace............ 4-19
Ball Joint Inspection 4-19

Page No.

Coil Spring, Replace.......... 4-19
Control Arm, Replace 4-20
Drag Link, Replace 4-21
Hub & Bearing, Replace 4-19
Pitman Arm, Replace 4-20
Power Steering 13-1
Power Steering Gear, Replace 4-21
Power Steering Pump, Replace 4-21
Power Steering System Bleed........................ 4-21
Precautions.................. 4-19
Shock Absorber, Replace 4-20
Stabilizer Bar, Replace........ 4-20
Steering Columns............. 12-1
Steering Knuckle, Replace.... 4-20
Tie Rod End, Replace 4-20
Tightening Specifications...... 4-22
NON-STANDARD TIRE & WHEEL SIZE ADJUSTMENT TO RIDE HEIGHT SPECIFICATIONS & TIRE SIZE CHART 0-61
REAR AXLE & SUSPENSION
Camber Strut, Replace........ 4-17
Coil Spring, Replace.......... 4-17
Control Arm, Replace 4-17
Differential Carrier, Replace... 4-16
Differential Housing, Replace . 4-16
Hub & Bearing, Replace 4-17
Lateral Link, Replace 4-18
Propeller Shaft, Replace 4-16
Rear Halfshaft, Replace....... 4-16
Shock Absorber, Replace 4-17
Spindle Knuckle, Replace..... 4-17
Tightening Specifications...... 4-18
Track Rod, Replace........... 4-18
Trailing Link, Replace......... 4-17
SERVICE REMINDER & WARNING LAMP RESET PROCEDURES 0-34
SPECIFICATIONS
Fluid Capacities & Cooling System Data.................. 4-2
Front Wheel Alignment Specifications............... 4-2
General Engine Specifications............... 4-2
Lubricant Data................ 4-3
Rear Wheel Alignment Specifications................. 4-2
Tune Up Specifications 4-2

Page No.

TIRE PRESSURE MONITORING SYSTEM 20-1
VEHICLE IDENTIFICATION 0-1
VEHICLE LIFT POINTS 0-51
VEHICLE MAINTENANCE SCHEDULES 0-73
WHEEL ALIGNMENT
Front Wheel Alignment........ 4-23
Preliminary Inspection 4-23
Rear Wheel Alignment........ 4-23
Wheel Alignment Specifications................. 4-2
WIRE COLOR CODE IDENTIFICATION 0-63
3.2L ENGINE
Belt Tension Data.............. 4-13
Camshaft, Replace 4-12
Compression Pressure........ 4-8
Cooling System Bleed 4-13
Crankshaft Damper, Replace.. 4-11
Crankshaft Rear Oil Seal, Replace 4-12
Crankshaft Seal, Replace..... 4-12
Cylinder Head, Replace....... 4-9
Engine Rebuilding Specifications.................. 21-1
Engine, Replace 4-8
Engine Mount, Replace 4-8
Exhaust Manifold, Replace.... 4-9
Front Cover, Replace 4-11
Fuel Filter, Replace........... 4-13
Fuel Pump, Replace........... 4-13
Intake Manifold, Replace...... 4-9
Main & Rod Bearings 4-12
Oil Pan, Replace.............. 4-12
Oil Pump, Replace............ 4-12
Oil Pump Service 4-12
Precautions................... 4-8
Radiator, Replace............. 4-13
Rocker Arms, Replace 4-10
Serpentine Drive Belt 4-13
Supercharger, Replace 4-14
Thermostat, Replace.......... 4-13
Tightening Specifications...... 4-15
Timing Chain, Replace........ 4-11
Timing Chain Tensioner, Replace 4-12
Valve Adjustment 4-10
Valve Cover, Replace......... 4-10
Valve Springs, Replace 4-10
Water Pump, Replace......... 4-13

Specifications

GENERAL ENGINE SPECIFICATIONS

Engine	Engine VIN Code①	Fuel System	Bore & Stroke, Inches	Compression Ratio	Net HP @ RPM	Maximum Torque, Ft. Lbs. @ RPM	Normal Oil Pressure, psi	
							Curb Idle	3000 RPM
3.2L	L	MPFI	3.54 x 3.31	10.1:1	215 @ 5700	230 @ 3000	5	45–105
	N	MPFI	3.54 x 3.31	9.0:1	330 @ 6100	310 @ 3500	5	45–105

① — Eighth digit of VIN denotes engine code.

TUNE UP SPECIFICATIONS

Engine	Spark Plug Gap, Inch	Ignition Timing		Curb Idle Speed	Fuel Pump Pressure, psi	Valve Clearance, Inch
		Firing Order	°BTDC			
3.2L	.035	1-4-3-6-2-5	①	③	54–61	②

BTDC — Before Top Dead Center
① — Twin Ignition System not adjustable.

② — Equipped with hydraulic valve adjusters. No valve adjustment is required.

③ — Controlled by PCM.

FRONT WHEEL ALIGNMENT SPECIFICATIONS

Year	Camber, Degrees		Caster, Degrees		Toe In, Degrees ①		Ball Joint Wear
	Limits	Desired	Limits	Desired	Limits	Desired	
2004–08	—	-1.22	—	5.2	—	+2.5	②

① — The flexible mount of the control arms results in a correspondingly large toe value which reduces to the correct dimension in the ready-to-drive condition.

② — Refer to Ball Joint Inspection in Front Suspension & Steering.

REAR WHEEL ALIGNMENT SPECIFICATIONS

Year	Camber Angle, Degrees		Total Toe, Degrees		Thrust Angle, Degrees
	Limits	Desired	Limits	Desired	
2004–08	—	-1.13	—	1.2	—

FLUID CAPACITIES & COOLING SYSTEM DATA

Year	Coolant Capacity, Qts.	Coolant Type	Radiator Cap Relief Pressure, Lbs.	Thermostat. Opening Temp., °F	Fuel Tank, Gals.	Engine Oil Refill, Qts.①	Auto. Transaxle Oil, Qts.②	Man. Transaxle Oil, Pts.
2004–08	11.8③	Ethylene Glycol	14–18	192–195	15.8	6.1④	8.5	3.2

① — Includes oil filter.

② — Approximate, make final inspection w/dipstick.

③ — With supercharger 15.3 Qts.
④ — With supercharger 8.5 Qts.

LUBRICANT DATA

Year	Transaxle		Power Steering	Brake System
	Automatic	Manual		
2004–08	Mopar ATF+4 Type 9602	Mopar ATF+4 Type 9602	Mopar ATF+4 Type 9602	DOT 3–4

Electrical

NOTE: On Air Bag Equipped Models, Refer To "Air Bag System Precautions" Located In The Front Of This Manual For System Disarming & Arming Procedures.

NOTE: Refer To "Computer Relearn Procedures" Located In The Front Of This Manual When Battery Power To The Computer Has Been Interrupted.

INDEX

	Page No.			Page No.			Page No.
Air Bag System (Volume 2)	4-1		Fuel Pump Relay Location	4-3		Radio, Replace	4-4
Air Conditioning	8-1		Fuse Panel & Flasher Location	4-3		Speed Controls (Volume 2)	2-1
Alternator, Replace	4-3		Headlamp Switch, Replace	4-4		Starter Motors	10-1
Alternators	11-1		Heater Core, Replace	4-5		Starter, Replace	4-3
Blower Motor, Replace	4-5		Ignition Lock, Replace	4-3		Steering Columns	12-1
Coil Pack, Replace	4-3		Ignition Switch, Replace	4-4		Steering Wheel, Replace	4-4
Cooling Fans	9-1		Instrument Cluster, Replace	4-4		Stop Light Switch, Replace	4-4
Cruise Control (Volume 2)	2-1		Multi-Function Switch, Replace	4-4		Turn Signal Switch, Replace	4-4
Dash Gauges (Volume 2)	1-1		Passive Restraint Systems			Wiper Motor, Replace	4-5
Dash Panel Service			(Volume 2)	4-1		Wiper Switch, Replace	4-5
(Volume 2)	5-1		Precautions	4-3		Wiper Systems (Volume 2)	3-1
Dimmer Switch, Replace	4-4		Air Bag Systems	4-3			
Evaporator Core, Replace	4-6		Battery Ground Cable	4-3			

PRECAUTIONS

Air Bag Systems

Refer to "Air Bag System Precautions" in the front of this manual for system disarming and arming procedures.

Battery Ground Cable

Prior to service, disconnect battery ground cable and isolate as required.

FUSE PANEL & FLASHER LOCATION

This vehicle is equipped with two fuse panels. The engine compartment fuse panel is located on the lefthand side of the engine compartment, between the brake master cylinder and front fender. The second instrument panel fuse panel is located behind an access door on the lefthand side of the instrument panel.

The turn indicator signals are controlled by an Erasable Electronic Programmable Read Only Memory (EEPROM) chip that is integrated into the instrument cluster. If the turn indicators fail and the EEPROM is found at fault the instrument cluster must be replaced.

FUEL PUMP RELAY LOCATION

The fuel pump relay is housed within the relay control module located on the righthand side of the engine compartment. The relay control module also contains the fuel pump relay fuse. If the fuel pump relay or circuitry fail the control module must be replaced as an assembly.

STARTER
REPLACE

1. Raise and support vehicle.
2. Remove lower engine panel.
3. Disconnect righthand O2 sensor electrical connector.
4. Remove righthand exhaust pipe from manifold and rear exhaust pipe.
5. Remove starter mounting bolts, then position starter to access posi-lock wiring connector.
6. Remove battery feed and solenoid wiring harness connectors.
7. Remove starter mounting bolts, then starter.
8. Reverse procedure to install. **Torque** starter mounting bolts to 31 ft. lbs.

ALTERNATOR
REPLACE

1. Remove righthand air inlet tube.
2. Rotate accessory drive belt tensioner

in a counterclockwise direction, then lock belt tensioner with a locking pin.
3. Remove protective cap from alternator electrical cable, then disconnect the electrical cable.
4. Position wire harness aside and remove alternator mounting bolts, then the alternator.
5. Reverse procedure to install. **Torque** alternator mounting bolts to 31 ft. lbs.

COIL PACK
REPLACE

1. Remove air cleaner housing.
2. Disconnect ignition coil harness connector.
3. Disconnect spark plug cables from spark plugs.
4. Remove coil pack mounting bolts, then the coil pack.
5. Reverse procedure to install. **Torque** coil pack mounting bolts to 71 inch lbs.

IGNITION LOCK
REPLACE

1. Press out ignition lock cylinder escutcheon with suitable trim tool.
2. Remove transponder coil off key lock cylinder with suitable plastic wedge tool.
3. With ignition key in lock cylinder, push sleeve onto lock cylinder cap.

4. Turn lock cylinder to position No. 1, using ignition key.
5. Rotate lock cylinder cap 90° counterclockwise to remove ignition lock cylinder.
6. Reverse procedure to install, noting the following:
   a. Lubricate outside of lock cylinder using suitable cylinder lock grease, then insert lock cylinder into cap.
   b. Push ignition key through lock cylinder cap until it stops.
   c. Rotate cap clockwise 90° until cylinder can be felt or heard lock into position.

IGNITION SWITCH

REPLACE

1. Remove lower lefthand instrument panel cover retaining clips, then lower cover.
2. Remove two instrument cluster bezel retaining screws, then the bezel.
3. Remove four instrument cluster retaining screws, then move instrument cluster outwards.
4. Disconnect instrument cluster electrical connectors and harness retaining clips from back of instrument cluster.
5. Remove instrument cluster from vehicle.
6. Remove A-pillar trim panel.
7. Remove lefthand and righthand fuse covers.
8. Remove retaining screw located within the lefthand and righthand air vents, **Fig. 1.**
9. Remove retaining screw from inside of fuse panel covers.
10. Remove retaining screws from center console to top on instrument panel.
11. Remove retaining screws from inside glove compartment.
12. Remove defroster grille screws, then the defroster outwards.
13. Remove bolts from lefthand and righthand side under defroster grille, **Fig. 2.**
14. Remove sheet metal clips from both A-pillars.
15. Remove top panel of instrument panel.
16. Insert suitable plastic wedge directly between, ignition switch cover sleeve and transponder coil. Press transponder coil off ignition switch cover sleeve using suitable plastic wedge, **Fig. 3.**
17. Disconnect 2–pin transponder coil electrical connector from control module.
18. **Steering lock and cylinder lock can only be installed in lock position. Never turn steering lock when ignition/starter switch is being installed.**
19. Remove ignition key cylinder.
20. Disconnect warning buzzer electrical contact and ignition/starter switch electrical contact.
21. Disconnect parking lock interlock cable.
22. Release locking pin clamp and pull steering lock from steering column.
23. Remove ignition switch.
24. Remove washer and parking lock valve.

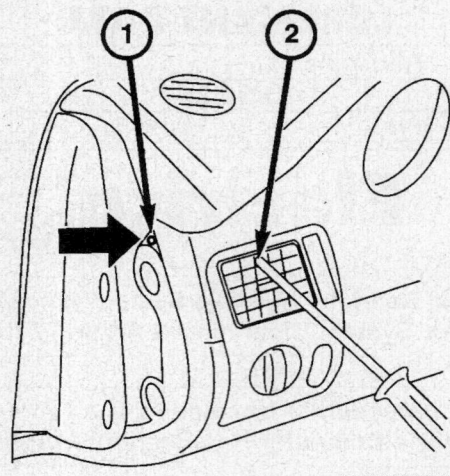

ARM030000000196

Fig. 1   Vent screw removal

25. Remove warning buzzer and contact switch.
26. Reverse procedure to install.

HEADLAMP SWITCH

REPLACE

1. Remove lower lefthand instrument panel cover retaining clips, then lower cover.
2. Disconnect electrical connectors at back of headlamp switch.
3. Remove headlamp switches from interior trim panel using suitable trim stick.
4. Remove two headlamp switch to trim panel retaining screws, then headlamp switch.
5. Reverse procedure to install.

STOP LIGHT SWITCH

REPLACE

1. Remove lower lefthand instrument panel cover retaining clips, then lower cover.
2. Disconnect electrical connectors at back of stop light switch.
3. Press stop light switch locking tabs, then rotate stop light switch clockwise to release from brake pedal brace.
4. Remove stop lamp switch.
5. Reverse procedure to install.

MULTI-FUNCTION SWITCH

REPLACE

1. Remove steering wheel as outlined in "Steering Wheel, Replace."
2. Remove lower instrument panel retainers, then lower instrument panel.
3. Remove cruise control to multi-function switch retaining screw.
4. Remove cruise control retaining screws from bracket below cruise control.
5. Remove multi-function switch to steering column retaining screws.
6. Disconnect multi-function switch electrical connectors and wire harness from steering column.

7. Remove multi-function switch.
8. Reverse procedure to install.

TURN SIGNAL SWITCH

REPLACE

Refer to "Multi-Function Switch, Replace" for procedure.

DIMMER SWITCH

REPLACE

Refer to "Multi-Function Switch, Replace" for procedure.

STEERING WHEEL

REPLACE

Refer to **Fig. 4** for exploded view of steering column to aid in replacement and installation. **Steering wheel does not require a wheel puller tool for removal.**

1. Place front wheels in straight ahead position.
2. Remove lefthand lower instrument panel fuse panel from below steering column.
3. Remove driver's air bag retaining screws, disconnect air bag electrical connector, then pass air bag connector wire through hole in steering column.
4. Remove driver's air bag module.
5. Remove steering wheel countersunk bolt, using a long Allen wrench, then steering wheel.
6. Remove clockspring screws.
7. Reverse procedure to install, noting the following:
   a. **Torque** steering wheel mounting hex bolt to 60 ft. lbs.
   b. If steering wheel is offset by more than one tooth, turn signal indicator is no longer aligned properly.

INSTRUMENT CLUSTER

REPLACE

Remove instrument cluster as outlined in "Ignition Switch, Replace."

RADIO

REPLACE

1. Record customers defined presets.
2. Insert radio removal tools No. 3291, or equivalents, into slots located on righthand and lefthand sides of radio, with jagged edge of tools facing inward toward center of radio unit, push forward until a slight click is heard.
3. Gently pull tool rings along with radio rearward until radio is clear of dash panel.
4. Press flexible detentes in sides of radio after it has been remove, then release tools.
5. Disconnect radio electrical connectors and antenna.
6. Remove radio unit from vehicle.
7. Reverse procedure to install, then enter customer preset stations.

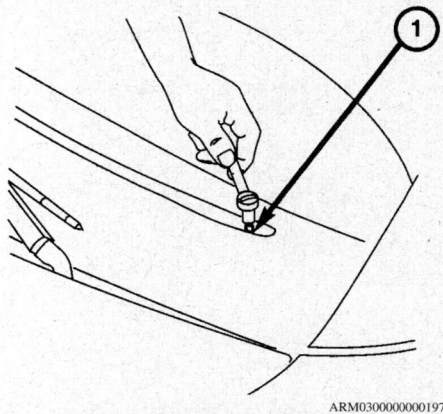

Fig. 2 Defroster grille bolt removal

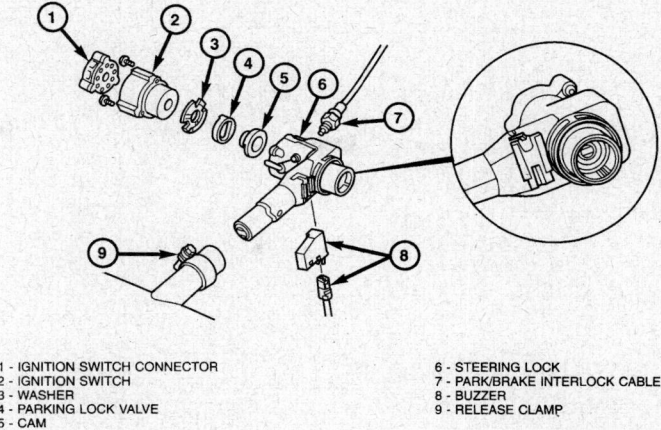

1 - IGNITION SWITCH CONNECTOR
2 - IGNITION SWITCH
3 - WASHER
4 - PARKING LOCK VALVE
5 - CAM
6 - STEERING LOCK
7 - PARK/BRAKE INTERLOCK CABLE
8 - BUZZER
9 - RELEASE CLAMP

ARM0300000000065

Fig. 3 Ignition switch replacement

WIPER MOTOR
REPLACE

1. Open hood, then extend hood prop fully open to support hood.
2. Lift wiper arm to its over-center position.
3. Remove plastic nut cap at pivot arm end of wiper arm.
4. Remove wiper arm retaining nut from wiper pivot shaft.
5. Remove wiper arm from pivot shaft using suitable battery terminal puller to release wiper arm from pivot shaft.
6. Remove cowl grille retaining screws, then pull back on cowl grille to release retaining clips.
7. Disconnect hoses from under side of cowl grille.
8. Remove cowl grille from vehicle.
9. Remove control module box cover.
10. Disconnect wiper motor electrical connector from Body Control Module (BCM).
11. Remove wiper motor wire harness rubber grommet from BCM box and cowl ledge.
12. Remove cowl drain by rotating drain insert counterclockwise, then lift drain upward to remove.
13. Remove lower wiper module retaining bolts located under cowl ledge.
14. Remove two upper wiper module retaining bolts, then wiper module and wiper motor assembly.
15. Remove wiper motor retaining bolts, then position wiper motor to access crank arm retaining nut, **Fig. 5.**
16. Remove crank arm retaining nut from wiper motor shaft.
17. Scribe a reference mark on both wiper motor and wiper crank arm to ensure proper alignment during reassembly.
18. Remove crank arm from wiper motor shaft, then remove wiper motor from wiper module.
19. Reverse procedure to install. **Torque** wiper motor retaining blots to 98 inch lbs.

WIPER SWITCH
REPLACE

Refer to "Multi-Function Switch, Replace" for procedure.

BLOWER MOTOR
REPLACE

1. Remove righthand lower instrument panel cover retainers, then lower instrument panel cover.
2. Disconnect blower motor electrical connector from relief in blower motor door.
3. Position blower motor door release catches to one side, then swing blower motor cover door downward.
4. Remove blower motor retaining screws, then blower motor.
5. Reverse procedure to install.

HEATER CORE
REPLACE

1. Recover refrigerant as outlined in "Air Conditioning" chapter.
2. Drain engine coolant into suitable container.
3. Remove top panel of dash panel as outlined in "Ignition Switch, Replace."
4. Remove air nozzles.
5. Remove steering column undercover attaching screw, then cover.
6. Remove fuse panel cover.
7. Remove lower instrument cover retaining screws from illumination control module, side of instrument panel and support bar, **Fig. 6.**
8. Remove illumination control module.
9. Remove underside cover screws from cover, **Fig. 7.**
10. Remove lefthand lower instrument panel cover to upper instrument panel cover retaining screws, then the panel cover, **Fig. 8.**
11. Remove hood latch release handle to lefthand lower instrument panel retaining screws, then guide handle through lower cover, **Fig. 9.**
12. Remove righthand lower instrument panel cover to upper instrument panel cover retaining screws, then lower cover.
13. Remove carpeting from righthand side passenger area.
14. Remove glove compartment to righthand lower instrument panel retaining screws, then glove compartment, **Fig. 10.**
15. Remove instrument cluster as outlined in "Ignition Switch, Replace."
16. Ensure all wire harness to instrument panel nylon retaining straps are removed.
17. Remove lower instrument panel from vehicle.
18. Disconnect hot water hose located on firewall near brake booster.
19. Disconnect heater core supply hoses located on righthand side of firewall.
20. Remove green insulating mats.
21. Disconnect Sentry Key Entry Module (SKREM) electrical connectors by depressing retaining tabs.
22. Remove SKREM retaining screws, then SKREM from mounting plate.
23. Ensure all wire harness to instrument panel support nylon retaining straps are removed.
24. Remove wire harness connectors and retainers from transmission tunnel.
25. Remove steering column to instrument panel support nuts, then position steering column aside.
26. Disconnect passenger's air bag module electrical connector.
27. Remove righthand and lefthand heater ducts to instrument panel support retaining screws, then heater ducts.
28. Remove HVAC case to instrument panel support and transmission tunnel mounting bolts.
29. Remove instrument panel support to front vehicle bulkhead mounting bolts.
30. Remove instrument panel support to A- pillar support bolts.

CROSSFIRE

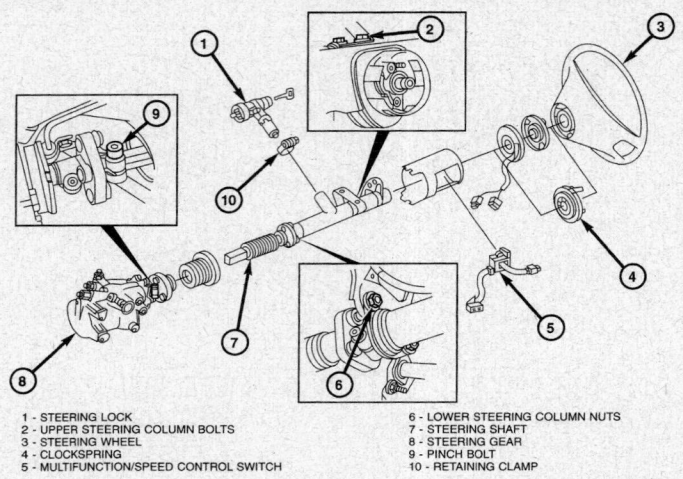

Fig. 4   Exploded view of steering column

1 - STEERING LOCK
2 - UPPER STEERING COLUMN BOLTS
3 - STEERING WHEEL
4 - CLOCKSPRING
5 - MULTIFUNCTION/SPEED CONTROL SWITCH
6 - LOWER STEERING COLUMN NUTS
7 - STEERING SHAFT
8 - STEERING GEAR
9 - PINCH BOLT
10 - RETAINING CLAMP

ARM0300000000018

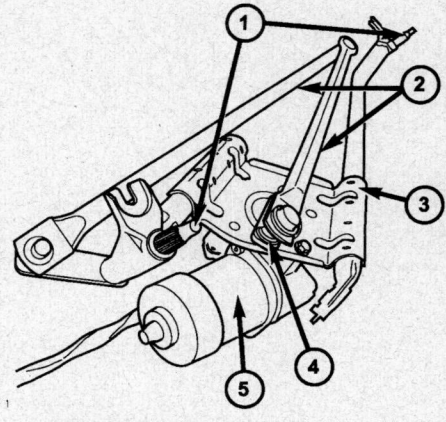

1 Wiper pivot shafts
2 Linkage
3 Module frame
4 Crank arm
5 Wiper motor

ARM0300000000582

Fig. 5   Wiper motor replacement

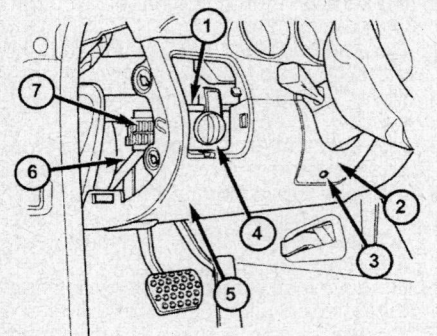

1- MOUNTING SCREW
2- STEERING COLUMN COVER
3- MOUNTING SCREW
4- ILLUMINATION CONTROL MODULE
5- LOWER INSTRUMENT COVER
6- SUPPORT BAR
7- ILLUMINATION CONTROL MODULE

ARM0300000000199

Fig. 6   Illumination control module removal

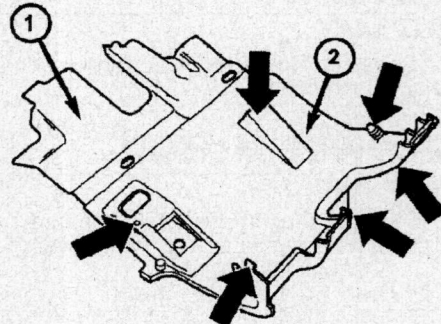

1- UPPER INSTRUMENT PANEL COVER
2- LOWER INSTRUMENT PANEL COVER

ARM0300000000200

Fig. 7   Underside cover screw removal

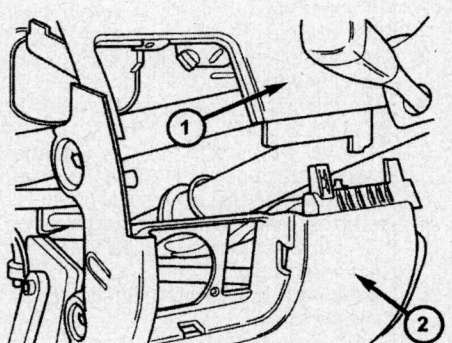

1- CLUSTER COVER
2- LOWER INSTRUMENT PANEL

ARM0300000000202

Fig. 8   Lefthand lower instrument panel removal

31. Disconnect vacuum reservoir connectors.
32. Disconnect heater core and evaporator core temperature sensor electrical connectors located on lefthand side of HVAC housing.
33. Disconnect fresh air/recirculating flap switch-over valve electrical and vacuum reservoir connectors located on front of HVAC housing.
34. Remove remaining wire harness to heater housing nylon retaining ties.
35. Ensure to cap or plug off any coolant fluid lines.
36. Tip heater core housing and instrument panel support assembly forward and carefully remove through passenger's door opening.
37. Remove heater core cover retaining screws located on righthand side of HVAC housing.
38. Release heater core cover retaining spring clamps.
39. Remove heater core cover.
40. Remove heater core water flow pipe guide to HVAC housing retaining bolt.
41. Remove heating water return line to heater core retaining clip, then return line from heater core.
42. Remove heater core to HVAC housing retaining screws, then heater core and flow tube as an assembly.
43. Remove heater core water flow pipe retaining clip, then flow pipe from heater core.
44. Reverse procedure to install.

EVAPORATOR CORE
REPLACE

1. Remove HVAC housing and heater core as outlined in "Heater Core, Replace."
2. Remove aluminum A/C lines from valve strip located on top of HVAC unit, **Fig. 11.**

3. Disconnect vacuum lines from reservoir element.
4. Separate blower housing from HVAC housing using suitable plastic trim stick to release sliding retaining clips, **Fig. 11.**
5. Remove blower motor housing to HVAC housing retaining spring clips, then separate blower motor housing from HVAC housing, **Fig. 12.**
6. Remove four expansion valve retaining screws and gasket located behind expansion valve.
7. Separate HVAC housing upper section by removing spring retainer clips.
8. Remove evaporator core from HVAC housing.
9. Reverse procedure to install.

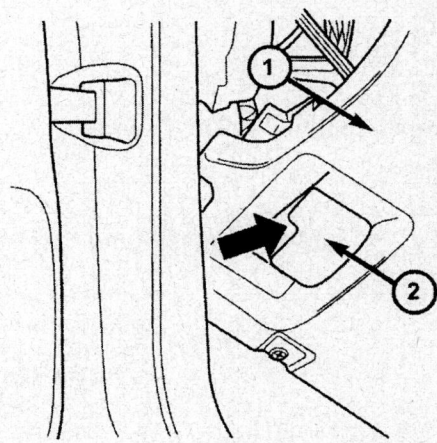

1- LOWER INSTRUMENT PANEL
2- HOOD RELEASE LEVER

ARM0300000000201

Fig. 9   Hood latch release removal

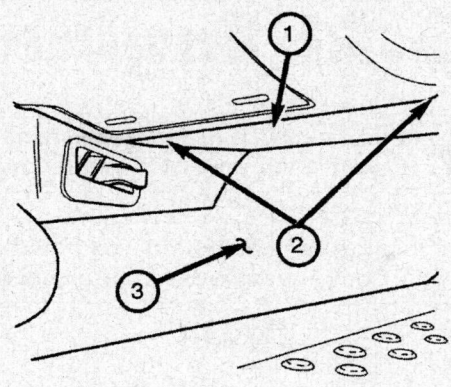

1- LOWER INSTRUMENT PANEL
2- MOUNTING SCREWS
3- CARPET

ARM0300000000203

Fig. 10   Righthand lower instrument panel removal

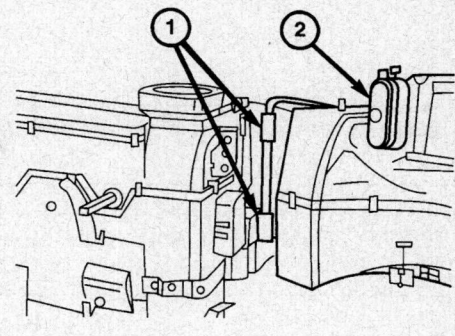

1 Sliding clips
2 Vacuum element

ARM0300000000583

Fig. 11   HVAC housing retaining clip & reservoir element locations

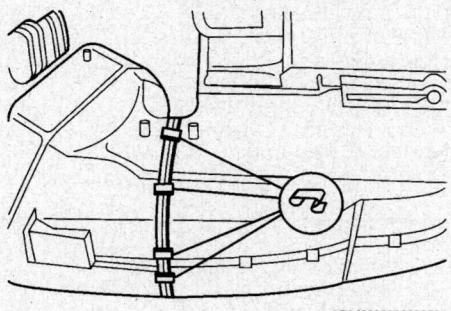

ARM0300000000584

Fig. 12   HVAC housing spring clip removal

3.2L Engine

NOTE: On Air Bag Equipped Models, Refer To "Air Bag System Precautions" Located In The Front Of This Manual For System Disarming & Arming Procedures.

NOTE: Refer To "Computer Relearn Procedures" Located In The Front Of This Manual When Battery Power To The Computer Has Been Interrupted.

INDEX

	Page No.
Belt Tension Data	4-13
Camshaft, Replace	4-12
Compression Pressure	4-8
Cooling System Bleed	4-13
Crankshaft Damper, Replace	4-11
Crankshaft Rear Oil Seal, Replace	4-12
Crankshaft Seal, Replace	4-12
Cylinder Head, Replace	4-9
Installation	4-10
Removal	4-9
Engine Rebuilding Specifications	21-1
Engine, Replace	4-8
Engine Mount, Replace	4-8
Front	4-8
Rear	4-8

	Page No.
Exhaust Manifold, Replace	4-9
Front Cover, Replace	4-11
Fuel Filter, Replace	4-13
Fuel Pump, Replace	4-13
Intake Manifold, Replace	4-9
Main & Rod Bearings	4-12
Oil Pan, Replace	4-12
Lower	4-12
Upper	4-12
Oil Pump, Replace	4-12
Oil Pump Service	4-12
Precautions	4-8
Air Bag Systems	4-8
Battery Ground Cable	4-8
Fuel System Pressure Relief	4-8
Radiator, Replace	4-13
Rocker Arms, Replace	4-10

	Page No.
Installation	4-10
Removal	4-10
Serpentine Drive Belt	4-13
Supercharger, Replace	4-14
Thermostat, Replace	4-13
Tightening Specifications	4-15
Timing Chain, Replace	4-11
Installation	4-11
Removal	4-11
Timing Chain Tensioner, Replace	4-12
Valve Adjustment	4-10
Valve Cover, Replace	4-10
Valve Springs, Replace	4-10
Water Pump, Replace	4-13
Less Supercharger	4-13
With Supercharger	4-13

PRECAUTIONS

Air Bag Systems

Refer to "Air Bag System Precautions" in the front of this manual for system disarming and arming procedures.

Battery Ground Cable

Prior to service, disconnect battery ground cable and isolate as required.

Fuel System Pressure Relief

1. Remove fuel pump relay form power distribution center.
2. Start and run engine until it stalls.
3. Attempt to start engine until it no longer runs.
4. Turn ignition switch to Off position.
5. Place suitable rag or shop towel under fuel line quick-connector fitting at fuel rail.
6. Install fuel pump relay.
7. One or more Diagnostic Trouble Codes (DTCs) may have been stored because of removing fuel pump relay. Clear these DTCs with suitably programmed scan tool.

COMPRESSION PRESSURE

1. Drive vehicle until engine reaches normal operating temperature.
2. Disconnect ignition coil cables from spark plugs.
3. Remove spark plugs from engine.
4. Inspect spark plugs for signs of abnormal firing or oil fouling.
5. Ensure throttle plate is fully open.
6. Install suitable compression gauge into number one spark plug hole.
7. Crank engine over with starter until maximum pressure is obtained. Repeat for remaining cylinders.
8. Compression pressure should be no less than 100 psi and maximum variation between cylinders should be no more than 25%.

ENGINE MOUNT
REPLACE

Front

1. Remove air cleaner housing.
2. Attach suitable engine support frame.
3. Remove upper engine mount bolt and heat shield, **Fig. 1.**
4. Slightly raise engine. Do not stretch hoses and lines while lifting engine.
5. Raise and support vehicle.
6. Remove lower splash shield mounting bolts, then splash shield.
7. Remove engine mount.
8. Reverse procedure to install. Ensure arrows on engine mounts are aligned with engine bracket retaining slots.

Rear

1. Raise and support vehicle.
2. Support transmission with suitable transmission jack.
3. Remove lower engine mount retaining bolts.
4. Raise transmission slightly off crossmember support.
5. Remove upper engine mount bolts.
6. Remove rear engine mount.
7. Reverse procedure to install.

ENGINE
REPLACE

1. Relieve fuel pressure as outlined in "Precautions."
2. Remove air cleaner assembly housing.
3. Drain engine coolant into suitable container.
4. Remove cooling fan assembly as outlined in "Cooling Fans" chapter.
5. Remove radiator as outlined in "Radiator, Replace."
6. Remove serpentine drive belt as outlined in "Serpentine Drive Belt."
7. Disconnect mass air flow sensor connector and retaining screws, then remove sensor.
8. Disconnect brake vacuum booster, intake manifold inspect valve and purge vacuum valve hoses.
9. Drain fluid from power steering pump reservoir using suitable fluid removal pump.

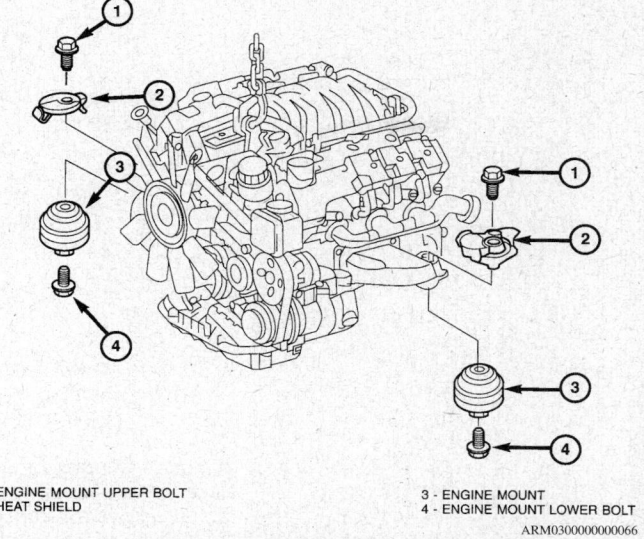

1 - ENGINE MOUNT UPPER BOLT
2 - HEAT SHIELD
3 - ENGINE MOUNT
4 - ENGINE MOUNT LOWER BOLT
ARM0300000000066

Fig. 1 Front engine mount replacement

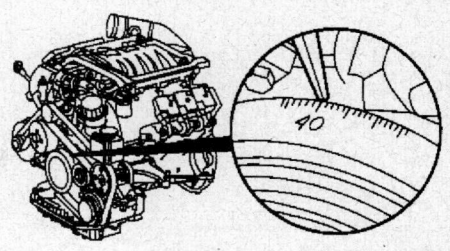

ARM0300000000070

Fig. 2 Crankshaft positioned at 40° ATDC

10. Disconnect ground lead at power steering pump.
11. Disconnect return and supply lines from power steering pump.
12. Disconnect fuel supply line at fuel rail.
13. Disconnect engine wire harness and connectors.
14. Raise and support vehicle.
15. Remove splash shield retaining bolts, then splash shield.
16. Drain engine oil into suitable container.
17. Remove transmission to rear drive axle propeller shaft as outlined in "Rear Axle & Suspension" section.
18. Disconnect transmission wire connectors and wiring harness from retainers at transmission, then position aside.
19. **On models equipped with automatic transmission,** disconnect gear selector cable from transmission shift lever.
20. **On models equipped with manual transmission,** disconnect pressure line at clutch slave cylinder, reverse lock-out cable and shift rod from ball stud.
21. **On all models,** disconnect starter motor connectors and wire harness from starter.
22. Remove front engine mount bolt.
23. Remove lower radiator hose and coolant bypass hose from water pump, then lower vehicle.
24. Remove upper radiator hose from thermostat housing.
25. Remove heater hoses from intake manifold and engine block.
26. Remove A/C compressor bolts, position compressor aside with lines attached.
27. Raise transmission slightly using suitable floor jack.
28. Remove transmission mount and crossmember mounting bolts, then crossmember and transmission mount as an assembly.
29. Attach suitable engine lifting hoist to engine removal eyelets located on engine.
30. Lower rear of transmission with floor jack.
31. Lift engine and transmission as an assembly from vehicle.
32. Separate engine and transmission after mounting onto suitable stand.
33. Reverse procedure to install.

INTAKE MANIFOLD
REPLACE

1. Relieve fuel pressure as outlined in "Precautions."
2. Remove air cleaner housing.
3. Disconnect mass air flow sensor electrical connector and retaining bolts, then sensor.
4. Disconnect EGR, brake booster and ventilator purge valve vacuum hoses from intake manifold.
5. Disconnect engine wiring connectors and harnesses, then position aside.
6. Remove fuel supply line from fuel rail.
7. Remove fuel rail and injectors as an assembly.
8. Disconnect EGR pipe at EGR valve.
9. Remove air pump switch over valves and retainers.
10. Remove intake manifold mounting bolts and gaskets.
11. Reverse procedure to install, noting the following:
    a. Clean all gasket surfaces thoroughly.
    b. Install new gaskets.
    c. Tighten intake manifold bolts to specification.

EXHAUST MANIFOLD
REPLACE

1. Remove air cleaner housing.
2. Raise and support vehicle.
3. Remove splash shield retaining bolts, then splash shield.
4. Disconnect catalytic converter sensor connector, then remove sensor and catalytic converter from vehicle.

5. Remove exhaust manifold nuts from cylinder head.
6. Lower vehicle.
7. Remove exhaust manifold and gasket from engine compartment.
8. Reverse procedure to install, noting the following:
    a. Clean all gasket surfaces thoroughly.
    b. Install new gaskets.
    c. Tighten exhaust manifold bolts to specification.

CYLINDER HEAD
REPLACE
Removal

1. Relieve fuel pressure as outlined in "Precautions."
2. Remove air cleaner housing.
3. Disconnect mass air flow sensor electrical connector, then remove sensor.
4. Drain engine oil and coolant into suitable containers.
5. Remove radiator as outlined in "Radiator, Replace."
6. Remove righthand and lefthand camshaft position sensor connectors and retaining bolts, then camshaft position sensors and wiring harnesses.
7. Remove drive belt as outlined in "Serpentine Drive Belt."
8. Remove intake manifold as outlined in "Intake Manifold, Replace."
9. Remove valve cover as outlined in "Valve Cover, Replace."
10. Disconnect righthand and lefthand exhaust system pipes at exhaust manifolds.
11. Position crankshaft at 40° ATDC, **Fig. 2.**
12. Lock camshafts in position using camshaft locating plate tool No. 9104 and locking pin tool No. 9105, or equivalents, place locating plate tool flush on cylinder head and insert locking pin tool into groove located on camshaft.
13. Remove timing chain tensioner, **Fig. 3.**
14. Secure timing chain to righthand camshaft sprocket using plastic tie strap, **Fig. 4.**
15. Remove camshaft sprocket bolts, then camshaft sprockets.
16. Remove camshaft locating plate tool No. 9104 and locking pin tool No. 9105, or equivalents.
17. Reverse sequence, **Figs. 5 and 6,** remove camshaft bearing bridge bolts in two steps.

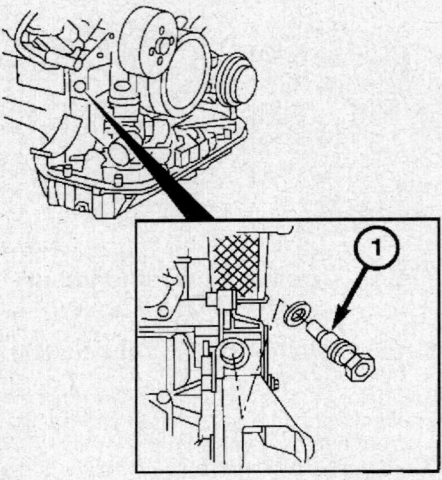

Fig. 3   Timing chain tensioner replacement

18. Remove camshaft bearing bridges and camshafts.
19. Reverse sequence, **Fig. 7,** remove cylinder head bolts.
20. Remove cylinder head and gasket.

Installation

1. Clean cylinder head and block gasket surfaces of any foreign material.
2. Position new gasket and cylinder head on engine block dowels.
3. Measure and inspect cylinder head bolts prior to reuse. Do not reuse bolts that exceed, 5.66 of an inch (144 mm) in length, **Fig. 8.**
4. Tighten cylinder head bolts in four steps using sequence, **Fig. 7.**
   a. Step one, **torque** head bolts 1–8 to 15 ft. lbs.
   b. Step two, **torque** head bolts 1–8 to 37 ft. lbs.
   c. Step three, tighten head bolts 1–8 an additional 60–70°.
   d. Step four, tighten head bolts 1–8 an additional 60–70°.
   e. Tighten timing chain cover bolts 9–10 to 18 ft. lbs.
5. Ensure crankshaft is at 40° ATDC, **Fig. 2.**
6. Position camshaft bearing bridge on camshaft.
7. Lock camshafts in position by using camshaft locating plate tool No. 9104 and locking pin tool No. 9105, or equivalents, place locating plate tool flush on cylinder head and inserting locking pin tool into grove located on camshaft.
8. **Torque** camshaft bridge bolts to 11 ft. lbs., then an additional 90° using sequence, **Figs. 5 and 6.**
9. Install camshaft sprockets and bolts, **torque** sprocket bolts to 37 ft. lbs., then tighten an additional 90°.
10. Install timing chain tensioner.
11. Remove plastic retaining tie from right-hand camshaft sprocket and chain.
12. Remove camshaft locating plate tool No. 9104 and locking pin tool No. 9105, or equivalents.

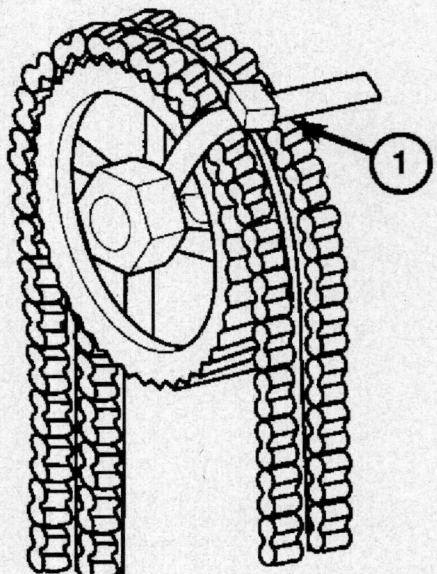

Fig. 4   Righthand timing chain & sprocket

13. Install valve cover as outlined in "Valve Cover, Replace."
14. Install air cleaner housing.
15. Install mass air flow sensor.

VALVE COVER
REPLACE

1. Remove air cleaner housing.
2. Disconnect ignition coil electrical connectors and harness to valve cover retaining clips, then position harness assembly aside.
3. Disconnect spark plug wires at spark plugs.
4. Disconnect PCV, vacuum hoses and retainers from valve covers, then position them aside.
5. Remove valve cover retaining bolts, then valve cover and gasket.
6. Reverse procedure to install, noting the following:
   a. Clean all gasket surfaces thoroughly.
   b. Install new gaskets.
   c. Tighten valve cover bolts to specification.

VALVE ADJUSTMENT

These engines are equipped with hydraulic lash adjusters. No adjustment required.

ROCKER ARMS
REPLACE
Removal

1. Remove camshaft bearing bridge as outlined in "Cylinder Head, Replace."
2. Remove rocker arm shaft from camshaft bearing bridge using a 16 mm drift to drive rocker arm shaft from

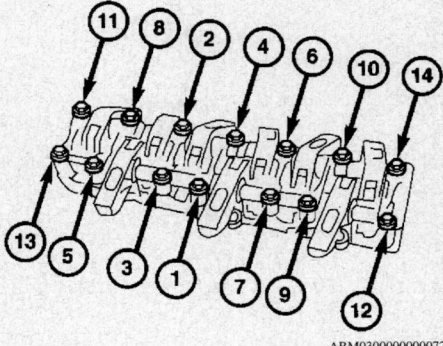

Fig. 5   Camshaft bearing bridge bolt tightening sequence (lefthand)

camshaft bearing bridge, **Fig. 9.** If resistance is encountered while driving rocker arm shaft from bearing bridge, bearing must be heated. **Do not exceed 320°F.**
3. Remove rocker arms, inspect rocker arm bearing surfaces. If longitudinal scoring is present on rocker arm bearing surface, replace effected rocker arms.

Installation

1. Allow rocker arm shaft and camshaft bearing bridge to cool.
2. Insert rocker arm shaft into camshaft bearing bridge and through rocker arms by gently tapping rocker arm shaft using suitable soft head mallet. Ensure rocker arms are aligned, **Fig. 10.**
3. Ensure oil supply holes in rocker arm shaft are facing downward, toward cylinder head.
4. Install camshaft bearing bridge as outlined in "Cylinder Head, Replace."

VALVE SPRINGS
REPLACE

1. Remove starter motor as outlined under "Starter, Replace" in "Electrical" section.
2. Remove camshafts as outlined in "Camshaft, Replace."
3. Remove spark plug from cylinder requiring valve spring replacement.
4. Position piston at TDC in cylinder requiring valve spring replacement.
5. Install flywheel locking tool No. 9102, or equivalent into starter motor opening.
6. Pressurize cylinder with compressed shop air using suitable adapter and air hose assembly.
7. Compress valve spring using suitable valve spring compression tool.
8. With valve spring compressed, remove collets.
9. Slowly release valve spring compression tool.

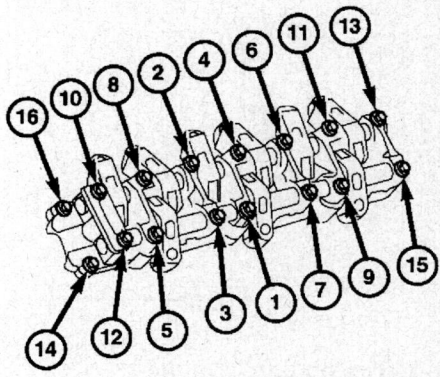

Fig. 6 Camshaft bearing bridge bolt tightening sequence (righthand)

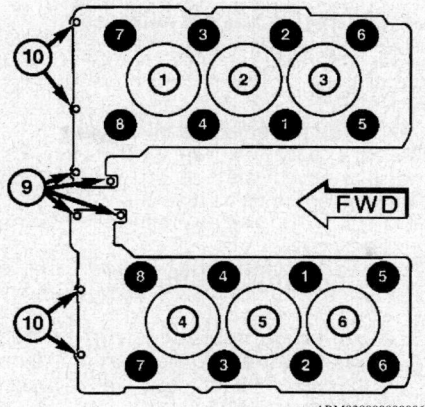

Fig. 7 Cylinder head bolt tightening sequence

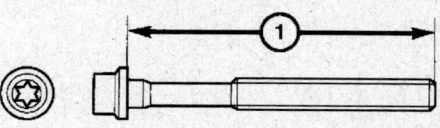

Fig. 8 Cylinder head bolt measurement

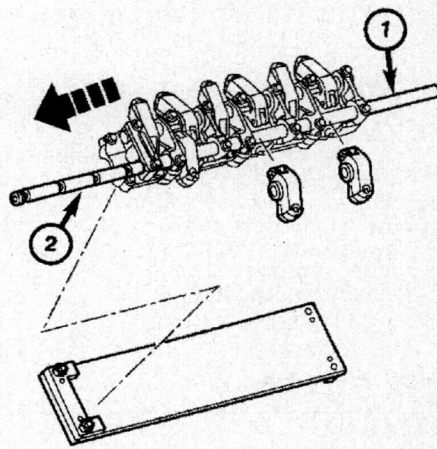

1 16mm Drift
2 Rocker arm shaft

Fig. 9 Rocker arms & shaft removal

10. Remove valve spring retainer, valve spring, valve stem seal and spring seat.
11. Reverse procedure to install. Always replace valve stem seal when replacing valve spring.

CRANKSHAFT DAMPER
REPLACE

1. Drain coolant into suitable container.
2. Remove radiator as outlined in "Radiator, Replace."
3. Remove drive belt as outlined in "Serpentine Drive Belt."
4. Remove starter motor as outlined under "Starter, Replace" in "Electrical" section.
5. Install flywheel locking tool No. 9102, or equivalent, into starter motor opening.
6. Remove crankshaft damper retaining bolt, then the crankshaft damper.
7. Reverse procedure to install. Replace damper retaining bolt if length exceeds 3.07 inch.

FRONT COVER
REPLACE

1. Remove engine as outlined in "Engine, Replace."
2. Separate transmission from engine, then mount engine on suitable engine stand.
3. **On models equipped with manual transmission,** remove clutch pressure plate, clutch disc and flywheel from engine crankshaft.
4. **On models equipped with automatic transmission,** remove drive flexplate from engine crankshaft.
5. **On all models,** remove upper and lower oil pan retaining bolts, then the upper and lower oil pans.
6. Remove drive belt as outlined in "Serpentine Drive Belt."
7. Remove power steering pump and idler pulley as outlined under "Power Steering Pump, Replace" in "Front Suspension & Steering" section.
8. Remove crankshaft damper as outlined in "Crankshaft Damper, Replace."
9. Remove alternator as outlined under "Alternator, Replace" in "Electrical" section.
10. Ensure crankshaft is at 40° ATDC, **Fig. 2.**
11. Remove starter motor as outlined under "Starter, Replace" in "Electrical" section.
12. Remove cylinder heads as outlined in "Cylinder Head, Replace."
13. Remove timing chain tensioner retaining bolt, then tensioner.
14. Remove front timing cover retaining bolts, then front timing chain cover.
15. Reverse procedure to install.

TIMING CHAIN
REPLACE

Removal

1. Remove timing chain cover as outlined in "Front Cover, Replace."
2. Remove oil pump drive chain and tensioner.

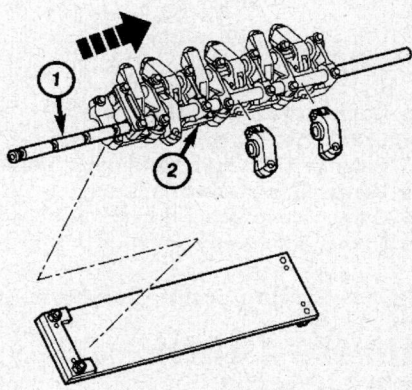

1 16mm Drift
2 Rocker arm shaft

Fig. 10 Rocker arms & shaft installation

3. Remove lefthand and righthand camshaft sprocket retaining bolts.
4. Remove timing chain and camshaft sprockets.
5. Remove timing chain crankshaft sprocket.
6. Clean and inspect all gasket surfaces, chain guides and sprockets for wear or damage replace as required.

Installation

1. Invert engine on engine stand.
2. Install crankshaft sprocket, **Fig. 11.**
3. Ensure crankshaft is at 40° ATDC, **Fig. 2.**
4. Align balance shaft sprocket timing mark with copper teeth on timing chain.
5. Insert camshaft sprockets into timing chain and align camshaft sprocket timing marks with copper teeth on timing chain.
6. Install timing chain with sprockets and route within timing chain guides, **Fig. 12.**
7. Lock camshaft sprockets into position using camshaft locating plate tool No. 9104 and locking pin tool No. 9105, or equivalents, place locating plate tool flush on cylinder head and insert locking pin tool into groove located on camshaft.
8. Install oil pump, oil pump drive chain and oil pump drive chain tensioner.
9. Rotate engine to upright position on engine stand.
10. Install timing chain front cover as outlined in "Front Cover, Replace."
11. Remove camshaft locating plate tool No. 9104 and locking pin tool No. 9105, or equivalents.

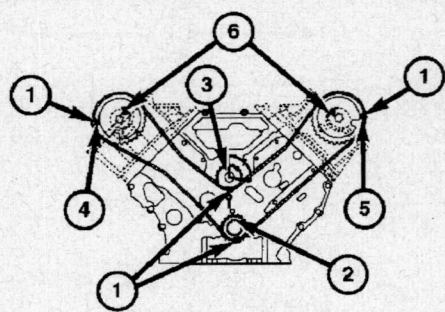

1 Copper teeth of timing chain
2 Crankshaft sprocket
3 Balance shaft sprocket timing mark
4 Camshaft sprocket timing mark
5 Camshaft sprocket timing mark
6 Camshaft sprockets

ARM0300000000080

Fig. 11   Timing chain replacement

TIMING CHAIN TENSIONER
REPLACE

1. Remove alternator as outlined under "Alternator, Replace" in "Electrical," section.
2. Remove timing chain tensioner retaining bolt, then timing chain tensioner.
3. Reverse procedure to install.

CAMSHAFT
REPLACE

Refer to "Cylinder Head, Replace" for camshaft replacement procedure.

MAIN & ROD BEARINGS

1. Tighten main journal cap bolts as follows using sequence, **Fig. 13.**
   a. **Torque** M8 bolts to 15 ft. lbs., then tighten an additional 90°.
   b. **Torque** M10 bolts to 22 ft. lbs., then tighten an additional 90°.
2. Tighten connecting rod bolts in three steps: First step, **torque** bolts to 44 inch lbs.; second step, **torque** bolts to 18 ft. lbs.; third step, tighten bolts an additional 90°.

CRANKSHAFT SEAL
REPLACE

1. Remove crankshaft damper as outlined in "Crankshaft Damper, Replace."
2. Remove crankshaft oil seal using suitable seal removal pry bar or screwdriver.
3. Reverse procedure to install. Lubricate crankshaft seal inner lips using suitable engine oil.

CRANKSHAFT REAR OIL SEAL
REPLACE

Crankshaft rear oil seal cannot be replaced separately. The end cover and seal are assembled at the factory and must be replaced as a set.
1. Remove engine as outlined in "Engine, Replace."
2. Separate transmission from engine, then mount engine on suitable engine stand.
3. **On models equipped with manual transmission,** remove clutch pressure plate, clutch disc and flywheel from engine crankshaft.
4. **On models equipped with automatic transmission,** remove drive flexplate from crankshaft.
5. **On all models,** remove crankshaft end cover retaining bolts, then end cover seal assembly.
6. Reverse procedure to install, noting the following:
   a. Install new end cover and gaskets (without new crankshaft seal installed).
   b. Apply a 2 mm bead of Loctite sealer No. 5203, or equivalent, to areas outlined, **Fig. 14. Components requiring sealer must be installed within 10 minutes after sealer is applied.**
   c. Clean engine block and oil pan sealing surfaces of gasket material.
   d. Ensure circumference of new crankshaft oil seal, sealing lips and crankshaft are oil and grease free.
   e. Position crankshaft seal at right-hand angles to crankshaft to ensure proper seal.
   f. Install new seal into crankshaft end cover using seal installation tool No. 9100, or equivalent.
   g. Measure between edge of end cover and crankshaft oil seal, distance must be approximately .039 inch, around entire circumference.

OIL PAN
REPLACE
Lower

1. Raise and support vehicle.
2. Drain engine oil into suitable container.
3. Remove lower splash shield retaining screws, then splash shield.
4. Remove transmission oil cooler line retaining bolts, then position oil cooler line aside.
5. Remove lower oil pan mounting bolts, then oil pan.
6. Reverse procedure to install.

Upper

1. Remove engine as outlined in "Engine, Replace."
2. Separate transmission from engine, then mount engine on suitable engine stand.
3. **On models equipped with manual**

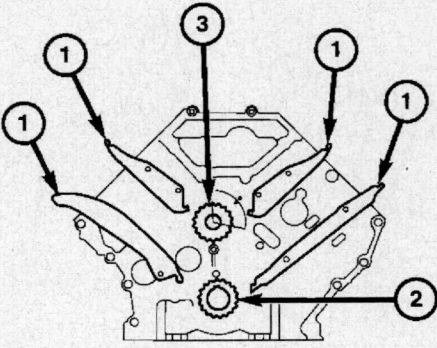

1 Timing chain guides
2 Crankshaft sprocket
3 Balance shaft sprocket timing mark

ARM0300000000081

Fig. 12   Timing chain guide locations

transmission, remove clutch pressure plate, clutch disc and flywheel from engine crankshaft.
4. **On models equipped with automatic transmission,** remove drive flexplate from engine crankshaft.
5. **On all models,** remove upper and lower oil pan retaining bolts, then upper and lower oil pans.
6. Reverse procedure to install.

OIL PUMP
REPLACE

1. Raise and support vehicle.
2. Drain engine oil into suitable container.
3. Remove lower engine splash shield retaining bolts then splash shield.
4. **On models equipped with automatic transmission,** remove transmission fluid cooler line retaining bolt, then position cooler lines aside.
5. **On all models,** remove lower oil pan retaining bolts, then lower oil pan.
6. Remove oil pump retaining bolts.
7. Release oil pump drive chain tensioner.
8. Remove oil pump from drive chain and engine block.
9. Reverse procedure to install, noting the following:
   a. Inspect oil pump check valve operation by pressing and releasing plunger to ensure free movement of plunger.
   b. Fill oil pump (prime) with new suitable engine oil.
   c. Inspect oil pump drive chain for wear or damaged components.
   d. Position oil pump driven sprocket in drive chain, install oil pump, tighten retaining bolts to specification.

OIL PUMP SERVICE

The oil pump is not serviceable and will require replacement should failure occur.

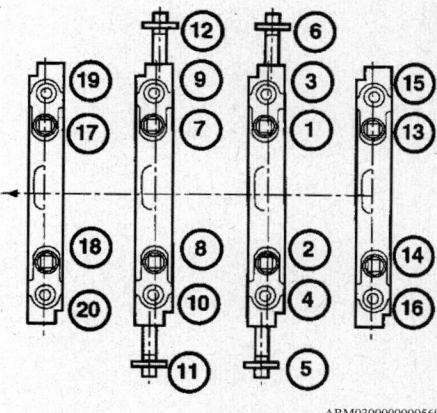

Fig. 13 Main bearing journal tightening sequence

BELT TENSION DATA

This engine is equipped with an automatic belt tensioner. Adjustment is not required.

SERPENTINE DRIVE BELT

For serpentine drive belt routing refer to **Fig. 15.**
1. Pull accessory drive belt tensioner in a counterclockwise direction using suitable pry tool.
2. Lock belt tensioner with a locking pin.
3. Remove drive belt.

COOLING SYSTEM BLEED

1. Close radiator drain hand tight.
2. Attach approximately 48 inches of ¼ inch I.D. clear hose to bleed valve.
3. Route hose away from drive belt, drive pulleys and electrical cooling fan and into a clean container.
4. Open cooling system bleed valve, then attach filling aid funnel tool No. 8195, or equivalent, to pressure bottle filler neck.
5. Pinch overflow hose between coolant bottle chambers.
6. Pour 50/50 mix of suitable coolant and distilled water into large section of filling funnel.
7. Slowly fill until steady stream of coolant flows from bleed valve hose.
8. Close bleed valve and continue filling system to top of funnel.
9. Remove overflow hose clip and allow funnel to drain into overflow chamber.
10. Remove funnel and install coolant pressure bottle cap.
11. Remove bleed valve hose, then start and run engine until it reaches operating temperature.
12. Shut off engine and allow to cool.
13. With engine cold, ensure pressure chamber level is between MIN and MAX marks.

THERMOSTAT
REPLACE

Thermostat and housing are serviced as an assembly.
1. Remove air cleaner housing.
2. Partially drain cooling system into suitable container.
3. Disconnect upper radiator hose at thermostat housing.
4. Remove thermostat housing retaining bolts, then thermostat and housing assembly.
5. Reverse procedure to install.

WATER PUMP
REPLACE

Less Supercharger

1. Remove air cleaner housing.
2. Drain engine coolant into suitable container.
3. Remove radiator as outlined in "Radiator, Replace."
4. Remove drive belt as outlined in "Serpentine Drive Belt."
5. Release belt tensioner locking pin.
6. Remove belt tensioner mounting bolts, then belt tensioner.
7. Disconnect lower radiator hose and coolant bypass hose.
8. Remove water pump drive and idler pulleys.
9. Remove water pump retaining bolts, then water pump and gasket, **Fig. 16.**
10. Reverse procedure to install, noting the following:
    a. Clean gasket surfaces.
    b. Position water pump with new gasket on locating pins.
    c. Ensure water pump retaining bolts are in correct locations, **Fig. 16.**

With Supercharger

1. Remove engine cover.
2. Drain coolant into suitable container.
3. Remove radiator as outlined in "Radiator, Replace."
4. Remove air pump mounting bolts, then air pump assembly.
5. Remove drive belt as outlined in "Serpentine Drive Belt."
6. Remove supercharger idler pulley upper and lower mounting bolts, then idler pulley.
7. Remove belt tensioner mounting bolts, then tensioner.
8. Remove coolant bypass hose.
9. Remove alternator as outlined under "Alternator, Replace."
10. Remove water pump drive and idler pulleys.
11. Remove water pump retaining bolts, then water pump and gasket, **Fig. 16.**
12. Reverse procedure to install.
    a. Clean gasket surfaces.
    b. Position water pump with new gasket on location pins.

RADIATOR
REPLACE

1. Remove radiator cooling fan as out-

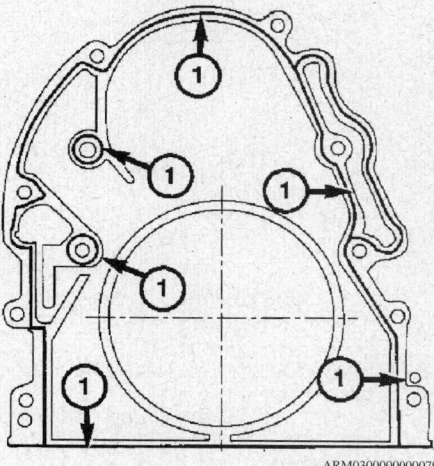

Fig. 14 End cover sealer locations

lined under "Cooling Fans, Replace" in "Cooling Fans" chapter.
2. Drain coolant into suitable container.
3. Remove air cleaner inlet tubes.
4. Disconnect upper, lower and coolant recovery reservoir hoses.
5. **On models equipped with automatic transmission,** disconnect transmission fluid cooler lines, then plug openings to prevent leakage and contamination.
6. **On all models,** remove two radiator hold-down clamps.
7. Tilt radiator forward and remove A/C condenser to radiator retaining bolts.
8. Remove radiator from vehicle.
9. Reverse procedure to install.

FUEL PUMP
REPLACE

1. Relieve fuel pressure as outlined in "Precautions."
2. Raise and support vehicle.
3. Remove under vehicle splash shield retaining screws, then splash shield.
4. Pinch off fuel suction hose and fuel supply hose, using suitable hose clamping pliers.
5. Disconnect fuel suction and supply hoses from fuel pump located on rear differential carrier.
6. Disconnect fuel pump electrical connector and harness at fuel pump.
7. Remove fuel pump to mounting bracket retaining clamp, then fuel pump.
8. Reverse procedure to install.

FUEL FILTER
REPLACE

1. Relieve fuel pressure as outlined in "Precautions."
2. Raise and support vehicle.
3. Remove under vehicle splash shield retaining screws, then splash shield.
4. Remove fuel filter/pressure regulator degassing line.
5. Remove fuel rail supply line at fuel filter/pressure regulator.

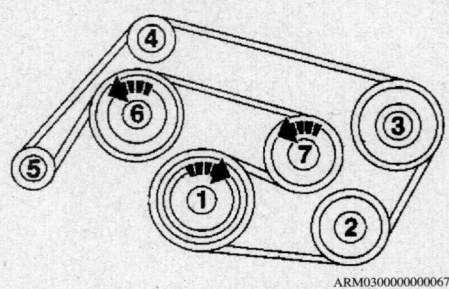

Fig. 15 Serpentine drive belt routing

ARM0300000000067

6. Remove fuel delivery hose at fuel filter/pressure regulator.
7. Remove fuel filter clamp retaining screw, then fuel filter/pressure regulator assembly.
8. Reverse procedure to install.

SUPERCHARGER
REPLACE

1. Drain coolant into suitable container.

2. Remove engine cover and air cleaner.
3. Disconnect throttle body wire harness electrical connector.
4. Disconnect vacuum line at throttle body.
5. Remove righthand and lefthand intake plenums.
6. Remove throttle body mounting bolts, then throttle body.
7. Remove supercharger outlet housing hose clamps, then housing.
8. Disconnect fuel supply line at fuel rail.
9. Disconnect fuel injector harness electrical connector.
10. Remove fuel rail mounting bolts, then fuel rail.
11. Disconnect charge air cooler coolant hoses from righthand front of engine.
12. Disconnect supercharger clutch electrical connector.
13. Remove secondary air injection valves.
14. Remove supercharger to cylinder head mounting bolts, then supercharger. Do not reuse gasket.
15. Reverse procedure to install. Torque

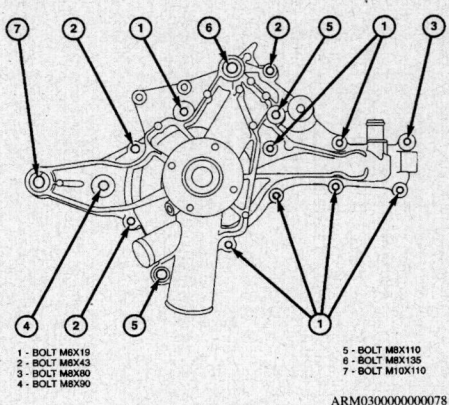

1 - BOLT M6X19
2 - BOLT M6X43
3 - BOLT M8X80
4 - BOLT M8X90

5 - BOLT M8X110
6 - BOLT M8X135
7 - BOLT M10X110

ARM0300000000078

Fig. 16 Water pump bolt identification & locations

supercharger mounting bolts to 17 ft. lbs.

TIGHTENING SPECIFICATIONS

Year	Component	Torque Ft. Lbs.
2004–08	A/C Compressor Bolts	15
	Balance Shaft Bolts	15
	Camshaft Bearing Bridge Bolts	③
	Camshaft Sprocket Bolts	④
	Connecting Rod Cap Bolts	②
	Cooler Lines	84①
	Crankshaft Damper Bolt	148⑥
	Crankshaft Main Bearing Cap bolts	⑤
	Crossmember To Body Bolts	30
	Cylinder Head Bolts	③
	Cylinder Head Cover Bolts	84①
	Engine Lower Mount Bolt	26
	Engine Mount Bolts	22
	Engine Mount To Axle Carrier Bolts	41
	Engine Mount To Transmission Bolts	37
	Engine Support Bolts	15
	Engine Upper Mount Bolt	41
	Exhaust Flange Bolts	15
	Exhaust Manifold Heat Shield Bolts	12
	Exhaust Manifold To Cylinder Head Bolts	26
	Intake Manifold Bolts	15
	Lower Splash Shield Bolts	60①
	Oil Cooler Bolts	96①
	Oil Filter Adapter Center Bolt	52
	Oil Pan Lower Bolts	10
	Oil Pan Upper 6mm Bolts	89①
	Oil Pan Upper 8mm Bolts	15
	Oil Pump Retaining Bolts	21
	Oil Spray Nozzle Bolts	11
	Power Steering Pump Ground Bolt	18
	Power Steering Pump High Pressure Line	33
	Radiator To Body Screws	90①
	Thermostat Housing Bolts	17
	Timing Chain Cover Bolts	15
	Timing Chain Tensioner Bolt	59
	Transmission Mount Bolts	30

① — Inch lbs.
② — Refer to Piston & Rod Assembly for tightening procedure.
③ — Refer to Cylinder Head, Replace for tightening procedure.
④ — Refer to Timing Chain, Replacefor tightening procedure.
⑤ — Refer to Main & Rod Bearings for tightening procedure.
⑥ — Plus 90°.

Rear Axle & Suspension

NOTE: On Air Bag Equipped Models, Refer To "Air Bag System Precautions" Located In The Front Of This Manual For System Disarming & Arming Procedures.

NOTE: Refer To "Computer Relearn Procedures" Located In The Front Of This Manual When Battery Power To The Computer Has Been Interrupted.

INDEX

	Page No.		Page No.		Page No.
Camber Strut, Replace	4-17	Hub & Bearing, Replace	4-17	Spindle Knuckle, Replace	4-17
Coil Spring, Replace	4-17	Lateral Link, Replace	4-18	Tightening Specifications	4-18
Control Arm, Replace	4-17	Propeller Shaft, Replace	4-16	Track Rod, Replace	4-18
Differential Carrier, Replace	4-16	Rear Halfshaft, Replace	4-16	Trailing Link, Replace	4-17
Differential Housing, Replace	4-16	Shock Absorber, Replace	4-17		

REAR HALFSHAFT

REPLACE

1. Raise and support vehicle.
2. Remove rear tire and wheel assemblies.
3. Remove exhaust muffler.
4. Index mark across halfshaft flange and differential flange to ensure proper alignment during installation.
5. Remove halfshaft outer retaining nut, then push halfshaft through wheel hub.
6. Remove halfshaft flange to differential flange retaining bolts, then halfshaft.
7. Reverse procedure to install. Ensure index markings are aligned properly.

DIFFERENTIAL HOUSING

REPLACE

1. Raise and support vehicle.
2. Remove propeller shaft as outlined in "Propeller Shaft, Replace."
3. Drain differential fluid into suitable container.
4. Support differential housing with suitable jack.
5. Separate halfshafts from rear differential as outlined in "Rear Halfshaft, Replace."
6. Remove front and rear differential housing to carrier mounting bolts.
7. Remove differential housing from vehicle.
8. Reverse procedure to install.

DIFFERENTIAL CARRIER

REPLACE

1. Remove righthand and lefthand brake caliper mounting bolts, then position calipers away from suspension components using suitable wire.
2. Remove rear portion of exhaust system including muffler.

3. Remove parking brake cable from brake cable equalizer.
4. Remove righthand and lefthand wheel speed sensor retaining bolts, then sensors.
5. Remove righthand and lefthand halfshaft as outlined in "Rear Halfshaft, Replace."
6. Remove coil spring as outlined in "Coil Spring, Replace."
7. Remove shock absorbers as outlined in "Shock Absorber, Replace."
8. Remove propeller shaft as outlined in "Propeller Shaft, Replace."
9. Remove fuel pump retaining bolts, then position pump away from axle carrier using suitable wire. **Do not remove any fuel lines.**
10. Remove differential housing as outlined in "Differential Housing, Replace."
11. Support differential carrier with suitable transmission jack.
12. Remove differential carrier mounting bolts, then lower carrier assembly from frame.

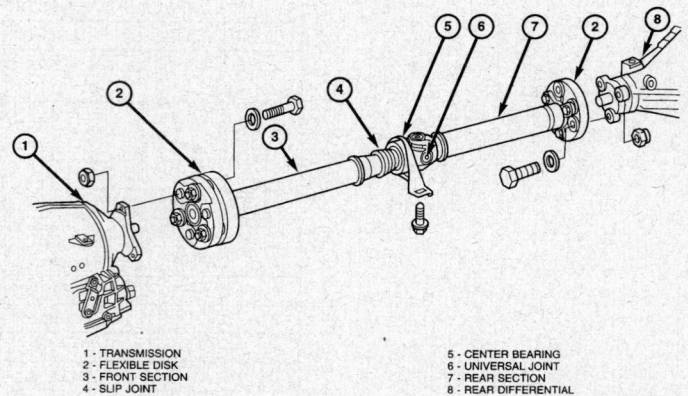

1 - TRANSMISSION
2 - FLEXIBLE DISK
3 - FRONT SECTION
4 - SLIP JOINT
5 - CENTER BEARING
6 - UNIVERSAL JOINT
7 - REAR SECTION
8 - REAR DIFFERENTIAL

ARM030000000580

Fig. 1 Exploded view of propeller shaft

13. Reverse procedure to install. Inspect rear wheel alignment.

PROPELLER SHAFT

REPLACE

When removing or servicing the propeller shaft, never allow shaft to drop or hang from universal joints. Suspend shafts to the underside of the vehicle using suitable wire, **Fig. 1.**

1. Raise and support vehicle.
2. Remove exhaust system.
3. Remove center exhaust heat shield retaining nuts, then heat shield.
4. Remove rear transmission tunnel support bracket bolts, then support bracket.
5. Support transmission using suitable jack stand.
6. Remove transmission mount and transmission crossmember retaining bolts, then crossmember.
7. Index mark across front driveshaft flange to transmission flange, and rear

axle pinion to drive shaft flange to en-sure proper alignment during installation.

8. Remove rear axle pinion to propeller shaft flange retaining bolts, then propeller shaft from pinion flange.
9. Remove front propeller shaft flange to transmission flange retaining bolts, then propeller shaft from transmission flange.
10. Remove center bearing retaining bolts, then propeller shaft from vehicle, **Fig. 1.**
11. Reverse procedure to install. Ensure index markings are aligned properly.

HUB & BEARING
REPLACE

1. Remove disc brake caliper and rotor as outlined in "Disc Brakes" chapter.
2. Remove parking brake shoes as outlined in "Disc Brakes" chapter.
3. Remove rear halfshaft as outlined in "Rear Halfshaft, Replace."
4. Remove snap ring from rear hub assembly.
5. Remove bearing on hub using bearing tool No. 9181, or equivalent.
6. Clamp rear axle halfshaft flange into suitable soft jawed vise.
7. Remove inner bearing race from rear axle halfshaft flange by screwing suitable pair of clamping pliers onto bearing tool No. 9181, or equivalent, then tighten pliers.
8. Place thrust piece with large diameter on rear axle halfshaft flange, then position complete bearing tool No. 9181, or equivalent, over bearing race.
9. Clamp bearing race firmly at upper grooves of clamping pliers, above sleeve of bearing tool No. 9181, or equivalent.
10. Remove inner bearing race from halfshaft using bearing tool No. 9181, or equivalent.
11. Inspect halfshaft flange runout, allowable lateral and radial runout is .001–.018 inch.
12. Reverse procedure to install, noting the following:
    a. Install bearing onto wheel carrier until it touches shoulder of wheel carrier using bearing tool No. 9181, or equivalent.
    b. Install washer, ensure snap ring is seated into wheel carrier retaining groove.
    c. Install halfshaft flange onto rear axle using soft faced mallet.

SPINDLE KNUCKLE
REPLACE

For component descriptions and locations when servicing wheel knuckle, refer to **Fig. 2.**
1. Remove disc brake caliper and rotor as outlined in "Disc Brakes" chapter.
2. Remove parking brake shoes as outlined in "Disc Brakes" chapter.
3. Remove parking brake cable retaining clip at caliper, then cable.

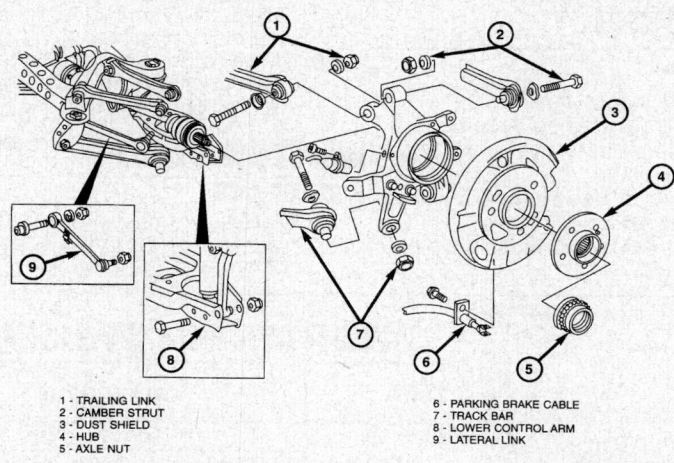

1 - TRAILING LINK
2 - CAMBER STRUT
3 - DUST SHIELD
4 - HUB
5 - AXLE NUT
6 - PARKING BRAKE CABLE
7 - TRACK BAR
8 - LOWER CONTROL ARM
9 - LATERAL LINK

ARM0300000000581

Fig. 2   Exploded view of rear wheel knuckle

4. Remove wheel speed sensor retaining bolt, then wheel speed sensor.
5. Remove halfshaft as outlined in "Rear Halfshaft, Replace."
6. Remove disc brake dust shield retaining bolts, then dust shield.
7. Remove camber strut, trailing link and lateral link bolts and nuts.
8. Remove track rod as outlined in "Track Rod, Replace."
9. Remove lower control arm as outlined in "Control Arm, Replace."
10. Remove wheel knuckle from vehicle.
11. Reverse procedure to install. Ensure rear axle halfshaft is horizontal before tightening bolts and nuts.

SHOCK ABSORBER
REPLACE

Vehicle must be standing with weight on all four wheels before removing shock absorber mounting hardware.
1. Remove upper shock absorber retaining nut and hardware.
2. Raise and support vehicle.
3. Remove lower control arm plastic protective cover retaining bolt, then protective cover.
4. Remove lower shock absorber to control arm mounting bolt and nut.
5. Remove shock absorber from lower control arm.
6. Reverse procedure to install.

COIL SPRING
REPLACE

1. Raise and support vehicle.
2. Remove tire and wheel assembly.
3. Remove lower control arm plastic shield retaining bolts, then plastic shield.
4. Remove shock absorber to control arm retaining bolts.
5. Raise control arm until axle shaft is in a horizontal position, using suitable floor jack.
6. Compress coil spring, using coil spring compressor tool No. 9152 and compressor plate tool No. 9150, or equivalents.

7. Remove control arm to frame retaining bolts.
8. Slowly lower control arm, then remove floor jack.
9. Swing control arm downward to release spring form mounting tabs.
10. Remove coil spring from vehicle.
11. Reverse procedure to install.

CONTROL ARM
REPLACE

1. Raise and support vehicle.
2. Remove tire and wheel assembly.
3. Remove coil spring as outlined in "Coil Spring, Replace."
4. Remove shock absorber as outlined in "Shock Absorber, Replace."
5. Remove stabilizer bar link to lower control arm retaining bolt, then stabilizer bar link.
6. Remove lower control arm to wheel carrier bolts, then lower control arm.
7. Reverse procedure to install.

CAMBER STRUT
REPLACE

1. Raise and support vehicle.
2. Remove tire and wheel assembly.
3. Remove camber strut to axle carrier retaining bolt.
4. Remove outer camber strut to wheel carrier retaining bolt.
5. Remove camber strut.
6. Reverse procedure to install. Vehicle must have full weight on four wheels before tightening retaining bolts.

TRAILING LINK
REPLACE

1. Raise and support vehicle.
2. Remove tire and wheel assembly.
3. Remove inner and outer trailing link to wheel carrier retaining bolts.
4. Remove trailing link from vehicle.
5. Reverse procedure to install. Vehicle must have full weight on four wheels before tightening retaining bolts.

CROSSFIRE

TRACK ROD

REPLACE

1. Raise and support vehicle.
2. Remove tire and wheel assembly.
3. Remove inner track bar to axle carrier retaining bolt.
4. Remove outer track bar wheel carrier retaining bolt.
5. Remove track bar using suitable plas-

tic headed hammer to loosen rubber mounts from guides.
6. Reverse procedure to install. Vehicle must have full weight on four wheels before tightening retaining bolts.

LATERAL LINK

REPLACE

1. Raise and support vehicle.
2. Remove tire and wheel assembly.

3. Remove lateral link to axle carrier retaining bolt.
4. Remove lateral link ball joint stud to wheel carrier retaining nut.
5. Remove lateral link ball joint stud from carrier using ball joint removal tool No. 9168, or equivalent.
6. Remove lateral link from vehicle.
7. Reverse procedure to install. Axle shaft must be horizontal before tightening retaining bolts.

TIGHTENING SPECIFICATIONS

Year	Component	Torque Ft. Lbs.
2004–08	Camber Strut Bolts	52
	Differential Housing To Carrier Bolt (Front)	82
	Differential Housing To Carrier Bolt (Rear)	33
	Differential Housing To Carrier Nut (Center)	66
	Halfshaft Connecting Flange Bolts	52
	Halfshaft Outer Nut	164
	Heat Shield Nuts	89①
	Lateral Link To Axle Carrier Bolt	52
	Lateral Link To Wheel Carrier Bolt	22
	Lower Control Arm To Axle Carrier Bolt	52
	Lower Control Arm To Wheel Carrier Bolt	88
	Pinion Shaft Nut	133
	Propeller Shaft Center Bearing Support Bolts	33
	Propeller Shaft To Axle Flange Bolts	44
	Propeller Shaft To Transmission Flange Bolts	44
	Shock Absorber (Lower) Bolt	41
	Shock Absorber (Upper) Nut	13
	Stabilizer Bar Clamp Bolts	15
	Stabilizer Bar To Stabilizer Link Nut	15
	Stabilizer Link To Stabilizer Bar Bolt	22
	Track Bar Bolts	52
	Trailing Arm Bolts	52
	Transmission Crossmember Bolts	33
	Transmission Mount Bolts	33
	Transmission Tunnel Bolts	15

① — Inch lbs.

Front Suspension & Steering

NOTE: On Air Bag Equipped Models, Refer To "Air Bag System Precautions" Located In The Front Of This Manual For System Disarming & Arming Procedures.

NOTE: Refer To "Computer Relearn Procedures" Located In The Front Of This Manual When Battery Power To The Computer Has Been Interrupted.

INDEX

	Page No.		Page No.		Page No.
Ball Joint, Replace	4-19	Drag Link, Replace	4-21	Battery Ground Cable	4-19
Lower	4-19	Hub & Bearing, Replace	4-19	Shock Absorber, Replace	4-20
Upper	4-19	Pitman Arm, Replace	4-20	Stabilizer Bar, Replace	4-20
Ball Joint Inspection	4-19	Power Steering Gear, Replace	4-21	Steering Knuckle, Replace	4-20
Coil Spring, Replace	4-19	Power Steering Pump, Replace	4-21	Tie Rod End, Replace	4-20
Control Arm, Replace	4-20	Power Steering System Bleed	4-21	Tightening Specifications	4-22
Lower	4-20	Precautions	4-19		
Upper	4-20	Air Bag Systems	4-19		

PRECAUTIONS
Air Bag Systems

Refer to "Air Bag System Precautions" in the front of this manual for system disarming and arming procedures.

Battery Ground Cable

Prior to service, disconnect battery ground cable and isolate as required.

HUB & BEARING
REPLACE

1. Raise and support vehicle.
2. Remove tire and wheel assembly.
3. Remove brake caliper retaining bolts, then suspend caliper aside using suitable wire.
4. Remove bearing hub center dust cap, **Fig. 1.**
5. Remove brake rotor retaining bolt, then brake rotor.
6. Remove bearing hub retaining nut, then hub and tapered roller bearing from spindle.
7. Reverse procedure to install, then adjust wheel bearing end play as follows:
   a. Ensure brake pads are pushed back and not in contact with brake rotor.
   b. Loosen hub nut until a slight amount of endplay is achieved.
   c. Attach a dial indicator as outlined, **Fig. 2.**
   d. Adjust wheel bearing endplay by turning hub nut in stages while pushing and puling firmly on brake rotor.
   e. Dial indicator should show endplay of .004–.008 inch.

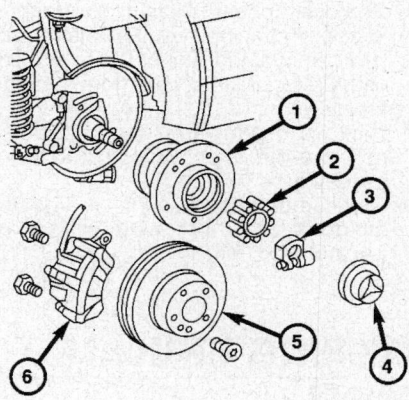

1 Front wheel hub
2 Tapered roller bearing
3 Hub nut and bolt
4 Dust cap
5 Brake rotor
6 Brake caliper

ARM0300000000575

Fig. 1   Hub & bearing replacement

BALL JOINT INSPECTION

The upper ball joint is serviced with the upper control arm.
1. Raise and support front of vehicle.
2. Grasp tire at top and bottom, then apply in and out force on wheel and tire assembly.
3. While applying force to tire, look for movement between upper or lower ball joint and control arm.
4. If there is any movement in upper or lower ball joints, replace ball joint as outlined in "Ball Joint, Replace."

BALL JOINT
REPLACE

Lower

1. Raise and support vehicle.
2. Remove tire and wheel assembly.
3. Remove front brake caliper retaining bolts, then position caliper aside using suitable wire to suspend caliper.
4. Remove one brake rotor to hub retaining bolt, then brake rotor.
5. Remove three retaining bolts from front hub dust shield, then dust shield.
6. Remove coil spring as outlined in "Coil Spring, Replace."
7. Remove ball joint retaining nuts, then using ball joint removal tool No. 9168, or equivalent, press ball joint from lower control arm and steering knuckle mountings.
8. Reverse procedure to install.

Upper

The upper ball joint is serviced with the upper control arm.

COIL SPRING
REPLACE

1. Remove tire and wheel assembly.
2. Remove shock absorber as outlined in "Shock Absorber, Replace."
3. Support lower control arm with suitable floor jack.
4. Raise lower control arm until arm is almost level.
5. Compress front spring carefully using spring compressor tools No. 9151 and 9152, or equivalent.

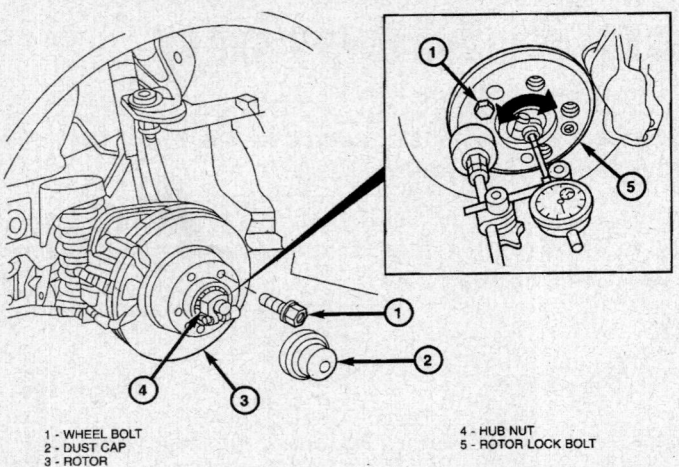

1 - WHEEL BOLT
2 - DUST CAP
3 - ROTOR
4 - HUB NUT
5 - ROTOR LOCK BOLT

ARM0300000000576

Fig. 2   Wheel bearing endplay adjustment

1 - UPPER CONTROL ARM
2 - TIE ROD END
3 - WHEEL SPEED SENSOR
4 - UPPER BALL JOINT NUT
5 - DUST SHIELD BOLT
6 - ROTOR LOCK BOLT
7 - ROTOR
8 - DUST CAP
9 - HUB NUT
10 - BEARING
11 - HUB
12 - DUST SHIELD
13 - TIE ROD END NUT
14 - LOWER BALL JOINT NUT
15 - CALIPER BOLT
16 - LOWER BALL JOINT

ARM0300000000574

Fig. 3   Steering knuckle replacement

6. Remove sway bar retaining clamp nuts, then position sway bar aside.
7. Remove nuts from lower control arm retaining nuts, then lower control arm while holding coil spring.
8. Slowly lower coil spring from vehicle.
9. Reverse procedure to install.

SHOCK ABSORBER
REPLACE

Vehicle must be standing with weight on all four wheels before removing shock absorber upper mounting hardware.
1. Remove upper shock absorber retaining nut, washer and rubber mount.
2. Raise and support vehicle.
3. Remove lower shock absorber to control arm mounting bolt and nut.
4. Remove shock absorber from lower control arm, then the shock absorber by pulling downward out form vehicle.
5. Remove mounting hardware from shock absorber.
6. Reverse procedure to install.

CONTROL ARM
REPLACE
Lower

Refer to "Coil Spring, Replace" for lower control arm replacement procedure.

Upper

The shock absorber must remain installed to remove the upper control arm.
1. Remove air cleaner housing to access upper control arm retaining bolt and nut located inside engine compartment.
2. Raise and support vehicle.
3. Remove tire and wheel assembly, then support lower control arm with suitable floor jack.
4. Raise floor jack to relieve any tension on brake lines or speed sensor electrical connection.

5. Secure steering knuckle to shock absorber using suitable wire.
6. Remove upper ball joint to steering knuckle retaining nut, then using ball joint removal tool No. 9168, or equivalent, press ball joint stud from steering knuckle.
7. Remove control arm upper retaining bolt and nut, then upper control arm assembly.
8. Reverse procedure to install. **Tighten all bolts and nuts with vehicle at normal ride height.**

STEERING KNUCKLE
REPLACE

The shock absorber must remain installed when removing the steering knuckle.
1. Raise and support vehicle.
2. Remove hub and bearing assembly as outlined in "Hub & Bearing, Replace."
3. Remove three disc brake dust shield hex bolts, then dust shield, **Fig. 3.**
4. Remove Wheel Speed Sensor (WSS) retaining bolt and pull sensor straight out of steering knuckle.
5. Remove tie rod end to steering knuckle retaining nut, then using tie rod end removal tool No. C-3894–A, or equivalent, press tie rod end stud from steering knuckle.
6. Remove lower ball joint to steering knuckle stud retaining nut, then using ball joint removal tool No. 9168, or equivalent, press ball joint stud from steering knuckle.
7. Remove upper ball joint to steering knuckle stud retaining nut, then using ball joint removal tool No. 9168, or equivalent, push upper ball joint stud from steering knuckle.
8. Remove steering knuckle.
9. Reverse procedure to install.

STABILIZER BAR
REPLACE

1. Remove righthand and lefthand stabilizer bar retaining nuts and clamps from lower control arms.
2. Remove righthand and lefthand stabilizer bar retaining nuts and clamps from front mounting brackets.
3. Remove stabilizer bar from vehicle.
4. Reverse procedure to install.

TIE ROD END
REPLACE

1. Raise and support vehicle, then remove tire and wheel assembly.
2. Loosen tie rod end locknut.
3. Remove outer tie rod to steering knuckle retaining nut.
4. Remove tie rod end from steering knuckle using tie rod end removal tool No. C-3894-A, or equivalent.
5. Remove tie rod end from drag link.
6. Reverse procedure to install. Inspect toe setting prior to tightening adjustment sleeve locknut.

PITMAN ARM
REPLACE

1. Raise and support vehicle.
2. Remove drag link to pitman arm retaining nut.
3. Remove drag link from pitman arm using ball joint removal tool No. 9168, or equivalent.
4. Measure and record distance between pitman arm and steering gear using suitable caliper gauge, **Fig. 4.**
5. Remove snap ring retainer from pitman arm shaft.
6. Remove pitman arm from gear box using suitable pitman arm removal tool.
7. Reverse procedure to install. Ensure distance between pitman arm and steering gear is same as recorded.

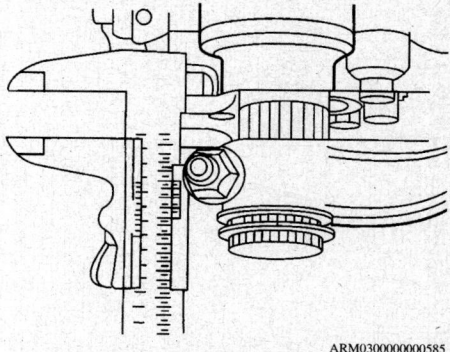

Fig. 4 Pitman arm measurement

DRAG LINK

REPLACE

1. Raise and support vehicle.
2. Remove steering damper to drag link bolt and nut, then position damper aside.
3. Remove pitman arm and idler arm to drag link retaining nuts.
4. Remove pitman arm and idler arm from drag link using ball joint removal tool No. 9168, or equivalent.
5. Remove tie rod end as outlined in "Tie Rod End, Replace."
6. Remove drag link.
7. Reverse procedure to install.

POWER STEERING GEAR

REPLACE

Refer to **Fig. 5** when replacing steering gear.

1. Lock steering wheel in straight ahead position. **Ensure steering wheel does not move when replacing steering gear or damage to clock spring will occur.**
2. Drain power steering fluid into suitable container.
3. Raise and support vehicle.
4. Remove drag link as outlined in "Drag Link, Replace."
5. Remove outer tie rod end as outlined in "Tie Rod End, Replace."
6. Remove pitman arm as outlined in "Pitman Arm, Replace."
7. Remove lefthand front cross brace, **Fig. 6.**
8. Remove steering fluid supply and return lines at steering gear.
9. Remove steering gear to steering shaft coupler pinch bolt.
10. Remove steering shaft from steering gear.
11. Remove engine ground strap from vehicle frame.
12. Remove lefthand and rigthand engine mount retaining bolts.
13. Raise engine approximately two inch-

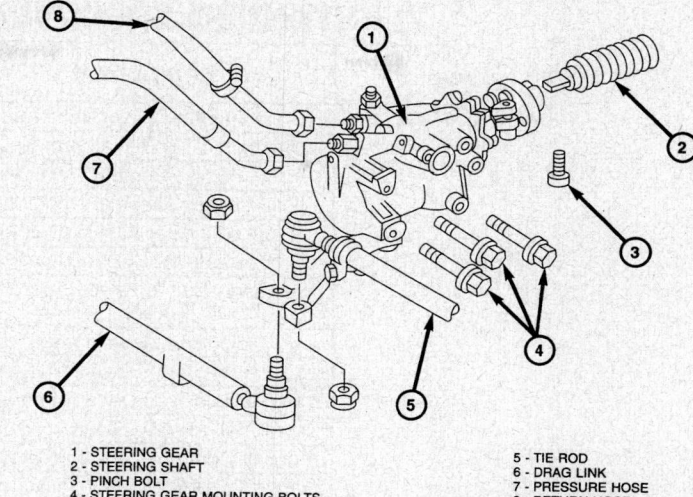

1 - STEERING GEAR
2 - STEERING SHAFT
3 - PINCH BOLT
4 - STEERING GEAR MOUNTING BOLTS
5 - TIE ROD
6 - DRAG LINK
7 - PRESSURE HOSE
8 - RETURN HOSE

Fig. 5 Exploded view of steering gear

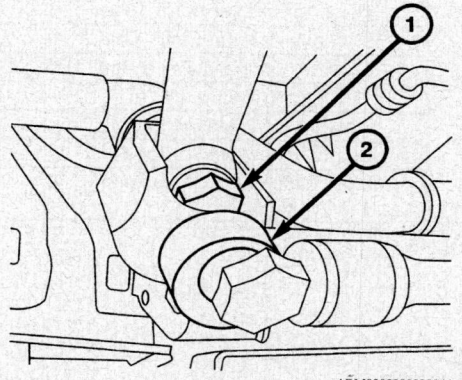

Fig. 6 Lefthand front cross brace replace

es using suitable transmission jack placed under lefthand side of engine.
14. Remove steering gear mounting bolts, carefully slide steering shaft from steering gear.
15. Remove steering gear from vehicle.
16. Reverse procedure to install, noting the following:
  a. Ensure steering gear is in center position, by aligning steering shaft and housing cover alignment marks.**Do not use force or damage will occur to lower steering shaft collapsible tubing.**
  b. Tighten mounting bolts and fluid lines.

POWER STEERING PUMP

REPLACE

1. Drain power steering fluid into suitable container.

2. Remove reservoir supply and return hoses.
3. Remove serpentine drive belt as outlined in "Engine" section.
4. Remove power steering pump to engine mounting bolts, then steering pump.
5. Remove steering fluid reservoir C-type retaining clip.
6. Remove steering fluid reservoir.
7. Reverse procedure to install.

POWER STEERING SYSTEM BLEED

1. Fill fluid reservoir to correct level, allow fluid to settle for at least two minutes.
2. Start and allow engine to run for a few seconds, then turn engine off.
3. When fluid level remains constant after running engine, raise front wheels off ground.
4. Turn steering wheel righthand and left, lightly contacting wheel stops at least 20 times.
5. Add steering fluid if required.
6. Lower vehicle.
7. Start engine and turn steering wheel from lock to lock 2–3 times.
8. Inspect steering fluid and add if required.
9. If fluid is foamy or looks milky, allow vehicle to stand a few minutes, then repeat procedure.

TIGHTENING SPECIFICATIONS

Year	Component	Torque Ft. Lbs.
2004–08	Drag Link To Idler Arm Nut	37
	Drag Link To Pitman Arm Nut	37
	Front Shock Absorber Lower Nut	41
	Front Shock Absorber Upper Nut	13
	Front Sway Bar Bushing Nut M8	15
	Front Sway Bar Bushing Nut M10	30
	Front Sway Bar To Lower Control Arm Nut	15
	Idler Arm Mounting Bolt	37
	Idler Arm Pinch Bolt	41
	Lower Ball Joint To Lower Control Arm	77
	Lower Ball Joint To Steering Knuckle	103
	Lower Control Arm To Frame Nut	88
	Outer Tie Rod To Steering Knuckle Nut	37
	Power Steering Fluid Pressure Hose	30
	Power Steering Pump Mounting	15
	Power Steering Return Tube	30
	Steering Column Pinch Bolt	22
	Steering Coupling Pinch Bolt	22
	Steering Gear Locknut	44
	Steering Gear Mounting Bolts	44
	Upper Control Arm To Body Nut	50
	Upper Control Arm To Steering Knuckle Bolt	33

Wheel Alignment

INDEX

	Page No.			Page No.			Page No.
Front Wheel Alignment	4-23		Preliminary Inspection	4-23		Toe	4-23
Camber	4-23		Rear Wheel Alignment	4-23		Wheel Alignment	
Caster	4-23		Camber	4-23		Specifications	4-2
Toe	4-23		Caster	4-23			

PRELIMINARY INSPECTION

Before any attempt is made to change or correct wheel alignment, the following inspections and required corrections must be made.
1. Ensure tire pressure is at recommended pressure, all tires should be same size and in good condition and have approximately same wear.
2. Inspect both front tire and wheel assemblies for radial runout.
3. Inspect lower ball joint and steering linkage for looseness.
4. Inspect for broken or damaged front and rear springs.
5. Just prior to each alignment reading, the vehicle should be bounced (rear first, then front) by grasping bumper at center and bouncing each end of vehicle an equal number of times. Always release bumpers at bottom of down cycle.

FRONT WHEEL ALIGNMENT

Caster

1. Prepare vehicle as outlined in "Preliminary Inspection."
2. Compress front coil spring as outlined in "Front Suspension & Steering" section.
3. Install adjusting bolt, **Fig. 1,** then hand tighten nut.
4. Release coil spring as outlined in "Front Suspension & Steering" section.
5. Lower vehicle, then bounce vehicle several times to settle suspension.
6. Adjust caster to specifications by turning adjusting bolt using suitable wrench.
7. **Torque** adjusting bolt and nut to 88 ft. lbs., counter bolt movement using suitable hex wrench.

Camber

1. Prepare vehicle as outlined in "Preliminary Inspection."
2. Compress front coil spring as outlined in "Front Suspension & Steering" section.
3. Install adjusting bolt, **Fig. 2,** then hand tighten nut.
4. Release coil spring as outlined in "Front Suspension & Steering" section.
5. Lower vehicle, then bounced vehicle several times to settle suspension.
6. Adjust camber to specifications by turning adjusting bolt using suitable wrench.
7. **Torque** adjusting bolt and nut to 88 ft. lbs., counter bolt movement using suitable hex wrench.

Toe

The steering wheel is in the center position when the separating joint of the steering coupler and the notch on the steering gear are aligned above each other. If required offset the steering wheel by one tooth maximum.
1. Prepare vehicle as outlined in "Preliminary Inspection."
2. Ensure steering wheel is in center position, then hold with steering wheel clamp.
3. Loosen tie rod adjustment sleeve locknut.
4. Rotate adjustment sleeve to align toe to specifications. When setting toe, maximum threads exposed on tie rod can not exceed .78 inch (20mm).
5. **Torque** adjustment locknut to 37 ft. lbs.

REAR WHEEL ALIGNMENT

Caster

Rear axle caster is not adjustable. If caster is not within specifications, inspect rear suspension components for damage or wear as outlined in "Preliminary Inspection."

Camber

Rear axle camber is not adjustable. If caster is not within specifications, inspect rear suspension components for damage or wear as outlined in "Preliminary Inspection."

Toe

1. Prepare vehicle as outlined in "Preliminary Inspection."
2. Adjust toe to specification using left-hand and righthand tie rod to carrier mounting cam bolt, **Fig. 3.**

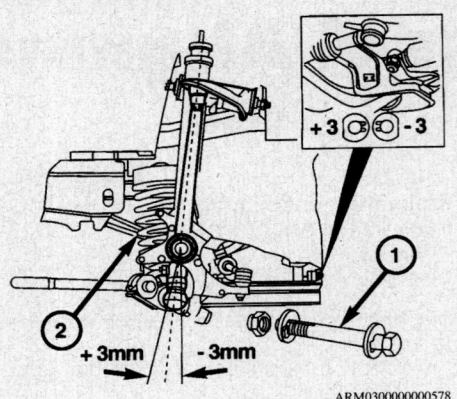

Fig. 1 Caster repair bolt installation

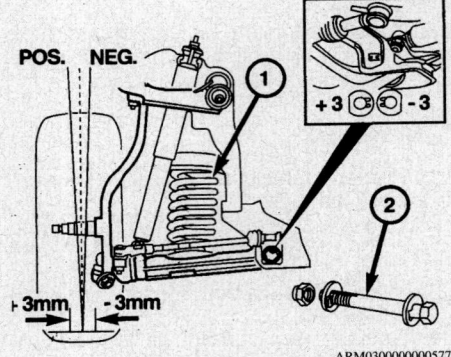

Fig. 2 Camber repair bolt installation

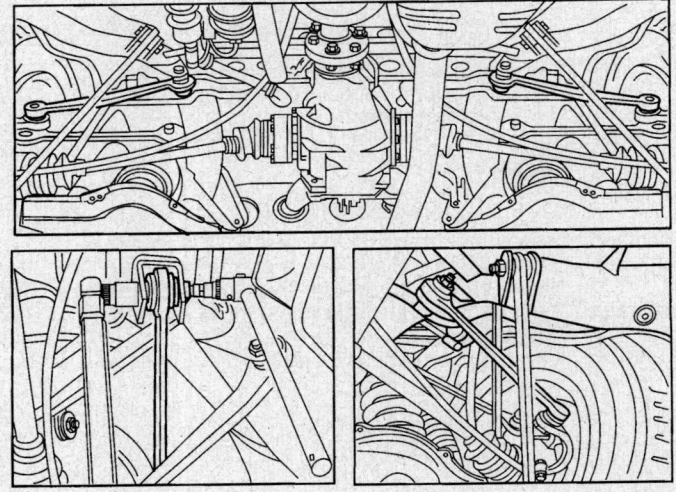

Fig. 3 Rear axle toe adjustment

NEON

NOTE: Refer To The Rear Of This Manual For Manufacturer's Special Service Tool Supplies.

INDEX OF SERVICE OPERATIONS

Page No.

**AIR BAG SYSTEM
PRECAUTIONS** 0-18
BRAKES
   Anti-Lock Brakes (Volume 2).. 6-1
   Disc Brakes.................... 14-1
   Drum Brakes 15-1
   Hydraulic Brake Systems 16-1
   Power Brake Units 17-1
**COMPUTER RELEARN
PROCEDURE** 0-31
ELECTRICAL
   Air Bag System (Volume 2) ... 4-1
   Air Conditioning 8-1
   Alternator, Replace 5-4
   Alternators.................... 11-1
   Blower Motor, Replace........ 5-6
   Clutch Start Switch, Replace.. 5-5
   Coil Pack, Replace 5-5
   Cooling Fans 9-1
   Cruise Control (Volume 2) ... 2-1
   Dash Gauges (Volume 2) 1-1
   Dash Panel Service
   (Volume 2) 5-1
   Dimmer Switch, Replace...... 5-5
   Evaporator Core, Replace 5-7
   Fuel Pump Relay Location 5-4
   Fuse Panel Location 5-4
   Headlamp Switch, Replace ... 5-5
   Heater Core, Replace......... 5-6
   Ignition Lock, Replace 5-5
   Ignition Switch, Replace 5-5
   Instrument Cluster, Replace... 5-5
   Multi-Function Switch,
   Replace 5-5
   Passive Restraint Systems
   (Volume 2) 4-1
   Precautions................... 5-4
   Radio, Replace 5-5
   Relay Center Location 5-4
   Starter, Replace 5-4
   Speed Controls (Volume 2) ... 2-1
   Starter Motors 10-1
   Steering Columns............. 12-1
   Steering Wheel, Replace...... 5-5
   Stop Light Switch, Replace ... 5-5
   Turn Signal Switch, Replace .. 5-5
   Wiper Motor, Replace......... 5-5
   Wiper Switch, Replace 5-6
   Wiper Systems (Volume 2).... 3-1
**ELECTRICAL SYMBOL
IDENTIFICATION** 0-63
FRONT DRIVE AXLES 18-1
**FRONT SUSPENSION &
STEERING**
   Ball Joint, Replace 5-31
   Ball Joint Inspection 5-31
   Control Arm, Replace 5-32
   Description 5-30
   Hub & Bearing, Replace 5-30
   Hub & Bearing Service....... 5-30
   Manual Steering Gear,
   Replace 5-33
   Power Steering 13-1
   Power Steering Gear,

Page No.

   Replace 5-32
   Power Steering Pump,
   Replace 5-33
   Steering Columns............ 12-1
   Steering Knuckle, Replace 5-32
   Strut, Replace 5-31
   Strut Service................. 5-32
   Tightening Specifications 5-34
**NON-STANDARD TIRE &
WHEEL SIZE
ADJUSTMENT TO RIDE
HEIGHT SPECIFICATIONS
& TIRE SIZE CHART** 0-61
REAR SUSPENSION
   Description 5-26
   Hub & Bearing, Replace 5-26
   Lateral Link, Replace 5-27
   Roll Bar, Replace 5-27
   Spindle Knuckle, Replace 5-26
   Strut, Replace 5-26
   Strut Service................. 5-27
   Tension Strut, Replace........ 5-27
   Tightening Specifications 5-29
**SERVICE REMINDER &
WARNING LAMP RESET
PROCEDURES** 0-34
SPECIFICATIONS
   Fluid Capacities & Cooling
   System Data................. 5-3
   Front Wheel Alignment
   Specifications................ 5-2
   General Engine
   Specifications................ 5-2
   Lubricant Data............... 5-3
   Rear Wheel Alignment
   Specifications................ 5-3
   Tune Up Specifications 5-2
   Vehicle Ride Height
   Specifications................ 5-3
**VEHICLE
IDENTIFICATION** 0-1
VEHICLE LIFT POINTS....... 0-51
**VEHICLE MAINTENANCE
SCHEDULES** 0-73
WHEEL ALIGNMENT
   Front Wheel Alignment........ 5-35
   Preliminary Inspection 5-35
   Rear Wheel Alignment 5-35
   Wheel Alignment
   Specifications................ 5-2
**WIRE COLOR CODE
IDENTIFICATION** 0-63
2.0L ENGINE
   Belt Tension Data............. 5-12
   Camshaft, Replace 5-10
   Camshaft Lobe Lift
   Specifications................ 5-10
   Compression Pressure........ 5-8
   Cooling System Bleed 5-12
   Crankshaft Rear Oil Seal,
   Replace 5-11
   Crankshaft Seal, Replace 5-11
   Cylinder Head, Replace 5-9

Page No.

   Engine Rebuilding
   Specifications................ 21-1
   Engine, Replace 5-8
   Engine Mount, Replace 5-8
   Exhaust Manifold, Replace.... 5-9
   Front Cover, Replace 5-10
   Fuel Filter, Replace 5-13
   Fuel Pump, Replace 5-13
   Intake Manifold, Replace...... 5-9
   Main & Rod Bearings 5-11
   Oil Pan, Replace............. 5-11
   Oil Pump, Replace 5-11
   Oil Pump Service 5-12
   Piston & Rod Assembly 5-11
   Precautions.................. 5-8
   Radiator, Replace 5-13
   Rocker Arms 5-10
   Serpentine Drive Belt 5-12
   Technical Service Bulletins.... 5-13
   Thermostat, Replace......... 5-12
   Tightening Specifications...... 5-15
   Timing Belt, Replace 5-10
   Valve Arrangement 5-10
   Valve Clearance
   Specifications................ 5-10
   Valve Cover, Replace........ 5-9
   Water Pump, Replace 5-12
2.4L ENGINE
   Accessory Drive Belts,
   Replace 5-22
   Balance Shaft, Replace 5-20
   Balance Shaft Carrier,
   Replace 5-21
   Camshaft, Replace 5-20
   Compression Pressure........ 5-16
   Cooling System Bleed 5-22
   Crankshaft Damper, Replace.. 5-19
   Crankshaft Rear Oil Seal,
   Replace 5-21
   Cylinder Head, Replace....... 5-18
   Cylinder Head Cover,
   Replace 5-19
   Engine Rebuilding
   Specifications................ 21-1
   Engine, Replace 5-17
   Engine Mount, Replace 5-16
   Exhaust Manifold, Replace.... 5-18
   Front Cover, Replace 5-19
   Fuel Pump, Replace 5-23
   Hydraulic Lash Adjusters,
   Replace 5-19
   Intake Manifold, Replace...... 5-18
   Main & Rod Bearings 5-21
   Oil Pan, Replace............. 5-22
   Oil Pump, Replace 5-22
   Piston & Rod Assembly 5-21
   Precautions.................. 5-16
   Radiator, Replace............ 5-23
   Rocker Arms, Replace 5-19
   Structural Collar, Replace 5-17
   Thermostat, Replace......... 5-23
   Tightening Specifications...... 5-25
   Timing Belt, Replace 5-19
   Timing Belt Rear Cover,
   Replace 5-20

NEON

	Page No.		Page No.		Page No.
Turbocharger, Replace	5-24	Valve Adjustment	5-19	Water Pump, Replace	5-23

Specifications

GENERAL ENGINE SPECIFICATIONS

Engine	Engine VIN Code[1]	Fuel System	Bore & Stroke, Inches	Compression Ratio	Net HP @ RPM	Maximum Torque, Ft. Lbs. @ RPM	Normal Oil Pressure, psi	
							Curb Idle	3000 RPM
2.0L SOHC	C	SMPI	3.45 X 3.27	9.8	132 @ 5600	130 @ 4600	4	25–80
2.0L SOHC	F	SMPI	3.45 X 3.27	9.8	150 @ 6500	135 @ 4400	4	25–80
2.4L DOHC	S	SMPI	3.45 X 3.98	8.1	220 @ 5100	245 @ 4400	4	25–80

DOHC — Dual Overhead Cam
SMPI — Sequential Multi-Port Fuel Injection

SOHC — Single Overhead Cam

[1] — Eighth digit of VIN denotes engine code.

TUNE UP SPECIFICATIONS

Engine	Spark Plug Gap, Inch	Ignition Timing		Curb Idle Speed	Fuel Pump Pressure, psi	Valve Clearance, Inch
		Firing Order [2]	°BTDC			
2.0L	.035	1-3-4-2	[1]	550–1300	49–50	[3]
2.4L	.050	1-3-4-2	[1]	—	—	[3]

BTDC — Before Top Dead Center
[1] — Direct Ignition System (DIS); not adjustable.

[2] — Refer to **Fig. A** for spark plug wire connections.
[3] — Equipped w/non-adjustable hydraulic lash adjusters.

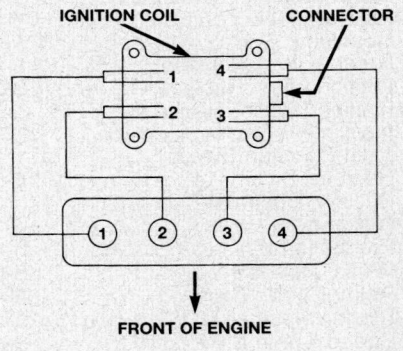

Fig. A

CR1139500468000A

FRONT WHEEL ALIGNMENT SPECIFICATIONS

Year	Camber, Degrees[1]		Caster, Degrees[1]		Toe In, Degrees		Ball Joint Wear
	Limits	Desired	Limits	Desired	Limits	Desired	
All	–.4 to +.4	0	+1.6 to +3.6[2]	+2.6	–.1 to +.3	+.1	[3]

[1] — Reference angle only; not adjustable.

[2] — Side to side differential not to exceed .1°.

[3] — Refer to Ball Joint Inspection in Front Suspension & Steering.

REAR WHEEL ALIGNMENT SPECIFICATIONS

Year	Camber Angle, Degrees①		Total Toe, Degrees①		Thrust Angle, Degrees①
	Limits	Desired	Limits	Desired	
All	−.65 to +.15	−.25	−.10 to +.50	+.30	−.10 to +.10

① — Reference angle only. Non-adjustable.

VEHICLE RIDE HEIGHT SPECIFICATIONS

Year	Body Style	Manufacturer's Original Tire Size	Measurement Points & Specifications					
			Front			Rear		
			Dim.,②	Specification		Dim.,②	Specification	
				Inches	mm		Inches	mm
All	Neon	①	A	26.14–26.78	664–680	B	26.41–27.05	671–687
	SRT-4	①	A	26.65–27.29	677–693	B	27.12–27.76	691–705

A Dim. — Ground to Lower Edge of Front Wheel Well

B Dim. — Ground to Lower Edge of Rear Wheel Well

① — See door sticker or inside of glove box for manufacturers original tire size specifications. If tires on vehicle do not match manufacturers original tire size & measurement is not within limits, it will be required to refer to the Non-Standard Tire & Wheel Size Adjustment To Ride Height Specification & Tire Size Adjustment Charts in the front of this manual for approximate changes in ride height specifications.

② — Refer to Fig. A.

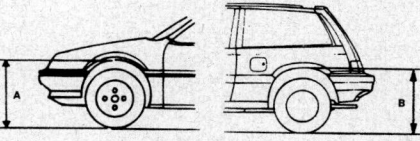

Fig. A   Dimensions A & B

FLUID CAPACITIES & COOLING SYSTEM DATA

Year	Engine	Coolant Capacity, Qts.	Coolant Type	Radiator Cap Relief Pressure, Lbs.	Thermo. Opening Temp., °F	Fuel Tank, Gals.	Engine Oil Refill, Qts.③	Auto. Transaxle Oil, Qts.②	Man. Transaxle Oil, Pts.
All	2.0L	6.5	Ethylene Glycol	14–18	192–199	12.5	4.5	①	5.0–5.6
	2.4L	6.5	Ethylene Glycol	14–18	192–199	12.5	5.0	①	4.8–5.2

① — Fluid change only, 4.0 qts. After overhaul, 8.6 qts.

② — Approximate. Make final inspection w/dipstick.

③ — Includes oil filter.

LUBRICANT DATA

Year	Transaxle		Power Steering	Brake System
	Automatic	Manual		
All	Mopar ATF+4 Type 9602	Mopar ATF+4 Type 9602	Mopar ATF+4 Type 9602	DOT 3

Electrical

NOTE: On Air Bag Equipped Models, Refer To "Air Bag System Precautions" Located In The Front Of This Manual For System Disarming & Arming Procedures.

NOTE: Refer To "Computer Relearn Procedures" Located In The Front Of This Manual When Battery Power To The Computer Has Been Interrupted.

INDEX

	Page No.
Air Bag System (Volume 2)	4-1
Air Conditioning	8-1
Alternator, Replace	5-4
2.0L Engine	5-4
2.4L Engine	5-4
Alternators	11-1
Blower Motor, Replace	5-6
Less A/C	5-6
With A/C	5-6
Clutch Start Switch, Replace	5-5
Coil Pack, Replace	5-5
Cooling Fans	9-1
Cruise Control (Volume 2)	2-1
Dash Gauges (Volume 2)	1-1
Dash Panel Service (Volume 2)	5-1

	Page No.
Dimmer Switch, Replace	5-5
Evaporator Core, Replace	5-7
Fuel Pump Relay Location	5-4
Fuse Panel Location	5-4
Headlamp Switch, Replace	5-5
Heater Core, Replace	5-6
Ignition Lock, Replace	5-5
Ignition Switch, Replace	5-5
Instrument Cluster, Replace	5-5
Multi-Function Switch, Replace	5-5
Passive Restraint Systems (Volume 2)	4-1
Precautions	5-4
Air Bag Systems	5-4
Battery Ground Cable	5-4
Radio, Replace	5-5

	Page No.
Relay Center Location	5-4
Speed Controls (Volume 2)	2-1
Starter Motors	10-1
Starter, Replace	5-4
Steering Columns	12-1
Steering Wheel, Replace	5-5
Stop Light Switch, Replace	5-5
Turn Signal Switch, Replace	5-5
Wiper Motor, Replace	5-5
Wiper Switch, Replace	5-6
Wiper Systems (Volume 2)	3-1

PRECAUTIONS

Air Bag Systems

Refer to "Air Bag System Precautions" in the front of this manual for system disarming and arming procedures.

Battery Ground Cable

Prior to service, disconnect battery ground cable and isolate as required.

FUSE PANEL LOCATION

The fuse block is positioned on a mounting bracket up and under the lefthand side of the instrument panel, secured by two screws. It can be accessed by removing the instrument panel end cap.

FUEL PUMP RELAY LOCATION

The fuel pump relay is located on the lefthand side of the engine compartment near the battery, in the Power Distribution Center (PDC).

RELAY CENTER LOCATION

The relay center is located on the lefthand side of the engine compartment, next to the battery.

STARTER

REPLACE

1. Raise and support vehicle using a suitable lift.
2. **On models equipped with 2.0L H/O engine and automatic transaxle,** disconnect inlet hose from intake manifold, then reposition air cleaner assembly.
3. **On models equipped with automatic transaxle,** remove two upper bracket bolts from intake support, then the oil pan and intake support brackets.
4. **On all models,** remove battery positive cable connector from starter assembly.
5. Disconnect latch and remove solenoid connector from starter assembly.
6. Remove starter attaching bolts, then the starter assembly.
7. Reverse procedure to install. **Torque** starter attaching bolts to 40 ft. lbs.

ALTERNATOR

REPLACE

2.0L Engine

1. Loosen alternator adjustment nut.
2. Raise and support vehicle.
3. Remove lower splash shield.
4. Disconnect alternator wiring.
5. Loosen alternator pivot bolt and remove alternator drive belt.
6. Remove pivot bracket mounting bolts.
7. Remove pivot nut from T-bolt while supporting alternator.
8. Lower alternator and remove through wheelwell.
9. Reverse procedure to install, noting the following:
   a. **Torque** alternator mounting bolts to 40 ft. lbs.
   b. **Torque** alternator feed terminal nut to 72 inch lbs.

2.4L Engine

1. Remove alternator heat shield attaching bolts.
2. Remove nut from upper T-bolt adjustment bracket.
3. Raise and support vehicle.
4. Remove right front wheel assembly.
5. Remove accessory drive splash shield from under righthand side of vehicle.
6. Remove drive axle retaining nut.
7. Remove lower control arm to steering knuckle retaining nut, then separate control arm from steering knuckle.
8. Remove axle shaft bearing support retaining bolts.
9. Remove axle shaft from transaxle. Place a suitable drain pan under transaxle to catch fluid.
10. Remove lower heat shield, then the alternator heat shield.
11. Disconnect alternator electrical connectors.
12. Loosen accessory drive belt T-bolt.
13. Remove pencil strut, **Fig. 1.**
14. Loosen lower alternator pivot bolt.
15. Remove alternator belt.
16. Remove alternator from lower mounting bracket and position aside.
17. Remove lower mounting bracket.

18. Remove alternator through axle shaft opening.
19. Reverse procedure to install, noting the following:
    a. **Torque** lower bracket mounting bolts to 40 ft. lbs.
    b. **Torque** axle shaft bearing support bolts to 40 ft. lbs.
    c. **Torque** control arm to steering knuckle nut to 70 ft. lbs.
    d. **Torque** axle shaft nut to 180 ft. lbs.
    e. **Torque** accessory drive belt T-bolt to 40 ft. lbs.
    f. **Torque** lower alternator pivot bolt to 40 ft. lbs.
    g. **Torque** heat shield bolts to 40 ft. lbs.
    h. **Torque** upper adjustment bracket nut to 18 ft. lbs.

COIL PACK

REPLACE

1. Disconnect coil pack electrical connector and remove mounting bolts.
2. Remove coil pack from valve cover.
3. Reverse procedure to install. **Torque** coil pack to valve cover bolts to 106 inch lbs.

IGNITION LOCK

REPLACE

Refer to "Ignition Switch, Replace" for ignition lock replacement procedure.

IGNITION SWITCH

REPLACE

1. Turn ignition to Run position.
2. Depress lock cylinder retaining tab through hole in lower column shroud and remove lock cylinder using suitable tool.
3. Remove steering column upper and lower shrouds as required.
4. Disconnect ignition switch electrical connectors.
5. Remove ignition switch mounting screw.
6. Depress retaining tabs and pull ignition switch from steering column.
7. Reverse procedure to install, ensuring ignition switch and actuator rod in lock housing are both in Run position.

CLUTCH START SWITCH

REPLACE

1. Remove lefthand lower instrument panel bezel.
2. Disconnect clutch master cylinder rod from clutch pedal pin. **Inspect plastic retainer upon removal, it must be replaced if damaged.**
3. Remove brake booster push rod retaining clip from brake pedal, then disengage rod from pedal.
4. Remove pedal assembly bracket to instrument panel nuts, then brake booster/pedal bracket to cowl nuts.
5. From under hood, pull brake master cylinder/booster forward enough to obtain pedal to bracket stud clearance.

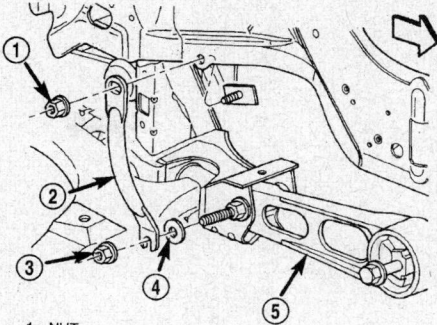

1 - NUT
2 - PENCIL STRUT
3 - NUT
4 - FLAT WASHER
5 - LOWER TORQUE STRUT

ARM0400000000242

Fig. 1   Pencil strut removal

6. Remove pedal bracket assembly, then the pedal pivot shaft and brake/clutch pedals.
7. Remove interlock/upstop switch assembly from brake/clutch pedal bracket assembly by depressing four plastic wing tabs on each switch.
8. Reverse procedure to install, noting the following:
    a. **Torque** pivot shaft nut, brake booster mounting nuts and pedal bracket to instrument panel nuts to 25 ft. lbs.
    b. **Torque** adjustment screw to 70 inch lbs.

HEADLAMP SWITCH

REPLACE

Refer to "Multi-Function Switch, Replace" for procedures.

STOP LIGHT SWITCH

REPLACE

1. Depress brake pedal and rotate switch counterclockwise approximately 30°.
2. Pull switch rearward and remove from mounting bracket.
3. Disconnect electrical connector.
4. Pull switch plunger head out until ratchet sound stops.
5. Reverse procedure to install.

MULTI-FUNCTION SWITCH

REPLACE

1. Remove steering column upper and lower shrouds.
2. Disconnect all multi-function switch electrical connectors.
3. Remove mounting screws and multi-function switch.
4. Reverse procedure to install.

TURN SIGNAL SWITCH

REPLACE

Refer to "Multi-Function Switch, Replace" for procedure.

DIMMER SWITCH

REPLACE

Refer to "Multi-Function Switch, Replace" for procedure.

STEERING WHEEL

REPLACE

1. Place front wheels in straight ahead position.
2. Rotate steering wheel 180° clockwise.
3. Lock steering with column lock cylinder.
4. Remove speed control switch and connector.
5. Remove air bag as outlined in "Passive Restraint Systems" chapter.
6. Remove steering wheel mounting nut and vibration damper, if equipped.
7. Remove steering wheel while avoiding damage to clockspring wiring using appropriate puller tool.
8. Reverse procedure to install, noting the following:
    a. Install steering wheel ensuring flats on hub align with clockspring.
    b. **Torque** steering wheel mounting nut to 40 ft. lbs.

INSTRUMENT CLUSTER

REPLACE

1. Remove A-pillar moldings using trim stick tool No. C-4755, or equivalent.
2. Remove instrument panel top cover and cluster bezel.
3. Remove cluster housing to base panel mounting screws.
4. Pull cluster rearward to disconnect from base panel.
5. Remove cluster assembly.
6. Reverse procedure to install.

RADIO

REPLACE

1. Remove instrument panel center module bezel.
2. Remove radio mounting screws and pull radio out of instrument panel.
3. Disconnect radio electrical connectors, ground wire and antenna lead.
4. Reverse procedure to install.

WIPER MOTOR

REPLACE

1. Remove wiper arms and blades.
2. Remove cowl cover to cowl screws at base of windshield opening.
3. Remove hood to cowl seal at leading edge of cowl cover. Pull seal toward front of vehicle.
4. Remove cowl cover.
5. Disconnect electrical connectors at wiper motor.
6. Remove windshield wiper module.
7. Remove motor crank linkage by inserting suitable screwdriver between crank and linkage, then twisting and lifting straight up.

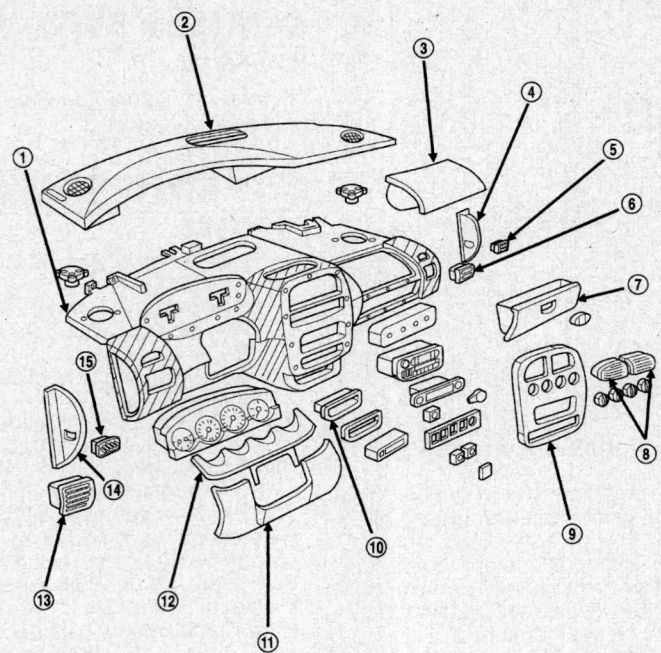

Fig. 2   Exploded view of instrument panel. Neon

1 - INSTRUMENT PANEL ASSEMBLY
2 - UPPER COVER INSTRUMENT PANEL
3 - MODULE, PASSENGER SIDE AIRBAG
4 - END CAP, RIGHT
5 - DEMISTER GRILLE, RIGHT
6 - LOUVER, AIR OUTLET, RIGHT
7 - DOOR, GLOVE BOX
8 - LOUVER, AIR OUTLET, CENTER

9 - BEZEL INSTRUMENT PANEL, CENTER
10 - BIN, LOWER STORAGE
11 - COVER, LOWER INSTRUMENT PANEL
12 - CLUSTER BEZEL
13 - LOUVER, AIR OUTLET, LEFT
14 - END CAP, LEFT
15 - DEMISTER GRILLE, LEFT

CR9140100078000X

8. Remove mounting screws and separate windshield wiper motor from linkage.
9. Reverse procedure to install, noting the following:
   a. Add suitable unilube grease to socket.
   b. **Torque** motor mounting screws to 45–55 inch lbs.
   c. **Torque** drive link nut to 98–106 inch lbs.

WIPER SWITCH

REPLACE

Refer to "Multi-Function Switch, Replace" for procedures.

BLOWER MOTOR

REPLACE

Less A/C

1. Disconnect blower motor electrical connector.
2. Turn blower motor approximately ⅛ turn counterclockwise while pulling down on locking tab.
3. Remove blower motor from housing.
4. Reverse procedure to install.

With A/C

1. Remove righthand side scuff plate and pull back carpet.

2. Disconnect blower motor wiring connector.
3. Remove mounting screws and lower blower motor from housing.
4. Reverse procedure to install, taping silencer in position.

HEATER CORE

REPLACE

1. Drain coolant into suitable container.
2. Move front seats as far rearward as possible.
3. Ensure front wheels are locked in straight-ahead position, to prevent clockspring damage.
4. Remove A-pillar trim using trim stick tool No. C-4755, or equivalent.
5. Remove instrument panel top cover, **Fig. 2.**
6. Remove instrument cluster bezel.
7. Remove lefthand lower instrument panel cover by gently pulling rearward.
8. Remove steering column lower cover.
9. **On models equipped with speed control,** remove speed control switches from steering wheel.
10. **On all models,** remove driver's side air bag module to steering wheel mounting screws.
11. Disconnect air bag module electrical connectors, then remove module from steering wheel.
12. Hold steering wheel firmly in place, then remove steering wheel retaining nut.
13. **On models equipped with steering**

wheel damper weight, remove weight from steering wheel.
14. **On all models,** remove steering wheel from steering column using a suitable steering wheel puller tool. **Do not pound on shaft.**
15. Remove key from ignition.
16. Remove steering column lower and upper shrouds.
17. Remove steering column coupler retaining pin.
18. Loosen pinch bolt nut, then remove coupling pinch bolt.
19. Separate upper and lower steering column couplings.
20. **On models equipped with automatic transaxle,** disconnect transaxle ignition interlock cable from column. Depress tab on top of cable connector and remove cable from rear side of ignition cylinder housing.
21. **On all models,** remove two column to instrument panel lower mounting nuts.
22. Remove two column to instrument panel upper mounting nuts.
23. Lower steering column away from instrument panel.
24. Disconnect air bag clockspring electrical connector.
25. Disconnect electrical connectors at multi-function, windshield wiper, ignition and Sentry Key Immobilizer Module (SKIM) switches.
26. Carefully remove steering column from vehicle.
27. Remove instrument panel lefthand and righthand end covers.
28. Remove lefthand and righthand cowl side panels.
29. Apply parking brake, then remove floor center console, **Fig. 3.**
30. Remove Data Link Connector (DLC) from instrument panel by depressing side tabs.
31. Remove four instrument panel to firewall retaining bolts.
32. Remove two bolts on top of brake pedal support bracket.
33. Remove two center support bolts.
34. Remove lefthand and righthand A-pillar mounting bolts.
35. Disconnect vanity and rearview mirror electrical connector at top lefthand side of instrument panel.
36. Disconnect two harness connectors to heater HVAC at top righthand of instrument panel.
37. Remove both A/C outlet barrels.
38. Remove heater and A/C control knobs.
39. Gently pry outward on center bezel and remove from instrument panel.
40. Remove two heater and A/C control head retaining screws.
41. Disconnect electrical and vacuum connectors at heater and A/C control head.
42. Pull heater and A/C control head out of instrument panel, twist 90° and push back through opening. **Leave control cables in place.**
43. Disconnect electrical connectors at Air Bag Control Module (ACM), parking brake warning lamp switch and PRNDL lamp.
44. Remove two bolts at top of brake pedal

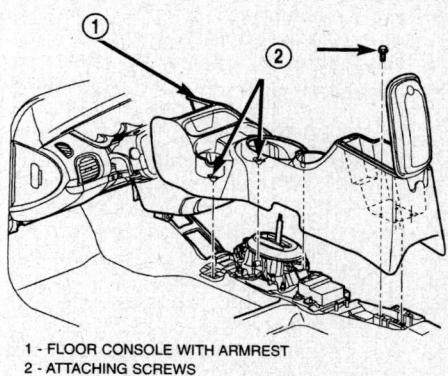

1 - FLOOR CONSOLE WITH ARMREST
2 - ATTACHING SCREWS

CR9140100079000X

Fig. 3   Floor center console. Neon

bracket, then carefully remove instrument panel from vehicle.
45. Disconnect heater hoses at dash panel.
46. Plug heater core outlets to prevent coolant spillage during housing removal.
47. **On models equipped with A/C,** evacuate and recover A/C refrigerant.
48. **On all models,** remove coolant reservoir fasteners and position reservoir aside.
49. Remove suction line at expansion

valve. Plug refrigerant lines to prevent contamination of system.
50. Remove expansion valve. Plug all fittings.
51. Remove rubber drain tube extension from evaporator drain.
52. Disconnect vacuum harness at brake booster.
53. Unsnap and remove defroster duct.
54. Remove engine side of firewall housing mounting nuts.
55. Remove righthand side mounting screw.
56. Remove one remaining nut located on dash panel stud.
57. Disconnect electrical connectors as required.
58. Remove unit housing.
59. Separate air distribution outlet foam seals at case halves.
60. Remove foam seals at evaporator and heater core tubes.
61. Remove retaining clips and screws holding halves together.
62. Separate housing halves.
63. Lift heater core out of housing.
64. Reverse procedure to install.

EVAPORATOR CORE
REPLACE

1. Remove unit housing as outlined in

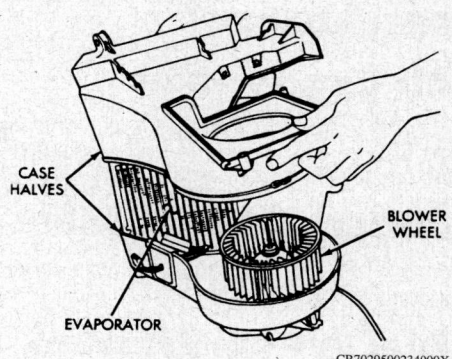

CR7029500234000X

Fig. 4   Evaporator case separation

"Heater Core, Replace."
2. Remove clips and screws to separate evaporator/blower case.
3. Remove evaporator case foam seal.
4. Remove mounting screws and air duct with recirculation door assembly.
5. Disconnect fin sensing switch.
6. Remove upper and lower clips and screws, then separate case halves, **Fig. 4.**
7. Remove evaporator.
8. Reverse procedure to install.

2.0L Engine

NOTE: On Air Bag Equipped Models, Refer To "Air Bag System Precautions" Located In The Front Of This Manual For System Disarming & Arming Procedures.

NOTE: Refer To "Computer Relearn Procedures" Located In The Front Of This Manual When Battery Power To The Computer Has Been Interrupted.

INDEX

	Page No.		Page No.		Page No.
Belt Tension Data	5-12	Front Cover, Replace	5-10	Air Conditioning Compressor &	
Camshaft, Replace	5-10	Fuel Filter, Replace	5-13	Alternator Belt	5-12
Camshaft Lobe Lift		Fuel Pump, Replace	5-13	Installation	5-12
Specifications	5-10	Intake Manifold, Replace	5-9	Removal	5-12
Compression Pressure	5-8	Main & Rod Bearings	5-11	Technical Service Bulletins	5-13
Cooling System Bleed	5-12	Oil Pan, Replace	5-11	Irregular Engine Snapping	
Crankshaft Rear Oil Seal,		Oil Pump, Replace	5-11	Sound	5-13
Replace	5-11	Oil Pump Service	5-12	Low Or No Cabin Heat	5-13
Crankshaft Seal, Replace	5-11	Assemble	5-12	Thermostat, Replace	5-12
Cylinder Head, Replace	5-9	Disassemble	5-12	Tightening Specifications	5-15
Engine Rebuilding		Inspection	5-12	Timing Belt, Replace	5-10
Specifications	21-1	Piston & Rod Assembly	5-11	Installation	5-10
Engine, Replace	5-8	Precautions	5-8	Removal	5-10
Engine Mount, Replace	5-8	Air Bag Systems	5-8	Valve Arrangement	5-10
Front	5-8	Battery Ground Cable	5-8	Valve Clearance Specifications	5-10
Lefthand	5-8	Fuel System Pressure Relief	5-8	Valve Cover, Replace	5-9
Rear	5-8	Radiator, Replace	5-13	Water Pump, Replace	5-12
Righthand	5-8	Rocker Arms	5-10		
Exhaust Manifold, Replace	5-9	Serpentine Drive Belt	5-12		

PRECAUTIONS

Air Bag Systems

Refer to "Air Bag System Precautions" in the front of this manual for system disarming and arming procedures.

Battery Ground Cable

Prior to service, disconnect battery ground cable and isolate as required.

Fuel System Pressure Relief

1. Remove fuel pump relay from Power Distribution Center (PDC).
2. Start and run engine until it stalls.
3. Attempt restarting engine until it will no longer run.
4. Turn ignition key to Off position.
5. Place a rag or shop towel below fuel line quick connect fitting at fuel rail.
6. Return fuel pump relay to (PDC).
7. One or more diagnostic trouble codes may have been stored in PCM memory due to fuel pump relay removal. Use suitable scan tool to erase codes.

COMPRESSION PRESSURE

Recommended compression pressures are 170–225 psi. Recommended pressures are used only as a guide to diagnosing engine problem. An engine should not be disassembled to determine the cause of low compression unless a fault is present.

1. Ensure battery is fully charged and starter is in good operating condition.
2. Inspect engine oil level and top up if required.
3. Drive vehicle until engine is at normal operating temperature.
4. Remove spark plugs from engine and inspect for abnormal firing indicators.
5. Disconnect coil wire from distributor and secure to good ground. For direct ignition system, disconnect coil connector.
6. Ensure throttle blade is fully open during compression test.
7. Insert compression gauge adapter tool No. 8116, or equivalent, into No. 1 cylinder spark plug hole.
8. Connect 0–500 psi (Blue) transducer with cable adapters to DRBIII.
9. Crank engine until maximum pressure is reached on gauge, repeat for all cylinders.
10. Compression should not be less than 100 psi or vary by more than 25 percent from cylinder to cylinder.

ENGINE MOUNT
REPLACE
Front

1. Raise and support vehicle.

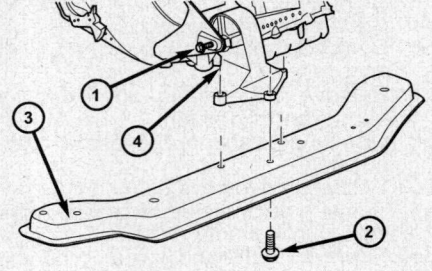

1 - HORIZONTAL THROUGH BOLT
2 - VERTICAL BOLT(S)
3 - LOWER RADIATOR CROSSMEMBER
4 - FRONT ENGINE MOUNT

CR1060100964000X

Fig. 1   Front engine mount replacement

2. Remove front mount to bracket horizontal through bolt, **Fig. 1.**
3. Remove vertical bolts and front mount.
4. Reverse procedure to install.

Lefthand

1. Support transaxle with suitable jack.
2. Remove three engine mount to transaxle mounting bolts, **Fig. 2.**
3. Remove mounting bolts and lefthand mount.
4. Reverse procedure to install.

Righthand

1. Raise and support vehicle, then remove inner splash guard.
2. Remove righthand engine support mounting bolts from frame rail, **Fig. 3.**
3. Lower vehicle and support engine with suitable floor jack.
4. Remove three engine support to engine bracket mounting bolts.
5. Reverse procedure to install.

Rear

1. Raise and support vehicle, then remove lefthand front tire and wheel assembly.
2. Support transaxle with suitable transaxle jack.
3. Remove mount and rear suspension crossover insulator mounting bolt, **Fig. 4.**
4. Remove four mounting bolts and transaxle mount.
5. Reverse procedure to install.

ENGINE
REPLACE

1. Relieve fuel system pressure as outlined under "Precautions."
2. Drain coolant into suitable container.
3. Recover refrigerant as outlined in "Air Conditioning" chapter.
4. Remove throttle body air inlet hose and air cleaner assembly.
5. Remove upper radiator crossmember, then the upper and lower radiator hoses.

6. Disconnect transaxle oil cooler lines at transaxle. Plug lines and fittings.
7. Disconnect air conditioning lines from condenser and remove cooling module.
8. Disconnect electrical harness from transaxle and shift cable.
9. Disconnect engine electrical harness from PCM and bulkhead connector.
10. Raise and support vehicle, then remove front tire and wheel assemblies.
11. Remove both splash shields.
12. Remove both drive axles as outlined in "Front Wheel Drive Axles" chapter.
13. Drain engine oil into suitable container and remove accessory drive belts.
14. Remove power steering pump from bracket and position aside.
15. Disconnect heater return hose from pipe connection.
16. Disconnect air conditioning compressor electrical connector.
17. Disconnect oxygen sensor electrical connector.
18. Remove exhaust pipe to manifold mounting nuts and catalytic convertor pipe band clamp.
19. Remove catalytic convertor pipe from resonator pipe.
20. Disconnect from hanger and remove catalytic convertor pipe.
21. Remove front and rear engine mount through bolts.
22. Remove rear mount bracket from transmission.
23. Remove structural collar and torque reaction bracket, **Fig. 5.**
24. Mark flex plate to torque converter position for installation alignment, then remove torque converter bolts.
25. Lower vehicle, then disconnect battery positive cable from Power Distribution Center (PDC).
26. Disconnect throttle and speed control cables, then the coolant recovery overflow hose.
27. Remove heater hose from thermostat housing and disconnect all engine ground straps.
28. Disconnect brake booster and vapor purge hoses, then the fuel line from fuel rail.
29. Remove intake manifold as outlined under "Intake Manifold, Replace."
30. Remove alternator.
31. Remove air conditioning suction line at compressor.
32. Remove compressor. Plug ports and lines.
33. Raise and support vehicle.
34. Support engine using dolly and cradle tool Nos. 6135 and 6710, or equivalents.
35. Install post tool No. 6848, or equivalent.
36. Loosen engine cradle mounts to position engine locating holes in bedplate.
37. Lower vehicle until engine rests on cradle mounts. Tighten mounts to cradle frame.
38. Lower vehicle so weight of engine and transaxle is only on cradle.
39. Remove left and righthand vertical mount mounting bolts.
40. Slowly raise and support vehicle.

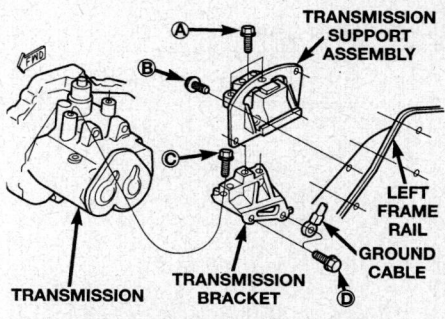

ITEM	DESCRIPTION	TORQUE
A	Bolt	61 N·m (45 ft. lbs.)
B	Bolt	33 N·m (24 ft. lbs.)
C	Bolt	61 N·m (45 ft. lbs.)
D	Bolt	61 N·m (45 ft. lbs.)

CR1069500597000X

Fig. 2   Lefthand engine mount replacement

41. Remove engine and transaxle on cradle around body flanges.
42. Reverse procedure to install, noting the following:
    a. Place structural collar into position between transaxle and oil pan, install transaxle bolt 1 hand tight, **Fig. 5.**
    b. Install collar to oil pan bolts 4 and 5 hand tight.
    c. Position torque reaction bracket in place, then install bolts 2 and 3 hand tight.
    d. **Torque** bolts 1–3 to 75 ft. lbs.
    e. Install bolts 6 and 7 through torque reduction bracket into block hand tight.
    f. **Torque** bolts 4 and 5 to 35 ft. lbs.
    g. **Torque** bolts 6 and 7 to 45 ft. lbs.
    h. **Torque** front engine mount through bolt to 45 ft. lbs.

INTAKE MANIFOLD
REPLACE

1. Relieve fuel system pressure as outlined under "Precautions."
2. Drain engine coolant into suitable container.
3. Remove throttle body air inlet hose and air cleaner housing assembly.
4. Remove throttle and speed control cables from throttle lever and bracket.
5. Remove EGR and oil dipstick tubes.
6. Disconnect vacuum hoses from intake manifold.
7. Disconnect fuel supply line at fuel rail.
8. Remove fastener holding fuel rail bracket to side of cylinder head.
9. Disconnect fuel injectors, then the knock and ECT sensors' electrical connectors.
10. Disconnect IAC, then the throttle position and MAP sensors' electrical connectors.
11. Disconnect air conditioning pressure switch and compressor clutch, then the alternator electrical connectors.

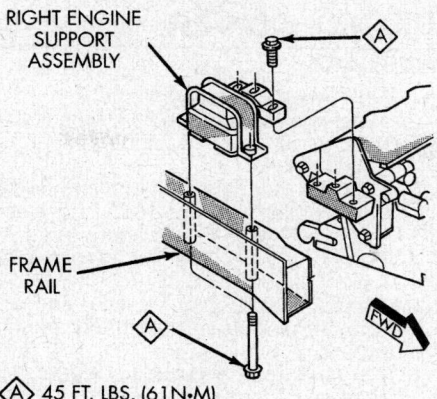

A   45 FT. LBS. (61 N·M)

CR1069500593000X

Fig. 3   Righthand engine mount replacement

12. Position wiring harness aside and remove fuel rail.
13. Remove coolant outlet connector.
14. Remove mounting bolts and intake manifold.
15. Reverse procedure to install, noting the following:
    a. Install new gasket.
    b. Tighten intake manifold bolts gradually in sequence, **Fig. 6.**

EXHAUST MANIFOLD
REPLACE

1. Raise and support vehicle.
2. Remove exhaust system, **Fig. 7.**
3. Raise and support vehicle, then remove lefthand front tire and wheel assembly.
4. Support transaxle with suitable transaxle jack.
5. Remove mount and rear suspension crossover insulator mounting bolt, **Fig. 4.**
6. Remove four mounting bolts and transaxle mount.
7. Remove exhaust manifold heat shield.
8. Disconnect oxygen sensor electrical connector.
9. Remove mounting bolts and exhaust manifold.
10. Reverse procedure to install noting the following:
    a. Install new gasket.
    b. Tighten bolts in sequence, **Fig. 8.**

CYLINDER HEAD
REPLACE

1. Relieve fuel system pressure as outlined under "Precautions."
2. Remove throttle body air inlet hose and air cleaner housing assembly.
3. Drain coolant into suitable container.
4. Remove intake manifold as outlined under "Intake Manifold, Replace."
5. Disconnect heater hose from thermostat housing.
6. Remove heater tube support bracket from cylinder head.
7. Disconnect Camshaft Position (CMP) sensor and EGR solenoid electrical connectors.

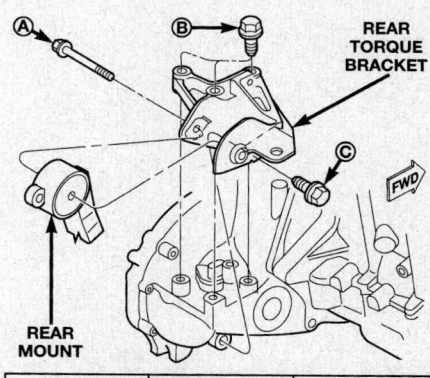

ITEM	DESCRIPTION	TORQUE
A	Bolt	61 N·m (45 ft. lbs.)
B & C	Bolt—w/Auto. Transaxle	110 N·m (80 ft. lbs.)
	Bolt—w/Manual Transaxle	61 N·m (45 ft. lbs.)

CR1069500599000X

Fig. 4   Rear engine mount replacement

8. Raise and support vehicle, then disconnect exhaust pipe from exhaust manifold.
9. Remove accessory drive belts and crankshaft damper.
10. Remove timing belt as outlined under "Timing Belt, Replace."
11. Remove camshaft sprockets.
12. Remove timing belt idler pulley and rear timing belt cover.
13. Remove air cleaner inlet duct.
14. Disconnect coil pack electrical connector.
15. Remove spark plug cables from coil pack by twisting cable and boot assembly, then pulling outward.
16. Remove mounting bolts and coil pack.
17. Remove mounting bolts and valve cover.
18. Remove valve cover as outlined under "Valve Cover, Replace."
19. Remove camshafts and rocker arms.
20. Remove mounting bolts and cylinder head.
21. Reverse procedure to install, noting the following:
    a. Apply oil to cylinder head bolts
    b. **Torque** cylinder head bolts to 25 ft. lbs., in sequence, **Fig. 9.**
    c. **Torque** head bolts to 50 ft. lbs., in sequence.
    d. **Torque** bolts to 50 ft. lbs., in sequence.
    e. Tighten bolts an additional 90° in sequence.

VALVE COVER
REPLACE

1. Remove air cleaner inlet duct.
2. Disconnect coil pack electrical connector.
3. Remove spark plug cables from coil pack by twisting cable and boot assembly, then pulling outward.
4. Remove mounting bolts and coil pack.
5. Remove mounting bolts and valve cover.

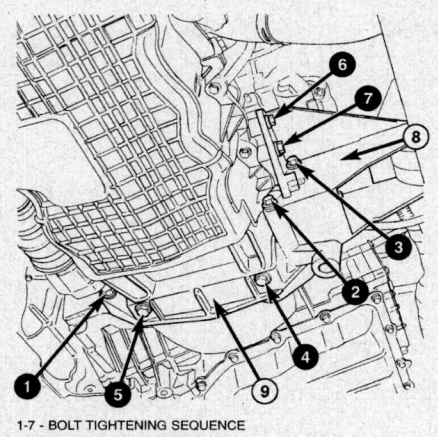

1-7 - BOLT TIGHTENING SEQUENCE
8 - TORQUE REACTION BRACKET
9 - STRUCTURAL COLLAR

CR1060100965000X

Fig. 5   Structural collar & torque reaction bracket replacement

6. Reverse procedure to install. Install new valve cover gasket.

VALVE ARRANGEMENT

Intake valves are located on intake manifold side of engine and exhaust valves are located on exhaust manifold side of engine.

CAMSHAFT LOBE LIFT SPECIFICATIONS

Engine	Lift, Inch	
	Intake	Exhaust
2.0L	.340	.312

VALVE CLEARANCE SPECIFICATIONS

These engines are equipped with hydraulic lash adjusters designed to maintain zero lash at all times.

ROCKER ARMS

1. Remove air cleaner inlet duct.
2. Disconnect coil pack electrical connector.
3. Remove spark plug cables from coil pack by twisting cable and boot assembly, then pulling outward.
4. Remove mounting bolts and coil pack.
5. Remove mounting bolts and valve cover.
6. Identify rocker arm shaft assemblies for installation in original positions.
7. Remove mounting bolts and rocker arm shaft.
8. Reverse procedure to install, noting the following:
   a. Install rocker arm and shaft assemblies with notches on shafts facing up and toward timing belt side of engine, **Fig. 10**.
   b. Tighten bolts in sequence, **Fig. 11**.
9. Install new valve cover gasket.

FRONT COVER
REPLACE

1. Remove accessory drive belts.
2. Raise and support vehicle on suitable hoist and remove righthand inner splash shield.
3. Remove mounting bolt and crankshaft using puller tool No. 1023 and insert tool No. C-4685-C2, or equivalents.
4. Lower vehicle and support engine using suitable jack.
5. Remove purge duty solenoid and wiring harness from righthand engine mount.
6. Remove righthand engine mount and bracket.
7. Remove mounting bolts and upper timing belt cover.
8. Remove mounting bolts and lower timing belt cover.
9. Reverse procedure to install.

TIMING BELT
REPLACE
Removal

1. Remove timing belt front cover as outlined under "Front Cover, Replace."
2. Align crankshaft and camshaft sprocket marks, **Fig. 12**, then loosen timing belt tensioner mounting bolts.
3. Remove timing belt. If belt is to be reused, mark running direction on belt for installation alignment.
4. Remove timing belt tensioner. **Fig. 13. Tensioner pivot bolt, should never be tightened, loosened or removed, as factory locking compound is not reusable. If pivot bolt is disturbed, entire pivot bracket assembly must be replaced.**
5. Inspect timing belt for cracks, missing teeth, rubber hardening and abnormal wear.

Installation

1. Position timing belt tensioner in suitable soft jawed vise, then slowly compress tensioner plunger into tensioner body.
2. With tensioner plunger compressed into body, insert ⁵⁄₆₄ inch hex wrench, or suitable locking pin, through holes in tensioner body, **Fig. 14**.
3. Align crankshaft sprocket mark with oil pump housing and back off to three sprocket teeth before Top Dead Center (TDC), **Fig. 15**.
4. Align camshaft sprocket mark with timing belt rear cover , **Fig. 12**.
5. Position crankshaft sprocket at ½ tooth before TDC, **Fig. 16**.
6. Position timing belt over crankshaft, around water pump and over camshaft sprockets, then around tensioner pulley.
7. Remove timing belt slack by placing crankshaft sprocket in TDC position.
8. Position timing belt tensioner on engine block and loosely install mounting bolts, **Fig. 13. Tensioner pivot bolt**

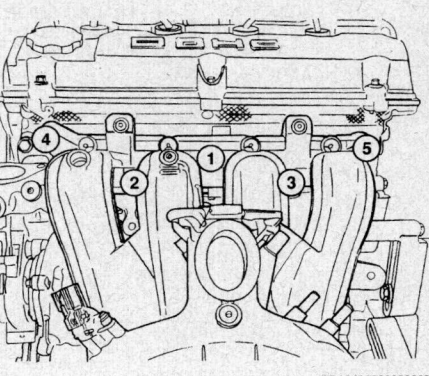

CR1060000928000X

Fig. 6   Intake manifold tightening sequence

should never be tightened, loosened or removed, as factory locking compound is not reusable. If pivot bolt is disturbed, entire pivot bracket assembly must be replaced.

9. Apply 20–21 ft. lbs., force to timing belt tensioner pulley using suitable torque wrench, **Fig. 12**.
10. While applying tension on tensioner pulley, move timing belt tensioner against tensioner pulley bracket and tighten mounting bolts.
11. Remove hex wrench or locking pin retaining tensioner plunger in body. Timing belt pretension is correct when wrench or pin can be freely removed and installed in tensioner body holes.
12. Rotate crankshaft two revolutions in normal rotation direction.
13. Inspect crankshaft and camshaft sprocket timing mark alignment, **Fig. 12**. If timing marks are not properly aligned, repeat belt installation procedure.
14. Install front cover as outlined under "Front Cover, Replace."
15. **After completing installation, perform camshaft and crankshaft alignment relearn procedure using suitably programmed scan tool and instructions.**
16. Remove park plug No. 1.
17. Set cylinder No. 1 at TDC on compression stroke using suitable dial indicator.
18. Remove timing belt front cover access plug.
19. Camshaft sprocket timing mark should be aligned with timing belt rear cover arrow, **Fig. 12**.

CAMSHAFT
REPLACE

1. Relieve fuel system pressure as outlined under "Precautions."
2. Remove cylinder head as outlined under "Cylinder Head, Replace."
3. Remove camshaft sensor and camshaft target magnet, then the camshaft sprocket bolt.
4. Remove sprocket from camshaft with modified sprocket removal tool No. C-4687-1, or equivalent, **Fig. 17**. Hold

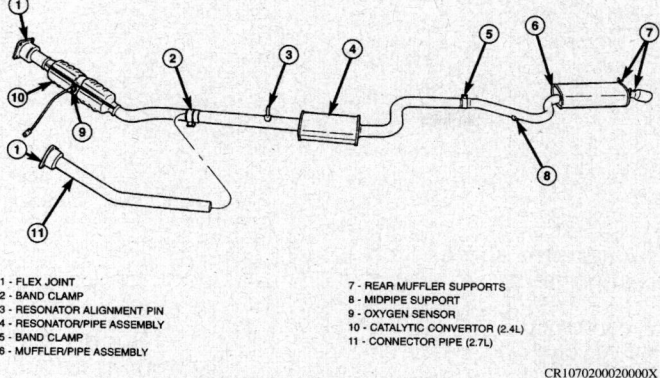

1 - FLEX JOINT
2 - BAND CLAMP
3 - RESONATOR ALIGNMENT PIN
4 - RESONATOR/PIPE ASSEMBLY
5 - BAND CLAMP
6 - MUFFLER/PIPE ASSEMBLY

7 - REAR MUFFLER SUPPORTS
8 - MIDPIPE SUPPORT
9 - OXYGEN SENSOR
10 - CATALYTIC CONVERTOR (2.4L)
11 - CONNECTOR PIPE (2.7L)

CR1070200020000X

Fig. 7 Exhaust system replacement

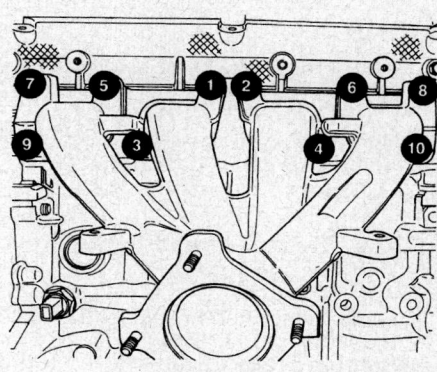

CR1060000929000X

**Fig. 8 Exhaust manifold
tightening sequence**

camshaft sprocket with modified tool while removing bolt.
5. Remove camshaft seal using camshaft seal remover tool No. C-4679, or equivalent.
6. Remove camshaft from rear of cylinder head.
7. Reverse procedure to install, noting the following:
   a. Install new camshaft seal with seal insertion tool No. MD998306, or equivalent.
   b. Hold camshaft sprocket with tool No. C-4687 and adapter tool No. C-4687-1, or equivalents, and tighten.

PISTON & ROD ASSEMBLY

1. L or H stamping on front portion of piston must face toward front of engine.
2. Connecting rod and cap are stamped on side with cylinder number identification.
3. Numbered side of connecting rod cap must be installed on same side as numbered side of rod.
4. **Torque** cap bolts to 20 ft. lbs.
5. Tighten bolts an additional 90°.

MAIN & ROD BEARINGS

All upper and lower bearing shells in the crankcase have oil grooves.

Upper and lower bearing No. 3 halves are flanged to carry the crankshaft thrust loads and are not interchangeable with any other bearing halves.

All bearing cap bolts removed during service procedures are to be cleaned and oiled before installation.

Bearing shells are available in standard and .001 and .010 inch undersized: **Never install an undersize bearing that will reduce clearance below specifications.**

Torque main bearing M8 cap bolts to 20–21 ft. lbs., and M11 bolts to 30 ft. lbs., plus an additional ¼ turn, in sequence.

1. Install main bearing shells with lubrication groove in cylinder block. Ensure oil holes in block line up with oil holes in bearings. Bearing tabs must seat in block tab slots.

2. Oil the bearings and journals, then install crankshaft. **Do not get oil on bedplate mating surface.**
3. Ensure both cylinder block and bedplate surfaces are clean.
4. Apply .059–.078 inch bead of anaerobic sealer Mopar Bed Plate Sealant, or equivalent, to cylinder block, **Fig. 18.**
5. Install lower main bearings into main bearing cap/bedplate. Ensure bearing tabs are seated into bedplate slots.
6. Position main bearing/bedplate onto engine block.
7. Lubricate bolt threads with suitable, clean engine oil. Wipe off any excess oil.
8. Install main bearing bedplate to engine block bolts 11, 17 and 20 hand tight, **Fig. 19.**
9. Tighten bolts down together until bedplate contacts cylinder block.
10. Rotate crankshaft until piston No. 4 is at TDC.
11. Move crankshaft rearward to limits of travel
12. Move crankshaft forward to limits of travel.
13. Hold crankshaft in it's furthest forward position by wedging an appropriate tool between rear of cylinder block (not bed plate) and rear crankshaft counterweight.
14. **Torque** mounting bolts 1–10 to 30 ft. lbs., in sequence, **Fig. 19.**
15. Remove wedge tool.
16. **Torque** bolts 1–10 to 30 ft. lbs., in sequence.
17. Tighten bolts and additional 90° in sequence.
18. Install main bearing bedplate engine block bolts 11–20.
19. **Torque** mounting bolts to 20 ft. lbs., in sequence.
20. After main bearing bedplate is installed, ensure crankshaft turning torque does not exceed 50 in. lbs.

CRANKSHAFT SEAL
REPLACE

1. Remove components to access crankshaft sprocket as outlined under "Timing Belt, Replace."
2. Remove crankshaft sprocket using sprocket remover tool No. 6793 and in-

sert tool No. C-4685-C2, or equivalents, **Fig. 20.**
3. Remove front crankshaft seal using oil seal remover tool No. 6771, or equivalent, **Fig. 21.**
4. Reverse procedure to install, noting the following:
   a. Install new seal using seal installation tool No. 6780-1, or equivalent.
   b. Install crankshaft sprocket using installed tool No. 6792, or equivalent.

CRANKSHAFT REAR OIL SEAL
REPLACE

1. Remove transaxle as outlined in **MOTOR's "Domestic Transmission Manual, In-Vehicle Service."**
2. Remove flex plate.
3. Insert suitable ³⁄₁₆ screwdriver between dust lip and metal case of seal seat. Pry out seal.
4. Reverse procedure to install, noting the following:
   a. Seal should be installed dry with THIS SIDE OUT mark facing away from block.
   b. Install seal flush with block surface using pilot tool No. 6926-1, seal installation tool No. 6926-2 and handle tool No. C-4171, or equivalents.

OIL PAN
REPLACE

1. Drain engine oil into suitable container.
2. Remove front engine mount bracket and bending strut.
3. Remove structural collar from oil pan to transaxle, then transaxle dust cover.
4. **On models equipped with air conditioning,** remove oil filter and adapter.
5. **On all models,** remove mounting bolts and oil pan.
6. Reverse procedure to install. Apply Molar silicone rubber adhesive sealant, or equivalent, at oil pump to engine block parting line, then to oil pan gasket to hold gasket in place.

OIL PUMP
REPLACE

1. Remove components to access oil

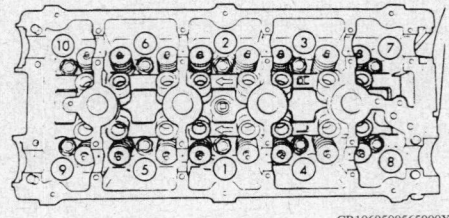

Fig. 9 Cylinder head tightening sequence

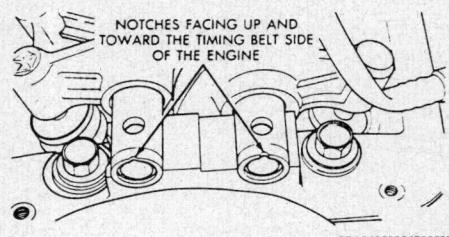

Fig. 10 Rocker arm shaft notch alignment

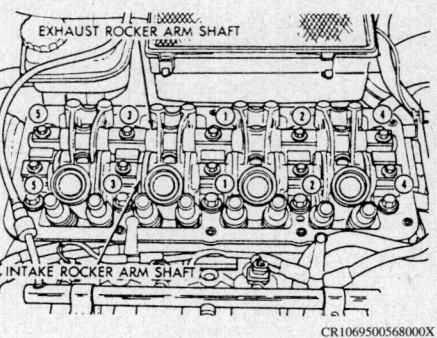

Fig. 11 Rocker arm shaft tightening sequence

pump as outlined under "Timing Belt, Replace."
2. Remove oil pick-up tube.
3. Remove mounting bolts and oil pump.
4. Reverse procedure to install.

OIL PUMP SERVICE
Disassemble

1. Remove relief valve plug and gasket, then spring and relief valve.
2. Remove mounting bolts and cover.
3. Remove pump rotors.

Inspection

1. Clean all components thoroughly in suitable solvent. Mating surface of oil pump should be smooth. Replace pump cover if scratched or grooved.
2. Measure clearance between suitable straightedge and pump cover. If measurement is more than .001 inch, replace cover.
3. Measure thickness and diameter of outer rotor. If outer rotor thickness is .301 inch or less, or if diameter is 3.148 inches or less, replace outer rotor.
4. If inner rotor measures .301 inch or less, replace inner rotor.
5. Place outer rotor into pump housing and press to one side. Measure clearance between rotor and housing. If measurement is .015 inch or more, replace housing.
6. Install inner rotor into pump housing. If clearance between inner and outer rotors is .008 inch or more, replace rotors.
7. Measure clearance between straightedge and pump housing face between bolt holes. If measurement is .004 inch, or more, replace pump.
8. Inspect oil pressure relief valve plunger for scoring and for free operation within its bore. Small marks may be removed with 400 grit wet/dry sandpaper.
9. Oil pump relief valve spring should be approximately 2.39 inches long, Spring should have 18–19 lbs., of resistance when compressed to 1.6 inches. Replace spring if it is not within specifications.

Assemble

1. Install inner rotor with chamfer facing cast iron oil pump cover.
2. Apply Molar gasket maker lightly to cover mounting surface on pump body.

3. Install cover and tighten.
4. Install relief valve, spring, gasket and cap, then tighten.
5. Prime oil pump by filling rotor cavity with suitable, clean engine oil.
6. Apply Molar gasket maker to oil pump.
7. Install oil-ring into counter bore on oil pump body discharge passage.
8. Install oil pump slowly onto crankshaft until seated to engine block.

BELT TENSION DATA

Refer to **Fig. 22** for belt tension data.

SERPENTINE DRIVE BELT

Air Conditioning Compressor & Alternator Belt

REMOVAL

1. Raise and support vehicle.
2. Remove righthand front tire and wheel assembly.
3. Remove drive belt splash shield.
4. Insert suitable ⅜ inch drive breaker bar into square opening of belt tensioner pivot plate.
5. Rotate belt tensioner clockwise until tensioner bottoms out, then remove belt from pulleys.

INSTALLATION

1. Insert suitable ⅜ inch drive breaker bar into square opening of belt tensioner pivot plate.
2. Install belt over all pulleys except air conditioning compressor drive pulley, **Fig. 23**.
3. Rotate belt tensioner clockwise until tensioner bottoms out and belt can be installed over air conditioning compressor pulley.
4. Gently release tensioner.
5. Install drive belt splash shield, then the tire and wheel assembly.

COOLING SYSTEM BLEED

This procedure has been revised by a Technical Service Bulletin.
1. Install cooling system filling aid (funnel type) tool No. 8195, or equivalent, to

filler neck in place of pressure cap along with attached hose clip.
2. Pinch off overflow hose attached to fill neck.
3. Attach 5–6.5 foot length of clear ¼ inch I.D. clear hose to bleed valve. Place other end of hose in suitable container.
4. Open cooling system bleed valve located on water outlet connector near front of engine.
5. Pour suitable coolant mixture into large side of filling aid tool.
6. Slowly fill cooling system, using large side of cooling aid.
7. When steady stream of coolant comes out of clear hose, close bleed valve. Continue filling to top of filling aid tool.
8. Remove overflow hose clip. Excess fluid will drain into coolant bottle overflow.
9. Remove filling aid.
10. Ensure pressure cap bottom seal and filler neck are clean and free of debris.
11. Install coolant bottle pressure cap.

THERMOSTAT
REPLACE

1. Drain coolant to below thermostat into suitable container.
2. Loosen clamp, then disconnect hoses at coolant outlet connector and thermostat housing.
3. Remove coolant outlet connector to thermostat housing mounting bolts.
4. Remove coolant outlet connector.
5. Remove thermostat and gasket.
6. Reverse procedure to install, noting the following:
   a. Install new gasket.
   b. Align air bleed with notch in coolant outlet connector.

WATER PUMP
REPLACE

1. Raise and support vehicle, then remove righthand inner splash shield.
2. Remove accessory drive belts.
3. Drain coolant into suitable container.
4. Support engine from bottom and remove righthand engine mount.
5. Remove mounting bolts, then position power steering pump and bracket aside. Power steering lines do not need to be disconnected.

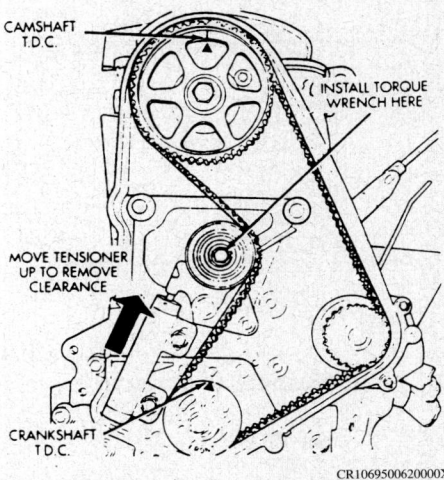

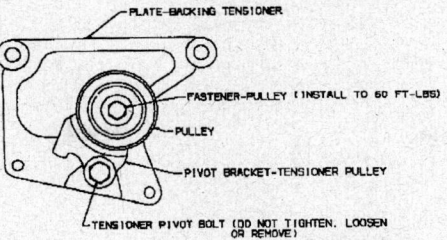

Fig. 13 Tensioner pivot bracket

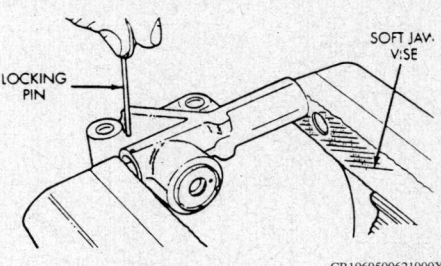

Fig. 14 Timing belt tensioner locking pin installation

Fig. 12 Crankshaft & camshaft timing mark alignment

6. Remove timing belt as outlined under "Timing Belt, Replace."
7. Remove mounting bolts water pump.
8. Reverse procedure to install. Install new O-ring gasket in water pump body O-ring groove.

RADIATOR
REPLACE

1. Drain coolant into suitable container, then remove upper radiator cross-member.
2. Disconnect electrical connector and remove radiator fan.
3. Disconnect hoses from radiator.
4. Remove screw holding support bracket for transmission cooler tubes to left-hand side of radiator.
5. Remove air conditioning lines support bracket.
6. Carefully lift out radiator.
7. Reverse procedure to install.

FUEL PUMP
REPLACE

The electric fuel pump is not serviceable. If fuel pump requires service, the entire fuel pump module must be replaced.

1. Remove fuel pump relay from power distribution center.
2. Start and run engine until it stalls.
3. Attempt to restart engine until it will no longer run, then turn ignition key to OFF position.
4. Install fuel pump relay, then erase any DTC's that may have been stored because of removing fuel pump relay.
5. Drain and remove fuel tank.
6. Disconnect fuel filter lines at fuel pump module.
7. Clean top of tank to remove dirt and debris.
8. Remove lockout securing pump module with fuel pump module ring spanner tool No. 6856, or equivalent, **Fig. 24.**

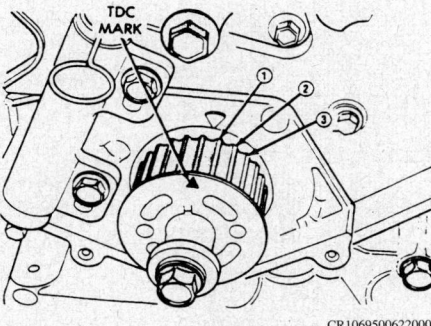

Fig. 15 Crankshaft sprocket & oil pump housing alignment

9. Remove fuel pump module and O-ring from tank. Discard O-ring.
10. Reverse procedure to install. Install new pump module O-ring.

FUEL FILTER
REPLACE

The fuel filter is part of the fuel pressure regulator and is located on top of the fuel pump module.

1. Relieve fuel system pressure as outlined under "Precautions."
2. Drain fuel tank into suitable container.
3. Raise and support vehicle on hoist.
4. Support fuel tank with suitable transmission jack.
5. Remove strap bolts lower tank slightly.
6. Disconnect fuel filler vent tube, fuel line and vapor line.
7. Disconnect vacuum line from LDP.
8. Loosen clamp and remove fuel filler tube.
9. Unlock and disconnect fuel pump module electrical connector.
10. Lower fuel tank.
11. Disconnect fuel supply line at filter/regulator nipple.
12. Depress locking spring tab on side of fuel regulator, rotate 90° counterclockwise and remove.
13. Reverse procedure to install.

TECHNICAL SERVICE BULLETINS
Irregular Engine Snapping Sound

On some of these models there may be

an irregular engine snapping sound. The sound is irregular, not periodic or harmonious. The sound is more higher pitch snapping, not low metallic knock. The sound may be noticed when the engine is idling in PARK between idle and 1400 RPM at normal operating temperature. The sound is on the upper end cylinder head toward the front righthand side.

This condition may be caused by the cam bearing caps.

To correct this condition, proceed as follows:

1. Remove valve cover as outlined under "Valve Cover, Replace."
2. Remove L2 cam bearing cap, **Fig. 25.**
3. **Do not remove L1/R1 or L6 cam bearing caps. Do not loosen L1/R1 or L6 cam bearing caps mounting bolts.**
4. **Remove one cam bearing cap at a time.**
5. Lightly chamfer two bores radius edges using suitable, small hand file, **Fig. 26.**
6. Create a 45° chamfer, .039–.059 inch wide along edge of each bore radios.
7. **Do not scratch bore surface.**
8. Clean part of aluminum filings.
9. Install L2 cam bearing cap and loosely install mounting bolts.
10. Twist cam bearing cap clockwise (as viewed from top of engine) by hand.
11. **Torque** bolts to 105 inch lbs while maintaining clockwise twisting force on cam bearing cap.
12. Repeat procedure on cam bearing caps L3, L4, L5, R2, R3, R4, R5 and R6.

Low Or No Cabin Heat

On some of these models there may be low or no cabin heat, engine overheating and/or coolant bottle damage after servicing the cooling system.

This condition may be caused by not filling cooling system completely.

To correct this condition, bleed cooling system as outlined under "Cooling System Bleed.'"

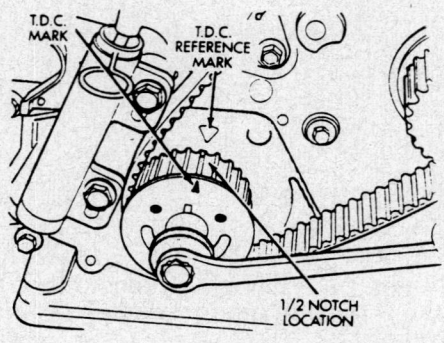

Fig. 16 Crankshaft sprocket ½ tooth rotation

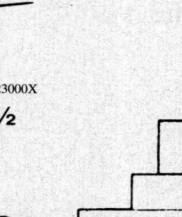

Fig. 17 Sprocket removal tool modification

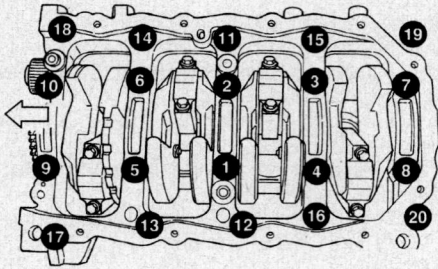

Fig. 19 Main bearing bolt tightening sequence

Accessory Drive Belt	Belt Tension		
Air Conditioning Compressor/ Generator	Dynamic Tensioned		
Power Steering Pump	New	120 - 180 lbs.	160 - 223 Hz
	Used*	70 - 115 lbs.	114 - 179 Hz
*A belt is considered used after 15 minutes of run-in time.			

CR1060200978000X

Fig. 22 Belt tension chart

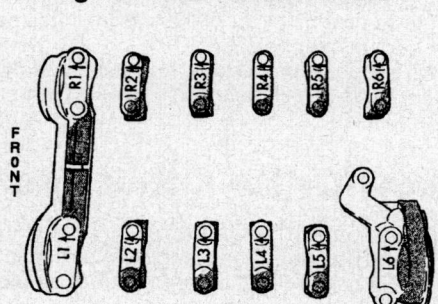

Fig. 25 Camshaft bearing cap identification

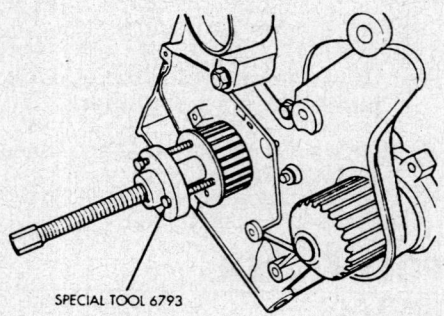

Fig. 20 Crankshaft sprocket replacement

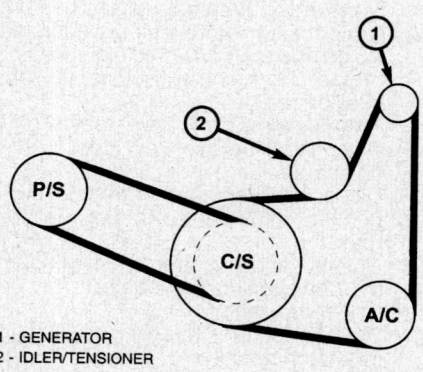

1 - GENERATOR
2 - IDLER/TENSIONER

CR1060100968000X

Fig. 23 Serpentine drive belt routing

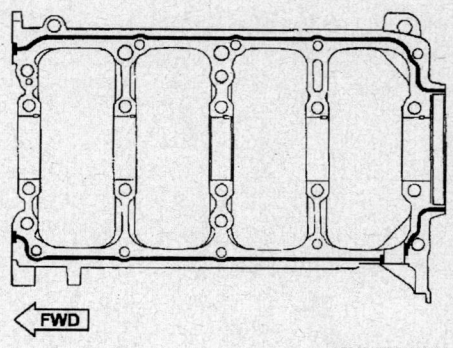

ARM0400000000989

Fig. 18 Sealer application

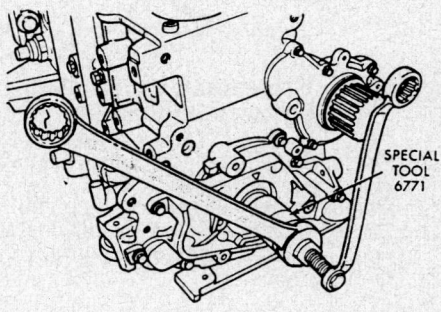

CR1069500577000X

Fig. 21 Front crankshaft oil seal replacement

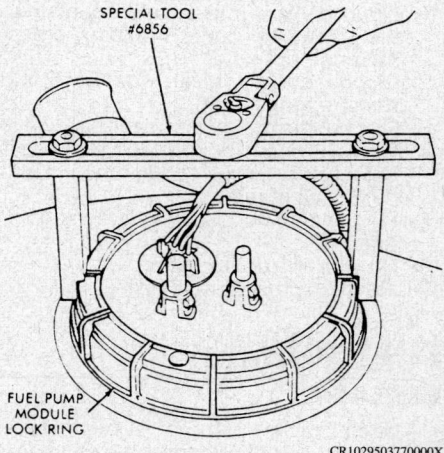

CR1029503770000X

Fig. 24 Fuel pump module lockout

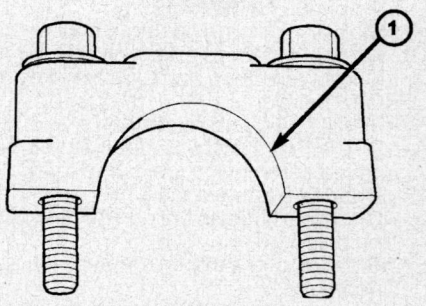

1- CAM BEARING CAP RADIUS

ARM0400000000984

Fig. 26 Camshaft bearing cap chamfer area

TIGHTENING SPECIFICATIONS

Year	Component	Torque Ft. Lbs.
All	Camshaft Sprocket	85
	Connecting Rod Cap	②
	Crankshaft Damper	105
	Crankshaft Main Bearing Bedplate (M8)	25
	Crankshaft Main Bearing Bedplate (M11)	60
	Cylinder Head	⑤
	Drive Plate	70
	Engine Mount	③
	Exhaust Manifold	17
	Exhaust Manifold Heat Shield	105①
	Fuel Pump Module Lock Ring	40
	Fuel Rail To Intake Manifold	16–17
	Fuel Tank Drain Plug	32①
	Hydraulic Timing Belt Tensioner	23
	Intake Manifold	105①
	Main Bearing Cap	④
	Oil Filter	15
	Oil Filter Adapter	40
	Oil Pan	105①
	Oil Pan Drain Plug	20
	Oil Pump	20
	Oil Pump Cover	105①
	Oil Pump Pickup Tube	20
	Oil Pump Relief Valve Retaining Cap	30
	PCV Valve	70①
	Spark Plugs	13
	Thermostat Housing	16–17
	Throttle Body Support Bracket	96–108①
	Throttle Body To Intake	16
	Timing Belt Cover	105①
	Timing Belt Tensioner	23
	Valve Cover	105①
	Water Pump	105①

① — Inch lbs.
② — Refer to Piston & Rod Assembly for tightening procedure & specifications.
③ — Refer to Engine Mount, Replace illustrations for tightening specifications.
④ — Refer to Main & Rod Bearings for tightening procedure & specifications.
⑤ — Refer to Cylinder Head, Replace for tightening procedure & specifications.

2.4L Engine

NOTE: On Air Bag Equipped Models, Refer To "Air Bag System Precautions" Located In The Front Of This Manual For System Disarming & Arming Procedures.

NOTE: Refer To "Computer Relearn Procedures" Located In The Front Of This Manual When Battery Power To The Computer Has Been Interrupted.

INDEX

	Page No.
Accessory Drive Belts, Replace.	5-22
A/C & Power Steering	5-22
Alternator	5-22
Balance Shaft, Replace	5-20
Balance Shafts	5-20
Installation	5-21
Balance Shaft Carrier, Replace.	5-21
Camshaft, Replace	5-20
Installation	5-20
Removal	5-20
Compression Pressure	5-16
Cooling System Bleed	5-22
Crankshaft Damper, Replace	5-19
Crankshaft Rear Oil Seal, Replace	5-21
Installation	5-22
Removal	5-21
Cylinder Head, Replace	5-18
Cylinder Head Cover, Replace	5-19
Engine Rebuilding Specifications	21-1

	Page No.
Engine, Replace	5-17
Engine Mount, Replace	5-16
Left	5-16
Right	5-16
Torque Struts	5-17
Adjustment Procedure	5-17
Lower	5-17
Upper	5-17
Exhaust Manifold, Replace	5-18
Front Cover, Replace	5-19
Lower	5-19
Upper	5-19
Fuel Pump, Replace	5-23
Hydraulic Lash Adjusters, Replace	5-19
Intake Manifold, Replace	5-18
Main & Rod Bearings	5-21
Oil Pan, Replace	5-22
Oil Pump, Replace	5-22
Piston & Rod Assembly	5-21

	Page No.
Precautions	5-16
Air Bag Systems	5-16
Battery Ground Cable	5-16
Fuel System Pressure Relief	5-16
Radiator, Replace	5-23
Rocker Arms, Replace	5-19
Structural Collar, Replace	5-17
Installation	5-17
Removal	5-17
Thermostat, Replace	5-23
Tightening Specifications	5-25
Timing Belt, Replace	5-19
Installation	5-19
Removal	5-19
Timing Belt Rear Cover, Replace	5-20
Turbocharger, Replace	5-24
Valve Adjustment	5-19
Water Pump, Replace	5-23

PRECAUTIONS

Air Bag Systems

Refer to "Air Bag System Precautions" in the front of this manual for system disarming and arming procedures.

Battery Ground Cable

Prior to service, disconnect battery ground cable and isolate as required.

Fuel System Pressure Relief

1. Remove fuel pump relay from Power Distribution Center (PDC).
2. Start and run engine until it stalls.
3. Attempt restarting engine until it will no longer run.
4. Turn ignition key to Off position.
5. Place a rag or shop towel below fuel line quick connect fitting at fuel rail.
6. Return fuel pump relay to (PDC).
7. One or more diagnostic trouble codes may have been stored in PCM memory due to fuel pump relay removal. Use suitable scan tool to erase codes.

COMPRESSION PRESSURE

Recommended compression pressures are 170–225 psi. Recommended pressures are used only as a guide to diagnosing engine problem. An engine should not be disassembled to determine the cause of low compression unless a fault is present.

1. Ensure battery is fully charged and starter is in good operating condition.
2. Inspect engine oil level and top up if required.
3. Drive vehicle until engine is at normal operating temperature.
4. Remove spark plugs from engine and inspect for abnormal firing indicators.
5. Disconnect coil wire from distributor and secure to good ground. For direct ignition system, disconnect coil connector.
6. Ensure throttle blade is fully open during compression test.
7. Insert compression gauge adapter tool No. 8116, or equivalent, into No. 1 cylinder spark plug hole.
8. Connect 0–500 psi (Blue) transducer with cable adapters to DRBIII.
9. Crank engine until maximum pressure is reached on gauge, repeat for all cylinders.
10. Compression should not be less than 100 psi or vary by more than 25 percent from cylinder to cylinder.

ENGINE MOUNT

REPLACE

Left

1. Remove air cleaner assembly.
2. Remove bolts attaching PDC bracket to left mount and battery tray.
3. Support transaxle with suitable jack.
4. Remove mount to transaxle bolts, **Fig. 1.**
5. Remove left mount bracket to body frame rail fasteners, then the motor mount.
6. Reverse procedure to install.

Right

Engine removal is required for required clearance to access the right motor mount. The right engine mount attaching holes are slightly oversize to compensate for manufacturing tolerances. The mount has been set at the factory for proper powertrain alignment. If mount is to be removed, it will be required to mark the position of the mount before removing the attaching bolts.

1. Remove engine assembly as outlined under "Engine, Replace."
2. Mark position of engine mount to body frame rail using a suitable permanent marker.

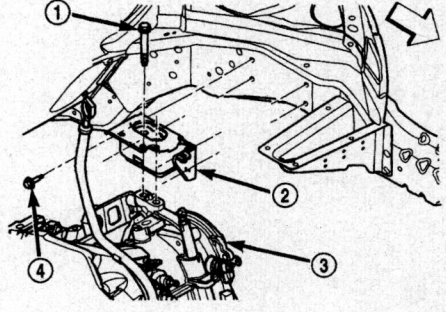

1 - BOLT
2 - LEFT MOUNT
3 - TRANSAXLE
4 - BOLT

ARM0400000000243

Fig. 1   Left engine mount

3. Remove bolts attaching mount to body, **Fig. 2,** then the mount.
4. Reverse procedure to install.

Torque Struts

UPPER

1. Remove bolts attaching strut to shock tower bracket and engine mount bracket, **Fig. 2.**
2. **On models equipped with A/C,** remove timing belt front upper cover.
3. **On all models,** remove upper torque strut.
4. Reverse procedure to install, adjust torque strut according to adjustment procedure.

LOWER

1. Raise and support vehicle.
2. Remove accessory belt splash shield.
3. Remove pencil strut, **Fig. 2.**
4. Remove bolts attaching lower strut to crossmember and strut bracket, then the lower torque strut.
5. Reverse procedure to install, adjust torque strut according to adjustment procedure.

ADJUSTMENT PROCEDURE

The upper and lower torque struts need to be adjusted together to assure proper engine mount load balance and engine positioning. Whenever a torque strut bolt is loosened, the following adjustment procedure must be performed.
1. Remove pencil strut.
2. Loosen upper and lower torque strut attaching bolt at suspension crossmember and shock tower bracket.
3. Position a suitable floor jack on forward edge of transmission bell housing, **Fig. 3.**
4. Floor jack must be positioned to prevent minimal upward lifting of engine.
5. Apply upward force, allowing upper engine to rotate rearward until distance between center or rearmost attaching bolt on engine mount bracket (point "A") and center of hole on shock tower bracket (point "B") is 4.70 inches, **Fig. 4.**
6. With engine held at proper position,

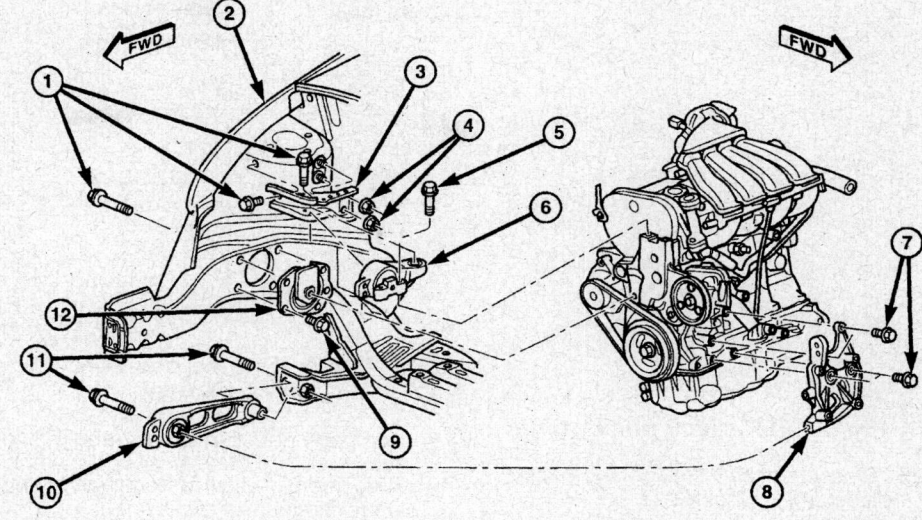

1 - BOLT
2 - RIGHT FENDER
3 - UPPER TORQUE STRUT BRACKET
4 - NUTS
5 - BOLT
6 - UPPER TORQUE STRUT

7 - BOLT
8 - LOWER TORQUE STRUT BRACKET
9 - BOLT
10 - LOWER TORQUE STRUT
11 - BOLT
12 - RIGHT ENGINE MOUNT

ARM0400000000244

Fig. 2   Right engine mount & torque struts

torque upper and lower torque strut bolts to 85 ft. lbs.
7. Remove floor jack.
8. Install pencil strut and **torque** nuts to 43 ft. lbs.

STRUCTURAL COLLAR
REPLACE
Removal

1. Raise and support vehicle.
2. Remove bolts attaching bending strut to engine and transaxle, **Fig. 5,** then the strut.
3. Remove bolts attaching collar and clutch slave cylinder to oil pan and transaxle, then the collar.

Installation

Torque procedure for structural collar and bending strut must be followed or damage could occur to oil pan, collar and/or bending strut. Refer to **Fig. 5** for bolt position when performing this procedure.
1. Place collar into position between transaxle and oil pan. Install collar to transaxle bolt (1), hand tighten only.
2. Position power steering hose support bracket and install collar to oil pan bolt (2), hand tighten only.
3. Position clutch slave cylinder into mounting position and install bolts (3) and (4), hand tighten only.
4. Position power steering hose support bracket and install remaining collar to oil pan bolt (5), hand tighten only.
5. Tighten all bolts in sequence as follows:
   a. **Torque** bolt (1) to 75 ft. lbs.
   b. **Torque** bolts (2) and (5) to 45 ft. lbs.
   c. **Torque** bolts (3) and (4) to 20 ft. lbs.

ENGINE
REPLACE

1. Relieve fuel system pressure as outlined under "Precautions."
2. Remove air cleaner housing assembly and clean air hose.
3. Disconnect both battery cables.
4. Remove battery and battery tray.
5. Drain cooling system into suitable container.
6. **On models equipped with A/C,** recover refrigerant as outlined in "Air Conditioning" chapter.
7. **On all models,** disconnect throttle and speed control cables.
8. Disconnect engine wiring harness at PCM connector.
9. Disconnect positive cable from PDC and ground wire from vehicle body.
10. Remove power distribution center attaching bolts and set PDC aside.
11. Disconnect wiring connectors at lower battery tray support.
12. Disconnect ground wire from vehicle body to engine at right side strut tower.
13. Disconnect brake booster vacuum hose from intake manifold.
14. Disconnect proportional purge hoses from intake manifold.
15. Disconnect coolant reserve/recovery hose from coolant outlet connector.
16. Disconnect heater hoses.
17. Remove upper radiator support crossmember.
18. Remove upper and lower radiator hoses.
19. Disconnect upper A/C line from condenser.
20. Disconnect A/C lines at junction near upper torque strut.
21. Disconnect electrical fan connector and remove cooling module assembly fan.

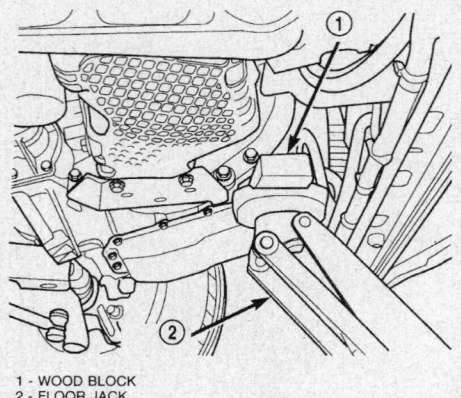

1 - WOOD BLOCK
2 - FLOOR JACK

ARM0400000000245

Fig. 3 Floor jack positioning

22. Disconnect shift linkage and transaxle electrical connectors.
23. Disconnect clutch hydraulic line at quick disconnect fitting using removal tool No. 6638, or equivalent.
24. Raise and support vehicle.
25. Remove front wheels, right inner splash shield and axle shafts.
26. Remove accessory drive belts, alternator and support brackets.
27. Remove charge air cooler hoses.
28. Drain engine oil into suitable container.
29. Disconnect downstream oxygen sensor connector.
30. Disconnect exhaust system from manifold.
31. Disconnect power steering pressure hose from steering gear.
32. Remove upper and lower heat shields, elbow support bracket, turbocharger support bracket and elbow.
33. Remove lower engine torque strut and structural collar.
34. Remove torque converter bolts.
35. Lower vehicle and remove A/C compressor.
36. Disconnect power steering fluid return line from reservoir.
37. Remove power steering pump.
38. Raise and support vehicle, and position engine dolly and cradle tool No. 6135 and tool No. 6710, or equivalents, **Fig. 6,** below engine and transaxle assembly.
39. Loosen engine support posts to allow movement for positioning onto engine locating holes and flange on engine bedplate.
40. Lower vehicle and position cradle until engine is resting on support posts.
41. Tighten mounts to cradle frame.
42. Install suitable safety straps around engine to cradle. Tighten straps and lock into position.
43. Raise vehicle enough to determine if straps are secure enough to hold cradle assembly to engine.
44. Lower vehicle so weight of engine and transmission is on cradle assembly.
45. Remove upper engine torque strut.
46. Remove right mount through bolt and left mount attaching bolt.
47. Raise vehicle slowly until engine/transaxle assembly clears engine

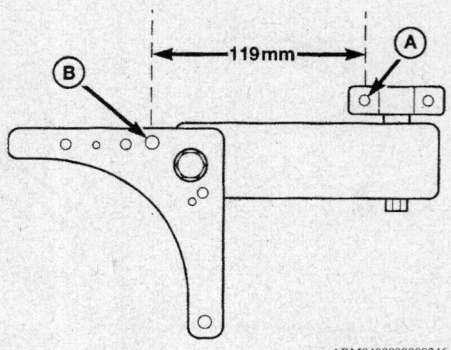

ARM0400000000246

Fig. 4 Engine position measurement

compartment. It may be required to move engine/transmission assembly with cradle to allow for removal around body flanges.
48. Reverse procedure to install.

INTAKE MANIFOLD
REPLACE

1. Relieve fuel system pressure as outlined under "Precautions."
2. Remove fuel rail trim cover.
3. Disconnect charge air cooler to throttle body hose.
4. Disconnect vacuum hoses from throttle body and intake manifold.
5. Disconnect throttle cable from throttle body.
6. Disconnect Throttle Position (TP) sensor and Idle Air Control (IAC) valve electrical connectors.
7. Remove intake manifold support bracket.
8. Disconnect fuel injector electrical connectors, then unclip wiring harness from fuel rail.
9. Disconnect Manifold Absolute Pressure (MAP) sensor electrical connector.
10. Disconnect fuel supply line quick connect at fuel rail assembly.
11. Remove intake manifold attaching bolts, then the intake manifold.
12. Reverse procedure to install.

EXHAUST MANIFOLD
REPLACE

The exhaust manifold must be serviced as an assembly with the turbocharger. Refer to "Turbocharger, Replace" for replacement procedure.

CYLINDER HEAD
REPLACE

1. Perform fuel system pressure relief procedure as outlined under "Precautions."
2. Remove clean air hose and air cleaner housing.
3. Drain cooling system into suitable container.
4. Disconnect fuel supply line quick connect at fuel rail assembly.

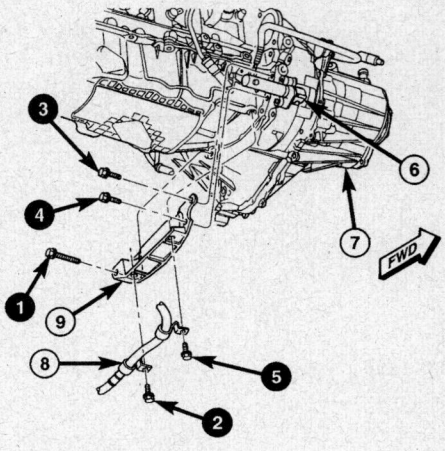

1–5 – BOLT TIGHTENING SEQUENCE
6 – HYDRAULIC CLUTCH SLAVE CYLINDER
7 – TRANSAXLE
8 – POWER STEERING HOSE
9 – COLLAR

ARM0400000000247

Fig. 5 Structural collar & bending strut. With manual transaxle

5. Remove heater tube support bracket from cylinder head.
6. Disconnect upper radiator and heater supply hoses from coolant outlet connections.
7. Disconnect Engine Coolant Temperature (ECT) sensor electrical connector.
8. Remove accessory drive belts.
9. Raise and support vehicle.
10. Disconnect exhaust pipe from manifold.
11. Remove turbocharger heat shields.
12. Remove elbow and turbocharger support brackets.
13. Remove oil supply and return lines.
14. Remove coolant supply and return lines.
15. Lower vehicle and disconnect ignition coil wiring connector.
16. Remove ignition coil and plug wires.
17. Disconnect Camshaft Position (CMP) sensor electrical connector.
18. Remove valve cover as outlined under "Valve Cover, Replace."
19. Remove timing belt and camshafts as outlined under "Timing Belt, Replace" and "Camshaft, Replace."
20. Remove rocker arms.
21. Remove cylinder head bolts in reverse order of tightening sequence, **Fig. 7.**
22. Remove cylinder head from engine block.
23. Reverse procedure to install, noting the following:
    a. Install new cylinder head gasket on cylinder block with part number facing up.
    b. Before installing bolts, lightly coat threads with engine oil.
    c. **Torque** cylinder head bolts in four steps using sequence, **Fig. 7,** First step, all bolts to 25 ft. lbs.; second step, all bolts to 50 ft. lbs.; third step, all bolts to 50 ft. lbs., again; fourth step, tighten all bolts an additional 90.°

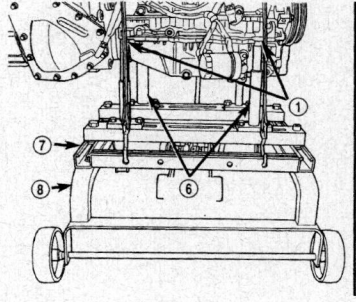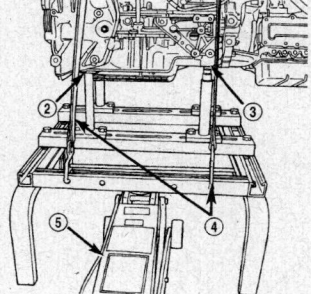

1 - POST LOCATING HOLES IN BLOCK
2 - POST POSITIONED UNDER BRACKET
3 - POST LOCATING HOLE IN STRUT
4 - SAFETY STRAPS
5 - FLOOR JACK
6 - SPECIAL TOOL 6848
7 - SPECIAL TOOL 6135
8 - SPECIAL TOOL 6710

ARM0400000000248

Fig. 6   Engine cradle support

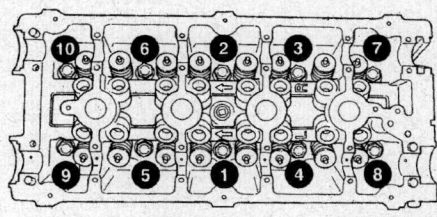

ARM0400000000249

Fig. 7   Cylinder head tightening sequence

CYLINDER HEAD COVER

REPLACE

1. Disconnect ignition coil connector.
2. Disconnect spark plug wires and remove ignition coil.
3. Disconnect PCV and make-up air hoses from cover.
4. Remove wire harness from cover studs.
5. Remove coolant return line bracket to cover stud retaining nut.
6. Remove remaining cover attaching bolts and nuts, then the cover.
7. Reverse procedure to install.

VALVE ADJUSTMENT

These engines use hydraulic lifters. No adjustment is required.

ROCKER ARMS

REPLACE

This procedure is for in-vehicle service with camshafts installed.
1. Remove valve cover as outlined under "Valve Cover, Replace."
2. Remove spark plugs.
3. Rotate engine until camshaft lobe, on follower being removed, is positioned on it's base circle (heel). Piston should be a minimum of .025 inch below TDC position.
4. If cam follower assemblies are to be reused, mark followers for installation reference.
5. Slowly depress valve assembly until cam follower can be removed using valve spring compressor tool No. 8215 and adapter tool No. 8436, or equivalent, **Fig. 8.**
6. It may be required to remove additional brackets to allow clearance for tool handle movement.
7. Reverse procedure to install.

CRANKSHAFT DAMPER

REPLACE

1. Raise and support vehicle.
2. Remove right front wheel.
3. Remove right splash shield.

4. Remove accessory drive belts.
5. Remove crankshaft damper retaining bolt.
6. Remove crankshaft damper using puller tool No. 1026, or equivalent.
7. Reverse procedure to install.

HYDRAULIC LASH ADJUSTERS

REPLACE

1. Remove rocker arm as outlined under "Rocker Arms, Replace."
2. Remove hydraulic lash adjusters from cylinder head. If reusing lash adjusters, mark each adjuster for installation reference.
3. Reverse procedure to install. Before installing, ensure lash adjuster is at least partially full of engine oil.

FRONT COVER

REPLACE

Upper

1. Remove upper torque strut as outlined under "Engine Mounts, Replace."
2. Remove upper timing belt cover attaching bolts, then the cover, **Fig. 9.**
3. Reverse procedure to install.

Lower

1. Remove crankshaft damper as outlined under "Crankshaft Damper, Replace."
2. Remove lower torque strut as outlined under "Engine Mounts, Replace."
3. Disconnect exhaust system from manifold.
4. Disconnect A/C pressure switch at rear of compressor housing.
5. Lower vehicle and support engine with suitable jack.
6. Remove upper torque strut.
7. Remove power steering pump and bracket. Set pump aside. Do not disconnect lines from pump.
8. Remove right engine mount through bolt.
9. Raise engine with suitable jack until engine support bracket bolts are accessible, **Fig. 10.**

10. Remove engine support bracket, then the lower timing belt cover.
11. Reverse procedure to install.

TIMING BELT

REPLACE

Removal

1. Raise and support vehicle.
2. Remove timing belt covers as outlined under "Front Cover, Replace."
3. Before removing timing belt, rotate crankshaft until TDC mark on oil pump housing aligns with TDC mark on crankshaft sprocket, **Fig. 11.**
4. When aligning crankshaft and camshaft timing marks, always rotate engine from crankshaft. **Do not rotate camshaft after timing belt has been removed.**
5. Install a 6mm Allen wrench into top plate of belt tensioner opening, **Fig. 12.**
6. Rotate top plate of belt tensioner clockwise, then remove timing belt.

Installation

1. Set crankshaft sprocket to TDC by aligning sprocket with arrow on oil pump housing, **Fig. 11.**
2. Set camshaft sprocket timing marks so exhaust camshaft timing mark is ½ notch below intake camshaft sprocket, **Fig. 13.**
3. Ensure arrows on both camshaft sprockets are facing up.
4. Install timing belt. Starting at crankshaft, go around water pump sprocket, idler pulleys, camshaft sprockets and tensioner.
5. Move exhaust camshaft sprocket counterclockwise to take up belt slack and align marks.
6. Install a 6mm Allen wrench into top plate of belt tensioner opening, **Fig. 12.**
7. Rotate top plate of belt tensioner counterclockwise. Tensioner pulley will move against belt and setting notch will start to move clockwise, **Fig. 14.**
8. Watching movement of setting notch, continue rotating top plate until setting notch is aligned with spring tang.
9. Use allen wrench to prevent top plate from moving, then **torque** tensioner bolt to 18 ft. lbs.
10. Remove allen wrench.
11. Rotate crankshaft two complete revolutions and verify camshaft and crankshaft timing marks are aligned, **Fig. 11.**

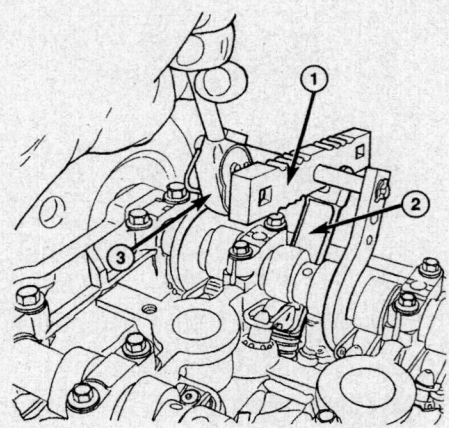

Fig. 8 Rocker arm (camshaft follower) replacement

1 - SPECIAL TOOL 8215A
2 - SPECIAL TOOL 8436
3 - 3/8" DRIVE RACHET

ARM0400000000250

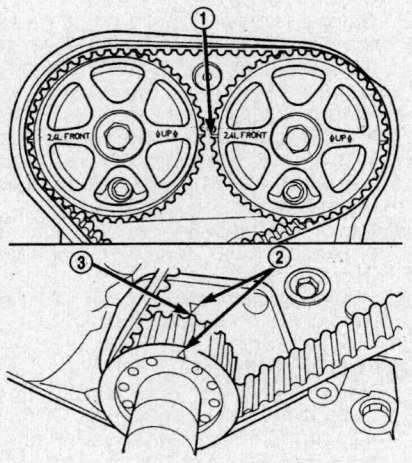

1 - CAMSHAFT TIMING MARKS
2 - CRANKSHAFT TDC MARKS
3 - TRAILING EDGE OF SPROCKET TOOTH

ARM0400000000253

Fig. 11 Crankshaft & camshaft timing marks

12. Ensure spring tang is within tolerance window, **Fig. 14.**
13. Install lower and upper timing belt covers as outlined under "Front Cover, Replace."

TIMING BELT REAR COVER
REPLACE

1. Remove timing belt as outlined under "Timing Belt, Replace."
2. Remove timing belt idler pulley retaining bolt, then the idler pulley.
3. Hold camshaft sprocket in place with holding tool No. 6847, or equivalent, then remove camshaft sprocket retaining bolt and sprocket.
4. Remove rear timing belt cover attaching bolts, then the rear cover.
5. Reverse procedure to install.

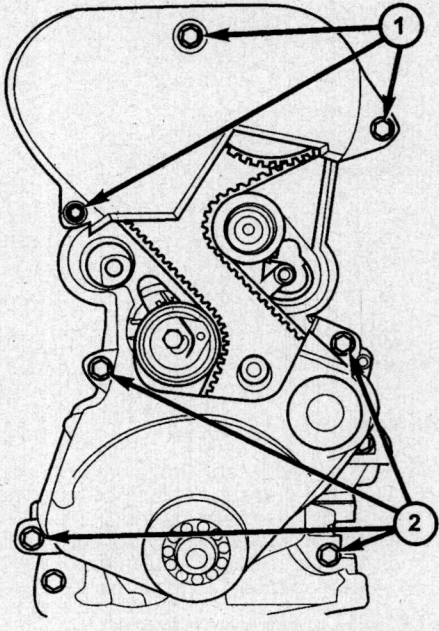

1 - UPPER COVER FASTENERS
2 - LOWER COVER FASTENERS

ARM0400000000251

Fig. 9 Upper & lower timing belt covers

CAMSHAFT
REPLACE
Removal

Camshafts are not interchangeable. The left (intake) camshaft thrust bearing face (No. 6) spacing is wider.
1. Remove cylinder head cover as outlined under "Cylinder Head Cover, Replace."
2. Remove camshaft position sensor and camshaft target magnet.
3. Remove timing belt as outlined under "Timing Belt, Replace."
4. Remove rear timing belt cover as outlined under "Timing Belt Rear Cover, Replace."
5. Bearing caps are identified for location, remove outside bearing caps first, **Fig. 15.**
6. Loosen camshaft bearing cap attaching bolts in sequence, **Fig. 16.**
7. Identify camshafts, then remove from cylinder head.

Installation

Ensure no piston is at TDC when installing camshafts.
1. Lubricate all camshaft bearing journals, cam followers and camshafts.
2. Install cam followers and camshafts.
3. Install right and left camshaft bearing caps No. 2–5 and right No. 6. **Torque** M6 fasteners to 105 inch lbs., in sequence, **Fig. 17.**
4. Apply Mopar Gasket Maker, or equivalent, to No. 1 and left No. 6 bearing caps. Install caps and tighten M8 fas-

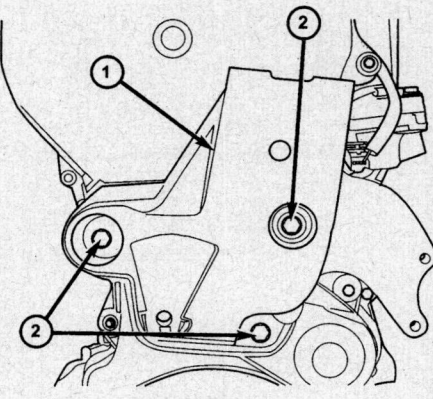

1 - ENGINE SUPPORT BRACKET
2 - BOLTS - 61 N·m (45 ft. lbs.)

ARM0400000000252

Fig. 10 Engine support bracket

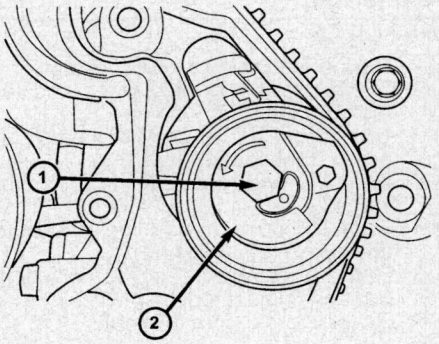

1 - LOCK BOLT
2 - TOP PLATE

ARM0400000000254

Fig. 12 Locking timing belt tensioner

teners to specification.
5. Camshaft end caps must be installed before camshaft seals are installed.
6. Install camshaft seals, rear timing belt cover, camshaft sprockets and timing belt as outlined under "Timing Belt, Replace."
7. Install camshaft target magnet and camshaft position sensor.
8. Install cylinder head cover.

BALANCE SHAFT
REPLACE
Balance Shafts

1. Drain engine oil into suitable container.
2. Remove oil pan and oil pickup tube.
3. Remove chain cover, guide and tensioner, **Fig. 18.**
4. Remove balance shaft drive sprocket retaining bolt, **Fig. 19.**
5. Remove chain and sprocket assembly. Using two wide pry bars, work sprocket back and forth until it is off of crankshaft.
6. Remove gear cover retaining stud (double ended to also retain chain guide), gear cover and balance shaft gears.

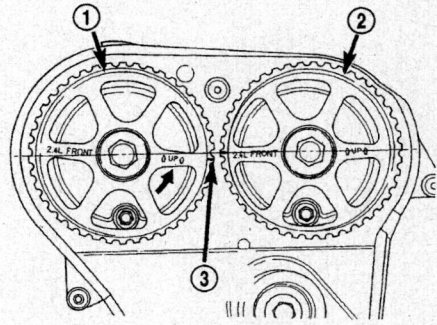

1 - CAMSHAFT SPROCKET-EXHAUST
2 - CAMSHAFT SPROCKET-INTAKE
3 - 1/2 NOTCH LOCATION

ARM0400000000255

Fig. 13 Camshaft sprocket alignment

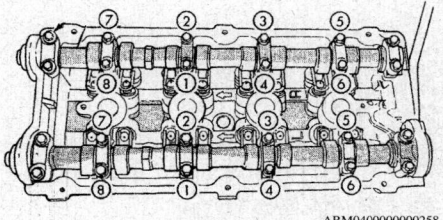

ARM0400000000258

Fig. 16 Camshaft bearing cap removal sequence

7. Remove gear cover and balance shafts.
8. Remove four carrier to crankcase attaching bolts to separate carrier from engine bedplate.

INSTALLATION

1. With balance shafts installed in carrier, **Fig. 18,** position carrier on crankcase and install four attaching bolts.
2. Turn balance shafts until both shaft keyways are up, parallel to vertical centerline of engine.
3. Install short hub drive gear on sprocket driven shaft and long hub gear on gear driven shaft.
4. Gear and balance shaft keyways must be up with gear timing marks meshed, **Fig. 20.**
5. Install gear cover and tighten double ended stud/washer to specification.
6. Align flat on balance shaft sprocket to flat on crankshaft, **Fig. 21.**
7. Install balance shaft drive sprocket on crankshaft using sprocket installer tool No. 6052, or equivalent.
8. Turn crankshaft until No. 1 cylinder is at TDC, timing marks on chain sprocket should align with parting line on left side of No. 1 main bearing cap, **Fig. 22.**
9. Place chain over crankshaft sprocket so that plated link of chain is over No. 1 cylinder timing mark on balance shaft crankshaft sprocket, **Fig. 22.**
10. Place balance shaft sprocket into timing chain and align timing mark on sprocket with lower plated link on chain, **Fig. 22.**

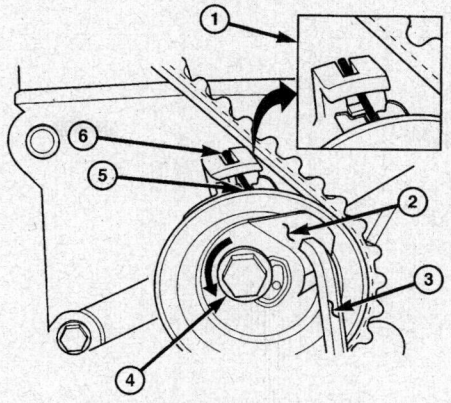

1 - ALIGN SETTING NOTCH WITH SPRING TANG
2 - TOP PLATE
3 - 6mm ALLEN WRENCH
4 - LOCK BOLT
5 - SETTING NOTCH
6 - SPRING TANG

ARM0400000000256

Fig. 14 Timing belt tension adjustment

11. Lower plated link is eight links from upper link.
12. With balance shaft keyways pointing up, slide balance shaft sprocket onto nose of balance shaft. Balance shaft may have to be pushed in slightly to allow for clearance.
13. Timing mark on sprocket, lower nickel plated link and arrow on side of gear cover should align when balance shafts are timed correctly.
14. Install balance shaft bolts. Place a wood block between crankcase and crankshaft counterbalance to prevent crankshaft and gear rotation.
15. Install chain tensioner loosely.
16. Position guide on double ended stud. Ensure tab on guide fits into slot on gear cover, then install nut and **torque** to 105 inch lbs.
17. Place a shim .039 inch thick and 2.75 inches long between tensioner and chain, **Fig. 23.**
18. Push tensioner and shim up against chain. Apply firm pressure (5.5–6.6 lbs.) directly behind adjustment slot to take up all slack.
19. Chain must have shoe radius contact, **Fig. 23.**
20. With load applied, tighten top bolt first, then the bottom pivot bolt. Tighten bolts to specification, then remove shim.
21. Install carrier covers, pickup tube and oil pan.

BALANCE SHAFT CARRIER
REPLACE

1. Remove oil pan and pickup tube as outlined under "Oil Pan, Replace."
2. Remove chain cover, guide and tensioner, **Fig. 18.**
3. Remove balance shaft drive sprocket retaining bolt, **Fig. 19.**
4. Move driven balance shaft inboard

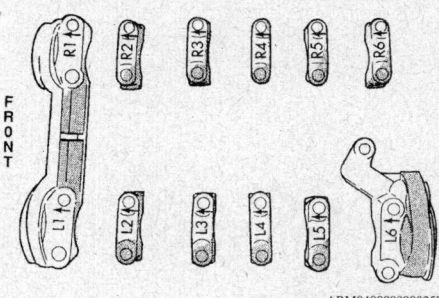

ARM0400000000257

Fig. 15 Camshaft bearing cap identification

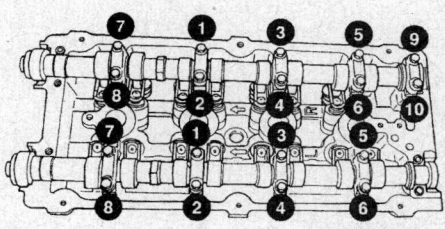

ARM0400000000259

Fig. 17 Camshaft bearing cap tightening sequence

through driven chain sprocket. Sprocket will hang in lower chain loop.
5. Remove carrier to crankcase attaching bolts, then the carrier.
6. Reverse procedure to install.

PISTON & ROD ASSEMBLY

The directional stamp on the piston should face toward the front of the engine.

MAIN & ROD BEARINGS

The crankshaft and main bearings are supported by a bedplate. When installing bedplate, refer to **Fig. 24** for bolt tightening sequence and identification. Tighten bedplate retaining bolts in five steps. First step, **torque** bolts numbered 1–10 to 30 ft. lbs.; second step, **torque** bolts numbered 1–10 to 30 ft. lbs.; Third step, **torque** bolts numbered 11–20 to 21 ft. lbs.; Fourth step, **torque** bolts numbered 1–10 to 55 ft. lbs.; Fifth step, **torque** bolts numbered 11–20 to 21 ft. lbs.

CRANKSHAFT REAR OIL SEAL
REPLACE
Removal

1. Remove transaxle and flexplate as outlined in **MOTOR'S "Domestic Transmission, In-Vehicle Service"** manual.
2. Insert a ³⁄₁₆ inch flat bladed screwdriver between dust lip and metal case of crankshaft seal.
3. Pry out seal.

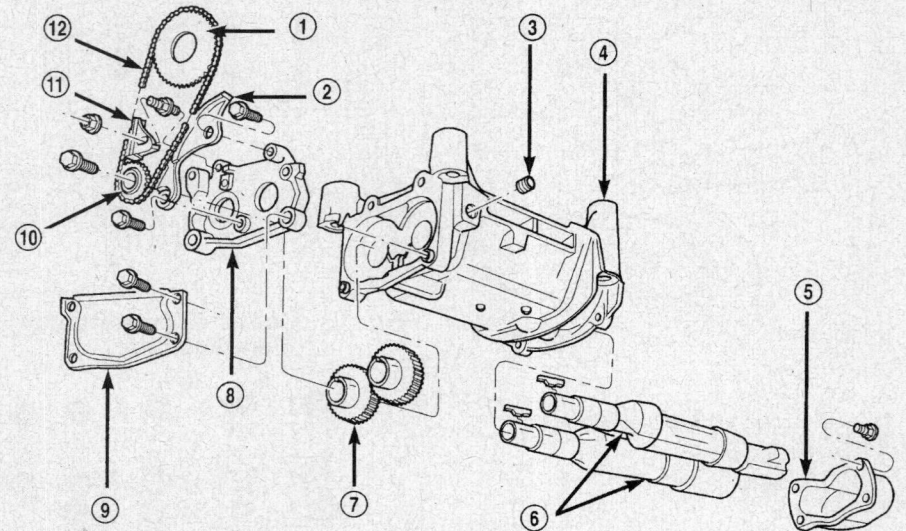

1 - SPROCKET
2 - TENSIONER
3 - PLUG
4 - CARRIER
5 - REAR COVER
6 - BALANCE SHAFTS

7 - GEARS
8 - GEAR COVER
9 - CHAIN COVER
10 - SPROCKET
11 - GUIDE
12 - CHAIN

ARM0400000000260

Fig. 18 Exploded view of balance shaft & carrier assembly

4. Do not allow screwdriver blade to contact crankshaft seal surface.
5. If burrs or scratches are present on crankshaft edge, polish with 400 grit sand paper to prevent seal damage during installation of new seal.

Installation

When installing new seal, no lube on seal is needed.
1. Place seal guide tool No. 6926–1, or equivalent, on crankshaft.
2. Position seal over guide tool, guide tool should remain on crankshaft during installation of seal.
3. Ensure lip of seal is facing toward crankcase during installation.
4. Drive seal into block using seal driver tool No. 6926–2 and handle tool No. C-4171, or equivalents, until tool bottoms out against block.
5. Install flexplate.
6. Apply Mopar Lock and Seal adhesive to bolt threads and tighten to specification.
7. Install transaxle as outlined in **MO-TOR'S "Domestic Transmission, In-Vehicle Service"** manual.

OIL PAN

REPLACE

1. Raise and support vehicle.
2. Drain engine oil into suitable container.
3. Remove oil filter.
4. Remove right inner splash shield.
5. Remove turbocharger to charge air cooler hose assembly.
6. Remove oil cooler connector bolt. **Do not disconnect coolant lines from oil cooler.**

7. Remove structural collar as outlined under "Structural Collar, Replace."
8. Remove lower torque strut.
9. Remove oil filter adapter and gasket.
10. Remove oil pan and gasket.
11. Reverse procedure to install, noting the following:
    a. Clean oil pan and all gasket surfaces.
    b. Apply Mopar Engine RTV GEN II, or equivalent, at oil pump to engine block parting lines.
    c. Install oil pan and gasket, tighten to specification.
    d. Install oil filter adapter and gasket, tighten to specification.

OIL PUMP

REPLACE

1. Remove timing belt and timing belt rear cover as outlined under "Timing Belt, Replace" and "Timing Belt Rear Cover, Replace."
2. Remove oil pan as outlined under "Oil Pan, Replace."
3. Remove crankshaft sprocket using puller tool Nos. 6793 and C-4685–C2, or equivalents.
4. Remove crankshaft key.
5. Remove oil pickup tube.
6. Remove oil pump and front crankshaft seal, **Fig. 25.**
7. Reverse procedure to install, noting the following:
    a. Ensure all surfaces are clean and free of oil and dirt.
    b. Apply Mopar Gasket Maker, or equivalent, to oil pump, **Fig. 26.**
    c. Install O-ring into oil pump body discharge passage.
    d. Prime oil pump with engine oil before installation.

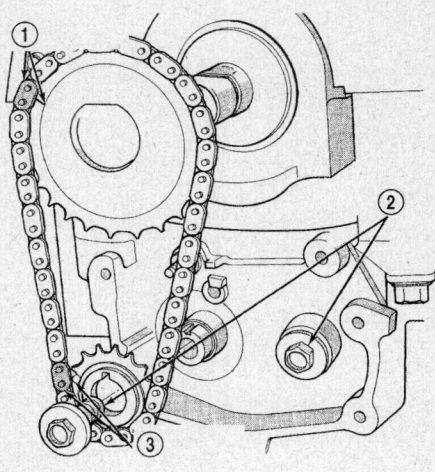

1 - NICKEL PLATED LINK AND MARK
2 - GEAR/SPROCKET SCREWS
3 - NICKEL PLATED LINK AND DOT

ARM0400000000261

Fig. 19 Drive chain & sprockets

ACCESSORY DRIVE BELTS

REPLACE

A/C & Power Steering

1. Raise and support vehicle.
2. Remove splash shield.
3. Rotate belt tensioner clockwise and remove belt from power steering and compressor pulleys.
4. Reverse procedure to install.

Alternator

1. Remove A/C and power steering pump belt.
2. Loosen alternator pivot bolt.
3. Loosen locking nut and adjusting bolt, then remove belt.
4. Reverse procedure to install.

COOLING SYSTEM BLEED

1. Open cooling system bleed valve, **Fig. 27.**
2. Attach a four foot length of clear hose to bleed valve, route hose away from accessory drive and radiator fan.
3. Place other end of hose into suitable container.
4. Fill cooling system with proper amount of recommended coolant.
5. Slowly continue filling system until a steady stream of coolant flows from attached hose on bleed valve.
6. Close bleed valve and remove hose.
7. Fill coolant level to top of pressure cap neck, then install pressure cap.
8. Fill coolant recovery bottle to at least Full Hot mark.
9. Perform 3–4 warm up and cool down cycles, top up coolant as required.

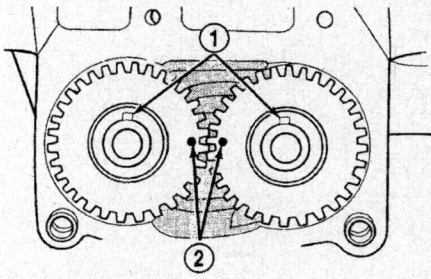

1 - KEY WAYS UP
2 - GEAR ALIGNMENT DOTS

ARM0400000000262

Fig. 20   Gear timing

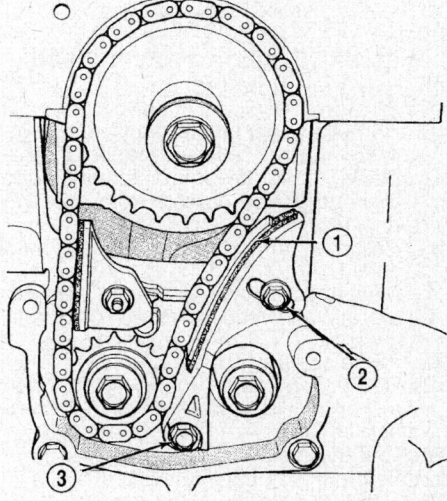

1 - 1MM (0.039 IN.) SHIM
2 - TENSIONER (ADJUSTER) BOLT
3 - PIVOT BOLT

ARM0400000000265

Fig. 23   Chain tension adjustment

THERMOSTAT
REPLACE

1. Remove upper intake manifold as outlined under "Intake Manifold, Replace."
2. Drain cooling system into suitable container to level below thermostat.
3. Remove upper radiator hose from outlet connector.
4. Remove coolant recovery system hose from outlet connector.
5. Remove thermostat/outlet connector.
6. Remove thermostat assembly.
7. Reverse procedure to install, noting the following:
    a. Clean sealing surfaces.
    b. Place new thermostat into coolant outlet connector aligning air bleed with location notch on outlet connector, **Fig. 28.**

WATER PUMP
REPLACE

1. Drain cooling system into suitable container.
2. Remove timing belt as outlined under "Timing Belt, Replace."

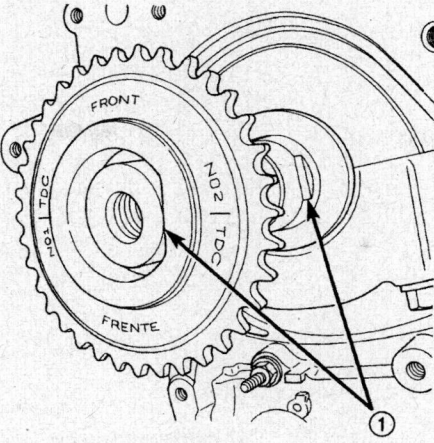

1 - ALIGN FLATS

ARM0400000000263

Fig. 21   Balance shaft sprocket to crankshaft alignment

3. Remove camshaft sprockets and rear timing belt cover as outlined under "Rear Timing Belt Cover, Replace."
4. Remove water pump attaching bolts, then the water pump.
5. Reverse procedure to install, noting the following:
    a. Apply Mopar Dielectric Grease, or equivalent, to new O-ring.
    b. Ensure O-ring seal is properly seated in water pump groove.

RADIATOR
REPLACE

1. Remove battery and battery tray.
2. Drain cooling system into suitable container.
3. Recover refrigerant as outlined under "Air Conditioning."
4. Remove grille and upper radiator support crossmember.
5. Remove upper radiator hose from radiator.
6. Raise and support vehicle.
7. Disconnect and cap automatic transmission cooler hoses.
8. Disconnect radiator fan motor electrical connector.
9. Remove lower radiator hose.
10. Lower vehicle, then remove A/C lines from condenser.
11. Remove cooling module assembly (radiator, fan and A/C condenser).
12. Place cooling module on workbench and remove radiator fan to radiator attaching bolts.
13. Remove A/C condenser and transmission oil cooler to radiator attaching bolts.
14. Remove lower air shield from radiator.
15. Reverse procedure to install.

FUEL PUMP
REPLACE

The fuel pump is part of the fuel pump module assembly which includes the fuel pump, fuel pump reservoir, inlet strainer, fuel pressure regulator, fuel gauge sending

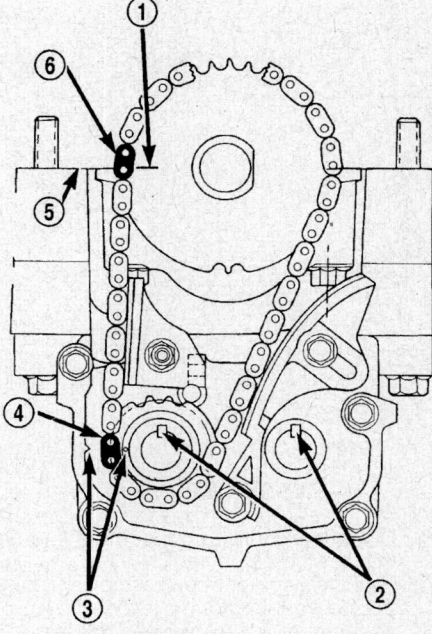

1 - MARK ON SPROCKET
2 - KEYWAYS UP
3 - ALIGN MARKS
4 - PLATED LINK
5 - PARTING LINE (BEDPLATE TO BLOCK)
6 - PLATED LINK

ARM0400000000264

Fig. 22   Balance shaft timing

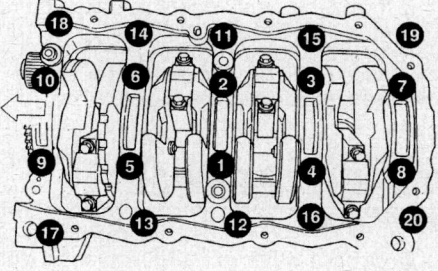

ARM0400000000266

Fig. 24   Bedplate bolt identification & tightening sequence

unit, fuel supply line connection and the fuel filter. The fuel pump module is located on the top of the fuel tank. The fuel level sensor is the only serviceable component on the fuel pump module. If any other components are faulty, the entire fuel pump module must be replaced.

1. Remove fuel filler cap and relieve fuel system pressure as outlined under "Precautions."
2. Remove air cleaner lid.
3. Disconnect inlet air temperature sensor and makeup air hose.
4. Raise and support vehicle.
5. Drain fuel into a suitable container.
6. Support fuel tank with a suitable jack.
7. Disconnect fuel tank rubber fill hose.
8. Remove bolts from fuel tank straps.
9. Lower fuel tank, then remove EVAP line and recirculation line.
10. Remove vacuum line from LDP.

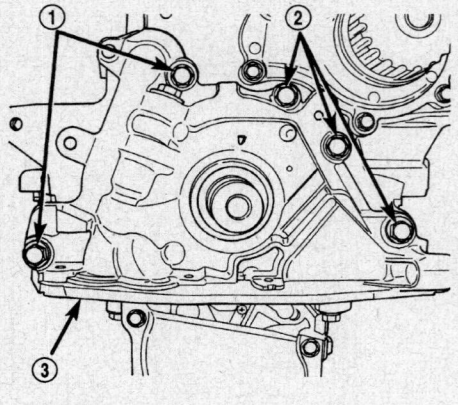

1 – BOLTS
2 – BOLTS
3 – OIL PUMP

CR1060000866000X

Fig. 25   Oil pump

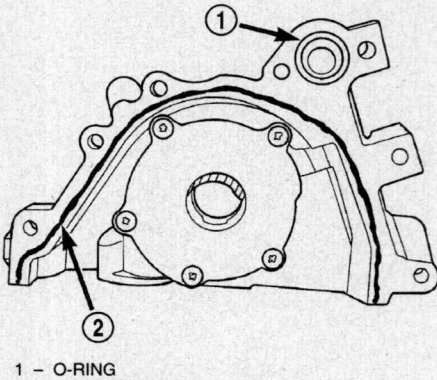

1 – O-RING
2 – SEALER LOCATION

CR1060000867000X

Fig. 26   Oil pump sealing

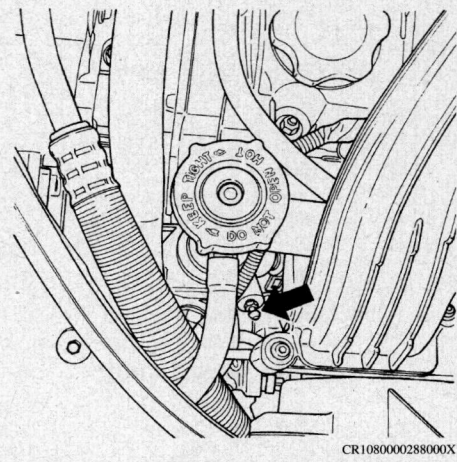

CR1080000288000X

Fig. 27   Cooling system bleed valve

11. Disconnect quick connect fuel line fitting in front of fuel tank.
12. Unlock electrical connector, then disconnect connector.
13. Remove hoses from EVAP canister.
14. Remove fuel tank from vehicle.
15. Clean top of fuel tank to remove loose dirt and debris.
16. Disconnect fuel lines from fuel pump module.
17. Remove fuel pump module locknut using spanner wrench tool No. 6856, or equivalent.
18. Remove fuel pump module and seal from tank. Fuel reservoir of fuel pump module does not empty out when fuel tank is drained. Ensure residual fuel does not spill onto vehicle surfaces.
19. Reverse procedure to install.

TURBOCHARGER

REPLACE

If turbocharger is being replaced due to a bearing failure, replacement of oil pressure feed line is required. Oil return tube should be cleaned also.

1. Drain engine cooling system.
2. Remove air cleaner housing and lid.
3. Disconnect clean air hose from turbocharger.
4. Disconnect throttle and speed control cables from throttle body.
5. Disconnect IAT, MAP, IAC motor, TP,

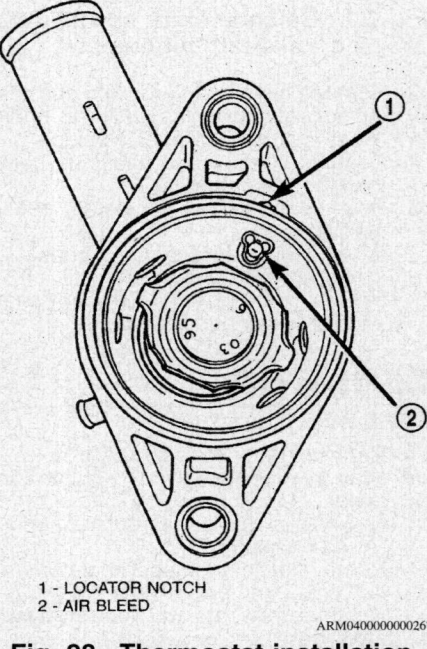

1 - LOCATOR NOTCH
2 - AIR BLEED

ARM0400000000267

Fig. 28   Thermostat installation

ignition coil capacitor and upstream HO2 sensor electrical connectors.
6. Disconnect air inlet hose from throttle body.
7. Disconnect vacuum hoses from throttle body and upper intake manifold.
8. Remove upper intake manifold support bracket.

9. Remove upper intake manifold as outlined under "Intake Manifold, Replace." Cover lower intake manifold to prevent foreign objects from entering engine.
10. Remove turbocharger upper heat shield.
11. Disconnect oil supply line, coolant return line and vacuum hoses from turbocharger.
12. Raise and support vehicle.
13. Remove muffler ground strap, then disconnect downstream oxygen sensor.
14. Remove bolts securing catalytic converter to exhaust manifold.
15. Remove catalytic converter and intermediate pipe as an assembly.
16. Remove turbocharger to charge air cooler hose assembly.
17. Remove turbocharger and elbow support brackets.
18. Remove oil return tube, then the turbocharger coolant supply line.
19. Remove turbocharger lower heat shield, then the elbow.
20. Remove lower exhaust manifold bolts, then lower vehicle.
21. Remove upper exhaust manifold bolts.
22. Remove turbocharger/exhaust manifold assembly from engine and cowl panel.
23. Reverse procedure to install. Install a new exhaust manifold gasket, position steel layer of gasket against cylinder head.

TIGHTENING SPECIFICATIONS

Year	Component	Torque Ft. Lbs.
All	Balance Shaft Carrier	40
	Balance Shaft Chain Tensioner	105①
	Balance Shaft Gear Cover	105①
	Balance Shaft Sprockets	21
	Camshaft Bearing Caps (M6)	105①
	Camshaft Bearing Caps (M8)	18
	Catalytic Converter To Exhaust Manifold	21
	Connecting Rod Cap	20②
	Coolant Line Banjo Bolt	22
	Coolant/Oil Line Brass Bolt	30
	Coolant/Oil Line Flared Fitting	23
	Crankshaft Damper	100
	Crankshaft Main Bearing Cap (Bedplate)	④
	Cylinder Head	③
	EGR Retainer Plate (Small Bolt)	95①
	EGR Retainer Plate (Large Bolt)	20
	Exhaust Manifold	17
	Exhaust Manifold/Turbocharger Assembly	21
	Exhaust Manifold Heat Shields	105①
	Exhaust Pipe To Manifold	21
	Flex Plate	70
	Fuel Pump Module Locknut	55
	Fuel Rail Assembly To Intake Manifold	18
	Intake Manifold	17
	Motor Mount (R)	21
	Motor Mount (L) Bracket To Body Rail	21
	Motor Mount (L) To Transaxle	87
	Oil Filter Adapter	105①
	Oil Pan	105①
	Thermostat Outlet	110①
	Turbocharger Support Bracket	40
	Water Pump	105①

① — Inch lbs.
② — Plus ¼ turn.
③ — Refer to Cylinder Head, Replace for bolt tightening sequence and procedure.
④ — Refer to Main & Rod Bearings for bolt tightening sequence and procedure.

Rear Suspension

NOTE: On Air Bag Equipped Models, Refer To "Air Bag System Precautions" Located In The Front Of This Manual For System Disarming & Arming Procedures.

NOTE: Refer To "Computer Relearn Procedures" Located In The Front Of This Manual When Battery Power To The Computer Has Been Interrupted.

INDEX

	Page No.		Page No.		Page No.
Description	5-26	Roll Bar, Replace	5-27	Strut Service	5-27
Hub & Bearing, Replace	5-26	Spindle Knuckle, Replace	5-26	Tension Strut, Replace	5-27
Lateral Link, Replace	5-27	Installation	5-26	Tightening Specifications	5-29
Installation	5-27	Removal	5-26		
Removal	5-27	Strut, Replace	5-26		

DESCRIPTION

Because the construction of this type of suspension, only frame contact or wheel lift type hoisting equipment should be used to raise vehicle.

Rear suspension components which become damaged must be replaced. No attempt should be made to repair these components.

The rear suspension is a fully independent strut type, **Fig. 1.** A forged spindle knuckle is bolted to the strut assembly. Lateral links and tension struts are used to control position and movement of the rear suspension.

HUB & BEARING
REPLACE

The rear hub and bearing are serviced as an assembly.
1. Raise and support vehicle, then remove wheel and tire.
2. **On models equipped with rear disc brakes,** remove caliper and disc as outlined in "Disc Brakes" chapter.
3. **On models equipped with rear drum brakes,** remove brake drum as outlined in "Drum Brakes" chapter of this manual.
4. **On all models,** remove mounting nut, hub and bearing assembly.
5. Reverse procedure to install.

SPINDLE KNUCKLE
REPLACE
Removal

1. Remove rear hub and bearing as outlined in "Hub & Bearing, Replace."
2. **On models equipped with ABS,** remove sensor bracket to strut screw.
3. **On models equipped with rear drum brakes,** proceed as follows:
   a. Remove four brake support plate to knuckle bolts.
   b. Remove brake support plate, brake

shoes and wheel cylinder as an assembly from knuckle. Leave brake hose intact.
   c. Tie assembly aside with suitable cord or string. **Avoid overextending brake hose.**
4. **On models equipped with rear disc brakes,** proceed as follows:
   a. Remove four brake adapter to knuckle bolts.
   b. Remove adapter, rotor shield, parking brake shoes and cable as an assembly.
   c. Tie assembly aside with suitable cord or string.
5. **On all models,** loosen, but do not completely remove, two knuckle to strut nuts and bolts. **These bolts are serrated and must not be turned during removal. Hold bolts in place in knuckle while removing nuts and tap bolts out using suitable pin punch.**
6. Remove rear knuckle to lateral arm nuts and bolt.
7. Remove tension strut rear nut using suitable wrench on strut's flat to prevent tension strut from turning.
8. Remove tension strut retainer.
9. Remove rear tension strut bayonet bushing from strut.
10. Remove rear knuckle to strut mounting nuts and bolts. Tap out bolts using suitable pin punch.
11. Remove knuckle.

Installation

1. Align hole in lower end of rear knuckle with forward bayonet bushing on tension strut. Ensure bushing's stepped area seats squarely into knuckle's hole.
2. Rotate knuckle until its upper mounting holes align with holes in strut's clevis bracket.
3. Install strut to rear knuckle mounting bolts from front side. Install nuts on bolts.
4. Align lateral arms with hole in center of

knuckle. Install arm to knuckle bolts. Start bolt from front side. Install nut, but do not tighten completely.
5. Install rear bayonet bushing onto tension strut. Ensure stepped area seats squarely into hole in knuckle.
6. Install rear tension strut retainer and nut. Tighten nut to specifications while holding strut in place with suitable wrench on flat area.
7. Install brake support plate or adapter onto knuckle.
8. **On models equipped with anti-lock brakes,** install sensor bracket to strut screw.
9. **On all models,** install tire and wheel. Tighten lugnuts in proper sequence to half specification. Repeat sequence again to full specification.
10. Lower vehicle to ground and rock to bring to curb height.
11. Tighten lateral arm to knuckle mounting bolt to specifications.
12. Inspect and adjust rear toe. Refer to "Rear Wheel Alignment Specifications" in "Specifications" section.

STRUT
REPLACE

1. Raise and support vehicle.
2. Remove wheel and tire.
3. **On models equipped with rear drum brakes,** remove brake hose bracket to strut screw.
4. **On models equipped with anti-lock brakes,** remove wheel speed sensor bracket to strut screw.
5. **On all models,** remove nut from end of rear stabilizer bar link bolt. Pull bolt out through top and remove link.
6. **On models equipped with rear disc brakes,** proceed as follows:
   a. Remove four brake adapter to knuckle bolts.
   b. Remove adapter, rotor shield, parking brake shoes and cable as an assembly.
   c. Tie assembly aside with suitable cord or string.

7. **On all models,** remove two knuckle to strut nuts and bolts. **These bolts are serrated and must not be turned during removal. Hold bolts in place in knuckle while removing nuts and tap bolts out using suitable pin punch.**
8. Lower vehicle only enough to climb into luggage compartment without tires reaching ground.
9. Remove carpeting from top of strut tower inside luggage compartment.
10. Loosen, but do not completely remove, three strut to tower nuts.
11. Hold strut firmly in place and remove mounting nuts.
12. Remove strut from knuckle by sliding it away from knuckle and lowering it between lateral arms, then angle top outward and out through wheelwell opening.
13. Reverse procedure to install, noting the following:
    a. Align holes in strut clevis bracket on strut's lower end with knuckle's mounting holes.
    b. Lower vehicle to ground and rock to bring to curb height.
    c. Inspect and adjust rear toe. Refer to "Rear Wheel Alignment Specifications" in "Specifications" section.

STRUT SERVICE

Coil springs on these models are available in different load rates. Spring rates may be different on each side of the vehicle depending on how the vehicle is equipped. Ensure proper spring rates are chosen during assembly.

The gas-charged strut damper cannot be rebuilt and is serviced as a unit.

1. Remove strut as outlined in "Strut, Replace."
2. Record orientation of all markings, letters and assembly tips before proceeding.
3. Place match marks on components to aid alignment.
4. Position strut in compressor tool No. PSE W-7200, or equivalent, following tool manufacturers instructions.
5. Compress coil spring until all spring tension is off upper mount.
6. Install strut nut socket tool No. 6864, or equivalent, on strut shaft mounting nut.
7. Install socket on shaft's end hex.
8. Remove shaft nut while preventing strut shaft from turning.
9. Remove upper mount from strut shaft.
10. Remove clamp from bottom of spring.
11. Pull strut through bottom of spring.
12. Remove dust shield and jounce bumper by pulling them straight up.
13. Remove lower spring isolator from strut's lower spring seat.
14. If coil spring is being replaced, proceed as follows:
    a. Record spring's position in compressor tool for easier assembly.
    b. Back off compressor drive completely to release spring tension.
    c. Push hooks back and remove spring.
15. Reverse procedure to install, noting the following:

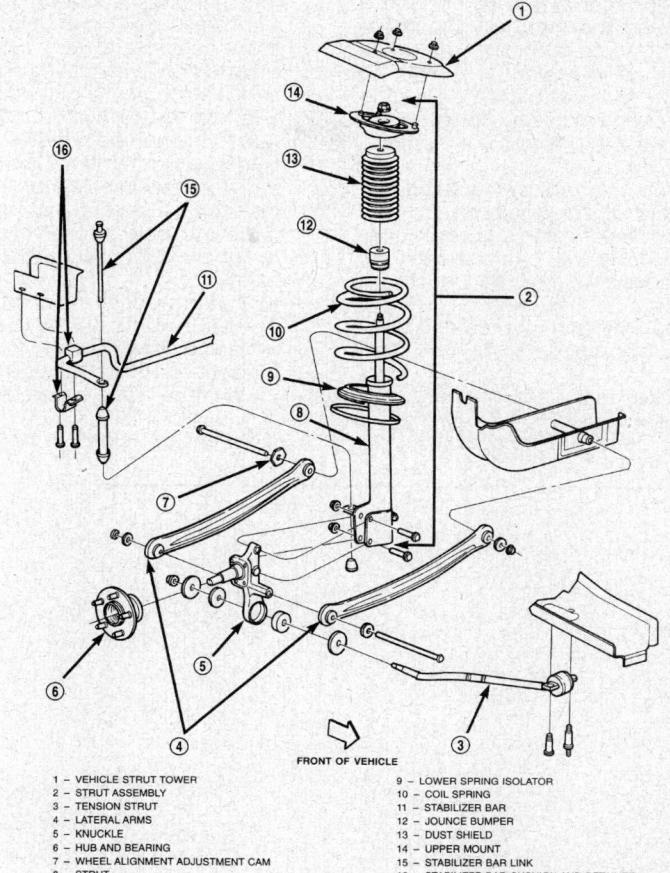

1 – VEHICLE STRUT TOWER
2 – STRUT ASSEMBLY
3 – TENSION STRUT
4 – LATERAL ARMS
5 – KNUCKLE
6 – HUB AND BEARING
7 – WHEEL ALIGNMENT ADJUSTMENT CAM
8 – STRUT
9 – LOWER SPRING ISOLATOR
10 – COIL SPRING
11 – STABILIZER BAR
12 – JOUNCE BUMPER
13 – DUST SHIELD
14 – UPPER MOUNT
15 – STABILIZER BAR LINK
16 – STABILIZER BAR CUSHION AND RETAINER

CR2039900089000X

Fig. 1   Exploded view of rear suspension

a. Mount coil spring into original position.
b. Inspect upper mount before installation. Ensure proper mount is being installed. Righthand mounts are marked R, while lefthand has L marking.

TENSION STRUT
REPLACE

1. Remove wheel and tire as required.
2. Remove nuts from both ends of tension strut using suitable wrench on flat to prevent tension strut from turning.
3. Record orientation of tension strut bushings and washers.
4. Remove bushings, washers and tension strut.
5. Reverse procedure to install noting. Inspect and adjust rear wheel alignment as outlined in "Wheel Alignment."

ROLL BAR
REPLACE

1. Raise and support vehicle, then remove both rear wheels.
2. Disconnect roll bar from mounting links at each side and swing bar down to clear links.
3. Remove mounting bracket and roll bar. **Record bushing orientation.**

4. Reverse procedure to install. Ensure bushings are installed in original positions.

LATERAL LINK
REPLACE
Removal

1. Raise and support vehicle.
2. Remove tire and wheel.
3. Remove lateral link to knuckle nut, bolt and washers.
4. Remove nut, washer, bolt and wheel alignment cam mounting lateral arms to rear crossmember.
5. Remove lateral arms.

Installation

The lateral arms have a specific installation orientation. The arm with identical size bushing sleeves on both ends must be mounted on the forward side of the crossmember and knuckle with the trimmed outer edge facing rearward. This front arm also displays the word FORWARD facing forward.

The arm with differing size bushing sleeves mounts on the rearward side of the crossmember and knuckle. Position the smaller sleeve end at the knuckle and the larger end at the rear crossmember. **If the rear arm will be mounted on the right-hand side,** the trimmed outer edge must face rearward. **If the rear arm will be mounted on the lefthand side,** the trimmed outer edge must face forward.

1. Place forward lateral arm against leading edge of knuckle.
2. Install short lateral arm mounting bolt with washer through lateral arm and knuckle and out trailing end of knuckle.
3. Install small sleeved end of rear lateral arm onto end of bolt previously installed.
4. Install washer and nut onto end of mounting bolt, but do not tighten completely.
5. Install alignment cam on long arm mounting bolt.
6. Hold rear lateral arm up against crossmember and install long mounting bolt with adjustment cam through lateral arm bushing and rear crossmember. Ensure bolt is installed with alignment cam's notch pointing straight up.
7. Position forward lateral arm against rear crossmember hole.
8. Route long mounting bolt through lateral arm bushing sleeve.
9. Install washer and nut onto end of mounting bolt at rear crossmember, but do not tighten completely. Note the following:
   a. When properly installed, each lateral arm will have bow in its length facing downward.
   b. Both righthand side arms will have trimmed outer edges facing rear of vehicle.
   c. Lefthand side arms will have trimmed outer edges facing each other.
   d. Mounting bolt at knuckle will have nut at rear, while mounting bolt at crossmember will have nut at front.
10. Install tire and wheel. Tighten lugnuts in proper sequence to half specification. Repeat sequence again to full specification.
11. Lower vehicle to ground and rock to bring to curb height.
12. Tighten lateral arm mounting bolt nut at knuckle to specifications.
13. Tighten lateral arm mounting bolt nut at crossmember to specifications.
14. Inspect and adjust rear toe. Refer to "Rear Wheel Alignment Specifications" in "Specifications" section.

TIGHTENING SPECIFICATIONS

Year	Component	Torque Ft. lbs.
All	Brake Hose Bracket	23
	Brake Support Plate	55
	Disc Brake Adapter	55
	Hub & Bearing To Knuckle	160
	Knuckle	65
	Lateral Arm Nut At Crossmember	65
	Lateral Arm Nut At Knuckle	70
	Parking Brake Cable	21
	Roll Bar Cushion Retainer	25
	Roll Bar Link	17
	Strut Assembly Shaft	55
	Tension Strut Frame Rail	70
	Tension Strut Rear	70
	Tower	25
	Wheel Lugnuts	100①

① — Tighten lugnuts in proper sequence to half specification. Repeat sequence again to full specification.

Front Suspension & Steering

NOTE: On Air Bag Equipped Models, Refer To "Air Bag System Precautions" Located In The Front Of This Manual For System Disarming & Arming Procedures.

NOTE: Refer To "Computer Relearn Procedures" Located In The Front Of This Manual When Battery Power To The Computer Has Been Interrupted.

NOTE: Prior To Performing Any Service Operations Listed In This Section, Consult The "Technical Service Bulletins" For Related Information.

INDEX

	Page No.		Page No.		Page No.
Ball Joint, Replace	5-31	Assemble	5-31	Strut, Replace	5-31
Installation	5-31	Disassemble	5-30	Installation	5-32
Removal	5-31	Manual Steering Gear, Replace	5-33	Removal	5-31
Ball Joint Inspection	5-31	Power Steering	13-1	Strut Service	5-32
Control Arm, Replace	5-32	Power Steering Gear, Replace	5-32	Installation	5-32
Description	5-30	Power Steering Pump, Replace	5-33	Removal	5-32
Hub & Bearing, Replace	5-30	Steering Columns	12-1	Tightening Specifications	5-34
Hub & Bearing Service	5-30	Steering Knuckle, Replace	5-32		

DESCRIPTION

This suspension is a gas pressurized strut system used in place of front suspension upper ball joint and upper control arm. The bottom of the strut is attached directly to the steering knuckle using two mounting bolts and nuts going through the clevis bracket and steering knuckle, **Fig. 1.**

A cast lower arm assembly is attached to the front suspension crossmember using two rubber isolator bushings and to the steering knuckle by means of a ball joint.

A sealed for life front hub and bearing assembly is attached to the front steering knuckle. The outer CV joint assembly is splined to the front hub and bearing assembly.

HUB & BEARING

REPLACE

The cartridge type front wheel bearing on these models is not transferable to a new knuckle. If a new knuckle does not arrive with a new bearing, a new bearing must be installed. This must be done before the knuckle is installed on the vehicle.

1. Raise and support vehicle.
2. Remove tire and wheel.
3. Remove cotter pin, locknut and spring washer from hub nut.
4. Apply brakes, then remove hub nut on end of driveshaft.
5. Remove caliper to knuckle guide pin bolts.
6. Remove caliper from knuckle and position aside with suitable cord or wire. **Do not let caliper hang by brake hose.**
7. Remove any clips from wheel studs.
8. Remove rotor from hub.

9. Remove outer tie rod to knuckle nut.
10. Remove tie rod end from knuckle using tie rod remover tool No. MB991113, or equivalent.
11. Remove tie rod heat shield.
12. Remove ball joint stud to knuckle nut and pinch bolt.
13. Remove two strut to knuckle bolts. **These bolts are serrated and must not be turned during removal. Hold bolts in place in knuckle while removing nuts and tap bolts out using suitable pin punch.**
14. Separate ball joint from knuckle by prying down on lower control arm and up against ball joint knuckle boss. **Do not cutting or tearing seal.**
15. Pull knuckle off driveshaft outer CV joint splines and remove knuckle. **Do not let driveshaft hang by inner CV joint. Support it with suitable cord.**
16. Refer to "Hub & Bearing Service" for continuation of bearing replacement procedure.

HUB & BEARING SERVICE

Disassemble

The cartridge type front wheel bearing on these models is not transferable to a new knuckle. If a new knuckle does not arrive with a new bearing, a new bearing must also be installed. This must be done before the knuckle is installed on the vehicle.

1. Press one wheel stud out of hub flange using stud remover tool No. 4150A, or equivalent.
2. Rotate hub until removed stud aligns with bearing retainer plate notch.

3. Remove stud from hub.
4. Rotate hub until open stud hole faces away from caliper lower rail on knuckle.
5. Install one half of bearing splitter tool No. 1130, or equivalent between hub and bearing plate.
6. Align threaded hole in first half of bearing splitter with caliper rail on knuckle.
7. Install remaining portions of splitter. Hand tighten nuts to hold splitter in place on knuckle.
8. Ensure retainer plate to knuckle bolts are contacting splitter. **Retainer plate should not support knuckle or contact splitter.**
9. Mount knuckle in suitable arbor press supported by bearing splitter.
10. Position driver tool No. 6644-2, or equivalent on hub's small end.
11. Remove hub from wheel bearing using arbor press. Outer race normally comes out of bearing when hub is pressed.
12. Remove bearing splitter tool from knuckle.
13. Remove mounting bolts and bearing retainer plate.
14. Mount knuckle in arbor press again, supported by press blocks. Ensure press blocks do not obstruct knuckle bore or bearing will not slide out.
15. Place bearing driver tool No. MB990799, or equivalent on bearing's outer race.
16. Press bearing out of knuckle.
17. Install bearing splitter tool on hub between hub flange and outer bearing race.
18. Place hub, race and splitter in arbor press.
19. Place driver tool on end of hub.
20. Press hub out of bearing race.

Assemble

The cartridge type front wheel bearing on these models is not transferable to a new knuckle. If a new knuckle does not arrive with a new bearing, a new bearing must also be installed. This must be done before the knuckle is installed on the vehicle.

1. Wipe knuckle bore clean with clean, dry lint free towel. Ensure no dirt or grease remains.
2. Place new bearing into knuckle bore, perfectly square.
3. Place knuckle in arbor press with receiver tool No. C-4698-2, or equivalent supporting knuckle.
4. Place driver tool 5052, or equivalent, on bearing outer race.
5. Press bearing into knuckle until it has fully bottomed. Remove knuckle from press.
6. Install bearing retainer plate onto knuckle with three original or exact replacement bolts. **Do not use substitutions.**
7. Place previously removed wheel stud back into hub flange.
8. Place hub in arbor press supported by tool No. C-4698-1, or equivalent.
9. Press stud into hub flange until it seats fully against flange's rear side. Remove hub from press.
10. Place knuckle with its newly installed bearing back into arbor press with receiver tool No. MB990799, or equivalent, supporting bearing inner race.
11. Place hub in bearing, ensuring it is square with inner race.
12. Press hub into bearing until it fully bottoms in bearing.
13. Remove knuckle from press.

BALL JOINT INSPECTION

With weight of vehicle resting on wheels, grasp grease fitting and, with no mechanical assistance or added force, attempt to move grease fitting, **Fig. 2.**

If the ball joint is worn the grease fitting will move easily. If there is movement replace ball joint as required.

BALL JOINT
REPLACE
Removal

1. Remove lower control arm following procedure outlined in "Control Arm, Replace."
2. Pry ball joint seal boot off ball joint using suitable screwdriver.
3. Position receiver tool No. 6908-2, or equivalent, on hydraulic press to support lower control arm while receiving ball joint.
4. Place control arm on top of receiver tool so bottom of ball joint sits in receiver cup.
5. Place larger end of adapter tool No. 6804, or equivalent, on top of ball joint.
6. Press ball joint completely out of control arm use hydraulic press.

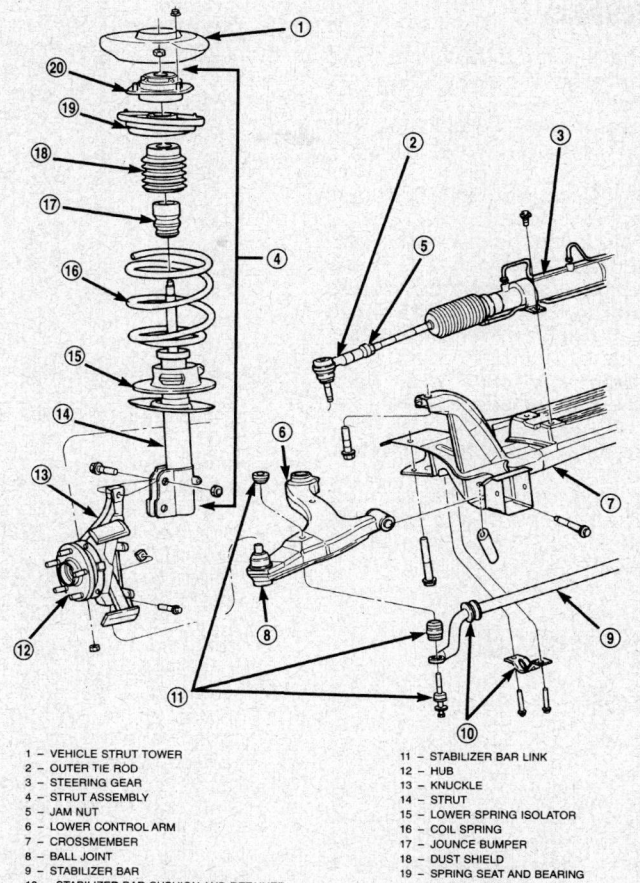

1 – VEHICLE STRUT TOWER
2 – OUTER TIE ROD
3 – STEERING GEAR
4 – STRUT ASSEMBLY
5 – JAM NUT
6 – LOWER CONTROL ARM
7 – CROSSMEMBER
8 – BALL JOINT
9 – STABILIZER BAR
10 – STABILIZER BAR CUSHION AND RETAINER
11 – STABILIZER BAR LINK
12 – HUB
13 – KNUCKLE
14 – STRUT
15 – LOWER SPRING ISOLATOR
16 – COIL SPRING
17 – JOUNCE BUMPER
18 – DUST SHIELD
19 – SPRING SEAT AND BEARING
20 – UPPER MOUNT

CR2029900153000X

Fig. 1 Exploded view of front suspension

7. Remove arm and all tools from press.

Installation

1. Position new ball joint by hand into its control arm bore, with notch in stud facing control arm front isolator bushing, to ease assembly. Ensure it moves in straight and square.
2. Position installer tool No. 6758, or equivalent on hydraulic press to support control arm. Place control arm on top of installer in upside-down position, aligning ball joint stud squarely with installer cup.
3. Place larger end of adapter tool No. 6804, or equivalent on top of ball joint.
4. Use hydraulic press to press ball joint into control arm until joint's shoulder bottoms in its bore. **Do not apply excessive pressure after joint has bottomed.**
5. Remove all tools and control arm from press.
6. Install new ball joint seal over stud. Position upward lip on outside perimeter of seal boot outward away from control arm once installed. Start installation by hand.
7. Position installer tool No. 6758, or equivalent over boot's outer diameter. Use hand pressure on top of tool until boot is pressed squarely down against

top surface of control arm.
8. Install lower control arm following procedure outlined in "Control Arm, Replace."

STRUT
REPLACE
Removal

1. Raise and support vehicle on hoist.
2. Remove tire and wheel.
3. Mark strut assemblies if both lefthand and righthand units will be replaced.
4. Remove ground wire screw at rear of strut.
5. **On models equipped with ABS,** remove ABS sensor bracket screw at rear of strut.
6. **On all models,** remove two strut to knuckle bolts. Hold bolts in place in knuckle while removing nuts and tap bolts out using suitable pin punch. **These bolts are serrated and must not be turned during removal.**
7. Lower vehicle enough to open hood, but do not let tires reach ground.
8. Remove three strut to tower mounting nuts.
9. Remove strut.

Installation

1. Install new strut into tower. Ensure three studs align with tower holes.
2. Close hood.
3. Position lower end of strut in line with upper end of knuckle and align mounting holes.
4. Install strut to knuckle bolts with nuts facing front of vehicle.
5. Tighten mounting nuts to specifications, then an additional 90.° **These bolts are serrated and must not be turned during removal. Hold bolts in place in knuckle while installing nuts.**
6. **On models equipped with ABS,** mount wheel speed sensor to rear ear of strut.
7. **On all models,** attach ground wire to rear of strut.
8. Install tire and wheel. Tighten lugnuts in proper sequence to half specification. Repeat sequence again to full specification.

STRUT SERVICE

Removal

1. Remove strut as outlined in "Strut, Replace."
2. Position strut into coil spring compressor tool No. PSE W-7200, or equivalent, following manufacturers instructions. Set lower and upper hooks.
3. Place clamp on lower end of spring to hold strut in place when shaft nut is removed. **Do not remove strut shaft nut until after spring has been compressed.**
4. Compress spring until all tension is gone from upper mount.
5. When spring has been sufficiently compressed, install strut nut socket tool No. 6864, or equivalent on nut.
6. Install suitable socket on strut shaft hex end, then hold shaft in place and remove nut.
7. Remove upper spring seat and bearing with upper spring isolator as a unit from top of coil spring by pulling straight up. Isolator can be separated after removal.
8. Remove dust shield and jounce bumper by pulling straight up.
9. If coil spring is being replaced, release spring tension by completely backing off compressor drive. Push hooks back and remove spring.

Installation

1. Place coil spring into compressor tool following manufacturers instructions.
2. Rotate spring so end of top coil is directly in rear.
3. Slowly compress spring until strut can be assembled.
4. Install lower spring isolator on strut's lower spring seat.
5. Install strut through bottom of spring until clevis bracket is positioned

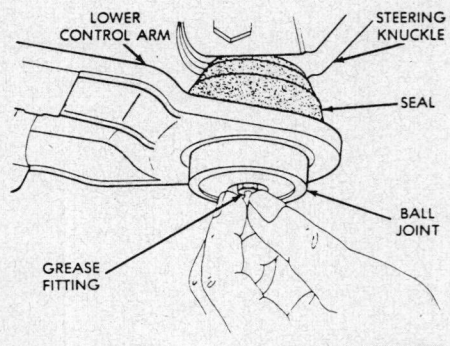

Fig. 2 Ball joint wear inspection

straight outward away from compressor.
6. Install clamp on lower end of spring and strut so strut stays in place.
7. Install jounce bumper on strut shaft, with smaller end pointing downward toward lower seat.
8. Install dust shield on strut shaft. Shield's bottom will snap past retainer on top of strut housing.
9. Install upper spring isolator on upper spring seat and bearing.
10. Install upper spring seat and bearing on top of spring. Position notch in upper edge of seat straight out away from compressor.
11. Install strut upper mount over strut shaft, onto top of upper spring seat and bearing.
12. Loosely install strut shaft mounting nut.
13. Install strut nut socket tool No. 6864, or equivalent, on strut shaft mounting nut.
14. Install suitable socket on hex end of strut shaft, hold shaft in place and tighten nut to specifications.
15. Slowly release coil spring tension by completely backing off tensioner drive. Ensure upper mount, seat and bearing properly align, and upper mount does not bind.
16. Remove clamp from lower end of spring and strut. Push hooks back and remove strut from compressor.
17. Install strut.

CONTROL ARM

REPLACE

This procedure has been revised by a Technical Service Bulletin.
1. Raise and support vehicle.
2. Remove tires and wheels.
3. Remove stabilizer links.
4. Rotate forward ends of stabilizer bar downward. Loosen bar cushion retainers if required.
5. Remove ball joint stud nut and pinch bolt at knuckle. **Do not pull outward on knuckle. This might separate inner CV joint on driveshaft.**
6. Separate ball joint stud from knuckle, avoiding seal cuts and tears. Pry downward on control arm and up against knuckle's ball joint boss.
7. On righthand control arm, remove mounting bolts and engine torque strut.

8. Remove control arm front pivot bolt at crossmember.
9. Remove control arm rear pivot bolt at crossmember and frame rail.
10. Remove control arm from crossmember.
11. Reverse procedure to install, noting the following:
    a. Position control arm into crossmember.
    b. Install rear pivot bolt at crossmember and frame rail, but do not fully tighten at this time.
    c. Install control arm front pivot bolt at crossmember.
    d. If righthand control arm was replaced, install engine torque strut and adjust as outlined in "Adjustment" in "Engine Mount, Replace" section.
    e. Install new ball joint pinch bolt.
    f. Lower vehicle to ground and rock to bring to curb height.
    g. If original stabilizer link bolts are being installed, clean all grease, oil and loose material, then apply two drops of Mopar Lock And Seal part No. 4318031, or equivalent, to last ½ inch of each bolt's threads.

STEERING KNUCKLE

REPLACE

Refer to "Hub & Bearing, Replace" for procedure.

POWER STEERING GEAR

REPLACE

1. Ensure front wheels are in straight ahead position and lock it using steering wheel holder tool.
2. Remove steering column coupler retainer pin inside passenger compartment.
3. Back nut off and remove coupling pinch bolt.
4. Separate steering column upper and lower couplings.
5. Raise and support vehicle.
6. Remove both front tires and wheels.
7. Remove both outer tie rod to knuckle nuts. Hold tie rods stationary while removing nuts.
8. Remove outer tie rods from knuckles using tie rod remover tool No. MB991113, or equivalent.
9. Remove tie rod heat shield.
10. Release locking tab and disconnect power steering fluid pressure switch wiring electrical connector.
11. Back out tube nut securing power steering fluid pressure hose to gear.
12. **On models less power steering fluid cooler,** disconnect fluid return hose from gear and remove hose from C-clamps on outside of two routing clips on gear's front side.
13. **On models equipped with power steering fluid cooler,** disconnect cooler hose from steering gear, then remove mounting screws and allow cooler to hang aside.

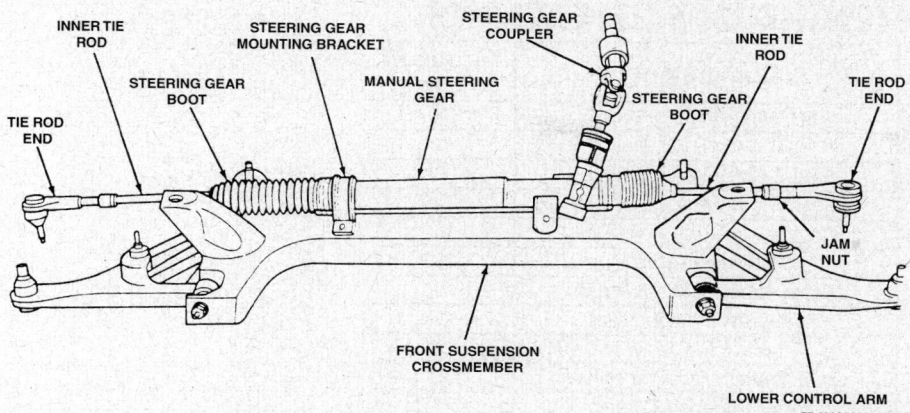

INNER TIE ROD — STEERING GEAR MOUNTING BRACKET — STEERING GEAR COUPLER — INNER TIE ROD — STEERING GEAR BOOT — MANUAL STEERING GEAR — STEERING GEAR BOOT — TIE ROD END — TIE ROD END — JAM NUT — FRONT SUSPENSION CROSSMEMBER — LOWER CONTROL ARM

CR6039500041000X

Fig. 3   Manual steering gear assembly

14. **On all models,** remove pressure hose from front of steering gear.
15. Remove engine torque strut to right-hand forward corner of crossmember.
16. Scribe alignment marks on crossmember and body for installation reference.
17. Support crossmember with suitable transmission jack under center.
18. Loosen and completely remove two front crossmember to frame rail bolts.
19. Loosen, but do not remove, two rear crossmember to frame rail bolts.
20. Lower front crossmember with jack enough to allow steering gear removal from rear of crossmember.
21. Remove roll pin where steering column lower coupling meets pinion shaft using suitable punch. Push lower coupling up and off pinion shaft.

22. Release pinion shaft firewall cover seal from tabs cast into steering gear housing and remove seal from gear.
23. Loosen and remove four steering gear to crossmember bolts.
24. Remove steering gear from front crossmember.
25. Reverse procedure to install, noting the following:
    a. Install front crossmember to frame rail mounting bolts.
    b. Temporarily tighten mounting bolts to 20 inch lbs.
    c. Tap crossmember back into place and align with marks made during removal using suitable soft-faced hammer.
    d. Ensure grease is present on dash to coupling seal lip where it meets

plastic collar.
    e. Fill and bleed power steering fluid system.
    f. Inspect and adjust front toe setting as outlined in "Wheel Alignment."

POWER STEERING PUMP
REPLACE

1. Siphon all possible power steering fluid from pump reservoir.
2. Remove steering pump drive belt.
3. Disconnect fluid return hose from reservoir.
4. Disconnect fluid pressure hose from steering pump.
5. Remove steering pump to rear support bracket bolt.
6. Loosen two support bracket to engine block bolts.
7. Working through pump pulley holes, remove three pump to cast bracket bolts.
8. Remove power steering pump with reservoir.
9. Reverse procedure to install, noting the following:
    a. Fill and bleed power steering fluid system.
    b. Inspect for and correct any leaks.

MANUAL STEERING GEAR
REPLACE

Refer to "Power Steering Gear, Replace" and **Fig. 3** for service procedures.

TIGHTENING SPECIFICATIONS

Year	Component	Torque Ft. Lbs.
All	ABS Wheel Speed Sensor	10
	Ball Joint Pinch Bolt	70
	Brake Caliper Guide Bolts	16
	Control Arm Front Pivot Bolt	120
	Control Arm Rear Pivot Bolt	150
	Driveshaft Hub	180
	Front Crossmember, Front	105
	Front Crossmember, Rear	150
	Ground Wire To Strut	10
	Hub Bearing Retainer Plate	21
	Power Steering Cooler	90①
	Power Steering Fluid Pressure Switch	70①
	Power Steering Hose Tube	25
	Power Steering Pump	21
	Power Steering Pump Pressure Fitting	65
	Power Steering Pump Pressure Hose Tube	25
	Power Steering Pump Rear Support Bracket To Engine	40
	Stabilizer Bar Cushion	21
	Stabilizer Link	22
	Steering Column Lower Coupling Pinch Bolt	21
	Strut Shaft	55
	Strut To Knuckle	40②
	Strut To Tower	25
	Wheel Lugnuts	100③

① — Inch lbs.
② — Tighten an additional 90°.
③ — Tighten lugnuts in proper sequence to half specification. Repeat sequence again to full specification.

Wheel Alignment

INDEX

	Page No.
Front Wheel Alignment	5-35
Camber	5-35
Caster	5-35
Toe	5-35

	Page No.
Preliminary Inspection	5-35
Rear Wheel Alignment	5-35
Camber	5-35
Caster	5-35

	Page No.
Toe	5-36
Wheel Alignment Specifications	5-2

PRELIMINARY INSPECTION

Ensure vehicle has a full tank of gas when wheel alignment specifications are inspected or adjusted. If tank is not full, this change in weight will affect curb height of vehicle and alignment specifications. Inspect and adjust tire pressure. Ensure all tires are the same size. Inspect all suspension components for looseness or damage. Components showing signs of wear or damage should be replaced before alignment.

FRONT WHEEL ALIGNMENT

Caster and camber settings are determined by the location of vehicle's suspension components, **Fig. 1.** No adjustment of caster and camber is possible after vehicle is built or when servicing suspension components. Caster and camber are not normally considered an adjustable specification when performing an alignment on these models.

Caster

If caster is not within specifications, inspect for damaged suspension components or body damage causing component locations to change. No adjustment is possible for caster.

Camber

1. Properly position vehicle on alignment rack and install all required equipment per alignment equipment specifications.
2. Center steering wheel and lock in place using steering wheel clamp.
3. Jounce vehicle, read front alignment settings and compare to specifications.
4. If camber readings obtained are not within specifications, Mopar Service Kit will be required. Different kits are designed for front and rear suspension.
5. Raise and support vehicle, then remove original front strut clevis bracket to steering knuckle upper mounting bolt. **These bolts are serrated and must not be turned during removal. Hold bolts in place in knuckle while** removing nuts and tap bolts out using suitable pin punch.
6. Loosen strut clevis bracket to steering knuckle mounting lower bolt enough to allow knuckle to move in clevis bracket.
7. Install bolt from service kit into upper strut clevis bracket to steering knuckle mounting hole.
8. Install nut provided by service kit on replacement bolt.
9. Tighten upper bolt and nut from service kit until snug, but still allowing movement between strut clevis bracket and knuckle.
10. Remove original lower bolt and install bolt from service kit into lower strut clevis bracket hole. Install nut and tighten until snug.
11. Lower vehicle until full weight is supported by suspension.
12. Jounce front and rear of vehicle equal number of times.
13. Adjust camber to preferred setting by pushing or pulling top of tire.
14. Tighten upper and lower strut clevis bracket bolts.
15. Jounce vehicle equal number of times and ensure rear camber setting. When vehicle is at proper setting, **torque** both front strut clevis brackets to 40 ft. lbs., plus additional ¼ turn.

Toe

Rear wheel toe must be set prior to setting front wheel toe. Proceed as follows:
1. Center steering wheel and lock in place using steering wheel clamp.
2. Loosen lefthand and righthand lateral links to rear crossmember mounting bolts' nuts, **Fig. 2.**
3. Rotate lateral link adjustment cams until preferred rear toe specification is obtained, **Fig. 3.**
4. Tighten righthand and lefthand lateral links to rear crossmember mounting bolt nuts while holding toe adjustment cams from turning. This will securely hold adjustment cams in position.
5. **Torque** lateral link mounting bolt to 70 ft. lbs., while prevent lateral link mounting bolt and adjustment cam from turning.
6. Loosen front inner tie rod end jam nuts and grasp inner tie rods at serration.
7. Rotate inner tie rods of steering gear and set front toe specifications.
8. **Torque** tie rod locknuts to 55 ft. lbs.

REAR WHEEL ALIGNMENT

Caster and camber settings are determined by the location of vehicle's suspension components, **Fig. 1.** No adjustment of caster is possible after vehicle is built or when servicing suspension components. Caster and camber are not normally considered an adjustable specification when performing an alignment on this vehicle.

Caster

If caster is not within specifications, inspect for damaged suspension components or body damage causing component locations to change. No adjustment is possible for caster.

Camber

1. Properly position vehicle on alignment rack and install all required equipment, per alignment equipment specifications.
2. Jounce vehicle and read rear alignment settings and compare to specifications.
3. If camber readings obtained are not within specifications, Mopar Service Kit will be required. Different kits are designed for front and rear suspension.
4. Raise and support vehicle, then remove original rear strut clevis bracket to rear knuckle upper mounting bolt. **These bolts are serrated and must not be turned during removal. Hold bolts in place in knuckle while removing nuts and tap bolts out using suitable pin punch.**
5. Loosen strut clevis bracket to rear knuckle lower mounting bolt enough to allow knuckle to move in clevis bracket.
6. Install bolt from service kit into upper strut clevis bracket to rear knuckle mounting hole.
7. Install nut provided by service kit on replacement bolt.
8. Tighten upper bolt and nut from service kit until snug, but still allowing movement between strut clevis bracket and knuckle.
9. Remove original lower bolt and install bolt from service kit into lower strut clevis bracket hole. Install nut and tighten until snug.

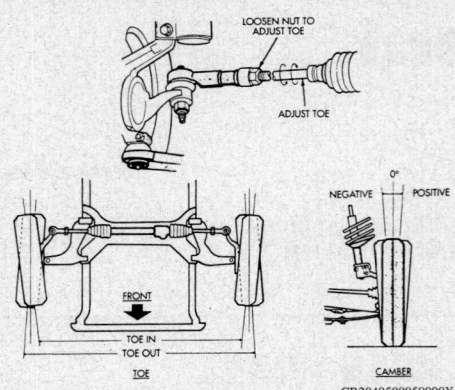

Fig. 1   Camber & toe alignment

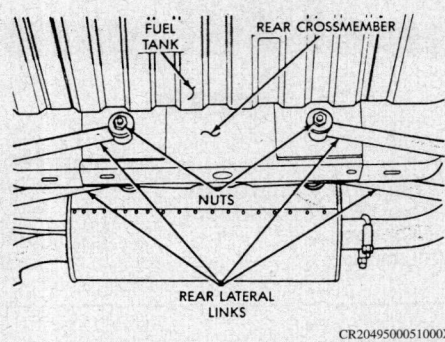

Fig. 2   Rear lateral link toe setting

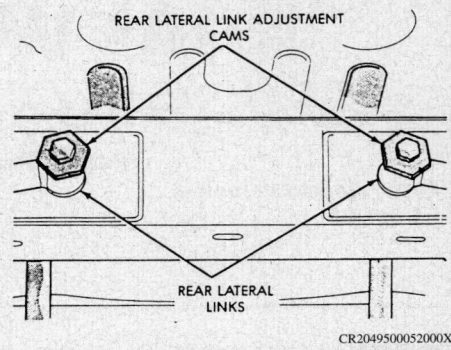

Fig. 3   Rear wheel toe adjustment cams

10. Lower vehicle until full weight is supported by suspension.
11. Jounce front and rear of vehicle equal number of times.
12. Adjust camber to preferred setting by pushing or pulling top of tire.
13. Tighten upper and lower strut clevis bracket bolts.

14. Jounce vehicle equal number of times and ensure rear camber setting. When vehicle is at proper setting, **torque** rear strut clevis brackets to 70 ft. lbs.

Toe

Rear wheel toe must be set prior to

setting front wheel toe. Refer to "Front Wheel Alignment" in this section for front and rear wheel toe setting procedures.

CHARGER, MAGNUM & 300

INDEX OF SERVICE OPERATIONS

Page No.

AIR BAG SYSTEM PRECAUTIONS 0-18
BRAKES
  Anti-Lock Brakes (Volume 2).. 6-1
  Disc Brakes................... 14-1
  Drum Brakes 15-1
  Hydraulic Brake Systems 16-1
  Power Brake Units............ 17-1
COMPUTER RELEARN PROCEDURE 0-31
ELECTRICAL
  Air Bag System (Volume 2) ... 4-1
  Air Conditioning.............. 8-1
  Alternator, Replace 6-6
  Alternators................... 11-1
  Blower Motor, Replace........ 6-8
  Cabin Air Filter, Replace 6-8
  Coil Pack, Replace 6-6
  Cooling Fans 9-1
  Cruise Control (Volume 2) 2-1
  Dash Gauges (Volume 2) 1-1
  Dash Panel Service (Volume 2) 5-1
  Dimmer Switch, Replace...... 6-8
  Evaporator Core, Replace 6-9
  Fuel Pump Relay Location.... 6-6
  Fuse Panel & Flasher Location 6-5
  Headlamp Switch, Replace ... 6-7
  Heater Core, Replace......... 6-9
  Ignition Lock, Replace 6-7
  Ignition Switch, Replace 6-7
  Instrument Cluster, Replace... 6-8
  Multi-Function Switch, Replace 6-7
  Neutral Safety Switch, Replace 6-7
  Passive Restraint Systems (Volume 2).................. 4-1
  Precautions.................. 6-5
  Radio, Replace 6-8
  Speed Controls (Volume 2) ... 2-1
  Starter Motors 10-1
  Starter, Replace 6-6
  Steering Columns............ 12-1
  Steering Wheel, Replace...... 6-8
  Stop Light Switch, Replace ... 6-7
  Technical Service Bulletins.... 6-9
  Turn Signal Switch, Replace .. 6-8
  Wiper Motor, Replace......... 6-8
  Wiper Switch, Replace........ 6-8
  Wiper Systems (Volume 2).... 3-1
  Wiper Transmission, Replace . 6-8
ELECTRICAL SYMBOL IDENTIFICATION 0-63
FRONT DRIVE AXLES 18-1
FRONT SUSPENSION & STEERING
  Ball Joint, Replace............ 6-47
  Coil Spring & Strut Service.... 6-48
  Coil Spring, Replace.......... 6-48
  Control Arm, Replace 6-49
  Description 6-46
  Driveshaft, Replace.......... 6-47

Page No.

  Hub & Bearing, Replace 6-47
  Power Steering 13-1
  Power Steering Gear, Replace 6-51
  Power Steering Pump, Replace 6-51
  Power Steering System Bleed.................... 6-51
  Precautions................. 6-46
  Stabilizer Bar, Replace....... 6-50
  Steering Columns........... 12-1
  Steering Knuckle, Replace.... 6-49
  Strut, Replace 6-48
  Tension Strut, Replace 6-50
  Tie Rod, Replace 6-51
  Tightening Specifications...... 6-52
NON-STANDARD TIRE & WHEEL SIZE ADJUSTMENT TO RIDE HEIGHT SPECIFICATIONS & TIRE SIZE CHART 0-61
REAR AXLE & SUSPENSION
  Camber Link, Replace 6-41
  Coil Spring, Replace.......... 6-41
  Compression Link, Replace ... 6-41
  Description 6-38
  Differential Carrier, Replace... 6-39
  Hub & Bearing, Replace 6-40
  Hub & Bearing Service........ 6-40
  Knuckle, Replace 6-43
  Precautions 6-38
  Propeller Shaft, Replace 6-39
  Rear Halfshaft, Replace....... 6-38
  Shock Absorber, Replace 6-40
  Spring Link, Replace.......... 6-42
  Stabilizer Bar, Replace....... 6-43
  Tension Link, Replace 6-42
  Tightening Specifications...... 6-45
  Toe Link, Replace 6-41
REAR DRIVE AXLE......... 19-1
SERVICE REMINDER & WARNING LAMP RESET PROCEDURES 0-34
SPECIFICATIONS
  Fluid Capacities & Cooling System Data 6-4
  Front Wheel Alignment Specifications.............. 6-3
  General Engine Specifications.............. 6-2
  Lubricant Data 6-4
  Rear Wheel Alignment Specifications.............. 6-3
  Tune Up Specifications....... 6-2
  Vehicle Ride Height Specifications.............. 6-3
TIRE PRESSURE MONITORING SYSTEM 20-1
VEHICLE IDENTIFICATION 0-1

Page No.

VEHICLE LIFT POINTS....... 0-51
VEHICLE MAINTENANCE SCHEDULES 0-73
WHEEL ALIGNMENT
  Front Wheel Alignment........ 6-53
  Preliminary Inspection 6-53
  Rear Wheel Alignment 6-55
  Technical Service Bulletins.... 6-55
  Wheel Alignment Specifications.............. 6-3
WIRE COLOR CODE IDENTIFICATION 0-63
2.7L ENGINE
  Belt Tension Data............. 6-18
  Camshaft, Replace 6-16
  Compression Pressure 6-11
  Cooling System Bleed 6-18
  Crankshaft Damper, Replace.. 6-15
  Crankshaft Rear Oil Seal, Replace 6-17
  Crankshaft Seal, Replace 6-17
  Cylinder Head, Replace 6-13
  Engine Rebuilding Specifications................ 21-1
  Engine, Replace 6-12
  Engine Mount, Replace 6-12
  Exhaust Manifold, Replace.... 6-13
  Front Cover, Replace 6-15
  Fuel Filter, Replace 6-19
  Fuel Pump, Replace 6-19
  Hydraulic Lifters, Replace 6-15
  Intake Manifold, Replace..... 6-13
  Main & Rod Bearings 6-17
  Oil Pan, Replace............. 6-17
  Oil Pump, Replace........... 6-18
  Oil Pump Service 6-18
  Piston & Rod Assembly 6-16
  Precautions................. 6-11
  Radiator, Replace 6-19
  Rocker Arms, Replace 6-15
  Serpentine Drive Belt 6-18
  Structural Collar, Replace 6-12
  Thermostat, Replace 6-19
  Tightening Specifications...... 6-20
  Timing Chain, Replace 6-15
  Timing Chain Tensioner, Replace 6-16
  Timing Chain Tensioner Bleed.................... 6-16
  Valve Adjustment 6-15
  Valve Clearance Specifications................ 6-15
  Valve Cover, Replace 6-14
  Water Pump, Replace 6-19
3.5L ENGINE
  Belt Tension Data............. 6-27
  Camshaft, Replace 6-25
  Camshaft Oil Seal, Replace... 6-25
  Compression Pressure........ 6-21
  Cooling System Bleed 6-27
  Crankshaft Damper, Replace.. 6-23
  Crankshaft Rear Oil Seal, Replace 6-26
  Crankshaft Seal, Replace 6-26

CHARGER, MAGNUM & 300

	Page No.		Page No.		Page No.
Cylinder Head, Replace	6-23	Tightening Specifications	6-29	Fuel Filter, Replace	6-36
Engine Rebuilding		Timing Belt, Replace	6-24	Fuel Pump, Replace	6-36
Specifications	21-1	Valve Adjustment	6-23	Hydraulic Lifters, Replace	6-33
Engine, Replace	6-22	Valve Clearance		Intake Manifold, Replace	6-31
Engine Mount, Replace	6-21	Specifications	6-23	Main & Rod Bearings	6-34
Exhaust Manifold, Replace	6-23	Valve Cover, Replace	6-23	Oil Pan, Replace	6-34
Front Cover, Replace	6-24	Water Pump, Replace	6-28	Oil Pump, Replace	6-35
Fuel Filter, Replace	6-28	**5.7L & 6.1L ENGINES**		Oil Pump Service	6-35
Fuel Pump, Replace	6-28	Belt Tension Data	6-35	Piston & Rod Assembly	6-34
Intake Manifold, Replace	6-22	Camshaft, Replace	6-33	Precautions	6-30
Main & Rod Bearings	6-25	Compression Pressure	6-30	Radiator, Replace	6-36
Oil Cooler, Replace	6-27	Cooling System Bleed	6-36	Rocker Arms, Replace	6-32
Oil Pan, Replace	6-26	Crankshaft Damper, Replace	6-33	Serpentine Drive Belt	6-35
Oil Pump, Replace	6-26	Crankshaft Rear Oil Seal,		Thermostat, Replace	6-36
Oil Pump Service	6-27	Replace	6-34	Tightening Specifications	6-37
Piston & Rod Assembly	6-25	Crankshaft Seal, Replace	6-34	Timing Chain, Replace	6-33
Precautions	6-21	Cylinder Head, Replace	6-32	Timing Chain Tensioner,	
Radiator, Replace	6-28	Engine Rebuilding		Replace	6-33
Rear Timing Belt Cover,		Specifications	21-1	Valve Adjustment	6-32
Replace	6-24	Engine, Replace	6-31	Valve Clearance	
Rocker Arms, Replace	6-23	Engine Mount, Replace	6-31	Specifications	6-32
Serpentine Drive Belt	6-27	Exhaust Manifold, Replace	6-31	Valve Cover, Replace	6-32
Thermostat, Replace	6-28	Front Cover, Replace	6-33	Water Pump, Replace	6-36

Specifications

GENERAL ENGINE SPECIFICATIONS

Engine	Engine Code①	Fuel System	Bore & Stroke, Inch	Comp. Ratio	Brake HP @ RPM	Maximum Torque, Ft. Lbs. @ RPM	Normal Oil Pressure, psi	
							Idle	3000 RPM
2.7L	R	MPI	3.386 x 3.091	9.67	190 @ 6400	190 @ 4000	5	45–105
3.5L	G	MPI	3.780 x 3.189	10.0	250 @ 6400	250 @ 3800	5	45–105
5.7L	H	MPI	3.910 x 3.580	9.6	340 @ 5000	390 @ 4000	4	25–110
6.1L	W	SMPI	4.055 x 3.58	10.3	425 @ 6000	420 @ 4800	4	25–110

MPI — Multi-Port Electronic Fuel Injection

SMPI — Sequential Multi-Port Electronic Fuel Injection

① — Eighth digit of VIN denotes engine code.

TUNE UP SPECIFICATIONS

Engine	Spark Plug Gap, Inch	Firing Order Fig.④	Ignition Timing		Idle Speed, RPM	Fuel Pump Pressure, psi⑥	Valve Clearance, Inch
			°BTDC	Mark			
2.7L	.048–.058	⑨	②	⑤	①	53–63	③
3.5L	.048–.053	⑨	②	⑤	①	53–63	③
5.7L	.045	A⑩	⑦	Damper	⑧	53–63	③
6.1L	.045	A⑩	⑦	—	⑧	53–63	③

BTDC — Before Top Dead Center

N — Neutral

① — Controlled by PCM.

② — Direct (Distributorless) Ignition System (DIS). Not adjustable.

③ — Equipped w/hydraulic lash adjusters. No adjustment is required.

④ — Before disconnecting wires from coil unit, determine location of No. 1 wire, as position may have been altered.

⑤ — Equipped w/crankshaft position sensor.

⑥ — Remove cover from service valve on fuel rail. Connect suitable fuel pressure test gauge to service valve. With ignition switch in Run position, use Diagnostic Read-Out Box to activate fuel pump & pressurize system.

⑦ — Non-adjustable.

⑧ — Controlled by an idle speed control motor.

⑨ — Firing order, 1-2-3-4-5-6.

⑩ — Firing order, 1-8-4-3-6-5-7-2.

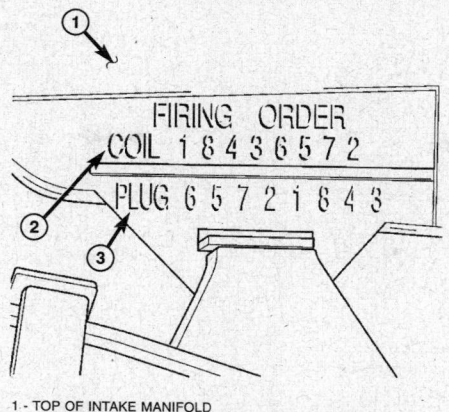

1 - TOP OF INTAKE MANIFOLD
2 - CYLINDER FIRING ORDER (IGNITION COIL NUMBER)
3 - CORRESPONDING SPARK PLUG NUMBER

LTV1900000000328

Fig. A

FRONT WHEEL ALIGNMENT SPECIFICATIONS

This chart has been revised by a Technical Service Bulletin.

Year	Camber Angle, Degrees⑤		Caster Angle, Degrees⑥		Toe In, Degrees④		Ball Joint Wear
	Limits	Desired	Limits	Desired	Limits	Desired	
2005–08	-.60 to +.40	-.10	+9.00 to +12.10	①	-.05 to +.15③	+.10②	.059

① — Lefthand, +10.30°; righthand, +11.10°.

② — Total toe, +.20°.

③ — Total toe, 0° to +.40°.

④ — Maximum side-to-side difference: desired, 0°; limits, +.06°.

⑤ — Maximum side-to-side difference: desired, +.20°; limits, -.30° to +.60°.

⑥ — Maximum side-to-side difference: desired, -.80°; limits, -1.30° to -.50°.

REAR WHEEL ALIGNMENT SPECIFICATIONS

This chart has been revised by a Technical Service Bulletin.

Year	Camber Angle, Degrees①②		Toe In, Degrees		Thrust Angle, Degrees	
	Limits	Desired	Limits	Desired	Limits	Desired
2005–08	-1.25 to -.25	-.75	-.05 to +.25	+.10	-.50 to +.50	0

① — Reference angle only; not adjustable.

② — Maximum side-to-side difference: desired, 0°; limits, -.50° to +.50°.

VEHICLE RIDE HEIGHT SPECIFICATIONS

This chart has been revised by a Technical Service Bulletin.

Model	Year	Drive	Manufacturer's Original Tire Size①	Measurement Points & Specifications②					
				Front③			Rear③		
				Dim., Fig.	Specification④		Dim., Fig.	Specification⑦	
					Inches	mm		Inches	mm
All	2005–08	AWD	—	A	13.9000⑧	353⑨	B	12.099⑩	307⑪
		RWD	—	A	12.9375②	328③	B	11.625⑤	296⑥

① — See door sticker or inside of glove compartment for manufacturers original tire size specifications. If tires on vehicle do not match manufacturers original tire size & measurement is not within limits, it will be required to refer to the Non-Standard Tire & Wheel Size Adjustment To Ride Height Specification & Tire Size Adjustment Charts in the front of this manual for approximate changes in ride height specifications.

② — Limits, 12.500–13.375 inches.

③ — Limits, 318–338 mm.

④ — Cross ride height, .5 inch or -12 to +12 mm.

⑤ — Limits, 11.25–12.00 inches.

⑥ — Limits, 286–306 mm.

⑦ — Cross ride height, 0 inch or -12 to +12 mm.

⑧ — Limits, 13.51–14.29 inches.

⑨ — Limits, 243–363 mm.

⑩ — Limits, 11.70–12.48 inches.

⑪ — Limits, 297–317 mm

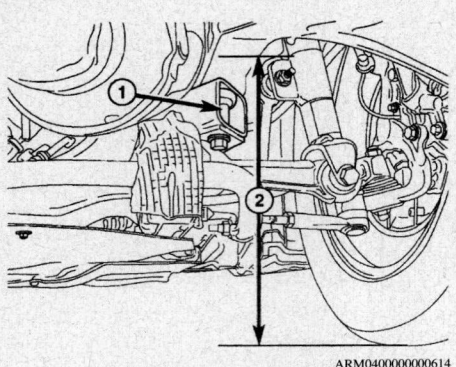

Fig. A Front ride height (1) Engine cradle rear mount (2) Dimension

ARM0400000000614

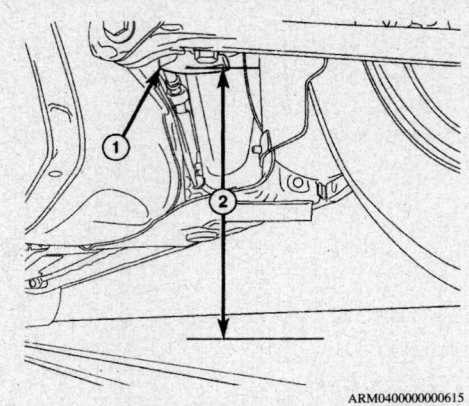

Fig. B Rear ride height (1) Travel limiter (2) Dimension

ARM0400000000615

FLUID CAPACITIES & COOLING SYSTEM DATA

Engine	Coolant Capacity, Qts.	Recommended Engine Coolant Type	Radiator Cap Relief Pressure, Lbs.	Thermostat. Opening Temp., °F	Fuel Tank, Gals.	Engine Oil Refill, Qts.①	Transmission Oil, Qts.②	Transfer Case, Pts	Differential Oil, Qts.	
									Front	Rear
2.7L	9.7	Ethylene Glycol	16	203–220	18	6.0	③⑤	1.3	—	⑦
3.5L	10.6	Ethylene Glycol	16	203–220	19	6.0	③⑥	1.3	.78	⑦
5.7L	14.6	Ethylene Glycol	16	195	19	7.0	③⑥	1.3	④	⑦
6.1L	14.8	Ethylene Glycol	16	192–199	19	7.0	③⑥	1.3	.64	⑦

① — Includes oil filter.
② — Approximate; make final inspection w/dipstick. Includes torque converter sump.
③ — 42RLE, overhaul fill, 12,0 pts,; Service fill, 3pts.

④ — 10 ½ inch, 4.75 pts.; 11 ½ inch, 7.65 pts.
⑤ — NAG1, overhaul fill, 17.1 pts., service fill, 14.8 pts.
⑥ — Dry fill capacity depends on type and size of internal cooler, length

and inside diameter of cooler lines, or use of an auxiliary cooler, these figures may vary.
⑦ — 198 mm RII Axle, 1.5 qts.; 210 MM RII Axle, 1.7 qts.; 215RII Axle, 1.3 qts.

LUBRICANT DATA

Year	Lubricant Type					
	Transmission	Transfer Case	Differential		Power Steering	Brake System
			Front	Rear		
2005–08	ATF+4 (MS9602)	Mopar Transfer Case Lubricant	Mopar Synthetic Gear & Axle Lubricant 75W-90	Mopar Synthetic Gear & Axle Lubricant 75W-140	ATF+4 (MS9602)	DOT 3

NOTE: On Air Bag Equipped Models, Refer To "Air Bag System Precautions" Located In The Front Of This Manual For System Disarming & Arming Procedures.

NOTE: Refer To "Computer Relearn Procedures" Located In The Front Of This Manual When Battery Power To The Computer Has Been Interrupted.

NOTE: Prior To Performing Any Service Operations Listed In This Section, Consult The "Technical Service Bulletins" Section For Related Information.

NOTE: Refer To The Rear Of This Manual For Vehicle Manufacturer's Special Tool Suppliers.

INDEX

	Page No.		Page No.		Page No.
Air Bag System (Volume 2)	4-1	Fuse Panel & Flasher Location	6-5	Steering Wheel, Replace	6-8
Air Conditioning	8-1	Headlamp Switch, Replace	6-7	Stop Light Switch, Replace	6-7
Alternator, Replace	6-6	Heater Core, Replace	6-9	Technical Service Bulletins	6-9
2.7L Engine	6-6	Ignition Lock, Replace	6-7	Audio System Intermittent	
3.5L Engine	6-6	Ignition Switch, Replace	6-7	Output	6-10
5.7L Engine	6-6	Instrument Cluster, Replace	6-8	Loss of Communications	
6.1L Engine	6-6	Multi-Function Switch, Replace	6-7	w/Multiple Module DTCs Set	6-10
Alternators	11-1	Neutral Safety Switch, Replace	6-7	Cavity 31 Dislodged	6-10
Blower Motor, Replace	6-8	Passive Restraint Systems		Cavity 32 Dislodged	6-10
Cabin Air Filter, Replace	6-8	(Volume 2)	4-1	Cavity 33 Dislodged	6-10
Coil Pack, Replace	6-6	Precautions	6-5	Radio DTC221E	6-9
2.7L Engine	6-6	Air Bag Systems	6-5	Rain Sensor Switch Setting Not	
3.5L Engine	6-7	Battery Ground Cable	6-5	Sensitive Enough	6-10
5.7L & 6.1L Engines	6-7	Recalibration	6-5	Wiper Linkage Contacts MAP	
Cooling Fans	9-1	Radio, Replace	6-8	Sensor Wiring	6-10
Cruise Control (Volume 2)	2-1	Speed Controls (Volume 2)	2-1	Turn Signal Switch, Replace	6-8
Dash Gauges (Volume 2)	1-1	Starter Motors	10-1	Wiper Motor, Replace	6-8
Dash Panel Service		Starter, Replace	6-6	Front	6-8
(Volume 2)	5-1	2.7L & 3.5L Engines	6-6	Rear	6-8
Dimmer Switch, Replace	6-8	5.7L Engine	6-6	Wiper Switch, Replace	6-8
Evaporator Core, Replace	6-9	6.1L Engine	6-6	Wiper Systems (Volume 2)	3-1
Fuel Pump Relay Location	6-6	Steering Columns	12-1	Wiper Transmission, Replace	6-8

PRECAUTIONS

Air Bag Systems

Refer to "Air Bag System Precautions" in the front of this manual for system disarming and arming procedures.

Battery Ground Cable

Prior to service, disconnect battery ground cable and isolate as required.

RECALIBRATION

Anytime the battery has been disconnect or has lost its charge, the following must be recalibrated:

EXPRESS WINDOW

1. Turn ignition switch to RUN position.
2. Move driver's window upward until it stalls in full up position. Allow window motor to stall for at least two seconds before releasing switch.
3. Move driver's window downward until it stalls in full down position. Allow window motor to stall for at least two seconds before releasing switch.
4. Move driver's window upward until it stalls in full up position. Allow window motor to stall for at least two seconds before releasing switch.
5. Move passenger's window upward until it stalls in full up position. Allow window motor to stall for at least two seconds before releasing switch.
6. Move passenger's window downward until it stalls in full down position. Allow window motor to stall for at least two seconds before releasing switch.
7. Move passenger's window upward until it stalls in full up position. Allow window motor to stall for at least two seconds before releasing switch.

ELECTRONIC STABILITY PROGRAM (ESP) STEERING ANGLE SENSOR

1. Start engine.
2. Turn steering wheel to righthand side until wheel locks full right.
3. Turn steering wheel to lefthand side until wheel locks full left.
4. Turn steering wheel to righthand until wheels are centered.
5. Cycle ignition switch OFF and ON. Do not start engine.

FUSE PANEL & FLASHER LOCATION

The majority of electrical system fuses and relays are housed in the two Power Distribution Centers (PDC). The engine compartment PDC and the Front Control Module (FCM) are combined to form the Integrated Power Module (IPM). The other PDC is located next to the battery, at the rear of the vehicle.

The FCM is a micro controller based module located in the righthand front corner of the engine compartment. The IPM connects directly to the battery and provides the primary means of circuit protection and power distribution for all vehicle electrical systems. The FCM controls power to some of these vehicle systems electrical and electromechanical loads based on inputs received from hard wired switch inputs and data received on the CAN bus circuit.

FUEL PUMP RELAY LOCATION

The fuel pump relay is located in the Power Distribution Center (PDC) in the righthand front corner of the engine compartment.

STARTER
REPLACE
2.7L & 3.5L Engines

1. Lock steering wheel in straight-ahead position using suitable wheel holder.
2. Raise vehicle and support.
3. Remove underbody splash shield.
4. Remove center pinch bolt, then separate intermediate steering shaft upper from lower shaft.
5. Disconnect starter electrical connector.
6. Remove three starter mounting bolts and wiring clip.
7. Pull starter forward and down, then around exhaust.
8. Move starter past intermediate steering shaft and remove.
9. Reverse procedure to install, noting the following:
   a. **Torque** starter mounting bolts 40 ft. lbs.
   b. **Torque** intermediate shaft pinch bolt to 32 ft. lbs.

5.7L Engine

1. Raise and support vehicle.
2. **On models equipped with AWD,** proceed as follows:
   a. Remove steering gear to steering column pinch bolt.
   b. Remove three mounting bolts and slightly lower steering gear.
   c. Temporarily support steering gear. **Do not disconnect any hydraulic hoses or remove steering linkage.**
   d. Remove steering gear heat-shield.
3. **On all models,** remove mounting bolts and move starter motor towards front of vehicle for nose to clear. **Support starter motor during process.**
4. Remove nut and solenoid wire from solenoid stud.**Do not let starter motor hang from wire harness.**
5. Remove starter motor.
6. Reverse procedure to install.

6.1L Engine

1. Raise and support vehicle.
2. Remove heat shield.
3. Remove mounting bolts and move

starter motor towards front of vehicle for nose to clear. **Support starter motor during process.**
4. Remove nut and solenoid wire from solenoid stud.
5. Remove starter motor.
6. Reverse procedure to install.

ALTERNATOR
REPLACE
2.7L Engine

1. Rotate belt tensioner counterclockwise until it contacts it's stop.
2. Remove belt and slowly rotate tensioner into freearm position. **Do not let tensioner arm snap back to freearm position.**
3. Disconnect field circuit plug.
4. Remove B+ terminal nut and wire.
5. Remove two lower mounting bolts, upper bolt and alternator.
6. Reverse procedure to install, noting the following:
   a. **Torque** alternator mounting bolts to 48 ft. lbs.
   b. **Torque** B+ terminal nut to 115 inch lbs.
   c. Route belt around all pulleys except idler pulley.
   d. Rotate tensioner arm until it contacts it's stop position.
   e. Route belt around idler and slowly let tensioner rotate into belt.
   f. Ensure belt is seated onto all pulleys.

3.5L Engine

1. Rotate belt tensioner counterclockwise until it contacts it's stop.
2. Remove belt and slowly rotate tensioner into freearm position. **Do not let tensioner arm snap back to freearm position.**
3. Remove bracket mounting bolts.
4. Remove alternator upper mounting bolt.
5. Raise and support vehicle.
6. Remove middle splash pan.
7. Disconnect field circuit plug.
8. Remove B+ terminal nut and wire.
9. Remove lower mounting bolts and alternator.
10. Reverse procedure to install, noting the following:
    a. **Torque** alternator mounting bolts to 48 ft. lbs.
    b. **Torque** B+ terminal nut to 115 in. lbs.
    c. **Torque** bracket mounting bolts to 40 ft. lbs.
    d. Route belt around all pulleys except idler pulley.
    e. Rotate tensioner arm until it contacts it's stop position.
    f. Route belt around idler and slowly let tensioner rotate into belt.
    g. Ensure belt is seated onto all pulleys.

5.7L Engine

1. Rotate belt tensioner counterclock-

wise until it contacts it's stop.
2. Remove belt and slowly rotate tensioner into freearm position. **Do not let tensioner arm snap back to freearm position.**
3. Raise and support vehicle.
4. Unsnap plastic insulator cap from B+ output terminal.
5. Remove B+ terminal mounting nut, then disconnect terminal and field wire connector.
6. Remove mounting nut, bolt and support bracket.
7. Remove two mounting bolts and alternator.
8. Reverse procedure to install, noting the following
   a. **Torque** alternator mounting bolts to 48 ft. lbs.
   b. **Torque** B+ terminal nut to 115 in. lbs.
   c. **Torque** bracket mounting bolts to 30 ft. lbs.
   d. Route belt around all pulleys except idler pulley.
   e. Rotate tensioner arm until it contacts it's stop position.
   f. Route belt around idler and slowly let tensioner rotate into belt.
   g. Ensure belt is seated onto all pulleys.

6.1L Engine

1. Rotate belt tensioner counterclockwise until it contacts it's stop.
2. Remove belt and slowly rotate tensioner into freearm position. **Do not let tensioner arm snap back to freearm position.**
3. Raise and support vehicle.
4. Drain enough coolant into suitable container to remove upper radiator hose.
5. Remove righthand engine mount heat shield.
6. Loosen, but do not remove, alternator support bracket retaining nut.
7. Remove alternator support bracket mounting bolt.
8. Unsnap plastic insulator cap from B+ output terminal.
9. Remove B+ terminal mounting nut, then disconnect terminal and field wire connector.
10. Lower vehicle.
11. Remove alternator mounting bolts, then alternator.
12. Reverse procedure to install, noting the following
    a. **Torque** alternator mounting bolts to 48 ft. lbs.
    b. **Torque** B+ terminal nut to 115 in. lbs.
    c. **Torque** bracket mounting bolts to 30 ft. lbs.

COIL PACK
REPLACE
2.7L Engine

1. Remove intake manifold as outlined under "Intake Manifold, Replace" in "2.7L Engine" section.

2. Clean around coil area and spark plug using suitable compressed air.
3. Remove electrical connector.
4. Remove two mounting screws and ignition coil.
5. Reverse procedure to install. **Torque** mounting screws to 57 inch lbs.

3.5L Engine

1. Remove intake manifold as outlined under "Intake Manifold, Replace" in "3.5L Engine" section.
2. Clean around coil area and spark plug using suitable compressed air.
3. Remove electrical connector.
4. Remove two mounting screws, loosen screws by alternating back and forth. **Do not lose spacers under coil**
5. Remove ignition coil.
6. Reverse procedure to install. **Torque** mounting screws to 60 inch lbs., alternating back and forth.

5.7L & 6.1L Engines

Before removing or disconnecting any spark plug cables, mark their original position for installation reference. Remove cables one-at-a-time. To prevent ignition crossfire, spark plug cables must be placed in cable tray (routing loom) into their original position.

1. Depending on which coil is being removed, the throttle body air intake tube or intake box may need to be removed to gain access.
2. Disconnect electrical connector by moving slide lock first.
3. Press release lock while pulling electrical connector from coil.
4. Disconnect secondary high-voltage cable from coil with twisting action.
5. Clean area at base of coil with suitable compressed air.
6. Remove two mounting bolts (mounting bolts are retained to coil).
7. Pull up and remove coil from cylinder head opening with slight twisting action.
8. Reverse procedure to install, noting the following:
   a. Apply dielectric grease to inside of boots.
   b. **Torque** mounting bolts to 105 inch lbs.

IGNITION LOCK

REPLACE

1. Remove bezel ignition switch ring.
2. Pull center console bezel loose from instrument panel.
3. Insert ignition key and turn to switch ON position.
4. Depress ignition switch housing locking tab.
5. Remove key cylinder from ignition switch housing.
6. Reverse procedure to install.

IGNITION SWITCH

REPLACE

1. Disconnect snap retainers using trim stick tool No. C-4755, or equivalent,

between ignition switch bezel and instrument cluster.
2. Remove ignition switch bezel.
3. Disconnect wire harness connector from headlamp switch and remove cluster bezel.
4. Remove side trim panel to steering column cover.
5. Remove steering column cover to instrument panel and relocate panel mounting screws.
6. Disconnect snap retainers by pulling steering column cover rearward at top and righthand side.
7. Remove instrument panel steering column cover reinforcement to bracket mounting screws.
8. Remove reinforcement.
9. Remove two front mounting nuts and lower mounting nut, then slide switch rearward.
10. Disconnect ignition switch and SKREEM module electrical connector.
11. Remove interlock cable by depressing locking tab and pulling straight out.
12. Remove mounting screw, squeeze two locking tabs and remove ignition switch.
13. Reverse procedure to install.

NEUTRAL SAFETY SWITCH

REPLACE

1. Place ignition key in ACC position.
2. Remove lower instrument panel trim and disconnect park lock cable from ignition cylinder.
3. Apply parking brake and turn ignition switch to ON position.
4. Apply brakes and place gear selector lever into Neutral position.
5. Turn ignition switch to OFF position and release brakes.
6. Remove floor console front cubby bin mat.
7. Open lid of console rear bin and remove mat.
8. Remove two front of console shifter bezel to console mountings screws.
9. Disconnect console bezel from console using suitable trim stick.
10. Remove shifter bezel from around gear selector lever.
11. Remove three console to floor panel transmission tunnel mounting bolts from rear bin.
12. Remove two front of console to instrument panel mounting screws.
13. Slide console rearward and disconnect accessory power outlet jumper wire connector.
14. Remove floor console.
15. Remove mounting bolts, then the shield covering gearshift and park lock cables.
16. Disconnect park lock cable from shift mechanism.
17. Reverse procedure to install.

HEADLAMP SWITCH

REPLACE

1. Remove steering column cover to instrument panel mounting screws.

2. Disconnect snap retainers from instrument panel by pulling steering column cover rearward at top and righthand side.
3. Disconnect trunk release switch wire harness connector.
4. Disconnect emergency bracket release handle release cable.
5. Remove steering column cover.
6. From underneath and behind instrument panel, push up on lower clip on headlamp switch, then wiggle it down and out of instrument panel.
7. Disconnect headlamp switch electrical connector.
8. Reverse procedure to install.

STOP LIGHT SWITCH

REPLACE

1. Depress and hold brake pedal.
2. Rotate stop lamp switch counterclockwise approximately 30° from its mounting position.
3. Pull switch rearward and remove it from mounting bracket.
4. Disconnect wiring harness connector.
5. Reverse procedure to install.

MULTI-FUNCTION SWITCH

REPLACE

The multi-function switch is located on the steering column, just below the steering wheel, within the Steering Column Control Module (SCCM). The only visible components of the multi-function switch are the control stalk and control knob that extend through the SCCM on the lefthand side of the column. The multi-function switch cannot be adjusted or repaired. If any function of the switch is faulty, or if the switch is damaged, the entire switch must be replaced.

1. Position front wheels straight-ahead.
2. Fully extend or pull out adjustable steering column.
3. Remove two driver's air bag module covers and mounting screws from behind steering wheel.
4. Pull air bag module rearward, then disconnect two air bag squib connectors and horn connector. **Do not pull on horn switch feed pigtail wire.**
5. Separate driver's air bag module from steering column.
6. Remove mounting bolt and slide steering wheel off shaft.
7. Back out set screw through access hole in bottom of SCCM.
8. Pull SCCM off steering column shaft.
9. Remove three clockspring screws.
10. Remove clockspring by pulling it straight up.
11. **On models equipped with ESP,** remove mounting screw at six o'clock position and remove steering angle sensor.
12. **On models less ESP,** lift out a plastic strengthening insert.
13. **On models equipped with manual telescoping column,** remove mounting screw at six o'clock position and strut.

14. **On models less electronic telescoping column,** remove mounting screw at six o'clock position, then the stalk and switch.
15. **On all models,** remove speed control switch.
16. Remove steering column tilt/telescoping lever mounting screw at six o'clock position.
17. Remove three mounting screws from bottom and separate multi-function switch from SCCM circuit board.
18. Reverse procedure to install, noting the following:
    a. **Torque** steering wheel mounting bolt to 52 ft. lbs.
    b. **Torque** driver' air bag module mounting screws to 89 inch lbs.

TURN SIGNAL SWITCH
REPLACE

Refer to "Multi-Function Switch, Replace" for the turn signal switch replacement procedure.

DIMMER SWITCH
REPLACE

Refer to "Multi-Function Switch, Replace" for the dimmer switch replacement procedure.

STEERING WHEEL
REPLACE

1. Position front wheels straight-ahead.
2. Fully extend or pull out adjustable steering column.
3. Remove two driver's air bag module mounting covers and mounting screws from behind steering wheel.
4. Pull air bag module rearward, then disconnect two air bag squib connectors and horn connector. **Do not pull on horn switch feed pigtail wire.**
5. Separate driver's air bag module from steering column.
6. Reverse procedure to install, noting the following:
    a. **Torque** steering wheel mounting bolt to 52 ft. lbs.
    b. **Torque** driver' air bag module mounting screws to 89 inch lbs.

INSTRUMENT CLUSTER
REPLACE

1. Disconnect snap retainers using trim stick tool No. C-4755, or equivalent, between ignition switch bezel and instrument cluster.
2. Remove ignition switch bezel.
3. Disconnect wire harness connector from headlamp switch and remove cluster bezel.
4. Remove four mounting screws and disconnect cluster electrical connectors.
5. Remove instrument cluster.
6. Reverse procedure to install

RADIO
REPLACE

1. Remove center bezel from instrument panel by releasing snap retainers using trim stick tool No. C-4755, or equivalent.
2. Disconnect air conditioning/heater control and switch pod electrical connectors.
3. Remove center bezel.
4. Remove mounting bolts.
5. Disconnect antenna cable by pulling locking antenna connector away from radio.
6. Disconnect electrical harness connector and remove radio.
7. Reverse procedure to install.

WIPER MOTOR
REPLACE
Front

1. Remove caps and mounting nuts, then separate wiper arm from pivot using suitable two-jaw puller.
2. Remove wiper arms.
3. Remove cowl top panel to each front fender push-pin.
4. Disconnect two ¼ turn fasteners securing cowl top panel to dash panel.
5. Remove six cowl top panel to strut tower support push-pins.
6. Disconnect integral cowl top panel to dash panel retaining clips.
7. Remove cowl panel.
8. Disconnect wiper motor electrical connector.
9. Remove two mounting bolts and wiper module.
10. Remove bellcrank to motor shaft mounting nut.
11. Pry bellcrank from wiper motor shaft using suitable, flat bladed tool.
12. Remove two motor mounting bolts.
13. Separate wiper motor from module/linkage. **Do not loose two pocket nuts.**
14. Reverse procedure to install, noting the following:
    a. **Torque** wiper module mounting bolts to 70 inch lbs.
    b. **Torque** wiper arm nuts to 13 ft. lbs.

Rear

1. Remove rear wiper arm caps and mounting nuts.
2. Remove wiper arm by rocking it from side to side.
3. Remove lamp from lower liftgate trim panel.
4. Remove two lower trim panel to inside of liftgate mounting screws in pull cup formation to right of latch.
5. Disconnect seven push-in plastic fasteners securing panel to liftgate by prying trim panel away from inside of liftgate using suitable trim stick.
6. Remove liftgate lower trim panel.
7. Remove two upper trim panel lower corner screws.

8. Disconnect eight panel to liftgate push-in plastic fasteners using suitable trim stick.
9. Remove liftgate upper trim panel.
10. Remove three mounting nuts and disconnect electrical harness connector.
11. Remove wiper motor.
12. Reverse procedure to install. **Torque** mounting nuts to 70 inch lbs.

WIPER SWITCH
REPLACE

Refer to "Multi-Function Switch, Replace" for the wiper switch replacement procedure.

WIPER TRANSMISSION
REPLACE

1. Remove caps and mounting nuts, then separate wiper arm from pivot using suitable two-jaw puller.
2. Remove wiper arms.
3. Remove cowl top panel to each front fender push-pin.
4. Disconnect two ¼ turn fasteners securing cowl top panel to dash panel.
5. Remove six cowl top panel to strut tower support push-pins.
6. Disconnect integral cowl top panel to dash panel retaining clips.
7. Remove cowl panel.
8. Disconnect wiper motor electrical connector.
9. Remove two mounting bolts and wiper module.
10. Reverse procedure to install, noting the following:
    a. **Torque** wiper module mounting bolts to 70 inch lbs.
    b. **Torque** wiper arm nuts to 13 ft. lbs.

BLOWER MOTOR
REPLACE

1. Remove two righthand side instrument panel silencer to instrument pane push-pins.
2. Disconnect brackets near dash panel by pulling instrument panel silencer rearward.
3. Remove instrument panel silencer.
4. Disconnect locking tab, wire harness connector and retainers.
5. Remove four blower motor mounting screws.
6. Reverse procedure to install. **Torque** mounting screws to 20 inch lbs.

CABIN AIR FILTER
REPLACE

1. Remove air inlet grille from wiper module screen.
2. Remove filter from housing located inside of dash panel plenum.
3. Reverse procedure to install, noting direction of air flow indicated by arrow on filter.

HEATER CORE
REPLACE

1. Drain engine cooling system into suitable container.
2. Disconnect heater hoses from core tubes.
3. Remove two lefthand side instrument panel silencer to bracket push-pins.
4. Disconnect brackets by pulling instrument panel silencer rearward.
5. Remove lefthand side instrument panel silencer.
6. Remove three mounting screws and lefthand blend door actuator from air distribution housing.
7. Disconnect HVAC wire harness connector and remove blend door actuator.
8. Remove two mounting screw and flange from front of HVAC housing.
9. Remove clamps and disconnect tubes from heater core. Discard O-ring seals.
10. Pull heater core tubes through dash panel. Plug or tape over opened heater core ports.
11. Remove mounting screw and heater core bracket.
12. Pull heater core out of air distribution housing.
13. Reverse procedure to install, noting the following:
    a. **Torque** heater core bracket mounting screws to 20 inch lbs.
    b. Install new rubber O-ring seals lubricated with suitable, clean engine coolant.
    c. **Torque** flange mounting screws to 20 inch lbs.
    d. **Torque** blend door mounting screws to 17 inch lbs.

EVAPORATOR CORE
REPLACE

1. Recover refrigerant as outlined in "Air Conditioning" chapter.
2. Drain engine cooling system into suitable container.
3. Remove caps and mounting nuts, then separate wiper arm from pivot using suitable two-jaw puller.
4. Remove wiper arms.
5. Remove cowl top panel to each front fender push-pin.
6. Disconnect two 1/4 turn fasteners securing cowl top panel to dash panel.
7. Remove six cowl top panel to strut tower support push-pins.
8. Disconnect integral cowl top panel to dash panel retaining clips.
9. Remove cowl panel.
10. Disconnect wiper motor electrical connector.
11. Remove two mounting bolts and wiper module.
12. Raise and support vehicle.
13. Remove front splash shields.
14. Remove mounting nut and disconnect air conditioning liquid line from condenser. Discard dual plane seal.
15. Install plugs, or tape over opened liquid line fitting and condenser outlet port.
16. Lower vehicle.

17. Remove mounting nut and disconnect front section of air conditioning liquid line from rear section. Discard dual plane seal.
18. Install plugs in, or tape over opened liquid line fittings.
19. **On models equipped with 2.7L engine,** proceed as follows:
    a. Remove front section of air conditioning liquid line.
    b. Disconnect Mass Air Flow (MAF) sensor electrical connector.
    c. Remove clean air duct between throttle body and air filter housing.
    d. Remove vent tube.
    e. Remove mounting bolt and air filter housing.
    f. Raise and support vehicle.
    g. Partially remove front fascia to gain access to air filter resonator.
    h. Remove mounting bolt and air cleaner resonator.
20. **On models equipped with 3.5L engine,** proceed as follows:
    a. Separate air inlet duct at element housing.
    b. Disconnect PCV hose at element housing.
    c. Remove housing mounting bolt.
    d. Pull housing up and off of locating pin.
    e. Remove element housing,
21. **On models equipped with 5.7L or 6.1L engines,** proceed as follows:
    a. Loosen clamp and disconnect air duct at air cleaner cover.
    b. Lift entire housing assembly from four locating pins.
22. **On all models,** disconnect air conditioning pressure transducer wire harness.
23. Remove refrigerant line mounting bracket to lefthand front shock tower mounting bolt.
24. Remove liquid and suction line tapping block to expansion valve mounting nut.
25. Disconnect rear section of air conditioning liquid and suction lines from expansion valve. Discard liquid line fittings and dual plane seal.
26. Install plugs in, or tape over opened suction and liquid line fittings, and expansion valve ports.
27. Remove rear section of air conditioning liquid and suction lines.
28. Disconnect hoses from heater core tubes.
29. Remove two mounting nuts and air inlet water separator, or cabin air filter and housing.
30. Remove HVAC housing mounting nut inside fresh air inlet housing.
31. Remove two HVAC housing engine compartment mounting nuts.
32. Remove instrument panel as outlined in "Dash Panel Service" chapter.
33. Remove floor console front cubby bin mat.
34. Open lid of console rear bin and remove rear bin mat.
35. Remove two front of console shifter bezel to console mountings screws.
36. Disconnect console bezel from console using suitable trim stick.
37. Remove shifter bezel from around gear selector lever.

38. Remove three console to floor panel transmission tunnel mounting bolts from rear bin.
39. Remove two front of console to instrument panel mounting screws.
40. Slide console rearward and disconnect accessory power outlet jumper wire connector.
41. Remove floor console.
42. Remove mounting bolts, then the shield covering gearshift and park lock cables.
43. Remove two duct to center floor panel mounting screws.
44. Disconnect and remove floor console ducts.
45. Remove six mounting screws and floor distribution duct.
46. Remove four mounting screws and defroster duct.
47. Remove two HVAC housing passenger compartment mounting nuts.
48. Pull HVAC housing rearward to clear mounting studs.
49. Lift housing so condensate drain tube clears floor panel grommet.
50. Remove HVAC housing.
51. Remove air distribution and inlet housings.
52. Remove two mounting screws, then the flange and heater core tubes.
53. Disconnect evaporator temperature sensor, blower motor resistor or power module, and blower motor wiring harnesses.
54. Disconnect two wire harness retainers and remove blower motor.
55. Remove blower motor resistor or power module.
56. Remove evaporator temperature sensor.
57. Remove two mounting bolts and expansion valve.
58. Discard evaporator tube fittings O-ring seals.
59. Install plugs in, or tape over opened evaporator tube fittings and all expansion valve ports.
60. Remove HVAC wiring harness.
61. Remove 10 mounting screws, then separate upper half from lower half of HVAC housing.
62. Lift evaporator and foam seal out of lower half of housing.
63. Reverse procedure to install, noting the following:
    a. **Torque** wiper module mounting bolts to 70 inch lbs.
    b. **Torque** wiper arm nuts to 13 ft. lbs.

TECHNICAL SERVICE BULLETINS

Radio DTC221E

On some of these models equipped with navigation radios, Diagnostic Trouble Code (DTC) B221E may be set when the ignition is turned ON.

This is an erroneous code. Do not replace the radio based solely on internal radio DTC B221.E.

Rain Sensor Switch Setting Not Sensitive Enough

On some of these models the rain sensor switch settings do not differ or are not sensitive enough.

These condition may be caused by the Light Rain Sensor Module (LRSM) programming.

To correct this situation, program LRSM with latest software version.

Wiper Linkage Contacts MAP Sensor Wiring

On some of these models built before April 14, 2004, with 5.7L engine, the wiper linkage may contact and move the MAP sensor wiring. Overtime, this may break the wires and/or the MAP sensor.

This condition may be caused by MAP sensor wiring.

To correct this condition, secure MAP sensor wiring to the purge solenoid vacuum line and away from wiper linkage using suitable tie strap, **Fig. 1**.

Audio System Intermittent Output

On some of these models built before May 10, 2004, and equipped with premium audio system. may occasionally not produce audio for an entire ignition cycle. The radio display and control may work normally, but no sound is produced.

These condition may be caused by Audio Amplifier (AMP) programming.

To correct this situation, program AMP with latest software version.

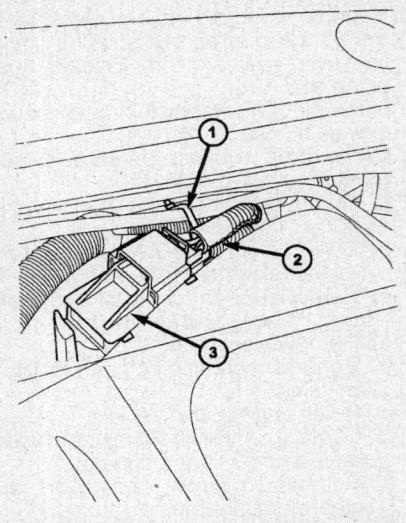

1 - TIE STRAP WIRING TO THE PURGE SOLENOID VACUUM LINE
2 - DO NOT PULL ON WIRING
3 - MAP SENSOR

ARM0400000000613

Fig. 1   MAP sensor wiring position

Loss of Communications w/Multiple Module DTCs Set

On some of these models there may be loss of communications and multitple module Diagnostic Trouble Codes (DTCs) set.

This condition may be caused by dislodged diodes in cavity 31, 32 and/or 33 in the Rear Power Distribution Center (RPDC), located in the truck next to the battery.

CAVITY 31 DISLODGED

If cavity 31 diode becomes dislodged, DTCs will be set for these modules, the air bag lamp will illuminate and the Front Control Module (FCM) will set DTC B2124, ignition run control circuit open.

If cavity 31 diode becomes dislodged, ignition run feed will be lost to the following modules/components:
1. Occupant Restraint Control (ORC) module.
2. Automatic Temperature Control (ATC) control head.
3. Manual Temperature Control (MTC) and ATC blower motor.
4. High Intensity Discharge (HID) module and associated sensors/headlamps.
5. Parktronics module.

CAVITY 32 DISLODGED

If cavity 32 diode becomes dislodged, the following will occur:
1. All modules capable will set loss of communication DTCs with Transmission Control Module.
2. Transmission will go into second gear limp-in mode.
3. Anti-Lock Brake System (ABS) lamp will illuminate.

CAVITY 33 DISLODGED

If cavity 33 diode becomes dislodged, no DTC or any noticeable functions are affected. Cavity 33 diode provides charging system over voltage protection.

To correct this condition, ensure all diodes and fuses are securely seated by pressing down on them. If diodes becomes complete separated from RPDC cavity, note the following:
1. Diodes are keyed and can only be install in one direction.
2. Diode arrow symbol on top of diodes in slots 31 and 32 point toward spare tire.
3. Diode arrow symbol on top of diode 33 points toward vehicle rear.
4. Ensure diode 33 is properly orientated as reverse terminal contact will cause fuse No. 5 to fail.

2.7L Engine

NOTE: On Air Bag Equipped Models, Refer To "Air Bag System Precautions" Located In The Front Of This Manual For System Disarming & Arming Procedures.

NOTE: Refer To "Computer Relearn Procedures" Located In The Front Of This Manual When Battery Power To The Computer Has Been Interrupted.

NOTE: Refer To The Rear Of This Manual For Vehicle Manufacturer's Special Tool Suppliers.

INDEX

	Page No.
Belt Tension Data	6-18
Camshaft, Replace	6-16
Installation	6-16
Removal	6-16
Compression Pressure	6-11
Cooling System Bleed	6-18
Crankshaft Damper, Replace	6-15
Crankshaft Rear Oil Seal, Replace	6-17
Crankshaft Seal, Replace	6-17
Cylinder Head, Replace	6-13
Engine Rebuilding Specifications	21-1
Engine, Replace	6-12
Engine Mount, Replace	6-12
Lefthand & Righthand	6-12
Rear	6-12
Exhaust Manifold, Replace	6-13
Lefthand	6-13
Righthand	6-13
Front Cover, Replace	6-15

	Page No.
Fuel Filter, Replace	6-19
Fuel Pump, Replace	6-19
Hydraulic Lifters, Replace	6-15
Intake Manifold, Replace	6-13
Lower	6-13
Upper	6-13
Main & Rod Bearings	6-17
Oil Pan, Replace	6-17
Oil Pump, Replace	6-18
Oil Pump Service	6-18
Assemble	6-18
Disassemble	6-18
Inspection	6-18
Piston & Rod Assembly	6-16
Precautions	6-11
Air Bag Systems	6-11
Battery Ground Cable	6-11
Recalibration	6-11
Fuel System Pressure Relief	6-11
Radiator, Replace	6-19
Rocker Arms, Replace	6-15

	Page No.
Serpentine Drive Belt	6-18
Replacement	6-18
Installation	6-18
Removal	6-18
Routing	6-18
Structural Collar, Replace	6-12
Thermostat, Replace	6-19
Tightening Specifications	6-20
Timing Chain, Replace	6-15
Installation	6-15
Removal	6-15
Timing Chain Tensioner, Replace	6-16
Timing Chain Tensioner Bleed	6-16
Valve Adjustment	6-15
Valve Clearance Specifications	6-15
Valve Cover, Replace	6-14
Lefthand	6-14
Righthand	6-15
Water Pump, Replace	6-19

PRECAUTIONS

Air Bag Systems

Refer to "Air Bag System Precautions" in the front of this manual for system disarming and arming procedures.

Battery Ground Cable

Prior to service, disconnect battery ground cable and isolate as required.

RECALIBRATION

Anytime the battery has been disconnect or has lost its charge, the following must be recalibrated.

EXPRESS WINDOW

1. Turn ignition switch to RUN position.
2. Move driver's window upward until it stalls in full up position. Allow window motor to stall for at least two seconds before releasing switch.
3. Move driver's window downward until it stalls in full down position. Allow window motor to stall for at least two seconds before releasing switch.
4. Move driver's window upward until it stalls in full up position. Allow window motor to stall for at least two seconds before releasing switch.
5. Move passenger's window upward until it stalls in full up position. Allow window motor to stall for at least two seconds before releasing switch.
6. Move passenger's window downward until it stalls in full down position. Allow window motor to stall for at least two seconds before releasing switch.
7. Move passenger's window upward until it stalls in full up position. Allow window motor to stall for at least two seconds before releasing switch.

ELECTRONIC STABILITY PROGRAM (ESP) STEERING ANGLE SENSOR

1. Start engine.
2. Turn steering wheel to righthand side until wheel locks full right.
3. Turn steering wheel to lefthand side until wheel locks full left.
4. Turn steering wheel to righthand side until wheels are centered.
5. Cycle ignition switch OFF and ON. Do not start engine.

Fuel System Pressure Relief

1. Remove fuel pump relay for Power Distribution Center (PDC).
2. Start and run engine until it stalls.
3. Attempt to start engine until it no longer runs.
4. Turn ignition switch to OFF position.
5. Install fuel pump relay.

COMPRESSION PRESSURE

1. Ensure battery is completely charged and engine starter motor is in good operating condition.
2. Ensure engine oil level is correct.
3. Drive vehicle until engine reaches normal operating temperature.
4. Remove all spark plugs. Inspect electrodes for abnormal firing indicators fouled, hot, oily, etc.
5. Record cylinder number of spark plug for future reference.
6. Remove Auto Shutdown (ASD) relay from PDC.

7. Ensure throttle blade is fully open during compression inspection.
8. Insert compression gauge adaptor tool No. 8116, or equivalent, into spark plug hole No. 1.
9. Connect suitable 0–500 psi pressure gauge.
10. Crank engine until maximum pressure is reached on gauge. Record this pressure.
11. Repeat previous step for all remaining cylinders.
12. Compression should not be less than 100 psi and not vary more than 25% from cylinder to cylinder.
13. If one or more cylinders have abnormally low compression pressures, repeat compression test.
14. If same cylinder, or cylinders, repeat an abnormally low reading on second compression test, it could indicate existence of problem in cylinder.

ENGINE MOUNT
REPLACE

Lefthand & Righthand

1. Disconnect Mass Air Flow (MAF) sensor electrical connector.
2. Remove clean air duct between throttle body and air filter housing.
3. Remove vent tube.
4. Remove mounting bolt and air filter housing.
5. Raise and support vehicle.
6. Remove three per side wheel house splash shield rivets.
7. Remove nine belly pan mounting screws.
8. Remove two fascia to fender mounting screw, one per side.
9. Open hood and remove upper push pin fasteners (four per sedan and six per wagon).
10. Partially remove front fascia to gain access to air filter resonator.
11. Remove air cleaner resonator.
12. Remove mounting bolts and lower splash shield.
13. Remove lefthand engine mount nuts and studs.
14. Place suitable wooden block under oil pan and raise engine with suitable jackstand.
15. Remove mounting bolts and engine mount isolator.
16. Reverse procedure to install. Do not do not let mount contact frame when lowering engine.

Rear

1. Raise and support vehicle on hoist.
2. Remove crossmember to mount bolts.
3. Raise transmission using suitable jack under transmission pan.
4. Remove mounting bolts and crossmember.
5. Remove mounting bolts and rear mount.
6. Reverse procedure to install.

STRUCTURAL COLLAR
REPLACE

1. Raise and support vehicle on hoist.
2. Remove mounting bolts and lower splash shield.
3. Remove transmission mount bolts.
4. Place suitable transmission jack under transmission pan, then raise engine and transmission.
5. Remove mounting bolts and structural collar to right, then rear.
6. Reverse procedure to install, noting the following:
   a. Hand tighten mounting bolts.
   b. Ensure structural collar is flush with oil pan and transmission bell housing.
   c. **Torque** vertical collar bolts to oil pan to 10 inch lbs.
   d. **Torque** horizontal collar bolts to transmission to 40 ft. lbs.
   e. **Torque** mounting bolts, starting with center vertical bolts and working outward to 40 ft. lbs.

ENGINE
REPLACE

1. Remove hood.
2. Relieve fuel system pressure as outlined under "Precautions."
3. Disconnect Intake Air Temperature (IAT) sensor electrical connector.
4. Disconnect Manifold Absolute Pressure (MAP) sensor electrical connector.
5. Remove clean air duct between throttle body and air filter housing.
6. Remove vent tube.
7. Remove mounting bolt and air filter housing.
8. Rotate belt tensioner counterclockwise until it contacts it's stop.
9. Remove belt and slowly rotate tensioner into freearm position. **Do not let tensioner arm snap back to freearm position.**
10. Disconnect power steering pump lines.
11. Remove mounting bolts and position power steering pump aside.
12. Recover refrigerant as outlined in "Air Conditioning" chapter.
13. Disconnect compressor electrical connectors.
14. Disconnect wire harness connector from air conditioning compressor clutch coil connector.
15. Remove mounting nuts, then disconnect suction and discharge lines from compressor. Discard dual plane seals. Install plugs in, or tape over all of opened refrigerant line fittings and compressor ports.
16. Raise and support vehicle.
17. Remove mounting bolts and splash shield.
18. Remove automatic transmission cooler line bracket and air conditioning compressor mounting bolts.
19. Position cooler lines aside and remove compressor.
20. Drain cooling system into suitable container.

21. Drain engine oil into suitable container and remove oil filter.
22. Disconnect downstream oxygen sensor connectors.
23. Disconnect exhaust pipes at manifolds.
24. Disconnect electrical connectors, then remove mounting bolts and position starter aside.
25. Disconnect coolant pipe near starter from hose.
26. Disconnect electrical connector, then remove mounting bolt and Crankshaft Position (CKP) sensor.
27. Disconnect ground strap.
28. Disconnect oil pressure sensor electrical connector.
29. Remove four engine mount nuts and studs.
30. Remove mounting bolts and lower steering gear for clearance.
31. Raise engine using suitable wooden block and lifting device under oil pan.
32. Remove mounting bolts and structural collar.
33. Remove lower bell housing bolts.
34. Lower engine and remove jack stand.
35. Mark flexplate to torque converter for installation alignment.
36. Remove torque converter mounting bolts.
37. Lower vehicle.
38. Remove caps and mounting bolts, then separate wiper arm from pivot using suitable two-jaw puller.
39. Remove wiper arms.
40. Remove two push pins securing front cowl top panel to righthand rear corner of engine compartment.
41. Remove front cowl top panel.
42. Remove push-pin securing each end of cowl top panel to each front fender.
43. Disconnect two ¼ turn fasteners securing cowl top panel to dash panel.
44. Remove six push-pins securing cowl top panel to strut tower support.
45. Disengage integral retaining clips securing cowl top panel to dash panel.
46. Remove cowl panel.
47. Remove strut tower support and position purge solenoid aside.
48. Remove intake manifold as outlined under "Intake Manifold, Replace."
49. Disconnect vacuum lines and electrical connectors.
50. Disconnect ground straps.
51. Disconnect fuel line at fuel rail.
52. Disconnect coil, injector, capacitor and knock sensor connectors.
53. Remove from bracket and position purge solenoid aside.
54. Unlock and disconnect EGR valve electrical connector.
55. Disconnect electrical connector, then remove two mounting bolts and wiper module.
56. Remove and position shock tower brace aside.
57. Remove upper intake manifold as outlined under "Intake Manifold, Replace."
58. Remove mounting bolts and EGR valve tube. **Do not drop silicone rubber seals into intake manifold.**
59. Remove mounting bolts and EGR valve.

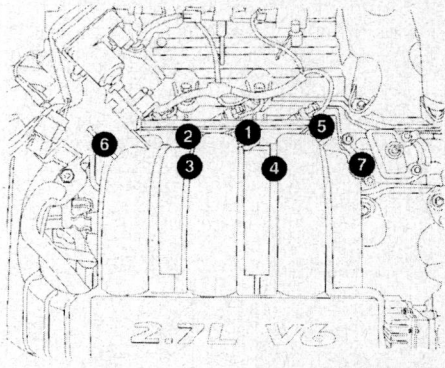

Fig. 1 Upper intake manifold tightening sequence

60. Remove upper bellhousing bolts and position electrical harness aside.
61. Attach suitable lifting fixture to front of lefthand cylinder head and rear of righthand cylinder head.
62. Support transmission with suitable wooden block and floor jack.
63. Remove engine.
64. Reverse procedure to install.

INTAKE MANIFOLD
REPLACE
Upper

1. Disconnect Manifold Absolute Pressure (MAP) sensor electrical connector.
2. Remove clean air duct between throttle body and air filter housing.
3. Remove vent tube.
4. Remove mounting bolt and air filter housing.
5. Disconnect electronic throttle control and manifold tuning valve electrical connectors.
6. Disconnect vapor purge, brake booster and Positive Crankcase Ventilation (PCV) hoses.
7. Remove manifold support brackets.
8. Remove mounting bolts, upper manifold and foam insulator.
9. Reverse procedure to install, noting the following:
   a. Ensure fuel injectors and wiring harnesses are in correct position to not interfere with upper manifold installation.
   b. Tighten mounting bolts in sequence, **Fig. 1**.

Lower

1. Relieve fuel system pressure as outlined under "Precautions."
2. Disconnect Manifold Absolute Pressure (MAP) sensor electrical connector.
3. Remove clean air duct between throttle body and air filter housing.
4. Remove vent tube.
5. Remove mounting bolt and air filter housing.
6. Disconnect electronic throttle control

and manifold tuning valve electrical connectors.
7. Disconnect vapor purge, brake booster hose and Positive Crankcase Ventilation (PCV) hoses.
8. Remove manifold support brackets.
9. Remove mounting bolts, upper manifold and foam insulator.
10. Disconnect injector electrical connectors.
11. Disconnect fuel supply hose from fuel rail.
12. Remove mounting bolts, then fuel rail and injectors.
13. Remove mounting bolts and lower manifold.
14. Remove fuel rail fuel supply hose, then fuel rail support bracket to throttle body support bracket mounting screw.
15. Reverse procedure to install, noting the following:
   a. Position manifold on cylinder head surfaces by installing upper intake manifold bolt 2–3 turns in rearmost hole.
   b. Install fuel rail with injectors and start bolts 1–4, **Fig. 2**.
   c. **Torque** mounting bolts in sequence, **Fig. 2**.

EXHAUST MANIFOLD
REPLACE
Lefthand

1. Disconnect Intake Air Temperature (IAT) sensor connector.
2. Disconnect Manifold Absolute Pressure (MAP) sensor electrical connector.
3. Remove clean air duct between throttle body and air filter housing.
4. Remove vent tube.
5. Remove mounting bolt and air filter housing.
6. Remove oil dipstick tube.
7. Disconnect and remove oxygen sensor.
8. Remove upper and lower heat shields.
9. Raise and support vehicle on hoist.
10. Disconnect downstream oxygen sensor connector.
11. Remove catalytic converter to muffler and resonator clamps.
12. Remove isolators, then muffler and tailpipe by twisting/turning while pulling assembly out of catalytic converters.
13. Remove ball flange nuts, then ball flange nut and catalytic converter.
14. Remove mounting bolts and exhaust manifold.
15. Reverse procedure to install, noting the following:
   a. Tighten exhaust manifold mounting bolts starting at center working outward.
   b. **Torque** manifold ball flange nut to 106 inch lbs.
   c. Measure exhaust module and fuel tank clearance. Clearance should be .62 inch.
   d. Measure clearance at rear tunnel reinforcement. Clearance .59–.78 inch.

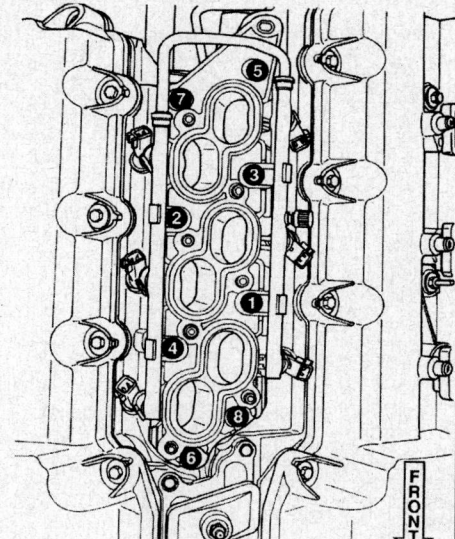

Fig. 2 Lower intake manifold tightening sequence

   e. **Torque** ball flange nuts to 25 ft. lbs.

Righthand

1. Disconnect and remove upstream oxygen sensor.
2. Raise and support vehicle.
3. Remove tube at EGR valve and manifold.
4. Disconnect downstream oxygen sensor electrical connector.
5. Remove catalytic converter to muffler and resonator clamps.
6. Remove isolators, then muffler and tailpipe by twisting/turning while pulling assembly out of catalytic converters.
7. Remove mounting nuts and crossbrace.
8. Remove ball flange nuts and catalytic converter.
9. Remove upper and lower heat shields.
10. Remove mounting bolts and exhaust manifold.
11. Reverse procedure to install, noting the following:
   a. Tighten exhaust manifold mounting bolts starting at center working outward.
   b. **Torque** manifold ball flange nut to 106 inch lbs.
   c. Measure exhaust module and fuel tank clearance. Clearance should be .62 inch.
   d. Measure clearance at rear tunnel reinforcement. Clearance .59–.78 in.
   e. **Torque** ball flange nuts to 25 ft. lbs.

CYLINDER HEAD
REPLACE

1. Relieve fuel system pressure as outlined under "Precautions."
2. Raise and support vehicle on hoist.
3. Drain cooling system into suitable container.

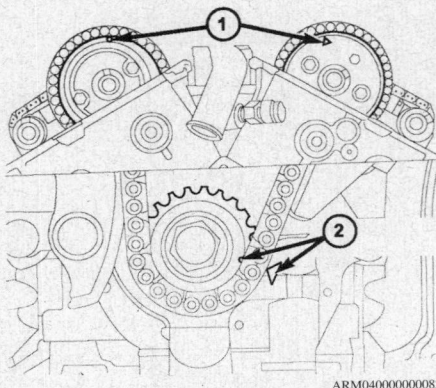

Fig. 3 Timing mark alignment

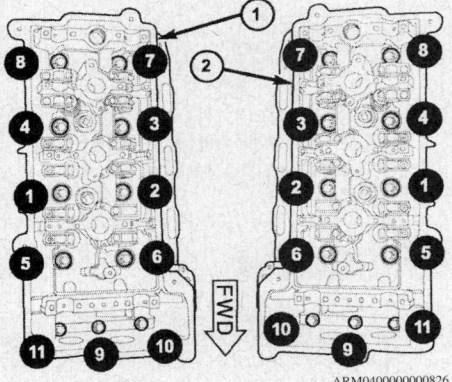

ARM0400000000826

Fig. 6 Cylinder head tightening sequence

4. Rotate belt tensioner counterclockwise until it contacts it's stop.
5. Remove belt and slowly rotate tensioner into freearm position. **Do not let tensioner arm snap back to freearm position.**
6. Hold damper using damper holder tool No. 9365, or equivalent, then remove damper mounting bolts.
7. Remove damper using suitable three-jaw puller.
8. Disconnect Camshaft Position (CMP) and coolant temperature sensors' connectors.
9. Remove upper and lower intake manifolds as outlined under "Intake Manifold, Replace."
10. Remove cylinder head covers as outlined under "Valve Cover, Replace."
11. Remove radiator as outlined under "Radiator, Replace."
12. Remove radiator upper hose at tube.
13. Remove heater hose from heater tube at rear of engine.
14. Disconnect heater tube from retaining clip at rear of engine.
15. Remove mounting screws, then disconnect and remove heater tube from outlet connector.
16. Rotate crankshaft until crankshaft sprocket timing mark aligns with timing mark on oil pump housing, **Fig. 3.** Mark on oil pump housing is 60° ATDC of cylinder No. 1.
17. Remove primary timing chain as out-

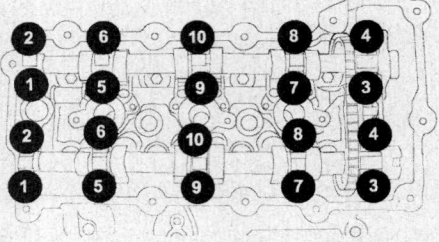

ARM0400000000824

Fig. 4 Camshaft loosening sequence

lined under "Timing Chain, Replace."
18. Remove upper primary timing chain guides.
19. Remove camshaft bearing caps gradually in sequence, **Fig. 4.**
20. Mark position for install alignment, then remove camshafts and valve train components from cylinder head.
21. **For lefthand cylinder head,** proceed as follows:
    a. Remove oil dipstick tube to cylinder head mounting bolt.
    b. Remove engine oil dipstick tube.
    c. Remove alternator.
22. **For righthand cylinder head,** proceed as follows:
    a. Remove cylinder head ground strap.
    b. Disconnect electrical connector and remove EGR valve from head.
23. **On all models,** ensure cylinder head bolts No. 1–3 are removed before attempting removal of cylinder head.
24. Remove cylinder head bolts in sequence, **Fig. 5.**
25. Reverse procedure to install, noting the following:
    a. Cylinder head bolts are tightened using torque plus angle procedure. Bolts with stretched threads must be replaced.
    b. Install new head gasket over locating dowels.
    c. Ensure head is properly positioned over locating dowels.
    d. Lubricate bolt threads with suitable, clean engine oil.
    e. **Torque** cylinder head bolts Nos. 1–8 in sequence to 35 ft. lbs., **Fig. 6.**
    f. **Torque** head bolts Nos. 1–8 in sequence to 55 ft. lbs.
    g. **Torque** bolts Nos. 1–8 in sequence to 55 ft. lbs.
    h. Tighten bolts Nos. 1–8 an additional 90° in sequence.
    i. **Torque** cylinder head bolts Nos. 9–11 in sequence to 21 ft. lbs.
    j. **Torque** cylinder head bolts 9–11 to 21 ft. lbs.
    k. Tighten camshaft bearing caps in sequence, **Fig. 7.**

VALVE COVER
REPLACE
Lefthand

1. Disconnect Manifold Absolute Pres-

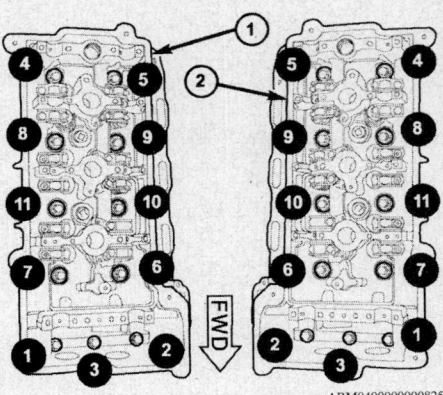

ARM0400000000825

Fig. 5 Cylinder head removal sequence

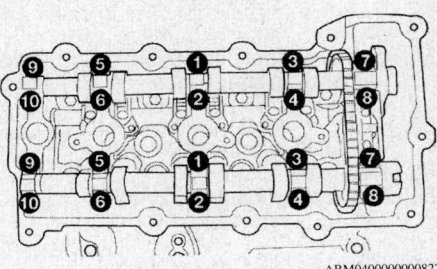

ARM0400000000827

Fig. 7 Camshaft bearing cap tightening sequence

sure (MAP) sensor electrical connector.
2. Remove clean air duct between throttle body and air filter housing.
3. Remove vent tube.
4. Remove mounting bolt and air filter housing.
5. Disconnect electronic throttle control and manifold tuning valve electrical connectors.
6. Disconnect vapor purge, brake booster hose and Positive Crankcase Ventilation (PCV) hoses.
7. Remove manifold support brackets.
8. Remove mounting bolts, upper manifold and foam insulator.
9. Disconnect ignition coils electrical connectors.
10. Remove ground strap from cylinder head cover stud and disconnect capacitor connector.
11. Position electrical harness aside.
12. Disconnect retaining clips from cylinder head cover studs and position electrical harness aside.
13. Remove make up air hose.
14. Remove capacitor mounting bolts and ignition coils.
15. Loosen valve cover mounting bolts, **Fig. 8. Cylinder head cover mounting bolts are captured in cover. Ensure double ended studs in center of cover are loose before attempting to remove cover.**
16. Remove valve cover.
17. Reverse procedure to install. Ensure double-ended studs are in correct locations.

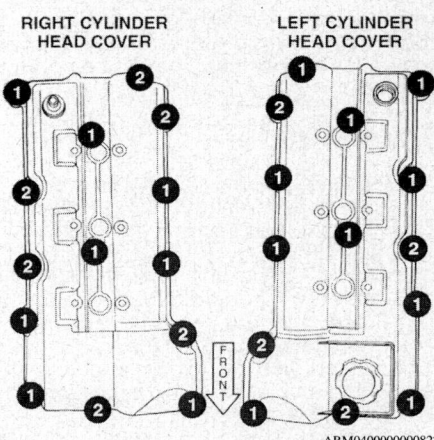

Fig. 8 Valve cover loosening & tightening sequence

ARM0400000000822

Righthand

1. Disconnect Manifold Absolute Pressure (MAP) sensor electrical connector.
2. Remove clean air duct between throttle body and air filter housing.
3. Remove vent tube.
4. Remove mounting bolt and air filter housing.
5. Disconnect electronic throttle control and manifold tuning valve electrical connectors.
6. Disconnect vapor purge, brake booster hose and Positive Crankcase Ventilation (PCV) hoses.
7. Remove manifold support brackets.
8. Remove mounting bolts, upper manifold and foam insulator.
9. Disconnect ignition coils electrical connectors.
10. Disconnect capacitor electrical connector.
11. Remove PCV hose from cylinder head cover grommet.
12. Remove ground strap from cylinder head cover stud.
13. Disconnect retaining clips from cylinder head cover studs and position electrical harness aside.
14. Remove ignition coil capacitor mounting bolts and ignition coils.
15. Remove foam insulator.
16. Loosen valve cover mounting bolts, **Fig. 8. Cylinder head cover mounting bolts are captured in cover.**
17. Remove valve cover.
18. Reverse procedure to install. Ensure double-ended studs are in correct locations.

VALVE CLEARANCE SPECIFICATIONS

This engine is equipped with hydraulic lifters and valves are lashed with zero clearance.

VALVE ADJUSTMENT

This engine is equipped with hydraulic lash adjusters. No adjustment is required.

ROCKER ARMS
REPLACE

1. Remove cylinder head cover(s) as outlined under "Valve Cover, Replace."
2. Rotate engine until cam lobe is on its base circle (heel), on rocker arm being removed.
3. Mark rocker arms for installation in original positions.
4. Depress valve spring using spring removal tools Nos. 8215 and 8216, suitable adaptor and ratchet.
5. Repeat procedure for each rocker arm removed.
6. Reverse procedure to install using spring installation tools Nos. 8215-A and 8216-A, suitable adaptor and ratchet.

HYDRAULIC LIFTERS
REPLACE

1. Remove rocker arm as outlined under "Rocker Arm, Replace."
2. Mark hydraulic lash adjuster for installation in original position.
3. Remove hydraulic lash adjuster.
4. Reverse procedure to install. Ensure adjuster is partially full of oil (little or no plunger travel when lash adjuster is depressed).

CRANKSHAFT DAMPER
REPLACE

1. Rotate belt tensioner counterclockwise until it contacts it's stop.
2. Remove belt and slowly rotate tensioner into freearm position. **Do not let tensioner arm snap back to freearm position.**
3. Hold damper using damper holder tool No. 9365, or equivalent, then remove damper mounting bolts.
4. Remove damper using suitable three-jaw puller.
5. Reverse procedure to install, using installer tool No. 6792-1, screw tool No. 8179, and nut and thrust bearing tool No. 6792, or equivalents.

FRONT COVER
REPLACE

1. Drain cooling system into suitable container.
2. Remove coolant pressure container.
3. Raise and support vehicle on hoist.
4. Remove mounting bolts and lower splash shield.
5. Rotate belt tensioner counterclockwise until it contacts it's stop.
6. Remove belt and slowly rotate tensioner into freearm position. **Do not let tensioner arm snap back to freearm position.**
7. Hold damper using damper holder tool No. 9365, or equivalent, then remove damper mounting bolts.
8. Remove damper using suitable three-jaw puller.
9. Lower vehicle.
10. Remove mounting bolts and timing

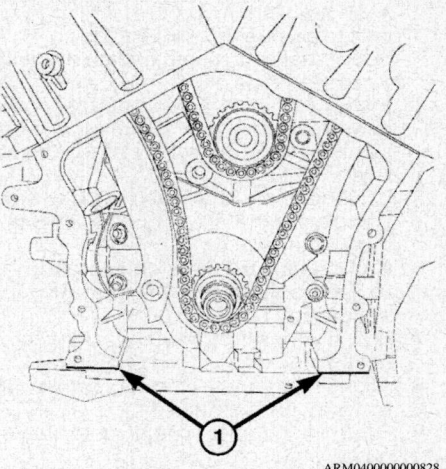

Fig. 9 Front cover RTV application

ARM0400000000828

chain cover. Discard timing chain cover gasket.
11. Remove front crankshaft oil seal from cover.
12. Reverse procedure to install. Apply 1/8 inch bead of Mopar Engine RTV GEN II, or equivalent, to the parting lines between oil pan and cylinder block, **Fig. 9.**

TIMING CHAIN
REPLACE

With the timing chain removed, avoid turning the camshaft or crankshaft. If movement is required, exercise extreme caution to avoid valve damage caused by piston contact.

Removal

1. Drain cooling system into suitable container.
2. Remove cylinder heads as outlined under "Cylinder Head, Replace."
3. Remove timing chain cover as outlined under "Front Cover, Replace."
4. Rotate crankshaft until crankshaft sprocket timing mark aligns with timing mark on oil pump housing, **Fig. 3.** Mark on oil pump housing is 60° ATDC of cylinder No. 1.
5. Remove cap and primary timing chain tensioner retainer cap from righthand cylinder head.
6. Disconnect and remove Camshaft Position (CMP) sensor from lefthand cylinder head.
7. Remove timing chain guide access plugs from cylinder heads.
8. Remove mounting bolts, righthand camshaft damper and sprocket. **When camshaft sprocket bolts are removed, camshafts rotate in clockwise direction.**
9. Remove mounting bolts and lefthand camshaft sprocket.

Installation

1. Install lefthand and righthand side short chain guides.

2. Align crankshaft sprocket timing to oil pump housing marks, **Fig. 10.**
3. Lubricate timing chain and guides with suitable engine oil.
4. Place lefthand side primary chain sprocket onto chain so timing mark is located between two (plated) timing links.
5. Lower primary chain with lefthand side sprocket through lefthand cylinder head opening.
6. **Camshaft sprockets can be allowed to float on camshaft hub during installation.**
7. Loosely position lefthand side camshaft sprocket over camshaft hub.
8. Align timing (plated) link to crankshaft sprocket timing mark.
9. Position primary chain onto water pump drive sprocket.
10. Align righthand camshaft sprocket timing mark to timing (plated) link on timing chain and loosely position over camshaft hub.
11. Ensure all chain timing (plated) links are properly aligned to timing marks on all sprockets.
12. Install lefthand side lower chain guide and tensioner arm.
13. Install chain guide access plugs to cylinder heads.
14. Place check ball end of tensioner into shallow end of timing chain tensioner reset gauge tool No. 8186, or equivalent.
15. Slowly depress tensioner using hand pressure until oil is purged from tensioner.
16. Position tensioner cylinder plunger into deeper end of tensioner reset gauge tool.
17. Apply downward force until tensioner is reset.
18. Install reset chain tensioner into righthand cylinder head, position tensioner retaining and tighten mounting bolts.
19. Starting at righthand cylinder bank, position camshaft damper on camshaft hub, then insert ⅜ inch square drive extension with breaker bar into intake camshaft drive hub.
20. Rotate camshaft until camshaft hub aligns to camshaft sprocket and damper attaching holes.
21. Install and tighten sprocket mounting bolts.
22. Turn lefthand side camshaft by inserting ⅜ inch square drive extension with breaker bar into intake camshaft drive hub until sprocket mounting bolts can be installed and tightened.
23. Remove timing chain slack by rotating engine slightly clockwise.
24. Activate timing chain tensioner by gently pry tensioner arm towards tensioner slightly using suitable flat bladed pry tool. Release tensioner arm.
25. Ensure tensioner is activated (extends).
26. Install CMP sensor and connect electrical connector.
27. Install cylinder heads as outlined under "Cylinder Head, Replace."
28. Install timing chain cover as outlined under "Front Cover, Replace."
29. After installation of reset tensioner, en-

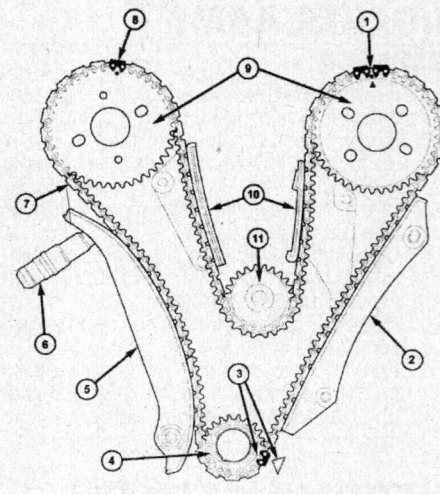

1- TWO (PLATED) TIMING LINKS
2- CHAIN GUIDE
3- OIL PUMP HOUSING
4- CRANKSHAFT SPROCKET
5- CHAIN GUIDE
6- CHAIN TENSIONER
7- TIMING CHAIN
8- TIMING (PLATED) LINK
9- CAMSHAFT SPROCKETS
10- CHAIN GUIDE
11- WATER PUMP DRIVE SPROCKET

ARM0400000000829

Fig. 10 Timing chain alignment

gine noise will occur after initial startup. Noise will normally disappear within 5–10 seconds.
30. Fill cooling system.

TIMING CHAIN TENSIONER
REPLACE

1. Remove timing chain cover as outlined under "Front Cover, Replace."
2. Align timing marks, **Fig. 10.**
3. Remove cover and timing chain tensioner.
4. Reverse procedure to install, noting the following:
   a. Ensure proper timing alignment prior to tensioner installation.
   b. Position tensioner cylinder plunger into deeper end of tensioner reset gauge tool No. 8186, or equivalent.
   c. Apply downward force until tensioner is reset.
   d. Tensioner retaining plate dowel pin must aligned with hole in cylinder head.

TIMING CHAIN TENSIONER BLEED

1. Place check ball end of tensioner into shallow end of timing chain tensioner reset gauge tool No. 8186, or equivalent.
2. Slowly depress tensioner using hand pressure until oil is purged from tensioner.

CAMSHAFT
REPLACE

With the timing chain removed, avoid

turning the camshaft or crankshaft. If movement is required, exercise caution to avoid valve damage caused by piston contact.

Removal

1. Remove primary timing chain as outlined under "Timing Chain, Replace."
2. Remove secondary chain tensioner mounting bolts.
3. Slowly loosen and remove camshaft bearing caps gradually in sequence, **Fig. 4.**
4. Camshaft bearing caps have been marked during engine manufacturing. For example, No. 1 exhaust camshaft bearing is marked 1E.
5. Remove intake camshaft, exhaust camshaft), secondary timing chain and secondary timing chain tensioner as an assembly.
6. Remove secondary timing chain tensioner and secondary timing chain from camshafts.

Installation

When the timing chain is removed and the cylinder heads are installed, do not rotate the camshafts or crankshaft without first locating the proper crankshaft position.
1. Assemble camshaft chain on cams.
2. Ensure plated links are facing toward front, **Fig. 11.**
3. Align plated links to camshaft sprockets' dots.
4. If camshaft chain tensioner is already in compressed and locked position, proceed to next step. When camshaft chain tensioner has been removed, proceed as follows:
   a. Place tensioner into suitable soft jaw vise.
   b. Slowly compress tensioner until fabricated lock pin can be inserted into locking holes.
5. Install compressed and locked camshaft chain tensioner between camshafts and chain.
6. Rotate cams so plated links and dots are facing 12 o'clock position.
7. Install cams to cylinder head. Ensure rocker arms are correctly seated and in proper positions.
8. Install camshaft bearing caps. Ensure bearing caps are installed in original positions.
9. Tighten camshaft bearing cap bolts gradually in sequence, **Fig. 7.**
10. Install and tighten secondary chain tensioner mounting bolts.
11. Remove locking pin from secondary tensioners.
12. Measure camshafts end play. Endplay should be .0051–.0110 inch.
13. Install primary timing chain as outlined under "Timing Chain, Replace."

PISTON & ROD ASSEMBLY

1. Position bearing onto connecting rod.

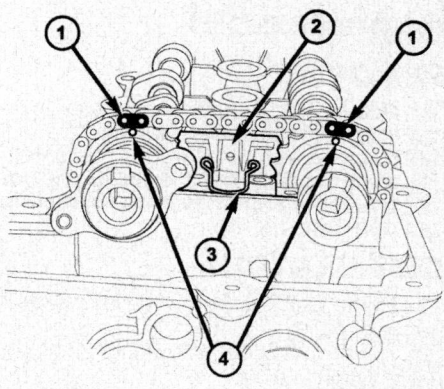

Fig. 11 Camshaft cam alignment

Ensure bearing half and connecting rod holes align.
2. Lubricate bearing surface with suitable, clean engine oil.
3. Install connecting rod guides tools No. 8189, or equivalent, into connecting rod.
4. Ensure pistons top mark arrow and F (front) above pin boss. pointing towards front of engine in both cylinder banks.
5. Connecting rod oil squirt hole faces major thrust (righthand) side of block.
6. Rotate crankshaft so connecting rod journal is on center of cylinder bore.
7. Insert rod and piston into cylinder bore, then guide rod over crankshaft journal.
8. **Do not interchange piston assemblies bank to bank.**
9. Tap piston down in cylinder bore, using suitable hammer handle while guide connecting rod into position on connecting rod journal.
10. Lubricate rod bolts and bearing surface with suitable engine oil.
11. Install and connecting rod cap and bearing, then tighten bolts.

MAIN & ROD BEARINGS

Upper and lower bearing halves are not interchangeable.
1. Refer to **Fig. 12** to select main bearings.
2. Install main bearing in block and main caps ensuring tangs engage slots in block and main caps.
3. Lubricate upper main bearing halves with suitable engine oil.
4. Install crankshaft. **Do not damage bearing surfaces on crankshaft.**
5. Ensure coated and oil groove side of crankshaft thrust washer faces crankshaft thrust surface.
6. Push crankshaft forward.
7. Lubricate and install front thrust washer by rolling thrust washer onto machined shelf between upper main bulk head No. 3 and crankshaft thrust surface.
8. Move crankshaft rearward.
9. Lubricate and install rear thrust washer by rolling thrust washer onto machined

Crankshaft Main Journal Grade Mark	Main Bearing Bore Grade Mark		
	1	2	3
1	(3) Standard	(2) +.0001 inch	(1) +.0002 inch
2	(4) -.0001 inch	(3) Standard	(2) +.0001 inch
3	(5) (-.0002 inch	(4) (-.0001 inch	(3) Standard

Fig. 12 Main bearing selection chart

shelf between upper main bulk head No. 3 and crankshaft thrust surface.
10. Lubricate lower main bearings with suitable engine oil.
11. Install main bearings caps.
12. Lubricate main bearing cap bolts with suitable engine oil.
13. **Torque** inner main cap bolts to 15 ft. lbs., then tighten additional 90°.
14. Measure crankshaft end play. End play should be .0019–.0108 inch.
15. Install connecting rods and measure side clearance. using plastigage. Side clearance should be .0052–.015 inch.
16. Install windage tray with slots to righthand side of engine.
17. Lubricate mounting bolts with suitable engine oil and **Torque** to 20 ft. lbs., then tighten additional 90°.
18. Install main cap tie (horizontal) bolts and **torque** to 20 ft. lbs.

CRANKSHAFT SEAL
REPLACE

1. Rotate belt tensioner counterclockwise until it contacts it's stop.
2. Remove belt and slowly rotate tensioner into freearm position. **Do not let tensioner arm snap back to freearm position.**
3. Hold damper using damper holder tool No. 9365, or equivalent, then remove damper mounting bolts.
4. Remove damper using suitable three-jaw puller.
5. Remove seal using remover tool Nos. 6771 and 8194, or equivalents.
6. Reverse procedure to install using crankshaft seal protector tool No. 6780-2, crankshaft seal and sprocket installer tool 6780-1 and crankshaft damper installer screw tool No. 8179, or equivalents.

CRANKSHAFT REAR OIL SEAL
REPLACE

The crankshaft rear oil seal is incorporated in the seal adapter and can not be removed from the adapter. The crankshaft rear oil seal/seal adapter are serviced as an assembly.

The integrated stamped steel rear crankshaft seal is not interchangeable with the cast aluminum rear seal adapter and seal assembly.
1. Raise and support vehicle.
2. Remove mounting bolts and splash shield.

3. Raise and support vehicle on hoist.
4. Remove mounting bolts and lower splash shield.
5. Remove transmission mount bolts.
6. Place suitable transmission jack under transmission pan, then raise engine and transmission.
7. Remove mounting bolts and structural collar to right, then rear.
8. Remove transmission as outlined in **MOTOR's "Domestic Transmission Manual, In-Vehicle Service" manual or "Transmission Service DVD."**
9. Remove mounting bolts, then backing and flex plates.
10. Remove oil pan as outlined under "Oil Pan, Replace."
11. Remove mounting screws and crankshaft rear oil seal/adapter.
12. Reverse procedure to install, noting the following:
   a. Install seal assembly using seal installer tool No. 6926-1, or equivalent.
   b. Install seal mounting bolts hand tight.
   c. Attach alignment tools No. 8225, or equivalent to pan rail.
   d. Ensure 2.7L stamped on special tool is facing cylinder block (flat side of tools against pan rail).
   e. Apply firm pressure to seal assembly against special tools and **torque** seal screws 105 inch lbs.

OIL PAN
REPLACE

1. Remove engine oil indicator.
2. Raise and support vehicle on hoist.
3. Remove mounting bolts and lower splash shield.
4. Drain engine oil into suitable container and remove oil filter.
5. Remove bolt and steering separate coupler from rack.
6. Disconnect power steering pressure switch electrical connector.
7. Remove steering rack mounting bolts and power steering line support from frame.
8. Position rack aside.
9. Raise and support vehicle on hoist.
10. Remove mounting bolts and lower splash shield.
11. Remove transmission mount bolts.
12. Place suitable transmission jack under transmission pan, then raise engine and transmission.
13. Remove mounting bolts and structural collar to right, then rear.

14. Remove alternator mounting bracket to oil pan lower bolt.
15. Remove air conditioning compressor bracket to oil pan lower bolt.
16. Remove lower timing chain cover to oil pan bolts.
17. Remove mounting bolts, oil pan and gasket. **Ensure four lower timing cover bolts are removed.**
18. Reverse procedure to install, noting the following:
    a. Apply ⅛ inch bead of Mopar Engine RTV GEN II, or equivalent, to front T-joints (oil pan gasket to timing cover gasket interface) and rear T-joints (oil pan gasket to crankshaft rear oil seal retainer gasket interface), **Fig. 13.**
    b. Install oil pan bolts and nuts, then hand tighten just tight enough to compress gasket's rubber seal.
    c. Line up front of oil pan to be flush with front face of block.
    d. Install lower timing chain cover bolts and **torque** to 105 inch lbs.
    e. **Torque** oil pan bolts to 20 ft. lbs.
    f. **Torque** oil pan nuts to 105 inch lbs.
    g. Hand tighten structural collar mounting bolts.
    h. Ensure structural collar is flush with oil pan and transmission bell housing.
    i. **Torque** vertical collar bolts to oil pan to 10 inch lbs.
    j. **Torque** horizontal collar bolts to transmission to 40 ft. lbs.
    k. **Torque** mounting bolts, starting with center vertical bolts and working outward to 40 ft. lbs.

OIL PUMP

REPLACE

1. Remove timing chain and sprockets as outlined under "Timing Chain, Replace."
2. Remove oil pan as outlined under "Oil Pan, Replace."
3. Remove oil pick-up tube and O-ring.
4. Ensure crankshaft position is at 60° ATDC of cylinder No. 1 or crankshaft sprocket and oil pimp marks align.
5. Remove mounting bolts and oil pump.
6. Reverse procedure to install, noting the following:
    a. Prime oil pump before installation by filling rotor cavity with suitable engine oil.
    b. Ensure crankshaft position is at 60° ATDC of cylinder No. 1 or crankshaft sprocket.
    c. Install new oil pick-up tube O-ring lubricated with suitable, clean engine oil.

OIL PUMP SERVICE

Do not remove oil pressure relief valve. If the oil pressure relief valve is suspect, replace the oil pump assembly.

Disassemble

1. Remove mounting screws and oil pump cover.
2. Remove inner and outer pump rotors.

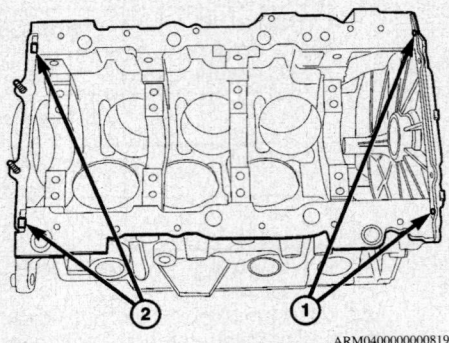

Fig. 13 Oil pan RTV application

Inspection

1. Wash all components in suitable solvent.
2. Inspect mating surface of oil pump housing and cover. Replace oil pump if deeply scratched or grooved.
3. Lay straightedge across pump cover surface. Replace cover is gap is .001 inch or more.
4. Measure thickness and diameter of outer rotor. If outer rotor thickness is .373 inch, or less, or if diameter is 3.5108 inches, or less, replace outer rotor.
5. Measure inner rotor. If inner rotor is .373 inch, or less, replace inner rotor.
6. Slide outer rotor into body, press to one side with fingers, then measure clearance between rotor and body. If measurement is 015 inch, or more, replace body only if outer rotor is within specifications.
7. Install inner rotor into body. If clearance between inner and outer rotors is .008 inch, or more, replace both rotors.
8. Place straightedge across face of body, between bolt holes. If clearance between rotors and straightedge is .003 inch, or more, replace pump assembly if rotors are within specification.

Assemble

1. Install rotor.
2. Tighten cover mounting screws.
3. Prime oil pump before installation by filling rotor cavity with suitable engine oil.

BELT TENSION DATA

Belt adjustment is maintained by an automatic (spring load) belt tensioner.

SERPENTINE DRIVE BELT

Routing

Refer to **Fig. 14** for serpentine drive belt routing.

Replacement

REMOVAL

1. Rotate belt tensioner counterclockwise until it contacts it's stop.
2. Remove belt and slowly rotate tensioner into freearm position. **Do not let tensioner arm snap back to freearm position.**

INSTALLATION

1. Route belt around all pulleys except idler pulley.
2. Rotate tensioner arm until it contacts it's stop position.
3. Route belt around idler and slowly let tensioner rotate into belt.
4. Ensure belt is seated onto all pulleys.
5. Tensioner is equipped with indexing tang on back and indexing stop on housing.
6. If new belt (used 15 minutes or less) is being installed, tang must be within approximately .24–.32 inch of indexing stop.

COOLING SYSTEM BLEED

1. Attach 4–6 feet long ¼ inch ID clear hose to bleeder fitting located on lower intake manifold, lefthand of center and below upper intake plenum, **Fig. 15. When installing drain hose to air bleed valve, route hose away from accessory drive belts, accessory drive pulleys, and electric cooling fan motors.**
2. Route hose away from accessory drive belt, drive pulleys and electric cooling fan.
3. Place other end of hose into clean container.
4. **Ensure cooling system air bleed valve is opened before any coolant is added to cooling system.**
5. Attach filling aid funnel tool No. 8195, or equivalent, to pressure bottle filler neck.
6. Pinch overflow hose that connects between two chambers of coolant bottle using suitable hose pinch-off pliers.
7. Open bleed fitting.
8. Pour suitable antifreeze mixture into larger section of filling aid funnel (smaller section of funnel is to allow air to escape).
9. Slowly fill cooling system until steady stream of coolant flows from hose attached to bleed valve.
10. Close bleed valve and continue filling system to top of filling aid funnel tool.
11. Remove pinch-off pliers from overflow hose.
12. Allow coolant in filling funnel to drain into overflow chamber of pressure bottle.
13. Remove funnel and install coolant pressure bottle cap.
14. Remove hose from bleed valve.
15. Start engine and run at 1500–2000 RPM for 30 minutes, noting the following:
    a. Engine cooling system will push

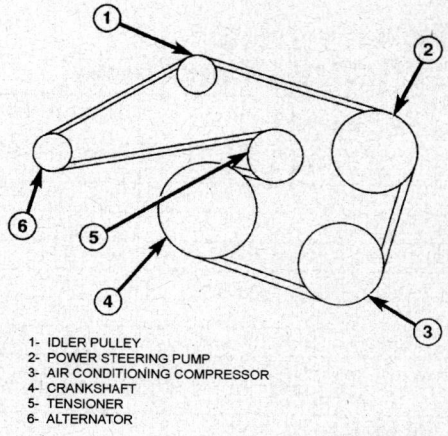

1- IDLER PULLEY
2- POWER STEERING PUMP
3- AIR CONDITIONING COMPRESSOR
4- CRANKSHAFT
5- TENSIONER
6- ALTERNATOR

ARM0400000000616

Fig. 14 Serpentine drive belt routing

any remaining air into coolant bottle within about an hour of normal driving. As a result, a drop in coolant level in pressure bottle may occur.

b. If engine cooling system overheats and pushes coolant into overflow side of coolant bottle, this coolant will be sucked back into cooling system, **only if pressure cap is left on bottle.**

c. Removing pressure cap breaks vacuum path between two bottle sections and coolant will not return to cooling system.

16. Shut off engine allow it to cool down for 30 minutes. This permits coolant to be drawn into pressure chamber.

17. With engine cold, ensure coolant level should be within MIN and MAX marks. Coolant will normally only be in inboard of coolant bottle two chambers. Outboard chamber is only to recover coolant in event of an overheat or after recent service fill.

THERMOSTAT
REPLACE

1. Drain cooling system into suitable container.
2. Remove radiator lower hose from thermostat housing.
3. Remove nuts from heater tube flange studs.
4. Loosen starter bolt at heater tube bracket.
5. Remove and position heater tube aside.
6. Remove mounting bolt, two studs, thermostat housing, O-ring and thermostat.

7. Remove thermostat housing bolts.
8. Reverse procedure to install, noting the following:
   a. Install thermostat with bleed valve located at 12 o'clock position, between tabs on seal.
   b. Lubricate new heater return tube O-ring.

WATER PUMP
REPLACE

1. Drain cooling system into suitable container.
2. Remove upper radiator hose.
3. Disconnect cooling fan electrical connector.
4. Remove mounting bolts and radiator cooling fan.
5. Rotate belt tensioner counterclockwise until it contacts it's stop.
6. Remove belt and slowly rotate tensioner into freearm position. **Do not let tensioner arm snap back to freearm position.**
7. Remove timing chain and guides as outlined under "Timing Chain, Replace."
8. Remove mounting bolts, water pump and gasket.
9. Reverse procedure to install.

RADIATOR
REPLACE

1. Drain cooling system into suitable container.
2. Remove upper radiator hose.
3. Remove upper radiator closure panels.
4. Disconnect cooling fan electrical connector, then remove mounting bolts and cooling fan.
5. Raise and support vehicle.
6. Remove lower splash shield.
7. Remove lower radiator hose.
8. Remove lower condenser mount bolts.
9. Lower vehicle.
10. Remove mounting bolts and upper radiator mounting brackets.
11. Remove upper condenser mounting bolts.
12. Separate condenser from radiator.
13. Tilt radiator toward engine and remove it.
14. Reverse procedure to install.

FUEL PUMP
REPLACE

1. Relieve fuel system pressure as outlined under "Precautions."
2. Drain partial fuel from fuel tank through

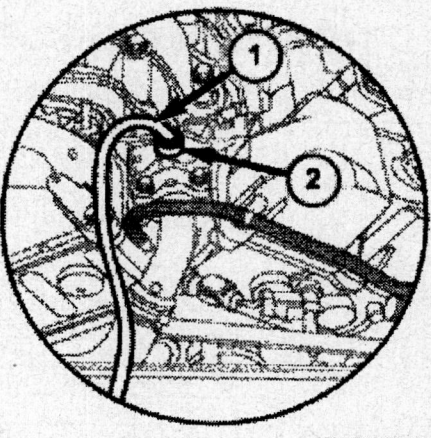

ARM0400000000803

Fig. 15 Cooling system bleed

filler tube using hard nylon tube, with 30° cut on end, to push check valve open to drain fuel from tank. **Fuel level of vehicle must be below 5/8 of tank before removing module lock-rings.**
3. Remove rear lower seat cushion by pushing seat back and up.
4. Fold back foam pad covering access cover for modules.
5. Disconnect electrical connector from lefthand side module.
6. Mark module orientation for installation alignment.
7. Remove lefthand side module lock ring use lock ring tool No. 9340, or equivalent.
8. Drain fuel from lefthand side of fuel tank. Lift module up enough to push hose into tank and drain. **Do not spill fuel in interior of vehicle.**
9. Disconnect electrical connectors from module top.
10. Remove module top half.
11. Remove module fuel level sending card, fuel return lines and supply line.
12. Press in fuel line release tab and remove fuel line by pulling it up.
13. Unsnap and remove fuel return line from lower module.
14. Tip module on its side and drain remaining fuel from reservoir.
15. Remove module.
16. Reverse procedure to install.

FUEL FILTER
REPLACE

The fuel filter is replaceable only as part of the fuel pump module.

TIGHTENING SPECIFICATIONS

Year	Component	Torque Ft. Lbs.
2005–08	Air Conditioning Compressor	21
	Alternator/Compressor Mounting Bracket, No. 1 &2	40
	Alternator/Compressor Mounting Bracket, No. 3	30
	Automatic Belt Tensioner	40
	Camshaft Bearing Cap	105①
	Camshaft Chain Tensioner	105①
	Camshaft Sprocket	20
	Connecting Rod Cap	20②
	Cooling Fan	50①
	Cooling System Bleed Screw	110①
	Crankshaft Damper	125
	Crankshaft Rear Seal Retainer	105①
	Cross-Brace	40
	Crossmember	50
	Cylinder Head	③
	Cylinder Head Cover	105①
	EGR Tube	95①
	Engine Mount	45
	Engine Mount Adapter	55
	Engine Mount Isolator	106
	Engine Mount, Rear	35
	Exhaust Manifold	17
	Exhaust Manifold Heat Shield	20
	Exhaust Manifold Ball Flange	
	Fan Blade	17
	Fan Shroud	50①
	Fuel Line Clamps	31①
	Heater Supply Tube	30①
	Hose Clamp	31①
	Idler Pulley	20
	Intake Manifold	105①
	Main Bearing Cap	⑤
	Oil Pan	④

TIGHTENING SPECIFICATIONS—Continued

Year	Component	Torque Ft. Lbs.
2005–08	Oil Pan Drain Plug	20
	Oil Pump	20
	Oil Pump Cover	105①
	Oil Pump Pick Up Tube	20
	Radiator to Support Bracket	105①
	Starter	30
	Steering Coupling	22
	Steering Gear	95
	Structural Collar	⑥
	Thermostat Housing	105①
	Thermostat Housing/Water Inlet Connector	105①
	Throttle Body	105①
	Timing Chain Cover, M6	105①
	Timing Chain Cover, M10	40
	Timing Chain Guide Access Plug	15
	Timing Chain Tensioner	105①
	Torque Converter	55
	Transmission Mount	35
	Upper Radiator Closure Panel	90①
	Water Pump	105①

① — Inch lbs.

② — Plus an additional 90°.

③ — Refer to Cylinder Head, Replace for tightening specifications and sequence.

④ — Refer to Oil Pan, Replace for tightening specifications and sequence.

⑤ — Refer to Main & Rod Bearings for tightening specifications and sequence.

⑥ — Refer to Structure Collar, Replace for tightening specifications and sequence.

2.7L ENGINE

NOTE: On Air Bag Equipped Models, Refer To "Air Bag System Precautions" Located In The Front Of This Manual For System Disarming & Arming Procedures.

NOTE: Refer To "Computer Relearn Procedures" Located In The Front Of This Manual When Battery Power To The Computer Has Been Interrupted.

NOTE: Refer To The Rear Of This Manual For Vehicle Manufacturer's Special Tool Suppliers.

INDEX

	Page No.		Page No.		Page No.
Belt Tension Data	6-27	Righthand	6-22	Battery Ground Cable	6-21
Camshaft, Replace	6-25	Exhaust Manifold, Replace	6-23	Recalibration	6-21
Camshaft Oil Seal, Replace	6-25	Lefthand	6-23	Fuel System Pressure Relief	6-21
Lefthand	6-25	Righthand	6-23	Radiator, Replace	6-28
Righthand	6-25	Front Cover, Replace	6-24	Rear Timing Belt Cover,	
Compression Pressure	6-21	Fuel Filter, Replace	6-28	Replace	6-24
Cooling System Bleed	6-27	Fuel Pump, Replace	6-28	Rocker Arms, Replace	6-23
Crankshaft Damper, Replace	6-23	Intake Manifold, Replace	6-22	Serpentine Drive Belt	6-27
Crankshaft Rear Oil Seal,		Lower	6-22	Replacement	6-27
Replace	6-26	Upper	6-22	Installation	6-27
Crankshaft Seal, Replace	6-26	Main & Rod Bearings	6-25	Removal	6-27
Cylinder Head, Replace	6-23	Oil Cooler, Replace	6-27	Routing	6-27
Engine Rebuilding		Oil Pan, Replace	6-26	Thermostat, Replace	6-28
Specifications	21-1	AWD	6-26	Tightening Specifications	6-29
Engine, Replace	6-22	RWD	6-26	Timing Belt, Replace	6-24
Engine Mount, Replace	6-21	Oil Pump, Replace	6-26	Installation	6-25
AWD	6-21	Oil Pump Service	6-27	Removal	6-24
Lefthand	6-21	Assemble	6-27	Valve Adjustment	6-23
Rear	6-22	Disassemble	6-27	Valve Clearance Specifications	6-23
Righthand	6-22	Inspect	6-27	Valve Clearance Specifications	6-23
RWD	6-22	Piston & Rod Assembly	6-25	Valve Cover, Replace	6-23
Lefthand	6-22	Precautions	6-21	Water Pump, Replace	6-28
Rear	6-22	Air Bag Systems	6-21		

PRECAUTIONS
Air Bag Systems

Refer to "Air Bag System Precautions" in the front of this manual for system disarming and arming procedures.

Battery Ground Cable

Prior to service, disconnect battery ground cable and isolate as required.

RECALIBRATION

Anytime the battery has been disconnect or has lost its charge, the following must be recalibrated:

EXPRESS WINDOW

1. Turn ignition switch to RUN position.
2. Move driver's window upward until it stalls in full up position. Allow window motor to stall for at least two seconds before releasing switch.
3. Move driver's window downward until it stalls in full down position. Allow window motor to stall for at least two seconds before releasing switch.
4. Move driver's window upward until it stalls in full up position. Allow window motor to stall for at least two seconds before releasing switch.
5. Move passenger's window upward until it stalls in full up position. Allow window motor to stall for at least two seconds before releasing switch.
6. Move passenger's window downward until it stalls in full down position. Allow window motor to stall for at least two seconds before releasing switch.
7. Move passenger's window upward until it stalls in full up position. Allow window motor to stall for at least two seconds before releasing switch.

ELECTRONIC STABILITY PROGRAM (ESP) STEERING ANGLE SENSOR

1. Start engine.
2. Turn steering wheel to righthand side until wheel locks full right.
3. Turn steering wheel to lefthand side until wheel locks full left.
4. Turn steering wheel to righthand side until wheels are centered.
5. Cycle ignition switch OFF and ON. Do not start engine.

Fuel System Pressure Relief

1. Remove fuel pump relay for Power Distribution Center (PDC).
2. Start and run engine until it stalls.
3. Attempt to start engine until it no longer runs.
4. Turn ignition switch to OFF position.
5. Install fuel pump relay.

COMPRESSION PRESSURE

Refer to "2.7L Engine" for compression pressure procedures.

ENGINE MOUNT
REPLACE
AWD
LEFTHAND

1. Raise and support vehicle, then remove lefthand front tire and wheel assembly.

2. Remove lefthand engine mount to cradle mounting bolt.
3. Support engine using suitable jack stand.
4. Remove mounting bolts and nuts, then engine mount.
5. Reverse procedure to install.

REAR

1. Raise and support vehicle on hoist.
2. Remove crossmember to mount bolts.
3. Raise transmission using suitable transmission jack.
4. Remove mounting bolts and crossmember.
5. Remove mounting bolts and rear mount.
6. Reverse procedure to install.

RIGHTHAND

1. Raise and support vehicle, then remove righthand front tire and wheel assembly.
2. Support engine using suitable jack stand.
3. Remove engine mount to cradle mounting bolt.
4. Raise and support engine with jack stand.
5. Remove mounting bolts and righthand engine mount.
6. Reverse procedure to install.

RWD

LEFTHAND

1. Raise and support vehicle, then remove both engine mount to cradle nuts and lefthand engine mount studs.
2. Raise engine approximately .20 inch using suitable jack and wooden block under oil pan.
3. Remove lefthand engine mount heat shield.
4. Remove mounting bolts and lefthand engine mount.
5. Reverse procedure to install.

REAR

1. Raise and support vehicle on hoist.
2. Remove crossmember to mount bolts.
3. Raise transmission using suitable transmission jack.
4. Remove mounting bolts and crossmember.
5. Remove mounting bolts and rear mount.
6. Reverse procedure to install.

RIGHTHAND

1. Raise and support vehicle, then remove both of engine mount to cradle nuts.
2. Remove both the engine mount through studs.
3. Raise engine approximately .20 inch using suitable jack stand and wooden block under oil pan.
4. Remove righthand mount heat shield mounting bolts.
5. Remove righthand engine mount.
6. Reverse procedure to install.

ENGINE
REPLACE

1. Relieve fuel system pressure as outlined under "Precautions."
2. Center and secure steering wheel.
3. Recover refrigerant as outlined in "Air Conditioning" chapter.
4. Remove hood.
5. Remove windshield cowl.
6. Raise and support vehicle.
7. Remove lower engine close out panel.
8. Drain cooling system into suitable container.
9. Disconnect lower radiator hose.
10. **On models equipped with AWD,** remove front drive axles and housing.
11. **On all models,** disconnect alternator electrical connectors.
12. Separate column coupling from steering gear.
13. Remove underbody splash shield.
14. Remove center bolt, then separate intermediate steering shaft upper and lower shaft.
15. Disconnect starter electrical connector.
16. Remove three starter mounting bolts and wiring clip.
17. Pull starter forward and down, then work it up and around exhaust.
18. Work starter past intermediate steering shaft and remove it.
19. Disconnect hose at oil cooler and remove cooler hose retainer at transmission.
20. Disconnect transmission line bracket at air conditioning compressor and allow bolt to rest on cradle.
21. Disconnect ground strap at righthand transmission housing.
22. Disconnect and position engine block heater wiring connector aside.
23. Disconnect connector, then remove mounting bolt and Crankshaft Position (CKP) sensor.
24. Disconnect lefthand No. 2 oxygen senor electrical connector and separate exhaust manifold from lefthand exhaust pipe.
25. Disconnect righthand No. oxygen senor electrical connector and separate exhaust manifold from righthand exhaust pipe.
26. Remove flex plate inspection cover and torque converter bolts.
27. Remove transmission housing to engine mounting bolts.
28. Remove engine mounting to cradle mounting bolts and nuts.
29. Lower vehicle.
30. Remove upper intake manifold as outlined under "Intake Manifold, Replace."
31. Disconnect heater and coolant reservoir hoses from rear coolant pipe.
32. Disconnect oxygen sensor connector and ground wire on lefthand cylinder head cover.
33. Disconnect coolant temperature, cam position, oil pressure sensors' electrical connectors.
34. Disconnect lefthand ignition coil and fuel injector harness connectors, then position wiring harness aside.

35. Remove righthand intake manifold support braces.
36. Disconnect capacitor and ground strap from righthand cylinder head cover.
37. Disconnect oxygen sensor, knock, EGR, injector and ignition coil harness connectors, then position wiring harness aside.
38. Disconnect engine wiring harness from transmission housing and remove remaining transmission housing bolts.
39. Connect driveline support fixture tool No. 8534B, or equivalent, engine lifting bracket to righthand rear of cylinder head outer most bolt access hole.
40. Install bolt into inner most bolt access hole next to engine lift bracket to assure lifting bracket positioning.
41. Connect suitable engine hoisting chain to lefthand timing chain cover engine lifting point and engine lift bracket.
42. Remove engine, constantly inspecting to ensure proper positioning and no damage to other components or wiring harnesses. As engine is hoisted from engine bay area, remove loosened air conditioning compressor bolt retaining transmission cooler lines and direct lines aside.
43. Reverse procedure to install. **Do not pinch power steering rack sensor with lefthand engine mount.**

INTAKE MANIFOLD
REPLACE
Upper

1. Disconnect Intake Air temperature (IAT) sensor electrical connector.
2. Remove air inlet hose from throttle body.
3. Disconnect Manifold Absolute Pressure (MAP) sensor electrical connector.
4. Disconnect engine electrical harness connectors from intake manifold.
5. Disconnect EGR tube, PCV, Purge and power brake booster vacuum hoses from upper intake manifold.
6. Disconnect throttle control electrical electronic connector.
7. Remove throttle bracket mounting bolts from throttle body and cylinder head.
8. Disconnect Manifold Tuning Valve (MTV) and Short Runner Valve (SRV) electrical connectors.
9. Remove righthand intake manifold support brackets.
10. Remove mounting bolts, insulation foam pad and upper intake manifold.
11. Reverse procedure to install, noting the following:
   a. Install new gasket.
   b. Tighten mounting bolts starting in center working outward in cross sequence pattern.

Lower

1. Relieve fuel system pressure as outlined under "Precautions."

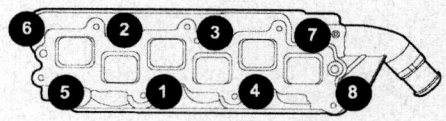

Fig. 1 Lower intake manifold tightening sequence

2. Drain cooling system into suitable container.
3. Disconnect upper radiator hose from thermostat housing.
4. Remove upper intake manifold as outlined under "Upper."
5. Position power steering fluid reservoir and bracket aside.
6. Disconnect fuel injectors and coolant temperature sensor electrical connectors.
7. Disconnect heater hose from rear intake manifold.
8. Disconnect coolant container hose at rear intake manifold.
9. Disconnect fuel supply hose from rail.
10. Remove mounting bolts, then the fuel rail and injectors as an assembly.
11. Remove mounting bolts and lower intake manifold.
12. Reverse procedure to install, noting the following:
    a. Install new gaskets.
    b. Gradually tighten intake manifold mounting bolts in sequence, **Fig. 1.**

EXHAUST MANIFOLD
REPLACE

Lefthand

1. Raise and support vehicle.
2. Separate front exhaust pipe to manifold union.
3. Lower vehicle.
4. Disconnect and remove oxygen sensor from exhaust manifold.
5. Remove shield mounting bolts and exhaust manifold. Discard gasket.
6. Reverse procedure to install. Tighten mounting bolts starting at center working outward.

Righthand

1. Disconnect upstream oxygen sensor electrical connector.
2. Raise and support vehicle.
3. Remove exhaust manifold to exhaust pipe flange mounting bolts.
4. Lower vehicle.
5. Remove heat shield and exhaust manifold manifold.
6. Remove oxygen sensor from exhaust manifold.
7. Reverse procedure to install. Tighten mounting bolts starting at center working outward.

CYLINDER HEAD
REPLACE

1. Remove upper radiator crossmember, then fan module and accessory drive belts.

2. Remove upper radiator crossmember and fan module.
3. Remove damper using crankshaft damper holder tool No. 8191, or equivalent, and three-jaw puller tool No. 1023, or equivalent.
4. Remove damper using crankshaft damper holder tool No. 8191, or equivalent, and three-jaw puller tool No. 1023, or equivalent.
5. Remove lower belt cover, stamped steel cover and lefthand cast cover.
6. Remove camshaft sprockets as outlined under "Camshaft Sprocket, Replace."
7. Remove upper and lower intake manifolds as outlined under "Intake Manifold, Replace."
8. Remove exhaust manifold to catalytic converter pipe connection V-band clamps.
9. Remove rear timing belt cover to cylinder head mounting bolts and rear covers.
10. Remove mounting bolts and cylinder heads.
11. Reverse procedure to install, noting the following:
    a. **Cylinder head bolts with stretched threads must be replaced.**
    b. Lubricate bolt threads with suitable, clean engine oil.
    c. **Torque** cylinder head bolts in sequence to 45 ft. lbs., **Fig. 2.**
    d. **Torque** head bolts in sequence to 65 ft. lbs.
    e. **Torque** bolts in sequence to 65 ft. lbs.
    f. Tighten bolts an additional 90° in sequence.
    g. If final cylinder head bolt **torque** is not 90 ft. lbs, replace bolts.
    h. Install new O-ring seal in righthand rear timing belt cover.

VALVE COVER
REPLACE

1. Remove upper intake manifold as outlined under "Intake Manifold, Replace."
2. Cover lower intake manifold.
3. Disconnect and remove three ignition coils.
4. Remove ground strap/resistor mounting bolt from cylinder head cover.
5. Lift wire harness track retaining tabs.
6. Loosen mounting bolts and remove cylinder head cover.
7. Reverse procedure to install. Install new spark plug tube seals using spark plug tube seal installation tool No. MD-998306, or equivalent.

VALVE CLEARANCE SPECIFICATIONS

This engine is equipped with hydraulic lifters and valves are lashed with zero clearance.

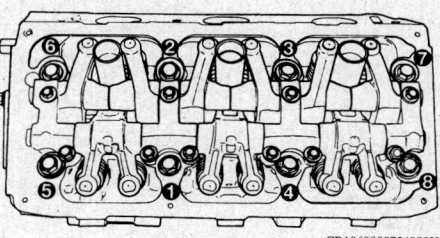

Fig. 2 Cylinder head bolt tightening sequence

VALVE ADJUSTMENT

Rocker arms are equipped with hydraulic lash adjusters. No adjustment is required.

ROCKER ARMS
REPLACE

The rocker arm and shaft assembly on the righthand side of the engine has an oil passage hole from the cylinder head to the third rocker shaft support. The rocker arm shaft assembly on the lefthand side of the engine has an oil passage hole from the cylinder head to the second rocker shaft support.

1. Remove upper intake manifold as outlined under "Intake Manifold, Replace."
2. Cover lower intake manifold.
3. Disconnect and remove three ignition coils.
4. Remove ground strap/resistor retaining bolt from cylinder head cover.
5. Lift up wire harness track retaining tabs.
6. Loosen mounting bolts and remove cylinder head cover.
7. Identify rocker arm assembly and rocker arms for installation alignment, **Fig. 3.**
8. Remove mounting bolts and rocker arm assembly. **Avoid turning rocker arm assembly upside down. Do not allow rocker arm assembly to rest on lash adjusters.**
9. Reverse procedure to install, noting the following:
    a. Rotate camshaft gears to timing position were lobes are in a neutral position (no load to the valve), **Fig. 4.**
    b. Install rocker arm and shaft assembly ensuring identification marks face toward front of engine for lefthand head and toward rear of engine for righthand head.
    c. Tighten rocker arm/shaft assembly bolts in sequence, **Fig. 5.**

CRANKSHAFT DAMPER
REPLACE

1. Rotate belt tensioner counterclockwise until it contacts it's stop.
2. Remove belt and slowly rotate tensioner into the freearm position. **Do not let tensioner arm snap back to freearm position.**
3. Raise and support vehicle on hoist.

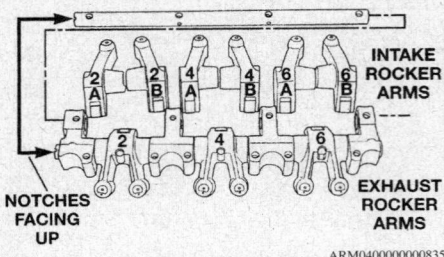

Fig. 3 Rock arm identification

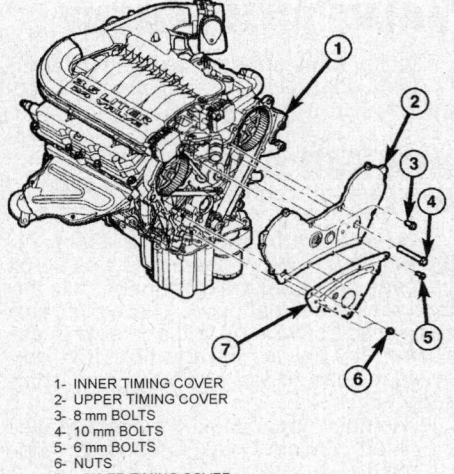

1- INNER TIMING COVER
2- UPPER TIMING COVER
3- 8 mm BOLTS
4- 10 mm BOLTS
5- 6 mm BOLTS
6- NUTS
7- LOWER TIMING COVER

ARM0400000000838

Fig. 6 Timing belt cover replacement

4. Remove crankshaft damper bolt.
5. Remove crankshaft damper using suitable three-jaw puller.
6. Reverse procedure to install, using damper install bolt tool No. C-4685-C1, with nut and thrust bearing from tools Nos. 6792 and 6792-1, or equivalents.

FRONT COVER

REPLACE

1. Relieve fuel system pressure as outlined under "Precautions."
2. Rotate belt tensioner counterclockwise until it contacts it's stop.
3. Remove belt and slowly rotate tensioner into the freearm position. **Do not let tensioner arm snap back to freearm position.**
4. Remove mounting bolts and position power steering pump aside.
5. Raise and support vehicle on hoist.
6. Remove crankshaft damper bolt.
7. Remove crankshaft damper using suitable three-jaw puller.
8. Remove lower front timing belt cover mounting bolts and nuts, Fig. 6.
9. Lower vehicle.
10. Remove upper mounting bolts and front timing belt cover.
11. Reverse procedure to install.

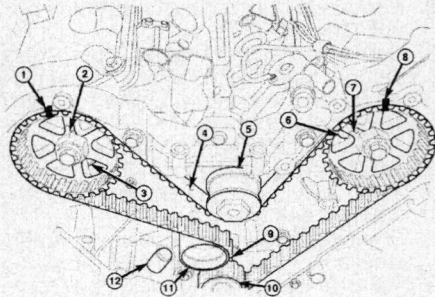

1- RIGHTHAND CAMSHAFT GEAR ALIGNMENT MARK
2- RIGHTHAND CAMSHAFT GEAR
3- CYLINDER HEAD TO INNER TIMING BELT COVERS BOLTS- RIGHTHAND
4- TIMING BELT
5- WATER PUMP PULLEY
6- CYLINDDER HEAD TO INNER TIMING BELT COVER BOLTS- LEFTHAND
7- LEFTHAND CAMSHAFT GEAR
8- LEFTHAND CAMSHAFT GEAR ALIGNMENT MARK
9- CRANKSHAFT GEAR ALIGNMENT MARK
10- CRANKSHAFT GEAR
11- TIMING BELT TENSIONER PULLEY
12- TIMING BELT TENSIONER

ARM0400000000836

Fig. 4 Camshaft timing position

REAR TIMING BELT COVER

REPLACE

With the timing belt removed, avoid turning the camshaft or crankshaft. If movement is required, exercise extreme caution to avoid valve damage caused by piston contact.

1. Relieve fuel system pressure as outlined under "Precautions."
2. Remove timing belt as outlined under "Timing Belt, Replace."
3. Camshaft timing gears are keyed to camshaft.
4. Hold lefthand camshaft sprocket with box end wrench.
5. Loosen and remove mounting bolt (bolt is 10 inches long) and washer, then camshaft sprocket.
6. Righthand camshaft must be pushed rearward approximately 3 ½ inches to remove camshaft gear retaining bolt and gear. **Do not scratch or nick camshaft or cylinder head journals when moving camshaft.**
7. Hold righthand camshaft sprocket with box end wrench.
8. Loosen and remove mounting bolt (righthand bolt is 8 ⅜ inches long) and washer, then righthand camshaft sprocket.
9. Remove mounting bolts and rear timing belt cover, Fig. 7.
10. Reverse procedure to install. Install new O-rings lubricates with Mopar Dielectric Grease, or equivalent.

TIMING BELT

REPLACE

With the timing belt removed, avoid turning the camshaft or crankshaft. If movement is required, exercise extreme caution to avoid valve damage caused by piston contact.

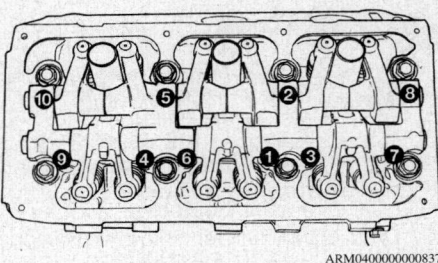

ARM0400000000837

Fig. 5 Rocker arm tightening sequence

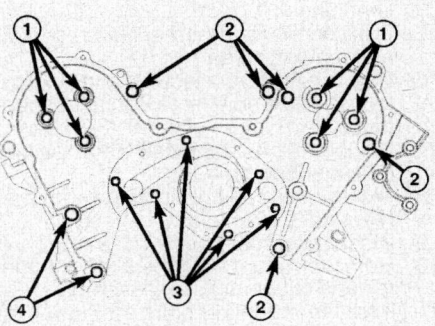

1- M8 FASTENERS (APPLY THREAD SEAALANT)
2- M10 FASTENERS
3- M6 FASTENERS
4- M10 FASTENERS (STUD/NUT)

ARM0400000000840

Fig. 7 Rear timing belt cover replacement

Removal

The 3.5L is not a freewheeling engine. Loosen the valve train rocker assemblies before servicing the timing drive.

1. Relieve fuel system pressure as outlined under "Precautions."
2. Remove both cylinder head covers as outlined under "Valve Cover, Replace" and loosen rocker arm assemblies as outlined under "Rocker Arm, Replace."
3. Remove front timing belt cover as outlined under "Front Cover, Replace."
4. Mark belt running direction if timing belt is to be reused.
5. Rotate engine clockwise by turning crankshaft until crankshaft mark aligns with TDC mark on oil pump housing and camshaft sprocket timing marks are aligned with marks on rear cover, Fig. 4.
6. Remove timing belt tensioner and timing belt.
7. Place tensioner into suitable vise. Index tensioner in vise same way it is installed on engine.
8. Compress plunger. Total bleed down of tensioner should take approximately five minutes.
9. When plunger is compressed into tensioner body install suitable pin through body and plunger to retain plunger in place for installation.

Installation

If camshafts have moved from the timing marks, always rotate camshaft towards the direction nearest to the timing marks, **Do not turn camshafts a full revolution or damage to valves and/or pistons could result.**

1. Align crankshaft sprocket with TDC mark on oil pump cover, **Fig. 4.**
2. Align camshaft sprockets timing reference marks with marks on rear cover.
3. Install timing belt starting at crankshaft sprocket going in counterclockwise direction.
4. Install belt around last sprocket. Maintain tension on belt as it is positioned around tensioner pulley.
5. If camshaft gears have been removed it is only required to have camshaft gear mounting bolts installed to snug torque at this time.
6. Holding tensioner pulley against belt, install tensioner into housing and tighten.
7. Each camshaft sprocket mark should remain aligned with cover marks.
8. When tensioner is in place pull retaining pin to allow tensioner to extend to pulley bracket.
9. Rotate crankshaft sprocket two revolutions and inspect timing marks on camshafts and crankshaft. If marks do not line up within their respective locations, repeat procedure.
10. If camshaft gears have been removed and timing is correct, counterhold and tighten camshaft gears to final specification.
11. Install front timing belt cover as outlined under "Front Cover, Replace."
12. Tighten the rocker arm assemblies as outlined under "Rocker Arm, Replace."
13. Install cylinder head covers as outlined under "Valve Cover, Replace."

CAMSHAFT

REPLACE

1. Remove cylinder head as outlined under "Cylinder Head, Replace."
2. Carefully remove camshaft from rear of cylinder head. **Do not to nick or scratch journals when removing camshaft.**
3. Reverse procedure to install. Lubricate camshaft bearing journals, lobes and seal with suitable, clean engine oil.

CAMSHAFT OIL SEAL

REPLACE

Lefthand

1. Drain cooling system into suitable container.
2. Remove front timing cover as outlined under "Front Cover, Replace."
3. Align camshaft gear and crankshaft gear timing marks to TDC, **Fig. 4.**
4. Remove rear timing cover as outlined under "Rear Timing Belt Cover, Replace."

Crankshaft Main Journal Grade Mark	Main Bearing Bore Grade Mark		
	1	2	3
A	(3) Standard	(2) +.0001 inch	(1) +.0002 inch
B	(4) -.0001 inch	(3) Standard	(2) +.0001 inch
C	(5) (-.0002 inch	(4) (-.0001 inch	(3) Standard

Fig. 8   Main bearing selection chart

5. Remove rocker arm assembly as outlined under "Rocker Arm, Replace."
6. Remove camshaft thrust plate from rear of cylinder head.
7. Maneuver camshaft rearward and out of cylinder head approximately 3.5 inches.
8. Remove camshaft oil seal using suitable driver. **Do no damage cylinder head to seal or camshaft journal surfaces.**
9. Reverse procedure to install, noting the following:
   a. Tap seal into place using camshaft seal installer tool No. MD-998306, or equivalent.
   b. Light coat camshaft oil seal lip and seal protector sleeve tool 6788, or equivalent, with suitable, clean engine oil.
   c. Install oil tool onto camshaft.
   d. Slide camshaft forward, inserting seal protector through camshaft seal until camshaft seats. Remove special tool.
   e. Install camshaft thrust plate and new seal.

Righthand

1. Remove timing belt as outlined under "Timing Belt, Replace."
2. Righthand camshaft must be pushed rearward approximately 3 ½ inches to remove camshaft gear retaining bolt and gear. **Do not scratch or nick camshaft or cylinder head journals when moving camshaft.**
3. Hold righthand camshaft sprocket with box end wrench.
4. Loosen and remove mounting bolt (righthand bolt is 8 ⅜ inches long) and washer, then righthand camshaft sprocket.
5. Remove EGR valve and camshaft thrust plate from rear of cylinder head.
6. Remove rocker arm assembly as outlined under "Rocker Arm, Replace."
7. Maneuver camshaft rearward and out of cylinder head approximately 3.5 inches.
8. Remove camshaft oil seal using suitable driver tool. **Do not damage cylinder head to seal or camshaft journal surfaces.**
9. Reverse procedure to install, noting the following:
   a. Tap seal into place using camshaft seal installer tool No. MD-998306, or equivalent.
   b. Light coat camshaft oil seal lip and seal protector sleeve tool 6788, or

equivalent, with suitable, clean engine oil.
   c. Install oil tool onto camshaft.
   d. Slide camshaft forward, inserting seal protector through camshaft seal until camshaft seats. Remove special tool.
   e. Install camshaft thrust plate and new seal.

PISTON & ROD ASSEMBLY

Refer to "2.7L Engine" for piston and rod assembly service.

MAIN & ROD BEARINGS

Bearing caps are not interchangeable and are marked to insure correct installation. Upper and lower bearing halves are not interchangeable.

1. Remove upper half of bearing by inserting main bearing tool No. C-3059, or equivalent, into crankshaft oil hole. Slowly rotate crankshaft clockwise, forcing out upper half of bearing shell.
2. Refer to **Fig. 8** to select main bearings.
3. Lubricate main bearing with suitable, clean engine oil.
4. Start bearing in place and insert main bearing tool C-3059, or equivalent, into crankshaft oil hole.
5. Slowly rotate crankshaft counterclockwise sliding bearing into position.
6. Move crankshaft forward to limit of travel.
7. Lubricate and install front thrust washer by rolling washer onto machined shelf between upper main bulk head No. 2 and crankshaft thrust surface.
8. Move crankshaft rearward to limit of travel.
9. Lubricate and install rear thrust washer by rolling washer onto machined shelf between upper main bulk head No. 2 and crankshaft thrust surface.
10. Install lower main bearings into main bearing caps.
11. Lubricate lower main bearings with suitable, clean engine oil.
12. Lubricate main bearing cap bolts with suitable engine oil.
13. Install each main cap and tighten bolts hand tight.
14. Install inside main bearing cap bolts and **torque** to 15 ft. lbs., then tighten an additional 90°.
15. Measure crankshaft end play. Endplay should be 004–.012 inch.

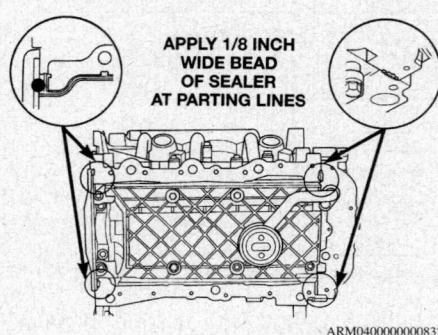

Fig. 9 Oil pan RTV application

16. Install connecting rods and measure side clearance. Maximum clearance is .153 inch.
17. Install windage tray.
18. Lubricate bolts with suitable engine oil and **torque** to 20 ft. lbs., then tighten an additional 90°.
19. Install main cap tie (horizontal) bolts and **torque** to 20 ft. lbs.

CRANKSHAFT SEAL
REPLACE

1. Drain cooling system into suitable container.
2. Remove timing belt as outlined under "Timing Belt, Replace."
3. Remove crankshaft sprocket using crankshaft sprocket removal tool No. L-4407-A, or equivalent.
4. Tap dowel pin out of crankshaft.
5. Remove crankshaft seal using crankshaft oil seal removal tool No. 6341A, or equivalent. **Do not nick shaft seal surface or seal bore.**
6. Reverse procedure to install noting the following:
   a. Install crankshaft seal using crankshaft oil seal installer tool No. 6342, or equivalent.
   b. Install dowel pin into crankshaft to .047 inch protrusion.

CRANKSHAFT REAR OIL SEAL
REPLACE

1. Remove engine oil pan as outlined under "Oil Pan, Replace."
2. Lower weight of engine back onto engine mounts.
3. Remove transmission as outlined in **MOTOR's "Domestic Transmission Manual, In-Vehicle Service" manual or "Transmission Service DVD."**
4. Remove flexplate.
5. Remove mounting bolts and rear crankshaft oil seal.
6. Reverse procedure to install, noting the following:
   a. **Do not separate seal protector from rear crankshaft oil seal before installation.**
   b. Position oil seal, retainer and seal protector on crankshaft, then push firmly into place on engine block (seal protector will be removed

from rear oil seal assembly as a result of installing rear oil seal).
   c. Hand tighten rear oil seal mounting bolts.
   d. Attach alignment tools No. 8225, or equivalent to pan rail. Tool notch should be located away seal retainer.
   e. While applying firm pressure to seal retainer against special tools, tighten seal retainer screws

OIL PAN
REPLACE

AWD

1. Drain cooling system into suitable container.
2. Remove oil dipstick tube mounting bolt at righthand exhaust manifold.
3. Raise and support vehicle.
4. Drain engine oil into suitable container and remove oil filter.
5. Remove lefthand axle shaft.
6. Disconnect power steering power steering rack.
7. Remove lefthand front axle intermediate shaft support bracket and housing.
8. Remove front drive shaft heat shield.
9. Mark for installation alignment and remove righthand front drive shaft.
10. Remove righthand catalytic converter.
11. Separate from cradle hold down and position power steering hose aside.
12. Remove lower engine mount to cradle mounting bolts and nuts.
13. Remove front sway bar.
14. Raise and support engine with suitable jack stand.
15. Remove front axle housing support bracket.
16. Remove mounting bolts, then rotate and remove front axle housing.
17. Lower engine and remove jack stand.
18. Remove hoses from and oil cooler.
19. Separate oil dipstick tube from oil pan.
20. Remove torque converter access cover.
21. Remove mounting bolts and oil pan.
22. Reverse procedure to install, noting the following:
   a. Install new oil dipstick tube seal.
   b. Apply ⅛ inch bead of Mopar Engine RTV GEN II, or equivalent, at parting line of oil pump housing and rear seal retainer, **Fig. 9.**
   c. Install oil pan mounting bolts hand tight.
   d. Ensure rear face of oil pan is flush to transmission bell housing.
   e. **Torque** horizontal rear oil pan to transmission bolts to 12 inch lbs.
   f. **Torque** lefthand M8 oil pan alignment bolt to 21 ft. lbs., **Fig. 10.**
   g. **Torque** righthand M8 oil pan alignment bolt to 21 ft. lbs.
   h. **Torque** remaining M8 bolts and nuts to 21 ft. lbs.
   i. **Torque** M6 bolts to 1 105 inch lbs.
   j. **Torque** four M10 oil pan to transmission bolts to 40 ft. lbs.

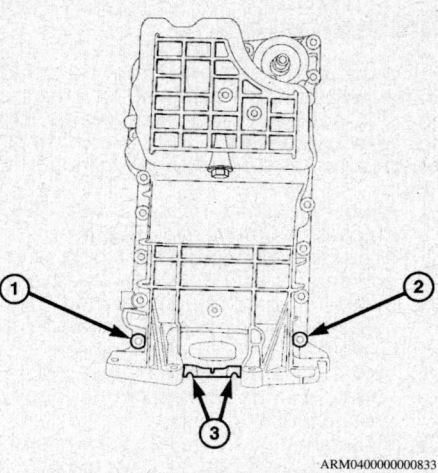

Fig. 10 Oil pan alignment tightening sequence

RWD

1. Lock steering wheel in center position.
2. Remove engine oil indicator.
3. Raise and support vehicle, then remove splash shield.
4. Drain engine oil into suitable container and remove oil filter.
5. Remove oil filter/oil cooler mounting stud and position oil cooler aside.
6. Separate steering column coupler from steering gear.
7. Remove steering gear to cradle mounting bolts and suspend steering gear aside.
8. Remove flexplate access cover.
9. Remove rear oil pan to transmission mounting bolts.
10. Remove two rear oil pan bolts.
11. Remove remaining oil pan bolts.
12. Loosen engine mount bolts at cradle.
13. Raise and support engine using suitable floor jack with wooden block at transmission housing.
14. Remove oil pan.
15. Reverse procedure to install, noting the following:
   a. Apply ⅛ inch bead of Mopar Engine RTV GEN II, or equivalent, at parting line of oil pump housing and rear seal retainer, **Fig. 9.**
   b. Install oil pan mounting bolts hand tight.
   c. Ensure rear face of oil pan is flush to transmission bell housing.
   d. **Torque** horizontal rear oil pan to transmission bolts to 12 inch lbs.
   e. **Torque** lefthand M8 oil pan alignment bolt to 21 ft. lbs., **Fig. 10.**
   f. **Torque** righthand M8 oil pan alignment bolt to 21 ft. lbs.
   g. **Torque** remaining M8 bolts and nuts to 21 ft. lbs.
   h. **Torque** M6 bolts to 1 105 inch lbs.
   i. **Torque** four M10 oil pan to transmission bolts to 40 ft. lbs.

OIL PUMP
REPLACE

1. Drain cooling system into suitable container.

2. Remove timing belt as outlined under "Timing Belt, Replace."
3. Remove crankshaft sprocket using crankshaft sprocket removal tool No. L-4407-A, or equivalent.
4. Remove oil pan as outlined under "Oil Pan, Replace."
5. Remove oil pickup tube.
6. Remove mounting bolts, oil pump and gasket.
7. Reverse procedure to install, noting the following:
   a. Prime oil pump before installation by filling rotor cavity with suitable, clean engine oil.
   b. Install new oil pickup tube O-ring.

OIL PUMP SERVICE

Disassemble

1. Remove mounting screws and oil pump cover.
2. Remove pump rotors.

Inspect

Do not inspect the oil relief valve assembly. If the oil relief valve is suspect, replace the oil pump.
1. Clean all components thoroughly.
2. Ensure mating surface of oil pump housing is smooth. Replace pump cover if scratched or grooved.
3. Lay straightedge across pump cover surface. If clearance is .001 inch or more between cover and straight edge, cover should be replaced.
4. Measure thickness and diameter of outer rotor. If outer rotor thickness is .563 inch, or less, or if diameter is 3.141 inches. or less, replace outer rotor.
5. If inner rotor measures .563 inch, or less, replace inner rotor.
6. Slide outer rotor into body, press to one side with fingers and measure clearance between rotor and body. If clearance is .015 inch, or more, replace body only if outer rotor is within specifications.
7. Install inner rotor into body. If clearance between inner and outer rotors is .008 inch, or more, replace both rotors.
8. Place straightedge across face of body, between bolt holes. If clearance is .003 inch, or more, between rotors and straightedge, replace pump assembly only if rotors are within specifications.

Assemble

Prime oil pump before installation by filling rotor cavity with engine oil.

OIL COOLER

REPLACE

1. Drain cooling system into suitable container.
2. Raise and support vehicle on hoist.
3. Disconnect coolant hoses from oil cooler.
4. Remove oil filter.

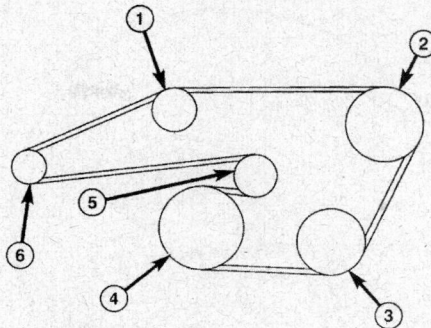

1- IDLER PULLEY
2- POWER STEERING PUMP
3- AIR CONDITIONING COMPRESSOR
4- CRANKSHAFT
5- TENSIONER
6- ALTERNATOR

ARM0400000000617

Fig. 11 Serpentine drive belt routing

5. Remove mounting bolts and oil cooler.
6. Reverse procedure to install, noting the following:
   a. Oil cooler seal retainer flange cut out section (top), must be aligned with tab on oil pan.
   b. Oil cooler must be prevented from turning during tightening.

BELT TENSION DATA

Belt adjustment is maintained by an automatic (spring load) belt tensioner.

SERPENTINE DRIVE BELT

Routing

Refer to **Fig. 11** for serpentine drive belt routing.

Replacement

REMOVAL

1. Rotate belt tensioner counterclockwise until it contacts it's stop.
2. Remove belt and slowly rotate tensioner into the freearm position. **Do not let tensioner arm snap back to freearm position.**

INSTALLATION

1. Route belt around all pulleys except idler pulley.
2. Rotate tensioner arm until it contacts it's stop position.
3. Route belt around idler and slowly let tensioner rotate into belt.
4. Ensure belt is seated onto all pulleys.
5. Tensioner is equipped with indexing tang on back and indexing stop on tensioner housing.
6. If new belt (used 15 minutes or less) is being installed, tang must be within approximately .24–.32 inch of indexing stop.

COOLING SYSTEM BLEED

1. Attach 4–6 feet long ¼ inch ID clear hose to bleeder fitting located on lower intake manifold, lefthand of center and below upper intake plenum, **Fig. 12. When installing drain hose to air bleed valve, route hose away from accessory drive belts, accessory drive pulleys, and electric cooling fan motors.**
2. Route hose away from accessory drive belt, drive pulleys and electric cooling fan.
3. Place other end of hose into clean container.
4. **Ensure cooling system air bleed valve is opened before any coolant is added to cooling system.**
5. Attach filling aid funnel tool No. 8195, or equivalent, to pressure bottle filler neck.
6. Pinch overflow hose that connects between two chambers of coolant bottle using suitable hose pinch-off pliers.
7. Open bleed fitting.
8. Pour suitable antifreeze mixture into larger section of filling aid funnel (smaller section of funnel is to allow air to escape).
9. Slowly fill cooling system until steady stream of coolant flows from hose attached to bleed valve.
10. Close bleed valve and continue filling system to top of filling aid funnel tool.
11. Remove pinch-off pliers from overflow hose.
12. Allow coolant in filling funnel to drain into overflow chamber of pressure bottle.
13. Remove funnel and install coolant pressure bottle cap.
14. Remove hose from bleed valve.
15. Start engine and run at 1500–2000 RPM for 30 minutes, noting the following:
    a. Engine cooling system will push any remaining air into coolant bottle within about an hour of normal driving. As a result, a drop in coolant level in pressure bottle may occur.
    b. If engine cooling system overheats and pushes coolant into overflow side of coolant bottle, this coolant will be sucked back into cooling system, **only if pressure cap is left on bottle.**
    c. Removing pressure cap breaks vacuum path between two bottle sections and coolant will not return to cooling system.
16. Shut off engine allow it to cool down for 30 minutes. This permits coolant to be drawn into pressure chamber.
17. With engine cold, ensure coolant level should be within MIN and MAX marks. Coolant will normally only be in inboard of coolant bottle two chambers. Outboard chamber is only to recover coolant in event of an overheat or after recent service fill.

THERMOSTAT
REPLACE

1. Drain cooling system into suitable container.
2. Remove radiator lower hose from thermostat housing.
3. Remove bypass hose.
4. Remove mounting bolts, housing and thermostat.
5. Reverse procedure to install.

WATER PUMP
REPLACE

1. Drain cooling system into suitable container.
2. Rotate belt tensioner counterclockwise until it contacts it's stop.
3. Remove belt and slowly rotate tensioner into the freearm position. **Do not let tensioner arm snap back to freearm position.**

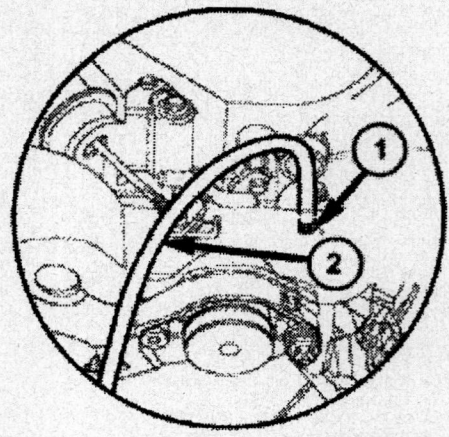

ARM0400000000804

Fig. 12   Cooling system bleed

4. Remove engine timing belt as outlined under "Timing Belt, Replace."
5. Remove mounting bolts and water pump. Record position of longer bolts for installation alignment.
6. Reverse procedure to install.

RADIATOR
REPLACE

Refer to "Radiator, Replace" in the "2.7L Engine" for radiator replacement procedure.

FUEL PUMP
REPLACE

Refer to "Fuel Pump, Replace" in "2.7L Engine" for fuel pump replacement procedure.

FUEL FILTER
REPLACE

The fuel filter is replaceable only as part of the fuel pump module.

TIGHTENING SPECIFICATIONS

Year	Component	Torque Ft. Lbs.
2005–08	Alternator/Compressor Mounting Bracket, Nos. 1 & 2	40
	Alternator/Compressor Mounting Bracket, No. 3	30
	Automatic Belt Tensioner	40
	Camshaft Sprocket	75②
	Camshaft Thrust Plate	20
	Connecting Rod Cap	20②
	Crankshaft Damper	70
	Crankshaft Main Bearing Cap	④
	Crankshaft Rear Seal Retainer	105①
	Cylinder Head	③
	Engine Mount Heat Shield	97①
	Engine Mount to Cradle	55
	Engine Mount to Mounting Bracket	55
	Engine Mount Through Studs	106
	Exhaust Manifold	17
	Exhaust Manifold Heat Shield	105①
	Fan Blade	17
	Fan Shroud	50①
	Flexplate Inspection Cover	97①
	Flexplate to Crankshaft	70
	Flexplate to Torque Converter	55
	Front Drive Axle Housing	48
	Front Drive Axle Intermediate Shaft Housing & Support Bracket, Lefthand	19
	Fuel Line Clamps	31①
	Heater Supply Tube	30①
	Idler Pulley	20
	Intake Manifold, Lower	20
	Intake Manifold, Upper	105①
	Main Bearings	④
	Oil Cooler Connector	55
	Oil Pan, M6	105①
	Oil Pan, M8	20
	Oil Pan Drain Plug	20
	Oil Pan to Transmission Bell Housing	40
	Oil Pump	20
	Oil Pump Cover	105①
	Oil Pump Pick Up Tube	20
	Radiator to Support Bracket	106①
	Rocker Shaft Pedestal Retaining	23
	Thermostat Housing	105①
	Timing Belt Cover, M6	105①
	Timing Belt Cover, M8	20
	Timing Belt Cover, M10	40
	Timing Belt Tensioner	20
	Timing Belt Tensioner Pulley	45
	Upper Radiator Closure Panel	90①
	Valve Cover	105①
	Water Pump	105①
	Windage Tray	④

① — Inch lbs.
② — Plus an additional 90°.
③ — Refer to Cylinder Head, Replace for tightening specifications and sequence.
④ — Refer to Main & Rod Bearings for tightening specifications and sequence.

5.7L & 6.1L Engines

NOTE: On Air Bag Equipped Models, Refer To "Air Bag System Precautions" Located In The Front Of This Manual For System Disarming & Arming Procedures.

NOTE: Refer To "Computer Relearn Procedures" Located In The Front Of This Manual When Battery Power To The Computer Has Been Interrupted.

NOTE: Refer To The Rear Of This Manual For Vehicle Manufacturer's Special Tool Suppliers.

INDEX

	Page No.		Page No.		Page No.
Belt Tension Data	6-35	6.1L Engine	6-31	Fuel System Pressure Relief	6-30
Camshaft, Replace	6-33	Lefthand	6-31	Radiator, Replace	6-36
Compression Pressure	6-30	Righthand	6-32	Rocker Arms, Replace	6-32
Cooling System Bleed	6-36	Front Cover, Replace	6-33	Serpentine Drive Belt	6-35
Crankshaft Damper, Replace	6-33	Fuel Filter, Replace	6-36	Replacement	6-35
Crankshaft Rear Oil Seal,		Fuel Pump, Replace	6-36	Installation	6-35
Replace	6-34	Hydraulic Lifters, Replace	6-33	Removal	6-35
Installation	6-34	Intake Manifold, Replace	6-31	Routing	6-35
Removal	6-34	Main & Rod Bearings	6-34	Thermostat, Replace	6-36
Crankshaft Seal, Replace	6-34	Oil Pan, Replace	6-34	Tightening Specifications	6-37
Cylinder Head, Replace	6-32	AWD	6-34	Timing Chain, Replace	6-33
Engine Rebuilding		RWD	6-35	Timing Chain Tensioner,	
Specifications	21-1	Oil Pump, Replace	6-35	Replace	6-33
Engine, Replace	6-31	Oil Pump Service	6-35	Valve Adjustment	6-32
Engine Mount, Replace	6-31	Piston & Rod Assembly	6-34	Valve Clearance Specifications	6-32
Front	6-31	Precautions	6-30	Valve Cover, Replace	6-32
Rear	6-31	Air Bag Systems	6-30	Water Pump, Replace	6-36
Exhaust Manifold, Replace	6-31	Battery Ground Cable	6-30		
5.7L Engine	6-31	Recalibration	6-30		

PRECAUTIONS

Air Bag Systems

Refer to "Air Bag System Precautions" in the front of this manual for system disarming and arming procedures.

Battery Ground Cable

Prior to service, disconnect battery ground cable and isolate as required.

RECALIBRATION

Anytime the battery has been disconnect or has lost its charge, the following must be recalibrated:

EXPRESS WINDOW

1. Turn ignition switch to RUN position.
2. Move driver's window upward until it stalls in full up position. Allow window motor to stall for at least two seconds before releasing switch.
3. Move driver's window downward until it stalls in full down position. Allow window motor to stall for at least two seconds before releasing switch.
4. Move driver's window upward until it stalls in full up position. Allow window motor to stall for at least two seconds before releasing switch.

5. Move passenger's window upward until it stalls in full up position. Allow window motor to stall for at least two seconds before releasing switch.
6. Move passenger's window downward until it stalls in full down position. Allow window motor to stall for at least two seconds before releasing switch.
7. Move passenger's window upward until it stalls in full up position. Allow window motor to stall for at least two seconds before releasing switch.

ELECTRONIC STABILITY PROGRAM (ESP) STEERING ANGLE SENSOR

1. Start engine.
2. Turn steering wheel to righthand side until wheel locks full right.
3. Turn steering wheel to lefthand side until wheel locks full left.
4. Turn steering wheel to righthand side until wheels are centered.
5. Cycle ignition switch OFF and ON. Do not start engine.

Fuel System Pressure Relief

1. Remove fuel pump relay for Power Distribution Center (PDC).
2. Start and run engine until it stalls.

3. Attempt to start engine until it no longer runs.
4. Turn ignition switch to OFF position.
5. Install fuel pump relay.

COMPRESSION PRESSURE

The minimum compression pressure should be no less than 100 psi and the maximum variation between cylinders should be no more than 25%.

1. Ensure battery is completely charged and engine starter motor is in good operating condition.
2. Clean spark plug recesses with compressed air.
3. Remove fuel pump relay for Power Distribution Center (PDC).
4. Start and run engine until it stalls.
5. Attempt to start engine until it no longer runs.
6. Turn ignition switch to OFF position.
7. Install fuel pump relay.
8. Remove Auto Shutdown (ASD) relay.
9. Insert suitable compression pressure gauge and rotate engine with engine starter motor for three revolutions.
10. Record compression pressure on third revolution.
11. Continue test for remaining cylinders.

ENGINE MOUNT
REPLACE
Front

1. Raise and support vehicle.
2. Remove mounting bolt, nut and alternator support bracket.
3. Remove hydromount to frame studs and nuts.
4. Raise engine using suitable jack.
5. Remove bracket mounting bolts and hydromount.
6. Mounting bolts and engine mount brackets.
7. Reverse procedure to install.

Rear

1. Raise and support vehicle on hoist, then support transmission using suitable jack.
2. Remove mounting bolts and crossmember.
3. Remove mounting bolts and transmission mount.
4. Remove mounting bolts and transmission mount bracket.
5. Reverse procedure to install.

ENGINE
REPLACE

1. Remove engine cover.
2. Relieve fuel system pressure as outlined under "Precautions."
3. Remove air cleaner resonator and duct work.
4. Remove caps and mounting nuts, then separate wiper arm from pivot using suitable two-jaw puller.
5. Remove wiper arms.
6. Remove cowl top panel to each front fender push-pin.
7. Disconnect two ¼ turn fasteners securing cowl top panel to dash panel.
8. Remove six cowl top panel to strut tower support push-pins.
9. Disconnect integral cowl top panel to dash panel retaining clips.
10. Remove cowl panel.
11. Drain cooling system into suitable container.
12. Rotate belt tensioner counterclockwise until it contacts it's stop.
13. Remove belt and slowly rotate tensioner into the freearm position. **Do not let tensioner arm snap back to freearm position.**
14. Remove upper radiator hose.
15. Remove upper radiator closure panels.
16. Disconnect cooling fan electrical connector, then remove mounting bolts and cooling fan.
17. Remove air conditioning compressor with lines attached and position aside.
18. Raise and support vehicle.
19. Unsnap plastic insulator cap from B+ output terminal.
20. Remove B+ terminal mounting nut, then disconnect terminal and field wire connector.

Fig. 1 Lefthand exhaust manifold tightening sequence. 5.7L engine

ARM0400000000810

21. Remove mounting nut, bolt and support bracket.
22. Remove two mounting bolts and alternator.
23. Remove intake manifold and IAFM as outlined under "Intake Manifold, Replace."
24. Remove ground wires from rear of each cylinder head.
25. Disconnect heater hoses.
26. Remove power steering pump and set aside. It is not required to disconnect hoses.
27. Disconnect fuel supply line.
28. Raise and support vehicle on hoist.
29. Drain engine oil into suitable container.
30. Remove mounting screws and front belly pan.
31. Remove engine front mount to frame nuts.
32. **On models equipped with AWD,** proceed as follows:
    a. Mark front driveshaft to flange at both ends for installation alignment.
    b. Remove front drive shaft mounting bolts from differential and transfer case.
    c. Remove driveshaft.
    d. Remove lefthand and righthand front drive axles.
    e. Remove support bracket from differential to engine block.
    f. Unbolt differential from oil pan.
    g. Rotate differential so drive flange is facing forward and oil pan side is facing up.
    h. Remove differential through opening at rear of cradle.
    i. Remove intermediate shaft from oil pan.
33. **On all models,** disconnect transmission oil cooler lines from oil pan bolts retainers.
34. Disconnect exhaust pipe at manifolds.
35. Disconnect wires and remove starter motor.
36. Remove torque converter access cover.
37. Remove drive plate to converter bolts.
38. Remove transmission bell housing to engine block bolts.
39. Lower vehicle.
40. Install engine lift fixture tool Nos. 8984 and 8984-UPD, or equivalents.
41. Separate engine from transmission, then remove engine and install it on suitable repair stand.
42. Reverse procedure to install.

INTAKE MANIFOLD
REPLACE

1. Remove engine cover.
2. Relieve fuel system pressure as outlined under "Precautions."
3. Remove air inlet hose.

Fig. 2 Righthand exhaust manifold tightening sequence. 5.7L engine

ARM0400000000811

4. Remove ignition wires from on top of intake manifold.
5. Disconnect Manifold Absolute Pressure (MAP) sensor, fuel injectors and Electric Throttle Control (ETC) electrical connectors.
6. Remove wire harness from intake manifold.
7. Disconnect brake booster, purge and Make Up Air (MUA) hoses.
8. Remove EGR tube from intake manifold.
9. Remove intake manifold mounting bolts in crisscross pattern starting from outside bolts and ending at middle bolts.
10. Remove intake manifold.
11. Reverse procedure to install.

EXHAUST MANIFOLD
REPLACE
5.7L Engine

1. Raise and support vehicle.
2. Remove exhaust pipe to manifold bolts.
3. Remove engine mount to frame mounting bolts.
4. Raise engine enough to remove exhaust manifolds using suitable jack. **Do not damage engine harness.**
5. Remove bracket mounting bolts and hydromount.
6. Mounting bolts and engine mount brackets.
7. Remove heat shield.
8. Remove exhaust manifold bolts, then the exhaust manifold, **Figs. 1 and 2.**
9. Reverse procedure to install, noting the following:
    a. **Torque** exhaust manifold bolts in sequence to 18 ft. lbs, **Figs. 1 and 2.**
    b. **Torque** manifold ball flange nut to 106 inch lbs.
    c. Measure exhaust module and fuel tank clearance. Clearance should be .55 inch.
    d. Measure clearance at rear tunnel reinforcement. Clearance .59–.78 in.
    e. **Torque** ball flange nuts to 25 ft. lbs.

6.1L Engine
LEFTHAND

1. Raise and support vehicle.
2. Remove exhaust pipe to manifold bolts.
3. Remove knock sensor.
4. Remove air cleaner assembly and coolant bottle.

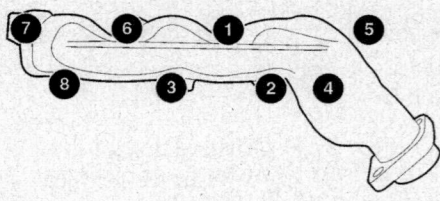

ARM0500000000562

Fig. 3 Lefthand exhaust manifold tightening sequence. 6.1L engine

INTAKE SIDE

EXHAUST SIDE

ARM0400000000813

Fig. 6 Rocker shaft loosening & tightening sequence

5. Remove exhaust manifold mounting bolts.
6. Remove exhaust manifold.
7. Reverse procedure to install, noting the following:
   a. **Torque** exhaust manifold bolts in sequence to 23 ft. lbs., **Fig. 3.**

RIGHTHAND

1. Raise and support vehicle.
2. Remove exhaust pipe to manifold bolts.
3. Remove knock sensor.
4. Remove starter as outlined under "Starter Motor, Replace" in "Electrical" section.
5. Disconnect wire harness on righthand inner fender panel.
6. Remove Power Distribution Center (PDC) box and bracket.
7. Remove exhaust manifold mounting bolts, then manifold.
8. Reverse procedure to install, noting the following:
   a. **Torque** exhaust manifold bolts in sequence to 23 ft. lbs., **Fig. 4.**

CYLINDER HEAD
REPLACE

The head gaskets are not interchangeable between lefthand and righthand sides. They are marked L and R to indicate lefthand and righthand sides.
1. Relieve fuel system pressure as outlined under "Precautions."
2. Disconnect fuel supply line.
3. Drain cooling system into suitable container.
4. Loosen clamp and disconnect air duct at air cleaner cover.
5. Remove air cleaner resonator and duct work from four locating pins.

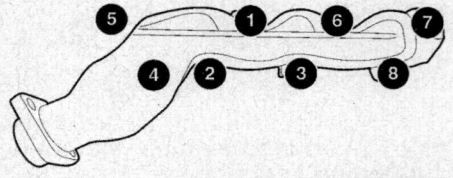

ARM0500000000563

Fig. 4 Righthand exhaust manifold tightening sequence. 6.1L engine

6. Remove closed crankcase ventilation system.
7. Disconnect exhaust at exhaust manifolds.
8. Disconnect evaporation control system.
9. Disconnect heater hoses.
10. Remove power steering pump.
11. Disconnect coil on plug electrical connectors.
12. Remove valve cover mounting bolts and ground straps, **Fig. 5. Ground straps must be installed in original locations.**
13. Remove valve cover.
14. Remove intake manifold and throttle body as outlined under "Intake Manifold, Replace."
15. Install pushrod retaining plate tool No. 9070, or equivalent.
16. Loosen rocker shafts in sequence, **Fig. 6.**
17. Mark locations for installation alignment and remove rocker shafts.
18. Mark locations for installation alignment and remove push rods.
19. **Do not remove retainers from rocker shaft.**
20. Remove head bolts in sequence and cylinder heads, **Fig. 7.**
21. Discard cylinder head gasket.
22. Reverse procedure to install, noting the following:
   a. Head gaskets are marked TOP to indicate which side goes up.
   b. **Torque** M12 cylinder head bolts in sequence to 25 ft. lbs., and M8 bolts to 15 ft. lbs., **Fig. 7.**
   c. **Torque** M12 cylinder head bolts in sequence to 40 ft. lbs., and ensure M8 bolts as at 15 ft. lbs.
   d. Tighten M12 cylinder head bolts and additional 90° in sequence.
   e. **Torque** M8 bolts to 25 ft. lbs.

VALVE COVER
REPLACE

1. Disconnect coil on plug electrical connectors.
2. Remove valve cover mounting bolts and ground straps, **Fig. 5. Ground straps must be installed in original locations.**
3. Remove valve cover.
4. Reverse procedure to install, noting the following:
   a. Hand start all valve cover mounting bolts.
   b. Ensure all double ended studs are in correct location.
   c. Righthand ground strap is located

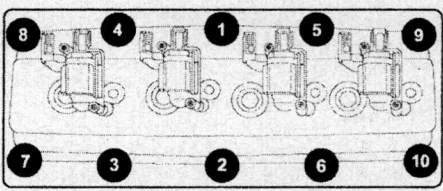

ARM0400000000812

Fig. 5 Valve cover loosening & tightening sequence

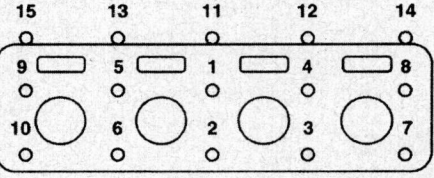

ARM0400000000814

Fig. 7 Cylinder head loosening & tightening sequence

on front inboard stud and lefthand is on rear inboard stud.
   d. Tighten valve cover bolts is sequence, **Fig. 5.**

VALVE CLEARANCE SPECIFICATIONS

This engine is equipped with hydraulic lifters and valves are lashed with zero clearance.

VALVE ADJUSTMENT

This engine is equipped with hydraulic lash adjusters. No adjustment is required.

ROCKER ARMS
REPLACE

The rocker arms are not interchangeable between intake and exhaust. The intake rocker arms are marked with an I.
1. Disconnect coil on plug electrical connectors.
2. Remove valve cover mounting bolts and ground straps, **Fig. 5. Ground straps must be installed in original positions.**
3. Remove valve cover.
4. Install pushrod retaining plate tool No. 9070, or equivalent.
5. Loosen rocker shafts in sequence, **Fig. 6.**
6. Mark locations for installation alignment and remove rocker shafts.
7. Mark locations for installation alignment and remove push rods.
8. **Do not remove retainers from rocker shaft.**
9. Reverse procedure to install, noting the following:
   a. Longer push rods are for exhaust side and shorter ones intake.
   b. Ensure retainers and rocker arms are not overlapped when tightening bolts.
   c. Ensure pushrod is installed into rocker arm and tappet correctly.

d. Tighten rocker shaft bolts in sequence, **Fig. 6.**
e. Do not rotate or crank engine during or immediately after rocker arm installation. Allow hydraulic tappets five minutes to bleed down.

HYDRAULIC LIFTERS
REPLACE

1. Remove cylinder head as outlined under "Cylinder Head, Replace."
2. Remove mounting bolt and tappet guide holder.
3. If all tappets are to be removed and reused, identify tappets to ensure installation in original location.
4. Pull tappet out of bore with twisting motion.
5. Reverse procedure to install.

CRANKSHAFT DAMPER
REPLACE

1. Rotate belt tensioner counterclockwise until it contacts it's stop.
2. Remove belt and slowly rotate tensioner into the freearm position. **Do not let tensioner arm snap back to freearm position.**
3. Drain cooling system into suitable container.
4. Remove radiator upper hose.
5. Remove upper radiator hose and disconnect cooling fan electrical connector.
6. Remove mounting bolts and cooling fan.
7. Remove crankshaft damper bolt.
8. Remove damper using suitable three-jaw puller tool.
9. Reverse procedure to install, using crankshaft, damper tool No. 8512-A, as follows:
   a. Thread nut onto shaft first.
   b. Place roller bearing onto threaded rod.
   c. Ensure hardened bearing surface of bearing faces nut.
   d. Slide hardened washer onto threaded rod.
   e. Coat threaded rod's threads with Mopar Nickel Anti-Seize, or Loctite No. 771, or equivalent.
   f. Press damper onto crankshaft.

FRONT COVER
REPLACE

1. Remove engine cover.
2. Loosen clamp and disconnect air duct at air cleaner cover.
3. Remove air cleaner resonator and duct work from four locating pins.
4. Drain cooling system into suitable container.
5. Rotate belt tensioner counterclockwise until it contacts it's stop.
6. Remove belt and slowly rotate tensioner into the freearm position. **Do not let tensioner arm snap back to freearm position.**
7. Remove upper radiator hose and disconnect cooling fan electrical connector.

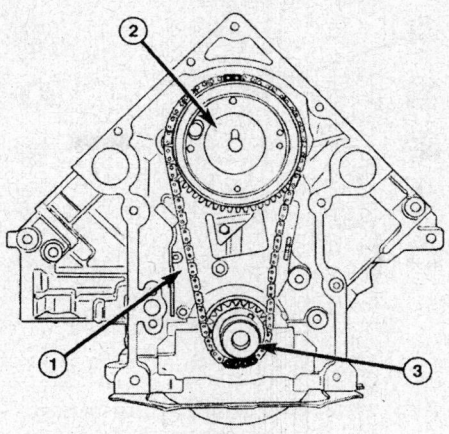

1. Crankshaft
2. Camshaft
3. Timing Chain

ARM0400000000815

Fig. 8   Timing chain alignment

8. Remove mounting bolts and cooling fan.
9. Remove thermostat housing radiator hose.
10. Remove coolant and washer bottles.
11. Remove fan shroud.
12. Remove air conditioning compressor and position it aside. **It is not required to disconnect lines or recover refrigerant.**
13. Remove alternator and upper radiator hose.
14. Disconnect both heater hoses at timing cover.
15. Disconnect lower radiator hose at engine.
16. Remove accessory drive belt tensioner and both idler pulleys.
17. Remove crankshaft damper bolt.
18. Remove damper using suitable three-jaw puller tool.
19. Remove power steering pump and position it aside. **Do not remove power steering pump hoses.**
20. Remove dipstick support bolt.
21. Remove oil pan and pick up tube as outlined under "Oil Pan, Replace."
22. Remove mounting bolts and timing cover. **It is not required to remove water pump for timing cover removal.**
23. Reverse procedure to install, noting the following:
   a. Ensure slide bushings are located in timing cover.
   b. Install new gasket.

TIMING CHAIN
REPLACE

1. Remove timing chain cover as outlined under "Front Cover, Replace."
2. Install vibration damper bolt hand tight.
3. Align timing chain sprockets and keyways using suitable socket and breaker bar to rotate crankshaft, **Fig. 8,** noting the following:
   a. Camshaft pin and slot in cam sprocket must be at 12 o'clock position.

b. Crankshaft keyway must be at 2 o'clock position.
c. Crankshaft sprocket must be installed so dots and or paint marking is at 6 o'clock position.
4. Remove four mounting bolts and oil pump.
5. Retract tensioner shoe until hole in shoe lines up with hole in bracket.
6. Slide suitable pin into holes.
7. Remove camshaft sprocket mounting bolt, then the timing chain with crankshaft and camshaft sprockets.
8. Reverse procedure to install, noting the following:
   a. Install timing chain with single plated link aligned with dot and or paint marking on camshaft sprocket.
   b. Crankshaft sprocket is aligned with dot and or paint marking on sprocket between two plated timing chain links.

TIMING CHAIN TENSIONER
REPLACE

1. Remove timing chain as outlined under "Timing Chain, Replace."
2. Remove mounting bolts and tensioner.
3. Reverse procedure to install.

CAMSHAFT
REPLACE

The 5.7L & 6.1L engines use a unique camshaft for use with the multi displacement system. When installing a new camshaft, the replacement camshaft must be compatible with the multi displacement system.

1. Remove cylinder heads as outlined under "Cylinder Head, Replace."
2. Remove oil pan as outlined under "Oil Pan, Replace."
3. Remove timing chain as outlined under "Timing Chain, Replace."
4. Remove camshaft tensioner/thrust plate.
5. Identify lifters for installation in original location.
6. Remove tappets and retainer.
7. Install long bolt into front of camshaft.
8. Remove camshaft. **Do not damage cam bearings with cam lobes.**
9. Reverse procedure to install, noting the following:
   a. Lubricate camshaft lobes and camshaft bearing journals.
   b. Measure camshaft end play. If measurement is not .0031–.0114 inch, install new thrust plate.
   c. This engine uses both standard roller tappets and deactivating roller tappets with the multi displacement system. Deactivating roller tappets must be used in cylinders Nos. 1, 4, 6 and 7.
   d. Deactivating tappets can be identified by two holes in side of tappet body, for latching pins.

GRADE	SIZE mm (in.)	FOR USE WITH
MARKING		JOURNAL SIZE
A	0.008 mm U/S	64.988–64.995 mm
	(0.0004 in.) U/S	(2.5585– 2.5588in.)
B	NOMINAL	64.996–65.004 mm
		(2.5588–2.5592 in.)
C	0.008 mm O/S	65.005–65.012 mm
	(0.0004 in.) O/S	(2.5592–2.5595 in.)

ARM0400000000816

Fig. 9 Main bearing selection chart

PISTON & ROD ASSEMBLY

Install pistons with raised mark or arrow facing toward front of engine.

Install connecting rod with oil slinger slot facing toward front of engine.

Connecting rod bolts are torque to yield **Install new bolts when they are loosened or removed.**

MAIN & ROD BEARINGS

1. Identify rod bearing caps for installation in original positions before removal.
2. Identify main bearing caps for installation in original positions before removal.
3. Select proper main bearings, **Fig. 9.**
4. Install main bearings in block and caps, then lubricate bearings.
5. Position crankshaft into cylinder block.
6. Install thrust washers.
7. Install new washer/seal on crossbolts.
8. Clean and oil all cap bolts.
9. Install all main bearing caps.
10. **Torque** cap bolts in sequence to 20 ft. lbs., **Fig. 10.**
11. Tighten main cap bolts an additional 90°.
12. Install crossbolts with new washer/gasket.
13. **Torque** crossbolts to 21 ft. lbs.
14. Repeat crossbolt tightening.
15. Measure crankshaft end play. End play should be 0031–.0114 inch.

CRANKSHAFT SEAL
REPLACE

1. Rotate belt tensioner counterclockwise until it contacts it's stop.
2. Remove belt and slowly rotate tensioner into the freearm position. **Do not let tensioner arm snap back to freearm position.**
3. Drain cooling system into suitable container.
4. Remove radiator upper hose.
5. Remove upper radiator hose and disconnect cooling fan electrical connector.
6. Remove mounting bolts and cooling fan.
7. Remove crankshaft damper bolt.
8. Remove damper using suitable three-jaw puller tool.

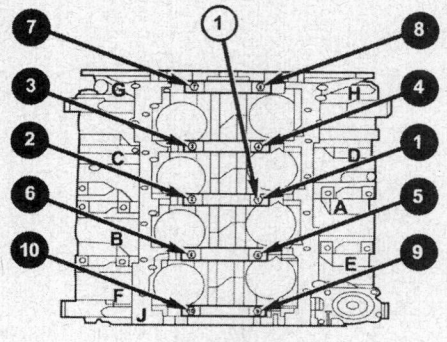

FRONT

ARM0400000000817

Fig. 10 Main bearing tightening sequence

9. Remove crankshaft front seal using seal tool No. 9071, or equivalent.
10. Reverse procedure to install:
    a. Front crankshaft seal must be installed dry. **Do not apply lubricant to sealing lip or to outer edge.**
    b. Install crankshaft front seal using driver tools Nos. 8348 and 8512A, or equivalents.

CRANKSHAFT REAR OIL SEAL
REPLACE

Removal

1. Remove transmission as outlined in **MOTOR's "Domestic Transmission Manual, In-Vehicle Service" manual or "Transmission Service DVD."**
2. Remove mounting bolts and flexplate.
3. Remove crankshaft rear oil seal using remover Tool No. 8506, or equivalent.

Installation

Rear seal must be installed dry. **Do not lubricate the seal lip or outer edge.**
1. Position plastic seal guide onto crankshaft rear face.
2. Position crankshaft rear oil seal onto guide.
3. Tap seal into place using crankshaft rear oil seal installer tool No. 8349 and driver handle tool No, C-4171, or equivalents.
4. Continue to tap on driver handle until seal installer seats against cylinder block crankshaft bore.
5. Tighten flexplate mounting bolts in sequence, **Fig. 11.**

OIL PAN
REPLACE

Gasket is integral to engine windage tray and does not come out with oil pan. When the oil pan is removed, a new oil pan gasket/windage tray assembly must be installed. The old gasket cannot be reused.

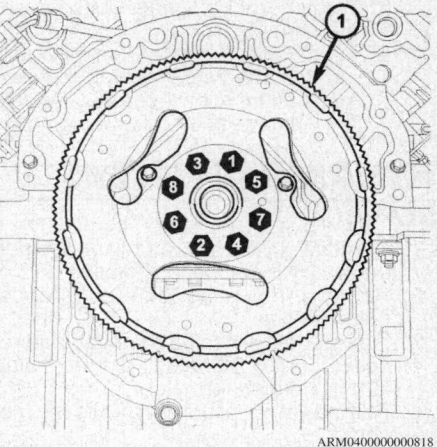

ARM0400000000818

Fig. 11 Flexplate tightening sequence

AWD

1. Remove engine cover.
2. Remove intake manifold as outlined under "Intake Manifold, Replace."
3. Install engine lift fixture tool No. 8984 and adapter No. 8984-UPD, or equivalent. **Do not use air tools when installing mounting bolts and nuts.**
4. Raise and support vehicle.
5. Remove mounting screws and front belly pan.
6. Remove lefthand and righthand side engine mount to frame mounting bolts.
7. Drain engine oil into suitable container and remove oil filter.
8. Remove mounting bolts and lower steering rack. **Do not remove power steering hoses, tie rod ends or disconnect steering column.**
9. Remove engine oil dipstick and tube from oil pan.
10. Disconnect downstream oxygen sensor connectors.
11. Remove catalytic converter to muffler and resonator clamps.
12. Remove mounting nuts and tunnel reinforcement.
13. Remove two mounting nuts and isolators, then the lefthand resonator and tailpipe.
14. Remove isolators, then the muffler and tailpipe by twisting/turning while pulling assembly out of catalytic converters.
15. Remove ball flange nuts and catalytic converter.
16. Mark front driveshaft to flange at both ends for installation alignment.
17. Remove front drive shaft mounting bolts from differential and transfer case.
18. Remove driveshaft.
19. Remove lefthand and righthand front drive axles.
20. Remove differential support bracket.
21. Remove mounting bolts and differential support bracket.
22. Turn differential so drive flange is facing forward and oil pan side is facing up.
23. Remove differential through opening

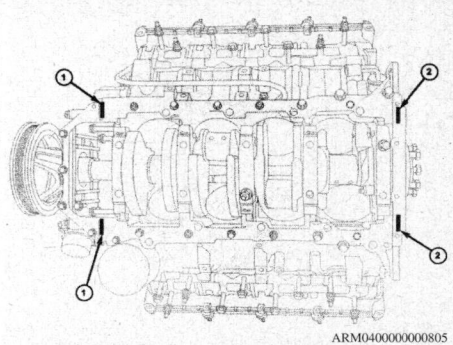

Fig. 12 Oil pan RTV sealing

at rear of cradle.

24. Remove intermediate shaft from oil pan.
25. Lower vehicle.
26. Install engine support fixture tool No. 8534, or equivalent. **Do not fasten fixture to vehicle body, or attach third support leg to radiator support.**
27. Raise engine to provide oil pan removal clearance.
28. Raise and support vehicle.
29. Mark oil pan mounting bolts for installation alignment. **Horizontal M10 fasteners are .20 inch longer and must be installed in original locations.**
30. Remove oil pan to transmission, then the engine rear vertical and horizontal mounting bolts.
31. Remove mounting bolts and oil pan. **Do not pry on oil pan or gasket.**
32. Discard integral windage tray and gasket.
33. Reverse procedure to install, noting the following:
    a. Apply .177 x .985 inch Mopar Engine RTV, or equivalent, bead to four T-joints, (area where front cover, rear retainer, block, and oil pan gasket meet). Bead should cover bottom of gasket, **Fig. 12.**
    b. Install new oil pan gasket/windage tray assembly.
    c. Horizontal M10 fasteners are .20 inch longer and must be installed in original locations.
    d. Align oil pan rear with engine block rear face.
    e. Install M10 and M6 oil pan fasteners hand tight.
    f. **Torque** M6 mounting bolts in sequence to 44 inch lbs., **Fig. 13.**
    g. **Torque** M10 oil pan mounting bolts in sequence to 39 ft. lbs.
    h. **Torque** M6 oil pan mounting bolts to 106 inch lbs.

RWD

1. Remove intake manifold as outlined under "Intake Manifold, Replace."
2. Install engine lift fixture tool No. 8984 and adapter No. 8984-UPD, or equivalent. **Do not use air tools when installing mounting bolts and nuts.**
3. Raise and support vehicle.
4. Remove mounting screws and front belly pan.
5. Drain engine oil into suitable container and remove oil filter.

6. Remove mounting bolts and lower steering rack. **Do not remove power steering hoses, tie rod ends or disconnect steering column.**
7. Remove lefthand and righthand side engine hydromount to frame nuts and studs.
8. Remove engine oil dipstick and tube from oil pan.
9. Lower vehicle.
10. Raise engine to provide oil pan removal clearance.
11. Raise and support vehicle.
12. Mark oil pan mounting bolts for installation alignment. **Horizontal M10 fasteners are .20 inch longer length and must be installed in original locations.**
13. Remove oil pan to transmission, then the engine rear vertical and horizontal mounting bolts.
14. Remove mounting bolts and oil pan. **Do not pry on oil pan or gasket.**
15. Discard integral windage tray and gasket.
16. Reverse procedure to install, noting the following:
    a. Apply .177 x .985 inch Mopar Engine RTV, or equivalent, bead to four T-joints, (area where front cover, rear retainer, block, and oil pan gasket meet). Bead should cover bottom of gasket, **Fig. 12.**
    b. Install new oil pan gasket/windage tray assembly.
    c. Horizontal M10 fasteners are .20 inch longer, and must be installed in original locations.
    d. Align oil pan rear with engine block rear face.
    e. Install M10 and M6 oil pan fasteners hand tight.
    f. **Torque** M6 mounting bolts in sequence to 44 inch lbs., **Fig. 13.**
    g. **Torque** M10 oil pan mounting bolts in sequence to 39 ft. lbs.
    h. **Torque** M6 oil pan mounting bolts to 106 inch lbs.

OIL PUMP

REPLACE

1. Remove oil pan as outlined under "Oil Pan, Replace."
2. Remove mounting bolt and pick-up tube.
3. Remove timing chain cover as outlined under "Front Cover, Replace."
4. Remove four mounting bolts and oil pump.
5. Reverse procedure to install.

OIL PUMP SERVICE

The oil pump pressure relief valve and spring should not be removed from the oil pump. If these components are disassembled and/or removed from the pump. The entire oil pump assembly must be replaced.

1. Remove pump cover.
2. Clean all components thoroughly.
3. Mating surface of oil pump housing should be smooth. If pump cover is scratched or grooved oil pump assembly should be replaced.
4. Slide outer rotor into body of oil pump.

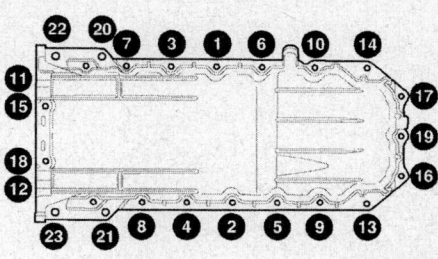

Fig. 13 Oil pan tightening sequence

5. Press outer rotor to one side of oil pump body and measure clearance between outer rotor and body, **Fig. 14.**
6. If clearance is .009 inch, or more, oil pump assembly must be replaced.
7. Install inner rotor in into oil pump body.
8. Measure clearance between inner and outer rotors, **Fig. 15.**
9. If clearance between rotors is .006 inch, or more, oil pump assembly must be replaced.
10. Place suitable straight edge across body of oil pump between bolt holes and measure clearance, **Fig. 16.**
11. If clearance is .0038 inch, or more, pump must be replaced.
12. Install pump cover.

BELT TENSION DATA

Belt adjustment is maintained by an automatic (spring load) belt tensioner.

SERPENTINE DRIVE BELT

Routing

Refer to **Fig. 17** for serpentine drive belt routing.

Replacement

REMOVAL

1. Rotate belt tensioner counterclockwise until it contacts it's stop.
2. Remove belt and slowly rotate tensioner into the freearm position. **Do not let tensioner arm snap back to freearm position.**

INSTALLATION

1. Route belt around all pulleys except idler pulley.
2. Rotate tensioner arm until it contacts it's stop position.
3. Route belt around idler and slowly let tensioner rotate into belt.
4. Ensure belt is seated onto all pulleys.
5. Tensioner is equipped with indexing tang on back and indexing stop on tensioner housing.
6. If new belt (used 15 minutes or less) is being installed, tang must be within approximately .24—.32 inch of indexing stop.

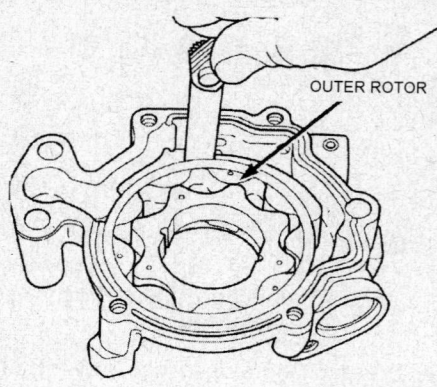

Fig. 14 Outer rotor to body clearance

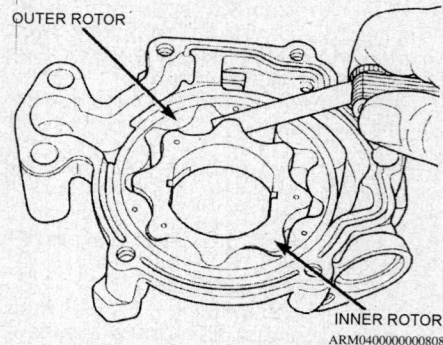

Fig. 15 Clearance between rotors

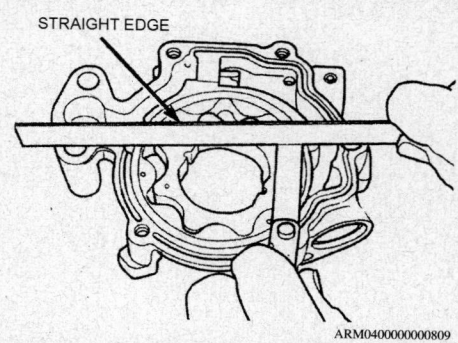

Fig. 16 Clearance over rotors

COOLING SYSTEM BLEED

1. Attach 4–6 feet long ¼ inch ID clear hose to bleeder fitting located on front of water outlet housing at front of engine, **Fig. 18.** It may be required to install bleed fitting. **When installing drain hose to air bleed valve, route hose away from accessory drive belts, accessory drive pulleys, and electric cooling fan motors.**
2. Route hose away from accessory drive belt, drive pulleys and electric cooling fan.
3. Place other end of hose into clean container.
4. **Ensure cooling system air bleed valve is opened before any coolant is added to cooling system.**
5. Install threaded and barbed fitting (¼ - 18 npt) into water pump housing.
6. Attach filling aid funnel tool No. 8195, or equivalent, to pressure bottle filler neck.
7. Pinch overflow hose that connects between two chambers of coolant bottle using suitable hose pinch-off pliers.
8. Open bleed fitting.
9. Pour suitable antifreeze mixture into larger section of filling aid funnel (smaller section of funnel is to allow air to escape).
10. Slowly fill cooling system until steady stream of coolant flows from hose attached to bleed valve.
11. Close bleed valve and continue filling system to top of filling aid funnel tool.
12. Remove pinch-off pliers from overflow hose.
13. Allow coolant in filling funnel to drain into overflow chamber of pressure bottle.
14. Remove funnel and install coolant pressure bottle cap.
15. Remove hose from bleed valve.
16. Install fitting into thermostat housing. Coat threads with Mopar Thread Sealant with Teflon, or equivalent.

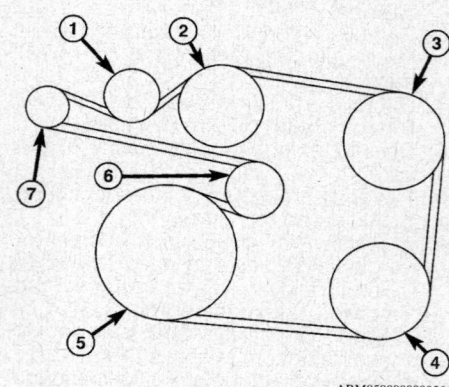

Fig. 17 Serpentine drive belt routing

17. Start engine and run at 1500–2000 RPM for 30 minutes, noting the following:
    a. Engine cooling system will push any remaining air into coolant bottle within about an hour of normal driving. As a result, a drop in coolant level in pressure bottle may occur.
    b. If engine cooling system overheats and pushes coolant into overflow side of coolant bottle, this coolant will be sucked back into cooling system, **only if pressure cap is left on bottle.**
    c. Removing pressure cap breaks vacuum path between two bottle sections and coolant will not return to cooling system.
18. Shut off engine allow it to cool down for 30 minutes. This permits coolant to be drawn into pressure chamber.
19. With engine cold, ensure coolant level should be within MIN and MAX marks. Coolant will normally only be in inboard of coolant bottle two chambers. Outboard chamber is only to recover coolant in event of an overheat or after recent service fill.

THERMOSTAT
REPLACE

1. Drain coolant into suitable container.

2. Remove thermostat housing radiator hose.
3. Remove mounting bolts, housing and thermostat.
4. Reverse procedure to install. Install thermostat (spring side down) into recessed machined groove on timing chain cover with bleed valve located at 12 o'clock position.

WATER PUMP
REPLACE

1. Drain coolant into suitable container.
2. Remove upper radiator hose and disconnect cooling fan electrical connector.
3. Remove mounting bolts and cooling fan.
4. Rotate belt tensioner counterclockwise until it contacts it's stop.
5. Remove belt and slowly rotate tensioner into the freearm position. **Do not let tensioner arm snap back to freearm position.**
6. Remove thermostat housing radiator hose.
7. Remove mounting bolts, housing and thermostat.
8. Mark location of different length water pump mounting bolts.
9. Remove mounting bolts and water pump.
10. Reverse procedure to install.

RADIATOR
REPLACE

Refer to "Radiator, Replace" in the "2.7L Engine" for radiator replacement procedure.

FUEL PUMP
REPLACE

Refer to "Fuel Pump, Replace" in "2.7L Engine" for fuel pump replacement procedure.

FUEL FILTER
REPLACE

The fuel filter is replaceable only as part of the fuel pump module.

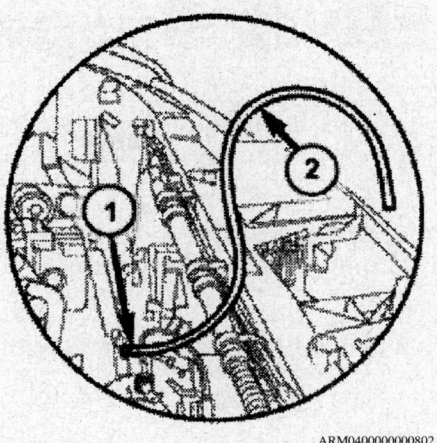

Fig. 18 Cooling system bleed

TIGHTENING SPECIFICATIONS

Year	Component	Torque Ft. Lbs.
2005–08	Air Cleaner	30①
	Alternator	40
	Automatic Belt Tensioner to Block	40
	Camshaft Sprocket	20
	Camshaft Tensioner Plate	20
	Connecting Rod Cap	15②
	Cooling Fan	50
	Crossbolts	20
	Cylinder Head	③
	Cylinder Head Cover	70①
	Exhaust Manifold	⑥
	Exhaust Manifold Ball Flange	⑥
	Exhaust Manifold Heat Shield	70①
	Fan Blade to Fan Motor	17
	Fan Shroud	50①
	Flexplate To Crankshaft	55
	Front Insulator	70
	Heater Supply Tube	30①
	Housing, Coolant Outlet	105①
	Idler Pulley	40
	Intake Manifold	105①
	Lifter Guide Holder	106
	Lifting Stud	40
	Main Bearing Cap	④
	Oil Dipstick Tube	105
	Oil Pan	⑤
	Oil Pan Drain Plug	20
	Oil Pump	20
	Oil Pump Pickup Tube	20
	Radiator to Support Bracket	106①

TIGHTENING SPECIFICATIONS—Continued

Year	Component	Torque Ft. Lbs.
2005–08	Rear Insulator to Bracket	50
	Rear Insulator to Crossmember	30
	Rear Insulator to Transmission	50
	Rear Insulator Bracket	50
	Rear Seal Retainer	11
	Rocker Arm	16
	Tappet Guide Yoke	106①
	Thermostat Housing	112
	Throttle Body	105①
	Timing Chain Case Cover	112①
	Upper Radiator Closure Panel	90①
	Vibration Damper	129
	Water Pump	20
	Water Pump to Timing Chain	20

① — Inch lbs.

② — Plus an additional 90°.

③ — Refer to Cylinder Head, Replace for tightening specifications and sequence.

④ — Refer to Main & Rod Bearings for tightening specifications and sequence.

⑤ — Refer to Oil Pan, Replace for tightening specifications and sequence.

⑥ — Refer to Exhaust Manifold, Replace for tightening specifications and sequence.

Rear Axle & Suspension

NOTE: On Air Bag Equipped Models, Refer To "Air Bag System Precautions" Located In The Front Of This Manual For System Disarming & Arming Procedures.

NOTE: Refer To "Computer Relearn Procedures" Located In The Front Of This Manual When Battery Power To The Computer Has Been Interrupted.

NOTE: Refer To The Rear Of This Manual For Vehicle Manufacturer's Special Tool Suppliers.

INDEX

	Page No.			Page No.			Page No.
Camber Link, Replace	6-41		Recalibration	6-38		**Stabilizer Bar, Replace**	6-43
Coil Spring, Replace	6-41		**Propeller Shaft, Replace**	6-39		Installation	6-44
Compression Link, Replace	6-41		**Rear Halfshaft, Replace**	6-38		Removal	6-43
Description	6-38		Installation	6-39		**Tension Link, Replace**	6-42
Differential Carrier, Replace	6-39		Removal	6-39		**Tightening Specifications**	6-45
Hub & Bearing, Replace	6-40		**Shock Absorber, Replace**	6-40		**Toe Link, Replace**	6-41
Hub & Bearing Service	6-40		Load-Leveling	6-40		Lefthand	6-41
Knuckle, Replace	6-43		Installation	6-40		Installation	6-41
Removal	6-43		Removal	6-40		Removal	6-41
Installation	6-43		Standard	6-41		Righthand	6-42
Precautions	6-38		**Spring Link, Replace**	6-42		Installation	6-42
Air Bag Systems	6-38		Installation	6-42		Removal	6-42
Battery Ground Cable	6-38		Removal	6-42			

PRECAUTIONS

Air Bag Systems

Refer to "Air Bag System Precautions" in the front of this manual for system disarming and arming procedures.

Battery Ground Cable

Prior to service, disconnect battery ground cable and isolate as required.

RECALIBRATION

Anytime the battery has been disconnect or has lost its charge, the following must be recalibrated.

EXPRESS WINDOW

1. Turn ignition switch to RUN position.
2. Move driver's window upward until it stalls in full up position. Allow window motor to stall for at least two seconds before releasing switch.
3. Move driver's window downward until it stalls in full down position. Allow window motor to stall for at least two seconds before releasing switch.
4. Move driver's window upward until it stalls in full up position. Allow window motor to stall for at least two seconds before releasing switch.
5. Move passenger's window upward until it stalls in full up position. Allow window motor to stall for at least two seconds before releasing switch.
6. Move passenger's window downward until it stalls in full down position. Allow window motor to stall for at least two seconds before releasing switch.
7. Move passenger's window upward until it stalls in full up position. Allow window motor to stall for at least two seconds before releasing switch.

ELECTRONIC STABILITY PROGRAM (ESP) STEERING ANGLE SENSOR

1. Start engine.
2. Turn steering wheel to righthand side until wheel locks full right.
3. Turn steering wheel to lefthand side until wheel locks full left.
4. Turn steering wheel to righthand side until wheels are centered.
5. Cycle ignition switch OFF and ON. Do not start engine.

DESCRIPTION

This vehicle utilizes a five-link rear suspension including the following major components: camber link, compression link, spring link, tension link, toe link, coil spring crossmember, hub and bearing, knuckle, shock absorber and stabilizer bar.

The knuckle, camber link, compression link and tension link are aluminum castings.

Both AWD and RWD models utilize a two-piece rear propeller shaft design to transmit torque to the rear axle assembly, **Fig. 1.** This two-piece design consists of: front and rear shaft segments, center support bearing/bracket assembly, single-cardan U-joint at rear segment/bearing interface, rubber couplers at transmission and rear axle flanges, and, on 2.7L and 3.5L models, fore-mounted vibration damper.

The front shaft segment is designed with a collapsing feature, consisting of two concentric tubes secured by shear pins. This feature allows the tubes to telescope up to eight inches during certain impacts. The flexible rubber couplers at the transmission and axle flanges absorb vibration. The low-travel single-cardan universal joint permits the minimal axial and angular variations that occur with independent rear suspension. Additionally, models equipped with 2.7L and 3.5L engines utilize a vibration damper which is designed to absorb and isolate driveline vibrations and harmonics. This damper is mounted to the front segment, sandwiched between the coupler and propeller shaft.

AWD models utilize a two-piece front propeller shaft design to transmit torque to the front axle assembly, **Fig. 2.** This two-piece design consists of: front and rear shaft segments, single-cardan U-joints at end flanges and rubber boot at front/rear segment interface.

REAR HALFSHAFT
REPLACE

This procedure requires the compression of the rear suspension to ride height. A drive-on hoist should be used. If a drive-on hoist is not used, screw-style under-hoist jack stands are required to compress the rear suspension, facilitating rear halfshaft removal.

Halfshaft inner and outer boots are not serviceable separately. Boot replacement requires entire shaft assembly replacement.

Removal

1. Raise and support vehicle on hoist.
2. Drain rear axle fluid into suitable container suitable. Install drain plug.
3. **On models equipped with 5.7L engine,** remove rear exhaust system.
4. **On all models,** remove tire an wheel assembly.
5. Remove wheel hub nut and discard.
6. Mark propeller shaft rubber coupler and axle flange for installation alignment.
7. Remove three propeller shaft coupler-to-axle flange bolt/nuts.
8. Partially disengage halfshaft from axle using suitable screwdriver.
9. **If drive-on hoist is not used,** compress rear suspension using screw-style under-hoist jack stands.
10. **On all models,** position transmission jack to rear axle.
11. Remove rear axle forward mount isolator bolt/nut.
12. Remove rear axle-to-crossmember bolts using short socket and flexible-head ratchet.
13. Lower rear axle. While lowering axle, separate propeller shaft from axle and support with suitable rope or wire.
14. Lower axle just enough to remove halfshafts one at a time.
15. Shift axle assembly in one direction, compressing one halfshaft while removing other. **Protect axle seal and journal.**
16. **Unequal-length halfshafts are used. Lefthand halfshaft is shorter. Identify and tag halfshafts upon removal to ensure proper installation.**
17. **Never grasp halfshaft assembly by inner or outer boots.**
18. Remove halfshaft from hub.
19. Remove and inspect rubber isolation washer.
20. Remove axle seals using suitable screwdriver.

Installation

1. Install new axle seal using driver tool No. 9223, or equivalent.
2. Install halfshaft isolation washer. Washer is bi-directional and can be installed in either direction.
3. Install halfshaft to wheel hub/knuckle assembly.
4. Install new hub nut by hand.
5. Lubricate halfshaft inner joint bearing journal with Mopar Gear and Axle Lubricant 75W-140, or equivalent.
6. Install halfshaft to rear axle using new circlip. **Do not damage axle seals.**
7. Ensure proper installation by pulling outward on joint by hand.
8. Raise rear axle into position.
9. Align propeller shaft and start propeller shaft coupler-to-axle bolt/nuts by hand.
10. Install two rear axle-to-crossmember bolts and tighten.

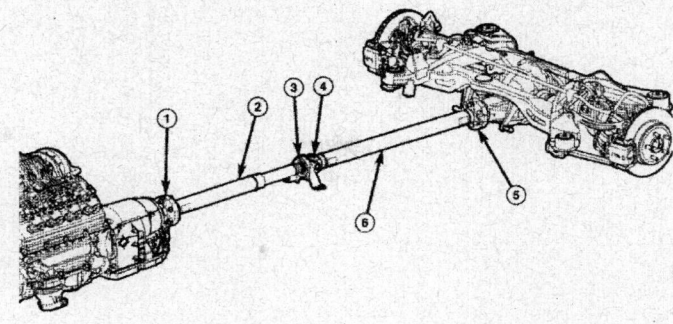

1- FRONT COUPLER
2- FRONT SEGMENT
3- BEARING/BRACKET ASSEMBLY
4- SINGLE-CARDAN U-JOINT
5- REAR COUPLER
6- REAR SEGMENT

ARM0400000000640

Fig. 1 Propeller shaft. Rear

11. Install rear axle front mount isolator and tighten.
12. Ensure halfshaft inner joints are fully engaged to axle.
13. Remove transmission jack and/or screw-type under-hoist jack stands.
14. Tighten propeller shaft coupler-to-axle flange bolt/nuts.
15. Remove rear axle fill plug and fill axle with Mopar 75W-140 Synthetic Gear & Axle Lubricant, or equivalent.
16. Install and tighten fill plug.
17. **On models equipped with 5.7L engine,** install exhaust system. Tighten band clamps
18. **On all models,** lower vehicle and tighten halfshaft hub nut.
19. Install wheel center cap.
20. Install tie and wheel assembly and tighten lug nuts.

DIFFERENTIAL CARRIER
REPLACE

This procedure requires the compression of the rear suspension to ride height. A drive-on hoist should be used. If a drive-on hoist is not used, screw-style under-hoist jack stands are required to compress the rear suspension, facilitating rear halfshaft removal.
Never grasp halfshaft assembly by inner or outer boots.
1. Raise and support vehicle on hoist.
2. Drain rear axle fluid in suitable container. Install drain plug.
3. **On models equipped with dual outlet exhaust,** remove rear exhaust system.
4. **On models less dual outlet exhaust,** lower exhaust system at rear hanger(s) to provide adequate clearance.
5. **On all models,** mark propeller shaft rubber coupler and axle flange for installation alignment.
6. Remove three propeller shaft coupler to axle flange bolt/nuts.
7. Partially disengage halfshaft from axle using suitable screwdriver.
8. **If a drive-on hoist is not used,** compress rear suspension using screw-style jack stands.
9. **On all models,** support rear axle with suitable transmission jack.
10. Remove rear axle forward mount isolator bolt/nut.
11. Remove two rear axle to crossmember bolts.
12. Lower rear axle. While lowering axle, separate propeller shaft from axle and support with suitable rope or wire.
13. Lower axle just enough to remove both halfshafts one at a time.
14. Shift axle assembly in one direction, compressing one halfshaft while removing the other. **Protect axle seal and journal.**
15. Remove axle assembly and transfer to bench.
16. Remove and discard axle seals using suitable screwdriver.
17. Reverse procedure to install, noting the following:
    a. Install new axle sea using driver tool No. 9223, or equivalent.
    b. Halfshaft installation angle should be minimized to avoid damage to seal.
    c. Use new circlip(s).

PROPELLER SHAFT
REPLACE

1. Raise and support vehicle on hoist.
2. Mark transmission and axle flanges and rubber couplers for installation alignment.
3. Remove crossmember, rear exhaust system and heat shield.
4. Remove propeller shaft front and rear coupler-to-flange bolts.
5. Remove center bearing mounting bolts.
6. Remove propeller shaft with aid of helper. **Never allow propeller shaft to hang from center bearing, or while only connected to transmission or rear axle flanges.**
7. Remove three coupler-to-propeller shaft bolt/nuts.

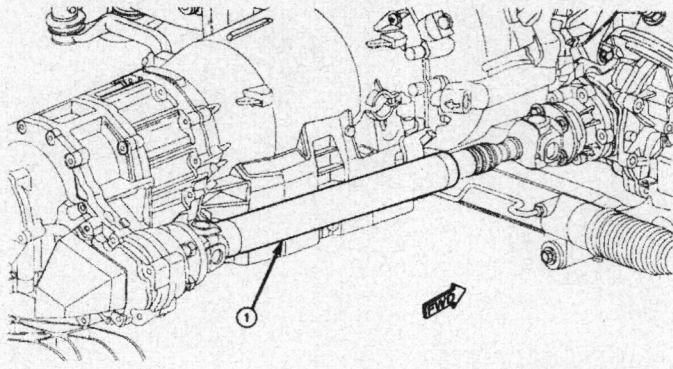

ARM0400000000641

Fig. 2   Propeller shaft. Front

8. Record orientation and direction of components for install alignment.
9. Separate coupler and damper from propeller shaft.
10. Reverse procedure to install.

HUB & BEARING
REPLACE

1. Raise and support vehicle, then remove tire and wheel assembly.
2. While helper applies brakes to keep hub from rotating, remove half shaft hub nut.
3. **On SRT8 models,** proceed as follows:
   a. Apply pressure against brake pad until both pistons are fully seated in bores of caliper using suitable trim stick or equivalent.
   b. Support spring link with a suitable transmission jack and raise spring link enough to access lower caliper mounting bolt from above compression link.
4. **On all models,** remove two mounting bolts, disc brake caliper and adapter.
5. Hang assembly aside using suitable wire. **Do not overextend brake hose.**
6. Remove clips, then slide brake rotor off hub and bearing.
7. Loosen each hub and bearing mounting bolt a turn or two at a time while pulling outward on hub and bearing to avoid bolt contact with half shaft outer joint.
8. Once removed from threads in hub and bearing (but not knuckle), allow bolts to stay in and protrude through knuckle and brake support plate.
9. Slide hub and bearing off knuckle and half shaft.
10. Reverse procedure to install. Ensure isolation washer is present on end of half shaft. Washer can be installed in either direction on shaft.

HUB & BEARING SERVICE

The rear wheel bearing and wheel hub are a one piece sealed unit or hub and bearing unit type assembly. The wheel mounting studs used to mount the tire and wheel to the vehicle are the only replaceable components of the hub and bearing. Otherwise, the hub and bearing is serviced only as a complete assembly.

SHOCK ABSORBER
REPLACE

Load-Leveling
REMOVAL

1. Raise and support vehicle, then remove both rear tire and wheel assemblies.
2. **If servicing lefthand side,** proceed as follows:
   a. Drain fuel from tank into suitable container.
   b. Open filler tube door and remove retaining wire from inside filler tube rubber.
   c. Start removing rubber from body sheet metal, squeeze rubber and push in.
   d. Remove lefthand inner splash shield.
   e. Disconnect filler tube vent line.
   f. Remove filler tube mounting bolt.
   g. Remove under body splash shield.
   h. Loosen filler tube hose clamp. Leave clamp tight on hose and fuel tank location.
   i. Move clamp toward fuel tank and remove filler tube.
3. **On all models,** position an extra pair of suitable jack stands under and support forward end of engine cradle.
4. **If servicing righthand side or on models with dual-exhaust,** proceed as follows:
   a. Position under-hoist utility jack or stand several inches below exhaust at muffler.
   b. Disconnect exhaust isolators at muffler and resonators hangers.
   c. Lower exhaust down to rest upon top of jack or stand.
5. **On all models,** position suitable under-hoist utility jack or transmission jack under center of rear axle differential.
6. Raise jack head to contact differential and secure in place. **Do not secure stabilizer bar.**
7. Remove shock absorber upper mounting screws, lower mounting bolt and nut.

8. Remove both front and rear crossmember mounting bolts on repair-side of vehicle. **Do not loosen or remove crossmember mounting bolts on opposite side of vehicle. On models equipped with AWD, do not misplace spacers between crossmember mounts and body.**
9. Slowly lower jack allowing repair-side of crossmember to drop. Lower jack just enough to allow top of shock absorber to clear body flange. **Do not lower crossmember any further than required to remove shock absorber.**
10. Remove shock absorber by tipping top outward and lifting lower end out of pocket in spring link.

INSTALLATION

1. Install shock absorber by setting lower end into pocket in spring link, then tipping top inward until aligned with upper mounting holes.
2. Install lower shock mounting bolt and nut. **Do not tighten now.**
3. **On models equipped with AWD,** ensure spacers on top of crossmember mount bushings.
4. **On all models,** raise jack, guiding coil spring and upper end of shock absorber into mounted positions.
5. Install and tighten shock absorber upper mounting screws.
6. Install crossmember mounting bolts. Snug, but do not fully tighten bolts now. **Rear crossmember mounting bolts are longer than front mounting bolts. Do not interchange mounting bolts.**
7. Measure distance between tension link and weld flange on body directly in front of it, just outboard of front mount bushing, **Fig. 3.**
8. This distance must be at least .47 inch to allow proper clearance for suspension movement, noting the following:
   a. If distance is less than specified on either side of vehicle, shift that side of rear crossmember directly rearward until distance is .47 inch, or more.
   b. To do so, loosen three mounting bolts slightly, leaving one on opposite side of shift snugged to pivot off of.
   c. Shift crossmember rearward and snug loosened bolts.
   d. Measure opposite side to ensure it still maintains minimum .47 inch distance.
9. Tighten all crossmember mounting bolts.
10. Remove jack from under rear axle differential.
11. If previously lowered, raise rear exhaust back to mounted position and connect exhaust isolators at muffler and resonators hangers. Remove jack or stand below exhaust muffler.
12. Insert filler tube into fuel tank rubber hose.
13. Slide hose clamp into place and tighten.
14. Hose clamp in place and tighten.

15. Install filler tube mounting bolt and vent line.
16. Install underbody splash shield.
17. Install lefthand inner splash shield.
18. Pull rubber through opening and install to body. Ensure sheet metal is in rubber groove.
19. Start metal wire retaining wire in groove on inside of filler tube rubber.
20. Work wire retaining wire around rubber and install wire retainer.
21. Install tire and wheel assemblies, then tighten wheel mounting nuts.
22. Lower and position vehicle on alignment rack/drive-on lift.
23. Raise lift as required to access lower mounting bolt.
24. Tighten shock absorber lower mounting bolt nut.

Standard

1. Raise and support vehicle, then remove tire and wheel assembly.
2. Position suitable under-hoist utility jack or jack stand under outer spring link adding just enough support to keep suspension from going into full-rebound when shock absorber mounting bolts.
3. Remove lower mounting bolt, nut, upper mounting bolts and shock absorber.
4. Reverse procedure to install, noting the following:
   a. Tighten upper mounting bolt when installed.
   b. **Do not tighten lower mounting bolt nut when installed.**
   c. Lower and position vehicle on alignment rack/drive-on lift.
   d. Raise lift as required to access lower mounting bolt.
   e. Tighten shock absorber lower mounting bolt nut.

COIL SPRING
REPLACE

Rear coil springs are interchangeable.
1. Remove shock absorber as outlined under "Shock Absorber, Replace," "Load-Leveling."
2. Disconnect brake hose at bracket mounted to body.
3. Slowly lower jack until crossmember is low enough to remove coil spring. **Do not lower jack any further than required to remove spring.**
4. Remove coil spring and isolators.
5. Reverse procedure to install, noting the following:
   a. Install upper and lower isolators on coil spring.
   b. Ensure isolators are completely installed on ends of spring.
   c. Install coil spring with isolators into spring pocket of spring link fitting lower isolator to shape of pocket, then align top of spring with body mount.

CAMBER LINK
REPLACE

1. Remove shock absorber as outlined

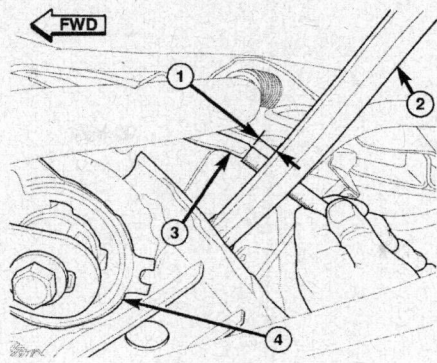

1- CLEARANCE
2- TENSION LINK
3- WELD FLANGE
4- FRONT MOUNT BUSHING

ARM0400000000638

Fig. 3   Suspension movement clearance

under "Shock Absorber, Replace."
2. Remove mounting link to knuckle nut and bolt, then the mounting link to crossmember nut bolt.
3. Remove link.
4. Reverse procedure to install, noting the following:
   a. Heavier, thicker end goes toward crossmember.
   b. Fore-or-aft bow faces forward (curves around coil spring).
   c. Up-or-down bow faces downward.

COMPRESSION LINK
REPLACE

1. Raise and support vehicle, then remove rear tire and wheel assembly.
2. Remove mounting link bolt and nut at knuckle, **Fig. 4.**
3. Remove mounting link bolt and nut at crossmember.
4. Remove link.
5. Reverse procedure to install, noting the following:
   a. Although compression link is different end-to-end, there is no top and bottom.
   b. **Do not tighten mounting bolts and nuts when installed.**
   c. Lower and position vehicle on alignment rack/drive-on lift.
   d. Raise vehicle as required to access link fasteners.
   e. Tighten crossmember bolt, then the knuckle bolt.

TOE LINK
REPLACE
Lefthand
REMOVAL

1. Raise and support vehicle, then remove both rear tire and wheel assemblies.
2. Drain fuel from tank into suitable container.

3. Open filler tube door and remove retaining wire from inside filler tube rubber.
4. Start removing rubber from body sheet metal, squeeze rubber and push in.
5. Remove lefthand inner splash shield.
6. Disconnect filler tube vent line.
7. Remove filler tube mounting bolt.
8. Remove under body splash shield.
9. Loosen filler tube hose clamp. Leave clamp tight on hose and fuel tank location.
10. Move clamp toward fuel tank and remove filler tube.
11. Position suitable extra pair of jack stands under and support forward end of engine cradle.
12. **On models equipped with dual-exhaust,** proceed as follows:
   a. Position under-hoist utility jack or stand several inches below exhaust at muffler.
   b. Disconnect exhaust isolators at muffler and resonators hangers.
   c. Lower exhaust down to rest upon top of jack or stand.
13. **On all models,** support rear axle differential by positioning suitable under-hoist utility jack or transmission jack under center.
14. Remove shock absorber lower mounting bolt and nut.
15. Remove both front and rear crossmember mounting bolts on repair-side of vehicle. **Do not loosen or remove crossmember mounting bolts on opposite side of vehicle. On models equipped with AWD, do not misplace spacers between crossmember mounts and body.**
16. Slowly lower jack allowing repair-side of crossmember to drop just enough to access toe link mounting bolt at crossmember.
17. Remove wheel speed sensor cable from toe link.
18. While holding toe adjustment cam bolt from rotating, remove nut securing toe link at crossmember.
19. Slide cam bolt rearward out of crossmember and link.
20. Remove mounting bolt and nut at knuckle, then the toe link.

INSTALLATION

1. Slide crossmember end of toe link into box bracket on crossmember.
2. Slide cam bolt through bracket and link from rear.
3. Install bolt and nut to knuckle. **Do not tighten bolt now.**
4. While holding toe adjustment cam bolt from rotating (cam facing upward), install cam washer and nut at crossmember. **Do not tighten nut now.**
5. Attach wheel speed sensor cable to toe link.
6. Carefully raise jack, guiding coil spring and lower end of shock absorber into mounted positions.
7. When lower shock mounting bolt holes line up, install bolt and nut. **Do not tighten now.**
8. Install crossmember mounting bolts. Snug, but do not fully tighten bolts now. **Rear crossmember mounting bolts**

are longer than front mounting bolts. **Do not interchange mounting bolts.**

9. Measure distance between tension link and weld flange on body directly in front of it, just outboard of front mount bushing, **Fig. 3.**

10. This distance must be at least .47 inch to allow proper clearance for suspension movement, noting the following:
   a. If distance is less than specified on either side of vehicle, shift that side of rear crossmember directly rearward until distance is .47 inch, or more.
   b. To do so, loosen three mounting bolts slightly, leaving one on opposite side of shift snugged to pivot off of.
   c. Shift crossmember rearward and snug loosened bolts.
   d. Measure opposite side to ensure it still maintains minimum .47 inch distance.

11. Tighten all crossmember mounting bolts.

12. Remove jack from under rear axle differential.

13. If previously lowered, raise rear exhaust back to mounted position and connect exhaust isolators at muffler and resonators hangers.

14. Remove jack or stand below exhaust muffler.

15. Insert filler tube into fuel tank rubber hose.

16. Slide hose clamp into place and tighten.

17. Hose clamp in place and tighten.

18. Install filler tube mounting bolt and vent line.

19. Install underbody splash shield.

20. Install lefthand inner splash shield.

21. Pull rubber through opening and install to body. Ensure sheet metal is in rubber groove.

22. Start metal wire retaining wire in groove on inside of filler tube rubber.

23. Work wire retaining wire around rubber and install wire retainer.

24. Install tire and wheel assemblies, then tighten wheel mounting nuts.

25. Lower and position vehicle on alignment rack/drive-on lift.

26. Raise vehicle as required to access mounting bolts.

27. Tighten shock absorber lower mounting bolt nut.

28. Tighten toe link nut at crossmember. This nut may be tightened after rear wheel alignment toe is set. **Do not tighten from bolt head end.**

29. Tighten tow link bolt at knuckle.

Righthand

REMOVAL

1. Raise and support vehicle, then remove rear tire and wheel assembly.

2. Remove wheel speed sensor cable from toe link.

3. While holding toe adjustment cam bolt from rotating, remove nut securing toe link at crossmember.

4. Slide cam bolt rearward out of cross-

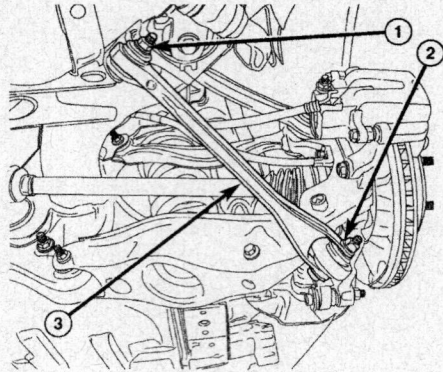

1- CROSSMEMBER BOLT & NUT
2- KNUCKLE BOLT & NUT
3- COMPRESSION LINK

ARM0400000000639

Fig. 4 Compression link replacement

member and link.

5. Remove mounting bolt and nut at knuckle, then the link.

INSTALLATION

1. Slide crossmember end of toe link into box bracket on crossmember.

2. Slide cam bolt through bracket and link from rear of vehicle.

3. Install bolt and nut securing link to knuckle. Do not tighten bolt now.

4. While holding toe adjustment cam bolt from rotating (cam facing upward), install cam washer and nut securing toe link at crossmember. **Do not tighten nut now.**

5. Attach wheel speed sensor cable to toe link.

6. Raise rear exhaust back to mounted position and connect exhaust isolators at muffler and resonators hangers.

7. Remove jack or stand below exhaust muffler.

8. Install tire and wheel assembly, then tighten wheel mounting nuts.

9. Lower and position vehicle on alignment rack/drive-on lift.

10. Raise vehicle as required to access mounting bolts.

11. Tighten toe link nut at crossmember. This nut may be tightened after rear wheel alignment toe is set. **Do not tighten from bolt head end.**

12. Tighten bolt at knuckle.

SPRING LINK
REPLACE

Removal

1. Raise and support vehicle.

2. **On SRT8 models,** remove rear spring on side of repair as outlined under "Coil Spring, Replace."

3. **On all models,** remove spring link-to-knuckle nut and bolt.

4. Place guide tool No. 9361-2, or equivalent, against sleeve in knuckle to keep tap tool No. 9361-1, or equivalent, straight.

5. Cut threads approximately halfway

through bushing (or about six complete threads) using tap with suitable handle.

6. Thread remover tool No. 9361, noting the following:
   a. **On models equipped with AWD, lefthand side,** use bolt No. 9361-3, nut, spherical washer, thrust bearing and sleeve tool No. 9361-5, or equivalents.
   b. **On models equipped with AWD, righthand side,** use bolt No. 9361-3, nut, spherical washer, thrust bearing and sleeve tool No. 9361-6, or equivalents.
   c. **On models equipped with RWD,** use bolt No. 9361-3, nut, spherical washer, thrust bearing and sleeve tool No. 9361-4, or equivalents.
   d. **On all models,** ensure to place hardened side against nut.

7. Rotate nut down, matching sleeve angled end with angled face of knuckle. Continue to rotate nut until knuckle sleeve is removed from knuckle. Discard knuckle sleeve.

8. Remove crossmember mounting bolt and nut, then spring link.

Installation

1. Guide ball joint end of spring link into mounting pocket of knuckle, then swing opposite end up to bushing in crossmember and install bolt and nut. **Do not tighten bolt now.**

2. Place new knuckle sleeve onto installer bolt tool No. 9361-7, or equivalent, slide it up to bolt's head.

3. Slide bolt tool with sleeve through knuckle and spring link ball joint, starting from knuckle forward end.

4. Install thrust bearing and nut on end of bolt tool.

5. While holding bolt head stationary, rotate nut (using hand tools) installing sleeve in knuckle. Install sleeve until nut stops turning. **Do not overtighten nut.**

6. Remove special tool.

7. Install spring link-to-knuckle bolt front-to-rear through knuckle and link, then install nut.

8. While holding bolt head stationary, tighten nut.

9. Lower and position vehicle on alignment rack/drive-on lift.

10. Raise vehicle as required to access mounting bolt.

11. Tighten spring link bolt at crossmember.

TENSION LINK
REPLACE

1. Remove shock absorber as outlined under "Shock Absorber, Replace."

2. Remove mounting link to knuckle nut and bolt, then the mounting link to crossmember nut bolt.

3. Remove link.

4. Reverse procedure to install, noting the following:
   a. Although link is same end-to-end, ensure that center bow is facing downward.

b. **Do not tighten mounting bolts and nuts when installed.**

c. Lower and position vehicle on alignment rack/drive-on lift.

d. Raise vehicle as required to access link fasteners.

e. Tighten crossmember bolt, then the knuckle bolt.

KNUCKLE

REPLACE

Removal

1. Raise and support vehicle.
2. Unclip wheel speed sensor cable at rear brake rotor shield.
3. Remove mounting screw and wheel speed sensor head from knuckle.
4. Remove tire and wheel assembly.
5. While helper applies brakes to keep hub from rotating, remove half shaft hub nut.
6. Remove two mounting bolts, disc brake caliper and adapter.
7. Hang assembly aside using suitable wire. **Do not overextend brake hose.**
8. Remove clips, then slide brake rotor off hub and bearing.
9. Loosen each hub and bearing mounting bolt a turn or two at a time while pulling outward on hub and bearing to avoid bolt contact with half shaft outer joint.
10. Once removed from threads in hub and bearing (but not knuckle), allow bolts to stay in and protrude through knuckle and brake support plate.
11. Slide hub and bearing off knuckle and half shaft.
12. Completely back off parking brake shoe adjustment.
13. Remove spring and parking brake shoe adjuster.
14. Remove hold-down clip and pin, then the upper brake shoe from return spring and shoe actuator lever.
15. Remove return spring from lower shoe.
16. Remove shoe actuator lever from end of cable.
17. Remove hold-down clip and pin, then the lower shoe.
18. If not removed, remove parking brake shoe actuator lever from end of cable and shoe support from knuckle.
19. Remove parking brake cable screw at knuckle and pull cable out.
20. Support contact spring link at shock mount using suitable under-hoist utility jack or jack stand under spring link.
21. Remove spring link-to-knuckle nut and bolt.
22. Place guide tool No. 9361-2, or equivalent, against sleeve in knuckle to keep tap tool No, 9361-1, or equivalent, straight.
23. Cut threads approximately halfway through bushing (or about six complete threads) using tap with suitable handle.
24. Thread remover tool No. 9361, noting the following:
    a. **On models equipped with AWD, lefthand side,** use bolt No. 9361-3,

nut, spherical washer, thrust bearing and sleeve tool No. 9361-5, or equivalents.

b. **On models equipped with AWD, righthand side,** use bolt No. 9361-3, nut, spherical washer, thrust bearing and sleeve tool No. 9361-6, or equivalents.

c. **On models equipped with RWD,** use bolt No. 9361-3, nut, spherical washer, thrust bearing and sleeve tool No. 9361-4, or equivalents.

d. **On all models,** ensure to place hardened side against nut.

25. Rotate nut down, matching sleeve angled end with angled face of knuckle. Continue to rotate nut until knuckle sleeve is removed from knuckle. Discard knuckle sleeve.
26. Remove compression link to knuckle mounting bolt and nut.
27. Remove toe link to knuckle mounting bolt.
28. Remove stabilizer link to knuckle mounting nut and bolt.
29. Remove tension link to knuckle mounting nut and bolt.
30. Remove camber link to knuckle mounting nut and bolt.
31. Remove knuckle and hub mounting bolts.

INSTALLATION

1. Install four hub mounting bolts through knuckle from inboard side allowing ends to protrude from opposite side.
2. Position knuckle, then install camber link to knuckle mounting bolt and nut. **Do not tighten bolt now.**
3. Install tension link to knuckle mounting bolt and nut. **Do not tighten bolt now.**
4. Install stabilizer link to knuckle mounting bolt and nut. **Do not tighten bolt now.**
5. Install toe link to knuckle mounting. **Do not tighten bolt now.**
6. Install compression link to knuckle mounting bolt and nut. **Do not tighten bolt now.**
7. Place new knuckle sleeve onto installer bolt tool No. 9361-7, or equivalent, slide it up to bolt's head.
8. Slide bolt tool with sleeve through knuckle and spring link ball joint, starting from knuckle forward end.
9. Install thrust bearing and nut on end of bolt tool.
10. While holding bolt head stationary, rotate nut (using hand tools) installing sleeve in knuckle. Install sleeve until nut stops turning. **Do not overtighten nut.**
11. Remove special tool.
12. Install spring link-to-knuckle bolt front-to-rear through knuckle and link, then install nut.
13. While holding bolt head stationary, tighten nut.
14. Remove under-hoist utility jack or jack stand from under spring link.
15. Insert end of cable through rear knuckle and install mounting screw.
16. Install parking brake shoe support over hub and bearing mounting screws and onto face of knuckle.
17. Install shoe actuator lever on end of

parking brake cable. Ensure actuator lever is positioned with word UP facing outward.

18. Install parking brake shoes as well as all components required to access them.
19. Ensure isolation washer is present on end of half shaft. Washer can be installed in either direction on shaft.
20. Install hub and bearing as well as all components required to access it.
21. Insert wheel speed sensor head into mounting hole in rear of knuckle and install mounting screw.
22. Install sensor cable at rear brake rotor shield.
23. Lower vehicle and adjust parking brake shoes as required.
24. Position vehicle on alignment rack/ drive-on hoist and raise vehicle as required to access mounting bolts.
25. Tighten mounting bolts and nuts at knuckle with vehicle at curb height in following order:
    a. Camber link
    b. Compression link
    c. Stabilizer link
    d. Tension Link
    e. Toe link

STABILIZER BAR

REPLACE

Removal

1. Raise and support vehicle, then remove both tire and wheel assemblies.
2. Remove rear exhaust system.
3. Mark to propeller shaft rubber coupler and axle flange for installation alignment.
4. Remove three propeller shaft coupler-to-axle flange bolts and nuts.
5. Support propeller shaft using suitable bungee cord attached to fuel tank straps.
6. Disconnect righthand rear front parking brake cable at connector.
7. Remove front parking brake cable from equalizer.
8. On each rear disc brake, while holding guide pins from turning, remove disc brake caliper guide pin bolts.
9. Remove brake caliper from brake adapter and pads.
10. Guide brake caliper up through suspension, following brake hose path.
11. Support caliper above rear suspension to keep caliper from overextending brake hose when crossmember is lowered.
12. Remove retaining clip, wheel speed sensor connector from body wiring harness connector and pull sensor connector outward.
13. Remove wheel speed sensor connectors from body wiring harness connector located in luggage compartment floor pan.
14. Unclip lefthand wheel speed sensor cable from routing clip near body connector.
15. Remove shock absorber lower mounting bolt and nut.
16. Mark location of rear crossmember on

body at all four mount (bushing) locations for installation alignment.

17. Support forward end of engine cradle by positioning an extra pair of suitable jack stands under.
18. Support rear axle differential with suitable under-hoist utility jack or transmission jack. **Do not secure stabilizer bar.**
19. Drain fuel from tank into suitable container.
20. Open filler tube door and remove retaining wire from inside filler tube rubber.
21. Start removing rubber from body sheet metal, squeeze rubber and push in.
22. Remove lefthand inner splash shield.
23. Disconnect filler tube vent line.
24. Remove filler tube mounting bolt.
25. Remove under body splash shield.
26. Loosen filler tube hose clamp. Leave clamp tight on hose and fuel tank location.
27. Move clamp toward fuel tank and remove filler tube.
28. Remove both front and rear crossmember mounting bolts. **On models equipped with AWD, do not misplace spacers between crossmember mounts and body.**
29. Slowly lower crossmember just enough to allow propeller shaft removal from rear axle differential.
30. Slide propeller shaft out of rear axle differential and support it with bungee cord.
31. Slowly lower crossmember several inches.
32. Remove front parking brake cable routing bracket to rear crossmember mounting screw.
33. Continue to lower jack until crossmember is at comfortable working level to access stabilizer bar.
34. On each end, remove stabilizer bar to stabilizer link mounting bolt and nut.
35. Remove each stabilizer bar isolator retainer to crossmember mounting bolt.
36. Remove stabilizer bar with isolators and retainers.
37. Remove retainers from isolators, then the isolators from stabilizer bar utilizing slits in bushings.

Installation

1. Install isolators on stabilizer bar utilizing slits in bushings.
2. Install each isolator so its slit faces forward and flat side is positioned toward crossmember.
3. Install retainers on isolators.
4. Install stabilizer bar with isolators and retainers on crossmember.
5. Install isolator retainer mounting bolts. **Do not tighten now.**
6. Install stabilizer bar ends to each stabilizer links mounting bolt and nut. **Do not tighten now.**
7. Tighten isolator retainer mounting bolts.
8. Remove coil springs with isolators from spring links.
9. Raise crossmember until there is approximately 10 inches clearance to body mounting points.

10. Install front parking brake cable routing bracket to rear crossmember screw.
11. Raise crossmember to body mounting points.
12. As crossmember is raised, slide propeller shaft onto rear axle differential flange and align shocks with pockets in spring links.
13. Continue to raise crossmember until crossmember mounting bolts can be installed.
14. Install lefthand side crossmember mounting bolts, but not righthand side bolts. Rear mounting bolts are longer than front mounting bolts. **Do not interchange mounting bolts. Do not tighten bolts now.**
15. Slowly lower jack allowing righthand side of crossmember to drop. Lower jack just enough to allow spring installation. **Do not lower jack any further than required.**
16. Ensure isolators are completely installed on ends of spring.
17. Install coil spring with isolators into spring pocket of spring link fitting lower isolator to shape of pocket, then align top of spring with body mount.
18. Carefully raise jack, guiding coil spring and lower end of shock absorber into mounted positions.
19. Once shock absorber lower mounting hole lines up with hole in spring link, stop jacking.
20. Install lower shock mounting bolt and nut. **Do not tighten now.**
21. **On models equipped with AWD,** insert spacers on top of righthand crossmember mount bushings before crossmember is raised into place.
22. **On all models,** raise righthand side of crossmember into mounted position.
23. Install righthand side crossmember mounting bolts. Rear mounting bolts are longer than front mounting bolts. **Do not interchange mounting bolts.**
24. Snug, but do not fully tighten bolts now.
25. Remove both lefthand side front and rear crossmember mounting bolts.
26. Slowly lower jack allowing lefthand side of crossmember to drop. Lower jack just enough to allow spring Installation. **Do not lower jack any further than required.**
27. Ensure isolators are completely installed on ends of spring.
28. Install coil spring with isolators into spring pocket of spring link fitting lower isolator to shape of pocket, then align top of spring with body mount.
29. Carefully raise jack, guiding coil spring and lower end of shock absorber into mounted positions.
30. Once shock absorber lower mounting hole lines up with hole in spring link, stop jacking.
31. Install lower shock mounting bolt and nut. **Do not tighten now.**
32. **On models equipped with AWD,** insert spacers on top of lefthand crossmember mount bushings before crossmember is raised into place.
33. **On all models,** raise lefthand side of crossmember into mounted position.
34. Install lefthand side crossmember mounting bolts. Rear mounting bolts

are longer than front mounting bolts. **Do not interchange mounting bolts.**
35. Snug, but do not fully tighten bolts now.
36. Shift crossmember to line up mounts with location marks.
37. Once mounts are lined up with location marks, on both sides of vehicle, measure distance between tension link and weld flange on body directly in front of it, just outboard of front mount bushing, **Fig. 3.**
38. This distance must be at least .47 inch to allow proper clearance for suspension movement, noting the following:
    a. If distance is less than specified on either side of vehicle, shift that side of rear crossmember directly rearward until distance is .47 inch, or more.
    b. To do so, loosen three mounting bolts slightly, leaving one on opposite side of shift snugged to pivot off of.
    c. Shift crossmember rearward and snug loosened bolts.
    d. Measure opposite side to ensure it still maintains minimum .47 inch distance.
39. Tighten four crossmember mounting bolts.
40. Remove jack from under rear axle differential.
41. Align propeller shaft index marks.
42. Install propeller shaft rear coupler to axle flange bolts and nuts by hand.
43. Tighten propeller shaft rear coupler to axle flange bolts.
44. Insert filler tube into fuel tank rubber hose.
45. Slide hose clamp into place and tighten.
46. Hose clamp in place and tighten.
47. Install filler tube mounting bolt and vent line.
48. Install underbody splash shield.
49. Install lefthand inner splash shield.
50. Pull rubber through opening and install to body. Ensure sheet metal is in rubber groove.
51. Start metal wire retaining wire in groove on inside of filler tube rubber.
52. Work wire retaining wire around rubber and install wire retainer.
53. Clip lefthand rear wheel speed sensor cable to routing clip near body connector.
54. Match lefthand rear wheel speed sensor connector to righthand sensor connector to make one connector.
55. Insert speed sensor connectors into body wiring harness connector in luggage compartment floor pan.
56. Ensure retaining clip on body connector is properly in place and sensor connector cannot be pulled out.
57. On each rear disc brake, push caliper guide pins into caliper adapter to clear caliper mounting bosses.
58. Guide caliper and brake hose down through rear suspension, then slide caliper over brake pads and onto caliper adapter.
59. Align caliper mounting holes with guide pins and install guide pin bolts. **Do not to cross-thread caliper guide pin bolts.**

60. While holding guide pins from turning, tighten bolts.
61. Ensure brake hose is properly routed and will not come in contact with suspension components.
62. Route parking brake cable above rear crossmember and slide cable through equalizer above rear differential.
63. Because of short travel and low spring tension, it is not required to lock-out parking brake lever to service parking brake components.
64. Connect front parking brake cable at connector to righthand rear parking brake cable.
65. Install rear exhaust system.
66. Install tire and wheel assemblies, then tighten wheel mounting nuts.
67. Lower vehicle until rear wheels are just above floor level.
68. Apply parking brake lever. Release lever and apply.
69. Ensure rear wheels will not rotate with lever applied.
70. Lower vehicle.
71. Connect battery ground cable to battery post.
72. Pump brake pedal several times to ensure vehicle has firm brake pedal before moving vehicle.
73. Position vehicle on alignment rack/drive-on hoist.
74. Raise vehicle as required to access mounting bolts.
75. Tighten shock absorber lower mounting bolt nuts and stabilizer link fasteners.

TIGHTENING SPECIFICATIONS

Year	Component	Torque Ft. Lbs.
2005–08	Axle Front Mount Isolator	48
	Axle Housing-to-Crossmember	162
	Axle Hub	157
	Brake Caliper Adapter Knuckle	88
	Camber Link Crossmember	63
	Camber Link Knuckle	72
	Center Bearing-To-Body (Rear)	20
	Compression Link Crossmember	63
	Compression Link Knuckle	60
	Coupler/Damper-To-Propeller Shaft (Rear)	43
	Crossmember	133
	Differential Cover (198 mm)	22①
	Differential Cover (210 mm)	37
	Exhaust System Band Clamp	45
	Front Propeller Shaft To Axle/Transfer Case Flange	22
	Hub	157
	Hub & Bearing	50
	Parking Brake Cable Knuckle	71
	Rear Axle Drain/Fill Plug (198 mm)	44
	Rear Axle Drain/Fill Plug (210 mm)	37
	Ring Gear-to-Differential Case	63
	Shaft Coupler-To-Rear Axle	43
	Shaft Coupler-To-Transmission	43
	Shock Absorber, Lower	53
	Shock Absorber, Upper	38
	Spring Link Crossmember	80
	Spring Link Knuckle	102
	Stabilizer Bar Isolator Retainer	45
	Stabilizer Link	45
	Tension Link Crossmember	63
	Tension Link Knuckle	72
	Toe Link Crossmember	80
	Toe Link Knuckle	60
	Wheel Lug Nut	110

① — Plus an additional 45°.

Front Suspension & Steering

NOTE: On Air Bag Equipped Models, Refer To "Air Bag System Precautions" Located In The Front Of This Manual For System Disarming & Arming Procedures.

NOTE: Refer To "Computer Relearn Procedures" Located In The Front Of This Manual When Battery Power To The Computer Has Been Interrupted.

NOTE: Refer To The Rear Of This Manual For Vehicle Manufacturer's Special Tool Suppliers.

INDEX

	Page No.		Page No.		Page No.
Ball Joint, Replace	6-47	AWD	6-47	Steering Columns	12-1
Lower	6-47	RWD	6-47	Steering Knuckle, Replace	6-49
Upper	6-48	Power Steering	13-1	AWD	6-49
Coil Spring, Replace	6-48	Power Steering Gear, Replace	6-51	RWD	6-50
Coil Spring & Strut Service	6-48	Power Steering Pump, Replace	6-51	Strut, Replace	6-48
Control Arm, Replace	6-49	Power Steering System Bleed	6-51	AWD	6-48
Lower	6-49	Precautions	6-46	RWD	6-48
AWD	6-49	Air Bag Systems	6-46	Tension Strut, Replace	6-50
RWD	6-49	Battery Ground Cable	6-46	Tie Rod, Replace	6-51
Upper	6-49	Recalibration	6-46	Outer	6-51
Description	6-46	Stabilizer Bar, Replace	6-50	Tightening Specifications	6-52
Driveshaft, Replace	6-47	AWD	6-50		
Hub & Bearing, Replace	6-47	RWD	6-50		

PRECAUTIONS

Air Bag Systems

Refer to "Air Bag System Precautions" in the front of this manual for system disarming and arming procedures.

Battery Ground Cable

Prior to service, disconnect battery ground cable and isolate as required.

RECALIBRATION

Anytime the battery has been disconnect or has lost its charge, the following must be recalibrated.

EXPRESS WINDOW

1. Turn ignition switch to RUN position.
2. Move driver's window upward until it stalls in full up position. Allow window motor to stall for at least two seconds before releasing switch.
3. Move driver's window downward until it stalls in full down position. Allow window motor to stall for at least two seconds before releasing switch.
4. Move driver's window upward until it stalls in full up position. Allow window motor to stall for at least two seconds before releasing switch.
5. Move passenger's window upward until it stalls in full up position. Allow window motor to stall for at least two seconds before releasing switch.

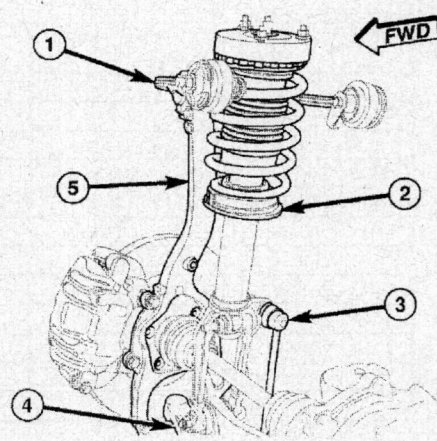

1- UPPER CONTROL ARM
2- STRUT
3- STABILIZER BAR AND LINK
4- LOWER CONTROL ARM
5- KNUCKLE

ARM0400000000630

Fig. 1 Front suspension. AWD

6. Move passenger's window downward until it stalls in full down position. Allow window motor to stall for at least two seconds before releasing switch.
7. Move passenger's window upward until it stalls in full up position. Allow window motor to stall for at least two seconds before releasing switch.

ELECTRONIC STABILITY PROGRAM (ESP) STEERING ANGLE SENSOR

1. Start engine.
2. Turn steering wheel to righthand side until wheel locks full right.
3. Turn steering wheel to lefthand side until wheel locks full left.
4. Turn steering wheel to righthand side until wheels are centered.
5. Cycle ignition switch OFF and ON. Do not start engine.

DESCRIPTION

The front suspension for both All-Wheel-Drive (AWD) and Rear-Wheel-Drive (RWD) vehicles is a long and short arm design.

On models equipped with AWD, the front suspension includes: hub and bearing knuckle, lower control arm, shock assembly, stabilizer bar and link, and upper control arm, **Fig. 1.**

On models equipped with RWD, the front suspension includes: hub and bearing knuckle, lower control arm, shock assembly, stabilizer bar and link, tension strut, and upper control arm, **Fig. 2.**

The power steering systems consist of: steering column rack and pinion steering gear, belt driven hydraulic steering pump, pump pressure, return and supply hoses, oil cooler, remote reservoir, and inner and outer tie rod ends, **Figs. 3 and 4.**

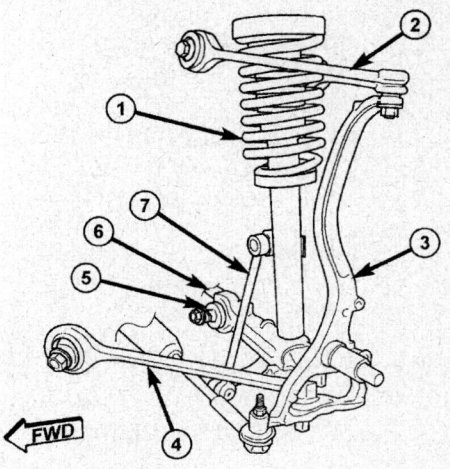

1- STRUT
2- UPPER CONTROL ARM
3- KNUCKLE
4- TENSION STRUT
5- LOWER CONTROL ARM
6- STABILIZER BAR
7- STABILIZER LINK (7)

ARM0400000000629

Fig. 2 Front suspension. RWD

HUB & BEARING
REPLACE

AWD

1. Raise and support vehicle, then remove tire and wheel assembly.
2. While a helper applies brakes to keep hub from rotating, remove hub nut from axle half shaft.
3. Remove two mounting bolts, then remove disc brake caliper and adapter from knuckle.
4. Hang assembly aside using suitable wire. **Do not overextend brake hose.**
5. Remove wheel studs' clips, then slide brake rotor off hub and bearing.
6. Remove four mounting bolts, then slide hub and bearing off axle half shaft and knuckle.
7. Reverse procedure to install. Ensure isolation washer is present on end of half shaft.

RWD

1. Raise and support vehicle, then remove tire and wheel assembly.
2. While a helper applies brakes to keep hub from rotating, remove hub nut from axle half shaft.
3. Remove two mounting bolts, then remove disc brake caliper and adapter from knuckle.
4. Hang assembly aside using suitable wire. **Do not overextend brake hose.**
5. Remove dust cap. **Do not damaging internal bore of hub.**
6. Remove hub nut, then slide hub and bearing off knuckle spindle.
7. Reverse procedure to install. Install new dust cap.

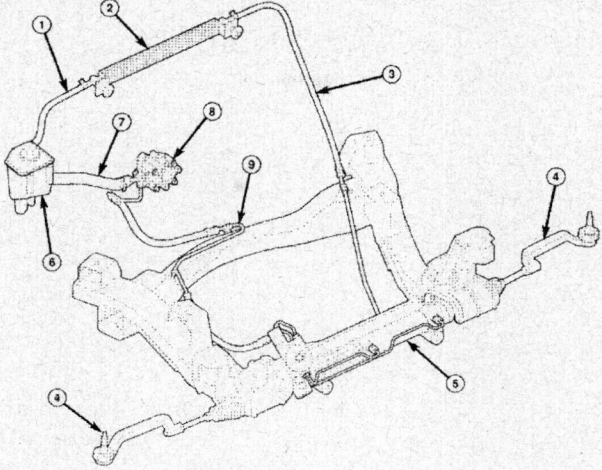

1- RETURN HOSES
2- OIL COOLER
3- RETURN HOSES
4- OUTER TIE ROD ENDS
5- RACK & PINION STEERING GEAR
6- REMOTE RESERVOIR
7- SUPPLY HOSES
8- BELT DRIVEN HYDRAULIC STEERING PUMP
9- PUMP PRESSURE HOSES

ARM0400000000631

Fig. 3 Power steering system. AWD

DRIVESHAFT
REPLACE

Halfshaft inner and outer boots are not serviceable separately. Boot replacement requires entire shaft assembly replacement.

Lefthand halfshaft is shorter than right. Identify and tag halfshafts upon removal to ensure proper installation.

1. Raise and support vehicle, then remove tire and wheel assembly.
2. While holding link ball joint stem from rotating, remove stabilizer link to shock clevis bracket nut.
3. Slide link ball joint stem from clevis bracket.
4. Remove clevis bracket to bottom of shock nut and pinch bolt.
5. Remove shock clevis bracket to lower control arm nut and bolt.
6. Pull lower end of clevis bracket outward away from lower control arm bushing, then slide it off shock.
7. While helper applies brakes to keep hub from rotating, remove hub nut from axle half shaft.
8. Remove two mounting bolts, then the disc brake caliper and adapter from knuckle.
9. Hang assembly aside using suitable wire. **Do not overextend brake hose.**
10. Remove wheel studs' clips, then slide brake rotor off hub and bearing.
11. Separate upper ball joint stud from knuckle using puller tool No. 9360, or equivalent, **Do not damage ball joint seal boot.**
12. Remove upper ball joint stud nut.

13. Remove wheel speed sensor to knuckle clip.
14. Disconnect righthand halfshaft from axle and remove.
15. Remove lefthand halfshaft.
16. Remove four assembly-to-oil pan mounting bolts and intermediate shaft.
17. Reverse procedure to install, noting the following:
    a. Install new axle seal using driver tool No. C-4193-A, or equivalent.
    b. Ensure isolation washer is present on end of half shaft. Washer is bi-directional and can be installed in either direction on shaft.
    c. Lubricate halfshaft inner joint bearing journal with Mopar Gear and Axle Lubricant 75W-140, or equivalent.
    d. Install new circlip(s).

BALL JOINT
REPLACE

Lower

1. Remove knuckle as outlined under "Steering Knuckle, Replace."
2. Remove bottom ball joint snap ring using suitable snap-ring pliers.
3. Support knuckle and ball joint using support clamp tool No. 9320-1, or equivalent.
4. Remove ball joint using press tool No. C-4212F, or equivalent, and suitable vice.
5. Reverse procedure to install.

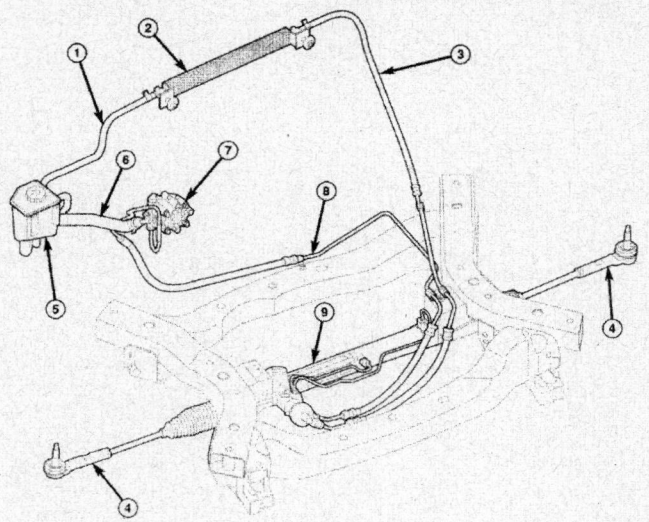

1- RETURN HOSES
2- OIL COOLER
3- RETURN HOSES
4- INNER & OUTER TIE ROD ENDS
5- REMOTE RESERVOIR
6- SUPPLY HOSES
7- BELT DRIVEN HYDRAULIC STEERING PUMP
8- PUMP PRESSURE HOSES
9- RACK & PINION STEERING GEAR

ARM0400000000632

Fig. 4   Power steering system. RWD

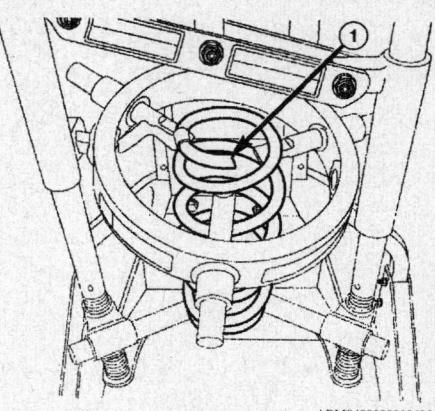

ARM0400000000635

Fig. 5   Coil spring alignment

Upper

The upper ball joint is pressed into the upper control arm. The ball joint is a sealed for life component and cannot be maintenance lubricated. Neither the upper ball joint, nor the seal boot can be serviced as a separate component. The entire upper control arm must be replaced if either are damaged.

COIL SPRING

REPLACE

Refer to "Coil Spring & Strut Service" for coil spring replacement procedure.

STRUT

REPLACE

AWD

1. Raise and support vehicle, then remove tire and wheel assembly.
2. While holding link ball joint stem from rotating, remove stabilizer link to shock clevis bracket nut.
3. Slide link ball joint stem from clevis bracket.
4. Remove clevis bracket to bottom of strut shock mounting nut and pinch bolt.

5. Remove strut clevis bracket to lower control arm mounting nut and bolt.
6. Pull lower end of clevis bracket outward away from lower control arm bushing, then slide it off strut.
7. Lower vehicle just enough to access upper strut mounting nuts.
8. Remove strut tower cap, three nuts and strut.
9. Reverse procedure to install.

RWD

1. Remove front strut tower cap and upper three mounting nuts.
2. Raise and support vehicle, then remove tire and wheel assembly.
3. Remove stabilizer link to strut mounting nut.
4. Slide link ball joint stem from strut.
5. Remove strut to lower control arm mounting bolt.
6. Disconnect wheel speed sensor cable routing clip at brake tube bracket.
7. Loosen upper ball joint stud to knuckle nut. Back nut off until nut is even with end of stud.
8. Separate upper ball joint stud from knuckle using puller tool No. 9360, or equivalent. **Do not damage ball joint seal boot.**
9. Remove end of upper ball joint stud nut and tip knuckle top outward. **Do not overextend brake flex hose.**
10. Remove strut.
11. Reverse procedure to install.

COIL SPRING & STRUT SERVICE

Left and righthand springs must not be interchanged.
1. Remove strut as outlined under "Strut, Replace."
2. Position strut coil spring on spring compressor tool No. W-7200, or equivalent, hooks.
3. Install clamp securing shock to lower spring coil.
4. Position compressor tool upper hooks on upper coil spring.
5. Rotate strut as required positioning shock in compressor so that upper spring coil ends (step in upper mount) at straight outward position from tool.
6. Compress coil spring until all spring tension is removed from upper mount.
7. Holding shaft from turning using position wrench tool No. 9362, or equivalent, remove shaft nut.
8. Remove clamp from bottom of coil spring, then the strut and lower isolator out through bottom of coil spring.
9. Remove upper mount from shaft and coil spring.
10. Mark lower spring coil end relationship to compressor for assembly alignment.
11. Back off compressor drive and releasing tension from coil spring.
12. Push back compressor upper hooks and remove coil spring from tool.
13. Remove jounce bumper from shaft by pulling straight up and off.
14. Remove lower isolator from body by pulling straight up and off shaft.
15. Reverse procedure to assemble, noting the following:
    a. Place coil spring with part number tag end upward in compressor lower hooks.
    b. Rotate coil spring around until upper coil ends at straight outward position from compressor, **Fig. 5.**
    c. Install jounce bumper on shock shaft, small end first.

CONTROL ARM
REPLACE

Lower

AWD

1. Raise and support vehicle, then remove tire and wheel assembly.
2. While helper applies brakes to keep hub from rotating, remove hub nut from the axle half shaft.
3. Remove mounting screws and belly pan.
4. Loosen lower control arm ball joint stud to knuckle nut. Back nut off until nut is even with end of stud.
5. Separate ball joint stud from knuckle using puller tool No. 9360, or equivalent. **Do not damage ball joint seal boot.**
6. Remove nut from end of ball joint stud.
7. Back off shock clevis bracket to lower control arm nut until it is flush with end of bolt.
8. Tap bolt out of clevis bracket until bolt serrations clear bracket using suitable brass drift punch.
9. Remove clevis bracket and control arm mounting nut and bolt.
10. Remove mounting screws and heat shields above both inner tie rod bellows.
11. On lefthand side arm, remove bolts (3) and (4), **Fig. 6.** Loosen, but do not remove bolt. **Do not drop gear too far.**
12. One righthand side arm, remove bolts (2) and (3). Loosen, but do not remove bolt (4).
13. Remove bolt and nut securing rearward end of lower control arm to engine cradle. If lower control arm bolt at engine cradle has lengthwise grooved shaft, note the following:
    a. Bolt is special wheel alignment adjustment bolt.
    b. Bolt head must not be rotated in vehicle or damage to bolt and engine cradle will result.
    c. While holding bolt in place with suitable wrench, remove nut.
    d. Slide bolt out of bushing and cradle recording of bolt positioning in engine cradle for installation alignment.
    e. Bolt needs to be installed in same position as removed to ensure wheel camber and caster return to adjusted position.
14. Slide lower control arm from engine cradle and knuckle.
15. Reverse procedure to install. Install new ball joint stud nuts.

RWD

1. Raise and support vehicle, then remove tire and wheel assembly.
2. Remove mounting screws and belly pan.
3. Remove stabilizer bar heat shield mounting screws on side of control arm repair.
4. Remove stabilizer bar bushing retainer mounting bolts on side of control arm repair.

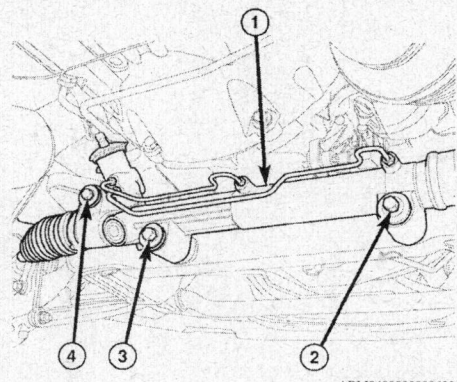

Fig. 6   Steering gear replacement. AWD

5. Remove retainer halves from around stabilizer bar bushing.
6. Utilizing slit, remove bushing from stabilizer bar.
7. Remove bolt and nut securing lower control arm to engine cradle. If lower control arm bolt at engine cradle has lengthwise grooved shaft, note the following:
    a. Bolt is special wheel alignment adjustment bolt.
    b. Bolt head must not be rotated in vehicle or damage to bolt and engine cradle will result.
    c. While holding bolt in place with suitable wrench, remove nut.
    d. Slide bolt out of bushing and cradle recording of bolt positioning in engine cradle for installation alignment.
    e. Bolt needs to be installed in same position as removed to ensure wheel camber and caster return to adjusted position.
8. Remove strut to lower control mounting bolt.
9. Remove wheel speed sensor to knuckle mounting screw. Remove sensor head.
10. Remove wheel speed sensor cable routing clip from brake flex hose routing bracket.
11. Loosen ball joint stud to lower control arm nut. Back nut off until nut is even with end of stud.
12. Separate ball joint stud from lower control arm using puller, tool No. 9360, or equivalent.
13. Remove nut from end of ball joint stud attaching lower control arm to knuckle.
14. Pry knuckle downward and slide ball joint stud out of lower control arm.
15. Position knuckle outward, away from lower control arm. Slide lower control arm out of engine cradle.
16. Reverse procedure to install.
    a. Measure height of ball joint seal boot mounted on knuckle, **Fig. 7.**
    b. If seal boot height is above 1.00 inch, any air inside seal boot must be expelled.
    c. Tip ball joint stud completely to one side. Using thumb and index finger, gently squeeze seal boot together at center expelling any air. **Do not**

allow grease to be release.
    d. Push down very top of seal boot.
    e. Return ball joint stud to original centered position.
    f. Install new ball joint stud nuts.

Upper

Although AWD and RWD upper control arms are similar, they are not interchangeable.

1. **When removing lefthand upper control arm,** proceed as follows:
    a. Remove coolant recovery container pressure cap.
    b. Remove and plug coolant recovery tube.
    c. Remove mounting nuts and position coolant recovery container aside.
2. **When removing rightright upper control arm,** proceed as follows:
    a. Open battery cable nut cover.
    b. Remove battery cable nut and cable from the Integrated Power Module (IPM).
    c. Disconnect outboard retaining clip and rotate IPM to access wire harness connectors.
    d. Disconnect wire harness connectors.
    e. Disconnect inboard retaining clips and remove IPM.
3. **On all models,** remove front shock tower cap and three upper strut mounting nuts.
4. Remove nuts from upper control arm mounting bolts.
5. Raise and support vehicle, then remove tire and wheel assembly.
6. Disconnect wheel speed sensor cable routing clip at brake tube bracket.
7. Loosen upper ball joint stud to knuckle mounting nut. Back nut off until nut is even with end of stud.
8. Separate upper ball joint stud from knuckle using puller tool No. 9360, or equivalent. **Do not damage ball joint seal boot.**
9. Remove nut from end of upper ball joint stud.
10. Pull strut downward until its clear shock tower, then pull it outward allowing access to upper control arm mounting bolts.
11. Remove mounting bolts and upper control arm.
12. Reverse procedure to install.

STEERING KNUCKLE
REPLACE

AWD

1. Raise and support vehicle, then remove tire and wheel assembly.
2. While helper applies brakes to keep hub from rotating, remove hub nut from axle half shaft.
3. Remove clip fastening wheel speed sensor to knuckle.

4. Remove screw fastening wheel speed sensor) to knuckle.
5. Pull sensor head out of knuckle.
6. Remove two mounting bolts, then the caliper and adapter. Hang assembly aside using suitable wire. **Do not overextend brake hose.**
7. Remove nut from outer tie rod end) stud.
8. Separate tie rod stud from knuckle using puller tool No. 9360, or equivalent.
9. Loosen lower control arm ball joint stud to knuckle nut. Back nut off until nut is even with end of stud.
10. Separate ball joint stud from knuckle using puller tool No. 9360, or equivalent. **Do not damage ball joint seal boot.**
11. Remove ball joint stud nut.
12. Loosen nut attaching upper ball joint stud to knuckle. Back nut off until nut is even with end of stud.
13. Separate ball joint stud from knuckle using puller tool No. 9360, or equivalent. **Do not damage ball joint seal boot.**
14. Remove nut from end of upper ball joint stud.
15. Slide knuckle off half shaft and remove.
16. If hub and bearing, and dust shield are to be removed, remove four mounting bolts, then slide hub and bearing out of knuckle along with shield.
17. Reverse procedure to install, noting the following:
    a. Ensure isolation washer is present on end of half shaft. Washer can be installed in either direction on shaft.
    b. Install new ball joint stud nuts.

RWD

1. Raise and support vehicle, then remove tire and wheel assembly.
2. Remove fastening wheel speed sensor to knuckle mounting screw. Pull sensor head out of knuckle
3. Remove wheel speed sensor cable routing clip from brake flex hose routing bracket.
4. Remove brake flex hose routing bracket to knuckle mounting screw.
5. Remove two mounting bolts, then the brake caliper and adapter. Hang assembly aside using suitable wire.
6. Remove nut from outer tie rod end stud.
7. Separate tie rod stud from knuckle using puller tool No. 9360, or equivalent.
8. Loosen nut attaching upper ball joint stud to knuckle. Back nut off until nut is even with end of stud.
9. Separate upper ball joint stud from knuckle using puller tool No. 9360, or equivalent. **Do not damage ball joint seal boot.**
10. Remove nut from end of upper ball joint stud.
11. Loosen nut attaching tension strut ball joint stud to knuckle. Back nut off until nut is even with end of stud.
12. Separate strut ball joint stud from knuckle using puller tool No. 9360, or

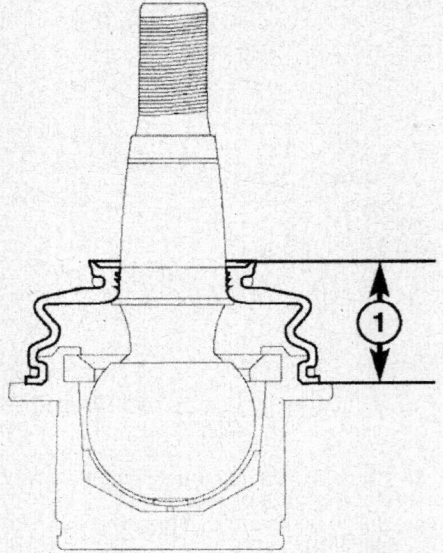

ARM0400000000634

Fig. 7 Ball joint seal boot measurement

equivalent. **Do not damage ball joint seal boot.**
13. Remove nut from end of tension strut ball joint stud.
14. Loosen nut attaching ball joint stud to lower control arm. Back nut off until nut is even with end of stud.
15. Separate ball joint stud from lower control arm using puller tool No. 9360, or equivalent. **Do not damage ball joint seal boot.**
16. Remove nut from end of ball joint stud attaching lower control arm to knuckle. Remove knuckle.
17. If hub and bearing, and dust shield are to be removed, remove four mounting bolts, then slide hub and bearing out of knuckle along with shield.
18. Reverse procedure to install.
    a. Install new dust cap.
    b. Measure height of ball joint seal boot mounted on knuckle, **Fig. 7.**
    c. If seal boot height is above 1.00 inch, any air inside seal boot must be expelled.
    d. Tip ball joint stud completely to one side. Using thumb and index finger, gently squeeze seal boot together at center expelling any air. **Do not allow grease to be release.**
    e. Push down very top of seal boot.
    f. Return ball joint stud to original centered position.
    g. Install new ball joint stud nuts.

STABILIZER BAR
REPLACE
AWD

1. Raise and support vehicle.
2. Remove mounting screws and belly pan.
3. On each side of vehicle, remove stabilizer link to stabilizer bar mounting nut.
4. Slide link ball joint stem from bar.

5. On each side of vehicle, remove stabilizer bar isolator retainer mounting bolts.
6. Remove stabilizer bar with isolators and retainers.
7. On each side of bar, remove stabilizer bar isolators retainers.
8. Utilizing slit and remove each isolator.
9. Reverse procedure to install, noting the following:
    a. Ensure isolator slit is positioned toward rear of vehicle.
    b. Ensure link ball joint stem is pointed inboard toward engine cradle.

RWD

1. Raise and support vehicle.
2. Remove mounting screws and belly pan.
3. On each side of vehicle, remove mounting screws and stabilizer bar heat shield.
4. On each side of vehicle, remove stabilizer bar isolator retainer mounting bolts.
5. On each side of vehicle, remove stabilizer bar isolator retainer halves.
6. Remove each isolator utilizing slit.
7. On each side of vehicle, remove stabilizer link to stabilizer bar mounting nut.
8. Slide link ball joint stem from bar and remove bar.
9. Reverse procedure to install, noting the following:
    a. Ensure link ball joint stem is pointed inboard toward engine cradle.
    b. Ensure sure slit in isolator is positioned toward rear of vehicle.

TENSION STRUT
REPLACE

1. Raise and support vehicle, then remove tire and wheel assembly.
2. Remove mounting screws and belly pan.
3. Loosen tension strut ball joint stud to knuckle mounting nut. Back nut off until nut is even with end of stud.
4. Separate tension strut ball joint stud from knuckle using puller special tool No. 9360, or equivalent. **Do not damage ball joint seal boot.**
5. Remove nut from end of tension strut ball joint stud.
6. Rotate knuckle outward and push ball joint upward, out of knuckle.
7. Remove bolt and nut securing tension strut to engine cradle. If lower tension strut bolt at engine cradle has lengthwise grooved shaft, note the following:
    a. Bolt is special wheel alignment adjustment bolt.
    b. Bolt head must not be rotated in vehicle or damage to bolt and engine cradle will result.
    c. While holding bolt in place with suitable wrench, remove nut.
    d. Slide bolt out of bushing and cradle recording of bolt positioning in engine cradle for installation alignment.

e. Bolt needs to be installed in same position as removed to ensure wheel camber and caster return to adjusted position.
8. Slide tension strut out of cradle bracket.
9. Reverse procedure to install. Install new ball joint stud nuts.

TIE ROD

REPLACE

Outer

1. Raise and support vehicle, then remove tire and wheel assembly.
2. Remove clamp at inner tie rod and ensuring bellows moves freely before rotating inner tie rod. **Do not twist bellows at inner tie rod.**
3. Loosen tie rod jam nut at outer tie rod.
4. Remove outer tie rod end nut at knuckle.
5. Separate outer tie rod end from knuckle using remover tool No. 9630, or equivalent.
6. Unthread outer tie rod from inner tie rod. Count number of turns when removing outer tie rod for good starting point when installing and setting toe.
7. Reverse procedure to install.

POWER STEERING GEAR

REPLACE

1. Center steering wheel and lock it with suitable steering wheel holder.
2. Siphon power steering fluid from pump reservoir.
3. Raise and support vehicle, then remove both front tire and wheel assemblies.
4. Remove clamp at inner tie rod and ensure bellows moves freely before rotating inner tie rod. **Do not twist bellows at inner tie rod.**
5. Loosen tie rod jam nut at each outer tie rod.
6. Remove outer tie rod end nut at each knuckle.
7. Separate outer tie rod from each knuckle using remover tool No. 9630, or equivalent.
8. Fully extend or pull out adjustable steering column.
9. Remove pinch bolt connecting steering shaft to lower steering coupling shaft.

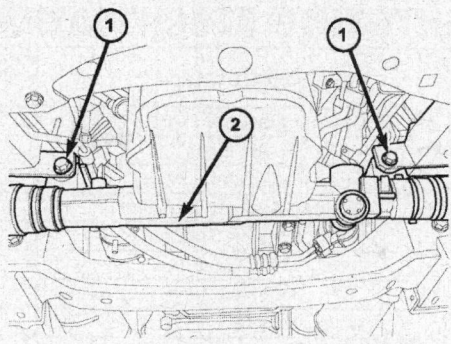

Fig. 8   Steering gear replacement. RWD

10. Separate lower coupling from steering shaft.
11. Remove pinch bolt from steering coupling at steering gear.
12. Slide coupling from steering gear.
13. Unthread tube nut from steering gear and remove return hose from steering gear.
14. Unthread tube nut and remove pressure hose from steering gear.
15. Remove mounting screws and heat shield above each inner tie rod bellows.
16. **On models equipped with AWD,** proceed as follows:
    a. Remove steering gear upper mounting bolt and nut, **Fig. 6.**
    b. Remove lower mounting bolts and steering gear.
17. **On models equipped with RWD,** remove mounting bolts and steering gear, **Fig. 8.**
18. **On all models,** reverse procedure to install.
    a. Install new O-ring lubricated with suitable, clean power steering fluid on steering hoses' ends.
    b. Install new pinch bolts to steering couplings.

POWER STEERING PUMP

REPLACE

1. Siphon power steering fluid from pump reservoir.
2. Disconnect Mass Air Flow (MAF) sensor electrical connector.
3. Remove clean air duct between throttle body and air filter housing.
4. Remove vent tube.

5. Remove mounting bolt and air filter housing.
6. Raise and support vehicle.
7. Remove wheel house splash shield rivets three per side.
8. Remove nine belly pan mounting screws.
9. Remove two fascia to fender screw (one per side).
10. Open hood and remove upper push pin fasteners (four per sedan and six per wagon), then partially remove front fascia.
11. Remove mounting bolt and air cleaner resonator.
12. Rotate belt tensioner counterclockwise until it contacts it's stop.
13. Remove belt and slowly rotate tensioner into **Do not let tensioner arm snap back to the freearm position.**
14. Remove hose clamp and supply hose from pump.
15. Unthread tube nut and remove pressure hose from pump.
16. Remove three mounting bolts through pulley access holes and pump from engine bracket.
17. Reverse procedure to install. Install new O-rings lubricated with suitable, clean power steering fluid

POWER STEERING SYSTEM BLEED

1. Wipe filler cap clean and inspect fluid level.
2. Turn steering wheel all way to left.
3. Fill pump fluid reservoir to proper level and let fluid settle for least two minutes.
4. Raise and support front wheels off ground.
5. Slowly turn steering wheel lock-to-lock 20 times with engine off while inspecting fluid level. Vehicles with long return lines or oil coolers turn wheel 40 times.
6. Start engine.
7. With engine idling maintain fluid level.
8. Lower front wheels and let engine idle for two minutes.
9. Turn steering wheel in both direction, and verify power assist and quiet operation of pump.
10. If fluid is extremely foamy or milky looking, allow vehicle to stand few minutes and repeat procedure. **Do not run vehicle with foamy fluid for an extended period.**

TIGHTENING SPECIFICATIONS

Year	Component	Torque Ft. Lbs.
2005–08	Air Cleaner Resonator (2.7L & 3.5L)	89①
	Air Filter	89①
	Ball Stud Joint	35②
	Caliper Adapter To Knuckle	125
	Engine Cradle	136
	Hub Bearing	50
	Hub Nut, AWD	157
	Hub Nut, RWD	184
	Intermediate Shaft-To-Oil Pan	18
	Knuckle Dust Shield	89①
	Lower Control Arm, Ball Joint (AWD)	90
	Lower Control Arm, Ball Joint (RWD)	50②
	Lower Control Arm, Cradle	130
	Outer Tie Rod Ball Joint	63
	Power Steering Gear (AWD)	75
	Power Steering Gear (RWD)	70
	Power Steering Hose Tube	35
	Power Steering Pump	21
	Stabilizer Bar, Heat Shield	62①
	Stabilizer Bar, Isolator Retainer	44
	Stabilizer Bar, Link (Lower)	95
	Stabilizer Bar, Link (Upper)	95
	Steering Coupling Lower Shaft Pinch Bolt	23
	Steering Coupling To Steering Gear Pinch Bolt	40
	Steering Gear	90
	Strut, Clevis Bracket (Lower)	128
	Strut, Clevis Bracket (Pinch)	45
	Strut, Lower (RWD)	128
	Strut, Shaft	70
	Strut, Upper	20
	Tension Strut, Cradle	130
	Tension Strut, Ball Joint	50②
	Tie Rod Jam Nut	55
	Upper Control Arm, Ball Joint	35②
	Wheel Lug Nut	110

① — Inch lbs.
② — Tighten an additional 90°.

Wheel Alignment

NOTE: On Air Bag Equipped Models, Refer To "Air Bag System Precautions" Located In The Front Of This Manual For System Disarming & Arming Procedures.

NOTE: Refer To "Computer Relearn Procedures" Located In The Front Of This Manual When Battery Power To The Computer Has Been Interrupted.

NOTE: Prior To Performing Any Service Operations Listed In This Section, Consult The "Technical Service Bulletins" Section For Related Information.

NOTE: Refer To The Rear Of This Manual For Vehicle Manufacturer's Special Tool Suppliers.

INDEX

	Page No.		Page No.		Page No.
Front Wheel Alignment	6-53	Toe	6-54	**Technical Service Bulletins**	6-55
Camber & Caster	6-53	**Preliminary Inspection**	6-53	Lead To Right	6-55
Adjustment Bolt Package		**Rear Wheel Alignment**	6-55	**Wheel Alignment**	
Installation	6-54	Toe	6-55	**Specifications**	6-3
Adjustment By Shifting					
Cradle	6-53				

PRELIMINARY INSPECTION

Before any attempt is made to change or correct the wheel alignment, the following inspection and required corrections must be made to ensure proper alignment.

1. Ensure fuel tank is full of fuel.
2. Ensure passenger and luggage compartments are free of any load that is not factory equipment.
3. Ensure all tires are same size and in good condition with approximately same amount of tread wear.
4. Inflate all tires to recommended air pressure.
5. Inspect wheel and tire assemblies for excessive radial runout.
6. Inspect lower ball joints and all steering linkage for looseness, binding, wear or damage.
7. Inspect suspension fasteners for proper torque.
8. Inspect all suspension component rubber bushings for signs of wear or deterioration.
9. Inspect vehicle's curb height to ensure it is within specifications.

FRONT WHEEL ALIGNMENT

On this vehicle, four-wheel alignment is recommended.

1. Position vehicle on alignment rack.
2. Install all required alignment equipment on vehicle per alignment equipment manufacturers instructions
3. Prior to reading vehicle's alignment readouts, front and rear of vehicle should be jounced (suspension compressed/released).
4. Induce jounce (rear first, then front) by grasping center of bumper and jouncing each end of vehicle an equal number of times.
5. Bumper should always be released when vehicle is at bottom of jounce cycle.
6. Record vehicle's current front and rear alignment settings. Compare settings to vehicle specifications for camber, caster and toe-in.
7. If caster and camber are within specifications, proceed to roe.
8. Rear camber and caster are not adjustable. If found not to be within specifications, inspect for damaged suspension or body components.
9. If rear toe is not within specifications, adjust rear toe before proceeding to adjust front toe.

Camber & Caster

Camber and caster settings on this vehicle are determined at the time the vehicle is designed, by the location of the vehicle's suspension components. This is referred to as net build. The result is no required adjustment of camber and caster after the vehicle is built or when servicing the suspension components. Thus, when performing a wheel alignment, caster and camber are not normally considered adjustable angles.

Camber and caster should be inspected to ensure they meet vehicle specifications.

If individual front camber or caster is found not to meet alignment specifications, each can be adjusted by shifting the engine cradle if cross-camber and cross-caster are within specifications, or by using an available service adjustment bolt package. Always try to shift the cradle first (if camber and caster are off slightly) to correct the misalignment before installing an adjustment bolt package. If an adjustment bolt package installation is required, inspect the suspension components for any signs of damage or bending first.

Do not attempt to adjust the vehicles wheel alignment by heating, bending or by performing any other modification to the vehicle's front suspension components or body.

ADJUSTMENT BY SHIFTING CRADLE

1. Loosen four engine cradle mounting bolts enough to allow movement of cradle, **Fig. 1**.
2. Shift cradle to bring camber or caster into specifications. **When shifting cradle, use care not to move other angles (camber or caster) that are within specifications, out of specifications.**
3. Tighten four mounting bolts.
4. Jounce rear, then front of vehicle an equal amount of times.
5. Measure camber and caster.
6. If camber and caster are within specifications, proceed to roe.
7. If camber or caster cannot be brought into specifications, perform the "Adjustment Bolt Package Installation."

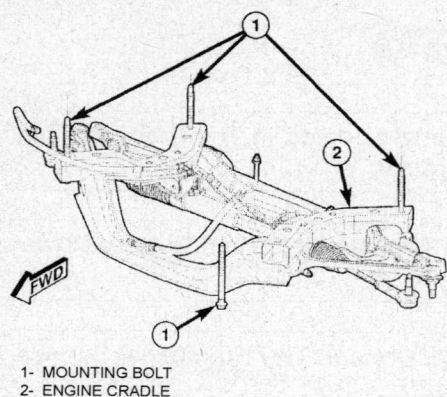

1- MOUNTING BOLT
2- ENGINE CRADLE

ARM0400000000619

Fig. 1 Engine cradle adjustment

ADJUSTMENT BOLT PACKAGE INSTALLATION

Adjustment bolts for AWD and RWD are not interchangeable.
1. Adjustment bolt package contains two special bolts, **Fig. 2.**
2. These bolts can be identified by offset grooves cut into thread section.
3. These bolts are designed to replace inboard mounting bolts of lower control arm at engine cradle.
4. Each bolt allows approximately .3° movement.
5. **To adjust camber only,** use both bolts, one at each leg of control arm.
6. **To adjust caster only,** use one bolt at front leg only.
7. **On all models,** raise and support vehicle by frame until tires are not supporting vehicle weight.
8. Remove mounting screws and front belly pan.
9. **On models equipped with AWD,** proceed as follows:
   a. Remove mounting screws and heat shields covering steering gear inner tie rod boots.
   b. Loosen (do not remove) steering gear mounting bolt furthest from side of adjustment bolt installation.
   c. Remove two remaining mounting bolts and allow steering gear to relax on side of adjustment bolt installation, proving access to lower control arm rear mounting bolt.
10. **On models equipped with RWD,** proceed as follows:
   a. Remove mounting screws and heat shields covering stabilizer bar bushing retainers to cradle.
   b. Remove four stabilizer bar bushing retainers mounting bolts, then position stabilizer bar rearward and down out of way of control arm mounting bolts.
11. **On all models,** hold head of control arm or tension strut mounting bolt stationary and remove nut. **Do not rotate bolt.**

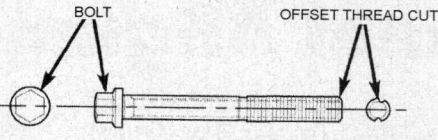

BOLT   OFFSET THREAD CUT

ARM0400000000620

Fig. 2 Adjustment bolt

12. Slide bolt straight out of bushing and discard. **Do not damage bat wings in bushing inner metal or cradle.**
13. **When installing an adjustment bolt, ensure it is install in correct direction. Lower control arm rear mounting bolts must be installed from rear-forward and lower control arm front mounting bolts must be installed from front-rearward.**
14. Grooves on adjustment bolts are off-center forcing bolt to be installed in one of two ways depending on whether more positive or negative camber or caster is required. Bolts must be rotated 180° to achieve either more positive or negative camber or caster.
15. **Do not force adjustment bolt.**
16. **To achieve more positive camber,** proceed as follows:
   a. Move control arm in desired direction.
   b. Insert adjustment bolt with washer installed through bat wing hole in engine cradle and round hole in bushing inner metal, **Fig. 3.**
17. **To achieve more negative camber,** proceed as follows:
   a. Move control arm in desired direction.
   b. Insert adjustment bolt with washer installed through bat wing hole in engine cradle and round hole in bushing inner metal, **Fig. 4.**
18. **To achieve more positive caster,** proceed as follows:
   a. Move lower control arm in desired direction.
   b. Insert adjustment bolt with washer installed through bat wing hole in engine cradle and round hole in bushing inner metal, **Fig. 3.**
19. **To achieve more negative caster,** proceed as follows:
   a. Move lower control arm in desired direction.
   b. Insert adjustment bolt with washer installed through bat wing hole engine cradle and round hole in bushing inner metal, **Fig. 4.**
20. **On all adjustments,** start new nut and washer (on RWD vehicles) on end of mounting bolt by hand, then while holding head of bolt stationary, install nut. **Do not tighten nut now.**
21. Install steering gear and heat shields.
22. Lower vehicle to curb position.
23. Jounce rear, then front of vehicle an equal amount of times.
24. **Torque** adjustment bolt nut using suitable crowfoot wrench to 130 ft. lbs., while holding bolt stationary. Socket on

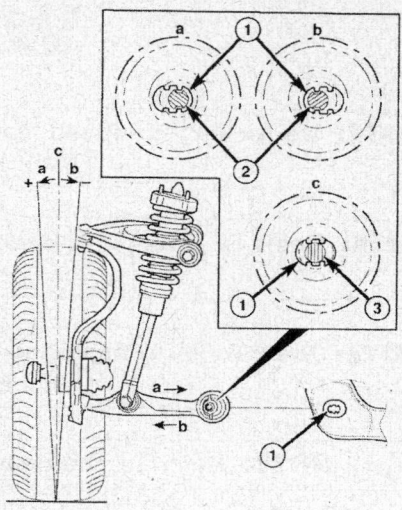

1- ENGINE CRADLE
2- ADJUSTMENT BOLT
3- ORIGINAL (NON-GROOVED) MOUNTING BOLT

ARM0400000000621

Fig. 3 Positive camber adjustment

end of breaker bar works well for holding rear bolt stationary with steering gear is installed.
25. Measure camber and caster.
26. If camber and caster are not within specifications, inspect suspension components for any signs of damage or bending.
27. If camber and caster (and cross-camber and cross-caster) are within specifications, proceed with toe to inspect and adjust toe.
28. Install the belly pan.

Toe

When performing the toe adjustment procedure, set rear toe to specifications before setting front toe.

Do not twist the inner tie rod-to-steering gear boots during front wheel toe adjustment.

Perform the following procedure to each side of the vehicle as required.
1. Center steering wheel and lock in place using suitable steering wheel clamp.
2. Remove boot clamps at inner tie rods and ensure boots move freely on inner tie rods.
3. Loosen jam nut at inner-to-outer tie rod connection, **Figs. 5 and 6.**
4. Grasp inner tie rod at hex and rotate as required to adjust front toe.
5. **Torque** tie rod jam nut to 55 ft. lbs.
6. Ensure inner tie rod-to-steering gear boot is not twisted, then install boot clamp at inner tie rod.
7. Adjust front toe on opposite side as outlined in previous steps.

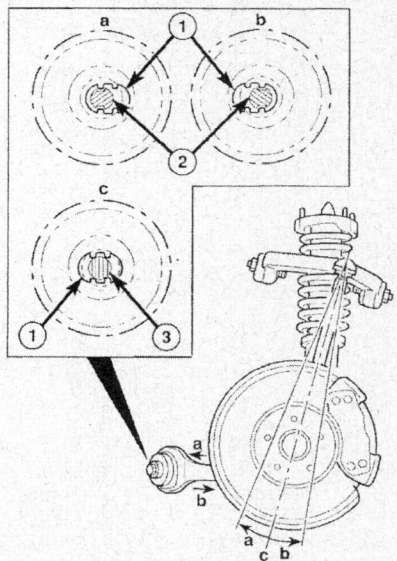

1- ENGINE CRADLE
2- ADJUSTMENT BOLT
3- ORIGINAL (NON-GROOVED) MOUNTING BOLT

ARM0400000000622

Fig. 4   Negative camber adjustment

REAR WHEEL ALIGNMENT

Rear camber and caster are not adjustable. If found not to be within specifications, inspect for damaged suspension or body components If rear toe is not within specifications, adjust rear toe before proceeding to adjust front toe.

Toe

When performing the toe adjustment procedure, set rear toe to specifications before setting front toe.

1. Center steering wheel and lock in place using suitable steering wheel clamp.
2. Loosen toe link to rear crossmember cam bolt nut (front of rear crossmember) just enough to rotate cam bolt, **Fig. 7.**

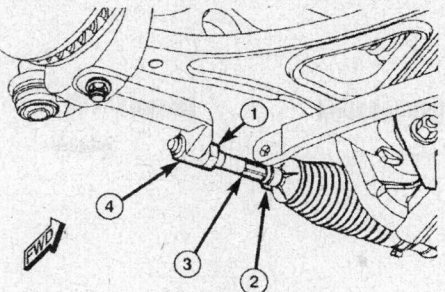

1- JAM NUT
2- CLAMP
3- INNER TIE ROD CONNECTION
4- OUTER TIE ROD CONNECTION

ARM0400000000626

Fig. 5   Jam nut. AWD

3. Rotate cam bolt head on opposite side (rear) of crossmember in either direction until preferred specification is obtained.**When adjusting rear toe, eccentric lobes on toe adjustment cam bolts and washers are not to be facing downward. Lobes should only be facing upward or up to 90° to one side or other from 12 O'clock position.**
4. While holding cam bolt from turning, tighten cam bolt nut.
5. Adjust rear toe on opposite side of vehicle as outlined in previous test.
6. Once rear toe is set, proceed to front toe to set vehicle's front toe.

TECHNICAL SERVICE BULLETINS

Lead To Right

Some of these vehicles built before April 25, 2004, may lead to right.

This condition may be caused by alignment bias.

To correct this condition, proceed as follows:

1. Ensure vehicle is not being affected by crown sensitivity (vehicle drives straight on flat road).
2. Adjust all four tire pressures to door placard standards.

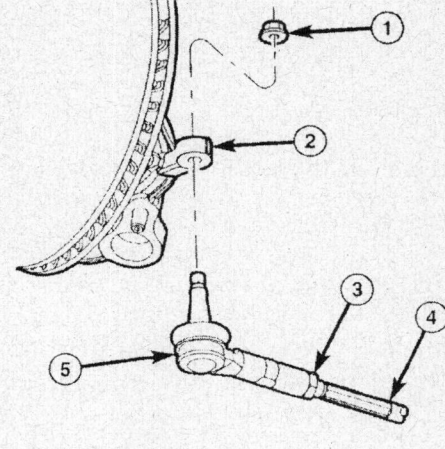

1- NUT
2- STEERING KNUCKLE
3- JAM NUT
4- INNER TIR ROD CONNECTION
5- OUTER TIE ROD CONNECTION

ARM0400000000627

Fig. 6   Jam nut. RWD

3. Ensure all four tires are same size and type.
4. Set alignment to specifications, noting the following:
   a. Set more caster on righthand side than on left.
   b. There will be more camber on left-hand side than right.
   c. Utilize cradle shift before using caster/camber adjustment bolt kit (part No. 05134117AA). adjustment bolts only provide approximately .2–.3° change.
   d. Shift cradle will move passenger's side forward and driver's side rearward.
   e. If installing adjustment bolt, do not allow bolt head to turn as cradle tension link joint or lower control arm bushing inner metal sleeve will be destroyed.
   f. Nut must be untorqued and removed before bolt.
   g. Once nut is removed, bolt can be slid out.

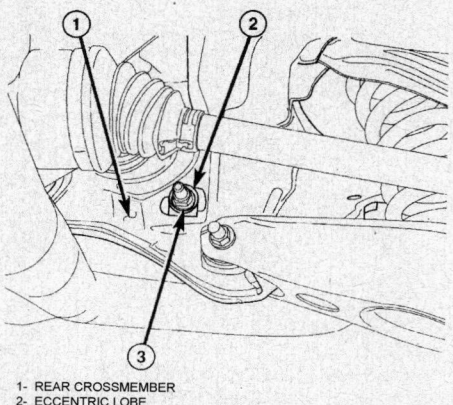

1- REAR CROSSMEMBER
2- ECCENTRIC LOBE
3- CAM BOLT

ARM0400000000623

**Fig. 7   Rear toe adjustment
(Part 1 of 2)**

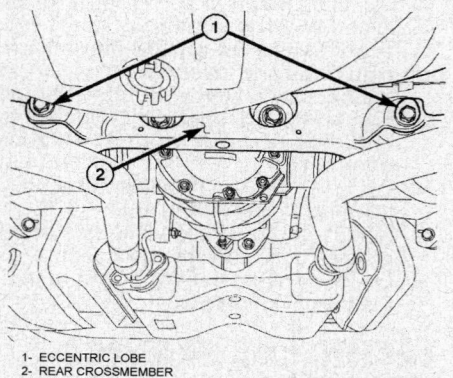

1- ECCENTRIC LOBE
2- REAR CROSSMEMBER

ARM0400000000624

**Fig. 7   Rear toe adjustment
(Part 2 of 2)**

CALIBER

INDEX OF SERVICE OPERATIONS

Page No.

**AIR BAG SYSTEM
PRECAUTIONS** 0-18
BRAKES
    Anti-Lock Brakes (Volume 2) .. 6-1
    Disc Brakes.............. 14-1
    Drum Brakes 15-1
    Hydraulic Brake Systems 16-1
    Power Brake Units 17-1
**COMPUTER RELEARN
PROCEDURE** 0-31
ELECTRICAL
    Air Bag System (Volume 2) ... 4-1
    Air Conditioning.............. 8-1
    Alternator, Replace 7-4
    Alternators 11-1
    Blower Motor, Replace........ 7-7
    Cabin Air Filter, Replace 7-7
    Cooling Fans 9-1
    Cruise Control (Volume 2) 2-1
    Dash Gauges (Volume 2) 1-1
    Dash Panel Service
    (Volume 2) 5-1
    Dimmer Switch, Replace...... 7-5
    Evaporator Core, Replace 7-8
    Fuel Pump Relay Location 7-4
    Fuse Panel & Flasher
    Location 7-4
    Headlamp Switch, Replace ... 7-5
    Heater Core, Replace......... 7-7
    Ignition Coil, Replace 7-4
    Ignition Lock, Replace 7-5
    Ignition Switch, Replace 7-5
    Instrument Cluster, Replace... 7-6
    Multi-Function Switch,
    Replace 7-5
    Neutral Safety Switch,
    Replace 7-5
    Passive Restraint Systems
    (Volume 2) 4-1
    Precautions.................... 7-4
    Radio, Replace 7-6
    Starter, Replace 7-4
    Speed Controls (Volume 2) ... 2-1
    Starter Motors 10-1
    Steering Columns............. 12-1
    Steering Wheel, Replace...... 7-5
    Stop Light Switch, Replace ... 7-5
    Technical Service Bulletins.... 7-8
    Turn Signal Switch, Replace .. 7-5
    Wiper Motor, Replace......... 7-6
    Wiper Switch, Replace........ 7-7
    Wiper Systems (Volume 2).... 3-1
    Wiper Transmission, Replace . 7-7
**ELECTRICAL SYMBOL
IDENTIFICATION** 0-63
FRONT DRIVE AXLES 18-1
**FRONT SUSPENSION &
STEERING**
    Ball Joint, Replace............ 7-27

Page No.

Coil Spring & Strut Service.... 7-27
Coil Spring, Replace 7-27
Control Arm, Replace 7-28
Description 7-26
Driveshaft, Replace 7-27
Hub & Bearing, Replace 7-26
Power Steering 13-1
Power Steering Gear,
Replace 7-28
Power Steering Pump,
Replace 7-29
Power Steering System
Bleed 7-29
Precautions................... 7-26
Stabilizer Bar, Replace........ 7-28
Steering Columns............. 12-1
Steering Knuckle, Replace.... 7-28
Strut, Replace 7-27
Tie Rod, Replace 7-28
Tightening Specifications...... 7-30
**NON-STANDARD TIRE &
WHEEL SIZE
ADJUSTMENT TO RIDE
HEIGHT SPECIFICATIONS
& TIRE SIZE CHART** 0-61
**REAR AXLE &
SUSPENSION**
    Coil Spring, Replace.......... 7-23
    Control Arm, Replace 7-23
    Description 7-22
    Differential Carrier, Replace... 7-22
    Hub & Bearing, Replace 7-22
    Hub & Bearing Service........ 7-22
    Precautions................... 7-22
    Propeller Shaft, Replace...... 7-22
    Rear Halfshaft, Replace....... 7-22
    Shock Absorber, Replace 7-22
    Stabilizer Bar, Replace........ 7-23
    Tightening Specifications...... 7-25
    Toe Link, Replace 7-23
    Trailing Link, Replace......... 7-23
**SERVICE REMINDER &
WARNING LAMP RESET
PROCEDURES** 0-34
SPECIFICATIONS
    Fluid Capacities & Cooling
    System Data................ 7-3
    Front Wheel Alignment
    Specifications................ 7-2
    General Engine
    Specifications................ 7-2
    Lubricant Data................ 7-3
    Rear Wheel Alignment
    Specifications................ 7-2
    Tune Up Specifications 7-2
    Vehicle Ride Height
    Specifications................ 7-3

Page No.

**TIRE PRESSURE
MONITORING SYSTEM** 20-1
**VEHICLE
IDENTIFICATION** 0-1
VEHICLE LIFT POINTS 0-51
**VEHICLE MAINTENANCE
SCHEDULES** 0-73
WHEEL ALIGNMENT
    Front Wheel Alignment........ 7-31
    Preliminary Inspection 7-31
    Rear Wheel Alignment 7-31
    Wheel Alignment
    Specifications................ 7-2
**WIRE COLOR CODE
IDENTIFICATION** 0-63
**1.8L, 2.0L & 2.4L
ENGINES**
    Belt Tension Data............. 7-17
    Camshaft, Replace 7-15
    Compression Pressure........ 7-11
    Cooling System Bleed 7-17
    Crankshaft Damper, Replace.. 7-14
    Crankshaft Rear Oil Seal,
    Replace 7-15
    Crankshaft Seal, Replace..... 7-15
    Cylinder Head, Replace....... 7-13
    Engine Rebuilding
    Specifications................ 21-1
    Engine, Replace 7-12
    Engine Mount, Replace 7-11
    Exhaust Manifold, Replace.... 7-13
    Front Cover, Replace 7-14
    Fuel Filter, Replace 7-18
    Fuel Pump, Replace 7-18
    Hydraulic Lifters, Replace..... 7-14
    Intake Manifold, Replace...... 7-12
    Main & Rod Bearings 7-15
    Oil Pan, Replace.............. 7-15
    Oil Pump, Replace............ 7-16
    Oil Pump Service 7-16
    Piston & Rod Assembly 7-15
    Precautions................... 7-11
    Radiator, Replace 7-18
    Rocker Arms, Replace 7-14
    Serpentine Drive Belt 7-17
    Thermostat, Replace.......... 7-17
    Tightening Specifications...... 7-21
    Timing Chain, Replace........ 7-14
    Timing Chain Tensioner,
    Replace 7-15
    Valve Adjustment 7-14
    Valve Clearance
    Specifications................ 7-14
    Valve Cover, Replace 7-13
    Water Pump, Replace 7-17

Specifications

GENERAL ENGINE SPECIFICATIONS

Engine	Engine Code①	Fuel System	Bore & Stroke, Inch	Comp. Ratio	Brake HP @ RPM	Maximum Torque, Ft. Lbs. @ RPM	Normal Oil Pressure, psi	
							Idle	3000 RPM
1.8L	C	MPI	3.386 x 3.047	10.5	148 @ 6500	125 @ 5200	4–6	25–80
2.0L	B	MPI	3.465 x 3.819	10.5	158 @ 6400	141 @ 5000	4–6	25–80
2.4L	K	MPI	3.465 x 3.819	10.5	172 @ 6000	165 @ 4400	4–6	25–80

MPI–Multi-Port Injection

① — Eighth digit of VIN denotes engine code.

TUNE UP SPECIFICATIONS

Engine	Spark Plug Gap, Inch	Firing Order Fig.	Ignition Timing		Idle Speed, RPM③	Fuel Pump Pressure, psi⑤	Valve Clearance, Inch
			°BTDC	Mark			
1.8L	.043	1–3–4–2	①	—	④	55–63	②
2.0L	.043	1–3–4–2	①	—	④	55–63	②
2.4L	.043	1–3–4–2	①	—	④	55–63	②

BTDC — Before Top Dead Center

① — Computer controlled. No adjustment.

② — Equipped w/hydraulic lifters. No adjustment is required.

③ — When inspecting idle speed, set parking brake & block drive wheels.

④ — Idle speed is controlled by an idle speed control motor.

⑤ — With shop towel wrapped around fuel pressure fitting to prevent fuel spillage, connect a suitable fuel pressure gauge. Inspect fuel pressure with ignition On, but engine not running.

FRONT WHEEL ALIGNMENT SPECIFICATIONS

Year	Manufacturer's Original Tire Size	Camber Angle, Degrees		Caster Angle, Degrees		Toe In, Degrees④		Ball Joint Wear
		Limits	Desired	Limits	Desired	Limits	Desired	
2007-08	15 Inch	−0.90 to −0.10	−0.50	①	②	0.00 to +0.40	+0.20	—
	17 Inch	−1.10 to −0.30	−0.70	①	②	0.00 to +0.40	+0.20	—
	18 Inch	−1.10 to −0.30	−0.70	③	④	0.00 to +0.40	+0.20	—

① — Left, +1.90° to +3.90°; Right, +1.60° to +3.60°.

② — Left, +2.90°; Right, +2.60°.

③ — Left, +2.00° to +4.00°; Right, +1.70° to +3.70°.

④ — Left, +3.00°; Right, +2.70°.

REAR WHEEL ALIGNMENT SPECIFICATIONS

Year	Manufacturer's Original Tire Size	Camber Angle, Degrees		Toe In, Degrees		Thrust Angle, Degrees	
		Limits	Desired	Limits	Desired	Limits	Desired
2007-08	15 Inch	−0.80 to 0.00	−0.40	0.00 to +0.40	+0.20	−0.10 to +0.10	0.00
	17 Inch	−1.00 to −0.20	−0.60	0.00 to +0.40	+0.20	−0.10 to +0.10	0.00
	18 Inch	−1.10 to −0.30	−0.70	0.00 to +0.40	+0.20	−0.10 to +0.10	0.00

VEHICLE RIDE HEIGHT SPECIFICATIONS

Model	Year	Body Style	Manufacturer's Original Tire Size	Measurement Points & Specifications①					
				Front			Rear		
				Fig.	Spec.		Fig.	Spec.	
					Inches	mm		Inches	mm
Caliber	2007-08	All	15 Inch	A	7.75–8.39	197–213	B	12.63–13.27	321–337
			17 & 18 Inch	A	8.11–8.75	206–222	B	12.99–13–63	330–346

Fig. — Figure

Fig. A. — On each side of the vehicle, measure the distance (2) from the center of the lower control arm pivot bolt head (1) to the floor or alignment rack/lift runway surface. It may be required to measure to the bottom of a straight edge (3), placed from lift runway to runway, to get an accurate measurement, **Fig. A.**

Fig. B. — On each side of the vehicle, measure the distance (2) from the center of the outboard trailing arm-to-body mounting bolt (1) to the floor or alignment rack/lift runway surface, **Fig. B.**

① — Measurement is with fuel, radiator coolant and engine oil full, spare tire, jack, hand tools and mats in designated positions and tires properly inflated.

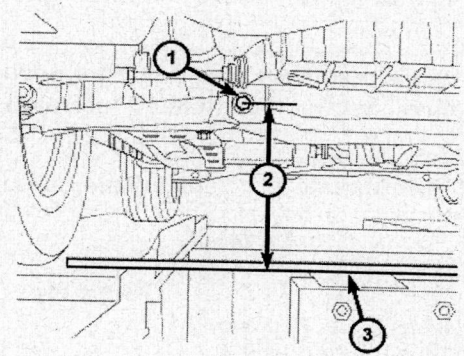

1. Lower control arm pivot bolt head
2. Ride height measurement (Front)
3. Straight edge

ARM0600000000166

Fig. A

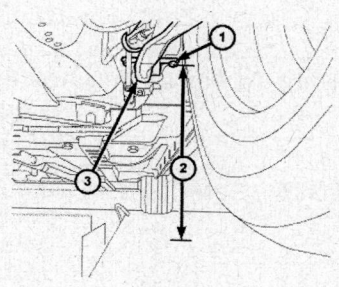

1. Center of the outboard trailing arm-to-body mounting bolt
2. Ride height measurement (Rear)
3. Outboard trailing arm

ARM0600000000167

Fig. B

FLUID CAPACITIES & COOLING SYSTEM DATA

Engine	Coolant Capacity, Qts.	Recommended Engine Coolant Type	Radiator Cap Relief Pressure, Lbs.	Thermostat. Opening Temp., °F	Fuel Tank, Gals.	Engine Oil Refill, Qts.①	Auto Transaxle, Qts.	Manual Transaxle Pts.	Transfer Case, Pts	Differential Oil, Pts.	
										Front	Rear
1.8L	7.2	③	14–15	179	13.5	4.2	②	④	1.0	—	1.1
2.0L	7.2	③	14–15	179	13.5	4.2	②	④	1.0	—	1.1
2.4L	7.2	③	14–15	179	13.5	4.2	②	④	1.0	—	1.1

① — With filter change.

② — Drain & refill, 4.0 qts.; Overhaul, 8.6 qts.

③ — Mopar Antifreeze/Coolant 5 Year/100,000 Mile (5 Year/160,000 km) Formula HOAT (Hybrid Organic Additive Technology) or equivalent.

④ — Manual transaxle model NV T355, 5.6 Pts.; Manual transaxle model BG6, 4.2 Pts.

LUBRICANT DATA

Year	Lubricant Type					
	Transmission	Transfer Case	Differential		Power Steering	Brake System
			Front	Rear		
2007-08	①	②	②	②	Mopar ATF+4	DOT 3

① — Automatic transaxle, MOPAR CVT+4,; Manual transaxle, MOPAR® ATF+4.

② — SAE 80W-90 API GL 5 or equivalent non-synthetic.

Electrical

NOTE: On Air Bag Equipped Models, Refer To "Air Bag System Precautions" Located In The Front Of This Manual For System Disarming & Arming Procedures.

NOTE: Refer To "Computer Relearn Procedures" Located In The Front Of This Manual When Battery Power To The Computer Has Been Interrupted.

NOTE: Prior To Performing Any Service Operations Listed In This Section, Consult The "Technical Service Bulletins" Section For Related Information.

NOTE: Refer To The Rear Of This Manual For Vehicle Manufacturer's Special Tool Suppliers.

INDEX

	Page No.		Page No.		Page No.
Air Bag System (Volume 2)	4-1	Heater Core, Replace	7-7	Steering Columns	12-1
Air Conditioning	8-1	Ignition Coil, Replace	7-4	Steering Wheel, Replace	7-5
Alternator, Replace	7-4	Ignition Lock, Replace	7-5	Stop Light Switch, Replace	7-5
Alternators	11-1	Ignition Switch, Replace	7-5	Technical Service Bulletins	7-8
Blower Motor, Replace	7-7	Instrument Cluster, Replace	7-6	Rear Wiper Stops Operating	
Cabin Air Filter, Replace	7-7	Multi-Function Switch, Replace	7-5	with Diagnostic Trouble Codes	
Cooling Fans	9-1	Neutral Safety Switch, Replace	7-5	B231B & B2215	7-8
Cruise Control (Volume 2)	2-1	Passive Restraint Systems		2007-08 Caliber	7-8
Dash Gauges (Volume 2)	1-1	(Volume 2)	4-1	Turn Signal Switch, Replace	7-5
Dash Panel Service		Precautions	7-4	Wiper Motor, Replace	7-6
(Volume 2)	5-1	Air Bag Systems	7-4	Front	7-6
Dimmer Switch, Replace	7-5	Battery Ground Cable	7-4	Rear	7-6
Evaporator Core, Replace	7-8	Radio, Replace	7-6	Wiper Switch, Replace	7-7
Fuel Pump Relay Location	7-4	Speed Controls (Volume 2)	2-1	Wiper Systems (Volume 2)	3-1
Fuse Panel & Flasher Location	7-4	Starter Motors	10-1	Wiper Transmission, Replace	7-7
Headlamp Switch, Replace	7-5	Starter, Replace	7-4		

PRECAUTIONS

Air Bag Systems

Refer to "Air Bag System Precautions" in the front of this manual for system disarming and arming procedures.

Battery Ground Cable

Prior to service, disconnect battery ground cable and isolate as required.

FUSE PANEL & FLASHER LOCATION

The fuse/relay block is located in the engine compartment on the lefthand frame rail.

The flashers are controlled by the Totally Integrated Power Module (TIPM) located in the engine compartment near the air cleaner assembly.

FUEL PUMP RELAY LOCATION

The fuel pump relay is located in the Totally Integrated Power Module (TIPM).

STARTER
REPLACE

1. Remove air cleaner box and air tube.
2. Remove three starter motor mounting bolts.
3. Disconnect electrical connector at throttle body.
4. Remove throttle body mounting bolts, then the throttle body.
5. Push starter under intake manifold.
6. Tip starter nose toward cooling module, then pull starter up and out.
7. Disconnect starter motor wiring connectors.
8. Remove starter motor from vehicle.
9. Reverse procedure to install, noting the following:
   a. **Torque** starter mounting bolts to 40 ft. lbs.
   b. **Torque** throttle body mounting bolts to 80 inch lbs.

ALTERNATOR
REPLACE

1. Raise and support vehicle.
2. Remove right front wheel.
3. Remove underbody air dam.
4. Remove accessory drive splash shield.
5. Remove accessory drive idler pulley.
6. Loosen lower mounting bolt.
7. Loosen A/C compressor and relocate, pull down and to outboard side of vehicle.
8. Unplug field circuit from alternator.
9. Remove B+ terminal nut and wire.
10. Remove upper mounting bolt.
11. Remove alternator lower mounting bolt.
12. Relocate battery stud to of A/C line for removal of alternator.
13. Rotate alternator pulley down.
14. Slide alternator down and out of vehicle.
15. Reverse procedure to install, noting the following:
   a. **Torque** alternator mounting bolt to 45 ft. lbs.
   b. **Torque** A/C Compressor bolts to 18 ft. lbs.
   c. **Torque** B+ terminal nut to 89 inch lbs.

IGNITION COIL
REPLACE

1. Remove engine compartment appearance cover.
2. Disconnect ignition coil electrical connector, **Fig. 1.**

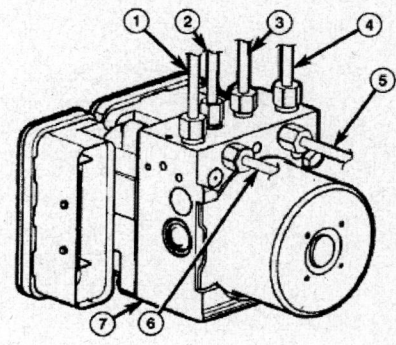

1. Secondary tube
2. Brake tube
3. Brake tube
4. Primary tube
5. Brake tube
6. Brake tube
7. Hydraulic Control Unit

ARM0600000000168

Fig. 1 Ignition coil replacement

3. Remove ignition coil mounting bolts, then the ignition coil.
4. Reverse procedure to install. **Torque mounting bolt to 80 inch lbs.**

IGNITION LOCK
REPLACE

1. Place ignition key cylinder in RUN position.
2. Working through access hole in lower shroud, depress lock cylinder retaining tab and remove key cylinder.
3. Reverse procedure to install, noting the following:
   a. Turn ignition key to RUN position allowing retaining tab on lock cylinder to be depressed.
   b. Shaft at end of lock cylinder aligns with socket in end of housing. To align socket with lock cylinder, ensure socket is in Run position.
   c. Align lock cylinder with grooves in housing, then slide lock cylinder into housing until tab sticks through opening in housing.
   d. Turn ignition key to Off position, then remove key.

IGNITION SWITCH
REPLACE

1. Ensure steering wheel is in straight-ahead position.
2. Remove driver's air bag.
3. Disconnect clockspring wiring connector.
4. Remove steering wheel mounting bolt, then using suitable steering wheel puller, remove steering wheel.
5. Remove upper and lower steering column shrouds.
6. Lock clockspring rotor in center position by using suitable pin inserted through hole in rotor located at the 10 o'clock position.
7. Remove three Steering Column Control Module (SCCM), **Fig. 2.**

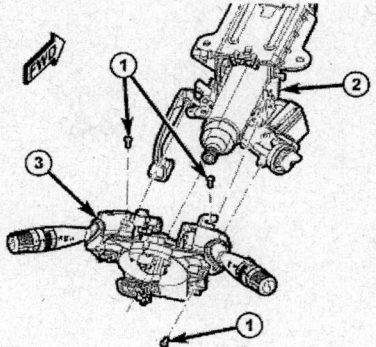

1. Mounting screws
2. Steering column
3. Steering Column Control Module (SCCM)

ARM0600000000169

Fig. 2 Steering Column Control Module (SCCM) removal

8. Disconnect SCCM three electrical connectors, then remove module from column.
9. Remove cylinder lock housing mounting screws.
10. Unhook ignition switch retaining fingers from lock cylinder housing and remove it.
11. Reverse procedure to install.

NEUTRAL SAFETY SWITCH
REPLACE

1. Remove nut holding shift lever to manual shaft, then the lever from shaft.
2. Disconnect neutral safety switch (range sensor) electrical connector.
3. Remove sensor to transaxle case mounting bolts then the range sensor.
4. Reverse procedure to install, noting the following:
   a. Ensure manual shaft is in N position, then using alignment tool No. 9876, or equivalent, **Fig. 3,** adjust position of sensor.
   b. Install and **torque** range sensor bolts to 49 inch lbs.
   c. Remove alignment tool.

HEADLAMP SWITCH
REPLACE

1. Remove upper and lower steering column shrouds.
2. Remove screw that secures righthand multi-function switch, **Fig. 4,** to righthand side of clockspring.
3. Pull switch straight away from clockspring far enough to access electrical connector.
4. Disconnect instrument panel wiring harness from back of multi-function switch.
5. Remove switch from clockspring.
6. Reverse procedure to install.

STOP LIGHT SWITCH
REPLACE

1. Remove silencer pad below located

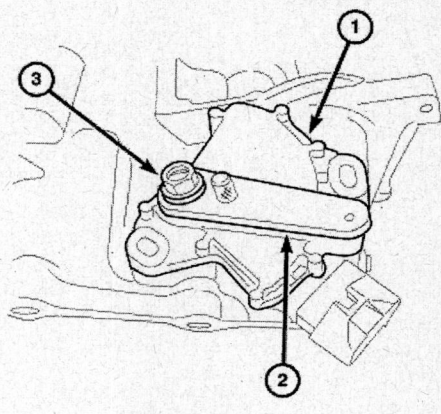

1. Range sensor
2. Alignment tool No. 9876, or equivalent
3. Lever retaining nut

ARM0600000000170

Fig. 3 Neutral safety switch (Range sensor) installation

steering column.
2. Disconnect stop light switch electrical connector.
3. Remove stop lamp switch from brake pedal bracket by rotating switch in a counterclockwise direction approximately 30 degrees, then pulling switch rearward.
4. Reverse procedure to install. **Do not reuse stop light switch, once removed it must be discarded.**

MULTI-FUNCTION SWITCH
REPLACE

Refer to "Headlamp Switch, Replace" for multi-function switch replacement procedure.

TURN SIGNAL SWITCH
REPLACE

Refer to "Headlamp Switch, Replace" for multi-function switch replacement procedure.

DIMMER SWITCH
REPLACE

Refer to "Headlamp Switch, Replace" for multi-function switch replacement procedure.

STEERING WHEEL
REPLACE

1. Ensure steering wheel is in straight-ahead position.
2. Working from behind steering wheel, gently pry off driver air bag bolt covers.
3. Remove two driver air bag mounting bolts.
4. Pull air bag rearward and disconnect two air bag squib connectors.

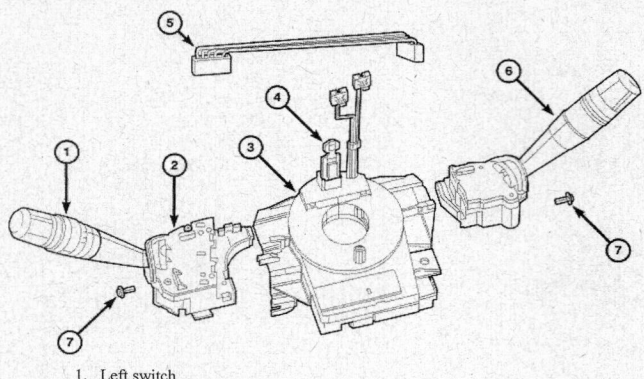

1. Left switch
2. Left multi-function switch
3. Clockspring
4. Alignment pin
5. Wire harness
6. Right multi-function switch
7. Screws

ARM0600000000171

Fig. 4   Righthand multi-function switch replacement

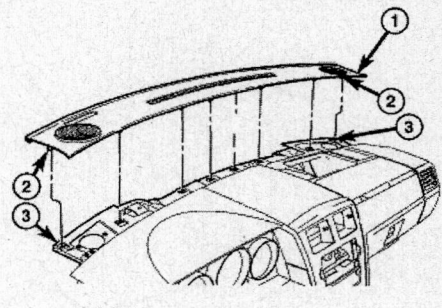

1. Trim panel cover
2. Panel clips
3. Inner instrument panel

ARM0600000000172

Fig. 5   Upper instrument panel trim removal

5. Disconnect wiring connector at clock-spring.
6. Holding steering wheel firmly in place, then remove mounting bolt.
7. Thread steering wheel retaining bolt back into end of shaft until approximately, 0.5 inches of thread is showing between wheel and head of bolt.
8. Remove screw form speed control switch in order to install steering wheel puller tool.
9. Install suitable three jawed steering wheel puller on steering wheel, then remove steering wheel from steering column shaft.
10. Remove wheel retaining bolt, then the steering wheel.
11. Reverse procedure to install. **Torque** steering wheel mounting bolt to 32 ft. lbs.

INSTRUMENT CLUSTER
REPLACE

1. Remove A-pillar trim using suitable trim removal tool.
2. Remove upper instrument panel trim panel using trim stick tool No. C-4755, or equivalent, **Fig. 5,** disengaging panel clips.
3. Remove four instrument cluster bezel retaining screws.
4. Pull instrument cluster rearward to expose four electrical connectors.
5. Disconnect electrical connectors, then remove cluster from instrument panel.
6. Separate cluster bezel from cluster by removing four retaining screws.
7. Reverse procedure to install.

RADIO
REPLACE

1. Remove center instrument panel trim bezel.
2. Remove radio retaining screws, then pull radio rearward to access wiring.
3. Disconnect electrical connectors and antenna cable.
4. Remove radio from vehicle.
5. Reverse procedure to install.

WIPER MOTOR
REPLACE

Front

Do not apply pressure to, or pry on, the plastic drive link bushings. When removing the drive link from, or installing the drive link to the ball stud on the wiper motor crank arm, apply pressure to, or pry on, only the metal portions of the drive link around the bushing. If the bushing is damaged, the entire front wiper module MUST be replaced.

Do not remove the crank arm nut from the wiper motor output shaft. The crank arm is indexed to the output shaft with the motor in the park position during the manufacturing process, but there are no provisions made for correctly indexing this connection in the field. If the crank arm to output shaft indexing is incorrect, the entire front wiper module MUST be replaced.

1. Remove both wiper arms from wiper pivots as follows:
   a. Lift front wiper arm to its over-center position to hold wiper blade off windshield and relieve spring tension on wiper arm to pivot shaft connection.
   b. Carefully pry plastic nut cap off of pivot end of wiper arm.
   c. Remove nut that secures wiper arm to wiper pivot shaft .
   d. Use a slight rocking motion to disengage front wiper arm pivot end from pivot shaft, then remove wiper arm.
2. Remove cowl plenum cover/grille panel from over front wiper motor module.
3. Disengage routing clip, from stud in cowl plenum, then disconnect wire harness connector from front wiper motor module.
4. Remove two screws, **Fig. 6,** that secure ends of front wiper motor module bracket to brackets within cowl plenum.

5. Pull front wiper motor module inboard far enough to disengage rubber isolator from slotted bracket located on forward wall of cowl plenum.
6. Remove front wiper motor module.
7. Disengage socket bushing from passenger side wiper drive link, **Fig. 7,** from ball stud on wiper motor crank arm using two large screwdrivers, one on each side of ball stud. Pry firmly and evenly between crank arm and metal portion of drive link until socket unsnaps from ball.
8. Remove sleeve bushing from driver side wiper drive link from ball stud on wiper motor crank arm.
9. Remove two screws that secure motor bracket to module bracket.
10. Remove wiper motor and crank arm as a unit from underside of module bracket.
11. Reverse procedure to install.

Rear

1. Lift front wiper arm to its over-center position to hold wiper blade off windshield and relieve spring tension on wiper arm to pivot shaft connection.
2. Carefully pry plastic nut cap off of pivot end of wiper arm.
3. Remove nut that secures wiper arm to wiper pivot shaft.
4. Use a slight rocking motion to disengage front wiper arm pivot end from pivot shaft, then remove wiper arm.
5. Remove liftgate inside trim panel using suitable trim removal tool.
6. Disconnect liftgate wire harness connector, **Fig. 8,** from rear wiper motor.
7. Remove three screws that secure motor mounting bracket to U-nuts, **Fig. 8,** on liftgate inner panel.
8. Pull wiper motor forward far enough to disengage output shaft from rubber grommet located in liftgate glass.
9. Remove wiper motor from liftgate.
10. Reverse procedure to install.

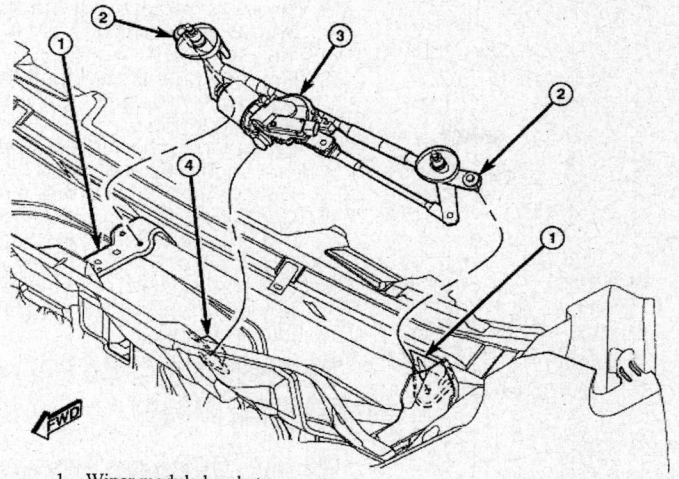

1. Wiper module bracket
2. Module to bracket mounting screws
3. Front wiper module
4. Rubber isolator

ARM0600000000173

Fig. 6   Front wiper motor replacement

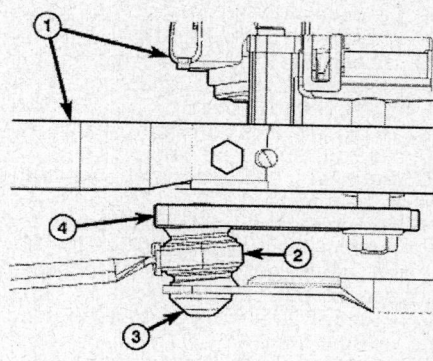

1. Front wiper module
2. Sleeve bushing
3. Socket bushing
4. Wiper motor crank arm

ARM0600000000174

Fig. 7   Front wiper motor crank arm to ball stud removal

WIPER SWITCH
REPLACE

1. Remove upper and lower steering column shrouds.
2. Remove screw that secures righthand multi-function switch, **Fig. 9,** to mounting bracket integral to righthand side of clockspring on steering column.
3. Slide switch away from clockspring, enough to disengage slide tab located on bottom of switch housing from channel formation in mounting bracket.
4. Disconnect jumper wire harness connector from receptacle on inboard end of righthand multi-function switch.
5. Remove switch from clockspring.
6. Reverse procedure to install.

WIPER TRANSMISSION
REPLACE

Refer to "Wiper Motor, Replace" for wiper transmission replacement procedures.

BLOWER MOTOR
REPLACE

1. Remove righthand instrument panel under cover.
2. Disengage connector lock, then disconnect instrument panel wire harness connector from blower motor.
3. Remove three blower motor to HVAC housing mounting bolts, wire lead bracket to bottom of HVAC housing, then the blower motor.
4. Reverse procedure to install.

CABIN AIR FILTER
REPLACE

1. Open glove compartment latch.
2. Unsnap glove compartment damper, **Fig. 10,** from glove box bin.
3. Flex glove compartment open position stops inboard, then rotate past stops.
4. Unsnap glove compartment door from base panel lower hinge pins.
5. Disengage four retaining tabs, **Fig. 11,** that secure cabin (particulate) air filter cover to passenger side of HVAC housing, then remove filter cover.
6. Remove cabin air filter from HVAC housing by pulling filter element straight out of housing.
7. Reverse procedure to install.

HEATER CORE
REPLACE

1. Recover air conditioning refrigerant as outlined in "Air Conditioning" chapter.
2. Drain cooling system.
3. Remove heater core hoses.
4. Remove heat shield located on bulkhead in engine compartment, **Fig. 12.**
5. Remove bolt that secures A/C liquid and suction line assembly to A/C evaporator core.
6. Disconnect A/C liquid and suction line assembly from A/C evaporator, then remove and discard dual-plane seals. Plug refrigerant line fittings.
7. Disconnect heater hoses from heater core tubes.
8. Remove five HVAC housing to instrument panel mounting bolts.
9. Remove lefthand and righthand instrument panel end caps.
10. Remove lefthand and righthand knee air bag covers.
11. Disconnect steering column wire harness.
12. Reposition floor carpeting to access steering column coupling located at base of column.
13. Ensure steering wheel is locked with wheel in straight-ahead position.
14. Remove intermediate shaft coupling bolt. **Do not separate intermediate shaft from steering gear pinion shaft at this time.**

15. Remove steering wheel as outlined under "Steering Wheel, Replace."
16. Position column tilt at full-upward position.
17. Remove four steering column cover reinforcement panel mounting bolts, then the reinforcement panel.
18. Remove two screws attaching upper shroud to lower shroud and then unclip shrouds from each other by applying hand pressure along seams where shrouds connect on sides, then remove upper shroud.
19. Push tilt lever downward.
20. Remove screw attaching lower shroud to steering column, then the lower shroud.
21. Push tilt lever upward, locking it in place.
22. Insert ignition key into key cylinder, then turn key to ON position.
23. Depress tab on top of interlock cable connector and pull cable out of lock cylinder housing.
24. Disconnect wiring harness connectors from Steering Column Control Module (SCCM).
25. Disconnect any remaining wiring harness connectors at column components.
26. Separate intermediate shaft from steering gear pinion shaft.
27. Remove steering column to instrument panel mounting bolts, then the steering column.
28. Remove rear center console, **Fig. 13.**
29. Remove shift knob and shift bezel from front center console.
30. Remove two front console mounting screws
31. Pull on side of console housing and unsnap housing tabs.
32. Disconnect console housing wire connector and instrument panel connector.
33. Remove front console from vehicle.
34. Remove center bezel using trim stick tool No. C-4755, or equivalent.

35. Disconnect wire harness from accessory switch bank, **Fig. 14**.
36. Disconnect HVAC control cables.
37. Remove fasteners attaching HVAC control head to bezel.
38. Remove switch bank from bezel.
39. Remove shifter assembly.
40. Remove lefthand and righthand A-pillar trim.
41. Remove upper instrument panel trim panel using trim stick tool No. C-4755, or equivalent, **Fig. 5,** disengaging panel clips.
42. Remove lefthand and righthand door sill scuff plates.
43. Remove lefthand and righthand cowl trim to dash mounting nuts, then remove trim panels using suitable trim tool.
44. Disconnect instrument panel wire harness connects located behind cowl panels.
45. Disconnect wire harness clipped along A - pillars.
46. Remove glove compartment as outlined under "Cabin Air Filter, Replace."
47. Disconnect antenna wire from radio harness.
48. Remove lefthand and righthand front seats as follows:
    a. Remove seat belt anchor trim using trim stick tool No. C-4755, or equivalent, to pry trim from seat.
    b. Remove seat belt anchor bolt, then separate seat belt anchor from seat.
    c. Remove seat to floor mounting bolts.
    d. Tilt seat backward and disconnect electrical connectors.
    e. Remove seats from vehicle. **No one should sit in front passenger seat after it has been removed from vehicle. This uneven force may damage the sensing ability of the seat weight sensors.**
49. Remove lefthand and righthand B-pillar trim panels.
50. Remove lefthand and righthand floor ducts.
51. Remove four bolts located behind center bezel, **Fig. 15**, and one behind glove compartment.
52. Remove three bolts located behind lefthand end cap, and one at bottom center of instrument panel.
53. Remove condensation drain tube from HVAC housing.
54. Remove two bolts located behind righthand end cap and four screws located under top cover near windshield.
55. Disconnect wire harness from HVAC housing.
56. Remove instrument panel through driver's door.
57. Remove foam seal, **Fig. 16**, from flange located on front of HVAC housing.
58. Remove screw that secures flange to front of HVAC housing, then remove flange.
59. Remove screw that secures retaining bracket for heater core tubes to left side of air distribution housing.

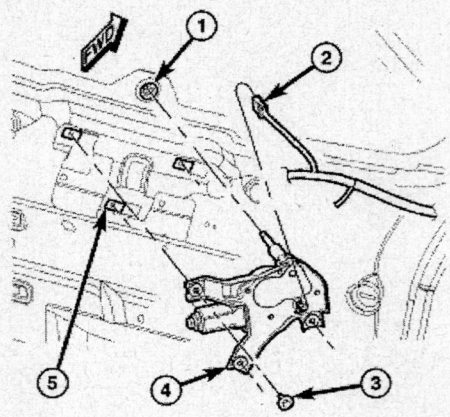

1. Rubber grommet
2. Wire harness connector
3. Mounting screws
4. Rear wiper motor
5. U-nuts

ARM0600000000175

Fig. 8   Rear wiper motor replacement

60. Carefully pull heater core out of lefthand side of air distribution housing.
61. Reverse procedure to install, noting the following:
    a. **Torque** A/C lines to evaporator to 105 inch lbs.
    b. **Torque** HVAC housing to dash panel nuts to 10 inch lbs.
    c. **Torque** Steering column mounting nuts and bolts to 21 ft. lbs.
    d. **Torque** Intermediate shaft coupling bolt to 35 ft. lbs.
    e. **Torque** Seat belt anchor bolts to 30 ft. lbs.
    f. **Torque** Seat track to floor pan bolts to 40 ft lbs.

EVAPORATOR CORE
REPLACE

1. Recover air conditioning refrigerant as outlined in "Air Conditioning" chapter.
2. Drain cooling system.
3. Remove heater core hoses.
4. Remove heat shield located on bulkhead in engine compartment, **Fig. 12**.
5. Remove HVAC housing as outlined under "Heater Core, Replace."
6. Remove two metal retaining clips, **Fig. 17**, that secure bottom of air distribution housing to HVAC housing.
7. Remove seven screws that secure air distribution housing to rear of HVAC housing.
8. Remove air distribution housing from HVAC housing.
9. Remove blower motor from HVAC housing.
10. Remove blower motor resistor from bottom of housing.
11. Disengage two retaining tabs that secure evaporator temperature sensor to lefthand side of HVAC housing, then remove sensor using needle nose pliers.

12. Carefully remove foam seal, **Fig. 18**, from front two halves of HVAC housing.
13. Remove nine screws and three metal clips that secure two halves of HVAC housing together.
14. Disengage nine plastic retaining tabs that secure two halves of HVAC housing together, then separate housing.
15. Carefully lift A/C evaporator core, **Fig. 19**, and foam insulator out of lower half of HVAC housing.
16. Reverse procedure to install. Replace any deformed or damaged foam insulators or seals.

TECHNICAL SERVICE BULLETINS

Rear Wiper Stops Operating with Diagnostic Trouble Codes B231B & B2215

2007-08 CALIBER

On some of these models the rear wiper may stop operating. Upon further investigation the technician may find that the following Diagnostic Trouble Codes (DTC's) are present:; B2215: front control module (FMC) internal or B2331B: rear wiper motor control circuit low.

This condition may be caused by an improperly programed FCM.

To correct this condition will require flash reprogramming the Totally Integrated Power Module (TIPM) with updated software. **Flash files for this bulletin must be retrieved from the internet.** Proceed as follows:

1. Connect StarSCAN tool programmed with software release level 6.06 or higher, to vehicle.
2. Turn ignition switch to On position.
3. Connect StarSCAN Ethernet cable to StarSCAN and dealer's network drop.
4. Retrieve old TIPM part number. Using StarSCAN at the "Home" screen.
5. Select "ECU View."
6. Touch screen to highlight appropriate ECU in list of modules.
7. Select "More Options."
8. Select "ECU Flash."
9. Record part number at top of "Flash ECU" screen for later reference.
10. Select "Browse for New File." Follow on screen instructions.
11. Highlight listed calibration.
12. Select "Download to Scan tool."
13. Select "Close" after download is complete, then select ""
14. Highlight listed calibration.
15. Select "Update Controller." Follow on screen instructions.
16. When update is complete, select "OK."
17. Verify part number at top of "Flash ECU" screen has updated to new part number.

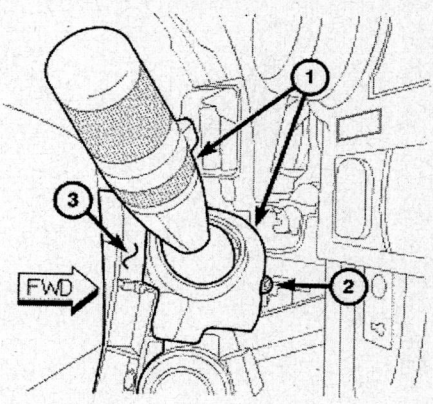

1. Righthand multi-function switch
2. Retaining screw
3. Clockspring

ARM0600000000176

Fig. 9   Righthand multi-function switch replacement

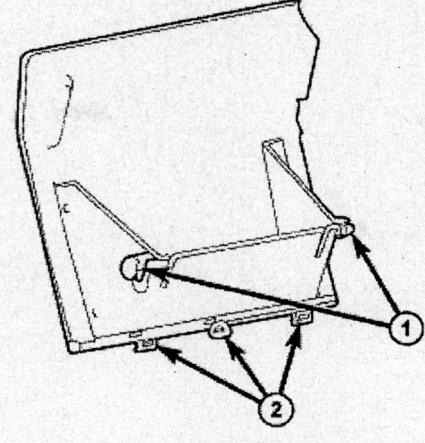

1. Compartment stops (dampers)
2. Lower hinge pins

ARM0600000000178

Fig. 10   Glove compartment removal

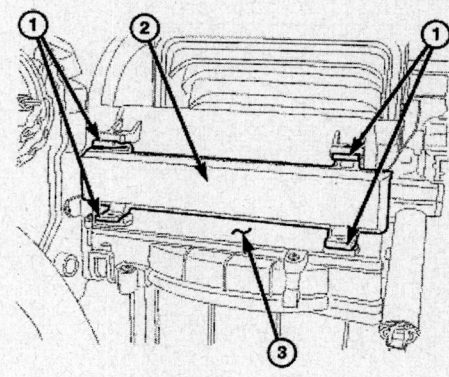

1. Retaining tabs
2. Filter cover
3. HVAC housing

ARM0600000000177

Fig. 11   Cabin air filter replacement

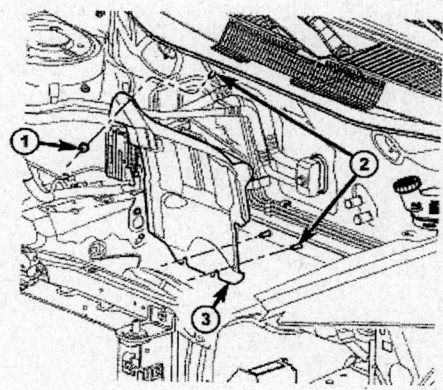

1. Mounting nuts
2. Heat shield
3. Studs

ARM0600000000180

Fig. 12   Heat shield removal.

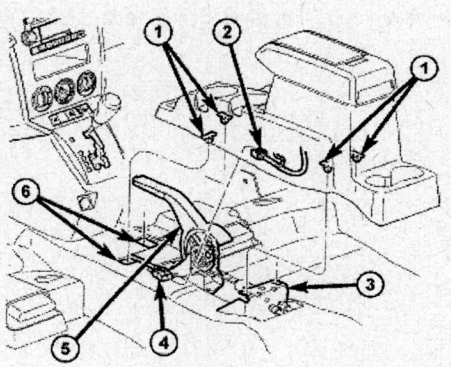

1. Front mounting screws
2. Wiring connector
3. Rear floor bracket
4. Brake lever electrical connector
5. Parking brake lever
6. Front floor bracket

ARM0600000000181

Fig. 13   Rear center console replacement

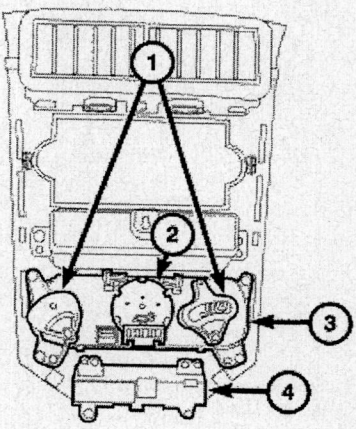

1. HVAC control cables
2. Accessory switch bank
3. Control head bezel
4. Bezel

ARM0600000000182

Fig. 14   Center HVAC switch bank removal

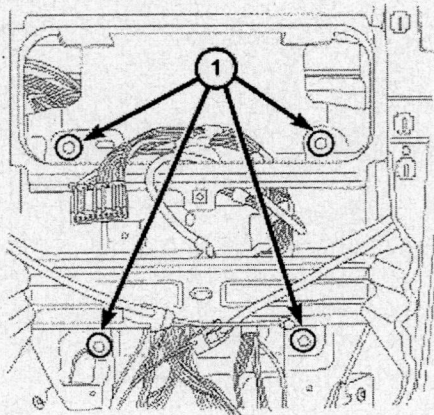

1. Bolt locations

ARM0600000000183

Fig. 15 Instrument panel bolt locations behind center bezel & glove compartment

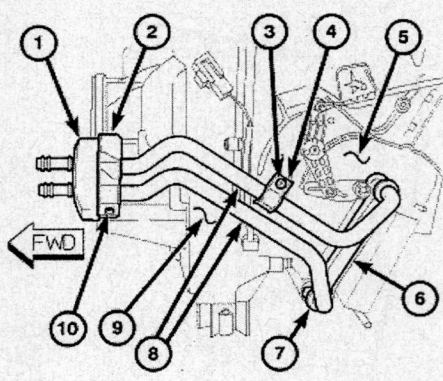

1. Foam seal
2. Front flange
3. Screw
4. Tube flange
5. Air distribution housing
6. Heater core
7. Foam tube seal
8. Heater core tubes
9. HVAC housing
10. Front flange retaining screw

ARM0600000000179

Fig. 16 Heater core removal

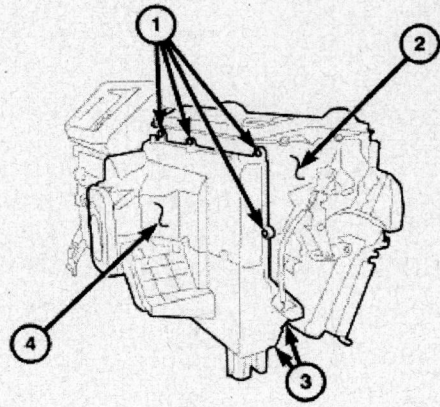

1. Seven retaining screws
2. Air distribution housing
3. Metal retaining clips
4. HVAC housing

ARM0600000000184

Fig. 17 Air distribution housing removal from HVAC housing

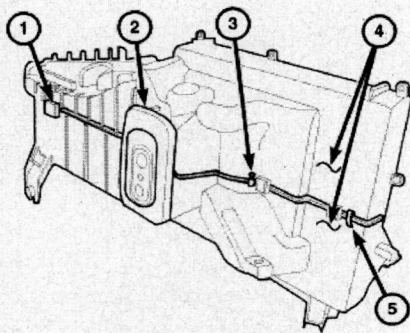

1. Plastic retaining tabs
2. Foam seal
3. Screws
4. HVAC housing
5. Metal retaining clips

ARM0600000000185

Fig. 18 HVAC housing disassemble

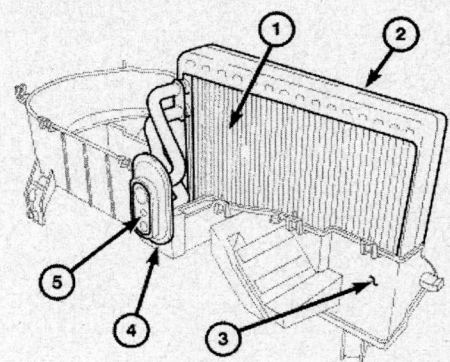

1. Evaporator core
2. Foam insulator
3. HVAC housing
4. Evaporator core seal
5. Evaporator tube tapping block

ARM0600000000186

Fig. 19 Evaporator core removal

1.8L, 2.0L & 2.4L Engines

NOTE: On Air Bag Equipped Models, Refer To "Air Bag System Precautions" Located In The Front Of This Manual For System Disarming & Arming Procedures.

NOTE: Refer To "Computer Relearn Procedures" Located In The Front Of This Manual When Battery Power To The Computer Has Been Interrupted.

NOTE: Refer To The Rear Of This Manual For Vehicle Manufacturer's Special Tool Suppliers.

INDEX

	Page No.
Belt Tension Data	7-17
Camshaft, Replace	7-15
Compression Pressure	7-11
Cooling System Bleed	7-17
Crankshaft Damper, Replace	7-14
Crankshaft Rear Oil Seal, Replace	7-15
Crankshaft Seal, Replace	7-15
Cylinder Head, Replace	7-13
Engine Rebuilding Specifications	21-1
Engine, Replace	7-12
Engine Mount, Replace	7-11
Front	7-11
Lefthand	7-11
Rear	7-11
Righthand	7-11
Exhaust Manifold, Replace	7-13
Front Cover, Replace	7-14
Fuel Filter, Replace	7-18
Fuel Pump, Replace	7-18

	Page No.
Hydraulic Lifters, Replace	7-14
Intake Manifold, Replace	7-12
Main & Rod Bearings	7-15
Oil Pan, Replace	7-15
Oil Pump, Replace	7-16
1.8L Engine	7-16
2.0L & 2.4L Engines	7-16
Installation	7-16
Removal	7-16
Oil Pump Service	7-16
1.8L Engine	7-16
Assemble	7-17
Disassemble	7-16
Inspection	7-16
2.0L & 2.4L Engines	7-17
Piston & Rod Assembly	7-15
Precautions	7-11
Air Bag Systems	7-11
Battery Ground Cable	7-11
Fuel System Pressure Relief	7-11
Radiator, Replace	7-18

	Page No.
Rocker Arms, Replace	7-14
Serpentine Drive Belt	7-17
Replacement	7-17
Installation	7-17
Removal	7-17
Routing	7-17
Thermostat, Replace	7-17
Primary	7-17
Secondary	7-17
Tightening Specifications	7-21
Timing Chain, Replace	7-14
Installation	7-14
Removal	7-14
Timing Chain Tensioner, Replace	7-15
Valve Adjustment	7-14
Valve Clearance Specifications	7-14
Valve Cover, Replace	7-13
Water Pump, Replace	7-17

PRECAUTIONS

Air Bag Systems

Refer to "Air Bag System Precautions" in the front of this manual for system disarming and arming procedures.

Battery Ground Cable

Prior to service, disconnect battery ground cable and isolate as required.

Fuel System Pressure Relief

1. Remove lower rear seat cushion.
2. Remove fuel pump module cover.
3. Disconnect electrical connector for fuel pump module.
4. Start and run engine until it stalls.
5. Attempt restarting engine until it will no longer run.
6. Turn ignition key to OFF position.
7. One or more Diagnostic Trouble Codes (DTC's) may have been stored in PCM memory. Use a properly programed scan tool to erase a DTC.

COMPRESSION PRESSURE

1. Crank engine until maximum pressure is reached on gauge. Record this pressure as No. 1 cylinder pressure.
2. Repeat previous step for all remaining cylinders.
3. Compression should not be less than 100 psi and should not vary more than 25 percent from cylinder to cylinder.

ENGINE MOUNT
REPLACE
Front

1. Raise and support vehicle.
2. Remove fore aft member, **Fig. 1,** to mount bolts.
3. Remove fore aft member mounting bolts, then the member.
4. Remove front engine mount.
5. Reverse procedure to install.

Lefthand

1. Remove air cleaner inlet and air cleaner housing.

2. Remove PCM and mounting bracket.
3. Disconnect negative cable from battery.
4. Support transaxle with a suitable jack.
5. Remove engine mount through bolt.
6. Remove engine mount bracket to body frame rail bolts, then the mount.
7. Reverse procedure to install.

Rear

1. Remove rear mount retaining bolts.
2. Remove rear mount through bolt.
3. Remove oxygen sensor connector from mount.
4. Remove rear mount.
5. Reverse procedure to install.

Righthand

1. Remove coolant reservoir, then position it aside.
2. Remove power steering reservoir, then position it aside.
3. Remove windshield washer bottle.
4. Remove power steering line support bracket from engine mount.
5. Support transaxle with a block of wood and a suitable jack.
6. Remove engine mount through bolt.

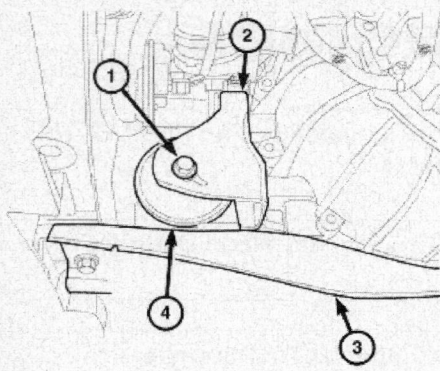

1. Through bolt
2. Mount bracket
3. Fore aft member
4. Front engine mount

ARM0600000000187

Fig. 1 Front engine mount replacement

7. Remove three engine mount bracket bolts.
8. Remove engine mount retaining bolts, then the mount.
9. Reverse procedure to install.

ENGINE
REPLACE

1. Remove engine cover.
2. Recover air conditioning refrigerant as outlined in "Air Conditioning" chapter.
3. Drain cooling system into suitable container.
4. Relieve fuel pressure as outlined under "Precautions."
5. Disconnect and remove fuel line.
6. Loosen retainers, then remove air inlet tube.
7. Disconnect intake air temperature sensor electrical connector.
8. Remove clean air tube from air cleaner housing.
9. Remove air cleaner housing assembly.
10. Disconnect cables from battery, then remove battery.
11. Remove battery tray.
12. Remove coolant reservoir.
13. Remove coolant hoses from coolant adapter.
14. Disconnect coolant temperature sensor and capacitor connectors.
15. Remove upper radiator hose support.
16. Disconnect coils, injectors, cam sensors, oil temperature sensor, coolant temperature sensor, and oil control valve electrical connectors, then reposition wiring harness aside.
17. Remove PCV hose from valve cover.
18. Remove harness retainer from intake manifold.
19. Remove throttle body support bracket.
20. Remove vacuum lines from throttle body and intake manifold.
21. Disconnect electronic throttle control and manifold flow control valve electrical connectors.
22. Remove oil dipstick and tube.

23. Remove intake manifold bolts in sequence, **Fig. 2.**
24. Disconnect coolant temperature sensor at block, then the knock sensor, oil pressure sensor, alternator, starter, block heater, A/C compressor, and block ground.
25. Remove accessory drive belt.
26. Remove power steering reservoir.
27. Remove power steering line support at engine mount.
28. Remove power steering hose support from exhaust manifold.
29. Remove power steering pump, then position it aside.
30. Remove shift linkage from transaxle by squeezing tabs of retainer, then lifting upwards on shift cable.
31. Remove ground strap from right strut tower.
32. Raise and support vehicle, then remove front wheels.
33. Remove righthand splash shield.
34. Remove front axle shafts.
35. Remove cotter pin, nut lock, spring washer and hub nut from end of outer C/V joint stub axle.
36. Disconnect front wheel speed sensor and secure harness aside.
37. Remove nut and bolt retaining ball joint stud into steering knuckle.
38. Separate ball joint stud from steering knuckle using suitable tool and prying downward on lower control arm. **Use caution when separating ball joint stud from steering knuckle, so ball joint seal does not get damaged.**
39. Remove halfshaft from steering knuckle, **Fig. 3,** by pulling outward on knuckle while pressing in on halfshaft, using hub removal tool No. 1026, or equivalent. Ensure to support outer end of halfshaft assembly.
40. Remove halfshaft bracket from upper and lower mounting bolts, then support outer end of halfshaft assembly.
41. Drain transaxle oil into suitable container.
42. Disengage inner tripod joints from side gears of transaxle using a suitable punch, **Fig. 4,** position punch to inner tripod joint extraction groove and strike punch sharply with a hammer to dislodge inner tripod joint retaining ring from transaxle side gear.
43. Remove inner tripod joint and halfshaft assembly from transaxle by pulling it straight out of transaxle side gear and transaxle.
44. Remove exhaust pipe to exhaust manifold bolts.
45. Disconnect oxygen sensor connector.
46. Pull exhaust pipe rearward, then secure with a suitable strap.
47. Remove front engine mount through bolt.
48. Remove fore aft member.
49. Remove front engine mount bracket.
50. Remove rear engine mount as outlined under "Engine Mount, Replace."
51. Remove inspection cover, then match mark clutch module to flywheel.
52. Remove modular clutch bolts.
53. Remove lower bellhousing bolts.
54. Disconnect A/C lines from compressor.

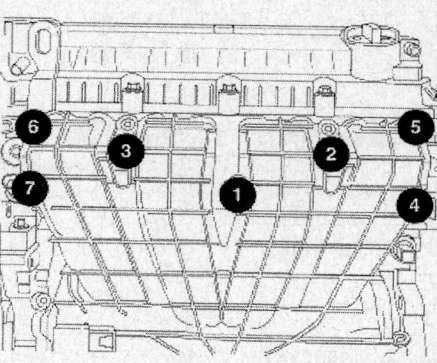

ARM0600000000188

Fig. 2 Intake manifold bolt removal sequence

55. Remove A/C compressor from mounting bracket.
56. Remove A/C compressor mounting bracket from engine.
57. Install adapter plate tool No. 9704, or equivalent, **Fig. 5,**
58. Remove alternator and lower idler pulley.
59. Disconnect transaxle electrical connector and harness retainer.
60. Disconnect CKP electrical connector.
61. Position dolly, **Fig. 6,** under engine and lower vehicle.
62. Install safety straps, **Fig. 6. Safety straps MUST be used.**
63. Remove PCM bracket retaining bolts, then the bracket.
64. Remove lefthand and righthand engine mount bracket retaining bolts.
65. Raise vehicle away from engine and transaxle.
66. Separate engine from transaxle.
67. Reverse procedure to install. Tighten intake manifold bolts in sequence, **Fig. 7,** to 18 ft. lbs.

INTAKE MANIFOLD
REPLACE

1. Remove engine cover.
2. Relieve fuel pressure as outlined under "Precautions."
3. Remove air cleaner inlet, then the air cleaner housing.
4. Disconnect fuel line at injector fuel rail.
5. Remove fuel injector electrical connectors.
6. Remove fuel rail retaining bolts, then the fuel rail.
7. Disconnect oil temperature sensor.
8. Disconnect variable valve timing solenoid electrical connector.
9. Disconnect intake camshaft position sensor electrical connector, then position harness aside.
10. Remove throttle body support bracket.
11. Disconnect electronic throttle control electrical connector.
12. Remove wiring harness retainer from intake manifold.
13. Disconnect MAP sensor electrical connector.
14. Disconnect vacuum lines at intake.
15. Remove upper radiator hose retaining bracket.

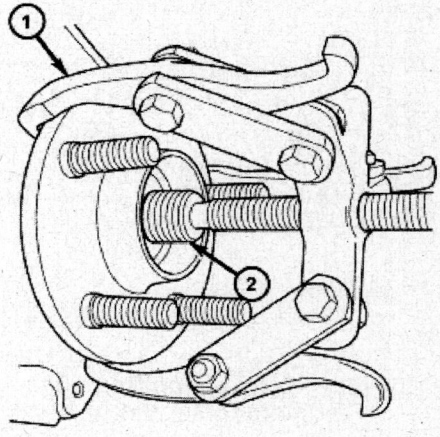

1. Hub puller tool No. 1026
2. Halfshaft

ARM0600000000189

Fig. 3 Halfshaft removal from steering knuckle

16. Remove intake manifold bolts in sequence, **Fig. 2.**
17. Remove intake manifold.
18. Reverse procedure to install. Tighten intake manifold bolts in sequence, **Fig. 7,** to 18 ft. lbs.

EXHAUST MANIFOLD
REPLACE

1. Remove engine cover.
2. Remove upper heat shield bolts, then the shield.
3. Disconnect exhaust pipe from manifold.
4. Remove manifold support bracket.
5. Remove four exhaust manifold heat shield retaining bolts, then the shield.
6. Disconnect oxygen sensor electrical connector.
7. Remove exhaust manifold retaining bolts in sequence, **Fig. 8,** then the manifold.
8. Reverse procedure to install. Tighten manifold bolts in sequence, **Fig. 8,** to 25 ft. lbs.

CYLINDER HEAD
REPLACE

1. Remove engine cover.
2. Relieve fuel pressure as outlined under "Precautions."
3. Drain engine coolant into suitable container.
4. Remove intake manifold as outlined under, "Intake Manifold, Replace."
5. Remove cylinder head cover bolts, then the cylinder head cover.
6. Remove exhaust manifold as outlined under, "Exhaust Manifold, Replace."
7. Raise and support vehicle.
8. Remove righthand splash shield.
9. Remove accessory drive belts.
10. Ensure engine is set at TDC, **Fig. 9.**

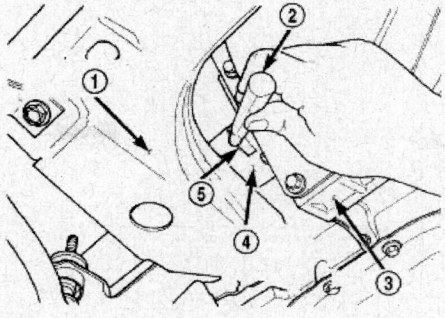

1. Cross member frame
2. Punch
3. Transaxle housing
4. Inner tripod joints
5. Extraction groove

ARM0600000000190

Fig. 4 Inner tripod joint removal from transaxle

11. Remove lower A/C compressor bolts, then the lower compressor mounting bracket.
12. Remove accessory drive belt lower idler pulley.
13. Remove crankshaft damper as outlined under "Crankshaft Damper, Replace."
14. Remove water pump pulley.
15. Remove righthand side engine mount bracket lower bolt.
16. Remove timing chain cover lower bolts.
17. Disconnect oxygen sensor electrical connector.
18. Remove oxygen sensor.
19. Remove exhaust pipe at exhaust manifold.
20. Lower vehicle.
21. Support engine with suitable jack.
22. Remove righthand engine mount as outlined under "Engine Mount, Replace."
23. Remove accessory drive upper idler pulley.
24. Remove righthand upper engine mount bracket.
25. Remove accessory drive belt tensioner.
26. Remove timing chain as outlined under "Timing Chain, Replace."
27. Disconnect top engine electrical connectors and reposition harness.
28. Remove coolant adapter and set aside.
29. Remove ground strap at right rear of cylinder head.
30. Insert wedge tool No.9701, or equivalent, **Fig. 10,** between camshaft phasers, (Variable Valve Timing VVT). Lightly tap wedge into place until it will no longer sink down.
31. Remove front camshaft bearing cap bolts in sequence, **Fig. 11.**
32. Slowly remove remaining intake and exhaust camshaft bearing cap bolts one turn at a time.
33. Remove intake camshaft by lifting rear of camshaft upward, then rotate camshaft counterclockwise while lifting out of front bearing cradle.

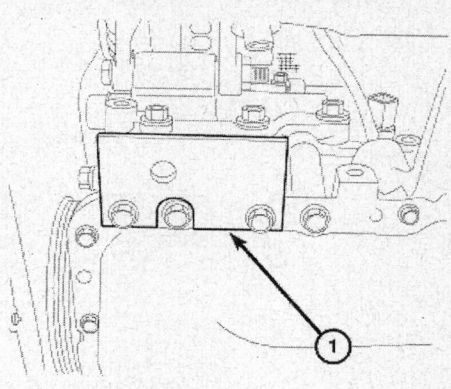

1. Adapter plate tool No. 9704

ARM0600000000191

Fig. 5 Adapter plate installation

34. Remove exhaust camshaft.
35. Remove cylinder head bolts. **All cylinder head bolts have captured washers EXCEPT the front two.**
36. Remove cylinder head from engine block.
37. Reverse procedure to install, noting the following:
   a. Always replace variable valve timing filter screen, **Fig. 12,** when servicing head gasket or engine damage could result.
   b. Place two pea size dots of RTV, **Fig. 13,** on cylinder block and head gasket.
   c. Front two cylinder head bolts do not have captured washers. Washers must be installed with bevel up towards bolt head.
   d. Lightly coat head bolts with clean engine oil.
   e. Tighten cylinder head bolts in sequence, **Fig. 14,** as follows: First step, **torque** bolts to 25 ft. lbs. Second step, **torque** bolts to 45 ft. lbs. Third step, lightly coated with engine oil, bolts to 45 ft. lbs. Fourth step, rotate bolts an additional 90 degrees.
   f. Install camshafts and tighten front cap bolts in reverse sequence of removal, **Fig. 11. Torque** M6 bolts to 105 inch lbs. **Torque** M8 bolts to 25 ft lbs.
   g. Install timing chain as outlined under "Timing Chain, Replace."
   h. Remove wedge tool No.9701, or equivalent, **Fig. 10,** installed between camshaft phasers.

VALVE COVER
REPLACE

1. Remove engine cover.
2. Disconnect ignition coil electrical connectors.
3. Disconnect PCV and make up air hoses from cylinder head cover.
4. Use compressed air to blow dirt and debris off cylinder head cover prior to removal.
5. Remove cylinder head cover bolts.
6. Remove cylinder head cover from cylinder head.

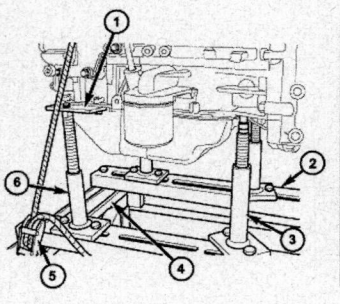

1. Adapter plate
2. Adjustable mounting plate
3. Hi-Lo screw jack No.1
4. Dolly No.1
5. Safety strap
6. Safety strap

7. Hi-Lo screw jack No. 3
8. Dolly No. 2
9. Safety strap
10. Floor jack mounting
11. Adjustable mounting plate
12. Hi-Lo screw jack No. 4

ARM0600000000192

Fig. 6   Engine removal dolly installation

7. Reverse procedure to install, noting the following:
   a. Install new cylinder head cover gaskets.
   b. Install studs in cover as indicated, **Fig. 15**.
   c. Tighten bolts in sequence, **Fig. 16**, in two steps: First step, **torque** bolts to 40 inch lbs. Second **torque** bolts to 90 inch lbs.

VALVE CLEARANCE SPECIFICATIONS

Intake valve lash clearance, .362 inch. Exhaust valve lash clearance, .331 inch.

VALVE ADJUSTMENT

1. Remove valve cover as outlined under "Valve Cover, Replace."
2. Rotate camshaft so lobes are vertical, **Fig. 17**.
3. Inspect clearance using feeler gauges, repeat for all tappets and record readings.
4. If valve clearance is not as specified, refer to "Valve Clearance Specifications," remove camshaft as outlined under "Cylinder Head, Replace."
5. If clearance is to small; Specification minus clearance = change: Decrease valve tappet bucket thickness by "change" figure.
6. If clearance is to large; Specification minus clearance = change: Increase valve tappet bucket thickness by "change" figure.

ROCKER ARMS
REPLACE

These engine are equipped with overhead camshafts and have no rocker arms.

HYDRAULIC LIFTERS
REPLACE

These engines are equipped with solid lifters (Tappets).

CRANKSHAFT DAMPER
REPLACE

1. Remove accessory drive belt as outlined under "Serpentine Drive Belt."
2. Install damper holder tool No. 9707, or equivalent.
3. Remove damper mounting bolt, then pull damper off crankshaft.
4. Reverse procedure to install.

FRONT COVER
REPLACE

1. Remove engine cover by pulling upward.
2. Relieve fuel pressure as outlined under "Precautions."
3. Remove cylinder head cover bolts, then the cylinder head cover.
4. Remove upper timing chain cover retaining bolts, then the upper cover.
5. Remove exhaust manifold as outlined under, "Exhaust Manifold, Replace."
6. Raise and support vehicle.
7. Remove righthand splash shield.
8. Remove accessory drive belts.
9. Ensure engine is set at TDC, **Fig. 9**.
10. Remove lower A/C compressor bolts, then the lower compressor mounting bracket.
11. Remove accessory drive belt lower idler pulley.
12. Remove crankshaft damper as outlined under "Crankshaft Damper, Replace."
13. Remove water pump pulley.
14. Remove righthand side engine mount bracket lower bolt.
15. Remove front engine cover to oil pan lower bolts.
16. Disconnect oxygen sensor electrical connector.
17. Remove oxygen sensor.
18. Remove exhaust pipe at exhaust manifold.
19. Lower vehicle.
20. Support engine with suitable jack.
21. Remove righthand engine mount as outlined under "Engine Mount, Replace."

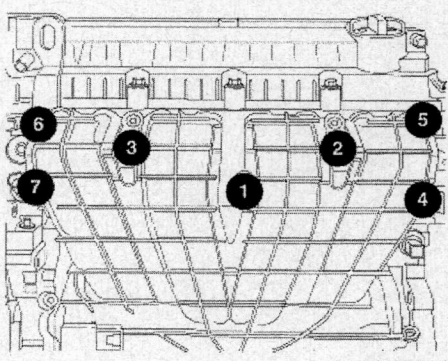

ARM0600000000193

Fig. 7   Intake manifold bolt tightening sequence

22. Remove accessory drive upper idler pulley.
23. Remove righthand upper engine mount bracket.
24. Remove accessory drive belt tensioner.
25. Insert small Allen wrench through timing tensioner plug hole and lift ratchet upward to release tensioner, then push Allen wrench inward. Leave Allen wrench installed during remainder of procedure.
26. Remove front engine cover mounting bolts, **Fig. 18**, then pry cover loose at pry points.
27. Remove front engine cover.
28. Reverse procedure to install, noting the following:
    a. Apply suitable engine sealant RTV at cylinder head to block parting line, corners of oil pan and block and front lip of oil pan.
    b. Apply 2 mm bead of suitable engine sealant RTV to engine block as indicated, **Fig. 19**.
    c. **Torque** M6 cover bolts to 105 inch lbs. **Torque** M8 cover bolts to 17 ft. lbs.

TIMING CHAIN
REPLACE

With the timing chain removed, avoid turning the camshaft or crankshaft. If movement is required, exercise extreme caution to avoid valve damage caused by piston contact.

Removal

1. Remove front engine cover as outlined under "Front Cover, Replace."
2. Ensure camshafts are aligned to marked chain links & corresponding camshaft timing marks, **Fig. 20**.
3. Ensure crankshaft is aligned to marked chain links & corresponding crankshaft timing mark, **Fig. 21**.
4. Remove timing chain tensioner, **Fig. 22**.
5. Remove timing chain.

Installation

1. Verify that crankshaft sprocket keyway is at 9 o'clock position, **Fig. 23**.

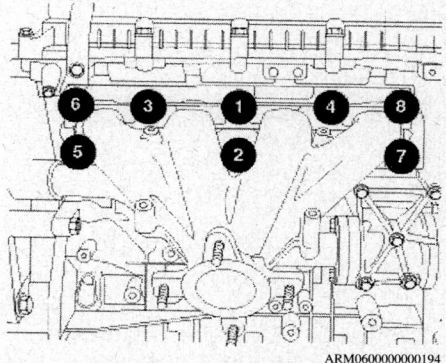

Fig. 8 Exhaust manifold bolt installation & removal sequence

2. Align camshaft timing marks so they are parallel to cylinder head and align each other as indicated, **Fig. 24.**
3. Install timing chain guide and tighten bolts to 105 inch lbs.
4. Install timing chain so plated links on chain align with timing marks on camshaft sprockets, **Fig. 25.**
5. Align timing mark on crankshaft sprocket with plated link on timing chain, **Fig. 26.** Position chain so slack will be on tensioner side.
6. Install moveable timing chain pivot guide. **Keep the slack in timing chain on tensioner side.**
7. Reset timing chain tensioner by lifting up on ratchet, **Fig. 27,** then pushing plunger inward towards tensioner body. Insert tensioner pin part No.8514, or equivalent, into slot to hold tensioner plunger in retracted position.
8. Install timing chain tensioner, then remove tensioner pin part No.8514, or equivalent.
9. Rotate crankshaft clockwise two complete revolutions until crankshaft is repositioned at TDC position, **Fig. 23,** with keyway at 9 o'clock position.
10. Verify that camshaft timing marks are in proper position, **Fig. 24.**
11. Install front cover as outlined under "Front Cover, Replace."

TIMING CHAIN TENSIONER
REPLACE
1. Remove timing chain as outlined under "Timing Chain, Replace."
2. Remove timing chain tensioner retaining bolts, then the tensioner.
3. Reverse procedure to install.

CAMSHAFT
REPLACE
Refer to "Cylinder head, Replace" for camshaft replacement procedures.

PISTON & ROD ASSEMBLY
There are three different sizes of rod bearings available.

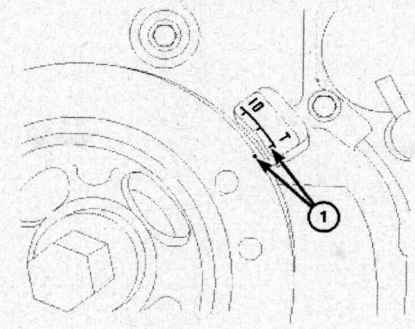

1. Timing marks

Fig. 9 Timing marks set at TDC

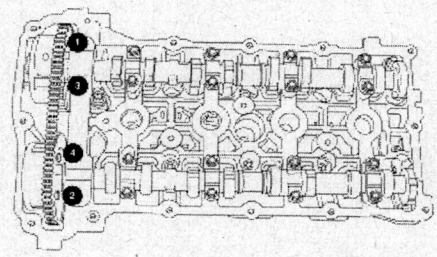

Fig. 11 Front camshaft cap bolt removal sequence

The front mark on piston must face timing belt side of engine. Connecting rods and caps must be installed in original positions. **Torque** bolts to 15 ft. lbs., then an additional 90°.

MAIN & ROD BEARINGS
There are three different possibilities for the upper main bearings and five different lower main bearings. The upper and lower bearing shells are not interchangeable.

There are three different sizes of rod bearings available.

1. Measure crankshaft journal diameter and select appropriate lower bearing from chart, **Fig. 28**
2. Measure crankshaft journal diameter and select appropriate upper bearing from chart, **Fig. 29.**
3. **Torque** bolts to 20 ft. lbs., in sequence, **Fig. 30,** then an additional 45°.

CRANKSHAFT SEAL
REPLACE
1. Remove accessory drive belt.
2. Install damper holder tool No. 9707, or equivalent, then remove damper retaining bolt.
3. Pull damper off crankshaft using suitable puller.
4. Remove front crankshaft oil seal by prying out with suitable screw driver.
5. Reverse procedure to install, noting the following:

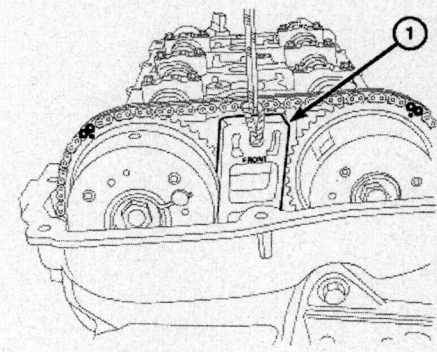

1. Wedge tool No. 9701

Fig. 10 Wedge tool installation

a. Place seal onto seal installer tool No. 9506, or equivalent, with seal spring facing towards inside of engine.

CRANKSHAFT REAR OIL SEAL
REPLACE
1. Remove transaxle assembly refer to, **MOTOR's "Domestic Transmission, In-Vehicle Service" or "Transmission Service DVD."**
2. Remove flex plate bolts, then the flex plate.
3. Insert a ³⁄₁₆ flat bladed screwdriver between dust lip and metal case of crankshaft seal. Angle screwdriver through dust lip against metal case of seal, then pry out seal.
4. Ensure oil seals garter spring is not on crankshaft.
5. Reverse procedure to install, noting the following:
   a. Place seal guide tool No. 9509, or equivalent, on crankshaft.
   b. Position seal over guide tool. Guide tool should remain on crankshaft during installation of seal. Ensure that lip of seal is facing towards crankcase during installation.
   c. Drive seal into block using seal driver tool No. 9706, and driver handle tool No. C-4171, or equivalents, until seal driver bottoms out against engine block.

OIL PAN
REPLACE
1. Raise and support vehicle.
2. Drain engine oil into suitable container.
3. Remove accessory drive belt splash shield.
4. Remove lower A/C compressor mounting bolt.
5. Remove A/C mounting bracket.
6. Remove oil pan retaining bolts.
7. Loosen seal around oil pan using a putty knife.
8. Remove oil pan from vehicle.
9. Reverse procedure to install, noting the following:

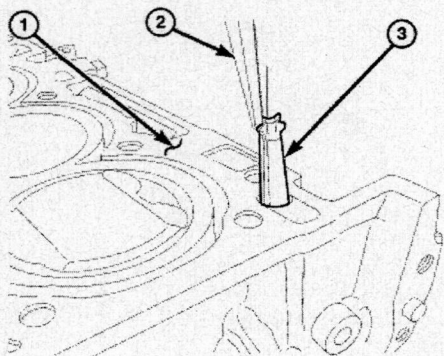

1. Engine block
2. Needle noise pliers
3. Variable valve timing filter screen

ARM0600000000202

Fig. 12   Variable valve timing filter screen replacement

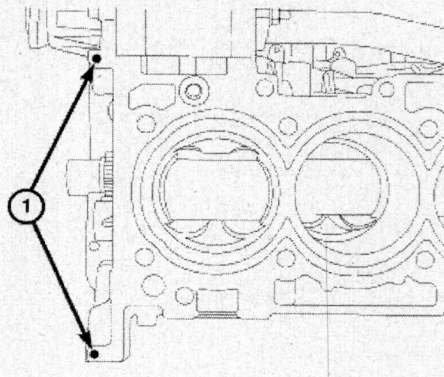

1. RTV placement location

ARM0600000000203

Fig. 13   RTV placement locations

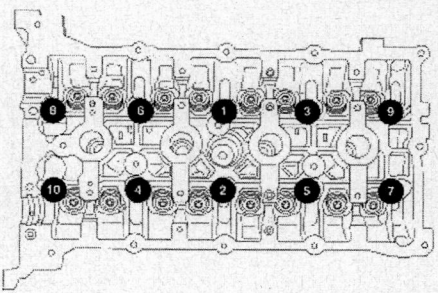

ARM0600000000204

Fig. 14   Cylinder head bolt tightening sequence

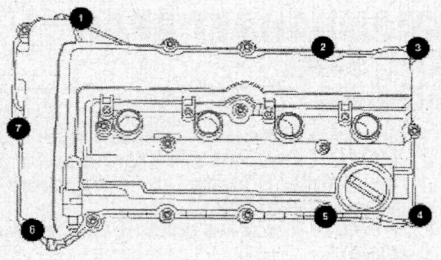

ARM0600000000205

Fig. 15   Valve cover stud installation locations

a. Apply a 2 mm bead of Mopar engine RTV GEN II, or equivalent, around oil pan as indicated, **Fig. 31.**
b. Tighten oil pan bolts in two steps; First step, **torque** small bolts to 105 inch lbs. Second step, **torque** two long bolts to 16 ft. lbs.

OIL PUMP

REPLACE

1.8L Engine

1. Remove timing chain cover as outlined under "Front Cover, Replace."
2. Remove engine oil pan as outlined under "Oil Pan, Replace."
3. Pull tensioner guide back and secure with suitable wire.
4. Remove oil pump mounting bolts.
5. Remove oil pump from sprocket and chain, then remove pump.
6. Reverse procedure to install. Remove wire from chain tensioner shoe.

2.0L & 2.4L Engines

INSTALLATION

1. Clean BSM mounting holes brake parts cleaner.

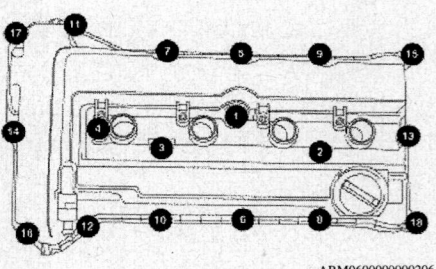

ARM0600000000206

Fig. 16   Valve cover bolt tightening sequence

2. Align marks on crankshaft sprocket and chain, **Fig. 32.**
3. Align marks on oil pump sprocket and chain, **Fig. 32.**
4. Install chain on sprocket.
5. Pivot BSM assembly upwards and position on ladder frame.
6. Start new BSM mounting bolts by hand.
7. Tighten BSM mounting bolts in three steps in sequence, **Fig. 33,** as follows:
   a. First step, **torque** BSM bolts to 11 ft. lbs.
   b. Second step, **torque** BSM bolts to 22 ft. lbs.
   c. Third step rotate bolts an additional 90°.
8. Remove tensioner pin tool No. 9703, or equivalent.
9. Install oil pan as outlined under "Oil Pan, Replace."
10. Install transaxle assembly refer to, **MOTOR's "Domestic Transmission, In-Vehicle Service"** or **"Transmission Service DVD."**

REMOVAL

The oil pump is integral to the Balance Shaft Module (BSM). The oil pump cannot be disassembled for inspection. The pressure relief valve is serviceable and can be removed and inspected. The BSM can be identified by the plastic end caps, **Figs. 34 and 35.**

1. Rotate engine to TDC on No. 1 compression stroke.
2. Remove transaxle assembly refer to, **MOTOR's "Domestic Transmission,**

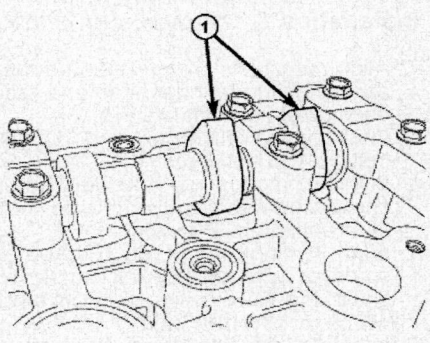

1. Cam lobes in vertical position

ARM0600000000207

Fig. 17   Camshaft lobe positioning

In-Vehicle Service" or **"Transmission Service DVD."**

3. Remove oil pan as outlined under "Oil Pan, Replace."
4. Mark chain and oil pump sprocket, **Fig. 32,** for reassembly.
5. Push tensioner piston back into tensioner body, then insert tensioner pin tool No. 9703, or equivalent, into tensioner body to hold piston in retracted position.
6. Remove Balance Shaft Module (BSM) mounting bolts and discard. **Do not remove sprocket from BSM.**
7. Lower back of BSM, **Fig. 32,** then remove chain from sprocket.
8. Remove BSM from engine block.

OIL PUMP SERVICE

1.8L Engine

DISASSEMBLE

1. Remove pressure relief valve and spring.
2. Remove oil pump drive sprocket using holder tool No. 9711, or equivalent.
3. Remove oil pump housing cover retaining bolts.
4. Remove housing cover.

INSPECTION

1. Inspect pressure relief valve for scoring or damage. If scored or damaged, replace valve.

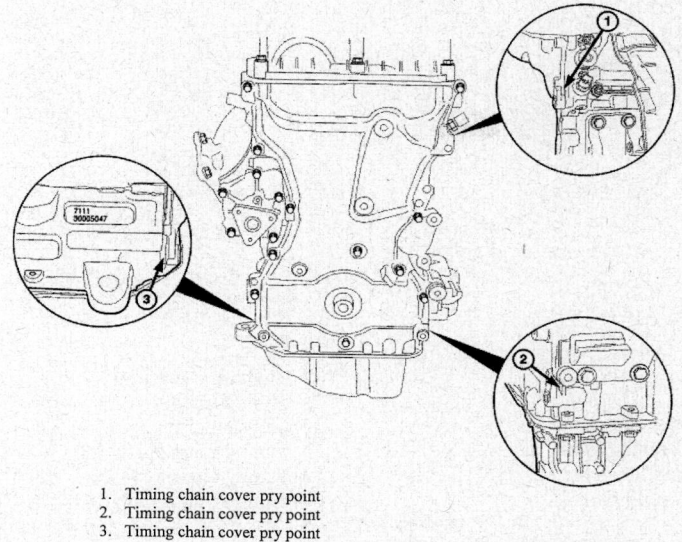

1. Timing chain cover pry point
2. Timing chain cover pry point
3. Timing chain cover pry point

ARM0600000000196

Fig. 18   Front engine cover bolt & pry locations

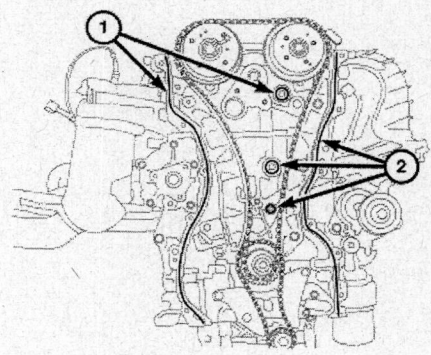

1-2. RTV sealant locations

ARM0600000000208

Fig. 19   RTV sealant locations

2. Inspect oil pump housing bore for damage or scoring, if scoring or damage is found replace pump.
3. Measure outer rotor to housing clearance with feeler gauge.
4. Measure tip clearance between outer and inner rotor.
5. Measure pump cover flatness with a straight edge and feeler gauge.
6. Measure clearance over rotors with a straight edge and feeler gauge.
7. Measure outer rotor thickness.
8. Measure inner rotor thickness.

ASSEMBLE

1. Install oil pump housing cover.
2. **Torque** cover bolts in sequence, **Fig. 36,** to 88 inch lbs.
3. Install pump drive sprocket using holder tool No. 9711, or equivalent.
4. Install pressure relief valve and spring.

2.0L & 2.4L Engines

The oil pump is integral to the Balance Shaft Module (BSM). The oil pump cannot be disassembled for inspection. The pressure relief valve is serviceable and can be removed and inspected. The BSM can be identified by the plastic end caps.

BELT TENSION DATA

Belt adjustment is maintained by an automatic (spring load) belt tensioner.

SERPENTINE DRIVE BELT

Routing

Refer to **Fig. 37** for serpentine drive belt routing.

Replacement

REMOVAL

1. Rotate accessory drive belt tensioner counterclockwise until accessory drive belt can be removed from pulleys, using a suitable wrench.
2. Remove accessory drive belt.

INSTALLATION

1. Install accessory drive belt around all pulleys, **Fig. 37,** except for alternator pulley.
2. Rotate accessory drive belt tensioner counterclockwise until accessory drive belt can be installed on alternator pulley, using a wrench.
3. Release spring tension onto accessory drive belt.

COOLING SYSTEM BLEED

This procedure has been revised by a Technical Service Bulletin.

1. Install cooling system filling aid tool No. 8195, or equivalent that looks like funnel that attaches to filler neck in place of pressure cap along with attached hose clip.
2. Pinch off overflow hose attach to fill neck.
3. Attach 5–6.5 foot length of clear ¼ inch I.D. clear hose to bleed valve. Pit other end of hose in suitable container.
4. Open cooling system bleed valve located on water outlet connector near front of engine.
5. Pour suitable coolant mixture into large side of filling aid tool.
6. Slowly fill cooling system, using large side of cooling aid.
7. When steady stream of coolant comes out of clear hose, close bleed valve. Continue filling to top of filling aid tool.

8. Remove overflow hose clip. Excess fluid will drain into coolant bottle overflow.
9. Remove filling aid.
10. Ensure pressure cap bottom seal and filler neck are clean and free of debris.
11. Install coolant bottle pressure cap.

THERMOSTAT
REPLACE
Primary

1. Partially drain cooling system into suitable container.
2. Remove air filter housing.
3. Disconnect coolant hose (1) from inlet housing
4. Remove inlet housing bolts.
5. Remove thermostat assembly, and clean sealing surfaces.
6. Reverse procedure to install. Ensure to bleed cooling system as outlined under, "Cooling system Bleed."

Secondary

1. Partially drain cooling system into suitable container.
2. Remove air filter housing.
3. Disconnect coolant hoses from rear of coolant adapter.
4. Remove radiator hose.
5. Remove radiator hose from front of coolant adapter.
6. Remove coolant adapter mounting bolts.
7. Carefully slide coolant adapter off water pump inlet tube and remove coolant adapter, then remove secondary thermostat.
8. Remove thermostat assembly, and clean sealing surfaces.
9. Reverse procedure to install. Ensure to bleed cooling system as outlined under, "Cooling system Bleed."

WATER PUMP
REPLACE

1. Drain cooling system into suitable container.
2. Remove accessory drive belt as outlined under "Serpentine Drive Belt."

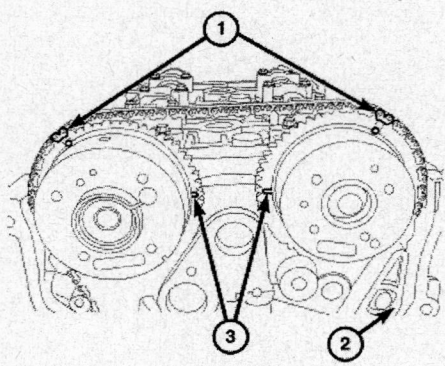

1. Chain link marks and alignment
2. Cylinder head
3. Timing gear alignment marks

ARM0600000000197

Fig. 20 Marked chain links & corresponding camshaft timing mark alignment

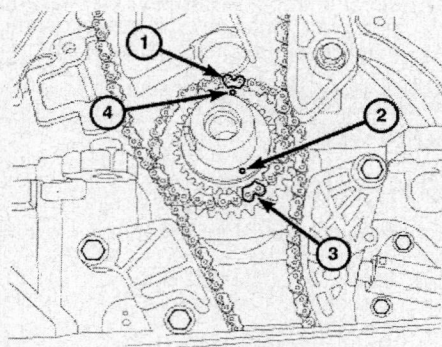

1. Marked chain link
2. Crankshaft timing mark
3. Marked chair link
4. Crankshaft keyway

ARM0600000000209

Fig. 23 Crankshaft sprocket keyway at 9 o'clock position

3. Raise and support vehicle.
4. Remove accessory drive belt splash shield.
5. Remove screws attaching water pump pulley, then the pulley.
6. Remove water pump mounting bolts, then the water pump.
7. Reverse procedure to install. Ensure to bleed cooling system as outlined under, "Cooling system Bleed."

RADIATOR
REPLACE

1. Drain engine coolant into suitable container.
2. Remove radiator core support.

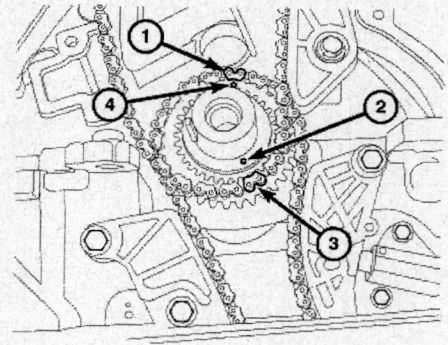

1. Marked chain link chain 1
2. Crankshaft timing mark
3. Marked chain link chain 2
4. Crankshaft timing mark

ARM0600000000198

Fig. 21 Marked chain links & corresponding crankshaft timing mark alignment

3. Disconnect upper radiator hose from radiator.
4. Remove wiring harness bracket.
5. Disconnect radiator fan electrical connector.
6. Remove radiator fan mounting screws.
7. Detach radiator fan assembly from retaining clips.
8. Remove radiator fan by lifting upward from engine compartment.
9. Disconnect lower radiator hose.
10. Remove fasteners attaching A/C condenser to radiator, then reposition A/C condenser aside.
11. Remove radiator assembly by lifting it upward from engine compartment.
12. Reverse procedure to install. Ensure to bleed cooling system as outlined under, "Cooling system Bleed."

FUEL PUMP
REPLACE

1. Remove air cleaner lid, disconnect inlet air temperature sensor and make-up air hose.
2. Remove rear seat cushion.
3. Remove plastic access cover located on floor pan.
4. Clean top of tank to remove loose dirt and debris.
5. Remove left side module lock ring using lock ring tool No. 9340, or equivalent. **Match mark fuel pump location on top of fuel tank.**
6. Disconnect fuel pump electrical connector.
7. Pull module upward out of fuel tank, make sure that you do not spill fuel inside of vehicle.

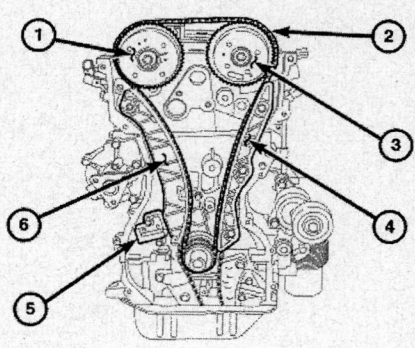

1. Right camshaft gear
2. Timing chain
3. Left cam gear
4. Timing chain guide
5. Timing chain tensioner
6. Timing chain guide

ARM0600000000199

Fig. 22 Timing chain removal

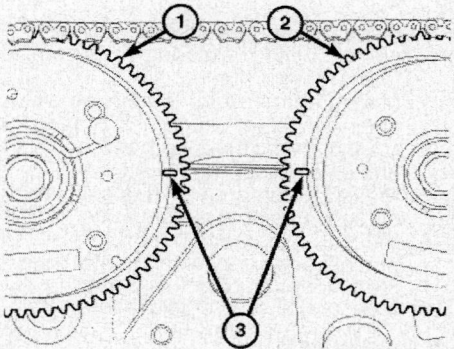

1-2. Camshaft gears
3. Camshaft gear timing marks

ARM0600000000210

Fig. 24 Camshaft timing marks aligned

8. Reverse procedure to install. Ensure to align position match marks.

FUEL FILTER
REPLACE

1. Remove fuel filter shield retaining bolt, then remove shield.
2. Remove air cleaner housing. Filter is located in engine compartment near brake master cylinder.
3. Disconnect fuel supply line from fuel tank, **Fig. 38.**
4. Disconnect fuel supply line to fuel pump.
5. Disconnect both fuel return lines from filter.
6. Remove filter retaining screw.
7. Remove retaining bracket and filter.
8. Reverse procedure to install.

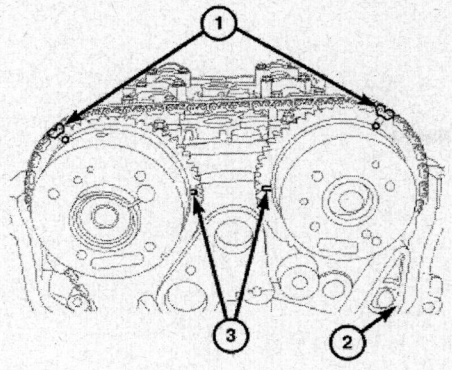

1. Plated chain links
2. Camshaft gear marks aligned
3. Chain tensioner

ARM0600000000211

Fig. 25 Timing chain plated link alignment with camshaft timing marks

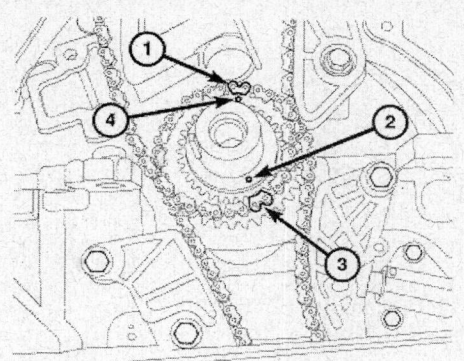

1. Plated link
2. Crankshaft timing mark
3. Plated link
4. Crankshaft keyway

ARM0600000000212

Fig. 26 Crankshaft sprocket plated chain link alignment

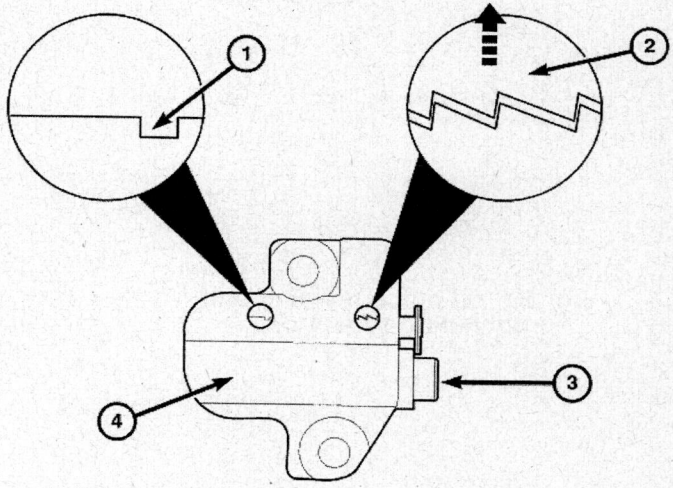

1. Pin slot
2. Ratchet
3. Plunger
4. Tensioner body

ARM0600000000213

Fig. 27 Resetting timing chain tensioner

CRANKSHAFT IDENTIFICATION		LOWER CRANKSHAFT BEARING SELECTION	
JOURNAL DIAMETER GRADE	DIMENSION	LOWER MAIN BEARING SIZE CLASSIFICATION	LOWER MAIN BEARING DIMENSION
0	52 mm, -0.012 to -0.015 mm	0 (Pink or Red)	2 mm, 0 to -0.003 mm
1	52 mm, -0.015 to -0.018 mm	1 (Black)	2 mm, +0.003 to 0 mm
2	52 mm, -0.018 to -0.021 mm	2 (No Color)	2 mm, +0.006 to +0.003 mm
3	52 mm, -0.021 to -0.024 mm	3 (Green)	2 mm, +0.009 to +0.006 mm
4	52 mm, -0.024 to -0.027 mm	4 (Blue)	2 mm, +0.012 to +0.009 mm

ARM0600000000214

Fig. 28 Lower main bearing identification

CYLINDER BLOCK IDENTIFICATION		UPPER CRANKSHAFT BEARING SELECTION	
MAIN BEARING GRADE	DIMENSION	UPPER MAIN BEARING SIZE CLASSIFICATION	UPPER MAIN BEARING DIMENSION
1	56.000<56.006 mm	1 (Black)	2 mm, 0 to -0.006 mm
2	56.006<56.012 mm	2 (No Color)	2 mm, +0.006 to 0 mm
3	56.012<56.018 mm	3 (Green)	2 mm, +0.012 to +0.006 mm

ARM0600000000215

Fig. 29 Upper main bearing identification

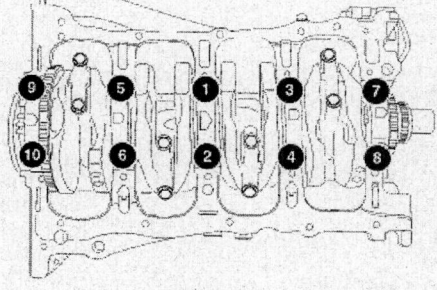

ARM0600000000216

Fig. 30 Main bearing tightening sequence

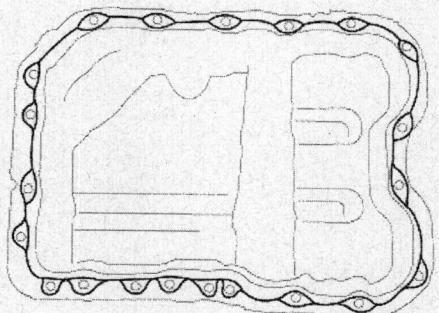

ARM0600000000217

Fig. 31 RTV placement on oil pan

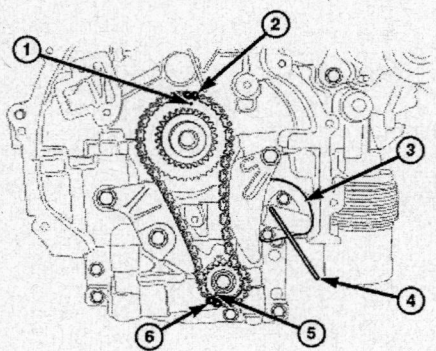

1. Balance shaft gear timing mark
2. Paint marked chain link
3. Chain tensioner
4. Tensioner pin tool No. 9703
5. Oil pump sprocket alignment mark
6. Paint marked chain link

ARM0600000000221

Fig. 32   Oil pump sprocket to balance shaft alignment

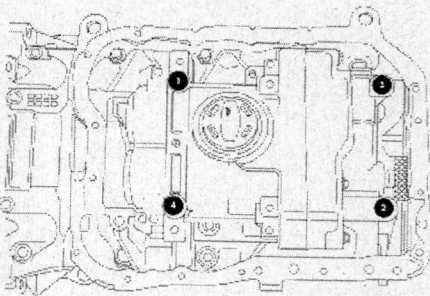

ARM0600000000222

Fig. 33   BSM mounting bolt tightening sequence

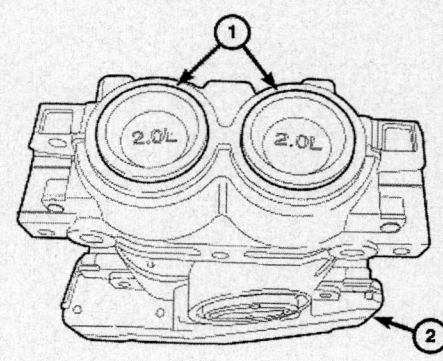

1. Balance Shaft Module (BSM)
2. Plastic end caps

ARM0600000000235

Fig. 34   Balance Shaft Module (BSM) identification. 2.0L engine

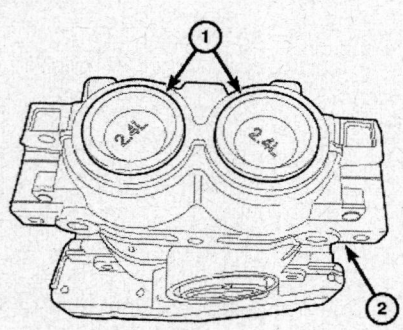

1. 1. Balance Shaft Module (BSM)
2. Plastic end caps

ARM0600000000236

Fig. 35   Balance Shaft Module (BSM) identification. 2.4L engine

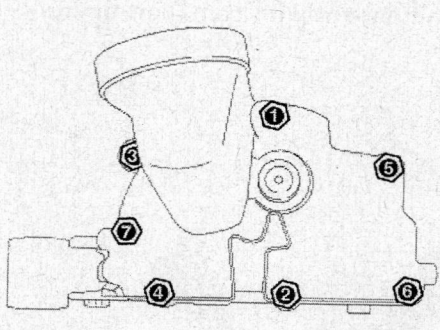

ARM0600000000218

Fig. 36   Oil pump housing bolt tightening sequence

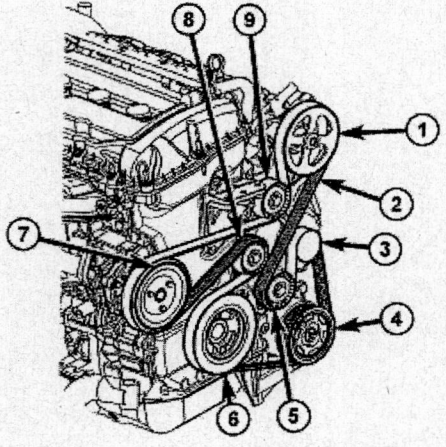

ARM0600000000219

Fig. 37   Serpentine drive belt routing

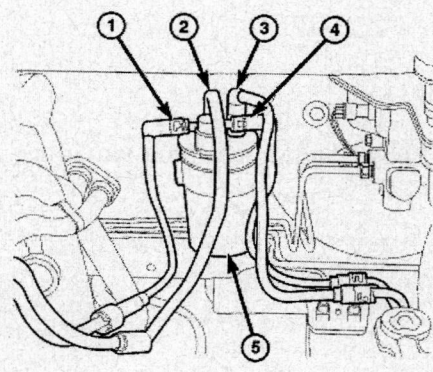

1. Fuel return line
2. Fuel supply line to fuel pump
3. Fuel supply line from fuel tank
4. Fuel return
5. Fuel Filter

ARM0600000000220

Fig. 38   Fuel line to fuel filter locations

TIGHTENING SPECIFICATIONS

Year	Component	Torque Ft. Lbs.
2007-08	Air Conditioning Accumulator Band	71①
	Air Conditioning Accumulator Bracket	11
	Air Conditioning Compressor	18
	Balance Shaft Module	⑥
	Bell Housing	35
	Camshaft Bearing Cap Bolts	③
	Camshaft Sprocket Bolt	44
	Condenser	70①
	Connecting Rod Caps	15②
	Crankshaft Damper	155
	Crankshaft Position Sensor	80①
	Cylinder Head	③
	Cylinder Head Cover	⑦
	Drive Belt Tensioner	18
	Engine Mount To Block R/H	55
	Engine Mount Bracket (All)	50
	Engine Mount Through Bolt L/H	74
	Engine Mount Through Bolt R/H	65
	Engine Mount Through Bolt (Rear)	55
	Engine Mount To Bracket (Front)	35
	Engine Mount To Frame L/H	55
	Engine Mount To Frame (Rear)	37
	Exhaust Manifold	25
	Flex Plate	70
	Fore Aft Member	74
	Fuel Rail Bolts	20
	Intake Manifold	⑧
	Ladder Frame	16
	Main Bearing Caps	⑤
	Manifold Tuning Valve	53①
	Oil Cooler Connector	36
	Oil Pan	④
	Oil Pan Drain Plug	30
	Oil Pump Cover	⑩
	Oil Pressure Switch	71①
	Oxygen Sensor	80①
	PCV Valve	40①
	Radiator Fan	55①
	Spark Plugs	20
	Thermostat Housing	70①
	Throttle Body	80①
	Timing Chain Cover	⑨
	Timing Chain Guides	105①
	Timing Chain Tensioner	105①
	Water Pump	18

① — Inch lbs.

② — Plus an additional 90°.

③ — Refer to "Cylinder Head, Replace" for tightening specifications and sequence.

④ — Refer to "Oil Pan, Replace" for tightening specifications and sequence.

⑤ — Refer to "Main & Rod Bearings" for tightening specifications and sequence.

⑥ — Refer to "Oil Pump, Replace" for tightening specifications and sequence.

⑦ — Refer to "Valve Cover, Replace" for tightening specifications and sequence.

⑧ — Refer to "Intake Manifold, Replace" for tightening specifications and sequence.

⑨ — Refer to "Front Cover, Replace" for tightening specifications and sequence.

⑩ — Refer to "Oil Pump Service" for tightening specifications and sequence.

Rear Axle & Suspension

NOTE: On Air Bag Equipped Models, Refer To "Air Bag System Precautions" Located In The Front Of This Manual For System Disarming & Arming Procedures.

NOTE: Refer To "Computer Relearn Procedures" Located In The Front Of This Manual When Battery Power To The Computer Has Been Interrupted.

NOTE: Refer To The Rear Of This Manual For Vehicle Manufacturer's Special Tool Suppliers.

INDEX

	Page No.
Coil Spring, Replace	7-23
Control Arm, Replace	7-23
Lower	7-23
Upper	7-23
Description	7-22
Differential Carrier, Replace	7-22
Hub & Bearing, Replace	7-22
Hub & Bearing Service	7-22
Precautions	7-22
Air Bag Systems	7-22
Battery Ground Cable	7-22
Propeller Shaft, Replace	7-22
Rear Halfshaft, Replace	7-22
Shock Absorber, Replace	7-22
Stabilizer Bar, Replace	7-23
Tightening Specifications	7-25
Toe Link, Replace	7-23
Trailing Link, Replace	7-23

PRECAUTIONS

Air Bag Systems

Refer to "Air Bag System Precautions" in the front of this manual for system disarming and arming procedures.

Battery Ground Cable

Prior to service, disconnect battery ground cable and isolate as required.

DESCRIPTION

This vehicle uses a multi-link rear suspension design, **Fig. 1.**

REAR HALFSHAFT
REPLACE

1. Raise and support vehicle.
2. Remove tire and wheel assembly.
3. Drain differential carrier oil into suitable container.
4. Mark rear propeller shaft and differential, **Fig. 2,** for proper installation.
5. Remove rear propeller shaft to rear axle retaining nuts.
6. Remove three bolts from center support heat shield, then the heat shield.
7. Remove center support mounting bolts. **Never allow propeller shaft to hang while connected to Power Transfer Unit (PTU), rear driveline module flanges or center bearings.**
8. Remove propeller shaft.
9. Remove righthand side sway bar nut if equipped.
10. Remove lefthand side sway bar nut.
11. Roll sway bar down and position aside.
12. Remove lefthand side stay bracket bolts.
13. Remove righthand side stay bracket bolts, **Fig. 3.**

14. Remove exhaust system up to catalytic converter.
15. Support rear driveline module with a suitable transmission jack.
16. Remove rear bolt and two side bolts at differential carrier.
17. Lower differential carrier enough to gain access to electrical connector and bracket.
18. Remove wire routing bracket bolt.
19. Disconnect electrical connector.
20. Lower differential carrier, **Fig. 4.**
21. Disengage axle shafts from carrier.
22. Remove cotter pins, nuts and washers from halfshafts to lefthand and righthand rear hubs.
23. Remove halfshafts from rear hubs. If halfshafts are hard to remove or sticking, use a suitable punch and hammer, then tap them out.
24. Reverse procedure to install.

DIFFERENTIAL CARRIER
REPLACE

Refer to "Rear Halfshaft, Replace" for differential carrier procedures.

PROPELLER SHAFT
REPLACE

Refer to "Rear Halfshaft, Replace" for propeller shaft procedures.

HUB & BEARING
REPLACE

1. Raise and support vehicle.
2. Remove tire and wheel assembly.
3. Remove cotter pin from hub nut on end of axle half shaft, then the hub nut.
4. Tap end of halfshaft inward, loosening it from hub and bearing.
5. Remove disc brake Caliper lower guide pin bolt.

6. Rotate Caliper upward hinging off upper guide pin bolt. Rotate Caliper upward just enough to allow brake rotor removal. Secure Caliper with suitable wire.
7. Slide brake rotor off hub and bearing.
8. Unclip wheel speed sensor head from retainer on rear of hub and bearing.
9. Remove four bolts securing hub and bearing to trailing link.
10. Remove hub and bearing.
11. Reverse procedure to install.

HUB & BEARING SERVICE

The rear wheel bearing and wheel hub are a one piece sealed unit or hub and bearing unit type assembly. The wheel mounting studs used to mount the tire and wheel to the vehicle are the only replaceable components of the hub and bearing. Otherwise, the hub and bearing is serviced only as a complete assembly.

SHOCK ABSORBER
REPLACE

1. Raise liftgate.
2. Remove liftgate scuff plate.
3. Remove cargo floor.
4. Remove B-pillar lower trim.
5. Remove scuff plate door sill.
6. Remove seat striker bezel using trim stick tool No. C-4755, or equivalent.
7. Remove rear quarter trim cargo loop fastener.
8. Remove rear quarter trim panel.
9. Remove two nuts, **Fig. 5,** securing shock assembly to upper body bracket.
10. Raise and support vehicle.
11. Remove tire and wheel assembly.
12. Remove lower shock mounting nut and bolt.

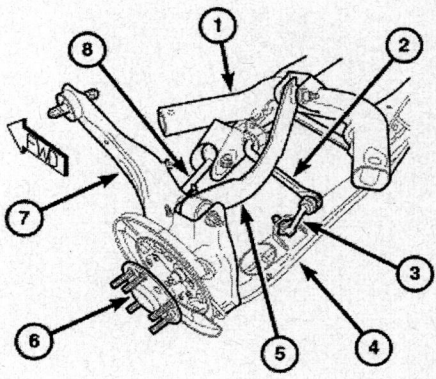

1. Rear crossmember
2. Stabilizer bar
3. Stabilizer link
4. Lower control arm
5. Upper control arm
6. Hub & bearing
7. Trailing arm
8. Toe link

ARM0600000000223

Fig. 1   Exploded view of rear suspension

13. Lower shock assembly out of body bracket and lift out over rear suspension.
14. Remove coil spring as outlined under, "Coil Spring, Replace."
15. Reverse procedure to install.

COIL SPRING
REPLACE

1. Remove shock absorber as outlined under "Shock Absorber, Replace."
2. Position shock assembly in suitable strut spring compressor following manufacturers instructions, then set lower and upper hooks of compressor on coil spring.
3. Once spring is sufficiently compressed, install Snap On shock absorber socket tool No. A139, or equivalent, on end of shock rod. While holding shock rod from turning, remove nut using suitable wrench, then remove washer.
4. Disassemble shock/coil spring assembly, **Fig. 6.**
5. Inspect coils spring and all components for any sign of damage.
6. Reverse procedure to install.

CONTROL ARM
REPLACE
Lower

1. Raise and support vehicle.
2. Remove tire and wheel assemblies.
3. While holding stabilizer bar link lower stud stationary, remove nut securing link to lower control arm.

4. Remove lower shock mounting nut and bolt.
5. Remove stay brace mounting screws, then the stay brace.
6. Remove nut and bolt securing lower control arm to trailing link.
7. Remove nut and bolt securing lower control arm to crossmember.
8. Remove lower control arm.
9. Reverse procedure to install, noting the following:
    a. Lower stabilizer bar link stud on righthand side link needs to point toward rear of vehicle, **Fig. 7,** when inserted through lower control arm mounting flange.
    b. Lefthand side link lower stud needs to point toward front of vehicle. **If links are not installed correctly suspension geometry will not function properly.**

Upper

1. Raise and support vehicle.
2. Remove tire and wheel assemblies.
3. Remove nut and bolt securing upper control arm, **Fig. 8,** to trailing link.
4. Remove bolt securing upper control arm to crossmember.
5. Remove upper control arm.
6. Reverse procedure to install, noting the following:
    a. Position vehicle on an alignment rack or drive on lift. Raise vehicle as required to access mounting bolts and nuts.
    b. First tighten control arm to crossmember bolt, second tighten control arm to trailing link bolt.

TOE LINK
REPLACE

1. Raise and support vehicle.
2. Remove bolt securing toe link to trailing link, **Fig. 9.**
3. Mark position of cam bolt cam on crossmember using a paint marker. This mark will be used during installation to help get alignment close prior to performing rear wheel alignment.
4. While holding cam bolt head stationary, loosen and remove toe link mounting cam bolt nut and washer, then remove cam bolt.
5. Remove toe link.
6. Reverse procedure to install. Ensure to align paint marks.

TRAILING LINK
REPLACE

1. Raise and support vehicle.
2. Remove tire and wheel assemblies.
3. Remove screw securing brake tube & flex hose to trailing link, **Fig. 10.**
4. Remove nut securing brake tube routing bracket to trailing link.
5. Remove brake tube from trailing link routing clip.
6. Remove disc brake Caliber adapter to brake support plate bolts.

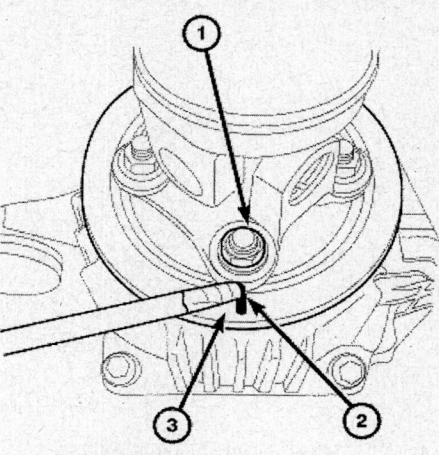

1. Retaining nut
2. Match mark
3. Differential flange

ARM0600000000228

Fig. 2   Propeller shaft removal

7. Remove Caliber and adapter as an assembly, then secure assembly aside using suitable wire.
8. Remove wheel speed sensor to trailing link mounting bolt, then sensor harness routing clip and position sensor aside.
9. Remove brake rotor, then hub and bearing assembly.
10. Disconnect parking brake cable from lever on parking brake shoe.
11. Remove hair pin securing parking brake cable to brake support plate.
12. Slide brake support plate with parking brake shoes, off end of parking brake cable.
13. Remove support plate and parking brake shoe.
14. Remove toe link to trailing link mounting bolt.
15. Remove lower control arm to trailing link mounting nut
16. Remove upper control arm to trailing link mounting nut
17. Remove two bolts, **Fig. 11,** mounting leading end of trailing link to body.
18. Remove trailing link.
19. Reverse procedure to install.

STABILIZER BAR
REPLACE

1. Raise an support vehicle.
2. Hold lefthand and righthand stabilizer bar link upper stud stationary, remove nut securing link to stabilizer bar.
3. **On models equipped with AWD,** remove differential carrier as out lined under "Differential Carrier, Replace."
4. **On all models,** remove stabilizer bar bushing retainer, **Fig. 12,** to crossmember mounting bolts.
5. Remove lefthand and righthand stabilizer bushing retainers.
6. Remove stabilizer bar from vehicle.
7. Reverse procedure to install.

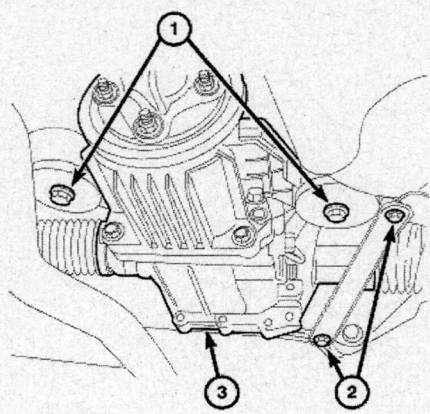

1. Differential carrier mounting bolts
2. Stay bracket bolts
3. Differential carrier

ARM0600000000227

Fig. 3 Stay bracket & carrier mounting bolt locations

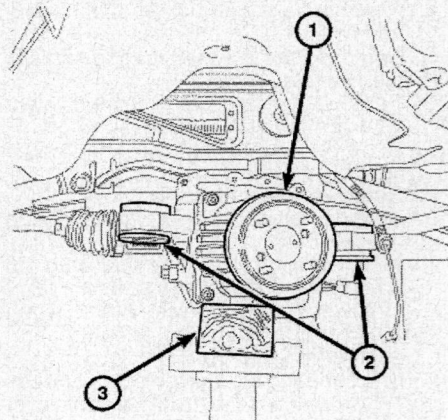

1. Differential carrier
2. Differential carrier mounts
3. Block of wood

ARM0600000000226

Fig. 4 Differential carrier removal.

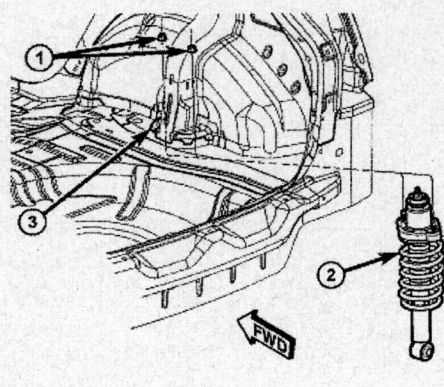

1. Shock mounting nuts
2. Shock assembly
3. Body bracket

ARM0600000000229

Fig. 5 Shock absorber removal

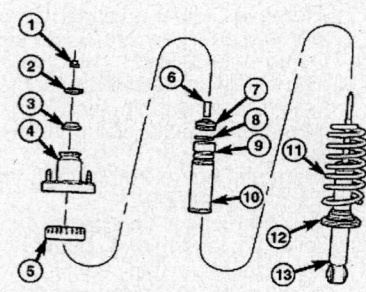

1. Nut
2. Washer
3. Bushing
4. Mounting bracket
5. Upper spring isolator
6. Sleeve
7. Bushing
8. Slide washer
9. Jounce bumper
10. Dust shield
11. Coil spring
12. Lower spring isolator
13. Shock absorber

ARM0600000000230

Fig. 6 Exploded view of shock/ coil spring assembly

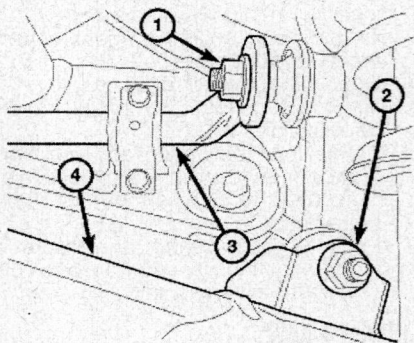

1. Stabilizer bar link Upper stud
2. Stabilizer bar link lower stud
3. Stabilizer bar
4. Lower control arm

ARM0600000000224

Fig. 7 Stabilizer bar link lower stud positioning

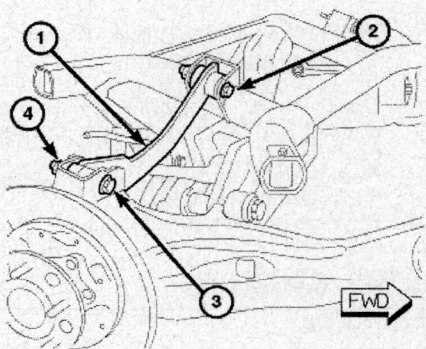

1. Upper control arm
2. Upper mounting bolt
3. Lower mounting bolt
4. Lower mounting nut

ARM0600000000225

Fig. 8 Upper control arm replacement

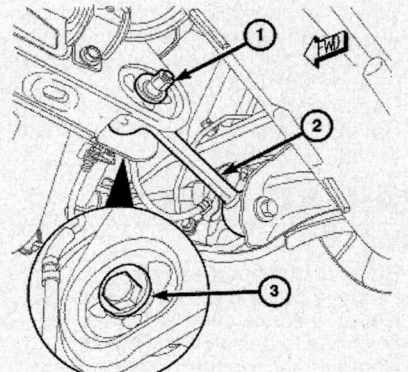

1. Cam bolt
2. Toe link
3. Cam bolt head (Index Mark Before Removing)

ARM0600000000231

Fig. 9 Toe link removal & cam bolt location

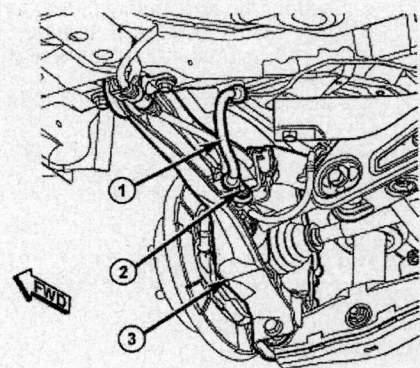

1. Flex brake hose
2. Flex hose mounting screw
3. Trailing link

ARM0600000000232

Fig. 10 Flex hose to trailing link removal

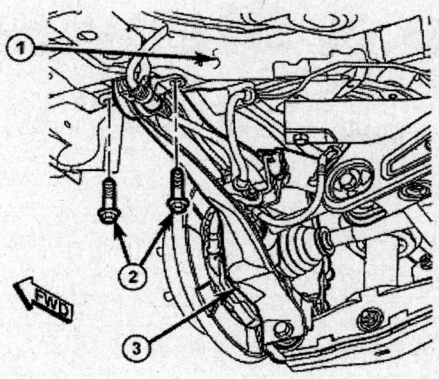

1. Vehicle body
2. Trailing link upper bolts
3. Trailing link

ARM0600000000233

Fig. 11   Trailing link removal

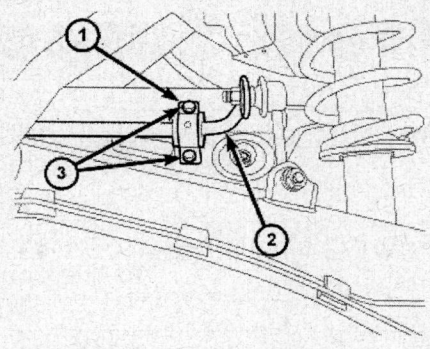

1. Crossmember
2. Stabilizer bar
3. Retaining bushing and bolts

ARM0600000000234

Fig. 12   Stabilizer bar retaining bushing removal

TIGHTENING SPECIFICATIONS

Year	Component	Torque/Ft. Lbs.
2007-08	Brake Flex Hose Nut	11
	Brake Flex Hose Screw	17
	Crossmember Stay Brace	18
	Differential Carrier Mounting Bolts	75
	Differential Carrier Stay Bracket Bolt	45
	Hub & Bearing Mounting Bolts	77
	Hub Nut	181
	Lower Control Arm To Crossmember Nut	70
	Lower Control Arm To Trailing Link	70
	Shock Absorber Lower Bolt & Nut	73
	Shock Absorber Upper Nuts	35
	Shock Rod Nut	18
	Stabilizer Bar Bushing Retainer Bolts	25
	Stabilizer Link Mounting Nuts	43
	Toe Link Cam Bolt & Nut	26
	Toe Link To Trailing Link Bolts	70
	Trailing Link To Body Bolts	81
	Upper Control Arm To Crossmember Bolts	70
	Upper Control Arm To Trailing Link Bolt	70
	Wheel Lug Nuts	100

Front Suspension & Steering

NOTE: On Air Bag Equipped Models, Refer To "Air Bag System Precautions" Located In The Front Of This Manual For System Disarming & Arming Procedures.

NOTE: Refer To "Computer Relearn Procedures" Located In The Front Of This Manual When Battery Power To The Computer Has Been Interrupted.

NOTE: Refer To The Rear Of This Manual For Vehicle Manufacturer's Special Tool Suppliers.

INDEX

	Page No.
Ball Joint, Replace	7-27
Coil Spring, Replace	7-27
Coil Spring & Strut Service	7-27
Control Arm, Replace	7-28
Description	7-26
Driveshaft, Replace	7-27
Hub & Bearing, Replace	7-26
Installation	7-26

	Page No.
Removal	7-26
Power Steering	13-1
Power Steering Gear, Replace	7-28
Power Steering Pump, Replace	7-29
Power Steering System Bleed	7-29
Precautions	7-26
Air Bag Systems	7-26
Battery Ground Cable	7-26

	Page No.
Re-calibration	7-26
Stabilizer Bar, Replace	7-28
Steering Columns	12-1
Steering Knuckle, Replace	7-28
Strut, Replace	7-27
Tie Rod, Replace	7-28
Tightening Specifications	7-30

PRECAUTIONS

Air Bag Systems

Refer to "Air Bag System Precautions" in the front of this manual for system disarming and arming procedures.

Battery Ground Cable

Prior to service, disconnect battery ground cable and isolate as required.

RE-CALIBRATION

Anytime the battery has been disconnect or has lost its charge, the following must be re-calibrated.

DESCRIPTION

This vehicle has a gas pressurized MacPherson strut type front suspension design. The front suspension consists of these major components, hub pressed into bearing, bearing pressed into knuckle, steering knuckle, lower control arm, stabilizer bar and strut assembly. The front suspension also includes a crossmember to support the lower half of the suspension.

HUB & BEARING

REPLACE

Installation

When installing the wheel bearing in knuckle it is important to place side of bearing with wheel speed sensor magnetic encoder ring (dark band) in knuckle first. Otherwise, wheel speed sensor will not operate correctly.

1. Wipe bearing bore of knuckle clean of any grease or dirt with a clean, dry shop towel.
2. Place knuckle in an arbor press supporting knuckle from underneath using cup No. tool 6310-1, equivalent, **Fig. 1.**
3. Place new wheel bearing magnetic encoder ring side down into bore of knuckle. Ensure wheel bearing is placed squarely into bore.
4. Place receiver tool No. 8498, or equivalent, larger inside diameter end down over outer race of wheel bearing.
5. Place disc tool No. 6310-2, or equivalent, into top of receiver tool No. 8498, or equivalent.
6. Lower arbor press ram and press wheel bearing into knuckle until it is bottomed in bore of knuckle.
7. Remove knuckle and tools from arbor press.
8. Install a new snap ring in knuckle using suitable pair of snap ring pliers. Ensure snap ring is fully seated.
9. Place knuckle in suitable arbor press. Support knuckle from underneath using Remover/Installer tool No. MB-99079, or equivalent, **Fig. 2,** smaller end up against wheel bearing inner race.
10. Place hub in wheel bearing making sure it is square with bearing inner race.
11. Position Remover/Installer tool 9712-2, or equivalent, in end of hub.
12. Lower arbor press ram and press hub into wheel bearing until it bottoms.
13. Remove knuckle and tools from press.
14. Verify hub turns smoothly without rubbing or binding.
15. Install steering knuckle as outlined under "Steering Knuckle, Replace."

Removal

1. Remove steering knuckle as outlined under.
2. Install knuckle in press fixture tool No. 9712, or equivalent, as follows:
   a. For lefthand side knuckles, place locator block to lefthand side on fixture, **Fig. 3.** For righthand side knuckles, place locator block to righthand side on fixture. Side of locator block with angle cut goes downward, toward fixture. Install mounting screws and tighten them to approximately 40 ft. lbs.
   b. Install knuckle in fixture as indicated, **Fig. 4,** guiding steering arm to rest on locator block and brake Caliber mounting bosses on two fixture pins.
   c. Place fixture with knuckle in suitable arbor press, **Fig. 5.**
3. Position Remover/Installer tool 9712-2, or equivalent, in small end of hub.
4. Lower arbor press ram and remove hub from wheel bearing and knuckle.
5. Bearing race will normally come out of wheel bearing with hub as it is pressed out of bearing.
6. Remove knuckle from fixture and turn it over.
7. Remove snap ring from knuckle using suitable pair of snap ring pliers.
8. Place knuckle back in fixture in arbor press ram.
9. Place Installer tool MD-998334, or equivalent, on outer race of wheel bearing.
10. Lower arbor press ram and remove wheel bearing from knuckle.
11. Remove knuckle and tools from arbor press.
12. If bearing race is still pressed onto hub, install bearing splitter tool No. 1130, or

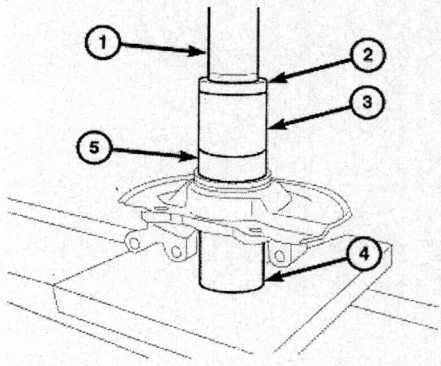

1. Press ram
2. Disc tool No. 6310-2
3. Receiver tool No. 8498
4. Cup tool No. 6310-1
5. Wheel bearing

ARM0600000000242

Fig. 1 Wheel bearing installation on hub

equivalent, between hub flange and bearing inner race.
13. Place hub, bearing race and Bearing Splitter in an arbor press.
14. Press support blocks must not obstruct wheel hub while it is being pressed out of bearing race.
15. Place Remover/Installer tool No. 9712-2, or equivalent, in end of hub.
16. Lower arbor press ram and remove hub from bearing race.

DRIVESHAFT
REPLACE

Halfshaft inner and outer boots are not serviceable separately. Boot replacement requires entire shaft assembly replacement.

Lefthand halfshaft is shorter than right. Identify and tag halfshafts upon removal to ensure proper installation.
1. Raise and support vehicle.
2. Remove tire and wheel assembly.
3. Remove cotter pin, nut lock, spring washer, and hub nut from end of outer C/V joint stub axle.
4. Disconnect front wheel speed sensor and secure harness aside.
5. Remove nut and bolt retaining ball joint stud into steering knuckle.
6. Separate ball joint stud from steering knuckle by prying down on lower control arm.
7. Remove halfshaft from steering knuckle by pulling outward on knuckle while pressing in on halfshaft. Ensure to support outer end of halfshaft assembly.
8. If difficulty in separating halfshaft from hub is encountered, use puller tool No. 1026, or equivalent, to separate halfshaft.
9. Remove halfshaft bracket to engine upper and lower mounting bolt. Support outer end of halfshaft assembly.
10. Remove inner tripod joints from side gears of transaxle using a suitable punch inserted into tripod joint extrac-

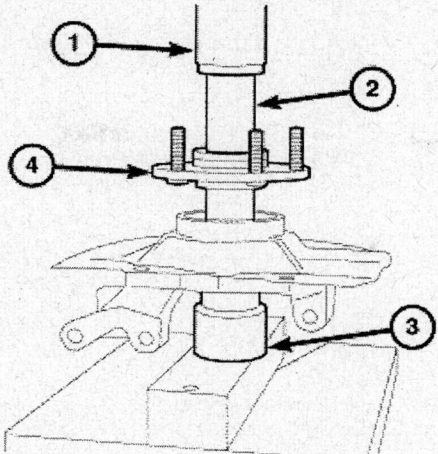

1. Press ram
2. Installation tool 9712-2
3. Installation tool MB-99079
4. Wheel hub

ARM0600000000243

Fig. 2 Hub installation on wheel bearing

tion groove, **Fig. 6,** to dislodge inner tripod joint retaining ring from transaxle side gear. Strike punch sharply with a hammer to dislodge inner joint from side gear.
11. Hold inner tripod joint and interconnecting shaft of halfshaft assembly.
12. Remove inner tripod joint from transaxle by pulling shaft straight out of transaxle side gear and transaxle oil seal.
13. Reverse procedure to install.

BALL JOINT
REPLACE

Lower ball joint is not serviced separately, control arm and ball joint must be replaced as an assembly.

COIL SPRING
REPLACE

Refer to "Coil Spring & Strut Service" for coil spring replacement procedure.

STRUT
REPLACE

1. Raise and support vehicle.
2. Remove tire and wheel assembly.
3. Remove screw securing flex hose routing bracket to strut.
4. While holding stabilizer bar link stud stationary, remove nut securing link to strut. **Strut assembly to knuckle attaching bolts are serrated and must not be turned during removal.**
5. While holding bolt heads stationary, remove two nuts from bolts attaching strut to knuckle.
6. Remove two bolts attaching strut to knuckle, **Fig. 7,** using suitable pin punch.

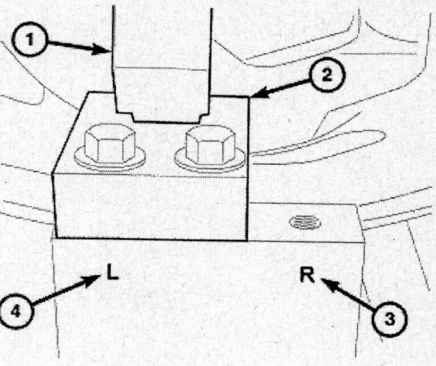

1. Fixture arm
2. Locator block
3. Lefthand side of fixture
4. Righthand side of fixture

ARM0600000000239

Fig. 3 Locator block location on special fixture

7. Remove two bolts attaching strut to knuckle using suitable pin punch.
8. Lower vehicle just enough to open hood without allowing tires to touch floor.
9. Remove three nuts attaching strut assembly upper mount to strut tower.
10. Remove strut assembly from vehicle.
11. Reverse procedure to install. Refer to "Coil Spring & Strut Service" for strut disassembly procedure.

COIL SPRING & STRUT SERVICE

The coil spring must be compressed, removing spring tension from the upper mount and bearing, before the strut rod nut is removed.
1. Remove strut spring assembly as outlined under "Strut, Replace."
2. Position strut assembly in suitable strut coil spring compressor following manufacturers instructions and set lower and upper hooks of compressor on coil spring.
3. Compress coil spring until all coil spring tension is removed from upper mount and bearing.
4. Install strut nut wrench tool No. 9362, or equivalent, on strut rod nut, then install strut shaft socket No. tool 9894, or equivalent, on end of strut rod.
5. While holding strut rod from turning, **Fig. 8,** remove nut using strut nut wrench.
6. Remove clamp from bottom of coil spring and remove strut damper out through bottom of coil spring.
7. Remove lower isolator from strut seat.
8. Slide dust shield and jounce bumper from strut rod.
9. Remove upper mount and bearing from top of upper spring seat and isolator.
10. Remove upper spring seat and isolator from top of coil spring.
11. Remove lower spring isolator from lower spring seat on strut.

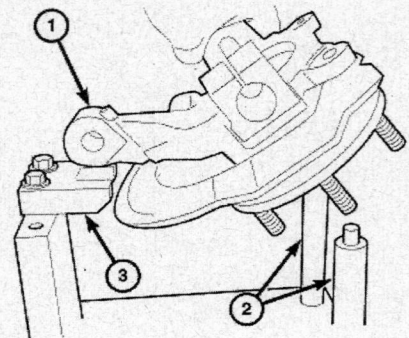

1. Knuckle
2. Fixture pins
3. Locator Block

ARM0600000000240

Fig. 4 Steering knuckle positioned in fixture

12. Release tension from coil spring by backing off compressor drive completely. Push back compressor hooks and remove coil spring.
13. Reverse procedure to install.

CONTROL ARM
REPLACE

1. Raise and support vehicle.
2. Remove tire and wheel assembly.
3. Remove nut and pinch bolt, **Fig. 9,** clamping ball joint stud to knuckle
4. Separate ball joint stud from knuckle by prying down on lower control arm and up against ball joint boss on knuckle, using suitable pry tool.
5. Remove front bolt attaching lower control arm to front suspension crossmember.
6. Remove nut on rear bolt attaching lower control arm to front suspension crossmember. Remove bolt.
7. Remove lower control arm from crossmember.
8. Reverse procedure to install.

STEERING KNUCKLE
REPLACE

1. Raise and support vehicle.
2. Remove tire and wheel assembly.
3. Remove cotter pin from hub nut.
4. Remove hub nut and washer from axle halfshaft.
5. Remove two bolts securing disc brake Caliber and adapter bracket to steering knuckle.
6. Remove disc brake Caliber adapter bracket as and assembly, then secure assembly aside using suitable wire.
7. Remove any clips retaining brake rotor to wheel studs, then slide rotor off hub.
8. Remove routing clip securing wheel speed sensor cable to knuckle.
9. Remove bolt retaining wheel speed sensor to knuckle, then the sensor from knuckle.
10. Remove outer tie rod to knuckle retaining nut.

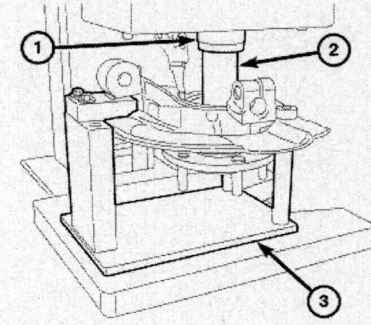

1. Press arm
2. Installer/Removal tool No. 9712-2
3. Fixture with knuckle

ARM0600000000241

Fig. 5 Fixture placement in arbor press.

11. Remove outer tie rod from knuckle using tie rod removal tool No. 9360, or equivalent.
12. Remove nut and pinch bolt, **Fig. 10,** clamping ball joint stud to knuckle.
13. While holding bolt heads stationary, remove two nuts from bolts attaching strut to knuckle. Strut assembly to knuckle attaching bolts are serrated and must not be turned during removal. **Strut to knuckle mounting bolts are serrated and must not be allowed turned during removal.**
14. Remove strut to knuckle mounting bolts using suitable pin punch.
15. Separate ball joint stud from knuckle by prying down, **Fig. 11,** on lower control arm and up against ball joint boss on knuckle.
16. Pull knuckle off halfshaft outer C/V joint splines.
17. Remove knuckle from vehicle.
18. Reverse procedure to install.

STABILIZER BAR
REPLACE

1. Raise and support vehicle.
2. Remove engine belly pan.
3. Remove rear engine mount as outlined "Engine Mount, Replace" in "1.8L, 2.0L & 2.4L Engines" section.
4. Remove front engine mount through bolt.
5. Remove bolts securing power steering hose routing clamps to crossmember.
6. Hold both ends of stabilizer bar link lower stud stationary, then remove nut securing link to stabilizer bar.
7. Remove screws securing stabilizer bushing retainers to crossmember.
8. Remove two stabilizer bushing retainers.
9. Utilizing slit cut into cushions (bushings), remove two cushions from stabilizer bar.
10. Mark location of front crossmember on body near each mounting bolt.
11. Support crossmember with suitable transmission jack.
12. Support steering gear using a bungee

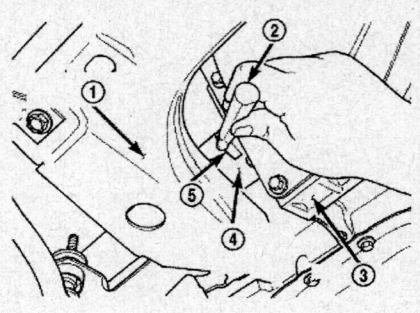

1. Crossmember
2. Punch
3. Transaxle case
4. Inner tripod joint
5. Joint extraction groove

ARM0600000000244

Fig. 6 Halfshaft removal from transaxle

cord or wire to keep steering gear from lowering when crossmember is lowered.
13. Slowly lower crossmember until there is enough space present to remove stabilizer bar between rear of crossmember and body. Due to fore-and-aft crossmember still being attached, do not lower crossmember any more than required to remove stabilizer bar.
14. Remove stabilizer bar over rear of crossmember.
15. Reverse procedure to install.

TIE ROD
REPLACE

1. Raise and support vehicle.
2. Remove tire and wheel assembly.
3. Loosen tie rod jam nut.
4. Remove nut attaching outer tie rod to knuckle.
5. Hold tie rod end stud with a wrench while loosening and removing nut with a standard wrench or crowfoot wrench.
6. Remove tie rod end from steering knuckle using removal tool No. 9360, or equivalent.
7. Remove outer tie rod from inner tie rod.
8. Reverse procedure to install. Adjust front wheel toe setting as outlined under "Toe" in "Wheel Alignment" section.

POWER STEERING GEAR
REPLACE

1. Siphon out as much power steering fluid as possible from pump.
2. Reposition floor carpeting to access intermediate shaft coupling at base of column.
3. Position front wheels of vehicle in straight-ahead position, then turn steering wheel to right until intermediate shaft coupling bolt at base of column can be accessed.
4. Remove intermediate shaft coupling

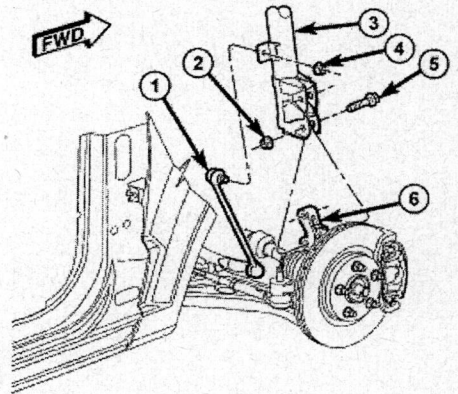

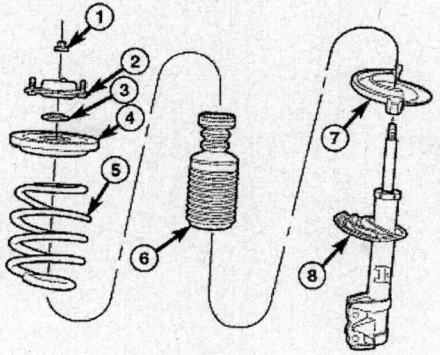

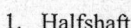

1. Shaft nut
2. Upper mount
3. Bearing
4. Upper spring seat isolator
5. Coil Spring
6. Jounce bumper
7. lower spring isolator
8. Strut

ARM0600000000247

Fig. 8   Exploded view of front strut/spring assembly

1. Halfshaft
2. Tie rod nut
3. Steering knuckle
4. Ball joint nut
5. Ball joint bolt
6. Ball joint
7. Tie rod end

ARM0600000000245

Fig. 9   Lower control arm replacement

1. Stabilizer bar link
2. Lower strut nut
3. strut assembly
4. upper strut nut
5. Serrated bolt
6. Steering knuckle

ARM0600000000246

Fig. 7   Strut spring assembly removal

bolt. **Do not separate intermediate shaft from steering gear pinion shaft at this time.**

5. Return front wheels of vehicle and steering wheel to straight-ahead position.
6. Lock steering wheel in place to keep it from rotating, using a steering wheel holder. This keeps clockspring in proper orientation.
7. Raise and support vehicle.
8. Remove tire and wheel assembly.
9. Remove lefthand and righthand out tie rod end retaining nuts at steering knuckle.
10. Separate tie rod ends from steering knuckles using removal tool No. 9360, or equivalent.
11. Remove engine belly pan.
12. Remove rear engine mount as outlined under "Engine Mount, Replace" in "1.8L, 2.0L & 2.4L Engines" section.
13. Remove front engine mount through bolt.
14. Remove three screws securing heat shield to crossmember, then the shield.
15. Remove return hose at steering gear.
16. Remove pressure hose at steering gear.
17. Remove fasteners securing power steering hose routing clamps to crossmember.
18. Remove screws securing stabilizer

bushing retainers to crossmember.
19. Remove two stabilizer bushing retainers.
20. Mark location of front crossmember on body near each mounting bolt using suitable paint marker.
21. Support front crossmember with suitable transmission jack.
22. Remove four mounting bolts mounting front crossmember to body.
23. Lower crossmember enough to access intermediate shaft coupling at steering gear pinion shaft. Slide coupling off pinion shaft.
24. Remove dash seals as required.
25. Remove two bolts securing steering gear to crossmember.
26. Rotate stabilizer bar upward in order to remove steering gear from vehicle.
27. Remove steering gear from crossmember, **Fig. 12.**
28. Reverse procedure to install.

POWER STEERING PUMP

REPLACE

1. Siphon as much fluid as possible from power steering fluid reservoir.
2. Remove engine appearance cover.
3. Remove pressure hose routing bracket bolt (2) at upper mount.
4. Remove pressure hose at pump pressure port.
5. Remove hose clamp securing supply hose at pump, then the supply hose.

6. Remove drive belt as outlined under "Serpentine Drive Belt" in "1.8L, 2.0L & 2.4L Engines" section.
7. Remove three pump mounting bolts working through pulley openings.
8. Remove power steering pump.
9. Reverse procedure to install.

POWER STEERING SYSTEM BLEED

1. Wipe filler cap clean and inspect fluid level.
2. Turn steering wheel all way to left.
3. Fill pump fluid reservoir to proper level and let fluid settle for least two minutes.
4. Raise and support front wheels off ground.
5. Slowly turn steering wheel lock-to-lock 20 times with engine off while inspecting fluid level. Vehicles with long return lines or oil coolers turn wheel 40 times.
6. Start engine.
7. With engine idling maintain fluid level.
8. Lower front wheels and let engine idle for two minutes.
9. Turn steering wheel in both direction, and verify power assist and quiet operation of pump.
10. If fluid is extremely foamy or milky looking, allow vehicle to stand few minutes and repeat procedure. **Do not run vehicle with foamy fluid for an extended period.**

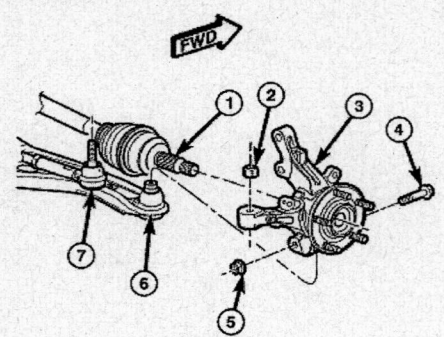

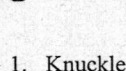

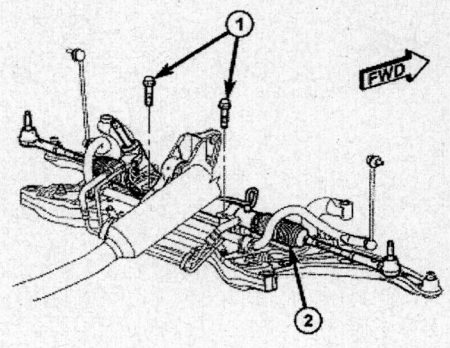

1. Halfshaft
2. Tie rod end nut
3. Knuckle
4. Ball joint stud bolt
5. Ball joint stud nut
6. Lower ball joint

ARM0600000000237

**Fig. 10   Steering knuckle
replacement**

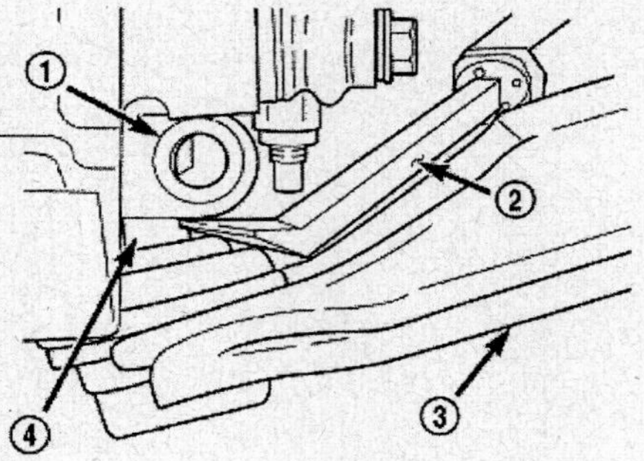

1. Knuckle
2. Pry Bar
3. Lower control arm
4. Ball joint stud

ARM0600000000238

**Fig. 11   Ball joint separated from
steering knuckle**

1. Mounting bolts
2. Steering gear on crossmember

ARM0600000000248

**Fig. 12   Steering gear removal
from crossmember**

TIGHTENING SPECIFICATIONS

Year	Component	Torque/Ft. Lbs.
2007-08	Ball Joint To Knuckle Pinch Bolt	60
	Bolt Intermediate Shaft Bracket Block	55
	Driveshaft To Hub Bearing Nut	181
	Gear Heat Shield To Crossmember	12
	Hose Routing Clamp	71①
	Hose Tube To Gear (Pressure)	24
	Hose Tube To Gear (Return)	15
	Hose Tube To Pump	24
	Hub Wheel To Hub Nut	95
	Intermediate Shaft Coupling Bolt	35
	Lower Control Arm Pivot Bolts	135
	Pump Mounting Bolts	19
	Reservoir Mounting Screws	106①
	Stabilizer Bar Cushion Retainer	22
	Stabilizer Bar Link	43
	Steering Gear To Crossmember	52
	Strut Rod Nut	55
	Strut To Tower Nuts	35
	Suspension To Crossmember	140
	Tie Rod End To Knuckle Nut	97
	Tie Rod Jam Nut	55
	Wheel Lug Nut	110

① — Inch lbs.

Wheel Alignment

NOTE: On Air Bag Equipped Models, Refer To "Air Bag System Precautions" Located In The Front Of This Manual For System Disarming & Arming Procedures.

NOTE: Refer To "Computer Relearn Procedures" Located In The Front Of This Manual When Battery Power To The Computer Has Been Interrupted.

NOTE: Prior To Performing Any Service Operations Listed In This Section, Consult The "Technical Service Bulletins" Section For Related Information.

NOTE: Refer To The Rear Of This Manual For Vehicle Manufacturer's Special Tool Suppliers.

INDEX

	Page No.		Page No.		Page No.
Front Wheel Alignment	7-31	Preliminary Inspection	7-31	Wheel Alignment	
Camber & Caster	7-31	Rear Wheel Alignment	7-31	Specifications	7-2
Toe	7-31	Toe	7-32		

PRELIMINARY INSPECTION

Before any attempt is made to change or correct the wheel alignment, the following inspection and required corrections must be made to ensure proper alignment.
1. Ensure fuel tank is full of fuel.
2. Ensure passenger and luggage compartments are free of any load that is not factory equipment.
3. Ensure all tires are same size and in good condition with approximately same amount of tread wear.
4. Inflate all tires to recommended air pressure.
5. Inspect wheel and tire assemblies for excessive radial runout.
6. Inspect lower ball joints and all steering linkage for looseness, binding, wear or damage.
7. Inspect suspension fasteners for proper torque.
8. Inspect all suspension component rubber bushings for signs of wear or deterioration.
9. Inspect vehicle's curb height to ensure it is within specifications.

FRONT WHEEL ALIGNMENT

On this vehicle, four-wheel alignment is recommended.
1. Position vehicle on alignment rack.
2. Install all required alignment equipment on vehicle per alignment equipment manufacturers instructions
3. Prior to reading vehicle's alignment readouts, front and rear of vehicle should be jounced (suspension compressed/released).
4. Induce jounce (rear first, then front) by

grasping center of bumper and jouncing each end of vehicle an equal number of times.
5. Bumper should always be released when vehicle is at bottom of jounce cycle.
6. Record vehicle's current front and rear alignment settings. Compare settings to vehicle specifications for camber, caster and toe-in.
7. If caster and camber are within specifications, proceed to roe.
8. Rear camber and caster are not adjustable. If found not to be within specifications, inspect for damaged suspension or body components.
9. If rear toe is not within specifications, adjust rear toe before proceeding to adjust front toe.

Camber & Caster

Camber and caster settings on this vehicle are determined at the time the vehicle is designed, by the location of the vehicle's suspension components. This is referred to as net build. The result is no required adjustment of camber and caster after the vehicle is built or when servicing the suspension components. Thus, when performing a wheel alignment, caster and camber are not normally considered adjustable angles.

Camber and caster should be inspected to ensure they meet vehicle specifications.

If individual front camber or caster is found not to meet alignment specifications, each can be adjusted by shifting the engine cradle if cross-camber and cross-caster are within specifications, or by using an available service adjustment bolt package. Always try to shift the cradle first (if camber and caster are off slightly) to correct the misalignment before installing an adjust-

ment bolt package. If an adjustment bolt package installation is required, inspect the suspension components for any signs of damage or bending first.

Do not attempt to adjust the vehicles wheel alignment by heating, bending or by performing any other modification to the vehicle's front suspension components or body.

Toe

When performing the toe adjustment procedure, set rear toe to specifications before setting front toe.

Do not twist the inner tie rod-to-steering gear boots during front wheel toe adjustment.

Perform the following procedure to each side of the vehicle as required.
1. Center steering wheel and lock in place using suitable steering wheel clamp.
2. Remove boot clamps at inner tie rods and ensure boots move freely on inner tie rods.
3. Loosen jam nut at inner-to-outer tie rod connection.
4. Grasp inner tie rod at hex and rotate as required to adjust front toe.
5. **Torque** tie rod jam nut to 55 ft. lbs.
6. Ensure inner tie rod-to-steering gear boot is not twisted, then install boot clamp at inner tie rod.
7. Adjust front toe on opposite side as outlined in previous steps.

REAR WHEEL ALIGNMENT

Rear camber and caster are not adjustable. If found not to be within specifications, inspect for damaged suspension or body

Toe

components If rear toe is not within specifications, adjust rear toe before proceeding to adjust front toe.

Toe

When performing the toe adjustment procedure, set rear toe to specifications before setting front toe.

1. Center steering wheel and lock in place using suitable steering wheel clamp.
2. Loosen toe link to rear crossmember cam bolt nut (front of rear crossmember) just enough to rotate cam bolt.
3. Rotate cam bolt head on opposite side (rear) of crossmember in either direction until preferred specification is obtained. **When adjusting rear toe, eccentric lobes on toe adjustment cam bolts and washers are not to be facing downward. Lobes should only be facing upward or up to 90° to one side or other from 12 O'clock position.**
4. While holding cam bolt from turning, tighten cam bolt nut.
5. Adjust rear toe on opposite side of vehicle as outlined in previous test.
6. Once rear toe is set, proceed to front toe to set vehicle's front toe.

AIR CONDITIONING

NOTE: Prior To Performing Any Service Operations Listed In This Section, Consult The "Technical Service Bulletins" Section For Related Information.

TABLE OF CONTENTS

	Page No.			Page No.
SPECIFICATIONS	8-7	**SYSTEM TESTING**		8-1
SYSTEM SERVICE	8-6			

System Testing

NOTE: On Air Bag Equipped Models, Refer To "Air Bag System Precautions" Located In The Front Of This Manual For System Disarming & Arming Procedures.

NOTE: Refer To "Computer Relearn Procedures" Located In The Front Of This Manual When Battery Power To The Computer Has Been Interrupted.

INDEX

	Page No.		Page No.		Page No.
Charging System	8-4	Performance Test	8-1	2004–06	8-2
Charger, Magnum & 300	8-4	Avenger Sedan & Sebring		Sebring Coupe & Stratus	
Concorde, Intrepid & 300M	8-4	Sedan	8-2	Coupe	8-3
Crossfire	8-4	2007–08	8-2	Precautions	8-1
Neon	8-4	Charger, Magnum & 300	8-2	Battery Ground Cable	8-1
Sebring Convertible, Sebring		Concorde, Intrepid & 300M	8-2	R-134a Systems	8-1
Sedan & Stratus Sedan	8-4	Crossfire	8-2	System Evacuation	8-3
Sebring Coupe & Stratus		Neon	8-2	Using Charging Station	8-3
Coupe	8-4	Sebring Convertible, Stratus		Using Vacuum Pump	8-3
Discharging System	8-3	Sedan & 2004–06 Sebring			
Exercise System	8-1	Sedan	8-2		
Leak Test	8-3				

PRECAUTIONS

Battery Ground Cable

Prior to service, disconnect battery ground cable and isolate as required.

R-134a Systems

R-134a refrigerant is a non-toxic, non-flammable, clear, colorless, odorless liquefied gas.

R-134a refrigerant is not compatible with R-12 refrigerant. Even small amounts of R-12 in an R-134a system will cause lubricant contamination, compressor failure, or improper air conditioning performance. Never add R-12 to an R-134a system.

New service ports have been added to the compressor to prevent charging the system with R-12 refrigerant. R-134a systems require a special compressor lubricant. Use PAG compressor oil when servicing system.

Avoid breathing air conditioning R-134a refrigerant and lubricant vapor or mist. Exposure may irritate eyes, nose and throat. Use only approved service equipment to discharge R-134a systems.

Always wear eye protection when servicing the air conditioning system. Serious injury may result from eye contact with refrigerant. If this happens, seek prompt medical attention.

EXERCISE SYSTEM

Air conditioning units must be used periodically. Manufacturers caution that when the air conditioner is not used regularly, particularly during cold months, it should be turned on for a few minutes once every two or three weeks while the engine is running. This keeps the system in good operating condition.

Inspecting the system for effects of infrequent usage before the onset of summer is one of the most important aspects of air conditioning servicing.

First, clean out the condenser core, in all cases in front of the radiator. All obstructions such as leaves, bugs and dirt must be removed, as they will reduce heat transfer and impair the efficiency of the system. Ensure the space between the condenser and the radiator is also free of foreign matter.

Ensure evaporator water drain is open. The evaporator cools and dehumidifies the air before it enters the passenger compartment. At that point, the refrigerant is changed from a liquid to a vapor. As the core cools the air, moisture condenses on it but is prevented from collecting in the evaporator by the water drain.

PERFORMANCE TEST

Vehicle should not be in sunlight when performing this test.

Ambient Temperature, Deg. F	70	80	90	100	110
Maximum Allowable Air Temperature At Center Left Panel Outlet, Deg. F	42	45	50	54	59
Compressor Discharge Pressure, psi	200–230	210–250	240–280	280–320	320–365
Compressor Suction Pressure, psi	15–25	20–30	25–35	30–40	35–45

Fig. 1 Performance temperature & pressure test. Concorde, Intrepid, 300M, 2004–06 Sebring Convertible, Sebring Sedan & Stratus Sedan

Concorde, Intrepid & 300M

1. Ensure ambient air temperature of vehicle and location are at least 70° F.
2. Ensure evaporator temperature sensor probe (between evaporator fins) is at least 65° F.
3. Connect suitable tachometer and manifold gauge set to vehicle.
4. **On models equipped with Manual Temperature Control (MTC),** set air conditioning controls as follows:
   a. Blower motor control to highest speed position.
   b. Temperature control to full cool position.
   c. Mode control to recirculation (MAX-A/C) position.
   d. Air conditioning switch to MAX A/C.
   e. A/C control to ON position.
5. **On models equipped with Automatic Temperature Control (ATC),** set air conditioning controls as follows:
   a. Blower motor control to highest speed position.
   b. Temperature control to LO position.
   c. Recirculation control ON (A/C and RECIRC symbols should be lit).
   d. Mode control to PANEL position.
   e. MANUAL should appear in ATC display, confirming system is set manually.
6. **On all models,** adjust idle to 1000 RPM with air conditioning clutch engaged. Engine should be at normal operating temperature. Doors and windows should be closed.
7. Insert thermometer in lefthand center air conditioning outlet and operate engine for 20 minutes.
8. Evaporator inlet line temperature should be no more than 10°F cooler than discharged air temperature.
9. If discharge air temperature fails to meet specifications, further diagnosis of air conditioning system should be performed.
10. Start engine and hold idle at 1000 RPM with compressor clutch engaged. If compressor does not engage, inspect pressure.
11. Engine should be warmed to operating temperature with doors closed and windows open.
12. Insert suitable thermometer in driver side center panel outlet and operate system until it stabilizes.
13. With compressor clutch engaged, compare air temperature at center panel outlet and compressor discharge pressure (high side) to chart, **Fig. 1.**
14. Compressor clutch may cycle, depending upon ambient temperature and humidity. If clutch cycles, use readings obtained before clutch disengaged.
15. If air outlet temperature fails to meet specifications, or if compressor discharge pressure is high, inspect pressure.

Crossfire

Air temperature in the test room must be at least 70° F.
1. Connect suitable manifold gauge set.
2. Set air conditioning heater mode control switch knob in Panel position.
3. Set temperature control knob to cool position, and A/C button to On position.
4. Rotate blower motor control knob to highest speed position.
5. Start engine and hold at 1300 RPM with compressor clutch engaged.
6. Ensure all vehicle windows and doors, then allow engine to reach operating temperature.
7. Insert suitable thermometer in lefthand center vent and allow engine to run for five minutes. Air conditioning clutch may cycle depending on ambient conditions.
8. With compressor clutch engaged, record discharge air temperature and compressor discharge pressure.
9. Compare discharge air temperature to chart, **Fig. 2.** Reading should be taken with compressor clutch engaged.

Charger, Magnum & 300

1. Connect suitable tachometer and manifold gauge set.
2. Set system control to recirculation mode (MAX-A/C) position, temperature control to full cool position and blower motor control to highest speed position.
3. Start engine and hold idle at 1000 RPM with compressor clutch engaged.
4. If compressor does not engage, diagnosis system.
5. Engine should be at operating temperature, doors closed and windows opened.
6. Insert suitable thermometer in driver side center panel outlet.
7. Operate system until it stabilizes.
8. With compressor clutch engaged, compare air temperature at center panel outlet and compressor discharge pressure (high side) to chart, **Fig. 3.**

9. Compressor clutch may cycle, depending upon ambient temperature and humidity. If clutch cycles, use readings obtained before clutch disengaged.

Neon

1. Connect suitable tachometer and manifold gauge set.
2. Attach suitable thermocouple to evaporator inlet line.
3. Set controls to A/C, RECIRC and PANEL Set temperature lever to full cool and blower on high.
4. Start and hold engine at 1000 RPM with compressor clutch engaged.
5. Engine should be warmed with doors close and windows open.
6. Insert suitable thermometer in lefthand center vent and operate engine for five minutes. If compressor clutch cycles, disconnect low pressure cycling clutch switch connector.
7. With clutch engaged, compare center panel outlet air temperature and compressor discharge pressure to chart, **Figs. 4 and 5.**
8. If clutch cycles, obtained reading before clutch disengaged.

Sebring Convertible, Stratus Sedan & 2004–06 Sebring Sedan

2004–06

Refer to "Concorde, Intrepid & 300M" for performance testing.

Avenger Sedan & Sebring Sedan

2007–08

1. Connect suitable tachometer and manifold gauge set.
2. Set control to A/C, RECIRC, and PANEL, temperature lever on full cool and blower on high.
3. Start engine and hold at 1000 RPM with air conditioning clutch engaged.
4. Engine should be warmed up with doors and windows closed.
5. Insert suitable thermometer in lefthand center air conditioning outlet and operate engine for five minutes.
6. Clutch may cycle depending on ambient conditions.
7. With compressor clutch engaged, compare discharge air temperature to evaporator inlet line temperature.
8. Evaporator outlet line temperature should be at least 10°F cooler than discharge air temperature.
9. If discharge air temperature fails to meet specifications, inspect for leaks, **Fig. 6.**

Sebring Coupe & Stratus Coupe

1. Ensure vehicle is not in direct sunlight.
2. Connect suitable gauge manifold to high and low-pressure valves.
3. Start engine.
4. Set system controls as follows:
   a. A/C switch to ON position.
   b. Model selection to FACE position.
   c. Temperature control to MAXIMUM COOLING position.
   d. Air selection to RECIRCULATION position.
   e. Blower switch to F (Fast) position.
5. Adjust engine sped to 1500 RPM with compressor clutch engaged.
6. Engine should be warmed with doors and windows closed.
7. Insert suitable thermometer in center air outlets and operate engine for 20 minutes.
8. Record discharge temperature.
9. If clutch cycles, take reading before clutch disengages.
10. Compare readings to chart, **Fig. 7.**

LEAK TEST

Do not pressure test R-134a systems with compressed air. Some mixtures of air and R-134a have been indicated to be combustible at higher pressures.

A leak detector designed for R-12 will not detect leaks in an R-134a system.

Park vehicle in a wind-free work area, then proceed as follows:

1. Inspect charge level as outlined under "Performance Test" in this section.
2. When performing this test with original discharge pressure less than 30 psi, reclaim remaining refrigerant, then connect suitable vacuum pump and evacuate system to lowest vacuum possible.
3. Ensure system holds vacuum reading for at least 15 minutes. If system holds vacuum for 15 minutes a leak is probably not present. If vacuum did not hold for 15 minutes proceed as follows:
   a. Ensure transaxle is in Park.
   b. Run engine for five minutes, then ensure engine is idling at 700 RPM.
   c. Charge system with 10 ounces of R-134a refrigerant.
   d. Set air conditioning control to 100% outside air.
   e. Set panel mode to full cool.
   f. Set blower to high speed.
   g. Place air conditioning button in ON position.
   h. Open vehicle windows.
4. Turn engine Off, wait approximately five minutes, then use suitable electronic leak detector designed for R-134a refrigerant systems and inspect system for leakage. If a leak is found repair as required. If no leak was found fill system as outlined under "Performance Test."

DISCHARGING SYSTEM

The use of refrigerant recovery and recycling stations allows the recovery and reuse of refrigerant after contaminants and moisture have been removed.

Follow the recovery or recycling station manufacturer's operating instructions.

SYSTEM EVACUATION

Using Vacuum Pump

Vacuum pumps suitable for removing air and moisture from air conditioning systems are commercially available. A specification for system pump-down used here is 26–29 ½ inches of vacuum. This reading can be attained at or near sea level only. For each 1000 feet of altitude this operation is being performed, the vacuum reading will be 1 inch lower. As an example, at 5000 feet elevation, only 21–24 ½ inches of vacuum can be obtained.

The system must be completely discharged before it can be evacuated. Damage to vacuum pump may result if pressurized refrigerant is allowed to enter.

1. With gauges connected into system, remove cap from vacuum hose connector. Install center hose from gauge manifold to vacuum pump connector. Mid-position high and low side compressor service valves (if used). Open high and low side gauge manifold hand valves.
2. Operate vacuum pump a minimum of 45 minutes for air and moisture removal. Watch compound gauge that system pumps down into a vacuum. System will reach 26–29 ½ inches vacuum in 5 minutes or less. If system does not pump down, inspect all connections and leak-test if required.
3. Close gauge manifold hand valves and shutoff vacuum pump.
4. Inspect ability of system to hold vacuum. Watch compound gauge to ensure gauge does not rise at a faster rate than 1 inch of vacuum every 4 or 5 minutes. If compound gauge rises at too rapid a rate, install partial charge and leak-test, then evacuate system as outlined above.
5. If system holds vacuum, charge system with refrigerant.

Using Charging Station

On systems using R-134a refrigerant use a charging station designed for R-134a refrigerant systems.

A vacuum pump is built into the charging station and is constructed to withstand repeated and prolonged use without damage. Complete moisture removal from the system is possible only with a vacuum pump constructed for the purpose.

The system must be completely discharged before it can be evacuated. Damage to the vacuum pump may result if pressurized refrigerant is allowed to enter.

1. Connect hose to vacuum pump if system was discharged through charging station.
2. Open high and low side gauge valves of charging station.
3. Connect station to proper electrical outlet.
4. Engage Off-On switch to vacuum pump according to directions of specific station being used.
5. System should pump down into a 28–29 ½ inches vacuum in 5 minutes or less. If system fails to meet this specification, repair as required.
6. Operate pump a minimum of 45 minutes to remove all air and moisture.
7. Close high and low side gauge valves. Open switch to turn off pump.
8. Inspect ability of system to hold vacuum by watching compound gauge to ensure it does not rise at a rate higher

Ambient Air Temperature, Deg F, & Humidity %	70 @ 80	80 @ 80	90 @ 80	100 @ 50	110 @ 20
Air Temperature at Center Panel Outlet, Deg. F①	50–55	58–63	60–65	63–68	58–63
Evaporator Inlet Pressure at Charge Port, psi	35–40	38–42	39–43	40–44	38–42
Compressor Discharge Pressure, psi	18–260	200–280	200–280	240–320	220–300

① — The discharge air temperatures will be lower if the humidity is less than the percentages outlined.

Fig. 2   Performance temperature & pressure chart. Crossfire

Ambient Temperature, Deg. F	70	80	90	100	110
Maximum Allowable Air Temperature At Center Left Panel Outlet, Deg. F	48	48	54	59	65
Compressor Suction Pressure, psi	20–30	20–30	30–40	30–40	35–45
Discharge Pressure at Service Port, psi	150–200	200–300	225–325	250–350	300–400

Fig. 3   Performance Temperature & Pressure. Charger, Magnum & 300

Ambient Temperature	21°C (70°F)	26.5°C (80°F)	32°C (90°F)	37°C (100°F)	43°C (110°F)
Air Temperature at Left Center Panel Outlet	1-8°C (34-46°F)	3-9°C (37-49°F)	4-10°C (39-50°F)	6-11°C (43-52°F)	7-18°C (45-65°F)
Compressor Discharge Pressure After the Filter Drier	1034-1724 kPa (150-250 PSI)	1517-2275 kPa (220-330 PSI)	1999-2620 kPa (290-380 PSI)	2068-2965 kPa (300-430 PSI)	2275-3421 kPa (330-496 PSI)
Evaporator Suction Pressure	103-207 kPa (15-30 PSI)	117-221 kPa (17-32 PSI)	138-241 kpa (20-35 PSI)	172-269 kpa (25-39 PSI)	207-345 kPa (30-50 PSI)

CR7020000584000X

Fig. 4 Performance temperature chart. Neon w/2.4L turbocharged engine

Ambient Temperature, Deg. F	70	80	90	100	110
Air Temperature At Lefthand Center Panel Outlet, Deg. F	42	48	53	57	69
Compressor Discharge Pressure, psi	125	150	215	275	350
Evaporator Suction Pressure, psi	26	35	38	45	57

Fig. 5 Performance temperature chart. Neon w/2.0L engine

than 1 inch of vacuum every 4 or 5 minutes. If rise rate is not within specifications, repair system as required. If rise rate is within specifications, charge system with refrigerant.

CHARGING SYSTEM
Concorde, Intrepid & 300M

Use a suitable refrigerant recovery station to discharge and charge system. Follow the station manufacturer's instructions.

Crossfire

1. Connect suitable pressure gauge to discharge side of compressor, then attach two thermocouple probes on evaporator coil inlet and outlet tubes just before refrigerant line connector fitting.
2. With transaxle in Park and engine idling at 1000 RPM, set air conditioning controls as follows:
   a. Air conditioning control set to outside air.
   b. Set panel mode to full cool.
   c. Blower to high speed.
   d. Air conditioning button in On position.
   e. Turn Recirc button Off.
3. Open all vehicle windows, operate system and allow to stabilize, then set system pressure to 260 psi by placing piece of cardboard over part of condenser to obtain specified gauge reading.
4. Observe discharge pressure and evaporator coil inlet and outlet tube temperature, then determine system charge, **Fig. 8.**
5. If charge is not within specification, add or reclaim two ounces of refrigerant at a time.
6. Read gauge pressure and liquid line

temperature. Continue procedure until proper charge is obtained.

Charger, Magnum & 300

1. Connect suitable manifold gauge set and R-134a refrigerant recovery/recycling/charging station.
2. Measure proper amount of refrigerant and heat it to 125° F with charging station.
3. Open both suction and discharge valves, then open charge valve to allow heated refrigerant to flow into system.
4. When transfer of refrigerant has stopped, close both suction and discharge valves.
5. If all of refrigerant charge did not transfer from dispensing device, open all of windows in vehicle and set system controls so that compressor is engaged and blower motor is operating at its lowest speed setting.
6. Run engine at steady high idle (more than 1400 RPM).
7. If compressor does not engage, test and repair compressor clutch control circuit.
8. Open low-side valve to allow remaining refrigerant to transfer to system.
9. **Do not open discharge (high pressure) valve now.**
10. Disconnect charging station and manifold gauge set from refrigerant system service ports.
11. Install caps onto refrigerant system service ports.

Neon

1. Connect suitable manifold gauge set to service ports.
2. Measure refrigerant.
3. Ensure engine is shut off.
4. Open suction and discharge valves.
5. Open charge valve to allow refrigerant to flow into system.

6. When transfer of refrigerant has stopped, close suction and discharge valve.
7. If all of charge did not transfer from dispensing device, put vehicle controls into following mode:
   a. Automatic transaxle in park or manual transaxle in neutral position.
   b. Engine idling at 700 RPM.
   c. Control set in 100 percent outside air, panel mode and Blower motor ON high speed with vehicle windows closed.
8. If compressor does not engage, test compressor clutch control circuit.
9. Open suction valve to allow remaining refrigerant to transfer to system.
10. Close all valves and test performance.
11. Disconnect charging station or manifold gauge set.
12. Install service port caps.

Sebring Convertible, Sebring Sedan & Stratus Sedan

1. Disconnect charging station or manifold gauge, install service port caps.
2. Measure proper amount of refrigerant and heat it to 125° F with charging station.
3. Open both suction and discharge valves, then open charge valve to allow heated refrigerant to flow into system.
4. When transfer of refrigerant has stopped, close both suction and discharge valves.
5. **If all refrigerant charge did not transfer from dispensing device,** proceed as follows:
   a. Open all windows.
   b. Set system controls so that compressor is engaged and blower motor is operating at its lowest speed setting.
   c. Run engine at steady high idle about 1400 RPM.
   d. If compressor does not engage, test and repair compressor clutch control circuit.
   e. Open low-side valve to allow remaining refrigerant to transfer to system.
6. **Do not to open discharge (high pressure) valve now.**
7. Disconnect charging station and manifold gauge set from refrigerant system service ports.
8. Install caps onto service ports.

Sebring Coupe & Stratus Coupe

Use a suitable refrigerant recovery station to discharge and charge the system. Follow the station manufacturer's instructions.

Ambient Temperature, Deg. F	70	80	90	100	110
Maximum Allowable Air Temperature At Center Left Panel Outlet, Deg. F	42–59	45–64	48–69	52–72	56–75
Compressor Discharge Pressure, psi	150–275	175–300	200–325	225–350	250–375
Compressor Suction Pressure, psi	31–53	36–59	41–69	46–70	52–72

Fig. 6 Performance temperature & pressure test. 2007–08 Avenger Sedan & Sebring Sedan

Ambient Temperature, Deg. F	68	77	95	104
Discharge Air Temperature. Deg F	42–50	43–51	46–54	46–55
Compressor High Pressure, psi	224–281	235–290	301–320	311–380
Compressor Low Pressure, psi	18–23	18–23	22–26	21–38

Fig. 7 Performance temperature & pressure test. Sebring Coupe & Stratus Coupe

Compressor Discharge Pressure Chart					
Ambient Temperature	16°C (60°F)	21°C (70°F)	27°C (80°F)	32°C (90°F)	38°C (100°F)	43°C (110°F)
Compressor Discharge Pressure	1378 kPa (200 psi)	1516 kPa (220 psi)	1723 kPa (250psi)	1930 kPa (280 psi)	2206 kPa (320 psi)	2413 kPa (350 psi)

ARM0300000000005

Fig. 8 Charge determination chart. Crossfire

AIR CONDITIONING

System Service

INDEX

Page No.
Oil Charge 8-6
Oil Level Check.................. 8-7

OIL CHARGE

To obtain proper oil fill capacities when replacing air conditioning compressors, measure the amount of oil removed from the failed compressor using a suitable measurement container, then add the same amount of manufactures recommended oil to the new compressor unit.

Model	Year	Compressor	Compressor Oil Viscosity	Component	Oil, Ounces
Avenger Sedan & Sebring Sedan	2007–08	Denso 5SE12C	ND-8 PAG	Accumulator	1.0
				Compressor	1.7
				Condenser	.3
				Evaporator	.3
Charger, Magnum & 300	2005–08	Denso 10S17	ND-8 PAG	Compressor	①
				Condenser	1.00
				Evaporator	2.00
				Lines	1.50
				Receiver-Dryer	1.00
Concorde, Intrepid & 300M②	2004	Nippondenso 10PA17	ND-8 PAG	Compressor	①
				Condenser	1.00
				Evaporator	2.00
				Lines	1.50
				Receiver-Dryer	1.00
Crossfire	2004–07	Nippondenso 10S17	ND-8 PAG	Compressor	①
				Condenser	.34
				Evaporator	1.69
				Lines	1.50
				Receiver-Dryer	2.37
Neon	2004–05 W/2.4L	Nippondenso 10S17	ND-8 PAG	Compressor	①
				Condenser	1.00
				Evaporator	2.00
				Lines	1.50
				Receiver-Dryer	1.00
Sebring Convertible, Sebring Sedan & Stratus Sedan	2004–05 (2.4L Turbo)	Sanden TRS -090	ND-15 PAG	Compressor	①
				Condenser	1.00
				Evaporator	2.00
				Filter/Drier	1.00
				Lines	1.50
	2004–06 (2.4L Non-Turbo & 2.7L)	Visteon HS-15	VC-46 PAG	Compressor	①
				Condenser	1.00
				Evaporator	2.00
				Filter/Drier	1.00
				Lines	1.50
Sebring Coupe & Stratus Coupe	2004–05	MSC90C Scroll Type	SUN PAG 56	Compressor	4.10
				Condenser	.50
				Evaporator	2.00
				Lines	.30
				Receiver	.30

① — Drained refrigerant oil from old compressor and measure. Drain all refrigerant oil from new compressor, then fill new compressor with same amount of refrigerant oil that was drained out of old compressor.

OIL LEVEL CHECK

The oil level of these compressors should be inspected whenever refrigerant has been lost due to leakage or through normal system servicing.

Specifications

INDEX

	Page No.
A/C Specifications	8-7
Belt Tension	8-8
Avenger Sedan & Sebring Sedan	8-8
2007–08	8-8
Charger, Magnum & 300	8-8
Concorde, Intrepid & 300M	8-8
Crossfire	8-8
Neon	8-8
Sebring Convertible, Stratus Sedan & 2004–06 Sebring Sedan	8-8
2.4L Engines	8-8
2.7L Engine	8-8
Sebring Coupe & Stratus Coupe	8-8
Charging Valve Location	8-8
Avenger Sedan & Sebring Sedan	8-8
2007–08	8-8
Charger, Magnum & 300	8-8
Concorde, Intrepid & 300M	8-8
Crossfire	8-8
Neon	8-8
Sebring Convertible, Stratus Sedan & 2004–06 Sebring Sedan	8-8
Sebring Coupe & Stratus Coupe	8-8
Technical Service Bulletins	8-9
Erratic Air Conditioning Operation	8-9
Concorde, Intrepid, Sebring Convertible, Sebring Sedan, Stratus Sedan & 300M	8-9
Window Fogging In Certain Climate Conditions	8-9
2004 Sebring Convertible/ Sebring Sedan & Stratus Sedan	8-9

A/C SPECIFICATIONS

Model	Year	Refrigerant		Compressor Oil Viscosity	Total System Capacity, Ounces	Compressor Clutch Air Gap, Inch
		Capacity, Lbs.	Type			
Avenger Sedan & Sebring Sedan	2007–08	1.0	R-134a	ND8 PAG	3.4	—
Concorde, Intrepid & 300M	2004	①	R-134a	ND8 PAG	5.0	.014–.026
Crossfire	2004–07	1.970	R-134a	ND8 PAG	4.4	.025–.035
Charger, Magnum & 300	2005–08	①	R-134a	ND8 PAG	6.1	014–.024
Neon	2004–05	①	R-134a	ND8 PAG	6.1	.014–.026
Sebring Convertible, Sebring Sedan & Stratus Sedan	2004–05 w/2.4L Turbo	①	R-134a	SP-15 PAG	5.0	.013–.025
	2004–06 w/2.4L Non-Turbo & 2.7L	①	R-134a	VC-46 PAG	5.0	.014–.030
Sebring Coupe & Stratus Coupe	2003–05	.880–.970	R-134a	SUN PAG 56	5.1	②

① — Refer to underhood label for refrigerant capacity.

② — 2.4L engine, .012–.020 inch; 3.0L engine, .016–.024.

CHARGING VALVE LOCATION

Concorde, Intrepid & 300M

On models equipped with 2.7L engines, the high pressure gauge port is located on the liquid line and the low pressure gauge port is located on the suction line.

On models equipped with 3.2L and 3.5L engines, the high and low side pressure connectors are located on the air conditioning compressor.

Crossfire

The high pressure service port is located on the liquid line near the front of the engine compartment behind the grille, **Fig. 1**.

The suction line is located on the lefthand side of the engine compartment near the strut mounting, **Fig. 2**.

Charger, Magnum & 300

The high side service port is located on the liquid line near lefthand shock tower.

The low side service port is located on the suction line near the lefthand shock tower.

Neon

On **2004–05 models with 2.0L engine**, the low side valve is located on the liquid line between the condenser and the evaporator. The high side valve is located on the discharge line fitting at condenser.

On **2003–05 models with 2.4L engine**, the low side valve is located on the suction line near the receiver/drier. The high side valve is located on the liquid line fitting at the receiver/drier outlet port.

Sebring Convertible, Stratus Sedan & 2004–06 Sebring Sedan

The high side service port is located on the receiver/drier. The low side service port is located on the suction line, near the righthand strut tower.

Avenger Sedan & Sebring Sedan

2007–08

The high side service port is located on the A/C discharge line in front of the engine, below the upper radiator hose. The low side service port is located on the A/C liquid line near the righthand front strut tower.

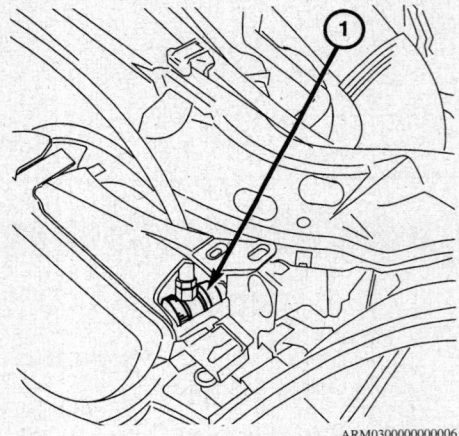

ARM0300000000006

Fig. 1 High pressure service port location. Crossfire

Sebring Coupe & Stratus Coupe

The low side valve is located on the suction line. The high side valve is located on the high pressure lines.

BELT TENSION

Concorde, Intrepid & 300M

1. Loosen tensioner pulley locking nut, **Figs. 3 and 4**.
2. Measure tension using belt tensioning tool No. C-7198, or equivalent, **Fig. 5**.
3. **Torque** locking nut to 40 ft. lbs.

Crossfire

Belt adjustment is maintained by an automatic (spring load) belt tensioner.

Charger, Magnum & 300

Belt adjustment is maintained by an automatic (spring load) belt tensioner.

Neon

1. Install drive belt over all pulleys except for power steering pump pulley.
2. Rotate belt tensioner clockwise using 17 mm wrench until belt can be installed on power steering pulley.
3. Release spring tension onto belt.
4. Inspect belt length indicator marks. Indicator mark should be within minimum belt length and maximum belt length marks, **Fig. 6**. On new belt, indicator mark should align approximately with nominal belt length mark.

Sebring Coupe & Stratus Coupe

1. Loosen tension pulley fixing nut A be-

hind tension pulley, **Figs. 7 and 8**.
2. Adjust belt tension amount using adjusting bolt B.
3. **Torque** fixing nut to 26–40 ft. lbs.
4. **If using scan tool,** proceed as follows:
   a. Connect belt tension meter set tool No. MB991668 to scan tool MUT-II No. MB991502, or equivalents.
   b. Connect scan tool to data Link Connector.
   c. Turn ignition switch to ON position and select belt tension measurement from menu screen,
   d. Hold microphone from tension meter drive belt center between pulleys approximately .4–.8 inch away from and perpendicular to rear surface of belt.
   e. Gently tap middle of belt with finger and measure vibration frequency, **Fig. 9**.
5. **If using tension gauge,** refer to **Figs. 10 and 11**.
6. **If measuring deflection,** apply 22 lbs., force in middle of drive belt between pulleys and measure, **Figs. 12 and 13**.

Sebring Convertible, Stratus Sedan & 2004–06 Sebring Sedan

2.4L ENGINES

Belt adjustment is maintained by an automatic (spring load) belt tensioner.

2.7L ENGINE

1. Engage suitable torque wrench, with maximum two-inch extension in ½ inch square opening of tensioner bracket.
2. Apply 104 ft. lbs., of torque, counterclockwise to tensioner bracket while tightening upper fastener.
3. **Torque** fastener to 20 ft. lbs.
4. Remove torque wrench from tensioner bracket and **torque** lower tensioner bracket fastener to 20 ft. lbs.
5. Connect belt tension gauge adapter tool No. 8371 to DRBIII following tool instructions.
6. Place end of microphone probe approximately 1 inch from belt at one of belt center span locations, **Fig. 14**.
7. Pluck belt at least three times using finger, or other suitable tool.
8. Adjust belt to obtain proper tension frequency hertz (Hz), **Fig. 15**.

Avenger Sedan & Sebring Sedan

2007–08

Belt tension for all engines is maintained by a non-adjustable automatic drive belt tensioner.

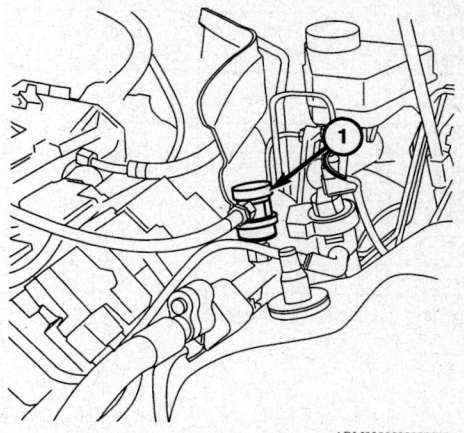

Fig. 2   Suction line service port location. Crossfire

Engine	Condition	Tension, Lbs.
2.7L	New	180–200
	Used	120
3.2L & 3.5L	New	150–170
	Used	120

Fig. 5   Belt tension. Concorde, Intrepid & 300M

TECHNICAL SERVICE BULLETINS

Erratic Air Conditioning Operation

CONCORDE, INTREPID, SEBRING CONVERTIBLE, SEBRING SEDAN, STRATUS SEDAN & 300M

On some of these models the air conditioning and heater systems may operate erratically to include: lack of cold air, lack of hot air, unrequested mode change on Automatic Temperature Control (ATC), no control of mode or temperature control or dithering/tapping blend door noise. These symptoms may be accompanied by the following Diagnostic Trouble Codes (DTCs) blend door feedback, blend door stall, air conditioning control mode door input shorted to battery, in-vehicle temperature sensor failure, ATC messages not received, or mode door stall.

This condition may be caused by the HVAC control assembly.

To correct this condition, proceed as follows:
1. Verify symptoms and inspect for DTCs using suitably programmed scan tool.

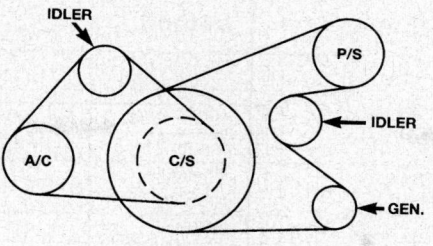

Fig. 3   Belt tension inspection. Concorde, Intrepid & 300M w/2.7L engine

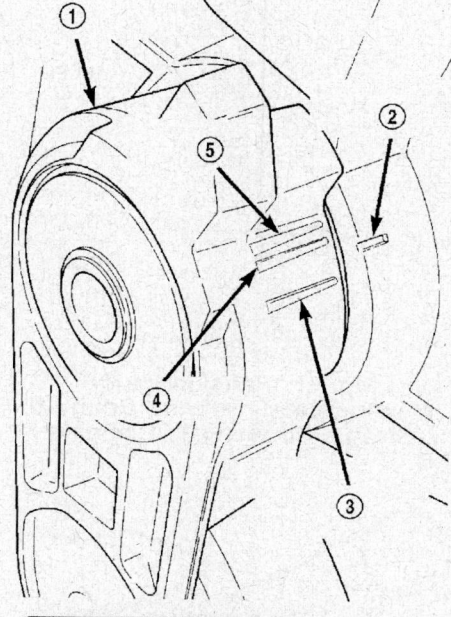

1 - AUTOMATIC BELT TENSIONER	
2 - BELT LENGTH INDICATOR	
3 - MAXIMUM BELT LENGTH	
4 - NOMINAL BELT LENGTH	
5 - MINIMUM BELT LENGTH	

Fig. 6   Belt tensioning. Neon

2. With vehicle at room temperature (50–80°F), remove fuse 19 from junction block M-1 circuit for 10 minutes to erase DTC's.
3. Replace fuse and start vehicle to calibrate HVAC system. Allow approximately five minutes for recalibration to complete.
4. Operate vehicle and air conditioning heater system to ensure symptoms and/or DTCs are gone.
5. If dithering/tapping noise is still present, additional diagnosis is required.

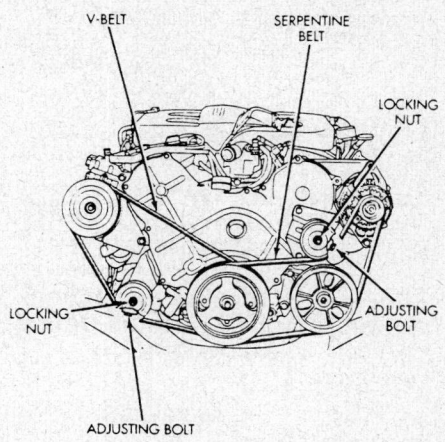

Fig. 4   Belt tension inspection. Concorde, Intrepid & 300M w/3.2L & 3.5L engines

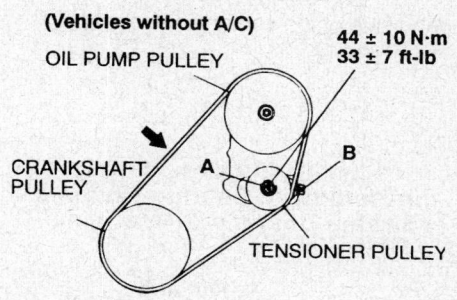

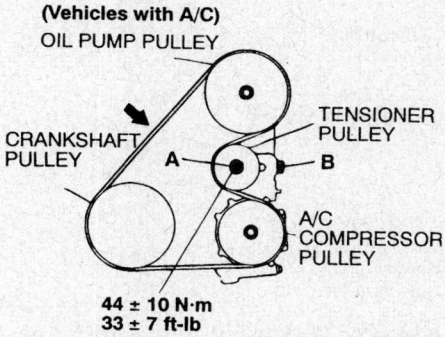

Fig. 7   Belt tension inspection. Sebring Coupe & Stratus Coupe w/2.4L engine

Window Fogging In Certain Climate Conditions

2004 SEBRING CONVERTIBLE/SEBRING SEDAN & STRATUS SEDAN

On some of these models the windows may fog with the HVAC system In Floor Mode.

This condition may be caused by the Body Control Computer (BCM) programing.

To correct this condition, program BCM with latest software.

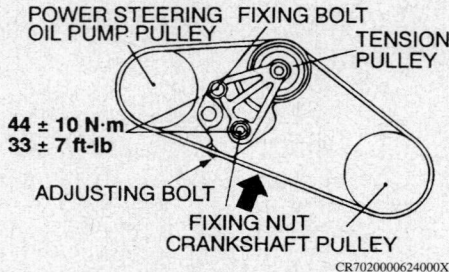

Fig. 8 Belt tension inspection. Sebring Coupe & Stratus Coupe w/3.0L engine

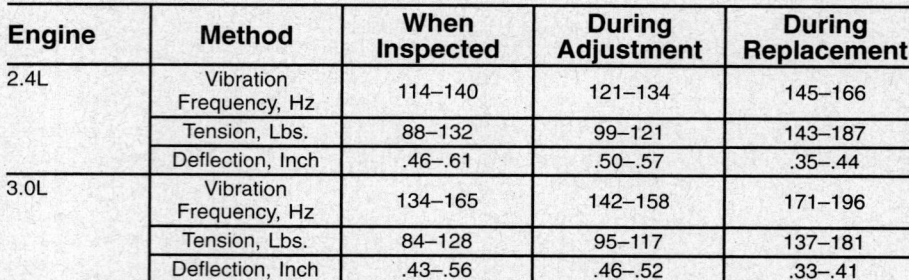

Engine	Method	When Inspected	During Adjustment	During Replacement
2.4L	Vibration Frequency, Hz	114–140	121–134	145–166
	Tension, Lbs.	88–132	99–121	143–187
	Deflection, Inch	.46–.61	.50–.57	.35–.44
3.0L	Vibration Frequency, Hz	134–165	142–158	171–196
	Tension, Lbs.	84–128	95–117	137–181
	Deflection, Inch	.43–.56	.46–.52	.33–.41

Fig. 9 Belt tension table. Sebring Coupe & Stratus Coupe

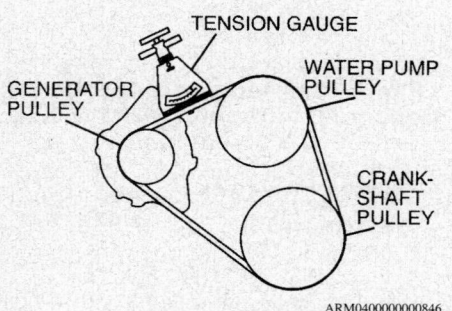

Fig. 10 Tension gauge measurement. Sebring Coupe & Stratus Coupe w/2.4L engine

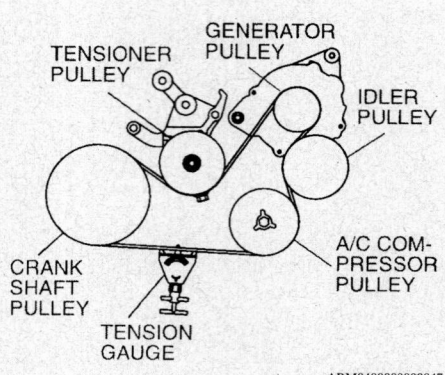

Fig. 11 Tension gauge measurement. Sebring Coupe & Stratus Coupe w/3.0L engine

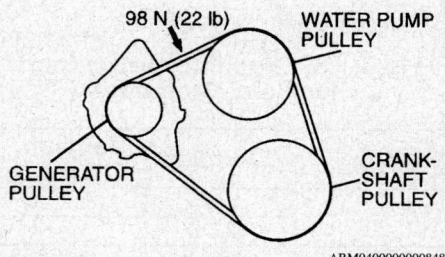

Fig. 12 Deflection measurement. Sebring Coupe & Stratus Coupe w/2.4L engine

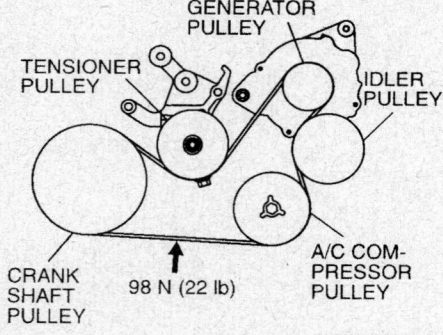

Fig. 13 Deflection measurement. Sebring Coupe & Stratus Coupe w/3.0L engine

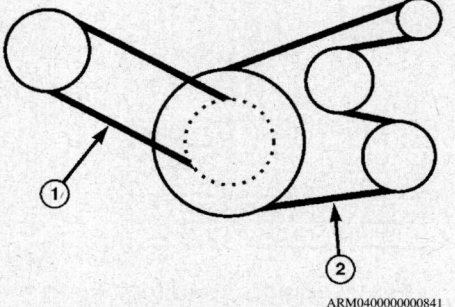

Fig. 14 Belt center span locations. 2.7L engine

Condition①	Lbs	Hz.
New	185–235	204–230
Used	110–160	157–190

① — A belt is considered used after 15 minutes of run-in time.

Fig. 15 Belt tension specifications. 2.7L engine

COOLING FANS

NOTE: On Air Bag Equipped Models, Refer To "Air Bag System Precautions" Located In The Front Of This Manual For System Disarming & Arming Procedures.

NOTE: Refer To "Computer Relearn Procedures" Located In The Front Of This Manual When Battery Power To The Computer Has Been Interrupted.

NOTE: "Electrical Symbol And Wire Color Code Identification" Located In Front Of This Manual Can Be Used As An Aid When Using Wiring Circuits Found In This Section.

INDEX

	Page No.
Component Diagnosis & Testing	9-51
Coolant Temperature Sensor	9-51
Caliber, Sebring Convertible, Sebring Sedan & Stratus Sedan	9-51
Concorde, Intrepid & 300M	9-51
Neon	9-51
Fan Control Module	9-51
Sebring Coupe & Stratus Coupe	9-51
Fan Control Relay	9-51
Caliber, Sebring Convertible, Sebring Sedan & Stratus Sedan	9-52
Concorde, Intrepid & 300M	9-51
Crossfire	9-51
Neon	9-51
Sebring Coupe & Stratus Coupe	9-52
Radiator Fan Motor	9-52
Caliber, Sebring Convertible, Sebring Sedan & Stratus Sedan	9-52
Concorde, Intrepid & 300M	9-52
Neon	9-52
Component Replacement	9-52
Fan Control Module	9-53
Crossfire	9-53

	Page No.
Fan Motor	9-52
Caliber	9-52
Charger, Magnum & 300	9-52
Concorde, Intrepid & 300M	9-52
Crossfire	9-52
Neon	9-53
Sebring Convertible, Sebring Sedan & Stratus Sedan	9-53
Sebring Coupe & Stratus Coupe	9-53
Description	9-1
Caliber & 2007–08 Avenger Sedan & Sebring Sedan	9-1
Concorde, Intrepid & 300M	9-1
Crossfire	9-1
Neon	9-2
Sebring Convertible, Stratus Sedan & 2004–06 Sebring Sedan	9-2
Sebring Coupe & Stratus Coupe	9-2
Diagnostic Chart Index	9-7
Precautions	9-1
Air Bag Systems	9-1
Battery Ground Cable	9-1
System Diagnosis & Testing	9-2
Accessing Diagnostic Trouble Codes	9-2

	Page No.
Clearing Diagnostic Trouble Codes	9-3
Diagnostic Tests	9-3
Caliber, Sebring Convertible, Sebring Sedan & Stratus Sedan	9-3
Charger, Magnum & 300	9-3
Concorde, Intrepid & 300M	9-3
Neon	9-3
Diagnostic Trouble Code Interpretation	9-2
Symptom Based Test	9-2
Crossfire	9-2
Sebring Coupe & Stratus Coupe	9-3
Wiring Diagrams	9-2
Caliber	9-2
Charger, Magnum & 300	9-2
Concorde, Intrepid & 300M	9-2
Crossfire	9-2
Neon	9-2
Sebring Convertible, Sebring Sedan & Stratus Sedan	9-2
Sebring Coupe & Stratus Coupe	9-2

PRECAUTIONS

Air Bag Systems

Refer to "Air Bag System Precautions" in the front of this manual for system disarming and arming procedures.

Battery Ground Cable

Prior to service, disconnect battery ground cable and isolate as required.

DESCRIPTION

CALIBER & 2007–08 AVENGER SEDAN & SEBRING SEDAN

The radiator cooling fans are dual-speed electric motor driven fans. The radiator fan assembly includes two electric motors, two five blade fans, and a support shroud that is attached to the radiator. The radiator fans are serviced as an assembly.

Concorde, Intrepid & 300M

Radiator fan control is accomplished in two ways. A pressure transducer on the compressor discharge line sends a signal to the Powertrain Control Module (PCM) which activates the fans. The fans are also activated when the coolant temperature sensor sends a signal to the PCM. The engine controller then sends a signal to the fan relay which turns the coolant fans on.

Radiator fan control can be accomplished five ways.
1. Pressure transducer on air conditioning compressor discharge line sends signal to Powertrain Control Module (PCM) which will activate both fans.
2. In addition to this control, fans are turned on based output to the PCM from:
   a. Coolant temperature sensor.
   b. Intake air temperature sensor.
   c. Output speed sensor.
   d. Transmission oil temperature sensor.
3. Regardless of coolant temperature fan will not run during cranking until engine starts.
4. Fans will run in accordance with specifications, **Figs. 1 and 2.**

Crossfire

The Radiator Cooling Fan System is comprised of the radiator fan control module, Powertrain Control Module (PCM) and the radiator fan motor. The Radiator fan

ENGINE COOLANT TEMPERATURE						INTAKE (CHARGE) TEMPERATURE	
	A/C Off		A/C On		Engine @ Idle < 13 Km/h (8 MPH) Vehicle Speed		Vehicle Speed < 45 Km/h (28 MPH)**	
Fan Speed	Low	High	Low	High	Low	High	Low	High
Fan On:	106°C (223°F)	110°C (230°F)	105°C (221°F)	110°C (230°F)	104°C (219°F) - After 1st Fan Cycle	110°C (230°F)	65°C (149°F) if coolant <93°C (199°F) 61°C (142°F) if coolant >105°C (221°F)	After Low Fan On for 8 minutes.
Fan Off:	102°C (216°F)	107°C (225°F)	102°C (216°F)	106°C (223°F)	Fan on time = 4 minutes*	105°C (221°F)	64°C (147°F) if coolant <92°C (197°F) 60°C (140°F) if coolant >104°C (219°F	Fan on time = 4 minutes*

*Minimum fan on time = 90 seconds

**Note: If low fan is on for 8 minutes, fan turns on high speed for 4 minutes, then goes back to low speed.

A/C PRESSURE			TRANSMISSION OIL TEMPERATURE	
Fan Speed	Low	High	Low	High
Fan On:	1,448 Kpa (210 psi)	1,717 Kpa (249 psi)	109°C (228°F)	111°C (232°F)
Fan Off:	1,207 Kpa (175 psi)	1,503 Kpa (218 psi)	104°C (220°F)	109°C (228°F)

CR1080200345000X

Fig. 1 Fan operating mode conditions. Concorde & Intrepid w/2.7L engine

ENGINE COOLANT TEMPERATURE					INTAKE (CHARGE) AIR TEMPERATURE	
	A/C Off/On		Engine @ Idle < 13 Km/h (8 MPH) Vehicle Speed		Vehicle Speed < 45 Km/h (28 MPH)	
Fan Speed	Low	High	Low	High	Low	High
Fan On:	102°C (216°F)	110°C (230°F)	99°C (210°F) - After 2nd Fan Cycle	110°C (230°F)	71°C (159°F) if coolant <93°C (199°F) 66°C (150°F) if coolant >99°C (210°F)	72°C (162°F)
Fan Off:	99°C (210°F)	105°C (221°F)	Fan on time = 4 minutes*	105°C (221°F)	Fan on time = 8 minutes*	Fan on time = 4 minutes*

*Minimum fan on time = 90 seconds

A/C PRESSURE			TRANSMISSION OIL TEMPERATURE	
Fan Speed	Low	High	Low	High
Fan On:	1,448 Kpa (210 psi)	1,717 Kpa (249 psi)	102°C (216°F)	109°C (228°F)
Fan Off:	1,207 Kpa (175 psi)	1,510 Kpa (219 psi)	98°C (208°F)	107°C (224°F)

CR1080200346000X

Fig. 2 Fan operating mode conditions. Concorde, Intrepid & 300M w/3.2L & 3.5L engines

control module acts as the relay for the cooling fan circuit. The module is mounted to the inner fender. The PCM acts as the input to the module to command the fan operation. The radiator cooling fan is made up of a multiple bladed fan. The cooling fan motor is a high speed DC type.

Neon

The radiator fan is a single speed electric motor driven fan.

Depending on engine/transmission combination, the vehicle may be equipped with a single fan or a dual fan. Vehicles equipped with dual fans, each fan blade is different from the other.

Sebring Convertible, Stratus Sedan & 2004–06 Sebring Sedan

Fan control is accomplished three ways.
1. Fan runs when air conditioning pressure reaches set psi.
2. In addition to this control, fan is turned on by temperature of coolant which is sensed by coolant temperature sensor which sends message to Powertrain Control Module (PCM). PCM turns on fan through fan relay.
3. On models equipped with automatic transmission, transmission fluid thermistor may have some influences on fan operation.

The PCM provides fan control for the following conditions:
1. Fan will not run during cranking until engine starts no matter what coolant temperature is.
2. Fan will run when air conditioning clutch is engaged, low pressure cutout switch is closed and once set compressor head pressure is reached.
3. Fan will run according to **Figs. 3 through 5**.

Sebring Coupe & Stratus Coupe

On models equipped with manual transaxle, the Engine Control Module (ECM) and on models equipped with automatic transaxle the Powertrain Control Module (PCM) judge radiator and condenser fan motors' required speed using input signals from the air conditioning switch, automatic compressor controller, vehicle or output shaft speed sensor and engine coolant temperature sensor. The ECM or PCM activates the fan control module to drive the radiator and condenser fan motors.

SYSTEM DIAGNOSIS & TESTING

Accessing Diagnostic Trouble Codes

Connect a suitably programmed scan tool to Data Link Connector (DLC), and follow manufacturer's instructions.

Diagnostic Trouble Code Interpretation

Refer to **Fig. 6** for Diagnostic Trouble Code (DTC) interpretation.

Wiring Diagrams

CALIBER

Refer to **Fig. 7** for engine cooling fan wiring diagram.

CHARGER, MAGNUM & 300

Refer to **Fig. 8** for engine cooling fan wiring diagram.

CONCORDE, INTREPID & 300M

Refer to **Figs. 9 and 10** for cooling fan wiring diagrams.

CROSSFIRE

Refer to **Fig. 11** for cooling fan wiring diagrams.

NEON

Refer to **Figs. 12 through 14** for cooling fan wiring diagrams.

SEBRING CONVERTIBLE, SEBRING SEDAN & STRATUS SEDAN

Refer to **Figs. 15 and 16** for cooling fan wiring diagram.

SEBRING COUPE & STRATUS COUPE

Refer to **Figs. 17 and 18** for cooling fan wiring diagrams.

Symptom Based Test

CROSSFIRE

RADIATOR COOLING FAN ALWAYS ON

1. Turn ignition Switch to ON position.
2. Inspect air conditioning switch using DRB III, or suitably programmed scan tool. If tool displays air conditioning off, proceed to next step. If tool displays air conditioning on, repair switch circuit.
3. Turn ignition switch to OFF position.
4. Disconnect radiator fan control module harness connector.
5. Disconnect radiator fan motor harness connector.
6. Turn ignition Switch to ON position.
7. Measure voltage on radiator fan control module output circuit. If measurement is less than 1 volt, proceed to next step. If voltage is not as specified, inspect for short to voltage in radiator fan control module output circuit.
8. Turn ignition switch to OFF position.
9. Disconnect Powertrain Control Module (PCM) harness connector.
10. Measure resistance between ground

Radiator Fan Control			A/C Pressure	
A/C Off	Low	High		
Fan On:	104°C (220°F)	110°C (230°F)		
Fan Off:	99°C (210°F)	104°C (220°F)		
A/C On	Low	High	Low	High
Fan On:	99°C (210°F)	110°C (230°F)	1,466 Kpa (209 psi)	1,717 Kpa (249 psi)
Fan Off:	93°C (200°F)	104°C (220°F)	1,172 Kpa (170 psi)	1,579 Kpa (229 psi)
EATX Fluid Temperature			Low Speed	High Speed
Fan On:			116°C (240°F)	120°C (248°F)
Fan Off:			109°C (228°F)	116°C (240°F)

CR1080100327000X

Fig. 3 Fan operating mode conditions. Sebring Sedan & Stratus Sedan w/2.0L engine

Radiator Fan Control			A/C Pressure	
A/C Off	Low	High		
Fan On:	104°C (219°F)	110°C (230°F)		
Fan Off:	99°C (210°F)	105°C (221°F)		
A/C On	Low	High	Low	High
Fan On:	99°C (210°F)	110°C (230°F)	1,448 Kpa (210 psi)	1,718 Kpa (249 psi)
Fan Off:	93°C (199°F)	105°C (221°F)	1,207 Kpa (175 Psi)	1,585 Kpa (229 Psi)
EATX Fluid Temperature			Low Speed	High Speed
Fan On:			109°C (228°F)	111°C (232°F)
Fan Off:			104°C (220°F)	109°C (228°F)

CR1080100325000X

Fig. 4 Fan operating mode conditions. Sebring Convertible, Sebring Sedan & Stratus Sedan w/2.4L engine

Radiator Fan Control			A/C Pressure	
A/C Off	Low	High		
Fan On:	104°C (220°F)	110°C (230°F)		
Fan Off:	98°C (208°F)	105°C (221°F)		
A/C On	Low	High	Low	High
Fan On:	99°C (210°F)	110°C (230°F)	1,448 Kpa (210 psi)	1,718 Kpa (249 psi)
Fan Off:	93°C (199°F)	105°C (221°F)	1,207 Kpa (175 psi)	1,585 kpa (229 psi)
EATX Fluid Temperature			Low Speed	High Speed
Fan On:			109°C (228°F)	111°C (232°F)
Fan Off:			104°C (220°F)	109°C (228°F)

CR1080100329000X

Fig. 5 Fan operating mode conditions. Sebring Convertible, Sebring Sedan & Stratus Sedan w/2.7L engine

and radiator fan control circuit. Is resistance more than 100 kohms, proceed to next step. If resistance is not as specified, inspect for short to ground in radiator fan control circuit.

11. Turn ignition switch to OFF position.
12. Connect PCM harness connector.
13. Measure resistance between ground and radiator fan control circuit at radiator fan control module harness connector. If resistance is more than 100 kohms, replace radiator fan control module. If resistance is not as specified, replace PCM.

RADIATOR COOLING FAN INOPERATIVE

1. Turn ignition Switch to ON position.
2. Actuate radiator cooling fan using DRB III, or suitably programmed scan tool. If fan is not operating, proceed to next step. If fan is operating, replace Powertrain Control Module (PCM).
3. Turn ignition Switch to OFF position.
4. Disconnect PCM harness connector.
5. Turn ignition Switch to ON position.
6. Connect suitable jumper wire between ground and radiator fan control circuit at PCM harness connector cavity 39. If cooling fan is running, replace PCM. If fan is not running, proceed to next step.
7. Turn ignition Switch to OFF position.
8. Disconnect radiator fan control module harness connector.
9. Turn ignition Switch to ON position.
10. Measure voltage of fused B + circuit at radiator fan control module harness connector. If measurement is more than 11 volts, proceed to next step. If measurement is not as specified, inspect for open in fused B + circuit.
11. Turn ignition switch to OFF position.
12. Measure resistance between ground

and module ground circuit. If resistance is less than 5. ohms, proceed to next step. If resistance is not as specified, inspect for open in module ground circuit.

13. Ensure ignition switch is in OFF position.
14. Disconnect PCM harness connector.
15. Measure resistance of radiator fan control circuit from radiator fan control module harness connector to PCM harness connector. If resistance is less than 5.0 ohms, go to next step, If resistance is not as specified, inspect for an open in radiator fan control circuit.
16. Ensure ignition switch is in OFF position.
17. Disconnect radiator fan motor harness connector.
18. Measure resistance of radiator fan control module output circuit from radiator fan control module harness connector to radiator fan motor harness connector. If resistance is less than 5 ohms, proceed to next step. If resistance is not as specified, inspect for open in radiator fan control module output circuit.
19. Ensure ignition switch is in OFF position.
20. Measure resistance of radiator fan control module ground circuit from radiator fan control module harness connector to radiator fan motor harness connector. If resistance is less than 5 ohms, proceed to next step. If resistance is not as specified, inspect for open in radiator fan control module ground circuit.
21. Ensure ignition switch is in OFF position.
22. Measure resistance of radiator fan motor. If resistance is less than 5

ohms, replace radiator fan control module. If resistance is not as specified, replace radiator fan motor.

SEBRING COUPE & STRATUS COUPE

Refer to **Figs. 19 through 22** for radiator and condenser fan motor troubleshooting.

Diagnostic Tests

CHARGER, MAGNUM & 300

Refer to **Figs. 23 through 33** for diagnostic tests.

CONCORDE, INTREPID & 300M

Refer to **Figs. 34 through 48** for diagnostic tests.

NEON

Refer to **Fig. 49 through 54** for diagnostic tests.

CALIBER, SEBRING CONVERTIBLE, SEBRING SEDAN & STRATUS SEDAN

Refer to **Figs. 55 through 68** for diagnostic test.

Clearing Diagnostic Trouble Codes

Connect a suitably programmed scan tool to Data Link Connector (DLC), and follow manufacturer's instructions.

Test	Description
P0110	Intake Air Temperature Sensor Stuck
P0111	Intake Air Temperature Sensor Performance
P0112	Intake Air Temperature Sensor Voltage Low
P0113	Intake Air Temperature Sensor Voltage High
P0116	Engine Coolant Temperature Performance
P0117	Engine Coolant Temperature Sensor Too Low
P0118	Engine Coolant Temperature Sensor Too High
P0480	Low Speed Fan Control Relay Circuit
P0481	High Speed Fan Control Relay Circuit
P0532	Air Conditioning Pressure Sensor Low
P0533	Air Conditioning Pressure Sensor High
P0711	Transmission Temperature Sensor Performance
P0712	Transmission Temperature Sensor Low
P0713	Transmission Temperature Sensor High
P0714	Transmission Temperature Sensor Intermittent
P0720	Output Speed Sensor Error
P1489	High Speed Fan Control Relay Circuit Test
P1490	Low Speed Fan Control Relay Circuit Test
P1491	Fan Control Relay Circuit Test
P1738	High Temperature Operation Activated

Fig. 6   DTC interpretation

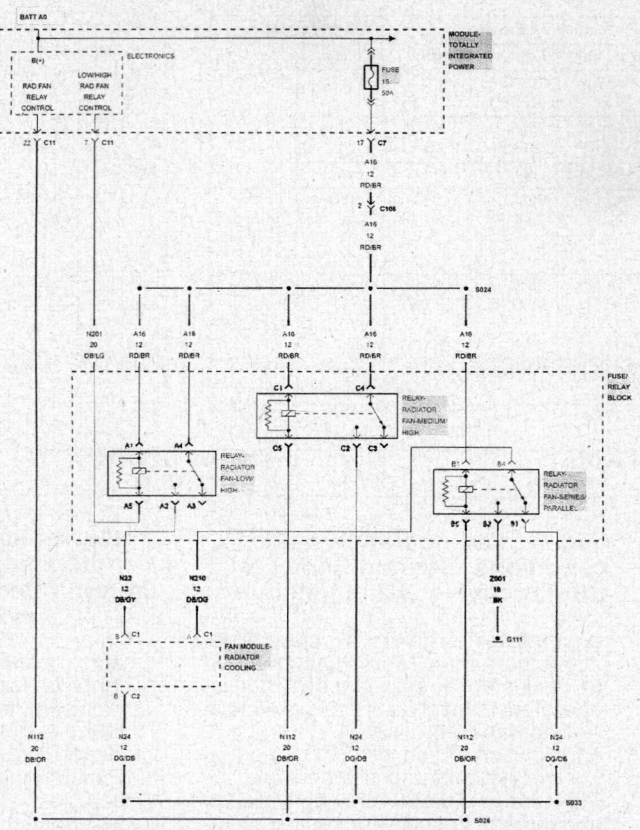

ARM0600000001235

Fig. 7   Engine cooling fan wiring diagram. Caliber

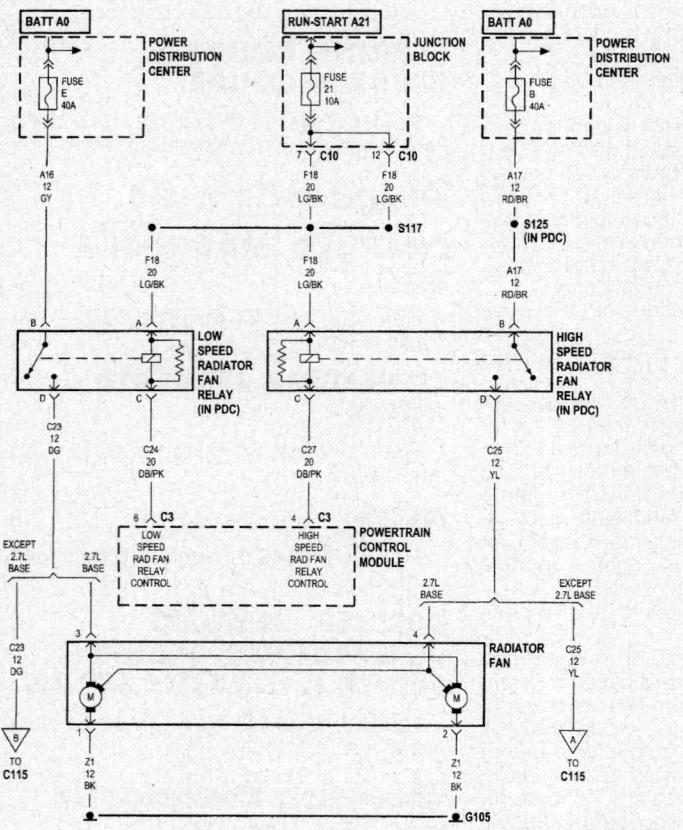

ARM0400000000915

Fig. 8   Engine cooling fan wiring diagram (Part 1 of 2). Charger, Magnum & 300

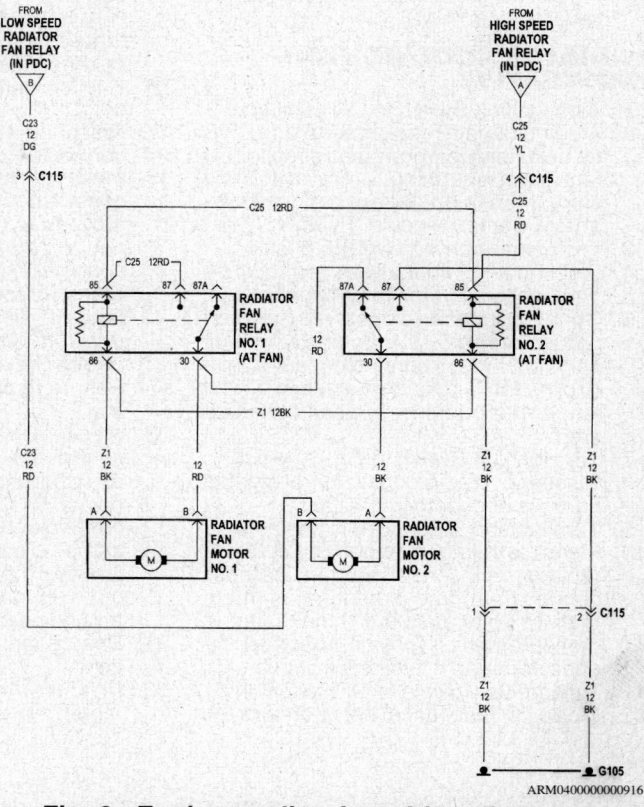

ARM0400000000916

Fig. 8   Engine cooling fan wiring diagram (Part 2 of 2). Charger, Magnum & 300

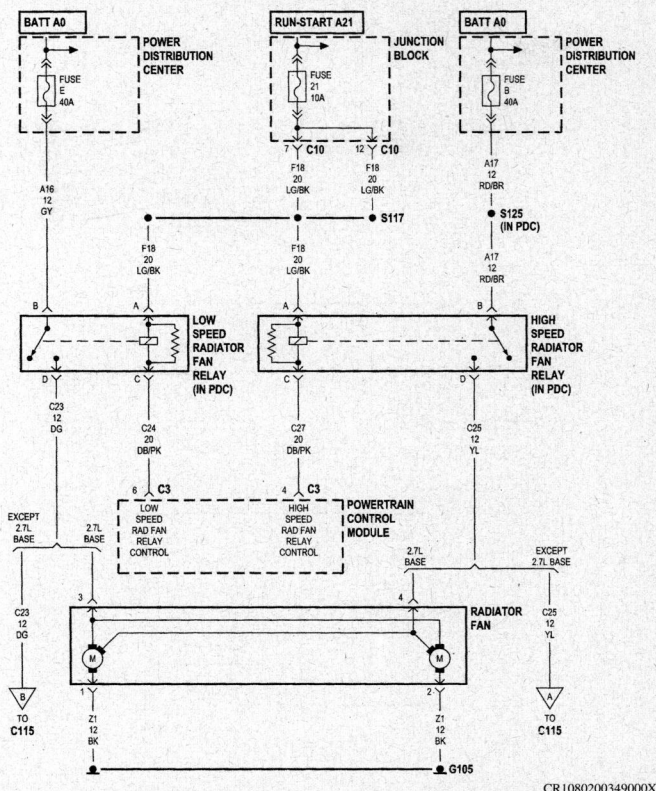

Fig. 9   Engine cooling fan wiring diagram. 2004 Concorde & Intrepid w/2.7L engine

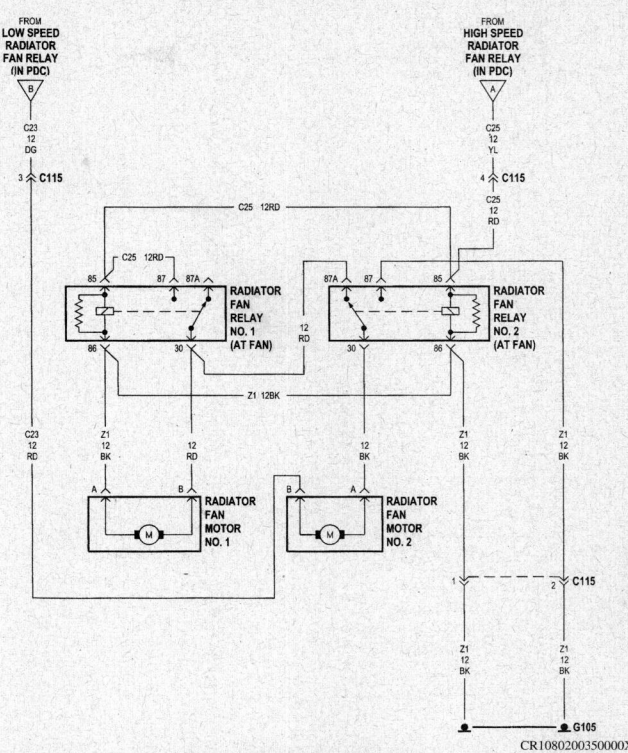

Fig. 10   Engine cooling fan wiring diagram. 2004 Concorde, Intrepid & 300M except 2.7L engine

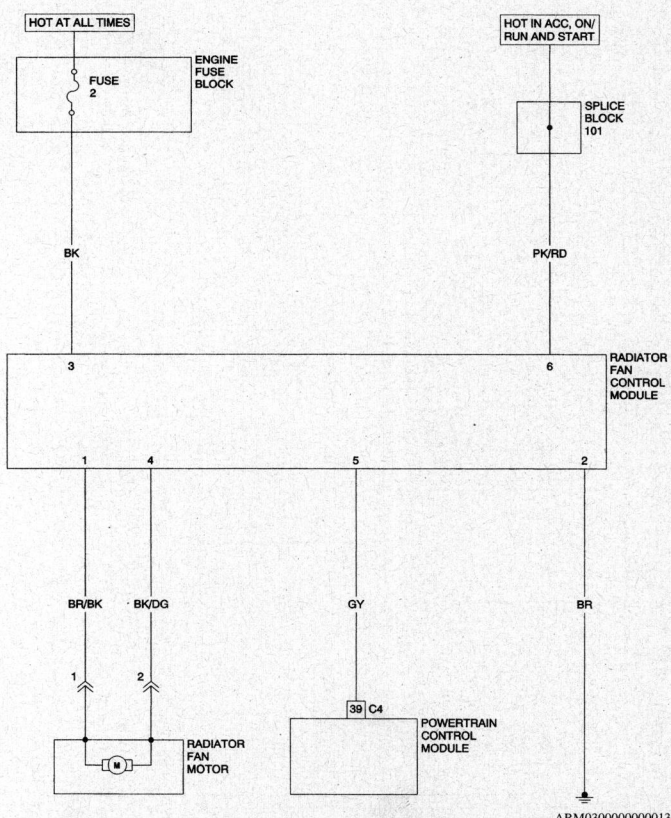

Fig. 11   Engine cooling fan wiring diagram. Crossfire

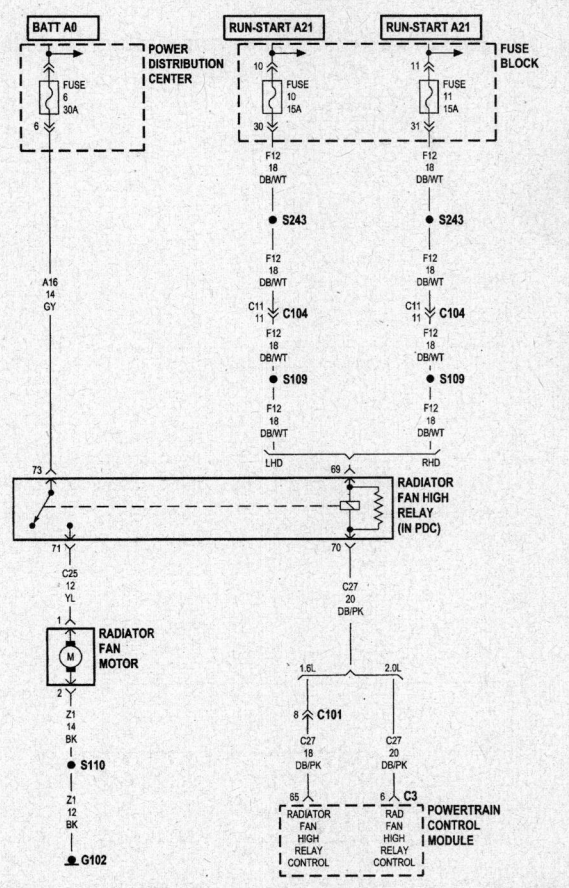

Fig. 12   Engine cooling fan wiring diagram. Neon w/2.0L engine

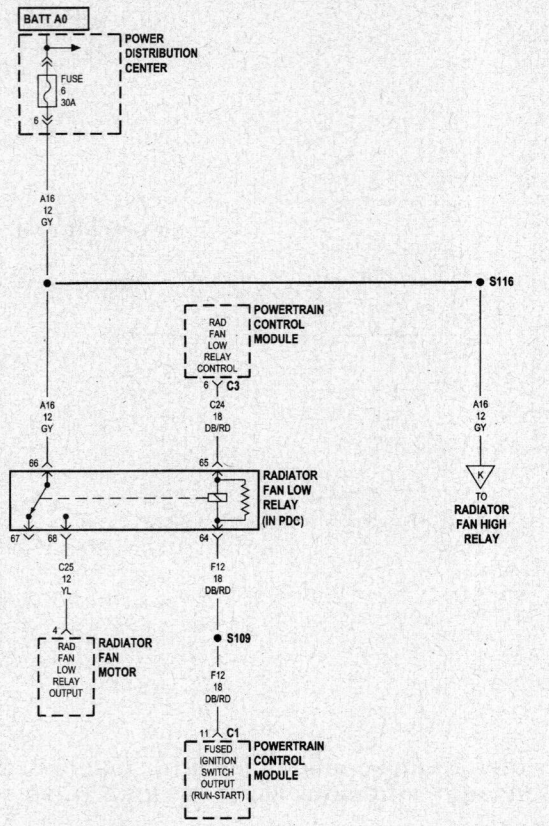

Fig. 13 Engine cooling fan wiring diagram. Neon w/2.4L engine

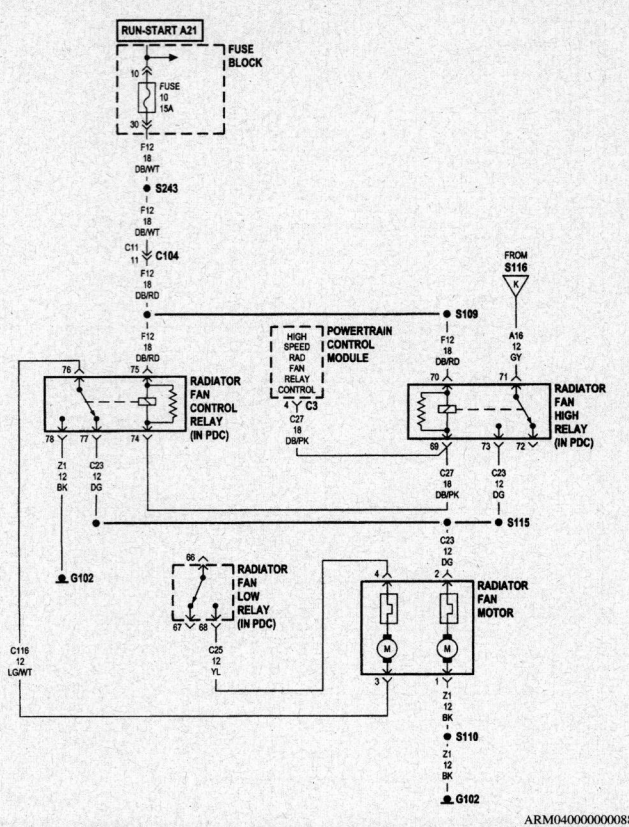

Fig. 14 Engine cooling fan wiring diagram. Neon w/2.4L engine

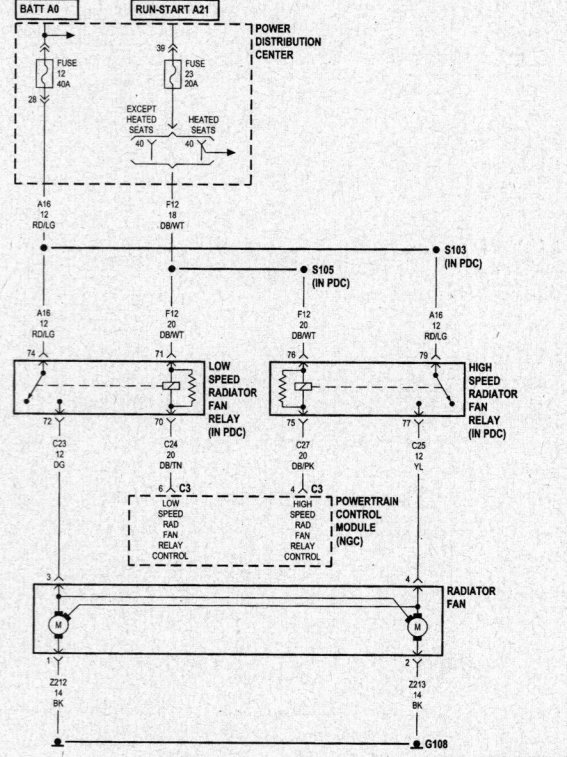

Fig. 15 Engine cooling fan wiring diagram. 2004–06 Sebring Convertible, Sebring Sedan & Stratus Sedan

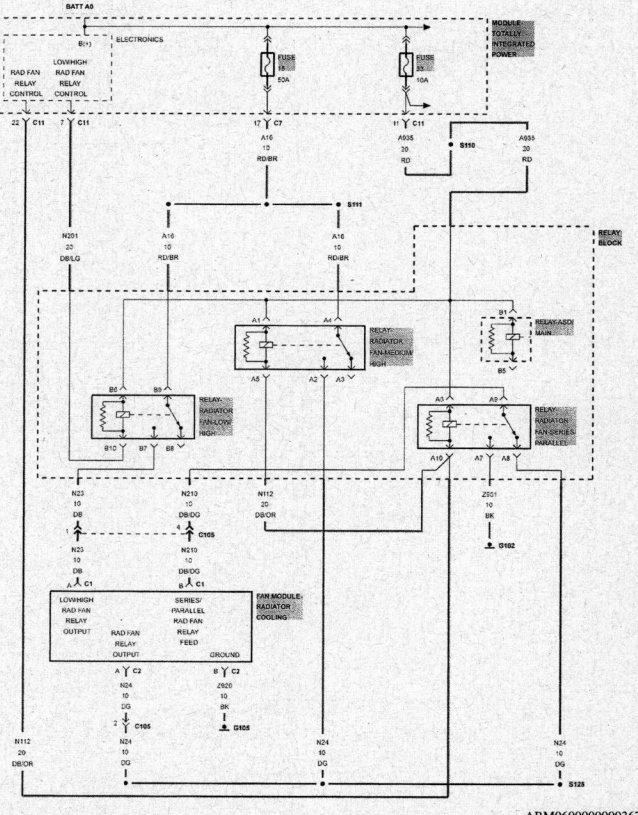

Fig. 16 Engine cooling fan wiring diagram. 2007-08 Avenger Sedan & Sebring Sedan

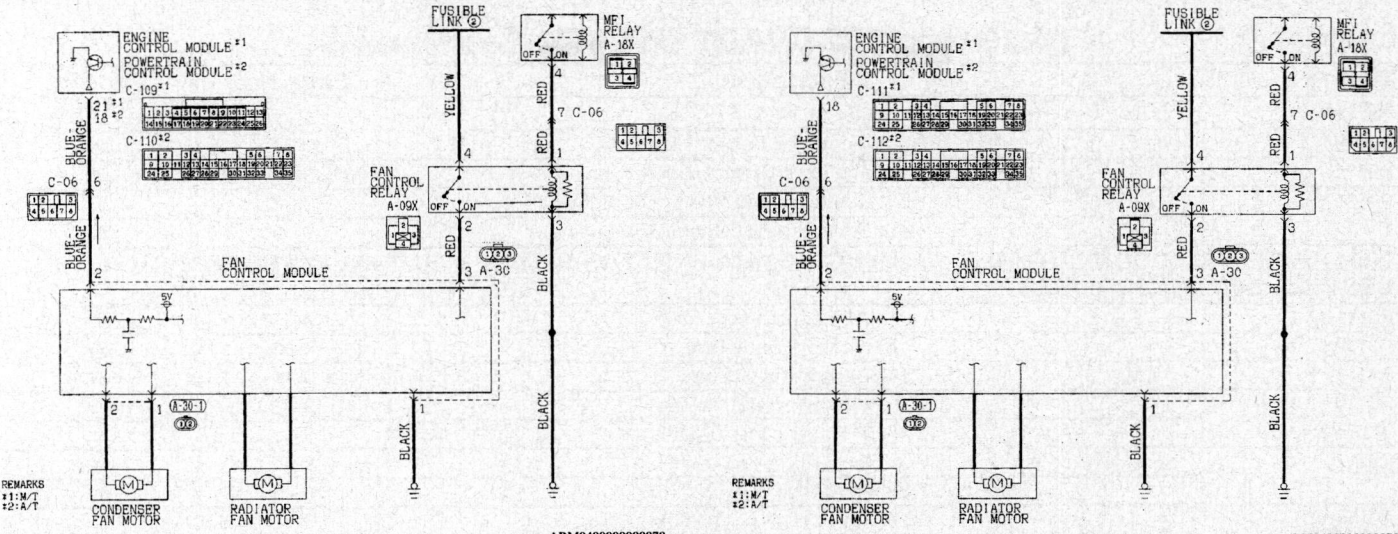

Fig. 17   Radiator & condenser fan wiring diagram.
Sebring Coupe & Stratus Coupe w/2.4L engine

ARM0400000000878

Fig. 18   Radiator & condenser fan wiring diagram.
Sebring Coupe & Stratus Coupe w/3.0L engine

ARM0400000000879

DIAGNOSTIC CHART INDEX

Test	Description	Page No.	Fig. No.
CHARGER, MAGNUM & 300			
P0111	IAT Sensor Rationality	9-12	23
P0112	IAT Sensor Circuit Low	9-13	24
P0113	IAT Sensor Circuit High	9-14	25
P0116	Engine Coolant Temperature Sensor Circuit Performance	9-15	26
P0117	Engine Coolant Temperature Sensor Circuit Low	9-16	27
P0118	Engine Coolant Temperature Sensor Circuit High	9-17	28
P0125	Insufficient Coolant Temp For Closed Loop Fuel Control	9-18	29
P0128	Thermostat Rationality	9-19	30
P0480	Cooling Fan 1 Control Circuit	9-22	31
P0481	Cooling Fan 2 Control Circuit	9-23	32
P2181	Cooling System Performance	9-24	33
CONCORDE, INTREPID & 300M			
P0110	IAT Sensor Stuck	9-26	34
P0111	IAT Sensor Performance	9-26	34
P0112	IAT Sensor Low	9-26	35
P0113	IAT Sensor High	9-27	36
P0116	ECT Performance	9-27	37
P0117	ECT Sensor Low	9-28	38
P0118	ECT Sensor High	9-29	39
P0480	Low Speed Fan Control Relay Circuit	9-29	40
P0481	High Speed Fan Control Relay Circuit	9-30	41
P0532	Air Conditioning Pressure Sensor Low	9-30	42
P0533	Air Conditioning Pressure Sensor High	9-31	43
P0711	Transmission Temperature Sensor Performance	9-32	44
P0712	Transmission Temperature Sensor Low	9-32	45
P0713	Transmission Temperature Sensor High	9-33	46
P0714	Transmission Temperature Sensor Intermittent	9-34	47
P0720	Output Speed Sensor Error	9-35	48
CROSSFIRE			
—	Refer to "Symptom Based Testing"	—	—
NEON			
P0116	ECT Performance (2004–05)	9-36	49
P0117	ECT Temperature Sensor Low	9-36	50

Continued

COOLING FANS

DIAGNOSTIC CHART INDEX—Continued

Test	Description	Page No.	Fig. No.
NEON			
P0118	ECT Temperature Sensor High	9-37	51
P0480	Cooling Fan No 1 Control Circuit	9-37	52
P0481	Cooling Fan No 2 Control Circuit Open (2.0L Engine)	9-38	53
	Cooling Fan No 2 Control Circuit Open (2.4L Engine)	9-38	54
2004–06 SEBRING CONVERTIBLE, SEBRING SEDAN, STRATUS SEDAN & 2007–08 AVENGER SEDAN, SEBRING SEDAN & CALIBER			
P0111	IAT Performance	9-39	55
P0112	IAT Sensor Circuit Low	9-40	56
P0113	IAT Sensor Circuit High	9-41	57
P0116	ECT Performance (2004–06)	9-42	58
	ECT Performance (2007-08)	9-43	59
P0117	ECT Sensor Low (2004–06)	9-44	60
	ECT Sensor Circuit Low (2007-08)	9-45	61
P0118	ECT Sensor High (2004–06)	9-46	62
	ECT Sensor Circuit High (2007-08)	9-46	63
P0480	Low Speed Fan Control Relay Circuit (2004–06)	9-47	64
	Cooling Fan 1 Control Circuit (2007-08)	9-48	65
P0481	Cooling Fan 2 Control Circuit	9-49	66
P1489	High Speed Fan Control Relay Circuit	9-50	67
P1490	Low Speed Fan Control Relay Circuit	9-50	68
2004–05 SEBRING COUPE & STRATUS COUPE			
—	Condenser Fan Does Not Operate	9-11	22
—	Radiator & Condenser Fans Do Not Change Speed Or Stop	9-10	20
—	Radiator & Condenser Fans Do Not Operate	9-8	19
—	Radiator Fan Does Not Operate	9-11	21

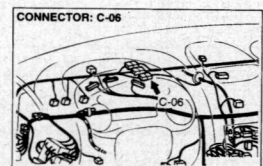

CIRCUIT OPERATION
- The fan control module is powered from fusible link number 2.
- The ECM <M/T> or PCM <A/T> judges the required revolution speed of radiator fan motor and condenser fan motor using the input signals transmitted from A/C switch, automatic compressor controller, vehicle speed sensor <M/T>, output shaft speed sensor <A/T> and engine coolant temperature sensor. The ECM <M/T> or PCM <A/T> activates the fan control module to drive the radiator fan motor and condenser fan motor.

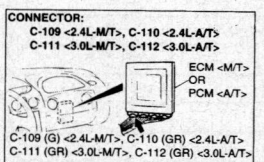

TECHNICAL DESCRIPTION
- The cause could be a malfunction of the fan control module power supply or ground circuit.
- The cause could also be a malfunction of the fan control module.

TROUBLESHOOTING HINTS
- Malfunction of fusible link
- Malfunction of fan control relay
- Malfunction of fan control module
- Malfunction of ECM <M/T> or PCM <A/T>
- Damaged wiring harness or connector

DIAGNOSIS

Required Special Tool:
MB991223: Harness Set

STEP 1. Check the fusible link number 2.
Q: Is the fusible link number 2 in good condition?
NO : Replace it. go to Step 13.
YES : Go to Step 2.

CR1080200343010X

Fig. 19   Radiator & Condenser Fans Do Not Operate (Part 1 of 8). 2004–05 Sebring Coupe & Stratus Coupe

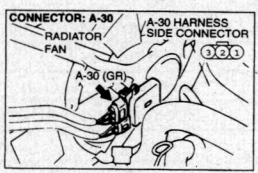

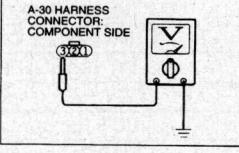

STEP 2. Measure the power supply voltage signal at fan control module connector A-30.
(1) Disconnect fan control module connector A-30.

(2) Measure the voltage between fan control module connector A-30 terminal number 3 and ground.
- The measured voltage should measure battery positive voltage. (When the ignition switch is turned to "ON" position).
(3) Connect fan control module connector A-30.
Q: Is the measured voltage battery positive voltage?
YES : Go to Step 8.
NO : Go to Step 3.

STEP 3. Check the fan control relay.
Refer to P.7-22.
Q: Is the fan control relay in good condition?
YES : Go to Step 4.
NO : Replace it. Go to Step 13.

CR1080200343020X

Fig. 19   Radiator & Condenser Fans Do Not Operate (Part 2 of 8). 2004–05 Sebring Coupe & Stratus Coupe

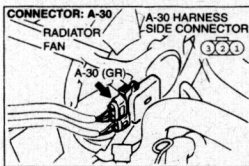

STEP 4. Check fan control relay connector A-09X and fan control module connector A-30 for loose, corroded or damaged terminals, or terminals pushed back in the connector.

Q: Are the connectors and terminals in good condition?

YES : Go to Step 5.

NO : Repair or replace the faulty components.

Go to Step 13.

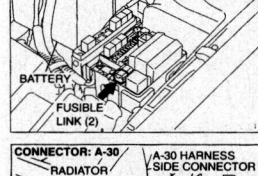

STEP 5. Check the harness wires between fusible link (2) and fan control module connector A-30 terminal 3 for damage.

Q: Are the harness wires between in good condition?

YES : It can be assumed that this malfunction is intermittent.

Go to Step 6.

NO : Repair the damaged harness wires. Go to Step 13.

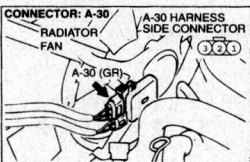

Fig. 19 Radiator & Condenser Fans Do Not Operate (Part 3 of 8). 2004–05 Sebring Coupe & Stratus Coupe

CR1080200343030X

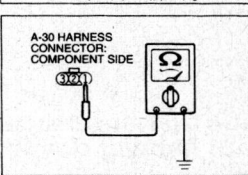

STEP 8. Measure the continuity between fan control module connector A-30 and ground.

(1) Disconnect fan control module connector A-30.

(2) Measure the resistance between fan control module connector A-30 terminal number 1 and ground.
• The measured resistance should be less than 2 ohms.

(3) Connect fan control module connector A-30.

Q: Is the measured resistance less than 2 ohms?

YES : Go to Step 11.

NO : Go to Step 9.

STEP 9. Check fan control module connector A-30 for loose, corroded or damaged terminals, or terminals pushed back in the connector.

Q: Is the connector and terminals in good condition?

YES : Go to Step 10.

NO : Repair or replace the faulty components.

2). Go to Step 13.

CR1080200343050X

Fig. 19 Radiator & Condenser Fans Do Not Operate (Part 5 of 8). 2004–05 Sebring Coupe & Stratus Coupe

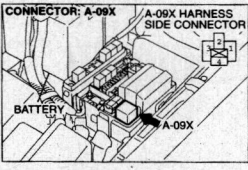

STEP 6. Check fan control relay connector A-09X and intermediate connector C-06 for loose, corroded or damaged terminals, or terminals pushed back in the connector.

Q: Are the connectors and terminals in good condition?

YES : Go to Step 7.

NO : Repair or replace the faulty components.

Go to Step 13.

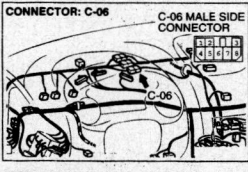

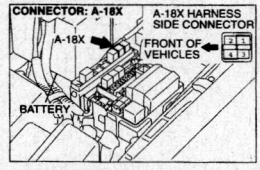

STEP 7. Check the harness wires between MFI relay connector A-18X terminal 4 and grounding point (2) for damage.

Q: Are the harness wires between in good condition?

YES : It can be assumed that this malfunction is intermittent.

Go to Step 13.

NO : Repair the damaged harness wires. Go to Step 13.

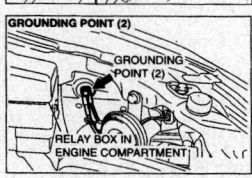

CR1080200343040X

Fig. 19 Radiator & Condenser Fans Do Not Operate (Part 4 of 8). 2004–05 Sebring Coupe & Stratus Coupe

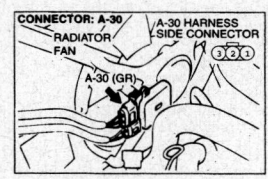

STEP 10. Check the harness wires between fan control module connector A-30 terminal 1 and grounding point (2) for damage.

Q: Are the harness wires between in good condition?

YES : It can be assumed that this malfunction is intermittent.

Go to Step 13.

NO : Repair the damaged harness wires. Go to Step 13.

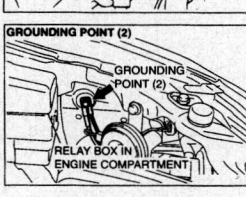

CR1080200343060X

Fig. 19 Radiator & Condenser Fans Do Not Operate (Part 6 of 8). 2004–05 Sebring Coupe & Stratus Coupe

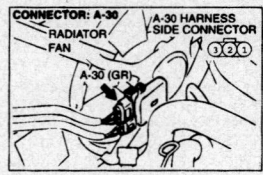

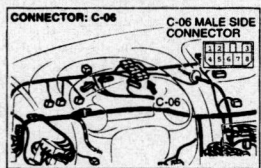

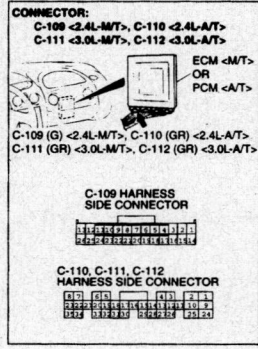

STEP 11. Check fan control module connector A-30, intermediate connector C-06 and ECM connector C-109 <2.4L-M/T> or C-111 <3.0L-M/T>, or PCM connector C-110 <2.4L-A/T> or C-112 <3.0L-A/T> for loose, corroded or damaged terminals, or terminals pushed back in the connector.

Q: Are the connectors and terminals in good condition?
> **YES :** Go to Step 12.
> **NO :** Repair or replace the faulty components.

Go to Step 13.

CR1080200343070X

Fig. 19 Radiator & Condenser Fans Do Not Operate (Part 7 of 8). 2004–05 Sebring Coupe & Stratus Coupe

STEP 12. Check the harness wires between fan control module connector A-30 terminal 2 and ECM connector C-109 terminal 21 <2.4L-M/T> or C-111 terminal 18 <2.4L-M/T>, or PCM connector C-110 terminal 18 <2.4L-A/T> or C-112 terminal 18 <3.0L-A/T> for damage.

Q: Are the harness wires between in good condition?
> **YES :** Check that the malfunction is eliminated. If the malfunction is eliminated, it can be assumed that this malfunction is intermittent. (Refer to INTRODUCTION, How to Use Trouble Inspection Service Points P.-6) If the malfunction is not eliminated, replace the fan control module.(Refer to P.7-23), then go to Step 13.
> **NO :** Repair the damaged harness wires. Go to Step 13.

STEP 13. Retest the system.

Q: Do the radiator fan and condenser fan operate correctly?
> **YES :** The procedure is complete.
> **NO :** Replace the ECM <M/T> or PCM <A/T>.

CR1080200343080X

Fig. 19 Radiator & Condenser Fans Do Not Operate (Part 8 of 8). 2004–05 Sebring Coupe & Stratus Coupe

NOTE: *If the engine coolant temperature reaches 110℃ (230℉) or higher, the radiator fan control rotates the radiator fan for up to 5 minutes even after the ignition switch is turned to the "LOCK" (OFF) position [the fan stops its rotation when the engine coolant temperature decreases to 110℃(230℉) or lower.]*

Radiator Fan and Condenser Fan Drive Circuit

CIRCUIT OPERATION
- The fan control module is powered from fusible link number 2.
- The ECM <M/T> or PCM <A/T> judges the required revolution speed of radiator fan motor and condenser fan motor using the input signals transmitted from A/C switch, automatic compressor controller, vehicle speed sensor <M/T>, output shaft speed sensor <A/T> and engine coolant temperature sensor. The ECM <M/T> or PCM <A/T> activates the fan control module to drive the radiator fan motor and condenser fan motor.

TECHNICAL DESCRIPTION
The fan control module has variable control of the radiator fan motor and the condenser fan motor speeds using signals transmitted from the ECM <M/T> or PCM <A/T>.

TROUBLESHOOTING HINTS
- Malfunction of fan control relay
- Malfunction of fan control module
- Malfunction of ECM <M/T> or PCM <A/T>
- Damaged wiring harness or connector

DIAGNOSIS

Required Special Tool:
MB991223: Harness Set

STEP 1. Check the fan control relay.

Q: Is the fan control relay in good condition?
> **YES :** Go to Step 2.
> **NO :** Replace it. Go to Step 5.

CR1080200344010X

Fig. 20 Radiator & Condenser Fans Do Not Change Speed Or Stop (Part 1 of 4). 2004–05 Sebring Coupe & Stratus Coupe

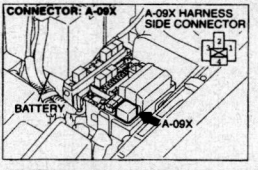

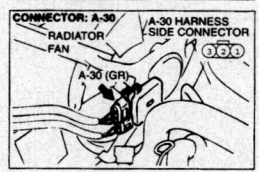

STEP 2. Check the harness wire between fan control relay connector A-09X terminal 2 and fan control module connector A-30 terminal 3 for damage.

Q: Is the harness wire in good condition?
> **YES :** Go to Step 3.
> **NO :** Repair the damaged harness wire. Go to Step 5.

CR1080200344020X

Fig. 20 Radiator & Condenser Fans Do Not Change Speed Or Stop (Part 2 of 4). 2004–05 Sebring Coupe & Stratus Coupe

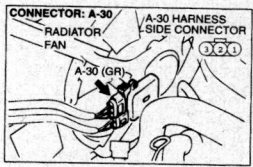

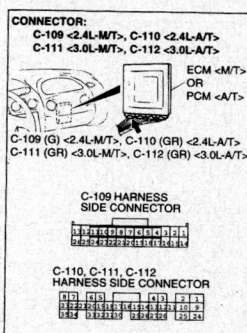

STEP 3. Check fan control module connector A-30, intermediate connector C-06 and ECM connector C-109 <2.4L-M/T> or C-111 <3.0L-M/T>, or PCM connector C-110 <2.4L-A/T> or C-112 <3.0L-A/T> for loose, corroded or damaged terminals, or terminals pushed back in the connector.

Q: Are the connectors and terminals in good condition?

YES : Go to Step 4.

NO : Repair or replace the faulty components.

Go to Step 5.

STEP 4. Check the harness wires between fan control module connector A-30 terminal 2 and ECM connector C-109 terminal 21 <2.4L-M/T> or C-111 terminal 18 <2.4L-M/T>, or PCM connector C-110 terminal 18 <2.4L-A/T> or C-112 terminal 18 <3.0L-A/T> for damage.

Q: Are the harness wires between in good condition?

YES : Check that the malfunction is eliminated. If the malfunction is eliminated, it can be assumed that this malfunction is intermittent.

If the malfunction is not eliminated, replace the fun control module then go to Step 5.

NO : Repair the damaged harness wires. Go to Step 5.

STEP 5. Retest the system.

Q: Do the radiator fan and condenser fan operate correctly?

YES : The procedure is complete.

NO : Replace the ECM <M/T> or PCM <A/T>.

CR1080200344040X

Fig. 20 Radiator & Condenser Fans Do Not Change Speed Or Stop (Part 4 of 4). 2004–05 Sebring Coupe & Stratus Coupe

CR1080200344030X

Fig. 20 Radiator & Condenser Fans Do Not Change Speed Or Stop (Part 3 of 4). 2004–05 Sebring Coupe & Stratus Coupe

TECHNICAL DESCRIPTION

The cause could be a malfunction of the radiator fan motor or an open circuit between the fan control module and the radiator fan motor.

TROUBLESHOOTING HINTS

- Malfunction of radiator fan motor
- Malfunction of fan control module

DIAGNOSIS

Replace the radiator fan motor and fan control module assembly.

Q: Does the radiator fan operate correctly?

YES : There is no action to be taken?

NO : Repair the wiring harness between the fan control module and the radiator fan motor.

CR1080200333000X

Fig. 21 Radiator Fan Does Not Operate. 2004–05 Sebring Coupe & Stratus Coupe

Radiator Fan and Condenser Fan Drive Circuit

CIRCUIT OPERATION

- The fan control module is powered from fusible link number 2.
- The ECM <M/T> or PCM <A/T> judges the required revolution speed of radiator fan motor and condenser fan motor using the input signals transmitted from A/C switch, automatic compressor controller, vehicle speed sensor <M/T>, output shaft speed sensor <A/T> and engine coolant temperature sensor. The ECM <M/T> or PCM <A/T> activates the fan control module to drive the radiator fan motor and condenser fan motor.

TECHNICAL DESCRIPTION

The cause could be a malfunction of the condenser fan motor or of the fan control module.

TROUBLESHOOTING HINTS

- Malfunction of condenser fan motor
- Malfunction of fan control module

DIAGNOSIS

STEP 1. Check the condenser fan motor.

Q: Is the condenser fan in good condition?

YES : Go to Step 2.

NO : Replace the condenser fan motor. Then go to Step 3.

STEP 2. Check the fan control module.

Q: Is the fan control module in good condition?

YES : Go to Step 3.

NO : Replace the fan control module, then go to Step 3.

CR1080200334010X

Fig. 22 Condenser Fan Does Not Operate (Part 1 of 2). 2004–05 Sebring Coupe & Stratus Coupe

STEP 3. Check the symptoms.

Q: Does the condenser fan operate correctly?

YES : This diagnosis is complete.

NO : Return to Step 1.

CR1080200334020X

Fig. 22 Condenser Fan Does Not Operate (Part 2 of 2). 2004–05 Sebring Coupe & Stratus Coupe

1. ACTIVE DTC

Ignition on, engine not running.
With a scan tool, read DTCs.

Is the DTC active at this time?

Yes

- Go To 2

No

- Diagnose INTERMITTENT CONDITION
- Perform the POWERTRAIN VERIFICATION TEST.

2. (K21) IAT SIGNAL CIRCUIT SHORTED TO BATTERY VOLTAGE

Turn the ignition off.
Disconnect the PCM harness connectors.
Disconnect the IAT Sensor harness connector.

NOTE: Visually inspect both the component and the PCM connectors. Look for damaged, partially broken wires, and backed out or corroded terminals.

Ignition on, engine not running.
Measure the voltage on the (K21) IAT Signal circuit in the IAT Sensor harness connector.

Is voltage present?

Yes

- Repair the short to battery voltage in the (K21) IAT Signal circuit.
- Perform the POWERTRAIN VERIFICATION TEST.

No

- Go To 3

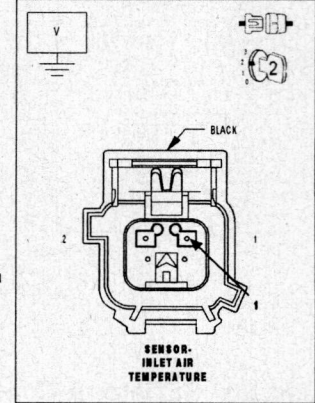

ARM0500000000565

Fig. 23 Code P0111: IAT Sensor Rationality (Part 1 of 6). Charger, Magnum & 300

5. (K21) IAT SIGNAL CIRCUIT OPEN

Turn the ignition off.
Disconnect the PCM harness connectors.

CAUTION: Do not probe the PCM harness connectors. Probing the PCM harness connectors will damage the PCM terminals resulting in poor terminal to pin connection. Install Miller Special Tool #8815 to perform diagnosis.

Measure the resistance of the (K21) IAT Signal circuit from the IAT Sensor harness connector to the appropriate terminal of special tool #8815.

Is the resistance below 5.0 ohms?

Yes

- Go To 6

No

- Repair the open in the (K21) IAT Signal circuit.
- Perform the POWERTRAIN VERIFICATION TEST.

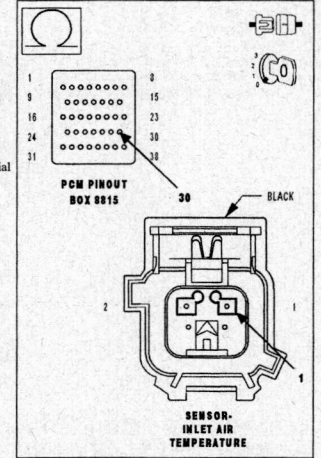

ARM0500000000567

Fig. 23 Code P0111: IAT Sensor Rationality (Part 3 of 6). Charger, Magnum & 300

3. IAT SENSOR VOLTAGE ABOVE 4.6 VOLTS

Turn the ignition off.
Connect the PCM harness connectors.
Ignition on, engine not running.
With a scan tool, read the IAT voltage.

Is the voltage above 4.6 volts?

Yes

- Go To 4

No

- Go To 7

4. IAT SENSOR

Connect a jumper wire between the (K21) IAT Signal circuit and the (K900) Sensor ground circuit in the IAT Sensor harness connector.
With a scan tool, read the IAT voltage.

Is the voltage below 1.0 volt with the jumper wire installed?

Yes

- Replace the IAT Sensor.
- Perform the POWERTRAIN VERIFICATION TEST.

No

- Go To 5

NOTE: Remove the jumper wire before continuing.

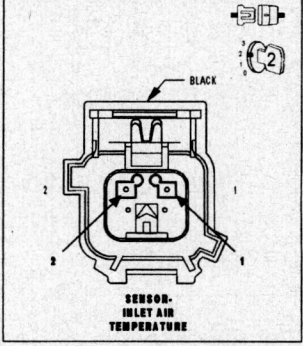

ARM0500000000566

Fig. 23 Code P0111: IAT Sensor Rationality (Part 2 of 6). Charger, Magnum & 300

6. (K900) SENSOR GROUND CIRCUIT OPEN

Measure the resistance of the (K900) Sensor ground circuit from the IAT Sensor harness connector to the appropriate terminal of special tool #8815.

Is the resistance below 5.0 ohms?

Yes

- Go To 9

No

- Repair the open in the (K900) Sensor ground circuit.
- Perform the POWERTRAIN VERIFICATION TEST.

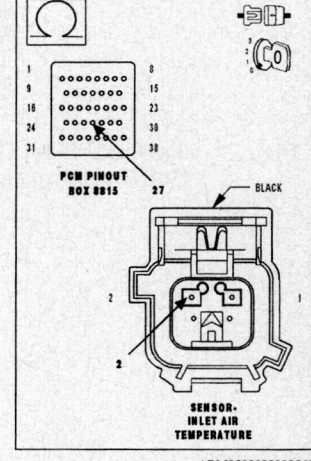

ARM0500000000568

Fig. 23 Code P0111: IAT Sensor Rationality (Part 4 of 6). Charger, Magnum & 300

7. (K21) IAT SIGNAL CIRCUIT SHORTED TO GROUND

Turn the ignition off.
Disconnect the PCM harness connectors.
Measure the resistance between ground and the (K21) IAT Signal circuit in the IAT Sensor harness connector.

Is the resistance below 100 ohms?

Yes

- Repair the short to ground in the (K21) IAT Signal circuit.
- Perform the POWERTRAIN VERIFICATION TEST.

No

- Go To 8

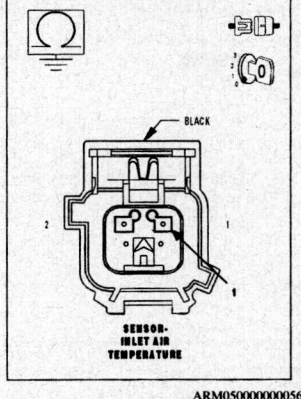

BLACK

SENSOR-
INLET AIR
TEMPERATURE

ARM0500000000569

**Fig. 23   Code P0111: IAT Sensor Rationality
(Part 5 of 6). Charger, Magnum & 300**

1. IAT SENSOR VOLTAGE BELOW 0.078 OF A VOLT

Ignition on, engine not running.
With a scan tool, read the IAT voltage.

Is the voltage below 0.078 of a volt?

Yes

- Go To 2

No

- Diagnose INTERMITTENT CONDITION
- Perform the POWERTRAIN VERIFICATION TEST.

2. IAT SENSOR

Turn the ignition off.
Disconnect the IAT Sensor harness connector.
Ignition on, engine not running.
With a scan tool, read IAT voltage.

Is the voltage above 4.5 of a volts?

Yes

- Replace the Intake Air Temperature Sensor.
- Perform the POWERTRAIN VERIFICATION TEST.

No

- Go To 3

ARM0500000000571

**Fig. 24   Code P0112: IAT Sensor Circuit Low
(Part 1 of 4). Charger, Magnum & 300**

3. (K21) IAT SENSOR SIGNAL SHORTED TO GROUND

Turn the ignition off.
Disconnect the PCM harness connectors.
Measure the resistance between ground and the (K21) IAT Sensor Signal circuit in the IAT Sensor harness connector.

Is the resistance below 100 ohms?

Yes

- Repair the short to ground in the (K21) IAT Sensor Signal circuit.
- Perform the POWERTRAIN VERIFICATION TEST.

No

- Go To 4

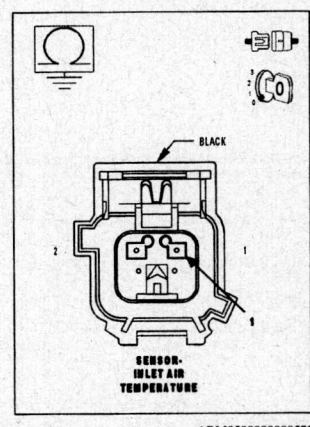

BLACK

SENSOR-
INLET AIR
TEMPERATURE

ARM0500000000572

**Fig. 24   Code P0112: IAT Sensor Circuit Low
(Part 2 of 4). Charger, Magnum & 300**

8. (K21) IAT SIGNAL SHORTED TO THE (K900) SENSOR GROUND

Measure the resistance between the (K21) IAT Signal circuit and the (K900) Sensor ground circuit in the IAT Sensor harness connector.

Is the resistance below 5.0 ohms?

Yes

- Repair the short between the (K900) Sensor ground and the (K21) IAT Signal circuit.
- Perform the POWERTRAIN VERIFICATION TEST.

No

- Go To 9

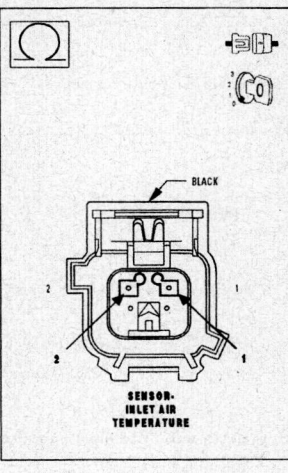

BLACK

SENSOR-
INLET AIR
TEMPERATURE

9. PCM

NOTE: Before continuing, check the PCM harness connector terminals for corrosion, damage, or terminal push out. Repair as necessary.

Using the schematics as a guide, inspect the wire harness and connectors. Pay particular attention to all Power and Ground circuits.

Were there any problems found?

Yes

- Repair as necessary.
- Perform the POWERTRAIN VERIFICATION TEST.

No

- Replace and program the Powertrain Control Module

ARM0500000000570

**Fig. 23   Code P0111: IAT Sensor Rationality
(Part 6 of 6). Charger, Magnum & 300**

4. (K21) IAT SENSOR SIGNAL SHORTED TO THE (K900) SENSOR GROUND CIRCUIT

Measure the resistance between the (K21) IAT Sensor Signal circuit and the (K900) Sensor ground circuit in the IAT Sensor harness connector.

Is the resistance below 100 ohms?

Yes

- Repair the short between the (K900) Sensor ground circuit and the (K21) IAT Sensor Signal circuit.
- Perform the POWERTRAIN VERIFICATION TEST.

No

- Go To 5

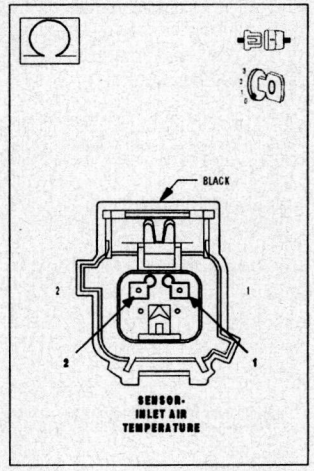

BLACK

SENSOR-
INLET AIR
TEMPERATURE

ARM0500000000573

**Fig. 24   Code P0112: IAT Sensor Circuit Low
(Part 3 of 4). Charger, Magnum & 300**

5. PCM

NOTE: Before continuing, check the PCM harness connector terminals for corrosion, damage, or terminal push out. Repair as necessary.

Using the schematics as a guide, inspect the wire harness and connectors. Pay particular attention to all Power and Ground circuits.

Were there any problems found?

Yes

- Repair as necessary.
- Perform the POWERTRAIN VERIFICATION TEST.

No

- Replace and program the Powertrain Control Module

ARM0500000000574

Fig. 24 Code P0112: IAT Sensor Circuit Low (Part 4 of 4). Charger, Magnum & 300

3. (K21) IAT SIGNAL CIRCUIT SHORTED TO BATTERY VOLTAGE

Ignition on, engine not running.
Measure the voltage on the (K21) IAT Signal circuit in the IAT Sensor harness connector.

Is the voltage above 5.2 volts?

Yes

- Repair the short to battery voltage in the (K21) IAT Signal circuit.
- Perform the POWERTRAIN VERIFICATION TEST.

No

- Go To 4

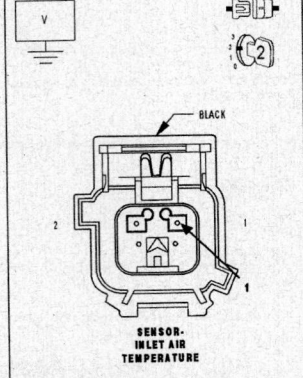

ARM0500000000576

Fig. 25 Code P0113: IAT Sensor Circuit High (Part 2 of 4). Charger, Magnum & 300

4. (K21) IAT SIGNAL CIRCUIT OPEN

Turn the ignition off.
Disconnect the PCM harness connector.

CAUTION: Do not probe the PCM harness connectors. Probing the PCM harness connectors will damage the PCM terminals resulting in poor terminal to pin connection. Install Miller Special Tool #8815 to perform diagnosis.

Measure the resistance of the (K21) IAT Signal circuit from the IAT Sensor harness connector to the appropriate terminal of special tool #8815.

Is the resistance below 5.0 ohms?

Yes

- Go To 5

No

- Repair the open in the (K21) IAT Signal circuit.
- Perform the POWERTRAIN VERIFICATION TEST.

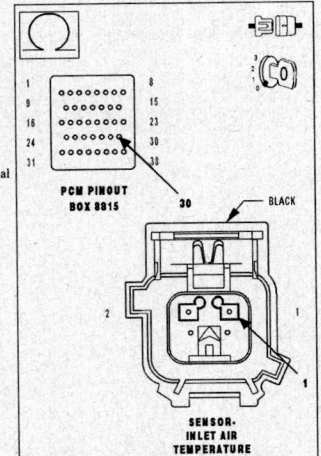

ARM0500000000577

Fig. 25 Code P0113: IAT Sensor Circuit High (Part 3 of 4). Charger, Magnum & 300

1. IAT SENSOR VOLTAGE ABOVE 4.98 VOLTS

Ignition on, engine not running.
With a scan tool, read the Intake Air Temperature Sensor voltage.

Is the voltage above 4.98 volts?

Yes

- Go To 2

No

- Diagnose INTERMITTENT CONDITION
- Perform the POWERTRAIN VERIFICATION TEST.

2. IAT SENSOR

Turn the ignition off.
Disconnect the Intake Air Temperature Sensor harness connector.
Connect a jumper wire between the (K21) IAT Signal circuit and the (K900) Sensor ground circuit in the IAT Sensor harness connector.
Ignition on, engine not running.
With a scan tool, read the IAT Sensor voltage.

Is the voltage below 1.0 volt with the jumper wire installed?

Yes

- Replace the IAT Sensor.
- Perform the POWERTRAIN VERIFICATION TEST.

No

- Go To 3

NOTE: Remove the jumper wire before continuing.

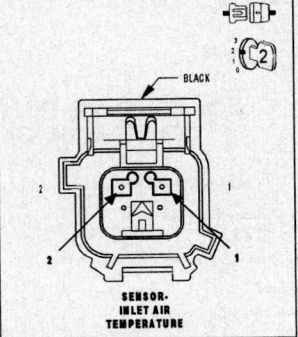

ARM0500000000575

Fig. 25 Code P0113: IAT Sensor Circuit High (Part 1 of 4). Charger, Magnum & 300

5. (K900) SENSOR GROUND CIRCUIT OPEN

Measure the resistance of the (K900) Sensor ground circuit from the IAT Sensor harness connector to the appropriate terminal of special tool #8815.

Is the resistance below 5.0 ohms?

Yes

- Go To 6

No

- Repair the open in the (K900) Sensor ground circuit.
- Perform the POWERTRAIN VERIFICATION TEST.

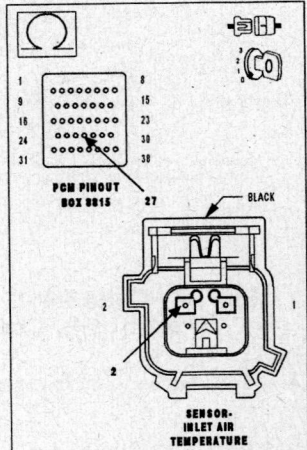

6. PCM

NOTE: Before continuing, check the PCM harness connector terminals for corrosion, damage, or terminal push out. Repair as necessary.

Using the schematics as a guide, inspect the wire harness and connectors. Pay particular attention to all Power and Ground circuits.

Were there any problems found?

Yes

- Repair as necessary.
- Perform the POWERTRAIN VERIFICATION TEST.

No

- Replace and program the Powertrain Control Module

ARM0500000000579

Fig. 25 Code P0113: IAT Sensor Circuit High (Part 4 of 4). Charger, Magnum & 300

1. ACTIVE DTC

Ignition on, engine not running.
With a scan tool, read DTCs.

Is the DTC active at this time?

Yes

- Go To 2

No

- Diagnose INTERMITTENT CONDITION
- Perform the POWERTRAIN VERIFICATION TEST.

ARM0500000000580

Fig. 26   Code P0116: Engine Coolant Temperature Sensor Circuit Performance (Part 1 of 7). Charger, Magnum & 300

4. ECT SENSOR

Connect a jumper wire between the (K2) ECT Signal circuit and the (K900) Sensor ground circuit in the ECT Sensor harness connector.
With a scan tool, read the ECT voltage.

Is the voltage below 1.0 volt with the jumper wire installed?

Yes

- Replace the ECT Sensor.
- Perform the POWERTRAIN VERIFICATION TEST.

No

- Go To 5

  NOTE: Remove the jumper wire before continuing.

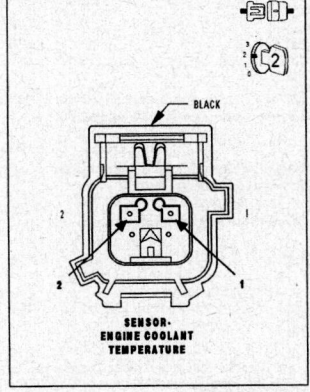

ARM0500000000582

Fig. 26   Code P0116: Engine Coolant Temperature Sensor Circuit Performance (Part 3 of 7). Charger, Magnum & 300

5. (K2) ECT SIGNAL CIRCUIT OPEN

Turn the ignition off.
Disconnect the PCM harness connectors.

CAUTION: Do not probe the PCM harness connectors. Probing the PCM harness connectors will damage the PCM terminals resulting in poor terminal to pin connection. Install Miller Special Tool #8815 to perform diagnosis.

Measure the resistance of the (K2) ECT Signal circuit from the ECT Sensor harness connector to the appropriate terminal of special tool #8815.

Is the resistance below 5.0 ohms?

Yes

- Go To 6

No

- Repair the open in the (K2) ECT Signal circuit.
- Perform the POWERTRAIN VERIFICATION TEST.

ARM0500000000583

Fig. 26   Code P0116: Engine Coolant Temperature Sensor Circuit Performance (Part 4 of 7). Charger, Magnum & 300

2. (K2) ECT SIGNAL CIRCUIT SHORTED TO BATTERY VOLTAGE

Turn the ignition off.
Disconnect the PCM harness connectors.
Disconnect the ECT Sensor harness connector.

NOTE: Visually inspect both the component and the PCM connectors. Look for damaged, partially broken wires, and backed out or corroded terminals.

Ignition on, engine not running.
Measure the voltage on the (K2) ECT Signal circuit in the ECT Sensor harness connector.

Is voltage present?

Yes

- Repair the short to battery voltage in the (K2) ECT Signal circuit.
- Perform the POWERTRAIN VERIFICATION TEST.

No

- Go To 3

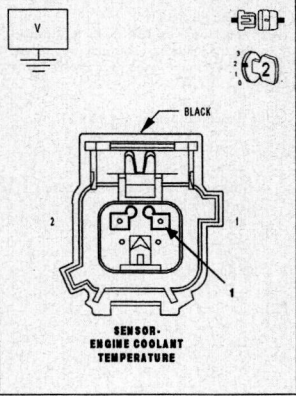

3. ECT SENSOR VOLTAGE ABOVE 4.6 VOLTS

Turn the ignition off.
Connect the PCM harness connectors.
Ignition on, engine not running.
With a scan tool, read the ECT voltage.

Is the voltage above 4.6 volts?

Yes

- Go To 4

No

- Go To 7

ARM0500000000581

Fig. 26   Code P0116: Engine Coolant Temperature Sensor Circuit Performance (Part 2 of 7). Charger, Magnum & 300

6. (K900) SENSOR GROUND CIRCUIT OPEN

Measure the resistance of the (K900) Sensor ground circuit from the ECT Sensor harness connector to the appropriate terminal of special tool #8815.

Is the resistance below 5.0 ohms?

Yes

- Go To 9

No

- Repair the open in the (K900) Sensor ground circuit.
- Perform the POWERTRAIN VERIFICATION TEST.

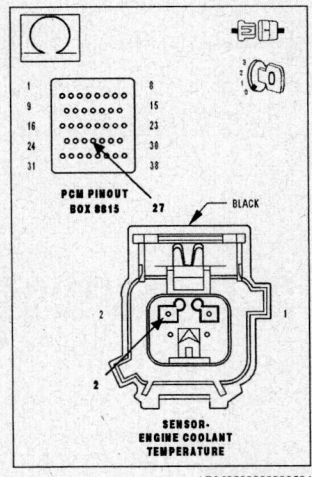

ARM0500000000584

Fig. 26   Code P0116: Engine Coolant Temperature Sensor Circuit Performance (Part 5 of 7). Charger, Magnum & 300

COOLING FANS

7. (K2) ECT SIGNAL CIRCUIT SHORTED TO GROUND

Turn the ignition off.
Disconnect the PCM harness connectors.
Measure the resistance between ground and the (K2)
ECT Signal circuit in the ECT Sensor harness
connector.

Is the resistance below 100 ohms?

Yes

- Repair the short to ground in the (K2) ECT
  Signal circuit.
- Perform the POWERTRAIN VERIFICATION
  TEST.

No

- Go To 8

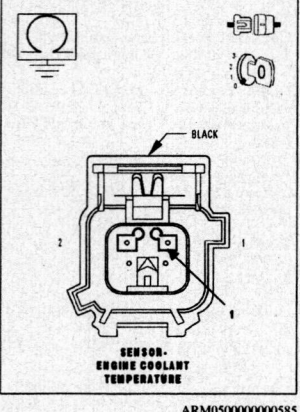

Fig. 26   Code P0116: Engine Coolant Temperature Sensor Circuit Performance (Part 6 of 7). Charger, Magnum & 300

1. ECT SENSOR VOLTAGE BELOW 0.078 OF A VOLT

Ignition on, engine not running.
With a scan tool, read the ECT voltage.

Is the voltage below 0.078 of a volt?

Yes

- Go To 2

No

- Diagnose INTERMITTENT CONDITION
- Perform the POWERTRAIN VERIFICATION TEST.

2. ECT SENSOR

Turn the ignition off.
Disconnect the ECT harness connector.
Ignition on, engine not running.
With a scan tool, read ECT voltage.

Is the voltage above 1.0 volt?

Yes

- Replace the ECT Sensor.
- Perform the POWERTRAIN VERIFICATION TEST.

No

- Go To 3

ARM0500000000587

Fig. 27   Code P0117: Engine Coolant Temperature Sensor Circuit Low (Part 1 of 3). Charger, Magnum & 300

8. (K2) ECT SIGNAL SHORTED TO THE (K900) SENSOR GROUND

Measure the resistance between the (K2) ECT Signal
circuit and the (K900) Sensor ground circuit in the ECT
Sensor harness connector.

Is the resistance below 5.0 ohms?

Yes

- Repair the short between the (K900) Sensor
  ground and the (K2) ECT Signal circuit.
- Perform the POWERTRAIN VERIFICATION
  TEST.

No

- Go To 9

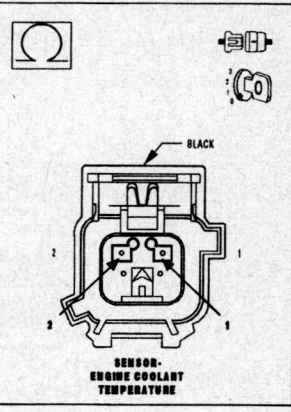

9. PCM

NOTE: Before continuing, check the PCM harness connector terminals for corrosion, damage, or terminal push out. Repair as necessary.

Using the schematics as a guide, inspect the wire harness and connectors. Pay particular attention to all
Power and Ground circuits.

Were there any problems found?

Yes

- Repair as necessary.
- Perform the POWERTRAIN VERIFICATION TEST.

No

- Replace and program the Powertrain Control Module
- Perform the POWERTRAIN VERIFICATION TEST.

ARM0500000000586

Fig. 26   Code P0116: Engine Coolant Temperature Sensor Circuit Performance (Part 7 of 7). Charger, Magnum & 300

3. (K2) ECT SIGNAL CIRCUIT SHORTED TO THE (K900) SENSOR GROUND CIRCUIT

Turn the ignition off.
Disconnect the PCM harness connectors.
Measure the resistance between the (K900) Sensor
ground circuit and the (K2) ECT Signal circuit in the
ECT Sensor harness connector.

Is the resistance below 5.0 ohms?

Yes

- Repair the short to between the (K900) Sensor
  ground circuit and the (K2) ECT Signal circuit.
- Perform the POWERTRAIN VERIFICATION
  TEST.

No

- Go To 4

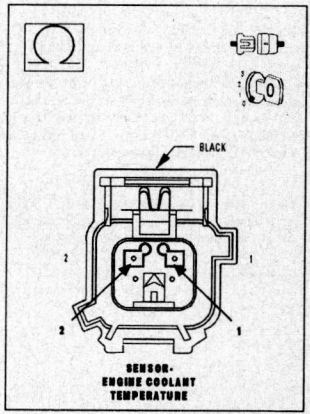

ARM0500000000588

Fig. 27   Code P0117: Engine Coolant Temperature Sensor Circuit Low (Part 2 of 3). Charger, Magnum & 300

4. (K2) ECT SIGNAL CIRCUIT SHORTED GROUND

Measure the resistance between ground and the (K2) ECT Signal circuit in the ECT Sensor harness connector.

Is the resistance below 100 ohms?

Yes

- Repair the short to ground in the (K2) ECT Signal circuit.
- Perform the POWERTRAIN VERIFICATION TEST.

No

- Go To 5

5. PCM

NOTE: Before continuing, check the PCM harness connector terminals for corrosion, damage, or terminal push out. Repair as necessary.

Using the schematics as a guide, inspect the wire harness and connectors. Pay particular attention to all Power and Ground circuits.

Were there any problems found?

Yes

- Repair as necessary.
- Perform the POWERTRAIN VERIFICATION TEST.

No

- Replace and program the Powertrain Control Module
- Perform the POWERTRAIN VERIFICATION TEST.

ARM0500000000589

Fig. 27   Code P0117: Engine Coolant Temperature Sensor Circuit Low (Part 3 of 3). Charger, Magnum & 300

2. ECT SENSOR

Turn the ignition off.
Disconnect the ECT harness connector.
Connect a jumper wire between the (K2) ECT Signal circuit and the (K900) Sensor ground circuit in the ECT harness connector.
Ignition on, engine not running.
With a scan tool, read ECT voltage.

Is the voltage below 1.0 volt with the jumper wire installed?

Yes

- Replace the ECT Sensor.
- Perform the POWERTRAIN VERIFICATION TEST.

No

- Go To 3

NOTE: Remove the jumper wire before continuing.

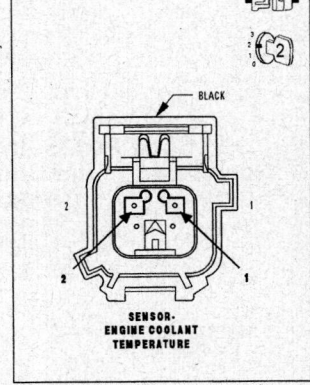

ARM0500000000591

Fig. 28   Code P0118: Engine Coolant Temperature Sensor Circuit High (Part 2 of 6). Charger, Magnum & 300

1. ECT SENSOR VOLTAGE ABOVE 4.98 VOLTS

Ignition on, engine not running.
With a scan tool, read the ECT voltage.

Is the voltage above 4.98 volts?

Yes

- Go To 2

No

- Diagnose INTERMITTENT CONDITION
- Perform the POWERTRAIN VERIFICATION TEST.

ARM0500000000590

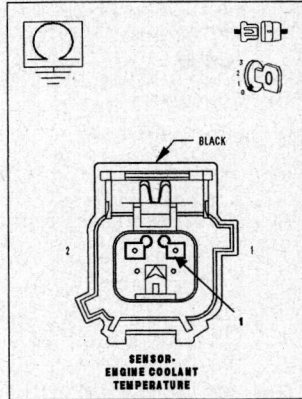

Fig. 28   Code P0118: Engine Coolant Temperature Sensor Circuit High (Part 1 of 6). Charger, Magnum & 300

3. (K2) ECT SIGNAL CIRCUIT SHORTED TO BATTERY VOLTAGE

Turn the ignition off.
Disconnect the PCM harness connectors.
Ignition on, engine not running.
Measure the voltage on the (K2) ECT Signal circuit in the ECT Sensor harness connector.

Is voltage present?

Yes

- Repair the short to battery voltage in the (K2) ECT Signal circuit.
- Perform the POWERTRAIN VERIFICATION TEST.

No

- Go To 4

ARM0500000000592

Fig. 28   Code P0118: Engine Coolant Temperature Sensor Circuit High (Part 3 of 6). Charger, Magnum & 300

4. (K2) ECT SIGNAL CIRCUIT OPEN

Turn the ignition off.

CAUTION: Do not probe the PCM harness connectors. Probing the PCM harness connectors will damage the PCM terminals resulting in poor terminal to pin connection. Install Miller Special Tool #8815 to perform diagnosis.

Measure the resistance of the (K2) ECT Signal circuit from the ECT Sensor harness connector to the appropriate terminal of special tool #8815.

Is the resistance below 5.0 ohms?

Yes

- Go To 5

No

- Repair the open in the (K2) ECT Signal circuit.
- Perform the POWERTRAIN VERIFICATION TEST.

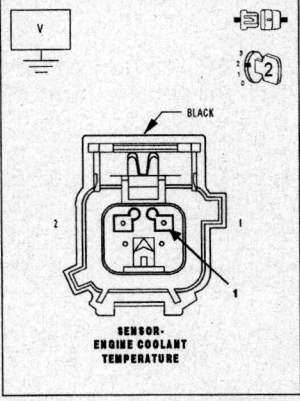

ARM0500000000593

Fig. 28   Code P0118: Engine Coolant Temperature Sensor Circuit High (Part 4 of 6). Charger, Magnum & 300

5. (K900) SENSOR GROUND CIRCUIT OPEN

Measure the resistance of the (K900) Sensor ground circuit from the ECT Sensor harness connector to the appropriate terminal of special tool #8815.

Is the resistance below 5.0 ohms?

Yes

- Go To 6

No

- Repair the open in the (K900) Sensor ground circuit.
- Perform the POWERTRAIN VERIFICATION TEST.

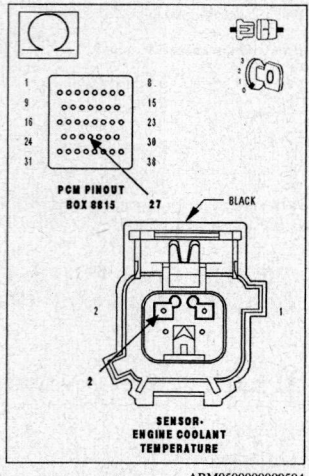

ARM0500000000594

Fig. 28 Code P0118: Engine Coolant Temperature Sensor Circuit High (Part 5 of 6). Charger, Magnum & 300

1. CHECKING COOLANT LEVEL AND CONDITION

Ignition on, engine not running.
With a scan tool, read DTCs.

NOTE: If an Engine Coolant Temperature (ECT) DTC is set along with this code, diagnose the ECT DTC first.

NOTE: Inspect the ECT terminals and related PCM terminals. Make sure the terminals are free from corrosion and damage.

NOTE: The best way to diagnose this DTC is to allow the vehicle to sit overnight outside in order to have a totally cold soaked engine.

NOTE: Extremely cold outside ambient temperatures may have caused this DTC to set.

WARNING: Never open the cooling system when the engine is hot. The system is under pressure. Extreme burns or scalding may result. Failure to follow these instructions can result in personal injury or death. Allow the engine to cool before opening the cooling system.

Inspect the coolant system for proper level and condition.

Is the coolant level and condition OK?

Yes

- Go To 2

No

- Inspect the vehicle for a coolant leak, make the appropriate repairs, and add the correct amount of coolant.
- Perform the POWERTRAIN VERIFICATION TEST.

ARM0500000000596

Fig. 29 Code P0125: Insufficient Coolant Temp For Closed-Loop Fuel Control (Part 1 of 3). Charger, Magnum & 300

6. PCM

NOTE: Before continuing, check the PCM harness connector terminals for corrosion, damage, or terminal push out. Repair as necessary.

Using the schematics as a guide, inspect the wire harness and connectors. Pay particular attention to all Power and Ground circuits.

Were there any problems found?

Yes

- Repair as necessary.
- Perform the POWERTRAIN VERIFICATION TEST.

No

- Replace and program the Powertrain Control Module
- Perform the POWERTRAIN VERIFICATION TEST.

ARM0500000000595

Fig. 28 Code P0118: Engine Coolant Temperature Sensor Circuit High (Part 6 of 6). Charger, Magnum & 300

2. THERMOSTAT OPERATION

NOTE: This test works best if performed on a cold engine (cold soak)

Ignition on, engine not running.
With a scan tool, read the Eng Coolant Temp Deg value. If the engine was allowed to sit overnight (cold soak), the temperature value should be a sensible value that is somewhere close to the ambient temperature.

NOTE: If engine coolant temperature is above 82°C (180°F), allow the engine to cool until 65°C (150°F) is reached.

Start the Engine.
During engine warm-up monitor the Eng Coolant Temp Deg value. The temp deg value change should be a smooth transition from start up to normal operating temp 82°C (180°F). Also monitor the actual coolant temperature with a thermometer.

NOTE: As the engine warms up to operating temperature, the actual coolant temperature (thermometer reading) and the scan tool Eng Coolant Temp Deg values should stay relatively close to each other.

Using the appropriate service information, determine the proper opening temperature of the thermostat.

Did the thermostat open at the proper temperature?

Yes

- Go To 3

No

- Replace the thermostat.
- Perform the POWERTRAIN VERIFICATION TEST.

ARM0500000000597

Fig. 29 Code P0125: Insufficient Coolant Temp For Closed-Loop Fuel Control (Part 2 of 3). Charger, Magnum & 300

3. ECT SENSOR OPERATION

Ignition on, engine not running.
With a scan tool, read the Eng Coolant Temp Deg value. If the engine was allowed to sit overnight (cold soak), the temperature value should be a sensible value that is somewhere close to the ambient temperature.

NOTE: If engine coolant temperature is above 82°C (180°F), allow the engine to cool until 65°C (150°F) is reached.

Start the Engine.
During engine warm-up monitor the Eng Coolant Temp Deg value. The temp deg value change should be a smooth transition from start up to normal operating temp 82°C (180°F). Also monitor the actual coolant temperature with a thermometer.

NOTE: As the engine warms up to operating temperature, the actual coolant temperature (thermometer reading) and the scan tools Eng Coolant Temp Deg value should stay relatively close to each other.

Is the thermometer reading relatively close to the scan tool ECT reading?

Yes

- Test Complete.

No

- Replace the Engine Coolant Temperature Sensor.
- Perform the POWERTRAIN VERIFICATION TEST.

ARM0500000000598

Fig. 29   Code P0125: Insufficient Coolant Temp For Closed-Loop Fuel Control (Part 3 of 3). Charger, Magnum & 300

2. LOW COOLANT LEVEL

NOTE: If an Engine Coolant Temperature (ECT) DTC is set along with this code, diagnose the ECT DTC first.

NOTE: Inspect the ECT terminals and related PCM terminals. Make sure the terminals are free from corrosion and damage.

NOTE: The best way to diagnose this DTC is to allow the vehicle to sit overnight outside in order to have a totally cold soaked engine.

NOTE: Extremely cold outside ambient temperatures may have caused this DTC to set.

WARNING: Never open the cooling system when the engine is hot. The system is under pressure. Failure to follow these instructions can result in personal injury including extreme burns, scalding, or death. Allow the engine to cool before opening the cooling system.

Check the coolant system to make sure that the coolant is in good condition and at the proper level.

Is the coolant level and condition OK?

Yes

- Go To 3

No

- Inspect the vehicle for a coolant leak and add the necessary amount of coolant.
- Perform the POWERTRAIN VERIFICATION TEST.

ARM0500000000600

Fig. 30   Code P0128: Thermostat Rationality (Part 2 of 12). Charger, Magnum & 300

1. ACTIVE DTC

NOTE: If any ECT, AAT, CMP or CKP sensor DTCs have set along with P0128, diagnose them before continuing.

NOTE: Make sure that the Pinion Factor has been programmed correctly into the PCM.

Ignition on, engine not running.
With a scan tool, read DTCs.

Is the DTC active at this time?

Yes

- Go To 2

No

- Diagnose INTERMITTENT CONDITION
- Perform the POWERTRAIN VERIFICATION TEST.

ARM0500000000599

Fig. 30   Code P0128: Thermostat Rationality (Part 1 of 12). Charger, Magnum & 300

3. THERMOSTAT OPERATION

NOTE: This test works best if performed on a cold engine (cold soak).

Ignition on, engine not running.
With a scan tool, read the ECT Deg value. If the engine was allowed to sit overnight (cold soak), the temperature value should be a sensible value that is somewhere close to the ambient temperature.

NOTE: If engine coolant temperature is above 82°C (180°F), allow the engine to cool until 65°C (150°F) is reached.

Start the Engine.
During engine warm-up, monitor the ECT Deg value. The temp deg value change should be a smooth transition from start up to normal operating temp 82°C (180°F). Also monitor the actual coolant temperature with a thermometer.

NOTE: As the engine warms up to operating temperature, the actual coolant temperature (thermometer reading) and the scan tool, ECT Temperature value should stay relatively close to each other.

Using the appropriate service information, determine the proper opening temperature of the thermostat.

Did the thermostat open at the proper temperature?

Yes

- Go To 4

No

- Replace the thermostat.
- Perform the POWERTRAIN VERIFICATION TEST.

ARM0500000000601

Fig. 30   Code P0128: Thermostat Rationality (Part 3 of 12). Charger, Magnum & 300

4. AMBIENT AIR TEMP SENSOR OPERATION

Ignition on, engine not running.
With a scan tool, read and record the AAT Sensor Temperature value.
Using the DRB Temperature Probe #CH7050, or an equivalent temperature measuring tool, measure the ambient air temperature near the AAT Sensor.

Is the AAT Sensor value with -15°C (5°F) of the temperature probe reading?

Yes

- Go To 5

No

- Go To 7

5. ECT SENSOR OPERATION

WARNING: Make sure the engine cooling system is cool before removing the pressure cap or any hose. The cooling system is pressurized when hot. Failure to follow these instructions can result in personal injury including extreme burns, scalding, or death.

With a scan tool, read and record the ECT Sensor Temperature value.
Use the DRB Temperature Probe #CH7050, or an equivalent temperature measuring tool, measure the engine coolant temperature.

Is the ECT Sensor value with -15°C (5°F) of the temperature probe reading?

Yes

- Go To 6

No

- Go To 7

ARM0500000000602

Fig. 30   Code P0128: Thermostat Rationality (Part 4 of 12). Charger, Magnum & 300

7. SIGNAL CIRCUIT SHORTED TO BATTERY VOLTAGE

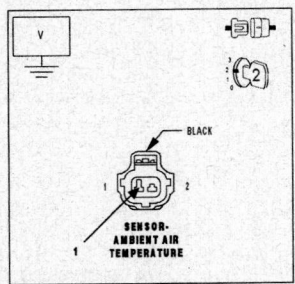

NOTE: Visually inspect both the component and the PCM/FCM connectors. Look for damage, partially broken wires and backed out or corroded terminals

Turn the ignition off.
Disconnect the applicable Temperature Sensor harness connector.
Disconnect the applicable controller harness connectors.

Ignition on, engine not running.
Measure the voltage on the Signal circuit at the Temperature Sensor harness connector.

Is voltage present?

Yes

- Repair the short to battery voltage in the Signal circuit.
- Perform the POWERTRAIN VERIFICATION TEST.

No

- Go To 8

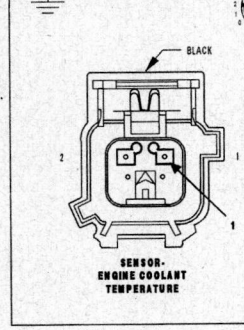

ARM0500000000604

Fig. 30   Code P0128: Thermostat Rationality (Part 6 of 12). Charger, Magnum & 300

6. OTHER POSSIBLE CAUSES

Inspect the Temperature Sensors for any physical damage.
Inspect the engine coolant. Make sure the coolant is at the proper level.

Make sure the Temperature Sensors are properly installed.
Make sure the CMP and CKP sensors are installed properly. Check the connectors for any signs of damage.

WARNING: When the engine is operating, do not stand in direct line with the fan. Do not put your hands near the pulleys, belts, or fan. Do not wear loose clothing. Failure to follow these instructions can result in personal injury or death.

Refer to any Technical Service Bulletins (TSBs) that may apply.
With the engine running at normal operating temperature, monitor the Temperature sensor parameters while wiggling the wire harness. Look for parameter values to change.
Visually inspect the related wire harness. Look for any chafed, pierced, pinched, partially broken wires and broken, bent, pushed out, or corroded terminals.

CAUTION: Do not probe the PCM harness connectors. Probing the PCM harness connectors will damage the PCM terminals resulting in poor terminal to pin connection. Install Miller Special Tool #8815 to perform diagnosis.

Inspect and clean all PCM, engine, and chassis grounds.

Were any problems found during the above inspections?

Yes

- Repair as necessary.
- Perform the POWERTRAIN VERIFICATION TEST.

No

- Test Complete.

ARM0500000000603

Fig. 30   Code P0128: Thermostat Rationality (Part 5 of 12). Charger, Magnum & 300

8. TEMPERATURE SENSOR

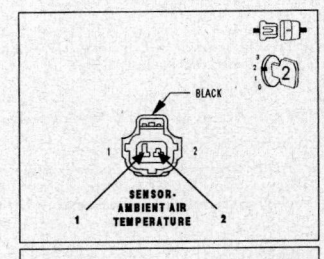

Turn the ignition off.
Connect the controller harness connectors.
Connect a jumper wire across Sensor harness connectors.
Ignition on, engine not running.
With a scan tool, read the Temperature Sensor voltage.

Does the voltage start at 5.0 volts and drop below 1.0 volt when the jumper wire is installed?

Yes

- Replace the appropriate Temperature Sensor.
- Perform the POWERTRAIN VERIFICATION TEST.

No

- Go To 9

NOTE: Disconnect the jumper wire before continuing.

ARM0500000000605

Fig. 30   Code P0128: Thermostat Rationality (Part 7 of 12). Charger, Magnum & 300

9. SIGNAL CIRCUIT OPEN

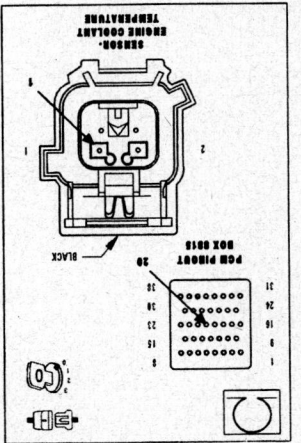

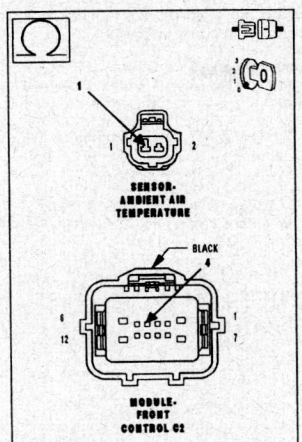

Turn the ignition off.

CAUTION: Do not probe the PCM harness connectors. Probing the PCM harness connectors will damage the PCM terminals resulting in poor terminal to pin connection. Install Miller Special Tool #8815 to perform diagnosis.

Measure the resistance of the Sensor Signal circuit Sensor harness connector to the appropriate terminal of special tool #8815 or the FCM.

Is the resistance below 5.0 ohms?

Yes

No

- Go To 10

- Repair the open in the Sensor Signal circuit.
- Perform the POWERTRAIN VERIFICATION TEST.

ARM0500000000606

Fig. 30   Code P0128: Thermostat Rationality (Part 8 of 12). Charger, Magnum & 300

---

11. SIGNAL CIRCUIT SHORTED TO GROUND

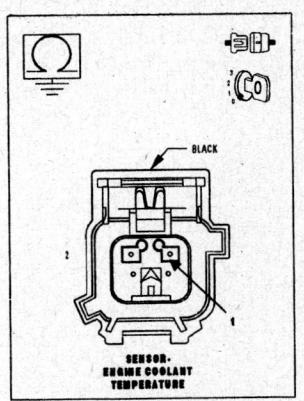

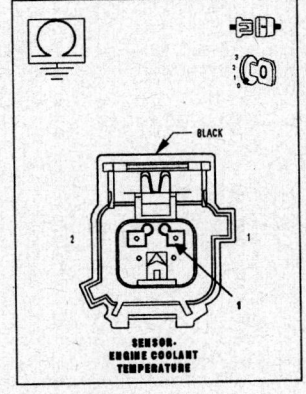

Measure the resistance between ground and the Sensor Signal circuit in the Temperature Sensor harness connector.

Is the resistance below 100 ohms?

Yes

- Repair the short to ground in the Signal circuit.
- Perform the POWERTRAIN VERIFICATION TEST.

No

- Go To 12

ARM0500000000608

Fig. 30   Code P0128: Thermostat Rationality (Part 10 of 12). Charger, Magnum & 300

---

10. SENSOR GROUND CIRCUIT OPEN

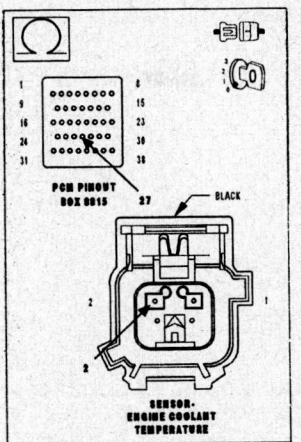

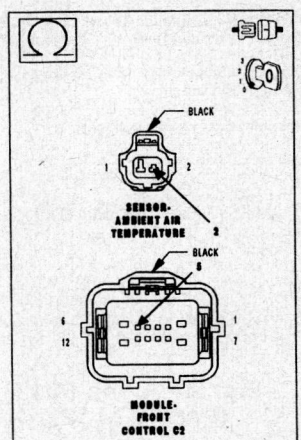

Measure the resistance of the Sensor ground circuit from the appropriate Temperature Sensor harness connector to the appropriate terminal of special tool #8815 or the FCM.

Is the resistance below 5.0 ohms?

Yes

- Go To 11

No

- Repair the open in the Sensor ground circuit.
- Perform the POWERTRAIN VERIFICATION TEST.

ARM0500000000607

Fig. 30   Code P0128: Thermostat Rationality (Part 9 of 12). Charger, Magnum & 300

---

12. SIGNAL CIRCUIT SHORTED TO SENSOR GROUND CIRCUIT

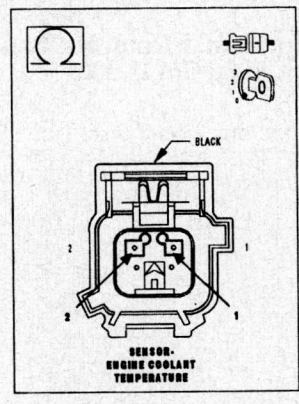

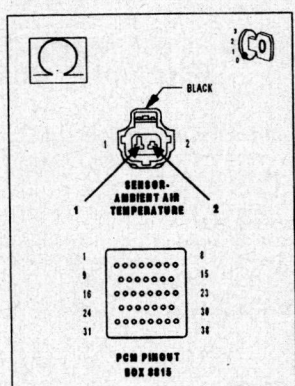

Measure the resistance between the Signal circuit and the Sensor ground circuit in the Sensor harness connector.

Is the resistance below 100 ohms?

Yes

- Repair the short between the Sensor ground circuit and the Sensor Signal circuit.
- Perform the POWERTRAIN VERIFICATION TEST.

No

- Go To 13

ARM0500000000609

Fig. 30   Code P0128: Thermostat Rationality (Part 11 of 12). Charger, Magnum & 300

13. FCM/PCM

NOTE: Before continuing, check the FCM/PCM harness connector terminals for corrosion, damage, or terminal push out. Repair as necessary.

Using the schematics as a guide, inspect the wire harness and connectors. Pay particular attention to all Power and Ground circuits.

Were there any problems found?

Yes

- Repair as necessary.
- Perform the POWERTRAIN VERIFICATION TEST.

No

- Replace applicable Control Module
- Perform the POWERTRAIN VERIFICATION TEST.

ARM0500000000610

Fig. 30   Code P0128: Thermostat Rationality (Part 12 of 12). Charger, Magnum & 300

3. RADIATOR FAN CONTROL RELAY CONTROL CIRCUIT

Turn the ignition on, engine not running.
With a scan tool, select Radiator Cooling Fan Relay #1 Control State, Toggle, to actuate the Radiator Fan Control Relay.
Using a 12-volt test light connected to battery voltage, probe the Radiator Control Relay Control circuit in the PDM.

Does the test light illuminate and flash on and off?

Yes

- Replace the Radiator Fan Control Relay.
- Perform BODY VERIFICATION TEST-VER 1.

No

- Go To 4

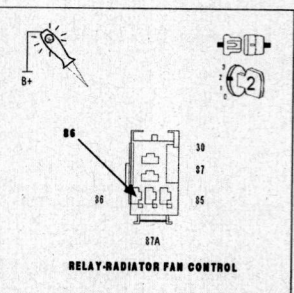

ARM0500000000612

Fig. 31   Code P0480: Cooling Fan 1 Control Circuit (Part 2 of 4). Charger, Magnum & 300

4. (N201) RADIATOR FAN CONTROL RELAY CONTROL CIRCUIT OPEN

Turn the ignition off.
Remove the FCM from the PDM.
Measure the resistance of the (N201) Radiator Fan Control Relay Control circuit from the Relay to the FCM PDM — 49 way connector.

Is the resistance below 5.0 ohms?

Yes

- Go To 5

No

- Replace the PDM
- Perform BODY VERIFICATION TEST-VER 1.

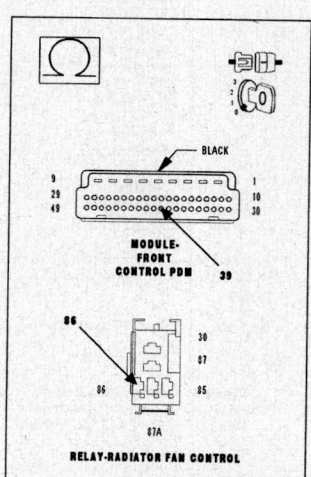

ARM0500000000613

Fig. 31   Code P0480: Cooling Fan 1 Control Circuit (Part 3 of 4). Charger, Magnum & 300

1. RADIATOR FAN CONTROL RELAY OPERATION

NOTE: When actuating the radiator fan relays, the Radiator Fan(s) may have a delay in operation and ramp up slowly.

Ignition on, engine not running.
With a scan tool, select Radiator Cooling Fan Relay #1 Control State to actuate the Radiator Fan Control Relay.

Is the Cooling Fan Relay operating?

Yes

- Diagnose INTERMITTENT CONDITION
- Perform the POWERTRAIN VERIFICATION TEST.

No

- Go To 2

2. (A201) FUSED B+ CIRCUITS

Turn the ignition off.
Remove the Radiator Fan Control Relay.
Using a 12-volt test light connected to ground, probe the (A201) Fused B+ circuits.

Is the voltage above 11.0 volts?

Yes

- Go To 3

No

- Repair the open or short to ground in the (A201) Fused B+ circuits. Inspect the related fuse and repair as necessary.

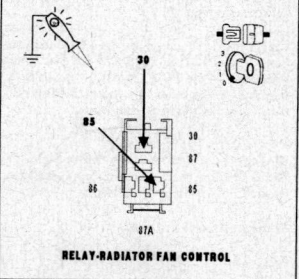

ARM0500000000611

Fig. 31   Code P0480: Cooling Fan 1 Control Circuit (Part 1 of 4). Charger, Magnum & 300

5. (N201) RADIATOR FAN CONTROL RELAY CONTROL CIRCUIT SHORTED TO GROUND

Measure the resistance between ground and the (N201) Radiator Fan Control Relay Control circuit at the Relay connection.

Is the resistance below 100 ohms?

Yes

- Replace the PDM
- Perform BODY VERIFICATION TEST-VER 1.

No

- Replace Front Control Module
- Perform BODY VERIFICATION TEST-VER 1.

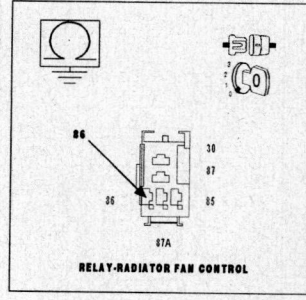

ARM0500000000614

Fig. 31   Code P0480: Cooling Fan 1 Control Circuit (Part 4 of 4). Charger, Magnum & 300

1. RADIATOR FAN HIGH RELAY OPERATION

Ignition on, engine not running.
With a scan tool, select Radiator Cooling Fan Relay #2 Control State, to actuate the Radiator Fan High Relay.

Is the Cooling Fan Relay operating?

Yes

- Diagnose INTERMITTENT CONDITION
- Perform the POWERTRAIN VERIFICATION TEST.

No

- Go To 2

2. (A16) FUSED B+ CIRCUITS

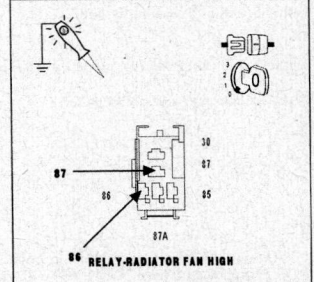

Turn the ignition off.
Remove the Radiator High Fan Relay.
Using a 12-volt test light connected to ground, probe the (A16) Fused B+ circuits in the Relay connection.

Does the test light illuminate brightly?

Yes

- Go To 4

No

- Go To 3

ARM0500000000615

Fig. 32 Code P0481: Cooling Fan 2 Control Circuit (Part 1 of 4). Charger, Magnum & 300

5. (N112) RADIATOR FAN HIGH RELAY CONTROL CIRCUIT OPEN

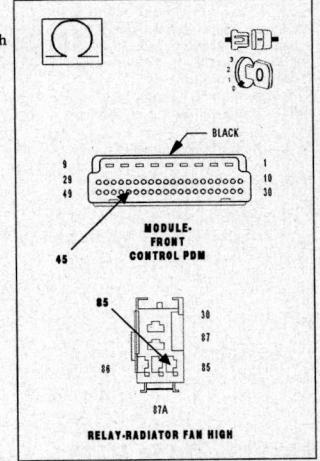

Remove the FCM from the PDM.
Measure the resistance of the (N112) Radiator Fan High Relay Control circuit from the Relay connection to the FCM PDM — 49 way connector.

Is the resistance below 5.0 ohms?

Yes

- Go To 6

No

- Replace the PDM
- Perform BODY VERIFICATION TEST-VER 1

ARM0500000000617

Fig. 32 Code P0481: Cooling Fan 2 Control Circuit (Part 3 of 4). Charger, Magnum & 300

3. RADIATOR FAN HI/LO CONTROL RELAY SHORTED INTERNALLY

With the test light still at the (A16) Fused B+ circuit (Radiator High Fan Relay), remove the Radiator Fan HI/LO Control Relay.

When the relay is removed, does the test light illuminate brightly?

Yes

- Replace the Radiator Fan HI/LO Control Relay.
- Perform BODY VERIFICATION TEST-VER 1.

No

- Repair the open or short to ground in the (A16) Fused B+ circuits. Inspect the related fuse and repair as necessary.
- Perform BODY VERIFICATION TEST-VER 1.

4. RADIATOR FAN HIGH RELAY CONTROL CIRCUIT

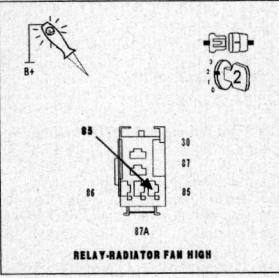

Turn the ignition on, engine not running.
With a scan tool, select Radiator Cooling Fan Relay #2 Control State and then Toggle, to actuate the Radiator Fan High Relay.
Using a 12-volt test light connected to battery voltage, probe the Radiator Fan High Relay Control circuit in the PDM.

Does the test light illuminate and flash on and off?

Yes

- Replace the Radiator Fan High Relay.
- Perform BODY VERIFICATION TEST-VER 1.

No

- Go To 5

ARM0500000000616

Fig. 32 Code P0481: Cooling Fan 2 Control Circuit (Part 2 of 4). Charger, Magnum & 300

6. (N112) RADIATOR FAN HIGH RELAY CONTROL CIRCUIT SHORTED TO GROUND

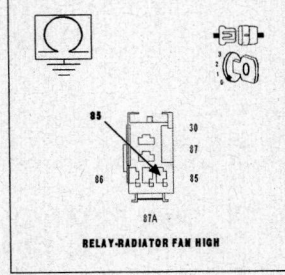

Measure the resistance between ground and the (N112) Radiator Fan High Control circuit at the Relay connection.

Is the resistance below 100 ohms?

Yes

- Go To 7

No

- Replace the Front Control Module
- Perform BODY VERIFICATION TEST-VER 1.

7. RADIATOR FAN HI/LO CONTROL RELAY SHORTED INTERNALLY

With the probe still at the (N112) Radiator Fan High Control circuit, remove the Radiator Fan HI/LO Control Relay.

Is the resistance still below 100 ohms?

Yes

- Repair the open or short to ground in the (N112) Radiator Fan High Control circuit.
- Perform BODY VERIFICATION TEST-VER 1.

No

- Replace the Radiator Fan HI/LO Control Relay.
- Perform BODY VERIFICATION TEST-VER 1

ARM0500000000618

Fig. 32 Code P0481: Cooling Fan 2 Control Circuit (Part 4 of 4). Charger, Magnum & 300

1. ACTIVE DTC

Ignition on, engine not running.

NOTE: If this code sets during extreme ambient temperatures, improper installation of a block heater could be the cause of this DTC.

With a scan tool, read DTCs.
Diagnose all other ECT and Cooling System codes before continuing.

Is the DTC active at this time?

Yes

- Go To 2

No

- Diagnose INTERMITTENT CONDITION
- Perform the POWERTRAIN VERIFICATION TEST.

ARM0500000000619

Fig. 33   Code P2181: Cooling System Performance (Part 1 of 10). Charger, Magnum & 300

3. THERMOSTAT

NOTE: This test works best if performed on a cold engine (cold soak).

Ignition on, engine not running.
With a scan tool, read the Eng Coolant Tmp Deg value. If the engine was allowed to sit overnight (cold soak), the temperature value should be a sensible value that is somewhere close to the ambient temperature.

NOTE: If engine coolant temperature is above 82°C (180°F), allow the engine to cool until 65°C (150°F) is reached.

Start the Engine.
During engine warm-up monitor the Eng Coolant Tmp Deg value. The temp deg value change should be a smooth transition from start up to normal operating temp 82°C (180°F) . Also monitor the actual coolant temperature with a thermometer.

NOTE: As the engine warms up to operating temperature, the actual coolant temperature (thermometer reading) and the Eng Coolant Tmp Deg on the scan tool should stay relatively close to each other.

Using the appropriate service information, determine the proper opening temperature of the thermostat.

Did the thermostat open at the proper temperature?

Yes

- Go To 4

No

- Replace the thermostat.
- Perform the POWERTRAIN VERIFICATION TEST.

ARM0500000000621

Fig. 33   Code P2181: Cooling System Performance (Part 3 of 10). Charger, Magnum & 300

2. LOW COOLANT LEVEL

NOTE: If a Engine Coolant Temperature (ECT) DTC is set along with this code, diagnose the ECT DTC first.

NOTE: Inspect the ECT terminals and related PCM terminals. Ensure the terminals are free from corrosion and damage.

NOTE: The best way to diagnose this DTC is to allow the vehicle to sit overnight outside in order to have a totally cold soaked engine.

NOTE: Extremely cold outside ambient temperatures may have caused this DTC to set.

NOTE: Need to make sure that no Cooling System DTCs are set or changes that would make the warm up much slower or much faster: broken water pump can set this, addition of aftermarket auxiliary cooler can set this DTC.

WARNING: Never open the cooling system when the engine is hot. The system is under pressure. Failure to follow these instructions can result in personal injury or death. Allow the engine to cool before opening the cooling system.

Inspect the coolant system for proper level and condition.

Is the coolant level and condition OK?

Yes

- Go To 3

No

- Inspect the vehicle for a coolant leak and add the necessary amount of coolant.
- Perform the POWERTRAIN VERIFICATION TEST.

ARM0500000000620

Fig. 33   Code P2181: Cooling System Performance (Part 2 of 10). Charger, Magnum & 300

4. ECT SENSOR

Connect a jumper between the (K2) ECT Signal circuit and the (K900) Sensor ground circuit in the ECT Sensor harness connector.
Turn the ignition off.
Disconnect the ECT Sensor harness connector.
With a scan tool, read the ECT voltage.

Is the voltage below 1.0 volt?

Yes

- Replace the ECT Sensor.
- Perform the POWERTRAIN VERIFICATION TEST.

No

- Go To 5

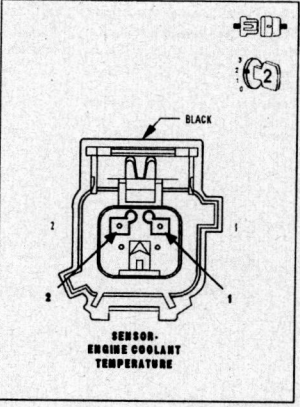

ARM0500000000622

Fig. 33   Code P2181: Cooling System Performance (Part 4 of 10). Charger, Magnum & 300

5. (K2) ECT SIGNAL CIRCUIT SHORTED TO BATTERY VOLTAGE

Turn the ignition off.
Disconnect the PCM harness connectors.
Ignition on, engine not running.
Measure the voltage on the (K2) ECT Signal circuit in the ECT Sensor harness connector.

Is the voltage above 5.2 volts?

Yes

- Repair the short to battery voltage in the (K2) ECT Signal circuit.
- Perform the POWERTRAIN VERIFICATION TEST.

No

- Go To 6

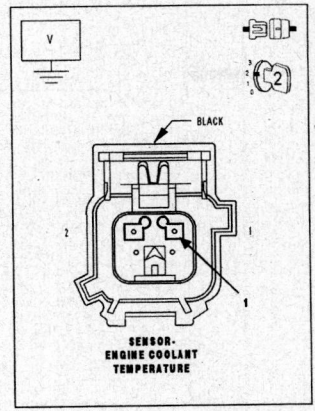

ARM0500000000623

Fig. 33   Code P2181: Cooling System Performance (Part 5 of 10). Charger, Magnum & 300

7. (K900) SENSOR GROUND CIRCUIT OPEN

Measure the resistance of the (K900) Sensor ground circuit from the ECT Sensor harness connector to the appropriate terminal of special tool #8815.

Is the resistance below 5.0 ohms?

Yes

- Go To 8

No

- Repair the open in the (K900) Sensor ground circuit.
- Perform the POWERTRAIN VERIFICATION TEST.

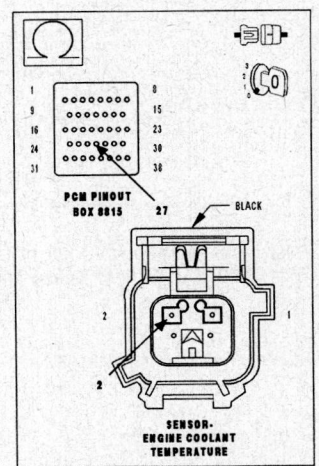

ARM0500000000625

Fig. 33   Code P2181: Cooling System Performance (Part 7 of 10). Charger, Magnum & 300

9. (K2) ECT SIGNAL CIRCUIT SHORTED TO THE (K900) SENSOR GROUND CIRCUIT

Measure the resistance between the (K2) ECT Signal circuit and the (K900) Sensor ground circuit in the ECT Sensor harness connector.

Is the resistance below 5.0 ohms?

Yes

- Repair the short between the (K900) Sensor ground and the (K2) ECT Signal circuit.
- Perform the POWERTRAIN VERIFICATION TEST.

No

- Go To 10

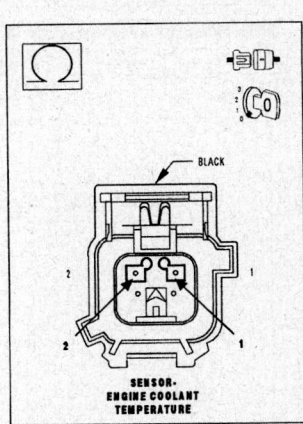

ARM0500000000627

Fig. 33   Code P2181: Cooling System Performance (Part 9 of 10). Charger, Magnum & 300

6. (K2) ECT SIGNAL CIRCUIT OPEN

Turn the ignition off.

CAUTION: Do not probe the PCM harness connectors. Probing the PCM harness connectors will damage the PCM terminals resulting in poor terminal to pin connection. Install Miller Special Tool #8815 to perform diagnosis.

Measure the resistance of the (K2) ECT Signal circuit from the ECT Sensor harness connector to the appropriate terminal of special tool #8815.

Is the resistance below 5.0 ohms?

Yes

- Go To 7

No

- Repair the open in the (K2) ECT Signal circuit.
- Perform the POWERTRAIN VERIFICATION TEST.

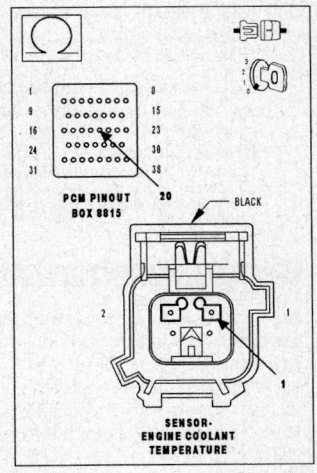

ARM0500000000624

Fig. 33   Code P2181: Cooling System Performance (Part 6 of 10). Charger, Magnum & 300

8. (K2) ECT SIGNAL CIRCUIT SHORTED TO GROUND

Measure the resistance between ground and the (K2) ECT Signal circuit in the ECT Sensor harness connector.

Is the resistance below 100 ohms?

Yes

- Repair the short to ground in the (K2) ECT Signal circuit.
- Perform the POWERTRAIN VERIFICATION TEST.

No

- Go To 9

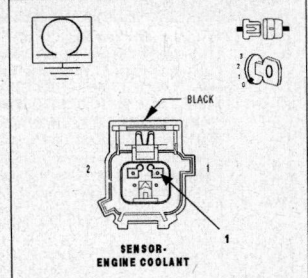

ARM0500000000626

Fig. 33   Code P2181: Cooling System Performance (Part 8 of 10). Charger, Magnum & 300

10. PCM

NOTE: Before continuing, check the PCM harness connector terminals for corrosion, damage, or terminal push out. Repair as necessary.

Using the schematics as a guide, inspect the wire harness and connectors. Pay particular attention to all Power and Ground circuits.

Were there any problems found?

Yes

- Repair as necessary.
- Perform the POWERTRAIN VERIFICATION TEST.

No

- Replace and program the Powertrain Control Module
- Perform the POWERTRAIN VERIFICATION TEST.

ARM0500000000628

Fig. 33   Code P2181: Cooling System Performance (Part 10 of 10). Charger, Magnum & 300

When Monitored and Set Condition:

P0110-INTAKE AIR TEMPERATURE SENSOR STUCK

When Monitored: Engine Running.

Set Condition: After 4 warm-up cycles, the PCM did not see a 2°C (6°F) change in the IAT Sensor voltage within 200 miles. Two Trip Fault

P0111-INTAKE AIR TEMPERATURE SENSOR PERFORMANCE

When Monitored: Engine off time is greater than 480 minutes. Ambient temperature is greater than -23°C (-10°F).

Set Condition: After a calibrated amount of cool down time, the PCM compares the ECT Sensor, IAT Sensor and the Ambient Air Temperature Sensor values. If the IAT Sensor value is not within calibrated temperature amount of the other two temperature sensors an error is detected. Two Trip Fault.

POSSIBLE CAUSES
GOOD TRIP EQUAL TO ZERO
(K21) IAT SIGNAL CIRCUIT SHORTED TO BATTERY VOLTAGE
IAT SENSOR VOLTAGE BELOW 1.0 VOLTS
(K21) IAT SIGNAL CIRCUIT OPEN
(K4) SENSOR GROUND CIRCUIT OPEN
(K21) IAT SIGNAL SHORTED TO GROUND
(K21) IAT SIGNAL CIRCUIT SHORTED TO (K4) SENSOR GROUND
PCM HIGH
PCM LOW

ARM0400000000938

Fig. 34   Code P0110 & P0111: IAT Sensor Stuck Or Performance (Part 1 of 3). Concorde, Intrepid & 300M

TEST	ACTION
6	Turn the ignition off. Disconnect the IAT Sensor harness connector. Disconnect the PCM harness connector. **CAUTION: DO NOT PROBE THE PCM HARNESS CONNECTORS. PROBING THE PCM HARNESS CONNECTORS WILL DAMAGE THE PCM TERMINALS RESULTING IN POOR TERMINAL TO PIN CONNECTION. INSTALL MILLER SPECIAL TOOL #8815 TO PERFORM DIAGNOSIS.** Measure the resistance of the (K4) Sensor ground circuit from the IAT Sensor harness connector to the appropriate terminal of special tool #8815. Is the resistance below 5.0 ohms? Yes → NOTE: Before continuing, check the PCM harness connector terminals for corrosion, damage, or terminal push out. Repair as necessary. Replace and program the Powertrain Control Module in accordance with the Service Information. No → Repair the open in the (K4) Sensor ground circuit.
7	Turn the ignition off. Disconnect the IAT Sensor harness connector. Disconnect the PCM harness connector. Measure the resistance between ground and the (K21) IAT Signal circuit in the IAT Sensor harness connector. Is the resistance below 100 ohms? Yes → Repair the short to ground in the (K21) IAT Signal circuit. No → Go To 8
8	Turn the ignition off. Disconnect the IAT Sensor harness connector. Disconnect the PCM harness connector. Measure the resistance between the (K4) Sensor ground circuit and the (K21) IAT Sensor Signal circuit at the IAT Sensor harness connector. Is the resistance below 5.0 ohms? Yes → Repair the (K4) Sensor ground circuit shorted to the (K21) IAT Signal circuit. No → NOTE: Before continuing, check the PCM harness connector terminals for corrosion, damage, or terminal push out. Repair as necessary. Replace and program the Powertrain Control Module

ARM0400000000940

Fig. 34   Code P0110 & P0111: IAT Sensor Stuck Or Performance (Part 3 of 3). Concorde, Intrepid & 300M

TEST	ACTION
1	Ignition on, engine not running. With the DRBIII®, read DTCs and record the related Freeze Frame data. Is the Good Trip Counter displayed and equal to zero? Yes → Go To 2 No → Diagnose intermittent condition.
2	Turn the ignition off. Disconnect the IAT Sensor harness connector. **NOTE: Visually inspect both the component and the PCM connectors. Look for damaged, partially broken wires, and backed out or corroded terminals.** Ignition on, engine not running. Measure the voltage on the (K21) IAT Signal circuit in the IAT Sensor harness connector. Is the voltage above 5.2 volts? Yes → Repair the short to battery voltage in the (K21) IAT Signal circuit. No → Go To 3
3	Turn the ignition off. Disconnect the IAT Sensor harness connector. Ignition on, engine not running. With the DRBIII®, read the IAT Sensor voltage. Is the voltage above 4.9 volts? Yes → Go To 4 No → Go To 7
4	Turn the ignition off. Disconnect the IAT Sensor harness connector. Using a jumper wire, jumper across the IAT Sensor harness connector. Ignition on, engine not running. With the DRBIII®, read the IAT Sensor voltage. Is the voltage below 1.0 volt? Yes → Replace the IAT Sensor. No → Go To 5
5	Turn the ignition off. Disconnect the IAT Sensor harness connector. Disconnect the PCM harness connector. **CAUTION: DO NOT PROBE THE PCM HARNESS CONNECTORS. PROBING THE PCM HARNESS CONNECTORS WILL DAMAGE THE PCM TERMINALS RESULTING IN POOR TERMINAL TO PIN CONNECTION. INSTALL MILLER SPECIAL TOOL #8815 TO PERFORM DIAGNOSIS.** Measure the resistance of the (K21) IAT Signal circuit from the IAT Sensor harness connector to the appropriate terminal of special tool #8815. Is the resistance below 5.0 ohms? Yes → Go To 6 No → Repair the open in the (K21) IAT Signal circuit.

ARM0400000000939

Fig. 34   Code P0110 & P0111: IAT Sensor Stuck Or Performance (Part 2 of 3). Concorde, Intrepid & 300M

When Monitored and Set Condition:

P0112-INTAKE AIR TEMPERATURE SENSOR LOW

When Monitored: With the ignition on. Battery voltage greater than 10 volts.

Set Condition: The Intake Air Temperature (IAT) sensor voltage is less than 0.0784 of a volt. One trip Fault.

POSSIBLE CAUSES
IAT SENSOR VOLTAGE BELOW 1.0 VOLT
IAT SENSOR INTERNAL FAILURE
(K21) IAT SIGNAL SHORTED TO GROUND
(K21) IAT SIGNAL SHORTED TO (K4) SENSOR GROUND CIRCUIT
PCM

TEST	ACTION
1	Ignition on, engine not running. With the DRBIII®, read the IAT Sensor voltage. Is the voltage below 1.0 volt? Yes → Go To 2 No → Diagnose intermittent condition.
2	Turn the ignition off. Disconnect the IAT harness connector. Ignition on, engine not running. With the DRBIII®, read IAT Sensor voltage. Is the voltage above 1.0 volt? Yes → Replace the IAT Sensor. No → Go To 3
3	Turn the ignition off. Disconnect the IAT Sensor harness connector. Disconnect the PCM harness connector. Measure the resistance between ground and the (K21) IAT Signal circuit at the IAT Sensor harness connector. Is the resistance below 100 ohms? Yes → Repair the short to ground in the (K21) IAT Signal circuit. No → Go To 4

ARM0400000000941

Fig. 35   Code P0112: IAT Sensor Low (Part 1 of 2). Concorde, Intrepid & 300M

TEST	ACTION
4	Turn the ignition off. Disconnect the IAT Sensor harness connector. Disconnect the PCM harness connector. Measure the resistance between the (K21) IAT Sensor Signal circuit and the (K4) Sensor ground circuit in the IAT Sensor harness connector. Is the resistance below 100 ohms? Yes → Repair the (K4) Sensor ground shorted to the (K21) IAT Signal circuit. No → Go To 5
5	NOTE: Before continuing, check the PCM harness connector terminals for corrosion, damage, or terminal push out. Repair as necessary. If there are no possible causes remaining, view repair. Repair Replace and program the Powertrain Control Module

ARM0400000000942

Fig. 35   Code P0112: IAT Sensor Low (Part 2 of 2). Concorde, Intrepid & 300M

TEST	ACTION
3	Turn the ignition off. Disconnect the IAT harness connector. Connect a jumper wire between the (K21) IAT Signal circuit and the (K4) Sensor ground circuit in the IAT harness connector. Ignition on, engine not running. With the DRBIII®, read IAT voltage. Is the voltage below 1.0 volt? Yes → Replace the IAT Sensor. No → Go To 4
4	Turn the ignition off. Disconnect the IAT Sensor harness connector. Disconnect the PCM harness connector. CAUTION: DO NOT PROBE THE PCM HARNESS CONNECTORS. PROBING THE PCM HARNESS CONNECTORS WILL DAMAGE THE PCM TERMINALS RESULTING IN POOR TERMINAL TO PIN CONNECTION. INSTALL MILLER SPECIAL TOOL #8815 TO PERFORM DIAGNOSIS. Measure the resistance of the (K21) IAT Signal circuit from the IAT Sensor harness connector to the appropriate terminal of special tool #8815. Is the resistance below 5.0 ohms? Yes → Go To 5 No → Repair the open in the (K21) IAT Signal circuit.
5	Turn the ignition off. Disconnect the IAT Sensor harness connector. Disconnect the PCM harness connector. CAUTION: DO NOT PROBE THE PCM HARNESS CONNECTORS. PROBING THE PCM HARNESS CONNECTORS WILL DAMAGE THE PCM TERMINALS RESULTING IN POOR TERMINAL TO PIN CONNECTION. INSTALL MILLER SPECIAL TOOL #8815 TO PERFORM DIAGNOSIS. Measure the resistance of the (K4) Sensor ground circuit from the IAT Sensor harness connector to the appropriate terminal of special tool #8815. Is the resistance below 5.0 ohms? Yes → Go To 6 No → Repair the open in the (K4) Sensor ground circuit.
6	NOTE: Before continuing, check the PCM harness connector terminals for corrosion, damage, or terminal push out. Repair as necessary. If there are no possible causes remaining, view repair. Repair Replace and program the Powertrain Control Module

ARM0400000000944

Fig. 36   Code P0113: IAT Sensor High (Part 2 of 2). Concorde, Intrepid & 300M

When Monitored and Set Condition:

P0113-INTAKE AIR TEMPERATURE SENSOR HIGH

When Monitored: With the ignition on. Battery voltage greater than 10 volts.

Set Condition: The Intake Air Temperature (IAT) sensor voltage at the PCM is greater than 4.98 volts. One trip Fault.

POSSIBLE CAUSES
IAT SENSOR VOLTAGE ABOVE 4.6 VOLTS
(K21) IAT SIGNAL CIRCUIT SHORTED TO BATTERY VOLTAGE
IAT SENSOR INTERNAL FAILURE
(K21) IAT SIGNAL CIRCUIT OPEN
(K4) SENSOR GROUND CIRCUIT OPEN
PCM

TEST	ACTION
1	Ignition on, engine not running. With the DRBIII®, read the IAT Sensor voltage. Is the voltage above 4.6 volts? Yes → Go To 2 No → Diagnose intermittent condition.
2	Turn the ignition off. Disconnect the IAT Sensor harness connector. Ignition on, engine not running. Measure the voltage of the (K21) IAT Signal circuit in the IAT Sensor harness connector. Is the voltage above 5.2 volts? Yes → Repair the short to battery voltage in the (K21) IAT Signal circuit. No → Go To 3

ARM0400000000943

Fig. 36   Code P0113: IAT Sensor High (Part 1 of 2). Concorde, Intrepid & 300M

When Monitored and Set Condition:

P0116-ENGINE COOLANT TEMPERATURE PERFORMANCE

When Monitored: Engine off time is greater than 480 minutes. Ambient temperature is greater than 4°C (39°F) 02 MY or -23°C (-10°F) 03 MY.

Set Condition: After a calibrated amount of cool down time, the PCM compares the ECT Sensor, IAT Sensor and the Ambient Air Temperature Sensor values. If the ECT Sensor value is not within calibrated temperature amount of the other two temperature sensors an error is detected. Two Trip Fault.

POSSIBLE CAUSES
GOOD TRIP EQUAL TO ZERO
(K2) ECT SIGNAL CIRCUIT SHORTED TO BATTERY VOLTAGE
ECT SENSOR VOLTAGE BELOW 1.0 VOLT
(K2) ECT SIGNAL CIRCUIT OPEN
(K4) SENSOR GROUND CIRCUIT OPEN
(K2) ECT SIGNAL CIRCUIT SHORTED TO GROUND
(K2) ECT SIGNAL SHORTED TO (K4) SENSOR GROUND
PCM HIGH
PCM LOW

TEST	ACTION
1	NOTE: Due to the fact that the PCM compares the IAT, AAT and ECT sensor to see if they are within a calibrated temp of one another, the use of a block heater can cause false readings for the PCM. Check with the customer to see if they use a block heater. Ignition on, engine not running. With the DRBIII®, read DTCs and record the related Freeze Frame data. Is the Good Trip Counter displayed and equal to zero? Yes → Go To 2 No → Diagnose intermittent condition.

ARM0400000000945

Fig. 37   Code P0116: ECT Performance (Part 1 of 3). Concorde, Intrepid & 300M

TEST	ACTION
2	Turn the ignition off. Disconnect the ECT Sensor harness connector. **NOTE: Visually inspect both the component and the PCM connectors. Look for damaged, partially broken wires, and backed out or corroded terminals.** Ignition on, engine not running. Measure the voltage on the (K2) ECT Signal circuit in the ECT Sensor harness connector. Is the voltage above 5.2 volts? Yes → Repair the short to battery voltage in the (K2) ECT Signal circuit. No → Go To 3
3	Turn the ignition off. Disconnect the ECT Sensor harness connector. Ignition on, engine not running. With the DRBIII®, read the ECT Sensor voltage. Is the voltage above 4.6 volts? Yes → Go To 4 No → Go To 7
4	Turn the ignition off. Disconnect the ECT Sensor harness connector. Using a jumper wire, jumper across the ECT Sensor harness connector. Ignition on, engine not running. With the DRBIII®, read the ECT Sensor voltage. Is the voltage below 1.0 volt? Yes → Replace the ECT Sensor. No → Go To 5
5	Turn the ignition off. Disconnect the ECT Sensor harness connector. Disconnect the PCM harness connector. **CAUTION: DO NOT PROBE THE PCM HARNESS CONNECTORS. PROBING THE PCM HARNESS CONNECTORS WILL DAMAGE THE PCM TERMINALS RESULTING IN POOR TERMINAL TO PIN CONNECTION. INSTALL MILLER SPECIAL TOOL #8815 TO PERFORM DIAGNOSIS.** Measure the resistance of the (K2) ECT Signal circuit from the ECT Sensor harness connector to the appropriate terminal of special tool #8815. Is the resistance below 5.0 ohms? Yes → Go To 6 No → Repair the open in the (K2) ECT Signal circuit.

Fig. 37 Code P0116: ECT Performance (Part 2 of 3). Concorde, Intrepid & 300M

ARM0400000000946

TEST	ACTION
6	Turn the ignition off. Disconnect the ECT harness connector. Disconnect the PCM harness connector. **CAUTION: DO NOT PROBE THE PCM HARNESS CONNECTORS. PROBING THE PCM HARNESS CONNECTORS WILL DAMAGE THE PCM TERMINALS RESULTING IN POOR TERMINAL TO PIN CONNECTION. INSTALL MILLER SPECIAL TOOL #8815 TO PERFORM DIAGNOSIS.** Measure the resistance of the (K4) Sensor ground circuit from the ECT Sensor harness connector to the appropriate terminal of special tool #8815. Is the resistance below 5.0 ohms? Yes → NOTE: Before continuing, check the PCM harness connector terminals for corrosion, damage, or terminal push out. Repair as necessary. Replace and program the Powertrain Control Module No → Repair the open in the (K4) Sensor ground circuit.
7	Disconnect the ECT Sensor harness connector. Turn the ignition off. Disconnect the PCM harness connector. Measure the resistance between ground and the (K2) ECT Signal circuit in the ECT Sensor harness connector. Is the resistance below 100 ohms? Yes → Repair the short to ground in the (K2) ECT Signal circuit. No → Go To 8
8	Turn the ignition off. Disconnect the ECT Sensor harness connector. Disconnect the PCM harness connector. Measure the resistance between the (K2) ECT Sensor Signal circuit and the (K4) Sensor ground circuit at the ECT Sensor harness connector. Is the resistance below 5.0 ohms? Yes → Repair the (K4) Sensor ground shorted to the (K2) ECT Sensor Signal circuit. No → NOTE: Before continuing, check the PCM harness connector terminals for corrosion, damage, or terminal push out. Repair as necessary. Replace and program the Powertrain Control Module

Fig. 37 Code P0116: ECT Performance (Part 3 of 3). Concorde, Intrepid & 300M

ARM0400000000947

When Monitored and Set Condition:

P0117-ENGINE COOLANT TEMPERATURE SENSOR LOW

When Monitored: With the ignition on. Battery voltage greater than 10 volts.

Set Condition: The Engine Coolant Temperature (ECT) sensor circuit voltage at the PCM is less than 0.0782 of a volt. One Trip Fault.

POSSIBLE CAUSES
ECT SENSOR VOLTAGE BELOW 1.0 VOLTS
ECT SENSOR INTERNAL FAILURE
(K2) ECT SIGNAL SHORTED TO GROUND
(K2) ECT SIGNAL SHORTED TO (K4) SENSOR GROUND CIRCUIT
PCM

TEST	ACTION
1	Ignition on, engine not running. With the DRBIII®, read the ECT Sensor voltage. Is the voltage below 1.0 volt? Yes → Go To 2 No → Diagnose intermittent condition.
2	Turn the ignition off. Disconnect the ECT harness connector. Ignition on, engine not running. With the DRBIII®, read ECT Sensor voltage. Is the voltage between 4.8 and 5.2 volts? Yes → Replace the ECT Sensor. No → Go To 3
3	Turn the ignition off. Disconnect the ECT Sensor harness connector. Disconnect the PCM harness connector. Measure the resistance between ground and the (K2) ECT Signal circuit in the ECT Sensor harness connector. Is the resistance below 100 ohms? Yes → Repair the ground shorted to the (K2) ECT Signal circuit. No → Go To 4

TEST	ACTION
4	Turn the ignition off. Disconnect the ECT Sensor harness connector. Disconnect the PCM harness connector. Measure the resistance between the (K2) ECT Sensor Signal circuit and the (K4) Sensor ground circuit in the ECT Sensor harness connector. Is the resistance below 100 ohms? Yes → Repair the (K4) Sensor ground shorted to the (K2) ECT Sensor Signal circuit. No → Go To 5
5	**NOTE: Before continuing, check the PCM harness connector terminals for corrosion, damage, or terminal push out. Repair as necessary.** If there are no possible causes remaining, view repair. Repair Replace and program the Powertrain Control Module

Fig. 38 Code P0117: ECT Sensor Low (Part 2 of 2). Concorde, Intrepid & 300M

ARM0400000000949

Fig. 38 Code P0117: ECT Sensor Low (Part 1 of 2). Concorde, Intrepid & 300M

ARM0400000000948

When Monitored and Set Condition:

P0118-ENGINE COOLANT TEMPERATURE SENSOR HIGH

When Monitored: With the ignition on. Battery voltage greater than 10 volts.

Set Condition: The Engine Coolant Temperature (ECT) sensor voltage at the PCM is greater than 4.9 volts. One trip Fault.

POSSIBLE CAUSES
ECT SENSOR VOLTAGE ABOVE 4.9 VOLTS
(K2) ECT SIGNAL CIRCUIT SHORTED TO BATTERY VOLTAGE
ECT SENSOR INTERNAL FAILURE
(K2) ECT SIGNAL CIRCUIT OPEN
(K4) SENSOR GROUND CIRCUIT OPEN
PCM

TEST	ACTION
1	Ignition on, engine not running. With the DRBIII®, read the ECT Sensor voltage. Is the voltage above 4.9 volts? Yes → Go To 2 No → Diagnose intermittent condition.
2	Turn the ignition off. Disconnect the ECT Sensor harness connector. Ignition on, engine not running. Measure the voltage of the (K2) ECT Signal circuit in the ECT Sensor harness connector. Is the voltage above 5.2 volts? Yes → Repair the short to battery voltage in the (K2) ECT Signal circuit. No → Go To 3

ARM0400000000950

Fig. 39   Code P0118: ECT Sensor High (Part 1 of 2). Concorde, Intrepid & 300M

When Monitored and Set Condition:

P0480-LOW SPEED FAN CONTROL RELAY CIRCUIT

When Monitored: With the ignition on. Battery voltage greater than 10 volts.

Set Condition: An open or shorted circuit is detected in the radiator fan relay control circuit. One Trip Fault.

POSSIBLE CAUSES
LOW SPEED RADIATOR FAN RELAY OPERATION
(A16) FUSED B+ FEED CIRCUITS
LOW SPEED RADIATOR FAN RELAY RESISTANCE
(C24) LOW SPEED RAD FAN RELAY CONTROL CIRCUIT OPEN
(C24) LOW SPEED RAD FAN RELAY CONTROL CIRCUIT SHORT TO GROUND
PCM

TEST	ACTION
1	Ignition on, engine not running. With the DRBIII®, actuate the Radiator Fan Relay. Is the Low Speed Radiator Fan Relay operating? Yes → Diagnose intermittent condition. No → Go To 2
2	Turn the ignition off. Remove the Low Speed Radiator Fan Relay from the PDC. Ignition on, engine not running. Measure the voltage of the (A16) Fused B+ Feed circuit in the PDC. Is the voltage above 11.0 volts? Yes → Go To 3 No → Repair the (A16) Fused B+ Output circuit. Inspect the related fuse and repair as necessary.

ARM0400000000928

Fig. 40   Code P0480: Low Speed Fan Control Relay Circuit (Part 1 of 2). Concorde, Intrepid & 300M

TEST	ACTION
3	Turn the ignition off. Disconnect the ECT harness connector. Connect a jumper wire between the (K2) ECT Signal circuit and the (K4) Sensor ground circuit in the ECT harness connector. Ignition on, engine not running. With the DRBIII®, read ECT Sensor voltage. Is the voltage below 1.0 volt? Yes → Replace the ECT Sensor. No → Go To 4
4	Turn the ignition off. Disconnect the ECT Sensor harness connector. Disconnect the PCM harness connector. CAUTION: DO NOT PROBE THE PCM HARNESS CONNECTORS. PROBING THE PCM HARNESS CONNECTORS WILL DAMAGE THE PCM TERMINALS RESULTING IN POOR CONNECTION. INSTALL MILLER SPECIAL TOOL #8815 TO PERFORM DIAGNOSIS. Measure the resistance of the (K2) ECT Signal circuit from the ECT Sensor harness connector to the appropriate terminal of special tool #8815. Is the resistance below 5.0 ohms? Yes → Go To 5 No → Repair the open in the (K2) ECT Signal circuit.
5	Turn the ignition off. Disconnect the ECT Sensor harness connector. Disconnect the PCM harness connector. CAUTION: DO NOT PROBE THE PCM HARNESS CONNECTORS. PROBING THE PCM HARNESS CONNECTORS WILL DAMAGE THE PCM TERMINALS RESULTING IN POOR TERMINAL TO PIN CONNECTION. INSTALL MILLER SPECIAL TOOL #8815 TO PERFORM DIAGNOSIS. Measure the resistance of the (K4) Sensor ground circuit from the ECT Sensor harness connector to the appropriate terminal of special tool #8815. Is the resistance below 5.0 ohms? Yes → Go To 6 No → Repair the open in the (K4) Sensor ground circuit.
6	NOTE: Before continuing, check the PCM harness connector terminals for corrosion, damage, or terminal push out. Repair as necessary. If there are no possible causes remaining, view repair. Repair Replace and program the Powertrain Control Module

ARM0400000000951

Fig. 39   Code P0118: ECT Sensor High (Part 2 of 2). Concorde, Intrepid & 300M

TEST	ACTION
3	Turn the ignition off. Remove the Low Speed Radiator Fan Relay from the PDC. Measure the resistance of the Low Speed Radiator Fan Relay between the Fused Ignition Switch Output terminal and the Low Speed Rad Fan Relay Control terminal. Is the resistance between 60 to 85 ohms? Yes → Go To 4 No → Replace the Low Speed Radiator Fan Relay.
4	Turn the ignition off. Remove the Low Speed Radiator Fan Relay from the PDC. Disconnect the PCM harness connector. CAUTION: DO NOT PROBE THE PCM HARNESS CONNECTORS. PROBING THE PCM HARNESS CONNECTORS WILL DAMAGE THE PCM TERMINALS RESULTING IN POOR TERMINAL TO PIN CONNECTION. INSTALL MILLER SPECIAL TOOL #8815 TO PERFORM DIAGNOSIS. Measure the resistance of the (C24) Low Speed Rad Fan Relay Control circuit from the PDC to the appropriate terminal of special tool #8815. Is the resistance below 5.0 ohms? Yes → Go To 5 No → Repair the open in the (C24) Low Speed Rad Fan Relay Control circuit.
5	Turn the ignition off. Remove the Low Speed Radiator Fan Relay from the PDC. Disconnect the PCM harness connector. Measure the resistance between ground and the (C24) Low Speed Rad Fan Control circuit at the PDC. Is the resistance below 100 ohms? Yes → Repair the short to ground in the (C24) Low Speed Rad Fan Relay Control circuit. No → Go To 6
6	NOTE: Before continuing, check the PCM harness connector terminals for corrosion, damage, or terminal push out. Repair as necessary. If there are no possible causes remaining, view repair. Repair Replace and program the Powertrain Control Module

ARM0400000000929

Fig. 40   Code P0480: Low Speed Fan Control Relay Circuit (Part 2 of 2). Concorde, Intrepid & 300M

When Monitored and Set Condition:

P0481-HIGH SPEED FAN CONTROL RELAY CIRCUIT

When Monitored: With the ignition on. Battery voltage greater than 10 volts.

Set Condition: An open or shorted circuit is detected in the radiator fan relay control circuit. One trip Fault.

POSSIBLE CAUSES
HIGH SPEED RADIATOR FAN RELAY OPERATION
(A16) FUSED IGNITION SWITCH OUTPUT CIRCUIT
HIGH SPEED RADIATOR FAN RELAY RESISTANCE
(C27) HIGH SPEED RAD FAN RELAY CONTROL CIRCUIT OPEN
(C27) HIGH SPEED RAD FAN RELAY CONTROL CIRCUIT SHORT TO GROUND
PCM

TEST	ACTION
1	Turn the ignition on. With the DRBIII®, actuate the High Speed Radiator Fan Relay. Is the High Speed Radiator Fan Relay operating? Yes → Diagnose intermittent condition. No → Go To 2
2	Turn the ignition off. Remove the High Speed Radiator Fan Relay from the PDC. Turn the ignition on. Measure the voltage of the (A16) Fused Ignition Switch Output circuit in the PDC. Is the voltage above 11.0 volts? Yes → Go To 3 No → Repair the (A16) Fused Ignition Switch Output circuit. Check and replace any open fuses.

ARM0400000000930

Fig. 41 Code P0481: High Speed Fan Control Relay Circuit (Part 1 of 2). Concorde, Intrepid & 300M

When Monitored and Set Condition:

P0532-A/C PRESSURE SENSOR LOW

When Monitored: The engine running. The A/C relay energized.

Set Condition: The A/C pressure sensor signal voltage at the PCM goes below 0.58 volts for 2.6 seconds. One Trip Fault.

POSSIBLE CAUSES
A/C PRESSURE SENSOR VOLTAGE BELOW 0.6 VOLTS
(K7) 5 VOLT SUPPLY CIRCUIT SHORTED TO GROUND
(K7) 5 VOLT SUPPLY CIRCUIT OPEN
A/C PRESSURE SENSOR INTERNAL FAILURE
(C18) A/C PRESSURE SIGNAL CIRCUIT SHORTED TO GROUND
(C18) A/C PRESSURE SIGNAL CIRCUIT SHORTED TO (K4) SENSOR GROUND CIRCUIT
PCM (K7) 5 VOLT SUPPLY CIRCUIT
PCM A/C PRESSURE SENSOR SIGNAL

TEST	ACTION
1	NOTE: Ensure the A/C refrigerant System is properly charged per the Service Information. Start the engine. With the DRBIII®, read the A/C Pressure Sensor voltage. Is the voltage below 0.6 of a volt? Yes → Go To 2 No → Diagnose intermittent condition.
2	Turn the ignition off. Disconnect the A/C Pressure Sensor harness connector. Turn the ignition on. Measure the voltage of the (K7) 5 Volt Supply circuit in the A/C Pressure Sensor harness connector. Is the voltage between 4.5 to 5.2 volts? Yes → Go To 3 No → Go To 7

ARM0400000000932

Fig. 42 Code P0532: Air Conditioning Pressure Sensor Low (Part 1 of 3). Concorde, Intrepid & 300M

TEST	ACTION
3	Turn the ignition off. Remove the High Speed Radiator Fan Relay from the PDC. Measure the resistance of the High Speed Radiator Fan Relay between the Fused Ignition Switch Output terminal and the High Speed Rad Fan Relay Control terminal. Is the resistance between 60 to 85 ohms? Yes → Go To 4 No → Replace the High Speed Radiator Fan Relay.
4	Turn the ignition off. Remove the High Speed Radiator Fan Relay from the PDC. Disconnect the PCM harness connector. CAUTION: DO NOT PROBE THE PCM HARNESS CONNECTORS. PROBING THE PCM HARNESS CONNECTORS WILL DAMAGE THE PCM TERMINALS RESULTING IN POOR TERMINAL TO PIN CONNECTION. INSTALL MILLER SPECIAL TOOL #8815 TO PERFORM DIAGNOSIS. Measure the resistance of the (C27) High Speed Rad Fan Relay Control circuit from the PDC to the appropriate terminal of special tool #8815. Is the resistance below 5.0 ohms? Yes → Go To 5 No → Repair the open in the (C27) High Speed Rad Fan Relay Control circuit.
5	Turn the ignition off. Remove the High Speed Radiator Fan Relay from the PDC. Disconnect the PCM harness connector. Measure the resistance between ground and the (C27) High Speed Rad Fan Relay Control circuit in the PDC. Is the resistance below 5.0 ohms? Yes → Repair the short to ground in the (C27) High Speed Rad Fan Relay Control circuit. No → Go To 6
6	NOTE: Before continuing, check the PCM harness connector terminals for corrosion, damage, or terminal push out. Repair as necessary. If there are no possible causes remaining, view repair. Repair NOTE: Before continuing, check the PCM harness connector terminals for corrosion, damage or terminal push out. Repair as necessary. Replace and program the Powertrain Control Module

ARM0400000000931

Fig. 41 Code P0481: High Speed Fan Control Relay Circuit (Part 2 of 2). Concorde, Intrepid & 300M

TEST	ACTION
3	Turn the ignition off. Disconnect the A/C Pressure Sensor harness connector. With the DRBIII®, monitor the A/C Pressure Sensor voltage. Turn the ignition on. Is the voltage above 0.6 of a volt? Yes → Replace the A/C Pressure Sensor. No → Go To 4
4	Turn the ignition off. Disconnect the A/C Pressure Sensor harness connector. Disconnect the PCM harness connector. Measure the resistance between ground and the (C18) A/C Pressure Signal circuit in the A/C Pressure Sensor harness connector. Is the resistance below 100 ohms? Yes → Repair the short to ground in the (C18) A/C Pressure Signal circuit. No → Go To 5
5	Turn the ignition off. Disconnect the A/C Pressure Sensor harness connector. Disconnect the PCM harness connector. Measure the resistance between the (C18) A/C Pressure Sensor Signal circuit and the (K4) Sensor ground circuit in the A/C Pressure Sensor harness connector. Is the resistance below 100 ohms? Yes → Repair the short to the (K4) Sensor ground circuit in the (C18) A/C Pressure Signal circuit. No → Go To 6
6	NOTE: Before continuing, check the PCM harness connector terminals for corrosion, damage, or terminal push out. Repair as necessary. If there are no possible causes remaining, view repair. Repair Replace and program the Powertrain Control Module
7	Turn the ignition off. Disconnect the A/C Pressure Sensor harness connector. Disconnect the PCM harness connector. Measure the resistance between ground and the (K7) 5 Volt Supply circuit in the A/C Pressure Sensor harness connector. Is the resistance below 100 ohms? Yes → Repair the short to ground in the (K7) 5 Volt Supply circuit. No → Go To 8

ARM0400000000933

Fig. 42 Code P0532: Air Conditioning Pressure Sensor Low (Part 2 of 3). Concorde, Intrepid & 300M

TEST	ACTION
8	Turn the ignition off. Disconnect the A/C Pressure Sensor harness connector. Disconnect the PCM harness connector. **CAUTION: DO NOT PROBE THE PCM HARNESS CONNECTORS. PROBING THE PCM HARNESS CONNECTORS WILL DAMAGE THE PCM TERMINALS RESULTING IN POOR TERMINAL TO PIN CONNECTION. INSTALL MILLER SPECIAL TOOL #8815 TO PERFORM DIAGNOSIS.** Measure the resistance of the (K7) 5 Volt Supply circuit from the A/C Pressure Sensor harness connector to the appropriate terminal of special tool #8815. Is the resistance below 5.0 ohms? Yes → Go To 9 No → Repair the open in the (K7) 5 Volt Supply circuit.
9	**NOTE: Before continuing, check the PCM harness connector terminals for corrosion, damage, or terminal push out. Repair as necessary.** If there are no possible causes remaining, view repair. Repair Replace and program the Powertrain Control Module

ARM0400000000934

Fig. 42 Code P0532: Air Conditioning Pressure Sensor Low (Part 3 of 3). Concorde, Intrepid & 300M

TEST	ACTION
3	Turn the ignition off. Disconnect the A/C Pressure Sensor harness connector. Turn the ignition on. Measure the voltage on the (C18) A/C Pressure Sensor Signal circuit at the A/C Pressure Sensor harness connector. Is the voltage above 5.2 volts? Yes → Repair the (C18) A/C Pressure Signal circuit for a short to battery voltage. No → Go To 4
4	Turn the ignition off. Disconnect the A/C Pressure Sensor harness connector. Connect a jumper wire between the (C18) A/C Pressure Signal circuit and the (K4) Sensor ground circuit. With the DRBIII®, monitor the A/C Pressure Sensor voltage. Turn the ignition on. Is the voltage below 1.0 volt? Yes → Replace the A/C Pressure Sensor. No → Go To 5
5	Turn the ignition off. Disconnect the A/C Pressure Sensor harness connector. Disconnect the PCM harness connector. **CAUTION: DO NOT PROBE THE PCM HARNESS CONNECTORS. PROBING THE PCM HARNESS CONNECTORS WILL DAMAGE THE PCM TERMINALS RESULTING IN POOR TERMINAL TO PIN CONNECTION. INSTALL MILLER SPECIAL TOOL #8815 TO PERFORM DIAGNOSIS.** Measure the resistance of the (C18) A/C Pressure Sensor Signal circuit from the A/C Pressure Sensor harness connector to the appropriate terminal of special tool #8815. Is the resistance below 5.0 ohms? Yes → Go To 6 No → Repair the (C18) A/C Pressure Signal circuit for an open.
6	Turn the ignition off. Disconnect the A/C Pressure Sensor harness connector. Disconnect the PCM harness connector. **CAUTION: DO NOT PROBE THE PCM HARNESS CONNECTORS. PROBING THE PCM HARNESS CONNECTORS WILL DAMAGE THE PCM TERMINALS RESULTING IN POOR TERMINAL TO PIN CONNECTION. INSTALL MILLER SPECIAL TOOL #8815 TO PERFORM DIAGNOSIS.** Measure the resistance of the (K4) Sensor ground circuit from the A/C Pressure Sensor harness connector to the appropriate terminal of special tool #8815. Is the resistance below 5.0 ohms? Yes → Go To 7 No → Repair the (K4) Sensor ground circuit for an open.

ARM0400000000936

Fig. 43 Code P0533: Air Conditioning Pressure Sensor High (Part 2 of 3). Concorde, Intrepid & 300M

When Monitored and Set Condition:

P0533-A/C PRESSURE SENSOR HIGH

When Monitored: The engine running. The A/C relay energized.

Set Condition: The A/C pressure sensor signal at the PCM goes above 4.92 volts. One trip Fault.

POSSIBLE CAUSES
A/C PRESSURE SENSOR VOLTAGE ABOVE 4.6 VOLTS
(C18) A/C PRESSURE SIGNAL CIRCUIT SHORTED TO (K7) 5 VOLT SUPPLY CIRCUIT
(C18) A/C PRESSURE SIGNAL CIRCUIT SHORTED TO BATTERY VOLTAGE
A/C PRESSURE SENSOR INTERNAL FAILURE
(C18) A/C PRESSURE SIGNAL CIRCUIT OPEN
(K4) SENSOR GROUND CIRCUIT OPEN
PCM

TEST	ACTION
1	**NOTE: Ensure the A/C refrigerant System is properly charged per the Service Information.** Start the engine. With the DRBIII®, read the A/C Pressure Sensor voltage. Is the voltage above 4.6 volts? Yes → Go To 2 No → Diagnose intermittent condition.
2	Turn the ignition off. Disconnect the A/C Pressure Sensor harness connector. Disconnect the PCM harness connector. Measure the resistance between the (C18) A/C Pressure Signal circuit and the (K7) 5 Volt Supply circuit in the A/C Pressure Sensor harness connector. Is the resistance below 5.0 ohms? Yes → Repair the (C18) A/C Pressure Signal circuit for a short to the (K7) 5 Volt Supply circuit. No → Go To 3

ARM0400000000935

Fig. 43 Code P0533: Air Conditioning Pressure Sensor High (Part 1 of 3). Concorde, Intrepid & 300M

TEST	ACTION
7	**NOTE: Before continuing, check the PCM harness connector terminals for corrosion, damage, or terminal push out. Repair as necessary.** If there are no possible causes remaining, view repair. Repair Replace and program the Powertrain Control Module

ARM0400000000937

Fig. 43 Code P0533: Air Conditioning Pressure Sensor High (Part 3 of 3). Concorde, Intrepid & 300M

When Monitored and Set Condition:

P0711-TRANSMISSION TEMPERATURE SENSOR PERFORMANCE

When Monitored: Continuously with the ignition on and engine running.

Set Condition: This DTC will set when the desired transmission temperature does not reach a normal operating temperature within a given time frame. Time is variable due to ambient temperature. Approximate times are starting temperature to warm up time: (-40° F / -40° C - 35 min) (-20° F / -28° C - 25 min) (20° F / -6.6° C - 20 min) (60° F / 15.5 ° C - 10 min)

POSSIBLE CAUSES
RELATED DTC'S PRESENT
TRANSMISSION TEMPERATURE SENSOR
POWERTRAIN CONTROL MODULE
INTERMITTENT WIRING AND CONNECTORS

TEST	ACTION
1	NOTE: Low fluid level can be the cause of many transmission problems. If the fluid level is low locate and repair the leak then check and adjust the fluid level per the Service Information. NOTE: Always perform diagnostics with a fully charged battery to avoid false symptoms. With the DRBIII®, read Engine DTC's. Check and repair all Engine DTC's prior to performing any transmission symptom diagnostics. With the DRBIII®, read Transmission DTC's. Record all DTC's and 1 Trip Failures. NOTE: Diagnose 1 Trip Failures as a fully matured DTC. Using the wiring diagram/schematic as a guide, inspect the wiring and connectors. Repair as necessary. Perform the Shift Lever Position Test. If the test does not pass, refer to Symptom test for P0706 Check Shifter Signal. For Gear Ratio DTC's, check and record all CVI's. Most DTC's set on start up but some must be set by driving the vehicle such that all diagnostic monitors have run. NOTE: Verify flash level of Powertrain Control Module. Some problems are corrected by software upgrades to the Transmission and Engine software. NOTE: Check for applicable TSB's related to the problem. Perform this procedure prior to Symptom diagnosis. Continue Go To 2

ARM0400000000952

Fig. 44 Code P0711: Transmission Temperature Sensor Performance (Part 1 of 3). Concorde, Intrepid & 300M

TEST	ACTION
7	The conditions necessary to set this DTC are not present at this time. Using the schematics as a guide, inspect the wiring and connectors specific to this circuit. Wiggle the wires while checking for shorted and open circuits. With the DRBIII®, check the EATX EVENT DATA to help identify the conditions in which the DTC was set. Were there any problems found? Yes → Repair as necessary. No → Test Complete.

ARM0400000000954

Fig. 44 Code P0711: Transmission Temperature Sensor Performance (Part 3 of 3). Concorde, Intrepid & 300M

TEST	ACTION
2	With the DRBIII®, check Transmission DTC's. Are there any other Transmission Temperature Sensor related DTCs present? Yes → Refer to the Transmission category and perform the appropriate symptom. No → Go To 3
3	With the DRBIII®, Check the STARTS SINCE SET counter for P0711. NOTE: This counter only applies to the last DTC set. Is the STARTS SINCE SET counter 2 or less? Yes → Go To 4 No → Go To 7
4	Turn the ignition off to the lock position. Remove the Starter Relay. CAUTION: Removal of the Starter Relay is to prevent a Transmission, NO RESPONSE, condition and disable the starter. Install the Transmission Simulator, Miller tool #8333 and the Electronic Transmission Adapter kit 8333-1A. Note: Check connectors - Clean/repair as necessary. Ignition on, engine not running. With the Transmission Simulator, turn the Input/Output switch to OFF. With the DRBIII®, monitor the TRANS TEMP VOLTS while turning the Thermistor Voltage switch to all three positions on the Transmission Simulator. Compare the DRBIII® readings with the numbers listed on the Transmission Simulator. Do the readings on the Transmission Simulator match the DRBIII® readings ± 0.2 volts? Yes → Go To 5 No → Go To 6
5	If there are no possible causes remaining, view repair. Repair Replace Transmission Solenoid/TRS assembly
6	Using the schematics as a guide, inspect the wiring and connectors. Repair as necessary. Pay particular attention to all power and ground circuits. If there are no possible causes remaining, view repair. Repair Replace the Powertrain Control Module

ARM0400000000953

Fig. 44 Code P0711: Transmission Temperature Sensor Performance (Part 2 of 3). Concorde, Intrepid & 300M

When Monitored and Set Condition:

P0712-TRANSMISSION TEMPERATURE SENSOR LOW

When Monitored: Continuously with the ignition on and engine running.

Set Condition: The DTC will set when the monitored Temperature Sensor voltage drops below 0.078 volts for the period of 0.45 seconds.

POSSIBLE CAUSES
RELATED DTC'S PRESENT
TRANSMISSION TEMPERATURE SENSOR SIGNAL CIRCUIT SHORT TO GROUND
TRANSMISSION TEMPERATURE SENSOR
POWERTRAIN CONTROL MODULE
INTERMITTENT WIRING AND CONNECTORS

TEST	ACTION
1	NOTE: Low fluid level can be the cause of many transmission problems. If the fluid level is low locate and repair the leak then check and adjust the fluid level per the Service Information. NOTE: Always perform diagnostics with a fully charged battery to avoid false symptoms. With the DRBIII®, read Engine DTC's. Check and repair all Engine DTC's prior to performing any transmission symptom diagnostics. With the DRBIII®, read Transmission DTC's. Record all DTC's and 1 Trip Failures. NOTE: Diagnose 1 Trip Failures as a fully matured DTC. Using the wiring diagram/schematic as a guide, inspect the wiring and connectors. Repair as necessary. Perform the Shift Lever Position Test. If the test does not pass, refer to Symptom test for P0706 Check Shifter Signal. For Gear Ratio DTC's, check and record all CVI's. Most DTC's set on start up but some must be set by driving the vehicle such that all diagnostic monitors have run. NOTE: Verify flash level of Powertrain Control Module. Some problems are corrected by software upgrades to the Transmission and Engine software. NOTE: Check for applicable TSB's related to the problem. Perform this procedure prior to Symptom diagnosis. Continue Go To 2
2	With the DRBIII®, check Transmission DTC's. Are there any Speed Sensor DTC's present? Yes → Refer to the Transmission category and perform the appropriate symptom. No → Go To 3

ARM0400000000955

Fig. 45 Code P0712: Transmission Temperature Sensor Low (Part 1 of 3). Concorde, Intrepid & 300M

TEST	ACTION
3	With the DRBIII®, Check the STARTS SINCE SET counter for P0712. **NOTE: This counter only applies to the last DTC set.** Is the STARTS SINCE SET counter 2 or less? Yes → Go To 4 No → Go To 8
4	Turn the ignition off to the lock position. Remove the Starter Relay. **CAUTION: Removal of the Starter Relay is to prevent a Transmission, NO RESPONSE, condition and disable the starter.** Install the Transmission Simulator, Miller tool #8333 and the Electronic Transmission Adapter kit 8333-1A. **Note: Check connectors - Clean/repair as necessary.** Ignition on, engine not running. With the Transmission Simulator, turn the Input/Output switch to OFF. With the DRBIII®, monitor the TRANS TEMP VOLTS while turning the Thermistor Voltage switch to all three positions on the Transmission Simulator. Compare the DRBIII® readings with the numbers listed on the Transmission Simulator. Do the readings on the Transmission Simulator match the DRBIII® readings ± 0.2 volts? Yes → Go To 5 No → Go To 6
5	If there are no possible causes remaining, view repair. Repair Replace Transmission Solenoid/TRS assembly
6	Turn the ignition off to the lock position. Disconnect the PCM C4 harness connector. Disconnect the Transmission Solenoid/TRS Assembly harness connector. **Note: Check connectors - Clean/repair as necessary.** **CAUTION: DO NOT PROBE THE PCM HARNESS CONNECTORS. PROBING THE PCM HARNESS CONNECTORS WILL DAMAGE THE PCM TERMINALS RESULTING IN POOR TERMINAL TO PIN CONNECTION. INSTALL MILLER SPECIAL TOOL #8815 TO PERFORM DIAGNOSIS.** Measure the resistance between ground and the Transmission Temperature Sensor Signal circuit. Is the resistance below 5.0 ohms? Yes → Repair the Transmission Temperature Sensor Signal circuit for a short to ground. No → Go To 7

ARM0400000000956

Fig. 45   Code P0712: Transmission Temperature Sensor Low (Part 2 of 3). Concorde, Intrepid & 300M

When Monitored and Set Condition:

P0713-TRANSMISSION TEMPERATURE SENSOR HIGH

When Monitored: Continuously with the ignition on and engine running.

Set Condition: The DTC will set when the monitored Temperature Sensor voltage rises above 4.94 volts for the period of 0.45 seconds.

POSSIBLE CAUSES
RELATED DTC'S PRESENT
TRANSMISSION TEMPERATURE SENSOR SIGNAL CIRCUIT OPEN
TRANSMISSION TEMPERATURE SENSOR SIGNAL CIRCUIT SHORT TO VOLTAGE
TRANSMISSION TEMPERATURE SENSOR
POWERTRAIN CONTROL MODULE
INTERMITTENT WIRING AND CONNECTORS

TEST	ACTION
1	**NOTE: Low fluid level can be the cause of many transmission problems. If the fluid level is low locate and repair the leak then check and adjust the fluid level per the Service Information.** **NOTE: Always perform diagnostics with a fully charged battery to avoid false symptoms.** With the DRBIII®, read Engine DTC's. Check and repair all Engine DTC's prior to performing any transmission symptom diagnostics. With the DRBIII®, read Transmission DTC's. Record all DTC's and 1 Trip Failures. **NOTE: Diagnose 1 Trip Failures as a fully matured DTC.** Using the wiring diagram/schematic as a guide, inspect the wiring and connectors. Repair as necessary. Perform the Shift Lever Position Test. If the test does not pass, refer to Symptom test for P0706 Check Shifter Signal. For Gear Ratio DTC's, check and record all CVI's. Most DTC's set on start up but some must be set by driving the vehicle such that all diagnostic monitors have run. **NOTE: Verify flash level of Powertrain Control Module. Some problems are corrected by software upgrades to the Transmission and Engine software.** **NOTE: Check for applicable TSB's related to the problem.** Perform this procedure prior to Symptom diagnosis. Continue Go To 2

ARM0400000000958

Fig. 46   Code P0713: Transmission Temperature Sensor High (Part 1 of 4). Concorde, Intrepid & 300M

TEST	ACTION
7	Using the schematics as a guide, inspect the wiring and connectors. Repair as necessary. Pay particular attention to all power and ground circuits. If there are no possible causes remaining, view repair. Repair Replace the Powertrain Control Module
8	The conditions necessary to set this DTC are not present at this time. Using the schematics as a guide, inspect the wiring and connectors specific to this circuit. Wiggle the wires while checking for shorted and open circuits. With the DRBIII®, check the EATX EVENT DATA to help identify the conditions in which the DTC was set. Were there any problems found? Yes → Repair as necessary. No → Test Complete.

ARM0400000000957

Fig. 45   Code P0712: Transmission Temperature Sensor Low (Part 3 of 3). Concorde, Intrepid & 300M

TEST	ACTION
2	With the DRBIII®, check Transmission DTC's. Are there any Speed Sensor DTCs present? Yes → Refer to the Transmission category and perform the appropriate symptom. No → Go To 3
3	With the DRBIII®, Check the STARTS SINCE SET counter for P0713. **NOTE: This counter only applies to the last DTC set.** Is the STARTS SINCE SET counter 2 or less? Yes → Go To 4 No → Go To 9
4	Turn the ignition off to the lock position. Remove the Starter Relay. **CAUTION: Removal of the Starter Relay is to prevent a Transmission, NO RESPONSE, condition and disable the starter.** Install the Transmission Simulator, Miller tool #8333 and the Electronic Transmission Adapter kit 8333-1A. **Note: Check connectors - Clean/repair as necessary.** Ignition on, engine not running. With the Transmission Simulator, turn the Input/Output switch to OFF. With the DRBIII®, monitor the TRANS TEMP VOLTS while turning the Thermistor Voltage switch to all three positions on the Transmission Simulator. Compare the DRBIII® readings with the numbers listed on the Transmission Simulator. Do the readings on the Transmission Simulator match the DRBIII® readings ± 0.2 volts? Yes → Go To 5 No → Go To 6
5	If there are no possible causes remaining, view repair. Repair Replace Transmission Solenoid/TRS assembly

ARM0400000000959

Fig. 46   Code P0713: Transmission Temperature Sensor High (Part 2 of 4). Concorde, Intrepid & 300M

TEST	ACTION
6	Turn the ignition off to the lock position. Disconnect the PCM C4 harness connector.. Disconnect the Transmission Solenoid /TRS Assembly harness connector **Note: Check connectors - Clean/repair as necessary.** **CAUTION: DO NOT PROBE THE PCM HARNESS CONNECTORS. PROBING THE PCM HARNESS CONNECTORS WILL DAMAGE THE PCM TERMINALS RESULTING IN POOR TERMINAL TO PIN CONNECTION. INSTALL MILLER SPECIAL TOOL #8815 TO PERFORM DIAGNOSIS.** Measure the resistance of the Transmission Temperature Sensor Signal circuit from the appropriate terminal of special tool #8815 to the Transmission Solenoid/TRS Assembly harness connector. Is the resistance above 5.0 ohms? Yes → Repair the Transmission Temperature Sensor Signal circuit for an open. No → Go To 7
7	Turn the ignition off to the lock position. Disconnect the PCM C4 harness connector. Remove the Transmission Control Relay. **Note: Check connectors - Clean/repair as necessary.** **CAUTION: DO NOT PROBE THE PCM HARNESS CONNECTORS. PROBING THE PCM HARNESS CONNECTORS WILL DAMAGE THE PCM TERMINALS RESULTING IN POOR TERMINAL TO PIN CONNECTION. INSTALL MILLER SPECIAL TOOL #8815 TO PERFORM DIAGNOSIS.** Connect a jumper wire between the Fused B+ circuit and the Transmission Control Relay Output circuit in the Transmission Control Relay connector. Ignition on, engine not running. Measure the voltage of the Transmission Temperature Sensor Signal circuit in the appropriate terminal of special tool #8815. Is the voltage above 0.5 volts? Yes → Repair the Transmission Temperature Sensor Signal circuit for a short to voltage. No → Go To 8
8	Using the schematics as a guide, inspect the wiring and connectors. Repair as necessary. Pay particular attention to all power and ground circuits. If there are no possible causes remaining, view repair. Repair Replace the Powertrain Control Module

ARM0400000000960

Fig. 46 Code P0713: Transmission Temperature Sensor High (Part 3 of 4). Concorde, Intrepid & 300M

When Monitored and Set Condition:

P0714-TRANSMISSION TEMPERATURE SENSOR INTERMITTENT

When Monitored: Continuously with the ignition on and engine running.

Set Condition: The DTC will set when the monitored Temperature Sensor voltage fluctuates or changes abruptly within a predetermined period of time.

POSSIBLE CAUSES
RELATED DTC'S PRESENT
TRANSMISSION TEMPERATURE SENSOR
POWERTRAIN CONTROL MODULE
INTERMITTENT WIRING AND CONNECTORS

TEST	ACTION
1	**NOTE: Low fluid level can be the cause of many transmission problems. If the fluid level is low locate and repair the leak then check and adjust the fluid level per the Service Information.** **NOTE: Always perform diagnostics with a fully charged battery to avoid false symptoms.** With the DRBIII®, read Engine DTC's. Check and repair all Engine DTC's prior to performing any transmission symptom diagnostics. With the DRBIII®, read Transmission DTC's. Record all DTC's and 1 Trip Failures. **NOTE: Diagnose 1 Trip Failures as a fully matured DTC.** Using the wiring diagram/schematic as a guide, inspect the wiring and connectors. Repair as necessary. Perform the Shift Lever Position Test. If the test does not pass, refer to Symptom test for P0706 Check Shifter Signal. For Gear Ratio DTC's, check and record all CVI's. Most DTC's set on start up but some must be set by driving the vehicle such that all diagnostic monitors have run. **NOTE: Verify flash level of Powertrain Control Module. Some problems are corrected by software upgrades to the Transmission and Engine software.** **NOTE: Check for applicable TSB's related to the problem.** Perform this procedure prior to Symptom diagnosis. Continue Go To 2
2	With the DRBIII®, check Transmission DTC's. Are there any Speed Sensor and/or other Temperature Sensor DTCs present? Yes → Refer to the Transmission category and perform the appropriate symptom. No → Go To 3

ARM0400000000962

Fig. 47 Code P0714: Transmission Temperature Sensor Intermittent (Part 1 of 2). Concorde, Intrepid & 300M

TEST	ACTION
9	The conditions necessary to set this DTC are not present at this time. Using the schematics as a guide, inspect the wiring and connectors specific to this circuit. Wiggle the wires while checking for shorted and open circuits. With the DRBIII®, check the EATX EVENT DATA to help identify the conditions in which the DTC was set. Were there any problems found? Yes → Repair as necessary. No → Test Complete.

ARM0400000000961

Fig. 46 Code P0713: Transmission Temperature Sensor High (Part 4 of 4). Concorde, Intrepid & 300M

TEST	ACTION
3	With the DRBIII®, Check the STARTS SINCE SET counter for P0714. **NOTE: This counter only applies to the last DTC set.** Is the STARTS SINCE SET counter 2 or less? Yes → Go To 4 No → Go To 7
4	Turn the ignition off to the lock position. Remove the Starter Relay. **CAUTION: Removal of the Starter Relay is to prevent a Transmission, NO RESPONSE, condition and disable the starter.** Install the Transmission Simulator, Miller tool #8333 and the Electronic Transmission Adapter kit 8333-1A. **Note: Check connectors - Clean/repair as necessary.** Ignition on, engine not running. With the Transmission Simulator, turn the Input/Output switch to OFF. With the DRBIII®, monitor the TRANS TEMP VOLTS while turning the Thermistor Voltage switch to all three positions on the Transmission Simulator. Compare the DRBIII® readings with the numbers listed on the Transmission Simulator. Do the readings on the Transmission Simulator match a non-fluctuating DRBIII® reading ± 0.2 volts? Yes → Go To 5 No → Go To 6
5	If there are no possible causes remaining, view repair. Repair Replace Transmission Solenoid/TRS assembly
6	Using the schematics as a guide, inspect the wiring and connectors. Repair as necessary. Pay particular attention to all power and ground circuits. If there are no possible causes remaining, view repair. Repair Replace the Powertrain Control Module
7	The conditions necessary to set this DTC are not present at this time. Using the schematics as a guide, inspect the wiring and connectors specific to this circuit. Wiggle the wires while checking for shorted and open circuits. With the DRBIII®, check the EATX EVENT DATA to help identify the conditions in which the DTC was set. Were there any problems found? Yes → Repair as necessary. No → Test Complete.

ARM0400000000963

Fig. 47 Code P0714: Transmission Temperature Sensor Intermittent (Part 2 of 2). Concorde, Intrepid & 300M

When Monitored and Set Condition:

P0720-OUTPUT SPEED SENSOR ERROR

When Monitored: The transmission gear ratio is monitored continuously while the transmission is in gear.

Set Condition: If there is an excessive change in the Output RPM in any gear.

POSSIBLE CAUSES
OUTPUT SPEED SENSOR SIGNAL CIRCUIT OPEN
SPEED SENSOR GROUND CIRCUIT OPEN
OUTPUT SPEED SENSOR SIGNAL CIRCUIT SHORT TO GROUND
OUTPUT SPEED SENSOR SIGNAL CIRCUIT SHORT TO VOLTAGE
SPEED SENSOR GROUND CIRCUIT SHORT TO VOLTAGE
OUTPUT SPEED SENSOR
POWERTRAIN CONTROL MODULE
INTERMITTENT WIRING AND CONNECTORS

TEST	ACTION
1	NOTE: Low fluid level can be the cause of many transmission problems. If the fluid level is low locate and repair the leak then check and adjust the fluid level per the Service Information. NOTE: Always perform diagnostics with a fully charged battery to avoid false symptoms. With the DRBIII®, read Engine DTC's. Check and repair all Engine DTC's prior to performing any transmission symptom diagnostics. With the DRBIII®, read Transmission DTC's. Record all DTC's and 1 Trip Failures. NOTE: Diagnose 1 Trip Failures as a fully matured DTC. Using the wiring diagram/schematic as a guide, inspect the wiring and connectors. Repair as necessary. Perform the Shift Lever Position Test. If the test does not pass, refer to Symptom test for P0706 Check Shifter Signal. For Gear Ratio DTC's, check and record all CVI's. Most DTC's set on start up but some must be set by driving the vehicle such that all diagnostic monitors have run. NOTE: Verify flash level of Powertrain Control Module. Some problems are corrected by software upgrades to the Transmission and Engine software. NOTE: Check for applicable TSB's related to the problem. Perform this procedure prior to Symptom diagnosis. Continue Go To 2

ARM0400000000964

Fig. 48   Code P0720: Output Speed Sensor Error (Part 1 of 4). Concorde, Intrepid & 300M

TEST	ACTION
6	Turn the ignition off to the lock position. Disconnect the PCM harness connector. Disconnect the Output Speed Sensor harness connector. Note: Check connectors - Clean/repair as necessary. CAUTION: DO NOT PROBE THE PCM HARNESS CONNECTORS. PROBING THE PCM HARNESS CONNECTORS WILL DAMAGE THE PCM TERMINALS RESULTING IN POOR TERMINAL TO PIN CONNECTION. INSTALL MILLER SPECIAL TOOL #8815 TO PERFORM DIAGNOSIS. Measure the resistance of the Speed Sensor Ground circuit from the appropriate terminal of special tool #8815 to the Output Speed Sensor harness connector. Is the resistance above 5.0 ohms? Yes → Repair the Speed Sensor Ground circuit for an open. No → Go To 7
7	Turn the ignition off to the lock position. Disconnect the PCM harness connector. Disconnect the Output Speed Sensor harness connector. Note: Check connectors - Clean/repair as necessary. CAUTION: DO NOT PROBE THE PCM HARNESS CONNECTORS. PROBING THE PCM HARNESS CONNECTORS WILL DAMAGE THE PCM TERMINALS RESULTING IN POOR TERMINAL TO PIN CONNECTION. INSTALL MILLER SPECIAL TOOL #8815 TO PERFORM DIAGNOSIS. Measure the resistance between ground and the Output Speed Sensor Signal circuit. Is the resistance below 5.0 ohms? Yes → Repair the Output Speed Sensor Signal circuit for a short to ground. No → Go To 8
8	Turn the ignition off to the lock position. Disconnect the PCM harness connector. Disconnect the Output Speed Sensor harness connector. Remove the Transmission Control Relay. Note: Check connectors - Clean/repair as necessary. Connect a jumper wire between the Fused B+ circuit and Transmission Control Relay Output circuit in the Transmission Control Relay connector. Ignition on, engine not running. CAUTION: DO NOT PROBE THE PCM HARNESS CONNECTORS. PROBING THE PCM HARNESS CONNECTORS WILL DAMAGE THE PCM TERMINALS RESULTING IN POOR TERMINAL TO PIN CONNECTION. INSTALL MILLER SPECIAL TOOL #8815 TO PERFORM DIAGNOSIS. Measure the voltage of the Output Speed Sensor Signal circuit. Is the voltage above 0.5 volt? Yes → Repair the Output Speed Sensor Signal circuit for a short to voltage. No → Go To 9

ARM0400000000965

Fig. 48   Code P0720: Output Speed Sensor Error (Part 3 of 4). Concorde, Intrepid & 300M

TEST	ACTION
2	Start the engine in park. Raise the drive wheels off of the ground. WARNING: PROPERLY SUPPORT THE VEHICLE. Firmly apply the brakes and place the transmission selector in drive. WARNING: BE SURE TO KEEP HANDS AND FEET CLEAR OF ROTATING WHEELS. Release the brakes and allow the drive wheels to spin freely. Note: The drive wheels must be turning at this point. With the DRBIII®, read the Output RPM Is the Output RPM below 100? Yes → Go To 3 No → Go To 11
3	Turn the ignition off to the lock position. Remove the Starter Relay. CAUTION: Removal of the Starter Relay is to prevent a Transmission, NO RESPONSE, condition and disable the starter. Install the Transmission Simulator, Miller tool #8333 and the Electronic Transmission Adapter kit 8333-1A. Ignition on, engine not running. With the Transmission Simulator, set the "Input/Output Speed" switch to "ON" and the rotary switch to the "3000/1250" position. With the DRBIII®, read the Input and Output RPM. Does the Input RPM read 3000 and the Output RPM read 1250 (within 50 RPM)? Yes → Go To 4 No → Go To 5
4	If there are no possible causes remaining, view repair. Repair Replace the Output Speed Sensor
5	Turn the ignition off to the lock position. Disconnect the PCM harness connector. Disconnect the Output Speed Sensor harness connector. Note: Check connectors - Clean/repair as necessary. CAUTION: DO NOT PROBE THE PCM HARNESS CONNECTORS. PROBING THE PCM HARNESS CONNECTORS WILL DAMAGE THE PCM TERMINALS RESULTING IN POOR TERMINAL TO PIN CONNECTION. INSTALL MILLER SPECIAL TOOL #8815 TO PERFORM DIAGNOSIS. Measure the resistance of the Output Speed Sensor Signal circuit from appropriate terminal of special tool #8815 to the Output Speed Sensor harness connector. Is the resistance above 5.0 ohms? Yes → Repair the Output Speed Sensor Signal circuit for an open. No → Go To 6

ARM0400000000967

Fig. 48   Code P0720: Output Speed Sensor Error (Part 2 of 4). Concorde, Intrepid & 300M

TEST	ACTION
9	Turn the ignition off to the lock position. Disconnect the PCM harness connector. Disconnect the TRS harness connector. Remove the Transmission Control Relay. Note: Check connectors - Clean/repair as necessary. Connect a jumper wire between the Fused B+ and Transmission Control Relay Output circuits in the Transmission Control Relay connector. Ignition on, engine not running. CAUTION: DO NOT PROBE THE PCM HARNESS CONNECTORS. PROBING THE PCM HARNESS CONNECTORS WILL DAMAGE THE PCM TERMINALS RESULTING IN POOR TERMINAL TO PIN CONNECTION. INSTALL MILLER SPECIAL TOOL #8815 TO PERFORM DIAGNOSIS. Measure the voltage of the Speed Sensor Ground circuit. Is the voltage above 0.5 volts? Yes → Repair the Speed Sensor Ground circuit for a short to voltage. No → Go To 10
10	Using the schematics as a guide, inspect the wiring and connectors. Repair as necessary. Pay particular attention to all power and ground circuits. If there are no possible causes remaining, view repair. Repair Replace the Powertrain Control Module
11	The conditions necessary to set the DTC are not present at this time. Using the schematics as a guide, inspect the wiring and connectors specific to this circuit. Wiggle the wiring and connectors while checking for shorted and open circuits. With the DRBIII®, check the EATX EVENT DATA to help identify the conditions in which the DTC was set. Were there any problems found? Yes → Repair as necessary. No → Test Complete.

ARM0400000000966

Fig. 48   Code P0720: Output Speed Sensor Error (Part 4 of 4). Concorde, Intrepid & 300M

When Monitored and Set Condition:

P0116-ENGINE COOLANT TEMPERATURE PERFORMANCE

When Monitored: Engine off time is greater than 480 minutes. Ambient temperature is greater than -23°C (-9°F).

Set Condition: After a calibrated amount of cool down time, the PCM compares the ECT Sensor, IAT Sensor and the Ambient Air Temperature Sensor values. If the ECT Sensor value is not within calibrated temperature amount of the other two temperature sensors an error is detected. Two Trip Fault.

POSSIBLE CAUSES
GOOD TRIP EQUAL TO ZERO
(K2) ECT SIGNAL CIRCUIT SHORTED TO BATTERY VOLTAGE
ECT SENSOR VOLTAGE BELOW 0.1 VOLT
(K2) ECT SIGNAL CIRCUIT OPEN
(K167) SENSOR GROUND CIRCUIT OPEN
(K2) ECT SIGNAL CIRCUIT SHORTED TO GROUND
(K2) ECT SIGNAL SHORTED TO (K167) SENSOR GROUND
PCM HIGH
PCM LOW

TEST	ACTION
1	NOTE: The PCM compares IAT, AAT and ECT to determine if they are within a calibrated temp of one another. Using a block heater that does not meet OEM specifications or that is not installed at the proper location can defeat the algorithm in the PCM. Ignition on, engine not running. NOTE: Check with the customer to determine if such a block heater is installed on the vehicle. With the DRBIII®, read DTCs and record the related Freeze Frame data. Is the Good Trip Counter displayed and equal to zero? Yes → Go To 2 No → Diagnose intermittent condition.

ARM0400000000905

Fig. 49   Code P0116: ECT Performance (Part 1 of 3). 2004–05 Neon

TEST	ACTION
6	Turn the ignition off. Disconnect the ECT harness connector. Disconnect the PCM harness connector. CAUTION: DO NOT PROBE THE PCM HARNESS CONNECTORS. PROBING THE PCM HARNESS CONNECTORS WILL DAMAGE THE PCM TERMINALS RESULTING IN POOR TERMINAL TO PIN CONNECTION. INSTALL MILLER SPECIAL TOOL #8815 TO PERFORM DIAGNOSIS. Measure the resistance of the (K167) Sensor ground circuit from the ECT Sensor harness connector to the appropriate terminal of special tool # 8815. Is the resistance below 5.0 ohms? Yes → NOTE: Before continuing, check the PCM harness connector terminals for corrosion, damage, or terminal push out. Repair as necessary. Replace and program the Powertrain Control Module No → Repair the open in the (K167) Sensor ground circuit.
7	Disconnect the ECT Sensor harness connector. Turn the ignition off. Disconnect the PCM harness connector. Measure the resistance between ground and the (K2) ECT Signal circuit in the ECT Sensor harness connector. Is the resistance below 100 ohms? Yes → Repair the short to ground in the (K2) ECT Signal circuit. No → Go To 8
8	Turn the ignition off. Disconnect the ECT Sensor harness connector. Disconnect the PCM harness connector. Measure the resistance between the (K2) ECT Sensor Signal circuit and the (K167) Sensor ground circuit at the ECT Sensor harness connector. Is the resistance below 5.0 ohms? Yes → Repair the (K167) Sensor ground shorted to the (K2) ECT Signal circuit. No → NOTE: Before continuing, check the PCM harness connector terminals for corrosion, damage, or terminal push out. Repair as necessary. Replace and program the Powertrain Control Module

ARM0400000000907

Fig. 49   Code P0116: ECT Performance (Part 3 of 3). 2004–05 Neon

TEST	ACTION
2	Turn the ignition off. Disconnect the ECT Sensor harness connector. NOTE: Visually inspect both the component and the PCM connectors. Look for damaged, partially broken wires, and backed out or corroded terminals. Ignition on, engine not running. Measure the voltage on the (K2) ECT Signal circuit in the ECT Sensor harness connector. Is the voltage above 5.2 volts? Yes → Repair the short to battery voltage in the (K2) ECT Signal circuit. No → Go To 3
3	Turn the ignition off. Disconnect the ECT Sensor harness connector. Ignition on, engine not running. With the DRBIII®, read the ECT Sensor voltage. Is the voltage above 4.9 volts? Yes → Go To 4 No → Go To 7
4	Turn the ignition off. Disconnect the ECT Sensor harness connector. Using a jumper wire, jumper across the ECT Sensor harness connector. Ignition on, engine not running. With the DRBIII®, read the ECT Sensor voltage. Is the voltage below 0.1 volt? Yes → Replace the ECT Sensor. No → Go To 5
5	Turn the ignition off. Disconnect the ECT Sensor harness connector. Disconnect the PCM harness connector. CAUTION: DO NOT PROBE THE PCM HARNESS CONNECTORS. PROBING THE PCM HARNESS CONNECTORS WILL DAMAGE THE PCM TERMINALS RESULTING IN POOR TERMINAL TO PIN CONNECTION. INSTALL MILLER SPECIAL TOOL #8815 TO PERFORM DIAGNOSIS. Measure the resistance of the (K2) ECT Signal circuit from the ECT Sensor harness connector to the appropriate terminal of special tool #8815. Is the resistance below 5.0 ohms? Yes → Go To 6 No → Repair the open in the (K2) ECT Signal circuit.

ARM0400000000906

Fig. 49   Code P0116: ECT Performance (Part 2 of 3). 2004–05 Neon

When Monitored and Set Condition:

P0117-ENGINE COOLANT TEMPERATURE SENSOR LOW

When Monitored: With the ignition on. Battery voltage greater than 10 volts.

Set Condition: The Engine Coolant Temperature (ECT) sensor circuit voltage at the PCM is less than 0.0782 of a volt. One Trip Fault.

POSSIBLE CAUSES
ECT SENSOR VOLTAGE BELOW 0.1 VOLTS
ECT SENSOR INTERNAL FAILURE
(K2) ECT SIGNAL SHORTED TO GROUND
(K2) ECT SIGNAL SHORTED TO (K167) SENSOR GROUND CIRCUIT
PCM

TEST	ACTION
1	Ignition on, engine not running. With the DRBIII®, read the ECT Sensor voltage. Is the voltage below 0.1 volt? Yes → Go To 2 No → Diagnose intermitten condition.
2	Turn the ignition off. Disconnect the ECT harness connector. Ignition on, engine not running. With the DRBIII®, read ECT Sensor voltage. Is the voltage between 4.8 and 5.2 volts? Yes → Replace the ECT Sensor. No → Go To 3
3	Turn the ignition off. Disconnect the ECT Sensor harness connector. Disconnect the PCM harness connector. Measure the resistance between ground and the (K2) ECT Signal circuit in the ECT Sensor harness connector. Is the resistance below 100 ohms? Yes → Repair the ground shorted to the (K2) ECT Signal circuit. No → Go To 4

ARM0400000000901

Fig. 50   Code P0117: ECT Temperature Sensor Low (Part 1 of 2). 2004–05 Neon

TEST	ACTION

4	Turn the ignition off.
	Disconnect the ECT Sensor harness connector.
	Disconnect the PCM harness connector.
	Measure the resistance between the (K2) ECT Sensor Signal circuit and the (K167) Sensor ground circuit in the ECT Sensor harness connector.
	Is the resistance below 100 ohms?
	
	      Yes → Repair the (K167) Sensor ground shorted to the (K2) ECT Sensor Signal circuit.
	
	      No → Go To 5

5	NOTE: Before continuing, check the PCM harness connector terminals for corrosion, damage, or terminal push out. Repair as necessary.
	If there are no possible causes remaining, view repair.
	
	      Repair
	          Replace and program the Powertrain Control Module

ARM0400000000902

Fig. 50 Code P0117: ECT Temperature Sensor Low (Part 2 of 2). 2004–05 Neon

TEST	ACTION

3	Turn the ignition off.
	Disconnect the ECT harness connector.
	Connect a jumper wire between the (K2) ECT Signal circuit and the (K4) Sensor ground circuit in the ECT harness connector.
	Ignition on, engine not running.
	With the DRBIII®, read ECT Sensor voltage.
	Is the voltage below 1.0 volt?
	
	      Yes → Replace the ECT Sensor.
	
	      No → Go To 4

4	Turn the ignition off.
	Disconnect the ECT Sensor harness connector.
	Disconnect the PCM harness connector.
	CAUTION: DO NOT PROBE THE PCM HARNESS CONNECTORS. PROBING THE PCM HARNESS CONNECTORS WILL DAMAGE THE PCM TERMINALS RESULTING IN POOR TERMINAL TO PIN CONNECTION. INSTALL MILLER SPECIAL TOOL #8815 TO PERFORM DIAGNOSIS.
	Measure the resistance of the (K2) ECT Signal circuit from the ECT Sensor harness connector to the appropriate terminal of special tool #8815.
	Is the resistance below 5.0 ohms?
	
	      Yes → Go To 5
	
	      No → Repair the open in the (K2) ECT Signal circuit.

5	Turn the ignition off.
	Disconnect the ECT Sensor harness connector.
	Disconnect the PCM harness connector.
	CAUTION: DO NOT PROBE THE PCM HARNESS CONNECTORS. PROBING THE PCM HARNESS CONNECTORS WILL DAMAGE THE PCM TERMINALS RESULTING IN POOR TERMINAL TO PIN CONNECTION. INSTALL MILLER SPECIAL TOOL #8815 TO PERFORM DIAGNOSIS.
	Measure the resistance of the (K167) Sensor ground circuit from the ECT Sensor harness connector to the appropriate terminal of special tool #8815.
	Is the resistance below 5.0 ohms?
	
	      Yes → Go To 6
	
	      No → Repair the open in the (K167) Sensor ground circuit.

6	NOTE: Before continuing, check the PCM harness connector terminals for corrosion, damage, or terminal push out. Repair as necessary.
	If there are no possible causes remaining, view repair.
	
	      Repair
	          Replace and program the Powertrain Control Module

ARM0400000000904

Fig. 51 Code P0118: ECT Temperature Sensor High (Part 2 of 2). 2004–05 Neon

When Monitored and Set Condition:

P0118-ENGINE COOLANT TEMPERATURE SENSOR HIGH

When Monitored: With the Ignition on. Battery voltage greater than 10 volts.

Set Condition: The Engine Coolant Temperature (ECT) sensor voltage at the PCM is greater than 4.9 volts. One trip Fault.

POSSIBLE CAUSES
ECT SENSOR VOLTAGE ABOVE 4.9 VOLTS
(K2) ECT SIGNAL CIRCUIT SHORTED TO BATTERY VOLTAGE
ECT SENSOR INTERNAL FAILURE
(K2) ECT SIGNAL CIRCUIT OPEN
(K167) SENSOR GROUND CIRCUIT OPEN
PCM

TEST	ACTION

1	Ignition on, engine not running.
	With the DRBIII®, read the ECT Sensor voltage.
	Is the voltage above 4.9 volts?
	
	      Yes → Go To 2
	
	      No → Diagnsoe intermittent condition.

2	Turn the ignition off.
	Disconnect the ECT Sensor harness connector.
	Ignition on, engine not running.
	Measure the voltage of the (K2) ECT Signal circuit in the ECT Sensor harness connector.
	Is the voltage above 5.2 volts?
	
	      Yes → Repair the short to battery voltage in the (K2) ECT Signal circuit.
	
	      No → Go To 3

ARM0400000000903

Fig. 51 Code P0118: ECT Temperature Sensor High (Part 1 of 2). 2004–05 Neon

When Monitored and Set Condition:

P0480-COOLING FAN 1 CONTROL CIRCUIT

When Monitored: With the ignition on. Battery voltage greater than 10 volts.

Set Condition: An open or shorted circuit is detected in the radiator fan relay control circuit. One Trip Fault.

POSSIBLE CAUSES
LOW SPEED RADIATOR FAN RELAY OPERATION
(A16) FUSED B+ FEED CIRCUITS
LOW SPEED RADIATOR FAN RELAY RESISTANCE
(C24) LOW SPEED RAD FAN RELAY CONTROL CIRCUIT OPEN
(C24) LOW SPEED RAD FAN RELAY CONTROL CIRCUIT SHORT TO GROUND
PCM

TEST	ACTION

1	Ignition on, engine not running.
	With the DRBIII®, actuate the Radiator Fan Relay.
	Is the Low Speed Radiator Fan Relay operating?
	
	      Yes → Diagnose intermittent condition.
	
	      No → Go To 2

2	Turn the ignition off.
	Remove the Low Speed Radiator Fan Relay from the PDC.
	Ignition on, engine not running.
	Measure the voltage of the (A16) Fused B+ Feed circuit in the PDC.
	Is the voltage above 11.0 volts?
	
	      Yes → Go To 3
	
	      No → Repair the (A16) Fused B+ Output circuit. Inspect the related fuse and repair as necessary.
	Perform POWERTRAIN VERIFICATION TEST VER - 5.

ARM0400000000908

Fig. 52 Code P0480: Cooling Fan No 1 Control Circuit (Part 1 of 2). 2004–05 Neon

TEST	ACTION
3	Turn the ignition off. Remove the Low Speed Radiator Fan Relay from the PDC. Measure the resistance of the Low Speed Radiator Fan Relay between the Fused Ignition Switch Output terminal and the Low Speed Rad Fan Relay Control terminal. Is the resistance between 60 to 85 ohms? Yes → Go To 4 No → Replace the Low Speed Radiator Fan Relay.
4	Turn the ignition off. Remove the Low Speed Radiator Fan Relay from the PDC. Disconnect the PCM harness connector. **CAUTION: DO NOT PROBE THE PCM HARNESS CONNECTORS. PROBING THE PCM HARNESS CONNECTORS WILL DAMAGE THE PCM TERMINALS RESULTING IN POOR TERMINAL TO PIN CONNECTION. INSTALL MILLER SPECIAL TOOL #8815 TO PERFORM DIAGNOSIS.** Measure the resistance of the (C24) Low Speed Rad Fan Relay Control circuit from the PDC to the appropriate terminal of special tool #8815. Is the resistance below 5.0 ohms? Yes → Go To 5 No → Repair the open in the (C24) Low Speed Rad Fan Relay Control circuit.
5	Turn the ignition off. Remove the Low Speed Radiator Fan Relay from the PDC. Disconnect the PCM harness connector. Measure the resistance between ground and the (C24) Low Speed Rad Fan Control circuit at the PDC. Is the resistance below 100 ohms? Yes → Repair the short to ground in the (C24) Low Speed Rad Fan Relay Control circuit. No → Go To 6
6	NOTE: Before continuing, check the PCM harness connector terminals for corrosion, damage, or terminal push out. Repair as necessary. If there are no possible causes remaining, view repair. Repair Replace and program the Powertrain Control Module

ARM0400000000909

Fig. 52 Code P0480: Cooling Fan No 1 Control Circuit (Part 2 of 2). 2004–05 Neon

TEST	ACTION
3	Turn the ignition off. Remove the High Speed Radiator Fan Relay from the PDC. Measure the resistance of the High Speed Radiator Fan Relay between the Fused Ignition Switch Output terminal and the High Speed Rad Fan Relay Control terminal. Is the resistance between 60 to 85 ohms? Yes → Go To 4 No → Replace the High Speed Radiator Fan Relay.
4	Turn the ignition off. Remove the High Speed Radiator Fan Relay from the PDC. Disconnect the PCM harness connector. **CAUTION: DO NOT PROBE THE PCM HARNESS CONNECTORS. PROBING THE PCM HARNESS CONNECTORS WILL DAMAGE THE PCM TERMINALS RESULTING IN POOR TERMINAL TO PIN CONNECTION. INSTALL MILLER SPECIAL TOOL #8815 TO PERFORM DIAGNOSIS.** Measure the resistance of the (C27) High Speed Rad Fan Relay Control circuit from the PDC to the appropriate terminal of special tool #8815. Is the resistance below 5.0 ohms? Yes → Go To 5 No → Repair the open in the (C27) High Speed Rad Fan Relay Control circuit.
5	Turn the ignition off. Remove the High Speed Radiator Fan Relay from the PDC. Disconnect the PCM harness connector. Measure the resistance between ground and the (C27) High Speed Rad Fan Relay Control circuit in the PDC. Is the resistance below 5.0 ohms? Yes → Repair the short to ground in the (C27) High Speed Rad Fan Relay Control circuit. No → Go To 6
6	NOTE: Before continuing, check the PCM harness connector terminals for corrosion, damage, or terminal push out. Repair as necessary. If there are no possible causes remaining, view repair. Repair NOTE: Before continuing, check the PCM harness connector terminals for corrosion, damage or terminal push out. Repair as necessary. Replace and program the Powertrain Control Module.

ARM0400000000911

Fig. 53 Code P0481: Cooling Fan No 2 Control Circuit Open (Part 2 of 2). 2004–05 Neon w/2.0L Engine

When Monitored and Set Condition:

P0481-COOLING FAN 2 CONTROL CIRCUIT (NON-TURBO)

When Monitored: With the ignition on. Battery voltage greater than 10 volts.

Set Condition: An open or shorted circuit is detected in the radiator fan relay control circuit. One trip Fault.

POSSIBLE CAUSES
HIGH SPEED RADIATOR FAN RELAY OPERATION
(A110) FUSED IGNITION SWITCH OUTPUT CIRCUIT
HIGH SPEED RADIATOR FAN RELAY RESISTANCE
(C27) HIGH SPEED RAD FAN RELAY CONTROL CIRCUIT OPEN
(C27) HIGH SPEED RAD FAN RELAY CONTROL CIRCUIT SHORT TO GROUND
PCM

TEST	ACTION
1	Turn the ignition on. With the DRBIII®, actuate the High Speed Radiator Fan Relay. Is the High Speed Radiator Fan Relay operating? Yes → Diagnose intermittent condition. No → Go To 2
2	Turn the ignition off. Remove the High Speed Radiator Fan Relay from the PDC. Turn the ignition on. Measure the voltage of the (A110) Fused Ignition Switch Output circuit in the PDC. Is the voltage above 11.0 volts? Yes → Go To 3 No → Repair the (A110) Fused Ignition Switch Output circuit. Check and replace any open fuses.

ARM0400000000910

Fig. 53 Code P0481: Cooling Fan No 2 Control Circuit Open (Part 1 of 2). 2004–05 Neon w/2.0L Engine

When Monitored and Set Condition:

P0481-COOLING FAN 2 CONTROL CIRCUIT (TURBO)

When Monitored: With the ignition on. Battery voltage greater than 10 volts.

Set Condition: An open or shorted circuit is detected in the radiator fan relay control circuits. One Trip Fault.

POSSIBLE CAUSES
RADIATOR FAN RELAYS 2 AND 3 OPERATION
FUSED IGNITION SWITCH OUTPUT CIRCUIT
RADIATOR FAN RELAY #2 CONTROL CIRCUIT OPEN BEFORE THE SPLICE
RADIATOR FAN RELAY #3 CONTROL CIRCUIT OPEN BEFORE SPLICE
RADIATOR FAN RELAY CONTROL CIRCUITS SHORT TO GROUND
RADIATOR FAN RELAY CONTROL CIRCUIT OPEN AFTER THE SPLICE
RADIATOR FAN RELAY #2 OR #3
PCM

TEST	ACTION
1	Turn the ignition on. With the DRBIII®, actuate the High Speed Radiator Fan Relay. Are both Radiator Fan operating at high speed? Yes → Refer to the INTERMITTENT CONDITION symptom in the Driveability category. No → Go To 2
2	Turn the ignition off. Remove both of the Radiator Fan Relays (#2 and #3) from the PDC. Turn the ignition on. NOTE: A voltage measurement must be taken at both Radiator Fan Relay Fused Ignition Switch Output circuits in the PDC. Measure the voltage of the Fused Ignition Switch Output circuit at the radiator Fan Relay connector in the PDC. Is the voltage above 11.0 volts at both relay connectors? Yes → Go To 3 No → Repair the Fused Ignition Switch Output circuit. Check and replace any open fuses.

ARM0400000000912

Fig. 54 Code P0481: Cooling Fan No 2 Control Circuit Open (Part 1 of 3). 2004–05 Neon w/2.4L Engine

TEST	ACTION
3	**NOTE: Both Radiator Fan Relays must be removed from the PDC during the following steps.** Turn the ignition on. Using the DRBIII®, actuate the High Speed Radiator Fan Relay. Using a test light connected to battery voltage, probe both of the Radiator Fan Relay Control circuits (relays #2 and #3). **NOTE: The test light should flash at both control circuits.** Choose a conclusion that best matches the result of the above test. Does NOT flash for Relay #2 (ONLY). Repair the open in the Radiator Fan Relay #2 Control circuit between the PDC and the splice. Does NOT flash for Relay #3 (ONLY). Repair the open in the Radiator Fan Relay #3 Control circuit between the PDC and the splice. Does NOT flash for both #2 and #3 Relays Go To **4** Flashes at both Relays. Install a substitute relay in place of the Radiator Fan Relays #2 and #3 to determine the faulty relay. Replace the appropriate Radiator Fan Relay.
4	**NOTE: Both Radiator Fan Relays must be removed from the PDC during the following steps.** Turn the ignition off. Disconnect the PCM harness connector. Measure the resistance between ground and the Radiator Fan Relay #2 Control circuit in the PDC. Is the resistance below 100 ohms? Yes → Repair the short to ground in the Radiator Fan Relay Control circuits. No → Go To **5**

ARM0400000000913

Fig. 54 Code P0481: Cooling Fan No 2 Control Circuit Open (Part 2 of 3). 2004–05 Neon w/2.4L Engine

Possible Causes
INTERMITTENT DTC
(K21) IAT SIGNAL CIRCUIT HIGH RESISTANCE
(K900) SENSOR GROUND CIRCUIT HIGH RESISTANCE
INTAKE AIR TEMPERATURE SENSOR
POWERTRAIN CONTROL MODULE (PCM)

Diagnostic Test

1. DTC IS ACTIVE

NOTE: Diagnose any CAN - C Communication DTCs before continuing.

Turn the ignition off.
If possible, allow the vehicle to sit with the ignition off for more than 480 minutes in an environment where the temperature is consistent and above - 7° C (19.4° F).
Test drive the vehicle. The vehicle must exceed 48 km/h (30 mph) during the test drive.
Do not cycle the ignition off when the test drive is completed.
With a scan tool, select View DTCs.

Is the status Active or Pending for this DTC?

Yes

- Go to 3

No

- Go to 2

ARM0600000000334

Fig. 55 Code P0111: IAT Performance. (Part 1 of 5). 2007–08 Caliber, Avenger Sedan & Sebring Sedan

TEST	ACTION
5	**NOTE: Both Radiator Fan Relays must be removed from the PDC during the following steps.** Turn the ignition off. Disconnect the PCM harness connector. **CAUTION: DO NOT PROBE THE PCM HARNESS CONNECTORS. PROBING THE PCM HARNESS CONNECTORS WILL DAMAGE THE PCM TERMINALS RESULTING IN POOR TERMINAL TO PIN CONNECTION. INSTALL MILLER SPECIAL TOOL #8815 TO PERFORM DIAGNOSIS.** Measure the resistance of the Radiator Fan Relay #3 Control circuit from the PDC to the appropriate terminal of special tool #8815. Is the resistance below 5.0 ohms? Yes → NOTE: Before continuing, check the PCM harness connector terminals for corrosion, damage or terminal push out. Repair as necessary. Replace and program the Powertrain Control Module No → Repair the open in the Radiator Fan Relay Control circuit.

ARM0400000000914

Fig. 54 Code P0481: Cooling Fan No 2 Control Circuit Open (Part 3 of 3). 2004–05 Neon w/2.4L Engine

2. AMBIENT AIR TEMPERATURE

Turn the ignition off.
Allow the vehicle to sit with the ignition off in an environment where the temperature is consistent and above - 7° C (19.4° F) until the engine coolant temperature is equal to ambient temperature.
Turn the ignition on.
With a scan tool, compare the AAT, ECT, and IAT sensor values.

Is the Intake Air Temperature Sensor value within 10° C (18° F) of the other two sensor values?

Yes

- Refer to the *CHECKING FOR AN INTERMITTENT DTC Diagnostic Procedure.

No

- Go to 3

3. INTAKE AIR TEMPERATURE SENSOR VOLTAGE

Turn the ignition off.
Disconnect the Intake Air Temperature Sensor harness connector.
Turn the ignition on.
With a scan tool, read the Intake Air Temperature Sensor voltage.

NOTE: The sensor voltage should be approximately 5.0 volts (plus or minus .1 volt) with the connector disconnected.

Does the scan tool display the voltage as described above?

Yes

- Go to 4

No

- Go to 5

ARM0600000000335

Fig. 55 Code P0111: IAT Performance. (Part 2 of 5). 2007–08 Caliber, Avenger Sedan & Sebring Sedan

COOLING FANS

4. INTAKE AIR TEMPERATURE SENSOR

Turn the ignition off.
Connect a jumper wire between the (K21) IAT Signal circuit and the (K900) Sensor Ground circuit in the Intake Air Temperature Sensor harness connector.
Turn the ignition on.
With a scan tool, read the Intake Air Temperature Sensor voltage.

NOTE: The sensor voltage should be approximately 0.0 volts (plus or minus .1 volt) with the jumper wire in place.

Does the scan tool display the voltage as described above?
Yes

- Replace the Intake Air Temperature Sensor.
- Perform the PCM Verification Test.

No

- Go to 5

5. (K21) IAT SIGNAL CIRCUIT HIGH RESISTANCE

Turn the ignition off.
Connect the Intake Air Temperature Sensor harness connector.

CAUTION: Do not probe the PCM harness connectors. Probing the PCM harness connectors will damage the PCM terminals resulting in poor terminal to pin connection. Install Miller Special Tool #8815 along with the #8815-1 to perform the diagnosis.

Using a voltmeter, perform a voltage drop test by backprobing the (K21) IAT Signal circuit at the Intake Air Temperature Sensor harness connector and probing the appropriate terminal of the special tool #8815. Make sure the voltmeter leads are connected so that positive polarity is displayed on the voltmeter.
Start the engine.
Is the voltage below 0.5 volts?
Yes

- Go to 6

No

- Repair the (K21) IAT Signal circuit for high resistance.
- Perform the PCM Verification Test.

ARM0600000000336

Fig. 55   Code P0111: IAT Performance. (Part 3 of 5). 2007–08 Caliber, Avenger Sedan & Sebring Sedan

7. POWERTRAIN CONTROL MODULE (PCM)

Using the wiring diagram/schematic as a guide, inspect the wiring and connectors between the Intake Air Temperature Sensor and the Powertrain Control Module (PCM).
Look for any chafed, pierced, pinched, or partially broken wires.
Look for broken, bent, pushed out or corroded terminals.
Monitor the scan tool data relative to this circuit and wiggle test the wiring and connectors.
Look for the data to change or for the DTC to reset during the wiggle test.
Refer to any Technical Service Bulletins that may apply.

Were any problems found?

Yes

- Repair as necessary.
- Perform the PCM Verification Test.

No

- Replace the Powertrain Control Module (PCM)
- Perform the PCM Verification Test.

ARM0600000000338

Fig. 55   Code P0111: IAT Performance. (Part 5 of 5). 2007–08 Caliber, Avenger Sedan & Sebring Sedan

6. (K900) SENSOR GROUND CIRCUIT HIGH RESISTANCE

Turn the ignition off.

CAUTION: Do not probe the PCM harness connectors. Probing the PCM harness connectors will damage the PCM terminals resulting in poor terminal to pin connection. Install Miller Special Tool #8815 along with the #8815-1 to perform the diagnosis.

Using a voltmeter, perform a voltage drop test by backprobing the (K900) Sensor Ground circuit at the Intake Air Temperature Sensor harness connector and probing the appropriate terminal of the special tool #8815. Make sure the voltmeter leads are connected so that positive polarity is displayed on the voltmeter.

WARNING: When the engine is operating, do not stand in direct line with the fan. Do not put your hands near the pulleys, belts, or fan. Do not wear loose clothing. Failure to follow these instructions can result in personal injury or death.

Start the engine.

Is the voltage below 0.5 volts?

Yes

- Go to 7

No

- Repair the (K900) Sensor Ground circuit for high resistance.
- Perform the PCM Verification Test.

ARM0600000000337

Fig. 55   Code P0111: IAT Performance. (Part 4 of 5). 2007–08 Caliber, Avenger Sedan & Sebring Sedan

Possible Causes
INTERMITTENT DTC
(K21) IAT SIGNAL CIRCUIT SHORTED TO GROUND
(K21) IAT SIGNAL CIRCUIT SHORTED TO (K900) SENSOR GROUND
(K21) IAT SIGNAL CIRCUIT OPEN OR HIGH RESISTANCE
INTAKE AIR TEMPERATURE SENSOR
POWERTRAIN CONTROL MODULE (PCM)

Diagnostic Test

1. DTC IS ACTIVE

Start the engine and allow it to reach normal operating temperature.

WARNING: When the engine is operating, do not stand in direct line with the fan. Do not put your hands near the pulleys, belts, or fan. Do not wear loose clothing. Failure to follow these instructions can result in personal injury or death.

NOTE: Diagnose and repair any system voltage DTCs before continuing with this test.

With the scan tool, select View DTCs.

Is the status Active for this DTC?

Yes

- Go to 2

No

- Refer to the *CHECKING FOR AN INTERMITTENT DTC Diagnostic Procedure.

ARM0600000000339

Fig. 56   Code P0112: IAT Sensor Circuit Low. (Part 1 of 4). 2007–08 Caliber, Avenger Sedan & Sebring Sedan

2. (K21) IAT SIGNAL CIRCUIT SHORTED TO GROUND

Turn the ignition off.
Disconnect the Intake Air Temperature Sensor connector.
Disconnect the Powertrain Control Module (PCM) connector.
Measure the resistance between ground and the (K21) IAT Signal circuit in the Intake Air Temperature Sensor harness connector.

Is the resistance above 100 ohms?

Yes

- Go to 3

No

- Repair the (K21) IAT Signal circuit for a short to ground.
- Perform the PCM Verification Test.

3. (K21) IAT SIGNAL CIRCUIT SHORTED TO (K900) SENSOR GROUND CIRCUIT

Measure the resistance between the (K21) IAT Signal circuit and the (K900) Sensor Ground circuit in the Intake Air Temperature Sensor harness connector.

Is the resistance above 100 ohms?

Yes

- Go to 4

No

- Repair the (K21) IAT Signal circuit for a short to the (K900) Sensor Ground circuit.
- Perform the PCM Verification Test.

ARM0600000000340

**Fig. 56 Code P0112: IAT Sensor Circuit Low.
(Part 2 of 4). 2007–08 Caliber, Avenger Sedan &
Sebring Sedan**

6. POWERTRAIN CONTROL MODULE (PCM)

Using the wiring diagram/schematic as a guide, inspect the wiring and connectors between the Intake Air Temperature Sensor and the Powertrain Control Module (PCM).
Look for any chafed, pierced, pinched, or partially broken wires.
Look for broken, bent, pushed out or corroded terminals.
Monitor the scan tool data relative to this circuit and wiggle test the wiring and connectors.
Look for the data to change or for the DTC to reset during the wiggle test.
Refer to any Technical Service Bulletins that may apply.

Were any problems found?

Yes

- Repair as necessary.
- Perform the PCM Verification Test.

No

- Replace and program the Powertrain Control Module (PCM)

- Perform the PCM Verification Test.

ARM0600000000342

**Fig. 56 Code P0112: IAT Sensor Circuit Low.
(Part 4 of 4). 2007–08 Caliber, Avenger Sedan &
Sebring Sedan**

4. (K21) IAT SIGNAL CIRCUIT OPEN CIRCUIT OR HIGH RESISTANCE

CAUTION: Do not probe the PCM harness connectors. Probing the PCM harness connectors will damage the PCM terminals, resulting in poor terminal to pin connection. Install Miller Special Tool #8815 to perform diagnosis.

Measure the resistance of the (K21) IAT Signal circuit between the Intake Air Temperature Sensor harness connector and the appropriate terminal of special tool #8815.

Is the resistance below 5.0 ohms?

Yes

- Go to 5

No

- Repair the (K21) IAT Signal circuit for an open circuit or high resistance.
- Perform the PCM Verification Test.

5. INTAKE AIR TEMPERATURE SENSOR

Turn the ignition off.
Connect the Powertrain Control Module (PCM) connector.
Turn the ignition on.
With the scan tool, read the Intake Air Temperature Sensor signal voltage.

NOTE: The sensor voltage should be approximately 5.0 volts (plus or minus .1 volt) with the connector disconnected.

Does the scan tool display the voltage as described above?

Yes

- Replace the Intake Air Temperature Sensor

- Perform the PCM Verification Test.

No

- Go to 6

ARM0600000000341

**Fig. 56 Code P0112: IAT Sensor Circuit Low.
(Part 3 of 4). 2007–08 Caliber, Avenger Sedan &
Sebring Sedan**

Possible Causes
INTERMITTENT DTC
(K21) IAT SIGNAL CIRCUIT SHORTED TO VOLTAGE
(K21) IAT SIGNAL CIRCUIT OPEN OR HIGH RESISTANCE
(K900) SENSOR GROUND CIRCUIT OPEN OR HIGH RESISTANCE
INTAKE AIR TEMPERATURE SENSOR
POWERTRAIN CONTROL MODULE (PCM)

Diagnostic Test

1. DTC IS ACTIVE

Start the engine and allow it to reach normal operating temperature.

WARNING: When the engine is operating, do not stand in direct line with the fan. Do not put your hands near the pulleys, belts, or fan. Do not wear loose clothing. Failure to follow these instructions can result in personal injury or death.

NOTE: Diagnose and repair any system voltage DTCs before continuing with this test.

With the scan tool, select View DTCs.

Is the status Active for this DTC?

Yes

- Go to 2

No

- Refer to the *CHECKING FOR AN INTERMITTENT DTC Diagnostic Procedure.

ARM0600000000343

**Fig. 57 Code P0113: IAT Sensor Circuit High.
(Part 1 of 4). 2007–08 Caliber, Avenger Sedan &
Sebring Sedan**

2. (K21) IAT SIGNAL CIRCUIT SHORTED TO VOLTAGE

Turn the ignition off.
Disconnect the Intake Air Temperature Sensor connector.
Disconnect the Powertrain Control Module (PCM) connector.
Turn the ignition on.
Measure the voltage of the (K21) IAT Signal circuit in the Intake Air Temperature Sensor harness connector.

Is there any voltage present?

Yes

- Repair the (K21) IAT Signal circuit for a short to voltage.
- Perform the PCM Verification Test.

No

- Go to 3

3. (K21) IAT SIGNAL OPEN OR HIGH RESISTANCE

Turn the ignition off.

CAUTION: Do not probe the PCM harness connectors. Probing the PCM harness connectors will damage the PCM terminals, resulting in poor terminal to pin connection. Install Miller Special Tool #8815 to perform diagnosis.

Measure the resistance of the (K21) IAT Signal circuit between the Intake Air Temperature Sensor harness connector and the appropriate terminal of special tool #8815.

Is the resistance below 5.0 ohms?

Yes

- Go to 4

No

- Repair the (K21) IAT Signal circuit for an open circuit or high resistance.
- Perform the PCM Verification Test.

ARM0600000000344

Fig. 57 Code P0113: IAT Sensor Circuit High. (Part 2 of 4). 2007–08 Caliber, Avenger Sedan & Sebring Sedan

6. POWERTRAIN CONTROL MODULE (PCM)

Using the wiring diagram/schematic as a guide, inspect the wiring and connectors between the Intake Air Temperature Sensor and the Powertrain Control Module (PCM).
Look for any chafed, pierced, pinched, or partially broken wires.
Look for broken, bent, pushed out or corroded terminals.
Monitor the scan tool data relative to this circuit and wiggle test the wiring and connectors.
Look for the data to change or for the DTC to reset during the wiggle test.
Refer to any Technical Service Bulletins that may apply.

Were any problems found?

Yes

- Repair as necessary.
- Perform the PCM Verification Test.

No

- Replace and program the Powertrain Control Module (PCM)
- Perform the PCM Verification Test.

ARM0600000000346

Fig. 57 Code P0113: IAT Sensor Circuit High. (Part 4 of 4). 2007–08 Caliber, Avenger Sedan & Sebring Sedan

4. (K900) SENSOR GROUND CIRCUIT OPEN OR HIGH RESISTANCE

CAUTION: Do not probe the PCM harness connectors. Probing the PCM harness connectors will damage the PCM terminals, resulting in poor terminal to pin connection. Install Miller Special Tool #8815 to perform diagnosis.

Measure the resistance of the (K900) Sensor Ground circuit between the Intake Air Temperature Sensor harness connector and the appropriate terminal of special tool #8815.

Is the resistance below 5.0 ohms?

Yes

- Go to 5

No

- Repair the (K900) Sensor Ground circuit for an open circuit or high resistance.
- Perform the PCM Verification Test.

5. INTAKE AIR TEMPERATURE SENSOR

Turn the ignition off.
Connect the Powertrain Control Module (PCM) connector.
Connect a jumper wire between the (K21) IAT Signal circuit and the (K900) Sensor Ground in the Intake Air Temperature Sensor harness connector.
Turn the ignition on.
With the scan tool, read the Intake Air Temperature Sensor signal voltage.

NOTE: The sensor voltage should be approximately 0.0 volts (plus or minus .1 volt) with the jumper wire in place.

Does the scan tool display the voltage as described above?

Yes

- Replace the Intake Air Temperature Sensor

- Perform the PCM Verification Test.

No

- Go to 6

ARM0600000000345

Fig. 57 Code P0113: IAT Sensor Circuit High. (Part 3 of 4). 2007–08 Caliber, Avenger Sedan & Sebring Sedan

When Monitored and Set Condition:

P0116-ENGINE COOLANT TEMPERATURE PERFORMANCE

When Monitored: Engine off time is greater than 480 minutes. Ambient temperature is greater than 4°C (39°F).

Set Condition: After a calibrated amount of cool down time, the PCM compares the ECT Sensor, IAT Sensor and the Ambient Air Temperature Sensor values. If the ECT Sensor value is not within calibrated temperature amount of the other two temperature sensors an error is detected. Two Trip Fault.

POSSIBLE CAUSES
GOOD TRIP EQUAL TO ZERO
(K2) ECT SIGNAL CIRCUIT SHORTED TO BATTERY VOLTAGE
ECT SENSOR VOLTAGE BELOW 1.0 VOLT
(K2) ECT SIGNAL CIRCUIT OPEN
(K4) SENSOR GROUND CIRCUIT OPEN
(K2) ECT SIGNAL CIRCUIT SHORTED TO GROUND
(K2) ECT SIGNAL SHORTED TO (K4) SENSOR GROUND
PCM HIGH
PCM LOW

TEST	ACTION
1	NOTE: Due to the fact that the PCM compares the IAT, AAT and ECT sensor to see if they are within a calibrated temp of one another, the use of a block heater can cause false readings for the PCM. Check with the customer to see if they use a block heater. Ignition on, engine not running. With the DRBIII®, read DTCs and record the related Freeze Frame data. Is the Good Trip Counter displayed and equal to zero? Yes → Go To 2 No → Diagnose intermittent condition.

ARM0400000000854

Fig. 58 Code P0116: ECT Performance. (Part 1 of 3). 2004–06 Sebring Convertible, Sebring Sedan & Stratus Sedan

TEST	ACTION
2	Turn the ignition off. Disconnect the ECT Sensor harness connector. **NOTE: Visually inspect both the component and the PCM connectors. Look for damaged, partially broken wires, and backed out or corroded terminals.** Ignition on, engine not running. Measure the voltage on the (K2) ECT Signal circuit in the ECT Sensor harness connector. Is the voltage above 5.2 volts? Yes → Repair the short to battery voltage in the (K2) ECT Signal circuit. No → Go To 3
3	Turn the ignition off. Disconnect the ECT Sensor harness connector. Ignition on, engine not running. With the DRBIII®, read the ECT Sensor voltage. Is the voltage above 4.6 volts? Yes → Go To 4 No → Go To 7
4	Turn the ignition off. Disconnect the ECT Sensor harness connector. Using a jumper wire, jumper across the ECT Sensor harness connector. Ignition on, engine not running. With the DRBIII®, read the ECT Sensor voltage. Is the voltage below 1.0 volt? Yes → Replace the ECT Sensor. No → Go To 5
5	Turn the ignition off. Disconnect the ECT Sensor harness connector. Disconnect the PCM harness connector. **CAUTION: DO NOT PROBE THE PCM HARNESS CONNECTORS. PROBING THE PCM HARNESS CONNECTORS WILL DAMAGE THE PCM TERMINALS RESULTING IN POOR TERMINAL TO PIN CONNECTION. INSTALL MILLER SPECIAL TOOL #8815 TO PERFORM DIAGNOSIS.** Measure the resistance of the (K2) ECT Signal circuit from the ECT Sensor harness connector to the appropriate terminal of special tool #8815. Is the resistance below 5.0 ohms? Yes → Go To 6 No → Repair the open in the (K2) ECT Signal circuit.

ARM0400000000855

Fig. 58 Code P0116: ECT Performance. (Part 2 of 3). 2004–06 Sebring Convertible, Sebring Sedan & Stratus Sedan

TEST	ACTION
6	Turn the ignition off. Disconnect the ECT harness connector. Disconnect the PCM harness connector. **CAUTION: DO NOT PROBE THE PCM HARNESS CONNECTORS. PROBING THE PCM HARNESS CONNECTORS WILL DAMAGE THE PCM TERMINALS RESULTING IN POOR TERMINAL TO PIN CONNECTION. INSTALL MILLER SPECIAL TOOL #8815 TO PERFORM DIAGNOSIS.** Measure the resistance of the (K4) Sensor ground circuit from the ECT Sensor harness connector to the appropriate terminal of special tool # 8815. Is the resistance below 5.0 ohms? Yes → NOTE: Before continuing, check the PCM harness connector terminals for corrosion, damage, or terminal push out. Repair as necessary. Replace and program the Powertrain Control Module No → Repair the open in the (K4) Sensor ground circuit.
7	Disconnect the ECT Sensor harness connector. Turn the ignition off. Disconnect the PCM harness connector. Measure the resistance between ground and the (K2) ECT Signal circuit in the ECT Sensor harness connector. Is the resistance below 100 ohms? Yes → Repair the short to ground in the (K2) ECT Signal circuit. No → Go To 8
8	Turn the ignition off. Disconnect the ECT Sensor harness connector. Disconnect the PCM harness connector. Measure the resistance between the (K2) ECT Sensor Signal circuit and the (K4) Sensor ground circuit at the ECT Sensor harness connector. Is the resistance below 5.0 ohms? Yes → Repair the (K4) Sensor ground shorted to the (K2) ECT Sensor Signal circuit. No → NOTE: Before continuing, check the PCM harness connector terminals for corrosion, damage, or terminal push out. Repair as necessary. Replace and program the Powertrain Control Module

ARM0400000000856

Fig. 58 Code P0116: ECT Performance. (Part 3 of 3). 2004–06 Sebring Convertible, Sebring Sedan & Stratus Sedan

Possible Causes

Possible Causes
INTERMITTENT DTC
(K2) ECT SIGNAL CIRCUIT HIGH RESISTANCE
(K900) SENSOR GROUND CIRCUIT HIGH RESISTANCE
ENGINE COOLANT TEMPERATURE SENSOR
POWERTRAIN CONTROL MODULE (PCM)

Diagnostic Test

1. DTC IS ACTIVE

NOTE: Diagnose any CAN - C Communication DTCs before continuing.

Turn the ignition off.
If possible, allow the vehicle to sit with the ignition off for more than 480 minutes in an environment where the temperature is consistent and above - 7° C (19.4° F).
Test drive the vehicle. The vehicle must exceed 48 km/h (30 mph) during the test drive.
Do not cycle the ignition off when the test drive is completed.
With a scan tool, select View DTCs.

Is the status Active or Pending for this DTC?

Yes

- Go to 3

No

- Go to 2

ARM0600000000347

Fig. 59 Code P0116: ECT Performance. (Part 1 of 5). 2007–08 Caliber, Avenger Sedan & Sebring Sedan

2. AMBIENT AIR TEMPERATURE

Turn the ignition off.
Allow the vehicle to sit with the ignition off in an environment where the temperature is consistent and above - 7° C (19.4° F) until the engine coolant temperature is equal to ambient temperature.
Turn the ignition on.
With a scan tool, compare the AAT, ECT, and IAT sensor values.

Is the Engine Coolant Temperature Sensor value within 10° C (18° F) of the other two sensor values?

Yes

- Refer to the *CHECKING FOR AN INTERMITTENT DTC Diagnostic Procedure.

No

- Go to 3

3. ENGINE COOLANT TEMPERATURE SENSOR VOLTAGE

Turn the ignition off.
Disconnect the Engine Coolant Temperature Sensor harness connector.
Turn the ignition on.
With a scan tool, read the Engine Coolant Temperature Sensor voltage.

NOTE: The sensor voltage should be approximately 5.0 volts (plus or minus .1 volt) with the connector disconnected.

Does the scan tool display the voltage as described above?

Yes

- Go to 4

No

- Go to 5

ARM0600000000348

Fig. 59 Code P0116: ECT Performance. (Part 2 of 5). 2007–08 Caliber, Avenger Sedan & Sebring Sedan

4. ENGINE COOLANT TEMPERATURE SENSOR

Turn the ignition off.
Connect a jumper wire between the (K2) ECT Signal circuit and the (K900) Sensor Ground circuit in the Engine Coolant Temperature Sensor harness connector.
Turn the ignition on.
With a scan tool, read the Engine Coolant Temperature Sensor voltage.

NOTE: The sensor voltage should be approximately 0.0 volts (plus or minus .1 volt) with the jumper wire in place.

Does the scan tool display the voltage as described above?

Yes

- Replace the Engine Coolant Temperature Sensor.
- Perform the PCM Verification Test.

No

- Go to 5

5. (K2) ECT SIGNAL CIRCUIT HIGH RESISTANCE

Turn the ignition off.
Connect the Engine Coolant Temperature Sensor harness connector.

CAUTION: Do not probe the PCM harness connectors. Probing the PCM harness connectors will damage the PCM terminals resulting in poor terminal to pin connection. Install Miller Special Tool #8815 along with the #8815-1 to perform the diagnosis.

Using a voltmeter, perform a voltage drop test by backprobing the (K2) ECT Signal circuit at the Engine Coolant Temperature Sensor harness connector and probing the appropriate terminal of the special tool #8815. Make sure the voltmeter leads are connected so that positive polarity is displayed on the voltmeter.
Start the engine.
Is the voltage below 0.5 volts?
Yes

- Go to 6

No

- Repair the (K2) ECT Signal circuit for high resistance.
- Perform the PCM Verification Test.

ARM0600000000349

Fig. 59   Code P0116: ECT Performance. (Part 3 of 5). 2007–08 Caliber, Avenger Sedan & Sebring Sedan

7. POWERTRAIN CONTROL MODULE (PCM)

Using the wiring diagram/schematic as a guide, inspect the wiring and connectors between the Engine Coolant Temperature Sensor and the Powertrain Control Module (PCM).
Look for any chafed, pierced, pinched, or partially broken wires.
Look for broken, bent, pushed out or corroded terminals.
Monitor the scan tool data relative to this circuit and wiggle test the wiring and connectors.
Look for the data to change or for the DTC to reset during the wiggle test.
Refer to any Technical Service Bulletins that may apply.

Were any problems found?

Yes

- Repair as necessary.
- Perform the PCM Verification Test.

No

- Replace the Powertrain Control Module (PCM)
- Perform the PCM Verification Test.

ARM0600000000351

Fig. 59   Code P0116: ECT Performance. (Part 5 of 5). 2007–08 Caliber, Avenger Sedan & Sebring Sedan

6. (K900) SENSOR GROUND CIRCUIT HIGH RESISTANCE

Turn the ignition off.

CAUTION: Do not probe the PCM harness connectors. Probing the PCM harness connectors will damage the PCM terminals resulting in poor terminal to pin connection. Install Miller Special Tool #8815 along with the #8815-1 to perform the diagnosis.

Using a voltmeter, perform a voltage drop test by backprobing the (K900) Sensor Ground circuit at the Engine Coolant Temperature Sensor harness connector and probing the appropriate terminal of the special tool #8815. Make sure the voltmeter leads are connected so that positive polarity is displayed on the voltmeter.

WARNING: When the engine is operating, do not stand in direct line with the fan. Do not put your hands near the pulleys, belts, or fan. Do not wear loose clothing. Failure to follow these instructions can result in personal injury or death.

Start the engine.

Is the voltage below 0.5 volts?

Yes

- Go to 7

No

- Repair the (K900) Sensor Ground circuit for high resistance.
- Perform the PCM Verification Test.

ARM0600000000350

Fig. 59   Code P0116: ECT Performance. (Part 4 of 5). 2007–08 Caliber, Avenger Sedan & Sebring Sedan

When Monitored and Set Condition:

P0117-ENGINE COOLANT TEMPERATURE SENSOR LOW

When Monitored: With the ignition on. Battery voltage greater than 10 volts.

Set Condition: The Engine Coolant Temperature (ECT) sensor circuit voltage at the PCM is less than 0.0782 of a volt. One Trip Fault.

POSSIBLE CAUSES
ECT SENSOR VOLTAGE BELOW 1.0 VOLTS
ECT SENSOR INTERNAL FAILURE
(K2) ECT SIGNAL SHORTED TO GROUND
(K2) ECT SIGNAL SHORTED TO (K4) SENSOR GROUND CIRCUIT
PCM

TEST	ACTION
1	Ignition on, engine not running. With the DRBIII®, read the ECT Sensor voltage. Is the voltage below 1.0 volt? Yes → Go To 2 No → Diagnose INTERMITTENT CONDITION
2	Turn the ignition off. Disconnect the ECT harness connector. Ignition on, engine not running. With the DRBIII®, read ECT Sensor voltage. Is the voltage between 4.8 and 5.2 volts? Yes → Replace the ECT Sensor. No → Go To 3
3	Turn the ignition off. Disconnect the ECT Sensor harness connector. Disconnect the PCM harness connector. Measure the resistance between ground and the (K2) ECT Signal circuit in the ECT Sensor harness connector. Is the resistance below 100 ohms? Yes → Repair the ground shorted to the (K2) ECT Signal circuit. No → Go To 4

ARM0400000000857

Fig. 60   Code P0117: ECT Sensor Low (Part 1 of 2). 2004–06 Sebring Convertible, Sebring Sedan & Stratus Sedan

TEST	ACTION

4	Turn the ignition off.
	Disconnect the ECT Sensor harness connector.
	Disconnect the PCM harness connector.
	Measure the resistance between the (K2) ECT Sensor Signal circuit and the (K4) Sensor ground circuit in the ECT Sensor harness connector.
	Is the resistance below 100 ohms?
	
	        Yes → Repair the (K4) Sensor ground shorted to the (K2) ECT Sensor Signal circuit.
	
	        No → Go To 5

5	NOTE: Before continuing, check the PCM harness connector terminals for corrosion, damage, or terminal push out. Repair as necessary.
	If there are no possible causes remaining, view repair.
	
	    Repair
	        Replace and program the Powertrain Control Module

ARM0400000000858

Fig. 60   Code P0117: ECT Sensor Low (Part 2 of 2). 2004–06 Sebring Convertible, Sebring Sedan & Stratus Sedan

2. (K2) ECT SIGNAL CIRCUIT SHORTED TO GROUND

Turn the ignition off.
Disconnect the Engine Coolant Temperature Sensor connector.
Disconnect the Powertrain Control Module (PCM) connector.
Measure the resistance between ground and the (K2) ECT Signal circuit in the Engine Coolant Temperature Sensor harness connector.

Is the resistance above 100 ohms?

Yes

- Go to 3

No

- Repair the (K2) ECT Signal circuit for a short to ground.
- Perform the PCM Verification Test.

3. (K2) ECT SIGNAL CIRCUIT SHORTED TO (K900) SENSOR GROUND CIRCUIT

Measure the resistance between the (K2) ECT Signal circuit and the (K900) Sensor Ground circuit in the Engine Coolant Temperature Sensor harness connector.

Is the resistance above 100 ohms?

Yes

- Go to 4

No

- Repair the (K2) ECT Signal circuit for a short to the (K900) Sensor Ground circuit.
- Perform the PCM Verification Test.

ARM0600000000353

Fig. 61   Code P0117: ECT Sensor Circuit Low. (Part 2 of 4). 2007–08 Caliber, Avenger Sedan & Sebring Sedan

Possible Causes
INTERMITTENT DTC
(K2) ECT SIGNAL CIRCUIT SHORTED TO GROUND
(K2) ECT SIGNAL CIRCUIT SHORTED TO (K900) SENSOR GROUND
(K2) ECT SIGNAL CIRCUIT OPEN OR HIGH RESISTANCE
ENGINE COOLANT TEMPERATURE SENSOR
POWERTRAIN CONTROL MODULE (PCM)

Diagnostic Test

1. DTC IS ACTIVE

Start the engine and allow it to reach normal operating temperature.

WARNING: When the engine is operating, do not stand in direct line with the fan. Do not put your hands near the pulleys, belts, or fan. Do not wear loose clothing. Failure to follow these instructions can result in personal injury or death.

NOTE: Diagnose and repair any system voltage DTCs before continuing with this test.

With the scan tool, select View DTCs.

Is the status Active for this DTC?

Yes

- Go to 2

No

- Refer to the *CHECKING FOR AN INTERMITTENT DTC Diagnostic Procedure.

ARM0600000000352

Fig. 61   Code P0117: ECT Sensor Circuit Low. (Part 1 of 4). 2007–08 Caliber, Avenger Sedan & Sebring Sedan

4. (K2) ECT SIGNAL CIRCUIT OPEN CIRCUIT OR HIGH RESISTANCE

CAUTION: Do not probe the PCM harness connectors. Probing the PCM harness connectors will damage the PCM terminals, resulting in poor terminal to pin connection. Install Miller Special Tool #8815 to perform diagnosis.

Measure the resistance of the (K2) ECT Signal circuit between the Engine Coolant Temperature Sensor harness connector and the appropriate terminal of special tool #8815.

Is the resistance below 5.0 ohms?

Yes

- Go to 5

No

- Repair the (K2) ECT Signal circuit for an open circuit or high resistance.
- Perform the PCM Verification Test.

5. ENGINE COOLANT TEMPERATURE SENSOR

Turn the ignition off.
Connect the Powertrain Control Module (PCM) connector.
Turn the ignition on.
With the scan tool, read the Engine Coolant Temperature Sensor signal voltage.

NOTE: The sensor voltage should be approximately 5.0 volts (plus or minus .1 volt) with the connector disconnected.

Does the scan tool display the voltage as described above?

Yes

- Replace the Engine Coolant Temperature Sensor
- Perform the PCM Verification Test.

No

- Go to 6

ARM0600000000354

Fig. 61   Code P0117: ECT Sensor Circuit Low. (Part 3 of 4). 2007–08 Caliber, Avenger Sedan & Sebring Sedan

6. POWERTRAIN CONTROL MODULE (PCM)

Using the wiring diagram/schematic as a guide, inspect the wiring and connectors between the Engine Coolant Temperature Sensor and the Powertrain Control Module (PCM).
Look for any chafed, pierced, pinched, or partially broken wires.
Look for broken, bent, pushed out or corroded terminals.
Monitor the scan tool data relative to this circuit and wiggle test the wiring and connectors.
Look for the data to change or for the DTC to reset during the wiggle test.
Refer to any Technical Service Bulletins that may apply.

Were any problems found?

Yes

- Repair as necessary.
- Perform the PCM Verification Test.

No

- Replace and program the Powertrain Control Module (PCM)

- Perform the PCM Verification Test.

ARM0600000000355

Fig. 61   Code P0117: ECT Sensor Circuit Low. (Part 4 of 4). 2007–08 Caliber, Avenger Sedan & Sebring Sedan

TEST	ACTION
3	Turn the ignition off. Disconnect the ECT harness connector. Connect a jumper wire between the (K2) ECT Signal circuit and the (K4) Sensor ground circuit in the ECT harness connector. Ignition on, engine not running. With the DRBIII®, read ECT Sensor voltage. Is the voltage below 1.0 volt? Yes → Replace the ECT Sensor. No → Go To 4
4	Turn the ignition off. Disconnect the ECT Sensor harness connector. Disconnect the PCM harness connector. CAUTION: DO NOT PROBE THE PCM HARNESS CONNECTORS. PROBING THE PCM HARNESS CONNECTORS WILL DAMAGE THE PCM TERMINALS RESULTING IN POOR TERMINAL TO PIN CONNECTION. INSTALL MILLER SPECIAL TOOL #8815 TO PERFORM DIAGNOSIS. Measure the resistance of the (K2) ECT Signal circuit from the ECT Sensor harness connector to the appropriate terminal of special tool #8815. Is the resistance below 5.0 ohms? Yes → Go To 5 No → Repair the open in the (K2) ECT Signal circuit.
5	Turn the ignition off. Disconnect the ECT Sensor harness connector. Disconnect the PCM harness connector. CAUTION: DO NOT PROBE THE PCM HARNESS CONNECTORS. PROBING THE PCM HARNESS CONNECTORS WILL DAMAGE THE PCM TERMINALS RESULTING IN POOR TERMINAL TO PIN CONNECTION. INSTALL MILLER SPECIAL TOOL #8815 TO PERFORM DIAGNOSIS. Measure the resistance of the (K4) Sensor ground circuit from the ECT Sensor harness connector to the appropriate terminal of special tool #8815. Is the resistance below 5.0 ohms? Yes → Go To 6 No → Repair the open in the (K4) Sensor ground circuit.
6	NOTE: Before continuing, check the PCM harness connector terminals for corrosion, damage, or terminal push out. Repair as necessary. If there are no possible causes remaining, view repair. Repair Replace and program the Powertrain Control Module

ARM0400000000860

Fig. 62   Code P0118: ECT Sensor High (Part 2 of 2). 2004–06 Sebring Convertible, Sebring Sedan & Stratus Sedan

When Monitored and Set Condition:

P0118-ENGINE COOLANT TEMPERATURE SENSOR HIGH

When Monitored: With the ignition on. Battery voltage greater than 10 volts.

Set Condition: The Engine Coolant Temperature (ECT) sensor voltage at the PCM is greater than 4.98 volts. One trip Fault.

POSSIBLE CAUSES
ECT SENSOR VOLTAGE ABOVE 4.9 VOLTS
(K2) ECT SIGNAL CIRCUIT SHORTED TO BATTERY VOLTAGE
ECT SENSOR INTERNAL FAILURE
(K2) ECT SIGNAL CIRCUIT OPEN
(K4) SENSOR GROUND CIRCUIT OPEN
PCM

TEST	ACTION
1	Ignition on, engine not running. With the DRBIII®, read the ECT Sensor voltage. Is the voltage above 4.9 volts? Yes → Go To 2 No → Diagnose INTERMITTENT CONDITION
2	Turn the ignition off. Disconnect the ECT Sensor harness connector. Ignition on, engine not running. Measure the voltage of the (K2) ECT Signal circuit in the ECT Sensor harness connector. Is the voltage above 5.2 volts? Yes → Repair the short to battery voltage in the (K2) ECT Signal circuit. No → Go To 3

ARM0400000000859

Fig. 62   Code P0118: ECT Sensor High (Part 1 of 2). 2004–06 Sebring Convertible, Sebring Sedan & Stratus Sedan

Possible Causes
INTERMITTENT DTC
(K2) ECT SIGNAL CIRCUIT SHORTED TO VOLTAGE
(K2) ECT SIGNAL CIRCUIT OPEN OR HIGH RESISTANCE
(K900) SENSOR GROUND CIRCUIT OPEN OR HIGH RESISTANCE
ENGINE COOLANT TEMPERATURE SENSOR
POWERTRAIN CONTROL MODULE (PCM)

Diagnostic Test

1. DTC IS ACTIVE

Start the engine and allow it to reach normal operating temperature.

WARNING: When the engine is operating, do not stand in direct line with the fan. Do not put your hands near the pulleys, belts, or fan. Do not wear loose clothing. Failure to follow these instructions can result in personal injury or death.

NOTE: Diagnose and repair any system voltage DTCs before continuing with this test.

With the scan tool, select View DTCs.

Is the status Active for this DTC?

Yes

- Go to 2

No

- Refer to the *CHECKING FOR AN INTERMITTENT DTC Diagnostic Procedure.

ARM0600000000356

Fig. 63   Code P0118: ECT Sensor Circuit High. (Part 1 of 4). 2007–08 Caliber, Avenger Sedan & Sebring Sedan

2. (K2) ECT SIGNAL CIRCUIT SHORTED TO VOLTAGE

Turn the ignition off.
Disconnect the Engine Coolant Temperature Sensor connector.
Disconnect the Powertrain Control Module (PCM) connector.
Turn the ignition on.
Measure the voltage of the (K2) ECT Signal circuit in the Engine Coolant Temperature Sensor harness connector.

Is there any voltage present?

Yes

- Repair the (K2) ECT Signal circuit for a short to voltage.
- Perform the PCM Verification Test.

No

- Go to 3

3. (K2) ECT SIGNAL OPEN OR HIGH RESISTANCE

Turn the ignition off.

CAUTION: Do not probe the PCM harness connectors. Probing the PCM harness connectors will damage the PCM terminals, resulting in poor terminal to pin connection. Install Miller Special Tool #8815 to perform diagnosis.

Measure the resistance of the (K2) ECT Signal circuit between the Engine Coolant Temperature Sensor harness connector and the appropriate terminal of special tool #8815.

Is the resistance below 5.0 ohms?

Yes

- Go to 4

No

- Repair the (K2) ECT Signal circuit for an open circuit or high resistance.
- Perform the PCM Verification Test.

ARM0600000000357

Fig. 63   Code P0118: ECT Sensor Circuit High. (Part 2 of 4). 2007–08 Caliber, Avenger Sedan & Sebring Sedan

6. POWERTRAIN CONTROL MODULE (PCM)

Using the wiring diagram/schematic as a guide, inspect the wiring and connectors between the Engine Coolant Temperature Sensor and the Powertrain Control Module (PCM).
Look for any chafed, pierced, pinched, or partially broken wires.
Look for broken, bent, pushed out or corroded terminals.
Monitor the scan tool data relative to this circuit and wiggle test the wiring and connectors.
Look for the data to change or for the DTC to reset during the wiggle test.
Refer to any Technical Service Bulletins that may apply.

Were any problems found?

Yes

- Repair as necessary.
- Perform the PCM Verification Test.

No

- Replace and program the Powertrain Control Module (PCM)
- Perform the PCM Verification Test.

ARM0600000000359

Fig. 63   Code P0118: ECT Sensor Circuit High. (Part 4 of 4). 2007–08 Caliber, Avenger Sedan & Sebring Sedan

4. (K900) SENSOR GROUND CIRCUIT OPEN OR HIGH RESISTANCE

CAUTION: Do not probe the PCM harness connectors. Probing the PCM harness connectors will damage the PCM terminals, resulting in poor terminal to pin connection. Install Miller Special Tool #8815 to perform diagnosis.

Measure the resistance of the (K900) Sensor Ground circuit between the Engine Coolant Temperature Sensor harness connector and the appropriate terminal of special tool #8815.

Is the resistance below 5.0 ohms?

Yes

- Go to 5

No

- Repair the (K900) Sensor Ground circuit for an open circuit or high resistance.
- Perform the PCM Verification Test.

5. ENGINE COOLANT TEMPERATURE SENSOR

Turn the ignition off.
Connect the Powertrain Control Module (PCM) connector.
Connect a jumper wire between the (K2) ECT Signal circuit and the (K900) Sensor Ground in the Engine Coolant Temperature Sensor harness connector.
Turn the ignition on.
With the scan tool, read the Engine Coolant Temperature Sensor signal voltage.

NOTE: The sensor voltage should be approximately 0.0 volts (plus or minus .1 volt) with the jumper wire in place.

Does the scan tool display the voltage as described above?

Yes

- Replace the Engine Coolant Temperature Sensor

- Perform the PCM Verification Test.

No

- Go to 6

ARM0600000000358

Fig. 63   Code P0118: ECT Sensor Circuit High. (Part 3 of 4). 2007–08 Caliber, Avenger Sedan & Sebring Sedan

When Monitored and Set Condition:

P0480-LOW SPEED FAN CONTROL RELAY CIRCUIT

When Monitored: With the ignition on. Battery voltage greater than 10 volts.

Set Condition: An open or shorted circuit is detected in the radiator fan relay control circuit. One Trip Fault.

POSSIBLE CAUSES
LOW SPEED RADIATOR FAN RELAY OPERATION
(A16) FUSED B+ FEED CIRCUITS
LOW SPEED RADIATOR FAN RELAY RESISTANCE
(C24) LOW SPEED RAD FAN RELAY CONTROL CIRCUIT OPEN
(C24) LOW SPEED RAD FAN RELAY CONTROL CIRCUIT SHORT TO GROUND
PCM

TEST	ACTION
1	Ignition on, engine not running. With the DRBIII®, actuate the Radiator Fan Relay. Is the Low Speed Radiator Fan Relay operating? Yes → Diagnose intermittent condition. No → Go To 2
2	Turn the ignition off. Remove the Low Speed Radiator Fan Relay from the PDC. Ignition on, engine not running. Measure the voltage of the (A16) Fused B+ Feed circuit in the PDC. Is the voltage above 11.0 volts? Yes → Go To 3 No → Repair the (A16) Fused B+ Output circuit. Inspect the related fuse and repair as necessary.

ARM0400000000861

Fig. 64   Code P0480: Low Speed Fan Control Relay Circuit (Part 1 of 2). 2004–06 Sebring Convertible, Sebring Sedan & Stratus Sedan

TEST	ACTION
3	Turn the ignition off. Remove the Low Speed Radiator Fan Relay from the PDC. Measure the resistance of the Low Speed Radiator Fan Relay between the Fused Ignition Switch Output terminal and the Low Speed Rad Fan Relay Control terminal. Is the resistance between 60 to 85 ohms? Yes → Go To 4 No → Replace the Low Speed Radiator Fan Relay.
4	Turn the ignition off. Remove the Low Speed Radiator Fan Relay from the PDC. Disconnect the PCM harness connector. **CAUTION: DO NOT PROBE THE PCM HARNESS CONNECTORS. PROBING THE PCM HARNESS CONNECTORS WILL DAMAGE THE PCM TERMINALS RESULTING IN POOR TERMINAL TO PIN CONNECTION. INSTALL MILLER SPECIAL TOOL #8815 TO PERFORM DIAGNOSIS.** Measure the resistance of the (C24) Low Speed Rad Fan Relay Control circuit from the PDC to the appropriate terminal of special tool #8815. Is the resistance below 5.0 ohms? Yes → Go To 5 No → Repair the open in the (C24) Low Speed Rad Fan Relay Control circuit.
5	Turn the ignition off. Remove the Low Speed Radiator Fan Relay from the PDC. Disconnect the PCM harness connector. Measure the resistance between ground and the (C24) Low Speed Rad Fan Control circuit at the PDC. Is the resistance below 100 ohms? Yes → Repair the short to ground in the (C24) Low Speed Rad Fan Relay Control circuit. No → Go To 6
6	NOTE: Before continuing, check the PCM harness connector terminals for corrosion, damage, or terminal push out. Repair as necessary. If there are no possible causes remaining, view repair. Repair Replace and program the Powertrain Control Module

ARM0400000000862

Fig. 64   Code P0480: Low Speed Fan Control Relay Circuit (Part 2 of 2). 2004–06 Sebring Convertible, Sebring Sedan & Stratus Sedan

3. LOW/HIGH RAD FAN CONTROL CIRCUIT

Turn the ignition on, engine not running.
With a scan tool, select Radiator Cooling Fan Relay #1 Control State, Toggle, to actuate the Cooling Fan (Low/High).
Using a 12-volt test light connected to battery voltage, probe the (N201) Low/High Rad Fan Control circuit in the Low/High Rad Relay harness connector.

Does the test light illuminate brightly and flash on and off?

Yes

- Replace the Low/High Rad Fan Relay.
- Perform the POWERTRAIN VERIFICATION TEST.

No

- Go To 4

4. (N201) LOW/HIGH RAD FAN CONTROL CIRCUIT SHORTED TO BATTERY VOLTAGE

Disconnect the TIPM C11 harness connector.
Using a voltmeter, measure the voltage of the (N201) Low/High Rad Fan Control circuit in the Low/High Rad Relay harness connector.

Is there voltage present?

Yes

- Repair the short to voltage in the (N201) Low/High Rad Fan Control circuit
- Perform the POWERTRAIN VERIFICATION TEST.

No

- Go To 5

ARM0600000000361

Fig. 65   Code P0480: Cooling Fan 1 Control Circuit. (Part 2 of 3). 2007–08 Caliber, Avenger Sedan & Sebring Sedan

Possible Causes
(A16) FUSED (B+) CIRCUITS
(N201) LOW/HIGH/HIGH RAD FAN CONTROL CIRCUIT SHORTED TO BATTERY VOLTAGE
(N201) LOW/HIGH RAD FAN CONTROL CIRCUIT OPEN
(N201) LOW/HIGH RAD FAN CONTROL CIRCUIT SHORTED TO GROUND
LOW/HIGH RAD FAN RELAY
TOTALLY INTEGRATED POWER MODULE

Diagnostic Test

1. RADIATOR COOLING FAN MODULE OPERATION

Ignition on, engine not running.
With a scan tool, select Radiator Cooling Fan Relay #1 Control State to actuate the Cooling Fan (Low/High).
Is the one Cooling Fan operating?

Yes

- Refer to the INTERMITTENT CONDITION Diagnostic Procedure.
- Perform the POWERTRAIN VERIFICATION TEST.

No

- Go To 2

2. (A16) FUSED B+ CIRCUIT

Ignition on.
Disconnect the Low/High Rad Relay harness connector.
Using a 12-volt test light connected to ground, probe the (A16) Fused B+ circuit in the Low/High Rad Relay harness connector.
Does the test light illuminate brightly?
Yes

- Go To 3

No

- Repair the (A16) Fused B+ circuit. Inspect the related fuse and repair as necessary.
- Perform the POWERTRAIN VERIFICATION TEST.

ARM0600000000360

Fig. 65   Code P0480: Cooling Fan 1 Control Circuit. (Part 1 of 3). 2007–08 Caliber, Avenger Sedan & Sebring Sedan

5. (N201) LOW/HIGH RAD FAN CONTROL CIRCUIT OPEN

Measure the resistance of the (N201) Low/High Fan Control circuit from the Low/High Rad Relay harness connector to the TIPM C11 harness connector.

Is the resistance below 5.0 ohms?

Yes

- Go To 6

No

- Repair the open in the (N201) Low/High Fan Control circuit.
- Perform the POWERTRAIN VERIFICATION TEST.

6. (N201) LOW/HIGH RAD FAN CONTROL CIRCUIT SHORTED TO GROUND

Measure the resistance between ground and the (N201) Low/High Fan Control circuit in the TIPM C11 harness connector.

Is the resistance below 100 ohms?

Yes

- Repair the short to ground in the (N201) Low/High Fan Control circuit.
- Perform the POWERTRAIN VERIFICATION TEST.

No

- Replace the Totally Integrated Power Module
- Perform the POWERTRAIN VERIFICATION TEST.

ARM0600000000362

Fig. 65   Code P0480: Cooling Fan 1 Control Circuit. (Part 3 of 3). 2007–08 Caliber, Avenger Sedan & Sebring Sedan

Possible Causes
(A16) FUSED (B+) CIRCUITS
(N112) RAD FAN RELAY CONTROL CIRCUIT SHORTED TO BATTERY VOLTAGE
(N112) RAD FAN RELAY CONTROL CIRCUIT OPEN
(N112) RAD FAN RELAY CONTROL CIRCUIT SHORTED TO GROUND
MED/HIGH RAD FAN RELAY
SERIES/PARALLEL RAD FAN RELAY
TOTALLY INTEGRATED POWER MODULE

Diagnostic Test

1. RADIATOR COOLING FAN MODULE OPERATION

Ignition on, engine not running.
With a scan tool, actuate both the Radiator Cooling Fan Relays #1 and #2.
Are both cooling fan operating at medium speed?
Yes

- Refer to the INTERMITTENT CONDITION Diagnostic Procedure.
- Perform the POWERTRAIN VERIFICATION TEST.

No

- Go To 2

2. (A16) FUSED B+ CIRCUIT

Ignition on.
Disconnect the Med/High Rad Fan Relay from the Fuse/Relay Block.
Disconnect the Series/Parallel Rad Fan Relay from the Fuse/Relay Block.
Using a 12-volt test light connected to ground, probe the (A16) Fused B+ circuit at both the Med/High Rad Fan Relay and the Series/Parallel Rad Fan Relay connectors.
Does the test light illuminate brightly at each terminal?
Yes

- Go To 3

No

- Repair the (A16) Fused B+ circuit. Inspect the related fuse and repair as necessary.
- Perform the POWERTRAIN VERIFICATION TEST.

ARM0600000000363

Fig. 66   Code P0481: Cooling Fan 2 Control Circuit. (Part 1 of 4). 2007–08 Caliber, Avenger Sedan & Sebring Sedan

5. (N112) RAD FAN RELAY CONTROL CIRCUIT SHORTED TO BATTERY VOLTAGE

Disconnect the TIPM C11 harness connector.
Using a voltmeter, measure the voltage of the (N112) Rad Fan Relay Control circuit in the Med/High Rad Fan Relay harness connector.

Is there voltage present?

Yes

- Repair the short to voltage in the (N112) Rad Fan Relay Control circuit.
- Perform the POWERTRAIN VERIFICATION TEST.

No

- Go To 6

6. (N112) RAD FAN RELAY CONTROL CIRCUIT OPEN

Measure the resistance of the (N112) Rad Fan Relay Control circuit from the Med/High Rad Fan Relay harness connector to the TIPM C11 harness connector.

Is the resistance below 5.0 ohms?

Yes

- Go To 7

No

- Repair the open in the (N112) Rad Fan Relay Control circuit.
- Perform the POWERTRAIN VERIFICATION TEST.

ARM0600000000365

Fig. 66   Code P0481: Cooling Fan 2 Control Circuit. (Part 3 of 4). 2007–08 Caliber, Avenger Sedan & Sebring Sedan

3. MED/HIGH RAD FAN RELAY

Install the Series/Parallel Rad Fan Relay.
Turn the ignition on, engine not running.
With a scan tool, select Radiator Cooling Fan Relay #2 Control State, Toggle, to actuate the Cooling Fan (Med/High Rad Fan Relay).
Using a 12-volt test light connected to battery voltage, probe the (N112) Rad Fan Relay Control circuit at the Med/High Rad Fan Relay.

Does the test light illuminate brightly and flash on and off?

Yes

- Replace the Med/High Rad Fan Relay.
- Perform the POWERTRAIN VERIFICATION TEST.

No

- Go To 4

4. SERIES/PARALLEL RAD FAN RELAY)

Remove the Series/Parallel Rad Fan Relay.
Install the Med/High Rad Fan Relay.
Turn the ignition on, engine not running.
With a scan tool, select Radiator Cooling Fan Relay #2 Control State, Toggle, to actuate the Cooling Fan (Series/Parallel Rad Fan Relay).
Using a 12-volt test light connected to battery voltage, probe the (N112) Rad Fan Relay Control circuit at the Series/Parallel Rad Fan Relay.

Does the test light illuminate brightly and flash on and off?

Yes

- Replace the Series/Parallel Rad Fan Relay.
- Perform the POWERTRAIN VERIFICATION TEST.

No

- Go To 5

ARM0600000000364

Fig. 66   Code P0481: Cooling Fan 2 Control Circuit. (Part 2 of 4). 2007–08 Caliber, Avenger Sedan & Sebring Sedan

7. (N112) RAD FAN RELAY CONTROL CIRCUIT SHORTED TO GROUND

Measure the resistance between ground and the (N112) Rad Fan Relay Control circuit in the TIPM C11 harness connector.

Is the resistance below 100 ohms?

Yes

- Repair the short to ground in the (N112) Rad Fan Relay Control circuit.
- Perform the POWERTRAIN VERIFICATION TEST.

No

- Replace the Totally Integrated Power Module
- Perform the POWERTRAIN VERIFICATION TEST.

ARM0600000000366

Fig. 66   Code P0481: Cooling Fan 2 Control Circuit. (Part 4 of 4). 2007–08 Caliber, Avenger Sedan & Sebring Sedan

P1489-HIGH SPEED FAN CONTROL RELAY CIRCUIT

When Monitored: With the ignition on. Battery voltage greater than 10.0 volts.

Set Condition: An open or shorted circuit is detected in the radiator fan relay control circuit.

POSSIBLE CAUSES
HIGH SPEED RADIATOR FAN RELAY OPERATION
FUSED IGNITION SWITCH OUTPUT CIRCUIT
HIGH SPEED RADIATOR FAN RELAY RESISTANCE
(C27) HIGH SPEED RADIATOR FAN RELAY CONTROL CIRCUIT OPEN
(C27) HIGH SPEED RADIATOR FAN RELAY CONTROL CIRCUIT SHORT TO GROUND
PCM

TEST	ACTION
1	Turn the ignition on. With the DRBIII®, actuate the High Speed Radiator Fan Relay. Is the High Speed Radiator Fan Relay operating? 　　Yes → Refer to the INTERMITTENT CONDITION symptom in the Driveability category. 　　Perform POWERTRAIN VERIFICATION TEST VER - 5. 　　No → Go To 2
2	Turn the ignition off. Remove the High Speed Radiator Fan Relay from the PDC. Turn the ignition on. Using a 12-volt test light connected to ground, probe the (F12) Fused Ignition Switch Output circuit in the PDC. Did the test light illuminate brightly? 　　Yes → Go To 3 　　No → Repair the Fused Ignition Switch Output circuit. Check and replace any open fuses. 　　Perform POWERTRAIN VERIFICATION TEST VER - 5.

CR1080200351010X

Fig. 67   Code P1489: High Speed Fan Control Relay Circuit (Part 1 of 2). 2004–06 Sebring Convertible, Sebring Sedan & Stratus Sedan

P1490-LOW SPEED FAN CONTROL RELAY CIRCUIT

When Monitored: With the ignition on. Battery voltage greater than 10 volts.

Set Condition: An open or shorted circuit is detected in the radiator fan relay control circuit.

POSSIBLE CAUSES
LOW SPEED RADIATOR FAN RELAY OPERATION
(F12) FUSED IGNITION SWITCH OUTPUT CIRCUIT
LOW SPEED RADIATOR FAN RELAY RESISTANCE
(C24) LOW SPEED RADIATOR FAN RELAY CONTROL CIRCUIT OPEN
(C24) LOW SPEED RADIATOR FAN RELAY CONTROL CIRCUIT SHORT TO GROUND
PCM

TEST	ACTION
1	Turn the ignition on. With the DRBIII®, actuate the Low Speed Radiator Fan Relay. Is the Low Speed Radiator Fan Relay operating? 　　Yes → 　　Perform POWERTRAIN VERIFICATION TEST 　　No → Go To 2
2	Turn the ignition off. Remove the Low Speed Radiator Fan Relay from the PDC. Turn the ignition on. using a 12-volt test light connected to ground, probe the (F12) Fused Ignition Switch Output circuit in the PDC. Did the test light illuminate brightly? 　　Yes → Go To 3 　　No → Repair the (F12) Fused Ignition Switch Output circuit. Check and replace any open fuses.

CR1080200352010X

Fig. 68   Code P1490: Low Speed Fan Control Relay Circuit (Part 1 of 2). 2004–06 Sebring Convertible, Sebring Sedan & Stratus Sedan

TEST	ACTION
3	Turn the ignition off. Remove the High Speed Radiator Fan Relay from the PDC. Measure the resistance of the High Speed Radiator Fan Relay between the Fused Ignition Switch Output terminal and the High Speed Radiator Fan Relay Control terminal. Is the resistance between 60 to 80 ohms? 　　Yes → Go To 4 　　No → Replace the High Speed Radiator Fan Relay.
4	Turn the ignition off. Remove the High Speed Radiator Fan Relay from the PDC. Disconnect the PCM harness connector. Measure the resistance of the (C27) High Speed Radiator Fan Relay Control circuit between the PDC and the PCM harness connector. Is the resistance below 5.0 ohms. 　　Yes → Go To 5 　　No → Repair the open in the (C27) High Speed Radiator Fan Relay Control circuit.
5	Turn the ignition off. Remove the High Speed Radiator Fan Relay from the PDC. Disconnect the PCM harness connector. Measure the resistance between ground and the (C27) High Speed Radiator Fan Relay Control circuit in the PDC. Is the resistance below 5.0 ohms? 　　Yes → Repair the short to ground in the (C27) High Speed Radiator Fan Relay Control circuit. 　　No → Go To 6
6	NOTE: Before Continuing: Disconnect the PCM harness connector and check the related wiring terminals for corrosion, damage or terminal push out. Repair as necessary. Using the schematics as a guide, inspect the wire harness and connectors. Pay particular attention to all Power and Ground circuits. If there are no possible causes remaining, view repair. 　　Repair 　　　Replace and program the Powertrain Control Module in accordance with the Service Information.

CR1080200351020X

Fig. 67   Code P1489: High Speed Fan Control Relay Circuit (Part 2 of 2). 2004–06 Sebring Convertible, Sebring Sedan & Stratus Sedan

TEST	ACTION
3	Turn the ignition off. Remove the Low Speed Radiator Fan Relay from the PDC. Measure the resistance of the Low Speed Radiator Fan Relay between the Fused Ignition Switch Output terminal and the Low Speed Radiator Fan Relay Control terminal. Is the resistance between 60 to 80 ohms? 　　Yes → Go To 4 　　No → Replace the Low Speed Radiator Fan Relay.
4	Turn the ignition off. Remove the Low Speed Radiator Fan Relay from the PDC. Disconnect the PCM harness connector. Measure the resistance of the (C24) Low Speed Radiator Fan Relay Control circuit between the PDC and the PCM harness connector. Is the resistance below 5.0 ohms? 　　Yes → Go To 5 　　No → Repair the open in the (C24) Low Speed Radiator Fan Relay Control circuit.
5	Turn the ignition off. Remove the Low Speed Radiator Fan Relay from the PDC. Disconnect the PCM harness connector. Measure the resistance of the (C24) Low Speed Radiator Fan Relay Control circuit in the PDC to ground. Is the resistance below 100 ohms? 　　Yes → Repair the short to ground in the (C24) Low Speed Radiator Fan Relay Control circuit. 　　No → Go To 6
6	NOTE: Before continuing, check the PCM harness connector terminals for corrosion, damage, or terminal push out. Repair as necessary. Using the schematics as a guide, inspect the wire harness and connectors. Pay particular attention to all Power and Ground circuits. If there are no possible causes remaining, view repair. 　　Repair 　　　Replace and program the Powertrain Control Module in accordance with the Service Information.

CR1080200352020X

Fig. 68   Code P1490: Low Speed Fan Control Relay Circuit (Part 2 of 2). 2004–06 Sebring Convertible, Sebring Sedan & Stratus Sedan

COMPONENT DIAGNOSIS & TESTING

Coolant Temperature Sensor

CONCORDE, INTREPID & 300M

1. Turn ignition switch to OFF position.
2. Disconnect coolant temperature sensor connector.
3. Measure resistance between sensor terminals when engine is at 200°F.
4. If resistance is not 700–1000 ohms, replace sensor.

NEON

1. Ensure ignition is in OFF position and disconnect coolant temperature sensor electrical connector.
2. Measure resistance between sensor terminals. Resistance should be 7–13 kohms.
3. Run engine until coolant temperature reaches approximately 200°F, then measure resistance. Resistance should be 700–1000 ohms.
4. Measure wiring harness resistance between Powertrain Control Module (PCM) terminal No. 28 and coolant sensor harness connector. Resistance should not exceed 1 ohm.
5. Measure wiring harness resistance between PCM terminal No. 51 and coolant sensor harness connector. Resistance should not exceed 1 ohm.
6. If resistance is not as specified, replace coolant sensor or repair wiring harness.

CALIBER, SEBRING CONVERTIBLE, SEBRING SEDAN & STRATUS SEDAN

Refer to appropriate Diagnostic Trouble Code (DTC) in "System Diagnosis & Testing" section for coolant temperature sensor testing.

Fan Control Module

SEBRING COUPE & STRATUS COUPE

1. Disconnect condenser fan motor electrical connector.
2. Start engine and allow it to idle.
3. Turn air conditioning switch on and maintain engine coolant temperature of 176°F, or less.
4. Measure voltage between fan control module side connector terminal, **Fig. 69.**
5. Ensure voltage changes repeatedly as follows:
   a. Zero volts.
   b. 5.6–10.8 volts.
   c. Battery positive voltage ± 2.6 volts.
6. If voltage does not repeatedly change as specified, replace radiator fan motor and control module.

Fig. 69 Fan control module terminal identification. Sebring Coupe & Stratus Coupe

CR1080000296000X

Fan Control Relay

CONCORDE, INTREPID & 300M

Refer to appropriate Diagnostic Trouble Code (DTC) in "System Diagnosis & Testing" section for fan control relay testing.

CROSSFIRE

1. Disconnect radiator fan electrical harness connector at fan motor.
2. Remove radiator cooling fan module retaining bolts.
3. Remove cooling fan module.
4. Reverse procedures to install. **Torque** module retaining bolts to 89 inch lbs.

NEON

NON-TURBO ENGINES

1. Turn ignition switch to ON position.
2. Actuate radiator fan relay using DRBIII, or suitably programmed scan tool.
3. If relay does not actuate, turn ignition switch to OFF position.
4. Disconnect radiator fan harness connector.
5. Measure resistance between ground circuit and fan harness connector to ground. If resistance is less than 5 ohms, proceed to next step. If resistance is not as specified, inspect ground circuit for open.
6. Turn ignition switch to ON position.
7. Actuate radiator fan relay using DRBIII, or suitably programmed scan tool.
8. Measure voltage of relay output circuit in harness connector. If measurement is note more than 11 volts, , proceed to next step. If measurement is more than 11 volts, replace fan motor.
9. Turn ignition switch to OFF position.
10. Remove radiator fan relay from PDC.
11. Probe fused B+ circuit in PDC using suitable 12-volt test light connected to ground. If test light illuminates brightly, proceed to next step. If light does not illuminate, repair fused B+ circuit, then inspect fuses.
12. Measure resistance of relay output circuit between PDC and fan harness connector. If resistance is less than 5 ohms, replace relay. If resistance is not less than 5 ohms, inspect circuit for open.

TURBO ENGINE

Low Speed

1. Turn ignition switch to ON position.
2. Actuate low speed radiator relay using DRBIII, or suitably programmed scan tool.
3. If only fan No. 2 is operating, proceed to next step. If fans are not operating, proceed as follows:
   a. Remove low speed relay No. 1 from PDC.
   b. Probe fused B+ circuit in PDC using suitable 12-volt test light connected to ground. If test light illuminates brightly, proceed to next step. If light does not illuminate, repair fused B+ circuit, then inspect fuses.
   c. Turn ignition switch to OFF position.
   d. Install substitute relay.
   e. Turn ignition switch to ON position.
   f. Actuate low speed radiator relay using DRBIII, or suitably programmed scan tool.
   g. If fan did not operate, proceed to next step. If fan did operate, replace relay.
   h. Turn ignition switch to OFF position.
   i. Disconnect radiator fan No. 1 harness connector.
   j. Measure resistance between fan No. 1 harness connector ground circuit and ground. If resistance is less than 5 ohms, proceed to next step. If resistance in not as specified, inspect for open in ground circuit.
   k. Remove radiator fan replay No. 3 from PDC.
   l. Turn ignition switch to ON position.
   m. Actuate low speed radiator relay No. 1 using DRBIII, or suitably programmed scan tool.
   n. Connect probe to low speed radiator relay output in control relay No. 3 using fused jumper wire.
   o. If radiator fan No. 2 operates, inspect for open between relay No. 3 and fan No. 1 in relay output circuit. If circuit is satisfactory, replace fan assembly.
   p. If radiator fan No. 2 does not operates, inspect for open between relay No. 2 and fan No. 3 in relay output circuit. If circuit is satisfactory, replace fan assembly.
4. Actuate low speed radiator relay No. 1 using DRBIII, or suitably programmed scan tool.
5. Turn ignition switch to ON position.
6. Remove relay control No. 3 from PDC. If fan No. 2 continued to operate, proceed to next step. If fan No. 2 stopped operating, replace relay control No. 3.
7. Turn ignition switch to OFF position.
8. Remove low speed radiator fan relay No. 1 from PDC.
9. Measure resistance between ground and low speed radiator fan relay out circuit at relay No. 1 connect in PDC. If resistance is not less than 5 ohms, proceed to next step. If resistance is 5 ohms, repair short to ground in low speed radiator fan output circuit.

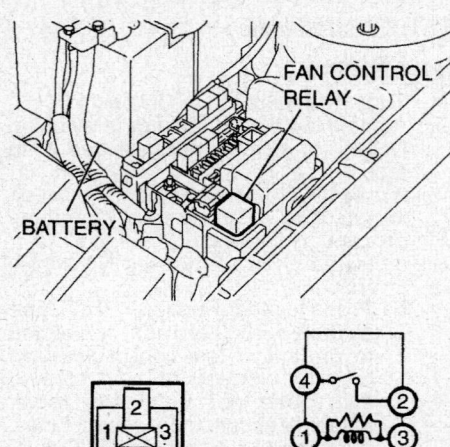

CR1080200348000X

10. Connect all relays and connectors.
11. Turn ignition switch to ON position.
12. Actuate low speed radiator relay using DRBIII, or suitably programmed scan tool.
13. Disconnect radiator fan No. 1 connector. If fan No. 2 still operates, inspect low speed radiator fan output circuit for short to ground. If fan does not operate, replace radiator fan assembly.

High Speed

The low speed fan operation must be inspected first.
1. Turn ignition switch to ON position.
2. Actuate high speed radiator fan relay using DRBIII, or suitably programmed scan tool.
3. If fan No. 1 does not operate, proceed to next step. If fan does operator, proceed as follows:
   a. Acutate low speed radiator fan relay No. 1 using DRBIII, or suitably programmed scan tool.
   b. Fan No. 2 should operate at high speed.
   c. If fan No. 2 does not operate on high speed, inspect radiator fan control relay No. 3 connector in PDC for open ground circuit.
   d. If circuit is satisfactory, replace radiator fan control relay No. 3.
4. Turn ignition switch to OFF position.
5. Disconnect radiator fan No. 1 harness connector.
6. Measure resistance between harness connector ground circuit and ground. If resistance is less than 5 ohms, proceed to next step. If resistance is not as specified, inspect ground circuit for open.
7. Turn ignition switch to ON position.
8. Actuate high speed radiator fan relay No. 2 using DRBIII, or suitably programmed scan tool.
9. Measure voltage of relay output circuit in harness connector. If measurement is not more than 11 volts, proceed to next step. If measurement is more than 11 volts, replace radiator fan assembly.

10. Turn ignition switch to OFF position.
11. Remove high speed radiator fan relay No. 2 from PDC.
12. Probe fused B+ circuit in PDC using suitable 12-volt test light connected to ground. If test light illuminates brightly, proceed to next step. If light does not illuminate, repair fused B+ circuit, then inspect fuses.
13. Remove high speed radiator fan relay from PDC.
14. Disconnect radiator fan No. 1 harness connector.
15. Measure resistance of high speed radiator fan relay output circuit between PDC and fan harness connector. If resistance is less than 5 ohms, replace relay. If resistance is not less than 5 ohms, inspect circuit for open.

CALIBER, SEBRING CONVERTIBLE, SEBRING SEDAN & STRATUS SEDAN

Refer to appropriate Diagnostic Trouble Code (DTC) in "System Diagnosis & Testing" section for fan control relay testing.

SEBRING COUPE & STRATUS COUPE

Refer to **Figs. 70 and 71** for fan control relay location and for continuity inspection.

Radiator Fan Motor

CONCORDE, INTREPID & 300M

Refer to appropriate Diagnostic Trouble Code (DTC) in "System Diagnosis & Testing" section for radiator fan motor testing.

NEON

1. Disconnect fan motor electrical connector.
2. Connect suitable 14 gauge jumper wire between battery positive terminal and fan motor terminal No. 1.
3. If fan motor does not operate normally, inspect circuit between fan motor electrical connector terminal No. 2 and ground.
4. If ground circuit is satisfactory, replace fan motor.

CALIBER, SEBRING CONVERTIBLE, SEBRING SEDAN & STRATUS SEDAN

Refer to appropriate Diagnostic Trouble Code (DTC) in "System Diagnosis & Testing" section for radiator fan motor testing.

COMPONENT REPLACEMENT

Fan Motor

CALIBER

1. Drain cooling system into suitable container below level of upper radiator hose.

TESTER CONNECTION	BATTERY VOLTAGE	SPECIFIED CONDITION
1 – 3	Not applied	Approximately 2 ohms
2 – 4	Not applied	Open circuit
	Applied (Connect "+" to the terminal 1 and "–" to the terminal 3.)	Less than 2 ohms

CR1080200347000X

Fig. 71 Fan control relay continuity inspection. 2004–05 Sebring Coupe & Stratus Coupe

2. Remove radiator core support.
3. Disconnect upper radiator hose from radiator.
4. Remove wiring harness bracket, then disconnect electrical connector.
5. Remove radiator fan assembly mounting screws.
6. Detach radiator fan assembly from retaining clips.
7. Remove fan assembly.
8. Reverse procedure to install.

CHARGER, MAGNUM & 300

1. Partially drain cooling system into suitable container.
2. Remove upper radiator hose and disconnect cooling fan electrical connector.
3. Remove mounting bolts and radiator cooling fan assembly.
4. Reverse procedure to install.

CONCORDE, INTREPID & 300M

1. Disconnect electrical connector, **Fig. 72**.
2. Remove fan module to radiator clips and bolts, **Fig. 72**.
3. Remove fan module from radiator.
4. Bench support motor and motor shaft.
5. Remove fan retaining clip or nut. Remove burrs before removing fans from shaft. **Do not let fan blades touch bench when removing.**
6. Remove mounting bolts and motor from support.
7. Reverse procedure to install, noting the following:
   a. **Torque** lefthand fan motor mounting bolts to 45 inch lbs., and righthand bolts to 25 inch lbs.
   b. **Torque** shroud to radiator mounting bolts to 45 inch lbs.

CROSSFIRE

1. Drain engine coolant into suitable container.
2. Loosen upper coolant hose clamp then, remove hose and position aside.
3. Disconnect radiator fan harness connector at fan motor.
4. Remove radiator fan hold-down clamps.
5. Lift radiator cooling fan assembly upward to remove from vehicle.
6. Reverse procedure to install noting the following:
   a. Lightly lubricate two lower retaining studs with suitable grease.
   b. Lower radiator cooling fan rubber

mounts onto retaining studs.

c. Install radiator fan hold-down clamps.
d. Connect upper coolant hose and tighten clamp.
e. Refill engine coolant, then inspect for leaks.

NEON

1. Drain cooling system to below upper radiator hose level into suitable container.
2. Remove upper hose from radiator.
3. Remove mounting bolts and nuts, then position air cleaner housing aside.
4. Raise and support vehicle.
5. Disconnect Powertrain Control Module (PCM) electrical connectors and remove wiring harness clip from bracket.
6. Remove mounting bolts and PCM with bracket.
7. Disconnect electrical connector from motor.
8. Lower vehicle.
9. Remove radiator upper support mounts.
10. Remove air conditioning line support bracket screw.
11. Remove radiator fan mounting screws.
12. Lift radiator fan assembly up and out of lower shroud clips.
13. Remove in-rush current suppressor

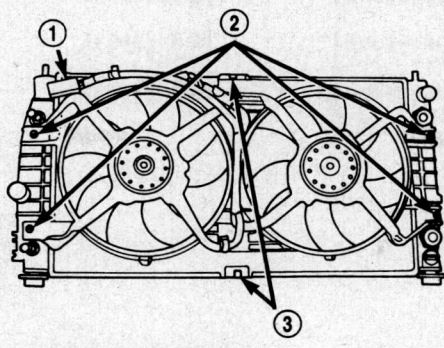

1 – ELECTRICAL CONNECTOR
2 – FASTENERS
3 – CLIPS

CR1080000273000X

Fig. 72   Fan module removal. Concorde, Intrepid & 300M

mounting screw.
14. Remove mounting screws and fan motor.
15. Remove hub mounting nut and fan from motor shaft.
16. Reverse procedure to install.

SEBRING CONVERTIBLE, SEBRING SEDAN & STRATUS SEDAN

1. Remove upper radiator crossmember.

2. Disconnect fan motor electrical connector.
3. Remove fan module to radiator mounting bolts.
4. Remove fan from motor shaft.
5. Remove mounting bolts and motor.
6. Reverse procedure to install. **Torque** mounting bolts to 45 inch lbs.

SEBRING COUPE & STRATUS COUPE

1. Drain cooling system into suitable container.
2. Remove upper radiator hose, **Fig. 73.**
3. Remove mounting bolts and condenser fan motor assembly.
4. Remove mounting bolts and radiator fan motor assembly.
5. Remove mounting nut and fan, then mounting bolts and motor.
6. Reverse procedure to install.

Fan Control Module

CROSSFIRE

1. Disconnect radiator fan control module harness connector.
2. Remove mounting and cooling fan module.
3. Reverse procedure to install.

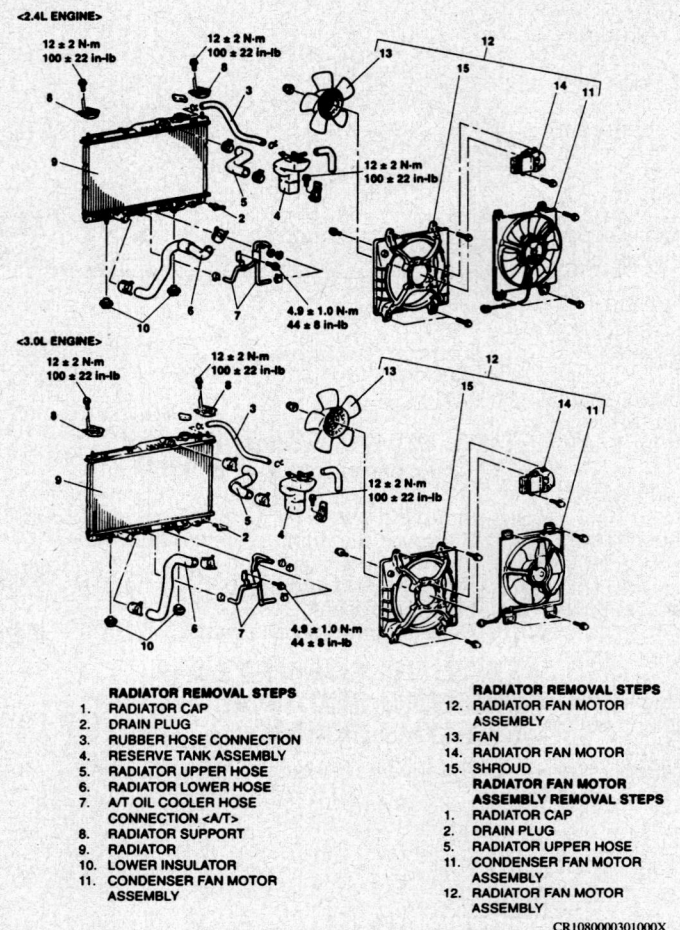

RADIATOR REMOVAL STEPS
1. RADIATOR CAP
2. DRAIN PLUG
3. RUBBER HOSE CONNECTION
4. RESERVE TANK ASSEMBLY
5. RADIATOR UPPER HOSE
6. RADIATOR LOWER HOSE
7. A/T OIL COOLER HOSE CONNECTION <A/T>
8. RADIATOR SUPPORT
9. RADIATOR
10. LOWER INSULATOR
11. CONDENSER FAN MOTOR ASSEMBLY

RADIATOR REMOVAL STEPS
12. RADIATOR FAN MOTOR ASSEMBLY
13. FAN
14. RADIATOR FAN MOTOR
15. SHROUD

RADIATOR FAN MOTOR ASSEMBLY REMOVAL STEPS
1. RADIATOR CAP
2. DRAIN PLUG
5. RADIATOR UPPER HOSE
11. CONDENSER FAN MOTOR ASSEMBLY
12. RADIATOR FAN MOTOR ASSEMBLY

CR1080000301000X

Fig. 73 Radiator fan replacement. Sebring Coupe & Stratus Coupe

STARTER MOTORS

TABLE OF CONTENTS

Page No.
APPLICATION CHART 10-1
BOSCH STARTER MOTORS 10-2
MELCO STARTER MOTORS 10-4

Page No.
MITSUBISHI STARTER MOTORS. 10-5
NIPPONDENSO STARTER
MOTORS 10-8

Application Chart

Model	Year	Engine	Starter Manufacturer	Starter Type
Avenger, Sebring Convertible, Sebring Sedan & Stratus Sedan	2004–08	2.4L	Nippondenso	Gear Reduction
		2.7L	Melco	Direct Drive
		3.5L	Nippondenso	Gear Reduction
Caliber	2007–08	2.0L	Nippondenso	Gear Reduction
		2.4L	Nippondenso	Gear Reduction
Charger, Magnum & 300	2005–08	2.7L	Melco	Direct Drive
		3.5L	Nippondenso	Gear Reduction
		5.7L	Nippondenso	Gear Reduction
Concorde, Intrepid & 300M	2004	2.7L	Melco	Direct Drive
		3.2L	Nippondenso	Gear Reduction
		3.5L	Nippondenso	Gear Reduction
Crossfire	2004–08	3.2L	Nippondenso	Gear Reduction
Neon	2004–05	2.0L & 2.4L	Bosch	Gear Reduction
Sebring Coupe & Stratus Coupe	2004–05	2.4L	Mitsubishi	Gear Reduction
		3.0L	Mitsubishi	Gear Reduction

Bosch Starter Motors

NOTE: On Air Bag Equipped Models, Refer To "Air Bag System Precautions" Located In The Front Of This Manual For System Disarming & Arming Procedures.

NOTE: Refer To "Computer Relearn Procedures" Located In The Front Of This Manual When Battery Power To The Computer Has Been Interrupted.

INDEX

	Page No.		Page No.		Page No.
Description	10-2	In-Vehicle Tests	10-2	Test	10-2
Diagnosis & Testing	10-2	Starter Control Circuit Test	10-2	Starter Feed Circuit Test	10-2
Bench Tests	10-3	Starter Feed Circuit		Starter Specifications	10-3
Starter Solenoid	10-3	Resistance (Voltage Drop)		Troubleshooting	10-2

DESCRIPTION

Bosch starter motor is a permanent magnet starter motor. The fields have six permanent magnets. A planetary gear train transmits power between starter motor and pinion shaft. The starter provides mechanical torque to rotate the crankshaft at an RPM (crank speed) required for self-sustained spark/ignition.

TROUBLESHOOTING

Refer to **Fig. 1** when troubleshooting the starting system.

DIAGNOSIS & TESTING

In-Vehicle Tests

Before starting any tests, ensure the battery is fully charged and all connections are secure.

The following tests will require a suitable volt-ohmmeter tester accurate to .10 volt.

On models equipped with manual transaxle, apply parking brake and depress clutch pedal whenever a test step calls for turning the ignition switch to START position.

STARTER FEED CIRCUIT TEST

1. Connect suitable tester to battery remote terminals following manufacturer's instructions.
2. Disable ignition and fuel systems by disconnecting Automatic Shutdown (ASD) relay in Power Distribution Center (PDC).
3. Ensure all electrical accessories are off, transmission is in Park or Neutral position and parking brake is set.
4. Turn ignition switch to START position.
5. If measurement is 9.6–12.4 volts and amperage draw more than 280 amps, perform test outlined under "Starter Feed Circuit Resistance Test."
6. If measurement is 12.4 volts. or more. and amperage 0–10 amps, perform "Starter Control Circuit Test."

7. After starting system conditions have been corrected, ensure battery is fully charged.
8. If voltage is less than 9.6 volts and amperage draw more than 300 amps, replace starter motor.

STARTER FEED CIRCUIT RESISTANCE (VOLTAGE DROP) TEST

1. Disable ignition and fuel system by disconnecting Automatic Shutdown (ASD) relay in power distribution center.
2. Connect negative lead of a suitable voltmeter to battery ground post and positive lead to battery ground clamp.
3. Turn ignition switch to START position.
4. If voltage is detected, correct poor contact between cable clamp and post.
5. Connect voltmeter positive lead to positive battery terminal and negative lead to battery positive cable clamp.
6. Turn ignition switch to START position.
7. If voltage is detected, correct poor contact between cable clamp and post.
8. Connect voltmeter negative lead to battery ground terminal and positive lead to engine block near battery cable attaching point.
9. Turn ignition switch to START position.
10. If measurement is more than .2 volt, correct poor contact at ground cable attaching point.
11. If measurement is still more than .2 volt, replace ground cable.
12. Remove starter heat shield.
13. Connect positive voltmeter lead to starter motor housing and negative lead to battery ground terminal.
14. Turn ignition switch to START position.
15. If measurement is more than .2 volt, correct poor starter to engine ground.
16. Connect positive voltmeter lead to battery positive terminal and negative lead to battery cable terminal on starter solenoid.
17. Turn ignition switch to START position.
18. If measurement is more than .2 volt correct poor contact at battery cable to solenoid connection.

19. If measurement is still more than .2 volt, replace battery positive cable.
20. If resistance tests do not detect feed circuit failures, replace starter motor.

STARTER CONTROL CIRCUIT TEST

Perform the starter solenoid test before performing the starter relay test.

STARTER SOLENOID TEST

1. Raise and support vehicle.
2. Inspect starter and starter solenoid for corrosion or loose wiring.
3. Lower vehicle and remove starter relay from connector.
4. Connect suitable remote starter switch or jumper wire between battery remote positive post and terminal 87 on starter relay connector.
5. If engine cranks, starter and starter solenoid are operating properly. Perform starter relay test as outlined under "Starter Relay Test."
6. If engine does not crank or solenoid chatters, inspect wiring and connectors from relay to starter for loose or corroded connections.
7. Repeat test and, if engine still does not crank properly, repair or replace starter or starter solenoid.

STARTER RELAY TEST

1. Remove starter relay from power distribution center.
2. With relay in de-energized position, continuity should exist between terminals 87A and 30, but not between terminals 87 and 30.
3. Measure resistance between terminals 85 and 86. Resistance should be 70–80 ohms.
4. Connect battery positive lead to terminal 86 and ground lead to terminal 85. Relay should click.
5. With relay in energized position, continuity should exist between terminals 30 and 87, but not between terminals 87A and 30.
6. If any one inspection failed, replace relay.

CONDITION	POSSIBLE CAUSE	CORRECTION
STARTER FAILS TO ENGAGE.	1. BATTERY DISCHARGED OR FAULTY.	1. REFER TO THE BATTERY SECTION FOR MORE INFORMATION. CHARGE OR REPLACE BATTERY, IF REQUIRED.
	2. STARTING CIRCUIT WIRING FAULTY.	2. REFER TO FEED CIRCUIT RESISTANCE TEST AND FEED CIRCUIT TEST IN THIS SECTION.
	3. STARTER RELAY FAULTY.	3. REFER TO RELAY TEST, IN THIS SECTION. REPLACE RELAY, IF NECESSARY.
	4. IGNITION SWITCH FAULTY.	4. REFER TO IGNITION SWITCH TEST, IN THE STEERING SECTION OR 8 WIRING DIAGRAMS. REPLACE SWITCH, IF NECESSARY.
	5. PARK/NEUTRAL POSITION SWITCH (AUTO TRANS) FAULTY OR MIS-ADJUSTED.	5. REFER PARK/NEUTRAL POSITION SWITCH TEST, IN THE TRANSAXLE. SECTION FOR MORE INFORMATION. REPLACE SWITCH, IF NECESSARY.
	6. CLUTCH INTERLOCK SWITCH (MAN TRANS) FAULTY.	6. REFER TO CLUTCH PEDAL POSITION SWITCH TEST, IN THE CLUTCH. SECTION. REPLACE SWITCH, IF NECESSARY.
	7. STARTER SOLENOID FAULTY.	7. REFER TO SOLENOID TEST, IN THIS SECTION. REPLACE STARTER ASSEMBLY, IF NECESSARY.
	8. STARTER ASSEMBLY FAULTY.	8. IF ALL OTHER STARTING SYSTEM COMPONENTS AND CIRCUITS CHECK OK, REPLACE STARTER ASSEMBLY.
	9. FAULTY TEETH ON RING GEAR.	9. ROTATE FLYWHEEL 360°, AND INSPECT TEETH AND RING GEAR REPLACED IF DAMAGED.
	10. PCM DOUBLE START OVERRIDE OUTPUT FAILURE.	10. REFER TO PCM DIAGNOSTIC. CHECK FOR CONTINUITY BETWEEN PCM AND TERMINAL 85. REPAIR OPEN CIRCUIT AS REQUIRED. IF OK, PCM MAY BE DEFECTIVE.
STARTER ENGAGES, FAILS TO TURN ENGINE.	1. BATTERY DISCHARGED OR FAULTY.	1. REFER TO THE BATTERY SECTION FOR MORE INFORMATION. CHARGE OR REPLACE BATTERY AS NECESSARY.

CR1120200465010X

Fig. 1 Starting system troubleshooting (Part 1 of 2)

IGNITION SWITCH TEST

After testing starter solenoid and relay, test ignition switch and wiring. Inspect all wiring for opens and shorts and all connectors for looseness or corrosion.

CONDITION	POSSIBLE CAUSE	CORRECTION
	2. STARTING CIRCUIT WIRING FAULTY.	2. REFER TO THE FEED CIRCUIT RESISTANCE TEST AND THE FEED CIRCUIT TEST IN THIS SECTION. REPAIR AS NECESSARY.
	3. STARTER ASSEMBLY FAULTY.	3. IF ALL OTHER STARTING SYSTEM COMPONENTS AND CIRCUITS CHECK OK, REPLACE STARTER ASSEMBLY.
	4. ENGINE SEIZED.	4. REFER TO THE ENGINE SECTION, FOR DIAGNOSTIC AND SERVICE PROCEDURES.
	5. LOOSE CONNECTION AT BATTERY, PDC, STARTER, OR ENGINE GROUND.	5. INSPECT FOR LOOSE CONNECTIONS.
	6. FAULTY TEETH ON RING GEAR.	6. ROTATE FLYWHEEL 360°, AND INSPECT TEETH AND RING GEAR REPLACED IF DAMAGED.
STARTER ENGAGES, SPINS OUT BEFORE ENGINE STARTS.	1. BROKEN TEETH ON STARTER RING GEAR.	1. REMOVE STARTER. INSPECT RING GEAR AND REPLACE IF NECESSARY.
	2. STARTER ASSEMBLY FAULTY.	2. IF ALL OTHER STARTING SYSTEM COMPONENTS AND CIRCUITS CHECK OK, REPLACE STARTER ASSEMBLY.
STARTER DOES NOT DISENGAGE.	1. STARTER IMPROPERLY INSTALLED.	1. INSTALL STARTER. TIGHTEN STARTER MOUNTING HARDWARE TO CORRECT TORQUE SPECIFICATIONS.
	2. STARTER RELAY FAULTY.	2. REFER TO RELAY TEST, IN THIS SECTION. REPLACE RELAY, IF NECESSARY.
	3. IGNITION SWITCH FAULTY.	3. REFER TO IGNITION SWITCH TEST, IN THE STEERING SECTION. REPLACE SWITCH, IF NECESSARY.
	4. STARTER ASSEMBLY FAULTY.	4. IF ALL OTHER STARTING SYSTEM COMPONENTS AND CIRCUITS CHECK OK, REPLACE STARTER ASSEMBLY.
	5. FAULTY TEETH ON RING GEAR.	5. ROTATE FLYWHEEL 360°, AND INSPECT TEETH AND RING GEAR REPLACED IF DAMAGED.

CR1120200465020X

Fig. 1 Starting system troubleshooting (Part 2 of 2)

Bench Tests

STARTER SOLENOID

1. Disconnect field coil wire from field coil terminal.
2. Inspect for continuity between solenoid terminal and field coil terminal. Continuity should exist.
3. Inspect for continuity between solenoid terminal and solenoid housing. Continuity should exist.
4. If continuity does not exist in either test, replace solenoid.

STARTER SPECIFICATIONS

Year	Free Speed Test			Minimum RPM	Cranking Amp Draw Test
	Power Rating, KW	Max. Amps	Volts		
2004–08	1.1	—	12	—	150–280

Melco Starter Motors

NOTE: On Air Bag Equipped Models, Refer To "Air Bag System Precautions" Located In The Front Of This Manual For System Disarming & Arming Procedures.

NOTE: Refer To "Computer Relearn Procedures" Located In The Front Of This Manual When Battery Power To The Computer Has Been Interrupted.

INDEX

	Page No.		Page No.		Page No.
Description	10-4	Diagnosis & Testing	10-4	Starter Specifications	10-4

DESCRIPTION

Melco starter is direct drive, **Fig. 1.** They have an overrunning clutch starter drive and a solenoid switch mounted on the starter motor.

DIAGNOSIS & TESTING

Refer to the "Nippondenso Starter Motors" section for Melco starter diagnosis and testing procedures.

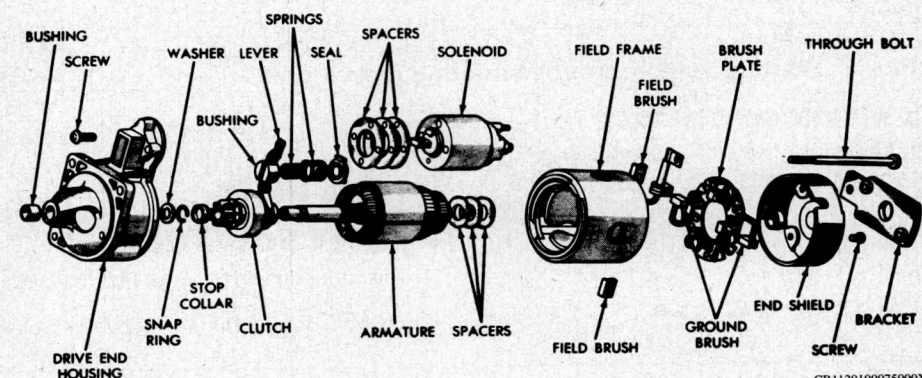

Fig. 1 Exploded view of direct drive starter

STARTER SPECIFICATIONS

Engine	Free Speed Test		Cranking Amp Draw Test
	Power Rating, KW	Volts	
2.7L	1.4	12	150–280

Mitsubishi Starter Motors

NOTE: On Air Bag Equipped Models, Refer To "Air Bag System Precautions" Located In The Front Of This Manual For System Disarming & Arming Procedures.

NOTE: Refer To "Computer Relearn Procedures" Located In The Front Of This Manual When Battery Power To The Computer Has Been Interrupted.

INDEX

	Page No.
Description	10-5
Diagnosis & Testing	10-5
Free Running Test	10-6
Magnetic Switch Hold-In Test	10-5
Magnetic Switch Pull-In Test	10-5

	Page No.
Magnetic Switch Return Test	10-6
Starter Relay Test	10-5
Theft Alarm Starter Relay Test	10-6
Starter Specifications	10-7
Troubleshooting	10-5

	Page No.
Starter Does Not Stop	10-5
Starter Motor Does Not Operate	10-5

DESCRIPTION

Mitsubishi starter is a gear reduction type utilizing a planetary gear assembly to obtain higher rotational speeds with the same torque output, **Fig. 1.**

TROUBLESHOOTING

Starter Motor Does Not Operate

1. Inspect starter coil.
2. Inspect for poor contact at battery terminals and starter.
3. **On models equipped with automatic transaxle,** inspect transmission range switch.
4. **On models equipped with manual transaxle,** inspect starter relay and interlock switch.

Starter Does Not Stop

Inspect the starter magnetic switch.

DIAGNOSIS & TESTING

Starter Relay Test

Refer to **Figs. 2 through 4** for starter relay continuity tests.

Magnetic Switch Pull-In Test

1. Disconnect field coil wire from M terminal, **Figs. 5 and 6.**
2. Connect 12-volt battery between terminals S and M. **This test must be performed in less than 10 seconds to prevent coil from burning.**
3. If pinion moves out, pull-in coil is satisfactory.

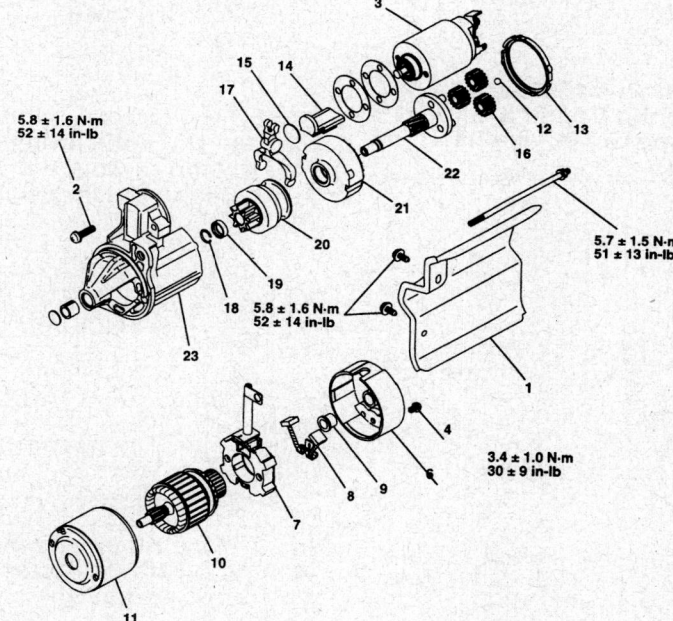

5.8 ± 1.6 N·m
52 ± 14 in-lb

5.7 ± 1.5 N·m
51 ± 13 in-lb

5.8 ± 1.6 N·m
52 ± 14 in-lb

3.4 ± 1.0 N·m
30 ± 9 in-lb

1. COVER	10. ARMATURE
2. SCREW	11. YOKE ASSEMBLY
3. MAGNETIC SWITCH	12. BALL
4. SCREW	13. PACKING A
5. SCREW	14. PACKING B
6. REAR BRACKET	15. PLATE
7. BRUSH HOLDER	16. PLANETARY GEAR
8. BRUSH	17. LEVER
9. REAR BEARING	18. SNAP RING
	19. STOP RING

CR1120000401000X

Fig. 1 Exploded view of Mitsubishi gear reduction starter

4. If pinion does not move out, replace magnetic switch.

Magnetic Switch Hold-In Test

1. Disconnect field coil wire from terminal M of switch, **Figs. 7 and 8.**
2. Connect 12-volt battery between terminal S and starter body. **This test must be performed in less than 10 seconds to prevent coil from burning.**
3. Pull out pinion by hand until it hits stopper.

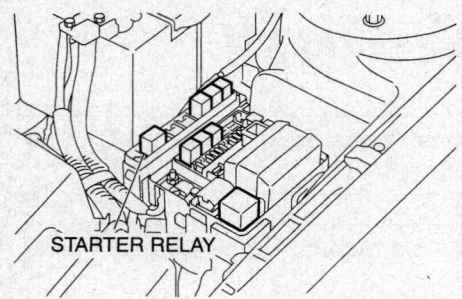

Fig. 2 Starter relay location. Sebring Coupe & Stratus Coupe

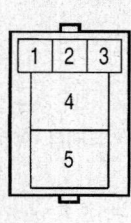
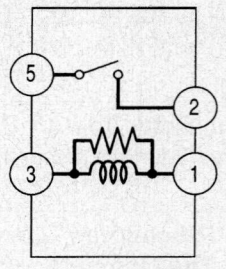

Fig. 3 Starter relay terminal identification. Sebring Coupe & Stratus Coupe

BATTERY VOLTAGE	TERMINAL NO. TO BE CONNECTED TO BATTERY	TERMINAL NO. TO PERFORM CONTINUITYTEST
Not applied	2 – 5	Open circuit
1 – Battery (–) terminal 3 – Battery (+) terminal	2 – 5	Less than 2 ohm

Fig. 4 Starter relay test. Sebring Coupe & Stratus Coupe

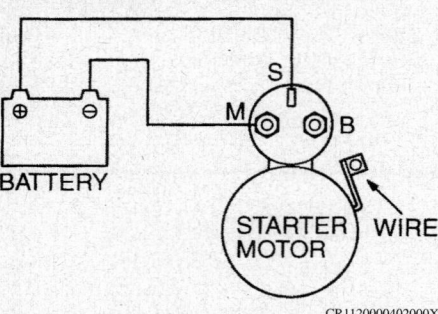

Fig. 5 Magnetic switch pull-in test. Sebring Coupe & Stratus Coupe w/2.4L engine

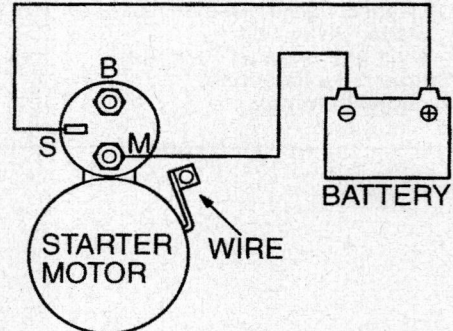

Fig. 6 Magnetic switch pull-in test. Sebring Coupe & Stratus Coupe w/3.0L engine

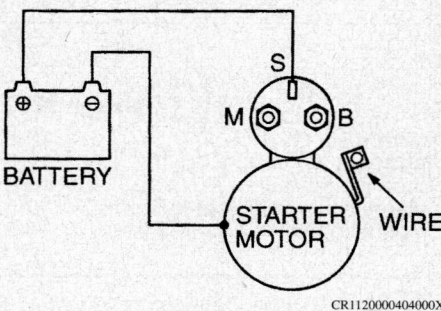

Fig. 7 Magnetic switch hold-in test. Sebring Coupe & Stratus Coupe w/2.4L engine

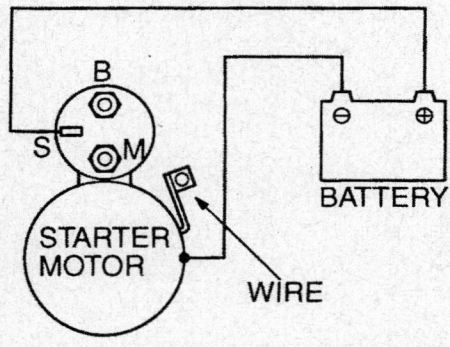

Fig. 8 Magnetic switch hold-in test. Sebring Coupe & Stratus Coupe w/3.0L engine

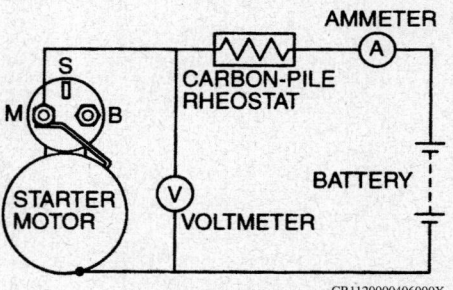

Fig. 9 Free running test. Sebring Coupe & Stratus Coupe w/2.4L engine

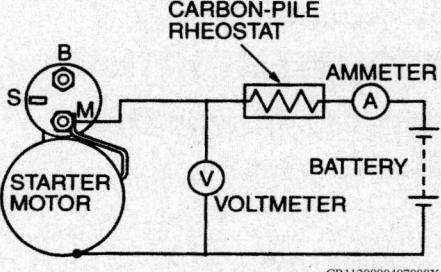

Fig. 10 Free running test. Sebring Coupe & Stratus Coupe w/3.0L engine

4. If pinion remains out, switch is operating properly.
5. If pinion moves in, hold-in circuit is open. Replace magnetic switch.

Free Running Test

1. Place starter motor assembly in suitable soft-jawed vise.
2. Connect suitable 100-amp scale test voltmeter and carbon pile rheostat in series with positive post of fully charged battery and starter motor terminal, **Figs. 9 and 10.**
3. Connect suitable 15-volt scale voltmeter across starter motor.
4. Rotate carbon pile to full resistance position.

5. Connect battery ground cable to starter body.
6. Adjust rheostat until battery voltage outlined by voltmeter matches voltage listed under "Starter Specifications."
7. Confirm amperage is as specified and starter motor turns smoothly and freely.

Magnetic Switch Return Test

1. Disconnect field coil wire from terminal M from magnetic switch, **Figs. 11 and 12.**

2. Connect 12-volt battery between terminals M and starter body. **This test must be performed in less than 10 seconds to prevent coil from burning.**
3. Pull pinion out and release.
4. If pinion quickly returns to original position, switch is operating properly.
5. If pinion does not quickly return to original position, replace magnetic switch.

Theft Alarm Starter Relay Test

Refer to **Figs. 13 through 16** for theft alarm starter relay continuity tests.

CR1120000408000X

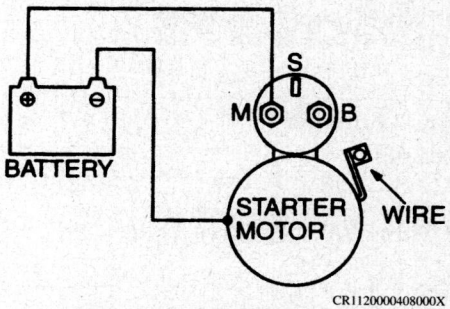

Fig. 11 Magnetic switch return test. Sebring Coupe & Stratus Coupe w/2.4L engine

CR1120000409000X

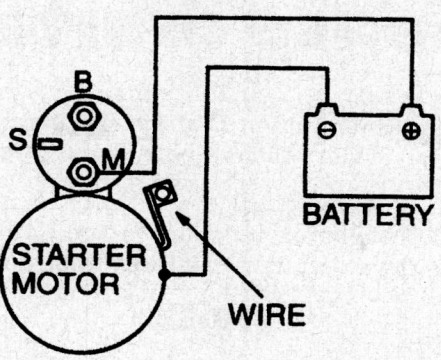

Fig. 12 Magnetic switch return test. Sebring Coupe & Stratus Coupe w/3.0L engine

Battery voltage	Terminal 1	2	3	5
Not applied	O————		————O	
Applied	⊖ - - - -		- - - - ⊕	
		O————	——	————O

NOTE
O—O indicates that there is continuity between the terminals.
⊕- -⊖ indicates terminals to which battery voltage is applied.

CR1129500201000X

Fig. 14 Theft alarm starter relay test. Manual transaxle

CR1129500199000X

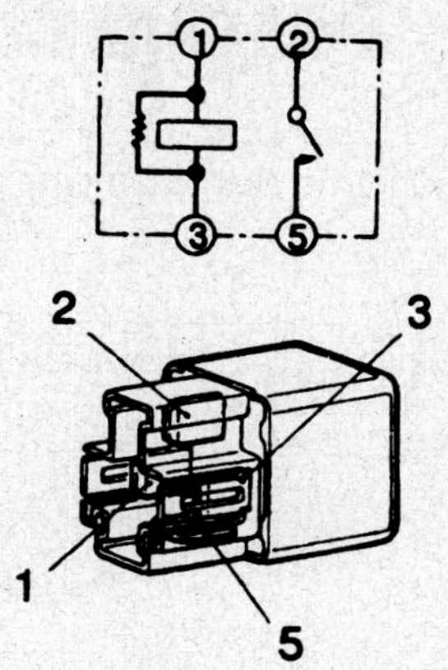

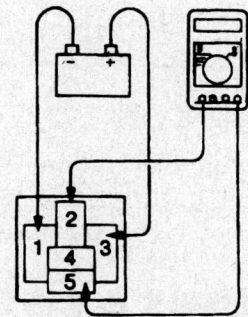

Fig. 13 Theft alarm starter relay terminal identification. Manual transaxle

CR1129500200000X

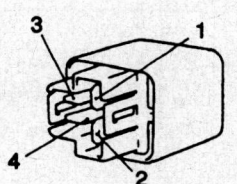

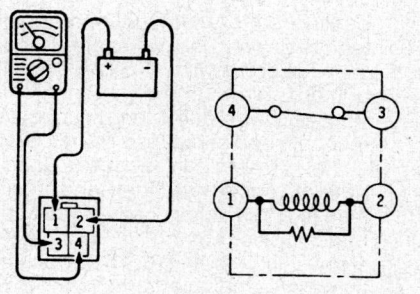

Fig. 15 Theft alarm starter relay terminal identification. Automatic transaxle

Battery voltage	Terminal 1	2	3	4
Not applied	O——	——O	O——	——O
Applied	⊕- - -	- - -⊖		

NOTE
O—O indicates that there is continuity between the terminals.
⊕- -⊖ indicates terminals to which battery voltage is applied.

CR1129500202000X

Fig. 16 Theft alarm starter relay test. Automatic transaxle

STARTER SPECIFICATIONS

Engine	Rated Output, kW/V	Free Speed Test			Pinion Gap, Inch	Commutator				Undercut Depth, Inch	
		Terminal Voltage	Currant, Amps	Speed, RPM		Run-Out, Inch		Diameter, Inch		Standard	Limit
						Standard	Limit	Standard	Limit		
2.4L	1.33	11	90	2400	.02–.07	.002	.004	1.16	1.13	.02	.008
3.0L	1.17	11	90	2800	.02–.07	.002	.004	1.16	1.13	.02	.008

Nippondenso Starter Motors

NOTE: On Air Bag Equipped Models, Refer To "Air Bag System Precautions" Located In The Front Of This Manual For System Disarming & Arming Procedures.

NOTE: Refer To "Computer Relearn Procedures" Located In The Front Of This Manual When Battery Power To The Computer Has Been Interrupted.

INDEX

	Page No.		Page No.		Page No.
Description	10-8	In-Vehicle Tests	10-8	Test	10-8
Diagnosis & Testing	10-8	Starter Control Circuit Test	10-8	Starter Feed Circuit Test	10-8
Bench Testing	10-9	Starter Feed Circuit		Starter Specifications	10-10
Starter Solenoid	10-9	Resistance (Voltage Drop)			

DESCRIPTION

Nippondenso starters are gear reduction types, **Fig. 1.** The structure of the gear reduction type starter differs from that of the direct drive type, but the electrical wiring is the same for both types.

DIAGNOSIS & TESTING

The following tests will require a voltmeter accurate to .10 volt.

Before starting any tests, ensure the battery is fully charged and that all connections are good. Disconnect ignition coils electrical connectors. Disconnect Automatic Shutdown (ASD) relay in Power Distribution Center (PDC).

On models equipped with manual transaxle, apply parking brake and depress clutch pedal whenever test step calls for turning the ignition switch to START position.

In-Vehicle Tests

STARTER FEED CIRCUIT TEST

1. Connect tester to battery terminals following manufacturer's instructions.
2. Ensure all electrical accessories are off, transmission is in Park or Neutral and parking brake is set.
3. Turn ignition switch to START position.
4. If measurement is more than 9.6 volts and amperage draw more than 280 amps, inspect for engine seizure or faulty starter.
5. If measurement is 12.4 volts, or more, and amperage is 0–10 amps, inspect and correct corroded cables and poor connections.
6. If measurement is less than 9.6 volts and amperage more than 300 amps, replace starter motor.

STARTER FEED CIRCUIT RESISTANCE (VOLTAGE DROP) TEST

1. Connect voltmeter negative lead to battery ground post and positive lead to battery ground clamp.
2. Turn ignition switch to START position.
3. If voltage is detected, correct poor contact between cable clamp and post.
4. Connect voltmeter positive lead to positive battery terminal and negative lead to battery positive cable clamp.
5. Turn ignition switch to START position and observe voltmeter.
6. If voltage is detected, correct poor contact between cable clamp and post.
7. Connect voltmeter negative lead to battery ground terminal, and positive lead to engine block near battery cable attaching point.
8. Turn ignition switch to START position.
9. If measurement is more than .2 volt, correct poor contact at ground cable attaching point.
10. If voltage reading is still more than .2 volt after correcting poor contacts, replace ground cable.
11. Remove starter heat shield if required.
12. Connect positive voltmeter lead to starter motor housing and negative lead to battery ground terminal.
13. Turn ignition switch to START position.
14. If measurement is more than .2 volt, correct poor starter to engine ground.
15. Connect positive voltmeter lead to battery positive terminal, and negative lead to battery cable terminal on starter solenoid.
16. Turn ignition switch to START position.
17. If measurement is more than .2 volt correct poor contact at battery cable to solenoid connection.

18. If reading is still more than .2 volt after correcting poor contacts, replace battery positive cable.
19. If resistance tests do not detect feed circuit failures, replace starter motor.

STARTER CONTROL CIRCUIT TEST

The starter control circuit consists of the starter solenoid, starter relay, ignition switch, neutral safety switch and all related wiring and connections.

On models equipped with manual transaxle, apply parking brake and depress clutch pedal whenever a test step calls for turning the ignition switch to START position.

STARTER RELAY TEST

1. Disconnect Automatic Shutdown (ASD) relay in Power Distribution Center (PDC).
2. Remove starter relay from power distribution center.
3. With relay in de-energized position, continuity should exist between terminals 87A and 30, but not between terminals 87 and 30.
4. Measure resistance between terminals 85 and 86, which should be 70–80 ohms.
5. Connect battery positive lead to terminal 86 and ground lead to terminal 85. Relay should click.
6. With relay in energized position, continuity should exist between terminals 30 and 87, but not between terminals 87A and 30.
7. If any one inspection failed, replace relay.

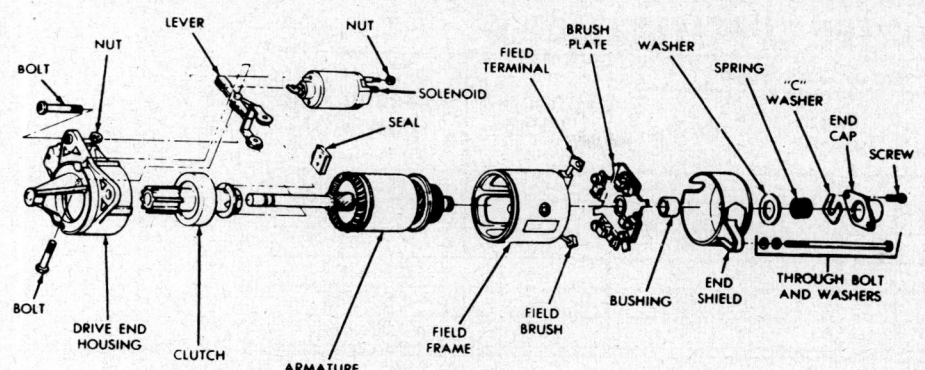

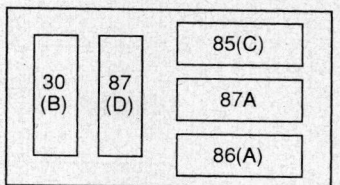

Fig. 1 Exploded view of Nippondenso gear reduction starter

STARTER SOLENOID TEST

1. Disconnect Automatic Shutdown (ASD) relay in Power Distribution Center (PDC).
2. Ensure battery is fully charged and in good condition.
3. Raise and support vehicle.
4. Inspect starter and starter solenoid for corrosion or loose wiring.
5. Lower vehicle.
6. Remove starter relay from connector.
7. Connect suitable remote starter switch or jumper wire between battery positive post and terminal 87, **Fig. 2**.
8. If engine cranks, starter and starter solenoid are operating properly.
9. Perform starter relay test as outlined under "Starter Control Circuit Test."
10. If engine does not crank or solenoid chatters, inspect wiring and connectors from relay to starter for loose or corroded connections.
11. Repeat test and, if engine still does not crank properly, repair or replace starter or starter solenoid as required.

IGNITION SWITCH TEST

After testing starter solenoid and relay,

Starter Relay Pinout

CAV	COLOR	FUNCTION
30 (B)	RD	B (+)
85 (C)	TN	P/N POSITION SW. SENSE (AUTO)
86 (A)	YL	IGNITION SWITCH OUTPUT
87 (D)	LG	STARTER RELAY OUTPUT

CR1129100065000X

Fig. 2 Starter relay terminal identification

test ignition switch and wiring. Inspect all wiring for opens or shorts and all connectors for looseness or corrosion.

Bench Testing

STARTER SOLENOID

Refer to "Bench Tests" in the "Bosch Starter Motors" section.

STARTER SPECIFICATIONS

Engine	Free Speed Test			Minimum RPM	Cranking Amp Draw Test
	Power Rating, KW	Max. Amps	Volts		
2.0L	1.2	—	12	—	150–280
2.4L	1.4	—	12	—	150–280
2.7L	1.4	—	12	—	150–280
3.2L	1.4	—	12	—	150–280
3.5L	1.4	—	12	—	150–280
5.7L	2.4	73	11	3601	125–250

ALTERNATORS

NOTE: On Air Bag Equipped Models, Refer To "Air Bag System Precautions" Located In The Front of This Manual For System Disarming & Arming Procedures.

NOTE: Refer To "Computer Relearn Procedure" Located In The Front of This Manual When Battery Power To The Computer Has Been Interrupted.

NOTE: "Electrical Symbol & Wire Color Code Identification" Located In The Front of This Manual May Be Used As An Aid When Using Wiring Circuits Found In This Section.

TABLE OF CONTENTS

	Page No.		Page No.
APPLICATION CHART	11-1	**MITSUBISHI**	11-26
BOSCH	11-2	**NIPPONDENSO**	11-3
MELCO	11-17		

Application Chart

Model	Year	Type
Avenger, Sebring Convertible & Sebring Sedan & Stratus Sedan	2004–06	Nippondenso
	2007–08	Melco
Caliber	2007–08	Melco
Charger, Magnum & 300	2005–08	Nippondenso
Concorde, Intrepid & 300M	2004	Nippondenso
Crossfire	2004–08	Bosch
Neon	2004–05	Mitsubishi
Sebring Coupe & Stratus Coupe	2004–05	Mitsubishi

Bosch

INDEX

	Page No.		Page No.		Page No.
Alternator Specifications	11-2	Diagnosis & Testing	11-2	Precautions	11-2
Description	11-2	Wiring Diagrams	11-2	Battery Ground Cable	11-2

PRECAUTIONS

Battery Ground Cable

Prior to service, disconnect battery ground cable and isolate as required.

DESCRIPTION

The alternator is belt-driven by the engine using a serpentine type accessory drive belt. It is serviced only as a complete assembly. If the alternator fails for any reason, the entire assembly must be replaced. The only component that is replaceable is the voltage regulator.

DIAGNOSIS & TESTING

Wiring Diagrams

Refer to **Fig. 1** for wiring diagrams.

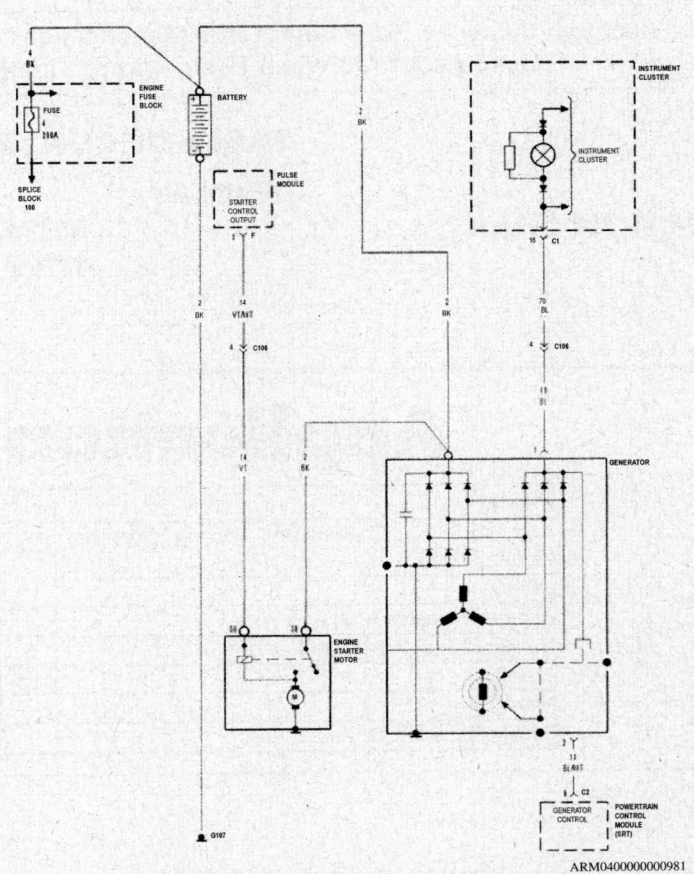

Fig. 1   Wiring diagram. Crossfire

ALTERNATOR SPECIFICATIONS

Model & Year	Engine	No.	Rated Output Amps
Crossfire	3.2L	05097756AA	120

Nippondenso

INDEX

	Page No.
Alternator Specifications	11-17
Application Chart	11-3
Description	11-3
Diagnosis & Testing	11-3
Diagnostic Tests	11-3
Charger, Magnum & 300	11-3
Concorde, Intrepid & 300M	11-3

	Page No.
Sebring Convertible, Sebring Sedan & Stratus Sedan	11-3
Wiring Diagrams	11-3
Charger, Magnum & 300	11-3
Concorde, Intrepid & 300M	11-3
Sebring Convertible, Sebring Sedan & Stratus Sedan	11-3

	Page No.
Diagnostic Chart Index	11-5
General Information	11-3
Diode Rectifiers	11-3
Precautions	11-3
Battery Ground Cable	11-3

APPLICATION CHART

Model	Engine	Type
Charger, Magnum & 300	2.7L, 3.5L, 5.7L & 6.1L	Nippondenso
Concorde, Intrepid & 300M	2.7L	Nippondenso
	3.2L & 3.5L	Nippondenso
Sebring Convertible & Sedan & Stratus Sedan	2.4L & 2.7L	Nippondenso

PRECAUTIONS

Battery Ground Cable

Prior to service, disconnect battery ground cable and isolate as required.

GENERAL INFORMATION

The power source of the charging system is the alternator. Current is transmitted from the field terminal of the regulator through a slip ring to the field coil and back to ground through another slip ring. The strength of the field regulates the output of the alternating current. This alternating current is then transmitted from the alternator to the rectifier where it is converted to direct current.

These alternators employ a three-phase stator winding in which the phase windings are electrically 120° apart. The rotor consists of a field coil encased between interleaved sections producing a magnetic field with alternate north and south poles. By rotating the rotor inside the stator, the alternating current is induced in the stator windings. This alternating current is rectified (changed to DC) by silicon diodes and sent to the output terminal of the alternator.

Diode Rectifiers

Six or more silicon diode rectifiers are used and act as electrical one-way valves.

One half of the diodes have ground polarity and are pressed or screwed into a heat sink which is grounded. The other diodes (ungrounded) are pressed or screwed into and insulated from the end head. These diodes are connected to the alternator output terminal.

Since the diodes have a high resistance to the flow of current in one direction and a low resistance in the opposite direction, they may be connected in a manner which allows current to flow from the alternator to the battery in the low resistance direction. The high resistance in the opposite direction prevents the flow of current from the battery to the alternator. Because of this feature no circuit breaker is required between the alternator and battery.

DESCRIPTION

The main components of the alternator are the rotor, stator, rectifier, end shields and drive pulley. Direct current is available at the output B terminal.

Alternator output is controlled by voltage regulator circuitry contained within the power and logic modules of the engine controller.

DIAGNOSIS & TESTING

Wiring Diagrams

CONCORDE, INTREPID & 300M

Refer to **Fig. 1** for wiring diagrams.

CHARGER, MAGNUM & 300

Refer to **Fig. 2** for wiring diagrams.

SEBRING CONVERTIBLE, SEBRING SEDAN & STRATUS SEDAN

Refer to **Figs. 3 and 4** for wiring diagrams.

Diagnostic Tests

CHARGER, MAGNUM & 300

Refer to **Figs. 5 through 8** for diagnostic tests.

CONCORDE, INTREPID & 300M

Refer to **Figs. 9 through 13** for diagnostic tests.

SEBRING CONVERTIBLE, SEBRING SEDAN & STRATUS SEDAN

Refer to **Figs. 14 through 20** for diagnostic tests.

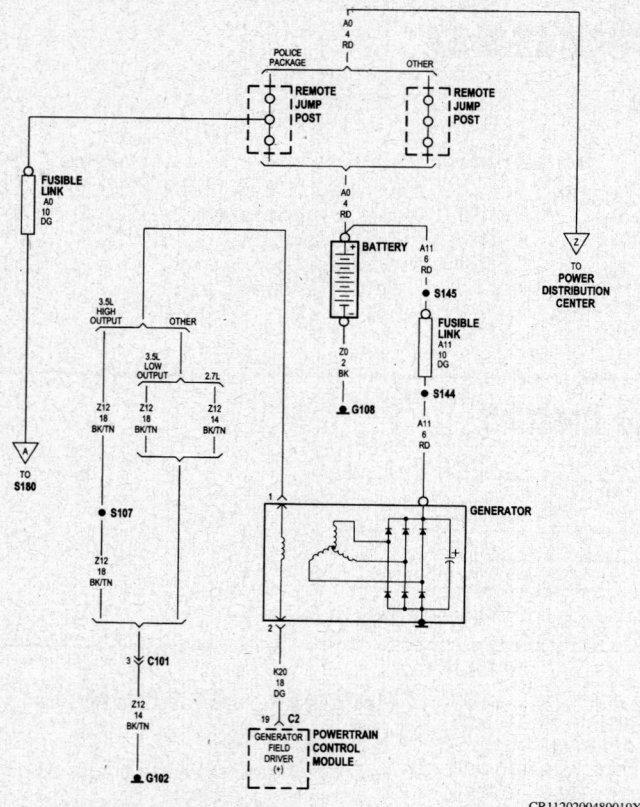

Fig. 1 Wiring diagram (Part 1 of 3). Concorde, Intrepid & 300M

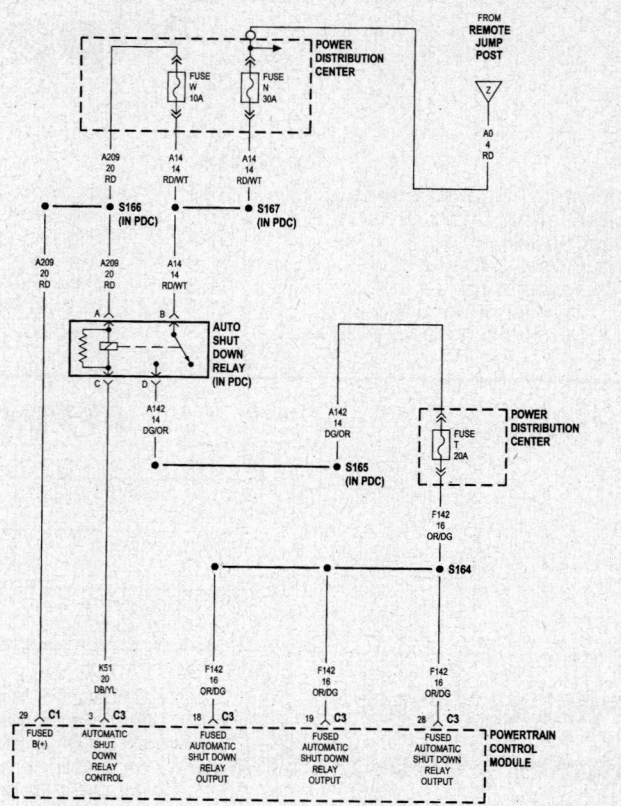

Fig. 1 Wiring diagram (Part 2 of 3). Concorde, Intrepid & 300M

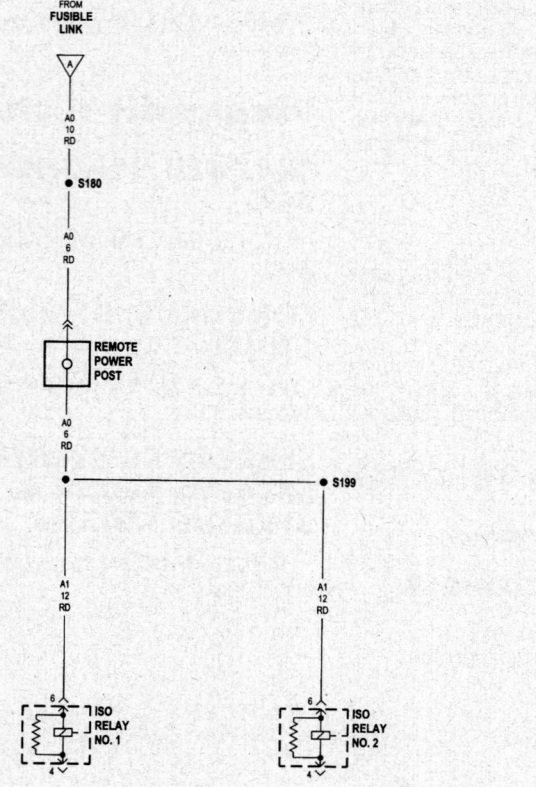

Fig. 1 Wiring diagram (Part 3 of 3). Concorde, Intrepid & 300M w/police package

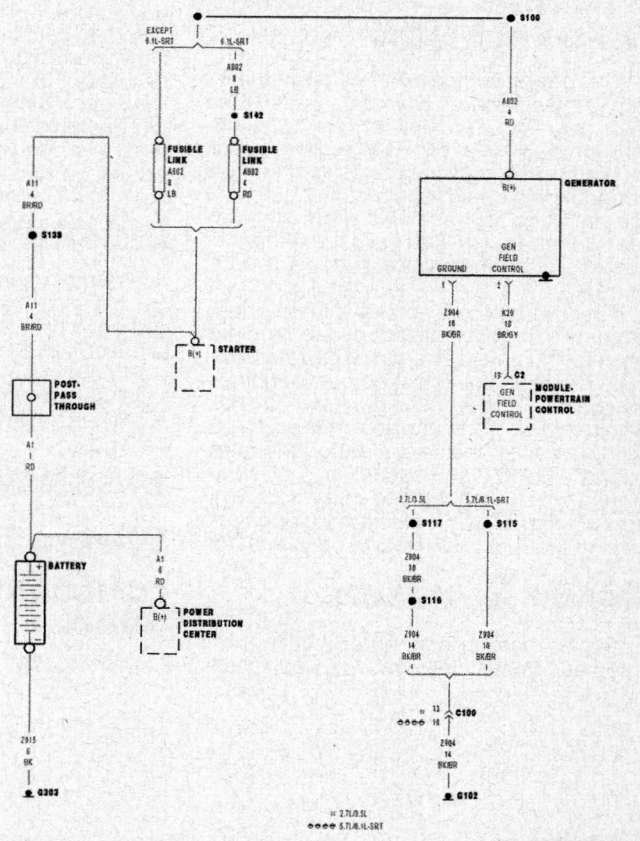

Fig. 2 Wiring diagram. Charger, Magnum & 300

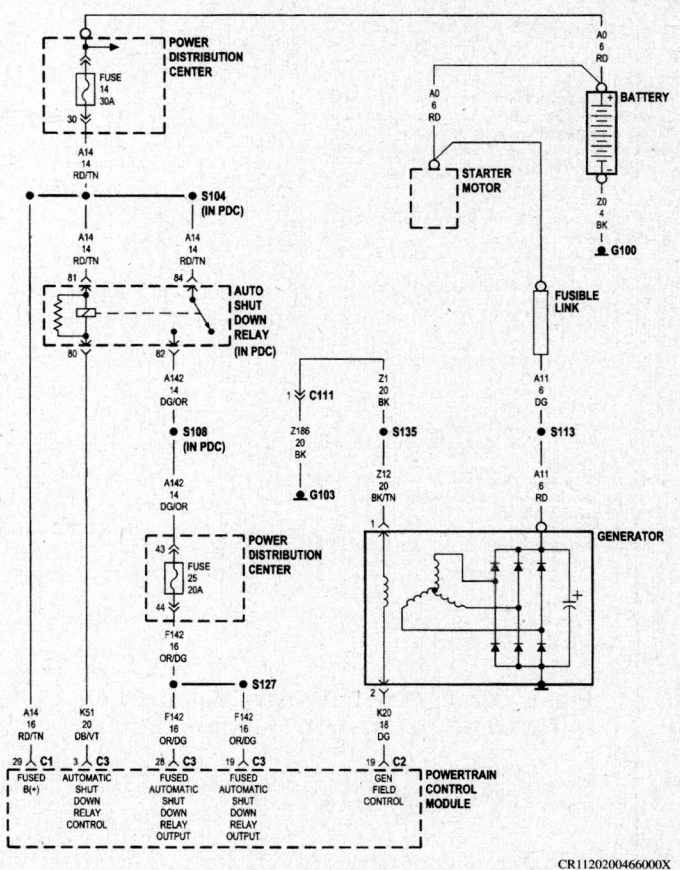

Fig. 3 Wiring diagram. Sebring Convertible, Sebring Sedan & Stratus Sedan w/2.4L engine

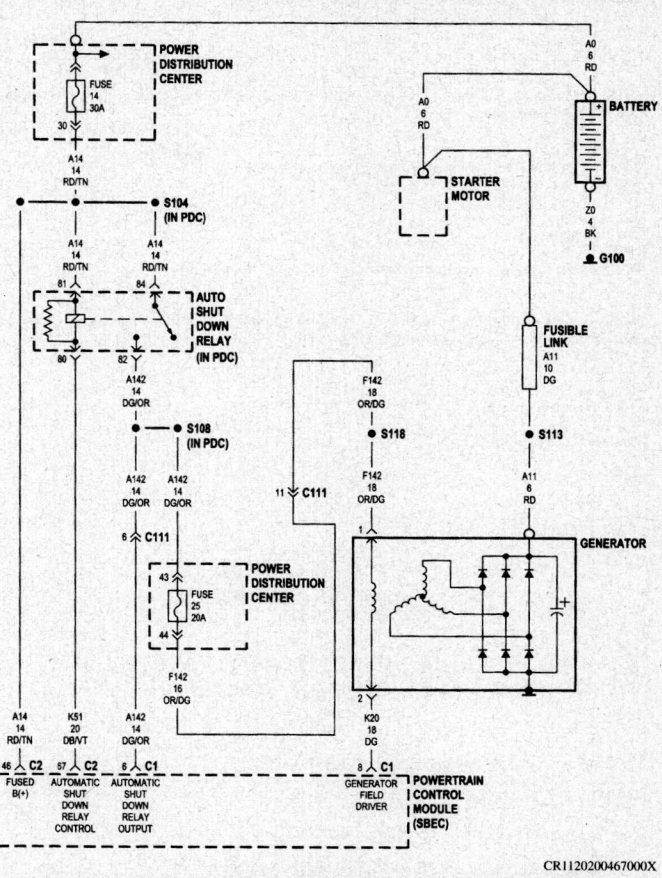

Fig. 4 Wiring diagram. Sebring Convertible, Sebring Sedan & Stratus Sedan w/2.7L engine

DIAGNOSTIC CHART INDEX

Code/Test	Description	Page No.	Fig. No.
CHARGER, MAGNUM & 300			
P0562	Battery Voltage Low	11-6	5
P0563	Battery Voltage High	11-7	6
P0622	Alternator Field Control Circuit	11-8	7
P2503	Charging System Output Low	11-9	8
CONCORDE, INTREPID & 300M			
—	Verification Test VER-3	11-13	13
P0562	Battery Voltage Low	11-10	9
P0563	Battery Voltage High	11-11	10
P0622	Alternator Field Control Circuit	11-12	11
P2503	Charging System Voltage Low	11-12	12
SEBRING CONVERTIBLE, SEBRING SEDAN & STRATUS SEDAN			
—	Verification Test VER-3	11-16	19
—	Verification Test VER-5	11-16	20
P0622	Alternator Field Not Switching Properly	11-13	14
P1492	Ambient/Battery Temperature Sensor Voltage Too High	11-14	15
P1493	Ambient/Battery Temperature Sensor Voltage Too Low	11-14	16
P1594	Charging System Voltage Too High	11-15	17
P1682	Charging System Voltage Too Low	11-15	18

1. ACTIVE DTC

NOTE: Make sure the Battery is in good condition. Using the Midtronics Battery Tester, test the Battery before continuing.

NOTE: Inspect the vehicle for after market accessories that may exceed the Generator System output.

Turn the ignition off.

NOTE: Make sure the generator drive belt is in good operating condition.

NOTE: Inspect the fuses in the IPM. If an open fuse is found, use the wire diagram/schematic as a guide, inspect the wiring and connectors for damage.

Ignition on, engine not running.
With the scan tool, read DTCs.

Is the DTC active at this time?

Yes

- Go To 2

No

- Refer to the INTERMITTENT CONDITION Diagnostic Procedure.
- Perform the POWERTRAIN VERIFICATION TEST.

ARM0500000000630

Fig. 5   Code P0562: Battery Voltage Low (Part 1 of 6). Charger, Magnum & 300

3. GENERATOR CASE GROUND HIGH RESISTANCE

Ignition on, engine not running.
Start the engine.
Allow the engine to reach normal operating temperature.

NOTE: Make sure all wires are clear of the engine's moving parts.

Measure the voltage between the Generator case and Battery ground post.

Is the voltage above 0.1 of a volt?

Yes

- Repair excessive resistance in the Generator Ground between the Generator Case and Battery ground side.
- Perform the POWERTRAIN VERIFICATION TEST.

No

- Go To 4

4. GENERATOR OPERATION

Turn the ignition off.
Disconnect the Generator Field harness connector.
Using a 12-volt test light, jump it across the Generator Field harness connector.
Ignition on, engine not running.
With the scan tool, actuate the Gen Field Control circuit.

Does the test light illuminate brightly and flash on and off?

Yes

- Replace the Generator.

No

- Go To 5

ARM0500000000632

Fig. 5   Code P0562: Battery Voltage Low (Part 3 of 6). Charger, Magnum & 300

2. (A1) B+ CIRCUIT HIGH RESISTANCE

WARNING: When the engine is operating, do not stand in direct line with the fan. Do not put your hands near the pulleys, belts, or fan. Do not wear loose clothing. Failure to follow these instructions can result in personal injury or death.

NOTE: Make sure all wires are clear of the engine's moving parts.

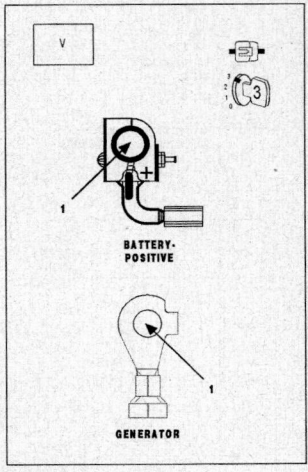

Measure the voltage between the (A802) B+ Terminal at the Generator and the (A1)Battery + Post. Start the engine.

Is the voltage above 0.4 of a volt?

Yes

- Repair the excessive resistance in the (A802/A11/A1) B+ circuit between the Generator and Battery.
- NOTE: Inspect the (A802) fuse link circuit and the Post Pass Through connection, ensure proper operation.
- Perform the POWERTRAIN VERIFICATION TEST.

No

- Go To 3

ARM0500000000631

Fig. 5   Code P0562: Battery Voltage Low (Part 2 of 6). Charger, Magnum & 300

5. (K20) GENERATOR FIELD CONTROL CIRCUIT OPEN

Turn the ignition off.
Disconnect the PCM harness connectors.

CAUTION: Do not probe the PCM harness connectors. Probing the PCM harness connectors will damage the PCM terminals resulting in poor terminal to pin connection. Install Miller Special Tool #8815 to perform diagnosis.

Measure the resistance of the (K20) Gen Field Control circuit from the Generator harness connector to the appropriate terminal of the special tool #8815.

Is the resistance below 5.0 ohms?

Yes

- Go To 6

No

- Repair the open in the (K20) Gen Field Control circuit.
- Perform the POWERTRAIN VERIFICATION TEST.

ARM0500000000633

Fig. 5   Code P0562: Battery Voltage Low (Part 4 of 6). Charger, Magnum & 300

6. (K20) GENERATOR FIELD CONTROL CIRCUIT SHORTED TO GROUND

Measure the resistance between the (K20) Gen Field Control circuit in the Generator Field harness connector and ground.

Is the resistance below 100 ohms?

Yes

- Repair the short to ground in the (K20) Gen Field Control circuit.
- Perform the POWERTRAIN VERIFICATION TEST.

No

- Go To 7

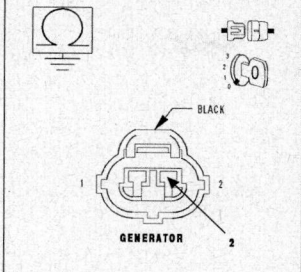

7. (Z20) GROUND CIRCUIT OPEN

Measure the resistance between the (Z20) Ground circuit in the Generator Field harness connector and ground.

Is the resistance below 5.0 ohms?

Yes

- Go To 8

No

- Repair the open in the (Z20) Ground circuit.
- Perform the POWERTRAIN VERIFICATION TEST.

ARM0500000000634

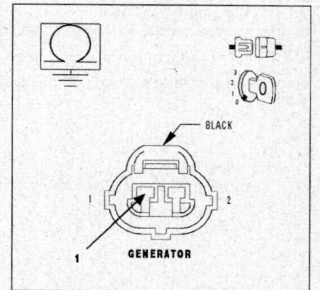

Fig. 5   Code P0562: Battery Voltage Low (Part 5 of 6). Charger, Magnum & 300

1. ACTIVE DTC

NOTE: Make sure the Battery is in good condition. Using the Midtronics Battery Tester, test the Battery before continuing.

NOTE: Inspect the vehicle for after market accessories that may exceed the Generator System output.

Turn the ignition off.

NOTE: Make sure the generator drive belt is in good operating condition.

NOTE: Inspect the fuses in the IPM. If a fuse is open use the wire diagram/schematic as a guide, inspect the wiring and connectors for damage.

Ignition on, engine not running.
With a scan tool, read DTCs.

Is the DTC active at this time?

Yes

- Go To 2

No

- Refer to the INTERMITTENT CONDITION Diagnostic Procedure.
- Perform the POWERTRAIN VERIFICATION TEST.

ARM0500000000636

Fig. 6   Code P0563: Battery Voltage High (Part 1 of 3). Charger, Magnum & 300

8. PCM

NOTE: Before continuing, check the PCM harness connector terminals for corrosion, damage, or terminal push out. Repair as necessary.

Using the schematics as a guide, inspect the wire harness and connectors. Pay particular attention to all Power and Ground circuits.

Were there any problems found?

Yes

- Repair as necessary.
- Perform the POWERTRAIN VERIFICATION TEST.

No

- Replace and program the Powertrain Control Module
- Perform the POWERTRAIN VERIFICATION TEST.

ARM0500000000635

Fig. 5   Code P0562: Battery Voltage Low (Part 6 of 6). Charger, Magnum & 300

2. GENERATOR OPERATION

Turn the ignition off.
Disconnect the Generator Field harness connector.
Using a 12-volt test light, jump across the Generator Field harness connector.
Ignition on, engine not running.
With the scan tool, actuate the Generator Field Driver.

Does the test light illuminate brightly and flash on and off?

Yes

- Replace the Generator.
- Perform the POWERTRAIN VERIFICATION TEST.

No

- Go To 3

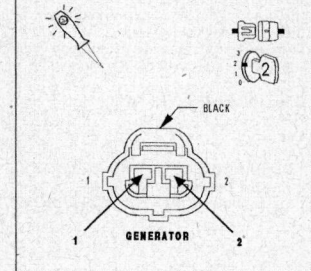

3. (K20) FIELD CIRCUIT SHORTED BATTERY VOLTAGE

Turn the ignition off.
Disconnect the PCM harness connectors.
Ignition on, engine not running.
Measure the voltage on the (K20) Gen Field Control circuit at the Generator Field harness connector.

Is the voltage above 1.0 volt?

Yes

- Repair the short to battery voltage in the (K20) Gen Field Control circuit.

No

- Go To 4

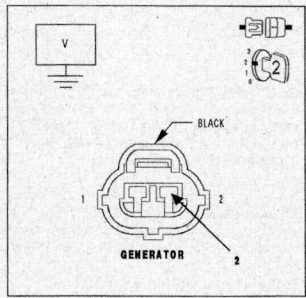

ARM0500000000637

Fig. 6   Code P0563: Battery Voltage High (Part 2 of 3). Charger, Magnum & 300

4. PCM

NOTE: Before continuing, check the PCM harness connector terminals for corrosion, damage, or terminal push out. Repair as necessary.

Using the schematics as a guide, inspect the wire harness and connectors. Pay particular attention to all Power and Ground circuits.

Were there any problems found?

Yes

- Repair as necessary.
- Perform the POWERTRAIN VERIFICATION TEST.

No

- Replace and program the Powertrain Control Module
- Perform the POWERTRAIN VERIFICATION TEST.

ARM0500000000638

Fig. 6 Code P0563: Battery Voltage High (Part 3 of 3). Charger, Magnum & 300

3. (K20) GEN FIELD CIRCUIT SHORTED BATTERY VOLTAGE

Turn the ignition off.
Disconnect the PCM harness connectors.
Ignition on, engine not running.
Measure the voltage on the (K20) Gen Field Control circuit in the Generator Field harness connector.

Is the voltage above 1.0 volt?

Yes

- Repair the short to battery voltage in the (K20) Gen Field Control circuit.
- Perform the POWERTRAIN VERIFICATION TEST.

No

- Go To 4

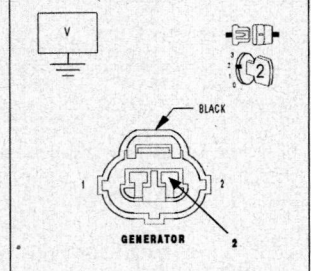

ARM0500000000640

Fig. 7 Code P0622: Alternator Field Control Circuit (Part 2 of 5). Charger, Magnum & 300

4. (K20) GEN FIELD CIRCUIT OPEN

Turn the ignition off.

CAUTION: Do not probe the PCM harness connectors. Probing the PCM harness connectors will damage the PCM terminals resulting in poor terminal to pin connection. Install Miller Special Tool #8815 to perform diagnosis.

Measure the resistance of the (K20) Gen Field Control circuit from the Generator Field harness connector to appropriate terminal of the special tool #8815.

Is the resistance below 5.0 ohms?

Yes

- Go To 5

No

- Repair the open in the (K20) Gen Field Control circuit.
- Perform the POWERTRAIN VERIFICATION TEST.

ARM0500000000641

Fig. 7 Code P0622: Alternator Field Control Circuit (Part 3 of 5). Charger, Magnum & 300

1. ACTIVE DTC

Ignition on, engine not running.
With a scan tool, read DTCs.

Is the DTC active at this time?

Yes

- Go To 2

No

- Refer to the INTERMITTENT CONDITION Diagnostic Procedure.
- Perform the POWERTRAIN VERIFICATION TEST.

2. GENERATOR OPERATION

Turn the ignition off.
Disconnect the Generator Field harness connector.
Using a 12-volt test light, jump it across the Generator Field harness connector.
Ignition on, engine not running.
With the scan tool, actuate the Generator Field Control circuit.

Does the test light illuminate brightly and flash on and off?

Yes

- Replace the Generator.
- Perform the POWERTRAIN VERIFICATION TEST.

No

- Go To 3

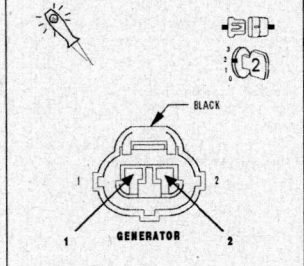

ARM0500000000639

Fig. 7 Code P0622: Alternator Field Control Circuit (Part 1 of 5). Charger, Magnum & 300

5. (K20) GEN FIELD CIRCUIT SHORTED TO GROUND

Measure the resistance between ground and the (K20) Gen Field Control circuit in the Generator Field harness connector.

Is the resistance below 100 ohms?

Yes

- Repair the short to ground in the (K20) Gen Field Control circuit.
- Perform the POWERTRAIN VERIFICATION TEST.

No

- Go To 6

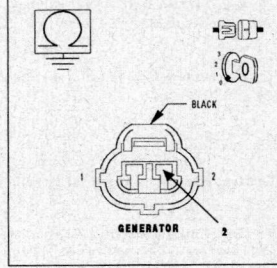

6. (Z20) GROUND CIRCUIT OPEN

Measure the resistance between the (Z20) Ground circuit in the Gen Field harness connector and ground.

Does the test light illuminate brightly?

Yes

- Go To 7

No

- Repair the open in the (Z20) Ground circuit.
- Perform the POWERTRAIN VERIFICATION TEST.

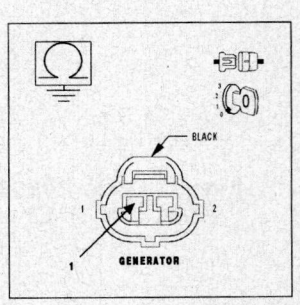

ARM0500000000962

Fig. 7 Code P0622: Alternator Field Control Circuit (Part 4 of 5). Charger, Magnum & 300

7. PCM

NOTE: Before continuing, check the PCM harness connector terminals for corrosion, damage, or terminal push out. Repair as necessary.

Using the schematics as a guide, inspect the wire harness and connectors. Pay particular attention to all Power and Ground circuits.

Were there any problems found?

Yes

- Repair as necessary.
- Perform the POWERTRAIN VERIFICATION TEST.

No

- Replace and program the Powertrain Control Module
- Perform the POWERTRAIN VERIFICATION TEST.

ARM0500000000963

Fig. 7   Code P0622: Alternator Field Control Circuit (Part 5 of 5). Charger, Magnum & 300

2. FUSED B+ CIRCUIT HIGH RESISTANCE

WARNING: When the engine is operating, do not stand in direct line with the fan. Do not put your hands near the pulleys, belts, or fan. Do not wear loose clothing. Failure to follow these instructions can result in personal injury or death.

Ignition on, engine not running.

NOTE: Make sure all wires are clear of the engine's moving parts.

Measure the voltage between the Generator B+ Output Terminal and the Battery+ Post.
Start the engine.

Is the voltage above 0.4 of a volt?

Yes

- Repair the excessive resistance in the battery positive circuit between the Generator and Battery.
- Perform the POWERTRAIN VERIFICATION TEST.

No

- Go To 3

ARM0500000000965

Fig. 8   Code P2503: Charging System Output Low (Part 2 of 7). Charger, Magnum & 300

3. EXCESSIVE RESISTANCE IN THE CASE GROUND

WARNING: When the engine is operating, do not stand in direct line with the fan. Do not put your hands near the pulleys, belts, or fan. Do not wear loose clothing. Failure to follow these instructions can result in personal injury or death.

Start the engine.
Warm the engine to operating temperature.

NOTE: Make sure all wires are clear of the engine's moving parts.

Measure the voltage between the Generator Case and Battery ground post.

Is the voltage above 0.1 of a volt?

Yes

- Repair the excessive resistance in the Generator Case Ground.
- Perform the POWERTRAIN VERIFICATION TEST.

No

- Go To 4

ARM0500000000966

Fig. 8   Code P2503: Charging System Output Low (Part 3 of 7). Charger, Magnum & 300

1. ACTIVE DTC

NOTE: Inspect the vehicle for aftermarket accessories that may exceed the Generator System output.

Ignition on, engine not running.

NOTE: The battery must be fully charged.

NOTE: The Generator belt tension and condition must be checked before continuing.

With a scan tool, read DTCs.
With a scan tool, erase DTCs.
Start the engine.
Allow the idle to stabilize.
With the scan tool, read DTCs.

Is the DTC active at this time?

Yes

- Go To 2

No

- Refer to the INTERMITTENT CONDITION Diagnostic Procedure.
- Perform the POWERTRAIN VERIFICATION TEST.

ARM0500000000964

Fig. 8   Code P2503: Charging System Output Low (Part 1 of 7). Charger, Magnum & 300

4. GENERATOR OPERATION

Turn the ignition off.
Disconnect the Generator Field harness connector.
Using a 12-volt test light, jump across the Generator Field harness connector.
Ignition on, engine not running.
With a scan tool, actuate the Generator Field Driver.

Does the test light illuminate brightly and flash on and off?

Yes

- Replace the Generator.
- Perform the POWERTRAIN VERIFICATION TEST.

No

- Go To 5

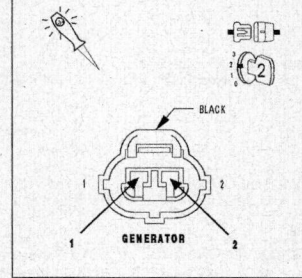

5. (K20) GEN FIELD CONTROL CIRCUIT SHORTED TO BATTERY VOLTAGE

Turn the ignition off.
Disconnect the PCM harness connectors.
Ignition on, engine not running.
Measure the voltage on the (K20) Gen Field Control circuit in the Generator Field harness connector.

Is the voltage above 1.0 volt?

Yes

- Repair the short to battery voltage in the (K20) Gen Field Control circuit.

No

- Go To 6

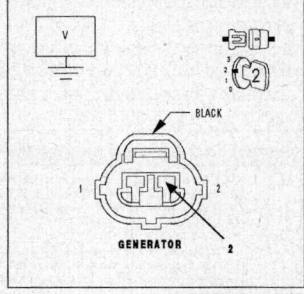

ARM0500000000967

Fig. 8   Code P2503: Charging System Output Low (Part 4 of 7). Charger, Magnum & 300

ALTERNATORS

6. (K20) FIELD CONTROL CIRCUIT OPEN

Turn the ignition off.

CAUTION: Do not probe the PCM harness connectors. Probing the PCM harness connectors will damage the PCM terminals resulting in poor terminal to pin connection. Install Miller Special Tool #8815 to perform diagnosis.

Measure the resistance of the (K20) Gen Field Control circuit from the Generator Field harness connector to the appropriate terminal of special tool #8815.

Is the resistance below 5.0 ohms?

Yes

- Go To 7

No

- Repair the open in the (K20) Gen Field Control circuit.
- Perform the POWERTRAIN VERIFICATION TEST.

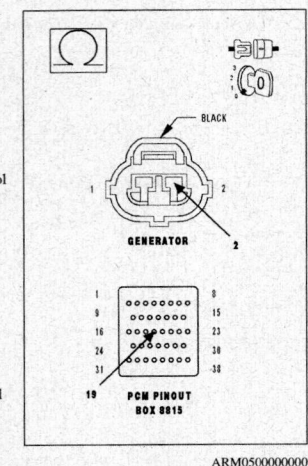

ARM0500000000968

Fig. 8   Code P2503: Charging System Output Low (Part 5 of 7). Charger, Magnum & 300

9. PCM

NOTE: Before continuing, check the PCM harness connector terminals for corrosion, damage, or terminal push out. Repair as necessary.

Using the schematics as a guide, inspect the wire harness and connectors. Pay particular attention to all Power and Ground circuits.

Were there any problems found?

Yes

- Repair as necessary.
- Perform the POWERTRAIN VERIFICATION TEST.

No

- Replace and program the Powertrain Control Module
- Perform the POWERTRAIN VERIFICATION TEST.

ARM0500000000970

Fig. 8   Code P2503: Charging System Output Low (Part 7 of 7). Charger, Magnum & 300

Set Condition: The battery sensed voltage is 1 volt below the charging goal for 13.47 seconds. The PCM senses the battery voltage turns off the field driver and senses the battery voltage again. If the voltages are the same, the code is set. One trip Fault.

POSSIBLE CAUSES
INTERMITTENT CONDITION
B+ CIRCUIT HIGH RESISTANCE
GENERATOR GROUND HIGH RESISTANCE
GENERATOR OPERATION
GENERATOR FIELD GROUND CIRCUIT OPEN
GENERATOR FIELD CONTROL CIRCUIT SHORTED TO GROUND
GENERATOR FIELD CONTROL CIRCUIT OPEN
PCM

TEST	ACTION
1	NOTE: Ensure the Battery is in good condition. Using the Midtronics Battery Tester, test the Battery before continuing. NOTE: Inspect the vehicle for aftermarket accessories that may exceed the Generator System output. Turn the ignition off. NOTE: Ensure the generator drive belt is in good operating condition. NOTE: Inspect the fuses in the PDC. If a fuse is found to be open use the wiring diagram/schematic as a guide, inspect the wiring and connectors for damage. Ignition on, engine not running. With the DRBIII®, read DTCs and record the related Freeze Frame data. Is the Good Trip Counter displayed and equal to zero? Yes → Go To 2 No → Go To 9

CR1120100445010X

Fig. 9   Code P0562: Battery Voltage Low (Part 1 of 3). Concorde, Intrepid & 300M

7. (K20) GEN FIELD CONTROL CIRCUIT SHORTED TO GROUND

Measure the resistance between ground and the (K20) Gen Field Control circuit in the Generator Field harness connector.

Is the resistance below 100 ohms?

Yes

- Repair the short to ground in the (K20) Gen Field Control circuit.
- Perform the POWERTRAIN VERIFICATION TEST.

No

- Go To 8

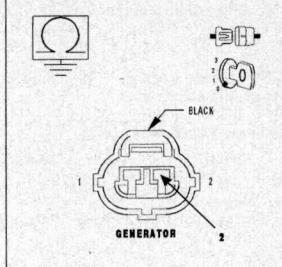

8. (Z904) GROUND CIRCUIT OPEN

Using a 12-volt test light connected to battery voltage, probe the (Z904) Ground circuit in the Generator Field harness connector.

Does the test light illuminate brightly?

Yes

- Go To 9

No

- Repair the open in the (Z904) Generator Ground circuit.
- Perform the POWERTRAIN VERIFICATION TEST.

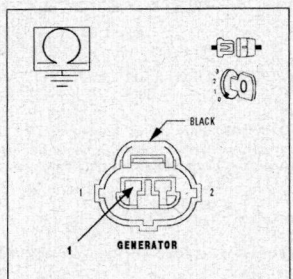

ARM0500000000969

Fig. 8   Code P2503: Charging System Output Low (Part 6 of 7). Charger, Magnum & 300

TEST	ACTION
2	WARNING: WHEN THE ENGINE IS OPERATING, DO NOT STAND IN A DIRECT LINE WITH THE FAN. DO NOT PUT YOUR HANDS NEAR THE PULLEYS, BELTS OR FAN. DO NOT WEAR LOOSE CLOTHING. Ignition on, engine not running. NOTE: Ensure all wires are clear of the engine's moving parts. Measure the voltage between the Generator B+ Terminal and the Battery+ Post. Start the engine. Is the voltage above 0.4 of a volt? Yes → Repair the B+ circuit for high resistance between the Generator and Battery. Perform POWERTRAIN VERIFICATION TEST VER - 3. No → Go To 3
3	WARNING: WHEN THE ENGINE IS OPERATING, DO NOT STAND IN A DIRECT LINE WITH THE FAN. DO NOT PUT YOUR HANDS NEAR THE PULLEYS, BELTS OR FAN. DO NOT WEAR LOOSE CLOTHING. Start the engine. Allow the engine to reach normal operating temperature. NOTE: Ensure all wires are clear of the engine's moving parts. Measure the voltage between the Generator case and Battery ground post. Is the voltage above 0.1 of a volt? Yes → Repair Generator Ground for high resistance, Generator Case to Battery ground side. Perform POWERTRAIN VERIFICATION TEST VER - 3. No → Go To 4
4	Turn the ignition off. Disconnect the Generator Field harness connector. Using a 12-volt test light, jumper it across the Generator Field harness connector. Ignition on, engine not running. With the DRBIII®, actuate the Generator Field Driver circuit. Does the test light illuminate brightly and flash on and off? Yes → Replace the Generator. Perform POWERTRAIN VERIFICATION TEST VER - 3. No → Go To 5
5	Turn the ignition off. Disconnect the Generator Field harness connector. Using a 12-volt test connected to battery voltage, probe the Generator Ground circuit in the Generator Field harness connector. Does the test light illuminate brightly? Yes → Go To 6 No → Repair the open in the Generator Field Ground circuit. Perform POWERTRAIN VERIFICATION TEST VER - 3.

CR1120100445020X

Fig. 9   Code P0562: Battery Voltage Low (Part 2 of 3). Concorde, Intrepid & 300M

TEST	ACTION
6	Ignition on, engine not running. Disconnect the Generator Field harness connector. Disconnect the PCM harness connector. Measure the resistance between ground and the Generator Field Control circuit in the Generator Field harness connector. Is the resistance below 100 ohms? Yes → Repair the Generator Field Control circuit for a short to ground. Perform POWERTRAIN VERIFICATION TEST VER - 3. No → Go To 7
7	Turn the ignition off. Disconnect the Generator Field harness connector. Disconnect the PCM harness connector. CAUTION: DO NOT PROBE THE PCM HARNESS CONNECTORS. PROBING THE PCM HARNESS CONNECTORS WILL DAMAGE THE PCM TERMINALS RESULTING IN POOR TERMINAL TO PIN CONNECTION. INSTALL MILLER SPECIAL TOOL #8815 TO PERFORM DIAGNOSIS. Measure the resistance of the Generator Field Control circuit from the Generator Field harness connector to the appropriate terminal of the special tool #8815. Is the resistance below 5.0 ohms? Yes → Go To 8 No → Repair the open in the Generator Field Control circuit. Perform POWERTRAIN VERIFICATION TEST VER - 3.

8	NOTE: Before continuing, check the PCM harness connector terminals for corrosion, damage or terminal push out. Repair as necessary.
	If there are no possible causes remaining, view repair.
	
	Repair
	    Replace and program the Powertrain Control Module in accordance with the Service Information.
	    Perform POWERTRAIN VERIFICATION TEST VER - 3.

9	NOTE: Ensure the Battery is in good condition. Using the Midtronics Battery Tester, test the Battery before continuing. NOTE: The conditions that set the DTC are not present at this time. The following list may help in identifying the intermittent condition. WARNING: WHEN THE ENGINE IS OPERATING, DO NOT STAND IN A DIRECT LINE WITH THE FAN. DO NOT PUT YOUR HANDS NEAR THE PULLEYS, BELTS OR FAN. DO NOT WEAR LOOSE CLOTHING. With the engine running at normal operating temperature, monitor the DRBIII® parameters related to the DTC while wiggling the wire harness. Look for parameter values to change and/or a DTC to set. Review the DRBIII® Freeze Frame information. If possible, try to duplicate the conditions under which the DTC was set. Refer to any Technical Service Bulletins (TSB) that may apply. Visually inspect the related wire harness. Look for any chafed, pierced, pinched, or partially broken wires. Visually inspect the related wire harness connectors. Look for broken, bent, pushed out, or corroded terminals. Were any of the above conditions present? Yes → Repair as necessary Perform POWERTRAIN VERIFICATION TEST VER - 3. No → Test Complete.

CR1120100445030X

Fig. 9   Code P0562: Battery Voltage Low (Part 3 of 3). Concorde, Intrepid & 300M

TEST	ACTION
3	Turn the ignition off. Disconnect the Generator Field harness connector. Disconnect the PCM harness connector. Measure the voltage on the Generator Field Control circuit at the Generator Field harness connector. Is the voltage above 1.0 volt? Yes → Repair the short to voltage in the Generator Field Control circuit. Perform POWERTRAIN VERIFICATION TEST VER - 3. No → Go To 4
4	Turn the ignition off. Disconnect the Generator Field harness connector. Using a 12-volt test connected to battery voltage, probe the Generator Ground circuit in the Generator Field harness connector. Does the test light illuminate brightly? Yes → Go To 5 No → Repair the open in the Generator Field Ground circuit. Perform POWERTRAIN VERIFICATION TEST VER - 3.
5	Ignition on, engine not running. Disconnect the Generator Field harness connector. Disconnect the PCM harness connector. Measure the resistance between ground and the Generator Field Control circuit in the Generator Field harness connector. Is the resistance below 100 ohms? Yes → Repair the Generator Field Control circuit for a short to ground. Perform POWERTRAIN VERIFICATION TEST VER - 3. No → Go To 6
6	Turn the ignition off. Disconnect the Generator Field harness connector. Disconnect the PCM harness connector. CAUTION: DO NOT PROBE THE PCM HARNESS CONNECTORS. PROBING THE PCM HARNESS CONNECTORS WILL DAMAGE THE PCM TERMINALS RESULTING IN POOR TERMINAL TO PIN CONNECTION. INSTALL MILLER SPECIAL TOOL #8815 TO PERFORM DIAGNOSIS. Measure the resistance of the Generator Field Control circuit from the Generator Field harness connector to the appropriate terminal of the special tool #8815. Is the resistance below 5.0 ohms? Yes → Go To 7 No → Repair the open in the Generator Field Control circuit. Perform POWERTRAIN VERIFICATION TEST VER - 3.

7	NOTE: Before continuing, check the PCM harness connector terminals for corrosion, damage or terminal push out. Repair as necessary.
	If there are no possible causes remaining, view repair.
	
	Repair
	    Replace and program the Powertrain Control Module in accordance with the Service Information.
	    Perform POWERTRAIN VERIFICATION TEST VER - 3.

CR1120100446020X

Fig. 10   Code P0563: Battery Voltage High (Part 2 of 3). Concord, Intrepid & 300M

When Monitored: The engine running. The engine speed greater than 380 RPM.

Set Condition: Battery voltage is 1 volt greater than desired system voltage. One Trip Fault

POSSIBLE CAUSES
GENERATOR FIELD CONTROL CIRCUIT SHORTED TO GROUND
GENERATOR FIELD CONTROL CIRCUIT OPEN
GENERATOR FIELD GROUND CIRCUIT OPEN
INTERMITTENT CONDITION
GENERATOR OPERATION
GENERATOR FIELD CONTROL CIRCUIT SHORTED TO BATTERY VOLTAGE
PCM

TEST	ACTION
1	NOTE: Ensure the Battery is in good condition. Using the Midtronics Battery Tester, test the Battery before continuing. NOTE: Inspect the vehicle for aftermarket accessories that may exceed the Generator System output. Turn the ignition off. NOTE: Ensure the generator drive belt is in good operating condition. NOTE: Inspect the fuses in the PDC. If a fuse is found to be open use the wiring diagram/schematic as a guide, inspect the wiring and connectors for damage. Ignition on, engine not running. With the DRBIII®, read DTCs and record the related Freeze Frame data. Is the Good Trip Counter displayed and equal to zero? Yes → Go To 2 No → Go To 8
2	Turn the ignition off. Disconnect the Generator Field harness connector. Using a 12-volt test light, jumper it across the Generator Field harness connector. Ignition on, engine not running. With the DRBIII®, actuate the Generator Field Driver circuit. Does the test light illuminate brightly and flash on and off? Yes → Go To 4 No → Go To 3

CR1120100446010X

Fig. 10   Code P0563: Battery Voltage High (Part 1 of 3). Concord, Intrepid & 300M

TEST	ACTION
8	NOTE: The conditions that set the DTC are not present at this time. The following list may help in identifying the intermittent condition. NOTE: Ensure the Battery is in good condition. Using the Midtronics Battery Tester, test the Battery before continuing. WARNING: WHEN THE ENGINE IS OPERATING, DO NOT STAND IN A DIRECT LINE WITH THE FAN. DO NOT PUT YOUR HANDS NEAR THE PULLEYS, BELTS OR FAN. DO NOT WEAR LOOSE CLOTHING. With the engine running at normal operating temperature, monitor the DRBIII® parameters related to the DTC while wiggling the wire harness. Look for parameter values to change and/or a DTC to set. Review the DRBIII® Freeze Frame information. If possible, try to duplicate the conditions under which the DTC was set. Refer to any Technical Service Bulletins (TSB) that may apply. Visually inspect the related wire harness. Look for any chafed, pierced, pinched, or partially broken wires. Visually inspect the related wire harness connectors. Look for broken, bent, pushed out, or corroded terminals. Were any of the above conditions present? Yes → Repair as necessary Perform POWERTRAIN VERIFICATION TEST VER - 3. No → Test Complete.

CR1120100446030X

Fig. 10   Code P0563: Battery Voltage High (Part 3 of 3). Concord, Intrepid & 300M

When Monitored: With the ignition on. Engine running.

Set Condition: When the PCM tries to regulate the generator field with no result during monitoring. One Trip Fault.

POSSIBLE CAUSES
WIRING HARNESS INTERMITTENT
GENERATOR OPERATION
GENERATOR FIELD GROUND CIRCUIT OPEN
GENERATOR FIELD CONTROL CIRCUIT SHORTED TO BATTERY VOLTAGE
GENERATOR FIELD CONTROL CIRCUIT SHORTED TO GROUND
GENERATOR FIELD CONTROL CIRCUIT OPEN
PCM

TEST	ACTION
1	Ignition on, engine not running. With the DRBIII®, read DTCs and record the related Freeze Frame data. Does the test light illuminate brightly and flash? Yes → Go To 2 No → Go To 3
2	With the DRBIII®, erase DTCs. **WARNING: WHEN THE ENGINE IS OPERATING, DO NOT STAND IN A DIRECT LINE WITH THE FAN. DO NOT PUT YOUR HANDS NEAR THE PULLEYS, BELTS OR FAN. DO NOT WEAR LOOSE CLOTHING.** Start the engine and allow it to idle. Wiggle the wire harness from the Generator to PCM. With the DRBIII®, read DTCs. Did the DTC reset? Yes → Repair as necessary. Perform POWERTRAIN VERIFICATION TEST VER - 3. No → Test Complete.

CR1120100447010X

Fig. 11 Code P0622: Alternator Field Control Circuit (Part 1 of 3). Concorde, Intrepid & 300M

TEST	ACTION
8	NOTE: **Before continuing, check the PCM connector terminals for corrosion, damage, or terminal push out. Repair as necessary.** If there are no possible causes remaining, view repair. Repair Replace and program the Powertrain Control Module in accordance with the Service Information. Perform POWERTRAIN VERIFICATION TEST VER - 3.

CR1120100447030X

Fig. 11 Code P0622: Alternator Field Control Circuit (Part 3 of 3). Concorde, Intrepid & 300M

When Monitored: The engine running. The engine speed greater than 1157 RPM.

Set Condition: The battery sensed voltage is 1 volt below the charging goal for 13.47 seconds. The PCM senses the battery voltage turns off the field driver and senses the battery voltage again. If the voltages are the same, the code is set.

POSSIBLE CAUSES
B+ CIRCUIT HIGH RESISTANCE
GENERATOR GROUND HIGH RESISTANCE
GENERATOR OPERATION
INTERMITTENT CONDITION
GENERATOR FIELD GROUND CIRCUIT OPEN
GENERATOR FIELD CONTROL CIRCUIT SHORTED TO BATTERY VOLTAGE
GENERATOR FIELD CONTROL CIRCUIT SHORTED TO GROUND
GENERATOR FIELD CONTROL CIRCUIT OPEN
PCM

TEST	ACTION
1	NOTE: **Inspect the vehicle for aftermarket accessories that may exceed the Generator System output.** Turn the ignition off. NOTE: **The battery must be fully charged.** NOTE: **The Generator belt tension and condition must be checked before continuing.** Start the engine. Allow the idle to stabilize. With the DRBIII®, read the Target Charging Voltage. Is the Target Charging Voltage above 15.1 volts? Yes → Go To 2 No → Go To 3

CR1120100448010X

Fig. 12 Code P2503: Charging System Voltage Low (Part 1 of 4). Concorde, Intrepid & 300M

TEST	ACTION
3	Turn the ignition off. Disconnect the Generator Field harness connector. Using a 12-volt test light, jumper it across the Generator Field harness connector. Ignition on, engine not running. With the DRBIII®, actuate the Generator Field Driver circuit. Does the test light illuminate brightly and flash on and off? Yes → Replace the Generator. Perform POWERTRAIN VERIFICATION TEST VER - 3. No → Go To 4
4	Turn the ignition off. Disconnect the Generator Field harness connector. Using a 12-volt test connected to battery voltage, probe the Generator Ground circuit in the Generator Field harness connector. Does the test light illuminate brightly? Yes → Go To 5 No → Repair the open in the Generator Field Ground circuit. Perform POWERTRAIN VERIFICATION TEST VER - 3.
5	Turn the ignition off. Disconnect the Generator Field harness connector. Disconnect the PCM harness connector. Measure the voltage on the Generator Field Control circuit in the Generator Field harness connector. Is the voltage above 1.0 volts? Yes → Repair the short to voltage in the Generator Field Control circuit. Perform POWERTRAIN VERIFICATION TEST VER - 3. No → Go To 6
6	Turn the ignition on. Disconnect the Generator Field harness connector. Disconnect the PCM harness connector. Measure the resistance between ground and the Generator Field Control circuit in the Generator Field harness connector. Is the resistance below 100 ohms? Yes → Repair the Generator Field Control circuit for a short to ground. Perform POWERTRAIN VERIFICATION TEST VER - 3. No → Go To 7
7	Turn the ignition off. Disconnect the Generator Field harness connector. Disconnect the PCM harness connector. CAUTION: **DO NOT PROBE THE PCM HARNESS CONNECTORS. PROBING THE PCM HARNESS CONNECTORS WILL DAMAGE THE PCM TERMINALS RESULTING IN POOR TERMINAL TO PIN CONNECTION. INSTALL MILLER SPECIAL TOOL #8815 TO PERFORM DIAGNOSIS.** Measure the resistance of the Generator Field Control circuit from the Generator Field harness connector to the appropriate terminal of the special tool #8815. Is the resistance below 5.0 ohms? Yes → Go To 8 No → Repair the open in the Generator Field Control circuit. Perform POWERTRAIN VERIFICATION TEST VER - 3.

CR1120100447020X

Fig. 11 Code P0622: Alternator Field Control Circuit (Part 2 of 3). Concorde, Intrepid & 300M

TEST	ACTION
2	NOTE: **The conditions that set the DTC are not present at this time. The following list may help in identifying the intermittent condition.** WARNING: **WHEN THE ENGINE IS OPERATING, DO NOT STAND IN A DIRECT LINE WITH THE FAN. DO NOT PUT YOUR HANDS NEAR THE PULLEYS, BELTS OR FAN. DO NOT WEAR LOOSE CLOTHING.** With the engine running at normal operating temperature, monitor the DRBIII® parameters related to the DTC while wiggling the wire harness. Look for parameter values to change and/or a DTC to set. Review the DRBIII® Freeze Frame information. If possible, try to duplicate the conditions under which the DTC was set. Refer to any Technical Service Bulletins (TSB) that may apply. Visually inspect the related wire harness. Look for any chafed, pierced, pinched, or partially broken wires. Visually inspect the related wire harness connectors. Look for broken, bent, pushed out, or corroded terminals. Were any of the above conditions present? Yes → Repair as necessary Perform POWERTRAIN VERIFICATION TEST VER - 3. No → Test Complete.
3	WARNING: **WHEN THE ENGINE IS OPERATING, DO NOT STAND IN A DIRECT LINE WITH THE FAN. DO NOT PUT YOUR HANDS NEAR THE PULLEYS, BELTS OR FAN. DO NOT WEAR LOOSE CLOTHING.** Ignition on, engine not running. NOTE: **Ensure all wires are clear of the engine's moving parts.** Measure the voltage between the Generator B+ Terminal and the Battery+ Post. Start the engine. Is the voltage above 0.4 of a volt? Yes → Repair the B+ circuit for high resistance between the Generator and Battery. Perform POWERTRAIN VERIFICATION TEST VER - 3. No → Go To 4
4	WARNING: **WHEN THE ENGINE IS OPERATING, DO NOT STAND IN A DIRECT LINE WITH THE FAN. DO NOT PUT YOUR HANDS NEAR THE PULLEYS, BELTS OR FAN. DO NOT WEAR LOOSE CLOTHING.** Start the engine. Warm the engine to operating temperature. NOTE: **Ensure all wires are clear of the engine's moving parts.** Measure the voltage between the Generator case and Battery ground post. Is the voltage above 0.1 of a volt? Yes → Repair Generator Ground for high resistance, Generator Case to Battery ground side. Perform POWERTRAIN VERIFICATION TEST VER - 3. No → Go To 5

CR1120100448020X

Fig. 12 Code P2503: Charging System Voltage Low (Part 2 of 4). Concorde, Intrepid & 300M

TEST	ACTION
5	Turn the ignition off. Disconnect the Generator Field harness connector. Using a 12-volt test light, jumper it across the Generator Field harness connector. Ignition on, engine not running. With the DRBIII®, actuate the Generator Field Driver circuit. Does the test light illuminate brightly and flash on and off? Yes → Replace the Generator. Perform POWERTRAIN VERIFICATION TEST VER - 3. No → Go To 6
6	Turn the ignition off. Disconnect the Generator Field harness connector. Using a 12-volt test connected to battery voltage, probe the Generator Ground circuit in the Generator Field harness connector. Does the test light illuminate brightly? Yes → Go To 7 No → Repair the open in the Generator Field Ground circuit. Perform POWERTRAIN VERIFICATION TEST VER - 3.
7	Turn the ignition off. Disconnect the Generator Field harness connector. Disconnect the PCM harness connector. Measure the voltage on the Generator Field Control circuit at the Generator Field harness connector. Is the voltage above 1.0 volt? Yes → Repair the short to voltage in the Generator Field Control circuit. Perform POWERTRAIN VERIFICATION TEST VER - 3. No → Go To 8
8	Turn the ignition on. Disconnect the Generator Field harness connector. Disconnect the PCM harness connector. Measure the resistance between ground and the Generator Field Control circuit in the Generator Field harness connector. Is the resistance below 100 ohms? Yes → Repair the Generator Field Control circuit for a short to ground. Perform POWERTRAIN VERIFICATION TEST VER - 3. No → Go To 9
9	Turn the ignition off. Disconnect the Generator Field harness connector. Disconnect the PCM harness connector. CAUTION: DO NOT PROBE THE PCM HARNESS CONNECTORS. PROBING THE PCM HARNESS CONNECTORS WILL DAMAGE THE PCM TERMINALS RESULTING IN POOR TERMINAL TO PIN CONNECTION. INSTALL MILLER SPECIAL TOOL #8815 TO PERFORM DIAGNOSIS. Measure the resistance of the Generator Field Control circuit from the Generator Field harness connector to the appropriate terminal of the special tool #8815. Is the resistance below 5.0 ohms? Yes → Go To 10 No → Repair the open in the Generator Field Control circuit. Perform POWERTRAIN VERIFICATION TEST VER - 3.

CR1120100448030X

Fig. 12   Code P2503: Charging System Voltage Low (Part 3 of 4). Concorde, Intrepid & 300M

POWERTRAIN VERIFICATION TEST VER - 3
1. NOTE: After completing the Powertrain Verification Test the Transmission Verification Test must be performed. 2. NOTE: If the PCM has been replaced and the correct VIN and mileage have not been programmed, a DTC will be set in the ABS Module, Airbag Module and the SKIM. 3. NOTE: If the vehicle is equipped with a Sentry Key Immobilizer System, Secret Key data must be updated. Refer to the Service Information for the PCM, SKIM and the Transponder (ignition key) for programming information. 4. Inspect the vehicle to ensure that all components related to the repair are connected properly. 5. With the DRBIII®, clear DTCs. 6. Perform generator output test. Refer to the appropriate service information as necessary. 7. Start the engine and set engine speed to 2000 RPM for at least thirty seconds. 8. Cycle the ignition key off and on. 9. With the DRBIII®, read the DTCs. If the DTC returns, or any other symptom or DTC is present, refer to the appropriate category and perform the corresponding symptom. 10. If there are no DTCs present and all components are functioning properly, the repair is complete. Are any DTCs present? Yes → Repair is not complete, refer to appropriate symptom. No → Repair is complete.

CR1120100449000X

Fig. 13   Verification Test VER-3. Concorde, Intrepid & 300M

TEST	ACTION
10	If there are no possible causes remaining, view repair. Repair Replace and program the Powertrain Control Module in accordance with the Service Information. Perform POWERTRAIN VERIFICATION TEST VER - 3.

CR1120100448040X

Fig. 12   Code P2503: Charging System Voltage Low (Part 4 of 4). Concorde, Intrepid & 300M

TEST	ACTION	APPLICABILITY
1	Turn the ignition on. With the DRBIII®, actuate the Generator Field Driver circuit. Using a 12-volt test light connected to ground, backprobe the Generator Field Driver circuit in the back of the Generator. Does the test light illuminate brightly and flash? Yes → Go To 2 No → Go To 4	All
2	Turn the ignition on. With the DRBIII® actuate the Generator Field Driver circuit. Wiggle the wiring harness from the Generator to PCM. With the DRBIII®, read DTC's. Did the DTC reset? Yes → Repair as necessary . Perform POWERTRAIN VERIFICATION TEST VER - 3. No → Go To 3	All
3	Turn the ignition off. Using the schematic as a guide, inspect the Wiring and Connectors. Were any problems found? Yes → Repair as necessary. Perform POWERTRAIN VERIFICATION TEST VER - 3. No → Test Complete.	All

CR1120100394010X

Fig. 14   Code P0622: Alternator Field Not Switching Properly (Part 1 of 2). Sebring Convertible, Sebring Sedan & Stratus Sedan

TEST	ACTION
4	NOTE: Carefully inspect all Connectors for corrosion or spread Terminals before continuing. Disconnect the Generator Field harness connector. Turn the ignition on. With the DRBIII® actuate the Generator Field Driver circuit. Using a 12-volt test light connected to ground, probe the ASD Relay Output circuit. Does the test light illuminate brightly? Yes → Go To 5 No → Repair the ASD Relay Output circuit. Perform POWERTRAIN VERIFICATION TEST VER - 3.
5	Turn the ignition off. Disconnect the PCM harness connector. Disconnect the Generator Field harness connector. Measure the resistance of the Generator Field Driver circuit from PCM harness connector to ground. Is the resistance below 5.0 ohms? Yes → Repair the Generator Field Driver circuit for a shorted to ground. Perform POWERTRAIN VERIFICATION TEST VER - 3. No → Go To 6
6	Turn the ignition off. Disconnect the PCM harness connector. Disconnect the Generator Field harness connector. Measure the resistance of the Generator Field Driver circuit from the PCM harness connector to the Generator Field harness connector. Is the resistance below 5.0 ohms? Yes → Go To 7 No → Repair the Generator Field Driver circuit for an open. Perform POWERTRAIN VERIFICATION TEST VER - 3.
7	Turn the ignition off. Disconnect the Generator Field harness connector. Measure the resistance across the Generator Field Terminals at the Generator. Is the resistance above 15.0 ohms? Yes → Replace the Generator. Perform POWERTRAIN VERIFICATION TEST VER - 3. No → Go To 8
8	Turn the ignition off. Disconnect the Generator Field harness connector. Measure the resistance across the Generator Field Terminals at the Generator. Is the resistance below 0.5 ohms? Yes → Replace the Generator. Perform POWERTRAIN VERIFICATION TEST VER - 3. No → Go To 9
9	If there is no more possible causes remaining, view repair. Repair Replace and program the Powertrain Control Module in accordance with the Service Information. Perform POWERTRAIN VERIFICATION TEST VER - 3.

CR1120100394020X

Fig. 14   Code P0622: Alternator Field Not Switching Properly (Part 2 of 2). Sebring Convertible, Sebring Sedan & Stratus Sedan

TEST	ACTION
1	Turn the ignition on. With the DRBIII®, read the Ambient Temperature Sensor voltage. Is the voltage above 4.8 volts? Yes → Go To 2 No → Go To 7
2	Turn the ignition off. Disconnect the Ambient Temperature Sensor harness connector. Turn the ignition on. Measure the voltage of the Ambient Temperature Sensor Signal circuit in the Ambient Temperature Sensor harness connector. Is the voltage above 5.2 volts? Yes → Repair the Ambient Temperature Sensor Signal circuit for a short to battery voltage. Perform POWERTRAIN VERIFICATION TEST VER - 5. No → Go To 3

CR1120100395010X

Fig. 15   Code P1492: Ambient/Battery Temperature Sensor Voltage Too High (Part 1 of 2). Sebring Convertible, Sebring Sedan & Stratus Sedan

TEST	ACTION
1	Turn the ignition on. With the DRBIII®, read the Ambient Temperature Sensor voltage. Is the voltage below 0.3 volt? Yes → Go To 2 No → Go To 6
2	Turn the ignition off. Disconnect the Ambient Temperature Sensor harness connector. Turn the ignition on. With the DRBIII®, read Ambient Temperature Sensor voltage. Is the voltage above 1.0 volt? Yes → Replace the Ambient Temperature Sensor. Perform POWERTRAIN VERIFICATION TEST VER - 5. No → Go To 3
3	Turn the ignition off. Disconnect the Ambient Temperature Sensor harness connector. Disconnect the PCM harness connector. Measure the resistance of the Ambient Temperature Sensor Signal circuit in the Ambient Temperature Sensor harness connector to chassis ground. Is the resistance below 100 ohms? Yes → Repair the Ambient Temperature Sensor Signal circuit for a short to ground. Perform POWERTRAIN VERIFICATION TEST VER - 5. No → Go To 4

CR1120100396010X

Fig. 16   Code P1493: Ambient/Battery Temperature Sensor Voltage Too Low (Part 1 of 2). Sebring Convertible, Sebring Sedan & Stratus Sedan

TEST	ACTION
3	Turn the ignition off. Disconnect the Ambient Temperature Sensor harness connector. Connect a jumper wire between the Ambient Temperature Sensor Signal circuit and the Sensor ground circuit in the Ambient Temperature Sensor harness connector. Turn the ignition on. With the DRBIII®, read Ambient Temperature Sensor voltage. Is the voltage below 1.0 volt? Yes → Replace the Ambient Temperature Sensor. Perform POWERTRAIN VERIFICATION TEST VER - 5. No → Go To 4
4	Turn the ignition off. Disconnect the Ambient Temperature Sensor harness connector. Disconnect the PCM harness connector. Measure the resistance of the Ambient Temperature Sensor Signal circuit between the Ambient Temperature Sensor harness connector and the PCM harness connector. Is the resistance below 5.0 ohms? Yes → Go To 5 No → Repair the Ambient Temperature Sensor Signal circuit for an open. Perform POWERTRAIN VERIFICATION TEST VER - 5.
5	Turn the ignition off. Disconnect the Ambient Temperature Sensor harness connector. Disconnect the PCM harness connector. Measure the resistance of the Sensor ground circuit between the Ambient Temperature Sensor harness connector and the PCM harness connector. Is the resistance below 5.0 ohms? Yes → Go To 6 No → Repair the Sensor ground circuit for an open. Perform POWERTRAIN VERIFICATION TEST VER - 5.
6	If there are no possible causes remaining, view repair. Repair Replace and program the Powertrain Control Module Perform POWERTRAIN VERIFICATION TEST VER - 5.

CR1120100395020X

Fig. 15   Code P1492: Ambient/Battery Temperature Sensor Voltage Too High (Part 2 of 2). Sebring Convertible, Sebring Sedan & Stratus Sedan

TEST	ACTION
4	Turn the ignition off. Disconnect the Ambient Temperature Sensor harness connector. Disconnect the PCM harness connector. Measure the resistance between the Ambient Temperature Sensor Signal circuit and the Sensor ground circuit in the Ambient Temperature Sensor harness connector. Is the resistance below 100 ohms? Yes → Repair the Ambient Temperature Sensor Signal circuit for a short to the Sensor ground circuit. Perform POWERTRAIN VERIFICATION TEST VER - 5. No → Go To 5
5	If there are no possible causes remaining, view repair. Repair Replace and program the Powertrain Control Module in accordance with the Service Information. Perform POWERTRAIN VERIFICATION TEST VER - 5.
6	WARNING: WHEN THE ENGINE IS OPERATING, DO NOT STAND IN A DIRECT LINE WITH THE FAN. DO NOT PUT YOUR HANDS NEAR THE PULLEYS, BELTS OR FAN. DO NOT WEAR LOOSE CLOTHING. NOTE: The conditions that set the DTC are not present at this time. The following list may help in identifying the intermittent condition. With the engine running at normal operating temperature, monitor the DRB parameters related to the DTC while wiggling the wiring harness. Look for parameter values to change and/or a DTC to set. Review the DRB Freeze Frame information. If possible, try to duplicate the conditions under which the DTC was set. Refer to any Technical Service Bulletins (TSB) that may apply. Visually inspect the related wiring harness. Look for any chafed, pierced, pinched, or partially broken wires. Visually inspect the related wiring harness connectors. Look for broken, bent, pushed out, or corroded terminals. Were any of the above conditions present? Yes → Repair as necessary Perform POWERTRAIN VERIFICATION TEST VER - 5. No → Test Complete.

CR1120100396020X

Fig. 16   Code P1493: Ambient/Battery Temperature Sensor Voltage Too Low (Part 2 of 2). Sebring Convertible, Sebring Sedan & Stratus Sedan

TEST	ACTION

1	Note: Battery must be fully charged.
	Note: Generator Belt tension and condition must be checked before continuing.
	Turn the ignition on.
	With DRBIII®, actuate the Generator Field Driver.
	With a 12-volt test light connected to ground, backprobe the Generator Field Driver circuit in the back of Generator Field harness connector.
	Does the test light illuminate brightly and flash?
	
	    Yes → Go To 2
	
	    No → Go To 5

2	With DRBIII®, stop all actuation.
	Turn the ignition on.
	With DRBIII®, read the Target Charging voltage.
	Is the Target Charging voltage above 13 volts?
	
	    Yes → Go To 3
	
	    No → Go To 4

3	Start the engine.
	With DRBIII®, manually set the engine speed to 1600 RPM.
	With DRBIII®, read both the Battery voltage and the Target Charging voltage.
	Compare the Target Charging Voltage to the Battery Voltage reading.
	Monitor voltage for 5 minutes, if necessary. Look for a 1.0 volt difference or more.
	Was there more than a 1.0 volt difference?
	
	    Yes → Replace the Powertrain Control Module in accordance with the Service Information.
	           Perform POWERTRAIN VERIFICATION TEST VER - 3.
	
	    No → Go To 4

CR1120100397010X

Fig. 17 Code P1594: Charging System Voltage Too High (Part 1 of 2). Sebring Convertible, Sebring Sedan & Stratus Sedan

TEST	ACTION

1	NOTE: Inspect the vehicle for aftermarket accessories that may exceed the Generator System output.
	Turn the ignition off.
	NOTE: The battery must be fully charged.
	NOTE: The Generator belt tension and condition must be checked before continuing.
	Start the engine.
	Allow the idle to stabilize.
	With the DRBIII®, read the Target Charging Voltage.
	Is the Target Charging Voltage above 15.1 volts?
	
	    Yes → Go To 8
	
	    No → Go To 2

2	WARNING: WHEN THE ENGINE IS OPERATING, DO NOT STAND IN A DIRECT LINE WITH THE FAN. DO NOT PUT YOUR HANDS NEAR THE PULLEYS, BELTS OR FAN. DO NOT WEAR LOOSE CLOTHING.
	Turn the ignition on.
	NOTE: Ensure all wires are clear of the engine's moving parts.
	Measure the voltage between the Generator B+ Terminal and the Battery+ Post.
	Start the engine.
	Is the voltage above 0.4 volt?
	
	    Yes → Repair the B+ circuit for high resistance between the Generator and Battery.
	           Perform POWERTRAIN VERIFICATION TEST VER - 3.
	
	    No → Go To 3

CR1120100398010X

Fig. 18 Code P1682: Charging System Voltage Too Low (Part 1 of 3). 2004–06 Sebring Convertible, Sebring Sedan & Stratus Sedan

TEST	ACTION

4	WARNING: WHEN THE ENGINE IS OPERATING, DO NOT STAND IN A DIRECT LINE WITH THE FAN. DO NOT PUT YOUR HANDS NEAR THE PULLEYS, BELTS OR FAN. DO NOT WEAR LOOSE CLOTHING.
	NOTE: The conditions that set the DTC are not present at this time. The following list may help in identifying the intermittent condition.
	With the engine running at normal operating temperature, monitor the DRB parameters related to the DTC while wiggling the wiring harness. Look for parameter values to change and/or a DTC to set.
	Review the DRB Freeze Frame information. If possible, try to duplicate the conditions under which the DTC was set.
	Refer to any Technical Service Bulletins (TSB) that may apply.
	Visually inspect the related wiring harness. Look for any chafed, pierced, pinched, or partially broken wires.
	Visually inspect the related wiring harness connectors. Look for broken, bent, pushed out, or corroded terminals.
	Were any of the above conditions present?
	
	    Yes → Repair as necessary
	           Perform POWERTRAIN VERIFICATION TEST VER - 3.
	
	    No → Test Complete.

5	Turn the ignition off.
	Disconnect the PCM harness connector.
	Disconnect the Generator Field harness connector.
	Measure the resistance of the Generator Field Driver circuit from the PCM harness connector to ground.
	Is the resistance below 5.0 ohms?
	
	    Yes → Repair the Generator Field Driver circuit shorted to ground.
	           Perform POWERTRAIN VERIFICATION TEST VER - 3.
	
	    No → Go To 6

6	Turn the ignition off.
	Disconnect the Generator Field harness connector.
	Measure resistance of the Generator Field Driver terminal on the Generator to ground.
	Is the resistance below 5.0 ohms?
	
	    Yes → Repair or replace the shorted Generator as necessary.
	           Perform POWERTRAIN VERIFICATION TEST VER - 3.
	
	    No → Go To 7

7	If there are no possible causes remaining, view repair.
	
	    Repair
	           Replace and program the Powertrain Control Module
	
	           Perform POWERTRAIN VERIFICATION TEST VER - 3.

CR1120100397020X

Fig. 17 Code P1594: Charging System Voltage Too High (Part 2 of 2). Sebring Convertible, Sebring Sedan & Stratus Sedan

TEST	ACTION

3	WARNING: WHEN THE ENGINE IS OPERATING, DO NOT STAND IN A DIRECT LINE WITH THE FAN. DO NOT PUT YOUR HANDS NEAR THE PULLEYS, BELTS OR FAN. DO NOT WEAR LOOSE CLOTHING.
	Start the engine.
	Warm the engine to operating temperature.
	NOTE: Ensure all wires are clear of the engine's moving parts.
	Measure the voltage between the Generator case and Battery ground post.
	Is the voltage above 0.1 volt?
	
	    Yes → Repair Generator Ground for high resistance, Generator Case to Battery ground side.
	           Perform POWERTRAIN VERIFICATION TEST VER - 3.
	
	    No → Go To 4

4	Start the engine.
	WARNING: WHEN THE ENGINE IS OPERATING, DO NOT STAND IN A DIRECT LINE WITH THE FAN. DO NOT PUT YOUR HANDS NEAR THE PULLEYS, BELTS OR FAN. DO NOT WEAR LOOSE CLOTHING.
	Turn on all accessories, manually set engine speed to 1600 RPM.
	With DRBIII®, read Target Charging and Charging voltage.
	Compare the two readings.
	Is there more than a 1.0 volt difference?
	
	    Yes → Go To 5
	
	    No → Go To 8

5	Turn the ignition off.
	Disconnect the PCM harness connector.
	Disconnect the Generator Field harness connector.
	Measure the resistance of the Generator Field Driver circuit from the PCM harness connector to Generator harness connector.
	Is the resistance below 5.0 ohms?
	
	    Yes → Go To 6
	
	    No → Repair the Generator Field Driver circuit for an open.
	           Perform POWERTRAIN VERIFICATION TEST VER - 3.

6	Disconnect the Generator Field harness connector.
	Turn the ignition on.
	With the DRBIII® actuate the Generator Field Driver.
	Using a 12-volt test light connected to ground, probe the ASD Relay Output circuit in the Generator harness connector.
	Does the test light illuminate brightly?
	
	    Yes → Go To 7
	
	    No → Repair the ASD Relay Output circuit.
	           Perform POWERTRAIN VERIFICATION TEST VER - 3.

7	If there is no possible causes remaining, view repair.
	
	    Yes → Repair or replace the Generator as necessary..
	           Perform POWERTRAIN VERIFICATION TEST VER - 3.

CR1120100398020X

Fig. 18 Code P1682: Charging System Voltage Too Low (Part 2 of 3). 2004–06 Sebring Convertible, Sebring Sedan & Stratus Sedan

TEST	ACTION
8	**WARNING: WHEN THE ENGINE IS OPERATING, DO NOT STAND IN A DIRECT LINE WITH THE FAN. DO NOT PUT YOUR HANDS NEAR THE PULLEYS, BELTS OR FAN. DO NOT WEAR LOOSE CLOTHING.** NOTE: The conditions that set the DTC are not present at this time. The following list may help in identifying the intermittent condition. With the engine running at normal operating temperature, monitor the DRB parameters related to the DTC while wiggling the wiring harness. Look for parameter values to change and/or a DTC to set. Review the DRB Freeze Frame information. If possible, try to duplicate the conditions under which the DTC was set. Refer to any Technical Service Bulletins (TSB) that may apply. Visually inspect the related wiring harness. Look for any chafed, pierced, pinched, or partially broken wires. Visually inspect the related wiring harness connectors. Look for broken, bent, pushed out, or corroded terminals. Were any of the above conditions present? Yes → Repair as necessary Perform POWERTRAIN VERIFICATION TEST VER - 3. No → Test Complete.

CR1120100398030X

Fig. 18   Code P1682: Charging System Voltage Too Low (Part 3 of 3). Sebring Convertible, Sebring Sedan & Stratus Sedan

POWERTRAIN VERIFICATION TEST VER - 3
1. **NOTE: If the PCM has been replaced and the correct VIN and mileage have not been programmed, a DTC will be set in the ABS Module, Airbag Module and the SKIM.** 2. **NOTE: If the vehicle is equipped with a Sentry Key Immobilizer System, Secret Key data must be updated. Refer to the Service Information for the PCM, SKIM and the Transponder (ignition key) for programming information.** 3. Inspect the vehicle to ensure that all components related to the repair are connected properly. 4. With the DRBIII®, clear DTCs. 5. Perform generator output test. Refer to the appropriate service information as necessary. 6. Start the engine and set engine speed to 2000 RPM for at least thirty seconds. 7. Cycle the ignition key off and on. 8. With the DRBIII®, read the DTCs. If the DTC returns, or any other symptom or DTC is present, refer to the appropriate category and perform the corresponding symptom. 9. If there are no DTCs present and all components are functioning properly, the repair is complete. Are any DTCs present? Yes → Repair is not complete, refer to appropriate symptom. No → Repair is complete.

CR1120100399000X

Fig. 19   Verification Test VER-3. Sebring Convertible, Sebring Sedan & Stratus Sedan

POWERTRAIN VERIFICATION TEST VER - 5
1. **NOTE: If the PCM has been replaced and the correct VIN and mileage have not been programmed, a DTC will be set in the ABS Module, Airbag Module and the SKIM.** 2. **NOTE: If the vehicle is equipped with a Sentry Key Immobilizer System, Secret Key data must be updated. Refer to the Service Information for the PCM, SKIM and the Transponder (ignition key) for programming information.** 3. Inspect the vehicle to ensure that all engine components are properly installed and connected. Reassemble and reconnect components as necessary. 4. Connect the DRBIII® to the data link connector. 5. Ensure the fuel tank has at least a quarter tank of fuel. Turn off all accessories. 6. If a Comprehensive Component DTC was repaired, perform steps 5 - 8. If a Major OBDII Monitor DTC was repaired skip those steps and continue verification. 7. After the ignition has been off for at least 10 seconds, restart the vehicle and run 2 minutes. 8. If the Good Trip counter changed to one or more and there are no new DTC's, the repair was successful and is now complete. Erase DTC's and disconnect the DRBIII®. 9. If the repaired DTC has reset, the repair is not complete. Check for any related TSB's or flash updates and return to the Symptom list. 10. If another DTC has set, return to the Symptom List and follow the path specified for that DTC. 11. With the DRBIII®, monitor the appropriate pre-test enabling conditions until all conditions have been met. Once the conditions have been met, switch screen to the appropriate OBDII monitor, (Audible beeps when the monitor is running). 12. If the monitor ran, and the Good Trip counter changed to one or more, the repair was successful and is now complete. Erase DTC's and disconnect the DRBIII®. 13. If the repaired OBDII trouble code has reset or was seen in the monitor while on the road test, the repair is not complete. Check for any related technical service bulletins or flash updates and return to Symptom List. 14. If another DTC has set, return to the Symptom List and follow the path specified for that DTC. Are any DTCs present? Yes → Repair is not complete, refer to appropriate symptom. No → Repair is complete.

CR1120100400000X

Fig. 20   Verification Test VER-5. Sebring Convertible, Sebring Sedan & Stratus Sedan

ALTERNATOR SPECIFICATIONS

Model & Year	Engine	Rated Output Amps
Charger, Magnum & 300	2.7L, 3.5L, 5.7L & 6.1L	—
Concorde, Intrepid & 300M	2.7L	105
	3.2L & 3.5L	125
Sebring Convertible, Sebring Sedan & Stratus Sedan	2.4L & 3.0L	135

Melco

INDEX

	Page No.
Alternator Specifications	11-26
Description	11-17
Diagnosis & Testing	11-17

	Page No.
Diagnostic Tests	11-17
Wiring Diagrams	11-17
Diagnostic Chart Index	11-18

	Page No.
Precautions	11-17
Battery Ground Cable	11-17

PRECAUTIONS

Battery Ground Cable

Prior to service, disconnect battery ground cable and isolate as required.

DESCRIPTION

The charging system is turned on and off with the ignition switch. This voltage is connected through the PCM and supplied to one of the alternator field terminals (Alt. Source +) at the back of the alternator. The alternator is internally grounded. The alternator regulates the field using Pin 1 of the field connector.

The PCM receives a voltage input from the alternator and also a battery voltage input from the TIPM, it then compares the voltages and if there is a difference it send a signal to the alternator EVR circuit to increase or decrease output. It uses a pulse width modulation (PWM) to send signals to the alternator circuitry to control the amount of output from the alternator. The amount of DC current produced by the alternator is controlled by the EVR (electronic voltage regulator) circuitry contained within the alternator.

DIAGNOSIS & TESTING

Wiring Diagrams

Refer to **Figs. 1 and 2** for wiring diagrams.

Diagnostic Tests

Refer to **Figs. 3 through 13** for diagnostic tests.

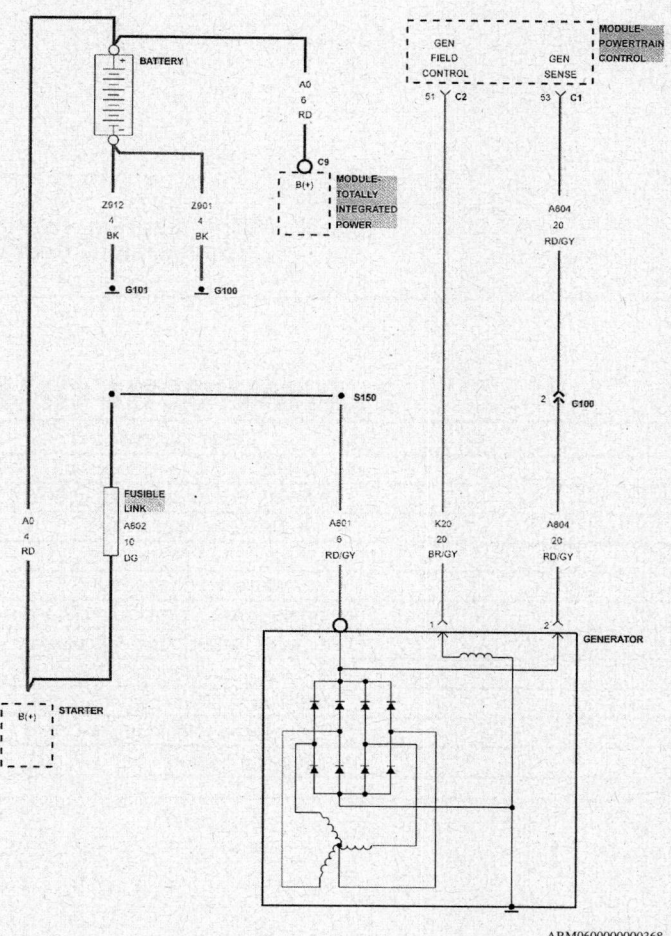

Fig. 1   Wiring diagram. Caliber

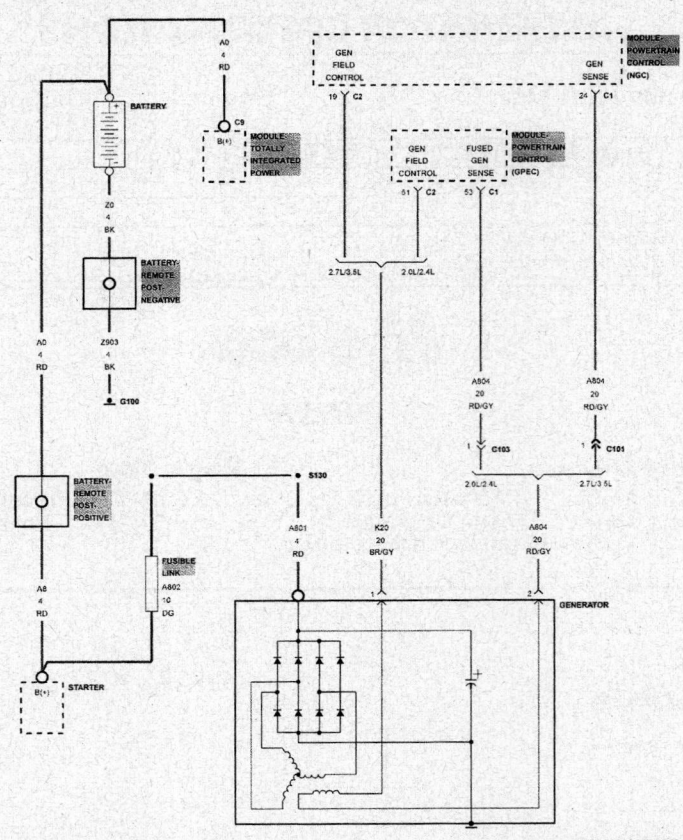

Fig. 2 Wiring diagram. Avenger Sedan, Sebring Convertible & Sebring Sedan

DIAGNOSTIC CHART INDEX

Code	Description	Page No.	Fig. No.
—	Charging System Operation	11-23	11
—	Checking For An Intermittent DTC	11-25	12
—	PCM Verification Test	11-25	13
P0562	Battery Voltage Low	11-19	3
P0563	Battery Voltage High	11-19	4
P0622	Alternator Field Control Circuit/Open	11-19	5
P0625	Alternator Field Control Circuit Low	11-20	6
P0626	Alternator Field Control Circuit High	11-21	7
P063A	Alternator Voltage Sense Circuit	11-21	8
P2503	Charging System Output Low	11-22	9
P2504	Charging System Output High	11-23	10

Diagnostic Test

1. DTC IS ACTIVE

Start the engine and allow it to reach operating temperature.

WARNING: When the engine is operating, do not stand in direct line with the fan. Do not put your hands near the pulleys, belts, or fan. Do not wear loose clothing. Failure to follow these instructions can result in personal injury or death.

With the scan tool, select View DTCs.

Is the status Active for this DTC?

Yes

- Go to 2

No

- Refer to the *CHECKING FOR AN INTERMITTENT DTC Diagnostic Procedure.

2. CHECKING THE CHARGING SYSTEM OPERATION

Perform the diagnostic procedure for CHECKING THE CHARGING SYSTEM OPERATION.

Were any problems found?

Yes

- Repair as necessary
- Perform the PCM Verification Test.

No

- Refer to the *CHECKING FOR AN INTERMITTENT DTC Diagnostic Procedure.

ARM0600000000370

Fig. 3   Code P0562: Battery Voltage Low

Diagnostic Test

1. DTC IS ACTIVE

Turn the ignition on.
With the scan tool, Clear DTCs in the Powertrain Control Module (PCM).
Start the engine and allow it to reach operating temperature.

WARNING: When the engine is operating, do not stand in direct line with the fan. Do not put your hands near the pulleys, belts, or fan. Do not wear loose clothing. Failure to follow these instructions can result in personal injury or death.

Increase engine speed by pressing the accelerator pedal. Do not exceed 3500 rpm.
With the scan tool, select View DTCs.

Is the status Active for this DTC?

Yes

- Go to 2

No

- Refer to the *CHECKING FOR AN INTERMITTENT DTC Diagnostic Procedure.

2. (K20) GEN FIELD CONTROL CIRCUIT SHORTED TO GROUND

Turn the ignition off.
Disconnect the Generator connector.
Disconnect the Powertrain Control Module (PCM) connector.
Measure the resistance between ground and the (K20) Gen Field Control circuit in the Generator harness connector.

Is the resistance above 100 ohms?

Yes

- Go to 3

No

- Repair the (K20) Gen Field Control circuit for a short to ground.
- Perform the PCM Verification Test.

ARM0600000000372

Fig. 5   Code P0622: Alternator Field Control Circuit/Open (Part 1 of 3)

Diagnostic Test

1. DTC IS ACTIVE

Start the engine and allow it to reach operating temperature.

WARNING: When the engine is operating, do not stand in direct line with the fan. Do not put your hands near the pulleys, belts, or fan. Do not wear loose clothing. Failure to follow these instructions can result in personal injury or death.

With the scan tool, select View DTCs.

Is the status Active for this DTC?

Yes

- Go to 2

No

- Refer to the *CHECKING FOR AN INTERMITTENT DTC Diagnostic Procedure.

2. CHECKING THE CHARGING SYSTEM OPERATION

Perform the diagnostic procedure for CHECKING THE CHARGING SYSTEM OPERATION.

Were any problems found?

Yes

- Repair as necessary
- Perform the PCM Verification Test.

No

- Refer to the *CHECKING FOR AN INTERMITTENT DTC Diagnostic Procedure.

ARM0600000000371

Fig. 4   Code P0563: Battery Voltage High

3. (K20) GEN FIELD CONTROL CIRCUIT OPEN OR HIGH RESISTANCE

CAUTION: Do not probe the PCM harness connectors. Probing the PCM harness connectors will damage the PCM terminals, resulting in poor terminal to pin connection. Install Miller Special Tool #8815 to perform diagnosis.

Measure the resistance of the (K20) Gen Field Control circuit between the Generator harness connector and the appropriate terminal of special tool #8815.

Is the resistance below 5.0 ohms?

Yes

- Go to 4

No

- Repair the (K20) Gen Field Control circuit for an open circuit or high resistance.
- Perform the PCM Verification Test.

4. GENERATOR

Connect the Powertrain Control Module (PCM) connector.
Turn the ignition on.
With the scan tool, actuate the Alternator Field Control State.
Using a 12 volt test light connected to ground, check the (K20) Gen Field Control circuit in the Generator harness connector.

NOTE: The voltage supplied to the solenoid circuit during the actuation will be less than battery voltage. The test light should be illuminated, but not as bright as a direct connection to the battery.

Is the test light illuminated during the actuation?

Yes

- Replace the Generator
- Perform the PCM Verification Test.

No

- Go to 5

ARM0600000000373

Fig. 5   Code P0622: Alternator Field Control Circuit/Open (Part 2 of 3)

5. POWERTRAIN CONTROL MODULE (PCM)

Using the wiring diagram/schematic as a guide, inspect the wiring and connectors between the Generator and the Powertrain Control Module (PCM).
Look for any chafed, pierced, pinched, or partially broken wires.
Look for broken, bent, pushed out or corroded terminals.
Refer to any Technical Service Bulletins that may apply.

Were any problems found?

Yes

- Repair as necessary.
- Perform the PCM Verification Test.

No

- Replace and program the Powertrain Control Module (PCM)

- Perform the PCM Verification Test.

ARM0600000000374

Fig. 5   Code P0622: Alternator Field Control Circuit/Open (Part 3 of 3)

3. (K20) GEN FIELD CONTROL CIRCUIT OPEN OR HIGH RESISTANCE

Measure the resistance of the (K20) Gen Field Control circuit between the Generator harness connector and the Powertrain Control Module (PCM) harness connector.

Is the resistance below 5.0 ohms?

Yes

- Go to 4

No

- Repair the (K20) Gen Field Control circuit for an open circuit or high resistance.
- Perform the PCM Verification Test Ver. 1

4. GENERATOR

Connect the Powertrain Control Module (PCM) connector.
Turn the ignition on.
With the scan tool, actuate the Generator field control to the ON (100%) position.
Using a 12 volt test light connected to ground, check the (K20) Gen Field Control circuit in the Generator harness connector.

NOTE: The test light should be illuminated and bright. Compare the brightness to that of a direct connection to the battery.

With the scan tool, actuate the Generator field control to the OFF (0%) position.
Using a 12 volt test light connected to ground, check the (K20) Gen Field Control circuit in the Generator harness connector.

NOTE: The test light should not be illuminated.

Is the test light illuminated and bright with the actuation ON (100%) and not illuminated with the actuation OFF (0%)?

Yes

- Replace the Generator
- Perform the PCM Verification Test Ver. 1

No

- Go to 5

ARM0600000000382

Fig. 6   Code P0625: Alternator Field Control Circuit Low (Part 2 of 3). Caliber

Diagnostic Test

1. DTC IS ACTIVE

Start the engine and allow it to reach normal operating temperature.

WARNING: When the engine is operating, do not stand in direct line with the fan. Do not put your hands near the pulleys, belts, or fan. Do not wear loose clothing. Failure to follow these instructions can result in personal injury or death.

With the scan tool, select View DTCs.

Is the status Active for this DTC?

Yes

- Go to 2

No

- Refer to the *CHECKING FOR AN INTERMITTENT DTC Diagnostic Procedure.

2. (K20) GEN FIELD CONTROL CIRCUIT SHORTED TO GROUND

Turn the ignition off.
Disconnect the Generator connector.
Disconnect the Powertrain Control Module (PCM) connector.
Measure the resistance between ground and the (K20) Gen Field Control circuit in the Generator harness connector.

Is the resistance below 100 ohms?

Yes

- Repair the (K20) Gen Field Control circuit for a short to ground.
- Perform the PCM Verification Test Ver. 1

No

- Go to 3

ARM0600000000381

Fig. 6   Code P0625: Alternator Field Control Circuit Low (Part 1 of 3). Caliber

5. POWERTRAIN CONTROL MODULE (PCM)

Using the wiring diagram/schematic as a guide, inspect the wiring and connectors between the Generator and the Powertrain Control Module (PCM).
Look for any chafed, pierced, pinched, or partially broken wires.
Look for broken, bent, pushed out or corroded terminals.
Refer to any Technical Service Bulletins that may apply.

Were any problems found?

Yes

- Repair as necessary.
- Perform the PCM Verification Test Ver. 1

No

- Replace and program the Powertrain Control Module (PCM)

- Perform the PCM Verification Test Ver. 1

ARM0600000000383

Fig. 6   Code P0625: Alternator Field Control Circuit Low (Part 3 of 3). Caliber

Diagnostic Test

1. DTC IS ACTIVE

Start the engine and allow it to reach normal operating temperature.

WARNING: When the engine is operating, do not stand in direct line with the fan. Do not put your hands near the pulleys, belts, or fan. Do not wear loose clothing. Failure to follow these instructions can result in personal injury or death.

With the scan tool, select View DTCs.

Is the status Active for this DTC?

Yes

- Go to 2

No

- Refer to the *CHECKING FOR AN INTERMITTENT DTC Diagnostic Procedure.

2. (K20) GEN FIELD CONTROL CIRCUIT SHORTED TO VOLTAGE

Turn the ignition off.
Disconnect the Generator connector.
Disconnect the Powertrain Control Module (PCM) connector.
Turn the ignition on.
Measure the voltage of the (K20) Gen Field Control circuit in the Generator harness connector.

Is there any voltage present?

Yes

- Repair the (K20) Gen Field Control circuit for a short to voltage.
- Perform the PCM Verification Test Ver. 1

No

- Go to 3

ARM0600000000384

Fig. 7 Code P0626: Alternator Field Control Circuit High (Part 1 of 3). Caliber

5. POWERTRAIN CONTROL MODULE (PCM)

Using the wiring diagram/schematic as a guide, inspect the wiring and connectors between the Generator and the Powertrain Control Module (PCM).
Look for any chafed, pierced, pinched, or partially broken wires.
Look for broken, bent, pushed out or corroded terminals.
Refer to any Technical Service Bulletins that may apply.

Were any problems found?

Yes

- Repair as necessary.
- Perform the PCM Verification Test Ver. 1

No

- Replace and program the Powertrain Control Module (PCM)

- Perform the PCM Verification Test Ver. 1

ARM0600000000386

Fig. 7 Code P0626: Alternator Field Control Circuit High (Part 3 of 3). Caliber

3. (K20) GEN FIELD CONTROL CIRCUIT OPEN OR HIGH RESISTANCE

Turn the ignition off.
Measure the resistance of the (K20) Gen Field Control circuit between the Generator harness connector and the Powertrain Control Module (PCM) harness connector.

Is the resistance below 5.0 ohms?

Yes

- Go to 4

No

- Repair the (K20) Gen Field Control circuit for an open circuit or high resistance.
- Perform the PCM Verification Test Ver. 1

4. GENERATOR

Connect the Powertrain Control Module (PCM) connector.
Turn the ignition on.
With the scan tool, actuate the Generator field control to the ON (100%) position.
Using a 12 volt test light connected to ground, check the (K20) Gen Field Control circuit in the Generator harness connector.

NOTE: The test light should be illuminated and bright. Compare the brightness to that of a direct connection to the battery.

With the scan tool, actuate the Generator field control to the OFF (0%) position.
Using a 12 volt test light connected to ground, check the (K20) Gen Field Control circuit in the Generator harness connector.

NOTE: The test light should not be illuminated.

Is the test light illuminated and bright with the actuation ON (100%) and not illuminated with the actuation OFF (0%)?

Yes

- Replace the Generator
- Perform the PCM Verification Test Ver. 1

No

- Go to 5

ARM0600000000385

Fig. 7 Code P0626: Alternator Field Control Circuit High (Part 2 of 3). Caliber

Diagnostic Test

1. DTC IS ACTIVE

Start the engine and allow it reach operating temperature.
With the scan tool, select View DTCs.

Is the status Active for this DTC?

Yes

- Go to 2

No

- Refer to the *CHECKING FOR AN INTERMITTENT DTC Diagnostic Procedure.

2. (A804) GENERATOR SENSE CIRCUIT SHORTED TO VOLTAGE

Turn the ignition off.
Disconnect the Generator connector.
Disconnect the Powertrain Control Module (PCM) connector.
Turn the ignition on.
Measure the voltage of the (A804) Generator Sense circuit in the Generator harness connector.

Is there any voltage present?

Yes

- Repair the (A804) Generator Sense circuit for a short to voltage.
- Perform the PCM Verification Test.

No

- Go to 3

ARM0600000000375

Fig. 8 Code P063A: Alternator Voltage Sense Circuit (Part 1 of 4)

3. (A804) GENERATOR SENSE CIRCUIT SHORTED TO GROUND

Turn the ignition off.
Measure the resistance between ground and the (A804) Generator Sense circuit in the Generator harness connector.

Is the resistance below 100 ohms?

Yes

- Repair the (A804) Generator Sense circuit for a short to ground.
- Perform the PCM Verification Test.

No

- Go to 4

4. (A804) GENERATOR SENSE CIRCUIT OPEN OR HIGH RESISTANCE

CAUTION: Do not probe the PCM harness connectors. Probing the PCM harness connectors will damage the PCM terminals, resulting in poor terminal to pin connection. Install Miller Special Tool #8815 to perform diagnosis.

Measure the resistance of the (A804) Generator Sense circuit between the Generator harness connector and the appropriate terminal of special tool #8815.

Is the resistance below 5.0 ohms?

Yes

- Go to 5

No

- Repair the (A804) Generator Sense circuit for an open circuit or high resistance.
- Perform the PCM Verification Test.

ARM0600000000376

Fig. 8 Code P063A: Alternator Voltage Sense Circuit (Part 2 of 4)

6. POWERTRAIN CONTROL MODULE (PCM)

Using the wiring diagram/schematic as a guide, inspect the wiring and connectors between the Generator and the Powertrain Control Module (PCM).
Look for any chafed, pierced, pinched, or partially broken wires.
Look for broken, bent, pushed out or corroded terminals.
Refer to any Technical Service Bulletins that may apply.

Were any problems found?

Yes

- Repair as necessary.
- Perform the PCM Verification Test.

No

- Replace and program the Powertrain Control Module (PCM)

- Perform the PCM Verification Test.

ARM0600000000378

Fig. 8 Code P063A: Alternator Voltage Sense Circuit (Part 4 of 4)

5. GENERATOR

WARNING: When the engine is operating, do not stand in direct line with the fan. Do not put your hands near the pulleys, belts, or fan. Do not wear loose clothing. Failure to follow these instructions can result in personal injury or death.

Connect the Generator connector.
Connect the Powertrain Control Module (PCM) connector.
Turn the ignition on.

CAUTION: Do not probe the PCM harness connectors. Probing the PCM harness connectors will damage the PCM terminals, resulting in poor terminal to pin connection. Install Miller Special Tool #8815 along with the #8815-1 to perform the diagnosis.

While backprobing, measure the voltage of the (A804) Generator Sense circuit in the appropriate terminal of special tool #8815-1.
Start the engine.
With the scan tool, perform the Generator Full Field test.
Monitor the voltage of the (A804) Generator Sense circuit with the Generator Full Field test actuated.

NOTE: The voltage should increase by more than 1 volt with the Generator fully fielded.

Does the voltage increase by at least 1 volt with the Generator Full Field Test on?

Yes

- Go to 6

No

- Replace the Generator
- Perform the PCM Verification Test.

ARM0600000000377

Fig. 8 Code P063A: Alternator Voltage Sense Circuit (Part 3 of 4)

Diagnostic Test

1. DTC IS ACTIVE

Start the engine and allow it to reach operating temperature.

WARNING: When the engine is operating, do not stand in direct line with the fan. Do not put your hands near the pulleys, belts, or fan. Do not wear loose clothing. Failure to follow these instructions can result in personal injury or death.

With the scan tool, select View DTCs.

Is the status Active for this DTC?

Yes

- Go to 2

No

- Refer to the *CHECKING FOR AN INTERMITTENT DTC Diagnostic Procedure.

2. CHECKING THE CHARGING SYSTEM OPERATION

Perform the diagnostic procedure for CHECKING THE CHARGING SYSTEM OPERATION.

Were any problems found?

Yes

- Repair as necessary.
- Perform the PCM Verification Test.

No

- Refer to the *CHECKING FOR AN INTERMITTENT DTC Diagnostic Procedure.

ARM0600000000379

Fig. 9 Code P2503: Charging System Output Low

Diagnostic Test

1. DTC IS ACTIVE

Start the engine and allow it to reach operating temperature.

WARNING: When the engine is operating, do not stand in direct line with the fan. Do not put your hands near the pulleys, belts, or fan. Do not wear loose clothing. Failure to follow these instructions can result in personal injury or death.

With the scan tool, select View DTCs.

Is the status Active for this DTC?

Yes

- Go to 2

No

- Refer to the *CHECKING FOR AN INTERMITTENT DTC Diagnostic Procedure.

2. CHECKING THE CHARGING SYSTEM OPERATION

Perform the diagnostic procedure for CHECKING THE CHARGING SYSTEM OPERATION.

Were any problems found?

Yes

- Repair as necessary
- Perform the PCM Verification Test.

No

- Refer to the *CHECKING FOR AN INTERMITTENT DTC Diagnostic Procedure.

ARM0600000000380

Fig. 10   Code P2504: Charging System Output High

2. CHARGING SYSTEM INSPECTION

Inspect and test the battery in accordance with the Service Information.
Inspect the generator drive belt for proper alignment and adjustment.
Inspect the vehicle for aftermarket accessories that may exceed the generator system output.
Inspect the fuses in the IPM. If an open fuse is found, use the wire diagram/schematics as a guide and inspect the wiring and connectors for a damaged or shorted circuit.

Were any problems found?

Yes

- Repair as necessary.

No

- Go to 3

3. BATTERY POSITIVE (+) CIRCUIT HIGH RESISTANCE

NOTE: Make sure all testing equipment and cables are clear of any engine parts before starting the engine.

Start the engine.

WARNING: When the engine is operating, do not stand in direct line with the fan. Do not put your hands near the pulleys, belts, or fan. Do not wear loose clothing. Failure to follow these instructions can result in personal injury or death.

Measure the voltage between the B (+) Terminal at the Generator and the Battery Positive (+) Post.

Is the voltage below 0.4 volts?

Yes

- Go to 4

No

- Repair the battery positive (+) circuit between the generator and battery for high resistance.
- Perform the PCM Verification Test.

ARM0600000000388

Fig. 11   Charging System Operation (Part 2 of 8)

Diagnostic Test

1. GENERATOR FULL FIELD TEST

NOTE: Diagnose and repair any generator sense or field control circuit DTCs before proceeding with this test.

Start the engine and allow it to reach operating temperature.

WARNING: When the engine is operating, do not stand in direct line with the fan. Do not put your hands near the pulleys, belts, or fan. Do not wear loose clothing. Failure to follow these instructions can result in personal injury or death.

With the scan tool, perform the Generator Full Field test. Follow the instructions displayed on the scan tool.
Monitor the system (battery) voltage and the generator sense voltage on the scan tool while performing the test.

NOTE: With the engine running, the difference between the system (battery) voltage and the generator sense voltage should be below .2 volts.

NOTE: With the generator field fully actuated, the system (battery) voltage should be above 14.0 volts.

NOTE: With the generator field actuated off, the system (battery) voltage should be below 13.0 volts, and eventually drop as battery load is increased.

Did the system voltage change as described above during the Generator Full Field test?

Yes

- Test complete.

No

- Go to 2

ARM0600000000387

Fig. 11   Charging System Operation (Part 1 of 8)

4. GENERATOR CASE GROUND HIGH RESISTANCE

NOTE: Make sure all testing equipment and cables are clear of any engine parts before starting the engine.

Start the engine.
Measure the voltage between the Generator case and the Battery Negative (-) post.

Is the voltage below 0.1 volt?

Yes

- Go to 5

No

- Repair the Generator Case ground for high resistance.
- Perform the PCM Verification Test.

5. (A109) FUSED B(+) CIRCUIT HIGH RESISTANCE

Turn the ignition off.

CAUTION: Do not probe the PCM harness connectors. Probing the PCM harness connectors will damage the PCM terminals resulting in poor terminal to pin connection. Install Miller Special Tool #8815 along with the #8815-1 to perform the diagnosis.

Using a voltmeter, perform a voltage drop test by probing the battery positive (+) terminal and the appropriate terminal(s) of the special tool #8815. Make sure the voltmeter leads are connected so that positive polarity is displayed on the voltmeter.

Start the engine.

Is the voltage below 0.5 volts?

Yes

- Go to 6

No

- Repair the (A109) Fused B(+) circuit(s) for high resistance.
- Perform the PCM Verification Test.

ARM0600000000389

Fig. 11   Charging System Operation (Part 3 of 8)

6. (A804) GENERATOR SENSE CIRCUIT HIGH RESISTANCE

Turn the ignition off.

CAUTION: Do not probe the PCM harness connectors. Probing the PCM harness connectors will damage the PCM terminals resulting in poor terminal to pin connection. Install Miller Special Tool #8815 along with the #8815-1 to perform the diagnosis.

Using a voltmeter, perform a voltage drop test by backprobing the (A804) Generator Sense circuit at the Generator harness connector and probing the appropriate terminal of the special tool #8815. Make sure the voltmeter leads are connected so that positive polarity is displayed on the voltmeter.

WARNING: When the engine is operating, do not stand in direct line with the fan. Do not put your hands near the pulleys, belts, or fan. Do not wear loose clothing. Failure to follow these instructions can result in personal injury or death.

Start the engine.

Is the voltage below 0.5 volts?

Yes

- Go to 7

No

- Repair the (A804) Generator Sense circuit for high resistance.
- Perform the PCM Verification Test.

ARM0600000000390

Fig. 11   Charging System Operation (Part 4 of 8)

9. (K20) GEN FIELD CONTROL CIRCUIT SHORTED TO VOLTAGE

Turn the ignition off.
Disconnect the Powertrain Control Module (PCM) connector.
Turn the ignition on.
Measure the voltage of the (K20) Gen Field Control circuit in the Generator harness connector.

Is there any voltage present?

Yes

- Repair the (K20) Gen Field Control circuit for a short to voltage.
- Perform the PCM Verification Test.

No

- Go to 10

10. (K20) GEN FIELD CONTROL CIRCUIT SHORTED TO GROUND

Turn the ignition off.
Measure the resistance between ground and the (K20) Gen Field Control circuit in the Generator harness connector.

Is the resistance below 100 ohms?

Yes

- Repair the (K20) Gen Field Control circuit for a short to ground.
- Perform the PCM Verification Test.

No

- Go to 11

ARM0600000000392

Fig. 11   Charging System Operation (Part 6 of 8)

7. (K20) GEN FIELD CONTROL CIRCUIT HIGH RESISTANCE

Turn the ignition off.
CAUTION: Do not probe the PCM harness connectors. Probing the PCM harness connectors will damage the PCM terminals resulting in poor terminal to pin connection. Install Miller Special Tool #8815 along with the #8815-1 to perform the diagnosis.
Using a voltmeter, perform a voltage drop test by backprobing the (K20) Gen Field Control circuit at the Generator harness connector and probing the appropriate terminal of the special tool #8815. Make sure the voltmeter leads are connected so that positive polarity is displayed on the voltmeter.
Start the engine.
Is the voltage below 0.5 volts?
Yes

- Go to 8

No

- Repair the (K20) Gen Field Control circuit for high resistance.
- Perform the PCM Verification Test.

8. GENERATOR

Turn the ignition off.
Disconnect the Generator harness connector.
Connect a 12 volt test light connected between ground and the (K20) Gen Field Control circuit in the Generator harness connector.
Turn the ignition on.
With the scan tool, actuate the Alternator Field Control State to toggle.

NOTE: The test light should toggle on and off with the actuation.

NOTE: If a DTC is active, the actuation test may not be allowed by the PCM. If may be necessary to clear DTCs before starting the actuation.

Does the test light illuminate on and off with the actuation?
Yes

- Replace the Generator
- Perform the PCM Verification Test.

No

- Go to 9

ARM0600000000391

Fig. 11   Charging System Operation (Part 5 of 8)

11. (K20) GEN FIELD CONTROL CIRCUIT OPEN OR HIGH RESISTANCE

CAUTION: Do not probe the PCM harness connectors. Probing the PCM harness connectors will damage the PCM terminals, resulting in poor terminal to pin connection. Install Miller Special Tool #8815 to perform diagnosis.

Measure the resistance of the (K20) Gen Field Control circuit between the Generator harness connector and the appropriate terminal of special tool #8815.

Is the resistance below 5.0 ohms?

Yes

- Go to 12

No

- Repair the (K20) Gen Field Control circuit for an open circuit or high resistance.
- Perform the PCM Verification Test.

12. CHECKING THE PCM POWER AND GROUND CIRCUITS

Perform the diagnostic procedure for CHECKING THE PCM POWER AND GROUND CIRCUITS.

Were any problems found?

Yes

- Repair the PCM power and ground circuit(s) as necessary.
- Perform the PCM Verification Test.

No

- Go to 13

ARM0600000000393

Fig. 11   Charging System Operation (Part 7 of 8)

13. POWERTRAIN CONTROL MODULE (PCM)

Using the wiring diagram/schematic as a guide, inspect the wiring and connectors between the Generator and the Powertrain Control Module (PCM).
Look for any chafed, pierced, pinched, or partially broken wires.
Look for broken, bent, pushed out or corroded terminals.
Refer to any Technical Service Bulletins that may apply.

Were any problems found?

Yes

- Repair as necessary.
- Perform the PCM Verification Test.

No

- Replace and program the Powertrain Control Module (PCM)

- Perform the PCM Verification Test.

ARM0600000000394

Fig. 11 Charging System Operation (Part 8 of 8)

Diagnostic Test

1. CHECKING FOR AN INTERMITTENT DTC

WARNING: When the engine is operating, do not stand in direct line with the fan. Do not put your hands near the pulleys, belts, or fan. Do not wear loose clothing. Failure to follow these instructions can result in personal injury or death.

CAUTION: Do not probe the PCM harness connectors. Probing the PCM harness connectors will damage the PCM terminals, resulting in poor terminal to pin connection. Install Miller Special Tool #8815 to perform diagnosis.

The conditions necessary to set this DTC are not present at this time.
Review the scan tool environmental data and Freeze Frame. If possible, try to duplicate the conditions under which the DTC set.
If applicable, actuate the component with the scan tool.
Monitor the scan tool data relative to this circuit and wiggle test the wiring and connectors.
Look for the data to change other than as expected, the actuation to be interrupted, or for the DTC to reset during the wiggle test.
Turn the ignition off.
Visually inspect the related wire harness. Disconnect all the related harness connectors.
Look for any chafed, pierced, pinched, partially broken wires and broken, bent, pushed out, or corroded terminals.
Perform a voltage drop test on the related circuits between the suspected component and the PCM.
Inspect and clean all PCM, engine, and chassis grounds that are related to the most current DTC.
If multiple trouble codes were set, use a schematic and inspect any common ground or supply circuits.
For intermittent misfire DTCs check for restrictions in the intake and exhaust system, proper installation of all sensors, vacuum leaks, and binding components that are run by the accessory drive belt.
Use the scan tool to perform a system test if one applies to the component.
A co-pilot, data recorder, and/or lab scope should be used to help diagnose intermittent conditions.
Were any problems found during the above inspections?

Yes

- Repair as necessary
- Perform the PCM Verification Test.

No

- Test Complete.

ARM0600000000396

Fig. 12 Checking For An Intermittent DTC

3. CHARGING SYSTEM VERIFICATION TEST

1. Inspect the vehicle to verify that all engine components are properly installed and connected. Reassemble and reconnect components as necessary.
2. With the scan tool, erase all diagnostic trouble codes (DTCs).
3. Start the engine.
4. Raise the engine speed to 2000 RPM for at least 30 seconds.
5. Allow the engine to idle.
6. Turn the ignition off for 20 seconds.
7. Turn the ignition on.
8. With the scan tool, read PCM DTCs.
9. If this DTC has set again, or another DTC has set, look for any Technical Service Bulletins (TSBs) that may relate to this condition. Return to the Symptom List if necessary.
10. If the charging system is functioning correctly and there are no DTCs, the repair is now complete.

Are any DTCs or symptoms remaining?

Yes

- Repair is not complete, refer to the appropriate diagnostic procedure.

No

- Repair is complete.

ARM0600000000395

Fig. 13 PCM Verification Test

ALTERNATOR SPECIFICATIONS

Model & Year	Engine	Rated Output Amps
Avenger, Sebring Convertible & Sebring Sedan	2.0L, 2.4L, 2.7L & 3.5L	120
Caliber	1.8L, 2.0L & 2.4L	120

Mitsubishi

INDEX

	Page No.
Alternator Specifications	11-34
Application Chart	11-26
Description	11-27
Diagnosis & Testing	11-27
Alternator Output Wire Voltage Drop Test	11-27
Sebring Coupe & Stratus Coupe	11-27

	Page No.
Current Output Test	11-28
Sebring Coupe & Stratus Coupe	11-28
Diagnostic Tests	11-27
Neon	11-27
Voltage Regulator Test	11-28
Sebring Coupe & Stratus Coupe	11-28

	Page No.
Wiring Diagrams	11-27
Diagnostic Chart Index	11-29
General Information	11-26
Diode Rectifiers	11-26
Service Precautions	11-26
Precautions	11-26
Battery Ground Cable	11-26
Service	11-26

APPLICATION CHART

Model	Year	Engine	Part No.
Neon	2004–05	2.0L	4794222AC
	2004–05	2.4L	—
Sebring Coupe & Stratus Coupe	2004–05	2.4L	MD362870
		3.0L	MD373093

PRECAUTIONS

Battery Ground Cable

Prior to service, disconnect battery ground cable and isolate as required.

Service

1. Ensure battery polarity is proper when servicing units. Reversed battery polarity will damage rectifiers and regulators.
2. If booster battery is used for starting, use proper polarity in hookup.
3. When a fast charger is used to charge a vehicle battery, vehicle battery cables should be disconnected unless fast charger is equipped with a special alternator protector, in which case vehicle battery cables need not be disconnected. Also, fast chargers should never be used to start a vehicle, as damage to rectifiers will result.
4. Lead connections to grounded rectifiers (negative) should never be soldered, as excessive heat may damage rectifiers.
5. Unless system includes a load relay or field relay, grounding alternator output terminal will damage alternator and/or circuits. This is true even when system is not in operation, since no circuit breaker is used and battery voltage is applied to alternator output terminal at all times. Field or load relay acts as a circuit breaker in that it is controlled by ignition switch.
6. Before making any in-vehicle tests of alternator or regulator, battery should be inspected and circuit inspected for faulty wiring or insulation, loose or corroded connections and poor ground circuits.
7. Inspect alternator belt tension to ensure belt is tight enough to prevent slipping under load.
8. To prevent system damage, turn ignition off before making any test connections.
9. Vehicle battery must be fully charged or a fully charged battery may be installed for test purposes.

GENERAL INFORMATION

The power source of the charging system is the alternator. Current is transmitted from the field terminal of the regulator through a slip ring to the field coil and back to ground through another slip ring. The strength of the field regulates the output of the alternating current. This alternating current is then transmitted from the alternator to the rectifier where it is converted to direct current.

These alternators employ a three-phase stator winding in which the phase windings are electrically 120° apart. The rotor consists of a field coil encased between interleaved sections producing a magnetic field with alternate north and south poles. By rotating the rotor inside the stator the alternating current is induced in the stator windings. This alternating current is rectified (changed to D.C.) by silicon diodes and brought out to the output terminal of the alternator.

Diode Rectifiers

Six or more silicon diode rectifiers are used and act as electrical one-way valves. One half of the diodes have ground polarity and are pressed or screwed into a heat sink which is grounded. The other diodes (ungrounded) are pressed or screwed into and insulated from the end head. These diodes are connected to the alternator output terminal.

Since the diodes have a high resistance to the flow of current in one direction and a low resistance in the opposite direction, they may be connected in a manner which allows current to flow from the alternator to the battery in the low resistance direction. The high resistance in the opposite direction prevents the flow of current from the battery to the alternator. Because of this feature, no circuit breaker is required between the alternator and battery.

Service Precautions

1. Ensure battery polarity is proper when servicing units. Reversed battery polarity will damage rectifiers and regulators.

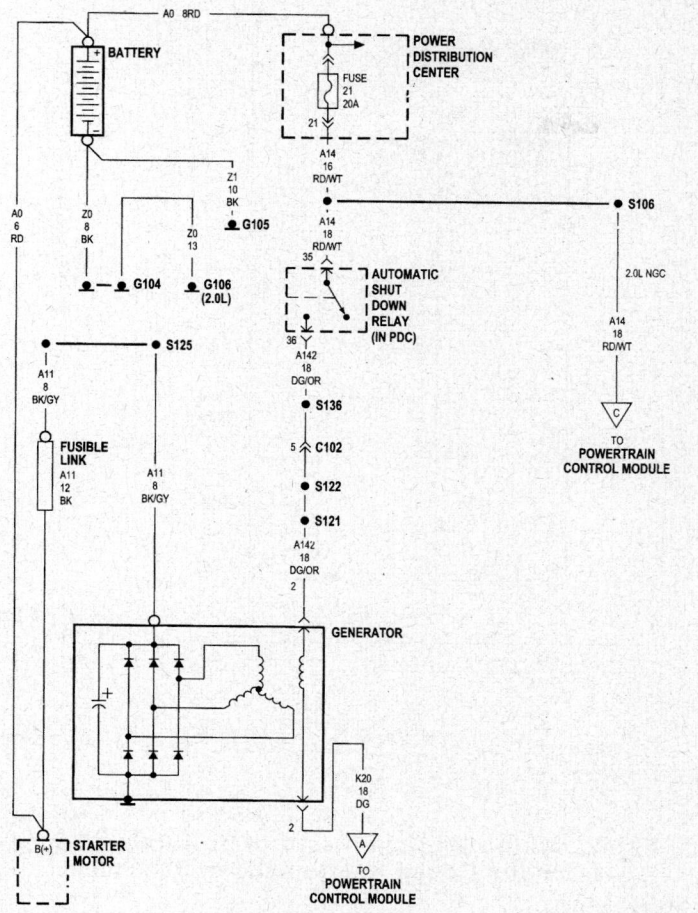

Fig. 1   Wiring diagram (Part 1 of 2). Neon

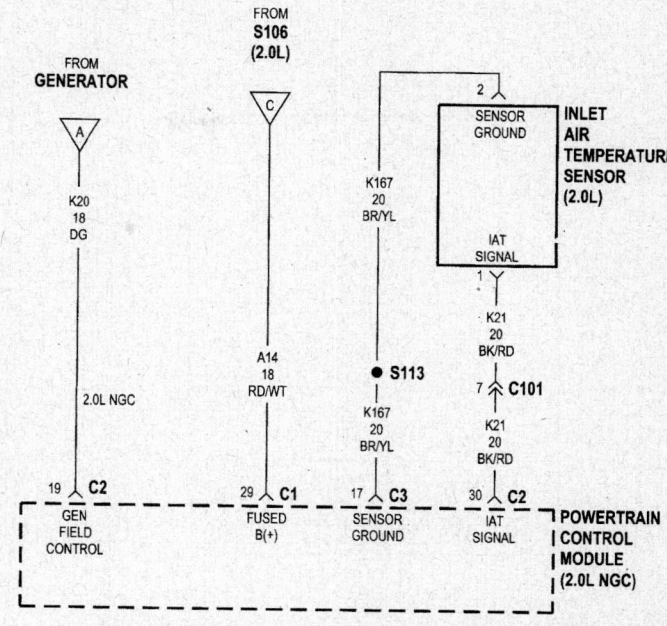

Fig. 1   Wiring diagram (Part 2 of 2). Neon

Alternator Output Wire Voltage Drop Test

SEBRING COUPE & STRATUS COUPE

1. Disconnect alternator output lead from alternator B terminal, then connect suitable 0–100 amp ammeter in series between terminal B and disconnected output lead, **Fig. 12.**
2. Connect suitable digital voltmeter between alternator B terminal and battery positive terminal.
3. Connect battery ground cable and leave hood open.
4. With engine running at approximately 2500 RPM, turn headlamps and other lamps on and off to adjust alternator load on ammeter to slightly more than 30 amps.
5. Decrease engine speed gradually until value displayed on ammeter is 30 amps and read voltmeter. Limit value should be .3 volts maximum.
6. If alternator output is high and value does not decrease to 30 amps, set value to 40 amps. Limit value should be .4 volts maximum.
7. If value is still more than limit value, a fault in alternator output wire may exist.
8. Inspect wiring between alternator B terminal and battery positive terminal, including fusible link.
9. If terminal is not sufficiently tight or if harness has become discolored because of overheating, repair and test again.

2. If booster battery is used for starting, use proper polarity in hookup.
3. When a fast charger is used to charge a vehicle battery, vehicle battery cables should be disconnected unless fast charger is equipped with a special alternator protector, in which case vehicle battery cables need not be disconnected. Also, fast chargers should never be used to start a vehicle, as damage to rectifiers will result.
4. Lead connections to grounded rectifiers (negative) should never be soldered, as excessive heat may damage rectifiers.
5. Unless system includes a load relay or field relay, grounding alternator output terminal will damage alternator and/or circuits. This is true even when system is not in operation, since no circuit breaker is used and battery is applied to alternator output terminal at all times. Field or load relay acts as a circuit breaker in that it is controlled by ignition switch.
6. Before making any in-vehicle tests of alternator or regulator, battery should be inspected and circuit inspected for faulty wiring or insulation, loose or corroded connections and poor ground circuits.
7. Inspect alternator belt tension to ensure belt is tight enough to prevent slipping under load.
8. To prevent system damage, turn ignition off before making any test connections.
9. Vehicle battery must be fully charged for test purposes.

DESCRIPTION

On these units, the regulator is incorporated into the alternator rear housing. The electronic voltage regulator has the ability to vary regulated system voltage upward or downward as temperature changes. No voltage regulator adjustments are required on these units.

DIAGNOSIS & TESTING
Wiring Diagrams

Refer to **Figs. 1 through 3** for wiring diagrams when diagnosing the charging system.

Diagnostic Tests
NEON

Refer to **Figs. 4 through 11** for diagnostic tests.

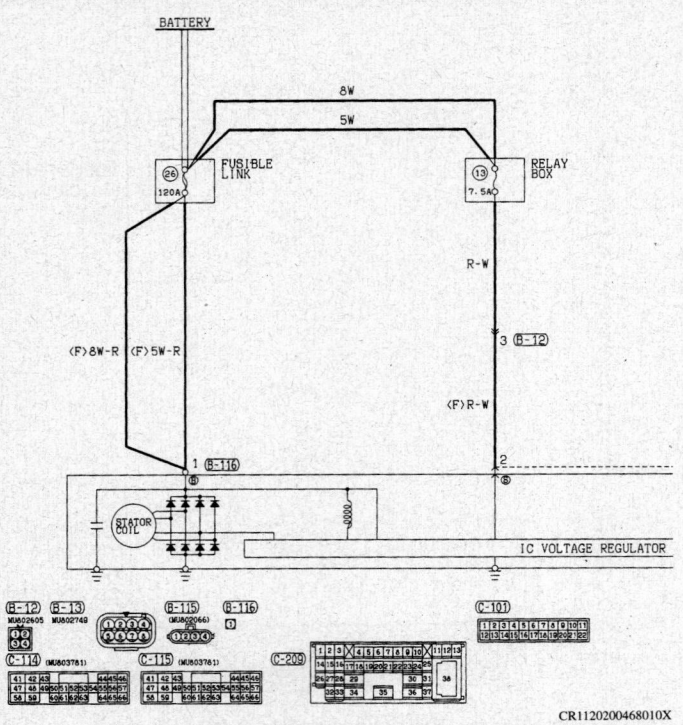

Fig. 2 Wiring diagram (Part 1 of 2). Sebring Coupe & Stratus Coupe w/automatic transmission

CR1120200468020X

Fig. 2 Wiring diagram (Part 2 of 2). Sebring Coupe & Stratus Coupe w/automatic transmission

Current Output Test

SEBRING COUPE & STRATUS COUPE

1. Disconnect wire from alternator terminal B then connect suitable 0–100 amp ammeter in series between B terminal and disconnected output wire, **Fig. 13.**
2. Connect suitable 0–20 volt voltmeter between alternator and ground, noting the following:
3. Connect battery ground cable. Leave hood open.
4. Ensure voltmeter reading is equal to battery voltage. If voltage is 0 volts, cause is probably an open circuit in wire or fusible link between alternator B terminal and battery positive terminal.
5. Turn headlamps on at low beam, then start engine.
6. Turn headlamps to high beam, HVAC blower switch to High, increase engine speed to approximately 2500 RPM and record maximum current output.

Limit should be 70% of nominal current output.
7. Reading should be more than limit value. If reading is below limit value and alternator output wire is in good condition, replace alternator.

Voltage Regulator Test

SEBRING COUPE & STRATUS COUPE

1. Connect suitable, digital voltmeter between alternator S terminal and ground using harness tool No. MB991519, or equivalent, **Fig. 14.**
2. Disconnect alternator output wire from alternator B terminal, then connect suitable 0–100 amp ammeter in series between B terminal and output wire.
3. Connect battery ground cable, then

ensure all lamps and accessories are off.
4. Connect suitable tachometer and turn ignition On.
5. Ensure voltmeter reading is equal to battery positive voltage. If voltage is 0 volts, cause is probably an open circuit in wire or fusible link between alternator S terminal and battery positive terminal.
6. Ensure all lights and accessories are turned off.
7. Start engine and increase speed to approximately 2500 RPM.
8. Read voltmeter when current output by alternator becomes 10 amps or less.
9. If voltage reading is as specified voltage regulator is operating properly, **Fig. 15.**
10. If voltage is not within specification, voltage regulator or alternator fault exists.

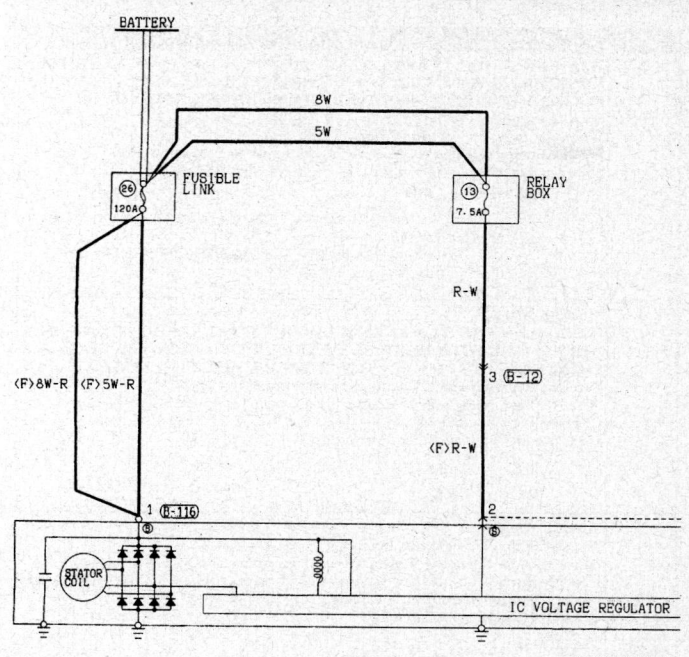

Fig. 3 Wiring diagram (Part 1 of 2). Sebring Coupe & Stratus Coupe w/manual transmission

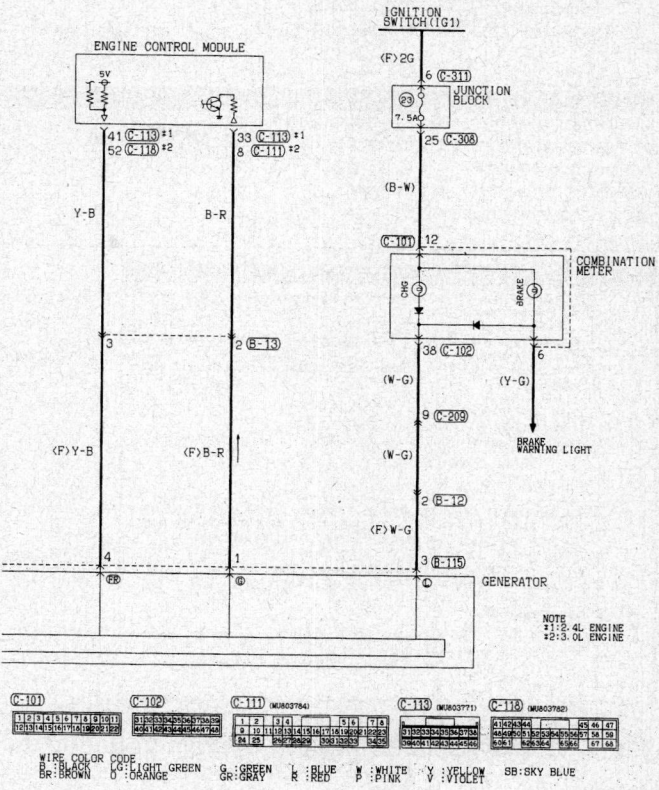

Fig. 3 Wiring diagram (Part 2 of 2). Sebring Coupe & Stratus Coupe w/manual transmission

DIAGNOSTIC CHART INDEX

Code/Test	Description	Page No.	Fig No.
NEON			
—	Verification Test VER-3	11-33	11
P0562	Charging System Voltage Too Low	11-30	4
P0563	Charging System Voltage Too High	11-30	5
P0622	Alternator Field Not Switching Properly	11-31	6
P0625	Alternator Field Control Circuit Low	11-31	7
P0626	Alternator Field Control High	11-32	8
P1594	Charging System Voltage Too High	11-32	9
P1682	Charging System Voltage Too Low	11-33	10

When Monitored: With the engine running for more than 30 seconds.

Set Condition: When battery voltage is less than 11.5 volts for more than 5 seconds.

POSSIBLE CAUSES
B+ CIRCUIT HIGH RESISTANCE
GENERATOR GROUND HIGH RESISTANCE
INTERMITTENT CONDITION
GENERATOR FIELD DRIVER CIRCUIT OPEN
ASD RELAY OUTPUT CIRCUIT OPEN
GENERATOR

TEST	ACTION
1	NOTE: Inspect the vehicle for aftermarket accessories that may exceed the Generator System output. Turn the ignition off. NOTE: Verify that the battery is fully charged and capable of passing a load test before continuing. NOTE: The Generator belt tension and condition must be checked before continuing. Start the engine. Allow the idle to stabilize. With the DRBIII®, read the Target Charging Voltage. Is the Target Charging Voltage above 15.1 volts? Yes → Go To 7 No → Go To 2
2	WARNING: WHEN THE ENGINE IS OPERATING, DO NOT STAND IN A DIRECT LINE WITH THE FAN. DO NOT PUT YOUR HANDS NEAR THE PULLEYS, BELTS OR FAN. DO NOT WEAR LOOSE CLOTHING. Turn the ignition on. NOTE: Ensure all wires are clear of the engine's moving parts. Measure the voltage between the Generator B+ Terminal and the Battery+ Post. Start the engine. Is the voltage above 0.4 volt? Yes → Repair the B+ circuit for high resistance between the Generator and Battery. Perform POWERTRAIN VERIFICATION TEST VER - 3. No → Go To 3

CR1120100434010X

Fig. 4   Code P0562: Charging System Voltage Too Low (Part 1 of 3). Neon

TEST	ACTION
7	WARNING: WHEN THE ENGINE IS OPERATING, DO NOT STAND IN A DIRECT LINE WITH THE FAN. DO NOT PUT YOUR HANDS NEAR THE PULLEYS, BELTS OR FAN. DO NOT WEAR LOOSE CLOTHING. NOTE: The conditions that set the DTC are not present at this time. The following list may help in identifying the intermittent condition. With the engine running at normal operating temperature, monitor the DRBIII® parameters related to the DTC while wiggling the wiring harness. Look for parameter values to change and/or a DTC to set. Review the DRBIII® Freeze Frame information. If possible, try to duplicate the conditions under which the DTC was set. Refer to any Technical Service Bulletins (TSB) that may apply. Visually inspect the related wiring harness. Look for any chafed, pierced, pinched, or partially broken wires. Visually inspect the related wiring harness connectors. Look for broken, bent, pushed out, or corroded terminals. Were any of the above conditions present? Yes → Repair as necessary Perform POWERTRAIN VERIFICATION TEST VER - 3. No → Test Complete.

CR1120100434030X

Fig. 4   Code P0562: Charging System Voltage Too Low (Part 3 of 3). Neon

TEST	ACTION
3	WARNING: WHEN THE ENGINE IS OPERATING, DO NOT STAND IN A DIRECT LINE WITH THE FAN. DO NOT PUT YOUR HANDS NEAR THE PULLEYS, BELTS OR FAN. DO NOT WEAR LOOSE CLOTHING. Start the engine. Warm the engine to operating temperature. NOTE: Ensure all wires are clear of the engine's moving parts. Measure the voltage between the Generator case and Battery ground post. Is the voltage above 0.1 volt? Yes → Repair Generator Ground for high resistance, Generator Case to Battery ground side. Perform POWERTRAIN VERIFICATION TEST VER - 3. No → Go To 4
4	Start the engine. WARNING: WHEN THE ENGINE IS OPERATING, DO NOT STAND IN A DIRECT LINE WITH THE FAN. DO NOT PUT YOUR HANDS NEAR THE PULLEYS, BELTS OR FAN. DO NOT WEAR LOOSE CLOTHING. Turn on all accessories, manually set engine speed to 1600 RPM. With DRBIII®, read Target Charging and Charging voltage. Compare the two readings. Is there more than a 1.0 volt difference? Yes → Go To 5 No → Go To 7
5	Turn the ignition off. Disconnect the PCM harness connector. Disconnect the Generator Field harness connector. Measure the resistance of the Generator Field Driver circuit from the PCM harness connector to Generator harness connector. Is the resistance below 5.0 ohms? Yes → Go To 6 No → Repair the Generator Field Driver circuit for an open. Perform POWERTRAIN VERIFICATION TEST VER - 3.
6	Disconnect the Generator Field harness connector. Turn the ignition off. With the DRBIII® actuate the Generator Field Driver. Using a 12-volt test light connected to ground, probe the ASD Relay Output circuit in the Generator harness connector. Does the test light illuminate brightly? Yes → Repair or replace the Generator as necessary. Perform POWERTRAIN VERIFICATION TEST VER - 3. No → Repair the ASD Relay Output circuit. Perform POWERTRAIN VERIFICATION TEST VER - 3.

CR1120100434020X

Fig. 4   Code P0562: Charging System Voltage Too Low (Part 2 of 3). Neon

When Monitored: With the engine running for more than 30 seconds.

Set Condition: When battery voltage is greater than 1 volt over target voltage for more than 5 seconds.

POSSIBLE CAUSES
TARGET VOLTAGE DIFFERS FROM BATTERY VOLTAGE
INTERMITTENT CONDITION
GENERATOR FIELD DRIVER CIRCUIT SHORTED TO GROUND
GENERATOR FIELD
POWERTRAIN CONTROL MODULE

TEST	ACTION
1	NOTE: Verify that the battery is fully charged and capable of pass a load test before continuing. Note: Generator Belt tension and condition must be checked before continuing. Turn the ignition on. With DRBIII®, actuate the Generator Field Driver. With a 12-volt test light connected to ground, backprobe the Generator Field Driver circuit in the back of Generator Field harness connector. Does the test light illuminate brightly and flash? Yes → Go To 2 No → Go To 5
2	With DRBIII®, stop all actuation. Turn the ignition on. With DRBIII®, read the Target Charging voltage. Is the Target Charging voltage above 13.0 volts? Yes → Go To 3 No → Go To 4

CR1120100435010X

Fig. 5   Code P0563: Charging System Voltage Too High (Part 1 of 2). Neon

TEST	ACTION
3	Start the engine. With the DRBIII®, manually set the engine speed to 1600 RPM. With DRBIII®, read both the Battery voltage and the Target Charging voltage. Compare the Target Charging Voltage to the Battery Voltage reading. Monitor voltage for 5 minutes, if necessary. Look for a 1.0 volt difference or more. Was there more than a 1.0 volt difference? Yes → Replace the Powertrain Control Module in accordance with the Service Information. Perform POWERTRAIN VERIFICATION TEST VER - 3. No → Go To 4
4	**WARNING: WHEN THE ENGINE IS OPERATING, DO NOT STAND IN A DIRECT LINE WITH THE FAN. DO NOT PUT YOUR HANDS NEAR THE PULLEYS, BELTS OR FAN. DO NOT WEAR LOOSE CLOTHING.** **NOTE: The conditions that set the DTC are not present at this time. The following list may help in identifying the intermittent condition.** With the engine running at normal operating temperature, monitor the DRBIII® parameters related to the DTC while wiggling the wiring harness. Look for parameter values to change and/or a DTC to set. Review the DRBIII® Freeze Frame information. If possible, try to duplicate the conditions under which the DTC was set. Refer to any Technical Service Bulletins (TSB) that may apply. Visually inspect the related wiring harness. Look for any chafed, pierced, pinched, or partially broken wires. Visually inspect the related wiring harness connectors. Look for broken, bent, pushed out, or corroded terminals. Were any of the above conditions present? Yes → Repair as necessary. Perform POWERTRAIN VERIFICATION TEST VER - 3. No → Test Complete.
5	Turn the ignition off. Disconnect the PCM harness connector. Disconnect the Generator Field harness connector. Measure the resistance of the Generator Field Driver circuit from the PCM harness connector to ground. Is the resistance below 5.0 ohms? Yes → Repair the Generator Field Driver circuit shorted to ground. Perform POWERTRAIN VERIFICATION TEST VER - 3. No → Go To 6
6	Turn the ignition off. Disconnect the Generator Field harness connector. Measure the resistance of the Generator Field Driver terminal pin to ground. Is the resistance below 5.0 ohms? Yes → Repair or replace the shorted Generator as necessary. Perform POWERTRAIN VERIFICATION TEST VER - 3. No → Replace and program the Powertrain Control Module in accordance with the Service Information. Perform POWERTRAIN VERIFICATION TEST VER - 3.

CR1120100435020X

Fig. 5   Code P0563: Charging System Voltage Too High (Part 2 of 2). Neon

TEST	ACTION
4	**NOTE: Carefully inspect all Connectors for corrosion or spread Terminals before continuing.** Disconnect the Generator Field harness connector. Turn the ignition on. With the DRBIII® actuate the Generator Field Driver circuit. Using a 12-volt test light connected to ground, probe the ASD Relay Output circuit. Does the test light illuminate brightly? Yes → Go To 5 No → Repair the ASD Relay Output circuit. Perform POWERTRAIN VERIFICATION TEST VER - 3.
5	Turn the ignition off. Disconnect the PCM harness connector. Disconnect the Generator Field harness connector. Measure the resistance of the Generator Field Driver circuit from PCM harness connector to ground. Is the resistance below 100 ohms? Yes → Repair the Generator Field Driver circuit for a shorted to ground. Perform POWERTRAIN VERIFICATION TEST VER - 3. No → Go To 6
6	Turn the ignition off. Disconnect the PCM harness connector. Disconnect the Generator Field harness connector. Measure the resistance of the Generator Field Driver circuit from the PCM harness connector to the Generator Field harness connector. Is the resistance below 5.0 ohms? Yes → Go To 7 No → Repair the Generator Field Driver circuit for an open. Perform POWERTRAIN VERIFICATION TEST VER - 3.
7	Turn the ignition off. Disconnect the Generator Field harness connector. Measure the resistance across the Generator Field Terminals at the Generator. Is the resistance above 15.0 ohms? Yes → Replace the Generator. Perform POWERTRAIN VERIFICATION TEST VER - 3. No → Go To 8
8	Turn the ignition off. Disconnect the Generator Field harness connector. Measure the resistance across the Generator Field Terminals at the Generator. Is the resistance below 0.5 ohms? Yes → Replace the Generator. Perform POWERTRAIN VERIFICATION TEST VER - 3. No → Go To 9
9	If there is no more possible causes remaining, view repair. Repair Replace and program the Powertrain Control Module in accordance with the Service Information. Perform POWERTRAIN VERIFICATION TEST VER - 3.

CR1120100436020X

Fig. 6   Code P0622: Alternator Field Not Switching properly (Part 2 of 2). Neon

When Monitored: With the ignition on. Engine running.

Set Condition: When the PCM tries to regulate the generator field with no result during monitoring.

POSSIBLE CAUSES
WIRING HARNESS INTERMITTENT
INSPECT WIRING HARNESS
ASD RELAY OUTPUT CIRCUIT OPEN
GENERATOR FIELD DRIVER CIRCUIT SHORTED TO GROUND
GENERATOR FIELD DRIVER CIRCUIT OPEN
GENERATOR FIELD COIL OPEN
GENERATOR FIELD COIL SHORTED
POWERTRAIN CONTROL MODULE

TEST	ACTION
1	Turn the ignition on. With the DRBIII®, actuate the Generator Field Driver circuit. Using a 12-volt test light connected to ground, backprobe the Generator Field Driver circuit in the back of the Generator. Does the test light illuminate brightly and flash? Yes → Go To 2 No → Go To 4
2	Turn the ignition on. With the DRBIII® actuate the Generator Field Driver cirtuit. Wiggle the wiring harness from the Generator to PCM. With the DRBIII®, read DTC's. Did the DTC reset? Yes → Repair as necessary. Perform POWERTRAIN VERIFICATION TEST VER - 3. No → Go To 3
3	Turn the ignition off. Using the schematic as a guide, inspect the Wiring and Connectors. Were any problems found? Yes → Repair as necessary. Perform POWERTRAIN VERIFICATION TEST VER - 3. No → Test Complete.

CR1120100436010X

Fig. 6   Code P0622: Alternator Field Not Switching Properly (Part 1 of 2). Neon

When Monitored: With the engine running for more than 25 seconds.

Set Condition: When the Generator Field Circuit is open or shorted to ground.

POSSIBLE CAUSES
WIRING HARNESS INTERMITTENT
GENERATOR FIELD DRIVER CIRCUIT SHORTED TO GROUND
GENERATOR FIELD
GENERATOR FIELD DRIVER CIRCUIT OPEN
GENERATOR FIELD COIL OPEN
POWERTRAIN CONTROL MODULE

TEST	ACTION
1	**NOTE: Verify that the battery is capable of passing a load test and is fully charged before continuing.** Turn the ignition on. With the DRBIII®, actuate the Generator Field Driver circuit. Using a 12-volt test light connected to ground, backprobe the Generator Field Driver circuit in the back of the Generator. Does the test light illuminate brightly and flash? Yes → Go To 2 No → Go To 3
2	Turn the ignition off. Using a schematic as a guide, inspect the related Wiring and Connectors. Turn the ignition on, engine not running. With the DRBIII® actuate the Generator Field Driver circuit. Wiggle the wiring harness from the Generator to PCM. With the DRBIII®, read DTC's. Did the DTC reset? Yes → Repair as necessary. Perform POWERTRAIN VERIFICATION TEST VER - 3. No → Test Complete.

CR1120100437010X

Fig. 7   Code P0625: Alternator Field Control Circuit Low (Part 1 of 2). Neon

TEST	ACTION
3	Turn the ignition off. Disconnect the PCM harness connector. Disconnect the Generator Field harness connector. Measure the resistance of the Generator Field Driver circuit from PCM harness connector to ground. Is the resistance below 5.0 ohms? Yes → Repair the Generator Field Driver circuit for a shorted to ground. Perform POWERTRAIN VERIFICATION TEST VER - 3. No → Go To 4
4	Turn the ignition off. Disconnect the Generator Field harness connector. Measure resistance of the Generator Field Driver terminal on the Generator to ground. Is the resistance below 5.0 ohms? Yes → Repair or replace the shorted Generator as necessary. Perform POWERTRAIN VERIFICATION TEST VER - 3. No → Go To 5
5	Turn the ignition off. Disconnect the PCM harness connector. Disconnect the Generator Field harness connector. Measure the resistance of the Generator Field Driver circuit from the PCM harness connector to the Generator Field harness connector. Is the resistance below 5.0 ohms? Yes → Go To 6 No → Repair the Generator Field Driver circuit for an open. Perform POWERTRAIN VERIFICATION TEST VER - 3.
6	Turn the ignition off. Disconnect the Generator Field harness connector. Measure the resistance across the Generator Field Terminals at the Generator. Is the resistance above 15.0 ohms? Yes → Replace the Generator. Perform POWERTRAIN VERIFICATION TEST VER - 3. No → Go To 7
7	If there is no more possible causes remaining, view repair. Repair Replace and program the Powertrain Control Module in accordance with the Service Information. Perform POWERTRAIN VERIFICATION TEST VER - 3.

CR1120100437020X

Fig. 7   Code P0625: Alternator Field Control Circuit Low (Part 2 of 2). Neon

When Monitored: The engine running. The engine speed greater than 380 RPM.

Set Condition: Battery voltage is 1 volt greater than desired system voltage.

POSSIBLE CAUSES
TARGET VOLTAGE DIFFERS FROM BATTERY VOLTAGE
INTERMITTENT CONDITION
GENERATOR FIELD DRIVER CIRCUIT SHORTED TO GROUND
GENERATOR FIELD
POWERTRAIN CONTROL MODULE

TEST	ACTION
1	Note: Battery must be fully charged. Note: Generator Belt tension and condition must be checked before continuing. Turn the ignition on. With DRBIII®, actuate the Generator Field Driver. With a 12-volt test light connected to ground, backprobe the Generator Field Driver circuit in the back of Generator Field harness connector. Does the test light illuminate brightly and flash? Yes → Go To 2 No → Go To 5
2	With DRBIII®, stop all actuation. Turn the ignition on. With DRBIII®, read the Target Charging voltage. Is the Target Charging voltage above 13.0 volts? Yes → Go To 3 No → Go To 4
3	Start the engine. With the DRBIII®, manually set the engine speed to 1600 RPM. With DRBIII®, read both the Battery voltage and the Target Charging voltage. Compare the Target Charging Voltage to the Battery Voltage reading. Monitor voltage for 5 minutes, if necessary. Look for a 1.0 volt difference or more. Was there more than a 1.0 volt difference? Yes → Replace the Powertrain Control Module in accordance with the Service Information. Perform POWERTRAIN VERIFICATION TEST VER - 3. No → Go To 4

CR1120100439010X

Fig. 9   Code P1594: Charging System Voltage Too High. (Part 1 of 2). Neon

When Monitored: With the engine running for more than 25 seconds.

Set Condition: When the Generator Field circuit is shorted to B+.

POSSIBLE CAUSES
WIRING HARNESS INTERMITTENT
GENERATOR FIELD CKT SHORT TO VOLTAGE
POWERTRAIN CONTROL MODULE

TEST	ACTION
1	NOTE: Verify that the battery is capable of passing a load test and is fully charged before continuing. Turn the ignition on. With the DRBIII®, actuate the Generator Field Driver circuit. Using a 12-volt test light connected to ground, backprobe the Generator Field Driver circuit in the back of the Generator. Does the test light illuminate brightly and flash? Yes → Go To 2 No → Go To 3
2	Turn the ignition off. Using a schematic as a guide, inspect the related Wiring and Connectors. Turn the ignition on, engine not running. With the DRBIII® actuate the Generator Field Driver circuit. Wiggle the wiring harness from the Generator to PCM. With the DRBIII®, read DTC's. Did the DTC reset? Yes → Repair as necessary. Perform POWERTRAIN VERIFICATION TEST VER - 3. No → Test Complete.
3	Turn the ignition off. Disconnect PCM harness connector. Using a 12-volt test light connect to Ground (B-), backprobe the Generator Field circuit at the PCM harness connector. Does the test light illuminate brightly? Yes → Repair the Generator Field Driver circuit short to B+. Perform POWERTRAIN VERIFICATION TEST VER - 3. No → Replace and program the Powertrain Control Module in accordance with the Service Manual. Perform POWERTRAIN VERIFICATION TEST VER - 3.

CR1120100438000X

Fig. 8   Code P0626: Alternator Field Control High. Neon

TEST	ACTION
4	WARNING: WHEN THE ENGINE IS OPERATING, DO NOT STAND IN A DIRECT LINE WITH THE FAN. DO NOT PUT YOUR HANDS NEAR THE PULLEYS, BELTS or FAN. DO NOT WEAR LOOSE CLOTHING. NOTE: The conditions that set the DTC are not present at this time. The following list may help in identifying the intermittent condition. With the engine running at normal operating temperature, monitor the DRBIII® parameters related to the DTC while wiggling the wiring harness. Look for parameter values to change and/or a DTC to set. Review the DRBIII® Freeze Frame information. If possible, try to duplicate the conditions under which the DTC was set. Refer to any Technical Service Bulletins (TSB) that may apply. Visually inspect the related wiring harness. Look for any chafed, pierced, pinched, or partially broken wires. Visually inspect the related wiring harness connectors. Look for broken, bent, pushed out, or corroded terminals. Were any of the above conditions present? Yes → Repair as necessary. Perform POWERTRAIN VERIFICATION TEST VER - 3. No → Test Complete.
5	Turn the ignition off. Disconnect the PCM harness connector. Disconnect the Generator Field harness connector. Measure the resistance of the Generator Field Driver circuit from the PCM harness connector to ground. Is the resistance below 5.0 ohms? Yes → Repair the Generator Field Driver circuit shorted to ground. Perform POWERTRAIN VERIFICATION TEST VER - 3. No → Go To 6
6	Turn the ignition off. Disconnect the Generator Field harness connector. Measure resistance of the Generator Field Driver terminal pin to ground. Is the resistance below 5.0 ohms? Yes → Repair or replace the shorted Generator as necessary. Perform POWERTRAIN VERIFICATION TEST VER - 3. No → Replace and program the Powertrain Control Module in accordance with the Service Information. Perform POWERTRAIN VERIFICATION TEST VER - 3.

CR1120100439020X

Fig. 9   Code P1594: Charging System Voltage Too High. (Part 2 of 2). Neon

When Monitored: With the ignition on. Engine RPM greater than 1152 RPM. With no other charging system codes set.

Set Condition: The battery sensed voltage is 1 volt below the charging goal for 13.47 seconds. The PCM senses the battery voltage, then turns off the field driver, and then senses the battery voltage again. If the voltages are the same, the code is set.

POSSIBLE CAUSES
B+ CIRCUIT HIGH RESISTANCE
GENERATOR GROUND HIGH RESISTANCE
INTERMITTENT CONDITION
GENERATOR FIELD DRIVER CIRCUIT OPEN
ASD RELAY OUTPUT CIRCUIT OPEN
GENERATOR

TEST	ACTION
1	NOTE: Inspect the vehicle for aftermarket accessories that may exceed the Generator System output. Turn the ignition off. NOTE: The battery must be fully charged. NOTE: The Generator belt tension and condition must be checked before continuing. Start the engine. Allow the idle to stabilize. With the DRBIII®, read the Target Charging Voltage. Is the Target Charging Voltage above 15.1 volts? Yes → Go To 7 No → Go To 2
2	WARNING: WHEN THE ENGINE IS OPERATING, DO NOT STAND IN A DIRECT LINE WITH THE FAN. DO NOT PUT YOUR HANDS NEAR THE PULLEYS, BELTS OR FAN. DO NOT WEAR LOOSE CLOTHING. Turn the ignition on. NOTE: Ensure all wires are clear of the engine's moving parts. Measure the voltage between the Generator B+ Terminal and the Battery+ Post. Start the engine. Is the voltage above 0.4 volt? Yes → Repair the B+ circuit for high resistance between the Generator and Battery. Perform POWERTRAIN VERIFICATION TEST VER - 3. No → Go To 3

CR1120100440010X

Fig. 10   Code P1682: Charging System Voltage Too Low (Part 1 of 3). Neon

TEST	ACTION
7	WARNING: WHEN THE ENGINE IS OPERATING, DO NOT STAND IN A DIRECT LINE WITH THE FAN. DO NOT PUT YOUR HANDS NEAR THE PULLEYS, BELTS OR FAN. DO NOT WEAR LOOSE CLOTHING. NOTE: The conditions that set the DTC are not present at this time. The following list may help in identifying the intermittent condition. With the engine running at normal operating temperature, monitor the DRBIII® parameters related to the DTC while wiggling the wiring harness. Look for parameter values to change and/or a DTC to set. Review the DRBIII® Freeze Frame information. If possible, try to duplicate the conditions under which the DTC was set. Refer to any Technical Service Bulletins (TSB) that may apply. Visually inspect the related wiring harness. Look for any chafed, pierced, pinched, or partially broken wires. Visually inspect the related wiring harness connectors. Look for broken, bent, pushed out, or corroded terminals. Were any of the above conditions present? Yes → Repair as necessary Perform POWERTRAIN VERIFICATION TEST VER - 3. No → Test Complete.

CR1120100440030X

Fig. 10   Code P1682: Charging System Voltage Too Low (Part 3 of 3). Neon

TEST	ACTION
3	WARNING: WHEN THE ENGINE IS OPERATING, DO NOT STAND IN A DIRECT LINE WITH THE FAN. DO NOT PUT YOUR HANDS NEAR THE PULLEYS, BELTS OR FAN. DO NOT WEAR LOOSE CLOTHING. Start the engine. Warm the engine to operating temperature. NOTE: Ensure all wires are clear of the engine's moving parts. Measure the voltage between the Generator case and Battery ground post. Is the voltage above 0.1 volt? Yes → Repair Generator Ground for high resistance, Generator Case to Battery ground side. Perform POWERTRAIN VERIFICATION TEST VER - 3. No → Go To 4
4	Start the engine. WARNING: WHEN THE ENGINE IS OPERATING, DO NOT STAND IN A DIRECT LINE WITH THE FAN. DO NOT PUT YOUR HANDS NEAR THE PULLEYS, BELTS OR FAN. DO NOT WEAR LOOSE CLOTHING. Turn on all accessories, manually set engine speed to 1600 RPM. With DRBIII®, read Target Charging and Charging voltage. Compare the two readings. Is there more than a 1.0 volt difference? Yes → Go To 5 No → Go To 7
5	Turn the ignition off. Disconnect the PCM harness connector. Disconnect the Generator Field harness connector. Measure the resistance of the Generator Field Driver circuit from the PCM harness connector to Generator harness connector. Is the resistance below 5.0 ohms? Yes → Go To 6 No → Repair the Generator Field Driver circuit for an open. Perform POWERTRAIN VERIFICATION TEST VER - 3.
6	Disconnect the Generator Field harness connector. Turn the ignition on. With the DRBIII® actuate the Generator Field Driver. Using a 12-volt test light connected to ground, probe the ASD Relay Output circuit in the Generator harness connector. Does the test light illuminate brightly? Yes → Repair or replace the Generator as necessary. Perform POWERTRAIN VERIFICATION TEST VER - 3. No → Repair the ASD Relay Output circuit. Perform POWERTRAIN VERIFICATION TEST VER - 3.

CR1120100440020X

Fig. 10   Code P1682: Charging System Voltage Too Low (Part 2 of 3). Neon

POWERTRAIN VERIFICATION TEST VER - 3
1. NOTE: If the PCM has been replaced and the correct VIN and mileage have not been programmed, a DTC will be set in the ABS Module, Airbag Module and the SKIM. 2. NOTE: If the vehicle is equipped with a Sentry Key Immobilizer System, Secret Key data must be updated. Refer to the Service Information for the PCM, SKIM and the Transponder (ignition key) for programming information. 3. Inspect the vehicle to ensure that all components related to the repair are connected properly. 4. With the DRBIII®, clear DTCs. 5. Perform generator output test. Refer to the appropriate service information as necessary. 6. Start the engine and set engine speed to 2000 RPM for at least thirty seconds. 7. Cycle the ignition key off and on. 8. With the DRBIII®, read the DTCs. If the DTC returns, or any other symptom or DTC is present, refer to the appropriate category and perform the corresponding symptom. 9. If there are no DTCs present and all components are functioning properly, the repair is complete. Are any DTCs present? Yes → Repair is not complete, refer to appropriate symptom. No → Repair is complete.

CR1120100442000X

Fig. 11   Verification Test VER-3. Neon

ALTERNATORS

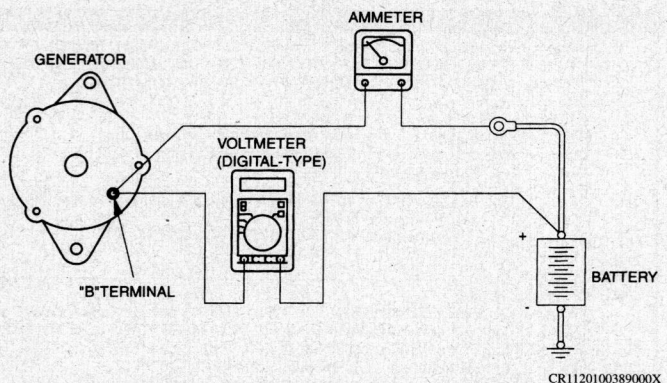

Fig. 12   Alternator output wire voltage drop test connection. Sebring Coupe & Stratus Coupe

CR1120100389000X

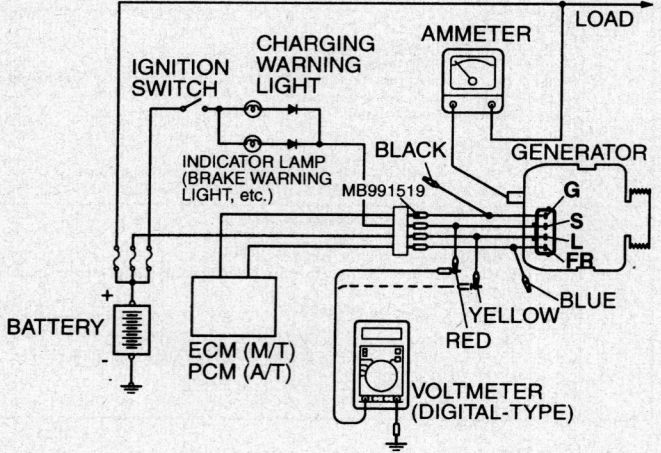

Fig. 14   Voltage regulator test connections. Sebring Coupe & Stratus Coupe

CR1120100391000X

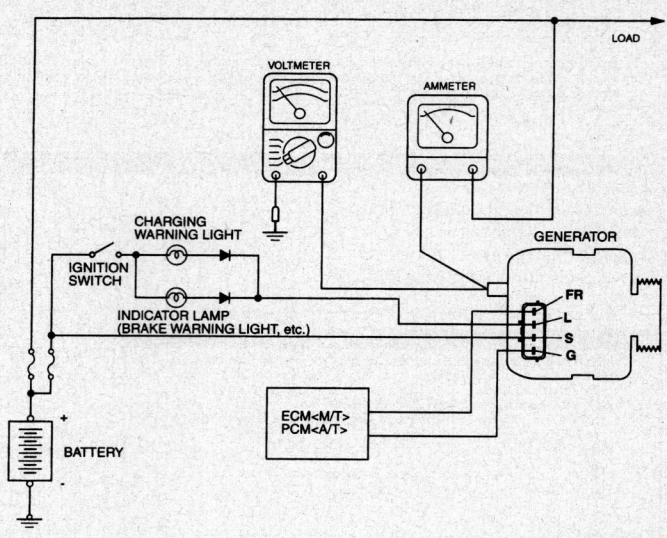

Fig. 13   Alternator output test connection. Sebring Coupe & Stratus Coupe

CR1120100390000X

INSPECTION TERMINAL	VOLTAGE REGULATOR AMBIENT TEMPERATURE [°C(°F)]	STANDARD VALUE (V)
Terminal "S"	-20 (-4)	14.2 - 15.4
	20 (68)	13.9 - 14.9
	60 (140)	13.4 - 14.5
	80 (176)	13.1 - 14.5

CR1120100392000X

Fig. 15   Regulated voltage specifications. Sebring Coupe & Stratus Coupe

ALTERNATOR SPECIFICATIONS

Model	Engine	Rated Output Amps
Neon	2.0L	85
Sebring Coupe & Stratus Coupe	2.4L	95
	3.0L	85

STEERING COLUMNS

NOTE: On Air Bag Equipped Models, Refer To "Air Bag System Precautions" Located In The Front Of This Manual For System Disarming & Arming Procedures.

NOTE: Refer To "Computer Relearn Procedures" Located In The Front Of This Manual When Battery Power To The Computer Has Been Interrupted.

NOTE: Prior To Performing Any Service Operations Listed In This Section, Consult The "Technical Service Bulletins" Section For Related Information.

INDEX

	Page No.
Diagnosis & Testing	12-1
Diagnostic Tests	12-1
Charger, Magnum & 300	12-1
Diagnostic Trouble Code Interpretation	12-1
Diagnostic Chart Index	12-3
Precautions	12-1
Air Bag Systems	12-1
Battery Ground Cable	12-1
Column Service	12-1
Steering Column, Replace	12-22
2004–06 Sebring Convertible, Sebring Sedan & Stratus Sedan	12-24

	Page No.
Caliber & 2007–08 Avenger & Sebring Sedan	12-22
Charger, Magnum & 300	12-22
Concorde, Intrepid & 300M	12-23
Crossfire	12-23
Neon	12-23
Sebring Coupe & Stratus Coupe	12-24
Steering Column Service	12-24
2004–06 Sebring Convertible, Sebring Sedan & Stratus Sedan	12-25
Caliber & 2007–08 Avenger Sedan & Sebring Sedan	12-24

	Page No.
Charger, Magnum & 300	12-25
Concorde, Intrepid & 300M	12-24
Crossfire	12-25
Assemble	12-25
Disassembly	12-25
Neon	12-25
Sebring Coupe & Stratus Coupe	12-25
Technical Service Bulletins	12-25
Steering Column Clicking	12-25
2004 Sebring Convertible, Sebring Sedan, Stratus Sedan	12-25

PRECAUTIONS

Air Bag Systems

Refer to "Air Bag System Precautions" in the front of this manual for system disarming and arming procedures.

Battery Ground Cable

Prior to service, disconnect battery ground cable and isolate as required.

Column Service

When servicing collapsible steering columns, care should be exercised since they are extremely susceptible to damage. Dropping of or leaning on column or striking sharp blows on end of steering shaft or shift levers could loosen or shear plastic fasteners which maintain column rigidity.

It is important only the specified screws, bolts and nuts be used during the assembly sequence and tightened to specifications to ensure proper breakaway action of column under impact. Avoid using excessively long bolts, as they may prevent a portion of the steering column from collapsing under impact.

If there is evidence of a sheared plastic shift tube injection, a new shift tube must be installed. If plastic injections are sheared but steering shaft is not bent, repairs may be possible using a service steering shaft repair kit containing instructions and dimensions for all steering columns. On some models, the mounting brackets will shear under impact and must also be replaced.

DIAGNOSIS & TESTING

Diagnostic Trouble Code Interpretation

Refer to **Fig. 1** for Diagnostic Trouble Code (DTC) interpretation.

Diagnostic Tests

CHARGER, MAGNUM & 300

Refer to **Figs. 2 through 24** for diagnostic tests.

Test	Description
B1489	Steering Wheel Control Audio Switch Circuit
B148A	Steering Wheel Control Menu Switch Circuit
B148B	Steering Wheel Control Up Switch Circuit
B148C	Steering Wheel Control Down Switch Circuit
B148D	Steering Wheel Control Side Switch Circuit
B148E	Steering Wheel Control + Switch Circuit
B148F	Steering Wheel Control - Switch Circuit
B1490	Steering Wheel Control C/T Switch Circuit
B1D8D	Steering Column Control Telescope Position Sensor Circuit Low
B1D8E	Steering Column Control Telescope Position Sensor Circuit High
B1D91	Steering Column Control Tilt Position Sensor Circuit Low
B1D92	Steering Column Control Tilt Position Sensor Circuit High
B1D93	Steering Column Control Telescope Motor Control Circuit Performance
B1D97	Steering Column Control Tilt Motor Control Circuit Performance
B1DA0	Steering Column Control Tilt Switch Circuit Stuck
B1DA5	Steering Column Control Telescope Switch Circuit Stuck
B2225	Steering Column Control Module Internal
B2332	Horn Switch Input Circuit/Performance
C1219	Steering Angle Sensor Erratic Performance
P0562	Battery Voltage Low
P0563	Battery Voltage High
P0585	Speed Control Multiplex Switch 1/2 Correlation
P1593	Speed Control Switch 1/2 Stuck

Fig. 1   DTC interpretation

2. (G206) EVIC MUX SIGNAL 2 CIRCUIT SHORT TO (G907) EVIC/NAV MUX RETURN CIRCUIT

Turn the ignition off.
Remove the Driver Airbag in accordance with the Service Information to gain access to the Steering Wheel Control Switches.
Disconnect the Left Steering Switch harness connector.
Disconnect the Right Steering Switch harness connector.

NOTE: Before proceeding, thoroughly inspect the wiring harness and connectors between the Left Steering Switch and the Right Steering Switch for a short to ground or to any other circuit.

Measure the resistance between the (G206) EVIC Mux Signal 2 circuit and the (G907) EVIC/NAV Mux Return circuit.

Is the resistance below 5.0 ohms?

Yes

- Repair the (G206) EVIC Mux Signal 2 circuit for a short to the (G907) EVIC/NAV Mux Return circuit.

No

- Go to 3

ARM0500000000972

Fig. 2   Code B1489: Steering Wheel Control Audio Switch Circuit (Part 2 of 4). Charger, Magnum & 300

1. DTC STATUS IS ACTIVE

NOTE: If U1109–LOST COMMUNICATION WITH LIN STEERING WHEEL CONTROLS is set along with this DTC, diagnose the communication DTC first.

NOTE: If P0562–BATTERY VOLTAGE LOW or P0563–BATTERY VOLTAGE HIGH is set along with this DTC, diagnose the battery voltage DTC first.

Ignition on, engine not running.
With the Scan Tool, select View DTCs in the Steering Control Module.

Is the DTC status Active at this time?

Yes

- Go to 2

No

- Go to 7

ARM0500000000971

Fig. 2   Code B1489: Steering Wheel Control Audio Switch Circuit (Part 1 of 4). Charger, Magnum & 300

3. (G206) EVIC MUX SIGNAL 2 CIRCUIT SHORT TO GROUND

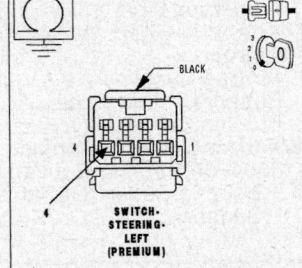

NOTE: Before proceeding, thoroughly inspect the wiring harness and connectors between the Left Steering Switch and the Right Steering Switch for a short to ground or to any other circuit.

Measure the resistance between the (G206) EVIC Mux Signal 2 circuit and ground.

Is the resistance below 5.0 ohms?

Yes

- Repair the (G206) EVIC Mux Signal 2 circuit for a short to ground.

No

- Go to 4

4. LEFT STEERING SWITCH

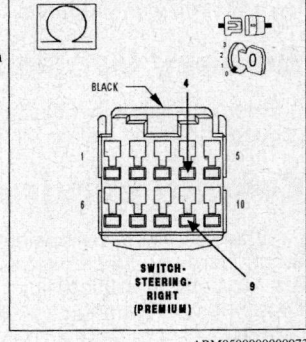

Reconnect the Left Steering Switch harness connector. Measure the resistance between the (G206) EVIC Mux Signal 2 circuit and the (G907) EVIC/NAV Mux Return circuit at the Right Steering Switch harness connector.

Is the resistance approximately 10.00 K ohms (+/- 10%)?

Yes

- Replace the Left Steering Switch

No

- Go to 5

ARM0500000000973

Fig. 2   Code B1489: Steering Wheel Control Audio Switch Circuit (Part 3 of 4). Charger, Magnum & 300

5. RIGHT STEERING SWITCH

Replace the Right Steering Switch in accordance with the Service Information.
Reconnect the C206 (LIN Bus) connector.
Turn the ignition on.
Press and release the Audio Switch several times.
With the scan tool, Clear Stored DTCs in the Steering Control Module.
With the scan tool, select Data Display and view the Audio switch data.
While monitoring the Audio switch data, press and release the Audio Switch several times.

Does the Audio switch data change from Set to Not Set as the switch is pressed and released?

Yes

- Test Complete.

No

- Go to 6

6. STEERING CONTROL MODULE (SCM)

View repair.

Repair

- Replace the Steering Control Module (SCM)

7. INTERMITTENT STEERING WHEEL CONTROL AUDIO SWITCH CIRCUIT DTC

The conditions necessary to set this DTC are not present at this time.
Using the wiring diagram/schematic as a guide, inspect the wiring and connectors.
While monitoring the scan tool data relative to this circuit, wiggle test the wiring and connectors.
Look for the data to change or for the DTC to reset during the wiggle test.

Were any problems found?

Yes

- Repair as necessary.

No

- Test complete.

ARM0500000000974

Fig. 2   Code B1489: Steering Wheel Control Audio Switch Circuit (Part 4 of 4). Charger, Magnum & 300

DIAGNOSTIC CHART INDEX

Code	Description	Page No.	Fig. No.
B148A	Steering Wheel Control Menu Switch Circuit	12-4	3
B148B	Steering Wheel Control Up Switch Circuit	12-4	4
B148C	Steering Wheel Control Down Switch Circuit	12-5	5
B148D	Steering Wheel Control Side Switch Circuit	12-6	6
B148E	Steering Wheel Control + Switch Circuit	12-7	7
B148F	Steering Wheel Control – Switch Circuit	12-8	8
B1489	Steering Wheel Control Audio Switch Circuit	12-2	2
B1490	Steering Wheel Control C/T Switch Circuit	12-8	9
B1D8D	Steering Wheel Control Telescope Position Sensor Circuit Low	12-9	10
B1D8E	Steering Wheel Control Telescope Position Sensor Circuit High	12-9	11
B1D91	Steering Wheel Control Tilt Position Sensor Circuit Low	12-11	12
B1D92	Steering Wheel Control Tilt Position Sensor Circuit High	12-11	13
B1D93	Steering Wheel Control Telescope Motor Control Circuit Performance	12-13	14
B1D97	Steering Wheel Control Tilt Motor Control Circuit Performance	12-15	15
B1DA0	Steering Column Control Tilt Switch Circuit Stuck	12-17	16
B1DA5	Steering Column Control Telescope Switch Circuit Stuck	12-17	17
B2225	Steering Column Control Module Internal	12-18	18
B2332	Horn Switch Input Circuit/Performance	12-18	19
C1219	Steering Angle Sensor Erratic Performance	12-19	20
P0562	Battery Voltage Low	12-20	21
P0563	Battery Voltage High	12-20	22
P0585	Speed Control Multiplex Switch 1/2 Correlation	12-21	23
P1593	Speed Control Switch 1/2 Stuck	12-22	24

1. DTC IS ACTIVE

NOTE: If U1109–LOST COMMUNICATION WITH LIN STEERING WHEEL CONTROLS is set along with this DTC, diagnose the communication DTC first.

NOTE: If P0562–BATTERY VOLTAGE LOW or P0563–BATTERY VOLTAGE HIGH is set along with this DTC, diagnose the battery voltage DTC first.

Ignition on, engine not running.
With the Scan Tool, select View DTCs in the Steering Control Module.

Is the DTC status Active at this time?

Yes

- Go to 2

No

- Go to 4

2. RIGHT STEERING SWITCH

Turn the ignition off.
Replace the Right Steering Switch in accordance with the Service Information.
Turn the ignition on.
Press and release the Menu Switch several times.
With the Scan Tool, Clear Stored DTCs in the Steering Control Module.
With the Scan Tool, select Data Display and view the Menu switch data.
While monitoring the Menu switch data, press and release the Menu Switch several times.

Does the Menu switch data change from Set to Not Set when the switch is pressed and released?

Yes

- Test complete.

No

- Go to 3

ARM0500000000975

Fig. 3   Code B148A: Steering Wheel Control Menu Switch Circuit (Part 1 of 2). Charger, Magnum & 300

1. DTC STATUS IS ACTIVE

NOTE: If U1109–LOST COMMUNICATION WITH LIN STEERING WHEEL CONTROLS is set along with this DTC, diagnose the communication DTC first.

NOTE: If P0562–BATTERY VOLTAGE LOW or P0563–BATTERY VOLTAGE HIGH is set along with this DTC, diagnose the battery voltage DTC first.

Ignition on, engine not running.
With the Scan Tool, select View DTCs in the Steering Column Control Module.

Is the DTC status Active at this time?

Yes

- Go to 2

No

- Go to 7

ARM0500000000977

Fig. 4   Code B148B: Steering Wheel Control Up Switch Circuit (Part 1 of 4). Charger, Magnum & 300

3. STEERING CONTROL MODULE (SCM)

View repair.

Repair

- Replace the Steering Control Module (SCM)

4. INTERMITTENT STEERING WHEEL CONTROL MENU SWITCH CIRCUIT DTC

The conditions necessary to set this DTC are not present at this time.
Using the wiring diagram/schematic as a guide, inspect the wiring and connectors.
While monitoring the scan tool data relative to this circuit, wiggle test the wiring and connectors.
Look for the data to change or for the DTC to reset during the wiggle test.

Were any problems found?

Yes

- Repair as necessary.

No

- Test complete.

ARM0500000000976

Fig. 3   Code B148A: Steering Wheel Control Menu Switch Circuit (Part 2 of 2). Charger, Magnum & 300

2. (G106) EVIC MUX SIGNAL 1 CIRCUIT SHORT TO (G907) EVIC/NAV MUX RETURN CIRCUIT

Turn the ignition off.
Remove the Driver Airbag in accordance with the Service Information.
Disconnect the Left Steering Switch harness connector.
Disconnect the Right Steering Switch harness connector.

NOTE: Before proceeding, thoroughly inspect the wiring harness and connectors between the Left Steering Switch and the Right Steering Switch for a short to ground or any other circuit.

Measure the resistance between the (G106) EVIC Mux Signal 1 circuit and the (G907) EVIC/NAV Mux Return circuit.

Is the resistance below 5.0 ohms?

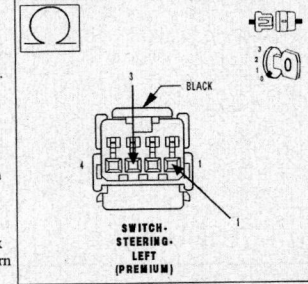

Yes

- Repair the (G106) EVIC Mux Signal 1 circuit for a short to the (G907) EVIC/NAV Mux Return circuit.

No

- Go to 3

ARM0500000000978

Fig. 4   Code B148B: Steering Wheel Control Up Switch Circuit (Part 2 of 4). Charger, Magnum & 300

3. (G106) EVIC MUX SIGNAL 1 CIRCUIT SHORT TO GROUND

NOTE: Before proceeding, thoroughly inspect the wiring harness and connectors between the Left Steering Switch and the Right Steering Switch for a short to ground or any other circuit.

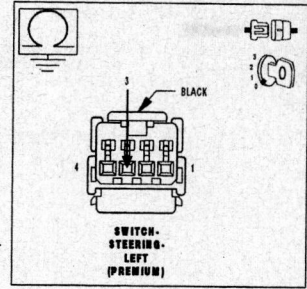

Measure the resistance between the (G106) EVIC Mux Signal 1 circuit and ground.

Is the resistance below 5.0 ohms?

Yes

- Repair the (G106) EVIC Mux Signal 1 circuit for a short to ground.

No

- Go to 4

4. LEFT STEERING SWITCH

Reconnect the Left Steering Switch harness connector. Measure the resistance between the (G106) EVIC Mux Signal 1 circuit and the (G907) EVIC/NAV Mux Return circuit at the Right Steering Switch harness connector.

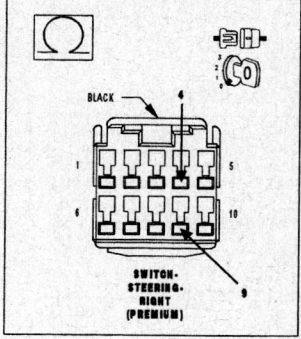

Is the resistance approximately .5 ohms (+/- 1 ohm)?

Yes

- Replace the Left Steering Switch

No

- Go to 5

ARM0500000000979

Fig. 4   Code B148B: Steering Wheel Control Up Switch Circuit (Part 3 of 4). Charger, Magnum & 300

1. DTC STATUS IS ACTIVE

NOTE: If U1109–LOST COMMUNICATION WITH LIN STEERING WHEEL CONTROLS is set along with this DTC, diagnose the communication DTC first.

NOTE: If P0562–BATTERY VOLTAGE LOW or P0563–BATTERY VOLTAGE HIGH is set along with this DTC, diagnose the battery voltage DTC first.

Ignition on, engine not running.
With the Scan Tool, select View DTCs in the Steering Control Module.

Is the DTC status Active at this time?

Yes

- Go to 2

No

- Go to 7

ARM0500000000981

Fig. 5   Code B148C: Steering Wheel Control Down Switch Circuit (Part 1 of 4). Charger, Magnum & 300

5. RIGHT STEERING SWITCH

Replace the Right Steering Switch in accordance with the Service Information.
Reconnect the C206 (LIN Bus) connector.
Turn the ignition on.
Press and release the Up Switch several times.
With the scan tool, Clear Stored DTCs in the Steering Column Control Module.
With the scan tool, select Data Display and view the Up switch data.
While monitoring the Up switch data, press and release the Up Switch several times.

Does the Up switch data change from Set to Not Set as the switch is pressed and released?

Yes

- Test complete.

No

- Go to 6

6. STEERING COLUMN CONTROL MODULE (SCCM)

View repair.

Repair

- Replace the Steering Column Control Module (SCCM)

7. INTERMITTENT STEERING WHEEL CONTROL UP SWITCH CIRCUIT DTC

The conditions necessary to set this DTC are not present at this time.
Using the wiring diagram/schematic as a guide, inspect the wiring and connectors.
While monitoring the scan tool data relative to this circuit, wiggle test the wiring and connectors.
Look for the data to change or for the DTC to reset during the wiggle test.

Were any problems found?

Yes

- Repair as necessary.

No

- Test complete.

ARM0500000000980

Fig. 4   Code B148B: Steering Wheel Control Up Switch Circuit (Part 4 of 4). Charger, Magnum & 300

2. (G106) EVIC MUX SIGNAL 1 CIRCUIT SHORT TO (G907) EVIC/NAV MUX RETURN CIRCUIT

Turn the ignition off.
Remove the Driver Airbag in accordance with the Service Information.
Disconnect the Left Steering Switch harness connector.
Disconnect the Right Steering Switch harness connector.

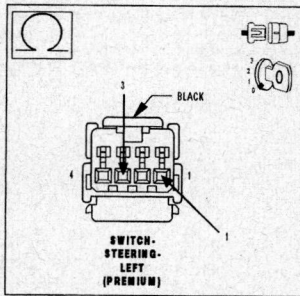

NOTE: Before proceeding, thoroughly inspect the wiring harness and connectors between the Left Steering Switch and the Right Steering Switch for a short to ground or any other circuit.

Measure the resistance between the (G106) EVIC Mux Signal 1 circuit and the (G907) EVIC/NAV Mux Return circuit.

Is the resistance below 5.0 ohms?

Yes

- Repair the (G106) EVIC Mux Signal 1 circuit for a short to the (G907) EVIC/NAV Mux Return circuit.

No

- Go to 3

ARM0500000000982

Fig. 5   Code B148C: Steering Wheel Control Down Switch Circuit (Part 2 of 4). Charger, Magnum & 300

3. (G106) EVIC MUX SIGNAL 1 CIRCUIT SHORT TO GROUND

NOTE: Before proceeding, thoroughly inspect the wiring harness and connectors between the Left Steering Switch and the Right Steering Switch for a short to ground or any other circuit.

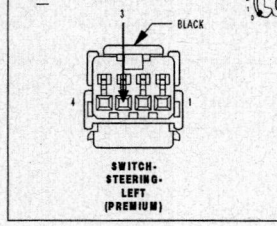

Measure the resistance between the (G106) EVIC Mux Signal 1 circuit and ground.

Is the resistance below 5.0 ohms?

Yes

- Repair the (G106) EVIC Mux Signal 1 circuit for a short to ground.

No

- Go to 4

4. LEFT STEERING SWITCH

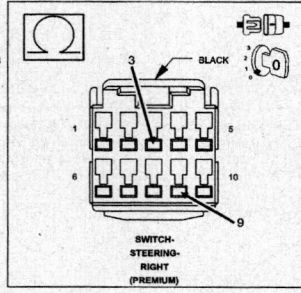

Reconnect the Left Steering Switch harness connector. Measure the resistance between the (G106) EVIC Mux Signal 1 circuit and the (G907) EVIC/NAV Mux Return circuit at the Right Steering Switch harness connector.

Is the resistance approximately 10 K ohms (+/- 10%)?

Yes

- Replace the Left Steering Switch

No

- Go to 5

ARM0500000000983

Fig. 5   Code B148C: Steering Wheel Control Down Switch Circuit (Part 3 of 4). Charger, Magnum & 300

1. DTC STATUS IS ACTIVE

NOTE: If U1109–LOST COMMUNICATION WITH LIN STEERING WHEEL CONTROLS is set along with this DTC, diagnose the communication DTC first.

NOTE: If P0562–BATTERY VOLTAGE LOW or P0563–BATTERY VOLTAGE HIGH is set along with this DTC, diagnose the battery voltage DTC first.

Ignition on, engine not running.
With the Scan Tool, select View DTCs in the Steering Control Module.

Is the DTC status Active at this time?

Yes

- Go to 2

No

- Go to 7

ARM0500000000985

Fig. 6   Code B148D: Steering Wheel Control Side Switch Circuit (Part 1 of 4). Charger, Magnum & 300

5. RIGHT STEERING SWITCH

Replace the Right Steering Switch in accordance with the Service Information.
Reconnect the C206 (LIN Bus) connector.
Turn the ignition on.
Press and release the Down Switch several times.
With the scan tool, Clear Stored DTCs in the Steering Control Module.
With the scan tool, select Data Display and view the Down switch data.
While monitoring the Down switch data, press and release the Down Switch several times.

Does the Down switch data change from Set to Not Set as the switch is pressed and released?

Yes

- Test complete.

No

- Go to 6

6. STEERING CONTROL MODULE (SCM)

View repair.

Repair

- Replace the Steering Control Module (SCM)

7. INTERMITTENT STEERING WHEEL CONTROL DOWN SWITCH CIRCUIT DTC

The conditions necessary to set this DTC are not present at this time.
Using the wiring diagram/schematic as a guide, inspect the wiring and connectors.
While monitoring the scan tool data relative to this circuit, wiggle test the wiring and connectors.
Look for the data to change or for the DTC to reset during the wiggle test.

Were any problems found?

Yes

- Repair as necessary.

No

- Test complete.

ARM0500000000984

Fig. 5   Code B148C: Steering Wheel Control Down Switch Circuit (Part 4 of 4). Charger, Magnum & 300

2. (G206) EVIC MUX SIGNAL 1 CIRCUIT SHORT TO (G907) EVIC/NAV MUX RETURN CIRCUIT

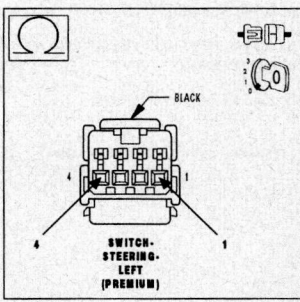

Turn the ignition off.
Remove the Driver Airbag in accordance with the Service Information.
Disconnect the Left Steering Switch harness connector.
Disconnect the Right Steering Switch harness connector.

NOTE: Before proceeding, thoroughly inspect the wiring harness and connectors between the Left Steering Switch and the Right Steering Switch for a short to ground or any other circuit.

Measure the resistance between the (G206) EVIC Mux Signal 1 circuit and the (G907) EVIC/NAV Mux Return circuit.

Is the resistance below 5.0 ohms?

Yes

- Repair the (G206) EVIC Mux Signal 1 circuit for a short to the (G907) EVIC/NAV Mux Return circuit.

No

- Go to 3

ARM0500000000986

Fig. 6   Code B148D: Steering Wheel Control Side Switch Circuit (Part 2 of 4). Charger, Magnum & 300

3. (G206) EVIC MUX SIGNAL 1 CIRCUIT SHORT TO GROUND

NOTE: Before proceeding, thoroughly inspect the wiring harness and connectors between the Left Steering Switch and the Right Steering Switch for a short to ground or any other circuit.

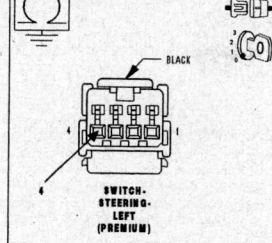

Measure the resistance between the (G206) EVIC Mux Signal 1 circuit and ground.

Is the resistance below 5.0 ohms?

Yes

- Repair the (G206) EVIC Mux Signal 1 circuit for a short to ground.

No

- Go to 4

4. LEFT STEERING SWITCH

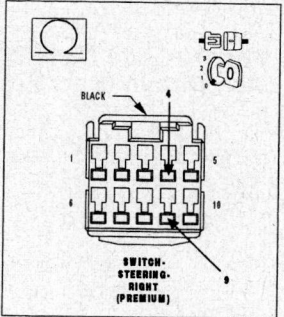

Reconnect the Left Steering Switch harness connector. Measure the resistance between the (G206) EVIC Mux Signal 1 circuit and the (G907) EVIC/NAV Return circuit at the Right Steering Switch harness connector.

Is the resistance approximately .5 ohms (+/- 1 ohm)?

Yes

- Replace the Left Steering Switch

No

- Go to 5

Fig. 6   Code B148D: Steering Wheel Control Side Switch Circuit (Part 3 of 4). Charger, Magnum & 300

ARM0500000000987

1. DTC IS ACTIVE

NOTE: If U1109–LOST COMMUNICATION WITH LIN STEERING WHEEL CONTROLS is set along with this DTC, diagnose the communication DTC first.

NOTE: If P0562–BATTERY VOLTAGE LOW or P0563–BATTERY VOLTAGE HIGH is set along with this DTC, diagnose the battery voltage DTC first.

Ignition on, engine not running.
With the Scan Tool, select View DTCs in the Steering Control Module.

Is the DTC status Active at this time?

Yes

- Go to 2

No

- Go to 4

2. RIGHT STEERING SWITCH

Turn the ignition off.
Replace the Right Steering Switch
Turn the ignition on.
Press and release the Plus (+) Switch several times.
With the Scan Tool, Clear Stored DTCs in the Steering Control Module.
With the Scan Tool, select Data Display and view the Plus (+) switch data.
While monitoring the Plus (+) switch data, press and release the Plus (+) Switch several times.

Does the Plus (+) switch data change from Set to Not Set when the switch is pressed and released?

Yes

- Test complete.

No

- Go to 3

ARM0500000000989

Fig. 7   Code B148E: Steering Wheel Control + Switch Circuit (Part 1 of 2). Charger, Magnum & 300

5. RIGHT STEERING SWITCH

Replace the Right Steering Switch
Reconnect the C206 (LIN Bus) connector.
Turn the ignition on.
Press and release the Side Switch several times.
With the scan tool, Clear Stored DTCs in the Steering Control Module.
With the scan tool, select Data Display and view the Side switch data.
While monitoring the Side switch data, press and release the Side Switch several times.

Does the Side switch data change from Set to Not Set as the switch is pressed and released?

Yes

- Test complete.

No

- Go to 6

6. STEERING CONTROL MODULE (SCM)

View repair.

Repair

- Replace the Steering Control Module (SCM)

7. INTERMITTENT STEERING WHEEL CONTROL SIDE SWITCH CIRCUIT DTC

The conditions necessary to set this DTC are not present at this time.
Using the wiring diagram/schematic as a guide, inspect the wiring and connectors.
While monitoring the scan tool data relative to this circuit, wiggle test the wiring and connectors.
Look for the data to change or for the DTC to reset during the wiggle test.

Were any problems found?

Yes

- Repair as necessary.

No

- Test complete.

ARM0500000000988

Fig. 6   Code B148D: Steering Wheel Control Side Switch Circuit (Part 4 of 4). Charger, Magnum & 300

3. STEERING CONTROL MODULE (SCM)

View repair.

Repair

- Replace the Steering Control Module (SCM)

4. INTERMITTENT STEERING WHEEL CONTROL [+] SWITCH CIRCUIT DTC

The conditions necessary to set this DTC are not present at this time.
Using the wiring diagram/schematic as a guide, inspect the wiring and connectors.
While monitoring the scan tool data relative to this circuit, wiggle test the wiring and connectors.
Look for the data to change or for the DTC to reset during the wiggle test.

Were any problems found?

Yes

- Repair as necessary.

No

- Test complete.

ARM0500000000990

Fig. 7   Code B148E: Steering Wheel Control + Switch Circuit (Part 2 of 2). Charger, Magnum & 300

1. DTC IS ACTIVE

NOTE: If U1109–LOST COMMUNICATION WITH LIN STEERING WHEEL CONTROLS is set along with this DTC, diagnose the communication DTC first.

NOTE: If P0562–BATTERY VOLTAGE LOW or P0563–BATTERY VOLTAGE HIGH is set along with this DTC, diagnose the battery voltage DTC first.

Ignition on, engine not running.
With the Scan Tool, select View DTCs in the Steering Control Module.

Is the DTC status Active at this time?

Yes

- Go to 2

No

- Go to 4

2. RIGHT STEERING SWITCH

Turn the ignition off.
Replace the Right Steering Switch
Turn the ignition on.
Press and release the Minus (-) Switch several times.
With the Scan Tool, Clear Stored DTCs in the Steering Control Module.
With the Scan Tool, select Data Display and view the Minus (-) switch data.
While monitoring the Minus (-) switch data, press and release the Minus (-) Switch several times.

Does the Minus (-) switch data change from Set to Not Set when the switch is pressed and released?

Yes

- Test complete.

No

- Go to 3

ARM0500000000991

Fig. 8   Code B148F: Steering Wheel Control – Switch Circuit (Part 1 of 2). Charger, Magnum & 300

1. DTC IS ACTIVE

NOTE: If U1109–LOST COMMUNICATION WITH LIN STEERING WHEEL CONTROLS is set along with this DTC, diagnose the communication DTC first.

NOTE: If P0562–BATTERY VOLTAGE LOW or P0563–BATTERY VOLTAGE HIGH is set along with this DTC, diagnose the battery voltage DTC first.

Ignition on, engine not running.
With the Scan Tool, select View DTCs in the Steering Control Module.

Is the DTC status Active at this time?

Yes

- Go to 2

No

- Go to 4

2. RIGHT STEERING SWITCH

Turn the ignition off.
Replace the Right Steering Switch
Turn the ignition on.
With the Scan Tool, Clear Stored DTCs in the Steering Control Module.
With the Scan Tool, select Data Display and view the Compass/Temperature switch data.
While monitoring the Compass/Temperature switch data, press and release the Compass/Temperature Switch several times.

Does the Compass/Temperature switch data change from Set to Not Set when the switch is pressed and released?

Yes

- Test complete.

No

- Go to 3

ARM0500000000993

Fig. 9   Code B1490: Steering Wheel Control C/T Switch Circuit (Part 1 of 2). Charger, Magnum & 300

3. STEERING CONTROL MODULE (SCM)

View repair.

Repair

- Replace the Steering Control Module (SCM)

4. INTERMITTENT STEERING WHEEL CONTROL [-] SWITCH CIRCUIT DTC

The conditions necessary to set this DTC are not present at this time.
Using the wiring diagram/schematic as a guide, inspect the wiring and connectors.
While monitoring the scan tool data relative to this circuit, wiggle test the wiring and connectors.
Look for the data to change or for the DTC to reset during the wiggle test.

Were any problems found?

Yes

- Repair as necessary.

No

- Test complete.

ARM0500000000992

Fig. 8   Code B148F: Steering Wheel Control – Switch Circuit (Part 2 of 2). Charger, Magnum & 300

3. STEERING CONTROL MODULE (SCM)

View repair.

Repair

- Replace the Steering Control Module (SCM)

4. INTERMITTENT STEERING WHEEL CONTROL C/T SWITCH CIRCUIT DTC

The conditions necessary to set this DTC are not present at this time.
Using the wiring diagram/schematic as a guide, inspect the wiring and connectors.
While monitoring the scan tool data relative to this circuit, wiggle test the wiring and connectors.
Look for the data to change or for the DTC to reset during the wiggle test.

Were any problems found?

Yes

- Repair as necessary.

No

- Test complete.

ARM0500000000994

Fig. 9   Code B1490: Steering Wheel Control C/T Switch Circuit (Part 2 of 2). Charger, Magnum & 300

1. DTC IS ACTIVE

Ignition on, engine not running.
With the Scan Tool, select Clear Stored DTCs in the Memory Seat Module.
Move the Steering Column Telescope Switch to the Forward and Rearward positions several times, holding the switch in position for at least 2 seconds each time.
With the Scan Tool, select View DTCs in the Memory Seat Module.

Does the DTC reset and/or remain active?

Yes

- Go to 2

No

- Go to 6

2. CHECK DTC WITH HARNESS DISCONNECTED

Turn the ignition off.
Disconnect the Steering Column Telescope Motor connector.
Turn the ignition on.
Move the Steering Column Telescope Switch to the Forward and Rearward positions several times.
With the Scan Tool, select Clear Stored DTCs in the Memory Seat Module.
Move the Steering Column Telescope Switch to the Forward and Rearward positions several times, holding the switch in position for at least 2 seconds each time.
With the Scan Tool, select View DTCs in the Memory Seat Module.

Does the DTC reset and/or remain active?

Yes

- Go to 4

No

- Go to 3

ARM0500000000995

Fig. 10   Code B1D8D: Steering Wheel Control Telescope Position Sensor Circuit Low (Part 1 of 3). Charger, Magnum & 300

5. MEMORY SEAT MODULE (MSM)

Inspect the wiring between the Memory Seat Module harness connector and the Steering Column Telescope Motor harness connector for a short to ground or to any other circuit. If any problems are found, repair as necessary. If no problems are found, view repair.

Repair

- Replace the Memory Seat Module (MSM)

6. INTERMITTENT STEERING COLUMN TELESCOPE POSITION SENSOR CIRCUIT LOW DTC

The conditions necessary to set this DTC are not present at this time.
While monitoring the scan tool data relative to this circuit, wiggle test the component and connectors and move the switch to each position.
Look for the data to change other than as expected or for the DTC to reset during the wiggle test.

Were any problems found?

Yes

- Repair as necessary.

No

- Test complete.

ARM0500000000997

Fig. 10   Code B1D8D: Steering Wheel Control Telescope Position Sensor Circuit Low (Part 3 of 3). Charger, Magnum & 300

3. STEERING COLUMN TELESCOPE MOTOR

View repair.

Repair

- Inspect the wiring between the Steering Column Telescope Motor and the harness connector (on the motor side) for a short to ground or to any other circuit. If any problems are found, repair as necessary. If no problems are found, replace the Steering Column Telescope Motor

4. (P152) TELESCOPE STEERING FORWARD/REARWARD POSITION SENSE CIRCUIT SHORT TO GROUND

Turn the ignition off.
Disconnect the Memory Seat Module (MSM) C1 connector.
Measure the resistance between ground and the (P152) Telescope Steering Forward/Rearward Position Sense circuit at the Steering Column Telescope Motor connector (harness side).

Is the resistance below 5.0 ohms?

Yes

- Repair the (P152) Telescope Steering Forward/Rearward Position Sense circuit for a short to ground.

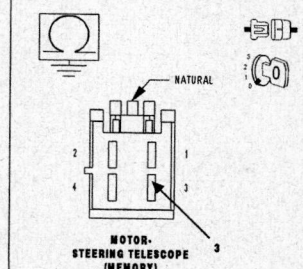

No

- Go to 5

ARM0500000000996

Fig. 10   Code B1D8D: Steering Wheel Control Telescope Position Sensor Circuit Low (Part 2 of 3). Charger, Magnum & 300

1. DTC IS ACTIVE

Ignition on, engine not running.
With the Scan Tool, select Clear Stored DTCs in the Memory Seat Module.
Move the Steering Column Telescope Switch to the Forward and Rearward positions several times, holding the switch in position for at least 2 seconds each time.
With the Scan Tool, select View DTCs in the Memory Seat Module.

Does this DTC reset and/or remain active?

Yes

- Go to 2

No

- Go to 10

2. CHECK DTC WITH HARNESS DISCONNECTED

Turn the ignition off.
Disconnect the Steering Telescope Motor harness connector.
Ignition on, engine not running.
Move the Steering Column Telescope Switch to the Forward and Rearward positions several times.
With the Scan Tool, select Clear Stored DTCs in the Memory Seat Module.
Move the Steering Column Telescope Switch to the Forward and Rearward positions several times, holding the switch in position for at least 2 seconds each time.
With the Scan Tool, select View DTCs in the Memory Seat Module.

Does this DTC reset and/or remain active?

Yes

- Go to 3

No

- Go to 8

ARM0500000000998

Fig. 11   Code B1D8E: Steering Wheel Control Telescope Position Sensor Circuit High (Part 1 of 5). Charger, Magnum & 300

3. (P152) TELESCOPE STEERING FORWARD/REARWARD POSITION SENSE CIRCUIT OPEN

Turn the ignition off.
Disconnect the Memory Seat Module (MSM) C1 connector.
Measure the resistance of the (P152) Telescope Steering Forward/Rearward Position Sense circuit.

Is the resistance above 5.0 ohms?

Yes

- Repair the (P152) Telescope Steering Forward/Rearward Position Sense circuit for an open.

No

- Go to 4

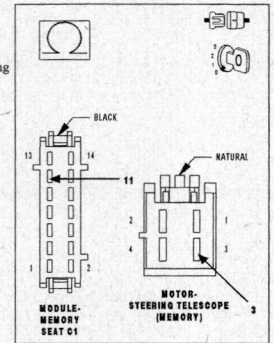

4. (P152) TELESCOPE STEERING FORWARD/REARWARD POSITION SENSE CIRCUIT SHORT TO VOLTAGE

Turn the ignition on.
Measure the voltage of the (P152) Telescope Steering Forward/Rearward Position Sense circuit.

Is there any voltage present?

Yes

- Repair the (P152) Telescope Steering Forward/Rearward Position Sense circuit for a short to voltage.

No

- Go to 5

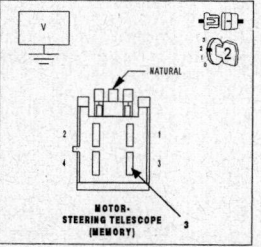

ARM0500000000999

Fig. 11 Code B1D8E: Steering Wheel Control Telescope Position Sensor Circuit High (Part 2 of 5). Charger, Magnum & 300

6. (G914) SENSOR RETURN CIRCUIT OPEN

Measure the resistance of the (G914) Sensor Return circuit.

Is the resistance above 5.0 ohms?

Yes

- Repair the (G914) Sensor Return circuit for an open.

No

- Go to 7

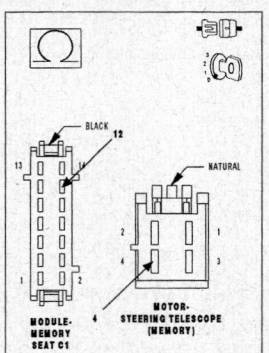

7. (G914) SENSOR RETURN CIRCUIT SHORT TO VOLTAGE

Turn the ignition on.
Measure the voltage of the (G914) Sensor Return circuit.

Is there any voltage present?

Yes

- Repair the (G914) Sensor Return circuit for a short to voltage.

No

- Go to 9

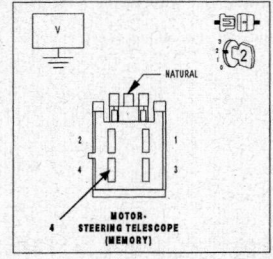

ARM0500000001001

Fig. 11 Code B1D8E: Steering Wheel Control Telescope Position Sensor Circuit High (Part 4 of 5). Charger, Magnum & 300

5. (P152) TELESCOPE STEERING FORWARD/REARWARD POSITION SENSE CIRCUIT SHORT TO TILT/TELESCOPE MOTOR CIRCUIT(S)

Turn the ignition off.
Measure the resistance between the following circuits at the Memory Seat Module (MSM) C1 connector :

- The (P152) Telescope Steering Forward/Rearward Position Sense circuit and the (P157) Telescope Steering Motor Forward/Rearward Driver circuit.
- The (P152) Telescope Steering Forward/Rearward Position Sense circuit and the (P153) Tilt Steering Motor Up/Down Driver circuit.
- The (P152) Telescope Steering Forward/Rearward Position Sense circuit and the (P953) Steering Motor Common circuit.

Is the resistance below 5.0 ohms for any of the circuit tests?

Yes

- Repair the (P152) Telescope Steering Forward/Rearward Position Sense circuit for a short to the motor circuit(s).

No

- Go to 6

ARM0500000001000

Fig. 11 Code B1D8E: Steering Wheel Control Telescope Position Sensor Circuit High (Part 3 of 5). Charger, Magnum & 300

8. STEERING COLUMN TELESCOPE MOTOR

Thoroughly inspect the wiring and connectors between the Memory Seat Module harness connector and the Steering Telescope Motor for a short to voltage or to any other circuit. If any problems are found, repair as necessary. If no other problems are found, view repair.

Repair

- Replace the Steering Column Telescope Motor

9. MEMORY SEAT MODULE (MSM)

Thoroughly inspect the wiring and connectors between the Memory Seat Module harness connector and the Steering Telescope Motor harness connector for a short to voltage or to any other circuit. If any problems are found, repair as necessary. If no other problems are found, view repair.

Repair

- Replace the Memory Seat Module (MSM)

10. INTERMITTENT STEERING COLUMN TELESCOPE POSITION SENSOR CIRCUIT HIGH DTC

The conditions necessary to set this DTC are not present at this time.
While monitoring the scan tool data relative to this circuit, wiggle test the component and connectors and move the switch to each position.
Look for the data to change other than as expected or for the DTC to reset during the wiggle test.

Were any problems found?

Yes

- Repair as necessary.

No

- Test complete.

ARM0500000001002

Fig. 11 Code B1D8E: Steering Wheel Control Telescope Position Sensor Circuit High (Part 5 of 5). Charger, Magnum & 300

1. DTC IS ACTIVE

Ignition on, engine not running.
With the Scan Tool, select Clear Stored DTCs in the Memory Seat Module.
Move the Steering Column Tilt Switch to the Up and Down positions several times, holding the switch in position for at least 2 seconds each time.
With the Scan Tool, select View DTCs in the Memory Seat Module.

Does the DTC reset and/or remain active?

Yes

- Go to 2

No

- Go to 6

2. CHECK DTC WITH HARNESS DISCONNECTED

Turn the ignition off.
Disconnect the Steering Column Tilt Motor connector.
Turn the ignition on.
Move the Steering Column Tilt Switch to the Up and Down positions several times.
With the Scan Tool, select Clear Stored DTCs in the Memory Seat Module.
Move the Steering Column Tilt Switch to the Up and Down positions several times, holding the switch in position for at least 2 seconds each time.
With the Scan Tool, select View DTCs in the Memory Seat Module.

Does the DTC reset and/or remain active?

Yes

- Go to 4

No

- Go to 3

ARM0500000001003

Fig. 12   Code B1D91: Steering Wheel Control Tilt Position Sensor Circuit Low (Part 1 of 3). Charger, Magnum & 300

5. MEMORY SEAT MODULE (MSM)

Inspect the wiring between the Memory Seat Module harness connector and the Steering Column Tilt Motor harness connector for a short to ground or to any other circuit. If any problems are found, repair as necessary. If no problems are found, view repair.

Repair

- Replace the Memory Seat Module (MSM)

6. INTERMITTENT STEERING COLUMN TILT POSITION SENSOR CIRCUIT LOW DTC

The conditions necessary to set this DTC are not present at this time.
While monitoring the scan tool data relative to this circuit, wiggle test the component and connectors and move the switch to each position.
Look for the data to change other than as expected or for the DTC to reset during the wiggle test.

Were any problems found?

Yes

- Repair as necessary.

No

- Test complete.

ARM0500000001005

Fig. 12   Code B1D91: Steering Wheel Control Tilt Position Sensor Circuit Low (Part 3 of 3). Charger, Magnum & 300

3. STEERING COLUMN TILT MOTOR

View repair.

Repair

- Inspect the wiring between the Steering Column Tilt Motor and the harness connector (on the motor side) for a short to ground or to any other circuit. If any problems are found, repair as necessary. If no problems are found, replace the Steering Column Tilt Motor in accordance with the Service Information.

4. (P151) TILT STEERING UP/DOWN POSITION SENSE CIRCUIT SHORT TO GROUND

Turn the ignition off.
Disconnect the Memory Seat Module (MSM) C1 connector.
Measure the resistance between ground and the (P151) Tilt Steering Up/Down Position Sense circuit at the Steering Column Tilt Motor connector (harness side).

Is the resistance below 5.0 ohms?

Yes

- Repair the (P151) Tilt Steering Up/Down Position Sense circuit for a short to ground.

No

- Go to 5

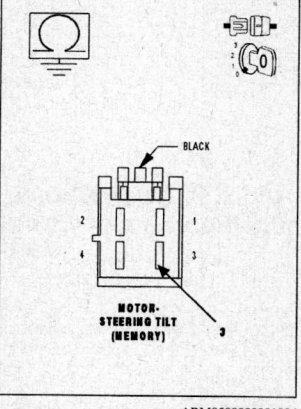

ARM0500000001004

Fig. 12   Code B1D91: Steering Wheel Control Tilt Position Sensor Circuit Low (Part 2 of 3). Charger, Magnum & 300

1. DTC IS ACTIVE

Ignition on, engine not running.
With the Scan Tool, select Clear Stored DTCs in the Memory Seat Module.
Move the Steering Column Tilt Switch to the Up and Down positions several times, holding the switch in position for at least 2 seconds each time.
With the Scan Tool, select View DTCs in the Memory Seat Module.

Does this DTC reset and/or remain active?

Yes

- Go to 2

No

- Go to 10

2. CHECK DTC WITH HARNESS DISCONNECTED

Turn the ignition off.
Disconnect the Steering Tilt Motor harness connector.
Ignition on, engine not running.
Move the Steering Column Tilt Switch to the Up and Down positions several times.
With the Scan Tool, select Clear Stored DTCs in the Memory Seat Module.
Move the Steering Column Tilt Switch to the Up and Down positions several times, holding the switch in position for at least 2 seconds each time.
With the Scan Tool, select View DTCs in the Memory Seat Module.

Does this DTC reset and/or remain active?

Yes

- Go to 3

No

- Go to 8

ARM0500000001006

Fig. 13   Code B1D92: Steering Wheel Control Tilt Position Sensor Circuit High (Part 1 of 7). Charger, Magnum & 300

3. (P151) TILT STEERING UP/DOWN POSITION SENSE CIRCUIT OPEN

Turn the ignition off.
Disconnect the Memory Seat Module (MSM) C1 connector.
Measure the resistance of the (P151) Tilt Steering Up/Down Position Sense circuit.

Is the resistance above 5.0 ohms?

Yes

- Repair the (P151) Tilt Steering Up/Down Position Sense circuit for an open.

No

- Go to 4

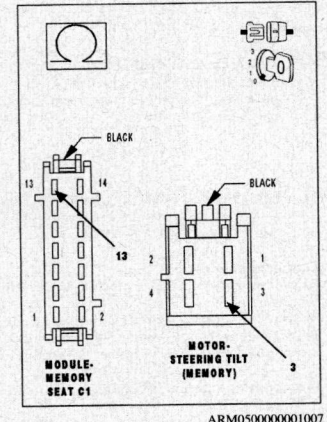

ARM0500000001007

Fig. 13   Code B1D92: Steering Wheel Control Tilt Position Sensor Circuit High (Part 2 of 7). Charger, Magnum & 300

4. (P151) TILT STEERING UP/DOWN POSITION SENSE CIRCUIT SHORT TO VOLTAGE

Turn the ignition on.
Measure the voltage of the (P151) Tilt Steering Up/Down Position Sense circuit.

Is there any voltage present?

Yes

- Repair the (P151) Tilt Steering Up/Down Position Sense circuit for a short to voltage.

No

- Go to 5

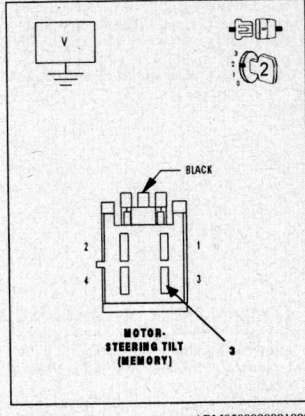

ARM0500000001008

Fig. 13   Code B1D92: Steering Wheel Control Tilt Position Sensor Circuit High (Part 3 of 7). Charger, Magnum & 300

5. (P151) TILT STEERING UP/DOWN POSITION SENSE CIRCUIT SHORT TO TILT/TELESCOPE MOTOR CIRCUIT(S)

Turn the ignition off.
Measure the resistance between the following circuits at the Memory Seat Module (MSM) C1 connector :

- The (P151) Tilt Steering Up/Down Position Sense circuit and the (P157) Telescope Steering Motor Forward/Rearward Driver circuit.

- The (P151) Tilt Steering Up/Down Position Sense circuit and the (P153) Tilt Steering Motor Up/Down Driver circuit.

- The (P151) Tilt Steering Up/Down Position Sense circuit and the (P953) Steering Motor Common circuit.

Is the resistance below 5.0 ohms for any of the circuit tests?

Yes

- Repair the (P151) Tilt Steering Up/Down Position Sense circuit for a short to the motor circuit(s).

No

- Go to 6

ARM0500000001009

Fig. 13   Code B1D92: Steering Wheel Control Tilt Position Sensor Circuit High (Part 4 of 7). Charger, Magnum & 300

6. (G914) SENSOR RETURN CIRCUIT OPEN

Measure the resistance of the (G914) Sensor Return circuit.

Is the resistance above 5.0 ohms?

Yes

- Repair the (G914) Sensor Return circuit for an open.

No

- Go to 7

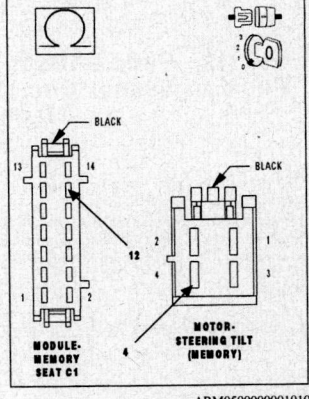

ARM0500000001010

Fig. 13   Code B1D92: Steering Wheel Control Tilt Position Sensor Circuit High (Part 5 of 7). Charger, Magnum & 300

7. (G914) SENSOR RETURN CIRCUIT SHORT TO VOLTAGE

Turn the ignition on.
Measure the voltage of the (G914) Sensor Return circuit.

Is there any voltage present?

Yes

- Repair the (G914) Sensor Return circuit for a short to voltage.

No

- Go to 9

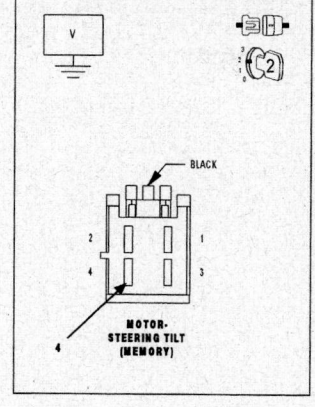

8. STEERING COLUMN TILT MOTOR

Thoroughly inspect the wiring and connectors between the Memory Seat Module harness connector and the Steering Tilt Motor for a short to voltage or to any other circuit. If any problems are found, repair as necessary. If no other problems are found, view repair.

Repair

- Replace the Steering Column Tilt Motor

ARM0500000001011

Fig. 13   Code B1D92: Steering Wheel Control Tilt Position Sensor Circuit High (Part 6 of 7). Charger, Magnum & 300

1. DTC IS ACTIVE

Ignition on, engine not running.

NOTE: If a DTC is set for B1D8D and/or B1D8E, perform the diagnostic procedure(s) before continuing.

With the Scan Tool, select Clear Stored DTCs in the Memory Seat Module.
Move the Steering Column Telescope Switch to the Forward and Rearward positions several times, holding the switch in position for at least 2 seconds each time.
With the Scan Tool, select View DTCs in the Memory Seat Module.

Does the DTC reset and/or remain active?

Yes

- Go to 2

No

- Go to 14

2. (P157) TELESCOPE STEERING MOTOR FORWARD/REARWARD DRIVER CIRCUIT — TEST TO GROUND

Turn the ignition off.
Disconnect the Steering Telescope Motor harness connector.
Turn the ignition on.
Using a 12–volt test light connected to 12–volts, check the (P157) Telescope Steering Motor Forward/Rearward Driver circuit.
Monitor the test light with the Steering Column Telescope Switch in the Forward position, the Rearward position and with the switch at rest.
The test light should be illuminated and bright only when the switch is in the Rearward position.

Does the test light illuminate as described?

Yes

- Go to 3

No

- Go to 6

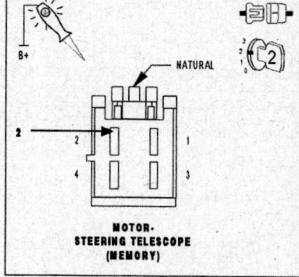

ARM0500000001013

Fig. 14   Code B1D93: Steering Wheel Control Telescope Motor Control Circuit Performance (Part 1 of 7). Charger, Magnum & 300

9. MEMORY SEAT MODULE (MSM)

Thoroughly inspect the wiring and connectors between the Memory Seat Module harness connector and the Steering Tilt Motor harness connector for a short to voltage or to any other circuit. If any problems are found, repair as necessary. If no other problems are found, view repair.

Repair

- Replace the Memory Seat Module (MSM)

10. INTERMITTENT STEERING COLUMN TILT POSITION SENSOR CIRCUIT HIGH DTC

The conditions necessary to set this DTC are not present at this time.
While monitoring the scan tool data relative to this circuit, wiggle test the component and connectors and move the switch to each position.
Look for the data to change other than as expected or for the DTC to reset during the wiggle test.

Were any problems found?

Yes

- Repair as necessary.

No

- Test complete.

ARM0500000001012

Fig. 13   Code B1D92: Steering Wheel Control Tilt Position Sensor Circuit High (Part 7 of 7). Charger, Magnum & 300

3. (P953) TELESCOPE STEERING MOTOR COMMON CIRCUIT — TEST TO GROUND

Using a 12–volt test light connected to 12–volts, check the (P953) Telescope Steering Motor Common circuit.
Monitor the test light with the Steering Column Telescope Switch in the Forward position, the Rearward position and with the switch at rest.
The test light should be illuminated and bright when the switch is in the Forward position and when the switch is at rest.

Does the test light illuminate as described?

Yes

- Go to 4

No

- Go to 9

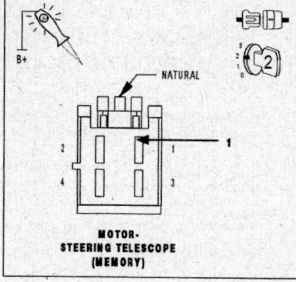

4. (P157) TELESCOPE STEERING MOTOR FORWARD/REARWARD DRIVER CIRCUIT- TEST TO VOLTAGE

Using a 12–volt test light connected to ground, check the (P157) Telescope Steering Motor Forward/Rearward Driver circuit.
Monitor the test light with the Steering Column Telescope Switch in the Forward position, the Rearward position and with the switch at rest.
The test light should be illuminated and bright only when the switch is in the Forward position.

Does the test light illuminate as described?

Yes

- Go to 5

No

- Go to 6

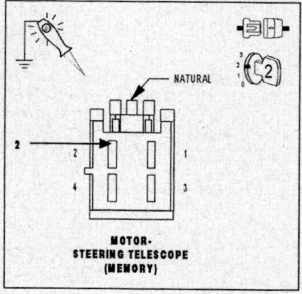

ARM0500000001014

Fig. 14   Code B1D93: Steering Wheel Control Telescope Motor Control Circuit Performance (Part 2 of 7). Charger, Magnum & 300

5. (P953) TELESCOPE STEERING MOTOR COMMON CIRCUIT — TEST TO VOLTAGE

Using a 12–volt test light connected to ground, check the (P953) Telescope Steering Motor Common circuit.
Monitor the test light with the Steering Column Telescope Switch in the Forward position, the Rearward position and with the switch at rest.
The test light should be illuminated and bright only when the switch is in the Rearward position.

Does the test light illuminate as described?

Yes

- Go to 12

No

- Go to 9

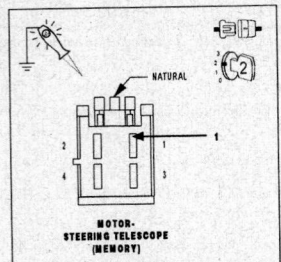

6. (P157) TELESCOPE STEERING MOTOR FORWARD/REARWARD DRIVER CIRCUIT SHORT TO GROUND

Turn the ignition off.
Disconnect the Memory Seat Module (MSM) C1 connector.
Turn the ignition on.
Using a 12–volt test light connected to 12–volts, check the (P157) Telescope Steering Motor Forward/Rearward Driver circuit.

Does the test light illuminate?

Yes

- Repair the (P157) Telescope Steering Motor Forward/Rearward Driver circuit for a short to ground.

No

- Go to 7

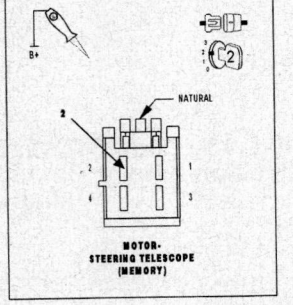

ARM0500000001015

Fig. 14   Code B1D93: Steering Wheel Control Telescope Motor Control Circuit Performance (Part 3 of 7). Charger, Magnum & 300

9. (P953) TELESCOPE STEERING MOTOR COMMON CIRCUIT SHORT TO GROUND

Turn the ignition off.
Disconnect the Memory Seat Module (MSM) C1 connector.
Turn the ignition on.
Using a 12–volt test light connected to 12–volts, check the (P953) Telescope Steering Motor Common circuit.

Does the test light illuminate?

Yes

- Repair the (P953) Telescope Steering Motor Common circuit for a short to ground.

No

- Go to 10

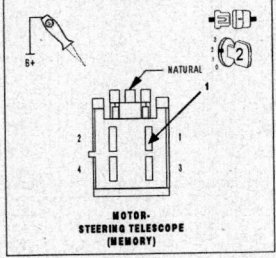

10. (P953) TELESCOPE STEERING MOTOR COMMON CIRCUIT OPEN

Turn the ignition off.
Measure the resistance of the (P953) Telescope Steering Motor Common circuit.

Is the resistance above 5.0 ohms?

Yes

- Repair the (P953) Telescope Steering Motor Common circuit for an open.

No

- Go to 11

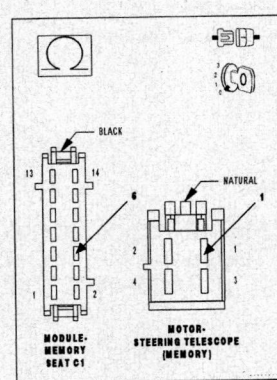

ARM0500000001017

Fig. 14   Code B1D93: Steering Wheel Control Telescope Motor Control Circuit Performance (Part 5 of 7). Charger, Magnum & 300

7. (P157) TELESCOPE STEERING MOTOR FORWARD/REARWARD DRIVER CIRCUIT OPEN

Turn the ignition off.
Measure the resistance of the (P157) Telescope Steering Motor Forward/Rearward Driver circuit.

Is the resistance above 5.0 ohms?

Yes

- Repair the (P157) Telescope Steering Motor Forward/Rearward Driver circuit for an open.

No

- Go to 8

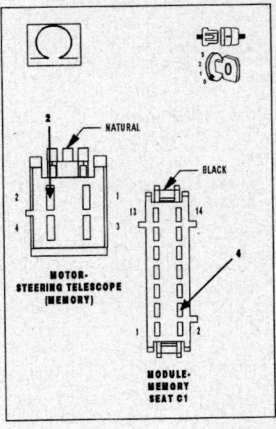

8. (P157) TELESCOPE STEERING MOTOR FORWARD/REARWARD DRIVER CIRCUIT SHORT TO VOLTAGE

Turn the ignition on.
Measure the voltage of the (P157) Telescope Steering Motor Forward/Rearward Driver circuit.

Is there any voltage present?

Yes

- Repair the (P157) Telescope Steering Motor Forward/Rearward Driver circuit for a short to voltage.

No

- Go to 13

ARM0500000001016

Fig. 14   Code B1D93: Steering Wheel Control Telescope Motor Control Circuit Performance (Part 4 of 7). Charger, Magnum & 300

11. (P953) TELESCOPE STEERING MOTOR COMMON CIRCUIT SHORT TO VOLTAGE

Turn the ignition on.
Measure the voltage of the (P953) Telescope Steering Motor Common circuit.

Is there any voltage present?

Yes

- Repair the (P953) Telescope Steering Motor Common circuit for a short to voltage.

No

- Go to 13

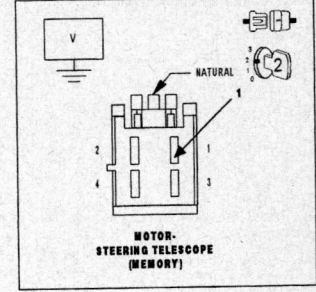

12. STEERING COLUMN TELESCOPE MOTOR

Inspect the wiring between the Memory Seat Module harness connector and the Steering Column Telescope Motor harness connector for a short to ground or to any other circuit. If any problems are found, repair as necessary. If no problems are found, view repair.

Repair

- Replace the Steering Column Telescope Motor

ARM0500000001018

Fig. 14   Code B1D93: Steering Wheel Control Telescope Motor Control Circuit Performance (Part 6 of 7). Charger, Magnum & 300

13. MEMORY SEAT MODULE (MSM)

Inspect the wiring between the Memory Seat Module harness connector and the Steering Column Telescope Motor harness connector for a short to ground or to any other circuit. If any problems are found, repair as necessary. If no problems are found, view repair.

Repair

- Replace the Memory Seat Module (MSM)

14. INTERMITTENT STEERING COLUMN TELESCOPE MOTOR CONTROL CIRCUIT PERFORMANCE DTC

The conditions necessary to set this DTC are not present at this time.
While monitoring the scan tool data relative to this circuit, wiggle test the component and connectors and move the switch to each position.
Look for the data to change other than as expected or for the DTC to reset during the wiggle test.

Were any problems found?

Yes

- Repair as necessary.

No

- Test complete.

ARM0500000001019

Fig. 14   Code B1D93: Steering Wheel Control Telescope Motor Control Circuit Performance (Part 7 of 7). Charger, Magnum & 300

3. (P953) TILT STEERING MOTOR COMMON CIRCUIT — TEST TO GROUND

Using a 12–volt test light connected to 12–volts, check the (P953) Tilt Steering Motor Common circuit.
Monitor the test light with the Steering Column Tilt Switch in the Up position, the Down position and with the switch at rest.
The test light should be illuminated and bright when the switch is in the Up position and when the switch is at rest.

Does the test light illuminate as described?

Yes

- Go to 4

No

- Go to 9

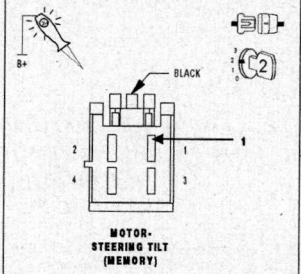

4. (P153) TILT STEERING MOTOR UP/DOWN DRIVER CIRCUIT- TEST TO VOLTAGE

Using a 12–volt test light connected to ground, check the (P153) Tilt Steering Motor Up/Down Driver circuit.
Monitor the test light with the Steering Column Tilt Switch in the Up position, the Down position and with the switch at rest.
The test light should be illuminated and bright only when the switch is in the Up position.

Does the test light illuminate as described?

Yes

- Go to 5

No

- Go to 6

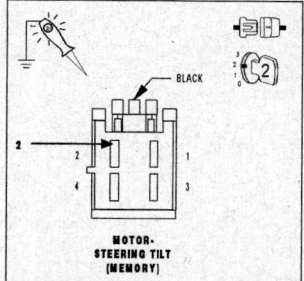

ARM0500000001021

Fig. 15   Code B1D97: Steering Wheel Control Tilt Motor Control Circuit Performance (Part 2 of 8). Charger, Magnum & 300

1. DTC IS ACTIVE

Ignition on, engine not running.

NOTE: If a DTC is set for B1D8D and/or B1D8E, perform the diagnostic procedure(s) before continuing.

With the Scan Tool, select Clear Stored DTCs in the Memory Seat Module.
Move the Steering Column Tilt Switch to the Forward and Rearward positions several times, holding the switch in position for at least 2 seconds each time.
With the Scan Tool, select View DTCs in the Memory Seat Module.

Does the DTC reset and/or remain active?

Yes

- Go to 2

No

- Go to 14

2. (P153) TILT STEERING MOTOR UP/DOWN DRIVER CIRCUIT — TEST TO GROUND

Turn the ignition off.
Disconnect the Steering Tilt Motor harness connector.
Turn the ignition on.
Using a 12–volt test light connected to 12–volts, check the (P153) Tilt Steering Motor Up/Down Driver circuit.
Monitor the test light with the Steering Column Tilt Switch in the Up position, the Down position and with the switch at rest.
The test light should be illuminated and bright only when the switch is in the Down position.

Does the test light illuminate as described?

Yes

- Go to 3

No

- Go to 6

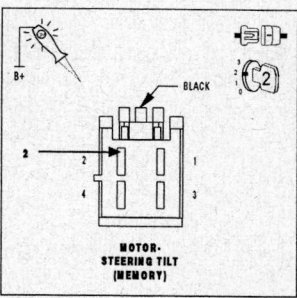

ARM0500000001020

Fig. 15   Code B1D97: Steering Wheel Control Tilt Motor Control Circuit Performance (Part 1 of 8). Charger, Magnum & 300

5. (P953) TILT STEERING MOTOR COMMON CIRCUIT — TEST TO VOLTAGE

Using a 12–volt test light connected to ground, check the (P953) Tilt Steering Motor Common circuit.
Monitor the test light with the Steering Column Tilt Switch in the Up position, the Down position and with the switch at rest.
The test light should be illuminated and bright only when the switch is in the Down position.

Does the test light illuminate as described?

Yes

- Go to 12

No

- Go to 9

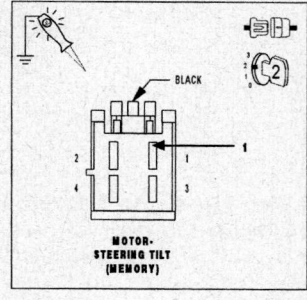

6. (P153) TILT STEERING MOTOR UP/DOWN DRIVER CIRCUIT SHORT TO GROUND

Turn the ignition off.
Disconnect the Memory Seat Module (MSM) C1 connector.
Turn the ignition on.
Using a 12–volt test light connected to 12–volts, check the (P153) Tilt Steering Motor Up/Down Driver circuit.

Does the test light illuminate?

Yes

- Repair the (P153) Tilt Steering Motor Up/Down Driver circuit for a short to ground.

No

- Go to 7

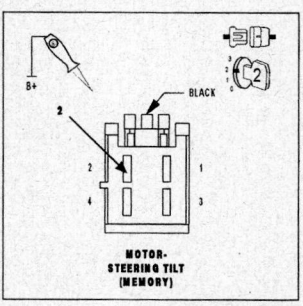

ARM0500000001022

Fig. 15   Code B1D97: Steering Wheel Control Tilt Motor Control Circuit Performance (Part 3 of 8). Charger, Magnum & 300

7. (P153) TILT STEERING MOTOR UP/DOWN DRIVER CIRCUIT OPEN

Turn the ignition off.
Measure the resistance of the (P153) Tilt Steering Motor Up/Down Driver circuit.

Is the resistance above 5.0 ohms?

Yes

- Repair the (P153) Tilt Steering Motor Up/Down Driver circuit for an open.

No

- Go to 8

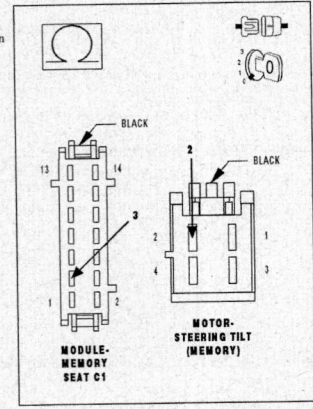

Fig. 15 Code B1D97: Steering Wheel Control Tilt Motor Control Circuit Performance (Part 4 of 8). Charger, Magnum & 300

10. (P953) TILT STEERING MOTOR COMMON CIRCUIT OPEN

Turn the ignition off.
Measure the resistance of the (P953) Tilt Steering Motor Common circuit.

Is the resistance above 5.0 ohms?

Yes

- Repair the (P953) Tilt Steering Motor Common circuit for an open.

No

- Go to 11

ARM0500000001025

Fig. 15 Code B1D97: Steering Wheel Control Tilt Motor Control Circuit Performance (Part 6 of 8). Charger, Magnum & 300

8. (P153) TILT STEERING MOTOR UP/DOWN DRIVER CIRCUIT SHORT TO VOLTAGE

Turn the ignition on.
Measure the voltage of the (P153) Tilt Steering Motor Up/Down Driver circuit.

Is there any voltage present?

Yes

- Repair the (P153) Tilt Steering Motor Up/Down Driver circuit for a short to voltage.

No

- Go to 13

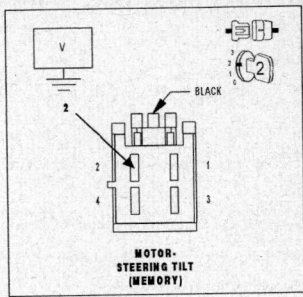

9. (P953) TILT STEERING MOTOR COMMON CIRCUIT SHORT TO GROUND

Turn the ignition off.
Disconnect the Memory Seat Module (MSM) C1 connector.
Turn the ignition on.
Using a 12–volt test light connected to 12–volts, check the (P953) Tilt Steering Motor Common circuit.

Does the test light illuminate?

Yes

- Repair the (P953) Tilt Steering Motor Common circuit for a short to ground.

No

- Go to 10

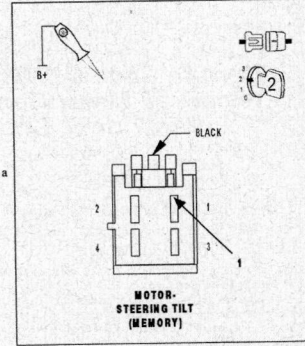

ARM0500000001024

Fig. 15 Code B1D97: Steering Wheel Control Tilt Motor Control Circuit Performance (Part 5 of 8). Charger, Magnum & 300

11. (P953) TILT STEERING MOTOR COMMON CIRCUIT SHORT TO VOLTAGE

Turn the ignition on.
Measure the voltage of the (P953) Tilt Steering Motor Common circuit.

Is there any voltage present?

Yes

- Repair the (P953) Tilt Steering Motor Common circuit for a short to voltage.

No

- Go to 13

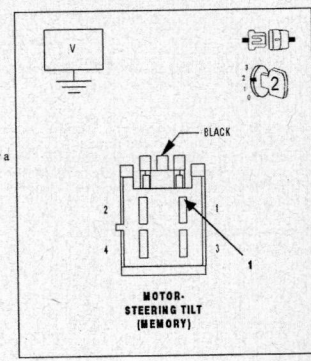

12. STEERING COLUMN TILT MOTOR

Inspect the wiring between the Memory Seat Module harness connector and the Steering Column Tilt Motor harness connector for a short to ground or to any other circuit. If any problems are found, repair as necessary. If no problems are found, view repair.

Repair

- Replace the Steering Column Tilt Motor

ARM0500000001026

Fig. 15 Code B1D97: Steering Wheel Control Tilt Motor Control Circuit Performance (Part 7 of 8). Charger, Magnum & 300

13. MEMORY SEAT MODULE (MSM)

Inspect the wiring between the Memory Seat Module harness connector and the Steering Column Tilt Motor harness connector for a short to ground or to any other circuit. If any problems are found, repair as necessary. If no problems are found, view repair.

Repair

- Replace the Memory Seat Module (MSM)

14. INTERMITTENT STEERING COLUMN TILT MOTOR CONTROL CIRCUIT PERFORMANCE DTC

The conditions necessary to set this DTC are not present at this time.
While monitoring the scan tool data relative to this circuit, wiggle test the component and connectors and move the switch to each position.
Look for the data to change other than as expected or for the DTC to reset during the wiggle test.

Were any problems found?

Yes

- Repair as necessary.

No

- Test complete.

ARM0500000001027

Fig. 15 Code B1D97: Steering Wheel Control Tilt Motor Control Circuit Performance (Part 8 of 8). Charger, Magnum & 300

3. STEERING CONTROL MODULE

View repair.

Repair

- Replace the Steering Control Module (SCM)

4. INTERMITTENT STEERING COLUMN TELESCOPE SWITCH CIRCUIT STUCK DTC

The conditions necessary to set this DTC are not present at this time.
While monitoring the scan tool data relative to this circuit, wiggle test the component and connectors and move the switch to each position.
Look for the data to change other than as expected or for the DTC to reset during the test.

Were any problems found?

Yes

- Repair as necessary.

No

- Test complete.

ARM0500000001029

Fig. 16 Code B1DA0: Steering Column Control Tilt Switch Circuit Stuck (Part 2 of 2). Charger, Magnum & 300

1. DTC IS ACTIVE

NOTE: If P0562–BATTERY VOLTAGE LOW or P0563–BATTERY VOLTAGE HIGH is set along with this DTC, diagnose the battery voltage DTC first.

Ignition on, engine not running.
With the Scan Tool, select View DTCs in the Steering Control Module.

Is the DTC status Active at this time?

Yes

- Go to 2

No

- Go to 4

2. STEERING COLUMN TILT/TELESCOPE SWITCH

Turn the ignition off.
Replace the Steering Column Tilt/Telescope Switch
Turn the ignition on.
Move the Steering column telescope switch forward and back several times.
With the Scan Tool, Clear Stored DTCs in the Steering Control Module.
With the Scan Tool, select Data Display and view the Steering column forward and Steering column back switch data.
While monitoring the Steering column forward and Steering column back switch data, move the Steering column telescope switch forward and back several times.

Does the Steering column switch data change from Set to Not Set as the switch is moved to each position?

Yes

- Test complete.

No

- Go to 3

ARM0500000001028

Fig. 16 Code B1DA0: Steering Column Control Tilt Switch Circuit Stuck (Part 1 of 2). Charger, Magnum & 300

1. DTC IS ACTIVE

NOTE: If P0562–BATTERY VOLTAGE LOW or P0563–BATTERY VOLTAGE HIGH is set along with this DTC, diagnose the battery voltage DTC first.

Ignition on, engine not running.
With the Scan Tool, select View DTCs in the Steering Control Module.

Is the DTC status Active at this time?

Yes

- Go to 2

No

- Go to 4

2. STEERING COLUMN TILT/TELESCOPE SWITCH

Turn the ignition off.
Replace the Steering Column Tilt/Telescope Switch
Turn the ignition on.
Move the Steering column tilt switch to the up and down positions several times.
With the Scan Tool, Clear Stored DTCs in the Steering Control Module.
With the Scan Tool, select Data Display and view the Steering column up and the Steering column down switch data.
While monitoring the Steering column up and the Steering column down switch data, move the Steering column tilt switch to the up and down positions several times.

Does the Steering column switch data change from Set to Not Set as the switch is moved to each position?

Yes

- Test complete.

No

- Go to 3

ARM0500000001030

Fig. 17 Code B1DA5: Steering Column Control Telescope Switch Circuit Stuck (Part 1 of 2). Charger, Magnum & 300

3. STEERING CONTROL MODULE (SCM)

View repair.

Repair

- Replace the Steering Control Module (SCM)

4. INTERMITTENT STEERING COLUMN TILT SWITCH CIRCUIT STUCK DTC

The conditions necessary to set this DTC are not present at this time.
While monitoring the scan tool data relative to this circuit, wiggle test the component and connectors and move the switch to each position.
Look for the data to change other than as expected or for the DTC to reset during the test.

Were any problems found?

Yes

- Repair as necessary.

No

- Test complete.

ARM0500000001031

Fig. 17   Code B1DA5: Steering Column Control Telescope Switch Circuit Stuck (Part 2 of 2). Charger, Magnum & 300

1. DTC IS ACTIVE

NOTE: If P0562–BATTERY VOLTAGE LOW or P0563–BATTERY VOLTAGE HIGH is set along with this DTC, diagnose the battery voltage DTC first.

Ignition on, engine not running.
With the Scan Tool, select View DTCs in the Steering Control Module.

Is the DTC status Active at this time?

Yes

- Go to 2

No

- Go to 7

ARM0500000001033

Fig. 19   Code B2332: Horn Switch Input Circuit/ Performance (Part 1 of 5). Charger, Magnum & 300

2. (X3) HORN SWITCH SIGNAL CIRCUIT SHORT TO (X903) HORN SWITCH RETURN CIRCUIT

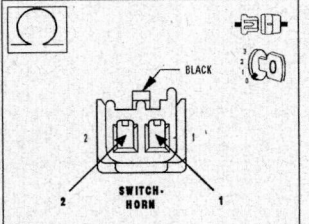

Turn the ignition off.
Remove the Driver Airbag
Disconnect the Horn Switch harness connector.
Disconnect the Right Steering Switch harness connector.

NOTE: Before proceeding, thoroughly inspect the wiring harness and connectors between the Horn Switch and the Right Steering Switch for a short to ground or any other circuit.

Measure the resistance between the (X3) Horn Switch circuit and the (X903) Horn Switch Return circuit.

Is the resistance below 5.0 ohms?

Yes

- Repair the (X3) Horn Switch circuit for a short to the (X903) Horn Switch Return circuit.
- Perform the VERIFICATION TEST-VER 1.

No

- Go to 3

ARM0500000001034

Fig. 19   Code B2332: Horn Switch Input Circuit/ Performance (Part 2 of 5). Charger, Magnum & 300

1. STEERING CONTROL MODULE (SCM)

The Steering Control Module (SCM) is reporting internal errors.

View repair.

Repair

- Replace the Steering Control Module (SCM)

ARM0500000001032

Fig. 18   Code B2225: Steering Column Control Module Internal. Charger, Magnum & 300

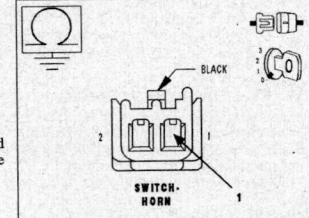

3. (X3) HORN SWITCH SIGNAL CIRCUIT SHORT TO GROUND

NOTE: Before proceeding, thoroughly inspect the wiring harness and connectors between the Horn Switch and the Right Steering Switch for a short to ground or to any other circuit.

Measure the resistance between the (X3) Horn Switch circuit at the harness connector to the Right Switch and ground (include the metal casing at the back side of the Airbag).

Is the resistance below 5.0 ohms?

Yes

- Repair the (X3) Horn Switch circuit for a short to ground.

No

- Go to 4

4. HORN SWITCH

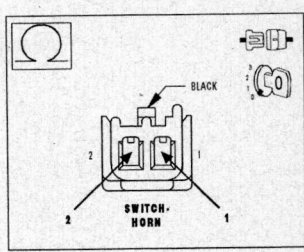

Measure the resistance between the (X3) Horn Switch circuit and the (X903) Horn Switch Return circuit at the harness connector to the horn switch.

Is the resistance below 5.0 ohms?

Yes

- Replace the Horn Switch

No

- Go to 5

ARM0500000001035

Fig. 19   Code B2332: Horn Switch Input Circuit/ Performance (Part 3 of 5). Charger, Magnum & 300

5. RIGHT STEERING SWITCH

Turn the ignition off.
Replace the Right Steering Switch
Turn the ignition on.

NOTE: The C206 (LIN bus) connector must be connected for this test.

Press and release the Horn Switch several times.
With the Scan Tool, Clear Stored DTCs in the Steering Control Module.
With the Scan Tool, select Data Display and view the Horn switch data.
While monitoring the Horn switch data, press and release the Horn Switch several times.

Does the Horn switch data change from Set to Not Set when the switch is pressed and released?

Yes

- Test Complete.

No

- Go to 6

ARM0500000001036

Fig. 19   Code B2332: Horn Switch Input Circuit/ Performance (Part 4 of 5). Charger, Magnum & 300

1. DTC IS ACTIVE

NOTE: If P0562–BATTERY VOLTAGE LOW or P0563–BATTERY VOLTAGE HIGH is set along with this DTC, diagnose the battery voltage DTC first.

Ignition on, engine not running.
Turn the steering wheel from stop to stop at least three times.
With the Scan Tool, select View DTCs in the Steering Control Module.

Is the DTC status Active at this time?

Yes

- Go to 2

No

- Go to 5

2. STEERING ANGLE SENSOR TONE WHEEL

Turn the ignition off.
Remove the steering wheel
Inspect the clockspring for loose mounting screws or damage.
Remove the clockspring in accordance with the Service Information.
Inspect the Steering Angle Sensor and Tone Wheel for damage, loose or missing mounting screws, etc.

Were any problems found?

Yes

- Repair or replace Sensor and/or Tone Wheel as necessary.

No

- Go To 3

ARM0500000001038

Fig. 20   Code C1219: Steering Angle Sensor Erratic Performance (Part 1 of 2). Charger, Magnum & 300

6. STEERING CONTROL MODULE (SCM)

View repair.

Repair

- Replace the Steering Control Module (SCM)

7. INTERMITTENT HORN SWITCH INPUT CIRCUIT/PERFORMANCE DTC

The conditions necessary to set this DTC are not present at this time.
Using the wiring diagram/schematic as a guide, inspect the wiring and connectors.
While monitoring the scan tool data relative to this circuit, wiggle test the wiring and connectors.
Look for the data to change or for the DTC to reset during the wiggle test.

Were any problems found?

Yes

- Repair as necessary.

No

- Test complete.

ARM0500000001037

Fig. 19   Code B2332: Horn Switch Input Circuit/ Performance (Part 5 of 5). Charger, Magnum & 300

3. STEERING ANGLE SENSOR

Replace the Steering Angle Sensor
Ignition on, engine not running.
Turn the steering wheel from stop to stop at least three times.
With the Scan Tool, Clear Stored DTCs in the Steering Control Module.
Turn the steering wheel from stop to stop at least three times.
With the Scan Tool, select View DTCs in the Steering Control Module.

Is the DTC status Active at this time?

Yes

- Go To 4

No

- Test Complete.

4. STEERING CONTROL MODULE (SCM)

View repair.

Repair

- Replace the Steering Control Module (SCM)

5. INTERMITTENT STEERING ANGLE SENSOR ERRATIC PERFORMANCE DTC

The conditions necessary to set this DTC are not present at this time.
Using the wiring diagram/schematic as a guide, inspect the wiring and connectors.
While monitoring the scan tool data relative to this circuit, wiggle test the wiring and connectors.
Look for the data to change or for the DTC to reset during the wiggle test.

Were any problems found?

Yes

- Repair as necessary.

No

- Test complete.

ARM0500000001039

Fig. 20   Code C1219: Steering Angle Sensor Erratic Performance (Part 2 of 2). Charger, Magnum & 300

STEERING COLUMNS

1. RELATED DTC(S) PRESENT IN PCM

Ignition on, engine not running.
With the scan tool, select View DTCs in the Powertrain Control Module.

Are there any charging system or related battery voltage DTCs present in the PCM?

Yes

- Refer to the appropriate symptom in the Driveability category.

No

- Go to 2

2. DTC STATUS IS ACTIVE

With the scan tool, select View DTCs in the Steering Control Module.

Is the DTC status Active at this time?

Yes

- Go to 3

No

- Go to 5

ARM0500000001040

Fig. 21   Code P0562: Battery Voltage Low (Part 1 of 3). Charger, Magnum & 300

4. (Z910) GROUND CIRCUIT HIGH RESISTANCE

Using a 12–volt test light connected to 12–volts, check the (Z910) Ground circuit in the Steering Control Module harness connector.

NOTE: The test light must illuminate brightly. Compare the brightness to that of a direct connection to the battery.

Does the test light illuminate brightly?

Yes

- Replace the Steering Control Module

No

- Repair the (Z910) Ground circuit.

5. INTERMITTENT BATTERY VOLTAGE LOW DTC

The conditions necessary to set this DTC are not present at this time.
Using the wiring diagram/schematic as a guide, inspect the wiring and connectors.
While monitoring the scan tool data relative to this circuit, wiggle test the wiring and connectors.
Look for the data to change or for the DTC to reset during the wiggle test.

Were any problems found?

Yes

- Repair as necessary.

No

- Test complete.

ARM0500000001042

Fig. 21   Code P0562: Battery Voltage Low (Part 3 of 3). Charger, Magnum & 300

3. (A913) FUSED B(+) CIRCUIT HIGH RESISTANCE

Turn the ignition off.
Remove the Steering Control Module
Turn the ignition on.
Using a 12–volt test light connected to ground, check the (A913) Fused B(+) circuit in the Steering Control Module harness connector.

NOTE: The test light must illuminate brightly. Compare the brightness to that of a direct connection to the battery.

Does the test light illuminate brightly?

Yes

- Go to 4

No

- Repair the (A913) Fused B(+) circuit.

ARM0500000001041

Fig. 21   Code P0562: Battery Voltage Low (Part 2 of 3). Charger, Magnum & 300

1. RELATED DTC(S) PRESENT IN THE PCM

Ignition on, engine not running.
With the scan tool, select View DTCs in the Powertrain Control Module.

Are there any charging system or related battery voltage DTCs present in the PCM?

Yes

- Refer to the appropriate symptom in the Driveability category.

No

- Go to 2

2. DTC IS ACTIVE

Start the engine. Allow the engine to idle for 2 minutes.
With the scan tool, select View DTCs in the Steering Control Module.

Is the DTC status Active at this time?

Yes

- Go to 3

No

- Go to 5

ARM0500000001043

Fig. 22   Code P0563: Battery Voltage High (Part 1 of 3). Charger, Magnum & 300

3. (A913) FUSED B(+) CIRCUIT HIGH RESISTANCE

Turn the ignition off.
Remove the Steering Control Module in accordance with the Service Information.
Start the engine. Allow the engine to idle.
Using a 12–volt test light connected to ground, check the (A913) Fused B(+) circuit in the Steering Control Module harness connector.

NOTE: The test light must illuminate brightly. Compare the brightness to that of a direct connection to the battery.

Does the test light illuminate brightly?

Yes

- Go to 4

No

- Repair the (A913) Fused B(+) circuit.

ARM0500000001044

Fig. 22 Code P0563: Battery Voltage High (Part 2 of 3). Charger, Magnum & 300

1. DTC IS ACTIVE

NOTE: If P0562–BATTERY VOLTAGE LOW or P0563–BATTERY VOLTAGE HIGH is set along with this DTC, diagnose the battery voltage DTC first.

Ignition on, engine not running.
With the Scan Tool, select View DTCs in the Steering Control Module.

Is the DTC status Active at this time?

Yes

- Go to 2

No

- Go to 4

2. SPEED CONTROL SWITCH

Turn the ignition off.
Replace the Speed Control Switch
Turn the ignition on.
Move the Speed Control Switch to each position several times.
With the Scan Tool, Clear Stored DTCs in the Steering Control Module.
With the Scan Tool, select View DTCs in the Steering Control Module.
Move the Speed Control Switch to each position several times while monitoring the Scan Tool.

Does this DTC reset?

Yes

- Go To 3

No

- Test Complete.

ARM0500000001046

Fig. 23 Code P0585: Speed Control Multiplex Switch 1/2 Correlation (Part 1 of 2). Charger, Magnum & 300

4. (Z910) GROUND CIRCUIT HIGH RESISTANCE

Using a 12–volt test light connected to 12–volts, check the (Z910) Ground circuit in the Steering Control Module harness connector.

NOTE: The test light must illuminate brightly. Compare the brightness to that of a direct connection to the battery.

Does the test light illuminate brightly?

Yes

- Replace the Steering Control Module (SCM)

No

- Repair the (Z910) Ground circuit.

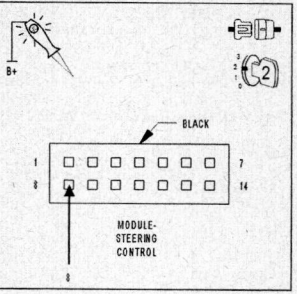

5. INTERMITTENT BATTERY VOLTAGE HIGH DTC

The conditions necessary to set this DTC are not present at this time.
Using the wiring diagram/schematic as a guide, inspect the wiring and connectors.
While monitoring the scan tool data relative to this circuit, wiggle test the wiring and connectors.
Look for the data to change or for the DTC to reset during the wiggle test.

Were any problems found?

Yes

- Repair as necessary.

No

- Test complete.

ARM0500000001045

Fig. 22 Code P0563: Battery Voltage High (Part 3 of 3). Charger, Magnum & 300

3. STEERING CONTROL MODULE (SCM)

View repair.

Repair

- Replace the Steering Control Module (SCM)

4. INTERMITTENT SPEED CONTROL SWITCH 1/2 STUCK DTC

The conditions necessary to set this DTC are not present at this time.
While monitoring the scan tool data relative to this circuit, move the Speed Control Switch to each position several times.
Look for the DTC to reset while the switch is being moved to each position.

Were any problems found?

Yes

- Repair as necessary.

No

- Test complete.

ARM0500000001047

Fig. 23 Code P0585: Speed Control Multiplex Switch 1/2 Correlation (Part 2 of 2). Charger, Magnum & 300

1. DTC IS ACTIVE

NOTE: If P0562–BATTERY VOLTAGE LOW or P0563–BATTERY VOLTAGE HIGH is set along with this DTC, diagnose the battery voltage DTC first.

Ignition on, engine not running.
With the Scan Tool, select View DTCs in the Steering Control Module.

Is the DTC status Active at this time?

Yes

- Go to 2

No

- Go to 4

2. SPEED CONTROL SWITCH

Turn the ignition off.
Replace the Speed Control Switch
Turn the ignition on.
Move the Speed Control Switch to each position several times.
With the Scan Tool, Clear Stored DTCs in the Steering Control Module.
With the Scan Tool, select View DTCs in the Steering Control Module.
Move the Speed Control Switch to each position several times while monitoring the Scan Tool.

Does this DTC reset?

Yes

- Go To 3

No

- Test Complete.

ARM0500000001048

Fig. 24 Code P1593: Speed Control Switch 1/2 Stuck (Part 1 of 2). Charger, Magnum & 300

3. Steering Control Module (SCM)

View repair.

Repair

- Replace the Steering Control Module (SCM)

4. INTERMITTENT SPEED CONTROL MULTIPLEXED SWITCH 1/2 CORRELATION DTC

The conditions necessary to set this DTC are not present at this time.
While monitoring the scan tool data relative to this circuit, move the Speed Control Switch to each position several times.
Look for the DTC to reset while the switch is being moved to each position.

Were any problems found?

Yes

- Repair as necessary.

No

- Test complete.

ARM0500000001049

Fig. 24 Code P1593: Speed Control Switch 1/2 Stuck (Part 2 of 2). Charger, Magnum & 300

STEERING COLUMN

REPLACE

Caliber & 2007–08 Avenger & Sebring Sedan

1. Position front wheels in straight ahead position.
2. Raise and support vehicle.
3. Turn steering wheel to right until intermediate shaft coupling bolt can be accessed.
4. Remove intermediate shaft coupling bolt. Do not separate intermediate shaft from pinion shaft at this time.
5. Return front wheels to straight ahead position.
6. Lower vehicle.
7. Remove steering wheel as outlined in "Electrical" section of appropriate chassis chapter.
8. Position column tilt at full-upward position.
9. Remove lower steering column cover, then the cover reinforcement.
10. Remove upper and lower steering column covers.
11. Disconnect steering column electrical connectors.
12. **On models equipped with manual transaxle,** remove clutch pedal blocker mounting screws and blocker.
13. **On all models,** separate intermediate shaft from steering gear pinion shaft.
14. Remove steering column to instrument panel mounting bolt.
15. Remove steering column to instrument panel retaining nuts.
16. Remove steering column, **Fig. 25.**
17. Reverse procedure to install, noting the following:
    a. **Torque** steering column retaining nuts and mounting bolt to 21 ft. lbs., in a clockwise pattern starting with upper left nut and ending with lower left bolt.
    b. **Torque** steering wheel retaining bolt to 32 ft. lbs.
    c. **Torque** intermediate shaft coupling bolt to 35 ft. lbs.

Charger, Magnum & 300

1. **On models equipped with electric telescoping column,** place column mid-tilt position.
2. **On all models,** removing steering wheel as outlined under "Electrical" section of "Charger, Magnum & 300" chapter.
3. Remove mounting screw, then disconnect steering column cover snap retainers by pulling it rearward at top and righthand side.
4. Disconnect wire harness connector from trunk release switch.
5. Disconnect emergency bracket release handle release cable and remove steering column cover.
6. Remove steering column opening reinforcement.
7. Remove at least one clockspring mounting screw.
8. **On models equipped with manual tilt and telescoping columns,** disconnect unlatch lever from column.
9. **On all models,** remove four mounting screws and roll top shroud.
10. Back set screw out through access hole and remove Steering Column Control Module (SCCM).
11. Remove two steering column mounting nuts at bulkhead.
12. Remove instrument cluster as outlined under "Electrical" section of "Charger, Magnum & 300" chapter.
13. Raise and support vehicle.
14. Remove lower coupling shaft pinch bolt.
15. Slide steering shaft out of lower coupling shaft.
16. Lower vehicle.
17. **On models equipped with electronic telescoping column,** remove mounting screws, brace and support beam bracket.
18. **On all models,** remove lower steering column mounting pivot bolt and nut.
19. Remove two upper mounting bolts and steering column.
20. Reverse procedure to install, noting the following:
    a. **Torque** steering column upper mounting screws to 22 ft. lbs.
    b. **Torque** pivot bolt to 22 ft. lbs.
    c. **Torque** support beam bracket mounting screw at column to 21 ft. lbs.
    d. **Torque** support beam bracket mounting screw at support beam to 106 in. lbs.
    e. **Torque** steering column to bulkhead to 62 inch lbs.
    f. **Torque** new pinch bolt to 23 ft. lbs.
    g. **Torque** new steering wheel nut to 52 ft. lbs.

Concorde, Intrepid & 300M

1. Remove instrument panel lefthand end fuse panel cover.
2. Remove lower instrument panel cover to instrument panel mounting bracket mounting screws from behind fuse panel cover.
3. Remove lower instrument panel cover.
4. Remove trunk release switch wiring harness connector.
5. Remove park release handle cable.
6. Remove mounting bolts and instrument panel reinforcement.
7. Remove diagnostic connector.
8. Ensure front wheels are in straight ahead position. If steering column is to be removed as one assembly, or without removing steering wheel, steering wheel must be turned to righthand 180° from straight ahead position and locked in place.
9. If removing steering wheel as outlined under "Electrical" section of "Concorde, Intrepid & 300M" chapter.
10. Push in righthand seam between upper and lower shrouds.
11. When upper shroud unsnaps, pull upper shroud away from lower.
12. Remove steering column upper shroud by repeating previous steps on lefthand side.
13. Remove tilt lever.
14. Remove mounting screws and lower steering column shroud.
15. Remove clockspring wiring harness connectors.
16. Remove mounting screws and clockspring.
17. Disconnect module wire harness connector.
18. Remove mounting screw and unclip module from key cylinder halo bezel.
19. Disconnect multi-function switch wiring harness from routing clip.
20. Remove mounting screws and multi-function switch.
21. Remove mounting screws and ignition switch.
22. **On models equipped with floor mounted shifter,** depress lock tab and remove shifter/ignition interlock cable from key lock housing.
23. **On models equipped with steering column mounted shifter,** proceed as follows:
    a. Remove cable from shifter mechanism.
    b. Unlock cable lock, then remove shift cable by inserting suitable screwdriver between shift cable and shifter mechanism, and prying cable off pin.
24. **On all models,** remove mounting screws and cable mounting bracket.
25. Remove air ducts under steering column.
26. Remove retaining pin and steering column coupler pinch bolt.
27. Remove mounting bracket to support bracket mounting nuts and loosen steering column lower mounting bracket to support bracket mounting bolts.

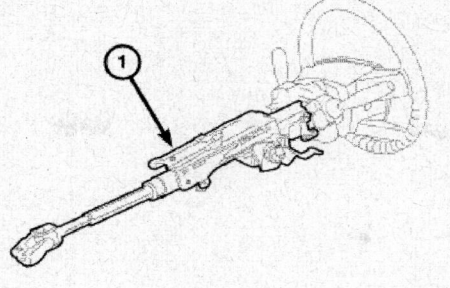

1- Steering Column

ARM0600000000397

Fig. 25 Steering column. Caliber & 2007–08 Avenger & Sebring Sedan

28. Remove steering column support bracket by pulling rearward and out.
29. Reverse procedure to install, noting the following:
    a. **Torque** bracket to support bracket fasteners to 96 inch lbs.
    b. **Torque** coupler pinch bolt to 20 ft. lbs.
    c. **Torque** steering wheel mounting nut to 45 ft. lbs.
    d. **Torque** air bag module bolts to 96 inch lbs.

Crossfire

1. Place front wheels in straight ahead position.
2. Remove lefthand lower instrument panel fuse panel from below steering column.
3. Remove driver's air bag screws, disconnect air bag electrical connector, then pass air bag connector wire through whole in steering column.
4. Remove air bag module.
5. Remove steering wheel countersunk bolt, **Fig. 26.**
6. Remove clockspring screws.
7. Remove mounting screws and instrument cluster.
8. Remove ashtray from center console, then press locking tabs together and push ignition lock cable from ignition starter switch.
9. Remove mounting screws and position center console bezel aside.
10. Turn ignition lock cable 90° to lefthand and pull cable straight out.
11. Remove mounting screws, electrical connector and speed control switch.
12. Remove mounting screws, electrical connector and multi-function switch.
13. Remove steering column trim ring.
14. Remove pinch bolt from steering column to steering gear coupling.
15. Remove lower steering column mounting nuts.
16. Remove upper steering column to instrument panel support bolts.
17. Slowly lower steering column, then pull column outward away from instrument panel.
18. Reverse procedure to install, noting the following:
    a. **Torque** lower steering column mounting nuts to 71 inch lbs.
    b. **Torque** upper steering column bolts to 15 ft. lbs.
    c. **Torque** steering column to steering gear pinch bolt to 22 ft. lbs.
    d. **Torque** steering wheel mounting hex bolt to 60 ft. lbs.
    e. If steering wheel is offset by more than one tooth, turn signal indicator is no longer aligned properly.

Neon

1. Ensure front wheels in straight-ahead position.
2. Remove instrument panel top cover lefthand end mounting just above lefthand instrument panel end cap.
3. Starting at lefthand end, push upward on instrument panel top cover, disconnecting its retainer clips along face. Disconnect just enough clips to allow access to upper ends of instrument cluster bezel.
4. Disconnect clips along outer edge and remove instrument cluster bezel.
5. Remove two mounting screws along bottom of steering column cover below instrument panel.
6. Disconnect upper end clips and remove steering column cover.
7. If removing steering wheel as outlined under "Electrical" section of "Neon" chapter.
8. Remove key from ignition cylinder.
9. Remove two lower shroud to steering column and upper shroud mounting screws.
10. Disconnect clips from each other, then remove lower shroud from upper shroud and column.
11. Remove upper shroud.
12. Remove steering column coupling retainer pin at base of column, back off pinch bolt nut and remove steering column coupling pinch bolt. Pinch bolt nut is caged to coupling and is not removable.
13. Separate upper and lower steering column couplings.
14. **On models equipped with automatic transaxle,** depress cable connector top tab and remove ignition interlock cable from back side of steering column ignition cylinder housing.
15. **On all models,** remove two lower and two upper steering column to instrument panel mounting nuts.
16. Lower steering column away from instrument panel.
17. Disconnect clockspring wiring harness electrical connector.
18. Disconnect multi-function, windshield wiper and ignition switches' wiring harness electrical connectors.
19. **On models equipped with Sentry Key Immobilizer Module (SKIM),** disconnect SKIM electrical connector.
20. **On all models,** remove steering column.

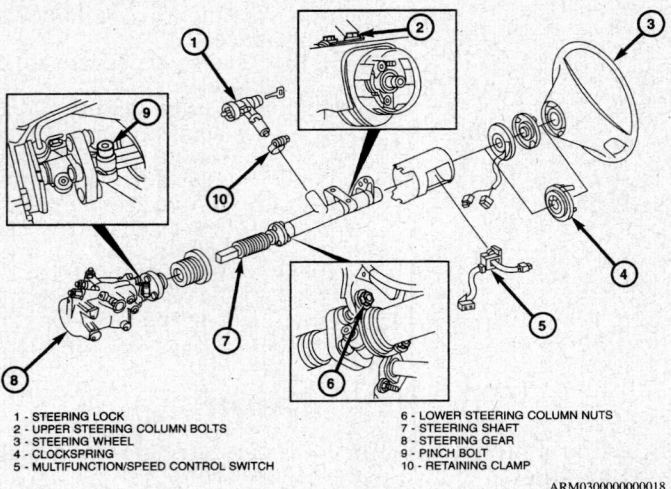

1 - STEERING LOCK
2 - UPPER STEERING COLUMN BOLTS
3 - STEERING WHEEL
4 - CLOCKSPRING
5 - MULTIFUNCTION/SPEED CONTROL SWITCH
6 - LOWER STEERING COLUMN NUTS
7 - STEERING SHAFT
8 - STEERING GEAR
9 - PINCH BOLT
10 - RETAINING CLAMP

ARM0300000000018

Fig. 26 Exploded view of steering column. Crossfire

21. If steering column is being replaced, proceed as follows:
    a. Insert key and turn ignition key cylinder to ON position.
    b. Depress retaining tab and remove Ignition key cylinder by pulling key and cylinder straight out of column.
    c. Disconnect latch hooks on back of clockspring by lifting clockspring slightly to clear column housing with top latch hook.
    d. Lower clockspring slightly and disconnect lower latch hook.
    e. Remove clockspring.
    f. Remove two mounting screws and multi-function/windshield wiper switch.
    g. **On models equipped with SKIM,** remove two mounting screws and slide SKIM off non-halo trim ring, then remove non-halo trim ring.
22. **On all models,** reverse procedure to install, noting the following:
    a. **Torque** SKIM mounting screws to 25 inch lbs.
    b. **Torque** steering column mounting nuts to 12 ft. lbs.
    c. **Do not tighten coupling pinch bolt anytime vehicle is not at curb riding height.**
    d. **Torque** coupling pinch bolt to 12 ft. lbs.

2004–06 Sebring Convertible, Sebring Sedan & Stratus Sedan

1. Place wheels in straight ahead position.
2. Remove fuse panel cover and instrument panel top cover mounting screws.
3. Remove radio bezel and climate control panel from top cover of instrument panel.
4. Remove instrument panel mounting screws from rear of climate control panel.
5. Remove knee bolster and cruise control switches from steering wheel.
6. Remove driver's air bag module and disconnect electrical connector from module, **Fig. 27.**
7. Remove steering wheel using suitable steering wheel puller.
8. Remove upper shroud by pressing inward on upper shroud while pulling apart upper and lower shrouds.
9. Place column tilt in highest position and remove lower shroud.
10. Remove electrical connectors from clockspring, ignition switch and multi-function switch.
11. **On models equipped with automatic transaxles,** proceed as follows:
    a. Place key cylinder in OFF position.
    b. Depress locking tab on shifter/ignition interlock cable, **Fig. 28.**
    c. Remove cable from key lock housing.
12. **On all models,** remove and position steering column wiring harness aside.
13. Remove pinch bolt from intermediate shaft and slide shaft up and off steering gear, **Fig. 29.**
14. Remove mounting bolts, nuts and steering column.
15. Reverse procedure to install, noting the following:
    a. **Torque** steering column mounting brackets nuts and bolts to 150 inch lbs.
    b. **Torque** intermediate shaft coupler pinch bolt to 32 ft. lbs.
    c. Depress plastic locking pin to disengage clockspring mechanism. Rotate clockspring clockwise to end of travel.
    d. Slowly rotate counterclockwise until yellow appears in centering window of clockspring and drive pin on rotor will be in front of arrow on clockspring label. Engage clockspring.
    e. **Torque** upper and lower shroud bolts to 17 inch lbs.

f. **Torque** steering wheel bolt to 40 ft. lbs.
g. **Torque** driver's air bag module mounting screws to 17 inch lbs.
h. **Torque** cruise control switch mounting screws to 12 inch lbs.

Sebring Coupe & Stratus Coupe

1. Remove mounting screws and driver's air bag module, **Fig. 30. Do not remove screws from holder.**
2. Disconnect driver's air bag module clockspring connect by pressing lock toward outer side using suitable flat-tipped screwdriver.
3. Remove mounting nut and steering wheel using puller tool No. MB-990803, or equivalent. **Do not hammer.**
4. Remove mounting screws and instrument panel under cover.
5. Remove mounting bolts, then the lower and upper column covers.
6. Remove mounting screws and clockspring.
7. Remove mounting bolts and column switch.
8. **On models equipped with automatic transaxle,** remove cover and disconnect key interlock cable.
9. **On all models,** remove mounting and pinch bolts, then the steering column.
10. Remove mounting bolt and steering cover.
11. Reverse procedure to install, noting the following:
    a. **Torque** steering cover mounting bolts to 36–52 inch lbs.
    b. **Torque** pinch bolt to 12–14 ft. lbs., and mounting bolts to 78–122 inch lbs.
    c. **Torque** install column switch mounting bolts to 14–22 ft. lbs.
    d. **Torque** steering wheel mounting nut to 26–36 ft. lbs.
    e. **Torque** air bag module mounting bolts to 61–95 inch lbs.

STEERING COLUMN SERVICE

Caliber & 2007–08 Avenger Sedan & Sebring Sedan

The steering column has been designed to be serviced as an assembly less wiring, switches, clockspring, gear shift lever, shift ignition interlock, brake lock solenoid, shrouds and steering wheel.

Concorde, Intrepid & 300M

The steering column has been designed to be serviced as an assembly less wiring, switches, clockspring, gear shift lever, shift ignition interlock, brake lock solenoid, shrouds and steering wheel, **Fig. 31.**

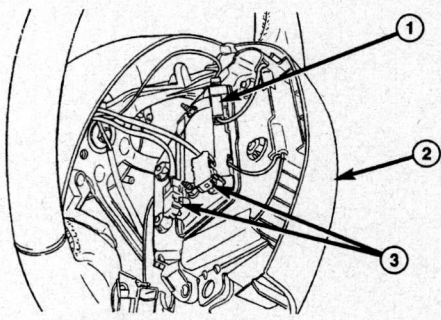

1 - HORN CONNECTOR
2 - DRIVER AIRBAG
3 - AIRBAG SQUIB CONNECTORS

CR6040100156000X

Fig. 27 Air bag electrical connector. Sebring Convertible, Stratus Sedan & 2004–06 Sebring Sedan

The steering column intermediate shaft must be replaced as an entire assembly.

Crossfire

The steering column has been designed to be serviced as an assembly less wiring, switches, clockspring, gear shift lever, shift ignition interlock, brake lock solenoid, shrouds and steering wheel.

DISASSEMBLY

1. Remove pinch bolt from intermediate shaft, then intermediate shaft, **Fig. 32.**
2. Remove retaining ring, disk spring and thrust ring.
3. Push intermediate shaft outward slightly.
4. Remove locking ring and thrust ring.
5. Press ball bearing from steering column using intermediate shaft.

ASSEMBLE

1. Press new bearing up to stop in steering column using suitable press tool.
2. Slide intermediate shaft into inner column tube, then press second bearing in using suitable press tool.
3. Ensure locking rings, position correctly in upper steering shaft lock grooves.
4. Push thrust and locking ring together onto intermediate shaft.
5. Slide thrust ring and disk spring into intermediate shaft.
6. Ensure disk spring is fully preloaded using lower steering shaft, if required.
7. If disk spring preload is to high, upper steering shaft will turn unevenly and bind.
8. If disk spring preload is to low, detectable movement will result when steering wheel jacket tube is installed.
9. Mount retaining ring on intermediate shaft, using suitable tool, push disk spring on until it is fully loaded.
10. Attach lower tube to upper tube by screwing countersunk screw to protect splines.
11. Slide lower intermediate shaft onto upper intermediate shaft, then install mounting nut and bolt.
12. Cover to protect lower intermediate shaft.

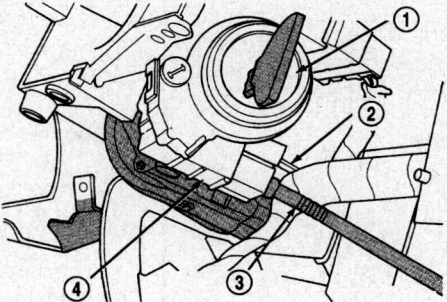

1 - KEY CYLINDER
2 - LOCKING TAB
3 - SHIFTER IGNITION INTERLOCK CABLE
4 - KEY LOCK HOUSING

CR6040100157000X

Fig. 28 Shifter/ignition interlock cable removal. Sebring Convertible, Stratus Sedan & 2004–06 Sebring Sedan

13. Install lower intermediate shaft onto upper shaft until disc spring is fully preloaded. Use a suitable press to fully preload intermediate shaft disc spring.
14. Inspect steering column for ease of movement, by turning steering wheel at same time, tighten nut and bolt in this position.

Charger, Magnum & 300

Do not attempt to remove or modify any component of the column.

Neon

The steering column on these models has been designed to be serviced as a complete assembly, only. The shaft, bearings and upper coupling are all serviced with the column.

The replaceable components on the steering column are the key cylinder, ignition switch, multi-function switch, trim shrouds, steering wheel, air bag module and the clockspring.

2004–06 Sebring Convertible, Sebring Sedan & Stratus Sedan

The steering column has been designed to be serviced as an assembly except for wiring, switches, key cylinder, shrouds and the steering wheel.

The only other serviceable component is the intermediate shaft. If the shaft requires replacement, proceed as follows:
1. Remove steering column as outlined under "Steering Column, Replace."
2. Remove roll pin from flex joint using remover/installer tool No. 6831-A, or equivalent, **Fig. 33.**
3. Pry intermediate shaft off steering column using a suitable screwdriver.
4. Reverse procedure to install.

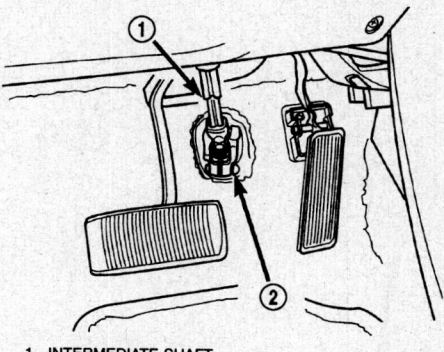

1 - INTERMEDIATE SHAFT
2 - PINCH BOLT

CR6040100158000X

Fig. 29 Intermediate shaft pinch bolt removal. Sebring Convertible, Stratus Sedan & 2004–06 Sebring Sedan

Sebring Coupe & Stratus Coupe

The steering column has been designed to be serviced as an assembly except for wiring, switches, shrouds and the steering wheel.

The only serviceable component is the steering lock cylinder, **Fig. 34.** To remove cylinder lock proceed as follows:
1. Cut bolts at steering column lock bracket, **Fig. 35.** Discard old bolts.
2. Remove bracket and cylinder lock.
3. Install new steering lock cylinder in alignment with column boss. Do not completely tighten new twist off bolts.
4. Ensure lock is working properly. Tighten new bolts until head twists off.

TECHNICAL SERVICE BULLETINS

Steering Column Clicking

2004 SEBRING CONVERTIBLE, SEBRING SEDAN, STRATUS SEDAN

Some of these models there maybe a clicking sound when the steering wheel is turned.

This condition may be caused by steering column alignment.

To correct this condition proceed as follows:
1. Remove steering column shrouds. If click sound remains, proceed to next step. If click sound is eliminated, inspect for steering column shroud interference.
2. Remove steering wheel as outlined under "Electrical" section of "Sebring Convertible, Sebring Sedan & Stratus Sedan" or "Neon" chapters.
3. Disconnect intermediate shaft to steering gear lower coupling.
4. Install steering wheel.

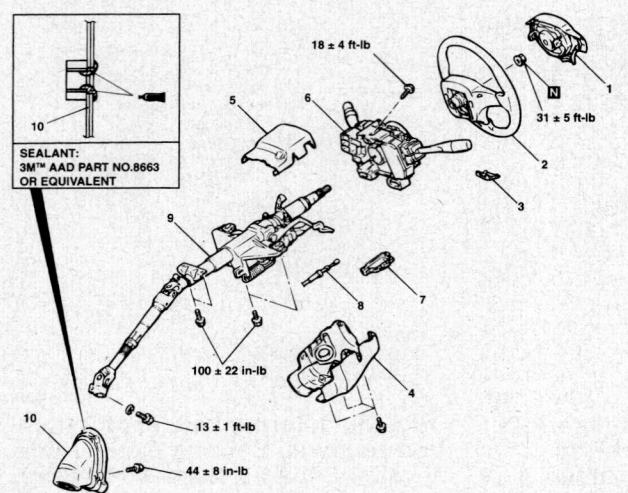

Fig. 30 Steering column replacement. Sebring Coupe & Stratus Coupe

1. AIR BAG MODULE
2. STEERING WHEEL
3. COVER
   - INSTRUMENT PANEL UNDER COVER
4. LOWER COLUMN COVER
5. UPPER COLUMN COVER
6. CLOCK SPRING AND COLUMN SWITCH ASSEMBLY
7. COVER <A/T>
8. KEY INTERLOCK CABLE <A/T>
9. STEERING SHAFT ASSEMBLY
10. STEERING COVER ASSEMBLY

CR6040000152000X

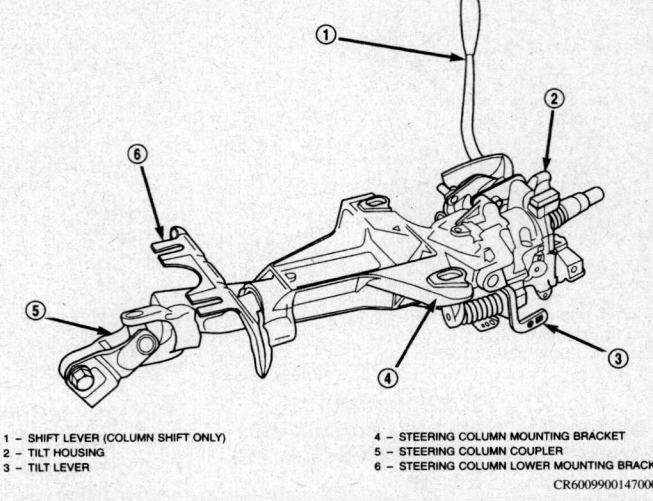

1 – SHIFT LEVER (COLUMN SHIFT ONLY)
2 – TILT HOUSING
3 – TILT LEVER
4 – STEERING COLUMN MOUNTING BRACKET
5 – STEERING COLUMN COUPLER
6 – STEERING COLUMN LOWER MOUNTING BRACKET

CR6009900147000X

Fig. 31 Steering column components. Concorde, Intrepid & 300M

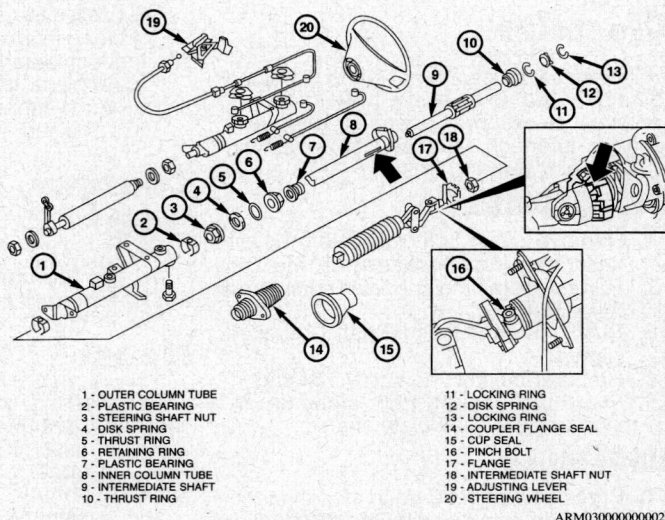

1 - OUTER COLUMN TUBE
2 - PLASTIC BEARING
3 - STEERING SHAFT NUT
4 - DISK SPRING
5 - THRUST RING
6 - RETAINING RING
7 - PLASTIC BEARING
8 - INNER COLUMN TUBE
9 - INTERMEDIATE SHAFT
10 - THRUST RING
11 - LOCKING RING
12 - DISK SPRING
13 - LOCKING RING
14 - COUPLER FLANGE SEAL
15 - CUP SEAL
16 - PINCH BOLT
17 - FLANGE
18 - INTERMEDIATE SHAFT NUT
19 - ADJUSTING LEVER
20 - STEERING WHEEL

ARM0300000000020

Fig. 32 Exploded view of steering column. Crossfire

5. Ensure clockspring is centered.
6. **Torque** coupling pinch bolt to 21 ft. lbs.
7. **Torque** steering wheel bolt to 40 ft. lbs.
8. If click sound returns, loosen lower coupling pinch bolt and four steering column mounting bracket nuts.
9. Jiggle steering column and **torque** coupling pinch bolt to 21 ft. lbs.
10. Hold steering column in place by tightening two lower mounting nuts.
11. Ensure both break-away capsules are fully seated in upper steering column mounting bracket slots.
12. Ensure mounting studs are centered fore-and-aft in plastic capsules.
13. Equally tighten both steering column mounting nuts, until upper steering column back is seated against support bracket.
14. **Torque** four steering column bracket to support bracket nuts to 12 ft. lbs.
15. If click sound remains, proceed to next step. If click sound is eliminated, replace lower coupling pinch bolt (part No. 06506382AA) and **torque** it to 21 ft. lbs.
16. Remove clockspring and disconnect lower coupling.
17. If click sound remains, proceed to next step. If click sound is eliminated, inspect for clockspring interference.
18. Remove steering column as outlined under "Steering Column, Replace."
19. Remove two mounting screws and separate multi-function switch from column.
20. Remove intermediate shaft universal joint roll pin using remover/installer

tool No. 6831-A, or equivalent.
21. Pry column intermediate shaft from steering column shaft using suitable screwdriver between universal joint and lower mounting bracket.
22. Remove spring retainer by pinching outside of retainer using suitable pliers and sliding it off steering column shaft , **Fig. 36.**
23. Remove spring, wedge and steering column shaft.
24. Inspect and replace bearings (upper part No. 04690507AB, lower part No. 04690344AB), as required.
25. Stand steering column on end with upper bearing outer race supported on 1¹⁄₁₆ inches socket.
26. Tap bearing downward several times until bearing is fully seated using ⅞ inch deep well socket, or suitable tool, against lower bearing outer race and

brass hammer.
27. Ensure there is no clearance between lower casting and lower bearing outer race using .005 inch feeler gauge.
28. Install original steering column shaft.
29. Thread steering wheel bolt into shaft.
30. Stand column on bolt head.
31. Install new retainer (part No. 04664130), onto shaft using ⅞ inch deep well socket and suitable small hammer to tap retainer into place, **Fig. 37.**
32. Ensure distance between lower housing and outside face of retainer is ¹⁵⁄₃₂–¹⁷⁄₃₂ inch, **Fig. 38.**
33. If distance is less than ¹⁵⁄₃₂–¹⁷⁄₃₂ inch, remove retainer and install new one until specified distance is obtained.
34. Ensure click sound is corrected. If should is still present, further diagnosis is required.

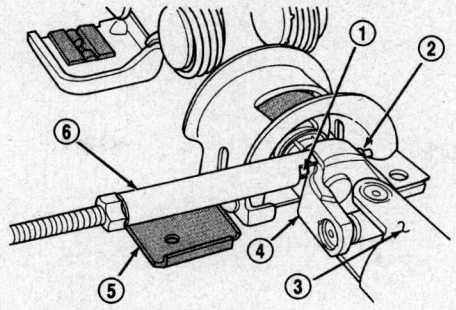

1 - ROLL PIN
2 - KNURLED NUT
3 - INTERMEDIATE SHAFT
4 - UNIVERSAL JOINT
5 - STEERING COLUMN LOWER MOUNTING BRACKET
6 - SPECIAL TOOL 6831–A

CR6040100162000X

Fig. 33 Roll pin removal. 2004–06 Sebring Convertible, Sebring Sedan & Stratus Sedan

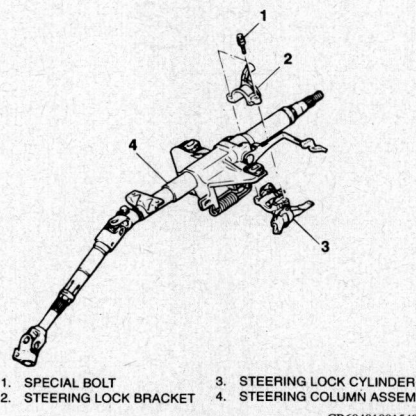

1. SPECIAL BOLT	3. STEERING LOCK CYLINDER
2. STEERING LOCK BRACKET	4. STEERING COLUMN ASSEMBLY

CR6040100154000X

Fig. 34 Steering lock cylinder & bracket. Sebring Coupe & Stratus Coupe

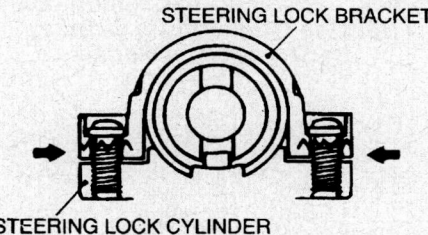

STEERING LOCK BRACKET

STEERING LOCK CYLINDER

CR6040100155000X

Fig. 35 Steering lock bracket bolts removal. Sebring Coupe & Stratus Coupe

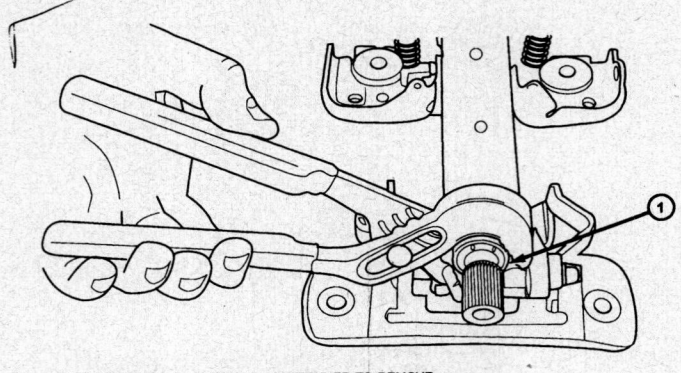

1 - DEFORM OUTSIDE DIAMETER OF RETAINER TO REMOVE

CR6040100159000X

Fig. 36 Spring retainer replacement. 2004 Sebring Convertible, Sebring Sedan, Stratus Sedan

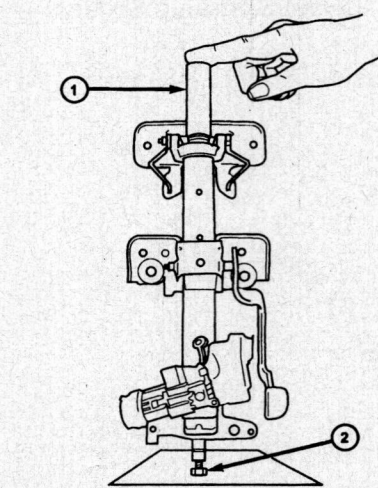

1 - 12-14 MM (15/32-17/32 IN.)

2 - INSURE SURFACE IS FLAT AND DOES NOT DAMAGE THE SHAFT

CR6040100160000X

Fig. 37 Retainer installation. 2004 Sebring Convertible, Sebring Sedan, Stratus Sedan

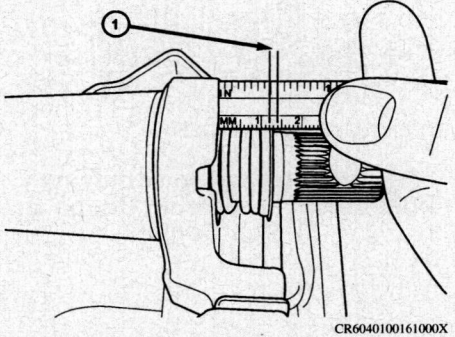

CR6040100161000X

Fig. 38 Spring retainer measurement. 2004 Sebring Convertible, Sebring Sedan, Stratus Sedan

POWER STEERING

TABLE OF CONTENTS

Page No.

CALIBER & 2007–08
AVENGER & SEBRING SEDAN ..   13-1
CHARGER, MAGNUM & 300 ...   13-15
CONCORDE, INTREPID &
300M   13-6

Page No.

CROSSFIRE   13-11
NEON & 2004–06 SEBRING
CONVERTIBLE, SEBRING
SEDAN & STRATUS SEDAN   13-17
SEBRING COUPE & STRATUS
COUPE   13-21

Caliber & 2007–08 Avenger & Sebring Sedan

NOTE: On Air Bag Equipped Models, Refer To "Air Bag System Precautions" Located In The Front Of This Manual For System Disarming & Arming Procedures.

NOTE: Refer To "Computer Relearn Procedures" Located In The Front Of This Manual When Battery Power To The Computer Has Been Interrupted.

NOTE: Prior To Performing Any Service Operations Listed In This Section, Consult The "Technical Service Bulletins" Section For Related Information.

INDEX

Page No.

Description 13-2
Diagnosis & Testing 13-2
  Accessing Diagnostic Trouble
    Codes 13-2
Power Steering Pressure
Specifications 13-1

Page No.

Power Steering System Bleed. . . 13-2
  Component Service 13-2
    Drive Pulley, Replace 13-2
    Fluid Cooler, Replace 13-2
    Reservoir, Replace. 13-2
  Manual 13-2

Page No.

  Mechanical 13-2
Precautions 13-2
  Air Bag Systems 13-2
  Battery Ground Cable 13-2
Tightening Specifications 13-5
Troubleshooting 13-2

POWER STEERING PRESSURE SPECIFICATIONS

| Model | Year | Power Steering Pump Pressure, psi | | Max Relief Pressure | Output Flow, Gallons Per Minute |
| | | Test Valve | | | |
		Open	Closed		
Caliber, Avenger & Sebring Sedan	2007–08	50–80	1392–1465	1392–1465	1.5–1.7

PRECAUTIONS

Air Bag Systems

Refer to "Air Bag System Precautions" in the front of this manual for system disarming and arming procedures.

Battery Ground Cable

Prior to service, disconnect battery ground cable and isolate as required.

DESCRIPTION

Power assist steering is provided by a belt driven rotary type pump. It directs fluid through power steering fluid hoses to the power steering gear where it is used to assist the driver's turning effort.

TROUBLESHOOTING

Refer to **Fig. 1** when troubleshooting the power steering system.

DIAGNOSIS & TESTING

Accessing Diagnostic Trouble Codes

Connect the DRB III, or suitably programmed scan tool, to the Data Link Connector (DLC), **Fig. 2**. The diagnostic cycle begins when the ignition is turned On.

POWER STEERING SYSTEM BLEED

MECHANICAL

1. Ensure power steering fluid remote reservoir is full.
2. Install power steering cap adapter tool No. 9688 or equivalent, on to reservoir.
3. Attach hand vacuum pump tool No. C-4207 or equivalent, to power steering cap adapter.
4. Apply 20-25 inch Hg of vacuum to system for a minimum of three minutes.
5. Slowly release vacuum and remove special tools.
6. Adjust fluid level as required and repeat steps 1–6 until fluid no longer drops when vacuum is applied.
7. Start engine and turn steering wheel lock to lock three times.
8. Stop engine and inspect for leaks at all connections.
9. Repeat procedure if there are any signs of air in reservoir.

MANUAL

1. Ensure power steering fluid remote reservoir is full, then start engine and turn steering wheel from stop to stop several times.

CONDITION	POSSIBLE CAUSES	EVALUATION/CORRECTION
OBJECTIONABLE HISS OR WHISTLE WHILE TURNING STEERING WHEEL WHEN STATIONARY OR MOVING SLOWLY*	1. Damaged or mispositioned steering column shaft/coupling dash boot seal.	1. Check to ensure boot is properly installed and seals against sheet metal. Reposition or replace steering column shaft/coupling dash boot seal as necessary.
	2. Mis-routed power steering hose.	2. Check routing of power steering hoses. Ensure hoses do not come in unwanted contact with other components and objects.
	3. Restriction in pressure or return hose.	3. Using an electronic listening tool, determine if noise is coming from either pressure or return hose. Replace hose that noise is present within.
	4. Noisy valve in power steering gear.	4. For evaluation and correction.
RATTLE OR EXCESSIVE CLUNK**	1. Power steering gear loose on engine cradle/crossmember.	1. Check fastener torque and tighten to specifications. Replace as necessary. Check steering wheel center following repair.
	2. Loose strut assembly mounting fasteners at tower or knuckle.	2. Check fastener torque and tighten to specifications.
	3. Excessive play in outer tie rod.	3. For evaluation and correction.
	4. Engine cradle/crossmember mounting fasteners loose at frame or bushings worn.	4. Check fastener torque and tighten to specifications. Inspect bushings and repair as necessary.
	5. Wheel mounting (lug) nuts loose.	5. Inspect wheel mounting (Lug) nuts and studs and repair as necessary. Tighten nuts to specifications.

ARM0600000000398

Fig. 1 Troubleshooting (Part 1 of 11)

2. Stop engine and inspect fluid level again. If required, add fluid until proper fluid level is reached.
3. Repeat procedure until fluid level is consistent. Inspect system for leaks.

Component Service

FLUID COOLER, REPLACE

1. Remove as much power steering fluid as possible from reservoir using suitable siphon pump.
2. Raise and support vehicle on suitable frame contact hoist or with suitable jack stands.
3. **On 300M models,** remove front fascia.
4. **On all models,** remove clamp and lower hose, then drain fluid into suitable container.
5. Remove clamp and upper hose.
6. Remove mounting clips and air dam from lower radiator support or bumper reinforcement.
7. Remove mounting nuts and cooler.

8. Reverse procedure to install, noting following:
   a. Install air dam with new retaining clips.
   b. Ensure clamps are installed on hoses past cooler retention beads.

RESERVOIR, REPLACE

1. Remove engine cover.
2. Disconnect coolant recovery bottle and position aside. Do not remove coolant hoses from bottle.
3. Remove as much power steering fluid as possible from reservoir using suitable siphon pump.
4. Remove cooler return hose from reservoir fitting.
5. Remove supply hose from reservoir fitting.
6. Remove reservoir mounting screw, then reservoir.
7. Reverse procedure to install.

DRIVE PULLEY, REPLACE

The pulley cannot be serviced separately. The power steering pump is serviced as a complete assembly.

	6. Power steering hose touching the body or frame of vehicle.	6. For evaluation and correction.
	7. Stabilizer bar link joints worn (occurs with steering input only when moving, not stationary).	7. At park, jounce only one side of vehicle front to exercise stabilizer bar. Replace stabilizer bar link.
	8. Loose lower control arm mounting bolts at engine cradle, frame or crossmember (occurs with steering input only when moving, not stationary).	8. Check control arm mounting bolts and tighten to specified torque.
	9. Loose intermediate shaft or column.	9. Rotate intermediate (steering) shaft in relationship to gear, checking for free-play. Check column fasteners and tighten to specifications as necessary.
	10. Lower control arm pivot bushing worn (occurs with steering input only when moving, not stationary).	10. Inspect bushings for wear and replace lower control arm as necessary.
	11. Internal power steering gear noise.	11. Drive vehicle on rough road, then steer rapidly back and forth when stopped. Replace power steering gear as necessary.
	12. Loose inner tie rod.	12. For evaluation and correction.
	13. Damaged engine cradle/crossmember.	13. Inspect the cradle/crossmember for cracks or other damage. Replace as necessary.
POPPING NOISE	1. Loose steering gear mounting fasteners.	1. Check fasteners for proper torque and retighten as necessary.

ARM0600000000399

Fig. 1 Troubleshooting (Part 2 of 11)

	2. Loose outer tie rod mounting nut or jam nut.	2. Check fastener torque. Replace nuts as necessary and tighten to specifications.
	3. Loose intermediate (steering) shaft coupling at gear input shaft.	3. Make sure coupling is fully seated on gear input shaft. Retighten or re-seat as necessary.
	4. Worn tie rod (outer or inner).	4. For evaluation and correction.
	5. Worn axle half-shaft.	5. For evaluation and correction.
CHIRP OR SQUEAL (POWER STEERING PUMP)	1. Loose power steering pump drive belt.	1. Inspect belt. Replace belt if worn or glazed. Tighten/adjust power steering pump drive belt if equipped with a manual tensioner.
	2. Pulley alignment incorrect.	2. Realign accessory drives.
	3. Malfunctioning belt auto-tensioner.	3. Verify belt tension. Replace belt auto-tensioner.
	4. Power steering pump noisy (worn bearing/bushing noise).	4. Using an electronic listening tool, determine if noise is coming from pump. Replace power steering pump as required.
	5. Generator or water pump noisy.	5. Using an electronic listening tool, determine if noise is coming from generator or water pump. Replace faulty component.
WHINE, GROWL, MOAN OR GROAN (POWER STEERING PUMP)***	1. Low power steering fluid level.	1. Fill power steering fluid reservoir to proper level and check for leaks (make sure all air is bled from the system fluid).
	2. Air in power steering fluid.	2. Inspect for excessive air bubbles in fluid (fluid will appear foamy and lighter in color). Inspect hoses for leaks and replace as necessary. Bleed air from fluid.
	3. Power steering hose touching body or frame of vehicle.	3. For evaluation and correction.

ARM0600000000400

Fig. 1 Troubleshooting (Part 3 of 11)

	4. Wear of power steering pump internal components.	4. For evaluation and correction.
COLD START WHINE OR MOAN (POWER STEERING PUMP)***	1. Low power steering fluid level.	1. Fill power steering fluid reservoir to proper level and check for leaks (make sure all air is bled from the system fluid).
	2. Extremely low ambient temperature (near 0 F° (-18 C°) or below).	2. Some noise is expected as pump attempts to pull cold, thick fluid. Noise should go away as vehicle warms up. Acceptable levels of excessive noise are one second at 0 F° (-18 C°) and 15 seconds at -20 F° (-29 C°). If noise is excessive, look for poor sealing on the return hose or a possible fluid leak.
SQUEAKING OR RUBBING SOUND	1. Steering column shroud or shaft rubbing.	1. While turning the steering wheel, listen down column to locate. Check interference between moving components. Move or realign shrouds or shaft as necessary. Replace components if this does not correct problem.
	2. Clockspring inside steering column noisy.	2. Remove clockspring and reinstall steering wheel for testing. If noise is gone, replace clockspring.
	3. Boot/dash seal lubrication inadequate.	3. Remove boot seal and recheck for noise. Lubricate seal as necessary.
	4. Steering gear outer tie rod noisy.	4. While a helper turns the steering wheel, use an electronic listening tool to determine if noise is coming from either outer tie rod. Replace outer tie rods as necessary.
	5. Steering gear internally noisy.	5. Remove dash seal boot, then exercise the steering wheel. If noise is still present at gear, replace steering gear.
SCRUBBING OR KNOCKING SOUND	1. Incorrect tire or wheel size.	1. Replace incorrect size tire or wheel with original equipment size.

ARM0600000000401

Fig. 1 Troubleshooting (Part 4 of 11)

	2. Worn motor or transmission mount.	2. Drive vehicle, moving accelerator pedal rapidly up and down attempting to locate noise. Try in both forward and reverse. Replace mounts as necessary.
	3. Tires contacting wheel well.	3. Make sure wheel house is properly positioned. If not, reposition as necessary. If steering wheel is properly centered, check steering gear travel left to right by rotating the steering wheel to each stop. Steering wheel should rotate the same amount in both directions from center. If not, replace steering gear.
	4. Interference between moving steering components and other components.	4. Check for bent or misaligned components. Correct or replace as necessary.
	5. Accessory drive pulley rubbing against another component.	5. Check pulleys for wear. Check for worn engine or transmission mount. Reposition components or replace mounts as necessary.

NOTE: * There is some noise in all power steering systems. One of the most common is a hissing sound evident when turning the steering wheel when at a standstill or when parking and the steering wheel is at the end of its travel. Hiss is a very high frequency noise similar to that experienced while slowly closing a water tap. The noise is present in every valve and results when high velocity fluid passes valve orifice edges. There is no relationship between this noise and the performance of the steering system.

NOTE: ** A light clunk may be felt or heard during steering wheel reversal while vehicle is stationary. This results from internal steering gear rack movement at the bushings and in no way affects the performance of the steering system. This movement may be felt in the steering components during steering wheel reversal.

NOTE: * Power steering pump growl/moan/groan results from the development of high pressure fluid flow. Normally this noise level should not be high enough to be objectionable.**

ARM0600000000402

Fig. 1 Troubleshooting (Part 5 of 11)

CONDITION	POSSIBLE CAUSES	EVALUATION/CORRECTION
STEERING WHEEL OR COLUMN HAS FREE-PLAY/LASH/LOOSENESS (CLUNKING OR RATTLING)	1. Loose coupling pinch bolt at gear input shaft.	1. Check pinch bolt torque. Replace pinch bolt if equipped with thread locker patch and tighten to specifications.
	2. Power steering gear loose on cradle/crossmember.	2. Inspect gear mounting bolts. Replace if necessary and tighten to specifications.
	3. Excessive free-play or noise from steering column bearings.	3. Replace steering column.
	4. Excessive intermediate (steering) shaft coupling U-joint free-play.	4. Rotate steering wheel back-and-forth while watching coupling. Observe for free-play. Replace steering column as necessary.
	5. Loose or worn outer tie rod.	5. For evaluation and correction.
	6. Lack of lubrication in lower ball joint or ball joint is damaged.	6. Lubricate ball joint if equipped with a zerk fitting and check for function . If not equipped with a zerk fitting, test and replace ball joint/lower control arm as necessary.
	7. Excessive lash inside steering gear.	7. Disconnect intermediate shaft and turn steering gear input shaft. Observe for any movement without a corresponding tire movement. Replace steering gear as necessary.
STEERING WHEEL HAS FORE AND AFT LOOSENESS	1. Steering wheel retaining bolt loose.	1. Check steering wheel retaining bolt torque and tighten to specifications as necessary.
	2. Loose steering column to instrument panel fasteners.	2. Check steering column to instrument panel fastener torque and tighten to specifications as necessary.

ARM0600000000403

Fig. 1   Troubleshooting (Part 6 of 11)

CONDITION	POSSIBLE CAUSES	EVALUATION/CORRECTION
	3. Steering column lower bearing spring retainer slipped on steering column shaft.	3. Pull steering wheel fore-and-aft while observing movement. Replace steering column as necessary.
STEERING WHEEL, DASH OR VEHICLE VIBRATES DURING STEERING MANEUVERS (ESPECIALLY AT LOW SPEED OR STANDSTILL)	1. Air in power steering fluid.	1. Inspect for excessive air bubbles in fluid (fluid will appear foamy and lighter in color). Inspect hoses for leaks and replace as necessary. Bleed air from fluid.
	2. Tire(s) not properly inflated.	2. Check and inflate tires to the specified pressure.
	3. Excessive engine vibration.	3. Ensure that the engine is tuned properly.
	4. Loose tie rod end jam nut.	4. Check torque and tighten the inner to outer tie rod jam nut to specifications.
	5. Overcharged air conditioning (A/C) system.	5. Turn A/C off and verify issue goes away. Repair A/C as necessary.
	6. Grounded, damaged or loose engine mount.	6. Visually inspect for damaged or misaligned mounts. Check fastener torque. Replace or realign as necessary.
	7. Loose or worn outer tie rod.	7. For evaluation and correction.
	8. Steering gear noisy.	8. During a parking event at 0 mph, verify there is vibration only with steering. Steer in both directions and verify that the noise follows the steering input. Check TSB's for any known issues. Replace steering gear as necessary.
STEERING CATCHES, SURGES OR STICKS IN CERTAIN POSITIONS OR IS DIFFICULT TO TURN	1. Low power steering fluid level.	1. Check fluid level and fill to proper level as necessary. Check for leaks. Make sure all air is bled from system.
	2. Tire(s) not properly inflated.	2. Check and inflate tires to the specified pressure.

ARM0600000000404

Fig. 1   Troubleshooting (Part 7 of 11)

	3. Loose or slipping power steering/accessory drive belt.	3. Verify belt tension. Replace belt auto-tensioner and belt as necessary.
	4. Lack of lubrication in lower ball joint or ball joint is damaged.	4. Lubricate ball joint if equipped with a zerk fitting and check for function . If not equipped with a zerk fitting, test and replace ball joint/lower control arm as necessary.
	5. Lack of lubrication in steering gear outer tie rod end(s).	5. For evaluation and correction.
	6. Faulty power steering pump.	6. Perform Power Steering Flow and Pressure Test. Look for low or erratic flow or pressure. Replace power steering pump as necessary.
	7. Excessive friction in intermediate shaft/coupler joint.	7. Disconnect intermediate shaft/coupler at steering gear and check joint for smooth operation in all directions. Replace steering column.
	8. Excessive friction in steering column.	8. Disconnect intermediate shaft/coupler at steering gear. Turn steering wheel two revolutions in either direction from on center and check for smooth operation. DO NOT turn past two revolutions. Damage to the clockspring may occur. Replace steering column as necessary.
	9. Worn or binding seat and bearing in front strut assembly.	9. Disconnect outer tie rod ends from knuckles, then turn tire and wheel assembly checking for smooth operation. Replace front strut assembly seat and bearing.
	10. Faulty steering gear.	10. With vehicle on hoist, tires unsupported and engine off, steer gear throughout travel and check for smooth operation. Replace steering gear.

ARM0600000000405

Fig. 1   Troubleshooting (Part 8 of 11)

STEERING WHEEL DOES NOT RETURN TO CENTER POSITION	1. Tire(s) not properly inflated.	1. Check and inflate tires to the specified pressure.
	2. Improper front wheel alignment.	2. Check and adjust wheel alignment as necessary.
	3. Lack of lubrication in lower ball joint or ball joint is damaged.	3. Lubricate ball joint if equipped with a zerk fitting and check for function . If not equipped with a zerk fitting, test and replace ball joint/lower control arm as necessary.
	4. Excessive friction in intermediate shaft/coupler joint.	4. Disconnect intermediate shaft/coupler at steering gear and check joint for smooth operation in all directions. Replace steering column.
	5. Excessive friction in steering column.	5. Disconnect intermediate shaft/coupler at steering gear. Turn steering wheel two revolutions in either direction from on center and check for smooth operation. DO NOT turn past two revolutions. Damage to the clockspring may occur. Replace steering column as necessary.
	6. Worn or binding seat and bearing in front strut assembly.	6. Disconnect steering gear outer tie rod ends at knuckles, then turn tire and wheel assembly in and out checking for smooth operation. Replace seat and bearing as necessary.
	7. Excessive friction in power steering gear.	7. With vehicle on hoist, tires unsupported and engine off, steer gear throughout travel and check for smooth operation. Replace steering gear (only after all previous components have been checked).
EXCESSIVE STEERING WHEEL KICKBACK FROM ROAD INPUTS	1. Air in power steering fluid.	1. Inspect for excessive air bubbles in fluid (fluid will appear foamy and lighter in color). Inspect hoses for leaks and replace as necessary. Bleed air from fluid.

ARM0600000000406

Fig. 1   Troubleshooting (Part 9 of 11)

	2. Power steering gear loose on cradle/crossmember.	2. Inspect gear mounting bolts. Replace if necessary and tighten to specifications.		
	3. Steering column, coupling or intermediate shaft worn or loose.	3. Rotate steering wheel back-and-forth while inspecting intermediate shaft going into steering gear. Look for excessive free-play. Retighten if loose bolt is found. Replace steering column, coupling or intermediate shaft if necessary.		
	4. Power steering pump flow is too low.	4. Perform Power Steering Flow and Pressure Test. Look for low or erratic flow or pressure. Replace power steering pump as necessary.		

AERATED FLUID*	1. Low power steering fluid level.	1. Check fluid level and fill to proper level as necessary. Check for leaks. Make sure all air is bled from system.
	2. Air leak at power steering supply hose, reservoir or pump.	2. Inspect components. Place a hand vacuum pump with Adapter 9688 on reservoir and verify that system can sustain vacuum. System should not lose more than 1 psi in 2 minutes (make sure vacuum pump is sealed well to the reservoir). Replace steering component as necessary.
RESERVOIR FLUID OVERFLOW OR FLUID THAT IS MILKY IN COLOR	1. Water contamination of power steering fluid.	1. Inspect fluid for milky appearance. Completely drain power steering fluid. Refill and bleed system.

ARM0600000000408

Fig. 1 Troubleshooting (Part 11 of 11)

FLUID ISSUES

CONDITION	POSSIBLE CAUSES	EVALUATION/CORRECTION
LOW FLUID LEVEL WITH VISIBLE LEAK	1. Loose power steering hose fittings or connections.	1. Check torque on all tube nuts (at gear and pump). Inspect clamps at all rubber hose connections for correct position, damage and tension. Tighten tube nuts to specifications as required. Reposition or replace clamps at hose connections. Clean joints and reinspect for leaks.
	2. Damaged or missing O-ring at power steering hose tube nuts.	2. Remove tube nut and inspect O-ring. If damaged or missing, replace O-ring. Clean joints and reinspect for leaks.
	3. Power steering line or hose failure.	3. Clean fluid from around suspect areas. Run vehicle and inspect for leaks. Look inside reservoir to see if air is being ingested. Replace hoses as necessary.
	4. Power steering component leaking (reservoir, pump, gear).	4. Clean fluid from around suspect areas. Run vehicle and inspect for leaks. Look inside reservoir to see if air is being ingested. Replace power steering component as necessary.

ARM0600000000407

Fig. 1 Troubleshooting (Part 10 of 11)

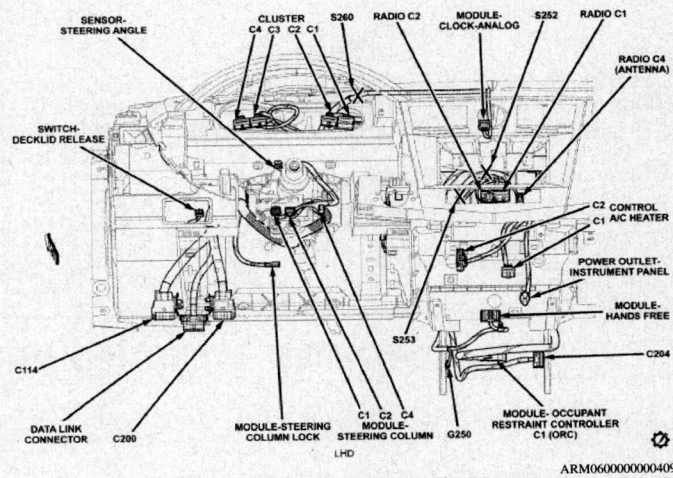

ARM0600000000409

Fig. 2 Data link connector location

TIGHTENING SPECIFICATIONS

Year	Component	Torque Ft. Lbs.
2007–08	Hose Tube Nuts	24
	Power Steering Gear Mounting	52
	Power Steering Pump	19
	Power Steering Pump Discharge Fitting	62
	Pump Mounting Bracket Bolts (2.7L Engine)	22
	Pump Pressure Fitting	65
	Reservoir	106①
	Suspension Crossmember Mounting Bolts	140
	Tie Rod Adjuster Pinch Bolt	28
	Tie Rod End Knuckle Nut	97
	Tie Rod Jam Nut	55

① — Inch lbs.

Concorde, Intrepid & 300M

NOTE: On Air Bag Equipped Models, Refer To "Air Bag System Precautions" Located In The Front Of This Manual For System Disarming & Arming Procedures.

NOTE: Refer To "Computer Relearn Procedures" Located In The Front Of This Manual When Battery Power To The Computer Has Been Interrupted.

NOTE: Prior To Performing Any Service Operations Listed In This Section, Consult The "Technical Service Bulletins" Section For Related Information.

INDEX

	Page No.		Page No.		Page No.
Description	13-6	Power Steering Pressure Specifications	13-6	Control Module, Replace	13-7
Diagnosis & Testing	13-6	Power Steering System Bleed	13-7	Solenoid Control Valve, Replace	13-7
Accessing Diagnostic Trouble Codes	13-6	Component Service	13-7	Precautions	13-6
Clearing Diagnostic Trouble Codes	13-6	Drive Pulley, Replace	13-7	Air Bag Systems	13-6
		Fluid Cooler, Replace	13-7	Battery Ground Cable	13-6
Connector Terminal Identification	13-6	Pressure Switch, Replace	13-7	Tightening Specifications	13-11
Diagnostic Tests	13-6	Reservoir, Replace	13-7	Troubleshooting	13-6
		Solenoid Control Valve			

POWER STEERING PRESSURE SPECIFICATIONS

Model	Year	Power Steering Pump Pressure, psi		Max Relief Pressure	Output Flow, Gallons Per Minute①
		Test Valve			
		Open	Closed		
Concorde, Intrepid & 300M	2004	50–125	1250–1350	1250–1350	2.1–2.5

① — At 1500 RPM & minimum pressure.

PRECAUTIONS

Air Bag Systems

Refer to "Air Bag System Precautions" in the front of this manual for system disarming and arming procedures.

Battery Ground Cable

Prior to service, disconnect battery ground cable and isolate as required.

DESCRIPTION

Power assist is provided by an open center, rotary type control valve. It is used to direct oil from the power steering pump to either side of the integral steering rack piston. These vehicles may be equipped with three different types of power steering. They are base, firm feel and speed proportional power steering.

TROUBLESHOOTING

Refer to **Fig. 1** when troubleshooting the power steering system.

DIAGNOSIS & TESTING

Accessing Diagnostic Trouble Codes

Connect the DRB III, or suitably programmed scan tool, to the Data Link Connector (DLC), **Fig. 2**. The diagnostic cycle begins when the ignition is turned On.

Connector Terminal Identification

Refer to **Fig. 3** for connector terminal identification.

Diagnostic Tests

Refer to **Figs. 4 through 7** for diagnostic tests.

Clearing Diagnostic Trouble Codes

Connect the DRB III, or suitably programmed scan tool, to the Data Link Connector (DLC), **Fig. 2**. The diagnostic cycle begins when the ignition is turned On.

CONDITION	POSSIBLE CAUSES	CORRECTION
OBJECTIONABLE HISS OR WHISTLE*	1. Damaged or mispositioned steering column shaft/coupling dash panel seal. 2. Noisy valve in power steering gear.	1. Reposition or replace steering column shaft/coupling dash panel seal. 2. Replace power steering gear.
RATTLE OR CLUNK	1. Power steering gear loose on front suspension crossmember. 2. Front suspension crossmember mounting fasteners loose at frame. 3. Loose tie rod (outer or inner). 4. Loose lower control arm mounting bolts at front suspension crossmember. 5. Loose shock assembly mounting fasteners at shock tower. 6. Power steering fluid pressure hose touching the body of the vehicle. 7. Internal power steering gear noise. 8. Damaged front suspension crossmember.	1. Inspect power steering gear mounting bolts. Replace as necessary. Tighten to the specified torque. 2. Tighten the front suspension crossmember mounting fasteners to the specified torque. 3. Check tie rod pivot points for wear. Replace worn/loose parts as required. 4. Tighten control arm mounting bolts to the specified torques. 5. Tighten shock assembly fasteners to the specified torques. 6. Adjust hose to proper position by loosening, repositioning, and tightening fitting to specified torque. Do not bend tubing. 7. Replace power steering gear. 8. Replace front suspension crossmember.

CR6029700192010X

Fig. 1 Troubleshooting (Part 1 of 6)

POWER STEERING SYSTEM BLEED

1. Ensure power steering fluid remote reservoir is full, then start engine and turn steering wheel from stop to stop several times.
2. Stop engine and inspect fluid level again. If required, add fluid until proper fluid level is reached.
3. Repeat procedure until fluid level is consistent. Inspect system for leaks.

Component Service

FLUID COOLER, REPLACE

1. Remove as much power steering fluid as possible from reservoir using suitable siphon pump.
2. Raise and support vehicle on suitable frame contact hoist or with suitable jack stands.
3. Remove front fascia.
4. Remove hose clamps attaching fluid return hoses to power steering fluid cooler line.
5. Remove mounting clips at bumper reinforcement.
6. Remove cooler line from vehicle.
7. Reverse procedure to install.

RESERVOIR, REPLACE

2.7L ENGINE

1. Remove power steering pump as outlined under "Power Steering Pump, Replace" in "Front Suspension & Steering" of "Concorde, Intrepid & 300M" chassis chapter.
2. Remove mounting bolts and reservoir.
3. Reverse procedure to install, noting following:
   a. Lubricate reservoir O-ring seal with suitable, fresh, clean power steering fluid.
   b. Press reservoir nipple straight into pump without rotating or twisting.

3.2L & 3.5L ENGINES

1. Raise and support vehicle on suitable frame contact hoist or with suitable jack stands.
2. Remove reservoir hoses and drain fluid into suitable container.
3. Lower vehicle, then rotate and remove reservoir's rear side toward engine, out of its bracket.
4. Reverse procedure to install, noting following:
   a. Ensure reservoir bottom tab is inserted into frame rail hole.
   b. Ensure clamps are installed on hoses past retention beads.

DRIVE PULLEY, REPLACE

REMOVAL

1. Remove power steering pump as outlined under "Power Steering Pump, Replace" in "Front Suspension & Steering" section of "Concorde, Intrepid & 300M." chassis chapter.
2. Mount pump by mounting boss in suitable vise. **Do not clamp pump body.**
3. Remove pulley using puller tool No. C-4333, or equivalent. **Do not use press or hammer on pump shaft.**

INSTALLATION

1. Place pulley squarely on shaft end and install spacer provided with pump or pulley into pulley hub.
2. Install spacer tool No. 6936, or equivalent, into pulley hub, **Fig. 8.**
3. Thread installer tool No. C-4063, or equivalent, into pump shaft.
4. Holding installer tool with one wrench, turn installer hex down threaded rod pushing pulley onto shaft. Ensure tool and pulley remain aligned.
5. Ensure spacer is fully seated against

CONDITION	POSSIBLE CAUSES	CORRECTION
POPPING NOISE	1. Worn outer tie rod.	1. Replace outer tie rod.
CHIRP OR SQUEAL (POWER STEERING PUMP)	1. Loose power steering pump drive belt.	1. Check and adjust power steering pump drive belt to specifications. Replace belt if worn or glazed.
WHINE OR GROWL (POWER STEERING PUMP)**	1. Low fluid level. 2. Power steering hose touching vehicle body or frame. 3. Extreme wear of power steering pump internal components.	1. Fill power steering fluid reservoir to proper level and check for leaks (make sure all air is bled from the system fluid). 2. Adjust hose to proper position by loosening, repositioning, and tightening fitting to specified torque. Do not bend tubing. Replace hose if damaged. 3. Replace power steering pump and flush system as necessary.
SUCKING AIR SOUND	1. Loose clamp on power steering fluid return hose. 2. Missing O-Ring on power steering hose connection. 3. Low power steering fluid level. 4. Air leak between power steering fluid reservoir and power steering pump.	1. Tighten or replace hose clamp. 2. Inspect connection and replace O-Ring as required. 3. Fill power steering fluid reservoir to proper level and check for leaks. 4. Replace power steering pump (with reservoir).
SQUEAK OR RUBBING SOUND	1. Steering column shroud rubbing. 2. Steering column shaft rubbing. 3. Clockspring noisy. 4. Steering gear internally noisy.	1. Realign shrouds as necessary. 2. Move or realign item rubbing shaft. 3. Remove clockspring. Reinstall wheel. If noise is gone, replace clockspring. 4. Replace steering gear.
SCRUBBING OR KNOCKING NOISE.	1. Incorrect tire or wheel size. 2. Interference between steering gear and other vehicle components. 3. Steering gear internal stops worn excessively allowing tires to be steered excessively far.	1. Replace incorrect size tire or wheel with size used as original equipment. 2. Check for bent or misaligned components and correct as necessary. 3. Replace steering gear.

CR6029700192020X

Fig. 1 Troubleshooting (Part 2 of 6)

shaft front, then remove tool and spacer.

PRESSURE SWITCH, REPLACE

1. **On models equipped with 3.2L and 3.5L engines,** raise and support vehicle.
2. **On all models,** disconnect electrical connector and remove power steering pressure switch.
3. Reverse procedure to install.

SOLENOID CONTROL VALVE CONTROL MODULE, REPLACE

1. Remove electrical connector from control module.
2. Depress two locking tabs on bottom of control module and disconnect control module from steering gear end cap.
3. Rotate control module upward, until retaining tabs can be removed from steering gear end cap.
4. Remove control module from steering gear.
5. Reverse procedure to install.

SOLENOID CONTROL VALVE, REPLACE

1. Remove solenoid control valve electrical connector.
2. Remove power steering pressure and return hoses from steering gear. Allowing fluid to drain into suitable container.
3. Loosen and remove solenoid control valve from steering gear using a suitable crowfoot wrench.
4. Reverse procedure to install.

CONDITION	POSSIBLE CAUSES	CORRECTION
STEERING WHEEL/ COLUMN CLICKING, CLUNKING OR RATTLING.	1. Steering column preload is not set properly.	1. Loosen steering column coupling pinch bolt to reset steering column preload. Replace pinch bolt and torque to specifications.
	2. Loose steering coupling pinch bolt.	2. Replace pinch bolt and torque to specifications.
	3. Steering column bearings.	3. Replace steering column.
STEERING WHEEL HAS FORE AND AFT LOOSENESS.	1. Steering wheel retaining nut not properly tightened and torqued.	1. Tighten the steering wheel retaining nut to its specified torque.
	2. Steering column preload is not set properly.	2. Loosen steering column coupling pinch bolt to reset steering column preload. Replace pinch bolt and torque to specifications.
	3. Steering column lower bearing spring retainer slipped on steering column shaft.	3. Replace steering column.
STEERING WHEEL OR DASH VIBRATES DURING LOW SPEED OR STANDSTILL STEERING MANEUVERS.	1. Air in the fluid of the power steering system.	1. Bleed air from system following the power steering pump initial operation service procedure.*
	2. Tires not properly inflated.	2. Inflate tires to the specified pressure.
	3. Excessive engine vibration.	3. Ensure that the engine is running properly.
	4. Loose tie rod end jam nut.	4. Tighten the inner to outer tie rod jam nut to the specified torque.
	5. Overcharged air conditioning system.	5. Check air conditioning pump head pressure and correct as necessary.
STEERING CATCHES, STICKS IN CERTAIN POSITIONS OR IS DIFFICULT TO TURN.	1. Low power steering fluid level.	1. Fill power steering fluid reservoir to specified level and check for leaks.
	2. Tires not inflated to specified pressure.	2. Inflate tires to the specified pressure.
	3. Lack of lubrication in front suspension control arm ball joints.	3. Lubricate ball joints if ball joints are not a lubricated-for-life type ball joint. If ball joint is a lubricated-for-life ball joint, replace ball joint or control arm.
	4. Worn upper or lower control arm ball joint.	4. Replace ball joint or control arm.
	5. Lack of lubrication in steering gear outer tie rod ends.	5. Lubricate tie rod ends if they are not a lubricated-for-life type. If tie rod end is a lubricated-for-life type, replace tie rod end.

CR6029700192030X

Fig. 1   Troubleshooting (Part 3 of 6)

CONDITION	POSSIBLE CAUSES	CORRECTION
	6. Loose power steering pump drive belt.	6. Tighten the power steering pump drive belt to specifications. If drive belt is worn or glazed, replace belt.
	7. Faulty power steering pump flow control (Perform Power Steering System Flow and Pressure Test).	7. Replace power steering pump.
	8. Excessive friction in steering column or intermediate shaft.	8. Isolate and correct condition.
	9. Binding upper or lower control arm ball joint.	9. Replace the upper or lower ball joint.
	10. Excessive friction in power steering gear.	10. Replace power steering gear.
STIFF, HARD TO TURN, SURGE, MOMENTARY INCREASE IN EFFORT WHEN TURNING.	1. Tires not properly inflated.	1. Inflate tires to specified pressure.
	2. Low power steering fluid level.	2. Add power steering fluid as required to power steering fluid reservoir to obtain proper level. Check for leaks.
	3. Loose power steering pump drive belt.	3. Tighten the power steering pump drive belt to specifications. If drive belt is worn or glazed, replace belt.
	4. Lack of lubrication in control arm ball joints.	4. Lubricate ball joints if ball joints are not a lubricated-for-life type ball joint. If ball joint is a lubricated-for-life ball joint, replace ball joint or control arm.
	5. Low power steering pump pressure (Perform Power Steering System Flow and Pressure Test).	5. Replace the power steering pump as necessary.
	6. High internal leak in power steering gear (Perform Power Steering System Flow and Pressure Test).	6. Replace power steering gear.
STEERING WHEEL DOES NOT RETURN TO CENTER POSITION.	1. Tires not inflated properly.	1. Inflate tires to specified pressure.
	2. Improper front wheel alignment.	2. Check and adjust wheel alignment as necessary.
	3. Lack of lubrication in front suspension control arm ball joints.	3. Lubricate ball joints if ball joints are not a lubricated for life type of ball joint. If ball joint is a lubricated for life ball joint, replace ball joint or control arm.
	4. Steering column coupling joints misaligned.	4. Realign steering column coupling joints.
	5. Steering wheel rubbing.	5. Adjust steering column shrouds to eliminate rubbing condition.

CR6029700192040X

Fig. 1   Troubleshooting (Part 4 of 6)

CONDITION	POSSIBLE CAUSES	CORRECTION
	6. Damaged, mis-positioned or un-lubricated steering column coupler to dash seal.**	6. Replace, reposition, or lubricate dash seal.
	7. Binding upper or lower control arm ball joint.	7. Replace the upper or lower control arm ball joint.
	8. Tight shaft bearing in steering column.	8. Replace the steering column.
	9. Excessive friction in steering column coupling.	9. Replace steering column coupling.
	10. Excessive friction in power steering gear.	10. Replace power steering gear.
EXCESSIVE STEERING WHEEL KICKBACK OR TOO MUCH STEERING WHEEL FREE PLAY.	1. Air in the fluid of the power steering system.	1. Bleed air from system following the the power steering pump initial operation service procedure. *
	2. Power steering gear loose on front suspension crossmember.	2. Inspect power steering gear mounting bolts. Replace as necessary. Tighten to the specified torque.
	3. Steering column coupling worn, broken or loose.	3. Replace steering column coupling.
	4. Free play in steering column.	4. Check all components of the steering system and repair or replace as required.
	5. Worn control arm ball joints.	5. Replace ball joint or control arm as required.
	6. Loose steering knuckle to ball joint stud pinch bolt.	6. Inspect pinch bolts, replace as necessary, and tighten to specified torque.
	7. Front wheel bearings loose or worn.	7. Replace wheel bearing or knuckle as necessary.
	8. Loose outer tie rod ends.	8. Replace outer tie rod ends that have excessive free play.
	9. Loose inner tie rod ends.	9. Replace power steering gear.
	10 Defective steering gear rotary valve.	10. Replace power steering gear.

NOTE: * Steering shudder can be expected in new vehicles and vehicles with recent steering system repairs. Shudder should dissipate after the vehicle has been driven several weeks.

CR6029700192050X

Fig. 1   Troubleshooting (Part 5 of 6)

CONDITION	POSSIBLE CAUSES	CORRECTION
LOW FLUID LEVEL WITH VISIBLE LEAK.	1. Loose power steering hose fittings.	1. Tighten the fitting to its specified torque.
	2. Damaged or missing fitting seal, gasket, or O-ring.	2. Replace as necessary.
	3. Power steering pump or power steering gear leaking.	3. Repair or replace the leaking component as required.
AERATED FLUID.	1. Low fluid level.*	1. Fill power steering fluid reservoir to proper level.
	2. Air leak between power steering fluid reservoir and pump.	2. Inspect for proper sealing. Replace the power steering pump (with reservoir).
	3. Cracked power steering pump housing.	3. Replace the power steering pump.
RESERVOIR FLUID OVERFLOW AND FLUID THAT IS MILKY IN COLOR	1. Water contamination.	1. Drain the power steering fluid from the system. Flush the system with fresh clean power steering fluid, drain, then refill to the proper level.

CR6029700192060X

Fig. 1   Troubleshooting (Part 6 of 6)

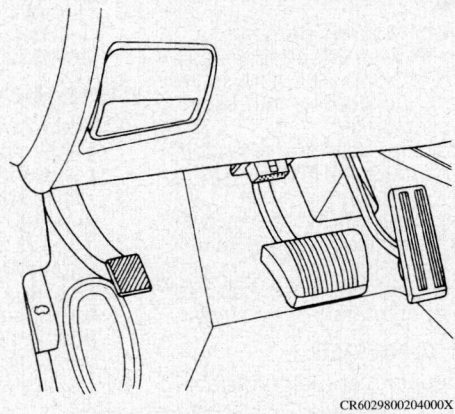

CR6029800204000X

Fig. 2   Data link connector location

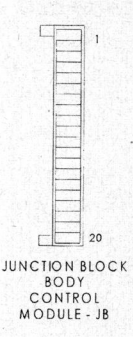

CAV	CIRCUIT	FUNCTION
1	Z20	GROUND
2	M2	COURTESY LAMP DRIVER
3	S76	SPEED PROPORTIONAL STEERING SOLENOID (-)
4	S77	SPEED PROPORTIONAL STEERING SOLENOID (+)
5	G5	FUSED IGNITION SWITCH OUTPUT (RUN-START)
6	L7	PARK LAMP RELAY OUTPUT
7	M1	FUSED B(+)
8	P2	DECKLID RELEASE CONTROL
9	-	-
10	D25	PCI BUS (OTIS)
11	-	-
12	-	-
13	P109	DRIVER DOOR UNLOCK RELAY CONTROL
14	L307	LOW BEAM RELAY CONTROL
15	P38	DOOR LOCK RELAY CONTROL
16	L308	PARK LAMP RELAY CONTROL
17	L26	FOG LAMP RELAY CONTROL
18	X3	HORN RELAY CONTROL
19	P36	DOOR UNLOCK RELAY CONTROL
20	Z2	GROUND

JUNCTION BLOCK
BODY
CONTROL
MODULE - JB

CR6020000214000X

Fig. 3 Connector terminal identification (Part 1 of 3)

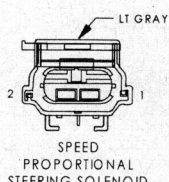

LT GRAY

SPEED
PROPORTIONAL
STEERING SOLENOID

CAV	CIRCUIT	FUNCTION
1	S76 18LG/PK	SPEED PROPORTIONAL STEERING SOLENOID (-)
2	S77 18VT/OR	SPEED PROPORTIONAL STEERING SOLENOID (+)

CR6020000216000X

Fig. 3 Connector terminal identification (Part 3 of 3)

TEST	ACTION
3	Turn the ignition off. Disconnect the Speed Pro Steering Solenoid harness connector. Start the engine. Measure the voltage of the Speed Pro Steering Solenoid (+) circuit in the Speed Pro Steering Solenoid harness connector. Is there any voltage present? Yes → Repair the Seed Pro Steering Solenoid (+) circuit for a short to voltage. Perform SPEED PRO STEERING VERIFICATION TEST - VER 1. No → Go To 4
4	Turn the ignition off. Disconnect the Speed Pro Steering Solenoid harness connector. Start the engine. Measure the voltage of the Speed Pro Steering Solenoid (-) circuit in the Speed Pro Steering Solenoid harness connector. Is there any voltage present? Yes → Repair the Speed Pro Steering Solenoid (-) circuit for a short to voltage and replace the Body Control Module (BCM will be damaged). Perform BODY VERIFICATION TEST - VER 1. No → Go To 5
5	Turn the ignition off. Disconnect the Speed Pro Steering Solenoid harness connector. Remove the Body Control Module from the Junction Block. Measure the resistance of the Speed Pro Steering Solenoid (+) circuit to the Speed Pro Steering Solenoid (-) circuit in the Junction Block BCM Internal connector. Is the resistance below 100.0 ohms Yes → Repair the Speed Pro Steering Solenoid (+) circuit for a short to the Speed Pro Steering Solenoid (-) circuit. Perform SPEED PRO STEERING VERIFICATION TEST - VER 1. No → Go To 6
6	If there are no possible causes remaining, view repair. Repair Replace the Body Control Module. Perform BODY VERIFICATION TEST - VER 1.

CR6020000217020X

Fig. 4 Speed Pro Steering Circuit Short to Voltage (Part 2 of 2)

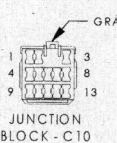

GRAY

JUNCTION
BLOCK - C10

CAV	CIRCUIT	FUNCTION
1	L60 18TN	RIGHT TURN SIGNAL
2	L61 18LG	LEFT TURN SIGNAL
3	G9 20GY/BK	RED BRAKE WARNING INDICATOR DRIVER
4	L34 20GY/OR	FUSED RIGHT HIGH BEAM OUTPUT
5	-	-
6	L1 20VT/BK	BACK-UP LAMP FEED
7	F18 20LG/BK	FUSED IGNITION SWITCH OUTPUT (RUN-START)
8	S77 18VT/OR (EXCEPT BUILT-UP EXPORT)	SPEED PROPORTIONAL STEERING SOLENOID (+)
9	-	-
10	S76 18LG/PK (EXCEPT BUILT-UP EXPORT)	SPEED PROPORTIONAL STEERING SOLENOID (-)

CR6020000215000X

Fig. 3 Connector terminal identification (Part 2 of 3)

TEST	ACTION
1	Start the engine. While turning the Steering Wheel, monitor the amount of force it takes to turn the Steering Wheel. With the DRBIII®, de-activate the Speed Pro Steering Solenoid for 15 seconds. Again turn the Steering Wheel and monitor the amount of force it takes to turn the Steering Wheel. Was the Steering Wheel harder to turn with the Speed Pro Steering Solenoid de-activated? Yes → System is operating properly at this time. Erase DTC, inspect the wiring and connectors and repair as necessary. Perform SPEED PRO STEERING VERIFICATION TEST - VER 1. No → Go To 2
2	Turn the ignition off. Disconnect the Speed Pro Steering Solenoid harness connector. Measure the resistance of the Speed Pro Steering Solenoid. Is the resistance between 5.7 and 6.3 ohms at 20 C (68° F)? Yes → Go To 3 No → Replace the Speed Pro Steering Solenoid. Perform SPEED PRO STEERING VERIFICATION TEST - VER 1.

CR6020000217010X

Fig. 4 Speed Pro Steering Circuit Short to Voltage (Part 1 of 2)

TEST	ACTION
1	Start the engine. While turning the Steering Wheel, monitor the amount of force it takes to turn the Steering Wheel With the DRBIII®, de-activate the Speed Pro Steering Solenoid for 15 seconds. Again turn the steering wheel and monitor the amount of force it takes to turn the Steering Wheel. Was the Steering Wheel harder to turn while the Speed Pro Steering Solenoid was de-activated? Yes → System is operating properly at this time. Erase the DTC, inspect the wiring and connectors and repair as necessary. Perform SPEED PRO STEERING VERIFICATION TEST - VER 1. No → Go To 2
2	Turn the ignition off. Disconnect the Speed Pro Steering Solenoid harness connector. Measure the resistance of the Speed Pro Steering Solenoid. Is the resistance between 5.7 and 6.3 ohms at 20 C (68° F)? Yes → Go To 3 No → Replace the Speed Pro Steering Solenoid. Perform SPEED PRO STEERING VERIFICATION TEST - VER 1.

CR6020000218010X

Fig. 5 Speed Pro Steering Solenoid Circuit Open/ Shorted to Ground (Part 1 of 2)

TEST	ACTION
3	Turn the ignition off. Disconnect the Speed Pro Steering Solenoid harness connector. Measure the resistance between ground and the Speed Pro Steering Solenoid (+) circuit in the Speed Pro Steering Solenoid harness connector. Is the resistance below 100 ohms? Yes → Repair the Speed Pro Steering (+) circuit for a short to ground. Perform SPEED PRO STEERING VERIFICATION TEST - VER 1. No → Go To 4
4	Turn the ignition off. Disconnect the Speed Pro Steering Solenoid harness connector. Measure the resistance between ground and the Speed Pro Steering Solenoid (-) circuit in the Speed Pro Steering Solenoid harness connector. Is the resistance below 100 ohms? Yes → Repair the Speed Pro Steering (-) circuit for a short to ground. Perform SPEED PRO STEERING VERIFICATION TEST - VER 1. No → Go To 5
5	Turn the ignition off. Disconnect the Speed Pro Steering Solenoid harness connector. Remove the Body Control Module from the Junction Block. Measure the resistance of the Speed Pro Steering Solenoid (-) circuit between the Junction Block BCM connector and the Speed Pro Steering Solenoid harness connector. Is the resistance below 5.0 ohms? Yes → Go To 6 No → Repair the open Speed Pro Steering Solenoid (-) circuit. Perform SPEED PRO STEERING VERIFICATION TEST - VER 1.
6	Turn the ignition off. Disconnect the Speed Pro Steering Solenoid harness connector. Remove the Body Control Module from the Junction Block. Measure the resistance of the Speed Pro Steering Solenoid (+) circuit to the Speed Pro Steering Solenoid (-) circuit in the Junction Block BCM Internal connector. Is the resistance below 100.0 ohms Yes → Repair the Speed Pro Steering Solenoid (+) circuit for a short to the Speed Pro Steering Solenoid (-) circuit. Perform SPEED PRO STEERING VERIFICATION TEST - VER 1. No → Go To 7
7	Turn the ignition off. Disconnect the Speed Pro Steering Solenoid harness connector. Remove the Body Control Module from the Junction Block. Measure the resistance of the Speed Pro Steering Solenoid (+) circuit between the Junction Block BCM connector and the Speed Pro Steering Solenoid connector. Is the resistance below 5.0 ohms? Yes → Go To 8 No → Repair the open Speed Pro Steering Solenoid (+) circuit. Perform SPEED PRO STEERING VERIFICATION TEST - VER 1.
8	If there are no possible causes remaining, view repair. Repair Replace the Body Control Module. Perform BODY VERIFICATION TEST - VER 1.

CR6020000218020X

Fig. 5   Speed Pro Steering Solenoid Circuit Open/ Shorted to Ground (Part 2 of 2)

TEST	ACTION
3	Using the wiring diagram/schematic as a guide, inspect the wiring and connectors from the BCM to the Speed Pro Steering Solenoid. Check for chafed, pinched, open or shorted wiring. Were there any problems found? Yes → Repair the Speed Pro Steering Solenoid wiring and/or connectors as necessary. Perform SPEED PRO STEERING VERIFICATION TEST - VER 1. No → Go To 4
4	If there are no possible causes remaining, view repair. Repair Replace the Body Control Module. Perform BODY VERIFICATION TEST - VER 1.

CR6020000219020X

Fig. 6   Speed Pro Steering Solenoid Over Temperature (Part 2 of 2)

TEST	ACTION
1	Start the engine. While turning the Steering Wheel, monitor the amount of force it takes to turn the Steering Wheel. With the DRBIII®, de-activate the Speed Pro Steering Solenoid for 15 seconds. Again turn the Steering Wheel and monitor the amount of force it takes to turn the Steering Wheel. Was the Steering Wheel harder to turn while the Speed Pro Steering Solenoid was de-activated? Yes → System is operating properly at this time. Erase the DTC, inspect the wiring and connectors and repair as necessary. Perform SPEED PRO STEERING VERIFICATION TEST - VER 1. No → Go To 2
2	Turn the ignition off. Disconnect the Speed Pro Steering Solenoid harness connector. Measure the resistance of the Speed Pro Steering Solenoid. Is the resistance between 5.7 and 6.3 ohms at 20 C (68° F)? Yes → Go To 3 No → Replace the Speed Pro Steering Solenoid. Perform SPEED PRO STEERING VERIFICATION TEST - VER 1.

CR6020000219010X

Fig. 6   Speed Pro Steering Solenoid Over Temperature (Part 1 of 2)

BODY VERIFICATION TEST - VER 1
1. Disconnect all jumper wires and reconnect all previously disconnected components and connectors. 2. If the Sentry Key Immobilizer Module (SKIM) or the Powertrain Control Module (PCM) was replaced, proceed to number 6. If the SKIM or PCM was not replaced, continue to the next number. 3. If the Body Control Module was replaced, turn the ignition on for 15 seconds (to allow the new BCM to learn VIN) or engine may not start (if VTSS equipped). If the vehicle is equipped with VTSS, use the DRBIII® and enable VTSS. 4. Program all other options as needed. 5. If any repairs were made to the HVAC System, disconnect the battery or, using the DRBIII®, recalibrate the HVAC doors. Proceed to number 13. 6. Obtain the Vehicle's unique PIN assigned to it's original SKIM from either the vehicle's invoice or from Chrysler's Customer Assistance Center (1-800-992-1997). 7. NOTE: Once Secured Access Mode is active, the SKIM will remain in that mode for 60 seconds. 8. With the DRBIII®, select THEFT ALARM, SKIM, MISCELLANEOUS and select SKIM REPLACED. Enter the 4 digit PIN to put the SKIM in Secured Access Mode. 9. The DRBIII® will prompt for the following steps. (1) Program the country code into the SKIM's memory. (2) Program the vehicle's VIN into the SKIM memory. (3) Transfer the vehicle's Secret Key data from the PCM. 10. Using the DRBIII®, program all customer keys into the SKIM memory. This requires that the SKIM be in Secured Access Mode, using the 4 digit PIN. 11. Note: If the PCM is replaced, the VIN and the unique Secret Key data must be transferred from the SKIM to the PCM. This procedure requires the SKIM to be placed in Secured Access Mode using the 4-digit PIN. 12. Note: If 3 attempts are made to enter Secured Access Mode using an incorrect PIN, Secured Access Mode will be locked out for 1 hour which causes the DRBIII® to display "Bus +\- Signals Open". To exit this mode, turn ignition to Run for 1 hour. 13. Ensure that all accessories are turned off and the battery is fully charged. 14. Ensure that the Ignition is on. 15. With the DRBIII®, record and erase all DTCs from ALL modules. Start and run the engine for 2 minutes. Operate all functions of the system that caused the original concern. 16. Turn the ignition off and wait 5 seconds. Turn the ignition on and using the DRBIII®, read DTCs from ALL modules. Are any DTC's present or is the original condition still present? Yes → Repair is not complete, refer to appropriate symptom. No → Repair is complete.

CR6020000220000X

Fig. 7   Verification Test VER-1

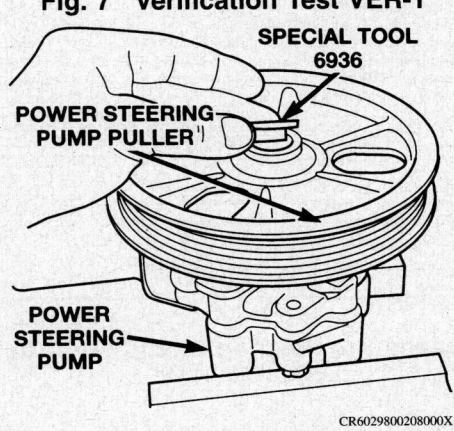

CR6029800208000X

Fig. 8   Spacer tool installation

TIGHTENING SPECIFICATIONS

Year	Component	Torque Ft. Lbs.
2004	Air Bag Module	75①
	Hose Tube Nuts	35
	Power Steering Gear Mounting	43
	Power Steering Pump	21
	Power Steering Pump Discharge Fitting	62
	Reservoir, Pulley Side	10
	Reservoir, Rear (2.7L)	18
	Speed Control Switch	13①
	Steering Column Coupler	20
	Steering Column	105①
	Steering Wheel	45
	Tie Rod Adjuster Pinch Bolt	28
	Tie Rod Steering Arm	27
	Tie Rod Steering Gear	74

① — Inch lbs.

Crossfire

NOTE: On Air Bag Equipped Models, Refer To "Air Bag System Precautions" Located In The Front Of This Manual For System Disarming & Arming Procedures.

NOTE: Refer To "Computer Relearn Procedures" Located In The Front Of This Manual When Battery Power To The Computer Has Been Interrupted.

INDEX

	Page No.
Description	13-11
Diagnosis & Testing	13-12
Accessing Diagnostic Trouble Codes	13-12
Clearing Diagnostic Trouble Codes	13-12
Component Testing	13-12
Power Steering Pump & Gear	13-12

	Page No.
Connector Terminal Identification	13-12
Diagnostic Tests	13-12
Power Steering Pressure Specifications	13-11
Power Steering System Bleed	13-12
Component Service	13-12
Drive Pulley, Replace	13-12

	Page No.
Idler Arm, Replace	13-12
Pitman Shaft & Seal, Replace.	13-12
Steering Damper, Replace	13-12
Precautions	13-11
Air Bag Systems	13-11
Battery Ground Cable	13-11
Tightening Specifications	13-15
Troubleshooting	13-12

POWER STEERING PRESSURE SPECIFICATIONS

Model	Year	Power Steering Pump Pressure, psi		Max Relief Pressure	Output Flow, Gallons Per Minute③
		Test Valve			
		Open①	Closed②		
Crossfire	2004–07	50–80	1250–1350	1250–1350	2.4–2.8

① — Initial pressure.

② — Do not leave valve closed for more than five seconds.

③ — At 1500 RPM & minimum pressure.

PRECAUTIONS

Air Bag Systems

Refer to "Air Bag System Precautions" in the front of this manual for system disarming and arming procedures.

Battery Ground Cable

Prior to service, disconnect battery ground cable and isolate as required.

DESCRIPTION

The power steering pump on this model, uses a constant flow rate displacement vane type pump with the fluid reservoir attached to the pump body, **Fig. 1.** The steering gear used is a recirculating ball type gear, input is provided by the steering column input, **Fig. 2.**

TROUBLESHOOTING

Refer to **Figs. 3 through 5** for steering system troubleshooting.

DIAGNOSIS & TESTING

Accessing Diagnostic Trouble Codes

Connect the DRB III, or suitably programmed scan tool, to the Data Link Connector (DLC) located near hood release, **Fig. 6.** The diagnostic cycle begins when the ignition is turned On.

Connector Terminal Identification

Refer to **Fig. 7** for connector terminal identification.

Diagnostic Tests

Refer to **MOTOR's** "Domestic Engine Performance & Driveability Manual" or "Engine Performance and Driveability DVD 1994–2005 v6.0" for DTC diagnostic test procedures.

Clearing Diagnostic Trouble Codes

Connect the DRB III, or suitably programmed scan tool, to the Data Link Connector (DLC) located near hood release, **Fig. 6.** The diagnostic cycle begins when the ignition is turned On.

Component Testing

POWER STEERING PUMP & GEAR

1. Connect pressure gauge hose from power steering analyzer to tube No. 6865, or equivalent, **Fig. 8.**
2. Connect adapter tool No. 6826, or equivalent, to steering analyzer test valve.
3. Disconnect high pressure hose from steering pump.

4. Connect tube 6865 onto pump hose fitting.
5. Connect power steering hose from steering gear to adapter tool No. 6826, or equivalent.
6. Fully open test valve.
7. Start engine and let idle long enough to circulate fluid pressure test gauge.
8. Turn engine off, then inspect and adjust fluid level.
9. Start engine and allow to idle.
10. If pressure is higher than specified, inspect hoses for restrictions.
11. Close valve fully three times, for no more than three seconds or pump damage could occur.
12. Record highest pressure indicated. All reading must be within 50 psi of each other.
13. Is pressure are not within 50 psi, replace power steering pump.
14. Open test valve and turn steering wheel to extreme lefthand and righthand positions against stops. **Do not force pump to operate against stops for more than 2–4 seconds at a time.**
15. Record highest pressure indicated at each steering stop position. All readings must be within 50 psi of each other. If pressure readings are not as specified, steering gear is leaking internally and must be repaired or replaced.

POWER STEERING SYSTEM BLEED

1. Ensure power steering fluid reservoir is full, then start engine and turn steering wheel from stop to stop approximately 20 times times.
2. Stop engine and inspect fluid level again. Add fluid until proper fluid level is reached.
3. Repeat procedure until fluid level is consistent. Inspect system for leaks.

Component Service

DRIVE PULLEY, REPLACE

REMOVAL

1. Remove power steering pump as outlined under "Power Steering Pump, Replace" in "Front Suspension & Steering" section of "Crossfire" chassis chapter.

2. Mount pump by mounting pump flange boss in suitable vise. **Do not clamp pump body or reservoir in vise.**
3. Remove mounting nut and drive pulley using drive pulley removal tool No. C-4333, or equivalent. **Do not use press or hammer on pump shaft.**

INSTALLATION

1. Place pulley squarely on shaft end and install spacer provided with pump or pulley.
2. Install spacer tool No. 6936, or equivalent, into pulley hub.
3. Thread spacer installation tool No. C-4063, or equivalent, into pump shaft.
4. Holding installer tool with one wrench, turn installer hex down threaded rod pushing pulley onto shaft. Ensure tool and pulley remain aligned.
5. Ensure spacer is fully seated against shaft front, then remove tool and spacer.

PITMAN SHAFT & SEAL, REPLACE

1. Measure distance of point (A) between pitman arm point (2) and steering gear point (1), using caliper gauge, **Fig. 9.**
2. Remove lower snap ring and pitman arm from shaft, **Fig. 10.**
3. Remove pitman shaft seal upper locking ring.
4. Remove pitman shaft seal from steering gear housing using suitable pry tool.
5. Install new seal using seal installer tool No. 9159, or equivalent, **Fig. 11.**
6. Reverse procedures to install.

IDLER ARM, REPLACE

1. Raise and support vehicle.
2. Remove mounting bolt and idler arm drag link, **Fig. 12.**
3. Remove steering linkage heat shield.
4. Remove mounting bolts and idler arm.
5. Remove pinch bolt, and idler arm bushing.
6. Reverse procedure to install.

STEERING DAMPER, REPLACE

1. Remove nut and bolt from steering damper mounting bracket, **Fig. 13.**
2. Remove drag link mounting nut and bolt.
3. Remove steering damper.
4. Reverse procedure to install.

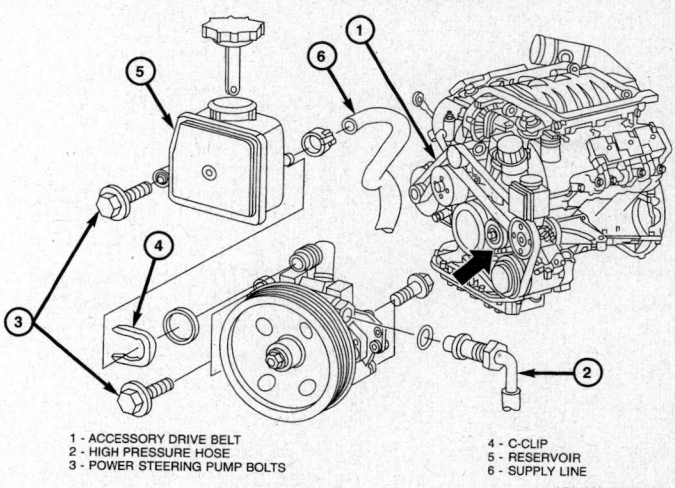

1 - ACCESSORY DRIVE BELT
2 - HIGH PRESSURE HOSE
3 - POWER STEERING PUMP BOLTS
4 - C-CLIP
5 - RESERVOIR
6 - SUPPLY LINE

ARM0300000000035

Fig. 1   Exploded view of power steering pump

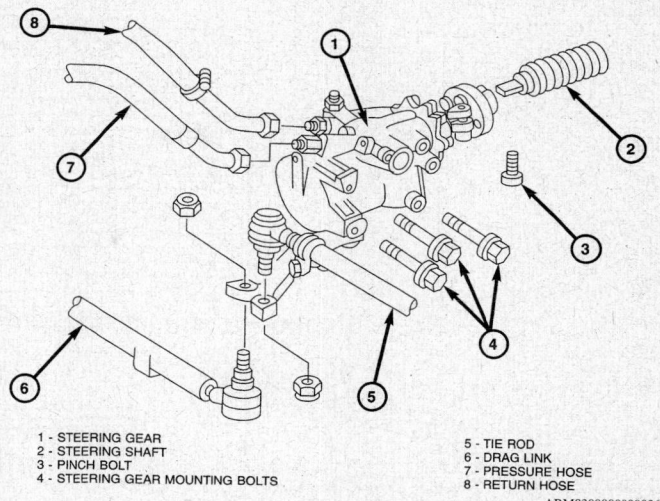

1 - STEERING GEAR
2 - STEERING SHAFT
3 - PINCH BOLT
4 - STEERING GEAR MOUNTING BOLTS
5 - TIE ROD
6 - DRAG LINK
7 - PRESSURE HOSE
8 - RETURN HOSE

ARM0300000000036

Fig. 2   Exploded view of power steering gear

STEERING NOISE

CONDITION	POSSIBLE CAUSES	CORRECTION
HISS OR WHISTLE	1. Steering intermediate shaft to dash panel seal.	1. Check and repair seal at dash panel.
	2. Noisy valve in power steering gear.	2. Replace steering gear.
RATTLE OR CLUNK	1. Gear mounting bolts loose.	1. Tighten bolts to specification.
	2. Loose or damaged suspension components.	2. Inspect and repair suspension.
	3. Loose or damaged steering linkage.	3. Inspect and repair steering linkage.
	4. Internal gear noise.	4. Replace gear.
	5. Pressure hose in contact with other components.	5. Reposition hose.
CHIRP OR SQUEAL	1. Loose belt.	1. Adjust or replace.
	2. Belt routing.	2. Verify belt routing is correct.
WHINE OR GROWL	1. Low fluid level.	1. Fill to proper level.
	2. Pressure hose in contact with other components.	2. Reposition hose.
	3. Internal pump noise.	3. Replace pump.
	4. Air in the system.	4. Perform pump initial operation.
SUCKING AIR SOUND	1. Loose return line clamp.	1. Replace clamp.
	2. O-ring missing or damaged on hose fitting.	2. Replace o-ring.
	3. Low fluid level.	3. Fill to proper level.
	4. Air leak between pump and reservoir.	4. Repair as necessary.
SCRUBBING OR KNOCKING	1. Wrong tire size.	1. Verify tire size.
	2. Wrong gear.	2. Verify gear.

ARM0300000000037

Fig. 3   Steering noise

BINDING AND STICKING

CONDITION	POSSIBLE CAUSE	CORRECTION
DIFFICULT TO TURN WHEEL STICKS OR BINDS	1. Low fluid level.	1. Fill to proper level.
	2. Tire pressure.	2. Adjust tire pressure.
	3. Steering component.	3. Inspect and lube.
	4. Loose belt.	4. Adjust or replace.
	5. Low pump pressure.	5. Pressure test and replace if necessary.
	6. Column shaft coupler binding.	6. Replace coupler.
	7. Steering gear worn or out of adjustment.	7. Repair or replace gear.
	8. Ball joints binding.	8. Inspect and repair as necessary.
	9. Belt routing.	9. Verify belt routing is correct.

INSUFFICIENT ASSISTANCE. OR POOR RETURN TO CENTER

CONDITION	POSSIBLE CAUSE	CORRECTION
HARD TURNING OR MOMENTARY INCREASE IN TURNING EFFORT	1. Tire pressure.	1. Adjust tire pressure.
	2. Low fluid level.	2. Fill to proper level.
	3. Loose belt.	3. Adjust or replace.
	4. Lack of lubrication.	4. Inspect and lubricate steering and suspension components.
	5. Low pump pressure or flow.	5. Pressure and flow test and repair as necessary.
	6. Internal gear leak.	6. Pressure and flow test, and repair as necessary.
	7. Belt routing.	7. Verify belt routing is correct.
STEERING WHEEL DOES NOT WANT TO RETURN TO CENTER POSITION	1. Tire pressure.	1. Adjust tire pressure.
	2. Wheel alignment.	2. Align front end.
	3. Lack of lubrication.	3. Inspect and lubricate steering and suspension components.
	4. High friction in steering gear.	4. Test and adjust as necessary.
	5. Ball joints binding.	5. Inspect and repair as necessary.

Note:
Some roads will cause a vehicle to drift, due to the crown in the road.

ARM0300000000038

Fig. 4   Binding & sticking

CONDITION	POSSIBLE CAUSE	CORRECTION
EXCESSIVE PLAY IN STEERING WHEEL	1. Worn or loose suspension or steering components.	1. Repair as necessary.
	2. Worn or loose wheel bearings.	2. Repair as necessary.
	3. Steering gear mounting.	3. Tighten gear mounting bolts to specification.
	4. Gear out of adjustment.	4. Adjust gear to specification.
	5. Worn or loose steering coupler.	5. Repair as necessary.
VEHICLE PULLS TO ONE SIDE DURING BRAKING	1. Tire Pressure.	1. Adjust tire pressure.
	2. Air in brake hydraulics system.	2. Bleed brake system.
	3. Worn brake components.	3. Repair as necessary.
VEHICLE LEADS OR DRIFTS FROM STRAIGHT AHEAD DIRECTION ON UNCROWNED ROAD.	1. Tire pressure.	1. Adjust tire pressure.
	2. Radial tire lead.	2. Cross front tires.
	3. Brakes dragging.	3. Repair as necessary.
	4. Wheel alignment.	4. Align vehicle.
	5. Weak or broken spring.	5. Replace spring.
	6. Loose or worn steering/suspension components.	6. Repair as necessary.

ARM0300000000039

Fig. 5   Loose steering & vehicle leads or drifts

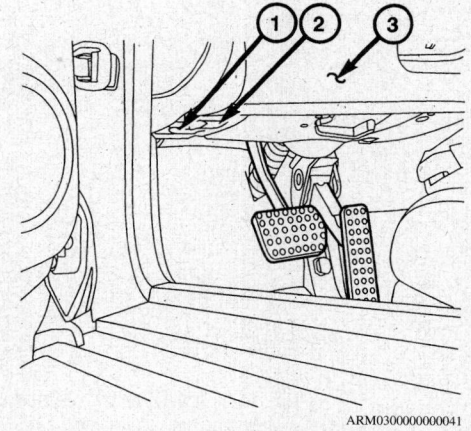

ARM0300000000041

Fig. 6   Data link connector location

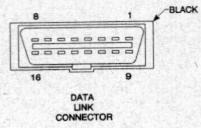

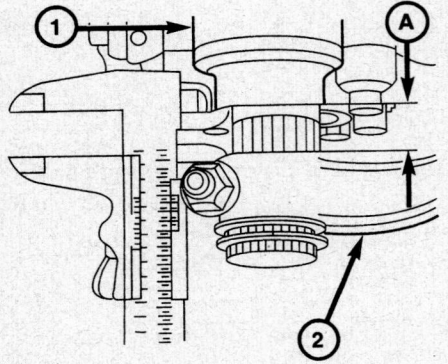

Fig. 7   Connector terminal identification

1. Caliper gauge
2. Steering gear
A. Distance pitman arm

ARM0300000000046

Fig. 9   Pitman arm measurement points

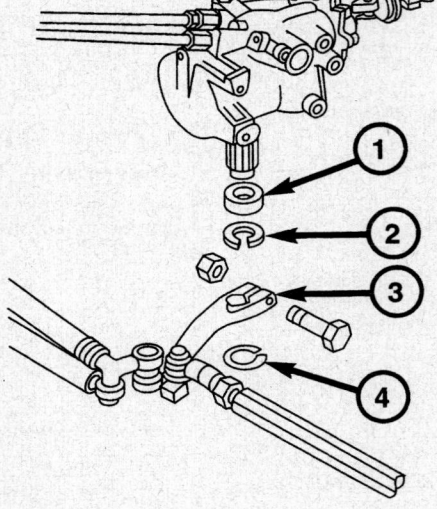
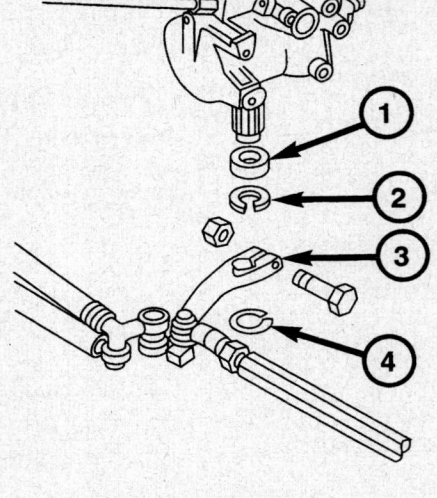

1. Pitman shaft seal
2. Upper locking ring
3. Pitman arm
4. lower snap ring

ARM0300000000047

Fig. 10   Pitman arm shaft & seal replacement

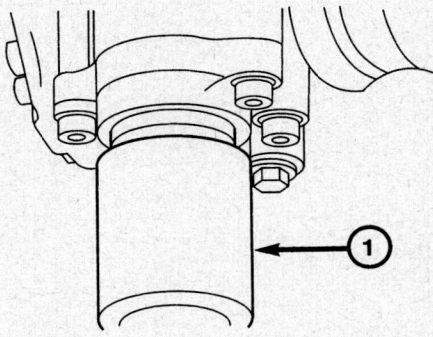

1 Gauge adapter
2 Test valve
3 Gauge assembly
4 Analyzer gauge tubr #6865

ARM0300000000040

Fig. 8   Power steering pump analyzer

1. Pitman seal installer tool No. 9159

ARM0300000000048

Fig. 11   Pitman shaft & seal installation

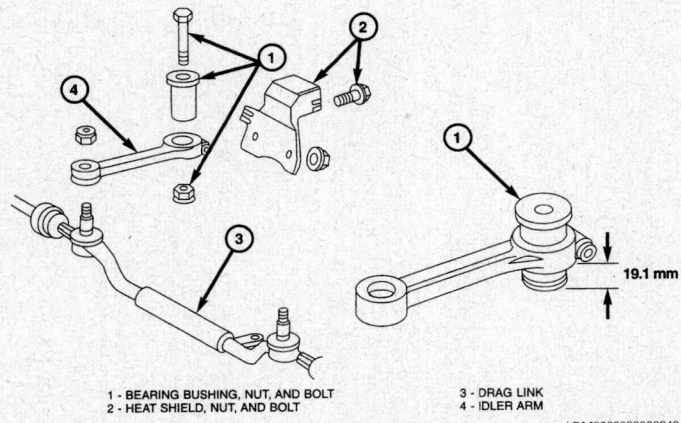

1 - BEARING BUSHING, NUT, AND BOLT
2 - HEAT SHIELD, NUT, AND BOLT
3 - DRAG LINK
4 - IDLER ARM

ARM0300000000049

Fig. 12   Idler arm replacement

19.1 mm

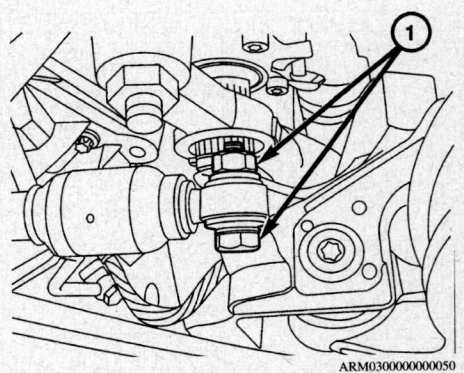

ARM0300000000050

Fig. 13   Steering damper replacement

TIGHTENING SPECIFICATIONS

Year	Component	Torque Ft. Lbs.
2004–07	Air Bag Module	71①
	Draglink To Idler Arm	37
	Draglink To Pitman Arm	37
	Engine Mount	18
	Hose Tube Nuts	22
	Idler Arm	37
	Idler Arm Pinch Bolt	22
	Pitman Arm Pinch Bolt	41
	Power Steering Gear	44
	Power Steering Pump	15
	Power Steering High Pressure Hose	22
	Power Steering Pump Discharge Fitting	30
	Steering Damper	29
	Tie Rod Steering Arm	37

① — Inch lbs.

Charger, Magnum & 300

NOTE: On Air Bag Equipped Models, Refer To "Air Bag System Precautions" Located In The Front Of This Manual For System Disarming & Arming Procedures.

NOTE: Refer To "Computer Relearn Procedures" Located In The Front Of This Manual When Battery Power To The Computer Has Been Interrupted.

INDEX

Page No.		Page No.		Page No.
Description 13-16		Oil Cooler, Replace 13-16		Air Bag Systems 13-16
Power Steering Pressure		Pump Pulley, Replace 13-16		Battery Ground Cable.......... 13-16
Specifications 13-15		Pump, Replace 13-16		**Tightening Specifications** 13-16
Power Steering System Bleed... 13-16		Reservoir, Replace........... 13-16		**Troubleshooting** 13-16
Component Service............. 13-16		**Precautions**....................... 13-16		

POWER STEERING PRESSURE SPECIFICATIONS

Model	Year	Power Steering Pump Pressure, psi		Output Flow, Gallons Per Minute①
		Test Valve	Max Relief Pressure	
		Open	Closed	
Charger, Magnum & 300	2005–08	50–125	1640–1740	1640–1740	2.2

① — At 1100 RPM & minimum pressure.

PRECAUTIONS

Air Bag Systems

Refer to "Air Bag System Precautions" in the front of this manual for system disarming and arming procedures.

Battery Ground Cable

Prior to service, disconnect battery ground cable and isolate as required.

DESCRIPTION

Hydraulic pressure for operation of the power steering gear is provided by a belt-driven all-aluminum power steering pump. A common power steering pump, mounted in a common location (lefthand front of engine), is standard on all models.

TROUBLESHOOTING

Refer to "Concorde, Intrepid & 300M" when troubleshooting the power steering system.

POWER STEERING SYSTEM BLEED

1. Wipe filler cap clean and adjust fluid level. Dipstick should indicate COLD when fluid is at normal temperature.
2. Turn steering wheel all way to left.
3. Adjust pump fluid reservoir to proper level and let fluid settle for at least two minutes.
4. Raise and support front wheels off ground.
5. Slowly turn steering wheel lock-to-lock 20 times with engine off while inspecting fluid level. On vehicles with long return lines or oil coolers turn wheel 40 times.
6. Start engine and idling maintain fluid level.
7. Lower front wheels and let engine idle for two minutes.
8. Turn steering wheel in both direction, then ensure power assist and quiet operation.
9. If fluid is extremely foamy or milky looking, allow vehicle to stand few minutes and repeat procedure.
10. **Do not run vehicle with foamy fluid for extended period.**

Component Service

PUMP, REPLACE

1. Siphon power steering fluid from pump reservoir.
2. Remove air cleaner housing and inlet tube to throttle body.
3. Remove serpentine drive belt as outlined under "Serpentine Drive Belt, Replace" in appropriate "Engine" section of "Charger, Magnum & 300" chassis chapter.
4. Remove pressure and supply hoses from pump.
5. Remove pump mounting bolts, then pump.
6. Reverse procedure to install.

PUMP PULLEY, REPLACE

DISASSEMBLY

1. Remove power steering pump as outlined under "Pump, Replace."
2. Secure pump in suitable vise.
3. Remove pulley from pump using tool No. C–4333, or equivalent puller.

ASSEMBLY

1. Place power steering pump pulley squarely on end of power steering pump shaft.
2. Install pulley on to pump using tool Nos. 6936 and C–4036C, or suitable pulley installation tool.
3. Install pump to engine.

OIL COOLER, REPLACE

1. Siphon power steering fluid from pump reservoir.
2. Raise and support vehicle.
3. Remove mounting screws and belly pan.
4. Remove clamps, then return hose from steering gear at cooler and to reservoir at cooler.
5. Push in on clip tabs and remove cooler from clips mounted to cooling module.
6. Reverse procedure to install.

RESERVOIR, REPLACE

1. Siphon power steering fluid from pump reservoir.
2. Remove air cleaner housing and inlet tube to throttle body.
3. Remove clamps, then the reservoir supply and return hoses.
4. Remove reservoir from coolant bottle by sliding it out of guide.
5. Reverse procedure to install.

TIGHTENING SPECIFICATIONS

Year	Component	Torque Ft. Lbs.
2005–08	Hose Tube	35
	Outer Tie Rod Ball Joint	63
	Power Steering Gear, AWD	75
	Power Steering Gear, RWD	70
	Power Steering Pump	21
	Tie Rod Jam Nut	55

Neon & 2004–06 Sebring Convertible, Sebring Sedan & Stratus Sedan

NOTE: On Air Bag Equipped Models, Refer To "Air Bag System Precautions" Located In The Front Of This Manual For System Disarming & Arming Procedures.

NOTE: Refer To "Computer Relearn Procedures" Located In The Front Of This Manual When Battery Power To The Computer Has Been Interrupted.

INDEX

	Page No.
Description	13-17
Diagnosis & Testing	13-17
Accessing Diagnostic Trouble Codes	13-17
Clearing Diagnostic Trouble Codes	13-18
Connector Terminal Identification	13-17
Diagnostic Tests	13-18

	Page No.
Power Steering Pressure Specifications	13-17
Power Steering System Bleed	13-18
Component Service	13-18
Power Steering Pressure Switch, Replace	13-18
Solenoid Control Module, Replace	13-18
Solenoid Control Valve, Replace	13-18

	Page No.
Pump Pressure Inspection	13-18
Non-Variable & Electronically Controlled Variable Assist	13-18
Precautions	13-17
Air Bag Systems	13-17
Battery Ground Cable	13-17
Tightening Specifications	13-20
Troubleshooting	13-17

POWER STEERING PRESSURE SPECIFICATIONS

Model	Year	Power Steering Pump Pressure, psi		Output Flow, Gallons Per Minute③
		Test Valve	Max Relief Pressure	
		Open①	Closed		
Neon	2004–05	50–80	1350–1450②	1350–1450	1.5–1.7
Sebring Convertible, Sebring Sedan & Stratus Sedan	2004–06	50–80	1195–1293	1195–1293	1.3–1.6

① — Initial pressure.

② — Do not leave valve closed for more than five seconds.

③ — At 1500 RPM & minimum pressure.

PRECAUTIONS

Air Bag Systems

Refer to "Air Bag System Precautions" in the front of this manual for system disarming and arming procedures.

Battery Ground Cable

Prior to service, disconnect battery ground cable and isolate as required.

DESCRIPTION

The steering gear is a rack and pinion type using power assist. These models have two versions depending upon production date. Early production models have two parallel flats on end where steering column intermediate shaft would bolt up. Later production models have two flats that are at 60° angles to one another where steering column intermediate shaft would bolt up.

The hydraulic pressure for operation of the power steering gear is provided by a belt driven power steering pump. Early production models are equipped with variable assist power steering pumps. Later production models are equipped with standard power steering pumps only.

TROUBLESHOOTING

Refer to "Concorde, Intrepid & 300M" when troubleshooting the power steering system.

DIAGNOSIS & TESTING

Accessing Diagnostic Trouble Codes

Connect DRB III, or suitable programmed scan tool, to the Data Link Connector (DLC), **Fig. 1.** The diagnostic cycle begins when the ignition is turned On.

Connector Terminal Identification

Refer to **Fig. 2** for connector terminal identification.

POWER STEERING

Diagnostic Tests

Refer to **Figs. 3 and 4** for diagnostic and testing procedures.

Clearing Diagnostic Trouble Codes

Connect DRB III, or suitable programmed scan tool, to the Data Link Connector (DLC), **Fig. 1**. The diagnostic cycle begins when the ignition is turned On.

POWER STEERING SYSTEM SERVICE

POWER STEERING SYSTEM BLEED

To avoid personal injury, power steering fluid level should be inspected with engine Off. Use only approved fluid. Do not use automatic transmission fluid. Do not overfill fluid system.

1. Wipe filler cap clean and inspect fluid level.
2. Dipstick should indicate Full Cold when fluid is at normal temperature, approximately 70–80° F.
3. Fill power steering pump fluid reservoir to proper level with approved power steering fluid.
4. Start and run engine for few seconds, then turn engine Off.
5. Adjust fluid level.
6. Repeat previous procedure until fluid level remains constant after running engine.
7. Raise front wheels off ground and start engine.
8. Slowly turn steering wheel to lefthand and righthand sides lightly contacting wheel stops.
9. Turn engine off and adjust fluid level.
10. Lower vehicle and start engine.
11. Turn steering wheel slowly from lock to lock.
12. Stop engine and adjust fluid level.
13. If fluid is extremely foamy, wait few minutes, then repeat entire bleeding procedure.

Pump Pressure Inspection

NON-VARIABLE & ELECTRONICALLY CONTROLLED VARIABLE ASSIST

1. Disconnect power steering fluid pressure hose at power steering pump.
2. Connect inlet hose on pressure gauge tool No. 6815, or equivalent, using suit-

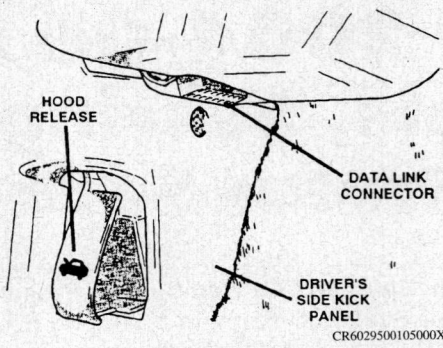

Fig. 1   DLC location

able adapter to pressure fitting on power steering pump.

3. Connect pressure hose power steering pump to outlet port of pressure gauge using suitable adapter fitting. **Pressure gauge is to be installed in series with power steering pressure hose, between pump and steering gear. It must also be installed so it is in proper direction of fluid flow.**
4. Completely open valve on gauge.
5. Start engine and let idle long enough to circulate fluid through flow/pressure test and get air out of fluid.
6. Turn off engine and adjust inspect fluid level.
7. Start engine. Pressure gauge should read less than 125 psi. If reading is more than specified, inspect hoses for restrictions.
8. Initial pressure reading should be 50–80 psi and flow meter should read 1.3–1.6 GPM.
9. Close pressure gauge valve fully three times and record highest pressure each time. Readings must be more than specified and within 50 psi of each other. **Do not leave valve closed for more than five seconds as pump could be damaged.**
10. Open test valve, then turn steering wheel to lefthand and righthand sides until it stops, recording highest pressure at each position. **Do not force pump to operate against stops for more than 2–4 seconds as pump damage will result.**
11. Compare pressure gauge readings to specifications.
12. If highest output pressures are not same against either stop, steering gear is leaking internally and must be replaced.

Component Service

POWER STEERING PRESSURE SWITCH, REPLACE

1. Raise and support vehicle.
2. Disconnect its electrical connector.

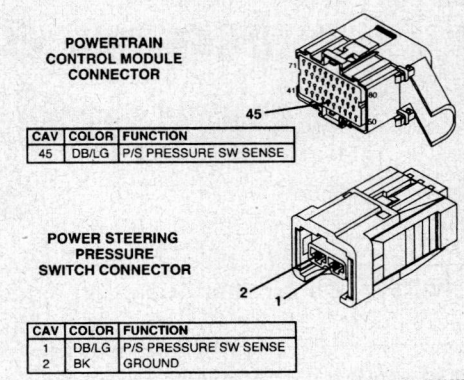

Fig. 2   Connector terminal identification

3. Remove pressure switch from steering gear using crowfoot and long extension, **Fig. 5**.
4. Reverse procedure to install, noting the following:
   a. Install and hand tighten switch into gear until fully seated.
   b. Tighten switch using crowfoot and extension. **Do not overtighten.**
   c. Connect pressure switch electrical connector, ensuring latch is securely engaged with locking tab.

SOLENOID CONTROL MODULE, REPLACE

1. Disconnect solenoid control module electrical connectors, **Fig. 6**.
2. Unclip locking tab, holding module to fluid lines, on bottom side of control module.
3. Rotate module upward and remove two upper attaching clips from steering gear, **Fig. 7**.
4. Reverse procedure to install.

SOLENOID CONTROL VALVE, REPLACE

1. Remove steering gear as outlined under "Power Steering Gear, Replace" in "Front Suspension & Steering" section of appropriate chassis chapter.
2. Disconnect solenoid control valve electrical connector at solenoid control module, **Fig. 7**.
3. Remove solenoid from steering gear using suitable crowfoot, **Fig. 8**.
4. Reverse procedure to install, noting the following:
   a. Coat O-ring seals with suitable, fresh, clean power steering fluid prior.
   b. Install solenoid control valve by hand until fully seated, then using crowfoot tool to tighten.

POSSIBLE CAUSES
POWER STEERING PRESSURE SWITCH OPERATION
GROUND CIRCUIT
POWER STEERING PRESSURE SWITCH SENSE CIRCUIT SHORTED TO GROUND
POWER STEERING PRESSURE SENSE CIRCUIT OPEN
PCM

TEST	ACTION
1	Turn the ignition off. Disconnect the Power Steering Pressure Switch harness connector. Turn the ignition on. With the DRBIII®, monitor the Power Steering Pressure Switch. Using a jumper wire, connect one end to the Power Steering Pressure Switch Sense circuit. With the other end of the jumper tap the ground circuit in the Power Steering Pressure Switch harness connector. Does the Power Steering Pressure Switch display change from HI to LOW? Yes → Replace the Power Steering Pressure Switch Perform POWERTRAIN VERIFICATION TEST VER - 5. No → Go To 2
2	Turn the ignition off. Disconnect Power Steering Pressure Switch harness connector. Using a 12-volt test light connected to 12-volts, probe the ground circuit in the Power Steering Pressure Switch harness connector. Does the test light illuminate? Yes → Go To 3 No → Repair the ground circuit for an open. Perform POWERTRAIN VERIFICATION TEST VER - 5.

CR6020100222010X

Fig. 3 DTC P0551: Power Steering Switch Failure (Part 1 of 2)

TEST	ACTION
3	Turn the ignition off. Disconnect the Power Steering Pressure Switch harness connector. Disconnect the PCM harness connector. Measure the resistance of the Power Steering Pressure Switch Sense circuit in the PSP Switch harness connector to ground. Is the resistance below 100 ohms? Yes → Repair the Power Steering Pressure Sense circuit for a short to ground. Perform POWERTRAIN VERIFICATION TEST VER - 5. No → Go To 4
4	Turn the ignition off. Disconnect the Power Steering Pressure Switch harness connector. Disconnect the PCM harness connector. Measure the resistance of the Power Steering Pressure Switch Sense circuit between the PSP Switch harness connector and the PCM harness connector. Is the resistance below 5.0 ohms? Yes → Go To 5 No → Repair the Power Steering Pressure Sense circuit for an open. Perform POWERTRAIN VERIFICATION TEST VER - 5.
5	If there are no possible causes remaining, view repair. Repair Replace and program the Powertrain Control Module in accordance with the Service Information. Perform POWERTRAIN VERIFICATION TEST VER - 5.

CR6020100222020X

Fig. 3 DTC P0551: Power Steering Switch Failure (Part 2 of 2)

POWERTRAIN VERIFICATION TEST VER - 5
1. NOTE: If the PCM has been replaced and the correct VIN and mileage have not been programmed, a DTC will be set in the ABS Module, Airbag Module and the SKIM. 2. NOTE: If the vehicle is equipped with a Sentry Key Immobilizer System, Secret Key data must be updated. Refer to the Service Information for the PCM, SKIM and the Transponder (ignition key) for programming information. 3. Inspect the vehicle to ensure that all engine components are properly installed and connected. Reassemble and reconnect components as necessary. 4. Connect the DRBIII® to the data link connector. 5. Ensure the fuel tank has at least a quarter tank of fuel. Turn off all accessories. 6. If a Comprehensive Component DTC was repaired, perform steps 5 - 8. If a Major OBDII Monitor DTC was repaired skip those steps and continue verification. 7. After the ignition has been off for at least 10 seconds, restart the vehicle and run 2 minutes. 8. If the Good Trip counter changed to one or more and there are no new DTC's, the repair was successful and is now complete. Erase DTC's and disconnect the DRBIII®. 9. If the repaired DTC has reset, the repair is not complete. Check for any related TSB's or flash updates and return to the Symptom list. 10. If another DTC has set, return to the Symptom List and follow the path specified for that DTC. 11. With the DRBIII®, monitor the appropriate pre-test enabling conditions until all conditions have been met. Once the conditions have been met, switch screen to the appropriate OBDII monitor, (Audible beeps when the monitor is running). 12. If the monitor ran, and the Good Trip counter changed to one or more, the repair was successful and is now complete. Erase DTC's and disconnect the DRBIII®. 13. If the repaired OBDII trouble code has reset or was seen in the monitor while on the road test, the repair is not complete. Check for any related technical service bulletins or flash updates and return to Symptom List. 14. If another DTC has set, return to the Symptom List and follow the path specified for that DTC. Are any DTCs present? Yes → Repair is not complete, refer to appropriate symptom. No → Repair is complete.

CR6020100223000X

Fig. 4 Verification Test VER-5

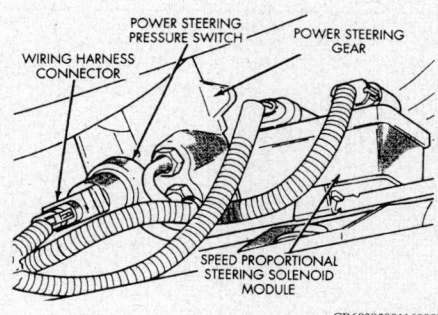

CR6029500116000X

Fig. 5 Pressure switch replacement

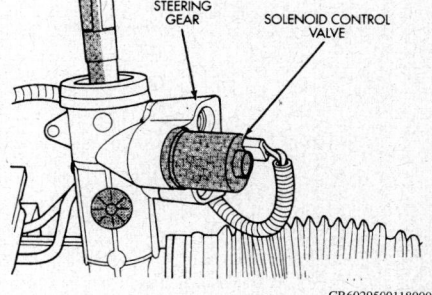

CR6029500118000X

Fig. 6 Solenoid module electrical connectors

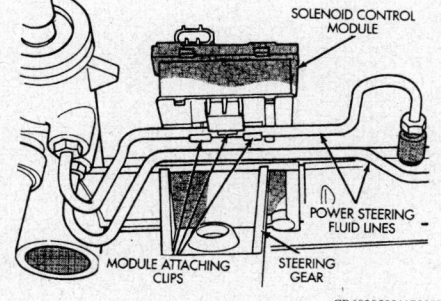

CR6029500117000X

Fig. 7 Solenoid control module replacement

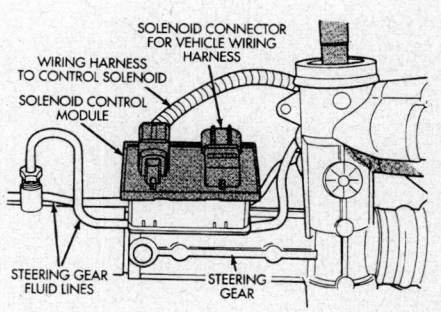

CR6029500119000X

Fig. 8 Solenoid control valve replacement

TIGHTENING SPECIFICATIONS

Year	Component	Torque Ft. Lbs.
2004–06	Air Bag Module	90①
	Flex Coupler	12
	Outer To Inner Tie Rod Jam Nut	55
	Power Steering Fluid Hose Banjo Fitting	33
	Power Steering Fluid Hose Pressure Hose To Return Hose Bracket	75①
	Power Steering Fluid Hose Return Hose Bracket To Head	21
	Power Steering Fluid Hose Tube Nuts	23
	Power Steering Fluid Reservoir	21
	Power Steering Pump Bracket To Engine	40
	Power Steering Pump Discharge Fitting	55
	Steering Column Mounting Bracket	105①
	Steering Gear To Crossmember	50
	Steering Wheel	45
	Tie Rod To Steering Knuckle	45

① — Inch lbs.

Sebring Coupe & Stratus Coupe

NOTE: On Air Bag Equipped Models, Refer To "Air Bag System Precautions" Located In The Front Of This Manual For System Disarming & Arming Procedures.

NOTE: Refer To "Computer Relearn Procedures" Located In The Front Of This Manual When Battery Power To The Computer Has Been Interrupted.

INDEX

	Page No.
Description	13-21
Diagnosis & Testing	13-21
Accessing Diagnostic Trouble Codes	13-21
Clearing Diagnostic Trouble Codes	13-21
Component Testing	13-21
No-Load Condition Pressure Test	13-21

	Page No.
Oil Pump Relief Pressure Test	13-21
Power Steering Pressure Switch Inspection	13-22
Steering Gear Retention Hydraulic Pressure Test	13-22
Connector Terminal Identification	13-21
Diagnostic Tests	13-21

	Page No.
Power Steering Pressure Specifications	13-21
Power Steering System Bleed	13-22
Precautions	13-21
Air Bag Systems	13-21
Battery Ground Cable	13-21
Tightening Specifications	13-24

POWER STEERING PRESSURE SPECIFICATIONS

Model	Year	Power Steering Pump Pressure, psi			Output Flow, Gallons Per Minute①
		Test Valve		Max Relief Pressure	
		Open	Closed②		
Sebring Coupe & Stratus Coupe	2004–05	116–145	1209–1280	1209–1280	—

① — At 1500 RPM & minimum pressure.

② — At 1000 RPM & minimum pressure.

PRECAUTIONS
Air Bag Systems

Refer to "Air Bag System Precautions" in the front of this manual for system disarming and arming procedures.

Battery Ground Cable

Prior to service, disconnect battery ground cable and isolate as required.

DESCRIPTION

The type of power steering which is responsive to engine speed has been added to all models. The steering column has a shock absorber mechanism and a tilt steering mechanism.

A vane type oil pump with fluid flow control system has been added to all models. The steering gear and linkage is an integral rack and pinion type.

DIAGNOSIS & TESTING
Accessing Diagnostic Trouble Codes

Connect DRB III, or suitable programmed scan tool, to the Data Link Connector (DLC) under the lefthand side of the instrument panel near the hood release. The diagnostic cycle begins when the ignition is turned On.

Connector Terminal Identification

Refer to **Fig. 1** for connector terminal identifications.

Diagnostic Tests

Refer to "Neon & 2004–06 Sebring Convertible, Sebring Sedan & Stratus Sedan" for power steering system diagnostic tests.

Clearing Diagnostic Trouble Codes

Connect DRB III, or suitable programmed scan tool, to the Data Link Connector (DLC) under the lefthand side of the instrument panel near the hood release. The diagnostic cycle begins when the ignition is turned On.

Component Testing
OIL PUMP RELIEF PRESSURE TEST

1. Disconnect pressure hose and connect oil pump pressure test tools, **Fig. 2**.
2. Bleed air, then turn steering wheel several times while vehicle is not moving.
3. Start engine and idle at 900–1100 RPM.
4. Fully close shutoff valve on pressure gauge, and measure oil pump relief pressure. **Pressure gauge shutoff valve must not remain closed for more than 10 seconds.**
5. If pressure is not as specified, replace oil pump.
6. Remove pressure test tools.

NO-LOAD CONDITION PRESSURE TEST

1. Disconnect pressure hose from oil pump and connect no-load condition pressure test tool, **Fig. 3**.
2. Bleed air, then turn steering wheel several times while vehicle is not moving so fluid temperature rises.
3. Start engine and idle at 900–1100 RPM.
4. Inspect and ensure hydraulic pressure is at standard value of 116–145 psi

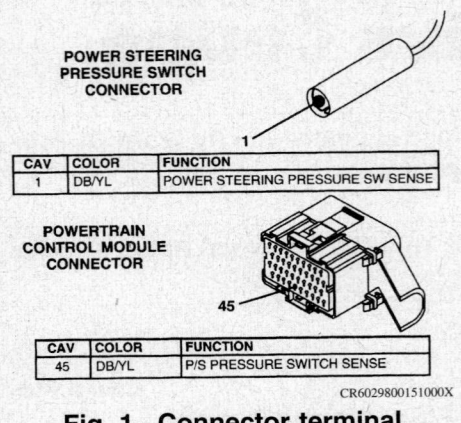

CAV	COLOR	FUNCTION
1	DB/YL	POWER STEERING PRESSURE SW SENSE

CAV	COLOR	FUNCTION
45	DB/YL	P/S PRESSURE SWITCH SENSE

CR6029800151000X

Fig. 1 Connector terminal identification

when no-load conditions are created by fully opening pressure gauge shut-off valve.
5. If pressure is not as specified, condition's probable cause is oil line or steering gearbox. Inspect and repair as required.

STEERING GEAR RETENTION HYDRAULIC PRESSURE TEST

1. Disconnect pressure hose from oil pump and connect retention hydraulic pressure test tools, **Fig. 4.**
2. Bleed air, then turn steering wheel several times while vehicle is not moving so fluid temperature rises.
3. Start engine, then idle at 900–1100 RPM.
4. Fully close, then fully open shutoff valve on pressure gauge.
5. Turn steering wheel all way to lefthand or righthand sides and record retention hydraulic pressure.
6. If pressure is not within standard value, overhaul steering gearbox.

POWER STEERING PRESSURE SWITCH INSPECTION

1. Disconnect pressure hose from oil pump and connect power steering pressure switch test tools, **Fig. 5.**
2. Bleed air, then turn steering wheel several times while vehicle is not moving so fluid temperature rises.
3. Idle engine.
4. Disconnect pressure switch connector and connect suitable ohmmeter.
5. Gradually close shutoff valve at pres-

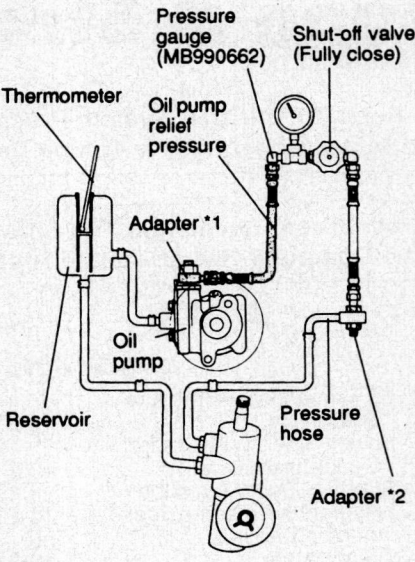

NOTE
*1: MB990993 or MB991217 <SOHC>
    MB991548 <DOHC>

*2: MB990994 <SOHC>
    MB991549 <DOHC>

CR6029500087000X

Fig. 2 Oil pump relief pressure test tool installation

sure gauge and increase hydraulic pressure.
6. Turn steering wheel all way to lefthand or righthand sides and record retention hydraulic pressure.
7. Ensure pressures are within specifications.
8. Gradually open shutoff valve and reduce hydraulic pressure.
9. Ensure hydraulic pressure deactivates switch at standard value of 116–348 psi.
10. Remove tools and tighten pressure hose.

POWER STEERING SYSTEM BLEED

1. Raise and support front wheels.
2. Manually turn oil pump pulley several times.
3. Turn steering wheel all way lefthand and righthand side 5–6 times.
4. Disconnect high-tension cable and crank starter motor intermittently, while

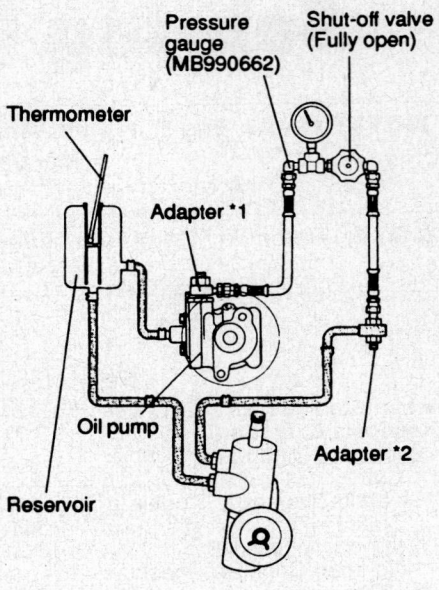

NOTE
*1: MB990993 or MB991217 <SOHC>
    MB991548 <DOHC>

*2: MB990994 <SOHC>
    MB991549 <DOHC>

CR6029500088000X

Fig. 3 No-load pressure test tool installation

turning steering wheel fully to lefthand and righthand sides 5–6 times for 15–20 seconds.
5. Refill fluid supply during air bleeding so level never falls below lower position of filter.
6. If air bleeding is done while engine is running, air will be broken up and absorbed into fluid. Ensure bleeding is done only while cranking.
7. Connect high-tension cable and start engine.
8. Turn steering wheel to lefthand and righthand sides until there are no air bubbles in reservoir.
9. Ensure fluid is not milky and adjust inspect fluid level.
10. Ensure level does not change when steering wheel is turned to lefthand or righthand sides.
11. Ensure level is within .2 inch when engine is stopped compared to when it is running.
12. If fluid level variation is more than .2 inch, air still exists in system, requiring additional bleeding.

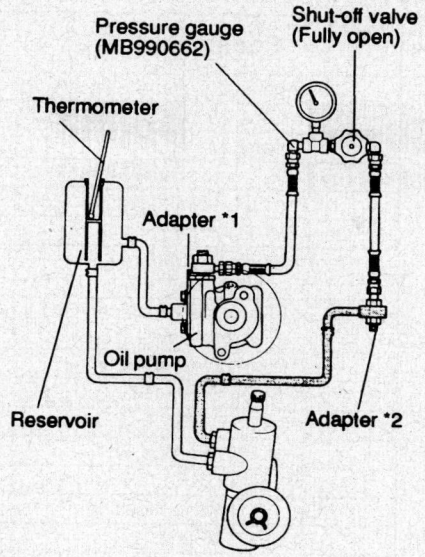

NOTE
*1: MB990993 or MB991217 <SOHC>
    MB991548 <DOHC>

*2: MB990994 <SOHC>
    MB991549 <DOHC>

CR6029500089000X

**Fig. 4 Retention pressure test
        tool installation**

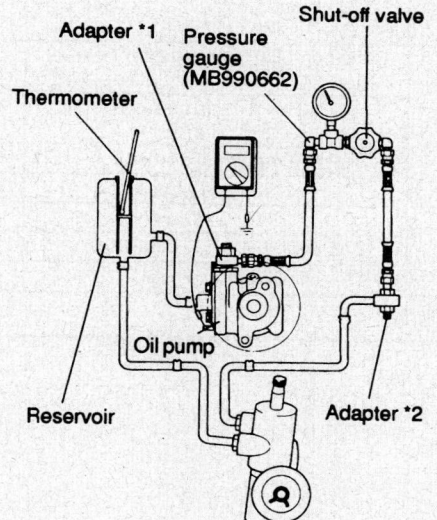

NOTE
*1: MB990993 or MB991217 <SOHC>
    MB991548 <DOHC>

*2: MB990994 <SOHC>
    MB991549 <DOHC>

CR6029500090000X

**Fig. 5 Pressure switch test tool
        installation**

TIGHTENING SPECIFICATIONS

Year	Component	Torque Ft. Lbs.
2004–05	Clockspring & Column Switch	18
	Gear Box Cylinder Clamp	51
	Gear Box End Plug	44
	Gear Box Feed Tube Flare	10
	Gear Box Pinion & Valve	18
	Gear Box Rack Support Cover	109①
	Gear Box Rack Support Cover, Jam Nut	44
	Gear Box Return & Pressure Hose Flare Nut	11
	Gear Box Stay (2.4L Engine)	55
	Gear Box Steering Shaft & Gear Box	13
	Gear Box Tie Rod	65
	Gear Box Tie Rod End	38
	Gear Box Tie Rod End To Knuckle	21
	Gear Box Valve Housing	14
	Hose Oil Pump Eye	42
	Hose Oil Reservoir & Pressure Hose	100①
	Hose Pressure Tube Flare, Gear Box Side	107①
	Hose Pressure Tube Flare, Pressure Hose Side	11
	Hose Return Tube & Cooler Tube	100①
	Oil Pump (3.0L Engine)	31
	Oil Pump Bracket (2.4L Engine)	36
	Oil Pump Bracket (3.0L Engine)	17
	Oil Pump Eye Bolt	42
	Oil Pump Front/Rear Bracket (3.0L Engine)	12
	Oil Pump Oil Pump Bracket Bolt M8 (2.4L)	21
	Oil Pump Pressure Hose (2.4L Engine)	100①
	Oil Pump Pressure Switch	15
	Steering Column	100①
	Steering Cover	44①
	Steering Shaft & Gear Box	13
	Steering Wheel	31

① — Inch lbs.

DISC BRAKES

TABLE OF CONTENTS

Page No.

CALIBER, 2007–08 AVENGER
SEDAN & SEBRING SEDAN 14-1
CHARGER, MAGNUM & 300 ... 14-12
CONCORDE, INTREPID &
300M 14-5
CROSSFIRE 14-9

Page No.

NEON 14-15
SEBRING CONVERTIBLE,
STRATUS SEDAN & 2004–06
SEBRING SEDAN 14-17
SEBRING COUPE & STRATUS
COUPE 14-20

Caliber, 2007–08 Avenger Sedan & Sebring Sedan

NOTE: On Air Bag Equipped Models, Refer To "Air Bag System Precautions" Located In The Front Of This Manual For System Disarming & Arming Procedures.

NOTE: Refer To "Computer Relearn Procedures" Located In The Front Of This Manual When Battery Power To The Computer Has Been Interrupted.

INDEX

Page No.

Adjustments 14-3
　Parking Brake 14-3
Brake Pad Service.............. 14-1
　Front 14-1
　Rear......................... 14-1
Brake System Bleed............. 14-1
Caliper Service 14-2

Page No.

Overhaul 14-2
　Assemble..................... 14-2
　Disassemble.................. 14-2
　Replacement 14-2
Description 14-1
Disc Brake Specifications 14-4
　Rotor Specifications 14-4

Page No.

Parking Brake Service........... 14-3
　Shoe 14-3
Rotor, Replace.................. 14-3
　Front 14-3
　Rear........................ 14-3
Tightening Specifications 14-4
Troubleshooting 14-1

DESCRIPTION

The hydraulic brake system is diagonally split for both the non-anti-lock and anti-lock braking systems. That means the left front and right rear brakes are on one hydraulic circuit and the right front and left rear are on the other.

Front disc brakes control the braking of the front wheels; rear braking is controlled by rear drum brakes as standard equipment. Rear disc brakes and anti-lock brakes with or without traction control are optional.

Vehicles equipped with the optional anti-lock brake system (ABS) use a system that shares most base brake hardware used on vehicles without ABS.

The parking brake system consists of a hand-operated lever mounted between the front seats that actuates parking brake cables connecting to the rear brakes.

TROUBLESHOOTING

Refer to **Fig. 1** for system troubleshooting.

BRAKE SYSTEM BLEED

Refer to "Hydraulic Brake Systems" chapter for brake system bleeding procedures.

BRAKE PAD SERVICE

FRONT

1. Raise and support vehicle, then remove wheel and tire assembly.
2. Retract caliper piston in bore by grasping rear of caliper and pulling outward working with guide pins. **Never push on piston directly.**
3. Remove two brake caliper guide pin bolts. When removing caliper guide pin bolts, note that upper bolt has a special sleeve on end. It important that this bolt be installed in the upper mounting hole when caliper is installed.
4. Remove brake caliper and position aside. **Do not overextend brake hose.**
5. Remove brake pads from caliper.
6. Reverse procedure to install, noting the following:
   a. Use hand pressure or suitable C-clamp to retract piston, first placing wood block over piston.
   b. Place pad with wear indicator attached on inboard side.

REAR

1. Raise and support vehicle, then remove wheel and tire assembly.

RED BRAKE WARNING INDICATOR

CONDITION	POSSIBLE CAUSES	CORRECTION
RED BRAKE WARNING INDICATOR ON	1. Parking brake lever not fully released.	1. Release parking brake lever.
	2. Parking brake warning switch on parking brake lever.	2. Inspect and replace switch as necessary.
	3. Brake fluid level low in reservoir.	3. Fill reservoir. Check entire system for leaks. Repair or replace as required.
	4. Brake fluid level switch.	4. Disconnect switch wiring connector. If lamp goes out, replace switch.
	5. Mechanical instrument cluster (MIC) problem.	5. Refer to appropriate diagnostic information.
	6. ABS EVBP malfunction.	6. Refer to ABS and appropriate diagnostic information.

BRAKE NOISE

CONDITION	POSSIBLE CAUSES	CORRECTION
DISC BRAKE CHIRP	1. Excessive brake rotor runout.	1. Diagnose and correct as necessary.
DISC BRAKE MOAN OR HOWL WHILE BRAKING IN REVERSE	1. Rear disc brake caliper guide pin bolts installed in incorrect locations.	1. Remove lower guide pin bolt and inspect for special sleeve on tip. If sleeve is present, remove upper and lower guide pin bolts and install special sleeved bolt in upper location and standard guide pin bolt in lower location. Perform on both sides of vehicle as necessary.
DISC BRAKE RATTLE OR CLUNK	1. Broken or missing spring clips.	1. Replace brake pads.
	2. Caliper guide pin bolts loose.	2. Tighten guide pin bolts.
	3. Missing abutment shims.	3. Replace missing abutment shims.

ARM0600000000410

Fig. 1   Brake system troubleshooting (Part 1 of 5)

	POSSIBLE CAUSES	CORRECTION
DISC BRAKE SQUEAK AT LOW SPEED (WHILE APPLYING LIGHT BRAKE PEDAL EFFORT)	1. Brake shoe linings.	1. Replace brake pads.
DRUM BRAKE CHIRP	1. Lack of lubricant on brake shoe support plate where shoes ride.	1. Lubricate shoe contact areas on brake shoe support plates.
	2. Wheel cylinder out of alignment.	2. Loosen wheel cylinder mounting bolts, realign wheel cylinder with brake shoes and tighten mounting bolts.
DRUM BRAKE CLUNK	1. Drum(s) have threaded machined braking surface.	1. Reface or replace brake drums as necessary.
DRUM BRAKE HOWL OR MOAN	1. Lack of lubricant on brake shoe support plate where shoes ride and at the anchor.	1. Lubricate shoe contact areas on brake shoe support plates and at the anchor.
	2. Rear brake shoes.	2. Replace rear brake shoes.
SCRAPING (METAL-TO-METAL).	1. Foreign object interference with brakes.	1. Inspect brakes and remove foreign object.
	2. Brake pads/shoes worn out.	2. Replace brake pads/shoes. Inspect rotors and drums. Reface or replace as necessary.
SCRAPING OR WHIRRING	1. ABS wheel speed sensor hitting tone wheel.	1. Inspect, correct or replace faulty component(s).

ARM0600000000411

Fig. 1   Brake system troubleshooting (Part 2 of 5)

9. Clean piston bore and drilled passage ways with alcohol, or suitable solvent.
10. Wipe it dry using only a lint-free cloth.
11. Inspect both piston and bore for scoring or pitting. **Do not hone caliper bore.**

ASSEMBLE

1. Lubricate caliper piston, piston seal and piston bore with suitable, clean, fresh brake fluid.
2. Install new piston seal in groove. Seal should be started at one area of groove and gently worked around and into groove using only clean fingers to seat it.
3. Install new dust boot on piston and work boot lip into groove at top of piston.
4. Stretch boot downward, straightening boot folds, then move boot back upward until folds snap uniformly into place.
5. Install piston into bore, pressing piston down to bottom of bore using hand-pressure.
6. Push piston in until it bottoms in caliper bore and dust boot lip seal falls into groove near top of piston.
7. Install caliper on vehicle and bleed brakes as required.

2. Remove disc brake caliper lower guide pin bolt.
3. Rotate caliper upward hinging off upper guide pin bolt. **Do not overextend brake hose.**
4. Remove inboard then outboard brake pads from caliper.
5. Reverse procedure to install.

CALIPER SERVICE

Replacement

1. Depress brake pedal past its first inch of travel and hold it in position using brake pedal holding tool.
2. Raise and support vehicle, then remove tire and wheel assembly.
3. Remove banjo bolt connecting flexible brake hose to caliper.
4. Remove caliper guide pin bolts, noting location for replacement.
5. Remove brake caliper from brake adapter and pads.
6. Reverse procedure to install, noting the following:
   a. Install new washers on each side of hose fitting as banjo bolt is placed through fitting.

Overhaul

DISASSEMBLE

1. Drain brake fluid from caliper into suitable container.
2. Mount caliper in suitable vise equipped with protective jaws.
3. Place suitable wooden block (padded with approximately one-inch thickness of shop towels) in front of caliper piston.
4. Padded block should be sized to allow piston to push out of bore far enough to be removed by hand after being loosened by air pressure, yet large enough to keep piston from coming completely out.
5. Apply low pressure compressed air to caliper fluid inlet in short spurts to ease piston out of bore. **Do not use high pressure.**
6. Remove piston from caliper.
7. Remove and discard dust boot using suitable tool.
8. Work piston seal out of groove caliper piston bore using suitable, soft tool such as plastic trim stick. **Do not use screw driver or other metal tool for seal removal.**

CONDITION	POSSIBLE CAUSES	CORRECTION
BRAKES CHATTER	1. Rear brake drum out of round or disc brake rotor has excessive thickness variation.	1. Isolate condition as rear or front. Reface or replace brake drums or rotors as necessary.
BRAKES DRAG (FRONT OR ALL)	1. Contaminated brake fluid.	1. Check for swollen seals. Replace all system components containing rubber.
	2. Binding caliper pins or bushings.	2. Replace pins and bushings
	3. Misadjusted brake lamp switch.	3. Replace brake lamp switch.
	4. Master cylinder not fully returning.	4. Inspect master cylinder and replace as necessary.
	5. Binding brake pedal.	5. Replace brake pedal/bushings.
BRAKES DRAG (REAR ONLY)	1. Parking brake cables binding or froze up.	1. Check cable routing. Replace cables as necessary.
	2. Parking brake cable return spring not returning shoes.	2. Replace cables as necessary.
	3. Service brakes not adjusted properly (rear drum brakes only).	3. Adjust rear brake shoes.
	4. Obstruction inside the center console preventing full return of the parking brake cables.	4. Remove console and remove obstruction.
BRAKES GRAB	1. Contaminated brake pad/shoe linings.	1. Inspect and clean, or replace pads/shoes. Repair source of contamination.
	2. Improper power brake booster assist.	2. Refer to Power Brake Booster
EXCESSIVE PEDAL EFFORT	1. Obstruction of brake pedal.	1. Inspect, remove or move obstruction.

ARM0600000000412

Fig. 1 Brake system troubleshooting (Part 3 of 5)

CONDITION	POSSIBLE CAUSES	CORRECTION
	2. Low power brake booster assist.	2. Refer to Power Brake Booster
	3. Glazed brake linings.	3. Reface or replace brake rotors as necessary. Replace brake shoes.
	4. Brake pad lining transfer to brake rotor.	4. Reface or replace brake rotors as necessary. Replace brake pads.
EXCESSIVE PEDAL EFFORT (HARD PEDAL - CAN'T SKID WHEELS)	1. Power brake booster runout (vacuum assist).	1. Check booster vacuum hose and engine tune for adequate vacuum supply. Refer to Power Brake Booster.
EXCESSIVE PEDAL TRAVEL (VEHICLE STOPS OK)	1. Air in brake lines.	1. Bleed brakes.
	2. Rear drum brake auto-adjuster malfunctioning.	2. Inspect and replace drum brake components as necessary. Adjust rear brakes.
EXCESSIVE PEDAL TRAVEL (ONE FRONT WHEEL LOCKS UP DURING HARD BRAKING)	1. One of the two hydraulic circuits is malfunctioning.	1. Inspect system for leaks. Check master cylinder for internal malfunction.
PEDAL PULSATES/SURGES DURING BRAKING	1. Rear brake drum out of round or disc brake rotor has excessive thickness variation.	1. Isolate condition as rear or front. Reface or replace brake drums or rotors as necessary.
PEDAL IS SPONGY	1. Air in brake lines.	1. Bleed brakes.
PREMATURE REAR WHEEL LOCKUP	1. Contaminated brake shoe linings.	1. Inspect and clean, or replace shoes. Repair source of contamination.
	2. Inoperative proportioning valve (non-ABS vehicles only).	2. Replace proportioning valves as necessary.
	3. ABS EVBP not functioning.	3. Refer to the ABS and appropriate diagnostic information.
STOP LAMPS STAY ON	1. Brake lamp switch out of adjustment.	1. Replace brake lamp switch.

ARM0600000000413

Fig. 1 Brake system troubleshooting (Part 4 of 5)

ROTOR
REPLACE
Front

1. Raise and support vehicle, then remove tire and wheel assembly.
2. Remove caliper and adapter bracket to steering knuckle mounting bolts.
3. Remove disc brake caliper and adapter from knuckle, then support it using suitable wire or bungee cord. **Do not to overextend brake hose.**
4. Slide brake rotor off hub and bearing.
5. Reverse procedure to install.

Rear

1. Raise and support vehicle, then remove tire and wheel assembly.
2. Remove brake caliper lower guide pin bolt.
3. Rotate caliper upward hinging off upper guide pin bolt enough to allow brake rotor removal.
4. Remove brake rotor off hub and bearing.
5. Reverse procedure to install.

PARKING BRAKE SERVICE
Shoe

1. Raise and support vehicle, then remove tire and wheel assembly.
2. Remove rear brake rotor as outlined under "Brake Rotor, Replace."
3. Turn brake shoe adjuster wheel until adjuster is at shortest length.
4. Remove upper return spring from anchor pin, then rear brake shoe.
5. Remove upper return spring from anchor pin, then front brake shoe.
6. Remove brake shoe hold down springs and pins. Rotate pins 90° to disengage.
7. Remove parking brake cable from lever on rear parking brake shoe.
8. Remove brake shoes, adjuster and lower return spring as an assembly from support plate.
9. Remove lower return spring and adjuster from shoes.
10. Reverse procedure to install.

ADJUSTMENTS
Parking Brake

1. Place parking brake lever in full released position.
2. Raise and support vehicle.
3. Remove rubber plug from hole in front of rotor.
4. Through access hole, rotate adjuster wheel to adjust shoes.
5. Reinstall rubber plug.
6. Lower vehicle far enough to access interior of vehicle.
7. Reach inside vehicle and cycle (fully apply and release) park brakes.
8. With parking brake lever in full released position, hand rotate each rear brake rotor to ensure that parking brake shoes are not dragging.
9. Repeat as needed.

	2. Brake pedal binding.	2. Inspect and replace as necessary.
	3. Power brake booster not allowing pedal to return completely.	3. Replace power brake booster.
VEHICLE PULLS TO RIGHT OR LEFT ON BRAKING	1. Frozen brake caliper piston.	1. Replace frozen piston or caliper. Bleed brakes.
	2. Contaminated brake pad/shoe lining (most likely front lining).	2. Inspect and clean, or replace pads/shoes. Repair source of contamination.
	3. Pinched brake lines.	3. Replace pinched line.
	4. Leaking piston seal.	4. Replace piston seal or brake caliper.
	5. Suspension problem.	5. Refer to the Suspension
PARKING BRAKE - EXCESSIVE HANDLE TRAVEL	1. Rear brakes out of adjustment.	1. Adjust rear drum brake shoes, or rear parking brake shoes on vehicles with rear disc brakes.

ARM0600000000414

Fig. 1 Brake system troubleshooting (Part 5 of 5)

DISC BRAKE SPECIFICATIONS
Rotor Specifications

Year/ Brake Size	Front Disc Brake						Rear Disc Brake					
	Brake Lining Wear Limit, Inch①	Rotor			Thickness Variation Parallelism, Inch	Lateral Run-Out (T.I.R.), Inch	Brake Lining Wear Limit, Inch①	Rotor			Thickness Variation Parallelism, Inch	Lateral Run-Out (T.I.R.), Inch
		Thickness, Inch						Thickness, Inch				
		Nominal	Min. Refinish	Discard Limit ②				Nominal	Min. Refinish	Discard Limit ②		
2007–08												
14-inch Brakes	—	1.020– 1.028	.961	—	.0002	.002	—	.386– .402	.331	—	.0006	.0024
16-inch Brakes	—	—	—	—	—	—	—	.386– .402	.331	—	.0006	.0016

① — Above rivet head or backing plate. Original equipment type brake lining.

② — Discard thickness is stamped on rotor.

TIGHTENING SPECIFICATIONS

Year	Component	Torque Ft. Lbs.
2007–08	Banjo Bolt	18
	Bleeder Screw	71①
	Brake Tube Nut	13
	Brake Hose-to-Front knuckle Bracket	97①
	Caliper Adapter, Front	80
	Caliper Adapter, Rear	52
	Caliper Guide Pin, Front	32
	Caliper Guide Pin	32
	Parking Brake Lever	21
	Wheel Lug Nuts	100

① — Inch lbs.

Concorde, Intrepid & 300M

NOTE: On Air Bag Equipped Models, Refer To "Air Bag System Precautions" Located In The Front Of This Manual For System Disarming & Arming Procedures.

NOTE: Refer To "Computer Relearn Procedures" Located In The Front Of This Manual When Battery Power To The Computer Has Been Interrupted.

INDEX

	Page No.		Page No.		Page No.
Adjustments	14-6	Front	14-5	Rotor Specifications	14-8
Parking Brake	14-6	Rear	14-5	Rotor, Replace	14-6
Brake Pad Service	14-5	Replacement	14-5	Tightening Specifications	14-8
Brake System Bleed	14-5	Description	14-5	Troubleshooting	14-5
Caliper Service	14-5	Disc Brake Specifications	14-8	Lateral Runout Inspection	14-5
Overhaul	14-5	Caliper Specifications	14-8	Parallelism Inspection	14-5

DESCRIPTION

The front single piston, floating caliper disc brake consists of rotor, caliper, pads and driving hub, **Fig. 1.** The caliper is mounted to steering knuckle using bushings, sleeves and two thru bolts which thread directly into steering knuckle.

This assembly has an anti-rattle clip attached to outer pad and an inner pad-piston retainer clip.

All of braking force is taken directly by adapter. The caliper is a one piece casting with inboard side containing a single piston cylinder bore.

A square cut rubber piston seal is located in a machined groove in caliper bore and provides a seal between piston and caliper bore.

A molded rubber dust boot installed in a groove in cylinder bore and piston keeps contamination from caliper bore and piston. The boot mounts in caliper bore and in a groove in piston.

The rear single piston, floating caliper rear disc brake includes a hub assembly, adapter, rotor, caliper, shoes and pads, **Fig. 2.** The parking brake system consists of a small duo-servo brake mounted to an adapter which expands out against the hat section on inside of rotor. The caliper has either a 1.338 or 1.420 inch piston located on inboard side.

The caliper floats on rubber bushings with metal sleeves on two bolts that are threaded into adapter. Two machined abutments on adapter position and align caliper and brake pads for movement fore and aft.

TROUBLESHOOTING

Refer to **Fig. 3** for system troubleshooting.

Lateral Runout Inspection

1. Raise and support vehicle, then remove wheel and tire assemblies.

2. Ensure wheel bearings are properly adjusted.
3. Install lug nuts or bolts.
4. Mount suitable dial indicator and position plunger so it contacts rotor at point one inch from outer edge.
5. Rotate rotor and note dial indicator readings. Perform this inspection on both inboard and outboard rotor faces.
6. If runout exceeds specifications, proceed as follows:
   a. Position rotor on hub and inspect runout.
   b. If runout still exceeds specifications, replace or machine rotor.

Parallelism Inspection

Measure the rotor at 12 equally spaced points at a radius approximately one inch from edge of disc using suitable micrometer.

BRAKE SYSTEM BLEED

Refer to "Hydraulic Brake Systems" chapter for brake system bleeding procedures.

BRAKE PAD SERVICE

1. Raise and support vehicle, then remove wheel and tire assembly.
2. Remove caliper assembly to steering knuckle guide pin bolts.
3. Rotate top of caliper away from steering knuckle.
4. Lift caliper off bottom machined abutment on steering knuckle.
5. Support caliper to prevent damage of flexible brake hose.
6. Remove outboard brake shoe by prying shoe retaining clip over raised area of caliper.
7. Pull inboard brake shoe away from piston until retaining clip is free from cavity in piston.

8. Reverse procedure to install, noting the following:
   a. Press caliper piston back into piston bore of caliper using suitable tool.
   b. Apply brake pedal several times, then inspect master cylinder brake fluid level and adjust fluid.

CALIPER SERVICE

Replacement

1. Remove caliper from brake rotor and brake pads from caliper as outlined under "Brake Pad Service."
2. Disconnect brake hose at brake caliper. Cap brake line.
3. Reverse procedure to install.

Overhaul

FRONT

DISASSEMBLE

1. Place suitable wood block between caliper piston and caliper fingers.
2. With brake hose attached to caliper, carefully depress brake pedal to push piston out of caliper bore.
3. Prop brake pedal to any position below first inch of brake pedal travel to prevent brake fluid loss.
4. If pistons are to be removed from both calipers, disconnect brake hose at frame bracket after removing piston, then cap brake line and repeat procedure to remove piston from other caliper.
5. Disconnect brake hose from caliper.
6. Mount caliper in suitable soft jawed vice.
7. Support caliper, then remove and discard dust boot.
8. Remove seal from groove in piston bore and discard using a small wooden or plastic stick. **Do not use screwdriver or other metal tool.**

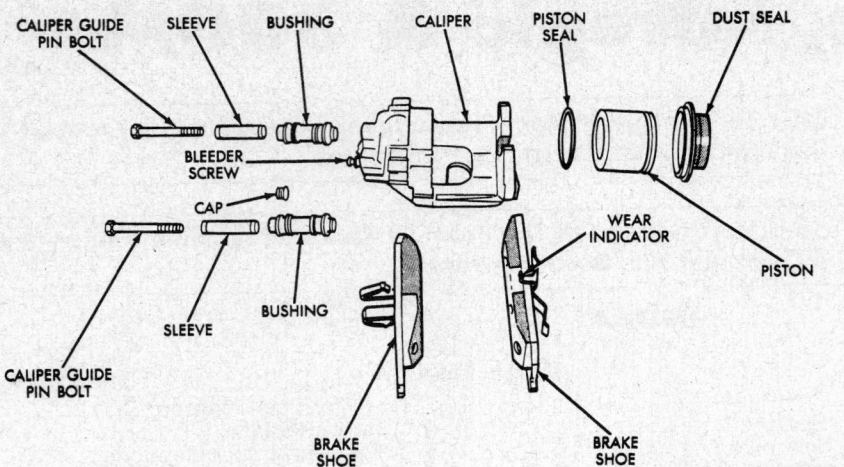

Fig. 1 Dual pin floating caliper disc brake. Front

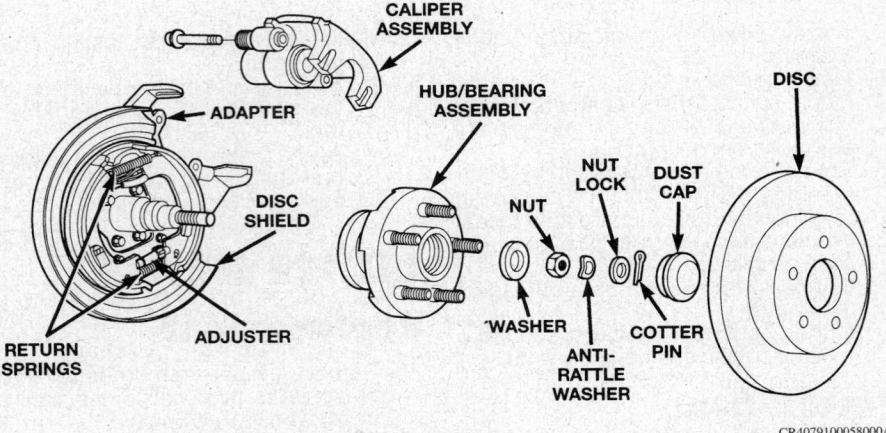

Fig. 2 Dual pin floating caliper disc brake. Rear

9. Remove caliper bushings.

ASSEMBLE

1. Mount caliper in suitable soft jawed vice.
2. Lubricate piston seal with clean brake fluid and install seal in caliper bore groove. Ensure seal is properly seated.
3. Lubricate piston boot with clean brake fluid and position over piston.
4. Install piston and boot assembly, pushing it past piston seal until it bottoms in caliper bore.
5. Drive dust boot into counterbore until properly seated using suitable hammer and dust boot installer No. C-4689 with handle No. C-4171 or equivalents.
6. Compress flanges of bushings and install on caliper housing. Ensure bushing flanges extend evenly over caliper housing on both sides.
7. Remove Teflon sleeves from guide pin bushings prior to installing bushings into caliper. After bushings are installed into caliper, install Teflon sleeves into bushings.
8. Connect brake hose to brake line at frame bracket.

REAR

1. Remove caliper from rotor as outlined under "Brake Pad Service."
2. Place a small piece of wood approximately 1 inch thick between piston and caliper fingers, then carefully depress brake pedal to hydraulically push piston out of bore. Prop brake pedal to any position below first inch of brake pedal travel to prevent brake fluid loss.
3. If pistons are to be removed from both calipers, disconnect brake hose at frame bracket after removing piston, then cap brake line and repeat procedure to remove piston from other caliper.
4. Disconnect brake hose from caliper.
5. Mount caliper in suitable soft jawed vice.
6. Support caliper, then remove and discard dust boot.
7. Remove seal from groove in piston bore and discard using a small wooden or plastic stick. **Do not use screwdriver or other metal tool.**
8. If required, remove bushing and sleeve assembly, as follows:
   a. Push inner sleeve until it pops out of

bushing, then pull inner sleeve completely out of bushing.
   b. Collapse one side of bushing. Pull opposite side of bushing to remove from caliper.
9. Thoroughly clean piston and caliper grooves, caliper housing and bushing mounting surfaces.
10. Dip new piston seal in clean brake fluid and install in groove in bore.
11. Coat new piston boot with clean brake fluid leaving a generous amount inside boot.
12. Coat piston with clean brake fluid, then position dust boot over piston.
13. Install piston into bore pushing it past piston seal until it bottoms in bore.
14. Position dust boot in counterbore, then using suitable hammer and installer No. C-4383-7 or equivalent, drive boot into counterbore of caliper.
15. If removed, install guide pin sleeve bushings as follows:
    a. Fold bushing in half lengthwise at solid middle section.
    b. Insert folded bushing into caliper. Do not use sharp object to perform this step.
    c. Unfold bushing until it is fully seated in caliper. Flanges should be seated evenly on both sides of bushing hole.
16. If removed, install guide pin sleeve as follows:
    a. Hold end of bushing, then push sleeve through bushing until end of bushing is fully seated into seal groove of sleeve.
    b. Holding sleeve in place, install other end of bushing into seal groove.
    c. Ensure bushing is in seal groove on both sides.
17. Install brake fluid line, then install caliper as outlined under "Brake Pad Service."

ROTOR
REPLACE

1. Remove caliper from brake rotor as outlined under "Brake Pad Service."
2. Remove parking brake adjustment hole plug from brake disc hub.
3. Remove rotor. Use suitable soft face hammer to tap rotor free of hub as required.
4. Reverse procedure to install.

ADJUSTMENTS
Parking Brake

1. Release parking brake.
2. Raise and support vehicle.
3. Adjust parking brake cable until there is slack in cable.
4. Tighten adjusting nut until slight drag is felt when rotating rear wheels.
5. Back off adjusting nut two full turns past point when both rear wheels rotate freely.
6. Inspect parking brake operation.

RED BRAKE WARNING LAMP

CONDITION	POSSIBLE CAUSES	CORRECTION
RED BRAKE WARNING LAMP ON	1. Parking brake lever not fully released.	1. Release parking brake lever.
	2. Parking brake warning lamp switch on parking brake lever.	2. Inspect and replace switch as necessary.
	3. Brake fluid level low in reservoir.	3. Fill reservoir. Check entire system for leaks. Repair or replace as required.
	4. Brake fluid level switch.	4. Disconnect switch wiring connector. If lamp goes out, replace switch.
	5. Mechanical instrument cluster (MIC) problem.	5. Refer to Chassis Diagnostic Procedures manual.

BRAKE NOISE

CONDITION	POSSIBLE CAUSES	CORRECTION
DISC BRAKE CHIRP	1. Excessive brake rotor runout.	1. Follow brake rotor diagnosis and testing. Correct as necessary.
	2. Lack of lubricant on brake caliper slides.	2. Lubricate brake caliper slides.
DISC BRAKE RATTLE OR CLUNK	1. Broken or missing anti-rattle spring clips on shoes.	1. Replace brake shoes.
	2. Caliper guide pins loose.	2. Tighten guide pins.
DISC BRAKE SQUEAK AT LOW SPEED (WHILE APPLYING LIGHT BRAKE PEDAL EFFORT)	1. Brake shoe linings.	1. Replace brake shoes.
SCRAPING (METAL-TO-METAL).	1. Foreign object interference with brakes.	1. Inspect brakes and remove foreign object.
	2. Brake shoes worn out.	2. Replace brake shoes. Inspect rotors. Reface or replace as necessary.

CR4079900136010X

Fig. 3   Brake system troubleshooting (Part 1 of 3)

OTHER BRAKE CONDITIONS

CONDITION	POSSIBLE CAUSES	CORRECTION
BRAKES CHATTER	1. Disc brake rotor has excessive thickness variation.	1. Isolate condition as rear or front. Reface or replace brake rotors as necessary.
BRAKES DRAG (FRONT OR ALL)	1. Contaminated brake fluid.	1. Check for swollen seals. Replace all system components containing rubber.
	2. Binding caliper pins or bushings.	2. Replace pins and bushings
	3. Binding master cylinder.	3. Replace master cylinder.
	4. Binding brake pedal.	4. Replace brake pedal.
BRAKES DRAG (REAR ONLY)	1. Parking brake cables binding or froze up.	1. Check cable routing. Replace cables as necessary.
	2. Parking brake cable return spring not returning shoes.	2. Replace cables as necessary.
	3. Obstruction inside the center console preventing full return of the parking brake cables.	3. Remove console and remove obstruction.
BRAKES GRAB	1. Contaminated brake shoe linings.	1. Inspect and clean, or replace shoes. Repair source of contamination.
	2. Improper power brake booster assist.	2. Refer to Power Brake Booster in the diagnosis and testing section.
EXCESSIVE PEDAL EFFORT	1. Obstruction of brake pedal.	1. Inspect, remove or move obstruction.
	2. Low power brake booster assist.	2. Refer to power brake booster in the diagnosis and testing section.
	3. Glazed brake linings.	3. Reface or replace brake rotors as necessary. Replace brake shoes.
	4. Brake shoe lining transfer to brake rotor.	4. Reface or replace brake rotors as necessary. Replace brake shoes.
EXCESSIVE PEDAL TRAVEL (VEHICLE STOPS OK)	1. Air in brake lines.	1. Bleed brakes.
EXCESSIVE PEDAL TRAVEL (PEDAL GOES TO FLOOR - CAN'T SKID WHEELS)	1. Power brake booster runout (vacuum assist).	1. Check booster vacuum hose and engine tune for adequate vacuum supply. Refer to power brake booster in the diagnosis and testing section.
EXCESSIVE PEDAL TRAVEL (ONE FRONT WHEEL LOCKS UP DURING HARD BRAKING)	1. One of the two hydraulic circuits to the front brakes is malfunctioning.	1. Inspect system for leaks. Check master cylinder for internal malfunction.
PEDAL PULSATES/ SURGES DURING BRAKING	1. Disc brake rotor has excessive thickness variation.	1. Isolate condition as rear or front. Reface or replace brake rotors as necessary.

CR4079900136020X

Fig. 3   Brake system troubleshooting (Part 2 of 3)

CONDITION	POSSIBLE CAUSES	CORRECTION
PEDAL IS SPONGY	1. Air in brake lines.	1. Bleed brakes.
	2. Power brake booster runout (vacuum assist).	2. Check booster vacuum hose and engine tune for adequate vacuum supply. Refer to power brake booster in the diagnosis and testing section.
PREMATURE REAR WHEEL LOCKUP	1. Contaminated brake shoe linings.	1. Inspect and clean, or replace shoes. Repair source of contamination.
	2. Inoperative proportioning valve.	2. Test proportioning valves folowing procedure listed in diagnosis and testing section. Replace valves as necessary.
	3. Improper power brake booster assist.	3. Refer to power brake booster in the diagnosis and testing section.
STOP LAMPS STAY ON	1. Brake lamp switch out of adjustment.	1. Adjust brake lamp switch.
	2. Brake pedal binding.	2. Inspect and replace as necessary.
	3. Obstruction in pedal linkage.	3. Remove obstruction.
	4. Power Brake Booster not allowing pedal to return completely.	4. Replace power brake booster.
VEHICLE PULLS TO RIGHT OR LEFT ON BRAKING	1. Frozen brake caliper piston.	1. Replace frozen piston or caliper. Bleed brakes.
	2. Contaminated brake shoe lining.	2. Inspect and clean, or replace shoes. Repair source of contamination.
	3. Pinched brake lines.	3. Replace pinched line.
	4. Leaking piston seal.	4. Replace piston seal or brake caliper.
	5. Suspension problem.	5. Refer to the Suspension group.
PARKING BRAKE - EXCESSIVE LEVER TRAVEL	1. Rear parking brake shoes out of adjustment.	1. Adjust rear parking brake shoes.

CR4079900136030X

Fig. 3   Brake system troubleshooting (Part 3 of 3)

DISC BRAKE SPECIFICATIONS
Rotor Specifications

Year	Front Disc Brake						Rear Disc Brake					
	Brake Lining Wear Limit, Inch③	Rotor			Thickness Variation Parallelism, Inch	Lateral Run-Out (T.I.R.), Inch	Brake Lining Wear Limit, Inch③	Rotor			Thickness Variation Parallelism, Inch	Lateral Run-Out (T.I.R.), Inch
		Thickness, Inch						Thickness, Inch				
		Nominal	Min. Refinish	Discard Limit ②				Nominal	Min. Refinish	Discard Limit ②		
2004	.312①	1.019–1.029	—	.960	.0005	.003	.281①	.458–.478	—	.409	.0005	.003

① — Includes backing plate.
② — Discard thickness is stamped on rotor.
③ — Above rivet head or backing plate. Original equipment type brake lining.

Caliper Specifications

Location, Type	Caliper Piston O.D., Inch
Front	2.36
Rear, Solid	1.34
Rear, Vented	1.42

TIGHTENING SPECIFICATIONS

Year	Component	Torque Ft. Lbs.
2004	Bearing Retainer	21
	Bleed Screws	10
	Brake Hose To Caliper Banjo Bolt	35
	Brake Line Fitting	12
	Caliper	16
	Caliper Guide Pins	30
	Front Brake Hose Intermediate Bracket	108①
	Support Plate To Rear Axle	80
	Wheel Lug Nuts	85–110

① — Inch lbs.

Crossfire

NOTE: On Air Bag Equipped Models, Refer To "Air Bag System Precautions" Located In The Front Of This Manual For System Disarming & Arming Procedures.

NOTE: Refer To "Computer Relearn Procedures" Located In The Front Of This Manual When Battery Power To The Computer Has Been Interrupted.

INDEX

	Page No.
Adjustments	14-10
Parking Brake	14-10
Brake Pad Service	14-9
Front	14-9
Rear	14-9
Brake System Bleed	14-9
Caliper Service	14-9

	Page No.
Overhaul	14-9
Replacement	14-9
Front	14-9
Rear	14-9
Description	14-9
Disc Brake Specifications	14-11
Caliper Specifications	14-11

	Page No.
Rotor Specifications	14-11
Parking Brake Service	14-10
Parking Brake Shoes, Replace	14-10
Rotor, Replace	14-10
Tightening Specifications	14-11
Troubleshooting	14-9

DESCRIPTION

On 2004 models, the rear disc brakes consist of fixed single piston style calipers with solid rotors.

On 2005–07 models, the rear disc brakes consist of fixed two piston style calipers with solid rotors.

On all models the rear caliper is mounted to the rear wheel hub. The calipers are directly bolted to the wheel hub with mounting bolts. The disc brake rotor dust shield is mounting to the hub.

The disc brake rotor has a built in drum used for the parking brakes. The parking brake shoes are mounted to the wheel hub.

TROUBLESHOOTING

Refer to "Concorde, Intrepid & 300M" for troubleshooting procedures.

BRAKE SYSTEM BLEED

Refer to "Hydraulic Brake Systems" chapter for brake system bleeding procedures.

BRAKE PAD SERVICE

Front

1. Raise and support vehicle, then remove front wheel and tire assemblies.
2. Drain small amount of brake fluid from master cylinder reservoir using suitable, clean suction gun.
3. Bottom caliper piston into bore by prying caliper body against rotor.
4. Remove caliper support spring by prying support spring from retaining holes located in caliper body, **Fig. 1.**
5. Disconnect brake pad wear indicator wiring harness connector.
6. Remove protective caps, caliper slide pins and caliper.
7. Support caliper using suitable wire.
8. Remove inboard and outboard pads.

9. Reverse procedure to install, noting the following:
   a. Bottom piston is caliper using suitable C-clamp.
   b. Lubricate slide pins with suitable silicone grease.

Rear

1. Raise and support vehicle, then remove rear wheel and tire assemblies.
2. Drain small amount of brake fluid from master cylinder reservoir using suitable, clean suction gun.
3. Remove mounting bolts and caliper from knuckle.
4. Remove brake hose by rotating caliper while holding brake hose with suitable line wrench.
5. Knock retaining pin out using suitable punch.
6. Remove anti-rattle clip and brake pads.
7. Reverse procedure to install. Bottom piston is caliper using suitable C-clamp.

CALIPER SERVICE

Replacement

FRONT

1. Raise and support vehicle, then remove front wheel and tire assemblies.
2. Drain small amount of fluid from master cylinder reservoir using suitable, clean suction gun.
3. Disconnect harness connector, then remove mounting bolt and brake pad wear indicator.
4. Bottom piston into caliper by prying caliper over.
5. Remove support spring by prying it out of caliper.
6. Remove caps, slide pins and caliper from mounting bracket.
7. Remove caliper brake hose.

8. Remove brake pads.
9. Reverse procedure to install. Lubricate slide pins with suitable silicone grease.

REAR

1. Raise and support vehicle, then remove rear wheel and tire assemblies.
2. Drain small amount of fluid from master cylinder reservoir using suitable, clean suction gun.
3. Remove mounting bolts and caliper.
4. Remove brake hose by rotating caliper while holding hose with suitable line wrench.
5. Knock pad retaining pin out using suitable punch.
6. Remove anti-rattle clip and brake pads.
7. Reverse procedure to install.

Overhaul

1. Place suitable small piece of wood pad with one-inch thickness of shop towels outboard of caliper in front of piston.
2. Remove caliper piston by apply short burst of low pressure air with suitable blow gun through brake hose port. **Do not attempt to catch piston. Do not use sustained air pressure.**
3. Remove piston dust boot with suitable pry tool.
4. Remove piston seal with suitable tool.
5. Remove bleed screw.
6. Clean caliper.
7. Lubricate piston, seals and bore with suitable, clean brake fluid.
8. Install new seal into groove. **Ensure seal is fully seated and not twisted.**
9. Install new dust boot and seat it into piston.
10. Stretch dust boot rearward to straighten folds, then move it forward until fold snaps into place.

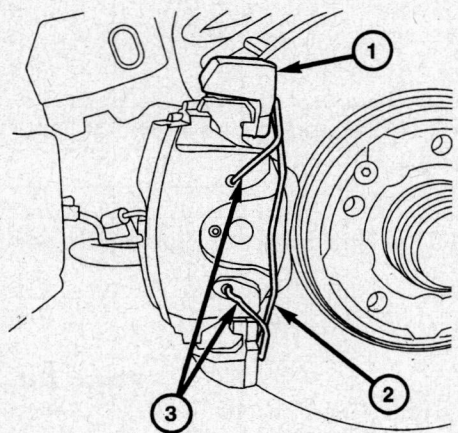

1 CALIPER
2 SUPPORT SPRING
3 SUPPORT SPRING RETAINING HOLE
  LOCATIONS

ARM0300000000052

Fig. 1 Front brake caliper retaining spring removal

11. Install piston into bore and press down to bottom of caliper by hand or with handle of suitable hammer.
12. Seat dust boot.
13. Install new bleed screw.

PARKING BRAKE SERVICE

Parking Brake Shoes, Replace

1. Raise and support vehicle, then remove tire and wheel assembly.
2. Remove rear disc brake caliper assembly as outlined under "Caliper Service."
3. Remove rear rotor from hub and dust cap.
4. Remove cotter pin, nut retainer, wave washer, rear hub/bearing retaining nut and washer from rear spindle.
5. Remove rear hub and bearing from rear spindle.
6. Release parking brake equalizer tensioning bolts.
7. Remove parking brake shoe lower return spring using suitable hooked pick spring release tool, **Fig. 2.**
8. Remove parking brake shoe hold-down spring using suitable needle-nose pliers.
9. Remove parking brake shoe lower return spring using suitable hooked pick spring release tool.
10. Remove parking brake expanding lock from lower parking brake shoes.

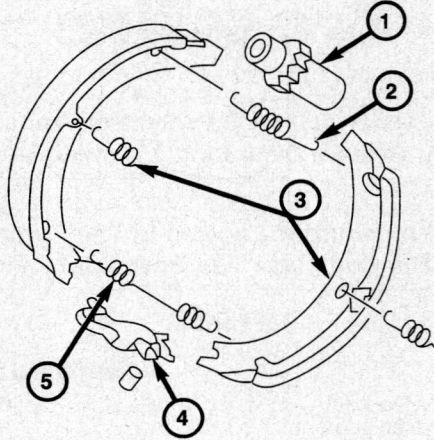

(1) Adjuster.
(2) Upper return spring.
(3) Hold down spring.
(4) Expanding lock.
(5) Lower return spring.

ARM0300000000055

Fig. 2 Exploded view of parking brake

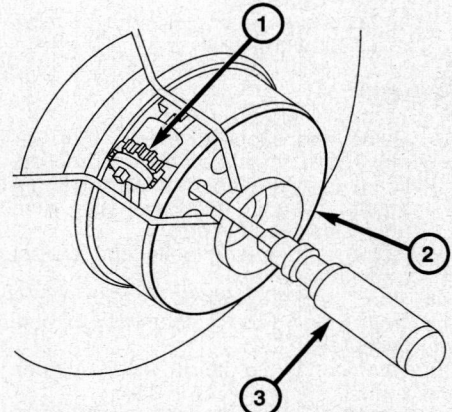

1 PARKING BRAKE ADJUSTER WHEEL
2 REAR WHEEL
3 SUITABLE SCREWDRIVER

ARM0300000000057

Fig. 4 Parking brake adjuster wheel

11. Remove parking brake shoes by lifting them over rear axle shaft flange.
12. Reverse procedure to install.

ADJUSTMENTS
Parking Brake

1. Raise and support vehicle.

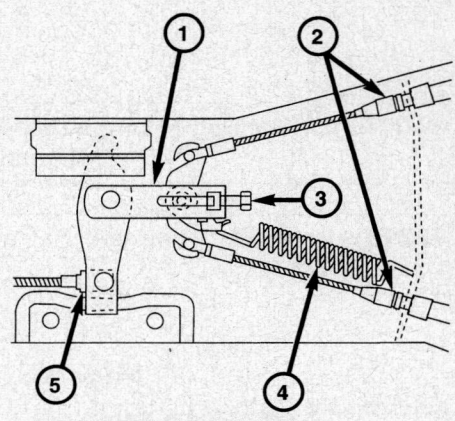

1 CABLE EQUALIZER MECHANISIM
2 PARKING BRAKE CABLES
3 EQUALIZER TENSIONER BOLT
4 RETURN RING
5 FRONT CABLE BOLTED TO EQUALIZER

ARM0300000000056

Fig. 3 Parking brake cable

2. Loosen parking brake cable tensioning bolt, **Fig. 3.**
3. Remove one wheel lug bolt on each rear wheel.
4. Rotate wheel until parking brake adjuster wheel can be seen through removed wheel bolt hole, **Fig. 4.**
5. **On righthand side,** turn adjusting wheel from bottom to top.
6. **On lefthand side,** turn adjusting wheel from top to bottom.
7. **On all sides,** turn adjusting wheel until parking brake shoes are applied and rear wheels no longer turn freely.
8. Tighten parking brake cable tensioning bolt until cables no longer sag and firmly apply parking brake several time.
9. To fine adjust parking brake, tighten parking brake cable tensioning bolt until parking brake lever can be moved one tooth with moderate effort of approximately, 66–88 ft. lbs.

ROTOR
REPLACE

1. Remove caliper from brake rotor as outlined under "Brake Pad Service."
2. Remove parking brake adjustment hole plug from brake disc hub.
3. Remove rotor. Use suitable soft face hammer to tap rotor free of hub as required.
4. Reverse procedure to install.

DISC BRAKE SPECIFICATIONS
Rotor Specifications

Engine	Front Disc Brake						Rear Disc Brake					
	Brake Lining Wear Limit, Inch[2]	Rotor					Brake Lining Wear Limit, Inch[2]	Rotor				
		Thickness, Inch			Thickness Variation Parallelism, Inch	Lateral Run-Out (T.I.R.), Inch		Thickness, Inch			Thickness Variation Parallelism, Inch	Lateral Run-Out (T.I.R.), Inch
		Nominal	Min. Refinish	Discard Limit [1]				Nominal	Min. Refinish	Discard Limit [1]		
3.2L	.55	1.10	1.02	.99	.0005	.002	.43	.35	.30	.29	.0005	.003

① — Discard thickness is stamped on rotor.

② — Above rivet head or backing plate. Original equipment type brake lining.

Caliper Specifications

Rotor Type	Caliper Piston O.D., Inch
Solid	1.34
Vented	1.42

TIGHTENING SPECIFICATIONS

Year	Component	Torque Ft. Lbs.
2004–07	Bearing Retainer	21
	Bleed Screw	62①
	Brake Hose To Caliper Banjo Bolt	35
	Brake Line Fitting	12
	Caliper Guide Pins	18
	Caliper Anchor, Front	85
	Caliper Anchor, Rear	41
	Support Plate To Rear Axle	80
	Wheel Lug Nuts	85–100

① — Inch lbs.

DISC BRAKES

Charger, Magnum & 300

NOTE: On Air Bag Equipped Models, Refer To "Air Bag System Precautions" Located In The Front Of This Manual For System Disarming & Arming Procedures.

NOTE: Refer To "Computer Relearn Procedures" Located In The Front Of This Manual When Battery Power To The Computer Has Been Interrupted.

INDEX

	Page No.
Adjustments	14-13
Parking Brake	14-13
Brake Pad Service	14-12
Except SRT8	14-12
SRT8	14-12
Brake System Bleed	14-12
Caliper Service	14-12

	Page No.
Overhaul	14-12
Assemble	14-13
Disassemble	14-12
Replacement	14-12
Description	14-12
Disc Brake Specifications	14-14
Rotor Specifications	14-14

	Page No.
Parking Brake Service	14-13
Shoe	14-13
Rotor, Replace	14-13
Tightening Specifications	14-14
Troubleshooting	14-12

DESCRIPTION

Four-wheel disc brakes are standard on these vehicle. There are two four-wheel disc brake systems available, a standard and a premium. The standard disc brake system is referred to as 17-inch. The premium disc brake system is referred to as 18-Inch.

Seventeen-inch four-wheel disc brakes (so called because they are designed to fit inside 17-inch wheels) are standard on rear-wheel drive models with V6 engines. They feature single-piston aluminum calipers and vented rotors in the front and single-piston aluminum calipers with solid rotors in the rear.

Eighteen-inch four-wheel disc brakes (so called because they are designed to fit inside 18-inch wheels) are standard on Chrysler 300 Hemi C and all international models, and optional on other models. They feature twin-piston aluminum calipers and vented rotors in the front and single-piston aluminum calipers with vented rotors in the rear.

Although the rear calipers appear the same as the 17-inch system, the rear calipers used with this system feature a wider jaw to compensate for the wider, vented brake rotors used.

Although the twin-piston caliper used is the same, Rear-Wheel-Drive (RWD) models mount the caliper to the rear (trailing end) of the knuckle while All-Wheel-Drive (AWD) models mount the caliper to the front (leading end) of the knuckle.

All calipers are aluminum construction and are the low-drag type, which allows minimal drag of the pads on the discs with low clearance to the rotors to maintain maximum pedal feel and responsiveness.

All calipers are anodized, giving them an off-black appearance. This coating offers corrosion protection and a long-term neat appearance. Phenolic pistons are used in all calipers. The premium twin caliper pistons have stainless steel caps for protection against damage because of contact with the brake pads. All brake rotors are fully coated with Geomet, a water-soluble, environmental friendly corrosion preventive. Both the friction surfaces and the vents are coated. During initial brake applications of a new rotor, the brake pads scrub the coating off the friction surfaces, ensuring that the remainder will be rust free. Coating the vents also ensures that there will not be a loss of heat capacity over time.

TROUBLESHOOTING

Refer to "Concorde, Intrepid & 300M" for troubleshooting procedures.

BRAKE SYSTEM BLEED

Refer to "Hydraulic Brake Systems" chapter for brake system bleeding procedures.

BRAKE PAD SERVICE

EXCEPT SRT8

1. Raise and support vehicle, then remove wheel and tire assembly.
2. Retract caliper piston in bore by grasping rear of caliper and pulling outward working with guide pins. **Never push on piston directly.**
3. Remove caliper guide pin bolt by holding it while turning bolt.
4. Rotate caliper upward. **Do not over-extend brake hose.**
5. Remove brake pads from caliper, then the anti-rattle clips.
6. Remove caliper to steering knuckle guide pin bolts.
7. Reverse procedure to install, noting the following:
   a. Use hand pressure or suitable C-clamp to retract piston, first placing wood block over piston.
   b. Inboard and outboard pads are interchangeable.

SRT8

1. Raise and support vehicle, then remove wheel and tire assembly.
2. Tap lower brake pad support pin out of caliper using hammer and suitable pin punch on outboard end, **Fig. 1.**
3. Remove brake pad spring clip, then remaining upper support pin, **Fig. 2.**
4. Pull pads back to seat caliper pistons into bores using hand pressure.
5. Remove brake pads through opening in caliper.
6. Reverse procedure to install.

CALIPER SERVICE

Replacement

1. Depress brake pedal past its first inch of travel and hold it in position using brake pedal holding tool.
2. Raise and support vehicle, then remove tire and wheel assembly.
3. Remove banjo bolt connecting flexible brake hose to caliper.
4. While holding guide pins from turning, remove caliper guide pin bolts.
5. Remove brake caliper from brake adapter and pads.
6. Reverse procedure to install, noting the following:
   a. Completely retract caliper piston back into bore of caliper using hand pressure or suitable C-clamp by first placing suitable wood block over piston.
   b. **Do not crossthread caliper guide pin bolts.**
   c. Install new washers on each side of hose fitting as banjo bolt is placed through fitting.

Overhaul

DISASSEMBLE

1. Drain brake fluid from caliper into suitable container.

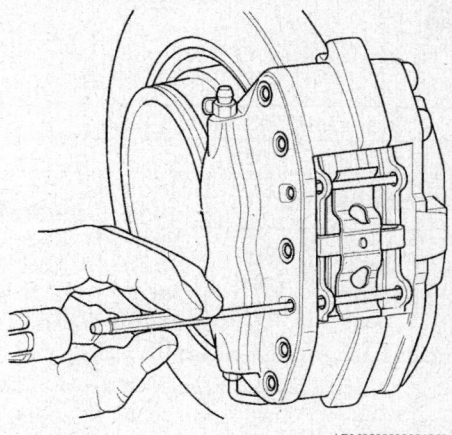

Fig. 1   Brake pad support pin. SRT8

2. Mount caliper in suitable vise equipped with protective jaws.
3. Place suitable wooden block (padded with approximately one-inch thickness of shop towels) in front of caliper piston.
4. Padded block should be sized to allow piston to push out of bore far enough to be removed by hand after being loosened by air pressure, yet large enough to keep piston from coming completely out.
5. Apply low pressure compressed air to caliper fluid inlet in short spurts to ease piston out of bore. **Do not use high pressure.**
6. Remove piston from caliper.
7. Remove and discard dust boot using suitable tool.
8. Work piston seal out of groove caliper piston bore using suitable, soft tool such as plastic trim stick. **Do not use screw driver or other metal tool for seal removal.**
9. Remove caliper bleeder screw.
10. Clean piston bore and drilled passage ways with alcohol, or suitable solvent.
11. Wipe it dry using only a lint-free cloth.
12. Inspect both piston and bore for scoring or pitting. **Do not hone caliper bore.**

ASSEMBLE

1. Lubricate caliper piston, piston seal and piston bore with suitable, clean, fresh brake fluid.
2. Install new piston sea in groove. Seal should be started at one area of groove and gently worked around and into groove using only clean fingers to seat it.

3. Install new dust boot on piston and work boot lip into groove at top of piston.
4. Stretch boot downward, straightening boot folds, then move boot back upward until folds snap uniformly into place.
5. Install piston into bore, pressing piston down to bottom of bore using hand-pressure. Dust boot will not seat now.
6. Seat dust boot in caliper counterbore using installer tool No. 9315, with handle tool No. C-4171, or equivalents.
7. Install dust boot until it bottoms. **Do not over-seat dust boot.**
8. Install bleeder screw in threaded hole that will be uppermost once caliper is installed.

ROTOR

REPLACE

1. Raise and support vehicle, then remove tire and wheel assembly.
2. Grasp rear of caliper and pull outward working with guide pins to retract piston. **Never push on piston directly.**
3. Remove disc brake caliper and adapter from knuckle, then support it using suitable wire or bungee cord. **Do not to overextend brake hose.**
4. Remove clips, then slide brake rotor off hub and bearing.
5. Reverse procedure to install.

PARKING BRAKE SERVICE

Shoe

1. Raise and support vehicle, then remove tire and wheel assembly.
2. While helper applies brakes, remove hub nut from half shaft.
3. Remove two mounting bolts, disc brake caliper and adapter. Suspend assembly aside using suitable wire or bungee cord. **Do not overextend brake hose.**
4. Remove clips and brake rotor.
5. Loosen each hub and bearing mounting bolt 1–2 turns at a time while pulling outward on hub and bearing.
6. Once removed from threads in hub and bearing, but not knuckle allow bolts to stay in and protrude through knuckle and brake support plate.
7. Slide hub and bearing off knuckle and half shaft.
8. Completely back off parking brake shoe adjustment.
9. Remove spring and parking brake shoe adjuster.

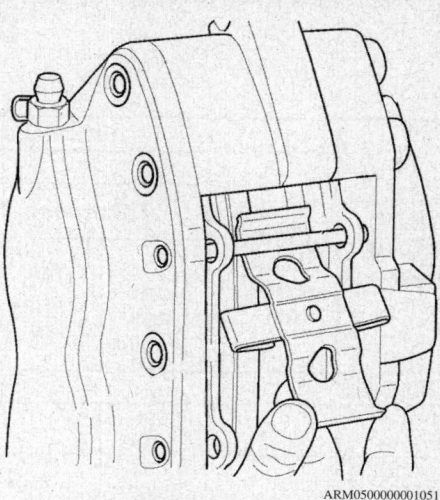

Fig. 2   Brake pad spring clip. SRT8

10. Remove shoe adjuster.
11. Remove upper brake shoe hold-down clip and pin.
12. Remove upper shoe from return spring and shoe actuator lever.
13. Remove return spring from lower shoe.
14. Remove lower brake shoe hold-down clip and pin.
15. Remove lower shoe.
16. Reverse procedure to install.

ADJUSTMENTS

Parking Brake

1. Place parking brake lever in full released position.
2. Raise and support vehicle.
3. Remove plug in parking brake shoe support to access adjuster star-wheel.
4. Through access hole, rotate adjuster star wheel to expand shoes outward against drum.
5. Turn adjuster star wheel until wheel will not rotate using suitable tool.
6. Back off adjuster six detents.
7. Rotate wheel to ensure light drag. If drag is too heavy, continue to back off adjuster one detent at a time until light drag is present. **Do not back off star-wheel more than 17 detents from wheel lock.**
8. Install access plug. Adjust opposite wheel parking brake shoes using same method.

DISC BRAKE SPECIFICATIONS
Rotor Specifications

Year/ Brake Size	Front Disc Brake						Rear Disc Brake					
	Brake Lining Wear Limit, Inch①	Rotor			Thickness Variation Parallelism, Inch	Lateral Run-Out (T.I.R.), Inch	Brake Lining Wear Limit, Inch①	Rotor			Thickness Variation Parallelism, Inch	Lateral Run-Out (T.I.R.), Inch
		Thickness, Inch						Thickness, Inch				
		Nominal	Min. Refinish	Discard Limit ②				Nominal	Min. Refinish	Discard Limit ②		
2005–08												
17-inch Brakes	—	1.097– 1.107	—	1.040	.0004	.0014	—	.389– .399	—	.335	.0004	.0014
18-inch Brakes	—	1.097– 1.107	—	1.040	.0004	.0014	—	.861– .871	—	807	.0004	.0014

① — Above rivet head or backing plate. Original equipment type brake lining.

② — Discard thickness is stamped on rotor.

TIGHTENING SPECIFICATIONS

Year	Component	Torque Ft. Lbs.
2005–08	Bleeder Screw	97①
	Brake Tube Nut	10
	Brake Hose Caliper Banjo Bolt	32
	Brake Hose-to-Front knuckle Bracket	97①
	Caliper Adapter, Front	70
	Caliper Adapter, Rear	85
	Caliper Guide Pin, Front	44
	Caliper Guide Pin	44
	Parking Brake Cable Knuckle	71①
	Wheel Lug Nuts	110

① — Inch lbs.

Neon

NOTE: On Air Bag Equipped Models, Refer To "Air Bag System Precautions" Located In The Front Of This Manual For System Disarming & Arming Procedures.

NOTE: Refer To "Computer Relearn Procedures" Located In The Front Of This Manual When Battery Power To The Computer Has Been Interrupted.

INDEX

	Page No.
Adjustments	14-16
Parking Brake	14-16
Brake Pad Service	14-15
Front	14-15
Rear	14-15
Brake System Bleed	14-15
Caliper Service	14-15

	Page No.
Overhaul	14-15
Assemble	14-16
Disassemble	14-15
Replace	14-15
Description	14-15
Disc Brake Specifications	14-16
Caliper Specifications	14-16

	Page No.
Rotor Specifications	14-16
Parking Brake Service	14-16
Parking Brake Shoes, Replace	14-16
Rotor, Replace	14-16
Tightening Specifications	14-17
Troubleshooting	14-15

DESCRIPTION

The front single piston, floating caliper disc brake consists of rotor, caliper, pads and driving hub. The caliper is mounted to steering knuckle using bushings, sleeves and two thru bolts which thread directly into steering knuckle.

This assembly has an anti-rattle clip attached to outer pad and an inner pad-piston retainer clip.

All of braking force is taken directly by adapter. The caliper is a one piece casting with inboard side containing a single piston cylinder bore.

A square cut rubber piston seal is located in a machined groove in caliper bore and provides a seal between piston and caliper bore.

A molded rubber dust boot installed in a groove in cylinder bore and piston keeps contamination from caliper bore and piston. The boot mounts in caliper bore and in a groove in piston.

The rear single piston, floating caliper rear disc brake includes a hub assembly, adapter, rotor, caliper, shoes and pads. The parking brake system consists of a small duo-servo brake mounted to an adapter which expands out against the hat section on inside of rotor. The caliper has either a 1.338 or 1.420 inch piston located on inboard side.

The caliper floats on rubber bushings with metal sleeves on two bolts that are threaded into adapter. Two machined abutments on adapter position and align caliper and brake pads for movement fore and aft.

TROUBLESHOOTING

Refer to "Concorde, Intrepid & 300M" for troubleshooting procedures.

BRAKE SYSTEM BLEED

Refer to "Hydraulic Brake Systems" chapter for brake system bleeding procedures.

BRAKE PAD SERVICE

Front

1. Raise and support vehicle, then remove front wheel and tire assemblies.
2. Remove caliper to steering knuckle guide pin bolts.
3. Rotate top of caliper away from steering knuckle.
4. Lift caliper off bottom machined abutment on steering knuckle.
5. Support caliper to prevent damage of flexible brake hose.
6. Remove outboard brake shoe by prying shoe retaining clip over raised area of caliper.
7. Pull inboard brake shoe away from piston until retaining clip is free from cavity in piston.
8. Reverse procedure to install, noting the following:
   a. Press caliper piston back into piston bore of caliper using suitable tool.
   b. Apply brake pedal several times, then inspect master cylinder brake fluid level and adjust fluid.

Rear

1. Raise and support vehicle, then remove rear wheels and tires.
2. Remove caliper guide pin bolts.
3. Rotate top of caliper away from adapter, then lift caliper off lower machined abutment on adapter.
4. Support caliper from rear strut using suitable wire.
5. Remove outboard brake pad from caliper by prying brake pad retaining clip over raised area on caliper.
6. Pull inboard pad away from caliper piston until retaining clip is free from piston cavity.
7. Press piston completely into caliper bore.
8. Lubricate adapter abutments with

Mopar multi-purpose grease, or equivalent.
9. Install inboard and outboard pads.
10. Place bottom of caliper over abutment, then rotate top of caliper into place.
11. Install caliper guide pin bolts.
12. Install tire and wheel assemblies, then lower vehicle and inspect brake fluid level.
13. Road test vehicle to remove any foreign material from brakes and seat brake pads.

CALIPER SERVICE

Replace

1. Remove caliper from brake rotor and brake pads from caliper as outlined under "Brake Pad Service."
2. Disconnect brake hose at brake caliper, then cap brake line.
3. Reverse procedure to install.

Overhaul

DISASSEMBLE

1. Place suitable wood block between caliper piston and caliper fingers.
2. With brake hose attached to caliper, depress brake pedal to push piston out of caliper bore.
3. Prop brake pedal to any position below first inch of brake pedal travel to prevent brake fluid loss.
4. If pistons are to be removed from both calipers, disconnect brake hose at frame bracket after removing piston. Cap brake line and repeat procedure to remove piston from other caliper.
5. Disconnect brake hose from caliper.
6. Mount caliper in suitable soft jawed vice.
7. Support caliper, then remove and discard dust boot.
8. Remove seal from groove in piston bore using suitable small wooden or

plastic stick. **Do not use screwdriver or other metal tool.**

9. Remove caliper bushings.

ASSEMBLE

1. Mount caliper in suitable soft jawed vice.
2. Lubricate piston seal with suitable, clean brake fluid.
3. Install seal in caliper bore groove. Ensure seal is properly seated.
4. Lubricate piston boot with suitable, clean brake fluid and position over piston.
5. Install piston and boot, pushing it past seal until it bottoms in caliper bore.
6. Drive dust boot into counterbore until properly seated using suitable hammer and dust boot installer No. C-4689 with handle No. C-4171, or equivalents.
7. Compress flanges of bushings and install on caliper housing.
8. Ensure bushing flanges extend evenly over caliper housing on both sides.
9. Remove Teflon sleeves from guide pin bushings prior to installing bushings into caliper.
10. After bushings are installed into caliper, install Teflon sleeves into bushings.

11. Connect brake hose to brake line at frame bracket.

ROTOR
REPLACE

1. Remove caliper from brake rotor as outlined under "Brake Pad Service."
2. Remove parking brake adjustment hole plug from brake disc hub.
3. Remove rotor using suitable soft face hammer to tap rotor free of hub as required.
4. Reverse procedure to install.

PARKING BRAKE SERVICE
Parking Brake Shoes, Replace

1. Remove rear disc brake caliper assembly as outlined under "Caliper Service."
2. Remove rear rotor and dust cap hub.
3. Remove cotter pin, nut retainer, wave washer and rear hub/bearing retaining nut and washer from rear spindle.
4. Remove rear hub and bearing.

5. Remove rear brake shoe hold-down clip.
6. Turn brake shoe adjuster wheel until adjuster is at shortest length.
7. Remove adjuster from parking brake.
8. Remove lower shoe to shoe spring.
9. Pull front parking brake shoe away from anchor pin, then remove front parking brake shoe and lower spring.
10. Pull rear brake shoe away from anchor.
11. Remove rear brake shoe and upper spring.
12. Remove hold-down clip and front brake shoe.
13. Reverse procedure to install.

ADJUSTMENTS
Parking Brake

1. Release parking brake.
2. Raise and support vehicle.
3. Adjust parking brake cable until there is slack in cable.
4. Tighten adjusting nut until slight drag is felt when rotating rear wheels.
5. Back off adjusting nut two full turns past point when both rear wheels rotate freely.
6. Inspect parking brake operation.

DISC BRAKE SPECIFICATIONS
Rotor Specifications

Year/ Engine	Front Disc Brake						Rear Disc Brake					
	Brake Lining Wear Limit, Inch①	Rotor			Thickness Variation Parallelism, Inch	Lateral Run-Out (T.I.R.), Inch	Brake Lining Wear Limit, Inch①	Rotor			Thickness Variation Parallelism, Inch	Lateral Run-Out (T.I.R.), Inch
		Thickness, Inch						Thickness, Inch				
		Nominal	Min. Refinish	Discard Limit ②				Nominal	Min. Refinish	Discard Limit ②		
2004–05												
2.0L	—	.861–.871	—	.803	.0005	.005	—	.344–.364	—	.285	.0005	.005
2.4L	—	1.1099–1.106	—	1.039	.0004	.005	—	.463–.482	—	.404	.0005	.005

① — Above rivet head or backing plate. Original equipment type brake lining.

② — Discard thickness is stamped on rotor.

Caliper Specifications

Location, Type	Caliper Piston O.D., Inch
Front	2.125
Rear, Solid	1.340
Rear, Vented	1.420

TIGHTENING SPECIFICATIONS

Year	Component	Torque Ft. Lbs.
2004–05	Bearing Retainer	21
	Bleed Screws	10
	Brake Hose To Caliper Banjo Bolt	18
	Brake Line Fitting	12
	Caliper	16
	Caliper Guide Pins	30
	Caliper Adapter (To Knuckle), Rear	55
	Front Brake Hose Intermediate Bracket	108①
	Support Plate To Rear Axle	80
	Wheel Lug Nuts	85–110

① — Inch lbs.

Sebring Convertible, Stratus Sedan & 2004–06 Sebring Sedan

NOTE: On Air Bag Equipped Models, Refer To "Air Bag System Precautions" Located In The Front Of This Manual For System Disarming & Arming Procedures.

NOTE: Refer To "Computer Relearn Procedures" Located In The Front Of This Manual When Battery Power To The Computer Has Been Interrupted.

INDEX

	Page No.
Adjustments	14-18
Parking Brake Lever	14-18
Parking Brake Shoe	14-18
Brake Pad Service	14-17
Front	14-17
Rear	14-17

	Page No.
Brake System Bleed	14-17
Caliper Service	14-18
Overhaul	14-18
Replacement	14-18
Disc Brake Specifications	14-19
Rotor Specifications	14-19

	Page No.
Rotor, Replace	14-18
Tightening Specifications	14-19
Troubleshooting	14-17
Lateral Runout Inspection	14-17
Parallelism Inspection	14-17

TROUBLESHOOTING

Lateral Runout Inspection

1. Remove caliper as outlined under "Brake Pad Service."
2. Inspect disc surface for grooves, cracks and rust.
3. Tighten rotor to hub.
4. Place suitable dial indicator approximately 1 inch from outer circumference of brake rotor, **Fig. 1.**
5. Measure brake rotor runout.
6. If runout of rotor is equal to or exceeds specifications, proceed as follows:
   a. Before removing brake rotor, chalk both sides of wheel stud on side at which runout is greatest.
   b. Remove brake rotor and place dial gauge, **Fig. 2.**
   c. Move hub in axial direction and measure play. If play exceeds .002 inch, disassemble hub knuckle and inspect each part.
   d. If play does not exceed specifications, install brake rotor 180° away from chalk marks.
   e. Inspect runout of brake rotor again.
   f. If runout cannot be corrected by changing phase of rotor, replace or machine rotor.

Parallelism Inspection

Measure the rotor thickness at 12 positions with suitable micrometer 1 inch in from outer edge of disc.

BRAKE SYSTEM BLEED

Refer to "Hydraulic Brake Systems" chapter for brake system bleeding procedures.

BRAKE PAD SERVICE

Front

1. Raise and support vehicle, then remove tire and wheel assemblies.
2. Remove anti-rattle spring from outboard side of caliper and adapter.
3. Remove caps, guide pin bolts and caliper.
4. Remove pads.
5. Reverse procedure to install, noting the following:
   a. Press caliper piston back into piston bore of caliper.
   b. Apply brake pedal several times, then inspect master cylinder brake fluid level and adjust fluid.

Rear

1. Raise and support vehicle, then rear wheel and tire assemblies.
2. Remove caliper guide pin bolts.

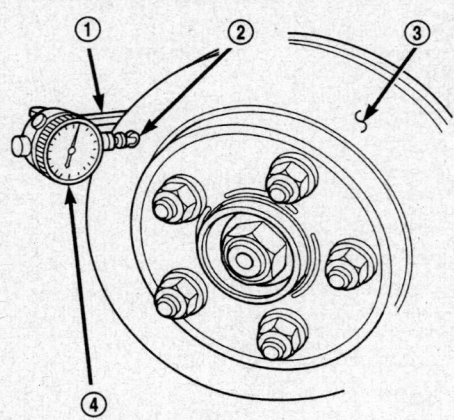

1 - SPECIAL TOOL SP-1910
2 - 25 mm FROM EDGE
3 - DISC SURFACE
4 - SPECIAL TOOL C-3339

CR4070100146000X

Fig. 1   Dial indicator mounting for rotor lateral runout

3. Rotate top of caliper away from adapter, then lift caliper off lower machined abutment on adapter.
4. Support caliper from rear strut assembly using suitable wire.
5. Remove outboard brake pad from caliper by prying brake pad retaining clip over raised area on caliper.
6. Pull inboard pad away from caliper piston until retaining clip is free from piston cavity.
7. Press piston completely into caliper bore.
8. Lubricate adapter abutments with Mopar multi-purpose grease, or equivalent.
9. Install inboard and outboard pads.
10. Place bottom of caliper over abutment, then rotate top of caliper into place.
11. Install caliper guide pin bolts.
12. Install tire and wheel assemblies, then lower vehicle and inspect brake fluid level.
13. Road test vehicle to remove any foreign material from brakes and seat brake pads.

CALIPER SERVICE

Replacement

1. Remove caliper from brake rotor and brake pads from caliper as outlined under "Brake Pad Service."
2. Disconnect brake hose at brake caliper. Cap brake line.
3. Reverse procedure to install.

Overhaul

1. Remove brake pads as outlined under "Brake Pad Service."
2. Hang caliper on suitable wire away from rotor.
3. Place suitable, small piece of wood between piston and caliper fingers.

4. Depress brake pedal to hydraulically push piston out of bore.
5. Apply and hold-down brake pedal to any position beyond first inch of brake travel to prevent master cylinder brake fluid loss.
6. Disconnect brake line from caliper. Plug brake line to avoid any additional brake fluid loss.
7. Mount brake caliper in suitable, soft jawed vise. **Excessive vise pressure will cause bore distortion and binding of piston.**
8. Remove guide pin bushings.
9. Remove and discard piston dust boot.
10. Work piston seal out of its groove using suitable plastic trim stick. **Do not use screw driver or other metal tool.**
11. Clean all components using alcohol, or suitable solvent, and wipe dry using a lint free cloth. **No lint residue can be left in caliper bore.**
12. Inspect piston bore for scoring or pitting. Light scratches or corrosion can usually be cleared from bores using crocus cloth. Bores that show deep scratches or scoring should be honed. **Bore diameter should not be honed more than .001 inch. If bore does not clean up within specification, replace caliper housing.**
13. When honing brake caliper housing, coat stones and bore with brake fluid.
14. After honing bore, clean seal and boot grooves with suitable, stiff non-metallic rotary brush.
15. Remove all dirt and grit by flushing caliper with brake fluid, wipe dry with lint free cloth.
16. Replace caliper piston if there is any pitting, scratches or physical damage.
17. Dip new piston seal in clean brake fluid and install in caliper bore groove. Seal should be positioned at one area in groove and gently worked around groove using only fingers until properly seated. **Never install old piston seal.**
18. Coat new piston boot with clean brake fluid leaving generous amount inside boot.
19. Coat dust boot with clean brake fluid and position over piston.
20. Install piston into caliper bore pushing it past piston seal until it bottoms in caliper bore.
21. Position dust boot in counterbore of caliper piston bore.
22. Drive boot into counterbore of caliper using suitable hammer and piston caliper boot installer No. C-4689 and handle No. C-4171, or equivalents, **Fig. 3.**
23. Install guide pin bushings and dust boots.
24. Attach hydraulic brake line to caliper. Use new seal washers when installing brake line to caliper.

ROTOR

REPLACE

1. Remove caliper from brake rotor as outlined under "Brake Pad Service."

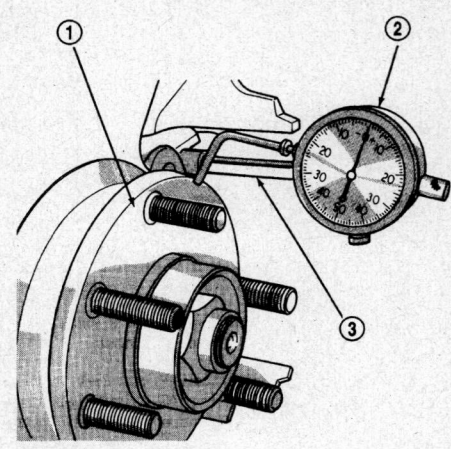

1 - HUB SURFACE
2 - SPECIAL TOOL C-3339
3 - SPECIAL TOOL SP-1910

CR4070100147000X

Fig. 2   Dial gauge mounting for hub lateral runout

2. Remove retaining clips and rotor. Use suitable soft face hammer to tap rotor free of hub as required.
3. Reverse procedure to install.

ADJUSTMENTS

Parking Brake Lever

1. Remove center floor console and lower parking brake handle.
2. Position lever to its fully released position.
3. Tighten adjusting nut on parking brake lever output cable until approximately 1.02 inch of thread is past edge of adjusting nut.
4. Actuate parking brake lever to its fully applied position (22 clicks) one time, then position lever to its fully released position.
5. Raise and support rear of vehicle.
6. Turn rear wheel with parking brake in released position to confirm rear brakes are not dragging.

Parking Brake Shoe

1. Raise and support vehicle, then remove rear wheels.
2. Remove adjusting hole plug from hub of brake disc.
3. Turn adjusting nut until brake disc cannot be turned by hand using suitable tool.
4. Back off adjusting nut five notches.
5. Firmly apply, then release parking brake lever several times to seat and center parking brake shoes.
6. Adjust parking brake lever as outlined under "Parking Brake Lever, Adjust."
7. Install rear wheels, then lower vehicle.

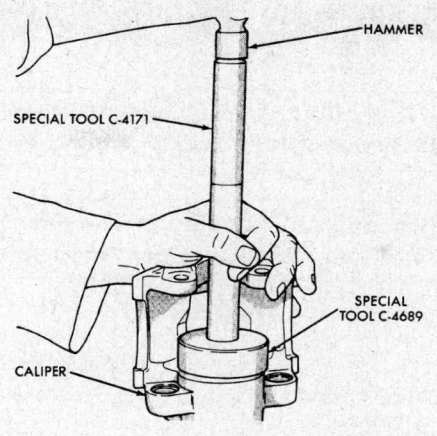

Fig. 3 Caliper piston boot installation

DISC BRAKE SPECIFICATIONS
Rotor Specifications

Year	Front Disc Brake						Rear Disc Brake					
	Brake Lining Wear Limit, Inch①	Rotor			Thickness Variation Parallelism, Inch	Lateral Run-Out (T.I.R.), Inch	Brake Lining Wear Limit, Inch①	Rotor			Thickness Variation Parallelism, Inch	Lateral Run-Out (T.I.R.), Inch
		Thickness, Inch						Thickness, Inch				
		Nominal	Min. Refinish	Discard Limit ②				Nominal	Min. Refinish	Discard Limit ②		
2004–06	—	.900–.911	—	.843	.0005	.004	—	.350–.360	—	.285	.0005	.005

① — Above rivet head or backing plate. Original equipment type brake lining.

② — Discard thickness is stamped on rotor.

TIGHTENING SPECIFICATIONS

Year	Component	Torque Ft. Lbs.
2004–06	Bleed Screws	10
	Brake Hose Intermediate Bracket	105①
	Brake Hose To Caliper (Banjo Bolt)	26
	Brake Tube	12
	Caliper Adapter	60
	Caliper Guide & Lockpins	26
	Wheel Lug Nuts	100

① — Inch lbs.

Sebring Coupe & Stratus Coupe

NOTE: On Air Bag Equipped Models, Refer To "Air Bag System Precautions" Located In The Front Of This Manual For System Disarming & Arming Procedures.

NOTE: Refer To "Computer Relearn Procedures" Located In The Front Of This Manual When Battery Power To The Computer Has Been Interrupted.

INDEX

	Page No.
Adjustments	14-21
Parking Brake Lever	14-21
Parking Brake Shoe	14-21
Brake Pad Service	14-20
Front	14-20
Rear	14-20
Brake System Bleed	14-20

	Page No.
Caliper Service	14-20
Overhaul	14-20
Front	14-20
Rear	14-20
Replacement	14-20
Disc Brake Specifications	14-25
Caliper Specifications	14-26

	Page No.
Rotor Specifications	14-25
Rotor, Replace	14-21
Tightening Specifications	14-26
Troubleshooting	14-20
Lateral Runout Inspection	14-20
Parallelism Inspection	14-20

TROUBLESHOOTING

Refer to **Fig. 1** for brake system troubleshooting.

Lateral Runout Inspection

1. Remove mounting bolts and caliper.
2. Inspect disc surface for grooves, cracks and rust.
3. Place suitable dial gauge approximately .2 inch from outer circumference of brake rotor.
4. Measure runout of rotor.
5. If runout of rotor is equal to or exceeds specifications, proceed as follows:
   a. Before removing brake rotor, chalk both sides of wheel stud on side at which runout is greatest.
   b. Remove brake rotor and place dial gauge as outlined, **Fig. 2.**
   c. Move hub in axial direction and measure play. If play exceeds .002 inch disassemble hub knuckle and inspect each part.
   d. If play does not exceed limit specification, install brake rotor 180° away from chalk marks.
   e. Inspect runout of brake rotor again.
   f. If runout cannot be corrected by changing phase of rotor, replace or machine rotor.

Parallelism Inspection

Measure the rotor thickness at eight positions approximately 45° apart and .39 inch in from outer edge of disc, using suitable micrometer.

BRAKE SYSTEM BLEED

Refer to "Hydraulic Brake Systems" chapter for brake system bleeding procedures.

BRAKE PAD SERVICE

Front

1. Raise and support vehicle, then remove tire and wheel assemblies.
2. Remove guide pin, lift caliper body upward and secure with suitable wire, **Fig. 3.**
3. Remove inner shims, anti-squeak shims, brake pad and clips from support mounting.
4. Reverse procedure to install, noting the following:
   a. Press caliper piston back into piston bore of caliper using suitable tool.
   b. Apply brake pedal several times, then inspect master cylinder brake fluid level and adjust fluid.

Rear

1. Raise and support vehicle, then remove rear wheel and tire assemblies.
2. Remove pin bolts and lift caliper from support.
3. Support caliper from rear strut using suitable wire.
4. Remove outboard brake pad and wear indicator.
5. Remove inner shims and inboard pad.
6. Remove outer shim and clip.
7. Reverse procedure to install.

CALIPER SERVICE

Replacement

1. Remove caliper from brake rotor and brake pads from caliper as outlined under "Brake Pad Service."
2. Disconnect brake hose at brake caliper. Cap brake line.
3. Reverse procedure to install.

Overhaul

FRONT

1. Remove caliper assembly as outlined under "Replacement."
2. Remove lockpin, bushing, caliper support, guide pin and lockpin boots, **Fig. 3.**
3. Remove boot ring using suitable flat blade screwdriver.
4. Position shop towel in caliper body, then apply compressed air through brake hose fitting hole to remove piston and dust boot. **Apply air gently.**
5. Remove piston seal using finger tips. **Do not use screwdriver or other tool.**
6. Reverse procedure to assemble, noting following:
   a. Inspect cylinder and piston for wear or damage and/or corrosion. Inspect caliper body and sleeve for wear.
   b. Apply suitable brake fluid to inner cylinder, then install piston seal into cylinder groove. **Do not wipe special grease from piston seal.**
   c. Apply suitable brake fluid to piston and insert into cylinder without twisting.
   d. Fill piston edge with grease from seal and boot repair kit, or equivalent, then install piston boot.
   e. Lubricate sliding surface of lockpin and guide pin boots, caliper support and bushing with grease from seal and boot repair kit.
   f. Install guide and lockpins with their head marks matched with identification marks on caliper body.

REAR

1. Remove caliper assembly as outlined under "Replacement."
2. Remove caliper support, **Fig. 4.**
3. Remove pin boots and boot ring.
4. Position suitable wood block in caliper body, then apply compressed air

through brake hose fitting hole to remove piston and dust boot. **Apply air gently.**

5. Remove piston seal using finger tip.
6. Reverse procedure to assemble, noting following:
   a. Inspect cylinder and piston for wear, damage and/or corrosion. Inspect caliper body and sleeve for wear.
   b. Apply brake fluid to inner cylinder, then install piston seal into cylinder groove. **Do not wipe grease from piston seal.**
   c. Apply brake fluid to pistons and insert into cylinders by pushing downward into caliper. **Do not twist pistons into caliper.**
   d. Fill piston edge with grease from seal and boot repair kit, then install piston boot.
   e. Lubricate bushing, pin boot and slide pins with grease from seal and boot repair kit.
   f. Install guide and lockpins. Ensure head marks match with identification marks on caliper body.

ROTOR
REPLACE

1. Remove caliper from brake rotor as outlined under "Brake Pad Service."
2. Remove rotor. Use suitable soft face hammer to tap rotor free of hub as required.
3. Reverse procedure to install.

ADJUSTMENTS
Parking Brake Lever

1. Pull parking brake lever with approximately 45 ft. lbs., force and count number of notches.
2. Standard value is 5–7 notches with drum brakes and 3–5 notches with disc brakes. If parking brake lever stroke is not as specified, proceed to next step.
3. Remove inner compartment mat of floor console.
4. Loosen adjusting nut to end of cable rod to free cable.
5. Remove adjustment hole plug and to turn adjuster using suitable flat tipped screwdriver.
6. Turn adjuster in direction which expands shoes so disc will not rotate.
7. Return adjuster five notches in opposite direction.
8. Turn adjusting nut to adjust parking brake lever stroke within standard

value. **If number of brake lever notches engaged is less than standard value, cable has been excessively pulled.**
9. Inspect to ensure there is no play between adjusting nut and pin.
10. Raise and support rear of vehicle.
11. Turn rear wheel with parking brake in released position to confirm rear brakes are not dragging.

Parking Brake Shoe

1. Raise and support vehicle, then remove rear wheels.

2. Firmly apply, then release parking brake lever several times to seat and center parking brake shoes.
3. Remove adjusting hole plug from hub of brake disc.
4. Turn adjusting nut until brake disc cannot be turned by hand using suitable tool.
5. Back off adjusting nut five notches.
6. Repeat above steps on opposite side.
7. Firmly apply, then release parking brake lever several times to seat and center parking brake shoes.

Symptom	Probable cause	Remedy
Vehicle pulls to one side when brakes are applied	Grease or oil on pad or lining surface	Replace
	Inadequate contact of pad or lining	Correct
	Auto adjuster malfunction	Adjust
	Drum out of round or uneven wear	Repair or replace as necessary
Insufficient braking power	Low or deteriorated brake fluid	Refill or change
	Air in brake system	Bleed air from system
	Overheated brake rotor due to dragging of pad or lining	Correct
	Inadequate contact of pad or lining	
	Brake booster malfunction	
	Clogged brake line	
	Grease or oil on pad or lining surface	Replace
	Proportioning valve malfunction	
	Auto adjuster malfunction	Adjust
Increased pedal stroke (Reduced pedal to floorboard clearance)	Air in brake system	Bleed air from system
	Worn lining or pad	Replace
	Broken vacuum hose	
	Faulty master cylinder	
	Brake fluid leaks	Correct
	Auto adjuster malfunction	Adjust
	Excessive push rod to master cylinder clearance	
Brake drag	Incomplete release of parking brake	Correct
	Clogged master cylinder return port	
	Incorrect parking brake adjustment	Adjust
	Incorrect push rod to master cylinder clearance	
	Faulty master cylinder piston return spring	Replace
	Worn brake pedal return spring	
	Broken rear drum brake shoe return spring	
	Lack of lubrication in sliding parts	Lubricate

CR4079100038010X

Fig. 1   Brake system troubleshooting (Part 1 of 3)

Symptom	Probable cause	Remedy
Insufficient parking brake function	Worn brake lining	Replace
	Grease or oil on lining surface	
	Parking brake cable sticking	
	Stuck wheel cylinder or caliper piston	
	Excessive parking brake lever stroke	Adjust the parking brake lever stroke or check the parking brake cable routing
	Auto adjuster malfunction	Adjust
Scraping or grinding noise when brakes are applied	Worn brake lining or pad	Replace
	Caliper to wheel interference	Correct or replace
	Dust cover to disc interference	
	Bent brake backing plate	
	Cracked drums or brake disc	
Squealing, groaning or chattering noise when brakes are applied	Missing or damaged brake pad anti-squeak shim	Replace
	Brake drums and linings, discs and pads worn or scored	Correct or replace
	Incorrect parts	
	Burred or rusted calipers	Clean or deburr
	Dirty, greased, contaminated or glazed linings	Clean or replace
	Drum brakes-weak, damaged or incorrect shoe hold-down springs, loose or damaged shoe hold-down pins and springs	Correct or replace
	Incorrect brake pedal or booster push rod setting	Adjust
Squealing noise when brakes are not applied	Bent or warped backing plate causing interference with drum	Replace
	Drum brakes-weak, damaged or incorrect shoe-to-shoe spring	
	Poor return of brake booster, master cylinder or wheel cylinder	
	Loose or extra brake parts	Retighten

CR4079100038020X

Fig. 1   Brake system troubleshooting (Part 2 of 3)

Symptom	Probable cause	Remedy
Squealing noise when brakes are not applied	Improper positioning of pads in caliper	Correct
	Improper installation of support mounting to caliper body	
	Improper machining of drum causing interference with backing plate or shoe	Replace drum
	Disc brakes-rusted, stuck	Lubricate or replace
	Worn, damaged or insufficiently lubricated wheel bearings	
	Incorrect brake pedal or booster push rod setting	Adjust
Groaning clicking or rattling noise when brakes are not applied	Stones or foreign material trapped inside wheel covers	Remove stones, etc.
	Loose wheel nuts	Retighten
	Disc brakes-loose installation bolt	
	Worn, damaged or dry wheel bearings	Lubricate or replace
	Disc brakes-failure of anti-rattle shim	Replace
	Disc brakes-wear on sleeve	
	Incorrect brake pedal or booster push rod setting	Adjust

CR4079100038030X

Fig. 1   Brake system troubleshooting (Part 3 of 3)

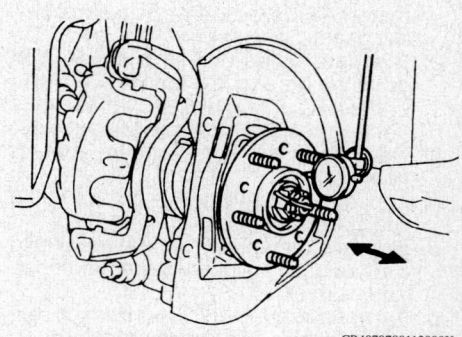

CR4079700112000X

Fig. 2   Dial gauge mounting

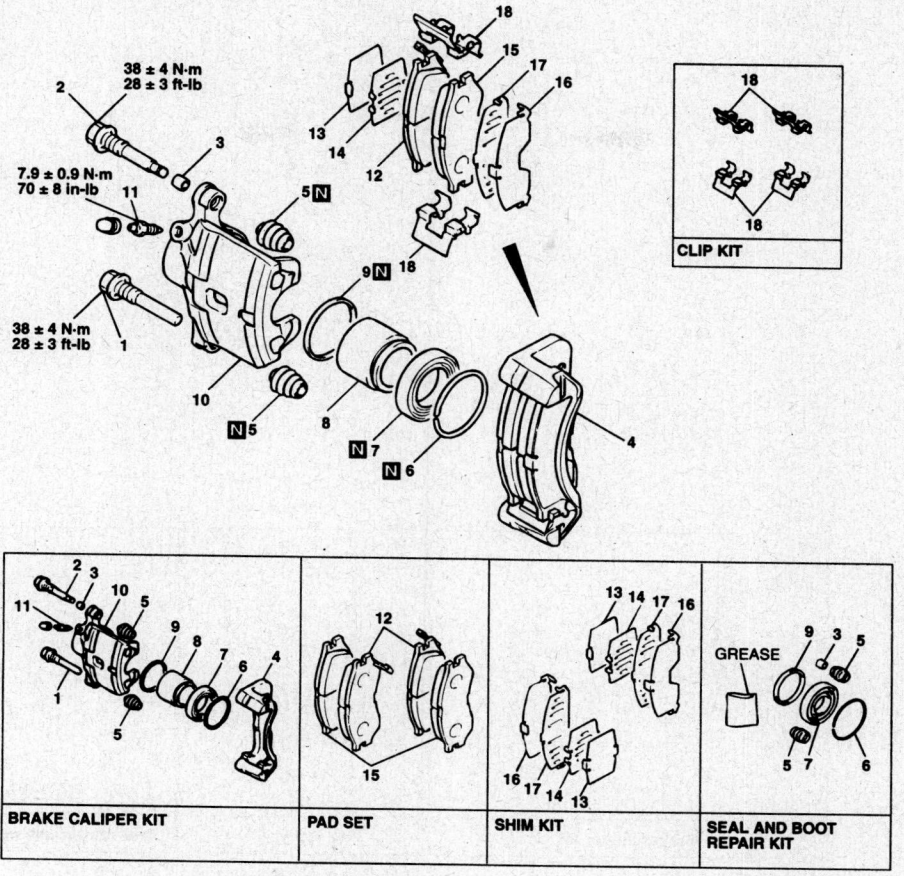

| BRAKE CALIPER KIT | PAD SET | SHIM KIT | SEAL AND BOOT REPAIR KIT |

CALIPER ASSEMBLY DISASSEMBLY STEPS
1. GUIDE PIN
2. LOCK PIN
3. BUSHING
4. CALIPER SUPPORT, PAD, CLIP AND SHIM ASSEMBLY
5. PIN BOOT
6. BOOT RING
7. PISTON BOOT
8. PISTON

9. PISTON SEAL
10. CALIPER BODY
11. BLEEDER SCREW

PAD ASSEMBLY DISASSEMBLY STEPS
1. GUIDE PIN
2. LOCK PIN
3. BUSHING
4. CALIPER SUPPORT, PAD, CLIP AND SHIM ASSEMBLY
12. PAD AND WEAR INDICATOR ASSEMBLY
13. INNER SHIM B
14. INNER SHIM A
15. PAD ASSEMBLY
16. OUTER SHIM B
17. OUTER SHIM A
18. CLIP

CR4070000144000X

Fig. 3   Disc brake

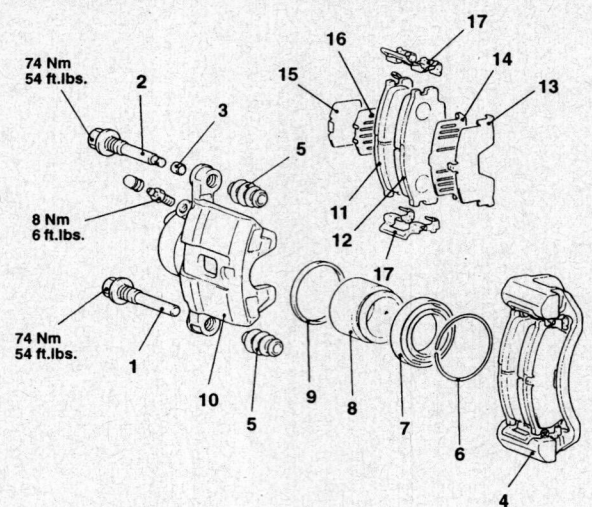

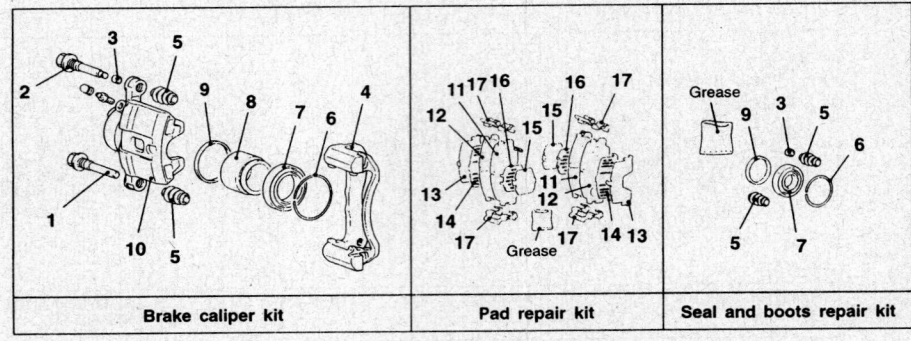

| Brake caliper kit | Pad repair kit | Seal and boots repair kit |

Caliper assembly

1. Guide pin
2. Lock pin
3. Bushing
4. Caliper support (pad, clip, shim)
5. Boot
6. Boot ring
7. Piston boot
8. Piston
9. Piston seal
10. Caliper body

Pad assembly

1. Guide pin
2. Lock pin
3. Bushing
4. Caliper support (pad, clip, shim)
11. Pad and wear indicator assembly
12. Pad assembly
13. Outer shim (stainless)
14. Outer shim (coated with rubber)
15. Inner shim (stainless)
16. Inner shim (coated with rubber)
17. Clip

CR4079100045000X

Fig. 4   Dual pin floating caliper disc brake. Rear

DISC BRAKE SPECIFICATIONS
Rotor Specifications

Year	Brake Lining Wear Limit, Inch[3]	Front Disc Brake					Brake Lining Wear Limit, Inch[3]	Rear Disc Brake				
		Rotor			Thickness Variation Parallelism, Inch	Lateral Run-Out (T.I.R.), Inch		Rotor			Thickness Variation Parallelism, Inch	Lateral Run-Out (T.I.R.), Inch
		Thickness, Inch						Thickness, Inch				
		Nominal	Min. Refinish	Discard Limit[2]				Nominal	Min. Refinish	Discard Limit[2]		
2004–05	.08	[1]	—	[4]	—	.002	.08	.40	—	.33	—	.003

[1] — 2.4L engine, .90 inch; 3.0L engine, 1.02 inches.
[2] — Discard thickness is stamped on rotor.
[3] — Above rivet head or backing plate. Original equipment type brake lining.
[4] — 2.4L engine, .88 inch; 3.0L engine, .96 inch.

Caliper Specifications

Location	Caliper Bore Dia. Inch
Front	2.375
Rear	1.375

TIGHTENING SPECIFICATIONS

Year	Component	Torque Ft. Lbs.
2004–05	Backing Plate	36–43
	Bleed Screws	50–84①
	Brake Hose To Rear Caliper Banjo Bolts	11–12
	Caliper Guide & Lockpins, Front	28–31
	Caliper Guide & Lockpins, Rear	32
	Caliper Support To Front Axle	65
	Caliper Support To Rear Axle	36–43
	Wheel Lug Nuts	87–101

① — Inch lbs.

DRUM BRAKES

TABLE OF CONTENTS

Page No.

CALIBER, 2007–08 AVENGER SEDAN & SEBRING SEDAN 15-1
NEON 15-4

Page No.

SEBRING CONVERTIBLE, STRATUS SEDAN & 2004–06 SEBRING SEDAN 15-7
SEBRING COUPE & STRATUS COUPE 15-9

Caliber, 2007–08 Avenger Sedan & Sebring Sedan

NOTE: On Air Bag Equipped Models, Refer To "Air Bag System Precautions" Located In The Front Of This Manual For System Disarming & Arming Procedures.

NOTE: Refer To "Computer Relearn Procedures" Located In The Front Of This Manual When Battery Power To The Computer Has Been Interrupted.

INDEX

Page No.

Adjustments 15-2
  Brake Shoe 15-2
Brake Service 15-2
  Shoe, Replace 15-2
  Wheel Cylinder, Replace 15-2

Page No.

Drum Brake Specifications 15-4
Inspection 15-1
  Adjuster Mechanism 15-2
  Backing Plate 15-2
  Brake Drums 15-1

Page No.

Brake Linings & Springs 15-1
  Parking Brake Cable 15-2
Precautions 15-1
Tightening Specifications 15-4
Troubleshooting 15-2

PRECAUTIONS

When working on or around brake assemblies, care must be taken to prevent breathing asbestos dust. During routine service operations, the amount of asbestos dust from brake lining wear is at a low level because of a chemical breakdown during use. A few precautions will minimize exposure.

Do not sand or grind brake linings unless suitable local exhaust ventilation equipment is used to prevent excessive asbestos exposure.

1. Wear suitable respirator approved for asbestos dust use during repair procedures.
2. When cleaning brake dust from brake components, use vacuum cleaner with highly efficient filter system. If suitable vacuum cleaner is not available, use water soaked rag. **Do not use compressed air or dry brush to clean brake components.**
3. Keep work area clean.
4. Properly dispose of rags and vacuum cleaner bags by placing them in plastic bags.
5. Do not smoke or eat while working on brake systems.
6. Never use any fluid containing mineral oil to clean brake system components.

INSPECTION

Brake Drums

When brake drums are removed for brake service, the braking surface diameter should be inspected with a suitable brake drum micrometer at several points to determine if they are within the safe oversize limit stamped on the brake drum outer surface. If the braking surface diameter exceeds specifications, the drum must be replaced. If the braking surface diameter is within specifications, drums should be cleaned and inspected for cracks, scores, deep grooves, taper, out of round and heat spotting. If drums are cracked or heat spotted, they must be replaced. Scoring and grooves in the braking surface can only be removed by machining with special equipment, as long as the braking surface is within specifications. Any brake drum showing taper or sufficiently out of round to cause vehicle vibration or noise while braking should also be machined, removing only enough stock to true up the drum.

After a brake drum is machined, wipe the braking surface diameter with a denatured alcohol soaked cloth. If one brake drum is machined, the other should also be machined to the same diameter to maintain equal braking forces.

Brake Linings & Springs

Inspect brake linings for excessive wear, damage, oil, grease or brake fluid contamination. If any of these conditions exist, brake linings should be replaced as an axle set to maintain equal braking forces. Examine brake shoe webbing, hold-down and return springs for signs of overheating indicated by a slight blue color. Any component which exhibits overheating signs should be replaced. Overheated springs lose their pull and could cause brake linings to wear out prematurely. Inspect springs for sags, bends and external damage and replace as required.

Inspect hold-down retainers and pins for

DRUM BRAKES

RED BRAKE WARNING INDICATOR

CONDITION	POSSIBLE CAUSES	CORRECTION
RED BRAKE WARNING INDICATOR ON	1. Parking brake lever not fully released.	1. Release parking brake lever.
	2. Parking brake warning switch on parking brake lever.	2. Inspect and replace switch as necessary.
	3. Brake fluid level low in reservoir.	3. Fill reservoir. Check entire system for leaks. Repair or replace as required.
	4. Brake fluid level switch.	4. Disconnect switch wiring connector. If lamp goes out, replace switch.
	5. Mechanical instrument cluster (MIC) problem.	5. Refer to appropriate diagnostic information.
	6. ABS EVBP malfunction.	6. Refer to ABS section and appropriate diagnostic information.

BRAKE NOISE

CONDITION	POSSIBLE CAUSES	CORRECTION
DISC BRAKE CHIRP	1. Excessive brake rotor runout.	1. Diagnose and correct as necessary.
DISC BRAKE MOAN OR HOWL WHILE BRAKING IN REVERSE	1. Rear disc brake caliper guide pin bolts installed in incorrect locations.	1. Remove lower guide pin bolt and inspect for special sleeve on tip. If sleeve is present, remove upper and lower guide pin bolts and install special sleeved bolt in upper location and standard guide pin bolt in lower location. Perform on both sides of vehicle. Replace rear brake pads.
DISC BRAKE RATTLE OR CLUNK	1. Broken or missing spring clips.	1. Replace brake pads.
	2. Caliper guide pin bolts loose.	2. Tighten guide pin bolts.
	3. Missing abutment shims.	3. Replace missing abutment shims.

ARM0600000001204

Fig. 1   Brake system troubleshooting (Part 1 of 5)

DISC BRAKE SQUEAK AT LOW SPEED (WHILE APPLYING LIGHT BRAKE PEDAL EFFORT)	1. Brake shoe linings.	1. Replace brake pads.
DRUM BRAKE CHIRP	1. Lack of lubricant on brake shoe support plate where shoes ride.	1. Lubricate shoe contact areas on brake shoe support plates.
	2. Wheel cylinder out of alignment.	2. Loosen wheel cylinder mounting bolts, realign wheel cylinder with brake shoes and tighten mounting bolts.
DRUM BRAKE CLUNK	1. Drum(s) have threaded machined braking surface.	1. Reface or replace drake drums as necessary.
DRUM BRAKE HOWL OR MOAN	1. Lack of lubricant on brake shoe support plate where shoes ride and at the anchor.	1. Lubricate shoe contact areas on brake shoe support plates and at the anchor.
	2. Rear brake shoes.	2. Replace rear brake shoes.
SCRAPING (METAL-TO-METAL).	1. Foreign object interference with brakes.	1. Inspect brakes and remove foreign object.
	2. Brake pads/shoes worn out.	2. Replace brake pads/shoes. Inspect rotors and drums. Reface or replace as necessary.
SCRAPING OR WHIRRING	1. ABS wheel speed sensor hitting tone wheel.	1. Inspect, correct or replace faulty component(s).

OTHER BRAKE CONDITIONS

CONDITION	POSSIBLE CAUSES	CORRECTION
BRAKES CHATTER	1. Rear brake drum out of round or disc brake rotor has excessive thickness variation.	1. Isolate condition as rear or front. Reface or replace brake drums or rotors as necessary.

ARM0600000001205

Fig. 1   Brake system troubleshooting (Part 2 of 5)

bends, rust and corrosion. If any of these are found, replace as required.

Backing Plate

Inspect backing plate shoe contact surface for grooves that may restrict shoe movement and cannot be removed by lightly sanding with emery cloth or other suitable abrasive. If backing plate exhibits these conditions, it should be replaced. Also inspect for signs of cracks, warpage and excessive rust, indicating need for replacement.

Adjuster Mechanism

Inspect components for rust, corrosion, bends and fatigue. Replace as required. On adjuster mechanism equipped with adjuster cable, inspect cable for kinks, fraying or elongation of eyelet and replace as required.

Parking Brake Cable

Inspect parking brake cable end for kinks, fraying and elongation and replace as required. Use a small hose clamp to compress clamp where it enters backing plate to remove.

TROUBLESHOOTING

Refer to **Fig. 1** for troubleshooting procedures.

BRAKE SERVICE
Shoe, Replace

1. Raise and support vehicle, then remove tire and wheel assembly.
2. Loosen parking brake cable nut, then remove brake drum, **Fig. 2.**
3. Remove brake drum.
4. Remove lower shoe spring.
5. Compress and remove hold-down spring retaining rear shoe to support plate.
6. Pull rear shoe away from anchor allowing access to parking brake cable lever connection.
7. Compress cable return spring, then remove parking brake cable from lever.
8. Compress and remove hold-down spring retaining front shoe to support plate.
9. Remove both brake shoes from wheel cylinder.
10. Remove both shoes and remaining parts as an assembly through opening

between wheel cylinder and support plate hub and bearing.
11. Reverse procedure to install.

Wheel Cylinder, Replace

1. Depress brake pedal past its first inch of travel and hold it in position using brake pedal holding tool.
2. Raise and support vehicle, then remove tire and wheel assembly.
3. Remove brake shoe as outlined under "Shoe, Replace."
4. Disconnect brake tube at wheel cylinder.
5. Remove wheel cylinder mounting bolts, then wheel cylinder.
6. Reverse procedure to install.

ADJUSTMENTS
Brake Shoe

1. Raise and support vehicle, then remove tire and wheel assembly.
2. Remove brake drum.
3. Measure inside diameter of brake

BRAKES DRAG (FRONT OR ALL)	1. Contaminated brake fluid.	1. Check for swollen seals. Replace all system components containing rubber.
	2. Binding caliper pins or bushings.	2. Replace pins and bushings
	3. Misadjusted brake lamp switch.	3. Replace brake lamp switch.
	4. Master cylinder not fully returning.	4. Inspect master cylinder and replace as necessary.
	5. Binding brake pedal.	5. Replace brake pedal/bushings.
BRAKES DRAG (REAR ONLY)	1. Parking brake cables binding or froze up.	1. Check cable routing. Replace cables as necessary.
	2. Parking brake cable return spring not returning shoes.	2. Replace cables as necessary.
	3. Service brakes not adjusted properly (rear drum brakes only).	3. Adjust rear brake shoes. Refer to Brake Pads/Shoes - Drum Brake.
	4. Obstruction inside the center console preventing full return of the parking brake cables.	4. Remove console and remove obstruction.
BRAKES GRAB	1. Contaminated brake pad/shoe linings.	1. Inspect and clean, or replace pads/shoes. Repair source of contamination.
	2. Improper power brake booster assist.	2. Refer to Power Brake Booster in this section.
EXCESSIVE PEDAL EFFORT	1. Obstruction of brake pedal.	1. Inspect, remove or move obstruction.
	2. Low power brake booster assist.	2. Refer to Power Brake Booster in this section.
	3. Glazed brake linings.	3. Reface or replace brake rotors as necessary. Replace brake shoes.
	4. Brake pad lining transfer to brake rotor.	4. Reface or replace brake rotors as necessary. Replace brake pads.

ARM0600000001206

Fig. 1 Brake system troubleshooting (Part 3 of 5)

EXCESSIVE PEDAL EFFORT (HARD PEDAL - CAN'T SKID WHEELS)	1. Power brake booster runout (vacuum assist).	1. Check booster vacuum hose and engine tune for adequate vacuum supply.
EXCESSIVE PEDAL TRAVEL (VEHICLE STOPS OK)	1. Air in brake lines.	1. Bleed brakes.
	2. Rear drum brake auto-adjuster malfunctioning.	2. Inspect and replace drum brake components as necessary. Adjust rear brakes.
EXCESSIVE PEDAL TRAVEL (ONE FRONT WHEEL LOCKS UP DURING HARD BRAKING)	1. One of the two hydraulic circuits is malfunctioning.	1. Inspect system for leaks. Check master cylinder for internal malfunction.
PEDAL PULSATES/SURGES DURING BRAKING	1. Rear brake drum out of round or disc brake rotor has excessive thickness variation.	1. Isolate condition as rear or front. Reface or replace brake drums or rotors as necessary.
PEDAL IS SPONGY	1. Air in brake lines.	1. Bleed brakes.
PREMATURE REAR WHEEL LOCKUP	1. Contaminated brake shoe linings.	1. Inspect and clean, or replace shoes. Repair source of contamination.
	2. Inoperative proportioning valve (non-ABS vehicles only).	2. Replace proportioning valves as necessary.
	3. ABS EVBP not functioning.	3. Refer to the ABS and appropriate diagnostic information.
STOP LAMPS STAY ON	1. Brake lamp switch out of adjustment.	1. Replace brake lamp switch.
	2. Brake pedal binding.	2. Inspect and replace as necessary.
	3. Power brake booster not allowing pedal to return completely.	3. Replace power brake booster.

ARM0600000001207

Fig. 1 Brake system troubleshooting (Part 4 of 5)

VEHICLE PULLS TO RIGHT OR LEFT ON BRAKING	1. Frozen brake caliper piston.	1. Replace frozen piston or caliper. Bleed brakes.
	2. Contaminated brake pad/shoe lining (most likely front lining).	2. Inspect and clean, or replace pads/shoes. Repair source of contamination.
	3. Pinched brake lines.	3. Replace pinched line.
	4. Leaking piston seal.	4. Replace piston seal or brake caliper.
	5. Suspension problem.	5. Refer to the Suspension
PARKING BRAKE - EXCESSIVE HANDLE TRAVEL	1. Rear brakes out of adjustment.	1. Adjust rear drum brake shoes, or rear parking brake shoes on vehicles with rear disc brakes.

ARM0600000001208

Fig. 1 Brake system troubleshooting (Part 5 of 5)

drum at center of shoe using a brake shoe gauge tool No. C-3919 or equivalent.

4. Adjust shoe diameter to setting on gauge by turning adjuster wheel in rear of shoe support plate.

5. Install brake drum and inspect operation.

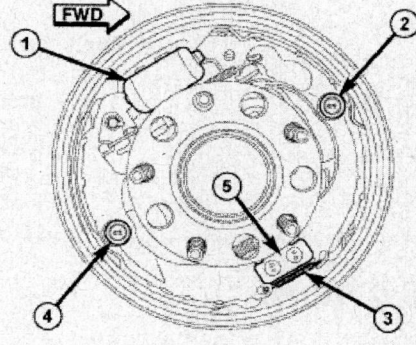

1- Wheel Cylinder
2- Hold Down Spring
3- Lower Shoe Spring
4- Hold Down Spring

ARM0600000001209

Fig. 2   View of brake drum

DRUM BRAKES

DRUM BRAKE SPECIFICATIONS

| Year | Brake Lining Wear Limit, Inch① | Brake Drum Inside Diameter, Inches | | | Drum Runout Limit, Inch | Drum Maximum Out Of Roundness, Inch |
		Nominal	Maximum Refinish	Maximum Inside Diameter (Discard Limit)		
2007–08	—	9.00	—	9.079	.002	—

① — Above rivet head or shoe. Original equipment type brake linings.

TIGHTENING SPECIFICATIONS

Year	Component	Torque Ft. Lbs.
2007–08	Brake Tube Nuts	13
	Disc Brake Caliper Guide Pin Bolts	32
	Front Caliper Adapter Mounting Bolts	80
	Parking Brake Lever Mounting Bolts	21
	Wheel Cylinder Bleeder Screw	10
	Wheel Cylinder Mounting Bolts	10

Neon

NOTE: On Air Bag Equipped Models, Refer To "Air Bag System Precautions" Located In The Front Of This Manual For System Disarming & Arming Procedures.

NOTE: Refer To "Computer Relearn Procedures" Located In The Front Of This Manual When Battery Power To The Computer Has Been Interrupted.

INDEX

	Page No.
Adjustments	15-5
Parking Brake	15-6
Service Brake	15-5
Brake Service	15-5
Installation	15-5
Removal	15-5
Drum Brake Specifications	15-6
Inspection	15-4
Adjuster Mechanism	15-5
Backing Plate	15-5
Brake Drums	15-4
Brake Linings & Springs	15-5
Parking Brake Cable	15-5
Wheel Cylinder	15-5
Precautions	15-4
Tightening Specifications	15-7
Troubleshooting	15-5

PRECAUTIONS

When working on or around brake assemblies, care must be taken to prevent breathing asbestos dust. During routine service operations, the amount of asbestos dust from brake lining wear is at a low level because of a chemical breakdown during use. A few precautions will minimize exposure.

Do not sand or grind brake linings unless suitable exhaust ventilation equipment is used to prevent excessive asbestos exposure.

1. Wear suitable respirator approved for asbestos dust use during repair procedures.
2. When cleaning brake dust from brake components, use vacuum cleaner with highly efficient filter system. If suitable vacuum cleaner is not available, use water soaked rag. **Do not use compressed air or dry brush to clean brake components.**
3. Keep work area clean.
4. Properly dispose of rags and vacuum cleaner bags by placing them in plastic bags.
5. Do not smoke or eat while working on brake systems.
6. Never use any fluid containing mineral oil to clean brake system components.

INSPECTION

Brake Drums

Any time the brake drums are removed for brake service, the braking surface diameter should be inspected with a suitable brake drum micrometer at several points to determine if they are within the safe oversize limit stamped on the brake drum outer surface. If the braking surface diameter exceeds specifications, the drum must be replaced. If the braking surface diameter is within specifications, drums should be cleaned and inspected for cracks, scores, deep grooves, taper, out of round and heat spotting. If drums are cracked or heat spotted, they must be replaced. Scoring and grooves in the braking surface can only be removed by machining with special equipment, as long as the braking surface is within specifications. Any brake drum showing taper or sufficient out of round to cause vehicle vibration or noise while braking should also be machined, removing only enough stock to true up the drum.

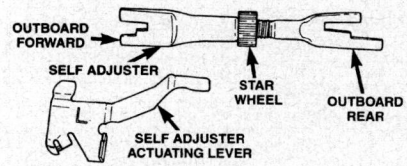

Fig. 1 Automatic self-adjuster mechanism

After a brake drum is machined, wipe the braking surface diameter with a denatured alcohol soaked cloth. If one brake drum is machined, the other should also be machined to the same diameter to maintain equal braking forces.

Brake Linings & Springs

Inspect brake linings for excessive wear, damage, oil, grease or brake fluid contamination. If any of these conditions exist, brake linings should be replaced as an axle set to maintain equal braking forces. Examine brake shoe webbing, hold-down and return springs for signs of overheating indicated by a slight blue color. Any component which exhibits overheating signs should be replaced. Overheated springs lose their pull and could cause brake linings to wear out prematurely. Inspect springs for sags, bends and external damage and replace as required.

Inspect hold-down retainers and pins for bends, rust and corrosion. Replace faulty components as required.

Wheel Cylinder

With brake drum removed, inspect the wheel cylinder for fluid leaks. Inspect wheel cylinder boots for cuts, tears, or heat cracks. Replace faulty components as required.

Backing Plate

Inspect backing plate shoe contact surface for grooves that may restrict shoe movement and cannot be removed by lightly sanding with emery cloth or other suitable abrasive. If backing plate exhibits these conditions, it should be replaced. Also inspect for signs of cracks, warpage and excessive rust, indicating need for replacement.

Adjuster Mechanism

1. Ensure quadrant rotates freely throughout its tooth contact range, **Fig. 1**.
2. Ensure quadrant slides freely entire length of its mounting slot.
3. Inspect quadrant spring for any signs of damage.
4. Ensure knurled pin is securely attached to adjuster mechanism and teeth are not damaged.
5. Examine adjuster mechanism for ex-

RED BRAKE WARNING LAMP

CONDITION	POSSIBLE CAUSES	CORRECTION
RED BRAKE WARNING LAMP ON	1. Parking brake lever not fully released.	1. Release parking brake lever.
	2. Parking brake warning lamp switch on parking brake lever.	2. Inspect and replace switch as necessary.
	3. Brake fluid level low in reservoir.	3. Fill reservoir. Check entire system for leaks. Repair or replace as required.
	4. Brake fluid level switch.	4. Disconnect switch wiring connector. If lamp goes out, replace switch.
	5. Mechanical instrument cluster (MIC) problem.	5. Diagnose Instrument Cluster Fault Condition.
	6. ABS EBD malfunction.	6. Refer to ABS section.

BRAKE NOISE

CONDITION	POSSIBLE CAUSES	CORRECTION
DISC BRAKE CHIRP	1. Excessive brake rotor runout.	1. Follow brake rotor diagnosis and testing. Correct as necessary.
	2. Lack of lubricant on brake caliper slides.	2. Lubricate brake caliper slides.
DISC BRAKE RATTLE OR CLUNK	1. Broken or missing anti-rattle spring clips on shoes.	1. Replace brake shoes.
	2. Caliper guide pins loose.	2. Tighten guide pins.
DISC BRAKE SQUEAK AT LOW SPEED (WHILE APPLYING LIGHT BRAKE PEDAL EFFORT)	1. Brake shoe linings.	1. Replace brake shoes.
DRUM BRAKE CHIRP	1. Lack of lubricant on brake shoe support plate where shoes ride.	1. Lubricate shoe contact areas on brake shoe support plates.
	2. Wheel cylinder out of alignment.	2. Loosen wheel cylinder mounting bolts, realign wheel cylinder with brake shoes and tighten mounting bolts.
DRUM BRAKE CLUNK	1. Drum(s) have threaded machined braking surface.	1. Reface or replace drake drums as necessary.
DRUM BRAKE HOWL OR MOAN	1. Lack of lubricant on brake shoe support plate where shoes ride and at the anchor.	1. Lubricate shoe contact areas on brake shoe support plates and at the anchor.
	2. Rear brake shoes.	2. Replace rear brake shoes.
DRUM BRAKE SCRAPING OR WHIRRING	1. ABS wheel speed sensor or tone wheel.	1. Inspect, correct or replace faulty component(s).
SCRAPING (METAL-TO-METAL).	1. Foreign object interference with brakes.	1. Inspect brakes and remove foreign object.
	2. Brake shoes worn out.	2. Replace brake shoes. Inspect rotors and drums. Reface or replace as necessary.

CR4089900044010X

Fig. 2 Brake system troubleshooting (Part 1 of 3)

cessive wear or damage. Replace as required.
6. If adjuster mechanism will be used again, apply light coat of suitable multi-purpose lubricant between quadrant and strut of adjuster mechanism.

Parking Brake Cable

Inspect parking brake cable end for kinks, fraying and elongation and replace as required. Use a small hose clamp to compress clamp where it enters backing plate during removal.

TROUBLESHOOTING

Refer to **Fig. 2** for brake system troubleshooting.

BRAKE SERVICE

Because of the automatic adjustment feature of the parking brake, only remove brake shoes from one side of the vehicle at a time.

Removal

1. Raise and support vehicle, then remove rear wheel and tire assembly.
2. Remove retaining clips, then the drum from hub and bearing.
3. Remove self-adjuster lever to brake shoe spring.
4. Remove self-adjustment lever from shoe.
5. Remove brake shoe to support plate hold-down clips and pins.
6. Remove lower brake shoe to anchor plate return spring.

7. Remove park brake lever pin to shoe retaining clip.
8. Remove leading and trailing brake shoes, upper return spring and self-adjuster screw from support plate.

Installation

1. Lubricate brake shoe contact areas on brake support plate and anchor, with suitable multi-purpose lubricant, **Fig. 3**.
2. Assemble front and rear shoes, self-adjuster screw and upper return spring.
3. Install brake shoe components.
4. Install wave washer on park brake lever pin.
5. Install both shoe to support plate hold-down pins and clips.
6. Install lower shoe to anchor plate return spring.
7. Install self-adjustment lever on leading brake shoe.
8. Install self-adjustment lever to shoe spring.
9. Adjust shoes out until drum drags lightly when installed. **Do not over-adjust.**
10. Install brake drum.

ADJUSTMENTS

Service Brake

1. Ensure parking brake is in its fully released position.
2. Raise and support vehicle.
3. Remove brake adjusting hole plug from rear brake shoe support plate.
4. Insert brake adjustment tool, or suitable thin screwdriver, through support

DRUM BRAKES

CONDITION	POSSIBLE CAUSES	CORRECTION
BRAKES CHATTER	1. Rear brake drum out of round or disc brake rotor has excessive thickness variation.	1. Isolate condition as rear or front. Reface or replace brake drums or rotors as necessary.
BRAKES DRAG (FRONT OR ALL)	1. Contaminated brake fluid.	1. Check for swollen seals. Replace all system components containing rubber.
	2. Binding caliper pins or bushings.	2. Replace pins and bushings
	3. Binding master cylinder.	3. Replace master cylinder.
	4. Binding brake pedal.	4. Replace brake pedal.
BRAKES DRAG (REAR ONLY)	1. Parking brake cables binding or froze up.	1. Check cable routing. Replace cables as necessary.
	2. Parking brake cable return spring not returning shoes.	2. Replace cables as necessary.
	3. Service brakes not adjusted properly (rear drum brakes only).	3. Follow the procedure listed in the adjustment section.
	4. Obstruction inside the center console preventing full return of the parking brake cables.	4. Remove console and remove obstruction.
BRAKES GRAB	1. Contaminated brake shoe linings.	1. Inspect and clean, or replace shoes. Repair source of contamination.
	2. Improper power brake booster assist.	2. Refer to power brake booster in the diagnosis and testing section.
EXCESSIVE PEDAL EFFORT	1. Obstruction of brake pedal.	1. Inspect, remove or move obstruction.
	2. Low power brake booster assist.	2. Refer to power brake booster in the diagnosis and testing section.
	3. Glazed brake linings.	3. Reface or replace brake rotors as necessary. Replace brake shoes.
	4. Brake shoe lining transfer to brake rotor.	4. Reface or replace brake rotors as necessary. Replace brake shoes.
EXCESSIVE PEDAL TRAVEL (VEHICLE STOPS OK)	1. Air in brake lines.	1. Bleed brakes.
	2. Rear drum brake auto-adjuster malfunctioning.	2. Inspect and replace drum brake components as necessary. Adjust rear brakes.
EXCESSIVE PEDAL TRAVEL (PEDAL GOES TO FLOOR - CAN'T SKID WHEELS)	1. Power brake booster runout (vacuum assist).	1. Check booster vacuum hose and engine tune for adequate vacuum supply. Refer to power brake booster in the diagnosis and testing section.
EXCESSIVE PEDAL TRAVEL (ONE FRONT WHEEL LOCKS UP DURING HARD BRAKING)	1. One of the two hydraulic circuits to the front brakes is malfunctioning.	1. Inspect system for leaks. Check master cylinder for internal malfunction.

CR4089900044020X

Fig. 2   Brake system troubleshooting (Part 2 of 3)

CONDITION	POSSIBLE CAUSES	CORRECTION
PEDAL PULSATES/SURGES DURING BRAKING	1. Rear brake drum out of round or disc brake rotor has excessive thickness variation.	1. Isolate condition as rear or front. Reface or replace brake drums or rotors as necessary.
PEDAL IS SPONGY	1. Air in brake lines.	1. Bleed brakes.
	2. Power brake booster runout (vacuum assist).	2. Check booster vacuum hose and engine tune for adequate vacuum supply. Refer to power brake booster in the diagnosis and testing section.
PREMATURE REAR WHEEL LOCKUP	1. Contaminated brake shoe linings.	1. Inspect and clean, or replace shoes. Repair source of contamination.
	2. Inoperative proportioning valve (non-ABS vehicles only).	2. Test proportioning valves folowing procedure listed in diagnosis and testing section. Replace valves as necessary.
	3. ABS EBD not functioning.	3. Refer to the ABS section.
	4. Improper power brake booster assist.	4. Refer to power brake booster in the diagnosis and testing section.
STOP LAMPS STAY ON	1. Brake lamp switch out of adjustment.	1. Adjust brake lamp switch.
	2. Brake pedal binding.	2. Inspect and replace as necessary.
	3. Obstruction in pedal linkage.	3. Remove obstruction.
	4. Power Brake Booster not allowing pedal to return completely.	4. Replace power brake booster.
VEHICLE PULLS TO RIGHT OR LEFT ON BRAKING	1. Frozen brake caliper piston.	1. Replace frozen piston or caliper. Bleed brakes.
	2. Contaminated brake shoe lining.	2. Inspect and clean, or replace shoes. Repair source of contamination.
	3. Pinched brake lines.	3. Replace pinched line.
	4. Leaking piston seal.	4. Replace piston seal or brake caliper.
	5. Suspension problem.	5. Refer to the Suspension section.
PARKING BRAKE - EXCESSIVE HANDLE TRAVEL	1. Rear brakes out of adjustment.	1. Adjust rear drum brake shoes, or rear parking brake shoes on vehicles with rear disc brakes.

CR4089900044030X

Fig. 2   Brake system troubleshooting (Part 3 of 3)

plate adjusting hole and against star wheel of adjustment screw.
5. Rotate adjuster downward until slight drag is felt when wheel is rotated.
6. Push adjustment lever out of engagement with star wheel using suitable thin screwdriver or welding rod through adjustment hole. **Do not bend adjusting lever or distort lever spring.**
7. If brakes are over-adjusted, insert second screwdriver and engage it with star wheel while holding adjuster actuator lever away from star wheel.
8. Back off star wheel until there is no brake shoe drag. Repeat adjustment procedure.
9. Install brake adjusting hole plug.
10. Repeat procedure at other rear wheel.

Parking Brake

Because of the self-adjusting feature of the parking brake lever, adjustment of the parking brake system relies on proper brake shoe adjustment. Refer to "Service Brake."

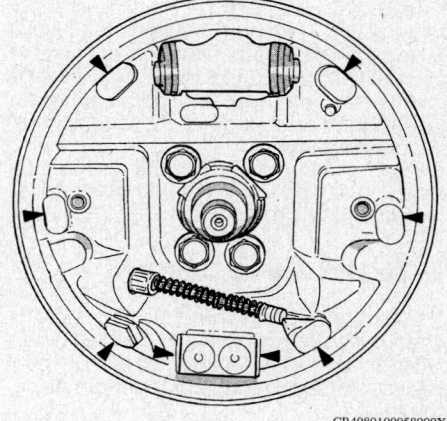

CR4080100058000X

Fig. 3   Brake shoe contact areas

DRUM BRAKE SPECIFICATIONS

Year	Brake Lining Wear Limit, Inch①	Brake Drum Inside Diameter, Inches			Drum Runout Limit, Inch	Drum Maximum Out Of Roundness, Inch③
		Nominal	Maximum Refinish④	Maximum Inside Diameter (Discard Limit)②		
2004–05	.030	7.875	7.904	7.921	.006	.0035

① — Above rivet head or shoe. Original equipment type brake linings.

② — Maximum brake drum inside diameter (discard limit) is stamped on drum.

③ — In 360°.

④ — Maximum refinishing diameter is stamped on outer face of drum.

TIGHTENING SPECIFICATIONS

Year	Component	Torque Ft. Lbs.
2004–05	Bearing Retainer	160
	Brake Line Fitting	12
	Support Plate To Rear Axle	55
	Wheel Cylinder Bleed Screw	80②
	Wheel Cylinder To Backing Plate	115②
	Wheel Lugnuts	100①

① — Tighten to half specification in star pattern, then to full specification in star pattern.
② — Inch lbs.

Sebring Convertible, Stratus Sedan & 2004–06 Sebring Sedan

NOTE: On Air Bag Equipped Models, Refer To "Air Bag System Precautions" Located In The Front Of This Manual For System Disarming & Arming Procedures.

NOTE: Refer To "Computer Relearn Procedures" Located In The Front Of This Manual When Battery Power To The Computer Has Been Interrupted.

INDEX

	Page No.
Adjustments	15-8
Parking Brake	15-8
Brake Service	15-8
Shoe, Replace	15-8
Wheel Cylinder, Replace	15-8

	Page No.
Drum Brake Specifications	15-9
Inspection	15-7
Adjuster Mechanism	15-8
Backing Plate	15-8
Brake Drums	15-7

	Page No.
Brake Linings & Springs	15-7
Parking Brake Cable	15-8
Precautions	15-7
Tightening Specifications	15-9
Troubleshooting	15-8

PRECAUTIONS

When working on or around brake assemblies, care must be taken to prevent breathing asbestos dust. During routine service operations, the amount of asbestos dust from brake lining wear is at a low level because of a chemical breakdown during use. A few precautions will minimize exposure.

Do not sand or grind brake linings unless suitable local exhaust ventilation equipment is used to prevent excessive asbestos exposure.

1. Wear suitable respirator approved for asbestos dust use during repair procedures.
2. When cleaning brake dust from brake components, use vacuum cleaner with highly efficient filter system. If suitable vacuum cleaner is not available, use water soaked rag. **Do not use compressed air or dry brush to clean brake components.**
3. Keep work area clean.
4. Properly dispose of rags and vacuum cleaner bags by placing them in plastic bags.
5. Do not smoke or eat while working on brake systems.
6. Never use any fluid containing mineral oil to clean brake system components.

INSPECTION

Brake Drums

When brake drums are removed for brake service, the braking surface diameter should be inspected with a suitable brake drum micrometer at several points to determine if they are within the safe oversize limit stamped on the brake drum outer surface. If the braking surface diameter exceeds specifications, the drum must be replaced. If the braking surface diameter is within specifications, drums should be cleaned and inspected for cracks, scores, deep grooves, taper, out of round and heat spotting. If drums are cracked or heat spotted, they must be replaced. Scoring and grooves in the braking surface can only be removed by machining with special equipment, as long as the braking surface is within specifications. Any brake drum showing taper or sufficiently out of round to cause vehicle vibration or noise while braking should also be machined, removing only enough stock to true up the drum.

After a brake drum is machined, wipe the braking surface diameter with a denatured alcohol soaked cloth. If one brake drum is machined, the other should also be machined to the same diameter to maintain equal braking forces.

Brake Linings & Springs

Inspect brake linings for excessive wear, damage, oil, grease or brake fluid contamination. If any of these conditions exist, brake linings should be replaced as an axle set to maintain equal braking forces. Examine brake shoe webbing, hold-down and return springs for signs of overheating indicated by a slight blue color. Any component which exhibits overheating signs should be replaced. Overheated springs lose their pull and could cause brake linings to wear out prematurely. Inspect springs for sags, bends and external damage and replace as required.

Inspect hold-down retainers and pins for

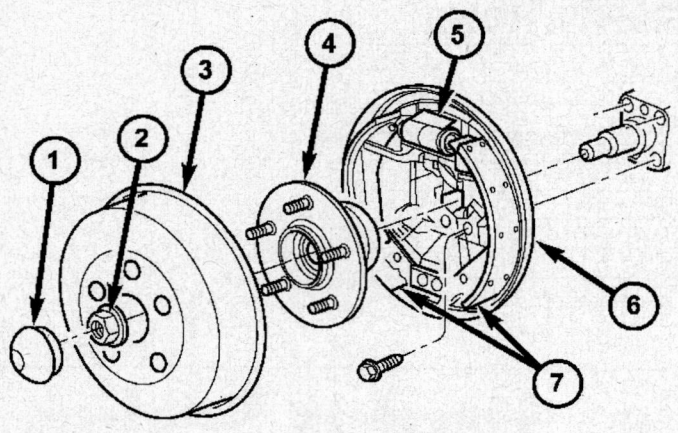

| 1 - DUST CAP |
| 2 - NUT |
| 3 - DRUM |
| 4 - HUB AND BEARING |
| 5 - WHEEL CYLINDER |
| 6 - SUPPORT PLATE |
| 7 - BRAKE SHOES |

ARM0500000001052

Fig. 1   Exploded view of brake drum

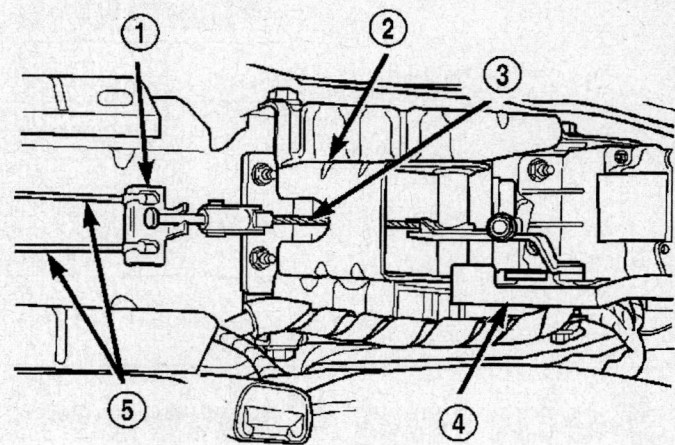

| 1 - PARK BRAKE CABLE TENSION EQUALIZER |
| 2 - PARK BRAKE MECHANISM |
| 3 - PARK BRAKE LEVER OUTPUT CABLE |
| 4 - PARK BRAKE LEVER |
| 5 - REAR PARK BRAKE CABLES |

ARM0500000001053

Fig. 2   Park brake cable tension equalizer

bends, rust and corrosion. If any of these are found, replace as required.

Backing Plate

Inspect backing plate shoe contact surface for grooves that may restrict shoe movement and cannot be removed by lightly sanding with emery cloth or other suitable abrasive. If backing plate exhibits these conditions, it should be replaced. Also inspect for signs of cracks, warpage and excessive rust, indicating need for replacement.

Adjuster Mechanism

Inspect components for rust, corrosion, bends and fatigue. Replace as required. On adjuster mechanism equipped with adjuster cable, inspect cable for kinks, fraying or elongation of eyelet and replace as required.

Parking Brake Cable

Inspect parking brake cable end for kinks, fraying and elongation and replace as required. Use a small hose clamp to compress clamp where it enters backing plate to remove.

TROUBLESHOOTING

Refer to "Sebring Coupe & Stratus Coupe" for troubleshooting procedures.

BRAKE SERVICE
Shoe, Replace

1. Raise and support vehicle, then remove tire and wheel assembly.
2. Loosen parking brake cable nut, then remove brake drum, **Fig. 1.**
3. Remove hub and bearing dust cap.
4. Remove hub and bearing retaining nut, then slide hub and bearing off spindle.
5. Compress cable return spring, then remove parking brake cable from parking brake lever.
6. Compress and remove shoe holddown springs.
7. Remove lower return spring, then both shoes and remaining components as an assembly from support plate.
8. Remove adjuster spring from leading shoe and lever pawl, then remove lever pawl from pivot on leading shoe and slide out from under adjuster.
9. Remove adjuster and upper spring.
10. Reverse procedure to install.

Wheel Cylinder, Replace

1. Depress brake pedal past its first inch of travel and hold it in position using brake pedal holding tool.
2. Raise and support vehicle, then remove tire and wheel assembly.
3. Unthread flex hose tube nut at wheel cylinder and remove hose, then cap end of hose.
4. Remove brake drum.
5. Remove wheel cylinder mounting bolts, then wheel cylinder.
6. Reverse procedure to install.

ADJUSTMENTS
Parking Brake

These vehicles use a bent nail type parking brake cable tension equalizer. The bent nail tension equalizer is to be used only one time to set the parking brake cable tension. If the parking brake cables require adjustment during the life of the vehicle, a **NEW** tension equalizer **MUST** be installed before doing the adjustment procedure.

1. Remove center floor console, then lower parking brake handle.
2. Loosen cable adjusting nut until it is flush with top of output cable end.
3. Unlatch park brake output cable retainer using a suitable screwdriver, then remove cable retainer from parking brake cable tension equalizer.
4. Remove parking brake cable tension equalizer from lever output cable and rear parking brake cables, **Fig. 2.**
5. Install a NEW parking brake cable tension equalizer and retaining clip on parking brake lever output cable and rear park brake cables.
6. Place park brake lever in fully released position.
7. Tighten adjusting nut on parking brake lever output cable until 26 millimeters of thread is out past top edge of adjustment nut.
8. Actuate parking brake lever to its fully applied position 15 clicks one time and then reposition lever to its fully released position.
9. Inspect rear wheels to ensure they move freely.

DRUM BRAKE SPECIFICATIONS

| Year | Brake Lining Wear Limit, Inch① | Brake Drum Inside Diameter, Inches | | | Drum Runout Limit, Inch | Drum Maximum Out Of Roundness, Inch |
		Nominal	Maximum Refinish	Maximum Inside Diameter (Discard Limit)		
2004–06	.040	9.00	—	9.08	—	—

① — Above rivet head or shoe. Original equipment type brake linings.

TIGHTENING SPECIFICATIONS

Year	Component	Torque Ft. Lbs.
2004–06	Brake Tube Nuts	12
	Disc Brake Caliper Guide Pin Bolts	26
	Front Caliper Adapter Mounting Bolts	80
	Parking Brake Lever Mounting Bolts	21
	Wheel Cylinder Bleeder Screw	10
	Wheel Cylinder Mounting Bolts	10

Sebring Coupe & Stratus Coupe

NOTE: On Air Bag Equipped Models, Refer To "Air Bag System Precautions" Located In The Front Of This Manual For System Disarming & Arming Procedures.

NOTE: Refer To "Computer Relearn Procedures" Located In The Front Of This Manual When Battery Power To The Computer Has Been Interrupted.

INDEX

	Page No.
Adjustments	15-10
Parking Brake	15-10
Brake Service	15-10
Shoe, Replace	15-10
Wheel Cylinder, Replace	15-10
Drum Brake Specifications	15-14

	Page No.
Drum Brake	15-14
Inspection	15-9
Adjuster Mechanism	15-10
Backing Plate	15-10
Brake Drums	15-9
Brake Linings & Springs	15-10

	Page No.
Parking Brake Cable	15-10
Precautions	15-9
Tightening Specifications	15-14
Troubleshooting	15-10

PRECAUTIONS

When working on or around brake assemblies, care must be taken to prevent breathing asbestos dust. During routine service operations, the amount of asbestos dust from brake lining wear is at a low level because of a chemical breakdown during use. A few precautions will minimize exposure.

Do not sand or grind brake linings unless suitable local exhaust ventilation equipment is used to prevent excessive asbestos exposure.

1. Wear suitable respirator approved for asbestos dust use during repair procedures.
2. When cleaning brake dust from brake components, use vacuum cleaner with highly efficient filter system. If suitable vacuum cleaner is not available, use water soaked rag. **Do not use compressed air or dry brush to clean brake components.**
3. Keep work area clean.
4. Properly dispose of rags and vacuum cleaner bags by placing them in plastic bags.
5. Do not smoke or eat while working on brake systems.
6. Never use any fluid containing mineral oil to clean brake system components.

INSPECTION

Brake Drums

Any time the brake drums are removed for brake service, the braking surface diameter should be inspected with a suitable brake drum micrometer at several points to determine if they are within the safe oversize limit stamped on the brake drum outer surface. If the braking surface diameter exceeds specifications, the drum must be replaced. If the braking surface diameter is within specifications, drums should be cleaned and inspected for cracks, scores, deep grooves, taper, out of round and heat spotting. If drums are cracked or heat spotted, they must be replaced. Scoring and grooves in the braking surface can only be removed by machining with special equipment, as long as the braking surface is within specifications. Any brake drum showing taper or sufficiently out of round to cause vehicle vibration or noise while braking should also be machined, removing only enough stock to true up the drum.

DRUM BRAKES

DIAGNOSIS

STEP 1. Check for oil, water, etc., on the pad or lining contact surface of all brakes.

Q: Is oil, water, etc., on the pad or lining contact surface?
YES : Replace the part and determine and repair source/ cause of foreign material. Then go to step 8.
NO : Go to Step 2.

STEP 2. Check the lining and brake drum contact (Vehicles equipped with rear drum brake).
(1) If equipped with rear disc brake, go to Step 5.
(2) Put chalk on the inner surface of the brake drum. Rub the lining against the drum inner surface.
NOTE: Clean off chalk after check.

Q: Does the lining wipe off or smudge the chalk across the full width of the lining?
YES : Go to Step 3.
NO : Replace the shoe and lining assemblies on both sides. Then go to Step 4.

CR4080100049010X

Fig. 1 Vehicle pulls to one side when brakes are applied (Part 1 of 2)

After a brake drum is machined, wipe the braking surface diameter with a denatured alcohol soaked cloth. If one brake drum is machined, the other should also be machined to the same diameter to maintain equal braking forces.

Brake Linings & Springs

Inspect brake linings for excessive wear, damage, oil, grease or brake fluid contamination. If any of these conditions exist, brake linings should be replaced as an axle set to maintain equal braking forces. Examine brake shoe webbing, hold-down and return springs for signs of overheating indicated by a slight blue color. Any component which exhibits overheating signs should be replaced. Overheated springs lose their pull and could cause brake linings to wear out prematurely. Inspect springs for sags, bends and external damage and replace as required.

Inspect hold-down retainers and pins for bends, rust and corrosion. If any of these are found, replace as required.

Backing Plate

Inspect backing plate shoe contact surface for grooves that may restrict shoe movement and cannot be removed by lightly sanding with emery cloth or other suitable abrasive. If backing plate exhibits these conditions, it should be replaced. Also inspect for signs of cracks, warpage and excessive rust, indicating need for replacement.

Adjuster Mechanism

Inspect components for rust, corrosion, bends and fatigue. Replace as required. On adjuster mechanism equipped with adjuster cable, inspect cable for kinks, fraying or elongation of eyelet and replace as required.

Parking Brake Cable

Inspect parking brake cable end for

STEP 3. Check the auto adjuster function

Q: Is there fault?
YES : Repair it. Then go to step 8.
NO : Go to Step 4.

STEP 4. Check the brake drum inside diameter

Q: Is the brake drum inside diameter outside of specifications?
YES : Replace the part. Then go to Step 8.
NO : Go to Step 5.

STEP 5. Check disc brake pistons for smooth operation.
(1) With engine not running, depress the brake pedal rapidly several times to deplete booster vacuum reserves.
(2) Test each disc brake assembly one at a time.
  a. 1) Remove the lower caliper bolt, then remove caliper from mount.
  b. 2) Have an assistant slowly depress the brake pedal. Confirm piston(s) extend slowly and smoothly with no jumpiness. Repeat for each disc brake assembly.

Q: Do (does) the piston(s) move correctly?
YES : Go to Step 6.
NO : Disassemble and inspect brake assembly Then go to Step 8.

STEP 6. Check brake disc(s) for run out

Q: Is runout outside of specifications?
YES : Repair and replace as necessary. Then go to Step 8.
NO : Go to Step 7.

STEP 7. Check brake discs for correct thickness

Q: Is the thickness outside of specifications?
YES : Repair or replace as necessary. Then go to Step 8.
NO : Go to Step 8.

STEP 8. Check symptoms.
Q: Is the symptom eliminated?
YES : Repair complete.
NO : Start over at Step 1. If a new symptom appears, refer to the symptom chart.

CR4080100049020X

Fig. 1 Vehicle pulls to one side when brakes are applied (Part 2 of 2)

kinks, fraying and elongation and replace as required. Use a small hose clamp to compress clamp where it enters backing plate to remove.

TROUBLESHOOTING

Refer to **Figs. 1 through 8** for brake system troubleshooting.

BRAKE SERVICE
Shoe, Replace

1. Raise and support vehicle, then remove tire and wheel assembly.
2. Loosen park brake cable adjusting nut.
3. Drain brake fluid into suitable container.
4. Remove brake drum, **Fig. 9.**
5. Remove shoe-to-lever spring, adjuster lever and auto adjuster assembly.
6. Remove retainer spring, then the hold-down cup, spring and cup.
7. Remove shoe-to-shoe spring, then the shoe and lining assemblies.
8. Remove retainer, wave washer and parking lever.
9. Remove hold-down pin, brake tube connection, snap ring and rear hub.
10. Reverse procedure to install.

DIAGNOSIS

STEP 1. Check whether the brake fluid is low, is the correct fluid (A/T fluid, engine oil, etc.) or is contaminated (debris, sand, etc.).
Q: Is there fault?
YES : Refill or replace with the specified brake fluid DOT 3 or DOT 4. Bleed the brakes if necessary Then go to Step 9.
NO : Go to Step 2.

STEP 2. Check for spongy (not firm brakes).
(1) With engine not running, depress the brake pedal rapidly several times to deplete booster vacuum reserve.
(2) With the brake pedal fully released, depress the brake pedal slowly until it stops.
(3) With a measuring stick (ruler, etc.) next to the brake pedal, depress the pedal firmly and measure the distance the pedal traveled.

Q: Is the distance greater than 20 mm (0.8 inch)?
YES : Bleed the brakes to remove air in the fluid. Then go to Step 9.
NO : Go to Step 3.

STEP 3. Check the lining and brake drum contact (Vehicles equipped with rear drum brake).
(1) If equipped with rear disc brake, go to Step 4.
(2) Put chalk on the inner surface of the brake drum. Rub the lining against the drum inner surface.
NOTE: Clean off chalk after check.

Q: Does the lining wipe off or smudge the chalk across the full width of the lining?
YES : Go to Step 5.
NO : Replace the shoe and lining assemblies on both sides. Go to Step 9.

STEP 4. Check the auto adjuster function.
Q: Is there fault?
YES : Repair it. Then go to Step 9.
NO : Go to Step 6.

STEP 5. Check the brake booster function.
Q: Is there fault?
YES : Replace the part. Then go to Step 9.
NO : Go to Step 5.

CR4080100050010X

Fig. 2 Insufficient braking power (Part 1 of 2)

Wheel Cylinder, Replace

1. Raise and support vehicle, then remove tire and wheel assembly.
2. Drain brake fluid into suitable container.
3. Remove brake drum, **Fig. 10.**
4. Remove shoe-to-lever and shoe-to-shoe springs.
5. Remove auto adjuster.
6. Remove connection pipe and wheel cylinder.
7. Reverse procedure to install.

ADJUSTMENTS
Parking Brake

These brakes are equipped with self adjusting mechanisms. Periodic adjustments are not required. If stopping power is insufficient, or if brake pedal travel is excessive, brakes and self adjusting mechanism should be cleaned and inspected.

After performing brake service, adjust parking brake as follows:
1. Apply parking brake lever with force of approximately 45 lbs. while counting clicks. Lever should click 5–7 times.
2. If not within specifications, release parking brake lever and remove center console.

STEP 6. Check for pinched or restricted brake tube or hose.

Q: Is there pinched or restricted brake tube or hose?

YES : Replace that complete section of brake tube or brake hose. Then go to Step 9.

NO : Go to Step 7.

STEP 7. Check for oil, water, etc., on the pad or lining contact surfaces of all brakes.

Q: Is oil, water, etc., on the pad or lining contact surface?

YES : replace the part and determine and repair source/cause of foreign material. Recheck symptom. Then go to Step 9.

NO : Diagnosis is complete. If condition persists, go to Step 8.

STEP 8. Check the proportioning valve operation.

Q: Is there fault?

YES : Replace the part. Then go to Step 9.

NO : Go to Step 9.

STEP 9. Recheck symptom.

Q: Is the symptom eliminated?

YES : Diagnosis is complete.

NO : Start over at step 1. If a new symptom surfaces, refer to the symptom chart.

CR4080100050020X

Fig. 2 Insufficient braking power (Part 2 of 2)

DIAGNOSIS

STEP 1. Check the parking brake lever return.

Q: Is there fault?

YES : Repair it. Then go to Step 10.

NO : Go to Step 2.

CR4080100052010X

Fig. 4 Brake drag (Part 1 of 3)

STEP 2. Check the parking brake pull amount.

Q: Is there fault?

YES : Adjust it. Then go to Step 10.

NO : Go to Step 3.

STEP 3. Check the brake pedal return spring for deterioration.

Q: Is there deterioration?

YES : Replace the spring. Then go to Step 10.

NO : Go to Step 4.

STEP 4. Check the brake shoe springs for breakage.

Q: Are the brake shoe springs broken?

YES : Replace the spring. Then go to Step 10.

NO : Go to Step 5.

STEP 5. Check the amount of grease at each sliding section.

Q: Is the grease amount low?

YES : Apply grease. Then go to Step 10.

NO : Go to Step 6.

CR4080100052020X

Fig. 4 Brake drag (Part 2 of 3)

3. Free parking brake cables by loosen parking brake lever adjusting nut.
4. Depress brake pedal several times to ensure shoe to drum clearance is properly maintained by self-adjusters.
5. Tighten adjusting nut until brake lever can be raised 5–7 notches with force of approximately 45 lbs. **If adjusting nut is tightened excessively, self-adjuster mechanism will be inoperative.**
6. Raise and support rear of vehicle, then ensure brakes do not drag with parking brake lever released.

DIAGNOSIS

STEP 1. Check for spongy (not firm brakes).

(1) With engine not running, depress the brake pedal rapidly several times to deplete booster vacuum reserve.

(2) With the brake pedal fully released, depress the brake pedal slowly until it stops.

(3) With a measuring stick (ruler, etc.) next to the brake pedal, depress the pedal firmly and measure the distance the pedal traveled.

Q: Is the distance greater than 20 mm (0.8 inch)?

YES : Bleed the brakes to remove air in the fluid. Then go to Step 8 .

NO : Go to Step 2.

Fig. 3 Increased pedal stroke (Part 1 of 2)

STEP 4. Check the master cylinder function.

Q: Is there fault?

YES : Repair it. Then go to Step 8.

NO : Go to Step 5.

STEP 5. Check for brake fluid leaks.

Q: Is there leaks?

YES : Check the connection for looseness, corrosion, etc. Clean and repair as necessary. If leaking in any tube or hose section, replace the complete tube or hose. Then go to Step 8.

NO : Go to Step 6.

Fig. 3 Increased pedal stroke (Part 2 of 2)

STEP 6. Check the clearance (too low) between the pushrod and primary piston.

Q: Is there fault?

YES : Adjust the clearance. Then go to Step 10.

NO : Go to Step 7.

STEP 7. Check the master cylinder piston return spring for damage and return port for clogging.

Q: Is there damage?

YES : Replace the part. Then go to Step 10.

NO : Go to Step 8.

STEP 8. Check port for clogging.

Q: Is the port clogged?

YES : Repair it. Then go to Step 10.

NO : Go to Step 9.

STEP 9. Check disc brake pistons for sticking.

Depress the brake pedal, then release. Confirm each wheel spins freely.

Q: Are all wheels stuck?

YES : Inspect that brake assembly. Then go to Step 10.

NO : Go to Step 10.

STEP 10. Recheck symptom.

Q: Is the symptom eliminated?

YES : Diagnosis is complete.

NO : Start over at step 1. If a new symptom surfaces, refer to the symptom chart.

CR4080100052030X

Fig. 4 Brake drag (Part 3 of 3)

STEP 2. Check the pad or lining for wear.

Q: Is the pad or lining thickness outside of specifications?

YES : Replace the part. Then go to Step 8.

NO : Go to Step 3.

STEP 3. Check the vacuum hose and check valve for damage.

Q: Is there damage?

YES : Replace the part. Then go to Step 8.

NO : Go to Step 4.

CR4080100051010X

STEP 6. Check the auto adjuster function.

Q: Is there fault?

YES : Repair the part. Then go to Step 8.

NO : Go to Step 7.

STEP 7. Check the clearance (too much) between the pushrod and primary piston.

Q: Is the clearance outside of specifications?

YES : Adjust the clearance. Then go to Step 8.

NO : Go to Step 8.

STEP 8. Recheck symptom.

Q: Is the symptom eliminated?

YES : Diagnosis is complete.

NO : Start over at step 1. If a new symptom surfaces, refer to the symptom chart.

CR4080100051020X

DIAGNOSIS

STEP 1. Check the front brakes, then rear brakes, for metal-to-metal condition.

Q: Is the metal-to-metal contact evicent?

YES : Repair or replace components. Then go to Step 6.

NO : Go to Step 2.

STEP 2. Check for interference between the caliper and wheel.

Q: Is there interference?

YES : Repair or replace the part. Then go to Step 6.

NO : Go to Step 3.

CR4080100053010X

Fig. 5 Scraping or grinding noise when brakes are applied (Part 1 of 2)

STEP 3. Check for interference between the dust cover and brake disc.

Q: Is there interference?

YES : Repair or replace the part. Then go to Step 6.

NO : Go to Step 4.

STEP 4. Check the brake drums or discs for cracks.

Q: Are there cracks?

YES : Repair or replace the part. Then go to Step 6.

NO : Go to Step 5.

STEP 5. Check for bent backing plate(s).

Q: Is(Are) the backing plate(s) bent?

YES : Repair or replace the part. Then go to Step 6.

NO : Go to Step 6.

STEP 6. Recheck symptom.

Q: Is the symptom eliminated?

YES : Diagnosis is complete.

NO : Start over at step 1. If a new symptom surfaces, refer to the symptom chart.

CR4080100053020X

Fig. 5 Scraping or grinding noise when brakes are applied (Part 2 of 2)

DRUM BRAKES

DIAGNOSIS

STEP 1. Check the brake drums and lining or brake disc and pads for wear or cutting.

Q: Is there wear or cutting?

YES : Repair or replace the part. Then go to Step 7.
NO : Go to Step 2.

STEP 2. Check the calipers for rust.

Q: Is there rust?

YES : Remove the rust. Then go to Step 7.
NO : Go to Step 3.

STEP 3. Check the lining parts for damage.
If equipped with rear disc brakes, go to Step 6.

Q: Is there damage?

YES : Repair or replace the part. Then go to Step 7.
NO : Go to Step 4.

STEP 4. Check whether the lining is dirty or greasy.

Q: Is the lining dirty or greasy?

YES : Clean or replace the part. Then go to Step 7.
NO : Go to Step 5.

STEP 5. Check whether the shoe hold-down springs are weak or the shoe-hold-down pins and springs are loose or damaged.

Q: Is there fault?

YES : Repair or replace the part. Then go to Step 7.
NO : Go to Step 6.

STEP 6. Adjust the brake pedal or brake booster pushrod.

Q: Is the adjustment value come?

YES : Adjust. Then go to Step 7.
NO : Go to Step 7.

STEP 7. Recheck symptom.

Q: Is the symptom eliminated?

YES : Diagnosis is complete.
NO : Start over at step 1. If a new symptom surfaces, refer to the symptom chart.

CR4080100054000X

Fig. 6   Squealing, groaning or chattering noise when brakes are applied

DIAGNOSIS

STEP 1. Check whether the backing plate is bent or loose and interfering with the drum

If equipped with rear disc brakes, go to Step 4.

Q: Is there fault?

YES : Replace the part. Then go to Step 10.
NO : Go to Step 2.

STEP 2. Check whether the drum is damaged due to interference with the backing plate or shoe.

Q: Is there damage?

YES : Replace the part. Then go to Step 10.
NO : Go to Step 3.

STEP 3. Check the brake drum for wear and the shoe-to-shoe spring for damage.

Q: Is there wear or damage?

YES : Replace the part. Then go to Step 10.
NO : Go to Step 4.

STEP 4. Check the brake discs for rust.

Q: Are the brake discs rusted?

YES : Remove the rust by using sand paper. If still rusted, turn the rotors with an on-the-car brake lathe. Then go to Step 10.
NO : Go to Step 5.

STEP 5. Check the brake pads for correct installation.

Q: Are the pads installed incorrectly?

YES : Repair it. Then go to Step 10.
NO : Go to Step 6.

STEP 6. Check the calipers for correct installation.

Q: Are the calipers installed incorrectly?

YES : Repair it. Then go to Step 10.
NO : Go to Step 7.

CR4080100055010X

Fig. 7   Squealing noise when brakes are not applied (Part 1 of 2)

STEP 7. Check the wheel bearings for deterioration or damage, and the quality and quantity.

Q: Are the wheel bearings damaged or out of grease?

YES : Apply grease or replace the part. Then go to Step 10.
NO : Go to Step 8.

STEP 8. Check whether the brake booster, master cylinder or wheel cylinder return is insufficient.

Q: Is the brake booster, master cylinder or wheel cylinder return insufficient?

YES : Replace the part. Then go to Step 10.
NO : Go to Step 9.

STEP 9. Adjust the brake pedal or brake booster pushrod.

Q: Is the adjustment value come?

YES : Adjust.Then go to Step 10.
NO : Go to Step 10.

STEP 10. Recheck symptom.

Q: Is the symptom eliminated?

YES : Diagnosis is complete.
NO : Start over at step 1. If a new symptom surfaces, refer to the symptom chart.

CR4080100055020X

Fig. 7   Squealing noise when brakes are not applied (Part 2 of 2)

DIAGNOSIS

STEP 1. Check whether foreign material has entered the wheel covers.

Q: Is there foreign material?

YES : Remove it. Then go to Step 5.
NO : Go to Step 2.

STEP 2. Check for looseness of the wheel nuts.

Q: Are the wheel nuts loose?

YES : Tighten to 98 ± 10 N·m (73 ± 7 ft-lb). Then go to Step 5.
NO : Go to Step 3.

STEP 3. Check for looseness of the caliper installation bolt.

Q: Is the caliper installation bolt loose?

YES : Tighten to 100 ± 10 N·m (74 ± 7 ft-lb) for the front caliper, or 60 ± 5 N·m (45 ± 3 ft-lb) for the rear caliper. Then go to Step 5.
NO : Go to Step 4.

CR4080100056010X

Fig. 8   Groaning, clicking or rattling noise when brakes are not applied (Part 1 of 2)

STEP 4. Check the wheel bearings for wear, damage or dryness.

Q: Is there fault?

YES : Apply grease or replace the part. Then go to Step 5.
NO : Go to Step 5.

STEP 5. Recheck symptom.

Q: Is the symptom eliminated?

YES : Diagnosis is complete.
NO : Start over at step 1. If a new symptom surfaces, refer to the symptom chart.

CR4080100056020X

Fig. 8   Groaning, clicking or rattling noise when brakes are not applied (Part 2 of 2)

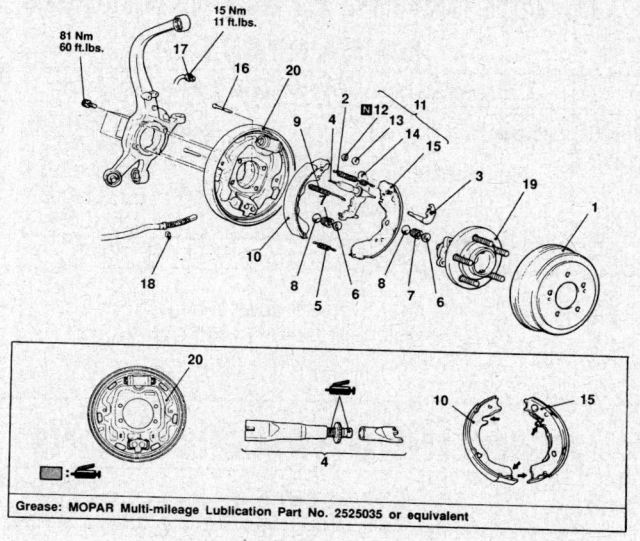

1. Brake drum
2. Shoe-to-lever spring
3. Adjuster lever
4. Auto adjuster assembly
5. Retainer spring
6. Shoe hold-down cup
7. Shoe hold-down spring
8. Shoe hold-down cup
9. Shoe-to-shoe spring
10. Shoe and lining assembly

11. Shoe and lever assembly
12. Retainer
13. Wave washer
14. Parking lever
15. Shoe and lining assembly
16. Shoe hold-down pin
17. Brake pipe connection
18. Snap ring
19. Rear hub assembly
20. Backing plate

CR4089500024000X

Fig. 9   Exploded view of drum brake

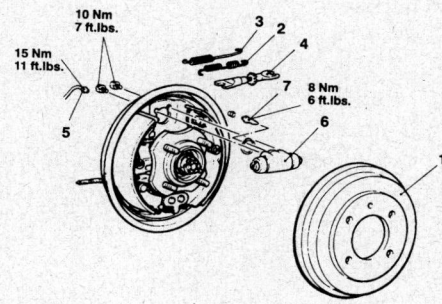

1. Brake drum
2. Retainer
3. Shoe-to-shoe spring
4. Auto adjuster assembly

5. Connection for the brake tube
6. Wheel cylinder
7. Bleeder screw

CR4089500023000X

Fig. 10   Rear drum brake wheel cylinder replacement

DRUM BRAKES

DRUM BRAKE SPECIFICATIONS
DRUM BRAKE

| Year | Brake Lining Wear Limit, Inch① | Brake Drum Inside Diameter, Inches | | | Drum Runout Limit, Inch | Drum Maximum Out Of Roundness, Inch③ |
		Nominal	Maximum Refinish	Maximum Inside Diameter (Discard Limit)②		
2004–05	.040	9.00	—	9.08	—	—

① — Above rivet head or shoe. Original equipment type brake linings.

② — Maximum brake drum inside diameter (discard limit) is stamped on drum.

③ — In 360°.

TIGHTENING SPECIFICATIONS

Year	Component	Torque Ft. Lbs.
2004–05	Backing Plate To Rear Axle	60
	Brake Line Fittings	11
	Wheel Cylinder Bleed Screw	96①
	Wheel Cylinder To Backing Plate	84①
	Wheel Lugnuts	65–80

① — Inch lbs.

HYDRAULIC BRAKE SYSTEMS

NOTE: On Air Bag Equipped Models, Refer To "Air Bag System Precautions" Located In The Front Of This Manual For System Disarming & Arming Procedures.

NOTE: Refer To "Computer Relearn Procedures" Located In The Front Of This Manual When Battery Power To The Computer Has Been Interrupted.

NOTE: Refer To "Anti-Lock Brakes" Chapter When Servicing ABS System.

INDEX

	Page No.		Page No.		Page No.
Brake System Bleed	16-5	Sedan & 2004–06 Sebring		Neon	16-5
Manual Bleed	16-6	Sedan	16-3	**Component Service**	16-5
Master Cylinder Bleed	16-6	Junction Block	16-3	**Description**	16-1
Bench Bleeding	16-6	Master Cylinder	16-4	Master Cylinder	16-1
On-Vehicle Bleeding	16-6	Caliber, 2007–08 Avenger		**Diagnosis & Testing**	16-1
Pressure Bleed	16-5	Sedan & Sebring Sedan	16-4	Proportioning Valve	16-1
Component Replacement	16-2	Charger, Magnum & 300	16-4	Concorde, Intrepid & 300M	16-1
Fluid Reservoir	16-2	Concorde, Intrepid & 300M	16-4	Crossfire	16-2
Caliber, 2007–08 Avenger		Crossfire	16-4	Neon	16-2
Sedan & Sebring Sedan	16-2	Neon	16-4	Sebring Coupe & Stratus	
Except Caliber & 2007–08		Sebring Convertible, Stratus		Coupe	16-2
Avenger Sedan & Sebring		Sedan & 2004–06 Sebring		**Hydraulic Brake Control**	
Sedan	16-2	Sedan	16-5	**Specifications**	16-7
Hydraulic Control Unit	16-3	Sebring Coupe & Stratus		**Hydraulic Brake System**	
Caliber, 2007–08 Avenger		Coupe	16-5	**Specifications**	16-6
Sedan & Sebring Sedan	16-3	Proportioning Valve	16-5	**Tightening Specifications**	16-8
Charger, Magnum & 300	16-3	Caliber, 2007–08 Avenger		**Troubleshooting**	16-1
Concorde, Intrepid & 300M	16-3	Sedan & Sebring Sedan	16-5		
Sebring Convertible, Stratus		Concorde, Intrepid & 300M	16-5		

DESCRIPTION

Master Cylinder

The master cylinder is a center valve master cylinder used for all applications. The brake fluid reservoir mounted on top and brake fluid level switch is mounted on the side of the reservoir.

The reservoir is indexed to prevent installation in the wrong direction. The cap diaphragm is slit to allow atmospheric pressure to equalize on both sides of diaphragm.

The primary and secondary outlet tubes of the master cylinder are connected to a junction block on non-ABS equipped vehicles. The master cylinder primary outlet port connects to the inboard port of the junction block and the secondary outlet port connects to the outboard port of the junction block. The inboard port of the junction block supplies the righthand front and lefthand rear brakes. The outboard port of the junction block supplies the lefthand front and righthand rear brakes.

On vehicles equipped with ABS the master cylinder primary outlet port outlet tubes connect to the inboard port of the ICU and the secondary outlet port outlet tubes connect to the outboard port of the ICU.

TROUBLESHOOTING

Refer to "Troubleshooting" in "Disc Brakes" chapter for troubleshooting of the hydraulic brake system.

DIAGNOSIS & TESTING

Proportioning Valve

CONCORDE, INTREPID & 300M

ABS

These models with ABS do not have proportioning valves to test, they use Electronic Variable Brake Proportioning which is built into the Integrated Control Unit (ICU).

NON-ABS

On early production non-ABS applications, refer to "ABS" for testing procedure.

On later production non-ABS applications, proceed as follows;
1. **If lefthand rear proportioning valve is suspect,** disconnect tube nut fitting at master cylinder primary port (port closest to power brake booster) and install adapter tool No. 8494-2, or equivalent, in its place on master cylinder.
2. **If righthand rear proportioning** valve is suspect, disconnect tube nut fitting at master cylinder secondary port (port furthest from power brake booster) and install adapter tool No. 8494-1, or equivalent, in its place on master cylinder.
3. **On all conditions,** connect primary brake tube to adapter.
4. Install pressure gauge tool No. C-4007-A, or equivalent, to adapter.
5. Remove speed control servo to upper radiator closure panel mounting screw.
6. Remove washer filler tube to upper radiator closure panel mounting screw.
7. Remove Transmission Control Module (TCM) mounting nut and screw. Position TCM with speed control servo attached aside ensure not to strain wires and speed control servo cable.
8. Clean any debris away from fittings on top of junction block.
9. Remove chassis brake tube leading to either lefthand or righthand rear brake at junction block.
10. **If lefthand rear proportioning valve is suspect,** install adapter tool No. 8494-3, or equivalent, in its place on junction block.
11. **If righthand rear proportioning valve is suspect,** install adapter tool No. 8494-4, or equivalent, in its place on junction block.
12. **On all conditions,** install pressure

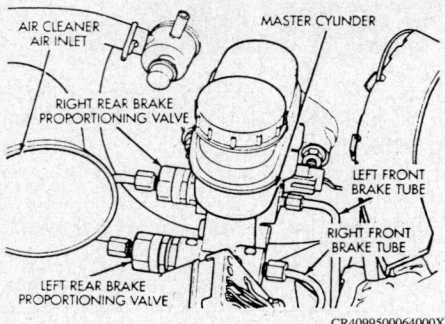

Fig. 1   Proportioning valve. Neon less ABS

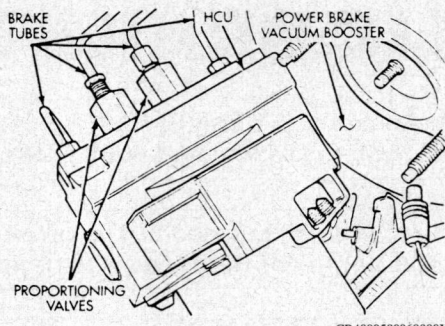

Fig. 2   Proportioning valve. Neon w/ABS

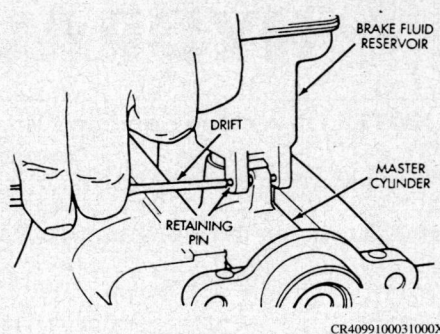

Fig. 3   Retaining pin removal

gauge tool No. C-4007-A, or equivalent, to adapter.

13. Bleed air out of system including air from hose between pressure test fitting and pressure gauge at pressure gauge.
14. With aid of a helper, apply pressure to brake pedal until reading on proportioning valve inlet gauge at master cylinder is at specifications.
15. Then inspect pressure reading on proportioning valve outlet gauge at junction block outlet to rear brake.
16. If proportioning valve outlet pressure is not within specifications once inlet pressure is obtained, replace junction block with internal proportioning valves.
17. Remove pressure gauge and adapter tools from junction block.
18. Install chassis brake tube to junction block port.
19. Install TCM with speed control servo attached.
20. Install washer filler tube to upper radiator closure panel mounting screw.
21. Install speed control servo to upper radiator closure panel mounting screw.
22. Remove pressure gauge and adapter tools from master cylinder.
23. Remove brake tube to master cylinder primary or secondary port.
24. Bleed affected brake line.

CROSSFIRE

These models are not equipped with a proportioning valve, junction block or splitter. The Hydraulic Control Unit (HCU) monitors and controls these functions.

NEON

LESS ANTI-LOCK BRAKE SYSTEM

1. Remove hydraulic brake line from proportioning valve to be tested, **Fig. 1**.
2. Remove master cylinder outlet port valve.
3. Install pressure test fitting tool No. 6805-1, 6805-2, or equivalent, into outlet port of master cylinder.
4. Install pressure test fitting tool No. 6805-1, 6805-2, or equivalent, into rear brake line.
5. Install proportioning valve into pressure test fitting.
6. Install pressure test fitting tool Nos. 6805-3 and 6805-4, or equivalents,

into outlet port or proportioning valve.
7. Connect brake hydraulic line onto pressure test fitting on proportioning valve.
8. Install pressure gauge set tool No. C-4007-A, or equivalent, into test fitting and bleed air from pressure gauge hose.
9. Apply pressure to brake pedal until proportioning valve inlet test fitting pressure is appropriate, then record outlet test fitting pressure.
10. If proportioning valve is not within specifications when inlet pressure is obtained, replace valve.
11. Install proportioning valve into master cylinder body until O-ring is seated.
12. Install brake tube onto proportioning valve.
13. Bleed brake line.

WITH ANTI-LOCK BRAKE SYSTEM

1. Remove hydraulic brake line from proportioning valve to be tested, **Fig. 2**.
2. Remove master cylinder outlet port valve.
3. Install pressure test fitting tool No. 6805-1 or 6805-2, or equivalent, into outlet port of master cylinder.
4. Install proportioning valve into pressure test fitting in master cylinder outlet port.
5. Install pressure test fitting tool No. 6805-3 or 6805-4, or equivalent, into outlet port of proportioning valve.
6. Connect brake hydraulic line onto pressure test fitting on proportioning valve.
7. Install pressure gauge set tool No. C-4007-A, or equivalent, into test fitting and bleed air from pressure gauge hose.
8. Apply pressure to brake pedal until proportioning valve inlet test fitting pressure is appropriate, then record outlet test fitting pressure.
9. If outlet test fitting pressure is not within specifications, replace proportioning valve.
10. Install proportioning valve into master cylinder body until O-ring is seated.
11. Install brake tube onto proportioning valve.
12. Bleed brake line.

SEBRING COUPE & STRATUS COUPE

1. Install suitable pressure gauges, one each on input and output side of proportioning valve.
2. Bleed brake line and pressure gauge, then gradually depress brake pedal and observe gauge.
3. Observe lefthand and righthand output pressures.
4. Pressure difference between lefthand and righthand sides should not be more than 57 psi.
5. If pressure is not within specifications, replace proportioning valve.

COMPONENT REPLACEMENT

Fluid Reservoir

CALIBER, 2007–08 AVENGER SEDAN & SEBRING SEDAN

1. Clean master cylinder housing and brake fluid reservoir.
2. Remove brake fluid reservoir cap, then siphon as much brake fluid as possible from reservoir.
3. Remove reservoir to master cylinder mounting screws.
4. Pull reservoir straight up to remove from master cylinder.
5. Remove brake fluid switch from reservoir.
6. Reverse procedure to install.

EXCEPT CALIBER & 2007–08 AVENGER SEDAN & SEBRING SEDAN

These models use ISO style flares that are of metric dimension. Use ISO style tubing flares and metric tubing when performing any repairs.
1. Remove reservoir caps.
2. Remove reservoir brake fluid.
3. Remove master cylinder as outlined in "Master Cylinder, Replace."
4. Secure master cylinder in suitable vise.
5. Remove two reservoir to master cylinder retaining pins, **Fig. 3**.
6. Rock reservoir side to side and remove

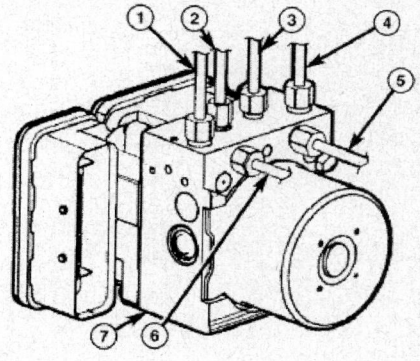

1- Secondary Brake Tube
2- Brake Tube
3- Brake Tube
4- Primary Brake Tube
5- Brake Tube
6- Brake Tube
7- Hydraulic Control Unit

ARM0600000001211

Fig. 4 HCU. Caliber, 2007–08 Avenger Sedan & Sebring Sedan

from master cylinder. **Do not use any tools when removing reservoir.**
7. Remove sealing grommets.
8. Reverse procedure to install, noting the following:
   a. Lubricate new sealing grommets with suitable brake fluid.
   b. Ensure reservoir is seated properly against sealing grommets.
   c. Bench bleed master cylinder as outlined in "Brake System Bleed."

Hydraulic Control Unit

The Hydraulic Control Unit (HCU) and the Anti-Lock Brake Module (ABM) used with this anti-lock brake system are combined (integrated) into one unit, which is called the Integrated Control Unit (ICU).

CALIBER, 2007–08 AVENGER SEDAN & SEBRING SEDAN

1. Depress pedal past its inch of travel and hold position using suitable tool.
2. Remove engine appearance cover.
3. Remove upper intake manifold as outlined under "Intake Manifold, Replace" in "Sebring Convertible & Sedan & Stratus Sedan" chassis chapter.
4. Remove primary and secondary brake tubes from master cylinder at hydraulic control unit (HCU), **Fig. 4.**
5. Remove remaining brake tubes at hydraulic control unit.
6. Pull brake tube bundle routing clip with tubes loose from stud on righthand side of dash panel.
7. Disconnect ABM harness electrical connector from Anti-lock Brake Module (ABM).
8. Loosen, but do not remove mounting screws attaching ICU mounting bracket to body.
9. Lift ICU and mounting bracket off mounting screws.

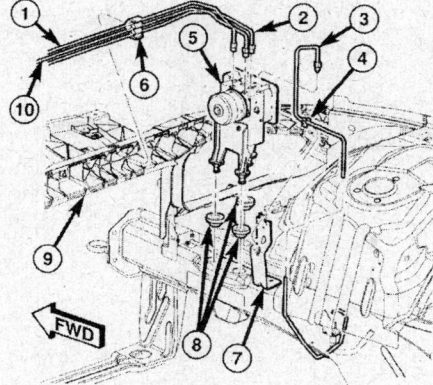

1- BRAKE TUBE
2- BRAKE TUBE
3- BRAKE TUBE
4- CLIP
5- INTEGRATED CONTROL UNIT
6- CLIP
7- MOUNTING BRACKET
8- RUBBER GROMMETS
9- BRAKE TUBE SUPPORT
10- BRAKE TUBE

ARM0500000001054

Fig. 5 Brake tube removal. Charger, Magnum & 300

10. Remove ICU with bracket through opening above rear valve cover.
11. Remove three attaching screws from ABM to HCU to separate.
12. Reverse procedure to install.

CHARGER, MAGNUM & 300

1. Depress pedal one inch down and hold in position using suitable tool.
2. Remove brake tubes at hydraulic control unit, **Fig. 5.**
3. Disconnect 47-way wiring electrical connector at ABM.
4. Pull up on unit to remove from mounting grommets.
5. Remove three attaching screws from ABM to HCU to separate.
6. Reverse procedure to install.

SEBRING CONVERTIBLE, STRATUS SEDAN & 2004–06 SEBRING SEDAN

1. Depress pedal one inch down and hold in position using suitable tool.
2. Remove air cleaner housing.
3. Remove brake tubes from master cylinder ports at ICU, **Figs. 6 and 7.**
4. Raise and support vehicle.
5. Disconnect 47-way connector from ABM by depressing tabs on each side of connector cover, then pulling outward and upward on lower half of cover until it locks into position pointing straight outward. The connector can then be pulled straight outward off ABM.
6. Remove three ICU to lower radiator support attaching screws.
7. Remove ICU from vehicle.
8. Remove four ABM to HCU attaching screws to separate.
9. Reverse procedure to install.

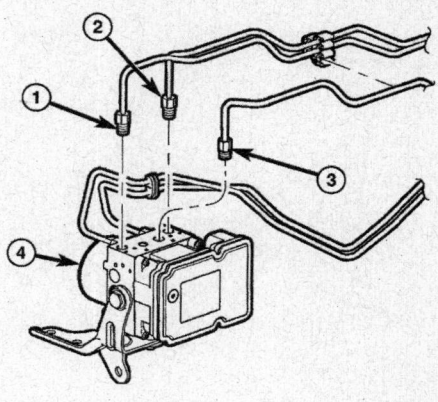

1 - PRIMARY BRAKE TUBE
2 - SECONDARY BRAKE TUBE
3 - LEFT FRONT CHASSIS BRAKE TUBE
4 - ICU

ARM0500000001055

Fig. 6 Brake tube removal. Sebring Convertible, Stratus Sedan & 2004–06 Sebring Sedan

CONCORDE, INTREPID & 300M

1. Depress pedal one inch down and hold in position using suitable tool.
2. Disconnect speed control servo wire harness electrical connection and mounting bolt and nuts, then position servo aside.
3. Remove washer bottle attaching screw and position washer bottle aside.
4. Remove transmission controller and bracket mounting bolt, then position controller and bracket aside.
5. Thoroughly clean all brake tube to HCU connections, then disconnect all brake tubes at HCU.
6. Disconnect 24-way wiring harness electrical connector from CAB.
7. Raise and support vehicle, then remove lefthand front tire and wheel assembly.
8. Remove inner fender splash shield.
9. Remove ICU attaching bolts, then ICU.
10. Remove CAB to HCU attaching bolts to separate units.
11. Reverse procedure to install.

Junction Block

1. Depress pedal one inch down and hold in position using suitable tool, **Fig. 8.**
2. **On Stratus Sedan & 2004–06 Sebring Sedan,** remove air cleaner housing.
3. **On all models,** raise and support vehicle.
4. Remove lefthand inner fender shield.
5. **On Concorde, Intrepid and 300M models,** proceed as follows:
   a. Remove speed control servo to upper radiator closure panel mounting screw, **Fig. 9.**
   b. Remove washer filler tube to upper radiator closure panel. mounting screw.
   c. Remove Transmission Control

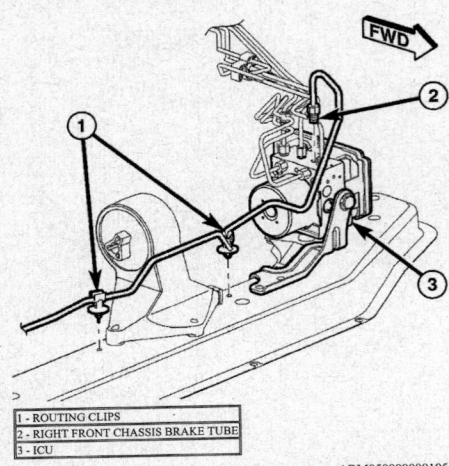

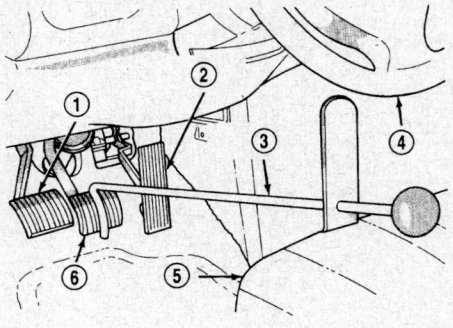

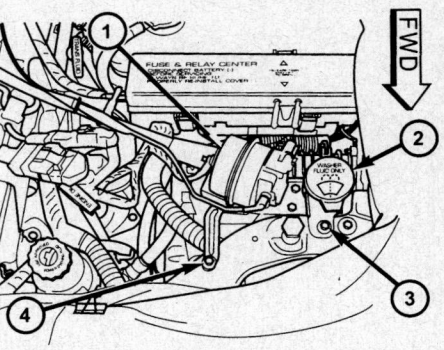

1 - ROUTING CLIPS
2 - RIGHT FRONT CHASSIS BRAKE TUBE
3 - ICU

ARM0500000001056

Fig. 7   Righthand front chassis brake tube. Sebring Convertible, Stratus Sedan & 2004–06 Sebring Sedan

1 – CLUTCH PEDAL (IF EQUIPPED WITH MANUAL TRANSAXLE)
2 – THROTTLE PEDAL
3 – BRAKE PEDAL HOLDING TOOL
4 – STEERING WHEEL
5 – DRIVER'S SEAT
6 – BRAKE PEDAL

CR4090000104000X

Fig. 8   Brake pedal holding tool

1 - SPEED CONTROL SERVO
2 - WINDSHIED WASHER FILLER TUBE
3 - SCREW
4 - SCREW

CR4090000105000X

Fig. 9   Speed control servo & filler tube replacement. Concorde, Intrepid & 300M

Module (TCM) mounting nut and screw.

d. Remove TCM with servo attached from mount and set aside with wiring harness connected.

e. Remove primary and secondary master cylinder ports tubes at junction block.

6. **On all models,** remove four chassis brake tubes mounted across front top of junction block.

7. Remove two brake tubes from primary and secondary ports, and top of junction block.

8. Remove three mounting bolts and junction block.

9. Reverse procedure to install.

Master Cylinder

CALIBER, 2007–08 AVENGER SEDAN & SEBRING SEDAN

WITH ABS

1. With engine not running, pump brake pedal 4-5 strokes until pedal feel is firm.

2. Disconnect wiring harness electrical connector from brake fluid level switch.

3. Disconnect primary and secondary brake tubes at master cylinder outlet ports. Plug open brake tube outlets.

4. **On models equipped with manual transaxle,** remove clamp and slide clutch actuator hose off reservoir port.

5. **On all models,** clean area around where master cylinder attaches to power brake booster.

6. Remove master cylinder to power brake booster attaching nuts.

7. Slide master cylinder straight out of power brake booster.

8. Reverse procedure to install.

WITHOUT ABS

1. With engine not running, pump brake pedal 4-5 strokes until pedal feel is firm.

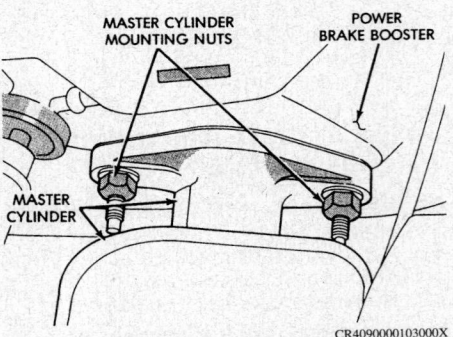

CR4090000103000X

Fig. 10   Master cylinder replacement. Concorde, Intrepid, Sebring Convertible, Stratus Sedan, 2004–06 Sebring Sedan & 300M

2. Disconnect wiring harness electrical connector from brake fluid level switch.

3. Disconnect two front brake tubes from master cylinder, then plug open tube outlets.

4. Disconnect two rear brake tubes from proportioning valves on master cylinder, then plug open tube outlets.

5. **On models equipped with manual transaxle,** remove clamp and slide clutch actuator hose off reservoir port.

6. **On all models,** clean area around where master cylinder attaches to power brake booster.

7. Remove master cylinder to power brake booster attaching nuts.

8. Slide master cylinder straight out of power brake booster.

9. Remove proportioning valves from master cylinder.

10. Reverse procedure to install.

CONCORDE, INTREPID & 300M

1. Disconnect brake fluid level sensor wire connector from reservoir side.

2. Disconnect master cylinder, primary and secondary brake lines. Plug or cap lines and openings.

3. Remove mounting nuts and slide mas-

ter cylinder away from brake booster, **Fig. 10.**

4. Reverse procedure to install.

CROSSFIRE

1. Disconnect brake fluid level sensor harness at brake fluid reservoir, **Fig. 11.**

2. Disconnect master cylinder brake fluid sensor harness connectors.

3. Disconnect master cylinder primary and secondary brake lines. Plug or cap lines and openings.

4. Remove mounting nuts and master cylinder. **Do not tilt master cylinder when removing from brake booster.**

5. Reverse procedure to install. Bench bleed master cylinder, **Fig. 12.**

CHARGER, MAGNUM & 300

1. Pump brake pedal with vehicle's engine not running until firm feeling brake pedal is achieved, 4–5 strokes.

2. Remove cowl area access panel.

3. Thoroughly clean all surfaces of brake fluid reservoir and master cylinder using suitable brake component cleaner.

4. Disconnect brake fluid level sensor wiring harness.

5. Disconnect Electronic Stability Program wiring harness connector.

6. Disconnect primary and secondary brake tubes from master cylinder. Plug or cap lines and openings.

7. Remove two mounting nuts and slide master cylinder straight out of power brake booster, then remove vacuum seal.

8. Reverse procedure to install using new vacuum seal.

NEON

LESS ANTI-LOCK BRAKE SYSTEM

1. Remove brake fluid level sensor wiring harness connector.

2. Disconnect master cylinder housing primary and secondary brake tubes. Plug or cap lines and openings.

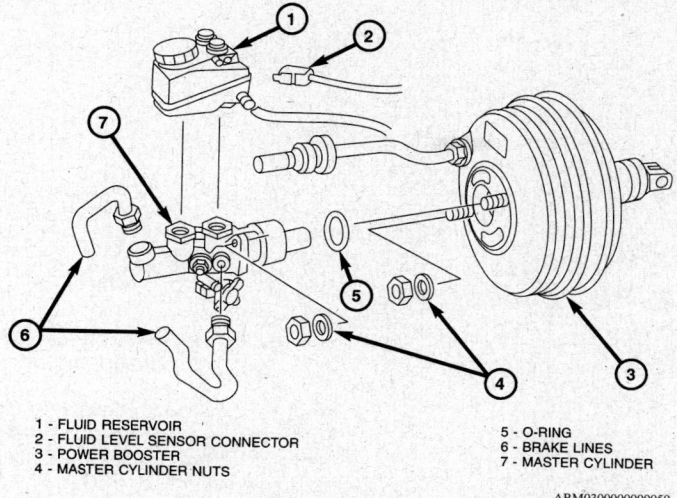

1 - FLUID RESERVOIR
2 - FLUID LEVEL SENSOR CONNECTOR
3 - POWER BOOSTER
4 - MASTER CYLINDER NUTS
5 - O-RING
6 - BRAKE LINES
7 - MASTER CYLINDER

ARM0300000000059

Fig. 11 Master cylinder components & locations. Crossfire

3. Remove master cylinder to power brake vacuum booster mounting nuts.
4. Slide master cylinder forward out of power brake vacuum booster.
5. Reverse procedure to install.

WITH ANTI-LOCK BRAKE SYSTEM

1. Ensure ignition switch is in OFF position.
2. Pumped down power booster vacuum by pumping brake pedal until it is firm.
3. Remove brake fluid level sensor wiring harness connector.
4. Disconnect master cylinder housing primary and secondary brake tubes. Plug or cap lines and openings.
5. Clean area where master cylinder attaches to power brake vacuum booster using suitable brake cleaner.
6. Remove master cylinder to power brake vacuum booster mounting nuts.
7. Slide master cylinder forward out of power brake vacuum booster.
8. Remove vacuum seal by carefully inserting suitable, small screwdriver between master cylinder push rod and vacuum seal.
9. Prying seal out of booster, **Fig. 13.**
10. **Do not attempt to pry seal out by inserting screwdriver between seal and booster.**
11. Reverse procedure to install, noting the following:
    a. Lubricate master cylinder push rod using suitable silicone lubricant.
    b. Slide vacuum seal onto master cylinder push rod with notches on seal pointing toward and seated against master cylinder housing.
    c. Slide master cylinder into power brake vacuum booster and position on mounting studs.

SEBRING CONVERTIBLE, STRATUS SEDAN & 2004–06 SEBRING SEDAN

Refer to "Concorde, Intrepid & 300M" for master cylinder replacement procedure.

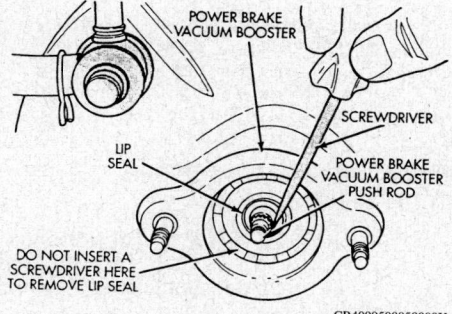

POWER BRAKE VACUUM BOOSTER

LIP SEAL

SCREWDRIVER

POWER BRAKE VACUUM BOOSTER PUSH ROD

DO NOT INSERT A SCREWDRIVER HERE TO REMOVE LIP SEAL

CR4099500058000X

Fig. 13 Vacuum seal removal. Neon w/ABS

SEBRING COUPE & STRATUS COUPE

1. Drain brake fluid into suitable container.
2. Disconnect brake tube connection, **Fig. 14.**
3. Remove mounting nuts and master cylinder.
4. Reverse procedure to install.

Proportioning Valve

CALIBER, 2007-08 AVENGER SEDAN & SEBRING SEDAN

1. Depress pedal past its inch of travel and hold position using suitable tool.
2. Disconnect brake tube from proportioning valve requiring removal.
3. Unscrew proportioning valve from master cylinder.
4. Reverse procedure to install.

CONCORDE, INTREPID & 300M

LESS ANTI-LOCK BRAKE SYSTEM

These models use a proportioning valve

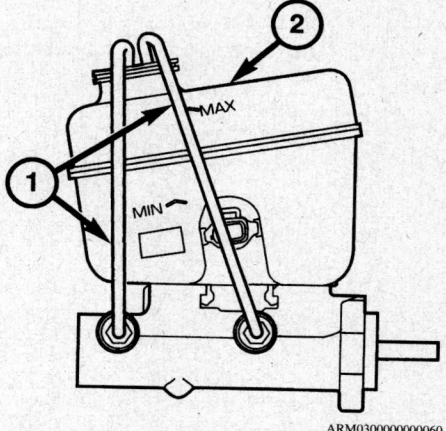

ARM0300000000060

Fig. 12 Bench bleeding master cylinder. Crossfire

that is integrated with the junction block. The proportioning valve cannot be serviced separately.

ANTI-LOCK BRAKE SYSTEM

These models use electronic variable brake proportioning built into the Integral Control Unit (ICU).

NEON

1. Depress brake pedal past its first one inch of travel and hold it in position using suitable brake pedal holder.
2. Disconnect brake tube from proportioning valve requiring removal.
3. Remove proportioning valve from master cylinder.
4. Reverse procedure to install. Lubricate new O-ring with suitable brake fluid.

COMPONENT SERVICE

The only serviceable component on master cylinder(s) are the reservoir and sealing grommets. The master cylinder(s) are not to be serviced, they must be replaced as an assembly.

BRAKE SYSTEM BLEED

Pressure Bleed

Use bleeder tank tool No. C-3496-B, or equivalent, and adapter tool No. BB400-9A, or equivalent, to pressurize hydraulic system.

Normal pressure bleeder pressure should not be more than 35 psi. **On models equipped with plastic reservoirs, do not exceed 25 psi bleeding pressure.**

1. Attach suitable clear plastic hose to bleeder screw and submerge other end into clear container with clean brake fluid.
2. Open bleeder screw at least one full turn.
3. Bleed 4–8 ounces of fluid through system until air free flow is maintained.
4. Repeat procedure at all screws.
5. If pedal travel is excessive or has not improved, repeat procedure.

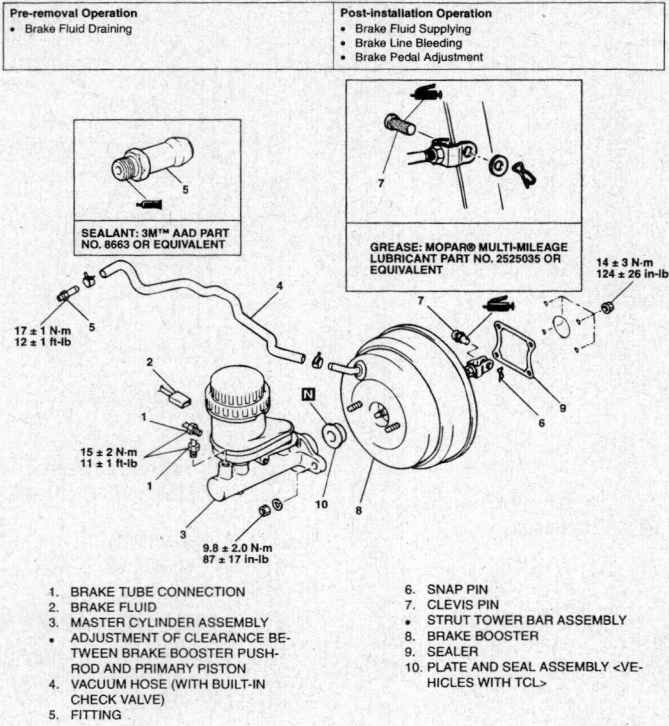

Pre-removal Operation
• Brake Fluid Draining

Post-installation Operation
• Brake Fluid Supplying
• Brake Line Bleeding
• Brake Pedal Adjustment

SEALANT: 3M™ AAD PART NO. 8663 OR EQUIVALENT

GREASE: MOPAR® MULTI-MILEAGE LUBRICANT PART NO. 2525035 OR EQUIVALENT

17 ± 1 N·m
12 ± 1 ft-lb

15 ± 2 N·m
11 ± 1 ft-lb

9.8 ± 2.0 N·m
87 ± 17 in-lb

14 ± 3 N·m
124 ± 26 in-lb

1. BRAKE TUBE CONNECTION
2. BRAKE FLUID
3. MASTER CYLINDER ASSEMBLY
• ADJUSTMENT OF CLEARANCE BE-
  TWEEN BRAKE BOOSTER PUSH-
  ROD AND PRIMARY PISTON
4. VACUUM HOSE (WITH BUILT-IN
   CHECK VALVE)
5. FITTING

6. SNAP PIN
7. CLEVIS PIN
• STRUT TOWER BAR ASSEMBLY
8. BRAKE BOOSTER
9. SEALER
10. PLATE AND SEAL ASSEMBLY <VE-
    HICLES WITH TCL>

CR4090000106000X

Fig. 14 Master cylinder replacement. Stratus Sedan & 2004–06 Sebring Sedan

Manual Bleed

On models with power brakes, if bleeding the hydraulic system without the engine running, first reduce vacuum in the power unit to zero by pumping the brake pedal several times with the engine off.

1. Remove four bleeder screws' rubber dust caps.
2. Attach suitable clear plastic tubing to bleeder screw and submerge other end of tube into clear container of clean brake fluid.
3. Pump brake pedal three or four times and hold it down.
4. Open bleeder screw at least one full turn.
5. Release brake pedal only after bleeder screw is closed.
6. Repeat procedure four or five times at all bleeder screw locations. Ensure fluid level in master cylinder stays at proper level.

Master Cylinder Bleed

BENCH BLEEDING

When clamping master cylinder in

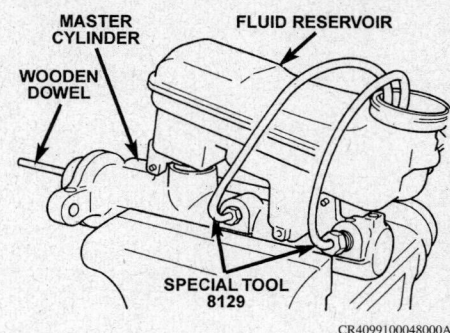

Fig. 15 Master cylinder bench bleeding

vise for bleeding, carefully tighten vise just enough to hold master cylinder from moving. Excessive pressure can damage master cylinder.

1. Support master cylinder and attach bleeding tubes, **Fig. 15**.
2. Fill reservoir with approved brake fluid.
3. Depress pushrod slowly using suitable wooden stick or dowel, then allow pistons to return under pressure of springs. Do this several times until all air bubbles are expelled.
4. Remove cylinder bleeding tubes and install reservoir cover.
5. Install master cylinder onto vehicle as outlined in "Component Replacement."
6. Bleed hydraulic system as outlined in "Brake System Bleed."

ON-VEHICLE BLEEDING

Master cylinders may be bled manually or by pressure bleeding. It is recommended that the master cylinder be bled before bleeding the wheel cylinders and calipers.

HYDRAULIC BRAKE SYSTEM SPECIFICATIONS

Model	Year	Master Cylinder Bore Dia., Inch	Booster to Primary Piston Clearance, Inch	Wheel Bleed Sequence
Caliber, Avenger Sedan & Sebring Sedan	2007–08	—	—	—
Charger, Magnum & 300	2005–08	—	—	—
Concorde, Intrepid & 300M	2004	.937	—	LR, RF, RR, LF
Crossfire	2004–07	.937	—	LR, RF, RR, LF
Neon	2004–05①	.875	—	LR, RF, RR, LF
	2004–05②	.937	—	LR, RF, RR, LF
Sebring Convertible, Sebring Sedan & Stratus Sedan	2004–06	—	—	LR, RF, RR, LF
Sebring Coupe & Stratus Coupe	2004–05	1.06	.404–.415	RR, LF, LR, RF

① — Less ABS.   ② — With ABS.

HYDRAULIC BRAKE CONTROL SPECIFICATIONS

| Model | Year | Valve Identifi-cation | Valve Tag Color① | Split Point | | Master Cylinder Inlet Pressure, psi | Rear Brake Outlet Pressure, psi |
				Pressure, psi	Slope		
LESS ABS							
Caliber, Avenger Sedan & Sebring Sedan	2007–08	③	—	—	—	—	—
Charger, Magnum & 300	2005–08	⑥	—	—	—	—	—
Concorde, Intrepid & 300M	2004	③	Bar Coded Label	400	.34	1000	525–625
Neon	2004–05②	③	Purple	350	.34	1000	525–625
	2004–05④	③	Red	300	.34	1000	480–580
Sebring Convertible, Sebring Sedan & Stratus Sedan	2004–06	⑥	—	—	—	—	—
Sebring Coupe & Stratus Coupe	2004–05	⑥	—	391–462	—	—	—
WITH ABS							
Caliber, Avenger Sedan & Sebring Sedan	2007–08	⑤	—	—	—	—	—
Charger, Magnum & 300	2005–08	⑤	—	—	—	—	—
Concorde, Intrepid & 300M	2004	③	Bar Code Label	400	.34	1000	525–625
Crossfire	2004–06	③	Bar Coded Label	400	.34	1000	525–625
Neon	2004–05	③	Black Band	300	.34	1000	550–650
Sebring Convertible, Sebring Sedan & Stratus Sedan	2004–06	⑤	—	—	—	—	—
Sebring Coupe & Stratus Coupe	2004–05	⑤	—	391–462	—	—	—

① — Color tag located under boot of valve stem.
② — 14-inch disc/disc.
③ — Proportioning valve.

④ — 14-inch disc/drum.
⑤ — Electronic variable brake proportioning.

⑥ — Proportioning valves are included in junction block, they are not serviceable.

TIGHTENING SPECIFICATIONS

Year	Component	Torque Ft. Lbs.
CALIBER, AVENGER SEDAN & SEBRING SEDAN		
2007–08	Brake Pedal/Booster Mounting Nuts	17
	Brake Tube Nuts	13
	Fluid Reservoir Mounting Screw	48①
	Master Cylinder Mounting Nuts	18
	Proportioning Valves	22
CHARGER, MAGNUM & 300		
2005–08	Booster	18
	Master Cylinder	19
	Tube	10
CONCORDE, INTREPID & 300M		
2004	Bleeder Screw	125①
	Brake Booster	21
	Brake Line	105①
	Junction Block	19
	Master Cylinder	21
	Tube	12
CROSSFIRE		
2004–07	Bleeder Screw	62①
	Brake Booster	15
	Brake Line	10
	Master Cylinder	15
NEON		
2004–05	Bleeder Screw	11
	Brake Booster	25
	Brake Line	13
	Master Cylinder	13
	Tube	12
SEBRING CONVERTIBLE, SEBRING SEDAN & STRATUS SEDAN		
2004–06	Bleeder Screw	11
	Brake Line	13
	Junction Block	21
	Master Cylinder	19
	Tube	12
SEBRING COUPE & STRATUS COUPE		
2004–05	Bleeder Screw	62–78①
	Brake Booster	11–17
	Brake Line	10–12
	Master Cylinder	70–104①

① — Inch lbs.

POWER BRAKE UNITS

NOTE: On Air Bag Equipped Models, Refer To "Air Bag System Precautions" Located In The Front Of This Manual For System Disarming & Arming Procedures.

NOTE: Refer To "Computer Relearn Procedures" Located In The Front Of This Manual When Battery Power To The Computer Has Been Interrupted.

INDEX

	Page No.			Page No.			Page No.
Description	17-1		Avenger, Caliber & 2007–08			Sebring Coupe & Stratus	
Operation	17-1		Sebring Sedan	17-2		Coupe	17-4
System	17-1		Charger, Magnum & 300	17-3		**Troubleshooting**	17-1
Diagnosis & Testing	17-1		Concorde, Intrepid & 300M	17-2		Decreasing Brake Pedal Travel	17-1
General Service	17-1		Crossfire	17-3		Dragging Brakes	17-1
Brake Booster Operation Test	17-2		Neon	17-3		Hard Brake Pedal	17-1
Check Valve Operation Test	17-2		Sebring Convertible, Stratus				
Power Brake Unit Service	17-2		Sedan & 2004–06 Sebring				
Power Booster, Replace	17-2		Sedan	17-4			

DESCRIPTION

System

These units are of the vacuum suspended type. Some units are of the single diaphragm type, while others are of the tandem diaphragm type, both single piston and double piston or split system type master cylinders are used, **Figs. 1 and 2.**

The vacuum suspended diaphragm type units utilize engine manifold vacuum and atmospheric pressure for its power. It consists of three basic elements combined into a single power unit. The three basic elements of the single diaphragm type are:

1. A vacuum power section which includes a front and rear shell, a power diaphragm, a return spring and a pushrod.
2. A control valve, built integral with power diaphragm and connected through a valve rod to brake pedal, controls degree of brake application or release in accordance with pressure applied to brake pedal.
3. A hydraulic master cylinder, attached to vacuum power section which contains all elements of conventional brake master cylinder except for pushrod, supplies fluid under pressure to wheel brakes in proportion to pressure applied to brake pedal.

Operation

Upon application of the brakes, the valve rod and plunger move to the left in the power diaphragm to close the vacuum port and open the atmospheric port to admit air through the air cleaner and valve at the rear diaphragm chamber. With vacuum present in the rear chamber, a force is developed to move the power diaphragm, hydraulic pushrod and hydraulic piston or pistons to close the compensating port or ports and

force fluid under pressure through the residual check valve or valves and lines into the front and rear wheel cylinders to actuate the brakes.

As pressure is developed within the master cylinder a counter force acting through the hydraulic pushrod and reaction disc against the vacuum power diaphragm and valve plunger sets up a reaction force opposing the force applied to the valve rod and plunger. This reaction force tends to close the atmospheric port and reopen the vacuum port. Since this force is in opposition to the force applied to the brake pedal by the driver it gives the driver a feel of the amount of brake applied. The proportion of reactive force applied to the valve plunger through reaction disc is designed into the Master-Vac to ensure maximum power consistent with maintaining pedal feel. The reaction force is in direct proportion to the hydraulic pressure developed within the brake system.

TROUBLESHOOTING

Decreasing Brake Pedal Travel

If a decreasing brake pedal is encountered, the power brake unit may be binding internally. To test the power brake unit for this condition proceed as follows:

1. Place transmission shift lever into Neutral and start engine.
2. Increase engine speed to approximately 1500 RPM, close throttle and completely depress brake pedal.
3. Slowly release brake pedal and stop engine.
4. Remove vacuum check valve and hose from power brake unit. Observe for backward movement of brake pedal.
5. If brake pedal moves backward, power

brake unit has internal binding. Replace power brake unit.

Hard Brake Pedal

An internal bind or a failed vacuum check valve would cause this condition. Refer to Previous to test power brake unit for an internal bind. To inspect for a failed vacuum check valve proceed as follows:

1. Start engine and increase engine speed to approximately 1500 RPM, then close throttle and stop engine.
2. Wait 90 seconds, then try brake action.
3. If brakes are not vacuum assisted for two or more applications, replace check valve.

Dragging Brakes

If slow or incomplete release of brakes (dragging brakes) is encountered the power brake unit has an internal bind condition. Test for an internal bind condition as outlined in "Decreasing Brake Pedal Travel."

DIAGNOSIS & TESTING

Refer to **Fig. 3** for power brake system diagnosis and testing.

GENERAL SERVICE

The BAS diaphragm travel sensor and the BAS control module are the only components that can be serviced. If any other repairs are required it will be required to replace the entire booster assembly, **Fig. 1.**

In order to properly service and repair available brake systems, a thorough understanding of the power assist systems is required. The vacuum assist diaphragm assembly multiplies the force exerted on the master cylinder piston in order to increase the hydraulic pressure delivered to

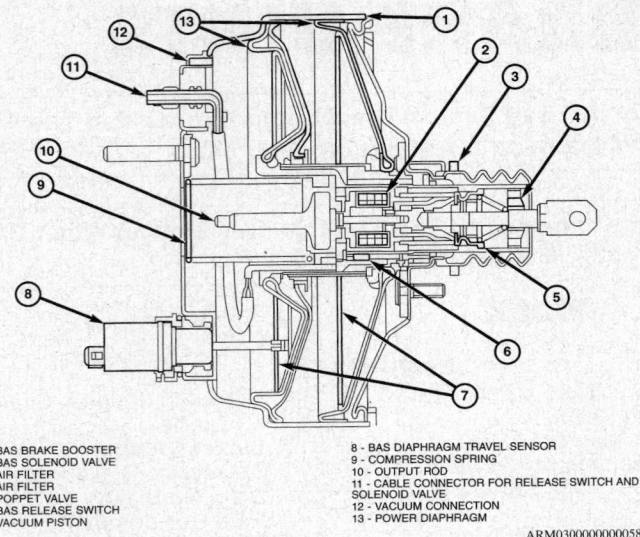

1 - BAS BRAKE BOOSTER
2 - BAS SOLENOID VALVE
3 - AIR FILTER
4 - AIR FILTER
5 - POPPET VALVE
6 - BAS RELEASE SWITCH
7 - VACUUM PISTON

8 - BAS DIAPHRAGM TRAVEL SENSOR
9 - COMPRESSION SPRING
10 - OUTPUT ROD
11 - CABLE CONNECTOR FOR RELEASE SWITCH AND SOLENOID VALVE
12 - VACUUM CONNECTION
13 - POWER DIAPHRAGM

ARM0300000000058

Fig. 1   Dual diaphragm vacuum power booster

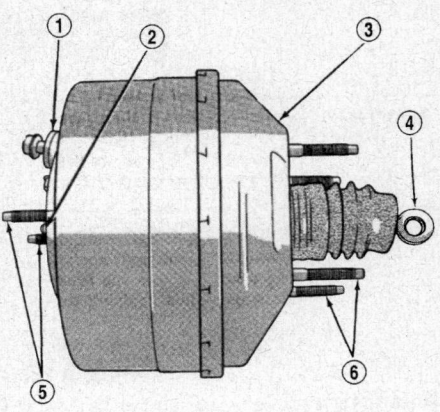

1 - VACUUM CHECK VALVE
2 - OUTPUT ROD
3 - POWER BRAKE BOOSTER ASSEMBLY
4 - INPUT ROD
5 - MASTER CYLINDER MOUNTING STUDS (2)
6 - POWER BOOSTER ASSEMBLY TO DASH PANEL MOUNTING STUDS (4)

ARM0300000000061

Fig. 2   Single diaphragm vacuum power booster

the wheel cylinders or calipers while decreasing the effort required to obtain acceptable stopping performance.

Vacuum assist units get their energy by opposing engine vacuum to atmospheric pressure. A piston, cylinder and flexible diaphragm utilize this energy to provide brake assistance. The diaphragm is balanced with engine vacuum until the brake pedal is depressed, allowing atmospheric pressure to unbalance the unit and apply force to the brake system.

Brakes will operate even if the power unit fails. This means the conventional brake system and the power assist system are completely separate. Troubleshooting conventional and power assist systems are exactly the same until the power unit is reached. As with conventional hydraulic brakes, a spongy pedal still means air is trapped in the hydraulic system. Power brakes give higher line pressure, making leaks more critical.

Brake Booster Operation Test

1. Start and run engine for one to two minutes, then shut engine off and inspect pedal operation as follows:
   a. If brake pedal depresses fully first time but gradually becomes higher when depressed succeeding times, booster is operating properly.
   b. If pedal height remains unchanged, booster is faulty.
2. With engine off, step on brake pedal several times, then step on brake pedal, start engine and inspect pedal operation as follows:
   a. If pedal moves downward slightly, booster is satisfactory.
   b. If pedal does not change position, booster is faulty.
3. Step on brake pedal and stop engine, continue to depress pedal for 30 seconds, then inspect brake operation as follows:
   a. If pedal height does not change,

booster is satisfactory.
   b. If pedal height rises, booster is faulty.
4. If brake booster does not pass all three tests, inspect check valve and vacuum hose as outlined in "Check Valve Operation Test." If check valve and vacuum hose are satisfactory, replace booster.

Check Valve Operation Test

1. Remove vacuum hose. **Check valve is press fitted inside vacuum hose.**
2. Inspect operation of check valve by using a vacuum pump. Refer to **Fig. 4** for vacuum pump connection locations.
3. Connect vacuum pump at brake booster side (A). A negative pressure (vacuum) should be created and held.
4. Connect vacuum pump at intake manifold side (B). A negative pressure (vacuum) is not created.
5. If check valve is faulty, replace it as an assembly unit together with vacuum hose.

POWER BRAKE UNIT SERVICE

Power Booster, Replace

AVENGER, CALIBER & 2007–08 SEBRING SEDAN

1. Remove PCM mounting fasteners, then position PCM aside.
2. Remove master cylinder as outlined under "Master Cylinder, Replace" in "Hydraulic Brake Systems" chapter.
3. Disconnect rear brake tubes at junction block. Plug all open brake tubes.
4. Disconnect vacuum hose from check valve on power brake booster.

5. Remove lower instrument panel/steering column cover.
6. Remove and discard brake lamp switch.
7. Remove brake booster push rod to brake pedal retaining clip. Discard clip.
8. Slide booster push rod off brake pedal pin.
9. Remove brake booster to dash panel retaining nuts.
10. Remove brake booster from engine compartment.
11. Reverse procedure to install, noting the following:
    a. Install new dash seal on booster mounting studs.
    b. **Torque** nuts in a crisscross pattern to 17 ft. lbs.

CONCORDE, INTREPID & 300M

Two different power brake vacuum booster designs are used, although externally they appear the same. On some models, use a Teves booster while others use a Bosch power brake booster, **Figs. 5 and 6.**

Do not attempt to disassemble or service power brake unit. Brake unit is serviced only as a complete unit.

1. Remove caps, mounting nuts and wiper arms, **Fig. 7.**
2. Remove wiper module and cowl cover, **Fig. 8.**
3. Remove eight reinforcement to strut towers mounting bolts and one wiper module to reinforcement mounting bolt, then the reinforcement, **Fig. 9.**
4. Disconnect brake fluid level sensor wire connector on righthand side of master cylinder reservoir.
5. Remove two mounting nuts and slide master cylinder off mounting studs with brake lines attached.
6. Position master cylinder backwards on lefthand engine valve cover.
7. Disconnect booster check valve vacuum hose. **Do not remove check valve from booster.**

8. Rotate windshield wiper motor crank lever until lever is at 12 o'clock position, **Fig. 10.**
9. From under instrument panel, position suitable, small screwdriver between center tang of booster input rod to brake pedal pin retaining clip, then rotate screwdriver so retainer clip center tang passes over end of brake pedal pin and pull retainer clip off. Discard old retainer clip.
10. From under instrument panel remove four mounting nuts, slide booster up and to righthand side on dash panel, then tilt outward and up to remove.
11. Reverse procedure to install noting following:
    a. **Torque** booster to dash panel and master cylinder to booster mounting nuts to 21 ft. lbs.
    b. Install new connecting booster input rod to brake pedal pin retainer clip.

CROSSFIRE

The BAS diaphragm travel sensor and the BAS control module are the only components that can be serviced. If any other repairs are required, replace the entire power booster assembly.
1. Remove master cylinder as outlined under "Master Cylinder, Replace" in "Hydraulic Brake Systems" chapter.
2. Disconnect power booster check valve vacuum hose, **Fig. 11.**
3. Remove retaining clip and slide booster push rod off brake pedal lever, **Fig. 12.**
4. Reverse procedure to install, noting the following:
    a. Install new gasket.
    b. Lubricate pushrod to brake pedal retaining pin with suitable multipurpose grease.
    c. Install new pushrod to brake pedal pin retainer clip.
    d. **Torque** power booster mounting nuts to 29 ft. lbs.

CHARGER, MAGNUM & 300

1. Move driver's seat to full rearward position.
2. Remove master cylinder as outlined under "Master Cylinder, Replace" in "Hydraulic Brake Systems" chapter.
3. **On models equipped with Electronic Stability Program (ESP),** disconnect wiring harness connectors at pedal travel sensor on power brake booster and at active brake booster solenoid.
4. **On all models,** disconnect check valve vacuum hose on face of booster. **Do not remove booster check valve.**
5. Remove brake lamp switch.
6. Remove booster push rod from pin on brake pedal by positioning suitable, small screwdriver between center tang on power brake booster brake pedal pin retaining clip. Rotate screwdriver enough to allow retaining clip center tang to pass over end of brake pedal pin, then slide retaining clip off brake pedal pin. Discard retaining clip.

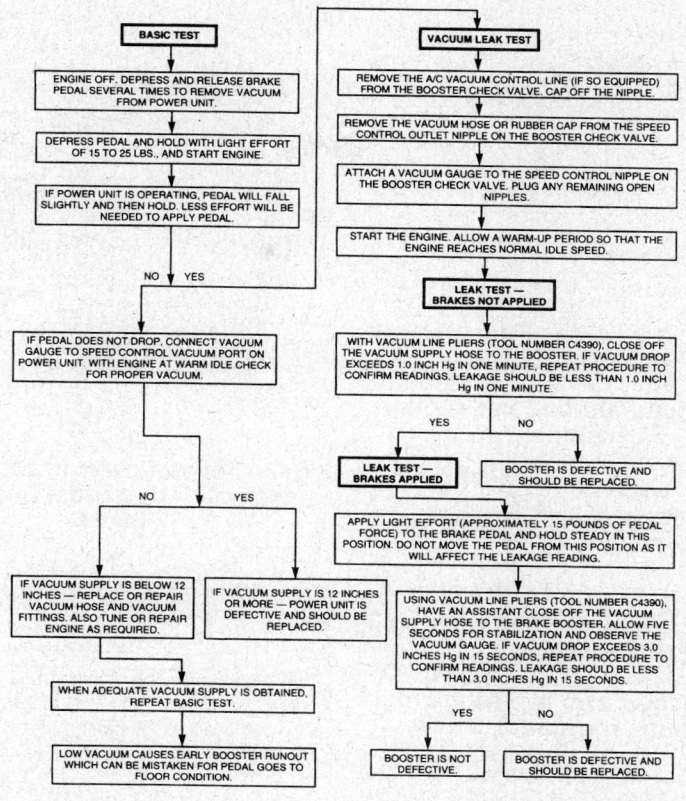

Fig. 3 Power brake system diagnosis

7. Slide booster push rod off brake pedal pin.
8. Remove four power brake booster mounting nuts and remove windshield wiper module.
9. Slide power brake booster forward out of dash panel and remove through opening between cross-brace and windshield.
10. Reverse procedure to install, noting the following:
    a. Install new booster seal.
    b. **Torque** power brake booster mounting nuts to 19 ft. lbs.

NEON

LESS ABS

1. Remove battery.
2. Remove air cleaner box mounting bolt and disconnect air inlet sensor electrical connector.
3. Lift air cleaner box upward to clear alignment post, then move air cleaner box forward to access battery tray mounting bolts and remove battery tray.
4. Disconnect brake fluid level sensor wiring harness on fluid reservoir.
5. Disconnect primary and secondary brake tubes from master cylinder housing. Plug or cap master cylinder outlets.
6. Remove mounting nuts and slide master cylinder forward out of booster.
7. Disconnect power booster check valve vacuum hoses. **Do not remove check valve from power booster.**
8. Position suitable small screwdriver between center tang on input rod to brake pedal pin retaining clip.
9. Rotate screwdriver to allow retaining clip center tang to pass over end of brake pedal pin. Discard retaining clip.
10. Remove mounting nuts and slide power booster forward until mounting studs clear dash, then tilt unit upward to remove.
11. Reverse procedure to install, noting the following:
    a. **Torque** power booster mounting nuts to 21 ft. lbs.
    b. **Torque** master cylinder mounting bolts to 13 ft. lbs.
    c. Install new brake booster input rod to brake pedal retaining clip.
    d. **Torque** master cylinder primary and secondary brake tube nuts to 12 ft. lbs.

WITH ABS

1. Pump brake with ignition off until firm pedal is achieved.
2. Ensure ignition switch is in Off position.
3. Remove battery.
4. Remove air cleaner box mounting bolt and disconnect air inlet sensor electrical connector.
5. Lift air cleaner box upward to clear alignment post, then move air cleaner box forward to access battery tray mounting bolts and remove battery tray.
6. Disconnect brake fluid level sensor wiring harness mounted on fluid reservoir.
7. Disconnect primary and secondary

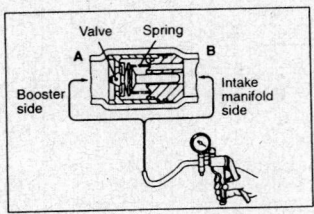

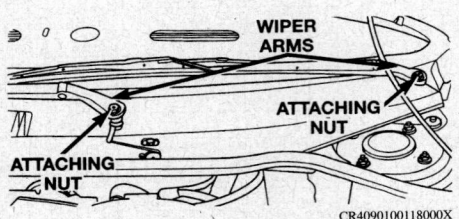

Vacuum pump connection	Accept/reject criteria
Connection at the brake booster side (A)	A negative pressure (vacuum) is created and held.
Connection at the intake manifold side (B)	A negative pressure (vacuum) is not created.

Fig. 4 Vacuum pump connection locations

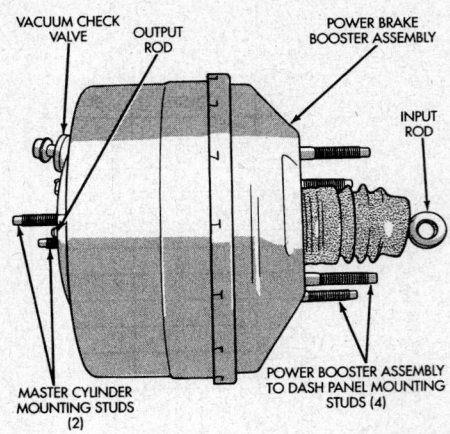

Fig. 5 Teves Power brake booster assembly. Concorde, Intrepid & 300M

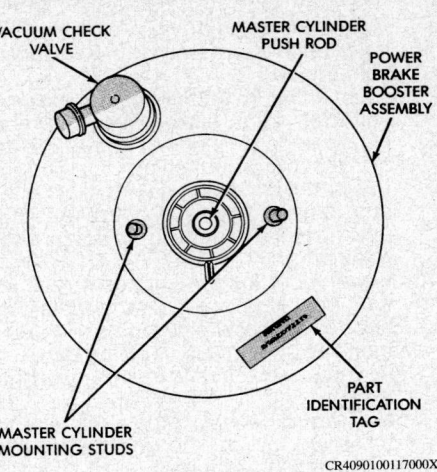

Fig. 6 Bosch Power brake booster identification. Concorde, Intrepid & 300M

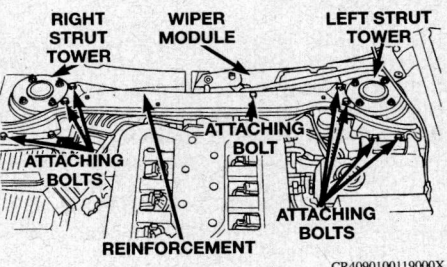

Fig. 7 Wiper arm replacement. Concorde, Intrepid & 300M

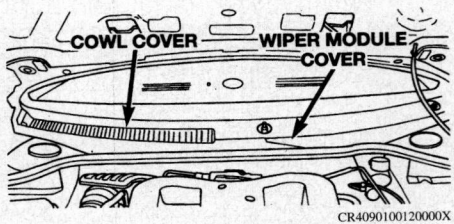

Fig. 8 Wiper module & cowl cover replacement. Concorde, Intrepid & 300M

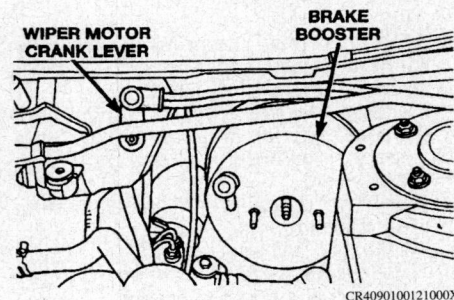

Fig. 10 Wiper crank lever position. Concorde, Intrepid & 300M

Fig. 9 Reinforcement & wiper module replacement. Concorde, Intrepid & 300M

brake tubes from master cylinder housing. Plug master cylinder outlets.

8. Clean area where master cylinder attaches to power booster using suitable cleaner.

9. Remove mounting nuts and slide master cylinder forward out of booster.

10. Remove vacuum seal in front of power brake vacuum booster by carefully inserting suitable, small screwdriver between master cylinder push rod and vacuum seal and prying seal out of booster. **Do not attempt to pry seal out by inserting screwdriver between seal and booster.**

11. Disconnect power booster check valve vacuum hoses. **Do not remove check valve from power booster.**

12. Remove Integrated Hydraulic Control Unit (ICU) and mounting bracket.

13. Position suitable, small screwdriver between center tang on input rod to brake pedal pin retaining clip.

14. Rotate screwdriver to allow retaining clip center tang to pass over end of brake pedal pin. Discard retaining clip.

15. Remove mounting nuts and slide power booster forward until mounting studs clear dash, then tilt unit upward to remove.

16. Reverse procedure to install, noting the following:
   a. Lubricate master cylinder push rod with suitable silicone lubricant.
   b. Install new vacuum seal onto push rod with notches on seal pointing toward master cylinder housing.
   c. **Torque** power booster mounting nuts to 21 ft. lbs.
   d. **Torque** master cylinder mounting bolts to 13 ft. lbs.

e. **Torque** master cylinder primary and secondary brake tube nuts to 12 ft. lbs.

SEBRING CONVERTIBLE, STRATUS SEDAN & 2004–06 SEBRING SEDAN

1. Disconnect speed control servo wiring harness connector and vacuum hose.
2. Remove speed control servo mounting nuts. Leave cable attached and position servo aside.
3. Remove master cylinder from booster as outlined under, "Hydraulic Brake Systems."
4. Remove vacuum booster check valve vacuum hoses.

5. Disconnect electrical connector, mounting screw and solenoid from frame rail, **Fig. 13.**
6. Insert small screwdriver between center tang on power brake booster input rod and brake pedal retaining clip, **Fig. 14.**
7. Rotate screwdriver to allow retaining clip center tang to pass over end of brake pedal pin, then pull retaining clip off brake pedal pin. **Discard retaining clip.**
8. Remove power brake vacuum booster to dash panel mounting nuts. Nuts are accessible from under dash panel, **Fig. 15.**
9. Slide power brake vacuum booster straight forward until mounting studs clear dash panel.
10. Reverse procedure to install, noting the following:
   a. **Torque** power booster mounting nuts to 21 ft. lbs.
   b. **Torque** speed control servo mounting nuts to 55 inch lbs.

SEBRING COUPE & STRATUS COUPE

Refer to **Fig. 16** for power booster removal procedures.

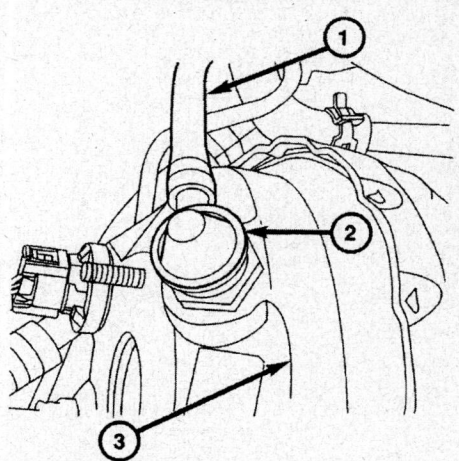

1- VACUUM HOSE
2- BOOSTER CHECK VALVE
3- BOOSTER

ARM0300000000062

Fig. 11 Power booster replacement. Crossfire

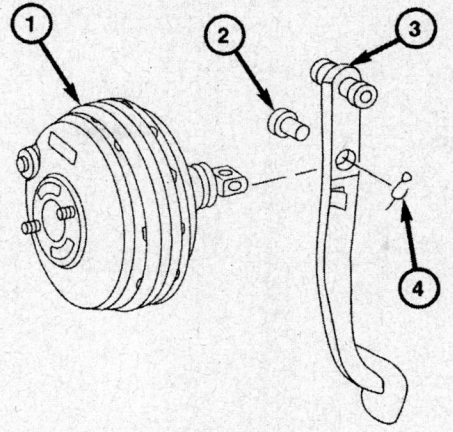

1- BOOSTER
2- BRAKE ROD PIN
3- BRAKE PEDAL
4- RETAINING CLIP

ARM0300000000063

Fig. 12 Power booster brake lever replacement. Crossfire

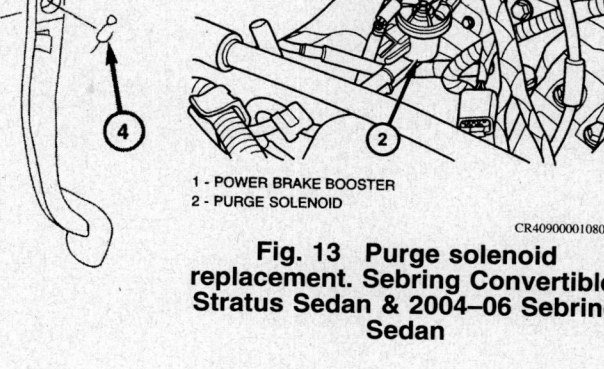

1 - POWER BRAKE BOOSTER
2 - PURGE SOLENOID

CR4090000108000X

Fig. 13 Purge solenoid replacement. Sebring Convertible, Stratus Sedan & 2004–06 Sebring Sedan

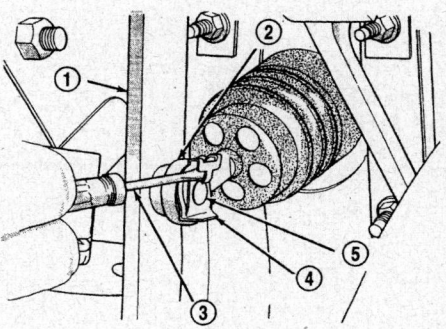

1 - BRAKE PEDAL
2 - INPUT ROD
3 - SCREWDRIVER
4 - RETAINING CLIP
5 - BRAKE PEDAL PIN

CR4090000109000X

Fig. 14 Input rod retaining pin replacement. Sebring Convertible, Stratus Sedan & 2004–06 Sebring Sedan

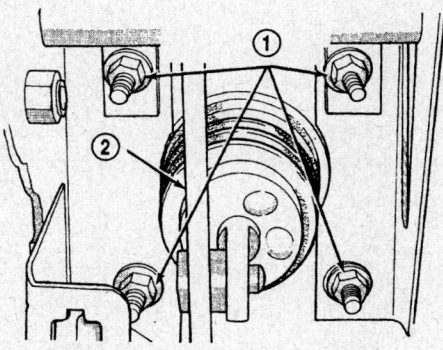

1 - POWER BRAKE BOOSTER MOUNTING NUTS
2 - BRAKE PEDAL

CR4090000110000X

Fig. 15 Power brake booster mounting nuts. Sebring Convertible, Stratus Sedan & 2004–06 Sebring Sedan

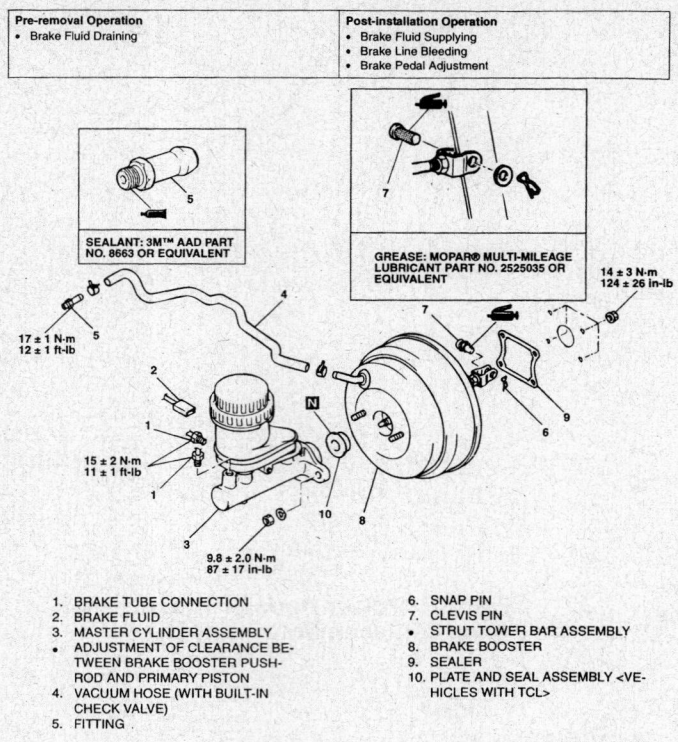

Fig. 16   Brake booster & master cylinder
replacement. Sebring Coupe & Stratus Coupe

Pre-removal Operation
- Brake Fluid Draining

Post-installation Operation
- Brake Fluid Supplying
- Brake Line Bleeding
- Brake Pedal Adjustment

SEALANT: 3M™ AAD PART
NO. 8663 OR EQUIVALENT

GREASE: MOPAR® MULTI-MILEAGE
LUBRICANT PART NO. 2525035 OR
EQUIVALENT

17 ± 1 N·m
12 ± 1 ft-lb

15 ± 2 N·m
11 ± 1 ft-lb

9.8 ± 2.0 N·m
87 ± 17 in-lb

14 ± 3 N·m
124 ± 26 in-lb

1. BRAKE TUBE CONNECTION
2. BRAKE FLUID
3. MASTER CYLINDER ASSEMBLY
• ADJUSTMENT OF CLEARANCE BE-
   TWEEN BRAKE BOOSTER PUSH-
   ROD AND PRIMARY PISTON
4. VACUUM HOSE (WITH BUILT-IN
   CHECK VALVE)
5. FITTING

6. SNAP PIN
7. CLEVIS PIN
• STRUT TOWER BAR ASSEMBLY
8. BRAKE BOOSTER
9. SEALER
10. PLATE AND SEAL ASSEMBLY <VE-
    HICLES WITH TCL>

CR4090000106000X

FRONT WHEEL DRIVE AXLES

TABLE OF CONTENTS

	Page No.		Page No.
APPLICATION CHART	18-1	**TYPE 2**............................	18-5
TYPE 1............................	18-1	**TYPE 3**............................	18-10

Application Chart

Model	Year	Type No.
Avenger & Sebring Sedan	2007–08	3
Caliber	2007–08	2
Charger, Magnum & 300	2005–08	3
Concorde, Intrepid & 300M	2004	2
Neon	2004–05	2
Sebring Convertible, Sebring Sedan & Stratus Sedan	2004–06	2
Sebring Coupe & Stratus Coupe	2004–05	1

Type 1

NOTE: On Air Bag Equipped Models, Refer To "Air Bag System Precautions" Located In The Front Of This Manual For System Disarming & Arming Procedures.

NOTE: Refer To "Computer Relearn Procedures" Located In The Front Of This Manual When Battery Power To The Computer Has Been Interrupted.

INDEX

	Page No.		Page No.		Page No.
Driveshaft, Replace.............	18-1	Assemble...................	18-2	Lefthand....................	18-2
Driveshaft Service..............	18-1	Disassemble................	18-2	Righthand	18-2
2.4L Engine...................	18-2	3.0L Engine.................	18-2	**Tightening Specifications**	18-4

DRIVESHAFT

REPLACE

1. Raise and support vehicle, then remove tire and wheel assembly.
2. **On models equipped with ABS,** disconnect speed sensor cable connector, **Fig. 1.**
3. **On all models,** disconnect brake hose clip.
4. Ensure vehicle weight is not applied to wheel bearing.
5. Remove cotter pin and driveshaft nut.
6. Loosen lower arm ball joint nut. **Do not remove nut.**
7. Disconnect lower arm ball joint using steering linkage puller tool No. MB99113, or equivalent, **Fig. 2.**
8. Remove cotter pin and loosen tie rod end nut. **Do not remove nut.**
9. Disconnect tie rod end using steering linkage puller.
10. Remove mounting nut and disconnect stabilizer link connector.
11. Push drive shaft from hub using axle puller tool No. MB990242, adapter MB991354 and end yoke holder tool No. MB990767, or equivalents, **Fig. 3,** noting the following:
    a. **On models equipped with ABS,** do not damage ABS rotor.
    b. **On all models,** do not pull driveshaft, use pry bar.
    c. Do inset pry bar deep enough to damage oil seal.
    d. Do not damage transaxle oil seal with driveshaft splines.
12. Remove driveshaft by inserting a suitable pry bar between transaxle case and driveshaft, **Fig. 4. Do damage transaxle oil seal with inner driveshaft spline.**
13. **On models equipped with 3.0L engine,** if righthand side inner shaft and transaxle are tightly joined, tap center bearing bracket lightly with suitable plastic hammer.
14. **On all models,** cover transaxle case with suitable shop towel.
15. Reverse procedure to install, noting the following:
    a. Washer convex side must face drive shaft nut.
    b. Use end yoke holder tool No. MB990767, or equivalent when tightening driveshaft nut.

DRIVESHAFT SERVICE

When servicing the drive axle, never disassemble the Birfield joint except when replacing the boot.

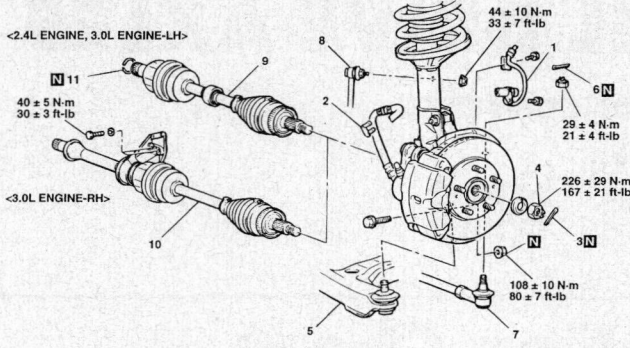

1. SPEED SENSOR CABLE CONNECTION <VEHICLES WITH ABS>
2. BRAKE HOSE CLIP
3. COTTER PIN
4. DRIVESHAFT NUT
5. LOWER ARM BALL JOINT CONNECTION
6. COTTER PIN
7. TIE ROD END CONNECTION
8. STABILIZER LINK CONNECTION
9. DRIVESHAFT
10. DRIVESHAFT AND INNER SHAFT
11. CIRCLIP

Required Special Tools:
- MB990242: Puller Bar
- MB990767: End Yoke Holder
- MB990998: Front Hub Remover and Installer
- MB991345: Puller Body

CR3030000478000X

Fig. 1   Exploded view of driveshaft

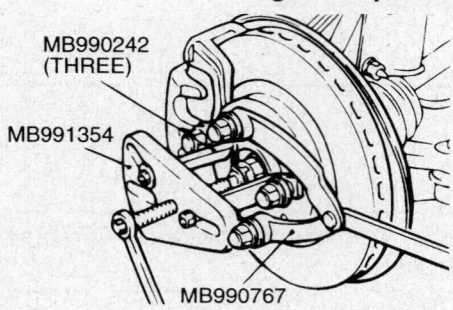

Fig. 3   Driveshaft replacement

2.4L Engine

DISASSEMBLE

1. Remove tripod joint bands, **Fig. 5.**
2. Remove circlip, snap ring and spider.
3. Wrap Birfield joint with suitable plastic tape.
4. Ensure plastic tape is around spline part on Birfield joint so tripod joint boot is not damaged when they are removed.
5. Remove bands and tripod boot.
6. Remove bands and dynamic damper.

ASSEMBLE

1. Install dynamic damper, **Fig. 6,** noting the following:
   a. **Ensure no grease adheres to rubber part of dynamic damper.**
   b. **Damper band and tripod joint boot band are different in shape, ensure proper band is installed.**

2. Wrap suitable plastic tape around shaft spline, then install tripod joint boot and band.
3. Apply drive axle repair kit grease to spider axles and rollers.
4. Install spider spline chamfered portion toward driveshaft and spider to driveshaft, **Fig. 7.**
5. Fill tripod joint with 3.1–3.9 ounces of repair kit grease, then install snap ring, case and circlip.

3.0L Engine

LEFTHAND

Refer to "2.4L Engine" for lefthand shaft replacement procedure.

RIGHTHAND

DISASSEMBLE

1. Disassemble outer shaft as outlined under "2.4L Engine,"
2. Remove tripod joint bands, **Fig. 5.**
3. Press and deform seal plate, then remove it with suitable press.
4. Remove inner shaft from tripod case using inner shaft remove tool No. MB991248, or MD998801, or equivalents, **Fig. 8.**
5. Remove dust covers.
6. Remove inner shaft and dust shields from center bearing bracket using inner shaft remove tool, **Fig. 9.**
7. Remove center bearing from bracket using adapter tool No. MB990930 and rear suspension bush base tool No. MB990938, or equivalents, **Fig. 10.**

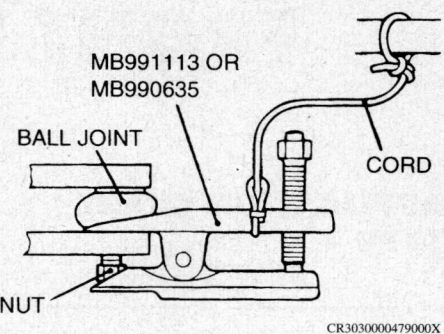

CR3030000479000X

Fig. 2   Ball joint/tie rod end disconnection

CR3030000481000X

Fig. 4   Pry bar installation

ASSEMBLE

1. Assemble outer shaft as outlined under "2.4L Engine."
2. Install center bearing into center bearing bracket using adapter tool No. MB990930 and rear suspension bush base tool No. MB990938, or equivalents, **Fig. 10.**
3. Pack .5–.7 ounces suitable multimileage grease into inner dust seal and .3–.4 ounces to outer, **Fig. 11.**
4. Install oil seal into center bearing bracket adapter and rear suspension bush base tools.
5. Apply suitable grease to dust seal lip of dust seal. **Do not damage outer dust seal surface rubber portion. Do not apply grease to outside of lip.**
6. Hold center bearing inner race using adapter tool No. MB991172, or equivalent, and press-in inner shaft, **Fig. 12.**
7. Install suitable grease to inner shaft serration and press inner shaft into tripod joint case.
8. Fill tripod joint with 3.3–4.1 ounces of repair kit grease, then install seal plate, case and circlip.
9. Position tripod joint outer race so distance between boot bands is 3.3 inches, **Fig. 13.**
10. Remove part of tripod joint outer race to release air pressure inside boot.

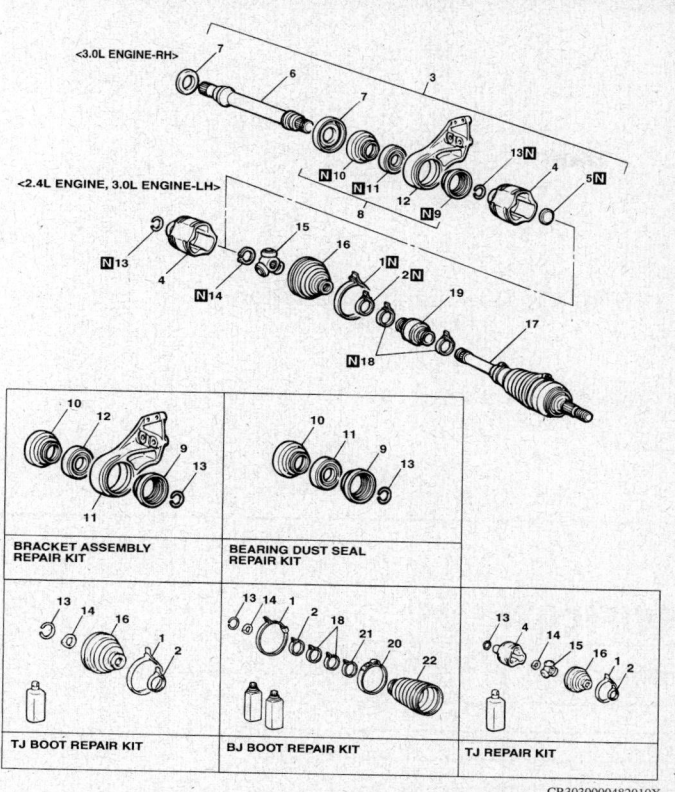

1. TJ BOOT BAND (LARGE)
2. TJ BOOT BAND (SMALL)
3. TJ CASE INNER SHAFT ASSEMBLY
4. TJ CASE
5. SEAL PLATE
6. INNER SHAFT
7. DUST COVER
8. BRACKET ASSEMBLY
9. DUST SEAL OUTER
10. DUST SEAL INNER
11. CENTER BEARING
12. CENTER BEARING BRACKET
13. CIRCLIP
14. SNAP RING
15. SPIDER ASSEMBLY
16. TJ BOOT
17. BJ ASSEMBLY
18. DAMPER BAND <2.4L ENGINE, 3.0L ENGINE-LH>
19. DYNAMIC DAMPER <2.4L ENGINE, 3.0L ENGINE-LH>
20. BJ BOOT BAND (LARGE)
21. BJ BOOT BAND (SMALL)
22. BJ BOOT

NOTE: BJ: Birfield Joint
      TJ: Tripod Joint

Required Special Tool:
- MB990890: Rear Suspension Bush Base
- MB990930: Installation Adapter
- MB990932: Installation Adapter
- MB990934: Installation Adapter
- MB990938: Installation Adapter
- MB991172: Adapter
- MB991248 or MD998801: Inner Shaft Remover
- MB991561: Boot Band Crimping Tool

CR3030000482020X

Fig. 5 Exploded view of driveshaft assembly (Part 2 of 2). 2.4L engine

CR3030000482010X

Fig. 5 Exploded view of driveshaft assembly (Part 1 of 2). 2.4L engine

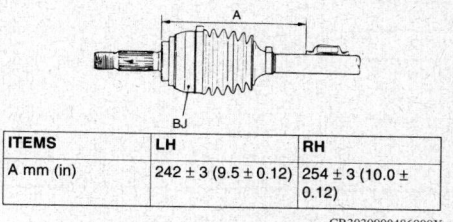

ITEMS	LH	RH
A mm (in)	242 ± 3 (9.5 ± 0.12)	254 ± 3 (10.0 ± 0.12)

CR3030000486000X

Fig. 6 Dynamic damper installation. 2.4L engine

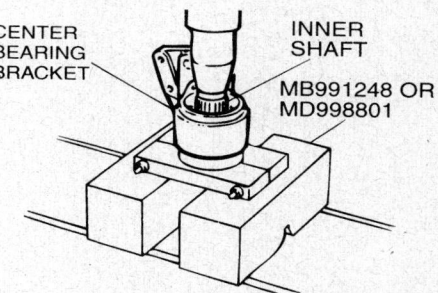

CR3030000484000X

Fig. 9 Inner shaft from center bearing bracket removal. Sebring Coupe & Stratus Coupe w/3.0L engine

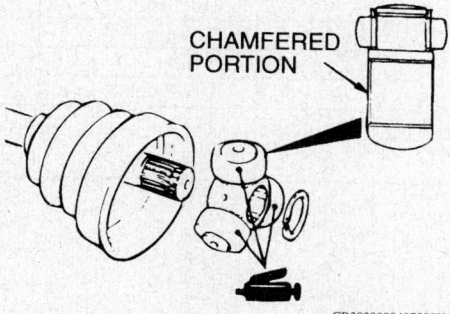

CHAMFERED PORTION

CR3030000487000X

Fig. 7 Spider installation. Sebring Coupe & Stratus Coupe w/2.4L engine

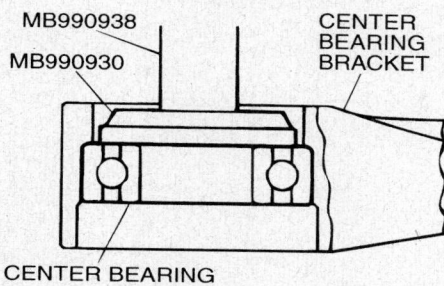

MB990938
MB990930
CENTER BEARING BRACKET
CENTER BEARING

CR3030000485000X

Fig. 10 Center bearing replacement. 3.0L engine

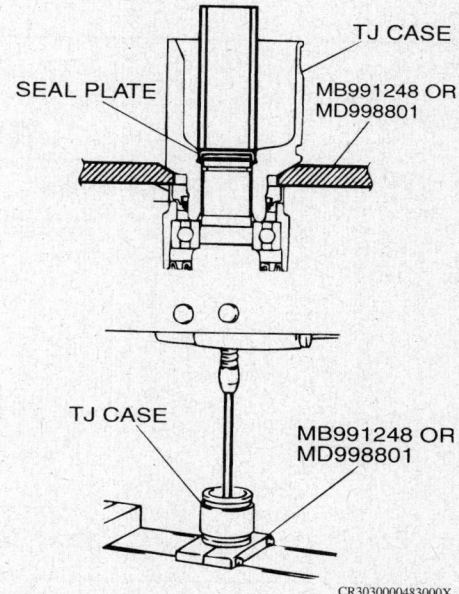

TJ CASE
SEAL PLATE
MB991248 OR MD998801
TJ CASE
MB991248 OR MD998801

CR3030000483000X

Fig. 8 Inner shaft from case removal. 3.0L engine

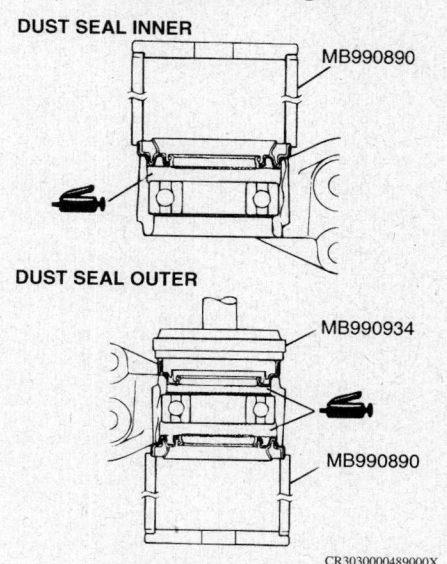

DUST SEAL INNER
MB990890
DUST SEAL OUTER
MB990934
MB990890

CR3030000489000X

Fig. 11 Dust seal installation. 3.0L engine

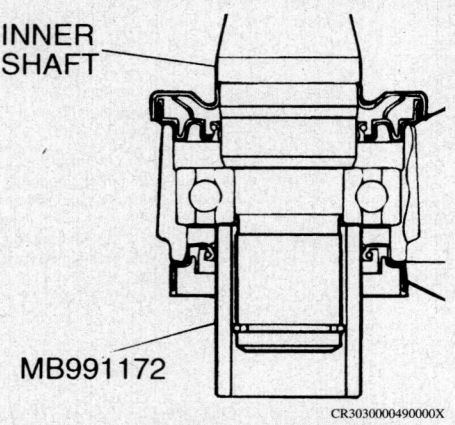
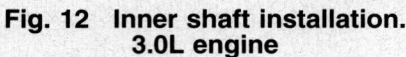

INNER SHAFT

MB991172

CR3030000490000X

**Fig. 12 Inner shaft installation.
3.0L engine**

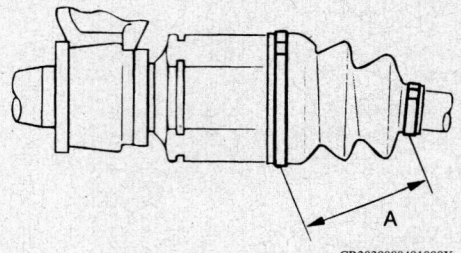

A

CR3030000491000X

**Fig. 13 Boot band installation.
3.0L engine**

TIGHTENING SPECIFICATIONS

Year	Component	Torque Ft. Lbs.
2004–05	Caliper	67–81
	Center Bearing	27–33
	Driveshaft Nut	146–188
	Driveshaft & Inner Shaft Bracket	27–33
	Dust Shield	61–95 ①
	Front Strut	203–239
	Knuckle To Front Hub	58–72
	Lower Arm Ball Joint	73–87
	Stabilizer Link	26–40
	Tie Rod End & Ball Joint	17–25

① — Inch lbs.

Type 2

NOTE: On Air Bag Equipped Models, Refer To "Air Bag System Precautions" Located In The Front Of This Manual For System Disarming & Arming Procedures.

NOTE: Refer To "Computer Relearn Procedures" Located In The Front Of This Manual When Battery Power To The Computer Has Been Interrupted.

INDEX

	Page No.
Driveshaft, Replace	18-5
Caliber, Neon, Sebring Convertible, Stratus Sedan & 2004–06 Sebring Sedan	18-5
Concorde, Intrepid & 300M	18-5
Driveshaft Identification	18-5
Driveshaft Service	18-6

	Page No.
Inner Driveshaft Boot, Replace	18-6
Installation	18-6
Removal	18-6
Outer Driveshaft Boot, Replace	18-6
Caliber, Neon, Sebring Convertible, Stratus Sedan & 2004–06 Sebring Sedan	18-7

	Page No.
Concorde, Intrepid & 300M	18-6
Tightening Specifications	18-9

DRIVESHAFT IDENTIFICATION

The unequal length system used on these models has a short solid interconnecting shaft on one side with a longer tubular interconnecting shaft on the other, **Figs. 1 and 2.**

DRIVESHAFT

REPLACE

Concorde, Intrepid & 300M

1. Raise and support vehicle, then remove wheel and tire assemblies.
2. Remove brake caliper as outlined in "Disc Brakes" chapter.
3. Remove brake rotor by pulling it straight off mounting studs.
4. Remove speed sensor cable routing bracket from strut.
5. Remove stub axle and hub mounting nut.
6. Install puller tool No. 6790, or equivalent, on hub and bearing assembly using wheel lugnuts.
7. Install lugnut on wheel stud to protect threads.
8. Prevent hub from turning. by inserting suitable flat-bladed pry tool.
9. Force outer stub axle from hub and bearing assembly using puller tool.
10. Disconnect inner tripod joint from transaxle stub shaft retaining ring.
11. Pry driveshaft from transmission by inserting suitable pry bar between transmission case and driveshaft, noting the following:
    a. **Do not pull on driveshaft.**
    b. **Do not insert pry bar deep enough to damage oil seal.**
    c. **Only pry inner joint from retaining snap ring.**

    d. **Do not attempt to remove inner tripod joint from transaxle stub shaft.**
12. Support steering knuckle, then disconnect and remove strut from steering knuckle.
13. Support outer CV joint assembly with one hand and grasp steering knuckle with other hand.
14. Rotate outer CV out and to rear, until it clears hub and bearing assembly.
15. Remove driveshaft inner tripod joint from transaxle stub shaft. **Do not pull on interconnecting shaft.**
16. Reverse procedure to install, noting the following:
    a. Install new O-ring seal and tripod joint retaining circlip.
    b. Apply thin, even bead suitable of multi-purpose lubricant grease around inner tripod joint splines where O-rings seats against joint.
    c. When installing outer CV joint into hub and bearing assembly, do not damage flinger disc, **Fig. 3.**
    d. **Ensure snap rings are securely seated in grooves because strut bolts have serrated shaft. Turn nut on bolts, but do not turn bolts.**
    e. Install new hub and bearing stub shaft mounting nut. Tighten, but do not torque nut now.
    f. Apply vehicle brakes, then tighten new hub and bearing stub shaft nut.

Caliber, Neon, Sebring Convertible, Stratus Sedan & 2004–06 Sebring Sedan

If the vehicle will be moved on its wheels when a driveshaft has been removed, install a properly sized bolt and

nut through the front hub. **Torque** to 180 ft. lbs., to ensure the hub bearing will not loosen.

1. Place transaxle in Park position.
2. Raise and support vehicle, then remove wheel and tire assembly.
3. **On models equipped with ABS,** disconnect front wheel speed sensor and position harness aside.
4. **On all models,** remove ball joint to knuckle mounting nut and bolt.
5. Separate ball joint stud from knuckle by prying down on lower control arm. **Avoid damaging joint seal.**
6. Remove driveshaft from knuckle by pulling outward on knuckle while pressing in on driveshaft. Support outer end of driveshaft. If separation is difficult, proceed as follows:
    a. Install puller tool No. 6790, or equivalent, on hub and bearing using lugnuts.
    b. Install axle nut to protect threads.
    c. Prevent hub from turning by inserting suitable flat-bladed pry tool.
    d. Force driveshaft outer stub axle from hub and bearing assembly using puller tool.
    e. Remove axle nut, then pull knuckle out and away from outer CV joint.
7. Support driveshaft outer end.
8. Remove inner tripod joints from transaxle side gears using suitable punch to disconnect inner joint retaining ring from side gear, noting the following:
    a. On righthand side joint, position punch against inner joint.
    b. On lefthand side joint, position punch in joint groove.
9. Position suitable oil resistant container under driveshaft where it enters transaxle.
10. Support inner tripod joint and driveshaft interconnecting shaft.
11. Remove inner joint from transaxle by pulling it straight out of side gear and oil seal. **Do not let spline or snap ring drag across oil sealing lip.**

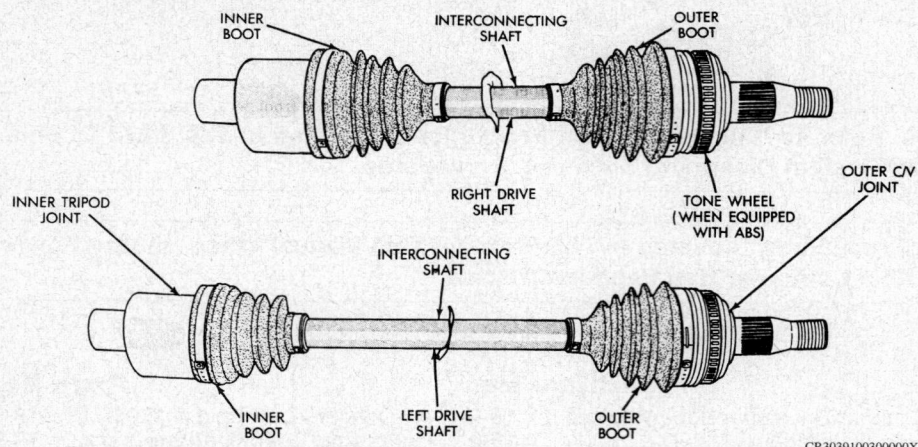

Fig. 1 Driveshaft identification. Concorde, Intrepid & 300M

12. Reverse procedure to install, noting the following:
    a. Thoroughly clean spline and oil sealing surface on tripod joint.
    b. Lubricate oil seal sealing surface with transaxle fluid.
    c. Ensure snap ring is fully seated in its groove. Tripod joint will not be removable by hand when snap ring is properly installed.
    d. Install new knuckle to ball joint stud bolt and nut.
    e. Clean dirt and debris from driveshaft outer stub shaft threads.
    f. Inspect transaxle fluid level.

DRIVESHAFT SERVICE

The driveshaft is a non-serviceable item, except for the inner and outer driveshaft boots, **Fig. 4.** If any failure of internal components is diagnosed, the driveshaft must be replaced as an assembly.

Inner Driveshaft Boot, Replace

REMOVAL

1. Remove driveshaft as outlined under "Driveshaft, Replace."
2. Remove inner joint boot clamps and slide boot down interconnecting shaft.
3. Remove joint housing interconnecting shaft and spider. **Do not pull on interconnecting shaft.**
4. Remove snap ring and spider from interconnecting shaft using suitable brass drift. **Hold bearings in place on spider trunnions to prevent them from falling away. Do not hit outer tripod bearings when removing spider.**
5. Remove interconnecting shaft joint boot.
6. Clean and inspect spider, tripod joint housing and interconnecting shaft for signs of excessive wear. **If excessive wear is present, replace entire driveshaft.**

INSTALLATION

Two different types of boots are used on these models. One is a high temperature, soft and pliable type, the other is a normal temperature, soft and rigid type. The replacement boot must be of the same type that was removed.

1. **On Concorde, Intrepid and 300M models,** install new boot clamps and boot onto interconnecting shaft. **Boot must be positioned on interconnecting shaft so only thinnest shaft groove is visible.**
2. **On Caliber, Neon, Sebring Convertible, Stratus Sedan & 2004–06 Sebring Sedan models,** install new boot clamps and boot onto interconnecting shaft. **Boot must be positioned so raised bead on inside of boot is in groove on interconnecting shaft.**
3. **On all models,** install spider onto interconnecting shaft and retaining snap ring. **Ensure retaining snap ring is fully installed and seated into shaft groove.**
4. Distribute ½ of grease provided in boot service package into tripod housing and remaining grease into boot. **Do not use any other type of grease.**
5. Install spider into tripod housing.
6. Position boot over boot retaining groove on interconnecting shaft and install boot retaining clamp using crimper tool No. C-4975-A, or equivalent.
7. Position boot into tripod housing retaining groove.
8. **On Caliber, Neon, Sebring Convertible, Stratus Sedan & 2004–06 Sebring Sedan models,** proceed as follows:
    a. Insert suitable trim stick between joint and boot to vent inner joint, **Fig. 5.** If inner joint has hard plastic boot, trim stick must be inserted between soft rubber insert and joint housing.
    b. With trim stick inserted between sealing boot and tripod joint housing, position interconnecting shaft in center of travel in tripod joint housing.
    c. On models equipped with Hytrel, hard plastic sealing boot, insert trim stick between soft rubber and tripod housing not hard plastic sealing boot and soft rubber insert.

d. **On all models,** position inner tripod joint on halfshaft until correct sealing boot edge to edge length is obtained, **Fig. 6.**
e. **On models with hard plastic sealing boot,** edge to edge length is 4.213 inches.
f. **On models with soft sealing boot,** edge to edge length is 4.134 inches.
g. **On all models,** position boot to interface with tripod housing. Boot lobes must be properly aligned with tripod housing recesses.
9. **On models equipped with crimp type boot clamp,** proceed as follows:
    a. Clamp sealing boot onto tripod housing using crimper tool No. C-4975-A, or equivalent.
    b. Place crimping tool over clamp bridge.
    c. Tighten nut on crimper tool until tool's jaws are completely closed together, face to face.
10. **On models equipped with latching type boot clamp,** proceed as follows:
    a. Clamp sealing boot onto tripod housing using clamp locking tool No. YA3050, or equivalent.
    b. Place tool's prongs in clamp hole.
    c. Squeeze tool together until clamp's top band is latched behind two tabs on lower clamp band.
11. **On all models,** install driveshaft as outlined under "Driveshaft, Replace."

Outer Driveshaft Boot, Replace

CONCORDE, INTREPID & 300M

REMOVAL

1. Remove driveshaft as outlined under "Driveshaft, Replace."
2. Remove outer joint boot clamps and slide boot down interconnecting shaft.
3. Remove grease to expose outer CV joint retaining ring, **Fig. 7.**
4. Spread retaining ring and slide CV joint off interconnecting shaft.
5. Remove and discard failed boot and clamps.
6. Clean and inspect spider, CV joint and interconnecting shaft for signs of excessive wear. **If excessive wear is present, entire driveshaft must be replacement.**

INSTALLATION

1. Install new boot clamps and boot onto interconnecting shaft.
2. Install CV joint onto interconnecting shaft by pushing shaft into CV joint until retaining snap ring is seated in shaft groove, **Fig. 7.**
3. Distribute ½ of grease provided in boot service package into CV joint and remaining grease into boot.
4. Position boot over boot retaining grove on interconnecting shaft with thinnest shaft groove is visible.
5. Install boot retaining clamp using

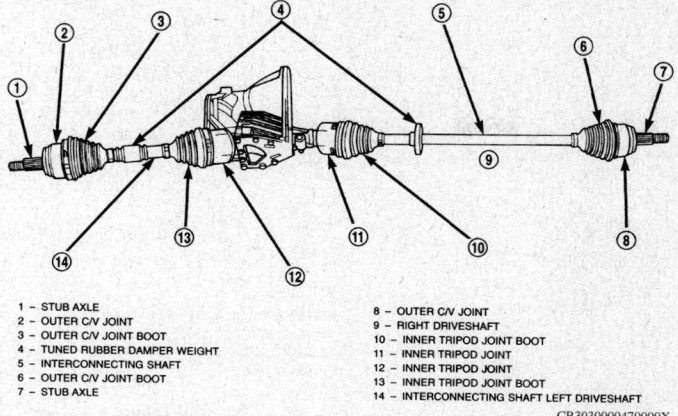

Fig. 2 Driveshaft identification. Neon, Sebring Convertible, Stratus Sedan & 2004–06 Sebring Sedan

1 – STUB AXLE
2 – OUTER C/V JOINT
3 – OUTER C/V JOINT BOOT
4 – TUNED RUBBER DAMPER WEIGHT
5 – INTERCONNECTING SHAFT
6 – OUTER C/V JOINT BOOT
7 – STUB AXLE

8 – OUTER C/V JOINT
9 – RIGHT DRIVESHAFT
10 – INNER TRIPOD JOINT BOOT
11 – INNER TRIPOD JOINT
12 – INNER TRIPOD JOINT
13 – INNER TRIPOD JOINT BOOT
14 – INTERCONNECTING SHAFT LEFT DRIVESHAFT

CR3030000470000X

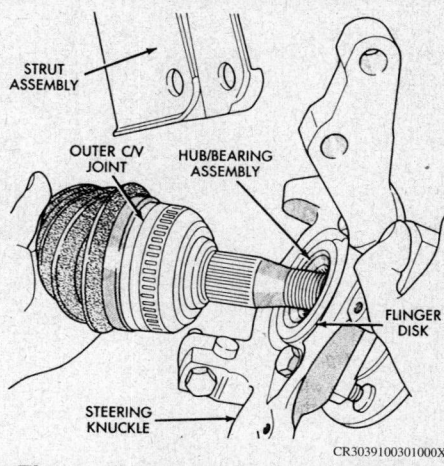

Fig. 3 Outer CV joint separation from hub. Concorde, Intrepid & 300M

CR3039100301000X

crimper tool No. C-4975-A, or equivalent.

6. Position boot over boot retaining grove on CV joint housing and install boot retaining clamp using crimper tool. Ensure seal is not dimpled, stretched or distorted.

7. Install driveshaft as outlined under "Driveshaft, Replace."

CALIBER, NEON, SEBRING CONVERTIBLE, STRATUS SEDAN & 2004–06 SEBRING SEDAN

REMOVAL

1. Remove driveshaft as outlined under "Driveshaft, Replace."
2. Remove and discard large boot clamp retaining CV joint sealing boot to CV joint housing.
3. Remove and discard small clamp retaining outer CV joint sealing boot to interconnecting shaft.
4. Slide outer CV joint housing sealing boot down interconnecting shaft.
5. Wipe away grease to expose outer CV joint and interconnecting shaft.

6. Support interconnecting shaft in suitable soft jawed vice with protective jaw caps.
7. Disconnect CV joint housing from interconnecting shaft internal circlip by strike end using suitable soft faced hammer.
8. CV joint may have to be tapped off interconnecting shaft using suitable soft faced hammer.
9. Remove interconnecting shaft large circlip.
10. Slide boot off interconnecting shaft.
11. Thoroughly clean and inspect outer CV and interconnecting joints for signs of excessive wear. **If components show signs of excessive wear, replace driveshaft.**

INSTALLATION

1. Slide new sealing boot to interconnecting shaft retaining clamp and onto interconnecting shaft, **Fig. 8. Ensure seal boot is positioned on interconnecting shaft so raised bead on inside of seal boot is in groove on interconnecting shaft.**
2. Align interconnecting shaft and outer CV joint cross splines, then start outer

CV joint onto interconnecting shaft.
3. Install outer CV joint assembly onto interconnecting shaft using suitable soft faced hammer, **Fig. 9.**
4. Distribute ½ of grease provided in seal boot service package into outer CV joint housing. **Do not use any other type of grease.**
5. Put remaining grease into sealing boot.
6. Install outer CV joint boot to interconnecting shaft clamp evenly on sealing boot.
7. Clamp sealing boot onto interconnecting shaft using clamp crimper tool No. C-4975-A, or equivalent, **Fig. 10.**
8. Position outer CV joint sealing boot into outer CV joint housing retaining groove.
9. Install sealing boot to outer CV joint retaining clamp evenly on sealing boot.
10. Clamp sealing boot onto CV joint housing using clamp crimper tool No. C-4975-A, or equivalent. **Ensure jaws of crimper tool are closed completely together.**
11. Install driveshaft as outlined under "Driveshaft, Replace."

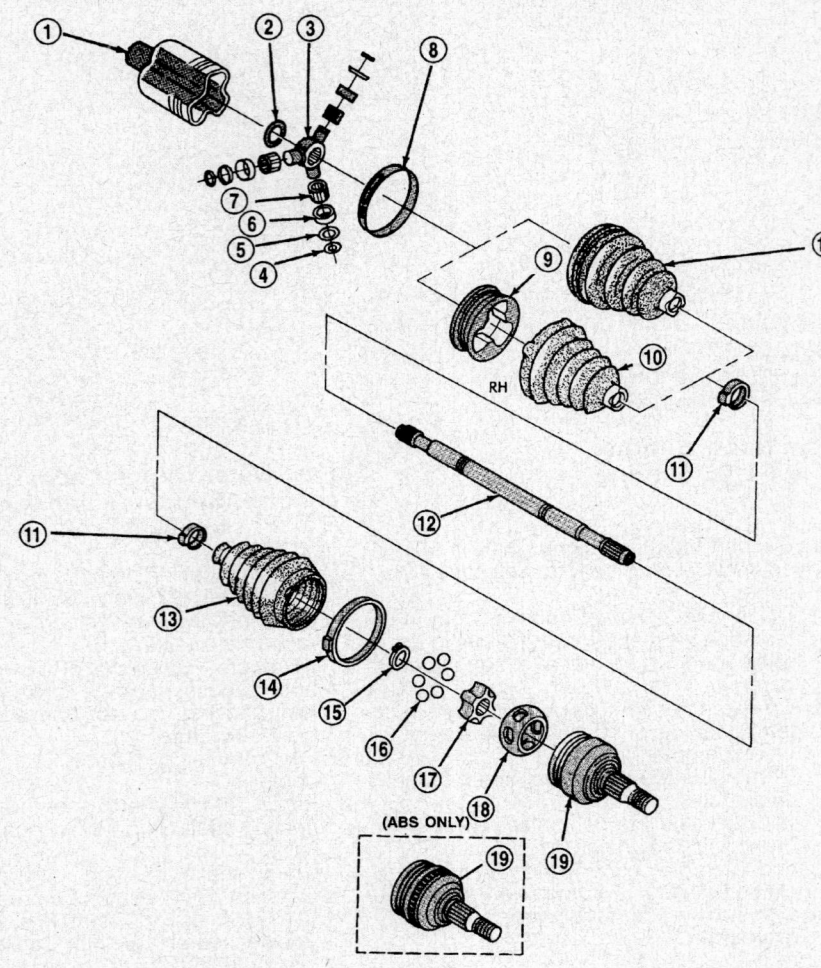

1 - HOUSING ASM, RETAINER
2 - RING, SPACER
3 - SPIDER, TRIPOD JOINT
4 - RING, RETAINING
5 - RETAINER, BALL & ROLLER
6 - BALL, TRIPOD JOINT
7 - ROLLER, NEEDLE
8 - CLAMP, SEAL RETAINING
9 - BUSHING, TRILOBAL TRIPOD
10 - SEAL, DRIVE AXLE INBOARD

11 - CLAMP, SEAL RETAINING
12 - SHAFT, AXLE (RH SHOWN, LH SIMILAR)
13 - SEAL, DRIVE AXLE OUTBOARD
14 - CLAMP, SEAL RETAINING
15 - RING, RACE RETAINING
16 - BALL, CHROME ALLOY
17 - RACE, C/V JOINT INNER
18 - CAGE, C/V JOINT
19 - RACE, C/V JOINT OUTER

CR3030000477000X

Fig. 4 Exploded view of driveshaft

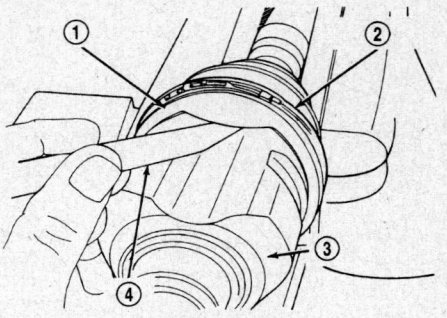

1 - INNER TRIPOD JOINT SEALING BOOT
2 - SEALING BOOT CLAMP
3 - INNER TRIPOD JOINT HOUSING
4 - TRIM STICK

CR3030100503000X

Fig. 5 Venting tripod joint assembly

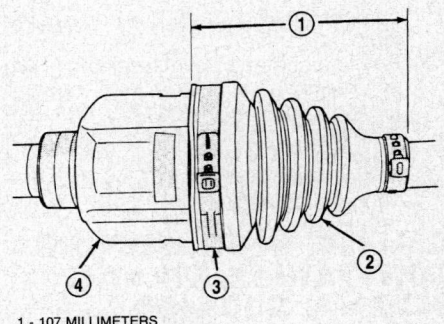

1 - 107 MILLIMETERS
2 - HYTREL SEALING BOOT
3 - SEALING BOOT CLAMP
4 - INNER TRIPOD JOINT

CR3030100504000X

Fig. 6 Sealing boot edge to edge length

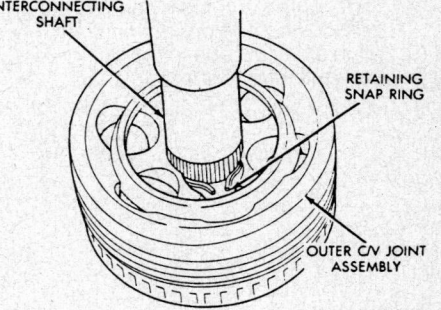

INTERCONNECTING SHAFT

RETAINING SNAP RING

OUTER C/V JOINT ASSEMBLY

CR3039100304000X

Fig. 7 Outer CV joint retaining snap ring location. Concorde, Intrepid & 300M

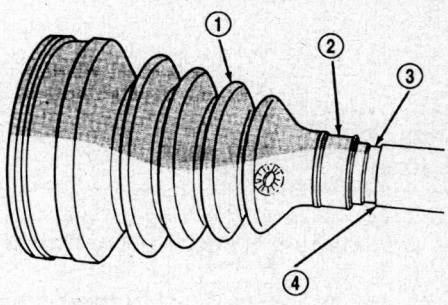

1 – SEALING BOOT
2 – RAISED BEAD IN THIS AREA OF SEALING BOOT
3 – GROOVE
4 – INTERCONNECTING SHAFT

CR3039800401000A

Fig. 8   Outer sealing boot installation. Caliber, Sebring Convertible, Stratus Sedan & 2004–06 Sebring Sedan

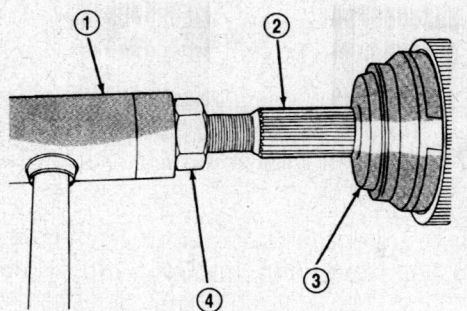

1 – SOFT FACED HAMMER
2 – STUB AXLE
3 – OUTER C/V JOINT
4 – NUT

CR3039800402000A

Fig. 9   Outer CV joint installation. Caliber, Neon, Sebring Convertible, Stratus Sedan & 2004–06 Sebring Sedan

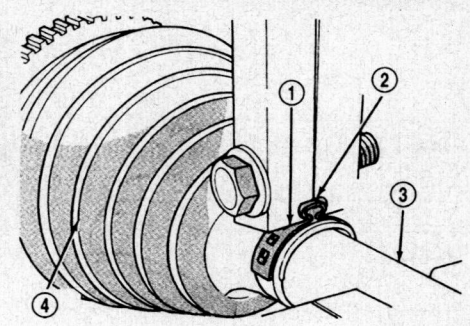

1 – CLAMP
2 – JAWS OF SPECIAL TOOL C-4975A MUST BE CLOSED COMPLETELY TOGETHER HERE
3 – INTERCONNECTING SHAFT
4 – SEALING BOOT

CR3039800403000A

Fig. 10   CV boot clamp installation. Caliber, Neon, Sebring Convertible, Stratus Sedan & 2004–06 Sebring Sedan

TIGHTENING SPECIFICATIONS

Year	Component	Torque Ft. Lbs.
CALIBER		
2007–08	Ball Joint Stud/Nut	70
	Halfshaft Bracket Bolts	55
	Hub Nut	180
	Wheel Lug Nut	95
CONCORDE, INTREPID & 300M		
2004	Halfshaft To Hub Bearing	105
	Knuckle To Ball Stud	70
	Knuckle To Strut Bolt	155
	Tie Rod End To Knuckle	27
	Wheel Lugnuts	100
NEON		
2004–05	Caliper To Knuckle	16
	Halfshaft To Hub Bearing	180
	Knuckle To Ball Joint Stud	70
	Knuckle To Strut Bolt	40①
	Tie Rod End To Knuckle	45
	Wheel Lugnuts	95
SEBRING CONVERTIBLE, SEBRING SEDAN & STRATUS SEDAN		
2004–06	Ball Joint To Knuckle	70
	Halfshaft To Hub Bearing	110
	Tie Rod To Knuckle	41
	Wheel Lugnuts	100

① — Final tighten an additional 90°.

Type 3

NOTE: On Air Bag Equipped Models, Refer To "Air Bag System Precautions" Located In The Front Of This Manual For System Disarming & Arming Procedures.

NOTE: Refer To "Computer Relearn Procedures" Located In The Front Of This Manual When Battery Power To The Computer Has Been Interrupted.

INDEX

	Page No.		Page No.		Page No.
Description	18-10	Removal	18-10	Inner	18-11
Driveshaft, Replace	18-10	Avenger & 2007–08 Sebring		Outer	18-11
Installation	18-10	Sedan	18-10	Intermediate Shaft, Replace	18-12
Avenger & 2007–08 Sebring		Except Avenger & 2007–08		Intermediate Shaft Service	18-12
Sedan	18-11	Sebring Sedan	18-10	Tightening Specifications	18-12
Except Avenger & 2007–08		Driveshaft Service	18-11		
Sebring Sedan	18-10	CV Boot	18-11		

DESCRIPTION

The inner joints of both half shaft assemblies are cross-groove joints. The outer joints of both assemblies are Rzeppa Joints. The cross-groove joints are true Constant Velocity (CV) joints, which allow for the changes in half shaft length through the jounce and rebound travel of the rear suspension.

The inner cross-groove joint of the lefthand halfshaft assembly is splined to the intermediate shaft and retained with a snap ring. The righthand halfshaft is splined to the front axle assembly and retained with a snap ring. The outer CV joint has a stub shaft that is splined into the wheel hub and retained by a steel hub nut.

DRIVESHAFT

REPLACE

Removal

EXCEPT AVENGER & 2007–08 SEBRING SEDAN

1. Raise and support vehicle, then remove tire and wheel assembly.
2. While holding link ball joint stem from rotating, remove stabilizer link (1) to shock clevis bracket nut.
3. Slide link ball joint stem from clevis bracket.
4. Remove clevis bracket to bottom of shock mounting nut and pinch bolt.
5. Remove shock clevis bracket to lower control arm mounting nut and bolt.
6. Pull lower end of clevis bracket outward away from lower control arm bushing, then slide it off shock. **If required, to use an appropriate prying tool to spread clamp area of clevis bracket.**
7. While helper applies brakes to keep hub from rotating, remove hub nut from axle half shaft.

8. Grasp rear of caliper and pull outward working with guide pins to retract caliper piston. **Never push on piston directly.**
9. Remove two disc brake caliper and adapter to knuckle mounting bolts.
10. Remove disc brake caliper and adapter from knuckle, then hang aside using suitable wire or bungee cord. **Do care not to overextend brake hose.**
11. Remove clips, then slide brake rotor off hub and bearing.
12. Separate upper ball joint stud from knuckle. using puller tool No. 9360, or equivalent. **Do not damage ball joint seal boot while sliding tool into place past seal boot.**
13. Remove tool and nut from end of upper ball joint stud.
14. Remove wheel speed sensor to knuckle clip.
15. Disconnect and remove righthand halfshaft from axle.
16. Remove lefthand halfshaft.

AVENGER & 2007–08 SEBRING SEDAN

1. Raise and support vehicle, then remove tire and wheel assembly.
2. Remove brake rotor as outlined under "Rotor, Replace" in "Disc Brake chapter."
3. Remove steering knuckle to strut mounting bolts.
4. Pull steering knuckle from strut clevis bracket.
5. Pull steering knuckle assembly down and away from outer C/V joint of half shaft assembly while pulling joint out of hub bearing.
6. Insert a pry bar between inner tripod joint and transaxle case. Pry against inner tripod joint, until tripod joint retaining snap-ring is disengaged from transaxle side gear.
7. Pull steering knuckle from strut clevis bracket.
8. Pull steering knuckle assembly down

and away from outer C/V joint of half shaft assembly while pulling joint out of intermediate shaft.
9. **On models equipped with a manual transaxle,** remove mid-shaft bearing to support bracket bolts from block, then remove intermediate shaft.
10. **On models equipped with 2.0L engine and manual transmission,** pull steering knuckle assembly down and away from outer C/V joint of half shaft assembly while pulling halfshaft out of transmission.
11. **On models with an automatic transmission,** remove heat shield.
12. **On all models,** remove mid-shaft to block mounting bolts.
13. Remove intermediate shaft.

Installation

EXCEPT AVENGER & 2007-08 SEBRING SEDAN

1. If previously removed, install and tighten intermediate shaft.
2. Install lefthand halfshaft.
3. Install new axle seal using seal installer tool No. C-4193-A, or equivalent.
4. Install righthand halfshaft.
5. Install halfshaft isolation washer. Washer is bi-directional and can be installed in either direction on shaft.
6. Install halfshaft into hub/bearing.
7. Loosely install halfshaft hub nut. **Do not tighten now.**
8. Place upper ball joint stud through hole in top of knuckle and install nut.
9. Tighten nut by holding ball joint stud with suitable hex wrench while turning nut with wrench. Tighten nut using crow foot wrench on torque wrench.
10. Clean hub face to remove dirt or corrosion where rotor mounts.
11. Install brake rotor over studs on hub and bearing.
12. Install disc brake caliper and adapter over brake rotor.
13. Install and tighten caliper adapter to

knuckle mounting bolts.

14. Pull lower end of shock outward, then slide clevis bracket onto lower end.
15. Slide clevis bracket onto shock until bracket contacts collar on shock housing.
16. Install clevis bracket to bottom of shock pinch bolt and nut. Install pinch bolt from rear. **Do not tighten now.**
17. Slide clevis bracket over bushing mounted in lower control arm.
18. Install shock clevis bracket to lower control arm bolt and nut. **Do not tighten now.**
19. Slide stabilizer link ball joint stem into clevis bracket.
20. Install link to clevis bracket nut.
21. Tighten ball joint stud turning nut using crow foot wrench on torque wrench.
22. Attach wheel speed sensor cable routing clip at knuckle.
23. Install hub nut on end of axle half shaft.
24. While helper applies brakes to keep hub from turning tighten hub nut.
25. Install tire and wheel assembly.
26. Lower vehicle.
27. Tighten lower shock clevis bracket bolt nut. **When tightening lower shock clevis mounting bolt, do not attempt rotating bolt. Bolt shaft is serrated. Turn nut only.**

AVENGER & 2007-08 SEBRING SEDAN

1. Install intermediate shaft into transaxle.
2. Install mid-shaft to block plate mounting bolts.
3. **On models equipped with a 2.0L engine and manual transmission,** install one piece righthand halfshaft.
4. **On models equipped with an automatic transmission,** install heat shield.
5. **On all models,** lightly lubricate oil seal sealing surface on tripod joint with fresh clean transmission lubricant and install rubber coated washer.
6. Install tripod joint into transaxle side gear as far as possible by hand, ensuring to engage splines before applying force.
7. Forcefully push tripod joint onto intermediate shaft, until snap-ring is engaged.
8. Slide half shaft back into front hub and bearing assembly.
9. Install steering knuckle in clevis bracket of strut damper assembly.
10. Install strut damper to steering knuckle attaching bolts. **Bolts are serrated and must not be turned during installation.**
11. Install rotor on hub and bearing assembly.
12. Install disc brake caliper assembly on steering knuckle.
13. Install halfshaft to hub/bearing assembly nut.
14. Install wheel and tire assembly.
15. Check for correct fluid level in transaxle assembly.

DRIVESHAFT SERVICE
CV Boot
INNER
REMOVAL

1. Remove large boot clamp which retains inner tripod joint sealing boot to tripod joint housing and discard.
2. Remove small clamp which retains inner tripod joint sealing boot to interconnecting shaft and discard.
3. Remove the sealing boot from the tripod housing and slide it down interconnecting shaft.
4. Slide tripod joint housing off spider assembly and interconnecting shaft. Hold bearings in place on spider trunnions.
5. Remove snap ring which retains spider assembly to interconnecting shaft.
6. Remove spider from interconnecting shaft. If spider will not come off interconnecting shaft by hand, remove it by tapping spider with suitable brass drift. **Do not hit outer tripod bearings.**
7. Slide sealing boot off interconnecting shaft.

INSTALLATION

1. Slide inner tripod joint seal boot retaining clamp, onto interconnecting shaft.
2. Slide replacement inner tripod joint sealing boot onto interconnecting shaft. Inner tripod joint seal boot must be positioned on interconnecting shaft, so raised bead on inside of seal boot is in groove on interconnecting shaft.
3. Install spider assembly onto interconnecting shaft. Spider must be installed on interconnecting shaft far enough to fully install spider retaining snap ring.
4. If spider will not fully install on interconnecting shaft by hand, it can be installed by tapping spider body with suitable brass drift. **Do not hit the outer tripod bearings.**
5. Install spider assembly to interconnecting shaft retaining snap ring into groove on end of interconnecting shaft. Ensure snap ring is fully seated into groove on interconnecting shaft.
6. Distribute half grease provided in seal boot service package into tripod housing. **Do not use any other type of grease.**
7. Put remaining amount into sealing boot.
8. Align tripod housing with spider, then slide tripod housing over spider and interconnecting shaft.
9. Install inner tripod joint seal boot to interconnecting shaft clamp evenly on sealing boot.
10. Place crimping tool C-4975-A, or equivalent, over bridge of clamp and tighten nut until tool jaws are closed, face to face.
11. **Seal must not be dimpled, stretched or out of shape.** If seal is not shaped correctly, equalize pressure in seal and shape it by hand.
12. Position sealing boot into tripod housing retaining groove.
13. Install seal boot retaining clamp evenly on sealing boot.
14. **Do not puncture or damage sealing boot.**
15. Insert suitable trim stick between tripod joint and sealing boot to vent inner tripod joint. Ensure trim stick is held flat and firmly against tripod housing. If inner tripod joint has Hytrel (hard plastic) sealing boot, ensure trim stick is inserted between soft rubber insert and tripod housing not hard plastic sealing boot and soft rubber insert.
16. Position interconnecting shaft so it is at center of its travel in tripod joint housing.
17. Remove trim stick from between sealing boot and tripod joint housing to equalize air pressure in tripod joint.
18. Position trilobal boot to interface with tripod housing. Boot lobes must be properly aligned with recess's of tripod housing.
19. **On models equipped with crimp type boot clamp,** place crimping tool C-4975-A, or equivalent, over bridge of clamp and tighten nut until tool jaws are closed, face to face.
20. **On models equipped with latching type boot clamp,** proceed as follows:
    a. Place prongs of Snap-On clamp locking tool No. YA3050, or equivalent, in clamp holes.
    b. Squeeze tool together until top band of clamp is latched behind two tabs on lower band.

OUTER

REMOVAL

1. Remove large boot clamp retaining C/V joint sealing boot to C/V joint housing and discard.
2. Remove small clamp that retains outer C/V joint sealing boot to interconnecting shaft and discard.
3. Remove sealing boot from outer C/V joint housing and slide it down interconnecting shaft.
4. Wipe away grease to expose outer C/V joint and interconnecting shaft.
5. Support interconnecting shaft in suitable vise equipped with protective caps on jaws.
6. Sharply hit end of C/V joint housing to dislodge housing from internal circlip on interconnecting shaft using suitable, soft-faced hammer.
7. Slide outer C/V joint off end of interconnecting shaft. Joint may have to be tapped off shaft using suitable, soft-faced hammer.
8. Remove large circlip from interconnecting shaft.
9. Slide sealing boot off interconnecting shaft.

INSTALLATION

1. Slide new sealing boot to interconnecting shaft retaining clamp onto interconnecting shaft.
2. Slide outer C/V joint sealing boot onto interconnecting shaft.
3. Seal boot be positioned on interconnecting shaft so raised bead on inside

FRONT WHEEL DRIVE AXLES

of seal boot is in groove on interconnecting shaft.

4. Align splines on interconnecting shaft with splines on cross of outer C/V joint assembly and start outer C/V joint onto interconnecting shaft.

5. Install outer C/V joint onto interconnecting shaft by using suitable, soft-faced hammer and tapping end of stub axle with nut installed until outer C/V joint is fully seated on interconnecting shaft.

6. Outer C/V joint must be installed on interconnecting shaft until cross of outer C/V joint is seated against circlip on interconnecting shaft.

7. Distribute half of grease provided in seal boot service package into outer C/V joint assembly housing. **Do not use any other type of grease.**

8. Put remaining grease into sealing boot.

9. Install outer C/V joint sealing boot to interconnecting shaft clamp evenly on sealing boot.

10. Place crimping tool C-4975-A, or equivalent, over bridge of clamp and tighten nut until tool jaws are closed, face to face.

11. **Seal must not be dimpled, stretched, or out-of-shape.** If seal is not shaped correctly, equalize pressure in seal and shape it by hand.

12. Position outer C/V joint sealing boot into its retaining groove on outer C/V joint housing.

13. Install sealing boot to outer C/V joint retaining clamp evenly on sealing boot.

14. Clamp sealing boot onto outer C/V joint housing using crimper tool.

15. Place tool over bridge of clamp and tighten nut until jaws are closed completely.

INTERMEDIATE SHAFT
REPLACE

1. Remove lefthand halfshaft as outlined under "Driveshaft, Replace."
2. Remove four intermediate shaft assembly-to-oil pan mounting bolts.
3. Remove intermediate shaft.
4. Reverse procedure to install. **Torque** intermediate shaft-to-oil pan bolts to 18 ft. lbs.

INTERMEDIATE SHAFT SERVICE

The intermediate shaft assembly is serviced only as an assembly.

TIGHTENING SPECIFICATIONS

Year	Component	Torque Ft. Lbs.
AVENGER & SEBRING SEDAN		
2007–08	Caliper Mounting Bolts	125
	Heat Shield Bolts	40③
	Hub Nut	118
	Midshaft To Block Plate Bolts	22
	Strut To Knuckle Bolts	65②
	Wheel Lug Nut	100
CHARGER, MAGNUM & 300		
2005–08	Caliper Adapter To Knuckle	125
	Clevis Bracket To Shock	45
	Hub Nut	157
	Intermediate Shaft-To-Oil Pan	18
	Lower Shock Clevis Bracket	128
	Stabilizer Link Ball Joint	108
	Upper Ball Joint Stud	35①
	Wheel Lug Nut	110

① — Final tighten an additional 90°.
② — Plus an additional ¼ turn.
③ — inch lbs.

DRIVE AXLES

NOTE: On Air Bag Equipped Models, Refer To "Air Bag System Precautions" Located In The Front Of This Manual For System Disarming & Arming Procedures.

NOTE: Refer To "Computer Relearn Procedures" Located In The Front Of This Manual When Battery Power To The Computer Has Been Interrupted.

NOTE: Prior To Performing Any Service Operations Listed In This Section, Consult The "Technical Service Bulletins" Section For Related Information.

INDEX

	Page No.		Page No.		Page No.
Driveshaft, Replace	19-1	Charger, Magnum & 300	19-1	Tightening Specifications	19-2
Avenger & 2007–08 Sebring		Identification	19-1	Troubleshooting	19-1
Sedan	19-1	Subassembly Service	19-1		
Caliber	19-1	CV Boot	19-1		

IDENTIFICATION

The inner joints of both half shaft assemblies are cross-groove joints and are splined to the differential side gears. The outer joints of both assemblies are Rzeppa Joints. The cross-groove joints are true constant velocity (CV) joint assemblies, which allow for the changes in half shaft length through the jounce and rebound travel of the rear suspension.

TROUBLESHOOTING

Refer to **Fig. 1** for halfshaft troubleshooting.

DRIVESHAFT

REPLACE

Caliber

1. Raise and support vehicle.
2. Mark propeller shaft and differential for proper installation.
3. Remove rear propeller shaft to rear axle retaining nuts.
4. Remove center support heat shield mounting bolts, then heat shield.
5. Remove center support mounting bolts.
6. Remove propeller shaft.
7. Reverse procedure to install.

Charger, Magnum & 300

1. With transmission in neutral, raise and support vehicle.
2. Drain rear axle fluid into a suitable container.
3. Remove crossmember.
4. Remove rear exhaust system, then heat shield.
5. Apply alignment index marks to propeller shaft rubber coupler and axle flange.
6. Remove propeller shaft front coupler-to-axle flange bolt.
7. Remove propeller shaft rear coupler-to-flange bolts.
8. Remove center bearing mounting bolts.
9. Remove propeller shaft assembly, **Fig. 2.**
10. Reverse procedure to install.

Avenger & 2007–08 Sebring Sedan

1. Raise and support vehicle.
2. Mark propeller shaft and differential for proper installation.
3. Remove rear propeller shaft to rear axle retaining nuts.
4. Remove center support heat shield mounting bolts, then heat shield.
5. Remove center support mounting bolts.
6. Remove propeller shaft to power transfer unit mounting bolts.
7. Remove propeller shaft.
8. Reverse procedure to install.

SUBASSEMBLY SERVICE

CV Boot

Refer to "Front Drive Axles, Type 3" for CV Boot replacement procedures.

DRIVE AXLES

VEHICLE INSPECTION

1. Check for grease in the vicinity of both the inboard and outboard joints. This is a sign of inner or outer joint seal boot or seal boot clamp damage.

NOISE AND/OR VIBRATION IN TURNS

A clicking noise and/or a vibration in turns could be caused by one of the following conditions:

- Damaged outer CV or inner cross-groove joint seal boot or seal boot clamps. This will result in the loss and/or contamination of the joint grease, resulting in inadequate lubrication of the joint.
- Noise may also be caused by another component of the vehicle coming in contact with the half shafts.

CLUNKING NOISE DURING ACCELERATION

This noise may be a result of one of the following conditions:

- A torn seal boot on the inner or outer joint of the half shaft assembly.
- A loose or missing clamp on the inner or outer joint of the half shaft assembly.
- A damaged or worn half shaft CV joint.
- A worn intermediate shaft bearing (AWD Models).

SHUDDER OR VIBRATION DURING ACCELERATION

This problem could be a result of:

- A worn or damaged half shaft inner cross-groove joint.
- A worn intermediate shaft bearing (AWD Models).
- Improper wheel alignment.

VIBRATION AT HIGHWAY SPEEDS

This problem could be a result of:

- Foreign material (mud, etc.) packed on the backside of the wheel(s).
- Out of balance tires or wheels.
- A worn intermediate shaft bearing (AWD Models).
- Improper tire and/or wheel runout.

ARM0500000001057

Fig. 1   Halfshaft troubleshooting

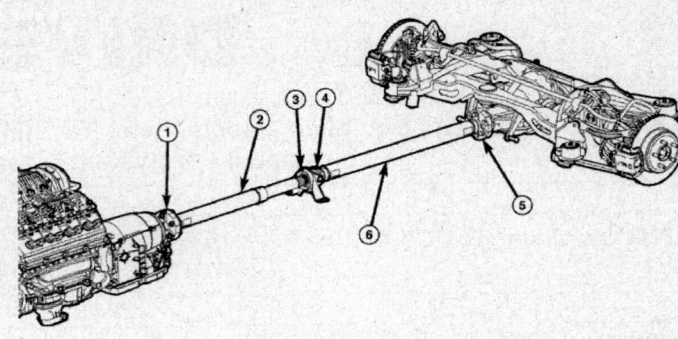

| 1 - FRONT COUPLER |
| 2 - FRONT SEGMENT |
| 3 - BEARING/BRACKET ASSEMBLY |
| 4 - SINGLE-CARDAN U-JOINT |
| 5 - REAR COUPLER |
| 6 - REAR SEGMENT |

ARM0600000001210

Fig. 2   Driveshaft assembly. Charger, Magnum & 300

TIGHTENING SPECIFICATIONS

Year	Component	Torque Ft. Lbs.
AVENGER & 2007–08 SEBRING SEDAN		
2007–08	Center Support Bearing Bolts	30
	Heat Shield Nuts	15
	Propeller Shaft To PTU Bolts	22
	Propeller Shaft To Rear Axle Flange Bolts	43
CALIBER		
2007–08	Center Support Bearing Bolts	30
	Heat Shield Nuts	15
	Propeller Shaft To Rear Axle Nuts	43
CHARGER, MAGNUM & 300		
2005–08	Axle Front Isolator Bolt	48
	Axle Housing To Crossmember Bolts	162
	Center Bearing To Body (Rear)	20
	Differential Drain Plug	37
	Hub Nut	157
	Intermediate Shaft-To-Engine	19
	Shaft Coupler To Rear Axle	43
	Shaft Coupler To Transmission	43

TIRE PRESSURE MONITORING SYSTEM

INDEX

	Page No.		Page No.		Page No.
Component Service	20-19	Installation	20-19	Intermittent & Poor	
Module, Replace	20-19	Removal	20-19	Connections	20-1
Crossfire	20-19	Transponder, Replace	20-19	Intermittents	20-1
Relearning Tire Pressure		**Description**	20-1	Poor Connections	20-1
Monitor System	20-19	**Diagnosis & Testing**	20-1	Wiring Diagrams	20-1
300M	20-19	Accessing Diagnostic Trouble		**Diagnostic Chart Index**	20-8
Charger, Magnum & 300	20-19	Codes	20-1	**Precautions**	20-1
Crossfire	20-19	Clearing Diagnostic Trouble		Air Bag Systems	20-1
Resetting Tire Pressure Monitor		Codes	20-1	Battery Ground Cable	20-1
Lamp	20-19	Crossfire	20-1	**Tightening Specifications**	20-22
TPM Sensor	20-19	Diagnostic Tests	20-1		

PRECAUTIONS

Air Bag Systems

Refer to "Air Bag System Precautions" in the front of this manual for system disarming and arming procedures.

Battery Ground Cable

Prior to service, disconnect battery ground cable and isolate as required.

DESCRIPTION

There are two types of Tire Pressure Monitoring (TPM) available, a base system and a premium system. The Base TPM system consists of tire pressure monitoring sensors attached to each road wheel through the valve stem mounting hole, a central receiver module and an indicator lamp. The Premium TPM system consists of tire pressure monitoring sensors attached to each road wheel through the valve stem mounting hole, a wireless control module (WCM) three wheel sensor transponders located in three of the four wheel wells, an electronic display, and an indicator lamp.

Upon detection of a warning or fault condition, the WCM will send a request to the module that controls the indicator lamp (and the text display if equipped with the Premium system) via the vehicle bus system to illuminate or flash the indicator lamp. Also, upon detection of a warning or fault condition, the electronic display will send a request to sound the "chime." A chime will only be requested once per ignition cycle per warning or fault condition detected.

DIAGNOSIS & TESTING

Accessing Diagnostic Trouble Codes

Connect a suitably programmed scan tool to Data Link Connector (DLC) and follow manufacturer's instructions.

Wiring Diagrams

Refer to **Figs. 1 through 21** for wiring diagrams.

Diagnostic Tests

Refer to **Figs. 22 through 29** for diagnostic tests.

Crossfire

Refer to **Figs. 30 through 40** for diagnostic tests.

Clearing Diagnostic Trouble Codes

Connect a suitably programmed scan tool to Data Link Connector (DLC), and follow manufacturer's instructions.

Intermittent & Poor Connections

INTERMITTENTS

Most intermittents are caused by faulty electrical connections or wiring. Inspect for the following:

1. Wiring broken inside insulation.
2. Poor connection between male and female terminal at connector.
3. Poor terminal to wire connection. Some conditions which fall under this are:
   a. Poor crimps.
   b. Poor solder joints.
   c. Crimping over wire insulation rather than wire.
   d. Corrosion in wire to terminal contact.
4. Wire insulation which is rubbed through. This causes an intermittent short as bare area touches other wiring or components.

POOR CONNECTIONS

1. It is important to test terminal contact at component and connectors before replacing suspect component.
2. Mating terminals must be inspected to ensure good terminal contact.
3. Poor connection between male and female terminal at a connector may be result of contamination or deformation.
4. Contamination may be caused by:
   a. Connector halves being improperly connected.
   b. Missing or damaged seal.
   c. Damaged connector.
   d. Exposing terminals to moisture and dirt.
5. Deformation is caused by:
   a. Probing connector terminal mating side without proper adapter.
   b. Improperly joining connector halves.
   c. Repeatedly separating and joining connector halves.

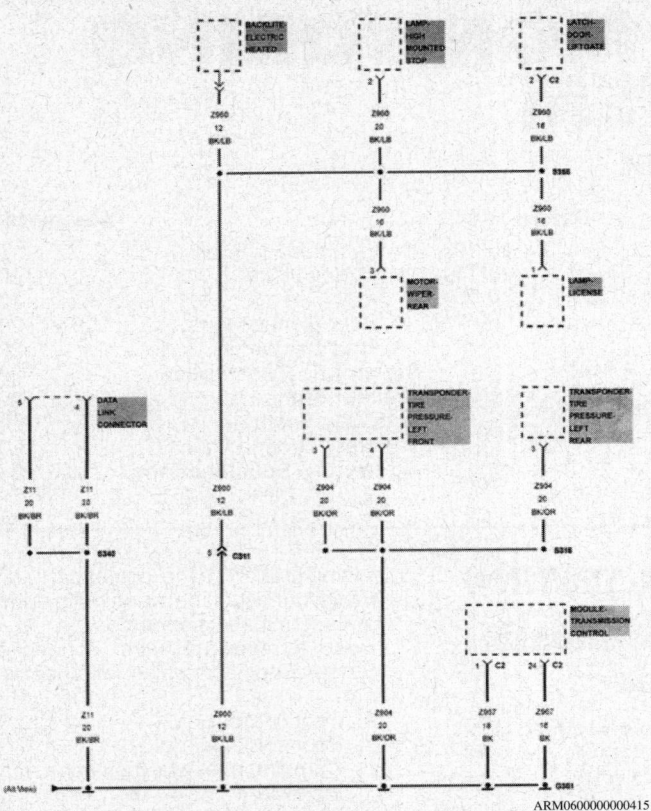

Fig. 1   TPM system (left front & left rear ground distribution). Caliber

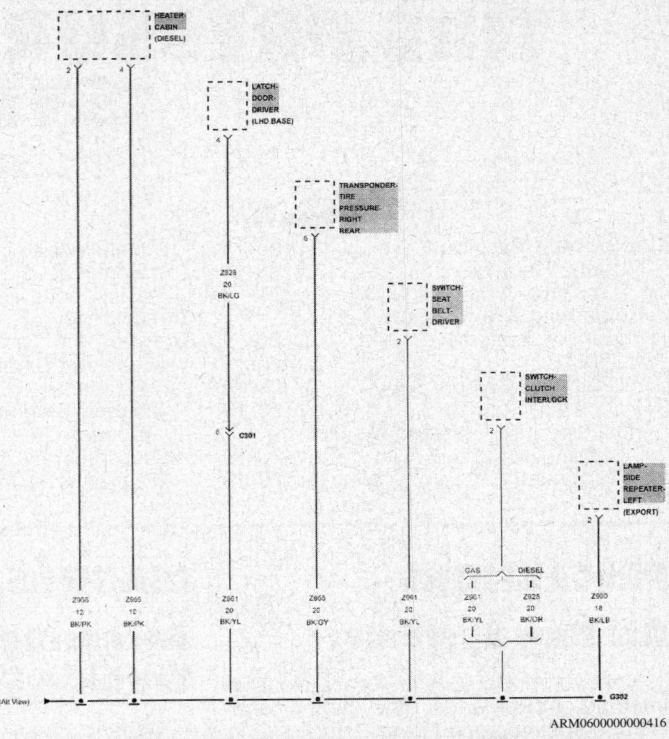

Fig. 2   TPM system (right rear ground distribution, Part 1 of 2). Caliber

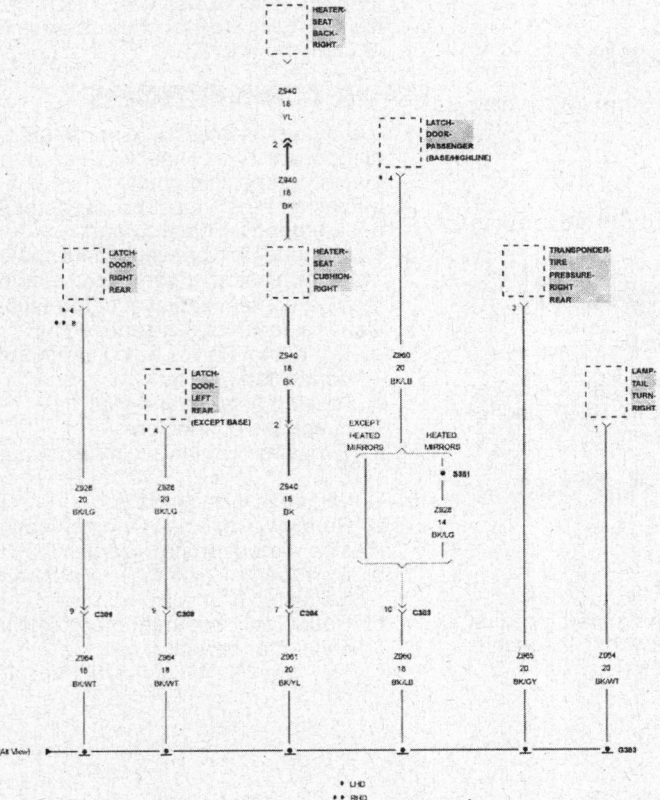

Fig. 2   TPM system (right rear ground distribution, Part 2 of 2). Caliber

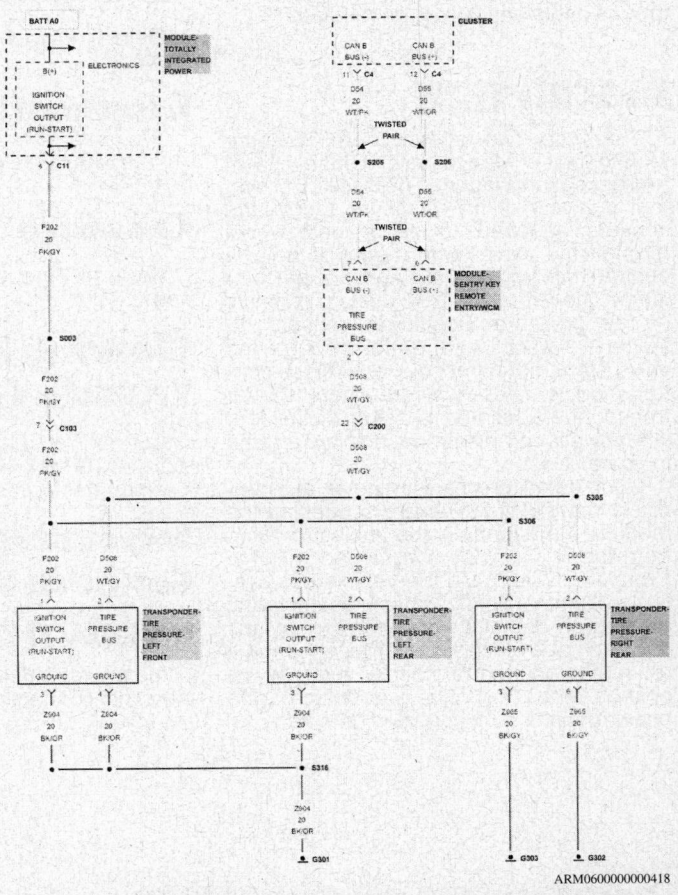

Fig. 3   TPM system (instrument cluster). Caliber

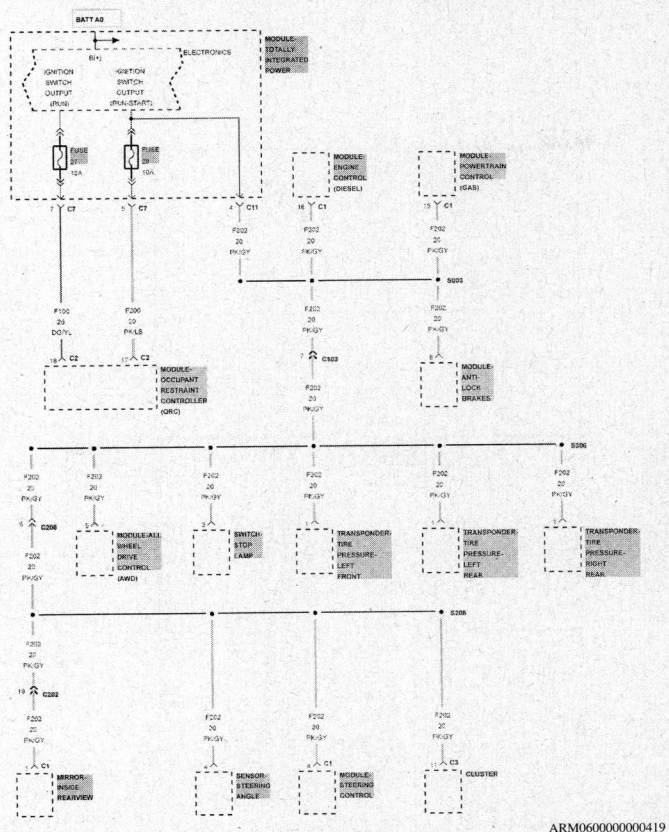

Fig. 4 TPM system (TIP module). Caliber

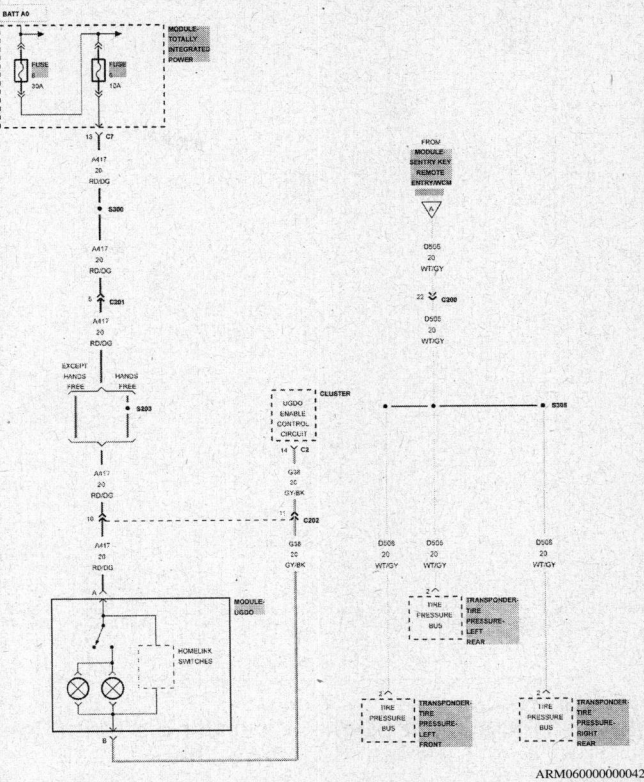

Fig. 5 TPM system (vehicle theft security). Caliber

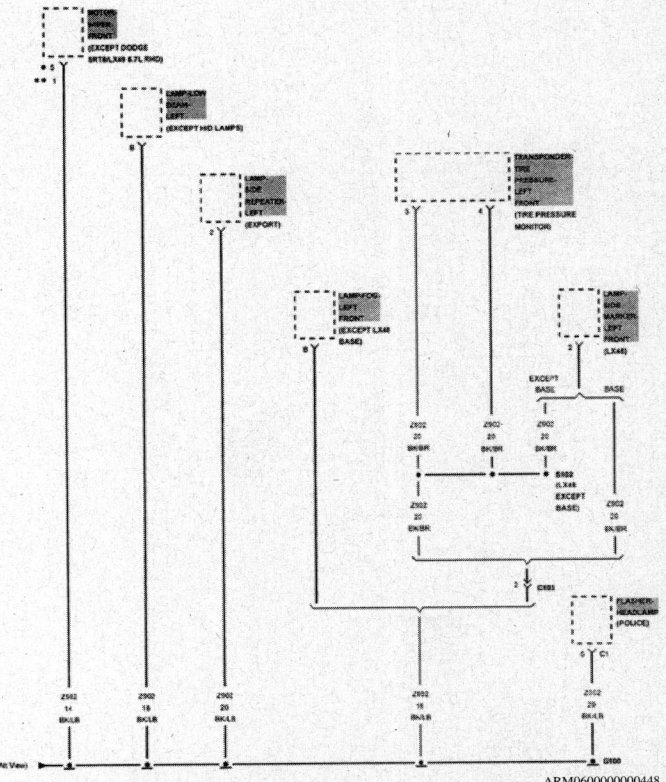

Fig. 6 TPM system (left front ground distribution). Charger, Magnum & 300

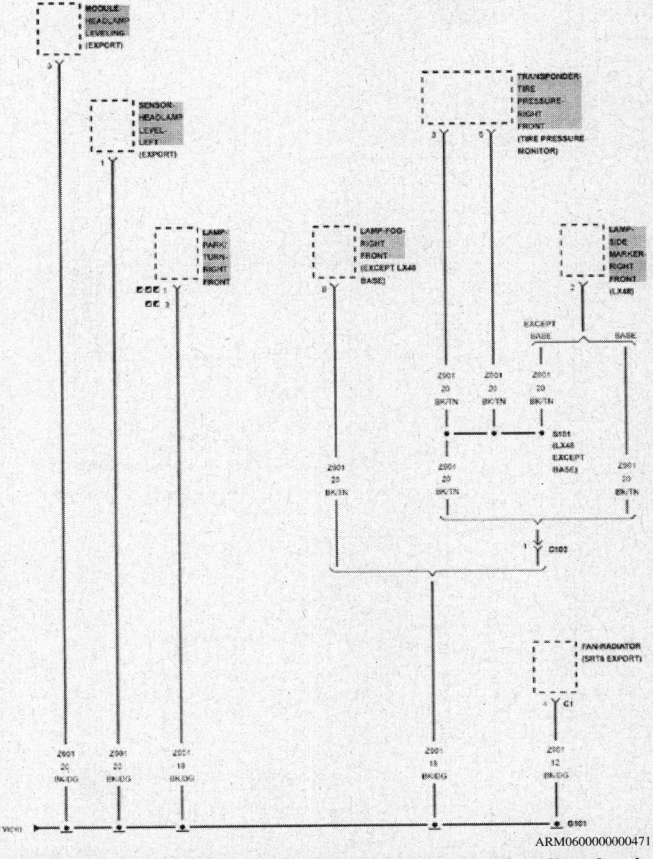

Fig. 7 TPM system (right front ground distribution). Charger, Magnum & 300

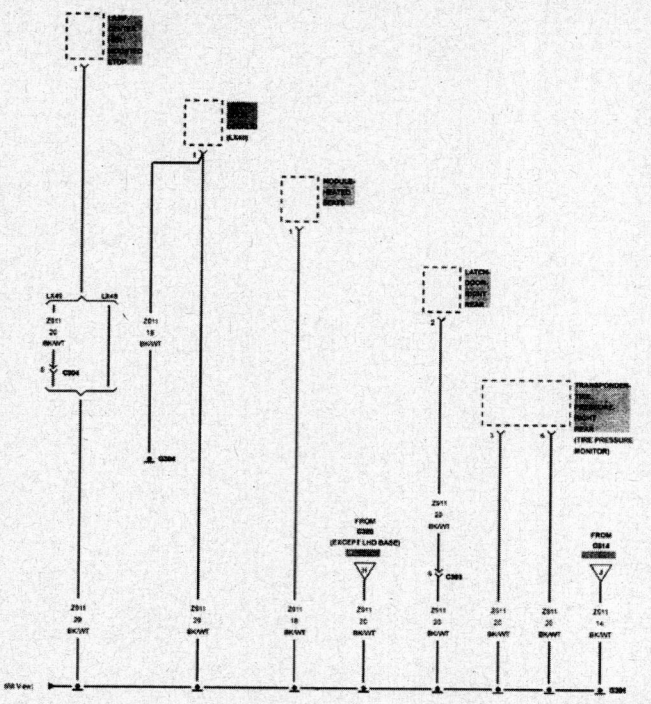

Fig. 8 TPM system (Right rear ground distribution). Charger, Magnum & 300

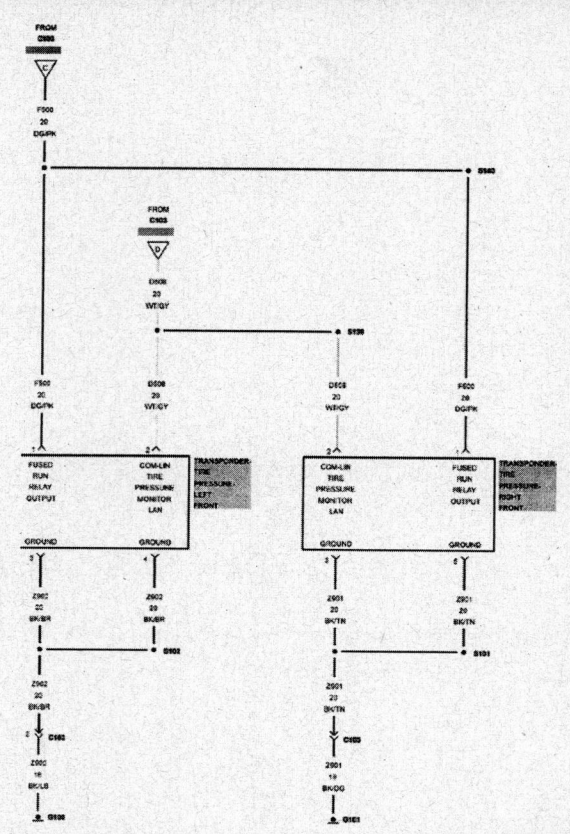

Fig. 9 TPM system (instrument cluster, left front & right front). Charger, Magnum & 300

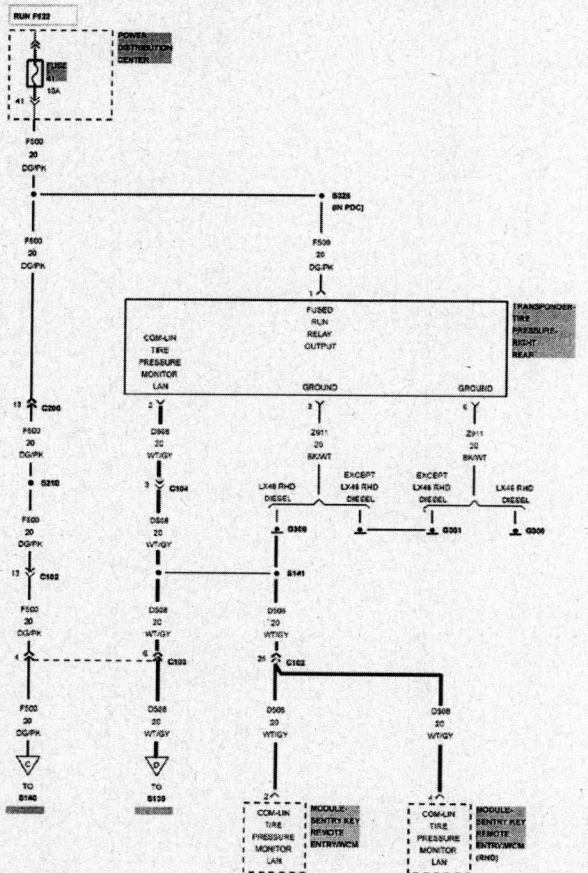

Fig. 10 TPM system (instrument cluster, right rear). Charger, Magnum & 300

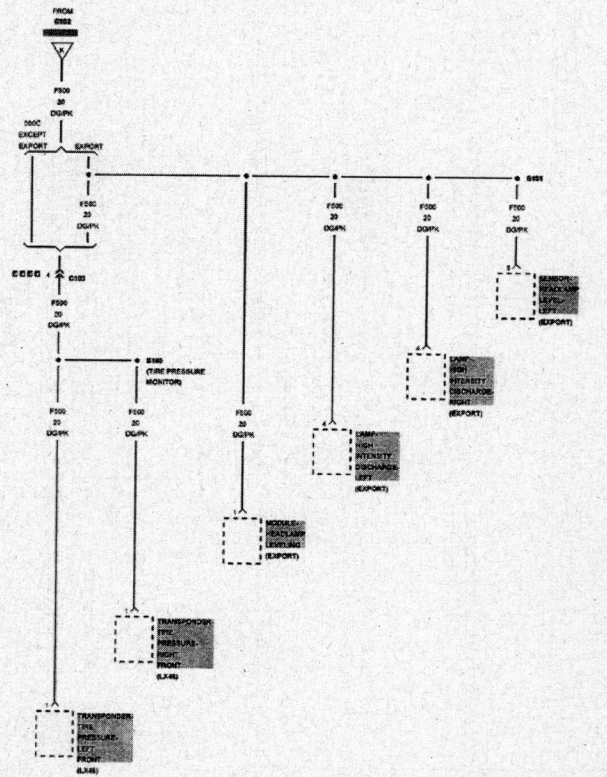

Fig. 11 TPM system (left front & right front power distribution). Charger, Magnum & 300

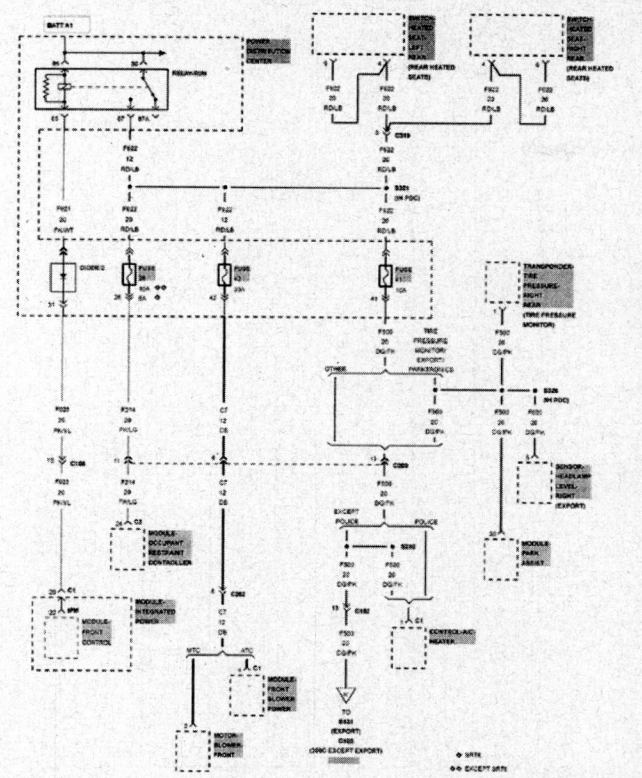

**Fig. 12   TPM system (right rear power distribution).
Charger, Magnum & 300**

ARM0600000000450

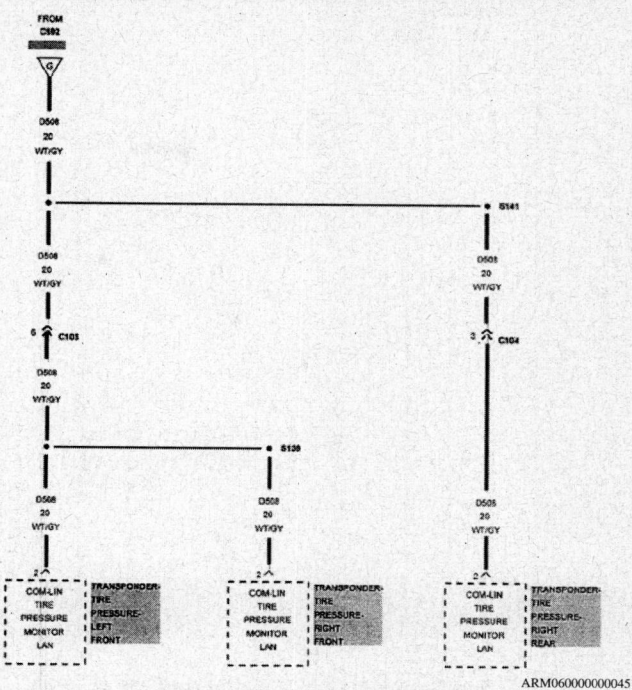

**Fig. 13   TPM system (vehicle theft security).
Charger, Magnum & 300**

ARM0600000000451

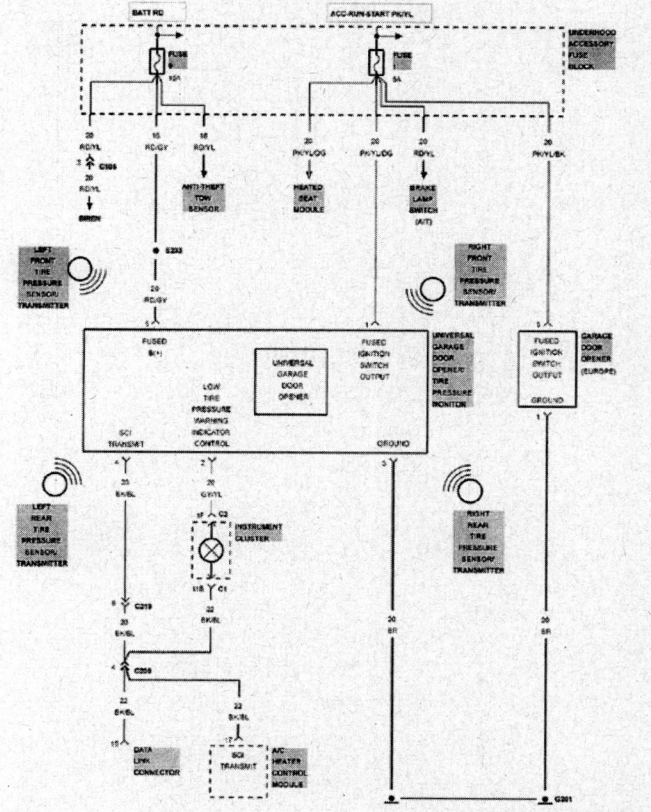

**Fig. 14   TPM system (TPM sensor/transmitter).
Crossfire**

ARM0600000001203

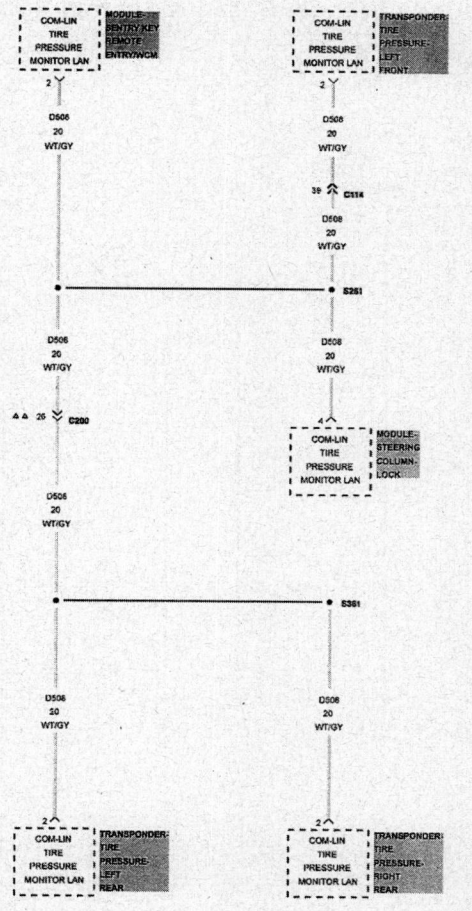

**Fig. 15   TPM system (Bus communication). 2007–08
Avenger Sedan & Sebring Sedan**

ARM0600000000475

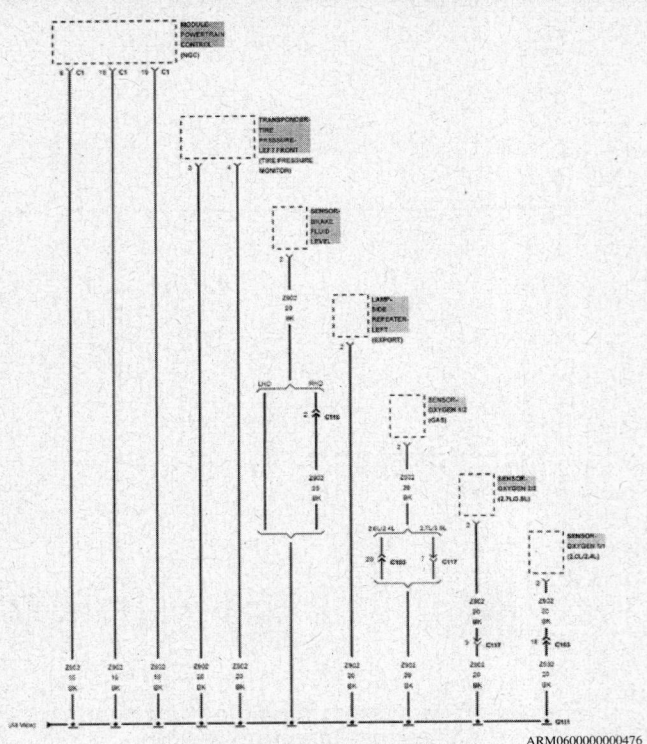

Fig. 16 TPM system (left front ground distribution). 2007–08 Avenger Sedan & Sebring Sedan

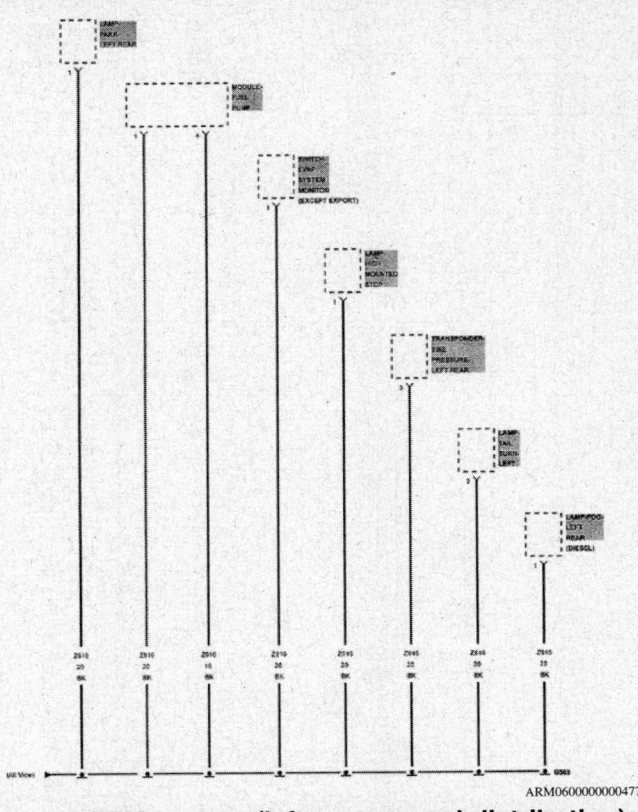

Fig. 17 TPM system (left rear ground distribution). 2007–08 Avenger Sedan & Sebring Sedan

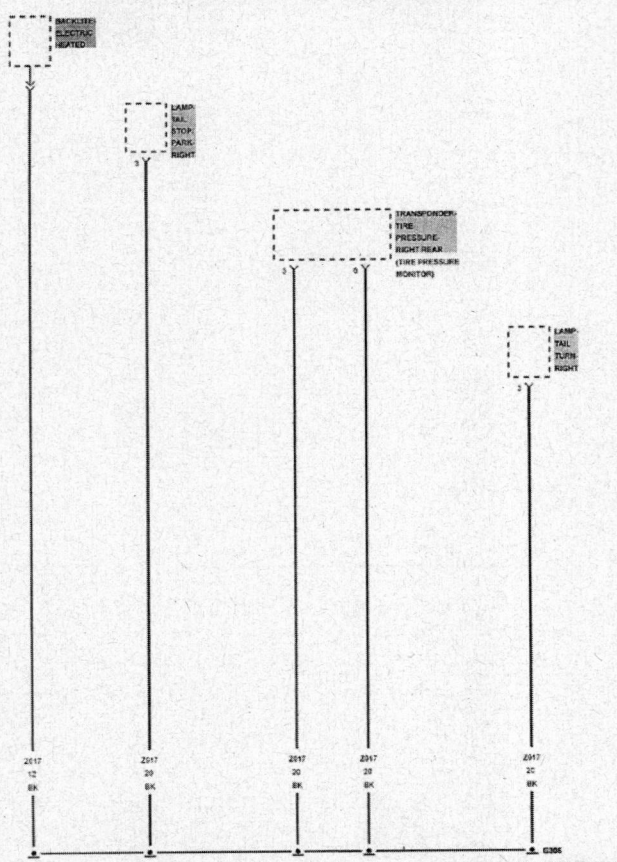

Fig. 18 TPM system (right rear ground distribution). 2007–08 Avenger Sedan & Sebring Sedan

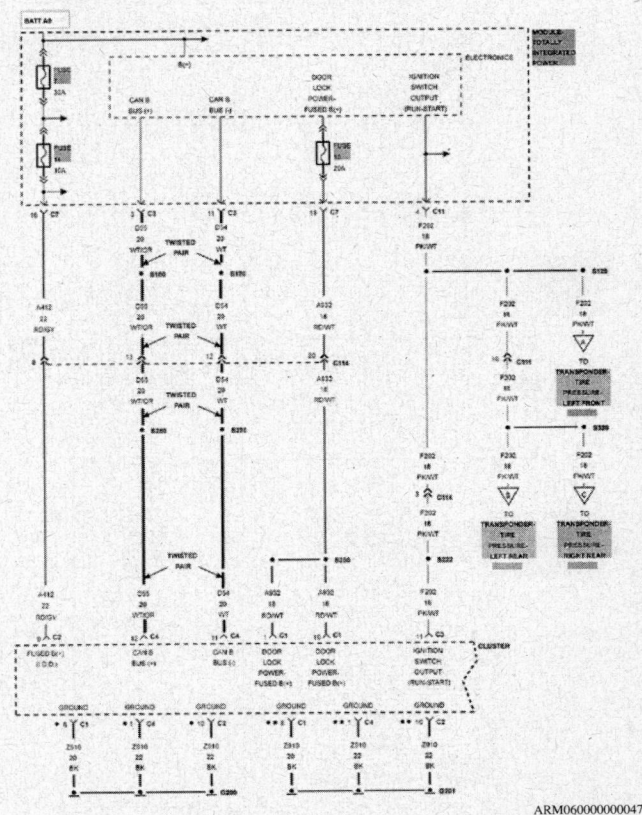

Fig. 19 TPM system (instrument cluster, Part 1 of 2). 2007–08 Avenger Sedan & Sebring Sedan

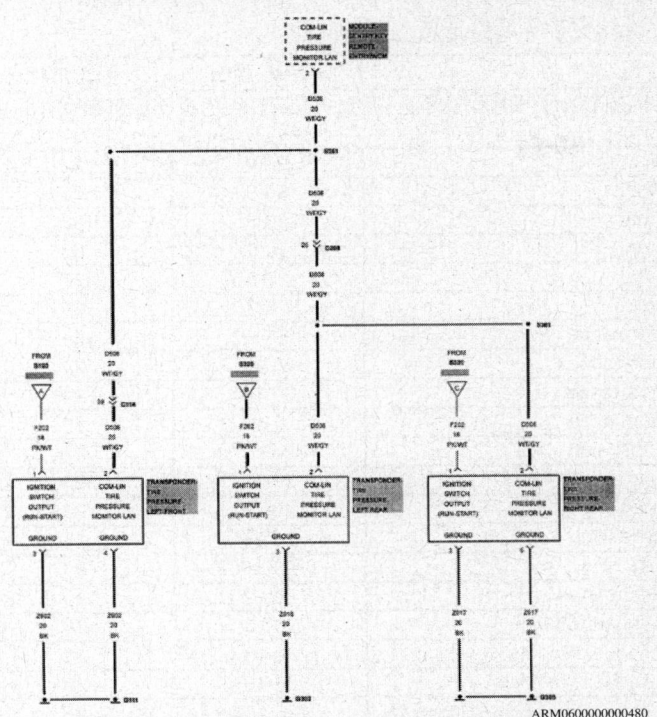

Fig. 19   TPM system (instrument cluster, Part 2 of 2). 2007–08 Avenger Sedan & Sebring Sedan

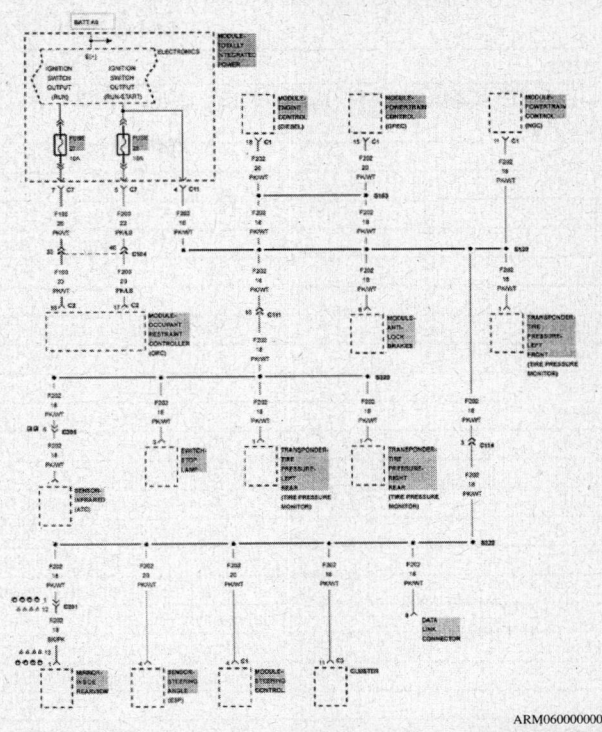

Fig. 20   TIPM system. 2007–08 Avenger Sedan & Sebring Sedan

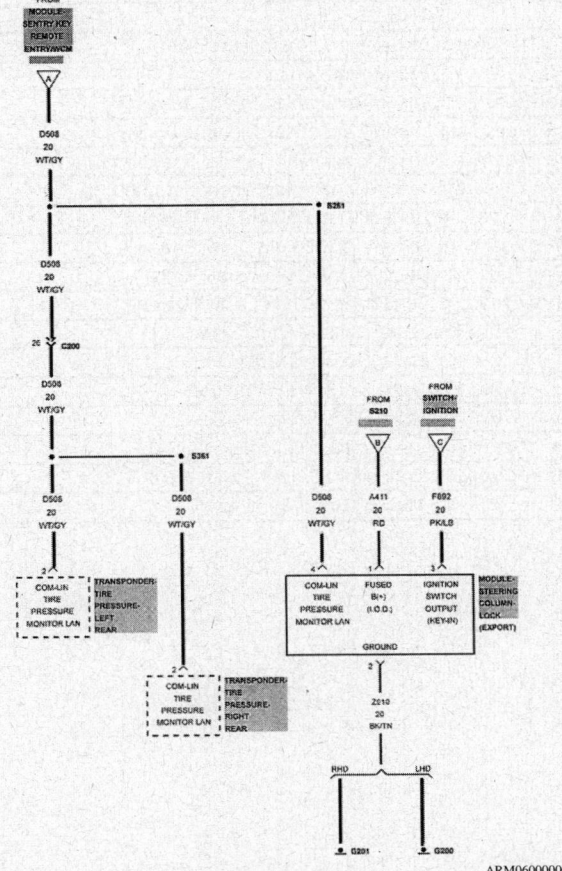

Fig. 21   TPM system (vehicle theft security). 2007–08 Avenger Sedan & Sebring Sedan

DIAGNOSTIC CHART INDEX

Code	Description	Page No.	Fig. No.
CALIBER, CHARGER, MAGNUM, 300, 2007–08 AVENGER SEDAN, SEBRING CONVERTIBLE & SEBRING SEDAN			
C0077	Low Tire Pressure	20-9	22
C1501	Tire Pressure Sensor 1 Internal	20-9	23
C1502	Tire Pressure Sensor 2 Internal	20-9	23
C1503	Tire Pressure Sensor 3 Internal	20-9	23
C1504	Tire Pressure Sensor 4 Internal	20-9	23
C1505	Tire Pressure Sensor 5 Internal	20-9	23
C1506	Tire Pressure Trigger Module Performance	20-10	24
C1507	Tire Pressure Trigger Module Performance	20-10	24
C1508	Tire Pressure Trigger Module Performance	20-10	24
C1509	Tire Pressure Trigger Module Performance	20-10	24
C150A	Tire Pressure Trigger Module Voltage High	20-11	25
C150B	Tire Pressure Trigger Module Voltage High	20-11	25
C150C	Tire Pressure Trigger Module Voltage High	20-11	25
C150D	Tire Pressure Trigger Module Voltage High	20-11	25
C151C	Tire Pressure Sensor Missing	20-11	26
C151D	Tire Pressure Sensor Location Undetermined	20-12	27
U1114	Lost Communication With Tire Pressure Trigger Module	20-13	28
U1116	Lost Communication With Tire Pressure Trigger Module	20-13	28
U1117	Lost Communication With Tire Pressure Trigger Module	20-13	28
—	TPM Verification	20-15	29
CROSSFIRE			
8001	Training Failed	20-15	30
8002	Tire Pressure Sensor/Transmitter Signal Jammed	20-16	31
8003	Battery Low	20-17	32
8004	Tire Pressure Sensor/Transmitter Failure	20-17	33
8005	TPM Module Failure	20-17	34
8009	Tire Pressure Sensor/Transmitter Signal Jammed	20-17	35
8010	Tire Pressure Sensor/Transmitter Signal Jammed	20-17	35
8011	Tire Pressure Sensor/Transmitter Signal Jammed	20-17	35
8012	Tire Pressure Sensor/Transmitter Signal Jammed	20-17	35
8013	Tire Pressure Sensor/Transmitter Low Battery	20-18	36
8014	Tire Pressure Sensor/Transmitter Low Battery	20-18	36
8015	Tire Pressure Sensor/Transmitter Low Battery	20-18	36
8016	Tire Pressure Sensor/Transmitter Low Battery	20-18	36
8017	Tire Pressure Sensor/Transmitter	20-18	37
8018	Tire Pressure Sensor/Transmitter	20-18	37
8019	Tire Pressure Sensor/Transmitter	20-18	37
8020	Tire Pressure Sensor/Transmitter	20-18	37
—	Tire Pressure Monitor Verification Test	20-18	38
—	Low Tire Pressure Indicator Light On With No DTC's	20-18	39
—	TPM Module Programming	20-19	40

Diagnostic Test

1. DTC STATUS IS ACTIVE

NOTE: If the incorrect Placard Values were programmed into the WCM/SKREEM, a DTC could be set. Before continuing with any TPM diagnostic test, using the scan tool, check that the correct Placard Values have been programmed in to the module.

NOTE:

If the following conditions are present:

- Low Tire Pressure DTC (C0077) (Active)

- Spare Tire is not equipped with a Tire Pressure Sensor

- Spare Tire is currently on the vehicle

Repair the tire and place it back on the vehicle.

Test drive the vehicle.

If the DTC(s) reset continue with the diagnostic procedure.

Turn the ignition on.
With the scan tool, select View DTCs in the Wireless Control Module (SKREEM).

Is the DTC status Active at this time?

Yes

- Go to 2

No

- Go to 4

ARM0600000000421

Fig. 22 Code C0077: Low Tire Pressure (Part 1 of 3). Except Crossfire

4. INTERMITTENT TIRE PRESSURE SENSOR DTC

The conditions necessary to set this DTC are not present at this time.
Refer to any Technical Service Bulletins that may apply to this condition.
With the scan tool, clear DTCs in the Wireless Control Module (SKREEM).
Test Drive the vehicle for a minimum of 10 minutes with vehicle speed greater than 15 MPH (24 km/h).
With the scan tool, select View DTCs in the Wireless Control Module (SKREEM).

Does the DTC reset or is the status Active for this DTC?

Yes

- Repair as necessary.
- Perform TPM VERIFICATION TEST.

No

- Test complete.
- Perform TPM VERIFICATION TEST.

ARM0600000000423

Fig. 22 Code C0077: Low Tire Pressure (Part 3 of 3). Except Crossfire

2. LOW TIRE PRESSURE

Correct all tire pressure to the recommended specifications and wait 2 minutes.
With the scan tool, clear DTCs in the Wireless Control Module (SKREEM).
Test Drive the vehicle for a minimum of 10 minutes with vehicle speed greater than 15 MPH (24 km/h).
With the scan tool, select View DTCs in the Wireless Control Module (SKREEM).

Does the DTC reset or is the status Active for this DTC?
Yes

- Go to 3

No

- Test Complete.
- Perform TPM VERIFICATION TEST.

3. TIRE PRESSURE SENSOR

NOTE: Before continuing, ensure the tire is free from any leaks or damage that would cause a low tire pressure condition. If a problem is found, repair as necessary and retest.

Turn the ignition off.
Replace the Tire Pressure Sensor in accordance with the Service Information.
With the scan tool, clear DTCs in the Wireless Control Module (SKREEM).
Test Drive the vehicle for a minimum of 10 minutes with vehicle speed greater than 15 MPH (24 km/h).
With the scan tool, select View DTCs in the Wireless Control Module (SKREEM).

Does the DTC reset or is the status Active for this DTC?

Yes

- Replace the Wireless Control Module (SKREEM)

- Perform TPM VERIFICATION TEST.

No

- Test Complete.
- Perform TPM VERIFICATION TEST.

ARM0600000000422

Fig. 22 Code C0077: Low Tire Pressure (Part 2 of 3). Except Crossfire

Diagnostic Test

1. DTC STATUS IS ACTIVE

NOTE:

If the following conditions are present:

- Tire Pressure Sensor Internal DTC (Active)

- Spare Tire is not equipped with a Tire Pressure Sensor

- Spare Tire is currently on the vehicle

Repair the tire and place it back on the vehicle .

Test drive the vehicle.

If the DTC(s) reset continue with the diagnostic procedure.

Turn the ignition on.
With the scan tool, select View DTCs in the Wireless Control Module (SKREEM).

Is the DTC status Active at this time?

Yes

- Go to 2

No

- Go to 4

ARM0600000000424

Fig. 23 Codes C1501–C1505: Tire Pressure Sensor Internal (Part 1 of 3). Except Crossfire

2. TIRE PRESSURE SENSOR

NOTE:

When working with vehicles equipped with the base tire pressure monitoring system the correct tire that set the fault must be identified. Following the below procedure will help in identifying the correct tire.

1. Set all tire pressures to the recommended specifications and recheck for fault/alert.

2. Turn the ignition on.

3. Starting with the left front wheel, deflate the tire to 20 PSI and wait 2 minutes. The fault will set once the pressure has reached 20 PSI within the 2 minute time frame.

4. If the TPM fault was detected and not associated to this Sensor/Transmitter, repeat the process until the faulty Sensor/Transmitter has been identified.

Once a fault/alert has set, it will establish the location of the tire pressure sensor/transmitter. Repeat steps until the applicable Tire Pressure Sensor/Transmitter has been located.

Turn the ignition off.
Replace the Tire Pressure Sensor in accordance with the Service Information.
With the scan tool, clear DTCs in the Wireless Control Module (SKREEM).
Test Drive the vehicle for a minimum of 10 minutes with vehicle speed greater than 15 MPH (24 km/h).
With the scan tool, select View DTCs in the Wireless Control Module (SKREEM).

Does the DTC reset or is the status Active for this DTC?

Yes

- Go to 3

No

- Test Complete.
- Perform TPM VERIFICATION TEST.

ARM0600000000425

Fig. 23   Codes C1501–C1505: Tire Pressure Sensor Internal (Part 2 of 3). Except Crossfire

Diagnostic Test

1. DTC STATUS IS ACTIVE

NOTE: If the incorrect Placard Values were programmed into the WCM/TPM, a DTC could be set. Before continuing with any TPM diagnostic test, using the scan tool, check that the correct Placard Values have been programmed in to the module.

Turn the ignition on.
With the scan tool, select View DTCs in the Wireless Control Module (TPM).

Is the DTC status Active at this time?
Yes

- Go to 2

No

- Go to 4

2. TIRE PRESSURE TRIGGER MODULE

Turn the ignition off.
Replace the appropriate Tire Pressure Trigger Module

With the scan tool, clear DTCs in the Wireless Control Module (TPM).
Test Drive the vehicle for a minimum of 10 minutes with vehicle speed greater than 15 MPH (24 km/h).
With the scan tool, select View DTCs in the Wireless Control Module (TPM).

Does the DTC reset or is the status Active for this DTC?

Yes

- Go to 3

No

- Test Complete.
- Perform TPM VERIFICATION TEST.

ARM0600000000427

Fig. 24   Codes C1506–C1509: Tire Pressure Trigger Module Performance (Part 1 of 2). Except Crossfire

3. WIRELESS CONTROL MODULE (SKREEM)

View repair.

Repair

- Replace the Wireless Control Module (SKREEM)

- Perform TPM VERIFICATION TEST.

4. INTERMITTENT TIRE PRESSURE SENSOR DTC

The conditions necessary to set this DTC are not present at this time.
Refer to any Technical Service Bulletins that may apply to this condition.
With the scan tool, clear DTCs in the Wireless Control Module (SKREEM).
Test Drive the vehicle for a minimum of 10 minutes with vehicle speed greater than 15 MPH (24 km/h).
With the scan tool, select View DTCs in the Wireless Control Module (SKREEM).

Does the DTC reset or is the status Active for this DTC?

Yes

- Return to the beginning of this test and perform the diagnostic procedure as necessary.

No

- Test complete.
- Perform TPM VERIFICATION TEST.

ARM0600000000426

Fig. 23   Codes C1501–C1505: Tire Pressure Sensor Internal (Part 3 of 3). Except Crossfire

3. WIRELESS CONTROL MODULE (TPM)

View repair.

Repair

- Replace the Wireless Control Module (TPM)

- Perform TPM VERIFICATION TEST.

4. INTERMITTENT TIRE PRESSURE TRIGGER MODULE DTC

The conditions necessary to set this DTC are not present at this time.
Using the wiring schematic as a guide, inspect the wiring and connectors relative to this circuit.
Refer to any Technical Service Bulletins that may apply to this condition.
With the scan tool, clear DTCs in the Wireless Control Module (TPM).
Test Drive the vehicle for a minimum of 10 minutes with vehicle speed greater than 15 MPH (24 km/h).
With the scan tool, select View DTCs in the Wireless Control Module (TPM).

Does the DTC reset or is the status Active for this DTC?

Yes

- Return to the first step of this test and perform the diagnostic procedure.

No

- Test complete.
- Perform TPM VERIFICATION TEST.

ARM0600000000428

Fig. 24   Codes C1506–C1509: Tire Pressure Trigger Module Performance (Part 2 of 2). Except Crossfire

Diagnostic Test

1. DTC STATUS IS ACTIVE

NOTE: If the incorrect Placard Values were programmed into the WCM/SKREEM, a DTC could be set. Before continuing with any TPM diagnostic test, using the scan tool, check that the correct Placard Values have been programmed in to the module.
Turn the ignition on.

NOTE: If a system or battery voltage high DTC is set in the Wireless Control Module (SKREEM) or in the PCM, repair the voltage DTC before continuing with this test.
With the scan tool, select View DTCs in the Wireless Control Module (SKREEM).

Is the DTC status Active at this time?

Yes

- Go to 2

No

- Go to 6

2. (F202) FUSED IGNITION SWITCH OUTPUT (RUN) CIRCUIT OPEN OR HIGH RESISTANCE

Turn the ignition on.
Using a 12-volt test light connect to ground, check the (F202) Fused Ignition Switch Output (Run) circuit.
NOTE: The test light should be illuminated and bright. Compare the brightness to that of a direct connection to the battery.

Is the test light illuminated and bright?

Yes

- Go to 3

No

- Repair the (F202) Fused Ignition Switch Output (Run) circuit for an open circuit or high resistance.
- Perform TPM VERIFICATION TEST.

ARM0600000000429

Fig. 25   Codes C150A, B, C & D: Tire Pressure Trigger Module Voltage High (Part 1 of 3). Except Crossfire

5. WIRELESS CONTROL MODULE (SKREEM)

View repair.

Repair

- Replace the Wireless Control Module (SKREEM)
- Perform TPM VERIFICATION TEST.

6. INTERMITTENT TIRE PRESSURE TRIGGER MODULE DTC

The conditions necessary to set this DTC are not present at this time.
Refer to any Technical Service Bulletins that may apply to this condition.
With the scan tool, clear DTCs in the Wireless Control Module (SKREEM).
Test Drive the vehicle for a minimum of 10 minutes with vehicle speed greater than 15 MPH (24 km/h).
With the scan tool, select View DTCs in the Wireless Control Module (SKREEM).

Does the DTC reset or is the status Active for this DTC?

Yes

- Return to the first step of this test and perform the diagnostic procedure.

No

- Test complete.
- Perform TPM VERIFICATION TEST.

ARM0600000000431

Fig. 25   Codes C150A, B, C & D: Tire Pressure Trigger Module Voltage High (Part 3 of 3). Except Crossfire

3. (Z904) GROUND CIRCUIT(S) OPEN OR HIGH RESISTANCE

Using a 12-volt test light connect to 12 volts, check each of the (Z904) Ground circuit(s).

NOTE: The test light should be illuminated and bright. Compare the brightness to that of a direct connection to the battery.

Is the test light illuminated and bright?

Yes

- Go to 4

No

- Repair the (Z904) Ground circuit(s) for an open circuit or high resistance.
- Perform TPM VERIFICATION TEST.

4. TIRE PRESSURE TRIGGER MODULE

Turn the ignition off.
Replace the appropriate Tire Pressure Trigger Module

With the scan tool, clear DTCs in the Wireless Control Module (SKREEM).
Test Drive the vehicle for a minimum of 10 minutes with vehicle speed greater than 15 MPH (24 km/h).
With the scan tool, select View DTCs in the Wireless Control Module (SKREEM).

Does the DTC reset or is the status Active for this DTC?

Yes

- Go to 5

No

- Test Complete.
- Perform TPM VERIFICATION TEST.

ARM0600000000430

Fig. 25   Codes C150A, B, C & D: Tire Pressure Trigger Module Voltage High (Part 2 of 3). Except Crossfire

Diagnostic Test

1. DTC STATUS

NOTE: This fault can be set if the wrong TPM sensor was installed on the vehicle, or that the wheel has a rubber valve stem. Check to make sure the vehicle is equipped with the correct sensors.

NOTE: If the vehicle is equipped with the remote start feature, check to make sure the antenna connector is properly connected to the WCM.

NOTE:

If the following conditions are present:

- Low Tire Pressure DTC

- Tire Pressure Sensor Internal DTC

- Spare Tire is not equipped with a Tire Pressure Sensor

- Spare Tire is currently on the vehicle

Repair the tire and place it back on the vehicle.

Test drive the vehicle.

If the DTC(s) reset continue with the diagnostic procedure.

Turn the ignition on.
With the scan tool, select View DTC's in the Wireless Control Module (SKREEM).

Is the DTC status Active at this time?

Yes

- Go to 2

No

- Go to 4

ARM0600000000452

Fig. 26   Code C151C: Tire Pressure Sensor Missing (Part 1 of 3). Except Crossfire

2. TIRE PRESSURE SENSOR

NOTE:

The following tests are used to locate the Tire Pressure Sensor/Transmitter that is setting the sensor internal fault. If the tires have been rotated, the Tire Pressure Sensor/Transmitter are no longer in sequence from the factory. Faults are linked to the sensor/transmitter IDs. You MUST locate the correct Tire Pressure Sensor/Transmitter that set the fault before continuing. Use one or more of the following methods below.

METHOD 1: Use a TPM-RKE Analyzer tool to scan each tire pressure sensor. If a suspected sensor has been located, lower the tire pressure to 20 PSI, wait for 2 minutes, and check the scan tool for changes to any compensated tire pressure values. If there was a pressure change to any compensated tire pressure values, check to make sure that the TPM-RKE Analyzer is set correctly, and repeat the process on each wheel on the vehicle until the faulty Sensor/Transmitter has been identified. On base systems starting with the left front wheel, deflate the tire to 20 PSI, wait 2 minutes, and check the scan tool for changes to any compensated tire pressure values or TPM lamp turning on. Look for NO pressure change to any compensated tire pressure value, or a pressure change corresponding to "Sensor 1 Identification".

NOTE: Compensated tire pressure values are only available on the premium TPM system. For a base TPM system lowering the tire pressure to 20 PSI will set DTC C0077 and turn on the TPM lamp.

NOTE: When scanning a sensor with a TPM-RKE Analyzer, replace the TPM sensor if the results show a "Damaged Accel", "Damaged Temp", or "Damaged Press".

Has the malfunctioning/faulty TPM sensor been located?

Yes

- Replace the Tire Pressure Sensor
- Perform TPM VERIFICATION TEST.

No

- Go to 3

ARM0600000000453

Fig. 26   Code C151C: Tire Pressure Sensor Missing (Part 2 of 3). Except Crossfire

Diagnostic Test

1. OTHER DTC'S SET

Repair all other DTC's first.

Is this DTC still active after all other DTC's repaired?

Yes

- Go To 2

No

- Test Complete.
- Perform TPM VERIFICATION TEST.

2. VERIFY DTC IS ACTIVE

NOTE: Ensure the IOD fuse is installed and battery voltage is between 10 and 16 volts before proceeding.

Turn the ignition on.
With the scan tool, read and record WCM DTCs.
With the scan tool, erase WCM DTCs.
Cycle the ignition switch.
With the scan tool, read WCM DTCs.

Does this DTC reset?

Yes

- Go To 3

No

- Perform the Stored Lost Communication test procedure.
- Perform BODY VERIFICATION TEST.

ARM0600000000432

Fig. 27   Code C151D: Tire Pressure Sensor Location Undetermined (Part 1 of 5). Except Crossfire

3. WIRELESS CONTROL MODULE (SKREEM)

Replace the Wireless Control Module (SKREEM).
Drive the vehicle for a minimum of 10 minutes while maintaining a continuous speed above 15 mph (24 km/h). During this time the system will learn the sensor IDs.
With the scan tool, read WCM/SKREEM DTC(s).

Are there any DTC(s) present?

Yes

- Repair the DTC.

No

- Repair complete.

4. INTERMITTENT TIRE PRESSURE SENSOR DTC

NOTE: The DTC can be caused by many different factors and might not be a sensor/transmitter or a WCM (SKREEM) fault. Interference from other elements will over power the sensor/transmitter RF frequency making erratic operation to the TPM system. Check the vehicle for aftermarket accessories that could compromise the RF frequency signal before diagnosing the TPM system.

The conditions necessary to set this DTC are not present at this time.
Refer to any Technical Service Bulletins that may apply to this condition.
With the scan tool, clear DTCs in the Wireless Control Module (SKREEM).
Test Drive the vehicle for a minimum of 10 minutes with vehicle speed greater than 15 m.p.h.
With the scan tool, select View DTCs in the Wireless Control Module (SKREEM).

Does the DTC reset or is the status Active for this DTC?

Yes

- Return to the beginning of this test and perform the diagnostic procedure as necessary.

No

- Test complete.

ARM0600000000454

Fig. 26   Code C151C: Tire Pressure Sensor Missing (Part 3 of 3). Except Crossfire

3. (D508) COM-LIN TIRE PRESSURE MONITOR LAN CIRCUIT OPEN

Turn the ignition off.
Disconnect the Tire Pressure Trigger Module.
Disconnect the WCM.
With an ohmmeter measure the resistance of the (D508) COM-LIN TIRE PRESSURE MONITOR LAN CIRCUIT.

Is the resistance below 5 Ohms?

Yes

- Go To 4

No

- Repair or replace the open circuit.
- Perform TPM VERIFICATION TEST.

4. FUSED IGNITION SWITCH OUTPUT (RUN) CIRCUIT OPEN OR HIGH RESISTANCE

Turn the ignition off.
Disconnect the Tire Pressure Transponder harness connector.
Disconnect the Sentry Key Remote Entry Module harness connector.
Turn the ignition on.
Using a 12-volt test light connect to ground, check the Fused Ignition Switch Output (Run) circuit.

NOTE: The test light should be illuminated and bright. Compare the brightness to that of a direct connection to the battery.

Is the test light illuminated and bright?

Yes

- Go to 5

No

- Repair the Fused Ignition Switch Output (Run) circuit for an open circuit or high resistance.
- Perform TPM VERIFICATION TEST.

ARM0600000000433

Fig. 27   Code C151D: Tire Pressure Sensor Location Undetermined (Part 2 of 5). Except Crossfire

5. GROUND CIRCUIT(S) OPEN OR HIGH RESISTANCE

Using a 12-volt test light connect to battery voltage, probe each of the Ground circuit(s).

NOTE: The test light should be illuminated and bright. Compare the brightness to that of a direct connection to the battery.

Does the test light illuminate brightly?

Yes

- Go to 6

No

- Repair the Ground circuit(s) for an open circuit or high resistance.
- Perform TPM VERIFICATION TEST.

6. (D508) COM - LIN TIRE PRESSURE MONITOR LAN CIRCUIT SHORT TO VOLTAGE

Turn the ignition on.
Measure the voltage of the (D508) COM - LIN Tire Pressure Monitor LAN circuit.

Is there any voltage present?

Yes

- Repair the (D508) COM - LIN Tire Pressure Monitor LAN circuit for a short to voltage.

No

- Go to 7
- Perform TPM VERIFICATION TEST.

ARM0600000000434

Fig. 27 Code C151D: Tire Pressure Sensor Location Undetermined (Part 3 of 5). Except Crossfire

9. POWER AND GROUND CIRCUIT OPEN

Turn the ignition on.
With a voltmeter measure the voltage between the power and ground circuit at the Trigger Module.

Is the voltage at least the same as battery voltage?

Yes

- Go To 10

No

- Repair the open circuit.
- Perform TPM VERIFICATION TEST.

10. CHECK FOR ADDITIONAL TRIGGER MODULE COMMUNICATION RELATED DTCs

With the scan tool, select Network View and select Advanced.

Is there more than one module with active DTCs "Logged Against" the WCM?

Yes

- Replace/update the WCM
- Perform TPM VERIFICATION TEST.

No

- Replace the Tire pressure trigger Module

- Perform TPM VERIFICATION TEST.

ARM0600000000436

Fig. 27 Code C151D: Tire Pressure Sensor Location Undetermined (Part 5 of 5). Except Crossfire

7. (D508) COM - LIN TIRE PRESSURE MONITOR LAN CIRCUIT SHORT TO GROUND

Turn the ignition off.
Measure the resistance between ground and the (D508) COM - LIN Tire Pressure Monitor LAN circuit.

Is the resistance below 5.0 ohms?

Yes

- Repair the (D508) COM - LIN Tire Pressure Monitor LAN circuit for a short to ground.
- Perform TPM VERIFICATION TEST.

No

- Go to 8

8. (D508) COM - LIN TIRE PRESSURE MONITOR LAN CIRCUIT OPEN OR HIGH RESISTANCE

Use a jumper wire with one end connected to ground and the other to the (D508) COM - LIN Tire Pressure Monitor LAN circuit in the Front Left Pressure Tire Transponder harness connector.
Using a 12-Volt test light connected to battery voltage, probe the (D508) COM - LIN Tire Pressure Monitor LAN circuit in the TPM harness connector.

NOTE: The test light should be illuminated and bright. Compared the brightness to that of a direct connection to the battery.

Does the test light illuminate bright?

Yes

- Go to 9

No

- Repair the (D508) COM - LIN Tire Pressure Monitor LAN circuit for an open circuit or high resistance.
- Perform TPM VERIFICATION TEST.

ARM0600000000435

Fig. 27 Code C151D: Tire Pressure Sensor Location Undetermined (Part 4 of 5). Except Crossfire

Diagnostic Test

1. VERIFY DTC IS ACTIVE

NOTE: Ensure the IOD fuse is installed and battery voltage is between 10 and 16 volts before proceeding.

Turn the ignition on.
With the scan tool, read and record WCM DTCs.
With the scan tool, erase WCM DTCs.
Cycle the ignition switch.
With the scan tool, read WCM DTCs.

Does this DTC reset?

Yes

- Go To 2

No

- Perform the Stored Lost Communication test procedure.

- Perform BODY VERIFICATION TEST.

2. (D508) COM-LIN TIRE PRESSURE MONITOR LAN CIRCUIT OPEN

Turn the ignition off.
Disconnect the Tire Pressure Trigger Module.
Disconnect the WCM.
With an ohmmeter measure the resistance of the (D508) COM-LIN TIRE PRESSURE MONITOR LAN CIRCUIT.

Is the resistance below 5 Ohms?

Yes

- Go To 3

No

- Repair or replace the open circuit.
- Perform TPM VERIFICATION TEST.

ARM0600000000437

Fig. 28 Codes U1114, U1116 & U1117: Lost Communication With Tire Pressure Trigger Module (Part 1 of 5). Except Crossfire

3. (F202) FUSED IGNITION SWITCH OUTPUT (RUN) CIRCUIT OPEN OR HIGH RESISTANCE

Turn the ignition off.
Disconnect the Tire Pressure Transponder harness connector.
Disconnect the Sentry Key Remote Entry Module harness connector.
Turn the ignition on.
Using a 12-volt test light connect to ground, check the (F202) Fused Ignition Switch Output (Run) circuit.

NOTE: The test light should be illuminated and bright. Compare the brightness to that of a direct connection to the battery.

Is the test light illuminated and bright?

Yes

- Go to 4

No

- Repair the (F202) Fused Ignition Switch Output (Run) circuit for an open circuit or high resistance.
- Perform TPM VERIFICATION TEST.

4. (Z904) GROUND CIRCUIT(S) OPEN OR HIGH RESISTANCE

Using a 12-volt test light connect to battery voltage, probe each of the (Z904) Ground circuit(s).

NOTE: The test light should be illuminated and bright. Compare the brightness to that of a direct connection to the battery.

Does the test light illuminate brightly?

Yes

- Go to 5

No

- Repair the (Z904) Ground circuit(s) for an open circuit or high resistance.
- Perform TPM VERIFICATION TEST.

ARM0600000000438

Fig. 28   Codes U1114, U1116 & U1117: Lost Communication With Tire Pressure Trigger Module (Part 2 of 5). Except Crossfire

7. (D508) COM - LIN TIRE PRESSURE MONITOR LAN CIRCUIT OPEN OR HIGH RESISTANCE

Use a jumper wire with one end connected to ground and the other to the (D508) COM - LIN Tire Pressure Monitor LAN circuit in the Front Left Pressure Tire Transponder harness connector.
Using a 12-Volt test light connected to battery voltage, probe the (D508) COM - LIN Tire Pressure Monitor LAN circuit in the TPM harness connector.

NOTE: The test light should be illuminated and bright. Compared the brightness to that of a direct connection to the battery.

Does the test light illuminate bright?

Yes

- Go to 8

No

- Repair the (D508) COM - LIN Tire Pressure Monitor LAN circuit for an open circuit or high resistance.
- Perform TPM VERIFICATION TEST.

8. POWER AND GROUND CIRCUIT OPEN

Turn the ignition on.
With a voltmeter measure the voltage between the power and ground circuit at the Trigger Module.

Is the voltage at least the same as battery voltage?

Yes

- Go To 9

No

- Repair the open circuit.
- Perform TPM VERIFICATION TEST.

ARM0600000000440

Fig. 28   Codes U1114, U1116 & U1117: Lost Communication With Tire Pressure Trigger Module (Part 4 of 5). Except Crossfire

5. (D508) COM - LIN TIRE PRESSURE MONITOR LAN CIRCUIT SHORT TO VOLTAGE

Turn the ignition on.
Measure the voltage of the (D508) COM - LIN Tire Pressure Monitor LAN circuit.

Is there any voltage present?

Yes

- Repair the (D508) COM - LIN Tire Pressure Monitor LAN circuit for a short to voltage.

No

- Go to 6
- Perform TPM VERIFICATION TEST.

6. (D508) COM - LIN TIRE PRESSURE MONITOR LAN CIRCUIT SHORT TO GROUND

Turn the ignition off.
Measure the resistance between ground and the (D508) COM - LIN Tire Pressure Monitor LAN circuit.

Is the resistance below 5.0 ohms?

Yes

- Repair the (D508) COM - LIN Tire Pressure Monitor LAN circuit for a short to ground.
- Perform TPM VERIFICATION TEST.

No

- Go to 7

ARM0600000000439

Fig. 28   Codes U1114, U1116 & U1117: Lost Communication With Tire Pressure Trigger Module (Part 3 of 5). Except Crossfire

9. CHECK FOR ADDITIONAL TRIGGER MODULE COMMUNICATION RELATED DTCs

With the scan tool, select Network View and select Advanced.

Is there more than one module with active DTCs "Logged Against" the WCM?

Yes

- Replace/update the WCM
- Perform TPM VERIFICATION TEST.

No

- Replace the Tire pressure trigger Module

- Perform TPM VERIFICATION TEST.

ARM0600000000441

Fig. 28   Codes U1114, U1116 & U1117: Lost Communication With Tire Pressure Trigger Module (Part 5 of 5). Except Crossfire

Diagnostic Test

1. TPM

Was the WCM/SKREEM replaced during the test procedure?
Yes

- Go to 2

No

- Go to 3

2. WCM/SKREEM

NOTE: When entering the PIN, care should be taken because the SKREEM will only allow three consecutive attempts to enter the correct PIN. If three consecutive incorrect PIN's are entered the SKREEM will Lock Out the scan tool. To exit Lock Mode, the ignition key must remain in the Run position for one hour. All accessories must be off.

1. Reconnect the previously removed and/or disconnected components and connectors.
2. Obtain the vehicle's unique Personal Identification Number (PIN) assigned to its original SKREEM.
3. With the scan tool, select Miscellaneous Functions, WCM/Wireless Control Module. Then select the desired procedure and follow the display on the scan tool.
4. If the WCM/SKREEM was replaced, all the customer's keys must be programmed to the new module. Use the scan tool and the Program Key procedure
5. With the scan tool, erase all DTCs. Perform 5 ignition key cycles, leaving the key on for at least 90 seconds per cycle.
6. Drive the vehicle for a minimum of 10 minutes while maintaining a continuous speed above 15 mph (24 km/h). During this time the system will learn the new sensor ID code and will clear any DTC(s) automatically.
7. With the scan tool, read WCM/SKREEM DTC(s).

Are there any DTC(s) present?
Yes

- Repair not complete, refer to the appropriate symptom.

No

- Repair is complete.

ARM0600000000442

Fig. 29   TPM Verification (Part 1 of 2). Except Crossfire

Diagnostic Test

1. VERIFY OPERATION OF LEFT FRONT TIRE PRESSURE SENSOR/TRANSMITTER

NOTE: DTC 8001 can ONLY be set during the tire training process. If while using the DRB III®, and for some reason the training process is interrupted (no signal from transmitter, transmitter time-out, etc.) the TPM will set this DTC.

NOTE: If the Tire Pressure Sensors/Transmitters prove to be operating correctly using the RF Signal Detector, and the TPM module still cannot identify a signal from one or more of the Tire Pressure Sensors/Transmitters during the training process, the vehicle should be moved a few feet. The location of the Tire Pressure Sensors/Transmitters could be in a position that does not allow a clear signal transmission. After moving the vehicle, again attempt to train the Tire Pressure Sensors/Transmitters.

NOTE: Use this test in conjunction with Miller Tool 9001 (RF Signal Detector) and Miller Tool 8821 (Re-Learn Magnet) to verify the operation of the Tire Pressure Sensors/Transmitters.

NOTE: This test will be used to verify the functionality of each Tire Pressure Sensor/Transmitter.

Turn the ignition OFF.
Place the 8821 Re-Learn Magnet over the valve stem of the Left Front Tire.
Hold the 9001 Radio Frequency Detector within one inch of the tire valve.
Monitor the Radio Frequency signal of the Tire Pressure Sensor/Transmitter.

Does the RF Detector detect a signal from the Left Front Tire Sensor?
No

- Replace the Left Front Tire Pressure Sensor/Transmitter

Yes

- Go to 2

ARM0600000000455

Fig. 30   Code 8001: Training Failed (Part 1 of 5). Crossfire

3. TIRE PRESSURE SENSOR/TIRE PRESSURE TRANSPONDER REPLACE

1. Reconnect the previously removed and/or disconnected components and connectors.
2. Drive the vehicle for a minimum of 10 minutes while maintaining a continuous speed above 15 mph (24 km/h). During this time the system will learn the new sensor ID code and will clear any DTC(s) automatically.
3. With the scan tool, read TPM DTC(s).

Are there any DTC(s) present?
Yes

- Repair not complete, refer to the appropriate symptom.

No

- Repair is complete.

ARM0600000000443

Fig. 29   TPM Verification (Part 2 of 2). Except Crossfire

2. VERIFY OPERATION OF RIGHT FRONT TIRE PRESSURE SENSOR/TRANSMITTER

With the ignition OFF.
Place the 8821 Re-Learn Magnet over the valve stem of the Right Front Tire.
Hold the 9001 Radio Frequency Detector within one inch of the tire valve.
Monitor the Radio Frequency signal of the Tire Pressure Sensor/Transmitter.

Does the RF Detector detect a signal from the Right Front Tire Sensor?
No

- Replace the Right Front Tire Pressure Sensor/Transmitter

Yes

- Go to 3

3. VERIFY OPERATION OF RIGHT REAR TIRE PRESSURE SENSOR/TRANSMITTER

With the ignition OFF.
Place the 8821 Re-Learn Magnet over the valve stem of the Right Rear Tire.
Hold the 9001 Radio Frequency Detector within one inch of the tire valve.
Monitor the Radio Frequency signal of the Tire Pressure Sensor/Transmitter.

Does the RF Detector detect a signal from the Right Rear Tire Sensor?
No

- Replace the Right Rear Tire Pressure Sensor/Transmitter

Yes

- Go to 4

ARM0600000000456

Fig. 30   Code 8001: Training Failed (Part 2 of 5). Crossfire

4. VERIFY OPERATION OF LEFT REAR TIRE PRESSURE
SENSOR/TRANSMITTER

With the ignition OFF.
Place the 8821 Re-Learn Magnet over the valve stem of the Left Rear Tire.
Hold the 9001 Radio Frequency Detector within one inch of the tire valve.
Monitor the Radio Frequency signal of the Tire Pressure Sensor/Transmitter.
Does the RF Detector detect a signal from the Left Rear Tire Sensor?
No

- Replace the Left Rear Tire Pressure Sensor/Transmitter

Yes

- Go to 5

5. RETRAINING THE LEFT FRONT TIRE PRESSURE
SENSOR/TRANSMITTER

NOTE: Use this test in conjunction with the DRB III® and Miller Tool 8821 (Re-Learn
Magnet) to attempt to Retrain all the Tire Pressure Sensors/Transmitters.
Turn the ignition ON.
With the DRB III®, read and record the TPM DTCs.
With the DRB III®, erase the TPM DTCs.
Using the DRB III®, navigate to the Chassis System of the DRB III® and begin
retraining by selecting the "Train All Mode".

**NOTE: While retraining, the TPM module must detect a signal within a one minute
time frame or the retraining process will time-out and the TPM module will store a
8001 DTC.**

Using the Miller Tool 8821 Re-Learn Magnet, start at the Left Front Tire Pressure
Sensor/Transmitter and attempt to retrain the Tire Pressure Sensors to the TPM module.
Does the DRB III® detect the Left Front Tire Sensor?
No

- Replace the TPM module

Yes

- Go to 6

ARM0600000000457

Fig. 30   Code 8001: Training Failed (Part 3 of 5). Crossfire

8. RETRAINING LEFT REAR TIRE PRESSURE TRANSMITTER

With the ignition on.
Move the magnet to the Left Rear Tire Pressure Sensor.

Does the DRB III® detect the Left Rear Tire Sensor?

No

- Replace the TPM module

Yes

- The training is now complete, and the DRB III® should display "Training
  Complete".

ARM0600000000459

Fig. 30   Code 8001: Training Failed (Part 5 of 5). Crossfire

6. RETRAINING RIGHT FRONT TIRE PRESSURE TRANSMITTER

With the ignition on.
Move the magnet to the Right Front Tire Pressure Sensor.

Does the DRB III® detect the Right Front Tire Sensor?

No

- Replace the TPM module

Yes

- Go to 7

7. RETRAINING RIGHT REAR TIRE PRESSURE TRANSMITTER

With the ignition on.
Move the magnet to the Right Rear Tire Pressure Sensor.

Does the DRB III® detect the Right Rear Tire Sensor?

No

- Replace the TPM module

Yes

- Go to 8

ARM0600000000458

Fig. 30   Code 8001: Training Failed (Part 4 of 5). Crossfire

Diagnostic Test

1. READING TPM DIAGNOSTIC TROUBLE CODES

NOTE: DTC 8002 will always be set in conjunction with one or more of the Tire
Pressure Sensor/Transmitter Signal Jammed DTCs. Either 8009 (LF Tire), 8010 (RF
Tire), 8011 (RR Tire), or 8012 (RF Tire) will be set along with the 8002 code.

**NOTE: Some environmental factors can cause a disruption in the RF frequency
signal. Check for RF frequency concerns and aftermarket accessories (cell phones,
two way transmitters, etc.) that would compromise the RF frequency signal.**

Turn the ignition on.
With the DRB III®, read and record the TPM DTCs.
Refer to the appropriate Tire Pressure Sensor/Transmitter Signal Jammed DTC for proper
diagnostic and repair procedures.

Tire Pressure Sensor/Transmitter Signal Jammed DTC List:

- 8009 - Left Front Tire Pressure Sensor/Transmitter Signal Jammed

- 8010 - Right Front Tire Pressure Sensor/Transmitter Signal Jammed

- 8011 - Right Rear Tire Pressure Sensor/Transmitter Signal Jammed

- 8012 - Left Rear Tire Pressure Sensor/Transmitter Signal Jammed

Are any of the above DTCs active along with 8002?

Yes

- Perform the diagnostics for the active DTCs.

No

- Test complete. Check for any TSBs that may apply.

ARM0600000000460

Fig. 31   Code 8002: Tire Pressure Sensor/ Transmitter Signal Jammed. Crossfire

Diagnostic Test

1. READING TPM DIAGNOSTIC TROUBLE CODES

NOTE: DTC 8003 will always be set in conjunction with one or more of the Tire Pressure Sensor/Transmitter Low Battery DTCs. Either 8013 (LF Tire), 8014 (RF Tire), 8015 (RR Tire), or 8016 (RF Tire) will be set along with the 8003 code.

NOTE: The Tire Pressure Sensor/Transmitters are equipped with a ten year battery. The battery is not serviceable, and the Tire Pressure Sensor/Transmitter must be replaced if the battery fails.

Turn the ignition on.
With the DRB III®, read and record the TPM DTCs.
Refer to the appropriate Tire Pressure Sensor/Transmitter Low Battery DTC for proper diagnostic and repair procedures.

Tire Pressure Sensor/Transmitter Low Battery DTC List:

- 8013 - Left Front Tire Pressure Sensor/Transmitter Low Battery

- 8014 - Right Front Tire Pressure Sensor/Transmitter Low Battery

- 8015 - Right Rear Tire Pressure Sensor/Transmitter Low Battery

- 8016 - Left Rear Tire Pressure Sensor/Transmitter Low Battery

Are any of the above DTCs active along with 8002?

Yes

- Perform the diagnostics for the active DTCs.

No

- Test complete.

ARM0600000000461

Fig. 32   Code 8003: Battery Low. Crossfire

Diagnostic Test

1. TIRE PRESSURE MONITOR MODULE

NOTE: This DTC will only be set if the TPM module has an internal failure.

The Tire Pressure Monitor Module is reporting internal errors, view repair to continue.

Repair

- Replace and program the TPM Module
- Perform TIRE PRESSURE MONITOR VERIFICATION TEST.

ARM0600000000463

Fig. 34   Code 8005: TPM Module Failure. Crossfire

Diagnostic Test

1. READING TPM DIAGNOSTIC TROUBLE CODES

NOTE: DTC 8004 will always be set in conjunction with one or more of the Tire Pressure Sensor/Transmitter Failure DTCs. Either 8017 (LF Tire), 8018 (RF Tire), 8019 (RR Tire), or 8020 (RF Tire) will be set along with the 8004 code.

NOTE: The Tire Pressure Sensor/Transmitters can set this DTC if the vehicle is sitting still for a prolonged period of time and the key is ON. The Tire Pressure Sensor/Transmitter must be tested properly prior to replacement.

Turn the ignition on.
With the DRB III®, read and record the TPM DTCs.
Refer to the appropriate Tire Pressure Sensor/Transmitter Failure DTC for proper diagnostic and repair procedures.

Tire Pressure Sensor/Transmitter Failure DTC List:

- 8017 - Left Front Tire Pressure Sensor/Transmitter Failure

- 8018 - Right Front Tire Pressure Sensor/Transmitter Failure

- 8019 - Right Rear Tire Pressure Sensor/Transmitter Failure

- 8020 - Left Rear Tire Pressure Sensor/Transmitter Failure

Are any of the above DTCs active along with 8002?
Yes

- Perform the diagnostics for the active DTCs.

No

- Test complete.

ARM0600000000462

Fig. 33   Code 8004: Tire Pressure Sensor/ Transmitter Failure. Crossfire

Diagnostic Test

1. READING TPM DIAGNOSTIC TROUBLE CODES

NOTE: DTC 8009 will always be set in conjunction with DTC 8004.

NOTE: Some environmental factors can cause a disruption in the Radio Frequency signal. Check for possible concerns and aftermarket accessories (cell phones, two way transmitters, etc.) that would compromise the Radio Frequency signal between the Tire Pressure Sensor and the TPM module.

Turn the ignition ON.
With the DRB III®, read and record the TPM DTCs.
Inspect the area around the Left Front Tire and repair any disruptions as necessary.

Were there any problems found?

NoPerform the TIRE PRESSURE MONITOR VERIFICATION TEST.
Yes

- Repair as necessary.
- Perform the TIRE PRESSURE VERIFICATION TEST.

ARM0600000000464

Fig. 35   Codes 8009–8012: Tire Pressure Sensor/ Transmitter Signal Jammed. Crossfire

Diagnostic Test

1. READING TPM DIAGNOSTIC TROUBLE CODES

NOTE: DTC 8013 will always be set in conjunction with DTC 8003.

NOTE: The Tire Pressure Sensor/Transmitter is equipped with a ten year battery. The battery is not serviceable, and the Tire Pressure Sensor/Transmitter must be replaced if the battery fails.

Turn the ignition ON.
With the DRB III®, read and record the TPM DTCs.
Replace the Left Front Tire Pressure Sensor/Transmitter
Retrain the Tire Pressure Sensor/Transmitter to the TPM module

Is the repair complete?

Yes

- Perform the TIRE PRESSURE MONITOR VERIFICATION TEST.

No

- Perform the necessary repair.
- Perform the TIRE PRESSURE MONITOR VERIFICATION TEST.

ARM0600000000465

Fig. 36   Codes 8013–8016: Tire Pressure Sensor/ Transmitter Low Battery. Crossfire

TIRE PRESSURE MONITOR VERIFICATION TEST

Ensure the air pressure is properly set in ALL tires.
Disconnect all jumper wires and reconnect all previously disconnected components and connectors.
With the DRB III® connected to the vehicle and an available assistant, monitor the Tire Pressure Transmitters on each tire.

- Drive the vehicle at 40 km/h (25 MPH) for at least 2 minutes.
- Verify the TPM module is receiving all Tire Pressure Sensor transmissions. If the Tire Sensors/Transmitters are operating properly, the following status will be displayed:
- LF TIRE MOVING: YES
- RF TIRE MOVING: YES
- RR TIRE MOVING: YES
- LR TIRE MOVING: YES
- ALL TIRES MOVING: YES
- With the DRB III®, confirm that no DTCs are present and that all components are functioning properly.
- If a DTC is present, refer to the appropriate category and select the corresponding symptom.

Are any DTCs present?
YES

- Repair is not complete, refer to appropriate symptom.

NO

- Repair is complete.

ARM0600000000467

Fig. 38   Tire Pressure Monitor Verification Test. Crossfire

Diagnostic Test

1. READING TPM DIAGNOSTIC TROUBLE CODES

NOTE: DTC 8017 will always be set in conjunction with DTC 8004.

NOTE: Under certain operating conditions (slow speed, stop-and-go driving, prolonged standing) the Tire Pressure Sensors can stop transmitting. This condition can be misdiagnosed as an inoperative Tire Pressure Sensor. Take care to fully diagnose any Sensor/Transmitter Failure code.

Turn the ignition ON.
With the DRB III®, read and record the TPM DTCs.
With the DRB III®, clear the TPM module DTCs.
Road test the vehicle.
Is the TPM Light on after the Road test?
Yes

- Go to 2

No

- The condition that caused this DTC to set is currently not present. Review the functionality for a possible intermittent condition.
- Perform the TIRE PRESSURE MONITOR VERIFICATION TEST.

2. CHECKING DTC RESET

Turn the ignition ON.
With the DRB III®, read the TPM DTCs.
Did DTC 8017 - LEFT FRONT TIRE PRESSURE SENSOR/TRANSMITTER reset?
Yes

- Replace the Left Front Tire Pressure Sensor/Transmitter. Retrain the Tire Pressure Sensor/Transmitter to the TPM module. Perform the TIRE PRESSURE MONITOR VERIFICATION TEST.

No

- The condition that caused this DTC to set is currently not present. Review the functionality for a possible intermittent condition.
- Perform the TIRE PRESSURE MONITOR VERIFICATION TEST.

ARM0600000000466

Fig. 37   Codes 8017–8020: Tire Pressure Sensor/ Transmitter. Crossfire

Diagnostic Test

1. LOW TIRE PRESSURE INDICATOR LIGHT

NOTE: The Low Tire Pressure Indicator Lamp will illuminate if the TPM module detects low tire pressure in one or more of the vehicle tires. Also, the TPM module will turn the light on if the module detects a lose of signal from one or more of the Tire Pressure Sensors/Transmitters during stop and go driving.
Turn the ignition OFF.
Inspect the tires for proper air pressure (refer to Tire Placard located in door opening).
Ensure the air pressure is properly set in ALL tires.
Turn the ignition ON.
Connect the DRB III® to the vehicle.
With the DRB III®, select "Chassis System" .
With the DRB III®, select "Input / Output" .
Verify the Tire Status of all tires (should be "NO" movement while parked).
With an available assistant, drive the vehicle at 40 km/h (25 MPH) for at least 2 minutes and monitor the Tire Status of all tires.

NOTE: The Tire Status must change when the vehicle is driven. The static reading will be "NO", and the dynamic reading will change to "YES".

If the Tire Sensors/Transmitters are operating properly, the following status will be displayed:

- LF TIRE MOVING: YES
- RF TIRE MOVING: YES
- RR TIRE MOVING: YES
- LR TIRE MOVING: YES
- ALL TIRES MOVING: YES

Are all the Tire Sensors/Transmitters reporting a YES status?

YES

- The TPM system is functioning properly.

NO

- Refer to the indicated tire to repair the sensor.

ARM0600000000468

Fig. 39   Low Tire Pressure Indicator Light On With No DTC's. Crossfire

COMPONENT SERVICE

Resetting Tire Pressure Monitor Lamp

The Low Pressure Tire Pressure indicator lamp will flash slowly and sound a single tone when tire pressure is low. If tire pressure drops lower, the indicator lamp will flash rapidly and the tone will be continuous. When the tire is inflated to the proper pressure the lamp and tone will turn off. If the lamp remains On, a problem in the low warning system is present and the low tire pressure system must be diagnosed and serviced to reset warning lamp.

Relearning Tire Pressure Monitor System

CHARGER, MAGNUM & 300

Drive vehicle for a minimum of 10 minutes while maintaining a continuous speed above 15 mph. During this time the system will learn the new sensor I.D. code and will clear any DTC's automatically.

CROSSFIRE

Do not rotate tires above five mph in the two minutes prior to programming.
1. Connect a suitably programmed scan tool to Data Link Connector (DLC).
2. Access "CHASSIS SYSTEMS."
3. Select "TIRE PRESSURE MONITOR."
4. Scan tool will display "PROGRAM TRANSMITTER COMPLETE" or direct you to next wheel.
5. Select appropriate function from menu.
6. Locate donut shaped training magnet located under spare tire cover.
7. Place magnet at valve stem of required wheel.
8. Exit function once programming is complete.
9. Verify module programming as indicated by sensor ID's in "SENSOR DISPLAY."

300M

To train the EVIC to recognize the source locations of the pressure sensor signals, proceed as follows:
1. Locate donut shaped training magnet located under spare tire cover.
2. Press EVIC MENU button until "RETAIN TIRE SENSORS-NO" is displayed.
3. Press STEP button to select "YES" retrain from TPM sensor.
4. Press MENU button to enter selection.
5. EVIC display will prompt "TRAIN LEFT FRONT TIRE."
6. Position training magnet over valve stem of lefthand front tire for at least five seconds.
7. When EVIC has received transmitted

STANDARD PROCEDURE - TPM MODULE PROGRAMMING

If the TPM module has been replaced, the TPM Module must be reprogrammed in order to identify the Tire Pressure Sensors/Transmitters. Proper identification of each of the Tire Pressure Sensors/Transmitters is necessary in order to identify which wheel is transmitting a signal to the TPM module.

NOTE: The TPM Module Programming procedure must use the DRB III® in conjunction with the Miller Tool 8821 Re-Learn Magnet.

NOTE: When reprogramming the TPM module, the magnet should be moved from wheel to wheel in a clockwise direction starting at the Left Front Wheel. There is a maximum time limit of 60 seconds for each tire. If the DRB III® cannot read the sensor within the 60 seconds, the DRB III® determines the time-out has been reached, and the module reprogramming will be discontinued. If the module reprogramming is not completed, the TPM module will then set the "Training Failed" DTC.

1. Connect a DRB III® scan tool to the vehicle's diagnostic connector beneath the Instrument Panel near the steering column.
2. Access the Chassis System using the DRB III®.
3. Once in the Chassis System, select "Miscellaneous Functions".
4. The following System Test menu selections will appear:
   - Train All Mode
   - Stop Train Mode
5. Select "Train All Mode" from the System Test menu selection.
6. Using the DRB III®, select "Yes" to continue.
7. Place the Special Tool 8821 Re-Learn Magnet, over the valve stem of the Left Front Wheel.
8. Each Tire Pressure Sensor/Transmitter will automatically sense the presence of the magnet and begin transmitting. When the pressure sensor/transmitter on each wheel has been programmed, the DRB III® will automatically BEEP and direct you to the next wheel to be programmed. Remove the magnet and move to each of the remaining wheels as directed by the DRB III®.
9. Remove the magnet from the Left Rear Wheel.
10. Once "Training Completed" is displayed, exit the program function screen and use the following to verify the TPM functionality:
    - Verify the TPM module programming is complete by viewing the **Input/Output Display** selection of the DRB III® and confirming the Tire Pressure Sensors are trained.
    - Verify the TPM module programming is complete by viewing the **Sensor Display** selection of the DRB III® and confirm the Tire Pressure Sensor pressure readings are accurate.

ARM0600000000470

Fig. 40   TPM Module Programming. Crossfire

message for Remote Tire Pressure Monitor (RTPM), it will chirp and display next train request.
8. There is a 60 second timer for learning tire location and 30 seconds between remaining tires. If timer expires, EVIC will abort training procedure and display "TRAINING ABORTED." Any ID's learned during current session will be discarded.
9. EVIC will request initiation of training sequence for each tire, one by one in a clockwise direction.

Module, Replace
CROSSFIRE

1. Pry Universal Garage Door Opener/Tire Pressure Monitor module from headliner using suitable plastic wedge or prying device, **Fig. 41.**
2. Disconnect module electrical connector.
3. Remove module.
4. Reverse procedure to install. Reprogram module as outlined under "Relearning Tire Pressure Monitor System."

TPM Sensor
REMOVAL

1. Raise and support vehicle.
2. Remove tire and wheel assembly.

3. Dismount tire from wheel, noting the following:
   a. When breaking tire bead loose from wheel, avoid using bead breaker in area of sensor.
   b. Separate tire from wheel, carefully insert mounting/dismounting tool at valve stem plus or minus 10°, **Fig. 42.**
4. Remove sensor retaining nut while holding pressure against metal valve stem to prevent damage to antenna strap, **Fig. 43.**
5. Remove sensor from wheel, **Fig. 44.**

INSTALLATION

1. Insert sensor through wheel, keep pressure against rear of metal valve stem. Potted side of sensor should be positioned toward wheel, **Fig. 45.**
2. Install sensor nut and pressed-in washer by hand.
3. Hold sensor flush with contour of wheel, then **torque** sensor nut to 71 inch lbs.
4. Mount tire to wheel.

Transponder, Replace

1. Remove wheel house splash shield.
2. Disconnect transponder electrical connection.
3. Remove mounting nuts, then transponder.
4. Reverse procedure to install.

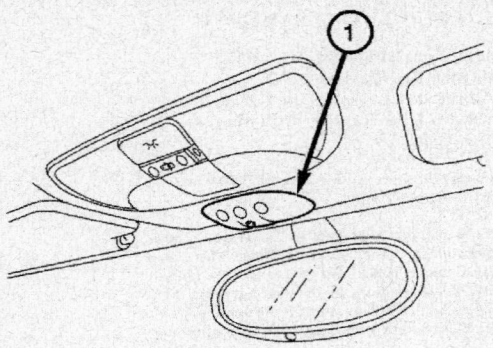

1- Universal Garage Door Opener/Tire Pressure Monitor

ARM0600000000469

Fig. 41   Universal garage door opener/tire pressure monitor. Crossfire

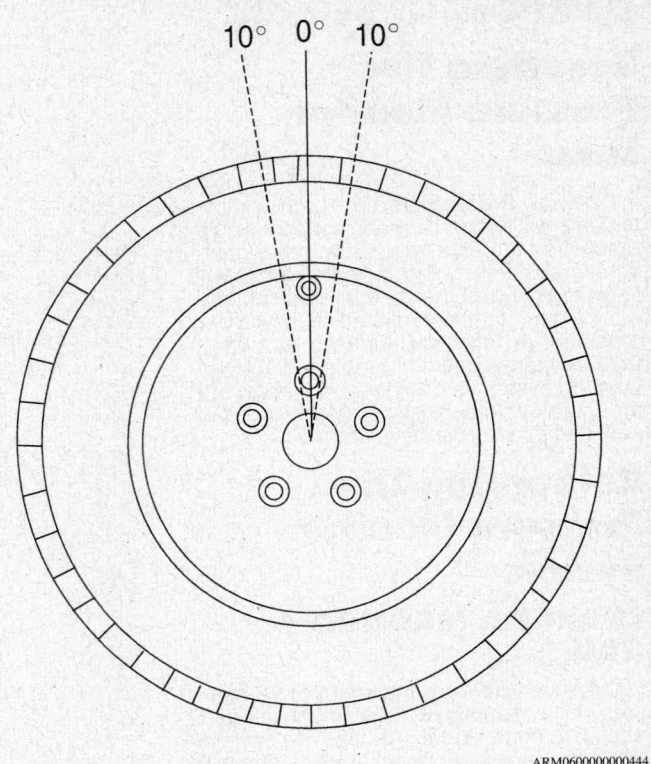

ARM0600000000444

Fig. 42   Tire removal

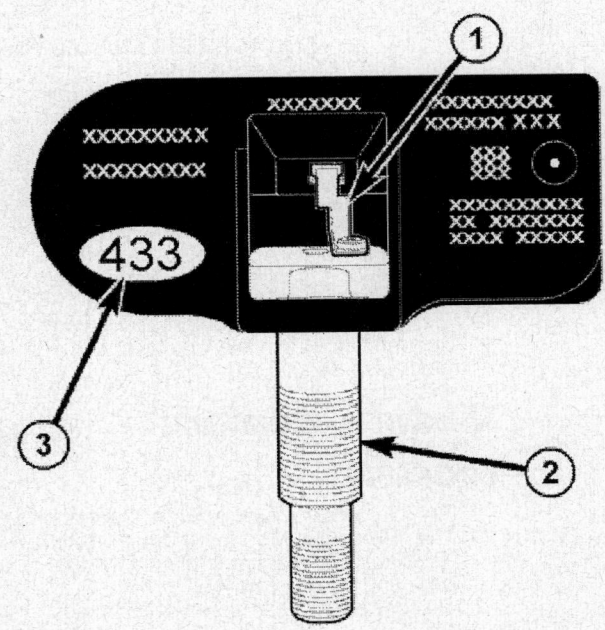

1-   Antenna Strap
2-   Valve Stem
3-   ID Insignia

ARM0600000000445

Fig. 43   Antenna strap

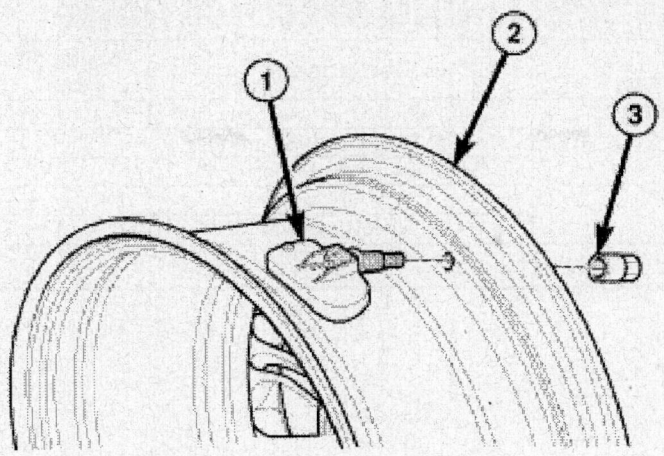

1- TPM Sensor
2- Wheel
3- Sensor Nut

ARM0600000000446

Fig. 44   TPM sensor

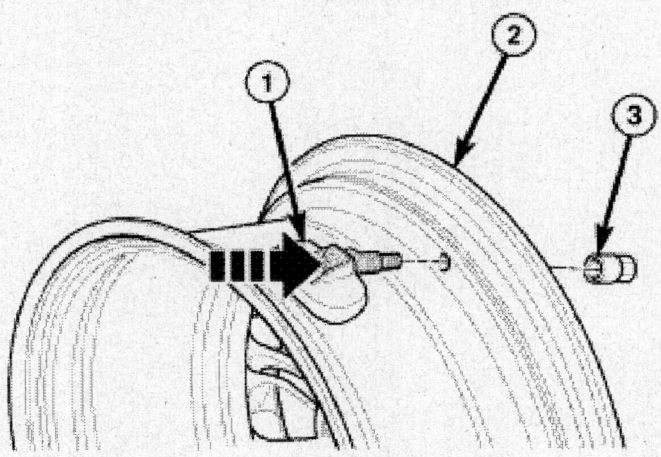

1- TPM Sensor
2- Wheel
3- Sensor Nut

ARM0600000000447

Fig. 45   TPM sensor installation

TIGHTENING SPECIFICATIONS

Year	Component	Torque Ft. Lbs.
2005–08	TPM Sensor Nut (Except Crossfire)	71①
	TPM Sensor Nut (Crossfire)	35①
	TMP Transponder Mounting Nut	26①
	Valve Core	4①
	Wheel Lug Nuts	100

① — Inch lbs.

ENGINE REBUILDING SPECIFICATIONS

NOTE: For Engine Tightening Specifications, Refer To The Engine Section In The Appropriate Chassis Chapter Of This Manual.

INDEX

	Page No.		Page No.		Page No.
Camshaft	21-3	Cylinder Head, Valve Guide & Valve Seats	21-1	Pistons, Pins & Rings	21-4
Crankshaft, Bearings & Rods	21-4			Valve Springs	21-2
Cylinder Block	21-5	Oil Pump	21-6	Valves	21-2

CYLINDER HEAD, VALVE GUIDE & VALVE SEATS

All measurements given in inches, unless otherwise specified.

Engine Liter	Year	Cylinder Head Warpage Limit①	Cylinder Head Overall Thickness②	Valve Guides (Standard)			Valve Seats			
				Inside Diameter	Stem To Guide Clearance		Angle, Degrees	Width		Runout
					Intake	Exhaust		Intake	Exhaust	
1.8L DOHC	2007–08	.004	—	.2165–.2170	.0018–.0025	.0029–.0037	44.75–45.10	.0456–.0574	.0531–.0649	.0020
2.0L DOHC	2007–08	.004	—	.2165–.2170	.0018–.0025	.0029–.0037	44.75–45.10	.0456–.0574	.0531–.0649	.0020
2.0L SOHC	2004–05	.004	—	.2350–.2360	.0018–.0030	.0029–.0040	44.5–45.0	.0350–.0790	.0350–.0980	.0020
2.4L DOHC	2004–06	.004	—	.2350–.2360	.0018–.0030	.0029–.0040	44.5–45.0	.0350–.0790	.0350–.0980	.0020
2.4L DOHC	2007–08	.004	—	.2165–.2172	.0008–.0021	.0012–.0024	45.25–45.75	.0456–.0574	.0531–.0649	.0020
2.4L SOHC	2004–05	.007	4.70	.2400	.0008–.0030	.0012–.0050	45.0–45.5	.0400–.0500	.0400–.0500	—
2.7L DOHC	2004	.008	—	.2353–.2363	.0009–.0114	.0020–.0146	45.0–45.5	.0394–.0591	.0492–.0689	.0020
2.7L DOHC ③	2007–08	.008	—	.2353–.2363	.0009–.0026	.0020–.0037	45.0–45.5	.0394–.0591	.0492–.0689	.0020
3.0L SOHC	2004–05	.007	4.70	.3200	.0008–.0030	.0016–.0050	45.0–45.5	.0400–.0500	.0490–.0690	—
3.2L SOHC 18-Valve	2004–06	.008	—	—	—	—	45.0	1.2200–1.2210	1.3780–1.3790	—
3.5L SOHC	2004–06	.008	—	.2746–.2756	.0009–.0114	.0020–.0146	45.0–45.5	.0295–.0492	.0492–.0689	.0020
3.5L SOHC③	2007–08	—	—	.2746–.2756	.0009–.0026	.0020–.0037	45.0–45.5	.0310–.0670	.0500–.0670	.0020
5.7L	2005–08	.002	—	.3130–.3140	.0080–.0025	.0019–.0037	44.5–45.0	.0464–.0637	.0582–.0755	.0019
6.1L	2006–08	—	—	.3130–.3140	.0008–.0025	.0010–.0028	44.5–45.0	.0464–.0637	.0582–.0755	.0019

DOHC — Dual Overhead Cam
SOHC — Single Overhead Cam
① — Measurement is a combined total dimension of stock removal limit from cylinder head and block surface (deck) together.
② — Overall thickness, less warpage limit.
③ — Avenger & 2007–08 Sebring Sedan.

ENGINE REBUILDING SPECIFICATIONS

VALVE SPRINGS

All measurements given in inches, unless otherwise specified.

Engine	Year	Free Length		Installed Height	Spring Pressure, Lbs. @ Inches		Maximum Straightness Deviation
		Intake	Exhaust		Intake	Exhaust	
1.8L DOHC	2007–08	1.8500	1.8500	1.3780	40.35 @ 2.0230	40.35 @ 2.0230	—
2.0L DOHC	2007–08	1.8500	1.8500	1.3780	40.35 @ 2.0230	40.35 @ 2.0230	—
2.0L SOHC	2004–05	①	①	1.5800	②	②	—
2.4L DOHC	2004–06	1.9430	1.9430	1.4960	70 @ 1.4960	70 @ 1.4960	—
2.4L DOHC	2007–08	1.8500	1.8500	1.3780	40.35 @ 1.3800	40.35 @1.3800	—
2.4L SOHC	2004–05	1.9600–2.0000	1.9600–2.0000	1.7400	60 @ 1.7400	60 @ 1.7400	4°
2.7L DOHC	2004	1.7965	1.7965	1.4961	56–64 @ 1.4961	56–64 @ 1.4961	—
2.7L DOHC ④	2007–08	1.7965	1.7965	1.4961	56–64 @ 1.4961	56–64 @ 1.4961	—
3.0L SOHC	2004–05	1.9700–2.0100	1.9700–2.0100	1.7400	60 @ 1.7400	60 @ 1.7400	4°
3.2L SOHC 18-Valve	2004–06	—	—	—	—	—	—
3.5L SOHC	2004–06	1.7195	1.7448	1.4961	19.5–80.5 @ 1.4961	71.0–79.0 @ 1.4961	—
3.5L SOHC ④	2007–08	1.7195	⑤	1.4961	70–81 @ 1.4961	⑥	—
5.7L	2005–08	2.2560	2.2560	1.8100	86–100 @ 1.8110	86–100 @ 1.8110	—
6.1L	2006–08	2.1330	2.0230	③	90–108 @ 1.8700	90–108 @ 1.7720	—

DOHC — Dual Overhead Cam
SOHC — Single Overhead Cam
① — Standard engine, 1.84 inches; High Output R/T engine, 2.13 inches.
② — Standard engine, 70 lbs. @ 1.57 inches; High Output R/T engine, 72 lbs. @ 1.57 inches.
③ — Intake 1.870, Exhaust 1.772.
④ — Avenger & 2007–08 Sebring Sedan.
⑤ — Yellow 1.8543 inch, White 1.9015 inch.
⑥ — Yellow 71–80 lbs. @ 1.496 inch, White 80–90 lbs. @ 1.496 inch.

VALVES

All measurements given in inches, unless otherwise specified.

Engine	Year	Stem Diameter		Clearance		Stem Tip Height		Maximum Tip Refinish	Face Angle, Degrees	Margin (Minimum)	
		Intake	Exhaust	Intake	Exhaust	Intake	Exhaust			Intake	Exhaust
1.8L DOHC	2007–08	.2151–.2157	.2148–.2153	—	—	1.89100	1.88900	—	45.25–45.75	.0246	.02629
2.0L DOHC	2007–08	.2151–.2157	.2148–.2153	—	—	1.89100	1.88900	—	45.25–45.75	.0246	.02629
2.0L SOHC	2004–05	.2337–.2344	.2326–.2333	.0460	.0500	1.7600–1.80000	1.7100–1.75000	—	45.0	.0380–.0580	.0420–.0710
2.4L DOHC	2004–06	.2337–.2344	.2326–.2333	—	—	1.89100	1.88900	—	44.5–45.0	.0470–.0660	.0380–.0510
2.4L DOHC	2007–08	.2151–.2157	.2148–.2153	—	—	1.89100	1.88900	—	45.25–45.75	.0246	.02629
2.4L SOHC	2004–05	.2400	.2300	—	—	1.94100–1.96000	1.94100–1.96000	—	45.0–45.5	.0400–.0500	.0400–.0500
2.7L DOHC	2004	.2337–.2344	.2326–.2333	—	—	1.83260–1.85694	1.91436–1.91804	—	44.5–45.0	—	—
2.7L DOHC ②	2007–08	.2337–.2344	.2326–.2333	.0009–.0026	.0020–.0037	1.85326–1.85694	1.91436–1.91804	—	44.5–45.5	—	—
3.0L SOHC	2004–05	.2400	.2400	.0008–.0030	.0016–.0050	1.94100–1.96000	1.94100–1.96000	—	45.0–45.5	.0200–.0400	.0300–.0500
3.2L SOHC 18-Valve	2004–06	.2740	.2740	.0009–.0025	.0020–.0037	—	—	—	45.0	.0470	.0620
3.5L SOHC	2004–06	.2730–.2737	.2719–.2726	—	—	1.66800–1.71870	1.76000–1.81050	—	44.5–45.0	.0329–.0459	.5670–.0697

Continued

VALVES—Continued

All measurements given in inches, unless otherwise specified.

Engine	Year	Stem Diameter		Clearance		Stem Tip Height		Maximum Tip Re-finish	Face Angle, De-grees	Margin (Mini-mum)	
		Intake	Exhaust	Intake	Exhaust	Intake	Exhaust			Intake	Exhaust
3.5L SOHC ②	2007–08	.2730–.2737	.2719–.2726	.0114	.0146	1.66800–1.71870	1.78000–1.83050	—	44.5–45.0	.0329–.0459	.0567–.0697
5.7L	2005–08	.3120–.3130	.3110–.3120	—	—	—	—	—	45.0–45.5	—	—
6.1L	2006–08	.3120–.3130	.3120–.3130	.0008–.0025	.0010–.0028	—	—	—	①	—	—

DOHC — Dual Overhead Cam
SOHC — Single Overhead Cam

① — Intake 45.5–46.0, Exhaust 45.0–45.5

② — Avenger & 2007–08 Sebring Sedan

CAMSHAFT

All measurements given in inches, unless otherwise specified.

Engine	Year	Camshaft Journal Diameter	Camshaft Bearing Clearance	Camshaft Endplay	Lifter Bore Diameter	Lifter Diameter	Lifter To Bore Clearance
1.8L DOHC	2007–08	⑤	⑥	.0040–.0090	—	—	—
2.0L DOHC	2007–08	⑤	⑥	.0040–.0090	—	—	—
2.0L SOHC	2004–05	①	.0021–.0047	.0020–.0150	—	—	—
2.4L DOHC	2004–06	1.0220–1.0230	.0009–.0025	.0019–.0066	—	—	—
2.4L DOHC	2007–08	⑤	⑥	.0040–.0090	—	—	—
2.4L SOHC	2004–05	1.8000	—	—	—	—	—
2.7L DOHC	2004	.9449–.9441	.0020–.0051	.0051–.0110	—	—	—
2.7L DOHC ④	2007–08	.9449–.9441	.0020–.0035	.0051–.0110	—	—	—
3.0L SOHC	2004–05	1.8000	—	—	—	—	—
3.2L SOHC 18-Valve	2004–06	—	—	—	—	—	—
3.5L SOHC	2004–06	1.6905–1.6913	.0030–.0059	.0040–.0140	—	—	—
3.5L SOHC④	2007–08	1.6905–1.6913	.0030–.0047	.0010–.0140	—	—	—
5.7L	2005–08	②	③	.0031–.0114	—	.8420–.8427	.0007–.0024
6.1L	2006–08	②	③	.0031–.0114	—	.8420–.8427	.0007–.0024

DOHC — Dual Overhead Cam
SOHC — Single Overhead Cam

① — Journal No. 1, 1.6190–1.6199 inches; No. 2, 1.634–1.635 inches; No. 3, 1.650–1.651 inches; No. 4, 1.666–1.668 inches; No. 5, 1.6820–1.6829 inches.

② — Journal No. 1, 2.29 inches; No. 2 2.27 inches; No. 3, 2.26 inches; No. 4, 2.24 inches; No. 5 1.72 inches.

③ — Journals Nos. 1, 3 & 5, .0015–.0030 inches; Journals Nos. 2 and 4, .0019–.0035 inch.

④ — Avenger & 2007–08 Sebring Sedan.

⑤ — Intake Cam, 1.1797–1.1803 inches; Exhaust Cam, 1.4166–1.4173 inches.

⑥ — Front Exhaust Journal, .0007–.0020 inch; Front Intake Journal, .0008–.0022 inch; All others, .0008–.0026 inch.

CRANKSHAFT, BEARINGS & RODS

All measurements given in inches, unless otherwise specified.

| Engine | Year | Crankshaft | | | | Bearing Clearance | | Connecting Rods | | Crank-shaft Endplay |
		Main Bearing Journal Diameter	Con-necting Rod Journal Diameter	Max. Out Of Round	Max. Taper	Main Bearings	Con-necting Rod Bearings	Pin Bore Diameter	Side Clear-ance	
1.8L DOHC	2007–08	②	③	.0001	.0002	.0011–.0018	.0012–.0023	—	—	.0019–.0098
2.0L DOHC	2007–08	②	③	.0001	.0002	.0011–.0018	.0012–.0023	—	—	.0019–.0098
2.0L SOHC	2004–05	2.0469–2.0475	1.8894–1.8900	.0001	.0001	.0008–.0024	.0010–.0023	.8252–.8260	.0050–.0150	.0035–.0150
2.4L DOHC	2004–06	2.3620–2.3625	1.9680–1.9685	.0003	.0001	.0007–.0024	.0009–.0027	.8264–.8267	.0051–.0160	.0035–.0150
2.4L DOHC	2007–08	②	③	.0001	.0002	.0011–.0018	.0012–.0023	—	—	.0019–.0098
2.4L SOHC	2004–05	2.2400	1.7700	—	—	.0008–.0030	.0004–.0150	—	.0040–.0150	.0020–.0150
2.7L DOHC	2004–04	2.4997–2.5004	2.1067–2.1060	.0006	.0006	.0014–.0034	.0010–.0026	.8665–.8668	.0052–.0170	.0019–.0170
2.7L DOHC①	2007–08	2.4997–2.5004	2.1067–2.106	.0006	.0006	.0034	.001–.0026	.8665–.8668	.0150	.0019–.018
3.0L SOHC	2004–05	2.4000	2.0000	—	—	.0008–.0030	.0008–.0030	—	—	.0020–.0100
3.2L SOHC 18-Valve	2004–06	—	—	.0006	.0006	.0030–.0100	.0030–.0100	—	—	—
3.5L SOHC	2004–06	2.5190–2.5200	2.2830–2.2840	.0006	.0006	.0007–.0034	.00075–.00340	.9452–.9455	.0153	.0040–.0170
3.5L SOHC①	2007–08	2.5190–2.5200	2.2820–2.2830	.0003	.0004	.0013–.0024	.0014–.0029	.9452–.9455	.0153	.0020–.0100
5.7L	2005–08	2.5585–2.5595	2.1250–2.1260	.0002	.0001	.0009–.0020	.0007–.0023	.9431–.9438	.0030–.0137	.0110
6.1L	2006–08	2.5585–2.5595	2.1250–2.1260	.0002	.0001	.0009–.002	.0007–.0029	.9431–.9438	.0030–.0137	.0020–.0110

DOHC — Dual Overhead Cam
SOHC — Single Overhead Cam
① — Avenger & 2007–08 Sebring Sedan.

② — Journal Grade; 0, 2.0466–2.0467 in.; 1, 2.0465–2.0466 in.; 2, 2.0464–2.0465 in.; 3, 2.0462–2.0464in. ; 4, 2.0461–2.0462 in.

③ — Journal Grade; 1, 1.8884–1.8886 in.; 2, 1.8884–1.8881 in.; 3, 1.8879–1.8881 in.

PISTONS, PINS & RINGS

All measurements given in inches, unless otherwise specified.

| Engine | Year | Piston Dia-meter (Std.) | Piston Clear-ance | Piston Pin Dia-meter | Piston Pin To Piston Clear-ance | Piston Ring End Gap (Minimum) | | | Piston Ring Side Clearance | | |
| | | | | | | Compression | | Oil | Compression | | Oil |
						Top	2nd		Top	2nd	
1.8L DOHC	2007–08	⑤	.0006	.8257–.8261	—	.0059–.0118	.0118–.0117	.0079–.0276	.1182–.0028	.1182–.0028	.0024–.0059
2.0L DOHC	2007–08	⑤	.0006	.8257–.8261	—	.0059–.0118	.0118–.0117	.0079–.0276	.1182–.0028	.1182–.0028	.0024–.0059
2.0L SOHC	2004–05	3.4432–3.4439	.0008–.0020②	.8268–.8269	.0003–.0006	.0900–.0310	.0190–.0390	.0090–.0390	.0010–.0040	.0010–.0040	.0002–.0070
2.4L DOHC	2004–06	3.4424–3.4431	.0009–.0022①	.8660–.8661	.0002–.0007	.0078–.0310	.0070–.0310	.0050–.0390	.0010–.0040	.0010–.0040	.0010–.0060
2.4L DOHC	2007–08	⑤	.0006	.8257–.8261	—	.0059–.0118	.0118–.0117	.0079–.0276	.1182–.0028	.1182–.0028	.0024–.0059
2.4L SOHC	2004–05	3.4000	.0008–.0015	.8700	.0008–.0030	.0100–.0300	.0160–.0300	.0040–.0300	.0008–.0030	.0012–.0030	—
2.7L DOHC	2004	3.3345–3.3868	.0003–.0016	.8661–.8662	.0002–.0005	.0080–.0140	.0146–.0240	.0100–.0300	.0013–.0032	.0016–.0031	.0022–.0080

Continued

PISTONS, PINS & RINGS—Continued

All measurements given in inches, unless otherwise specified.

Engine	Year	Piston Diameter (Std.)	Piston Clearance	Piston Pin Diameter	Piston Pin To Piston Clearance	Piston Ring End Gap (Minimum)			Piston Ring Side Clearance		
						Compression		Oil	Compression		Oil
						Top	2nd		Top	2nd	
2.7L DOHC ④	2007–08	3.3834–3.3868	.0003–.0016	.8661–.8662	.0002–.0005	.0080–.014	.0146–.0249	.010–.030	.0013–.0032	.0016–.0031	.0022–.0080
3.0L SOHC	2004–05	3.5800	.0008–.0015	.8700	—	.0120–.0030	.0180–.0300	.0080–.0300	.0012–.0030	.0080–.0030	—
3.2L SOHC 18-Valve	2004–06	3.5380–3.5390	.0003–.0018	—	—	.0070–.0130	.0070–.0150	—	.0016–.0031	.0016–.0031	.0015–.0073
3.5L SOHC	2004–06	3.7780–3.7796	.0000–.0018	.9448–.9449	.0002–.0006	.0080–.0140	.0091–.0197	.0100–.0300	.0016–.0031	.0016–.0031	.0015–.0073
3.5L SOHC ④	2007–08	3.7780–3.7796	.003–.0018	—	.0002–.0006	.008–.014	.0078–.0157	.010–.030	.0016–.0031	.0016–.0031	.0015–.0073
5.7L	2005–08	—	.0008–.0019③	.9448–.9449	.00035–.00070	.0090–.0149	.0137–.0236	.0059–.0259	.0007–.0026	.0007–.0026	.0007–.0091
6.1L	2006–08	—	.00096–.0020	.9843–.9844	.00023–.00059	.0118–.0157	.0137–.0236	.0079–.028	.0007–.0026	.0007–.0022	.0007–.0091

DOHC — Dual Overhead Cam

SOHC — Single Overhead Cam

① — Measured at .866 inch from bottom of skirt.

② — Measured at .42 inch from bottom of skirt.

③ — Measure 1.5 inches below deck.

④ — Avenger & 2007–08 Sebring Sedan.

⑤ — A, 3.4644–3.4652 in.; B, 3.4648–3.4656 in.; C, 3.4652–3.4659 in.

CYLINDER BLOCK

All measurements given in inches, unless otherwise specified.

Engine	Year	Cylinder Bore Diameter (Std.)	Cylinder Bore Taper (Max.)	Cylinder Bore Out Of Round (Max.)
1.8L DOHC	2007–08	②	.002	.0002
2.0L DOHC	2007–08	②	.001	.0008
2.0L SOHC	2004–05	3.4446–3.4452	.0020	.0020
2.4L DOHC	2004–05	3.4446–3.4452	.0020	.0020
2.4L DOHC	2007–08	②	.001	.0008
2.4L SOHC	2004–05	3.4100–3.4110	.0003	.00003
2.7L DOHC	2004	3.3856–3.3862	.0020	.0030
2.7L DOHC ①	2007–08	3.3856–3.3862	.002	.003
3.0L SOHC	2004–05	3.5900–3.5910	.0003	.0003
3.2L SOHC 18-Valve	2004–05	3.5390–3.5400	.0110	.0050
3.5L SOHC	2004–05	3.7797–3.7803	.0020	.0030
3.5L SOHC ①	2008	3.780–3.783	.002	.003
5.7L	2005–08	3.9170	.0005	.0003
6.1L	2006–08	4.055	.0005	.0003

DOHC — Dual Overhead Cam

SOHC — Single Overhead Cam

① — Avenger & 2007–08 Sebring Sedan

② — Bore A, 3.4645–3.4649 in.; B, 3.4649–3.4653 in.; C, 3.4653–3.4657 in.

ENGINE REBUILDING SPECIFICATIONS

OIL PUMP

All measurements given in inches, unless otherwise specified.

Engine	Year	Rotor Backlash	Rotor To Body Clearance②	Rotor Endplay ①	Rotor Thickness (Minimum)		Outer Rotor Diameter (Minimum)	Maximum Cover Flatness Variation	Relief Spring Free Length	Relief Spring Pressure, Lbs. @ Inches
					Inner	Outer				
1.8L DOHC	2007–08 ⑤	—	—	—	—	—	—	—	—	—
2.0L DOHC	2007–08 ⑤	—	—	—	—	—	—	—	—	—
2.0L SOHC	2004–05	.0080	.0040	.0040	.3010	.3010	3.1480	.003	2.390	18.0–19.0 @ 1.600
2.4L DOHC	2004–06	.0080	.0040	.0040	.4210	.4210	3.3830	.001	—	—
2.4L DOHC	2007–08⑤	—	—	—	—	—	—	—	—	—
2.4L SOHC	2004–05	—	③	—	—	—	—	—	—	—
2.7L DOHC	2004	.0080	.0030	—	.3731–.3741	.3731–.3741	3.5109	.001	—	—
2.7L DOHC ④	2007–08	.0080	.0030	—	.3731–.3741	.3731–.3741	3.5109	.001	—	—
3.0L SOHC	2004–05	.0030–.0070	.0040–.0130	.0020–.0030	—	—	—	—	—	—
3.2L SOHC 18-Valve	2004–06	—	—	—	—	—	—	—	—	—
3.5L SOHC	2004–06	.0030	.0150	.0030	.5630	.5630	3.1490	.001	—	—
3.5L SOHC ④	2007–08	.003	—	—	—	—	3.149	.001	—	—
5.7L	2005–08	.0060	.0038	.0090	—	—	—	—	—	—
6.1L	2006–08	.006	.0038	.009	—	—	—	—	—	—

DOHC — Dual Overhead Cam

SOHC — Single Overhead Cam

① — Measured between pump cover mounting surface & end of gear using straightedge & feeler gauge.

② — Maximum inner & outer rotor tip clearance.

③ — Drive gear, .004–.006 inch. Driven gear, .003–.004 inch.

④ — Avenger & 2007–08 Sebring Sedan.

⑤ — The oil pump is integral to the balance shaft module BSM. The oil pump cannot be disassembled for inspection.

FORD MOTOR COMPANY

Page No.   Page No.

FORD

Crown Victoria	2-1
Focus	6-1
Freestyle	7-1
Fusion	1-1
Mustang	4-1
Taurus (2004-07)	5-1
Taurus & Taurus X (2008)	7-1
Thunderbird	3-1
500	7-1

LINCOLN

LS	3-1
MKZ	1-1
Town Car	2-1
Zephyr	1-1

MERCURY

Grand Marquis	2-1
Marauder	2-1
Milan	1-1
Montego	7-1
Sable (2004-07)	5-1
Sable (2008)	7-1

GENERAL SERVICE

Active Suspension Systems (Volume 2)	7-1
Air Bag Systems (Volume 2)	4-1
Air Conditioning	8-1
Alternators	11-1
Anti-Lock Brakes (Volume 2)	6-1
Cooling Fans	9-1
Cruise Control (Volume 2)	2-1
Dash Gauges (Volume 2)	1-1
Dash Panel Service (Volume 2)	5-1
Disc Brakes	14-1
Drum Brakes	15-1
Engine Rebuilding Specifications	21-1
Front Drive Axles	18-1
Gauges, Dash (Volume 2)	1-1
Hydraulic Brake Systems	16-1
Machine Shop Specifications	21-1
Passive Restraint Systems (Volume 2)	4-1
Power Brake Units	17-1
Power Steering	13-1
Rear Drive Axles	19-1
Speed Controls (Volume 2)	2-1
Starter Motors	10-1
Steering Columns	12-1
Supplemental Restraint Systems (Volume 2)	4-1
Tire Pressure Monitoring Systems	20-1
Wiper Systems (Volume 2)	3-1

FORD MOTOR COMPANY

Page No.

Page No.

FORD

Crown Victoria 2-1
Focus. 6-1
Freestyle 7-1
Fusion 1-1
Mustang 4-1
Taurus (2004-07) 5-1
Taurus & Taurus X (2008) 7-1
Thunderbird. 3-1
500 7-1

LINCOLN

LS. 3-1
MKZ 1-1
Town Car 2-1
Zephyr 1-1

MERCURY

Grand Marquis 2-1
Marauder 2-1
Milan 1-1
Montego 7-1
Sable (2004-07) 5-1
Sable (2008). 7-1

GENERAL SERVICE

Active Suspension Systems (Volume 2). 7-1
Air Bag Systems (Volume 2) 4-1
Air Conditioning 8-1
Alternators 11-1
Anti-Lock Brakes (Volume 2). 6-1
Cooling Fans 9-1
Cruise Control (Volume 2) 2-1
Dash Gauges (Volume 2) 1-1
Dash Panel Service (Volume 2) 5-1
Disc Brakes. 14-1
Drum Brakes. 15-1
Engine Rebuilding Specifications 21-1
Front Drive Axles 18-1
Gauges, Dash (Volume 2) 1-1
Hydraulic Brake Systems 16-1
Machine Shop Specifications 21-1
Passive Restraint Systems (Volume 2). 4-1
Power Brake Units. 17-1
Power Steering. 13-1
Rear Drive Axles. 19-1
Speed Controls (Volume 2) 2-1
Starter Motors 10-1
Steering Columns. 12-1
Supplemental Restraint Systems (Volume 2) 4-1
Tire Pressure Monitoring Systems 20-1
Wiper Systems (Volume 2) 3-1

FUSION, MILAN, MKZ & ZEPHYR

NOTE: Refer To The Rear Of This Manual For Vehicle Manufacturer's Special Service Tools.

INDEX OF SERVICE OPERATIONS

Page No.

AIR BAG SYSTEM
PRECAUTIONS 0-18
BRAKES
  Anti-Lock Brakes (Volume 2) .. 6-1
  Disc Brakes 14-1
  Drum Brakes 15-1
  Hydraulic Brake Systems 16-1
  Power Brake Units 17-1
COMPUTER RELEARN
PROCEDURE 0-31
ELECTRICAL
  Air Bag System (Volume 2) ... 4-1
  Air Conditioning 8-1
  Alternator, Replace 1-4
  Alternators 11-1
  Blower Motor, Replace 1-7
  Cooling Fans 9-1
  Cruise Control (Volume 2) 2-1
  Dash Gauges (Volume 2) 1-1
  Dash Panel Service
  (Volume 2) 5-1
  Evaporator Core, Replace 1-7
  Fuel Pump Relay Location 1-4
  Fuse Panel & Flasher
  Location 1-4
  Headlamp Switch, Replace ... 1-5
  Heater Core, Replace 1-7
  Ignition Lock, Replace 1-5
  Ignition Switch, Replace 1-5
  Instrument Cluster, Replace ... 1-5
  Multi-Function Switch,
  Replace 1-5
  Neutral Safety Switch,
  Replace 1-5
  Passive Restraint Systems
  (Volume 2) 4-1
  Precautions 1-4
  Radio, Replace 1-6
  Speed Controls (Volume 2) ... 2-1
  Starter Motors 10-1
  Starter, Replace 1-4
  Steering Columns 12-1
  Steering Wheel, Replace 1-5
  Stop Light Switch, Replace ... 1-5
  Wiper Motor, Replace 1-6
  Wiper Switch, Replace 1-7
  Wiper Systems (Volume 2) 3-1
  Wiper Transmission, Replace . 1-7
ELECTRICAL SYMBOL
IDENTIFICATION 0-63
FRONT DRIVE AXLES 18-1
NON-STANDARD TIRE &
WHEEL SIZE
ADJUSTMENT TO RIDE
HEIGHT SPECIFICATIONS
& TIRE SIZE CHART 0-61
FRONT SUSPENSION &
STEERING
  Ball Joint, Replace 1-48
  Ball Joint Inspection 1-48

Page No.

  Coil Spring & Strut Service 1-48
  Control Arm, Replace 1-49
  Power Steering 13-1
  Power Steering Gear,
  Replace 1-50
  Power Steering Pump,
  Replace 1-50
  Stabilizer Bar, Replace 1-49
  Stabilizer Bar Link, Replace ... 1-49
  Steering Columns 12-1
  Steering Knuckle, Replace 1-49
  Strut, Replace 1-48
  Technical Service Bulletins 1-51
  Tightening Specifications 1-57
  Wheel Bearing, Replace 1-48
REAR SUSPENSION
  Coil Spring, Replace 1-40
  Control Arm, Replace 1-40
  Hub & Bearing, Replace 1-39
  Shock Absorber, Replace 1-39
  Stabilizer Bar, Replace 1-40
  Tightening Specifications 1-47
  Toe Link, Replace 1-40
  Trailing Arm, Replace 1-40
  Wheel Bearing, Adjust 1-39
  Wheel Knuckle, Replace 1-39
  Wheel Spindle, Replace 1-39
  Wheel Spindle, Replace 1-40
SERVICE REMINDER &
WARNING LAMP RESET
PROCEDURES 0-34
SPECIFICATIONS
  Fluid Capacities & Cooling
  System Data 1-3
  Front Wheel Alignment
  Specifications 1-2
  General Engine
  Specifications 1-2
  Lubricant Data 1-3
  Rear Wheel Alignment
  Specifications 1-2
  Tune Up Specifications 1-2
  Vehicle Ride Height
  Specifications 1-3
VEHICLE
IDENTIFICATION 0-1
VEHICLE LIFT POINTS 0-51
VEHICLE MAINTENANCE
SCHEDULES 0-73
WHEEL ALIGNMENT
  Front Wheel Alignment 1-58
  Preliminary Inspection 1-58
  Rear Wheel Alignment 1-58
  Wheel Alignment
  Specifications 1-2
WIRE COLOR CODE
IDENTIFICATION 0-63
2.3L ENGINE
  Compression Pressure 1-9
  Cooling System Bleed 1-11

Page No.

  Engine Rebuilding
  Specifications 21-1
  Engine, Replace 1-9
  Engine Mount, Replace 1-9
  Fuel Filter, Replace 1-11
  Fuel Pump, Replace 1-11
  Precautions 1-9
  Radiator, Replace 1-11
  Tightening Specifications 1-15
3.0L ENGINE
  Compression Pressure 1-16
  Engine Rebuilding
  Specifications 21-1
  Engine, Replace 1-17
  Engine Mount, Replace 1-16
  Fuel Filter, Replace 1-18
  Fuel Pump, Replace 1-18
  Precautions 1-16
  Radiator, Replace 1-18
  Tightening Specifications 1-20
3.5L ENGINE
  Camshaft, Replace 1-29
  Camshaft Lobe Lift
  Specifications 1-27
  Compression Pressure 1-21
  Cooling System Bleed 1-30
  Crankshaft Damper, Replace .. 1-27
  Cylinder Head, Replace 1-25
  Engine Rebuilding
  Specifications 21-1
  Engine, Replace 1-22
  Engine Mount, Replace 1-22
  Exhaust Manifold, Replace 1-24
  Front Cover, Replace 1-27
  Front Cover Seal, Replace 1-28
  Fuel Pump, Replace 1-31
  Intake Manifold, Replace 1-24
  Oil Pan, Replace 1-29
  Oil Pump, Replace 1-30
  Power Transfer Unit Seal,
  Replace 1-24
  Precautions 1-21
  Radiator, Replace 1-31
  Serpentine Drive Belt 1-30
  Thermostat, Replace 1-30
  Tightening Specifications 1-38
  Timing Chain, Replace 1-29
  Valve Adjustment 1-27
  Valve Clearance
  Specifications 1-27
  Valve Cover, Replace 1-26
  Water Pump, Replace 1-30

FUSION, MILAN, MKZ & ZEPHYR

Specifications

GENERAL ENGINE SPECIFICATIONS

Engine	Year	Fuel System	Bore & Stroke	Comp. Ratio	Net H.P. @ RPM	Maximum Torque/Ft. Lbs. @ RPM	Normal Oil Pressure, psi
2.3L	2006–08	SFI	3.44 x 3.70	9.7	151 @ 5750	154 @ 4250	29–39
3.0L	2006–08	SFI	3.50 x 3.13	10.0	200 @ 5700	200 @ 4400	11①
3.5L	2007–08	SFI	3.64 x 3.41	10.3	250 @ 6250	240 @ 4500	—

SFI — Sequential Fuel Injection   ① — At 1500 RPM with engine hot.

TUNE UP SPECIFICATIONS

Liter	Spark Plug Gap	Ignition Timing, °BTDC				Curb Idle Speed, RPM		Fast Idle Speed, RPM		Fuel Pump Pressure, psi	Valve Clearance
		Firing Order Fig. ②	Man. Trans.	Auto. Trans.	Mark	Man. Trans.	Auto. Trans.	Man. Trans.	Auto. Trans.		
2.3L	.049–.053	⑧	⑦	—	⑧	④	④	④	④	57	⑤
3.0L	.054	③	—	⑦	①	—	④	—	④	65	⑥
3.5L	.051–.057	⑨	—	⑦	—	—	④	—	④	65	⑩

BTDC — Before Top Dead Center

① — Equipped w/crankshaft position sensor.

② — Before disconnecting wires from distributor cap or coil, determine location of wire, as position may have been altered from that mounting at end of this chart.

③ — Coil on plug ignition system. Cylinder numbering front to rear, **Fig. A**, righthand bank, 1, 2, 3 ; lefthand bank, 4, 5, 6. Firing order 1-4-2-5-3-6.

④ — Idle speed is controlled by an automatic idle control system.

⑤ — Intake, .008–.011 inch; exhaust, .010–.023 inch.

⑥ — Equipped w/hydraulic valve lifters; no provision for adjustment.

⑦ — Non-adjustable.

⑧ — Cylinder numbering from front to rear of engine, 1-2-3-4. Firing order, 1-3-4-2.

⑨ — Firing order 1-4-2-3-5-6.

⑩ — Intake, .006–.010 inch; exhaust, .0118–.0157 inch.

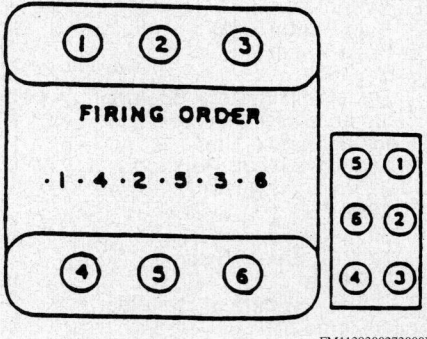

FIRING ORDER

· 1 · 4 · 2 · 5 · 3 · 6

FM1139300273000X

Fig. A

FRONT WHEEL ALIGNMENT SPECIFICATIONS

Model	Caster Angle°		Camber Angle°		Total Toe°		Ball Joint Wear
	Limits	Desired	Limits	Desired	Limits	Desired	
All	−1.0 to +1.0	0	−1.0 to +1.0	0	.0 to +.40	+.20	①

① — Refer to Ball Joint Inspection in Front Suspension & Steering section.

REAR WHEEL ALIGNMENT SPECIFICATIONS

Model	Camber°		Total Toe-In°	
	Limits	Desired	Limits	Desired
All	−1.0 to +1.0	0	+.04 to +.44	+.24

VEHICLE RIDE HEIGHT SPECIFICATIONS

Model	Year	Manufacturer's Original Tire Size	Front				Rear			
					Measurement Points & Specifications					
			Dim.	Specification			Dim.	Specification		
				Inches	mm			Inches	mm	
All (AWD)	2006–08	①	②	1.93–3.41	49–47		③	1.95–2.13	29–75	
All (FWD)	2006–08	①	②	1.93–3.41	49–47		③	2.46–2.64	42–88	

AWD — All Wheel Drive

FWD — Front Wheel Drive

Dim. — Dimension

① — See door sticker or inside of glove box for manufacturers original tire size specifications. If tires on vehicle do not match manufacturers original tire size & measurement is not within limits, it will be required to refer to the Non-Standard Tire & Wheel Size Adjustment To Ride Height Specification & Tire Size Adjustment Charts.

② — Front ride height is the difference between dimension A and B, **Fig. A.**

③ — Rear ride height is the difference between dimension A and B, **Fig. B.**

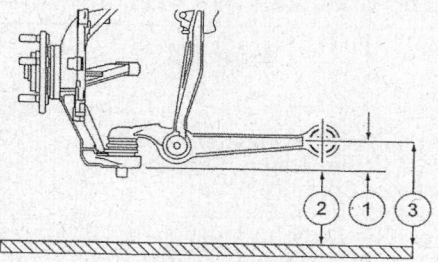

Item	Description
1	Ride height = B - A
2	Measurement A
3	Measurement B

ARM0500000000105

Fig. A Front ride height measurement

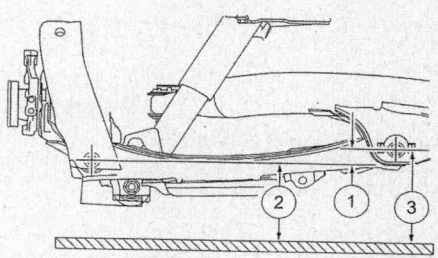

Item	Description
1	Ride height = B - A
2	Measurement A
3	Measurement B

ARM0500000000106

Fig. B Rear ride height measurement

FLUID CAPACITIES & COOLING SYSTEM DATA

Model	Engine Liter	Coolant Capacity, Qts.	Coolant Type	Radiator Cap Relief Pressure, Lbs.	Thermo. Opening Temp. °F	Fuel Tank Gals.	Engine Oil Refill, Qts.①	Rear Axle (AWD) Pints	Transfer Case., Oz.	Auto. Trans., Qts.④
2006–08	2.3L	8.6	②	13.0–18.0	176–183	17.5	4.8	—	—	③
	3.0L	9.7	②	13.0–18.0	180–203	17.5	6.0	2.4⑥	18⑤	③
2007–08	3.5L	10.0	②	13.0–18.0	187	17.5⑦	5.5	2.4⑥	18⑤	③

① — Includes filter.

② — Motorcraft premium gold part No. VC-7-B/WSS-M97B51-A1, or equivalent.

③ — 5 speed automatic transaxle – 7.0 qts., use Motorcraft FNR5 ATF/XT-9-QMM5 or equivalent; 6 speed automatic transaxle; 7.4 qts., use Motorcraft Premium ATF/XT-8-QAW.

④ — Approximate; make final inspection w/dipstick.

⑤ — Motorcraft SAE 75W-140 Synthetic rear axle lubricant XY-75W140-QL.

⑥ — Motorcraft SAE 80W-90 Premium rear axle lubricant XY-80W90-QL.

⑦ — FWD 17.5 gallons: AWD 16.5 gallons.

LUBRICANT DATA

Engine	Year	Transaxle		Power Steering	Brake System
		Manual/Transfer Case	Automatic		
2.3L	2006–08	③	—	①	DOT 3
3.0L	2006–08	②	⑤	①	DOT 3
3.5L	2007–08	④	⑤	①	DOT 3

① — Motorcraft MERCON Multi-Purpose ATF part No. XT-2-QDX, or equivalent.

② — SAE 80W-90 premium rear axle lubricant part No. XY-80W-90–QL, or equivalent.

③ — Transaxle fluid meeting Ford specification WSD-M2C200–C.

④ — Transfer case use Motorcraft SAE 75W-140 Synthetic rear axle lubricant XY-75W140-QL.

⑤ — 5 speed automatic transaxle use Motorcraft FNR5 ATF/XT-9-QMM5 or equivalent; 6 speed automatic transaxle use Motorcraft Premium ATF/XT-8-QAW.

Electrical

NOTE: On Air Bag Equipped Models, Refer To "Air Bag System Precautions" Located In The Front Of This Manual For System Disarming & Arming Procedures.

NOTE: Refer To "Computer Relearn Procedures" Located In The Front Of This Manual When Battery Power To The Computer Has Been Interrupted.

INDEX

	Page No.		Page No.		Page No.
Air Bag System (Volume 2)	4-1	Fuse Panel & Flasher Location	1-4	MKZ & Zephyr	1-6
Air Conditioning	8-1	Headlamp Switch, Replace	1-5	Fusion & Milan	1-6
Alternator, Replace	1-4	Heater Core, Replace	1-7	Speed Controls (Volume 2)	2-1
2.3L Engine	1-4	Ignition Lock, Replace	1-5	Starter Motors	10-1
3.0L Engine	1-5	Ignition Switch, Replace	1-5	Starter, Replace	1-4
3.5L Engine	1-5	Instrument Cluster, Replace	1-5	2.3L Engine	1-4
Alternators	11-1	Multi-Function Switch, Replace	1-5	3.0L & 3.5L Engines	1-4
Blower Motor, Replace	1-7	Neutral Safety Switch, Replace	1-5	Steering Columns	12-1
Cooling Fans	9-1	Passive Restraint Systems		Steering Wheel, Replace	1-5
Cruise Control (Volume 2)	2-1	(Volume 2)	4-1	Stop Light Switch, Replace	1-5
Dash Gauges (Volume 2)	1-1	Precautions	1-4	Wiper Motor, Replace	1-6
Dash Panel Service		Air Bag Systems	1-4	Wiper Switch, Replace	1-7
(Volume 2)	5-1	Battery Ground Cable	1-4	Wiper Systems (Volume 2)	3-1
Evaporator Core, Replace	1-7	Fuel Pressure Relief	1-4	Wiper Transmission, Replace	1-7
Fuel Pump Relay Location	1-4	Radio, Replace	1-6		

PRECAUTIONS

Air Bag Systems

Refer to "Air Bag System Precautions" in the front of this manual for system disarming and arming procedures.

Battery Ground Cable

Prior to service, disconnect battery ground cable and isolate as required.

Fuel Pressure Relief

1. Remove fuel pump relay.
2. Start engine, then allow engine to idle until it stalls.
3. After engine stalls, crank engine for approximately 5 seconds to make sure fuel injection supply manifold pressure has been released.
4. When fuel system service is complete, install fuel pump relay.
5. Cycle ignition key and wait 3 seconds to pressurize fuel system. Inspect for leaks before starting engine.

FUSE PANEL & FLASHER LOCATION

The engine compartment power distribution center is located on the front lefthand side of the engine compartment. The fuse panel is located under the instrument panel, left of the steering column. The combination turn signal/hazard flasher is located behind the lefthand side of the instrument panel reinforcement, in the Smart Junction Box (SJB).

FUEL PUMP RELAY LOCATION

On 2006 models, the fuel pump relay is located in the engine compartment, in the battery junction box, relay/fuse number 30.
On 2007–08 models, the fuel pump relay is located in the engine compartment, in the battery junction box, relay number 54.

STARTER
REPLACE

The heavy gauge input lead connected to the starter solenoid is hot at all times. Ensure the protective cap is installed over the terminal and is replaced after service.

2.3L Engine

1. Raise and support vehicle.
2. Remove seven underbody cover mounting screws, then the cover.
3. Remove starter motor solenoid wire nut and position wire aside.
4. Position starter motor solenoid battery cable terminal cover aside.
5. Disconnect wiring harness retainer from top and bottom starter motor stud bolt and position wiring harness aside.
6. Remove two starter motor stud bolts, then the starter.
7. Reverse procedure to install. **Torque** starter mounting bolts to 18 ft. lbs.

3.0L & 3.5L Engines

1. Remove air cleaner outlet pipe.
2. Remove battery tray.
3. Remove starter motor solenoid wire nut and position wire aside.
4. Remove starter solenoid safety cap.
5. Remove starter solenoid and ground stud cables.
6. Remove mounting bolts, stud and starter.
7. Reverse procedure to install. **Torque** starter mounting bolts to 20 ft. lbs.

ALTERNATOR
REPLACE

2.3L Engine

1. Remove bolt, two nuts and alternator upper air duct.
2. Rotate accessory drive belt tensioner clockwise, then position accessory drive belt aside.
3. Remove two nuts and alternator shield.
4. Press locking tabs and remove alternator intermediate air duct.
5. Position alternator protective cover aside, remove nuts and position alternator terminal wires aside.
6. Release alternator harness locator from engine block.
7. Disconnect CKP sensor connector, then position alternator harness aside.
8. Remove three bolts, then alternator lower air duct.

9. Remove two alternator mounting bolts, then the alternator.
10. Reverse procedure to install. **Torque** alternator mounting bolts to 18 ft. lbs.

3.0L Engine

1. Remove accessory drive belt.
2. Remove A/C compressor mounting bolts, then position compressor with lines attached aside.
3. Remove mounting nut, then position engine control sensor wiring and hose bracket aside.
4. Remove inboard upper alternator mounting bolt.
5. Loosen outboard upper alternator bolt.
6. Disconnect electrical harness connector and output terminal wiring.
7. Remove alternator splash shield and outboard upper alternator bolt.
8. Remove lower alternator bolt.
9. Remove alternator.
10. Reverse procedure to install, noting the following:
    a. **Torque** alternator mounting bolts to 35 ft. lbs.
    b. **Torque** alternator output terminal nut to 80–106 inch lbs.

3.5L Engine

1. Remove accessory drive belt.
2. Remove A/C compressor mounting bolts, then position compressor with lines attached aside.
3. Position alternator protective cover aside. Remove B+ terminal nut, place terminal wire aside.
4. Remove pin type alternator retainer and wiring harness.
5. Remove oil filter.
6. Remove alternator mounting nut and bolt, then alternator.
7. Reverse procedure to install, noting the following:
    a. **Torque** alternator mounting bolts to 35 ft. lbs.
    b. **Torque** alternator output B+ terminal nut to 108 inch lbs.

IGNITION LOCK

REPLACE

1. Remove three lower steering column shroud screws, then the lower shroud.
2. Place upper steering column shroud aside.
3. Disconnect Passive Anti-Theft System (PATS) transceiver electrical connector, then the PATS transceiver.
4. Turn ignition switch to ON position.
5. Using a suitable tool press ignition lock cylinder release button, remove ignition lock.
6. Reverse procedure to install.

IGNITION SWITCH

REPLACE

The instrument panel steering column cover is held in place by tabs that clip to the instrument panel.
1. Remove instrument panel steering column cover by pulling straight outward.

2. Release upper steering column shroud, by pressing inward on sides of shroud and lifting upward.
3. Release tilt lever, then remove lower steering column shroud screws and shroud.
4. Lower steering column to lowest tilt position.
5. Disconnect ignition switch electrical connector.
6. Press two tabs and remove ignition switch.
7. Reverse procedure to install. Ensure proper installation by rotating ignition switch through it's travel range.

NEUTRAL SAFETY SWITCH

REPLACE

Neutral safety switch functions are incorporated into the Transaxle Range (TR) sensor.
1. Place manual control lever in Neutral position.
2. Remove engine air cleaner and outlet tube.
3. Disconnect TR sensor electrical connector.
4. Remove manual control lever from transaxle.
5. Remove mounting bolts and TR sensor.
6. Reverse procedure to install, noting the following:
    a. Ensure manual control lever is in Neutral position.
    b. Install transaxle range sensor and mounting bolts loosely.
    c. Align position sensor using manual lever position sensor alignment tool No. T92P-70010-AH, or equivalent.
    d. **Torque** sensor mounting bolts to 89 inch lbs.
    e. **Torque** manual lever mounting nut to 16 ft. lbs.

HEADLAMP SWITCH

REPLACE

1. Remove lefthand instrument panel side, finish panel.
2. Release tabs and remove headlamp switch by pushing from behind.
3. Disconnect headlamp switch electrical connectors.
4. Reverse procedure to install.

STOP LIGHT SWITCH

REPLACE

The stop light switch is self-adjusting. Do not press the brake pedal during installation. Initial installation of the stop light switch allows for one adjustment. If additional adjustments are required, install a new stop light switch.
1. Disconnect stop light switch electrical connector.
2. Rotate switch clockwise 45°, then remove the switch.
3. Reverse procedure to install.

MULTI-FUNCTION SWITCH

REPLACE

The Multi-Function Switch contains the windshield wiper, turn signal, flash-to-pass and high and low beam switches.

The instrument panel steering column cover is held in place by tabs that clip to the instrument panel.
1. Place ignition switch in RUN position.
2. Remove instrument panel steering column cover by pulling straight outward.
3. Release upper steering column shroud, by pressing inward on sides of shroud and lifting upward.
4. Release tilt lever, then remove lower steering column shroud screws and shroud.
5. Lower steering column to lowest tilt position.
6. Disconnect multi-function switch electrical connector.
7. Remove two multi-function switch screws, then the switch.
8. Reverse procedure to install.

STEERING WHEEL

REPLACE

1. Place front wheels in straight-ahead position.
2. Remove driver's side air bag module as outlined in "Passive Restraints Systems" chapter.
3. Mark steering wheel and column shaft for installation reference. Remove steering wheel mounting nut.
4. Remove steering wheel using suitable steering wheel puller.
5. Reverse procedure to install, noting the following:
    a. Align steering shaft alignment marks.
    b. **Torque** steering wheel mounting nut to 26 ft. lbs.

INSTRUMENT CLUSTER

REPLACE

Module configuration is only required if a new instrument cluster is being installed.
1. If a new instrument cluster is being installed proceed as follows:
    a. Connect suitably programed scan tool to DLC.
    b. Upload module configuration information to diagnostic tool, following manufacturers instructions.
2. Tilt steering wheel to its lowest possible position.
3. **On MKZ and Zephyr models,** proceed as follows:
    a. Remove instrument finish panel mounting screws, then the finish panel.
    b. Remove instrument cluster mounting screws and pull top of cluster toward steering wheel.
    c. Disconnect electrical connectors behind instrument cluster.
    d. Remove instrument cluster.
4. **On Fusion and Milan models,** proceed as follows:

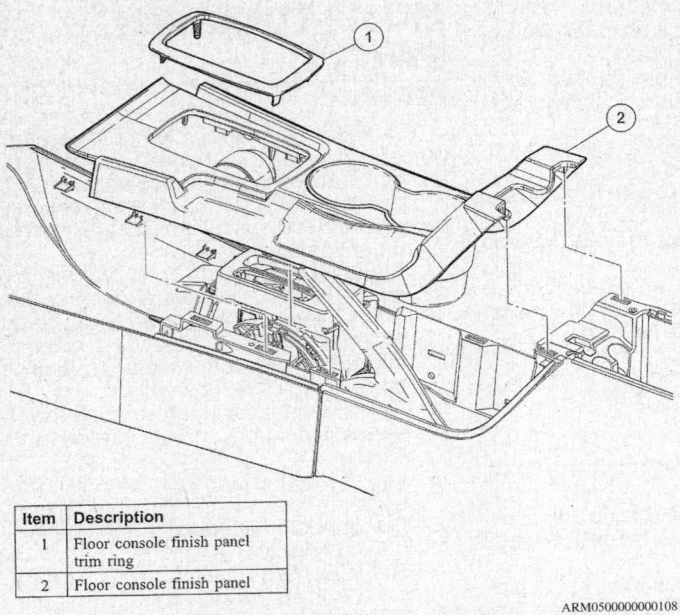

Item	Description
1	Floor console finish panel trim ring
2	Floor console finish panel

ARM0500000000108

Fig. 1   Floor console finish panel replacement. MKZ & Zephyr

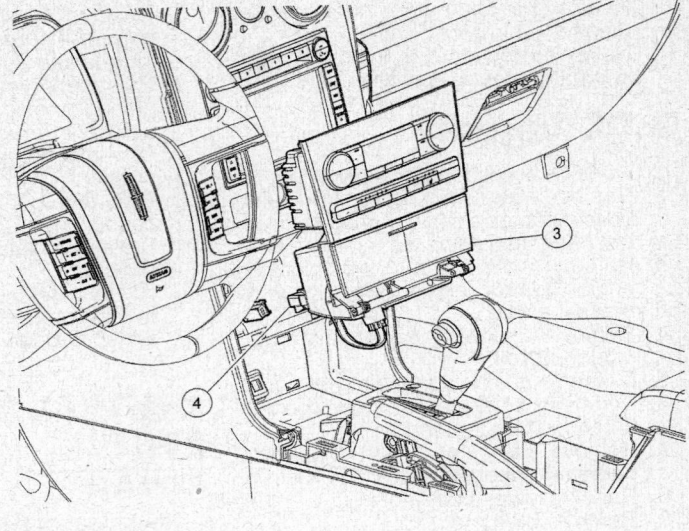

Item	Description
3	Climate control and bezel assembly
4	Climate control and bezel assembly electrical connectors

ARM0500000000109

Fig. 2   Climate control and bezel assembly replacement. MKZ & Zephyr

a. Remove finish panel by pull upward to release from spring clips.
b. Remove two instrument cluster attaching screws from bottom of instrument cluster.
c. Insert a suitable tool between instrument panel and top of instrument cluster. Use a slight outward motion until top of cluster is released.
d. Disconnect electrical connectors behind instrument cluster.
e. Remove instrument cluster.
5. **On all models,** reverse procedure to install noting the following:
   a. If a new instrument cluster is installed download the instrument cluster configuration information.

RADIO

REPLACE

Fusion & Milan

Module configuration is only required if a new audio unit is being installed.
1. Connect suitably programed scan tool to DLC.
2. Upload audio unit configuration information to diagnostic tool, following manufacturers instructions.
3. Disengage retaining clips, then remove center instrument cluster finish panel.
4. Remove four audio unit mounting screws.
5. Disconnect audio unit electrical connectors and antenna lead-in cable.
6. Remove audio unit.
7. Reverse procedure to install. If a new unit was installed, download configuration information from scan tool to audio unit.

MKZ & Zephyr

Module configuration is only required if a new audio unit is being installed.
1. Connect suitably programed scan tool to DLC.
2. Upload audio unit configuration information to diagnostic tool, following manufacturers instructions.
3. **On models equipped with navigation audio unit,** remove navigation digital versatile disc (DVD) before installing a new audio unit.
4. **On all models,** disengage floor console finish panel trim ring clips, **Fig. 1,** then the finish panel. Position parking brake lever all the way back to ease removal.
5. Remove ash tray receptacle to access climate control and bezel assembly retaining screws, **Fig. 2.**
6. Disconnect climate control electrical connectors.
7. Remove climate control and bezel assembly.
8. Remove center A/C duct vents by opening vents and pulling them straight out.
9. Remove center A/C duct retainers using suitable tool to release tabs, then pull retainers out.
10. Remove audio unit and bezel assembly retaining screws.
11. Disconnect audio unit electrical connectors and antenna lead-in cable.
12. Remove audio unit.
13. Reverse procedure to install. If a new unit was installed, download configuration information from scan tool to audio unit.

WIPER MOTOR

REPLACE

The wiper mounting arm and pivot shafts are connected with non-removable plastic ball joints. Except for the wiper motor, the entire wiper transmission assembly is non-serviceable.
1. Note normal park position of wiper arms and blades for installation alignment.
2. Remove upper cowl panel grille as follows:
   a. Remove two wiper pivot arm nuts, then the right and left wiper pivot arms, **Fig. 3.**
   b. Remove two pin type retainers, two bolts and two retaining clips from upper cowl panel grille.
   c. **On models with 3.5L engines,** insert a flat blade screwdriver behind power steering reservoir, then push retainer rearward to remove power steering reservoir.
   d. Place reservoir aside.
   e. Remove brake fluid reservoir nuts, then brake fluid reservoir. Place aside.
3. **On all models,** disconnect windshield wiper motor electrical connector.
4. Remove two windshield wiper mounting arm and pivot shaft assembly bolts, then the windshield wiper mounting arm and pivot shaft assembly.
5. Reverse procedure to install. **Torque** wiper motor pivot shaft assembly bolts to 44 inch lbs.

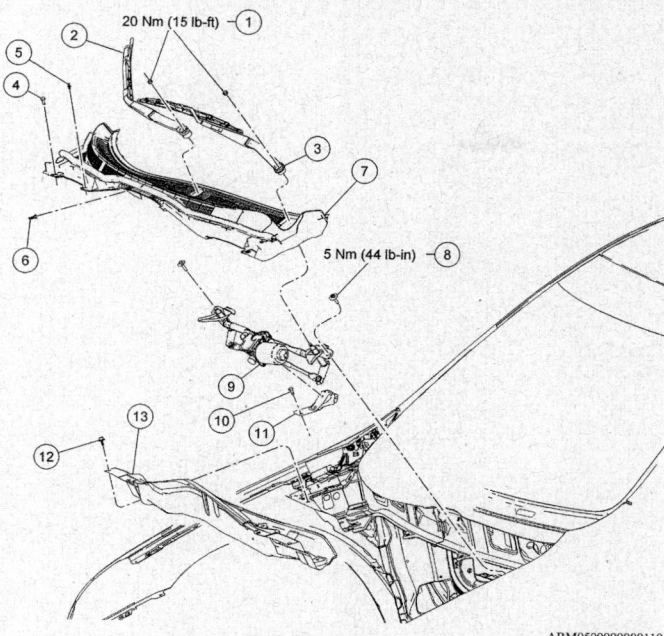

Fig. 3 Cowl panel & wiper motor pivot shaft assembly replacement (Part 1 of 2)

ARM0500000000110

Item	Description
1	Wiper pivot arm nuts (2 required)
2	Wiper pivot arm
3	Wiper pivot arm
4	Cowl panel grille bolt (2 required)
5	Pin-type retainer (2 required)
6	Cowl panel retaining clip (2 required)
7	Upper cowl panel grille
8	Wiper mounting arm and pivot shaft assembly bolt (2 required)
9	Wiper mounting arm and pivot shaft assembly
10	Cowl panel center brace bolt (3 required)
11	Cowl panel center brace
12	Lower cowl panel grille bolt (10 required)
13	Lower cowl panel grille

ARM0500000000111

Fig. 3 Cowl panel & wiper motor pivot shaft assembly replacement (Part 2 of 2)

14. Remove heater core from housing.
15. Reverse procedure to install. **Torque** evaporator and heater core housing assembly mounting bolts to 80 inch lbs.

WIPER SWITCH

REPLACE

Refer to "Multi-Function Switch, Replace" for wiper switch replacement procedure.

WIPER TRANSMISSION

REPLACE

The wiper mounting arm and pivot shafts are connected with non-removable plastic ball joints. Except for the wiper motor, the entire wiper transmission assembly is non-serviceable.
Refer to "Wiper Motor, Replace" for wiper transmission replacement procedure.

BLOWER MOTOR

REPLACE

1. **On MKZ & Zephyr models,** remove righthand lower instrument panel insulator panel.
2. **On all models,** disconnect blower motor electrical connector.
3. Remove mounting screws and blower motor from heater housing.
4. Remove blower motor wheel retaining clip, then the wheel.
5. Reverse procedure to install.

HEATER CORE

REPLACE

1. Remove upper cowl panel grill as outlined under "Wiper Motor Replace."
2. Remove lower cowl panel grill as follows:
   a. Remove wiper mounting arm and pivot shaft assembly.
   b. Remove three lower cowl panel center brace bolt, then the center brace, **Fig. 3.**
   c. Remove ten lower cowl panel grille bolts, then lower panel grille.
3. Drain coolant into suitable container.
4. Recover refrigerant as outlined in "Air Conditioning" chapter.
5. Remove instrument panel as outlined in "Dash Panel Service" chapter.
6. Disconnect heater hoses from core. Plug heater core tubes.
7. Disconnect A/C pressure transducer electrical connector and disconnect wire harness from Thermostatic Expansion Valve (TXV) stud.
8. Remove TXV fitting nut, then disconnect fitting.
9. Remove six evaporator and heater core housing nuts, **Fig. 4.**
10. Remove evaporator and heater core housing.
11. Disconnect wire harness from heater core cover.
12. Remove heater core cover retaining screws, then the cover.
13. Remove dash panel seal from heater core tubes.

EVAPORATOR CORE

REPLACE

1. Remove upper cowl panel grill as outlined under "Wiper Motor Replace."
2. Remove lower cowl panel grill as follows:
   a. Remove wiper mounting arm and pivot shaft assembly.
   b. Remove three lower cowl panel center brace bolt, then the center brace, **Fig. 3.**
   c. Remove ten lower cowl panel grille bolts, then lower panel grille.
3. Recover refrigerant as outlined in "Air Conditioning" chapter.
4. Drain coolant into suitable container.
5. Remove instrument panel as outlined in "Dash Panel Service" chapter.
6. Disconnect wire harness from heater core and evaporator core housing.
7. Remove evaporator core cover screws, **Fig. 5.**
8. Separate both halves of heater core and evaporator core housing.
9. Remove dash panel seal from housing.
10. Remove evaporator core from housing.
11. Reverse procedure to install, noting the following:
   a. Install a new dash panel seal.
   b. **Torque** evaporator and heater core housing assembly mounting bolts to 80 inch lbs.

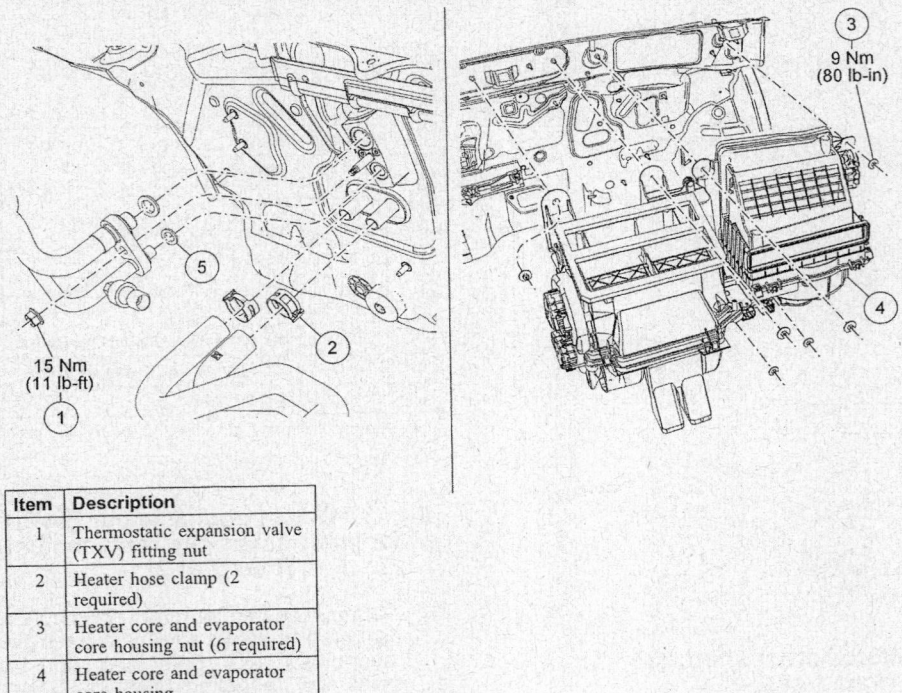

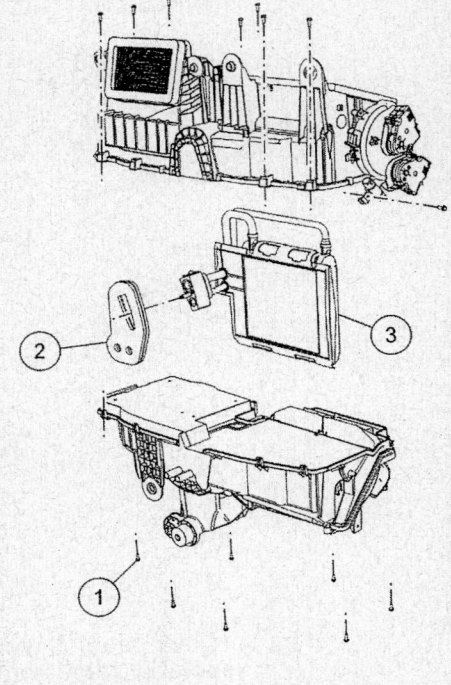

Item	Description
1	Thermostatic expansion valve (TXV) fitting nut
2	Heater hose clamp (2 required)
3	Heater core and evaporator core housing nut (6 required)
4	Heater core and evaporator core housing
5	Gasket seal (2 required)

ARM0500000000112

Fig. 4 Evaporator & heater core housing replacement

Item	Description
1	Evaporator core cover screw (15 required)
2	Dash panel seal
3	Evaporator core

ARM0500000000113

Fig. 5 Evaporator core replacement

NOTE: Refer To The "2.0L (Vin N) & 2.3L (Vin Z) DOHC Engines" Section In The "Focus" Chapter For Procedures Not Found In This Section.

NOTE: On Air Bag Equipped Models, Refer To "Air Bag System Precautions" Located In The Front Of This Manual For System Disarming & Arming Procedures.

NOTE: Refer To "Computer Relearn Procedures" Located In The Front Of This Manual When Battery Power To The Computer Has Been Interrupted.

INDEX

	Page No.
Compression Pressure	1-9
Cooling System Bleed	1-11
Engine Rebuilding Specifications	21-1
Engine, Replace	1-9
Engine Mount, Replace	1-9

	Page No.
Fuel Filter, Replace	1-11
Fuel Pump, Replace	1-11
Precautions	1-9
Air Bag Systems	1-9
Battery Ground Cable	1-9
Fuel Pressure Relief	1-9

	Page No.
Quick Disconnect Hoses	1-9
R-Clip	1-9
Spring Lock	1-9
Vapor Tube	1-9
Radiator, Replace	1-11
Tightening Specifications	1-15

PRECAUTIONS

Air Bag Systems

Refer to "Air Bag System Precautions" in the front of this manual for system disarming and arming procedures.

Battery Ground Cable

Prior to service, disconnect battery ground cable and isolate as required.

Fuel Pressure Relief

1. Remove fuel pump relay.
2. Start engine, then allow engine to idle until it stalls.
3. After engine stalls, crank engine for approximately 5 seconds to ensure fuel injection supply manifold pressure has been released.
4. When fuel system service is complete, install fuel pump relay.
5. Cycle ignition key and wait 3 seconds to pressurize fuel system. Inspect for leaks before starting engine.

Quick Disconnect Hoses

R-CLIP

When working with R-clip type connections, do not use tools to disconnect. Use of tools may deform clip components and could cause leaks.

DISCONNECT

1. Bend shipping tab downward.
2. Spread R-clip and push clip into fitting.
3. Separate fitting from tube.

CONNECT

1. Inspect fitting and tube for damage and ensure connections are clean.
2. Apply light coat of suitable, clean engine oil to male end of tube.
3. Insert R-clip into fitting.
4. Align tube and fitting, then insert tube into fitting and push together until click is heard.
5. Pull on connection to ensure it is fully engaged.

SPRING LOCK

When working with spring lock type connections, spring lock tool set No. T84L-19623-B, or equivalent, must be used to disconnect fittings.

When connecting spring lock type fittings, proceed as follows:
1. Inspect and clean both coupling ends.
2. Lubricate fuel line O-ring seals with suitable, clean engine oil.
3. When connection is made, pull on line to ensure it is fully engaged.

VAPOR TUBE

To disconnect vapor tube connections, squeeze fitting and disconnect vapor tube from fitting.

To connect, proceed as follows:
1. Ensure fittings are clean and free from damage.
2. Push tube onto fitting until it snaps into place.
3. Pull on connection to verify fitting is secure.

COMPRESSION PRESSURE

1. Ensure crankcase oil is of correct viscosity and at correct level.
2. Ensure battery is fully charged and engine is at normal operating temperature.
3. Turn ignition switch to OFF position.
4. Remove spark plugs.
5. Set throttle plates to wide open position.
6. Install suitable compression gauge in cylinder No. 1.
7. Install auxiliary starter switch in starting circuit.
8. With ignition switch off, crank engine at least five compression strokes using auxiliary starter switch.
9. Record number of compression strokes required to reach highest reading, then record highest reading.
10. Repeat test on each cylinder, cranking engine same number of compression strokes.
11. Lowest cylinder reading must be within 75% of highest reading.

ENGINE MOUNT
REPLACE

1. Remove mounting bolts and position expansion tank aside.
2. Support engine using three-bar engine support tool No. 303–F072, or equivalent.
3. Remove mounting nuts, **Fig. 1,** bolts and engine mount.
4. Remove procedure to install.

ENGINE
REPLACE

1. Relieve fuel system pressure as outlined under "Precautions."
2. Recover air conditioning refrigerant as outlined in "Air Conditioning" chapter.
3. Place steering wheel in straight ahead position and ignition key in Off position.

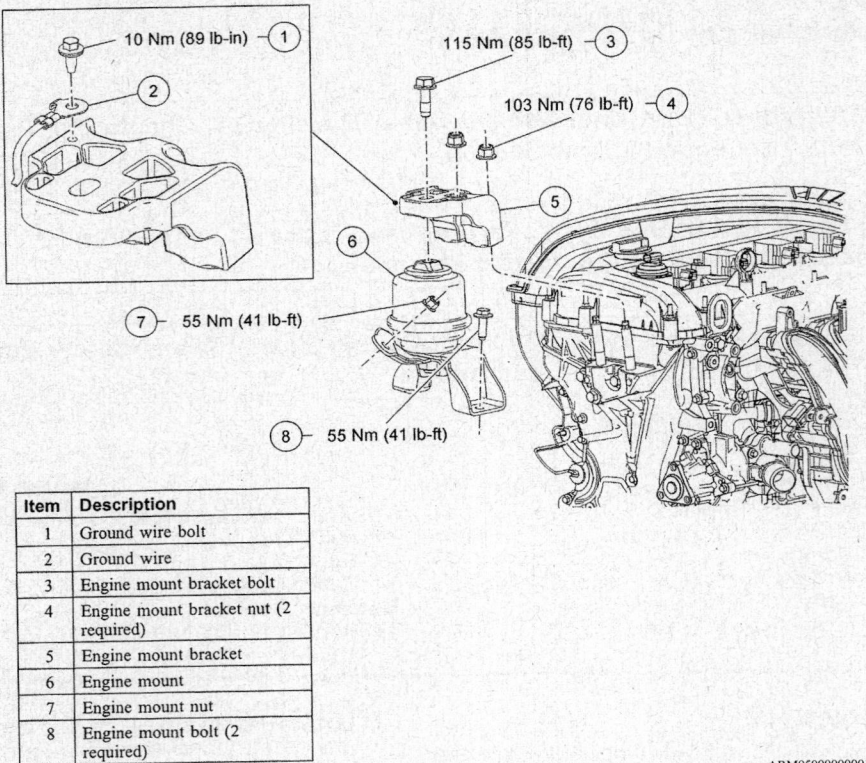

Item	Description
1	Ground wire bolt
2	Ground wire
3	Engine mount bracket bolt
4	Engine mount bracket nut (2 required)
5	Engine mount bracket
6	Engine mount
7	Engine mount nut
8	Engine mount bolt (2 required)

ARM0500000000114

Fig. 1 Engine mount replacement

4. Remove two steering joint cover retaining nuts, then the cover.
5. Index steering column shaft position to steering gear for reference during installation.
6. Remove steering column shaft to steering gear bolt, then disconnect shaft from gear box. **Do not allow intermediate shaft to rotate while it is disconnected from gear or damage to clockspring can occur.**
7. Remove bolt and disconnect power steering pressure (PSP) tube from power steering pump.
8. Drain engine coolant into suitable container.
9. Remove seven underbody cover screws, then cover if equipped.
10. Remove exhaust flexible pipe.
11. Release four clips, then slide steering gear to dash seal off of steering gear and into the passenger compartment. **Steering gear to dash seal must be removed or it will be damaged when lowering subframe.**
12. Remove engine roll restrictor mounting bolts, then the roll restrictor.
13. Remove righthand fender splash shield screws and position shield aside.
14. Remove 6 pin-type retainers, then righthand underbody splash shield.
15. Remove lefthand fender splash shield screws and position shield aside.
16. Remove 6 pin-type retainers, then lefthand underbody splash shield.
17. Remove cotter pins and nuts from both tie-rod ends.
18. Separate tie rod ends from steering knuckles using tie rod removal tool No.

211–105, or equivalent.
19. Disconnect power steering cooler tube.
20. Remove nuts and separate righthand and lefthand sway bar links from struts.
21. **Place a suitable block of wood, or equivalent, between righthand and lefthand lower arm and outer CV joints to prevent lower arm from striking outer CV joint.**
22. Remove lower ball joint nuts.
23. Separate ball joints from lower control arms using ball joint removal tool No. 205–592, or equivalent.
24. Remove lower control arm through bolts.
25. Position powertrain lift tool No. 014–00765, or equivalent, under subframe assembly.
26. Remove righthand and lefthand subframe bracket to body mounting bolts.
27. Remove two righthand and lefthand subframe bracket to body bolts.
28. Remove righthand and lefthand subframe nuts to subframe brackets, then the subframe brackets.
29. Remove front subframe nuts, then lower subframe from vehicle.
30. Drain engine oil into suitable container. Remove and discard oil filter.
31. Remove alternator air inlet duct, then engine air cleaner and air cleaner outlet pipe.
32. Remove battery, then battery tray.
33. Disconnect two main engine wiring harness electrical connectors, **Fig. 2.**
34. Disconnect engine to strut tower ground strap, then position strap aside.
35. Disconnect Powertrain Control Mod-

ule (PCM) electrical connector and pin-type retainer.
36. Disconnect fuel supply tube quick disconnect coupler from fuel rail as outlined under "Quick Disconnect Hoses."
37. Remove crankcase vent tube from valve cover.
38. Depress locking ring on brake booster vacuum supply tube, remove from intake manifold.
39. Remove evaporative emissions tube from intake manifold.
40. Remove evaporative emissions tube from retaining clip and position aside.
41. Remove upper and lower radiator hose from coolant bypass.
42. Disconnect engine block heater electrical connector, if equipped.
43. Disconnect heater hose inline connection.
44. **On models equipped with automatic transaxle,** proceed as follows:
    a. Disconnect transaxle control cable from transaxle selector lever.
    b. Remove transaxle control cable bracket bolts and position cable aside.
    c. Remove radio frequency interference capacitor attaching bolt from engine block, then capacitor and ground wire. Place aside.
    d. Remove coolant vent hose retaining clip from A/C tube.
    e. Remove power steering cooler tube.
45. **On models equipped with manual transaxle,** proceed as follows:
    a. Remove two clutch tube bracket bolts.
    b. Remove clutch slave cylinder attaching bolts, then the clutch slave cylinder.
    c. Disconnect transaxle control cables from control levers, then remove cables from bracket.
    d. Remove power steering cooler tube.
    e. Remove radio frequency interference capacitor attaching bolt from engine block, then capacitor and ground wire. Place aside.
    f. Remove coolant vent hose retaining clip from A/C tube.
46. **On all models,** remove A/C tube bracket bolts.
47. Remove A/C tube to condenser nuts, then the tube.
48. Remove radio frequency interference capacitor from engine mount bracket.
49. Remove retaining clip from lower radiator hose, then the lower radiator hose.
50. Separate lefthand halfshaft from transaxle, then support halfshaft with a piece of suitable wire.
51. Remove two righthand halfshaft carrier bearing bracket bolts.
52. Separate righthand halfshaft from transaxle, then support halfshaft with a piece of suitable wire.
53. Remove one bellhousing to oil pan and two oil pan to bellhousing bolts.
54. **On models equipped with Secondary Air Injection (AIR),** disconnect AIR pump electrical connector.
55. Remove AIR pump attaching bolt, then

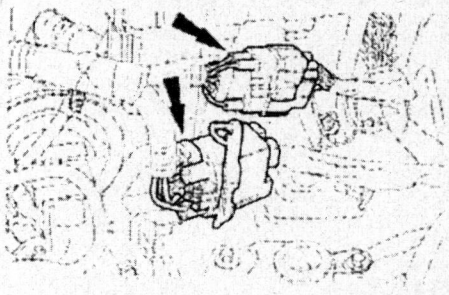

Fig. 2 Engine wiring harness electrical connector. 2.3L engine

the pump. Place aside.

56. **On all models,** install universal adapter brackets tool No. 014–0001 and lifting bracket set tool No. 303–D095, or equivalents, to powertrain lift and engine, **Fig. 3.**
57. Position a suitable block of wood on engine lift, **Fig. 3.**
58. Raise engine lift about one inch to relieve pressure from engine mounts.
59. Remove two transaxle mounting bolts.
60. Remove nuts and bolt from engine mount bracket.
61. Lower engine/transaxle from vehicle.
62. Disconnect starter electrical connectors.
63. Remove starter attaching bolts, then starter.
64. **On models equipped with automatic transaxle,** remove flywheel to torque converter nuts.
65. **On all models,** remove engine ground wire, place aside.
66. **On models equipped with automatic transaxle,** proceed as follows:
    a. Disconnect Transmission Range (TR) sensor and primary control solenoid electrical connector.
    b. Disconnect Transaxle Control electrical connector.
    c. Disconnect Turbine Shaft Speed (TSS) electrical connector.
    d. Disconnect Output Shaft Speed (OSS) electrical connector.
    e. Disconnect Transaxle Pressure switch electrical connector.
67. **On models equipped with manual transaxle,** proceed as follows:
    a. Disconnect backup lamp electrical connector.
    b. Disconnect Vehicle Speed Sensor (VSS) connector.
68. **On all models,** install spreader bar tool No. 303–D089, or equivalent, **Fig. 4.**
69. Remove transaxle to engine mounting bolts.
70. Separate engine and transaxle.

RADIATOR
REPLACE

1. Drain cooling system into suitable container.

2. Remove alternator air inlet duct.
3. Disconnect block heater wiring harness retainers, **Fig. 5,** from cooling fan shroud and position aside.
4. Ensure transmission is in Neutral position, then raise and support vehicle.
5. Remove under body splash shield.
6. Disconnect lower radiator hose bracket from cooling fan motor and shroud.
7. **On models equipped with automatic transaxle,** disconnect lower radiator hose bracket from cooling fan motor and shroud.
8. **On all models,** disconnect four wiring harness retainers and position the harness aside.
9. Disconnect cooling fan electrical connector.
10. Release two retaining tabs, then remove cooling fan motor and shroud.
11. Disconnect power steering hose retainer from radiator, **Fig. 6.**
12. Disconnect upper and lower radiator hose.
13. Disconnect radiator to degas bottle hose and retainer from radiator.
14. **On models equipped with automatic transaxle,** disconnect transmission cooling tubes from radiator.
15. **On all models,** disconnect lower radiator hose.
16. Lift and remove lock tabs from upper radiator support, then position radiator toward engine.
17. Remove A/C condenser to radiator pushpin-type retainer.
18. Squeeze radiator to support retaining tabs and separate A/C condenser from radiator.
19. Remove radiator from vehicle.
20. Reverse procedure to install. Fill and bleed cooling system as outlined under "Cooling System Bleed."

COOLING SYSTEM BLEED

If engine overheats or fluid level drops below minimum fill line during this procedure, turn engine off and add fluid to degas bottle maximum fill line after the engine has cooled.

1. Open degas bottle, then the bleed valve back of engine water outlet, **Fig. 7.**
2. Ensure coolant flows from radiator through upper radiator hose and fills engine. Coolant should flow from bleed hole when full.
3. Fill degas bottle to "MAX" line.
4. Close degas bottle cap and bleed valve.
5. Start engine and run at idle for 30 minutes or until engine reaches normal operating temperature.
6. Let engine cool and repeat procedure as necessary.
7. Start engine and turn heater to "MAX" setting.
8. Operate engine at 2500 RPM for ten minutes and repeat as necessary.

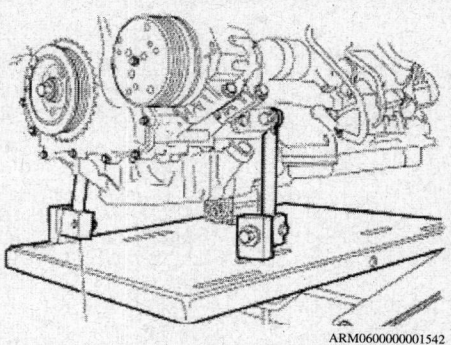

Fig. 3 Engine support lift. 2.3L engine

9. Ensure coolant level of degas bottle is at "MAX" line.

FUEL PUMP
REPLACE

1. Relieve fuel system pressure as outlined under "Precautions."
2. Ensure transmission is in Neutral position, then raise and support vehicle.
3. Remove rear seat lower cushion as follows:
    a. Fully release two latches and slightly raise rear seat cushion front edge to disengage from floor.
    b. Push rear seat cushion slightly rearward to disengage rear edge of cushion from rear retainers, then remove cushion.
4. **On FWD models,** remove four fuel pump module access cover mounting screws, **Fig. 8,** then the cover.
5. **On AWD models,** remove three fuel pump module access cover mounting screws, **Fig. 9,** then the cover.
6. **On all models,** disconnect fuel pump module electrical connector.
7. Press quick release tabs, then disconnect vent and fuel feed hoses.
8. Turn lock ring counterclockwise using fuel tank lock ring wrench too No. 310–123, or equivalent, then remove fuel pump module.
9. Reverse procedure to install, noting the following:
    a. Install new locking ring and seal.
    b. Lubricate fuel tube fittings with clean engine oil.
    c. Ensure alignment tab on fuel pump module and fuel tank meet before tightening fuel pump module lock ring.
    d. Ensure safety belts and buckles are accessible to occupants after installation of rear seat cushion.

FUEL FILTER
REPLACE

The fuel filter is part of the Fuel Pump Module. Refer to "Fuel Pump Replace" for procedure.

ARM0600000001543

Fig. 4 Engine lifting brackets & spreader installation

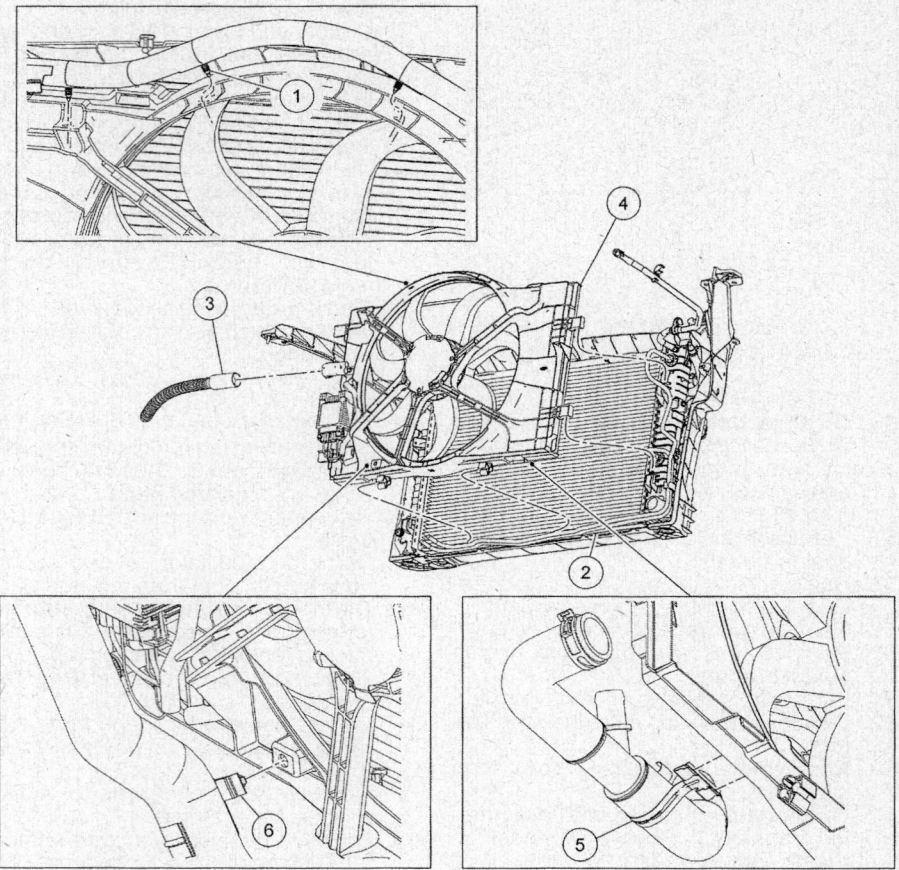

Item	Description
1	Wiring harness retainer (4 required)
2	Transmission cooler tubes (automatic transmission only)
3	Cooling fan motor and shroud electrical connector

Item	Description
4	Cooling fan motor and shroud
5	Lower radiator hose bracket
6	Lower radiator hose retainer (3.0L only)

ARM0500000000115

Fig. 5 Cooling fan motor & shroud replacement

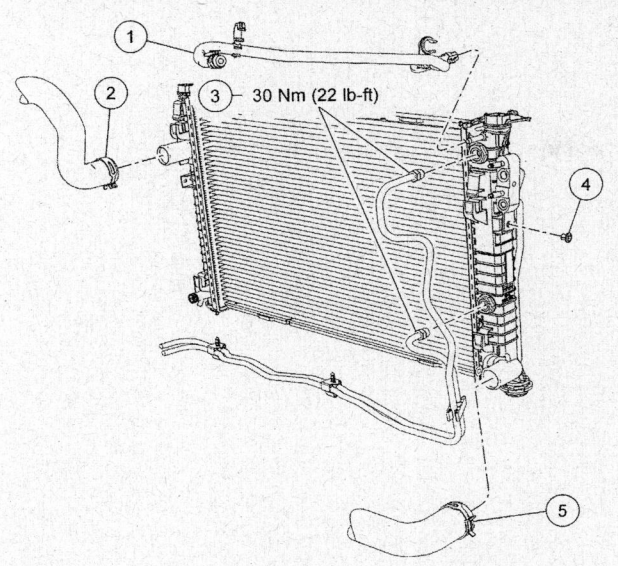

Item	Description
1	Radiator-to-degas bottle hose (3.0L only)
2	Upper radiator hose
3	Transmission cooler tubes (automatic transmission only)(2 required)

Item	Description
4	A/C condenser-to-radiator pushpin-type retainer
5	Lower radiator hose

ARM0500000000116

Fig. 6   Radiator replacement (Part 1 of 2)

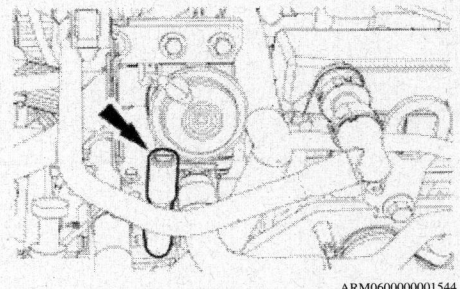

ARM0600000001544

Fig. 7   Thermostat housing bleed valve. 2.3L engine

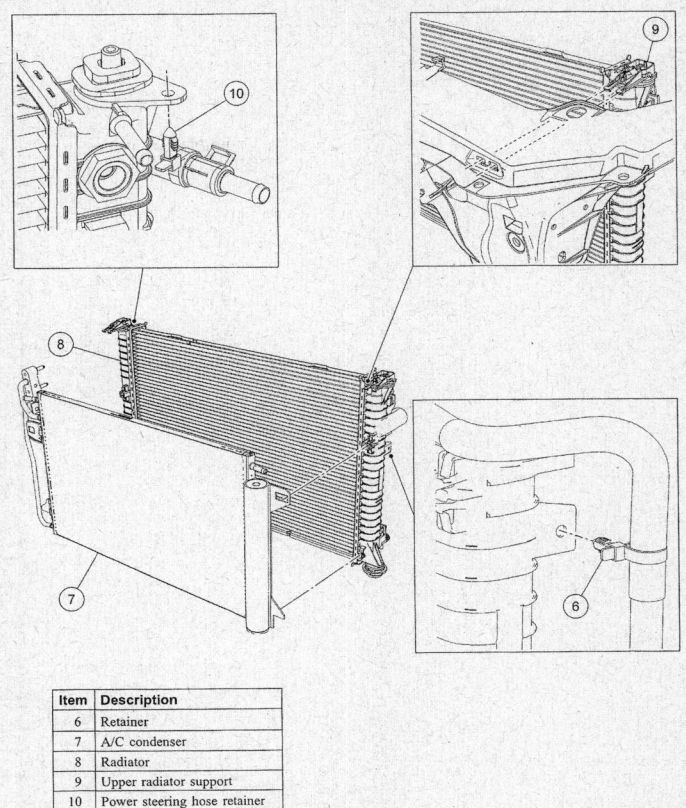

Item	Description
6	Retainer
7	A/C condenser
8	Radiator
9	Upper radiator support
10	Power steering hose retainer

ARM0500000000117

Fig. 6   Radiator replacement (Part 2 of 2)

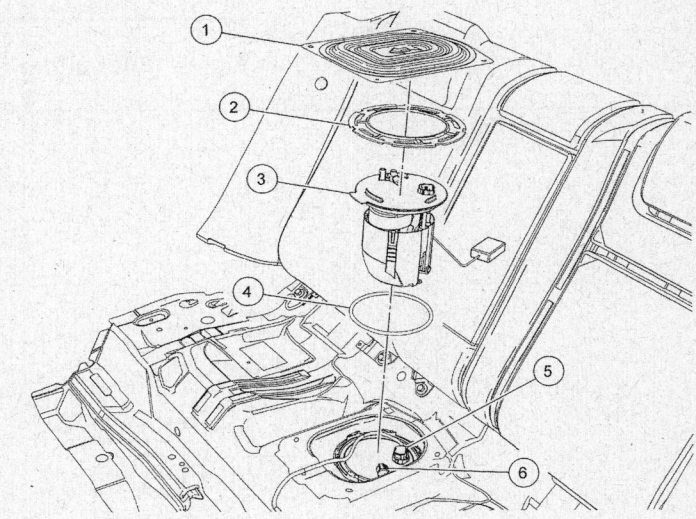

Item	Description
1	Fuel pump (FP) module access cover
2	FP module lock ring
3	FP module
4	FP module O-ring seal
5	FP module electrical connector
6	Fuel supply tube quick connect coupling

ARM0500000000118

Fig. 8   Fuel pump module replacement

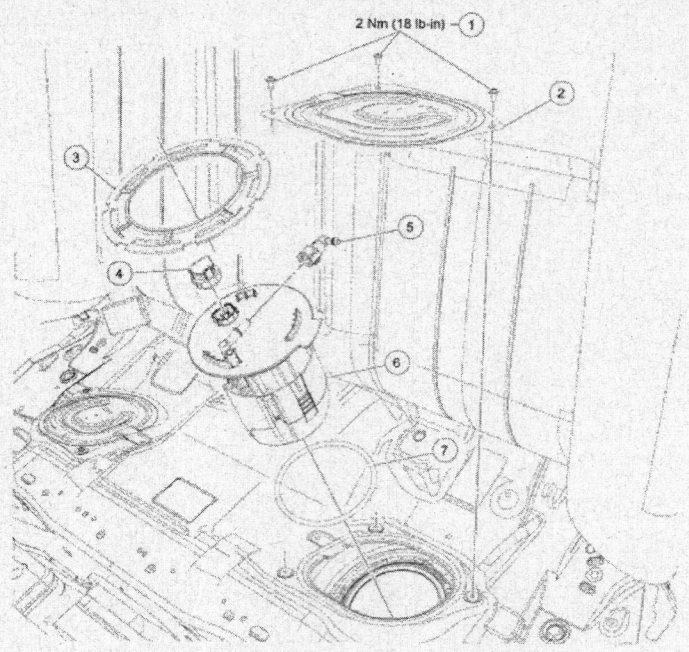

Item	Description
1	Fuel pump (FP) module access cover retainer screws (3 required)
2	FP module access cover
3	FP module lock ring
4	FP module electrical connector
5	Fuel supply tube-to-FP module quick connect coupling
6	FP module
7	FP module O-ring seal

ARM0600000001547

Fig. 9 Fuel pump module replacement

TIGHTENING SPECIFICATIONS

Year	Component	Torque, Ft. Lbs.
2006–08	Accessory Belt Tensioner	18
	Accessory Drive Belt Idler Pulley	18
	Air Conditioning Compressor	18
	Air Conditioning Compressor Manifold	18
	Alternator Mounting Bolts	35
	Bell Housing	35
	Camshaft	③
	Catalytic Converter To Cylinder Head Studs	13
	Catalytic Converter Heat Shield	89①
	Coil-On-Plug Bolts	71①
	Coolant Outlet Bolts	89①
	Coolant Pump Bolts	89①
	Crankshaft Damper	②
	Crankshaft Pulley	②
	Crankshaft Rear Oil Seal	②
	Cylinder Head	⑤
	EGR Tube	41
	Engine Mount Bolts	41
	Engine Mount Nuts	41
	Engine Mount Bracket Bolt	85
	Engine Mount Bracket Nuts	76
	Flexplate	④
	Flywheel	④
	Fuel Rail	17
	Ground Eyelet	89①
	Intake Manifold	13
	Intermediate Steering Shaft Bolt	17
	Lower Ball Joint Nuts	148
	Lower Control Arm To Strut Through Bolt	76
	Oil Adapter Bolt	18
	Oil Filter Cover	24
	Oil Filter Drain Plug	89①
	Oil Pressure Sender	11
	Oil Pan Drain Plug	27
	Power Steering Pump Bolts	18
	Power Steering Pressure Tube Bolts	26
	Radio Interference Capacitor Bracket	89①
	Spark Plugs	108①
	Starter Motor	18
	Sway Bar Link Nuts	30
	Thermostat Housing	89①
	Throttle Body Bolts	89①
	Tie Rod End	35
	Timing Chain Guide	89①
	Timing Chain Tensioner	89①
	Torque Converter To Flywheel	26
	Transaxle Mount Bolt	66

① — Inch lbs.
② — Refer to "Crankshaft Damper, Replace" for tightening specifications and sequence.
③ — Refer to "Camshaft, Replace" for tightening specifications and sequence.
④ — Refer to "Crankshaft Rear Oil Seal, Replace" for tightening specifications and sequence.
⑤ — Refer to "Cylinder Head, Replace" for tightening specifications and sequence.

3.0L Engine

NOTE: Refer To The "3.0L Engine" Section In The "Five-Hundred, Freestyle & Montego" Chapter For Procedures Not Found In This Section.

NOTE: On Air Bag Equipped Models, Refer To "Air Bag System Precautions" Located In The Front Of This Manual For System Disarming & Arming Procedures.

NOTE: Refer To "Computer Relearn Procedures" Located In The Front Of This Manual When Battery Power To The Computer Has Been Interrupted.

INDEX

	Page No.		Page No.		Page No.
Compression Pressure	1-16	Fuel Pump, Replace	1-18	R-Clip	1-16
Engine Rebuilding Specifications	21-1	Precautions	1-16	Spring Lock	1-16
Engine, Replace	1-17	Air Bag Systems	1-16	Vapor Tube	1-16
Engine Mount, Replace	1-16	Battery Ground Cable	1-16	Radiator, Replace	1-18
Fuel Filter, Replace	1-18	Fuel Pressure Relief	1-16	Tightening Specifications	1-20
		Quick Disconnect Hoses	1-16		

PRECAUTIONS

Air Bag Systems

Refer to "Air Bag System Precautions" in the front of this manual for system disarming and arming procedures.

Battery Ground Cable

Prior to service, disconnect battery ground cable and isolate as required.

Fuel Pressure Relief

1. Remove the fuel pump relay.
2. Start engine, then allow engine to idle until it stalls.
3. After engine stalls, crank engine for approximately 5 seconds to make sure fuel injection supply manifold pressure has been released.
4. When fuel system service is complete, install fuel pump relay.
5. Cycle ignition key and wait 3 seconds to pressurize fuel system. Inspect for leaks before starting engine.

Quick Disconnect Hoses

R-CLIP

When working with R-clip type connections, do not use tools to disconnect. Use of tools may deform clip components and could cause leaks.

DISCONNECT

1. Bend shipping tab downward.
2. Spread R-clip and push clip into fitting.
3. Separate fitting from tube.

CONNECT

1. Inspect fitting and tube for damage and ensure connections are clean.
2. Apply light coat of suitable, clean engine oil to male end of tube.
3. Insert R-clip into fitting.
4. Align tube and fitting, then insert tube into fitting and push together until click is heard.
5. Pull on connection to ensure it is fully engaged.

SPRING LOCK

When working with spring lock type connections, spring lock tool set No. T84L-19623-B, or equivalent, must be used to disconnect fittings.

When connecting spring lock type fittings, proceed as follows:
1. Inspect and clean both coupling ends.
2. Lubricate fuel line O-ring seals with suitable, clean engine oil.
3. When connection is made, pull on line to ensure it is fully engaged.

VAPOR TUBE

To disconnect vapor tube connections, squeeze fitting and disconnect vapor tube from fitting, proceed as follows:
1. Ensure fittings are clean and free from damage.
2. Push tube onto fitting until it snaps into place.
3. Pull on connection to verify fitting is secure.

COMPRESSION PRESSURE

1. Ensure crankcase oil is of correct viscosity and at correct level.
2. Ensure battery is fully charged and engine is at normal operating temperature.
3. Turn ignition switch to OFF position.
4. Remove spark plugs.
5. Set throttle plates to wide open position.
6. Install suitable compression gauge in cylinder No. 1.
7. Install auxiliary starter switch in starting circuit.
8. With ignition switch off, crank engine at least five compression strokes using auxiliary starter switch.
9. Record number of compression strokes required to reach highest reading, then record highest reading.
10. Repeat test on each cylinder, cranking engine same number of compression strokes.
11. Lowest cylinder reading must be within 75% of highest reading.

ENGINE MOUNT

REPLACE

1. Relieve fuel system pressure as outlined under "Precautions."
2. Drain engine coolant into suitable container.
3. Remove lower intake manifold as outlined under "Intake Manifold, Replace."
4. Remove engine coolant degas bottle.
5. Remove engine ground wire and position wire aside.
6. Remove three engine mount bracket to engine block mounting nuts, **Fig. 1.**
7. Remove two bracket to engine mount insulator bolts, then the mount bracket.
8. Install two universal adapter brackets tool No. 014–0001 and two lifting brackets tool No. 134–200243, or equivalents, **Fig. 2,** on top of cylinder block.
9. Install three bar engine support tool No. 33–F072, or equivalent, **Fig. 3,** to

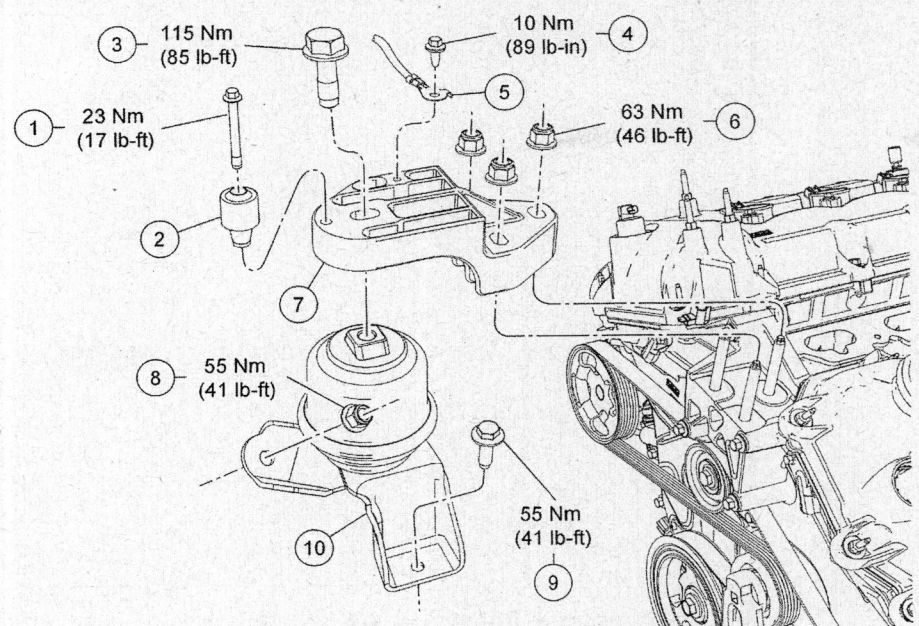

Item	Description
1	Damper bolt
2	Damper
3	Engine mount bracket bolt
4	Ground wire bolt
5	Ground wire
6	Engine support insulator bracket nuts (3 required)
7	Engine mount bracket
8	Engine mount nut
9	Engine mount bolts (2 required)
10	Engine mount

ARM0500000000119

Fig. 1 Engine mount replacement

lifting brackets, raise engine approximately one inch.
10. Remove engine mount insulator mounting bolts, **Fig. 1,** then the engine mount.
11. Reverse procedure to install.

ENGINE
REPLACE

1. Relieve fuel system pressure as outlined under "Precautions."
2. Recover air conditioning refrigerant as outlined in "Air Conditioning" chapter.
3. Drain engine coolant and oil into suitable containers.
4. Place steering wheel in straight ahead position and ignition key in Off position.
5. Remove two steering joint cover retaining, then the cover.
6. Index mark steering column shaft position to steering gear for reference during installation.
7. Remove steering column shaft to steering gear bolt, then disconnect shaft from gear box. **Do not allow intermediate shaft to rotate while it is disconnected from gear or damage to clockspring can occur.**
8. Remove exhaust flexible pipe.
9. Release four clips, then slide steering gear to dash seal off of steering gear and into the passenger compartment. **Steering gear to dash seal must be removed or it will be damaged when lowering subframe.**
10. Remove power steering pressure (PSP) hose bracket mounting bolt.
11. Remove and discard PSP hose banjo bolt and seals from steering gear.
12. Remove heat shield mounting bolts, then the shield.
13. Remove engine roll restrictor mounting bolts, then the roll restrictor.
14. Remove righthand fender splash shield screws and position shield aside.
15. Remove 6 pin-type retainers, then righthand underbody splash shield.
16. Remove lefthand fender splash shield screws and position shield aside.
17. Remove 6 pin-type retainers, then lefthand underbody splash shield.
18. Remove cotter pins and nuts from both tie-rod ends.

19. Separate tie rod ends from steering knuckles using ball joint/tie rod removal tool No. 205–592, or equivalent.
20. Disconnect power steering cooler tube.
21. Remove nuts and separate righthand and lefthand sway bar links from struts.
22. Place a suitable block of wood, or similar item, between righthand and lefthand lower arm and outer CV joints to prevent lower arm from striking outer CV joint , then remove lower ball joint nuts.
23. Separate ball joints from lower control arms using ball joint/tie rod removal tool No. 205–592, or equivalent.
24. Position powertrain lift tool No. 014–00765, or equivalent, under subframe assembly.
25. Remove righthand and lefthand lower control arm to subframe through bolts.
26. Remove righthand and lefthand subframe bracket to body mounting bolts.
27. Remove two righthand and lefthand subframe bracket to body bolts, **Fig. 4.**
28. Remove righthand and lefthand subframe nuts to subframe brackets, **Fig. 5,** then the subframe brackets.
29. Remove front subframe nuts, then lower subframe from vehicle.
30. Disconnect transaxle cooler hoses.
31. Remove and discard engine oil filter.
32. Remove engine air cleaner and air cleaner outlet pipe.
33. Remove battery, then battery tray.
34. Disconnect two main engine wiring harness electrical connectors.
35. Disconnect engine to strut tower ground strap, then position strap aside.
36. Disconnect Powertrain Control Module (PCM) electrical connector and pin-type retainer.
37. Disconnect fuel supply tube quick disconnect coupler from fuel rail as outlined under "Quick Disconnect Hoses."
38. Disconnect heater hose from thermostat housing.
39. Disconnect heater hose inline connection.
40. Disconnect evaporative emissions (EVAP) hose.
41. Disconnect upper and lower radiator hoses.
42. **On models equipped with, automatic transaxle,** proceed as follows:
    a. Disconnect transaxle control cable from transaxle selector lever.
    b. Remove transaxle control cable bracket bolts and position cable aside.
    c. Disconnect transaxle wiring harness connectors and retaining brackets, then position harness aside.
43. **On models equipped with manual transaxle,** proceed as follows:
    a. Disconnect hydraulic clutch hoses and plug openings.
    b. Disconnect speed sensor connector and retaining clamp, then position connector harness aside.
    c. Disconnect shift cable, remove bracket and position aside.
44. **On all models,** remove vacuum tube bracket bolt, then disconnect tube from

intake manifold and position tube aside.

45. Disconnect block heater cable retaining clips from cooling fan shroud.
46. Disconnect power steering hose from power steering reservoir.
47. Disconnect power steering hose retaining clip from lefthand valve cover stud bolt and engine wiring harness.
48. Disconnect coolant hose from degas bottle.
49. Detach coolant hose retaining clip and position coolant hose aside.
50. Remove A/C tube to radiator support bracket bolts.
51. Disconnect A/C tubes from condenser, then position tubes aside.
52. Remove bolt and ground wire from engine mount bracket.
53. Remove bolt and separate A/C manifold from compressor.
54. Separate lefthand halfshaft from transaxle using slide hammer tool No. 100—001 and halfshaft adapter tools No 205—243 and 205—832, or equivalents, then support halfshaft with a length of mechanic's wire.
55. Disconnect Crankshaft Position (CKP) sensor electrical connector and pin-type retainer.
56. Disconnect Power Steering Pressure (PSP) switch electrical connector.
57. Disconnect Catalyst Monitor Sensor (CMS) electrical connector and pin-type retainer.
58. Remove two righthand halfshaft carrier bearing bracket bolts.
59. Separate rightand halfshaft from transaxle, then support halfshaft with a length of mechanic's wire.
60. Remove torque converter nut access plug.
61. Remove three torque converter mounting nuts.
62. Remove two oil pan to transaxle mounting bolts.
63. Position a suitable block of wood under transaxle.
64. Remove engine mount as outlined under "Engine Mount, Replace."
65. Remove transaxle mount to transaxle assembly bolts.
66. Disconnect Heated Oxygen Sensor (HO2S) electrical connector from PSP bracket.
67. Remove PSP hose bracket from cylinder head.
68. Remove PSP hose bracket from power steering reservoir.
69. Remove PSP hose banjo bolt to steering pump, discard banjo bolt and 2 seals.
70. Disconnect Exhaust Gas Recirculation (EGR) valve electrical connector.
71. Loosen EGR tube to EGR valve nut.
72. Remove EGR valve mounting bolts and discard gasket.
73. Loosen EGR tube to catalytic converter nut, then remove EGR tube.
74. Remove catalytic converter heat shield and mounting bracket.
75. Install universal adapter brackets tool No. 303–D95, 014–0001, 303–1140

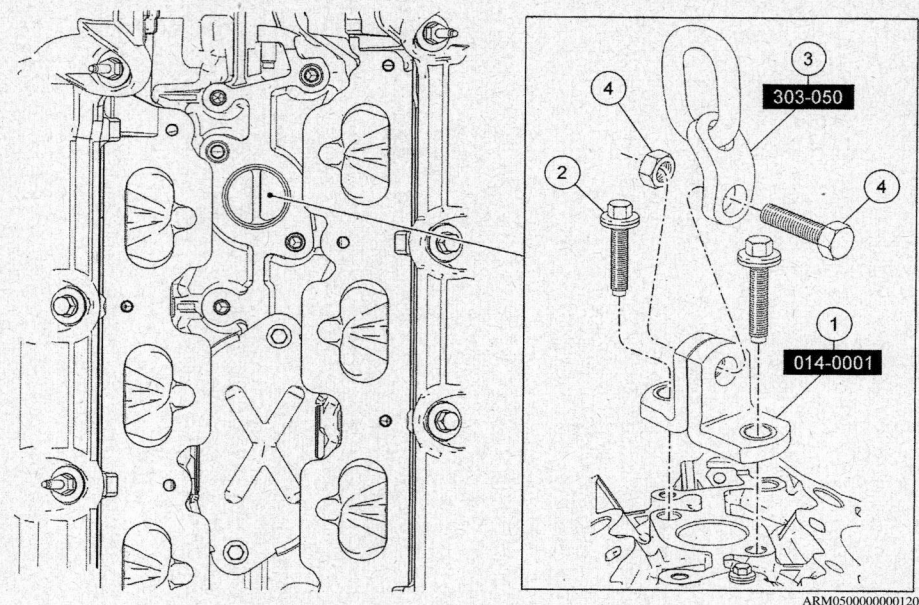

Fig. 2 Adapter & lifting bracket installation

and lifting brackets tool No. 134–00243 and 303–050 or equivalents, as outlined, **Fig. 6.**
76. Install engine lift spreader tool No. D93P-6001–A3, or equivalent, **Fig. 6,** and a suitable engine hoist, then raise engine and transaxle from powertrain lift tool No. 014–00765, or equivalent.
77. Remove Catalyst Monitor Sensor (CMS) electrical connector bracket.
78. Disconnect Transmission Control Module (TCM) electrical connector and wiring harness pin-type retainer.
79. Remove starter motor electrical connectors.
80. Remove starter motor mounting bolts, then the starter motor.
81. Ensure all wiring harness connectors and harness to engine retainers are disconnected.
82. Remove transaxle to engine mounting bolts.
83. Separate engine and transaxle.
84. Reverse procedure to install. Replace all discarded bolts, nuts and gaskets with OEM replacements.

RADIATOR
REPLACE

1. Drain cooling system into suitable container.
2. Disconnect block heater wiring harness retainers, from cooling fan shroud and position aside.
3. Ensure transmission is in Neutral position, then raise and support vehicle.
4. Remove under body splash shield.
5. Disconnect lower radiator hose bracket from cooling fan motor and shroud.
6. Disconnect retainer on lower radiator hose to cooling fan motor and shroud.
7. **On models equipped with automatic transaxle,** disconnect lower radiator hose bracket from cooling fan motor and shroud.
8. **On all models,** disconnect four wiring harness retainers and position the harness aside.
9. Disconnect cooling fan electrical connector.
10. Release two retaining tabs, then remove cooling fan motor and shroud.
11. Disconnect power steering hose retainer from radiator.
12. Disconnect upper and lower radiator hose.
13. Disconnect radiator to degas bottle hose and retainer from radiator.
14. **On models equipped with automatic transaxle,** disconnect transmission cooling tubes from radiator.
15. **On all models,** disconnect lower radiator hose.
16. Lift and remove lock tabs from upper radiator support, then position radiator toward engine.
17. Remove A/C condenser to radiator pushpin-type retainer.
18. Squeeze radiator to support retaining tabs and separate A/C condenser from radiator.
19. Remove radiator from vehicle.
20. Reverse procedure to install. Fill and bleed cooling system as outlined under "Cooling System Bleed."

FUEL PUMP
REPLACE

Refer to "2.3L Engine" section for fuel pump replacement procedure.

FUEL FILTER
REPLACE

Refer to "2.3L Engine" section for fuel filter replacement procedure.

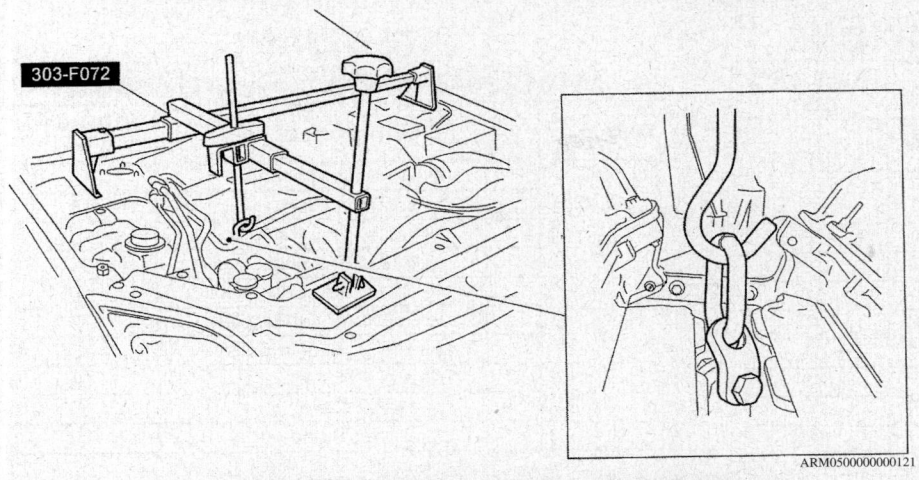

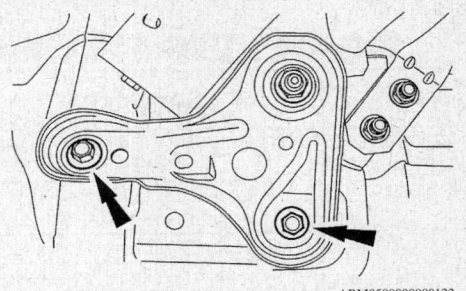

Fig. 4 Subframe bracket to body bolt locations

Fig. 3 Three bar engine support tool installation

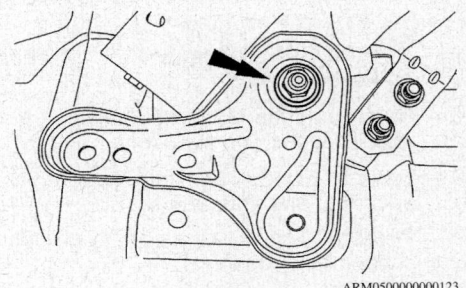

Fig. 5 Subframe nuts to subframe bracket locations

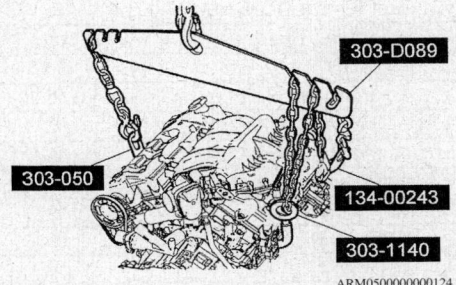

Fig. 6 Engine lifting brackets & spreader installation. 3.0L engine

TIGHTENING SPECIFICATIONS

Year	Component	Torque/Ft. Lbs.
2006–08	Accessory Drive Belt Idler (Grooved) Pulley	18
	Accessory Drive Belt Idler (Non-Grooved) Pulley	35
	Accessory Drive Belt Tensioner Bolt	33
	Air Conditioning Compressor	18
	Air Conditioning Manifold	11
	Air Conditioning Tube Connections	71①
	Alternator Mounting	35
	Block Heater	15
	Camshaft Cap Bolts	⑨
	Camshaft Position Sensor	108①
	Camshaft Oil Seal Retainer	89①
	Catalytic Converter To Engine Bracket Bolts	26
	Coolant Bypass Tube Nut	15
	Cylinder Head	②
	EGR Tube	30
	EGR Valve	18
	Engine Mount Bracket Bolt	85
	Engine Mount Bracket Nuts	46
	Engine Mount Nuts & Bolts	41
	Engine Roll-Restrictor Bolts	66
	Exhaust Manifold	⑤
	Flexplate	59
	Front Cover	⑧
	Fuel Rail Bolts	89①
	Intermediate Steering Shaft Bolt	17
	Intake Manifold	④
	Knock Sensor	15
	Lower Ball Joint Nuts	148
	Oil Pan	③
	Oil Pan Drain Plug	19
	Oil Pan To Engine Front Bolt Cover	18
	Oil Pan To Transaxle	35
	Oil Pump Screen & Pickup Tube Bolts	89①
	Oil Separator	89①
	Power Steering Pump Bolts	18
	Spark Plugs	11

TIGHTENING SPECIFICATIONS—Continued

Year	Component	Torque/Ft. Lbs.
2006–08	Steering Shaft Pinch Bolt	18
	Subframe Bolts	76
	Throttle Body Bolts	89①
	Tie Rod End Nuts	35
	Timing Chain Tensioner Bolts	18
	Torque Converter To Flexplate	27
	Transaxle To Engine Bolts	35
	Transaxle Mount Bolts	66
	Valve Cover	⑥
	Water Pump	⑦

① — Inch lbs.

② — Refer to Cylinder Head, Replace for tightening specifications and sequence.

③ — Refer to Oil Pan, Replace for tightening specifications and sequence.

④ — Refer to Intake Manifold, Replace for tightening specifications and sequence.

⑤ — Refer to Exhaust Manifold, Replace for tightening specifications and sequence.

⑥ — Refer to Valve Cover, Replace for tightening specifications and sequence.

⑦ — Refer to Water Pump, Replace for tightening specifications and sequence.

⑧ — Refer to Front Cover, Replace for tightening specifications and sequence.

⑨ — Refer to Camshaft, Replace for tightening specifications and sequence.

NOTE: On Air Bag Equipped Models, Refer To "Air Bag System Precautions" Located In The Front Of This Manual For System Disarming & Arming Procedures.

NOTE: Refer To "Computer Relearn Procedures" Located In The Front Of This Manual When Battery Power To The Computer Has Been Interrupted.

INDEX

	Page No.
Camshaft, Replace	1-29
Installation	1-29
Removal	1-29
Camshaft Lobe Lift Specifications	1-27
Compression Pressure	1-21
Cooling System Bleed	1-30
Crankshaft Damper, Replace	1-27
Cylinder Head, Replace	1-25
Lefthand	1-25
Righthand	1-25
Engine Rebuilding Specifications	21-1
Engine, Replace	1-22
Engine Mount, Replace	1-22
Exhaust Manifold, Replace	1-24
Lefthand	1-24
Righthand	1-24
Front Cover, Replace	1-27

	Page No.
Installation	1-28
Removal	1-27
Front Cover Seal, Replace	1-28
Fuel Pump, Replace	1-31
Intake Manifold, Replace	1-24
Lower	1-24
Upper	1-24
Oil Pan, Replace	1-29
Oil Pump, Replace	1-30
Power Transfer Unit Seal, Replace	1-24
Installation	1-24
Removal	1-24
Precautions	1-21
Air Bag Systems	1-21
Battery Ground Cable	1-21
Fuel Pressure Relief	1-21
Quick Disconnect Hoses	1-21
R-Clip	1-21

	Page No.
Spring Lock	1-21
Vapor Tube	1-21
Radiator, Replace	1-31
Serpentine Drive Belt	1-30
Belt Routing	1-30
Belt Tensioner, Replace	1-30
Belts, Replace	1-30
Thermostat, Replace	1-30
Tightening Specifications	1-38
Timing Chain, Replace	1-29
Valve Adjustment	1-27
Valve Clearance Specifications	1-27
Valve Cover, Replace	1-26
Lefthand	1-26
Righthand	1-26
Water Pump, Replace	1-30
Installation	1-31
Removal	1-30

PRECAUTIONS

Air Bag Systems

Refer to "Air Bag System Precautions" in the front of this manual for system disarming and arming procedures.

Battery Ground Cable

Prior to service, disconnect battery ground cable and isolate as required.

Fuel Pressure Relief

1. Remove the fuel pump relay.
2. Start engine, then allow engine to idle until it stalls.
3. After engine stalls, crank engine for approximately 5 seconds to make sure fuel injection supply manifold pressure has been released.
4. When fuel system service is complete, install fuel pump relay.
5. Cycle ignition key and wait 3 seconds to pressurize fuel system. Inspect for leaks before starting engine.

Quick Disconnect Hoses

R-CLIP

When working with R-clip type connections, do not use tools to disconnect. Use of tools may deform clip components and could cause leaks.

DISCONNECT

1. Bend shipping tab downward.
2. Spread R-clip and push clip into fitting.
3. Separate fitting from tube.

CONNECT

1. Inspect fitting and tube for damage and ensure connections are clean.
2. Apply light coat of suitable, clean engine oil to male end of tube.
3. Insert R-clip into fitting.
4. Align tube and fitting, then insert tube into fitting and push together until click is heard.
5. Pull on connection to ensure it is fully engaged.

SPRING LOCK

When working with spring lock type connections, spring lock tool set No. T84L-19623-B, or equivalent, must be used to disconnect fittings.

When connecting spring lock type fittings, proceed as follows:
1. Inspect and clean both coupling ends.
2. Lubricate fuel line O-ring seals with suitable, clean engine oil.
3. When connection is made, pull on line to ensure it is fully engaged.

VAPOR TUBE

To disconnect vapor tube connections, squeeze fitting and disconnect vapor tube from fitting, proceed as follows:
1. Ensure fittings are clean and free from damage.
2. Push tube onto fitting until it snaps into place.
3. Pull on connection to verify fitting is secure.

COMPRESSION PRESSURE

1. Ensure crankcase oil is of correct viscosity and at correct level.
2. Ensure battery is fully charged and engine is at normal operating temperature.
3. Turn ignition switch to OFF position.
4. Remove spark plugs.
5. Set throttle plates to wide open position.
6. Install suitable compression gauge in cylinder No. 1.
7. Install auxiliary starter switch in starting circuit.
8. With ignition switch off, crank engine at least five compression strokes using auxiliary starter switch.
9. Record number of compression strokes required to reach highest reading, then record highest reading.
10. Repeat test on each cylinder, cranking engine same number of compression strokes.
11. Lowest cylinder reading must be within 75% of highest reading.

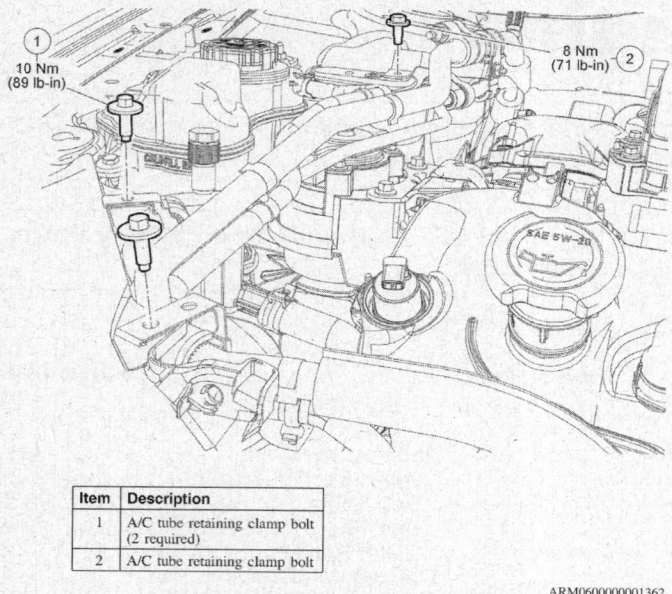

Item	Description
1	A/C tube retaining clamp bolt (2 required)
2	A/C tube retaining clamp bolt

Fig. 1   A/C line bolt locations. 3.5L Engine

ENGINE MOUNT
REPLACE

1. Raise and support vehicle.
2. Drain coolant into a suitable container, then lower vehicle.
3. Disconnect wiring harness retainer from coolant overflow bottle, then the overflow bottle vent hose.
4. Disconnect lower hose from coolant overflow bottle and position aside.
5. Remove coolant overflow bottle.
6. Remove upper intake manifold as outlined under "Intake Manifold, Replace."
7. Install engine lifting bracket tool No. 303–1245 or equivalent to lefthand cylinder head.
8. Install 3 bar engine support tool No. 303–F-072 or equivalent to support engine assembly.
9. Remove 3 A/C line retaining bolts, **Fig. 1.**
10. Disconnect power steering hose from engine mount brace, **Fig. 2.**
11. Disconnect ground wire from engine mount brace, then remove brace and engine mount, **Fig. 2.**
12. Reverse procedure to install.

ENGINE
REPLACE

1. Relieve fuel pressure as outlined under "Precautions."
2. Recover refrigerant as outlined in "Air Conditioning" chapter of this manual.
3. Remove accessory drive belts as outlined under "Serpentine Drive Belt."
4. Remove the underbody splash shield, **Fig. 3.**
5. Disconnect power steering cooler lines and drain fluid into a suitable container.
6. Disconnect wiring harness retainer from coolant overflow bottle, then the overflow bottle vent hose.

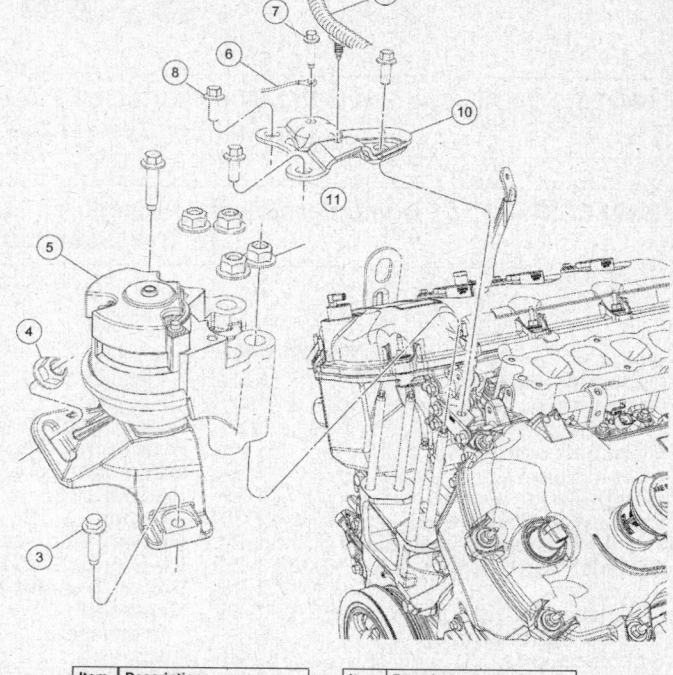

Item	Description
3	Engine mount-to-frame bolt (2 required)
4	Engine mount-to-frame nut
5	Engine mount
6	Ground wire
7	Ground wire bolt
8	Engine mount brace bolt (3 required)
9	Power steering hose retainer
10	Engine mount brace

Item	Description
11	Engine mount-to-engine nut (4 required)

Fig. 2   Engine mount. 3.5L engine

7. Disconnect lower hose from coolant overflow bottle and position aside.
8. Remove coolant overflow bottle.
9. Remove air cleaner and outlet tube, then the battery and battery tray.
10. Disconnect 2 main engine wiring harness connectors.
11. Disconnect harness retainers from transmission mount and battery tray bracket.
12. Disconnect power feed from battery terminal.
13. Disconnect ground straps as shown in **Fig. 4.**
14. Disconnect vacuum hoses and EVAP tube from upper intake manifold.
15. Raise and support vehicle.
16. Drain coolant into a suitable container, then lower vehicle.
17. Disconnect upper and lower radiator hoses, then the heater hoses from thermostat housing.
18. Disconnect transaxle control cable from control lever.
19. Remove transaxle control cable bracket and position aside.
20. **On models equipped with engine block heater,** disconnect engine block heater harness from radiator support, power steering hose, A/C tube and engine wiring harness.
21. **On all models,** disconnect coolant tube retainer clips from A/C tube.

22. Disconnect A/C tube from condenser. Discard O-ring seals.
23. Remove 2 A/C tube bracket bolts.
24. Disconnect A/C lines from evaporator, then all remaining wiring harness retainers and engine harness connectors.
25. Remove oil level indicator.
26. Disconnect hose from power steering reservoir and drain fluid into a suitable container.
27. Remove power steering reservoir from cowl.
28. Disconnect fuel supply line from fuel rail as outlined under "Precautions."
29. Remove ground strap from engine mount brace, then the brace.
30. Disconnect PCM electrical connectors and pin-type retainers.
31. Remove power steering pressure line bracket bolt.
32. Disconnect power steering pressure hose from steering gear. Power steering pressure hose bolt and seals should not be reused.
33. Ensure front wheels are in straight ahead position and that ignition key is OFF.
34. Remove steering joint cover, then place alignment marks on steering column shaft and steering gear for installation reference.
35. Disconnect steering column shaft from

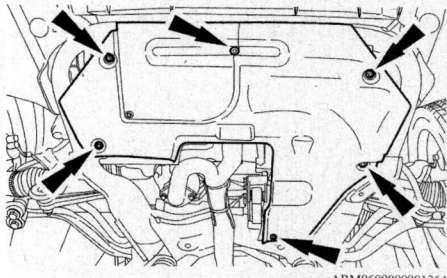

Fig. 3 Underbody splash shield. 3.5L engine

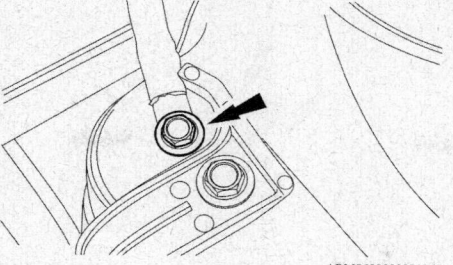

Fig. 4 Ground strap removal (Part 1 of 2). 3.5L engine

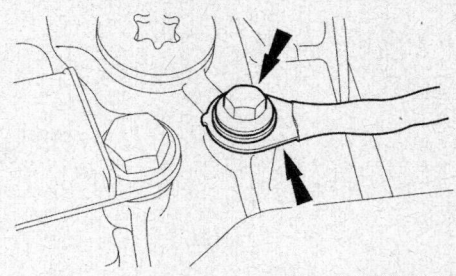

Fig. 4 Ground strap removal (Part 2 of 2). 3.5L engine

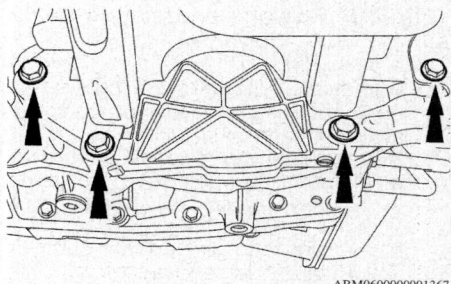

Fig. 5 Oil pan to transaxle bolt locations. 3.5L engine

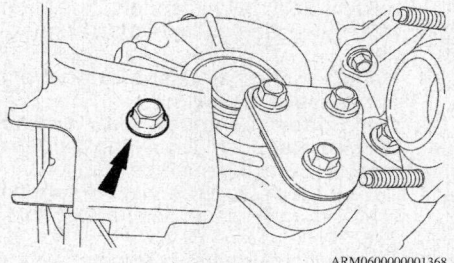

Fig. 6 Roll restrictor removal. 3.5L engine

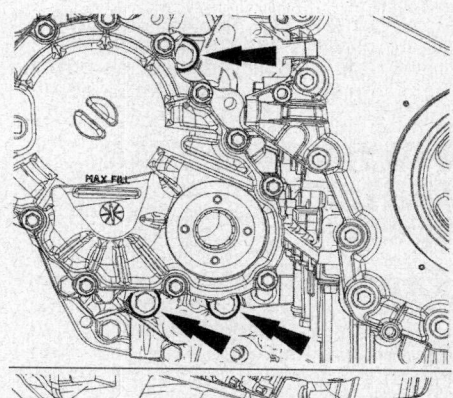

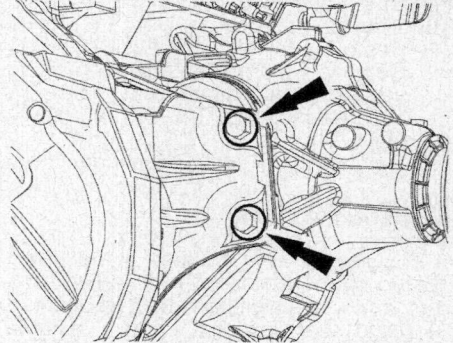

Fig. 7 Power transfer unit removal. 3.5L engine

steering gear. Discard steering column to steering gear bolt. **Ensure that steering column shaft does not rotate or damage to clockspring may occur.**

36. Remove lefthand fender splash shield.
37. Remove steering gear-to-dash seal from steering gear and slide into passenger compartment.
38. Disconnect transaxle cooler hoses and drain fluid into a suitable container.
39. Drain engine oil into a suitable container.
40. Remove and discard engine oil filter.
41. Remove and discard 6 exhaust Y-pipe nuts, then remove Y-pipe.
42. Remove 4 oil pan to transaxle bolts, **Fig. 5.**
43. Remove flywheel inspection cover.
44. Remove and discard 4 torque converter to flywheel nuts.
45. **On models equipped with AWD,** place alignment marks on driveshaft and mounting flange for installation reference.
46. **On models equipped with AWD,** remove 4 driveshaft attaching bolts and support driveshaft with suitable mechanics wire.
47. **On all models,** remove engine roll restrictor to subframe through-bolt, **Fig. 6.**
48. Remove cotter pins and attaching nuts from tie rod ends, then separate from steering knuckles using tie rod end remover tool No. 211–105 or equivalent.
49. Detach stabilizer bar links from struts, then remove 4 lower ball joint nuts.
50. Place a suitable block of wood between lower arm and outer CV joint to prevent lower arm from contacting outer CV joint.
51. Separate right and left lower ball joints from control arms using ball joint separa-

rator tool No. 205–592 or equivalent.
52. Support subframe assembly using powertrain lift tool No. 014–00765 or equivalent.
53. Remove subframe to body brackets.
54. Lower subframe assembly from vehicle enough to access halfshafts.
55. Separate lefthand halfshaft from transaxle using slide hammer tool No. 100–001, halfshaft remover tool Nos. 205–243 and 205–832 or equivalents. Support halfshaft using suitable mechanics wire.
56. Remove 2 righthand catalytic converter bracket bolts.
57. **On models equipped with FWD,** remove righthand catalytic converter bracket, then the halfshaft carrier bearing. Support halfshaft using suitable mechanics wire.
58. **On models equipped with AWD,** proceed as follows:
    a. Remove righthand halfshaft carrier bearing bolts.
    b. Separate halfshaft from transaxle and support using suitable mechanics wire.
    c. Disconnect righthand catalyst monitor sensor.
    d. Remove righthand catalytic converter, then the power transfer unit bracket.
    e. Remove power transfer unit, **Fig. 7.**
59. **On all models,** position a suitable block of wood beneath transaxle.
60. Install engine lifting bracket set tool No. D94L-6001-A or equivalent to powertrain lift, **Fig. 8.**
61. Remove transaxle mount, then the engine mount.
62. Lower engine and transaxle assembly from vehicle.
63. Disconnect wiring harness fasteners from transaxle to engine stud bolt and starter.

64. Disconnect ground wire, **Fig. 9.**
65. Disconnect transmission control module, then remove starter.
66. Install engine lift bracket tool No. 303–1245 or equivalent to cylinder head.
67. Remove engine from powertrain lift table using a suitable floor crane.
68. Suitably support engine and transaxle assembly.
69. Remove engine to transaxle attaching bolts and separate engine from transaxle if necessary.
70. Reverse procedure to install noting the following:
    a. Replace power transfer unit seal as outlined under "Power Transfer Unit Seal, Replace."
    b. Inspect halfshaft sealing surface for wear or damage. Replace as necessary.
    c. Ensure that new torque converter nuts are used.
    d. Ensure that new A/C O-ring seals are installed where A/C lines were disconnected.

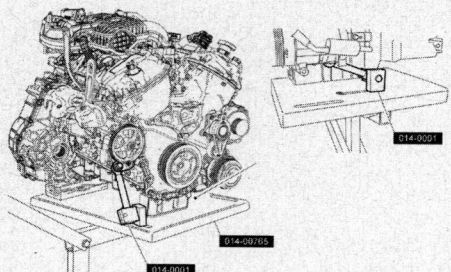

Fig. 8 Engine support bracket installation. 3.5L engine

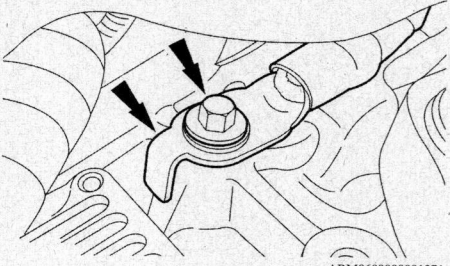

Fig. 9 Ground wire location. 3.5L engine

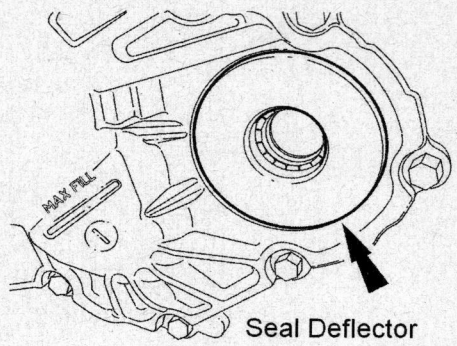

Seal Deflector

Fig. 10 Power transfer unit seal deflector

e. Ensure that all fluids are refilled to capacity and specifications.

f. Bleed cooling system as outlined under "Cooling System Bleed."

POWER TRANSFER UNIT SEAL
REPLACE
Removal

The seal deflector will be damaged during removal. Ensure that the seal directly behind the deflector is not damaged when removing the deflector.

1. Remove seal deflector, **Fig. 10.**
2. Remove intermediate shaft seal using a suitable slide hammer and bearing cup puller tool No. 308–047 or equivalents.
3. Remove cover seal if necessary.

Installation

Ensure that heat deflector is not overheated during installation. If damage occurs, a new seal deflector must be used.

1. Heat seal deflector using a suitable heat gun. Direct heat across the back of seal deflector near white tabs.
2. Install seal deflector immediately after heating using seal installer tool Nos. 308–430 and 308–431 or equivalents.
3. Ensure seal deflector is fully seated and that there are no cracks on face or inner diameter white tab.
4. If cover seal was removed, install a new one using seal installer tool Nos. 308–430 and 308–431 or equivalents.
5. Install a new intermediate shaft seal using bearing cup installer tool No. 204–038 and handle tool No. 205–153 or equivalents.

INTAKE MANIFOLD
REPLACE
Upper

1. Remove air cleaner outlet tube.
2. Disconnect throttle body electrical connector.
3. Disconnect EVAP tube from intake manifold as outlined under "Precautions."
4. Disconnect brake booster vacuum

hose from intake manifold, then the PCV valve tube and electrical connector.

5. Detach wiring harness retainers from upper intake manifold.
6. **On models equipped with engine block heater,** detach wiring harness retainer from upper intake manifold.
7. **On all models,** disconnect 2 support brackets from upper intake manifold, **Fig. 11.**
8. Remove six upper intake manifold attaching bolts, then the manifold.
9. Reverse procedure to install. Tighten manifold to specifications in sequence as shown in **Fig. 12.**

Lower

1. Raise and support vehicle.
2. Drain coolant into a suitable container, then lower vehicle.
3. Relieve fuel pressure as outlined under "Precautions."
4. Remove upper intake manifold as outlined under "Intake Manifold Replace," "Upper."
5. Disconnect fuel line from fuel rail as outlined under "Precautions."
6. Disconnect fuel injector electrical connectors.
7. Remove fuel rail attaching bolts.
8. Remove fuel injectors together with fuel rail.
9. Remove two thermostat housing to lower intake bolts, **Fig. 13.**
10. Remove ten lower intake manifold attaching bolts, then the lower intake manifold.
11. Reverse procedure to install noting the following:
    a. Tighten manifold to specifications in sequence as shown in **Fig. 14.**
    b. Install new fuel injector O-rings and lubricate with suitable clean engine oil.
    c. Fill all fluids to proper capacity and specifications.
    d. Bleed cooling system as outlined under "Cooling System Bleed."

EXHAUST MANIFOLD
REPLACE
Lefthand

1. Raise and support vehicle.
2. Disconnect catalyst monitor sensor.
3. Remove underbody splash shield.

4. Remove and discard two Y-pipe to resonator nuts, then the four Y-pipe to catalytic converter nuts.
5. Remove catalytic converter as follows:
    a. Remove two catalytic converter support bracket to transmission bolts.
    b. Remove and discard four catalytic converter nuts and gasket.
6. Remove and discard four catalytic converter to exhaust manifold studs.
7. Disconnect HO2S sensor and remove using HO2S sensor socket tool No. 303–476 or equivalent.
8. Remove exhaust manifold heat shield.
9. Remove and discard six exhaust manifold attaching nuts.
10. Remove exhaust manifold and discard gasket.
11. Remove and discard six exhaust manifold studs.
12. Reverse procedure to install noting the following:
    a. Clean exhaust manifold mating surface of cylinder head using a suitable metal surface prep.
    b. Inspect exhaust manifold gasket surface using a suitable straight edge and feeler gauge. Warpage limit is .030.
    c. Tighten manifold to specifications in sequence as shown in **Fig. 15.**
    d. Apply a thin coating of suitable anti-seize lubricant to HO2S threads before installation.

Righthand

1. Raise and support vehicle.
2. Disconnect catalyst monitor sensor.
3. Remove underbody splash shield.
4. Remove and discard two Y-pipe to resonator nuts, then the four Y-pipe to catalytic converter nuts.
5. Remove power steering gear heat shield.
6. Remove catalytic converter as follows:
    a. Remove roll restrictor bolt and rotate engine forward.
    b. Disconnect catalyst monitor sensor.
    c. Remove two catalytic converter support bracket to engine block nuts.
    d. Remove and discard four catalytic converter nuts and gasket.
7. Remove and discard four catalytic

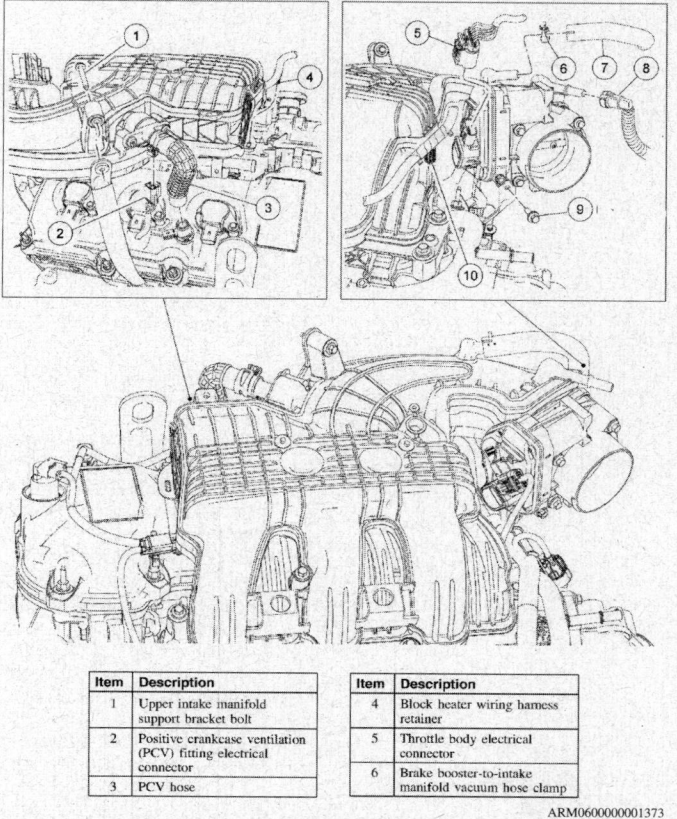

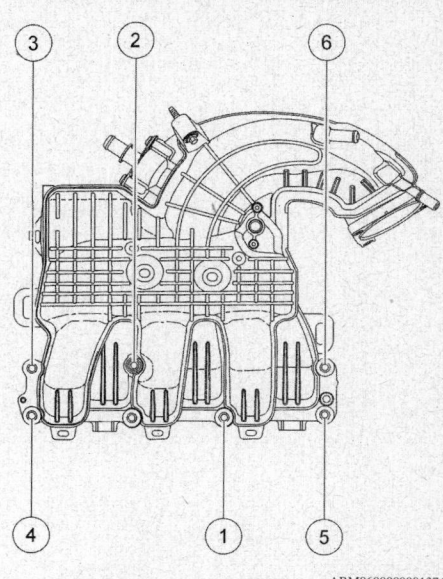

ARM0600000001374

Fig. 12 Upper intake manifold tightening sequence. 3.5L engine

Item	Description
1	Upper intake manifold support bracket bolt
2	Positive crankcase ventilation (PCV) fitting electrical connector
3	PCV hose

Item	Description
4	Block heater wiring harness retainer
5	Throttle body electrical connector
6	Brake booster-to-intake manifold vacuum hose clamp

ARM0600000001373

Fig. 11 Upper intake manifold support brackets. 3.5L engine

converter to exhaust manifold studs.
8. Disconnect righthand HO2S sensor.
9. Remove and discard six exhaust manifold attaching nuts.
10. Remove exhaust manifold.
11. Remove and discard six exhaust manifold studs.
12. Reverse procedure to install noting the following:
   a. Clean exhaust manifold mating surface of cylinder head using a suitable metal surface prep.
   b. Inspect exhaust manifold gasket surface using a suitable straight edge and feeler gauge. Warpage limit is .030.
   c. Tighten manifold to specifications in sequence as shown in **Fig. 16.**
   d. Apply a thin coating of suitable anti-seize lubricant to HO2S threads before installation.

CYLINDER HEAD
REPLACE
Lefthand

1. Remove camshafts as outlined under "Camshaft, Replace."
2. **On models equipped with engine block heater,** proceed as follows:
   a. Remove engine block heather heat shield.
   b. Disconnect engine block heater and remove harness from engine.

3. **On all models,** disconnect A/C compressor electrical connector.
4. Disconnect alternator electrical connectors.
5. Detach wiring harness from alternator.
6. Remove alternator, then disconnect oil pressure sensor and harness.
7. Disconnect fuel injector electrical connectors, then the cylinder head temperature sensor.
8. Remove radio interference capacitor and position aside.
9. Disconnect CMP sensor, then the lefthand HO2S sensor and catalyst monitor sensor.
10. Remove wiring harness retaining bolt from rear of cylinder head.
11. Remove exhaust manifold as outlined under "Exhaust Manifold, Replace."
12. Remove lefthand engine block drain plug, **Fig. 17.**
13. **On models equipped with AWD,** remove righthand catalytic converter bracket bolts.
14. **On all models,** remove righthand catalytic converter. Discard nuts and gasket.
15. Remove coolant drain plug or cylinder block heater from right side of engine block, **Fig. 18.**
16. Remove lower intake manifold as outlined under "Intake Manifold, Replace."
17. Remove lefthand CMP sensor, then the valve tappets from cylinder head. If valve tappets are to be reused, ensure that components are marked for instal-

lation reference.
18. Remove secondary timing chain tensioner.
19. Remove and discard "M6" bolt, **Fig. 19.**
20. Remove and discard 8 cylinder head bolts.
21. Remove cylinder head and gasket.
22. Reverse procedure to install noting the following:
   a. Install new gasket, cylinder head and 8 new bolts.
   b. Tighten in five stages using sequence shown in **Fig. 20** as follows: step 1, 15 ft. lbs.; step 2, 26 ft. lbs.; step 3, tighten an additional 90°; step 4, tighten an additional 90°; step 5, tighten an additional 90°.
   c. Install "M6" cylinder head bolt and **torque** to 89 inch lbs., **Fig. 19.**
   d. Apply suitable clean engine oil to tappets prior to installation.

Righthand

1. Remove camshafts as outlined under "Camshaft, Replace."
2. **On models equipped with engine block heater,** proceed as follows:
   a. Remove engine block heather heat shield.
   b. Disconnect engine block heater and remove harness from engine.
3. **On all models,** remove radio interference capacitor and position aside.
4. Disconnect CMP sensor, then the righthand HO2S sensor and catalyst monitor sensor.
5. Remove power steering tube and bracket and position aside.
6. Disconnect fuel injector electrical connectors, then the cylinder head temperature sensor.
7. Remove lefthand catalytic converter bracket bolts.
8. Remove and discard lefthand catalytic

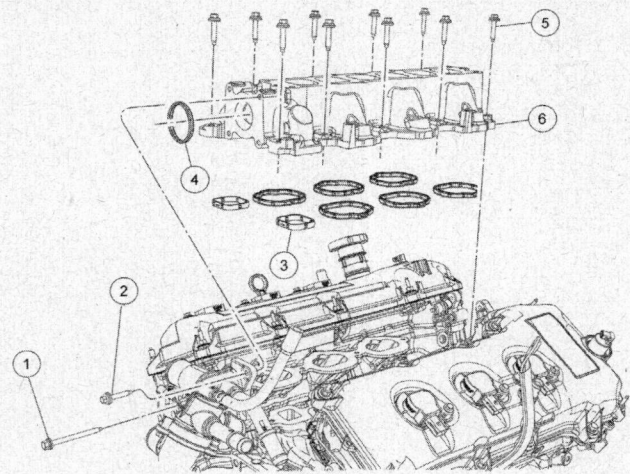

Item	Description
1	Thermostat housing-to-lower intake manifold bolt
2	Thermostat housing-to-lower intake manifold bolt
3	Lower intake manifold gasket (8 required)
4	Thermostat housing gasket
5	Lower intake manifold bolt (10 required)
6	Lower intake manifold

Fig. 13 Lower intake manifold removal. 3.5L engine

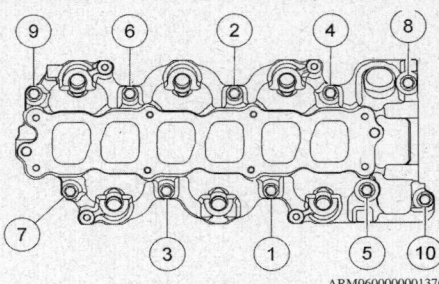

Fig. 14 Lower intake manifold tightening sequence. 3.5L engine

converter nuts and gasket.
9. Remove lefthand catalytic converter.
10. Remove lefthand engine block drain plug and drain coolant into a suitable container, **Fig. 17.**
11. Remove righthand exhaust manifold as outlined under "Exhaust Manifold, Replace."
12. Remove coolant drain plug or cylinder block heater from right side of engine block and drain coolant into a suitable container, **Fig. 18.**
13. Remove lower intake manifold as outlined under "Intake Manifold, Replace."
14. Remove secondary timing chain tensioner.
15. Remove engine lift bracket and upper intake manifold bracket from cylinder head.
16. Remove lefthand CMP sensor, then the valve tappets from cylinder head. If valve tappets are to be reused, ensure that components are marked for installation reference.
17. Remove cylinder head temperature sensor jumper harness.
18. Remove and discard "M6" bolt, **Fig. 21.**
19. Remove and discard 8 cylinder head bolts.
20. Remove cylinder head and gasket.
21. Reverse procedure to install noting the following:
   a. Install new gasket, cylinder head and 8 new bolts.
   b. Tighten in five stages using sequence shown in **Fig. 22** as follows: step 1, 15 ft. lbs.; step 2, 26 ft. lbs.; step 3, tighten an additional 90°; step 4, tighten an additional 90°; step 5, tighten an additional 90°.
   c. Install "M6" cylinder head bolt and **torque** to 89 inch lbs., **Fig. 21.**
   d. Apply suitable clean engine oil to tappets prior to installation.

VALVE COVER
REPLACE
Lefthand

1. Remove air cleaner outlet tube.
2. Disconnect crankcase vent tube from valve cover. Refer to "Precautions" for quick connect fitting procedures.
3. Disconnect coil on plug electrical connectors.
4. Remove ignition coils from spark plugs.
5. Remove dipstick, then disconnect lefthand variable cam timing solenoid.
6. Detach wiring harness retainers from hold down positions.
7. Disconnect two main engine control harness connectors, **Fig. 23.**
8. Remove wiring harness retaining bracket.
9. Detach wiring harness retainers from valve cover studs.
10. Disconnect fuel injector electrical connectors.
11. Remove valve cover attaching bolts, then the valve cover.
12. Inspect spark plug and variable cam timing solenoid seals in valve cover. If any are damaged, proceed as follows:
   a. Remove damaged seals using seal

removal tool No. 303–1247/1 and handle tool No. 205–153 or equivalents.
   b. Install new seal using seal installer tool No. 303–1247/2 and handle tool No. 205–153 or equivalents.
13. Reverse procedure to install noting the following:
   a. Apply a .310 inch bead of suitable silicone gasket and sealant on engine front cover to cylinder head joints.
   b. Ensure that valve cover is installed and tightened to specifications within 5 minutes of silicone gasket application.
   c. Tighten valve cover to specifications in sequence as shown in **Fig. 24.**

Righthand

1. Remove upper intake manifold as outlined under "Intake Manifold, Replace."
2. Disconnect coil on plug electrical connectors.
3. Remove ignition coils from spark plugs.
4. Siphon fluid from power steering reservoir using a suitable suction device.
5. Disconnect return hose from power steering fluid reservoir.
6. Remove power steering fluid reservoir from bracket by using a suitable screwdriver to depress and release retaining clip.
7. Disconnect power steering pressure switch, then the righthand catalyst monitor sensor.
8. Remove power steering pressure hose bracket from valve cover and position aside.
9. Disconnect righthand HO2S sensor, then the variable cam timing solenoid.
10. Disconnect fuel injectors, then the heated PCV valve electrical connector.
11. Detach wiring harness retainers from valve cover studs.
12. Remove A/C tube clamps and position aside.
13. Remove valve cover attaching bolts, then the valve cover.
14. Inspect spark plug and variable cam timing solenoid seals in valve cover. If any are damaged, proceed as follows:
   a. Remove damaged seals using seal removal tool No. 303–1247/1 and handle tool No. 205–153 or equivalents.

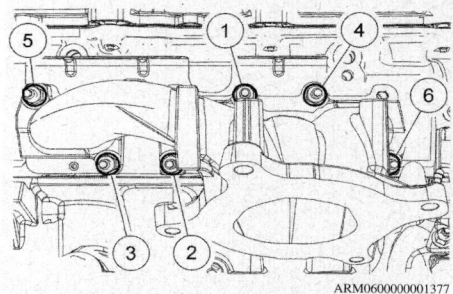

Fig. 15 Lefthand exhaust manifold tightening sequence. 3.5L engine

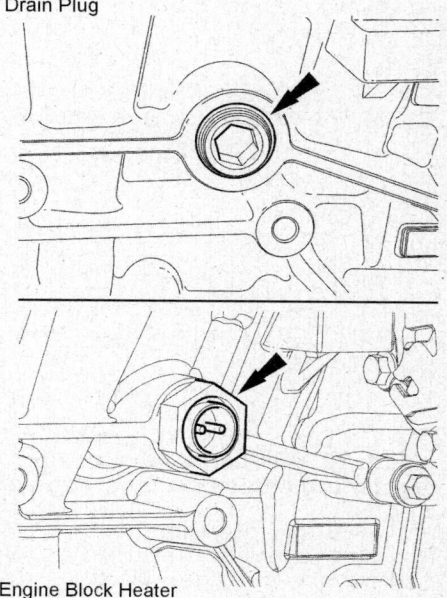

Drain Plug

Engine Block Heater

Fig. 18 Righthand engine block drain plug & block heater. 3.5L engine

b. Install new seal using seal installer tool No. 303–1247/2 and handle tool No. 205–153 or equivalents.
15. Reverse procedure to install noting the following:
   a. Apply a .310 inch bead of suitable silicone gasket and sealant on engine front cover to cylinder head joints.
   b. Ensure that valve cover is installed and tightened to specifications within 5 minutes of silicone gasket application.
   c. Tighten valve cover to specifications in sequence as shown in **Fig. 25.**

CAMSHAFT LOBE LIFT SPECIFICATIONS

Lobe Lift, Inch	
Intake	Exhaust
.380	.380

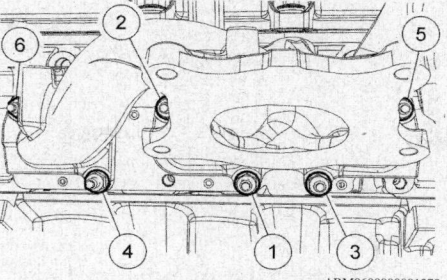

Fig. 16 Righthand exhaust manifold tightening sequence. 3.5L engine

VALVE CLEARANCE SPECIFICATIONS

Valve	Clearance, Inch
Exhaust	.012–.016
Intake	.006–.010

VALVE ADJUSTMENT

1. Remove valve covers as outlined under "Valve Cover, Replace."
2. Rotate crankshaft until base circle of camshaft lobe is resting on valve tappet, **Fig. 26.**
3. Using a suitable feeler gauge, inspect clearance between base circle of camshaft lobe and valve tappet. For intake valves, clearance should be .006–.010 inch. For exhaust valves, clearance should be .012–.016 inch.
4. Repeat procedure for remaining valves and record results.
5. If clearance is not within specifications, install new valve tappets where necessary.
6. To calculate required thickness of new tappet, proceed as follows:
   a. Inspect valve tappet for a number. For example, a valve tappet with a number of 3.51 has a thickness of 3.51 millimeters or .138 inch.
   b. For tappets where clearance is not within specifications, select a new tappet using the following formula: "Tappet Thickness = Measured Clearance + Base Tappet Thickness – Most Desirable Thickness."
   c. Select tappets and mark installation location.
7. If new tappet installation is necessary, remove camshafts as outlined under "Camshaft, Replace."
8. Remove valve tappets to be replaced.
9. Apply suitable clean engine oil to new tappets and install to cylinder head.
10. Install camshafts as outlined under "Camshaft replace."
11. Recheck valve clearance and ensure all are within specifications.
12. Install valve covers as outlined under "Valve Cover, Replace."

CRANKSHAFT DAMPER
REPLACE

1. Raise and support vehicle.
2. Remove accessory drive belt as outlined under "Serpentine Drive Belt."

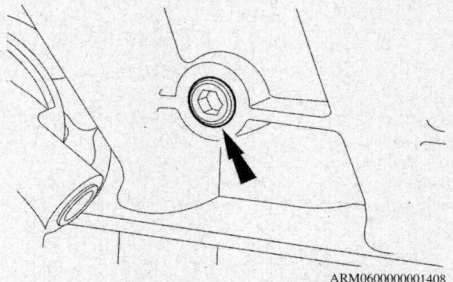

Fig. 17 Lefthand engine block drain plug. 3.5L engine

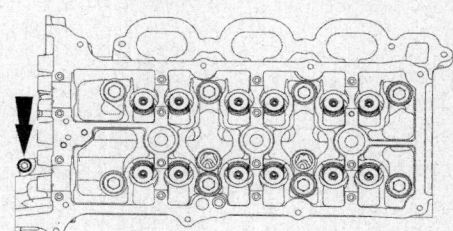

Fig. 19 Cylinder head M6 bolt location. 3.5L engine

3. Hold crankshaft damper using strap wrench tool No. 303–D055 or equivalent, then remove and discard crankshaft pulley bolt.
4. Remove crankshaft pulley using puller tool No. 303–D121 or equivalent, **Fig. 27.**
5. Reverse procedure to install noting the following:
   a. Lubricate crankshaft seal inner lip and outside diameter sealing surfaces using suitable engine oil.
   b. Install crankshaft pulley using threaded installer tool No. 303–102 and seal installer tool No. 303–335 or equivalents.
   c. Hold crankshaft pulley using strap wrench tool No. 303–D055 or equivalent, then tighten new pulley bolt in 4 stages as follows: Step 1, 89 ft. lbs.; step 2, loosen bolt 360°; step 3, 37 ft. lbs.; step 4, tighten an additional 90°.

FRONT COVER
REPLACE
Removal

1. Remove engine assembly as outlined under "Engine, Replace."
2. **On models equipped with engine block heater,** detach block heater wiring harness from upper intake manifold, power steering pressure hose and power steering reservoir hose.
3. **On all models,** disconnect PCV valve electrical connector.
4. Disconnect PCV hose from PCV valve.
5. Disconnect throttle body electrical connector.
6. Detach all wiring harness retainers from upper intake manifold.

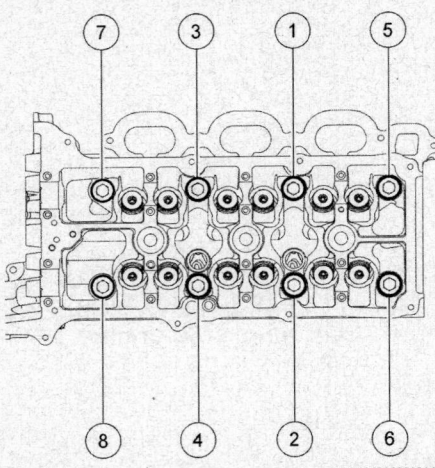

Fig. 20 Lefthand cylinder head tightening sequence. 3.5L engine

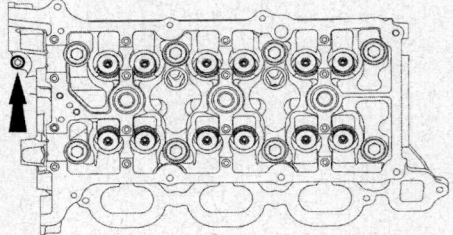

Fig. 21 Righthand cylinder head M6 bolt location. 3.5L engine

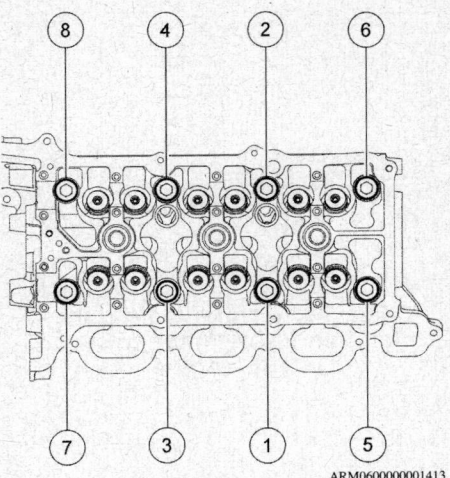

Fig. 22 Righthand cylinder head tightening sequence. 3.5L engine

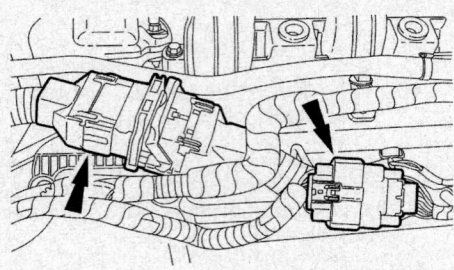

Fig. 23 Engine control main harness connectors. 3.5L engine

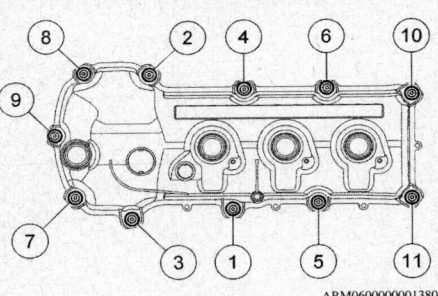

Fig. 24 Lefthand valve cover tightening sequence. 3.5L engine

must be used to ensure that all oil, gasket and foreign debris is removed from gasket surfaces.

Ensure that bolts 7, 8, 17, 18, 21, 22, 23, 24 and 25 are installed and tightened within 10 minutes of applying silicone gasket sealer to the front cover. If more than 10 minutes elapses, sealant must be removed and reapplied.

Ensure that the remainder of the front cover bolts (1, 2, 3, 4, 5, 6, 9, 10, 11, 12, 13, 14, 15, 16, 19, and 20) are installed and tightened to specifications within 60 minutes of initial sealant application. If more than 60 minutes elapses, sealant must be removed and reapplied.

1. Apply a .110 inch bead of suitable silicone gasket and sealant to front cover sealing surfaces, including the three engine mount bracket bosses, **Fig. 31.**
2. Apply a .210 inch bead of suitable silicone gasket and sealant on oil pan to engine block joints.
3. Install front cover and bolts 7, 8, 17, 18, 21 and 22, **Fig. 32. Torque** to 89 inch lbs.
4. Install engine mount bracket and three bolts. **Torque** in sequence shown in **Fig. 33** to 11 ft. lbs.
5. **Torque** bolts 7, 8, 17, 18, 21 and 22 to 18 ft. lbs., **Fig. 34.**
6. **Torque** bolts 23, 24 and 25 to 55 ft. lbs., **Fig. 34.**
7. Install bolts 1, 2, 3, 4, 5, 6, 9, 10, 11, 12, 13, 14, 15, 16, 19, and 20 and tighten in sequence, **Fig. 35,** as follows:
   a. Step 1, 89 inch lbs.
   b. Step 2, 18 ft. lbs.
8. Install 2 engine mount studs.
9. Apply suitable clean engine oil to crankshaft seal bore in front cover.
10. Install crankshaft front cover seal using seal installer tool No. 303–1251 and threaded installer tool No. 303–102 or equivalents.
11. Apply suitable clean engine oil to sealing surfaces of crankshaft pulley.
12. Install crankshaft pulley using threaded installer tool No. 303–102 and seal installer tool No. 303–335 or equivalents.
13. Hold crankshaft pulley using strap wrench tool No. 303–D055 or equivalent, then tighten new pulley bolt in 4 stages as follows:
   a. Step 1, 89 ft. lbs.
   b. Step 2, loosen bolt 360°.
   c. Step 3, 37 ft. lbs.
   d. Step 4, tighten an additional 90°.
14. Install valve covers as outlined under

7. Remove upper intake manifold as outlined under "Intake Manifold, Replace."
8. Remove right and left valve covers as outlined under "Valve Cover, Replace."
9. Remove power steering pump and position aside.
10. Remove three belt tensioner bolts, then the tensioner.
11. Attach strap wrench tool No. 303–D055 or equivalent to crankshaft pulley.
12. Hold crankshaft pulley using strap wrench tool No. 303–D055 or equivalent, then remove and discard crankshaft pulley bolt.
13. Remove crankshaft pulley using puller tool No. 303–D121 or equivalent, **Fig. 27.**
14. Remove and discard crankshaft front seal using oil seal removal tool No. 303–409 or equivalent.
15. Remove two engine mount studs shown in **Fig. 28.**
16. Remove engine mount bracket.
17. Remove 22 front cover bolts, **Fig. 29.**
18. Install bolts into four threaded holes in front cover, **Fig. 30.**
19. Tighten bolts one turn at a time using a criss-cross pattern until the front cover to cylinder block seal is released, then remove front cover.

Installation

A suitable gasket and oil removing agent

"Valve Cover, Replace."
15. Install upper intake manifold as outlined under "Intake Manifold, Replace."
16. Attach all wiring harness retainers from upper intake manifold.
17. Reconnect throttle body electrical connector.
18. Connect PCV hose from PCV valve.
19. **On models equipped with engine block heater,** attach block heater wiring harness from upper intake manifold, power steering pressure hose and power steering reservoir hose.
20. **On all models,** connect PCV valve electrical connector.
21. Install engine assembly as outlined under "Engine, Replace."

FRONT COVER SEAL
REPLACE

1. Remove crankshaft damper as outlined under "Crankshaft Damper, Replace."
2. Remove front cover seal using oil seal removal tool No. 303–409 or equivalent.
3. Reverse procedure to install. Apply suitable clean engine oil to new seal and install using seal installer tool No. 303–1251 or equivalent.

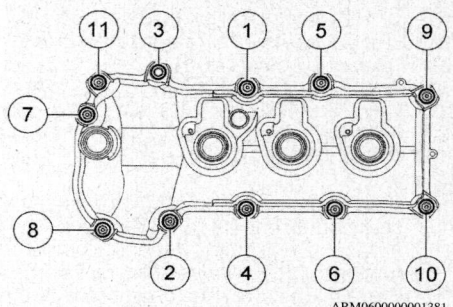

Fig. 25 Righthand valve cover tightening sequence. 3.5L engine

TIMING CHAIN

REPLACE

Refer to "Camshaft, Replace" for procedure.

CAMSHAFT

REPLACE

Removal

1. Remove front cover as outlined under "Front Cover, Replace."
2. Rotate crankshaft clockwise and align timing marks on variable cam timing assemblies as shown in **Fig. 36.**
3. Install camshaft alignment tool No. 303–1248 or equivalent to flats of camshafts, **Fig. 37.**
4. Remove variable cam timing housing from each cylinder head, **Fig. 38.**
5. Remove and discard variable cam timing housing seals.
6. Remove primary timing chain tensioner and tensioner arm, **Fig. 39.**
7. Remove lefthand lower primary timing chain guide, then the primary timing chain, **Fig. 39.**
8. Compress secondary timing chain tensioner, then install a suitable lockpin to retain tensioner in collapsed position, **Figs. 40 and 41.**
9. Remove and discard variable cam timing and exhaust camshaft sprocket bolts.
10. Remove variable cam timing sprocket, secondary timing chain and exhaust camshaft sprocket as an assembly.
11. Remove camshaft alignment tool from camshafts. When alignment tool is removed, valve spring pressure will rotate camshafts approximately 3° to a neutral position.
12. Verify that camshafts are in neutral position, **Figs. 42 and 43.**
13. Remove camshaft bearing caps, then the camshafts. Note position of caps for installation reference. Caps should already be marked to verify correct installation.

Installation

Crankshaft must remain in 9 O'clock position until after camshafts are installed and valve clearance is inspected, Fig. 44. Failure to do this will result in severe engine damage.

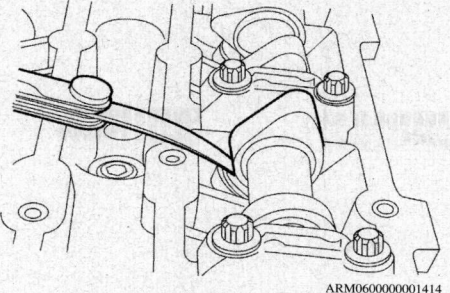

Fig. 26 Valve clearance measurement. 3.5L engine

1. Apply suitable clean engine oil to valve tappets and camshafts.
2. Position camshafts onto each cylinder head ensuring that each is in the neutral position as shown in **Figs. 42 and 43.**
3. Install camshaft bearing caps and tighten to specifications in sequence shown in **Figs. 45 and 46.**
4. Inspect valve clearance as outlined under "Valve Adjustment."
5. Install a camshaft sprocket bolt to each camshaft and finger tighten.
6. Rotate camshafts to TDC position using cam sprocket bolt, then install camshaft alignment tool No. 303–1248 or equivalent.
7. Assemble variable camshaft timing assembly ensuring that colored links are aligned with timing marks, **Figs. 47 and 48.**
8. Install secondary timing assembly to camshafts.
9. Install new camshaft sprocket bolts and tighten in sequence as follows:
   a. Step 1, 30 ft. lbs.
   b. Step 2, loosen 360°.
   c. Step 3, 89 inch lbs.
   d. Step 4, tighten an additional 90°.
10. Remove lockpin from secondary timing chain tensioner.
11. Rotate crankshaft clockwise 60° to TDC position. Crankshaft key should be at 11 O'clock position, **Fig. 49.**
12. Install primary timing chain ensuring that colored links are aligned with timing marks, **Fig. 50.**
13. Install lefthand primary timing chain guide, then the primary timing chain tensioner arm, **Fig. 39.**
14. Reset primary timing chain tensioner as follows:
   a. Rotate actuating lever counterclockwise, **Fig. 51.**
   b. Compress tensioner plunger using a suitable soft jawed vise.
   c. Align actuating lever with hole in tensioner housing and install a suitable lockpin.
15. Install primary timing chain tensioner and remove lockpin.
16. Ensure that timing marks are still aligned as shown in **Fig. 50.**
17. Install new variable cam timing control housing seals.
18. Install variable cam timing control housings and tighten in sequence, **Figs. 52 and 53.** Ensure that dowels of variable cam timing control as-

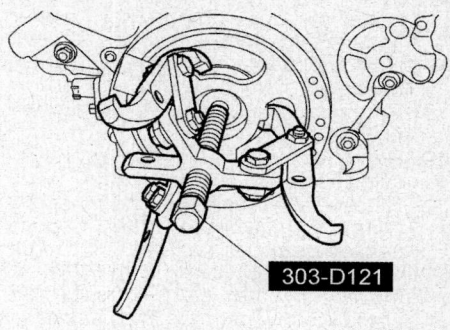

Fig. 27 Crankshaft pulley removal. 3.5L engine

sembly housing are fully engaged into cylinder head before tightening.
19. Install front cover as outlined under "Front Cover, Replace."

OIL PAN

REPLACE

The oil pan must be installed and aligned to cylinder block and A/C compressor within 5 minutes of sealant application. Final tightening of oil pan bolts must be carried out within 60 minutes of sealant application.

1. Remove engine as outlined under "Engine, Replace."
2. Remove flywheel, then the crankshaft sensor ring.
3. Mount engine to a suitable engine stand.
4. **On models equipped with engine block heater,** proceed as follows:
   a. Disconnect engine block heater harness retainer from upper intake manifold.
   b. Remove heat shield and disconnect harness connector from engine block heater.
5. **On all models,** disconnect PCV electrical connector, then the PCV hose from PCV valve.
6. Disconnect throttle body electrical connector.
7. Detach all wiring harness retainers from upper intake manifold.
8. Remove upper intake manifold support bracket bolts.
9. Remove six bolts, then the upper intake manifold.
10. Disconnect power steering pressure switch.
11. **On models equipped with FWD,** disconnect righthand catalyst monitor sensor.
12. **On all models,** disconnect right and left variable camshaft timing solenoids.
13. Disconnect coil on plug electrical connectors, then the lefthand catalyst monitor sensor.
14. Disconnect wire harness retainers from right and left valve covers.
15. Remove A/C compressor nut and stud, **Fig. 54.**
16. Remove accessory drive belt and

17. Remove power steering pump belt as outlined under "Serpentine Drive Belt."
18. Remove power steering hose retainer from engine lifting eye.
19. Remove power steering hose bracket nut.
20. Remove power steering pump and position aside.
21. Remove drive belt tensioner, then the lefthand catalytic converter. Discard converter nuts and gasket.
22. **On models equipped with FWD,** remove righthand catalytic converter. Discard converter nuts and gasket.
23. **On models less engine block heater,** remove righthand engine block drain plug and drain coolant into a suitable container, **Fig. 18.**
24. **On models equipped with engine block heater,** remove block heater and drain coolant into a suitable container, **Fig. 18.**
25. **On all models,** remove lefthand drain plug from engine block and drain coolant into a suitable container.
26. Remove valve covers as outlined under "Valve Cover, Replace."
27. Remove front cover as outlined under "Front Cover, Replace."
28. Install two oil pan bolts to locations shown in **Fig. 55.**
29. Alternately tighten bolts one turn at a time until oil pan to cylinder block seal is released, then remove oil pan.
30. Reverse procedure to install noting the following:
   a. Apply a .110 inch bead of suitable silicone gasket and sealant to sealing surface of oil pan, then apply a .210 inch bead of silicone gasket sealant to two crankshaft seal retainer plate to engine block joint areas on sealing surface of oil pan, **Fig. 56.**
   b. Install oil pan and **torque** in sequence to 27 inch lbs., **Fig. 57.**
   c. Loosen bolts 180°.
   d. Position oil pan mounting boss against A/C compressor. Align oil pan flush with rear of cylinder block using a suitable straightedge, **Fig. 58.**
   e. **Torque** bolts 1–14 to 18 ft. lbs., **Fig. 57.**
   f. **Torque** bolts 15 and 16 to 89 inch lbs.

OIL PUMP
REPLACE

1. Remove front cover as outlined under "Front Cover, Replace."
2. Remove primary timing chain as outlined under "Camshafts, Replace."
3. Remove crankshaft timing chain sprocket.
4. Remove oil pump screen and pickup tube bolts.
5. Remove three oil pump attaching bolts.
6. Rotate oil pump clockwise and separate oil pump from pickup screen, then remove oil pump.
7. Discard oil pump screen and pickup tube O-ring seal.

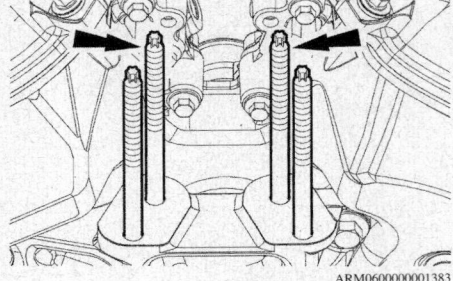

Fig. 28 Engine mount stud removal. 3.5L engine

8. Reverse procedure to install. Install a new oil pump screen and pickup tube O-ring seal.

SERPENTINE DRIVE BELT
Belt Routing

Refer to **Figs. 59 through 61** for serpentine drive belt routing.

Belts, Replace

1. Rotate belt tensioner clockwise using a suitable belt tension release tool, **Fig. 59.**
2. Remove belt from alternator pulley.
3. Raise and support vehicle.
4. Remove four screws and 6 pin-type retainers, then the righthand fender splash shield.
5. Remove accessory drive belt.
6. Install power steering belt removal tool No. 303–1252/1 between power steering pump belt and pulley, **Fig. 62.**
7. Rotate crankshaft clockwise to remove power steering belt.
8. Reverse procedure to install noting the following:
   a. Install power steering belt around crankshaft pulley first, then around bottom of power steering pump pulley.
   b. Install power steering belt installation tool No. 303–1252/2 or equivalent to power steering pulley, then rotate crankshaft clockwise to install belt, **Fig. 63.**
   c. Ensure accessory belt routing is as shown in **Fig. 60.**

Belt Tensioner, Replace

1. Remove accessory drive belt as outlined under "Serpentine Drive Belt", "Belts, Replace."
2. Remove three belt tensioner bolts, then the tensioner.
3. Reverse procedure to install.

COOLING SYSTEM BLEED

If engine overheats or fluid level drops below minimum fill line during this procedure, turn engine off and add fluid to degas bottle maximum fill line after the engine has cooled.

1. Open degas bottle, then the bleed valve on thermostat housing, **Fig. 64.**
2. Fill degas bottle to "MAX" line.
3. Close degas bottle cap and bleed valve.
4. Start engine and run at idle for ten minutes or until engine reaches normal operating temperature. Open thermostat housing bleed valve two full turns, **Fig. 64,** for two of the ten minutes, then close bleed valve.
5. Let engine cool and repeat procedure as necessary.
6. Start engine and turn heater to "MAX" setting.
7. Open thermostat housing bleed valve two full turns and let engine idle for two minutes, then close bleed valve.
8. Let engine idle for an additional eight minutes.
9. Operate engine at 2500 RPM for ten minutes and repeat as necessary.
10. Ensure coolant level of degas bottle is at "MAX" line.

THERMOSTAT
REPLACE

1. Release pressure in cooling system by slowly turning pressure relief cap ½ turn counterclockwise. When pressure is released, remove cap.
2. Open radiator draincock and drain coolant into a suitable container.
3. Disconnect lower radiator hose from thermostat housing and position aside, **Fig. 65.**
4. Remove thermostat housing cover, then the thermostat.
5. Reverse procedure to install. Lubricate thermostat O-ring seal with clean engine coolant before installation.

WATER PUMP
REPLACE
Removal

1. Remove front cover as outlined under "Front Cover, Replace."
2. Disconnect lefthand catalyst monitor sensor.
3. Remove lefthand catalytic converter bracket bolts, then the converter to exhaust manifold attaching nuts. Discard converter to manifold nuts.
4. Remove lefthand engine block drain plug and drain coolant into a suitable container, **Fig. 17.**
5. **On models equipped with AWD,** remove two righthand catalytic converter bracket bolts.
6. **On all models,** remove righthand catalytic converter from exhaust manifold and discard attaching nuts.
7. **On models equipped with engine block heater,** proceed as follows:
   a. Remove engine block heater heat shield.
   b. Disconnect engine block heater.
   c. Remove engine block heater and

drain coolant into a suitable container, **Fig. 18.**

8. **On models less engine block heater,** remove righthand engine block drain plug and drain coolant into a suitable container, **Fig. 18.**
9. **On all models,** rotate crankshaft clockwise and align timing marks on variable cam timing assemblies as shown in **Fig. 36.**
10. Install camshaft alignment tool No. 303–1248 or equivalent to flats of camshafts, **Fig. 37.**
11. Remove variable cam timing housing from each cylinder head, **Fig. 38.**
12. Remove and discard variable cam timing housing seals.
13. Remove primary timing chain tensioner and tensioner arm, **Fig. 39.**
14. Remove lefthand lower primary timing chain guide, then the primary timing chain, **Fig. 39.**
15. Remove lefthand upper primary timing chain guide, **Fig. 39.**
16. Remove righthand timing chain guide lower bolt.
17. Loosen righthand timing chain guide upper bolt, rotate guide, then tighten bolt.
18. Remove eight water pump attaching bolts, then the water pump, **Fig. 66.**

Installation

1. Install water pump and tighten to specifications in sequence, **Fig. 66.**
2. Loosen righthand primary timing chain guide upper bolt, align guide, then reinstall lower bolt. Tighten to specifications.
3. Install primary timing chain ensuring that colored links are aligned with timing marks, **Fig. 50.**
4. Install lefthand upper and lower timing chain guides.
5. Install primary timing chain tensioner arm.
6. Reset primary timing chain tensioner as follows:
   a. Rotate actuating lever counterclockwise, **Fig. 51.**
   b. Compress tensioner plunger using a suitable soft jawed vise.
   c. Align actuating lever with hole in tensioner housing and install a suitable lockpin.
7. Install primary timing chain tensioner and remove lockpin.
8. Ensure that timing marks are still aligned as shown in **Fig. 50.**
9. Install new variable cam timing control housing seals.
10. Install variable cam timing control housings and tighten in sequence, **Figs. 52 and 53. Ensure that dowels of variable cam timing control assembly housing are fully engaged into cylinder head before tightening.**
11. **On models equipped with engine block heater,** install engine block heater, then connect wiring harness

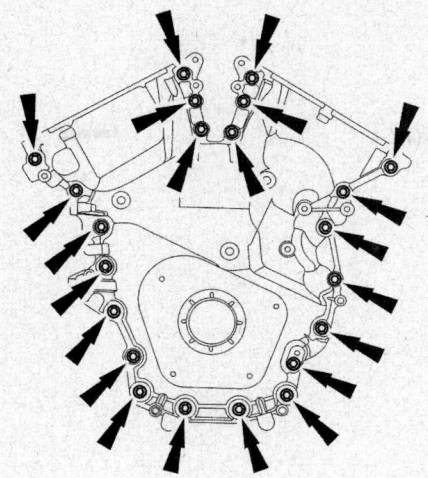

Fig. 29 Front cover bolt location. 3.5L engine

ARM0600000001384

and heat shield.

12. **On models less engine block heater,** install engine block drain plug.
13. **On FWD models,** install catalytic converter using new nuts and gasket.
14. **On AWD models,** proceed as follows:
   a. Install righthand catalytic converter using new nuts and gasket. Do not tighten until support bracket is installed.
   b. Install catalytic converter support bracket
15. **On all models,** install lefthand cylinder block drain plug.
16. Install lefthand catalytic converter using new nuts and gasket.
17. Install lefthand catalytic converter bracket.
18. Connect catalyst monitor sensors.
19. Install front cover as outlined under "Front Cover, Replace."

RADIATOR

REPLACE

1. Release pressure in cooling system by slowly turning pressure relief cap ½ turn counterclockwise. When pressure is released, remove cap.
2. Open radiator draincock and drain coolant into a suitable container.
3. Disconnect MAF sensor, then remove air filter outlet tube.
4. Remove air cleaner housing assembly, then the air filter housing bracket.
5. **On models equipped with engine block heater,** disconnect three wiring harness retainers from cooling fan motor and shroud and position aside.
6. **On all models,** raise and support vehicle, then remove under vehicle splash shield.
7. Disconnect lower radiator hose from cooling fan and shroud.
8. Detach transmission cooler lines and four wiring harness retainers from cooling fan shroud and position aside.

9. Disconnect cooling fan electrical connector.
10. Lower vehicle, then release two cooling fan shroud clips and remove shroud, **Fig. 67.**
11. Detach power steering hose retainer from radiator.
12. Disconnect upper radiator hose from radiator, then the degas bottle hose.
13. Disconnect transaxle cooler lines and lower radiator hose from radiator.
14. Disengage radiator securing clips from upper radiator support.
15. Disconnect A/C condenser to radiator pushpin retainer.
16. Depress tabs, then separate A/C condenser from radiator.
17. Remove radiator from vehicle.
18. Reverse procedure to install. Bleed cooling system as outlined under "Cooling System Bleed."

FUEL PUMP

REPLACE

1. Relieve fuel pressure as outlined under "Precautions."
2. Remove fuel tank filler cap and position aside.
3. Insert fuel draining hose tool No. 310–102 or equivalent into fuel filler neck, then down into fuel tank.
4. Attach fuel storage tank tool No. 164–R3202 or equivalent to fuel drain hose and remove as much fuel as possible from fuel tank.
5. Push rear seat cushion rearward far enough to disengage seat retainers, then lift up on seat and remove from vehicle.
6. Lift carpet and position aside to access fuel pump access cover, **Fig. 68.**
7. **On FWD models,** remove four access cover screws, then the access cover.
8. **On AWD models,** remove 3 access cover screws, then the access cover.
9. **On all models,** disconnect fuel pump electrical connector.
10. Disconnect fuel supply tube as outlined under "Precautions", "Quick Disconnect Hoses.".
11. Remove fuel pump lockring using lock ring wrench tool No. 310–123 or equivalent.
12. **On AWD models,** lift fuel pump from fuel tank enough to access and release fuel crossover tube. Refer to "Precautions", "Quick Disconnect Hoses" for quick disconnect procedures.
13. **On all models,** remove fuel pump from tank.
14. Drain residual fuel from fuel pump into a suitable container.
15. Reverse procedure to install noting the following:
   a. Inspect fuel pump and tank sealing surfaces for damage and replace as necessary.
   b. Apply suitable clean engine oil to new O-ring seal before installation.

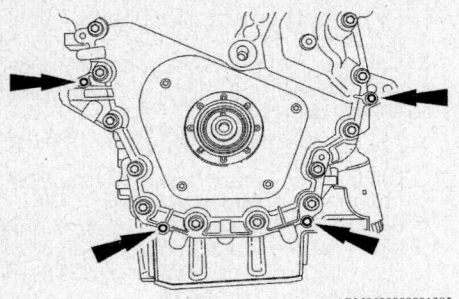

Fig. 30 Front cover removal hole locations. 3.5L engine

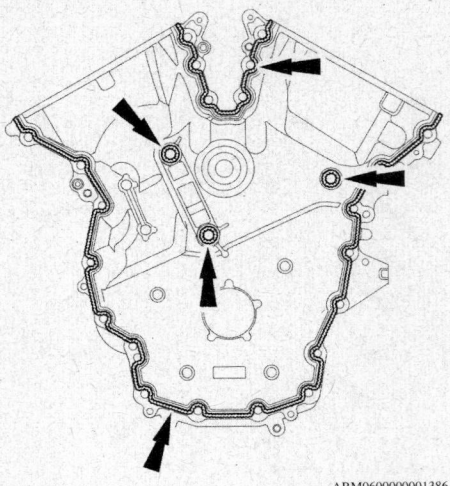

Fig. 31 Front cover sealant application. 3.5L engine

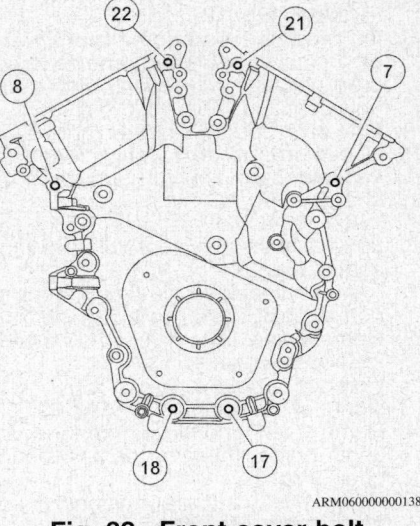

Fig. 32 Front cover bolt installation (Sequence 1). 3.5L engine

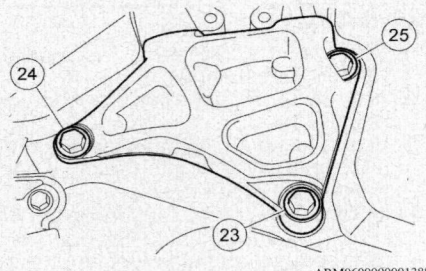

Fig. 33 Front cover bolt installation (Sequence 2). 3.5L engine

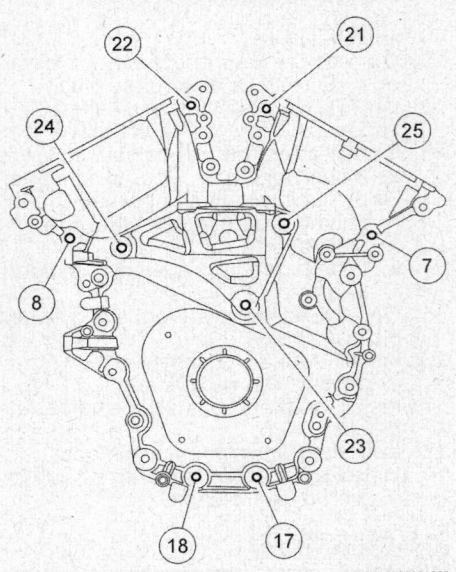

Fig. 34 Front cover bolt installation (Sequence 3). 3.5L engine

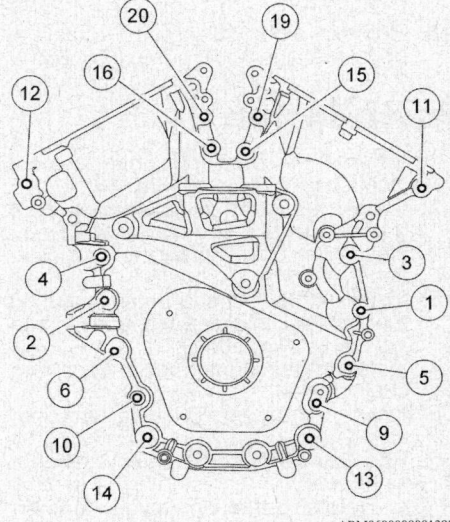

Fig. 35 Front cover bolt installation (Sequence 4). 3.5L engine

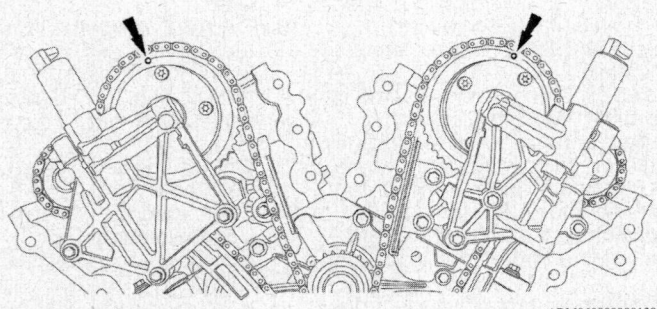

Fig. 36 Variable camshaft timing assembly timing mark alignment. 3.5L engine

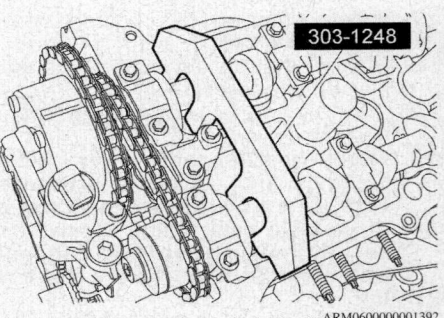

Fig. 37 Camshaft alignment tool installation. 3.5L engine

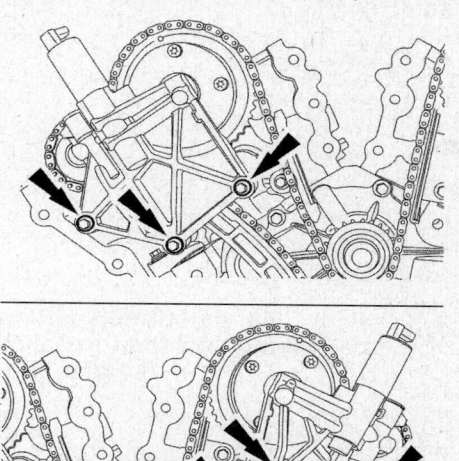

Fig. 38 Variable cam timing housing removal

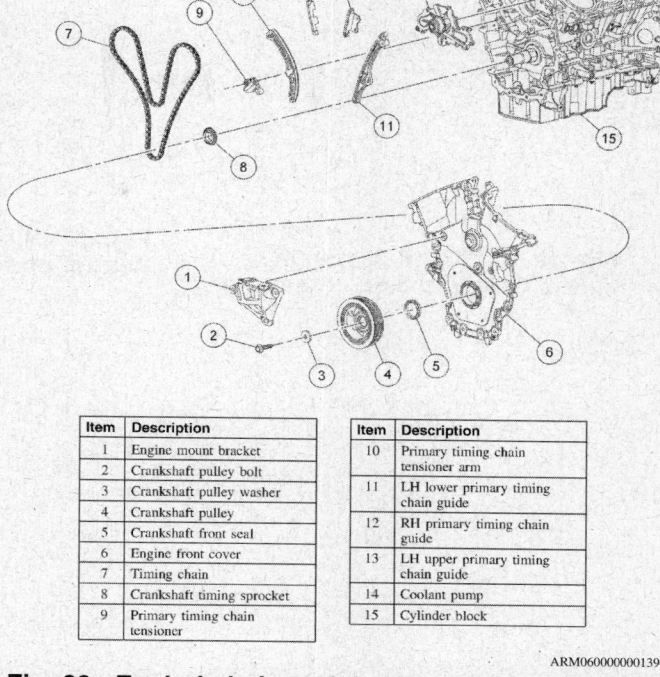

Item	Description
1	Engine mount bracket
2	Crankshaft pulley bolt
3	Crankshaft pulley washer
4	Crankshaft pulley
5	Crankshaft front seal
6	Engine front cover
7	Timing chain
8	Crankshaft timing sprocket
9	Primary timing chain tensioner

Item	Description
10	Primary timing chain tensioner arm
11	LH lower primary timing chain guide
12	RH primary timing chain guide
13	LH upper primary timing chain guide
14	Coolant pump
15	Cylinder block

Fig. 39 Exploded view of timing components. 3.5L engine

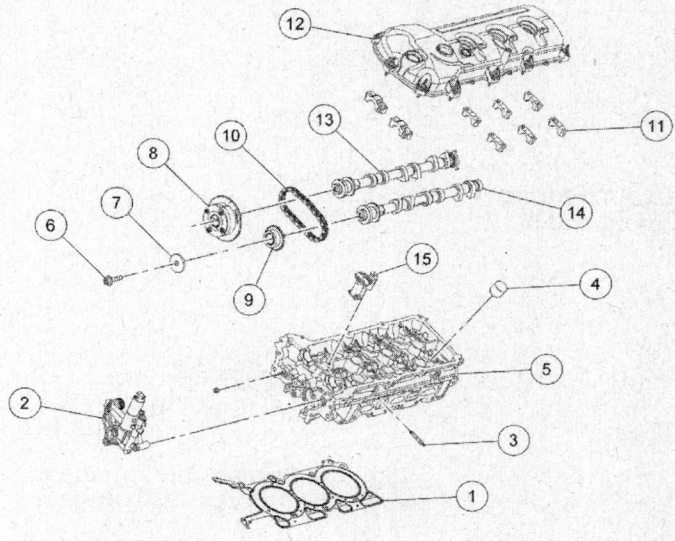

Item	Description
1	LH cylinder head gasket
2	LH variable camshaft timing (VCT) housing
3	LH exhaust manifold stud (6 required)
4	Valve tappet (32 required)
5	LH cylinder head
6	LH camshaft bolt (2 required)
7	LH exhaust camshaft sprocket washer

Item	Description
8	LH VCT assembly
9	LH exhaust camshaft sprocket
10	LH secondary timing chain
11	LH camshaft cap (8 required)
12	LH valve cover
13	LH intake camshaft
14	LH exhaust camshaft
15	LH secondary timing chain tensioner

Fig. 40 Exploded view of lefthand camshafts & secondary timing components. 3.5L engine

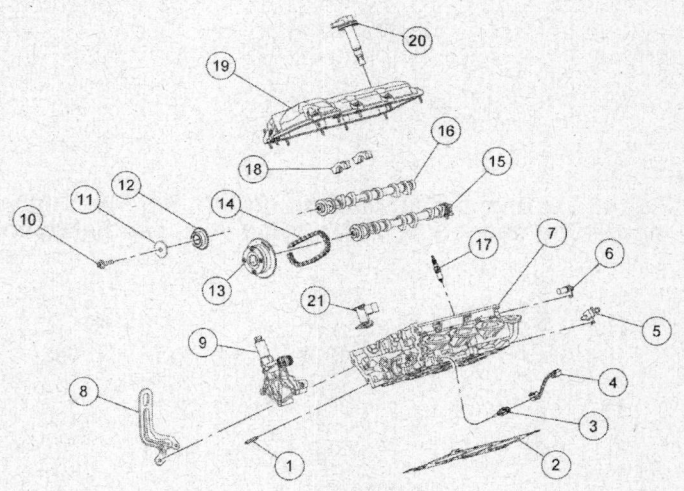

Item	Description
1	RH exhaust manifold stud (6 required)
2	RH cylinder head gasket
3	Cylinder head temperature (CHT) sensor
4	CHT sensor jumper harness
5	Radio interference capacitor (2 required)
6	Camshaft position sensor (2 required)
7	RH cylinder head
8	Engine lift eye
9	RH variable camshaft timing (VCT) housing

Item	Description
10	RH camshaft bolt (2 required)
11	RH exhaust camshaft sprocket washer
12	RH exhaust camshaft sprocket
13	RH VCT assembly
14	RH secondary timing chain
15	RH intake camshaft
16	RH exhaust camshaft
17	Spark plug (6 required)
18	RH camshaft cap (8 required)
19	RH valve cover
20	Coil-on-plug (6 required)
21	RH secondary timing chain tensioner

Fig. 41 Exploded view of righthand camshafts & secondary timing components. 3.5L engine

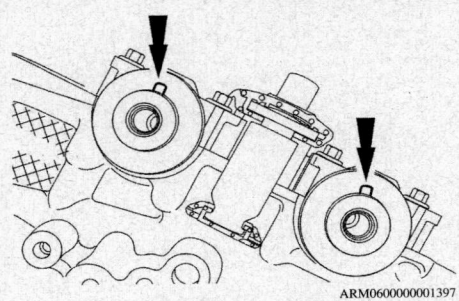

Fig. 42 Lefthand camshaft neutral position. 3.5L engine

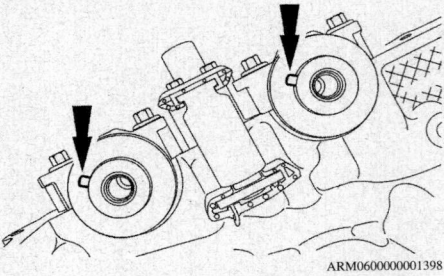

Fig. 43 Righthand camshaft neutral position. 3.5L engine

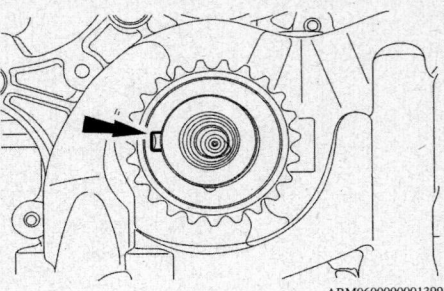

Fig. 44 Crankshaft position during camshaft installation. 3.5L engine

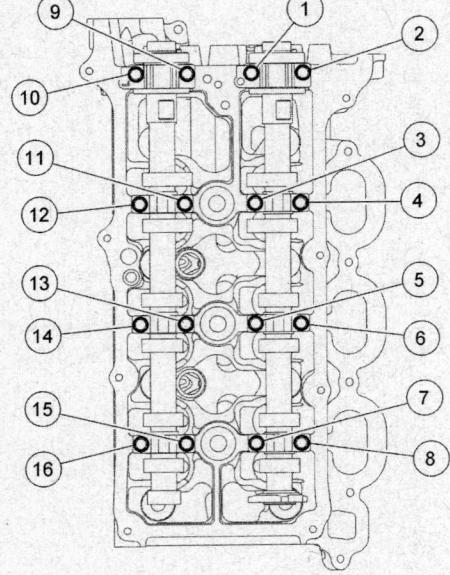

Fig. 45 Lefthand cam bearing cap tightening sequence. 3.5L engine

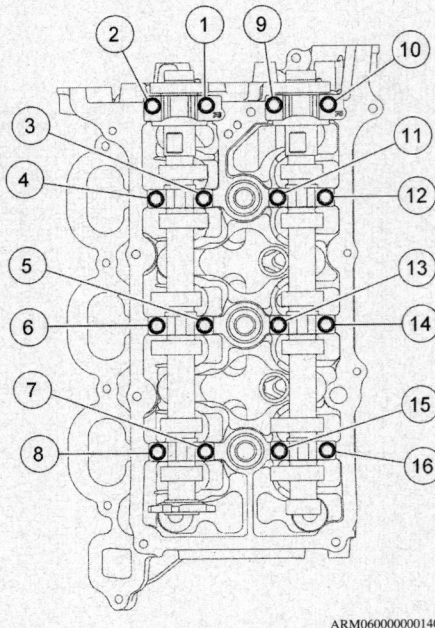

Fig. 46 Righthand cam bearing cap tightening sequence. 3.5L engine

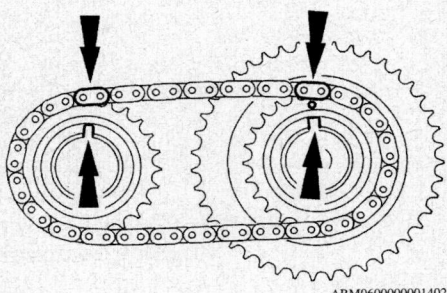

Fig. 47 Lefthand variable timing assembly timing marks. 3.5L engine

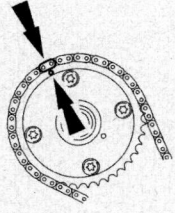

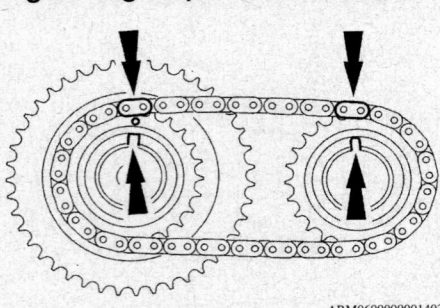

Fig. 48 Righthand variable timing assembly timing marks. 3.5L engine

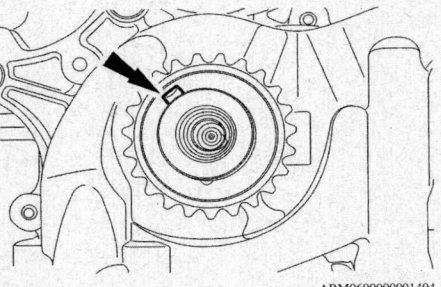

Fig. 49 Alignment of crankshaft to TDC. 3.5L engine

Fig. 50 Primary timing chain alignment marks. 3.5L engine

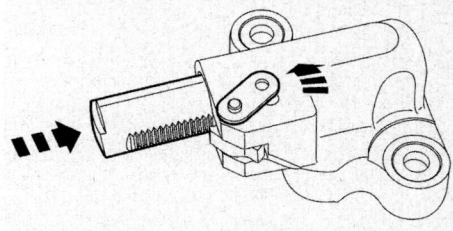

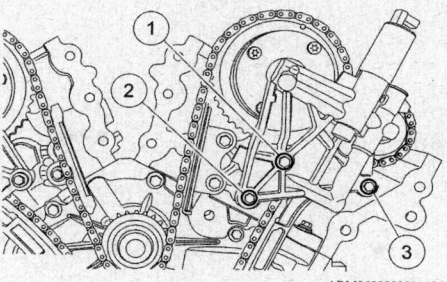

ARM0600000001406

Fig. 52 Lefthand variable cam timing control housing tightening sequence. 3.5L engine

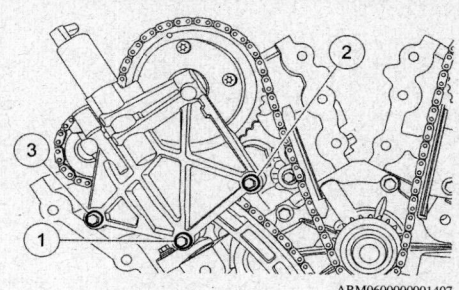

ARM0600000001407

Fig. 53 Righthand variable cam timing control housing tightening sequence. 3.5L engine

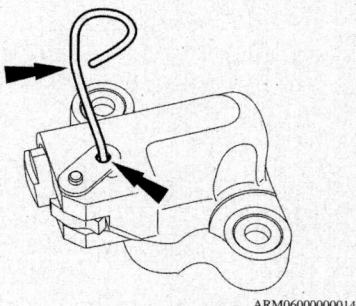

ARM0600000001405

Fig. 51 Primary timing chain reset. 3.5L engine

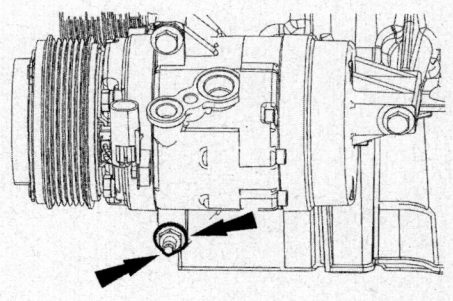

ARM0600000001426

Fig. 54 A/C compressor fastener removal. 3.5L engine

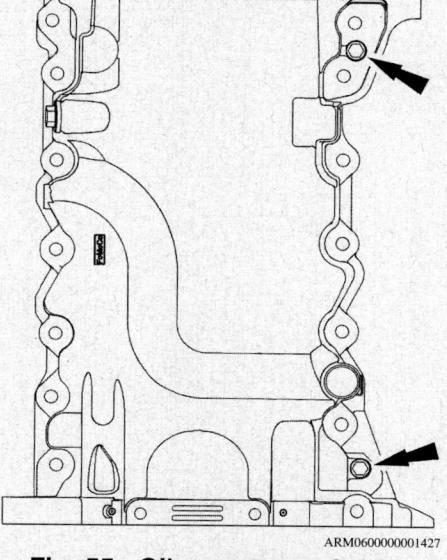

ARM0600000001427

Fig. 55 Oil pan removal. 3.5L engine

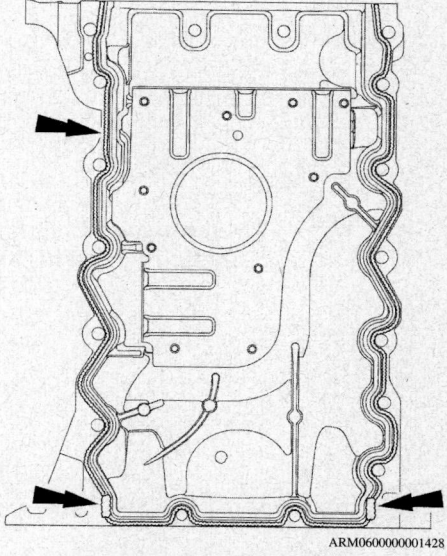

ARM0600000001428

Fig. 56 Oil pan sealant application. 3.5L engine

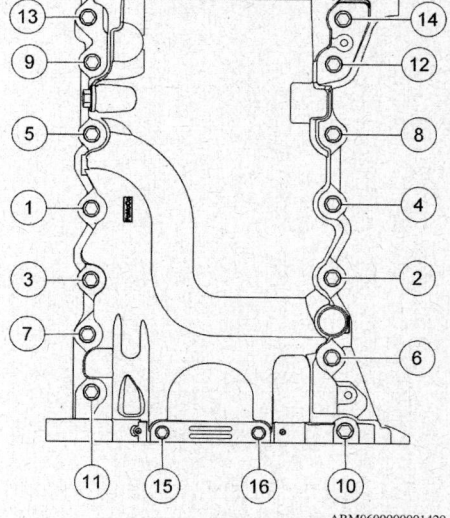

ARM0600000001429

Fig. 57 Oil pan tightening sequence. 3.5L engine

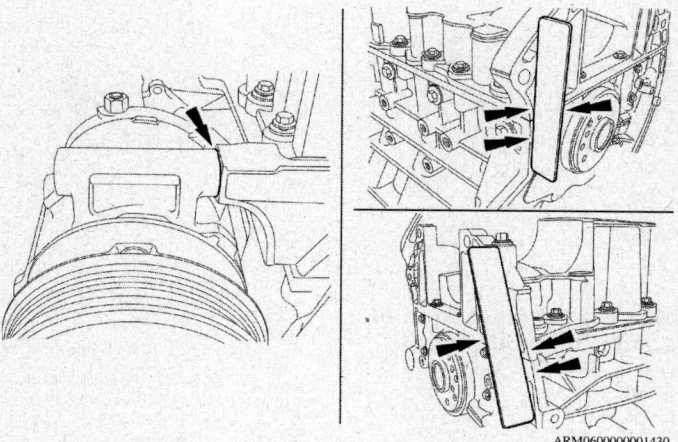

ARM0600000001430

Fig. 58 Oil pan alignment. 3.5L engine

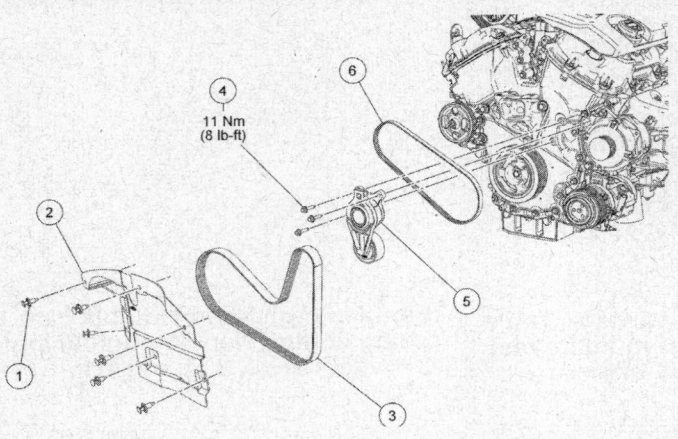

11 Nm
(8 lb-ft)

ARM0600000001417

Item	Description
1	Pin-type retainer (6 required)
2	RH splash shield
3	Accessory drive belt
4	Accessory drive belt tensioner bolt (3 required)

Item	Description
5	Accessory drive belt tensioner
6	Power steering pump drive belt

Fig. 59 Exploded view of accessory drive belt system. 3.5L engine

ARM0600000001418

Item	Description
1	Accessory drive belt tensioner pulley
2	Generator pulley
3	A/C clutch pulley

Item	Description
4	Accessory drive belt
5	Crankshaft pulley

Fig. 60 Accessory drive belt routing. 3.5L engine

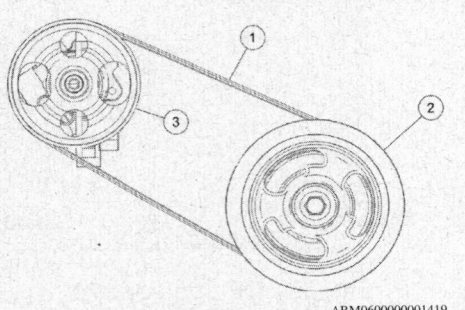

ARM0600000001419

Fig. 61 Power steering belt routing. 3.5L engine

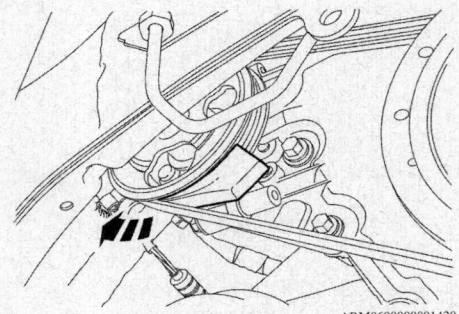

ARM0600000001420

Fig. 62 Power steering belt removal. 3.5L engine

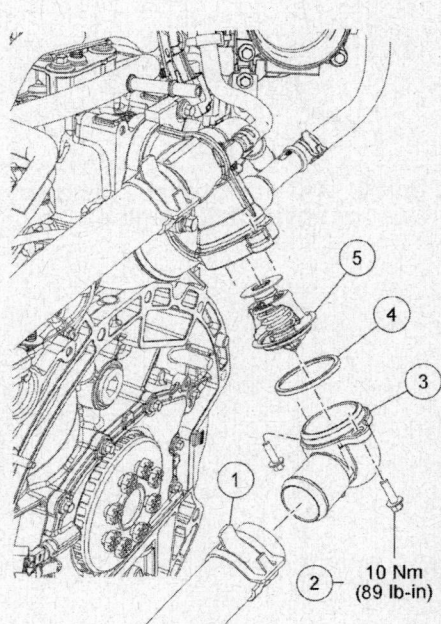

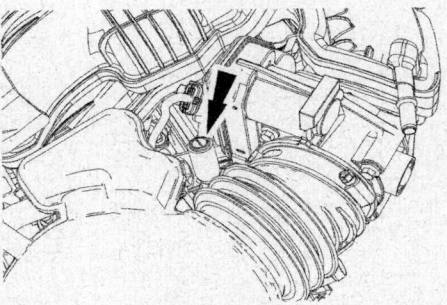

ARM0600000001421

Fig. 63 Power steering belt installation. 3.5L engine

ARM0600000001416

Fig. 64 Thermostat housing bleed valve. 3.5L engine

10 Nm
(89 lb-in)

ARM0600000001415

Item	Description
1	Lower radiator-to-thermostat housing cover hose
2	Thermostat housing cover bolt (2 required)
3	Thermostat housing cover
4	O-ring seal
5	Thermostat

Fig. 65 Thermostat removal. 3.5L engine

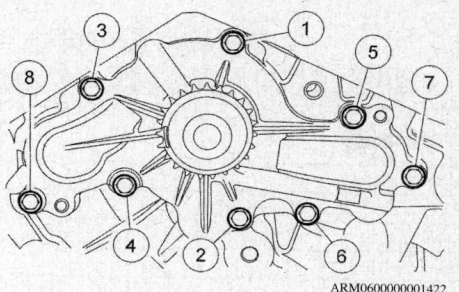

Fig. 66 Water pump bolt location & tightening sequence. 3.5L engine

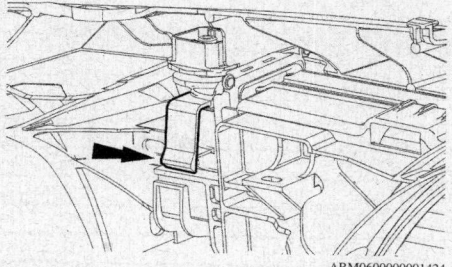

Fig. 67 Cooling fan removal. 3.5L engine

1. Fuel pump access cover screws
2. Access cover
3. Lock ring
4. Fuel pump
5. O-ring seal
6. Electrical connector
7. Fuel supply line

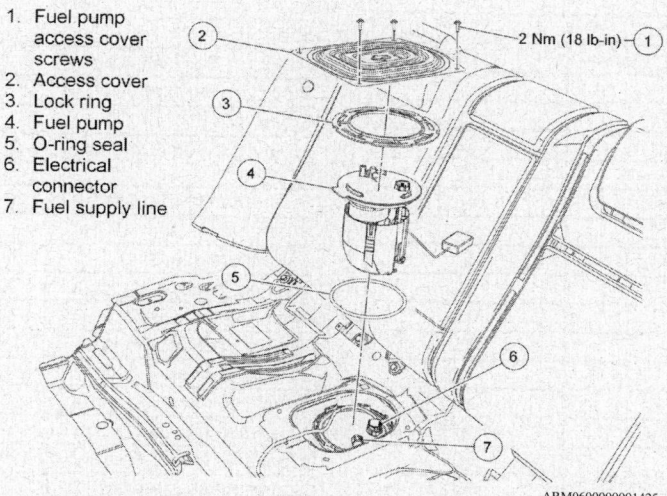

Fig. 68 Fuel pump replacement. 3.5L engine

TIGHTENING SPECIFICATIONS

Component	Torque Ft. Lbs.
Accessory Drive Belt Tensioner	89①
A/C Compressor Mounting Stud	80①
A/C Compressor Mounting Nut	18
A/C Tube To Condenser	71①
Alternator	35
Alternator "B" Terminal	53①
Belt Tensioner	96①
Camshaft Bearing Cap	89①
Camshaft Position Sensor	89①
Camshaft Sprocket	⑧
Catalytic Converter Nuts	30
Catalytic Converter To Exhaust Manifold Studs	18
Catalytic Converter To Bracket Bolts	15
Cylinder Head	⑤
Driveshaft To PTU Flange	52
Engine Block Heater	30
Engine Mount	46
Engine Mount Brace	18
Engine Mount Bolts	41
Engine Mount Nuts	46
Engine Mount Studs	13
Engine To Transaxle Bolts	35
Exhaust Manifold Nuts	15
Exhaust Manifold Heat Shield	18
Exhaust Manifold Studs	108①
Exhaust Y-Pipe	30
Flexplate	59
Front Cover	④
Fuel Rail	89①
Halfshaft To Transaxle (Righthand)②	17
Halfshaft To Transaxle (Righthand)③	41
Ignition Coil	53①
Lefthand Engine Block Drain Plug	15⑥
Lower Ball Joint Nut	148
Lower Control Arm Through Bolt	76
Lower Intake Manifold	89①
Oil Pan Drain Plug	20
Oil Pan To Engine Block	⑦
Oil Pan To Transaxle	35
Oil Pump To Engine Block	89①
Oil Pump Pickup Screen To Oil Pump	89①

TIGHTENING SPECIFICATIONS—Continued

Component	Torque Ft. Lbs.
Oxygen Sensor	35
Power Feed To Battery Cable	53①
Power Steering Pressure Line To Steering Gear	27
Power Steering Pump	18
Power Transfer Unit	66
Power Transfer Unit Support Bracket	52
Radio Interference Capacitor	89①
Righthand Engine Block Drain Plug	30
Roll Restrictor Through Bolt	66
Spark Plug	11
Stabilizer Bar Link (Lower)	31
Stabilizer Bar Link (Upper)	30
Starter Motor	19
Steering Column Intermediate Shaft To Steering Gear	17
Subframe Bracket Nuts	111
Subframe To Body Bolts	76
Thermostat Housing	89①
Tie Rod To Steering Knuckle	35
Timing Chain Guide	89①
Timing Chain Tensioner	89①
Torque Converter Nuts	27
Transaxle Cooler Lines	22
Transaxle Mount Bracket	59
Transaxle Mount Through Bolt	66
Upper Intake Manifold	89①
Valve Cover	89①
Variable Cam Timing Control Assembly	89①
Water Pump	89①

PTU — Power Transfer Unit
① — Inch lbs.
② — AWD models.
③ — FWD models.
④ — Refer to Front Cover, Replace for tightening specifications.
⑤ — Refer to Cylinder Head, Replace for tightening specifications.
⑥ — Tighten an additional 180°.
⑦ — Refer to Oil Pan, Replace for tightening specifications.
⑧ — Refer to Camshaft, Replace for tightening specifications.

NOTE: On Air Bag Equipped Models, Refer To "Air Bag System Precautions" Located In The Front Of This Manual For System Disarming & Arming Procedures.

NOTE: Refer To "Computer Relearn Procedures" Located In The Front Of This Manual When Battery Power To The Computer Has Been Interrupted.

INDEX

	Page No.
Coil Spring, Replace	1-40
Installation	1-40
Removal	1-40
Control Arm, Replace	1-40
Lower	1-40
Upper	1-40

	Page No.
Hub & Bearing, Replace	1-39
AWD	1-39
FWD	1-39
Shock Absorber, Replace	1-39
Stabilizer Bar, Replace	1-40
Tightening Specifications	1-47

	Page No.
Toe Link, Replace	1-40
Trailing Arm, Replace	1-40
Wheel Bearing, Adjust	1-39
Wheel Knuckle, Replace	1-39
Wheel Spindle, Replace	1-39
Wheel Spindle, Replace	1-40

HUB & BEARING
REPLACE

FWD

1. Raise and support vehicle, then remove tire/wheel assembly.
2. Remove wheel speed sensor bolt, **Fig. 1,** then position sensor aside.
3. Remove retaining clip, then disconnect parking brake cable from brake caliper.
4. Remove caliper anchor plate bolts, then position caliper and anchor plate assembly aside.
5. Remove two brake disc rotor mounting bolts, then the rotor.
6. Remove and discard wheel hub nut, then remove wheel hub and bearing assembly. Wheel bearing and hub are replaced as an assembly.
7. Reverse procedure to install.

AWD

1. Raise and support vehicle, then remove tire/wheel assembly.
2. Remove wheel speed sensor and position aside.
3. Disconnect parking brake cable from caliper.
4. Remove and discard wheel hub nut, **Fig. 2.**
5. Remove anchor plate bolts and position brake caliper and anchor plate assembly aside. Support anchor plate assembly using suitable mechanics wire.
6. Remove brake disc attaching bolts, then the brake disc.
7. Separate halfshaft from wheel hub using hub remover tool No. 205–D070 or equivalent.
8. Remove and discard shock absorber lower bolt and nut.
9. Raise lower suspension arm using a suitable jack.
10. Remove and discard upper arm bolts.

11. Remove and discard four trailing arm to knuckle nuts, then the wheel knuckle.
12. Remove wheel hub from wheel bearing using a suitable press and step plate tool No. 205–117 or equivalent.
13. If inner wheel bearing race remains in wheel knuckle after removing hub, remove race from hub using a suitable press and pinion bearing cone remover tool No. 205–D002 or equivalent.
14. Remove bearing snap ring from knuckle.
15. Remove wheel bearing from knuckle using a suitable press and bearing remover/installer tool No. 204–020 or equivalent.
16. Reverse procedure to install noting the following:
    a. Install new bearing to knuckle using a suitable press and bearing installer tool No. 205–147 or equivalent.
    b. Install wheel hub to bearing using a suitable press, step plate tool No. 205–117 and bearing installer tool No. 205–147 or equivalents.

WHEEL KNUCKLE
REPLACE

1. Raise and support vehicle, then remove tire/wheel assembly.
2. Remove wheel speed sensor and position aside.
3. Disconnect parking brake cable from caliper.
4. Remove and discard wheel hub nut, **Fig. 2.**
5. Remove anchor plate bolts and position brake caliper and anchor plate assembly aside. Support anchor plate assembly using suitable mechanics wire.
6. Remove brake disc attaching bolts, then the brake disc.
7. Separate halfshaft from wheel hub using hub remover tool No. 205–D070 or equivalent.

8. Remove and discard shock absorber lower bolt and nut.
9. Raise lower suspension arm using a suitable jack.
10. Remove and discard upper arm bolts.
11. Remove and discard four trailing arm to knuckle nuts, then the wheel knuckle.
12. Reverse procedure to install.

WHEEL SPINDLE
REPLACE

1. Remove wheel bearing and hub as outlined under "Hub & Bearing, Replace."
2. Remove three brake disc dust shield bolts, then the dust shield.
3. Remove four wheel spindle bolts, then the wheel spindle, **Fig. 3.**
4. Reverse procedure to install.

WHEEL BEARING
ADJUST

The rear wheel bearings are of a sealed cartridge design and are not adjustable.

SHOCK ABSORBER
REPLACE

The new shock absorber is shipped with a strap securing it in the compressed position. Do not remove this strap until the shock absorber and bracket assembly are in position and the three bracket bolts have been installed.

After removal discard all suspension component mounting bolts and nuts. Replace discarded fasteners.

1. Remove upper control arm as outlined under "Upper Control Arm, Replace."
2. Remove and discard shock absorber lower bolt and flag nut, **Fig. 4.**
3. Compress shock absorber and secure it in fully compressed position using tie straps.
4. Remove discarded shock absorber upper mounting bracket bolts.

5. Remove shock absorber and bracket assembly by guiding it between trailing arm and coil spring.
6. Index mark shock absorber to bracket, then separate shock absorber from upper bracket.
7. Reverse procedure to install, noting the following:
   a. Copy index mark from shock absorber that was removed to shock absorber that is being installed.
   b. Position shock absorber into upper bracket and loosely install a new upper bolt and nut.
   c. Align index marks so center line of shock absorber is approximately 118°, **Fig. 5,** from alignment tab on upper bracket, then tighten shock absorber upper nut.

COIL SPRING
REPLACE
Removal

After removal discard all suspension component mounting bolts and nuts. Replace discarded fasteners.
1. Index mark lower control arm cam bolt and cam adjuster, **Fig. 6,** then loosen cam adjuster nut.
2. Remove stabilizer bar link lower bolt.
3. Position suitable jack under lower control arm, then raise the lower arm. **The spring is under extreme compression, care must be taken at all times.**
4. Remove lower arm outboard bolt.
5. Slowly lower control arm and remove coil spring.

Installation

1. Position spring upper seat onto spring, **Fig. 7.** End of spring should be 0-.39 inch from step on seat.
2. Position coil spring lower seat into lower control arm, **Fig. 8,** aligning recess in seat with projection on lower arm.
3. Position coil spring onto lower arm with end of spring 0-.39 inch, **Fig. 9,** from step on spring seat.
4. Raise lower control arm using suitable jack, then install lower arm outboard bolt.
5. Raise suspension until distance between center of the hub, **Fig. 10,** and lip of fender is equal to 15.55 inch, then tighten lower control arm outboard bolt.
6. Install stabilizer bar link lower bolt.
7. Align index mark on cam bolt and cam

adjuster with index mark on lower control arm, then tighten cam adjuster nut.
8. Inspect rear wheel alignment.

CONTROL ARM
REPLACE
Lower

Refer to "Coil Spring, Replace." for lower control arm procedures.

Upper

After removal, discard all suspension component mounting bolts and nuts. Replace discarded fasteners.
1. Remove shock absorber lower mounting bolt and flag nut.
2. Raise trailing arm using suitable jack.
3. Remove upper control arm outboard bolt, **Fig. 11.**
4. Carefully lower trailing arm and remove jack.
5. Position shock absorber as required to remove upper control arm.
6. Remove upper control arm inboard bolt, then the upper control arm.
7. Reverse procedure to install, noting the following:
   a. Raise suspension until distance between center of the hub, **Fig. 10,** and lip of fender is equal to 15.55 inch, then tighten upper control arm outboard bolt.
   b. Inspect rear wheel alignment.

WHEEL SPINDLE
REPLACE

After removal, discard all suspension component mounting bolts and nuts. Replace discarded fasteners.
1. Remove wheel bearing and wheel hub assembly as outlined under "Hub & Bearing, Replace."
2. Remove three brake disc shield bolts, **Fig. 12,** then the brake disc shield.
3. Remove four wheel spindle bolts, then the wheel spindle.
4. Reverse procedure to install.

TRAILING ARM
REPLACE

After removal discard all suspension component mounting bolts and nuts. Replace discarded fasteners.
1. Remove wheel spindle as outlined under "Wheel Spindle, Replace."
2. Remove parking brake cable bracket bolt, then position parking brake cable aside.

3. Disconnect wheel speed sensor harness from trailing arm.
4. Position suitable jack under trailing arm, then raise arm upward.
5. Remove lower control arm outboard bolt, **Fig. 13.**
6. Remove upper control arm outboard bolt.
7. Carefully lower trailing arm and remove jack.
8. Remove shock absorber lower bolt and flag nut.
9. Remove toe link outboard bolt.
10. Remove two trailing arm forward bolts, then the trailing arm.
11. Reverse procedure to install, noting the following:
    a. Raise suspension until distance between center of the hub, **Fig. 10,** and lip of fender is equal to 15.55 inch, then tighten all bolts.
    b. Inspect rear wheel alignment.

STABILIZER BAR
REPLACE

After removal discard all suspension component mounting bolts and nuts. Replace discarded fasteners.
1. Remove stabilizer bar link upper nuts, **Fig. 14.**
2. Remove stabilizer bar mounting bracket nuts.
3. Remove stabilizer bar bracket bolts, stabilizer bar brackets, then the stabilizer bar.
4. Remove stabilizer bar link lower bolts, then the stabilizer bar links.
5. Reverse procedure to install, noting the following:
   a. Raise suspension until distance between center of the hub, **Fig. 10,** and lip of fender is equal to 15.55 inch, then tighten all bolts and nuts.
   b. Inspect rear wheel alignment.

TOE LINK
REPLACE

After removal discard all suspension component mounting bolts and nuts. Replace discarded fasteners.
1. Remove toe link shield bolt, **Fig. 15,** then the pushpin and shield.
2. Remove toe link inboard nut and bolt.
3. Remove toe link outboard bolt, then the toe link.
4. Reverse procedure to install, noting the following:
   a. Raise suspension until distance between center of the hub, **Fig. 10,** and lip of fender is equal to 15.55 inch, then tighten toe link bolts and nuts.
   b. Inspect rear wheel alignment.

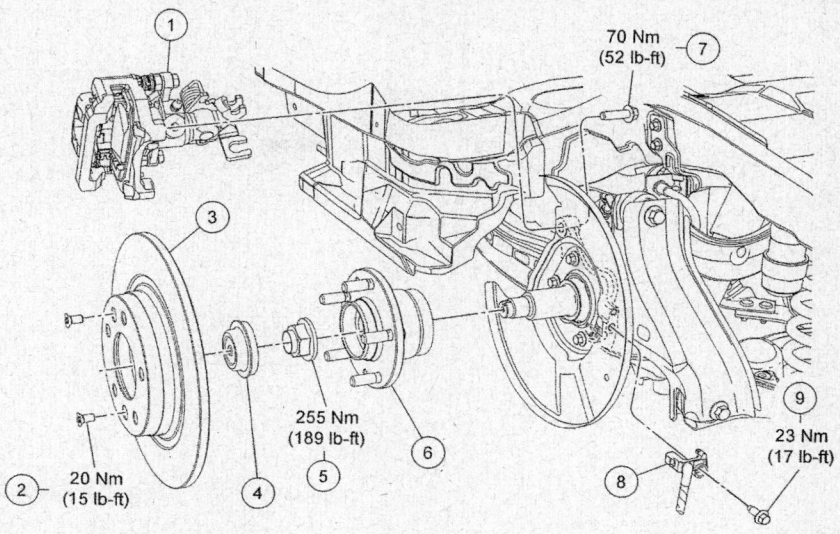

Item	Description
1	Caliper and anchor plate assembly
2	Brake disc bolt (2 required)
3	Brake disc
4	Grease cap
5	Wheel hub nut
6	Wheel hub and bearing assembly
7	Anchor plate bolt (2 required)
8	Wheel speed sensor
9	Wheel speed sensor bolt

ARM0500000000125

Fig. 1   Hub & bearing replacement

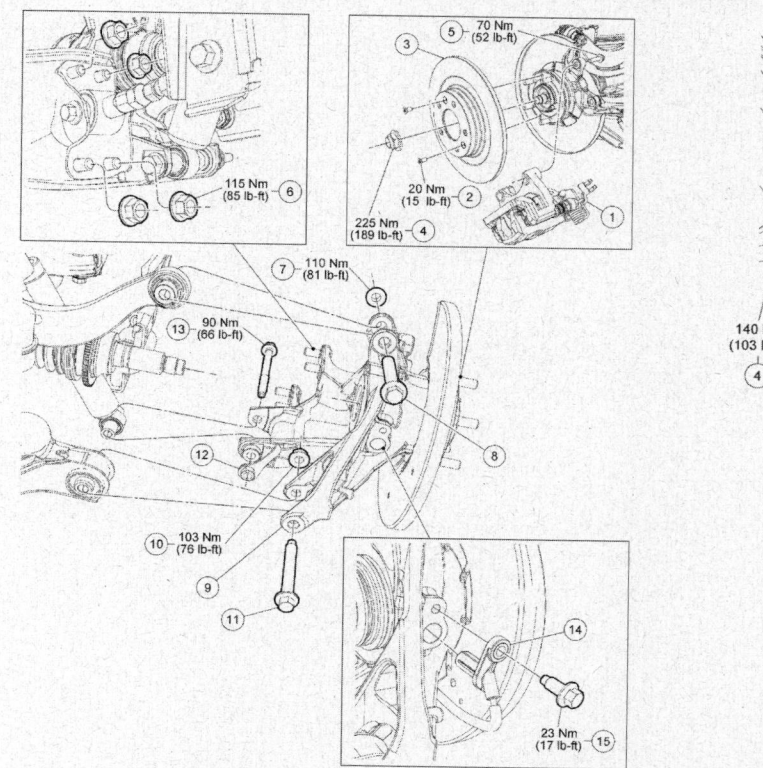

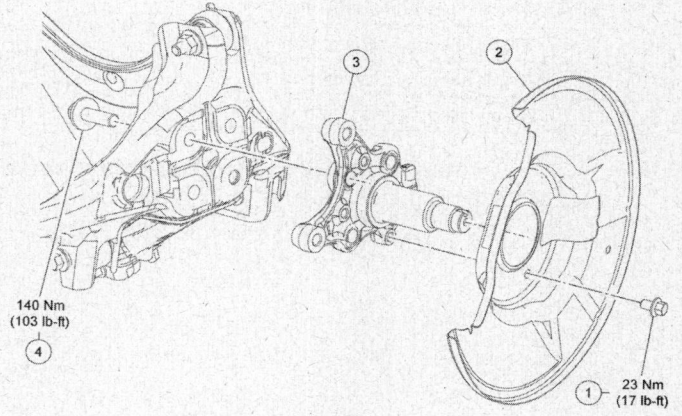

Item	Description
1	Brake disc shield bolt (3 required)
2	Brake disc shield
3	Wheel spindle
4	Wheel spindle bolt (4 required)

ARM0600000001432

Fig. 3   Rear spindle removal

ARM0600000001431

Fig. 2   Wheel knuckle removal. AWD

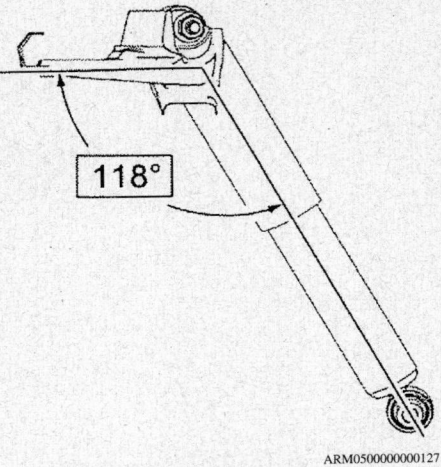

Fig. 5 Shock absorber alignment

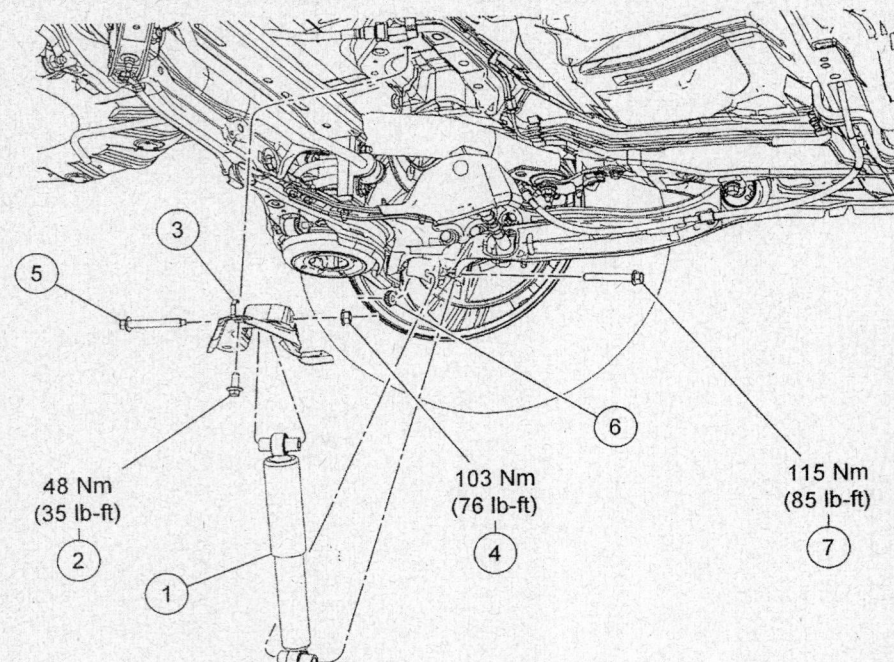

48 Nm
(35 lb-ft)

103 Nm
(76 lb-ft)

115 Nm
(85 lb-ft)

Item	Description
1	Shock absorber
2	Bracket bolt (3 required)
3	Shock absorber bracket
4	Shock absorber upper nut
5	Shock absorber upper bolt
6	Shock absorber lower flag nut
7	Shock absorber lower bolt

Fig. 4 Shock absorber replacement

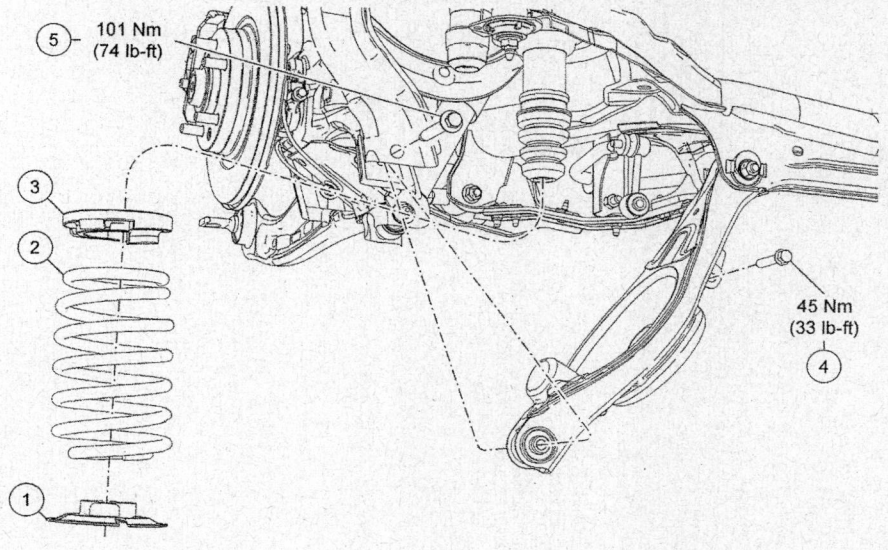

Fig. 6   Coil spring replacement

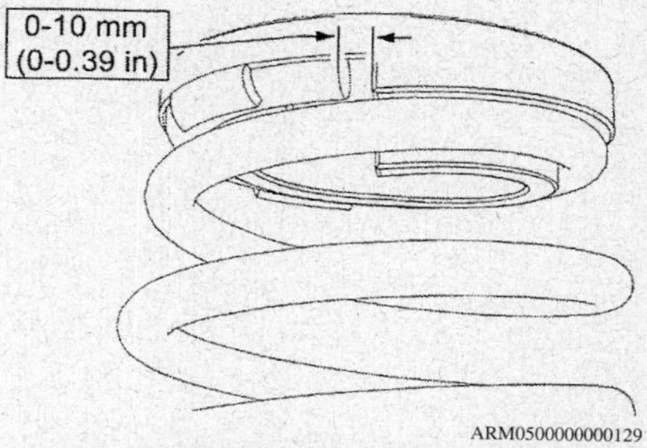

Item	Description
1	Spring lower seat
2	Spring
3	Spring upper seat
4	Stabilizer bar link lower bolt
5	Lower arm outboard bolt

ARM0500000000128

Fig. 7   Coil spring to upper seat measurement

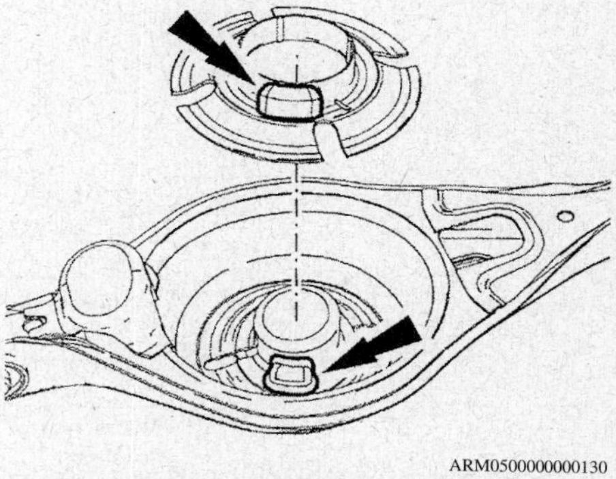

ARM0500000000129

Fig. 8   Coil spring lower seat alignment

ARM0500000000130

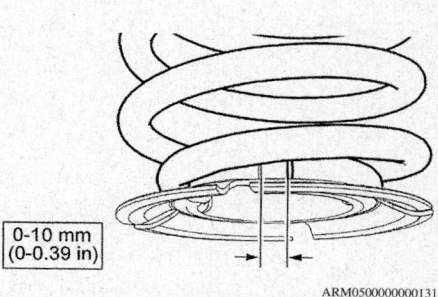

Fig. 9   Coil spring to lower seat measurement

ARM0500000000131

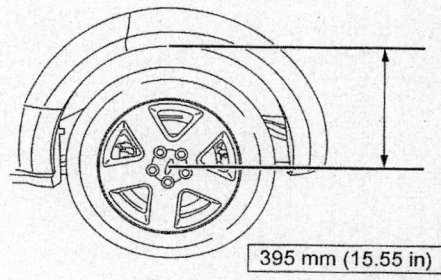

Fig. 10   Static ground position (curb height) measurement

395 mm (15.55 in)

ARM0500000000132

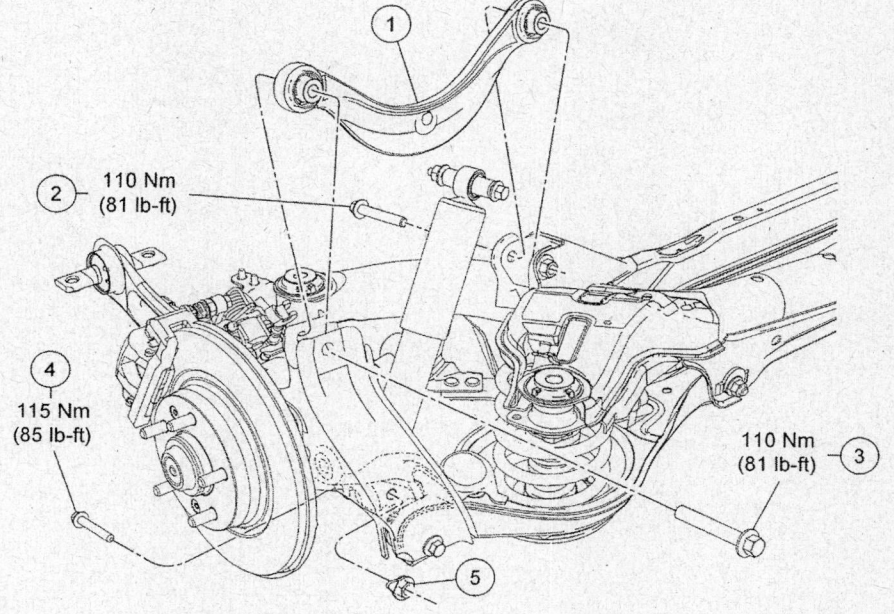

Item	Description
1	Upper arm
2	Upper arm inboard bolt
3	Upper arm outboard bolt
4	Shock absorber lower bolt
5	Shock absorber lower flag nut

ARM0500000000133

Fig. 11   Upper control arm replacement

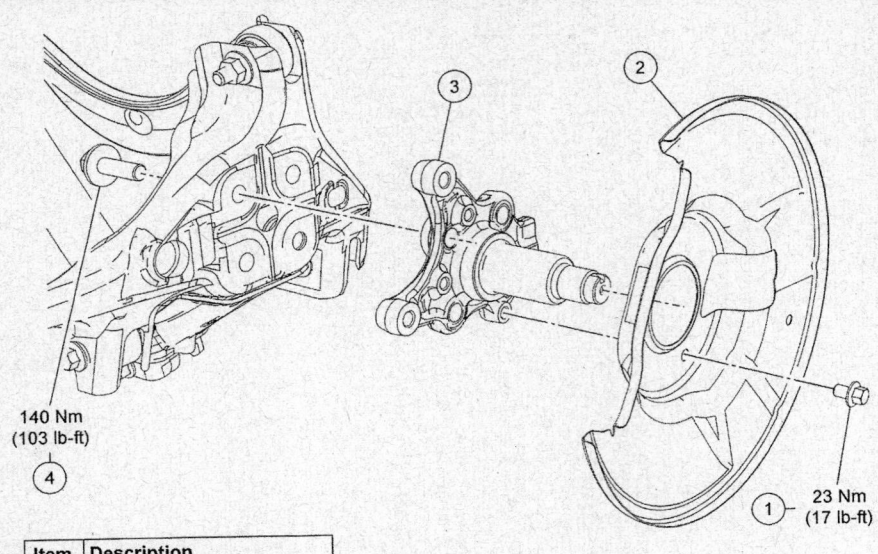

Item	Description
1	Brake disc shield bolt (3 required)
2	Brake disc shield
3	Wheel spindle
4	Wheel spindle bolt (4 required)

ARM0500000000134

Fig. 12 Wheel spindle replacement

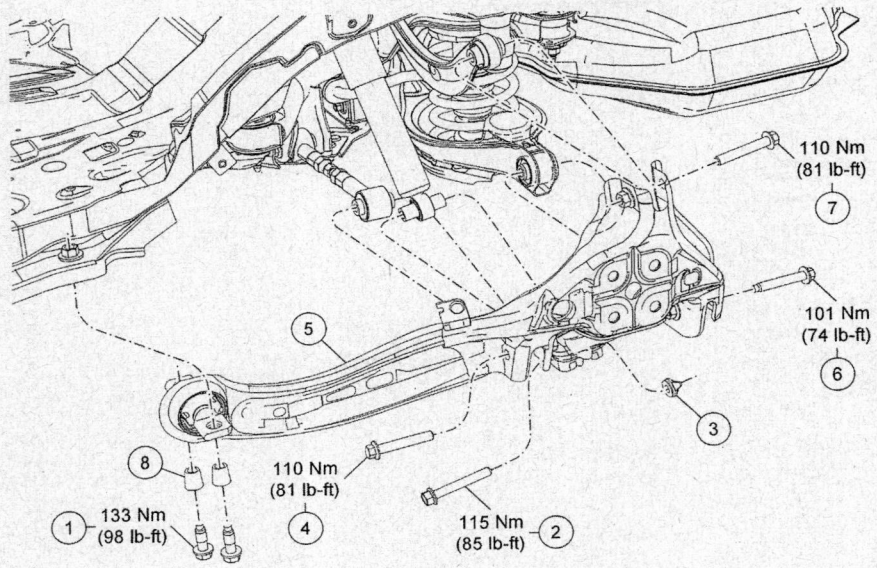

Item	Description
1	Trailing arm forward bolt (2 required)
2	Shock absorber lower bolt
3	Shock absorber lower flag nut
4	Toe link outboard bolt
5	Trailing arm
6	Lower arm outboard bolt
7	Upper arm outboard bolt
8	Cone washer (2 required)

ARM0500000000135

Fig. 13 Trailing arm replacement

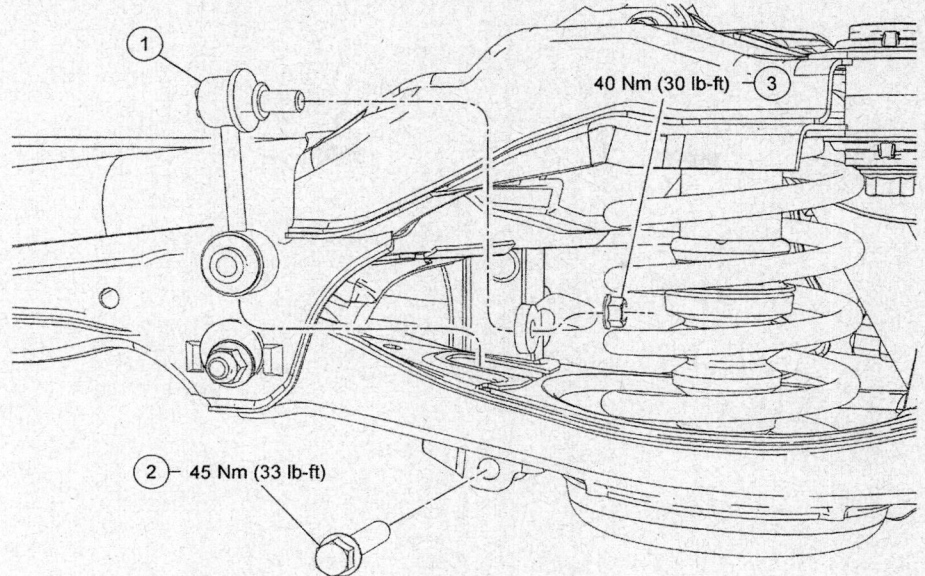

Item	Description
1	Stabilizer bar link
2	Stabilizer bar link lower bolt
3	Stabilizer bar link upper nut

ARM0500000000136

Fig. 14   Stabilizer bar replacement (Part 1 of 2)

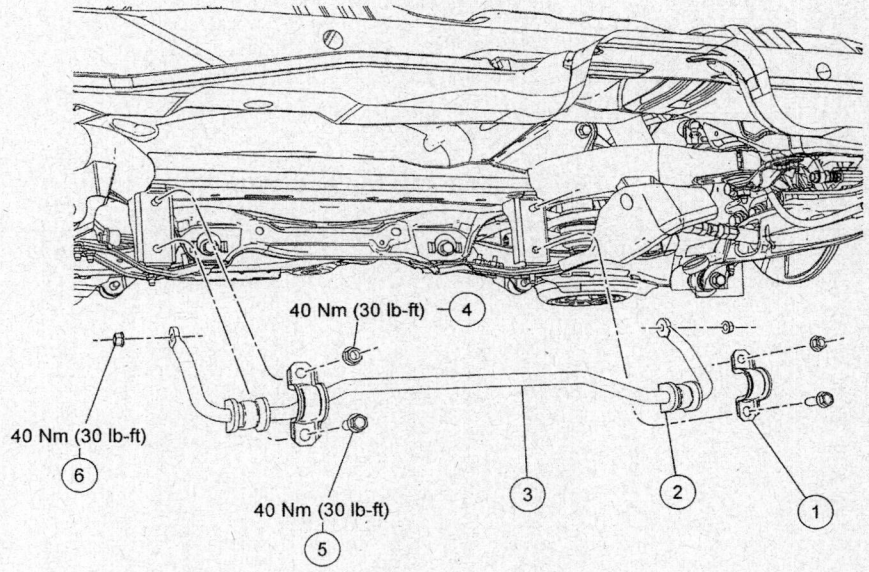

Item	Description
1	Stabilizer bar bracket (2 required)
2	Stabilizer bar bushing (2 required)
3	Stabilizer bar
4	Stabilizer bar bracket nut (2 required)
5	Stabilizer bar bracket bolt (2 required)
6	Stabilizer bar link upper nut (2 required)

ARM0500000000137

Fig. 14   Stabilizer bar replacement (Part 2 of 2)

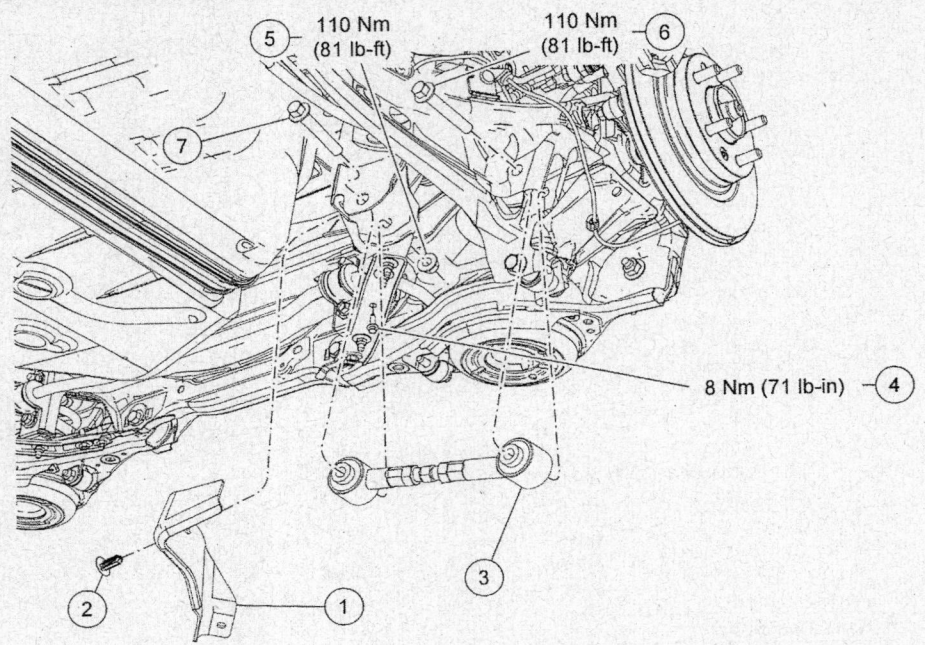

Fig. 15 Toe link replacement

Item	Description
1	Toe link shield
2	Pushpin
3	Toe link
4	Toe link shield bolt
5	Toe link inboard nut
6	Toe link outboard bolt
7	Toe link inboard bolt

ARM0500000000138

TIGHTENING SPECIFICATIONS

Component	Torque/Ft. Lbs.
Brake Caliper Anchor Plate	52
Brake Disc (Rotor)	15
Brake Disc Shield	17
Jounce Stop	41
Lower Control Arm Cam Adjuster	74
Lower Control Arm Outboard	②
Parking Brake Cable Bracket	89①
Shock Absorber Bracket	③
Shock Absorber Lower	④
Shock Absorber Upper	76
Stabilizer Bar Bracket	30
Stabilizer Bar Link Lower	33
Stabilizer Bar Link Upper	30
Toe Link Inboard	81⑤
Toe Link Outboard	81⑤
Toe Link Nut	52⑥
Toe Link Bolt	81⑥
Toe Link Shield	71①
Trailing Arm Forward Bolt	98⑤
Trailing Arm To Knuckle	85⑥
Upper Control Arm Inboard	81
Upper Control Arm Outboard	81
Wheel Hub Nut	189
Wheel Speed Sensor	89①
Wheel Spindle	103

① — Inch lbs.
② — On 2006 models, 74 ft. lbs. On 2007–08 models, 76 ft. lbs.
③ — On 2006 models, 35 ft. lbs. On 2007–08 models, 30 ft. lbs.
④ — On 2006 models, 85 ft. lbs. On 2007–08 models, 66 ft. lbs.
⑤ — 2006 models.
⑥ — 2007–08 models.

Front Suspension & Steering

NOTE: On Air Bag Equipped Models, Refer To "Air Bag System Precautions" Located In The Front Of This Manual For System Disarming & Arming Procedures.

NOTE: Refer To "Computer Relearn Procedures" Located In The Front Of This Manual When Battery Power To The Computer Has Been Interrupted.

INDEX

	Page No.		Page No.		Page No.
Ball Joint, Replace	1-48	Upper	1-49	Steering Knuckle, Replace	1-49
Ball Joint Inspection	1-48	Power Steering	13-1	Strut, Replace	1-48
Coil Spring & Strut Service	1-48	Power Steering Gear, Replace	1-50	Technical Service Bulletins	1-51
Assemble	1-48	Power Steering Pump, Replace	1-50	Noise On Lefthand Turns	1-51
Disassemble	1-48	2.3L Engine	1-50	2006–07 Fusion & Milan	1-51
Control Arm, Replace	1-49	3.0L & 3.5L Engines	1-51	Tightening Specifications	1-57
Lower	1-49	Stabilizer Bar, Replace	1-49	Wheel Bearing, Replace	1-48
Front	1-49	Stabilizer Bar Link, Replace	1-49		
Rear	1-49	Steering Columns	12-1		

WHEEL BEARING

REPLACE

1. Raise and support vehicle.
2. Remove wheel speed sensor bolt, **Fig. 1,** then the sensor.
3. Remove wheel speed sensor harness bolt, then position wheel speed sensor and harness aside.
4. Remove caliper anchor plate bolts, then position caliper and anchor plate assembly aside.
5. Remove two brake disc to hub mounting bolts, then the brake disc.
6. Remove and discard halfshaft nut.
7. Separate halfshaft from wheel hub using front hub removal tool No. D93P-1175–B, or equivalent.
8. Remove upper ball joint nut, then separate upper ball joint from steering knuckle using steering arm removal tool No.T64P-3590–F, or equivalent.
9. Remove tie rod end cotter pin and nut, then separate tie rod end from steering knuckle.
10. Remove two lower ball joint retaining nuts, then separate lower ball joints from steering knuckle using ball joint removal tool No. 204–592, or equivalent.
11. Remove steering knuckle from vehicle.
12. Press wheel hub from wheel bearing using suitable press and stop plate tool No. 205–117, or equivalent, **Fig. 2.**
13. Press inner wheel bearing race from wheel hub using suitable press and pinion bearing cone removal tool No. D79L-4621–A, or equivalent.
14. Remove snap ring, then press outer wheel bearing race from steering knuckle using suitable press and wheel hub cup tool No. 204–020, or equivalent.
15. Install wheel bearing into steering knuckle using suitable press and wheel hub bearing installation tool No. 205–147, or equivalent.
16. Install snap ring. Ensure snap ring is fully seated.
17. Install wheel hub into wheel bearing using suitable press, stop plate tool No. 205–117 and wheel hub bearing installation tool No. 205–147, or equivalents.
18. Reverse procedure to install.

BALL JOINT INSPECTION

1. Raise and support vehicle with wheels in full down position.
2. Grasp lower edge of tire, then move wheel assembly in and out.
3. As wheel is being moved, observe lower end of knuckle and lower control arm.
4. If movement is observed, replace lower control arm.

BALL JOINT

REPLACE

The ball joints must be replaced with the control arm as an assembly.

STRUT

REPLACE

1. Place ignition switch in OFF position and ensure steering wheel is not locked.
2. Remove three strut upper mount nuts, **Fig. 3.**
3. Remove wheel speed sensor bolt.
4. Remove speed sensor harness bolt, then position speed sensor aside.
5. Remove bolts, **Fig. 1,** then position caliper and anchor plate assembly aside. Support caliper and anchor plate assembly using suitable mechanic's wire.
6. Support wheel knuckle at lower ball joints by positioning suitable jack under control arm.
7. Remove stabilizer bar link upper nut.
8. Remove lower strut mounting bolt, flag nut and damper.
9. Slowly lower wheel knuckle and remove strut/spring assembly.
10. Reverse procedure to install.

COIL SPRING & STRUT SERVICE

Disassemble

1. Compress strut spring with Rotunda coil spring compressor tool No. 164-R3571, or equivalent.
2. Hold strut shaft with suitable box wrench and remove strut mounting nut, **Fig. 4,** using suitable crowfoot socket. **Do not allow strut shaft to rotate.**
3. Loosen compressor tool, then remove strut top mount bracket, bearing and seat assembly, and spring.

Assemble

1. Position end of spring, **Fig. 5,** within 0-.39 inch of step on spring mount.
2. Compress strut spring with Rotunda coil spring compressor tool No. 164-R3571, or equivalent.
3. Install spring over strut into lower seat, then install upper strut mounting plate with spring seat. Ensure spring is correctly seated in both upper and lower spring seats.

4. Hold strut shaft with suitable box wrench and install upper strut mounting plate retaining nut using suitable crowfoot socket. **Do not allow strut shaft to rotate.**

5. Carefully release tension on spring compressor.

CONTROL ARM

REPLACE

Lower

FRONT

1. Support front wheel knuckle at rear lower ball joint using suitable jack. **Place a block of wood, or similar item, between lower arm and outer CV joint to prevent damage to CV boot.**
2. Remove lower front control arm to subframe bolt and washer, **Fig. 6,** then separate lower front control arm from subframe.
3. Remove damper fork to lower arm bolt flag nut.
4. Remove front lower ball joint to steering knuckle nut.
5. Separate front lower ball joint from steering using ball joint removal tool No. 204–592, or equivalent.
6. Remove front lower arm and ball joint assembly.
7. Reverse procedure to install, noting the following:
   a. Raise suspension until distance between center of the hub, **Fig. 7,** and lip of fender is equal to 15.83 inch, then tighten lower control arm mounting bolts.
   b. Inspect front wheel alignment.

REAR

1. Support front wheel knuckle at rear lower ball joint using suitable jack. **Place a block of wood, or similar item, between lower arm and outer CV joint to prevent damage to CV boot.**
2. Remove lower rear control arm ball joint nut, **Fig. 8,** then separate rear lower ball joint from steering knuckle using ball joint removal tool No. 204–592, or equivalent.
3. Remove lower rear control arm to subframe bolt and washer.
4. Remove control arm ball joint assembly.
5. Reverse procedure to install, noting the following:
   a. Raise suspension until distance between center of the hub, **Fig. 7,** and lip of fender is equal to 15.83 inch, then tighten lower control arm mounting bolts.
   b. Inspect front wheel alignment.

Upper

1. Remove three upper strut mount nuts.
2. Remove wheel speed sensor mounting bolt, **Fig. 9,** then the sensor.
3. Remove wheel speed sensor harness

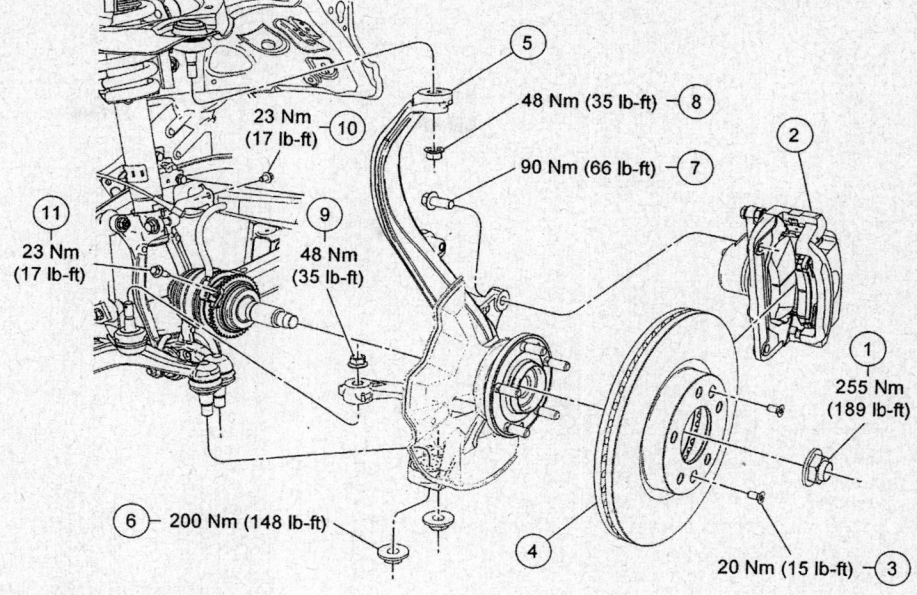

Item	Description
1	Halfshaft nut
2	Brake caliper and anchor plate assembly
3	Brake disc bolt (2 required)
4	Brake disc
5	Wheel knuckle
6	Lower ball joint nut (2 required)
7	Anchor plate bolt (2 required)
8	Upper ball joint nut
9	Tie-rod end nut
10	Wheel speed sensor harness bolt
11	Wheel speed sensor bolt

ARM0500000000140

Fig. 1   Steering knuckle replacement

bolt, then position wheel speed sensor and harness aside.

4. Remove upper ball joint to steering knuckle nut.
5. Separate upper ball joint from steering knuckle using steering arm removal tool No. T64P-3590–F, or equivalent.
6. Position strut/spring assembly toward steering knuckle to access upper control arm to body mounting bolts.
7. Remove two upper control arm to body bolts and remove the upper arm.
8. Remove upper control arm.
9. Reverse procedure to install, noting the following:
   a. Raise suspension until distance between center of the hub, **Fig. 7,** and lip of fender is equal to 15.83 inch, then tighten lower control arm mounting bolts.
   b. Inspect front wheel alignment.

STEERING KNUCKLE

REPLACE

Refer to "Wheel Bearing, Replace" for steering knuckle replacement procedure.

STABILIZER BAR LINK

REPLACE

1. Remove stabilizer bar link upper nut, **Fig. 10.**
2. Remove stabilizer bar link lower nut.
3. Remove stabilizer bar link.
4. Reverse procedure to install.

STABILIZER BAR

REPLACE

1. Place steering wheel in straight ahead position and ignition key in OFF position.
2. Raise and support vehicle.
3. Remove two steering joint cover retaining screws, then the cover.
4. Index mark steering column shaft position to steering gear for reference during installation.
5. Remove steering column shaft to steering gear bolt, then disconnect shaft from gear box. **Do not allow intermediate shaft to rotate while it is disconnected from gear or damage to clockspring can occur.**

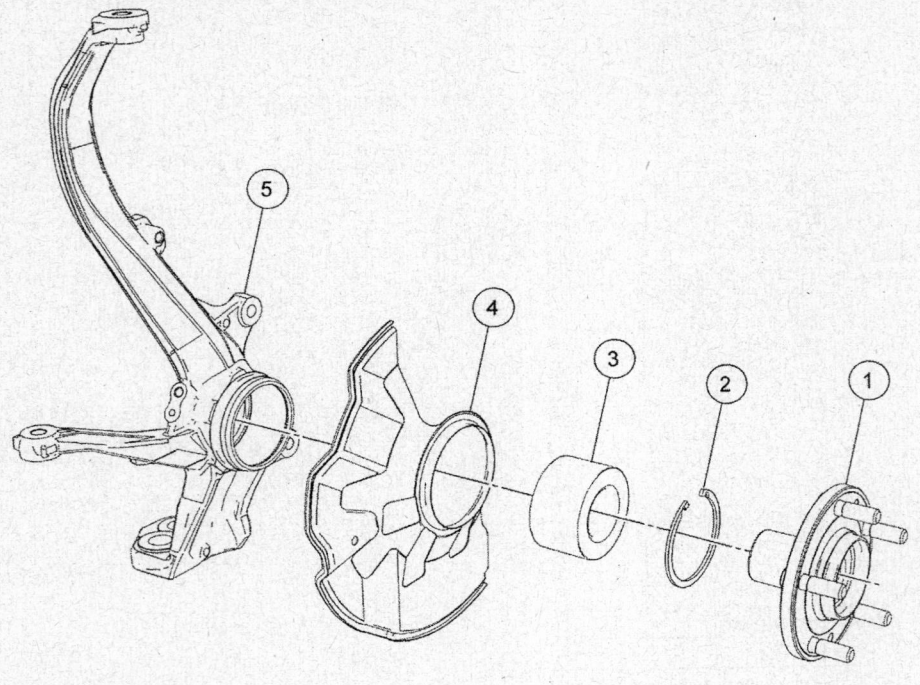

Item	Description
1	Wheel hub
2	Snap ring
3	Wheel bearing
4	Disc brake shield
5	Wheel knuckle

ARM0500000000139

Fig. 2 Wheel hub & bearing replacement

6. Release four clips, then slide steering gear to dash seal off of steering gear and into the passenger compartment. **Steering gear to dash seal must be removed or it will be damaged when lowering subframe.**
7. Remove seven screws, then the underbody cover.
8. Remove righthand fender splash shield screws and position shield aside.
9. Remove 6 pin-type retainers, then righthand underbody splash shield.
10. Remove lefthand fender splash shield screws and position shield aside.
11. Remove 6 pin-type retainers, then lefthand underbody splash shield.
12. Remove cotter pins and nuts from both tie-rod ends.
13. Separate both tie rod ends from steering knuckles using ball joint/tie rod removal tool No. T85M-3395–A, or equivalent.
14. Remove two stabilizer bar link lower nuts, **Fig. 11,** then disconnect both stabilizer bar links from stabilizer bar.
15. Remove front exhaust pipe heat shields.
16. Remove two engine roll restrictor bracket bolts.

17. Position two suitable jack stands to support rear of subframe assembly.
18. Remove four subframe bracket to body bolts, two subframe bracket to subframe nuts, then lower rear of subframe approximately three inches.
19. Remove steering gear to subframe mounting bolts, then position steering gear aside to access stabilizer bar mounting bracket nuts.
20. Remove stabilizer bar brackets and bushings.
21. Remove stabilizer bar through lefthand wheel opening.
22. Reverse procedure to install, noting the following:
    a. Raise suspension until distance between center of the hub, **Fig. 7,** and lip of fender is equal to 15.83 inch, then tighten lower control arm mounting bolts.
    b. Inspect front wheel alignment.

POWER STEERING GEAR

REPLACE

1. Place steering wheel in straight ahead position and ignition key in OFF position.

2. Raise and support vehicle.
3. Remove two steering joint cover retaining screws, **Fig. 12,** then the cover.
4. Index mark steering column shaft position to steering gear for reference during installation.
5. Remove steering column shaft to steering gear bolt, then disconnect shaft from gear box. **Do not allow intermediate shaft to rotate while it is disconnected from gear or damage to clockspring can occur.**
6. Release four clips, then slide steering gear to dash seal off of steering gear and into the passenger compartment. **Steering gear to dash seal must be removed or it will be damaged when lowering subframe.**
7. Remove seven screws, then the underbody cover.
8. Remove righthand fender splash shield screws and position shield aside.
9. Remove 6 pin-type retainers, then righthand underbody splash shield.
10. Remove lefthand fender splash shield screws and position shield aside.
11. Remove 6 pin-type retainers, then lefthand underbody splash shield.
12. Remove cotter pins and nuts from both tie-rod ends.
13. Separate both tie rod ends from steering knuckles using ball joint/tie rod removal tool No. T85M-3395–A, or equivalent.
14. Remove two engine roll restrictor bracket bolts.
15. Position two suitable jack stands to support rear of subframe assembly.
16. Remove four subframe bracket to body bolts, two subframe bracket to subframe nuts, then lower rear of subframe approximately three inches.
17. Remove clamp, then remove steering gear to fluid cooler return hose.
18. Remove power steering pressure line bracket to steering gear bolt.
19. Remove power steering pressure line banjo bolt and seals.
20. Remove steering gear to subframe mounting bolts.
21. Remove steering gear from lefthand side of vehicle.
22. Reverse procedure to install, noting the following:
    a. Raise suspension until distance between center of the hub, **Fig. 7,** and lip of fender is equal to 15.83 inch, then tighten lower control arm mounting bolts.
    b. Inspect front wheel alignment.

POWER STEERING PUMP

REPLACE

2.3L Engine

The power steering pump can only be replaced as a complete assembly. The pump has no serviceable components.

1. Siphon power steering fluid from steering fluid reservoir using suitable suction device.

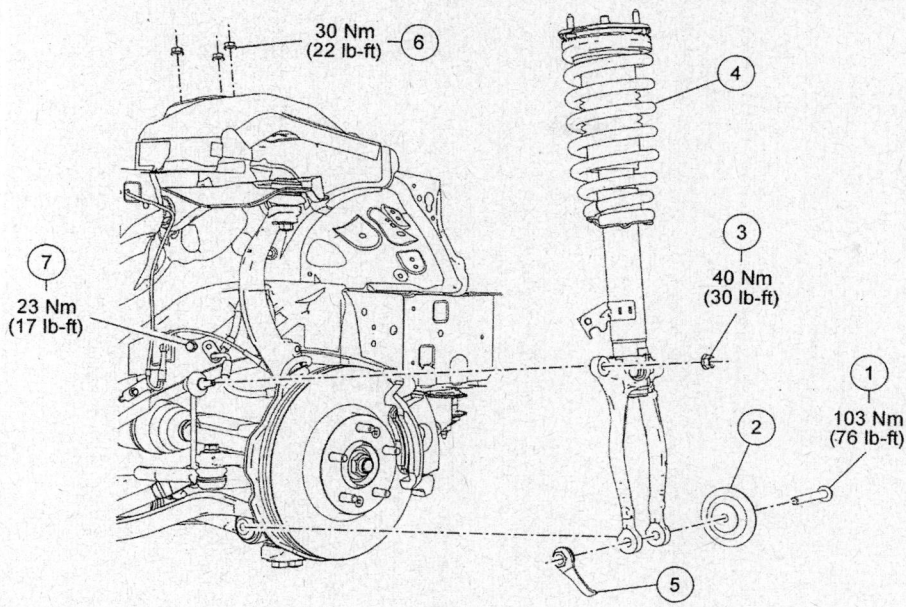

Item	Description
1	Damper fork-to-lower arm bolt
2	Damper
3	Stabilizer bar link upper nut
4	Shock absorber and spring assembly
5	Damper fork-to-lower arm flag nut
6	Shock absorber upper mount nut (3 required)
7	Brake line bracket bolt

Fig. 3   Strut assembly replacement

ARM0500000000141

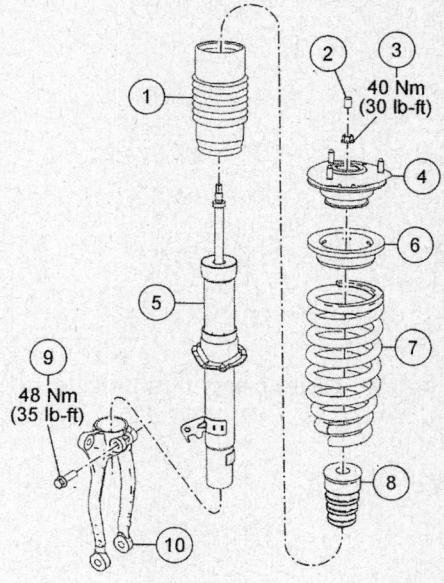

Item	Description
1	Dust boot
2	Shock absorber rod protective cap
3	Shock absorber rod nut
4	Shock absorber upper mount
5	Shock absorber and lower mount assembly
6	Spring upper seat
7	Spring
8	Jounce bumper
9	Shock absorber-to-damper fork
10	Damper fork

ARM0500000000142

Fig. 4   Exploded view strut & coil spring

2. Remove four screws, then position righthand fender splash shield aside.
3. Remove six pin type retainers, then the righthand splash shield.
4. Rotate accessory drive belt tensioner clockwise using pulley bolt, then remove accessory drive belt.
5. Remove clamp, **Fig. 13,** then disconnect power steering return hose from power steering fluid reservoir.
6. Disconnect power steering pressure switch electrical connector.
7. Remove power steering pressure line banjo bolt, then disconnect line from power steering pump.
8. Remove three power steering pump mounting bolts, then the power steering pump.
9. Reverse procedure to install.

3.0L & 3.5L Engines

The power steering pump can only be replaced as a complete assembly. The pump has no serviceable components.

1. Siphon power steering fluid from steering fluid reservoir using suitable suction device.
2. Rotate accessory drive belt tensioner counterclockwise using pulley bolt, then remove accessory drive belt.
3. Remove four screws, then position righthand fender splash shield aside.
4. Remove six pin type retainers, then the righthand splash shield.
5. Remove clamp, **Figs. 14 and 15,** then disconnect power steering supply hose from power steering pump.
6. **On models equipped with 3.5L engine,** remove power steering fluid reservoir.
7. Remove power steering pump drive belt.
8. **On all models,** disconnect power steering pressure switch electrical connector.
9. Remove electrical harness from stud on power steering pump.
10. Remove power steering pressure line fitting banjo bolt, then disconnect line from power steering pump.

11. Remove three power steering pump mounting bolts, then the power steering pump.
12. Reverse procedure to install.

TECHNICAL SERVICE BULLETINS

Noise On Lefthand Turns

2006-07 FUSION & MILAN

Models equipped with the 2.3L engine may exhibit a steering noise when turning left. To correct this condition, a revised power steering return line part No. 7E5Z–3A713–A should be installed.

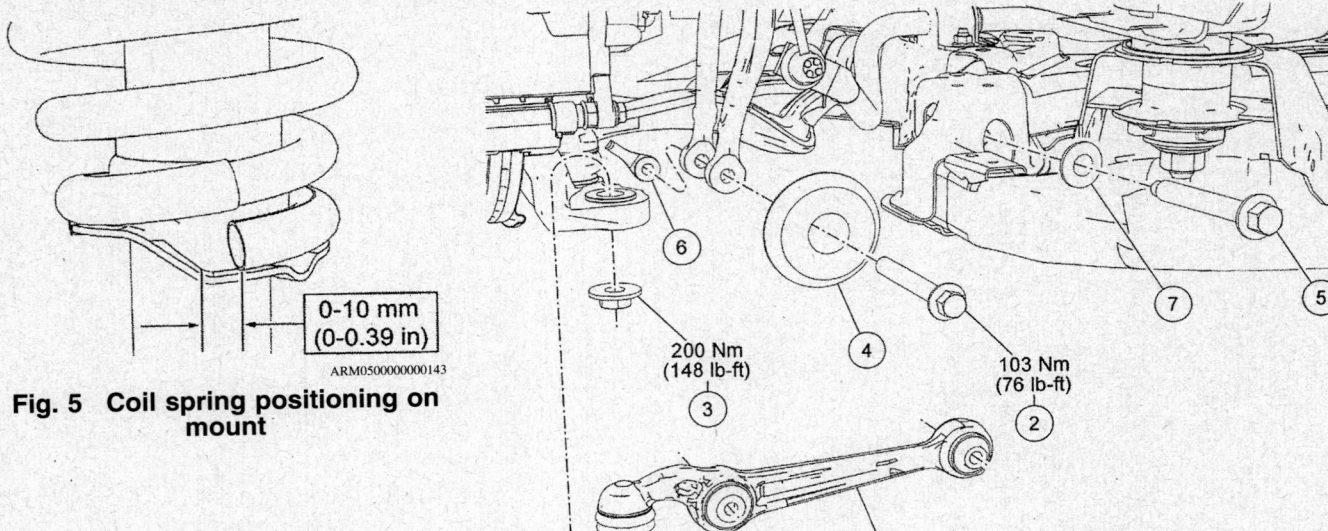

ARM0500000000143

Fig. 5 Coil spring positioning on mount

0-10 mm
(0-0.39 in)

200 Nm
(148 lb-ft)

103 Nm
(76 lb-ft)

ARM0500000000144

Fig. 6 Lower front control arm replacement (Part 1 of 2)

Item	Description
1	Lower arm (front)
2	Damper fork-to-lower arm bolt
3	Lower ball joint nut (front)
4	Damper
5	Front lower arm-to-subframe bolt
6	Damper fork-to-lower arm flag nut
7	Washer

ARM0500000000145

**Fig. 6 Lower front control arm replacement
(Part 2 of 2)**

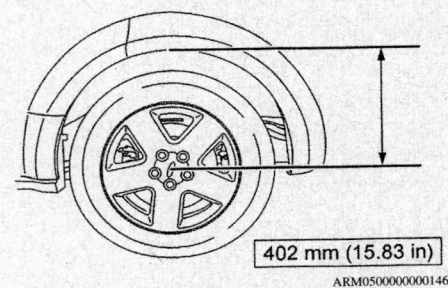

402 mm (15.83 in)

ARM0500000000146

**Fig. 7 Static ground position
(curb height) measurement**

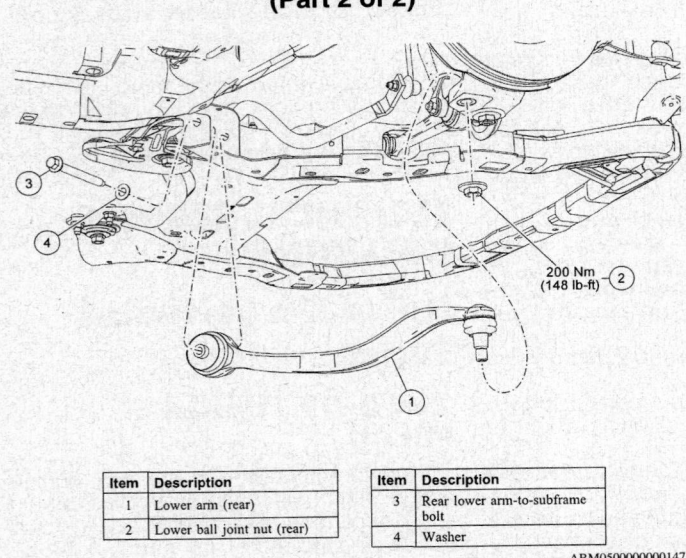

200 Nm
(148 lb-ft)

Item	Description		Item	Description
1	Lower arm (rear)		3	Rear lower arm-to-subframe bolt
2	Lower ball joint nut (rear)		4	Washer

ARM0500000000147

Fig. 8 Lower rear control arm replacement

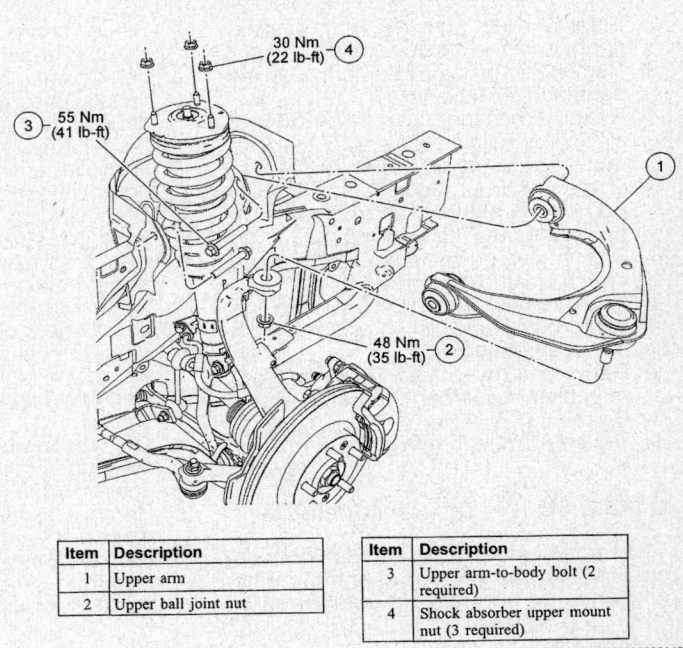

30 Nm
(22 lb-ft)

55 Nm
(41 lb-ft)

48 Nm
(35 lb-ft)

Item	Description		Item	Description
1	Upper arm		3	Upper arm-to-body bolt (2 required)
2	Upper ball joint nut		4	Shock absorber upper mount nut (3 required)

ARM0500000000148

Fig. 9 Upper control arm replacement

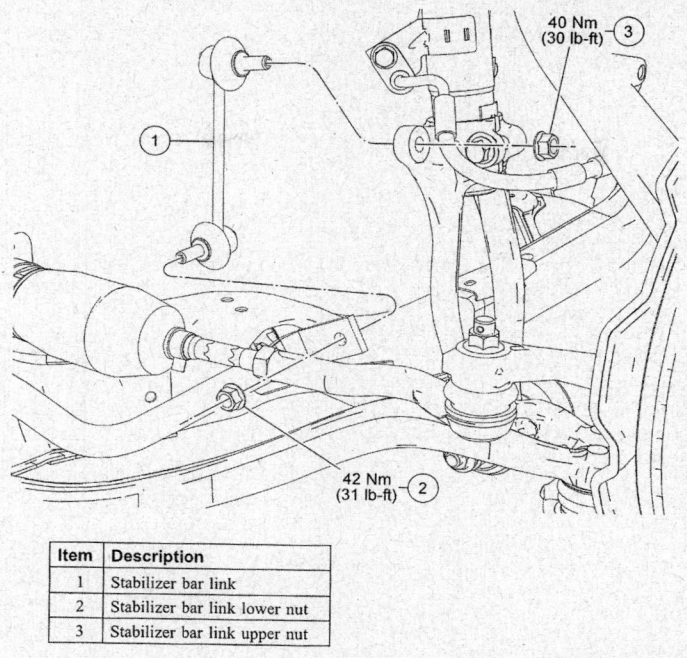

Item	Description
1	Stabilizer bar link
2	Stabilizer bar link lower nut
3	Stabilizer bar link upper nut

ARM0500000000149

Fig. 10 Stabilizer bar link replacement

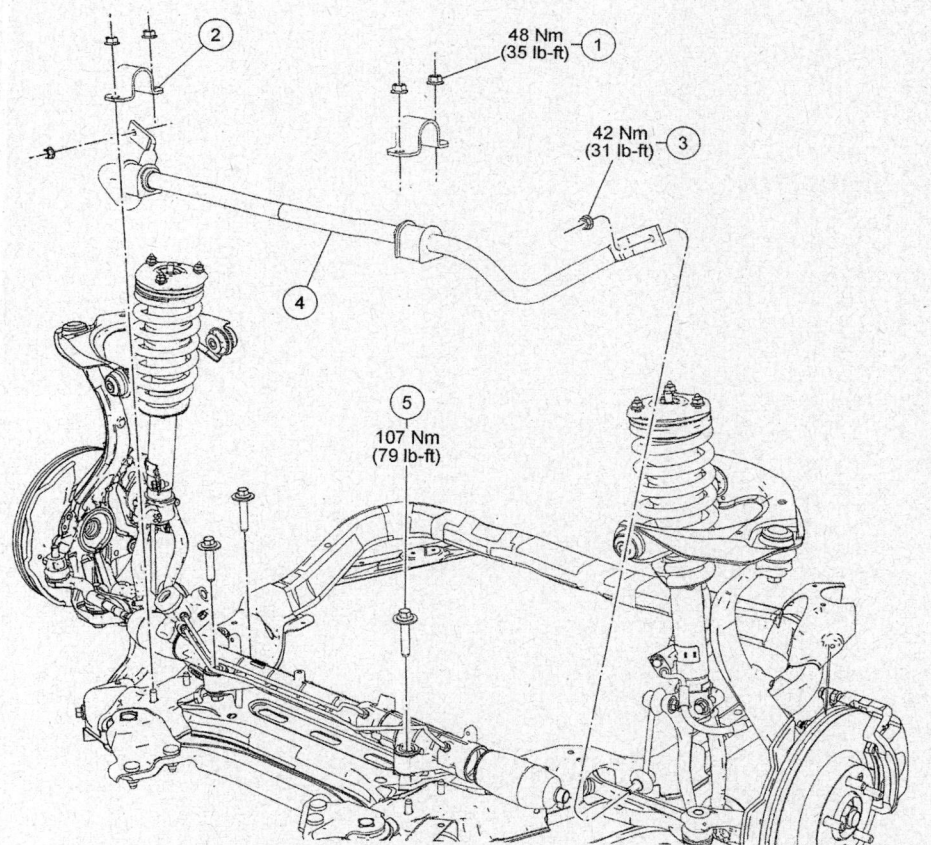

Item	Description
1	Stabilizer bar bracket nut (4 required)
2	Stabilizer bar bracket (2 required)
3	Stabilizer bar link lower nut (2 required)
4	Stabilizer bar
5	Steering gear-to-subframe bolt (3 required)

ARM0500000000151

Fig. 11 Stabilizer bar replacement (Part 2 of 2)

ARM0500000000150

Fig. 11 Stabilizer bar replacement (Part 1 of 2)

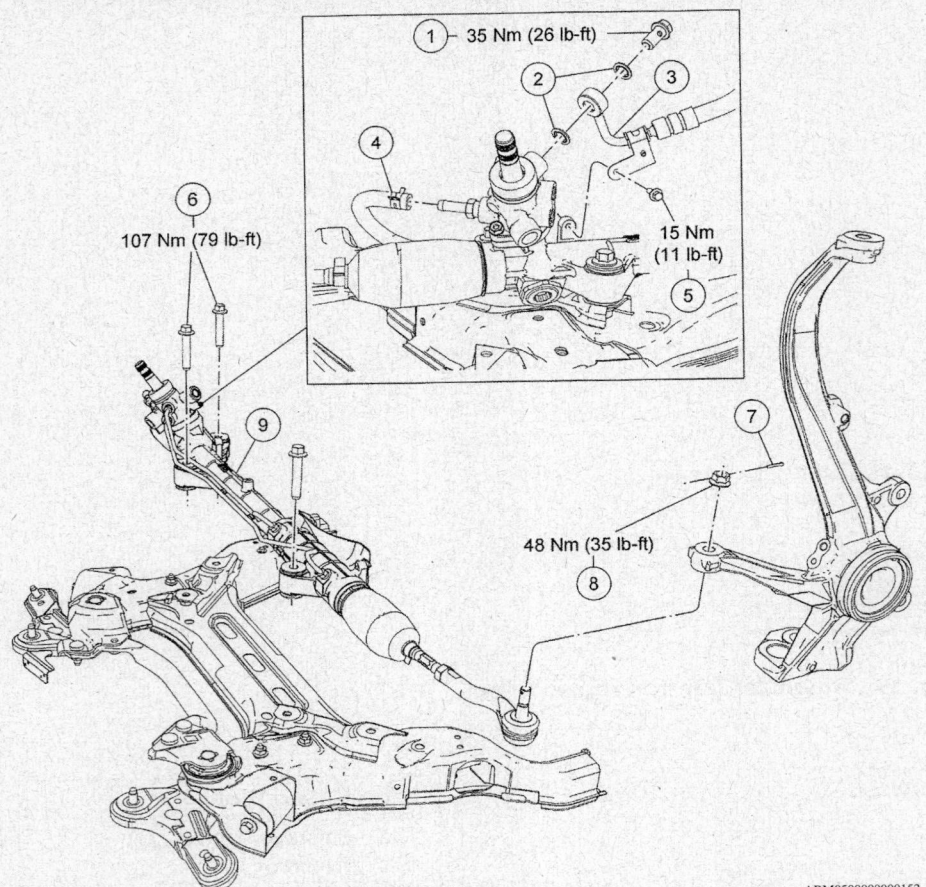

Item	Description
1	Power steering pressure line-to-steering gear banjo bolt
2	Power steering pressure line seals (2 required)
3	Power steering pressure line
4	Power steering return hose
5	Power steering line bracket-to-steering gear bolt
6	Steering gear bolts (3 required)
7	Cotter pin (2 required)
8	Tie-rod-to-wheel knuckle nut (2 required)
9	Steering gear

ARM0500000000153

Fig. 12 Steering gear replacement (Part 2 of 2)

ARM0500000000152

Fig. 12 Steering gear replacement (Part 1 of 2)

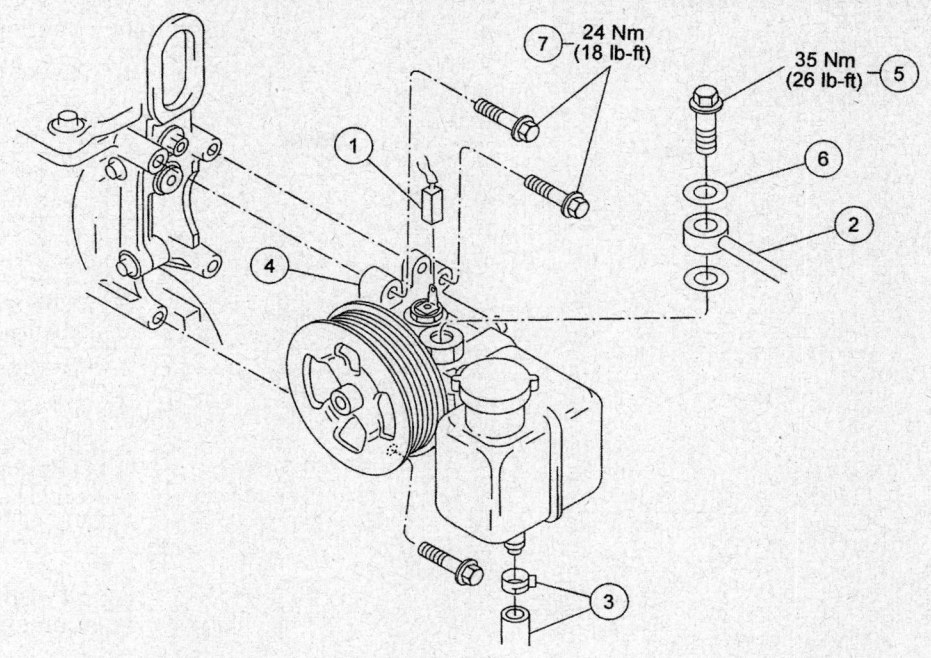

Item	Description
1	Power steering pressure switch electrical connector
2	Power steering pressure line
3	Power steering return hose
4	Power steering pump
5	Power steering pressure line banjo bolt
6	Power steering pressure line seal (2 required)
7	Power steering pump bolts (3 required)

ARM0500000000154

Fig. 13 Power steering pump replacement. 2.3L engine

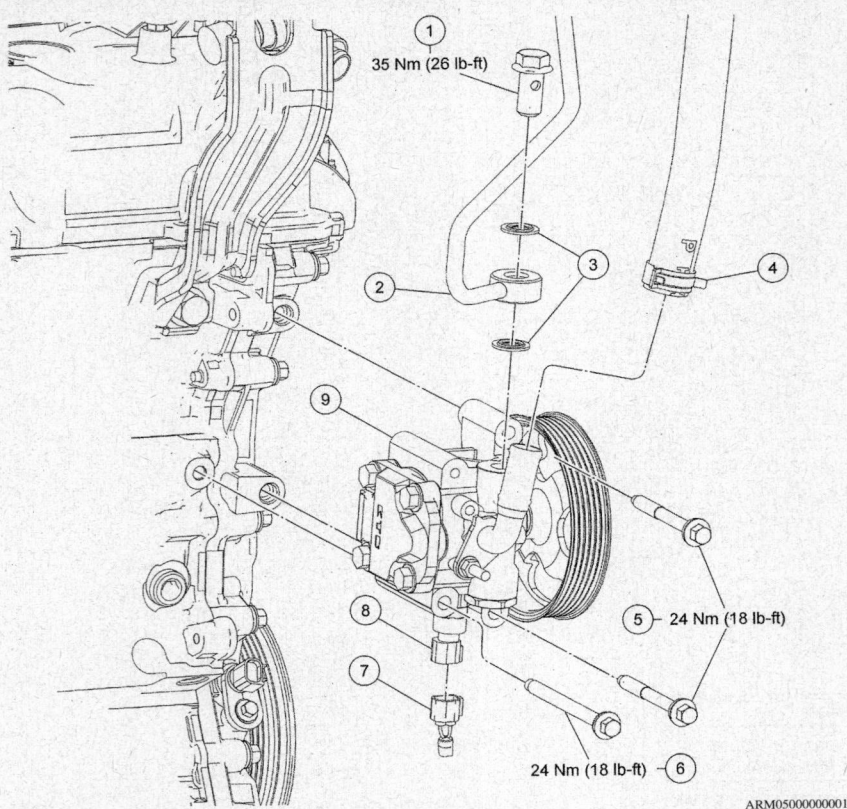

Item	Description
1	Power steering pressure line banjo bolt
2	Power steering pressure line
3	Power steering pressure line seals (2 required)
4	Power steering pump supply hose
5	Power steering pump bolts (2 required)
6	Power steering pump bolt
7	Power steering pressure switch electrical connector
8	Power steering pressure switch
9	Power steering pump

ARM0500000000156

Fig. 14 Power steering pump replacement (Part 2 of 2). 3.0L engine

ARM0500000000155

Fig. 14 Power steering pump replacement (Part 1 of 2). 3.0L engine

Item	Description
1	Power steering pressure line banjo bolt
2	Power steering pressure line
3	Power steering pressure line seals (2 required)
4	Power steering fluid reservoir-to-pump supply hose
5	Power steering pump bolts (2 required)
6	Power steering pump bolt
7	Power steering pressure switch electrical connector
8	Power steering pressure switch
9	Power steering pump

ARM0600000001549

Fig. 15 Power steering pump replacement (Part 2 of 2). 3.5L engine

ARM0600000001548

Fig. 15 Power steering pump replacement (Part 1 of 2). 3.5L engine

FUSION, MILAN, MKZ & ZEPHYR

TIGHTENING SPECIFICATIONS

Year	Component	Torque/Ft. Lbs.
2006–08	Axle Shaft Wheel Hub Nut	189
	Brake Caliper Anchor Plate	66
	Brake Disc Rotor	15
	Brake Disc Shield	17
	Brake Line Bracket	17
	Damper Fork To Front Lower Control Arm	76
	Front Lower Control Arm To Subframe	48
	Inner Tie Rod	70
	Lower Ball Joint Nut	148
	Power Steering Pressure Line Banjo Bolt	26
	Power Steering Pressure Line Bracket	80①
	Power Steering Fluid Reservoir Nuts (3.0L)	80①
	Power Steering Fluid Reservoir Nuts (3.5L)	62①
	Power Steering Pump Bolts	18
	Rear Lower Control Arm To Subframe	48
	Stabilizer Bar Bracket	35
	Stabilizer Bar Link Lower Nut	31
	Stabilizer Bar Link Upper Nut	30
	Steering Column Shaft	15
	Steering Gear To Subframe	79
	Strut Rod To Upper Mount Nut	30
	Strut To Damper Fork	35
	Strut Upper Mount To Body	22
	Subframe Bracket To Body Bolt	76
	Subframe Bracket To Subframe Nut	111
	Tie Rod End Jam Nut	55
	Tie Rod End Nut	35
	Upper Ball Joint Nut	35
	Upper Control Arm To Body	②
	Wheel Speed Sensor	17
	Wheel Speed Sensor Harness	17

① — Inch lbs.
② — 2006 torque to 41 ft. lbs.; 2007 torque to 35 ft. lbs.

Wheel Alignment

INDEX

	Page No.		Page No.		Page No.
Front Wheel Alignment	1-58	Preliminary Inspection	1-58	Wheel Alignment	
Camber	1-58	Rear Wheel Alignment	1-58	Specifications	1-2
Caster	1-58	Camber	1-58		
Toe-In	1-58	Caster	1-58		
		Toe-In	1-58		

PRELIMINARY INSPECTION

1. Ensure tires are inflated to proper pressure.
2. Inspect tires for wear patterns that may indicate improper wheel alignment, tire imbalance or damage because bulges or separations.
3. Inspect suspension for modifications such as trailer towing equipment or heavy duty handling components.
4. Inspect vehicle for signs of overloading or sagging. Ensure luggage compartment does not contain heavy objects.
5. Road test vehicle to isolate area of concern.

FRONT WHEEL ALIGNMENT

Camber

Front camber is not adjustable on these vehicles. If camber is not within specifications, inspect vehicle for suspension component damage, deteriorated bushings or distorted body mounting points.

Caster

If caster adjustment is required to resolve a vehicle alignment issue, then installing a revised upper control arm(s) is an acceptable method. This procedure should not be routinely performed with all alignments and only after all other possible sources have been inspected and corrected as required.

The revised upper control arms have the same base part number but are identified by the amount of caster they change (i.e. + .4° or - .4°).

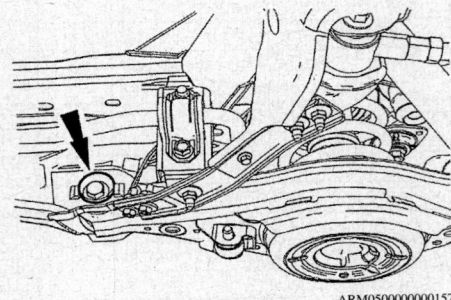

Fig. 1   Rear camber adjustment

Toe-In

1. Start engine and center steering wheel.
2. Turn ignition to Off position, then lock steering wheel in straight ahead position using suitable steering wheel holder.
3. Remove steering gear bellows clamps.
4. Loosen tie rod jam nut, then adjust left-hand and righthand tie rods until each wheel has half desired total toe specification. **Do not allow steering bellows to become twisted.**
5. Tighten tie rod adjusting nuts and install clamps.
6. Remove steering wheel holding tool.

REAR WHEEL ALIGNMENT

Camber

1. Install suitable alignment equipment, then following manufacturers instructions, measure rear camber.

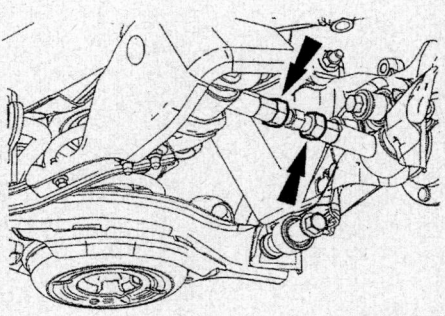

Fig. 2   Rear toe-in adjustment

2. Loosen rear camber adjustment nut, **Fig. 1.**
3. Rotate camber adjustment bolt until camber setting is within specifications as outlined in "Specifications."
4. **Torque** camber adjustment nut to 74 ft. lbs. **Do not allow camber adjustment bolt to rotate while tightening nut.**
5. Inspect rear camber and adjust as required.

Caster

The caster angles are factory set and cannot be adjusted.

Toe-In

Loosen toe link jam nuts, **Fig. 2,** approximately one full turn.

Adjust toe-in by rotating the toe link bolt from the opposite side. Rotate to link bolt to achieve the correct specifications as outlined in "Specifications." **Torque** toe link nut to 59 ft. lbs.

CROWN VICTORIA, GRAND MARQUIS, MARAUDER & TOWN CAR

NOTE: Refer To Rear Of This Manual For Vehicle Manufacturer's Special Service Tool Suppliers.

INDEX OF SERVICE OPERATIONS

Page No.

ACTIVE SUSPENSION 7-1
AIR BAG SYSTEM
PRECAUTIONS 0-18
BRAKES
  Anti-Lock Brakes (Volume 2).. 6-1
  Disc Brakes................. 14-1
  Drum Brakes................ 15-1
  Hydraulic Brake Systems..... 16-1
  Power Brake Units........... 17-1
COMPUTER RELEARN
PROCEDURE 0-31
ELECTRICAL
  Air Bag System (Volume 2) ... 4-1
  Air Conditioning.............. 8-1
  Alternators................... 11-1
  Blower Motor, Replace........ 2-6
  Cabin Air Filter, Replace 2-7
  Coil Pack, Replace 2-5
  Coil Units, Replace 2-5
  Cooling Fans 9-1
  Cruise Control (Volume 2) ... 2-1
  Dash Gauges (Volume 2) 1-1
  Dash Panel Service
  (Volume 2)................... 5-1
  Evaporator Core, Replace 2-7
  Fuel Pump Relay Location.... 2-5
  Fuse Panel & Flasher
  Location 2-5
  Headlamp Switch, Replace ... 2-6
  Heater Core, Replace........ 2-6
  Ignition Lock, Replace 2-5
  Ignition Switch, Replace 2-6
  Instrument Cluster, Replace... 2-6
  Multi-Function Switch,
  Replace 2-6
  Passive Restraint Systems
  (Volume 2) 4-1
  Precautions................. 2-5
  Radio, Replace 2-6
  Relay Center Location 2-5
  Speed Controls (Volume 2) ... 2-1
  Starter Motors 10-1
  Starter, Replace 2-5
  Steering Columns............ 12-1
  Steering Wheel, Replace...... 2-6
  Stop Light Switch, Replace ... 2-6
  Technical Service Bulletins.... 2-7
  Turn Signal Switch, Replace .. 2-6
  Wiper Motor, Replace........ 2-6
  Wiper Switch, Replace........ 2-6
  Wiper Systems (Volume 2).... 3-1
ELECTRICAL SYMBOL
IDENTIFICATION 0-63

Page No.

FRONT SUSPENSION &
STEERING
  Ball Joint, Replace........... 2-36
  Ball Joint Inspection 2-36
  Coil Spring, Replace......... 2-36
  Control Arm, Replace 2-37
  Power Steering............. 13-1
  Power Steering Gear,
  Replace 2-37
  Power Steering Pump,
  Replace 2-37
  Precautions................. 2-36
  Shock Absorber, Replace 2-36
  Stabilizer Bar, Replace........ 2-37
  Steering Columns............ 12-1
  Tightening Specifications...... 2-37
  Wheel Bearing, Adjust 2-36
  Wheel Bearing, Replace...... 2-36
NON-STANDARD TIRE &
WHEEL SIZE
ADJUSTMENT TO RIDE
HEIGHT SPECIFICATIONS
& TIRE SIZE CHART 0-61
REAR AXLE &
SUSPENSION
  Air Spring, Replace 2-33
  Coil Spring, Replace......... 2-33
  Control Arm, Replace 2-33
  Description 2-32
  Lateral Control Arm, Replace . 2-34
  Precautions................. 2-32
  Propeller Shaft, Replace 2-33
  Rear Axle, Replace 2-32
  Rear Axle Shaft, Replace 2-32
  Shock Absorber, Replace 2-33
  Stabilizer Bar, Replace 2-35
  Tightening Specifications...... 2-35
REAR DRIVE AXLE 19-1
SERVICE REMINDER &
WARNING LAMP RESET
PROCEDURES 0-34
SPECIFICATIONS
  Fluid Capacities & Cooling
  System Data................. 2-4
  Front Wheel Alignment
  Specifications................ 2-2
  General Engine
  Specifications................ 2-2
  Lubricant Data.............. 2-4
  Tune Up Specifications....... 2-2
  Vehicle Ride Height
  Specifications................ 2-3

Page No.

VEHICLE
IDENTIFICATION 0-1
VEHICLE LIFT POINTS...... 0-51
VEHICLE MAINTENANCE
SCHEDULES 0-73
WHEEL ALIGNMENT
  Front Wheel Alignment....... 2-38
  Preliminary Inspection 2-38
  Wheel Alignment
  Specifications................ 2-2
WIRE COLOR CODE
IDENTIFICATION 0-63
4.6L ENGINE
  Belt Tension Data............. 2-24
  Camshaft, Replace 2-22
  Camshaft Lobe Lift
  Specifications................ 2-19
  Compression Pressure........ 2-12
  Cooling System Bleed 2-24
  Crankshaft Rear Oil Seal,
  Replace 2-23
  Cylinder Head, Replace....... 2-16
  Engine Rebuilding
  Specifications................ 21-1
  Engine, Replace 2-12
  Engine Mount, Replace 2-12
  Exhaust Manifold, Replace.... 2-16
  Front Cover, Replace 2-20
  Front Cover Seal, Replace.... 2-21
  Fuel Filter, Replace 2-25
  Fuel Pump, Replace 2-24
  Hydraulic Lifters, Replace..... 2-19
  Intake Manifold, Replace...... 2-14
  Main & Rod Bearings 2-23
  Oil Pan, Replace............ 2-23
  Oil Pump, Replace........... 2-23
  Piston & Rod Assembly 2-23
  Precautions................. 2-9
  Radiator, Replace........... 2-24
  Rocker Arms, Replace 2-19
  Serpentine Drive Belt 2-24
  Technical Service Bulletins.... 2-25
  Thermostat, Replace......... 2-24
  Tightening Specifications...... 2-31
  Timing Chain, Replace........ 2-21
  Valve Adjustment 2-19
  Valve Arrangement........... 2-19
  Valve Cover, Replace 2-18
  Valve Spring & Valve Stem Oil
  Seal, Replace 2-20
  Water Pump, Replace 2-24

Specifications

GENERAL ENGINE SPECIFICATIONS

Engine Liter (VIN)①	Fuel System	Bore & Stroke	Compression Ratio	Net H.P. @ RPM	Maximum Torque Ft. Lbs. @ RPM	Normal Oil Pressure, psi
4.6L (V)	SEFI	3.60 x 3.60	9.85	302 @ 5700	318 @ 4300	20–45③
4.6L (W)	SEFI	3.55 x 3.54	9.40	224 @ 4800	②	40–70③
4.6L (W)④	SEFI	3.55 x 3.54	9.40	239 @ 4900	287 @ 4100	40–70③
4.6L (9)⑤	SEFI	3.55 x 3.54	10.00	175 @ 4500	235 @ 3500	40–70③

SEFI — Sequential Multi-Port Electronic Fuel Injection
① — The eighth digit of VIN denotes engine code.

② — 272 @ 4100 RPM w/single exhaust; 287 @ 4100 RPM w/dual exhaust.
③ — At 200°F.

④ — Sport.
⑤ — Natural Gas Vehicle (NGV).

TUNE UP SPECIFICATIONS

Engine Liter (VIN)①	Spark Plug Gap	Ignition Timing, BTDC				Curb Idle Speed, RPM③		Fast Idle Speed, RPM③		Fuel Pump Pressure, psi	Valve Clearance, Inch
		Firing Order Fig.	Man. Trans.	Auto. Trans.	Mark Fig.	Man. Trans.	Auto. Trans.	Man. Trans.	Auto. Trans.		
4.6L (V,W)	.052–.056	A⑦	—	8–12⑤	②	—	⑥	—	⑥	④	⑧
						—	⑥	—	⑥	④	⑧
4.6L (9)⑨	.052–.056	A⑦	—	⑤	②	—	⑥	—	⑥	④	⑧

BTDC — Before Top Dead Center
① — The eighth digit of Vehicle Identification Number (VIN) denotes engine code.
② — Equipped w/crankshaft sensor.
③ — When inspecting idle speed, set parking brake & block drive wheels.
④ — Key On, Engine Off, 35–45 psi. Key On, Engine Running, 30–45 psi.
⑤ — Non-adjustable.

⑥ — Idle speed is controlled by an automatic idle speed control. No adjustment is required.
⑦ — Equipped w/coil on spark plug ignition. Cylinder numbering front to rear, righthand bank, 1-2-3-4; lefthand bank 5-6-7-8. Firing order, 1-3-7-2-6-5-4-8.
⑧ — Equipped w/hydraulic lifters.
⑨ — Natural Gas Vehicle.

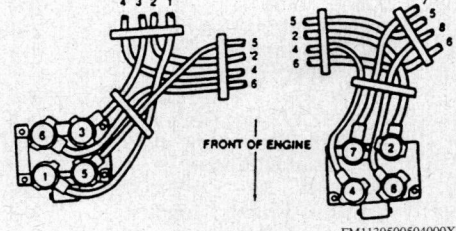

FRONT OF ENGINE

FM1139500504000X

Fig. A

FRONT WHEEL ALIGNMENT SPECIFICATIONS

Model	Caster Angle, Degrees		Camber Angle, Degrees		Total Toe, Inch①		Toe-Out On Turns, Degrees		Ball Joint Wear, Inch
	Limits	Desired	Limits	Desired	Limits	Desired	Outer Wheel	Inner Wheel	
Crown Victoria & Grand Marquis	+5.35 to +6.85	+6.1	-.75 to +.55	-.1	-.07 to +1.90	+.06	—	—	①
Marauder	+4.75 to +6.25	+5.5	-1.45 to +.05	-.7	-.18 to +.06	-.06	—	—	①
Town Car	+5.45 to +6.95	+6.2	-1.35 to +.15	-.6	②	③	—	—	①

① — Refer to "Ball Joint Inspection" in "Front Suspension & Steering" section.
② — +.13 to +37°.
③ — +.12°.

VEHICLE RIDE HEIGHT SPECIFICATIONS

Model	Year	Body Style	Manufacturer's Original Tire Size	Measurement Points & Specifications②					
				Front③			Rear③		
				Dim.	Specification⑤		Dim.	Specification④	
					Inches	mm		Inches	mm
Crown Victoria	2004	All	①	2⑧	2.4	60.0	2⑦	4.74	120.0
	2005–06	All	①	2⑧	2.6	66.0⑥	2⑦	4.64	118.0
Grand Marquis	2004	All	①	2⑧	2.4	60.0	2⑦	4.70	120.0
	2005–06	All	①	2⑧	2.6	66.0⑥	2⑦	4.64	118.0
Marauder	2004	All	①	2⑧	2.4	60.0	2⑦	4.70	118.0
Town Car	2004–06	All	P225/60R17	1⑧	+2.0 to +2.8	+50.0 to +70.0	2⑦	+4.40 to +5.00	+110.4 to +125.6

1 Dim. — Distance from lower control arm bolt head center to ground minus distance from ball stud center to ground

2 Dim. — 2004–06 distance from ground to center of lower control arm mounting bolt minus distance from ground to center of shock absorber mounting bolt

Dim. — Dimension

① — See door sticker or inside of glove box for manufacturer's original tire size specifications. If tires on vehicle do not match manufacturer's original tire size & measurement is not within limits, it will be required to refer to the "Non-Standard Tire & Wheel Size Adjustment To Ride Height Specification & Tire Size Adjustment Charts" in the front of this manual for approximate changes in ride height specifications.

② — Measurement is with fuel, radiator coolant and engine oil full, spare tire, jack, hand tools and mats in designated positions and tires properly inflated.

③ — Ride height lean (side to side) should be within .50 inch (12.7 mm).

④ — ± .3 inch (7.6 mm).

⑤ — ± .5 inch (12.7 mm)

⑥ — ± .23 inch (6.0 mm)

⑦ — Refer to **Fig. B**

⑧ — Refer to **Fig. A**

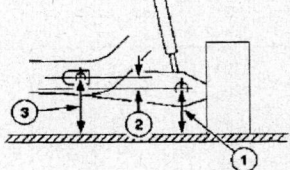

Item	Description
1	Distance between the ground and the center of the shock absorber mounting bolt
2	Ride height = 3-1
3	Distance between the ground and the center of the lower arm mounting bolt

ARM66FM000000041

Fig. A Front ride height measurement

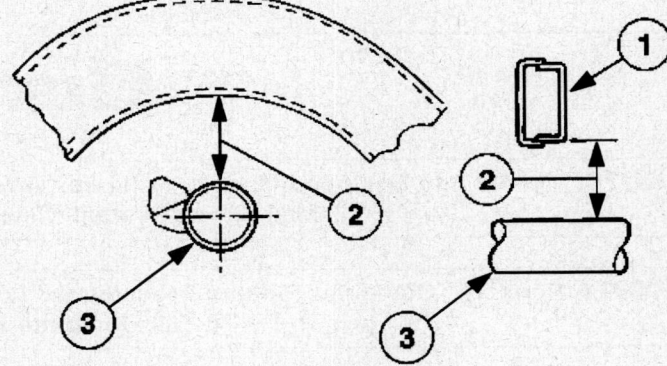

Item	Description
1	Inner frame reinforcement
2	Ride height
3	Rear axle

FM2030100153000X

Fig. B Rear ride height measurement

FLUID CAPACITIES & COOLING SYSTEM DATA

Engine	Coolant Capacity, Qts.	Coolant Type	Radiator Cap Relief Pressure, psi	Thermo. Opening Temp.	Fuel Tank Gals.	Engine Refill Qts.	Transmission Oil		
							Man. Trans. Pts.	Auto. Trans. Qts.①	Rear Axle Oil Pts.
4.6 DOHC	14.5	④	13–18	183–190	19	6.0②	—	11.9③	3.75
4.6 SOHC	15.8	④	13–18	188–193	19	5.0②	—	11.9③	3.75

EG — Ethylene Glycol

① — Approximate, make final inspection w/dipstick.

② — Includes filter. Final inspection is made w/dipstick.

③ — Police model, 12.8 qts.

④ — Always fill cooling system with same coolant that is present in the system. Do not mix coolant types. For models w/green coolant use ethylene glycol, Motorcraft Premium Engine Coolant VC-4 (in Oregon VC-5), or equivalent meeting Ford specification ESE-M97B44-A. For models w/orange coolant use coolant Motorcraft Premium Gold Engine Coolant VC-7-A meeting Ford specifications WSS-M97B51-A1.

LUBRICANT DATA

Year	Model	Lubricant Type				
		Transmission		Rear Axle	Power Steering	Brake System
		Manual	Automatic			
2004–06	All	—	Mercon V	80-90W GL-5①②	Mercon ATF	DOT 3

① — Premium thermally stable rear axle lubricant P/N XY-80–90W-QL, or equivalent, meeting Ford specification WSP-M2C197-A.

② — Traction-Lok axles, add 4 oz. of Ford Motor Co. Friction Modifier No. C8AZ-19B546-A, or equivalent.

Electrical

NOTE: On Air Bag Equipped Models, Refer To "Air Bag System Precautions" Located In The Front Of This Manual For System Disarming & Arming Procedures.

NOTE: Refer To "Computer Relearn Procedures" Located In The Front Of This Manual When Battery Power To The Computer Has Been Interrupted.

NOTE: Prior To Performing Any Service Operations Listed In This Section, Consult The "Technical Service Bulletins" Section For Related Information.

INDEX

	Page No.
Air Bag System (Volume 2)	4-1
Air Conditioning	8-1
Alternators	11-1
Blower Motor, Replace	2-6
Cabin Air Filter, Replace	2-7
Coil Pack, Replace	2-5
Crown Victoria, Grand Marquis & Marauder	2-5
Town Car	2-5
Coil Units, Replace	2-5
Cooling Fans	9-1
Cruise Control (Volume 2)	2-1
Dash Gauges (Volume 2)	1-1
Dash Panel Service (Volume 2)	5-1
Evaporator Core, Replace	2-7
Crown Victoria, Grand Marquis	

	Page No.
& Marauder	2-7
Town Car	2-7
Fuel Pump Relay Location	2-5
Crown Victoria, Grand Marquis & Marauder	2-5
Town Car	2-5
Fuse Panel & Flasher Location	2-5
Crown Victoria, Grand Marquis & Marauder	2-5
Town Car	2-5
Headlamp Switch, Replace	2-6
Heater Core, Replace	2-6
Crown Victoria, Grand Marquis & Marauder	2-6
Town Car	2-7
Ignition Lock, Replace	2-5
Functional Lock	2-5

	Page No.
Non-Functional Lock	2-5
Ignition Switch, Replace	2-6
Instrument Cluster, Replace	2-6
Multi-Function Switch, Replace	2-6
Passive Restraint Systems (Volume 2)	4-1
Precautions	2-5
Air Bag Systems	2-5
Battery Ground Cable	2-5
Radio, Replace	2-6
Relay Center Location	2-5
Speed Controls (Volume 2)	2-1
Starter Motors	10-1
Starter, Replace	2-5
Steering Columns	12-1
Steering Wheel, Replace	2-6
Stop Light Switch, Replace	2-6

	Page No.		Page No.		Page No.
Technical Service Bulletins	2-7	Crown Victoria, Grand Marquis & Marauder.........	2-8	**Wiper Switch, Replace**	2-6
Repeated Heater Core Failure ..	2-7	**Turn Signal Switch, Replace**	2-6	**Wiper Systems (Volume 2)**	3-1
White Flakes Coming From A/C Vents	2-8	**Wiper Motor, Replace**............	2-6		

PRECAUTIONS

Air Bag Systems

Refer to "Air Bag System Precautions" in the front of this manual for system disarming and arming procedures.

Battery Ground Cable

Prior to service, disconnect battery ground cable and isolate as required.

FUSE PANEL & FLASHER LOCATION

Crown Victoria, Grand Marquis & Marauder

The fuse panel is located behind the lefthand side of the instrument panel.

The emergency flashers are located on the lefthand rear of the trunk, front flasher is located in righthand rear of engine compartment and the rear flasher is located center rear of trunk.

Town Car

The instrument panel fuse panel is located behind the lefthand side of the instrument panel to the lefthand side of the steering column.

The engine compartment power distribution box is located next to the battery on the righthand front of the engine compartment.

The turn signal and hazard flashers are a component of the Lighting Control Module (LCM), located behind the lefthand side of instrument panel.

FUEL PUMP RELAY LOCATION

Crown Victoria, Grand Marquis & Marauder

The fuel pump relay is located on the righthand side of the engine compartment, in the relay center.

Town Car

The fuel pump relay is located on the righthand side of the engine compartment, in the relay center.

RELAY CENTER LOCATION

The relay center is located on the right-hand side of the engine compartment.

STARTER

REPLACE

1. Raise and support front of vehicle.
2. Remove starter motor solenoid terminal cover and disconnect cables.
3. Remove bolt, then position transmission cooler lines and bracket aside.
4. Remove two upper mounting bolts, lower bolt and starter motor.
5. Reverse procedure to install, noting the following:
   a. **Torque** starter bolts to 15–20 ft. lbs.
   b. **Torque** S-terminal cable eyelet with washer nut to 40–57 inch lbs.
   c. **Torque** starter cable B-terminal nut to 72–120 inch ft. lbs.
   d. **Torque** transmission cooler line bracket bolt to 84 inch lbs.

COIL PACK

REPLACE

Crown Victoria, Grand Marquis & Marauder

1. Disconnect engine control sensor wiring from ignition coil and radio ignition interference capacitor.
2. Disconnect ignition wires by squeezing locking tabs and twisting while pulling upward.
3. Remove ignition coil mounting screws and ignition coil with radio ignition interference capacitor.
4. Reverse procedure to install, noting the following:
   a. **Torque** coil pack mounting bolts to 40–61 inch lbs.
   b. Apply dielectric compound No. D7AZ-19A331-A, or equivalent, to ignition wire boots.

Town Car

1. Remove air cleaner outlet tube.
2. Disconnect coil electrical connector.
3. Remove bolt and coil.
4. Reverse procedure to install. **Torque** mounting bolts to 89 inch lbs.

COIL UNITS

REPLACE

1. Remove air cleaner outlet tube.
2. **On models equipped with DOHC engine,** remove coil cover bolts.

3. **On all models,** disconnect coil electrical connector.
4. Remove mounting bolt and coil.
5. Reverse procedure to install. **Torque** mounting bolts to 89 inch lbs.

IGNITION LOCK

REPLACE

Functional Lock

The following procedures are for vehicles that have a functioning ignition switch lock cylinder, ignition key is available, or the lock cylinder key numbers are known and key can be made.

1. Turn lock cylinder to Run position.
2. Insert 1/8 inch diameter wire pin or small drift punch in hole in trim shroud under lock cylinder.
3. Depress retaining pin while pulling out on lock cylinder to remove from column housing.
4. Install lock cylinder by turning to Run position and depressing retaining pin.
5. Insert lock cylinder into housing.
6. Ensure cylinder is fully seated and aligned in interlocking washer before turning key to OFF position. This will permit cylinder retaining pin to extend into cylinder housing hole.
7. Lock cylinder using key.
8. Ensure correct mechanical operation in all positions.

Non-Functional Lock

The following procedure is for vehicles that have a inoperative ignition lock cylinder and the ignition switch cannot be rotated because of a lost or broken lock cylinder key, unknown key number, or an ignition switch cap that has been damaged to the extent that the key cannot be rotated.

1. Center front wheels to straight ahead position.
2. Remove driver's air bag module as outlined in "Passive Restraint Systems" chapter.
3. Disconnect speed control wire harness from steering wheel.
4. Remove and discard steering wheel mounting bolt.
5. Remove steering wheel using suitable steering wheel puller.
6. Route contact wire harness through steering wheel as wheel is lifted off of shaft.
7. Twist ignition cap or bezel using suitable channel lock or vise-grip type pliers until it separates from ignition switch.
8. Drill down middle of key slot approximately 1¾ inches using suitable ⅜ inch diameter drill until ignition switch

lock cylinder breaks loose from breakaway base of ignition switch lock cylinder.

9. Remove lock cylinder and drill shavings from steering column tube flange.
10. Remove steering column upper bearing retainer, steering column lock housing bearing, ignition switch lock cylinder and steering column lock gear. Thoroughly clean drill shavings and other foreign material from casting.
11. Install new ignition lock cylinder as outlined under "Lock Cylinder, Functioning."

IGNITION SWITCH
REPLACE

1. Remove pin-type retainers and position lefthand instrument panel insulator aside.
2. Disconnect courtesy lamp and remove lefthand instrument panel insulator.
3. Remove lower instrument panel steering column opening cover.
4. Remove five bolts and instrument panel steering column opening cover reinforcement.
5. Disconnect ignition switch electrical connector.
6. Ensure ignition key is in Off position.
7. Remove ignition switch bolts and switch.
8. Reverse procedure to install.

HEADLAMP SWITCH
REPLACE

1. Remove instrument panel cluster finish panel.
2. Unclip switch and remove headlamp switch.
3. Reverse procedure to install.

STOP LIGHT SWITCH
REPLACE

1. Remove pin-type retainers and lefthand instrument panel insulator.
2. Disconnect stop light switch electrical connector.
3. Remove stop light switch self locking pin and brake master cylinder push rod spacer.
4. Remove stop light switch from brake master cylinder push rod.
5. Reverse procedure to install.

MULTI-FUNCTION SWITCH
REPLACE

1. Tilt column to lowest position and remove tilt lever, as required.
2. Remove ignition lock cylinder.
3. Remove mounting screws, then the upper and lower shrouds.
4. Remove two multi-function switch to steering column casting mounting screws.
5. Disconnect switch.
6. Disconnect two electrical connectors.

7. Reverse procedure to install. **Torque** mounting screws to 18–26 inch lbs.

TURN SIGNAL SWITCH
REPLACE

1. Tilt column to lowest position and remove tilt lever, as required.
2. Remove ignition lock cylinder.
3. Remove mounting screws, then the upper and lower shrouds.
4. Remove two multi-function switch to steering column casting mounting screws.
5. Disconnect switch.
6. Disconnect two electrical connectors.
7. Reverse procedure to install. **Torque** mounting screws to 18–26 inch lbs.

STEERING WHEEL
REPLACE

1. Center front wheels to straight ahead position.
2. Remove driver's air bag module as outlined in "Passive Restraint Systems" chapter.
3. Disconnect speed control wire harness from steering wheel.
4. Remove and discard steering wheel mounting bolt.
5. Remove steering wheel using suitable steering wheel puller.
6. Route contact wire harness through steering wheel as wheel is lifted off of shaft.
7. Reverse procedure to install, noting the following:
   a. Align steering wheel and shaft marks.
   b. Route contact wire harness through steering wheel opening at three o'clock position.
   c. Ensure air bag contact wire is not pinched and speed control wiring does not get trapped between steering wheel and contact.
   d. **Torque** steering wheel mounting bolt to 25–34 ft. lbs.
   e. **Torque** air bag module mounting nuts to 108 inch lbs.

INSTRUMENT CLUSTER
REPLACE

1. Remove instrument cluster finish panel.
2. **On Crown Victoria and Grand Marquis models,** proceed as follows:
   a. Remove lower steering column cover.
   b. Remove lower steering column reinforcement.
   c. Disconnect transmission range indicator cable and position aside.
3. **On models equipped with electronic cluster,** loosen steering column assembly.
4. **On all models,** remove instrument cluster, pull cluster out from instrument panel and disconnect electrical connectors.
5. Reverse procedure to install. **Torque** steering column to 11 ft. lbs.

RADIO
REPLACE

1. Release retaining clips by pushing radio removal tools No. T87P-19061-A, or equivalents, into face plate.
2. Slightly spread tools and pull radio from dash.
3. Disconnect power, antenna and speaker leads.
4. Reverse procedure to install. Ensure rear bracket is engaged on lower support rail.

WIPER MOTOR
REPLACE

1. Remove cowl top vent panel.
2. Remove mounting bolts, then position mounting arm and pivot shaft aside.
3. Remove wiper motor cover.
4. Remove clip and disconnect linkage from wiper motor.
5. Remove mounting bolts and wiper motor.
6. Reverse procedure to install.

WIPER SWITCH
REPLACE

1. Tilt column to lowest position and remove tilt lever, as required.
2. Remove ignition lock cylinder.
3. Remove mounting screws, then the upper and lower shrouds.
4. Remove two multi-function switch to steering column casting mounting screws.
5. Disconnect switch.
6. Disconnect two electrical connectors.
7. Reverse procedure to install. **Torque** mounting screws to 18–26 inch lbs.

BLOWER MOTOR
REPLACE

1. Remove mounting nut and position windshield washer fluid reservoir aside.
2. Remove righthand fender apron mounting screws and position apron aside.
3. Disconnect wire harness connector from retainer and blower motor electrical connector.
4. Disconnect blower motor rubber hose.
5. Remove mounting screws and blower motor.
6. Reverse procedure to install.

HEATER CORE
REPLACE

Crown Victoria, Grand Marquis & Marauder

1. Remove instrument panel as outlined in "Dash Panel Service" chapter.
2. Clamp off and disconnect heater hoses.
3. Remove plenum chamber nuts from

inside vehicle and disconnect electrical connectors.

4. **On five-passenger models,** loosen center console rear footwell duct nuts.
5. **On six-passenger models,** position back carpet from plenum chamber. Cut each side of rear footwell duct and bend back. **Only cut footwell duct enough to allow heater flow duct to be removed with plenum chamber as an assembly.**
6. **On all models,** remove in-vehicle temperature sensor hose.
7. Remove plenum chamber, then the heater core mounting screws.
8. Carefully cut seal above heater core inlet and outlet tubes, then remove heater core.
9. Reverse procedure to install.

Town Car

1. Remove instrument panel as outlined in "Dash Panel Service" chapter.
2. Remove evaporator core housing as outlined under "Evaporator Core, Replace."
3. Disconnect electrical connectors.
4. Position seal aside, the remove mounting screws and rear seat duct.
5. Remove air cleaner outlet pipe.
6. Disconnect wiring clip and remove dash panel nut.
7. Remove mounting nuts and heater core housing.
8. Remove mounting screws and heater core tube cover.
9. Remove mounting screws and floor duct.
10. Remove mounting screws, cover and heater core.
11. Reverse procedure to install.

EVAPORATOR CORE
REPLACE

Crown Victoria, Grand Marquis & Marauder

1. Recover air conditioning refrigerant system as outlined in "Air Conditioning" chapter.
2. Raise and support vehicle, then remove righthand front wheel and tire.
3. Remove mounting screws and righthand fender apron.
4. Remove evaporator core mounting nuts, **Fig. 1.**
5. Lower vehicle.
6. **On models equipped with manual air conditioning,** disconnect blower motor resister electrical connector.
7. **On models equipped with automatic temperature control,** disconnect blower motor speed control electrical connector.
8. **On all models,** disconnect evaporator air discharge temperature sensor electrical connector.
9. Disconnect evaporator inlet and outlet spring lock couplings. Discard O-ring seals.

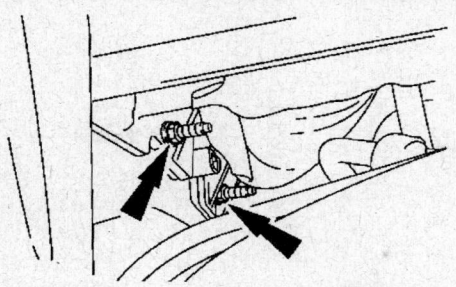

ARM66FM000000002

Fig. 1 Nut removal. Crown Victoria, Grand Marquis & Marauder

10. Remove mounting nuts, then position purge valve and bracket away from evaporator core housing.
11. Clamp off and disconnect heater hoses at heater core.
12. Disconnect electrical connectors from bracket, **Fig. 2.**
13. Disconnect blower motor electrical connector.
14. Remove mounting nut and position wire harness away from evaporator housing.
15. Disconnect wire harness from bracket.
16. Remove retainers and instrument panel lower insulator.
17. Fold back carpet and remove mounting screw.
18. From inside vehicle remove mounting screw, **Fig. 3.**
19. Remove evaporator core housing mounting bolts.
20. **On models equipped with automatic temperature control,** remove in-vehicle temperature sensor hose and elbow from evaporator housing.
21. **On all models,** remove evaporator core housing.
22. Reverse procedure to install using new O-rings lubricated with clean PAG oil.

Town Car

The evaporator core is not available separately. It is serviced only with the evaporator core housing assembly. The old evaporator core housing components will have to be transfer to the new one.

1. Recover air conditioning refrigerant system as outlined in "Air Conditioning" chapter.
2. Drain engine coolant into suitable container.
3. Disconnect spring lock couplings and discard O-ring seals.
4. Remove mounting screws and righthand cowl vent screen.
5. Remove cowl mounting bolts.
6. Disconnect EVAP canister purge valve vacuum hoses and wire harness connector.
7. Remove evaporator core engine compartment mounting nuts.
8. Disconnect evaporator core electrical connectors.
9. Disconnect clamps and heater core hoses.
10. Disconnect clamp and engine heater hose.

11. Remove nuts, then position purge valve and bracket away from evaporator core housing.
12. Remove mounting nuts, stud and position windshield washer fluid reservoir aside.
13. Loosen mounting bolts and position junction box aside.
14. Remove evaporator core mounting bolts.
15. Raise and support vehicle, then remove righthand tire and wheel assembly.
16. Remove mounting screws and fender apron, then disconnect wiring harness retainers.
17. Remove lower evaporator core housing mounting nuts.
18. Lower vehicle.
19. Remove upper evaporator core housing mounting nuts.
20. Remove evaporator core housing.
21. Reverse procedure to install using new O-rings lubricated with clean PAG oil.

CABIN AIR FILTER
REPLACE

Under normal operating conditions, cabin air filter should be replaced every 15,000 miles. Under severe operating conditions replace, cabin air filter should be replaced every 12,000 miles.

1. Open hood.
2. Pull hood pad away from righthand cowl vent screen.
3. Remove righthand cowl vent screen.
4. Remove water shield.
5. Remove cabin air filter element from filter housing, **Fig. 4.**
6. Reverse procedure to install.

TECHNICAL SERVICE BULLETINS

Repeated Heater Core Failure

On some of these models there may be repeated heater core leaks.

This condition may be caused by a chemical reaction (electrolysis).

To correct this condition, proceed as follows:

1. Place positive probe of suitable digital volt/ohm meter in engine coolant and negative probe on battery ground terminal.
2. Adjust engine to 2000 RPM.
3. If more than .4 volt is recorded, flush coolant and measure voltage, again.
4. If voltage is still excessive, inspect body/battery grounds.
5. If condition still exists, add extra grounds to heater core and engine, as follows:
   a. Secure 16 gauge stranded copper wire to heater core inlet tube using suitable hose clamp.
   b. Secure other end of wire to existing body sheet metal fastener.

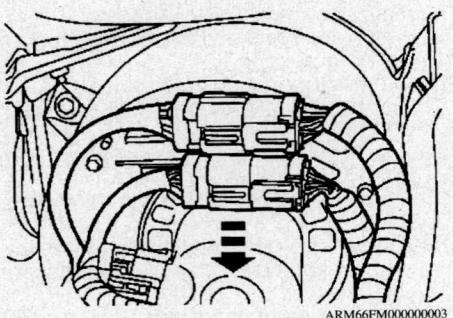

Fig. 2 Electrical connectors. Crown Victoria, Grand Marquis & Marauder

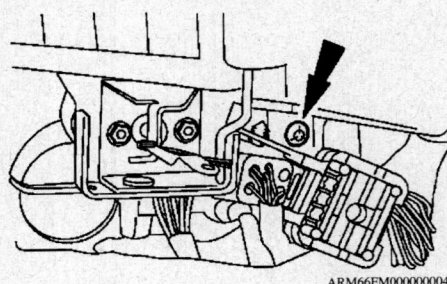

Fig. 3 Screw removal. Crown Victoria, Grand Marquis & Marauder

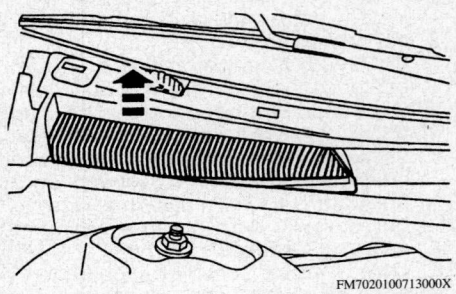

Fig. 4 Cabin air filter replacement

c. Secure another extra ground between existing engine and body sheet metal fasteners.

d. Ensure there is continuity between added grounds and battery ground terminal.

6. If condition still exists, install restrictor as follows:
   a. Cut line as close to engine block as possible.
   b. Install restrictor (P/N F1UZ-18D406-A) on inlet hose with arrow facing coolant flow direction (toward heater core).
   c. Secure with two suitable hose clamps.

7. Bleed cooling system trapped air as follows:
   a. Disconnect heater hose at right-hand front or rear of engine.
   b. Remove thermostat and housing.
   c. Fill engine with suitable coolant until mixture is seen at engine side heater hose connection.
   d. Connect heater hose, then install thermostat and housing.
   e. Fill degas bottle to coolant fill level mark.
   f. Fun engine to normal operating temperature.
   g. Select MAX heat and blower speeds

White Flakes Coming From A/C Vents

CROWN VICTORIA, GRAND MARQUIS & MARAUDER

Some of these models may exhibit white flakes coming from the A/C vents when the blower motor is engaged.

This condition may be caused by brazing flux utilized in the manufacturing process of the evaporator core.

To correct this condition, clean the A/C ducts through the registers and blow off the evaporator core through the blower motor opening as follows:

1. Evaporator core surface must be dry for best results.
2. Remove floor duct trim
3. Connect one end of vacuum cleaner hose to floor duct on driver side using masking tape.
4. Tape closed all other floor duct openings.
5. Obtain about two feet of rubber vacuum line large enough to fit end of a small shop air blowgun. Secure hose to end of blowgun using a suitable clamp.
6. Close all instrument panel registers.
7. Set temperature setting to full cold.
8. Place mode switch in Floor/Panel.

9. Turn on vacuum cleaner.
10. Working with one register at a time insert vacuum line down each duct, blow shop air through each duct for 30 seconds. Be sure to close each register before moving on to the next register.
11. Change mode switch to Floor/Defrost.
12. Blow shop air down each defroster duct for 30 seconds.
13. Alternate mode door between Floor and Floor/Defrost three times, giving door time to move between each mode change.
14. Turn off vacuum cleaner.
15. Remove blower motor.
16. Turn on vacuum cleaner.
17. Reach into blower opening with vacuum line and proceed to blow shop air for a minimum of 5 minutes, utilizing a very slow sweeping action.
18. Blow entire core face in up and down direction, then repeat moving from side to side.
19. Reinstall blower motor.
20. Open all registers.
21. Operate system with A/C on and blower on Max in each mode setting with temperature full Cold and then full Warm. Be sure to stay in each mode position for at least 30 seconds to ensure removal of any residual flakes/dust.
22. Disconnect vacuum cleaner and remove tape from floor duct.
23. Reassemble floor duct trim.

4.6L Engine

NOTE: On Air Bag Equipped Models, Refer To "Air Bag System Precautions" Located In The Front Of This Manual For System Disarming & Arming Procedures.

NOTE: Refer To "Computer Relearn Procedures" Located In The Front Of This Manual When Battery Power To The Computer Has Been Interrupted.

NOTE: Prior To Performing Any Service Operations Listed In This Section, Consult The "Technical Service Bulletins" Section For Related Information.

INDEX

	Page No.
Belt Tension Data	2-24
Camshaft, Replace	2-22
DOHC	2-22
SOHC	2-23
Camshaft Lobe Lift Specifications	2-19
Compression Pressure	2-12
Cooling System Bleed	2-24
DOHC	2-24
SOHC	2-24
Crankshaft Rear Oil Seal, Replace	2-23
Cylinder Head, Replace	2-16
DOHC	2-16
SOHC	2-17
Engine Rebuilding Specifications	21-1
Engine, Replace	2-12
DOHC	2-12
SOHC	2-13
Engine Mount, Replace	2-12
Crown Victoria, Grand Marquis & Marauder	2-12
Town Car	2-12
Lefthand	2-12
Exhaust Manifold, Replace	2-16
DOHC	2-16
SOHC	2-16
Front Cover, Replace	2-20
DOHC	2-20
SOHC	2-21
Front Cover Seal, Replace	2-21
Fuel Filter, Replace	2-25

	Page No.
Fuel Pump, Replace	2-24
Hydraulic Lifters, Replace	2-19
Intake Manifold, Replace	2-14
Gasoline Engine	2-14
DOHC	2-14
SOHC	2-14
Natural Gas Engine	2-15
Main & Rod Bearings	2-23
DOHC	2-23
Main	2-23
SOHC	2-23
Main	2-23
Oil Pan, Replace	2-23
Oil Pump, Replace	2-23
Piston & Rod Assembly	2-23
DOHC	2-23
SOHC	2-23
Precautions	2-9
Air Bag Systems	2-9
Battery Ground Cable	2-9
Fuel System Pressure Relief	2-9
Gasoline Engine	2-9
Natural Gas Engine	2-10
Radiator, Replace	2-24
Rocker Arms, Replace	2-19
DOHC	2-19
SOHC	2-19
Serpentine Drive Belt	2-24
Belt Routing	2-24
Replacement	2-24
Technical Service Bulletins	2-25
Engine - Exhaust - Knock During Initial Cold Start	2-25

	Page No.
2004	2-25
Engine Tick	2-25
2004	2-25
Engine Tick	2-25
2004–05 SOHC Engine	2-25
Idle Or Low Speed Engine Vibration	2-25
2004 Town Car	2-25
Thermostat, Replace	2-24
DOHC	2-24
SOHC	2-24
Tightening Specifications	2-31
Timing Chain, Replace	2-21
Removal	2-21
Installation	2-22
Valve Adjustment	2-19
Valve Arrangement	2-19
DOHC	2-19
Front To Rear	2-19
SOHC	2-19
Front To Rear	2-19
Valve Cover, Replace	2-18
DOHC	2-18
Lefthand	2-18
Righthand	2-18
SOHC	2-18
Lefthand	2-18
Righthand	2-18
Valve Spring & Valve Stem Oil Seal, Replace	2-20
Installation	2-20
Removal	2-20
Water Pump, Replace	2-24

PRECAUTIONS

Air Bag Systems

Refer to "Air Bag System Precautions" in the front of this manual for system disarming and arming procedures.

Battery Ground Cable

Prior to service, disconnect battery ground cable and isolate as required.

Fuel System Pressure Relief

GASOLINE ENGINE

The fuel system remains under high pressure even when the engine is not running. To avoid injury or fire, release pressure from the fuel system before disconnecting any fuel line. Proceed as follows:

1. Ensure ignition switch is in Off position.
2. Remove fuel tank cap to release residual fuel pressure.
3. Connect fuel pressure gauge tool No. T80L-9974-B, or equivalent, to fuel rail valve located on fuel rail.
4. Gradually open testing kit valve to relieve fuel pressure in system.
5. Drain fuel into suitable container or return to fuel tank.
6. When repair is completed, turn ignition On and Off several times to pressurize fuel system. **Do not start engine.**

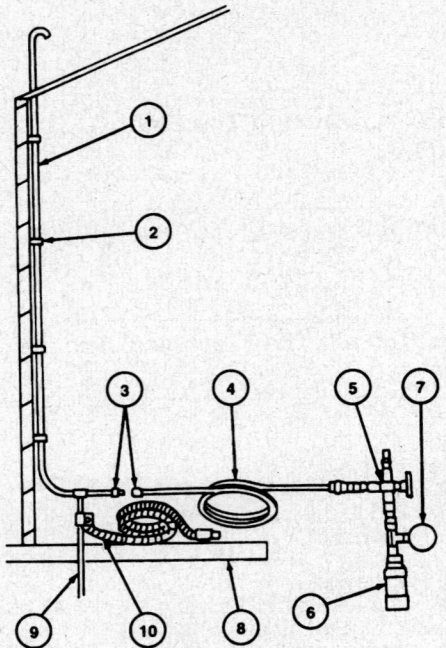

Item	Description
1	1/2 Inch Pipe
2	Vent Stack Support
3	Vent Stack Connectors
4	Rotunda Venting Hose
5	Rotunda Fuel Filter Neck Venting Kit
6	Fill Valve Connector
7	Gauge
8	Building Floor
9	Support / Grounding Rod
10	Grounding Cable

FM1029900308000X

Fig. 1 Typical vent stack installation

7. Inspect for fuel leaks at pressure regulator, fuel injectors and fuel fittings. Repair as required.

NATURAL GAS ENGINE

SYSTEM

When servicing any component of the fuel charging system, fuel pressure should be released using the following procedures.

When venting fuel system, venting into a vent stack is recommended, **Fig. 1.** If using a vent stack, ensure local regulations are followed. Before venting occurs, battery should be disconnected and isolated, as required.

Natural gas O-rings are identified with a yellow stripe. Do not use unapproved O-rings.

Before performing pressure relief procedures, refer to "Fuel Tank Solenoid Valve Test" to determine status of fuel tank solenoid valves.

If a manual override tool has been used to open fuel tank solenoid valve, solenoid valve must be replaced, **Fig. 2.**

Do not vent fuel tank unless tank or

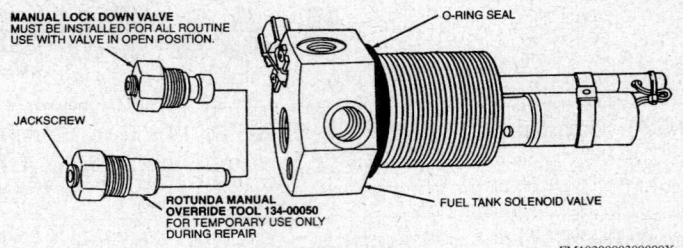

Fig. 2 Fuel tank solenoid valve replacement

Condition	Possible Source	Action
• Unable to Vent Fuel Tanks or Fuel Lines	• Damaged fuel tank solenoids. • Damaged lines or hoses. • Circuitry.	• GO to Pinpoint Test A.

FM1029900301000X

Fig. 3 NGV fuel tank solenoid valve symptom chart

fuel tank solenoid valve is being replaced. Venting of good tanks will damage fuel tank solenoid valve.

FUEL TANK SOLENOID VALVE TEST

Prior to relieving fuel pressure on NGV vehicles, the following diagnosis should be performed to determine whether or not the fuel tank solenoid valve is stuck open or closed.

1. Inspect fuel system and determine if any of the following apply:
   a. Damaged fuel tanks.
   b. Damaged fuel tank solenoid valve.
   c. Damaged lines or hoses.
   d. Damaged fuse or relay.
   e. Damaged power distribution box.
   f. Damaged, loose or corroded electrical connections.
2. If any of preceding conditions were found during visual inspection, repair as require.
3. If none of preceding conditions were found during visual inspection, refer to symptom chart, **Fig. 3.**
4. Refer to **Fig. 4** for pinpoint tests A.
5. If fuel tank solenoid valve requires replacement, refer to **MOTOR's "Domestic Engine Performance & Driveability Manual" or "Engine Performance & Driveability 1994–2005 v6.0."**

LINE PRESSURE

1. Connect grounding cable tool No. 134-00121, or equivalent, to fuel supply manifold and ground.
2. Ensure bleed valve on fuel rail pressure test kit is closed before installing.
3. Install fuel rail pressure test kit tool No. 134-00116, or equivalent, to fuel supply manifold Schraeder valve.
4. Connect vent hose to pressure test kit and vent stack.
5. Slowly open bleed valve of fuel rail pressure tester and allow fuel lines to vent to atmosphere for one minute. If pressure gauge still registers 95–125 psi, refer to **MOTOR's "Domestic Engine Performance & Driveability Manual" or "Engine Performance & Driveability 1994–2005 v6.0."**

TANK PRESSURE

Solenoid Normally Operating

1. Remove vapor vent box from fuel tank, as required.
2. Disconnect fuel tank electrical connectors and **torque** manual lockdown jackscrews to 80 inch lbs., on fuel tanks not to be vented. If neither of rear or upper tanks need to be vented, rear upper fuel tank rack harness connector may be disconnected without removing rear or upper fuel tank rack vent box.
3. Connect grounding cable 134-00121, or equivalent, to back side of fuel fill valve at fuel line connection and ground.
4. Ensure manual bleed valve on fuel vent kit is closed before connecting to fuel filler valve.
5. Connect fuel filler neck venting kit tool No. 134-00117, or equivalent, to fuel filler valve.
6. Connect vent hose tool No. 134-00118, or equivalent, to filler neck vent kit and vent stack.
7. Remove fuel valve relay from power distribution box.
8. Connect wire sockets Nos. 87 and 30 in fuel pump relay socket of power distribution box using suitable jumper wire constructed of six inches of 18 gauge wire and two spade terminals.
9. Slowly open manual backflow valve on fuel filler valve using suitable ³⁄₁₆ inch Allen wrench.
10. Ensure gauge on fuel filler neck vent kit indicates tank pressure.
11. Slowly open bleed valve on fuel filler neck vent kit and allow fuel tank to vent to atmosphere. Venting process may take one hour or more.
12. Close bleed valve on fuel filler neck vent kit. Ensure gauge pressure is zero psi.
13. Remove fuel tank solenoid manual lockdown valve.
14. **Ensure jackscrew in manual override tool is retracted fully (counter-clockwise) prior to installation into fuel tank solenoid valve. If tool is installed in vent position, fuel will be immediately released.**
15. Install Rotunda manual override tool

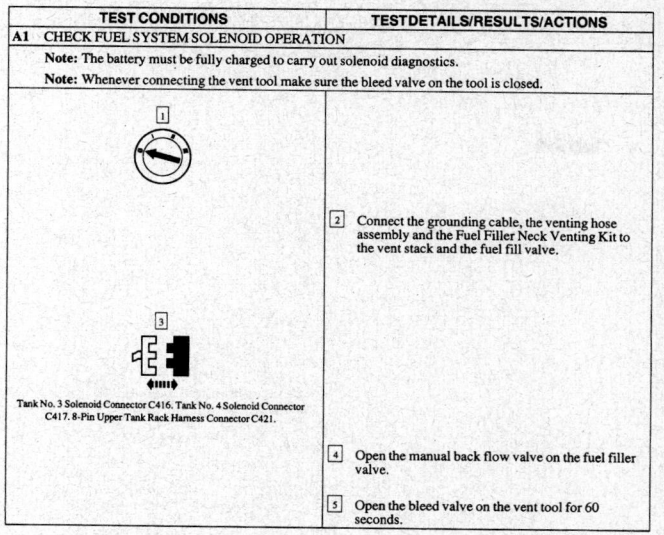

TEST CONDITIONS	TEST DETAILS/RESULTS/ACTIONS
A1 CHECK FUEL SYSTEM SOLENOID OPERATION	
Note: The battery must be fully charged to carry out solenoid diagnostics.	
Note: Whenever connecting the vent tool make sure the bleed valve on the tool is closed.	
	2 Connect the grounding cable, the venting hose assembly and the Fuel Filler Neck Venting Kit to the vent stack and the fuel fill valve.
Tank No. 3 Solenoid Connector C416. Tank No. 4 Solenoid Connector C417. 8-Pin Upper Tank Rack Harness Connector C421.	
	4 Open the manual back flow valve on the fuel filler valve.
	5 Open the bleed valve on the vent tool for 60 seconds.

FM1029900362010X

Fig. 4   Pinpoint Test A: Fuel tank solenoid valve diagnosis (Part 1 of 26)

No. 134-00050, or equivalent, to tank solenoid and **torque** to 30 ft. lbs.
16. Turn override tool jackscrew clockwise until fuel flows.
17. Vent system until fuel flow stops.
18. Close manual backflow valve on fuel filler valve after tank has been vented.
19. Vent fuel lines.
20. Remove manual override tool from fuel tank solenoid valve.
21. Install fuel tank solenoid manual lockdown valve and **torque** to 30 ft. lbs.
22. **Torque** manual lockdown valve jackscrew on fuel tank solenoid valve to 80 inch lbs.
23. Repeat procedure until affected tanks are vented.

Solenoid Stuck Open

1. Disconnect fuel tank electrical connectors and **torque** manual lockdown jackscrews to 80 inch lbs., on fuel tanks not to be vented. If neither of rear or upper tanks need to be vented, rear upper fuel tank rack harness connector may be disconnected without removing rear or upper fuel tank rack vent box.
2. Remove vent box from upper fuel tank rack, as required.
3. Connect grounding cable tool No. 134-00121, or equivalent, to back side of fuel fill valve and ground.
4. Ensure manual bleed valve on fuel filler neck vent kit is closed before connecting to fuel filler valve.
5. Connect fuel filler vent kit tool No. 134-00117, or equivalent, to fuel filler valve.
6. Connect vent hose tool No. 134-00118, or equivalent, to filler neck vent kit and vent stack.
7. Slowly open manual backflow valve on fuel filler valve.
8. Ensure filler neck vent kit pressure gauge indicates tank pressure.
9. Slowly open bleed valve on filler neck vent kit and allow contents of fuel tank to vent to atmosphere. Vent process

may take one hour or more.
10. Close bleed valve on fuel filler neck vent kit. Ensure pressure is zero psi.
11. Remove fuel tank solenoid manual lockdown valve.
12. **Ensure jackscrew in manual override tool is retracted fully (counter-clockwise) prior to installation into fuel tank solenoid valve. If tool is installed in vent position, fuel will be immediately released.**
13. Install Rotunda manual override tool No. 134-00050, or equivalent, to tank solenoid and **torque** to 30 ft. lbs.
14. Turn override tool jackscrew clockwise until fuel flows.
15. Open manual bleed valve on fuel filler neck vent kit and vent system until fuel flow stops.
16. Close manual backflow valve on fuel filler valve after tank has been vented.
17. Vent fuel lines.
18. Remove manual override tool from fuel tank solenoid valve.
19. Install fuel tank solenoid manual lockdown valve and **torque** to 30 ft. lbs.
20. **Torque** manual lockdown valve jackscrew on fuel tank solenoid valve to 80 inch lbs.
21. Repeat procedure until affected tanks are vented.

Solenoid Stuck Closed

1. Disconnect fuel tank electrical connectors and **torque** manual lockdown jackscrews to 80 inch lbs., on fuel tanks not to be vented. If neither of rear or upper tanks need to be vented, rear

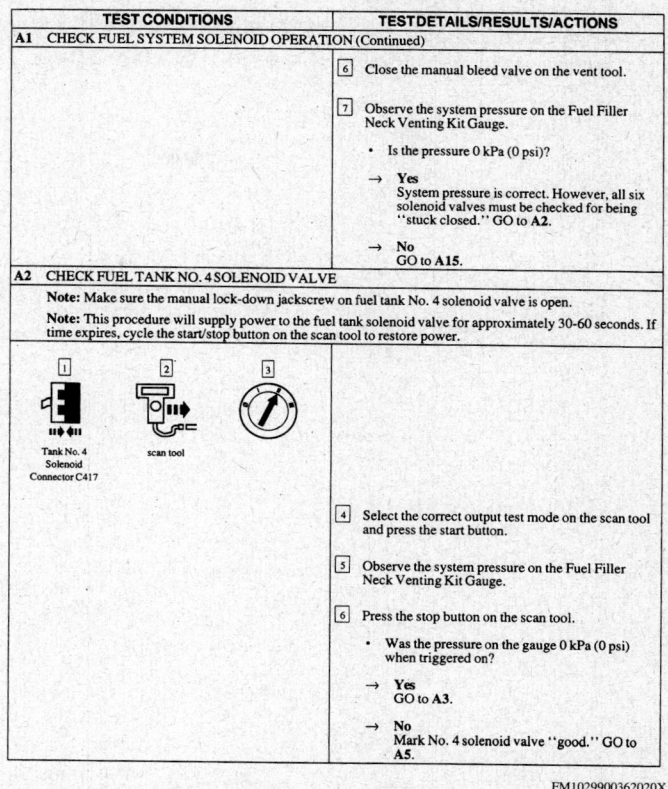

TEST CONDITIONS	TEST DETAILS/RESULTS/ACTIONS
A1 CHECK FUEL SYSTEM SOLENOID OPERATION (Continued)	
	6 Close the manual bleed valve on the vent tool.
	7 Observe the system pressure on the Fuel Filler Neck Venting Kit Gauge.
	• Is the pressure 0 kPa (0 psi)?
	→ Yes System pressure is correct. However, all six solenoid valves must be checked for being "stuck closed." GO to A2.
	→ No GO to A15.
A2 CHECK FUEL TANK NO. 4 SOLENOID VALVE	
Note: Make sure the manual lock-down jackscrew on fuel tank No. 4 solenoid valve is open.	
Note: This procedure will supply power to the fuel tank solenoid valve for approximately 30-60 seconds. If time expires, cycle the start/stop button on the scan tool to restore power.	
Tank No. 4 Solenoid Connector C417 scan tool	
	4 Select the correct output test mode on the scan tool and press the start button.
	5 Observe the system pressure on the Fuel Filler Neck Venting Kit Gauge.
	6 Press the stop button on the scan tool.
	• Was the pressure on the gauge 0 kPa (0 psi) when triggered on?
	→ Yes GO to A3.
	→ No Mark No. 4 solenoid valve "good." GO to A5.

FM1029900362020X

Fig. 4   Pinpoint Test A: Fuel tank solenoid valve diagnosis (Part 2 of 26)

upper fuel tank rack harness connector may be disconnected without removing rear or upper fuel tank rack vent box.
2. Remove vent box from upper fuel tank rack, as required.
3. Connect grounding cable tool No. 134-00121, or equivalent, to back side of fuel fill valve and ground.
4. Ensure manual bleed valve on fuel filler neck vent kit is closed before connecting to fuel filler valve.
5. Connect fuel filler vent kit tool No. 134-00117, or equivalent, to fuel filler valve.
6. Connect vent hose tool No. 134-00118, or equivalent, to filler neck vent kit and vent stack.
7. Open manual bleed valve on fuel filler neck vent kit for one minute to bleed residual fuel system pressure. Close manual bleed valve.
8. Remove manual lockdown valve from fuel tank solenoid valve of fuel tank to be vented.
9. **Ensure jackscrew in manual override tool is retracted fully (counter-clockwise) prior to installation into fuel tank solenoid valve. If tool is installed in vent position, fuel will be immediately released.**
10. Install Rotunda manual override tool No. 134-00050, or equivalent, to tank solenoid and **torque** to 30 ft. lbs.
11. Turn override tool jackscrew clockwise until fuel flows.
12. Slowly open manual backflow valve on fuel filler valve and ensure pressure gauge on vent kit reads tank pressure.

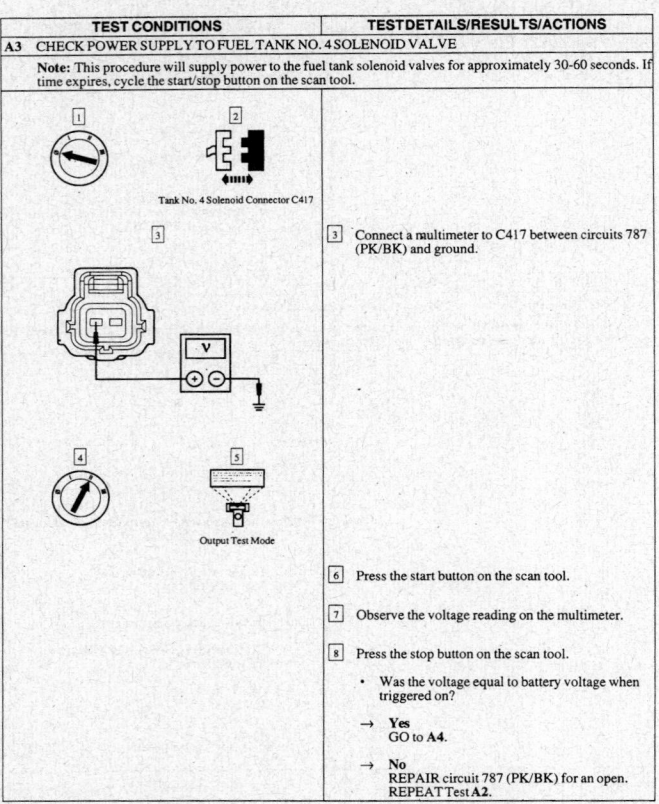

TEST CONDITIONS	TESTDETAILS/RESULTS/ACTIONS
A3 CHECK POWER SUPPLY TO FUEL TANK NO. 4 SOLENOID VALVE	

Note: This procedure will supply power to the fuel tank solenoid valves for approximately 30-60 seconds. If time expires, cycle the start/stop button on the scan tool.

Tank No. 4 Solenoid Connector C417

Output Test Mode

③   Connect a multimeter to C417 between circuits 787 (PK/BK) and ground.

⑥   Press the start button on the scan tool.

⑦   Observe the voltage reading on the multimeter.

⑧   Press the stop button on the scan tool.

- Was the voltage equal to battery voltage when triggered on?

→   **Yes**
GO to **A4**.

→   **No**
REPAIR circuit 787 (PK/BK) for an open.
REPEAT Test **A2**.

FM1029900362030X

Fig. 4   Pinpoint Test A: Fuel tank solenoid valve diagnosis (Part 3 of 26)

TEST CONDITIONS	TESTDETAILS/RESULTS/ACTIONS
A4 CHECK FUEL TANK NO. 4 SOLENOID VALVE CIRCUIT 57 (BK) FOR AN OPEN	

③   Measure the resistance between C417, circuit 57 (BK) and ground.

- Is resistance less than 5 ohms?

→   **Yes**
Mark fuel tank No. 4 solenoid valve ''stuck closed.'' A new solenoid valve will be installed after completing diagnostics. GO to **A5**.

→   **No**
REPAIR Circuit 57 (BK) for an open.
REPEAT Test **A2**.

FM1029900362040X

Fig. 4   Pinpoint Test A: Fuel tank solenoid valve diagnosis (Part 4 of 26)

2. Raise and support vehicle.
3. Remove mounting nut, bolts and right-hand engine mount.
4. Reverse procedure to install.

13. Slowly open bleed valve on fuel filler neck vent kit and allow tank to vent to atmosphere. Vent process may take one hour or more.
14. Vent tank until fuel flow stops.
15. Close manual backflow valve on fuel filler valve when tank venting is complete.
16. Vent fuel lines.
17. Remove manual override tool from fuel tank solenoid valve.
18. Install fuel tank solenoid manual lockdown valve and **torque** to 30 ft. lbs.
19. **Torque** manual lockdown valve jackscrew on fuel tank solenoid valve to 80 inch lbs.
20. Repeat procedure until affected tanks are vented.

COMPRESSION PRESSURE

Cylinder compression pressure should be 134–250 psi at an engine cranking speed of 180 RPM minimum. The compression in each cylinder should fall within the specified compression pressure range with no more than a 75% variance in compression.

ENGINE MOUNT
REPLACE

Crown Victoria, Grand Marquis & Marauder

1. Support vehicle engine with suitable engine support device.
2. Remove mounting bolts and mount(s).
3. Reverse procedure to install.

Town Car
LEFTHAND

1. Support with engine lift bracket tool No. 303-F047 and support bar tool No. 3030-D063, or equivalents.
2. Raise and support vehicle.
3. Remove oil filter.
4. Remove mounting nut, bolts and left-hand engine mount.
5. Reverse procedure to install.

RIGHTHAND

1. Support with engine lift bracket tool No. 303-F047 and support bar tool No. 3030-D063, or equivalents.

ENGINE
REPLACE

DOHC

1. Remove hood.
2. Remove air cleaner outlet tube.
3. Drain coolant into suitable container.
4. Remove fan shroud assembly.
5. Remove pin retainers, nuts and bolts, then the righthand cowl extension.
6. Disconnect electrical connector, then remove bolts and lefthand extension cover.
7. Disconnect power distribution power supply electrical connector.
8. Disconnect ground wire and air conditioning electrical connector.
9. Disconnect fuel hose spring lock coupling.
10. Remove accelerator controls splash shield.
11. Disconnect accelerator cable, speed control cable and return spring.
12. Remove accelerator and speed control cables from bracket.
13. Disconnect vacuum hoses and EAR system module electrical connector.
14. Remove mounting bolt and position accelerator cables aside.
15. Disconnect coolant hoses.
16. Disconnect engine bulkhead electrical connectors.

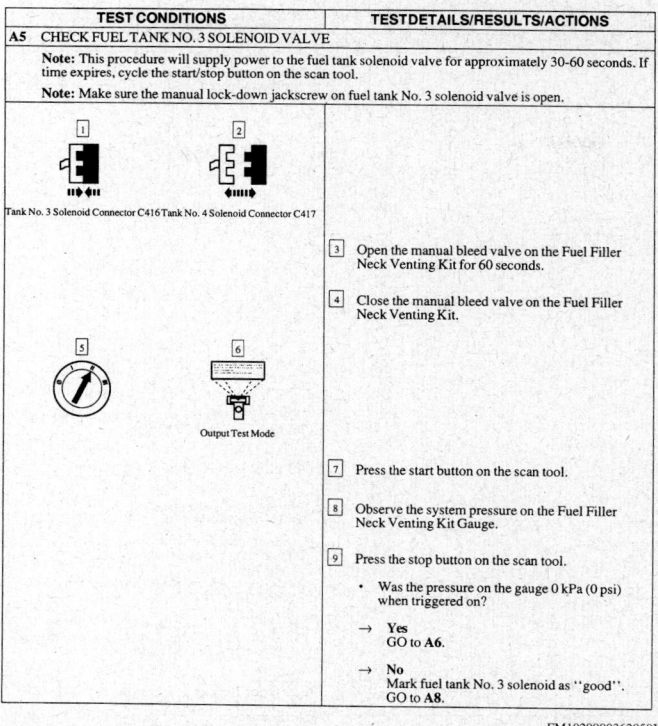

TEST CONDITIONS	TESTDETAILS/RESULTS/ACTIONS
A5 CHECK FUEL TANK NO. 3 SOLENOID VALVE	

Note: This procedure will supply power to the fuel tank solenoid valve for approximately 30-60 seconds. If time expires, cycle the start/stop button on the scan tool.

Note: Make sure the manual lock-down jackscrew on fuel tank No. 3 solenoid valve is open.

Tank No. 3 Solenoid Connector C416   Tank No. 4 Solenoid Connector C417

Output Test Mode

3 Open the manual bleed valve on the Fuel Filler Neck Venting Kit for 60 seconds.

4 Close the manual bleed valve on the Fuel Filler Neck Venting Kit.

7 Press the start button on the scan tool.

8 Observe the system pressure on the Fuel Filler Neck Venting Kit Gauge.

9 Press the stop button on the scan tool.

- Was the pressure on the gauge 0 kPa (0 psi) when triggered on?

→ **Yes**
  GO to **A6**.

→ **No**
  Mark fuel tank No. 3 solenoid as "good".
  GO to **A8**.

FM1029900362050X

Fig. 4 Pinpoint Test A: Fuel tank solenoid valve diagnosis (Part 5 of 26)

17. Disconnect lower radiator hose from oil filter adapter.
18. Raise and support vehicle, then drain engine oil into suitable container.
19. Disconnect power steering and power steering pressure switch electrical connectors.
20. Remove mounting nut and transmission cooler tube support bracket.
21. Disconnect CKP electrical connector.
22. Disconnect engine wiring harness retainers from air conditioning compressor.
23. Disconnect air conditioning compressor electrical connector.
24. Remove bolts, then position air conditioning compressor and power steering pump aside.
25. Remove starter motor and engine oil cooler tubes bracket.
26. Disconnect transmission and heated oxygen sensors electrical connectors.
27. Remove four exhaust pipe to manifold mounting nuts.
28. Remove inspection cover and torque converter nut access plug.
29. Remove engine support insulator nuts and lower vehicle.
30. Support transmission using suitable transmission jack.
31. Remove mounting bolts and separate transmission from engine.
32. Install engine lift bracket set tool No. D93P-6001-A, or equivalent.
33. Lift and remove engine.
34. Reverse procedure to install.

SOHC

1. Remove hood.
2. Evacuate air conditioning system as

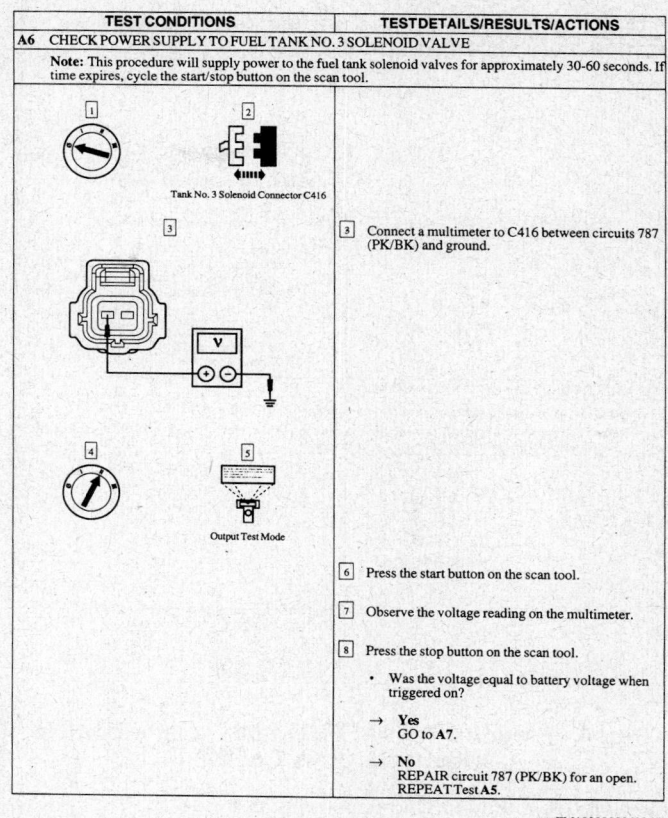

TEST CONDITIONS	TESTDETAILS/RESULTS/ACTIONS
A6 CHECK POWER SUPPLY TO FUEL TANK NO. 3 SOLENOID VALVE	

Note: This procedure will supply power to the fuel tank solenoid valves for approximately 30-60 seconds. If time expires, cycle the start/stop button on the scan tool.

Tank No. 3 Solenoid Connector C416

3 Connect a multimeter to C416 between circuits 787 (PK/BK) and ground.

Output Test Mode

6 Press the start button on the scan tool.

7 Observe the voltage reading on the multimeter.

8 Press the stop button on the scan tool.

- Was the voltage equal to battery voltage when triggered on?

→ **Yes**
  GO to **A7**.

→ **No**
  REPAIR circuit 787 (PK/BK) for an open.
  REPEAT Test **A5**.

FM1029900362060X

Fig. 4 Pinpoint Test A: Fuel tank solenoid valve diagnosis (Part 6 of 26)

outlined in "Air Conditioning" chapter.
3. Remove air cleaner outlet tube.
4. Relieve fuel pressure as outlined under "Precautions."
5. Remove wiper arm and pivot shaft.
6. Rotate tensioner clockwise and remove accessory drive belt.
7. Remove lefthand and righthand cowl extensions.
8. Drain engine coolant into suitable container.
9. Remove accelerator splash shield and disconnect vacuum hose.
10. Disconnect EVAP canister purge valve hoses and electrical connector, then remove EVAP canister purge valve.
11. Disconnect accelerator cable and speed control actuator cable.
12. Remove accelerator and speed control actuator cables from clips, then position them aside.
13. Disconnect fuel spring lock connector.
14. Disconnect power distribution power supply electrical connector.
15. Disconnect ground wire, **Fig. 5**.
16. Disconnect air conditioning electrical connector and heater water hoses.
17. Remove ground strap, **Fig. 6**.
18. Disconnect engine bulkhead electrical connectors.
19. Remove mounting bolt and position power steering pump reservoir aside.
20. Disconnect upper radiator hose and secure it to radiator assembly.
21. Disconnect lower radiator hose from oil filter adapter.

22. Remove cooling fan, then raise and support vehicle.
23. Drain engine oil into suitable container.
24. Disconnect power steering and power steering pressure switch electrical connectors.
25. Remove mounting nut and the transmission cooler tube support bracket.
26. Disconnect CKP electrical connector.
27. Disconnect engine wiring harness retainers from air conditioning compressor, then the air conditioning compressor electrical connector.
28. Remove mounting bolts and position air conditioning compressor aside.
29. Remove mounting bolts and position power steering pump aside.
30. Remove starter motor and lower vehicle.
31. Remove and discard pinch bolt, then disconnect lower intermediate steering shaft from upper intermediate shaft.
32. Remove and discard pinch bolt, then disconnect upper intermediate steering shaft from isolator.
33. Remove mounting nuts, bearing and seal, then the upper intermediate steering shaft.
34. Remove and discard pinch bolt, then remove lower intermediate steering shaft. **Do not allow steering wheel to rotate while steering shaft is removed.**
35. Disconnect transmission and heated oxygen sensors electrical connectors.

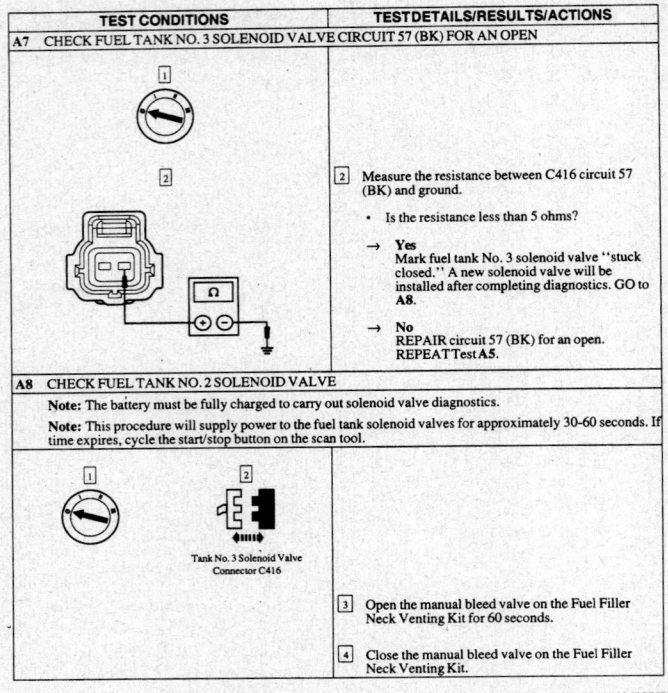

Fig. 4 Pinpoint Test A: Fuel tank solenoid valve diagnosis (Part 7 of 26)

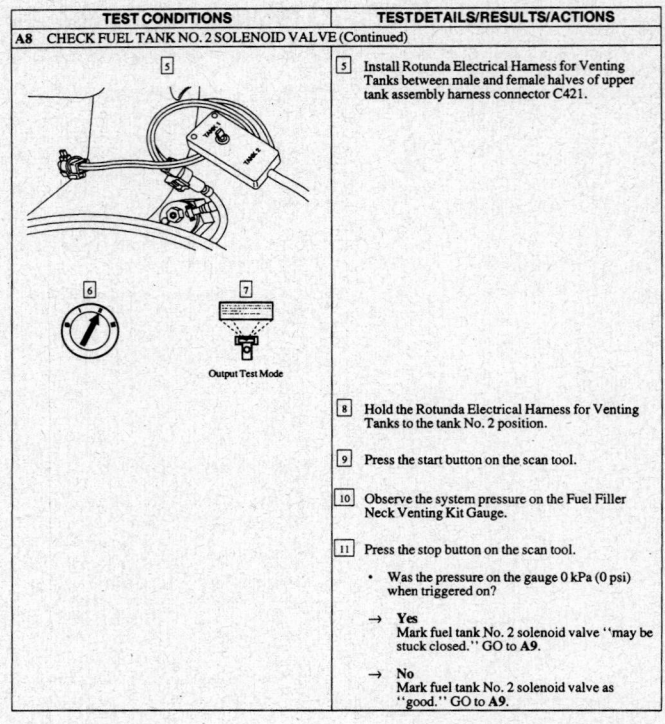

Fig. 4 Pinpoint Test A: Fuel tank solenoid valve diagnosis (Part 8 of 26)

36. Remove four mounting nuts from front exhaust pipes.
37. Remove mounting bolts inspection cover.
38. Remove torque converter nut access plug.
39. Remove lower engine to transmission mounting bolts.
40. Remove engine support insulator mounting nuts.
41. Install engine lifting bracket set tool No. 303-DS086, or equivalent.
42. Remove remaining engine to transmission bolts and engine.
43. Reverse procedure to install.

INTAKE MANIFOLD
REPLACE

Gasoline Engine
DOHC
LOWER

1. Drain engine coolant into suitable container.
2. Remove upper intake manifold as outlined under "Upper."
3. Disconnect engine coolant temperature sensor electrical connector and coolant hoses.
4. Remove serpentine drive belt and crossover tube.
5. Remove mounting bolts and alternator support bracket.
6. Remove mounting bolts and alternator.
7. Disconnect electrical connector and vacuum hose from fuel pressure sensor.

8. Separate wiring harness from fuel injection supply manifold studs in four places.
9. Disconnect eight fuel injector electrical connectors.
10. Remove lower intake manifold bolts in sequence, then raise slightly, **Fig. 7.**
11. Disconnect fuel charging wiring harness from rear of lower intake manifold.
12. Remove lower intake manifold.
13. Reverse procedure to install. **Torque** lower intake manifold bolts to 89 inch lbs., in sequence, **Fig. 8.**

UPPER

1. Remove air cleaner outlet tube and accelerator control splash shield.
2. Disconnect accelerator cable, speed control cable and return spring.
3. Disconnect fuel vapor hose.
4. Remove accelerator and speed control cables from bracket.
5. Disconnect vacuum hoses.
6. Remove mounting bolt and position accelerator control cables aside.
7. Disconnect EAR system module tube from EAR system module.
8. Disconnect throttle position sensor and IAC sensor electrical connectors.
9. Disconnect PCV ventilation tube.
10. Disconnect EAR system module electrical connector.
11. Disconnect vacuum hoses and PCV coolant hoses.
12. Remove mounting bolts in sequence and upper intake manifold, **Fig. 9.**
13. Reverse procedure to install, noting the following:
   a. Inspect and clean sealing surfaces,

then install new upper intake manifold gasket.
   b. **Torque** upper intake manifold bolts to 89 inch lbs., in sequence, **Fig. 10.**

SOHC

1. Drain engine coolant into suitable container.
2. Remove air cleaner outlet tube.
3. Relieve fuel pressure as outlined under "Precautions."
4. Remove wiper arm and pivot shaft.
5. Remove drive belt.
6. Raise and support vehicle.
7. Disconnect electrical connectors at crankshaft position sensor and air conditioning compressor.
8. Remove oil filter.
9. Disconnect oil pressure sensor electrical connector and power steering switch electrical connector.
10. Disconnect EAR valve from manifold.
11. Disconnect two differential pressure feedback hoses.
12. Disconnect righthand heated oxygen sensor electrical connector.
13. Disconnect fuel charging wiring electrical connectors from ignition coils and fuel injectors.
14. Disconnect accelerator cable and speed control actuator cable.
15. Remove cables from EAR tube heat shield and position aside.
16. Remove EAR tube heat shield.
17. Disconnect evaporative emissions return tube, main chassis vacuum supply line and EAR valve vacuum supply.
18. Disconnect PCV tube at two locations and remove.

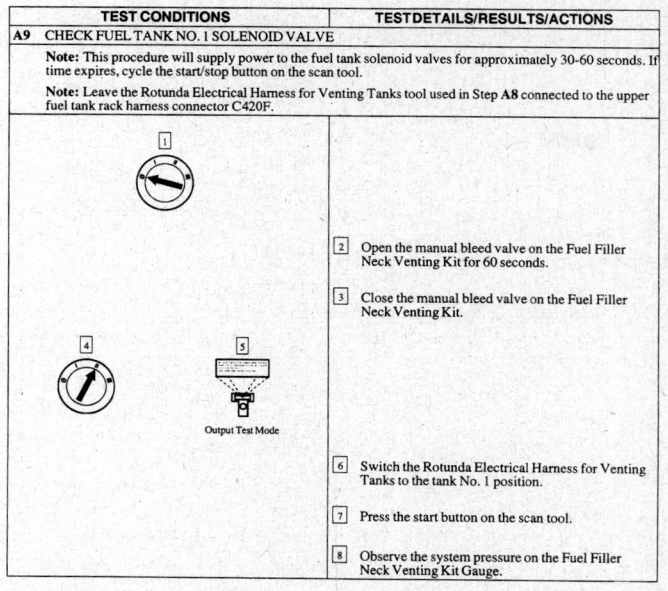

TEST CONDITIONS	TESTDETAILS/RESULTS/ACTIONS
A9 CHECK FUEL TANK NO. 1 SOLENOID VALVE	
Note: This procedure will supply power to the fuel tank solenoid valves for approximately 30-60 seconds. If time expires, cycle the start/stop button on the scan tool.	
Note: Leave the Rotunda Electrical Harness for Venting Tanks tool used in Step A8 connected to the upper fuel tank rack harness connector C420F.	
	2 Open the manual bleed valve on the Fuel Filler Neck Venting Kit for 60 seconds.
	3 Close the manual bleed valve on the Fuel Filler Neck Venting Kit.
	Output Test Mode
	6 Switch the Rotunda Electrical Harness for Venting Tanks to the tank No. 1 position.
	7 Press the start button on the scan tool.
	8 Observe the system pressure on the Fuel Filler Neck Venting Kit Gauge.

FM1029900362090X

Fig. 4 Pinpoint Test A: Fuel tank solenoid valve diagnosis (Part 9 of 26)

TEST CONDITIONS	TESTDETAILS/RESULTS/ACTIONS
A9 CHECK FUEL TANK NO. 1 SOLENOID VALVE (Continued)	
	9 Press the stop button on the scan tool. • Was the pressure on the gauge 0 kPa (0 psi) when triggered on? → **Yes** Fuel tank No. 1 solenoid valve "may be stuck closed." GO to **A10**. → **No** Mark fuel tank No. 1 solenoid valve "good." To complete diagnostics, install a new solenoid valve if the solenoid valve is marked "stuck closed." If fuel tank No. 2 solenoid valve was marked "may be stuck closed," GO to **A10** . If all solenoid valves were marked "good," diagnostics are complete. RESTORE the vehicle and test the system for normal operation.
A10 CHECK UPPER AND REAR TANK RACK CIRCUIT 57 (BK)	
Note: At this point in the diagnostics it is necessary to access the upper and rear fuel tank rack harness connections. Due to packaging considerations, it will be necessary to remove the upper and rear tank rack assemblies to remove the upper and rear tank rack vent boxes.	
	2 Disconnect and remove the Rotunda Electrical Harness for Venting Tanks from the upper and rear tank rack assembly harness connectors C420F.
	3 Open the manual bleed valve on the Fuel Filter Neck Venting Kit and vent system pressure to 0 kPa (0 psi).
	4 Close the manual bleed valve on the Fuel Filter Neck Venting Kit.
	5 Remove the upper and rear fuel tank rack assemblies.

FM1029900362100X

Fig. 4 Pinpoint Test A: Fuel tank solenoid valve diagnosis (Part 10 of 26)

19. Disconnect electrical connector from EAR vacuum regulator.
20. Disconnect vacuum line from evaporative emission canister purge valve.
21. Disconnect alternator cable and position aside.
22. Remove upper mounting bracket and electrical connector from alternator.
23. Remove upper radiator and heater hose.
24. Disconnect electrical connector from idle air control valve and throttle position sensor.
25. Disconnect EAR tube from EAR valve.
26. Remove lefthand oxygen sensor and transmission electrical connectors from wiring bracket, then the bracket.
27. Remove throttle body.
28. Separate fuel charging wiring pushpin connector from crash bracket, then remove bolt, stud and crash bracket.
29. Disconnect vacuum lines and remove vacuum harness.
30. Remove fuel injection supply manifold and fuel injectors as an assembly.
31. Remove eight ignition coils.
32. Remove water outlet adapter, thermostat and gasket.
33. Remove intake manifold and gaskets, clean gasket sealing surfaces.
34. Reverse procedure to install, noting the following:
    a. Install new gaskets.
    b. Install intake manifold and hand tighten bolts, **Fig. 11.**
    c. Install ignition coils and tighten bolts.
    d. Install fuel injection supply manifold and tighten studs.
    e. Install crash bracket loosely.
    f. Install thermostat and water outlet adapter loosely with bolts.
    g. **Torque** intake manifold bolts to 15–22 ft. lbs., in sequence, **Fig. 12.**

Natural Gas Engine

1. Remove wiper arm & pivot shaft.
2. Remove air cleaner outlet tube.
3. Relieve fuel pressure as outlined under "Precautions."
4. Disconnect fuel charging wiring electrical connectors from ignition coils and fuel injectors.
5. Disconnect fuel charging electrical connectors from fuel pressure, fuel pump temperature and engine coolant temperature sensors.
6. Remove isolation valve wiring lead from upper alternator support bracket and disconnect connector.
7. Disconnect alternator battery cable.
8. Remove power distribution box access cover, nut and wiring.
9. Disconnect fuel charging wiring electrical connectors from the following components:
    a. Inner fender splash shield connectors.
    b. Air conditioning pressure transducer.
    c. Cylinder head temperature sensor jumper.
    d. Camshaft position sensor.
    e. Alternator.
    f. Throttle position sensor.
    g. Radio ignition interference capacitor.
    h. EAR vacuum regulator solenoid.
    i. Differential pressure feedback EAR.
    j. Idle air control valve.
10. Disconnect throttle cable and speed control actuator cable from throttle body.
11. Remove mounting bolt, then position cables and bracket aside.
12. Remove fuel charging wiring mounting bolts and position harness aside.
13. Disconnect fuel lines and hoses from differential pressure feedback EAR and vacuum line from EAR valve.
14. Disconnect main chassis vacuum line.
15. Disconnect crankcase vent tube at two locations and remove.
16. Disconnect vacuum lines from throttle body adapter and EAR vacuum regulator solenoid.
17. Disconnect EAR tube from EAR valve.
18. Remove isolation valve bolts.
19. Remove fuel injection supply manifold and fuel injectors as an assembly.
20. Disconnect heater hose from intake manifold.
21. Disconnect upper radiator hose from water outlet adapter.
22. Remove eight ignition coils.
23. Remove upper alternator support bracket.
24. Remove water outlet adapter, thermostat and O-ring.
25. Remove mounting bolts and intake manifold.
26. Remove intake manifold gaskets and clean all surfaces.
27. Reverse procedure to install, noting the following:
    a. Install new intake manifold gaskets.
    b. **Torque** bolts to 15–22 ft. lbs., in sequence, **Fig. 13.**

TEST CONDITIONS	TEST DETAILS/RESULTS/ACTIONS
A10 CHECK UPPER AND REAR TANK RACK CIRCUIT 57 (BK) (Continued)	
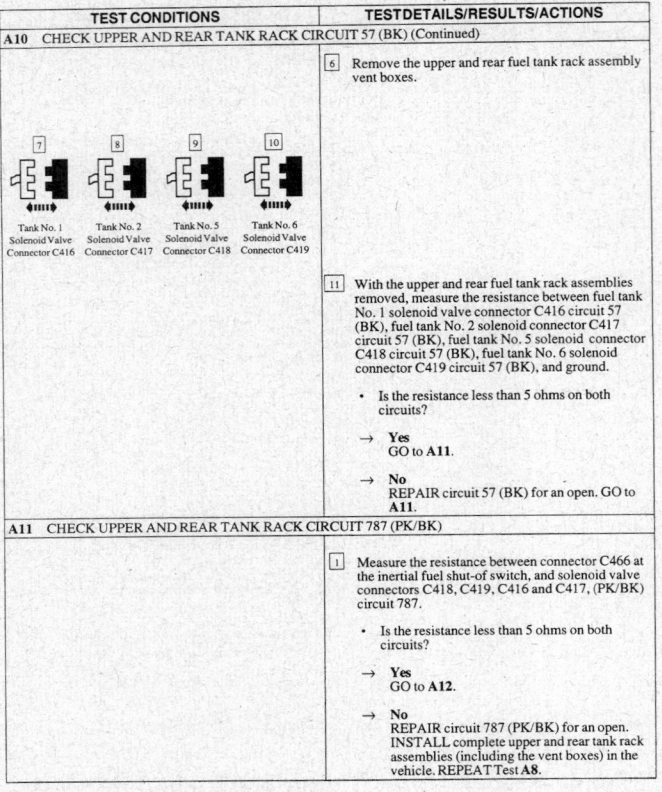 Tank No. 1 Solenoid Valve Connector C416 Tank No. 2 Solenoid Valve Connector C417 Tank No. 5 Solenoid Valve Connector C418 Tank No. 6 Solenoid Valve Connector C419	**6** Remove the upper and rear fuel tank rack assembly vent boxes.
	11 With the upper and rear fuel tank rack assemblies removed, measure the resistance between fuel tank No. 1 solenoid valve connector C416 circuit 57 (BK), fuel tank No. 2 solenoid connector C417 circuit 57 (BK), fuel tank No. 5 solenoid connector C418 circuit 57 (BK), fuel tank No. 6 solenoid connector C419 circuit 57 (BK), and ground. • Is the resistance less than 5 ohms on both circuits? → **Yes** GO to **A11**. → **No** REPAIR circuit 57 (BK) for an open. GO to **A11**.
A11 CHECK UPPER AND REAR TANK RACK CIRCUIT 787 (PK/BK)	
	1 Measure the resistance between connector C466 at the inertial fuel shut-of switch, and solenoid valve connectors C418, C419, C416 and C417, (PK/BK) circuit 787. • Is the resistance less than 5 ohms on both circuits? → **Yes** GO to **A12**. → **No** REPAIR circuit 787 (PK/BK) for an open. INSTALL complete upper and rear tank rack assemblies (including the vent boxes) in the vehicle. REPEAT Test **A8**.

FM1029900362110X

Fig. 4 Pinpoint Test A: Fuel tank solenoid valve diagnosis (Part 11 of 26)

TEST CONDITIONS	TEST DETAILS/RESULTS/ACTIONS
A12 CHECK UPPER FUEL TANK RACK ASSEMBLY MANUAL LOCK-DOWNS	
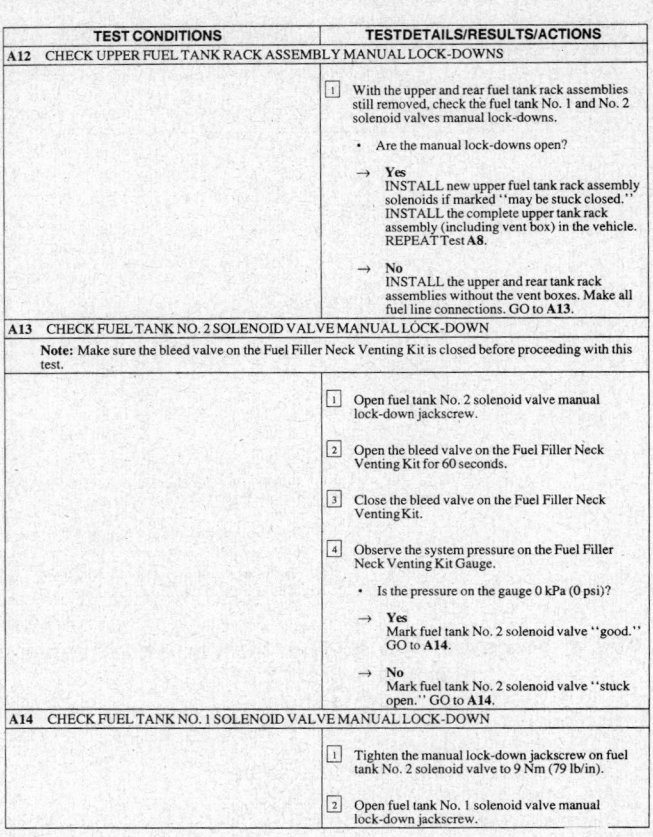	**1** With the upper and rear fuel tank rack assemblies still removed, check the fuel tank No. 1 and No. 2 solenoid valves manual lock-downs. • Are the manual lock-downs open? → **Yes** INSTALL new upper fuel tank rack assembly solenoids if marked "may be stuck closed." INSTALL the complete upper tank rack assembly (including vent box) in the vehicle. REPEAT Test **A8**. → **No** INSTALL the upper and rear tank rack assemblies without the vent boxes. Make all fuel line connections. GO to **A13**.
A13 CHECK FUEL TANK NO. 2 SOLENOID VALVE MANUAL LOCK-DOWN	
Note: Make sure the bleed valve on the Fuel Filler Neck Venting Kit is closed before proceeding with this test.	
	1 Open fuel tank No. 2 solenoid valve manual lock-down jackscrew. **2** Open the bleed valve on the Fuel Filler Neck Venting Kit for 60 seconds. **3** Close the bleed valve on the Fuel Filler Neck Venting Kit. **4** Observe the system pressure on the Fuel Filler Neck Venting Kit Gauge. • Is the pressure on the gauge 0 kPa (0 psi)? → **Yes** Mark fuel tank No. 2 solenoid valve "good." GO to **A14**. → **No** Mark fuel tank No. 2 solenoid valve "stuck open." GO to **A14**.
A14 CHECK FUEL TANK NO. 1 SOLENOID VALVE MANUAL LOCK-DOWN	
	1 Tighten the manual lock-down jackscrew on fuel tank No. 2 solenoid valve to 9 Nm (79 lb/in). **2** Open fuel tank No. 1 solenoid valve manual lock-down jackscrew.

FM1029900362120X

Fig. 4 Pinpoint Test A: Fuel tank solenoid valve diagnosis (Part 12 of 26)

EXHAUST MANIFOLD
REPLACE
DOHC

1. Remove front tire and wheel assembly.
2. Disconnect exhaust pipe from exhaust manifold.
3. Disconnect EAR system module tube from exhaust manifold.
4. Remove exhaust manifold heat shield.
5. Remove eight mounting nuts and exhaust manifold.
6. Reverse procedure to install. **Torque** bolts to 108 inch lbs., in sequence, **Figs. 14 and 15.**

SOHC

1. Raise and support vehicle.
2. Disconnect oxygen sensor connectors.
3. Remove exhaust manifold to catalytic converter nuts and disconnect converters at exhaust inlet pipes.
4. Remove catalytic converters.
5. Disconnect EAR tube at exhaust manifold connector.
6. Remove nuts, exhaust manifolds and gaskets.
7. Reverse procedure to install. **Torque** manifold nuts to 14–16 ft. lbs., in sequence, **Figs. 16 and 17.**

CYLINDER HEAD
REPLACE
DOHC

1. Remove engine as outlined under "Engine, Replace."
2. Remove flexplate and engine/transmission spacer plate.
3. Mount engine on suitable work stand.
4. Remove engine lift bracket tools.
5. Remove mounting bolts and righthand engine mount.
6. Remove engine block drain plug and drain coolant into suitable container. Install drain plugs.
7. Disconnect PCV tube, then the vacuum and PCV valve coolant hoses.
8. Remove mounting bolt and EAR system module bracket, then disconnect module tube.
9. Disconnect EAR system module tube.
10. Disconnect Throttle Position (TP) and Idle Air Control (IAC) sensor electrical connectors.
11. Remove mounting bolts in sequence and upper intake manifold, **Fig. 9.**
12. Disconnect electrical connector, alternator cable and harness retainer.
13. Remove mounting bolts and alternator bracket.
14. Disconnect Engine Coolant Temperature (ECT) sensors.
15. Remove crossover tube.
16. Remove mounting bolts and alternator.
17. Disconnect fuel pressure sensor electrical connector and vacuum hose.
18. Disconnect fuel charging wiring from fuel injection supply manifold studs.
19. Disconnect fuel injector electrical connectors.
20. Remove mounting bolts and studs in sequence, then slightly raise lower intake manifold, **Fig. 7.**
21. Disconnect fuel charging wiring harness from lower intake manifold rear, the remove manifold and gaskets.
22. Remove covers and disconnect ignition coil electrical connectors.
23. Remove ignition coils.
24. Disconnect Knock Sensor (KC) jumper harness from fuel charging harness.
25. Remove mounting bolts and water pump pulley.
26. Remove mounting bolt and crankshaft pulley using crankshaft vibration damper tool No. 303-009, or equivalent.
27. Remove crankshaft front seal using crankshaft front oil seal remover tool No. 303-107, or equivalent.
28. Remove belt idler pulleys.
29. Disconnect Camshaft Position (CMP) sensor and engine wiring harness retainers.
30. Disconnect oil pressure sensor electrical connector.
31. Disconnect electrical connectors, then

TEST CONDITIONS	TESTDETAILS/RESULTS/ACTIONS
A14 CHECK FUEL TANK NO. 1 SOLENOID VALVE MANUAL LOCK-DOWN (Continued)	
	3 Open the bleed valve on the Fuel Filler Neck Venting Kit for 60 seconds.
	4 Close the bleed valve on the Fuel Filler Neck Venting Kit.
	5 Observe the system pressure on the Fuel Filler Neck Venting Kit Gauge.
	• Is the system pressure on the Fuel Filler Neck Venting Kit Gauge 0 kPa (0 psi)?
	→ Yes Mark fuel tank No. 1 solenoid valve "good." GO to A8 to retest the upper tank rack.
	→ No MARK fuel tank No. 1 solenoid valve "stuck open." INSTALL new upper fuel tank rack assembly solenoid valves if marked "stuck open." GO to A8.
A15 CHECK ALL SOLENOID CIRCUITS 787 (PK/BK) FOR A SHORT TO B+	

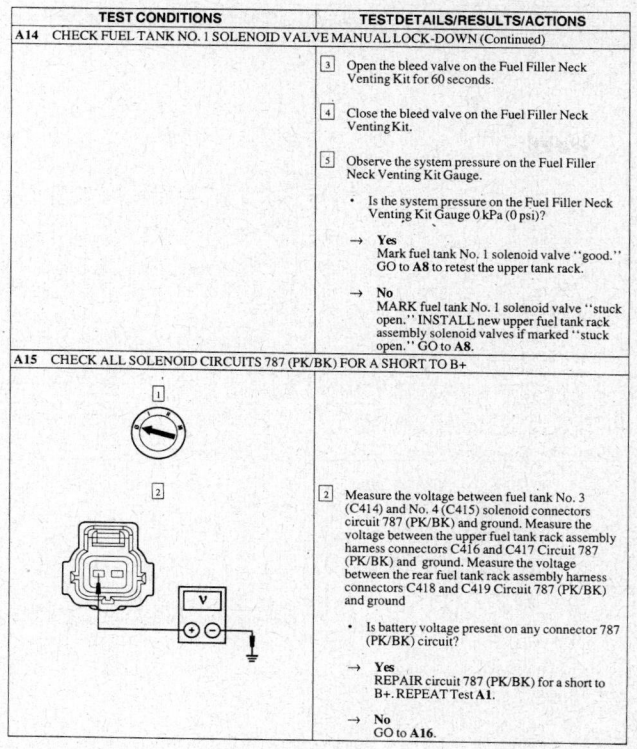

	2 Measure the voltage between fuel tank No. 3 (C414) and No. 4 (C415) solenoid connectors circuit 787 (PK/BK) and ground. Measure the voltage between the upper fuel tank rack assembly harness connectors C416 and C417 Circuit 787 (PK/BK) and ground. Measure the voltage between rear fuel tank rack assembly harness connectors C418 and C419 Circuit 787 (PK/BK) and ground
	• Is battery voltage present on any connector 787 (PK/BK) circuit?
	→ Yes REPAIR circuit 787 (PK/BK) for a short to B+. REPEAT Test A1.
	→ No GO to A16.

FM1029900362130X

Fig. 4   Pinpoint Test A: Fuel tank solenoid valve diagnosis (Part 13 of 26)

TEST CONDITIONS	TESTDETAILS/RESULTS/ACTIONS
A16 ISOLATE UPPER AND LOWER TANK RACK ASSEMBLIES	
Note: At this point in the diagnostics it is necessary to remove the rear rack assembly.	
	1 Tighten the manual lock-down jackscrew on fuel tank No. 3 and No. 4 solenoid valves to 9 Nm (79 lb/in).
	2 Open the manual bleed valve on the Fuel Filler Neck Venting Kit for 60 seconds.
	3 Close the manual bleed valve on the Fuel Filler Neck Venting Kit.
	4 Observe the system pressure on the Fuel Filler Neck Venting Kit Gauge.
	• Is the pressure on the gauge 0 kPa (0 psi)?
	→ Yes GO to A21.
	→ No GO to A17.
A17 CHECK FUEL TANK NO. 1 CIRCUIT 787 (PK/BK)	
Note: At this point in the diagnostics it is necessary to access the upper fuel tank rack harness connectors. Due to packaging considerations, it will be necessary to remove the upper tank rack assembly to remove the upper tank rack vent box.	
	2 Make sure the manual lock-downs on fuel tank No. 3 and No. 4 are still closed from Step A16.
	3 Open the manual bleed valve on the Fuel Filler Neck Venting Kit and vent the system pressure to 0 kPa (0 psi).
	4 Close the manual bleed valve on the Fuel Filler Neck Venting Kit.
	5 Remove the upper tank rack assembly.

FM1029900362140X

Fig. 4   Pinpoint Test A: Fuel tank solenoid valve diagnosis (Part 14 of 26)

remove mounting nuts and radio capacitors.

32. Disconnect retainers and remove fuel charging wiring harness.
33. Remove spark plugs.
34. Remove mounting bolts, valve covers and gaskets.
35. Remove mounting nuts, lefthand exhaust manifold and gaskets.
36. Remove oil dipstick tube.
37. Remove mounting nuts, righthand exhaust manifold and gaskets.
38. Remove mounting nut, ground strap and coolant bypass tube.
39. Remove mounting nut and position wiring harness bracket aside.
40. Remove front cover lower mounting bolts.
41. Remove mounting bolts and front cover.
42. Position piston at bottom of stroke and camshaft lobe at base circle.
43. Compress intake valve spring using intake valve spring compressor tool No. 303-452, or equivalent, and remove roller follower.
44. Compress exhaust valve spring using exhaust valve spring compressor tool No. 303-4567, or equivalent, and remove roller follower.
45. Repeat previous steps on all cylinders.
46. Remove mounting bolts, timing chain tensioners and tensioner arms.
47. Remove lefthand and righthand timing chains, then the crankshaft sprocket.
48. Remove lefthand and righthand timing chain guides.
49. Mark for installation alignment, then remove hydraulic lash adjusters.
50. Remove mounting bolts, cylinder head and gasket. Discard cylinder head bolts.
51. Reverse procedure to install, noting the following:
   a. **Torque** new cylinder head bolt to 30 ft. lbs., in sequence, **Fig. 18.**
   b. Tighten an additional 90° in sequence.
   c. Loosen bolts minimum of one full turn.
   d. **Torque** to 30 ft. lbs., in sequence.
   e. Tighten an additional 90° in sequence.
   f. Tighten an additional 90° in sequence.
   g. Align timing chain and sprockets as outlined under "Timing Chain, Replace."

SOHC

1. Remove engine as outlined under "Engine, Replace."
2. Remove mounting bolts and flexplate.
3. Remove eight mounting bolts and crankcase rear oil seal retainer.
4. Install engine on suitable engine stand.
5. Disconnect EAR system module tube from exhaust manifold connector.
6. Remove intake manifold as outlined under "Intake Manifold, Replace."
7. Remove valve cover as outlined under "Valve Cover, Replace."
8. Remove mounting bolts, water pump pulley and water pump.
9. Remove crankshaft pulley using removal tool No. 303-009, or equivalent.
10. Remove crankshaft front seal using removal tool No. 303-107, or equivalent.
11. Remove front cover as outlined under "Front Cover, Replace."
12. Remove timing chain as outlined under "Timing Chain, Replace."
13. Remove mounting nuts and exhaust manifold and gasket.
14. Remove cylinder head bolts in three one turn loosening passes in sequence, **Fig. 19.**
15. Remove cylinder head and gasket.
16. Reverse procedure to install noting the following:
   a. **Torque** cylinder head bolts to 30 ft. lbs., in sequence, **Figs. 20 and 21.**
   b. Tighten cylinder head bolts an additional 85–95° in sequence.
   c. Loosen cylinder head bolts a minimum of one full turn.
   d. Tighten cylinder head bolts an additional 85–95° in sequence.
   e. Tighten cylinder head bolts an additional 85–95° in sequence.
   f. **Torque** crankshaft pulley bolt to 66 ft. lbs.
   g. Loosen crankshaft pulley bolt 360°.
   h. **Torque** crankshaft pulley bolt to 37 ft. lbs, then rotate and additional 85–90°
   i. Tighten flexplate bolts in sequence, **Fig. 22.**

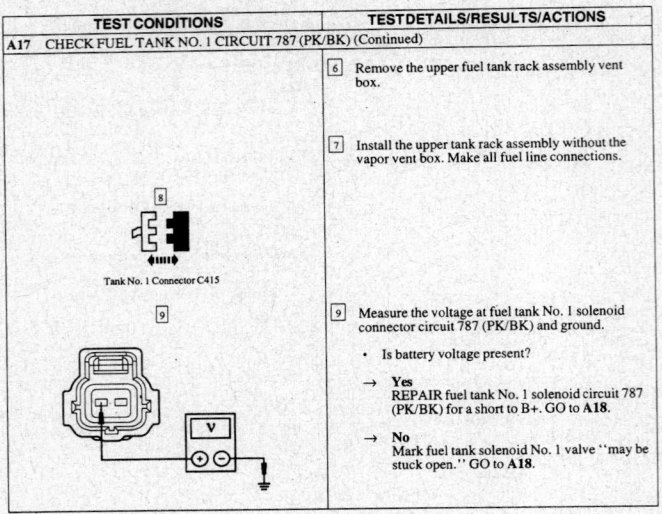

TEST CONDITIONS	TESTDETAILS/RESULTS/ACTIONS
A17 CHECK FUEL TANK NO. 1 CIRCUIT 787 (PK/BK) (Continued)	

6 Remove the upper fuel tank rack assembly vent box.

7 Install the upper tank rack assembly without the vapor vent box. Make all fuel line connections.

Tank No. 1 Connector C415

9 Measure the voltage at fuel tank No. 1 solenoid connector circuit 787 (PK/BK) and ground.

- Is battery voltage present?
  → **Yes**
    REPAIR fuel tank No. 1 solenoid circuit 787 (PK/BK) for a short to B+. GO to **A18**.
  → **No**
    Mark fuel tank solenoid No. 1 valve "may be stuck open." GO to **A18**.

FM1029900362150X

Fig. 4 Pinpoint Test A: Fuel tank solenoid valve diagnosis (Part 15 of 26)

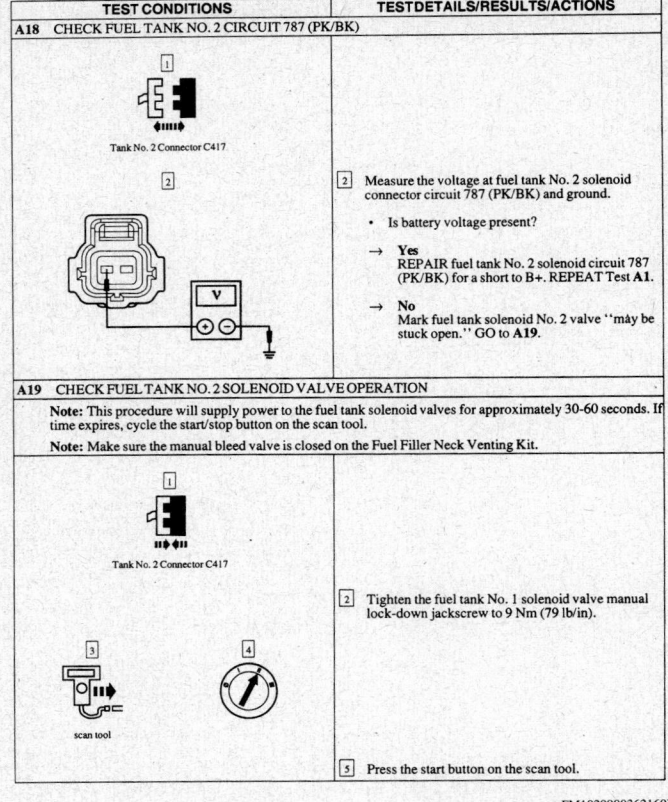

TEST CONDITIONS	TESTDETAILS/RESULTS/ACTIONS
A18 CHECK FUEL TANK NO. 2 CIRCUIT 787 (PK/BK)	

Tank No. 2 Connector C417

2 Measure the voltage at fuel tank No. 2 solenoid connector circuit 787 (PK/BK) and ground.

- Is battery voltage present?
  → **Yes**
    REPAIR fuel tank No. 2 solenoid circuit 787 (PK/BK) for a short to B+. REPEAT Test **A1**.
  → **No**
    Mark fuel tank solenoid No. 2 valve "may be stuck open." GO to **A19**.

A19 CHECK FUEL TANK NO. 2 SOLENOID VALVE OPERATION
Note: This procedure will supply power to the fuel tank solenoid valves for approximately 30-60 seconds. If time expires, cycle the start/stop button on the scan tool. **Note:** Make sure the manual bleed valve is closed on the Fuel Filler Neck Venting Kit.

Tank No. 2 Connector C417

scan tool

2 Tighten the fuel tank No. 1 solenoid valve manual lock-down jackscrew to 9 Nm (79 lb/in).

5 Press the start button on the scan tool.

FM1029900362160X

Fig. 4 Pinpoint Test A: Fuel tank solenoid valve diagnosis (Part 16 of 26)

VALVE COVER
REPLACE
DOHC
LEFTHAND

1. Remove throttle body and ignition coils.
2. Disconnect camshaft position sensors and engine wiring harness retainers.
3. Remove mounting nut and position oil lever indicator aside.
4. Remove mounting bolts and lefthand valve cover.
5. Reverse procedure to install noting the following:
   a. Apply silicone gasket and sealant No. F7AZ-19554-EA, or equivalent, **Fig. 23**.
   b. **Torque** bolts to 89 inch lbs., in sequence, **Fig. 24**.

RIGHTHAND

1. Drain engine cooling system into suitable container.
2. Disconnect fuel hose spring lock coupling.
3. Disconnect coolant hose and EVAP tube, then position aside.
4. Disconnect engine wiring harness retainer.
5. Remove righthand ignition coils.
6. Remove mounting bolts and righthand valve cover.
7. Reverse procedure to install noting the following:
   a. Apply silicone gasket and sealant No. F7AZ-19554-EA, or equivalent, **Fig. 23**.
   b. **Torque** bolts to 89 inch lbs., in sequence, **Fig. 24**.

SOHC
LEFTHAND

1. Raise and support vehicle.
2. Remove oil bypass filter.
3. Disconnect Power Steering Pressure (PSP) switch and oil pressure sensor connectors.
4. Lower vehicle.
5. Disconnect cylinder head temperature sensor jumper wire connector.
6. Remove bolt and two studs and position bracket aside.
7. Disconnect Camshaft Position (CMP) sensor connector.
8. Disconnect alternator connector and fuel charging wiring connectors from coils and fuel injectors.
9. Disconnect Idle Air Control (IAC) valve and Throttle Position (TP) sensor connector.
10. Disconnect 42-pin connector, 16-pin connector and transmission connector.
11. Remove six bolts, five studs and cam cover.
12. Reverse procedure to install, noting the following:
    a. Apply silicone gasket and sealant No. F7AZ-19554-EA, or equivalent, **Fig. 25**.
    b. Adjust engine oil level.
13. **Torque** bolts to 89 inch lbs., in se-

quence, **Fig. 26**.

RIGHTHAND

1. Raise and support vehicle.
2. Disconnect Crankshaft Position (CKP) sensor and air conditioning compressor electrical connectors.
3. Lower vehicle and disconnect air conditioning cycling switch connector.
4. Relieve fuel pressure as outlined under "Precautions."
5. Disconnect fuel lines.
6. Disconnect ignition coils and fuel injector connectors.
7. Disconnect fuel injector electrical connectors.
8. Remove Positive Crankcase Ventilation (PCV) tube and position aside.
9. Remove Evaporative Emission (EVAP) canister purge valve.
10. Position hold-down clamp and remove hose from bypass tube.
11. Disconnect harness retainers from valve cover and position harness aside.
12. Remove studs, bolts and cam cover.
13. Reverse procedure to install, noting the following:
    a. Apply silicone gasket and sealant No. F7AZ-19554-EA, or equivalent, **Fig. 25**.
    b. **Torque** bolts 89 inch lbs., in sequence, **Fig. 27**.

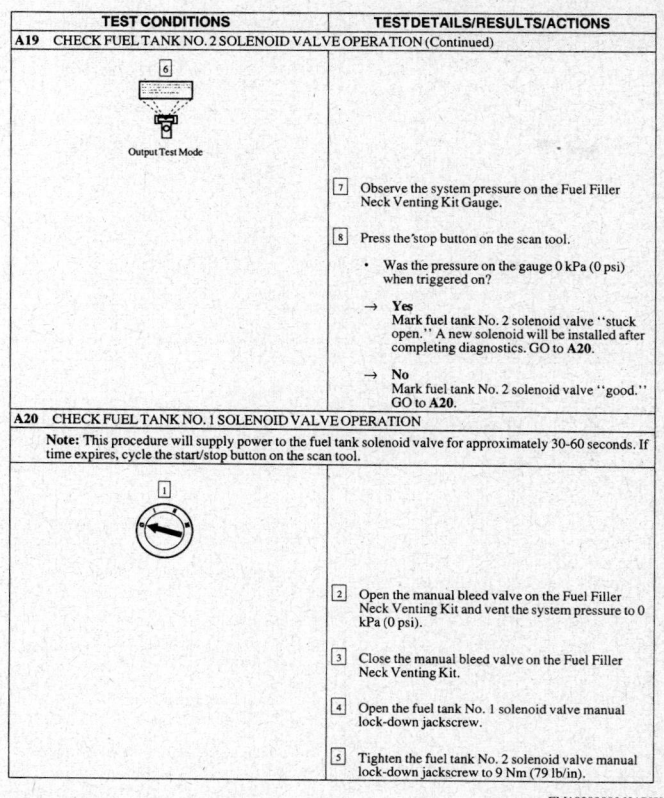

TEST CONDITIONS	TEST DETAILS/RESULTS/ACTIONS
A19 CHECK FUEL TANK NO. 2 SOLENOID VALVE OPERATION (Continued)	

Output Test Mode

⑦ Observe the system pressure on the Fuel Filler Neck Venting Kit Gauge.

⑧ Press the stop button on the scan tool.
- Was the pressure on the gauge 0 kPa (0 psi) when triggered on?
  → **Yes**
  Mark fuel tank No. 2 solenoid valve "stuck open." A new solenoid will be installed after completing diagnostics. GO to **A20**.
  → **No**
  Mark fuel tank No. 2 solenoid valve "good." GO to **A20**.

| A20 CHECK FUEL TANK NO. 1 SOLENOID VALVE OPERATION | |

Note: This procedure will supply power to the fuel tank solenoid valve for approximately 30-60 seconds. If time expires, cycle the start/stop button on the scan tool.

② Open the manual bleed valve on the Fuel Filler Neck Venting Kit and vent the system pressure to 0 kPa (0 psi).

③ Close the manual bleed valve on the Fuel Filler Neck Venting Kit.

④ Open the fuel tank No. 1 solenoid valve manual lock-down jackscrew.

⑤ Tighten the fuel tank No. 2 solenoid valve manual lock-down jackscrew to 9 Nm (79 lb/in).

FM1029900362170X

Fig. 4 Pinpoint Test A: Fuel tank solenoid valve diagnosis (Part 17 of 26)

TEST CONDITIONS	TEST DETAILS/RESULTS/ACTIONS
A20 CHECK FUEL TANK NO. 1 SOLENOID VALVE OPERATION (Continued)	

Tank No. 2 Connector C417   Tank No. 1 Connector C416   Output Test Mode

⑩ Press the start button on the scan tool.

⑪ Observe the system pressure on the Fuel Filler Neck Venting Kit Gauge.

⑫ Press the stop button on the scan tool.
- Was the pressure on the gauge 0 kPa (0 psi) when triggered on?
  → **Yes**
  Mark fuel tank No. 1 solenoid valve "stuck open." INSTALL new upper tank rack assembly valves if marked "stuck open." GO to **A21**.
  → **No**
  Mark fuel tank No. 1 solenoid valve "good." GO to **A21**.

| A21 CHECK FUEL TANK NO. 3 SOLENOID VALVE FOR STUCK OPEN CONDITION | |

② Open the manual lock-down jackscrew on fuel tank No. 3 solenoid valve.

③ Make sure the manual lock-down jackscrew on fuel tank No. 4 solenoid valve is still closed from Step A16.

④ Open the manual bleed valve on the Fuel Filler Neck Venting Kit for 60 seconds.

⑤ Close the manual bleed valve on the Fuel Filler Neck Venting Kit.

FM1029900362180X

Fig. 4 Pinpoint Test A: Fuel tank solenoid valve diagnosis (Part 18 of 26)

VALVE ARRANGEMENT

DOHC

FRONT TO REAR
Righthand ....S-P-E-E-S-P-E-E-S-P-E-E-S-P-E-E①
Lefthand.................E-E-P-S-E-E-P-S-E-E-P-S-E-E-P-S

①—S-Secondary Intake; P-Primary Intake; E-Exhaust.

SOHC

FRONT TO REAR
Righthand Bank ....I-E-I-E-I-E-I-E
Lefthand Bank ....E-I-E-I-E-I-E-I

CAMSHAFT LOBE LIFT SPECIFICATIONS

Engine	Intake, Inch	Exhaust, Inch
DOHC	.2200	.2186
SOHC	.2591	.2597

VALVE ADJUSTMENT

These engines are equipped with hydraulic valve lash adjusters. The intake and exhaust valves cannot be adjusted.

ROCKER ARMS
REPLACE
DOHC

1. Remove valve covers as outlined under "Valve Cover, Replace."
2. Position piston of cylinder being repaired at bottom of stroke and camshaft lobe at base circle.
3. Compress valve spring and remove roller follower using valve spring compressor tool No. T93P-6565-AR, or equivalent.
4. Repeat previous steps for remaining cylinders.
5. Reverse procedure to install.

SOHC

1. Remove camshaft covers as outlined under "Valve Cover, Replace."

2. Position piston of cylinder at bottom of stroke and camshaft lobe at base circle.
3. Install valve spring spacer tool No. T91P-6565-AH, or equivalent, between spring coils.
4. Compress valve spring using valve spring compressor tool No. T91P-6565-AH, or equivalent, and remove rocker arm, **Fig. 28.**
5. Remove valve spring compressor and spacer.
6. Repeat previous steps for remaining cylinders.
7. Reverse procedure to install. Apply clean engine oil to valve stem and tip, rocker arm roller contact surfaces and valve tappet.

HYDRAULIC LIFTERS
REPLACE

1. Remove rocker arms as outlined under "Rocker Arms, Replace."
2. Remove valve tappets from cylinder heads.
3. Clean and inspect valve tappets.
4. Reverse procedure to install, noting the following:
   a. Apply clean engine oil to valve stem

TEST CONDITIONS	TEST DETAILS/RESULTS/ACTIONS
A21 CHECK FUEL TANK NO. 3 SOLENOID VALVE FOR STUCK OPEN CONDITION (Continued)	

6 Observe the system pressure on the Fuel Filler Neck Venting Kit Gauge.
- Is the pressure on the gauge 0 kPa (0 psi)?
→ **Yes**
 Mark fuel tank No. 3 solenoid valve "good." GO to **A22**.
→ **No**
 Mark fuel tank No. 3 solenoid valve "stuck open." A new solenoid valve will be installed when diagnostics are complete. GO to **A22**.

TEST CONDITIONS	TEST DETAILS/RESULTS/ACTIONS
A22 CHECK FUEL TANK NO. 4 SOLENOID FOR STUCK OPEN CONDITION	

2 Close the manual lock-down jackscrew fuel tank No. 3 solenoid valve to 9 Nm (79 lb/in).

3 Open the manual bleed valve on the Fuel Filler Neck Venting Kit and vent the system pressure to 0 kPa (0 psi).

4 Close the manual bleed valve on the Fuel Filler Neck Venting Kit.

5 Open the manual lock-down jackscrew on fuel tank No. 4 solenoid valve.

6 Open the manual bleed valve on the Fuel Filler Neck Venting Kit for 60 seconds.

7 Close the manual bleed valve on the Fuel Filler Neck Venting Kit.

FM1029900362190X

Fig. 4   Pinpoint Test A: Fuel tank solenoid valve diagnosis (Part 19 of 26)

TEST CONDITIONS	TEST DETAILS/RESULTS/ACTIONS
A22 CHECK FUEL TANK NO. 4 SOLENOID FOR STUCK OPEN CONDITION (Continued)	

8 Observe the system pressure on the Fuel Filler Neck Venting Kit Gauge.
- Is the pressure on the gauge 0 kPa (0 psi)?
→ **Yes**
 Mark fuel tank No. 4 solenoid valve "good." If No. 3 solenoid valve was marked "stuck open," INSTALL a new solenoid valve at this time. GO to **A23**.
→ **No**
 Fuel tank No. 4 solenoid valve is stuck open. INSTALL a new fuel tank No. 4 solenoid valve. GO to **A23**.

TEST CONDITIONS	TEST DETAILS/RESULTS/ACTIONS
A23 CHECK FUEL TANK NO. 6 SOLENOID VALVE	

Note: Install the rear rack assembly fuel without the vent boxes. Make sure the manual lock-down jackscrew on fuel tank No. 6 solenoid valve is open.

Note: This procedure will supply power to the fuel tank solenoid valve for approximately 30-60 seconds. If time expires, cycle the start/stop button on the scan tool to restore power.

1 Tank No. 6 Solenoid Connector C419   2 scan tool   3

4 Select the correct output test mode on the scan tool and press the start button.

5 Observe the system pressure on the Fuel Filler Neck Venting Kit Gauge.

6 Press the stop button on the scan tool.
- Was the pressure on the gauge 0 kPa (0 psi) when triggered on?
→ **Yes**
 Fuel tank no. 6 solenoid may be "stuck closed." GO to **A24**.
→ **No**
 Mark No. 6 solenoid valve "good." GO to **A24**.

FM1029900362200X

Fig. 4   Pinpoint Test A: Fuel tank solenoid valve diagnosis (Part 20 of 26)

and tip, rocker arm roller contact surfaces and valve tappets and cylinder head valve tappet bore.

b. Valve tappets must have no more than .039 inches of plunger travel prior to installation.

VALVE SPRING & VALVE STEM OIL SEAL
REPLACE
Removal

If, during this procedure, air pressure has forced the piston to the bottom of the cylinder, any loss of air pressure will allow the valve to fall into the cylinder. A rubber band, tape or string wrapped around the end of the valve stem will prevent this and still allow enough travel to inspect the valve for binding and excess guide to valve stem clearance.

1. Remove camshaft covers as outlined under "Valve Cover, Replace."
2. Remove rocker arms/roller followers as outlined under "Rocker Arms, Replace."
3. Remove spark plug and position piston at top of stroke with both valves closed.
4. Install suitable air line with adapter in spark plug opening and apply air pressure.
5. Install valve spring spacer tool No. T91P-6565-AH, or equivalent, between valve spring coils.
6. Compress valve spring using valve spring compressor tool No. T91P-6565-A, or equivalent.
7. Remove keys, retainer and valve spring.
8. Remove valve stem seal using suitable locking pliers.
9. Repeat previously steps as required until all seals are removed.

Installation

Piston must be at Top Dead Center (TDC) of cylinder being serviced.

1. Remove air pressure and inspect valve stem for damage. Rotate valve and inspect valve stem tip eccentric movement during rotation.
2. Position valve up and down through normal travel and inspect stem for binding. **If valve has been damaged, it will be required to remove cylinder head for service.**
3. If valve condition is good, apply engine oil to valve stem and hold valve closed.
4. Apply air pressure in cylinder.
5. Install valve stem seal using valve stem seal replacer tool No. T91P-6571-A, or equivalent.
6. Position valve spring and retainer over valve stem.
7. Compress valve spring using valve spring spacer tool No. T91P-6565-AH, or equivalent, between coils.
8. Install valve spring retainer key using valve spring compressor tool No. T91P-6565-A, or equivalent.
9. Turn off air supply and remove adapter from spark plug opening.
10. Install spark plug, roller follower and camshaft cover.
11. Start engine and inspect for leaks.

FRONT COVER
REPLACE
DOHC

1. Remove valve covers as outlined under "Valve Cover, Replace."
2. Remove cooling fan.
3. Remove mounting bolts and water pump pulley.
4. Remove crankshaft front seal as outlined under "Front Cover Seal, Replace."
5. Remove mounting bolts and position power steering pump aside.
6. Disconnect air conditioning compressor and crankshaft position sensor electrical connectors.
7. Disconnect engine wiring harness retainers from air conditioning compressor.
8. Remove mounting bolts and position air conditioning compressor aside.
9. Drain engine oil into suitable container.
10. Remove four front oil pan mounting bolts.
11. Remove serpentine belt idler pulleys.
12. Remove mounting bolts, studs and front cover.
13. Reverse procedure to install, noting the following:
   a. Clean and inspect sealing surfaces. **Do not use metal scrapers, wire brushes or other abrasive means to clean sealing surfaces.**
   b. Apply silicone and gasket sealant

TEST CONDITIONS	TEST DETAILS/RESULTS/ACTIONS
A24 CHECK FUEL TANK NO. 5 SOLENOID VALVE	

Note: This procedure will supply power to the fuel tank solenoid valves for approximately 30–60 seconds. If time expires, cycle the start/stop button on the scan tool.

Note: Install the Rotunda Electrical Harness for Venting Tanks 134-00120 or equivalent to the rear fuel tank rack harness connector C420F.

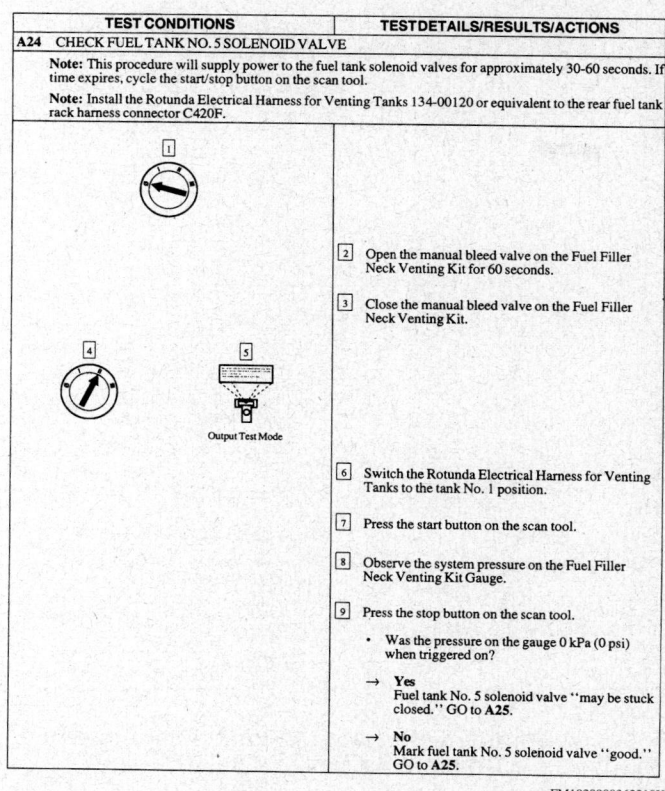

Output Test Mode

2	Open the manual bleed valve on the Fuel Filler Neck Venting Kit for 60 seconds.
3	Close the manual bleed valve on the Fuel Filler Neck Venting Kit.
6	Switch the Rotunda Electrical Harness for Venting Tanks to the tank No. 1 position.
7	Press the start button on the scan tool.
8	Observe the system pressure on the Fuel Filler Neck Venting Kit Gauge.
9	Press the stop button on the scan tool.

• Was the pressure on the gauge 0 kPa (0 psi) when triggered on?

→ **Yes**
Fuel tank No. 5 solenoid valve "may be stuck closed." GO TO **A25**.

→ **No**
Mark fuel tank No. 5 solenoid valve "good." GO TO **A25**.

FM1029900362210X

Fig. 4   Pinpoint Test A: Fuel tank solenoid valve diagnosis (Part 21 of 26)

TEST CONDITIONS	TEST DETAILS/RESULTS/ACTIONS
A25 CHECK REAR FUEL TANK RACK ASSEMBLY MANUAL LOCK-DOWNS	

1	With the rear fuel tank rack assembly installed without the vent box, check the fuel tank No. 5 and No. 6 solenoid valves manual lock-downs.

• Are the manual lock-downs open?

→ **Yes**
INSTALL new solenoids for those marked "stuck closed." If no. 5 or 6 solenoid valve was marked maybe be "stuck closed," INSTALL a new solenoid at this time. RESTORE the vehicle. RETEST the system for normal operation.

→ **No**
GO to **A26**.

TEST CONDITIONS	TEST DETAILS/RESULTS/ACTIONS
A26 CHECK FUEL TANK NO. 6 SOLENOID VALVE MANUAL LOCK-DOWN	

Note: Make sure the bleed valve on the Fuel Filler Neck Venting Kit is closed before proceeding with this test.

1	Open fuel tank No. 6 solenoid valve manual lock-down jackscrew.
2	Open the bleed valve on the Fuel Filler Neck Venting Kit for 60 seconds.
3	Close the bleed valve on the Fuel Filler Neck Venting Kit.
4	Observe the system pressure on the Fuel Filler Neck Venting Kit Gauge.

• Is the pressure on the gauge 0 kPa (0 psi)?

→ **Yes**
If fuel tank no. 5 solenoid valve manual lock down is open GO to **A23**. If closed GO to **A27**.

→ **No**
Mark fuel tank No. 6 solenoid valve "stuck open." GO to **A15**.

TEST CONDITIONS	TEST DETAILS/RESULTS/ACTIONS
A27 CHECK FUEL TANK NO. 5 SOLENOID VALVE MANUAL LOCK-DOWN	

1	Tighten the manual lock-down jackscrew on fuel tank No.6 solenoid valve to 9 Nm (79 lb/in).
2	Open fuel tank No. 5 solenoid valve manual lock-down jackscrew.

FM1029900362220X

Fig. 4   Pinpoint Test A: Fuel tank solenoid valve diagnosis (Part 22 of 26)

No. F7AZ-19554-EA, or equivalent, **Fig. 29.**
c. **Torque** front cover mounting bolts Nos. 1–7 to 15–22 ft. lbs., in sequence, **Fig. 30.**
d. **Torque** bolts Nos. 6–15 to 29–40 ft. lbs., in sequence.
e. **Torque** oil pan front mounting bolts to 18 inch lbs., in sequence, **Fig. 31.**
f. **Torque** mounting bolts to 15 ft. lbs., in sequence.
g. Final tighten an additional 60°.

SOHC

1. Remove both cam covers and water pump.
2. Raise and support vehicle.
3. Remove power steering bolts and position pump aside.
4. Drain engine oil into suitable container.
5. Remove oil pan to front cover bolts.
6. Remove crankshaft front seal.
7. Remove belt idler pulley.
8. Remove front cover bolts and stud bolts.
9. Remove engine front cover from front cover to cylinder block dowel.
10. Reverse procedure to install, noting the following:
    a. If engine front cover is not secured within four minutes, sealant must be removed and sealing area cleaned with metal surface cleaner No. F4AZ-19A536-RA , or equivalent. Allow to dry until there is no sign of wetness, or for four minutes,

whichever is longer.
b. Apply silicone along cylinder head-to-block surface and oil pan-to-cylinder block surface.
c. Use silicone gasket and sealant No. F7AZ-19554-EA, or equivalent.
d. Ensure crankshaft key and keyway are aligned, using crankshaft damper replacer tool No. T74P-6316-B, or equivalent.
e. Install crankshaft pulley.
f. **Torque** bolts Nos. 1–7 to 15–22 ft. lbs., in sequence, **Fig. 32.**
g. **Torque** bolts Nos. 6–15 to 29–40 ft. lbs., in sequence.
h. **Torque** four oil pan to engine front cover bolts to 15 ft. lbs., in sequence, **Fig. 33.**
i. Final tighten bolts an additional 60° in sequence.

FRONT COVER SEAL
REPLACE

1. Release belt tensioner and remove serpentine drive belt.
2. Raise and support vehicle, then remove crankshaft damper mounting bolt and washer.
3. Remove crankshaft damper using crankshaft damper removal tool No. T58P-6316-D, or equivalent.
4. Remove front cover seal using front cover seal removal tool No. T74P-6700-A, or equivalent.

5. Reverse procedure to install, noting the following:
   a. Install front cover seal using replacement tool No. T88T-6701-A, or equivalent.
   b. Apply silicone gasket and sealant P/N F6AZ-19562-AA, or equivalent, in damper keyway.
   c. Ensure crankshaft key and keyway are aligned.
   d. Install crankshaft damper using crankshaft damper replacer tool No. T74P-6316-B, or equivalent.
   e. **Torque** bolt to 66 ft. lbs.
   f. Loosen one complete turn.
   g. **Torque** bolts to 35–39 ft. lbs.
   h. Final tighten bolts an additional 85–95°.

TIMING CHAIN
REPLACE
Removal

Do not rotate the crankshaft and/or camshaft with the timing chains removed and the cylinder heads installed. Rotation of camshaft or crankshaft may result in valve and/or piston damage.

If engine has jumped time, cylinder heads must be removed to repair damage to valves and/or pistons.

1. Remove front cover as outlined under "Front Cover, Replace."

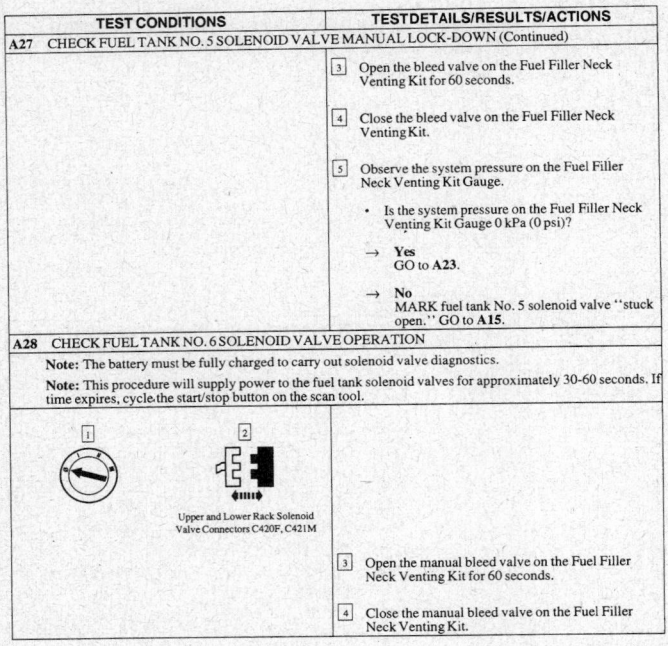

Fig. 4 Pinpoint Test A: Fuel tank solenoid valve diagnosis (Part 23 of 26)

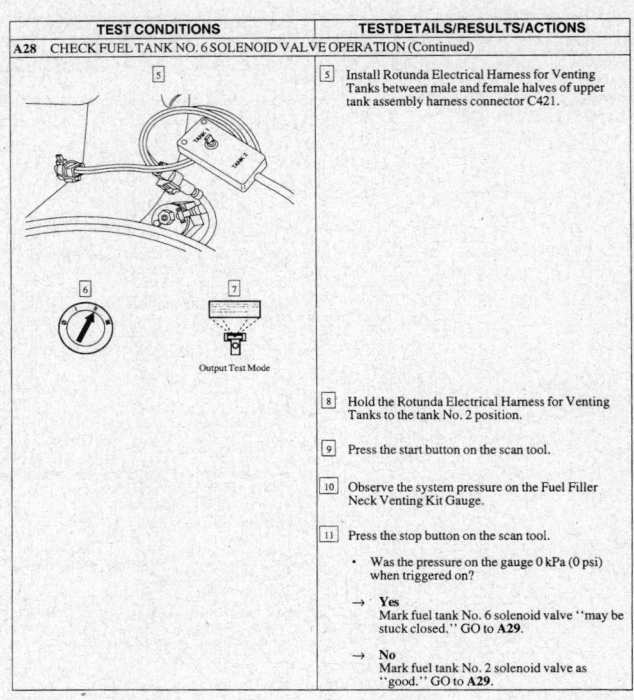

Fig. 4 Pinpoint Test A: Fuel tank solenoid valve diagnosis (Part 24 of 26)

2. Remove rocker arms as outlined under "Rocker Arms, Replace."
3. Remove crankshaft sensor ring from crankshaft.
4. Install camshaft aligner tool No. T91P-6256-A, or equivalent, **Fig. 34.**
5. Rotate crankshaft until timing mark on righthand camshaft sprocket is approximately at 11 o'clock position and timing mark on lefthand camshaft sprocket is approximately at 12 o'clock position, **Fig. 35.**
6. Inspect correct positioning of camshaft sprockets by install crankshaft holding tool No. T93P-6303-A, or equivalent, **Fig. 36.**
7. Remove crankshaft holding tool, then the timing chain tensioners and arms.
8. Remove righthand timing chain from camshaft and crankshaft sprockets.
9. Remove lefthand timing chain from camshaft and crankshaft sprockets.
10. Remove mounting bolts, then the lefthand and righthand timing chain guides.

INSTALLATION

1. Compress tensioner plunger using suitable vise and hold plunger in place by installing retaining clip.
2. If copper links on timing chain are not visible, mark one link on one end and one link on opposite end to use as timing marks, **Fig. 37.**
3. Rotate crankshaft until timing mark on righthand camshaft sprocket is approximately at 11 o'clock position and timing mark on lefthand camshaft sprocket is approximately at 12 o'clock position, **Fig. 35.**
4. Remove camshaft alignment tools.
5. Install crankshaft sprocket ensuring flange faces forward, **Fig. 38.**

6. Install timing chain guides.
7. Position crankshaft so cylinder No. 1 is at TDC using crankshaft holding tool No. T93P-6303-A, or equivalent, **Fig. 39.** Cylinder No. 1 is at TDC when stud on engine block fits into slot on holding tool.
8. Remove crankshaft holding tool.
9. Position lefthand timing chain on crankshaft sprocket aligning copper (marked) link with timing mark on sprocket, **Fig. 40.**
10. Install lefthand timing chain on camshaft sprocket aligning copper (marked) link with timing marks on sprocket, **Fig. 41.**
11. Position lefthand timing chain tensioner arm on dowel pin and install timing chain tensioner. Remove retaining clip from tensioner.
12. Position righthand timing chain on crankshaft sprocket aligning copper (marked) link with timing mark on sprocket, **Fig. 42.**
13. Install righthand timing chain on camshaft sprocket, aligning copper (marked) link with timing marks on sprocket, **Fig. 43.**
14. Position righthand timing chain tensioner arm on dowel pin and install timing chain tensioner. Remove retaining clip from tensioner.
15. Install crankshaft sensor ring on crankshaft.
16. Install rocker arms as outlined under "Rocker Arms, Replace."
17. Install front cover as outlined under "Front Cover, Replace."

CAMSHAFT
REPLACE
DOHC

1. Remove rocker arms as outlined under "Rocker Arms, Replace."
2. Remove timing chains as outlined under "Timing Chain, Replace."
3. Install camshaft holding tool No. T93P-6256-AHR, or equivalent, onto camshafts.
4. Remove exhaust camshaft sprocket, then the intake camshaft bolt, washer and spacer.
5. Remove camshaft holding tool.
6. Compress chain tensioner and install lock pin.
7. Remove timing chain, intake camshaft sprocket and spacer.
8. Remove timing chain tensioner bolts.
9. Mark camshaft bearing caps for installation alignment. Caps are not interchangeable.
10. Remove mounting bolts and camshaft bearing cap. **Outer bolts on outer cam bearing cap (exhaust) are longer and must be installed in same location.**
11. Remove camshafts.
12. Reverse procedure to install, noting the following:
   a. Lubricate camshafts with clean engine oil.
   b. Tighten camshaft bearing cap bolts to 14 ft. lbs., in sequence, **Fig. 44.**
   c. Align camshaft sprockets timing marks to 12 o'clock position, **Fig. 45,** then install camshaft sprockets and chain as assembly.

TEST CONDITIONS	TEST DETAILS/RESULTS/ACTIONS
A29 CHECK FUEL TANK NO. 5 SOLENOID VALVE OPERATION	

Note: This procedure will supply power to the fuel tank solenoid valves for approximately 30-60 seconds. If time expires, cycle the start/stop button on the scan tool.

Note: Leave the Rotunda Electrical Harness for Venting Tanks tool used in Step **A28** connected to the upper fuel tank rack harness connector C420F.

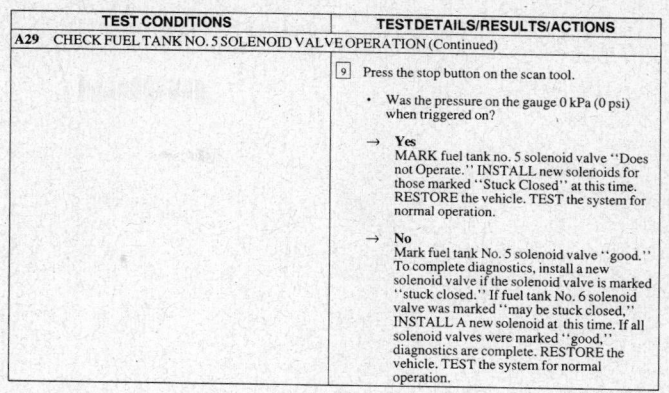

2. Open the manual bleed valve on the Fuel Filler Neck Venting Kit for 60 seconds.

3. Close the manual bleed valve on the Fuel Filler Neck Venting Kit.

Output Test Mode

6. Switch the Rotunda Electrical Harness for Venting Tanks to the tank No. 1 position.

7. Press the start button on the scan tool.

8. Observe the system pressure on the Fuel Filler Neck Venting Kit Gauge.

FM1029900362250X

Fig. 4 Pinpoint Test A: Fuel tank solenoid valve diagnosis (Part 25 of 26)

TEST CONDITIONS	TEST DETAILS/RESULTS/ACTIONS
A29 CHECK FUEL TANK NO. 5 SOLENOID VALVE OPERATION (Continued)	

9. Press the stop button on the scan tool.

• Was the pressure on the gauge 0 kPa (0 psi) when triggered on?

→ **Yes**
MARK fuel tank no. 5 solenoid valve "Does not Operate." INSTALL new solenoids for those marked "Stuck Closed" at this time. RESTORE the vehicle. TEST the system for normal operation.

→ **No**
Mark fuel tank No. 5 solenoid valve "good." To complete diagnostics, install a new solenoid valve if the solenoid valve is marked "stuck closed." If fuel tank No. 6 solenoid valve was marked "may be stuck closed," INSTALL A new solenoid at this time. If all solenoid valves were marked "good," diagnostics are complete. RESTORE the vehicle. TEST the system for normal operation.

FM1029900362260X

Fig. 4 Pinpoint Test A: Fuel tank solenoid valve diagnosis (Part 26 of 26)

No. T95P-6701-AH and slide hammer tool No. T50T-100-A, or equivalents.

4. Remove crankshaft rear oil seal using rear crankshaft seal remover tool No. T95P-6701-EH and slide hammer tool No. T50T-100-A, or equivalents.

5. Remove crankshaft rear oil seal retainer, as required.

6. Reverse procedure to install, noting the following:

a. Use suitable plastic scraping tool to remove all traces of old sealant. **Do not use metal scrapers, wire brushes, power abrasive discs or other abrasive means to clean sealing surfaces.**

b. Clean sealing surfaces with metal surface cleaner No. F4AZ-19A536-RA, or equivalent. Allow to dry until there is no sign of wetness, or four minutes, whichever is longer.

c. Use silicone gasket and sealant No. F7AZ-19554-EA, or equivalent.

SOHC

1. Remove rocker arms as outlined under "Rocker Arms, Replace."
2. Remove timing chain as outlined under "Timing Chain, Replace."
3. Remove mounting bolt, camshaft sprocket and spacer.
4. Remove 13 camshaft bearing cap bolts.
5. Remove bearing cap ladders and camshaft.
6. Reverse procedure to install noting the following:
   a. Lubricate camshaft journals and bearing cap ladders with clean engine oil.
   b. Tighten bearing cap bolts to 89 inch lbs., in sequence, **Fig. 46.**

PISTON & ROD ASSEMBLY

DOHC

1. Rod bearing cap bolts are torque-to-yield bolts, **Do not reuse bolts.**
2. Install connecting rod to piston with marks facing toward front of engine.
3. Install piston with arrow facing toward front of engine.

SOHC

If old pistons are serviceable, ensure they are installed on original rods. Inspect side clearance between connecting rods and crankshaft journal. Correct clearance is .00059–.01772 inch.

1. Assemble pistons, pins, bearings, caps, nuts and bolts in original positions.
2. Install pistons with notch to front of engine.

3. Alternatively tighten connecting rod caps.
4. Rotate crankshaft to ensure smooth operation.

MAIN & ROD BEARINGS

DOHC

MAIN

1. **Torque** vertical main bearing bolts to 89 inch lbs., in sequence, **Fig. 47.**
2. **Torque** vertical bolts to 18 ft. lbs., in sequence.
3. **Torque** vertical bolts to 30 ft. lbs., in sequence.
4. Tighten vertical bolts an additional 90° in sequence.
5. **Torque** cross mounted bolts to 30 ft. lbs., then an additional 90°.

SOHC

MAIN

1. **Torque** cross mounted bolts to 89 inch lbs., in sequence, **Fig. 48.**
2. **Torque** cross mounted bolts to 15 ft. lbs., in sequence.
3. **Torque** vertical bolts to 30 ft. lbs., in sequence, **Fig. 49.**
4. Then tighten an additional 90°.

CRANKSHAFT REAR OIL SEAL

REPLACE

1. Lower transmission and support using suitable jack.
2. Remove flywheel.
3. Remove crankshaft oil slinger using rear crankshaft slinger remover tool

OIL PAN

REPLACE

1. Remove engine as outlined under "Engine, Replace."
2. Remove mounting bolts and flywheel.
3. Mount engine on suitable engine stand.
4. Remove oil pan mounting bolts in sequence, **Fig. 50.**
5. Remove oil pan and gasket.
6. Reverse procedure to install, noting the following:
7. **On models equipped with DOHC engine, torque** oil pan mounting bolts to 15 ft. lbs., in sequence, **Fig. 50.**
8. **On models equipped with SOHC engine, torque** oil pan mounting bolts to 108 inch lbs., in sequence, **Fig. 50.**

OIL PUMP

REPLACE

1. Remove camshaft covers as outlined under "Valve Cover, Replace."
2. Remove front cover as outlined under "Front Cover, Replace."
3. Remove oil pan as outlined under "Oil Pan, Replace."

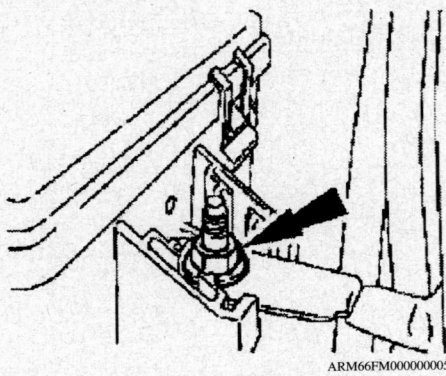

Fig. 5 Ground wire removal. SOHC engine

4. Remove timing chains as outlined under "Timing Chain, Replace."
5. Remove mounting bolts and oil pump, **Fig. 51.**
6. Reverse procedure to install. Align oil pump inner rotor with flat of crankshaft.

BELT TENSION DATA

Automatic belt tensioners are spring loaded devices which set and maintain drive belt tension. The drive belt should not require tension adjustment . Automatic tensioners have belt wear indicator marks. If indicator mark is not between indicator lines, belt is worn or an incorrect belt is installed.

SERPENTINE DRIVE BELT

Belt Routing

Refer to **Fig. 52** for drive belt routing.

Replacement

1. Rotate tensioner away from belt using suitable breaker bar installed in ½ inch square hole in tensioner arm.
2. Lift old belt over alternator pulley flange and remove.
3. When installing, position new belt over pulleys. Ensure all V-grooves make proper contact with pulley.
4. Ensure belt is properly installed on each pulley.

COOLING SYSTEM BLEED

DOHC

1. Remove coolant bleed plug from coolant bypass tube, **Fig. 53.**
2. Disconnect heater core coolant supply hose.
3. Add coolant through water bypass tube opening until coolant appears at heater core coolant supply hose.
4. Install heater hose and bypass bleed plug.
5. Fill coolant over flow bottle to COOL-

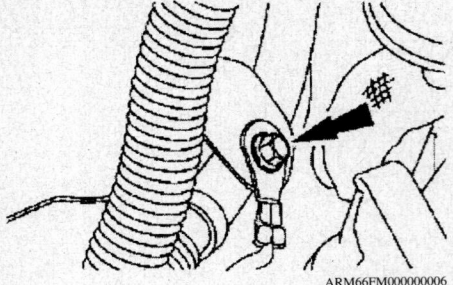

Fig. 6 Ground strap removal. SOHC engine

ANT FILL LEVEL marks and install pressure cap.
6. Select maximum heater temperature and blower speed settings, then position control to discharge air at air conditioning vents.
7. Run engine until it reaches operating temperature.
8. Fill coolant over flow bottle to COOLANT FILL LEVEL marks.
9. Repeat two previous steps until coolant level is between COOLANT FILL LEVEL on over flow bottle.

SOHC

1. Place heater temperature switch in maximum heat position.
2. Start engine and allow to idle. While engine is idling, feel for hot air at air conditioning vents.
3. If air discharge remains cool and engine coolant temperature gauge does not move, engine coolant level is low in engine and must be filled.
4. Stop engine, allow to cool and fill cooling system.
5. Start engine and allow to idle until normal operating temperature is reached, noting the following:
   a. Hot air should discharge from air conditioning vents.
   b. Engine coolant temperature gauge should maintain stabilized reading in middle of NORMAL range.
   c. Upper radiator hose should feel hot to touch.
6. Shut engine off and allow to cool.
7. Inspect engine for coolant leaks.
8. Adjust engine coolant level in overflow bottle, as required.

THERMOSTAT

REPLACE

DOHC

1. Drain cooling system into suitable container, then raise and support vehicle.
2. Disconnect coolant hose.
3. Remove mounting bolts and coolant outlet.
4. Remove thermostat and O-ring seal.
5. Reverse procedure to install using new hose clamps.

SOHC

1. Drain coolant into suitable container

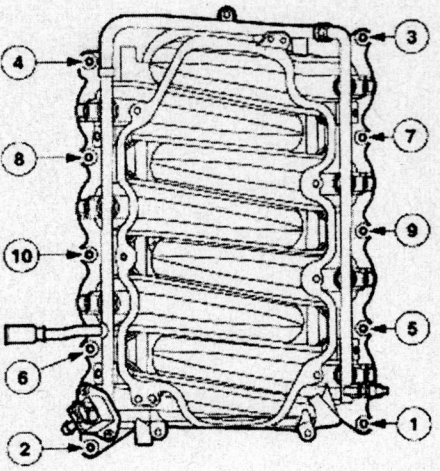

Fig. 7 Lower intake manifold bolt removal sequence. DOHC engine

until level is below upper radiator hose and thermostat housing.
2. Remove engine appearance cover.
3. Disconnect upper radiator hose at thermostat housing.
4. Remove two thermostat housing mounting bolts.
5. Remove O-ring seal and thermostat from intake manifold. Replace O-ring, as required.
6. Reverse procedure to install.

WATER PUMP

REPLACE

1. Drain coolant into suitable container.
2. Loosen water pump mounting bolts, release belt tensioner and remove accessory drive belt.
3. Remove mounting bolts and water pump pulley.
4. Loosen mounting bolts and remove water pump.
5. Reverse procedure to install. Replace O-ring.

RADIATOR

REPLACE

1. Raise and support vehicle.
2. Drain engine coolant into suitable container.
3. Remove fan blade, motor and shroud.
4. Release three hold downs and remove radiator sight shield.
5. Remove upper and lower radiator hoses from radiator.
6. Remove radiator support bolts and supports.
7. Remove bolts and position air conditioning condenser core and transmission oil cooler away from radiator.
8. Reverse procedure to install.

FUEL PUMP

REPLACE

1. Relieve fuel system pressure as outlined under "Precautions."

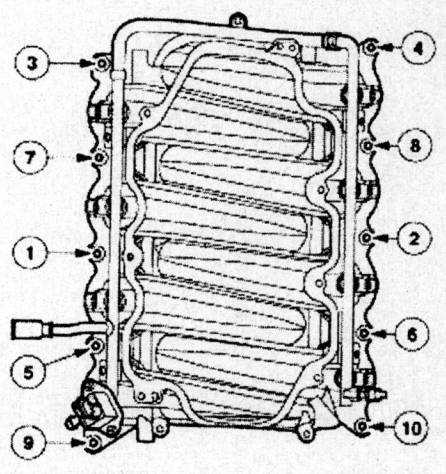

Fig. 8 Lower intake manifold tightening sequence. DOHC engine

2. Drain fuel tank into suitable container, then raise and support vehicle.
3. Remove fuel tank and disconnect pressure transducer connector on top rear corner of fuel tank.
4. Remove six mounting bolts and fuel pump module.
5. Reverse procedure to install, noting the following:
   a. Turn ignition from Off to On position for three seconds using fuel pressure gauge tool No. T80L-9974-B, or equivalent, on fuel charging Schraeder valve.
   b. Repeat off to on switching 5–10 times until pressure gauge shows at least 35 psi.

FUEL FILTER
REPLACE

1. Turn engine off and relieve fuel system pressure as outlined under "Precautions."
2. Raise and support vehicle.
3. Remove push connect fittings at both ends of filter. Install new retainer clips in each push connect fitting.
4. Remove two mounting bolts and fuel filter from metal bracket.
5. Remove filter from retainer. Record direction of flow. Arrow points to open end of retainer.
6. Remove rubber insulator rings from filter.
7. Reverse procedure to install, noting the following:
   a. Replace insulator if filter moves freely.
   b. Start engine and inspect for fuel leaks.

TECHNICAL SERVICE BULLETINS
Engine Tick
2004

Some of these models equipped with the Romeo, may exhibit an engine tick noise that is present at all temperatures during idle. The noise may be emanating from the valve guide area in the cylinder head. The noise may be more prevalent in the front wheel well area and may not be heard with the hood open.

This condition may be caused by the cylinder head valve guide area.

To correct this condition, proceed as follows:
1. Ensure noise is coming from back of cylinder head near exhaust ports by listening with suitable stethoscope.
2. Ensure noise is heard in wheel well or catalytic converter and from under vehicle.
3. Ensure there are no exhaust manifold leaks.
4. Ensure noise is present when canceling each cylinder by unplugging injectors one at a time.
5. Ensure camshaft spacers are in place.
6. Ensure cam sprocket is tightened to specifications.
7. Inspect hydraulic lash adjusters for spongy condition.
8. Ensure timing chain tensioner pin has been removed.
9. Replace cylinder head and cam (P/N 4L3Z-6049-AA-RH, P/N 4L3Z-6049-BA-LH).

Engine - Exhaust - Knock During Initial Cold Start
2004

On some of these models this condition may be caused by a loose exhaust shield.

To correct this condition, install exhaust shield kit (P/N 3W7Z-5E258-AA). Refer to **Fig. 54** when installing exhaust shield kit.

Idle Or Low Speed Engine Vibration
2004 TOWN CAR

On some of these models there may be an engine vibration at idle and/or low engine speeds. This condition may be more pronounced when the engine is cold. The vibration may be felt through the steering wheel, brake pedal or floor.

To correct this condition, proceed as follows:

This condition may be caused by the engine mounts, idle speed strategy and exhaust damper turning.
1. Remove and replace engine mounts

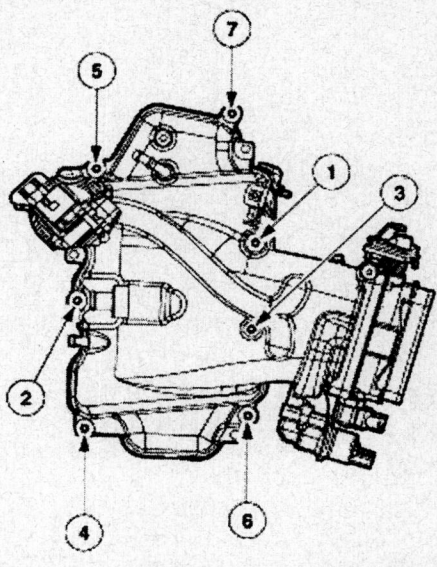

Fig. 9 Upper intake manifold bolt removal sequence. DOHC engine

(P/N 3W1Z-6038-EA, P/N 3W1Z-6038-DB).
2. Remove and discard one original rubber damper from each muffler.
3. Remove and discard lefthand front muffler to exhaust pipe clamps.
4. Install muffler damper (P/N 4W1Z-5F240-AA) using U-bolt (P/N W710145-S306). **Torque** to 33 ft. lbs.
5. Program Powertrain Control Module (PCM) with latest calibration.

Engine Tick
2004–05 SOHC ENGINE

On some of these models, there may be an engine tick noise at all temperatures during idle. The noise may be prevalent in the front wheel well area, but may be heard with the hood open.

This condition may be caused by the cylinder head valve guide area.

To correct this condition, proceed as follows:
1. Ensure noise is coming from back of cylinder head near exhaust ports by listening with suitable stethoscope.
2. Ensure noise is heard in wheel well or catalytic converter and from under vehicle.
3. Ensure there are no exhaust manifold leaks.
4. Ensure noise is present when canceling each cylinder by unplugging injectors one at a time.
5. Ensure camshaft spacers are in place.
6. Ensure cam sprocket is tightened to specifications.
7. Inspect hydraulic lash adjusters for spongy condition.
8. Ensure timing chain tensioner pin been removed.
9. Replace cylinder head and cam (P/N 1L2Z-6049-LA).

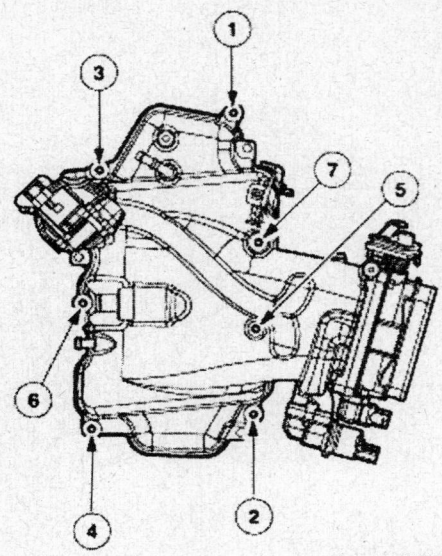

Fig. 10 Upper intake manifold tightening sequence. DOHC engine

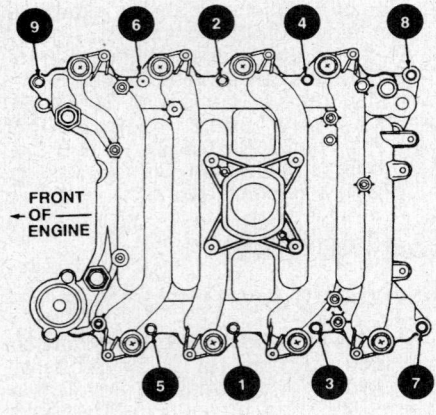

Installation Sequence — Gasoline Engine

FRONT OF ENGINE

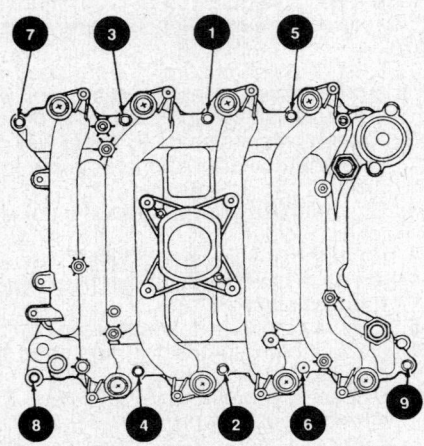

Installation Sequence — Natural Gas Engine

Fig. 13 Intake manifold tightening sequence. SOHC natural gas engine

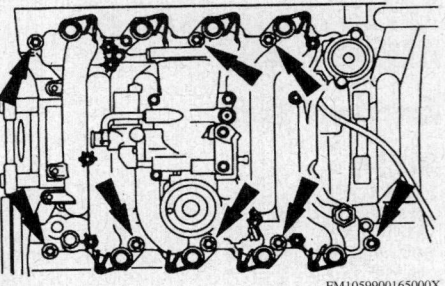

Fig. 11 Intake manifold initial tightening sequence. SOHC gasoline engine

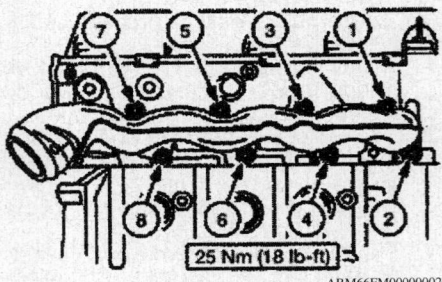

25 Nm (18 lb-ft)

Fig. 14 Righthand exhaust manifold tightening sequence. DOHC engine

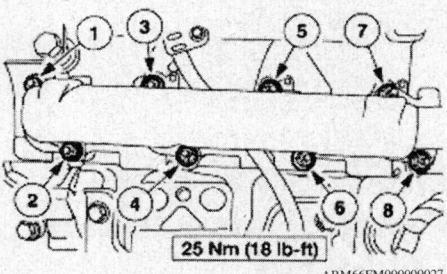

25 Nm (18 lb-ft)

Fig. 15 Lefthand exhaust manifold tightening sequence. DOHC engine

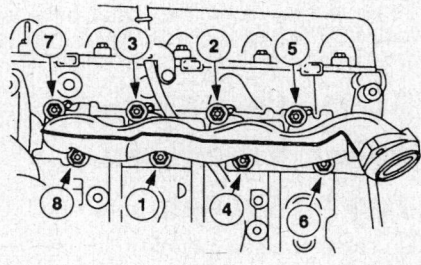

Fig. 17 Lefthand exhaust manifold tightening sequence. SOHC engine

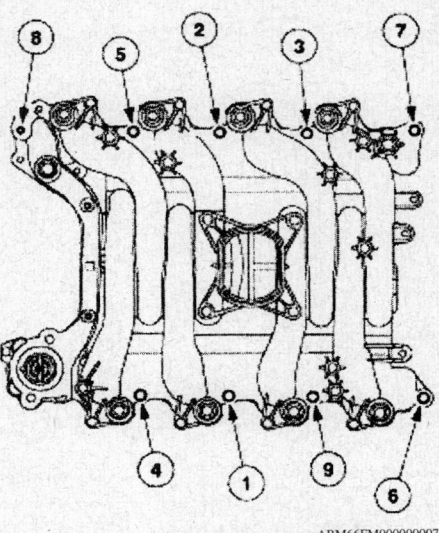

Fig. 12 Intake manifold bolt tightening sequence. SOHC gasoline engine

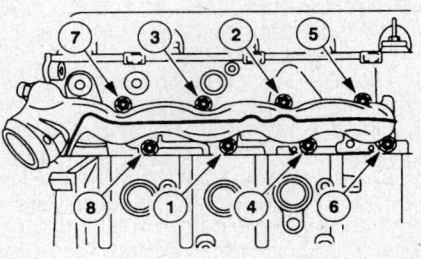

Fig. 16 Righthand exhaust manifold tightening sequence. SOHC engine

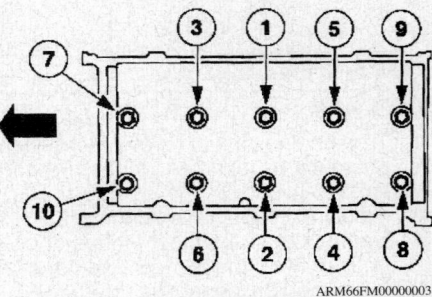

Fig. 18 Cylinder head tightening sequence. DOHC engine

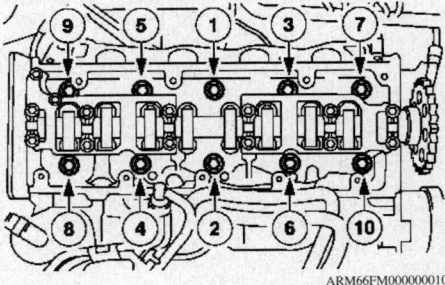

Fig. 19 Cylinder head bolt loosening sequence. SOHC engine

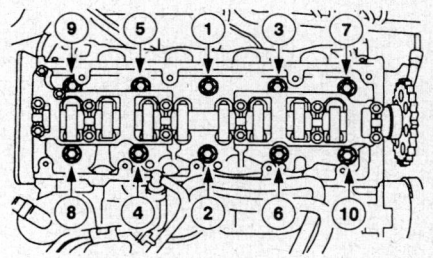

FM1069901036000X

Fig. 20 Righthand cylinder head bolt tightening sequence. SOHC engine

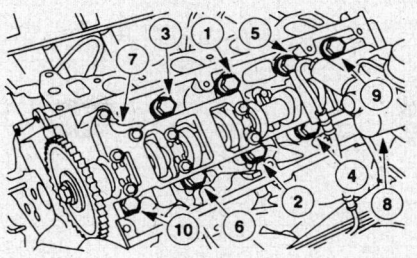

FM1069901037000X

Fig. 21 Lefthand cylinder head bolt tightening sequence. SOHC engine

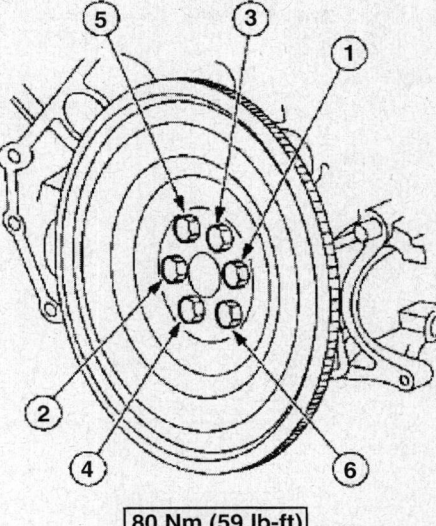

80 Nm (59 lb-ft)

ARM66FM000000011

Fig. 22 Flexplate bolt tightening sequence. SOHC engine

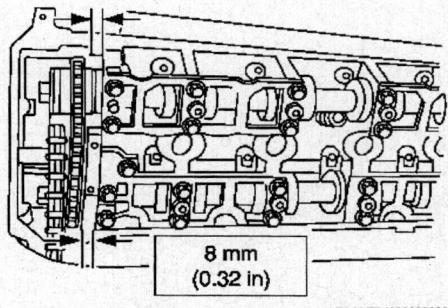

8 mm (0.32 in)

ARM66FM000000028

Fig. 23 Sealant location. DOHC engine

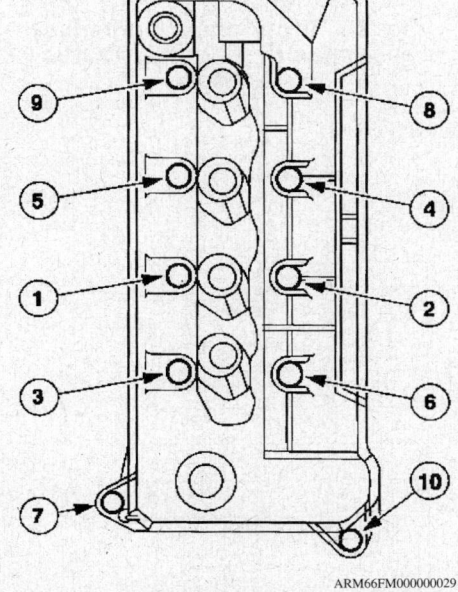

ARM66FM000000029

Fig. 24 Valve cover tightening sequence. DOHC engine

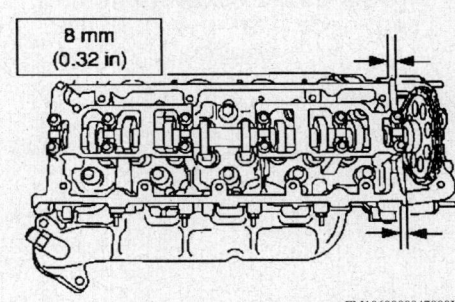

8 mm (0.32 in)

FM1069900847000X

Fig. 25 Sealant application locations. SOHC engine

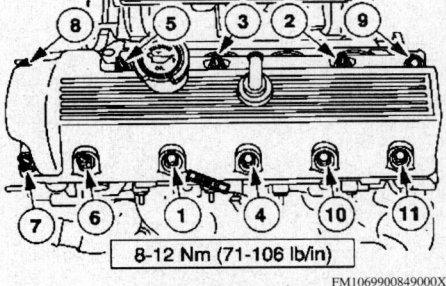

8-12 Nm (71-106 lb/in)

FM1069900849000X

Fig. 26 Lefthand cam cover bolt tightening sequence. SOHC engine

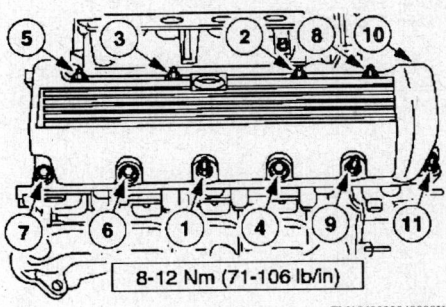

8-12 Nm (71-106 lb/in)

FM1069900848000X

Fig. 27 Righthand cam cover tightening sequence. SOHC engine

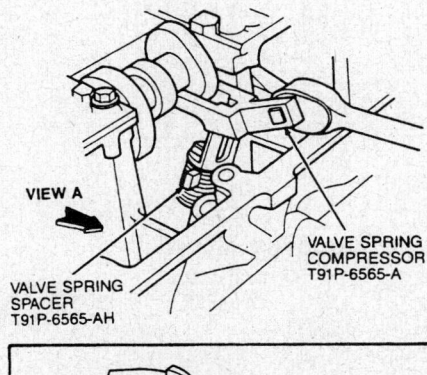

VIEW A

VALVE SPRING COMPRESSOR T91P-6565-A

VALVE SPRING SPACER T91P-6565-AH

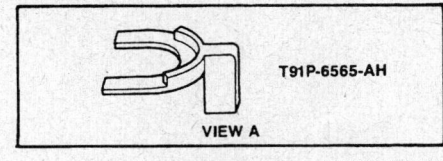

T91P-6565-AH

VIEW A

FM1069100137000X

Fig. 28 Valve spring compression. SOHC engine

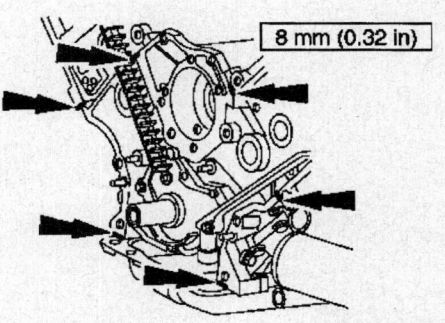

8 mm (0.32 in)

ARM66FM000000030

Fig. 29 Front cover sealant application. DOHC engine

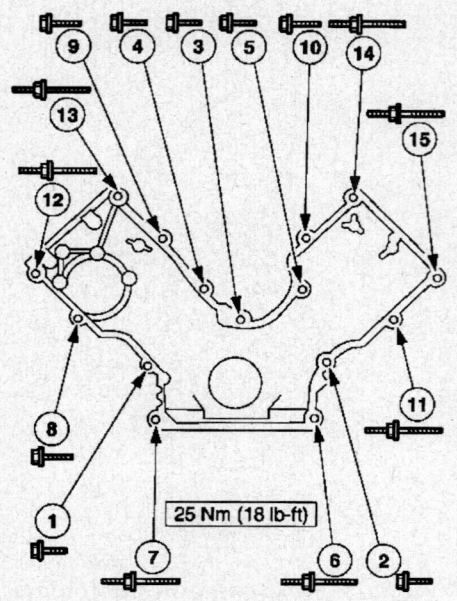

25 Nm (18 lb-ft)

Fig. 30 Front cover tightening sequence (Part 1 of 2). DOHC engine

ARM66FM000000031

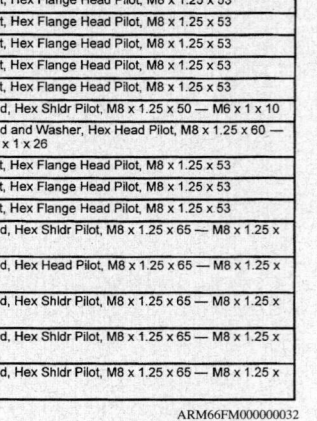

Item	Part Number	Description
1	N806177	Bolt, Hex Flange Head Pilot, M8 x 1.25 x 53
2	N806177	Bolt, Hex Flange Head Pilot, M8 x 1.25 x 53
3	N806177	Bolt, Hex Flange Head Pilot, M8 x 1.25 x 53
4	N806177	Bolt, Hex Flange Head Pilot, M8 x 1.25 x 53
5	N806177	Bolt, Hex Flange Head Pilot, M8 x 1.25 x 53
6	W706508	Stud, Hex Shldr Pilot, M8 x 1.25 x 50 — M6 x 1 x 10
7	N808586	Stud and Washer, Hex Head Pilot, M8 x 1.25 x 60 — M6 x 1 x 26
8	N806177	Bolt, Hex Flange Head Pilot, M8 x 1.25 x 53
9	N806177	Bolt, Hex Flange Head Pilot, M8 x 1.25 x 53
10	N806177	Bolt, Hex Flange Head Pilot, M8 x 1.25 x 53
11	N806300	Stud, Hex Shldr Pilot, M8 x 1.25 x 65 — M8 x 1.25 x 26
12	W706560	Stud, Hex Head Pilot, M8 x 1.25 x 65 — M8 x 1.25 x 16
13	W706560	Stud, Hex Shldr Pilot, M8 x 1.25 x 65 — M8 x 1.25 x 26
14	W706560	Stud, Hex Shldr Pilot, M8 x 1.25 x 65 — M8 x 1.25 x 26
15	N806300	Stud, Hex Shldr Pilot, M8 x 1.25 x 65 — M8 x 1.25 x 26

ARM66FM000000032

Fig. 30 Front cover tightening sequence (Part 2 of 2). DOHC engine

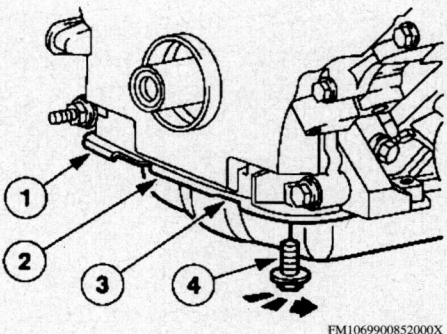

ARM66FM000000033

Fig. 31 Oil pan front bolts tightening sequence. DOHC engine

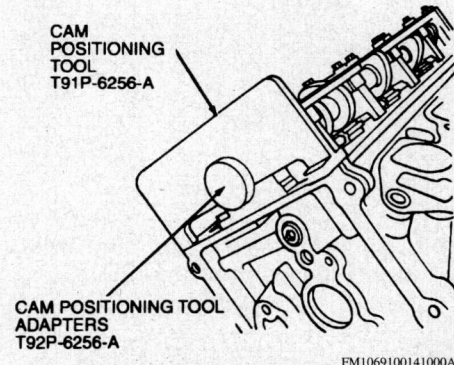

FM1069900852000X

Fig. 33 Oil pan to front cover bolt tightening sequence

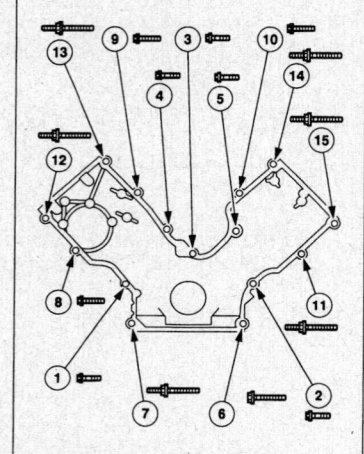

FM1069901038000X

Fig. 32 Front cover tightening sequence. SOHC engine

Item	Description
4	Bolt, Hex Flange Head Pilot, M8 x 1.25 x 53
5	Bolts, Hex Flange Head Pilot, M8 x 1.25 x 53
6	Bolt, Hex-Head Pilot, M10 x 1.5 x 1.5 x 103.1
7	Stud, Hex-Head Pilot, M10 x 1.5 x 1.5 x 103.1
8	Screw and Washer, Hex Pilot, M10 x 1.5 x 57.5
9	Screw and Washer, Hex Pilot, M10 x 1.5 x 57.5
10	Screw and Washer, Hex Pilot, M10 x 1.5 x 57.5
11	Stud and Washer, Hex Head Pilot, M10 x 1.5 x M8 x 1.25 x 109.6
12	Stud and Washer, Hex Head Pilot, M10 x 1.5 x M8 x 1.25 x 109.6
13	Stud and Washer, Hex Head Pilot, M10 x 1.5 x M8 x 1.25 x 109.6
14	Stud and Washer, Hex Head Pilot, M10 x 1.5 x M8 x 1.25 x 109.6
15	Stud and Washer, Hex Head Pilot, M10 x 1.5 x M8 x 1.25 x 109.6

Item	Description
1	Bolt, Hex Flange Head Pilot, M8 x 1.25 x 53
2	Bolt, Hex Flange Head Pilot, M8 x 1.25 x 53
3	Bolt, Hex Flange Head Pilot, M8 x 1.25 x 53

CAM POSITIONING TOOL T91P-6256-A

CAM POSITIONING TOOL ADAPTERS T92P-6256-A

FM1069100141000A

Fig. 34 Camshaft aligner tool

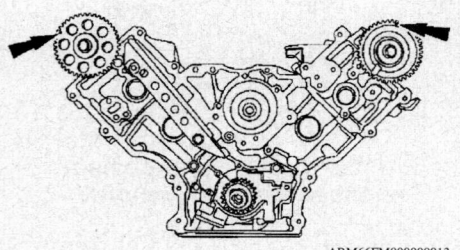

ARM66FM000000013

Fig. 35 Camshaft timing marks

303-448

ARM66FM000000009

Fig. 36 Crankshaft holding tool

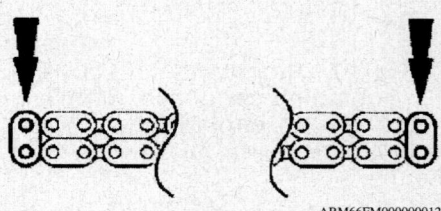

ARM66FM000000012

Fig. 37 Timing chain marks

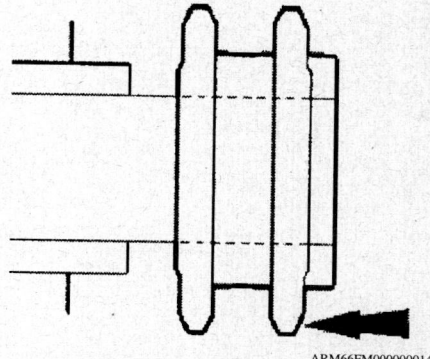

Fig. 38 Crankshaft sprocket installation

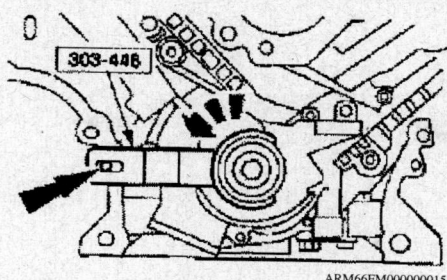

Fig. 39 Crankshaft holding tool installation

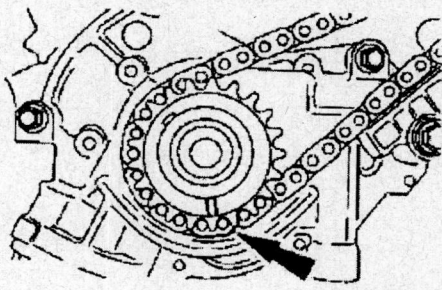

Fig. 40 Lefthand timing chain to crankshaft sprocket alignment

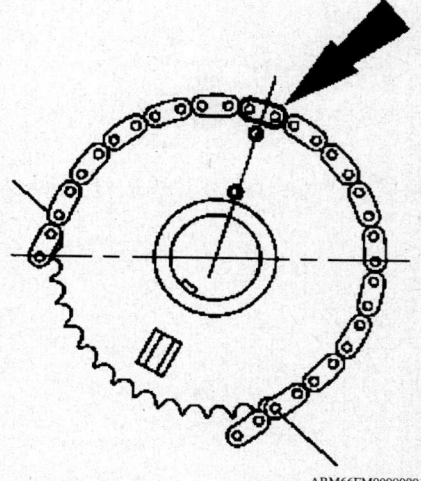

Fig. 41 Lefthand timing chain to camshaft sprocket alignment

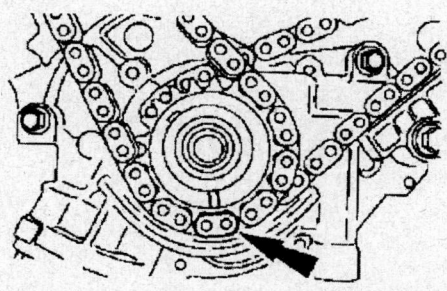

Fig. 42 Righthand timing chain to crankshaft sprocket alignment

Fig. 45 Camshaft timing marks. DOHC engine

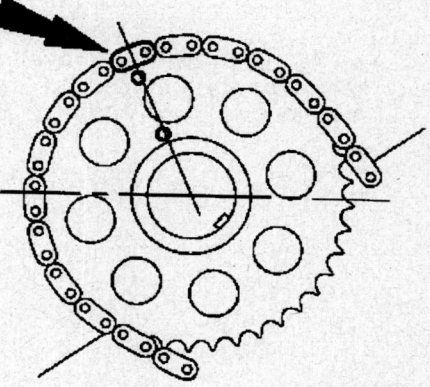

Fig. 43 Righthand timing chain to camshaft sprocket alignment

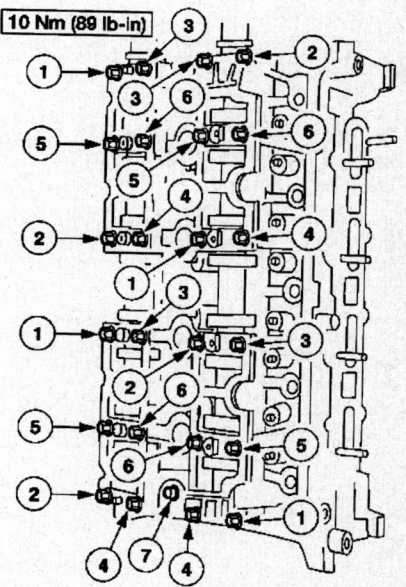

Fig. 44 Camshaft bearing tightening sequence. DOHC engine

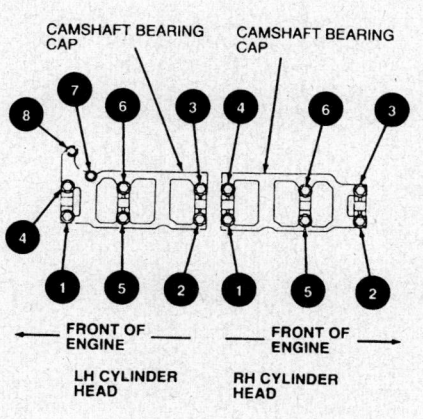

Fig. 46 Camshaft cap cluster tightening sequence. SOHC engine

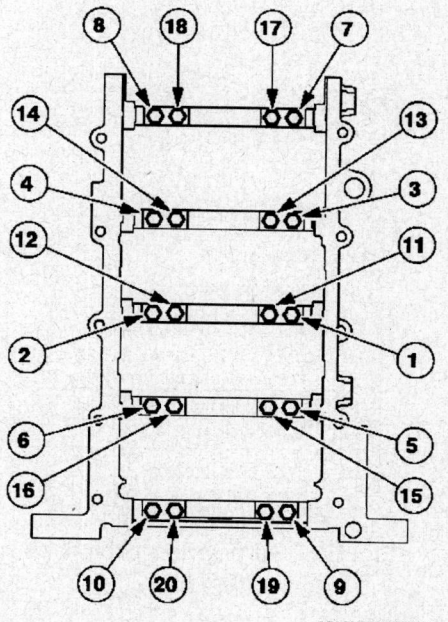

Fig. 47 Main bearing vertical bolts tightening sequence. DOHC engine

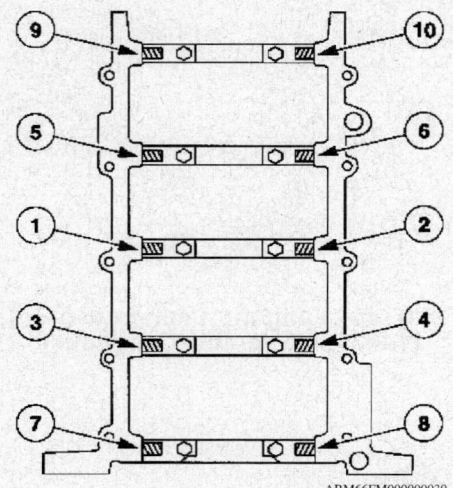

Fig. 48 Main bearing cross mounted bolts tightening sequence. SOHC engine

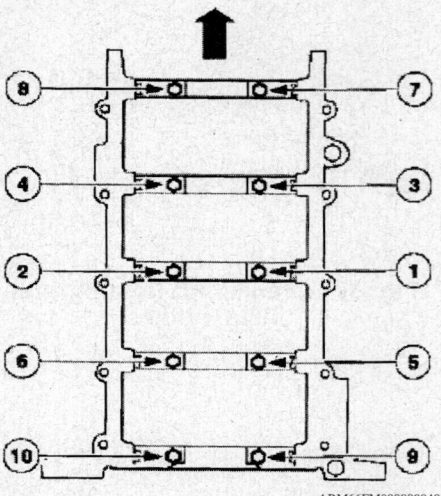

Fig. 49 Main bearing vertical mounted bolts tightening sequence. SOHC engine

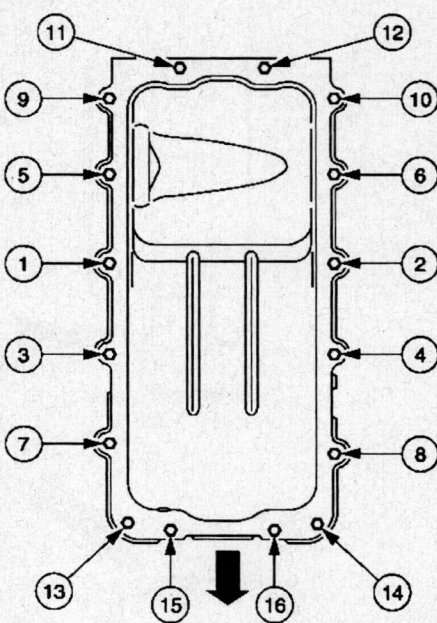

Fig. 50 Oil pan tighten sequence

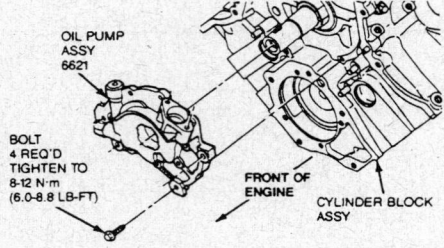

Fig. 51 Oil pump assembly

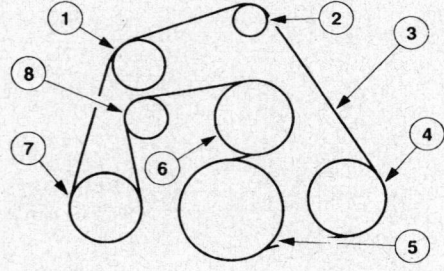

Item	Description
1	Belt idler pulley
2	Generator pulley
3	Drive belt
4	Power steering pump pulley
5	Crankshaft pulley
6	Water pump pulley
7	A/C clutch pulley
8	Drive belt tensioner pulley

FM1069901042000X

Fig. 52 Serpentine drive belt routing

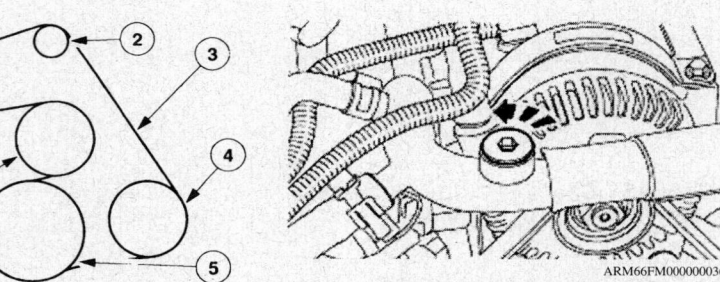

Fig. 53 Coolant bleed plug. DOHC engine

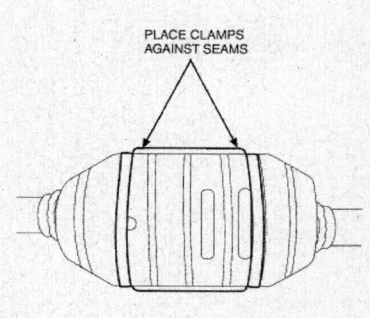

Fig. 54 Exhaust shield kit installation

TIGHTENING SPECIFICATIONS

Year	Component	Torque Ft. Lbs.
DOHC ENGINE		
2004–06	Air Conditioning Compressor	18
	Alternator Mounting Bracket	89①
	Camshaft Cap	④
	Camshaft Sprocket	85
	Connecting Rod	⑦
	Cylinder Head	⑤
	EAR Valve To Exhaust Manifold Tube	30
	Engine Mount	52
	Exhaust Manifold	⑩
	Flex Plate	59
	Front Cover	⑥
	Heater Coolant Outlet To Cylinder Head	89①
	Lower Intake Manifold	⑨
	Main Rod Bearing Cap	⑦
	Oil Filter Adapter	18
	Oil Pan	⑧
	Oil Pump Screen Cover & Tube To Oil Pump	89①
	Oil Pump Screen & Pickup Tube To Main Bearing Cap Stud Spacer	18
	Oil Pump To Cylinder Block	89①
	Outlet Heater Water Hose To Engine Front Cover	18
	Power Steering Pump	18
	Serpentine Belt Idler Pulley	18
	Serpentine Belt Tensioner	18
	Thermostat	18
	Timing Chain Guide	89
	Timing Chain Tensioner (Primary)	18
	Timing Chain Tensioner (Secondary)	89①
	Upper Intake Manifold	⑨
	Valve Cover	⑪
	Water Pump	18
	Water Pump Pulley	18
SOHC ENGINE		
2004–06	Camshaft Bearing Cap	④
	Camshaft Sprocket	89
	Connecting Rod Bearing Cap	③
	Crankshaft Main Bearings	②
	Cylinder Head	⑤
	EAR Tube	30
	Engine Mount	52
	Exhaust Manifold	25⑩
	Exhaust Manifold To Converter	25
	Flywheel	59

TIGHTENING SPECIFICATIONS—Continued

Year	Component	Torque Ft. Lbs.
SOHC ENGINE		
2004–06	Front Cover	⑥
	Fuel Injection Supply Manifold Studs	89①
	Idler Pulley	18
	Intake Manifold	18⑨
	Motor Mount To Crossmember	44
	Oil Filter Adapter	18
	Oil Pan	⑧
	Oil Pan Drain Plug	10①
	Oil Pump	89①
	Oil Pump Screen Cover & Tube Bolts	89①
	Oil Pump Screen Cover & Tube To Oil Pump Screen Cover & Tube Spacer	18
	Oil Pump Screen Cover & Tube Spacer	18
	Power Steering High Pressure Line	18
	Power Steering Pump	18
	Rear Main Seal Retainer Plate	89①
	Starter Motor	18
	Thermostat	18
	Throttle Body	89①
	Timing Chain Guide	89①
	Timing Chain Tensioner	18
	Torque Converter	27
	Transmission Mount	76
	Valve Cover	⑪
	Water Bypass Tube Stud	18
	Water Outlet Adapter	18
	Water Pump	18
	Water Pump Pulley	18

① — Inch lbs.
② — Torque to 30 ft. lbs., and final tighten an additional 90°.
③ — Torque to 30–33 ft. lbs., and final tighten an additional 90–120°.
④ — Refer to "Camshaft, Replace" for tightening specifications and sequence.
⑤ — Refer to "Cylinder Head, Replace" for tightening specifications and sequence.
⑥ — Refer to "Front Cover, Replace" for tightening specifications and sequence.
⑦ — Refer to "Main & Rod Bearings" for tightening specifications and sequence.
⑧ — Refer to "Oil Pan, Replace" for tightening specifications and sequence.
⑨ — Refer to "Intake Manifold, Replace" for tightening specifications and sequence.
⑩ — Refer to "Exhaust Manifold, Replace" for tightening specifications and sequence.
⑪ — Refer to "Valve Cover, Replace" for tightening specifications and sequence.

Rear Axle & Suspension

NOTE: On Air Bag Equipped Models, Refer To "Air Bag System Precautions" Located In The Front Of This Manual For System Disarming & Arming Procedures.

NOTE: Refer To "Computer Relearn Procedure" Located In The Front Of This Manual When Battery Power To The Computer Has Been Interrupted.

INDEX

	Page No.
Air Spring, Replace	2-33
Coil Spring, Replace	2-33
Control Arm, Replace	2-33
Lower	2-33
Upper	2-34
Description	2-32
Crown Victoria, Grand Marquis & Marauder	2-32

	Page No.
Town Car	2-32
Lateral Control Arm, Replace	2-34
Precautions	2-32
Air Bag Systems	2-32
Air Suspension Pressure Relief	2-32
Battery Ground Cable	2-32
Propeller Shaft, Replace	2-33
Rear Axle, Replace	2-32

	Page No.
Rear Axle Shaft, Replace	2-32
Installation	2-32
Removal	2-32
Shock Absorber, Replace	2-33
Stabilizer Bar, Replace	2-35
Tightening Specifications	2-35

PRECAUTIONS

Air Bag Systems

Refer to "Air Bag System Precautions" in the front of this manual for system disarming and arming procedures.

Air Suspension Pressure Relief

Before servicing any air suspension components, disconnect power to system by turning air suspension switch OFF or by disconnecting battery ground cable.

Do not remove an air spring under any circumstances when there is pressure in the air spring. Do not remove any component supporting an air spring without either exhausting the air or providing support for air spring. Refer to the "Active Suspension Systems" chapter to vent air from spring.

Battery Ground Cable

Prior to service, disconnect battery ground cable and isolate as required.

DESCRIPTION

Crown Victoria, Grand Marquis & Marauder

The rear suspension is composed of the upper and lower suspension arms, lateral arm, Watts link pivot, rear stabilizer bar and air or coil springs, **Fig. 1.**

Town Car

The rear suspension is composed of the upper and lower suspension arms, lateral arm, Watts link pivot, rear stabilizer bar and air or coil springs, **Fig. 2.**

REAR AXLE
REPLACE

1. **On models equipped with air suspension,** turn air suspension switch to Off position, then vent air from system as outlined in "Active Suspension Systems" chapter.
2. **On all models,** raise and support vehicle and position safety stands below rear frame crossmember.
3. Mark driveshaft flange and pinion flange for correct alignment during installation.
4. Remove four mounting bolts and disconnect driveshaft.
5. Remove rear wheels, calipers and brake discs. Support caliper with suitable wire.
6. Remove rear disc rotor, parking brake rear cable and conduit from parking brake cable equalizer. Reroute parking brake rear cable and conduit aside.
7. Remove anti-lock brake sensors. Reroute anti-lock brake sensor wiring.
8. Remove rear stabilizer bar from rear stabilizer bar link and bushing.
9. Remove rear stabilizer bar bracket bolts, rear stabilizer bar brackets and rear stabilizer bar.
10. Remove rear air springs height sensor, as required.
11. Separate Watts linkage from rear axle housing.
12. Remove bellcrank stud nut. **Do not damage bellcrank stud threads.**
13. Secure rear axle to jack using additional support straps.
14. Support rear axle housing with suitable jack.
15. Remove lower mounting nuts and shock absorbers from brackets.
16. Remove lower control arm retainer, then the upper control arm mounting nuts and bolts.
17. Unseat air springs and lower rear axle.
18. Reverse procedure to install.

REAR AXLE SHAFT
REPLACE

Removal

1. **On models equipped with air suspension,** turn air suspension switch to Off position, then vent air from system as outlined in "Active Suspension Systems" chapter.
2. **On all models,** raise and support vehicle, then remove rear wheel and tire assembly.
3. Remove disc brake calipers and rotors, then the rear anti-lock brake sensor.
4. Drain rear axle fluid into suitable container by removing cover.
5. Remove differential pinion shaft lock bolt and differential pinion shaft, **Fig. 3.**
6. Push flanged end of axle shafts toward center of vehicle and remove C-lock from button end of axle shaft, **Fig. 4.**
7. Remove axle shaft from housing. **Do not damage oil seal and ABS sensor ring.**

Installation

1. Ensure O-ring is present on spline end of axle shaft.
2. Slide axle shaft into axle housing. **Do not damage bearing seal or ABS sensor ring.**
3. Start splines into side gear and push firmly until button end of axle shaft can be seen in differential case.
4. Install C-lock on button end of axle shaft splines. Push shaft outboard until splines engage and C-lock seats in counterbore of differential side gear.
5. Position differential pinion shaft

through case and pinion gears, aligning hole in shaft with lock bolt hose.

6. Apply rear axle lubricant No. E0AZ-19554-BA, or equivalent, to pinion shaft lock bolt and tighten.
7. Install cover and tighten.
8. Install ABS speed sensor, rotors and calipers.

PROPELLER SHAFT
REPLACE

To maintain proper drive line balance, mark the driveshaft, universal joints, slip yoke and companion flange before removing the shaft so it can be installed in its original position.

1. Remove companion flange to drive pinion flange mounting bolts.
2. Pull driveshaft rearward until slip yoke clears transmission extension housing.
3. Reverse procedure to install.

SHOCK ABSORBER
REPLACE

1. **On models equipped with air suspension,** turn air suspension switch to Off position, then vent air from system as outlined in "Active Suspension Systems" chapter.
2. **On all models,** raise and support vehicle.
3. **On models equipped with plastic dust tube,** place suitable open end wrench on hex stamped into dust tube's metal cap.
4. **On models equipped with steel dust tube,** grasp tube to prevent stud rotation when loosening mounting nut.
5. **On all models,** remove shock absorber mounting nut, washer and insulator from stud on upper side of frame.
6. Compress shock absorber to clear hole in frame, then remove inner insulator and washer from upper stud.
7. Remove self-locking nut and disconnect shock absorber lower stud from mounting bracket on rear axle tube.
8. Reverse procedure to install.

COIL SPRING
REPLACE

1. Mark rear shock absorber relative to protective sleeve with vehicle in static, level ground position (curb height).
2. Raise and support vehicle on suitable hoist.
3. Remove both wheel and tire assemblies.
4. Remove nuts and bushings, then rotate stabilizer bar off links.
5. Support rear axle.
6. All vehicles are equipped with gas pressurized shock absorbers which will extend unassisted. **Do not apply heat or flame to shock absorbers during removal or component servicing.**
7. Remove nuts and disconnect shock absorbers. Discard nuts.

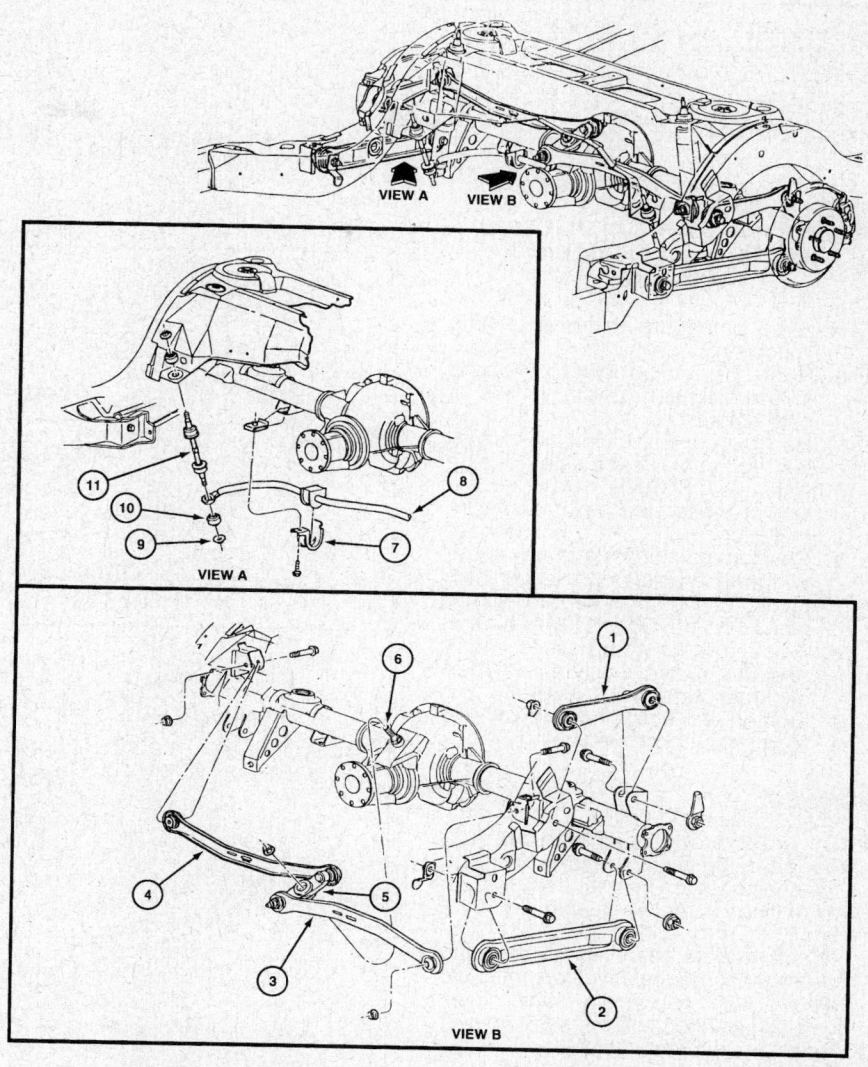

Fig. 1   Exploded view of rear suspension (Part 1 of 2). Crown Victoria, Grand Marquis & Marauder

8. Lower axle, then remove springs and spring insulators.
9. Reverse procedure to install.

AIR SPRING
REPLACE

Do not remove an air spring when there is pressure in the air spring.
Do not attempt to install any air spring that has become unfolded.

1. Raise and support vehicle until tires are slightly above ground.
2. Vent air springs as outlined in "Active Suspensions" chapter.
3. Remove air spring retainer, then detach air spring from rear axle.
4. Disconnect air spring electrical connector, then quick connect locking ring and pull out air line.
5. Remove air spring.
6. Reverse procedure to install.

CONTROL ARM
REPLACE

Lower

1. **On models equipped with air suspension,** turn air suspension switch to Off position, then vent air from system as outlined in "Active Suspension Systems" chapter.
2. **On all models,** mark rear suspension shock tube relative to protective sleeve with vehicle on level ground.
3. Raise and support vehicle, then remove wheel and tire assembly.
4. Support rear axle.
5. Remove and discard rear suspension lower arm pivot bolt and nut from axle bracket.
6. Remove and discard rear suspension lower arm pivot bolt and nut from frame bracket.
7. Remove rear suspension lower arm.

Item	Description	Item	Description
1	Rear Suspension Upper Arm	6	Watts Link Pivot Stud
2	Rear Suspension Lower Arm	7	Stabilizer Bar Bracket
3	Lateral Arm, LH (Part of 4264)	8	Stabilizer Bar and Isolator Assy
4	Lateral Arm, RH (Part of 4264)	9	Stabilizer Bar Link Retaining Nut
5	Watts Link Pivot (Part of 4264)	10	Stabilizer Bar Bushing
		11	Stabilizer Bar Link

FM2039800059020X

Fig. 1 Exploded view of rear suspension (Part 2 of 2). Crown Victoria, Grand Marquis & Marauder

8. Reverse procedure to install, noting the following:
   a. Rear suspension lower arm bolts must be tightened with vehicle at curb height.
   b. Rear suspension lower arms are interchangeable from side to side with "OUTBOARD" stamped on side of arm for positioning during installation.
   c. Position rear suspension lower arm to frame bracket and install new pivot bolt and nut. Insert bolt so nut faces inboard. **Do not tighten now.**
   d. Raise axle to compresses shock absorber to previously established alignment mark (curb height).
   e. Tighten rear suspension lower arm to frame bracket pivot bolt.

Upper

1. **On models equipped with air suspension,** turn air suspension switch to Off position, then vent air from system as outlined in "Active Suspension Systems" chapter.
2. **On all models,** mark rear suspension shock absorber relative to protective sleeve with vehicle in static, level ground position (curb height).
3. Raise and support vehicle.
4. Support rear axle.
5. Remove and discard rear suspension upper arm pivot bolt and nut from axle bracket. **Do not use excessive force when removing pivot bolt and flag nut on righthand upper suspension arm to axle bracket.**
6. Remove and discard rear suspension upper arm pivot bolt and nut from frame bracket.
7. Remove rear suspension upper arm.
8. Reverse procedure to install, noting the following:
   a. Rear suspension upper arm bolts must be tightened with vehicle at curb height.
   b. Rear suspension upper arms are interchangeable from side to side with "FRONT" and "OUTBOARD" stamped on side of arms for positioning during installation.
   c. Position rear suspension upper arm to frame bracket and install new pivot bolt and nut. Insert bolt so nut faces inboard. **Do not tighten now.**
   d. Raise axle to compresses shock absorber to previously established alignment mark (curb height).

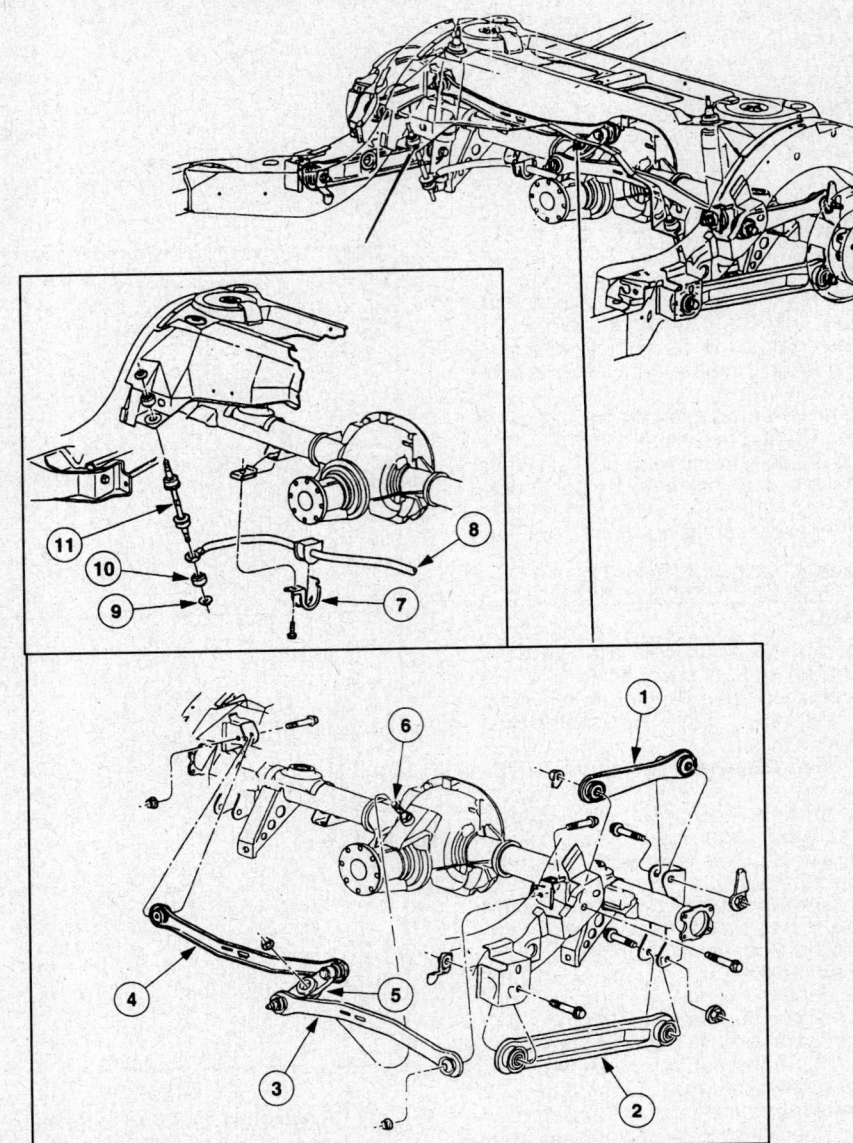

Item	Description	Item	Description
1	Rear Suspension Upper Arm	6	Watts Link Pivot Stud
2	Rear Suspension Lower Arm	7	Stabilizer Bar Bracket
3	Lateral Arm, LH	8	Stabilizer Bar and Isolator Assy
4	Lateral Arm, RH	9	Stabilizer Bar Link Retaining Nut
5	Watts Link Pivot	10	Stabilizer Bar Bushing
		11	Stabilizer Bar Link

FM20398000062000X

Fig. 2 Exploded view of rear suspension. Town Car

   e. Tighten bolts.

LATERAL CONTROL ARM
REPLACE

1. **On models equipped with air suspension,** turn air suspension switch to Off position, then vent air from system as outlined in "Active Suspension Systems" chapter.
2. **On all models,** mark rear suspension shock absorber relative to protective sleeve with vehicle in static, level ground position (curb height).
3. Raise and support vehicle.
4. Support rear axle.
5. Disconnect height sensor from mounting bracket.

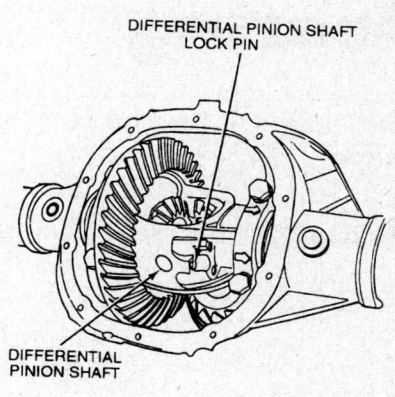

Fig. 3 Differential pinion shaft replacement

6. Remove and discard both lateral arm pivot bolts and nuts.
7. Watts link pivot stud is coated with dry adhesive and must be replaced whenever pivot nut or stud is loosened or removed using new Watts link pivot nut and stud service kit.
8. If Watts link pivot stud on axle loosens while removing pivot nut, continue to

loosen pivot stud until open end wrench can inserted to hold pivot stud. While holding pivot stud, remove and discard pivot nut.
9. Lower axle until Watts link is free of pivot stud. Remove lateral arm.
10. Remove and discard Watts link pivot stud.
11. Reverse procedure to install, noting the following:
   a. Install new Watts link pivot stud.
   b. Rear suspension lateral arm pivot bolts and Watts link pivot nut must be tightened with vehicle at curb height.
   c. Install lateral arm on pivot stud ensuring righthand arm flange faces front of vehicle.
   d. Raise axle until lateral arm aligns with frame brackets and install new pivot bolts and nuts. **Do not tighten now.**
   e. Raise axle to compresses shock absorber to previously established alignment mark (curb height). Tighten bolts.

STABILIZER BAR
REPLACE

1. **On models equipped with air suspension,** turn air suspension switch to

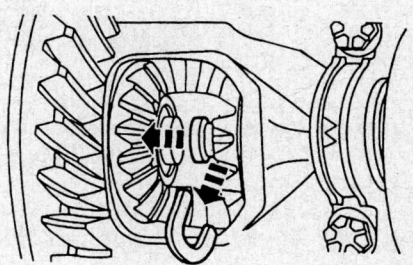

Fig. 4 Axle shaft C-lock replacement

Off position, then vent air from system as outlined in "Active Suspension Systems" chapter.
2. **On all models,** raise and support vehicle.
3. Support rear axle using hi-lift jack tool No. 014-00942, or equivalent.
4. Remove both stabilizer bar link lower mounting nuts and bushings.
5. Remove upper mounting nuts, bushings and both stabilizer bar links.
6. Remove mounting bolts, both stabilizer bars and brackets.
7. Reverse procedure to install.

TIGHTENING SPECIFICATIONS

Year	Component	Torque Ft. Lbs.
2004–06	Caliper Locating Pin	21–26
	Driveshaft Flange Bolt	70–95
	Height Sensor Mounting Bracket To Lateral Arm	9–12
	Lateral Arm To Frame Bracket	65–88
	Lateral Arm To Watts Link Pivot	60–77
	Lower Arm To Axle & Frame	95–127
	Lower Arm To Frame	120–150
	Pinion Shaft Lock Bolt	15–29
	Rear Cover	25–34
	Shock Absorber To Axle Bracket	57–75
	Shock Absorber Upper	26–34
	Stabilizer Bar Bracket Bolt To Axle	16–21
	Stabilizer Link Nut To Stabilizer Bar	13–16
	Upper Arm To Axle	65–88
	Upper Arm To Frame	95–127
	Watts Link Pivot, Nut	158–212
	Watts Link Pivot, Stud	189–211
	Wheel Lug Nut	80–106

Front Suspension & Steering

NOTE: On Air Bag Equipped Models, Refer To "Air Bag System Precautions" Located In The Front Of This Manual For System Disarming & Arming Procedures.

NOTE: Refer To "Computer Relearn Procedure" Located In The Front Of This Manual When Battery Power To The Computer Has Been Interrupted.

INDEX

	Page No.		Page No.		Page No.
Ball Joint, Replace	2-36	Power Steering Gear, Replace	2-37	Stabilizer Bar, Replace	2-37
Ball Joint Inspection	2-36	Power Steering Pump, Replace	2-37	Steering Columns	12-1
Coil Spring, Replace	2-36	Precautions	2-36	Tightening Specifications	2-37
Control Arm, Replace	2-37	Air Bag Systems	2-36	Wheel Bearing, Adjust	2-36
Lower	2-37	Air Suspension Pressure Relief	2-36	Wheel Bearing, Replace	2-36
Upper	2-37	Battery Ground Cable	2-36		
Power Steering	13-1	Shock Absorber, Replace	2-36		

PRECAUTIONS

Air Bag Systems

Refer to "Air Bag System Precautions" in the front of this manual for system disarming and arming procedures.

Air Suspension Pressure Relief

Before servicing any air suspension components, disconnect power to system by turning air suspension switch OFF or by disconnecting battery ground cable.

Do not remove an air spring under any circumstances when there is pressure in the air spring. Do not remove a component supporting an air spring without either exhausting the air or providing support for air spring. Refer to the "Active Suspension Systems" chapter to vent air from spring.

Battery Ground Cable

Prior to service, disconnect battery ground cable and isolate as required.

WHEEL BEARING
ADJUST

These models are equipped with sealed bearing units which do not require adjustment or maintenance. If the bearing is found to be faulty, then the hub and bearing must be replaced as an assembly.

WHEEL BEARING
REPLACE

1. Remove tire and wheel assembly.
2. Remove bolts, then position brake caliper, pads and anchor plate aside.
3. Remove brake rotor.

4. Disconnect electrical connector and unclip retainers.
5. Remove bolts, then the wheel bearing and hub assembly.
6. Reverse procedure to install.

BALL JOINT INSPECTION

On models equipped with air suspension, turn switch to Off position prior to raising and supporting vehicle.

Refer to "Specifications" section maximum backlash and endplay measurements.

1. Raise and support vehicle.
2. Inspect ball joint boos for tears. Replace ball joint as required.
3. Inspect wheel bearings.
4. Support lower control arm with suitable safety stand.
5. While assistant pushes and pulls equally on top and bottom of tire, observe any relative lateral backlash between upper control arm and front wheel spindle. Replace ball joint if lateral backlash is at or exceeds specifications.
6. While assistant moves tire up and down, observe any relative endplay between upper arm and front wheel spindle. Replace ball joint if endplay is at or exceeds specifications.
7. Remove tire and wheel assembly.
8. Separate lower arm from front wheel spindle. Disconnect mounting bolts and nuts.
9. Measure lateral backlash using suitable dial indicator while moving ball joint side to side. Replace ball joint if lateral backlash is at or exceeds specifications.
10. Measure endplay using suitable dial indicator while moving ball joint up and down. Replace ball joint if endplay is at or exceeds specifications.

BALL JOINT
REPLACE

The ball joint is not serviced separately. If the ball joint requires service, the lower or upper control arm will need to be replaced.

COIL SPRING
REPLACE

1. Remove and discard three upper shock absorber nuts.
2. Remove tire and wheel assembly.
3. Remove bolts, then position brake caliper, pads and anchor plate aside.
4. Remove brake rotor.
5. Remove nuts, then the stabilizer link. Discard nuts.
6. Remove and discard remaining shock absorber nuts.
7. Remove shock absorber and spring assembly.
8. Mount shock absorber and spring assembly in suitable holding device, then mark upper mount, spring and shock absorber for reference during assembly.
9. Compress spring using suitable spring compressor.
10. While holding shock absorber rod, remove and discard nut.
11. Remove upper mount and dust boot assembly.
12. Carefully remove spring and spring compressor.
13. Reverse procedure to install.

SHOCK ABSORBER
REPLACE

1. Remove and discard three upper shock absorber nuts.
2. Remove tire and wheel assembly.
3. Remove bolts, then position brake caliper, pads and anchor plate aside.
4. Remove brake rotor.
5. Remove nuts, then the stabilizer link. Discard nuts.

6. Remove and discard remaining shock absorber nuts.
7. Remove shock absorber and spring assembly.
8. Reverse procedure to install.

CONTROL ARM

REPLACE

Lower

1. Remove tire and wheel assembly.
2. Remove and discard lower nut.
3. Remove nut and flag bolt. Discard nut.
4. Remove and discard nuts and bolts.
5. Remove studs, then position steering gear upward to access cam bolt.
6. Remove cam bolt, then the lower control arm.
7. Reverse procedure to install. Do not tighten nuts and bolts until weight of vehicle is resting on control arm.

UPPER

1. Remove tire and wheel assembly.
2. Remove bolts, then position brake caliper, pads and anchor plate aside.
3. Remove brake rotor.
4. Raise suspension arms until pressure is released from stabilizer bar links using suitable jack stand.
5. Remove stabilizer bar nuts, then the stabilizer bar. Discard nuts.

6. Detach electrical retainers from arm and wheel knuckle.
7. Remove nuts, bolts and upper arm. Discard nuts.
8. Reverse procedure to install, noting the following:
   a. Do not tighten upper arm to crossmember nuts until weight of vehicle is resting on tire and wheel assemblies.
   b. Inspect wheel alignment.

STABILIZER BAR

REPLACE

1. Remove tire and wheel assemblies.
2. Remove bolts, then position brake caliper, pads and anchor plate aside.
3. Remove brake rotor.
4. Raise suspension arms until pressure is released from stabilizer bar links using suitable jack stand.
5. Remove nuts, then the stabilizer bar links. Discard nuts.
6. Remove nuts, brackets and stabilizer bar. Discard nuts.
7. Reverse procedure to install.

POWER STEERING GEAR

REPLACE

1. Hold steering wheel in straight ahead position using suitable holding device.

2. Remove tire and wheel assemblies.
3. Remove nuts, then detach tie rods from wheel knuckles.
4. Remove bolt, then detach intermediate shaft from steering gear. **Do not allow intermediate shaft to rotate while it is disconnected from steering gear.**
5. Disconnect power steering lines and drain fluid into suitable container.
6. Disconnect electrical connector.
7. Remove nuts, studs and power steering gear.
8. Reverse procedure to install.

POWER STEERING PUMP

REPLACE

1. Disconnect power steering pump return line and allow power steering pump fluid to drain into suitable container.
2. Disconnect power steering pump pressure hose from pump fitting.
3. Disconnect drive belt, then remove pulley and power steering pump.
4. Reverse procedure to install, noting the following:
   a. **Do not overtighten pressure hose fitting.**
   b. Swivel and/or endplay of fitting is normal and does not indicate loose fitting.

TIGHTENING SPECIFICATIONS

Year	Component	Torque Ft. Lbs
2004–06	Brake Caliper Anchor Plate To Wheel Knuckle	118
	Hub To Wheel Knuckle	74
	Lower Arm To Crossmember To Cam Bolt	166
	Lower Arm To Frame	85
	Lower Ball Joint To Wheel Knuckle Nut	111
	Power Steering Pump	18
	Shock Absorber To Crossmember Upper Nuts	22
	Shock Absorber To Lower Arm Nut & Flag Bolt	166
	Shock Absorber Top Stud Nut	37
	Stabilizer Bar Bracket To Frame	46
	Stabilizer Bar Links	46
	Steering Gear To Crossmember Stud Nuts	76
	Steering Gear To Crossmember Studs	13
	Tie Rod End To Wheel Knuckle	59
	Upper Arm To Crossmember	111
	Upper Ball Joint To Wheel Knuckle	111
	Wheel Bearing	74

Wheel Alignment

INDEX

	Page No.
Front Wheel Alignment	2-38
Caster & Camber	2-38

	Page No.
Toe-In & Steering Wheel Spoke Position	2-38

	Page No.
Preliminary Inspection	2-38
Wheel Alignment Specifications	2-2

PRELIMINARY INSPECTION

Prior to performing the front wheel alignment, a preliminary inspection should be made to determine the condition of the vehicle's suspension components. The following inspections and procedures should be made prior to performing front wheel alignment:

1. Vehicle must be leveled by performing air suspension system test. as outlined in "Active Suspensions" chapter.
2. Inflate tires to specified pressure (cold).
3. Measure vehicle ride height.
4. Inspect suspension and steering components for looseness.
5. Inspect existing caster, camber and toe settings prior to alignment.
6. Inspect suspension mounting bolts for proper tightness.
7. Alignment equipment must be capable of four wheel alignment.
8. Alignment rack must be leveled to 1/16 inch, side to side and front to rear, and be equipped with wheel runout compensation.

FRONT WHEEL ALIGNMENT

Caster & Camber

1. Remove and discard cam bolt retainer flag or lefthand caster bushing centering washer.
2. Inspect caster and chamber and record readings.
3. Loosen cam bolt nut, then rotate cam bolt to adjust camber, **Fig. 1.**
4. While holding cam bolt, **torque** nut to 166 ft. lbs.
5. Loosen nut and move arm inward to decrease caster and outward to increase caster, **Fig. 2.**
6. While holding arm **torque** nut to 111 ft. lbs.

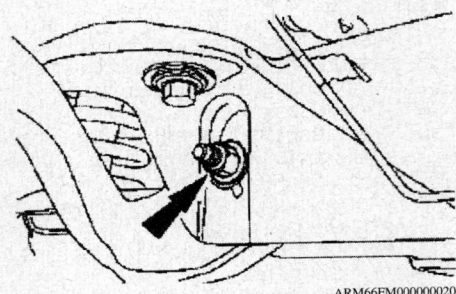

Fig. 1   Camber adjustment

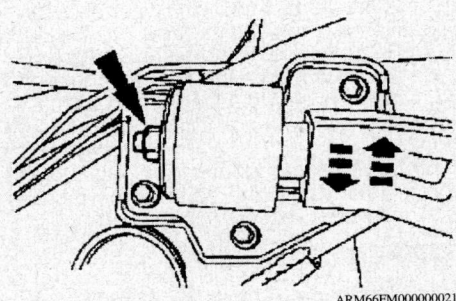

Fig. 2   Caster adjustment

Toe-In & Steering Wheel Spoke Position

After adjusting caster and camber, inspect steering wheel spoke position with front wheels in straight ahead position. If spokes are not in normal position, adjusted while toe is being adjusted.

1. Loosen two clamp bolts on each front wheel spindle tie rod adjusting sleeve, **Fig. 3.**
2. Adjust toe-in. If steering wheel spokes are in normal position, lengthen or shorten both rods equally to obtain correct toe.
3. If steering wheel spokes are not correct, make required rod adjustments to obtain correct toe-in and steering wheel alignment.
4. When toe-in and steering wheel position are both correct, lubricate clamp, bolts and nuts.
5. **Torque** clamp bolts on both connecting rod sleeves to 20–22 ft. lbs.
6. Sleeve position should not be changed when clamp bolts are tightened for proper clamp bolt orientation.

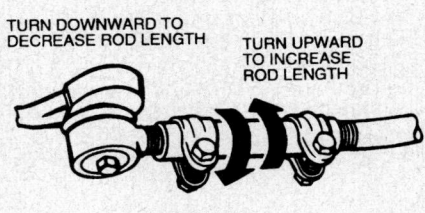

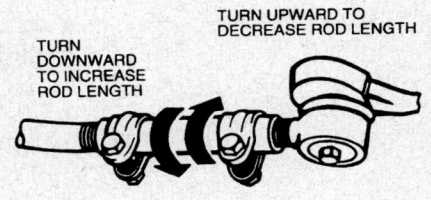

Fig. 3   Toe adjustment

LS & THUNDERBIRD

NOTE: Refer To Rear Of This Manual For Vehicle Manufacturer's Special Service Tool Suppliers.

INDEX OF SERVICE OPERATIONS

Page No.

AIR BAG SYSTEM
PRECAUTIONS 0-18
BRAKES
   Anti-Lock Brakes (Volume 2).. 6-1
   Disc Brakes.................. 14-1
   Drum Brakes 15-1
   Hydraulic Brake Systems 16-1
   Power Brake Units........... 17-1
COMPUTER RELEARN
PROCEDURE 0-31
ELECTRICAL
   Air Bag System (Volume 2) ... 4-1
   Air Conditioning.............. 8-1
   Alternator, Replace 3-6
   Alternators.................. 11-1
   Auxiliary Coolant Flow Pump,
   Replace 3-10
   Blower Motor, Replace........ 3-9
   Cabin Air Filter, Replace 3-9
   Clutch Start Switch, Replace.. 3-7
   Cooling Fans 9-1
   Cruise Control (Volume 2) 2-1
   Dash Gauges (Volume 2) 1-1
   Dash Panel Service
   (Volume 2) 5-1
   Digital Transmission Range
   (TR) Sensor, Replace......... 3-7
   Dual Coolant Flow Valve,
   Replace 3-10
   Evaporator Core, Replace 3-10
   Fuel Pump Relay Location 3-6
   Fuse Panel & Flasher
   Location 3-6
   Headlamp Switch, Replace ... 3-7
   Heater Core, Replace......... 3-9
   Ignition Coil, Replace 3-6
   Ignition Lock, Replace 3-6
   Ignition Switch, Replace 3-7
   Instrument Cluster, Replace... 3-8
   Module Configuration 3-5
   Multi-Function Switch,
   Replace 3-8
   Neutral Safety Switch,
   Replace 3-7
   Passive Restraint Systems
   (Volume 2)................... 4-1
   Precautions................. 3-5
   Radio, Replace 3-8
   Speed Controls (Volume 2) ... 2-1
   Starter Motors 10-1
   Starter, Replace 3-6
   Steering Columns............ 12-1
   Steering Wheel, Replace...... 3-8
   Stop Light Switch, Replace ... 3-8
   Technical Service Bulletins.... 3-10
   Wiper Motor, Replace......... 3-8
   Wiper Switch, Replace........ 3-9
   Wiper Systems (Volume 2).... 3-1
   Wiper Transmission, Replace . 3-9
ELECTRICAL SYMBOL
IDENTIFICATION 0-63

Page No.

NON-STANDARD TIRE &
WHEEL SIZE
ADJUSTMENT TO RIDE
HEIGHT SPECIFICATIONS
& TIRE SIZE CHART 0-61
FRONT SUSPENSION &
STEERING
   Ball Joint Inspection 3-47
   Coil Spring & Strut Service.... 3-47
   Control Arm, Replace 3-48
   Description 3-47
   Hub & Bearing, Replace 3-47
   Power Steering 13-1
   Power Steering Control Valve
   Actuator, Replace 3-50
   Power Steering Fluid Cooler,
   Replace 3-50
   Power Steering Gear,
   Replace 3-49
   Power Steering Pump,
   Replace 3-49
   Power Steering System
   Bleed 3-49
   Precautions................. 3-47
   Stabilizer Bar, Replace........ 3-49
   Steering Columns............ 12-1
   Steering Knuckle, Replace 3-48
   Steering Wheel Rotation
   Sensor, Replace 3-50
   Strut, Replace 3-47
   Tie Rod, Replace 3-49
   Tightening Specifications...... 3-53
   Wheel Bearing Inspection..... 3-47
REAR AXLE &
SUSPENSION
   Ball Joint, Replace............ 3-43
   Ball Joint Inspection 3-42
   Control Arm, Replace 3-43
   Description 3-39
   Driveline Angle Measurement . 3-40
   Hub & Bearing, Replace 3-42
   Knuckle, Replace 3-43
   Pinion Flange & Seal,
   Replace 3-40
   Precautions................. 3-39
   Propeller Shaft, Replace 3-41
   Propeller Shaft Alignment
   Bushing 3-42
   Propeller Shaft Center
   Bearing, Replace 3-41
   Rear Axle, Replace 3-39
   Rear Halfshaft, Replace....... 3-40
   Stabilizer Bar, Replace........ 3-44
   Stabilizer Bar Link, Replace... 3-44
   Strut, Replace 3-43
   Strut Service................. 3-43
   Stub Shaft Bearing & Seal,
   Replace 3-39
   Technical Service Bulletins 3-44
   Tightening Specifications...... 3-46
   Toe Link, Replace 3-43
   U-joint, Replace............. 3-41
   Wheel Bearing Inspection..... 3-43

Page No.

REAR DRIVE AXLE.......... 19-1
SERVICE REMINDER &
WARNING LAMP RESET
PROCEDURES 0-34
SPECIFICATIONS
   Fluid Capacities & Cooling
   System Data................. 3-4
   Front Wheel Alignment
   Specifications............... 3-2
   General Engine
   Specifications............... 3-2
   Lubricant Data.............. 3-4
   Rear Wheel Alignment
   Specifications............... 3-3
   Tune Up Specifications 3-2
   Vehicle Ride Height
   Specifications............... 3-3
TIRE PRESSURE
MONITORING SYSTEM 20-1
VEHICLE
IDENTIFICATION 0-1
VEHICLE LIFT POINTS....... 0-51
VEHICLE MAINTENANCE
SCHEDULES 0-73
WHEEL ALIGNMENT
   Front Wheel Alignment 3-54
   Preliminary Inspection 3-54
   Rear Wheel Alignment 3-54
   Wheel Alignment
   Specifications............... 3-2
WIRE COLOR CODE
IDENTIFICATION 0-63
3.0L ENGINE
   Camshaft, Replace 3-17
   Compression Pressure........ 3-12
   Cooling System Bleed 3-19
   Crankshaft Damper, Replace.. 3-15
   Crankshaft Rear Oil Seal,
   Replace 3-18
   Cylinder Head, Replace....... 3-14
   Engine Rebuilding
   Specifications................. 21-1
   Engine, Replace 3-13
   Engine Mount, Replace....... 3-12
   Exhaust Manifold, Replace.... 3-14
   Front Cover, Replace 3-15
   Front Cover Seal, Replace.... 3-16
   Fuel Filter, Replace 3-20
   Fuel Pump, Replace.......... 3-20
   Hydraulic Cooling Fan Pump,
   Replace 3-20
   Hydraulic Fan Motor, Replace. 3-20
   Intake Manifold, Replace...... 3-14
   Main & Rod Bearings 3-17
   Oil Cooler, Replace 3-18
   Oil Pan, Replace............. 3-18
   Oil Pump, Replace........... 3-18
   Piston & Rod Assembly 3-17
   Precautions................. 3-12
   Quick Disconnect Hoses...... 3-12
   Radiator, Replace 3-19
   Serpentine Drive Belt 3-18

LS & THUNDERBIRD

	Page No.		Page No.		Page No.
Thermostat, Replace	3-19	Cylinder Head, Replace	3-27	Oil Pan, Replace	3-30
Tightening Specifications	3-24	Engine Rebuilding Specifications	21-1	Oil Pump, Replace	3-31
Timing Chain, Replace	3-16	Engine, Replace	3-26	Precautions	3-25
Valve Adjustment	3-15	Engine Mount, Replace	3-25	Quick Disconnect Hoses	3-25
Valve Arrangement	3-15	Exhaust Manifold, Replace	3-27	Radiator, Replace	3-31
Valve Cover, Replace	3-15	Front Cover, Replace	3-28	Serpentine Drive Belt	3-31
Water Pump, Replace	3-19	Front Cover Seal, Replace	3-29	Thermostat, Replace	3-31
3.9L ENGINE		Fuel Filter, Replace	3-32	Tightening Specifications	3-38
Camshaft, Replace	3-30	Fuel Pump, Replace	3-32	Timing Chain, Replace	3-29
Compression Pressure	3-25	Hydraulic Cooling Fan Pump, Replace	3-32	Timing Chain Tensioner, Replace	3-30
Cooling System Bleed	3-31	Hydraulic Fan Motor, Replace	3-32	Valve Adjustment	3-28
Crankshaft Damper, Replace	3-28	Intake Manifold, Replace	3-26	Valve Arrangement	3-28
Crankshaft Rear Oil Seal, Replace	3-30	Oil Cooler, Replace	3-31	Valve Cover, Replace	3-27
				Water Pump, Replace	3-31

Specifications

GENERAL ENGINE SPECIFICATIONS

Year	Engine (Code)①	Fuel System	Bore x Stroke, Inches	Comp. Ratio	Net HP @ RPM	Maximum Torque, Ft. Lbs. @ RPM	Normal Oil Pressure, psi
2004–06	3.0L (S)	SFI	3.50 x 3.13	10.5	232 @ 6750	220 @ 4500	20–45②
	3.9L (A)	SFI	3.38 x 3.35	10.8	280 @ 6000	286 @ 4000	61–73③

① — The eighth digit of the VIN denotes engine code.

② — At operating temperature & 1500 RPM.

③ — At operating temperature & 400 RPM.

TUNE UP SPECIFICATIONS

Year & Engine (Code)①	Spark Plug Gap, Inch	Ignition Timing BTDC			Idle Speed⑩		Fuel Pump Pressure	Valve Lash, Inch
		Firing Order ⑨	BTDC°	Mark	Curb	Fast		
3.0L	.051–.057	④	⑤	⑥	②	②	30–65	⑦
3.9L	.039–.043	⑧	⑤	⑥	②	②	30–65	③

BTDC — Before Top Dead Center

D — Drive.

① — Eighth digit of Vehicle Identification Number (VIN) denotes engine code.

② — Idle speed is electronically controlled and is not adjustable.

③ — Intake, .007–.009 inch. Exhaust, .009–.011 inch.

④ — Cylinder numbering from front to rear of engine, righthand bank, 1-2-3; lefthand bank, 4-5-6. Firing order, 1-4-2-5-3-6.

⑤ — Not adjustable.

⑥ — Equipped w/crankshaft sensor.

⑦ — Intake, .007–.009 inch. Exhaust, .012–.015 inch.

⑧ — Equipped with coil on plug ignition system. Firing order, 1-5-4-2-6-3-7-8.

⑨ — Before disconnecting wires from coil unit, determine location of ignition wires, as position may have been altered from that outlined at end of this chart.

⑩ — When adjusting idle speed, set parking brake & chock drive wheels.

FRONT WHEEL ALIGNMENT SPECIFICATIONS

Year	Caster Angle°				Camber Angle°				Toe-In°	Ball Joint Wear, Inch①
	Limits	Desired	Split		Limits	Desired	Split			
			Limits	Desired			Limits	Desired		
2004–06	+7.6 to +8.6	+8.1	-.7 to +.7	0	-.65 to +.35	-.15	-.7 to +.7	0	-.09 to +.41	1/32

① — Radial play.

REAR WHEEL ALIGNMENT SPECIFICATIONS

Year	Camber°		Toe-In°				Ball Joint Wear, Inch①
	Limits	Desired	Limits	Desired	Split		
					Limits	Desired	
2004–06	-1.75 to -.25	-1	-.13 to +.37	+.12	-.01 to +.49	+.24	1/32

① — Radial play.

VEHICLE RIDE HEIGHT SPECIFICATIONS

Year	Front, Inches①	Rear, Inches①	Ride Height Difference, Inches	
			Side To Side	Front To Rear
LS				
2004–06	1.5–1.7②	.4–1.4③	.5	.6
THUNDERBIRD				
2004–05	2.1–2.7②	.7–1.3③	.5	.6

① — See door sticker or inside of glove box for manufacturers original tire size specifications. If tires on vehicle do not match manufacturers original tire size & measurement is not within limits, it will be required to refer to the "Non-Standard Tire & Wheel Size Adjustment To Ride Height Specification & Tire Size Adjustment Charts" in the front of this manual for approximate changes in ride height specifications.

② — Measure front vehicle ride height, **Fig. A.**

③ — Measure rear vehicle ride height, **Fig. B.**

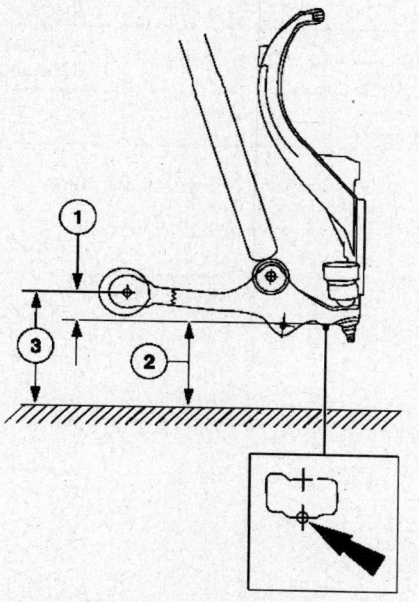

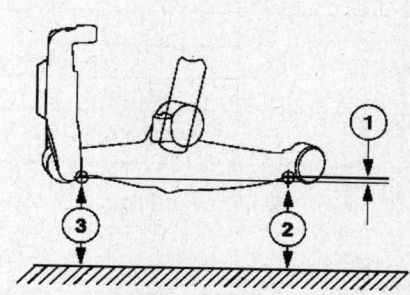

Item	Description
1	Ride height = A-B
2	Measurement A
3	Measurement B

FM2049900064000X

Fig. B Rear ride height measurement

Item	Description
1	Ride height = B-A
2	Measurement A
3	Measurement B

FM2049900063000X

Fig. A Front ride height measurement

LS & THUNDERBIRD

FLUID CAPACITIES & COOLING SYSTEM DATA

Year	Engine	Coolant Capacity, Qts.		Coolant Type	Radiator Cap Relief Pressure, Lbs.	Thermo. Opening Temp.	Fuel Tank, Gals.	Engine Oil Refill, Qts.④	Rear Axle, Pts.③	Transmission Oil	
		Less A/C	With A/C							Man. Trans., Pts.	Auto. Trans., Qts.
2004–06	3.0L	10.6	10.6	Ethylene Glycol	16	①	18	6.9	3	②	11.9
	3.9L	11.3	11.3	Ethylene Glycol	16	①	18	6.0	3	—	11.9

① — Thermostat begins to open at 192–199°F and is fully open at 219°F.

② — Fill transmission to .02 inch below lower edge of fill plug bore.

③ — Fill ⅛–³⁄₁₆ inch from bottom of filler hole.

④ — Includes engine oil filter.

LUBRICANT DATA

Year	Lubricant Type					
	Transmission		Rear Axle	Power Steering	Brake System	Hydraulic Clutch Fluid
	Manual	Automatic				
2004–06	Mercon ATF	Mercon V XT-5-Q-M	①	②	DOT 3	DOT 3

① — Use 75W-140 synthetic rear axle lubricant F1TZ-19580-B, or equivalent, meeting Ford specification WSL-M2C192-A.

② — Use Motorcraft Mercon multi-purpose ATF transmission fluid XT-2-QDX, or equivalent, meeting Ford specification Mercon.

Electrical

NOTE: On Air Bag Equipped Models, Refer To "Air Bag System Precautions" Located In The Front Of This Manual For System Disarming & Arming Procedures.

NOTE: Refer To "Computer Relearn Procedures" Located In The Front Of This Manual When Battery Power To The Computer Has Been Interrupted.

INDEX

	Page No.
Air Bag System (Volume 2)	4-1
Air Conditioning	8-1
Alternator, Replace	3-6
3.0L Engine	3-6
3.9L Engine	3-6
Alternators	11-1
Auxiliary Coolant Flow Pump, Replace	3-10
Blower Motor, Replace	3-9
Cabin Air Filter, Replace	3-9
LS	3-9
Thunderbird	3-9
Clutch Start Switch, Replace	3-7
Cooling Fans	9-1
Cruise Control (Volume 2)	2-1
Dash Gauges (Volume 2)	1-1
Dash Panel Service (Volume 2)	5-1
Digital Transmission Range (TR) Sensor, Replace	3-7
Installation	3-7
Removal	3-7
Dual Coolant Flow Valve, Replace	3-10

	Page No.
Evaporator Core, Replace	3-10
Fuel Pump Relay Location	3-6
Fuse Panel & Flasher Location	3-6
Battery Junction Box	3-6
Central Junction Box	3-6
Flasher	3-6
Interior Auxiliary Junction Box	3-6
Trailer Tow Auxiliary Junction Box	3-6
Underhood Auxiliary Junction Box	3-6
Headlamp Switch, Replace	3-7
Heater Core, Replace	3-9
LS	3-9
Thunderbird	3-10
Ignition Coil, Replace	3-6
3.0L Engine	3-6
3.9L Engine	3-6
Ignition Lock, Replace	3-6
Ignition Switch, Replace	3-7
Instrument Cluster, Replace	3-8
Module Configuration	3-5
Multi-Function Switch, Replace	3-8
Neutral Safety Switch, Replace	3-7

	Page No.
Passive Restraint Systems (Volume 2)	4-1
Precautions	3-5
Air Bag Systems	3-5
Battery Ground Cable	3-5
Electrostatic Discharge	3-5
Radio, Replace	3-8
Speed Controls (Volume 2)	2-1
Starter Motors	10-1
Starter, Replace	3-6
Steering Columns	12-1
Steering Wheel, Replace	3-8
Stop Light Switch, Replace	3-8
Technical Service Bulletins	3-10
Blower Motor Inoperative	3-10
2005 LS & Thunderbird models	3-10
Wiper Motor, Replace	3-8
LS	3-8
Thunderbird	3-9
Wiper Switch, Replace	3-9
Wiper Systems (Volume 2)	3-1
Wiper Transmission, Replace	3-9

PRECAUTIONS

Air Bag Systems

Refer to "Air Bag System Precautions" in the front of this manual for system disarming and arming procedures.

Battery Ground Cable

Prior to service, disconnect battery ground cable and isolate as required.

Electrostatic Discharge

Electronic modules are sensitive to electrical charges. Ensure modules are not exposed to these charges or damage may result.

MODULE CONFIGURATION

Newly released modules will require configuration after being installed on the vehicle. All configurable modules will be packaged in a kit which contains a warning label and multi-language sheet which lists requirements to configure the modules.

There are two types of configuration data. The first type is used by the module so that it can interact with the vehicle correctly. The second type is customer preference driven. These are items that the customer may or may not want to have enabled. To program customer driven preferences, a Ford Service Function (FSF) card and the New Generation Star Tester (NGS), tool No. 007-00500, or equivalents, must be used to toggle preferences on or off.

The New Generation Star Tester (NGS), tool No. 007-00500, or equivalent, must be used to retrieve configuration data from the old module before it is removed from the vehicle. This information will be transferred into the new module so that the new module will contain the same settings as the old module.

The following modules require configuration when being replaced: Anti-Lock Brake System (ABS) module, ABS module with traction control, Interactive Vehicle Dynamic (IVD) module, Instrument Cluster Module (ICM), ICM with message center, Message Center Module (MCM), Rear Electronic Module (REM), Front Electronic Module (FEM), Driver Door Module (DDM), Dual Automatic Temperature Control (DATC) module, Remote Emergency Satellite Cellular Unit (RESCU) module, Audio Control Module (ACM), Steering Column Lock Module (SCLM) and the Powertrain Control Module (PCM) when it is replaced on models equipped with a manual transmission. If configuring the PCM, a NGS tester flash cable tool No. 007-00531, or equivalent, must be used.

To perform the configuration process, proceed as follows:
1. Connect New Generation Star Tester tool No. 007-00500 with Ford Service Function (FSF) card, or equivalents, to vehicle DLC.
2. Follow scan tool instructions to upload configuration data.
3. Install new module. **NGS will not retain configuration data for more than 24 hours.**
4. Download stored configuration information to new module using FSF card and NGS tester.
5. If unable to carry out configuration process, proceed as follows:
   a. Inspect for signs of electrical damage.
   b. If NGS does not communicate with vehicle, ensure program card is correctly installed, vehicle connections are secure and ignition switch is in run position.

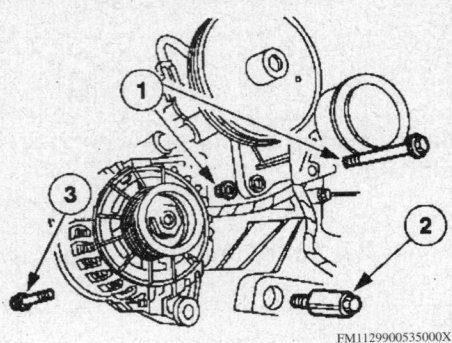

Fig. 1   Alternator bolt tightening sequence. 3.9L engine

c. If NGS still does not communicate with vehicle, diagnose module communications network concern.

FUSE PANEL & FLASHER LOCATION

Battery Junction Box

The battery junction box is located under the rear righthand side of the luggage compartment floor lining.

Central Junction Box

The central junction box is located under the righthand side of the instrument panel.

Interior Auxiliary Junction Box

The interior auxiliary junction box is located under the lefthand side of the instrument panel. This junction box contains a power junction stud and the DLC.

Underhood Auxiliary Junction Box

The underhood auxiliary junction box is located on the rear righthand side of the engine compartment.

Trailer Tow Auxiliary Junction Box

The trailer tow auxiliary junction box is located in the rear center of the luggage compartment.

Flasher

The flashing function is controlled by the front electronic module. The module is located at the lefthand A pillar.

FUEL PUMP RELAY LOCATION

The fuel pump relay is located under the luggage compartment floor lining in the battery junction box.

STARTER
REPLACE

1. Raise and support vehicle.
2. Remove ground strap from starter mounting stud.
3. Remove start cover and cables.
4. Remove mounting bolts and starter.
5. Reverse procedure to install. **Torque** starter mounting bolts to 18 ft. lbs.

ALTERNATOR
REPLACE
3.0L Engine

1. Remove accessory drive belt.
2. Raise and support vehicle.
3. Remove lower splash shield.
4. Support alternator, then remove mounting bolts.
5. Disconnect alternator electrical connections and remove alternator.
6. Reverse procedure to install, noting the following:
   a. **Torque** alternator electrical connectors to 71 inch lbs.
   b. **Torque** alternator mounting bolts to 33 ft. lbs.

3.9L Engine

1. Remove engine appearance cover.
2. Disconnect IAT sensor, breather hose and idle air control valve inlet tube.
3. Remove air intake tube support nut and washer.
4. Loosen tube clamps and remove tube.
5. Remove accessory drive belt.
6. Raise and support vehicle, then remove front lower splash shield.
7. Support alternator, then remove mounting bolts.
8. Turn alternator and remove positive cable.
9. Lower alternator and disconnect electrical connector.
10. Turn and remove alternator.
11. Reverse procedure to install, noting the following:
    a. **Torque** alternator electrical connector to 71 inch lbs.
    b. **Torque** alternator mounting bolts to 15 ft. lbs., then tighten an additional 90°, in sequence, **Fig. 1.**

IGNITION COIL
REPLACE

These engines use a coil on plug ignition system with an individual coil mounted on top of each spark plug.

3.0L Engine

1. Remove engine appearance cover.
2. If replacing righthand ignition coils, remove upper intake manifold as outlined under "Intake Manifold, Replace" in "3.0L Engine" section.
3. Disconnect coil electrical connector, **Fig. 2.**
4. Remove mounting bolts and ignition coil.

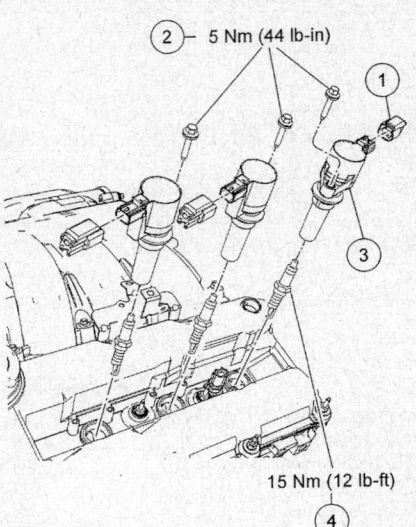

Item	Description
1	Ignition coil electrical connectors (3 required)
2	Ignition coil bolts (3 required)
3	Ignition coils (3 required)
4	Spark plugs (3 required)

Fig. 2   Ignition coil replacement. 3.0L engine

5. Reverse procedure to install, noting the following:
   a. Ensure coils are seated and boot is not damaged. If boot is damaged, coil must be replaced.
   b. **Torque** coil mounting bolts to 53 inch lbs.

3.9L Engine

1. Remove engine appearance cover.
2. Disconnect IAT sensor, breather hose and idle air control valve inlet tube.
3. Remove air intake tube support nut and washer.
4. Loosen tube clamps and remove tube.
5. Remove ignition coil cover, **Fig. 3.**
6. Disconnect coil electrical connectors.
7. Remove mounting bolts and ignition coils.
8. Reverse procedure to install. **Torque** mounting bolts to 44 inch lbs.

IGNITION LOCK
REPLACE

1. Remove steering column lower cover.
2. Remove mounting bolts and hood release handle.
3. Remove lower dash heater duct from below steering column.
4. Remove steering column opening cover reinforcement.
5. Place ignition switch in run position.
6. Depress ignition switch lock cylinder tab using suitable screwdriver, **Fig. 4.**
7. Remove ignition switch lock cylinder.
8. Reverse procedure to install.

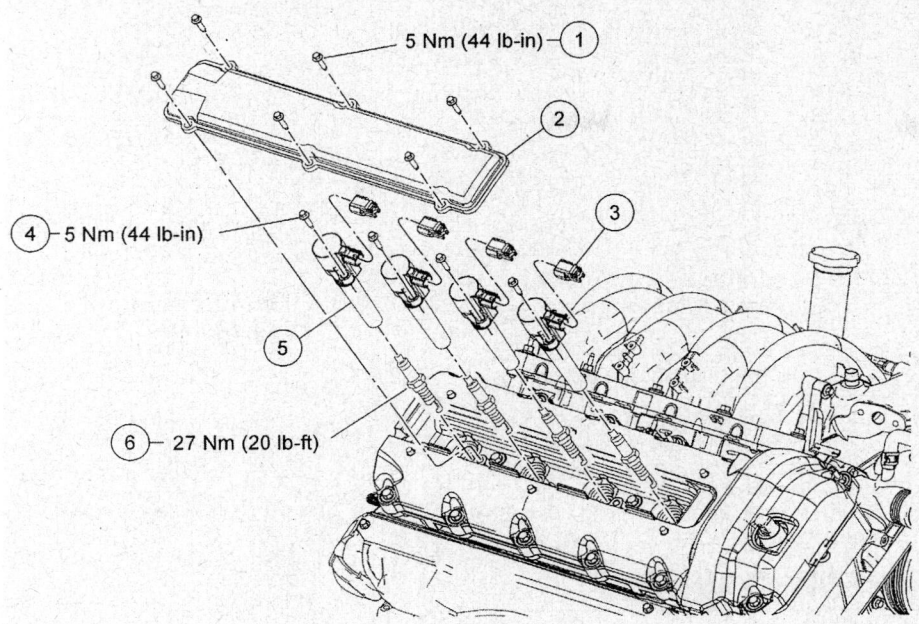

Fig. 3   Ignition coil replacement. 3.9L engine

Item	Description
1	Ignition coil cover bolt (6 required)
2	Ignition coil cover (2 required)
3	Ignition coil electrical connector (8 required)

Item	Description
4	Ignition coil bolt (8 required)
5	Ignition coil (8 required)
6	Spark plug (8 required)

ARM0500000000090

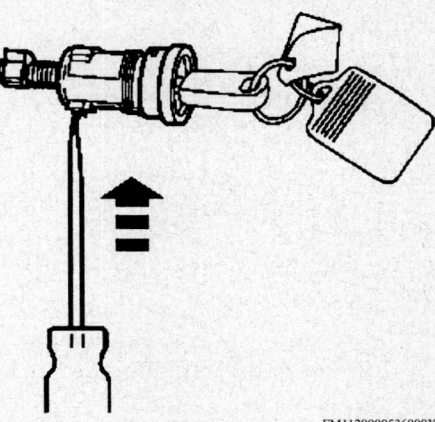

FM1129900536000X

Fig. 4   Ignition lock cylinder replacement

IGNITION SWITCH

REPLACE

1. Adjust steering column to full tilt down and full extended position.
2. Remove mounting bolts and hood release handle.
3. Disconnect electrical connectors, then remove lower steering column cover.
4. Disconnect electrical connectors and remove outer instrument panel finish panel, **Fig. 5.**
5. Remove inner instrument panel finish panel and instrument cluster finish panel mounting screws.
6. Disconnect in-vehicle air temperature sensor electrical connector and remove instrument cluster finish panel.
7. Remove mounting bolts and steering column reinforcement.
8. Disconnect ignition switch electrical connector and remove ignition switch lock cylinder mounting screws.
9. Remove ignition switch lock cylinder, **Fig. 6.**
10. With ignition switch in OFF position, remove set screw and ignition switch, **Fig. 7.**
11. Reverse procedure to install.

CLUTCH START SWITCH

REPLACE

1. Disconnect clutch pedal position switch electrical connector.

2. Lift retaining tag and remove switch, **Fig. 8.**
3. Reverse procedure to install.

NEUTRAL SAFETY SWITCH

REPLACE

Refer to "Digital Transmission Range (TR) Sensor, Replace" for neutral safety switch replacement procedure.

DIGITAL TRANSMISSION RANGE (TR) SENSOR

REPLACE

Removal

1. Raise and support vehicle.
2. Disconnect oxygen sensor and catalyst monitor electrical connectors.
3. Remove mounting nuts and three-way catalytic converter.
4. Remove mounting nuts and heat shield.
5. Make index marks on bolts, washers and nuts, to indicate installation position of driveshaft flex coupling to transmission flange and pinion flanges.
6. Make index marks on front driveshaft companion flange and transmission

flange, then remove companion flange to transmission flange mounting bolts. **Do not remove driveshaft flex coupling mounting bolts.**
7. Slide front driveshaft rearward and support transmission with suitable transmission jack. Secure transmission to jack using suitable safety chain.
8. Remove transmission mount, then lower transmission to gain access to digital TR sensor.
9. Disconnect shift cable.
10. Disconnect TR sensor electrical connector, then remove sensor.

Installation

1. Place TR sensor flush against boss on transmission case, then loosely install sensor mounting bolts.
2. Place manual lever in neutral position.
3. Align TR sensor using sensor alignment tool No. T97L-70010-A, or equivalent.
4. **Torque** sensor screws evenly to 89 inch lbs., then connect TR sensor electrical connector.
5. Connect shift cable and install rear transmission support.
6. Adjust shift cable as outlined in **MOTOR's "Domestic Transmission, In-Vehicle Service." or "Transmission Service DVD."**
7. Align index marks and **torque** companion flange to transmission flange bolts to 60 ft. lbs.
8. Install heat shield and catalytic converter, lower vehicle.

HEADLAMP SWITCH

REPLACE

1. Remove lower instrument panel steering column cover.
2. Remove outer instrument panel finish panel located on lefthand side of steering column.
3. Release four retaining clips, then remove headlamp switch from outer instrument panel finish panel.
4. Reverse procedure to install.

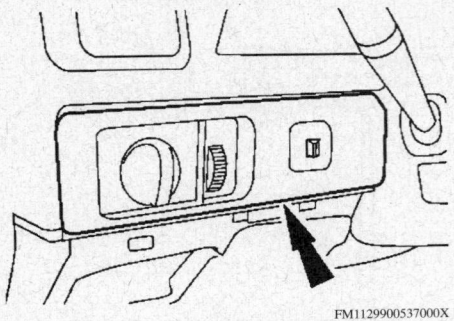

Fig. 5 Outer instrument panel finish panel replacement

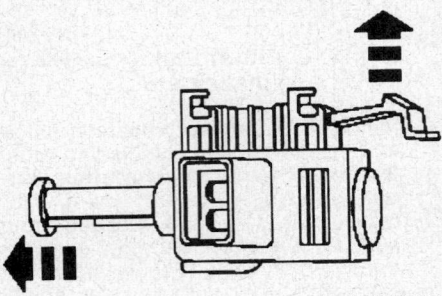

Fig. 8 Clutch pedal position switch

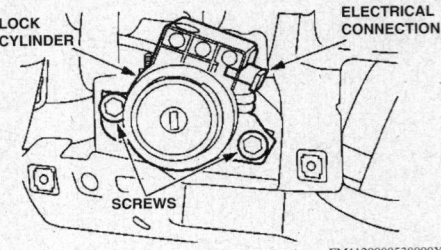

Fig. 6 Ignition switch lock cylinder replacement

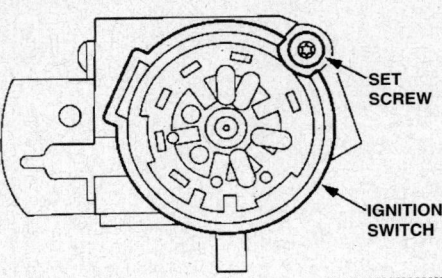

Fig. 7 Ignition switch replacement

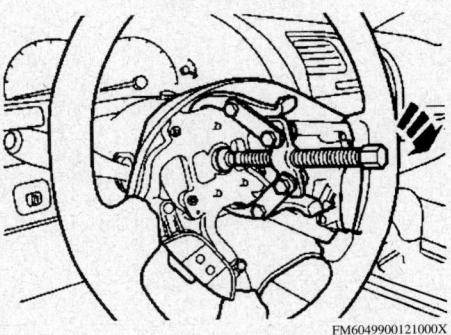

Fig. 9 Steering wheel replacement

STOP LIGHT SWITCH
REPLACE

1. Remove instrument panel insulator.
2. Disconnect and remove brake pedal position switch.
3. Reverse procedure to install.

MULTI-FUNCTION SWITCH
REPLACE

1. Ensure front wheels are in straight ahead position.
2. Remove driver's air bag module as outlined in "Passive Restraints Systems" chapter.
3. Remove horn switch.
4. Loosen steering wheel mounting bolt.
5. Loosen steering wheel using differential bearing cone removal tool No. T77F-4220-B1, or equivalent, **Fig. 9.**
6. Remove steering wheel puller, steering wheel mounting bolt and steering wheel. Discard steering wheel mounting bolt.
7. Remove mounting bolts and hood release handle.
8. Disconnect electrical connectors, then remove lower steering column cover.
9. Disconnect electrical connectors and remove outer instrument panel finish panel, **Fig. 5.**
10. Remove inner instrument panel finish panel and instrument cluster finish panel mounting screws.
11. Disconnect in-vehicle air temperature sensor electrical connector and remove instrument cluster finish panel.

12. Apply two strips of masking tape across air bag sliding contact to prevent rotation.
13. Depress three clips and position air bag sliding contact aside.
14. Disconnect multi-function switch electrical connector, then remove switch.
15. Reverse procedure to install. **Torque** steering wheel bolt to 30 ft. lbs.

STEERING WHEEL
REPLACE

1. Ensure front wheels are in straight ahead position.
2. Remove driver's air bag module as outlined in "Passive Restraints Systems" chapter.
3. Remove horn switch.
4. Loosen steering wheel mounting bolt.
5. Loosen steering wheel using differential bearing cone removal tool No. T77F-4220-B1, or equivalent, **Fig. 9.**
6. Remove steering wheel puller, steering wheel mounting bolt and steering wheel. Discard steering wheel mounting bolt.
7. Reverse procedure to install. **Torque** new steering wheel mounting bolt to 30 ft. lbs.

INSTRUMENT CLUSTER
REPLACE

Prior to instrument cluster removal, module configuration must be retrieved. Refer to "Module Configuration" for procedure.
1. Remove mounting bolts and hood release handle.
2. Disconnect electrical connectors, then remove lower steering column cover.
3. Disconnect electrical connectors and remove outer instrument panel finish panel, **Fig. 5.**
4. Remove inner instrument panel finish panel and instrument cluster finish panel mounting screws.
5. Disconnect in-vehicle air temperature sensor electrical connector and remove instrument cluster finish panel.
6. Remove floor heat duct.
7. Remove steering column reinforcement.
8. Loosen steering column mounting bolts and lower steering column.
9. Place suitable cloth over upper steering column cover to prevent damage to instrument cluster lens.
10. Remove mounting bolts and instrument cluster.
11. Reverse procedure to install. Down-

load module configuration from NGS tester into new module.

RADIO
REPLACE

Prior to radio removal, module configuration must be retrieved. Refer to "Module Configuration" for procedure.
1. Remove air conditioning register finish panel.
2. Remove ash tray finish panel.
3. Remove audio/climate control mounting bolts.
4. Disconnect electrical connectors and antenna cable.
5. Remove audio/climate control unit.
6. Separate audio unit from audio/climate control assembly.
7. Reverse procedure to install. Download module configuration from NGS tester into new module.

WIPER MOTOR
REPLACE

LS

1. Remove mounting nuts and wiper pivot arms.
2. Remove two part pin retainers and separate Velcro attachment of rubber hinge cover to rear outboard corner of cowl vent screen.
3. Lift cowl vent screen to release clips.
4. Remove cowl vent screen.
5. Remove strut tower support brace.
6. Remove coolant overflow bottle and position aside.
7. Remove wiper mounting arm and pivot shaft bolts.

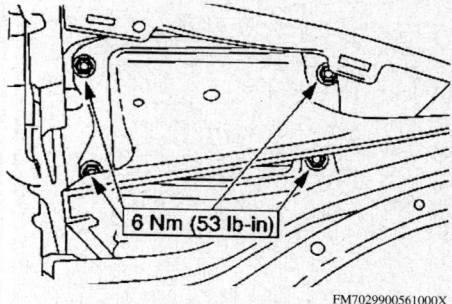

Fig. 10 Cabin air filter housing bolt locations

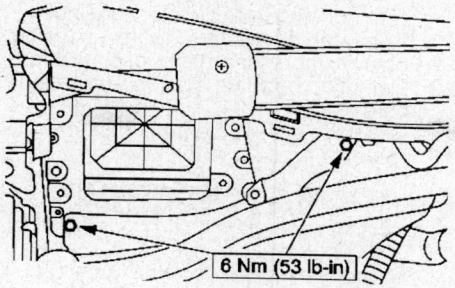

Fig. 11 Plenum panel replacement

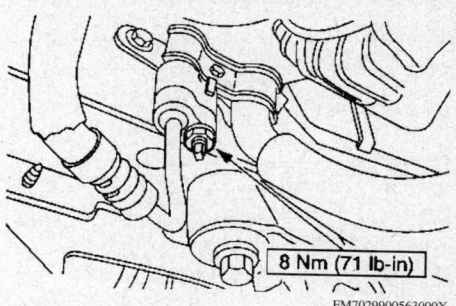

Fig. 12 Peanut fitting location

8. Disconnect drain boot from windshield wiper mounting arm and pivot shaft.
9. Position windshield wiper mounting arm and pivot shaft aside, then loosen upper windshield wiper motor bolt.
10. Turn wiper output arm to 6 o'clock position.
11. Remove lower wiper motor bolts.
12. Turn bottom of wiper mounting arm and pivot shaft upward.
13. Remove windshield wiper mounting arm and pivot shaft.
14. Remove remaining mounting bolts and wiper motor.
15. Reverse procedure to install, noting the following:
    a. **Torque** wiper pivot arm nuts to 18 ft. lbs.
    b. **Torque** strut support brace bolts to 15 ft. lbs.
    c. **Torque** mounting arm and pivot shaft bolts to 108 inch lbs.
    d. **Torque** wiper motor crank bolt and mounting bolts to 108 inch lbs.

Thunderbird

1. Remove mounting nuts and wiper arm pivot arms.
2. Remove lefthand and righthand cowl vent screen extension panels.
3. Disconnect windshield washer nozzle hoses from engine main wiring harness at lower righthand side of engine compartment.
4. Remove pin-type retainers and cowl vent screen.
5. Remove strut tower support brace.
6. Remove degas bottle and position aside. Route degas bottle lower hose in front of brake booster.
7. Remove wiper mounting arm and pivot shaft mounting bolts.
8. Disconnect drain boot from wiper mounting arm and pivot shaft,
9. Position wiper arm and pivot shaft aside, then loosen wiper motor mounting bolt.
10. Turn wiper output arm to 6 o'clock position, then remove lower wiper motor bolts.
11. Remove wiper mounting arm and pivot shaft by rotating upward.
12. Remove upper mounting and crank bolts, then the wiper motor.
13. Reverse procedure to install, noting the following:
    a. **Torque** wiper motor mounting bolts to 11 ft. lbs.

b. **Torque** wiper motor crank bolt and to 13 ft. lbs.
c. **Torque** strut support brace bolts to 15 ft. lbs.
d. **Torque** mounting arm and pivot shaft bolts to 108 inch lbs.

WIPER SWITCH
REPLACE

Refer to "Multi-Function Switch, Replace" for wiper switch replacement procedure.

WIPER TRANSMISSION
REPLACE

Refer to "Wiper Motor, Replace" for wiper transmission replacement procedure.

BLOWER MOTOR
REPLACE

1. Remove passenger side floor duct.
2. Remove blower motor cover.
3. Disconnect blower motor electrical connector.
4. Remove blower motor.
5. Reverse procedure to install.

CABIN AIR FILTER
REPLACE
LS

1. Remove mounting nuts and wiper pivot arms.
2. Remove two part pin retainers and separate Velcro attachment of rubber hinge cover to rear outboard corner of cowl vent screen.
3. Lift cowl vent screen to release clips.
4. Remove righthand cowl cover.
5. Push on righthand corner of filter to release clip.
6. Release lefthand clip and remove cabin air filter.
7. Reverse procedure to install.

Thunderbird

1. Remove left and righthand cowl side trim pieces.
2. Remove mounting nuts and wiper arms.
3. Remove pin-type retainers and cowl vent screen.

4. Push on righthand corner of cabin air filter and release righthand clip.
5. Release lefthand clip and cabin air filter.
6. Reverse procedure to install.

HEATER CORE
REPLACE
LS

1. Recover air conditioning refrigerant as outlined in "Air Conditioning" chapter.
2. Disconnect heater hose from heater core.
3. Remove mounting nuts and wiper pivot arms.
4. Remove two part pin retainers and separate Velcro attachment of rubber hinge cover to rear outboard corner of cowl vent screen.
5. Lift cowl vent screen to release clips.
6. Remove righthand cowl cover.
7. Push on righthand corner of filter to release clip.
8. Release lefthand clip and remove cabin air filter.
9. Remove strut tower support brace.
10. Remove cabin air filter housing mounting bolts, **Fig. 10**.
11. Remove mounting bolts and plenum panel, **Fig. 11**.
12. Disconnect coolant recovery line.
13. Remove forward heater hose mounting bolt at righthand shock tower.
14. Raise and support vehicle.
15. Remove rear heater hose mounting bolt from body side and position heater hose aside.
16. Disconnect spring lock coupling using spring lock coupling tool T84L-19623-B, or equivalent.
17. Remove nut and disconnect peanut fitting, **Fig. 12**.
18. Remove peanut fitting bracket bolt.
19. Remove air conditioning line bracket bolts, **Fig. 13**.
20. Remove thermostatic expansion valve manifold and tube.
21. Remove instrument panel as outlined in "Dash Panel Service" chapter.
22. Disconnect electrical connector at top of evaporator core housing.
23. Remove cowl top mounting bolt.
24. Remove evaporator housing attachment bolt.
25. Remove engine compartment nuts, **Fig. 14**.
26. Remove evaporator core housing.

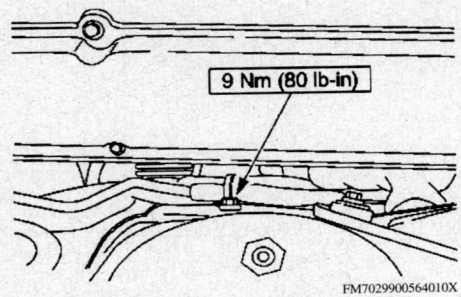

Fig. 13 Air conditioning line bracket location (Part 1 of 2)

27. Remove evaporator core housing to air inlet housing screws, **Fig. 15.**
28. Disconnect clip and separate evaporator core housing from air inlet housing.
29. Remove housing gasket.
30. Remove nine screws, then disconnect clip and separate evaporator core housing halves.
31. Disconnect bypass door connector and position harness aside.
32. Remove mounting screws, **Fig. 16.**
33. Remove heater core.
34. Reverse procedure to install noting the following:
    a. Lubricate air conditioning O-ring seal using PAG refrigerant oil YN-12-C, F7AZ-19589-DA, or equivalent.
    b. **Torque** air conditioning peanut fitting to 71 inch lbs.
    c. **Torque** expansion valve fitting to 15 ft. lbs.
    d. **Torque** evaporator housing to engine compartment nuts and cowl top attachment bolt to 62 inch lbs.
    e. **Torque** evaporator housing bolt to 44 inch lbs.
    f. Ensure heater hoses are correctly connected to heater core.

Thunderbird

1. Recover refrigerant as outlined in "Air Conditioning" chapter.
2. Partially drain cooling system into suitable container, then disconnect heater hose from heater core.
3. Remove manifold and tube to expansion valve mounting bolt, then disconnect assembly from expansion valve. Discard O-rings.
4. Remove instrument panel as outlined in "Dash Panel Service" chapter.
5. Disconnect electrical connector located on top of evaporator core housing.
6. Remove cowl top and evaporator housing mounting bolts.
7. Remove evaporator housing to bulkhead mounting nuts and washers from engine compartment side of bulkhead.
8. Remove evaporator housing to bulkhead mounting nut and washer from passenger compartment side of bulkhead.
9. Remove evaporator core housing.
10. Remove evaporator core housing to air inlet housing mounting screws.
11. Release clip and separate evaporator

core housing from air inlet housing.
12. Remove evaporator core housing screws, then separate housing halves.
13. Remove mounting screws and heater core.
14. Remove heater core tube gasket.
15. Reverse procedure to install.

EVAPORATOR CORE
REPLACE

1. Remove evaporator housing and separate housing halves as outlined under "Heater Core, Replace."
2. Remove evaporator core from housing.
3. Remove evaporator core to thermostatic expansion valve fittings and expansion valve from evaporator core.
4. Reverse procedure to install.

DUAL COOLANT FLOW VALVE
REPLACE

1. Ensure engine is cold.
2. Wrap suitable shop towel around pressure relief cap, then remove cap. **Ensure coolant does not come into contact with accessory drive belt.**
3. Drain radiator coolant into suitable container.
4. **On models equipped with oil cooler,** disconnect coolant return hose at oil cooler.
5. **On models equipped with 3.9L engine,** remove auxiliary coolant pump as follows:
    a. Ensure engine is cold.
    b. Wrap suitable shop towel around pressure relief cap, then remove cap.
    c. **Ensure coolant does not come into contact with accessory drive belt.**
    d. **On models equipped with oil cooler,** disconnect coolant return hose at oil cooler.
    e. **On all models,** disconnect auxiliary coolant pump electrical connector.
    f. Remove coolant pump to fan shroud mounting bolts, **Fig. 17.**
    g. Disconnect coolant pump hoses, then remove pump.
6. **On all models,** disconnect coolant valve electrical connector.
7. Place identification marks on dual coolant flow valve for installation alignment, **Fig. 18.**
8. Raise and support vehicle.
9. Remove coolant valve mounting nut and bolt.
10. Raise valve and disconnect coolant supply and return lines.
11. Remove coolant flow valve.
12. Reverse procedure to install.

AUXILIARY COOLANT FLOW PUMP
REPLACE

1. Ensure engine is cold.

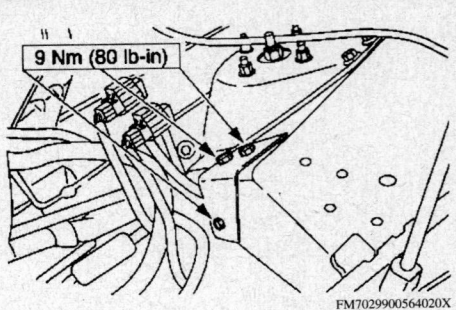

Fig. 13 Air conditioning line bracket location (Part 2 of 2)

2. Wrap suitable shop towel around pressure relief cap, then remove cap.
3. **Ensure coolant does not come into contact with accessory drive belt.**
4. Drain radiator coolant into suitable container.
5. **On models equipped with oil cooler,** disconnect coolant return hose at oil cooler.
6. **On all models,** disconnect auxiliary coolant pump electrical connector.
7. Remove coolant pump to fan shroud mounting bolts, **Fig. 17.**
8. Disconnect coolant pump hoses, then remove pump.
9. Reverse procedure to install. **Torque** auxiliary coolant pump mounting bolts to 53 inch lbs.

TECHNICAL SERVICE BULLETINS

Blower Motor Inoperative

2005 LS & THUNDERBIRD MODELS

Some of these models may exhibit an inoperative blower motor condition.

This condition may be caused by the blower motor speed controller.

To determine if this condition is caused by the controller, refer to the following:

1. With the ignition key off, disconnect blower motor speed controller connector.
2. Connect a 30 amp fused jumper lead between Pin-1 and Pin-2, **Fig. 19,** then turn the ignition key on.
3. If blower does not operate, follow normal diagnostics procedures.
4. If blower does operate, obtain a new blower motor speed controller part No. 3W4Z-19E624-AB. With ignition key On and Dual Automatic Temperature Control (DATC) Off, plug new controller into Connector, turn on DATC.
5. If blower motor now operates, install a new blower speed controller. Verify operation.

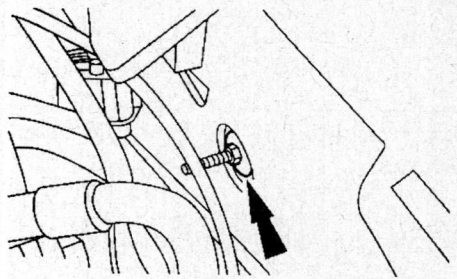

Fig. 14 Engine compartment evaporator housing bolt location (Part 1 of 3)

FM7029900565010X

Fig. 14 Engine compartment evaporator housing bolt location (Part 2 of 3)

FM7029900565020X

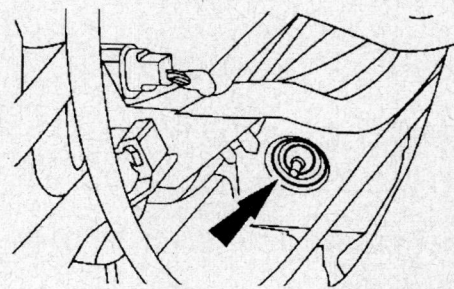

Fig. 14 Engine compartment evaporator housing bolt location (Part 3 of 3)

FM7029900565030X

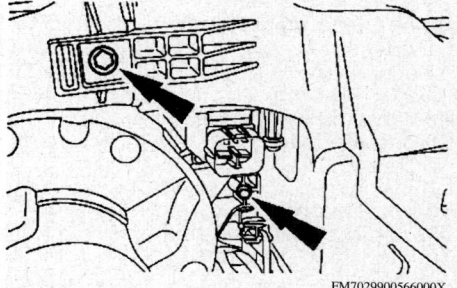

Fig. 15 Evaporator housing to air inlet housing screw location

FM7029900566000X

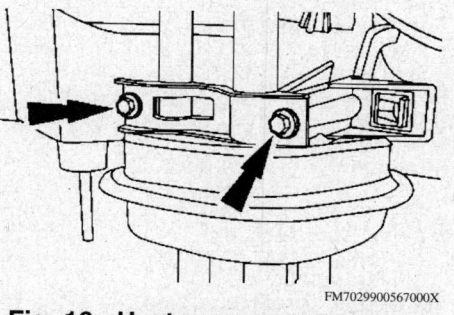

Fig. 16 Heater core cover screw location

FM7029900567000X

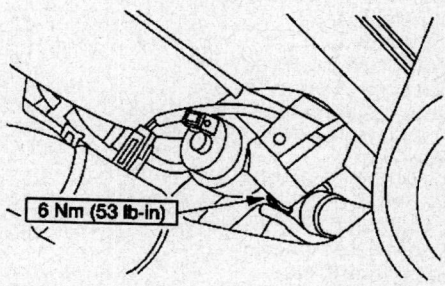

6 Nm (53 lb-in)

Fig. 17 Auxiliary coolant pump replacement

FM1069901007000X

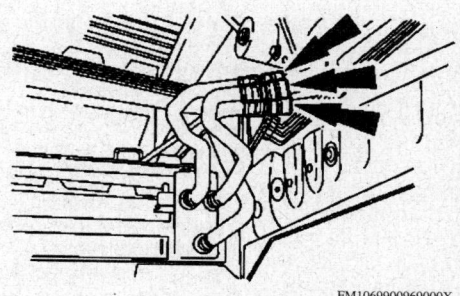

Fig. 18 Dual coolant flow valve

FM1069900969000X

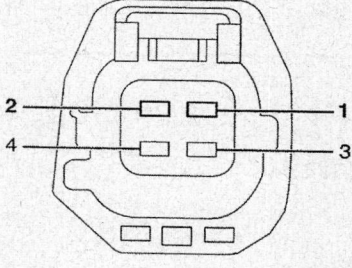

ARM0500000000097

Fig. 19 Blower motor speed controller connector terminal identification

3.0L Engine

NOTE: On Air Bag Equipped Models, Refer To "Air Bag System Precautions" Located In The Front Of This Manual For System Disarming & Arming Procedures.

NOTE: Refer To "Computer Relearn Procedures" Located In The Front Of This Manual When Battery Power To The Computer Has Been Interrupted.

INDEX

	Page No.
Camshaft, Replace	3-17
Installation	3-17
Removal	3-17
Compression Pressure	3-12
Cooling System Bleed	3-19
Crankshaft Damper, Replace	3-15
Crankshaft Rear Oil Seal, Replace	3-18
Cylinder Head, Replace	3-14
Lefthand	3-14
Righthand	3-14
Engine Rebuilding Specifications	21-1
Engine, Replace	3-13
Engine Mount, Replace	3-12
Exhaust Manifold, Replace	3-14
Lefthand	3-14
Righthand	3-14
Front Cover, Replace	3-15
Front Cover Seal, Replace	3-16

	Page No.
Fuel Filter, Replace	3-20
Fuel Pump, Replace	3-20
Fuel Delivery Module	3-20
Jet (Transfer) Pump	3-20
Hydraulic Cooling Fan Pump, Replace	3-20
Hydraulic Fan Motor, Replace	3-20
Intake Manifold, Replace	3-14
Lower	3-14
Upper	3-14
Main & Rod Bearings	3-17
Connecting Rod Bearings	3-17
Main Bearings	3-17
Oil Cooler, Replace	3-18
Oil Pan, Replace	3-18
Oil Pump, Replace	3-18
Piston & Rod Assembly	3-17
Precautions	3-12
Air Bag Systems	3-12
Battery Ground Cable	3-12

	Page No.
Fuel System Pressure Relief	3-12
Quick Disconnect Hoses	3-12
R-Clip	3-12
Spring Lock	3-12
Vapor Tube	3-12
Radiator, Replace	3-19
Serpentine Drive Belt	3-18
Routing	3-18
Tension	3-18
Thermostat, Replace	3-19
Tightening Specifications	3-24
Timing Chain, Replace	3-16
Installation	3-16
Removal	3-16
Valve Adjustment	3-15
Valve Arrangement	3-15
Valve Cover, Replace	3-15
Lefthand	3-15
Righthand	3-15
Water Pump, Replace	3-19

PRECAUTIONS

Air Bag Systems

Refer to "Air Bag System Precautions" in the front of this manual for system disarming and arming procedures.

Battery Ground Cable

Prior to service, disconnect battery ground cable and isolate as required.

Fuel System Pressure Relief

1. Remove Schraeder valve cap and install fuel pressure gauge tool No. T80L-9974-B, or equivalent, to Schraeder valve.
2. Slowly open manual valve on pressure gauge and drain fuel into suitable container.

QUICK DISCONNECT HOSES

R-Clip

When working with R-clip type connections do not use tools to disconnect, **Fig. 1.** Use of tools may deform clip components and could cause leaks.

To disconnect, bend shipping tab downward, **Fig. 1.** Spread R-clip and push clip into fitting. Separate fitting from tube.

To install, first inspect fitting and tube for damage and ensure connections are clean. Apply a light coat of clean 5W-30 motor oil to male end of tube. Insert R-clip into fitting. Align tube and fitting, then insert tube into fitting and push together until a click is heard. Pull on connection to ensure it is fully engaged.

Spring Lock

When working with spring lock type connections spring lock tool set No. T84L-19623-B, or equivalent, must be used to disconnect fittings, **Fig. 2.** When connecting spring lock type fittings, inspect and clean both coupling ends. Lubricate fuel line O-ring seals with clean 5W-30 motor oil. When connection is made, pull on line to ensure it is fully engaged.

Vapor Tube

To disconnect vapor tube connections, squeeze fitting and disconnect vapor tube from fitting, **Fig. 3.** To connect, ensure fittings are clean and free from damage. Push tube onto fitting until it snaps into place. Pull on connection to ensure fitting is secure.

COMPRESSION PRESSURE

Before performing compression test, ensure the crankcase oil is of correct viscosity and at correct level. Ensure battery is fully charged and engine is at normal operating temperature.

1. Turn ignition switch to OFF position.
2. Remove spark plugs.
3. Set throttle plates to wide open position.
4. Install suitable compression gauge in cylinder No. 1.
5. Install auxiliary starter switch in starting circuit.
6. With ignition switch in OFF position, use auxiliary starter switch to crank engine at least five compression strokes.
7. Count number of compression strokes required to reach highest reading and record highest reading.
8. Repeat test on each cylinder, cranking engine same number of compression strokes.
9. Indicated compression pressures are considered within specifications if lowest reading cylinder is within 75 percent of highest reading.

ENGINE MOUNT
REPLACE

1. Remove cowl vent screen as outlined

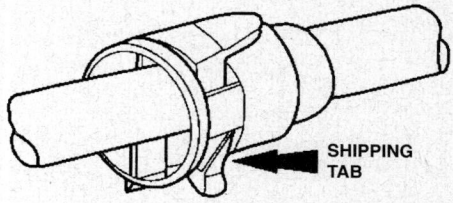

Fig. 1 R-clip connection

FM1069900923000X

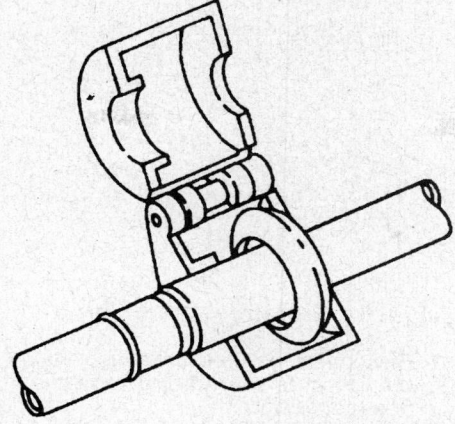

FM1069900924000X

Fig. 2 Spring lock connection

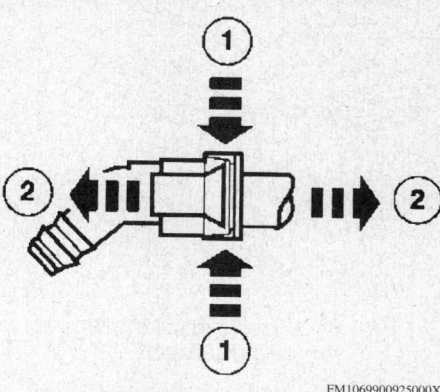

FM1069900925000X

Fig. 3 Vapor tube connection

under "Wiper Motor, Replace" in "Electrical" section.
2. Remove strut brace.
3. Remove wire harness bracket, **Fig. 4.**
4. Disconnect intake manifold tuning valve electrical connector.
5. Remove mounting bolts and intake manifold tuning valve.
6. Remove cabin air filter plenum as outlined under "Heater Core, Replace" in "Electrical" section.
7. Remove engine mount upper nut.
8. Raise and support vehicle.
9. Remove engine mount lower nut.
10. Raise engine and remove mount.
11. Reverse procedure to install, noting the following:
    a. **Ensure intake manifold tuning valve is fully seated into intake before installing bolts.**
    b. **Torque** intake manifold tuning valve to 89 inch lbs.
    c. **Torque** upper mount nut to 30 ft. lbs.
    d. **Torque** lower mount nut to 46 ft. lbs.

ENGINE
REPLACE

When carrying out operations which involve the removal and installation of the driveshaft, always inspect the joint angles and adjust as outlined under "Driveline Angle Measurement" in "Rear Axle & Suspension" section.
1. Disconnect IAT sensor electrical connector.
2. Disconnect aspirator and PCV hose from air cleaner outlet tube.
3. Remove air cleaner outlet tube.
4. Remove engine appearance cover.
5. Ensure engine is cold.
6. Wrap suitable shop towel around pressure relief cap, then remove cap.
7. **Ensure coolant does not come into contact with accessory drive belt.**
8. Open radiator draincock and drain coolant into suitable container.
9. **On models equipped with oil cooler,** disconnect coolant return hose at oil cooler.
10. **On all models,** recover air conditioning refrigerant as outlined in "Air Conditioning" chapter.
11. Remove upper radiator sight shield and upper radiator support brackets.
12. Disconnect air conditioning pressure switch connector.
13. Remove power steering reservoir bolts and position reservoir aside.
14. Disconnect fuel lines.
15. Disconnect brake aspirator vacuum

hose, then remove left and righthand cowl trim panels.
16. Unclip chassis vacuum lines from support bracket, then disconnect lines.
17. Remove strut brace support.
18. Remove cabin air filter plenum as outlined under "Heater Core, Replace" in "Electrical" section.
19. Disconnect main vacuum hose from rear of intake manifold.
20. Disconnect throttle and speed control cables and unclip from bracket.
21. Disconnect ground strap bolt, **Fig. 5.**
22. Disconnect main engine wiring harness and transmission harness connectors, **Figs. 6 and 7.**
23. Disconnect fuel charging wiring, **Fig. 8.**
24. Disconnect wiring harness retainer from bracket.
25. Remove air conditioning line mounting bracket.
26. Remove hydraulic cooling fan reservoir and position aside.
27. Unclip line from frame, **Fig. 9.**
28. Raise and support vehicle.
29. Drain engine oil into suitable container.
30. Remove left and righthand splash shields.
31. Remove air conditioning manifold bolt, then position manifold aside.
32. Place reference marks on dual coolant flow valve coolant lines for installation alignment.
33. Disconnect coolant hoses from dual coolant flow valve using quick disconnect tool No. T85T-18539-AH, or equivalent, **Fig. 10.**
34. Remove exhaust system and heat shields.
35. Remove driveshaft as outlined in "Rear Axle & Suspension" section
36. Disconnect shift cable at transmission.
37. Remove shift cable bracket bolt.
38. Remove front tires.
39. Disconnect left and righthand front ABS sensors.
40. Remove bolts, then position from brake calipers aside.
41. Disconnect stabilizer link lower mounts and upper ball joints.
42. Remove lower strut mount bolts.
43. Disconnect starter wiring harness at starter.

44. Disconnect power steering pressure electrical connectors.
45. Remove steering shaft clamp bolt.
46. Remove torque converter nuts.
47. Disconnect hose, **Fig. 11.**
48. Support rear of vehicle using suitable safety stands.
49. Support engine, transmission, front and center crossmembers and cooling system with suitable powertrain lift and transmission support bracket.
50. Remove four transmission crossmember bolts.
51. Remove four front and four center crossmember bolts.
52. Lower engine and transmission.
53. Install two engine lifting brackets tool No. 303-050, or equivalent, to engine.
54. Support engine and transmission in front subframe using suitable engine lift and spreader bar.
55. Disconnect two wire harness retainers and position harness aside.
56. Remove starter and oxygen sensor bracket.
57. Remove upper then lower transmission to engine mounting bolts.
58. Remove left and righthand engine mount upper mounting nuts.
59. Remove accessory drive belt.
60. Disconnect power steering pump electrical connector.
61. Remove power steering pump and position aside.
62. Disconnect hydraulic cooling fan pump electrical connector.
63. Remove hydraulic cooling fan pump and position aside.
64. Disconnect upper radiator hose.
65. **On models equipped with automatic transmission,** disconnect cooler line bracket from oil pan, then remove transmission cooler lines from transmission and plug fittings.
66. **On models equipped with oil cooler,** disconnect oil cooler hoses.
67. **On all models,** remove remaining transmission to engine mounting bolts and separate transmission from engine.
68. **On models equipped with manual transmission,** remove clutch.
69. **On all models,** remove flywheel.
70. Unclip left and righthand wire harness retainers.
71. Remove rear separator plate.
72. Mount engine to suitable work stand,

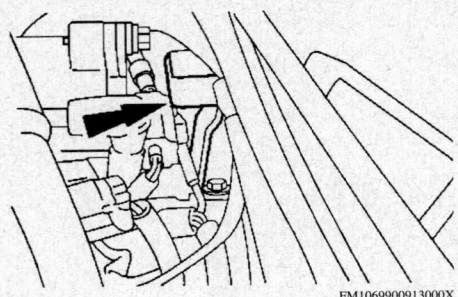

Fig. 4   Wire harness bracket replacement

then remove lifting equipment.
73. Reverse procedure to install.

INTAKE MANIFOLD
REPLACE
Upper

1. Ensure engine is cold.
2. Wrap suitable shop towel around pressure relief cap, then remove cap.
3. **Ensure coolant does not come into contact with accessory drive belt.**
4. Open radiator draincock and drain coolant into suitable container.
5. **On models equipped with oil cooler,** disconnect coolant return hose at oil cooler.
6. **On all models,** remove air cleaner outlet tube.
7. Disconnect TP sensor and IAC electrical connectors.
8. Disconnect speed control and accelerator cables and position aside.
9. Disconnect coolant hoses, PCV hose and vapor purge hose from throttle body.
10. Disconnect EGR vacuum hose and EGR tube.
11. Remove cowl vent screen.
12. Remove vacuum hoses and cruise control cables from mounting brackets.
13. Disconnect differential pressure feedback EGR electrical connector.
14. Remove differential pressure feedback EGR transducer and position aside.
15. Remove fuel pressure sensor shield.
16. Disconnect vacuum hose from rear of intake manifold.
17. Disconnect intake manifold tuning valve electrical connector.
18. Disconnect exhaust vacuum regulator electrical connector and vacuum line.
19. Remove upper intake support bolt.
20. Remove mounting bolts and upper intake manifold.
21. Reverse procedure to install. **Torque** manifold bolts to 89 inch lbs., in sequence, **Fig. 12.**

Lower

1. Remove upper intake manifold as outlined under "Upper."
2. Disconnect fuel lines.
3. Remove fuel line bracket bolt.

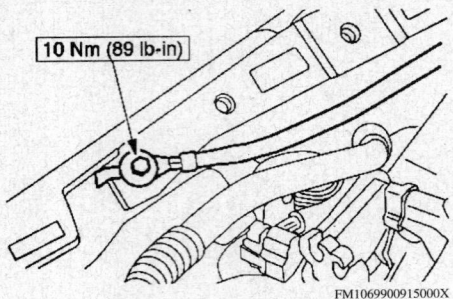

Fig. 5   Ground strap location

4. Disconnect fuel pressure sensor vacuum line and fuel charging wiring harness connector.
5. Disconnect crankcase ventilation tube and position aside.
6. Remove mounting bolts and lower intake manifold. **Fuel injection supply manifold and lower intake manifold must be removed as an assembly.**
7. Reverse procedure to install, noting the following:
   a. Inspect fuel injector O-rings.
   b. Inspect lower intake manifold gaskets.
   c. **Torque** mounting bolts to 89 inch lbs., in sequence, **Fig. 13.**

EXHAUST MANIFOLD
REPLACE
Lefthand

1. Remove heat shield.
2. Remove three upper nuts on manifold.
3. Remove secondary air tube from exhaust manifold.
4. Remove dual converter Y-pipe.
5. Remove three lower nuts and exhaust manifold.
6. Reverse procedure to install. Install new gasket and **torque** mounting nuts to 15 ft. lbs., in sequence, **Fig. 14.**

Righthand

1. Remove heat shield.
2. Remove secondary air tube from exhaust manifold.
3. Remove dual Y-pipe.
4. Disconnect EGR valve to exhaust manifold tube.
5. Remove mounting nuts and manifold.
6. Reverse procedure to install. Install new gasket and **torque** mounting nuts to 15 ft. lbs in sequence, **Fig. 14.**

CYLINDER HEAD
REPLACE

When cleaning cylinder head surfaces, do not use metal scrapers, wires brushes, power abrasive discs or other abrasive methods to clean sealing surfaces. Use only a plastic scraping tool to remove all traces of gasket material.

Cylinder head bolts are of torque-to-yield style and must be replaced when removed.

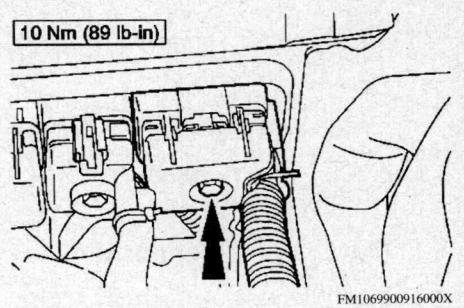

Fig. 6   Main engine harness connector

Lefthand and righthand cylinder head gaskets are not interchangeable.

Lefthand

1. Remove camshafts as outlined under "Camshaft, Replace."
2. Remove exhaust manifold as outlined under "Exhaust Manifold, Replace."
3. Remove lower intake manifold as outlined under "Intake Manifold, Replace."
4. Remove cylinder head ground strap, stud and bolt, **Fig. 15.**
5. Remove noise suppressor bolt, **Fig. 16.**
6. Disconnect coolant outlet hose from thermostat housing.
7. Remove thermostat housing.
8. Remove oil dipstick tube stud bolt.
9. Remove cylinder head bolts in sequence, **Fig. 17.**
10. Reverse procedure to install, noting the following:
    a. **Torque** cylinder head bolts to 22 ft. lbs., in sequence, **Fig. 18.**
    b. Tighten head bolts an additional 90° in sequence.
    c. Loosen bolts 360° in sequence.
    d. **Torque** to 22 ft. lbs., in sequence.
    e. Tighten an additional 90° in sequence.
    f. Tighten an additional 90° in sequence.

Righthand

1. Remove camshafts as outlined under "Camshaft, Replace."
2. Remove exhaust manifold as outlined under "Exhaust Manifold, Replace."
3. Remove lower intake manifold as outlined under "Intake Manifold, Replace."
4. Remove noise suppressor bolt, **Fig. 19.**
5. Disconnect outlet hose from thermostat housing.
6. Remove thermostat housing.
7. Remove cylinder head bolts in sequence, **Fig. 17.**
8. Reverse procedure to install, noting the following:
   a. **Torque** cylinder head bolts to 22 ft. lbs., in sequence, **Fig. 18.**
   b. Tighten head bolts an additional 90° in sequence.
   c. Loosen bolts 360° in sequence.
   d. **Torque** to 22 ft. lbs., in sequence.

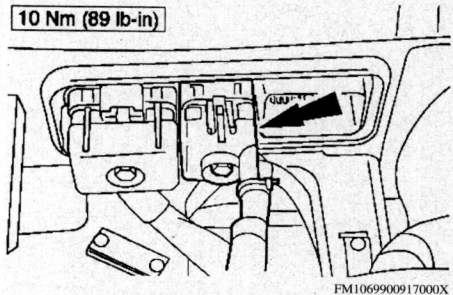

Fig. 7   Main transmission harness connector

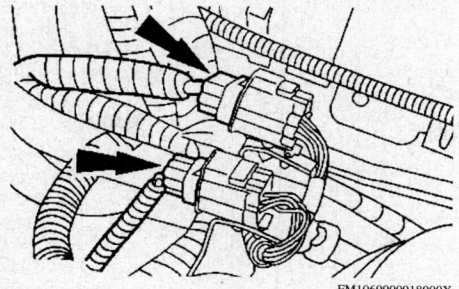

Fig. 8   Fuel charging wiring connectors

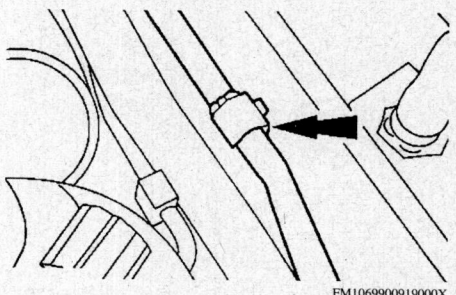

Fig. 9   Frame line location

   e. Tighten an additional 90° in sequence.
   f. Tighten an additional 90° in sequence.

VALVE COVER
REPLACE
Lefthand

1. Remove engine appearance cover.
2. Disconnect coil electrical connector.
3. Remove mounting bolts and ignition coil.
4. Remove cylinder head temperature sensor.
5. Remove vacuum hoses from appearance cover support bracket.
6. Remove appearance cover support bracket.
7. Disconnect PCV tube and position aside.
8. Remove ignition coil harness from retainers.
9. Remove studs, bolts and valve cover.
10. Reverse procedure to install, noting the following:
   a. Apply .2 inch bead of silicone gasket sealant part No. F7AZ-19554-EA, or equivalent, to front cover joints.
   b. **Torque** mounting bolts to 89 inch lbs., in sequence, **Fig. 20**.

Righthand

1. Remove upper intake manifold as outlined under "Intake Manifold, Replace."
2. Disconnect PCV tube and position aside.
3. Disconnect coil electrical connector.
4. Remove mounting bolts and ignition coil.
5. Remove wiring harness retainer from stud.
6. Remove upper intake manifold support bracket and position aside.
7. Remove wiring harness bracket nuts and position aside.
8. Remove mounting bolts, studs and valve cover.
9. Reverse procedure to install, noting the following:
   a. Apply .2 inch bead of silicone gasket sealant part No. F7AZ-19554-EA, or equivalent, to front cover joints.

   b. **Torque** mounting bolts to 89 inch lbs., in sequence, **Fig. 20**.

VALVE ARRANGEMENT
Inner .... I-I-I-I-I-I
Outer .... E-E-E-E-E-E

VALVE ADJUSTMENT

Rotating the engine in a counterclockwise direction will cause engine damage.

Mark shims with permanent marker. Scratches or paint on shim will cause incorrect lash adjustment and severe engine damage.

When measuring valve lash, ensure camshaft lobes are 180° away from each valve tappet.

1. Remove left and righthand valve covers as outlined under "Valve Cover, Replace."
2. Turn engine clockwise to position camshaft lobe away from shim surface.
3. Measure clearance between camshaft and shim surface using feeler gauge set tool No. D81L-4201-A, or equivalent, **Fig. 21**. Refer to "Specifications" section for correct valve clearance.
4. Mark position of timing chain in relation to camshaft sprockets to ensure timing remains correct.
5. Place alignment marks on camshaft caps for installation alignment. Caps should be marked for location and orientation.
6. Remove camshaft thrust cap and rear camshaft cap from camshaft that requires adjustment.
7. Install camshaft lift tools, tool No. 303-659, or equivalents, and hand tighten. Taller tool should be installed in place of rear camshaft cap to allow camshaft to be lifted for shim removal.
8. Remove center camshaft caps.
9. Mark location of each shim.
10. Remove shims that require adjustment using rubber tipped air gun and compressed air.
11. Measure and record thickness of each shim to correspond with valve clearance.
12. Calculate required shim thickness by adding original shim thickness to measured clearance and subtracting desired clearance.
13. Reverse procedure to install, noting the following:

   a. Apply coat of clean 5W-30 motor oil to replacement shims and install shims.
   b. Apply coat of clean 5W-30 motor oil to camshaft journals and bearing caps.
   c. Turn crankshaft in clockwise direction to turn camshafts two full revolutions. Inspect valve clearance and timing.

CRANKSHAFT DAMPER
REPLACE

1. Remove accessory drive belt.
2. Remove secondary air valve, bracket and tube.
3. Raise and support vehicle.
4. Remove front center splash panel.
5. Remove crankshaft pulley bolt and washer.
6. Remove crankshaft damper using damper removal tool No. 303-D121, or equivalent. **Ensure removal tool grabs inside of damper or damage will occur.**
7. Reverse procedure to install, noting the following:
   a. Ensure damper and crankshaft surfaces are clean.
   b. Apply silicone gasket and sealant part No. F7AZ-19554-EA, or equivalent, to end of keyway slot.
   c. Lubricate outside sealing surface of crankshaft pulley with clean 5W-30 motor oil.
   d. Install damper using damper installer tool No. T74P-6316-B, or equivalent.
   e. **Torque** crankshaft pulley bolt to 89 ft. lbs.
   f. Loosen pulley bolt 360°.
   g. **Torque** bolt to 37 ft. lbs.
   h. Tighten bolt an additional 90°.

FRONT COVER
REPLACE

1. Remove left and righthand valve covers as outlined under "Valve Cover, Replace."
2. Support engine with three bar engine support kit tool No. 303-F072, or equivalent.
3. Raise and support vehicle.
4. Remove splash shields.
5. Ensure engine is cold, then wrap suitable shop towel around pressure relief cap and remove cap. **Ensure coolant**

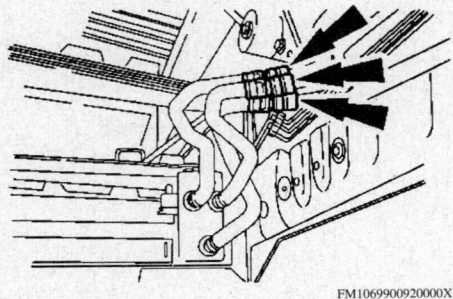

Fig. 10 Dual coolant flow valve

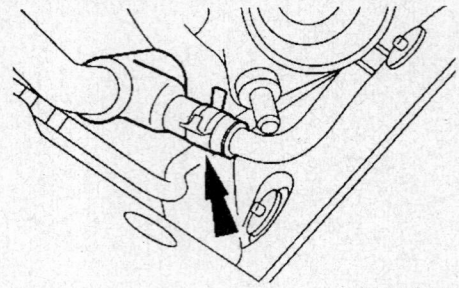

Fig. 11 Hose disconnect location

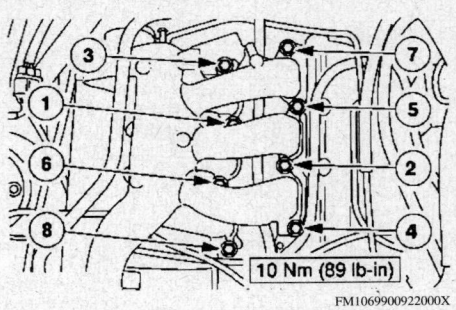

10 Nm (89 lb-in)

Fig. 12 Upper intake manifold bolt tightening sequence

does not come into contact with accessory drive belt.

6. Drain radiator coolant into suitable container.
7. **On models equipped with oil cooler,** disconnect coolant return hose at oil cooler.
8. **On all models,** disconnect upper water pump hose, then the upper and lower radiator hoses.
9. Disconnect and remove radiator hose.
10. Disconnect lower water pump hose.
11. Remove accessory drive belt.
12. Remove water pump as outlined under "Water Pump, Replace."
13. Remove oil pan as outlined under "Oil Pan, Replace."
14. Remove power steering pump as outlined under "Power Steering Pump, Replace" in "Front Suspension & Steering" section.
15. Remove lower cooling fan pump bolt, then disconnect hose.
16. Disconnect cooling fan pump electrical connector.
17. Remove high pressure line bracket.
18. Disconnect high pressure line.
19. Remove two upper mounting bolts and cooling fan pump.
20. Remove idler pulley and belt tensioner.
21. Remove secondary air valve, bracket and tube.
22. Remove crankshaft pulley bolt and washer.
23. Remove crankshaft damper using damper removal tool No. 303-D121, or equivalent. **Ensure removal tool grabs inside of damper or damage will occur.**
24. Remove crankshaft front oil seal using seal removal tool No. T92C-6700-CH, or equivalent.
25. Remove mounting bolts and front cover.
26. Reverse procedure to install, noting the following:
    a. Apply .24 inch diameter dot of silicone gasket and sealant part No. F7AZ-19554-EA, or equivalent, **Fig. 22.** Ensure front cover is installed within 6 minutes of sealer application.
    b. **Torque** front cover mounting bolts to 18 ft. lbs., in sequence, **Fig. 23.**
    c. Install front crankshaft seal using seal installer tool No. T88T-6701-1, or equivalent.
    d. Ensure all damper and crankshaft surfaces are clean.

    e. Apply silicone gasket and sealant part No. F7AZ-19554-EA, or equivalent, to end of keyway slot.
    f. Lubricate outside sealing surface of crankshaft pulley with clean 5W-30 motor oil.
    g. Install damper using damper installer tool No. T74P-6316-B, or equivalent.
    h. **Torque** crankshaft pulley bolt to 89 ft. lbs.
    i. Loosen pulley bolt 360°.
    j. **Torque** bolt to 37 ft. lbs.
    k. Tighten bolt an additional 90°.

FRONT COVER SEAL

REPLACE

1. Remove accessory drive belt.
2. Remove secondary air valve, bracket and tube.
3. Raise and support vehicle.
4. Remove front center splash panel.
5. Remove crankshaft pulley bolt and washer.
6. Remove crankshaft damper using damper removal tool No. 303-D121, or equivalent. **Ensure removal tool grabs inside of damper or damage will occur.**
7. Remove front cover seal using seal remover tool No. T92C-6700-CH, or equivalent.
8. Reverse procedure to install, noting the following:
   a. Lubricate inside diameter of seal using clean 5W-30 motor oil.
   b. Install front cover seal using seal installer tool No. T88T-6701-A, or equivalent.
   c. Ensure all damper and crankshaft surfaces are clean.
   d. Apply silicone gasket and sealant part No. F7AZ-19554-EA, or equivalent, to end of keyway slot.
   e. Lubricate outside sealing surface of crankshaft pulley with clean 5W-30 motor oil.
   f. Install damper using damper installer tool No. T74P-6316-B, or equivalent.
   g. **Torque** crankshaft pulley bolt to 89 ft. lbs.
   h. Loosen pulley bolt 360°.
   i. **Torque** bolt to 37 ft. lbs.
   j. Tighten bolt an additional 90°.

TIMING CHAIN

REPLACE

Rotating the engine in a counterclockwise direction will cause engine damage.

Removal

1. Remove front cover as outlined under "Front Cover, Replace."
2. Remove ignition pulse ring.
3. Install crankshaft damper bolt and washer.
4. Turn crankshaft clockwise until keyway is positioned in 9 o'clock position, **Fig. 24.**
5. If timing chain tensioner and chain are to be reused, place identification marks on them for installation alignment. **Do not interchange left and righthand timing components.**
6. Place suitable paper clip into righthand timing chain tensioner before removing bolts, **Fig. 25.**
7. Remove righthand timing chain tensioner and arm.
8. Remove righthand timing chain and chain guide.
9. Install suitable paper clip into lefthand timing chain tensioner.
10. Remove lefthand timing chain tensioner and arm, then the timing chain and guide.

Installation

Ensure crankshaft keyway remains in 9 o'clock position until cams are properly positioned or valve damage will occur.

1. Ensure crankshaft keyway is in 9 o'clock position, **Fig. 24.**
2. Turn left and righthand camshafts to locate them to neutral positions, **Fig. 26.**
3. Place lefthand chain tensioner into suitable soft-jawed vise.
4. Hold tensioner ratchet lock mechanism away from ratchet stem using suitable pick, **Fig. 27.**
5. **During tensioner compression, do not release ratchet stem until tensioner piston is fully bottomed in bore or stem will become damaged.** Slowly compress chain tensioner.
6. Retain lefthand tensioner piston using suitable paper clip, **Fig. 28.**
7. Turn crankshaft clockwise to 11 o'clock position.

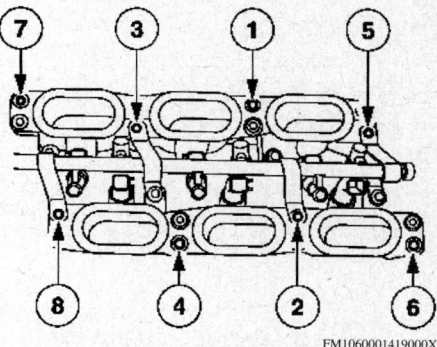

Fig. 13 Lower intake manifold tightening sequence

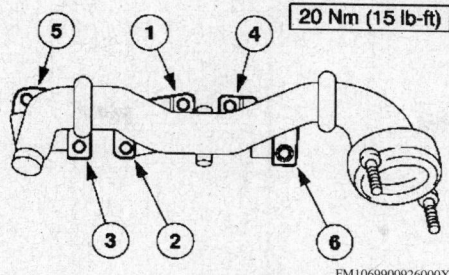

Fig. 14 Exhaust manifold tightening sequence

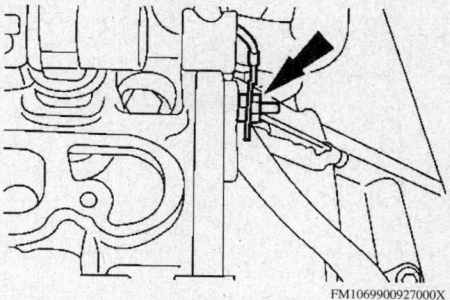

Fig. 15 Lefthand cylinder head ground strap location

8. Remove crankshaft damper bolt and washer.
9. Install lefthand timing chain guide and tighten. Ensure short bolt is installed into upper hole and long bolt into lower hole.
10. Install lefthand timing chain. Align gold timing chain index link with marks on camshaft and crankshaft sprockets, **Fig. 29.**
11. Install lefthand timing chain tensioner and tighten. Ensure tensioner piston is fully engaged in tensioner arm.
12. Remove paper clip from lefthand tensioner and install crankshaft damper bolt and washer.
13. Turn crankshaft clockwise until keyway is positioned between 2 and 3 o'clock position.
14. Ensure gold timing chain index links on lefthand timing chain are still aligned with timing index marks on crankshaft and camshaft sprockets, **Fig. 30.**
15. Place righthand chain tensioner into suitable soft-jawed vise.
16. Hold tensioner ratchet lock mechanism away from ratchet stem using suitable pick, **Fig. 27.**
17. **During tensioner compression, do not release ratchet stem until tensioner piston is fully bottomed in bore or stem will become damaged.** Slowly compress chain tensioner.
18. Retain righthand tensioner piston using suitable paper clip, **Fig. 28.**
19. Install righthand timing chain guide and tighten.
20. Install righthand timing chain. Align gold chain index marks with camshaft and crankshaft alignment marks, **Fig. 31.**
21. Install righthand timing chain tensioner and tighten.
22. Remove paper clip from righthand tensioner.
23. Ensure gold timing index links on righthand timing chain are still aligned with timing index marks on camshaft and crankshaft sprockets, **Fig. 32.**
24. Remove crankshaft damper bolt and washer.
25. Install ignition pulse ring.
26. Install front cover as outlined under "Front Cover, Replace."

CAMSHAFT
REPLACE

When removing camshafts, camshaft journal thrust caps must be removed prior to loosening other camshaft journal cap bolts.

When installing camshafts, camshaft bearing caps must be installed prior to installing thrust caps.

Camshaft journal caps and cylinder heads are numbered to ensure they are installed in original positions.

Removal

1. Remove upper intake manifold as outlined under "Intake Manifold, Replace."
2. Remove front cover as outlined under "Front Cover, Replace."
3. Remove timing chains as outlined under "Timing Chain, Replace."
4. Remove camshaft journal thrust caps, **Fig. 33.**
5. Remove remaining journal caps and camshafts.

Installation

1. Ensure bearing caps are installed to original positions.
2. Lubricate camshafts and bearing surfaces with clean 5W-30 motor oil.
3. Install camshaft bearing caps. **Do not tighten bolts now.**
4. Install camshaft thrust caps. **Do not tighten bolts now.**
5. **Torque** camshaft bearing caps to 89 inch lbs., in sequence, **Figs. 34 and 35.**
6. If new camshafts were installed, adjust valve lash as outlined under "Valve Adjustment."
7. **Ensure crankshaft keyway is in 9 o'clock position before rotating camshafts or engine damage will result.**
8. Turn camshafts to ensure they are not binding. If binding occurs, ensure bearing caps are in original positions. Loosen bearing caps in reverse order and tighten.
9. Install timing chains as outlined under "Timing Chain, Replace."
10. Install front cover as outlined under "Front Cover, Replace."
11. Install upper intake manifold as outlined under "Intake Manifold, Replace."

PISTON & ROD ASSEMBLY

When removing pistons and connecting rods, place reference marks on components involved for installation alignment.

When installing pistons, ensure arrow on piston is facing toward front of engine.

MAIN & ROD BEARINGS

Connecting Rod Bearings

Connecting rod bearing caps are cracked and split from connecting rods during the manufacturing process. When assembling components, ensure mating surfaces are clean and ensure identification marks on cap and rod are aligned.

Connecting rod bolts are of torque-to-yield design and must be replaced when removed.
1. **Torque** new bolts to 17 ft. lbs.
2. **Torque** bolts to 32 ft. lbs.
3. Final tighten bolts additional 90°.

Main Bearings

When cleaning gasket surfaces, do not use metal scrapers, wires brushes, power abrasive discs or other abrasive methods to clean sealing surfaces. Use only a plastic scraping tool to remove all traces of gasket material.

Lower cylinder block bolts and studs are of torque-to-yield design and must be replaced when removed.

To select and install main bearings, proceed as follows:
1. Read crankshaft flange and engine block rear face codes, **Fig. 36.**
2. First two numbers after asterisk are code for main No. 1 and next two numbers for main No. 2.
3. First two numbers after second asterisk are code for main No. 3 and last two numbers for main No. 4.
4. Refer to **Fig. 37** for bearing grade selection chart.
5. For example, if block code is *0609*0711* and crankshaft code is *8480*8082*, main No. 1 will use grade 1 bearings as determined by intersection of 06 block column and 84

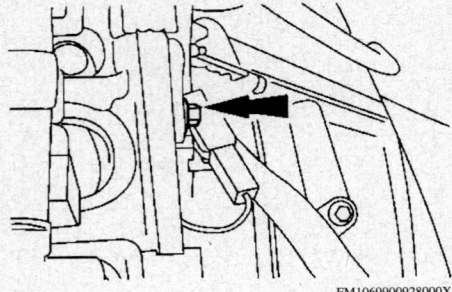

Fig. 16 Lefthand noise suppressor bolt location

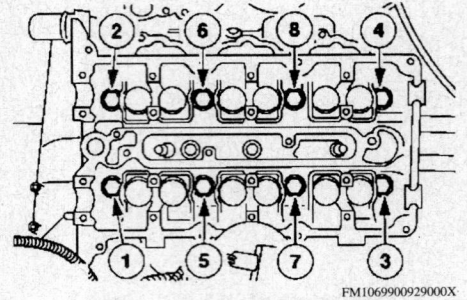

Fig. 17 Cylinder head bolt loosening sequence

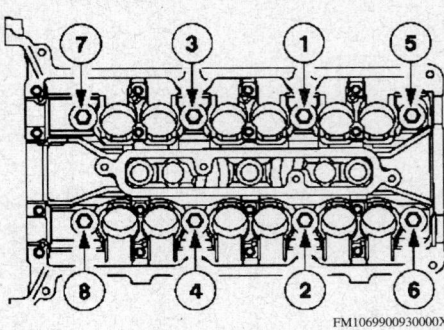

Fig. 18 Cylinder head bolt tightening sequence

crankshaft row, **Fig. 37.** Using these codes as, main Nos. 2, 3 and 4 will use grade 2.

6. Install upper main bearing and upper thrust bearing to cylinder block in proper locations.
7. Lubricate bearings using clean 5W-30 motor oil, then install crankshaft to cylinder block.
8. Install lower main bearings and lower thrust bearing into lower cylinder block in proper locations.
9. Ensure all gasket surfaces are clean using Ford Metal Surface Cleaner part No. F4AZ-19A536-RA, or equivalent. Allow to dry until there is no sign of wetness present.
10. Apply .12 inch bead of silicone gasket sealant part No. F7AZ-19554-EA, or equivalent, to lower cylinder block. End bead of gasket material .24 inch from rear crankshaft seal bore on both sides, **Fig. 38.** Bolts and studs must be tightened within four minutes of applying sealant.
11. Install lower cylinder block studs and bolts, **Fig. 39.**
12. Install new bolts and studs.
13. **Torque** bolts 1–8 to 18 ft. lbs., in sequence, **Fig. 40.**
14. **Torque** bolts 9–16 to 30 ft. lbs., in sequence.
15. Tighten bolts 1–16 an additional 90° in sequence.
16. **Torque** bolts 17–22 to 18 ft. lbs., in sequence.
17. Remove excess sealer from front cover and rear seal bore inner diameter areas.
18. Turn crankshaft in clockwise direction to ensure free rotation.

CRANKSHAFT REAR OIL SEAL

REPLACE

1. Remove transaxle as outlined in **MOTOR's "Domestic Transmission, In-Vehicle Service." or "Transmission Service DVD."**
2. Remove flywheel.
3. Remove rear crankshaft seal using seal removal tool No. T95P-6701-EH and slide hammer tool No. 307-005, or equivalents.
4. Lubricate outer lips and inner seal of new crankshaft rear seal with clean 5W-30 motor oil.
5. Install rear oil seal using seal installer

tool No. T82L-6701-A and rear adapter bolts tool No. T91P-6701-A, or equivalents.

6. Install flywheel with elongated hole over crankshaft dowel.
7. **Torque** flywheel bolts to 59 ft. lbs., in sequence, **Fig. 41.**
8. **On models equipped with automatic transmissions,** install transmission as outlined in **MOTOR's "Domestic Transmission, In-Vehicle Service." or "Transmission Service DVD."**
9. **On models equipped with manual transmissions,** install transmission as outlined in **MOTOR's "Domestic Transmission, In-Vehicle Service." or "Transmission Service DVD."**

OIL PAN

REPLACE

1. Support engine using three bar engine support tool No. 303-F072, or equivalent.
2. Remove accessory drive belt.
3. Raise and support vehicle.
4. Drain engine oil into suitable container.
5. Remove lower splash shield.
6. Support alternator, then remove mounting bolts.
7. Disconnect alternator electrical connections and remove alternator.
8. Remove air conditioning compressor mounting bolts, then support compressor aside using suitable mechanics wire.
9. Remove electronic thermactor air bracket bolts.
10. Remove power steering line from oil pan stud.
11. Remove steering gear mounting nuts and support steering gear.
12. Remove left and righthand control arm through bolts, then the left and righthand motor mount nuts.
13. Remove left and righthand subframe bolts, **Figs. 42 and 43.**
14. Remove transmission cooler line bracket nut.
15. Remove transmission to oil pan bolts.
16. Remove oil pan mounting bolts.
17. Pry subframe downward and remove oil pan.
18. Reverse procedure to install, noting the following:
    a. Install new gasket to oil pan.
    b. Apply .4 inch dot of silicone gasket sealant part No. F7AZ-19554-EA, or equivalent, to oil pan, **Fig. 44.**

c. Oil pan must be installed and bolts tightened within six minutes of sealant application.
d. **Torque** oil pan mounting bolts to 18 ft. lbs., in sequence, **Fig. 45.**
e. Ensure vehicle suspension alignment is within specifications. Refer to "Specifications" section.

OIL PUMP

REPLACE

1. Remove timing chains as outlined under "Timing Chain, Replace."
2. Remove oil pan as outlined under "Oil Pan, Replace."
3. Remove oil pump screen tube.
4. Remove mounting bolts and oil pump, **Fig. 46.**
5. Reverse procedure to install.

OIL COOLER

REPLACE

1. Ensure engine is cold.
2. Wrap suitable shop towel around pressure relief cap, then remove cap. **Ensure coolant does not come into contact with accessory drive belt.**
3. Drain radiator coolant into suitable container.
4. Disconnect coolant hoses at oil cooler.
5. Remove mounting bolt and oil cooler.
6. Reverse procedure to install, noting the following:
    a. Position oil cooler and gasket.
    b. Install mounting bolt, then turn cooler clockwise until locating pin hits stop.

SERPENTINE DRIVE BELT

Tension

Vehicle is equipped with an automatic belt tensioner and tension is not adjustable. Refer to **Fig. 47** to inspect tensioner.

Routing

Refer to **Fig. 48** for serpentine drive belt routing.

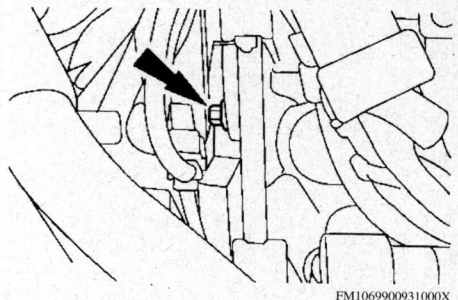

Fig. 19 Righthand noise suppressor bolt location

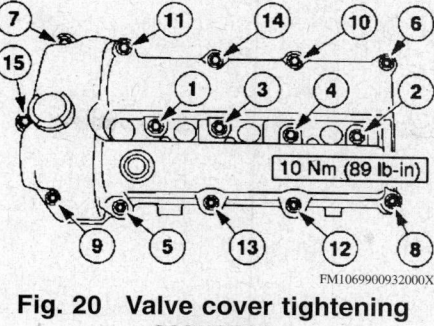

Fig. 20 Valve cover tightening sequence

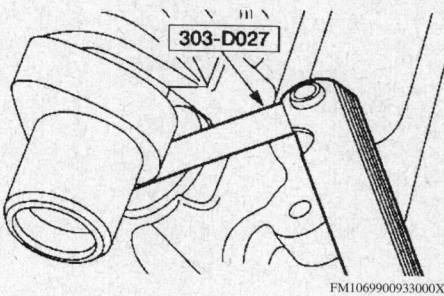

Fig. 21 Valve lash measurement

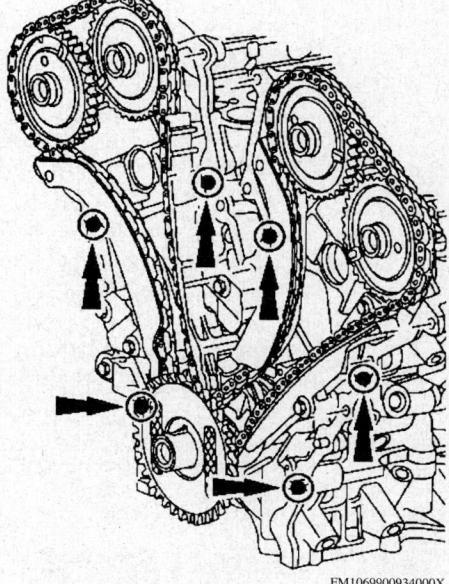

Fig. 22 Front cover sealant application points

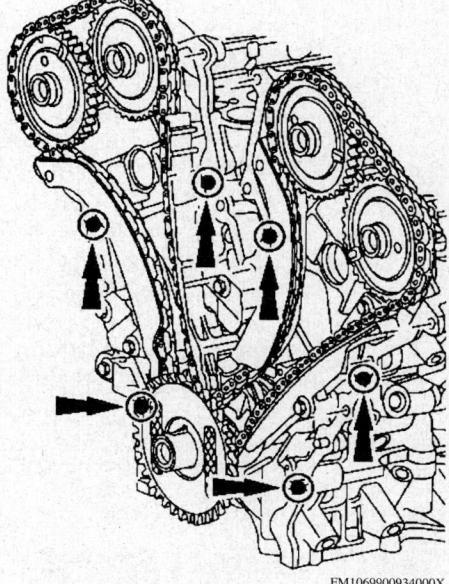

Fig. 23 Front cover tightening sequence

overflow bottle to bring level to MAX cold fill mark.

Fig. 24 Crankshaft keyway alignment

6. Disconnect engine vent hose, **Fig. 49.**
7. Disconnect upper and lower radiator hoses, then the heater supply and water pump hoses.
8. Remove water crossover.
9. Disconnect water inlet hose from coolant outlet tube.
10. Disconnect and remove water inlet hose from pump.
11. Remove serpentine drive belt.
12. Remove water pump mounting bolts, studs and water pump. Record location of water pump studs for installation alignment.
13. Reverse procedure to install.

COOLING SYSTEM BLEED

1. Open engine air bleed fitting, **Fig. 49.**
2. Open heater air bleed fitting, **Fig. 50.**
3. Add coolant to overflow bottle. Allow system to equalize until no more coolant can be added.
4. Close engine air bleed when coolant begins to escape.
5. Install cap to overflow bottle.
6. Start and run engine at idle speed with heater air bleed open. Turn heater to MAX position.
7. Close heater air bleed when steady stream of coolant starts to flow.
8. Allow engine to idle for 5 minutes, then add coolant to overflow bottle until it reaches MAX mark.
9. Reopen heater air bleed to release any trapped air, then close.
10. Operate engine at 1500 RPM for 3–5 minutes or until hot air comes from heater.
11. Return to idle and ensure hot air is still coming from heater.
12. Turn engine off and allow to cool. After engine has cooled, add coolant to

THERMOSTAT
REPLACE

1. Ensure engine is cold.
2. Wrap suitable shop towel around pressure relief cap, then remove cap. **Ensure coolant does not come into contact with accessory drive belt.**
3. Drain radiator coolant into suitable container.
4. Disconnect coolant hoses at oil cooler.
5. Remove air cleaner outlet tube.
6. Disconnect hoses from thermostat housing, **Fig. 51.**
7. Remove housing, thermostat and seal.
8. Reverse procedure to install.

WATER PUMP
REPLACE

1. Ensure engine is cold.
2. Wrap suitable shop towel around pressure relief cap, then remove cap. **Ensure coolant does not come into contact with accessory drive belt.**
3. Drain radiator coolant into suitable container.
4. Disconnect coolant hoses at oil cooler.
5. Remove air cleaner outlet tube.

RADIATOR
REPLACE

1. Ensure engine is cold.
2. Wrap suitable shop towel around pressure relief cap, then remove cap. **Ensure coolant does not come into contact with accessory drive belt.**
3. Drain radiator coolant into suitable container.
4. Disconnect coolant hoses at oil cooler.
5. Remove upper radiator sight shield.
6. Remove air cleaner outlet tube.
7. Remove radiator support brackets and upper radiator hose.
8. Remove receiver drier mounting bolt and position receiver drier aside.
9. Disconnect high pressure cooling fan line and return hose.
10. Separate return hose from fan shroud and position aside.
11. Remove fan shroud.
12. Support air conditioning condenser using suitable mechanics wire.
13. Raise and support vehicle.
14. Remove left and righthand splash shields, then the radiator air deflector.
15. Disconnect lower radiator hose.

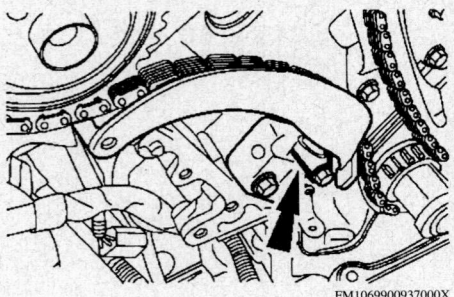

Fig. 25 Timing chain tensioner retention

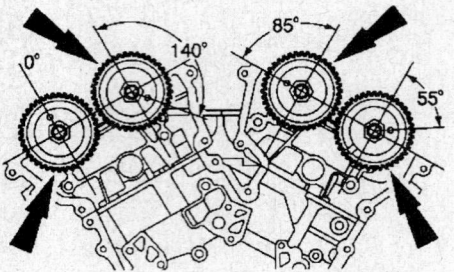

Fig. 26 Camshaft neutral positions

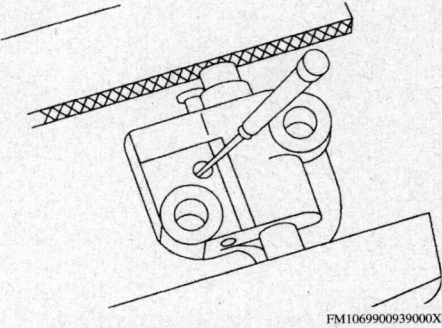

Fig. 27 Timing chain tensioner ratchet lock access hole

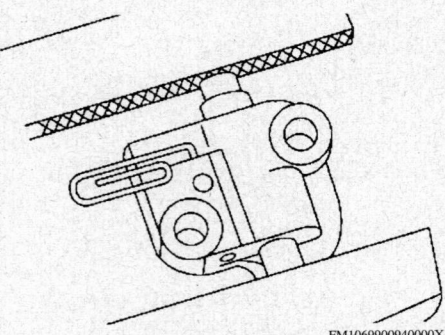

Fig. 28 Timing chain tensioner piston retention

16. Remove condenser to radiator mounting bolts.
17. Remove condenser support brackets and radiator through bottom of vehicle.
18. Reverse procedure to install.

HYDRAULIC FAN MOTOR
REPLACE

Refer to "Radiator, Replace" for hydraulic fan motor replacement procedure.

HYDRAULIC COOLING FAN PUMP
REPLACE

1. Remove accessory drive belt.
2. Remove lower cooling fan pump bolt.
3. Disconnect hose and allow to drain into suitable container, **Fig. 52**.
4. Disconnect cooling fan pump electrical connector.
5. Remove high pressure line bracket.
6. Disconnect high pressure line.
7. Remove two upper mounting bolts and cooling fan pump.
8. Reverse procedure to install.

FUEL PUMP
REPLACE

The fuel system contains two pumps. One is the "fuel delivery module" which pro-vides fuel pressure to the engine. The second pump is a jet pump or transfer pump which maintains fuel levels in both sides of the fuel tank.

The jet pump is located on the lefthand side of the fuel tank and contains a fuel level sensor and a check valve which maintains system pressure after the pump is shut off.

The fuel delivery module is located on the righthand side of the fuel tank and contains a fuel level sensor and an inlet screen on the bottom of the pump.

To disconnect fuel lines from pumps, press down on fuel line connector while pressing release tabs. Pull straight up to remove.

Whenever fuel pumps are removed, new fuel pump gaskets must be installed.

Fuel Delivery Module

1. Relieve fuel pressure as outlined under "Precautions."
2. Release rear seat mini-buckle.
3. Depress two seat cushion latches, then remove rear seat cushion and insulation.
4. Remove fuel pump access covers. Ensure fuel pump connectors are fully seated.
5. Remove black connector elbow on transfer pump, **Fig. 53**.
6. Attach fuel line draining connector to suitable fuel storage tanker hose and outlet fitting on transfer pump.
7. Siphon fuel until tank side is empty.
8. Attach fuel draining connector to fuel delivery module and repeat previous three steps, **Fig. 54**.
9. Disconnect remaining fuel line from fuel delivery module.
10. Disconnect fuel delivery module electrical connector.
11. Loosen fuel pump lockring using fuel sender wrench tool No. 310-069, or equivalent.
12. Remove fuel delivery module lockring.
13. Position pump flange clear of pump opening, then press lock tabs and release pump from tank mounting flange.
14. Lift pump straight up and out of retainer cup, then tilt while in tank to drain fuel

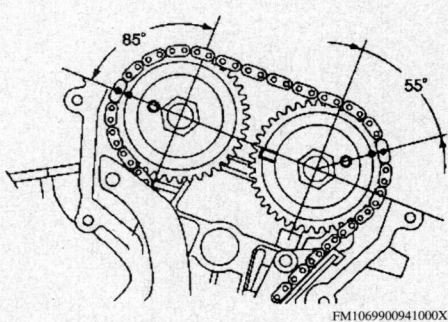

Fig. 29 Primary lefthand timing chain alignment mark inspection

from reservoir.
15. Straighten and lift straight up and out of tank. Drain excess fuel into suitable container.
16. Reverse procedure to install.

Jet (Transfer) Pump

1. Relieve fuel pressure as outlined under "Precautions."
2. Drain fuel tank as outlined under "Fuel Delivery Module."
3. Ensure fuel line connectors are fully seated prior to pressing release tabs.
4. Disconnect fuel lines from transfer pump.
5. Disconnect electrical connector from transfer pump.
6. Loosen transfer pump lockring using fuel sender wrench tool No. 310-069, or equivalent.
7. Remove lockring and transfer pump.
8. Reverse procedure to install.

FUEL FILTER
REPLACE

1. Relieve fuel pressure as outlined under "Precautions."
2. Raise and support vehicle.
3. Remove lefthand front tire and wheel assembly.
4. Remove splash shield fasteners.
5. Disconnect fuel line R-clip fittings, **Fig. 55**.
6. Remove mounting bolt and filter.
7. Reverse procedure to install.

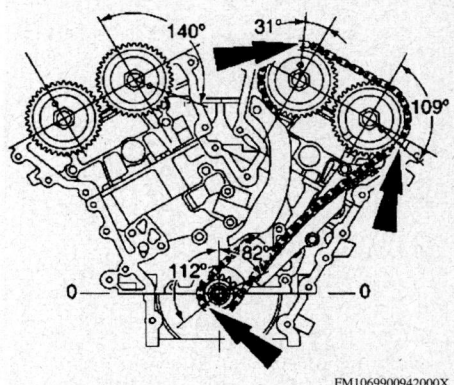

Fig. 30 Secondary lefthand timing chain alignment mark inspection

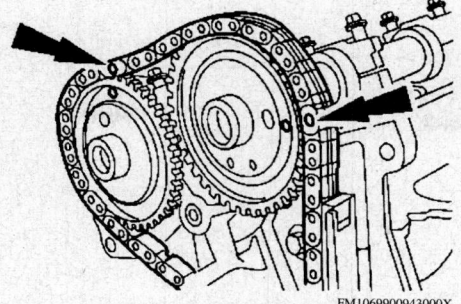

Fig. 31 Primary righthand timing chain alignment mark inspection

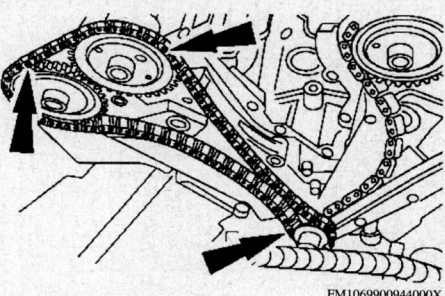

Fig. 32 Secondary righthand timing chain alignment mark inspection

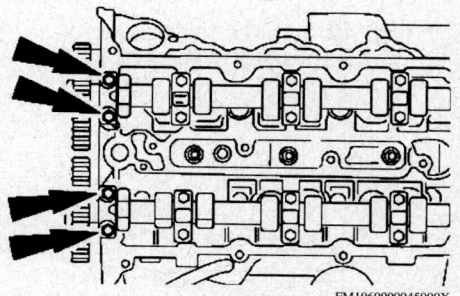

Fig. 33 Camshaft journal thrust cap location

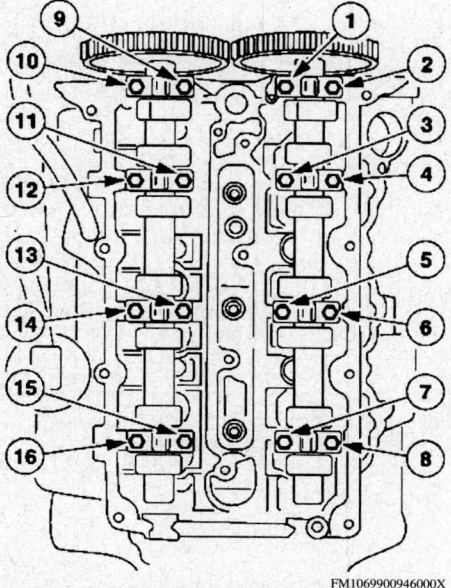

Fig. 34 Lefthand camshaft bearing cap tightening sequence

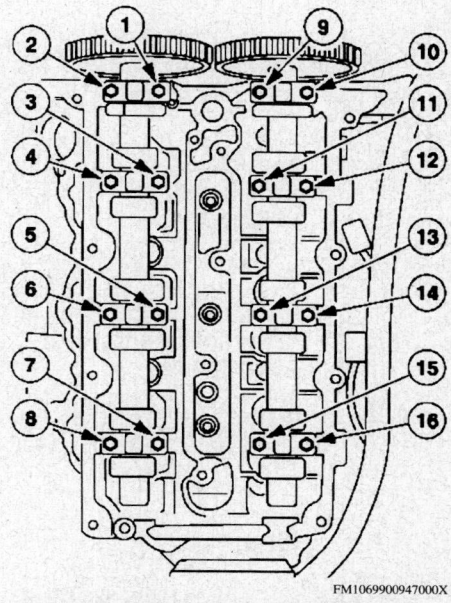

Fig. 35 Righthand camshaft bearing cap tightening sequence

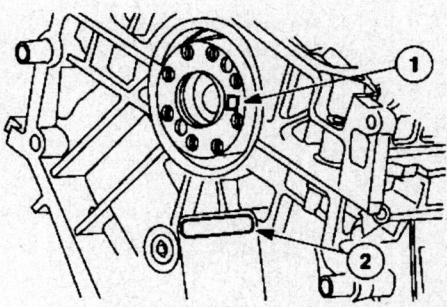

Fig. 36 Cylinder block and crankshaft bearing reference marks

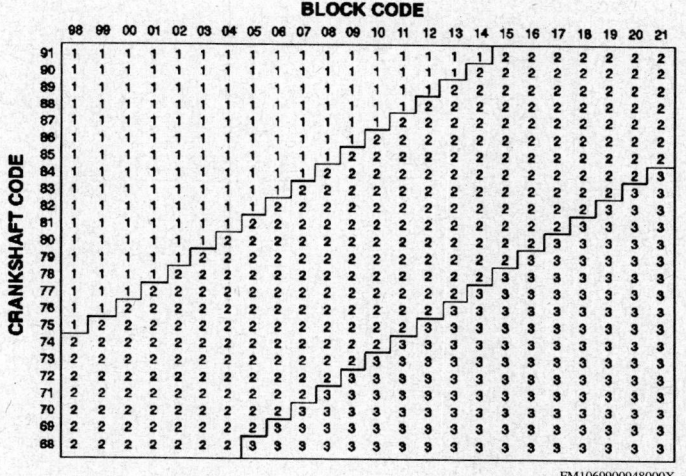

Fig. 37 Bearing grade selection chart

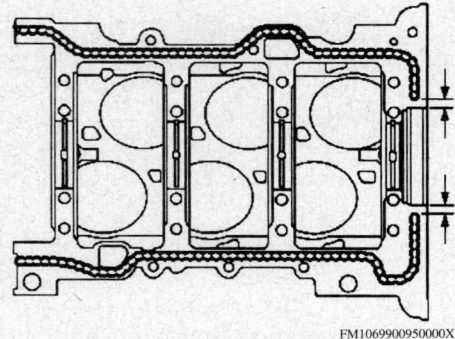

Fig. 38 Lower cylinder block sealant application

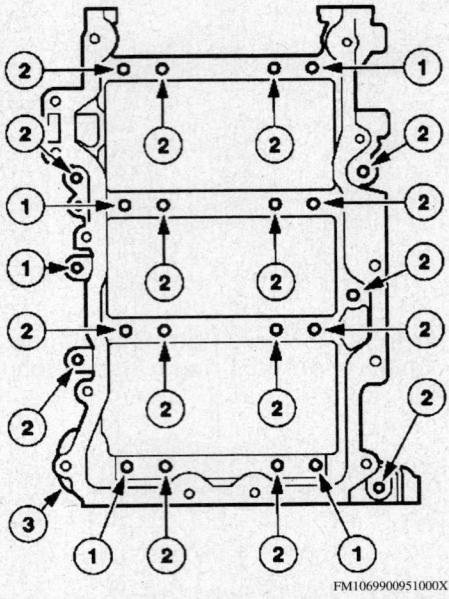

Fig. 39 Lower cylinder block bolt identification

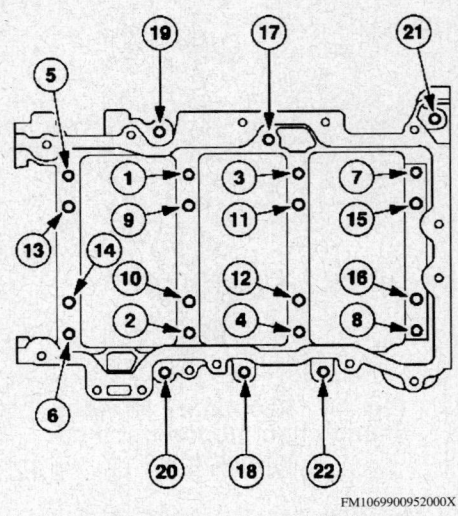

Fig. 40 Lower cylinder block tightening sequence

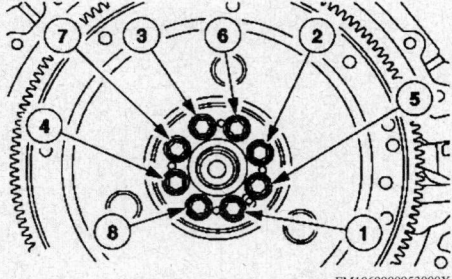

Fig. 41 Flywheel tightening sequence

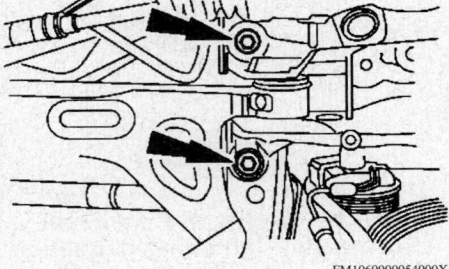

Fig. 42 Lefthand subframe bolt location

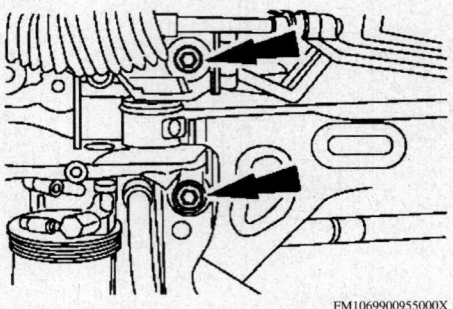

Fig. 43 Righthand subframe bolt location

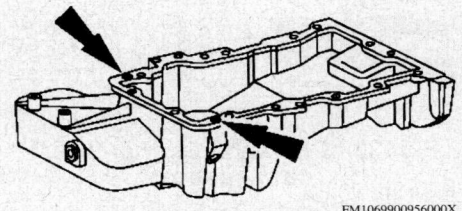

Fig. 44 Oil pan sealant application points

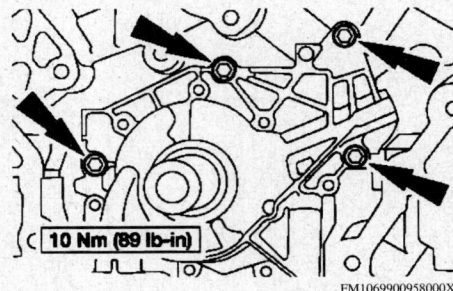

Fig. 46 Oil pump replacement

10 Nm (89 lb-in)

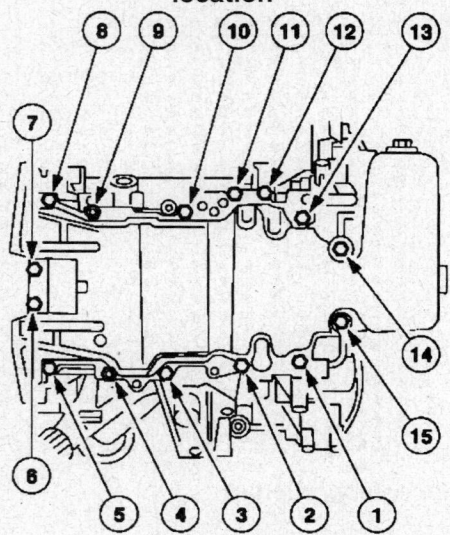

Fig. 45 Oil pan tightening sequence

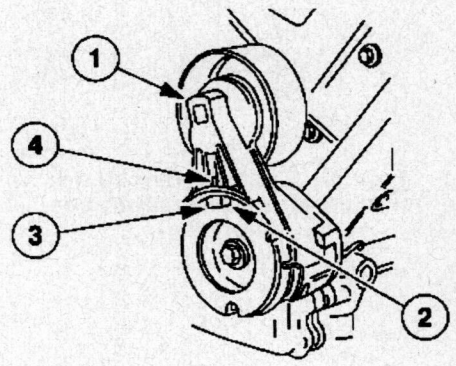

Item	Description
1	Belt tension relief point
2	Unacceptable belt wear range
3	Acceptable belt installation and wear range
4	Belt length indicator

Fig. 47 Belt tensioner inspection

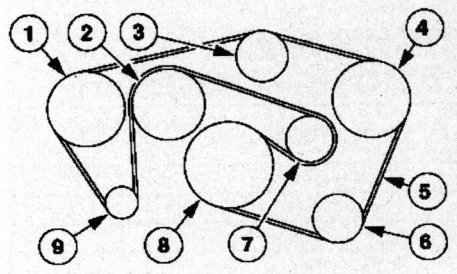

Item	Description
1	Hydraulic fan pump pulley
2	Water pump pulley
3	Belt idler pulley
4	Power steering pump pulley
5	Drive belt
6	A/C clutch pulley
7	Drive belt tensioner
8	Crankshaft vibration damper
9	Generator pulley

FM1069900960000X

Fig. 48   Serpentine drive belt routing

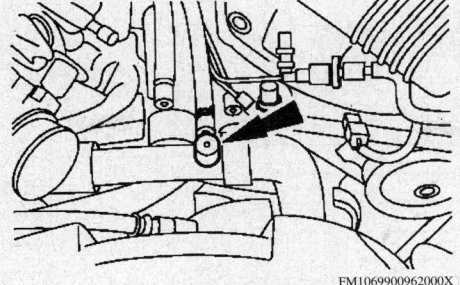

FM1069900962000X

Fig. 49   Engine air bleed location

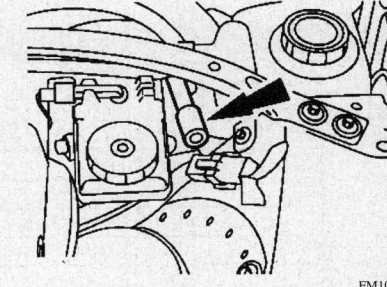

FM1069900963000X

Fig. 50   Heater air bleed location

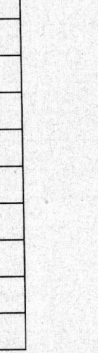

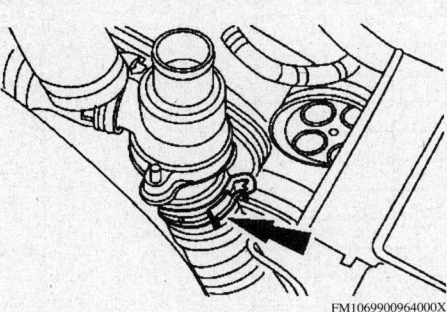

FM1069900964000X

Fig. 51   Thermostat housing location

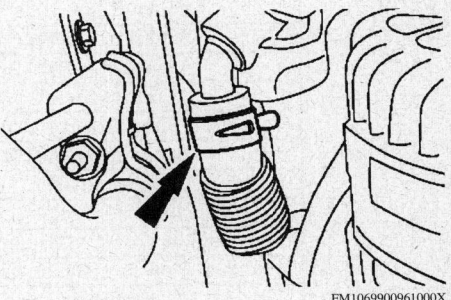

FM1069900961000X

Fig. 52   Hose location

FM1069900965000X

Fig. 53   Transfer pump fuel line connections

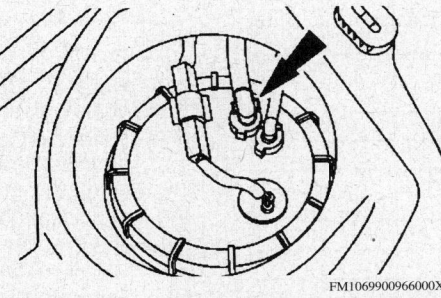

FM1069900966000X

Fig. 54   Fuel delivery module fuel line connections

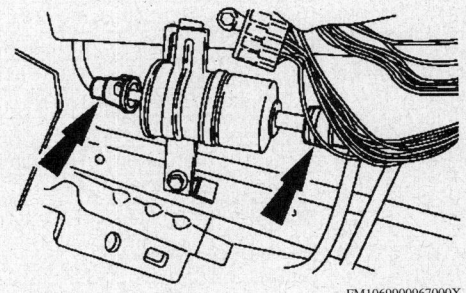

FM1069900967000X

Fig. 55   Fuel filter

TIGHTENING SPECIFICATIONS

Year	Component	Torque Ft. Lbs.
2004–06	Air Conditioning Compressor	18
	Alternator	35
	Belt Tensioner	35
	Camshaft Bearing Caps	⑨
	CKP Sensor	89①
	CMP Sensor	89①
	Connecting Rod	②
	Coolant Inlet Tube	18
	Coolant Outlet Tube	18
	Crankshaft Damper	③
	Cylinder Head	④
	Dipstick Tube	89①
	EGR Tube To EGR Valve	30
	Engine Appearance Cover Bracket	53
	Engine Mount	46
	Exhaust Manifold Heat Shield	89①
	Exhaust Manifold To Cylinder Head	⑥
	Exhaust Pipe To Exhaust Manifold	30
	Flywheel	⑩
	Front Brake Caliper	76
	Front Cover	⑦
	Front & Center Crossmember, Bolts	76
	Front Intake Manifold Support, Nut	89①
	Hydraulic Cooling Fan Pump	18
	Hydraulic Cooling Fan Reservoir	108①
	Idler Pulley	18
	Lower Control Arm, Through Bolt	129
	Lower Cylinder Block	②
	Lower Intake Manifold To Cylinder Head	⑤
	Lower Stabilizer Link	41
	Lower Strut Mount Bolts	129
	Main Bearing Cap	②
	Oil Cooler	42
	Oil Pan	⑧
	Oil Pan To Transmission	35
	Oil Pump	89①
	Oil Pump Screen	89①
	Power Steering Pump	18
	Power Steering Reservoir	108①
	Radiator Support Brackets	89①

TIGHTENING SPECIFICATIONS—Continued

Year	Component	Torque Ft. Lbs.
2004–06	Starter Motor	18
	Steering Gear	76
	Steering Shaft Clamp Bolt	18
	Subframe	77
	Thermostat Housing	96①
	Timing Chain Guide	18
	Timing Chain Tensioner	18
	Torque Converter	23–28
	Transmission Crossmember	41
	Transmission Cooler Lines	15
	Transmission To Engine	35
	Transmission To Oil Pan	35
	Upper Ball Joint	66
	Upper Intake Manifold Support Bracket, Bolt	89①
	Upper Intake Manifold Support Bracket, Nut	53①
	Upper Intake Manifold To Lower Intake Manifold	⑤
	Valve Cover	⑦
	Water Pump	18
	Wheel Lug Nuts	100

① — Inch lbs.

② — Refer to "Main & Rod Bearings" for tightening specifications & sequence.

③ — Refer to "Crankshaft Damper, Replace" for tightening specifications & sequence.

④ — Refer to "Cylinder Head, Replace" for tightening specifications & sequence.

⑤ — Refer to "Intake Manifold, Replace" for tightening specifications & sequence.

⑥ — Refer to "Exhaust Manifold, Replace" for tightening specifications & sequence.

⑦ — Refer to "Valve Cover, Replace" for tightening specifications & sequence.

⑧ — Refer to "Oil Pan, Replace" for tightening specifications & sequence.

⑨ — Refer to "Camshaft, Replace" for tightening specifications & sequence.

⑩ — Refer to "Crankshaft Rear Oil Seal, Replace" for tightening specifications & sequence.

3.9L Engine

NOTE: On Air Bag Equipped Models, Refer To "Air Bag System Precautions" Located In The Front Of This Manual For System Disarming & Arming Procedures.

NOTE: Refer To "Computer Relearn Procedures" Located In The Front Of This Manual When Battery Power To The Computer Has Been Interrupted.

INDEX

	Page No.		Page No.		Page No.
Camshaft, Replace	3-30	Fuel Filter, Replace	3-32	Serpentine Drive Belt	3-31
Installation	3-30	Fuel Pump, Replace	3-32	Routing	3-31
Removal	3-30	Hydraulic Cooling Fan Pump,		Tension Data	3-31
Compression Pressure	3-25	Replace	3-32	Thermostat, Replace	3-31
Cooling System Bleed	3-31	Hydraulic Fan Motor, Replace	3-32	Tightening Specifications	3-38
Crankshaft Damper, Replace	3-28	Intake Manifold, Replace	3-26	Timing Chain, Replace	3-29
Crankshaft Rear Oil Seal,		Oil Cooler, Replace	3-31	Primary	3-29
Replace	3-30	Oil Pan, Replace	3-30	Installation	3-29
Cylinder Head, Replace	3-27	Oil Pump, Replace	3-31	Removal	3-29
Engine Rebuilding		Precautions	3-25	Secondary	3-30
Specifications	21-1	Air Bag Systems	3-25	Timing Chain Tensioner,	
Engine, Replace	3-26	Battery Ground Cable	3-25	Replace	3-30
Engine Mount, Replace	3-25	Fuel System Pressure Relief	3-25	Valve Adjustment	3-28
Exhaust Manifold, Replace	3-27	Quick Disconnect Hoses	3-25	Valve Arrangement	3-28
Lefthand	3-27	R-Clip	3-25	Valve Cover, Replace	3-27
Righthand	3-27	Spring Lock	3-25	Lefthand	3-27
Front Cover, Replace	3-28	Vapor Tube	3-25	Righthand	3-28
Front Cover Seal, Replace	3-29	Radiator, Replace	3-31	Water Pump, Replace	3-31

PRECAUTIONS

Air Bag Systems

Refer to "Air Bag System Precautions" in the front of this manual for system disarming and arming procedures.

Battery Ground Cable

Prior to service, disconnect battery ground cable and isolate as required.

Fuel System Pressure Relief

1. Remove Schraeder valve cap and install fuel pressure gauge tool No. T80L-9974-B, or equivalent, to Schraeder valve.
2. Slowly open manual valve on pressure gauge and drain fuel into suitable container.

QUICK DISCONNECT HOSES

R-Clip

When working with R-clip type connections, do not use tools to disconnect, **Fig. 1.** Use of tools may deform clip components and could cause leaks.

To disconnect, bend shipping tab downward, **Fig. 1.** Spread R-clip and push clip into fitting. Separate fitting from tube.

To install, first inspect fitting and tube for damage and ensure connections are clean. Apply a light coat of clean 5W-30 motor oil to male end of tube. Insert R-clip into fitting. Align tube and fitting, then insert tube into fitting and push together until a click is heard. Pull on connection to ensure it is fully engaged.

Spring Lock

When working with spring lock type connections, spring lock tool set No. T84L-19623-B, or equivalent, must be used to disconnect fittings, **Fig. 2.** When connecting spring lock type fittings, inspect and clean both coupling ends. Lubricate fuel line O-ring seals with clean 5W-30 motor oil. When connection is made, pull on line to ensure it is fully engaged.

Vapor Tube

To disconnect vapor tube connections, squeeze fitting and disconnect vapor tube from fitting, **Fig. 3.** To connect, ensure fittings are clean and free from damage. Push tube onto fitting until it snaps into place. Pull on connection to ensure fitting is secure.

COMPRESSION PRESSURE

Before performing compression test, ensure crankcase oil is of correct viscosity and at correct level. Ensure battery is fully charged and engine is at normal operating temperature.

1. Turn ignition switch to OFF position.
2. Remove spark plugs.
3. Set throttle plates to wide open position.
4. Install suitable compression gauge in cylinder No. 1.
5. Install auxiliary starter switch in starting circuit.
6. With ignition switch in OFF position, use auxiliary starter switch to crank engine at least five compression strokes.
7. Count number of compression strokes required to reach highest reading and record highest reading.
8. Repeat test on each cylinder, cranking engine same number of compression strokes.
9. Indicated compression pressures are considered within specifications if lowest reading cylinder is within 75 percent of highest reading.

ENGINE MOUNT

REPLACE

1. Support engine using engine lifting eye kit tool No. D81L-6001-D and three bar

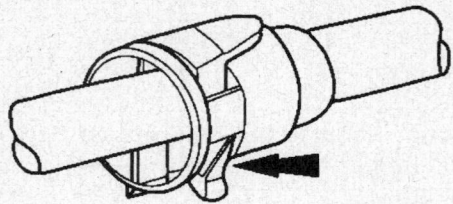

Fig. 1   R-clip connection

engine support kit tool No. D88L-6000-A, or equivalents.
2. Raise and support vehicle.
3. Remove upper and lower engine mount nuts.
4. Remove engine mount and bracket.
5. Reverse procedure to install.

ENGINE
REPLACE

When carrying out operations which involve the removal and installation of the driveshaft, always inspect the joint angles and adjust as outlined under "Driveline Angle Measurement" in "Rear Axle & Suspension" section.
1. Remove air cleaner and outlet tube.
2. Remove engine appearance cover.
3. Ensure engine is cold.
4. Wrap suitable shop towel around pressure relief cap, then remove cap.
5. **Ensure coolant does not come into contact with accessory drive belt.**
6. Open radiator draincock and drain coolant into suitable container.
7. **On models equipped with oil cooler,** disconnect coolant return hose at oil cooler.
8. **On all models,** remove upper radiator sight shield.
9. Remove upper radiator support brackets.
10. Recover refrigerant as outlined in "Air Conditioning" chapter.
11. Disconnect air conditioning pressure switch.
12. Release power steering line from frame rail.
13. Remove power steering reservoir and position aside.
14. Disconnect fuel lines.
15. Disconnect evaporative canister purge hose and main vacuum supply hose.
16. Remove cowl panels.
17. Remove cowl panel support bracket.
18. Disconnect throttle and speed control cables, then the engine ground strap.
19. Remove cabin air filter and plenum as outlined under "Heater Core, Replace" in "Electrical" section.
20. Disconnect powertrain bulkhead connectors located on rear side of righthand strut tower and position aside.
21. Remove cowl to engine insulation panel.
22. Disconnect remaining bulkhead connectors.
23. Place reference marks on heater hoses for installation alignment.
24. Disconnect four heater hoses at water control valve.
25. Remove hydraulic cooling fan reservoir and position aside.

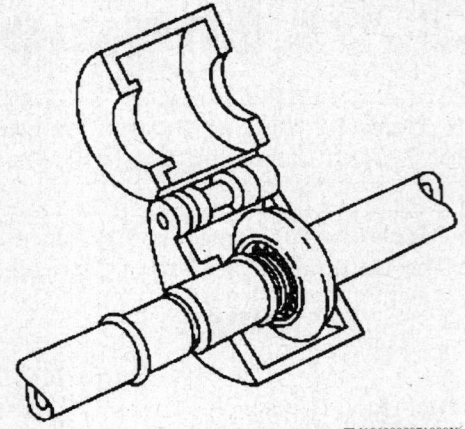

Fig. 2   Spring lock connection

26. Disconnect water valve electrical connector from radiator support and position harness aside.
27. Raise and support vehicle.
28. Remove front wheels.
29. Remove front anti-lock brake sensors.
30. Remove front calipers as outlined in "Disc Brakes" chapter and position aside.
31. Remove two sway bar link lower bolts.
32. Hold ball joint external hex, then remove upper ball joint nuts.
33. Separate upper ball joints from spindles.
34. Remove lower strut mount bolts.
35. Remove left, righthand and center splash shields.
36. Remove mounting nut, then disconnect air conditioning high pressure line.
37. Disconnect low pressure air conditioning quick disconnect coupler.
38. Remove exhaust system.
39. Remove driveshaft as outlined under "Propeller Shaft, Replace" in "Rear Axle & Suspension" section.
40. Disconnect shift cable and shift cable bracket bolt.
41. Disconnect hydraulic cooling fan lines from righthand frame rail.
42. Disconnect power steering lines from lefthand frame rail.
43. Disconnect steering gear electrical connectors.
44. Disconnect steering coupling.
45. Disconnect starter motor and alternator electrical connectors.
46. Remove flywheel inspection cover, **Fig. 4.**
47. Place reference marks on torque converter stud, nut and adapter plate for installation alignment.
48. Remove eight torque converter nuts from flywheel spacer.
49. **On models equipped with engine block heater,** disconnect engine block heater plug at grille opening.
50. **On all models,** support rear of vehicle using suitable safety stands.
51. Support engine transmission, front suspension, front and center crossmembers and cooling system using suitable powertrain lift and transmission support bracket. Disconnect

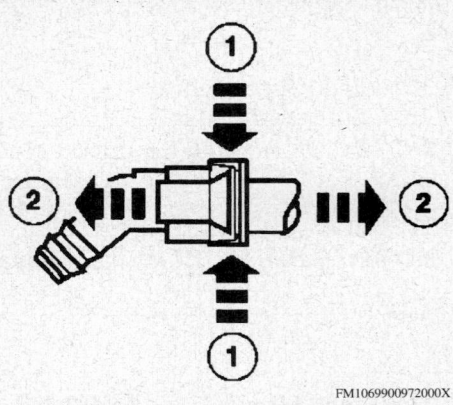

Fig. 3   Vapor tube connection

transmission support system.
52. Remove four front and four center support bolts, **Fig. 5.**
53. Lower powertrain assembly.
54. Disconnect engine block heater.
55. Disconnect air conditioning manifold hose from compressor.
56. Disconnect power steering pump and hydraulic cooling fan return hoses. Drain fluid into suitable container.
57. Remove lower radiator hose bolts.
58. Disconnect radiator and heater hoses.
59. Remove transmission cooler line bracket nut.
60. Disconnect transmission cooler and power steering pressure lines.
61. Remove power steering line bracket.
62. Install engine lifting eye kit tool No. D81L-6001-D, or equivalent, to engine.
63. Remove six lower transmission bolts.
64. Install spreader bar tool No. D93P-6001-A3, or equivalent, to engine lifting eyes.
65. Attach suitable engine crane to spreader bar and support engine and transmission.
66. Remove engine mount upper nuts.
67. Remove engine and transmission from subframe and place on floor.
68. Remove wiring harness mounting nuts and remaining transmission to engine mounting bolts.
69. Separate engine from transmission, then mount engine to suitable stand.
70. Reverse procedure to install.

INTAKE MANIFOLD
REPLACE

When cleaning cylinder head surfaces, do not use metal scrapers, wires brushes, power abrasive discs or other abrasive methods to clean sealing surfaces. Use only a plastic scraping tool to remove all traces of gasket material.
1. Remove air cleaner outlet tube.
2. Ensure engine is cold.
3. Wrap suitable shop towel around pressure relief cap, then remove cap. **Ensure coolant does not come into contact with accessory drive belt.**
4. Drain radiator coolant into suitable container.
5. Disconnect coolant return hose at oil cooler.

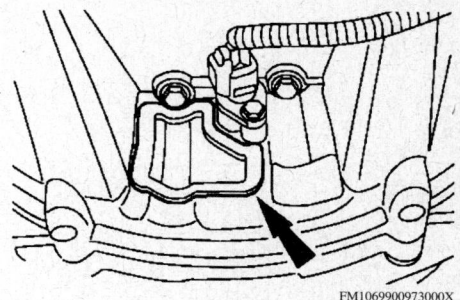

Fig. 4 Flywheel inspection cover

6. Remove wiper motor and arm as outlined under "Wiper Motor, Replace" in "Electrical" section.
7. Remove engine compartment brace.
8. Disconnect accelerator and speed control cables.
9. Disconnect main vacuum hose and vacuum harness.
10. Disconnect EGR vacuum line and EGR valve to exhaust manifold tube.
11. Disconnect camshaft position sensor and evaporative emission canister purge valve line.
12. Remove fuel pressure sensor connector.
13. Disconnect inline vacuum connector to fuel pressure sensor.
14. Relieve fuel pressure as outlined under "Precautions."
15. Disconnect fuel line, then the knock sensor and cylinder head temperature sensor connectors from bracket.
16. Raise wiring harness, then disconnect lefthand fuel injector connectors.
17. Disconnect idle air control, TP sensor and crankcase ventilation tube.
18. Disconnect coolant hoses from throttle body.
19. Raise wiring harness and disconnect righthand fuel injectors.
20. Remove manifold mounting bolts in sequence, **Fig. 6.**
21. Reverse procedure to install. **Torque** intake manifold bolts to 15 ft. lbs., in sequence, **Fig. 6.**

EXHAUST MANIFOLD
REPLACE
Lefthand

1. Remove dipstick tube.
2. Raise and support vehicle.
3. Remove exhaust catalyst pipe.
4. Remove eight mounting bolts and exhaust manifold.
5. Reverse procedure to install.

Righthand

1. Raise and support vehicle.
2. Disconnect exhaust catalyst from manifold.
3. Disconnect starter motor electrical connectors.
4. Disconnect EGR tube from exhaust manifold.
5. Remove eight mounting bolts and exhaust manifold.
6. Reverse procedure to install.

Fig. 5 Front & center support bolt location

CYLINDER HEAD
REPLACE

When cleaning cylinder head surfaces, do not use metal scrapers, wires brushes, power abrasive discs or other abrasive methods to clean sealing surfaces. Use only a plastic scraping tool to remove all traces of gasket material.

Cylinder head bolts should be replaced when removed.

Marking shims with permanent marker. Scratches or paint on shim will cause incorrect lash adjustment and severe engine damage.

1. Remove intake manifold as outlined under "Intake Manifold, Replace."
2. Remove engine sound insulator.
3. Remove camshafts as outlined under "Camshaft, Replace."
4. Place reference marks on bucket and shim tappets for installation alignment, then remove.
5. Remove water crossover tube.
6. Disconnect cylinder head temperature and camshaft position sensors.
7. Raise and support vehicle.
8. Disconnect exhaust system from exhaust manifolds.
9. Disconnect EGR tube from exhaust manifold, then lower vehicle.
10. Remove left and righthand front cylinder head bolts, **Fig. 7.**
11. Remove righthand cylinder head bolts in sequence, **Fig. 8.**
12. Remove righthand cylinder head and gasket.
13. Remove lefthand cylinder head bolts in sequence, **Fig. 9. If bolt 2 cannot be fully removed, hold bolt above decking surface using suitable rubber band when removing cylinder head.**
14. Remove lefthand cylinder head and gasket.
15. Reverse procedure to install, noting the following:
    a. Hand tighten cylinder head bolts.
    b. **Torque** cylinder head bolts to 15 ft. lbs., in sequence, **Figs. 10 and 11.**
    c. **Torque** head bolts to 26 ft. lbs., in sequence.
    d. **Torque** bolts to 33 ft. lbs., in sequence.
    e. Tighten an additional 90° in sequence

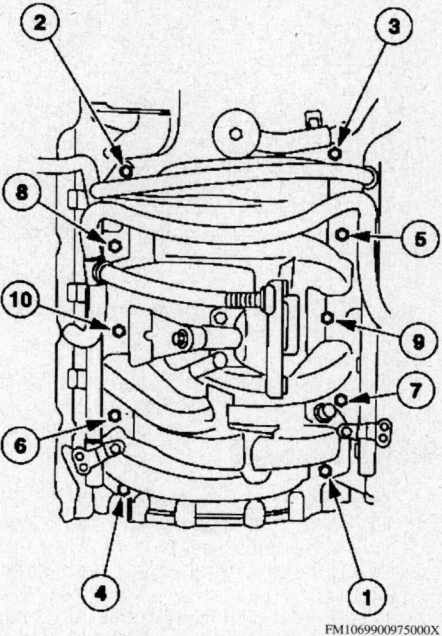

Fig. 6 Intake manifold loosening & tightening sequence

    f. Tighten an additional 90° in sequence.
    g. **Torque** front cylinder head bolts to 15 ft. lbs., then tighten an additional 90°.

VALVE COVER
REPLACE
Lefthand

1. Remove engine appearance cover.
2. Remove air cleaner housing.
3. Disconnect crankcase ventilation tube.
4. Relieve fuel system pressure as outlined under "Precautions."
5. Disconnect fuel line.
6. Disconnect evaporative emission canister purge valve hose, then the air assist tube.
7. Remove vapor management valve appearance cover and disconnect hose.
8. Position evaporative emission canister purge valve, engine vacuum regulator and bracket aside.
9. Position engine wiring harness upward, then remove ignition coil cover and ignition coils.
10. Disconnect three front and one rear wiring harness retainers.
11. Remove fuel line bracket bolt.
12. Remove reservoir mounting bolts and position aside.
13. Remove oil dipstick tube.
14. Remove brake line bracket, then the lefthand valve cover mounting bolts in sequence, **Fig. 12.**
15. Reverse procedure to install, noting the following:
    a. Apply .12 inch bead of silicone gasket and sealant part No. F7AZ-19554-EA, or equivalent, to cover joints, **Fig. 13.**

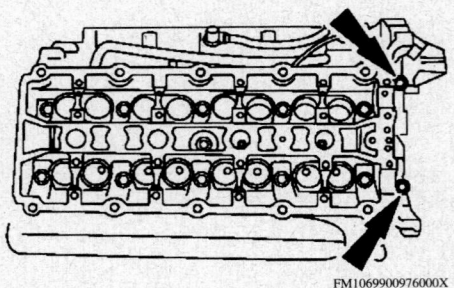

Fig. 7 Front cylinder head bolt location

b. **Torque** mounting bolts to 89 inch lbs., in sequence, **Fig. 12.**

Righthand

1. Remove air cleaner outlet tube.
2. Remove hydraulic cooling fan reservoir and position aside.
3. Disconnect crankcase ventilation hose.
4. Disconnect wiring harness brackets and position aside.
5. Remove ignition coil cover, then disconnect ignition coils.
6. Raise engine wiring harness and disconnect fuel injectors.
7. Disconnect three front and one rear wiring harness retainer, then remove ignition coils.
8. Remove righthand valve cover mounting bolts in sequence, then the valve cover, **Fig. 14.**
9. Reverse procedure to install, noting the following:
   a. Apply silicone gasket and sealant part No. F7AZ-19554-EA, or equivalent, to cover joints, **Fig. 13.**
   b. **Torque** valve cover mounting bolts to 89 inch lbs., in sequence, **Fig. 14.**

VALVE ARRANGEMENT

Inner..I-I-I-I-I-I-I-I
Outer............................E-E-E-E-E-E-E-E

VALVE ADJUSTMENT

1. Remove valve covers as outlined under "Valve Cover, Replace."
2. Remove spark plugs.
3. When measuring valve clearance, ensure camshaft is on base circle, **Fig. 15.**
4. Measure and record valve clearances using suitable feeler gauge. Refer to "Specifications" section for valve clearance.
5. If adjustment is required, remove camshafts as outlined under "Camshaft, Replace."
6. Remove shims from bucket tappet. Shims are marked for thickness (for example, 222 equals 2.22 mm shim.)
7. Select shims by adding base shim thickness to measured clearance, then subtract desirable clearance (intake, .006 inch; exhaust, .012 inch).

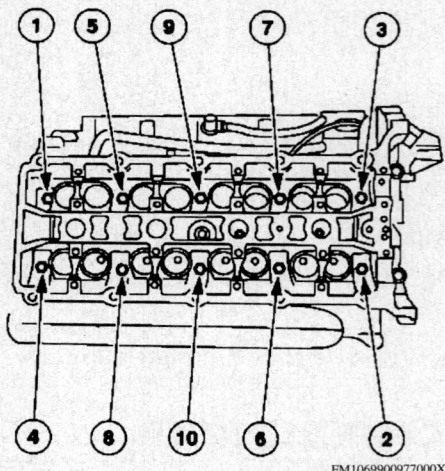

Fig. 8 Righthand cylinder head loosening sequence

8. Reverse procedure to install. Ensure new valve clearance is within specifications.

CRANKSHAFT DAMPER
REPLACE

1. Remove hydraulic cooling fan as outlined under "Radiator, Replace."
2. Remove accessory drive belt.
3. Remove crankshaft pulley mounting bolt.
4. Remove crankshaft damper using damper remover tool No. T58P-6316-D, or equivalent.
5. Reverse procedure to install, noting the following:
   a. Apply silicone gasket and sealant part No. F7AZ-19554-EA, or equivalent, to damper keyway.
   b. Install damper using damper installation tool No. T74P-6316-B, or equivalent.
   c. **Torque** crankshaft damper bolt to 59 ft. lbs.
   d. Loosen damper bolt two full turns.
   e. **Torque** bolt to 37 ft. lbs.
   f. Tighten an additional 90°.

FRONT COVER
REPLACE

1. Ensure engine is cold.
2. Wrap suitable shop towel around pressure relief cap, then remove cap. **Ensure coolant does not come into contact with accessory drive belt.**
3. Drain radiator coolant into suitable container.
4. **On models equipped with oil cooler,** disconnect coolant return hose at oil cooler.
5. **On all models,** remove valve covers as outlined under "Valve Cover, Replace."
6. Remove cooling fan as outlined under "Radiator, Replace."
7. Loosen water pump bolts.
8. Remove accessory drive belts.
9. Remove water pump pulley, then cover alternator.

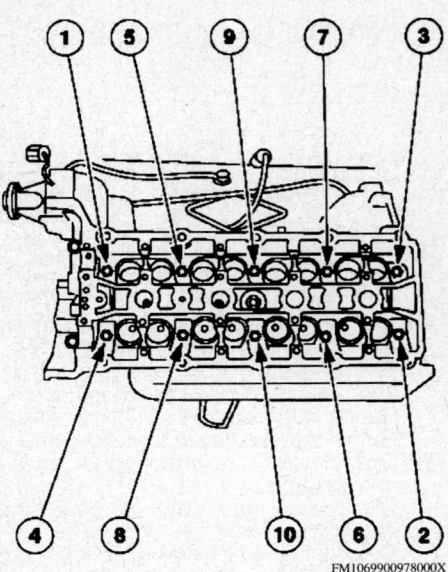

Fig. 9 Lefthand cylinder head loosening sequence

10. Remove lower radiator hose bolts.
11. Disconnect upper radiator hose from water crossover.
12. Disconnect heater hose.
13. Remove idler pulleys.
14. Remove crankshaft pulley mounting bolt.
15. Remove crankshaft damper using damper remover tool No. T58P-6316-D, or equivalent.
16. Recover refrigerant as outlined in "Air Conditioning" chapter.
17. Raise and support vehicle.
18. Remove splash shields.
19. Remove power steering hose bracket and position aside.
20. Remove air conditioning compressor manifold from compressor.
21. Disconnect compressor electrical connector.
22. Remove mounting bolts and air conditioning compressor.
23. Drain power steering reservoir into suitable container, then disconnect reservoir hose.
24. Remove power steering pump and position aside.
25. Remove power steering pump bracket.
26. Remove alternator as outlined under "Alternator, Replace" in "Electrical" section.
27. Drain hydraulic cooling fan reservoir into suitable container and disconnect hydraulic fan pump reservoir hose.
28. Remove hydraulic cooling fan pump and pump bracket.
29. Remove front cover bolts in sequence, **Fig. 16.** Clean gasket surfaces using suitable plastic scraper.
30. Reverse procedure to install, noting the following:
    a. Inspect front cover gaskets.
    b. Apply .12 inch wide bead of silicone gasket and sealant part No. F7AZ-19554-EA, or equivalent, to eight points, **Fig. 17.**
    c. **Torque** front cover mounting bolts

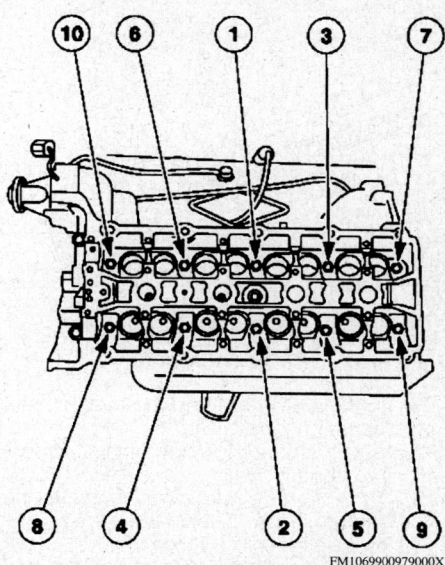

Fig. 10 Lefthand cylinder head tightening sequence

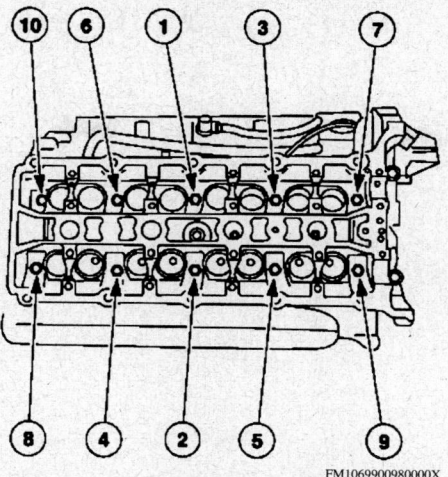

Fig. 11 Righthand cylinder head tightening sequence

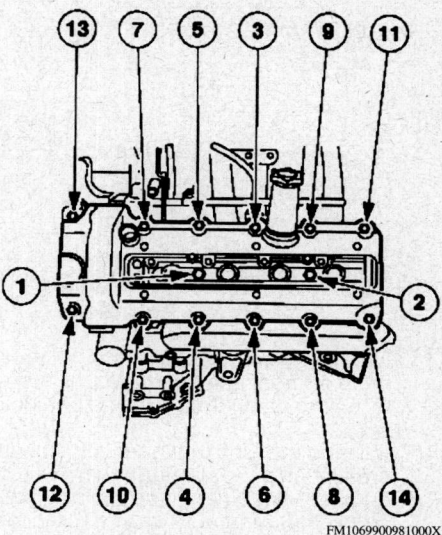

Fig. 12 Lefthand valve cover loosening & tightening sequence

to 44 inch lbs., in sequence **Fig. 18.**
d. **Torque** mounting bolts to 89 inch lbs., in sequence
e. Apply silicone gasket and sealant part No. F7AZ-19554-EA, or equivalent, to damper keyway.
f. Install damper using damper installation tool No. T74P-6316-B, or equivalent.
g. **Torque** crankshaft damper bolt to 59 ft. lbs.
h. Loosen damper bolt two full turns.
i. **Torque** bolt to 37 ft. lbs.
j. Tighten an additional 90°.

FRONT COVER SEAL
REPLACE

1. Remove hydraulic cooling fan as outlined under "Radiator, Replace."
2. Remove accessory drive belt.
3. Remove crankshaft pulley mounting bolt.
4. Remove crankshaft damper using damper remover tool No. T58P-6316-D, or equivalent.
5. Remove front seal using seal removal tool No. 303-409, or equivalent.
6. Reverse procedure to install, noting the following:
   a. Install new seal using seal installer tool No. 303-646, or equivalent.
   b. Apply silicone gasket and sealant part No. F7AZ-19554-EA, or equivalent, to damper keyway.
   c. Install damper using damper installation tool No. T74P-6316-B, or equivalent.
   d. **Torque** crankshaft damper bolt to 59 ft. lbs.
   e. Loosen damper bolt two full turns.
   f. **Torque** bolt to 37 ft. lbs.
   g. Tighten an additional 90°.

TIMING CHAIN
REPLACE
Primary
REMOVAL

There are no timing alignment marks for this engine. The proper alignment is achieved using suitable crankshaft locking tool and camshaft positioning/locking tools.
1. Remove front cover as outlined under "Front Cover, Replace."
2. Raise and support vehicle.
3. Remove crankshaft position sensor and torque converter access cover.
4. Turn crankshaft to 45° ATDC and ensure crankshaft keyway is at 6 o'clock position.
5. Install crankshaft positioning tool No. 303-645, or equivalent, to ignition pulse wheel.
6. Lower vehicle, then install camshaft locking tool No. 303-530, or equivalent, to righthand cylinder head.
7. Loosen outer camshaft bolt, **Fig. 19.**
8. Loosen camshaft damper bolt and slide camshaft sprockets forward on bolts, **Fig. 20.**
9. Remove righthand timing chain tensioner and blanking plate.
10. Remove tensioner arm and timing chain guide.
11. Remove righthand primary timing chain and crankshaft sprocket as an assembly.
12. Remove camshaft locking tool from righthand cylinder head.
13. Install camshaft locking tool to lefthand cylinder head.
14. Loosen outer camshaft bolt, **Fig. 21.**
15. Loosen lefthand camshaft damper bolt and slide camshaft sprockets forward on bolts, **Fig. 22.**
16. Remove lefthand timing chain tensioner and blanking plate, then the tensioner arm.
17. Remove lefthand timing chain guide.

18. Remove lefthand timing chain and crankshaft gear as an assembly.

INSTALLATION

There are no timing alignment marks for this engine. The proper alignment is achieved using suitable crankshaft locking tool and camshaft positioning/locking tools.
1. Insert suitable wire into timing chain tensioner and dislodge check ball, **Fig. 23.**
2. Compress tensioner using hand pressure and remove wire.
3. If timing mark on lefthand timing chain crankshaft gear is facing toward rear of engine, install righthand timing chain crankshaft gear with mark facing forward. If timing mark on lefthand timing chain crankshaft gear is facing toward front of engine, install righthand timing chain crankshaft gear with mark facing toward rear of engine.
4. Ensure camshaft holding tool is installed on lefthand cylinder head.
5. Position timing chain over lefthand intake camshaft sprocket.
6. Position crankshaft gear into timing chain.
7. Position timing chain and crankshaft gear over crankshaft as an assembly.
8. Install lefthand timing chain guide and tensioner arm.
9. Position lefthand blanking plate, **Fig. 24. If blanking plate is not positioned properly, oil galley will not seal resulting in low oil pressure and engine damage.**
10. Install lefthand timing chain tensioner and blanking plate.
11. Install suitable tie strap to take up timing chain slack, **Fig. 25.**
12. Apply tension to lefthand exhaust camshaft sprocket using timing chain tensioning tool No. 303-532, or equivalent.
13. **Torque** camshaft sprocket bolts to 15 ft. lbs., then tighten an additional 90°.

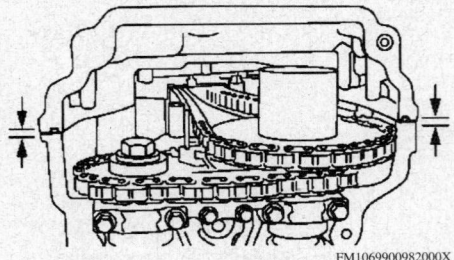

Fig. 13 Valve cover sealant application points

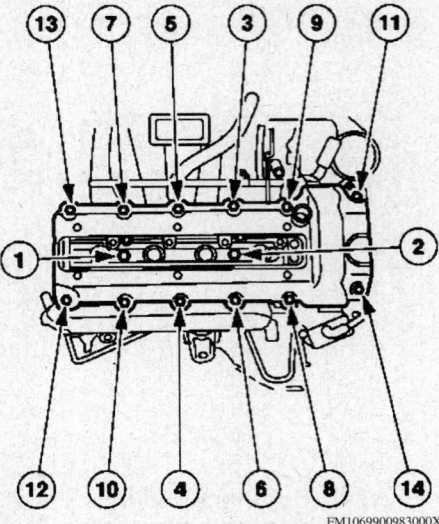

Fig. 14 Righthand valve cover loosening & tightening sequence

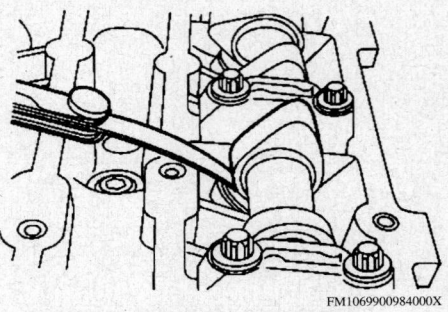

Fig. 15 Valve clearance measurement

14. Install camshaft holding tool to righthand cylinder head. It may be required to adjust camshafts to install holding tool.
15. If timing mark on lefthand timing chain crankshaft gear is facing toward rear of engine, install righthand timing chain crankshaft gear with mark facing forward. If timing mark on lefthand timing chain crankshaft gear is facing toward front of engine, install righthand timing chain crankshaft gear with mark facing toward rear of engine.
16. Position timing chain over righthand intake camshaft sprocket.
17. Place crankshaft gear into timing chain.
18. Install timing chain and crankshaft gear over crankshaft as an assembly.
19. Install righthand chain guide and tensioner arm.
20. Position righthand blanking plate, **Fig. 26. If blanking plate is not positioned properly, oil galley will not seal resulting in low oil pressure and engine damage.**
21. Install righthand timing chain tensioner and blanking plate.
22. Install suitable tie strap to take up timing chain slack, **Fig. 25.**
23. Exhaust camshaft sprocket bolt must be fully tightened before tightening intake camshaft sprocket bolt.
24. Apply tension to righthand exhaust camshaft sprocket using timing chain tensioning tool No. 303-532, or equivalent.
25. **Torque** sprocket bolts to 15 ft. lbs., then tighten an additional 90°.
26. Remove camshaft locking tool and tie straps.
27. Raise and support vehicle.
28. Remove crankshaft locking tool.
29. Install crankshaft position sensor and torque converter cover.
30. Lower vehicle.
31. Install front cover as outlined under "Front Cover, Replace."

Secondary

There are no timing alignment marks for this engine. The proper alignment is achieved using suitable crankshaft locking tool and camshaft positioning/locking tools.
1. Remove primary timing chains as outlined under "Primary."
2. Remove exhaust camshaft sprocket and intake camshaft sprocket bolts.
3. Remove sprockets, damper and chain as an assembly.

4. Remove secondary timing chain tensioner.
5. Reverse procedure to install, noting the following:
   a. Insert suitable wire into tensioner check valve.
   b. Apply hand pressure until tensioner is fully collapsed, then remove wire.
   c. When installing secondary timing chains, ensure camshaft holding tool No. 303-530, or equivalent, is in place.

TIMING CHAIN TENSIONER
REPLACE

Refer to "Timing Chain, Replace" for timing chain tensioner replacement procedure.

CAMSHAFT
REPLACE
Removal

1. Remove primary and secondary timing chains as outlined under "Timing Chain, Replace."
2. Remove camshaft locking tool.
3. Place reference marks on camshaft bearing caps and record locations for installation alignment.
4. Remove left and righthand camshaft bearing caps, then the camshafts.
5. Place reference marks on shims and bucket tappets, then record for installation alignment. **Mark shims and bucket tappets with permanent marker. Scratches or paint on shims will result in incorrect lash adjustments and engine damage.**

Installation

1. Apply clean 5W-30 motor oil to cam-

shaft journals, camshaft caps and camshaft lobes.
2. Install left and righthand cylinder head camshafts.
3. Hand tighten mounting bolts in sequence, **Figs. 27 and 28.**
4. **Torque** bolts to 53 inch lbs.
5. Final tighten bolts an additional 90°.
6. If any valve train components were replaced, perform valve lash adjustment as outlined under "Valve Adjustment."
7. Install camshaft locking tool No. 303-530, or equivalent, to lefthand cylinder head.
8. Install primary and secondary timing chains as outlined under "Timing Chain, Replace."

CRANKSHAFT REAR OIL SEAL
REPLACE

1. Raise and support vehicle.
2. Remove transaxle as outlined in **MOTOR's "Domestic Transmission, In-Vehicle Service." or "Transmission Service DVD."**
3. Remove flywheel.
4. Remove rear crankshaft oil seal using screw tool No. T95T-5310-AR2 and seal remover/installer tool No. 303-647, or equivalents.
5. Reverse procedure to install, noting the following:
   a. Lubricate outer lips and inner seal of new oil seal before installation.
   b. Install new seal using seal remover/installer tool No. 303-647, or equivalent.
   c. **Torque** flywheel mounting bolts to 11 ft. lbs., in sequence, **Fig. 29.**
   d. **Torque** mounting bolts to 81 ft. lbs., in sequence.

OIL PAN
REPLACE

1. Raise and support vehicle.
2. Drain engine oil into suitable container.
3. Remove mounting bolts and oil pan.
4. Reverse procedure to install, noting the following:
   a. Inspect oil pan gasket.
   b. **Torque** mounting bolts to 44 inch lbs., in sequence, **Fig. 30.**
   c. **Torque** mounting bolts to 108 inch lbs., in sequence.

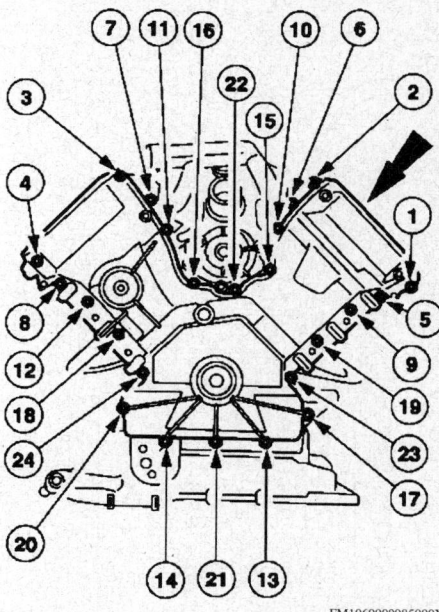

Fig. 16 Front cover removal sequence

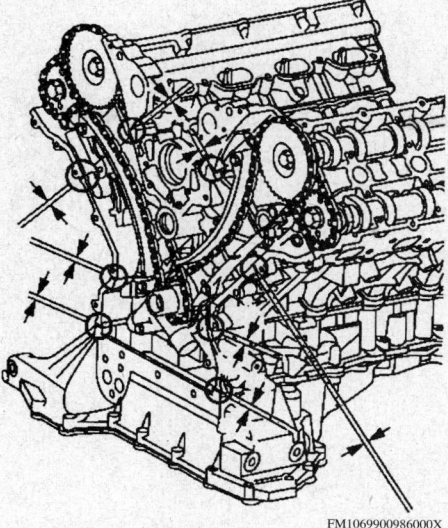

Fig. 17 Front cover sealant application points

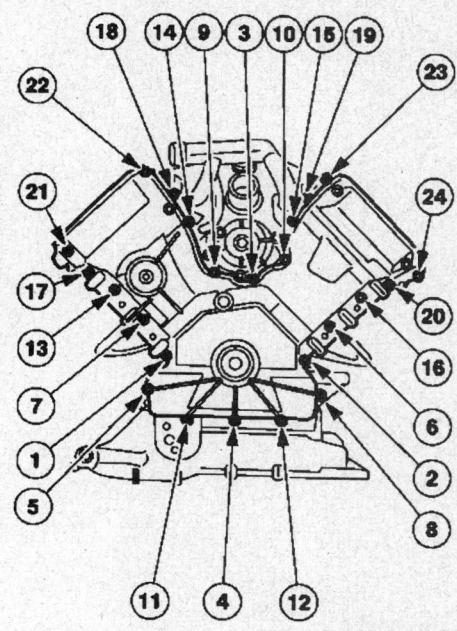

Fig. 18 Front cover tightening sequence

OIL PUMP

REPLACE

1. Remove primary timing chains as outlined under "Timing Chain, Replace."
2. Remove mounting bolts and oil pump.
3. Reverse procedure to install.

OIL COOLER

REPLACE

1. Ensure engine is cold.
2. Wrap suitable shop towel around pressure relief cap, then remove cap. **Ensure coolant does not come into contact with accessory drive belt.**
3. Drain radiator coolant into suitable container.
4. Disconnect coolant return hose at oil cooler.
5. Remove center air deflector and oil filter.
6. Disconnect oil cooler coolant hoses.
7. Remove mounting bolts and oil cooler.
8. Reverse procedure to install.

SERPENTINE DRIVE BELT

Tension Data

Vehicle is equipped with an automatic belt tensioner. Belt tension is not adjustable. Refer to **Fig. 31** to inspect tensioner.

Routing

Refer to **Fig. 32** for serpentine drive belt routing.

COOLING SYSTEM BLEED

1. Remove engine fill cap, **Fig. 33.**

2. Open heater air bleed, **Fig. 34.**
3. Add coolant to overflow bottle allowing system to equalize until no more coolant can be added.
4. Install overflow bottle cap.
5. Add as much coolant as possible to engine fill cap opening. Ensure coolant does not come in contact with accessory drive belt.
6. Install engine fill cap.
7. Start engine and turn heater to Max position.
8. Close heater bleed when steady stream of coolant is present.
9. Allow engine to idle for five minutes adding coolant to overflow bottle to maintain cold fill Max mark.
10. Open heater air bleed to release any trapped air and close again.
11. Operate engine at 2000 RPM for 3–5 minutes or until hot air comes from heater.
12. Return engine to idle and ensure hot air is still coming from heater.
13. Turn engine off and allow to cool.
14. Add coolant to overflow bottle to bring level to cold fill Max level.

THERMOSTAT

REPLACE

1. Ensure engine is cold.
2. Wrap suitable shop towel around pressure relief cap, then remove cap. **Ensure coolant does not come into contact with accessory drive belt.**
3. Drain radiator coolant into suitable container.
4. **On models equipped with oil cooler,** disconnect coolant return hose at oil cooler.
5. **On all models,** remove air cleaner outlet tube.
6. Remove coolant tube from front of engine, **Fig. 35.**
7. Remove coolant tube bracket studs.
8. Disconnect lower radiator hose from thermostat housing.

9. Remove housing cover and thermostat, **Fig. 36.**
10. Reverse procedure to install.

WATER PUMP

REPLACE

1. Ensure engine is cold.
2. Wrap suitable shop towel around pressure relief cap, then remove cap. **Ensure coolant does not come into contact with accessory drive belt.**
3. Drain radiator coolant into suitable container.
4. **On models equipped with oil cooler,** disconnect coolant return hose at oil cooler.
5. **On all models,** loosen water pump pulley bolts.
6. Remove accessory drive belt.
7. Remove mounting bolts and water pump pulley.
8. Remove mounting bolts and water pump. Inspect water pump O-ring seal.
9. Reverse procedure to install, noting the following:
   a. Lubricate water pump O-ring using premium engine coolant part No. E2FZ-19549-AA, or equivalent.
   b. Bleed cooling system as outlined under "Cooling System Bleed."

RADIATOR

REPLACE

1. Ensure engine is cold.
2. Wrap suitable shop towel around pressure relief cap, then remove cap. **Ensure coolant does not come into contact with accessory drive belt.**
3. Drain radiator coolant into suitable container.

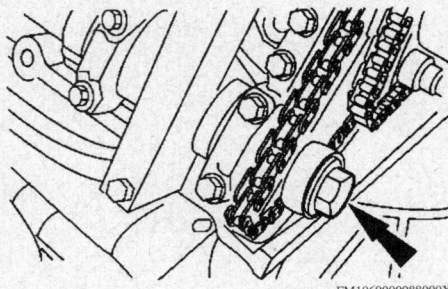

Fig. 19 Righthand outer camshaft bolt

FM1069900988000X

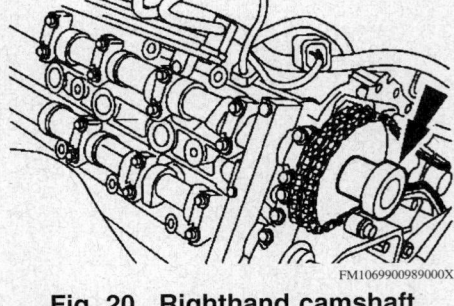

Fig. 20 Righthand camshaft damper bolt

FM1069900989000X

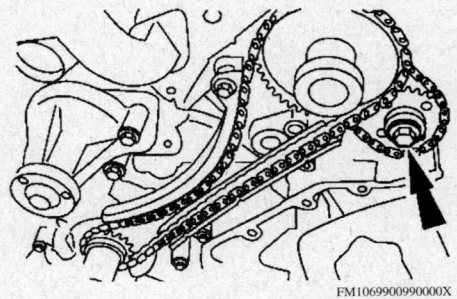

Fig. 21 Lefthand outer camshaft bolt

FM1069900990000X

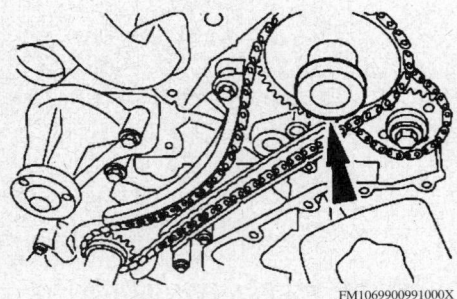

Fig. 22 Lefthand camshaft damper bolt

FM1069900991000X

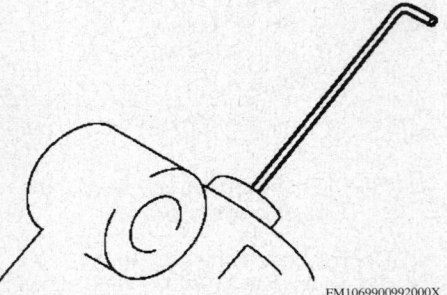

Fig. 23 Timing chain tensioner reset

FM1069900992000X

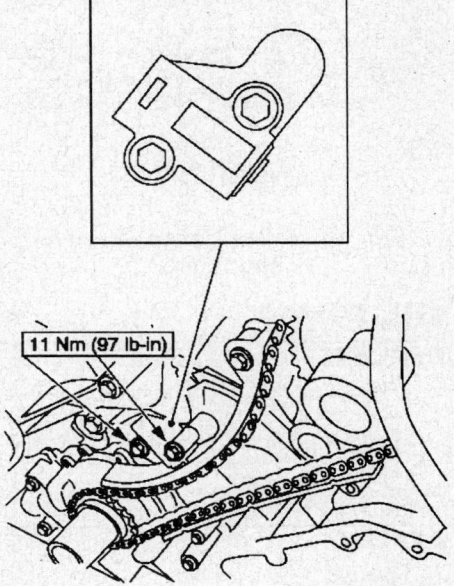

Fig. 24 Lefthand blanking plate installation

FM1069900993000X

4. **On models equipped with oil cooler, Fig. 37,** disconnect coolant hoses at oil cooler.
5. **On all models,** remove upper radiator sight shield.
6. Remove air cleaner outlet tube.
7. Remove radiator support brackets and upper radiator hose.
8. Remove receiver drier mounting bolt and position receiver drier aside.
9. Remove auxiliary coolant pump bolt and position aside.
10. Disconnect high pressure cooling fan line and return hose.
11. Separate return hose from fan shroud and position aside.
12. Remove fan shroud.
13. Support air conditioning condenser using suitable mechanics wire.
14. Raise and support vehicle.
15. Remove left and righthand splash shields, then the radiator air deflector.
16. Disconnect lower radiator hose.
17. Remove condenser to radiator mounting bolts.
18. Remove condenser support brackets and radiator through bottom of vehicle.
19. Reverse procedure to install.

HYDRAULIC FAN MOTOR
REPLACE

Refer to "Radiator, Replace" for hydraulic fan motor replacement procedure.

HYDRAULIC COOLING FAN PUMP
REPLACE

1. Remove engine appearance cover.
2. Disconnect IAT sensor, breather hose and idle air control valve inlet tube.
3. Remove air intake tube support nut and washer.
4. Loosen tube clamps and remove tube.
5. Remove accessory drive belt.
6. Raise and support vehicle, then remove mounting bolts.
7. Turn alternator and remove positive cable from alternator.
8. Lower alternator and disconnect electrical connector.
9. Turn alternator and remove.
10. Disconnect hose and drain fluid into suitable container, **Fig. 38.**
11. Disconnect fan pump electrical connector.
12. Remove high pressure line bracket and disconnect high pressure line.
13. Remove pump mounting bolts and cooling fan.

14. Reverse procedure to install.

FUEL PUMP
REPLACE

Refer to "Fuel Pump, Replace" in the "3.0L Engine" section for fuel pump replacement procedures.

FUEL FILTER
REPLACE

1. Relieve fuel pressure as outlined under "Precautions."
2. Raise and support vehicle.
3. Remove lefthand front tire and wheel assembly.
4. Remove splash shield fasteners.
5. Disconnect fuel line R-clip fittings.
6. Remove mounting bolt and filter.
7. Reverse procedure to install.

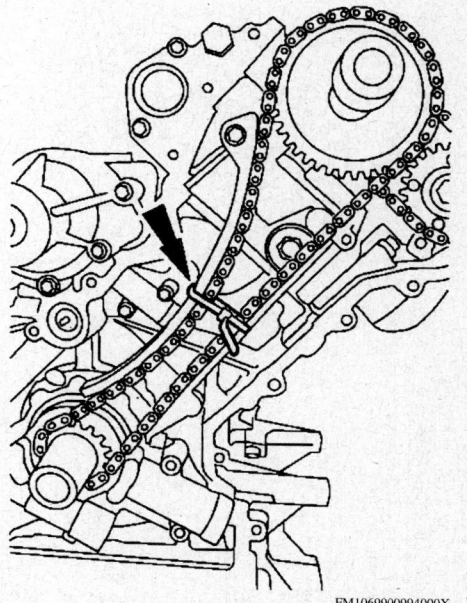

Fig. 25 Timing chain installation

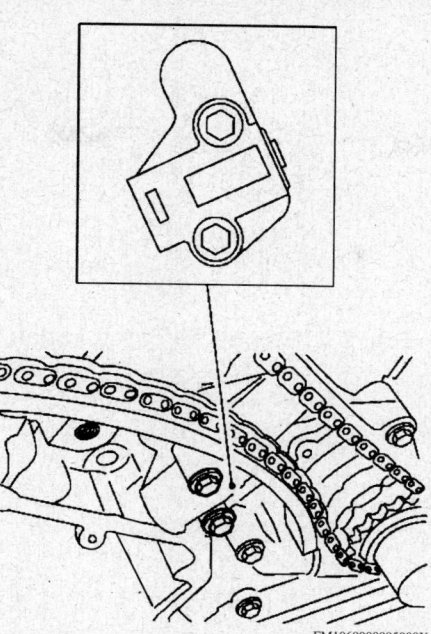

Fig. 26 Righthand blanking plate installation

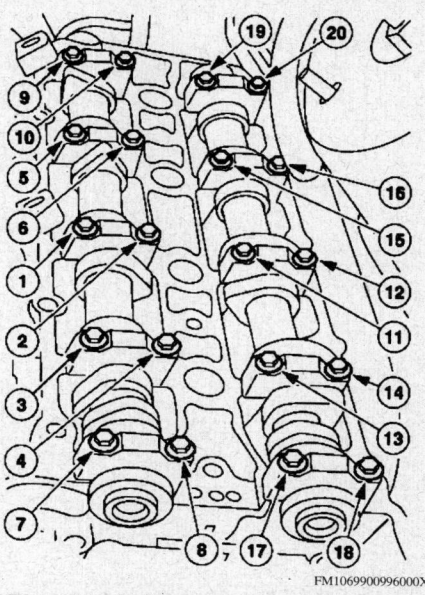

Fig. 27 Lefthand cylinder head camshaft tightening sequence

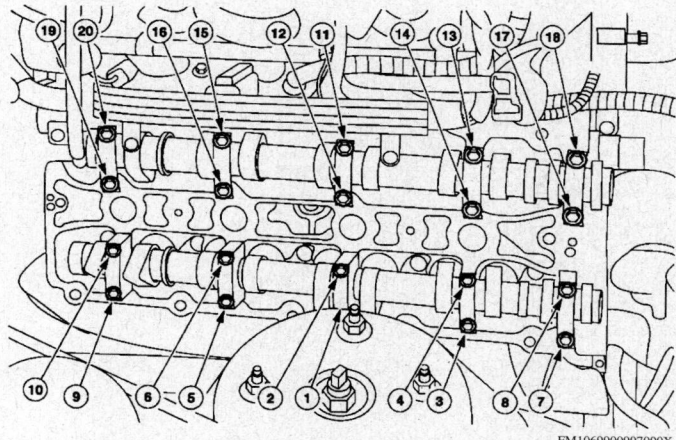

Fig. 28 Righthand cylinder head camshaft tightening sequence

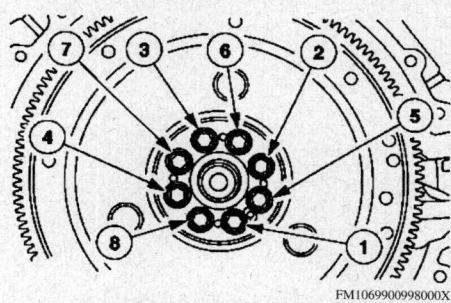

Fig. 29 Flywheel tightening sequence

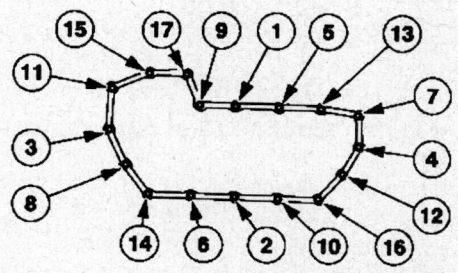

Fig. 30 Oil pan tightening sequence

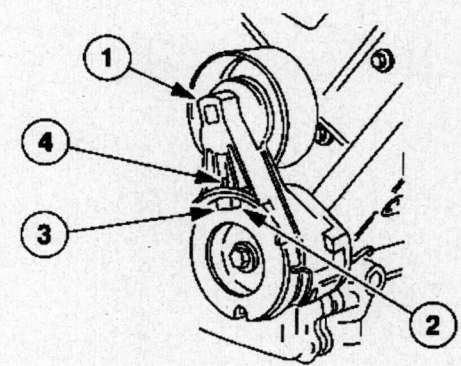

Item	Description
1	Belt tension relief point
2	Unacceptable belt wear range
3	Acceptable belt installation and wear range
4	Belt length indicator

Fig. 31 Belt tensioner inspection

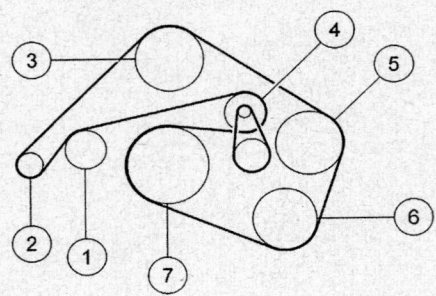

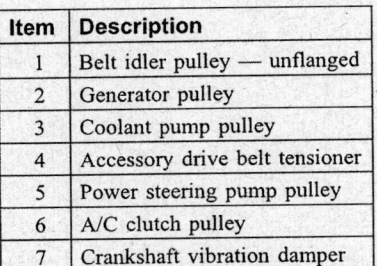

Item	Description
1	Belt idler pulley — unflanged
2	Generator pulley
3	Coolant pump pulley
4	Accessory drive belt tensioner
5	Power steering pump pulley
6	A/C clutch pulley
7	Crankshaft vibration damper

ARM0500000000082

Fig. 32 Serpentine drive belt routing

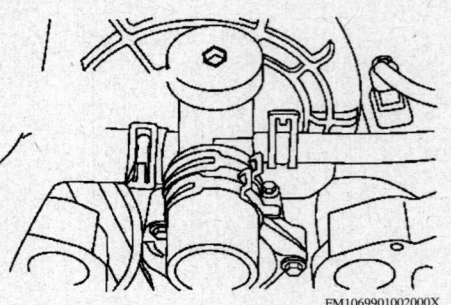

FM1069901002000X

Fig. 33 Engine fill cap location

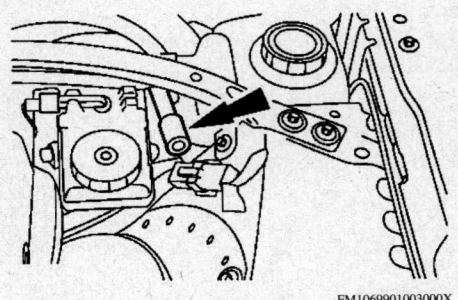

FM1069901003000X

Fig. 34 Heater air bleed location

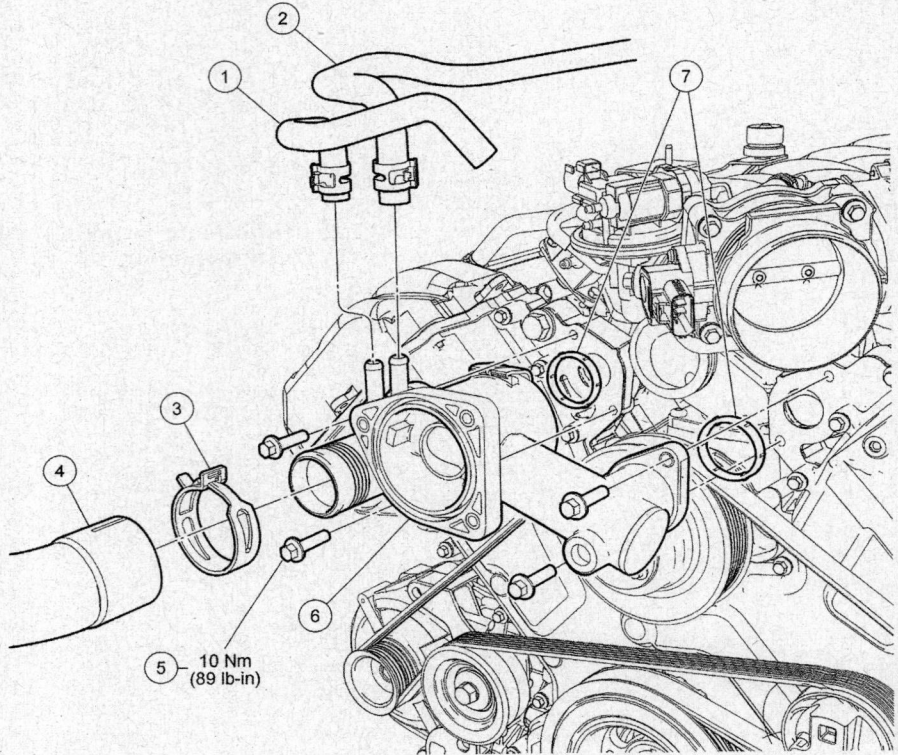

5 10 Nm (89 lb-in)

Item	Description		Item	Description
1	Throttle body heater hose		5	Coolant outlet pipe bolts (4 required)
2	Degas bottle hose		6	Coolant outlet pipe
3	Upper radiator hose clamp		7	Coolant outlet pipe seals (2 required)
4	Upper radiator hose			

ARM0500000000085

Fig. 35 Coolant tube replacement

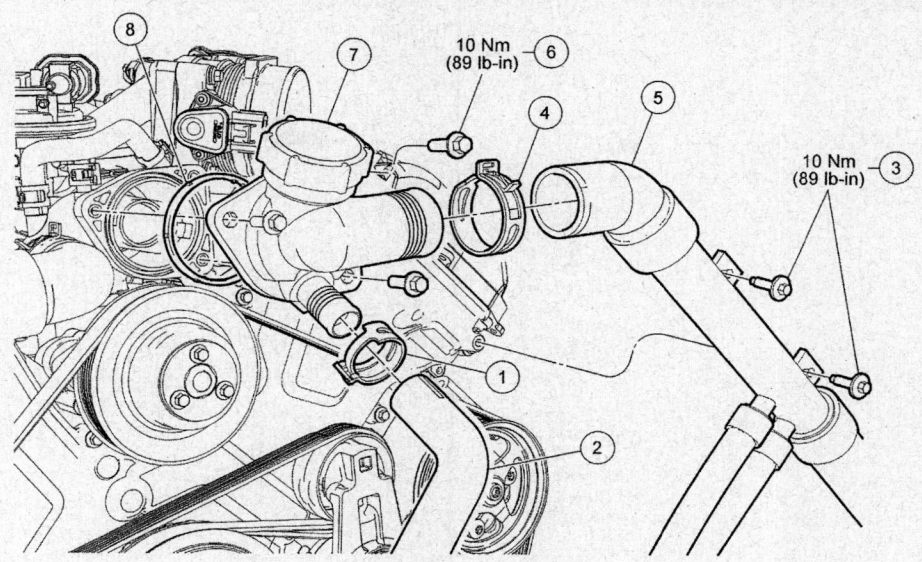

Item	Description
1	Auxiliary coolant pump-to-thermostat housing hose clamp
2	Auxiliary coolant pump-to-thermostat housing hose
3	Lower radiator hose support bracket bolts (2 required)
4	Lower radiator-to-thermostat housing hose clamp

Item	Description
5	Lower radiator-to-thermostat housing hose
6	Thermostat housing bolts (3 required)
7	Thermostat housing
8	Thermostat housing O-ring seal

ARM0500000000083

Fig. 36   Thermostat housing cover replacement (Part 1 of 2)

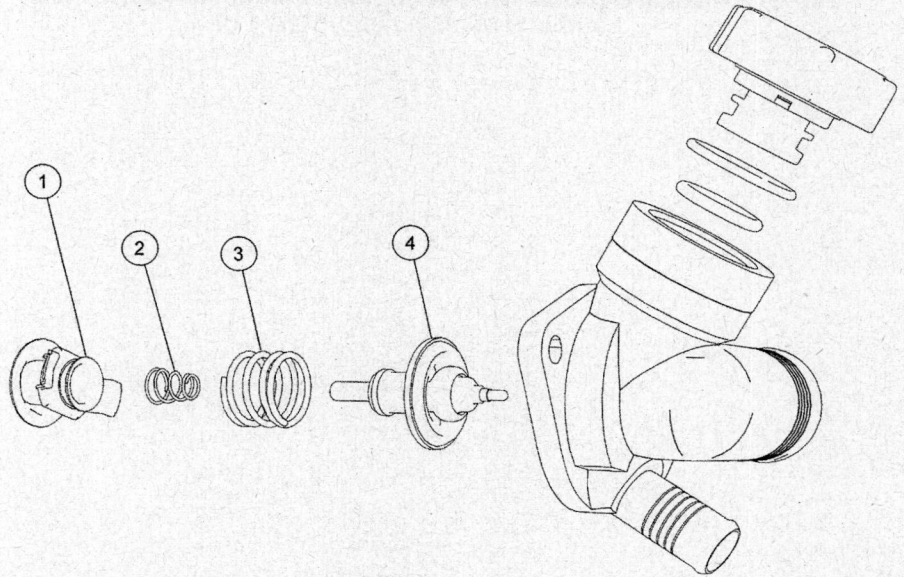

Item	Description
1	Thermostat-to-thermostat housing retainer
2	Thermostat spring
3	Thermostat main spring
4	Thermostat element

ARM0500000000084

Fig. 36   Thermostat housing cover replacement (Part 2 of 2)

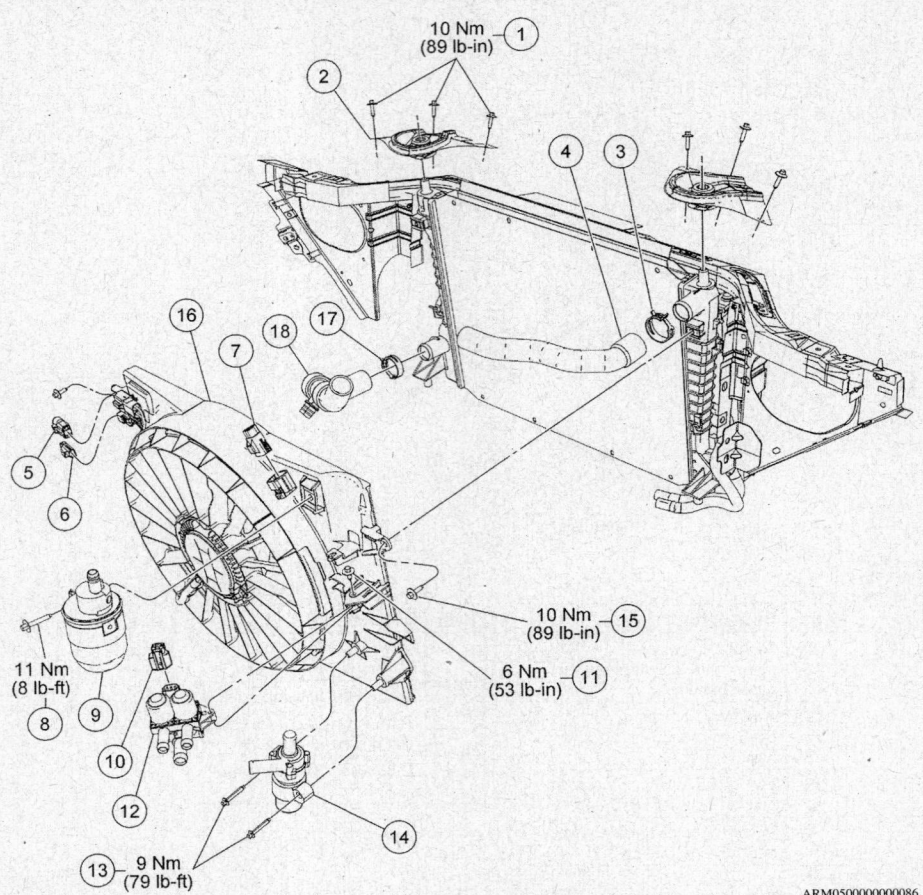

Fig. 37 Auxiliary coolant pump, combination cooler, condenser, fan & radiator replacement (Part 1 of 3)

ARM0500000000086

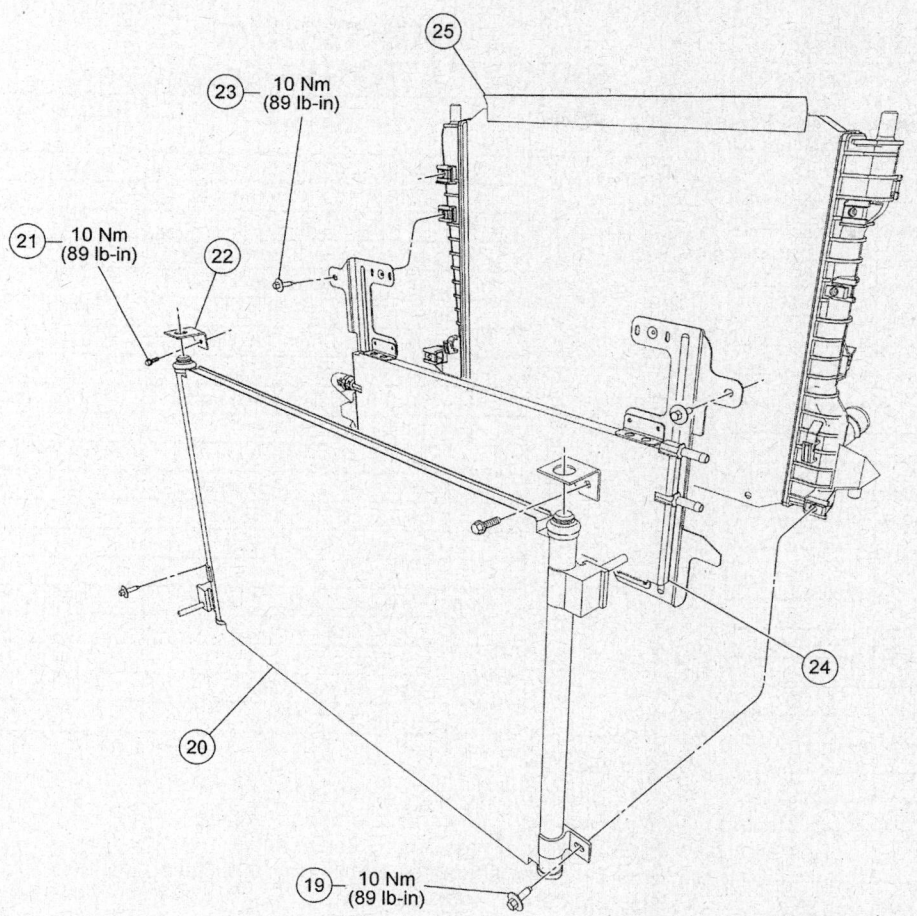

23 10 Nm (89 lb-in)

25

21 10 Nm (89 lb-in)

22

24

20

19 10 Nm (89 lb-in)

ARM0500000000087

Fig. 37 Auxiliary coolant pump, combination cooler, condenser, fan & radiator replacement (Part 2 of 3)

Item	Description
1	Upper radiator support bracket bolts (6 required)
2	Upper radiator support bracket (2 required)
3	Upper radiator hose clamp
4	Upper radiator hose
5	Electric cooling fan electrical connector
6	Electric cooling fan electrical connector
7	Coolant control valve jumper harness electrical connector
8	Receiver/drier bolt
9	Receiver/drier and bracket
10	Coolant control valve electrical connector
11	Coolant control valve bolt
12	Coolant control valve
13	Auxiliary coolant pump bolts (2 required)
14	Auxiliary coolant pump
15	Cooling fan motor and shroud bolt (2 required)
16	Cooling fan motor and shroud
17	Lower radiator hose clamp
18	Lower radiator hose
19	A/C condenser bolts (2 required)
20	A/C condenser
21	A/C condenser upper bracket bolt (2 required)
22	A/C condenser upper bracket (2 required)
23	Combination cooler bolt (2 required)
24	Combination cooler
25	Radiator

ARM0500000000088

Fig. 37 Auxiliary coolant pump, combination cooler, condenser, fan & radiator replacement (Part 3 of 3)

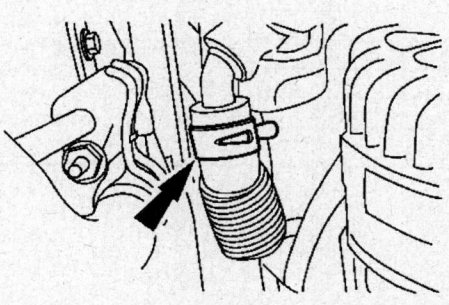

FM1069901008000X

Fig. 38 Fan pump hose location

TIGHTENING SPECIFICATIONS

Year	Component	Torque Ft. Lbs.
2004–06	Air Conditioning Compressor	18
	Air Conditioning Manifold To Compressor	15
	Alternator	⑤
	Belt Tensioner	37
	Camshaft Bearing Caps	⑩
	Camshaft Sprockets	15⑦
	Condenser To Radiator	89①
	Cowl Panel Support Bracket	80①
	Crankshaft Damper	③
	Crankshaft Position Sensor	89①
	Cylinder Head	②
	EGR Tube To EGR Valve	30
	EGR Tube To Exhaust Manifold	30
	Electric Water Pump	89①
	Engine Mount Bracket To Cylinder Block	34
	Engine Mount	30
	Exhaust Catalyst To Exhaust Manifold	30
	Exhaust Manifold To Cylinder Head	18
	Flywheel	⑧
	Front Cover	④
	Front & Center Support Bolts	76
	Hydraulic Cooling Fan Pump	18
	Hydraulic Cooling Fan Pump Bracket	18
	Hydraulic Cooling Fan Reservoir, Lower	106①
	Hydraulic Cooling Fan Reservoir, Upper	53①
	Idler Pulley	18
	Intake Manifold	⑫
	Lower Strut	129
	Lower Sway Bar Link	41
	Oil Cooler	43
	Oil Pan	⑨
	Oil Pump	53①⑦

TIGHTENING SPECIFICATIONS—Continued

Year	Component	Torque Ft. Lbs.
2004–06	Power Steering Pressure Line	89①
	Power Steering Pump Bracket	18
	Power Steering Pump To Bracket	18
	Power Steering Reservoir, Lower	106①
	Power Steering Reservoir, Upper	53①
	Primary Timing Chain Guide	97①
	Primary Timing Chain Tensioner	97①
	Receiver/Drier Bracket	8
	Secondary Timing Chain Tensioner	97①
	Steering Coupling	26
	Thermostat Housing	80①
	Torque Converter To Flywheel	28
	Transmission Cooler Lines	89①
	Transmission To Engine	35
	Upper Ball Joint	66
	Upper Radiator Support Brackets	89①
	Valve Cover	⑪
	Water Pump	71①⑦
	Water Pump Pulley	89①⑥
	Wheel Lug Nuts	100

① — Inch lbs.
② — Refer to "Cylinder Head, Replace."
③ — Refer to "Crankshaft Damper, Replace."
④ — Refer to "Front Cover, Replace."
⑤ — Refer to "Alternator, Replace" in "Electrical" section.
⑥ — Tighten an additional 45°.
⑦ — Tighten an additional 90°.
⑧ — Refer to "Crankshaft Rear Oil Seal, Replace" for tightening procedure.
⑨ — Refer to "Oil Pan, Replace" for tightening procedure.
⑩ — Refer to "Camshaft, Replace."
⑪ — Refer to "Valve Cover, Replace," for tightening specifications and sequence.
⑫ — Refer to "Intake Manifold, Replace," for tightening specifications and sequence.

Rear Axle & Suspension

NOTE: On Air Bag Equipped Models, Refer To "Air Bag System Precautions" Located In The Front Of This Manual For System Disarming & Arming Procedures.

NOTE: Refer To "Computer Relearn Procedures" Located In The Front Of This Manual When Battery Power To The Computer Has Been Interrupted.

NOTE: Prior To Performing Any Service Operations Listed In This Section, Consult The "Technical Service Bulletins" Section For Related Information.

INDEX

	Page No.
Ball Joint, Replace	3-43
Ball Joint Inspection	3-42
Control Arm, Replace	3-43
Lower	3-43
Installation	3-43
Removal	3-43
Upper	3-43
Installation	3-43
Removal	3-43
Description	3-39
Driveline Angle Measurement	3-40
Hub & Bearing, Replace	3-42
Knuckle, Replace	3-43
Pinion Flange & Seal, Replace	3-40
Installation	3-40
Removal	3-40
Precautions	3-39
Air Bag Systems	3-39
Battery Ground Cable	3-39
Propeller Shaft, Replace	3-41
Propeller Shaft Alignment Bushing	3-42
Installation	3-42
Removal	3-42
Propeller Shaft Center Bearing, Replace	3-41
Rear Axle, Replace	3-39
Rear Halfshaft, Replace	3-40
Stabilizer Bar, Replace	3-44
Stabilizer Bar Link, Replace	3-44
Strut, Replace	3-43
Strut Service	3-43
Assemble	3-43
Disassemble	3-43
Stub Shaft Bearing & Seal, Replace	3-39
Technical Service Bulletins	3-44
Droning Noise On Acceleration At Highway Speeds	3-44
Tightening Specifications	3-46
Toe Link, Replace	3-43
U-Joint, Replace	3-41
Wheel Bearing Inspection	3-43

PRECAUTIONS

Air Bag Systems

Refer to "Air Bag System Precautions" in the front of this manual for system disarming and arming procedures.

Battery Ground Cable

Prior to service, disconnect battery ground cable and isolate as required.

DESCRIPTION

The rear axle is an integral-type housing hypoid gear design, **Fig. 1.** The ring and pinion consists of an eight inch ring gear and an overhung drive pinion which is supported by two opposed tapered roller bearings. Pinion preload is maintained by a drive pinion collapsible spacer on the pinion shaft and is adjusted by the pinion nut. Differential bearing preload and ring gear backlash are adjusted by differential bearing shims located between differential bearing cup and rear axle housing.

Halfshafts are held in the differential case by a driveshaft bearing retainer circlip which engages a step in the differential side gear.

The suspension is an independent design featuring upper and lower control arms, shock absorber and spring, adjustable toe links, stabilizer bar and wheel knuckles, **Fig. 2.**

When servicing suspension components, always use new nuts and bolts when removed.

When carrying out operations which involve the removal and installation of the driveshaft, always inspect the joint angles and adjust as outlined under "Driveline Angle Measurement."

REAR AXLE
REPLACE

1. Remove halfshafts as outlined under "Rear Halfshaft, Replace."
2. Remove exhaust system and heat shield.
3. Place reference marks on pinion flange, flex coupling and driveshaft to pinion flange bolts, nuts, washers and weighted washers for installation alignment.
4. Support driveshaft, then remove driveshaft to flex coupling bolts and nuts. **Do not remove flex coupling on driveshaft flange.**
5. Position and secure driveshaft aside using mechanics wire.
6. Position suitable jack under axle housing and secure axle to jack using suitable strap.
7. Remove three axle mounting nuts, **Fig. 3.**

8. Lower axle housing.
9. Reverse procedure to install, noting the following:
   a. Add one gram of premium long life grease XG-1-C, or equivalent, to both alignment bushing cavities.
   b. Apply Threadlock type 262 E2FZ-19554-B, or equivalent, to driveshaft to flange nuts and bolts.

STUB SHAFT BEARING & SEAL
REPLACE

1. Remove halfshaft as outlined under "Rear Halfshaft, Replace."
2. Remove stub shaft bearing housing seal and bearing using bearing cup remover tool No. T77F-1102-A and slide hammer tool No. T50T-100-A, or equivalents.
3. Lubricate new bearing with SAE 75W-140 synthetic rear axle lubricant F1TZ-19580-B, or equivalent.
4. Install bearing into rear axle housing bore using bearing replacer tool No. T89P-1244-A and handle tool No. T80T-4000-W, or equivalents.
5. Lubricate lip of seal with premium long life grease XG-1-C, or equivalent.
6. Install seal using seal replacer tool No. T89P-4850-A and handle tool No. T80T-4000-W, or equivalents.
7. Install halfshaft as outlined under "Rear Halfshaft, Replace."

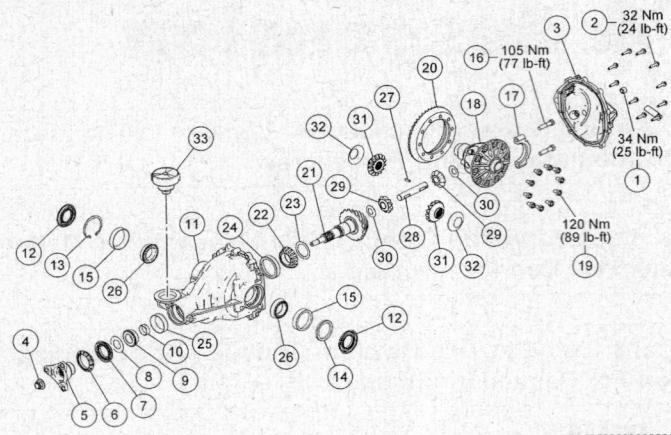

ARM0500000000091

Fig. 1 Exploded view of rear axle (Part 1 of 2)

Item	Description
1	Lubricant fill plug
2	Differential housing cover bolts
3	Differential housing cover
4	Differential drive pinion nut
5	Rear axle pinion flange
6	Rear pinion oil seal deflector
7	Rear pinion oil seal
8	Rear pinion oil seal slinger
9	Outer pinion bearing
10	Drive pinion collapsible spacer
11	Differential housing
12	Halfshaft housing seals
13	Selective snap ring
14	Differential bearing shim
15	Differential bearing cups
16	Bearing cap bolt
17	Bearing cap
18	Differential case
19	Differential ring gear bolts
20	Differential ring gear
21	Differential pinion gear
22	Inner pinion bearing
23	Differential pinion bearing adjustment shim
24	Inner pinion bearing cup
25	Outer pinion bearing cup
26	Differential bearings
27	Differential pinion shaft roll pin
28	Differential pinion shaft
29	Differential pinion gears
30	Differential pinion gear thrust washers
31	Differential side gears
32	Differential side gear thrust washers
33	Rear axle housing support insulator

ARM0500000000092

Fig. 1 Exploded view of rear axle (Part 2 of 2)

PINION FLANGE & SEAL

REPLACE

Removal

1. Raise and support vehicle, then remove rear wheels.
2. Remove mounting bolts and rear brake calipers. Position calipers aside.
3. Disconnect propeller shaft as outlined under "Propeller Shaft, Replace."
4. Record torque required to maintain rotation of pinion gear using suitable inch lb. torque wrench.
5. Install flange holding tool No. 205-478, or equivalent, and cotter pin, **Fig. 4.**
6. Remove and discard pinion nut using suitable breaker bar.
7. Place reference mark on pinion flange in relation to drive pinion stem for installation alignment, **Fig. 5.**
8. Remove flange from axle using flange removal tool No. 307-408, or equivalent.
9. Remove pinion seal.

Installation

1. Lubricate new seal using premium long life grease XG-1-C, or equivalent.
2. Install seal using seal installer tool No. T79P-4676-A, or equivalent.
3. Lubricate pinion flange spines using SAE 75W-140 synthetic rear axle lubricant F1TZ-19580-B, or equivalent.
4. Polish pinion flange seal journal using suitable crocus cloth.
5. Align pinion flange with drive pinion shaft.
6. Install flange using holding tool No. 205-478 and pinion flange installer tool No. 205-479, or equivalent.
7. Install cotter pin, **Fig. 4.**
8. Install new pinion nut.
9. Hold pinion flange using suitable flange holding tool as follows:
   a. Tighten new pinion nut until proper preload with used bearings, 8–10 inch lbs.
   b. Tighten new pinion nut until proper preload with new bearings, 16–29 inch lbs.
   c. **New collapsible spacer and pinion nut must be installed to reduce preload.**

REAR HALFSHAFT

REPLACE

Halfshafts are not serviceable. If wear or damage is present, replace entire halfshaft. When servicing halfshafts, ensure excessive angle is not applied to CV joints and that joints are not pulled apart or separated.

The halfshafts on models equipped with 3.9L engine are larger in diameter and are not interchangeable with halfshafts on models equipped with a 3.0L engine.

1. Raise and support vehicle.
2. Remove rear tires.
3. Remove and discard axle wheel hub nut.
4. Remove rear brake rotors as outlined in "Disc Brakes" chapter.
5. Remove ABS sensors as outlined in "Anti-Lock Brakes" chapter.
6. Remove lower knuckle mounting bolt.
7. Press CV joint from hub using hub remover/replacer tool No. T81P-1104-C, hub remover adapter tool No. T86P-1104-A1 and hub remover adapter tool No. T83P-1104-BH, or equivalents.
8. Raise and support knuckle, then remove CV joint from hub.
9. Separate CV joint from differential side gear using halfshaft removal tool No. 205-472, or equivalent. Ensure crown of tool forks face away from axle housing.
10. Remove halfshaft from axle housing.
11. Install differential plug tool No. T89P-4850-B, or equivalent, to differential.
12. Reverse procedure to install, noting the following:
   a. Install new axleshaft circlip.
   b. Before installing halfshaft into differential housing, install seal protector tool No. 205-461, or equivalent.
   c. Slide CV joint into housing until splines are past seal, then remove seal protector tool.
   d. Ensure halfshaft is fully seated into differential.
   e. Install new wheel hub nut.

DRIVELINE ANGLE MEASUREMENT

1. Park vehicle on level surface.
2. Remove mounting bolts and slide exhaust heat shield as far forward as possible to expose driveshaft to axle coupling.
3. Turn driveshaft several times by hand to neutralize center support bearing and flex couplings.
4. Place pinion angle level gauge tool No. T86P-4602-A, or equivalent, on left-hand frame rail with tool facing passenger side, **Fig. 6.**
5. Zero angle gauge tool using thumbscrew.
6. Mark location where tool was zeroed. **Do not remove flange bolts when measuring driveline angle.**

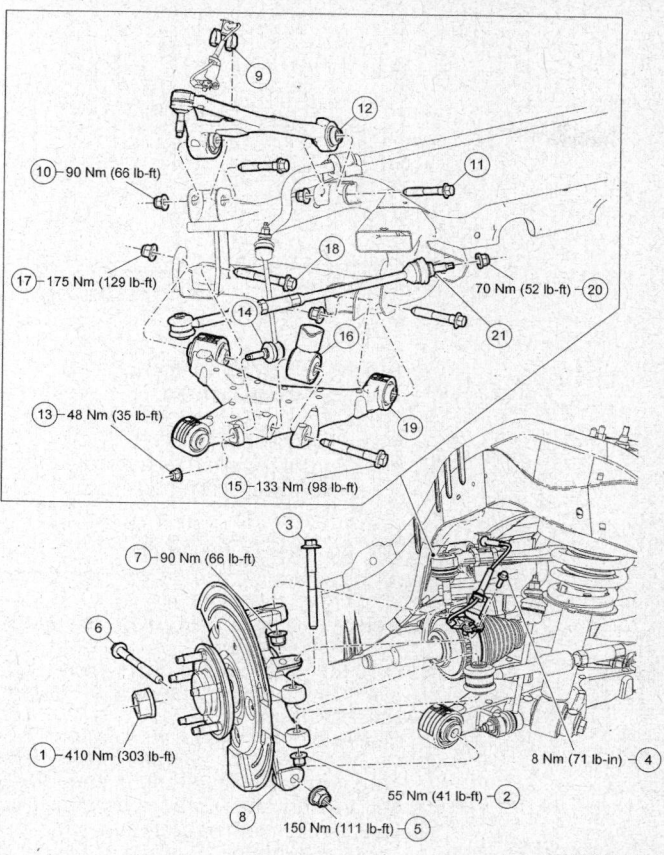

Fig. 2   Rear suspension components (Part 1 of 2)

Item	Description	Item	Description
1	Axle shaft nut	12	Upper arm
2	Toe link outboard nut	13	Stabilizer bar link lower nut
3	Toe link outboard bolt	14	Stabilizer bar link
4	Wheel speed sensor bolt	15	Shock absorber lower bolt
5	Lower arm-to-wheel knuckle nut	16	Shock absorber
6	Lower arm-to-wheel knuckle bolt	17	Lower arm-to-subframe nut (2 required)
7	Upper ball joint nut	18	Lower arm-to-subframe bolt (2 required)
8	Wheel knuckle and wheel hub assembly	19	Lower arm
9	Speed sensor retainer clip (part of 2C190)	20	Toe link inboard nut
10	Upper arm-to-subframe nut (2 required)	21	Toe link
11	Upper arm-to-subframe bolt (2 required)		

ARM0500000000094

Fig. 2   Rear suspension components (Part 2 of 2)

6. Support driveshaft using suitable strap.
7. Remove front and rear flex coupling to flange bolts and nuts, **Fig. 8. Do not remove flex coupling to driveshaft mounting bolts.**
8. Remove center bearing support brace nuts and driveshaft.
9. Reverse procedure to install, noting the following:
   a. Add one gram of premium long life grease XG-1-C, or equivalent, to both alignment bushing cavities.
   b. Apply Threadlock type 262 E2FZ-19554-B, or equivalent, to driveshaft to flange nuts and bolts.

U-JOINT
REPLACE

The single center U-joint is of a lubricated for life design that requires no periodic lubrication. This U-joint is staked to the yoke and is not removable.

PROPELLER SHAFT CENTER BEARING
REPLACE

1. Remove propeller shaft as outlined under "Propeller Shaft, Replace."
2. Place alignment marks on driveshaft for installation alignment.
3. Loosen adjustment nut, then separate front and rear shaft.
4. Place propeller shaft in suitable vise and clamp at driveshaft weld yoke.
5. Remove retaining ring, center bearing and bracket using two-jaw puller tool No. D80L-1002-L and bearing puller tool No. D84L-1123-A, or equivalents.
6. Reverse procedure to install. Install center bearing and retaining ring to driveshaft using driveshaft alignment bushing remover tube tool No. 205-D073, or equivalent, and suitable hammer.

7. Remove one nut from flex coupling to transmission flange.
8. Install driveline adapter tool No. 205-449, or equivalent, to front of flex coupling and tighten nut. Ensure adapter contacts flex coupling bolt sleeve to obtain accurate reading.
9. Place pinion angle gauge in angle adapter with angle gauge facing passenger side and record transmission angle A, **Fig. 7.**
10. Remove one nut from flex coupling to front driveshaft connection.
11. Install driveline adapter tool No. 205-449, or equivalent, to front of flex coupling and tighten nut. Ensure adapter contacts flex coupling bolt sleeve to obtain accurate reading.
12. Place pinion angle gauge in angle adapter with angle gauge facing passenger side and record front driveshaft angle B.
13. Remove one nut from flex coupling to rear driveshaft connection.
14. Install driveline adapter tool No. 205-449, or equivalent, to front of flex coupling and tighten nut. Ensure adapter contacts flex coupling bolt sleeve to obtain accurate reading.
15. Place pinion angle gauge in angle adapter with angle gauge facing passenger side and record rear driveshaft angle C.
16. Remove one nut from flex coupling to pinion flange connection.
17. Install driveline adapter tool No. 205-449, or equivalent, to front of flex coupling and tighten nut. Ensure adapter contacts flex coupling bolt sleeve to obtain accurate reading.
18. Place pinion angle gauge in angle adapter with angle gauge facing passenger side and record differential pinion angle D.
19. Calculate joint 1 angle by subtracting front driveshaft angle B from transmission angle A.
20. Calculate joint 2 angle by subtracting rear driveshaft angle C from front driveshaft angle B.
21. Calculate joint 3 angle by subtracting differential pinion angle D from rear driveshaft angle C
22. If adjustment is required, install suitable center support bearing adjusting washers. Ensure left and righthand washers are of equal thickness.

PROPELLER SHAFT
REPLACE

1. Raise and support vehicle.
2. Remove muffler, extension pipe and body brace.
3. Remove heat shield.
4. Inspect and record driveline angles as outlined under "Driveline Angle Measurement."
5. Place reference marks on bolts, washers, nuts and flex coupling to transmission flange and pinion flange for installation alignment.

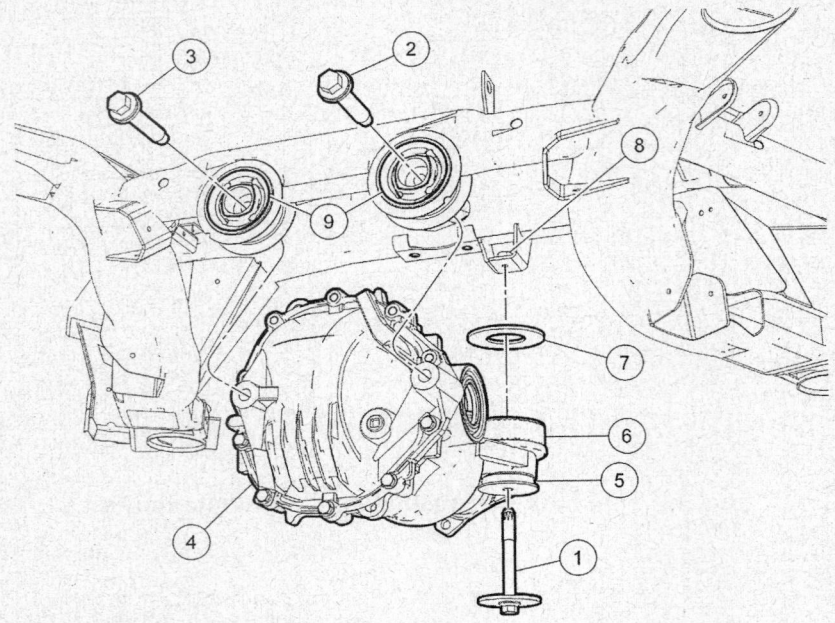

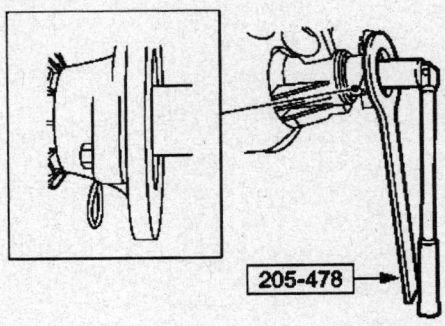

Item	Description
1	Rear axle housing support insulator front bolt
2	Rear axle housing support insulator rear bolt
3	Rear axle housing support insulator rear bolt
4	Rear axle assembly
5	Rear axle housing support insulator snubber
6	Rear axle housing support insulator bushing

Item	Description
7	Shim
8	Rear axle housing support insulator nut
9	Rear axle housing support insulator

ARM0500000000095

Fig. 3 Axle mounting nuts

Fig. 4 Flange holding tool installation

FM2039900075000X

PROPELLER SHAFT ALIGNMENT BUSHING

Removal

1. Remove propeller shaft as outlined under "Propeller Shaft, Replace."
2. Place alignment marks on front and rear driveshafts for installation alignment.
3. Loosen length adjustment nut, then separate front and rear shaft.
4. Remove mounting nuts, bolts and flex coupling.
5. Place driveshaft end yoke into suitable vise.
6. Remove alignment bushing inner core using blind hole puller set tool No. D80L-100A, driveshaft alignment bushing remover tube tool No. 205-D073 and handle tool No. T80T-4000-W, or equivalents, **Fig. 9**.
7. Remove bushing shell using removal tools, **Fig. 10**.

Installation

There are six bushings in each flex coupling. **Three bushings protrude from each side of coupling. Arrows on the side of coupling point toward protruding end of bushing. When installing flex coupling, protruding end of bushing must seat in driveshaft flange counterbore or damage will occur to coupling during operation.**

1. Align bushing with propeller shaft, then install using handle tool No. T80T-4000-W and alignment bearing installer tool No. 205-D074, or equivalents.
2. Install flex coupling as follows:
   a. Position protruding end of bushing against driveshaft flange, **Fig. 11.**
   b. Apply Threadlock type 262 E2FZ-19554-B, or equivalent, to flex coupling bolts and nuts, then install. Ensure bolt heads seat against driveshaft flange and nuts against flex coupling. Bolt heads are serrated and must be held in place while nut is tightened.
3. Align front and rear propeller shaft reference marks, then assemble both shafts. Hand tighten nut to prevent separation of shaft.
4. Add one gram of premium long life grease XG-1-C, or equivalent, to both alignment bushing cavities before installing propeller shaft.
5. Install propeller shaft as outlined under "Propeller Shaft, Replace."

HUB & BEARING
REPLACE

1. Remove knuckle as outlined under "Knuckle, Replace."
2. Drill out dust shield rivets using .23 inch drill bit. **Do not use drill bit larger than .24 inch.**
3. Remove dust shield.
4. Place knuckle in suitable press. Ensure knuckle is level and is supported as close to bearing bore as possible. Knuckle extremities should not be used for support.
5. Remove hub from knuckle using step plate adapter set tool No. D80L-630-A and bearing puller tool No. T71P-4621-B, or equivalents. When hub is pressed from bearing, bearing inner race will also be removed. **Do not install race back into bearing.**
6. Remove bearing retaining snap ring.
7. Support knuckle in press as close to bearing bore as possible.
8. Remove bearing from knuckle using suitable step plate adapter.
9. If hub is reused, remove inner bearing race from hub using suitable press and bearing puller tool No. T71P-4621-B, or equivalent.
10. Reverse procedure to install, noting the following:
    a. Attach dust shield using aluminum rivets.
    b. When installing hub to bearing, ensure bearing inner race is properly supported.

BALL JOINT INSPECTION

1. Raise and support vehicle.
2. Ensure brake pads are retracted enough to allow free movement of tire.
3. Grasp tire at top and bottom and move wheel inward and outward while lifting weight of tire off bearing.
4. If tire is loose on spindle or does not turn freely, install new hub and bearing.
5. Position suitable safety stand under lower suspension arm.

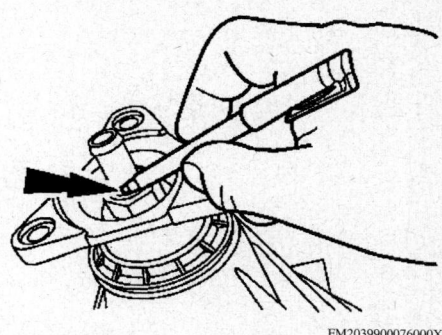

Fig. 5 Pinion flange marks

6. Grasp tire at top and bottom and attempt to move inward and outward.
7. If movement is more than 1/32 inch replace control arm.

WHEEL BEARING INSPECTION

1. Raise and support vehicle.
2. Ensure brake pads are retracted enough to allow free movement of tire.
3. Grasp tire at top and bottom and move wheel inward and outward while lifting weight of tire off bearing.
4. If tire is loose on spindle or does not turn freely, install new hub and bearing.

STRUT
REPLACE

When working with strut, do not apply heat during removal or service.
1. Open luggage compartment.
2. Remove carpet and spare tire.
3. Remove trim covers to access strut upper mounting bolts.
4. Remove four strut upper mounting nuts and discard, **Fig. 12.**
5. Raise and support vehicle.
6. Remove strut lower mounting bolt and nut and discard.
7. Remove strut.
8. Reverse procedure to install.

STRUT SERVICE
Disassemble

When working with strut, do not apply heat during removal or service.
If reusing components, place alignment marks for installation alignment.
1. Place strut into suitable vise, **Fig. 13.**
2. Compress spring using suitable spring compressor.
3. Remove center nut while holding shock absorber rod, **Fig. 14.**
4. Remove upper mount and dust boot.
5. Release spring and remove from strut.

Assemble

1. Inspect strut components for damage or wear. If spring paint is damaged, new spring should be installed.

2. Compress spring using suitable spring compressor.
3. Position upper mount and dust boot on spring. Ensure components are properly aligned.
4. Install new upper strut mount nut.
5. Remove strut from spring compressor and vise.

BALL JOINT
REPLACE

Refer to "Control Arm, Replace" for ball joint replacement procedure.

CONTROL ARM
REPLACE
Lower
REMOVAL

If lower arm bushings require service, entire lower control arm must be replaced.
1. With vehicle at static level position, remove hub cap and measure distance from center of hub to lip of fender, **Fig. 15.**
2. Raise and support vehicle, then remove rear wheels.
3. Remove rear brake rotor as outlined in "Disc Brakes" chapter.
4. Remove lower strut to control arm mounting bolt and nut, discard nut and bolt.
5. Remove lower stabilizer link to control arm mounting nut, discard nut.
6. Remove lower knuckle to control arm mounting nut and bolt, discard nut and bolt.
7. Remove lower arm to subframe mounting bolts and nuts, discard nuts and bolts.
8. Remove lower control arm.

INSTALLATION

Do not tighten lower arm to subframe or knuckle bolts and nuts until curb height is at correct level.
1. Connect lower arm to subframe.
2. Install knuckle to lower arm.
3. Connect stabilizer bar link to lower suspension arm.
4. Install strut to lower control arm.
5. Position suitable jackstand under lower arm and raise suspension until distance between center of hub and lip of fender is as recorded during removal procedure.
6. Tighten lower arm mounting nuts and remove jackstand.
7. Install rear rotors as outlined in "Disc Brakes" chapter.
8. Install wheels, then lower vehicle.

Upper
REMOVAL

If upper arm bushings and ball joints require service, entire upper control arm must be replaced.
1. With vehicle at static level position, re-

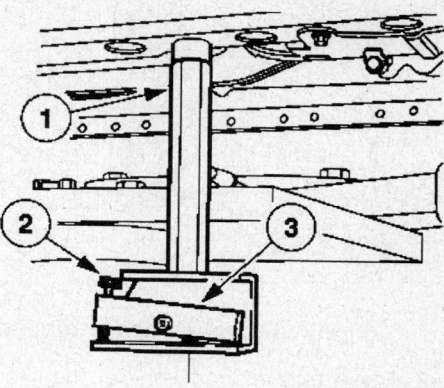

Fig. 6 Pinion angle gauge setup

move hub cap and measure distance from center of hub to lip of fender, **Fig. 15.**
2. Raise and support vehicle.
3. Remove rear wheels.
4. Unclip ABS sensor wire retainer from suspension arm.
5. Disconnect and remove ABS sensor and position aside.
6. Remove and discard upper ball joint to knuckle nut, then separate knuckle from ball joint.
7. Remove upper arm to subframe nuts and bolts, discard nuts and bolts.
8. Remove upper suspension arm.

INSTALLATION

Do not tighten upper arm to subframe or knuckle nuts and bolts until suspension is at proper curb height.
1. Install upper arm to subframe and knuckle.
2. Clip ABS sensor wire to upper suspension arm.
3. Position suitable jack under suspension lower arm.
4. Raise suspension until distance between center of hub and lip of fender is as recorded during removal procedure.
5. Tighten upper arm to subframe and knuckle mounting nuts.
6. Lower suspension and remove jack.
7. Install wheels and lower vehicle.

TOE LINK
REPLACE

1. Raise and support vehicle.
2. Remove rear wheels.
3. Disconnect toe link from knuckle, **Fig. 16.**
4. Remove toe link.
5. Reverse procedure to install. Use new toe link mounting nuts and ensure wheel alignment is within specifications. Refer to "Specifications" section.

KNUCKLE
REPLACE

1. With vehicle at static level position, remove hub cap, then measure and record distance from center of hub to lip of fender, **Fig. 15.**

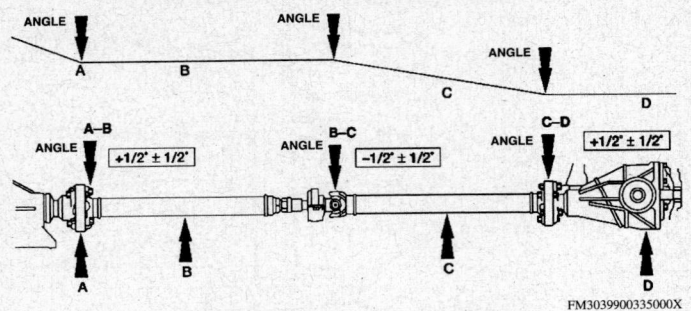

Fig. 7 Driveline angle inspection points

2. Raise and support vehicle, then remove rear wheels.
3. Remove and discard hub nut.
4. Remove rear rotors as outlined in "Disc Brakes" section.
5. Disconnect toe link from knuckle.
6. Remove ABS sensor and position aside.
7. Disconnect lower suspension arm from knuckle.
8. Support axleshaft.
9. Remove axleshaft from hub using hub remover/replacer tool No. T81P-1104-C, hub remover adapter tool No. T86P-1104-A and hub remover adapters tool No. T83P-1104-BH, or equivalents.
10. Remove upper ball joint and knuckle.
11. Reverse procedure to install, noting the following:
   a. Before tightening knuckle mounting bolts, raise suspension and ensure distance between center of hub and lip of fender is as recorded.
   b. When servicing suspension components, always use new nuts and bolts.

STABILIZER BAR
REPLACE

1. With vehicle at static level position, remove hub cap, then measure and record distance from center of hub to lip of fender, **Fig. 15.**
2. Raise and support vehicle, then remove wheels.
3. Disconnect propeller shaft from axle as outlined under "Propeller Shaft, Replace."
4. Place Rotunda powertrain lift tool No. 014-00765, or equivalent, under rear subframe.
5. Place reference marks on subframe mounting bolts for installation alignment.
6. Remove subframe mounting bolts and lower subframe eight inches.
7. Remove stabilizer link caps from left and righthand stabilizer links.
8. Disconnect left and righthand stabilizer links from stabilizer bar.
9. Remove stabilizer bar brackets and bushings.
10. Secure left and righthand knuckles to subframe using suitable mechanics wire.
11. Disconnect left and righthand upper control arms from subframe.

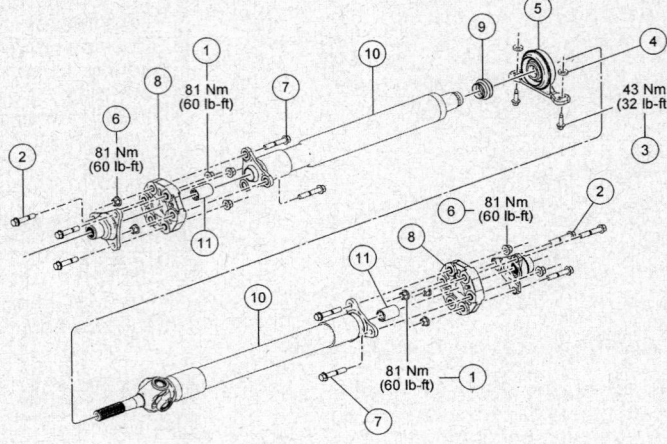

Fig. 8 Exploded view of driveshaft components

Item	Description
1	Flex coupling-to-flange bolt nuts (3 required)
2	Flex coupling-to-flange bolts (3 required)
3	Center support bearing bolts (2 required)
4	Center support adjusting washer (selective)
5	Center bearing and bracket assembly

Item	Description
6	Flex coupling-to-driveshaft bolt nuts (3 required)
7	Flex coupling-to-driveshaft bolts (3 required)
8	Flex coupling (2 required)
9	Driveshaft slip yoke boot
10	Driveshaft assembly
11	Alignment bushing (2 required)

ARM0500000000096

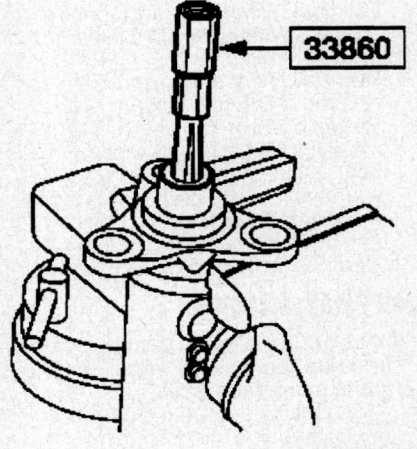

Fig. 9 Propeller shaft bushing inner core removal (Part 1 of 4)

12. Remove stabilizer bar.
13. Reverse procedure to install, noting the following:
   a. Before tightening knuckle mounting bolts, raise suspension and ensure distance between center of hub and lip of fender is as recorded.
   b. When servicing suspension components, always use new nuts and bolts.

STABILIZER BAR LINK
REPLACE

1. Raise and support vehicle, then remove rear wheels.
2. Disconnect stabilizer bar link from suspension lower arm.
3. Remove protective cap from stabilizer bar link.
4. Remove stabilizer link from stabilizer bar.
5. Reverse procedure to install. When servicing suspension components, always use new nuts and bolts.

TECHNICAL SERVICE BULLETINS

Droning Noise On Acceleration At Highway Speeds

Some vehicles may exhibit a moaning or droning noise during light acceleration while transmission is in 5th gear at highway speeds. Noise will disappear if the transmission is shifted to 4th gear or when lifting the throttle. The noise may be because of the body reacting to a resonant frequency generated by the powertrain. To correct this condition, install revised larger diameter rear halfshafts. Larger diameter halfshafts will reduce the resonant frequencies generated by the powertrain.

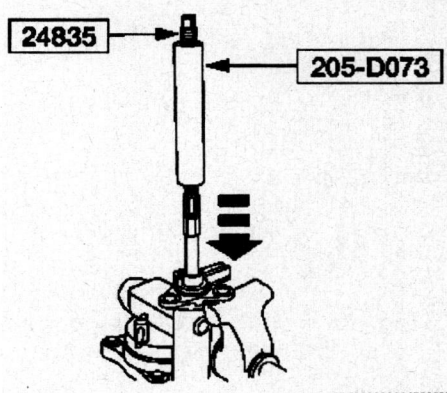

Fig. 9 Propeller shaft bushing inner core removal (Part 2 of 4)

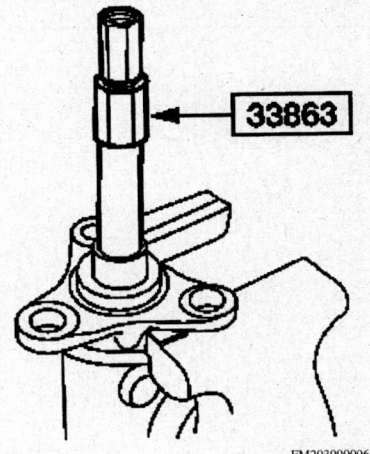

Fig. 10 Propeller shaft bushing shell removal (Part 1 of 4)

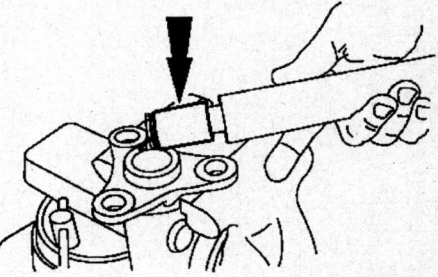

Fig. 10 Propeller shaft bushing shell removal (Part 4 of 4)

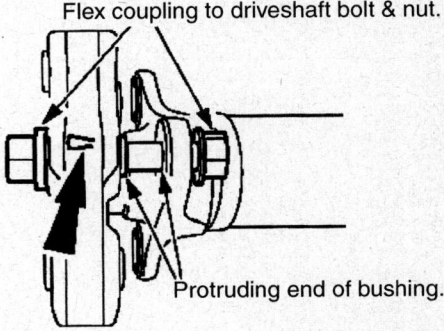

Flex coupling to driveshaft bolt & nut.

Protruding end of bushing.

Fig. 11 Flex coupling installation

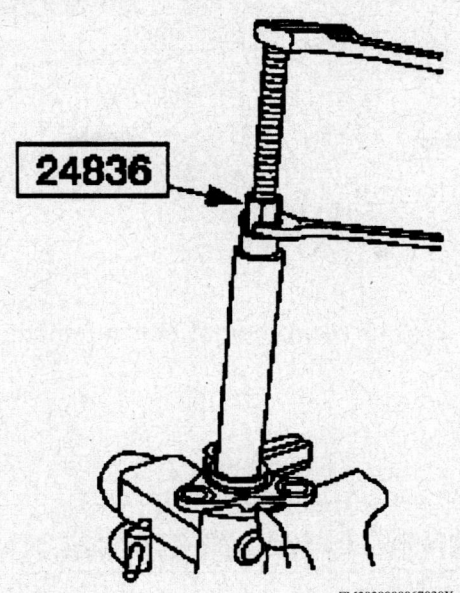

Fig. 9 Propeller shaft bushing inner core removal (Part 3 of 4)

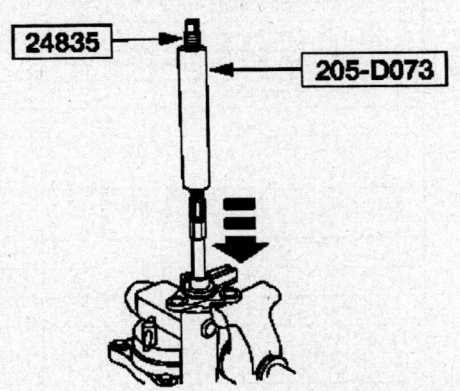

Fig. 10 Propeller shaft bushing shell removal (Part 2 of 4)

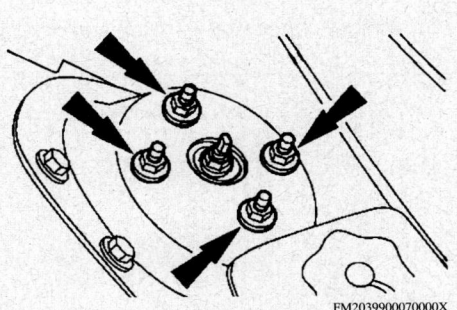

Fig. 12 Strut upper mounting nuts

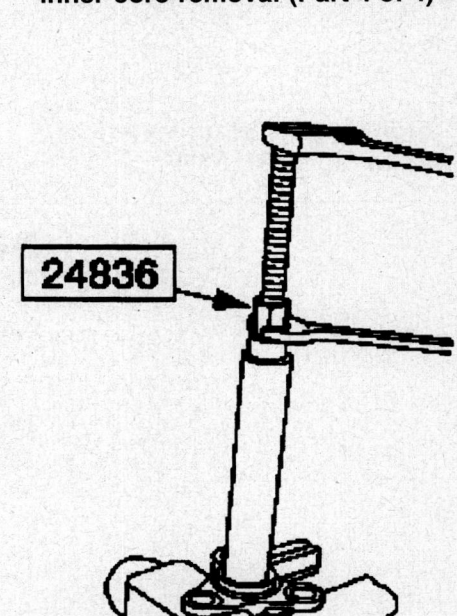

Fig. 9 Propeller shaft bushing inner core removal (Part 4 of 4)

Fig. 10 Propeller shaft bushing shell removal (Part 3 of 4)

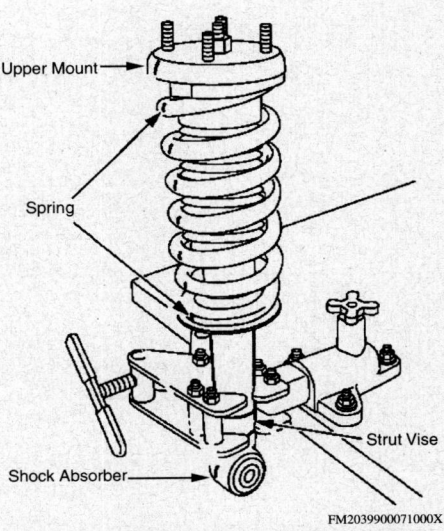

Upper Mount

Spring

Shock Absorber

Strut Vise

Fig. 13 Rear strut components

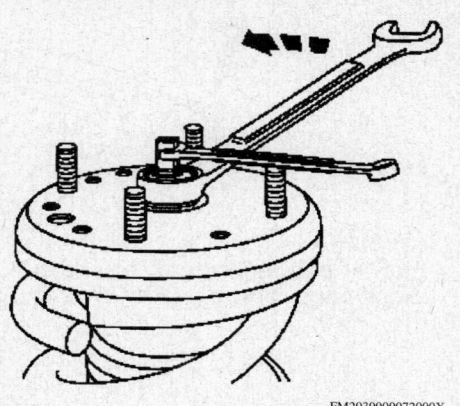

Fig. 14 Rear strut center nut replacement

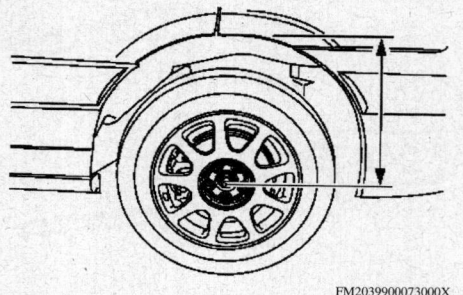

Fig. 15 Curb height measurement

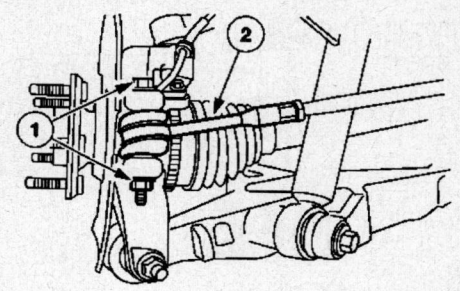

Fig. 16 Toe link replacement

TIGHTENING SPECIFICATIONS

Year	Component	Torque Ft. Lbs.
2004–06	Anti-Lock Brake Sensor	71①
	Axle Fill Plug	25
	Center Bearing	32
	Flex Coupling To Driveshaft	60
	Front Differential	52
	Hub Nut	221
	Lower Arm & Bushing To Knuckle Pivot	111
	Lower Arm & Bushing To Subframe Pivot	129
	Pinion Nut	②
	Rear Differential	76
	Rear Differential Insulator	111
	Shock & Spring To Lower Arm	98
	Stabilizer Bar Bracket	41
	Stabilizer Bar Link	35
	Subframe To Body	76
	Toe Link	41
	Upper Arm & Bushing To Subframe Pivot	66
	Upper Ball Joint	66
	Upper Shock Absorber Mount To Body	21
	Upper Shock Absorber Rod To Upper Shock Mount	37
	Wheel Lug Nuts	100
	Yoke Adjuster	66

① — Inch lbs.
② — Refer to "Pinion Flange & Seal, Replace" for proper preload.

Front Suspension & Steering

NOTE: On Air Bag Equipped Models, Refer To "Air Bag System Precautions" Located In The Front Of This Manual For System Disarming & Arming Procedures.

NOTE: Refer To "Computer Relearn Procedures" Located In The Front Of This Manual When Battery Power To The Computer Has Been Interrupted.

INDEX

	Page No.		Page No.		Page No.
Ball Joint Inspection	3-47	Power Steering	13-1	Air Bag Systems	3-47
Coil Spring & Strut Service	3-47	Power Steering Control Valve		Battery Ground Cable	3-47
Control Arm, Replace	3-48	Actuator, Replace	3-50	Stabilizer Bar, Replace	3-49
Lower	3-48	Power Steering Fluid Cooler,		Steering Columns	12-1
Installation	3-48	Replace	3-50	Steering Knuckle, Replace	3-48
Removal	3-48	Power Steering Gear, Replace	3-49	Steering Wheel Rotation	
Upper	3-48	Power Steering Pump, Replace	3-49	Sensor, Replace	3-50
Lefthand	3-48	3.0L Engine	3-49	Strut, Replace	3-47
Righthand	3-48	3.9L Engine	3-49	Tie Rod, Replace	3-49
Description	3-47	Power Steering System Bleed	3-49	Tightening Specifications	3-53
Hub & Bearing, Replace	3-47	Precautions	3-47	Wheel Bearing Inspection	3-47

PRECAUTIONS

Air Bag Systems

Refer to "Air Bag System Precautions" in the front of this manual for system disarming and arming procedures.

Battery Ground Cable

Prior to service, disconnect battery ground cable and isolate as required.

DESCRIPTION

The front suspension is an aluminum short-arm-long-arm that features struts, stabilizer bar and stabilizer bar links, **Fig. 1.**
When servicing suspension components, always use new nuts and bolts.

HUB & BEARING

REPLACE

1. Raise and support vehicle.
2. Remove front wheels.
3. Remove brake rotor as outlined in "Disc Brakes" chapter.
4. Remove inner fender splash shield and position aside.
5. Disconnect ABS wheel speed sensor and separate from wire retainers. **Do not remove ABS sensor from hub unless new sensor and wire are being installed.**
6. Remove wheel hub and bearing mounting bolts and discard, **Fig. 2.**
7. Remove wheel hub and bearing from knuckle. **Do not use suitable slide hammer or strike back of wheel hub and bearing to remove. Hub and bearing should slide out from knuckle.**

8. Reverse procedure to install, noting the following:
   a. Ensure knuckle bore is clean enough to allow hub and bearing to be seated by hand.
   b. Apply Motorcraft high temperature nickel anti-seize lubricant F6AZ-9L494-AA, or equivalent, to bearing carrier and wheel knuckle.
   c. Install new suspension mounting bolts and nuts.

BALL JOINT INSPECTION

1. Raise and support vehicle.
2. Ensure brake pads are retracted enough to allow free movement of tire.
3. Grasp tire at top and bottom and move wheel inward and outward while lifting weight of tire off bearing.
4. If tire is loose on spindle or does not turn freely, install new hub and bearing.
5. Position suitable safety stand under lower suspension arm.
6. Grasp tire at top and bottom and attempt to move inward and outward.
7. If movement is more than 1/32 inch on upper or lower ball joint, replace control arm.

WHEEL BEARING INSPECTION

1. Raise and support vehicle.
2. Ensure brake pads are retracted enough to allow free movement of tire.
3. Grasp tire at top and bottom and move wheel inward and outward while lifting weight of tire off bearing.

4. If tire is loose on spindle or does not turn freely, install new hub and bearing.

STRUT

REPLACE

Do not use heat to remove strut mounting bolts.
1. Raise and support vehicle, then remove front wheels.
2. Disconnect stabilizer bar link from control arm and discard nut.
3. Remove and discard strut to lower control arm mounting bolt.
4. Remove strut to body mounting bolts, **Fig. 3. Do not remove strut center nut.**
5. Reverse procedure to install. Install new suspension mounting bolts and nuts.

COIL SPRING & STRUT SERVICE

Do not use heat to remove strut mounting bolts.
1. Raise and support vehicle, then remove front wheels.
2. Disconnect stabilizer bar link from control arm and discard nut.
3. Remove and discard strut to lower control arm mounting bolt.
4. Remove strut to body mounting bolts, **Fig. 3. Do not remove strut center nut.**
5. Mount strut in suitable vise, **Fig. 4.**
6. Place reference marks on strut components for assembly alignment.
7. Compress spring using suitable spring compressor.
8. Hold shock absorber center rod and remove center nut from strut.
9. Remove upper mount and dust boot.

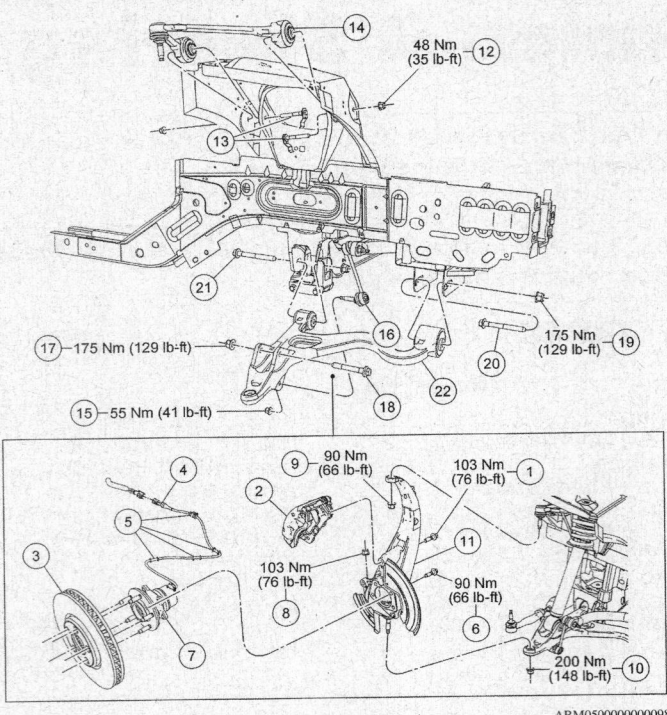

Fig. 1 Exploded view of front suspension components (Part 1 of 2)

10. Release pressure from spring and remove from spring compressor.
11. Reverse procedure to install, noting the following:
    a. Inspect spring, upper and lower spring seats, mount and insulator for damage. If spring coating is damaged, replace spring.
    b. Install new strut mounting nuts and bolts.

CONTROL ARM
REPLACE

Lower
REMOVAL

1. Ensure ignition switch is off in unlocked position.
2. Raise and support vehicle, then remove wheels.
3. Remove splash shields.
4. Disconnect stabilizer bar link from lower control arm and discard nut.
5. Disconnect strut from lower control arm, then discard nut and bolt.
6. Disconnect lower control arm from steering knuckle and discard nut.
7. Remove front lower control arm bolt and nut, then discard nut and bolt.
8. Remove two nuts and bolts, then loosen nut and bolt and turn steering gear rack to access lower control arm rear bolt, **Fig. 5.**
9. Remove and discard rear lower control arm nut and bolt.

INSTALLATION

1. Position lower control arm and install

new caster adjustment cam bolt with cam lobe pointed downward, ensure cam is seated between cam guides on crossmember No. 1, **Fig. 6.**
2. Install nut. **Do not fully tighten nut until wheel alignment is performed.**
3. Install new camber adjustment cam bolt with cam lobe pointed downward, ensure cam is seated in groove of crossmember No. 2 and nut, **Fig. 7.**
4. Install nut. **Do not fully tighten nut until wheel alignment is performed.**
5. Connect lower ball joint to control arm. Ensure tapered washer is installed on ball joint.
6. Connect stabilizer link and strut to lower arm.
7. Install splash shields.
8. Tighten bolts and nuts loosened when positioning steering gear.
9. Install wheels, then lower vehicle and ensure wheel alignment is within specifications.

Upper
LEFTHAND

1. Remove hub cap.
2. Measure and record distance from lip of fender to center of wheel hub, **Fig. 8.**
3. Remove air cleaner.
4. Remove upper control arm nut and discard, **Fig. 9.**
5. Raise and support vehicle, then remove front wheel.
6. Disconnect stabilizer bar link from control arm and discard nut.
7. Remove and discard strut to lower control arm mounting bolt.
8. Remove strut to body mounting bolts,

Fig. 3. Do not remove strut center nut.
9. Secure knuckle to body using suitable mechanics wire.
10. Disconnect upper control arm from steering knuckle and discard nut.
11. Remove control arm from body and discard nuts and bolts.
12. Reverse procedure to install, noting the following:
    a. Ensure suspension is at recorded distance, before tightening control arm mounting bolts.
    b. When servicing suspension components, always use new nuts and bolts.

RIGHTHAND

1. Remove hub cap.
2. Measure and record distance from lip of fender to center of wheel hub, **Fig. 8.**
3. Remove and discard nut from engine compartment, **Fig. 10.**
4. Disconnect wiring harness and brackets to access control arm mounting bolts and nuts.
5. Remove upper control arm mounting nut and discard.
6. Disconnect stabilizer bar link from control arm and discard nut.
7. Remove and discard strut to lower control arm mounting bolt.
8. Remove strut to body mounting bolts, **Fig. 3. Do not remove strut center nut.**
9. Secure knuckle to body using suitable mechanics wire.
10. Disconnect upper ball joint from steering knuckle and discard nut.
11. Remove upper arm mounting bolts, nuts and upper arm. Discard mounting bolts and nuts.
12. Reverse procedure to install, noting the following:
    a. Ensure suspension is at recorded distance, before tightening control arm mounting bolts.
    b. When servicing suspension components, always use new nuts and bolts.

STEERING KNUCKLE
REPLACE

1. Raise and support vehicle.
2. Remove front wheels.
3. Remove brake rotor as outlined in "Disc Brakes" chapter.
4. Remove inner fender splash shield and position aside.
5. Disconnect ABS wheel speed sensor and separate from wire retainers. **Do not remove ABS sensor from hub unless new sensor and wire are being installed.**
6. Remove wheel hub and bearing mounting bolts and discard, **Fig. 2.**
7. Remove wheel hub and bearing from knuckle. **Do not use slide hammer or strike back of wheel hub and bearing to remove. Hub and bearing should slide out from knuckle.**
8. Disconnect tie rod, upper control arm

and lower control arm from steering knuckle and discard nuts.

9. Remove steering knuckle.
10. Reverse procedure to install, noting the following:
    a. Support steering knuckle using suitable jackstand during installation.
    b. Ensure knuckle bore is clean enough to allow hub and bearing to be seated by hand.
    c. Apply Motorcraft high temperature nickel anti-seize lubricant F6AZ-9L494-AA, or equivalent, to bearing carrier and wheel knuckle
    d. When servicing suspension components always use new nuts and bolts.

STABILIZER BAR
REPLACE

1. Remove air cleaner.
2. Remove stabilizer bracket bolt, **Fig. 11.**
3. Raise and support vehicle, then remove front wheels.
4. Remove left, righthand and center splash shields.
5. Disconnect stabilizer bar link from control arm and stabilizer bar, discard nuts.
6. Disconnect strut from lefthand lower control arm, discard bolt and nut.
7. Disconnect lower control arm from lefthand steering knuckle, discard nut.
8. Remove heater water valve bracket and position valve aside.
9. Remove stabilizer bar brackets and bushings. Remove righthand front bolt first.
10. Remove stabilizer bar through lefthand wheel well.
11. Reverse procedure to install. When servicing suspension components, always use new nuts and bolts.

TIE ROD
REPLACE

Refer to "Power Steering" chapter for inner and outer tie rod replacement procedures.

POWER STEERING GEAR
REPLACE

1. Raise and support vehicle, then remove front wheels.
2. Disconnect tie rod ends, **Fig. 12,** from steering knuckles and discard nuts.
3. Disconnect variable assist power steering (VAPS) actuator electrical connector.
4. Loosen steering shaft bolt.
5. Remove pinch bolt and disconnect intermediate shaft.
6. Remove power steering hose bracket.
7. Disconnect power steering hoses from steering gear. Plug hose ends at gear.
8. Remove steering gear to crossmember mounting bolts and nuts.

Item	Description
1	Anchor plate bolt (2 required)
2	Brake caliper assembly
3	Brake disc
4	Speed sensor electrical connector
5	Speed sensor harness retainers
6	Wheel hub bolt (4 required)
7	Wheel bearing and hub assembly
8	Tie-rod end nut
9	Upper ball joint nut
10	Lower ball joint nut
11	Wheel knuckle
12	Upper arm-to-body nut (2 required)
13	Upper arm-to-body bolts (2 required)
14	Upper arm
15	Stabilizer bar link lower nut
16	Stabilizer bar link
17	Shock absorber lower nut
18	Shock absorber lower bolt
19	Lower arm-to-frame nut (2 required)
20	Lower arm-to-frame bolt
21	Lower arm-to-frame bolt
22	Lower arm

ARM0500000000099

Fig. 1 Exploded view of front suspension components (Part 2 of 2)

9. Remove steering gear assembly. Discard mounting bolts and nuts.
10. Reverse procedure to install, noting the following:
    a. Install new seal to power steering lines using Teflon seal replacer set tool No. D90P-3517-A, or equivalent.
    b. When servicing suspension components, always use new nuts and bolts.
    c. Fill system and inspect for leaks. Ensure wheel alignment is within specifications.

POWER STEERING PUMP
REPLACE
3.0L Engine

1. Remove engine appearance cover.
2. Remove air cleaner and outlet tube.
3. Remove accessory drive belt.
4. Disconnect power steering reservoir to pump hose and drain fluid into suitable container.
5. Raise and support vehicle, then remove front wheels.
6. Remove lower power steering pump shield, **Fig. 13.**
7. Remove power steering hose bracket bolt, then disconnect hose from pump.
8. Remove mounting bolts and pump.

9. Reverse procedure to install, noting the following:
   a. Install new O-rings to power steering hoses using Teflon seal replacer set tool No. D90P-3517-A, or equivalent.
   b. Tighten upper pump mounting bolts after lower bolts are installed.
   c. Fill power steering system and inspect for leaks.

3.9L Engine

1. Remove engine appearance cover.
2. Remove air cleaner and outlet tube.
3. Remove coolant tube mounting bolts, **Fig. 14.**
4. Rotate tensioner and remove accessory drive belt from power steering pump pulley.
5. Disconnect power steering reservoir to pump hose and drain fluid into suitable container.
6. Remove power steering reservoir mounting bolts and position reservoir aside.
7. Raise and support vehicle, then remove front wheels.
8. Remove pump line bracket bolt, **Fig. 15.**
9. Disconnect power steering pump electrical connector and wire retainer.
10. Remove air conditioning compressor mounting bolts and position compressor aside.
11. Disconnect power steering pressure hose from pump.
12. Remove pump mounting bolts.
13. Lower vehicle, then remove remaining pump mounting bolts and pump.
14. Reverse procedure to install, noting the following:
    a. Install new O-ring seals to power steering lines using Teflon seal replacer set tool No. D90P-3517-A, or equivalent.
    b. Tighten upper pump mounting bolts after lower bolts are installed.

POWER STEERING SYSTEM BLEED

1. Ensure power steering reservoir is filled to proper level.
2. Install vacuum tester tool No. 014-R1054, or equivalent, to reservoir, **Fig. 16.**
3. Start and run engine at idle speed.
4. Apply maximum vacuum for at least three minutes. Maintain vacuum with vacuum pump.
5. Remove vacuum tester.
6. Add Motorcraft Mercon multi-purpose ATF transmission fluid XT-2-QDX, or equivalent, fluid to bring reservoir to proper level.
7. Attach vacuum tester to reservoir and apply maximum vacuum. Cycle steering wheel from stop to stop every 30 seconds for 5 minutes. **Do not hold steering wheel against stops for more than 5 seconds.**
8. Remove vacuum tester and install reservoir cap.

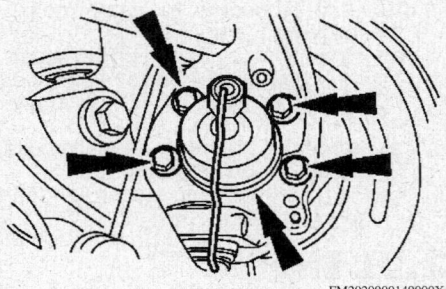

Fig. 2 Wheel hub & bearing replacement

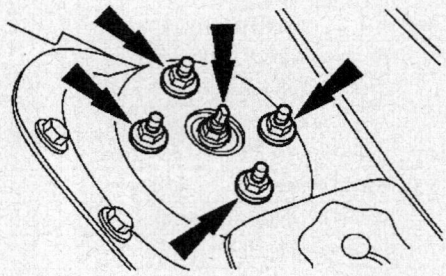

Fig. 3 Strut mounting bolts

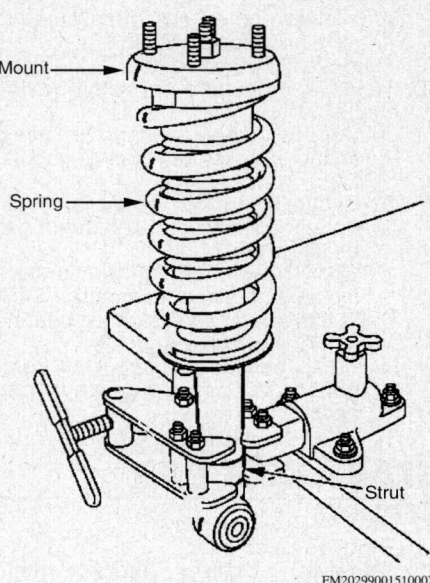

Fig. 4 Front strut components

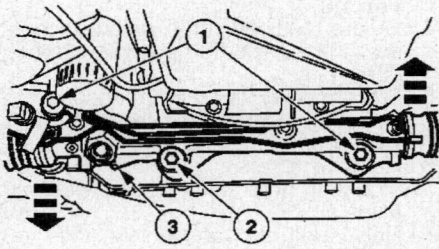

Fig. 5 Steering gear bolts

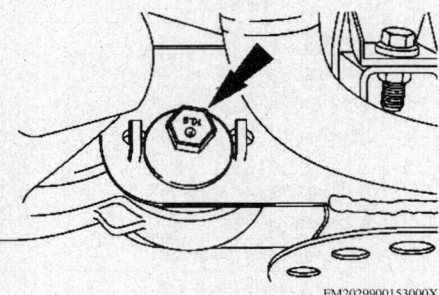

Fig. 6 Caster adjustment bolt installation

9. Ensure fluid is at proper level and inspect system for leaks.
10. Repeat procedure.

POWER STEERING FLUID COOLER

REPLACE

1. Recover refrigerant as outlined in "Air Conditioning" chapter.
2. Remove left, righthand and center splash shields.
3. **On models equipped with 3.9L engine,** disconnect air intake tube and position aside.
4. **On all models,** disconnect air conditioning lines from condenser.
5. Support condenser, then remove condenser mounting bolts and condenser.
6. Remove and discard fluid cooler clamps, **Fig. 17.**
7. Disconnect fluid cooler hoses and drain into suitable container.
8. Remove mounting bolts and cooler.
9. Reverse procedure to install. Tighten fluid cooler clamps using CV boot clamp tool No. T95P-3514-A, or equivalent.

POWER STEERING CONTROL VALVE ACTUATOR

REPLACE

1. Raise and support vehicle.
2. Disconnect steering control valve electrical connector.

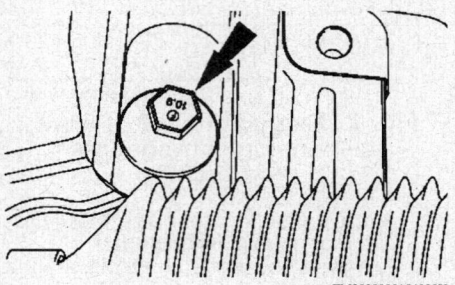

Fig. 7 Camber adjustment bolt installation

3. Remove power steering hose bracket and position aside.
4. Disconnect and plug power steering hoses.
5. Remove control valve actuator, **Fig. 18.**
6. Reverse procedure to install. Install new O-rings to power steering lines using Teflon seal replacer set tool No. D90P-3517-A, or equivalent.

STEERING WHEEL ROTATION SENSOR

REPLACE

1. Ensure wheels are in straight ahead position, then center steering wheel.
2. Remove driver air bag module as outlined in "Passive Restraint Systems" chapter.

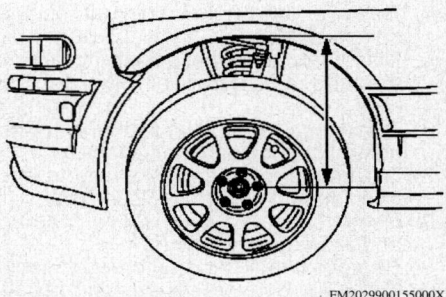

Fig. 8 Curb height measurement

3. Remove lower steering column opening finish panel and hood release.
4. Remove lefthand lower heater duct.
5. Pull carpet away from console tunnel and remove bracket bolts.
6. Remove steering column opening reinforcement.
7. Disconnect steering wheel rotation sensor and electric tilt/telescoping motor electrical connectors.
8. Disconnect lower steering column electrical connectors.
9. Secure steering column and shaft using suitable mechanics wire. **Ensure steering column and shaft do not turn.**
10. Remove and discard steering column shaft pinch bolt and disconnect shaft.
11. Support steering column, then remove and discard column locknuts.
12. Lower steering column, then remove sensor mounting screws and sensor, **Fig. 19.**
13. Reverse procedure to install. Install new steering column locknuts and pinch bolt.

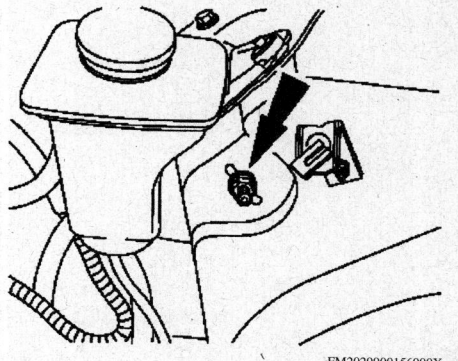

Fig. 9 Upper control arm mounting nut location

FM2029900156000X

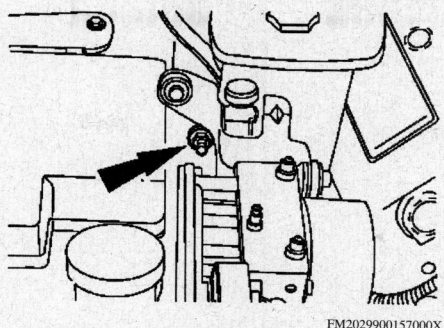

FM2029900157000X

Fig. 10 Engine compartment nut location

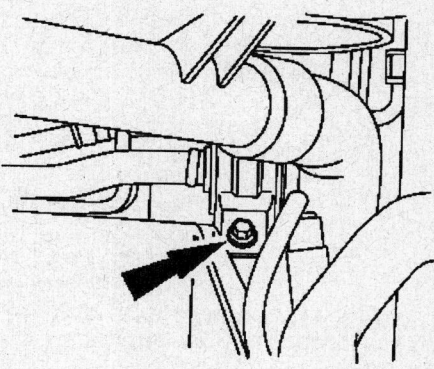

FM2029900158000X

Fig. 11 Stabilizer bracket bolt replacement

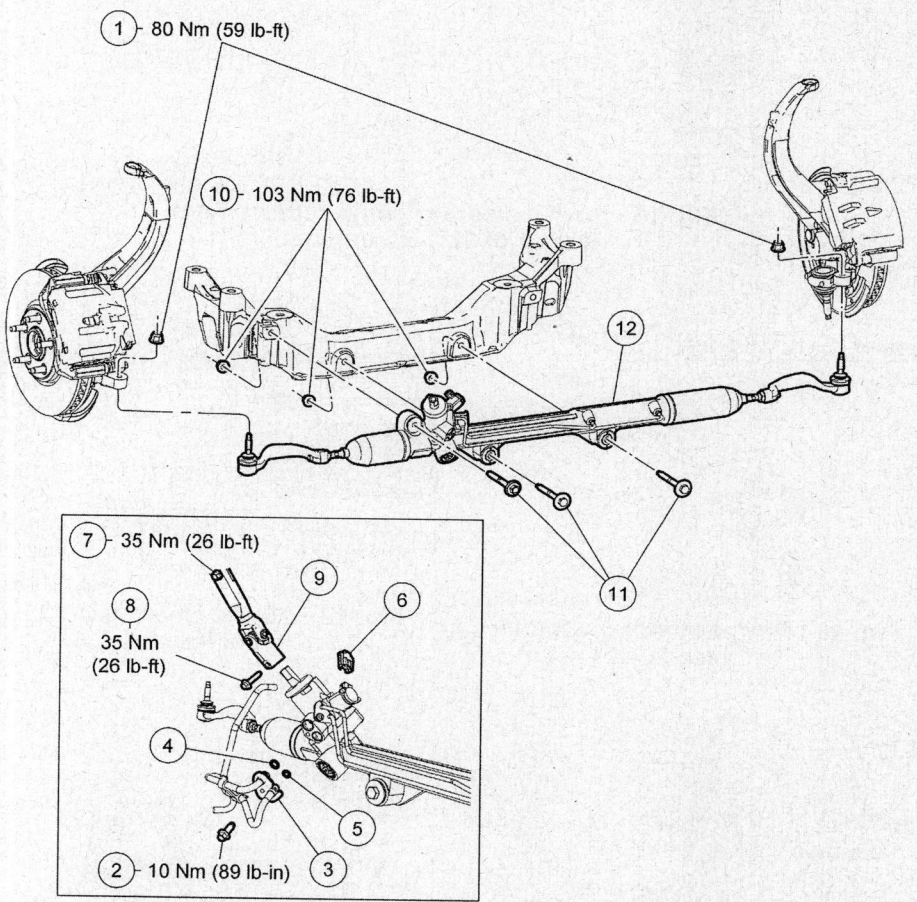

ARM0500000000100

Fig. 12 Power steering gear replacement (Part 1 of 2)

Item	Description
1	Tie-rod end nuts (2 required)
2	Steering line clamp plate bolt
3	Steering line (pressure/return)
4	O-ring (pressure line)
5	O-ring (return line)
6	Variable assist power steering (VAPS) actuator electrical connector
7	Intermediate shaft slider bolt
8	Intermediate shaft-to-steering gear bolt
9	Intermediate shaft
10	Steering gear-to-crossmember nuts (3 required)
11	Steering gear-to-crossmember bolts (3 required)
12	Steering gear

ARM0500000000101

Fig. 12 Power steering gear replacement (Part 2 of 2)

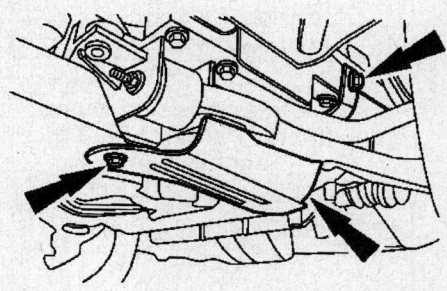

FM2029900159010X

Fig. 13 Power steering pump shield (Part 1 of 2). 3.0L engine

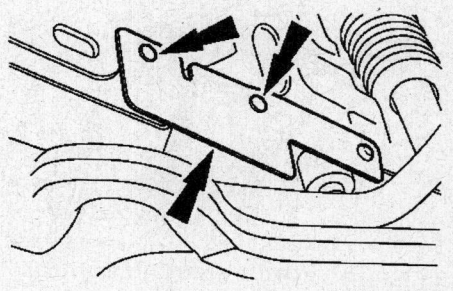

FM2029900159020X

Fig. 13 Power steering pump shield (Part 2 of 2). 3.0L engine

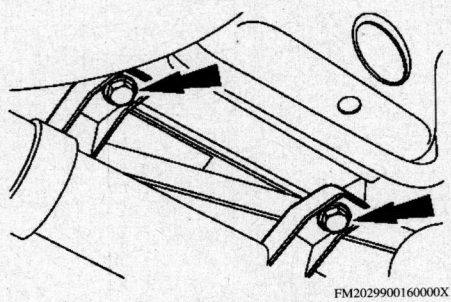

FM2029900160000X

Fig. 14 Coolant tube bolt location. 3.9L engine

Item	Description
1	Engine accessory drive belt
2	Air conditioning compressor electrical connector (3.9L only)
3	Air conditioning compressor bolt (3.9L only, 4 required)
4	Air conditioning compressor (3.9L only)
5	Reservoir-to-pump supply hose clamp
6	Reservoir-to-pump supply hose
7	Lower pump bolt (2 required)
8	Pressure line fitting
9	Teflon® seal
10	Upper pump bolt (2 required)
11	Radiator hose tube-to-engine bolt (3.9L engine only, 2 required)
12	Power steering pump

ARM0500000000103

Fig. 15 Power steering pump replacement (Part 2 of 2). 3.9L engine

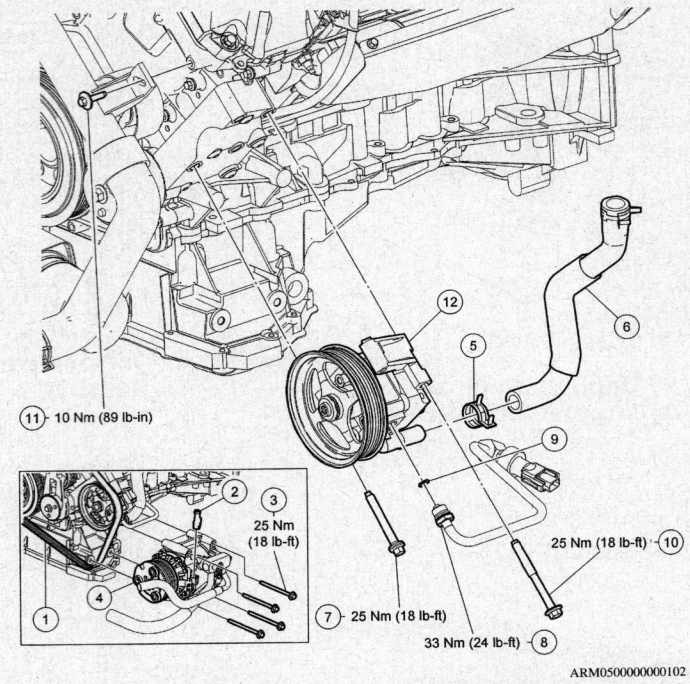

(11) 10 Nm (89 lb-in)

25 Nm (18 lb-ft)

25 Nm (18 lb-ft) (10)

(7) 25 Nm (18 lb-ft)

33 Nm (24 lb-ft) (8)

ARM0500000000102

Fig. 15 Power steering pump replacement (Part 1 of 2). 3.9L engine

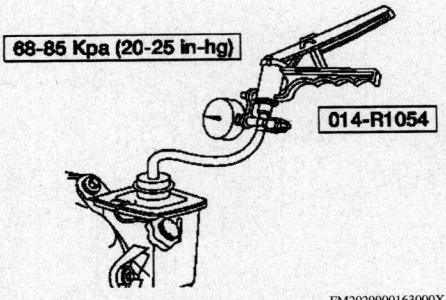

68-85 Kpa (20-25 in-hg)

014-R1054

FM2029900163000X

Fig. 16 Power steering vacuum bleed

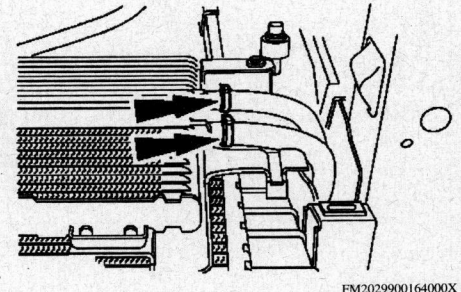

FM2029900164000X

Fig. 17 Power steering fluid cooler

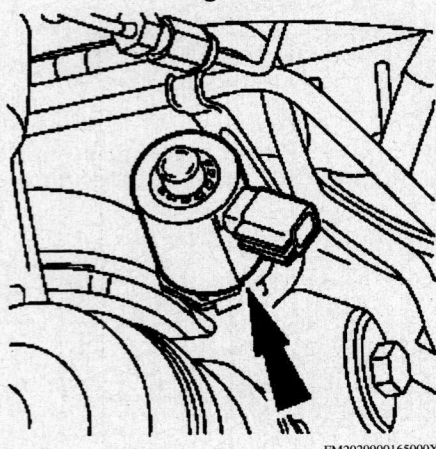

FM2029900165000X

Fig. 18 Power steering control valve actuator

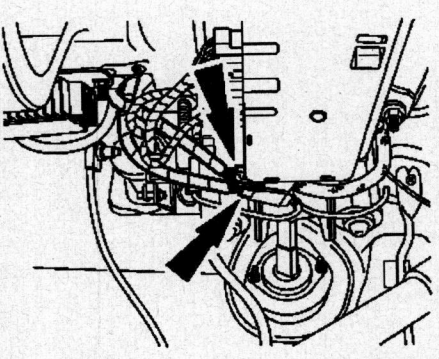

FM2029900166010X

Fig. 19 Steering wheel rotation sensor replacement (Part 1 of 2)

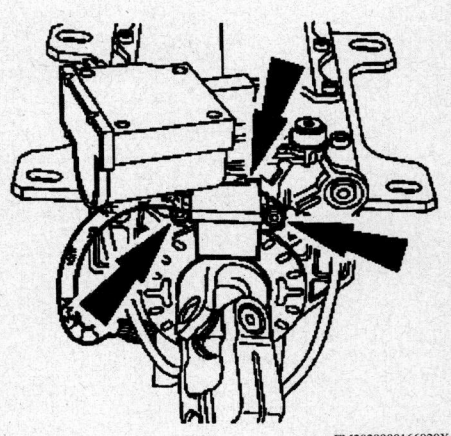

FM2029900166020X

Fig. 19 Steering wheel rotation sensor replacement (Part 2 of 2)

TIGHTENING SPECIFICATIONS

Year	Component	Torque Ft. Lbs.
2004–06	Air Conditioning Compressor	18
	Anchor Plate Bolt	76
	Control Valve Actuator	22
	Engine Control Wiring Bracket	44①
	Heater Water Valve Bracket	44①
	Hub & Bearing To Knuckle	66
	Intermediate Shaft	18
	Intermediate Shaft To Gear Pinch Bolt	26
	Lower Arm To Frame	129
	Lower Arm To Knuckle	148
	Power Steering Cooler To Radiator	89①
	Power Steering Gear To Crossmember	66
	Power Steering Hose Brackets	89①
	Power Steering Pressure Hose	24
	Power Steering Pump	18
	Power Steering Return Hose To Gear	24
	Power Steering Reservoir, Lower	90①
	Power Steering Reservoir, Upper	53①
	Radiator Tube To Engine	89①
	Stabilizer Bar Bracket	41
	Stabilizer Bar Link	41
	Steering Column Lock Nut	30
	Steering Column Opening Reinforcement	15
	Steering Column Shaft To Intermediate Shaft Pinch Bolt	26
	Steering Gear Lock Nut	76
	Strut To Body	21
	Strut To Lower Arm	129
	Tie Rod End To Knuckle	59
	Upper Control Arm To Body	35
	Upper Control Arm To Knuckle	66
	Upper Strut Rod To Upper Mount	37
	Variable Assist Power Steering Actuator (VAPS)	27①
	Wheel Lug Nut	100

① — Inch lbs.

Wheel Alignment

INDEX

	Page No.		Page No.		Page No.
Front Wheel Alignment	3-54	Preliminary Inspection	3-54	Toe	3-54
Caster & Camber	3-54	Rear Wheel Alignment	3-54	Wheel Alignment	
Toe	3-54	Caster & Camber	3-54	Specifications	3-2

PRELIMINARY INSPECTION

1. Inspect suspension and steering components for looseness and wear.
2. Inspect tires for similar tread and proper air pressure.
3. Ensure vehicle ride height is within specifications.

FRONT WHEEL ALIGNMENT

Caster & Camber

If vehicle is equipped with hex head bolts in lower control arm, new cam bolts and lock nuts must be installed before adjusting suspension. If new bolts are to be installed, refer to "Control Arm, Replace" in "Front Suspension & Steering" chapter for replacement procedure.

1. In order to turn camber and caster cams, loosen lower control arm mounting nuts, **Figs. 1 and 2.**
2. Turn caster adjustment bolt until caster is within specifications.
3. Turn camber adjustment bolt while supporting lower control arm by hand until camber is within specifications. Adjustments to camber may affect toe setting. Toe and camber may be adjusted at same time. Refer to "Toe" to adjust toe settings.
4. Tighten lower control arms and inspect alignment.

Toe

1. Start engine and center steering wheel.

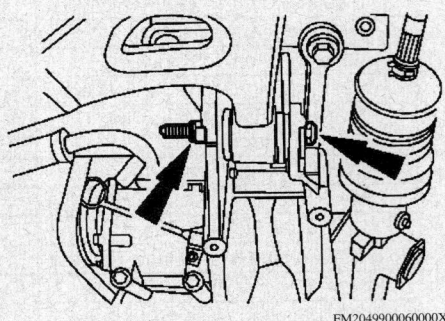

Fig. 1   Camber adjustment bolt

2. Turn engine off and hold steering wheel in straight ahead position by attaching suitable rigid link from steering wheel to brake pedal.
3. Remove tie rod boot clamps, then loosen jam nuts, **Fig. 3.**
4. Clean and lubricate nuts and tie rod threads.
5. Turn inner tie rod link to adjust to. Do not allow bellows to twist when tie rod is rotated.
6. Ensure toe is within specifications and tighten jam nuts.
7. Inspect alignment settings.

REAR WHEEL ALIGNMENT

Caster & Camber

Caster and camber are not adjustable on the rear suspension.

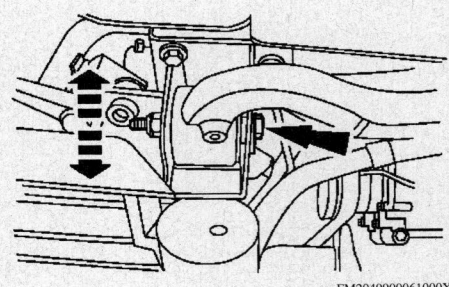

Fig. 2   Caster adjustment bolt

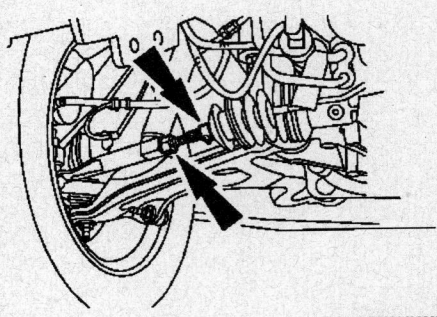

Fig. 3   Tie rod adjustment

Toe

1. Clean toe link threads and nut.
2. Loosen toe link jam nut and turn toe link until alignment is within specifications.
3. Tighten jam nut.
4. Ensure alignment is within specifications.

MUSTANG

NOTE: Refer To The Rear Of This Manual For Vehicle Manufacturer's Special Service Tool Suppliers.

INDEX OF SERVICE OPERATIONS

Page No.

AIR BAG SYSTEM
PRECAUTIONS 0-18
BRAKES
    Anti-Lock Brakes (Volume 2).. 6-1
    Disc Brakes.................... 14-1
    Drum Brakes 15-1
    Hydraulic Brake Systems 16-1
    Power Brake Units........... 17-1
COMPUTER RELEARN
PROCEDURE 0-31
ELECTRICAL
    Air Bag System (Volume 2) ... 4-1
    Air Conditioning.............. 8-1
    Alternator, Replace 4-7
    Alternators 11-1
    Blower Motor, Replace 4-11
    Clutch Start Switch, Replace.. 4-9
    Cooling Fans 9-1
    Cruise Control (Volume 2) 2-1
    Dash Gauges (Volume 2) 1-1
    Dash Panel Service
    (Volume 2)................. 5-1
    Evaporator Core, Replace 4-11
    Fuel Pump Relay Location.... 4-7
    Fuse Panel & Flasher
    Location 4-7
    Headlamp Switch, Replace ... 4-10
    Heater Core, Replace 4-11
    Ignition Coil Pack, Replace ... 4-8
    Ignition Lock, Replace 4-8
    Ignition Switch, Replace 4-9
    Instrument Cluster, Replace... 4-10
    Multi-Function Switch,
    Replace 4-10
    Neutral Safety Switch,
    Replace 4-9
    Passive Restraint Systems
    (Volume 2).................. 4-1
    Precautions 4-7
    Radio, Replace 4-10
    Relay Center Location 4-7
    Speed Controls (Volume 2) ... 2-1
    Starter Motors 10-1
    Starter, Replace 4-7
    Steering Columns............. 12-1
    Steering Wheel, Replace...... 4-10
    Stop Light Switch, Replace ... 4-10
    Technical Service Bulletins.... 4-12
    Wiper Motor, Replace........ 4-10
    Wiper Switch, Replace 4-11
    Wiper Systems (Volume 2) ... 3-1
    Wiper Transmission, Replace . 4-11
ELECTRICAL SYMBOL
IDENTIFICATION 0-63
FRONT SUSPENSION &
STEERING
    Ball Joint, Replace........... 4-94
    Ball Joint Inspection 4-94
    Coil Spring, Replace......... 4-94
    Control Arm, Replace 4-95
    Description 4-93
    Front Wheel Spindle,
    Replace 4-93
    Hub & Bearing, Replace 4-93

Page No.

Power Steering 13-1
Power Steering Gear,
    Replace 4-96
Power Steering Pump,
    Replace 4-96
    Precautions 4-93
    Stabilizer Bar, Replace....... 4-95
    Stabilizer Bar Bushing,
    Replace 4-95
    Steering Columns............. 12-1
    Strut, Replace 4-94
    Technical Service Bulletins.... 4-97
    Tightening Specifications...... 4-98
    Wheel Bearing, Adjust 4-93
NON-STANDARD TIRE &
WHEEL SIZE
ADJUSTMENT TO RIDE
HEIGHT SPECIFICATIONS
& TIRE SIZE CHART 0-61
REAR AXLE &
SUSPENSION
    Axle Damper, Replace 4-85
    Coil Spring, Replace 4-87
    Control Arm, Replace 4-88
    Control Arm Bushing,
    Replace 4-89
    Description 4-82
    Lateral Rod, Replace 4-90
    Precautions 4-82
    Propeller Shaft, Replace 4-86
    Rear Axle, Replace 4-82
    Rear Axle Shaft, Replace 4-85
    Shock Absorber, Replace 4-87
    Stabilizer Bar, Replace 4-89
    Technical Service Bulletins.... 4-90
    Tightening Specifications...... 4-92
REAR DRIVE AXLES 19-1
SERVICE REMINDER &
WARNING LAMP RESET
PROCEDURES 0-34
SPECIFICATIONS
    Fluid Capacities & Cooling
    System Data................. 4-5
    Front Wheel Alignment
    Specifications................. 4-4
    General Engine
    Specifications................. 4-3
    Lubricant Data............... 4-6
    Rear Wheel Alignment
    Specifications................. 4-4
    Tune Up Specifications 4-3
    Vehicle Ride Height
    Specifications................. 4-4
VEHICLE
IDENTIFICATION 0-1
VEHICLE LIFT POINTS...... 0-51
VEHICLE MAINTENANCE
SCHEDULES 0-73
WHEEL ALIGNMENT
    Front Wheel Alignment........ 4-99
    Preliminary Inspection 4-99
    Rear Wheel Alignment 4-99
    Wheel Alignment

Page No.

Specifications.................. 4-4
WIRE COLOR CODE
IDENTIFICATION 0-63
3.8L ENGINE
    Camshaft, Replace 4-17
    Camshaft Lobe Lift
    Specifications................. 4-16
    Compression Pressure........ 4-13
    Cooling System Bleed 4-19
    Crankshaft Rear Oil Seal,
    Replace 4-18
    Cylinder Head, Replace....... 4-15
    Engine Rebuilding
    Specifications................. 21-1
    Engine, Replace 4-13
    Engine Mount, Replace 4-13
    Exhaust Manifold, Replace.... 4-14
    Front Cover, Replace 4-17
    Fuel Filter, Replace 4-20
    Fuel Pump, Replace 4-20
    Hydraulic Lifters, Replace 4-16
    Intake Manifold, Replace...... 4-14
    Main & Rod Bearings 4-18
    Oil Pan, Replace............. 4-18
    Oil Pump, Replace........... 4-18
    Oil Pump Service............ 4-18
    Piston & Rod Assembly 4-18
    Pistons, Pins & Rings 4-18
    Precautions.................. 4-13
    Radiator, Replace 4-19
    Rocker Arms................. 4-16
    Serpentine Drive Belt 4-18
    Technical Service Bulletins.... 4-20
    Thermostat, Replace......... 4-19
    Tightening Specifications...... 4-21
    Timing Chain, Replace........ 4-17
    Valve Adjustment 4-16
    Valve Clearance
    Specifications................. 4-16
    Valve Cover, Replace 4-16
    Valve Guides 4-16
    Water Pump, Replace 4-19
4.0L ENGINE
    Balance Shaft, Replace 4-28
    Belt Tension Data............. 4-31
    Camshaft, Replace 4-27
    Camshaft Lobe Lift
    Specifications................. 4-26
    Camshaft Roller Follower,
    Replace 4-25
    Camshaft Timing............. 4-27
    Compression Pressure........ 4-22
    Cooling System Bleed 4-31
    Crankshaft Damper, Replace.. 4-26
    Crankshaft Rear Oil Seal,
    Replace 4-30
    Crankshaft Seal, Replace 4-30
    Cylinder Head, Replace....... 4-24
    Engine Rebuilding
    Specifications................. 21-1
    Engine, Replace 4-23
    Engine Mount, Replace 4-22
    Exhaust Manifold, Replace.... 4-24
    Front Cover, Replace 4-26

	Page No.
Front Cover Seal, Replace....	4-26
Fuel Filter, Replace...........	4-32
Fuel Pump, Replace...........	4-32
Hydraulic Lash Adjuster, Replace........................	4-26
Intake Manifold, Replace......	4-24
Main & Rod Bearings.........	4-30
Oil Pan, Replace..............	4-30
Oil Pump, Replace.............	4-30
Piston & Rod Assembly.......	4-29
Precautions....................	4-22
Radiator, Replace..............	4-31
Serpentine Drive Belt.........	4-31
Thermostat, Replace...........	4-31
Tightening Specifications......	4-36
Timing Chain, Replace........	4-27
Valve Adjustment	4-26
Valve Cover, Replace.........	4-25
Water Pump, Replace.........	4-31

4.6L DOHC ENGINE
Belt Tension Data..............	4-42
Camshaft, Replace	4-41
Camshaft Lobe Lift Specifications..................	4-40
Compression Pressure........	4-38
Cooling System Bleed........	4-43
Crankshaft Seal, Replace.....	4-42
Cylinder Head, Replace.......	4-39
Engine Rebuilding Specifications..................	21-1
Engine, Replace..............	4-38
Engine Mount, Replace.......	4-38
Exhaust Manifold, Replace....	4-39
Front Cover, Replace.........	4-40
Front Cover Seal, Replace....	4-40
Fuel Filter, Replace...........	4-43
Fuel Pump, Replace...........	4-43
Intake Manifold, Replace......	4-38
Main & Rod Bearings.........	4-42
Oil Pan, Replace..............	4-42
Oil Pump, Replace.............	4-42
Piston & Rod Assembly.......	4-42
Precautions....................	4-37
Radiator, Replace..............	4-43
Serpentine Drive Belt.........	4-42
Supercharger, Replace.......	4-43
Thermostat, Replace...........	4-43
Tightening Specifications......	4-45
Timing Chain, Replace........	4-41
Timing Chain Tensioner Bleed........................	4-41
Valve Adjustment	4-40
Valve Cover, Replace.........	4-39
Water Pump, Replace.........	4-43

	Page No.
4.6L SOHC (VIN H) ENGINE	
Belt Tension Data..............	4-64
Camshaft, Replace	4-61
Camshaft Lobe Lift Specifications..................	4-59
Compression Pressure........	4-54
Cooling System Bleed........	4-64
Crankshaft Damper, Replace..	4-59
Crankshaft Rear Oil Seal, Replace........................	4-63
Crankshaft Seal, Replace.....	4-62
Cylinder Head, Replace.......	4-57
Engine Rebuilding Specifications..................	21-1
Engine, Replace..............	4-55
Engine Mount, Replace.......	4-54
Exhaust Manifold, Replace....	4-56
Front Cover, Replace.........	4-60
Front Cover Seal, Replace....	4-60
Fuel Filter, Replace...........	4-65
Fuel Pump, Replace...........	4-65
Hydraulic Lash Adjuster, Replace........................	4-59
Intake Manifold, Replace......	4-56
Main & Rod Bearings.........	4-62
Oil Pan, Replace..............	4-63
Oil Pump, Replace.............	4-64
Piston & Rod Assembly.......	4-62
Precautions....................	4-54
Radiator, Replace..............	4-65
Serpentine Drive Belt.........	4-64
Technical Service Bulletins....	4-65
Thermostat, Replace...........	4-65
Tightening Specifications......	4-72
Timing Chain, Replace........	4-60
Valve Adjustment	4-59
Valve Cover, Replace.........	4-59
Water Pump, Replace.........	4-65

4.6L SOHC (VIN X) ENGINE
Belt Tension Data..............	4-51
Camshaft, Replace	4-50
Camshaft Lobe Lift Specifications..................	4-49
Compression Pressure........	4-47
Cooling System Bleed........	4-51
Crankshaft Seal, Replace.....	4-50
Cylinder Head, Replace.......	4-48
Engine Rebuilding Specifications..................	21-1
Engine, Replace..............	4-47
Engine Mount, Replace.......	4-47
Exhaust Manifold, Replace....	4-48
Front Cover, Replace.........	4-49

	Page No.
Front Cover Seal, Replace....	4-49
Fuel Filter, Replace...........	4-51
Fuel Pump, Replace...........	4-51
Intake Manifold, Replace......	4-47
Main & Rod Bearings.........	4-50
Oil Pan, Replace..............	4-51
Oil Pump, Replace.............	4-51
Piston & Rod Assembly.......	4-50
Precautions....................	4-46
Radiator, Replace..............	4-51
Serpentine Drive Belt.........	4-51
Technical Service Bulletins....	4-52
Thermostat, Replace...........	4-51
Tightening Specifications......	4-53
Timing Chain, Replace........	4-49
Timing Chain Tensioner Bleed........................	4-50
Valve Adjustment	4-49
Valve Cover, Replace.........	4-48
Water Pump, Replace.........	4-51

5.4L ENGINE
Belt Tension Data..............	4-79
Camshaft, Replace	4-77
Camshaft Lobe Lift Specifications..................	4-76
Compression Pressure........	4-73
Cooling System Bleed........	4-79
Crankshaft Damper, Replace..	4-76
Crankshaft Rear Oil Seal, Replace........................	4-78
Cylinder Head, Replace.......	4-75
Engine Rebuilding Specifications..................	21-1
Engine, Replace..............	4-74
Engine Mount, Replace.......	4-73
Exhaust Manifold, Replace....	4-74
Front Cover, Replace.........	4-77
Fuel Filter, Replace...........	4-79
Fuel Pump, Replace...........	4-79
Hydraulic Lash Adjuster, Replace........................	4-76
Intake Manifold, Replace......	4-74
Main & Rod Bearings.........	4-78
Oil Pan, Replace..............	4-78
Oil Pump, Replace.............	4-79
Piston & Rod Assembly.......	4-77
Precautions....................	4-73
Radiator, Replace..............	4-79
Serpentine Drive Belt.........	4-79
Thermostat, Replace...........	4-79
Tightening Specifications......	4-81
Timing Chain, Replace........	4-77
Valve Adjustment	4-76
Valve Cover, Replace.........	4-75
Water Pump, Replace.........	4-79

Specifications

GENERAL ENGINE SPECIFICATIONS

Year	Engine Liter (VIN)①	Fuel System	Bore & Stroke	Compression Ratio	Net H.P. @ RPM	Maximum Torque Ft. Lbs. @ RPM	Normal Oil Pressure, psi
2004	3.8L (4)	SEFI	3.81 × 3.39	9.4	193 @ 5500	225 @ 2800	40–125③
	4.6L (R) DOHC	SEFI	3.55 × 3.54	10.1	305 @ 5800	320 @ 4200	20–45④
	4.6L (X) SOHC	SEFI	3.55 × 3.54	9.4	260 @ 5250	302 @ 4000	20–45④
2005–08	4.0L (N) SOHC	SEFI	3.95 x 3.32	9.7	210 @ 5250	240 @ 3500	15②
	4.6L (H) OHC	SEFI	3.55 x 3.54	9.8	300 @ 5750	320 @ 4500	75②
	5.4L (S) DOHC	SEFI	3.55 x 4.16	8.4	500 @ 6000	480 @ 4500	40–60②

DOHC — Double overhead cams, four valves per cylinder

SEFI — Sequential Multi-Port Electronic Fuel Injection

SOHC — Single overhead cam, two valves per cylinder

OHV — Overhead valve, two valves per cylinder

① — Eighth digit denotes engine code.
② — Engine hot @ 2000 RPM.
③ — Engine hot @ 2500 RPM.
④ — Engine hot @ 1500 RPM.

TUNE UP SPECIFICATIONS

Year & Engine (Code①)	Spark Plug Gap	Firing Order Fig.	Ignition Timin, Deg. BTDC Man. Trans.	Ignition Timin, Deg. BTDC Auto. Trans.	Mark	Curb Idle Speed Man. Trans.	Curb Idle Speed Auto Trans.	Fast Idle Speed Man. Trans.	Fast Idle Speed Auto. Trans.	Fuel Pump Pressure, psi⑧	Valve Lash, Inch
2004											
3.8L (4)	.052–.056	②	⑥	⑥	⑦	⑤	⑤	⑤	⑤	35–50	④
4.6L (R) DOHC	.052–.056	③	⑥	⑥	⑦	⑤	⑤	⑤	⑤	35–50	④
4.6L (X) SOHC	.052–.056	③	⑥	⑥	⑦	⑤	⑤	⑤	⑤	35–50	④
2005–06											
4.0L (N) SOHC	.052–.056	②	⑥	⑥	⑦	⑤	⑤	⑤	⑤	27–37⑨	④
4.6L (H) OHC	—	⑥	10⑥	10⑦	⑤	⑤	⑤	⑤	⑤	27–37⑨	④
5.4L (S) DOHC	.041–.047	③	10⑥	10⑦	⑤	⑤	⑤	⑤	⑤	27–37⑨	④
2007–08											
4.0L (N) SOHC	.052–.056	②	⑥	⑥	⑦	⑤	⑤	⑤	⑤	27–37⑨	④
4.6L (H) OHC	—	⑥	10⑥	10⑦	⑤	⑤	⑤	⑤	⑤	27–37⑨	④
5.4L (S) DOHC	.041–.047	③	10⑥	10⑦	⑤	⑤	⑤	⑤	⑤	27–37⑨	④

BTDC — Before Top Dead Center
① — Eighth digit denotes engine code.
② — Cylinder numbering front to rear, righthand bank, 1, 2, 3 ; lefthand bank, 4, 5, 6. Firing order 1-4-2-5-3-6.
③ — Cylinder numbering front to rear: righthand bank 1, 2, 3, 4; lefthand bank 5, 6, 7, 8. Firing order 1-3-7-2-6-5-4-8. Refer to **Fig. A**, for ignition coil tower terminal numbering.
④ — Equipped w/hydraulic valve tappets.
⑤ — Idle speed controlled by an automatic idle speed control.

⑥ — Non-adjustable.
⑦ — Equipped w/crankshaft position sensor.
⑧ — Wrap shop towel around fitting to prevent fuel spillage, then connect

suitable fuel pressure gauge to fuel diagnostic valve on fuel rail assembly. Gradually open fuel pressure gauge test valve to relieve fuel system pressure & drain fuel into suitable container. Close fuel pressure gauge test valve. Turn ignition On. Access output test mode on scan tool & operate fuel pump to obtain maximum fuel pressure. Fuel pump will operate for approximately 8 seconds. Inspect fuel pressure gauge reading.

⑨ — Engine running @ idle.

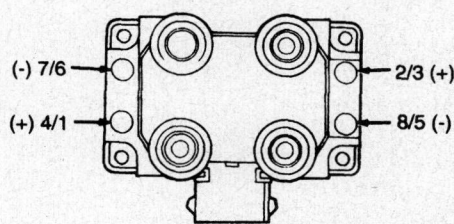

(-) 7/6
(+) 4/1
2/3 (+)
8/5 (-)

FM1139600469000X

Fig. A

FRONT WHEEL ALIGNMENT SPECIFICATIONS

Model	Caster Angle, Degrees①		Camber Angle, Degrees		Total Toe, Inches②	
	Limits	Desired	Limits	Desired	Limits	Desired
2004						
Base & GT	+2.45 to +3.95	+3.2	-1.25 to +.25	-.5	0 to +.26	+.13
Cobra	+2.45 to +3.95	+3.2	-1.30 to -.50	-.9	0 to +.26	+.13
2005–08						
All	+7.05 to +7.15	+7.10	-.25 to -1.25	-.75	-.10 to +.30	+.10

① — Difference side to side, lefthand minus righthand should not be more than .75°.

② — Toe-In (+). Toe-Out (–).

REAR WHEEL ALIGNMENT SPECIFICATIONS

Model	Caster Angle, Degrees	Camber Angle, Degrees		Toe-In, Inches	
		Limits	Desired	Limits	Desired
2004 Cobra	—	-1.0 to -.6	-.8	-.02 to +.18	+.08
2005–08	—	—	—	—	—

VEHICLE RIDE HEIGHT SPECIFICATIONS

Year	Body Style	Manufacturer's Original Tire Size	Measurement Points & Specifications②					
			Front③			Rear③		
			Dimension	Specification		Dimension	Specification	
				Inches	mm		Inches	mm
2004	Base & GT	①	1④	.2	4	2⑤	5.00	128
	Cobra	①	1④	.2	4	2⑥	1.40	36
2005–08	All	①	1④	1.2–1.8	31–45	2⑤	4.30–4.90	115–121

1 Dim. — Front suspension: Height from ground to center of lower control arm mounting bolt minus height from ground to bottom of steering knuckle

1 Dim. — Rear suspension: Height from ground to center of lower control arm mounting bolt minus height from ground to center of steering knuckle lower mounting bolt

2 Dim. — Rear axle arch center to body reinforcement at closest point

① — See door sticker or inside of glove compartment for manufacturers original tire size specifications. If tires on vehicle do not match manufacturers original tire size & measurement is not within limits, it will be required to refer to the "Non-Standard Tire & Wheel Size Adjustment To Ride Height Specification & Tire Size Adjustment Charts" in the front of this manual for approximate changes in ride height specifications.

② — Measurement is with fuel, radiator coolant and engine oil full, spare tire, jack, hand tools and mats in designated positions and tires properly inflated.

③ — Ride height side to side should be within .50 inch (13 mm). Ride height front to rear should be within .75 inch (19 mm).

④ — Refer to **Fig. A**.

⑤ — Refer to **Fig. B**.

⑥ — Refer to **Fig. C**.

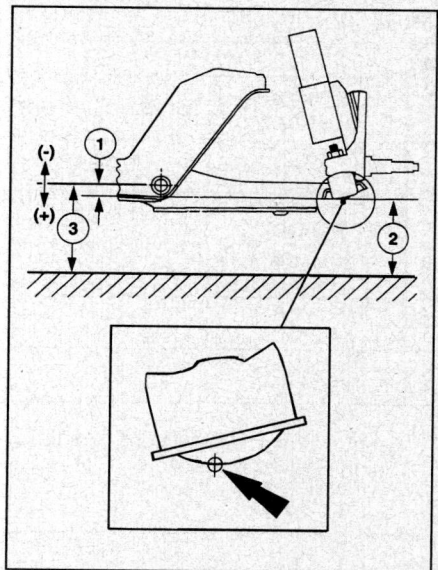

Item	Description
1	Ride height = B - A
2	Measurement A
3	Measurement B

FM2020100207000X

Fig. A   Front ride height

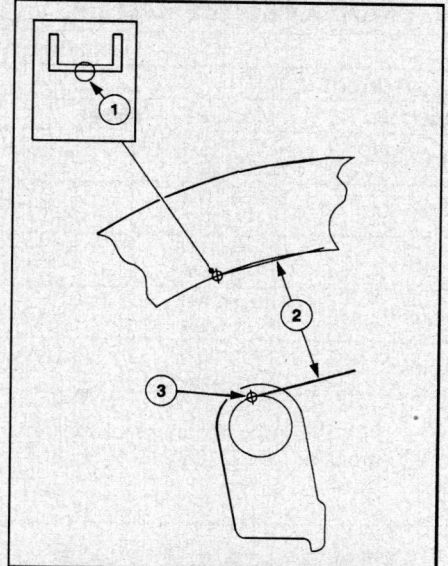

Item	Description
1	Body reinforcement
2	Ride height (shortest distance)
3	Rear axle

FM2030100158000X

Fig. B   Rear ride height. Base & GT

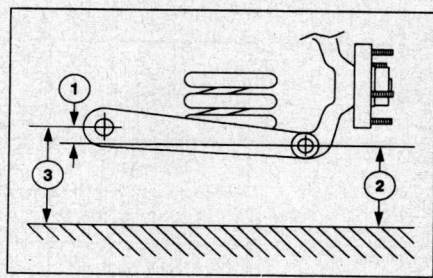

Item	Description
1	Ride height = B - A
2	Measurement A
3	Measurement B

FM2030100159000X

Fig. C   Rear ride height. Cobra

FLUID CAPACITIES & COOLING SYSTEM DATA

Year	Engine (VIN①)	Cooling Capacity, Qts.		Cool-ant Type	Radiator Cap Relief Pres-sure, Lbs.	Thermo. Open-ing Temp. Deg. F	Fuel Tank Gals.	Engine Oil Refill Qts.②	Transmission Oil		Rear Axle Oil Pints
		Less Air Condi-tioning	With Air Con-dition-ing						Man. Trans. Pints	Auto. Trans. Qts.③	
2004	3.8L (4)	11.8	11.8	⑤	13–18	189–196	15.7	5.0	5.6	5.0	3.50
	4.6L (R) DOHC	16.0	16.0	⑤	13–18	175–182	15.7	6.0	8.2	5.0	2.60–2.90
	4.6L (X) SOHC	14.1	14.1	⑤	13–18	192–199	15.7	5.0	7.5	5.0	4.00
2005–08	4.0L (N) SOHC	16.1	16.1	⑥	16	194–201	16.0	5.0	5.6	11.9	3.00④
	4.6L (H) SOHC	16.1	16.1	⑥	16	175–182	16.0	6.5	7.5	11.9	3.15④
	5.4L (S) DOHC	16.0	16.0	⑥	16	176–184	16.0	6.5	7.5	11.9	3.00④

EG — Ethylene Glycol
① — Eighth digit of Vehicle Identification Number (VIN) denotes engine code.
② — Includes filter.
③ — Approximate. Make final inspection w/dipstick.

④ — Models equipped with Traction-Lok axle, add 4 ounces of additive friction modifier.
⑤ — Always fill cooling system with same coolant that is present in the system. Do not mix coolant types. For models w/green coolant use ethylene glycol, Premium Engine

Coolant Fluid VC-4-A (in Oregon VC-5), or equivalent meeting Ford specifications ESE-M97B44-A.
⑥ — Motorcraft Premium Gold (Yellow) Engine Coolant VC-7-A (California, Oregon & New Mexico, VC-7-B), or equivalent.

LUBRICANT DATA

Year	Model	Lubricant Type				
		Transmission		Rear Axle	Power Steering	Brake System
		Automatic	Manual			
2004	3.8L Engine	Mercon V	Mercon ATF XT-2-QDX	80W-90①	Mercon ATF XT-2-QDX	DOT 3
	4.6L Engine	Mercon V	Mercon ATF XT-2-QDX	75W-140②	Mercon ATF XT-2-QDX	DOT 3
2005–08	4.0L (N) SOHC	Mercon V	Mercon ATF XT-2-QDX	75W-140②	Mercon ATF XT-2-QDX	DOT 3
	4.6L (H) SOHC	Mercon V	Mercon ATF XT-2-QDX	75W-140②	Mercon ATF XT-2-QDX	DOT 3
	5.4L	Mercon V	Mercon ATF XT-2-QDX	75W-140②	Mercon ATF XT-2-QDX	DOT 3

① — Thermally Stable Rear Axle Lubricant XY-80W90-QL.
② — On models equipped w/Traction-Lok axle, add 4 ounces of friction modifier C8AZ-19B546-A, or equivalent meeting Ford specification EST-M2C118-A.

Electrical

NOTE: On Air Bag Equipped Models, Refer To "Air Bag System Precautions" Located In The Front Of This Manual For System Disarming & Arming Procedures.

NOTE: Refer To "Computer Relearn Procedures" Located In The Front Of This Manual When Battery Power To The Computer Has Been Interrupted.

NOTE: Prior To Performing Any Service Operations Listed In This Section, Consult The "Technical Service Bulletins" Section For Related Information.

INDEX

	Page No.
Air Bag System (Volume 2)	4-1
Air Conditioning	8-1
Alternator, Replace	4-7
2004	4-7
2005–08	4-7
4.0L	4-7
4.6L	4-7
5.4L Engine	4-7
Alternators	11-1
Blower Motor, Replace	4-11
2004	4-11
2005–08	4-11
Clutch Start Switch, Replace	4-9
2004	4-9
2005–08	4-9
Cooling Fans	9-1
Cruise Control (Volume 2)	2-1
Dash Gauges (Volume 2)	1-1
Dash Panel Service (Volume 2)	5-1
Evaporator Core, Replace	4-11
2004	4-11
2005–08	4-11
Fuel Pump Relay Location	4-7
Fuse Panel & Flasher Location	4-7
Headlamp Switch, Replace	4-10
Heater Core, Replace	4-11
2004	4-11
2005–08	4-11

	Page No.
Ignition Coil Pack, Replace	4-8
2004	4-8
3.8L Engine	4-8
4.6L Engine	4-8
2005–08	4-8
4.0L Engine	4-8
4.6L Engine	4-8
5.4L Engine	4-8
Ignition Lock, Replace	4-8
2004	4-8
Functioning	4-8
Non-Functioning	4-8
2005–08	4-9
Ignition Switch, Replace	4-9
2004	4-9
2005–08	4-9
Instrument Cluster, Replace	4-10
2004	4-10
2005–08	4-10
Multi-Function Switch, Replace	4-10
2004	4-10
2005–08	4-10
Neutral Safety Switch, Replace	4-9
2004	4-9
2005–08	4-10
Installation	4-10
Removal	4-10
Passive Restraint Systems (Volume 2)	4-1

	Page No.
Precautions	4-7
Air Bag Systems	4-7
Battery Ground Cable	4-7
Radio, Replace	4-10
Relay Center Location	4-7
Speed Controls (Volume 2)	2-1
Starter Motors	10-1
Starter, Replace	4-7
2004	4-7
2005–08	4-7
4.0L Engine	4-7
4.6L & 5.4L Engines	4-7
Steering Columns	12-1
Steering Wheel, Replace	4-10
Stop Light Switch, Replace	4-10
Technical Service Bulletins	4-12
Repeated Heater Core Failure	4-12
Wiper Motor, Replace	4-10
2004	4-10
2005–08	4-11
Wiper Switch, Replace	4-11
2004	4-11
2005–08	4-11
Wiper Systems (Volume 2)	3-1
Wiper Transmission, Replace	4-11
2004	4-11
2005–08	4-11

PRECAUTIONS

Air Bag Systems

Refer to "Air Bag System Precautions" in front of this manual for system disarming and arming procedures.

Battery Ground Cable

Prior to service, disconnect battery ground cable and isolate as required.

FUSE PANEL & FLASHER LOCATION

The fuse panel is located below and to the lefthand of the steering column near the brake pedal. To access these fuses, remove the panel cover.

There is also a power distribution and relay box located in the engine compartment, adjacent to the battery.

RELAY CENTER LOCATION

A relay and power distribution box is located under the hood. Ensure its cover is intact when filling fluid reservoirs or servicing the battery.

FUEL PUMP RELAY LOCATION

The fuel pump relay is located in the underhood relay and power distribution box.

STARTER
REPLACE
2004

1. Raise and support vehicle.
2. **On models equipped with 3.8L engine,** remove ground cable nut.
3. **On models equipped with 4.6L engine,** HO2S wire harness and bracket.
4. **On all models,** remove solenoid protective cap and wiring nuts. Position wiring aside.
5. Remove mounting bolts and starter motor.
6. Reverse procedure to install, noting the following:
   a. **Torque** starter mounting bolts to 17 ft. lbs.
   b. **Torque** solenoid B-terminal nut to 108 inch lbs.
   c. **Torque** solenoid terminal nut to 53 inch lbs.
   d. **On models equipped with 3.8L engine, torque** ground cable nut to 17 ft. lbs.
   e. **On models equipped with 4.6L engine, torque** HO2S bracket nut to 18 ft. lbs.

2005-08
4.0L ENGINE

1. Raise and support vehicle.
2. Remove starter solenoid terminal cap, **Fig. 1.**
3. Remove two terminal nuts and position starter solenoid wires aside.
4. Remove two mounting bolts and starter motor.
5. Reverse procedure to install, noting the following:
   a. **Torque** starter motor mounting bolts to 18 ft. lbs.
   b. **Torque** solenoid B+ terminal nut to 106 inch lbs.
   c. **Torque** solenoid S-terminal nut 53 inch lbs.

4.6L & 5.4L ENGINES

1. Ensure anti-theft system is deactivated.
2. Raise and support vehicle.
3. Remove starter solenoid terminal cap, **Fig. 2.**
4. Remove two terminal nuts and position wires aside.
5. Remove three mounting bolts and starter motor.
6. Reverse procedure to install, noting the following:
   a. **Torque** mounting bolts to 18 ft. lbs.
   b. **Torque** B+ terminal nut to 108 inch lbs.
   c. **Torque** S terminal nut to 53 inch lbs.

ALTERNATOR
REPLACE
2004

1. Remove serpentine drive belt from alternator pulley. Leave belt in place to ease installation.
2. **On models equipped with 4.6L SOHC engine,** remove mounting bolts and alternator upper bracket, then disconnect alternator electrical connector by pressing tab. **Do not pull on tab.**
3. **On all models,** disconnect alternator electrical connections.
4. Remove mounting bolts and alternator.
5. Reverse procedure to install, noting the following:
   a. **On models equipped with 3.8L engine, torque** alternator lower mounting bolt to 35 ft. lbs., and upper bolt to 18 ft. lbs.
   b. **On models equipped with 4.6L engines, torque** alternator lower mounting bolts to 18 ft. lbs., and upper bolts to 89 inch lbs.
   c. **On all models, torque** battery positive cable nut to solenoid to 72 inch lbs.

2005-08
4.0L

1. Rotate tensioner counterclockwise and position front end accessory drive belt aside.
2. Disconnect alternator electrical connector.
3. Position boot aside, remove the remove nut and position B+ terminal aside.
4. Remove two mounting nuts and position shield aside.
5. Remove two stud nuts, mounting bolt and alternator.
6. Reverse procedure to install, noting the following:
   a. **Torque** B+ terminal nut to 71 inch lbs.
   b. **Torque** shield nuts to 26 ft. lbs.
   c. **Torque** stud nuts and mounting bolt to 35 ft. lbs.

4.6L

1. Press lock tab, remove crankcase vent tube from air cleaner outlet pipe and position it aside.
2. Loosen clamp, remove air cleaner outlet pipe from throttle body and position it aside.
3. Rotate tensioner clockwise and position front end accessory drive belt aside.
4. Remove two mounting bolts.
5. Remove two outer bracket bolts and position alternator aside.
6. Remove two inner bracket bolts.
7. Remove harness locator and bracket.
8. Disconnect electrical connector.
9. Position B+ protective boot aside, then remove nut and position alternator B+ terminal aside.
10. Remove alternator.
11. Reverse procedure to install, noting the following:
    a. **Torque** mounting bolts to 18 ft. lbs.
    b. **Torque** bracket bolts to 89 inch lbs.
    c. **Torque** terminal nut to 71 inch lbs.

5.4L ENGINE

1. Rotate tensioner clockwise and position front end accessory drive belt aside.
2. Remove alternator upper mounting bolts.
3. Remove power steering line bracket nut and position bracket aside.
4. Remove alternator lower mounting bolt.
5. Disconnect alternator electrical connector.
6. Position B+ protective boot aside, then remove nut and position alternator B+ terminal aside.
7. Remove alternator.
8. Reverse procedure to install, noting the following:
   a. **Torque** mounting bolts to 35 ft. lbs.
   b. **Torque** bracket bolts to 18 ft. lbs.
   c. **Torque** terminal nut to 71 inch lbs.

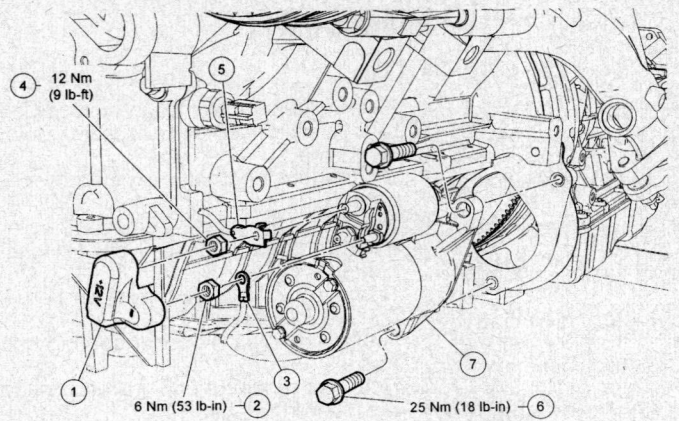

Item	Description
1	Starter solenoid terminal cover
2	Starter solenoid S-terminal nut
3	Starter solenoid S-terminal eyelet
4	Starter solenoid B+ terminal nut
5	Starter solenoid B+ terminal eyelet
6	Starter motor mounting bolt (2 required)
7	Starter motor

ARM0400000000594

Fig. 1   Starter replacement. 4.0L engine. 2005–08

Item	Description
1	Starter solenoid terminal cover
2	Starter solenoid S-terminal nut
3	Starter solenoid S-terminal eyelet
4	Starter solenoid B+ terminal nut
5	Starter solenoid B+ terminal eyelet
6	Starter motor mounting bolt (3 required)
7	Starter motor

ARM0400000000524

Fig. 2   Starter motor replacement. 2005–08 w/4.6L & 5.4L engines

IGNITION COIL PACK
REPLACE
2004

3.8L ENGINE

1. Disconnect electrical connectors.
2. Tag spark plug wires, squeeze locking tabs and disconnect. Position wires aside.
3. Record radio ignition interference capacitor location.
4. Remove mounting bolts and coil.
5. Reverse procedure to install, noting the following:
   a. Ensure radio ignition interference capacitor is located under proper coil mounting bolt.
   b. **Torque** coil mounting bolts to 53 inch lbs.
   c. Apply silicone brake caliper grease and dielectric compound No. D7AZ-19A331-A, or equivalent, to inside of each wire coil boot.

4.6L ENGINE

1. Remove air cleaner outlet tube.
2. Disconnect ignition coil.
3. Remove mounting bolt and ignition coil.
4. Reverse procedure to install, noting the following:
   a. Ensure ignition coil spring is correctly located inside boot and tip is not damaged.
   b. **Torque** mounting bolts to 89 inch lbs.

2005-08
4.0L ENGINE

1. Disconnect ignition coil electrical connector.
2. Disconnect six spark plug wires from ignition coil.
3. Remove four mounting bolts and ignition coil.
4. Reverse procedure to install. **Torque** mounting bolts to 53 inch lbs.

4.6L ENGINE

1. Disconnect ignition coil electrical connector.
2. Remove mounting bolts and ignition coil.
3. Reverse procedure to install, noting the following:
   a. Apply light film of suitable silicone brake caliper great and dielectric compound to inside of coil boots.
   b. **Torque** mounting bolts to 44 inch lbs.

5.4L ENGINE

1. Remove air cleaner outlet tube.
2. Disconnect ignition coil.
3. Remove mounting bolt and ignition coil.
4. Reverse procedure to install, noting the following:
   a. Ensure ignition coil spring is correctly located inside boot and tip is not damaged.
   b. **Torque** mounting bolts to 89 inch lbs.

IGNITION LOCK
REPLACE
2004
FUNCTIONING

1. Turn ignition to switch to Run position.
2. Remove ignition switch by depressing retaining pin with suitable drift punch in hole in upper steering column shroud under switch.
3. Reverse procedure to install. Ensure lock cylinder operates properly.

NON-FUNCTIONING

1. Remove driver's air bag module as outlined in "Passive Restraint Systems" chapter.
2. Remove and discard steering wheel mounting bolt.
3. Remove steering wheel using suitable puller tool.
4. Twist ignition switch lock cylinder cap with suitable locking-type pliers until it separates from ignition switch lock cylinder.
5. Center punch retaining pin with suitable small pilot punch through access hole in lower steering column shroud and drill it out with ⅛ inch diameter drill.
6. Drill down middle of key slot using ⅜ inch diameter bit approximately 1¾ inches until lock cylinder breaks loose.
7. Remove ignition switch lock cylinder.
8. Record positions of column lock gear, bearing and retainer.

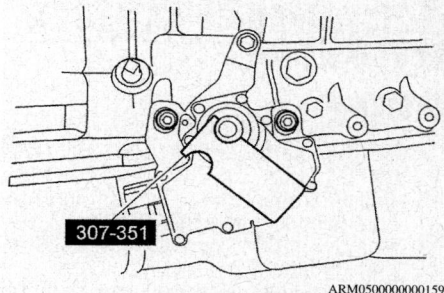

Fig. 3 Digital TR sensor alignment. 2005–08

9. Remove bearing retainer, steering column lock housing bearing, ignition switch lock cylinder and steering column lock gear.
10. Reverse procedures to install, noting the following:
   a. Repair steering column lock cylinder housing.
   b. Ensure components are properly aligned and oriented.
   c. Coat lock gear and housing with ignition lock grease No. F0AZ-19584-A, or equivalent.
   d. Install new steering wheel mounting bolt.
   e. **Torque** mounting bolt to 23–32 ft. lbs.

2005–08

1. Remove steering column cover.
2. Remove three mounting screws and lower steering column shroud.
3. Turn key to RUN position.
4. Insert suitable, small punch into hole and remove ignition lock cylinder.
5. Reverse procedure to install.

IGNITION SWITCH
REPLACE
2004

1. Remove mounting screws and steering column lower cover.
2. Remove mounting screws and instrument panel reinforcement.
3. Loosen mounting bolt and disconnect ignition switch electrical connector.
4. Ensure ignition switch is in OFF position.
5. Remove mounting screws and ignition switch.
6. Reverse procedure to install, noting the following:
   a. **Torque** ignition switch mounting screws to 53 inch lbs.
   b. **Torque** instrument panel reinforcement mounting screws to 80 inch lbs.
   c. **Torque** steering column lower cover mounting screws to 80 inch lbs.

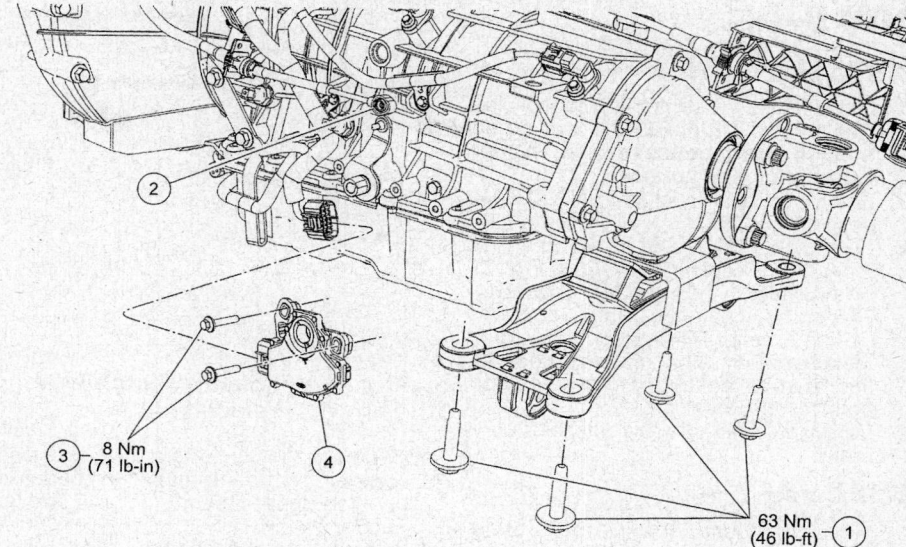

Item	Description
1	Transmission crossmember-to-floor pan screws
2	Transmission selector lever cable
3	Digital transmission range (TR) sensor screws
4	Digital TR sensor

Fig. 4 Digital TR sensor replacement. 2005–08

2005–08

1. Disarm air bag system as outlined under "Air Bag System Precautions" in front of this manual.
2. Remove upper steering column shroud by carefully pressing sides inward.
3. Remove three mounting screws and lower steering column shroud.
4. Disconnect ignition switch electrical connector, release two locking tabs and remove ignition switch.
5. Reverse procedure to install.

CLUTCH START SWITCH
REPLACE
2004

1. Disconnect clutch pedal position switch electrical connector.
2. Record switch's positioning.
3. Remove mounting bolt and switch.
4. Reverse procedure to install.

2005–08

1. Disconnect Clutch Pedal Position (CPP) switch electrical connector.
2. Release CPP switch from clutch pedal bracket.
3. Reverse procedure to install.

NEUTRAL SAFETY SWITCH
REPLACE
2004

On these models the neutral safety switch is incorporated into the digital Transmission Range (TR) sensor.

1. Apply parking brake and place transmission in Neutral position.
2. Raise and support vehicle.
3. Disconnect TR sensor electrical connector.
4. Disconnect range selector cable.
5. Remove mounting bolts and TR sensor.
6. Reverse procedure to install, noting the following:
   a. Ensure shift lever shaft is in Neutral position.
   b. Align sensor slots using TR sensor alignment tool No. T97L-70010-A, or equivalent.
   c. **Torque** sensor mounting bolts to 62–89 inch lbs.
   d. Ensure starter cranks in Park or Neutral position, only.

2005-08

INSTALLATION

1. Install digital TR sensor and loosely install screws. **Digital TR sensor must fit flush against boss on case to prevent damage to sensor.**
2. Ensure manual lever is in NEUTRAL position.
3. Align digital TR sensor using TR alignment gauge tool No. 307-351, **Fig. 3,** or equivalent, then **torque** screws to 71 inch lbs in an alternating sequence.
4. Connect digital TR sensor connector.
5. Install transmission crossmember to floor pan bolts. **Torque** crossmember bolts to 46 ft. lbs.
6. Verify that shift cable is adjusted correctly.

REMOVAL

On these models the neutral safety switch is incorporated into digital Transmission Range (TR) sensor.

1. Raise and support vehicle.
2. Support transmission using suitable transmission jack.
3. Remove transmission crossmember to floor pan bolts, **Fig. 4,** then lower transmission enough to gain access to digital TR sensor.
4. Disconnect digital TR sensor connector.
5. Disconnect transmission shift cable from manual control lever.
6. Remove digital TR sensor mounting screws, then the digital TR sensor.

HEADLAMP SWITCH

REPLACE

1. Pull headlamp switch to full ON position.
2. Pull and remove knob by inserting suitable thin tool into slot, **Fig. 5.**
3. Remove mounting screws and instrument cluster finish retaining panel.
4. Remove mounting screws and headlamp switch.
5. Disconnect headlamp switch electrical connector.
6. Reverse procedure to install.

STOP LIGHT SWITCH

REPLACE

1. Remove stop lamp switch linkage clip and retainer.
2. Disconnect switch electrical connector and remove switch.
3. Reverse procedure to install. Do not press brake pedal during installation. Initial installation of stop light switch allows for one adjustment. If additional adjustments are required, install a new switch.

MULTI-FUNCTION SWITCH

REPLACE

2004

1. Turn ignition to switch to Run position.

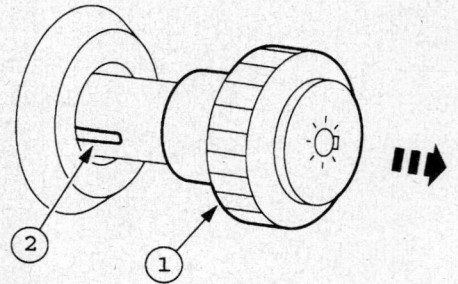

1. Knob
2. Slot

FM9019900384000X

Fig. 5 Headlamp switch knob replacement

2. Remove ignition switch by depressing retaining pin with suitable drift punch in hole in upper steering column shroud under switch.
3. Remove tilt wheel handle.
4. Remove mounting screws, then the steering column upper and lower shrouds.
5. Remove multi-function switch mounting screws.
6. Disconnect electrical connectors and remove multi-function switch.
7. Reverse procedure to install. **Torque** multi-function switch mounting screws to 18-26 inch lbs.

2005-08

1. Remove steering wheel as outlined under "Steering Wheel, Replace."
2. Remove and discard steering wheel mounting bolt.
3. Remove steering wheel using suitable puller tool.
4. Remove upper steering column shroud by carefully pressing sides inward.
5. Remove three mounting screws and lower steering column shroud.
6. Disconnect four lower multifunction switch electrical connectors.
7. Disconnect upper multifunction switch electrical connector.
8. Remove four mounting screws and multifunction switch.
9. Reverse procedure to install.

STEERING WHEEL

REPLACE

1. Remove driver's air bag module as outlined in "Passive Restraint Systems" chapter.
2. Remove and discard steering wheel mounting bolt.
3. Remove steering wheel using suitable puller tool.
4. Reverse procedure to install, noting the following:
   a. Install new steering wheel mounting bolt.
   b. **On 2004 models, torque** mounting bolt to 23-32 ft. lbs.
   c. **On 2005-08 models, torque** mounting bolt to 41 ft. lbs.

INSTRUMENT CLUSTER

REPLACE

2004

1. Pull headlamp switch to full ON position.
2. Pull and remove knob by inserting suitable thin tool into slot, **Fig. 5.**
3. Remove mounting screws and instrument cluster finish retaining panel.
4. Remove mounting screws and cluster out.
5. Disconnect electrical connector.
6. Remove instrument cluster.
7. Reverse procedure to install.

2005-08

Prior to removal of the instrument cluster, upload the instrument cluster configuration information to a suitable diagnostic tool.

1. Disarm supplemental restraint system as outlined under "Air Bag System Precautions" in the front of this manual.
2. Remove instrument cluster finish panel.
3. Remove four mounting screws and instrument cluster, then disconnect electrical connector.
4. Reverse procedure to install.

RADIO

REPLACE

1. Remove instrument panel center finishing panel.
2. Remove mounting screws and radio.
3. Disconnect electrical connector and antenna lead-in cable.
4. Reverse procedure to install.

WIPER MOTOR

REPLACE

2004

The internal permanent magnets used in the windshield wiper motor are of a ceramic material. Care must be exercised in handling the motor to avoid damaging the magnets. **Do not strike or tap motor with a hammer or other object.**

1. Turn windshield wipers on. When blades reach full upright travel on glass, turn ignition switch Off.
2. Remove windshield wiper pivot arms and blades.
3. Remove cowl top vent grille.
4. Disconnect wiper motor adapter and connecting linkage clip from motor arm.
5. Remove linkage drive arm from windshield wiper motor.
6. Disconnect wiper motor electrical connector and remove motor to cowl mounting fasteners.
7. Remove wiper motor.
8. Reverse procedures to install. **Torque** wiper motor mounting screws to 10-12 ft. lbs.

2005-08

1. Remove two covers, two mounting nuts and two wiper pivot arms.
2. Remove four cowl vent screen pin-type retainers.
3. Remove righthand and lefthand cowl vent screen overlaps. Righthand screen overlaps left.
4. Remove three mounting bolts, windshield wiper mounting arm and pivot shaft.
5. Remove mounting bolt, then disconnect mounting arm and pivot shaft linkage from wiper motor output shaft.
6. Remove three mounting bolts and windshield wiper motor.
7. Reverse procedure to install, noting the following:
   a. **Torque** wiper motor mounting bolt to 11 ft. lbs.
   b. **Torque** arm mounting bolt to 13 ft. lbs. If reusing mounting bolt, apply suitable Threadlock to bolt.
   c. **Torque** windshield wiper mounting arm and pivot shaft mounting bolts to 62 inch lbs.

WIPER SWITCH
REPLACE
2004

1. Turn ignition to switch to Run position.
2. Remove ignition switch by depressing retaining pin with suitable drift punch in hole in upper steering column shroud under switch.
3. Remove tilt wheel handle.
4. Remove mounting screws, then the steering column upper and lower shrouds.
5. Remove multi-function switch mounting screws.
6. Disconnect electrical connectors and remove multi-function switch.
7. Reverse procedure to install. **Torque** multi-function switch mounting screws to 18–26 inch lbs.

2005-08

1. Remove three lower steering column shroud screws, then shroud.
2. Remove two windshield wiper/washer switch mounting screws.
3. Disconnect electrical connector and remove windshield wiper/washer switch.
4. Reverse procedure to install.

WIPER TRANSMISSION
REPLACE
2004

1. Turn windshield wipers on. When blades reach full upright travel on glass, turn ignition Off.
2. Remove windshield wiper pivot arms and blades.
3. Remove cowl top vent grille.
4. Remove linkage drive arm from windshield wiper motor.

5. Lower hood, then remove mounting bolts and wiper transmission through righthand cowl chamber opening.
6. Reverse procedure to install, noting the following:
   a. Install retaining clip onto end of wiper transmission linkage.
   b. **Torque** transmission mounting bolts to 11 ft. lbs.
   c. Cycle wipers back to park position, then install arms and blades.

2005-08

1. Remove two covers, two mounting nuts and two wiper pivot arms.
2. Remove four cowl vent screen pin-type retainers.
3. Remove righthand and lefthand cowl vent screen overlaps. Righthand screen overlaps left.
4. Remove three mounting bolts, windshield wiper mounting arm and pivot shaft.
5. Reverse procedure to install, noting the following:
   a. **Torque** wiper motor mounting bolt to 11 ft. lbs.
   b. **Torque** arm mounting bolt to 13 ft. lbs. If reusing mounting bolt, apply suitable Threadlock to bolt.
   c. **Torque** windshield wiper mounting arm and pivot shaft mounting bolts to 62 inch lbs.

BLOWER MOTOR
REPLACE
2004

1. Disconnect jumper wire harness from main harness electrical connector.
2. Disconnect main harness at blower motor resistor.
3. Remove blower motor mounting screws.
4. Separate cover and motor.
5. Disconnect blower motor jumper harness.
6. Remove blower motor.
7. Reverse procedure to install.

2005-08

1. Disconnect blower motor electrical connector.
2. Remove three mounting screws and blower motor.
3. Remove clip and blower motor wheel.
4. Reverse procedure to install.

HEATER CORE
REPLACE
2004

1. Remove evaporator core housing as outlined under "Evaporator Core, Replace."
2. Remove foam sealing strip.
3. Remove mounting screws and heater core cover.
4. Remove heater core.
5. Reverse procedure to install.

2005-08

1. Drain engine coolant into suitable container.
2. Recover refrigerant as outlined in "Air Conditioning" chapter.
3. Remove instrument panel as outlined in "Dash Panel Service" chapter.
4. **On models equipped with 5.4L engine,** disconnect heater hose fittings at back of righthand cylinder head.
5. **On all models,** clamp off and disconnect heater core inlet and outlet hoses at core.
6. Remove two nuts and disconnect evaporator core fitting.
7. Remove two exterior heater and evaporator core housing nuts at dash panel.
8. Disconnect antenna cable from heater and evaporator core housing.
9. Remove interior heater and evaporator core housing nut.
10. Remove heater and evaporator core housing.
11. Reverse procedure to install, noting the following:
   a. Install new O-ring seals.
   b. Lubricate refrigerant system with correct amount of suitable, clean PAG oil.
   c. **Torque** interior heater and evaporator core housing nut to 44 inch lbs.
   d. **Torque** exterior heater and evaporator core housing nuts to 62 inch lbs.
   e. Install new evaporator core O-ring seals and **torque** mounting nuts to 71 inch lbs.

EVAPORATOR CORE
REPLACE
2004

1. Recover refrigerant as outlined in "Air Conditioning" chapter.
2. Drain coolant into suitable container.
3. Remove instrument panel as outlined in "Dash Panel Service" chapter.
4. Place suitable container in heater water hose connections.
5. Disconnect heater hoses at underhood core fittings.
6. Disconnect vacuum connector near firewall.
7. Remove air conditioning accumulator.
8. Disconnect air conditioning liquid line.
9. Remove evaporator core housing nuts and screws at firewall.
10. Remove evaporator core housing bolts from inside passenger compartment.
11. Remove evaporator core housing.
12. Reverse procedure to install. **Torque** evaporator core housing bolts to 71 inch lbs.

2005-08

1. Drain engine coolant into suitable container.
2. Recover refrigerant as outlined in "Air Conditioning" chapter.

3. Remove instrument panel as outline in "Dash Panel Service" chapter.
4. **On models equipped with 5.4L engine,** disconnect heater hose fittings at back of righthand cylinder head.
5. **On all models,** clamp off and disconnect heater core inlet and outlet hoses at core.
6. Remove two nuts and disconnect evaporator core fitting.
7. Remove two exterior heater and evaporator core housing nuts at dash panel.
8. Disconnect antenna cable from heater and evaporator core housing.
9. Remove interior heater and evaporator core housing nut.
10. Remove heater and evaporator core housing.
11. Reverse procedure to install, noting the following:
    a. Install new O-ring seals.
    b. Lubricate refrigerant system with correct amount of suitable, clean PAG oil.
    c. **Torque** interior heater and evaporator core housing nut to 44 inch lbs.
    d. **Torque** exterior heater and evaporator core housing nuts to 62 inch lbs.
    e. Install new evaporator core O-ring seals and **torque** mounting nuts to 71 inch lbs.

TECHNICAL SERVICE BULLETINS

Repeated Heater Core Failure

On some of these models there may be repeated heater core leaks.

This condition may be caused by a chemical reaction (electrolysis).

To correct this condition, proceed as follows:

1. Place positive probe of suitable digital volt/ohm meter in engine coolant and negative probe on battery ground terminal.
2. Adjust engine to 2000 RPM.
3. If more than .4 volt is recorded, flush coolant and inspect voltage, again.
4. If voltage is still excessive, inspect body/battery grounds.
5. If condition still exists, add extra grounds to heater core and engine, as follows:
    a. Secure 16 gauge stranded copper wire to heater core inlet tube using suitable hose clamp.
    b. Secure other end of wire to existing body sheet metal fastener.
    c. Secure another extra ground between existing engine and body sheet metal fasteners.
    d. Ensure there is continuity between added grounds and battery ground terminal.
6. If condition still exists, install restrictor as follows:
    a. Cut line as close to engine block as possible.
    b. Install restrictor (part No. F1UZ-18D406-A) on inlet hose with arrow facing coolant flow direction (toward heater core).
    c. Secure with two suitable hose clamps.
7. Bleed cooling system trapped air as follows:
    a. Disconnect heater hose at righthand front or rear of engine.
    b. Remove thermostat and housing.
    c. Fill engine with suitable coolant until mixture is seen at engine side heater hose connection.
    d. Connect heater hose, then install thermostat and housing.
    e. Fill degas bottle to coolant fill level mark.
    f. Fun engine to normal operating temperature.
    g. Select max heat and blower speeds.

3.8L Engine

NOTE: On Air Bag Equipped Models, Refer To "Air Bag System Precautions" Located In The Front Of This Manual For System Disarming & Arming Procedures.

NOTE: Refer To "Computer Relearn Procedures" Located In The Front Of This Manual When Battery Power To The Computer Has Been Interrupted.

NOTE: Prior To Performing Any Service Operations Listed In This Section, Consult The "Technical Service Bulletins" Section For Related Information.

INDEX

	Page No.
Camshaft, Replace	4-17
Camshaft Lobe Lift	
Specifications	4-16
Compression Pressure	4-13
Cooling System Bleed	4-19
Crankshaft Rear Oil Seal,	
Replace	4-18
Installation	4-18
Removal	4-18
Cylinder Head, Replace	4-15
Lefthand	4-15
Righthand	4-15
Engine Rebuilding	
Specifications	21-1
Engine, Replace	4-13
Engine Mount, Replace	4-13
Exhaust Manifold, Replace	4-14
Lefthand	4-14

	Page No.
Righthand	4-14
Front Cover, Replace	4-17
Fuel Filter, Replace	4-20
Fuel Pump, Replace	4-20
Hydraulic Lifters, Replace	4-16
Installation	4-17
Removal	4-16
Intake Manifold, Replace	4-14
Lower	4-14
Upper	4-14
Main & Rod Bearings	4-18
Oil Pan, Replace	4-18
Oil Pump, Replace	4-18
Oil Pump Service	4-18
Piston & Rod Assembly	4-18
Pistons, Pins & Rings	4-18
Precautions	4-13
Air Bag Systems	4-13

	Page No.
Battery Ground Cable	4-13
Fuel System Pressure Relief	4-13
Quick Disconnect Hoses	4-13
R-Clip	4-13
Spring Lock	4-13
Vapor Tube	4-13
Radiator, Replace	4-19
Rocker Arms	4-16
Installation	4-16
Removal	4-16
Serpentine Drive Belt	4-18
Belt Replacement	4-19
Belt Routing	4-18
Technical Service Bulletins	4-20
Righthand Exhaust Leak	4-20
2004	4-20
Thermostat, Replace	4-19
Tightening Specifications	4-21

	Page No.
Timing Chain, Replace	4-17
Installation	4-17
Removal	4-17
Valve Adjustment	4-16

	Page No.
Valve Clearance Specifications	4-16
Valve Cover, Replace	4-16
Lefthand	4-16
Righthand	4-16

	Page No.
Valve Guides	4-16
Water Pump, Replace	4-19

PRECAUTIONS
Air Bag Systems

Refer to "Air Bag System Precautions" in the front of this manual for system disarming and arming procedures.

Battery Ground Cable

Prior to service, disconnect battery ground cable and isolate as required.

Fuel System Pressure Relief

Fuel supply tubes will remain pressurized for long periods of time after engine shutdown. This pressure must be relieved before beginning fuel system service or personal injury or damage to vehicle may occur. A valve is provided on fuel injection supply manifold for this purpose.
1. Connect EFI/CFI fuel pressure gauge tool No. T80L-9974-B, or equivalent, to fuel pressure relief valve on fuel injection supply manifold.
2. Place outlet hose of tool into suitable fuel container.
3. Open manual valve on fuel pressure gauge tool to relieve fuel system pressure.

Quick Disconnect Hoses

R-CLIP

When working with R-clip type connections, do not use tools to disconnect. Use of tools may deform clip components and could cause leaks.

DISCONNECT
1. Bend shipping tab downward.
2. Spread R-clip and push clip into fitting.
3. Separate fitting from tube.

CONNECT
1. Inspect fitting and tube for damage and ensure connections are clean.
2. Apply light coat of suitable, clean engine oil to male end of tube.
3. Insert R-clip into fitting.
4. Align tube and fitting, then insert tube into fitting and push together until click is heard.
5. Pull on connection to ensure it is fully engaged.

SPRING LOCK

When working with spring lock type connections, spring lock tool set No. T84L-19623-B, or equivalent, must be used to disconnect fittings.

When connecting spring lock type fittings, proceed as follows:
1. Inspect and clean both coupling ends.
2. Lubricate fuel line O-ring seals with suitable, clean engine oil.
3. When connection is made, pull on line to ensure it is fully engaged.

VAPOR TUBE

To disconnect vapor tube connections, squeeze fitting and disconnect vapor tube from fitting.

To connect, proceed as follows:
1. Ensure fittings are clean and free from damage.
2. Push tube onto fitting until it snaps into place.
3. Pull on connection to verify fitting is secure.

COMPRESSION PRESSURE

When inspecting cylinder compression, lowest cylinder must be within 75% of highest cylinder. Perform compression test with engine at normal operating temperature, spark plugs and air cleaner removed and the throttle propped wide open.

ENGINE MOUNT
REPLACE

Whenever self-locking mounting bolts and nuts are removed, they must be replaced with new self-locking bolts and nuts.
1. Remove fan shroud mounting screws and air tube from remote air cleaner.
2. Raise and support vehicle, then support engine using suitable jack and wood block placed below engine.
3. Remove insulator to front subframe through bolts, **Fig. 1.**
4. Disconnect shift linkage and raise engine enough to clear front subframe brackets.
5. Remove accessories and oil cooler line attaching clips from engine support brackets.
6. Remove mounting bolts, insulator and bracket.
7. Reverse procedure to install.

ENGINE
REPLACE

1. Recover air conditioning refrigerant as outlined in "Air Conditioning" chapter.
2. Drain coolant into suitable container.
3. Relieve fuel system pressure as outlined under "Precautions."
4. Disconnect hood ground strap and underhood lamp electrical connector.
5. Mark hinge positions, then remove bolts and hood.
6. Disconnect vacuum hose near firewall.
7. Disconnect battery positive cable at alternator and alternator electrical connectors.
8. Disconnect power steering pump fluid lines and drain into suitable container.
9. Disconnect lower radiator hose at water pump.
10. Disconnect upper radiator hose at coolant outlet.
11. Remove coolant reservoir.
12. Disconnect accelerator cable.
13. Remove mounting bolt and position accelerator cable bracket aside.
14. Remove air cleaner and outlet tube.
15. Disconnect air conditioning manifold and tube.
16. Disconnect air conditioning compressor electrical connector.
17. Disconnect fuel supply line using fuel line disconnection set tool No. T90T-9550-S, or equivalent.
18. Disconnect vacuum hose at righthand rear corner of engine compartment.
19. Disconnect heater hoses at underhood core fittings and drain into suitable containers.
20. Disconnect 42-pin electrical connector at righthand rear corner of engine compartment and position wiring harness aside.
21. Disconnect vacuum tube and connector at rear of TBI.
22. Disconnect EVAP return tube.
23. Raise and support vehicle.
24. Remove ground cable nut.
25. Remove solenoid protective cap and wiring nuts. Position wiring aside.
26. Remove mounting bolts and starter motor.
27. Disconnect electrical connectors at lefthand and righthand O2 sensors.
28. Remove dual converter mounting nuts.
29. Remove lefthand and righthand exhaust manifold flange nuts.
30. Remove Y-pipe.
31. Disconnect engine ground strap.
32. Drain engine oil into suitable container.
33. **On models equipped with automatic transmission,** remove inspection cover and four torque converter to flexplate nuts. Discard nuts.
34. **On all models,** remove bellhousing upper and lower bolts.
35. **On models equipped with automatic transmission,** remove transmission fluid filler tube.
36. **On all models,** remove lefthand and righthand engine mount nuts.
37. Lower vehicle.
38. Support transmission using suitable floor jack and block of wood.
39. Install engine lifting brackets tool No. D94L-6001-A, or equivalent.

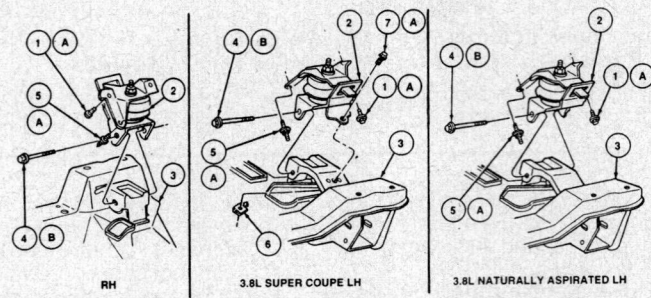

Item	Part Number	Description
1	N803098-S100	Bolt (2 Req'd)
2	6038	Front Engine Support Insulator
3	5C145	Front Sub-Frame
4	N805748-S36	Bolt
5	N805803-S36	Stud

Item	Part Number	Description
6	N805968-S36	U-Nut
7	N605918-S56	Bolt
A	—	Tighten to 34-47 N·m (25-35 Lb-Ft)
B	—	Tighten to 47-68 N·m (35-50 Lb-Ft)

FM1069100113000X

Fig. 1 Engine mount replacement

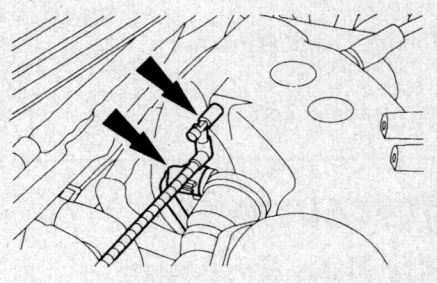

FM1059900167000X

Fig. 2 Vacuum tube at upper intake manifold replacement

40. Connect spreader bar tool No. D93L-6001-A3, or equivalent, to brackets.
41. Remove engine, then mount on suitable stand using suitable engine lift.
42. Reverse procedure to install, noting the following:
    a. **On models equipped with automatic transmission,** install four new torque converter to flexplate nuts.
    b. **On all models,** install oil pan drain plug and close radiator petcock.

INTAKE MANIFOLD
REPLACE
Upper

1. Remove air cleaner outlet tube.
2. Disconnect vacuum tube and Idle Air Control (IAC) solenoid, **Fig. 2.**
3. Disconnect Throttle Position (TP) sensor and EVAP return tube.
4. Disconnect accelerator cable from TBI and position aside.
5. Remove solenoid bracket bolts, **Fig. 3.**
6. Disconnect PCV tube and vacuum tubes.
7. Remove mounting bolts and position ignition coil aside.
8. Record remove upper intake manifold mounting bolts' locations.
9. Remove upper intake manifold. Discard gasket.
10. Reverse procedure to install, noting the following:
    a. Install new upper to lower intake manifold gasket.
    b. Ensure mounting bolts are in original proper locations.
    c. **Torque** manifold mounting bolts in sequence to 89 inch lbs., **Fig. 4.**
    d. Final tighten bolts an additional 90° in sequence.

Lower

1. Drain coolant into suitable container.
2. Remove upper intake manifold as outlined under "Upper."
3. Relieve fuel system pressure as outlined under "Precautions."
4. Disconnect fuel pressure sensor electrical connector.
5. Disconnect fuel injection supply manifold.
6. Disconnect engine wiring harness and position it aside.
7. Disconnect heater hose at rear of engine.
8. Position spark plug wire loom aside and remove stud bolt.
9. Disconnect EGR valve vacuum tube.
10. **On models equipped with exhaust air supply valve,** proceed as follows:
    a. Loosen tube nut, **Fig. 5.**
    b. Disconnect air tube.
    c. Disconnect vacuum tube.
    d. Remove nuts.
11. **On all models,** loosen EGR hex tube nut and disconnect tube.
12. Disconnect radiator upper hose and bypass hose.
13. Disconnect electrical connectors.
14. Remove bypass tube bolt.
15. Remove mounting bolts, then the fuel injection supply manifold and injectors.
16. Record lower intake manifold mounting bolts' locations.
17. Remove mounting bolts and lower intake manifold. Discard gaskets and end seals.
18. Reverse procedure to install, noting the following:
    a. Apply beads of silicone gasket sealant No. F7AZ-19554-EA, or equivalent, to end seal mounting points, **Fig. 6.**
    b. Apply beads of sealant to lower intake manifold mounting locations, **Fig. 7.**
    c. **Install lower intake manifold within four minutes of sealant**

application.
    d. Ensure manifold mounting bolts are installed in original locations.
    e. **Torque** manifold mounting bolts in sequence to 44 inch lbs., **Fig. 8.**
    f. **Torque** mounting bolts to 89 inch lbs., in sequence.

EXHAUST MANIFOLD
REPLACE
Lefthand

1. Raise and support vehicle.
2. Remove lefthand manifold flange nuts and lower vehicle.
3. Remove engine oil dipstick tube.
4. **On models equipped with exhaust air supply valve,** loosen tube nut at front of exhaust manifold.
5. **On all models,** remove mounting nuts and exhaust manifold. Discard gasket.
6. Reverse procedure to install, noting the following:
    a. Install new exhaust manifold gasket.
    b. **Torque** exhaust manifold mounting nuts in sequence to 24 ft. lbs., **Fig. 9.**

Righthand

1. Remove air cleaner outlet tube.
2. Disconnect two TBI hoses, **Fig. 10.**
3. **On models equipped with exhaust air supply valve,** proceed as follows:
    a. Loosen tube nut, **Fig. 5.**
    b. Disconnect air tube.
    c. Disconnect vacuum tube.
    d. Remove nuts and valve.
4. **On all models,** loosen EGR hex tube nut, disconnect vacuum lines and remove tube.
5. Raise and support vehicle.
6. Remove righthand manifold flange nuts and lower vehicle.
7. **On models equipped with exhaust air supply valve,** loosen tube nut at front of righthand exhaust manifold.
8. **On all models,** remove mounting nuts and manifold. Discard gasket.
9. Reverse procedure to install, noting the following:

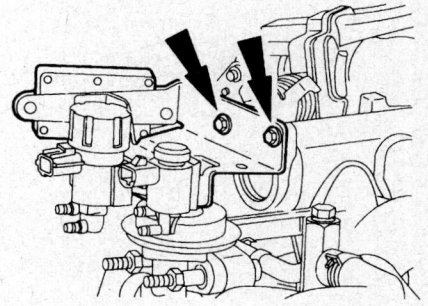

Fig. 3 Solenoid bracket replacement

a. Install new exhaust manifold gasket.
b. **Torque** exhaust manifold mounting nuts in sequence to 24 ft. lbs., **Fig. 11.**

CYLINDER HEAD
REPLACE
Lefthand

1. Drain coolant into suitable container.
2. Remove exhaust manifold as outlined under "Exhaust Manifold, Replace."
3. Remove lower intake manifold as outlined under "Intake Manifold, Replace."
4. Mark locations and position spark plug wires aside.
5. Disconnect PCV valve.
6. Remove mounting bolts and position ignition coil aside.
7. Remove lefthand valve cover. Discard gasket.
8. Keeping in order for installation in original position, remove mounting bolts, rocker arms and pushrods.
9. Remove serpentine belt.
10. Remove power steering pump pulley using pulley remover tool No. T69L-10300-B, or equivalent.
11. Remove power steering pump and alternator mounting brackets.
12. Remove exhaust manifold mounting studs.
13. Record long and short cylinder head bolts' locations.
14. Remove and discard cylinder head bolts.
15. Remove cylinder head.
16. Reverse procedure to install, noting the following:
    a. Install new head gaskets with small hole to front of engine, **Fig. 12.**
    b. Lubricate new cylinder head bolts with clean 5W-30 engine oil.
    c. Place cylinder head in position.
    d. Install new long cylinder head bolts, then the short ones.
    e. **Torque** cylinder head bolts in sequence to 15 ft. lbs., **Fig. 13.**
    f. **Torque** bolts in sequence to 30 ft. lbs.
    g. **Torque** bolts in sequence to 37 ft. lbs.
    h. **Perform following cylinder head**

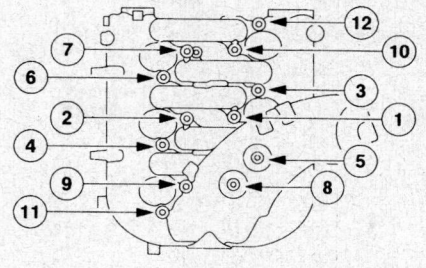

Fig. 4 Upper intake manifold bolt tightening sequence

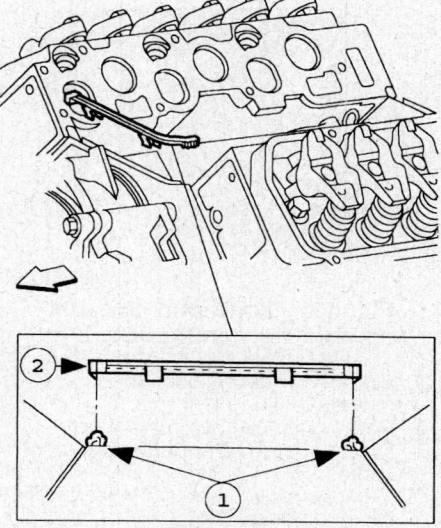

1. Sealant Beads
2. End Seals

Fig. 6 Lower intake manifold end seals bead locations

bolt steps on each bolt before moving to next bolt in sequence.
i. Back off cylinder head bolts 2–3 turns
j. **Torque** long bolt to 33 ft. lbs.
k. **Torque** short bolt to 18 ft. lbs.
l. Tighten bolt an additional 180°.
m. **Torque** rocker arm bolts to 44 inch lbs.
n. **Torque** arm bolts to 26 ft. lbs.
o. Install TBI with new mounting gasket.
p. **Torque** TBI mounting nuts and bolts to 80 inch lbs.
q. Tighten nuts and bolts an additional 85–90°.

Righthand

1. Drain coolant into suitable container.
2. Remove exhaust manifold as outlined under "Exhaust Manifold, Replace."
3. Remove lower intake manifold as outlined under "Intake Manifold, Replace."
4. Disconnect crankcase ventilation hose.
5. Disconnect transducer vacuum hoses.
6. **On models equipped with exhaust**

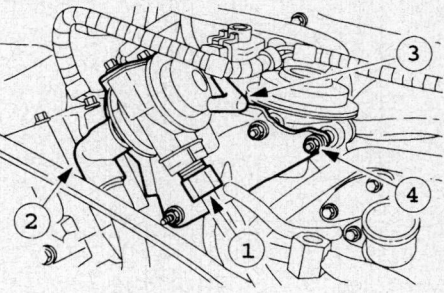

1. Tube Nut
2. Air Tube
3. Vacuum Tube
4. Nut

Fig. 5 Exhaust air supply valve replacement

air supply valve proceed as follows:
a. Loosen tube nut.
b. Disconnect air and vacuum tubes.
c. Remove nuts valve.
7. **On all models,** disconnect and remove EGR tube.
8. Mark locations and position spark plug wires aside.
9. Remove air cleaner outlet tube.
10. Disconnect throttle and speed control cables.
11. Remove mounting nuts, bolts and TBI. Discard gasket.
12. Remove righthand valve cover. Discard gasket.
13. Remove serpentine belt.
14. Recover air conditioning refrigerant as outlined in "Air Conditioning" chapter.
15. Disconnect air conditioning manifold and tube.
16. Disconnect air conditioning compressor clutch electrical connector.
17. Remove air conditioning compressor mounting bracket.
18. Remove exhaust manifold mounting studs.
19. Record long and short cylinder head bolts' locations.
20. Remove and discard cylinder head bolts.
21. Remove cylinder head.
22. Reverse procedure to install, noting the following:
    a. Install new head gaskets with small hole to front of engine, **Fig. 12.**
    b. Lubricate new cylinder head bolts with clean 5W-30 engine oil.
    c. Place cylinder head in position.
    d. Install new long cylinder head bolts, then the short ones.
    e. **Torque** cylinder head bolts in sequence to 15 ft. lbs., **Fig. 13.**
    f. **Torque** bolts in sequence to 30 ft. lbs.
    g. **Torque** bolts in sequence to 37 ft. lbs.
    h. **Perform following cylinder head bolt steps on each bolt before moving to next bolt in sequence.**
    i. Back off cylinder head bolts 2–3 turns.
    j. **Torque** long bolt in sequence to 33 ft. lbs.

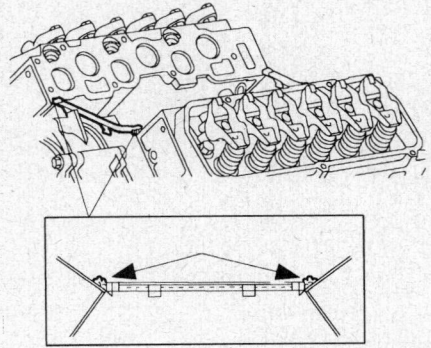

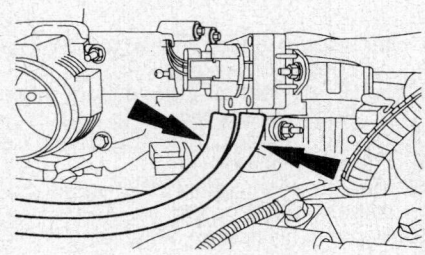

Fig. 7 **Lower intake manifold sealant bead locations**

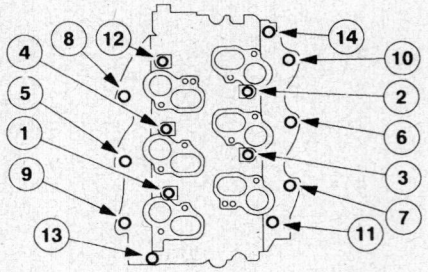

Fig. 8 **Lower intake manifold bolt tightening sequence**

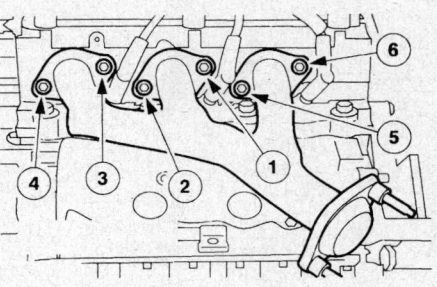

Fig. 9 **Lefthand exhaust manifold tightening sequence**

Fig. 10 **TBI hose replacement**

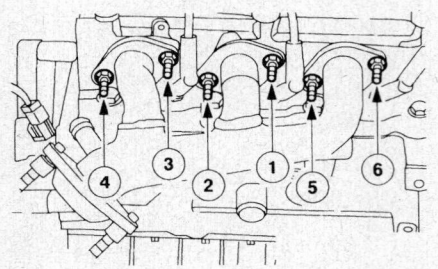

Fig. 11 **Righthand exhaust manifold tightening sequence**

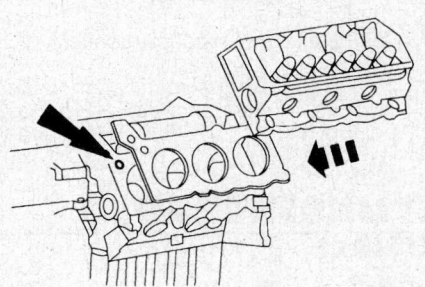

Fig. 12 **Cylinder head gasket orientation**

k. **Torque** short bolt in sequence to 18 ft. lbs.
l. Tighten bolt an additional 180°.
m. **Torque** rocker arm bolts to 44 inch lbs.
n. **Torque** bolts to 26 ft. lbs.
o. Install TBI with new mounting gasket.
p. **Torque** TBI mounting nuts and bolts to 80 inch lbs.
q. Tighten nuts and bolts an additional 85–90°.

VALVE COVER
REPLACE

Lefthand

1. Mark and position spark plug wires aside.
2. Disconnect PCV valve.
3. Remove mounting bolts and position ignition coil aside.
4. Remove cover and discard gasket.
5. Reverse procedure to install.

Righthand

1. Mark and position spark plug wires aside.
2. Disconnect crankcase ventilation hose.
3. Disconnect transducer vacuum hoses.
4. **On models equipped with exhaust air supply valve,** proceed as follows:
   a. Loosen tube nut.
   b. Disconnect air and vacuum tubes.
   c. Remove nuts and valve.

5. **On all models,** disconnect and remove EGR tube.
6. Remove air cleaner outlet tube.
7. Disconnect throttle and speed control cables.
8. Remove mounting nuts, bolts and TBI. Discard gasket.
9. Remove cover and discard gasket.
10. Reverse procedure to install.

CAMSHAFT LOBE LIFT SPECIFICATIONS

Engine	Intake, Inch	Exhaust, Inch
3.8L	.257	.259

VALVE CLEARANCE SPECIFICATIONS

Correct valve clearance is .09–.19 inch.

VALVE ADJUSTMENT

This engine is equipped with hydraulic valve lash adjusters. No adjustment is required.

ROCKER ARMS
Removal

1. Remove valve covers.
2. Remove seat mounting bolts and rocker arms.

Installation

1. Lubricate rocker arms with engine assembly lubricant D9AZ-19579-D, or equivalent.
2. **Rocker arm seats must be fully seated in cylinder head and pushrods must be seated in rocker arm sockets prior to final tightening.**
3. Rotate crankshaft until valve tappet rests onto heel (base circle) of camshaft lobe.
4. Position rocker arms over pushrods.
5. Install rocker arm seats.
6. Tighten rocker arm seat mounting bolts.
7. Repeat procedure for each rocket arm.
8. Final tighten with camshaft in any position.
9. Install valve cover.

VALVE GUIDES

Valve guides consist of holes bored in the cylinder head. For service the guide holes can be reamed oversize to accommodate valves with oversize stems of .015 and .030 inch.

HYDRAULIC LIFTERS
REPLACE

Before replacing a lifter for noisy operation, ensure the noise is not caused by improper valve to rocker arm clearance or by worn rocker arms or pushrods.

Removal

1. Disconnect ignition wires at spark

plugs using spark plug wire remover tool No. T74P-666-A, or equivalent.
2. Remove ignition wire routing clips from studs on valve cover mounting bolts. Lay ignition wires with routing clips toward front of engine.
3. Remove upper intake manifold as outlined under "Intake Manifold, Replace."
4. Remove valve covers and lower intake manifold as outlined under "Intake Manifold, Replace."
5. Loosen rocker arms seat mounting bolt sufficiently to allow rocker arm to be lifted off pushrod and rotated to one side.
6. Remove pushrods and mark for installation in original positions.
7. Remove four bolts holding two tappet guide plates and retainers in place (bolts are held captive in retainers).
8. Remove six valve tappet guide plates from adjacent valve tappets.
9. Remove lifters using suitable magnet and mark for installation in original positions.
10. If lift is stuck in bores because excessive varnish or gum deposits, rotate it back and forth using suitable claw-type tool.

Installation

1. Lean cylinder head and valve sealing surfaces using suitable solvent.
2. Lightly oil bolts and stud threads before installation, except those specifying special sealant.
3. Lubricate each lift and bore with engine assembly lubricant No. D9AZ-19579-D, or equivalent.
4. Install each lifer in bore from which it was removed.
5. If new lifters are being installed, inspect for free fit in bore.
6. Align flats on side of lifter and install six valve tappet guide plates between adjacent valve lifters (ensure word UP is showing).
7. Install two tappet guide plates and retainers, then tighten four captive bolts.
8. Dip each push rod end in engine assembly lubricant No. D9AZ-19579-D, or equivalent.
9. Install pushrods in original positions.
10. Lubricate rocker arms with engine assembly lubricant No. D9AZ-19579-D, or equivalent.
11. **Rocker arm seats must be fully seated in cylinder heads and pushrods must be seated in rocker arm sockets prior to final tightening.**
12. Rotate crankshaft until valve tappet rests onto heel (base circle) of camshaft lobe.
13. Position rocker arms over push rods.
14. Tighten rocker arm seat mounting bolts.
15. Repeat procedure for each rocker arm.
16. Final tighten with camshaft in any position.
17. Tighten rocker arm seat mounting bolts.
18. Repeat procedure for each rocker arm.
19. Final tighten with camshaft in any position.

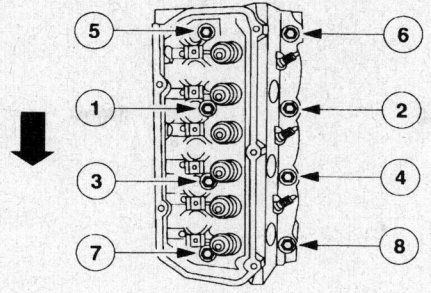

Fig. 13 Cylinder head bolt tightening sequence

20. Install lower intake manifold.
21. Install upper intake manifold.
22. Install routing clips and connect ignition wires to spark plugs.

FRONT COVER
REPLACE

1. Drain coolant into suitable container.
2. Remove serpentine belt.
3. Raise and support vehicle.
4. Rotate crankshaft pulley in engine's normal running direction until piston No. 1 reaches TDC mark.
5. Remove bolt and pulley using crankshaft pulley remover tool Nos. T58P-6316-D and T82L-6316-B, or equivalents.
6. Remove bolts and water pump pulley.
7. Remove power steering pump and bracket with hoses intact. Position pump aside.
8. Loosen nut and disconnect EGR valve tube.
9. Disconnect upper radiator and bypass hoses above front cover.
10. Disconnect connector, then remove mounting bolts and Camshaft Position (CMP) sensor.
11. Remove heater water outlet tube.
12. Ensure piston No. 1 is still at TDC.
13. Remove camshaft synchronizer mounting bolt, washer and sensor. **Oil pump intermediate shaft should be removed with synchronizer.**
14. Disconnect radiator lower hose at water pump.
15. Disconnect crankshaft position (CKP) sensor.
16. Remove engine front wiring harness pin-style retainer.
17. Record locations, types and sizes of front cover mounting bolts, nuts and screws. Pay attention to hidden cap screw, **Fig. 14.**
18. Slide front cover off alignment dowels. Discard gasket.
19. Reverse procedure to install, noting the following:
   a. Ensure gasket surfaces are clean and flat.
   b. Before installing front cover gasket, apply small portion of silicone gasket sealant No. F7AZ-19554-EA, or equivalent, **Fig. 15.**
   c. Install new front cover gasket.
   d. After installing front cover gasket,

apply silicone gasket sealant to top of oil pan surface, **Fig. 16.**
   e. Install cover mounting bolts are in original positions.
   f. **Torque** cover mounting bolt No. 12 to 89 inch lbs., and remaining bolts in sequence to 18 ft.-lbs., **Fig. 17.**
   g. Coat camshaft synchronizer gear with clean 10W-30 engine oil.
   h. Install synchro positioning tool No. 303-630, or equivalent, by rotating tool until it engages synchronizer housing notch and armature.
   i. Install synchronizer housing with tool's arrow at 54° from engine centerline, **Fig. 18.**

TIMING CHAIN
REPLACE

The front cover contains the oil pump gears and the water pump. If a new front cover is to be installed, remove water pump and oil pump gears from old front cover.

Removal

1. Remove front cover as outlined under "Front Cover, Replace."
2. Remove mounting bolt and camshaft position sensor drive gear.
3. Rotate crankshaft until timing marks and keyways align, **Fig. 19.**
4. Compress timing chain tensioner and install suitable retaining pin.
5. Remove camshaft sprocket, crankshaft sprocket and timing chain as an assembly.
6. Remove mounting bolts and timing chain tensioner.

Installation

1. Install timing chain tensioner.
2. Rotate crankshaft so piston No. 1 is at TDC and key is at 12 o'clock position, **Fig. 20.**
3. Turn camshaft sprocket so timing mark is on bottom of balance shaft, **Fig. 21.**
4. Install timing chain, camshaft sprocket and crankshaft sprocket.
5. Ensure timing marks and keyways are aligned, **Fig. 19.**
6. Install camshaft position sensor drive gear.
7. Remove retaining pin from timing chain tensioner.
8. Install front cover as outlined under "Front Cover, Replace."

CAMSHAFT
REPLACE

1. Remove lifter as outlined under "Hydraulic Lifter, Replace."
2. Remove timing chain as outlined under "Timing Chain, Replace."
3. Remove radiator fan and shroud.
4. Remove camshaft key and engine balance shaft drive gear.
5. Remove mounting bolts and camshaft thrust plate.
6. Remove spacer and camshaft.
7. Reverse procedure to install. Lubricate camshaft with clean engine oil.

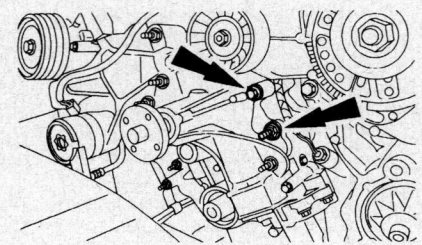

FM1069901045000X

Fig. 14 Front cover cap screw location

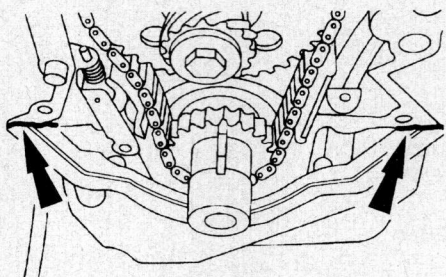

FM1069901046000X

Fig. 15 Sealant application before gasket installation

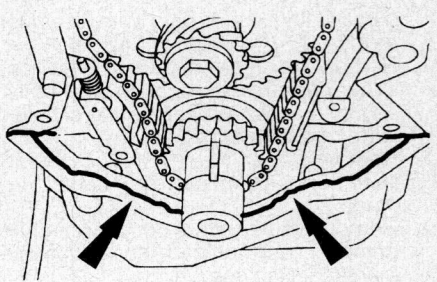

FM1069901047000X

Fig. 16 Sealant application gasket installation

PISTON & ROD ASSEMBLY

When installed, piston and rod should have the notch or arrow in piston head toward front of engine, **Fig. 22**. Side clearance between connecting rods at each crankshaft journal should be .0047–.0193 Inch.

PISTONS, PINS & RINGS

Pistons are available in standard sizes and oversizes of .003, .020, .030 and .040 inch. Piston rings are available in standard sizes and oversizes of .020, .030 and .040 inch. Piston pins are available in standard size and oversizes of .001 and .002 inch.

MAIN & ROD BEARINGS

Main and rod bearings are available in standard sizes and undersizes of .001, .002, .010, .020 and .030 inch.

CRANKSHAFT REAR OIL SEAL

REPLACE

Removal

1. Remove transmission as outlined in **MOTOR's "Domestic Transmission, In-Vehicle Service." or "Transmission Service DVD."**
2. Remove crankshaft rear oil seal using crankshaft rear seal remover tool No. T95T-6701-AR, or equivalent.

Installation

1. Lubricate new seal with clean engine oil.
2. Install crankshaft rear oil seal using crankshaft rear oil seal installation tool No. T95P-6701-EH, or equivalent. **MOTOR's "Domestic Transmission, In-Vehicle Service." or "Transmission Service DVD."**

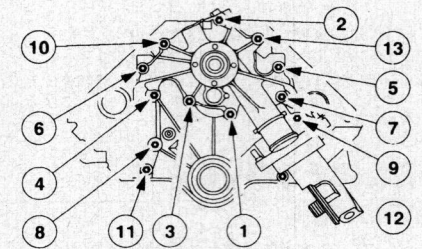

FM1069901048000X

Fig. 17 Front cover bolt tightening sequence

OIL PAN

REPLACE

1. Remove air cleaner outlet tube.
2. Remove radiator upper sight shield and coolant reservoir.
3. Raise and support vehicle using engine lift bracket tool set No. D94L-6001-A and engine support tool No. 303-F072, or equivalents, and suitable hoist.
4. Remove lefthand and righthand engine mount nuts, then lower vehicle.
5. Raise engine with engine support, then raise and support vehicle.
6. Drain engine oil into suitable oil pan.
7. Remove solenoid protective cap and wiring nuts. Position wiring aside.
8. Remove mounting bolts and starter motor.
9. Remove ground cable nut.
10. Position wiring harness bracket aside.
11. Remove bellhousing lower bolts.
12. Remove oil pan bolts.
13. Support front subframe with suitable jack.
14. Remove four lower and two upper front subframe bolts.
15. Loosen two forward front subframe bolts.
16. Lower front subframe.
17. Remove oil pan. Empty residual oil into suitable container.
18. Reverse procedure to install, noting the following:
    a. Apply silicone gasket sealant No. F7AZ-19554-EA, or equivalent, to oil pan and block sealing surfaces, **Fig. 23. Assembly must occur within 15 minutes of sealer application.**
    b. Install oil and loosely install bolts.

c. **Torque** oil pan mounting bolts in sequence to 44 inch lbs., **Fig. 24.**
d. **Torque** mounting bolts in sequence to 89 inch lbs.

OIL PUMP

REPLACE

1. Raise and support vehicle.
2. Drain engine oil into suitable container.
3. Remove engine oil filter.
4. Remove oil pump cover, mounting bolts and filter pad housing.
5. Separate oil pump drive and driven gears from cover. Discard O-ring.
6. Measure warpage across oil pump cover and front cover mounting surfaces, **Fig. 25.** If surface is warped more than .0016 inch, replace oil pump cover or front cover.
7. Remove front cover as outlined under "Front Cover, Replace."
8. Reverse procedure to install, noting the following:
    a. Clean components in suitable solvent.
    b. Lubricate oil pump components with clean 5W-30 engine oil.
    c. Assemble pressure relief valve ball and spring with new plug.

OIL PUMP SERVICE

Refer to "Oil Pump, Replace" for procedure.

SERPENTINE DRIVE BELT

Conditions requiring belt replacement are excessive wear, rib chunk-out, severe glazing and frayed cords. Replace any belt exhibiting any one of these conditions. Cracks on rib side of a belt are considered acceptable.

If the belt has chunks missing from its ribs, it should be replaced. If two or more adjacent ribs have lost sections ½ inch or longer, or if missing chunks are creating a noise or vibration condition, replace the belt.

Belt Routing

Refer to **Fig. 26** for serpentine drive belt routing.

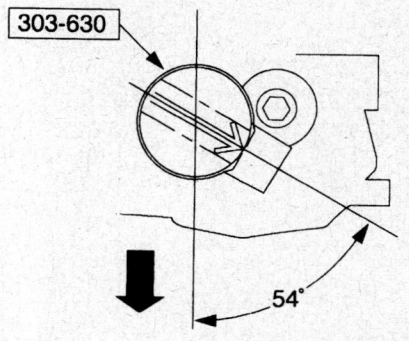

Fig. 18 Camshaft synchronizer installation

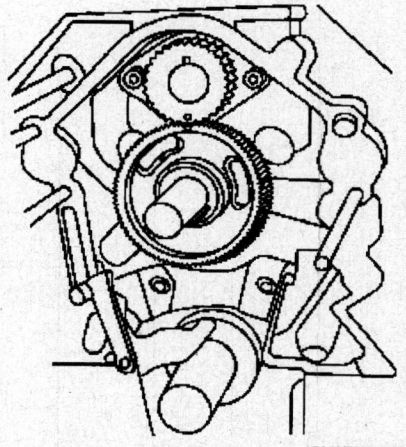

Fig. 21 Camshaft timing mark alignment

Belt Replacement

1. Lift or rotate automatic tensioner.
2. Remove belt.
3. Install new belt over pulleys. Ensure V-grooves make proper contact with pulley.
4. Rotate tensioner over belt.

COOLING SYSTEM BLEED

1. Remove vent plug, **Fig. 27**.
2. Fill radiator completely and install radiator cap.
3. Fill coolant reservoir and degas bottle to full cold mark.
4. Set heater control to full hot, high fan and set controls so air vents from dash vents.
5. Start and operate engine until fully warmed up while observing water temperature gauge as follows:
   a. If system is functioning properly, temperature will indicate normal and hot air will be felt at dash outlets.
   b. If system is not functioning properly, temperature gauge will not read and/or no hot air will be felt at dash vents.

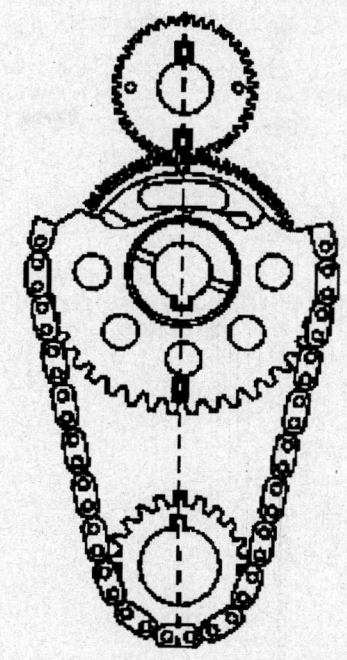

Fig. 19 Timing chain alignment marks

6. If system is not functioning properly, allow engine to cool and repeat procedure.
7. If system is functioning properly, allow engine to cool and fill coolant reservoir to full cold mark.
8. Install vent plug.

THERMOSTAT
REPLACE

1. Partially drain cooling system into suitable container.
2. Disconnect upper radiator hose at thermostat housing.
3. Remove two mounting bolts, housing and gaskets.
4. Reverse procedure to install.

WATER PUMP
REPLACE

1. Drain coolant into suitable container.
2. Loosen water pump pulley bolts.
3. Remove serpentine belt.
4. Remove power steering pump pulley using pulley remover tool No. T69L-10300-B, or equivalent.
5. Remove bolts and water pump pulley.
6. Remove mounting bolts and position power steering pump aside with hoses attached.
7. Remove mounting bolts and power steering pump mounting bracket.
8. Disconnect radiator lower hose at water pump.
9. Remove mounting bolts and position power steering fluid reservoir aside with hoses attached.
10. Disconnect camshaft position (CMP) sensor electrical connector.

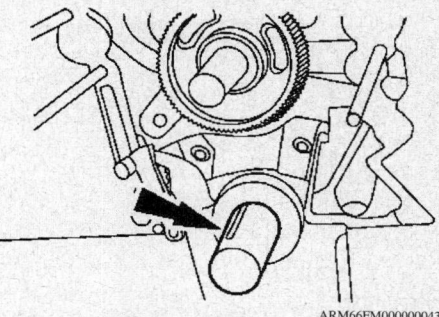

Fig. 20 Crankshaft key alignment

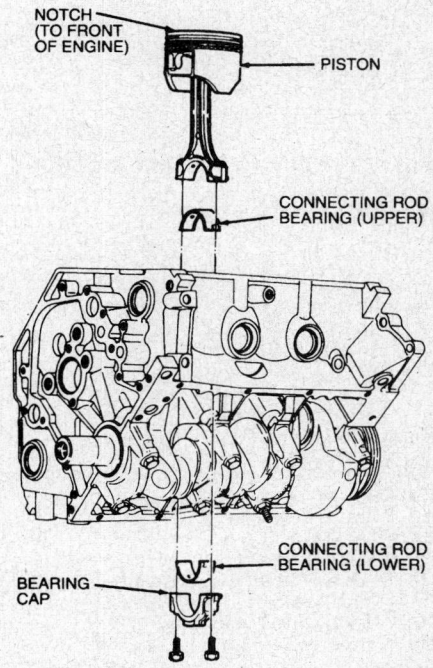

Fig. 22 Piston & rod assembly

11. Remove mounting bolt and CMP sensor.
12. Remove stud, bolts and nuts and water pump.
13. Reverse procedure to install, noting the following:
   a. Install new water pump gasket.
   b. Tighten stud, bolts and nuts in sequence to 18 ft. lbs., **Fig. 28**.

RADIATOR
REPLACE

1. Drain radiator and degas bottle coolant into suitable container.
2. Disconnect cooling fan motor electrical connector and separate fan harness from shroud.
3. Remove fan shroud lefthand and righthand mounting bolts.
4. Remove cooling fan, motor and shroud.
5. Remove radiator sight shield.
6. Disconnect radiator upper hose at radiator.
7. **On models equipped with automatic transmission,** remove lower and

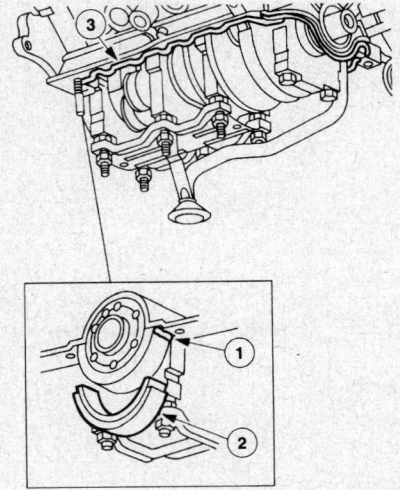

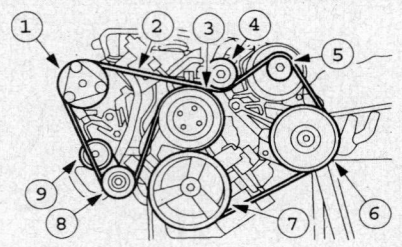

Fig. 23 Oil pan sealant locations

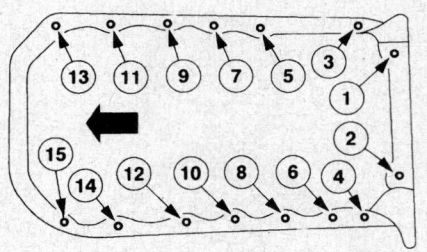

Fig. 24 Oil pan bolt tightening sequence

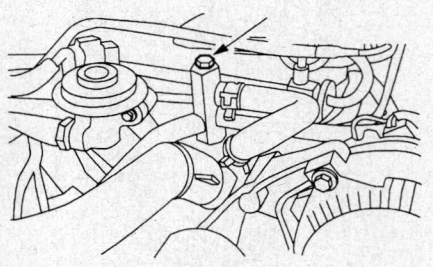

Fig. 27 Cooling system vent plug

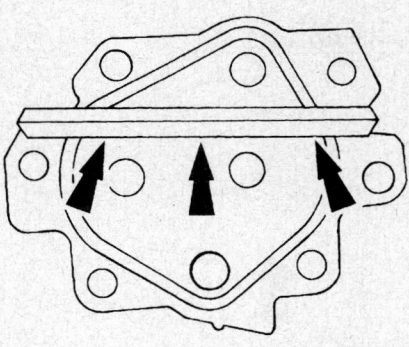

Fig. 25 Oil pump cover & front cover surface inspections

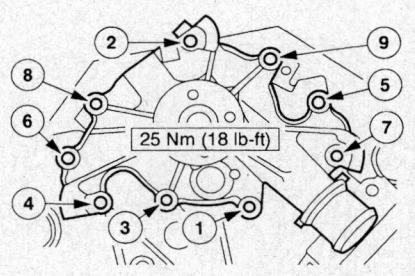

Fig. 28 Water pump tightening sequence

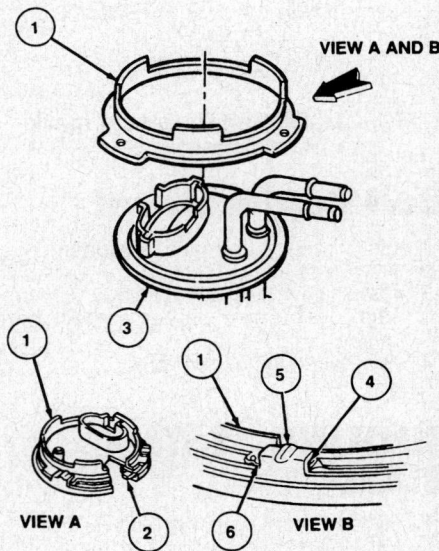

Fig. 29 Fuel pump ring replacement

Item	Description
1	Fuel Pump Locking Retainer Ring
2	Fuel Pump Mounting Gasket
3	Fuel Pump Module
4	Stop
5	Tab
6	Detent

1. Air Conditioning Compressor
2. Belt
3. Water Pump
4. Idler
5. Alternator
6. Power Steering Pump
7. Crankshaft
8. Tensioner Pulley
9. Tensioner

Fig. 26 Serpentine drive belt routing

upper cooler tube fittings.
8. **On all models,** raise and support vehicle.
9. Disconnect radiator lower hose at radiator and lower vehicle.
10. Remove supports and radiator.
11. Reverse procedure to install.

FUEL PUMP

REPLACE

1. Relieve fuel pressure as outlined under "Precautions."
2. Drain fuel tank into suitable container.
3. Raise and support vehicle.
4. Mark lines to be installed in original positions.
5. Disconnect and cap fuel tank fuel and vent lines.
6. Remove exhaust pipe and shield to gain access to fuel tank.
7. Mark electrical connections to be installed in original positions.
8. Disconnect electrical connectors from fuel sender and pump.

9. Disconnect fuel filler tube.
10. Remove support straps and fuel tank.
11. Remove fuel pump by rotating lock ring counterclockwise using fuel tank sender wrench No. T74P-9275-A, or equivalent, **Fig. 29.**
12. Reverse procedure to install.

FUEL FILTER
REPLACE

1. Relieve fuel system pressure as outlined under "Precautions."
2. Raise and support vehicle.
3. Remove push connect fittings at both ends of filter.
4. Remove fuel filter from bracket by loosening worm gear clamp. Record direction of flow arrow as installed in bracket to ensure proper direction of fuel flow through replacement filter.
5. Reverse procedure to install.

TECHNICAL SERVICE BULLETINS

Righthand Exhaust Leak

2004

On some of these models there may be a exhaust leak from the righthand exhaust pipe.

This condition may be caused by the inlet pipe.

To correct this condition, install new inlet pipe, condensation shield and exhaust hanger included in kit (manual transmission part No. 3R3Z-5H264-MT, or automatic transmission part No. 3R3Z-5H264-AT).

TIGHTENING SPECIFICATIONS

Year	Component	Torque/Ft. Lbs.
2004	Accelerator Cable Bracket	89①
	Air Conditioning Compressor Bracket, Bolt & Nut	35
	Air Conditioning Compressor Bracket, Stud	18
	Alternator Bracket	18
	Alternator Bracket To Head	30
	Alternator Positive Cable	89①
	Automatic Transmission Oil Cooler Tube Bracket	20
	Bulkhead 42-Pin Electrical Connector	89①
	Camshaft Position Sensor	27①
	Camshaft Synchronizer Drive Gear To Camshaft	33
	Camshaft Synchronizer To Front Cover	18
	Camshaft Thrust Plate	108①
	Connecting Rod Cap	⑤
	Coolant Reservoir To Head	89①
	Coolant Reservoir To Bracket	80①
	Cooling System Vent Plug	108①
	Crankshaft Main Bearing	⑥
	Crankshaft Pulley	118
	Cylinder Head	④
	EGR Transducer Bracket	89①
	EGR Tube	30
	Engine Mount	52
	Engine Mount Bracket	52
	Engine Mount Ground Strap	20
	Engine Mount To Subframe Nut	85
	Engine To Transmission	30
	Exhaust Air Supply Tube	22
	Exhaust Air Supply Valve	89①
	Exhaust Manifold, Nut	⑦
	Exhaust Manifold, Stud	71①
	Fan Shroud	80①
	Flywheel	59
	Front Cover	⑧
	Front Subframe To Body	66
	Front Subframe To Shock Tower	85
	Fuel Supply Manifold	89①
	Hood Ground Strap	108①
	Hood Hinge	108①
	Ignition Coil To Intake Manifold	53①
	Intake Manifold, Lower	③

TIGHTENING SPECIFICATIONS—Continued

Year	Component	Torque/Ft. Lbs.
2004	Intake Manifold, Upper	③
	Main Bearing Bridge	24
	Motor Mount Bracket	52
	Motor Mount To Motor Mount	52
	Motor Mount To Subframe	85
	Oil Dipstick Tube	89①
	Oil Pan Baffle	35
	Oil Pan Drain Plug	19
	Oil Pan To Block	②
	Oil Pan To Bellhousing	33
	Oil Pickup Tube To Baffle	35
	Oil Pickup Tube To Block	18
	Oil Pump Cover To Front Cover	18
	Power Steering Pressure Tube	30
	Power Steering Pump	18
	Power Steering Pump Bracket	71①
	Power Steering Pump Bracket To Block	15
	Radiator Support	22
	Rocker Arm Pivot	④
	Steering Column Pinch	35
	Throttle Body	④
	Throttle Cable Bracket	89①
	Timing Chain Tensioner	108①
	Torque Converter	27
	Valve Cover	89①
	Valve Lifter Guide Plate	108①
	Water Outlet Tube	89①
	Water Pump Pulley	⑨
	Wire Harness	20
	42-Pin Connector	89①

① — Inch lbs.
② — Refer to "Oil Pan, Replace" for tightening specifications and sequence.
③ — Refer to "Intake Manifold, Replace" for tightening specifications and sequence.
④ — Refer to "Cylinder Head, Replace" for tightening specifications and sequence.
⑤ — Torque to 33 ft. lbs.; then final tighten additional 105°.
⑥ — Torque to 37 ft. lbs., then tighten an additional 90°.
⑦ — Refer to "Exhaust Manifold, Replace" for tightening specifications and sequence.
⑧ — Refer to "Front Cover, Replace" for tightening specifications and sequence.
⑨ — Refer to "Water Pump, Replace" for tightening specifications and sequence.

4.0L Engine

NOTE: On Air Bag Equipped Models, Refer To "Air Bag System Precautions" Located In The Front Of This Manual For System Disarming & Arming Procedures.

INDEX

	Page No.
Balance Shaft, Replace	4-28
Belt Tension Data	4-31
Camshaft, Replace	4-27
Camshaft Lobe Lift Specifications	4-26
Camshaft Roller Follower, Replace	4-25
Camshaft Timing	4-27
Compression Pressure	4-22
Cooling System Bleed	4-31
Crankshaft Damper, Replace	4-26
Crankshaft Rear Oil Seal, Replace	4-30
Crankshaft Seal, Replace	4-30
Cylinder Head, Replace	4-24
Engine Rebuilding Specifications	21-1

	Page No.
Engine, Replace	4-23
Engine Mount, Replace	4-22
Exhaust Manifold, Replace	4-24
Front Cover, Replace	4-26
Front Cover Seal, Replace	4-26
Fuel Filter, Replace	4-32
Fuel Pump, Replace	4-32
Hydraulic Lash Adjuster, Replace	4-26
Intake Manifold, Replace	4-24
Main & Rod Bearings	4-30
Oil Pan, Replace	4-30
Oil Pump, Replace	4-30
Piston & Rod Assembly	4-29
Precautions	4-22
Air Bag Systems	4-22
Battery Ground Cable	4-22

	Page No.
Fuel System Pressure Relief	4-22
Quick Disconnect Hoses	4-22
R-Clip	4-22
Spring Lock	4-22
Vapor Tube	4-22
Radiator, Replace	4-31
Serpentine Drive Belt	4-31
Replacement	4-31
Routing	4-31
Thermostat, Replace	4-31
Tightening Specifications	4-36
Timing Chain, Replace	4-27
Valve Adjustment	4-26
Valve Cover, Replace	4-25
Lefthand	4-25
Righthand	4-25
Water Pump, Replace	4-31

PRECAUTIONS

Air Bag Systems

Refer to "Air Bag System Precautions" in front of this manual for system disarming and arming procedures.

Battery Ground Cable

Prior to service, disconnect battery ground cable and isolate as required.

Fuel System Pressure Relief

1. Remove fuel pump relay.
2. Start engine, then allow engine to idle until it stalls.
3. After engine stalls, crank engine for approximately 5 seconds to ensure fuel injection supply manifold pressure has been released.
4. When fuel system service is complete, install fuel pump relay.
5. Cycle ignition key and wait 3 seconds to pressurize fuel system. Inspect for leaks before starting engine.

Quick Disconnect Hoses

R-CLIP

When working with R-clip type connections, do not use tools to disconnect. Use of tools may deform clip components and could cause leaks.

DISCONNECT

1. Bend shipping tab downward.
2. Spread R-clip and push clip into fitting.
3. Separate fitting from tube.

CONNECT

1. Inspect fitting and tube for damage and ensure connections are clean.
2. Apply light coat of suitable, clean engine oil to male end of tube.
3. Insert R-clip into fitting.
4. Align tube and fitting, then insert tube into fitting and push together until click is heard.
5. Pull on connection to ensure it is fully engaged.

SPRING LOCK

When working with spring lock type connections, spring lock tool set No. T84L-19623-B, or equivalent, must be used to disconnect fittings.

When connecting spring lock type fittings, proceed as follows:
1. Inspect and clean both coupling ends.
2. Lubricate fuel line O-ring seals with suitable, clean engine oil.
3. When connection is made, pull on line to ensure it is fully engaged.

VAPOR TUBE

To disconnect vapor tube connections, squeeze fitting and disconnect vapor tube from fitting.

To connect, proceed as follows:
1. Ensure fittings are clean and free from damage.
2. Push tube onto fitting until it snaps into place.
3. Pull on connection to verify fitting is secure.

COMPRESSION PRESSURE

1. Ensure crankcase oil is correct viscosity and correct level, and battery is fully charged.
2. Operate vehicle until engine at normal operating temperature.
3. Turn ignition switch to OFF position and remove all spark plugs.
4. Set throttle plates in wide-open position.
5. Install suitable compression gauge in cylinder No. 1.
6. Install suitable auxiliary start switch.
7. Turn ignition switch to ON position.
8. Crank engine at least five compression strokes using auxiliary starter switch.
9. Record highest reading and approximate number of compression strokes required to obtain highest reading.
10. Repeat test on each cylinder.
11. Compression pressures are within specifications is the lowest cylinder reading is at least 75% of highest.

ENGINE MOUNT

REPLACE

1. Raise and support vehicle.
2. **If removing lefthand engine mount,** disconnect crankcase vent tube from air cleaner outlet pipe.
3. **On all engine mounts,** disconnect two throttle body electrical connectors, **Fig. 1.**
4. Disconnect two throttle body coolant hoses from coolant tube. Plug coolant hoses.

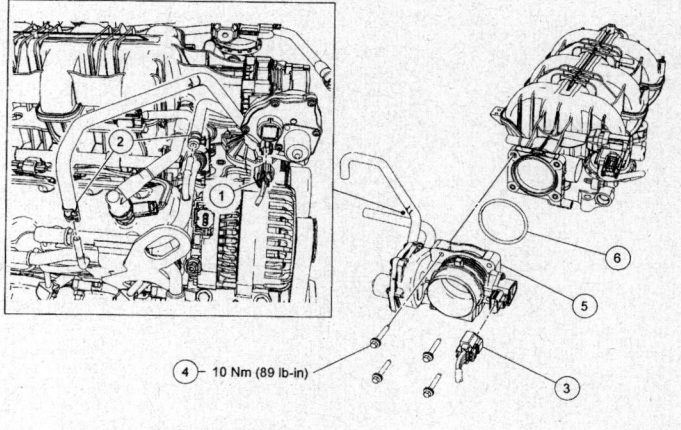

Item	Description
1	Throttle body (TB) electrical connector
2	TB coolant hoses (2 required)
3	Throttle position (TP) sensor electrical connector
4	TB bolts (4 required)
5	TB
6	TB gasket

ARM0400000000562

Fig. 1   Throttle body replacement

ARM0400000000554

Fig. 2   Engine mount replacement (Part 1 of 2). Lefthand

5. Remove four mounting bolts and throttle body.
6. Remove front end accessory drive bracket bolt and install engine lifting bracket tool No. D70P-6000, or equivalent.
7. Remove six pin-type retainers and radiator sight shield.
8. Support engine using suitable three-bar engine support tool.
9. Remove engine mount bracket-to-engine mount nut, **Figs. 2 and 3.**
10. Remove three mounting nuts and engine mount bracket.
11. Remove two mounting bolts and engine mount.
12. Reverse procedure to install.

ENGINE
REPLACE

1. Raise and support vehicle.
2. Remove fuel pump relay.
3. Start engine and allow it idle until is stalls.
4. Crank engine for approximately five seconds to ensure fuel injection supply manifold pressure has been released.
5. Turn ignition switch to OFF position.
6. Loosen clamp and disconnect a outlet pipe from air cleaner.
7. Disconnect Mass Air Flow (MAF) sensor electrical connector.
8. Remove mounting bolts and air cleaner assembly bolt. Ensure two rubber grommets are retained to air cleaner feet.
9. Mark hood hinge location for installation alignment.
10. Remove four bolts and hood.
11. Drain cooling system into suitable container.
12. **On models equipped with automatic transmission,** remove transmission as outlined in **MOTOR's** "Domestic Transmission, In-Vehicle Service." or "Transmission Service DVD."
13. **On models equipped with manual transmission,** remove clutch as outlined in **MOTOR's "Domestic Transmission, In-Vehicle Service." or "Transmission Service DVD."**
14. **On all models,** disconnect two Heated Oxygen Sensor (HO2S) and two catalyst monitor sensor electrical connectors.
15. Remove four catalytic converter-to-exhaust manifold nuts.
16. Remove stud bolt, then disconnect and position aside.
17. Drain engine oil into suitable container.
18. Disconnect upper radiator hose from thermostat housing.
19. Disconnect lower radiator hose from water pump.
20. Remove mounting bolt and disconnect power steering supply hose bracket from Front Engine Accessory Drive (FEAD) bracket.
21. Remove mounting bolt and disconnect Power Steering Pressure (PSP) tube bracket from crossmember.
22. Disconnect PSP switch electrical connector.
23. Disconnect the air conditioning compressor and high pressure switch electrical connectors.
24. Disconnect two wiring retainers from FEAD bracket.
25. Disconnect fuel supply tube coupling.
26. Rotate accessory drive belt tensioner counterclockwise and remove accessory drive belt.
27. Remove three mounting bolts and power steering pump pulley.
28. Remove three mounting bolts and position power steering pump aside.
29. Remove three mounting bolts and stud bolt, then position FEAD bracket and air conditioning compressor aside.
30. Disconnect two heater hoses from coolant tube.
31. Disconnect heater hose bracket from righthand valve cover.
32. Remove three coolant tube bracket bolts.
33. Disconnect six spark plug wires from spark plugs using suitable spark plug wire remover.
34. Disconnect spark plug wire retainer from intake manifold.
35. Disconnect radio ignition interference capacitor electrical connector.
36. Disconnect ignition coil electrical connector.
37. Remove two upper ignition coil bracket bolts.
38. Remove three lower ignition coil bracket bolts, then the ignition coil and spark plug wires.
39. Disconnect and remove crankcase vent tube from lefthand valve cover.
40. Disconnect brake booster vacuum hose from upper intake manifold.
41. Disconnect vapor tube from upper intake manifold.
42. Disconnect upper and lower Powertrain Control Module (PCM) electrical connectors.
43. Disconnect 16-pin electrical connector, two wiring retainers and three wiring harness retainers.
44. Remove power distribution box cover.
45. Remove mounting bolt and disconnect power distribution box B+ terminal.
46. Disconnect pin type retainer from strut tower.
47. Disconnect power distribution box upper housing from lower housing.
48. Loosen bolt and disconnect 68-pin connector from power distribution box.
49. Remove mounting bolt and disconnect ground cable from righthand strut tower.
50. Install suitable lifting brackets on cylinder heads.
51. Remove lefthand and righthand engine mounts' nuts.
52. Remove engine using suitable spread bar.
53. Reverse procedure to install.

Item	Description
1	LH engine mount bracket bolt (3 required)
2	LH engine mount bracket-to-engine mount nut
3	LH engine mount bracket
4	LH engine mount bolt (2 required)
5	LH engine mount

ARM0400000000555

Fig. 2 Engine mount replacement (Part 2 of 2). Lefthand

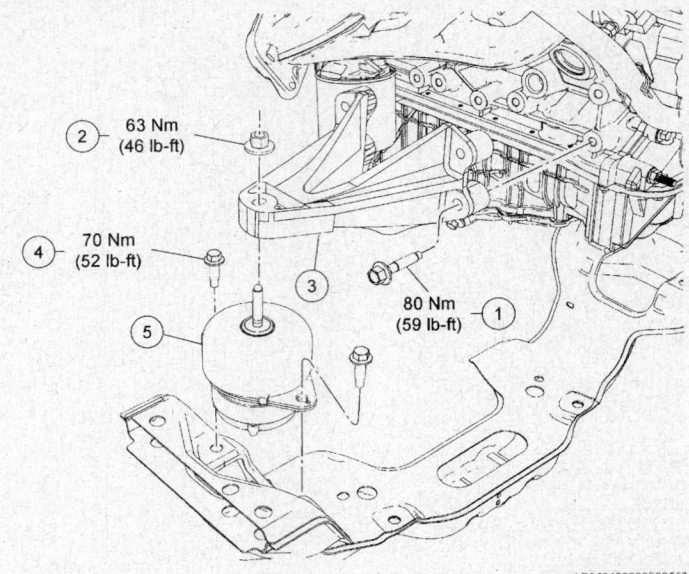

ARM0400000000563

Fig. 3 Engine mount replacement (Part 1 of 2). Righthand

INTAKE MANIFOLD
REPLACE

1. Disconnect righthand spark plug wires from ignition coil and spark plug wire retainer from intake manifold, **Fig. 4.**
2. Remove two ignition coil bracket upper bolts and three lower bolts.
3. Position ignition coil and bracket aside.
4. Disconnect Exhaust Gas Recirculation (EGR) system module electrical connector.
5. Disconnect tube from EGR system module.
6. Disconnect brake booster vacuum hose from intake manifold.
7. Disconnect vacuum tube from fuel rail pressure and temperature sensor.
8. Disconnect vapor tube from intake manifold.
9. Remove Positive Crankcase Ventilation (PCV) tube.
10. Disconnect Knock Sensor (KS) electrical connector retainer from intake manifold.
11. Disconnect Throttle Position (TP) sensor and throttle body electrical connectors.
12. Disconnect and plug two throttle body coolant hoses.
13. Remove eight mounting bolts and intake manifold.
14. Reverse procedure to install. Using sequence, **Fig. 5, torque** intake manifold mounting bolts to 89 inch lbs.

EXHAUST MANIFOLD
REPLACE

1. Raise and support vehicle.
2. Remove two catalytic converter-to-exhaust manifold nuts.
3. **If removing lefthand exhaust manifold,** disconnect Exhaust Gas Recirculation (EGR) system module tube.
4. **On all manifolds,** remove six nuts, exhaust manifold and gasket.
5. Reverse procedure to install.

CYLINDER HEAD
REPLACE

Lefthand and righthand camshaft timing procedure must be performed when either camshaft is serviced.
1. Raise and support vehicle.

2. Drain engine cooling system into suitable container.
3. Remove intake manifold as outlined under "Intake Manifold, Replace."
4. Remove valve covers as outlined under "Valve Cover, Replace."
5. Rotate crankshaft until camshaft for cylinder being serviced is at base circle.
6. Mark position of camshaft roller followers so they can be installed in original positions.
7. Remove camshaft roller followers using valve spring compressor tool No. T97T-6565-A, or equivalent.
8. Rotate accessory drive belt tensioner counterclockwise and remove accessory drive belt.
9. **On righthand side,** proceed as follows:
   a. Disconnect alternator electrical connector, then remove mounting nut and disconnect B+ terminal.
   b. Disconnect pin-type retainer.
   c. Remove mounting bolt and accessory drive belt tensioner.
   d. Remove mounting nut, two bolts and alternator mounting bracket .
   e. Disconnect heater hose from thermostat housing.
   f. Disconnect Engine Coolant Temperature (ECT) sensor electrical connector.
   g. Disconnect upper radiator hose.
   h. Position coolant bypass hose clamp aside.
   i. Remove three mounting bolts and thermostat housing.
10. **On lefthand side,** proceed as follows:
   a. Remove mounting bolt and oil dipstick tube.
   b. Remove mounting bolt and disconnect power steering supply hose bracket from Front Engine Accessory Drive (FEAD) bracket.
   c. Remove mounting bolt and disconnect Power Steering Pressure

(PSP) tube bracket from crossmember.
   d. Remove three mounting bolts and power steering pump pulley.
   e. Remove three mounting bolts and position power steering pump aside.
   f. Remove three mounting bolts, stud bolt and position FEAD bracket and air conditioning compressor aside.
   g. Remove mounting bolt and disconnect starter motor wiring retainer bracket.
   h. Remove ground strap bolt and disconnect wiring harness retainer from backside of cylinder head.
   i. Remove mounting bolt and disconnect starter motor wiring bracket.
11. **On all heads,** remove spark wire using suitable spark plug wire remover tool.
12. Remove four mounting bolts and fuel rail and injectors.
13. Separate fuel injectors from fuel rail and discard O-ring seals.
14. Remove four catalytic converter-to-manifold nuts.
15. Remove 12 mounting nuts, exhaust manifolds and gaskets.
16. **On righthand side,** proceed as follows:
   a. Remove righthand hydraulic chain tensioner.
   b. Install camshaft sprocket holding tool No. T97T-6256-B and adapter tool T97T-6256-A, or equivalents.
   c. Remove righthand camshaft bolt using torque wrench extension tool No. T97T-6256-F and camshaft sprocket nut socket tool No. 303-565, or equivalents.
   d. Remove righthand cassette bolt.
   e. Remove righthand camshaft sprocket from timing chain.
   f. Install suitable rubber band around cassette and timing chain.

Item	Description
1	RH engine mount bracket bolt (3 required)
2	RH engine mount bracket-to-engine mount nut
3	RH engine mount bracket
4	RH engine mount bolt (2 required)
5	RH engine mount

ARM0400000000564

Fig. 3 Engine mount replacement (Part 2 of 2). Righthand

17. **On lefthand side,** proceed as following:
    a. Remove lefthand hydraulic chain tensioner camshaft sprocket holding tool No. T97T-2656-B and adapter tool T97T-6256-A, or equivalents.
    b. Remove lefthand camshaft sprocket bolt.
    c. Remove lefthand cassette bolt.
    d. Remove lefthand camshaft sprocket from timing chain.
    e. Install suitable rubber band around cassette and timing chain.
18. **On all heads,** remove cylinder head bolts in sequence, **Fig. 6.**
19. Remove cylinder head with assistance and gaskets. **On righthand side, avoid contacting air conditioning tube.**
20. Reverse procedure to install, noting the following:
    a. Install new, torque-to-yield cylinder head bolts.
    b. Install eight new M12 bolts and tighten in sequence to 106 inch lbs., **Fig. 7.**
    c. **Torque** head bolts to 18 ft. lbs.
    d. Install two new M8 bolts and **torque** to 24 ft. lbs., **Fig. 8.**
    e. Tighten eight M12 bolts an additional 90° in sequence.
    f. Final tighten M12 bolts an additional 90° in sequence.

VALVE COVER
REPLACE
Lefthand

1. Disconnect ignition coil electrical connector, **Fig. 9.**
2. Disconnect six spark plug wires from ignition coil.
3. Remove four mounting bolts and ignition coil.
4. Remove fuel rail supply tube bracket-to-cylinder head bolt and cover bolt, then position fuel rail supply tube aside.
5. Disconnect crankcase ventilation tube

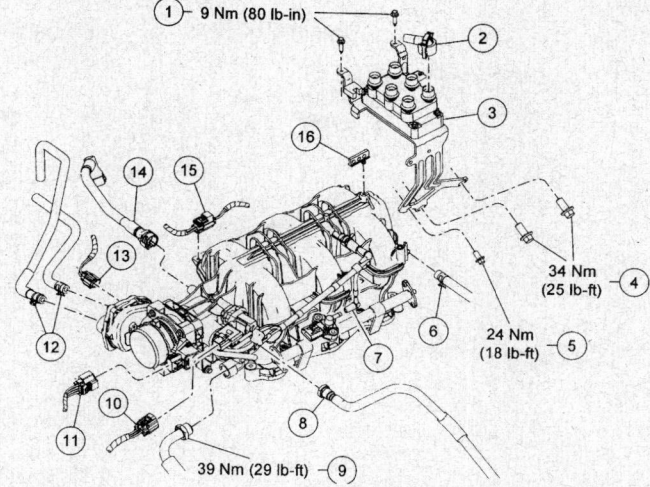

Item	Description
1	Ignition coil bracket upper bolts (2 required)
2	RH spark plug wire-to-ignition coil connectors (3 required)
3	Ignition coil and bracket assembly
4	Ignition coil bracket lower bolts (M12) (2 required)
5	Ignition coil bracket lower bolt (M8)
6	Brake booster vacuum hose
7	Vacuum harness fitting
8	Vapor tube
9	Exhaust gas recirculation (EGR) system module tube fitting

Item	Description
10	EGR system module electrical connector
11	Throttle position (TP) sensor electrical connector
12	Throttle body coolant hoses (2 required)
13	Throttle body electrical connector
14	Positive crankcase ventilation (PCV) tube
15	Knock sensor (KS) electrical connector
16	RH spark plug wire retainer

ARM0400000000566

Fig. 4 Intake manifold replacement (Part 1 of 2)

from valve cover and position tube aside.
6. Disconnect Camshaft Position (CMP) sensor electrical connector.
7. Disconnect fuel rail pressure and temperature sensor electrical connector.
8. Disconnect three lefthand fuel injector electrical connectors.
9. Disconnect wiring retainer from valve cover stud bolt and position it aside.
10. Disconnect spark plug wire retainer from valve cover stud bolt.
11. Remove three mounting bolts, three stud bolts and lefthand valve cover.
12. Reverse procedure to install, tighten valve cover mounting bolts in sequence, **Fig. 10.**

Righthand

1. Remove Positive Crankcase Ventilation (PCV) tube and disconnect PCV valve electrical connector, **Fig. 11.**
2. Disconnect heater hose retainer from valve cover.
3. Remove wiring harness bracket bolt from back of righthand cylinder head and disconnect bracket from valve cover stud bolt.
4. Disconnect engine wiring and spark plug wiring retainers from two valve cover stud bolts.
5. Remove two mounting bolts, four stud bolts and righthand valve cover.
6. Reverse procedure to install.

CAMSHAFT ROLLER FOLLOWER
REPLACE

1. Remove valve covers as outlined under "Valve Cover, Replace."
2. Rotate crankshaft until camshaft for cylinder being serviced is at base circle.
3. Mark position of camshaft roller followers so they can be installed in original positions.
4. Remove camshaft roller followers using valve spring compressor tool No. T97T-6565-A, or equivalent.
5. Reverse procedure to install. Lubricate camshaft roller followers with suitable, clean engine oil.

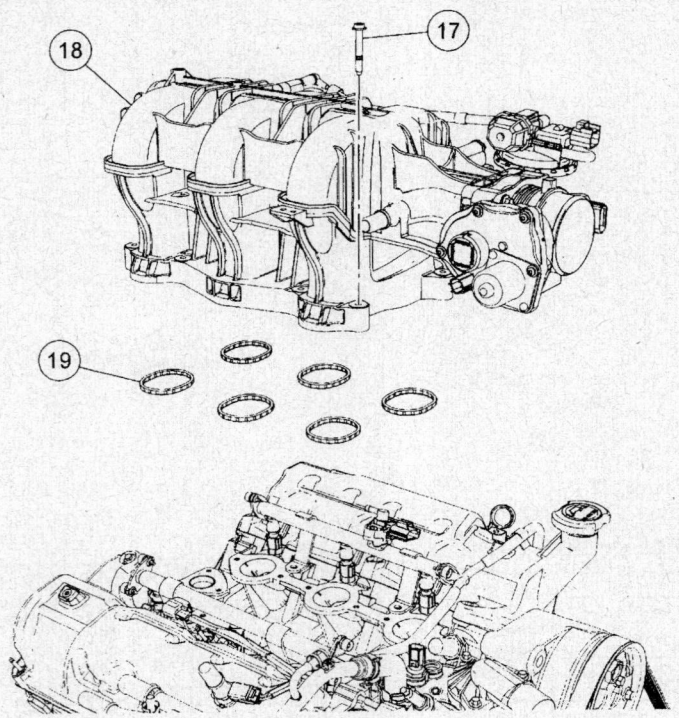

Item	Description
17	Intake manifold bolts (8 required)
18	Intake manifold
19	Intake manifold gaskets

ARM0400000000567

Fig. 4 Intake manifold replacement (Part 2 of 2)

CAMSHAFT LOBE LIFT SPECIFICATIONS

Engine	Intake, Inch	Exhaust, Inch
4.0L	.259	.259

VALVE ADJUSTMENT

These engine are equipped with hydraulic valve lash adjusters. No valve adjustment is required.

HYDRAULIC LASH ADJUSTER

REPLACE

1. Mark position of camshaft roller followers so they can be installed in original positions.
2. Remove valve covers as outlined under "Valve Cover, Replace."
3. Rotate crankshaft until camshaft for cylinder being serviced is at base circle.
4. Mark position of camshaft roller followers so they can be installed in original positions.
5. Remove camshaft roller followers

using valve spring compressor tool No. T97T-6565-A, or equivalent.
6. Mark position of hydraulic lash adjusters so they can be installed in original positions.
7. Remove hydraulic lash adjusters.
8. Reverse procedure to install. Lubricate hydraulic lash adjusters and camshaft roller followers with suitable, clean engine oil

CRANKSHAFT DAMPER

REPLACE

1. Raise and support vehicle.
2. Disconnect crankcase vent tube from air cleaner outlet pipe.
3. Loosen two clamps and remove air cleaner outlet pipe.
4. Rotate accessory drive belt tensioner clockwise with suitable belt tensioner release tool and remove belt.
5. Remove crankshaft pulley bolt using suitable strap wrench.
6. Install crankshaft pulley bolt 2–3 turns, then remove crankshaft pulley using crankshaft vibration damper remover tool No. T74P-3616-A, or equivalent.
7. Reverse procedure to install, noting the following:
   a. Install crankshaft pulley using

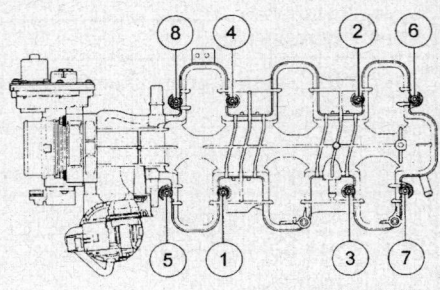

ARM0400000000568

Fig. 5 Intake manifold tightening sequence

crankshaft vibration damper installer tool No. T74P-6316-B, or equivalent.
   b. **Torque** new torque-to-yield crankshaft pulley bolt to 33 ft. lbs.
   c. Tighten pulley bolt an additional 85°.

FRONT COVER

REPLACE

1. Drain cooling system into suitable container.
2. Remove crankshaft pulley as outlined under "Crankshaft Damper, Replace."
3. Remove crankshaft front seal using crankshaft front oil seal remover tool No. T74P-6700-A and aligner tool No, T74P-6019-A, or equivalent.
4. Disconnect upper radiator hose, **Fig. 12.**
5. Disconnect water pump water heater and lower radiator hoses.
6. Remove mounting bolt and accessory drive belt idler pulley.
7. Disconnect Crankshaft Position (CKP) sensor and two 2 wiring retainers.
8. Remove five engine block cradle-to-engine front cover bolts.
9. Remove engine front cover five mounting bolts and 5 stud bolts.
10. Disconnect water pump coolant by-pass hose.
11. Remove engine front cover.
12. Drain engine oil into suitable container.
13. Reverse procedure to install, noting the following:
    a. Clean sealing area using suitable silicone gasket remover and metal surface prep.
    b. Apply suitable silicone gasket and sealant to oil pan and engine block mating surfaces, **Fig. 13. Front cover must be secured within four minutes of sealant application.**
    c. Apply thread sealant to stud bolts and ensure bolts are installed in original positions.
    d. Loosely install five mounting bolts and five stud bolts, then align front cover using front cover aligner tool No. T74P-6019-A, or equivalent, and tighten bolts and stud bolts to 14 ft. lbs.

FRONT COVER SEAL

REPLACE

1. Remove crankshaft pulley as outlined

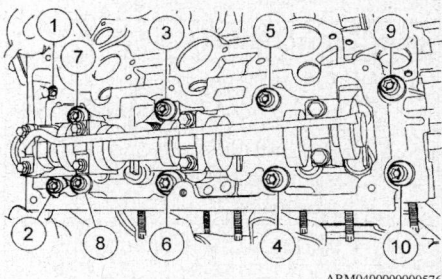

Fig. 6 Cylinder head removal sequence

Fig. 7 Cylinder head tightening sequence

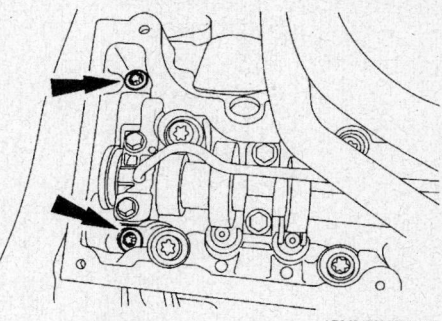

Fig. 8 M8 cylinder head bolts

under "Crankshaft Damper, Replace."

2. Remove crankshaft front seal using crankshaft front oil seal remover tool No. T74P-6700-A and aligner tool No, T74P-6019-A, or equivalent.
3. Reverse procedure to install using aligner tool and crankshaft vibration damper installer tool No. T74P-6316-B, or equivalent.

TIMING CHAIN
REPLACE

These engines have an interference fit design. If engine has jumped time cylinder heads must be removed to repair damage to valves and/or pistons.

At no time, when the timing chains are removed and the cylinder heads are installed, may the crankshaft and/or camshaft be rotated unless all rocker arms have been removed. Rotation may result in valve and/or piston damage.

Lefthand and righthand camshaft timing procedure must be performed when either camshaft is serviced.

1. Remove intake manifold as outlined under "Intake Manifold, Replace."
2. Remove engine front cover as outlined under "Front Cover, Replace."
3. Remove valve covers as outlined under "Valve Cover, Replace."
4. Rotate crankshaft until camshaft for cylinder being serviced is at base circle.
5. Mark position of camshaft roller followers so they can be installed in original positions.
6. Remove camshaft roller followers using valve spring compressor tool No. T97T-6565-A, or equivalent.
7. Turn crankshaft clockwise to position cylinder No. 1 at top dead center.
8. Remove lefthand hydraulic chain tensioner and camshaft sprocket bolt, **Fig. 14.**
9. Install camshaft sprocket holding tool No. T97T-6256-B, and adapter tool No. T97T-6256-A, or equivalent, on front of lefthand cylinder head.
10. Remove lefthand camshaft sprocket bolt.
11. Prevent crankshaft from turning using crankshaft holding tool No. 303-674, or equivalent, and remove jackshaft sprocket bolt.
12. Remove two mounting bolts and primary chain tensioner.
13. Remove primary chain and sprockets as assembly.

14. Remove upper mounting bolt and lefthand cassette.
15. Reverse procedure to install, noting the following:
    a. Ensure camshaft chain sprockets are oriented correctly, **Fig. 15.**
    b. **Torque** jackshaft sprocket bolt to 33 ft. lbs.
    c. Tighten an additional 90°.

CAMSHAFT
REPLACE

These engines have an interference fit design. If engine has jumped time cylinder heads must be removed to repair damage to valves and/or pistons.

At no time, when the timing chains are removed and the cylinder heads are installed, may the crankshaft and/or camshaft be rotated unless all rocker arms have been removed. Rotation may result in valve and/or piston damage.

Lefthand and righthand camshaft timing procedure must be performed when either camshaft is serviced.

1. Remove valve covers as outlined under "Valve Cover, Replace."
2. Rotate crankshaft until camshaft for cylinder being serviced is at base circle.
3. Mark position of camshaft roller followers so they can be installed in original positions.
4. Remove camshaft roller followers using valve spring compressor tool No. T97T-6565-A, or equivalent.
5. Rotate crankshaft clockwise to position cylinder No. 1 at TDC and lock damper in place using crankshaft TDC timing tool No. T97T-6303-A, or equivalent. Ensure tool contacts engine block. **Do not rotate engine counterclockwise.**
6. **On righthand camshaft,** proceed as follows:
    a. Install camshaft sprocket holding tool No. T97T-6256-B, and adapter tool No. T97T-6256-A, or equivalent, on rear of righthand cylinder head.
    b. Loosen camshaft sprocket bolt using torque wrench extension tool No. T97T-6256-F, and camshaft sprocket nut socket tool No. T97T-6256-G, or equivalents. **Righthand camshaft sprocket is lefthandthreaded bolt.**
    c. Position righthand camshaft sprocket aside.

7. **On lefthand camshaft,** proceed as follows:
    a. Install camshaft sprocket holding tool No. T97T-6256-B, and adapter tool No. T97T-6256-A, or equivalent, on front of lefthand cylinder head.
    b. Loosen camshaft sprocket bolt using torque wrench extension tool No. T97T-6256-F, and camshaft sprocket nut socket tool No. T97T-6256-G, or equivalents.
    c. Position lefthand camshaft sprocket aside.
8. **On all camshafts,** mark camshaft bearing caps positions for installation in original positions.
9. Remove mounting bolts sequence, **Fig. 16.**
10. Remove bearing caps and oil supply tube, then the camshaft.
11. Reverse procedure to install, noting the following:
    a. Lubricate camshafts and camshaft bearing caps with suitable, clean engine oil.
    b. Ensure camshaft has free rotation.
    c. **Torque** camshaft bearing caps bolts in sequence to 53 inch lbs., **Fig. 17.**
    d. **Torque** bolts to 12 ft. lbs.

CAMSHAFT TIMING

Lefthand and righthand camshaft timing procedure must be performed when either camshaft is serviced.

1. Remove valve covers as outlined under "Valve Cover, Replace."
2. Rotate crankshaft until camshaft for cylinder being serviced is at base circle.
3. Mark position of camshaft roller followers so they can be installed in original positions.
4. Remove camshaft roller followers using valve spring compressor tool No. T97T-6565-A, or equivalent.
5. Rotate crankshaft clockwise to position cylinder No. 1 at TDC and lock damper in place using crankshaft TDC timing tool No. T97T-6303-A, or equivalent. Ensure tool contacts engine block. **Do not rotate engine counterclockwise.**
6. Install camshaft sprocket holding tool No. T97T-6256-B, and adapter tool No. T97T-6256-A, or equivalent, on rear of righthand cylinder head.

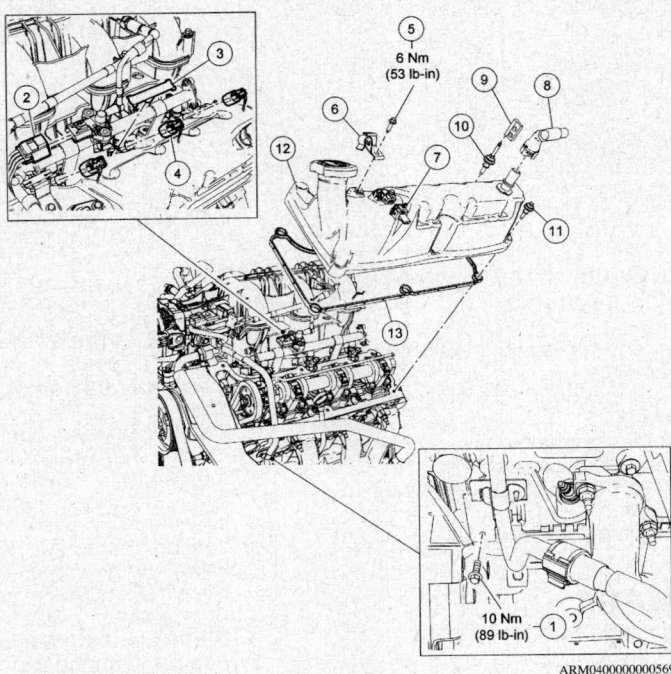

Fig. 9   Valve cover replacement (Part 1 of 2). Lefthand

Item	Description
1	Fuel rail supply tube bracket-to-cylinder head bolt
2	Fuel rail pressure and temperature sensor electrical connector
3	Wiring harness retainer
4	Fuel injector electrical connector (3 required)
5	Fuel rail supply tube bracket
6	Fuel rail supply tube bracket-to-valve cover bolt
7	Camshaft position (CMP) sensor electrical connector
8	Crankcase ventilation tube
9	Spark plug wire retainer
10	LH valve cover stud bolt (3 required)
11	LH valve cover bolt (3 required)
12	LH valve cover
13	LH valve cover gasket

ARM0400000000570

Fig. 9   Valve cover replacement (Part 2 of 2). Lefthand

7. Loosen camshaft sprocket bolt using torque wrench extension tool No. T97T-6256-F, and camshaft sprocket nut socket tool No. T97T-6256-G, or equivalents. **Righthand camshaft sprocket is lefthand-threaded bolt.**
8. Loosen top two camshaft sprocket holding tool clamp bolts.
9. Position camshaft timing slots below centerline of camshaft **Camshaft timing slots are off-center.**
10. Install camshaft holding tool No. T97T-6303-C and adapter tool No. T97T-6256-D, or equivalents, on front of righthand cylinder head.
11. Remove righthand camshaft tensioner.
12. Install timing chain tensioner tool No. T97T-6K254-A, or equivalent.
13. Tighten camshaft sprocket bolt and holding tool clamp bolts.
14. Tighten camshaft bolt using torque wrench extension and camshaft sprocket nut socket tools.
15. Remove special tool.
16. Install new O-ring seal on tensioner and lubricate it with suitable, clean engine oil.
17. Install righthand camshaft tensioner.
18. Remove righthand cylinder head special tools.
19. Install camshaft sprocket holding tool No. T97T-6256-B, and adapter tool No. T97T-6256-A, or equivalent, on front of lefthand cylinder head.
20. Loosen camshaft sprocket bolt using torque wrench extension tool No. T97T-6256-F, and camshaft sprocket nut socket tool No. T97T-6256-G, or equivalents.
21. Loosen top two camshaft sprocket holding tool clamp bolts and allow camshaft sprocket to rotate freely
22. Position camshaft timing slots below

centerline of camshaft **Camshaft timing slots are off-center.**
23. Install camshaft holding tool No. T97T-6303-C and adapter tool No. T97T-6256-D, or equivalents, on rear of lefthand cylinder head.
24. Remove lefthand camshaft tensioner.
25. Install timing chain tensioner tool No. T97T-6K254-A, or equivalent.
26. Tighten camshaft sprocket bolt and holding tool clamp bolts.
27. Tighten camshaft bolt.
28. Remove special tool.
29. Install new O-ring seal on tensioner and lubricated with suitable, clean engine oil.
30. Install lefthand camshaft tensioner.
31. Remove special tools from lefthand cylinder head.
32. Install camshaft roller followers.

BALANCE SHAFT
REPLACE

Balance shaft is on engines equipped with manual transmission only.
Complete engine disassembly is required to access the balance shaft.
1. Remove engine as outlined under "Engine, Replace."
2. Remove eight mounting bolts and flexplate/flywheel.
3. Remove spacer plate and flexplate-to-crankshaft spacer.
4. Mount engine on suitable engine stand.
5. Disconnect alternator throttle body electrical connectors.
6. Remove mounting nut and disconnect alternator B+ terminal.
7. Disconnect wiring retainer coolant tube bracket.

8. Disconnect vacuum tubes, then fuel rail pressure and temperature sensor electrical connector.
9. Disconnect Exhaust Gas Recirculation (EGR) system module and Throttle Position (TP) sensor electrical connectors.
10. Disconnect tube fitting from EGR system module.
11. Disconnect EGR tube fitting from lefthand exhaust manifold and remove the tube.
12. Disconnect two throttle body coolant hoses from coolant tube.
13. Disconnect Positive Crankcase Ventilation (PCV) tube fittings and remove the tube.
14. Disconnect Knock Sensor (KS) electrical connector and wiring retainer.
15. Remove eight mounting bolts and intake manifold.
16. Remove two fuel supply tube bracket bolts.
17. Disconnect Camshaft Position (CMP) electrical connector.
18. Disconnect oil pressure sensor electrical connector and wiring retainer.
19. Remove mounting bolt and belt tensioner.
20. Remove two mounting bolts, nu, alternator and bracket.
21. Disconnect Crankshaft Position (CKP) sensor electrical connector and two wiring retainers.
22. Disconnect Engine Coolant Temperature (ECT) sensor electrical connector.

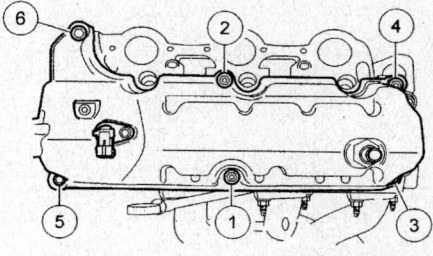

Fig. 10 Valve cover tightening sequence

23. Disconnect PCV valve electrical connector.
24. Disconnect fuel injector electrical connectors and wiring retainer from valve cover stud bolts.
25. Remove three bolts, disconnect wiring retainers and remove the main engine wiring harness.
26. Remove four mounting bolts, fuel rail and injectors.
27. Remove mounting and knock sensor.
28. Remove mounting bolt, then disconnect coolant bypass and heater hose from water pump.
29. Remove three mounting bolts, thermostat housing, hoses and coolant tube.
30. Remove three mounting bolts, three stud bolts and lefthand valve cover.
31. Remove two mounting bolts, four stud bolts and righthand valve cover.
32. Remove bolt and oil dipstick tube.
33. Remove six mounting nuts, lefthand exhaust manifold. and gasket.
34. Remove three mounting bolts and lefthand engine mount bracket.
35. Remove six mounting nuts, righthand exhaust manifold and gasket.
36. Remove four mounting bolts and righthand engine mount bracket.
37. Rotate crankshaft until cam lobe is in up position.
38. Mark each camshaft roller follower for installation in original position.
39. Remove camshaft roller followers using valve spring compressor tool No. T97T-6565-A, or equivalent.
40. Remove righthand hydraulic chain tensioner.
41. Install camshaft sprocket holding tool No. T97T-6256-B and adapter tool No. T97T-6256-A, or equivalent, on righthand cylinder head.
42. Remove righthand camshaft sprocket bolt. **Righthand camshaft sprocket bolt is lefthand-threaded bolt.**
43. Remove righthand cassette bolt.
44. Remove righthand camshaft sprocket from timing chain.
45. Hold timing chain and cassette with suitable rubber band
46. Remove lefthand hydraulic chain tensioner.
47. Install camshaft sprocket holding tool No. T97T-6256-B and adapter tool No. T97T-6256-A, or equivalent, on lefthand cylinder head.
48. Remove lefthand camshaft sprocket bolt.
49. Remove lefthand cassette bolt.
50. Remove lefthand camshaft sprocket

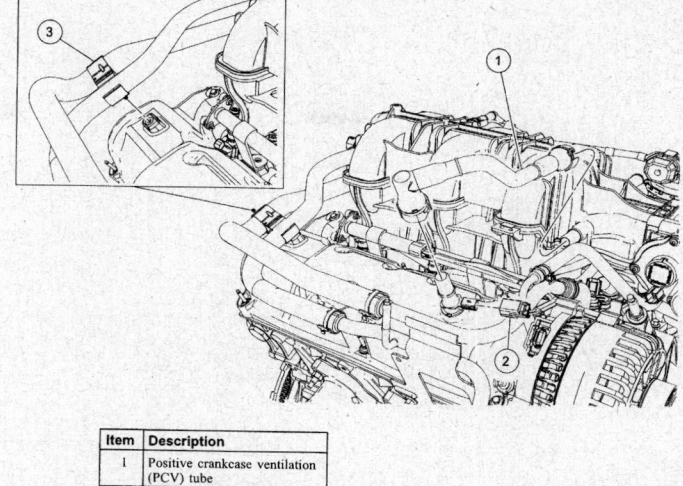

Item	Description
1	Positive crankcase ventilation (PCV) tube
2	PCV valve electrical connector
3	Heater hose retainer bracket

Fig. 11 Valve cover replacement (Part 1 of 2). Righthand

from timing chain.
51. Hold cassette and timing chain with suitable rubber band.
52. Remove mounting bolts in sequence, then the cylinder heads and gaskets, **Fig. 6.**
53. Remove mounting bolts and CKP sensor.
54. Remove mounting bolt and washer using suitable strap wrench, then the crankshaft pulley using crankshaft vibration damper remover tools Nos. T74P-3616-A and D85L-6000-A, or equivalent
55. Remove crankshaft front oil seal using crankshaft front oil seal remover tool No. T74P-6700-A, or equivalent.
56. Remove five cylinder block cradle-to-engine front cover bolts.
57. Remove five mounting bolts, five stud bolts and engine front cover.
58. Remove engine oil filter.
59. Remove mounting bolts and oil pan.
60. Remove mounting bolt, oil pump screen cover and tube.
61. Record location of two silver-colored bolts with washer seals for installation in original positions.
62. Remove cylinder block cradle inner bolts and washers.
63. Remove two cylinder block cradle Torx bolts.
64. Remove 15 mounting bolts, two nuts and cylinder block cradle.
65. Remove two bolts, oil pump pickup tube and intermediate shaft.
66. Remove oil filter adapter.
67. Remove rear jackshaft plug.
68. Hold crankshaft using crankshaft socket tool No. 303-674, or equivalent.
69. Remove rear jackshaft sprocket-retaining bolt and spacer.
70. Remove mounting bolt and righthand cassette.
71. Remove mounting bolt, retainer and oil pump drive.
72. Hold crankshaft using crankshaft

socket tool No. 303-674, or equivalent.
73. Loosen front sprocket retaining bolt, then remove bolts and chain tensioner.
74. Remove chain guide.
75. Remove mounting bolt, jackshaft sprocket and chain.
76. Remove mounting bolt and lefthand cassette.
77. Remove thrust plate and jackshaft.
78. Install suitable pin in balance shaft tensioner.
79. Remove two mounting bolts and balance shaft tensioner.
80. Remove two mounting bolts and Balance Shaft Chain Guide.
81. **Do not remove balance shaft sprocket bolt.**
82. Remove balance shaft chain and crankshaft sprocket.
83. Remove two mounting and balance shaft.
84. Reverse procedure to install

PISTON & ROD ASSEMBLY

Position the piston with the indentation arrow toward the front of the cylinder block.
1. Install connecting rod bearings.
2. Install rubber hose pieces on connecting rod bolts to protect crankshaft.
3. Install pistons using suitable piston ring compressor tool rotating crankshaft as required.
4. Inspect clearance of each connecting rod bearing using old nuts and bolts.
5. Rotate crankshaft until piston is at bottom of its stroke.
6. For cylinders Nos. 1, 2 and 3, remove connecting rod nut at oil split hole side first
7. For cylinders Nos. 4, 5 and 6, remove opposite nut first.
8. Loosen first nut until face is approximately .08 inch over end of bolt, **Fig. 18.**

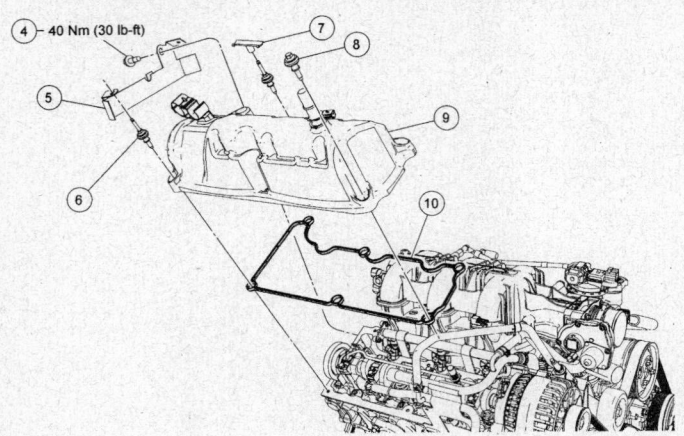

ARM0400000000573

Fig. 11   Valve cover replacement (Part 2 of 2). Righthand

Item	Description
4	Wiring harness bracket bolt
5	Wiring harness bracket
6	RH valve cover stud bolt (4 required)
7	Wiring retainer
8	RH valve cover bolt (2 required)
9	RH valve cover
10	RH valve cover gasket

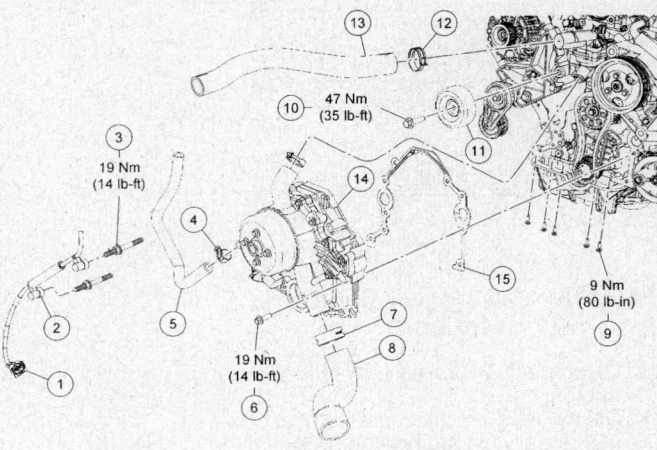

ARM0400000000583

Fig. 12   Front cover replacement (Part 1 of 2)

Item	Description
1	Crankshaft position (CKP) sensor electrical connector
2	Wiring retainers (part of
3	Engine front cover stud bolt (5 required)
4	Clamp

Item	Description
5	Coolant hose
6	Engine front cover bolt (5 required)
7	Clamp
8	Lower radiator hose
9	Block cradle-to-engine front cover bolts (5 required)

9. Tap on nut until bolt can be removed by hand.
10. Repeat previous steps for opposite bolt.
11. Install new bolts ensure head is parallel to sideward face of connecting rod, **Fig. 19.**
12. Install connecting rod cap in its original position.
13. Install and tighten connecting rod nuts finger-tight.
14. **Torque** connecting rod nuts to 15 ft. lbs.
15. Tighten bolts an additional 90°.

MAIN & ROD BEARINGS

1. Lubricate crankshaft main bearings with suitable, clean engine oil.
2. Install crankshaft main bearings and the thrust bearing.
3. Install lower main bearings in bearing caps.
4. Install crankshaft.
5. Apply silicone gasket and sealant to rear main bearing cap to cylinder block parting line, **Fig. 20. Cap must be secured within four minutes and seal application.**
6. Install main bearing caps in order in which they were removed.
7. **Torque** main bearing cap bolts in sequence to 26 ft. lbs, **Fig. 21.**
8. Tighten cap bolts an additional 57° in sequence.

CRANKSHAFT SEAL
REPLACE

1. Remove crankshaft pulley as outlined under "Crankshaft Damper, Replace."

2. Remove crankshaft front seal using crankshaft front oil seal remover tool No. T74P-6700-A and aligner tool No, T74P-6019-A, or equivalent.
3. Reverse procedure to install using aligner tool and crankshaft vibration damper installer tool No. T74P-6316-B, or equivalent.

CRANKSHAFT REAR OIL SEAL
REPLACE

1. **On models equipped with automatic transmission,** remove transmission as outlined in **MOTOR's "Domestic Transmission, In-Vehicle Service." or "Transmission Service DVD."**
2. **On models equipped with manual transmission,** remove clutch as outlined in **MOTOR's "Domestic Transmission, In-Vehicle Service." or "Transmission Service DVD."**
3. **On all models,** remove eight mounting bolts and flexplate/flywheel.
4. Remove spacer plate.
5. Remove crankshaft rear seal using oil seal remover too No. T92C-6700-CH, or equivalent. **Do not scratch or damage crankshaft rear seal running surface.**
6. Reverse procedure to install, noting the following:
   a. Lubricate crankshaft rear oil seal with suitable, clean engine oil
   b. Install seal using crankshaft rear oil seal tool No. T95T-6701-AR, or equivalent.
   c. **Torque** flexplate/flywheel mounting bolts in sequence to 115 inch lbs., **Fig. 22.**

d. **Torque** mounting bolts in sequence to 52 ft. lbs.

OIL PAN
REPLACE

1. Raise and support vehicle.
2. Drain engine oil into suitable container.
3. Remove mounting bolts, oil pan and gasket.
4. Reverse procedure to install.

OIL PUMP
REPLACE

1. Raise and support vehicle.
2. Disconnect two throttle body electrical connectors, **Fig. 1.**
3. Disconnect two throttle body coolant hoses from coolant tube. Plug coolant hoses.
4. Remove four mounting bolts and throttle body.
5. Remove front end accessory drive bracket bolt and install engine lifting bracket tool No. D70P-6000, or equivalent.
6. Remove six pin-type retainers and radiator sight shield.
7. Support engine using suitable three-bar engine support tool.
8. Remove lefthand and righthand engine mount nuts.
9. Drain engine oil into suitable container.
10. Remove mounting bolts, oil pan and gasket.
11. Remove mounting bolt, the oil pump screen and pickup tube.
12. Remove mounting bolt and disconnect steering column intermediate shaft from steering gear. **Do not allow steering wheel to rotate while steering column intermediate shaft is disconnected.**

Item	Description
10	Accessory drive belt idler pulley bolt
11	Accessory drive belt idler pulley
12	Clamp
13	Upper radiator hose
14	Engine front cover
15	Engine front cover gasket

ARM0400000000584

Fig. 12 Front cover replacement (Part 2 of 2)

13. Remove two steering gear-to-crossmember bolts and disconnect gear from crossmember.
14. Record positions and remove two cylinder block cradle rear Torx bolts.
15. Remove 20 mounting bolts and two nuts along outside of cylinder block cradle.
16. Remove with cylinder block cradle inner bolts and two washer seals. **Record location two silver-colored bolts that have washer seals for installation in original position.**
17. Raise engine and remove lower block cradle.
18. Remove two mounting bolts and oil pump.
19. Reverse procedure to install, noting the following:
    a. Back set screws off until they are below cylinder block cradle boss.
    b. Clean gasket mating surfaces using suitable silicone gasket remover and metal surface prep.
    c. Apply silicone, **Fig. 23. Cylinder block cradle must be secured within four minutes of sealant application.**
    d. Position new gasket and cylinder block cradle.
    e. Install outer 20 mounting bolts, two nuts finger, two rear Torx bolts and two bell housing-to-cylinder block cradle bolts finger tight.
    f. **Torque** two bell housing-to-cylinder block cradle bolts to 35 ft. lbs.
    g. **Torque** outer 20 mounting bolts and two nuts to 89 inch lbs.
    h. **Torque** cylinder block cradle rear Torx bolts to 71 inch lbs.
    i. **Torque** eight inserts to 27 inch lbs.
    j. Install two silver-colored bolts and new washer seals finger tight.
    k. Install six remaining inner bolts finger tight.
    l. **Torque** eight inner bolts in sequence to 11 ft. lbs., **Fig. 24.**
    m. **Torque** bolts in sequence to 25 ft. lbs.

BELT TENSION DATA

These models are equipped with an automatic drive belt tensioner. No adjustment or maintenance is required.

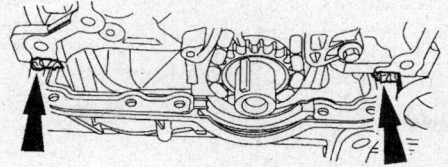

Fig. 13 Oil pan & block silicone sealant (Part 1 of 2)

SERPENTINE DRIVE BELT

Always use square drive tool in hole in tensioner to move tensioner. Never pry on tensioner pulley. When releasing drive belt tensioner, never allow tensioner to snap back. Damage to tensioner or personal injury could result.

Do not allow engine coolant to remain on serpentine belt or pulleys. If required, remove belt and flush with clean water.

Routing

Refer to **Fig. 25** for serpentine drive belt routing.

Replacement

Rotate the accessory drive belt tensioner clockwise with suitable belt tensioner release tool and remove the belt.

COOLING SYSTEM BLEED

1. Fill radiator through degas bottle until the coolant level is between the COOLANT FILL LEVEL marks.
2. Select maximum heater temperature and blower motor speed settings.
3. Position control to discharge air at air conditioning vents in instrument panel.
4. Start engine and allow to idle.
5. While engine is idling, feel for hot air at air conditioning vents.
6. **If air discharge remains cool and engine coolant temperature gauge does not move, engine coolant level is low and must be filled. Stop engine, allow it to cool and fill cooling system.**
7. Allow engine to idle until normal operating temperature is reached. Hot air should discharge from air conditioning vents.
8. Engine coolant temperature gauge should maintain stabilized reading in middle of NORMAL range.
9. Upper radiator hose should feel hot to touch.
10. Shut engine off and allow it to cool.
11. Inspect engine for coolant leaks.
12. Inspect and adjust engine coolant level in degas bottle.

THERMOSTAT
REPLACE

1. Drain cooling system into suitable container.

ARM0400000000586

Fig. 13 Oil pan & block silicone sealant (Part 2 of 2)

2. Disconnect crankcase vent tube from air cleaner outlet pipe.
3. Loosen two clamps and remove air cleaner outlet pipe.
4. Disconnect two throttle body electrical connectors, **Fig. 1.**
5. Disconnect two throttle body coolant hoses from coolant tube. Plug coolant hoses.
6. Remove four mounting bolts and throttle body.
7. Remove three upper mounting bolts and position thermostat housing aside.
8. Reverse procedure to install, using new thermostat O-ring seal and lubricate with suitable, clean engine coolant.

WATER PUMP
REPLACE

1. Drain engine coolant into suitable container.
2. Disconnect crankcase vent tube from air cleaner outlet pipe.
3. Loosen two clamps and remove air cleaner outlet pipe.
4. Loosen for water pump pulley mounting bolts, **Fig. 26.**
5. Rotate accessory drive belt tensioner clockwise with suitable belt tensioner release tool and remove belt.
6. Remove four mounting bolts and water pump pulley.
7. Disconnect thermostat housing-to-coolant pump hose and position aside.
8. Disconnect heater hose and position aside.
9. Disconnect radiator-to-coolant pump hose and position aside.
10. Remove 12 mounting bolts, water pump and gasket.
11. Reverse procedure to install using new gasket.

RADIATOR
REPLACE

1. Drain cooling system into suitable container.
2. Remove four push pin retainers and air deflector.
3. Disconnect crankcase vent tube from air cleaner outlet pipe.
4. Loosen two clamps and remove air cleaner outlet pipe.
5. Remove mounting bolt and position power steering reservoir aside, **Fig. 27.**
6. Remove two mounting bolts and position degas bottle aside.

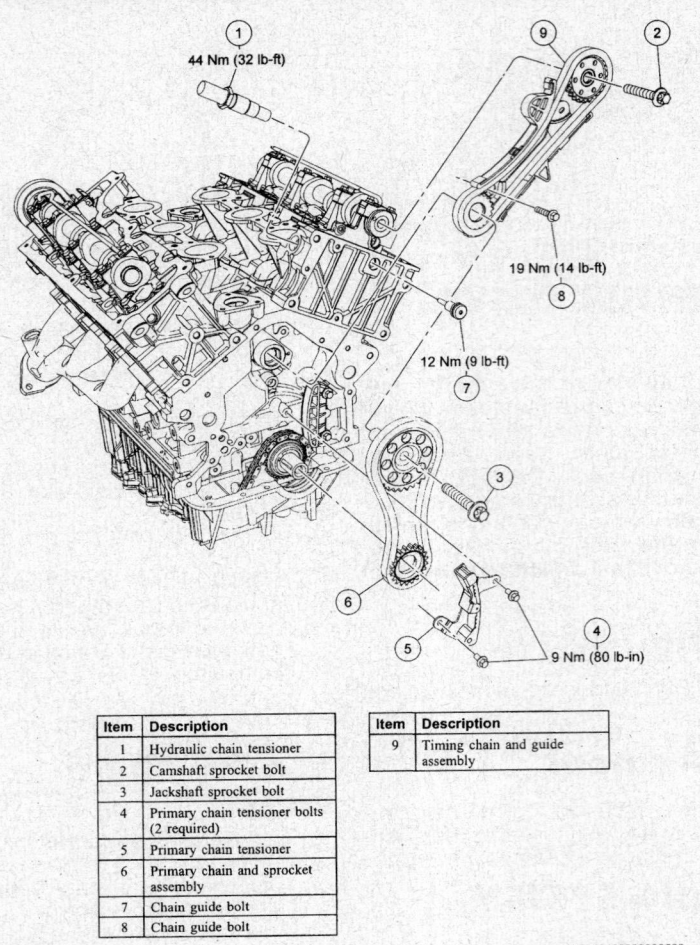

44 Nm (32 lb-ft)

19 Nm (14 lb-ft)

12 Nm (9 lb-ft)

9 Nm (80 lb-in)

Item	Description
1	Hydraulic chain tensioner
2	Camshaft sprocket bolt
3	Jackshaft sprocket bolt
4	Primary chain tensioner bolts (2 required)
5	Primary chain tensioner
6	Primary chain and sprocket assembly
7	Chain guide bolt
8	Chain guide bolt

Item	Description
9	Timing chain and guide assembly

ARM0400000000589

Fig. 14   Timing chain replacement

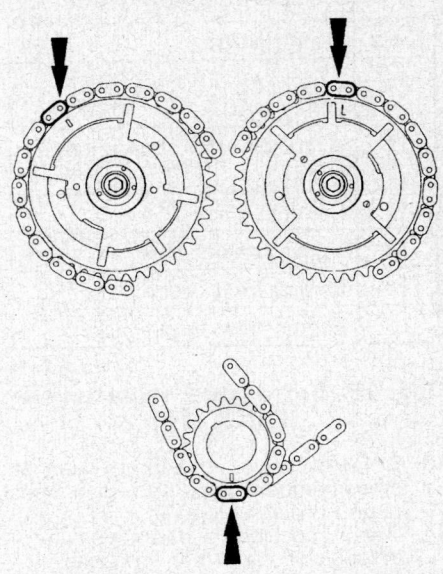

ARM0400000000590

Fig. 15   Camshaft chain sprocket orientation

7. Detach and position lower degas bottle hose aside.
8. Disconnect cooling fan motor and shroud electrical connector, **Fig. 28**.
9. Remove two mounting bolts, cooling fan motor and shroud.
10. Disconnect upper and lower radiator hoses from radiator, then position aside, **Fig. 29**.
11. Remove four mounting bolts and radiator support brackets.
12. Remove two power steering tubes and air conditioning condenser retaining nuts, then position power steering tubes aside.
13. Remove two condenser bolts and remove radiator.
14. Reverse procedure to install.

FUEL PUMP
REPLACE

1. Remove fuel pump relay.
2. Start engine and allow it idle until is stalls.
3. Crank engine for approximately five seconds to ensure fuel injection supply manifold pressure has been released.
4. Turn ignition switch to OFF position.
5. Remove fuel tank filler cap and insert suitable fuel tank drain hose into filler neck.
6. Insert chamfered end of hose into filler pipe through guide tube.
7. Attach suitable fuel recovery system to hose and remove fuel from tank. **Ensure to drain ⅛ of fuel capacity through filler pipe prior to removing pumps.**
8. Remove rear seat bottom and fuel pump module insulation padding.
9. Remove fuel pump module access cover.
10. Disconnect electrical connector and release fuel tube quick connect coupling on fuel pump module.
11. Remove fuel pump module lock retaining ring using suitable fuel tank locking wrench.
12. Position fuel pump module askew, then install suitable hose and fuel recovery system.
13. Completely drain fuel pump side of fuel tank.

14. Lift fuel pump module out of fuel tank allowing access to quick connect coupling.
15. Disconnect quick connect coupling from bottom of fuel pump module.
16. Remove fuel pump module. **Do not damage float arm.**
17. Reverse procedure to install, noting the following:
    a. Install new O-ring seal and lock ring.
    b. Apply suitable, clean engine oil to O-ring seal.
    c. Ensure alignment arrows on fuel pump module and fuel tank meet before tightening lock ring.

FUEL FILTER
REPLACE

1. Raise and support vehicle.
2. Remove fuel pump relay.
3. Start engine and allow it idle until is stalls.
4. Crank engine for approximately five seconds to ensure fuel injection supply manifold pressure has been released.
5. Turn ignition switch to OFF position.
6. Remove fuel bundle shield mounting bolts and nuts.
7. Remove fuel bundle shield pin-type retainer.
8. Release four mounting nuts and fuel bundle shield. **Nuts are encapsulated as part of fuel bundle shield and should only be removed as part of shield.**
9. Disconnect fuel tube quick connect couplings from both sides of fuel filter.
10. Release bracket mounting bolt and remove fuel filter.
11. Reverse procedure to install.

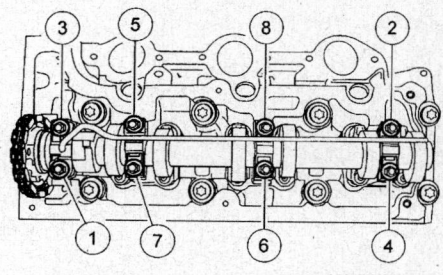

Fig. 16 Camshaft bearing cap remove sequence

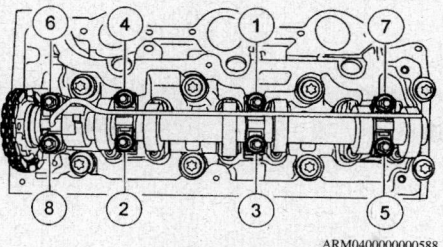

Fig. 17 Camshaft tightening sequence

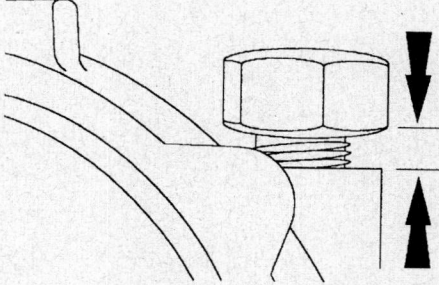

Fig. 18 Connecting rod nut removal

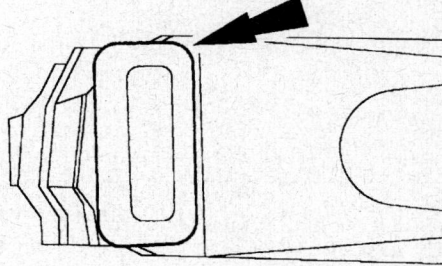

Fig. 19 Connecting rod bolt installation

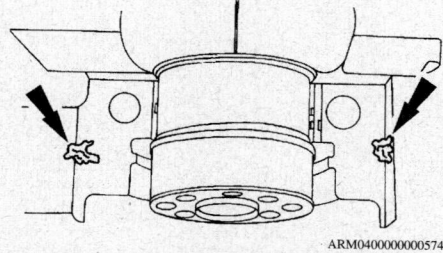

Fig. 20 Cylinder block sealant

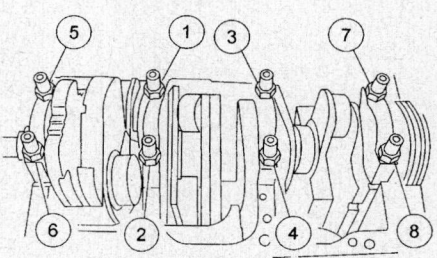

Fig. 21 Main bearing cap tightening sequence

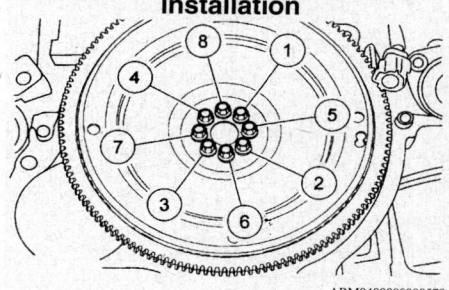

Fig. 22 Flexplate/flywheel tightening sequence

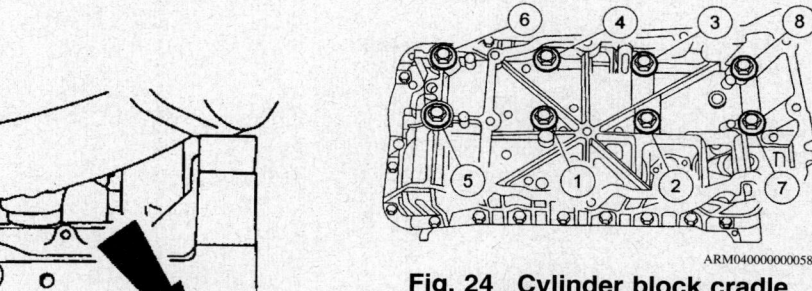

Fig. 24 Cylinder block cradle tightening sequence

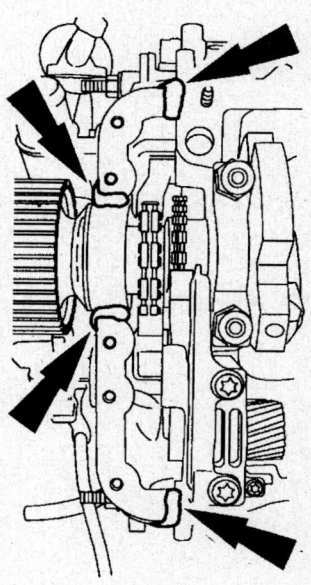

Fig. 23 Engine cradle silicone application (Part 1 of 2)

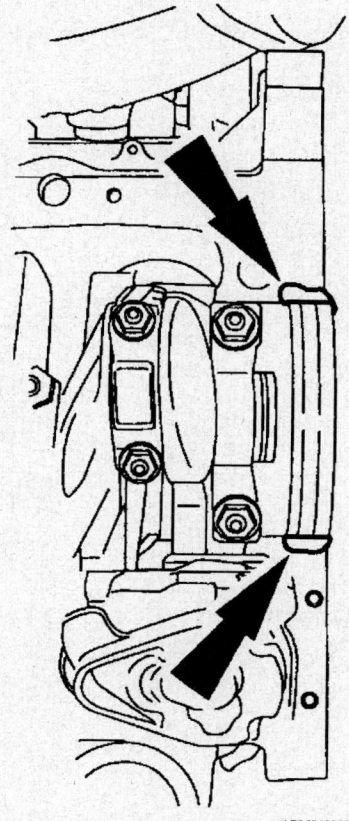

Fig. 23 Engine cradle silicone application (Part 2 of 2)

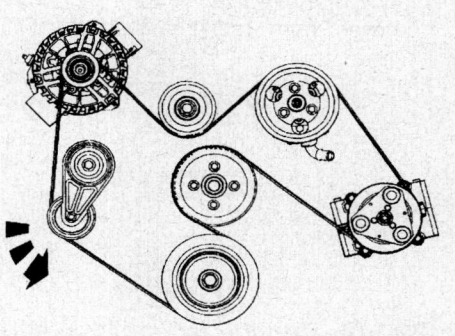

Fig. 25 Serpentine drive belt routing

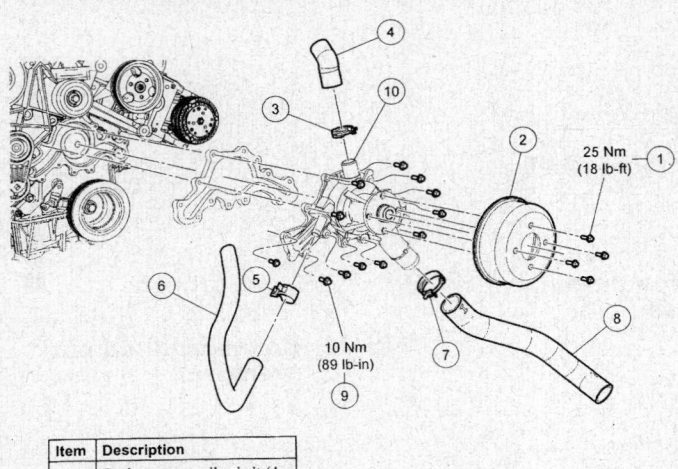

Item	Description
1	Coolant pump pulley bolt (4 required)
2	Coolant pump pulley
3	Hose clamp
4	Thermostat housing-to-coolant pump hose
5	Hose clamp
6	Heater hose
7	Hose clamp
8	Radiator-to-coolant pump hose
9	Coolant pump bolts (12 required)
10	Coolant pump

ARM0400000000593

Fig. 26　Water pump replacement

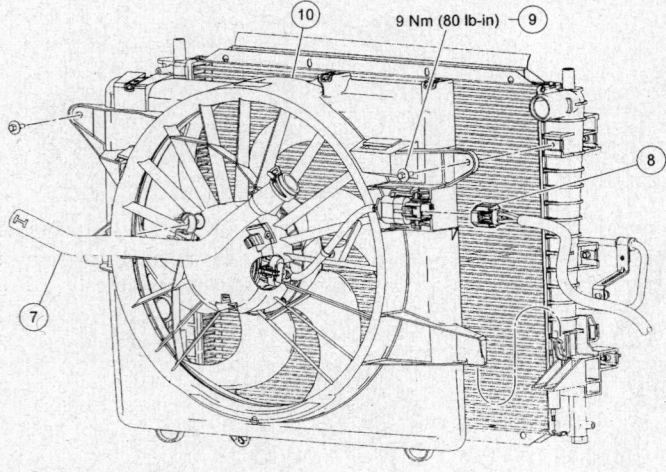

Item	Description
7	Lower degas bottle hose
8	Cooling fan motor and shroud electrical connector
9	Cooling fan motor and shroud bolt (2 required)
10	Cooling fan motor and shroud

ARM0400000000560

Fig. 28　Cooling fan motor & shroud replacement

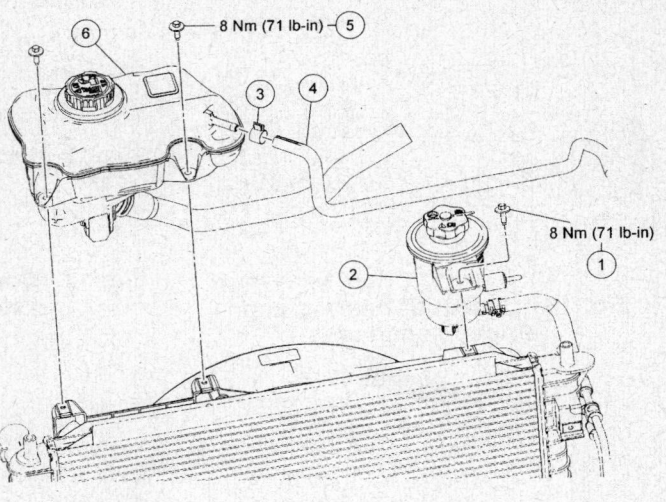

Item	Description	Item	Description
1	Power steering reservoir bolt	4	Upper degas bottle hose
2	Power steering reservoir	5	Degas bottle bolt (2 required)
3	Upper degas bottle hose clamp	6	Degas bottle

ARM0400000000559

Fig. 27　Degas bottle replacement

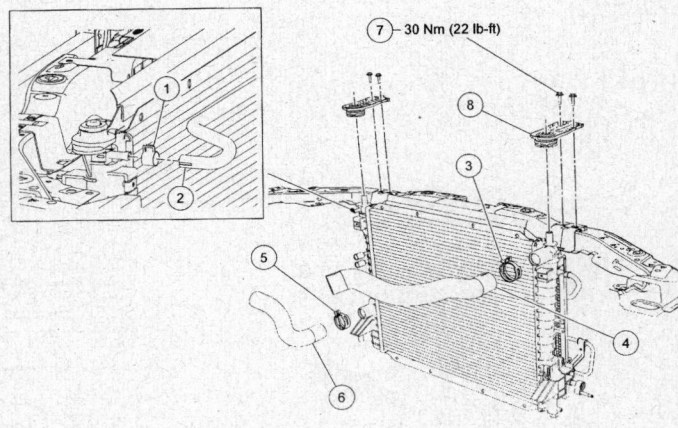

Item	Description	Item	Description
1	Hose clamp	6	Lower radiator hose
2	Degas bottle-to-radiator hose	7	Radiator support bracket bolt (4 required)
3	Hose clamp	8	Radiator support bracket (2 required)
4	Upper radiator hose		
5	Hose clamp		

ARM0400000000557

Fig. 29　Radiator replace (Part 1 of 2)

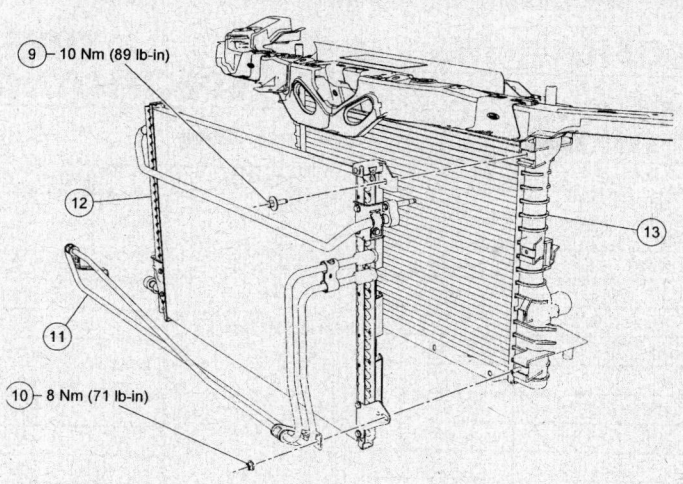

Item	Description
9	A/C condenser bolt (2 required)
10	Power steering tubes and A/C condenser retaining nut (2 required)
11	Power steering tubes
12	A/C condenser
13	Radiator

ARM0400000000558

Fig. 29 Radiator replace (Part 2 of 2)

MUSTANG

TIGHTENING SPECIFICATIONS

Year	Component	Torque/Ft. Lbs.
2005–07	Accessory Drive Belt Idler Pulley	35
	Air Cleaner Outlet Pipe	27①
	Air Conditioning Condenser	89①
	Alternator	35
	Balance Shaft	20
	Balance Shaft Chain Guide.	89①
	Balance Shaft Tensioner	21
	Belt Tensioner	35
	Camshaft	⑦
	Camshaft Cassette, Lefthand Lower	106①
	Camshaft Cassette, Lefthand Upper	14①
	Camshaft Cassette, Righthand	89①
	Camshaft Sprocket	63
	Camshaft Sprocket Holding Tool	89①
	Camshaft Tensioner	32
	Catalytic Converter-To-Exhaust Manifold	30
	Connecting Rod	④
	Cooling Fan Motor & Shroud	80①
	Crankshaft Damper	②
	Crankshaft Position (CKP) Sensor	89①
	Cylinder Block Cradle	⑥
	Cylinder Head	⑩
	EGR System Module Tube	29
	Engine Lifting Bracket	35
	Engine Mount	52
	Engine Mount Bracket	57
	Engine Mount Bracket-To-Engine	46
	Exhaust Gas Recirculation (EGR) System Module Tube	29
	Exhaust Manifold	17
	Flexplate/Flywheel	⑤
	Front Cassette	14
	Front Cover	14
	Front End Accessory Drive (FEAD) Bracket	35
	Fuel Bundle Shield	62①
	Fuel Filter	44①
	Fuel Rail	17
	Fuel Rail Supply Tube Bracket, Lower	89①
	Fuel Rail Supply Tube Bracket, Upper	53①
	Ignition Coil & Bracket, M8	18
	Ignition Coil & Bracket, M12	25

TIGHTENING SPECIFICATIONS—Continued

Year	Component	Torque/Ft. Lbs.
2005–07	Ignition Coil Bracket Upper	89①
	Intake Manifold	89①
	Jackshaft	⑨
	Jackshaft Cassette, Righthand	107①
	Jackshaft Chain Guide	14
	Jackshaft Chain Tensioner	89①
	Jackshaft Rear Sprocket	15⑧
	Jackshaft Thrust Plate	97①
	Knock Sensor	15
	Main Bearings	③
	Main Engine Wiring Harness	30
	Oil Dipstick Tube	97①
	Oil Filter Adapter	42
	Oil Pan	80①
	Oil Pan Drain Plug	19
	Oil Pump	15
	Oil Pump Drive	14
	Oil Pump Intermediate Shaft	14
	Oil Pump Screen & Pickup Tube	97①
	Power Steering Reservoir	71①
	Radiator Support Bracket	22
	Steering Gear	86
	Steering Column Intermediate Shaft	18
	Thermostat Housing	89①
	Throttle Body	89①
	Timing Chain Tensioner, Primary	80①
	Water Pump	89①
	Water Pump Pulley	18

① — Inch pounds.
② — Refer to "Crankshaft Damper, Replace" for tightening specifications and sequence.
③ — Refer to "Main & Rod Bearings" for tightening specifications and sequence.
④ — Refer to "Piston & Rod Assembly" for tightening specifications and sequence.
⑤ — Refer to "Crankshaft Rear Oil Seal, Replace" for tightening specifications and sequence.
⑥ — Refer to "Oil Pump, Replace" for tightening specifications and sequence.
⑦ — Refer to "Camshaft, Replace" for tightening specifications and sequence.
⑧ — Tighten an additional 90°.
⑨ — Refer to "Timing Chain, Replace" for tightening specifications and sequence.
⑩ — Refer to "Cylinder Head, Replace" for tightening specifications and sequence.

4.6L DOHC Engine

NOTE: For Procedures Not Found In This Section, Refer To "4.6L DOHC Engine" Section In "Continental" Chapter.

NOTE: On Air Bag Equipped Models, Refer To "Air Bag System Precautions" Located In The Front Of This Manual For System Disarming & Arming Procedures.

NOTE: Refer To "Computer Relearn Procedures" Located In The Front Of This Manual When Battery Power To The Computer Has Been Interrupted.

NOTE: Prior To Performing Any Service Operations Listed In This Section, Consult The "Technical Service Bulletins" Section For Related Information.

INDEX

	Page No.
Belt Tension Data	4-42
Camshaft, Replace	4-41
Camshaft Lobe Lift Specifications	4-40
Compression Pressure	4-38
Cooling System Bleed	4-43
Crankshaft Seal, Replace	4-42
Cylinder Head, Replace	4-39
Engine Rebuilding Specifications	21-1
Engine, Replace	4-38
Engine Mount, Replace	4-38
Exhaust Manifold, Replace	4-39
Lefthand	4-39
Righthand	4-39
Front Cover, Replace	4-40
Front Cover Seal, Replace	4-40
Fuel Filter, Replace	4-43
Fuel Pump, Replace	4-43
Intake Manifold, Replace	4-38
Lower	4-39
Upper	4-38
Main & Rod Bearings	4-42
Less Supercharger	4-42
With Supercharger	4-42
Oil Pan, Replace	4-42
Oil Pump, Replace	4-42
Piston & Rod Assembly	4-42
Precautions	4-37
Air Bag Systems	4-37
Battery Ground Cable	4-37
Fuel System Pressure Relief	4-37
2004	4-37
2005–08	4-37
Quick Disconnect Hoses	4-37
R-Clip	4-37
Spring Lock	4-38
Vapor Tube	4-38
Radiator, Replace	4-43
Serpentine Drive Belt	4-42
Installation	4-43
Removal	4-42
Routing	4-43
Supercharger, Replace	4-43
Thermostat, Replace	4-43
Tightening Specifications	4-45
Timing Chain, Replace	4-41
Installation	4-41
Removal	4-41
Timing Chain Tensioner Bleed	4-41
Valve Adjustment	4-40
Valve Cover, Replace	4-39
Lefthand	4-39
Righthand	4-40
Water Pump, Replace	4-43

PRECAUTIONS

Air Bag Systems

Refer to "Air Bag System Precautions" in front of this manual for system disarming and arming procedures.

Battery Ground Cable

Prior to service, disconnect battery ground cable and isolate as required.

Fuel System Pressure Relief

2004

Fuel supply tubes will remain pressurized for long periods of time after engine shutdown. This pressure must be relieved before beginning fuel system service or personal injury or damage to vehicle may occur. A valve is provided on fuel injection supply manifold for this purpose.

1. Connect EFI/CFI fuel pressure gauge tool No. T80L-9974-B, or equivalent, to fuel pressure relief valve on fuel injection supply manifold.
2. Place outlet hose of tool into suitable fuel container.
3. Open manual valve on fuel pressure gauge tool to relieve fuel system pressure.

2005–08

1. Remove fuel pump relay.
2. Start engine, then allow engine to idle until it stalls.
3. After engine stalls, crank engine for approximately 5 seconds to ensure fuel injection supply manifold pressure has been released.
4. When fuel system service is complete, install fuel pump relay.
5. Cycle ignition key and wait 3 seconds to pressurize fuel system. Inspect for leaks before starting engine.

Quick Disconnect Hoses

R-CLIP

When working with R-clip type connections, do not use tools to disconnect. Use of tools may deform clip components and could cause leaks.

DISCONNECT

1. Bend shipping tab downward.
2. Spread R-clip and push clip into fitting.
3. Separate fitting from tube.

CONNECT

1. Inspect fitting and tube for damage and ensure connections are clean.
2. Apply light coat of suitable, clean engine oil to male end of tube.
3. Insert R-clip into fitting.
4. Align tube and fitting, then insert tube into fitting and push together until click is heard.
5. Pull on connection to ensure it is fully engaged.

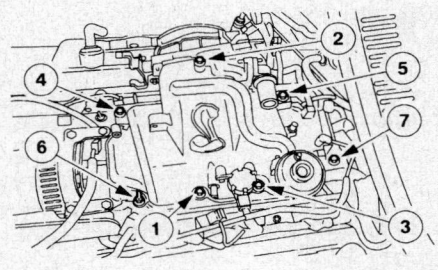

Fig. 1 Upper intake manifold bolt tightening sequence

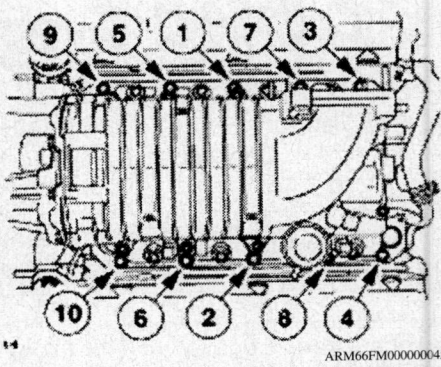

Fig. 2 Lower intake manifold tightening sequence

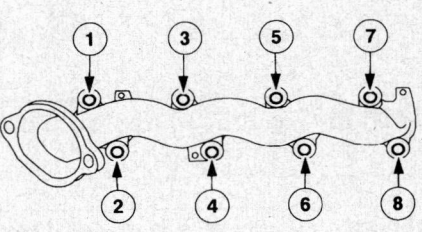

Fig. 3 Righthand exhaust manifold nut tightening sequence

SPRING LOCK

When working with spring lock type connections, spring lock tool set No. T84L-19623-B, or equivalent, must be used to disconnect fittings.

When connecting spring lock type fittings, proceed as follows:
1. Inspect and clean both coupling ends.
2. Lubricate fuel line O-ring seals with suitable, clean engine oil.
3. When connection is made, pull on line to ensure it is fully engaged.

VAPOR TUBE

To disconnect vapor tube connections, squeeze fitting and disconnect vapor tube from fitting.

To connect, proceed as follows:
1. Ensure fittings are clean and free from damage.
2. Push tube onto fitting until it snaps into place.
3. Pull on connection to verify fitting is secure.

COMPRESSION PRESSURE

When inspecting cylinder compression, lowest cylinder must be within 75% of highest cylinder. Perform compression test with engine at normal operating temperature, spark plugs and air cleaner removed and the throttle propped wide open.

ENGINE MOUNT

REPLACE

1. Install lift bracket tool No. D93P-6001-A3, or equivalent.
2. Install engine support tool No. 303-290-A, or equivalent.
3. Raise and support vehicle.
4. Remove solenoid protective cap and wiring nuts. Position wiring aside.
5. Remove mounting bolts and starter motor.
6. Remove engine mount nuts and lower vehicle.
7. Raise engine using support tool.
8. Raise vehicle and remove engine mount.
9. Reverse procedure to install.

ENGINE

REPLACE

1. Drain coolant into suitable container.

2. Recover air conditioning refrigerant as outlined in "Air Conditioning" chapter.
3. Remove air cleaner and outlet tube.
4. Relieve fuel system pressure as outlined under "Precautions."
5. Disconnect fuel lines.
6. Remove radiator upper hose.
7. Disconnect throttle and speed control cables, then the return spring.
8. Remove bracket mounting bolts, then the throttle and speed control cables aside.
9. Disconnect EVAP emissions return line.
10. Disconnect 16- and 42-pin electrical connectors.
11. Separate wiring harness at three firewall locations.
12. Disconnect TBI electrical connectors.
13. Disconnect HVAC vacuum supply hoses.
14. Place suitable container firewall fittings and disconnect heater hoses.
15. Remove nuts and wiring support bracket.
16. Disconnect electrical connectors near underhood power distribution box.
17. Slide underhood power distribution box access cover up, then remove nut and battery cables.
18. Disconnect low coolant sensor electrical connector.
19. Disconnect coolant hose at bypass tube.
20. Remove transmission shift lever knob.
21. Remove console panel shifter plate. Lift boot over lever.
22. Remove mounting bolts and shift lever.
23. Remove mounting screws inner boot.
24. Remove four mounting bolts and shifter.
25. Raise and support vehicle.
26. Remove front wheels and tires assemblies.
27. Disconnect front wheel speed sensor electrical connectors.
28. Remove mounting bolts and position front brake caliper aside with suitable wire or rope.
29. Remove mounting fasteners and three-way catalytic converter.
30. Disconnect air conditioning compressor inlet and outlet lines.
31. Position air conditioning muffler aside.
32. Raise and support vehicle.
33. Remove solenoid protective cap and

wiring nuts. Position wiring aside.
34. Remove mounting bolts and starter motor.
35. Position wiring harness at front of engine aside.
36. Disconnect engine oil pressure sensor electrical connector.
37. Remove mounting nut and engine power ground cable.
38. Disconnect hose oil filter adapter.
39. Remove radiator lower hose.
40. Disconnect clutch cable at transmission.
41. Disconnect power steering high pressure line.
42. Disconnect lower power steering line from fluid cooler.
43. Disconnect hose at power steering fluid reservoir.
44. Remove mounting bolt and power steering pump anti-rotation clip.
45. Disconnect power steering pump high pressure line fitting.
46. Separate steering shaft from steering gear, discarding bolt.
47. Remove pin-style retainers, then position lefthand and righthand splash shields aside.
48. Remove stabilizer bar clamp nuts.
49. Remove mounting bolts and inspection cover.
50. Remove exhaust air supply valve tube nuts at exhaust manifolds.
51. Position universal powertrain lift and extension.
52. Mark crossmember for installation alignment.
53. Remove crossmember to body and frame bolts.
54. Remove engine and transmission.
55. Install engine righthand lifting bracket tool No. D93P-6001-A1 and lefthand lifting bracket tool No. D93P-6002-A2, or equivalents.
56. Install suitable engine lifting crane.
57. Remove motor mount nuts.
58. Disconnect transmission wiring.
59. Remove transmission to engine bolts.
60. Raise and separate engine from front A-frame.
61. Reverse procedure to install.

INTAKE MANIFOLD

REPLACE

Upper

1. Remove air cleaner outlet tube.

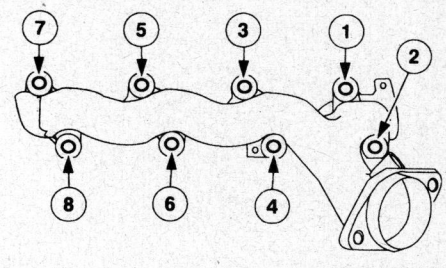

Fig. 4 Lefthand exhaust manifold nut tightening sequence

2. Disconnect accelerator and speed control cables, then the return spring.
3. Remove accelerator and speed control cable bracket bolts, then position cables aside.
4. Disconnect TPS electrical connector.
5. Disconnect EVAP emissions return hose.
6. Disconnect idle air control (IAC) valve electrical connector.
7. Disconnect differential pressure feedback EGR.
8. Disconnect main vacuum supply and EGR vacuum lines.
9. Disconnect differential pressure feedback EGR hoses.
10. Disconnect EGR valve to exhaust tube from EGR valve.
11. Disconnect EGR vacuum regulator solenoid vacuum lines and electrical connector.
12. Remove PCV valve and tube.
13. Remove upper intake manifold mounting bolts in sequence, **Fig. 1.**
14. Remove upper intake manifold. Discard gasket.
15. Reverse procedure to install, noting the following:
   a. Install new upper to lower intake gasket.
   b. **Torque** upper intake manifold mounting bolts in sequence to 89 inch lbs., **Fig. 1.**

Lower

1. Drain engine and supercharger coolant into suitable container.
2. Relieve fuel system pressure as outlined under "Precautions."
3. Disconnect radiator upper and lower hoses, then the supercharger degas hose.
4. Remove supercharger drive belt.
5. Disconnect coolant hose.
6. Remove air cleaner outlet tube.
7. Disconnect throttle position (TP) sensor and idle air control (IAC) valve electrical connectors.
8. Disconnect vacuum hoses from lower intake manifold.
9. Disconnect fuel hose spring lock coupling.
10. Disconnect accelerator and speed control cables.
11. Remove accelerator cable bracket bolts, then release clip and position bracket and cables aside.
12. Disconnect electrical connector from fuel pulse damper, EGR regulator so-

lenoid, super charger bypass vacuum solenoid and differential pressure feedback EGR system.
13. Disconnect vacuum hoses from differential pressure feedback EGR system.
14. Disconnect vacuum hoses from supercharger bypass vacuum solenoid and actuator.
15. Disconnect vacuum hoses from fuel pulse damper and EGR vacuum regulator solenoid.
16. Disconnect vacuum hoses from back of supercharger and position aside.
17. Remove mounting bolts and vacuum accessory bracket.
18. Disconnect exhaust manifold to EGR valve tube.
19. Disconnect barometric pressure sensor electrical connector and PCV ventilation hose.
20. Separate fuel charging wiring harness from fuel injection supply manifold in four places and position aside.
21. Remove ten mounting bolts, then the lower intake manifold, supercharger and fuel supply manifold as an assembly.
22. Reverse procedure to install, noting the following:
   a. Install new bypass tube O-rings and lubricate them with clean engine oil.
   b. Tighten intake manifold bolts in sequence, **Fig. 2.**

EXHAUST MANIFOLD
REPLACE
RIGHTHAND

1. Raise and support vehicle, then remove dual converter Y-pipe.
2. Remove solenoid protective cap and wiring nuts. Position wiring aside.
3. Remove mounting bolts and starter motor.
4. Remove mounting nuts and exhaust manifold.
5. Reverse procedure to install with new exhaust manifold gasket. **Torque** mounting nuts in sequence to 18 ft. lbs., **Fig. 3.**

LEFTHAND

1. Position steering wheel straight ahead and lock.
2. Raise and support vehicle, then remove dual converter Y-pipe.
3. Remove and discard steering pinch bolt, then separate steering coupler.
4. Disconnect EGR tube at exhaust manifold.
5. Remove oil dipstick tube.
6. Remove mounting nuts and exhaust manifold.
7. Reverse procedure to install with new exhaust manifold gasket. **Torque** mounting nuts in sequence to 18 ft. lbs., **Fig. 4.**

CYLINDER HEAD
REPLACE

1. Remove intake manifold as outlined under "Intake Manifold, Replace."

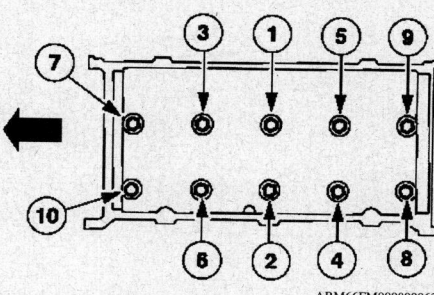

Fig. 5 Cylinder head tightening sequence

2. Remove valve covers as outlined under "Valve Covers, Replace."
3. Remove exhaust manifolds as outlined under "Exhaust Manifold, Replace."
4. Remove timing chains as outlined under "Timing Chain, Replace."
5. Remove mounting bolts and cylinder head.
6. Reverse procedure to install, noting the following:
   a. Lubricate cylinder head bolts and threads with clean engine oil.
   b. **Torque** cylinder head bolts in sequence to 30 ft. lbs., **Fig. 5.**
   c. Tighten bolts an additional 90° in sequence.
   d. Loosen bolts at least of one full turn.
   e. **Torque** bolts in sequence to 30 ft. lbs.
   f. Tighten bolts an additional 90° in sequence.
   g. Tighten bolts an additional 90° in sequence.

VALVE COVER
REPLACE
Lefthand

1. Turn engine off and depress brake pedal several times.
2. Disconnect brake fluid level sensor electrical connector.
3. Position suitable drain pan and disconnect brake fluid lines on lower side of master cylinder.
4. Position suitable drain pan and disconnect power steering fluid return line hose.
5. Disconnect power steering pressure lines at hydro-booster. Discard Teflon seals.
6. Remove self-locking pin in hydro-booster linkage.
7. Remove stop lamp switch and hydro-booster pushrod from brake pedal pin.
8. Remove hydro-booster mounting nuts at firewall.
9. Remove brake hydro-booster unit.
10. Remove lefthand ignition coils.
11. Unclip wiring harness from power steering bracket.
12. Disconnect electrical connectors from fuel pulse damper, EGR vacuum regulator solenoid, supercharger bypass vacuum solenoid and differential pressure feedback EGR system.

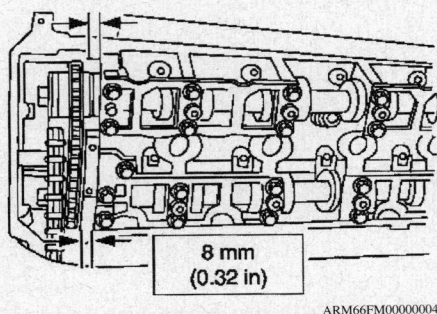

Fig. 6   Sealant application

13. Disconnect vacuum hoses from differential pressure feedback EGR system.
14. Disconnect vacuum hoses from supercharger bypass vacuum solenoid and actuator.
15. Disconnect vacuum hoses from fuel pulse damper and EGR vacuum regulator solenoid, then position vacuum harness aside.
16. Remove mounting bolts and vacuum accessory bracket.
17. Disconnect camshaft position (CMP) sensor electrical connector.
18. Remove mounting bolts and position power steering reservoir aside.
19. Remove mounting bolt and position oil dipstick tube aside.
20. Disconnect PCV valve and position aside.
21. Remove mounting bolts and valve cover.
22. Reverse procedure to install, noting the following:
   a. Apply bead of silicone gasket and sealant No. F7AZ-19554-EA, or equivalent, **Fig. 6**.
   b. **Install and tighten cover and mounting bolts within four minutes.**
   c. **Torque** valve cover bolts and studs in sequence to 89 inch lbs., **Fig. 7**.

Righthand

1. Remove righthand ignition coils.
2. Remove air conditioning condenser to evaporator tube.
3. Remove air conditioning manifold and tube.
4. Disconnect throttle position sensor and idle air control (IAC) valve electrical connectors.
5. Disconnect fuel hose spring lock coupling.
6. Disconnect accelerator and speed control cables.
7. Remove accelerator cable bracket bolts, then release clip and position bracket and cables aside.
8. Remove throttle body and spacer.
9. Remove mounting bolts and valve cover.
10. Reverse procedure to install, noting the following:
   a. Apply bead of silicone gasket and sealant No. F7AZ-19554-EA, or equivalent, **Fig. 6**.
   b. **Install and tighten cover and mounting bolts within four minutes.**
   c. **Torque** valve cover bolts and studs in sequence to 89 inch lbs., **Fig. 7**.

CAMSHAFT LOBE LIFT SPECIFICATIONS

Engine	Intake, Inch	Exhaust, Inch
4.6L DOHC	.2200	.2186

VALVE ADJUSTMENT

These engine are equipped with hydraulic valve lash adjusters. No valve adjustment is required.

FRONT COVER
REPLACE

1. Remove front seal as outlined under "Front Cover Seal, Replace."
2. Remove oil filter adapter.
3. Remove mounting bolts and position power steering pump aside.
4. Remove air conditioning muffler bracket nut.
5. Remove mounting bolts and position air conditioning compressor aside.
6. Disconnect crankshaft position sensor electrical connector.
7. Remove four front oil pan bolts.
8. Disconnect alternator electrical connectors.
9. Remove mounting bolts and alternator.
10. Remove alternator support bracket.
11. Drain coolant into suitable container.
12. Remove coolant bypass tube.
13. Remove valve covers as outlined under "Valve Cover, Replace."
14. Disconnect supercharger coolant hose and remove coolant hose mounting bolt.
15. Disconnect supercharger coolant hoses, then remove supercharger hose and tube.
16. Disconnect camshaft position sensor electrical connector and unclip wiring harness from power steering bracket.
17. Disconnect power steering hoses and drain power steering fluid into suitable container.
18. Remove mounting bolts and power steering reservoir.
19. Remove mounting nut and position power steering hose aside.
20. Remove mounting bolts and supercharger belt idler support bracket.
21. Remove wiring harness bracket.
22. Remove water pump pulley.
23. Remove mounting bolts and engine front cover.
24. Reverse procedure to install, noting the following:
   a. Apply silicone gasket sealer part No. F7AZ-19554-EA, or equivalent, **Fig. 8**.
   b. Ensure front cover bolts and studs are installed in original locations, **Fig. 9**.
   c. Tighten front cover bolts in sequence, **Fig. 9**.

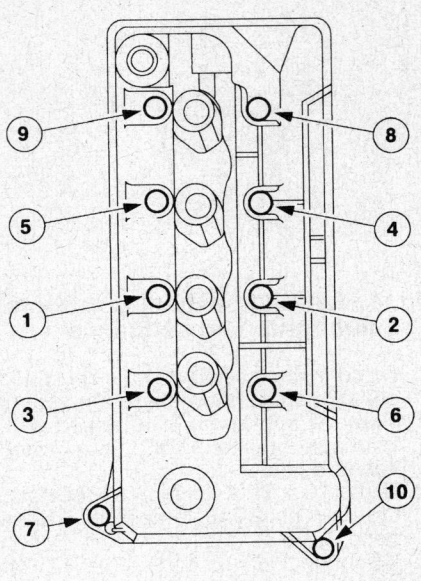

Fig. 7   Valve cover bolt tightening sequence

   d. **Torque** oil pan front bolts in sequence, to 18 inch lbs., **Fig. 10**.
   e. **Torque** pan front bolts in sequence to 15 ft. lbs.
   f. Tighten front bolts an additional 60° in sequence.

FRONT COVER SEAL
REPLACE

1. Remove cooling fan and supercharger drive belt.
2. Remove coolant hose bolt.
3. Raise and support vehicle.
4. Remove solenoid protective cap and wiring nuts. Position wiring aside.
5. Remove mounting bolts and starter motor.
6. Install flywheel lock tool No. 303-673, or equivalent.
7. Remove mounting bolts and alternator support bracket.
8. Remove stud and position coolant hose aside.
9. Remove auxiliary crankshaft pulley. Auxiliary crankshaft pulley is lefthand threaded.
10. Insert suitable square drive tool into square hole in tensioner arm and rotate tensioner away from belt.
11. Lift belt from pulley and slowly release tensioner.
12. Remove belt.
13. Remove crankshaft pulley using crankshaft vibration damper remover tool No. T58P-6316-D, or equivalent.
14. Remove front seal using front seal remover tool No. T74P-6700-A, or equivalent.
15. Reverse procedure to install, noting the following:
   a. Lubricate engine front cover and front seal with clean engine oil.
   b. Install front seal using seal installer tool No. T88T-6701-A, or equivalent.

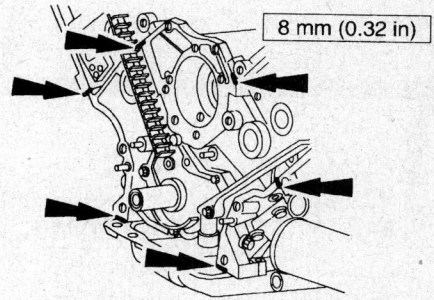

FM1069901063000X

Fig. 8 Front cover sealant application locations

c. Apply suitable sealant to Woodriff key slot on crankshaft pulley.
d. Install crankshaft pulley using crankshaft vibration damper installer tool No. T74P-6316-B, or equivalent.
e. **Torque** crankshaft pulley bolt to 66 ft. lbs.
f. Loosen pulley bolt one full turn.
g. **Torque** bolt to 37 ft. lbs.
h. Tighten bolt an additional 85–95°.

TIMING CHAIN
REPLACE

Removal

Unless otherwise instructed, at no time when timing chains are removed and the cylinder heads are installed is the crankshaft or camshaft to be rotated.

1. Remove front cover as outlined under "Front Cover, Replace."
2. Remove crankshaft sensor ring from crankshaft.
3. Install crankshaft holding tool No. T93P-6303-A, or equivalent, **Fig. 11.**
4. Align camshaft timing marks, **Fig. 12.** Copper links on timing chain may not line up with timing marks on sprockets. If required, turn crankshaft one full turn clockwise.
5. Remove two mounting bolts, timing chain tensioner and arm.
6. Remove crankshaft holding tool.
7. Remove righthand timing chain from camshaft and crankshaft sprocket.
8. Remove lefthand timing chain from camshaft and crankshaft sprocket.
9. Remove mounting bolts and timing chain guides. **Bolts are different lengths and must be installed in original locations.**

Installation

1. Compress tensioner plunger using suitable soft jawed vise and install retaining clip to hold plunger.
2. If copper links are not visible, mark links on opposite ends of timing chain to use as timing marks, **Fig. 13.**
3. Install timing chain guides.
4. Rotate lefthand camshaft sprocket

Item	Part Number	Description
1	N806177	Bolt, Hex Flange Head Pilot, M8 x 1.25 x 53
2	N806177	Bolt, Hex Flange Head Pilot, M8 x 1.25 x 53
3	N806177	Bolt, Hex Flange Head Pilot, M8 x 1.25 x 53
4	N806177	Bolt, Hex Flange Head Pilot, M8 x 1.25 x 53
5	N806177	Bolt, Hex Flange Head Pilot, M8 x 1.25 x 53
6	N806300	Stud, Hex Shldr Pilot, M8 x 1.25 x 1.25 x 91.1
7	N806300	Stud, Hex Shldr Pilot, M8 x 1.25 x 1.25 x 91.1
8	N806177	Bolt, Hex Flange Head Pilot, M8 x 1.25 x 53
9	N806177	Bolt, Hex Flange Head Pilot, M8 x 1.25 x 53
10	N806177	Bolt, Hex Flange Head Pilot, M8 x 1.25 x 53
11	N806177	Bolt, Hex Flange Head Pilot, M8 x 1.25 x 53
12	W706560	Stud, Hex Head Pilot, M8 x 1.25 x 65 — M8 x 1.25 x 16
13	N806300	Stud, Hex Shldr Pilot, M8 x 1.25 x 1.25 x 91.1
14	N806300	Stud, Hex Shldr Pilot, M8 x 1.25 x 1.25 x 91.1
15	N806300	Stud, Hex Shldr Pilot, M8 x 1.25 x 1.25 x 91.1

ARM66FM000000047

Fig. 9 Front cover bolt location & tightening sequence

until timing mark is approximately at 12 o'clock position, **Fig. 12.**
5. Rotate righthand camshaft sprocket until timing mark is approximately at 11 o'clock position.
6. Install crankshaft holding tool No. T93P-6303-A, or equivalent, to position crankshaft. **Fig. 11.**
7. Remove crankshaft holding tool.
8. Install crankshaft sprocket with flange facing forward, **Fig. 14.**
9. Install lefthand timing chain onto crankshaft sprocket, aligning one copper link on timing chain with slot on crankshaft sprocket.
10. Install righthand timing chain onto crankshaft sprocket, aligning one copper link on timing chain with slot on crankshaft sprocket.
11. Ensure camshaft sprockets and timing chain copper links are aligned.
12. Install timing chain tensioners and arms.
13. Remove retaining clips from timing chain tensioners.
14. Install crankshaft sensor ring on crankshaft.
15. Install engine front cover as outlined under "Front Cover, Replace."

TIMING CHAIN TENSIONER BLEED

1. Position timing chain tensioner in suitable soft-jawed vise.
2. Lock ratchet stem mechanism position using suitable tool and slowly compress tensioner plunger by rotating vise handle. **Tensioner must be compressed slowly.**

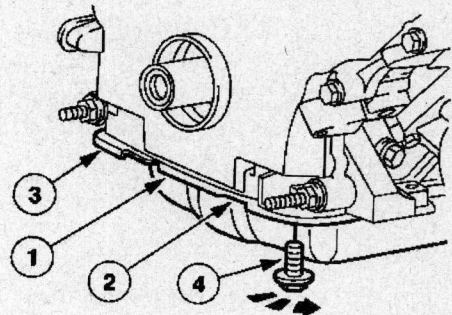

ARM66FM000000048

Fig. 10 Oil pan front bolts tightening sequence

3. When tensioner plunger bottoms in bore, continue holding ratchet lock mechanism and push ratchet mechanism down until flush with tensioner face.
4. While holding ratchet stem flush to tensioner face, release ratchet lock mechanism and install paper clip or suitable tool to lock tensioner in collapsed position.
5. **Do not remove paper clip or suitable tool until timing chain, tensioner arm, tensioner and timing chain guide are installed on engine.**

CAMSHAFT
REPLACE

1. Remove valve covers as outlined under "Valve Cover, Replace."
2. Position piston being worked on at bottom of stroke and camshaft lobe at base of circle.
3. Compress valve spring and remove roller followers using valve spring compressor tool No. T93P-6565-AR, or equivalent.
4. Remove timing chains as outlined under "Timing Chain, Replace."
5. Install camshaft holding tool No. T93P-6256-AHR, or equivalent.
6. Remove exhaust camshaft sprocket, then the intake camshaft bolt, washer and spacer.
7. Remove camshaft holding tool.
8. Compress chain tensioner and install suitable lock pin.
9. Remove chain, sprocket and intake camshaft sprocket spacer.
10. Remove chain tensioner bolts.
11. Remove bolts and camshaft bearings. Identify cap locations for installation alignment. **Outer exhaust cam bearing cap bolts are longer and must be installed in original location or engine damage may occur.**
12. Remove camshafts.
13. Reverse procedure to install, noting the following:
    a. Lubricate camshafts with clean engine oil.
    b. Tighten camshaft bearing caps in sequence to 89 inch lbs., **Fig. 15.**
    c. Install camshaft sprockets and chain as an assembly.
    d. Align timing marks to 12 o'clock position and index at 6 o'clock position, **Fig. 16.**

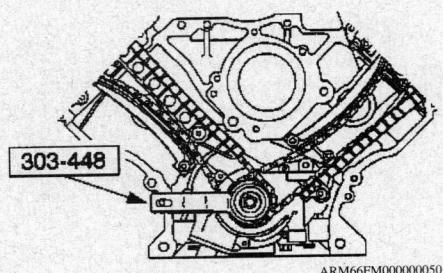

Fig. 11 Crankshaft holding tool installation

ARM66FM000000050

e. **Torque** camshaft sprocket bolt to 30 ft. lbs., then tighten an additional 90°.

PISTON & ROD ASSEMBLY

1. Rod bearing cap bolts are torque-to-yield bolts, do not reuse bolts.
2. Install connecting rod to piston with marks facing toward front of engine.
3. Install piston with arrow facing toward front of engine.
4. **Torque** connecting rod bearing cap bolts to 18 ft. lbs.
5. **On models equipped less supercharger, torque** cap bolts to 33 ft. lbs.
6. **On models equipped with supercharger, torque** cap bolts to 59 ft. lbs.
7. **On all models,** final tighten bolts an additional 90°.

MAIN & ROD BEARINGS

LESS SUPERCHARGER

1. **Torque** main bearing bolts in sequence to 89 inch lbs., **Fig. 17.**
2. **Torque** bearing bolts in sequence. to 18 ft. lbs.
3. **Torque** bolts in sequence to 30 ft. lbs.
4. Final tighten bolts an additional 90° in sequence.
5. **Torque** side bolts to 30 ft. lbs., then tighten an additional 90°.

WITH SUPERCHARGER

1. **Torque** vertical main bearing cap bolts in sequence to 30 ft. lbs., **Fig. 18.**
2. Tighten bolts an additional 85–95° in sequence.
3. **Torque** jackscrews against cylinder block in sequence to 44 inch lbs., **Fig. 19.**
4. **Torque** jackscrews against cylinder block in sequence to 89 inch lbs.
5. **Torque** main bearing cap side bolts in sequence to 15 ft. lbs., **Fig. 20.**

CRANKSHAFT SEAL

REPLACE

1. Remove transmission as outlined in **MOTOR's "Domestic Transmission, In-Vehicle Service." or "Transmission Service DVD."**
2. Remove flywheel.
3. Remove crankshaft oil slinger using

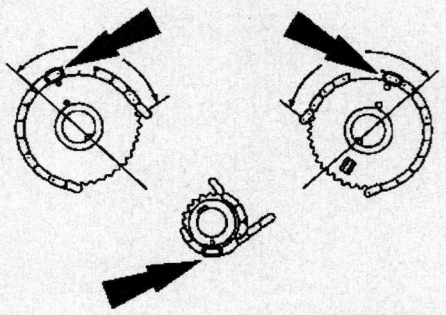

ARM66FM000000051

Fig. 12 Camshaft timing marks

rear crankshaft slinger remover tool No. T-95P-6701-AH, or equivalent, and suitable slide hammer.
4. Remove crankshaft rear oil seal using rear crankshaft seal remover tool No. T95P-6701-BH, or equivalent, and suitable slide hammer.
5. Reverse procedure to install, noting the following:
   a. Install rear oil seal using crankshaft seal replacer tool No. T-95P-6701-AH and rear crankshaft seal adapter tool No. T-95P-6701-DH, or equivalents.
   b. With rear crankshaft seal adapter still installed, use rear crankshaft slinger replacer and rear crankshaft seal replacer to install crankshaft oil slinger.

OIL PAN

REPLACE

1. Remove transmission.
2. Remove air cleaner outlet tube and radiator sight shield.
3. Remove accumulator to compressor manifold and tube.
4. Remove air conditioning line.
5. Install engine support tool No. 303-F072, or equivalent.
6. Raise and support vehicle.
7. Remove lefthand and righthand engine mount nuts, then lower vehicle.
8. Raise engine 2.5 inches using engine support tool.
9. Raise and support vehicle, then drain engine oil into suitable container.
10. Compress coil springs using coil spring compressor tool No. D78P-5310-A, or equivalent.
11. Position suitable jack stand under subframe.
12. Loosen but do not remove subframe bolts.
13. Lower subframe and remove brace.
14. Remove mounting nuts and position starter wiring harness aside.
15. Remove mounting bolts and oil pan.
16. Reverse procedure to install, noting the following:
    a. Apply silicone gasket sealant No. F7AZ-19554-EA, or equivalent, to rear oil seal retainer to block sealing surface and at front cover to block mating surface.
    b. **Install and tighten cover and mounting bolts within four minutes.**

ARM66FM000000052

Fig. 13 Timing chain timing marks

c. Move oil pan into position and loosely install bolts.
d. **Torque** oil pan bolts in sequence to 18 inch lbs., **Fig. 21.**
e. **Torque** pan bolts in sequence. to 15 ft. lbs.
f. Final tighten bolts an additional 60° in sequence.

OIL PUMP

REPLACE

This procedure has been revised by a Technical Service Bulletin.

1. Remove valve covers as outlined under "Valve Cover, Replace."
2. Remove front cover as outlined under "Front Engine Cover, Replace."
3. Remove oil pan as outlined under "Oil Pan, Replace."
4. Remove timing chains as outlined under "Timing Chain, Replace."
5. Remove mounting bolts and oil pump.
6. Reverse procedure to install, noting the following:
   a. Align oil pump inner rotor with flat of crankshaft.
   b. Prime oil pump and system prior to starting engine.

BELT TENSION DATA

These models are equipped with an automatic drive belt tensioner. No adjustment or maintenance is required.

SERPENTINE DRIVE BELT

Always use square drive tool in hole in tensioner to move tensioner. Never pry on tensioner pulley. When releasing drive belt tensioner, never allow tensioner to snap back. Damage to tensioner or personal injury could result.

Do not allow engine coolant to remain on serpentine belt or pulleys. If required, remove belt and flush with clean water.

Removal

1. Insert suitable square drive tool into square hole in tensioner arm and rotate tensioner away from belt.
2. Lift belt from pulley and slowly release tensioner.
3. Remove belt.

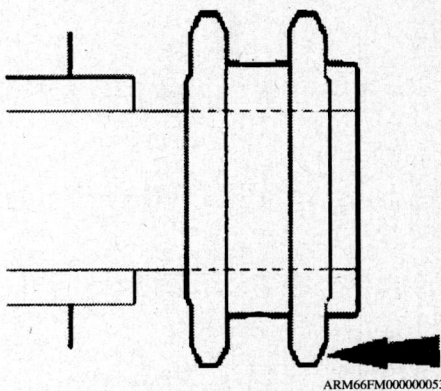

Fig. 14 Crankshaft sprocket installation

Routing

Refer to **Fig. 22** for belt routing.

Installation

1. Route belt.
2. Ensure belt is properly seated in pulley grooves.
3. Insert suitable square drive tool into square hole in tensioner arm and rotate tensioner away from belt.
4. Position belt under tensioner and slowly release tensioner onto belt.

COOLING SYSTEM
BLEED

1. Fill radiator completely full and install radiator cap.
2. Fill coolant reservoir and degas bottle to full cold mark.
3. Set heater control to full hot, high fan and set controls so air vents from dash vents.
4. Start and operate engine until fully warmed up while observing water temperature gauge.
5. If system is functioning properly, temperature will indicate normal and hot air will be felt at dash outlets.
6. If system is not functioning properly, temperature gauge will not read and/or no hot air will be felt at dash vents.
7. If system is not functioning properly, allow engine to cool and repeat procedure.
8. If system is functioning properly, allow engine to cool and fill coolant reservoir to full cold mark.

THERMOSTAT
REPLACE

1. Drain engine coolant into suitable container.
2. Remove thermostat housing bolts.
3. Remove thermostat and O-ring seal.
4. Reverse procedure to install. Thermostat is indexed and must be installed to original position.

WATER PUMP
REPLACE

1. Drain engine coolant into suitable container.
2. **On supercharged models,** remove supercharger drive belt.
3. **On all models,** loosen water pump pulley mounting bolts.
4. Insert suitable square drive tool into square hole in tensioner arm and rotate tensioner away from belt.
5. Lift belt from pulley and slowly release tensioner.
6. Remove belt.
7. Remove mounting bolts, water pump and gasket. Discard gasket.
8. Reverse procedure to install.

RADIATOR
REPLACE

1. Drain coolant from radiator and degas bottle into suitable container.
2. Disconnect cooling fan motor electrical connector and separate fan harness from shroud.
3. Remove fan shroud lefthand and righthand mounting bolts.
4. Remove cooling fan, motor and shroud.
5. Remove radiator sight shield.
6. Disconnect radiator upper hose at radiator.
7. **On models equipped with automatic transmission,** remove lower and upper cooler tube fittings.
8. **On all models,** raise and support vehicle.
9. Disconnect radiator lower hose at radiator. Lower vehicle.
10. Remove supports and radiator.
11. Reverse procedure to install.

FUEL PUMP
REPLACE

1. Relieve fuel system pressure as outlined under "Precautions."
2. Drain fuel from fuel tank into suitable container using draining tool No. 310-F013 and storage tanker tool No. 164-R3202, or equivalents.
3. Raise and support vehicle.
4. Remove filler pipe mounting bolt and disconnect pipe hose connections to tank.
5. Disconnect fuel tank electrical connector.
6. Disconnect vapor tube fitting at lefthand front side of tank.
7. Place suitable jack stand under tank.
8. Remove front two bolts from fuel tank support straps and position lefthand strap aside.
9. Remove righthand rear bolt and support strap.
10. Partially lower tank and disconnect fuel lines using suitable spring lock coupler tools.
11. Cut pipe-to-tank grommet's outer edge and remove grommet.

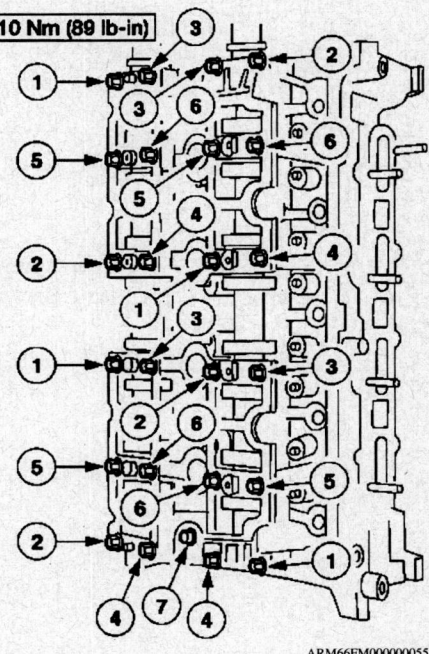

10 Nm (89 lb-in)

Fig. 15 Camshaft bearing cap tightening sequence

12. Lower and remove tank. Move tank to suitable bench.
13. Remove sender unit orientation for installation alignment and remove mounting bolts.
14. Pull sender unit up until locking tabs are accessible. **Avoid damaging filter, float arm, tubing and wiring.**
15. Remove sender by reaching through opening and squeeze locking tabs together.
16. Reverse procedure to install, noting the following:
    a. Install mounting bolts hand tight and tighten in sequence, **Fig. 23.**
    b. Lubricate filler pipe check valve area and new tank-to-filler pipe grommet with Serfactant (Merpol), or equivalent.

FUEL FILTER
REPLACE

1. Relieve fuel system pressure as outlined under "Precautions."
2. Raise and support vehicle.
3. Remove push connector fittings from fuel filter ends using suitable spring lock coupler tools.
4. Loosen worm gear clamp and remove filter from bracket. Record flow arrow to ensure proper direction of fuel flow through filter.
5. Reverse procedure to install using new retainer clips in each fitting.

SUPERCHARGER
REPLACE

Refer to "Intake Manifold, Replace" for supercharger replacement.

Fig. 16 Camshaft sprocket timing marks

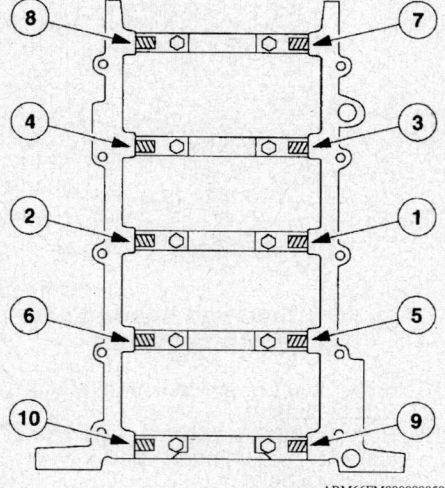

Fig. 19 Jackscrew tightening sequence. Supercharged engines

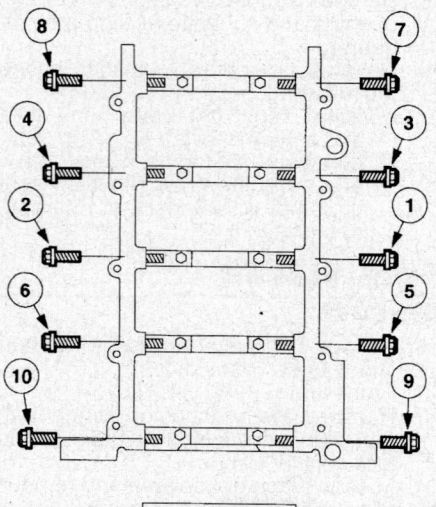

21 Nm (15 lb-ft)

Fig. 20 Main bearing cap side bolt tightening sequence. Supercharged engines

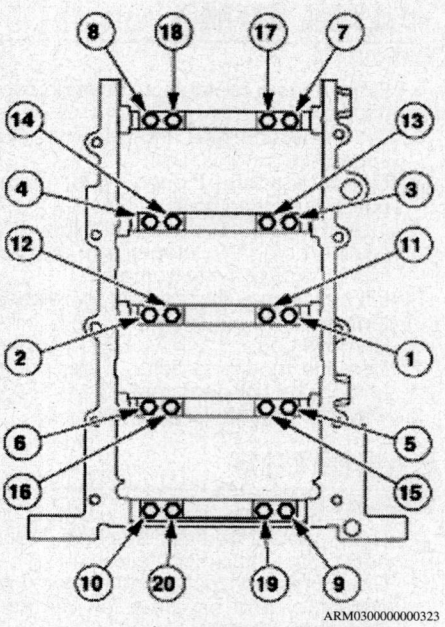

Fig. 17 Main bearing bolt tightening sequence. less supercharger

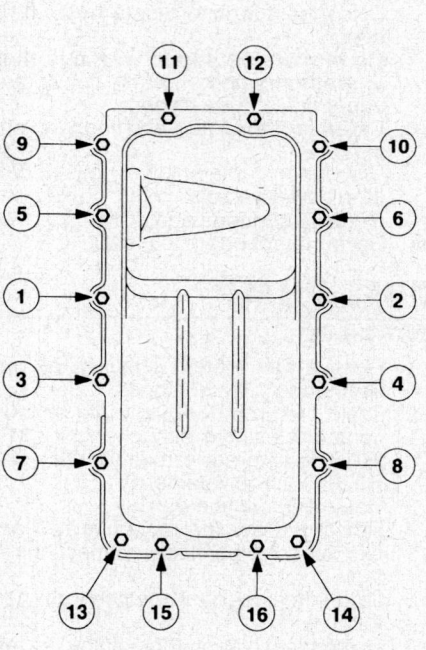

Fig. 21 Oil pan bolt tightening sequence

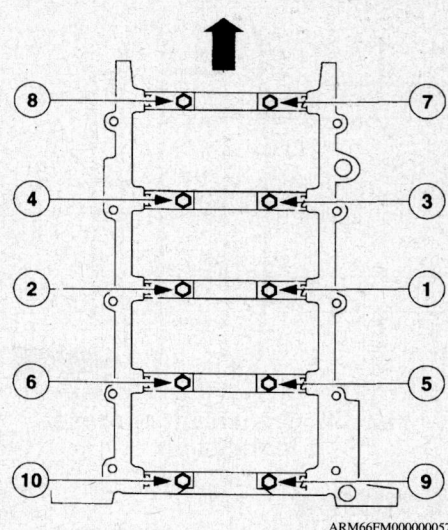

Fig. 18 Main bearing vertical cap bolt tightening sequence. Supercharged engines

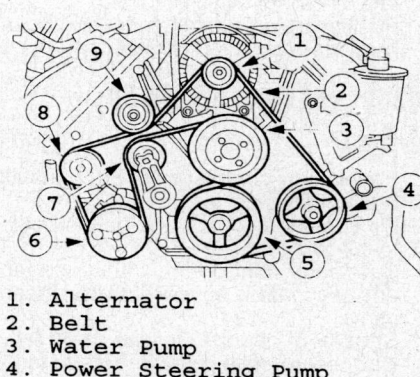

1. Alternator
2. Belt
3. Water Pump
4. Power Steering Pump
5. Crankshaft
6. Air Conditioning Compressor
7. Tensioner
8 & 9. Idler Pulleys

Fig. 22 Serpentine belt routing

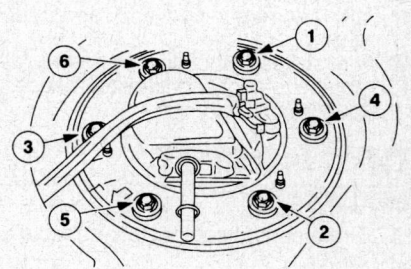

Fig. 23 Fuel tank sender unit bolt tightening sequence

TIGHTENING SPECIFICATIONS

Year	Component	Torque/Ft. Lbs.
2004	Accelerator Bracket	89①
	Air Conditioning Compressor	18
	Air Conditioning Muffler Nut	18
	Alternator	18
	Belt Idler Pulley	18
	Belt Idler Support Bracket	18
	Camshaft Cap	⑨
	Camshaft Sprocket	⑨
	Connecting Rod	⑪
	Coolant Bypass Tube	18
	Crankshaft Pulley	⑩
	Cylinder Head	③
	Drive Belt Tensioner	18
	Engine Mount Bolts	52
	Engine Mount Nuts	111
	Exhaust Manifold	⑥
	Front Cover	④
	Heater Water Inlet Tube	89①
	Heater Water Outlet Tube	18
	Idler Pulley Bracket	18
	Intake Manifold	⑤
	Main Bearing Cap	⑧
	Oil Dipstick Tube	89①
	Oil Filter Adapter	18
	Oil Pan	②
	Oil Pump Screen Cover	89①
	Oil Pump Screen & Pickup Tube Spacer To Main Bearing Stud	18
	Oil Pump To Cylinder Block	89①
	Power Steering Hose Bracket	89①
	Power Steering Hose Fitting	48

TIGHTENING SPECIFICATIONS—Continued

Year	Component	Torque/Ft. Lbs.
2004	Power Steering Pump	18
	Power Steering Pump To Cylinder Block	18
	Primary Timing Chain Guide	89①
	Subframe Brace	30
	Thermostat Housing	18
	Throttle Body	⑤
	Throttle Body Spacer	18
	Timing Chain Tensioner (Primary)	18
	Timing Chain (Secondary)	89①
	Valve Cover	⑦
	Water Pump Pulley	18
	Water Pump To Cylinder Block	18

① — Inch pounds.
② — Refer to "Oil Pan, Replace" for tightening specifications and sequence.
③ — Refer to "Cylinder Head, Replace" for tightening specifications and sequence.
④ — Refer to "Front Cover, Replace" for tightening specifications and sequence.
⑤ — Refer to "Intake Manifold, Replace" for tightening specifications and sequence.
⑥ — Refer to "Exhaust Manifold, Replace" for tightening specifications and sequence.
⑦ — Refer to "Valve Cover, Replace" for tightening specifications and sequence.
⑧ — Refer to "Main & Rod Bearings" for tightening specifications and sequence.
⑨ — Refer to "Camshaft, Replace" for tightening specifications and sequence.
⑩ — Refer to "Front Cover Seal, Replace" for tightening specifications and sequence.
⑪ — Refer to "Piston & Rod Assembly" for tightening specifications and sequence.

4.6L SOHC (VIN X) Engine

NOTE: For Procedures Not Found In This Section, Refer To "4.6L DOHC Engine" Section.

NOTE: On Air Bag Equipped Models, Refer To "Air Bag System Precautions" Located In The Front Of This Manual For System Disarming & Arming Procedures.

NOTE: Refer To "Computer Relearn Procedures" Located In The Front Of This Manual When Battery Power To The Computer Has Been Interrupted.

NOTE: Prior To Performing Any Service Operations Listed In This Section, Consult The "Technical Service Bulletins" Section For Related Information.

INDEX

	Page No.		Page No.		Page No.
Belt Tension Data	4-51	Fuel Pump, Replace	4-51	Routing	4-51
Camshaft, Replace	4-50	Intake Manifold, Replace	4-47	Technical Service Bulletins	4-52
Camshaft Lobe Lift		Main & Rod Bearings	4-50	Engine Tick	4-52
Specifications	4-49	Oil Pan, Replace	4-51	2004 SOHC Engine	4-52
Compression Pressure	4-47	Oil Pump, Replace	4-51	Fuel Pump Whining/Buzzing	
Cooling System Bleed	4-51	Piston & Rod Assembly	4-50	Through Radio Speaker	4-52
Crankshaft Seal, Replace	4-50	Precautions	4-46	Thermostat, Replace	4-51
Cylinder Head, Replace	4-48	Air Bag Systems	4-46	Tightening Specifications	4-53
Engine Rebuilding		Battery Ground Cable	4-46	Timing Chain, Replace	4-49
Specifications	21-1	Fuel System Pressure Relief	4-46	Installation	4-50
Engine, Replace	4-47	Quick Disconnect Hoses	4-46	Removal	4-50
Engine Mount, Replace	4-47	R-Clip	4-46	Timing Chain Tensioner Bleed	4-50
Exhaust Manifold, Replace	4-48	Spring Lock	4-46	Valve Adjustment	4-49
Lefthand	4-48	Vapor Tube	4-47	Valve Cover, Replace	4-48
Righthand	4-48	Radiator, Replace	4-51	Lefthand	4-48
Front Cover, Replace	4-49	Serpentine Drive Belt	4-51	Righthand	4-49
Front Cover Seal, Replace	4-49	Installation	4-51	Water Pump, Replace	4-51
Fuel Filter, Replace	4-51	Removal	4-51		

PRECAUTIONS

Air Bag Systems

Refer to "Air Bag System Precautions" in front of this manual for system disarming and arming procedures.

Battery Ground Cable

Prior to service, disconnect battery ground cable and isolate as required.

Fuel System Pressure Relief

Fuel supply tubes will remain pressurized for long periods of time after engine shutdown. This pressure must be relieved before beginning fuel system service or personal injury or damage to vehicle may occur. A valve is provided on fuel injection supply manifold for this purpose.
1. Connect EFI/CFI fuel pressure gauge tool No. T80L-9974-B, or equivalent, to fuel pressure relief valve on fuel injec-

tion supply manifold.
2. Place outlet hose of tool into suitable fuel container.
3. Open manual valve on fuel pressure gauge tool to relieve fuel system pressure.
4. Remove fuel pump relay.
5. Start engine, then allow engine to idle until it stalls.
6. After engine stalls, crank engine for approximately 5 seconds to ensure fuel injection supply manifold pressure has been released.
7. When fuel system service is complete, install fuel pump relay.
8. Cycle ignition key and wait 3 seconds to pressurize fuel system. Inspect for leaks before starting engine.

Quick Disconnect Hoses

R-CLIP

When working with R-clip type connections, do not use tools to disconnect. Use of tools may deform clip components and could cause leaks.

DISCONNECT
1. Bend shipping tab downward.
2. Spread R-clip and push clip into fitting.
3. Separate fitting from tube.

CONNECT
1. Inspect fitting and tube for damage and ensure connections are clean.
2. Apply light coat of suitable, clean engine oil to male end of tube.
3. Insert R-clip into fitting.
4. Align tube and fitting, then insert tube into fitting and push together until click is heard.
5. Pull on connection to ensure it is fully engaged.

SPRING LOCK

When working with spring lock type connections, spring lock tool set No. T84L-19623-B, or equivalent, must be used to disconnect fittings.
When connecting spring lock type fittings, proceed as follows:
1. Inspect and clean both coupling ends.
2. Lubricate fuel line O-ring seals with suitable, clean engine oil.
3. When connection is made, pull on line to ensure it is fully engaged.

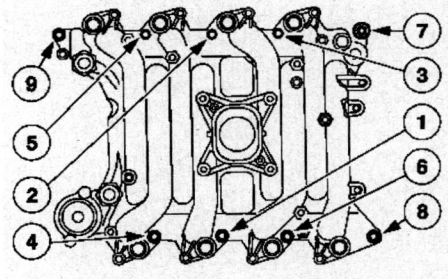

Fig. 1 Intake manifold bolt tightening sequence

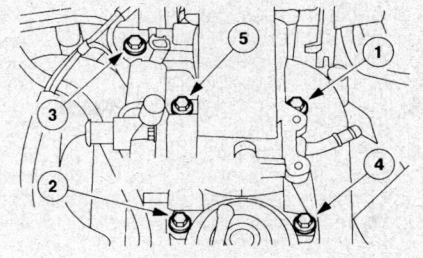

Fig. 2 TBI bolt tightening sequence

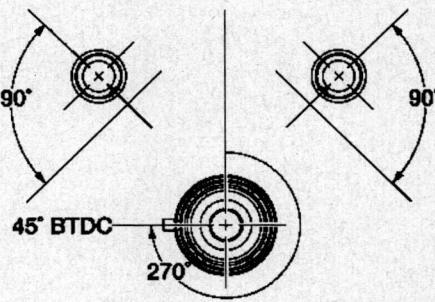

Fig. 3 Camshaft & Crankshaft keyway alignment

VAPOR TUBE

To disconnect vapor tube connections, squeeze fitting and disconnect vapor tube from fitting.

To connect, proceed as follows:
1. Ensure fittings are clean and free from damage.
2. Push tube onto fitting until it snaps into place.
3. Pull on connection to verify fitting is secure.

COMPRESSION PRESSURE

When inspecting cylinder compression, lowest cylinder must be within 75% of highest cylinder. Perform compression test with engine at normal operating temperature, spark plugs and air cleaner removed and the throttle propped wide open.

ENGINE MOUNT
REPLACE

1. Install lift bracket tool No. D93P-6001-A3, or equivalent.
2. Install engine support tool No. 303-290-A, or equivalent.
3. Raise and support vehicle.
4. Remove solenoid protective cap and wiring nuts. Position wiring aside.
5. Remove mounting bolts and starter motor.
6. Remove engine mount nuts and lower vehicle.
7. Raise engine using support tool.
8. Raise vehicle and remove engine mount.
9. Reverse procedure to install.

ENGINE
REPLACE

1. Drain coolant into suitable container.
2. Recover air conditioning refrigerant as outlined in "Air Conditioning" chapter.
3. Mark hinge locations, then disconnect ground strap and underhood lamp electrical connector.
4. Remove hood and battery.
5. Remove air cleaner and outlet tube.
6. Remove degas bottle.
7. Relieve fuel system pressure as outlined under "Precautions."
8. Disconnect fuel lines.

9. Disconnect radiator upper hose at water outlet.
10. Disconnect throttle and speed control cables, then the return spring.
11. Remove bracket mounting bolts, then position throttle and speed control cables aside.
12. Disconnect HVAC vacuum supply hoses.
13. Place suitable drain pan under firewall fittings and disconnect heater hoses.
14. Remove mounting bolt and disconnect bulkhead multi-pin electrical connector.
15. Separate wiring harness at three firewall locations.
16. Disconnect TBI electrical connectors.
17. Remove safety clip and disconnect manifold suction tube.
18. Disconnect air conditioning pressure cycling switch electrical connector.
19. Separate liquid tube from air conditioning condenser.
20. Disconnect power steering hose from fluid reservoir.
21. Disconnect engine to body or frame ground wires.
22. Disconnect fusible link and electrical connector near battery tray.
23. Disconnect ground connector near washer fluid reservoir.
24. Slide underhood power distribution box access cover up, then remove nut and battery cables.
25. Separate degas sensor electrical connector from battery tray.
26. Raise and support vehicle.
27. Disconnect HO2S electrical connectors.
28. Remove exhaust pipe to manifold flange nuts.
29. Remove solenoid protective cap and wiring nuts. Position wiring aside.
30. Remove mounting bolts and starter motor.
31. Remove nine bellhousing to engine bolts.
32. Disconnect engine to body lower ground strap.
33. Remove serpentine belt.
34. Position suitable drain pan under power steering pump.
35. Disconnect power steering fluid lines at pump.
36. Remove power steering pump pulley using power steering pump pulley remover tool No. T69L-10300-B, or equivalent.
37. Remove mounting bolts and power

steering pump.
38. Lower vehicle.
39. Remove safety clip and disconnect receiver-dryer suction tube.
40. Remove safety clip and disconnect evaporator core line.
41. Disconnect air conditioning line at rear of condenser.
42. Remove two nuts at righthand exhaust manifold.
43. Raise and support vehicle.
44. Remove six remaining righthand exhaust manifold nuts. **Do not remove exhaust manifold now.**
45. Lower vehicle.
46. Remove mounting bolts and alternator upper bracket, then disconnect alternator electrical connector by pressing tab. **Do not pull on tab.**
47. Disconnect alternator electrical connections.
48. Remove mounting bolts and alternator.
49. Install engine lifting bracket tool No. 303-639, or equivalent.
50. Raise engine using suitable lifting crane.
51. Remove righthand exhaust manifold from bottom of engine compartment.
52. Install engine lifting brackets tool No. 303-D074, or equivalent.
53. Support transmission with suitable floor jack and wooden block.
54. Connect spreader bar tool No. D93P-6001-A3, or equivalent, to suitable lifting crane.
55. Connect spreader bar to lifting brackets.
56. Raise engine slightly and disconnect transmission wiring pin at support bracket.
57. Remove engine.
58. If engine will be mounted on stand, remove rear seal as outlined under "Crankshaft Seal, Replace"
59. Reverse procedure to install.

INTAKE MANIFOLD
REPLACE

1. Drain coolant into suitable container.
2. Remove air cleaner outlet tube.
3. Relieve fuel system pressure as outlined under "Precautions."
4. Disconnect fuel lines.
5. Remove radiator upper hose.
6. Disconnect accelerator and speed control cables, then the return spring.

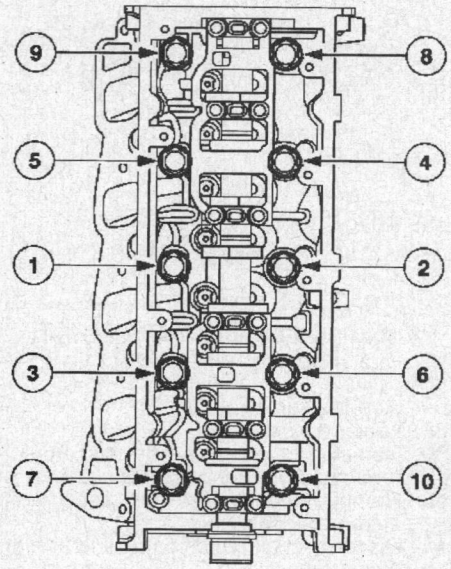

Fig. 4 Lefthand cylinder head tightening sequence

7. Remove accelerator and speed control cable bracket bolts, then position cables aside.
8. Remove breather tube at valve cover.
9. Disconnect EVAP emissions return line.
10. Disconnect differential pressure feedback EGR electrical connector.
11. Disconnect differential pressure feedback EGR transducer hoses.
12. Disconnect EGR vacuum regulator solenoid electrical connector and vacuum supply.
13. Remove EGR vacuum regulator solenoid bracket from intake manifold.
14. Disconnect EGR tube from EGR valve.
15. Remove PCV valve and hose.
16. Disconnect EGR valve vacuum lines.
17. Disconnect idle air control (IAC) valve electrical connector.
18. Disconnect main vacuum supply from TBI base adapter.
19. Disconnect TPS electrical connector.
20. Remove mounting bolts, TBI and adapter. Replace gasket.
21. Disconnect fuel pressure sensor electrical connector and fuel charging ground wire.
22. Disconnect ignition coil and fuel injector electrical connectors.
23. Disconnect HVAC vacuum supply lines and remove harness.
24. Remove four fuel supply manifold mounting studs.
25. Remove injectors and supply manifold.
26. Remove mounting bolts and ignition coils.
27. Remove mounting bolts and alternator upper bracket, then disconnect alternator electrical connector by pressing tab. **Do not pull on tab.**
28. Disconnect alternator electrical connections.
29. Remove mounting bolts and alternator.
30. Disconnect heater hose at rear of intake manifold.
31. Unclip harness at manifold and position engine wiring harness aside.
32. Disconnect coolant temperature sender electrical connector.
33. Remove thermostat housing, thermostat and O-ring.
34. Remove intake manifold mounting bolts in sequence, **Fig. 1. Gaskets can be used again if not damaged.**
35. Reverse procedure to install, noting the following:
    a. **Torque** intake manifold mounting bolts in sequence to 18 ft. lbs., **Fig. 1.**
    b. Tighten TBI mounting bolts in sequence to 89 inch lbs., **Fig. 2.**

EXHAUST MANIFOLD
REPLACE
Righthand

1. Raise and support vehicle, then remove dual converter Y-pipe.
2. Remove solenoid protective cap and wiring nuts. Position wiring aside.
3. Remove mounting bolts and starter motor.
4. Remove mounting nuts and exhaust manifold.
5. Reverse procedure to install with new exhaust manifold gasket. **Torque** mounting nuts in sequence to 18 ft. lbs., **Fig. 3.**

Lefthand

1. Position steering wheel straight ahead and lock.
2. Raise and support vehicle, then remove dual converter Y-pipe.
3. Remove and discard steering pinch bolt, then separate steering coupler.
4. Disconnect EGR tube at exhaust manifold.
5. Remove oil dipstick tube.
6. Remove mounting nuts and exhaust manifold.
7. Reverse procedure to install with new exhaust manifold gasket. **Torque** mounting nuts in sequence to 18 ft. lbs., **Fig. 4.**

CYLINDER HEAD
REPLACE

1. Remove intake manifold as outlined under "Intake Manifold, Replace."
2. Remove timing chains as outlined under "Timing Chain, Replace."
3. Disconnect oxygen sensor electrical connectors and remove H-pipes.
4. Remove exhaust manifold as outlined under "Exhaust Manifold, Replace."
5. Remove oil dipstick tube.
6. Remove bolt and position water bypass tube aside.
7. Remove cylinder head bolts supporting lower bolts with rubber band.
8. Remove cylinder head.
9. Reverse procedure to install, noting the following:
    a. **Camshaft keyways must maintain** 90° clocked position relative to valve cover rail, **Fig. 3.**

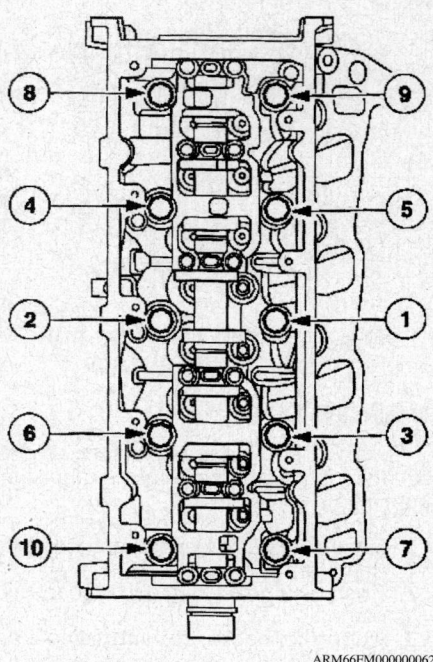

Fig. 5 Righthand cylinder head tightening sequence

    b. **Crankshaft keyway must be clocked at 270° (45° BTDC) before installation of cylinder head, Fig. 3.** Rotate crankshaft clockwise only.
    c. **Torque** cylinder head bolts in sequence to 30 ft. lbs., **Figs. 4 and 5.**
    d. Tighten head bolts an additional 90° in sequence.
    e. Loosen bolts at least of one full turn.
    f. **Torque** bolts to 30 ft. lbs., in sequence.
    g. Tighten an additional 90° in sequence.
    h. Tighten an additional 90° in sequence.

VALVE COVER
REPLACE
Lefthand

1. Remove bracket bolt and position oil dipstick tube aside.
2. Disconnect breather tube at valve cover grommet.
3. Disconnect engine wiring harness at valve cover retaining clips.
4. Remove bolts, studs and valve cover.
5. Reverse procedure to install, noting the following:
    a. Apply .32 inch bead of silicone gasket sealant No. F7AZ-19554-EA, or equivalent, to valve cover sealing surfaces.
    b. **Install and tighten cover and mounting bolts within four minutes.**
    c. **Torque** valve cover bolts and studs in sequence to 89 inch lbs., **Fig. 6.**

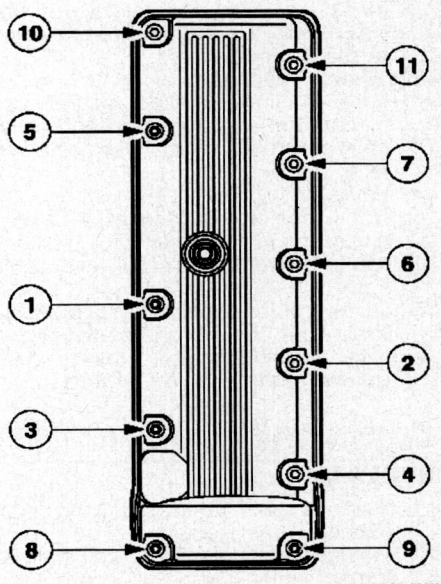

Fig. 6 Lefthand valve cover bolt tightening sequence

Righthand

1. Remove air cleaner outlet tube.
2. Relieve fuel system pressure as outlined under "Precautions."
3. Disconnect fuel lines.
4. Disconnect engine wiring harness at valve cover retaining clips.
5. Disconnect PCV valve and hose at valve cover grommet. Position them aside.
6. Remove bolts, studs and valve cover.
7. Reverse procedure to install, noting the following:
   a. Apply .32 inch bead of silicone gasket sealant No. F7AZ-19554-EA, or equivalent, to valve cover sealing surfaces.
   b. **Install and tighten cover and mounting bolts within four minutes.**
   c. **Torque** valve cover bolts and studs in sequence to 89 inch lbs., **Fig. 7.**

CAMSHAFT LOBE LIFT SPECIFICATIONS

Engine	Intake, Inch	Exhaust, Inch
4.6L SOHC	.2591	.2597

VALVE ADJUSTMENT

These engine are equipped with hydraulic valve lash adjusters. No valve adjustment is required.

FRONT COVER

REPLACE

1. Remove mounting nuts and position RFI capacitor aside.
2. Remove valve covers as outlined under "Valve Cover, Replace."

3. Drain coolant from radiator and degas bottle into suitable container.
4. Disconnect cooling fan motor electrical connector and separate fan harness from shroud.
5. Remove fan shroud lefthand and righthand mounting bolts.
6. Remove cooling fan, motor and shroud.
7. Remove serpentine belt.
8. Remove mounting bolts and water pump pulley.
9. Remove mounting nut and position air conditioning muffler aside.
10. Raise and support vehicle.
11. Drain engine oil into suitable container.
12. Position power steering pump aside.
13. Disconnect crankshaft position (CKP) sensor electrical connector.
14. Remove battery cable support nuts at front of engine.
15. Remove bolt and crankshaft pulley using puller tool No. T58P-6316-D, or equivalent.
16. Remove crankshaft front seal using seal remover tool No. T74P-6700-A, or equivalent.
17. Remove oil pan to front cover bolts.
18. Lower vehicle.
19. Position suitable drain pan under and remove power steering fluid reservoir.
20. Disconnect camshaft position (CMP) sensor electrical connector.
21. Remove serpentine belt idler pulley.
22. Mark locations for installation alignment, then remove front cover mounting bolts and studs.
23. Remove front cover. Discard gaskets.
24. Reverse procedure to install, noting the following:
   a. Apply silicone gasket sealer part No. F7AZ-19554-EA, or equivalent.
   b. Ensure bolts and studs are in original locations, **Fig. 8.**
   c. **Torque** oil pan to front cover bolts to 18 inch lbs.
   d. **Torque** oil pan to cover mounting bolts to 15 ft. lbs.
   e. Final tighten mounting bolts an additional 60°.
   f. Install new crankshaft pulley oil seal using installer and aligner tool No. T88T-6701-A, or equivalent.
   g. Apply silicone gasket sealer to crankshaft pulley keyway slot.
   h. **Install and tighten pulley and mounting bolt within four minutes.**
   i. Install crankshaft pulley using installer tool No. T74P-6316-B, or equivalent.
   j. **Torque** crankshaft pulley bolt to 66 ft. lbs., then loosen one full turn.
   k. **Torque** pulley bolt to 37 ft. lbs.
   l. Final tighten bolt an additional 90°.

FRONT COVER SEAL

REPLACE

1. Insert suitable square drive tool into square hole in tensioner arm and rotate tensioner away from belt.
2. Lift belt from pulley and slowly release tensioner.
3. Remove belt.

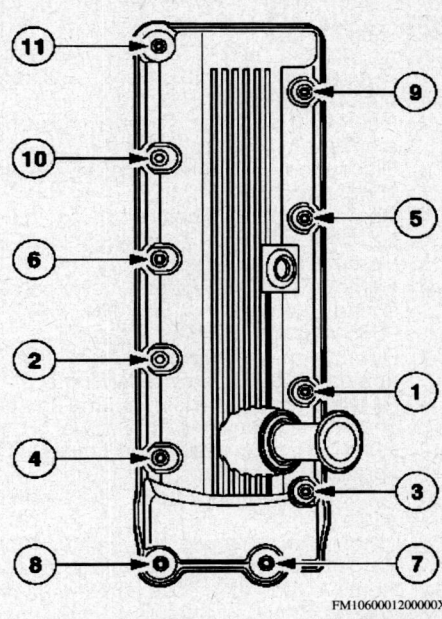

Fig. 7 Righthand valve cover bolt tightening sequence

4. Raise and support vehicle, then remove crankshaft pulley bolt.
5. Remove crankshaft pulley using crankshaft vibration damper remover tool No. T58P-6316-D, or equivalent.
6. Remove front seal using front seal remover tool No. T74P-6700-A, or equivalent.
7. Reverse procedure to install, noting the following:
   a. Lubricate engine front cover and front seal with clean engine oil.
   b. Install front seal using seal installer tool No. T88T-6701-A, or equivalent.
   c. Apply suitable sealant to Woodriff key slot on crankshaft pulley.
   d. Install crankshaft pulley using crankshaft vibration damper installer tool No. T74P-6316-B, or equivalent.
   e. **Torque** crankshaft pulley bolt to 66 ft. lbs.
   f. Loosen crankshaft pulley bolt one full turn.
   g. **Torque** pulley bolt to 37 ft. lbs.
   h. Tighten bolt an additional 90°.

TIMING CHAIN

REPLACE

These engines have an interference fit design. If engine has jumped time cylinder heads must be removed to repair damage to valves and/or pistons.

At no time, when the timing chains are removed and the cylinder heads are installed, may the crankshaft and/or camshaft be rotated unless all rocker arms have been removed. Rotation may result in valve and/or piston damage.

Before loosening or tightening camshaft sprocket nuts and bolts, ensure camshaft positioning and locking devices are in place.

Removal

1. Remove engine front cover as outlined under "Front Cover, Replace."
2. Remove crankshaft sensor ring from crankshaft.
3. Disconnect eight ignition coil electrical connectors.
4. Remove mounting bolts and eight ignition coils.
5. Remove spark plugs.
6. Remove 16 roller followers using valve spring compressor tool No. T97P-6565-AH, or equivalent.
7. Remove mounting bolts, lefthand and righthand timing chain tensioners.
8. Remove lefthand and righthand timing chain tensioner arms from dowel pins.
9. Remove timing chains and crankshaft sprocket.
10. Remove mounting bolts and timing chain guides.
11. Install camshaft position aligner tool No. T96T-6256-B, or equivalent.
12. Remove mounting bolts and camshaft gears.

Installation

1. Compress tensioner plunger using suitable soft jawed vise.
2. While holding ratchet mechanism, push ratchet arm back into tensioner housing.
3. Install paper clip into hole in tensioner housing to hold ratchet and plunger in during installation.
4. If copper links are not visible, mark links on opposite ends of timing chain to use as timing marks.
5. Install camshaft sprockets.
6. **Torque** bolts to 30 ft. lbs., then tighten an additional 90°.
7. Remove camshaft position aligner tool.
8. Position crankshaft with cylinder No. 1 at TDC using crankshaft holding tool No. T93P-6303-A, or equivalent.
9. Install crankshaft sprocket with flange facing forward.
10. Install lefthand and righthand timing chain guides.
11. Install lefthand timing chain on crankshaft sprocket, aligning copper link with dot on crankshaft sprocket.
12. Install lefthand timing chain on camshaft sprocket, aligning copper link with dot on camshaft sprocket.
13. Install righthand timing chain on crankshaft sprocket, aligning copper link with dot on crankshaft sprocket.
14. Install righthand timing chain on camshaft sprocket, aligning copper link with dot on camshaft sprocket.
15. Ensure copper links are aligned with dots on crankshaft and camshaft sprockets, **Fig. 9.**
16. Install lefthand and righthand timing chain tensioner arms on dowel pins. Lefthand tensioner arm has bump near dowel hole.
17. Install timing chain tensioners and remove paper clip.
18. Install 16 roller followers using valve spring compressor tool No. T97P-

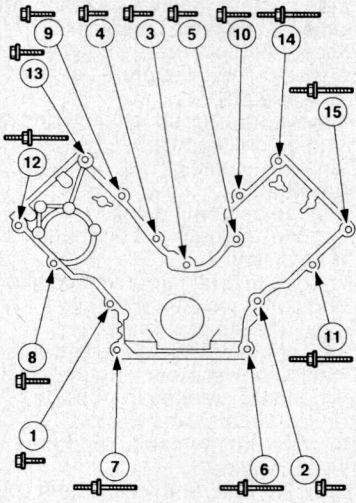

Item	Description
1	Bolt, Hex Flange Head Pilot, M8 x 1.25 x 53
2	Bolt, Hex Flange Head Pilot, M8 x 1.25 x 53
3	Bolt, Hex Flange Head Pilot, M8 x 1.25 x 53
4	Bolt, Hex Flange Head Pilot, M8 x 1.25 x 53
5	Bolt, Hex Flange Head Pilot, M8 x 1.25 x 53
6	Stud, Hex-Head Pilot, M10 x 1.5 x 1.5 x 103.1
7	Stud, Hex-Head Pilot, M10 x 1.5 x 1.5 x 103.1
8	Screw and Washer, Hex Pilot, M10 x 1.5 x 57.5
9	Screw and Washer, Hex Pilot, M10 x 1.5 x 57.5
10	Screw and Washer, Hex Pilot, M10 x 1.5 x 57.5
11	Stud and Washer, Hex-Head Pilot, M10 x 1.5 x M8 x 1.25 x 109.6
12	Stud and Washer, Hex-Head Pilot, M10 x 1.5 x M8 x 1.25 x 109.6
13	Stud and Washer, Hex-Head Pilot, M10 x 1.5 x M8 x 1.25 x 109.6
14	Stud and Washer, Hex-Head Pilot, M10 x 1.5 x M8 x 1.25 x 109.6
15	Stud and Washer, Hex-Head Pilot, M10 x 1.5 x M8 x 1.25 x 109.6

FM1069901064000X

Fig. 8 Front cover mounting locations

6565-AH, or equivalent.
19. Install spark plugs and ignition coils.
20. Install crankshaft sensor ring on crankshaft.
21. Install engine front cover as outlined under "Front Cover, Replace."

TIMING CHAIN TENSIONER BLEED

1. Position timing chain tensioner in suitable soft-jawed vise.
2. Lock ratchet stem mechanism position using suitable tool and slowly com-

press tensioner plunger by rotating vise handle. **Tensioner must be compressed slowly.**
3. When tensioner plunger bottoms in bore, continue holding ratchet lock mechanism and push ratchet mechanism down until flush with tensioner face.
4. While holding ratchet stem flush to tensioner face, release ratchet lock mechanism and install paper clip or suitable tool to lock tensioner in collapsed position.
5. **Do not remove paper clip or suitable tool until timing chain, tensioner arm, tensioner and timing chain guide are installed on engine.**

CAMSHAFT
REPLACE

1. Remove rocker arms as outlined under "Rocker Arms, Replace."
2. Remove timing chain as outlined under "Timing Chain, Replace."
3. Remove bolt, then the camshaft sprocket and spacer.
4. Remove 13 camshaft bearing cap bolts.
5. Remove camshaft bearing cap ladders, then the camshaft.
6. Reverse procedure to install noting the following:
   a. Lubricate camshaft journals and bearing cap ladders with clean engine oil.
   b. Tighten bearing cap bolts in sequence, **Fig. 10.**

PISTON & ROD ASSEMBLY

Ensure side clearance between connecting rods and crankshaft journal is .00059–.01772 inch.
1. Assemble pistons, pins, bearings, caps, nuts and bolts in original positions.
2. Install pistons with notch to front of engine.
3. **Torque** connecting rod bearing cap bolts to 18 ft. lbs.
4. **Torque** cap bolts to 30 ft. lbs.
5. Final tighten bolts an additional 90°.
6. Rotate crankshaft to ensure smooth operation.

MAIN & ROD BEARINGS

Refer to "DOHC" for main bearing tightening sequences.

CRANKSHAFT SEAL
REPLACE

1. Remove transmission as outlined in **MOTOR's "Domestic Transmission, In-Vehicle Service." or "Transmission Service DVD."**
2. Remove flywheel.
3. Remove crankshaft oil slinger using rear crankshaft slinger remover tool

No. T-95P-6701-AH, or equivalent, and suitable slide hammer.

4. Remove crankshaft rear oil seal using rear crankshaft seal remover tool No. T95P-6701-BH, or equivalent, and suitable slide hammer.
5. Reverse procedure to install, noting the following:
   a. Install rear oil seal using crankshaft seal replacer tool No. T-95P-6701-AH and rear crankshaft seal adapter tool No. T-95P-6701-DH, or equivalents.
   b. With rear crankshaft seal adapter still installed, use rear crankshaft slinger replacer and rear crankshaft seal replacer to install crankshaft oil slinger.

OIL PAN
REPLACE

1. Remove air cleaner outlet tube.
2. Remove radiator sight shield.
3. Support engine with engine lifting bracket tool No. D93P-6001-A2 and support tool No. 303-290-A, or equivalents.
4. Raise and support vehicle.
5. Drain engine oil into suitable container.
6. Remove lefthand and righthand engine mount nuts.
7. Lower vehicle.
8. Raise engine using support tool.
9. Raise and support vehicle.
10. Compress front coil springs using compressor tool No. D78P-5310-A, or equivalent.
11. Position suitable jack stand under subframe.
12. Remove four engine mount bolts.
13. Loosen front subframe bolts. **Do not completely remove bolt.**
14. Lower front subframe.
15. Remove mounting bolts and pan. **If gasket is in good condition it may be used again.**
16. Reverse procedure to install, noting the following:
   a. Apply silicone gasket sealant No. F7AZ-19554-EA, or equivalent, to rear oil seal retainer to block sealing surface and at front cover to block mating surface.
   b. **Install and tighten cover and mounting bolts within four minutes.**
   c. Move oil pan into position and loosely install bolts.
   d. **Torque** oil pan bolts in sequence to 18 inch lbs.
   e. **Torque** pan bolts in sequence 15 ft. lbs.
   f. Final tighten bolts an additional 60° in sequence.

OIL PUMP
REPLACE

This procedure has been revised by a Technical Service Bulletin.
1. Remove valve covers as outlined under "Valve Cover, Replace."
2. Remove front cover as outlined under "Front Engine Cover, Replace."

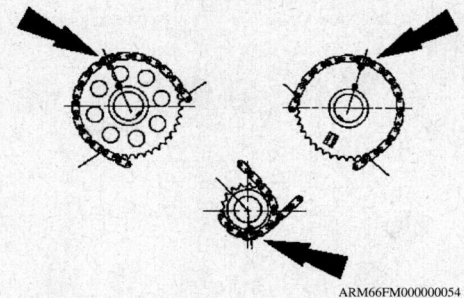

ARM66FM000000054

Fig. 9   Timing chain timing marks

3. Remove oil pan as outlined under "Oil Pan, Replace."
4. Remove timing chains as outlined under "Timing Chain, Replace."
5. Remove mounting bolts and oil pump.
6. Reverse procedure to install, noting the following:
   a. Align oil pump inner rotor with flat of crankshaft.
   b. Prime oil pump and system prior to starting engine.

BELT TENSION DATA

These models are equipped with an automatic drive belt tensioner. No adjustment or maintenance is required.

SERPENTINE DRIVE BELT

Always use square drive tool in hole in tensioner to move tensioner. Never pry on tensioner pulley. When releasing drive belt tensioner, never allow tensioner to snap back. Damage to tensioner or personal injury could result.

Do not allow engine coolant to remain on serpentine belt or pulleys. If required, remove belt and flush with clean water.

Removal

1. Insert suitable square drive tool into square hole in tensioner arm and rotate tensioner away from belt.
2. Lift belt from pulley and slowly release tensioner.
3. Remove belt.

Routing

Refer to "4.6L DOHC Engine" section for belt routing.

Installation

1. Route belt.
2. Ensure belt is properly seated in pulley grooves.
3. Insert suitable square drive tool into square hole in tensioner arm and rotate tensioner away from belt.
4. Position belt under tensioner and slowly release tensioner onto belt.

COOLING SYSTEM BLEED

1. Fill radiator completely full and install radiator cap.
2. Fill coolant reservoir and degas bottle to full cold mark.
3. Set heater control to full hot, high fan and set controls so air vents from dash vents.
4. Start and operate engine until fully warmed up while observing water temperature gauge.
5. If system is functioning properly, temperature will indicate normal and hot air will be felt at dash outlets.
6. If system is not functioning properly, temperature gauge will not read and/or no hot air will be felt at dash vents.
7. If system is not functioning properly, allow engine to cool and repeat procedure.
8. If system is functioning properly, allow engine to cool and fill coolant reservoir to full cold mark.

THERMOSTAT
REPLACE

1. Drain engine coolant into suitable container.
2. Remove mounting bolts and water outlet connection.
3. Position water outlet connection and upper radiator hose aside.
4. Remove thermostat and ring seal.
5. Reverse procedure to install.

WATER PUMP
REPLACE

1. Drain engine coolant into suitable container.
2. Loosen water pump pulley mounting bolts.
3. Insert suitable square drive tool into square hole in tensioner arm and rotate tensioner away from belt.
4. Lift belt from pulley and slowly release tensioner.
5. Remove belt.
6. Remove mounting bolts, water pump and gasket. Discard gasket.
7. Reverse procedure to install.

RADIATOR
REPLACE

Refer to "4.6L DOHC Engine" section for radiator replacement procedure

FUEL PUMP
REPLACE

Refer to "4.6L DOHC Engine" section for fuel pump replacement procedure

FUEL FILTER
REPLACE

1. Relieve fuel system pressure as outlined under "Precautions."
2. Raise and support vehicle.
3. Remove push connector fittings from

MUSTANG

fuel filter ends using suitable spring lock coupler tools.

4. Loosen worm gear clamp and remove filter from bracket. Record flow arrow to ensure proper direction of fuel flow through filter.

5. Reverse procedure to install using new retainer clips in each fitting.

TECHNICAL SERVICE BULLETINS

Fuel Pump Whining/ Buzzing Through Radio Speaker

Engine Tick

2004 SOHC ENGINE

On some of these models, there may be an engine tick noise at all temperatures

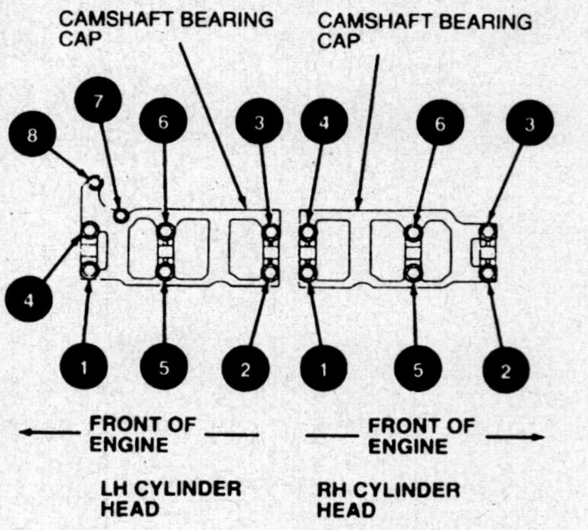

Fig. 10   Camshaft cap cluster tightening sequence

during idle. The noise may be prevalent in the front wheel well area, but may be heard with the hood open.

This condition may be caused by the cylinder head valve guide area.

To correct this condition, proceed as follows:

1. Ensure noise is coming from back of cylinder head near exhaust ports by listening with suitable stethoscope.

2. Ensure noise is heard in wheel well or catalytic converter and from under vehicle.

3. Ensure there are no exhaust manifold leaks.

4. Ensure noise is present when canceling each cylinder by unplugging injectors one at a time.

5. Ensure camshaft spacers are in place.

6. Ensure cam sprocket is tightened.

7. Inspect hydraulic lash adjusters for spongy condition.

8. Ensure timing chain tensioner pin been removed.

9. Replace cylinder head and cam (left-hand, part No. 4L3Z-6049-AA; right-hand part No. 4L3Z-4069-BA).

TIGHTENING SPECIFICATIONS

Year	Component	Torque/Ft. Lbs.
2004	Accelerator Bracket	89①
	Air Conditioning Compressor	18
	Air Conditioning Muffler Nut	18
	Alternator	18
	Belt Idler Pulley	18
	Belt Idler Support Bracket	18
	Camshaft Cap	⑨
	Camshaft Sprocket	⑨
	Connecting Rod	⑪
	Coolant Bypass Tube	18
	Crankshaft Pulley	⑩
	Cylinder Head	③
	Drive Belt Tensioner	18
	Engine Mount Bolts	52
	Engine Mount Nuts	111
	Exhaust Manifold	⑥
	Front Cover	④
	Heater Water Inlet Tube	89①
	Heater Water Outlet Tube	18
	Idler Pulley Bracket	18
	Intake Manifold	⑤
	Main Bearing Cap	⑧
	Oil Dipstick Tube	89①
	Oil Filter Adapter	18
	Oil Pan	②
	Oil Pump Screen Cover	89①
	Oil Pump Screen & Pickup Tube Spacer To Main Bearing Stud	18
	Oil Pump To Cylinder Block	89①
	Power Steering Hose Bracket	89①
	Power Steering Hose Fitting	48
	Power Steering Pump	18
	Power Steering Pump To Cylinder Block	18
	Primary Timing Chain Guide	89①
	Subframe Brace	30
	Thermostat Housing	18
	Throttle Body	⑤
	Throttle Body Spacer	18
	Timing Chain Tensioner (Primary)	18
	Timing Chain (Secondary)	89①
	Valve Cover	⑦
	Water Pump Pulley	18
	Water Pump To Cylinder Block	18

① — Inch lbs.
② — Refer to "Oil Pan, Replace" for tightening specifications and sequence.
③ — Refer to "Cylinder Head, Replace" for tightening specifications and sequence.
④ — Refer to "Front Cover, Replace" for tightening specifications and sequence.
⑤ — Refer to "Intake Manifold, Replace" for tightening specifications and sequence.
⑥ — Refer to "Exhaust Manifold, Replace" for tightening specifications and sequence.
⑦ — Refer to "Valve Cover, Replace" for tightening specifications and sequence.
⑧ — Refer to "Main & Rod Bearings" for tightening specifications and sequence.
⑨ — Refer to "Camshaft, Replace" for tightening specifications and sequence.
⑩ — Refer to "Front Cover Seal, Replace" for tightening specifications and sequence.
⑪ — Refer to "Piston & Rod Assembly" for tightening specifications and sequence.

4.6L SOHC (VIN H) Engine

NOTE: For Procedures Not Found In This Section, Refer To "4.6L SOHC (VIN X) Engine" Section.

NOTE: On Air Bag Equipped Models, Refer To "Air Bag System Precautions" Located In The Front Of This Manual For System Disarming & Arming Procedures.

INDEX

	Page No.
Belt Tension Data	4-64
Camshaft, Replace	4-61
Lefthand	4-62
Righthand	4-61
Camshaft Lobe Lift Specifications	4-59
Compression Pressure	4-54
Cooling System Bleed	4-64
Crankshaft Damper, Replace	4-59
Crankshaft Rear Oil Seal, Replace	4-63
Crankshaft Seal, Replace	4-62
Cylinder Head, Replace	4-57
Engine Rebuilding Specifications	21-1
Engine, Replace	4-55
Engine Mount, Replace	4-54
Exhaust Manifold, Replace	4-56
Lefthand	4-56

	Page No.
Righthand	4-56
Front Cover, Replace	4-60
Front Cover Seal, Replace	4-60
Fuel Filter, Replace	4-65
Fuel Pump, Replace	4-65
Hydraulic Lash Adjuster, Replace	4-59
Intake Manifold, Replace	4-56
Main & Rod Bearings	4-62
Oil Pan, Replace	4-63
Oil Pump, Replace	4-64
Piston & Rod Assembly	4-62
Precautions	4-54
Air Bag Systems	4-54
Battery Ground Cable	4-54
Fuel System Pressure Relief	4-54
Quick Disconnect Hoses	4-54
R-Clip	4-54
Spring Lock	4-54

	Page No.
Vapor Tube	4-54
Radiator, Replace	4-65
Serpentine Drive Belt	4-64
Replacement	4-64
Routing	4-64
Technical Service Bulletins	4-65
Ticking And/Or Knocking Noise From Engine	4-65
2005 Mustang	4-65
Thermostat, Replace	4-65
Tightening Specifications	4-72
Timing Chain, Replace	4-60
Removal	4-60
Installation	4-61
Valve Adjustment	4-59
Valve Cover, Replace	4-59
Lefthand	4-59
Righthand	4-59
Water Pump, Replace	4-65

PRECAUTIONS

Air Bag Systems

Refer to "Air Bag System Precautions" in front of this manual for system disarming and arming procedures.

Battery Ground Cable

Prior to service, disconnect battery ground cable and isolate as required.

Fuel System Pressure Relief

1. Remove fuel pump relay.
2. Start engine, then allow engine to idle until it stalls.
3. After engine stalls, crank engine for approximately 5 seconds to ensure fuel injection supply manifold pressure has been released.
4. When fuel system service is complete, install fuel pump relay.
5. Cycle ignition key and wait 3 seconds to pressurize fuel system. Inspect for leaks before starting engine.

Quick Disconnect Hoses

R-CLIP

When working with R-clip type connec-

tions, do not use tools to disconnect. Use of tools may deform clip components and could cause leaks.

DISCONNECT

1. Bend shipping tab downward.
2. Spread R-clip and push clip into fitting.
3. Separate fitting from tube.

CONNECT

1. Inspect fitting and tube for damage and ensure connections are clean.
2. Apply light coat of suitable, clean engine oil to male end of tube.
3. Insert R-clip into fitting.
4. Align tube and fitting, then insert tube into fitting and push together until click is heard.
5. Pull on connection to ensure it is fully engaged.

SPRING LOCK

When working with spring lock type connections, spring lock tool set No. T84L-19623-B, or equivalent, must be used to disconnect fittings.

When connecting spring lock type fittings, proceed as follows:
1. Inspect and clean both coupling ends.
2. Lubricate fuel line O-ring seals with suitable, clean engine oil.
3. When connection is made, pull on line to ensure it is fully engaged.

VAPOR TUBE

To disconnect vapor tube connections, squeeze fitting and disconnect vapor tube from fitting.

To connect, proceed as follows:
1. Ensure fittings are clean and free from damage.
2. Push tube onto fitting until it snaps into place.
3. Pull on connection to verify fitting is secure.

COMPRESSION PRESSURE

1. Ensure crankcase oil is correct viscosity and correct level, and battery is fully charged.
2. Operate vehicle until engine at normal operating temperature.
3. Turn ignition switch to OFF position and remove all spark plugs.
4. Set throttle plates in wide-open position.
5. Install suitable compression gauge in cylinder No. 1.
6. Install suitable auxiliary start switch.
7. Turn ignition switch to ON position.
8. Crank engine at least five compression strokes using auxiliary starter switch.
9. Record highest reading and approximate number of compression strokes required to obtain highest reading.
10. Repeat test on each cylinder.
11. Compression pressures are within specifications is the lowest cylinder reading is at least 75% of highest.

ENGINE MOUNT

REPLACE

1. Raise and support vehicle.

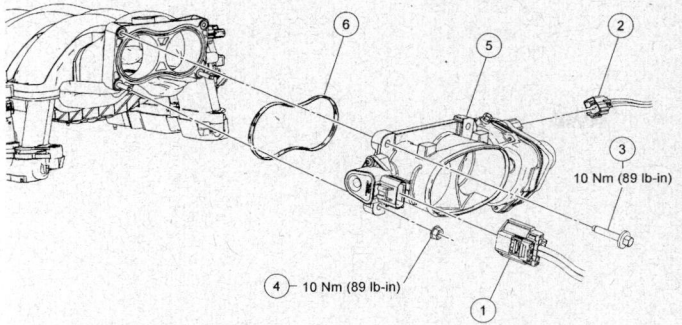

Item	Description
1	Electronic throttle control electrical connector
2	Throttle position (TP) sensor electrical connector
3	Throttle body bolts (2 required)
4	Throttle body nuts (2 required)
5	Throttle body
6	Throttle body gasket

ARM0400000000517

Fig. 1 Throttle body replacement

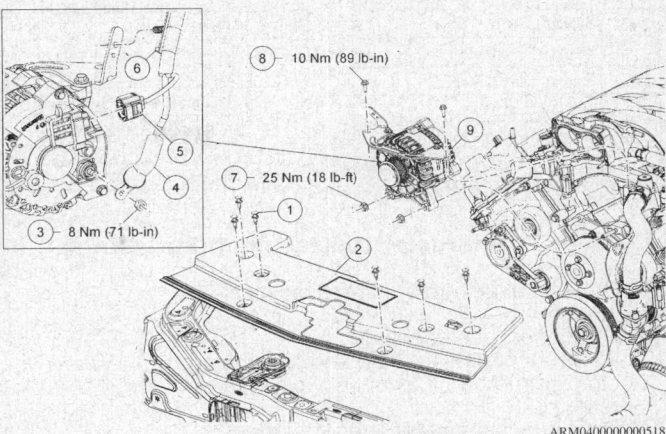

ARM0400000000518

Fig. 2 Alternator replacement (Part 1 of 2)

2. Loosen clamp and disconnect air cleaner outlet pipe.
3. Disconnect Mass Air Flow (MAF) sensor electrical connector.
4. Remove mounting bolt and air cleaner. Ensure two rubber grommets are retained to feet.
5. Disconnect Throttle Position (TP) sensor and electronic throttle control electrical connectors, **Fig. 1.**
6. Remove mounting bolts, nuts and throttle body.
7. Remove fix pin-type retainers and radiator sight shield, **Fig. 2.**
8. Remove two outer bracket mounting bolts and two lower mounting nuts, then disconnect alternator electrical connector and pin-type retainer.
9. Position cover aside, then remove B+ terminal nut and alternator.
10. Support engine using suitable engine lifting brackets and three-bar engine support tools.
11. Remove lefthand and righthand engine support insulator nuts, **Figs. 3 and 4.**
12. Raise engine approximately 1.57 inches.
13. Remove two mounting bolts and righthand engine support insulator.
14. Remove four mounting bolts and lefthand engine support engine support bracket.
15. Remove two mounting bolts and lefthand engine support insulator.
16. Reverse procedure to install.

ENGINE
REPLACE

1. Raise and support vehicle.
2. Remove fuel pump relay.
3. Start engine and allow it idle until is stalls.
4. Crank engine for approximately five seconds to ensure fuel injection supply manifold pressure has been released.
5. Turn ignition switch to OFF position.
6. Mark hood hinge location for installation alignment.
7. Remove four mounting bolts and hood.
8. Remove two cover, mounting nuts and wiper pivot arms
9. Remove four cowl vent screen pin-type retainers.
10. Remove righthand, then the lefthand vent screen.
11. Loosen clamp and disconnect air cleaner outlet pipe.
12. Disconnect Mass Air Flow (MAF) sensor electrical connector.
13. Remove mounting bolt and air cleaner. Ensure two rubber grommets are retained to feet.
14. Drain engine cooling system into suitable container.
15. Remove intake manifold as outlined under "Intake Manifold, Replace."
16. Remove four mounting bolts and position alternator support bracket aside, **Fig. 5.**
17. Disconnect, then position coolant crossover assembly-to-thermostat housing and assembly-to-radiator hoses aside.
18. Disconnect quick connect fitting, then position heater return and supply hose aside.
19. Remove two mounting bolts, coolant crossover and gasket.
20. Disconnect, the position upper and lower degas bottle hoses aside.
21. Remove two mounting bolts and degas bottle.
22. Remove fix pin-type retainers and radiator sight shield, **Fig. 2.**
23. Rotate accessory drive belt tensioner clockwise with suitable belt tensioner release tool and remove belt.
24. Disconnect air conditioning pressure transducer electrical connector.
25. Disconnect coolant hose from oil filter adapter.
26. Drain engine oil into suitable container.
27. Disconnect degas bottle hose from cooling fan.
28. Disconnect lower radiator hose from thermostat housing.
29. Remove thermostat housing and coolant hoses.
30. Disconnect oil temperature sensor electrical connector and two pin-type retainers.
31. Remove mounting nut and ground wire from stud bolt.
32. Disconnect pin-type retainer from air conditioning compressor.
33. Disconnect air conditioning clutch and Crankshaft Position (CKP) sensor electrical connectors.
34. Disconnect retainers and position wiring harness aside.
35. Remove mounting bolt and three nuts, then position and support air conditioning compressor aside.
36. Remove two mounting nuts and power steering pulley shield.
37. Remove wiring harness retainer, nut and tube retaining clip from power steering stud bolt.
38. Remove three stud bolts, then position and support power steering pump aside.
39. Support engine using suitable engine lifting brackets and three-bar engine support tools. **Do not position engine support legs on fenders. Legs should be positioned on body structure near suspension strut tower.**
40. **On models equipped with automatic transmission,** proceed as follows:
    a. Remove mounting nut and position transmission cooler tube bracket aside.
    b. Remove transmission as outlined in **MOTOR's "Domestic Transmission, In-Vehicle Service." or "Transmission Service DVD."**
41. **On models equipped with manual transmission,** remove clutch as outlined in **MOTOR's "Domestic Transmission, In-Vehicle Service." or "Transmission Service DVD."**
42. **On all models,** remove four catalytic converter flange nuts.
43. Disconnect righthand Heated Oxygen Sensor (HO2S) electrical connector.
44. Disconnect lefthand and righthand Catalyst Monitor Sensor (CMS).

Item	Description
1	Pin-type retainer
2	Radiator sight shield
3	B+ terminal nut
4	B+ terminal cover
5	Generator electrical connector

Item	Description
6	Wiring harness pin-type retainer
7	Generator nut (2 required)
8	Generator bracket bolt (2 required)
9	Generator

ARM0400000000519

Fig. 2 Alternator replacement (Part 2 of 2)

45. Remove engine-to-transmission spacer plate.
46. Disconnect heater hoses.
47. Remove mounting bolt and ground strap from cowl. Disconnect pin-type retainer.
48. Disconnect alternator jumper harness electrical connector.
49. Remove two mounting nuts, then position alternator and harness aside.
50. Disconnect upper and lower Powertrain Control Module (PCM) electrical connectors.
51. Disconnect 16-pin electrical connector and two wiring retainers.
52. Remove power distribution box cover.
53. Disconnect power distribution box upper housing from lower housing.
54. Loosen bolt and disconnect 68-pin connector from power distribution box.
55. Remove mounting nut, radio interference capacitor and J-bracket from engine front cover stud bolt.
56. Remove lefthand and righthand engine support insulator nuts.
57. Attach suitable floor crane and engine lifting bracket modular tool No. 014-00073, or equivalent, to engine.
58. Remove three-bar support.
59. Remove engine.
60. Reverse procedure to install.

INTAKE MANIFOLD
REPLACE

1. Remove fuel pump relay.
2. Start engine and allow it idle until is stalls.
3. Crank engine for approximately five seconds to ensure fuel injection supply manifold pressure has been released.
4. Turn ignition switch to OFF position.
5. Disconnect crankcase vent tube from air cleaner outlet pipe.
6. Loosen two clamps and remove air cleaner outlet pipe.
7. Disconnect fuel supply tube spring lock coupling.
8. Disconnect two retainers from fuel rail stud bolts and position wiring harness aside.
9. Disconnect fuel rail pressure and temperature sensor electrical connector and vacuum hose.
10. Disconnect eight fuel injection electrical connectors.
11. Remove four fuel rail stud bolts.
12. Remove fuel rail and injectors.
13. Disconnect Evaporative Emissions (EVAP) tube from intake manifold and position it aside, **Fig. 6**.
14. Disconnect Positive Crankcase Ventilation (PCV) tube from intake manifold and position it aside.

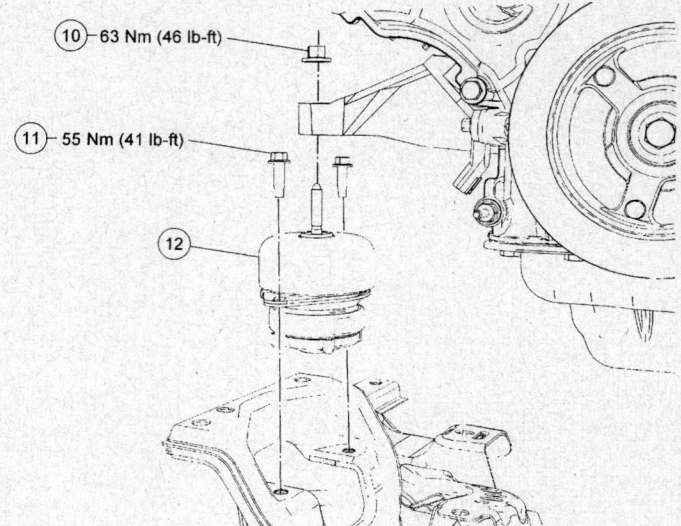

Item	Description
10	RH engine support insulator nut
11	RH engine support insulator bolt (2 required)
12	RH engine support insulator

ARM0400000000533

Fig. 3 Engine mounting replacement. Righthand

15. Disconnect Throttle Position (TP) sensor and electronic throttle body electrical connectors.
16. Disconnect Charge Motion Control Valve (CMCV) electrical connector.
17. Disconnect wiring retainers from intake manifold stud bolt and CMCV bracket. Position wiring harness aside.
18. Disconnect vacuum hose from T fitting.
19. Remove nine mounting bolts, stud bolt, intake manifold and gasket.
20. Reverse procedure to install, noting the following:
    a. Install new gasket.
    b. Tighten mounting bolts in sequence, **Fig. 7**.
    c. Install new upper and lower fuel injector O-ring seals lubricated with suitable, clean engine oil.

EXHAUST MANIFOLD
REPLACE
Lefthand

1. Raise and support vehicle.
2. Loosen clamp and disconnect air cleaner outlet pipe.
3. Disconnect Mass Air Flow (MAF) sensor electrical connector.
4. Remove mounting bolt and air cleaner. Ensure two rubber grommets are retained to feet.
5. Disconnect Throttle Position (TP) sensor and electronic throttle control electrical connectors, **Fig. 1**.
6. Remove mounting bolts, nuts and throttle body.
7. Disconnect lefthand Heated Oxygen

Sensor (HO2S) electrical connector and wiring harness retainer.
8. Remove two righthand catalytic converter to exhaust manifold nuts, **Fig. 8**.
9. Remove two lefthand catalytic converter-to-exhaust manifold nuts.
10. Remove fix pin-type retainers and radiator sight shield, **Fig. 2**.
11. Remove two outer bracket mounting bolts and two lower mounting nuts, then disconnect alternator electrical connector and pin-type retainer.
12. Position cover aside, then remove B+ terminal nut and alternator.
13. Support engine using suitable engine lifting brackets and three-bar engine support tools.
14. Remove lefthand and righthand engine support insulator nuts.
15. Raise engine approximately 1.57 inches.
16. Remove bolt and disconnect steering coupling. **Do not rotate steering wheel when steering column intermediate shaft is disconnected.**
17. Remove four bolts and lefthand engine support insulator bracket.
18. Remove eight nuts, exhaust manifold and gasket.
19. Reverse procedure to install, noting the following:
    a. Install new exhaust manifold gaskets.
    b. Tighten exhaust manifold mounting nuts in sequence, **Fig. 9**.

Righthand

1. Raise and support vehicle.
2. Loosen clamp and disconnect air

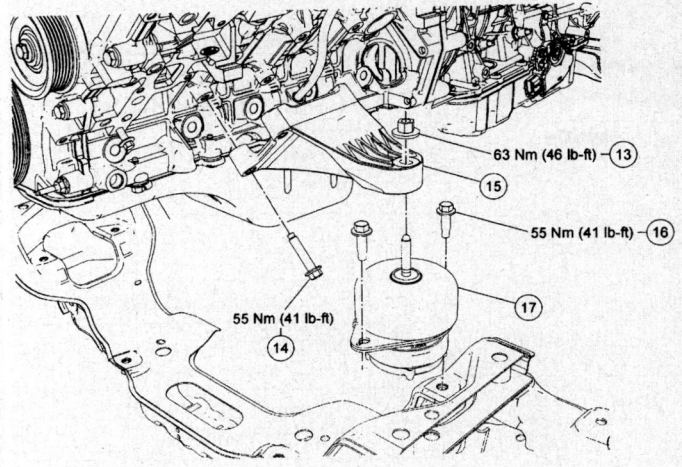

Item	Description
13	LH engine support insulator nut
14	LH engine support bracket bolt (4 required)
15	LH engine support bracket
16	LH engine support insulator bolt (2 required)
17	LH engine support insulator

ARM0400000000534

Fig. 4 Engine mount replacement. Lefthand

cleaner outlet pipe.
3. Disconnect Mass Air Flow (MAF) sensor electrical connector.
4. Remove mounting bolt and air cleaner. Ensure two rubber grommets are retained to feet.
5. Disconnect Throttle Position (TP) sensor and electronic throttle control electrical connectors, **Fig. 1.**
6. Remove mounting bolts, nuts and throttle body.
7. Ensure anti-theft system is deactivated.
8. Raise and support vehicle.
9. Remove starter solenoid terminal cap.
10. Remove two nuts terminal nuts and position wires aside.
11. Remove three mounting bolts and starter motor.
12. Disconnect lefthand Heated Oxygen Sensor (HO2S) electrical connector and wiring harness retainer.
13. Remove two righthand catalytic converter to exhaust manifold nuts, **Fig. 10.**
14. Remove two lefthand catalytic converter-to-exhaust manifold nuts.
15. Remove six pin-type retainers and radiator sight shield, **Fig. 2.**
16. Remove two outer bracket mounting bolts and two lower mounting nuts, then disconnect alternator electrical connector and pin-type retainer.
17. Position cover aside, then remove B+ terminal nut and alternator.
18. Support engine using suitable engine lifting brackets and three-bar engine support tools.
19. Remove lefthand and righthand engine support insulator nuts.
20. Raise engine approximately 1.57 inches.

21. Remove nut and ground wire from stud bolt.
22. **On models equipped with automatic transmission,** remove mounting nut and position transmission cooler tube bracket aside.
23. **On all models,** remove two bolts, two stud bolts and righthand engine support insulator bracket.
24. Remove eight nuts, exhaust manifold and gasket.
25. Reverse procedure to install, noting the following:
    a. Install new exhaust manifold gaskets.
    b. Tighten exhaust manifold mounting nuts in sequence, **Fig. 11.**

CYLINDER HEAD
REPLACE

1. Remove engine as outlined under "Engine. Replace."
2. Mount the engine on suitable work stand and remove special tools.
3. Disconnect lefthand and righthand Camshaft Position (CMP) sensor electrical connectors.
4. Disconnect lefthand and righthand Variable Camshaft Timing (VCT) solenoid electrical connectors.
5. Disconnect engine wiring harness pin-type retainers.

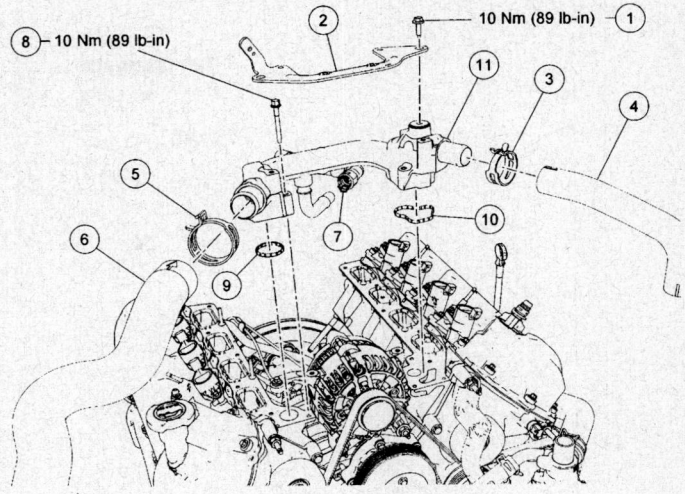

Item	Description
1	Alternator support bracket bolt (4 required)
2	Alternator support bracket
3	Hose clamp
4	Coolant crossover assembly-to-thermostat housing hose
5	Hose clamp
6	Coolant crossover assembly-to-radiator hose
7	Heater return and supply hose
8	Coolant crossover assembly bolt (2 required)
9	Gasket
10	Gasket
11	Coolant crossover assembly

ARM0400000000535

Fig. 5 Coolant crossover replacement

6. Remove mounting nut and righthand radio ignition interference capacitor.
7. Remove Positive Crankcase Ventilation (PCV) tubes from lefthand and righthand valve covers.
8. Disconnect ignition coils' electrical connectors.
9. Disconnect two engine wiring harness retainers from righthand and lefthand valve cover studs.
10. Disconnect engine wiring harness pin-type retainers.
11. Disconnect Cylinder Head Temperature (CHT) sensor electrical connector and jumper harness electrical connector pin-type retainer.
12. Disconnect Knock Sensor (KS) electrical connector and pin-type retainer.
13. Disconnect lefthand Heated Oxygen Sensor (HO2S) electrical connector.
14. Disconnect engine wiring harness retainer from stud bolt.
15. Disconnect engine oil pressure sensor electrical connector.
16. Remove engine wiring harness.
17. Remove oil filter.
18. Remove mounting bolt and oil dipstick tube.
19. Remove mounting bolts, then the lefthand and righthand CMP sensors.
20. Remove eight mounting bolts and ignition coils.
21. Loosen 29 mountings bolts and valve

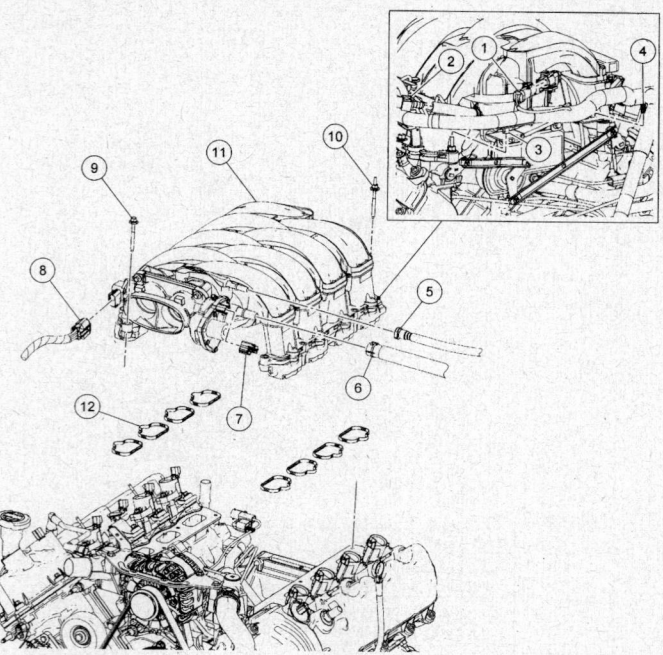

Fig. 6   Intake manifold replacement (Part 1 of 2)

Item	Description
1	Charge motion control valve (CMCV) electrical connector
2	Vacuum hose T-fitting
3	Wiring harness retainer
4	Wiring harness pin-type retainer
5	Evaporative emissions
6	Positive crankcase ventilation (PCV) tube
7	Electronic throttle body electrical connector
8	Throttle position (TP) sensor electrical connector
9	Intake manifold bolt (9 required)
10	Intake manifold stud bolt
11	Intake manifold
12	Intake manifold gasket (8 required)

Fig. 6   Intake manifold replacement (Part 2 of 2)

covers. **Mounting bolts are part of valve cover and should not be removed.**

22. Remove five mounting bolts, water pump pulley and righthand side accessory drive belt idler pulley.
23. Remove crankshaft pulley mounting bolt and washer.
24. Remove crankshaft pulley using suitable three-jaw puller tool.
25. Remove four oil pan-to-engine front cover mounting bolts.
26. Record front cover mounting bolt locations for installation alignment.
27. Remove mounting bolts and front cover.
28. Remove crankshaft sensor ring.
29. Position crankshaft keyway at 12 o'clock position, **Fig. 12,** noting the following:
    a. If camshaft lobes are not exactly positioned, **Fig. 13,** crankshaft will require one full additional rotation to 12 o'clock position.
    b. Cylinder No. 1 camshaft exhaust lobe must be coming up on exhaust stroke.
    c. Ensure positioning of two intake lobes and exhaust lobe on cylinder No. 1.
30. Mark components for installation into original locations.
31. Remove only three roller followers righthand cylinder head using valve spring compressor tool No. 303-1039, or equivalent, **Fig. 14. Do not allow valve keepers to fall off valve or valve may drop into cylinder.**
32. Remove only three roller followers lefthand cylinder head using valve spring compressor tool No. 303-1039, or equivalent, **Fig. 15. Do not allow valve keepers to fall off valve or valve may drop into cylinder.**

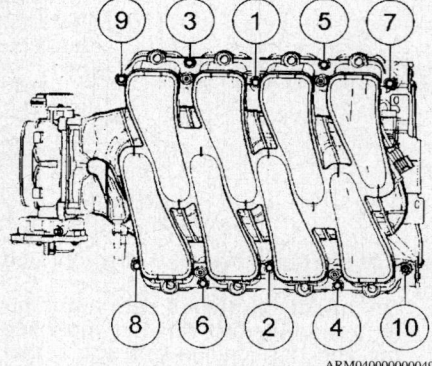

Fig. 7   Intake manifold tightening sequence

33. Rotate crankshaft clockwise and position crankshaft keyway at 6 o'clock position. **Do not move crankshaft past 6 o'clock position.**
34. Remove mounting bolts, then the lefthand and righthand timing chain tensioners and tensioner arms.
35. Remove righthand timing chain from camshaft and crankshaft sprockets.
36. Remove lefthand timing chain from the camshaft and crankshaft sprockets.
37. Remove two mounting bolts and both timing chain guides.
38. Remove mounting bolts, then the lefthand and righthand camshaft phaser sprocket using camshaft phase locking tool No. 303-1046, or equivalent. **Only use hand tools.**
39. Mark camshaft bearing caps for installation original locations.
40. Remove camshaft bearing caps bolts in sequence, **Fig. 16.**
41. **Remove front thrust camshaft bearing cap straight upward from bear-**

ing towers. Remove remaining bearing caps.
42. Remove camshaft.
43. Mark components for installation into original locations.
44. Remove all remaining roller followers.
45. Remove hydraulic lash adjusters.
46. Install cylinder head remover/installer tool No. T97T-6000-A, or equivalent.
47. Remove eight mounting nuts and exhaust manifold.
48. Remove nut and ground strap from lefthand cylinder head stud bolt.
49. Remove stud bolt and coolant tube from righthand cylinder head.
50. Place suitable, clean shop towels over exposed engine cavities.
51. Remove 20 mounting bolts, cylinder heads and gaskets.
52. Reverse procedure to install, noting the following:
    a. **Ensure all coolant residue and foreign material are cleaned from block surface and cylinder bore.**
    b. **Do not use sealing aids (aviation cement, copper spray and glue).** Gasket must be installed dry.
    c. **Cylinder head bolts are tighten-to-yield must be discarded and new bolts installed.**
    d. **Do not turn the crankshaft until instructed to do so.**
    e. Position cylinder head gaskets and cylinder heads over the dowels using cylinder head alignment pin tools No. SR-015486, or equivalent, and install cylinder head bolts loosely.

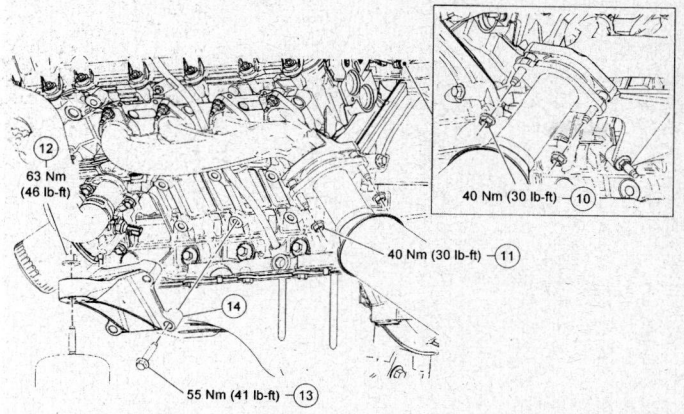

Item	Description
10	RH catalytic converter-to-exhaust manifold nuts (2 required)
11	LH catalytic converter-to-exhaust manifold nuts (2 required)
12	LH engine support insulator nut

Item	Description
13	LH engine support insulator bracket bolt (4 required)
14	LH engine support insulator bracket

ARM0400000000521

Fig. 8   Exhaust manifold replacement (Part 2 of 2), Lefthand

ARM0400000000520

Fig. 8   Exhaust manifold replacement (Part 1 of 2). Lefthand

f. **Torque** cylinder head bolts in sequence to 30 ft. lbs., **Fig. 17.**
g. Tighten head bolts an additional 90° in sequence.
h. Final tighten bolts an additional 90° in sequence.

VALVE COVER
REPLACE
Lefthand

1. Disconnect crankcase vent tube from air cleaner outlet pipe.
2. Loosen two clamps and remove air cleaner outlet pipe.
3. Disconnect ignition coil electrical connector.
4. Remove mounting bolts and ignition coil.
5. Raise and support vehicle.
6. Disconnect Evaporative Emissions (EVAP) canister purge valve from bracket and position it aside, **Fig. 18.**
7. Remove oil dipstick and tube mounting bolt.
8. Remove oil dipstick tube and O-ring.
9. Disconnect EVAP tube from Intake manifold, **Fig. 19.**
10. Remove Positive Crankcase Ventilation (PCV) tube.
11. Disconnect Variable Camshaft Timing (VCT) solenoid electrical connector and two wiring harness pin-type retainers.
12. Disconnect two wiring harness retainers from valve cover stud bolts.
13. Loosen 15 mounting bolts, then remove valve cover and gasket. **Mounting bolts are part of valve cover and should not be removed.**
14. Clean cylinder head valve cover mating surfaces with suitable silicone gasket remover.
15. Clean valve cover gasket groove with soap and water, or suitable solvent.
16. Reverse procedure to install, noting the following:
    a. **Valve cover must be secured within four minutes of sealant application.**

b. Apply .32 inch bead of suitable silicone gasket and sealant to where engine front cover meets cylinder head, **Fig. 20.**
c. Tighten mounting bolts in sequence, **Fig. 21.**
d. Lubricate new oil dipstick tube O-ring seal with suitable, clean engine oil.
e. Apply light film of suitable silicone brake caliper great and dielectric compound to inside of coil boots.

Righthand

1. Disconnect ignition coil electrical connector.
2. Remove mounting bolts and ignition coil.
3. Disconnect two wiring harness retainers from valve cover stud bolts.
4. Disconnect Variable Camshaft Timing (VCT) solenoid electrical connector, **Fig. 22.**
5. Disconnect Positive Crankcase Ventilation (PCV) tube.
6. Disconnect for wiring harness retainers from valve cover stud bolts.
7. Loosen 14 mounting bolts, then remove valve cover and gasket. **Mounting bolts are part of valve cover and should not be removed.**
8. Clean cylinder head valve cover mating surfaces with suitable silicone gasket remover.
9. Clean valve cover gasket groove with soap and water, or suitable solvent.
10. Reverse procedure to install, noting the following:
    a. **Valve cover must be secured within four minutes of sealant application.**
    b. Apply .32 inch bead of suitable silicone gasket and sealant to where engine front cover meets cylinder head, **Fig. 23.**
    c. Tighten mounting bolts in sequence, **Fig. 24.**
    d. Apply light film of suitable silicone brake caliper great and dielectric compound to inside of coil boots.

CAMSHAFT LOBE LIFT SPECIFICATIONS

Engine	Intake, Inch	Exhaust, Inch
4.6L SOHC (VIN H)	.217	.217

VALVE ADJUSTMENT

These engine are equipped with hydraulic valve lash adjusters. No valve adjustment is required.

HYDRAULIC LASH ADJUSTER
REPLACE

1. Remove camshafts as outlined under "Camshaft, Replace."
2. Rotate crankshaft until piston for valve being service is at top of stroke with intake and exhaust valves closed.
3. Compress spring and remove camshaft roller follower using valve spring compressor tool No. 303-1029, or equivalent.
4. Mark hydraulic lash adjusters for installation in original positions,
5. Remove hydraulic lash adjusters.
6. Reverse procedure to install.

CRANKSHAFT DAMPER
REPLACE

1. Raise and support vehicle.
2. Disconnect crankcase vent tube from air cleaner outlet pipe.
3. Loosen two clamps and remove air cleaner outlet pipe.
4. Rotate accessory drive belt tensioner clockwise with suitable belt tensioner release tool and remove belt.
5. Remove crankshaft pulley mounting bolt and washer.
6. Remove crankshaft pulley using suitable three-jaw puller tool.
7. Reverse procedure to install, noting the following:
    a. **Pulley must be secured within four minutes of sealant application.**
    b. Apply suitable silicone gasket and sealant to crankshaft pulley Woodruff key slot,
    c. Install crankshaft pulley using crankshaft vibration damper installer tool No. T74P-6316-B, or equivalent.

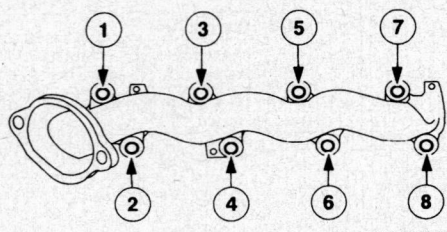

Fig. 9 Exhaust manifold tightening sequence. Lefthand

d. **Torque** next crankshaft pulley bolt to 66 ft. lbs.
e. Loosen crankshaft pulley bolt 360°.
f. **Torque** pulley bolt to 37 ft. lbs.
g. Tighten bolt an additional 90°.

FRONT COVER
REPLACE

1. Raise and support vehicle.
2. Drain engine oil into suitable container.
3. Drain engine coolant into suitable container.
4. Disconnect, the position upper and lower degas bottle hoses aside.
5. Remove two mounting bolts and degas bottle.
6. Rotate accessory drive belt tensioner clockwise with suitable belt tensioner release tool and remove belt.
7. Remove mounting bolt and righthand belt idler pulley.
8. Remove valve covers as outlined under "Valve Cover, Replace."
9. Disconnect two coolant hoses from crossover, **Fig. 25.**
10. Remove mounting nut and position righthand radio ignition interference capacitor aside.
11. Disconnect righthand Camshaft Position (CMP) sensor electrical connector.
12. Remove mounting nut and position lefthand radio ignition interference capacitor aside.
13. Remove J bracket from engine front cover stud bolt.
14. Disconnect lefthand CMP sensor electrical connector.
15. Remover four mounting bolts and water pump pulley.
16. Remove two mounting nuts and power steering pulley shield.
17. Remove wiring harness, retainer, nut and tube clip from power steering stud bolt.
18. Remove three stud bolts and support power steering pump aside.
19. Disconnect Crankshaft Position (CKP) sensor connector.
20. Remove crankshaft pulley mounting bolt and washer.
21. Remove crankshaft pulley using suitable three-jaw puller tool.
22. Remove crankshaft seal using crankshaft front seal remover tool No. T74P-66700-A, or equivalent.
23. Remove four front oil pan mounting bolts.
24. Record front cover mounting bolt locations for installation alignment.

25. Remove mounting bolts, studs and front cover.
26. Clean mating surfaces with suitable silicone gasket remover.
27. Reverse procedure to install, noting the following:
   a. **Front cover must be secured within four minutes of sealant application.**
   b. Apply silicone gasket and sealant along cylinder head-to-cylinder block and oil pan-to-cylinder block surfaces, **Fig. 26.**
   c. Install new front cover gasket and tighten mounting bolts and studs in sequence to 15 ft. lbs., **Fig. 27.**
   d. Tighten bolts and studs an additional 60° in sequence.

FRONT COVER SEAL
REPLACE

1. Remove crankshaft pulley as outlined under "Crankshaft Damper, Replace,"
2. Remove crankshaft seal using crankshaft front seal remover tool No. T74P-66700-A, or equivalent.
3. Reverse procedure to install, noting the following:
   a. Lubricate engine front cover and crankshaft front seal inner lip with suitable, clean engine oil.
   b. Install seal using crankshaft front seal installer tool No. 303-635, front cover seal installer tool No. T88T-6701-A and crankshaft vibration damper installer tool No. T74P-6316-B, or equivalents.

TIMING CHAIN
REPLACE

These engines have an interference fit design. If engine has jumped time cylinder heads must be removed to repair damage to valves and/or pistons.

At no time, when the timing chains are removed and the cylinder heads are installed, may the crankshaft and/or camshaft be rotated unless all rocker arms have been removed. Rotation may result in valve and/or piston damage.

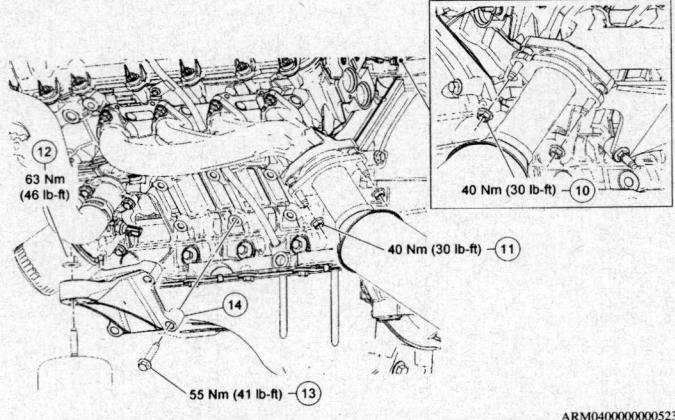

Fig. 10 Exhaust manifold replacement. Righthand

Before loosening or tightening camshaft sprocket nuts and bolts, ensure camshaft positioning and locking devices are in place.

Removal

1. Remove engine front cover as outlined under "Front Cover, Replace."
2. Remove crankshaft sensor ring.
3. Position crankshaft keyway at 12 o'clock position, **Fig. 12,** noting the following:
   a. If camshaft lobes are not exactly positioned, **Fig. 13,** crankshaft will require one full additional rotation to 12 o'clock position.
   b. Cylinder No. 1 camshaft exhaust lobe must be coming up on exhaust stroke.
   c. Ensure positioning of two intake lobes and exhaust lobe on cylinder No. 1.
4. Remove only three roller followers righthand cylinder head using valve spring compressor tool No. 303-1039, or equivalent, **Fig. 14. Do not allow valve keepers to fall off valve or valve may drop into cylinder.**
5. Remove only three roller followers lefthand cylinder head using valve spring compressor tool No. 303-1039, or equivalent, **Fig. 15. Do not allow valve keepers to fall off valve or valve may drop into cylinder.**
6. Rotate crankshaft clockwise and position crankshaft keyway at 6 o'clock position. **Do not move crankshaft past 6 o'clock position.**
7. Remove mounting bolts, then the lefthand and righthand timing chain tensioners and tensioner arms.
8. Remove righthand timing chain from camshaft and crankshaft sprockets.
9. Remove lefthand timing chain from the camshaft and crankshaft sprockets.
10. Remove two mounting bolts and both timing chain guides.
11. Remove mounting bolts, then the lefthand and righthand camshaft phaser

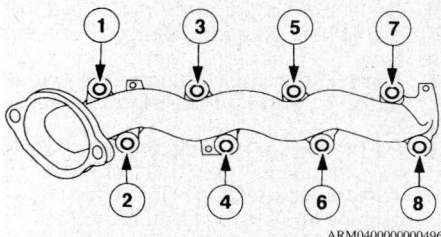

Fig. 11   Exhaust manifold tightening sequence. Righthand

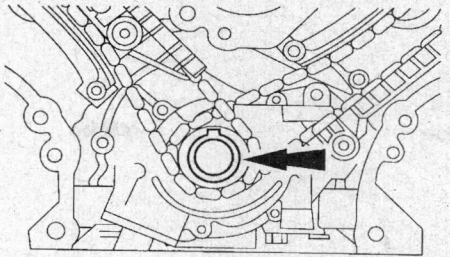

Fig. 12   Crankshaft keyway 12 o'clock position

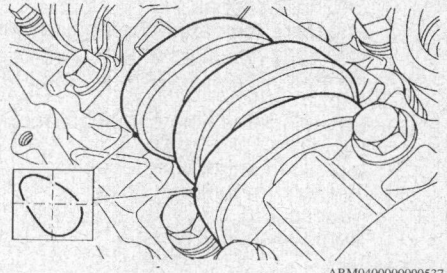

Fig. 13   Camshaft lobe positioning

sprocket using camshaft phase locking tool No. 303-1046, or equivalent. **Only use hand tools.**

12. Mark camshaft bearing caps for installation original locations.
13. Remove camshaft bearing caps bolts in sequence, **Fig. 16.**
14. **Remove front thrust camshaft bearing cap straight upward from bearing towers.** Remove remaining bearing caps.
15. Mark components for installation into original locations.
16. Remove all remaining roller followers.

INSTALLATION

1. Install camshafts as outlined under "Camshaft, Replace."
2. Install camshaft phaser sprockets and new mounting bolts finger tight.
3. **Torque** camshaft phaser sprocket bolts using camshaft phase locking tool No. 303-1046, or equivalent. to 30 ft. lbs. **Only use hand tools.**
4. Tighten sprocket bolts an additional 90°.
5. Install crankshaft sprocket, making sure the flange faces forward.
6. Rotate crankshaft to position crankshaft sprocket timing mark in 6 o'clock position, **Fig. 28.**
7. Compress tensioner plunger, using suitable vise.
8. Install suitable retaining clip to hold plunger in place.
9. If copper links are not visible, mark one 1 link on one end and one link on other end and use as timing marks.
10. Install timing chain guides and four mounting bolts.
11. Position lower end of lefthand (inner) timing chain on crankshaft sprocket, aligning timing mark on outer flange of crankshaft sprocket with single copper (marked) link on chain, **Fig. 29.**
12. Ensure upper half of timing chain is below tensioner arm dowel.
13. Position lefthand timing chain on camshaft sprocket. Ensure camshaft sprocket timing mark is aligned with copper (marked) chain link, **Fig. 30.**
14. Position lefthand timing chain tensioner arm on dowel pin, then install lefthand timing chain tensioner and mounting bolts. Lefthand timing chain tensioner arm has bump near dowel hole for identification.
15. Remove retaining clip from lefthand timing chain tensioner.
16. Position lower end of righthand (outer) timing chain on crankshaft sprocket, aligning timing mark on sprocket with

single copper (marked) chain link, **Fig. 31.**
17. Lower half of timing chain must be positioned above tensioner arm dowel.
18. Position righthand timing chain on camshaft sprocket. Ensure camshaft sprocket timing mark is aligned with copper (marked) chain link, **Fig. 32.**
19. Position righthand timing chain tensioner arm on dowel pin, then install righthand timing chain tensioner and mounting bolts.
20. Remove retaining clip from righthand timing chain tensioner.
21. Righthand and lefthand camshaft phaser sprockets are similar. Righthand camshaft phaser sprocket has single timing mark to identify, while L timing mark identifies lefthand camshaft phaser sprocket. Ensure timing marks on sprockets align, **Fig. 33.**
22. Install crankshaft sensor ring.
23. Lubricate roller followers with suitable, clean engine oil.
24. Rotate engine to position camshaft lobes at base circle and install all camshaft roller followers.
25. Install engine front cover as outlined under "Front Cover, Replace."

CAMSHAFT
REPLACE

These engines have an interference fit design. If engine has jumped time cylinder heads must be removed to repair damage to valves and/or pistons.

At no time, when the timing chains are removed and the cylinder heads are installed, may the crankshaft and/or camshaft be rotated unless all rocker arms have been removed. Rotation may result in valve and/or piston damage.

Before loosening or tightening camshaft sprocket nuts and bolts, ensure camshaft positioning and locking devices are in place.

If removing both camshafts, righthand camshaft must be removed first.

Righthand

1. Position crankshaft damper spoke at 12 o'clock position and timing mark indentation at 1 o'clock position, **Fig. 34.**
2. Remove righthand valve cover as outlined under "Valve Cover, replace."
3. Loosen and back off righthand camshaft phaser bolt one full turn.

4. Disconnect righthand Camshaft Position (CMP) sensor electrical connector.
5. Remove mounting bolt and righthand CMP sensor.
6. If camshaft lobes are not exactly positioned, **Fig. 13,** crankshaft will require one full additional rotation to 12 o'clock position.
7. Cylinder No. 1 camshaft exhaust lobe must be coming up on exhaust stroke.
8. Ensure positioning of two intake lobes and exhaust lobe on cylinder No. 1.
9. Remove only three roller followers righthand cylinder head using valve spring compressor tool No. 303-1039, or equivalent, **Fig. 14. Do not allow valve keepers to fall off valve or valve may drop into cylinder.**
10. Rotate crankshaft clockwise, as viewed from front, positioning crankshaft damper spoke at 6 o'clock position and timing mark indentation at 7 o'clock position, **Fig. 35. Crankshaft cannot be moved past 6 o'clock position once set.**
11. Install timing chain wedge tool No. 303-636 and handle tool No. 303-637, or equivalents, square to timing chain and engine block, **Fig. 36.**
12. **If timing chain wedge is removed or out of placement, engine front cover must be removed and engine must be timed.**
13. Mark timing chain and camshaft phaser sprocket for installation alignment.
14. Mark camshaft bearing caps for installation original locations.
15. Remove camshaft bearing caps bolts in sequence, **Fig. 16.**
16. **Remove front thrust camshaft bearing cap straight upward from bearing towers.** Remove remaining bearing caps.
17. Remove mounting bolt and withdraw camshaft from phaser sprocket leaving sprocket in place.
18. Reverse procedure to install, noting the following:
    a. Lubricate camshaft and camshaft journals with suitable, clean engine oil.
    b. Ensure camshaft phaser sprocket and timing chain scribe marks are still in alignment.
    c. **Do not allow roller followers to move out of position when installing camshaft.**
    d. Install camshaft bearing caps in

original locations.

e. Lubricate camshaft bearing caps with suitable, clean engine oil.

f. Position front camshaft bearing cap.

g. Position remaining camshaft bearing caps.

h. Install mounting bolts loosely.

i. Tighten mounting bolts in sequence, **Fig. 37.**

j. Remove special tools.

Lefthand

1. Position crankshaft damper spoke at 12 o'clock position and timing mark indentation at 1 o'clock position, **Fig. 34.**
2. Remove lefthand valve cover as outlined under "Valve Cover, replace."
3. Loosen and back off lefthand camshaft phaser bolt one full turn.
4. Disconnect lefthand Camshaft Position (CMP) sensor electrical connector.
5. Remove mounting bolt and lefthand CMP sensor.
6. If camshaft lobes are not exactly positioned, **Fig. 38,** crankshaft keyway will require one full additional rotation to 12 o'clock position.
7. Cylinder No. 5 cylinder must be coming up on exhaust stroke.
8. Ensure positioning of two intake lobes and exhaust lobe on cylinder No. .5.
9. Remove only three roller followers lefthand cylinder head using valve spring compressor tool No. 303-1039, or equivalent, **Fig. 15. Do not allow valve keepers to fall off valve or valve may drop into cylinder.**
10. Rotate crankshaft clockwise, as viewed from front, positioning crankshaft damper spoke at 6 o'clock position and timing mark indentation at 7 o'clock position, **Fig. 35. Crankshaft cannot be moved past 6 o'clock position once set.**
11. Install timing chain wedge tool No. 303-636 and handle tool No. 303-637, or equivalents, square to timing chain and engine block, **Fig. 39.**
12. **If timing chain wedge is removed or out of placement, engine front cover must be removed and engine must be timed.**
13. Mark timing chain and camshaft phaser sprocket for installation alignment.
14. Mark camshaft bearing caps for installation original locations.
15. Remove camshaft bearing caps bolts in sequence, **Fig. 16.**
16. **Remove front thrust camshaft bearing cap straight upward from bearing towers.** Remove remaining bearing caps.
17. Remove mounting bolt and withdraw camshaft from phaser sprocket leaving sprocket in place.
18. Reverse procedure to install, noting the following:

    a. Lubricate camshaft and camshaft journals with suitable, clean engine oil.

    b. Ensure camshaft phaser sprocket and timing chain scribe marks are

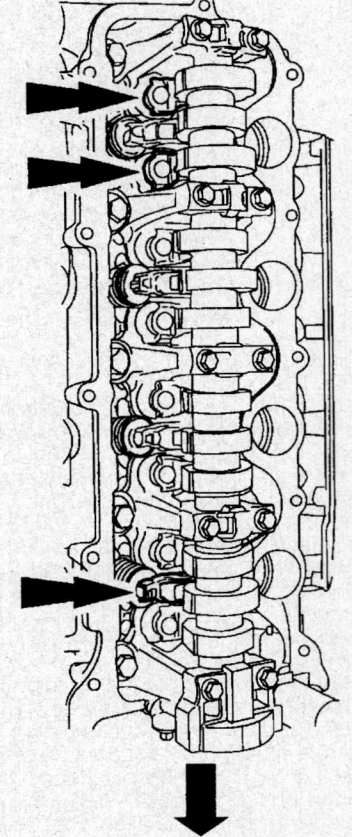

Fig. 14 Roller follower removal. Righthand

still in alignment.

c. **Do not allow roller followers to move out of position when installing camshaft.**

d. Install camshaft bearing caps in original locations.

e. Lubricate camshaft bearing caps with suitable, clean engine oil.

f. Position front camshaft bearing cap.

g. Position remaining camshaft bearing caps.

h. Install mounting bolts loosely.

i. Tighten mounting bolts in sequence, **Fig. 37.**

j. Remove special tools.

PISTON & ROD ASSEMBLY

The connecting rod must be installed into the connecting rod with identification markings toward the front, **Fig. 40.**

1. Lubricate piston and ring with suitable, clean engine oil.
2. Lubricate rod bearings with suitable, clean engine oil.
3. Install piston and connecting rod with upper connecting rod bearing in place using suitable piston ring compressor tool and connecting rod installer tools No. T93P-6136-A, or equivalent.

4. Once connecting rod is seated on crankshaft journal, remove special tools.
5. **The rod cap must be in same orientation as marked during disassembly.**
6. Position lower bearing and connecting rod , then install new bolts loosely.
7. **Torque** connecting rod bolts in sequence to 32 ft. lbs., **Fig. 41.**
8. Tighten bolts and additional 105° in sequence.

MAIN & ROD BEARINGS

1. Install crankshaft main bearings.
2. Install crankshaft upper main bearings into cylinder block.
3. Install crankshaft lower main bearings into bearing caps.
4. Ensure all oil passages are aligned.
5. Lubricate all main bearings with suitable, clean engine oil.
6. Lubricate crankshaft bearing journals with suitable, clean engine oil
7. Install crankshaft onto upper crankshaft main bearings.
8. **Oil groove on thrust washer must face toward rear of engine (against crankshaft thrust surface).**
9. Push crankshaft rearward and install rear crankshaft upper thrust washer at back of main boss No. 5.
10. Install rear (No. 5) main bearing cap.
11. Install crankshaft lower main bearings into main bearing caps and lubricate them with suitable, clean engine oil.
12. Locate main bearing cap on cylinder block and, keeping cap as square as possible, alternately draw cap down evenly using cap fasteners.
13. Push crankshaft forward to seat crankshaft thrust washer. Hold crankshaft in forward position.
14. Install vertical main bearing cap nuts and bolts, then tighten in sequence, **Fig. 42.**
15. **Torque** 1–20 in sequence to 89 inch lbs.
16. **Torque** 1–10 in sequence to 18 ft. lbs.
17. **Torque** 11–20 in sequence to 30 ft. lbs.
18. Tighten 1–20 an additional 90@ in sequence.
19. Install cross-mounted main bearing cap bolts and tighten in sequence, **Fig. 43.**
20. **Torque** in sequence to 30 ft. lbs.
21. Tighten an additional 90° in sequence.
22. Inspect crankshaft end play.
23. Ensure crankshaft torque-to-turn does not exceed 53 inch lbs.

CRANKSHAFT SEAL
REPLACE

1. Remove crankshaft pulley as outlined under "Crankshaft Damper, Replace,"
2. Remove crankshaft seal using crankshaft front seal remover tool No. T74P-66700-A, or equivalent, **Fig. 44.**
3. Reverse procedure to install, noting the following:

    a. Lubricate engine front cover and

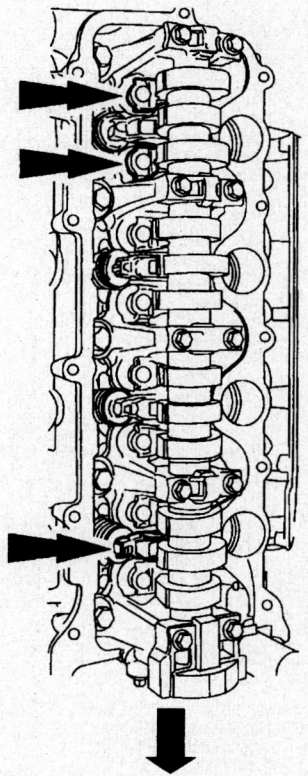

ARM0400000000539

Fig. 15 Roller follower removal. Lefthand

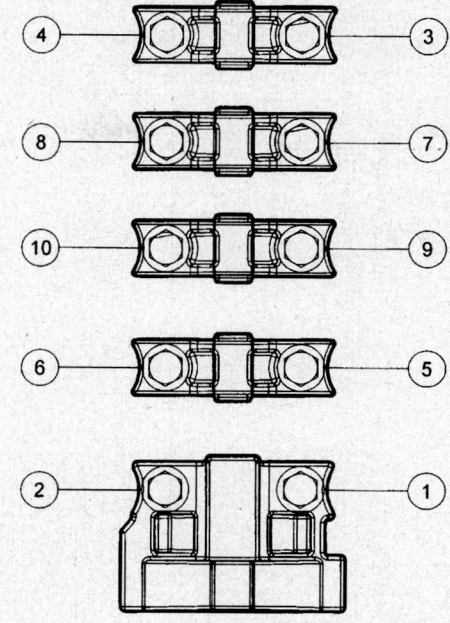

ARM0400000000540

Fig. 16 Camshaft bearing cap removal sequence

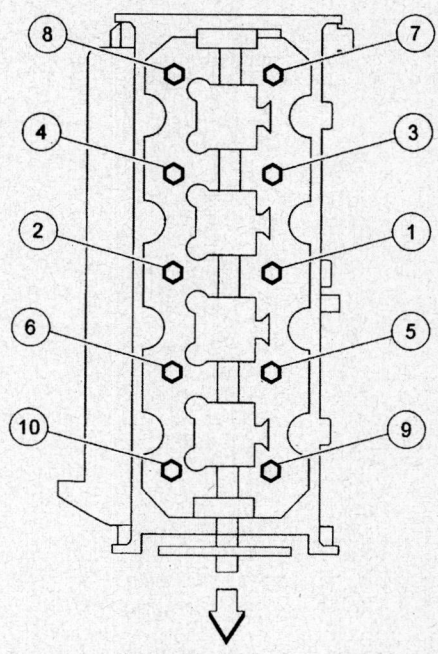

ARM0400000000541

Fig. 17 Cylinder head tightening sequence

crankshaft front seal inner lip with suitable, clean engine oil.
b. Install seal using crankshaft front seal installer tool No. 303-635, front cover seal installer tool No. T88T-6701-A and crankshaft vibration damper installer tool No. T74P-6316-B, or equivalents.

CRANKSHAFT REAR OIL SEAL
REPLACE

1. Remove automatic transmission or manual transmission and clutch as outlined in **MOTOR's "Domestic Transmission, In-Vehicle Service." or "Transmission Service DVD."**
2. Remove six mounting bolts and flywheel/flexplate, **Fig. 45.**
3. Remove engine-to-transmission spacer plate.
4. Remove crankshaft oil slinger using crankshaft rear oil seal slinger remover tool No. T95P-6701-AH, or equivalent, and suitable impact slide hammer.
5. Remove crankshaft rear seal using crankshaft rear seal remover tool No. T95P-6701-EH, or equivalent, and suitable impact slide hammer.
6. Remove two oil pan-to-crankshaft rear seal retainer plate bolts.
7. Remove six mounting bolts and crankshaft rear seal retainer plate.
8. Clean sealing surfaces with suitable silicone gasket remover.

9. Reverse procedure to install, noting the following:
   a. **Rear crankshaft seal retainer plate must be secured within four minutes of sealant application.**
   b. Apply .16 inch bead of silicone gasket and sealant around crankshaft rear seal retainer plate sealing surface.
   c. Tighten mounting bolts in sequence, **Fig. 46.**
   d. Tighten flywheel/flexplate mounting bolts in sequence, **Fig. 47.**
   e. **Torque** retainer plate-to-oil pan bolts to 15 ft. lbs., then tighten an additional 60°.
   f. Lubricate crankshaft rear seal with suitable, clean engine oil, then install using crankshaft rear seal installer tools Nos. T95P-6701-BH and T95P-6701-DH, or equivalents.
   g. Install crankshaft real oil slinger using crankshaft rear oil slinger tool No. T95P-6501-BH, crankshaft rear seal installer tools Nos. T95P-6701-BH and T95P-6701-DH, or equivalents.

OIL PAN
REPLACE

1. Raise and support vehicle.
2. Drain engine oil into suitable container.
3. Loosen clamp and disconnect air cleaner outlet pipe.
4. Disconnect Mass Air Flow (MAF) sensor electrical connector.
5. Remove mounting bolt and air cleaner. Ensure two rubber grommets are retained to feet.
6. Disconnect Throttle Position (TP) sen-

sor and electronic throttle control electrical connectors, **Fig. 1.**
7. Remove mounting bolts, nuts and throttle body.
8. Remove six pin-type retainers and radiator sight shield, **Fig. 2.**
9. Remove two outer bracket mounting bolts and two lower mounting nuts, then disconnect alternator electrical connector and pin-type retainer.
10. Position cover aside, then remove B+ terminal nut and alternator.
11. Support engine using suitable engine lifting brackets and three-bar engine support tools.
12. Remove lefthand and righthand engine support insulator nuts.
13. Raise engine approximately 1.57 inches.
14. Position suitable adjustable jack stand under subframe.
15. Mark position of four subframe mounting nuts and four mounting bolts for installation alignment.
16. Remove subframe mounting nuts and bolts.
17. Lower subframe approximately 1.96 inches.
18. Disconnect oil temperature sensor electrical connector and two pin-type retainers.
19. Remove six mounting bolts, oil pan and gasket. **Oil pan gasket is reusable if it is not damaged.**
20. Reverse procedure to install, noting the following:
   a. Clean oil pan mating surface with suitable silicone gasket remover and metal surface prep.
   b. **Oil pan must be secured within four minutes of sealant application.**
   c. Apply silicone gasket and sealant

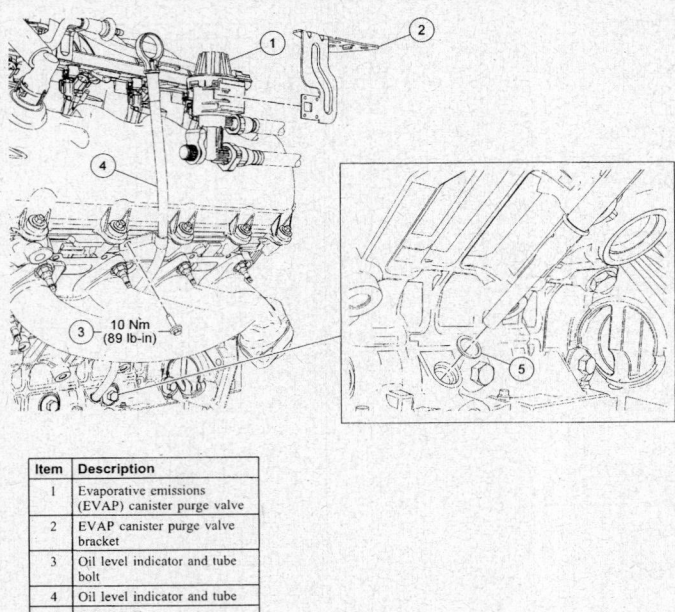

Fig. 18   Oil Dipstick tube replacement

Item	Description
1	Evaporative emissions (EVAP) canister purge valve
2	EVAP canister purge valve bracket
3	Oil level indicator and tube bolt
4	Oil level indicator and tube
5	O-ring seal

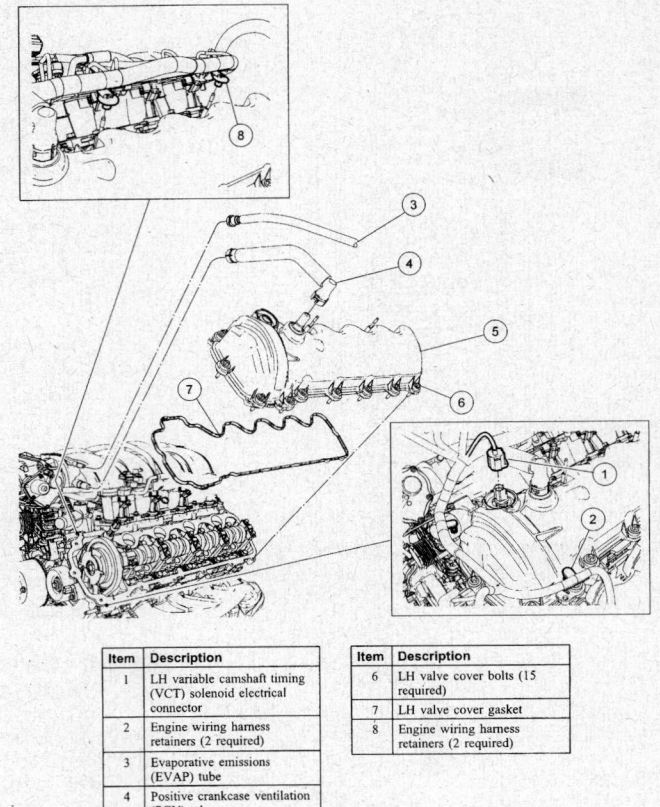

Item	Description	Item	Description
1	LH variable camshaft timing (VCT) solenoid electrical connector	6	LH valve cover bolts (15 required)
2	Engine wiring harness retainers (2 required)	7	LH valve cover gasket
3	Evaporative emissions (EVAP) tube	8	Engine wiring harness retainers (2 required)
4	Positive crankcase ventilation (PCV) tube		
5	LH valve cover		

ARM0400000000500

Fig. 19   Valve cover replacement. Lefthand

at crankshaft rear seal retainer plate-to-cylinder block sealing surface, **Fig. 48.**

d. Apply silicone gasket and sealant at engine front cover-to-cylinder block sealing surface, **Fig. 48.**

e. Install gasket and the oil pan, then loosely install 16 mounting bolts.

f. **Torque** oil pan mounting bolts in sequence to 18 inch lbs., **Fig. 49.**

g. **Torque** pan mounting bolts in sequence to 15 ft. lbs.

h. Tighten mounting bolts an additional 60° in sequence.

OIL PUMP
REPLACE

1. Remove oil pan as outlined under "Oil Pane, Replace."
2. Remove timing chain as outlined under "Timing Chain, Replace."
3. Remove mounting bolts, then the oil pump screen and pickup tube.
4. Remove three mounting bolts and oil pump.
5. Reverse procedure to install.

BELT TENSION DATA

These models are equipped with an automatic drive belt tensioner. No adjustment or maintenance is required.

SERPENTINE DRIVE BELT

Always use square drive tool in hole in tensioner to move tensioner. Never pry on tensioner pulley. When releasing drive belt tensioner, never allow tensioner to snap back. Damage to tensioner or personal injury could result.

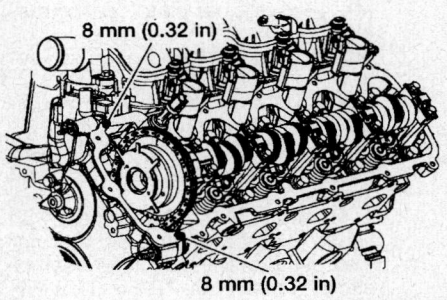

Fig. 20   Valve cover silicone gasket & sealant. Lefthand

Do not allow engine coolant to remain on serpentine belt or pulleys. If required, remove belt and flush with clean water.

Routing

Refer to **Fig. 50** for serpentine drive belt routing.

Replacement

Rotate the accessory drive belt tensioner clockwise with suitable belt tensioner release tool and remove the belt.

COOLING SYSTEM BLEED

1. Fill radiator through degas bottle until the coolant level is between the COOLANT FILL LEVEL marks.
2. Select maximum heater temperature and blower motor speed settings.
3. Position control to discharge air at air conditioning vents in instrument panel.
4. Start engine and allow to idle.
5. While engine is idling, feel for hot air at air conditioning vents.
6. **If air discharge remains cool and engine coolant temperature gauge does not move, engine coolant level is low and must be filled. Stop engine, allow it to cool and fill cooling system.**
7. Allow engine to idle until normal operating temperature is reached. Hot air should discharge from air conditioning vents.
8. Engine coolant temperature gauge should maintain stabilized reading in middle of NORMAL range.
9. Upper radiator hose should feel hot to touch.
10. Shut engine off and allow it to cool.
11. Inspect engine for coolant leaks.
12. Inspect and adjust engine coolant level in degas bottle.

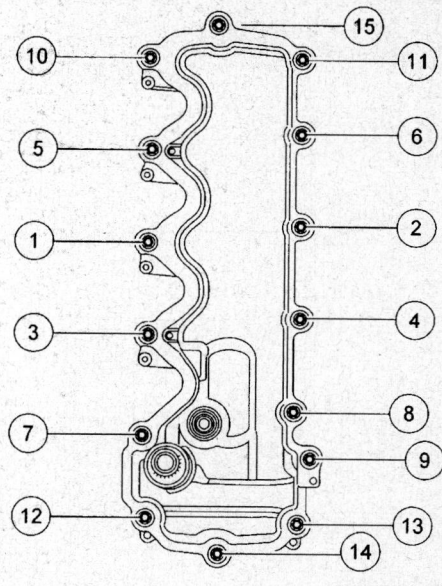

Fig. 21 Valve cover tightening sequence. Lefthand

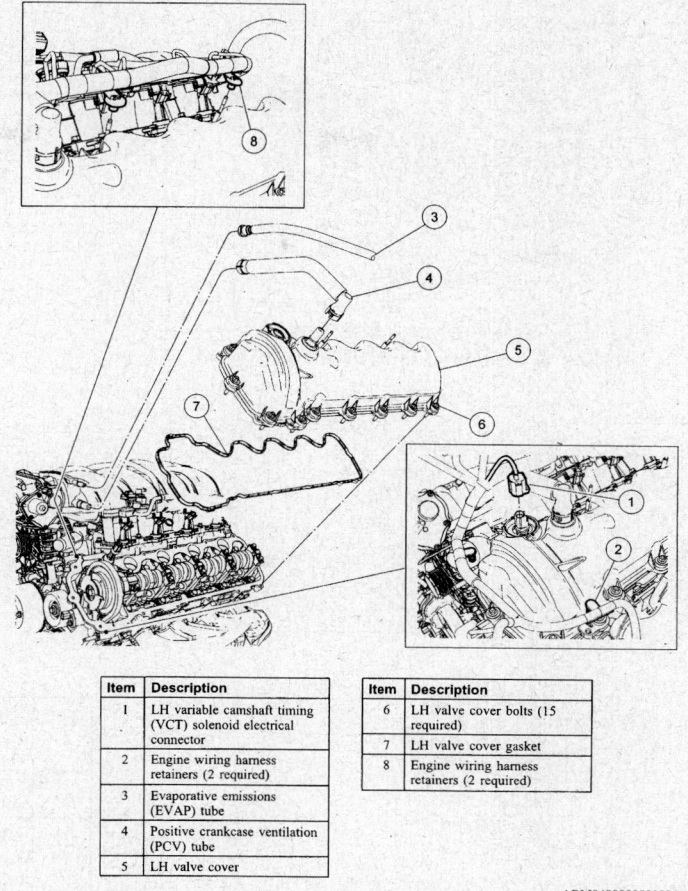

Item	Description
1	LH variable camshaft timing (VCT) solenoid electrical connector
2	Engine wiring harness retainers (2 required)
3	Evaporative emissions (EVAP) tube
4	Positive crankcase ventilation (PCV) tube
5	LH valve cover

Item	Description
6	LH valve cover bolts (15 required)
7	LH valve cover gasket
8	Engine wiring harness retainers (2 required)

Fig. 22 Valve cover replacement. Righthand

THERMOSTAT

REPLACE

1. Drain engine cooling system into suitable container.
2. Loosen clamp and disconnect air cleaner outlet pipe.
3. Remove two housing mounting bolts, thermostat. and O-ring seal.
4. Reverse procedure to install using new thermostat O-ring seal and lubricate with suitable, clean engine coolant.

WATER PUMP

REPLACE

1. Drain engine cooling system into suitable container.
2. Loosen clamp and disconnect air cleaner outlet pipe.
3. Loosen four coolant pump pulley bolts, **Fig. 51**.
4. Rotate accessory drive belt tensioner clockwise with suitable belt tensioner release tool and remove belt.
5. Remove four mounting bolts and water pump pulley.
6. Remove four mounting bolts, water pump and O-ring seal.
7. Reverse procedure to install, install new coolant pump O-ring seal and lubricate with suitable, clean engine coolant.

RADIATOR

REPLACE

Refer to "4.0L Engine" for radiator replacement procedure.

FUEL PUMP

REPLACE

Refer to "4.0L Engine" for fuel pump replacement procedure

FUEL FILTER

REPLACE

Refer to "4.0L Engine" for fuel pump replacement procedure

TECHNICAL SERVICE BULLETINS

Ticking And/Or Knocking Noise From Engine

2005 MUSTANG

This condition may be caused by a leaking lash adjuster or a faulting Variable Cam Timing (VCT) cam phaser.

To correct this condition proceed with the following procedures.

LASH ADJUSTER

1. Ensure engine oil is full and vehicle is at curb idle and operating temperature.
2. Use a stethoscope on top of cam cover bolt heads to confirm which bank is affected.
3. Move probe from front to rear and isolate affected cylinder.
4. Replace both intake and exhaust lash adjusters of the affected cylinder with revised lash adjuster part No. 5L1Z-6500-AA.

VCT CAM PHASER

1. Place transmission in park or neutral.
2. Bring engine oil temperature to 160° F.
3. Set engine speed to over 1200 RPM, if noise is a VCT knock, the noise should disappear.
4. If noise intensity is more than a lightly audible knock at hot idle under 1200 RPM at engine operating temperature, replace VCT cam phaser with revised cam phaser Part No. 3R2Z-6A257-DA.

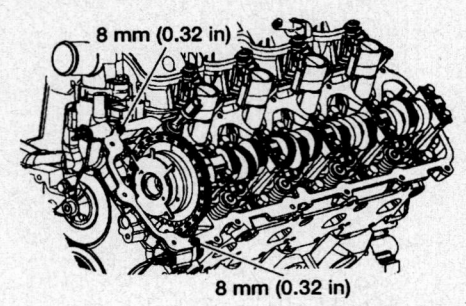

Fig. 23 Valve cover silicone gasket & sealant. Righthand

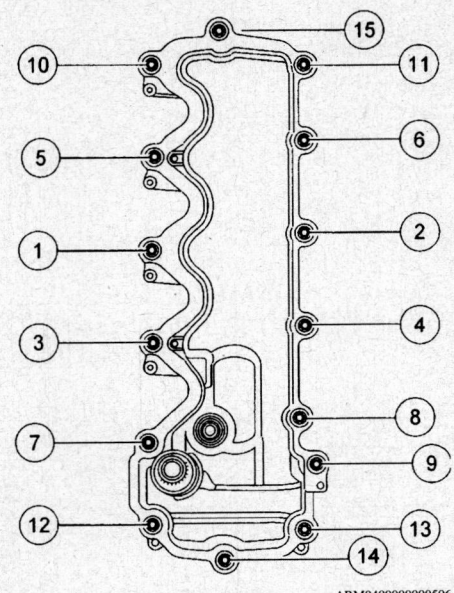

Fig. 24 Valve cover tightening sequence. Righthand

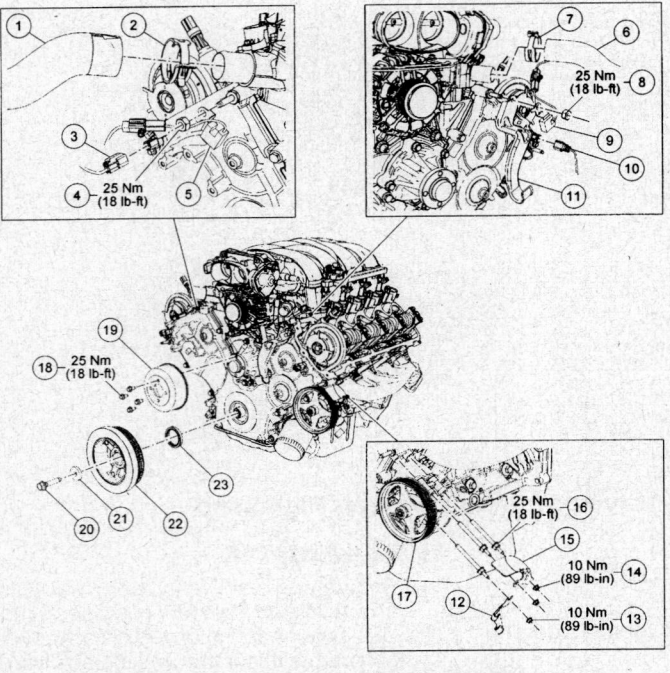

Item	Description
1	Coolant hose
2	Hose clamp
3	RH camshaft position (CMP) sensor electrical connector
4	RH radio ignition interference capacitor nut
5	RH radio ignition interference capacitor
6	Coolant hose

Item	Description
7	Hose clamp
8	LH radio ignition interference capacitor nut
9	LH radio ignition interference capacitor
10	LH CMP sensor electrical connector
11	J-bracket
12	Power steering tube retaining clip

Fig. 25 Front cover replacement (Part 1 of 3)

Item	Description
13	Power steering tube retaining clip nut
14	Power steering pulley shield nut (2 required)
15	Power steering pulley shield
16	Power steering pump stud bolt (3 required)
17	Power steering pump

Item	Description
18	Coolant pump pulley bolts (4 required)
19	Coolant pump pulley
20	Crankshaft pulley bolt
21	Crankshaft pulley bolt washer
22	Crankshaft pulley
23	Crankshaft front oil seal

Fig. 25 Front cover replacement (Part 2 of 3)

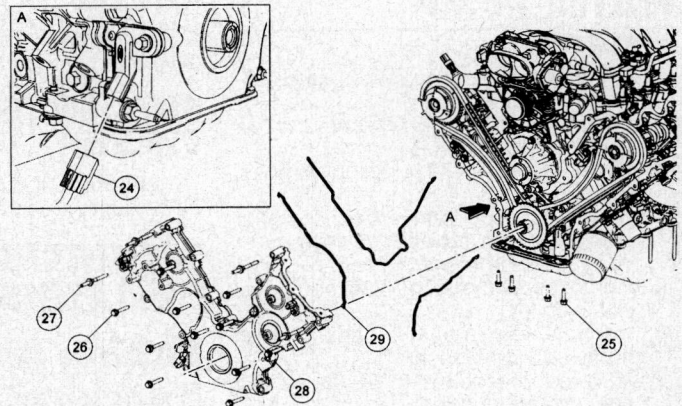

Item	Description
24	Crankshaft position (CKP) sensor electrical connector
25	Oil pan bolts (4 required)
26	Engine front cover bolts (11 required)
27	Engine front cover studs (4 required)
28	Engine front cover
29	Engine front cover gaskets (3 required)

Fig. 25 Front cover replacement (Part 3 of 3)

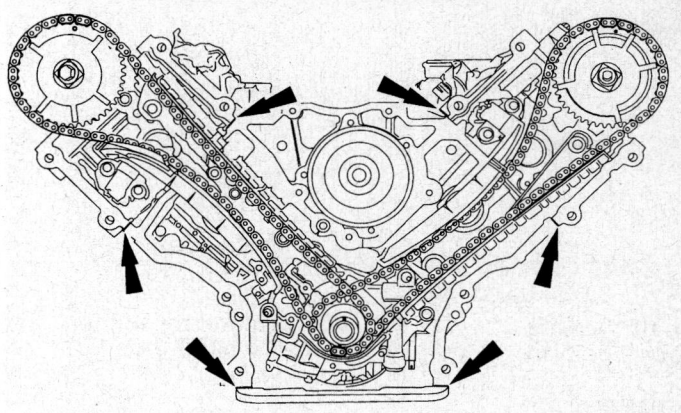

Fig. 26 Front cover sealing

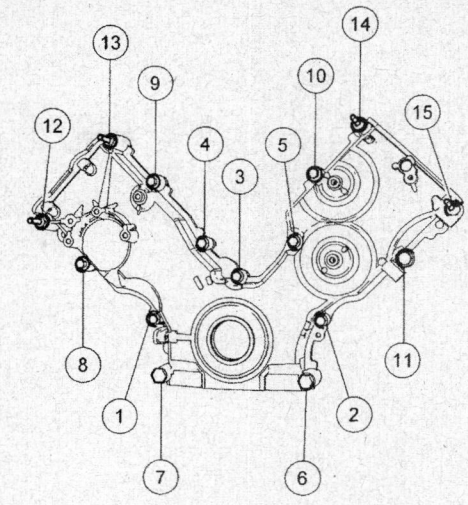

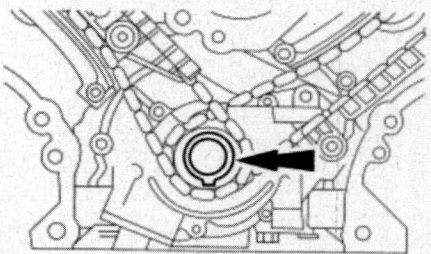

Fig. 28 Crankshaft keyway 6 o'clock position

Item	Description	Item	Description
1	Bolt, Hex Flange Head Pilot, M8 x 1.25 x 53	10	Bolt, Hex Flange Head Pilot, M8 x 1.25 x 53
2	Bolt, Hex Flange Head Pilot, M8 x 1.25 x 53	11	Bolt, Hex Flange Head Pilot, M8 x 1.25 x 53
3	Bolt, Hex Flange Head Pilot, M8 x 1.25 x 53	12	Stud, Hex Shoulder Pilot, M8 x 1.25 x 1.25 x 91.1
4	Bolt, Hex Flange Head Pilot, M8 x 1.25 x 53	13	Stud, Hex Shoulder Pilot, M8 x 1.25 x 1.25 x 91.1
5	Bolt, Hex Flange Head Pilot, M8 x 1.25 x 53	14	Stud, Hex Shoulder Pilot, M8 x 1.25 x 1.25 x 91.1
6	Bolt, Hex Flange Head Pilot, M8 x 1.25 x 53	15	Stud, Hex Shoulder Pilot, M8 x 1.25 x 1.25 x 91.1
7	Bolt, Hex Flange Head Pilot, M8 x 1.25 x 53		
8	Bolt, Hex Flange Head Pilot, M8 x 1.25 x 53		
9	Bolt, Hex Flange Head Pilot, M8 x 1.25 x 53		

Fig. 27 Front cover tightening sequence

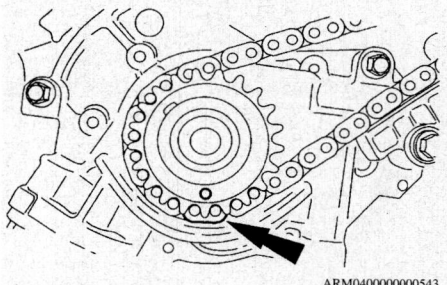

Fig. 29 Lefthand timing chain & crankshaft sprocket alignment

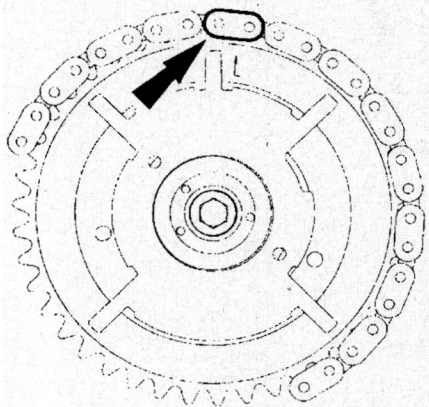

Fig. 30 Lefthand timing chain & camshaft sprocket alignment

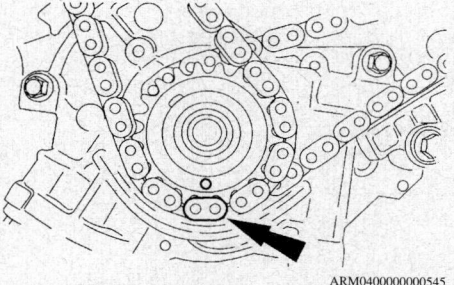

Fig. 31 Righthand timing chain & crankshaft sprocket alignment

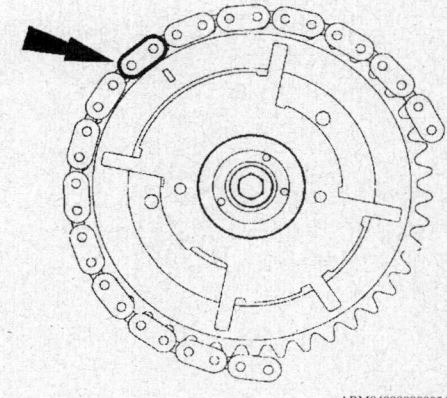

Fig. 32 Righthand timing chain & camshaft sprocket alignment

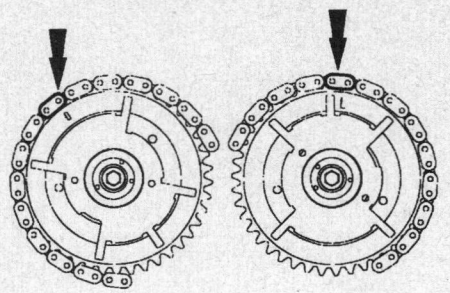

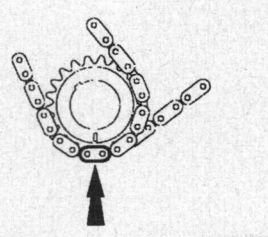

Fig. 33 Timing chain alignment

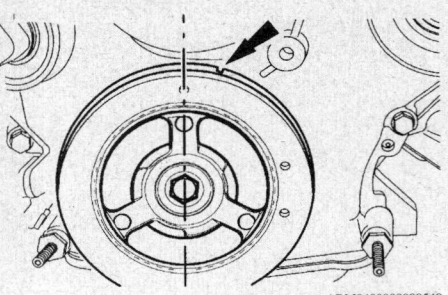

Fig. 34 Crankshaft damper position 12 o'clock position

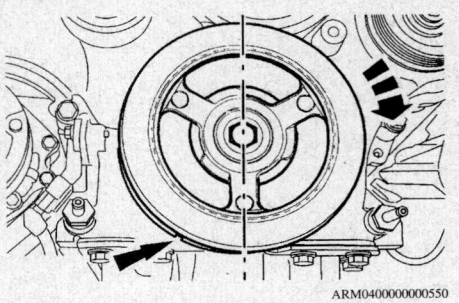

Fig. 35 Crankshaft damper position 6 o'clock position

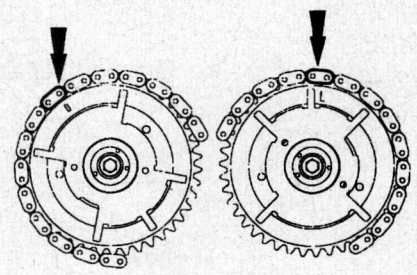

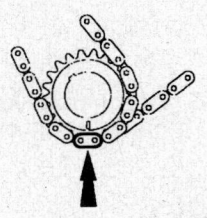

Fig. 38 Lefthand camshaft lobe positioning

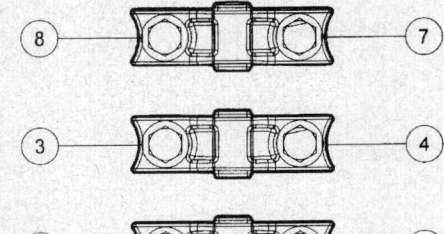

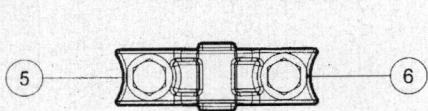

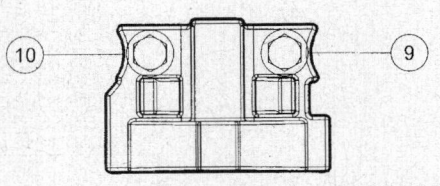

Fig. 37 Camshaft bearing cap tightening sequence

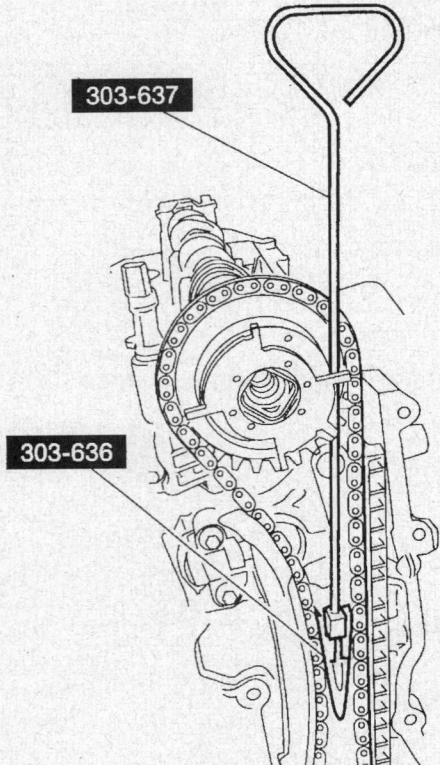

Fig. 36 Timing chain wedge installation. Righthand

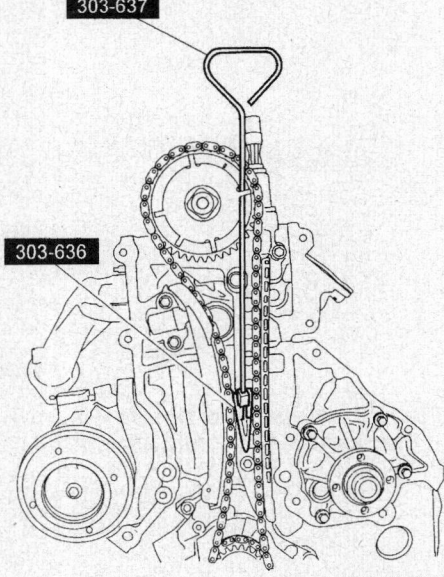

Fig. 39 Timing chain wedge installation. Lefthand

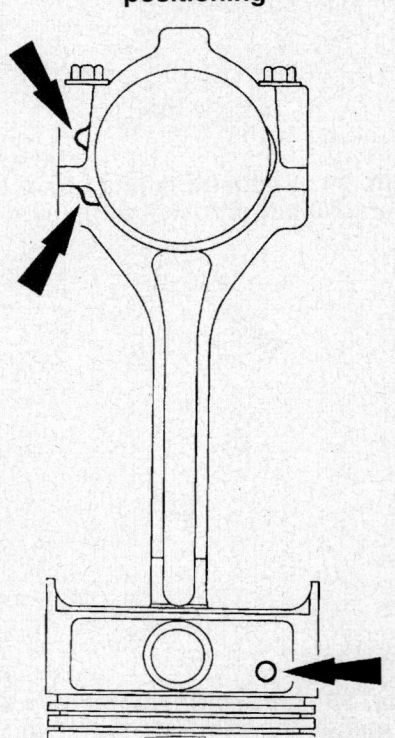

Fig. 40 Piston & connecting rod

4.6L SOHC (VIN H) ENGINE

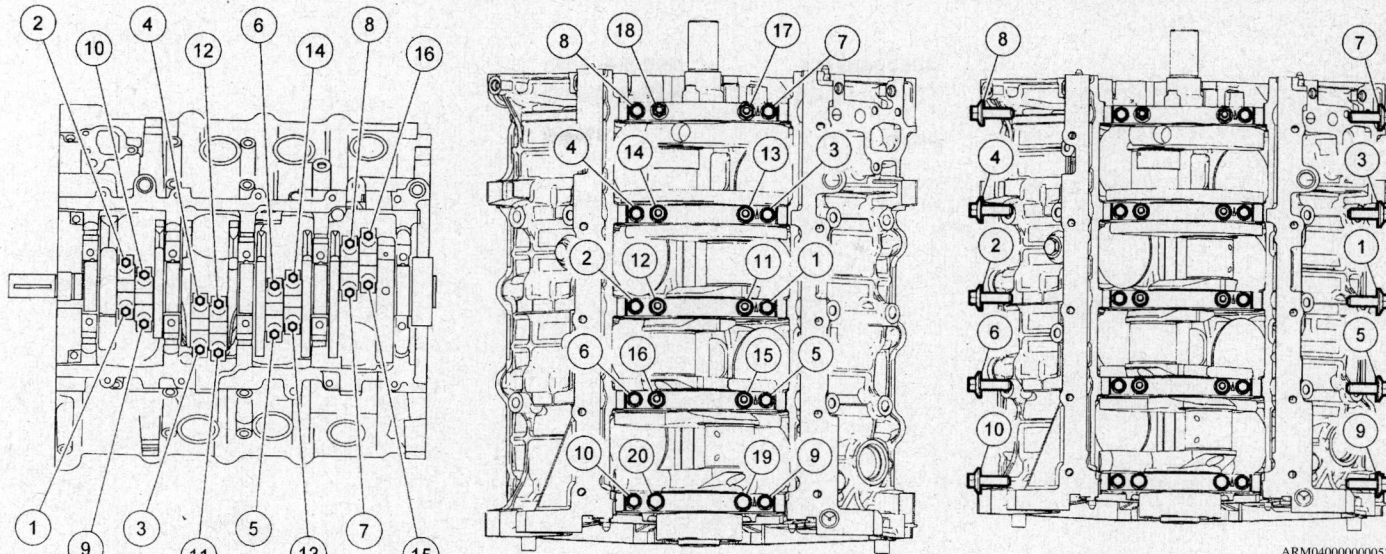

Fig. 41 Connecting rod bearing
tightening sequence

ARM0400000000532

Fig. 42 Vertical main bearing cap
tightening sequence

ARM0400000000530

Fig. 43 Cross-mounted main
bearing cap tightening sequence

ARM0400000000531

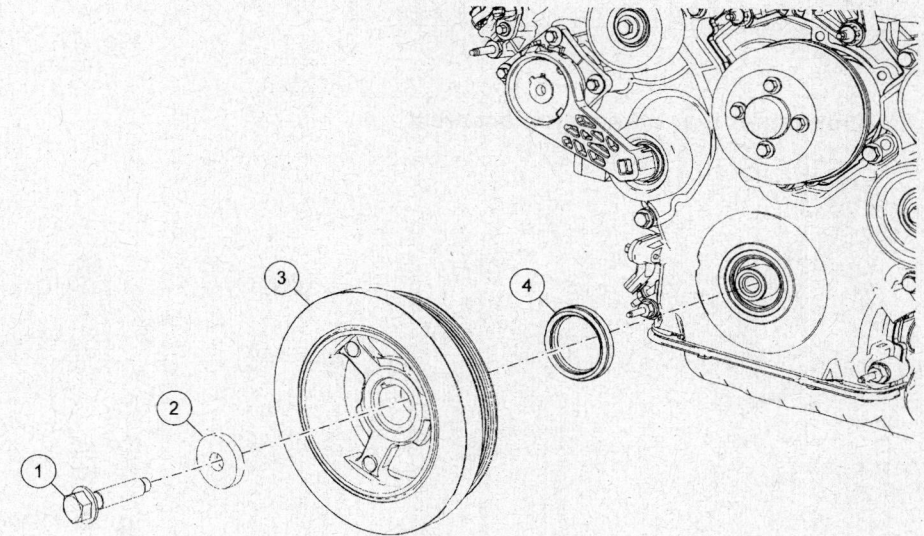

Item	Description
1	Crankshaft pulley bolt
2	Crankshaft pulley bolt washer
3	Crankshaft pulley
4	Crankshaft front oil seal

ARM0400000000513

Fig. 44 Front crankshaft seal replacement

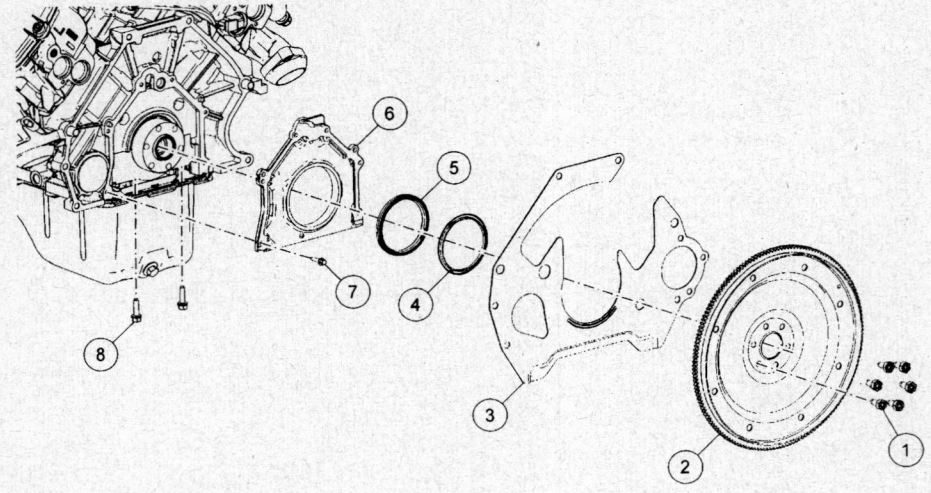

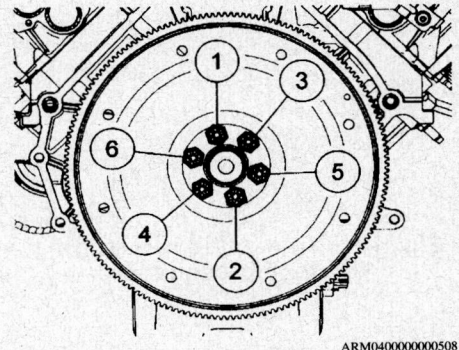

ARM0400000000509

Fig. 46 Rear crankshaft seal retaining plate tightening sequence

Item	Description
1	Flywheel/flexplate bolts (6 required)
2	Flywheel/flexplate
3	Engine-to-transmission spacer plate
4	Crankshaft oil slinger
5	Crankshaft rear seal

Item	Description
6	Crankshaft rear seal retainer plate
7	Crankshaft rear seal retainer plate bolts (6 required)
8	Oil pan bolts (2 required)

ARM0400000000514

Fig. 45 Crankshaft rear oil seal replacement

ARM0400000000508

Fig. 47 Flywheel/flexplate tightening sequence

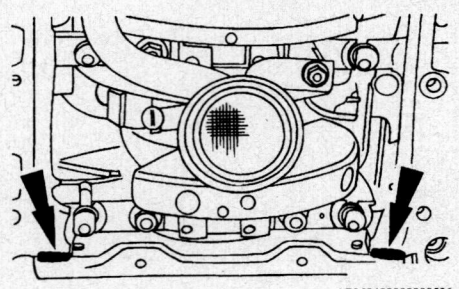

ARM0400000000526

Fig. 48 Oil pan sealing (Part 1 of 2)

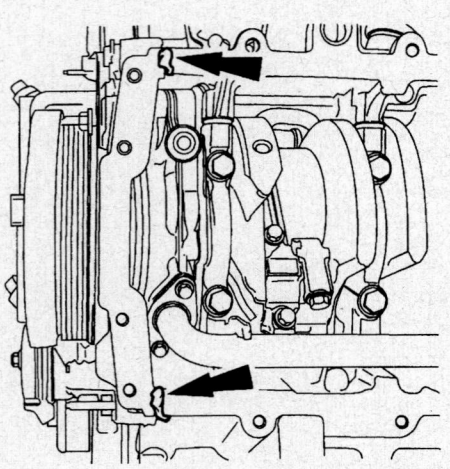

ARM0400000000527

Fig. 48 Oil pan sealing (Part 2 of 2)

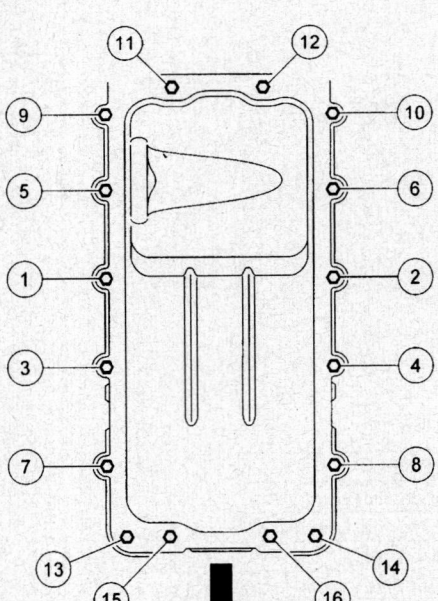

ARM0400000000528

Fig. 49 Oil pan tightening sequence

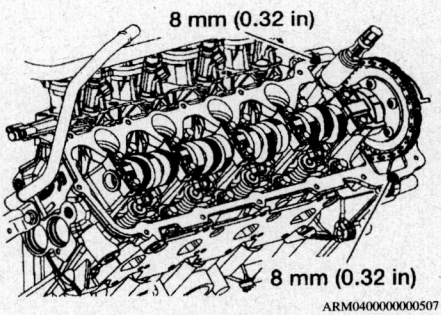

8 mm (0.32 in)

8 mm (0.32 in)

ARM0400000000507

Fig. 50 Serpentine drive belt routing

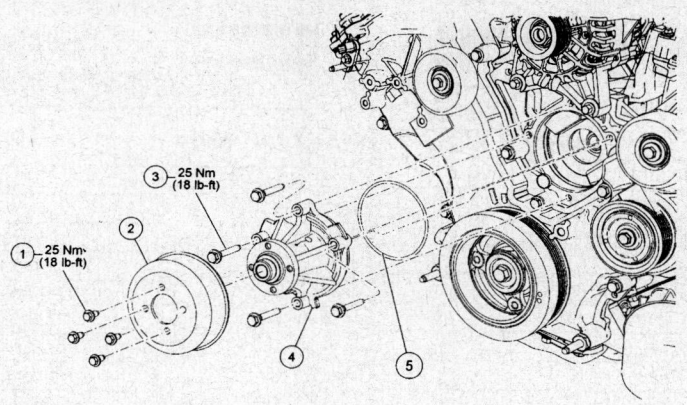

Item	Description
1	Coolant pump pulley bolts (4 required)
2	Coolant pump pulley
3	Coolant pump bolts (4 required)
4	Coolant pump
5	Coolant pump O-ring seal

ARM0400000000561

Fig. 51   Water pump replacement

TIGHTENING SPECIFICATIONS

Year	Component	Torque/Ft. Lbs.
2005–08	Air Cleaner	71①
	Air Cleaner Outlet Pipe	27①
	Air Conditioning Compressor	18
	Air Conditioning Condenser	89①
	Alternator, Lower	18
	Alternator, Upper	89①
	Alternator B+ Terminal	71①
	Alternator Support Bracket	89①
	Belt Idler Pulley	18
	Camshaft Bearing Cap	89①
	Camshaft Phaser Sprocket	⑧
	Catalytic Converter-To-Exhaust Manifold	30
	Coolant Crossover	89①
	Cooling Fan Motor & Shroud	80①
	Connecting Rod	⑥
	Crankshaft Pulley	②
	Crankshaft Rear Seal Retainer Plate	89①
	Crankshaft Rear Seal Retainer Plate To Oil Pan	③
	Cylinder Head	⑦
	Degas Bottle	71①
	Engine Support Insulator, Bolt	41
	Engine Support Insulator, Nut	46
	Exhaust Manifold	41
	Flywheel/Flexplate	59
	Front Cover	④
	Fuel Bundle Shield	62①
	Fuel Filter	44①
	Fuel Rail	89①
	Ground Wire	18
	Ignition Coil	44①
	Intake Manifold	89①
	Main Bearings	⑤

TIGHTENING SPECIFICATIONS—Continued

Year	Component	Torque/Ft. Lbs.
2005–08	Oil Dipstick Tube	89①
	Oil Pan	⑨
	Oil Pan Drain Plug	19
	Oil Pump	89①
	Oil Pump Screen & Pickup Tube-To-Oil Pump	89①
	Power Steering Pulley Shield	89①
	Power Steering Pump	18
	Power Steering Tube	89①
	Radiator Support Bracket	22
	Radio Ignition Interference Capacitor	18
	Steering Coupling	18
	Thermostat	89①
	Throttle Body	89①
	Timing Chain Guide	89①
	Timing Chain Tensioner	18
	Transmission Cooler Tube Bracket	18
	Valve Cover	89①
	Valve Cover Wiring Harness Bracket	30
	Water Pump	18
	Water Pump Pulley	18

① — Inch pounds.
② — Refer to "Crankshaft Damper, Replace" for tightening specifications and sequence.
③ — Refer to "Crankshaft Rear Oil Seal, Replace" for tightening specifications and sequence.
④ — Refer to "Front Cover, Replace" for tightening specifications and sequence.
⑤ — Refer to "Main & Rod Bearings" for tightening specifications and sequence.
⑥ — Refer to "Piston & Rod Assembly" for tightening specifications and sequence.
⑦ — Refer to "Cylinder Head, Replace" for tightening specifications and sequence.
⑧ — Refer to "Timing Chain, Replace" for tightening specifications and sequence.
⑨ — Refer to "Oil Pan, Replace" for tightening specifications and sequence.

5.4L Engine

NOTE: For Procedures Not Found In This Section, Refer To "4.6L SOHC (VIN X) Engine" Section.

NOTE: On Air Bag Equipped Models, Refer To "Air Bag System Precautions" Located In The Front Of This Manual For System Disarming & Arming Procedures.

INDEX

	Page No.
Belt Tension Data	4-79
Camshaft, Replace	4-77
Camshaft Lobe Lift Specifications	4-76
Compression Pressure	4-73
Cooling System Bleed	4-79
Crankshaft Damper, Replace	4-76
Crankshaft Rear Oil Seal, Replace	4-78
Cylinder Head, Replace	4-75
Installation	4-75
Removal	4-75
Engine Rebuilding Specifications	21-1
Engine, Replace	4-74
Engine Mount, Replace	4-73
Exhaust Manifold, Replace	4-74

	Page No.
Lefthand	4-74
Righthand	4-74
Front Cover, Replace	4-77
Fuel Filter, Replace	4-79
Fuel Pump, Replace	4-79
Hydraulic Lash Adjuster, Replace	4-76
Intake Manifold, Replace	4-74
Main & Rod Bearings	4-78
Oil Pan, Replace	4-78
Oil Pump, Replace	4-79
Piston & Rod Assembly	4-77
Precautions	4-73
Air Bag Systems	4-73
Battery Ground Cable	4-73
Fuel System Pressure Relief	4-73
Quick Disconnect Hoses	4-73

	Page No.
R-Clip	4-73
Spring Lock	4-73
Vapor Tube	4-73
Radiator, Replace	4-79
Serpentine Drive Belt	4-79
Replacement	4-79
Routing	4-79
Thermostat, Replace	4-79
Tightening Specifications	4-81
Timing Chain, Replace	4-77
Installation	4-77
Removal	4-77
Valve Adjustment	4-76
Valve Cover, Replace	4-75
Lefthand	4-75
Righthand	4-76
Water Pump, Replace	4-79

PRECAUTIONS

Air Bag Systems

Refer to "Air Bag System Precautions" in front of this manual for system disarming and arming procedures.

Battery Ground Cable

Prior to service, disconnect battery ground cable and isolate as required.

Fuel System Pressure Relief

1. Remove fuel pump relay.
2. Start engine, then allow engine to idle until it stalls.
3. After engine stalls, crank engine for approximately 5 seconds to ensure fuel injection supply manifold pressure has been released.
4. When fuel system service is complete, install fuel pump relay.
5. Cycle ignition key and wait 3 seconds to pressurize fuel system. Inspect for leaks before starting engine.

Quick Disconnect Hoses

R-CLIP

When working with R-clip type connections, do not use tools to disconnect. Use of tools may deform clip components and could cause leaks.

DISCONNECT

1. Bend shipping tab downward.
2. Spread R-clip and push clip into fitting.
3. Separate fitting from tube.

CONNECT

1. Inspect fitting and tube for damage and ensure connections are clean.
2. Apply light coat of suitable, clean engine oil to male end of tube.
3. Insert R-clip into fitting.
4. Align tube and fitting, then insert tube into fitting and push together until click is heard.
5. Pull on connection to ensure it is fully engaged.

SPRING LOCK

When working with spring lock type connections, spring lock tool set No. T84L-19623-B, or equivalent, must be used to disconnect fittings.

When connecting spring lock type fittings, proceed as follows:
1. Inspect and clean both coupling ends.
2. Lubricate fuel line O-ring seals with suitable, clean engine oil.
3. When connection is made, pull on line to ensure it is fully engaged.

VAPOR TUBE

To disconnect vapor tube connections, squeeze fitting and disconnect vapor tube from fitting.

To connect, proceed as follows:
1. Ensure fittings are clean and free from damage.
2. Push tube onto fitting until it snaps into place.
3. Pull on connection to verify fitting is secure.

COMPRESSION PRESSURE

1. Ensure crankcase oil is correct viscosity and correct level, and battery is fully charged.
2. Operate vehicle until engine is at normal operating temperature.
3. Turn ignition switch to OFF position and remove all spark plugs.
4. Set throttle plates in wide-open position.
5. Install suitable compression gauge in cylinder No. 1.
6. Install suitable auxiliary start switch.
7. Turn ignition switch to ON position.
8. Crank engine at least five compression strokes using auxiliary starter switch.
9. Record highest reading and approximate number of compression strokes required to obtain highest reading.
10. Repeat test on each cylinder.
11. Compression pressures are within specifications is the lowest cylinder reading is at least 75% of highest.

ENGINE MOUNT

REPLACE

1. Remove 2 dash boot nuts.
2. Remove battery and tray.
3. Remove air cleaner outlet pipe.

4. Install engine lifting tool Nos. 303-D087, 303-F070 and 303-F072, or suitable equivalents.
5. Remove lefthand and righthand engine mount nuts, then raise engine.
6. For righthand mount, remove mount to subframe bolts, then mount.
7. For lefthand mount, remove steering coupler to intermediate shaft bolt and position shaft aside. **Do not allow the steering wheel to rotate while the steering column intermediate shaft is disconnected or damage to the clockspring can result.**
8. Remove lefthand engine support bracket bolts, then bracket.
9. Remove oil filter and discard.
10. Remove engine mount to subframe bolts, then mount.
11. Reverse procedure to install.

ENGINE
REPLACE

1. Disconnect washer nozzles and hose from hood.
2. Mark hood hinges for installation reference, then remove hood.
3. Relieve fuel system pressure as outlined under "Precautions."
4. Recover air conditioning refrigerant as outlined in "Air Conditioning" chapter.
5. Remove battery and tray.
6. Remove air cleaner and outlet pipe.
7. Remove steering column dash boot nuts.
8. Raise and support vehicle.
9. Drain engine oil and coolant into suitable containers.
10. Remove engine coolant degas bottle.
11. Remove supercharger coolant degas bottle.
12. Disconnect upper radiator hose from thermostat housing.
13. Disconnect cooling fan electrical connector.
14. Remove cooling fan mounting bolts, then fan assembly.
15. Disconnect coolant hoses from charge air cooler, coolant tube, thermostat housing and coolant pump.
16. Disconnect fuel supply tube.
17. Disconnect EVAP tube and brake booster vacuum supply tube from throttle body.
18. Disconnect lower EVAP tube and electrical connector from EVAP canister purge valve.
19. Remove EVAP canister purge valve.
20. Disconnect heater hoses from coolant tube assembly at rear of engine.
21. Disconnect wire harness pin retainers.
22. Disconnect 68 pin connector from power distribution box.
23. Disconnect PCM electrical connectors.
24. Drain power steering fluid into suitable container.
25. Disconnect hose from power steering reservoir.
26. Disconnect A/C pressure transducer electrical connector.
27. Rotate drive belt tensioner clockwise and remove belt from pulley.
28. Disconnect coolant hose from oil cooler.

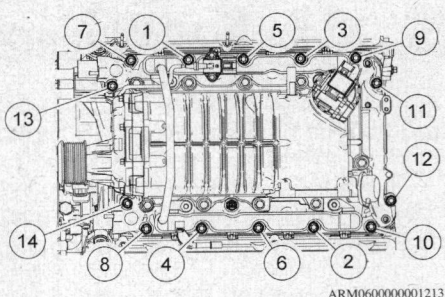

Fig. 1 Intake manifold tightening sequence. 5.4L engine

29. Disconnect lower radiator hose from radiator, then remove hose.
30. Disconnect power steering pressure tube fitting and discard teflon seal.
31. Disconnect power steering return hose.
32. Disconnect B+ wire from alternator.
33. Disconnect wiring harness retainers from oil pan stud bolts.
34. Disconnect CKP sensor electrical connector.
35. Disconnect A/C compressor electrical connector.
36. Disconnect wire harness retainers from A/C compressor stud bolts.
37. Remove A/C compressor mounting bolts, then position compressor aside.
38. Remove ground wire from righthand engine mount bracket stud bolt.
39. Remove starter as outlined under "Starter, Replace."
40. Remove ground wire from lefthand cylinder head.
41. Install engine lifting tool Nos. 303-D087, 303-D089 and 014-00071, or suitable equivalent.
42. Remove engine mount retaining nuts.
43. Remove engine.
44. Reverse procedure to install.

INTAKE MANIFOLD
REPLACE

1. Relieve fuel system pressure as outlined under "Precautions."
2. Drain coolant from engine and supercharger into suitable container.
3. Remove air cleaner outlet pipe.
4. Remove EGR tube.
5. Disconnect TP sensor electrical connector.
6. Remove throttle body mounting bolts, then position throttle body aside.
7. Disconnect IAT sensor electrical connector.
8. Disconnect fuel supply tube.
9. Disconnect lefthand fuel injector electrical connectors.
10. Remove wire harness retainers from rear of intake manifold.
11. Disconnect fuel rail pressure and temperature sensor electrical connector.
12. Disconnect righthand fuel injector electrical connectors.
13. Disconnect EGR system module electrical connector.
14. Disconnect crankcase ventilation tube from supercharger.

15. Disconnect supercharger bubbler hose from rear of supercharger.
16. Rotate supercharger drive belt tensioner clockwise and remove drive belt from drive pulley.
17. Disconnect upper radiator and coolant hoses from intake manifold.
18. Disconnect coolant hoses from charge air cooler.
19. Disconnect heater hose located below rear of intake manifold.
20. Remove intake manifold mounting bolts, then manifold.
21. Reverse procedure to install, noting the following:
    a. Install intake manifold using new gaskets.
    b. **Torque** mounting bolts in sequence to 89 inch lbs., **Fig. 1.**

EXHAUST MANIFOLD
REPLACE

Lefthand

1. Remove EVAP canister purge valve.
2. Remove 2 dash boot nuts.
3. Remove catalytic convertor.
4. Disconnect lefthand heated oxygen sensor electrical connector.
5. Remove and discard engine oil filter.
6. Remove upper bolt from intermediate shaft and position shaft aside. **Do not allow the steering wheel to rotate while the steering column intermediate shaft is disconnected or damage to the clockspring can result.**
7. Remove exhaust manifold retaining nuts, then manifold.
8. Reverse procedure to install, noting the following:
    a. Install manifold with new gaskets.
    b. **Torque** new retaining nuts in sequence to 15 ft. lbs., **Fig. 2.**
    c. **Torque** intermediate shaft bolt to 35 ft. lbs.

Righthand

1. Remove exhaust gas recirculation tube.
2. Remove catalytic convertor.
3. Remove battery and tray.
4. Rotate supercharger drive belt tensioner clockwise and remove drive belt from drive pulley.
5. Install engine lifting tool Nos. 303-D087, 303-F070 and 303-F072, or suitable equivalent.
6. Remove righthand engine mount nut.
7. Raise righthand side of engine.
8. Remove supercharger drive belt from A/C compressor pulley.
9. Remove wiring harness retainers from A/C compressor stud bolts and position wiring harness aside.
10. Loosen A/C compressor stud bolts for access to manifold bolts.
11. Remove exhaust manifold nuts, then manifold.
12. Reverse procedure to install, noting the following:
    a. Install manifold with new gaskets.
    b. **Torque** new retaining nuts in sequence to 15 ft. lbs., **Fig. 3.**

CYLINDER HEAD
REPLACE

Removal

1. Remove engine as outlined under "Engine, Replace."
2. Remove flywheel mounting bolts and then flywheel.
3. Remove engine/transmission spacer plate.
4. Mount engine on a suitable work stand.
5. Disconnect coolant hose from thermostat housing.
6. Remove coolant tube bracket nut.
7. Disconnect coolant vent hoses from intake manifold.
8. Disconnect upper radiator hoses from intake manifold.
9. Disconnect ECT sensor electrical connector.
10. Remove thermostat housing assembly.
11. Disconnect coolant hose from charge air cooler.
12. Loosen water pump pulley bolts.
13. Rotate accessory drive belt tensioner clockwise and remove accessory drive belt.
14. Remove mounting bolt, supercharger drive belt tensioner, then drive belt.
15. Remove power steering tube bracket nut.
16. Disconnect power steering pressure switch electrical connector.
17. Remove power steering tube bracket bolt.
18. Remove power steering pump mounting bolts, then pump and reservoir assembly.
19. Remove alternator as outlined under "Alternator, Replace."
20. Remove accessory drive belt tensioner.
21. Remove accessory drive belt idler pulley's.
22. Remove water pump as outlined under "Water Pump, Replace."
23. Disconnect EGR tube fittings, then remove tube.
24. Remove crankcase ventilation tube.
25. Disconnect TPS and throttle body electrical connectors.
26. Remove throttle body and discard gasket.
27. Disconnect cylinder head temperature sensor electrical connector.
28. Detach wiring harness retainer from coolant tube assembly bracket.
29. Disconnect lefthand heated oxygen sensor electrical connector.
30. Disconnect bubbler tube from supercharger.
31. Remove wiring harness retaining bracket.
32. Disconnect PCV valve electrical connector.
33. Disconnect righthand fuel injector electrical connectors.
34. Disconnect fuel rail pressure and temperature sensor electrical connectors.
35. Remove righthand radio interference capacitor.

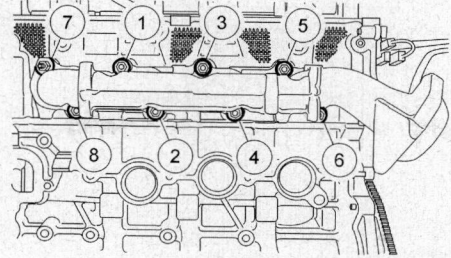

Fig. 2 Lefthand exhaust manifold tightening sequence. 5.4L engine

36. Disconnect EGR valve electrical connector.
37. Detach wiring harness righthand coil on plug cover stud bolt.
38. Remove righthand coil on plug cover.
39. Detach wiring harness retainers righthand valve cover bolts.
40. Disconnect righthand coil on plug electrical connections, then remove coil on plugs.
41. Disconnect electrical connections from CMP, IAT and engine oil pressure sensors.
42. Disconnect lefthand fuel injector electrical connectors.
43. Remove lefthand radio interference capacitor.
44. Remove lefthand coil on plug cover.
45. Disconnect lefthand coil on plug electrical connections, then remove coil on plugs.
46. Remove wiring harness assembly from engine.
47. Disconnect intake manifold to coolant tube assembly hose.
48. Remove intake manifold as outlined under "Intake Manifold, Replace."
49. Remove coolant tube assembly bolts.
50. Remove oil cooler mounting bolts, then oil cooler.
51. Remove oil filter adapter.
52. Remove oil level indicator and tube.
53. Remove righthand engine mount bracket for access to engine block drain plug.
54. Remove left and right engine block drain plugs.
55. Remove valve covers as outlined under "Valve Cover, Replace."
56. Remove crankshaft position sensor.
57. Remove water pump as outlined under "Water Pump, Replace."
58. Remove crankshaft pulley bolt using tool No. 303-D055, or equivalent.
59. Remove crankshaft pulley using tool No. 303-009, or equivalent.
60. Remove front crankshaft seal using tool No. 303-107, or equivalent.
61. Remove oil pan to engine front cover bolts, then oil pan to engine front cover bolts.
62. Remove engine front cover as outlined under "Front Cover, Replace."
63. Remove spark plugs.
64. Compress valve springs and remove roller followers using tool No. 303-452, or equivalent.
65. Remove hydraulic lash adjusters, noting locations for installation.
66. Remove crankshaft sensor ring.

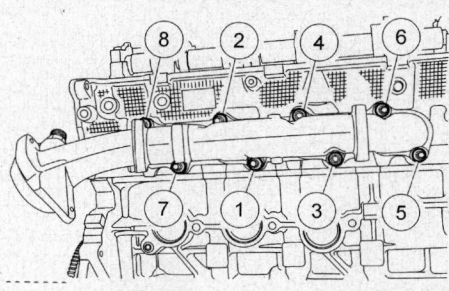

Fig. 3 Righthand exhaust manifold tightening sequence. 5.4L engine

67. Remove righthand primary timing chain tensioner, then timing chain.
68. Remove righthand primary timing chain guide.
69. Remove lefthand primary timing chain tensioner and tensioner arm.
70. Remove lefthand primary timing chain and guide.
71. Remove crankshaft sprocket.
72. **For lefthand cylinder head removal,** remove lefthand exhaust manifold as oulined under "Exhaust Manifold, Replace."
73. **For righthand cylinder head removal,** remove righthand exhaust manifold as outlined under "Exhaust Manifold, Replace."
74. Remove coolant tube assembly bolts.
75. Remove cylinder head mounting bolts, then cylinder head.

Installation

1. Install head gasket over dowel pins.
2. Install cylinder head on dowels and head gasket.
3. New cylinder head bolts must be lightly oiled with a rag, and allowed to drain for a few minutes prior to installation.
4. **Torque** cylinder head bolts in sequence, **Figs. 4 and 5** in following steps:
   a. Step one, **torque** to 15 ft. lbs.
   b. Step two, **torque** to 37 ft. lbs.
   c. Step three, **torque** to 59 ft. lbs.
   d. Step four, tighten and additional 90°.
   e. Step five, tighten and additional 90°.
5. Install timing chain as outlined under "Timing Chain, Replace."

VALVE COVER
REPLACE

Lefthand

1. Relieve fuel system pressure as outlined under "Precautions."
2. Remove power brake booster as outlined under "Power Booster, Replace" in "Power Brake Units" chapter.
3. Remove air cleaner assembly and outlet pipe.
4. Remove lefthand ignition coils as outlined under "Ignition Coil Pack, Replace" in "Electrical" section.

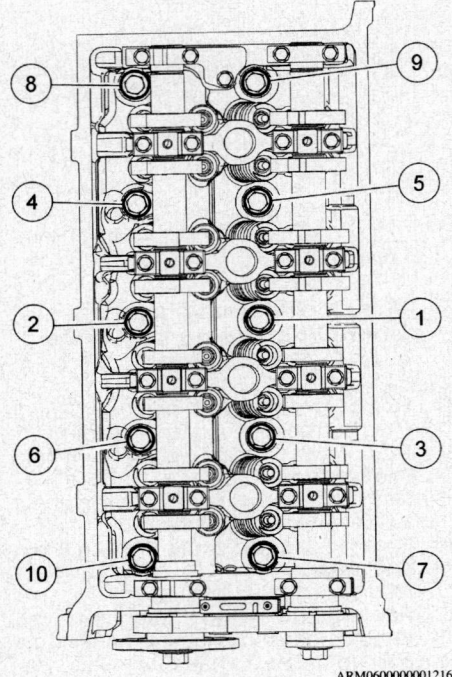

Fig. 4   Righthand cylinder head tightening sequence. 5.4L engine

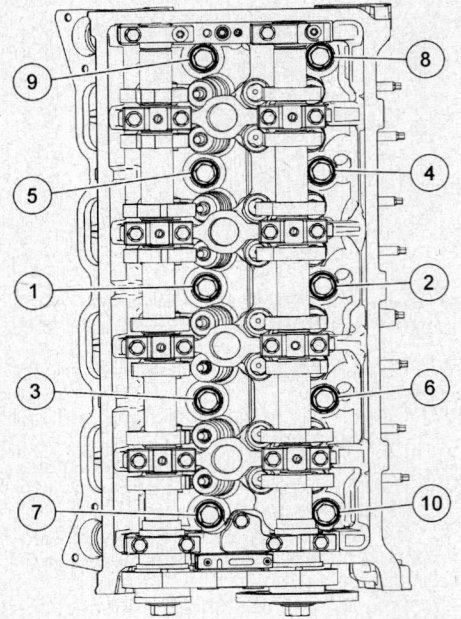

Fig. 5   Lefthand cylinder head tightening sequence. 5.4L engine

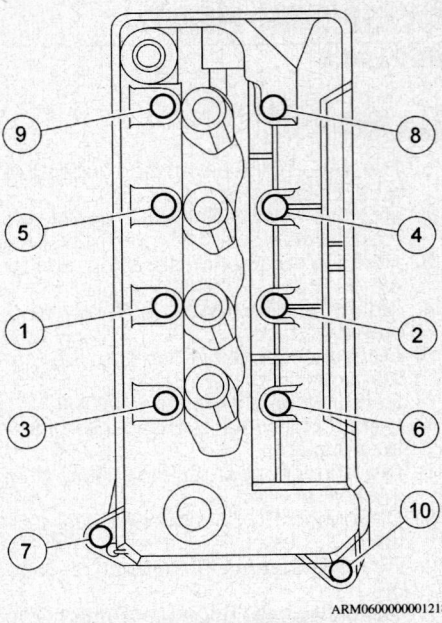

Fig. 6   Lefthand valve cover tightening sequence. 5.4L engine

5. Disconnect TP sensor electrical connection.
6. Disconnect electronic throttle control electrical connector.
7. Disconnect brake booster vacuum hose from throttle body spacer.
8. Disconnect EVAP hose from throttle body spacer.
9. Remove throttle body mounting bolts, then throttle body and spacer.
10. Disconnect lefthand fuel injector electrical connectors.
11. Disconnect fuel supply tube.
12. Remove lefthand radio interference capacitor.
13. Disconnect CMP sensor electrical connector.
14. Remove power steering reservoir bracket bolts and position reservoir aside.
15. Detach harness retainers from lefthand valve cover studs.
16. Remove bolt and position oil level indicator tube aside.
17. Remove valve cover mounting bolts, then valve cover.
18. Reverse procedure to install, noting the following:
    a. Install new gaskets on valve cover.
    b. Apply a bead two places where engine front cover meets cylinder head.
    c. **Torque** valve cover mounting bolts in sequence to 89 inch lbs., **Fig. 6**.

Righthand

1. Remove righthand ignition coils.
2. Remove crankcase ventilation tube.
3. Disconnect PCV valve electrical connector.

4. Remove righthand radio interference capacitor.
5. Disconnect righthand fuel injector electrical connectors.
6. Disconnect fuel rail pressure and temperature sensor electrical connectors.
7. Disconnect ECT sensor electrical connector.
8. Detach harness retainers from righthand valve cover studs.
9. Remove valve cover mounting bolts, then valve cover.
10. Reverse procedure to install, noting the following:
    a. Install new gaskets on valve cover.
    b. Apply a bead two places where engine front cover meets cylinder head.
    c. **Torque** valve cover mounting bolts in sequence to 89 inch lbs., **Fig. 7**.

CAMSHAFT LOBE LIFT SPECIFICATIONS

Engine	Intake, Inch	Exhaust, Inch
5.4L DOHC (VIN S)	.242	.259

VALVE ADJUSTMENT

These engine are equipped with hydraulic valve lash adjusters. No valve adjustment is required.

HYDRAULIC LASH ADJUSTER
REPLACE

1. Remove valve cover as outlined under "Valve Cover, Replace."
2. Position camshaft lobe at base circle.
3. Compress valve spring and remove

roller follower using tool No. 303-452, or equivalent.
4. Repeat step three for each additional follower.
5. Remove lash adjusters.
6. Reverse procedure to install.

CRANKSHAFT DAMPER
REPLACE

1. Remove cooling fan assembly.
2. Rotate supercharger drive belt tensioner clockwise and remove drive belt from drive pulley.
3. Rotate accessory drive belt tensioner clockwise and remove accessory drive belt from power steering pump pulley.
4. Position accessory drive belt and supercharger drive belt away from crankshaft pulley.
5. Remove crankshaft pulley mounting bolt using tool No. 303-D055, or equivalent.
6. Remove crankshaft pulley using tool No. 303-009, or equivalent.
7. Reverse procedure to install, noting the following:
    a. **Pulley must be secured within four minutes of sealant application.**
    b. Apply suitable silicone gasket and sealant to crankshaft pulley Woodruff key slot,
    c. Install crankshaft pulley using crankshaft vibration damper installer tool No. 303-102, or equivalent.
    d. **Torque** next crankshaft pulley bolt to 88 ft. lbs.
    e. Loosen crankshaft pulley bolt one full turn.
    f. **Torque** pulley bolt to 37 ft. lbs.
    g. Tighten bolt an additional 90°.

FRONT COVER
REPLACE

1. Relieve fuel system pressure as outlined under "Precautions."
2. Remove engine coolant degas bottle.
3. Remove supercharger coolant degas bottle.
4. Remove battery and tray.
5. Remove valve covers as outlined under "Valve Cover, Replace."
6. Loosen water pump pulley mounting bolts.
7. Remove accessory drive belt, accessory drive belt idler pulleys and accessory drive belt tensioner.
8. Remove water pump pulley.
9. Remove supercharger drive belt, drive belt tensioner and drive belt idler pulleys.
10. Remove thermostat housing.
11. Remove front crank seal using toll No. 303-107, or suitable equivalent.
12. Disconnect coolant vent hoses from intake manifold.
13. Disconnect upper radiator hoses from intake manifold.
14. Disconnect coolant hoses from charge air cooler.
15. Remove lower radiator hose assembly from water pump, radiator, oil filter adapter and coolant tube assembly.
16. Disconnect A/C pressure transducer electrical connector.
17. Disconnect power steering pressure switch electrical connector.
18. Remove power steering tube bracket nut from alternator bolt.
19. Remove power steering tube bracket bolt from engine front cover.
20. Remove power steering pump mounting bolts, then position power steering pump and reservoir aside.
21. Disconnect CKP sensor electrical connector.
22. Install engine lift tool Nos. 303-D087, 303-F070 and 303-F072, or equivalent.
23. Remove left and right engine mount retaining nuts.
24. Raise engine.
25. Remove alternator as outlined under "Alternator, Replace."
26. Disconnect coolant hose from oil filter adapter.
27. Remove oil cooler mounting bolts, then oil cooler.
28. Drain engine oil into a suitable container, then remove and discard oil filter.
29. Remove coolant tube assembly to oil filter adapter bolts.
30. Disconnect engine oil pressure sensor electrical connector.
31. Remove oil filter adapter mounting bolts, then adapter.
32. Remove water pump as outlined under "Water Pump, Replace."
33. Remove front cover mounting bolts, then front cover.
34. Reverse procedure to install, noting the following:
    a. Install front cover and mounting bolts.
    b. **Torque** bolts 1–14 in sequence to 18 ft. lbs., **Fig. 8.**

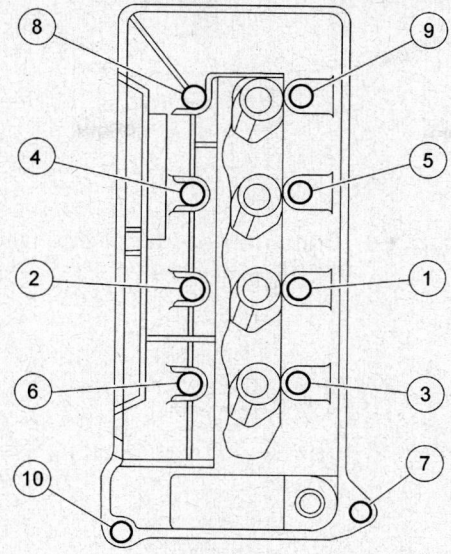

ARM0600000001219

Fig. 7   Righthand valve cover tightening sequence. 5.4L engine

c. **Torque** bolts 15 and 16 to 37 ft. lbs.
d. Install oil filter adapter and bolts in sequence, **Fig. 9.**
e. **Torque** bolts 1-6 to 18 ft. lbs.
f. **Torque** bolts 7 and 8 to 37 ft. lbs.

TIMING CHAIN
REPLACE

Removal

1. Remove camshaft followers as outlined under "Hydraulic Lash Adjuster, Replace."
2. Remove engine front cover as outlined under "Front Cover, Replace."
3. Remove crankshaft sensor ring.
4. Remove righthand primary timing chain tensioner and tensioner arm.
5. Remove righthand primary timing chain, then chain guide.
6. Remove lefthand primary timing chain tensioner and tensioner arm.
7. Remove lefthand primary timing chain, then chain guide.

Installation

1. Place tensioner arm in suitable vise and compress plunger.
2. Push back and hold ratchet mechanism using pick or suitable screw driver.
3. Push ratchet arm back into tensioner while holding ratchet mechanism.
4. Install suitable pin in hole of tensioner during installation.
5. Install lefthand primary timing chain guide and bolts.
6. Position camshaft sprocket timing marks as shown, **Fig. 10.**
7. Position lefthand inner timing chain onto crankshaft sprocket, aligning one colored link on timing chain with slot on crankshaft sprocket, **Fig. 11.**
8. Install lefthand timing chain on cam-

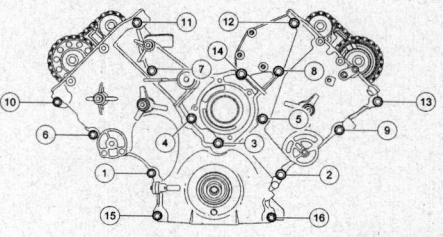

ARM0600000001220

Fig. 8   Front cover tightening sequence. 5.4L engine

shaft sprocket, aligning two colored links with timing mark on sprocket, **Fig. 12.**
9. Install lefthand primary timing chain tensioner arm.
10. Install lefthand timing chain tensioner and bolts, then remove pin from tensioner.
11. Position righthand outer timing chain on crankshaft sprocket, aligning colored link with timing marks on sprocket, **Fig. 13.**
12. Install righthand timing chain on camshaft sprocket, aligning two colored links with timing mark on sprocket, **Fig. 14.**
13. Install righthand primary timing chain tensioner arm.
14. Install righthand timing chain tensioner and bolts, then remove pin from tensioner.
15. Install crankshaft sensor ring.
16. Install engine front cover.
17. Install camshaft roller followers.

CAMSHAFT
REPLACE

1. Remove timing chain as outlined under "Timing Chain, Replace."
2. Install camshaft holding tool No. 303-446.
3. Remove camshaft drive sprocket.
4. Remove camshaft sprocket spacer.
5. Compress secondary timing chain tensioner and install a lockpin, **Fig. 15.**
6. Remove timing chain and camshaft sprockets.
7. Remove secondary timing chain tensioner.
8. Remove camshaft bearing cap bolts in sequence shown, **Fig. 16.**
9. Remove camshaft bearing caps, then camshafts.
10. Reverse procedure to install, noting the following:
    a. Lubricate camshafts with clean engine oil prior to installation.
    b. **Torque** camshaft bearing cap bolts in sequence to 89 inch lbs., **Fig. 17.**
    c. Index keyways on camshafts to 6 o'clock position.
    d. Install camshaft sprockets and chain as an assembly.

PISTON & ROD ASSEMBLY

The connecting rod must be installed into the connecting rod with identification markings toward the front, **Fig. 18.**

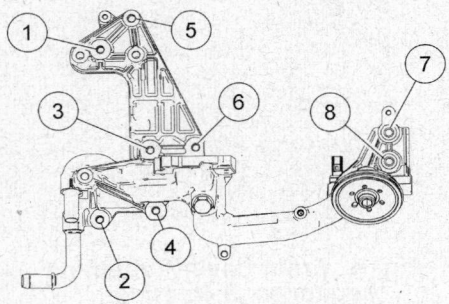

Fig. 9 Oil filter adapter tightening sequence. 5.4L engine

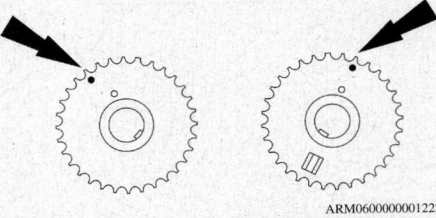

Fig. 10 Camshaft sprocket timing marks. 5.4L engine

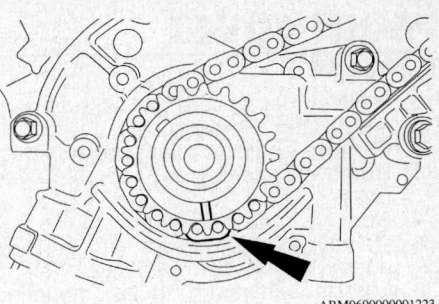

Fig. 11 Lefthand timing chain mark. 5.4L engine

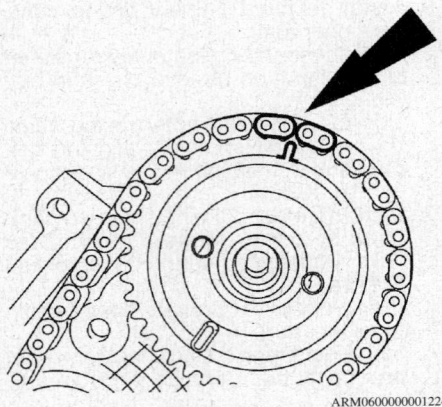

Fig. 12 Lefthand timing chain mark on camshaft. 5.4L engine

1. Lubricate piston and ring with suitable, clean engine oil.
2. Lubricate rod bearings with suitable, clean engine oil.
3. Install piston and connecting rod with upper connecting rod bearing in place using suitable piston ring compressor tool and connecting rod installer tool.
4. Once connecting rod is seated on crankshaft journal, remove special tools.
5. **The rod cap must be in same orientation as marked during disassembly.**
6. Position lower bearing and connecting rod , then install new bolts loosely.
7. **Torque** connecting rod bolts in to 30 ft. lbs. Then tighten bolts and additional 90°.

MAIN & ROD BEARINGS

1. Install crankshaft main bearings.
2. Install crankshaft upper main bearings into cylinder block.
3. Install crankshaft lower main bearings into bearing caps.
4. Ensure all oil passages are aligned.
5. Lubricate all main bearings with suitable, clean engine oil.
6. Lubricate crankshaft bearing journals with suitable, clean engine oil
7. Install crankshaft onto upper crankshaft main bearings.
8. **Make sure the side of the thrust**

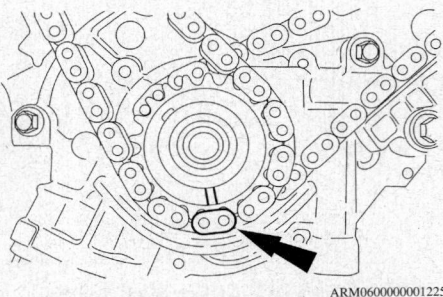

Fig. 13 Righthand timing chain marks on crankshaft sprocket. 5.4L engine

washer, with three 5-mm wide oil grooves, faces the crankshaft thrust surface.
9. Push crankshaft rearward and install rear crankshaft upper thrust washer at back of main boss No. 5.
10. Install rear (No. 5) main bearing cap.
11. Install crankshaft lower main bearings into main bearing caps and lubricate them with suitable, clean engine oil.
12. Locate main bearing cap on cylinder block and, keeping cap as square as possible, alternately draw cap down evenly using cap fasteners.
13. Push crankshaft forward to seat crankshaft thrust washer. Hold crankshaft in forward position.
14. Install vertical main bearing cap nuts and bolts, then tighten in sequence, **Fig. 19.**
15. **Torque** cap bolts in sequence to 89 inch lbs.
16. **Torque** cap bolts in sequence to 30 ft. lbs. Then tighten an additional 90° in sequence.
17. Install side bolt main bearing cap bolts and tighten in sequence, **Fig. 20.**
18. **Torque** in sequence to 30 ft. lbs.
19. Tighten an additional 90° in sequence.
20. Inspect crankshaft end play.
21. Ensure crankshaft torque-to-turn does not exceed 53 inch lbs.

CRANKSHAFT REAR OIL SEAL

REPLACE

1. Remove transmission as outlined in **MOTOR's "Domestic Transmission, In Vehicle Service"** or **"Transmission Service DVD."**
2. Remove flywheel.

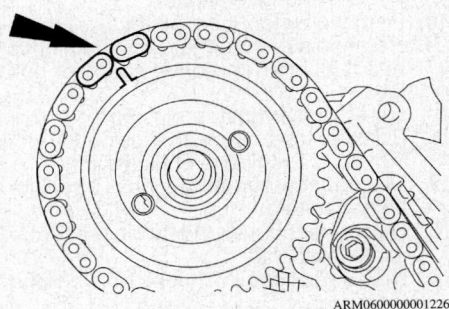

Fig. 14 Righthand timing chain mark on camshaft. 5.4L engine

3. Remove rear slinger using tool Nos. 303-514 and 100-001, or equivalent.
4. Remove crankshaft rear seal using tool Nos. 303-519 and 100-001, or equivalent.
5. Reverse procedure to install.

OIL PAN

REPLACE

1. Remove battery and tray.
2. Remove air cleaner outlet pipe.
3. Install engine lifting tool Nos. 303-D087, 303-F072 and 303-F070, or suitable equivalent.
4. Remove lefthand and righthand engine mount nuts.
5. Raise engine.
6. Raise and support vehicle.
7. Drain engine oil into suitable container.
8. Remove subframe cross brace.
9. Position a suitable jackstand under subframe.
10. Remove upper bolt from intermediate steering shaft.
11. Mark position of subframe nuts and bolts for referencing during assembly.
12. Lower subframe 1.96 inch using suitable jackstand.
13. Detach wiring harness retainers from oil pan stud bolts.
14. Remove oil pan mounting bolts, then oil pan.
15. Reverse procedure to install, noting the following:
    a. Clean oil pan mating surface with suitable silicone gasket remover and metal surface prep.
    b. **Oil pan must be secured within four minutes of sealant application.**
    c. Apply silicone gasket and sealant

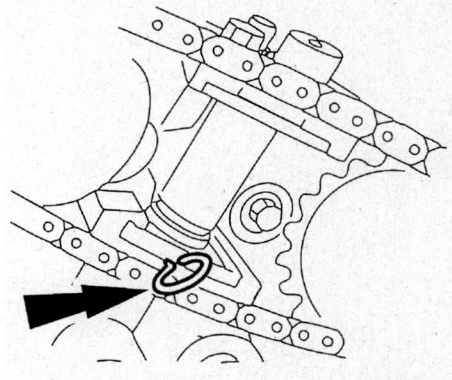

Fig. 15 Secondary timing chain tensioner

at engine front cover-to-cylinder block sealing surface.

d. Install gasket and the oil pan, then loosely install 16 mounting bolts.

e. **Torque** oil pan mounting bolts in sequence to 18 ft. lbs., **Fig. 21.**

OIL PUMP

REPLACE

1. Remove timing chain as outlined under "Timing Chain, Replace."
2. Remove oil pump screen and pickup tube.
3. Remove oil pump mounting bolts, then oil pump.
4. Reverse procedure to install, noting the following:
   a. Install oil pump and mounting bolts.
   b. **Torque** bolts to 89 inch lbs. in a clockwise pattern starting at top.

BELT TENSION DATA

These models are equipped with an automatic drive belt tensioner. No adjustment or maintenance is required.

SERPENTINE DRIVE BELT

Always use square drive tool in hole in tensioner to move tensioner. Never pry on tensioner pulley. When releasing drive belt tensioner, never allow tensioner to snap back. Damage to tensioner or personal injury could result.

Do not allow engine coolant to remain on serpentine belt or pulleys. If required, remove belt and flush with clean water.

Routing

Refer to **Fig. 22** for serpentine drive belt routing.

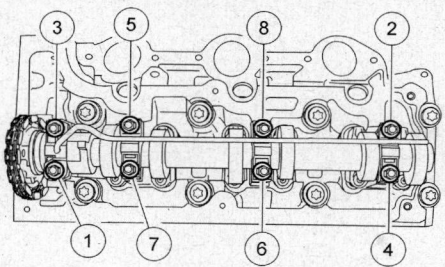

Fig. 16 Camshaft bearing cap bolt removal sequence. 5.4L engine

Replacement

Rotate the accessory drive belt tensioner clockwise with suitable belt tensioner release tool and remove the belt.

COOLING SYSTEM BLEED

1. Fill radiator through degas bottle until the coolant level is between the COOLANT FILL LEVEL marks.
2. Select maximum heater temperature and blower motor speed settings.
3. Position control to discharge air at air conditioning vents in instrument panel.
4. Start engine and allow to idle.
5. While engine is idling, feel for hot air at air conditioning vents.
6. **If air discharge remains cool and engine coolant temperature gauge does not move, engine coolant level is low and must be filled. Stop engine, allow it to cool and fill cooling system.**
7. Allow engine to idle until normal operating temperature is reached. Hot air should discharge from air conditioning vents.
8. Engine coolant temperature gauge should maintain stabilized reading in middle of NORMAL range.
9. Upper radiator hose should feel hot to touch.
10. Shut engine off and allow it to cool.
11. Inspect engine for coolant leaks.
12. Inspect and adjust engine coolant level in degas bottle.

THERMOSTAT

REPLACE

1. Drain coolant into a suitable container.
2. Remove thermostat housing cover mounting bolts, then position housing cover and hose assembly aside.
3. Remove o-ring seal and thermostat.
4. Reverse procedure to install.

WATER PUMP

REPLACE

1. Drain coolant from engine and super-

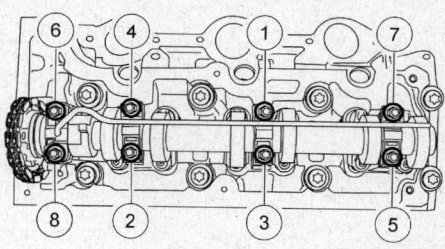

Fig. 17 Camshaft bearing cap bolt tightening sequence. 5.4L engine

charger into a suitable container.

2. Disconnect upper hose from degas bottle, and position bottle aside.
3. Disconnect upper hose from supercharger degas bottle, then position supercharger degas bottle aside.
4. Loosen water pump pulley mounting bolts.
5. Remove serpentine drive belt.
6. Rotate supercharger belt tensioner clockwise and remove belt off supercharger.
7. Remove water pump pulley mounting bolts, then pulley.
8. Reverse procedure to install.

RADIATOR

REPLACE

1. Drain coolant into a suitable container.
2. Remove lower radiator air deflector.
3. Remove upper air deflector.
4. Remove cooling fan motor and shroud.
5. Disconnect degas bottle to radiator hose and position aside.
6. Disconnect upper radiator hose from radiator.
7. Disconnect lower radiator hose from radiator.
8. Remove radiator support bracket mounting bolts and brackets.
9. Remove power steering tube and A/C condenser retaining nuts, then position power steering tubes aside.
10. Remove A/C condenser mounting bolts.
11. **On models equipped with transmission cooler,** remove mounting bolts and position cooler aside.
12. **On all models,** remove radiator.
13. Reverse procedure to install.

FUEL PUMP

REPLACE

Refer to "4.0L Engine" for fuel pump replacement procedure

FUEL FILTER

REPLACE

Refer to "4.0L Engine" for fuel pump replacement procedure.

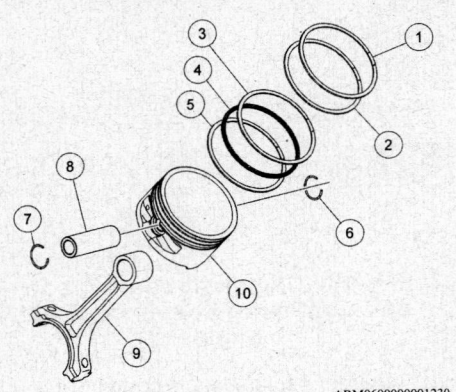

Fig. 18 Piston & connecting rod

ARM0600000001230

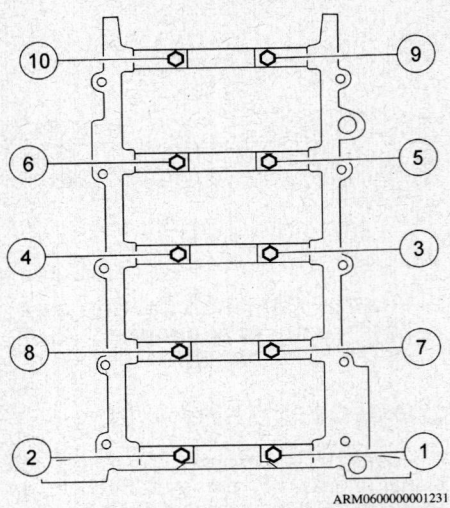

ARM0600000001231

**Fig. 19 Vertical main bearing cap
tightening sequence**

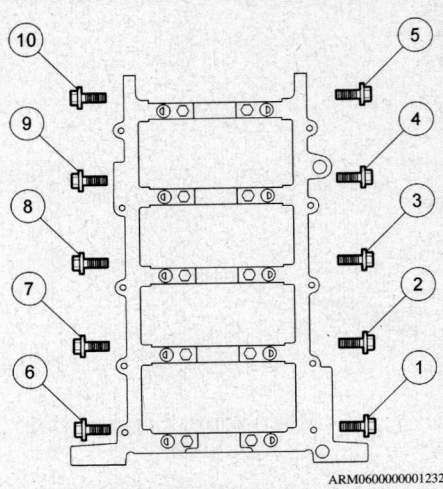

ARM0600000001232

**Fig. 20 Side bolt main bearing
tightening sequence**

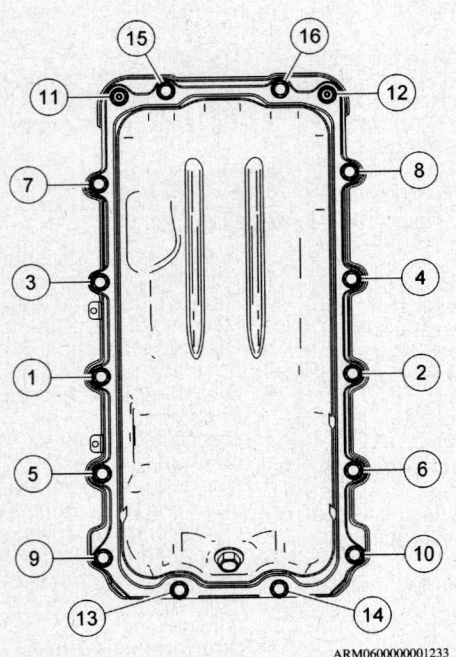

ARM0600000001233

**Fig. 21 Oil pan tightening
sequence**

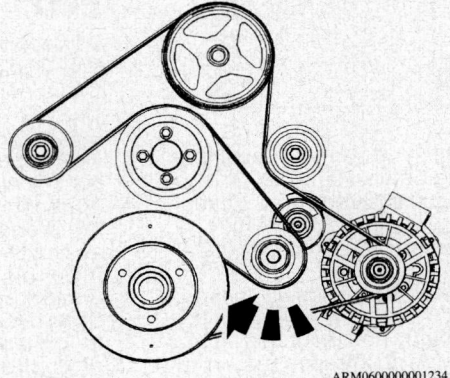

ARM0600000001234

**Fig. 22 Serpentine drive belt
routing. 5.4L engine**

TIGHTENING SPECIFICATIONS

Year	Component	Torque/Ft. Lbs.
2007–08	Air Cleaner	71①
	Air Cleaner Outlet Pipe	27①
	Air Conditioning Compressor	18
	Air Conditioning Condenser	89①
	Alternator, Lower	18
	Alternator, Upper	35
	Alternator B+ Terminal	71①
	Belt Idler Pulley	18
	Camshaft Bearing Cap	89①
	Camshaft Phaser Sprocket	⑧
	Catalytic Converter-To-Exhaust Manifold	30
	Cooling Fan Motor & Shroud	80①
	Connecting Rod	⑥
	Crankshaft Pulley	②
	Crankshaft Rear Seal Retainer Plate	89①
	Crankshaft Rear Seal Retainer Plate To Oil Pan	③
	Cylinder Head	⑦
	Degas Bottle	71①
	Engine Support Insulator, Bolt	41
	Engine Support Insulator, Nut	46
	Exhaust Manifold	41
	Flywheel/Flexplate	59
	Front Cover	④
	Fuel Rail	89①
	Ground Wire	18
	Ignition Coil	44①
	Intake Manifold	89①
	Main Bearings	⑤
	Oil Dipstick Tube	89①
	Oil Pan	⑨
	Oil Pan Drain Plug	19
	Oil Pump	89①

TIGHTENING SPECIFICATIONS—Continued

Year	Component	Torque/Ft. Lbs.
2007–08	Oil Pump Screen & Pickup Tube-To-Oil Pump	89①
	Power Steering Pulley Shield	89①
	Power Steering Pump	18
	Power Steering Tube	89①
	Radiator Support Bracket	22
	Radio Ignition Interference Capacitor	18
	Steering Coupling	18
	Subframe Bolts/nuts	85
	Supercharger Belt Tensioner	35
	Supercharger Idler Pulley	18
	Thermostat Cover	89①
	Thermostat Housing	18
	Throttle Body	89①
	Timing Chain Guide	89①
	Timing Chain Tensioner	18
	Transmission Cooler Tube Bracket	18
	Valve Cover	89①
	Valve Cover Wiring Harness Bracket	30
	Water Pump	18
	Water Pump Pulley	18

① — Inch pounds.
② — Refer to "Crankshaft Damper, Replace" for tightening specifications and sequence.
③ — Refer to "Crankshaft Rear Oil Seal, Replace" for tightening specifications and sequence.
④ — Refer to "Front Cover, Replace" for tightening specifications and sequence.
⑤ — Refer to "Main & Rod Bearings" for tightening specifications and sequence.
⑥ — Refer to "Piston & Rod Assembly" for tightening specifications and sequence.
⑦ — Refer to "Cylinder Head, Replace" for tightening specifications and sequence.
⑧ — Refer to "Timing Chain, Replace" for tightening specifications and sequence.
⑨ — Refer to "Oil Pan, Replace" for tightening specifications and sequence.

Rear Axle & Suspension

NOTE: On Air Bag Equipped Models, Refer To "Air Bag System Precautions" Located In The Front Of This Manual For System Disarming & Arming Procedures.

NOTE: Refer To "Computer Relearn Procedures" Located In The Front Of This Manual When Battery Power To The Computer Has Been Interrupted.

NOTE: Prior To Performing Any Service Operations Listed In This Section, Consult The "Technical Service Bulletins" Section For Related Information.

INDEX

	Page No.
Axle Damper, Replace	4-85
Coil Spring, Replace	4-87
2004	4-87
Cobra	4-87
Except Cobra	4-87
2005–08	4-88
Control Arm, Replace	4-88
2004	4-88
Cobra	4-88
Except Cobra	4-88
2005–08	4-89
Lower	4-89
Upper	4-89
Control Arm Bushing, Replace	4-89
2004	4-89
Cobra	4-89
Except Cobra	4-89
2005–08	4-89
Description	4-82
Cobra	4-82

	Page No.
Except Cobra	4-82
Lateral Rod, Replace	4-90
Precautions	4-82
Shock Absorber	4-82
Propeller Shaft, Replace	4-86
2004	4-86
Cobra	4-86
Except Cobra	4-86
2005–08	4-86
4.0L Engine	4-86
4.6L & 5.4L Engines	4-86
Rear Axle, Replace	4-82
2004	4-82
Cobra	4-83
Except Cobra	4-82
2005–08	4-84
Rear Axle Shaft, Replace	4-85
2004	4-85
Cobra	4-85
Except Cobra	4-85

	Page No.
2005–08	4-85
Shock Absorber, Replace	4-87
2004	4-87
Cobra	4-87
Except Cobra	4-87
2005–08	4-87
Stabilizer Bar, Replace	4-89
2004	4-89
Cobra	4-90
Except Cobra	4-89
2005–08	4-90
Technical Service Bulletins	4-90
Axle Whine	4-90
2005 Mustang	4-90
Limited Slip Axle Chatter, Shudder, Binding Sensation, Or Vibration During Low Speed Turning Maneuvers	4-90
2004–05 Mustang	4-90
Tightening Specifications	4-92

PRECAUTIONS
Shock Absorber

These vehicles are equipped with gas pressurized shock absorbers which will extend unassisted. Do not apply heat or flame to shock absorber.

DESCRIPTION
Except Cobra

This rear axle is an integral design hypoid with center line of pinion set below center line of ring gear, **Figs. 1 through 3.** Semi-floating axle shafts are retained in housing by ball bearings and bearing retainers at axle ends.

The differential is mounted on two opposed tapered roller bearings which are retained in housing by removable caps. The differential bearing preload and drive gear backlash is adjusted by nuts located behind each differential bearing cup.

The drive pinion is mounted on two opposed tapered roller bearings. The pinion bearing preload is adjusted by a collapsible spacer on pinion shaft. The pinion and ring gear tooth contact is adjusted by shims between rear bearing cone and pinion gear.

Cobra

On these models the hypoid type axle has an 8.8 inch ring gear and a one-piece differential case, **Fig. 4.** Two opposed pinion bearings support the drive pinion gear in the differential housing. Two pinion gears engage the differential side gears with half-shaft splines.

REAR AXLE
REPLACE
2004
EXCEPT COBRA

1. Raise and support vehicle, then position safety stands under rear frame crossmember.
2. Drain axle lubricant into suitable container by removing axle housing cover.
3. Remove wheels, rear disc brake calipers and rear disc brake rotors as outlined in "Disc Brakes" chapter.
4. Remove lockpin and differential pinion shaft.
5. Remove rear brake anti-lock sensor.
6. Remove rear axle shaft U-washers by pushing axle shafts inward.
7. Remove axle shafts.
8. Remove brake junction block to axle housing cover bolt and brake hose support bracket from clips. Position hose aside.
9. Mark driveshaft centering socket yoke and rear axle universal joint flange for installation alignment.
10. Disconnect driveshaft at rear axle universal joint flange and wire it to underbody.
11. Support rear axle housing with suitable jackstands or hoist.
12. Disconnect rear brake hose from rear brake hose to rear axle housing clips.
13. Disconnect rear axle housing vent from rear axle housing.
14. Disconnect lower shock absorber studs from rear shock absorber lower mounting bracket.
15. Remove rear suspension arm and bushing nuts and bolts from axle housing rear bracket mountings.
16. Lower rear axle housing until rear springs are released and remove rear springs.

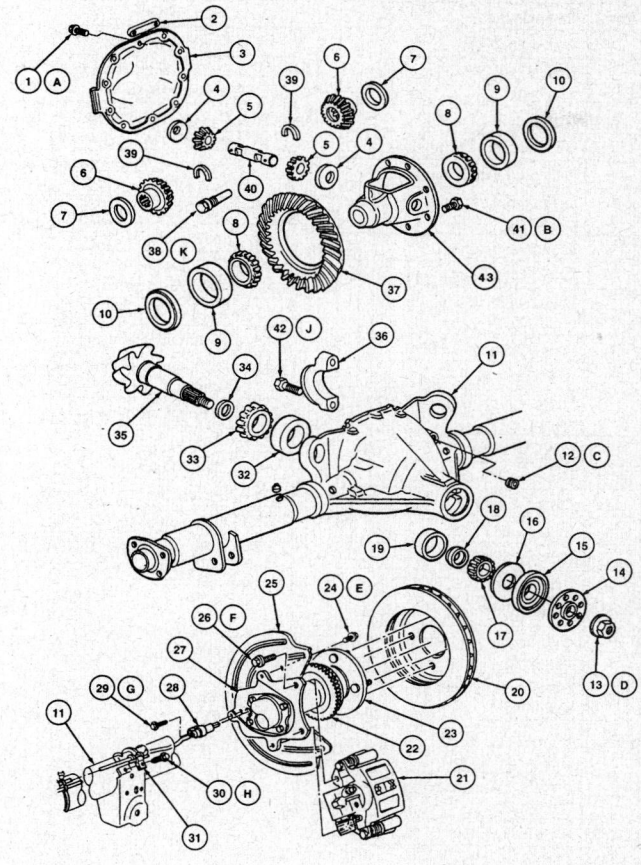

Fig. 1 Exploded view of integral rear axle (Part 1 of 2). 7.5 inch ring gear less Traction-Lock or except Cobra

FM3039400270010X

Item	Description
1	Bolt
2	Rear Axle Brake Line Clip
3	Axle Housing Cover
4	Differential Pinion Thrust Washer
5	Differential Pinion Gear
6	Differential Side Gear
7	Differential Side Gear Thrust Washer
8	Differential Bearing
9	Differential Bearing Cup
10	Differential Bearing Shim
11	Rear Axle Housing
12	Filler Plug
13	Pinion Nut
14	Rear Axle Universal Joint Flange
15	Rear Axle Drive Pinion Seal
16	Rear Axle Drive Pinion Shaft Oil Slinger
17	Differential Pinion Bearing
18	Differential Drive Pinion Collapsible Spacer
19	Differential Drive Pinion Bearing Cup
20	Rear Disc Brake Rotor
21	Rear Disc Brake Caliper
22	Rear Brake Anti-Lock Sensor Indicator
23	Axle Shaft Flange (Part of 4234)
24	Bolt (3 Req'd)
25	Rear Wheel Disc Brake Shield
26	Caliper Anchor Bolt
27	Left Hand Rear Disc Brake Adapter
	Right Hand Rear Disc Brake Adapter

Item	Description
28	Rear Brake Anti-Lock Sensor
29	Bolt
30	Bolt
31	Clip
32	Rear Axle Pinion Bearing Cup
33	Differential Pinion Bearing
34	Drive Pinion Bearing Adjustment Shim
35	Drive Pinion (Part of 4209)
36	Bearing Cap (Part of 4010)
37	Ring Gear (Part of 4209)
38	Differential Pinion Shaft Lock Pin
39	U-Washer
40	Differential Pinion Shaft
41	Rear Axle Differential Gear Case Bolt
42	Bolt (Part of 4010)
43	Differential Case
A	Tighten to 24-38 N·m (18-28 Lb-Ft)
B	Tighten to 95-115 N·m (70-85 Lb-Ft)
C	Tighten to 20-41 N·m (15-30 Lb-Ft)
D	Tighten to 190 N·m (140 Lb-Ft)
E	Tighten to 8-12 N·m (6-9 Lb-Ft)
F	Tighten to 87-119 N·m (64-87.7 Lb-Ft)
G	Tighten to 5-7 N·m (40-60 Lb-In)
H	Tighten to 10-14 N·m (7-10 Lb-Ft)
J	Tighten to 102-122 N·m (75-90 Lb-Ft)
K	Tighten to 20-41 N·m (15-30 Lb-Ft)

FM3039400270020X

Fig. 1 Exploded view of integral rear axle (Part 2 of 2). 7.5 inch ring gear less Traction-Lock or except Cobra

17. Remove rear suspension lower arm to rear axle housing nuts and bolts, then disconnect both rear suspension lower arms from rear axle housing.
18. Lower rear axle housing and remove it.
19. Reverse procedure to install, noting the following:
    a. Tighten differential pinion shaft lockpin using stud and bearing mount tool No. E0AZ-19554-BA, or equivalent.
    b. Tighten axle housing cover bolt in crosswise pattern.
    c. Apply threadlock and sealer E0AZ-19554-AA, or equivalent, to rear axle housing vents threads.

COBRA

1. Park vehicle at curb height and on level ground.
2. Mark rear shock absorber positions relative to upper sleeves for installation alignment.
3. Raise and safely support vehicle, then remove rear wheel and tire assemblies.
4. Remove exhaust system.
5. Record transverse bar fastener for installation alignment.
6. Remove mounting nuts and pinion nose crossmember.
7. Mark driveshaft companion flange to pinion flange for installation alignment.
8. Remove and discard companion flange to pinion flange bolts.
9. Position driveshaft aside with suitable wire or rope.
10. Disconnect parking brake cables and conduits from parking brake lever and calipers.
11. Separate parking brake cables and conduits from knuckles.
12. Remove rear brake rotors.
13. Remove rear brake calipers and support brackets from knuckles as an assembly. Position calipers aside with suitable wire or rope.
14. Remove rear brake anti-lock sensors and position aside.
15. Support lower suspension arm and bushing with suitable jack stand.
16. Remove and discard lower suspension arm nuts and bolts.
17. Remove and discard toe link cotter pins and nuts.
18. Disconnect toe links from knuckles using separator tool No. T64P-3590-F, or equivalent.
19. Mark cam bolt to upper control arms and bushings for installation alignment.
20. Remove and discard lower control arm bushing nuts and bolts.
21. Disconnect knuckles from lower control arms.
22. Mark upper control arm cam bolts for installation alignment.
23. Remove and discard upper control arm bushing nuts and bolts.
24. Disconnect knuckles from upper control arms.
25. Separate CV joint from side gear using halfshaft removal tool No. 205-475, or equivalent, to overcome circlip. **Ensure tool fork crowns face away from differential housing. Position tool between CV joint and housing.**
26. Install seal protector tool No. 205-461, or equivalent.
27. Remove halfshaft and knuckle assemblies.
28. Install differential plug tool No. T89P-4850-B, or equivalent, into housing bores.
29. Support differential housing with suitable transmission jack.
30. Remove differential to frame mounting bolts.
31. Lower and remove axle.
32. Reverse procedure to install, noting the following:

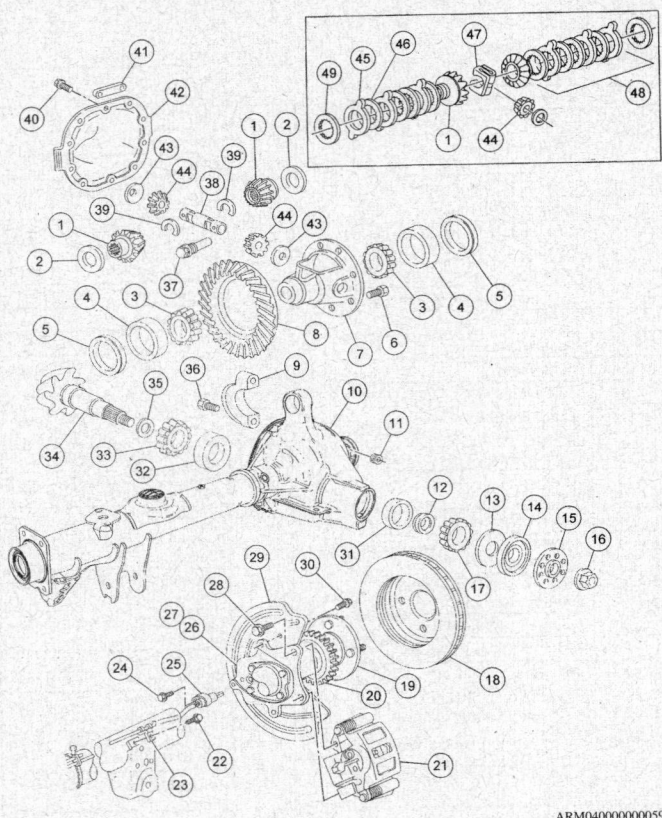

Fig. 2 Exploded view of integral rear axle (Part 1 of 2). 8.8 inch ring gear except Cobra

a. Install seal protector tool No. 205-461, or equivalent, before install halfshafts.
b. Ensure inboard CV joints circlips are properly seated.
c. Ensure transverse bar is in place and bolt passes through it. **Do not tighten until vehicle is on ground and shock absorber marks are aligned.**
d. Install new cam bolts and nuts at control arms and bushings. **Do not tighten until vehicle is on ground and shock absorber marks are aligned.**
e. Apply high temperature nickel anti-seize lubricant part No. F6AZ-9L494-AA, or equivalent, to rear brake anti-lock sensors at axle housing contact points.
f. Adjust wheel alignment.

2005-08

1. Mark rear shock absorbers relative to their protective sleeve for installation alignment with vehicle on level ground and at curb height.
2. Raise and support vehicle.
3. Remove rear wheel and tire assemblies.
4. **On convertible models,** proceed as follows:
   a. Remove four rear support brace bolts.
   b. Remove two upper support brace bolts.
   c. Remove four front support brace bolts.
5. **On all models,** depress tabs of trackbar cover retaining clip using two screwdrivers through access hole and remove trackbar cover.
6. Remove mounting bolts, flag nuts and Trackbar.
7. Support and secure differential housing to suitable transmission jack.
8. Remove shock absorber mounting nuts and bolts.
9. Remove upper suspension arm mounting nut and bolt.
10. Lower axle slightly and remove springs.
11. Remove trailing arm mounting nuts and bolts.
12. Disconnect lower suspension arms from axle housing.
13. Lower and remove axle housing.
14. Reverse procedure to install, noting the following:
    a. Raise suspension to reference mark before tightening suspension mounting nuts and bolts.
    b. Install new rear, upper and front support brace mounting bolts.
    c. Install new trackbar mounting bolts and flag nuts.
    d. Install new shock absorber mounting bolts and nuts
    e. Install new upper suspension and trailing arm mounting bolts and nuts.

Item	Description
1	Differential side gear
2	Differential side gear thrust washer
3	Differential bearing
4	Differential bearing cup
5	Differential bearing shim
6	Differential ring gear bolt (10 required)
7	Differential case
8	Differential ring gear (part of
9	Differential bearing cap (2 required
10	Axle housing
11	Filler plug
12	Drive pinion collapsible spacer
13	Drive pinion shaft oil slinger
14	Drive pinion seal
15	Pinion flange
16	Pinion nut
17	Drive pinion bearing (outer)
18	Brake disc
19	Axle shaft flange (2 required)
20	Anti-lock sensor indicator (2 required)
21	Disc brake caliper (2 required)
22	Brake line clip bolt
23	Brake line clip
24	Anti-lock sensor bolt (2 required)
25	Anti-lock sensor (2 required)
26	LH disc brake adapter
27	RH disc brake adapter
28	Disc brake caliper anchor bolt (4 required)
29	Brake disc shield (2 required)
30	Brake disc shield bolt (6 required)
31	Drive pinion bearing cup (outer)
32	Drive pinion bearing cup (inner)
33	Drive pinion bearing (inner)

Item	Description
34	Drive pinion gear
35	Drive pinion bearing adjustment shim
36	Differential bearing cap bolt (4 required
37	Differential pinion shaft lock bolt
38	Differential pinion shaft
39	Axle shaft U-washer
40	Differential housing cover bolt (10 required)
41	Axle identification tag
42	Differential housing cover
43	Differential pinion gear thrust washer
44	Differential pinion gear
45	Steel plate
46	Clutch disc
47	Differential clutch spring
48	Differential clutch pack
49	Rear axle differential clutch shim

ARM0400000000596

Fig. 2 Exploded view of integral rear axle (Part 2 of 2). 8.8 inch ring gear except Cobra

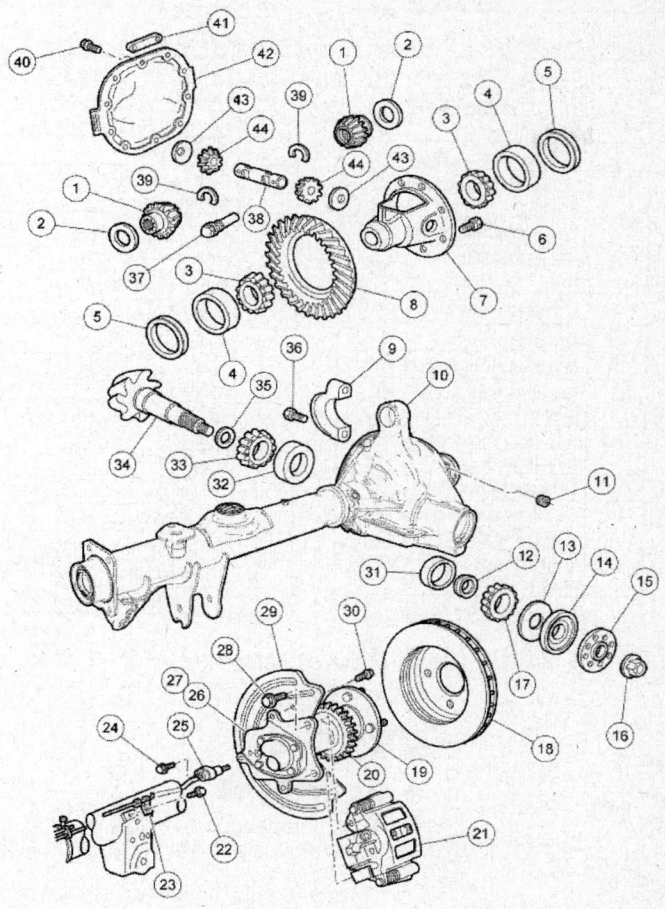

Fig. 3 Exploded view of integral rear axle (Part 1 of 2). 7.5 inch ring gear 5.4L engine

ARM06A0000001237

Item	Description	Item	Description
1	Differential side gears	31	Drive pinion bearing cup (outer)
2	Differential side gear thrust washers	32	Drive pinion bearing cup (inner)
3	Differential bearings	33	Drive pinion bearing (inner)
4	Differential bearing cups	34	Drive pinion gear (part of 4209)
5	Differential bearing shims	35	Drive pinion bearing adjustment shim
6	Differential ring gear bolt (10 required)	36	Differential bearing cap bolt (4 required) (part of 4010)
7	Differential case	37	Differential pinion shaft lock bolt
		38	Differential pinion shaft
8	Differential ring gear (part of 4209)	39	Axle shaft U-washers
		40	Differential housing cover bolt (10 required)
9	Differential bearing cap (2 required) (part of 4010)	41	Axle identification tag
		42	Differential housing cover
10	Axle housing	43	Differential pinion gear thrust washers
11	Filler plug	44	Differential pinion gears
14	Drive pinion seal		
15	Pinion flange		
16	Pinion nut		
17	Drive pinion bearing (outer)		
18	Brake disc		
19	Axle shaft flange (2 required) (part of 4234)		
20	Anti-lock sensor indicator (2 required)		
21	Disc brake caliper (2 required)		
22	Brake line clip bolt		
23	Brake line clip		
24	Anti-lock sensor bolt (2 required)		
25	Anti-lock sensor (2 required)		
26	LH disc brake adapter		
27	RH disc brake adapter		
28	Disc brake caliper anchor bolt (4 required)		
29	Brake disc shield (2 required)		
30	Brake disc shield bolt (6 required)		

ARM06A0000001238

Fig. 3 Exploded view of integral rear axle (Part 2 of 2). 7.5 inch ring gear 5.4L engine

REAR AXLE SHAFT
REPLACE
2004
EXCEPT COBRA

1. Raise and support vehicle, then remove rear wheel and tire assembly.
2. Remove brake drum as outlined in "Drum Brakes" chapter or rear disc brake calipers and rear disc brake rotors as outlined in "Disc Brakes" chapter.
3. Remove axle housing cover and drain axle lubricant into suitable container.
4. Remove lockpin and differential pinion shaft.
5. Remove rear brake anti-lock sensor.
6. Push axle shaft flanged end toward vehicle center and remove C-lock from axle shaft button end.
7. Remove axle shaft from housing. **Do not damage oil seal.**
8. Reverse procedure to install.

COBRA

Refer to "Rear Axle, Replace" for rear axle shaft replacement procedure.

2005-08

1. Raise and support vehicle, then remove rear wheel and tire assembly.
2. Remove 10 differential cover mounting bolts and drain lubricant from axle housing into suitable container.
3. Remove differential housing cover.
4. Remove two mounting bolts, then position and support disc brake caliper aside.
5. Remove disc brake pads.
6. Remove two mounting bolts and disc brake caliper anchor.
7. Remove brake disc.
8. Remove mounting bolt and anti-lock sensor from hub.
9. Remove lock bolt and differential pinion shaft.
10. Push in on axle shaft and U-washer. **Do not damage rubber O-ring in axle shaft grooves.**
11. Remove the axle shaft. **Do not damage axle shaft oil seal.**
12. Reverse procedure to install, noting the following:

a. Lubricate lip of axle shaft oil seal with grease.
b. If new differential pinion shaft lock bolt is unavailable, coat threads of old differential pinion shaft lock bolt with suitable Threadlock and Sealer.
c. Install new differential pinion shaft lock bolt.
d. Apply anti-seize lubricant to Anti-Lock Sensor body where it will contact .
e. Apply new continuous bead of suitable silicone sealant to differential housing cover.
f. **Differential housing cover must be installed within 15 minutes of application of silicone sealant.**

AXLE DAMPER
REPLACE

1. Raise vehicle and support rear axle, then remove rear wheel and tire assembly.

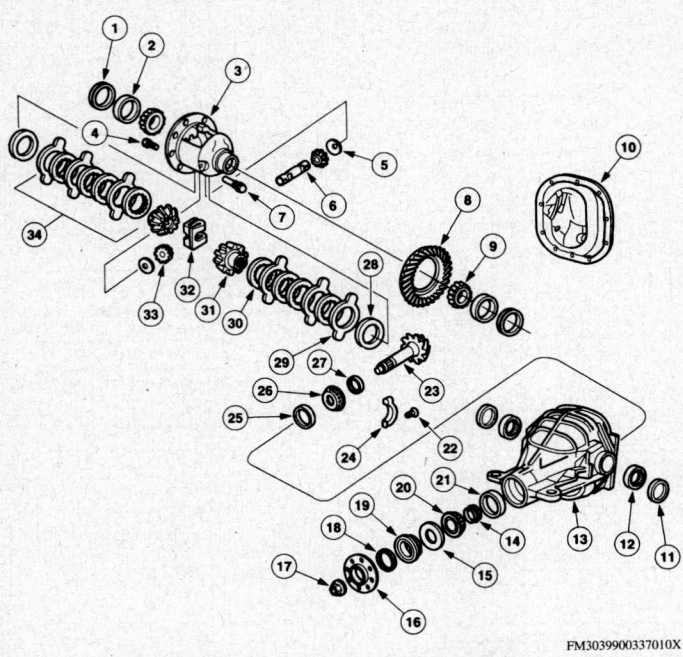

Item	Description
1	Differential bearing shim
2	Differential bearing cup
3	Differential case
4	Differential ring gear case bolt
5	Differential pinion thrust washer
6	Differential pinion shaft
7	Differential pinion shaft lock bolt
8	Differential ring gear
9	Differential bearing
10	Differential housing cover
11	Inboard CV joint stub shaft pilot bearing housing seal
12	Inboard CV joint stub shaft pilot bearing
13	Differential housing
14	Differential drive pinion collapsible spacer
15	Rear axle drive pinion shaft oil slinger
16	Rear axle pinion flange

Item	Description
17	Pinion nut
18	Drive pinion oil seal deflector
19	Rear axle drive pinion seal
20	Pinion bearing
21	Differential drive pinion bearing cup
22	Bolt
23	Drive pinion gear
24	Differential bearing cap
25	Rear axle pinion bearing cup
26	Pinion bearing
27	Drive pinion bearing adjustment shim
28	Rear axle differential clutch shim
29	Clutch plate
30	Clutch disc
31	Differential side gear
32	Differential clutch spring
33	Differential pinion gear
34	Differential clutch pack

FM3039900337010X

Fig. 4   Exploded view of rear axle (Part 1 of 2). Cobra

FM3039900337020X

Fig. 4   Exploded view of rear axle (Part 2 of 2). Cobra

2. Remove axle damper front retaining pivot bolt and rear mounting nut, **Fig. 5.**
3. Remove damper and washers.
4. Reverse procedure to install.

PROPELLER SHAFT

REPLACE

2004

EXCEPT COBRA

REMOVAL

1. Mark rear driveshaft yoke and drive pinion flange relationship for installation alignment.
2. Disconnect rear U-joint from companion flange, **Fig. 6.**
3. Wrap tape around loose bearing caps to prevent them from falling off spider.
4. Pull driveshaft toward rear of vehicle until slip yoke clears transmission extension housing and seal.
5. Install suitable plug into extension housing to prevent lubricant leakage.

INSTALLATION

1. Lubricate slip yoke splines with suitable grease and remove transmission extension plug.
2. Inspect housing seal for damage.
3. Align slip yoke index mark with transmission output shaft mark and install driveshaft. **Do not allow slip yoke to bottom on output shaft with excessive force.**
4. Install driveshaft so index mark on rear flange is aligned with index mark on axle companion flange to ensure original driveline balance.
5. When installing new driveshaft, align factory made yellow paint mark at rear

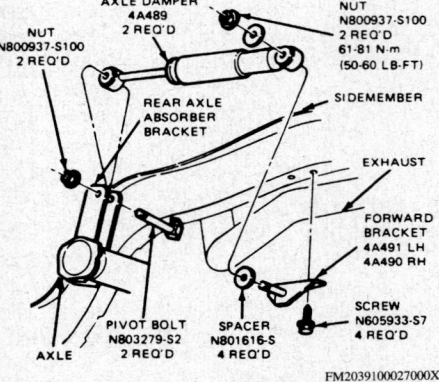

Fig. 5   Axle damper replacement

of driveshaft tube with factory made yellow paint mark on axle companion flange.

COBRA

1. Raise and support vehicle.
2. Remove exhaust hangers from rubber mounts.
3. Remove two mounting nuts on left-hand side exhaust flange.
4. Lower muffler pipe to clear flange and move muffler forward to disconnect third exhaust hanger.
5. Mark driveshaft companion flange to pinion flange for installation alignment.
6. Mark driveshaft yoke to transmission tailshaft for installation alignment.
7. Remove and discard companion flange to pinion flange bolts.
8. Lower driveshaft rear it clears axle housing.
9. Pull driveshaft rearward out of transmission.
10. Reverse procedure to install.

2005-08

4.0L ENGINE

1. Raise and support vehicle.
2. Mark driveshaft for installation alignment.
3. Remove eight driveshaft flange bolts, **Fig. 7.**
4. Disconnect driveshaft flanges from pilots and remove driveshaft using suitable tool, **Fig. 8. Driveshaft flanges fits tightly on pilots. Never hammer on driveshaft or any of its components to disconnect flanges from pilots. Pry only in area with suitable tool, to disconnect driveshaft flanges from flange pilots.**
5. Reverse procedure to install, noting the following:
   a. Install new mounting bolts.
   b. If new driveshaft flange bolts are not available, coat threads of original driveshaft flange bolts with Medium Strength Threadlocker TA-25, or equivalent meeting Ford specification WSK-M2G351-A5.

4.6L & 5.4L ENGINES

1. Raise and support vehicle.
2. Remove two exhaust hangers from rubber mounts.
3. Loosen two Exhaust Pipe nuts on left-hand side and disconnect lefthand muffler.
4. Lower muffler to clear exhaust pipe, then position muffler assembly forward and disconnect third exhaust hanger.
5. Mark driveshaft for installation alignment .
6. Remove six mounting bolts and washers, then disconnect Constant Velocity (CV) joint from pinion flange, **Fig. 9.**
7. Remove four driveshaft flange bolts.
8. Disconnect driveshaft flanges from

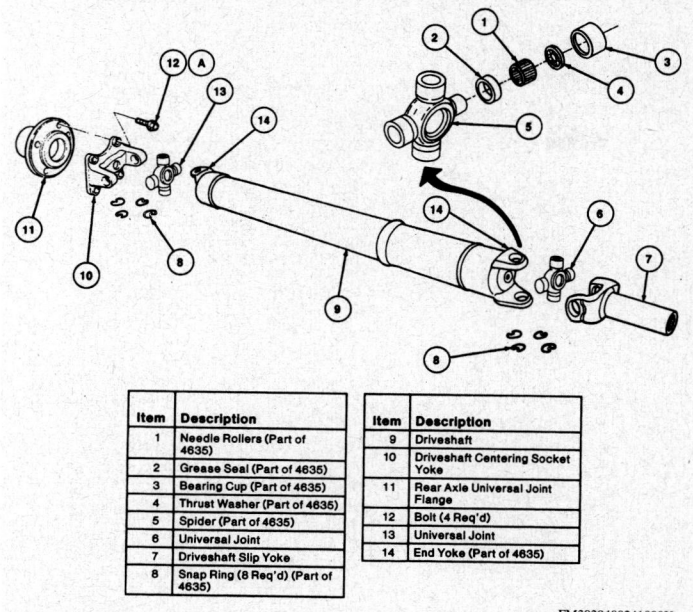

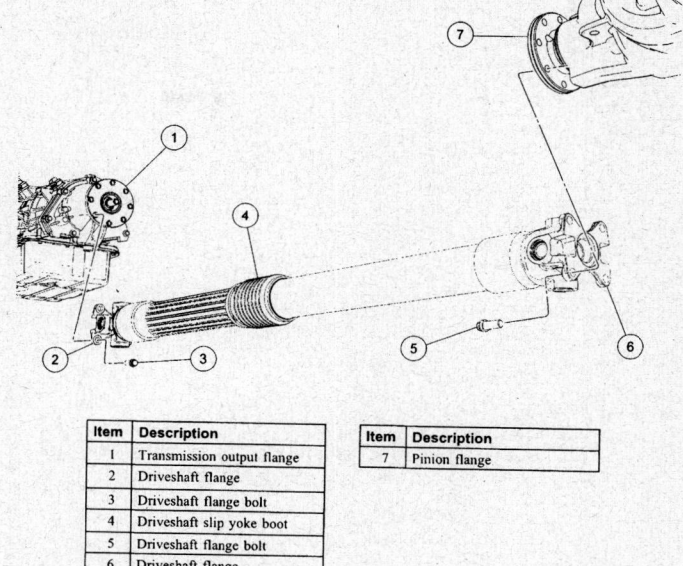

Item	Description
1	Needle Rollers (Part of 4635)
2	Grease Seal (Part of 4635)
3	Bearing Cup (Part of 4635)
4	Thrust Washer (Part of 4635)
5	Spider (Part of 4635)
6	Universal Joint
7	Driveshaft Slip Yoke
8	Snap Ring (8 Req'd) (Part of 4635)

Item	Description
9	Driveshaft
10	Driveshaft Centering Socket Yoke
11	Rear Axle Universal Joint Flange
12	Bolt (4 Req'd)
13	Universal Joint
14	End Yoke (Part of 4635)

FM3039400241000X

Fig. 6 Driveshaft & universal joint replacement. Single Cardan type U-joint

Item	Description
1	Transmission output flange
2	Driveshaft flange
3	Driveshaft flange bolt
4	Driveshaft slip yoke boot
5	Driveshaft flange bolt
6	Driveshaft flange

Item	Description
7	Pinion flange

ARM0400000000597

Fig. 7 Drive shaft replacement. 2005–06 w/4.0L engine

transmission flange pilot, **Fig. 8.** **Driveshaft flanges fits tightly on pilots. Never hammer on driveshaft or any of its components to disconnect flanges from pilots. Pry only in area with suitable tool, to disconnect driveshaft flanges from flange pilots.**
9. Remove two center bearing bolts and spacers, then remove driveshaft.
10. Reverse procedure to install, noting the following:
    a. Install new mounting bolts.
    b. If new driveshaft flange bolts are not available, coat threads of original driveshaft flange bolts with Medium Strength Threadlocker TA-25, or equivalent meeting Ford specification WSK-M2G351-A5.
    c. Tighten CV joint bolts evenly in star pattern.

SHOCK ABSORBER
REPLACE
2004
EXCEPT COBRA
1. Open luggage compartment and remove rubber cap.
2. Remove shock absorber upper stud nut, washer and insulator.
3. Raise and support vehicle, then support rear axle.
4. Remove shock absorber lower stud nut, washer and insulator.
5. Compress shock absorber to clear upper shock tower.
6. Remove shock absorber.
7. Reverse procedure to install.

COBRA
1. Open luggage compartment and position carpet aside.

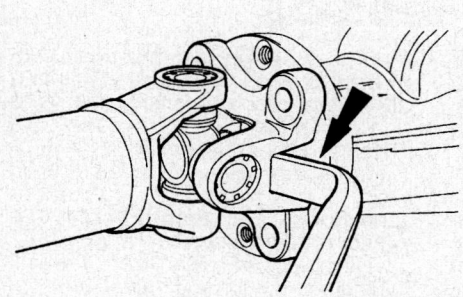

ARM0400000000598

Fig. 8 Driveshaft flange pry area. 2005–08 w/4.0L & 4.6L engine

2. Remove and discard shock absorber mounting nut, washer and insulator.
3. Raise and support vehicle.
4. Remove and discard shock absorber lower mounting bolt and nut.
5. Remove shock absorber insulator and washer.
6. Reverse procedure to install, noting the following:
    a. Install new lower insulator and washer onto shock absorber.
    b. **Ensure hardened washer sits between lower control arm and bushing and absorber.**
    c. Install new upper insulator, washer and nut.

2005–08
1. Open luggage compartment lid and position carpet aside.
2. Raise and support vehicle.
3. Support the rear axle with a jack stand. **Do not support rear axle at differential housing. Do not allow axle to be supported by upper or lower control arms.**
4. Remove mounting nut, washer and in-

sulator assembly, **Fig. 10.**
5. **On models equipped with rear stabilizer bar,** proceed as follows:
    a. Remove both stabilizer bar link bolts and nuts.
    b. Position stabilizer bar to access shock absorber lower bolt.
6. **On all models,** remove lower bolt and nut, then remove shock absorber.
7. Reverse procedure to install using new mounting nuts and bolts.

COIL SPRING
REPLACE
2004
EXCEPT COBRA
1. Raise rear of vehicle and support at rear body crossmember.
2. Remove stabilizer bar.
3. Lower axle housing until shock absorbers are fully extended. Support axle housing with suitable jack.
4. Support control arm with suitable jack under lower control arm rear pivot bolt. Remove pivot bolt.
5. Lower control arm until spring tension is relieved, then remove coil spring and insulator, **Fig. 11.**
6. Reverse procedure to install. Tighten lower control arm pivot bolt with suspension at curb height.

COBRA
1. Raise and support vehicle.
2. Support No. 1 crossmember with suitable jack stand.
3. Remove rear tire and wheel assemblies.
4. Remove both mufflers.
5. Mark rear driveshaft yoke and drive

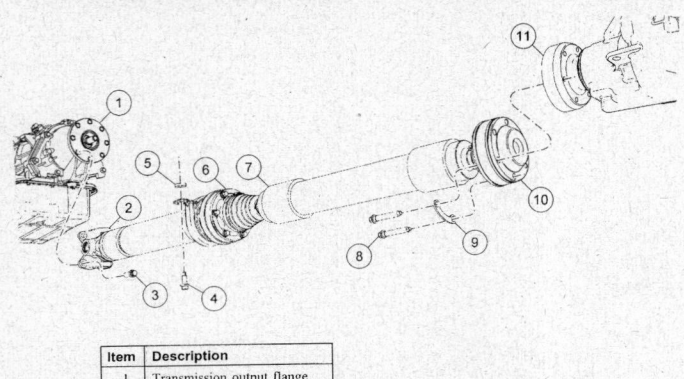

Item	Description
1	Transmission output flange
2	Driveshaft flange
3	Driveshaft flange bolt
4	Center bearing bolt
5	Spacer
6	Center bearing
7	Driveshaft assembly
8	Constant velocity (CV) joint bolts (6 required)
9	CV joint washer (3 required)
10	CV joint
11	Pinion flange

ARM0400000000599

Fig. 9 Drive shaft replacement. 2005–08 w/4.6L & 5.4L engines

Item	Description		Item	Description
1	Upper nut, washer and insulator		3	Shock flag nut
2	Shock lower bolt		4	Shock

ARM0400000000600

Fig. 10 Shock absorber replacement. 2005–08

40 Nm (30 lb-ft) — 1

115 Nm (85 lb-ft) — 2

pinion flange relationship for installation alignment.

6. Disconnect rear U-joint from companion flange, **Fig. 6.**
7. Wrap tape around loose bearing caps to prevent them from falling off spider.
8. Pull driveshaft toward rear of vehicle until slip yoke clears transmission extension housing and seal.
9. Install suitable plug into extension housing to prevent lubricant leakage.
10. Disconnect parking brake cables and conduits at parking brake levers, rear brake calipers and rear knuckles.
11. Remove parking brake cable brackets at coil spring seats.
12. Remove rear brake line to axle mounting bolts and position lines aside.
13. Remove mounting bolts and rear wheel speed sensors.
14. Disconnect ABS sensor wiring harness at subframe.
15. Support lower control arms and bushings with suitable jack stands.
16. Discard shock absorber lower mounting nuts and bolts.
17. Lower control arms and bushings, then remove jack stands.
18. Support rear subframe using powertrain lift tool No. 014-00765, or equivalent.
19. Remove and discard subframe front mounting nuts.
20. Remove and discard subframe rear mounting nuts and bolts.
21. Lower subframe and allow it to pivot on its front bolts.
22. Remove springs and insulators.
23. Reverse procedure to install, noting the following:
    a. Install new lower insulator and washer onto shock absorber.
    b. **Ensure hardened washer sits between lower control arm and bushing and absorber.**
    c. Adjust wheel alignment.

2005–08

1. Mark rear shock absorber relative to protective sleeve with the vehicle in a static, level ground position for installation alignment.
2. Raise and support vehicle.
3. Support rear axle with suitable hi-lift jack .
4. **One models equipped with rear stabilizer bar,** proceed as follows:
    a. Remove both stabilizer bar link mounting bolts and nuts.
    b. Position stabilizer bar to gain access to shock absorber lower bolt.
5. **On all models,** remove shock absorber lower mounting bolt and nut.
6. Lower rear axle and remove spring, **Fig. 12.**
7. Reverse procedure to install, noting the following:
    a. Use new mounting nuts and bolts
    b. When installing new spring, ensure tag is toward axle.

CONTROL ARM

REPLACE

2004

EXCEPT COBRA

LOWER

1. Raise and support vehicle, then support body at rear crossmember.
2. Lower hoist until rear shock absorbers are fully extended and place suitable transmission jack under lower arm to axle pivot bolt.
3. Remove and discard lower control arm front pivot bolt and nut, **Fig. 11.**
4. Remove control arm.
5. Reverse procedure to install.

UPPER

Removal

1. Raise rear of vehicle and support at rear body crossmember.
2. Remove rear and front pivot bolts, then the upper control arm.

Installation

1. Position upper control arm into side rail bracket and install front pivot bolt. **Do not tighten bolt now.**
2. Raise rear axle until upper control arm rear pivot bolt hole is aligned with hole in axle housing and install rear pivot bolt. **Do not tighten bolt now.**
3. Position suspension at curb height and tighten front pivot bolt.

COBRA

UPPER

1. Park vehicle at curb height and on level ground.
2. Mark rear shock absorber positions relative to upper sleeves.
3. Raise and support vehicle, then remove rear wheel and tire assemblies.
4. Remove rear brake rotor.
5. Remove coil springs as outlined under "Coil Spring, Replace."
6. Raise subframe into position, then remove and discard front bolts.
7. Mark upper control arm and bushing cam bolt position for installation alignment.
8. Remove and discard upper control arm bushing nut and bolt.
9. Disconnect knuckle from upper control arm.
10. Remove and discard upper control arm nut and bolt.
11. Remove upper control arm.
12. Reverse procedure to install, noting the following:
    a. Install new cam bolts and nuts at control arms and bushings. **Do not**

tighten until vehicle is on ground and shock absorber marks are aligned.

b. Adjust wheel alignment.

LOWER

1. Park vehicle at curb height and on level ground.
2. Mark rear shock absorber positions relative to upper sleeves.
3. Mark transverse bar fastener for installation alignment.
4. Remove coil springs as outlined under "Coil Spring, Replace."
5. Disconnect lower control arm from knuckle. Discard nut and bolt.
6. Disconnect lower control arm from subframe. Discard nuts and bolts.
7. Reverse procedure to install, noting the following:
   a. Install lower control arm with new fasteners. **Do not tighten until vehicle is on ground and shock absorber marks are aligned.**
   b. Ensure transverse bar is in place and bolt passes through it. **Do not tighten until vehicle is on ground and shock absorber marks are aligned.**
   c. Adjust wheel alignment.

2005-08
LOWER

1. Raise and support vehicle, then remove tire and wheel assembly.
2. Remove clip and disconnect parking brake cable from rear caliper.
3. Remove parking brake cable bracket.
4. Support rear axle with suitable jack stand. **Do not support rear axle at differential housing.**
5. Remove lower arm front mounting bolt and nut, **Fig. 12.**
6. Remove lower arm rear mounting bolt and flag nut.
7. Remove lower arm.
8. Reverse procedure to install, noting the following:
   a. Install new mounting nuts and bolts.
   b. Tighten lower arm mounting bolts while suspension is at curb height.

UPPER

1. Remove rear seat cushion.
2. Remove upper control arm front mounting bolt, **Fig. 12.**
3. Mark rear shock absorber relative to protective sleeve with vehicle in static, level ground position (curb height) for installation alignment,
4. Raise and support vehicle.
5. Place suitable safety support under fuel tank.
6. Remove two rear bolts and position both fuel tank support straps aside.
7. Partially lower fuel tank to access to upper control arm.
8. Remove two upper control arm rear mounting bolts, then the arm bushing flag bolt and nut.
9. Remove upper control arm.
10. Reverse procedure to install using new mounting nuts and bolts.

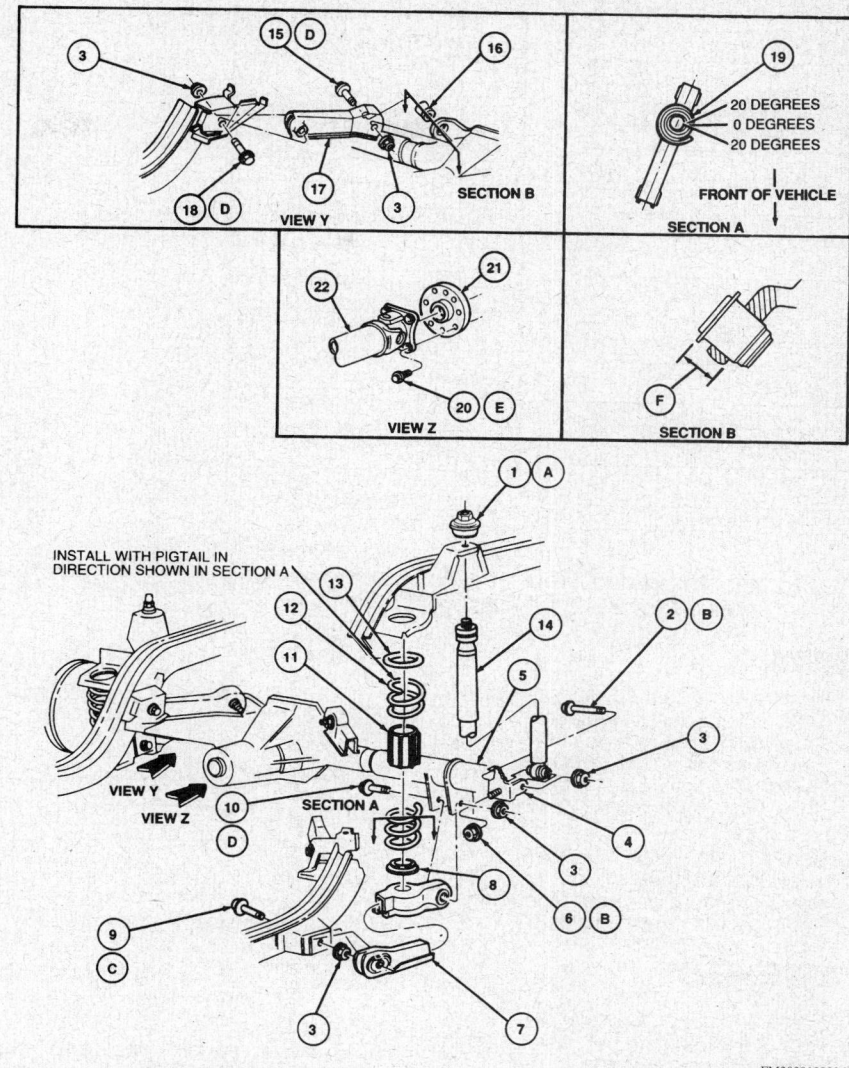

INSTALL WITH PIGTAIL IN DIRECTION SHOWN IN SECTION A

20 DEGREES
0 DEGREES
20 DEGREES
FRONT OF VEHICLE
SECTION A

SECTION B

VIEW Y

VIEW Z

VIEW Y
VIEW Z
SECTION A

FM2039100026010X

Fig. 11 Exploded view of rear suspension (Part 1 of 2). 2004 Except Cobra

CONTROL ARM BUSHING
REPLACE
2004
EXCEPT COBRA

1. Remove control arm as outlined under "Control Arm, Replace."
2. Remove bushing using bushing remover and installer set tool No. T78P-5638-A, or equivalent, **Fig. 13.**
3. Reverse procedure to install using suitable installer tool, **Fig. 14.**

COBRA

1. Remove upper control arm as outlined under "Control Arm, Replace."
2. Remove bushing using bushing remover and installer set tool No. T79P-5638-A, or equivalent.
3. Reverse procedure to install. Ensure bushing is properly installed, **Fig. 15.**

2005-08

1. Remove upper control arm as outlined under "Control Arm, Replace."
2. Remove upper arm bushing using C-frame and screw installer/remover tool T74P-4635-C, or equivalent.
3. Reverse proceed to install.

STABILIZER BAR
REPLACE
2004
EXCEPT COBRA

1. Raise and support rear of vehicle.
2. Remove four bolts attaching stabilizer bar to brackets on lower control arms.
3. Remove stabilizer bar.
4. Reverse procedure to install.

Item	Description
1	Nut, Insulator Assy (Part of 18198)
2	Bolt (2 Req'd)
3	Nut (2 Req'd)
4	Rear Shock Absorber Lower Mounting Bracket (2 Req'd)
5	Axle
6	Nut (2 Req'd)
7	Rear Suspension Lower Arm (2 Req'd)
8	Rear Spring Insulator (2 Req'd)
9	Bolt (2 Req'd)
10	Bolt
11	Rear Spring Damper (2 Req'd)
12	Rear Spring (2 Req'd)
13	Rear Spring Insulator (2 Req'd)
14	Rear Shock Absorber (2 Req'd)
15	Bolt (2 Req'd)

Item	Description
16	Rear Suspension Arm Bushing (2 Req'd)
17	Rear Suspension Arm and Bushing (2 Req'd)
18	Bolt (2 Req'd)
19	Pigtail
20	Bolt (4 Req'd)
21	Rear Axle Universal Joint Flange
22	Driveshaft
A	Tighten to 34-46 N·m (25-34 Lb-Ft)
B	Tighten to 76-103 N·m (57-75 Lb-Ft)
C	Tighten to 98-132 N·m (71-79 Lb-Ft)
D	Tighten to 98-132 N·m (71-79 Lb-Ft)
E	Tighten to 56-77 N·m (41-56 Lb-Ft)
F	Install to 35.5-36.5 mm (1.39-1.43 In)

FM2039100026020X

Fig. 11 Exploded view of rear suspension (Part 2 of 2). 2004 Except Cobra

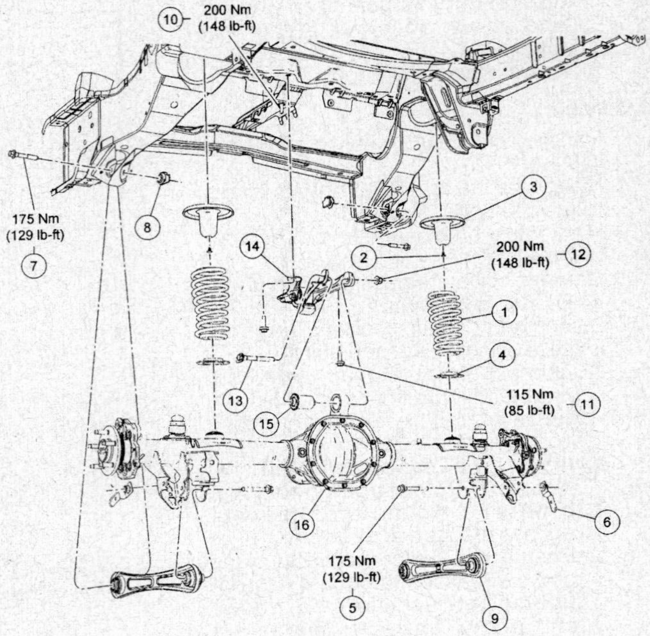

COBRA

1. Remove rear coil springs as outlined under "Coil Spring, Replace."
2. Raise subframe into position, then remove and discard its front bolts.
3. Lower subframe.
4. Remove stabilizer link and nuts. Discard nuts.
5. Remove stabilizer bar brackets and bolts. Discard bolts.
6. Remove stabilizer bar and bushings.
7. Reverse procedure to install.

2005-08

1. Raise and support vehicle.
2. Remove stabilizer bar link mounting bolts and nuts, **Fig. 16**.
3. Remove stabilizer bar bracket mounting nuts and studs.
4. Remove stabilizer bar and brackets.
5. Reverse procedure to install, noting the following:
   a. When installing new stabilizer bar, ensure tag is on lefthand side of vehicle.
   b. Stabilizer bar for convertible will have a B suffix in part number and it will have green-colored tag
   c. Stabilizer bar for coupe will have an A suffix in part number and it will have yellow-colored tag.
   d. Install new mounting nuts and bolts.

LATERAL ROD

REPLACE

1. Raise and support vehicle.
2. Support rear axle with suitable jack stand. **Do not support rear axle at differential housing.**
3. Loosen panard rod-to-body mount nut, then remove lateral stiffener bar-to-body mount nut and flag bolt, **Fig. 17**.
4. Remove laterals stiffener bar-to-body bolts.
5. Remove panard rod arm support bracket.
6. Reverse procedure to install, noting the following:
   a. Tighten panard rod fasteners while suspension is at curb height.
   b. Install new mounting nuts and bolts.

Item	Description
1	Spring (2 required)
2	Pin-type fastener (2 required)
3	Upper insulator (2 required)
4	Lower insulator (2 required)
5	Lower control arm rear bolt (2 required)
6	Lower control arm rear nut (2 required)
7	Lower control arm front bolt (2 required)

Item	Description
8	Lower control arm front nut (2 required)
9	Lower control arm (2 required)
10	Upper control arm front bolt
11	Upper control arm rear bolt (2 required)
12	Upper control arm rear nut
13	Upper control arm flag bolt
14	Upper control arm
15	Upper control arm bushing
16	Rear axle assembly

ARM0400000000601

Fig. 12 Coil spring and control arm replacement. 2005-08

TECHNICAL SERVICE BULLETINS

Axle Whine

2005 MUSTANG

Models built before 11/16/2004 may exhibit an axle whine noise.

This condition may be caused by faulty dampers on the axle assembly.

To correct this condition, install axle damper kit part No. 5R3Z-3C246-A.

Limited Slip Axle Chatter, Shudder, Binding Sensation, Or Vibration During Low Speed Turning Maneuvers

2004-05 MUSTANG

On some of these models equipped with 8.8 inch limited slip rear axle, may exhibit a chatter, shudder, a binding sensation, or a vibration during low speed turns.

This condition may be caused by a faulty limited slip clutch pack.

To correct this condition, install clutch pack service kit Part No. 3L1Z-4947-BC.

Axle fluid requirements have been changed. All vehicles being repaired by this TSB must have rear axle lube Part No. XY-75W140-QL installed. Additionally, remove the multi-colored label which is located on the righthand side axle tube, or block out any/all "FEHP" OR "75W90" references on the label.

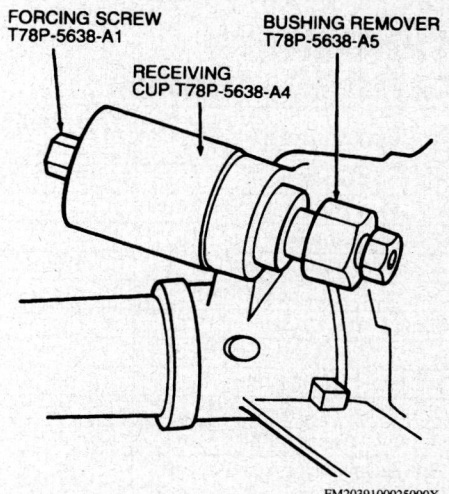

FORCING SCREW
T78P-5638-A1

RECEIVING
CUP T78P-5638-A4

BUSHING REMOVER
T78P-5638-A5

FM2039100025000X

Fig. 13 Upper control arm axle bracket bushing removal. Except Cobra

BUSHING REPLACER
T78P-5638-A3

REPLACER RECEIVING
CUP T78P-5638-A2

FORCING SCREW
T78P-5638-A1

FM2039100024000X

Fig. 14 Upper control arm axle bracket bushing installation. Except Cobra

36 mm (1.417 in)

FM2039900078000X

Fig. 15 Upper control arm bushing installation. Cobra

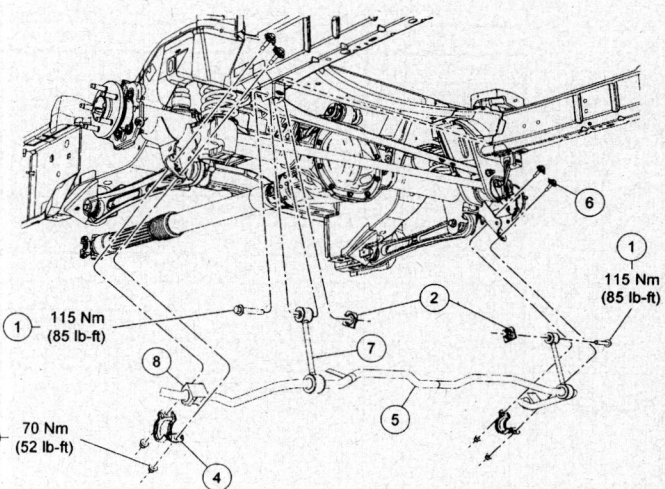

115 Nm (85 lb-ft)

115 Nm (85 lb-ft)

70 Nm (52 lb-ft)

Item	Description
1	Link bolt (2 required)
2	Clip nut (2 required)
3	Bracket nut (4 required)
4	Stabilizer bar bracket (2 required)
5	Stabilizer bar

Item	Description
6	Clip studs (4 required)
7	Stabilizer bar link (2 required)
8	Stabilizer bar bushing (2 required)

ARM0400000000602

Fig. 16 Stabilizer bar replacement. 2005–08

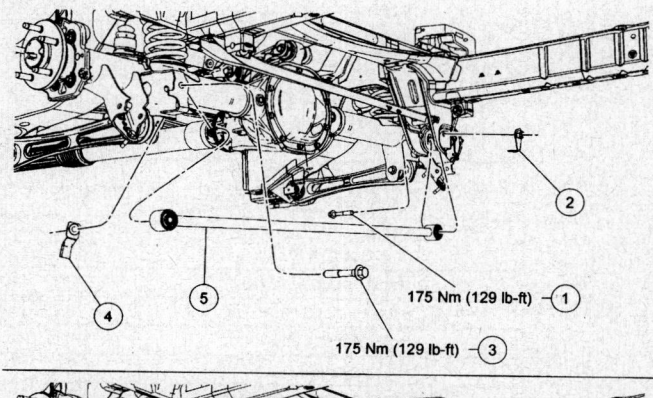

175 Nm (129 lb-ft)

175 Nm (129 lb-ft)

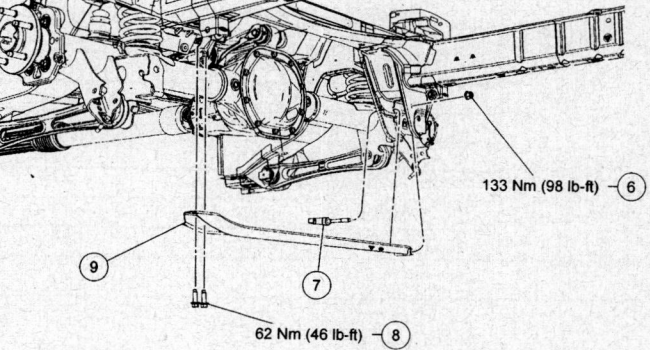

133 Nm (98 lb-ft)

62 Nm (46 lb-ft)

Item	Description
1	Panard rod bolt (RH)
2	Panard rod flag nut (RH)
3	Panard rod bolt (LH)
4	Panard rod flag nut (LH)
5	Panard rod

Item	Description
6	Lateral stiffener bar nut
7	Lateral stiffener bar flag bolt
8	Lateral stiffener bar-to-body bolts (2 required)
9	Lateral stiffener bar

ARM0400000000603

Fig. 17 Panard rod replacement. 2005–08

MUSTANG

TIGHTENING SPECIFICATIONS

Year	Component	Torque/Ft. Lbs.
2004	ABS Sensor	17
	Axle Damper	66
	Axle Damper Bracket	59
	Axle Shaft To Hub	240
	Bracket To Differential Housing	35
	Brake Fluid Line To Caliper	30
	Brake Rotor Dust Shield	89①
	Differential Insulator, Front	52
	Differential Insulator, Rear	76
	Differential Pinion Shaft Lockpin	15–30
	Driveshaft To Companion Flange	83
	Lower Control Arm	111
	Lower Control Arm & Bushing To Subframe (Cobra)	184
	Lower Control Arm & Bushing To Knuckle (Cobra)	85
	Lubricant Filler Plug	25
	Parking Brake Cable Bracket (Cobra)	11
	Parking Brake Cable Bracket (Except Cobra)	41
	Pinion Bumper	10
	Pinion Nose Crossmember	184
	Shock Absorber, Lower (Cobra)	98
	Shock Absorber, Lower (Except Cobra)	59
	Shock Absorber, Upper	30
	Shock Absorber Clevis Bracket	80
	Stabilizer Bar	41
	Stabilizer Bar Link	35
	Subframe Rear Bracket	59
	Subframe To Body	76
	Subframe To Rear Bracket	76
	Toe Link	35
	Upper Control Arm (Cobra)	66
	Upper Control Arm To Axle	82
	Upper Control Arm To Frame	72
	Wheel Hub Retainer	251
	Wheel Lug Nuts	95

TIGHTENING SPECIFICATIONS—Continued

Year	Component	Torque/Ft. Lbs.
2005–08	Anti-Lock Sensor	62①
	Center Bearing	35
	Control Arm Bushing	148
	Control Arm, Lower	129
	Control Arm, Upper (Front)	148
	Control Arm, Upper (Rear)	85
	CV Joint	41
	Differential Filler Plug	22
	Differential Housing Cover	33
	Differential Pinion Shaft Lock	22
	Disc Brake Caliper Anchor Plate To Knuckle	76
	Disc Brake Caliper To Anchor Plate	24
	Driveshaft Flange	76
	Exhaust Pipe	35
	Front Support Brace	46
	Laterals Stiffener Bar-To-Body	46
	Lateral Stiffener Bar-To-Body Mount	98
	Panard Rod-To-Body Mount	129
	Parking Brake Cable Bracket	26
	Shock Absorber, Lower	85
	Shock Absorber, Upper	30
	Stabilizer Bar Bracket	52
	Stabilizer Bar Link	85
	Rear Support Brace (Convertible)	46
	Trackbar	129
	Trailing Arm	129
	Upper Suspension Arm	129

① — Inch lbs.

Front Suspension & Steering

NOTE: On Air Bag Equipped Models, Refer To "Air Bag System Precautions" Located In The Front Of This Manual For System Disarming & Arming Procedures.

NOTE: Refer To "Computer Relearn Procedures" Located In The Front Of This Manual When Battery Power To The Computer Has Been Interrupted.

INDEX

	Page No.
Ball Joint, Replace	4-94
Ball Joint Inspection	4-94
Coil Spring, Replace	4-94
2004	4-94
2005–08	4-94
Control Arm, Replace	4-95
2004	4-95
2005–08	4-95
Description	4-93
Front Wheel Spindle, Replace	4-93
2004	4-93
2005–08	4-93
Hub & Bearing, Replace	4-93
2004	4-93
2005–08	4-93
Power Steering	13-1

	Page No.
Power Steering Gear, Replace	4-96
2004	4-96
2005–08	4-96
Power Steering Pump, Replace	4-96
2004	4-96
Type CII	4-96
Type CIII	4-96
2005–08	4-97
4.0L Engine	4-97
4.6L Engine	4-97
5.4L Engine	4-97
Precautions	4-93
Strut	4-93
Stabilizer Bar, Replace	4-95
2004	4-95
2005–07	4-95

	Page No.
Stabilizer Bar Bushing, Replace	4-95
2004	4-95
2005–08	4-95
Steering Columns	12-1
Strut, Replace	4-94
2004	4-94
2005–08	4-95
Technical Service Bulletins	4-97
Front Suspension Popping Noise While Turning Right Or Left	4-97
2005 Mustang	4-97
Tightening Specifications	4-98
Wheel Bearing, Adjust	4-93

PRECAUTIONS

Strut

These vehicles are equipped with gas pressurized strut which will extend unassisted. Do not apply heat or flame to shock absorber.

DESCRIPTION

The front suspension is of a modified McPherson strut design using shock struts and coil springs, **Fig. 1**. The springs are mounted between the lower control arm and a crossmember spring pocket.

WHEEL BEARING

ADJUST

Wheel bearings are not adjustable.

HUB & BEARING

REPLACE

2004

1. Raise and support vehicle, then remove wheel and tire assembly.
2. Remove and discard front hub cap grease seal.
3. Remove two mounting bolts and front disc brake caliper. **Do not let front disc brake caliper hang by front brake hose. Suspend it with suitable wire or rope.**
4. Remove front disc brake rotor. Discard factory push-on nuts.
5. Remove and discard front axle wheel hub retainer.
6. Remove wheel hub and bearing. If assembly cannot be removed by hand, use front hub remover/replacer tool No. T81P-1104-C, or equivalent.
7. Reverse procedure to install. Install new wheel hub retainer and hub cap grease seal.

2005–08

1. Raise and support vehicle, then remove wheel and tire assembly.
2. Remove two mounting bolts, then position and support brake caliper and anchor plate aside, **Fig. 2. Never allow brake caliper and anchor plate to hang from brake flexible hose.**
3. Remove brake disc.
4. Remove front hub cap grease seal.
5. Remove wheel hub retainer.
6. Remove front wheel hub and bearing.
7. Reverse procedure to install using new front hubcap grease seal and wheel hub retainer.

FRONT WHEEL SPINDLE

REPLACE

2004

1. Raise and support vehicle, then remove front wheel and tire assembly.
2. Remove front brake anti-lock sensor from spindle.
3. Remove disc brake caliper, rotor and dust shield.
4. Remove wheel hub and front stabilizer bar from lower arm.
5. Remove tie rod end from wheel spindle using tie rod end remover tool No. 3290-D, or equivalent. **Do not remove nut from ball joint stud now.**
6. Loosen ball joint nut one or two turns and tap spindle boss sharply to relieve stud pressure.
7. Compress front coil spring using suitable floor jack under front suspension lower arm as outlined under "Coil Spring, Replace."
8. Remove stud nut and front anti-lock sensor bracket.
9. Remove two mounting bolts and front wheel spindle.
10. Reverse procedures to install.

2005–08

1. Raise and support vehicle, then remove wheel and tire assembly.
2. Remove two mounting bolts, then position and support brake caliper and anchor plate aside, **Fig. 3. Never allow brake caliper and anchor plate to hang from brake flexible hose.**
3. Remove brake disc.
4. Remove front hub cap grease seal.
5. Remove wheel hub retainer.
6. Remove front wheel hub and bearing.
7. Remove three mounting bolts and brake disc dust shield.
8. Remove mounting bolt and ABS sensor.
9. Remove brake line bracket bolt and

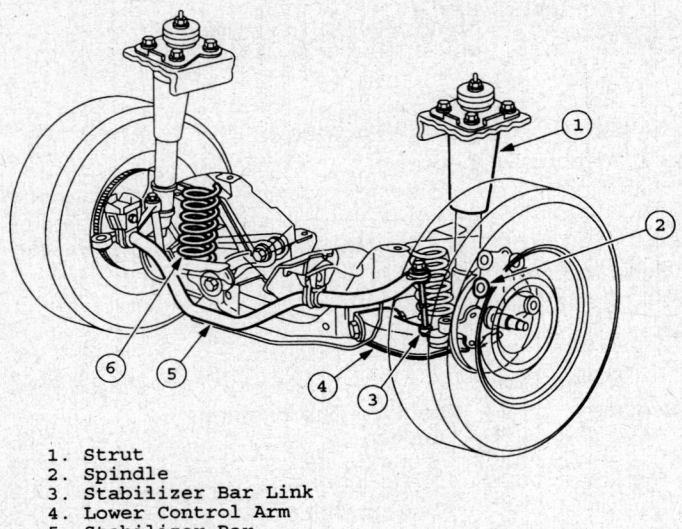

1. Strut
2. Spindle
3. Stabilizer Bar Link
4. Lower Control Arm
5. Stabilizer Bar
6. Spring

FM2029700167000X

Fig. 1 Exploded view of front suspension

133 Nm (98 lb-ft) — ①

20 Nm (15 lb-ft) — ⑥

300 Nm (221 lb-ft) — ⑤

Item	Description
1	Brake caliper bracket bolt (2 required)
2	Brake caliper assembly
3	Brake disc
4	Wheel hub grease cap

Item	Description
5	Wheel hub retainer nut
6	Dust shield bolt (3 required)
7	Dust shield
8	Wheel hub assembly (ABS/non-ABS)

ARM0400000000604

Fig. 2 Front wheel bearing replacement. 2005–08

disconnect ABS sensor wire from bracket.
10. Remove outer tie rod end nut.
11. Disconnect tie rod end from front wheel spindle using tie-rod end remover tool No. Tool-3290-D, or equivalent. **do not damage tie rod end dust boot.**
12. Support front suspension lower arm with suitable jack stand.
13. Remove pinch bolt and nut.
14. Separate lower control arm and wheel spindle. **Do not damage lower ball joint boot.**
15. Mark two strut-to-spindle bolts for installation alignment, then remove mounting bolts and nuts.
16. Remove wheel spindle.
17. Reverse procedure to install, noting the following:
    a. Install new outer tie rod end nut.
    b. Install new front hubcap grease seal and wheel hub retainer.

BALL JOINT INSPECTION

1. Raise and support front of vehicle.
2. Ensure front wheel hub and bearing are in good condition.
3. Place suitable jack stands under lower control arms.
4. Position suitable dial indicator between spindle and ball joint.
5. Grasp tire at top and bottom, then slowly move inward and outward.
6. Replace lower control arm if movement more than .031 inch.

BALL JOINT
REPLACE

On these models the ball joint and lower control arm must be replaced as an assembly.

COIL SPRING
REPLACE
2004

1. Park vehicle at curb height and on level ground.
2. Mark front strut positions to upper sleeves for installation alignment.
3. Raise and support vehicle.
4. Allowing front suspension lower arms to hang free, then remove wheel and tire assembly.
5. Remove brake caliper and support aside using suitable wire or rope.
6. Disconnect front wheel spindle connecting rod or end from front wheel spindle using tie rod end remover tool No. 3290-D, or equivalent.
7. Disconnect stabilizer bar link from lower control arm.
8. Remove mounting bolts and position steering gear so suspension arm bolt may be removed.
9. Compress coil spring using coil spring compressor tool No. D78P-5310-A, or equivalent.
10. Remove suspension arm-to-crossmember nuts and bolts.
11. Remove compression rod and coil spring.
12. Reverse procedure to install. Ensure lower spring end is positioned between two holes in lower control arm spring pocket.

2005–08

1. Raise and support vehicle, then remove wheel and tire assembly.
2. Remove mounting bolt and ABS sensor, **Fig. 4.**
3. Remove brake line bracket bolt and disconnect ABS sensor wire from bracket.
4. Remove stabilizer bar link upper nut,

Use hex-holding feature to prevent studs from turning while removing or installing stabilizer bar link nuts.
5. Disconnect link from strut.
6. Support lower control arm using suitable jack stand.
7. Mark two strut bolts for installation alignment, then remove strut bolts and nuts.
8. Lower front suspension lower arm and remove four strut-to-body nuts.
9. Remove strut and spring.
10. Compress spring until tension is released from strut using suitable spring compressor.
11. Holding strut rod and remove strut upper nut.
12. Remove strut, dust boot, jounce bumper, washer and upper bearing.
13. Release tension and remove spring.
14. Reverse procedure to install, noting the following:
    a. Align notch on upper bearing with clevis at bottom of strut.
    b. Install new strut upper nut.
    c. Notch and arrow etched into upper bearing must face outboard side of vehicle.
    d. Install new stabilizer bar link upper nut.

STRUT
REPLACE
2004

1. Place ignition in unlocked position.
2. Raise and support vehicle.
3. Remove front wheel and tire assembly.
4. Remove disc brake caliper and position aside with suitable wire or rope.
5. Remove mounting bolt and ABS wheel speed sensor.
6. Disconnect ABS sensor wiring harness at bracket.
7. Support lower control arm with suitable jack stand.

8. Remove two strut to front wheel spindle mounting nuts.
9. Lower control arm and remove jack stand.
10. Lower vehicle.
11. Remove strut upper mounting nuts and bolts. Discard nuts.
12. Remove strut.
13. Reverse procedures to install.

2005–08

1. Raise and support vehicle, then remove wheel and tire assembly.
2. Remove mounting bolt and ABS sensor, **Fig. 4.**
3. Remove brake line bracket bolt and disconnect ABS sensor wire from bracket.
4. Remove stabilizer bar link upper nut, Use hex-holding feature to prevent studs from turning while removing or installing stabilizer bar link nuts.
5. Disconnect link from strut.
6. Support lower control arm using suitable jack stand.
7. Mark two strut bolts for installation alignment, then remove strut bolts and nuts.
8. Lower front suspension lower arm and remove four strut-to-body nuts.
9. Remove strut and spring.
10. Reverse procedure to install, noting the following:
    a. Notch and arrow etched into upper bearing must face outboard side of vehicle.
    b. Install new stabilizer bar link upper nut.

CONTROL ARM
REPLACE
2004

1. Park vehicle at curb height and on level ground.
2. Mark front strut positions to upper sleeves for installation alignment.
3. Raise and support vehicle. Allowing front suspension lower arms to hang free.
4. Remove wheel and tire assembly.
5. Remove front disc brake caliper and position it aside with suitable wire or rope.
6. Remove front disc brake rotor and front disc brake rotor shield as outlined in "Disc Brakes" chapter.
7. Disconnect front wheel spindle connecting rod or end from front wheel spindle using tie rod end remover tool No. 3290-D, or equivalent.
8. Remove mounting bolts and steering gear so front suspension lower arm bolt is accessible.
9. Disconnect front stabilizer link from front suspension lower arm.
10. Loosen ball joint nut one or two turns and tap spindle boss sharply to relieve stud pressure. **Do not remove ball joint nut now.**
11. Compress spring using spring compressor tool No. D78P-5310-A, or equivalent.

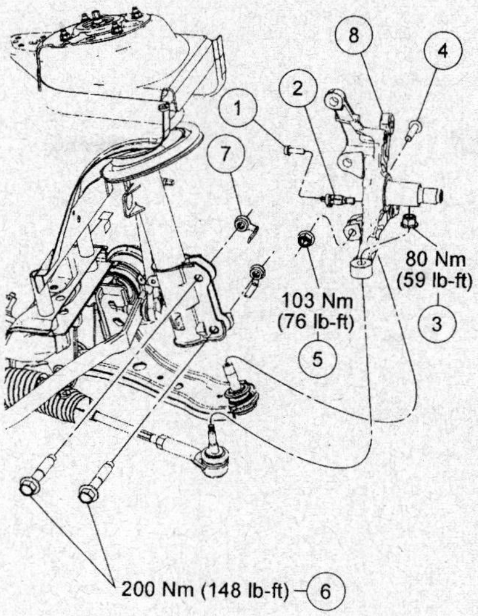

80 Nm (59 lb-ft)

103 Nm (76 lb-ft)

200 Nm (148 lb-ft) — 6

Item	Description
1	Wheel speed sensor bolt
2	Wheel speed sensor
3	Outer tie rod end nut
4	Wheel spindle pinch bolt
5	Wheel spindle pinch nut
6	Strut-to-wheel spindle bolt (2 required)
7	Strut-to-wheel spindle flag nut (2 required)
8	Wheel spindle (RH/LH)

ARM0400000000605

Fig. 3   Front wheel spindle replacement. 2005–08

12. Remove and discard ball joint stud nut.
13. Remove front shock absorber and spindle. Wire aside to obtain working room.
14. Remove and discard front suspension lower arm to crossmember nuts and bolts.
15. Remove front suspension lower arm and coil spring.
16. Reverse procedure to install, noting the following:
    a. Ensure spring end is positioned between two holes in front suspension lower arm pocket.
    b. Adjust wheel alignment.

2005–08

1. Raise and support vehicle, then remove wheel and tire assembly.
2. Remove pinch bolt and nut.
3. Separate lower control arm and wheel spindle.
4. Remove mounting bolts and position steering gear to access to lower control arm forward bolt.
5. Remove lower control arm forward bolt and nut, **Fig. 5. Do not damage steering gear boot while removing or installing lower control arm forward bolt.**
6. Remove lower control arm rearward nuts and flag bolts.

7. Remove lower control arm and bracket.
8. Remove three mounting and heat shield.
9. Reverse procedure to install, noting the following:
    a. Install new mounting bolts and nuts.
    b. To ease installation, position of lower control arm nut and flag bolt can be reversed to allow installation of nut from underneath vehicle.

STABILIZER BAR
REPLACE
2004

1. Raise and support vehicle.
2. Disconnect stabilizer bar from each link.
3. Remove insulator clamps, insulators and stabilizer bar.
4. Reverse procedure to install.

2005–07

1. Raise and support vehicle.
2. Remove both stabilizer bar link lower nuts, **Fig. 4. Use hex-holding feature to prevent studs from turning while removing or installing stabilizer bar link nuts. Boot seal must not be allowed to twist at all while tightening nut.**
3. Disconnect both links from stabilizer bar.
4. Remove four stabilizer bracket nuts.
5. Remove stabilizer bar and brackets.
6. Reverse procedure to install.

STABILIZER BAR BUSHING
REPLACE
2004

1. Raise and support vehicle.
2. Disconnect stabilizer bar from each link.
3. Remove insulator clamps, insulators and stabilizer bar.
4. Reverse procedure to install.

2005–08

1. Raise and support vehicle.
2. Disconnect stabilizer bar from each link.
3. Remove insulator clamps, insulators and stabilizer bar.
4. Coat front stabilizer bar and inside diameter of stabilizer bar bushing with suitable silicone spray lubricant.
5. Remove stabilizer bar bushing by sliding if off stabilizer bar.
6. Reverse procedure to install.

POWER STEERING GEAR
REPLACE

2004

1. Place front wheels in straight-ahead position. **Do not lock steering column.**
2. Raise and support vehicle, then remove front wheel and tire assemblies.
3. Remove tie rod end to spindle nut. Discard cotter pin.
4. Separate tie rod end from spindle using tie rod end separator tool No. 3290-D, or equivalent.
5. Remove and discard steering column intermediate shaft pinch bolt.
6. Lower vehicle.
7. Place front wheels in straight-ahead position and lock steering column. **Do not rotate steering wheel when lower column shaft is disconnected.**
8. Disconnect intermediate shaft coupling.
9. Remove steering gear mounting nuts, washers and bolts. Position gear forward.
10. Position drain pan to catch power steering lines' fluid.
11. Disconnect power steering hoses, remove and discard O-rings. Plug open ports.
12. Remove steering gear.
13. Reverse procedure to install, noting the following:
    a. Install new O-rings using seal replacement tool set No. D90P-3517-A, or equivalent.
    b. Install new shaft coupling pinch bolt.

2005–08

1. **On models equipped with 5.4L engine**, install engine lifting tool Nos. 303-D087 and 303-F070, or suiatble equivalent.
2. **On models equipped with 5.4L engine**, remove lefthand engine mount nut.
3. **On models equipped with 5.4L engine**, raise lefthand side of engine.
4. **On all models**, place steering wheel in straight-ahead position and turn ignition switch to OFF position.
5. Raise and support vehicle.
6. Remove two nuts and disconnect tie-rod ends from wheel knuckles, **Fig. 6. Use hex holding feature to prevent the tie-rod end stud from turning.**
7. Remove steering column coupling-to-steering gear bolt and disconnect coupling from steering gear.
8. Remove power steering line clamp plate bolt, then disconnect power steering pressure and return lines. Allow fluid to drain into suitable container.
9. Remove two pressure line bracket-to-crossmember bolts and position pressure line aside.

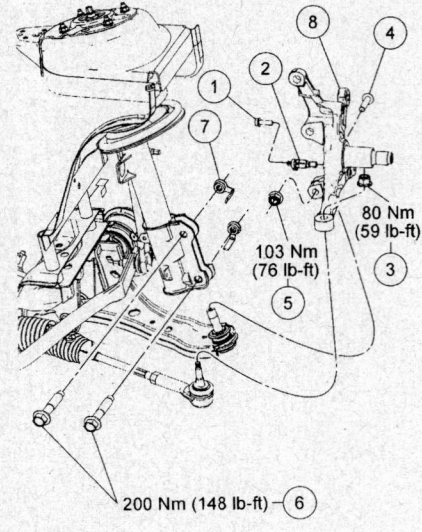

Item	Description
1	Wheel speed sensor bolt
2	Wheel speed sensor
3	Outer tie rod end nut
4	Wheel spindle pinch bolt
5	Wheel spindle pinch nut
6	Strut-to-wheel spindle bolt (2 required)
7	Strut-to-wheel spindle flag nut (2 required)
8	Wheel spindle (RH/LH)

ARM0400000000606

Fig. 4 Strut & coil spring replacement. 2005–08

10. Remove two mounting bolts and steering gear.
11. Reverse procedure to install. Install new O-ring seals.

POWER STEERING PUMP
REPLACE

2004

TYPE CII

1. Remove serpentine drive belt.
2. Position drain pan to catch power steering lines' fluid.
3. Disconnect power steering hose, remove and discard O-ring. Plug open ports.
4. Remove pump pulley using removal tool No. T69L-10300-B, or equivalent.
5. Remove mounting bolts and power steering pump.
6. Reverse procedure to install, noting the following:
    a. Install pump pulley using installer tool No. T65P-3A733-C, or equivalent.
    b. Install new O-ring using seal replacement tool set No. D90P-3517-A, or equivalent.

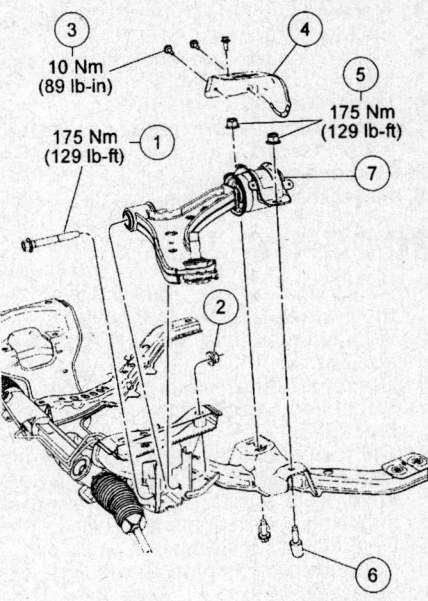

Item	Description
1	Lower control arm forward bolt
2	Lower control arm forward nut
3	Heat shield bolt (3 required)
4	Heat shield
5	Lower control arm rearward nut (2 required)
6	Lower control arm rearward flag bolt (2 required)
7	Lower control arm (LH/RH)

ARM0400000000607

Fig. 5 Lower control arm replacement. 2005–08

TYPE CIII

1. Remove serpentine drive belt.
2. Raise and support vehicle.
3. Remove pump pulley using removal tool No. T69L-10300-B, or equivalent.
4. Remove mounting bolt and bracket.
5. Position drain pan to catch power steering lines' fluid.
6. Disconnect power steering hoses, remove and discard O-rings. Plug open ports.
7. Remove mounting bolts and power steering pump.
8. Reverse procedure to install, noting the following:
    a. Inspect pump pulley for paint marks in hub web area. **If two paint marks are visible, discard pulley and install new one.**
    b. If there is only one or no mark, mark web area and pulley.
    c. Install pump pulley using installer tool No. T91P-3A733-A, or equivalent.
    d. Install new O-ring using seal replacement tool set No. D90P-3517-A, or equivalent.

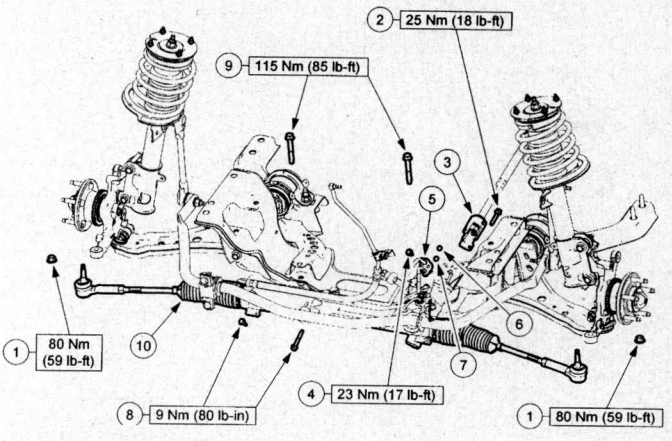

Fig. 6   Steering gear replacement. 2005–08

Item	Description
1	Tie-rod end nuts (2 required)
2	Steering column coupling-to-steering gear bolt
3	Steering column coupling
4	Power steering line clamp plate bolt
5	Power steering lines (pressure/return)
6	Pressure line O-ring seal
7	Return line O-ring seal
8	Pressure line bracket-to-crossmember bolts (2 required)
9	Steering gear bolts (2 required)
10	Steering gear

ARM0400000000608

Fig. 7   Power steering pump replacement. 2005–08

ARM0400000000609

2005–08

4.0L ENGINE

1. Rotate tensioner counterclockwise and remove accessory drive belt from power steering pump pulley.
2. Remove three mounting bolts and power steering pump pulley, **Fig. 7.**
3. Disconnect clamp and suction hose from power steering pump.
4. Disconnect pressure line fitting.
5. Remove suction hose bracket bolt.
6. Remove three mounting bolts and power steering pump.
7. Reverse procedure to install. Install new Teflon® seal on power steering pressure line fitting nut using Teflon seal replacer set tool No. D90P-3517-A, or equivalent.

4.6L ENGINE

1. Rotate tensioner counterclockwise and remove accessory drive belt from the power steering pump pulley.
2. Raise and support vehicle.
3. Remove power steering pump pulley using pump pulley remover tool No. T69L-10300-B, or equivalent, **Fig. 7.**

4. Disconnect clamp and suction hose from power steering pump.
5. Disconnect pressure line fitting.
6. Remove pressure line bracket nut.
7. Remove three bolts and power steering pump.
8. Reverse procedure to install, noting the following:
   a. Install new Teflon® seal on power steering pressure line fitting nut using Teflon seal replacer set tool No. D90P-3517-A, or equivalent.
   b. Install pulley using pump pulley replacer tool No. T91P-3A733-A, or equivalent.

5.4L ENGINE

1. Remove power steering pump pulley.
2. Separate power steering reservoir from reservoir bracket.
3. Disconnect power steering pump supply hose from power steering pump.
4. Remove pressure line bracket to engine bolt.
5. Disconnect power steering pressure line from pump, **Fig. 8.**
6. Remove power steering pump mounting bolts, then pump.
7. Reverse procedure to install.

TECHNICAL SERVICE BULLETINS

Front Suspension Popping Noise While Turning Right Or Left

2005 MUSTANG

Some models built before 4/8/2005 may exhibit an intermittent popping noise from the front of the vehicle while turning left or right. The noise will typically occur during low speed maneuvers and may occur multiple times while turning.

This condition may be caused by binding upper strut bearing assembly. If the vehicle was built before February, 2005 it may also be required to install a lower spring seat isolator.

To correct this condition, install a revised strut mount bearing Part No. 5R3Z-18183-A and a revised spring isolator part No. 5R3Z-5L302-A .

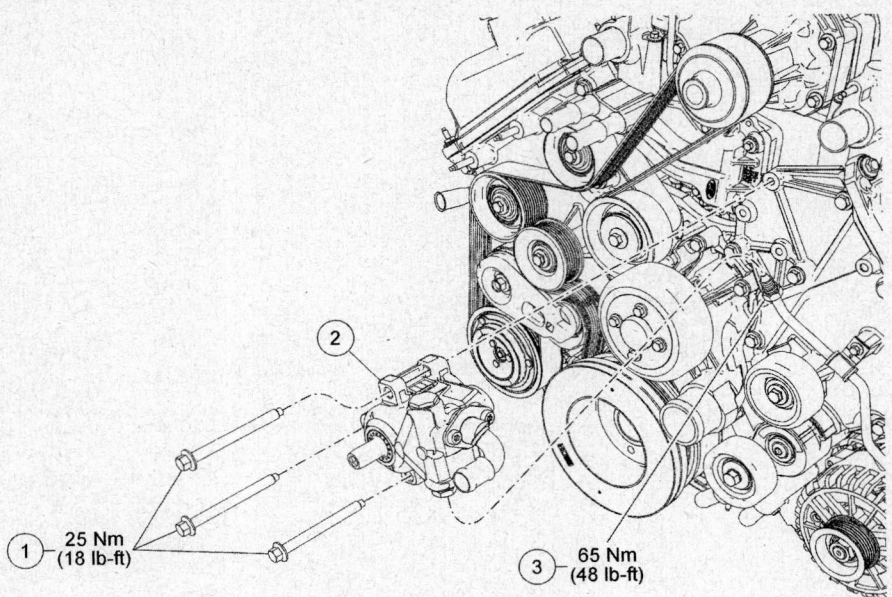

1- Power steering pump bolts
2- Power steering pump
3- Power steering pressure line

ARM0600000001236

Fig. 8 Power steering pump replacement. 5.4L engine

TIGHTENING SPECIFICATIONS

Year	Component	Torque/Ft. Lbs.
2004	ABS Sensor	53①
	ABS Sensor Wire Bracket	21
	Ball Joint To Spindle	129
	Lower Control Arm	148
	Stabilizer Bar Bracket	52
	Stabilizer Bar Link	14
	Steering Gear To Crossmember	52
	Strut To Spindle	148
	Strut Upper Mount	30
	Strut, Upper	74
	Tie Rod To Spindle	41
	Wheel Hub & Bearing Retainer	258
	Wheel Lug Nuts	95
2005–08	Brake Caliper & Anchor Plate	86
	Brake Disc Dust Shield	15
	Brake Line Bracket	15
	Control Arm Pinch	76
	Heat Shield	89①
	Lower Control Arm	129
	Outer Tie Rod End	59
	Pinch Bolt	76
	Power Steering Line Clamp	17
	Power Steering Pump	18
	Power Steering Pump Pressure Line	48
	Power Steering Pump Pulley	18

TIGHTENING SPECIFICATIONS—Continued

Year	Component	Torque/Ft. Lbs.
2005–08	Power Steering Suction Hose Bracket	71①
	Pressure Line Bracket	62①
	Pressure Line Bracket-To-Crossmember	80①
	Stabilizer Bar Link	85
	Stabilizer Bracket	52
	Steering Column Coupling-To-Steering Gear	18
	Steering Gear	85
	Strut	148
	Strut-To-Body	35
	Strut-To-Spindle	148
	Strut, Upper Nit	46
	Wheel Hub Retainer	221

① — Inch lbs.

Wheel Alignment

INDEX

	Page No.
Front Wheel Alignment	4-99
Basic Inspection	4-99
Camber	4-99
2004	4-99
2005–07	4-99

	Page No.
Caster	4-99
2004	4-99
2005–07	4-99
Toe-In	4-99
Preliminary Inspection	4-99

	Page No.
Rear Wheel Alignment	4-99
Cobra	4-99
Wheel Alignment	
Specifications	4-4

PRELIMINARY INSPECTION

1. Inspect tires for proper inflation and similar tread wear.
2. Inspect hub and bearing for excessive wear.
3. Inspect ball joints.
4. Inspect tie rod ends for excessive looseness.
5. Measure wheel and tire runout.
6. Inspect rack and pinion for looseness at frame.
7. Ensure proper strut operation.
8. Inspect suspension and steering components for damage.
9. Inspect vehicle ride height.

FRONT WHEEL ALIGNMENT

Basic Inspection

Inspect front wheel alignment under following curb load conditions:
1. Spare tire, wheel, jack and jack handle in proper positions.
2. Front seats in rearmost positions.
3. All other loading and aftermarket equipment removed.
4. All tires inflated to specified cold pressure.
5. All excessive mud, dirt and road deposit accumulation removed from chassis and underbody.

Caster

2004

Caster angle is preset during production and not adjustable. **However, if caster is still not within specifications by .6° after other sources have been inspected and corrected, perpendicular slot cutting is allowed at the tops of the strut towers. Each millimeter of adjustment will yield approximately .12° in caster change. Do not cut any slots longer than .2 inch in any direction.**

2005-07

If caster adjustment is required, slot the subframe and install cam bolts. This procedure should only be performed after all other possible sources have been inspected and corrected as required.
1. Remove front lower control arm as outlined in "Front Suspension & Steering" section.
2. Elongate lower control arm rear outboard mounting hole as indicated by etchings in subframe using suitable grinding tool, **Fig. 1.**
3. Do not elongate hole any more than indicated by etchings on subframe.
4. Remove any burrs, then clean and paint any exposed metal.
5. Install front lower control arm using cam bolt (part No. 4R33-2B236-BA) and new nut in rear inboard mounting hole.
6. Do not tighten cam bolt until alignment has been corrected.
7. Adjust the front caster using cam bolt until it is within specifications
8. **Torque** nut 129 ft. lbs.

Camber

2004

1. Remove camber plate pop rivet.
2. Loosen two strut mount to body apron nuts and one strut mount to body apron bolt.
3. Move top of shock strut to bring camber angle within specifications.
4. **Pop rivet replacement is not required.**

2005-07

If caster adjustment is required, slot the strut at the lower mounting plate and install cam bolts. This procedure should only be performed after all other possible sources have been inspected and corrected as required.
1. Remove strut and spring as outlined in "Front Suspension & Steering" section.
2. Enlarge strut-to-wheel spindle lower mounting holes as indicated by etchings in strut lower mount using suitable grinding tool, **Fig. 2.**
3. Do not enlarge holes any more than indicated by etchings on strut mount.
4. Remove any burrs, then clean and paint any exposed metal.
5. Install strut and spring using cam bolts (part No. 4R33-2B236-AA) and new nuts in place of regular strut-to-wheel spindle bolts and flag nuts.
6. Do not tighten cam bolts until alignment has been corrected.
7. Adjust front camber using cam bolts until it is within specifications.
8. **Torque** nuts 148 ft. lbs.

Toe-In

1. Determine if steering shaft and steering wheel marks are in alignment and in top position.
2. Loosen clamp screw on tie rod bellows and free seal on rod to prevent bellows from twisting.
3. Loosen tie rod jam nut.
4. Turn tie rod inner end to correct adjustment to specifications using suitable pliers, **Do not use pliers on tie rod threads.** Turning to reduce number of threads showing will increase toe-in. Turning in opposite direction will reduce toe-in.
5. Tighten nut.

REAR WHEEL ALIGNMENT

Cobra

On these models the independent rear suspension alignment is adjustable for camber and toe. Performing preliminary inspections, then proceed as follows:
1. Loosen upper control arm pivot nuts.
2. Rotate bolts and cams until camber is within range.
3. Tighten nuts.
4. Loosen toe control jam nuts and rotate toe link until toe is within range.
5. Tighten nuts.

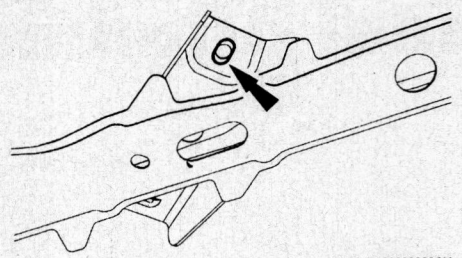

ARM0400000000611

**Fig. 1   Subframe hole elongating.
2005–07**

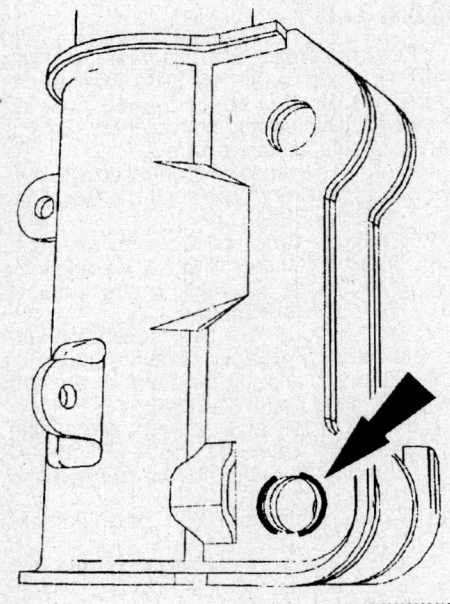

ARM0400000000612

**Fig. 2   Strut-to-wheel spindle
lower mounting hole elongating.
2005–07**

2004-07 SABLE & TAURUS

NOTE: Refer To The Rear Of This Manual For Vehicle Manufacturer's Special Service Tools.

INDEX OF SERVICE OPERATIONS

Page No.

AIR BAG SYSTEM PRECAUTIONS 0-18

BRAKES
Anti-Lock Brakes (Volume 2).. 6-1
Disc Brakes.................. 14-1
Drum Brakes................. 15-1
Hydraulic Brake Systems 16-1
Power Brake Units........... 17-1

COMPUTER RELEARN PROCEDURE 0-31

ELECTRICAL
Air Bag System (Volume 2) ... 4-1
Air Conditioning.............. 8-1
Alternators................... 11-1
Cooling Fans 9-1
Cruise Control (Volume 2) ... 2-1
Dash Gauges (Volume 2) 1-1
Dash Panel Service (Volume 2)................. 5-1
Passive Restraint Systems (Volume 2)................. 4-1
Speed Controls (Volume 2) ... 2-1
Starter Motors 10-1
Steering Columns............. 12-1
Wiper Systems (Volume 2).... 3-1
Alternator, Replace 5-4
Blower Motor, Replace........ 5-8
Cabin Air Filter, Replace 5-8
Evaporator Core, Replace 5-8
Fuel Pump Relay Location 5-4
Fuse Panel & Flasher Location 5-4
Headlamp Switch, Replace ... 5-5
Heater Core, Replace......... 5-8
Ignition Lock, Replace 5-5
Ignition Switch, Replace 5-5
Instrument Cluster, Replace... 5-6
Multi-function Switch, Replace 5-5
Neutral Safety Switch, Replace 5-5
Precautions.................. 5-4
Radio, Replace 5-6
Relay Center Location 5-4
Starter, Replace 5-4
Steering Wheel, Replace...... 5-6
Stop Light Switch, Replace ... 5-5
Wiper Motor, Replace......... 5-7
Wiper Switch, Replace........ 5-7
Wiper Transmission, Replace . 5-7

ELECTRICAL SYMBOL IDENTIFICATION 0-63

Page No.

FRONT DRIVE AXLES 18-1

FRONT SUSPENSION & STEERING
Ball Joint, Replace............ 5-29
Ball Joint Inspection 5-29
Coil Spring & Strut Service.... 5-29
Control Arm, Replace 5-30
Description 5-29
Power Steering 13-1
Power Steering Gear, Replace 5-31
Power Steering Pump, Replace 5-31
Stabilizer Bar, Replace........ 5-30
Steering Columns............ 12-1
Steering Knuckle, Replace.... 5-30
Strut, Replace 5-29
Tightening Specifications...... 5-31
Wheel Bearing, Replace 5-29

NON-STANDARD TIRE & WHEEL SIZE ADJUSTMENT TO RIDE HEIGHT SPECIFICATIONS & TIRE SIZE CHART 0-61

REAR SUSPENSION
Coil Spring, Replace 5-25
Control Arm, Replace 5-25
Description 5-23
Rear Wheel Spindle, Replace . 5-23
Shock Absorber, Replace 5-24
Stabilizer Bar, Replace........ 5-26
Strut, Replace 5-23
Strut Service................. 5-24
Tension Strut, Replace........ 5-24
Tightening Specifications...... 5-28
Wheel Bearing, Adjust 5-23

SERVICE REMINDER & WARNING LAMP RESET PROCEDURES 0-34

SPECIFICATIONS
Fluid Capacities & Cooling System Data.................. 5-3
Front Wheel Alignment Specifications................. 5-2
General Engine Specifications................. 5-2
Lubricant Data 5-3
Rear Wheel Alignment Specifications................. 5-2
Tune Up Specifications 5-2
Vehicle Ride Height Specifications................. 5-3

Page No.

TIRE PRESSURE MONITORING SYSTEM 20-1

VEHICLE IDENTIFICATION 0-1

VEHICLE LIFT POINTS 0-51

VEHICLE MAINTENANCE SCHEDULES 0-73

WHEEL ALIGNMENT
Front Wheel Alignment........ 5-32
Preliminary Inspection 5-32
Rear Wheel Alignment 5-32
Wheel Alignment Specifications................. 5-2

WIRE COLOR CODE IDENTIFICATION 0-63

3.0L ENGINE
Belt Tension Data.............. 5-18
Camshaft, Replace 5-17
Camshaft Lobe Lift Specifications................. 5-15
Compression Pressure........ 5-10
Cooling System Bleed 5-18
Crankshaft Rear Oil Seal, Replace 5-17
Cylinder Head, Replace....... 5-12
Engine Rebuilding Specifications................. 21-1
Engine, Replace 5-10
Engine Mount, Replace 5-10
Exhaust Manifold, Replace.... 5-12
Front Cover, Replace 5-15
Front Cover Seal, Replace.... 5-16
Fuel Filter, Replace 5-20
Fuel Pump, Replace.......... 5-20
Hydraulic Lifters, Replace..... 5-15
Intake Manifold, Replace...... 5-11
Main & Rod Bearings 5-17
Oil Pan, Replace.............. 5-18
Oil Pump, Replace........... 5-18
Oil Pump Service............. 5-18
Piston & Rod Assembly....... 5-17
Precautions.................. 5-9
Radiator, Replace............. 5-19
Serpentine Drive Belt 5-18
Thermostat, Replace.......... 5-19
Tightening Specifications...... 5-21
Timing Chain, Replace........ 5-16
Valve Adjustment............. 5-15
Valve Arrangement........... 5-15
Valve Clearance Specifications................. 5-15
Valve Cover, Replace 5-14
Water Pump, Replace 5-19

Specifications

GENERAL ENGINE SPECIFICATIONS

Liter (Code①)	Fuel System	Bore & Stroke	Comp. Ratio	Net H.P. @ RPM	Maximum Torque/Ft. Lbs. @ RPM	Normal Oil Pressure, psi
3.0L DOHC (S)	SFI	3.50 x 3.13	10:1	200 @ 5700	200 @ 4400	11③
3.0L OHV (U)	SFI	3.50 x 3.14	9.3:1	155 @ 4900	185 @ 3950	40–60②

DOHC — Dual Overhead Cam
OHV — Overhead Valve
SFI — Sequential Fuel Injection

① — The eighth digit of the VIN denotes engine code.
② — At 2500 RPM w/engine at operating temperature.

③ — At 1500 RPM with engine hot.

TUNE UP SPECIFICATIONS

Liter (Code①)	Spark Plug Gap	Ignition Timing, °BTDC				Curb Idle Speed, RPM		Fast Idle Speed, RPM		Fuel Pump Pressure, psi	Valve Clearance
		Firing Order ②	Man. Trans.	Auto. Trans.	Mark	Man. Trans.	Auto. Trans.	Man. Trans.	Auto. Trans.		
3.0L DOHC (S)	.054	⑤	—	⑦	—	—	④	—	④	③	⑥
3.0L OHV (U)	.044	⑤	—	10⑦	—	—	④	—	④	③	⑥

BTDC — Before Top Dead Center
D — Drive
① — The eighth digit of the VIN denotes engine code.
② — Before disconnecting wires from distributor cap or coil, determine location of wire, as position may have been altered from that mounting at end of this chart.
③ — Key on engine off, 37–45 psi. Key on engine running, 26–45 psi.
④ — Idle speed is controlled by an automatic idle control system.
⑤ — Coil on plug ignition system. Cylinder numbering front to rear, righthand bank, 1, 2, 3; lefthand bank, 4, 5, 6. Firing order 1-4-2-5-3-6.
⑥ — Equipped w/hydraulic valve lifters; no provision for adjustment.
⑦ — Non-adjustable.

FRONT WHEEL ALIGNMENT SPECIFICATIONS

Model	Caster Angle, Degrees		Camber Angle, Degrees		Total Toe, Inches		Ball Joint Wear
	Limits	Desired	Limits Left	Desired Left	Limits	Desired	
2004-07	+2.8 to +4.8	+3.8	-1.1 to +.1	-.5	-.22 to +.02	-.1	①

① — Refer to "Ball Joint Inspection" in "Front Suspension & Steering" section.

REAR WHEEL ALIGNMENT SPECIFICATIONS

Model	Camber Angle, Degrees①		Total Toe-In, Inches	
	Limits	Desired	Limits	Desired
Sedan	-1.7 to -.3	-1.0	+.05 to +.23	+.18
Wagon	-.1 to +1.3	+.6	+.05 to +.23	+.18

① — Not adjustable.

VEHICLE RIDE HEIGHT SPECIFICATIONS

Model	Year	Body Style	Manufacturer's Original Tire Size ①	Front Dim.②	Front Specification Inches	Front Specification mm	Rear Dim.②	Rear Specification Inches	Rear Specification mm
Sable	2004–05	Sedan	①	E	27.89–28.27	703–723	G	27.22–27.60	686–706
		Wagon	①	E	27.80–28.15	700–720	G	27.47–27.85	692–712
Taurus	2004–07	Sedan	①	E	27.89–28.27	703–723	G	27.22–27.60	686–706
		Wagon	①	E	27.80–28.15	700–720	G	27.47–27.85	692–712

A Dim. — Distance from Front Rocker Panel to Ground

B Dim. — Distance from Rear Rocker Panel to Ground

E Dim. — Ground to Front Wheel Opening Through Centerline of Wheel

G Dim. — Ground to Rear Wheel Opening Through Centerline of Wheel

Dim. — Dimension

① — See door sticker or inside of glove box for manufacturers original tire size specifications. If tires on vehicle do not match manufacturers original tire size & measurement is not within limits, it will be required to refer to the Non-Standard Tire & Wheel Size Adjustment To Ride Height Specification & Tire Size Adjustment Charts.

② — Refer to **Fig. A**.

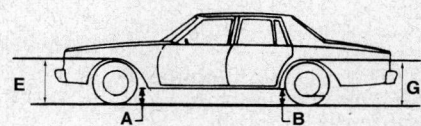

CRQ166

Fig. A   Dimensions A, B, E & G

FLUID CAPACITIES & COOLING SYSTEM DATA

Model	Engine Liter (Code①)	Coolant Capacity, Qts.	Coolant Type	Radiator Cap Relief Pressure, Lbs.	Thermo. Opening Temp. °F	Fuel Tank Gals.	Engine Oil Refill, Qts.②	Transaxle Capacity Manual Trans., Pts.	Transaxle Capacity Auto. Trans., Qts.④
2004-07	3.0L OHV (U)	11.6	⑤	13–18	183–190	16	4.5	—	③
	3.0L DOHC (S)	10.6	⑤	13–18	183–190	16	5.5	—	③

EG — Ethylene Glycol

① — The eighth digit of the VIN denotes engine code.

② — Includes filter.

③ — Models w/AX4S transaxle, 12.25 qts.; models w/AX4N transaxle, 13.50 qts.

④ — Approximate; make final inspection w/dipstick.

⑤ — For models w/green coolant use ethylene glycol. For models w/orange coolant use coolant meeting Ford specifications.

LUBRICANT DATA

Year	Transaxle Manual	Transaxle Automatic	Power Steering	Brake System
2004–07	—	Mercon V	①	DOT 3

① — Motorcraft MERCON Multi-Purpose ATF part No. XT-2-QDX, or equivalent.

Electrical

NOTE: On Air Bag Equipped Models, Refer To "Air Bag System Precautions" Located In The Front Of This Manual For System Disarming & Arming Procedures.

NOTE: Refer To "Computer Relearn Procedures" Located In The Front Of This Manual When Battery Power To The Computer Has Been Interrupted.

INDEX

	Page No.		Page No.		Page No.
Air Bag System (Volume 2)	4-1	Heater Core, Replace	5-8	Relay Center Location	5-4
Air Conditioning	8-1	Ignition Lock, Replace	5-5	Speed Controls (Volume 2)	2-1
Alternator, Replace	5-4	Ignition Switch, Replace	5-5	Starter Motors	10-1
DOHC Engine	5-4	Instrument Cluster, Replace	5-6	Starter, Replace	5-4
OHV Engine	5-4	Analog	5-6	Steering Columns	12-1
Alternators	19-1	Column Shift	5-6	Steering Wheel, Replace	5-6
Blower Motor, Replace	5-8	Floor Shift	5-6	Stop Light Switch, Replace	5-5
Cabin Air Filter, Replace	5-8	Multi-Function Switch, Replace	5-5	Installation	5-5
Cooling Fans	9-1	Neutral Safety Switch, Replace	5-5	Removal	5-5
Cruise Control (Volume 2)	2-1	Passive Restraint Systems		Wiper Motor, Replace	5-7
Dash Gauges (Volume 2)	1-1	(Volume 2)	4-1	Front	5-7
Dash Panel Service		Precautions	5-4	Rear	5-7
(Volume 2)	5-1	Air Bag Systems	5-4	Wiper Switch, Replace	5-7
Evaporator Core, Replace	5-8	Battery Ground Cable	5-4	Front	5-7
Fuel Pump Relay Location	5-4	Radio, Replace	5-6	Rear	5-7
Fuse Panel & Flasher Location	5-4	Integrated Control Panel (ICP)	5-6	Wiper Systems (Volume 2)	3-1
Headlamp Switch, Replace	5-5	Radio	5-6	Wiper Transmission, Replace	5-7

PRECAUTIONS

Air Bag Systems

Refer to "Air Bag System Precautions" in the front of this manual for system disarming and arming procedures.

Battery Ground Cable

Prior to service, disconnect battery ground cable and isolate as required.

FUSE PANEL & FLASHER LOCATION

The fuse panel is located under the instrument cluster or instrument panel, left-hand of the steering column. The combination turn signal/hazard flasher is located behind on the lefthand side instrument panel reinforcement above the fuse panel.

RELAY CENTER LOCATION

The relay panel/power distribution center is located at the front center of the engine compartment, attached to the radiator support. This panel contains the PCM relay, low fan control relay, high fan control relay and air conditioning WAC relay.

FUEL PUMP RELAY LOCATION

The fuel pump relay is located at the front center of the engine compartment, in the power distribution center.

STARTER
REPLACE

The heavy gauge input lead connected to the starter solenoid is hot at all times. Ensure the protective cap is installed over the terminal and is replaced after service.
1. Raise and support vehicle.
2. Remove lower air deflector.
3. Remove starter solenoid safety cap.
4. Remove starter solenoid and ground stud cables.
5. Remove mounting bolts, stud and starter.
6. Reverse procedure to install.

ALTERNATOR
REPLACE

DOHC Engine

1. Remove accessory drive belt from alternator.
2. Remove mounting nut, then position engine control sensor wiring and hose bracket aside.

3. Loosen alternator pulley nut and remove inboard upper alternator mounting bolt.
4. Loosen outboard upper alternator bolt.
5. Disconnect electrical harness connector and output terminal wiring.
6. Raise and support vehicle, then remove wheel and tire assembly.
7. Remove alternator splash shield and outboard upper alternator bolt.
8. Remove lower alternator bolt.
9. Remove pulley nut and alternator.
10. Reverse procedure to install, noting the following:
    a. **Torque** alternator mounting bolts to 15–22 ft. lbs.
    b. **Torque** alternator output nut to 80–106 inch lbs.
    c. **Torque** alternator pulley nut to 60–100 ft. lbs.

OHV Engine

The alternator is not internally service-able.
1. Disconnect integral alternator/voltage regulator electrical connectors.
2. Loosen alternator pivot bolt and remove mounting alternator brace bolt.
3. Disconnect accessory drive belt from alternator pulley.
4. Remove alternator brace.
5. Remove alternator pivot bolt and alternator/voltage regulator.
6. Reverse procedure to install, noting the following:
    a. **Torque** mounting nut and brace bolt to 15–22 ft. lbs.

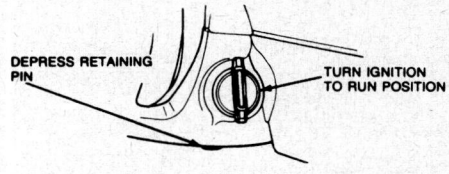

Fig. 1 Ignition lock cylinder replacement

b. **Torque** alternator brace bolts to 72–96 inch lbs.
c. **Torque** pivot bolt to 30–40 ft. lbs.
d. **Torque** alternator output nut (B+) to 60–84 inch lbs.

IGNITION LOCK

REPLACE

1. Place ignition switch in RUN position.
2. Depress lock cylinder retaining pin with suitable ⅛ inch drill or drift punch while working through steering column lower shroud, **Fig. 1.**
3. Pull ignition lock cylinder from housing.
4. Reverse procedure to install. Ensure proper installation by rotating ignition switch through travel.

IGNITION SWITCH

REPLACE

1. Remove lower instrument panel steering column cover, **Fig. 2.**
2. Turn ignition lock to RUN position.
3. Disconnect ignition switch electrical connector.
4. Remove mounting screws and ignition switch.
5. Reverse procedure to install, noting the following:
   a. Ensure ignition lock is in RUN position when installing ignition switch.
   b. **Torque** ignition switch mounting screws to 50–69 inch lbs.

NEUTRAL SAFETY SWITCH

REPLACE

Neutral safety switch functions are incorporated into the Transaxle Range (TR) sensor.

1. Place manual control lever in Neutral position.
2. Remove engine air cleaner and outlet tube.
3. Disconnect TR sensor electrical connector.
4. Remove manual control lever from transaxle.
5. Remove mounting bolts and TR sensor.
6. Reverse procedure to install, noting the following:
   a. Ensure manual control lever is in Neutral position.
   b. Install transaxle range sensor and mounting bolts loosely.
   c. Align position sensor using manual lever position sensor alignment tool No. T92P-70010-AH, or equivalent.

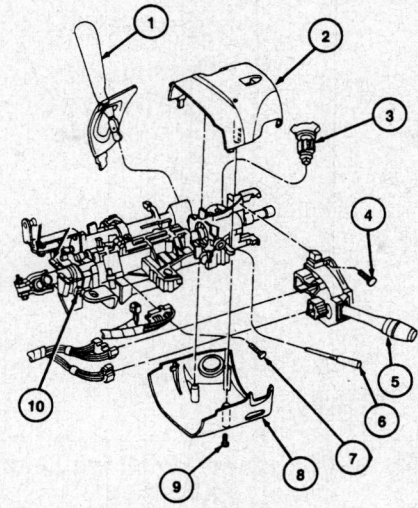

Item	Description
1	Gearshift Lever
2	Upper Steering Column Shroud
3	Ignition Lock Assy
4	Screw (2 Req'd)
5	Multi-Function Switch
6	Tilt Steering Column Lock Lever
7	Screw
8	Steering Column Shroud
9	Screw (3 Req'd)
10	Ignition Switch

Fig. 2 Ignition switch replacement

d. **Torque** sensor mounting bolts to 84–106 inch lbs.
e. **Torque** manual lever mounting bolts to 96–132 inch lbs.

HEADLAMP SWITCH

REPLACE

1. Pry headlamp switch housing from instrument panel.
2. Depress release button and pull headlamp switch away from instrument panel.
3. Disconnect electrical connectors and remove headlamp switch.
4. Reverse procedure to install.

STOP LIGHT SWITCH

REPLACE

Removal

1. Lift stop lamp switch harness wiring connector locking tab and remove connector.
2. Remove hairpin retainer and white nylon washer.
3. Slide switch and pushrod assembly away from brake pedal.
4. Remove switch, **Fig. 3. Removing master cylinder pushrod, black bushing or one white bushing near-**

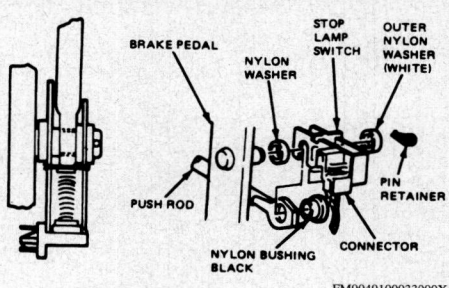

Fig. 3 Stop lamp switch replacement

est brake pedal from brake pedal pin is not required.

Installation

1. Position switch so U-shaped side is nearest brake pedal and directly over brake pedal pin. **Black bushing must be in position in pushrod eyelet with washer face on side away from pedal arm.**
2. Slide switch up and down to trap black plastic bushing and pushrod between two switch side plates.
3. Push switch and pushrod assembly towards brake pedal arm.
4. Install white nylon washer on pedal pin and hairpin retainer. **Do not substitute another type of pin retainer.**
5. Connect wire harness connector to switch and inspect brake lamps for proper operation. Brake lamps should illuminate with less than six pounds of force applied at brake pedal pad.

MULTI-FUNCTION SWITCH

REPLACE

1. **On models equipped with tilt steering column,** move column to lowest position, then remove tilt and key release levers.
2. **On all models,** place ignition switch in RUN position, then depress lock cylinder retaining pin with suitable ⅛ inch drill or drift punch while working through steering column lower shroud, **Fig. 1.**
3. Pull ignition lock cylinder from housing.
4. Rotate replacement lock cylinder to RUN position, depressing retaining pin and insert lock cylinder into housing. Ensure proper installation by rotating ignition switch through travel.
5. Remove upper and lower steering column shrouds.
6. Remove multi-function switch mounting screws and disconnect switch from casting.
7. Disconnect electrical connectors and remove switch.
8. Reverse procedure to install. noting the following:
   a. **Torque** multi-function switch mounting screws to 18–27 inch lbs.
   b. **Torque** tilt lever mounting screw to 6–8 inch lbs.

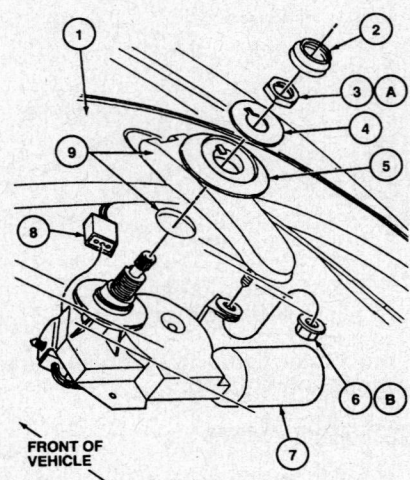

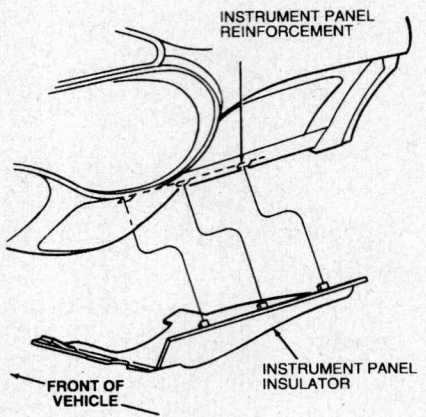

Fig. 5 Instrument panel insulator panel replacement

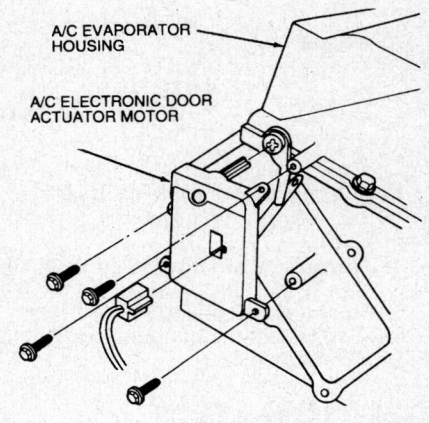

Fig. 6 Air conditioning electronic door actuator motor replacement

Item	Description
1	Liftgate
2	Windshield Wiper Output Arm Cover
3	Nut
4	Washer
5	Bezel
6	Nut and Washer
7	Windshield Wiper Motor
8	Rear Window Wiper / Washer Wire
9	Liftgate Window
A	Tighten to 15-20 N·m (11-15 Lb-Ft)
B	Tighten to 5-7 N·m (44-62 Lb-In)

Fig. 4 Rear wiper motor replacement

STEERING WHEEL
REPLACE

1. Center front wheels to straight-ahead position.
2. Disconnect speed control wire harness from steering wheel.
3. Remove driver's side air bag module as outlined in "Passive Restraint Systems" chapter.
4. Remove and discard steering wheel mounting bolt.
5. Remove steering wheel using steering wheel puller tool No. T67L-3600-A, or equivalent. Route contact assembly wire harness through steering wheel as wheel is lifted off shaft.
6. Reverse procedure to install, noting the following:
   a. Ensure front wheels are in straight-ahead position.
   b. Route contact assembly wire harness through steering column opening at three o'clock position.
   c. Align steering shaft alignment marks.
   d. **Torque** new steering wheel mounting bolt to 26-34 ft. lbs.

INSTRUMENT CLUSTER
REPLACE
Analog
COLUMN SHIFT

1. Pull ignition lock cylinder from housing.
2. Rotate replacement lock cylinder to RUN position, depressing retaining pin and insert lock cylinder into housing. Ensure proper installation by rotating ignition switch through travel.
3. Remove upper and lower steering column shrouds.
4. Remove instrument panel steering column cover.
5. Remove integrated control panel.
6. Tilt steering wheel to its lowest possible position.
7. Remove instrument panel. finish panel.
8. Disconnect PRNDL cable loop from column shift selector tube.
9. Remove adjustment nut and PRNDL cable from bracket.
10. Remove mounting screws and pull cluster toward steering wheel.
11. Disconnect three electrical connectors behind instrument cluster.
12. Remove instrument cluster.
13. Reverse procedure to install.

FLOOR SHIFT

1. Pull ignition lock cylinder from housing.
2. Rotate replacement lock cylinder to RUN position, depressing retaining pin and insert lock cylinder into housing. Ensure proper installation by rotating ignition switch through travel.
3. Remove upper and lower steering column shrouds.
4. Remove mounting screws and instrument finish panel.
5. Tilt steering wheel to its lowest possible position.
6. Remove instrument cluster mounting screws and pull top of cluster toward steering wheel.

7. Disconnect three electrical connectors behind instrument cluster.
8. Remove instrument cluster.
9. Reverse procedure to install.

RADIO
REPLACE

Each audio control is part of the Integrated Control Panel (ICP) and cannot be repaired separately. On the sedan model, the CD changer is located in the lefthand side of the luggage compartment. On the wagon, it is located in the righthand side of the rear quarter panel. On the six-passenger model it is located in the center console.

Integrated Control Panel (ICP)

1. Release mounting clips by install radio removal tool No. T87P-19061-A, or equivalent, to face plate and pushing tool inward approximately 1-1½ inches. **Do not push tool with excessive force.**
2. Apply light even force on tool and remove radio.
3. **On models equipped with automatic temperature control,** disconnect sensor hose and elbow.
4. **On all models,** disconnect radio electrical connectors and antenna lead.
5. Reverse procedure to install.

Radio

1. **On sedan models,** remove lefthand luggage compartment trim panel.
2. **On wagon models,** remove lefthand spare tire trim panel and spare tire.
3. **On all models,** disconnect wiring connectors and antenna lead in cable.
4. Remove mounting screws, nut and radio.
5. Reverse procedure to install.

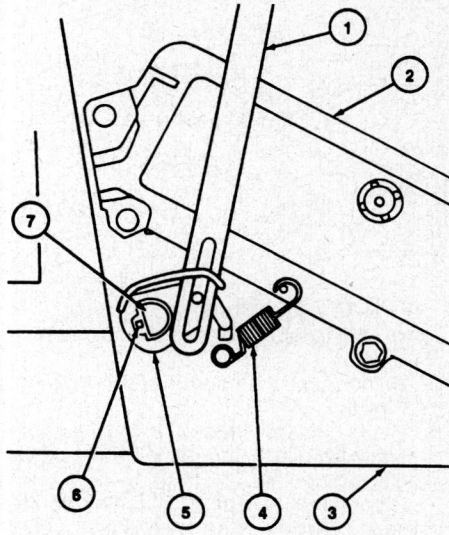

Item	Description
1	Metal Link
2	Heater Core Cover
3	A/C Evaporator Housing
4	Spring
5	Lever
6	Locking Ramp (Part of Secondary A/C Air Temperature Control Door Shaft)
7	Secondary A/C Air Temperature Control Door Shaft

FM7029600239000X

Fig. 7 Spring & metal link replacement

WIPER MOTOR
REPLACE

Front

The wiper mounting arm and pivot shafts are connected with non-removable plastic ball joints. Except for the wiper motor, the entire wiper transmission assembly is non-serviceable.

1. **Record normal park positions of wiper arms and blades for installation alignment.**
2. Remove wiper arm mounting nuts from pivot shafts.
3. Turn ignition switch to ON position and wiper switch to LO.
4. Turn ignition switch to OFF position when arms and blades to move to straight up-and-down position.
5. Remove wiper arms from pivot shafts.
6. Turn eight plastic cowl vent screen nuts ¼ turn counterclockwise.
7. Remove clips mounting vent screen to inner panels.
8. Remove mounting screws and wiper assembly.
9. Reverse procedure to install, noting the following:
   a. Turn ignition switch to ON position

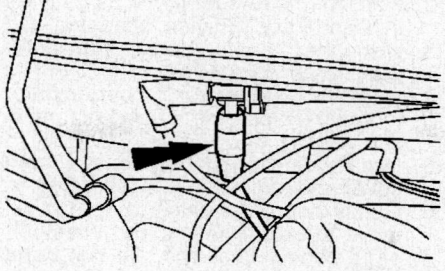

FM7020100681000X

Fig. 8 Vacuum supply hose replacement

and wiper control switch to Low or High.
   b. Turn wiper control switch to OFF position after wipers have cycled once or twice.
   c. **Torque** wiper assembly screws to 84-120 inch lbs.
   d. Install wiper arms and blades in their previously recorded park positions.
   e. **Torque** pivot arm nuts to 22-29 ft. lbs.

Rear

1. Open liftgate and remove window wiper motor cover, **Fig. 4.**
2. Disconnect rear window wiper/washer electrical connector.
3. Remove windshield wiper output arm cover.
4. Remove outside mounting nut, washer and bezel.
5. Remove wiper motor to liftgate window hinge mounting nut.
6. Remove wiper motor.
7. Reverse procedure to install.

WIPER SWITCH
REPLACE

Front

The windshield wiper switch is an integral component of the multi-function switch.

1. **On models equipped with tilt steering column,** move column to lowest position, then remove tilt and key release levers.
2. **On all models,** place ignition switch in RUN position, then depress lock cylinder retaining pin with suitable ⅛ inch drill or drift punch while working through steering column lower shroud, **Fig. 1.**
3. Pull ignition lock cylinder from housing.
4. Rotate replacement lock cylinder to RUN position, depressing retaining pin and insert lock cylinder into housing. Ensure proper installation by rotating ignition switch through travel.
5. Remove upper and lower steering column shrouds.
6. Remove multi-function switch mounting screws and disconnect switch from casting.
7. Disconnect electrical connectors and remove switch.

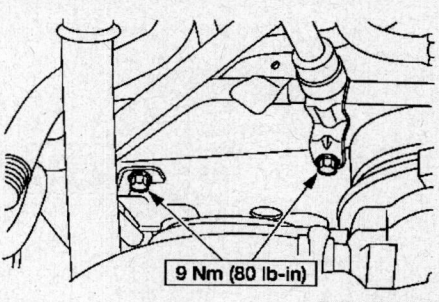

9 Nm (80 lb-in)

FM7020100682000X

Fig. 9 Air conditioning clamp hold-down bolts replacement

8. Reverse procedure to install. noting the following:
   a. **Torque** multi-function switch mounting screws to 18-27 inch lbs.
   b. **Torque** tilt lever mounting screw to 6-8 inch lbs.

Rear

1. Pull rear wiper/washer switch straight out of instrument panel.
2. Disconnect electrical connector and remove switch.
3. Reverse procedure to install.

WIPER TRANSMISSION
REPLACE

The wiper mounting arm and pivot shafts are connected with non-removable plastic ball joints. Except for the wiper motor, the entire wiper transmission assembly is non-serviceable.

1. **Record normal park positions of wiper arms and blades for installation alignment.**
2. Remove wiper arm mounting nuts from pivot shafts.
3. Turn ignition switch to ON position and wiper switch to LO.
4. Turn ignition switch to OFF position when arms and blades to move to straight up-and-down position.
5. Remove wiper arms from pivot shafts.
6. Turn eight plastic cowl vent screen nuts ¼ turn counterclockwise.
7. Remove clips mounting vent screen to inner panels.
8. Remove mounting screws and wiper assembly.
9. Reverse procedure to install, noting the following:
   a. Turn ignition switch to ON position and wiper control switch to Low or High.
   b. Turn wiper control switch to OFF position after wipers have cycled once or twice.
   c. **Torque** wiper assembly screws to 84-120 inch lbs.
   d. Install wiper arms and blades in their previously recorded park positions.
   e. **Torque** pivot arm nuts to 22-29 ft. lbs.

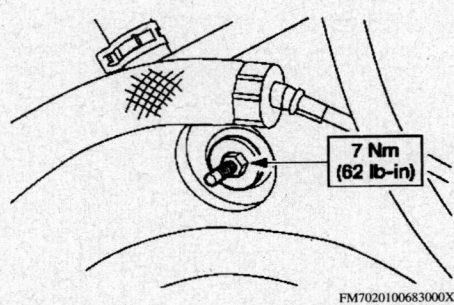

FM7020100683000X

Fig. 10 Evaporator housing replacement

BLOWER MOTOR
REPLACE

1. Pull instrument panel insulator from lower righthand side instrument panel reinforcement, **Fig. 5.**
2. Disconnect blower motor electrical connector.
3. Remove mounting screws and blower motor from evaporator housing.
4. Reverse procedure to install.

CABIN AIR FILTER
REPLACE

1. Remove righthand cowl vent screen.
2. Remove water shield.
3. Remove cabin air filter.
4. Reverse procedure to install.

HEATER CORE
REPLACE

1. Drain coolant into suitable container.

2. Remove instrument panel as outlined in "Dash Panel Service" chapter.
3. Disconnect heater hoses from core. Plug heater core tubes.
4. Remove four electronic door actuator motor to evaporator housing mounting screws, **Fig. 6.**
5. Disconnect spring from heater core cover and remove it from lever, **Fig. 7.**
6. Gently depress locking ramp and remove lever from secondary air temperature control door end. **Do not bend any part of lever.**
7. Rotate primary air temperature door shaft downward, swing metal link and remove from pin.
8. Remove three mounting screws, heater core cover and seal from evaporator housing.
9. Remove heater core and seal by pushing on tubes.
10. Reverse procedure to install.

EVAPORATOR CORE
REPLACE

The evaporator core is serviced as a core and housing assembly. The evaporator core, internal doors, seals and door linkage are included with the housing. Transfer the blower motor and wheel assembly, heater core and cover, dash panel seals and vacuum actuators to the new housing.

1. Recover refrigerant as outlined in "Air Conditioning" chapter.
2. Drain coolant into suitable container.
3. Remove instrument panel as outlined in "Dash Panel Service" chapter.
4. Remove righthand cowl vent screen and water shield.

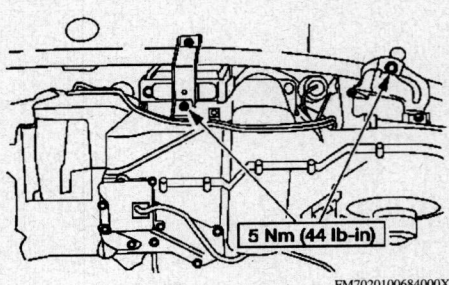

FM7020100684000X

Fig. 11 Evaporator housing mounting support replacement

5. Disconnect vacuum supply hose, **Fig. 8.**
6. Clamp heater hoses using suitable pinching pliers and disconnect hoses. Cap fittings.
7. Disconnect evaporator outlet spring lock coupling. Cap evaporator outlet tube and suction accumulator tube.
8. Remove air conditioning pipe clamps' hold-down bolts, **Fig. 9.**
9. Disconnect evaporator inlet spring lock coupling. Cap evaporator inlet tube and condenser to evaporator line tube.
10. Remove three evaporator housing mounting nuts, **Fig. 10.**
11. Remove heater outlet floor duct.
12. Remove evaporator housing support bracket mounting nuts, **Fig. 11.**
13. Remove heater/evaporator core housing.
14. Reverse procedure to install.

3.0L Engine

NOTE: On Air Bag Equipped Models, Refer To "Air Bag System Precautions" Located In The Front Of This Manual For System Disarming & Arming Procedures.

NOTE: Refer To "Computer Relearn Procedures" Located In The Front Of This Manual When Battery Power To The Computer Has Been Interrupted.

NOTE: Prior To Performing Any Service Operations, Consult The "Technical Service Bulletins" Section For Related Information.

INDEX

	Page No.
Belt Tension Data	5-18
Camshaft, Replace	5-17
DOHC Engine	5-17
OHV Engine	5-17
Camshaft Lobe Lift Specifications	5-15
DOHC Engine	5-15
OHV Engine	5-15
Compression Pressure	5-10
Cooling System Bleed	5-18
Crankshaft Rear Oil Seal, Replace	5-17
Cylinder Head, Replace	5-12
DOHC Engine	5-12
Lefthand	5-12
Righthand	5-13
OHV Engine	5-13
Lefthand	5-13
Righthand	5-14
Engine, Replace	5-10
Engine Mount, Replace	5-10
Engine & Transaxle	5-10
Front	5-10
Engine Rebuilding Specifications	21-1
Exhaust Manifold, Replace	5-12
DOHC Engine	5-12
Lefthand	5-12
Righthand	5-12
OHV Engine	5-12
Lefthand	5-12
Righthand	5-12
Front Cover, Replace	5-15

	Page No.
DOHC Engine	5-15
OHV Engine	5-16
Front Cover Seal, Replace	5-16
OHV Engine	5-16
Installation	5-16
Removal	5-16
Fuel Filter, Replace	5-20
Fuel Pump, Replace	5-20
Hydraulic Lifters, Replace	5-15
OHV Engine	5-15
Intake Manifold, Replace	5-11
DOHC Engine	5-11
Lower	5-11
Upper	5-11
OHV Engine	5-11
Lower	5-11
Upper	5-11
Main & Rod Bearings	5-17
DOHC Engine	5-17
Connecting Rod	5-17
Main Bearings	5-17
OHV	5-17
Main Bearings	5-17
Oil Pan, Replace	5-18
DOHC Engine	5-18
OHV Engine	5-18
Oil Pump, Replace	5-18
DOHC Engine	5-18
OHV Engine	5-18
Oil Pump Service	5-18
OHV Engine	5-18
Piston & Rod Assembly	5-17
Precautions	5-9

	Page No.
Air Bag Systems	5-9
Battery Ground Cable	5-10
Flexible Fuel Models	5-9
Fuel System Pressure Relief	5-9
Radiator, Replace	5-19
Serpentine Drive Belt	5-18
Belt Routing	5-18
Belt, Replace	5-18
Thermostat, Replace	5-19
Installation	5-19
Removal	5-19
Tightening Specifications	5-21
Timing Chain, Replace	5-16
DOHC Engine	5-16
OHV Engine	5-16
Valve Adjustment	5-15
Valve Arrangement	5-15
OHV Engine	5-15
Front To Rear	5-15
Valve Clearance Specifications	5-15
OHV Engine	5-15
Valve Cover, Replace	5-14
DOHC Engine	5-14
Lefthand	5-14
Righthand	5-14
OHV Engine	5-14
Lefthand	5-14
Righthand	5-15
Water Pump, Replace	5-19
DOHC Engine	5-19
OHV Engine	5-19

PRECAUTIONS

Air Bag Systems

Refer to "Air Bag System Precautions" in the front of this manual for system disarming and arming procedures.

Flexible Fuel Models

Flexible Fuel (FF) vehicles use unique methanol-compatible components. Certain gasoline-only components may appear identical to these FF vehicle components.

Under no circumstances should these components be interchanged.

Fuel System Pressure Relief

When releasing fuel pressure on flexible fuel vehicles, use methanol resistant gloves and eye protection. Avoid prolonged skin contact with liquid or breathing of vapors.

If methanol fuel should be spilled on paint, flush immediately with cold water. **Do not wipe, or paint damage may occur.**

Fuel supply lines will remain pressur- ized for long periods of time after engine shutdown. This pressure must be relieved before any service is attempted. A valve is provided on the fuel rail assembly for this purpose.

1. Remove air cleaner assembly.
2. Connect pressure gauge tool No. T80L-9974-A or T80L-9974-B, or equivalent, onto fuel rail assembly fuel valve.
3. Open manual valve on pressure gauge tool.
4. To pressurize fuel system, proceed as follows:
   a. Install pressure gauge tool onto fuel rail pressure fitting.

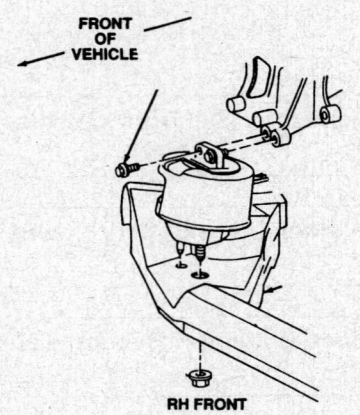

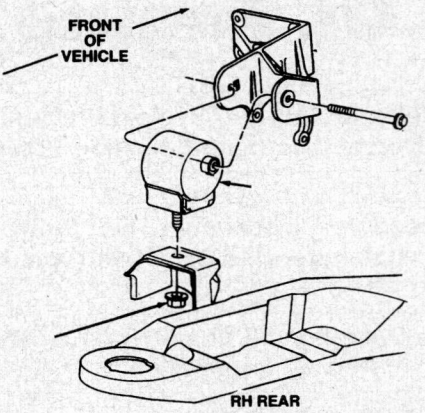

FM1069600478000X

Fig. 1 Engine mount replacement. DOHC engine

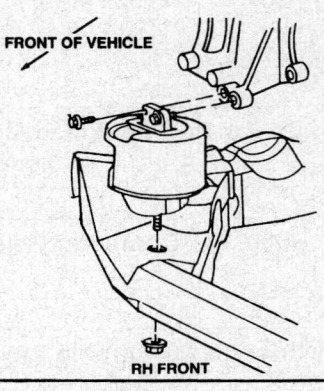

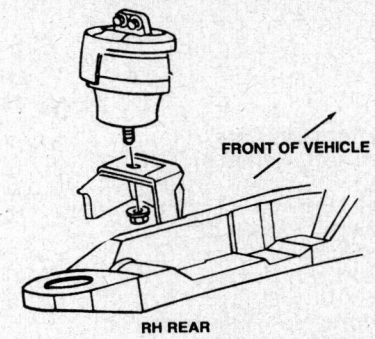

FM1069600477000X

Fig. 2 Engine mount replacement. OHV engine

b. Turn ignition switch to ON position for three seconds, 5–10 times until pressure gauge indicates 13 psi.

Battery Ground Cable

Prior to service, disconnect battery ground cable and isolate as required.

COMPRESSION PRESSURE

Perform compression inspection with engine at normal operating temperature, spark plugs removed and throttle wide open.

The lowest cylinder must be within 75 percent of the highest cylinder.

ENGINE MOUNT
REPLACE
Front

1. Raise and support vehicle.
2. Place suitable jack and wood block under engine block.
3. Remove lefthand and righthand front engine support insulator to subframe mounting nuts, **Figs. 1 and 2.**
4. Raise jack enough to remove load from support insulators.
5. Remove mounting bolts, then lefthand and righthand engine support insulators.
6. Reverse procedure to install.

Engine & Transaxle

1. Raise and support vehicle. Remove lefthand front tire and wheel assembly.
2. Support transaxle with suitable transaxle jack.
3. Remove engine and transaxle support insulator to rear engine and transaxle bracket mounting nut, **Fig. 3.**
4. Remove two engine and transaxle support insulator to subframe through bolts.
5. Raise transaxle enough to remove

load from engine and transaxle support insulator.
6. Remove support insulator.
7. Reverse procedure to install.

ENGINE
REPLACE

1. Drain cooling system into suitable container.
2. Remove cowl vent screen and cowl vent extension.
3. Remove engine air cleaner and outlet tube.
4. Recover refrigerant as outlined in "Air Conditioning" chapter.
5. Relieve fuel system pressure as outlined in "Precautions."
6. Disconnect and position steering column input shaft coupling aside.
7. Remove snow shield, **Fig. 4.**
8. Disconnect accelerator and speed control actuator cables, then the throttle return spring from throttle body. Position accelerator cable bracket aside.
9. Disconnect chassis vacuum hose, **Fig. 5.**
10. Disconnect manual control lever cable from lever and bracket, then set it aside.
11. Disconnect 42-pin and transaxle range sensor electrical connectors.
12. Disconnect upper radiator and heater hoses from thermostat housing.
13. Remove battery.
14. Remove nut and ground strap electrical connector, **Fig. 6.**
15. Disconnect lefthand exhaust manifold flange.
16. Disconnect power steering return hose.
17. Disconnect alternator electrical connectors and position wire harness aside.
18. Disconnect air condition suction tube from accumulator drier.
19. Disconnect fuel supply hose.
20. Remove engine roll restrictor brace and restrictor.
21. Disconnect hose from degas bottle.
22. Disconnect heater water hose.

23. Disconnect electrical ground connectors, **Fig. 7.**
24. Disconnect evaporative emissions canister purge valve electrical connector.
25. Disconnect powertrain control module electrical connector.
26. Raise and support vehicle.
27. Remove valance panel.
28. Disconnect catalyst monitor sensor electrical connector.
29. Remove catalytic converters and Y-pipe assemblies.
30. Remove front wheels.
31. Disconnect air conditioning discharge tube.
32. Disconnect water pump lower radiator hose and radiator support bracket.
33. Disconnect lower radiator hose from radiator and degas bottle supply hose.
34. Disconnect transaxle oil cooler hose.
35. Disconnect wire harness electrical connector.
36. Disconnect auxiliary oil cooler.
37. Drain engine oil into suitable container.
38. Remove starter motor, engine rear plate and torque converter nuts.
39. Disconnect stabilizer links from stabilizer bar and separate lower control arms from steering knuckles.
40. Separate tie rod ends from steering knuckles.
41. Remove both halfshafts from steering knuckles.
42. Support engine with cradle tool No. 014-00765, or equivalent.
43. Remove four subframe to body bolts, **Fig. 8.**

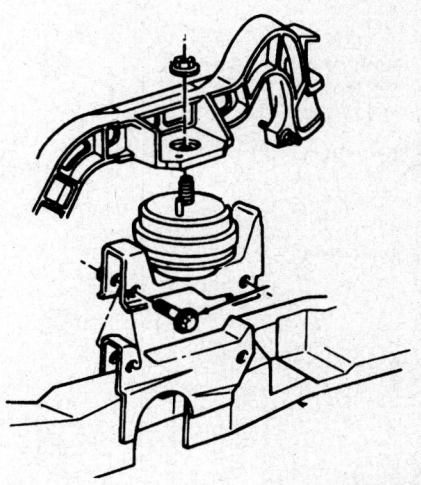

Fig. 3   Engine & transaxle mount replacement

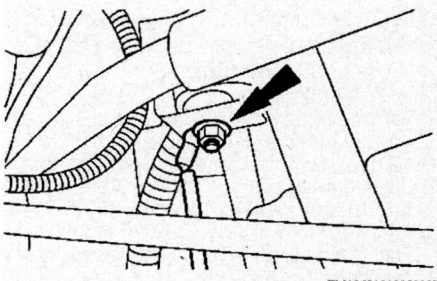

Fig. 6   Ground strap electrical connector replacement

44. Lower engine, transaxle and subframe assembly.
45. Reverse procedure to install.

INTAKE MANIFOLD
REPLACE
DOHC Engine
UPPER

1. Remove air cleaner outlet tube.
2. Remove accelerator cable splash shield.
3. Disconnect throttle and cruise control cables.
4. Disconnect throttle position sensor and idle air control valve electrical connectors, then the harness from throttle body.
5. Disconnect Exhaust Gas Recirculation (EGR) vacuum regulator and vacuum supply hoses.
6. Disconnect PCV and EVAP vacuum hoses.
7. Remove EGR valve and vacuum regulator valve.
8. Remove eight mounting bolts and upper intake manifold.
9. Reverse procedure to install, noting the following:
   a. Install new gaskets.
   b. **Torque** upper intake manifold

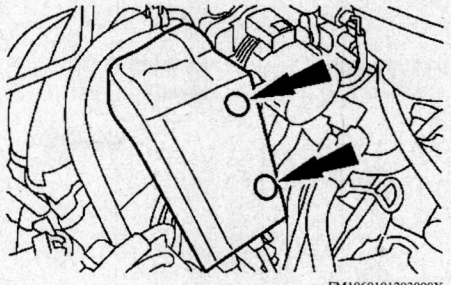

Fig. 4   Snow shield replacement

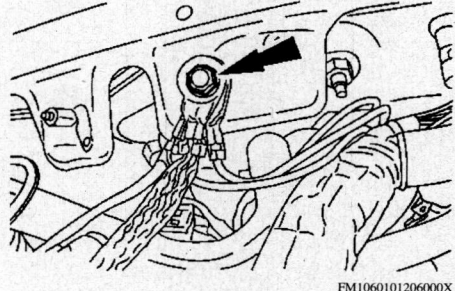

Fig. 7   Ground electrical connectors replacement

mounting bolts to 89 inch lbs., in sequence, **Fig. 9**.

LOWER

1. Relieve fuel system pressure as outlined in "Precautions."
2. Remove upper intake manifold as outlined in "Upper."
3. Disconnect fuel line spring lock coupling.
4. Disconnect fuel injector electrical connectors.
5. Remove mounting bolts in sequence, **Fig. 10**.
6. Remove lower intake manifold.
7. Remove fuel rail and injectors.
8. Reverse procedure to install, noting the following:
   a. Install new gaskets.
   b. Lubricate new O-ring seals lightly with suitable motor oil. **Do not use silicone grease.**
   c. **Torque** bolts to 89 inch lbs., in sequence, **Fig. 11**.

OHV Engine
UPPER

1. Remove air cleaner and outlet tube.
2. Remove snow shield, then the accelerator and speed control actuator cables.
3. Remove throttle return spring from throttle body.
4. Remove accelerator cable bracket and position aside.
5. Disconnect vacuum hoses and evaporative emissions return tube.
6. Disconnect idle air control valve and throttle position sensor.
7. Disconnect engine wiring harness from intake manifold support bracket.

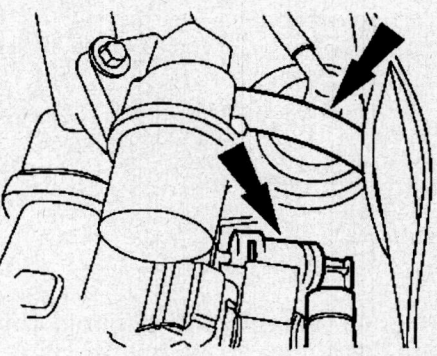

Fig. 5   Chassis vacuum hose replacement

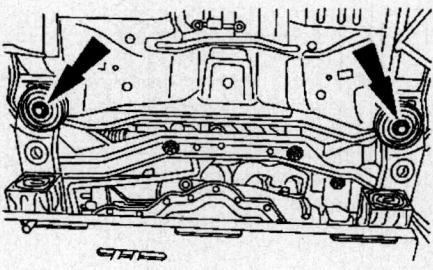

Fig. 8   Subframe to body bolts replacement

8. Remove upper intake manifold support bracket.
9. Disconnect Positive Crankcase Ventilation (PCV) tube from upper intake manifold.
10. Disconnect EGR tube from valve.
11. Disconnect vacuum tube from EGR valve.
12. Disconnect vacuum tube from upper intake manifold and Electronic Vacuum Regulator (EVR).
13. Disconnect electrical connector from EVR.
14. Disconnect wiring harness retaining clip and spark plug wire holder.
15. Remove mounting bolts and upper intake manifold.
16. Reverse procedure to install, noting the following:
   a. Hand tighten mounting bolts in sequence, **Fig. 12**.
   b. **Torque** mounting bolts to 89 inch lbs., in sequence.

LOWER

1. Disconnect fuel supply line.
2. Remove upper intake manifold as outlined in "Upper."
3. Remove both valve covers.
4. Disconnect engine control sensor wiring harness from fuel injectors.
5. Remove fuel injection supply manifold and fuel injectors as an assembly.
6. Disconnect heater hose and coolant temperature sender.
7. Disconnect engine coolant temperature sensor and degas bottle hose.
8. Disconnect upper radiator hose from thermostat housing.

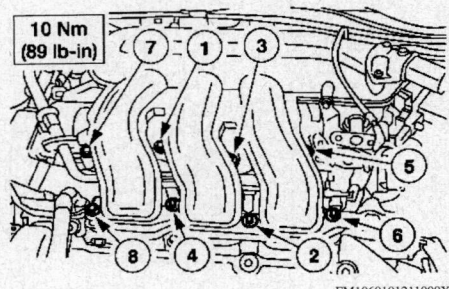

Fig. 9 Upper intake manifold bolt tightening sequence. DOHC engine

9. Remove Camshaft Position (CMP) sensor.
10. Remove lower intake manifold.
11. Reverse procedure to install, noting the following:
    a. Apply a drop of silicone gasket and sealant at four cylinder block to cylinder head seams, **Fig. 13.**
    b. Position gaskets and end seals.
    c. **Torque** mounting bolts to 11 ft. lbs., in sequence, **Fig. 14.**
    d. **Torque** bolts to 24 ft. lbs., in sequence, **Fig. 14.**

EXHAUST MANIFOLD
REPLACE
DOHC Engine
LEFTHAND

1. Remove lefthand exhaust manifold to pipe nuts.
2. Remove coolant tube bracket bolt.
3. Disconnect lefthand heated oxygen sensor electrical connector from coolant tube.
4. Raise and support vehicle.
5. Remove pin type retainers, mounting bolts and front splash shield.
6. Remove lower exhaust manifold nuts.
7. Remove coolant tube lower bracket.
8. Lower vehicle.
9. Remove upper mounting nuts and exhaust manifold.
10. Reverse procedure to install, noting the following:
    a. Install new exhaust manifold gasket.
    b. **Torque** nuts to 13–16 ft. lbs., in sequence, **Fig. 15.**
    c. **Torque** manifold to pipe nuts to 30 ft. lbs.

RIGHTHAND

1. Remove cowl panel grille.
2. Remove righthand valve cover.
3. Disconnect exhaust gas recirculation tube from exhaust manifold.
4. Raise and support vehicle.
5. Remove manifold to Y-pipe nuts.
6. Remove engine support insulator nut.
7. Lower vehicle.
8. Raise engine until exhaust manifold can be removed using suitable engine lifting device.
9. Remove nuts in sequence, **Fig. 16.**

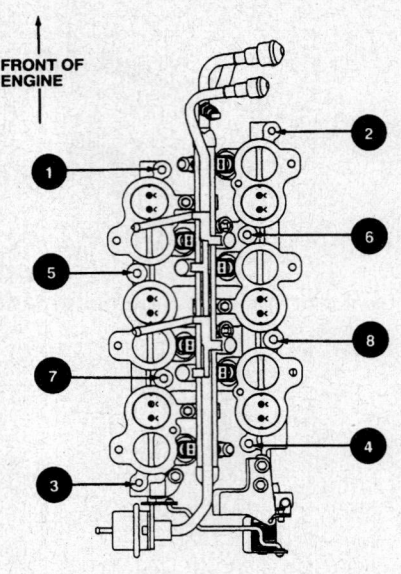

Fig. 10 Lower intake manifold bolt removal sequence. DOHC engine

10. Remove exhaust manifold.
11. Reverse procedure to install, noting the following:
    a. Install new exhaust manifold gasket.
    b. **Torque** exhaust manifold nuts to 13–16 ft. lbs., in sequence, **Fig. 17.**

OHV Engine
LEFTHAND

1. Disconnect heated oxygen sensor electrical connector.
2. Remove oil dipstick tube.
3. Disconnect power steering pressure line from power steering pump.
4. Remove nut from power steering line hold-down bracket and position hose aside.
5. Disconnect secondary air injection tube from exhaust manifold.
6. Separate dual converter Y-pipe from exhaust manifold.
7. Remove four exhaust manifold bolts and two stud bolts.
8. Remove exhaust manifold and gasket.
9. Reverse procedure to install, noting the following:
    a. Install new gasket.
    b. **Torque** mounting bolts to 89 inch lbs., in sequence, **Fig. 18.**
    c. **Torque** bolts to 16 ft. lbs., in sequence.

RIGHTHAND

1. Remove cowl vent screen and cowl extension.
2. Disconnect oxygen sensor electrical connector.
3. Remove exhaust manifold to exhaust gas recirculation tube.
4. Remove exhaust manifold heat shield.
5. Disconnect catalytic converter from exhaust manifold.

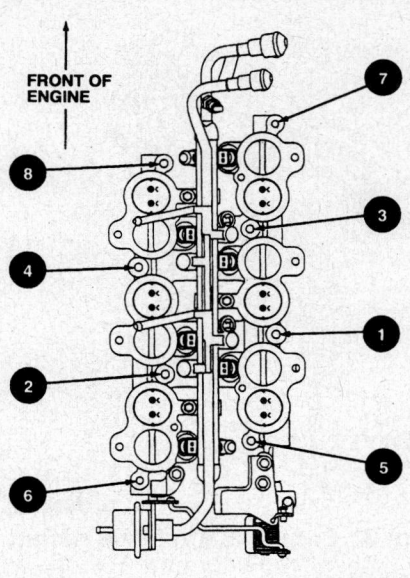

Fig. 11 Lower intake manifold bolt tightening sequence. DOHC engine

6. Remove six mounting bolts and exhaust manifold.
7. Reverse procedure to install, noting the following:
    a. Install new exhaust manifold gasket.
    b. **Torque** bolts to 89 inch lbs., in sequence, **Fig. 19.**
    c. **Torque** bolts to 16 ft. lbs., in sequence.

CYLINDER HEAD
REPLACE
DOHC Engine
LEFTHAND

1. Remove coolant bypass tube.
2. Remove exhaust manifold.
3. Remove water pump as outlined in "Water Pump, Replace."
4. Remove timing chain and gears as outlined in "Timing Chain, Replace."
5. Remove air cleaner outlet tube.
6. Remove accelerator cable splash shield.
7. Disconnect throttle and cruise control cables.
8. Disconnect throttle position sensor and idle air control valve electrical connectors, then the harness from throttle body.
9. Disconnect Exhaust Gas Recirculation (EGR) vacuum regulator and vacuum supply hoses.
10. Disconnect PCV and EVAP vacuum hoses.
11. Remove EGR valve and vacuum regulator valve.
12. Remove eight mounting bolts and upper intake manifold.
13. Remove both valve covers as outlined in "Valve Cover, Replace."

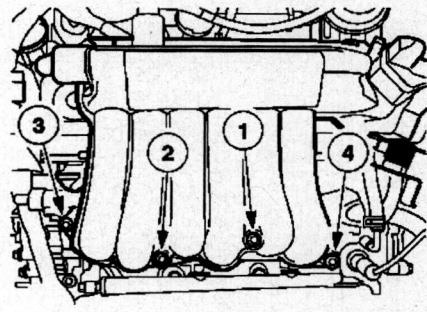

Fig. 12 Upper intake manifold bolt tightening sequence. OHV engine

FM1060101210000X

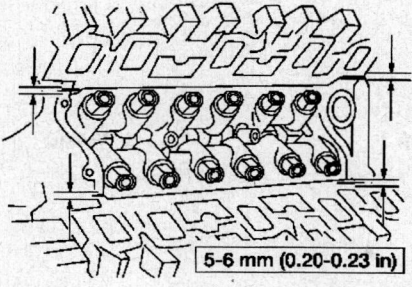

Fig. 13 Lower intake manifold silicone gasket sealant placement. OHV engine

5-6 mm (0.20-0.23 in)

FM1060101212000X

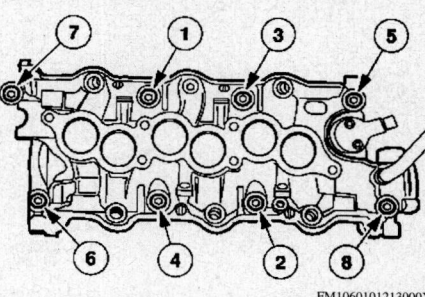

Fig. 14 Lower intake manifold bolt tightening sequence. OHV engine

FM1060101213000X

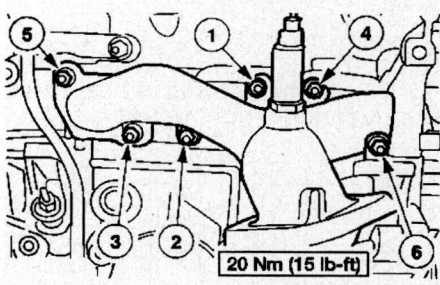

Fig. 15 Lefthand exhaust manifold tightening sequence. DOHC engines

20 Nm (15 lb-ft)

FM1060101216000X

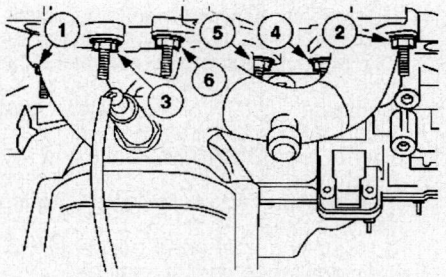

Fig. 16 Righthand exhaust manifold bolt loosening sequence. DOHC engine

FM1060101217000X

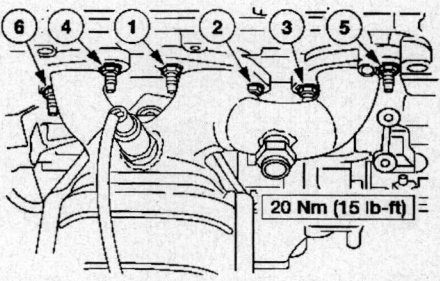

Fig. 17 Righthand exhaust manifold bolt tightening sequence. DOHC engine

20 Nm (15 lb-ft)

FM1060101218000X

14. Remove camshaft journal cap bolts in sequence, **Fig. 20.**
15. Remove camshafts and rocker arms. Mark rocker arms for installation alignment.
16. Remove camshaft followers and hydraulic lash adjusters.
17. Remove exhaust manifold.
18. Remove cylinder head bolts in sequence, **Fig. 21.**
19. Remove cylinder head. Discard gasket and bolts.
20. Reverse procedure to install, noting the following:
    a. Install new head gasket and bolts. **Bolts are torque to yield design and cannot be reused.**
    b. **Torque** cylinder head bolts to 30 ft. lbs., in sequence, **Fig. 22.**
    c. Tighten head bolts and additional 90° in sequence.
    d. Loosen bolts one full turn.
    e. **Torque** cylinder head bolts to 30 ft. lbs., in sequence.
    f. Tighten bolts an additional 90° in sequence.
    g. Final tighten bolts an additional 90° in sequence.

RIGHTHAND

1. Remove coolant bypass tube.
2. Remove timing chain and gears as outlined in "Timing Chain, Replace."
3. Remove air cleaner outlet tube.
4. Remove accelerator cable splash shield.
5. Disconnect throttle and cruise control cables.
6. Disconnect throttle position sensor

and idle air control valve electrical connectors, then the harness from throttle body.
7. Disconnect Exhaust Gas Recirculation (EGR) vacuum regulator and vacuum supply hoses.
8. Disconnect PCV and EVAP vacuum hoses.
9. Remove EGR valve and vacuum regulator valve.
10. Remove eight mounting bolts and upper intake manifold.
11. Remove both valve covers as outlined in "Valve Cover, Replace."
12. Remove camshaft journal cap bolts in sequence, **Fig. 20.**
13. Remove camshafts and rocker arms. Mark rocker arms for installation alignment.
14. Raise and support vehicle.
15. Remove righthand exhaust manifold to pipe bolts.
16. Lower vehicle.
17. Disconnect Exhaust Gas Recirculation (EGR) tube from exhaust manifold.
18. Remove camshaft followers and hydraulic lash adjusters.
19. Remove exhaust manifold as outlined in "Exhaust Manifold, Replace"
20. Remove cylinder head bolts in sequence, **Fig. 21.**
21. Remove cylinder head. Discard gasket and bolts.
22. Reverse procedure to install, noting the following:
    a. Install new head gasket and bolts. **Bolts are torque to yield design and cannot be reused.**
    b. **Torque** cylinder head bolts to 30 ft. lbs., in sequence, **Fig. 22.**
    c. Tighten head bolts and additional

90° in sequence.
d. Loosen bolts one full turn.
e. **Torque** cylinder head bolts to 30 ft. lbs., in sequence.
f. Tighten bolts an additional 90° in sequence.
g. Final tighten bolts an additional 90° in sequence.

OHV Engine

LEFTHAND

1. Remove lower intake manifold as outlined "Intake Manifold, Replace."
2. Remove accessory drive belt.
3. Remove engine anti-roll strut brace.
4. Disconnect alternator electrical connector.
5. Remove alternator.
6. Remove accessory drive belt idler and tensioner pulleys.
7. Remove spark plug wires.
8. Disconnect heated oxygen sensor electrical connector.
9. Remove oil dipstick tube.
10. Disconnect power steering pressure line from power steering pump.
11. Remove nut from power steering line hold-down bracket and position hose aside.
12. Disconnect secondary air injection tube from exhaust manifold.
13. Separate dual converter Y-pipe from exhaust manifold.
14. Remove four exhaust manifold bolts and two stud bolts.
15. Remove exhaust manifold and gasket.
16. Remove power steering pump and bracket assembly.

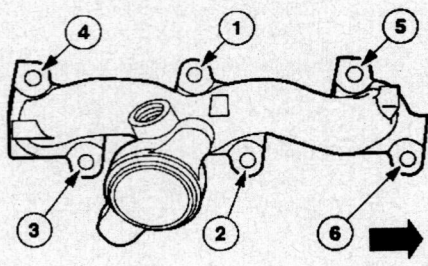

Fig. 18 Lefthand exhaust manifold bolt tightening sequence. OHV engine

FM1060101214000X

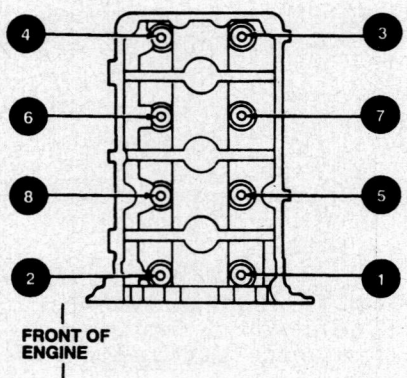

FRONT OF ENGINE

Fig. 21 Cylinder head bolt removal sequence. DOHC engine

FM1069600488000X

17. Remove eight mounting bolts and cylinder head.
18. Reverse procedure to install, noting the following:
   a. Installing new head gasket with V notch faces front of engine.
   b. **Torque** cylinder head bolts to 37 ft. lbs., in sequence, **Fig. 23.**
   c. Loosen cylinder head bolts one full turn in sequence.
   d. **Torque** head bolts to 22 ft. lbs., in sequence.
   e. Tighten bolts an additional 90° in sequence.
   f. Tighten bolts an additional 90° in sequence.

RIGHTHAND

1. Remove lower intake manifold as outlined in "Intake Manifold, Replace."
2. Disconnect Crankshaft Position (CKP) sensor electrical connector.
3. Disconnect oxygen sensor electrical connector.
4. Disconnect wire harness ground connections.
5. Disconnect Powertrain Control Module (PCM) electrical connectors.
6. Disconnect evaporative emissions canister purge valve electrical connector.
7. Position spark plug wires aside.
8. Disconnect Exhaust Gas Recirculation (EGR) tube.
9. Remove exhaust manifold heat shield.
10. Loosen exhaust manifold to catalytic

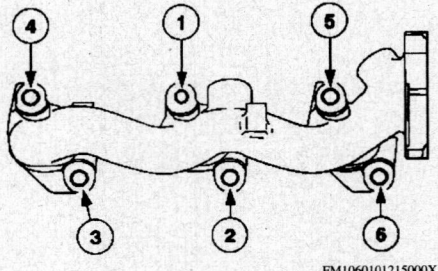

Fig. 19 Righthand exhaust manifold tightening sequence. OHV engine

FM1060101215000X

converter bolts.
11. Remove six exhaust manifold to cylinder head bolts.
12. Disconnect engine wire harness locator.
13. Separate catalytic converter heat shield from cylinder head.
14. Remove eight mounting bolts and cylinder head.
15. Reverse procedure to install, noting the following:
   a. Installing new head gasket with V notch faces front of engine.
   b. **Torque** cylinder head bolts to 37 ft. lbs., in sequence, **Fig. 23.**
   c. Loosen cylinder head bolts one full turn in sequence.
   d. **Torque** head bolts to 22 ft. lbs., in sequence.
   e. Tighten bolts an additional 90° in sequence.
   f. Tighten bolts an additional 90° in sequence.

VALVE COVER

REPLACE

DOHC Engine

LEFTHAND

1. Disconnect crankcase ventilation tube from valve cover.
2. Remove water pump drive belt cover.
3. Remove spark plug wire using a slight twisting motion to break seal.
4. Disconnect spark plug wire holder and position aside.
5. Disconnect wiring harness from valve cover and position aside.
6. Remove mounting bolts, studs and valve cover.
7. Reverse procedure to install, noting the following:
   a. Install new valve cover gasket.
   b. Apply 5 mm dot of silicone gasket sealant to front cover to cylinder head joints.
   c. **Torque** valve cover mounting bolts to 89 inch lbs., in sequence, **Fig. 24.**

RIGHTHAND

1. Remove upper intake manifold as outlined in "Intake Manifold, Replace."
2. Remove ignition coil and bracket.
3. Remove spark plug wires.
4. Disconnect differential pressure feed-

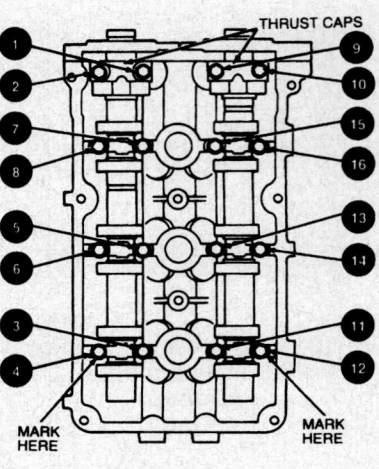

THRUST CAPS

MARK HERE   MARK HERE

FM1069600487000X

Fig. 20 Camshaft journal cap bolt removal sequence. DOHC engine

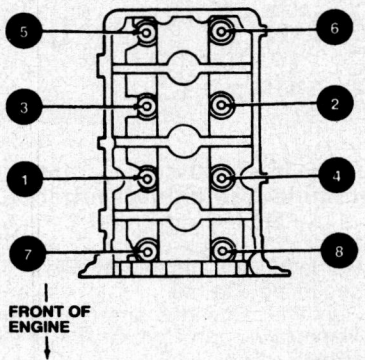

FRONT OF ENGINE

FM1069600490000X

Fig. 22 Cylinder head bolt tightening sequence. DOHC engine

back exhaust gas recirculation electrical connector.
5. Remove wiring harness nut and position harness aside.
6. Disconnect crankcase ventilation tube from valve cover.
7. Remove mounting bolts, studs and valve cover.
8. Reverse procedure to install, noting the following:
   a. Install new valve cover gasket.
   b. Apply 5 mm dot of silicone gasket and sealant to front cover cylinder head joints.
   c. **Torque** valve cover mounting bolts to 89 inch lbs., in sequence, **Fig. 25.**

OHV Engine

LEFTHAND

1. Remove ignition coil.
2. Disconnect crankcase ventilation hose.
3. Position engine wiring harness from front and back of valve cover aside.
4. Remove radio suppressor.
5. Remove retainers and position spark

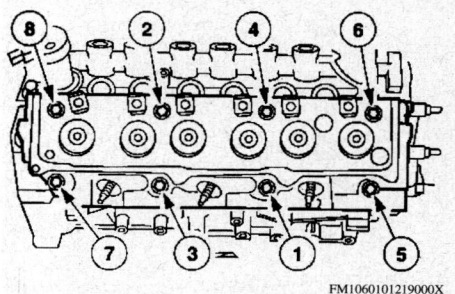

Fig. 23 Cylinder head bolt torque sequence. OHV engine

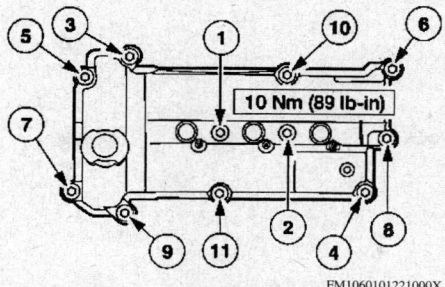

Fig. 24 Lefthand valve cover tightening sequence. DOHC engine

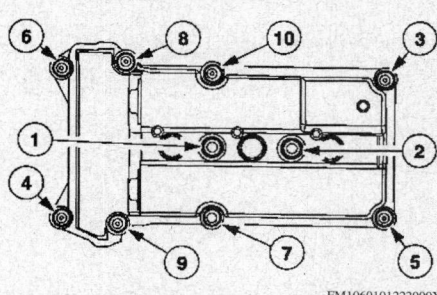

Fig. 25 Righthand valve cover tightening sequence. DOHC engine

plug wires aside.
6. Remove valve cover.
7. Reverse procedure to install, noting the following:
   a. **Do not clean valve cover with solvent.**
   b. Apply bead of silicone gasket and sealant in two places where cylinder head and intake manifold meet.

RIGHTHAND

1. Remove air cleaner outlet tube.
2. Remove accelerator cable splash shield.
3. Disconnect throttle and cruise control cables.
4. Disconnect throttle position sensor and idle air control valve electrical connectors, then the harness from throttle body.
5. Disconnect Exhaust Gas Recirculation (EGR) vacuum regulator and vacuum supply hoses.
6. Disconnect PCV and EVAP vacuum hoses.
7. Remove EGR valve and vacuum regulator valve.
8. Remove eight mounting bolts and upper intake manifold.
9. Position degas bottle aside.
10. Position fuel charge harness aside.
11. Position spark plug wires aside.
12. Remove valve cover.
13. Reverse procedure to install, noting the following:
   a. **Do not clean valve cover with solvent.**
   b. Apply bead of silicone gasket and sealant in two places where cylinder head and intake manifold meet.

VALVE ARRANGEMENT

OHV Engine

FRONT TO REAR

Righthand I-E-I-E-I-E
Lefthand E-I-E-I-E-I

CAMSHAFT LOBE LIFT SPECIFICATIONS

DOHC Engine

Exhaust .188 inch
Intake .188 inch

OHV Engine

Exhaust .264 inch
Intake .251 inch

VALVE CLEARANCE SPECIFICATIONS

OHV Engine

If any valve train component is replaced or if valve train components become intermixed, valve clearance will have to be inspected on those valves.
1. Apply pressure to push rod side of rocker arm until hydraulic lifter has bled down and bottomed out using suitable pry bar.
2. Ensure clearance between valve stem and rocker arm is .085–.185 inch.

VALVE ADJUSTMENT

Hydraulic valve lifters are used in this engine. No adjustment is required.

HYDRAULIC LIFTERS

REPLACE

OHV Engine

Before replacing a hydraulic valve lifter for noisy operation, ensure the noise is not caused by improper rocker arm to stem clearance, worn rocker arms, pushrods or valve tips.
1. Set engine to cylinder No. 1 TDC compression.
2. Remove intake manifold as outlined in "Intake Manifold, Replace."
3. Loosen remaining rocker arm fulcrum mounting bolts enough to swing rocker arm aside to allow pushrods to be removed and remove pushrods. Keep pushrods in order so they can be returned to original positions.
4. Remove mounting bolts and roller lifter guide retainer plate, **Fig. 26.**
5. Remove roller lifter guide from lifter pair by lifting straight up.
6. **If lifters are stuck in their bores by excessive varnish or gum buildup, use suitable claw type puller to remove roller lifters with a rocking and twisting motion.**

7. Place roller lifter lifters in rack so they can be installed in original positions.
8. Reverse procedure to install, noting the following:
   a. Ensure word UP and/or button is facing upward when installing roller lifter guide plates.
   b. Lubricate lifters, lifter bores, rocker arms and pushrods with oil conditioner part No. D9AZ-19579-A, or suitable heavy engine oil.
   c. Starting with engine at cylinder No. 1 TDC compression.
   d. Rotate crankshaft one full turn clockwise.
   e. Install exhaust No. 2 and No. 5, intake No. 1 and No. 4 intake push rod, then the rocker arm assembly.
   f. **Torque** rocker arm mounting bolts to 6–11 ft. lbs.
   g. **Torque** mounting bolts 20–28 ft. lbs.
   h. Rotate crankshaft ⅓ turn clockwise.
   i. Install remaining push rod and rocker arm assemblies.
   j. **Torque** rocker arm mounting bolts to 6–11 ft. lbs.
   k. **Torque** mounting bolts 20–28 ft. lbs.
   l. Ensure rocker arm bolts are fully seated to their shoulder after tightening.
   m. If any valve train components were replaced or intermixed, inspect valve clearance as outlined in "Valve Clearance Specifications."

FRONT COVER

REPLACE

DOHC Engine

1. Remove lefthand and righthand valve covers as outlined in "Valve Cover, Replace."
2. Remove power steering pump.
3. Raise and support vehicle.
4. Remove righthand front wheel and inner splash shield.
5. Remove dual converter Y-pipe.
6. Drain engine oil into suitable container.
7. Remove engine to transaxle bracket.
8. Remove torque converter inspection cover.
9. Remove oil pan.

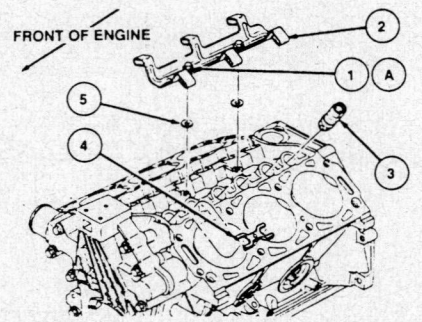

FRONT OF ENGINE

Item	Description
1A	Bolt (2 Req'd) (Part of 6K654)
2	Tappet Guide Plate and Retainer
3	Valve Tappet (12 Req'd)
4	Valve Tappet Guide Plate (6 Req'd)
5	Washer (2 Req'd) (Part of 6K564)
A	Tighten to 10-14 N·m (8-10 Lb-Ft)

FM1069500392000X

Fig. 26 Roller lifter replace. OHV engine

10. Remove mounting nut, then position power steering pressure line and muffler aside.
11. Remove alternator, crankshaft pulley and Crankshaft Position (CKP) sensor.
12. Remove air conditioning compressor to front cover bracket.
13. Disconnect Camshaft Position (CMP) sensor.
14. Remove belt tensioner.
15. Remove engine cooling fan.
16. Install suitable engine support tool.
17. Remove upper air conditioning compressor bolts and position air conditioning compressor aside.
18. Lower vehicle.
19. Remove air conditioning bracket.
20. Remove mounting bolts, studs and front cover.
21. Reverse procedure to install, noting the following:
    a. Install new gaskets in front cover.
    b. Apply .24 inch bead of gasket and sealer to cylinder block to lower block and cylinder head mating surfaces. Front cover must be installed and bolts tightened within six minutes of applying sealant.
    c. **Torque** front cover mounting bolt to 18 ft. lbs., in sequence, **Fig. 27**.

OHV Engine

1. Drain coolant into suitable container.
2. Remove engine anti-roll strut brace.
3. Remove engine roll restrictor.
4. Remove coolant expansion tank.
5. Loosen water pump pulley bolts.
6. Raise and support vehicle.
7. Remove crankshaft damper.
8. Disconnect lower radiator hose.
9. Remove Crankshaft Position (CKP) sensor.
10. Raise and support vehicle.
11. Remove starter motor.

12. Remove engine rear plate.
13. Drain engine oil into suitable container.
14. Remove oil pan.
15. Remove alternator and support brace.
16. Remove accessory drive belt, drive belt idler pulley and drive belt tensioner.
17. Remove air conditioning compressor bracket.
18. Disconnect heater hose.
19. Remove water pump pulley.
20. Remove engine front cover and water pump as an assembly.
21. Reverse procedure to install, noting the following:
    a. Apply pipe sealant with Teflon to bolts No. 1, 2, 3, 6 and 7, **Fig. 28**.
    b. **Torque** front cover mounting bolts to 18 ft. lbs., in sequence, **Fig. 28**.

FRONT COVER SEAL
REPLACE

OHV Engine

REMOVAL

1. Loosen accessory drive belts and remove righthand front wheel.
2. Remove four crankshaft pulley to damper mounting bolts, then the remove accessory drive belt and pulley.
3. Remove mounting bolt, and vibration damper using suitable puller.
4. Pry seal from front timing cover using flat bladed screwdriver, or other suitable tool. **Do not damage front cover or crankshaft.**

INSTALLATION

1. Lubricate replacement seal lip with suitable, clean engine oil and install seal with suitable seal installer.
2. Lubricate inner hub surface of vibration damper with suitable clean engine oil and apply RTV sealant to keyway of inner hub surface of vibration damper.
3. Install vibration damper and tighten mounting bolt.
4. Install crankshaft pulley and tighten bolts.
5. Install accessory drive belts and righthand front wheel.

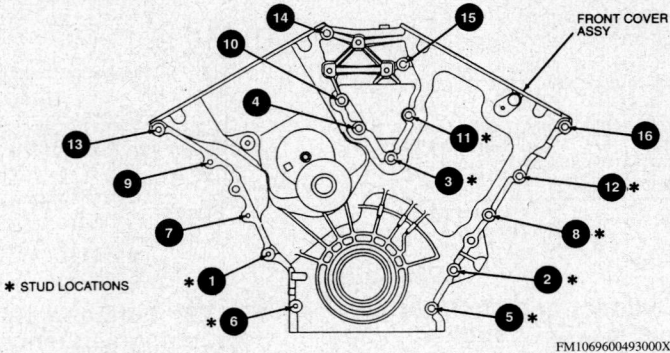

* STUD LOCATIONS

FM1069600493000X

Fig. 27 Front cover bolt tightening sequence. DOHC engine

TIMING CHAIN
REPLACE

DOHC Engine

1. Remove engine front cover as outlined in "Front Cover, Replace."
2. Remove ignition pulse wheel.
3. Install damper bolt, remove spark plugs and rotate crankshaft clockwise to position crankshaft keyway in 11 o'clock position.
4. Ensure camshaft are correctly located in cylinder No. 1 TDC position. If not, rotate crankshaft one additional turn and inspect.
5. Rotate crankshaft clockwise 120° to 3 o'clock position to place righthand camshafts in neutral position. Ensure camshafts are correctly positioned.
6. Remove righthand timing chain tensioner arm, timing chain guide and timing chain.
7. Rotate crankshaft clockwise two times to position crankshaft keyway in 11 o'clock position and ensure camshafts in neutral position.
8. Remove lefthand timing chain tensioner, tensioner arm and timing chain.
9. Remove crankshaft damper bolt.
10. Reverse procedure to install, noting the following:
    a. Position chain tensioner in suitable soft jawed vise.
    b. Hold chain tensioner ratchet lock mechanism away from ratchet stem with suitable small pick and slowly compress timing chain tensioner.
    c. Retain tensioner piston with .06 inch wire, or paper clip, **Fig. 29**.
    d. Ensure timing marks on sprockets and timing chain are aligned, **Fig. 30**.

OHV Engine

1. Remove front engine cover as outlined in "Front Cover, Replace"
2. Rotate crankshaft until piston No. 1 is at TDC and timing marks are aligned, **Fig. 31**.
3. Remove camshaft sprocket mounting bolt and washer.
4. Slide sprockets and timing chain forward, then remove as an assembly.

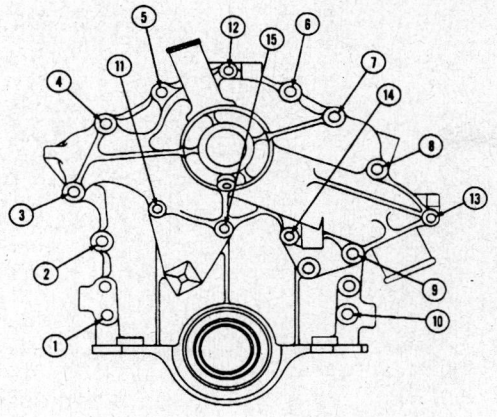

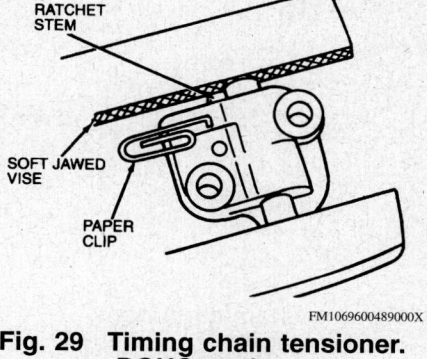

Fig. 29 Timing chain tensioner. DOHC engine

FASTENER AND HOLE NO.	FASTENERS		
	PART NO.	SIZE	FASTENER APPLICATION
1	N804113-S8	M8 x 1.25 x 43.5	F/C TO BLOCK
2	N804113-S100	M8 x 1.25 x 43.5	F/C TO BLOCK
3	N804811-S100	M8 x 1.25 x 70	W/P & F/C TO BLOCK
4	N804811-S8	M8 x 1.25 x 70	W/P & F/C TO BLOCK
5	N605909-S8	M8 x 1.25 x 42	F/C TO BLOCK
6	N804811-S8	M8 x 1.25 x 70	W/P & F/C TO BLOCK
7	N804811-S8	M8 x 1.25 x 70	W/P & F/C TO BLOCK
8	N804811-S8	M8 x 1.25 x 70	W/P & F/C TO BLOCK
9	N804811-S8	M8 x 1.25 x 70	W/P & F/C TO BLOCK
10	N605909-S8	M8 x 1.25 x 42	F/C TO BLOCK
11	N804166-S8	M6 x 1 x 25	W/P TO F/C
12	N804166-S8	M6 x 1 x 25	W/P TO F/C
13	N804166-S8	M6 x 1 x 25	W/P TO F/C
14	N804166-S8	M6 x 1 x 25	W/P TO F/C
15	N804166-S8	M6 x 1 x 25	W/P TO F/C

W/P — Water Pump Assy
F/C — Front Cover Assy
T/P — Timing Pointer

Fig. 28 Timing cover & water pump replacement. OHV engine

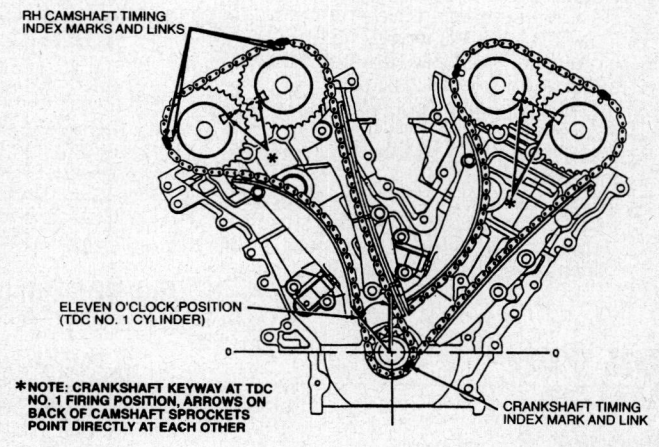

*NOTE: CRANKSHAFT KEYWAY AT TDC NO. 1 FIRING POSITION, ARROWS ON BACK OF CAMSHAFT SPROCKETS POINT DIRECTLY AT EACH OTHER

Fig. 30 Timing mark alignment. DOHC engine

5. Reverse procedure to install, noting the following:
   a. Slide timing chain and sprockets on with timing marks aligned, **Fig. 32.**
   b. Camshaft bolt is special oil transferring part. **Do not replace with standard bolt.**

CAMSHAFT
REPLACE
DOHC Engine

1. Remove timing chain and gears as outlined in "Timing Chain, Replace."
2. Remove upper intake manifold as outlined in "Intake Manifold, Replace."
3. Remove both valve covers as outlined in "Valve Cover, Replace."
4. Remove camshaft journal cap bolts in sequence, **Fig. 20.**
5. Remove camshafts and rocker arms. Mark rocker arms for installation alignment.
6. Reverse procedure to install.

OHV Engine

1. Remove engine and mount in suitable work stand.
2. Remove front cover and timing chain as outlined in "Timing Chain, Replace."
3. Remove intake manifolds and hydraulic valve lifters as outlined in "Hydraulic Lifters, Replace."
4. Remove camshaft thrust plate and pull

camshaft from cylinder block. **Do not damage bearings, journals and lobes.**
5. Reverse procedure to install. Lubricate lifters, lifter bores, rocker arms and pushrods with oil conditioner part No. D9AZ-19579-A, or suitable heavy engine oil.

PISTON & ROD ASSEMBLY

Assemble the rod to the piston with the notch on the piston dome on the same side as the button on the connecting rod identification marks. Assemble piston and rod assembly in engine with notch in dome facing front of engine, **Fig. 33.**

After installation, inspect connecting rod big end side clearance. Clearance should be .006–.014 inch.

MAIN & ROD BEARINGS

Main bearings are available in standard sizes and undersizes of .001 and .002 inch.

DOHC Engine
CONNECTING ROD

1. **Torque** connecting rod caps and bolts to 17 ft. lbs.

2. **Torque** caps and bolts to 32 ft. lbs.

MAIN BEARINGS

The bolts and studs vary in size and length. Ensure bolts and studs are installed in correct position.
1. **Torque** bolts and studs 1–8 to 18 ft. lbs., in sequence, **Fig. 34.**
2. **Torque** bolts and studs 9–16 to 30 ft. lbs.
3. Tighten bolts and studs 1–16 an additional 90° in sequence.
4. **Torque** bolts and studs 17–22 to 18 ft. lbs., in sequence.

OHV
MAIN BEARINGS

Torque bolts to 59 ft. lbs., in pairs sequence, **Fig. 35.**

CRANKSHAFT REAR OIL SEAL
REPLACE

1. Remove transaxle as outlined in MOTOR's "Domestic Transmission, In-Vehicle Service" manual or "Transmission Service DVD."
2. Remove flywheel.
3. Remove rear cover plate.

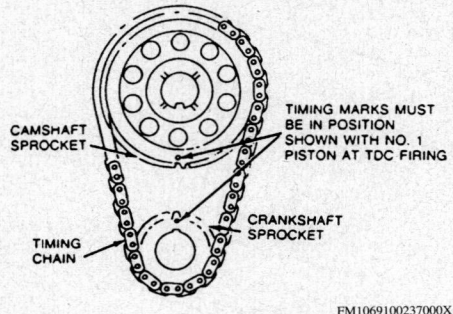

Fig. 31 Timing chain alignment. OHV engine

4. Punch hole into seal metal surface between lip and block using suitable tool.
5. Remove seal using slide hammer tool No. T77L-9533-B, or equivalent.
6. Coat crankshaft seal area and lip with suitable engine oil.
7. Install seal using tool No. T82L-6701-A, or equivalent.
8. Install rear cover plate and two dowels.
9. Install flywheel.
10. Install transaxle as outlined in **MOTOR's "Domestic Transmission, In-Vehicle Service" manual** or **"Transmission Service DVD."**

OIL PAN
REPLACE
DOHC Engine

1. Raise and support vehicle.
2. Remove righthand front wheel and inner splash shield.
3. Remove dual converter Y-pipe.
4. Drain engine oil into suitable container.
5. Remove engine to transaxle bracket.
6. Remove torque converter inspection cover.
7. Remove oil pan.
8. Reverse procedure to install, noting the following:
   a. Apply .40 inch diameter dot of suitable silicone gasket and sealer to areas indicated, **Fig. 36.**
   b. **Torque** oil pan mounting bolts to 18 ft. lbs., in sequence, **Fig. 37.**

OHV Engine

This procedure has been modified by a Technical Service Bulletin.
1. Raise and support vehicle.
2. Remove dual converter Y-pipe.
3. Remove starter motor.
4. Remove engine rear plate.
5. Drain engine oil into suitable container.
6. Remove oil pan.
7. Reverse procedure to install, noting the following:
   a. Apply bead of silicone gasket and sealant to front cover and in rear main bearing cap-to-block parting lines.
   b. Install new, longer mounting bolts (kit part No. 2U7Z-6710-AA, includes new gasket).

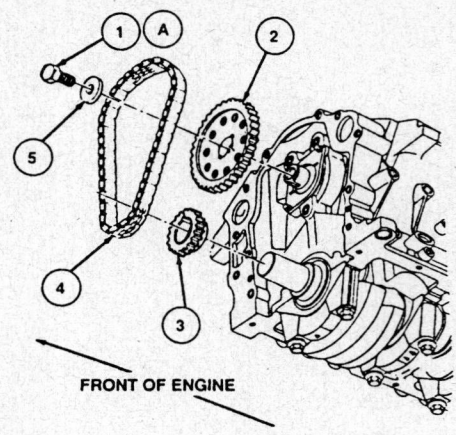

FRONT OF ENGINE

Item	Description
1A	Bolt
2	Camshaft Sprocket
3	Crankshaft Sprocket
4	Timing Chain Lubricate With Oil
5	Washer-Cam Sprocket
A	Tighten to 50-70 N·m (37-51 Lb-Ft)

Fig. 32 Timing chain installation. OHV engine

c. **Torque** four corner mounting bolts to 106 inch lbs.
d. **Torque** remaining 16 mounting bolts from back to front to 106 inch lbs.
e. After engine has run and cooling fan cycles at least once, stop engine and **torque** mounting bolts to 106 inch lbs.

OIL PUMP
REPLACE
DOHC Engine

1. Remove timing chains as outlined in "Timing Chain, Replace."
2. Remove mounting bolts and oil pump from crankshaft.
3. Reverse procedure to install.

OHV Engine

1. Remove oil pan as outlined in "Oil Pan, Replace."
2. Remove oil pump mounting bolts, **Fig. 38.**
3. Remove oil pump and intermediate shaft.
4. Pull intermediate shaft from oil pump.
5. Reverse procedure to install. Ensure intermediate shaft retainer clicks into position.

OIL PUMP SERVICE
OHV Engine

1. Wash all components in suitable solvent and dry with compressed air.

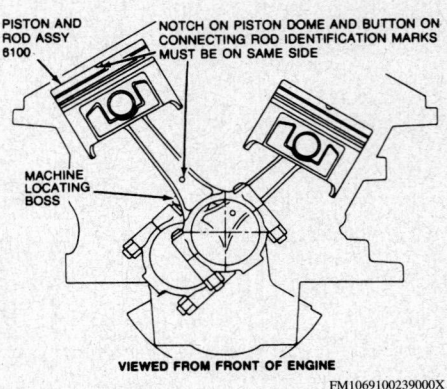

Fig. 33 Piston & rod assembly

2. Ensure all dirt and particles are removed.
3. Inspect inner pump housing for wear or damage.
4. Inspect pump cover mating surface for wear. Scuff marks are normal. If surface is worn or grooved, replace pump.
5. Inspect rotor for nicks, burrs or score marks, and remove imperfections with suitable oil stone.
6. Measure inner tip to outer rotor tip clearance using suitable feeler gauge, **Fig. 39.** Clearance should be .0024–.0071 inch.
7. Install suitable straightedge and measure rotor endplay, **Fig. 40.** Clearance should be .0012–.0035 inch.
8. If any clearance does not meet specifications, replace oil pump.

BELT TENSION DATA

Belt	New, Lbs.	Used, Lbs.
Five-Rib	140–160	110–130
Six-Rib	①	①

① — Automatic tensioner.

SERPENTINE DRIVE BELT

Belt Routing

Refer to **Figs. 41 and 42** for serpentine drive belt routing.

Belt, Replace

1. **On models equipped with DOHC engine,** rotate drive belt tensioner counterclockwise.
2. **On models equipped with OHV engine,** rotate drive belt tensioner clockwise.
3. **On all models,** remove serpentine drive belt.
4. Reverse procedure to install. Ensure spring keeper releases.

COOLING SYSTEM BLEED

1. Select maximum blower motor and heater temperature settings.

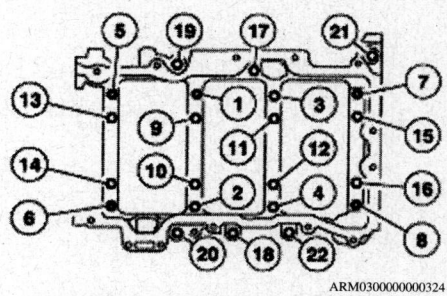

Fig. 34 Main bearing tighten sequence. DOHC engine

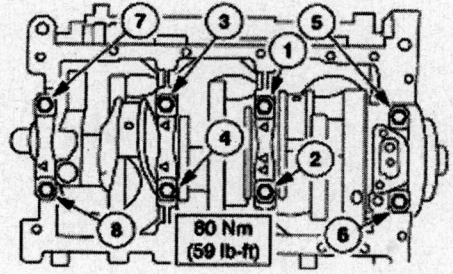

Fig. 35 Main bearing tightening sequence. OHV engine

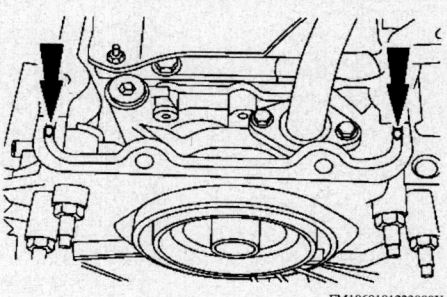

Fig. 36 Silicone gasket and sealer placement. DOHC engine

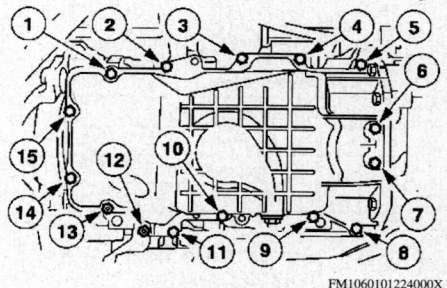

Fig. 37 Oil pan bolt tightening sequence. DOHC engine

2. Set controls to discharge air through instrument panel air conditioning vents.
3. Start engine and allow to idle until operating temperature is reached.
4. Hot air should now blow through air conditioning vents, temperature gauge should rest in NORMAL range and upper radiator hose should feel hot to touch. **If air discharge remains cool and engine coolant temperature gauge does not move, coolant level is low and must be filled, as follows:**
   a. Stop engine, allow to cool.
   b. Add coolant to bring level to top of Cold Fill mark on de-gas bottle.
   c. Start engine and allow it to idle. Feel for hot air at vents.
5. Stop engine and allow to cool. Inspect for leaks.
6. When engine coolant level indicator flashes, approximately one to 1 ½ quarts of coolant may now be added to de-gas bottle after proper refill.

THERMOSTAT
REPLACE
Removal

1. Drain cooling system into suitable container to below level of upper radiator hose.
2. Remove upper radiator hose.
3. Remove mounting bolts, then the housing and thermostat as an assembly. Discard gasket.

Installation

1. Install thermostat into housing. Ensure jiggle valve is up in relation to housing.

2. Install gasket onto housing using bolts to hold position.
3. Install housing and thermostat assembly and mounting bolts.
4. Install upper radiator hose.
5. Fill and bleed cooling system as outlined in "Cooling System Bleed."

WATER PUMP
REPLACE
DOHC Engine

1. Raise and support vehicle.
2. Drain cooling system into suitable container.
3. Remove splash shield.
4. Disconnect water hose from bottom of water pump.
5. Remove radiator lower tube bolt.
6. Lower vehicle.
7. Remove air cleaner, battery and battery tray.
8. Remove water pump belt.
9. Remove radiator upper front tube bolt.
10. Disconnect upper radiator hose and engine vent hose.
11. Disconnect transaxle 10-pin connector.
12. Remove radiator bypass hose assembly.
13. Disconnect thermostat housing and position aside.
14. Disconnect hose from water pump.
15. Remove water pump.
16. Reverse procedure to install, noting the following:
    a. **Torque** water pump mounting bolts to 89 inch lbs.
    b. Tighten mounting bolts an additional 90°.

OHV Engine

1. Drain cooling system into suitable container.
2. Remove accessory drive belt.
3. Remove engine anti roll strut brace and strut.
4. Remove accessory drive belt tensioner.
5. Remove roll restrictor bracket.
6. Remove bolts and water pump pulley.
7. Disconnect water pump inlet hose and Crankshaft Position (CKP) sensor.
8. Remove support bracket.
9. Remove water pump.
10. Reverse procedure to install, noting the following:

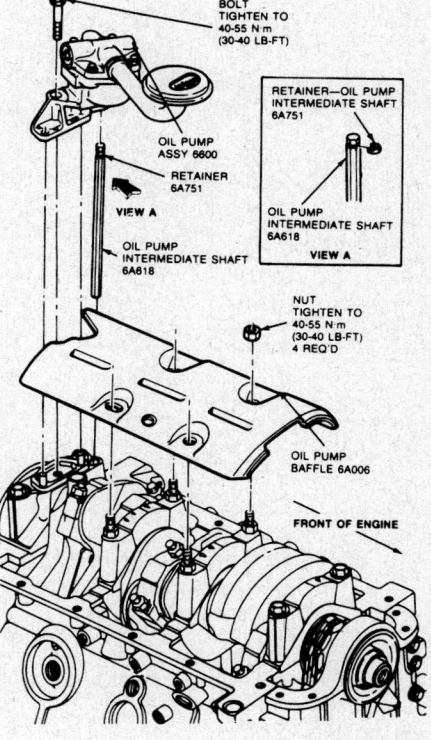

Fig. 38 Oil pump replacement. OHV engine

a. **Torque** numbers 1–7 to 18 ft. lbs., in sequence, **Fig. 43**.
b. **Torque** numbers 8–12 to 89 inch lbs., in sequence.

RADIATOR
REPLACE

1. Remove battery and battery tray.
2. Drain cooling system into suitable container.
3. Disconnect upper radiator hose.
4. Disconnect degas return hose.
5. Disconnect upper transaxle cooler line using suitable disconnect tool.
6. Remove air conditioning condenser mounting bolts.
7. Raise and support vehicle.
8. Disconnect lower radiator hose and transaxle cooler line.
9. Remove condenser to radiator mounting bolts.

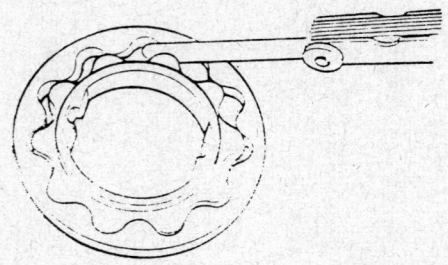

Fig. 39 Oil pump tip clearance. OHV engine

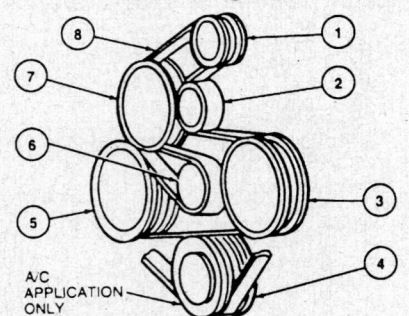

Fig. 42 Serpentine belt routing. OHV engine

Item	Description
1	Generator
2	Drive Belt Tensioner
3	Power Steering Pump
4	A/C Compressor
5	Crankshaft Pulley
6	Idler Pulley
7	Water Pump
8	Drive Belt

10. Remove power steering cooler to radiator mounting bolts.
11. Remove nuts and radiator support bracket.
12. Remove radiator.
13. Reverse procedure to install.

FUEL PUMP

REPLACE

1. Relieve fuel system pressure as outlined in "Precautions."
2. **On models equipped with flexible fuel,** remove fuel from tank as follows:
   a. Remove foam and rubber protective cover from special quick disconnect fitting on fuel drain tube found on righthand side of fuel tank.
   b. Attach adapter hose tool No. 034-00020, or equivalent, to suitable fuel storage tank.
   c. Pump fuel from tank.
3. **On models equipped with non-flexible fuel,** remove fuel from fuel tank by pumping it out filler neck using suitable fuel storage tanker.
4. **On all models,** raise and support vehicle.
5. Disconnect and remove fuel filler neck.
6. Support fuel tank and remove tank support straps.

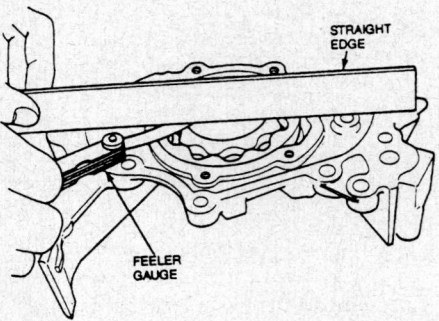

Fig. 40 Oil pump rotor endplay. OHV engine

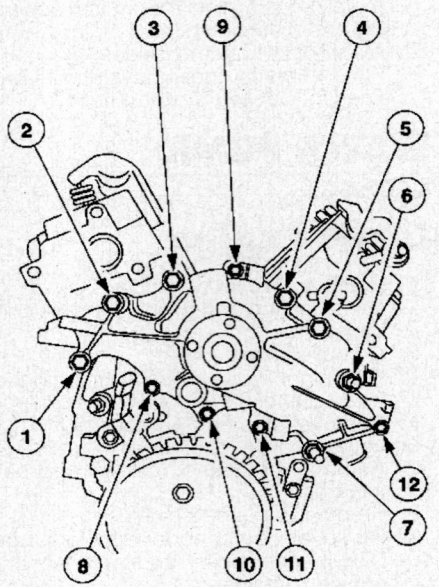

Fig. 43 Water pump bolt tightening sequence. OHV engine

7. Lower fuel tank partially, then remove fuel lines, electrical connectors and vent lines.
8. Remove tank and place on suitable workbench.
9. Remove fuel pump locking ring by turning it counterclockwise.
10. Remove fuel pump, bracket and gasket assembly.
11. Reverse procedure to install.

FUEL FILTER

REPLACE

1. Relieve fuel system pressure as outlined in "Precautions."
2. Twist push connect fittings at each end of filter until they move freely on tube.
3. Bend and break shipping tab from hairpin clip and spread two clip legs approximately ⅛ inch, **Fig. 44.**
4. Remove clip from tube and fitting by pulling gently on triangular end.
5. Separate fitting and hose assembly from fuel filter.

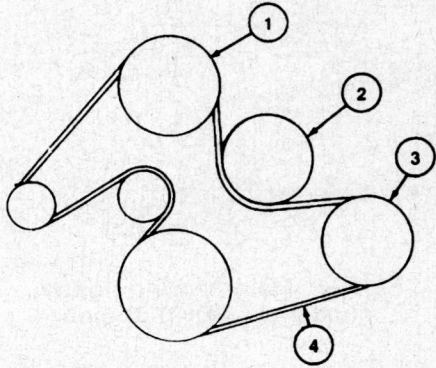

Item	Description
1	Power Steering Pump
2	Water Pump
3	A/C Compressor
4	Drive Belt

Fig. 41 Serpentine belt routing. DOHC engine

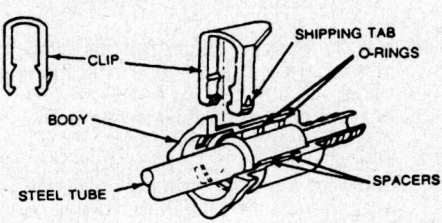

Fig. 44 Push connect fitting removal

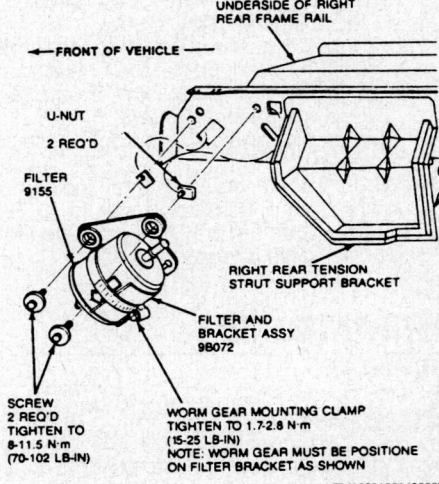

Fig. 45 Fuel filter replacement

6. Install retainer clips in each connect fitting.
7. Loosen worm gear mounting clip and remove filter from bracket, **Fig. 45.**
8. Reverse procedure to install.

TIGHTENING SPECIFICATIONS

Year	Component	Torque Ft. Lbs.
DOHC ENGINE		
2004–07	Air Conditioning Compressor	18
	Alternator Mounting	18
	Ball Joint Nuts	59
	Camshaft Cap Bolt	89①
	Camshaft Oil Seal Retainer	89①
	Camshaft Position Sensor	89①
	Connecting Rod	⑩
	Crankshaft Position Sensor	89①
	Cylinder Head	②
	EGR Tube	30
	EGR Valve	18
	Engine Mount	52
	Exhaust Manifold	⑤
	Flexplate	59
	Front Cover	⑧
	Fuel Rail	89①
	Halfshaft	191
	Intake Manifold	④
	Knock Sensor	13
	Lefthand Engine Support Insulator, Bolt	52
	Lefthand Engine Support Insulator, Nut	66
	Main Bearing Cap	⑩
	Oil Pan	③
	Oil Pan To Transaxle	30
	Oil Pump	89①
	Oil Separator	89①
	Power Steering Pressure Line	27
	Power Steering Pump	18
	Righthand Engine Support Insulator, Nut	66
	Righthand Engine Support Insulator, Through Bolt	89
	Shifter Cable	13
	Spark Plugs	11
	Steering Shaft Pinch Bolt	18
	Subframe Bolts	76
	Timing Chain Guide	18
	Timing Chain Tensioner	18
	Torque Converter To Flex Plate	27
	Valve Cover	⑥
	Water Pump	⑨
	Y-Pipe Nuts	30
	Y-Pipe To Exhaust Manifold	30
OHV ENGINE		
2004–07	Accelerator Cable Bracket	13
	Accessory Drive Belt Idler Pulley	35
	Accessory Drive Belt Tensioner	18
	Accessory Drive Belt Tensioner Pulley	35
	Air Conditioning Compressor To Bracket	18
	Air Conditioning Compressor Bracket To Engine	35

TIGHTENING SPECIFICATIONS—Continued

Year	Component	Torque Ft. Lbs.
OHV ENGINE		
2004–07	Air Conditioning Compressor Bracket Stabilizer	18
	Air Conditioning Manifold & Tube	89①
	Camshaft Position Sensor	18①
	Camshaft Sprocket	46
	Camshaft Synchronizer Clamp	18
	Camshaft Thrust Plate	89①
	Connecting Rod	26
	Crankshaft Damper	107
	Crankshaft Pulley	35
	Cylinder Head	②
	EGR Tube, Righthand Exhaust	30
	EGR Tube, EGR Valve	30
	EGR Valve	18
	Engine Rear Insulator To Front Subframe	40
	Engine Rear Insulator To Transaxle Bracket	72
	Engine Rear Plate	106①
	Engine Roll Restrictor	35
	Engine Roll Restrictor To Front Cover & Alternator	18
	Exhaust Manifold	⑤
	Exhaust Manifold Heat Shield	89①
	Flywheel	59
	Front Cover	⑧
	Fuel Injection Supply Manifold	89①
	Halfshaft To Steering Knuckle	190
	Intake Manifold	④
	Lower Control Arm To Steering Knuckle	59
	Main Bearing Cap	⑩
	Oil Filter Mounting Boss	25
	Oil Pan	③
	Oil Pan Drain Plug	10
	Oil Pump	35
	Power Steering Pressure Line	35
	Power Steering Pump Bracket	35
	Righthand Engine Insulator Bracket To Transaxle	44
	Righthand Engine Insulator Through Bolt	89
	Righthand Engine Insulator To Front Subframe	66
	Rocker Arm	⑦
	Secondary Air Injection Tube	30
	Spark Plugs	11
	Starter Motor	18
	Transaxle to Engine	37
	Valve Cover	106①
	Water Pump	⑨

① — Inch lbs.
② — Refer to "Cylinder Head, Replace" for tightening specifications and sequence.
③ — Refer to "Oil Pan, Replace" for tightening specifications and sequence.

④ — Refer to "Intake Manifold, Replace" for tightening specifications and sequence.

⑤ — Refer to "Exhaust Manifold, Replace" for tightening specifications and sequence.

⑥ — Refer to "Valve Cover, Replace" for tightening specifications and sequence.

⑦ — Refer to "Hydraulic Lifters, Replace" for tightening specifications and sequence.

⑧ — Refer to "Front Cover, Replace" for tightening specifications and sequence.

⑨ — Refer to "Water Pump, Replace" for tightening specifications and sequence.

⑩ — Refer to "Main & Rod Bearings" for tightening specifications and sequence.

Rear Suspension

NOTE: On Air Bag Equipped Models, Refer To "Air Bag System Precautions" Located In The Front Of This Manual For System Disarming & Arming Procedures.

NOTE: Refer To "Computer Relearn Procedures" Located In The Front Of This Manual When Battery Power To The Computer Has Been Interrupted.

INDEX

	Page No.
Coil Spring, Replace	5-25
Installation	5-25
Removal	5-25
Control Arm, Replace	5-25
Lower	5-25
Sedan	5-25
Wagon	5-25
Upper	5-25
Installation	5-26
Removal	5-25

	Page No.
Description	5-23
Sedan	5-23
Wagon	5-23
Rear Wheel Spindle, Replace	5-23
Sedan	5-23
Wagon	5-23
Shock Absorber, Replace	5-24
Stabilizer Bar, Replace	5-26
Sedan	5-26
Wagon	5-26

	Page No.
Strut, Replace	5-23
Strut Service	5-24
Tension Strut, Replace	5-24
Sedan	5-24
Wagon	5-24
Installation	5-24
Removal	5-24
Tightening Specifications	5-28
Wheel Bearing, Adjust	5-23

DESCRIPTION

Sedan

These models utilize an independent rear suspension. Each side consists of a McPherson strut, an upper mount and washers, two parallel lower control arms, a tension strut, a spindle and a stabilizer bar mounted on the strut.

The top of the McPherson strut is attached to the inner body side panel, while the lower end of the strut is attached to the spindle with a pinch clamp and bolt. The parallel lower control arms attach to the underbody with nuts and bolts. The tension strut attaches to the lower part of the spindle and to the underbody, **Fig. 1.**

Wagon

These models also utilize an independent rear suspension. Each side consists of an upper and lower control arm, a shock absorber, a two-piece spindle tension control strut and a coil spring.

The top of the shock absorber is attached to the body side panel by a rubber insulated top mount and to the lower control arms by two nuts. The upper control arm attaches to the crossmember and the upper part of the spindle. The lower control arm attaches to the underbody and lower part of the spindle. The coil spring operates against the lower control arm and is located inboard of the shock absorber, **Fig. 2.**

WHEEL BEARING

ADJUST

The rear wheel bearings are of a sealed cartridge design and are not adjustable.

REAR WHEEL SPINDLE

REPLACE

Sedan

1. Remove hub cap or wheel cover.
2. Measure distance from center of hub to lip of fender with vehicle in level static ground position.
3. Remove wheel hub and bearing.
4. Remove brake hose from shock absorber.
5. Remove rear anti-lock brake sensor.
6. **Do not allow brake components to hang from brake hose.**
7. Remove brake backing plate and support with suitable mechanics wire.
8. Remove lower control arm nuts, washers and flag bolts.
9. Remove and discard spindle pinch bolt.
10. Spread pinch joint with suitable large screwdriver.
11. Remove rear spindle.
12. Reverse procedure to install, noting the following:
    a. Cupped side of lower arm mounting washers must face away from bushing.
    b. Install nuts and bolts loosely.
    c. Position suitable floor jack under rear suspension and raise to previously measured height.
    d. Tighten suspension nuts and bolts.

Wagon

1. Remove hub cap or wheel cover.
2. Measure distance from center of hub to lip of fender with vehicle in a level static ground position.
3. Remove wheel hub and bearing.
4. Remove disc brake shield and anti-lock wheel sensor.

5. Place suitable jack stand under lower control arm and slightly raise suspension.
6. Remove and discard bolt and nut, **Fig. 3.**
7. Disconnect shock absorber, then remove washer and bushing.
8. Disconnect upper arm using suitable joint removal tool.
9. Remove wheel spindle. Discard nuts and flag bolts.
10. Reverse procedure to install, noting the following:
    a. Install new flag bolts, nuts and washers.
    b. Before tightening suspension nuts and bolts, raise suspension with suitable floor jack to previous height.

STRUT

REPLACE

1. Position suitable jack or hoist under vehicle, and raise just enough to contact body. **Do not raise vehicle by tension strut.**
2. Remove rear parcel shelf.
3. Raise and support vehicle. Remove tire and wheel assembly.
4. Remove brake differential valve to control arm mounting bolt.
5. Suspend control arm to body using suitable wire.
6. Remove brake hose to shock strut bracket mounting clip and position hose aside.
7. Remove U-bracket, stabilizer bar mounting nut, washer and insulator. Separate stabilizer bar from link.
8. Remove tension strut to spindle mounting nut, washer and insulator.
9. Separate spindle from tension strut by moving it rearward.
10. Remove strut to spindle pinch bolt.

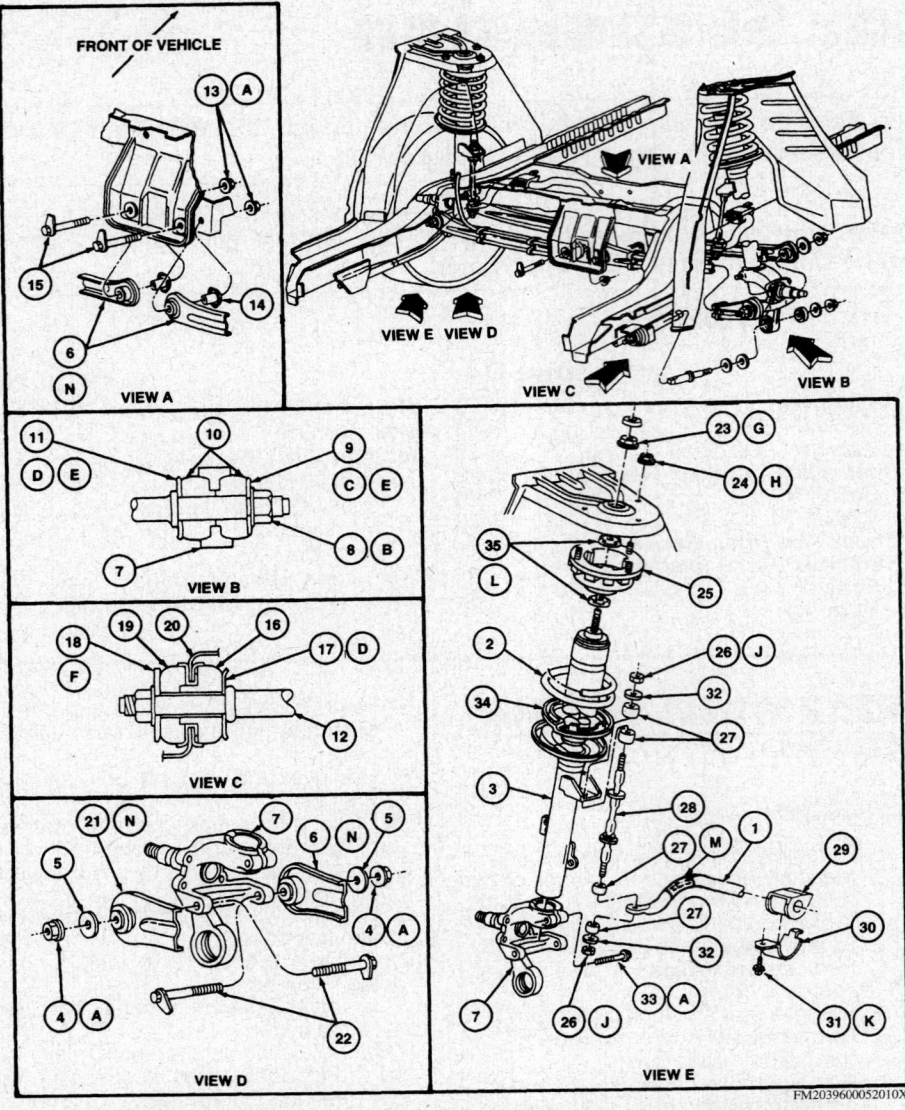

Fig. 1 Exploded view of rear suspension (Part 1 of 2). Sedan

11. Separate pinch joint using pry bar, or other suitable tool.
12. Remove strut from pinch joint then lower vehicle to allow removal of three strut to inner body mounting bolts.
13. Remove strut. **Do not stretch rear brake hose or kink steel brake line.**
14. Reverse procedure to install, noting the following:
    a. Install new mounting components.
    b. Tighten in order: stabilizer link to strut, strut pinch bolt, tension strut to spindle, stabilizer link to stabilizer bar, stabilizer bar U-bracket and strut top mount.

STRUT SERVICE

1. Remove mounting nut, washer, insulator and link.
2. Mark location of insulator to top mount for assembly alignment.
3. Place strut, spring and upper mount assembly in suitable spring compressor. Compress spring.

4. While preventing strut shaft from turning with suitable six-point deep well socket on top of shaft, remove mounting nut with oxygen sensor wrench tool No. T94P-9472-A, or equivalent. **Do not use vise grips or pliers to hold strut shaft.**
5. Loosen spring compressor tool, then remove top mount bracket assembly, spring insulator and spring, **Fig. 4.**
6. Reverse procedure to install. Ensure spring is properly located in upper and lower spring seats, **Fig. 5.**

TENSION STRUT
REPLACE
Sedan

1. Raise vehicle on frame contact hoist using lift pads located rearward of front wheels and forward of rear wheels. Raise hoist only enough to contact body.

2. Working inside trunk, loosen, but do not remove, three strut to inner body mounting nuts.
3. Raise vehicle, and remove tire and wheel assembly.
4. Remove and discard tension strut to spindle mounting nut.
5. Remove and discard tension strut to body mounting nut.
6. While moving spindle rearward, remove tension strut.
7. Install new inner washers and bushings on both ends of tension strut, **Fig. 6.**
8. Install tension strut end into body bracket, outer bushing, washers and nut. **Do not tighten nut now.**
9. While moving spindle rearward, install tension strut in spindle, outer bushing, washer and nut.
10. Ensure bushings are properly seated in mountings, **Fig. 6.**
11. Support spindle with suitable jack stand, and working inside trunk, remove three strut to inner body mounting nuts. Install new nuts and tighten.
12. Remove jack stand, and install tire and wheel assembly.
13. Lower vehicle.

Wagon
REMOVAL

1. Raise vehicle on frame contact hoist.
2. Remove wheel and tension strut to lower control arm mounting nut and bolt.
3. Remove tension strut to body bracket mounting nut and bolt, and tension strut.

INSTALLATION

1. Insert front end of replacement torsion strut in body bracket, then install new mounting nut and bolt. **Do not tighten now.**
2. Position rear end of torsion strut in lower control arm, then install new mounting nut and bolt.
3. Tighten torsion strut to body bracket mounting nut and bolt.
4. Install wheel and tire assembly.

SHOCK ABSORBER
REPLACE

1. Raise and support rear of vehicle. **If a frame contact hoist is used, support lower control arm with floor jack. If a twin post lift is used, support body with floor jacks on lifting pads forward of tension strut body bracket.**
2. Remove tire and wheel assembly.
3. Loosen shock absorber to lower control arm mounting nuts. **Do not remove nuts now.**
4. Lower vehicle and remove rear compartment access panels.
5. Remove shock absorber top mounting nut, washer and insulator.
6. Raise and support vehicle.
7. Remove absorber to lower control arm mounting nuts and absorber. **Shock**

absorbers are gas filled and will require effort to collapse.

8. **Do not grip shock absorber shafts with pliers or vise grips.**
9. Reverse procedure to install. **Use new bushing repair kit.**

COIL SPRING

REPLACE

Removal

1. Raise vehicle on frame contact hoist.
2. Raise lower control arm to normal curb height using suitable floor jack.
3. Remove tire and wheel assembly.
4. Remove brake hose bracket from body.
5. Remove shock absorber.
6. Install spring cage tool No. 164-R3555, or equivalent, on spring.
7. Remove and discard upper ball joint nut, then separate joint from spindle.
8. Slowly lower rear suspension arm and bushing, then remove spring and its insulators.

Installation

1. Install lower spring insulator on control arm. Ensure insulator is seated properly.
2. Position upper insulator on spring and install spring on lower control arm. Ensure spring is properly seated.
3. Slowly raise suspension arm and bushing, guiding upper insulator onto upper spring seat on underbody.
4. Position upper ball joint into suspension arm and bushing.
5. Install shock absorber, stabilizer bar and bracket.
6. Remove spring cage tool.
7. Install brake hose bracket to body.
8. Install tire and wheel assembly.
9. Lower vehicle and inspect rear wheel alignment.

CONTROL ARM

REPLACE

Lower

SEDAN

REMOVAL

1. Raise and support vehicle. **Do not support tension strut and bushing.**
2. Disconnect brake proportioning valve from lefthand front control arm, parking brake cable and conduit from control arms.
3. Remove control arm to spindle mounting bolt, nut and washer.
4. Remove body bracket mounting bolt, nut and control arm.

INSTALLATION

1. Position control arm at body bracket, **Fig. 7.**
2. **Offset must face up (the arms are stamped bottom on lower edge).** Flange edge of righthand rear arm

Item	Description	Item	Description
1	Rear Stabilizer Bar	29	Lower Suspension Arm Stabilizer Bar Insulator (2 Req'd)
2	Rear Spring	30	Stabilizer Bar Bracket (2 Req'd)
3	Shock Absorber	31	Bolt (2 Req'd)
4	Nut (4 Req'd)	32	Washer (4 Req'd)
5	Washer (4 Req'd)	33	Bolt (2 Req'd)
6	Rear Lower Suspension Arm (2 Req'd)	34	Rear Spring Center Mounting Insulator (Part of 18080)
7	Rear Wheel Spindle	35	Washer (2 Req'd)
8	Nut (4 Req'd)	A	Tighten to 68-92 N·m (50-68 Lb-Ft)
9	Washer (2 Req'd)	B	Tighten to 47-63 N·m (35-46 Lb-Ft)
10	Rear Suspension Tie Rod Bushing (4 Req'd)	C	Stamped Rear
11	Washer (2 Req'd)	D	Stamped This Side Out
12	Rear Suspension Tension Strut (2 Req'd)	E	Assemble N802855-S36 and N801335-S36 As Shown
13	Nut (4 Req'd)	F	Assemble 5B536 and 5B537 As Shown
14	Rear Suspension Arm Adjusting Cam Kit (4 Req'd)	G	Tighten to 53-71 N·m (39-53 Lb-Ft)
15	Bolt (4 Req'd)	H	Tighten to 25-34 N·m (19-26 Lb-Ft)
16	Rear Strut Body End Bushing Inner (2 Req'd)	J	Tighten to 7-9 N·m (62-79 Lb-In)
17	Washer (2 Req'd)	K	Tighten to 34-46 N·m (25-33 Lb-Ft)
18	Washer (2 Req'd)	L	Dished-Side Down
19	Bushing - Outer (2 Req'd)	M	Color Code Must Be Installed on RH Side Of Vehicle
20	Body	N	Arm Assemblies Must Be Installed As Shown. Trim Flange To Be Rearward On Front Arms And Left Rear Arm. Trim Flange To Be Forward On Right Rear Arm All Arms Are Stamped Bottom On Lower Surface
21	Forward Lower Suspension Arm (2 Req'd)		
22	Bolt (4 Req'd)		
23	Nut (2 Req'd)		
24	Nut (6 Req'd)		
25	Rear Shock Absorber Bracket (2 Req'd)		
26	Nut (4 Req'd)		
27	Lower Suspension Arm Stabilizer Bar Insulator (8 Req'd)		
28	Rear Stabilizer Bar Link (2 Req'd)		

FM2039600052020X

Fig. 1 Exploded view of rear suspension (Part 2 of 2). Sedan

stamping must face front of vehicle. Other three must face rear of vehicle.
3. **Control arms have two adjustment cams that fit inside bushings at control arm to body attachment. Cam is installed from rear on lefthand arm and from front on righthand arm.**
4. Install new nut and bolt. **Do not tighten now.**
5. Position outer end of arm at spindle, then install new bolt, washer and nut.
6. Attach parking brake cables and brake proportioning valve to control arms.
7. Lower vehicle and inspect rear toe.

WAGON

REMOVAL

1. Raise and support rear of vehicle.
2. Remove tire and wheel assembly.
3. Remove rear spring as outlined in "Coil Spring, Replace."
4. Remove lower control arm to body bracket mounting bolt and control arm.

INSTALLATION

1. Position lower control arm in body bracket.

2. Install new nut and bolt with bolt head toward front of vehicle. **Do not tighten now.**
3. Install rear spring as outlined in "Coil Spring, Replace."
4. Support lower control arm at normal curb height and tighten control arm to body bracket mounting bolt.
5. Tighten lower control arm to spindle mounting bolt.
6. Install tire and wheel assembly.

Upper

REMOVAL

1. Raise and support vehicle.
2. Raise lower control arm to normal curb height using suitable floor jack.
3. Remove wheel and tire assembly, then the brake hose bracket from body.
4. Loosen spindle to lower and upper control arms mounting nuts.
5. Remove and discard upper ball joint nut.
6. Separate joint from spindle.
7. Remove upper control arms to body brackets mounting nuts and bolts. **Ensure spindle does not fall outward.**

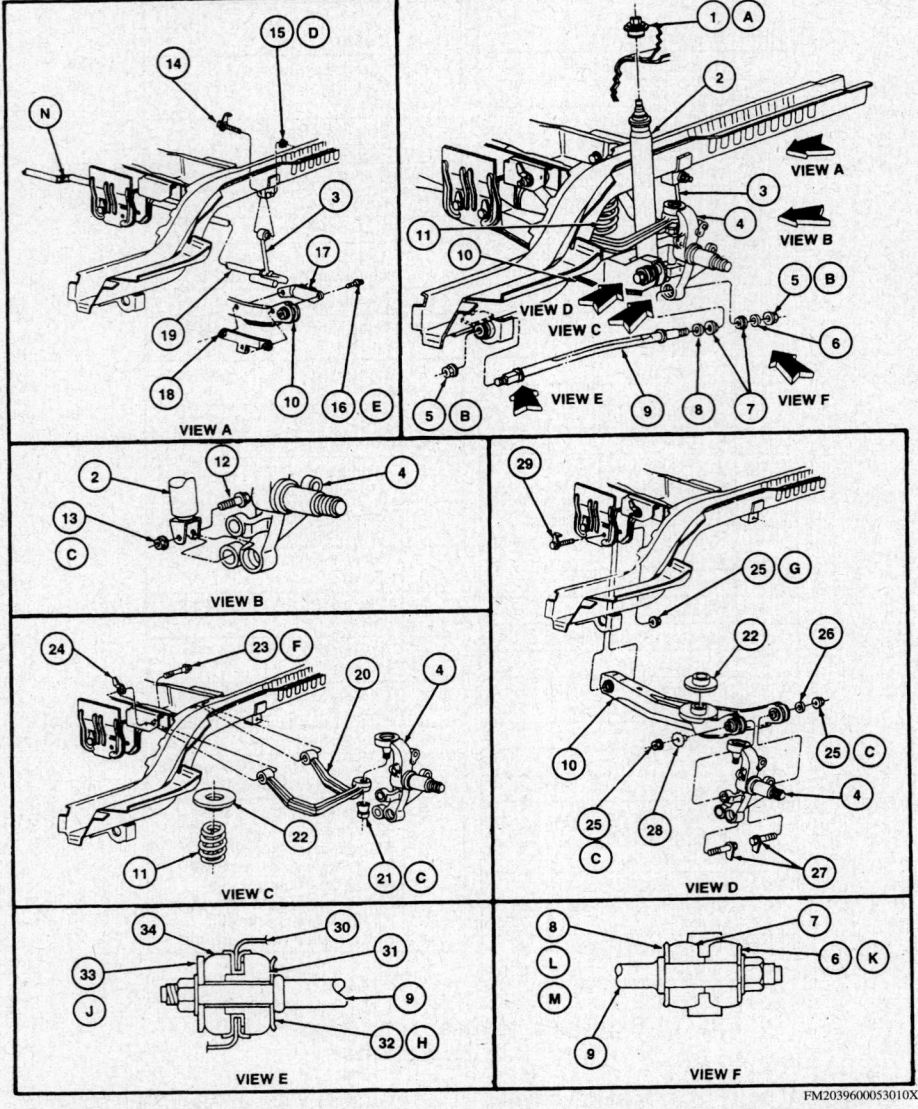

Fig. 2 Exploded view of rear suspension (Part 1 of 2). Wagon

8. Tilt upper part of spindle outward until upper control arms are clear of body brackets. Wire spindle in position.
9. Remove mounting nut and upper control arms.

INSTALLATION

1. Install upper control arms on spindle and install new nut. **Do not tighten now.**
2. Position upper control arms in body

brackets, and install new nuts and bolts. Remove support wire.
3. Tighten control arms to spindle mounting nuts.
4. Install brake hose bracket on body, and tire and wheel assembly.
5. Remove floor jack and lower vehicle.
6. Inspect rear wheel alignment.

STABILIZER BAR
REPLACE

Sedan

1. Raise and support vehicle. **Do use tension strut and bushing for support.**
2. Remove stabilizer bar to link mounting nuts, washers and insulators from both sides.
3. Remove U-bracket mounting bolts and stabilizer bar.
4. Remove link to strut mounting nuts, washers and insulators.
5. Reverse procedure to install. Use new mounting components.

Wagon

1. Raise and support vehicle.
2. Place jack stands under rear suspension arm and bushings so bar links and bushings are neutralized.
3. Remove U-bracket mounting nuts and bolts from either side, and slide U-brackets and insulators from stabilizer bar.
4. Remove link to body bracket mounting nuts and bolts, then the stabilizer and link assemblies.
5. Slide link assemblies from stabilizer bar.
6. Reverse procedure to install. Use new mounting components.

FM2039600053010X

Item	Description
1	Upper Shock Absorber Nut (2 Req'd)
2	Shock Absorber (2 Req'd)
3	Rear Stabilizer Bar Link and Bushing
4	Rear Wheel Spindle
5	Nut (4 Req'd)
6	Washer (2 Req'd)
7	Rear Suspension Tie Rod Bushing (4 Req'd)
8	Washer (2 Req'd)
9	Rear Suspension Tension Strut and Bushing (2 Req'd)
10	Rear Suspension Arm and Bushing
11	Rear Spring (2 Req'd)
12	Bolt (2 Req'd)
13	Nut (2 Req'd)
14	Bolt (2 Req'd)
15	Nut (2 Req'd)
16	Bolt (4 Req'd)
17	Stabilizer Bar Bracket
18	Nut and Retainer Assembly (2 Req'd)
19	Rear Stabilizer Bar
20	Rear Suspension Arm and Bushing
21	Nut (2 Req'd)
22	Rear Spring Insulators (4 Req'd)
23	Bolt (4 Req'd)
24	Nut (4 Req'd)
25	Nut (2 Req'd)

Item	Description
26	Washer (2 Req'd)
27	Bolt (4 Req'd)
28	Rear Suspension Arm Adjusting Cam Kit (2 Req'd)
29	Bolt (2 Req'd)
30	Body
31	Rear Strut Body End Bushing Inner (2 Req'd)
32	Washer (2 Req'd)
33	Sleeve (2 Req'd)
34	Bushing Outer (2 Req'd)
A	Tighten to 25-34 N·m (19-25 Lb-Ft)
B	Tighten to 47-63 N·m (35-46 Lb-Ft)
C	Tighten to 68-92 N·m (50-67 Lb-Ft)
D	Tighten to 60-80 N·m (45-59 Lb-Ft)
E	Tighten to 19-26 N·m (14-19 Lb-Ft)
F	Tighten to 98-132 N·m (73-97 Lb-Ft)
G	Tighten to 54-71 N·m (40-52 Lb-Ft)
H	Stamped "This Side Out"
J	Assemble 5B536 and 5B537 As Shown
K	Stamped "Rear"
L	Stamped "This Side Out"
M	Assemble N802855-S36 and N801335-S36 As Shown
N	Color Code Must Be Installed On

FM2039600053020X

Fig. 2 Exploded view of rear suspension (Part 2 of 2). Wagon

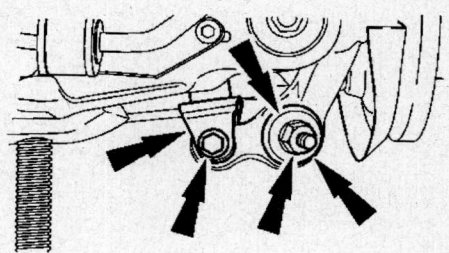

FM1060101226000X

Fig. 3 Rear spindle replacement. Wagon

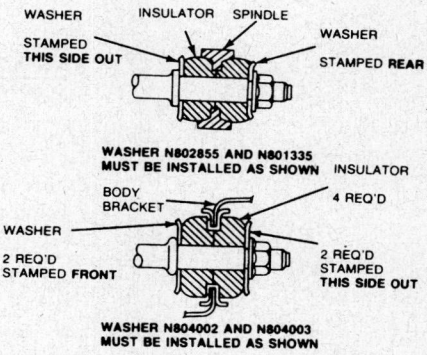

FM2039100032000X

Fig. 6 Tension strut bushing installation. Sedan

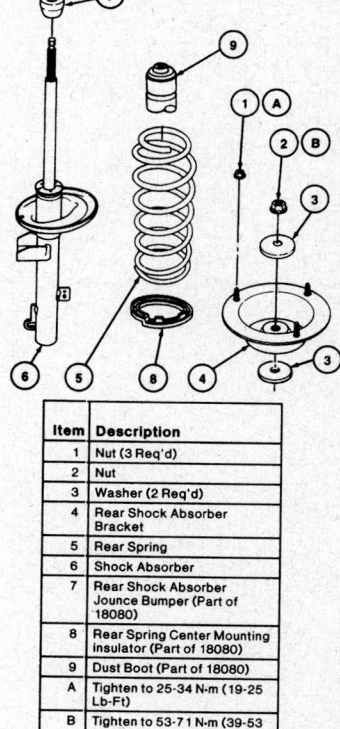

Item	Description
1	Nut (3 Req'd)
2	Nut
3	Washer (2 Req'd)
4	Rear Shock Absorber Bracket
5	Rear Spring
6	Shock Absorber
7	Rear Shock Absorber Jounce Bumper (Part of 18080)
8	Rear Spring Center Mounting Insulator (Part of 18080)
9	Dust Boot (Part of 18080)
A	Tighten to 25-34 N·m (19-25 Lb-Ft)
B	Tighten to 53-71 N·m (39-53 Lb-Ft)

FM2039600054000X

Fig. 4 Exploded view of rear strut & spring

Fig. 5 Spring & seat positioning

REAR SPRING END

STEP IN SPRING SEAT POCKET

SHOCK ABSORBER 18080

SPRING END MUST BE WITHIN 10 mm (0.39 INCH) OF STEP IN SPRING SEAT

FM2039600055000X

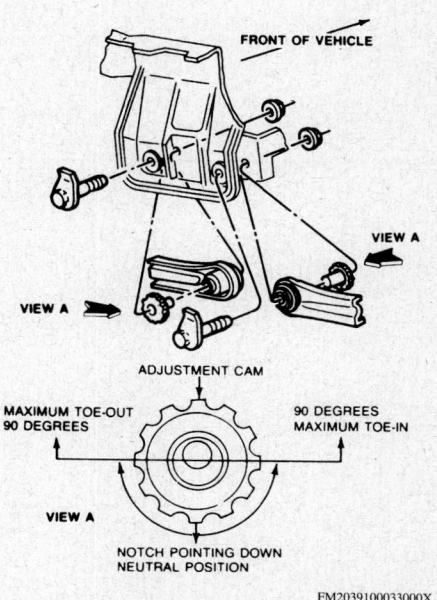

FRONT OF VEHICLE

VIEW A

VIEW A

ADJUSTMENT CAM

MAXIMUM TOE-OUT 90 DEGREES

90 DEGREES MAXIMUM TOE-IN

VIEW A

NOTCH POINTING DOWN NEUTRAL POSITION

FM2039100033000X

Fig. 7 Lower control arm bushing & cam installation. Sedan

TIGHTENING SPECIFICATIONS

Year	Component	Torque Ft. Lbs.
SEDAN		
2004–07	Brake Hose Bracket	9–12
	Control Arm To Body	73–97
	Control Arm To Spindle	50–67
	Stabilizer Bar Link To Stabilizer Bar	60–84①
	Stabilizer Bar Link To Strut	60–84①
	Stabilizer U-Bracket To Body	25–34
	Strut Rod Nut	39–53
	Strut Top Mount To Body	19–26
	Strut To Spindle	50–67
	Strut To Top Mount	35–50
	Tension Strut To Body	35–50
	Tension Strut To Spindle	35–50
	Wheel Bearing	188–254
	Wheel Lug	85–105
WAGON		
2004–06	Brake Hose Bracket	9–12
	Lower Control Arm To Body	40–52
	Shock Absorber To Body	19–27
	Shock Absorber To Lower Suspension Arm	12–20
	Shock Absorber To Lower Suspension Spindle	50–67
	Spindle To Lower Control Arm	50–67
	Stabilizer Bar U-Bracket To Lower Suspension Arm	20–30
	Stabilizer Link	44–59
	Tension Strut To Body	35–46
	Tension Strut To Spindle	35–46
	Upper Ball Joint	50–68
	Upper Control Arms To Body	70–95
	Upper Control Arms To Spindle	150–190
	Upper Suspension Arm To Spindle	40–55
	Wheel Bearing	188–254
	Wheel Lug	85–105

① — Inch lbs.

REAR SUSPENSION

Front Suspension & Steering

NOTE: On Air Bag Equipped Models, Refer To "Air Bag System Precautions" Located In The Front Of This Manual For System Disarming & Arming Procedures.

NOTE: Refer To "Computer Relearn Procedures" Located In The Front Of This Manual When Battery Power To The Computer Has Been Interrupted.

INDEX

	Page No.
Ball Joint, Replace	5-29
Ball Joint Inspection	5-29
Coil Spring & Strut Service	5-29
Control Arm, Replace	5-30
Description	5-29
Power Steering	13-1

	Page No.
Power Steering Gear, Replace	5-31
DOHC Engine	5-31
OHV Engine	5-31
Power Steering Pump, Replace	5-31
DOHC Engine	5-31
OHV Engine	5-31

	Page No.
Stabilizer Bar, Replace	5-30
Steering Columns	12-1
Steering Knuckle, Replace	5-30
Strut, Replace	5-29
Tightening Specifications	5-31
Wheel Bearing, Replace	5-29

DESCRIPTION

This suspension is a gas filled McPherson strut type, **Fig. 1.** The strut top mount consists of a rubber insulated bearing and seat and coil spring insulator. The top mount is attached to the body side apron by three bolts. The lower part of the strut is mounted in the steering knuckle and is retained by a pinch bolt. A forged lower control arm is attached to the subframe and to the steering knuckle. A tension strut is connected to the lower control arm and to the forward part of the subframe.

WHEEL BEARING
REPLACE

1. Turn ignition switch to OFF position and place steering column in unlocked position.
2. Remove wheel hub nut, then raise and support vehicle.
3. Remove cotter pin and nut from tie rod end stud. Discard cotter pin and nut.
4. Remove tie rod end from front wheel knuckle using tie rod end remover tool No. 3290-D, and tie rod adapter tool No. T81P-3504-W, or equivalents. **Do not use power tools to remove nut. Avoid damaging rod boot seal.**
5. Remove stabilizer bar link from front wheel knuckle.
6. Remove disc brake caliper and support it aside.
7. Remove anti-lock brake sensor.
8. Remove and discard lower ball joint nut.
9. Compress front coil spring until lower ball joint clears front suspension lower arm using Rotunda spring compressor tool No. 164-R-3571, or equivalent.
10. Push front axle from hub using suitable service tools.
11. Remove and discard three hub and bearing mounting bolts from front wheel knuckle.
12. **Wheel hub is not pressed into front wheel knuckle. Do not use slide hammer to remove stuck wheel hub. Do not strike back of inner bearing race.**
13. If bearing carrier is corroded to front wheel knuckle, apply rust penetrant part No. D7AZ-19A501-AA, or equivalent, to inboard and outboard wheel hub/knuckle mating surface and allow to soak. Pry wheel hub from knuckle assembly using suitable pry bar.
14. Reverse procedure to install, noting the following:
    a. If wheel hub is damaged, or if any endplay is detectable, replace wheel hub.
    b. Remove any foreign material from knuckle bearing bore.
    c. Lightly lubricate mating surfaces of bearing and front wheel knuckle.

BALL JOINT INSPECTION

1. Raise and support vehicle with wheels in full down position.
2. Grasp lower edge of tire, then move wheel assembly in and out.
3. As wheel is being moved, observe lower end of knuckle and lower control arm.
4. If movement is observed, replace lower control arm.

BALL JOINT
REPLACE

The ball joint must be replaced with the control arm as an assembly.

STRUT
REPLACE

1. Place ignition switch in OFF position and ensure steering wheel is not locked.
2. Remove hub nut and loosen three strut mounting nuts.
3. Raise and support vehicle. **Do not raise vehicle with lower control arm.**
4. Remove wheel and tire assembly.
5. Remove brake caliper and position it aside.
6. Remove brake rotor and tie rod end. **Do not use power tools to remove tie rod nut. Avoid damaging boot seal.**
7. Remove nut and stabilizer bar link from strut.
8. Remove lower control arm to steering knuckle pinch nut and bolt, slightly spread joint and remove lower control arm.
9. Press axle from hub using suitable hub remover/installer.
10. Wire axle shaft to body to maintain level position. **Do not allow axle shaft to move outward.**
11. Remove strut to steering knuckle pinch bolt and spread joint slightly.
12. Remove steering knuckle and hub.
13. Remove mounting nuts and strut.
14. Reverse procedure to install, noting the following:
    a. Tighten in following order: strut to steering knuckle pinch bolt, lower control arm to steering knuckle pinch bolt, stabilizer bar assembly to strut, tie rod end mounting nut and strut mounting nuts.
    b. Tighten hub nut with vehicle on ground.

COIL SPRING & STRUT SERVICE

1. Compress strut spring with Rotunda coil spring compressor tool No. 164-R3571, or equivalent.
2. Hold strut shaft with suitable box wrench and remove strut mounting nut using suitable crowfoot socket. **Do not allow strut shaft to rotate.**
3. Loosen compressor tool, then remove strut top mount bracket, bearing and seat assembly, and spring, **Fig. 2.**
4. Reverse procedure to install.

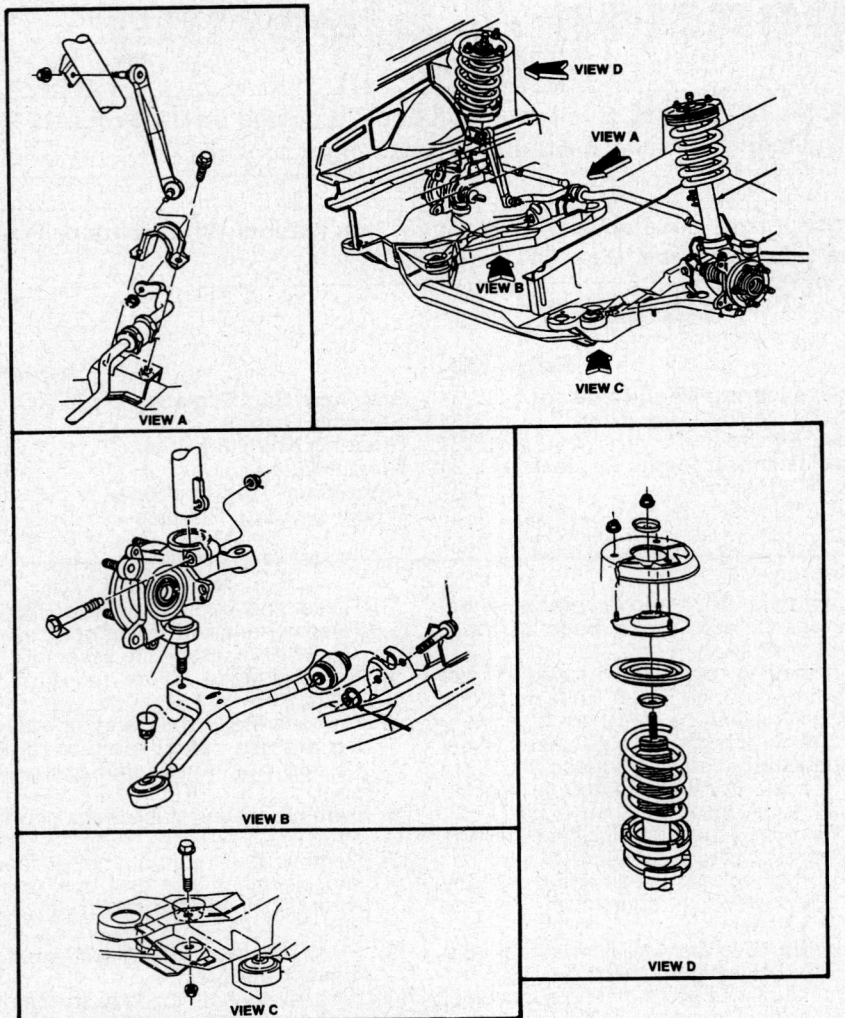

Fig. 1 Exploded view of front suspension

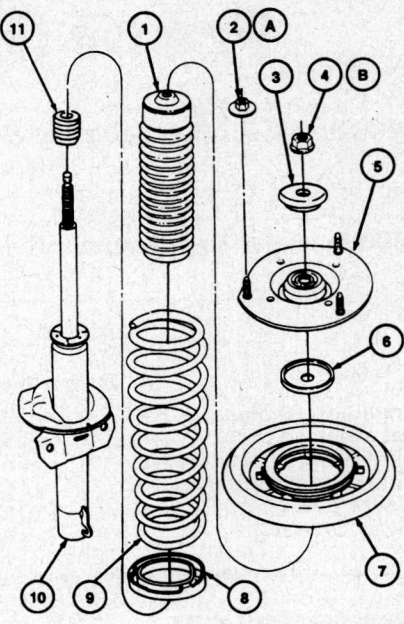

Item	Description
1	Dust Boot
2	Nut (3 Req'd)
3	Washer
4	Nut
5	Front Shock Absorber Mounting Bracket
6	Washer
7	Front Suspension Bearing and Seal
8	Front Spring Insulator
9	Front Coil Spring
10	Front Spring and Shock
11	Jounce Bumper
A	Tighten to 30-40 N·m (23-29 Lb-Ft)
B	Tighten to 53-72 N·m (40-53 Lb-Ft)

Fig. 2 Exploded view of McPherson strut

CONTROL ARM
REPLACE

1. Turn ignition switch to OFF position and place steering column in unlocked position.
2. Raise and support vehicle.
3. Remove and discard lower ball joint nut.
4. Separate ball joint from knuckle using ball joint remover tool No. T96P-3010-A and tie rod end remover tool No. T81P-3504-W, or equivalents.
5. Compress front coil spring until lower ball joint clears front suspension lower arm using Rotunda spring compressor tool No. 164-R-3571, or equivalent.
6. Remove forward lower suspension arm mounting nut and bolt.
7. Remove rear lower suspension arm mounting nut, bolt and suspension arm.
8. Reverse procedure to install.

STEERING KNUCKLE
REPLACE

Wheel hub retainer is a torque prevailing design and cannot be reused. If loosened, retainer must be replaced.

1. Ensure steering wheel in unlocked position.
2. Remove hub cap or wheel cover, wheel hub retainer and washer. Discard retainer.
3. Remove steering knuckle tie rod end using suitable joint removal tool.
4. Remove anti-lock brake sensor.
5. Disconnect ABS sensor wire retainer and position sensor aside.
6. Remove knuckle to shock mounting bolt and nut. Discard nut.
7. Disconnect ball joint from lower arm using suitable joint removal tool.
8. Push lower arm down until ball joint is free from arm using suitable pry bar.
9. Press halfshaft from wheel bearing

and hub using front wheel hub installation tool No. T81P-1104-C, or equivalent.
10. Support halfshaft in level position.
11. Remove flag bolt and steering knuckle.
12. Reverse procedure to install.

STABILIZER BAR
REPLACE

1. Raise and support vehicle. Place safety stands behind front subframe.
2. Remove stabilizer bar link to strut mounting nuts.
3. Remove stabilizer bar link to bar mounting nuts.
4. Remove mounting bolts and move steering gear off subframe.
5. Support subframe with second set of safety stands and remove rear subframe mounting bolts.

6. Lower rear part of subframe to access to stabilizer bar mounting brackets.
7. Remove mounting brackets and stabilizer bar.
8. Reverse procedure to install.

POWER STEERING GEAR
REPLACE

DOHC Engine

1. Turn steering wheel ¼ turn and turn ignition switch to OFF position.
2. Remove both front wheel and tire assemblies.
3. Remove tie rod end jam nuts. Discard tie rod end cotter pins and nuts.
4. Record of turns required to remove tie rod ends from steering gear for installation alignment.
5. Remove tie rod ends from steering knuckle with suitable joint removal tool.
6. Remove tie rod ends.
7. Remove nuts and disconnect both stabilizer bar links from stabilizer bar.
8. Remove bolt and disconnect intermediate shaft coupling.
9. **Do not allow steering wheel to rotate while steering column intermediate shaft is disconnected.**
10. Remove catalytic converter.
11. Remove and discard both steering gear mounting nuts.
12. Remove bolts and lower rear of front subframe approximately 4 inches.
13. Disconnect power steering pressure switch and remove pressure hose.
14. Remove bracket/heat shield.
15. Remove power steering lines from steering gear.
16. Remove brackets, pipes and steering gear through lefthand fender well.
17. Reverse procedure to install.

OHV Engine

1. Turn steering wheel ½ turn to righthand and turn ignition switch to OFF position.
2. Remove air cleaner outlet pipe.
3. Remove power steering pressure hose. Discard seals.
4. Remove intermediate shaft pinch bolt. Discard bolt.
5. Center steering wheel and turn ignition switch to OFF position.
6. **Do not allow steering wheel to rotate while steering column intermediate shaft is disconnected.**
7. Disconnect intermediate shaft from steering gear.
8. Remove front wheel and tire assemblies.
9. Loosen tie rod jam nuts, then remove tie rod end cotter pins and nuts. Discard tie rod end cotter pins and nuts.
10. Remove tie rod ends from steering knuckle using suitable joint removal tool.
11. Record number of turns required to remove tie rod ends for installation alignment.
12. Remove tie rod ends.
13. Remove nuts and disconnect both stabilizer bar links from stabilizer bar.
14. Remove catalytic converter.
15. Remove and discard steering gear mounting nuts.
16. Remove remaining steering gear brackets and pipes.
17. Support rear of front subframe with suitable jack stands.
18. Remove mounting bolts and lower subframe approximately four inches.
19. Remove steering gear through lefthand fender well.
20. Reverse procedure to install.

POWER STEERING PUMP
REPLACE

Power steering pumps are replaced only as complete assemblies. They have no serviceable components.

DOHC Engine

1. Drain and remove coolant recovery reservoir.
2. Remove drive belt.
3. Remove power steering reservoir pump hose from between pump and reservoir. Drain fluid into suitable container.
4. Remove pulley using pump pulley remover tool No. T69L-10300-B, or equivalent.
5. Disconnect power steering lefthand turn pressure hose from pump.
6. Remove three pump mounting bolts and pump.
7. Reverse procedure to install.

OHV Engine

1. Remove drive belt and alternator.
2. Drain and remove coolant recovery reservoir.
3. Remove power steering return hose from pump and drain fluid into suitable container.
4. Remove idler pulley from power steering pump support.
5. Remove power steering bracket mounting bolt from under tensioner mounting.
6. Remove power steering pump support with pump attached.
7. Remove pulley using pump pulley remover tool No. T69L-10300-B, or equivalent.
8. Reverse procedure to install.

TIGHTENING SPECIFICATIONS

Year	Component	Torque Ft. Lbs.
2004–07	Control Arm Pivot Bolt	72–97
	Control Arm To Subframe	72–97
	Hub Nut	170–202
	Stabilizer Bar Bracket To Subframe	22–39
	Stabilizer Bar Link To Stabilizer Bar	35–48
	Stabilizer Bar Link To Shock Strut	57–75
	Steering Gear	85–100
	Strut Top Mount To Body	30–40
	Strut To Top Mount	39–53
	Strut To Knuckle	72–97
	Tension Strut To Control Arm	70–95
	Tension Strut To Subframe	70–95
	Tie Rod End To Steering Knuckle	35–46
	Wheel Lug	85–105

Wheel Alignment

INDEX

	Page No.		Page No.		Page No.
Front Wheel Alignment	5-32	Preliminary Inspection	5-32	Toe-In	5-32
Caster & Camber	5-32	Rear Wheel Alignment	5-32	Wheel Alignment	
Toe-In	5-32	Caster & Camber	5-32	Specifications	5-2

PRELIMINARY INSPECTION

1. Ensure tires are inflated to proper pressure.
2. Inspect tires for wear patterns that may indicate improper wheel alignment, tire imbalance or damage because bulges or separations.
3. Inspect suspension for modifications such as trailer towing equipment or heavy duty handling components.
4. Inspect vehicle for signs of overloading or sagging. Ensure luggage compartment does not contain heavy objects.
5. Road test vehicle to isolate area of concern.

FRONT WHEEL ALIGNMENT

Caster & Camber

Caster is not adjustable. If caster is not be within specifications, inspect vehicle for suspension component damage, deteriorated bushings or distorted body mounting points.

1. Loosen subframe to body mounting bolts.
2. Install ¾ inch outside diameter pipe, or similar tool, into lefthand front subframe and body alignment holes, **Fig. 1.**
3. Align lefthand front subframe and body alignment holes and slightly tighten lefthand front subframe mounting bolt.
4. Repeat previous alignment steps on righthand front alignment holes.
5. Inspect lefthand front alignment again.
6. Tighten subframe mounting bolts.
7. Center punch spot welds on both strut alignment plates and loosen strut mounting nuts, **Fig. 2.**
8. Remove spot welds using Rotunda Spot-Eze, or equivalent. **Do not drill deeper than thickness of alignment plates.**
9. Remove strut mounting nuts and alignment plates.
10. Remove burrs from strut towers and alignment plates. Paint all exposed metal on strut towers and alignment plates.

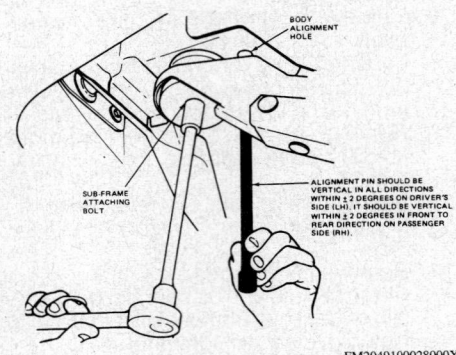

FM2049100028000X

Fig. 1 Front suspension alignment

11. Install alignment plates and loosely install strut mounting nuts.
12. Align front end and tighten strut mounting nuts.
13. Drill three ⅛ inch holes through alignment plates and strut towers, then paint exposed metal, **Fig. 3. Do not drill deeper than ⅜ inch into strut tower.**
14. Install three ⅛ inch diameter pop rivets with grip range of ¼ inch into alignment plate/strut tower.

Toe-In

1. Lock steering wheel in straight ahead position using suitable steering wheel holder.
2. Loosen and slide small outer clamps from off steering boot.
3. Loosen tie rod adjusting, then adjust lefthand and righthand tie rods until each wheel has half desired total toe specification.
4. Tighten tie rod adjusting nuts and install clamps.
5. Remove steering wheel holding tool.

REAR WHEEL ALIGNMENT

Caster & Camber

The caster and camber angles are factory set and cannot be adjusted. However,

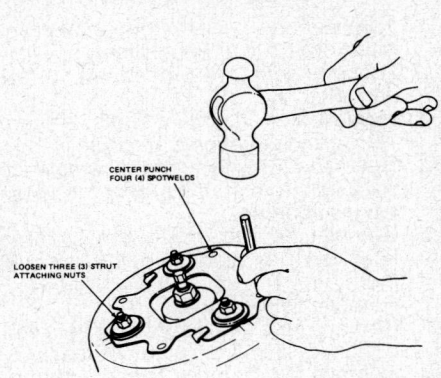

FM2049100029000X

Fig. 2 Alignment plate loosening

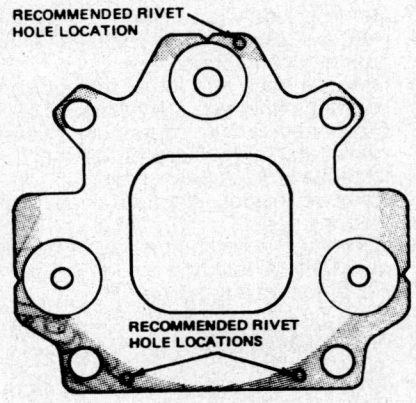

DRILL THREE (3) HOLES IN ALIGNMENT PLATE FOR 1/8 INCH RIVETS.

DRILL IN SHADED AREA ONLY.

FM2049100030000X

Fig. 3 Rivet hole location

rear camber adjustment kit part No. E7DZ-5K751-B, or an equivalent, may be installed to allow for adjustment.

Toe-In

On sedan models, toe-in is adjusted by rotating the cams located inside the rear inner lower control arm bushings.

On wagon models, toe-in is adjusted by rotating the cams located inside the outer lower control arm bushings.

FOCUS

NOTE: Refer To The Rear Of This Manual For Manufacturer's Special Service Tool Suppliers.

INDEX OF SERVICE OPERATIONS

Page No.

AIR BAG SYSTEM
PRECAUTIONS 0-18
BRAKES
   Anti-Lock Brakes (Volume 2)..   6-1
   Disc Brakes...................   14-1
   Drum Brakes   15-1
   Hydraulic Brake Systems   16-1
   Power Brake Units............   17-1
COMPUTER RELEARN
PROCEDURE 0-31
ELECTRICAL
   Air Bag System (Volume 2) ...   4-1
   Air Conditioning...............   8-1
   Alternator, Replace   6-5
   Alternators...................   11-1
   Blower Motor, Replace........   6-6
   Cabin Air Filter, Replace   6-6
   Cooling Fans   9-1
   Cruise Control (Volume 2)   2-1
   Dash Gauges (Volume 2)   1-1
   Dash Panel Service
   (Volume 2)...................   5-1
   Evaporator Core, Replace   6-7
   Fuel Pump Relay Location   6-4
   Fuse Panel & Flasher
   Location   6-4
   Headlamp Switch, Replace ...   6-5
   Heater Core, Replace.........   6-6
   Ignition Coil, Replace   6-5
   Ignition Lock, Replace   6-5
   Ignition Switch, Replace   6-5
   Instrument Cluster, Replace...   6-6
   Neutral Safety Switch,
   Replace   6-5
   Passive Restraint Systems
   (Volume 2)...................   4-1
   Precautions..................   6-4
   Radio, Replace   6-6
   Speed Controls (Volume 2) ...   2-1
   Starter Motors   10-1
   Starter, Replace   6-4
   Steering Columns   12-1
   Steering Wheel, Replace......   6-6
   Technical Service Bulletins....   6-7
   Wiper Motor, Replace.........   6-6
   Wiper Systems (Volume 2)....   3-1
ELECTRICAL SYMBOL
IDENTIFICATION 0-63
FRONT DRIVE AXLES 18-1
FRONT SUSPENSION &
STEERING
   Ball Joint, Replace............   6-35
   Coil Spring & Strut Service....   6-35
   Coil Spring, Replace..........   6-35
   Control Arm, Replace   6-35
   Description   6-34
   Hub & Bearing, Replace   6-35
   Power Steering   13-1
   Power Steering Fluid Cooler,
   Replace   6-37
   Power Steering Gear,
   Replace   6-36
   Power Steering Pump,
   Replace   6-36

Page No.

   Power Steering System
   Bleed........................   6-37
   Precautions..................   6-34
   Stabilizer Bar, Replace........   6-35
   Steering Columns.............   12-1
   Steering Knuckle, Replace   6-35
   Strut, Replace   6-35
   Technical Service Bulletins....   6-37
   Tie Rod, Replace   6-36
   Tie Rod End, Replace   6-36
   Tightening Specifications......   6-38
   Wheel Bearing, Adjust   6-34
NON-STANDARD TIRE &
WHEEL SIZE
ADJUSTMENT TO RIDE
HEIGHT SPECIFICATIONS
& TIRE SIZE CHART 0-61
REAR SUSPENSION
   Coil Spring, Replace..........   6-32
   Control Arm, Replace   6-32
   Description   6-31
   Hub & Bearing, Replace   6-31
   Precautions..................   6-31
   Rear Crossmember, Replace .   6-33
   Rear Wheel Spindle, Replace.   6-31
   Shock Absorber, Replace   6-31
   Stabilizer Bar, Replace........   6-33
   Tie-Bar, Replace   6-33
   Tightening Specifications......   6-34
SERVICE REMINDER &
WARNING LAMP RESET
PROCEDURES 0-34
SPECIFICATIONS
   Fluid Capacities & Cooling
   System Data..................   6-3
   Front Wheel Alignment
   Specifications.................   6-3
   General Engine
   Specifications.................   6-2
   Lubricant Data...............   6-3
   Rear Wheel Alignment
   Specifications.................   6-3
   Tune Up Specifications.......   6-2
VEHICLE
IDENTIFICATION 0-1
VEHICLE LIFT POINTS 0-51
VEHICLE MAINTENANCE
SCHEDULES 0-73
WIRE COLOR CODE
IDENTIFICATION 0-63
WHEEL ALIGNMENT
   Front Wheel Alignment........   6-39
   Preliminary Inspection   6-39
   Rear Wheel Alignment........   6-39
   Ride Height   6-39
   Technical Service Bulletins....   6-39
   Wheel Alignment
   Specifications.................   6-3
2.0L (VIN N) & 2.3L
(VIN Z) DOHC ENGINES
   Camshaft, Replace   6-27
   Camshaft Lobe Lift
   Specifications.................   6-26

Page No.

   Compression Pressure........   6-23
   Cooling System Bleed   6-28
   Crankshaft Damper, Replace..   6-26
   Crankshaft Rear Oil Seal,
   Replace   6-27
   Crankshaft Seal, Replace   6-27
   Cylinder Head, Replace.......   6-25
   Engine Rebuilding
   Specifications.................   21-1
   Engine, Replace   6-24
   Engine Mount, Replace   6-24
   Front Cover, Replace   6-26
   Fuel Filter, Replace   6-28
   Fuel Pump, Replace   6-28
   Intake Manifold, Replace......   6-25
   Oil Pan, Replace..............   6-27
   Precautions..................   6-23
   Radiator, Replace............   6-28
   Serpentine Drive Belt   6-27
   Technical Service Bulletins....   6-28
   Thermostat, Replace.........   6-28
   Tightening Specifications......   6-30
   Timing Chain, Replace........   6-26
   Valve Adjustment   6-26
   Valve Clearance
   Specifications.................   6-26
   Valve Cover, Replace   6-26
   Water Pump, Replace   6-28
2.0L (VIN P) SOHC
ENGINE
   Camshaft, Replace   6-20
   Compression Pressure........   6-17
   Crankshaft Rear Oil Seal,
   Replace   6-20
   Crankshaft Seal, Replace   6-20
   Cylinder Head, Replace.......   6-19
   Engine Rebuilding
   Specifications.................   21-1
   Engine, Replace   6-17
   Exhaust Manifold, Replace.....   6-19
   Fuel Filter, Replace   6-21
   Fuel Pump, Replace   6-21
   Intake Manifold, Replace......   6-18
   Oil Pan, Replace..............   6-20
   Oil Pump, Replace............   6-20
   Precautions..................   6-17
   Radiator, Replace............   6-21
   Serpentine Drive Belt   6-21
   Technical Service Bulletins....   6-21
   Thermostat, Replace.........   6-21
   Tightening Specifications......   6-22
   Timing Belt, Replace.........   6-19
   Valve Adjustment   6-19
   Water Pump, Replace   6-21
2.0L (VINS 3 & 5) DOHC
ENGINES
   Camshaft, Replace   6-13
   Compression Pressure........   6-8
   Crankshaft Damper, Replace..   6-12
   Crankshaft Rear Oil Seal,
   Replace   6-13
   Crankshaft Seal, Replace   6-13
   Cylinder Head, Replace.......   6-11
   Engine Rebuilding
   Specifications.................   21-1

	Page No.		Page No.		Page No.
Engine, Replace	6-9	Precautions	6-8	Timing Belt, Replace	6-12
Exhaust Manifold, Replace	6-11	Radiator, Replace	6-14	Valve Adjustment	6-12
Fuel Filter, Replace	6-14	Serpentine Drive Belt	6-14	Valve Clearance	
Fuel Pump, Replace	6-14	Technical Service Bulletins	6-14	Specifications	6-12
Intake Manifold, Replace	6-10	Thermostat, Replace	6-14	Valve Cover, Replace	6-12
Oil Pan, Replace	6-13	Tightening Specifications	6-16	Water Pump, Replace	6-14

Specifications

GENERAL ENGINE SPECIFICATIONS

Year	Engine Liter (Code①)	Fuel System	Bore x Stroke, Inches	Comp. Ratio	Net HP @ RPM	Maximum Torque, Ft. Lbs. @ RPM	Oil Pressure, psi
2004	2.0L DOHC (3)	SFI	3.34 x 3.46	9.6:1	130 @ 5300	135 @ 4500	②
	2.0L DOHC SVT (5)	SFI	3.34 x 3.46	10.2:1	170 @ 7000	145 @ 5500	②
	2.0L SOHC (P)	SFI	3.34 x 3.46	9.35:1	110 @ 5000	125 @ 3750	③
2005–07	2.0L (N) DOHC	SFI	3.34 x 3.45	10.0:1	130 @ 4500	129 @ 45000	29–39
	2.3L (Z) DOHC	SFI	3.44 x 3.70	9.7:1	151 @ 5750	154 @ 4250	29–39

SFI — Sequential Electronic Fuel Injection
① — The eighth digit of the VIN denotes engine code.

② — Pressure at normal operating temperature should be 18.9–36.3 psi @ 800–850 RPM and 53.7–79.8 psi @ 4000 RPM.

③ — Pressure at normal operating temperature should be 34.8–65.3 psi @ 2000 RPM.

TUNE UP SPECIFICATIONS

Year & Engine (Code①)	Spark Plug Gap	Ignition Timing BTDC				Curb Idle Speed⑩		Fast Idle Speed⑩		Fuel Pump Pressure, psi.	Valve Lash, Inch
		Firing Order④	Man. Trans.	Auto. Trans.	Mark	Man. Trans.	Auto Trans.	Man. Trans.	Auto. Trans.		
2004											
2.0L DOHC (3 & 5)	.052–.056	③	②	②	⑧	⑨	⑨	⑨	⑨	30–65⑦	⑥
2.0L SOHC (P)	.044	③	②	②	⑧	⑨	⑨	⑨	⑨	30–65⑦	⑤
2005–07											
2.0L DOHC (N)	.049–.053	③	②	②	⑧	⑨	⑨	⑨	⑨	30–65⑦	⑪
2.3L (Z) DOHC	.049–.053	③	②	—	⑧	⑨	—	⑨	—	30–65⑦	⑪

BTDC — Before Top Dead Center
N — Neutral
① — The eighth digit of the VIN denotes engine code.
② — Non-adjustable.
③ — Cylinder numbering from front to rear of engine, 1-2-3-4. Firing order, 1-3-4-2.
④ — Before disconnecting wires from distributor cap or coil unit, determine location of ignition wires.
⑤ — Equipped w/hydraulic lash adjusters.

⑥ — Measured at 59–77°F. Intake, .0043–.0071 inch; exhaust, .0106–.0134 inch.
⑦ — Wrap shop towel around fitting to prevent fuel spillage, then connect suitable fuel pressure gauge to fuel diagnostic valve on fuel rail assembly. Gradually open fuel pressure gauge test valve to relieve fuel system pressure & drain fuel into suitable container. Close fuel pressure gauge test valve. Place ignition switch in On position. Access output test mode on scan tool &

operate fuel pump to obtain maximum fuel pressure. Fuel pump will operate for approximately 8 seconds. Inspect fuel pressure gauge reading.
⑧ — Equipped w/crankshaft position sensor.
⑨ — Idle speed controlled by an automatic idle speed control.
⑩ — When adjusting idle speed, set parking brake & chock drive wheels.
⑪ — Intake, .008–.011 inch; exhaust, .010–.023 inch.

FRONT WHEEL ALIGNMENT SPECIFICATIONS

Year	Vehicle	Caster Angle, Degrees		Camber Angle, Degrees		Toe-In, Inches	
		Limits	Desired	Limits	Desired	Limits	Desired
2004	Coupe & Sedan	+1.97 to +4.09	+3.03	-1.82 to +.70	-.56	-.10 to +.10	0
	SVT	+1.97 to +4.09	+3.03	-1.82 to +.70	-.56	-.13 to +.13	0
	Wagon	+1.87 to +3.89	+2.88	-1.89 to +.63	-.63	-.10 to +.10	0
2005–07	All	+1.75 to +3/75	+2.75	-1.75 to +.75	-.50	-.20 to +2.0	0

REAR WHEEL ALIGNMENT SPECIFICATIONS

Year	Vehicle	Camber, Degrees		Toe-In, Inches	
		Limits	Desired	Limits	Desired
2004	Coupe & Sedan	-2.33 to +.30	-1.02	+.15 to +.35	+.25
	SVT	-2.33 to +.30	-1.02	+.25 to +.29	+.27
	Wagon	-2.22 to +.34	-.94	+.15 to +.35	+.25
2005–07	Sedan	-2.27 to +.23	-1.02	+.30 to +.70	+.50
	Wagon	-2.19 to +.31	-.94	+.30 to +.70	+.50

FLUID CAPACITIES & COOLING SYSTEM DATA

Year	Engine (Code①)	Coolant Capacity, Qts.	Coolant Type	Radiator Cap Relief Pressure, lbs.	Thermo. Opening Temp., Deg. F	Fuel Tank, Gals.	Engine Oil Refill, Qts.②	Transmission Fluid	
								Man. Trans., Pts	Auto. Trans., Qts.
2004	2.0L DOHC (3)	6.1	③	14.4–17.6	194–201	13.2	4.5	4.0	6.9
	2.0L DOHC (5)	6.1	③	14.4–17.6	194–201	13.2	4.5	3.6	—
	2.0L SOHC (P)	6.1	③	14.4–17.6	188–195	13.2	4.0	4.9	6.9
2005–07	2.0L DOHC (H)	6.1	④	17.4–21.7	194	14.0	4.5	3.3	7.0
	2.3L (Z) DOHC	7.6	④	17.4–21.7	194	14.0	4.5	3.3	7.0

EG — Ethylene Glycol
① — The eighth digit of the VIN denotes engine code.
② — Including oil filter.

③ — For models w/green coolant use ethylene glycol. For models w/orange coolant use coolant meeting Ford specifications.

④ — Motorcraft Premium Gold Engine Coolant VC-7-A (Oregan, VC-7-B), or equivalent, (yellow).

LUBRICANT DATA

Year	Lubricant Type					
	Transmission			Power Steering	Brake System	Hydraulic Clutch Fluid
	Manual		Automatic			
	IB5	MTX 75				
2004	①	②	Mercon V XT-5-QM	③	DOT 3④	DOT 3
2005–07	—	②	Mercon V XT-5-QM	Mercon (ATF) XT-2-QDX	DOT 3	DOT 3

① — Transaxle fluid meeting Ford specification WSD-M2C200-C.
② — Transaxle fluid meeting Ford specification ESD-M2C186-A.

③ — Power steering fluid meeting Ford specification WSA-M2C195-A.
④ — The use of super DOT 4 brake fluid meeting Ford specification

Delta ESD-M6C57-A is recommended for all vehicles equipped with manual transaxles.

Electrical

NOTE: On Air Bag Equipped Models, Refer To "Air Bag System Precautions" Located In The Front Of This Manual For System Disarming & Arming Procedures.

NOTE: Refer To "Computer Relearn Procedures" Located In The Front Of This Manual When Battery Power To The Computer Has Been Interrupted.

NOTE: Prior To Performing Any Service Operations Listed In This Section, Consult The "Technical Service Bulletins" Section For Related Information.

INDEX

	Page No.		Page No.		Page No.
Air Bag System (Volume 2)	4-1	Ignition Coil, Replace	6-5	VIN 3	6-4
Air Conditioning	8-1	DOHC Engine	6-5	VIN 5	6-4
Alternator, Replace	6-5	SOHC Engine	6-5	VINs N & Z	6-4
DOHC Engine	6-5	Ignition Lock, Replace	6-5	SOHC Engine	6-4
SOHC Engine	6-5	Ignition Switch, Replace	6-5	Steering Columns	12-1
Alternators	12-1	Instrument Cluster, Replace	6-6	Steering Wheel, Replace	6-6
Blower Motor, Replace	6-6	Neutral Safety Switch, Replace	6-5	Technical Service Bulletins	6-7
Cabin Air Filter, Replace	6-6	Passive Restraint Systems		Loss of Intermittent Wiper Or	
Cooling Fans	9-1	(Volume 2)	4-1	Park Function	6-7
Cruise Control (Volume 2)	2-1	Precautions	6-4	2004–05	6-7
Dash Gauges (Volume 2)	1-1	Air Bag Systems	6-4	White Flakes Coming From A/C	
Dash Panel Service		Battery Ground Cable	6-4	Vents	6-7
(Volume 2)	5-1	Electrostatic Discharge	6-4	2004–05	6-7
Evaporator Core, Replace	6-7	Radio, Replace	6-6	Wiper Motor, Replace	6-6
Fuel Pump Relay Location	6-4	Speed Controls (Volume 2)	2-1	Front	6-6
Fuse Panel & Flasher Location	6-4	Starter Motors	10-1	Rear	6-6
Headlamp Switch, Replace	6-5	Starter, Replace	6-4	Wiper Systems (Volume 2)	3-1
Heater Core, Replace	6-6	DOHC Engine	6-4		

PRECAUTIONS

Air Bag Systems

Refer to "Air Bag System Precautions" in the front of this manual for system disarming and arming procedures.

Battery Ground Cable

Prior to service, disconnect battery ground cable and isolate as required.

Electrostatic Discharge

Electronic modules are sensitive to electrical charges. Ensure modules are not exposed to these charges.

FUSE PANEL & FLASHER LOCATION

The central junction box is located in the lefthand footwell, **Fig. 1.**

The fuse box is located under the lefthand side of instrument panel, **Fig. 2.**

FUEL PUMP RELAY LOCATION

The fuel pump relay is located in the battery junction box in the engine compartment, **Fig. 3.**

STARTER

REPLACE

DOHC Engine

VINS N & Z

1. Ensure transmission is in Neutral position, then raise and support vehicle.
2. Remove terminal nuts and disconnect starter motor wiring.
3. Remove mounting nut and disconnect Power Steering Pressure (PSP) tube brackets from stud bolts.
4. Remove mounting bolts and starter motor.
5. Reverse procedure to install.

VIN 3

1. Disconnect Mass Air Flow (MAF) sensor.
2. Disconnect breather pipe.

3. Disconnect air cleaner outlet tube from throttle body and remove air cleaner.
4. Remove starter motor upper mounting bolts.
5. Raise and support vehicle.
6. Disconnect starter motor electrical connector.
7. Remove lower mounting bolts and starter motor.
8. Reverse procedure to install.

VIN 5

1. Remove intake manifold as outlined under "Intake Manifold, Replace" in "2.0L (VINs 3 & 5) DOHC Engines" section.
2. Disconnect starter motor electrical connectors.
3. Remove mounting bolts and starter motor.
4. Reverse procedure to install.

SOHC Engine

1. Remove air cleaner outlet tube.
2. Remove starter motor mounting bolts.
3. Raise and support vehicle.
4. Disconnect starter motor electrical connector.
5. Remove starter motor.
6. Reverse procedure to install.

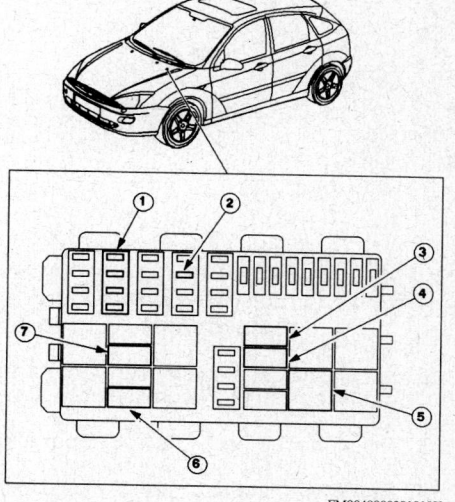

Fig. 1 Central junction box (Part 1 of 2)

Item	Description
1	Fuse F16 (10 A) for dipped beam, left
2	Fuse F17 (10 A) for dipped beam, right
3	Fuse F26 (10 A) main beam, left
4	Fuse F27 (10 A) main beam, right
5	Fuse F22 (15 A) - Dipped beam /daytime running lights
6	Main beam relay
7	Dipped beam relay
8	Headlamp washer system relay
9	Brake light relay
10	Daytime running lights relay

FM9049900301020X

Fig. 1 Central junction box (Part 2 of 2)

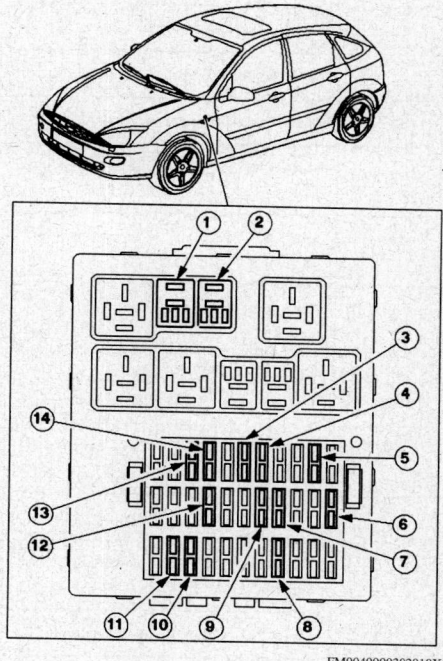

Fig. 2 Fuse box (Part 1 of 2)

FM9049900302010X

ALTERNATOR
REPLACE

DOHC Engine

1. Remove drive belt.
2. Remove cover and disconnect electrical connectors.
3. Remove mounting bolt and secure coolant expansion tank aside.
4. Secure power steering reservoir aside.
5. Remove mounting bolt and secure engine wiring bracket aside.
6. Disconnect ground cable.
7. Remove mounting nuts and secure evaporative emission canister purge valve aside.
8. Remove righthand mounting bolt and fully loosen lefthand bolt. Lefthand bolt cannot be remove at this time.
9. Remove alternator.
10. Reverse procedure to install.

SOHC Engine

1. Remove cooling fan motor and shroud.
2. Remove drive belt.
3. Remove power steering pipe support brackets.
4. Remove exhaust manifold heat shield.
5. Raise and support vehicle.
6. Disconnect alternator electrical connectors.
7. Remove alternator lower mounting bolt.
8. Lower vehicle.
9. Remove clip and two upper mounting bolts.
10. Remove alternator.
11. Reverse procedure to install.

IGNITION COIL
REPLACE

DOHC Engine

1. Remove ignition coil cover.

2. Disconnect spark plug wires and electrical connectors from ignition coil.
3. Remove mounting bolts and ignition coil.
4. Reverse procedure to install.

SOHC Engine

1. Disconnect spark plug wires from ignition coil.
2. Disconnect electrical connectors from ignition coil and capacitor.
3. Remove mounting bolts, ignition coil, capacitor and bracket.
4. Reverse procedure to install.

IGNITION LOCK
REPLACE

1. Remove mounting screws, fastener and instrument panel lower panel.
2. Disconnect steering column upper shroud using suitable thin bladed screwdriver to release clip on each side.
3. Remove audio control switch using suitable thin bladed screwdriver to release locking tang and disconnect electrical connector.
4. Release locking lever, then remove mounting screws and steering column lower shroud.
5. Disconnect electrical connector, then remove mounting screw and passive anti-theft system transceiver.
6. Insert key and turn ignition switch to accessory position No. 1.
7. Depress detent using suitable thin bladed screwdriver.
8. Remove lock cylinder.
9. Reverse procedure to install.

IGNITION SWITCH
REPLACE

1. Remove mounting screws, fastener

and instrument panel lower panel.
2. Disconnect steering column upper shroud using suitable thin bladed screwdriver to release clip on each side.
3. Release locking lever, then remove mounting screws, ignition key and steering column lower shroud.
4. Disconnect electrical connectors.
5. Release clips and remove ignition switch.
6. Reverse procedure to install.

NEUTRAL SAFETY SWITCH
REPLACE

1. Disconnect Transmission Range (TR) sensor electrical connector and selector lever cable.
2. Remove manual control lever. **Shift lever must be held while loosening manual shaft lever.**
3. Remove mounting bolts and TR sensor.
4. Reverse procedure to install. Align TR sensor using alignment tool No. 307-415, or equivalent.

HEADLAMP SWITCH
REPLACE

1. Remove lefthand side lower footwell trim.
2. Remove mounting screws and disconnect lamp switch bezel.
3. Remove mounting screws and disconnect electrical connectors.
4. Remove headlamp switch.
5. Reverse procedure to install.

Item	Description
1	Rear wiper relay
2	Windscreen wiper relay
3	Fuse F35 (7,5 A) - Interior lights
4	Fuse F36 (7,5 A) - Interior lights
5	Fuse F39 (10A) - reversing lights
8	Fuse F59 (7,5 A) - Direction indicators, electronic module
9	Fuse F47 (7,5A) - left-hand side lights
10	Fuse F54 (15 A) - Brake light
11	Fuse F53 (10A) - reversing lights
12	Fuse F44 (20 A) - Fog lamps
13	Fuse F32 (10 A) for instrument cluster illumination
14	Fuse F33 (15 A) - Hazard warning lights switch

FM9049900302020X

Fig. 2 Fuse box (Part 2 of 2)

STEERING WHEEL
REPLACE

1. Remove air bag module as outlined in "Passive Restraint Systems" chapter.
2. Ensure steering wheel is centered.
3. Remove ignition key to lock steering in position.
4. Disconnect speed control electrical connector.
5. Remove mounting bolt and steering wheel.
6. Reverse procedure to install, noting the following:
   a. Ensure air bag sliding contact is centralized.
   b. Turn steering wheel counterclockwise to ensure location.

INSTRUMENT CLUSTER
REPLACE

1. Disconnect instrument cluster bezel.
2. Disconnect luggage compartment release switch electrical connector and remove instrument cluster bezel.
3. Remove instrument cluster mounting screws.
4. Release locking tang and disconnect electrical connector.
5. Remove instrument cluster. **Instrument cluster must be kept upright to avoid leaking silicone liquid from gauges.**
6. Reverse procedure to install.

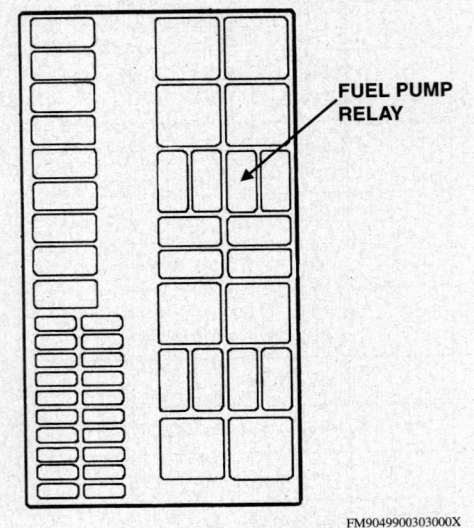

FM9049900303000X

Fig. 3 Battery junction box

FUEL PUMP RELAY

RADIO
REPLACE

1. Install radio remover tools No. T87P-19061-A, or equivalent, into locating holes until they click into place.
2. Pull tools gently left and right until locking tangs release.
3. Slide radio out of instrument panel.
4. Disconnect electrical connectors and remove radio.
5. Reverse procedure to install.

WIPER MOTOR
REPLACE

Front

1. Ensure wiper motor is in park position.
2. Lift plastic caps and loosen wiper arm mounting nuts approximately two turns.
3. Disconnect wiper arms from taper and position aside.
4. Remove mounting nuts and wiper arms.
5. Remove caps, mounting bolts and air cowl grille.
6. Remove wiper motor protective cap and disconnect electrical connector.
7. Remove mounting bolts, wiper motor and linkage.
8. Mark lever to assembly plate position for installation alignment.
9. Remove mounting nut and bolts, then the wiper motor from plate and lever.
10. Reverse procedure to install, noting the following:
    a. Ensure wiper motor is in park position.
    b. Fit guide pins before fitting mounting bolts when installing wiper linkage.
    c. Ensure wiper blades do not touch air cowl griller or molding.

Rear

1. Ensure wiper motor is in park position.

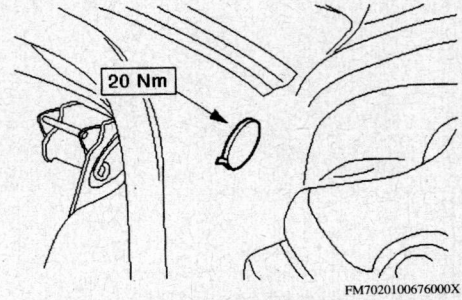

FM7020100676000X

Fig. 4 Cross-vehicle blind bolt replacement

20 Nm

2. Lift plastic caps and loosen wiper arm mounting nuts approximately two turns.
3. Disconnect wiper arms from taper and position aside.
4. Remove mounting nuts and wiper arms.
5. Remove two mounting bolts, 10 clips and cover.
6. Disconnect wiper motor electrical connector and ground lead.
7. Remove mounting bolts and wiper motor from bracket.
8. Reverse procedure to install. Ensure wiper motor is in park position.

BLOWER MOTOR
REPLACE

1. Remove righthand footwell lower trim.
2. Open glove compartment.
3. Disconnect hose and remove footwell vent air duct.
4. Close glove compartment.
5. Disconnect electrical connector.
6. Remove mounting screws and blower motor.
7. Reverse procedure to install.

CABIN AIR FILTER
REPLACE

1. Position wipers vertically.
2. Disconnect two clips, then remove mounting bolt and righthand air cowl grille.
3. Open service flap and remove cabin air filter.
4. Reverse procedure to install, noting the following:
   a. Ensure filter is installed in correct direction flow.
   b. Clean grille rubber edging between wiper motor and filter housing.
   c. Install new air cowl grille gasket.
   d. Ensure air cowl grille gasket for windscreen is seated correctly.

HEATER CORE
REPLACE

1. Install radio remover tools No. T87P-19061-A, or equivalent, into locating holes until they click into place.
2. Pull tools gently left and right until locking tangs release.
3. Slide radio out of instrument panel.
4. Disconnect electrical connectors and remove radio.

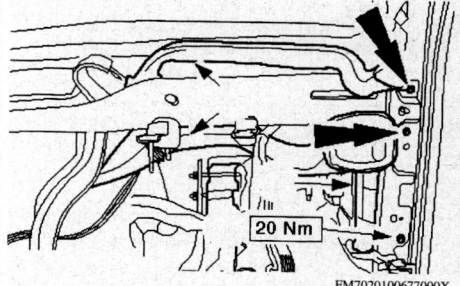

Fig. 5 Ventilation hoses & wiring harness replacement

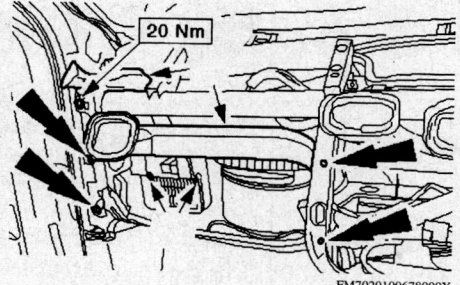

Fig. 6 Central junction box and ventilation hose replacement

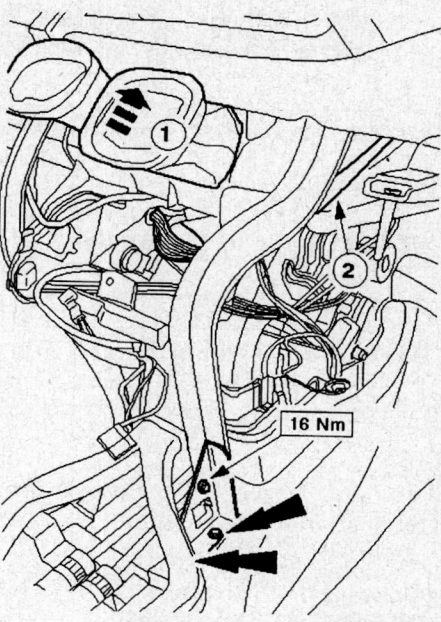

Fig. 7 Cross-vehicle beam replacement

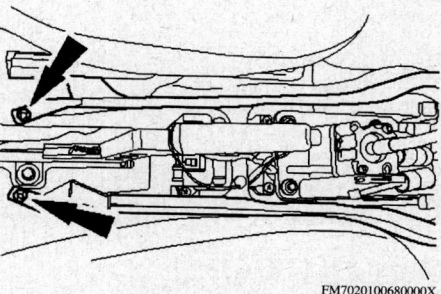

Fig. 8 Rear footwell ventilation hoses replacement

5. Recover air conditioning refrigerant as outlined in "Air Conditioning" chapter.
6. Drain cooling system into suitable container.
7. Remove instrument panel as outlined in "Dash Panel Service" chapter.
8. Disconnect heat exchanger take off connection coolant hoses.
9. Disconnect evaporator refrigerant lines using suitable air conditioning fitting removal tool.
10. Remove cap and mounting bolt, **Fig. 4.**
11. Remove ventilation hoses and mounting screws, then disconnect wiring harnesses from beam, **Fig. 5.**
12. Remove ventilation hoses and mounting screws, then disconnect junction box from cross-vehicle beam, **Fig. 6.**
13. Remove ventilation hose and disconnect wiring harnesses from beam.
14. Remove bracket and cross-vehicle beam, **Fig. 7.**
15. Remove rear footwell ventilation hoses, **Fig. 8.**
16. Disconnect wiring harnesses from heater housing.
17. Remove heater housing mounting nuts from passenger and engine compartments.
18. Remove heater housing.
19. Reverse procedure to install.

EVAPORATOR CORE
REPLACE

Refer to "Heater Core, Replace" for evaporator core replacement.

TECHNICAL SERVICE BULLETINS

Loss of Intermittent Wiper Or Park Function

2004-05

On some of these models the wipers may intermittently be inoperative, one sweep function may stop in the middle of glass when the stalk is released or the wipers may jump when parked from intermittent mode.

This condition may be caused by the wiper relay.

To correct this condition, replace the wiper relay.

White Flakes Coming From A/C Vents

2004-05

Some models may exhibit white flakes coming from the A/C vents when the blower motor is engaged.

This condition may be caused by brazing flux utilized in the manufacturing process of the evaporator core.

To correct this condition, clean the A/C ducts through the registers and blow off the evaporator core through the blower motor opening as follows:

1. Evaporator core surface must be dry for best results.
2. Remove floor duct trim
3. Connect one end of vacuum cleaner hose to floor duct on driver side using masking tape.
4. Tape closed all other floor duct openings.
5. Obtain about two feet of rubber vacuum line large enough to fit end of a small shop air blowgun. Secure hose to end of blowgun using a suitable clamp.
6. Close all instrument panel registers.
7. Set temperature setting to full cold.
8. Place mode switch in Floor/Panel.
9. Turn on vacuum cleaner.
10. Working with one register at a time insert vacuum line down each duct, blow shop air through each duct for 30 seconds. Be sure to close each register before moving on to the next register.
11. Change mode switch to Floor/Defrost.
12. Blow shop air down each defroster duct for 30 seconds.
13. Alternate mode door between Floor and Floor/Defrost three times, giving door time to move between each mode change.
14. Turn off vacuum cleaner.
15. Remove blower motor.
16. Turn on vacuum cleaner.
17. Reach into blower opening with vacuum line and proceed to blow shop air for a minimum of 5 minutes, utilizing a very slow sweeping action.
18. Blow entire core face in up and down direction, then repeat moving from side to side.
19. Reinstall blower motor.
20. Open all registers.
21. Operate system with A/C on and blower on Max in each mode setting with temperature full Cold and then full Warm. Be sure to stay in each mode position for at least 30 seconds to ensure removal of any residual flakes/dust.
22. Disconnect vacuum cleaner and remove tape from floor duct.
23. Reassemble floor duct trim.

2.0L (VINs 3 & 5) DOHC Engines

NOTE: On Air Bag Equipped Models, Refer To "Air Bag System Precautions" Located In The Front Of This Manual For System Disarming & Arming Procedures.

NOTE: Refer To "Computer Relearn Procedures" Located In The Front Of This Manual When Battery Power To The Computer Has Been Interrupted.

NOTE: Prior To Performing Any Service Operations Listed In This Section, Consult The "Technical Service Bulletins" Section For Related Information.

INDEX

	Page No.		Page No.		Page No.
Camshaft, Replace	6-13	VIN 3	6-11	Serpentine Drive Belt	6-14
Installation	6-13	VIN 5	6-11	Replace	6-14
Removal	6-13	Fuel Filter, Replace	6-14	Routing	6-14
Compression Pressure	6-8	Fuel Pump, Replace	6-14	Technical Service Bulletins	6-14
Crankshaft Damper, Replace	6-12	Intake Manifold, Replace	6-10	Engine Vibration At Idle	6-14
Crankshaft Rear Oil Seal,		VIN 3	6-10	2004–05	6-14
Replace	6-13	VIN 5	6-10	Thermostat, Replace	6-14
Crankshaft Seal, Replace	6-13	Oil Pan, Replace	6-13	Tightening Specifications	6-16
Cylinder Head, Replace	6-11	Precautions	6-8	Timing Belt, Replace	6-12
VIN 3	6-11	Air Bag Systems	6-8	Installation	6-12
VIN 5	6-11	Battery Ground Cable	6-8	Removal	6-12
Engine Rebuilding		Fuel System Pressure Relief	6-8	Valve Adjustment	6-12
Specifications	21-1	Quick Disconnect Hoses	6-8	Valve Clearance Specifications	6-12
Engine, Replace	6-9	R-Clip	6-8	Valve Cover, Replace	6-12
VIN 3	6-9	Spring Lock	6-8	Water Pump, Replace	6-14
VIN 5	6-9	Vapor Tube	6-8		
Exhaust Manifold, Replace	6-11	Radiator, Replace	6-14		

PRECAUTIONS

Air Bag Systems

Refer to "Air Bag System Precautions" in the front of this manual for system disarming and arming procedures.

Battery Ground Cable

Prior to service, disconnect battery ground cable and isolate as required.

Fuel System Pressure Relief

1. Remove fuel pump fuse.
2. Start engine and idle until engine stalls.
3. Crank engine for approximately five seconds to ensure fuel supply manifold pressure has been relieved.
4. Install fuel pump fuse.

Quick Disconnect Hoses

R-CLIP

When working with R-clip type connections, do not use tools to disconnect, **Fig. 1.**

Use of tools may deform clip components and could cause leaks.
To disconnect, proceed as follows:
1. Bend shipping tab downward.
2. Spread R-clip and push clip into fitting.
3. Separate fitting from tube.
To connect, proceed as follows:
1. Inspect fitting and tube for damage and ensure connections are clean.
2. Apply light coat of suitable, clean engine oil to male end of tube.
3. Insert R-clip into fitting.
4. Align tube and fitting, then insert tube into fitting and push together until click is heard.
5. Pull on connection to ensure it is fully engaged.

SPRING LOCK

When working with spring lock type connections, spring lock tool set No. T84L-19623-B, or equivalent, must be used to disconnect fittings, **Fig. 2.**
When connecting spring lock type fittings, proceed as follows:
1. Inspect and clean both coupling ends.
2. Lubricate fuel line O-ring seals with suitable, clean engine oil.
3. When connection is made, pull on line to ensure it is fully engaged.

VAPOR TUBE

To disconnect vapor tube connections,

squeeze fitting and disconnect vapor tube from fitting, **Fig. 3.**
To connect, proceed as follows:
1. Ensure fittings are clean and free from damage.
2. Push tube onto fitting until it snaps into place.
3. Pull on connection to verify fitting is secure.

COMPRESSION PRESSURE

1. Ensure crankcase oil is of correct viscosity and at correct level.
2. Ensure battery is fully charged and engine is at normal operating temperature.
3. Turn ignition switch to OFF position.
4. Remove spark plugs.
5. Set throttle plates to wide open position.
6. Install suitable compression gauge in cylinder No. 1.
7. Install auxiliary starter switch in starting circuit.
8. With ignition switch off, use to crank engine at least five compression strokes using auxiliary starter switch.
9. Record number of compression strokes required to reach highest reading and record highest reading.

10. Repeat test on each cylinder, cranking engine same number of compression strokes.
11. Lowest cylinder reading must be within 75% of highest reading.

ENGINE
REPLACE

VIN 3

1. Relieve fuel system pressure as outlined under "Precautions."
2. Ensure engine is cool, then open coolant expansion tank.
3. Remove battery and tray, then disconnect ground cable.
4. Disconnect Mass Air Flow (MAF) sensor, Positive Crankcase Ventilation (PCV) hose and intake hose from air cleaner housing.
5. Remove air cleaner housing.
6. Disconnect body ground cables.
7. Remove air cleaner intake hose from core support.
8. Raise and support vehicle.
9. Drain engine coolant into suitable container. Install drain plug.
10. Drain engine oil into suitable container. Install drain plug.
11. Partially lower vehicle.
12. Loosen lefthand and righthand suspension strut center nuts five turns. Prevent strut piston rod from turning by using suitable Allen key.
13. Loosen lefthand and righthand front wheel nuts.
14. **On models equipped with manual transaxle,** proceed as follows:
    a. Move shift lever to neutral position.
    b. Remove shift lever cover.
    c. Attach gearshift alignment tool No. T97P-7025-A, or equivalent, to gearshift lever.
15. **On all models,** disconnect speed control and accelerator cables.
16. Disconnect ignition coil, radio interference filter and heated oxygen sensor connectors.
17. Disconnect cooling fan, duel injector, alternator and engine harness connectors.
18. **On models equipped with manual transaxle,** disconnect clutch slave cylinder high pressure line.
19. **On all models,** raise and support vehicle.
20. **On models equipped with manual transaxle,** disconnect reverse lamp switch.
21. **On all models,** disconnect Vehicle Speed Sensor (VSS) and Crankshaft Position (CKP) sensor.
22. Remove air deflector and cooling fan.
23. Partially lower vehicle.
24. Disconnect engine and brake servo vacuum hoses.
25. Disconnect fuel lines and coolant hoses.
26. **On models equipped with automatic transaxle,** proceed as follows:
    a. Disconnect selector lever cable from transaxle.
    b. Remove oil filler pipe/selector cable bracket.

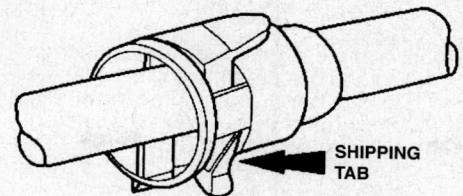

FM1069900923000X

Fig. 1 R-clip connection

c. Mark location of transaxle cooling lines for installation alignment, then remove.
27. **On models equipped with manual transaxle,** proceed as follows:
    a. Disconnect shift cable from gear lever.
    b. Pretension abutment collars by turning counterclockwise and remove cable assembly from bracket.
    c. Disconnect selector cable from selector lever.
    d. Pretension abutment collars by turning counterclockwise and remove cable assembly from bracket.
    e. Release adjustment mechanism by pressing inward.
28. **On all models,** raise and support vehicle.
29. Remove drive belt cover.
30. Disconnect Power Steering Pressure (PSP) switch and remove accessory drive belt.
31. **On models equipped with air conditioning,** remove compressor from mounting bracket, and attach it to radiator crossmember.
32. **On all models,** disconnect coolant hose and remove power steering pump bolts.
33. Lower vehicle, then disconnect coolant expansion tank and position aside.
34. Remove power steering reservoir and position aside.
35. Disconnect bracket of power steering high pressure pipe.
36. Remove power steering pump.
37. Raise and support vehicle.
38. Remove flexible exhaust pipe.
39. Remove engine roll restrictor.
40. Remove mounting bolts and disconnect lower ball joint from steering knuckle.
41. Disconnect intermediate shaft bearing cap and discard nuts and bearing cap. **Do not bend inner joint more than 18° or outer joint more than 45°.**
42. Pull intermediate shaft with front halfshaft from transmission and support using suitable mechanics wire.
43. Remove lefthand driveshaft from transaxle and support using suitable mechanics wire.
44. Install plug tool No. T81P-4026-A, or equivalent, to both sides of differential.
45. Place suitable assembly table with wooden blocks under vehicle.
46. Lower vehicle until engine and transmission assembly is on assembly stand.
47. Secure engine and transmission assembly to assembly stand using suitable safety strap.
48. Remove rear and front engine mounts.

49. Raise and support vehicle.
50. Install engine lift brackets tool No. T70P-6000 and spreader bar tool No. D93P-6001-A3, or equivalents to engine.
51. Attaching suitable lifting crane to spreader bar.
52. Remove starter motor and ground cable.
53. Remove engine to transmission mounting bolts and separate engine from transmission.
54. Reverse procedure to install noting the following:
    a. When installing driveshafts, use new snap rings, center bearing caps and bolts.
    b. Install righthand, then lefthand halfshaft.

VIN 5

1. Relieve fuel system pressure as outlined under "Precautions."
2. Ensure engine is cool, then open coolant expansion tank.
3. Remove battery, then battery tray.
4. Disconnect upper clip on air cleaner outlet tube.
5. Disconnect Mass Air Flow (MAF) sensor electrical connector and breather pipe from air cleaner housing.
6. Remove air cleaner.
7. Disconnect ground cable from inner fender.
8. Remove air cleaner intake hose and resonator.
9. Raise and support vehicle.
10. Drain engine coolant into suitable container. Install drain plug.
11. Drain engine oil into suitable container. Install drain plug.
12. Partially lower vehicle.
13. Loosen lefthand and righthand suspension strut center nuts five turns. Use suitable Allen key to prevent strut piston rod from turning.
14. Disconnect speed control and accelerator cables from throttle body.
15. Remove electronic ignition coil cover.
16. Disconnect fuel injector wiring harness.
17. Disconnect ground cable from engine lifting eye.
18. Disconnect alternator electrical connector.
19. Disconnect high pressure line from clutch slave cylinder.
20. Raise and support vehicle.
21. Disconnect Vehicle Speed Sensor (VSS).
22. Disconnect reverse lamp switch electrical connector.
23. Partially lower vehicle.
24. Disconnect engine vacuum hoses from intake manifold.
25. Release quick release coupling and disconnect brake booster pipe from intake manifold.
26. Disconnect fuel lines and coolant hoses.
27. Disconnect shift and selector cables from selector levers.
28. Disconnect retaining bracket from transaxle.
29. Raise and support vehicle.

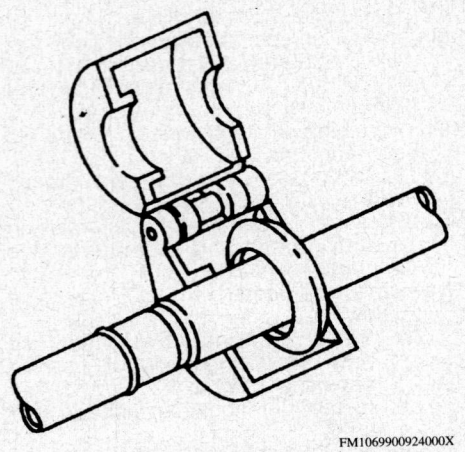

Fig. 2 Spring lock connection

30. Remove drive belt cover, rotate tensioner clockwise. Remove accessory drive belt.
31. **On models equipped with air conditioning,** remove compressor from mounting bracket, and attach to radiator crossmember.
32. **On all models,** disconnect radiator lower coolant hose from radiator.
33. Disconnect coolant hose from oil cooler.
34. Lower vehicle, disconnect coolant expansion tank and position aside.
35. Ensure road wheels are in straight ahead position and lock them in position.
36. Disconnect steering column from steering gear pinion extension.
37. Drain power steering reservoir into suitable container.
38. Remove power steering reservoir and position aside.
39. Raise and support vehicle.
40. Remove flexible exhaust pipe.
41. Remove front tire and wheel assemblies.
42. Loosen tie-rod end mounting nut on both sides. **Leave tie-rod end mounting nuts in place.**
43. Disconnect tie-rod end from wheel knuckle on both sides using tie-rod end remover tool No. TOOL-3290-D, or equivalent. **Protect ball joint seal with soft cloth.** Discard tie-rod end mounting nuts.
44. Disconnect stabilizer bar connecting link from stabilizer bar on both sides. Use 5 mm Allen Key to prevent ball joint from rotating.
45. Remove heat shields.
46. Disconnect lower arm ball joint from wheel knuckle on both sides. **Protect ball joint seal with soft cloth.**
47. Remove engine support insulator to transaxle center mounting bolt.
48. Remove steering gear heat shield.
49. Disconnect power steering line to clamp.
50. Remove power steering line clamp mounting bolt.
51. Rotate power steering clamp clockwise. Drain oil into suitable container.
52. Support crossmember with suitable transmission jack.

53. Remove c mounting bolts and cross-member.
54. Disconnect intermediate shaft bearing cap and discard nuts and bearing cap. **Do not bend inner joint more than 18° or outer joint i more than 45°.**
55. Pull intermediate shaft with front half-shaft from transmission and support using suitable mechanics wire.
56. Remove lefthand driveshaft from transaxle using halfshaft remover tool No. T86P-3514-A, or equivalent. Support it aside using mechanics wire and discard snap ring.
57. Place suitable assembly table with wooden blocks under vehicle.
58. Lower vehicle until engine and transmission assembly is on assembly stand.
59. Secure engine and transmission assembly to assembly stand using suitable safety strap.
60. Remove rear and front engine mounts.
61. Raise and support vehicle.
62. Install engine lift brackets tool No. T70P-6000 and spreader bar tool No. D93P-6001-A3, or equivalents, to engine.
63. Attaching suitable lifting crane to spreader bar.
64. Remove catalyst monitor sensor.
65. Support catalytic convertor and remove support bracket.
66. Remove heated oxygen sensor.
67. Disconnect catalytic convertor from exhaust manifold. Discard gaskets and nuts.
68. Remove engine to transmission upper mounting bolts.
69. Disconnect ground cable from transaxle.
70. Remove starter motor and secure aside.
71. Remove engine to transmission mounting bolts, then separate engine from transmission.
72. Reverse procedure to install. noting the following:
   a. Install new exhaust flange gasket and nuts.
   b. Installing new front driveshaft snap rings, center bearing caps and bolts.
   c. Install righthand, then lefthand half-shaft.
   d. Bleed hydraulic clutch system.

INTAKE MANIFOLD
REPLACE
VIN 3

1. Relieve fuel system pressure as outlined under "Precautions."
2. Remove alternator.
3. Disconnect Mass Air Flow (MAF) sensor electrical connector, crankcase ventilation hose and air intake hose from air cleaner housing.
4. Remove air cleaner housing.
5. Disconnect accelerator and speed control cables from throttle body.
6. Remove fuel pressure sensor.
7. Remove Exhaust Gas Recirculation (EGR) valve and EGR pipe bracket.

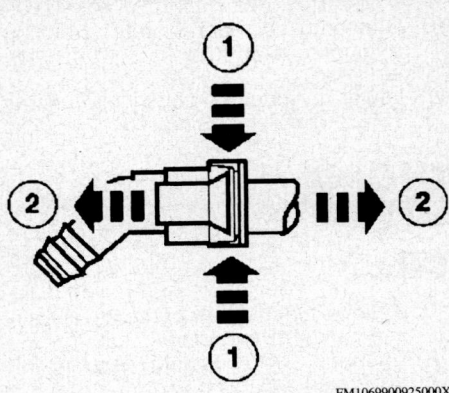

Fig. 3 Vapor tube connection

8. Disconnect vacuum hoses from throttle body.
9. Disconnect fuel injector and Camshaft Position (CMP) sensor electrical connectors.
10. Remove fuel line from throttle body.
11. Remove engine lifting eye.
12. Remove intake manifold studs from front of engine.
13. Remove intake manifold mounting bolts, nuts and intake manifold.
14. Reverse procedure to install.

VIN 5

1. Relieve fuel system pressure as outlined under "Precautions."
2. Raise and support vehicle.
3. Remove intake manifold lower mounting bolt.
4. Lower vehicle.
5. Disconnect inner cable from throttle body.
6. Disconnect Vehicle Speed Sensor (VSS) from throttle body.
7. Remove retaining clip and disconnect inner cable from throttle body.
8. Rotate outer cable.
9. Disconnect accelerator from throttle body.
10. Remove air cleaner outlet tube.
11. Disconnect fuel injector electrical connectors.
12. Remove fuel injection supply manifold.
13. Disconnect upper clip on air cleaner outlet tube.
14. Disconnect Mass Air Flow (MAF) Sensor and breather pipe from air cleaner housing.
15. Remove air cleaner housing.
16. Disconnect throttle Position Sensor (TPS) electrical connector.
17. Rotate Intake Manifold Runner Control (IMRC) lever.
18. Remove IMRC actuator cable.
19. Release IMRC actuator cable locking tangs.
20. Disconnect IRMC actuator from intake manifold.
21. Disconnect vacuum hoses from throttle body.
22. Release quick release coupling and pull out brake booster pipe.
23. Disconnect brake booster pipe from intake manifold.
24. Remove fuel line from throttle body.

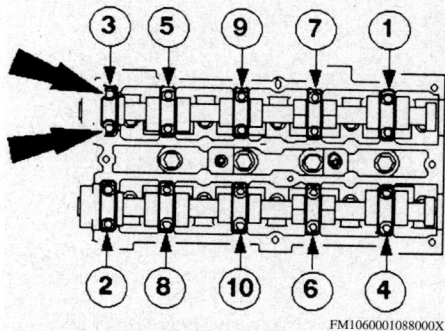

Fig. 4 Camshaft bearing cap bolt loosening sequence

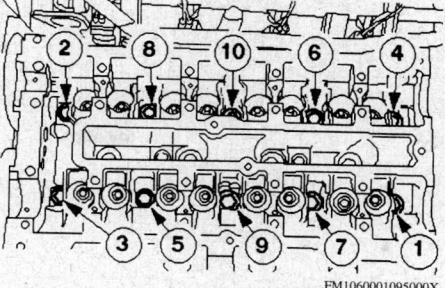

Fig. 5 Cylinder head bolt loosening sequence

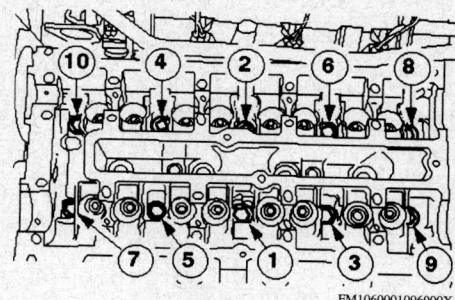

Fig. 6 Cylinder head bolt tightening sequence

25. Separate two sections of intake manifold.
26. Remove manifold inner section mounting nuts and bolt.
27. Remove intake manifold inner section retaining stud.
28. Remove intake manifold section.
29. Reverse procedure to install.

EXHAUST MANIFOLD
REPLACE

VIN 3

1. Raise and support vehicle.
2. Remove catalyst bracket and disconnect heated oxygen sensor electrical connectors.
3. Lower vehicle and remove heat shield from side of engine.
4. Disconnect Mass Air Flow (MAF) sensor.
5. Disconnect Positive Crankcase Ventilation (PCV) hose.
6. Disconnect air inlet hose and remove air cleaner housing.
7. Remove Exhaust Gas Recirculation (EGR) tube.
8. Remove catalytic converter to exhaust manifold mounting bolts.
9. Remove manifold to cylinder head mounting bolts and exhaust manifold.
10. Reverse procedure to install.

VIN 5

1. Remove oil dipstick.
2. Disconnect cooling fan motor electrical connectors.
3. Remove two pin-type retainers.
4. Raise and support vehicle.
5. Disconnect radiator top clip. then remove cooling fan motor and shroud.
6. Raise vehicle and support.
7. Remove heat shield lower mounting bolts.
8. Disconnect exhaust manifold from catalytic converter.
9. Lower vehicle.
10. Remove exhaust manifold heat shield.
11. Remove exhaust manifold and discard gaskets.
12. Reverse procedure to install.

CYLINDER HEAD
REPLACE

VIN 3

1. Raise and support vehicle.
2. Drain engine coolant into suitable container. Install drain plug after draining.
3. Release quick release coupling and disconnect brake booster pipe from intake manifold.
4. Disconnect oil pressure switch connector.
5. Lower vehicle and remove intake manifold as outlined under "Intake Manifold, Replace."
6. Remove exhaust manifold heat shield, then catalytic converter to exhaust manifold mounting bolts.
7. Remove thermostat housing mounting bolts, then thermostat housing.
8. Remove power steering pipe bracket and oil dipstick tube.
9. Disconnect bracket from power steering pump.
10. Loosen lefthand side bolt and remove righthand side bolt of alternator.
11. Remove upper bolt from alternator bracket.
12. Remove timing belt as outlined under "Timing Belt, Replace."
13. Remove air intake pipe.
14. To prevent camshaft pulley from turning, attach camshaft pulley remover tool No. T74P-6256-B, or equivalent, to camshaft pulley.
15. Remove camshaft pulleys mounting bolts, then camshaft pulleys.
16. Remove camshaft bearing cap mounting bolts in several steps in sequence, **Fig. 4.**
17. Remove oil seals and camshafts.
18. Remove cylinder head mounting bolts in sequence, **Fig. 5.**
19. Remove cylinder head.
20. Reverse procedure to install, noting the following:
    a. **Torque** new cylinder head bolts in sequence to 15 ft. lbs., **Fig. 6.**
    b. **Torque** head bolts in sequence to 30 ft. lbs.
    c. Tighten bolts an additional 90° in sequence.

VIN 5

1. Relieve fuel system pressure as outlined under "Precautions."

2. Relieve cooling system pressure by turning expansion tank cap ¼ turn. Remove cap when pressure has been released.
3. Raise and support vehicle.
4. Drain cooling system into suitable container.
5. Install radiator drain plug after draining coolant.
6. Release quick release coupling and disconnect brake booster pipe from intake manifold.
7. Disconnect oil pressure switch electrical connector.
8. Lower vehicle.
9. Remove air cleaner.
10. Disconnect accelerator cable from throttle body.
11. Disconnect vacuum hoses from intake manifold.
12. Disconnect fuel injector wiring harness.
13. Disconnect Camshaft Position (CMP) sensor electrical connector.
14. Disconnect fuel lines and ground cable.
15. Remove exhaust manifold as outlined under "Exhaust Manifold, Replace."
16. Disconnect thermostat housing.
17. Disconnect power steering pipe bracket from cylinder head.
18. Disconnect power steering pump bracket from cylinder head and cylinder block.
19. Loosen lefthand bolt and remove righthand alternator mounting bolt.
20. Disconnect wiring harness from Electronic Ignition (EI) coil and from Engine Coolant Temperature (ECT) sensor.
21. Remove alternator bracket upper mounting bolt.
22. Remove timing belt as outlined under "Timing Belt, Replace."
23. Hold camshafts by hexagon with an open ended wrench to prevent them from rotating.
24. Remove mounting bolts camshaft pulleys.
25. Remove oil feed flange and discard camshaft oil seals and oil feed flange oil seal.
26. Remove camshaft bearing cap mounting bolts in several steps in sequence, **Fig. 4.**
27. Remove camshaft.
28. Remove cylinder head mounting bolts in sequence, **Fig. 5.**
29. Remove cylinder head.

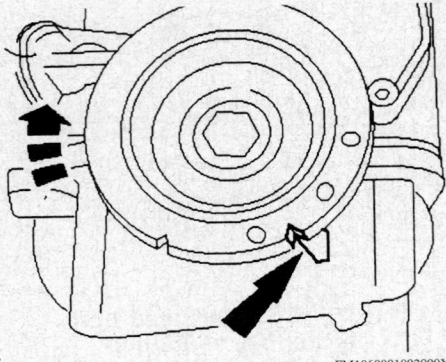

FM1060001092000X

Fig. 7 Crankshaft timing mark alignment

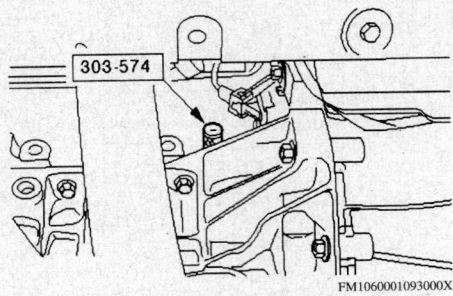

FM1060001093000X

Fig. 8 Crankshaft TDC timing peg installation

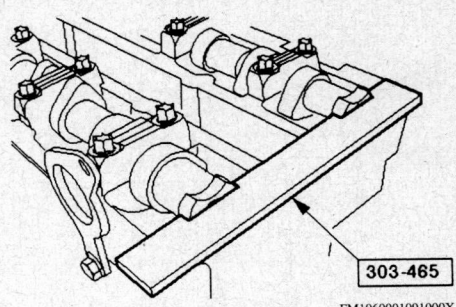

FM1060001091000X

Fig. 9 Camshaft alignment

30. Reverse procedure to install, noting the following:
   a. **Torque** new torque-to-yield cylinder head bolts in sequence to 15 ft. lbs., **Fig. 6.**
   b. **Torque** head bolts in sequence to 30 ft. lbs
   c. Tighten bolts an additional 90° in sequence.

VALVE COVER
REPLACE

1. Remove air inlet hose from throttle body and air cleaner housing.
2. Remove upper timing belt cover mounting bolts. Do not remove timing belt cover.
3. Disconnect spark plug connectors and crankcase ventilation hose.
4. Remove valve cover mounting bolts from outside to inside, working diagonally.
5. Remove valve cover.
6. Reverse procedure to install.

VALVE CLEARANCE SPECIFICATIONS

Valve	Clearance, Inches①
Intake	.0043–.0071
Exhaust	.0106–.0134

① — At 59–77°F.

VALVE ADJUSTMENT

1. Remove air inlet hose from throttle body and air cleaner housing.
2. Remove upper timing belt cover mounting bolts. Do not remove timing belt cover.
3. Disconnect spark plug connectors and crankcase ventilation hose.
4. Remove valve cover mounting bolts from the outside to the inside, working diagonally.
5. Remove valve cover.
6. Turn crankshaft to cylinder No. 1 Top Dead Center (TDC).
7. Measure valve clearance on cylinder No. 1, using suitable feeler gauge.
8. Rotate engine 180°, then measure valve clearance on cylinder No. 3.
9. Rotate engine 180°, then measure valve clearance on cylinder No. 4.
10. Rotate engine 180°, then measure valve clearance on cylinder No. 2.
11. If valve adjustment is required, remove camshafts as outlined under "Camshaft, Replace."
12. Each tappet is marked with number that indicates its thickness in millimeters.
13. To determine correct size tappet required, add tappet size to measured clearance.
14. Select and install a tappet that will bring clearance within specifications. Refer to "Valve Clearance Specifications."
15. Install camshafts as outlined under "Camshaft, Replace."

CRANKSHAFT DAMPER
REPLACE

1. Move serpentine belt tensioner in clockwise to relieve accessory belt tension.
2. Remove serpentine belt.
3. Remove crankshaft pulley/vibration damper.
4. Reverse procedure to install.

TIMING BELT
REPLACE
Removal

1. Loosen righthand front wheel lug nuts.
2. Raise and support vehicle.
3. Remove righthand front tire and wheel assembly.
4. Remove serpentine drive belt cover.
5. Loosen water pump pulley bolts.
6. Move serpentine belt tensioner in clockwise to relieve accessory belt tension.
7. Remove serpentine belt.
8. Remove water pump pulley.
9. Remove serpentine drive belt idler pulley.
10. Remove crankshaft pulley mounting bolt.
11. Remove crankshaft pulley using suitable puller tool.
12. Remove lower portion of engine front cover.
13. Lower vehicle.
14. Remove fasteners and position coolant expansion tank aside.

15. Disconnect power steering fluid reservoir and position it aside with hose attached.
16. Position suitable floor jack and wooden block under engine oil pan.
17. Mark engine front support insulator mounting position for installation alignment.
18. Take pressure off engine front support insulator by raising floor jack slightly. Remove insulator.
19. Remove upper timing belt cover mounting bolts.
20. Remove center cover and front engine mounting bracket bolts.
21. Remove timing belt cover upper and center portions.
22. Remove engine appearance cover.
23. Mark spark plug wires, and disconnect them at spark plugs.
24. Disconnect crankcase ventilation hose.
25. Remove mounting bolts working diagonally from outside to inside and valve cover.
26. Remove spark plugs.
27. Rotate crankshaft until cylinder No. 1 is approximately at TDC position.
28. Record timing belt tensioner alignment marks and loosen tensioner bolt.
29. Rotate belt tensioner clockwise to release tension.
30. Loosen belt tensioner bolt four turns and disconnect tensioner.
31. Remove timing belt.

Installation

1. Loosen exhaust camshaft sprocket and intake camshaft sprocket using holding tool No. T74P-6256-B, or equivalent, to prevent camshaft sprockets from turning when loosening bolts.
2. Rotate crankshaft until cylinder No. 1 reaches TDC, **Fig. 7.**
3. Remove engine block slide blanking plug and install timing peg tool No. T97P-6000-A, or equivalent, **Fig. 8.**
4. Hold camshafts by hexagons and turn them in direction of engine rotation.
5. Install camshaft alignment tool No. T94P-6256-CH, or equivalent, **Fig. 9.**
6. Ensure crankshaft is still resting against timing peg. **Do not rotate crankshaft.**
7. With timing belt tensioner bolt backed out four full turns, position tensioner so location tab is at approximately four o'clock position, **Fig. 10.** Line up hex

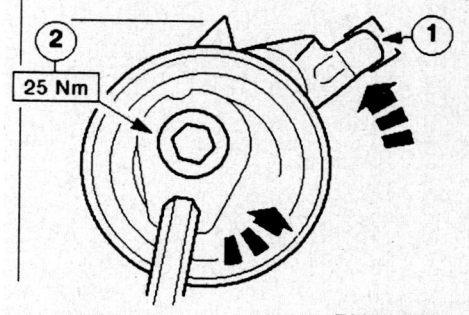

FM1060001094000X

Fig. 10 Timing belt tensioner alignment

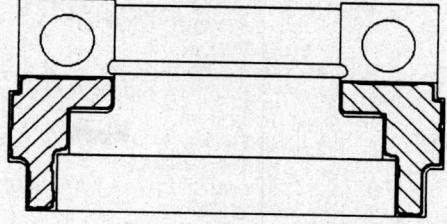

FM1060001089000X

Fig. 11 Camshaft bearing cap sealant application

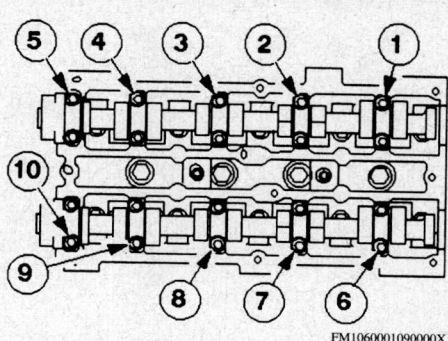

FM1060001090000X

Fig. 12 Camshaft bearing cap bolt tightening sequence

key slot in tensioner adjusting washer with pointer which is located behind pulley.

8. Starting at crankshaft and working counterclockwise, install timing belt.
9. Rotate timing belt tensioner locating tab counterclockwise and insert locating tab into slot in rear timing cover.
10. Position hex key slot in tensioner adjusting washer to 4 o'clock position.
11. Tighten tensioner bolt enough to seat tensioner firmly against rear timing belt cover, but still loose enough to allow tensioner adjusting washer to be rotated with 6 mm hex wrench.
12. Rotate adjusting washer counterclockwise until notch in pointer is centered over index line on locating tab using 6 mm hex wrench. During adjustment pointer will move in clockwise direction.
13. While holding adjusting washer in position, tighten tensioner mounting bolt.
14. After tightening tensioner mounting bolt, ensure tensioner pointer is still aligned with index line. If not, repeat previous steps.
15. Prevent camshaft sprockets from turning, by using holding tool No. T74P-6256-B, or equivalent. Tighten intake and exhaust camshaft sprockets.
16. Remove timing peg.
17. Remove camshaft locking tool.
18. Rotate crankshaft two revolutions in direction of engine rotation to cylinder No. 1 TDC compression stroke.
19. Install timing peg and ensure crankshaft timing is properly set.
20. Ensure camshaft timing is properly set by installing aligning tool No. T94P-6256-CH, or equivalent, onto camshafts. If aligning tool refuses to fit into both slots, loosen tensioner and both camshaft sprocket bolts, then tension timing belt again.
21. Remove alignment tool from camshafts and timing peg for crankshaft. Install blanking plug in crankshaft timing peg hole.
22. Install valve cover.
23. Install spark plugs.
24. Connect crankcase ventilation hose.
25. Connect spark plug wires.
26. Install engine appearance cover.
27. Install center and upper portions of engine front cover and engine support bracket.
28. Raise floor jack slightly and install engine support insulator.
29. Install coolant expansion tank.
30. Raise and support vehicle.
31. Install lower portion of timing belt cover.
32. Install crankshaft pulley.
33. Install serpentine belt idler and water pump pulleys.
34. Rotate serpentine belt tensioner clockwise and install belt.
35. Tighten water pump pulley bolts.
36. Install serpentine drive belt cover.
37. Install righthand front tire and wheel assembly.
38. Lower vehicle.
39. Tighten righthand front wheel lug nuts.
40. **Some abnormal drive symptoms may appear for approximately 10 miles while vehicle relearns its adaptive strategy.**

CAMSHAFT
REPLACE
Removal

1. Remove air intake pipe.
2. Disconnect accelerator and speed control cables from throttle body.
3. Remove timing belt as outlined under "Timing Belt, Replace."
4. Prevent camshaft pulley from turning, by installing camshaft pulley remover tool No. T74P-6256-B, or equivalent, to camshaft pulley.
5. Remove mounting bolts and camshaft pulleys.
6. Remove camshaft bearing cap mounting bolts in several steps in sequence, **Fig. 4.**
7. Remove oil seals and camshafts.

Installation

1. Camshaft bearing caps have identification numbers stamped on outer face. Apply suitable sealant to bearing caps marked 0 and 5, **Fig. 11.**
2. Turn crankshaft to approximately 60° Before Top Dead Center (BTDC) on cylinder No. 1.
3. Lubricate camshafts and bearing caps with suitable, clean engine oil.
4. Place camshafts into position so none of cams are at full lift.
5. Tighten camshaft bearing cap bolts evenly ½ turn at a time in sequence, **Fig. 12.**
6. **Torque** bolts in sequence to 88 inch lbs.
7. **Torque** bolts in sequence to 14 ft. lbs.

8. Lubricate camshaft and new camshaft oil seal lip with suitable, clean engine oil, then install oil seal.
9. Install camshaft timing pulleys. **Do not tighten pulley bolts fully at this time. Pulleys must be able to turn freely on camshafts.**
10. Install timing belt as outlined under "Timing Belt, Replace."
11. Connect accelerator and speed control cables to throttle body.
12. Install air intake pipe.

CRANKSHAFT SEAL
REPLACE

1. Remove crankshaft timing belt as outlined under "Timing Belt, Replace."
2. Remove crankshaft pulley hub.
3. Remove timing belt thrust washer. Record position of thrust washer for installation alignment.
4. Remove crankshaft front oil seal using oil seal remover tool No. T81P-6700-A, or equivalent.
5. Reverse procedure to install. Lubricate new oil seal and crankshaft running surface with suitable, clean engine oil.

CRANKSHAFT REAR OIL SEAL
REPLACE

1. Remove transaxle as outlined in **MOTOR's** "Domestic Transmission, In-Vehicle Service" manual or "Transmission Service DVD."
2. **On models with manual transaxle,** remove clutch pressure plate and clutch disc as outlined in **MOTOR's** "Domestic Transmission, In-Vehicle Service" manual or "Transmission Service DVD."
3. **On all models,** remove flywheel using flywheel locking tool No. T74P-6375-A, or equivalent.
4. Remove crankshaft rear seal using seal remover tool No. T92C-6700-CH, or equivalent.
5. Reverse procedure to install. Install oil seal using crankshaft rear oil installer tool No. T88P-6701B-1, or equivalent.

OIL PAN
REPLACE

1. Raise and support vehicle, then drain engine oil into suitable container.

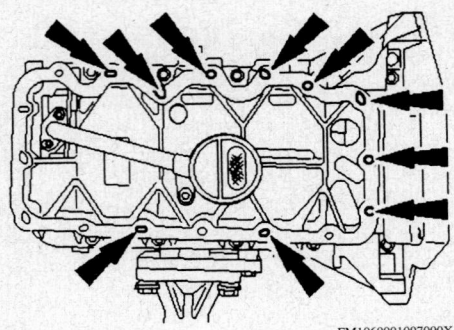

Fig. 13 Lower crankcase dead end bore stud installation

2. Remove catalytic converter.
3. Remove oil pan mounting bolts.
4. Separate oil pan from lower crankcase with suitable sharp tool.
5. Reverse procedure to install, noting the following:
   a. Install 10 M6 X 20 studs into dead end bores, **Fig. 13.**
   b. Apply suitable sealant to oil pan mating surface.
   c. **Install oil pan within 10 minutes of applying sealant.**
   d. **Torque** oil pan bolts in sequence to 53 inch lbs., **Fig. 14.**
   e. **Torque** bolts in sequence to 89 inch lbs.

SERPENTINE DRIVE BELT

Routing

Refer to **Figs. 15 and 16** for serpentine belt routing.

Replace

1. Raise and support vehicle.
2. Remove drive belt cover.
3. Loosen bolts on coolant pump pulley.
4. Rotate belt tensioner counterclockwise, and remove belt.
5. Reverse procedure to install.

THERMOSTAT

REPLACE

1. Drain engine cooling system into suitable container.
2. Disconnect thermostat housing coolant hoses.
3. Remove mounting bolts and thermostat housing.
4. Remove thermostat and discard rubber seal.
5. Reverse procedure to install.

WATER PUMP

REPLACE

1. Drain engine cooling system into suitable container.
2. Loosen water pump pulley mounting bolts.
3. Remove drive belt cover.

4. Loosen bolts on coolant pump pulley.
5. Rotate belt tensioner counterclockwise, and remove belt.
6. Remove water pump pulley.
7. Remove timing belt as outlined under "Timing Belt, Replace."
8. Remove timing belt idler pulley.
9. Disconnect water pump hose.
10. Remove lower and upper mounting bolts, then water pump.
11. Remove and discard water pump sealing ring.
12. Reverse procedure to install.

RADIATOR

REPLACE

1. Disconnect cooling fan motor electrical connectors.
2. Remove two pin-type retainers.
3. Raise and support vehicle.
4. Disconnect radiator top clip. then remove cooling fan motor and shroud.
5. Drain coolant into suitable container.
6. Remove four pin-type retainers from radiator air deflector.
7. Lower vehicle and disconnect upper radiator hose.
8. Raise and support vehicle.
9. **On models equipped with air conditioning,** support condenser and transaxle oil cooler.
10. **On all models,** disconnect radiator upper coolant hose.
11. Disconnect radiator lower coolant hoses.
12. Disconnect horn electrical connector.
13. Remove mounting bolts and radiator support bracket bolts.
14. Remove radiator.
15. Reverse procedure to install.

FUEL PUMP

REPLACE

1. Relieve fuel system pressure as outlined under "Precautions."
2. Drain fuel tank into suitable container.
3. Disconnect exhaust pipe from rear hanger insulator.
4. Disconnect center muffler from hanger.
5. Remove mounting nuts and disconnect exhaust pipe from remaining hangers. Position exhaust pipe aside.
6. Remove heat shield.
7. Disconnect fuel tank vent and filler pipes.
8. Disconnect inline fuel coupling as outlined under "Precautions."
9. Disconnect evaporative emission pipe and rollover valve connector.
10. Support fuel tank with suitable jack, then remove support strap bolt.
11. Partially lower tank and disconnect rollover valve hose.
12. Disconnect fuel pump electrical connector.
13. Disconnect fuel pressure sensor electrical connector.
14. Remove fuel tank.
15. Pull red fuel line clip fully towards fuel pump module.
16. Disconnect fuel supply line from mod-

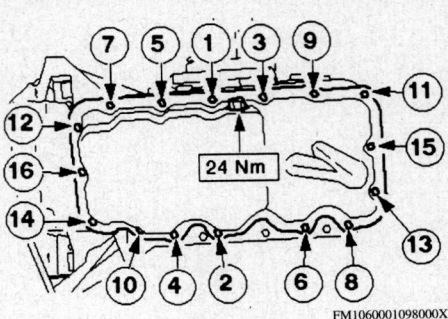

Fig. 14 Oil pan bolt tightening sequence

24 Nm

ule, by holding red fuel line clip against fuel pump module and firmly pulling line.
17. Remove locking ring using fuel tank sender unit wrench tool No. 310-069, or equivalent.
18. Rotate fuel pump module counterclockwise and remove it from tank. **Do not damage float or arm.**
19. Reverse procedure to install, noting the following:
    a. **Ensure red fuel line clip i clicks into place.**
    b. **Ensure that fuel line is fully seated by pulling on line. Clip should move slightly away from module and fuel line should not be able to be removed.**
    c. Ensure new fuel pump module seal is seated correctly on fuel tank prior to tightening locking ring.

FUEL FILTER

REPLACE

1. Relieve fuel system pressure as outlined under "Precautions."
2. Raise and support vehicle.
3. Disconnect evaporative emission pipe.
4. Remove fuel filter outlet pipe and disconnect inlet pipe.
5. Remove fuel filter and bracket.
6. Separate filter from bracket.
7. Reverse procedure to install.

TECHNICAL SERVICE BULLETINS

Engine Vibration At Idle

2004-05

Some models may have an excessive engine vibration at idle, most noticeable when the transmission is engaged in reverse.

This condition may be caused by small stones, road debris, ice or snow packed/lodged in the rear engine roll restrictor.

To correct this condition remove debris from rear engine roll restrictor and install service shield (P/N 2M5Z-16102-AA).

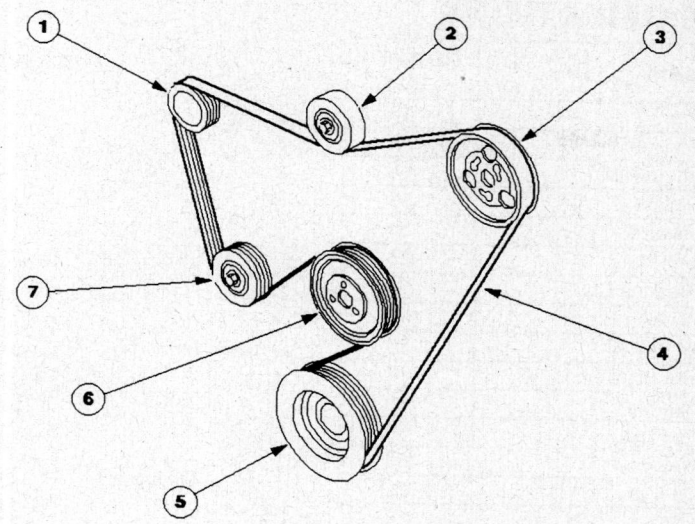

Item	Description
1	Generator pulley
2	Belt idler pulley
3	Power steering pump pulley
4	Accesory drive belt
5	Crankshaft pulley
6	Water pump pulley
7	Belt tensioner

FM1060001106000X

Fig. 15 Serpentine drive belt routing. Less air conditioning

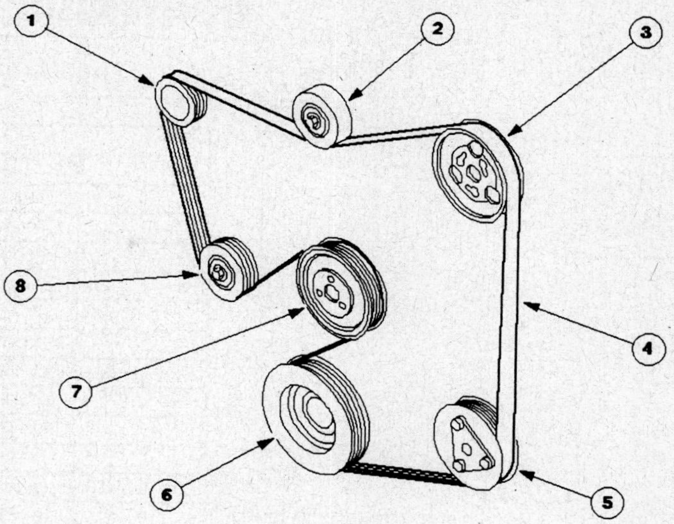

Item	Description
1	Generator pulley
2	Belt idler pulley
3	Power steering pump pulley
4	Accessory drive belt
5	A/C compressor pulley
6	Crankshaft pulley
7	Water pump pulley
8	Belt tensioner

FM1060001107000X

Fig. 16 Serpentine drive belt routing. With air conditioning

TIGHTENING SPECIFICATIONS

Year	Component	Torque Ft. Lbs.
2004–07	Alternator	18
	Alternator Bracket	48
	Camshaft Bearing Cap	③
	Camshaft Pulleys	50
	Catalytic Converter	35
	Clutch Pressure Plate	21
	Connecting Rod Bearing Cap	②
	Crankcase Ventilation Pipe Bracket	17
	Crankshaft Belt Pulley	85
	Cylinder Block Oil Gallery Blanking Plugs	17
	Cylinder Head	⑦
	Drive Belt Idler Pulley	30
	Driveplate	83
	EGR Pipe To Ignition Coil Bracket	53①
	EGR Valve	18
	Engine Roll Restrictor	35
	Exhaust Manifold Heat Shield	89①
	Exhaust Manifold Nuts	12
	Exhaust Manifold Studs	44①
	Flywheel	83
	Front Engine Lifting Eye	35
	Front Engine Mounting To Engine	59
	Fuel Pump Module	59
	Fuel Rail	89①
	Idler Pulley	17
	Ignition Coil Bracket	15
	Intake Manifold, Bolts & Nuts	13
	Intake Manifold, Studs	44①
	Lower Crankcase To Cylinder Block	16
	Main Bearing	⑤
	Oil Drain Plug	18
	Oil Intake Pipe To Oil Pump	89①
	Oil Pan	④
	Oil Pressure Switch	20
	Oil Pump	96①
	Power Steering Pump	18
	Rear Crankshaft Oil Seal Carrier	13
	Rear Engine Lifting Eye	35
	Rear Engine Mounting To Body	35
	Spark Plugs	11
	Starter Motor To Transmission	26
	Thermostat Housing	15
	Timing Belt Cover	89①
	Timing Belt Tensioner	18
	Transaxle Oil Drain Plug	33
	Valve Cover	⑥
	Water Pump Pulley	18
	Wheel Lug Nuts	63

① — Inch lbs.
② — Torque to 26 ft. lbs., then tighten an additional 90°.
③ — Refer to "Camshaft, Replace" for tightening specifications and sequence.
④ — Refer to "Oil Pan, Replace" for tightening specifications and sequence.
⑤ — Torque to 18 ft. lbs., then tighten an additional 60°.
⑥ — Refer to "Valve Cover, Replace" for tightening specifications and sequence.
⑦ — Refer to "Cylinder Head, Replace" for tightening specifications and sequence.

2.0L (VIN P) SOHC Engine

NOTE: On Air Bag Equipped Models, Refer To "Air Bag System Precautions" Located In The Front Of This Manual For System Disarming & Arming Procedures.

NOTE: Refer To "Computer Relearn Procedures" Located In The Front Of This Manual When Battery Power To The Computer Has Been Interrupted.

INDEX

	Page No.
Camshaft, Replace	6-20
Compression Pressure	6-17
Crankshaft Rear Oil Seal, Replace	6-20
Crankshaft Seal, Replace	6-20
Cylinder Head, Replace	6-19
Engine Rebuilding Specifications	21-1
Engine, Replace	6-17
Automatic Transaxle	6-17
Manual Transaxle	6-18
Exhaust Manifold, Replace	6-19
Fuel Filter, Replace	6-21
Fuel Pump, Replace	6-21

	Page No.
Intake Manifold, Replace	6-18
Oil Pan, Replace	6-20
Oil Pump, Replace	6-20
Precautions	6-17
Air Bag Systems	6-17
Battery Ground Cable	6-17
Fuel System Pressure Relief	6-17
Quick Disconnect Hoses	6-17
R-Clip	6-17
Spring Lock	6-17
Vapor Tube	6-17
Radiator, Replace	6-21
Serpentine Drive Belt	6-21
Replace	6-21

	Page No.
Routing	6-21
Tensioner	6-21
Technical Service Bulletins	6-21
Engine Vibration At Idle	6-21
2004–05	6-21
Thermostat, Replace	6-21
Tightening Specifications	6-22
Timing Belt, Replace	6-19
Installation	6-19
Removal	6-19
Valve Adjustment	6-19
Water Pump, Replace	6-21

PRECAUTIONS

Air Bag Systems

Refer to "Air Bag System Precautions" in the front of this manual for system disarming and arming procedures.

Battery Ground Cable

Prior to service, disconnect battery ground cable and isolate as required.

Fuel System Pressure Relief

1. Remove fuel pump fuse.
2. Start engine and idle until engine stalls.
3. Crank engine for approximately five seconds to ensure fuel supply manifold pressure has been relieved.
4. Install fuel pump fuse.

Quick Disconnect Hoses

R-CLIP

When working with R-clip type connections, do not use tools to disconnect, **Fig. 1.** Use of tools may deform clip components and could cause leaks.
To disconnect, proceed as follows:
1. Bend shipping tab downward.
2. Spread R-clip and push clip into fitting.
3. Separate fitting from tube.
To connect, proceed as follows:
1. Inspect fitting and tube for damage and ensure connections are clean.
2. Apply light coat of suitable, clean engine oil to male end of tube.
3. Insert R-clip into fitting.
4. Align tube and fitting, then insert tube into fitting and push together until click is heard.
5. Pull on connection to ensure it is fully engaged.

SPRING LOCK

When working with spring lock type connections, spring lock tool set No. T84L-19623-B, or equivalent, must be used to disconnect fittings, **Fig. 2.**
When connecting spring lock type fittings, proceed as follows:
1. Inspect and clean both coupling ends.
2. Lubricate fuel line O-ring seals with suitable, clean engine oil.
3. When connection is made, pull on line to ensure it is fully engaged.

VAPOR TUBE

To disconnect vapor tube connections, squeeze fitting and disconnect vapor tube from fitting, **Fig. 3.**
To connect, proceed as follows:
1. Ensure fittings are clean and free from damage.
2. Push tube onto fitting until it snaps into place.
3. Pull on connection to verify fitting is secure.

COMPRESSION PRESSURE

1. Ensure crankcase oil is of correct viscosity and at correct level.
2. Ensure battery is fully charged and engine is at normal operating temperature.
3. Turn ignition switch to OFF position.
4. Remove spark plugs.
5. Set throttle plates to wide open position.
6. Install suitable compression gauge in cylinder No. 1.
7. Install auxiliary starter switch in starting circuit.
8. With ignition switch off, use to crank engine at least five compression strokes using auxiliary starter switch.
9. Record number of compression strokes required to reach highest reading and record highest reading.
10. Repeat test on each cylinder, cranking engine same number of compression strokes.
11. Lowest cylinder reading must be within 75 percent of highest reading.

ENGINE

REPLACE

Automatic Transaxle

1. Relieve fuel system pressure as outlined under "Precautions."
2. Open coolant expansion tank.
3. Disconnect ground lead and remove battery tray.
4. Disconnect chassis ground cable.
5. Drain coolant into suitable container.
6. Loosen strut piston nuts five turns on both sides using suitable Allen wrench to prevent rod from turning.
7. Disconnect Mass Air Flow (MAF) sensor electrical connector and intake air

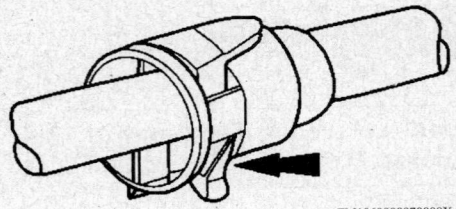

Fig. 1 R-clip connection

hose, then remove air cleaner housing from rubber bushing.

8. Remove air cleaner intake pipe, then the accelerator and speed control cables.
9. Disconnect power steering pump pressure switch, alternator and heated oxygen sensor electrical connectors.
10. Disconnect both Powertrain Control Module (PCM) connectors.
11. Remove EVAP, brake servo, delta pressure feedback electronic system sensor and EGR valve vacuum hoses.
12. Disconnect intake manifold vacuum hoses.
13. Disconnect fuel hose and drain excess fuel into suitable container.
14. Disconnect intake manifold coolant hose.
15. Remove water pump and coolant pipe coolant hoses, then disconnect coolant expansion tank and position it aside.
16. Remove power steering reservoir and position it aside.
17. Remove radiator fan.
18. Remove starter motor upper mounting bolts.
19. Remove accessory drive belt.
20. Remove power steering pump pulley using universal flange holding wrench tool No. 15-031A, or equivalent.
21. Remove power steering pump and position it aside.
22. Remove alternator and alternator bracket.
23. Remove coolant pipe bolt.
24. Raise and support vehicle.
25. Disconnect both lower suspension arms.
26. Disconnect oxygen sensor electrical connectors and remove drive belt cover.
27. **On models equipped with air conditioning,** remove compressor and tie it to radiator crossmember.
28. **On all models,** disconnect exhaust pipe.
29. Remove cover bolts and disconnect torque converter from engine drive plate.
30. Remove transaxle lower flange bolts.
31. Disconnect righthand front drive halfshaft from intermediate shaft.
32. Remove lefthand front drive halfshaft from tripod housing.
33. Remove intermediate shaft and secure aside with suitable cable tie.
34. Disconnect electrical connectors and remove starter motor.
35. Remove crankshaft pulley, righthand engine support insulator, then the lefthand and righthand transaxle flange bolts.

36. Lower vehicle.
37. Disconnect fuel line and drain excess fuel into suitable container.
38. Support transaxle with suitable jack. **Install wooden block between jack and transaxle.**
39. Relieve support insulators' pressure by raising engine slightly with suitable engine lifting device.
40. Remove engine front mounting, **Fig. 4.**
41. Disconnect Crankshaft Position (CKP) sensor electrical connector.
42. Remove upper transaxle flange bolts and separate engine from transaxle.
43. Remove engine.
44. Hold torque converter in transaxle using torque converter holding tool No. T96T-7902-A, or equivalent.
45. Reverse procedure to install.

Manual Transaxle

1. Relieve fuel system pressure as outlined under "Precautions."
2. Open coolant expansion tank.
3. Disconnect ground lead and remove battery tray.
4. Disconnect chassis ground cable.
5. Drain coolant into suitable container.
6. Loosen strut piston nuts five turns on both sides using suitable Allen wrench to prevent rod from turning.
7. Disconnect Mass Air Flow (MAF) sensor electrical connector and intake air hose, then remove air cleaner housing from rubber bushing.
8. Remove air cleaner intake pipe, then the accelerator and speed control cables.
9. Disconnect power steering pump pressure switch, alternator and heated oxygen sensor electrical connectors.
10. Disconnect both Powertrain Control Module (PCM) connectors.
11. Disconnect Vehicle Speed Sensor (VSS) and reverse lamp switch electrical connectors.
12. Remove high pressure pipe from clutch slave cylinder.
13. Remove EVAP, brake servo, delta pressure feedback electronic system sensor and EGR valve vacuum hoses.
14. Disconnect intake manifold vacuum hoses.
15. Disconnect intake manifold coolant hose.
16. Remove water pump and coolant pipe coolant hoses, then disconnect coolant expansion tank and position it aside.
17. Remove accessory drive belt.
18. Remove power steering pump pulley using universal flange holding wrench tool No.15-031-A, or equivalent.
19. Remove power steering pump and position it aside.
20. Remove powers steering reservoir and position it aside.
21. Remove radiator fan, catalytic converter, flexible exhaust pipe and drive belt cover.
22. Remove shift and selector cable covers, then the cables.
23. **On models equipped with air conditioning,** remove compressor and tie it to radiator crossmember.

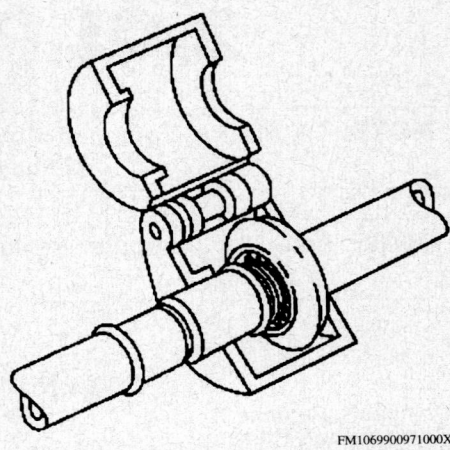

Fig. 2 Spring lock connection

24. **On all models,** remove righthand engine support insulator,
25. Remove both lower suspension arms.
26. Remove righthand front drive halfshaft from intermediate shaft. **Do not bend Inner joint more than 18° or outer joint more than 45°.**
27. Remove lefthand front drive halfshaft from tripod housing.
28. Position suitable engine assembly stand with wooden blocks under vehicle.
29. Lower vehicle until engine and transaxle assembly is on engine stand.
30. Remove engine rear mount, **Fig. 5.**
31. Remove front engine mount, **Fig. 4.**
32. Secure engine and transaxle assembly with suitable restraining strap to assembly table.
33. Raise vehicle, then pull assembly stand forward with engine and transaxle assembly.
34. Separate engine from transaxle using suitable lifting device.
35. Reverse procedure to install.

INTAKE MANIFOLD
REPLACE

1. Relieve fuel system pressure as outlined under "Precautions."
2. Raise and support vehicle.
3. Remove intake manifold bracket.
4. Disconnect Mass Air Flow (MAF) sensor, electrical connector.
5. Remove intake hose and air cleaner housing from rubber bushing.
6. Disconnect accelerator and speed control cables, then the plastic clips and position cables aside.
7. Disconnect Positive Crankcase Ventilation (PCV) hoses.
8. Remove EVAP system, brake servo, Delta pressure feedback electronic system sensor and EGR valve vacuum hoses.
9. Remove EGR valve.
10. Clamp coolant hoses to prevent leakage and remove from intake manifold.
11. Remove vacuum hose assembly.
12. Disconnect Throttle Position Sensor (TP) and Idle Air Control (IAC) valve.
13. Remove mounting bolt and oil dipstick tube bracket.

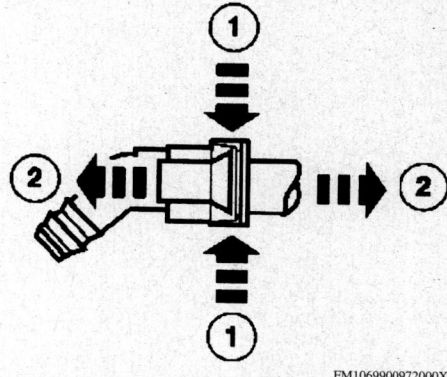

Fig. 3 Vapor tube connection

14. Remove intake manifold upper support bracket.
15. Disconnect fuel injector electrical connectors from intake manifold.
16. Disconnect Intake Manifold Runner Control (IMRC) electrical connector.
17. Disconnect Camshaft Position (CMP) sensor.
18. Disconnect ignition coil electrical connector.
19. Disconnect fuel lines from fuel rail.
20. Remove intake manifold retainers and position manifold to rear of engine compartment.
21. Remove two studs and Intake Manifold Runner Control (IMRC) manifolds.
22. Remove intake manifold.
23. Reverse procedure to install. **Torque** intake manifold mounting bolts and nuts 89 inch lbs., then tighten an additional 180°.

EXHAUST MANIFOLD
REPLACE

1. Disconnect Mass Air Flow (MAF) electrical connector.
2. Disconnect air intake hose.
3. Remove air cleaner housing from rubber bushing.
4. Disconnect heated oxygen sensor electrical connector.
5. Remove power steering high pressure tube.
6. Remove exhaust manifold heat shield.
7. Remove EGR tube at exhaust manifold, then loosen tube nut approximately three turns at valve.
8. Remove catalytic converter.
9. Remove mounting nuts and exhaust manifold.
10. Reverse procedure to install.

CYLINDER HEAD
REPLACE

1. Disconnect Mass Air Flow (MAF) sensor and intake air hose, then remove air cleaner housing from rubber bushing.
2. Disconnect battery ground cable and remove battery tray.
3. Disconnect accelerator and speed control cables, then the plastic clips and position cables aside.

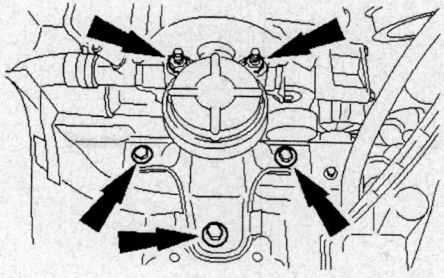

Fig. 4 Engine front mount replacement

4. Disconnect both Powertrain Control Module (PCM) connectors.
5. Disconnect heated oxygen sensor electrical connector.
6. Disconnect EVAP, brake servo, delta pressure feedback electronic system sensor and EGR valve vacuum hoses.
7. Remove nut and oil dipstick tube bracket.
8. Drain coolant into suitable container and remove thermostat housing coolant hoses.
9. Disconnect fuel line and drain excess fuel into suitable container.
10. Raise and support vehicle.
11. Disconnect knock sensor and oil pressure sensor electrical connectors.
12. Remove intake manifold bracket.
13. Remove catalyst monitor sensor electrical connector.
14. Lower vehicle, then remove power steering high pressure tube.
15. Remove exhaust manifold heat shield.
16. Remove catalytic converter from exhaust manifold.
17. Remove timing belt as outlined under "Timing Belt, Replace."
18. Disconnect Crankshaft Position (CKP) sensor electrical connector.
19. Disconnect PCV and fresh air hoses.
20. Remove valve cover.
21. Loosen cylinder head bolts in sequence, **Fig. 6.**
22. Remove cylinder head.
23. Reverse procedure to install, noting the following:
    a. Lubricate cylinder head bolts with suitable, clean engine oil.
    b. **Torque** new cylinder head bolts in sequence, **Fig. 7,** to 37 ft. lbs.
    c. Back head bolts off ½ turn.
    d. **Torque** cylinder head bolts in sequence, **Fig. 7,** to 37 ft. lbs.
    e. Tighten head bolt an additional 90° in sequence.
    f. Final tighten bolts an additional 90° in sequence.

VALVE ADJUSTMENT

Valve clearance is hydraulically controlled and is not adjustable.

TIMING BELT
REPLACE
Removal

1. Remove mounting bolt and expansion tank aside with hose attached.

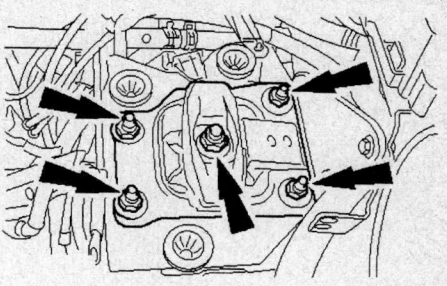

Fig. 5 Rear engine mount replacement

2. Disconnect power steering reservoir and position aside with hose attached.
3. Turn engine accessory drive belt tensioner clockwise and remove drive belt.
4. Raise and support vehicle.
5. Remove mounting screws and drive belt cover.
6. Lower vehicle.
7. Disconnect cables from spark plugs. Mark cables for installation alignment.
8. Remove two spark plug cable separators from valve cover.
9. Remove spark plugs. Note location of spark plugs so can be installed at same cylinders.
10. Position suitable jack under engine oil pan. Place wooden block between oil pan and jack.
11. Relieve weight from engine mounts by raising jack slightly.
12. Remove mounting bolts, nuts and front engine mount.
13. Remove three mounting bolts and timing belt lower cover.
14. Remove four mounting bolts and front engine mounting bracket.
15. Align crankshaft and camshaft sprocket timing marks, **Fig. 8.**
16. Insert 8 mm hex head wrench into tensioner pulley bore, then rotate timing belt tensioner ¼ turn counterclockwise.
17. Insert ⅛ inch drill bit, or similar item, through timing belt tensioner pulley hole to hold pulley in place.
18. Remove timing belt from crankshaft and camshaft sprockets.

Installation

1. Ensure crankshaft and camshaft sprocket timing marks are aligned, **Fig. 8.**
2. Install new timing belt in counterclockwise direction, over crankshaft sprocket, over camshaft sprocket, under timing belt tensioner, then over water pump sprocket. **Keep belt span taut between crankshaft and camshaft sprockets.**
3. Remove item holding timing belt tensioner pulley in position and allow tensioner to tension timing belt.
4. Rotate crankshaft two turns in normal direction of rotation.
5. Inspect crankshaft and camshaft sprocket timing marks for proper alignment, **Fig. 8.** If marks are improperly

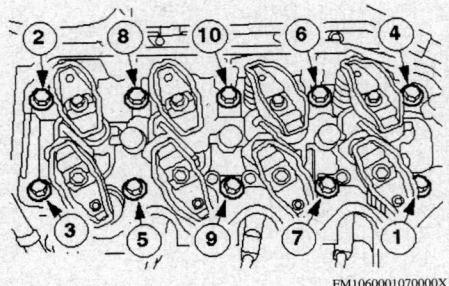

Fig. 6 Cylinder head bolt loosening sequence

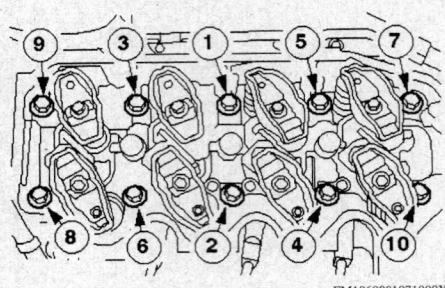

Fig. 7 Cylinder head bolt tightening sequence

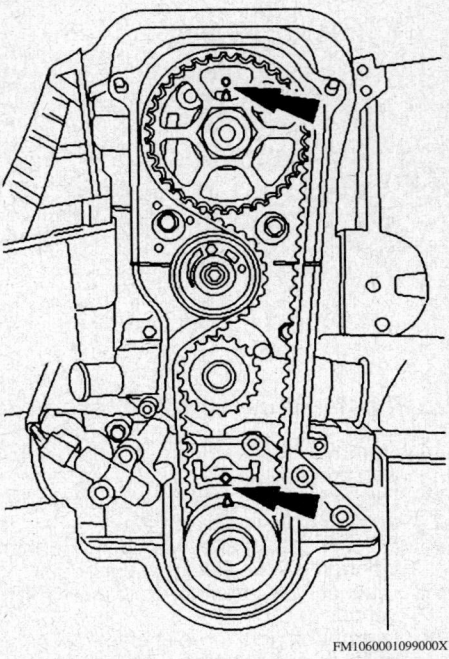

Fig. 8 Timing mark alignment

aligned, timing belt must be removed and installed.

6. Install front engine mounting bracket.
7. Install timing belt lower cover.
8. Install front engine mounting.
9. Remove jack and wooden block supporting engine.
10. Install spark plugs.
11. Install two spark plug cable wire separators to valve cover.
12. Apply suitable silicone grease to inside of spark plug connector boot, then spark plugs cables to spark plugs.
13. Raise and support vehicle.
14. Install crankshaft pulley.
15. Position accessory drive belt on crankshaft pulley.
16. Install drive belt cover.
17. Lower vehicle, then Install accessory drive belt.
18. Install power steering reservoir.
19. Install coolant expansion tank and mounting bolt.

CAMSHAFT
REPLACE

1. Disconnect battery ground cable and remove battery tray.
2. Disconnect Mass Air Flow (MAF) sensor and air cleaner outlet pipe, then remove air cleaner housing from rubber bushing.
3. Remove air cleaner intake pipe.
4. Remove ignition coil.
5. Disconnect PCV hoses.
6. Remove valve cover and rocker arms.
7. Remove plate retainers, plates and valve tappets. Keep tappets in order for reassembly.
8. Remove timing belt as outlined under "Timing Belt, Replace."
9. Remove camshaft timing belt pulley using wrench tool No. T74P-6256-B, or equivalent.
10. Remove and camshaft oil seal using seal remover tool No. T92C-6700-CH, or equivalent.
11. Support engine with suitable engine lifting device.
12. Remove rear engine mount.
13. Disconnect air cleaner housing bracket and position it aside.
14. Remove camshaft thrust plate.
15. Remove and discard blanking plug from rear of cylinder head.
16. Remove camshaft from rear of cylinder head.

17. Reverse procedure to install, noting the following:
   a. Coat cylinder head bore with suitable, clean engine oil prior to camshaft installation.
   b. Install camshaft through rear of cylinder head.
   c. Install new camshaft oil seal using oil seal installer tool No. T81P-6292-A, or equivalent, and draw seal into place with timing belt pulley bolt.
   d. Install camshaft timing pulley. using camshaft pulley wrench tool No. T74P-6256-B, or equivalent.

CRANKSHAFT SEAL
REPLACE

1. Remove timing belt as outlined under "Timing Belt, Replace."
2. Support engine using suitable floor jack and wooden block under oil pan.
3. Support engine using engine support tool Nos. 303-290, 303-050, 303-290-01 and 303-290-03, or equivalents.
4. Remove floor jack.
5. Raise and support vehicle.
6. Remove crankshaft timing belt pulley.
7. Remove crankshaft seal using seal remover tool No. T92C-6700-CH, or equivalent.
8. Reverse procedure to install, noting the following:
   a. Lubricate new crankshaft seal and crankshaft surface with suitable, clean engine oil.
   b. Install crankshaft front seal using seal installer tool No. 303-164, or equivalent.

CRANKSHAFT REAR OIL SEAL
REPLACE

1. Remove transaxle as outlined in **MOTOR's "Domestic Transmission, In-Vehicle Service" manual or "Transmission Service DVD."**
2. **On models equipped with manual transaxle,** remove clutch pressure plate and clutch disc as outlined in **MOTOR's "Domestic Transmission, In-Vehicle Service" manual or "Transmission Service DVD."**
3. **On all models,** remove flywheel using flywheel locking tool No. T74P-6375-A, or equivalent.
4. Remove crankshaft rear seal using

seal remover tool No. T92C-6700-CH, or equivalent.
5. Reverse procedure to install. Install oil seal using crankshaft rear oil installer tool No. T88P-6701B-1, or equivalent.

OIL PAN
REPLACE

1. Remove three-way catalytic converter.
2. Remove mounting bolts and two exhaust brackets.
3. Remove mounting bolts and intake manifold bracket.
4. Remove bolts and axle shaft bracket clamp.
5. Remove mounting bolts and axle shaft bracket.
6. Remove coolant tube mounting bolt.
7. Drain engine oil into suitable container.
8. Record oil pan stud bolts locations for installation alignment.
9. Remove mounting bolts and oil pan.
10. Reverse procedure to install, noting the following:
   a. Apply .12 inch wide bead of suitable silicone gasket sealant at oil pump to block joints and crankshaft rear seal retainer to block joints.
   b. **Oil pan must be installed within 10 minutes of sealant application.**
   c. Ensure press fit tabs fully engage in oil pan gasket channel.
   d. **Torque** oil pan bolts in sequence to 18 ft. lbs., **Fig. 9.**

OIL PUMP
REPLACE

1. Remove timing belt as outlined under "Timing Belt, Replace."
2. Support engine using suitable floor jack and wooden block under oil pan.
3. Support engine using engine support

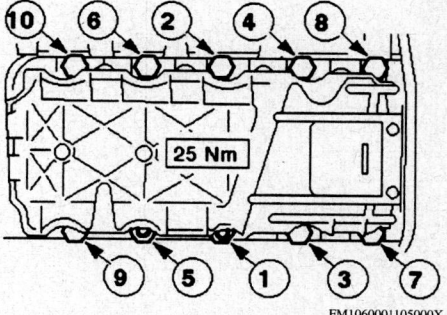

Fig. 9 Oil pan fastener tightening sequence

FM1060001105000X

tool Nos. 303-290, 303-050, 303-290-01 and 303-290-03, or equivalents.
4. Remove floor jack.
5. Remove crankshaft timing belt pulley.
6. Remove three-way catalytic converter.
7. Remove mounting bolts and two exhaust brackets.
8. Remove mounting bolts and intake manifold bracket.
9. Remove bolts and axle shaft bracket clamp.
10. Remove mounting bolts and axle shaft bracket.
11. Remove coolant tube mounting bolt.
12. Drain engine oil into suitable container.
13. Record oil pan stud bolts locations for installation alignment.
14. Remove mounting bolts and oil pan.
15. Remove Crankshaft Position (CKP) sensor.
16. Remove two mounting bolts, oil pump screen cover and tube.
17. Remove mounting bolts and oil pump.
18. Reverse procedure to install noting the following:
   a. Install oil pump seal using crankshaft front oil seal installer tool No. T81P-6700-A, or equivalent.
   b. Install new gasket.

SERPENTINE DRIVE BELT

Routing

Refer to **Figs. 10 and 11** for serpentine drive belt routing.

Replace

1. Raise and support vehicle.
2. Remove serpentine drive belt splash shield.
3. Lower vehicle.
4. Rotate tensioner clockwise using suitable ⅜ inch drive breaker bar.
5. Remove serpentine drive belt.
6. Reverse procedure to install.

Tensioner

1. Raise and support vehicle.
2. Remove serpentine drive belt splash shield.

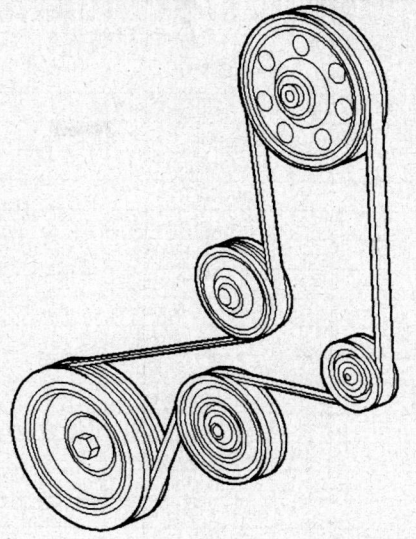

FM1060001080000X

Fig. 10 Serpentine belt routing. Less air conditioning

3. Lower vehicle.
4. Rotate tensioner clockwise using suitable ⅜ inch drive breaker bar.
5. Remove serpentine drive belt.
6. Remove power steering pipe to exhaust manifold bracket nuts and position pipe aside.
7. Remove mounting bolts and exhaust manifold heat shield.
8. Remove mounting bolts and serpentine drive belt tensioner.
9. Reverse procedure to install.

THERMOSTAT
REPLACE

1. Drain coolant into suitable container.
2. Disconnect thermostat housing coolant hoses.
3. Remove mounting bolts and thermostat housing.
4. Reverse procedure to install. Install new O-rings.

WATER PUMP
REPLACE

1. Drain cooling system into suitable container.
2. Remove timing belt as outlined under "Timing Belt, Replace."
3. Remove timing belt tensioner.
4. Disconnect coolant hoses.
5. Remove water pump.
6. Reverse procedure to install. using new gasket.

RADIATOR
REPLACE

Refer to "Radiator, Replace" in "2.0L (VINs 3 & 5) DOHC Engines" section for radiator replacement procedure.

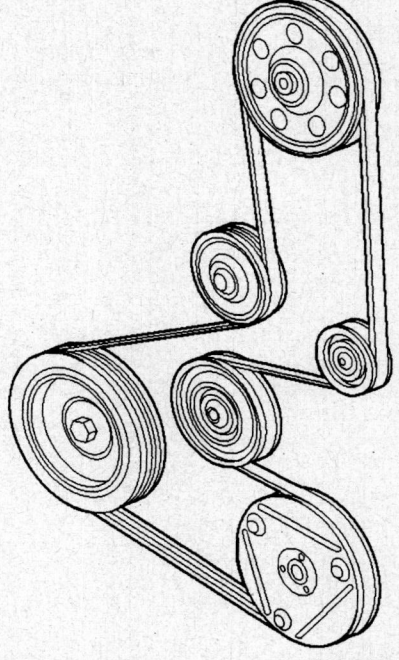

FM1060001079000X

Fig. 11 Serpentine belt routing. With air conditioning

FUEL PUMP
REPLACE

Refer to "Fuel Pump, Replace" in "2.0L (VINs 3 & 5) DOHC Engines" section for fuel pump replacement procedure.

FUEL FILTER
REPLACE

1. Relieve fuel system pressure as outlined under "Precautions."
2. Raise and support vehicle.
3. Disconnect evaporative emission pipe.
4. Remove fuel filter outlet pipe and disconnect inlet pipe.
5. Remove fuel filter and bracket.
6. Separate filter from bracket.
7. Reverse procedure to install.

TECHNICAL SERVICE BULLETINS

Engine Vibration At Idle

2004–05

Some models may have an excessive engine vibration at idle, most noticeable when the transmission is engaged in reverse.

This condition may be caused by small stones, road debris, ice or snow packed/lodged in the rear engine roll restrictor.

To correct this condition remove debris from rear engine roll restrictor and install service shield (P/N 2M5Z-16102-AA).

TIGHTENING SPECIFICATIONS

Year	Component	Torque Ft. Lbs.
2004	Accessory Drive Bracket	35
	Air Conditioning Compressor	18
	Alternator	35
	Battery Tray	18
	Camshaft Position Sensor	18
	Camshaft Pulley	77
	Camshaft Thrust Plate	89①
	Catalytic Converter To Exhaust Manifold	30
	Crankshaft Position Sensor	53①
	Crankshaft Pulley	89
	Cylinder Head	②
	EGR Manifold Tube To Exhaust Manifold	53①
	EGR Valve To EGR Manifold Tube	18
	EGR Valve To Intake Manifold	53①
	Engine Oil Drain Plug	18
	Engine Roll Restrictor To Subframe	35
	Engine Roll Restrictor To Transaxle	35
	Exhaust Manifold	20
	Flexible Exhaust Pipe	35
	Front Engine Mounting To Body	35
	Front Engine Mounting To Engine	59
	Intake Manifold	③
	Intake Manifold Bracket	89①
	Intermediate Shaft Bracket	35
	Knock Sensor	10
	Lefthand Transaxle Flange Bolts	35
	Lower Ball Joint To Spindle Carrier	35
	Lower Transaxle Flange Bolts	35
	Oil Intake Pipe To Oil Pump	89①
	Oil Pan	④
	Oil Pan Baffle	18
	Oil Pump	10
	Oil Pump Tube	89①
	Power Steering Pump	17
	Radiator Bracket	19
	Rear Crankshaft Oil Seal Retainer	18
	Rear Engine Mounting (Nut On Transaxle Mounting Bracket)	98
	Rear Engine Mounting To Body	35
	Rocker Arms	18
	Starter Motor To Transaxle	26
	Thermostat Housing	10
	Timing Belt Cover (Lower)	89①
	Timing Belt Cover (Upper)	35
	Timing Belt Tensioner	18
	Upper Transaxle Flange Bolts	35
	Valve Cover Bolts	80①
	Water Pump	18
	Wheel Lug Nuts	63

① — Inch lbs.
② — Refer to "Cylinder Head, Replace" for tightening specifications and sequence.
③ — Refer to "Intake Manifold, Replace" for tightening specifications and sequence.
④ — Refer to "Oil Pan, Replace" for tightening specifications and sequence.

2.0L (VIN N) & 2.3L (VIN Z) DOHC Engines

NOTE: On Air Bag Equipped Models, Refer To "Air Bag System Precautions" Located In The Front Of This Manual For System Disarming & Arming Procedures.

NOTE: Refer To "Computer Relearn Procedures" Located In The Front Of This Manual When Battery Power To The Computer Has Been Interrupted.

INDEX

	Page No.
Camshaft, Replace	6-27
Camshaft Lobe Lift Specifications	6-26
Compression Pressure	6-23
Cooling System Bleed	6-28
Crankshaft Damper, Replace	6-26
Installation	6-26
Removal	6-26
Crankshaft Rear Oil Seal, Replace	6-27
Crankshaft Seal, Replace	6-27
Cylinder Head, Replace	6-25
Engine Rebuilding Specifications	21-1
Engine, Replace	6-24

	Page No.
Engine Mount, Replace	6-24
Front Cover, Replace	6-26
Fuel Filter, Replace	6-28
Fuel Pump, Replace	6-28
Intake Manifold, Replace	6-25
Oil Pan, Replace	6-27
Precautions	6-23
Air Bag Systems	6-23
Battery Ground Cable	6-23
Fuel System Pressure Relief	6-23
Quick Disconnect Hoses	6-23
R-Clip	6-23
Spring Lock	6-23
Vapor Tube	6-23
Radiator, Replace	6-28

	Page No.
Serpentine Drive Belt	6-27
Replace	6-27
Routing	6-27
Technical Service Bulletins	6-28
Engine Vibration At Idle	6-28
2004–05	6-28
Thermostat, Replace	6-28
Tightening Specifications	6-30
Timing Chain, Replace	6-26
Valve Adjustment	6-26
Valve Clearance Specifications	6-26
Valve Cover, Replace	6-26
Water Pump, Replace	6-28

PRECAUTIONS

Air Bag Systems

Refer to "Air Bag System Precautions" in the front of this manual for system disarming and arming procedures.

Battery Ground Cable

Prior to service, disconnect battery ground cable and isolate as required.

Fuel System Pressure Relief

1. Remove fuel pump fuse.
2. Start engine and idle until engine stalls.
3. Crank engine for approximately five seconds to ensure fuel supply manifold pressure has been relieved.
4. Install fuel pump fuse.

Quick Disconnect Hoses

R-CLIP

When working with R-clip type connections, do not use tools to disconnect. Use of tools may deform clip components and could cause leaks.

DISCONNECT

1. Bend shipping tab downward.
2. Spread R-clip and push clip into fitting.
3. Separate fitting from tube.

CONNECT

1. Inspect fitting and tube for damage and ensure connections are clean.
2. Apply light coat of suitable, clean engine oil to male end of tube.
3. Insert R-clip into fitting.
4. Align tube and fitting, then insert tube into fitting and push together until click is heard.
5. Pull on connection to ensure it is fully engaged.

SPRING LOCK

When working with spring lock type connections, spring lock tool set No. T84L-19623-B, or equivalent, must be used to disconnect fittings.

When connecting spring lock type fittings, proceed as follows:
1. Inspect and clean both coupling ends.
2. Lubricate fuel line O-ring seals with suitable, clean engine oil.
3. When connection is made, pull on line to ensure it is fully engaged.

VAPOR TUBE

To disconnect vapor tube connections, squeeze fitting and disconnect vapor tube from fitting.

To connect, proceed as follows:

1. Ensure fittings are clean and free from damage.
2. Push tube onto fitting until it snaps into place.
3. Pull on connection to verify fitting is secure.

COMPRESSION PRESSURE

1. Ensure crankcase oil is of correct viscosity and at correct level.
2. Ensure battery is fully charged and engine is at normal operating temperature.
3. Turn ignition switch to OFF position.
4. Remove spark plugs.
5. Set throttle plates to wide open position.
6. Install suitable compression gauge in cylinder No. 1.
7. Install auxiliary starter switch in starting circuit.
8. With ignition switch off, use to crank engine at least five compression strokes using auxiliary starter switch.
9. Record number of compression strokes required to reach highest reading and record highest reading.
10. Repeat test on each cylinder, cranking engine same number of compression strokes.
11. Lowest cylinder reading must be within 75% of highest reading.

FOCUS

ENGINE MOUNT

REPLACE

1. Remove mounting bolts and position expansion tank aside.
2. Support engine using three-bar engine support tool No. 303-F072, or equivalent.
3. Remove mounting nuts, bolts and engine mount.
4. Remove procedure to install.

ENGINE

REPLACE

1. Ensure transmission is in Neutral position, then raise and support vehicle.
2. Relieve fuel system pressure as outlined under "Precautions."
3. Remove battery, then the mounting bolts and tray.
4. Recover air conditioning refrigerant as outlined in "Air Conditioning" chapter.
5. Drain engine cooling system into suitable container.
6. Drain engine oil into suitable container.
7. Remove mounting bolts and accessory drive belt splash shield.
8. Turn tensioner clockwise and remove accessory drive belt.
9. Remove mounting nuts and disconnect catalytic converter from muffler.
10. Remove mounting bolts and catalytic converter support bracket.
11. Remove mounting bolts and position catalytic converter heat shield aside.
12. Disconnect exhaust sensor electrical connector.
13. Disconnect upper exhaust sensor electrical connector and retainer.
14. Disconnect Secondary Air Injection (AIR) hose.
15. Remove catalytic converter-to-engine mounting nuts, then position converter aside using suitable mechanics wire. Remove gasket.
16. Loosen clamp and disconnect air cleaner outlet pipe vent tube.
17. Remove mounting bolts and disconnect air intake resonator from grommets. Remove resonator and outlet pipe.
18. Disconnect evaporative emissions hose pin-type retainer.
19. Remove mounting screw, pin-type retainer and accelerator control snow shield.
20. Disconnect accelerator and speed control cables from throttle body.
21. Remove mounting bolts, then position accelerator and speed control cables and bracket aside.
22. Disconnect quick release coupling from fuel rail and position fuel tube aside.
23. Disconnect evaporative emissions tube.
24. Disconnect AIR hose and vacuum regulator electrical connector.
25. Depress quick release locking ring and disconnect power brake booster vacuum tube.
26. Disconnect Exhaust Gas Recirculation (EGR) valve electrical connector.

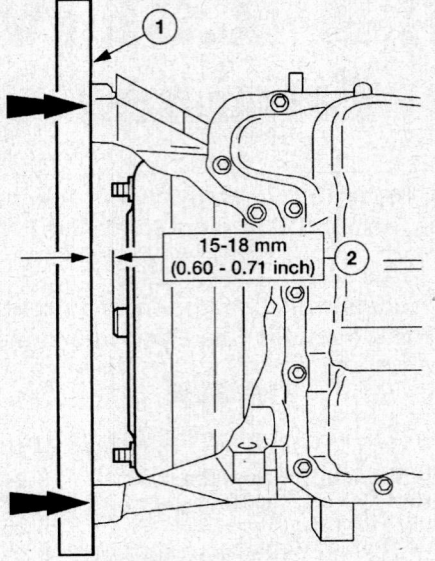

1- Straightedge
2- Torque converter centering spigot

ARM0400000000482

Fig. 1 Torque converter installation depth. 2.0L (VIN N) engine

27. Disconnect upper radiator, heater and coolant vent hoses from coolant bypass.
28. Remove mounting bolt and ground eyelet.
29. Disconnect fuel charging wiring harness electrical connectors and retainer.
30. Disconnect power distribution wiring harness.
31. Disconnect wiring harness retainers.
32. Remove mounting nut and power distribution wiring harness eyelet.
33. Disconnect three main engine wiring harness electrical connectors. Disconnect connectors from bracket.
34. **On models equipped with manual transaxle,** proceed as follows:
    a. Disconnect shifter cable from transaxle.
    b. Disconnect selector cable from lever.
    c. Disconnect shifter cable from retaining bracket, turning abutment sleeves counterclockwise.
    d. Disconnect selector cable from retaining bracket, turning abutment sleeves counterclockwise.
    e. Remove clip and clutch slave cylinder supply tube. Position tube aside using suitable cable ties.
    f. Disconnect back-up lamp switch electrical connector.
35. **On models equipped with 2.0L engine and automatic transaxle,** proceed as follows:
    a. Disconnect and position shifter cable aside.
    b. Disconnect transaxle cooler lines.
36. **On all models,** disconnect heater hose from "T" fitting and position it aside.

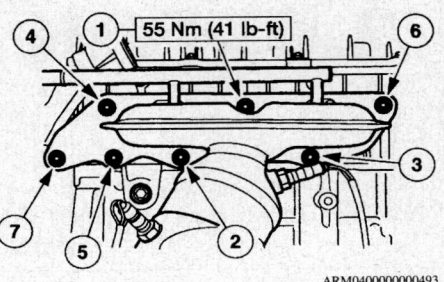

ARM0400000000493

Fig. 2 Catalytic converter flange tightening sequence. 2.0L (VIN N) & 2.3L (VIN Z) DOHC engines

37. Disconnect hoses from coolant expansion tank.
38. Remove mounting bolt and coolant expansion tank.
39. Remove power steering pump pulley using power steering pump pulley remover tool No. T69L-10300-8, or equivalent.
40. Disconnect Power Steering Pressure (PSP) switch electrical connector.
41. Disconnect PSP tube.
42. Remove mounting bolts and position power steering pump aside.
43. Disconnect cooling fan electrical connectors.
44. Disconnect top clips and remove cooling fan.
45. Disconnect lower radiator hose.
46. Remove mounting bolt and ground cable.
47. Remove alternator cooling pipe.
48. Disconnect starter motor electrical terminals.
49. Remove mounting bolts and disconnect power steering pressure tube brackets from stud bolts.
50. Disconnect air conditioning compressor electrical connector.
51. Remove three compressor mounting bolts.
52. Lower compressor, then remove fourth mounting bolt and compressor.
53. Disconnect lefthand brake hose from support bracket.
54. Remove covers, mounting bolts and lefthand caliper. Support caliper aside.
55. Loosen lefthand strut and spring top mount nuts four turns.
56. Remove mounting nut and disconnect lefthand stabilizer bar at strut.
57. Remove lefthand and righthand tie-end nuts.
58. Disconnect tie-rods from knuckles using tie-rod end remover tool, No. 393-050, or equivalent.
59. Remove mounting bolts and disconnect both lower control arms from knuckles.
60. Remove mounting nuts and intermediate shaft bearing bracket.
61. Remove intermediate shaft and righthand front drive halfshaft. Position aside shaft using suitable mechanics wire.
62. Install transaxle plug tools No. T88C-7025-AH, or equivalent, into transaxle housing.
63. Remove lefthand front drive halfshaft using front drive halfshaft remover tool

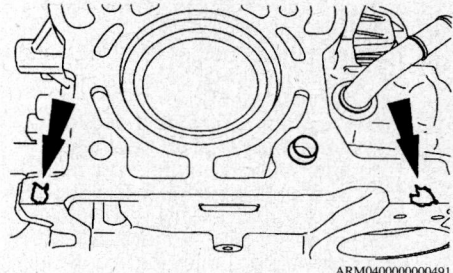

Fig. 3 Head silicone gasket & sealant installation

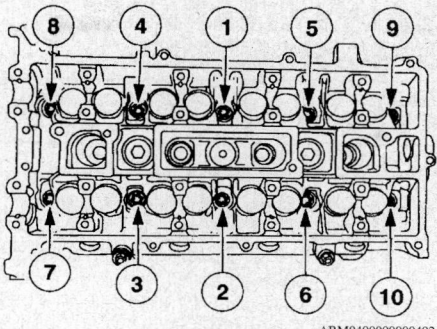

Fig. 4 Cylinder head bolt tightening sequence

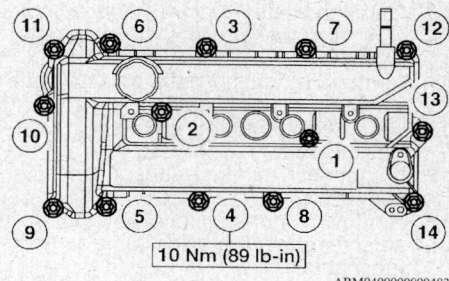

Fig. 5 Valve cover bolt tightening sequence

No. D93P-1175-B, or equivalent. Position shaft aside using suitable mechanics's wire.

64. Remove mounting bolts and transaxle roll restrictor.
65. Remove three mounting bolts and starter motor.
66. Remove start isolator.
67. Remove two lower bell housing bolts.
68. Remove two oil pan-to-bell housing mounting bolts.
69. Attach engine to suitable lift table using universal adaptor bracket tools No. 014-0001, or equivalent.
70. Remove mounting mount nuts.
71. Remove transaxle mount center nut.
72. Lower engine and transaxle.
73. **On models equipped with manual transaxle,** disconnect Vehicle Speed Sensor (VSS) electrical connector.
74. **On models equipped with 2.0L engine and automatic transaxle,** proceed as follows:
    a. Mark one stud and flexplate from installation alignment.
    b. Remove four torque converter mounting nuts.
    c. Disconnect Output Shaft Speed (OSS) sensor electrical connector.
    d. Disconnect Turbine Shaft Speed (TSS) sensor electrical connector.
    e. Disconnect solenoid body and Transmission Range (TR) sensor electrical connectors.
75. **On all models,** lower engine to within inches of floor.
76. Remove engine from lift table using suitable engine crane and spreader bar tool No. D93P-6001-A3, or equivalent.
77. Remove remaining bell housing bolts and separate engine and transaxle.
78. Remove dowel pins.
79. Lock torque converter in place using torque converter holding tool No. T96T-7902-A, or equivalent.
80. Reverse procedure to install, noting the following:
    a. Install new dowel pins.
    b. Ensure transaxle flange and torque converter centering spigot clearance is .60–.71 inch, **Fig. 1.**
    c. Install new front driveshaft snap rings.
    d. Install new air conditioning compressor manifold and tube O-ring seals.
    e. Install new power steering pump union O-ring seal.
    f. Install new catalytic converter

flange if it is wrapped more than .0295 inch.
    g. Install catalytic converter flange using new gasket and mounting nuts.
    h. Tighten catalytic converter flange mounting nuts in sequence, **Fig. 2.**
    i. Install new catalytic converter to muffler gasket and mounting nuts.

INTAKE MANIFOLD
REPLACE

1. Ensure transmission is in Neutral position, then raise and support vehicle.
2. Disconnect dual electric cooling fan electrical connector.
3. Remove cooling fan motors and shroud from bracket, then lower assembly from vehicle.
4. Remove lower intake manifold mounting bolt.
5. Loosen clamps, then disconnect and remove air cleaner outlet pipe.
6. Disconnect evaporative emissions hose pin-type retainer.
7. Remove mounting screw, pin-type retainer and accelerator control snow shield.
8. Disconnect accelerator and speed control cables from throttle body.
9. Remove mounting bolts, then position accelerator and speed control cables and bracket aside.
10. Disconnect Throttle Position (TP) sensor electrical connector and wiring harness pin-type retainer.
11. Disconnect Idle Air Control (IAC) valve electrical connector and wiring harness pin-type retainer.
12. Disconnect evaporative emissions hose.
13. Depress quick release locking ring and disconnect power brake booster vacuum tube.
14. Disconnect fuel rail pressure and temperature sensor vacuum hose.
15. Disconnect wiring harness pin-type retainer.
16. Disconnect Intake Manifold Runner Control (IMRC) actuator electrical connector.
17. Disconnect Manifold Absolute Pressure (MAP) sensor electrical connector.
18. **On models equipped with 2.0L engine,** proceed as follows:

a. Disconnect Secondary Air Injection (AIR) vacuum supply hose.
    b. Disconnect swirl control valve electrical connector.
19. **On models equipped with 2.3L engine,** disconnect swirl control valve electrical connectors and pin-type retainers.
20. **On all models,** remove mounting bolt and oil dipstick tube.
21. Mark mounting bolts for installation alignment.
22. Remove seven intake manifold mounting bolts.
23. Raise intake manifold and disconnect Knock Sensor (KS) electrical connector.
24. Disconnect Positive Crankcase Ventilation (PCV) hose.
25. Remove intake manifold.
26. Remove Exhaust Gas Recirculation (EGR) tube.
27. Reverse procedure to install, noting the following:
    a. Install new intake manifold gaskets.
    b. **On models equipped with 2.3L engine,** use 6 inch long, 5/16 inch diameter hose to install lower center mounting bolt.

CYLINDER HEAD
REPLACE

1. Drain cooling system into suitable container.
2. Remove camshaft as outlined under "Camshaft, Replace."
3. Relieve fuel system pressure as outlined under "Precautions."
4. Disconnect quick release coupling from fuel rail and position fuel tube aside.
5. Disconnect fuel injector electrical connector.
6. Disconnect fuel rail pressure and temperature sensor electrical connector, then the vacuum tube.
7. Remove mounting bolts, fuel rail, injectors and spacers.
8. Remove intake manifold as outlined under "Intake Manifold, Replace."
9. **On models equipped with 2.0L engine,** proceed as follows:
    a. Disconnect Secondary Air Injection (AIR) vacuum regulator electrical connector and vacuum hose.
    b. Disconnect AIR control valve hoses.
    c. Disconnect upper exhaust sensor electrical connector and retainer.

10. **On all models,** remove mounting nuts and disconnect catalytic converter from muffler.
11. Remove mounting bolts and catalytic converter support bracket.
12. Remove four mounting bolts and catalytic converter heat shield.
13. Disconnect exhaust sensor electrical connector.
14. Remove mounting nuts and position catalytic converter aside using suitable mechanic's wire.
15. Remove Exhaust Gas Recirculation (EGR) valve electrical connector.
16. Disconnect coolant bypass hoses.
17. Remove mounting bolts, coolant bypass and gasket.
18. Disconnect EGT coolant hose.
19. Remove mounting bolts, cylinder head and gasket.
20. Reverse procedure to install, noting the following:
    a. Apply suitable silicone gasket and sealant, **Fig. 3.**
    b. Tighten new torque-to-yield bolts in five steps using sequence, **Fig. 4.** First step, **torque** bolts to 44 inch lbs.; second step, **torque** bolts to 11 ft. lbs.; third step, **torque** bolts to 33 ft. lbs.; fourth step, tighten bolts an additional 90°; fifth step, tighten bolts an additional 90.°
    c. Install new fuel injector O-ring seals lubricated with suitable, clean engine oil.

VALVE COVER
REPLACE

1. Disconnect Camshaft Position (CMP) sensor electrical connector.
2. Lift connector boot and disconnect Cylinder Head Temperature (CHT) sensor electrical connector.
3. Disconnect coil-on-plug electrical connectors.
4. Remove mounting bolts, the rotate and remove ignition coils.
5. Disconnect breather tube.
6. Disconnect fuel rail pressure and temperature sensor, then the fuel injector electrical connectors. Disconnect wiring harness retainers.
7. Remove mounting bolt and position radio interference capacitor bracket aside.
8. Disconnect Heated Oxygen Sensor (HO2S) electrical connector.
9. Disconnect wiring harness retainer and position it aside.
10. Remove mounting bolts and valve cover.
11. Reverse procedure to install. **Torque** bolts in sequence, **Fig. 5.** to 89 inch lbs.

CAMSHAFT LOBE LIFT SPECIFICATIONS

Engine	Lobe Lift, Inch	
	Intake	Exhaust
2.0L	.324	.307
2.3L	.324	.307

VALVE CLEARANCE SPECIFICATIONS

Valve	Clearance, Inch
Intake	.008–.011
Exhaust	.010–.023

VALVE ADJUSTMENT

1. Remove valve cover as outlined under "Valve Cover, Replace."
2. Measure and record each valve clearance at base circle with lobe pointed away from tappet.
3. Select tappets based on (tappet thickness = measured clearance + base tappet thickness - most desirable thickness.)
4. Tappets are mark with digits following decimal, For example, tappet marked .650 is 3.650 mm thick.

CRANKSHAFT DAMPER
REPLACE
Removal

1. Disconnect dual electric cooling fan electrical connector.
2. Remove cooling fan motors and shroud from bracket, then lower assembly from vehicle.
3. Remove mounting bolts and accessory drive belt splash shield.
4. Turn tensioner clockwise and remove accessory drive belt.
5. Remove valve cover as outlined under "Valve Cover, Replace."
6. Remove mounting bolts and position expansion tank aside.
7. Remove battery, then the mounting bolts and tray.
8. Turn crankshaft pulley clockwise and position piston No. 1 at TDC.
9. Install camshaft alignment plate too No. T94P-6256-CH, or equivalent, in slots at rear of both camshafts. If timing slots are offset, rotate crankshaft pulley clockwise one complete revolution.
10. Install crankshaft timing peg tool No. 303-507, or equivalent.
11. Support engine using three-bar engine support tool No. 303-F072, or equivalent.
12. Remove transaxle mount center nut.
13. Remove engine mount nuts.
14. Loosen lower transaxle mount nuts.
15. Lower engine for clearance.
16. Install drive pinion flange holding fixture tool No. T78P-4851-A, or equivalent.
17. Remove mounting bolt, special tool and crankshaft pulley.

Installation

1. Apply suitable, clean engine oil to seal area.
2. Install crankshaft pulley and new damper bolt finger tight.
3. Install standard .23 by .7 inch bolt through pulley into front cover.
4. Hold crankshaft pulley in place using holding fixture tool No. T78P-4851-A, or equivalent.
5. **Torque** damper bolt to 74 ft. lbs., then tighten an additional 90°.
6. Remove standard bolt.
7. Remove crankshaft timing peg tool.
8. Remove camshaft alignment plate.
9. Turn engine two complete revolutions clockwise until piston No. 1 is at TDC.
10. Install crankshaft timing peg tool.
11. Attempt to install standard .23 by .7 inch bolt through pulley into front cover. If bolt cannot be installed, engine is timed correctly.
12. Inspect camshaft positions with camshaft alignment plate. If plate cannot be installed, engine is timed correctly.
13. Remove standard bolt and special tools.
14. Raise engine.
15. Install engine mount nuts, then the transaxle mount center nut.
16. Tighten lower transaxle mount nuts.
17. Install battery tray and coolant expansion tank.
18. Install valve cover and accessory drive belt.
19. Install fan and shroud.

FRONT COVER
REPLACE

1. Remove crankshaft pulley as outlined under "Crankshaft Damper, Replace."
2. Disconnect Crankshaft Position (CKP) sensor electrical connector and wiring harness pin-type retainer.
3. Disconnect Power Steering Pressure (PSP) electrical connector.
4. Remove mounting nut and disconnect PSP tube bracket.
5. Disconnect PSP tube.
6. Remove four mounting bolts and position power steering pump aside.
7. Remove mounting bolts and water pump pulley.
8. Remove mounting bolt and accessory drive belt idler pulley.
9. Remove mounting bolts and front cover.
10. Reverse procedure to install, noting the following:
    a. **Front cover must be installed and bolts tighten within four minutes of applying silicone gasket and sealant.**
    b. Apply .098 inch bead of suitable silicone gasket and sealant to cylinder head and oil pan joint areas.
    c. Apply .098 inch bead of suitable silicone gasket and sealant to front cover, **Fig. 6.**
    d. Tighten mounting bolts in sequence, **Fig. 7.**
    e. Install new PSP tube O-ring.

TIMING CHAIN
REPLACE

1. Ensure transmission is in Neutral position, then raise and support vehicle.
2. Relieve fuel system pressure as outlined under "Precautions."
3. Remove cooling fan motors and

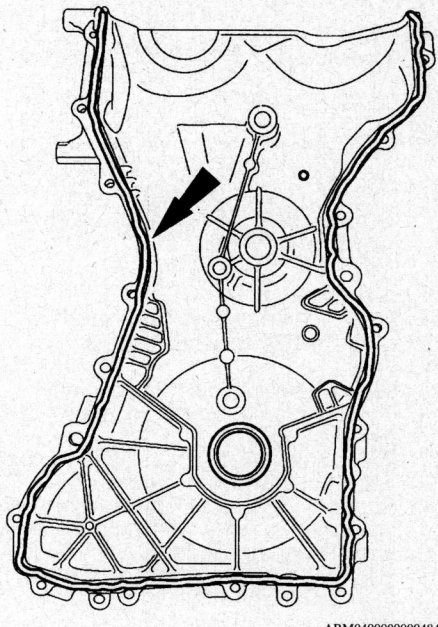

Fig. 6 Front cover sealant application

shroud from bracket, then lower assembly from vehicle.

4. Turn tensioner clockwise and remove accessory drive belt.
5. Remove valve cover as outlined under "Valve Cover, Replace."
6. Disconnect hoses from coolant expansion tank.
7. Remove mounting bolt and coolant expansion tank.
8. Remove battery, then the mounting bolts and tray.
9. Disconnect Crankshaft Position (CKP) sensor electrical connector and wiring harness pin-type retainers.
10. Remove crankshaft pulley as outlined under "Crankshaft Damper, Replace."
11. Remove mounting bolts and accessory belt tensioner.
12. Remove front cover as outlined under "Front Cover, Replace."
13. Compress timing chain tensioner and hold in place by installing suitable paper clip into hole.
14. Remove mounting bolts and timing chain tensioner.
15. Remove mounting bolts and righthand timing chain guide.
16. Remove timing chain.
17. Remove mounting bolts and lefthand timing chain guide.
18. Prevent camshaft rotation by holding at flats, then remove mounting bolts and camshaft sprockets.
19. Reverse procedure to install. Do not tighten camshaft sprockets mounting bolts until after guides, timing chain and tensioner have been installed.

CAMSHAFT

REPLACE

1. Remove valve cover as outlined under "Valve Cover, Replace."
2. Measure and record each valve clear-

ance at base circle with lobe pointed away from tappet.
3. Remove timing chain and sprockets as outlined under "Timing Chain, Replace."
4. Remove camshaft alignment plate tool.
5. Mark position of camshaft lobes on cylinder No. 1 for installation alignment.
6. Loosen camshaft bearing cap bolts one turn at a time in sequence, **Fig. 8.**
7. Repeat one turn removal sequence until all camshaft bearing cap tension is removed.
8. Remove bearing caps and camshaft.
9. Reverse procedure to install, noting the following:
   a. Lubricate camshaft journals and bearing caps with suitable, clean engine oil.
   b. Tighten camshaft bearing cap bolts one turn at a time until tight in sequence, **Fig. 9.**
   c. **Torque** bolts in sequence to 61 inch lbs.
   d. **Torque** bolts in sequence to 12 ft. lbs.

CRANKSHAFT SEAL

REPLACE

1. Remove crankshaft pulley as outlined under "Crankshaft Damper, Replace."
2. Remove crankshaft front oil seal using front oil seal remover tool No. T92C-6700-CH, or equivalent. **Do not damage front cover or crankshaft.**
3. Reverse procedure to install, noting the following:
   a. Lubricate new seal with suitable, clean engine oil.
   b. Use front oil seal installer tool No. T74P-6150-A, or equivalent.

CRANKSHAFT REAR OIL SEAL

REPLACE

1. Ensure transmission is in Neutral position, then raise and support vehicle.
2. Remove automatic transaxle or manual transaxle and clutch as outlined in **MOTOR's "Domestic Transmission, In-Vehicle Service"** manual.
3. Lock flywheel/flexplate in position using locking tool No. T74P-8375-A. or equivalent.
4. Remove mounting bolts and flywheel/flexplate.
5. Drain engine oil into suitable container.
6. Remove engine oil dipsticks, then the mounting bolt and tube.
7. Disconnect pin-type retainers and position wiring harness aside.
8. Remove mounting bolts and oil pan.
9. Remove mounting bolts and crankshaft rear oil seal.
10. Reverse procedure to install, noting the following:
    a. Install seal using crankshaft rear main oil seal installer tool No. T88P-6701-B1, or equivalent.
    b. Tighten bolts in sequence, **Fig. 10.**
    c. Tighten flywheel/flexplate mounting bolts in three steps using se-

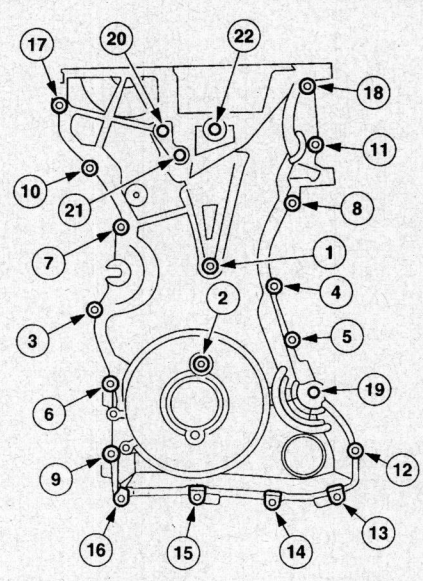

Fig. 7 Front cover tightening sequence

quence, **Fig. 11.** First step, **torque** bolts 37 ft. lbs.; second step, **torque** bolts to 50 ft. lbs.; third step, **torque** bolts to 83 ft. lbs.

OIL PAN

REPLACE

1. Ensure transmission is in Neutral position, then raise and support vehicle.
2. Drain engine oil into suitable container.
3. Remove engine oil dipsticks, then the mounting bolt and tube.
4. Disconnect pin-type retainers and position wiring harness aside.
5. Remove mounting bolts and oil pan.
6. Reverse procedure to install, noting the following:
   a. **Oil pan must be installed and bolts tighten within four minutes of applying silicone gasket and sealant.**
   b. Apply .098 inch bead of suitable silicone gasket and sealant to oil pan.
   c. Tighten mounting bolts in sequence, **Fig. 12.**

SERPENTINE DRIVE BELT

Routing

Refer to **Fig. 13** for serpentine belt routing.

Replace

1. Ensure transmission is in Neutral position, then raise and support vehicle.
2. Remove mounting bolts and accessory drive belt splash shield.
3. Turn tensioner clockwise and remove accessory drive belt.
4. Reverse procedure to install.

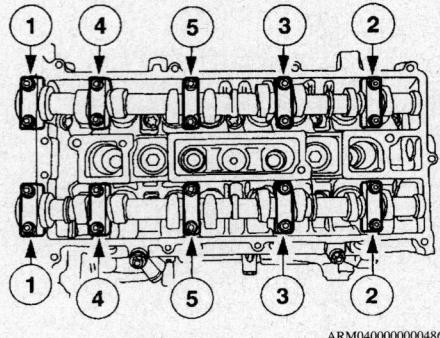

Fig. 8 Camshaft removal sequence

ARM0400000000486

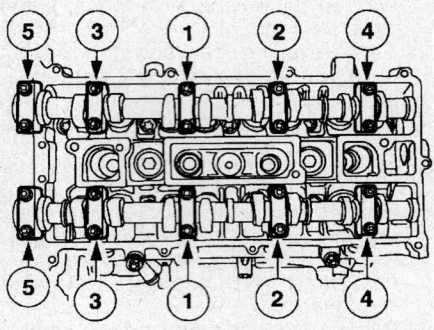

Fig. 9 Camshaft bearing cap bolt tightening sequence

ARM0400000000487

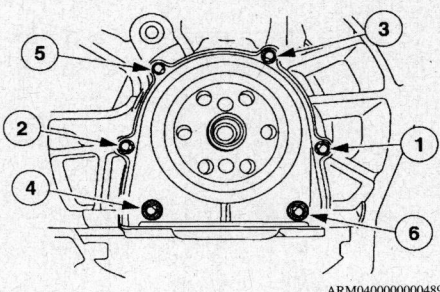

ARM0400000000489

Fig. 10 Crankshaft rear main oil seal tighten sequence

COOLING SYSTEM
BLEED

1. Disconnect heater inlet hose from engine.
2. Fill cooling system through inlet hose using suitable funnel until coolant starts trickling from engine.
3. Connect heater inlet hose.
4. Ensure heater temperature control is in HOT position.
5. Ensure blower switch and air conditioning switched are OFF.
6. Fill degas bottle to MAX mark with engine off.
7. Start and run engine for two fan cycles.
8. Allow engine to cool, then inspect and adjust coolant level to MAX mark.

THERMOSTAT
REPLACE

1. Ensure transmission is in Neutral position, then raise and support vehicle.
2. Remove cooling fan motors and shroud from bracket, then lower assembly from vehicle.
3. Remove mounting bolts, cover and air conditioning compressor drive belt.
4. Disconnect compressor field coil electrical connector.
5. Remove mounting bolts and position power steering line aside.
6. Remove three mounting bolts and position air conditioning compressor aside.
7. Drain cooling system into suitable container.
8. Disconnect clamps and remove thermostat housing hoses.
9. Remove mounting bolts, housing and thermostat.
10. Reverse procedure to install. Lubricate housing O-ring with clean engine oil.

WATER PUMP
REPLACE

1. Ensure transmission is in Neutral position, then raise and support vehicle.
2. Remove mounting bolts and accessory drive belt splash shield.

3. Turn tensioner clockwise and remove accessory drive belt.
4. Drain cooling system into suitable container.
5. Remove mounting bolts and water pump pulley.
6. Remove mounting bolts and water pump.
7. Reverse procedure to install. Install new O-ring lubricated with suitable, clean engine oil.

RADIATOR
REPLACE

1. Ensure transmission is in Neutral position, then raise and support vehicle.
2. Disconnect dual electric cooling fans electrical connector.
3. Drain cooling system into suitable container.
4. Remove cooling fan motors and shroud from retainer bracket, then lower and remove.
5. Disconnect horn electrical connector.
6. Disconnect clamps, then the radiator upper and lower hoses.
7. Remove push-pins and lower radiator splash shield.
8. **On models equipped with air conditioning,** disconnect and support condenser aside.
9. **On all models,** disconnect radiator support bracket wiring harness retaining clip.
10. **On models equipped with automatic transaxle,** disconnect fluid cooler from two righthand and one lefthand bracket. Support cooler aside.
11. **On all models,** remove mounting bolts and lower core support.
12. Remove radiator.
13. Reverse procedure to install.

FUEL PUMP
REPLACE

1. Ensure transmission is in Neutral position, then raise and support vehicle.
2. Relieve fuel system pressure as outlined under "Precautions."
3. Drain fuel tank into suitable container.
4. Disconnect fuel pump module electrical connector.

5. Remove heat shield mounting nut.
6. Loosen clamp and disconnect filler pipe.
7. Press quick release tabs, then disconnect vent and fuel feed hoses.
8. Support fuel tank with suitable high-lift jack using suitable packing material to prevent damage to tank.
9. Remove mounting bolt and position fuel tank straps aside.
10. Remove fuel tank.
11. Press quick release tab and disconnect fuel tube.
12. Turn lock ring counterclockwise using suitable fuel pump lock ring remover and remove fuel pump module.
13. Reverse procedure to install, noting the following:
    a. Install new locking ring and seal.
    b. Lubricate fuel tube fittings with clean engine oil.

FUEL FILTER
REPLACE

1. Ensure transmission is in Neutral position, then raise and support vehicle.
2. Relieve fuel system pressure as outlined under "Precautions."
3. Press quick release tabs, then disconnect filter inlet and outlet tubes.
4. Loosening mounting bolt and remove fuel filter.
5. Reverse procedure to install. Lubricate fuel tube fittings with clean engine oil.

TECHNICAL SERVICE BULLETINS

Engine Vibration At Idle

2004-05

Some models may have an excessive engine vibration at idle, most noticeable when the transmission is engaged in reverse.

This condition may be caused by small stones, road debris, ice or snow packed/lodged in the rear engine roll restrictor.

To correct this condition remove debris from rear engine roll restrictor and install service shield (P/N 2M5Z-16102-AA).

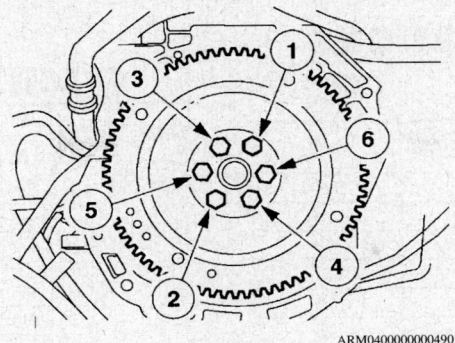

Fig. 11 Flywheel/flexplate bolt tightening sequence

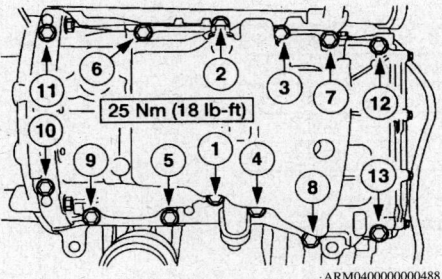

25 Nm (18 lb-ft)

Fig. 12 Oil pan bolt tightening sequence

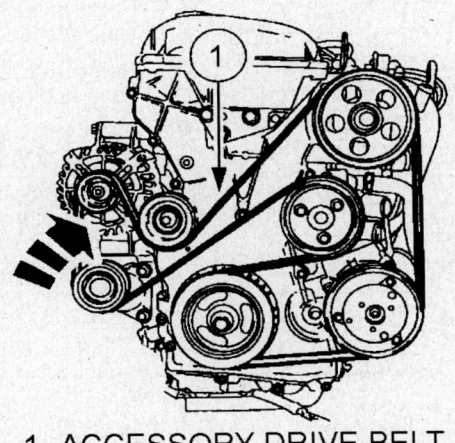

1- ACCESSORY DRIVE BELT

Fig. 13 Serpentine drive belt routing

TIGHTENING SPECIFICATIONS

Year	Component	Torque Ft. Lbs.
2005–06	Accelerator & Speed Control Cables' Bracket	89①
	Accelerator Control Snow Shield	89①
	Accessory Belt Tensioner	18
	Accessory Drive Belt Idler Pulley	18
	Air Cleaner Pipe	35①
	Air Conditioning Compressor	18
	Air Conditioning Compressor Manifold	15
	Bell Housing	35
	Caliper	21
	Camshaft	③
	Catalytic Converter Flange	41
	Catalytic Converter Heat Shield	89①
	Catalytic Converter Support Bracket;	35
	Catalytic Converter To Muffler	35
	Coil	89①
	Coolant Expansion Tank	89①
	Crankshaft Damper	②
	Crankshaft Pulley	②
	Crankshaft Rear Oil Seal	89①
	Cylinder Head	⑤
	EGR Tube	41
	Flexplate	④
	Flywheel	④
	Front Cover, 8 mm	89①
	Front Cover, 13 mm	35
	Fuel Rail	18
	Fuel Tank Strap	18
	Ground Bolt	35
	Ground Eyelet	89①
	Intake Manifold	18
	Intermediate Shaft Bearing Bracket	18
	Lower Control Arm To Knuckle	37
	Motor Mount	59
	Oil Indicator Tube	89①

TIGHTENING SPECIFICATIONS—Continued

Year	Component	Torque Ft. Lbs.
2005–06	Oil Pan	18
	Oil Pan Drain Plug	21
	Power Distribution Harness Eyelet	89①
	Power Steering Pressure Tube	44
	Radiator Bracket	18
	Radio Interference Capacitor Bracket	89①
	Stabilizer Bar	37
	Starter Motor	18
	Strut & Spring Top Mount	18
	Thermostat Housing	89①
	Tie Rod End	35
	Timing Chain Guide	89①
	Timing Chain Sprocket	48
	Timing Chain Tensioner	89①
	Torque Converter	26
	Transaxle Mount	98
	Transaxle Roll Restrictor	35
	Valve Cover	89①
	Water Pump	89①
	Water Pump Pulley	18

① — Inch lbs.

② — Refer to "Crankshaft Damper, Replace" for tightening specifications and sequence.

③ — Refer to "Camshaft, Replace" for tightening specifications and sequence.

④ — Refer to "Crankshaft Rear Oil Seal, Replace" for tightening specifications and sequence.

⑤ — Refer to "Cylinder Head, Replace" for tightening specifications and sequence.

Rear Suspension

NOTE: On Air Bag Equipped Models, Refer To "Air Bag System Precautions" Located In The Front Of This Manual For System Disarming & Arming Procedures.

NOTE: Refer To "Computer Relearn Procedures" Located In The Front Of This Manual When Battery Power To The Computer Has Been Interrupted.

INDEX

	Page No.		Page No.		Page No.
Coil Spring, Replace	6-32	Upper	6-33	Rear Wheel Spindle, Replace	6-31
Coupe & Sedan	6-32	Description	6-31	Shock Absorber, Replace	6-31
Wagon	6-32	Hub & Bearing, Replace	6-31	Coupe & Sedan	6-31
Control Arm, Replace	6-32	Precautions	6-31	Wagon	6-31
Lower	6-32	Air Bag Systems	6-31	Stabilizer Bar, Replace	6-33
Front	6-32	Battery Ground Cable	6-31	Tie-Bar, Replace	6-33
Rear	6-32	Rear Crossmember, Replace	6-33	Tightening Specifications	6-34

PRECAUTIONS

Air Bag Systems

Refer to "Air Bag System Precautions" in the front of this manual for system disarming and arming procedures.

Battery Ground Cable

Prior to service, disconnect battery ground cable and isolate as required.

DESCRIPTION

Refer to **Figs. 1 and 2** for exploded view of rear suspension.

HUB & BEARING
REPLACE

1. Release parking brake, then remove tire and wheel assembly.
2. Remove dust cap.
3. **On models equipped with rear disc brakes,** proceed as follows:
   a. Disconnect caliper parking brake cable.
   b. Disconnect brake caliper and anchor plate from wheel knuckle.
   c. Suspend brake caliper and anchor plate aside.
   d. Remove brake disc.
4. **On all models,** remove mounting nut and wheel hub.
5. **On models equipped with Anti-Lock Brake System (ABS),** remove ABS sensor ring.
6. **On all models,** remove circlip and press out bearing using suitable drift.
7. Reverse procedures to install noting the following:
   a. Install new bearing using axle bearing installer tool No. T80T-4000N, or equivalent.
   b. **On models equipped with ABS,** install new ABS sensor ring. Ensure

ABS sensor ring is pressed on slowly and squarely.
   c. **On models equipped with rear drum brakes,** rotate drum in opposite direction when tightening wheel hub mounting nut.
   d. **On models equipped with rear disc brakes,** rotate hub assembly 10 times in opposite direction when tightening wheel hub mounting nut.

REAR WHEEL SPINDLE
REPLACE

1. Release parking brake adjuster.
2. Loosen wheel nuts, then raise and support vehicle Remove tire and wheel assembly.
3. **On models equipped with anti-lock brakes,** disconnect wheel speed sensor.
4. **On models equipped with rear disc brakes,** proceed as follows:
   a. Disconnect caliper parking brake cable.
   b. Disconnect brake caliper and anchor plate from wheel knuckle.
   c. Suspend brake caliper and anchor plate aside.
   d. Remove brake disc.
5. **On all models equipped with rear drum brakes,** remove mounting nut, and wheel hub.
6. **On models equipped with Anti-lock Brake System (ABS),** ensure ABS sensor ring is not knocked or damaged and is kept free from metallic fragments when removing brake drum.
7. **On all models,** remove wheel spindle.
8. Reverse procedures to install noting the following:
   a. Install new bearing using axle bearing installer tool No. T80T-4000N, or equivalent.
   b. **On models equipped with ABS,** install new ABS sensor ring. Ensure ABS sensor ring is pressed on slowly and squarely.

   c. **On models equipped with rear drum brakes,** rotate drum in opposite direction when tightening wheel hub mounting nut.
   d. **On models equipped with rear disc brakes,** rotate hub assembly 10 times in opposite direction when tightening wheel hub mounting nut.

SHOCK ABSORBER
REPLACE

Coupe & Sedan

1. Raise and support vehicle.
2. Remove luggage compartment interior trim panel.
3. Remove shock absorber upper mounting nut using suitable spanner to prevent piston rod from rotating.
4. Remove lower mounting bolt and shock absorber.
5. Reverse procedure to install. Final suspension component tightening must be performed with vehicle weight on road wheels.

Wagon

1. Raise and support vehicle, then remove rear tire and wheel assembly.
2. When removing lefthand shock absorber, disconnect exhaust system from rear hanger insulator and remove exhaust heat shield.
3. Support lower arm using suitable transmission jack,
4. Remove shock absorber upper mounting bolt.
5. Remove lower mounting bolt and shock absorber.
6. Reverse procedure to install. Final suspension component tightening must be performed with vehicle weight on road wheels.

COIL SPRING
REPLACE
Coupe & Sedan

1. Remove rear tire and wheel.
2. Compress coil spring. using suitable compressor tool.
3. Disconnect shock absorber from wheel knuckle.
4. Mark position of coil spring compressor to coil spring for installation alignment.
5. Remove coil spring. **Coil spring is under extreme tension.**
6. If coil spring is to be removed from coil spring compressor, mark position of coil spring compressor to coil spring to aid installation.
7. Reverse procedure to install noting the following:
   a. Final tightening of shock absorber lower mounting bolt should be carried out when vehicle weight is on road wheels.
   b. Ensure top seat mounting is installed, and spring ends butt correctly against upper and lower spring seats.

Wagon

1. Remove rear tire and wheel assembly.
2. Disconnect stabilizer bar from rear lower arms.
3. Raise rear lower arm 1.25 inches using suitable transmission jack.
4. Disconnect rear lower arm from wheel knuckle.
5. Lower and remove transmission jack.
6. With the aid of another technician, pull stabilizer bar away from rear lower arm, lower rear lower arm and remove spring. **Coil spring is under extreme tension.**
7. Reverse procedure to install noting the following:
   a. Final tightening of shock absorber lower mounting bolt should be carried out when vehicle weight is on road wheels.
   b. Ensure top seat mounting is installed, and spring ends butt correctly against upper and lower spring seats.

CONTROL ARM
REPLACE
Lower
FRONT

1. Remove coil spring as outlined under "Coil Spring, Replace."
2. Set suspension ride height as outlined in "Wheel Alignment" section.
3. Record position of arm for installation alignment.

4. Remove mounting bolts and front lower arm.
5. Reverse procedures to install. Final tightening of rear suspension components should be carried out at ride height setting.

REAR

1. Remove coil spring as outlined under "Coil Spring, Replace"
2. Set suspension ride height as outlined in "Wheel Alignment" section.
3. Mark position of rear lower arm adjustment cam on crossmember for installation alignment.
4. Remove mounting bolts and rear lower arm.
5. Reverse procedure to install. Final tightening of rear suspension components should be carried out at ride height setting.

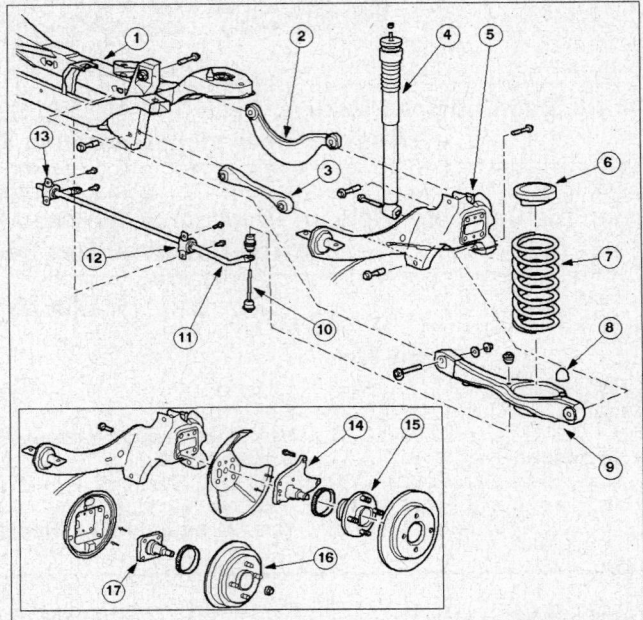

Item	Description
1	Crossmember
2	Upper arm
3	Front lower arm
4	Shock absorber assembly
5	Tie-bar and knuckle
6	Spring pad
7	Spring
8	Bump stop
9	Rear lower arm
10	Stabilizer bar link
11	Stabilizer bar
12	Stabilizer bar bushing
13	Stabilizer bar bushing clamp
14	Wheel spindle (disc brakes)
15	Wheel hub (disc brakes)
16	Drum and hub assembly (drum brakes)
17	Wheel spindle (drum brakes)

FM20399000095000X

Fig. 1   Rear suspension. Coupe & sedan

Upper

1. Remove coil spring as outlined under "Coil Spring, Replace."
2. Set suspension ride height as outlined in "Wheel Alignment" section.
3. Record position of upper arm for installation alignment.
4. Remove outer bolt and disconnect upper arm from wheel knuckle.
5. Remove inner bolt and upper arm.
6. Reverse procedures to install. Final tightening of rear suspension components should be carried out at ride height setting.

TIE-BAR
REPLACE

1. **On models equipped with rear disc brakes,** remove brake disc shield.
2. **On models equipped with rear drum brakes,** remove brake drum.
3. **On all models,** disconnect rear brake hose using suitable clamp, then the pipe at union.
4. Disconnect parking brake sleeve and cable.
5. Disconnect cable guide, then pull cable and guide through tie-bar.
6. Set suspension ride height as outlined in "Wheel Alignment" section.
7. Remove shock absorber lower mounting bolt, then the outer mount bolts and front lower arm.
8. Remove rear lower arm bolts.
9. Remove spring using suitable coil spring compressor.
10. Disconnect and remove upper arm.
11. Remove front mounting bolts and tie-bar.
12. Reverse procedures to install noting the following:
    a. Bleed brake system.
    b. Inspect rear wheel alignment.

REAR CROSSMEMBER
REPLACE

1. Set suspension ride height as outlined in "Wheel Alignment" section.
2. Remove mounting bolts, clamps and stabilizer bar.
3. Remove bushings.
4. Remove rear lower arms, front lower arms and upper arms as outlined under "Control Arm, Replace." Ensure wheel knuckles are supported before removing arms.
5. Support exhaust system, and bracket.
6. Support rear crossmember with suitable jack, then remove three mounting bolts from either side.
7. Lower and remove crossmember.

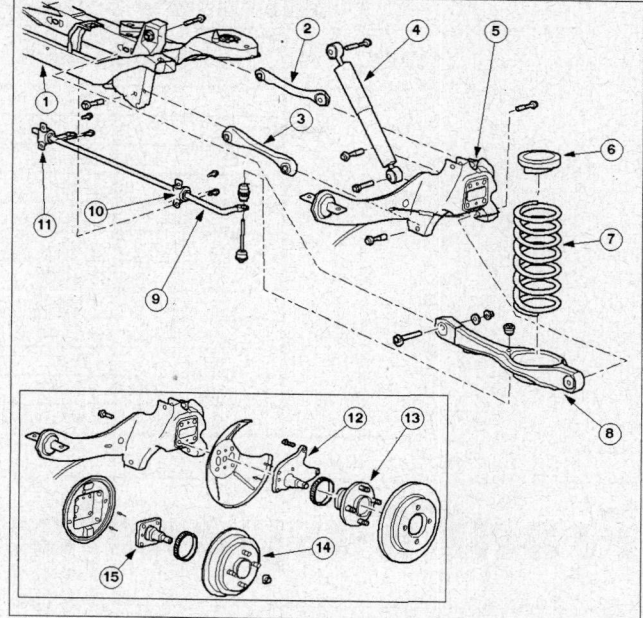

Item	Description
1	Crossmember
2	Upper arm
3	Front lower arm
4	Shock absorber
5	Tie-bar and knuckle
6	Spring pad
7	Spring
8	Rear lower arm
9	Stabilizer bar
10	Stabilizer bar bushing
11	Stabilizer bar bushing clamp
12	Wheel spindle (disc brakes)
13	Wheel hub (disc brakes)
14	Drum and hub assembly (drum brakes)
15	Wheel spindle (drum brakes)

FM20399000096000X

Fig. 2   Rear suspension. Wagon

8. Reverse procedures to install noting the following:
    a. Do not lower suspension from ride height.
    b. Inspect rear wheel alignment.

STABILIZER BAR
REPLACE

1. Set suspension ride height as outlined in "Wheel Alignment" section.
2. Remove mounting bolts, clamps and remove stabilizer bar.
3. Remove bushings.
4. Reverse procedures to install noting the following:
    a. Ensure bushing nipple is on left-hand side when installing onto stabilizer bar.
    b. Apply water to clamp to assist installation.

TIGHTENING SPECIFICATIONS

Year	Component	Torque Ft. Lbs.
2004–07	Control Arm	85
	Crossmember	85
	EVAP Canister	84①
	Lug Nut	94
	Shock Absorber, Lower	85
	Shock Absorber, Top	13
	Spindle Bolt	49
	Stabilizer Bar Link	11
	Stabilizer Bracket	35
	Tie Bar	85
	Wheel Hub Nut	173
	Wheel Speed Sensor	84①

① — Inch lbs.

Front Suspension & Steering

NOTE: On Air Bag Equipped Models, Refer To "Air Bag System Precautions" Located In The Front Of This Manual For System Disarming & Arming Procedures.

NOTE: Refer To "Computer Relearn Procedures" Located In The Front Of This Manual When Battery Power To The Computer Has Been Interrupted.

NOTE: Prior To Performing Any Service Operations Listed In This Section, Consult The "Technical Service Bulletins" Section For Related Information.

INDEX

	Page No.
Ball Joint, Replace	6-35
Coil Spring, Replace	6-35
Coil Spring & Strut Service	6-35
Control Arm, Replace	6-35
Description	6-34
Hub & Bearing, Replace	6-35
Power Steering	13-1
Power Steering Fluid Cooler, Replace	6-37
Power Steering Gear, Replace	6-36
Power Steering Pump, Replace	6-36

	Page No.
2.0L DOHC Engine	6-36
VIN 3	6-36
VIN 5	6-36
VINs N & Z	6-36
2.0L SOHC Engine	6-37
Power Steering System Bleed	6-37
Precautions	6-34
Air Bag Systems	6-34
Battery Ground Cable	6-34
Stabilizer Bar, Replace	6-35
Steering Columns	12-1

	Page No.
Steering Knuckle, Replace	6-35
Strut, Replace	6-35
Technical Service Bulletins	6-37
Front Suspension Creaking, Crunching, Grinding Or Rattle. 2004	6-37
Tie Rod, Replace	6-36
Tie Rod End, Replace	6-36
Tightening Specifications	6-38
Wheel Bearing, Adjust	6-34

PRECAUTIONS

Air Bag Systems

Refer to "Air Bag System Precautions" in the front of this manual for system disarming and arming procedures.

Battery Ground Cable

Prior to service, disconnect battery ground cable and isolate as required.

DESCRIPTION

Refer to **Fig. 1** for exploded view of front suspension.

WHEEL BEARING

ADJUST

Wheel bearing cannot be adjusted.
1. Raise and support vehicle.
2. Rock tire and wheel assembly at top and bottom to inspect for bearing looseness.
3. Spin wheel quickly by hand. Ensure wheel turns smoothly without noise from bearing.
4. Remove tire and wheel assembly, then brake caliper anchor plate.
5. Position dial indicator gauge bracket and gauge Nos. 100-D004 and 100-D005, or equivalent, against wheel hub, then push and pull wheel hub.
6. If end play exists, replace bearing.

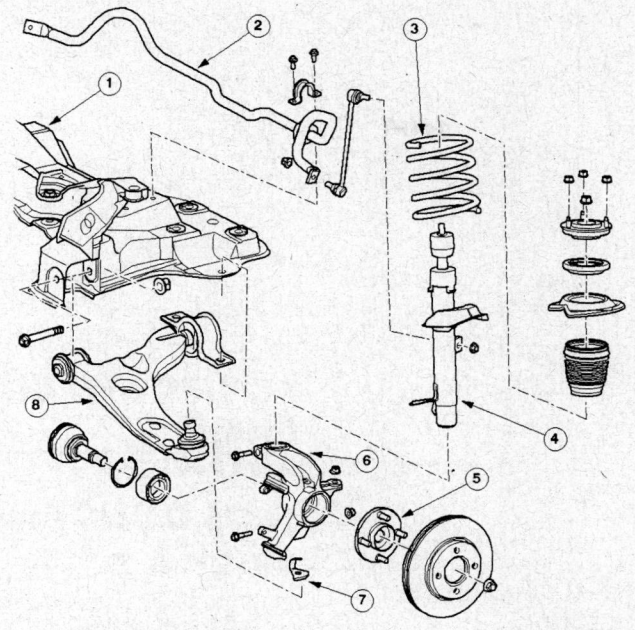

FM2020000172010X

**Fig. 1   Exploded view of front suspension
(Part 1 of 2)**

Item	Description
1	Crossmember
2	Stabilizer bar
3	Spring
4	Strut
5	Wheel hub
6	Wheel knuckle
7	Lower arm ball joint heat shield
8	Lower arm

FM2020000172020X

**Fig. 1   Exploded view of front
suspension (Part 2 of 2)**

HUB & BEARING
REPLACE

1. Remove knuckle as outlined under "Steering Knuckle, Replace."
2. Remove wheel hub and outer bearing race using bearing puller No. 205-D064, or equivalent, and suitable drift, **Fig. 2.**
3. Remove bearing circlip.
4. Remove inner bearing using suitable drift.
5. Reverse procedure to install. Install new bearing using bearing cup installer No. 205-139, or equivalent.

BALL JOINT
REPLACE

1. Raise and support vehicle, then remove tire and wheel assembly.
2. Remove mounting bolt and ball joint from knuckle.
3. Reverse procedure to install.

COIL SPRING
REPLACE

1. Raise and support vehicle, then remove tire and wheel assembly.
2. Remove knuckle as outlined under "Steering Knuckle, Replace."
3. Remove mounting nuts, strut and spring assembly.
4. Compress coil spring using suitable compressor tool.
5. Remove thrust bearing nut using suitable Allen key to prevent piston rod rotation.
6. Disassemble strut and spring assembly, **Fig. 3.**
7. Reverse procedure to assemble.

STRUT
REPLACE

1. Raise and support vehicle, then remove tire and wheel assembly.
2. Remove knuckle as outlined under "Steering Knuckle, Replace."
3. Remove mounting nuts, strut and spring assembly.
4. Reverse procedure to install.

COIL SPRING & STRUT SERVICE

1. Compress coil spring using suitable compressor tool.
2. Remove thrust bearing nut using suitable Allen key to prevent piston rod rotation.
3. Disassemble strut and spring assembly, **Fig. 3.**
4. Reverse procedure to assemble.

CONTROL ARM
REPLACE

1. Raise and support vehicle, then remove tire and wheel assembly.
2. Remove mounting bolt and ball joint from knuckle.
3. Remove mounting bolts and lower arm.
4. Reverse procedure to install, noting the following.
   a. Install lower arm nuts, bolts and washers.
   b. **Torque** nut 1 to 74 ft. lbs., **Fig. 4.**
   c. Tighten nut 1 an additional 60°.
   d. **Torque** nut 2 to 89 ft. lbs.
   e. **Torque** bolt 3 to 89 ft. lbs.
   f. Tighten bolt 3 an additional 90°.
   g. Ensure bolt 3 is **torqued** to 125–170 ft. lbs.

STEERING KNUCKLE
REPLACE

1. Loosen wheel hub mounting nut.
2. Loosen wheel nuts.
3. Loosen strut tower nuts at least five turns.
4. Raise and support vehicle, then remove tire and wheel assembly.
5. Disconnect brake hose from support bracket.
6. Disconnect wheel speed sensor, then remove and support brake caliper aside.
7. Remove brake rotor.
8. Remove tie rod end using tie rod end remover tool No. TOOL-3290-D, or equivalent.
9. Remove ball joint from knuckle.
10. Remove hub mounting nut.
11. Separate wheel hub from halfshaft using puller tools Nos. 204-067 and 204-069, or equivalents. **Ensure halfshaft does not disconnected from inner constant velocity joint.**
12. Remove pinch bolt and knuckle from strut.
13. Reverse procedure to install.

STABILIZER BAR
REPLACE

1. Center and lock steering wheel in position.
2. Disconnect steering column shaft from pinion extension.
3. Raise and support vehicle, then remove tire and wheel assemblies.
4. Remove tie rod end nuts, then using tie rod end remover No. TOOL-3290-D, or equivalent.
5. Disconnect tie rod ends from knuckles.
6. Disconnect stabilizer bar links.
7. Remove ball joints from knuckles.
8. Remove support insulator to transaxle center bolt, **Fig. 5.**
9. Support crossmember using suitable transmission jack.
10. Remove six crossmember mounting bolts, **Fig. 6.**
11. Lower crossmember.

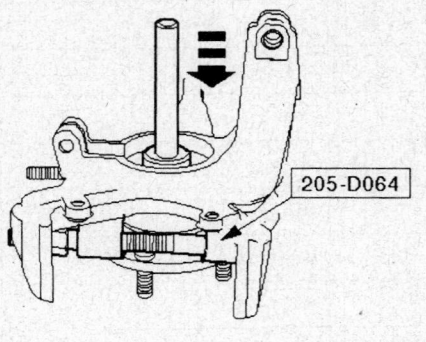

Fig. 2 Hub & outer race removal

12. Remove bolts, clamps and stabilizer bar.
13. Reverse procedure to install, noting the following:
    a. Install bushings onto stabilizer bar. **Do not use lubricant.**
    b. Support stabilizer bar to design height, **Fig. 7.**
    c. Tighten upper and lower clamp mounting bolts to specifications.
    d. Insert alignment tool No. 502-002, or equivalent, guide pins through crossmember alignment holes, **Fig. 8.**
    e. Slide locking plates into grooves and tighten guide pin sleeve.
    f. Raise crossmember, engaging guide pins into chassis aligning holes.

TIE ROD
REPLACE

1. Remove steering gear as outlined under "Power Steering Gear, Replace."
2. Remove tie rod end and locknut.
3. Remove steering gear boot.
4. Rotate pinion to expose rack gear teeth.
5. Secure steering gear in suitable vise.
6. Remove tie rod using suitable pipe wrench.
7. Remove thread locking compound.
8. Reverse procedure to install. Apply thread locking compound to new tie rod inner threads.

TIE ROD END
REPLACE

1. Raise and support vehicle, then remove tire and wheel assembly.
2. Loosen tie rod end lock nut, then remove mounting nut.
3. Disconnect tie rod end from knuckle using tie rod end remover tool No. TOOL-3290-D, or equivalent.
4. Note number of turns required to remove tie rod end.
5. Remove tie rod end and lock nut.
6. Reverse procedure to install. Inspect toe.

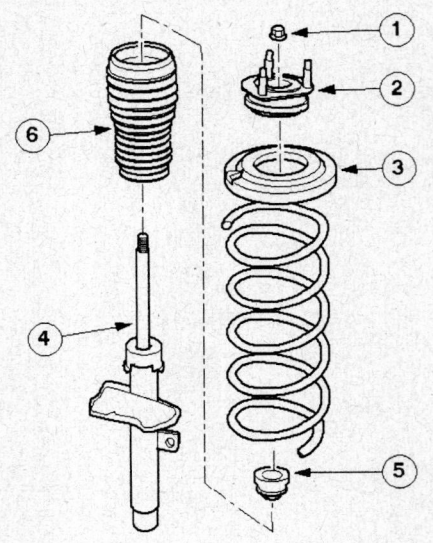

Fig. 3 Exploded view of strut & spring.

POWER STEERING GEAR
REPLACE

1. Center and lock steering wheel into position.
2. Remove instrument panel lower cover.
3. Disconnect steering column shaft from pinion extension.
4. Raise and support vehicle, then remove front tire and wheel assemblies.
5. Remove tie rod ends from knuckles using tie rod end removal tool No. TOOL-3290-D, or equivalent.
6. Disconnect stabilizer bar links from struts.
7. Disconnect fluid cooler hose using coupling tool No. 310-041, or equivalent. Drain fluid into suitable container.
8. Remove support insulator to transaxle center bolt, **Fig. 5.**
9. Remove steering gear heat shield.
10. Disconnect support clamp and remove steering gear hoses. Drain fluid into suitable container.
11. Support crossmember using suitable transmission jack.
12. Remove six mounting bolts and lower crossmember, **Fig. 6.**
13. Remove steering column coupling shaft and floor seal.
14. Move floor seal upwards.
15. Remove mounting bolts and steering gear.
16. Reverse procedure to install, noting the following:
    a. Insert alignment tool No. 502-002, or equivalent, guide pins through crossmember alignment holes, **Fig. 8.**
    b. Slide locking plates into grooves and tighten guide pin sleeve.
    c. Raise crossmember, engaging guide pins into chassis aligning holes.

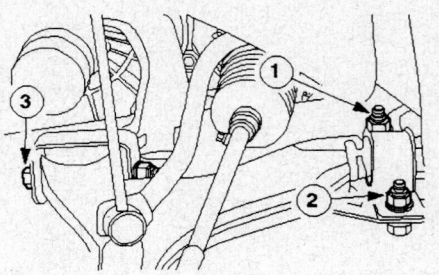

Fig. 4 Lower arm tightening sequence

POWER STEERING PUMP
REPLACE

2.0L DOHC Engine
VINS N & Z

1. Turn tensioner clockwise and remove accessory drive belt.
2. Disconnect Power Steering Pressure (PSP) switch electrical connector.
3. Remove clamp, disconnect steering fluid suction line from pump. Drain fluid into suitable container.
4. Disconnect power steering pressure line fitting nut.
5. Raise and support vehicle.
6. Remove mounting nuts and position power steering pressure line bracket aside.
7. Remove power steering pump lower mounting bolts.
8. Lower vehicle.
9. Remove upper mounting bolts and power steering pump.
10. Reverse procedure to install.

VIN 3

1. Remove accessory drive belt, then raise and support vehicle.
2. Disconnect fluid cooler hose using coupling tool No. 310-041, or equivalent. Drain fluid into suitable container.
3. Disconnect power steering pump line.
4. Lower vehicle, then disconnect pressure line support brackets.
5. Disconnect speed control cable.
6. Disconnect Power Steering Pressure (PSP) switch electrical connector.
7. Disconnect power steering pump hose. Drain fluid into suitable container.
8. Remove four mounting bolts power steering pump.
9. Remove PSP switch.
10. Reverse procedure to install. Install new O-ring seal onto pressure line using Teflon seal installer tool No. D90P-3517-A, or equivalent.

VIN 5

1. Remove accessory drive belt.
2. Disconnect fender splash shield from front bumper cover.
3. Remove righthand headlamp assembly lower mounting bolt.
4. Disconnect power steering fluid cooler

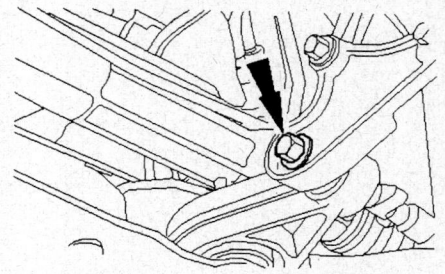

FM2020000174000X

Fig. 5 Support insulator bolt replacement

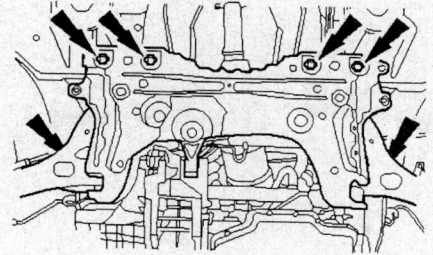

FM2020000175000X

Fig. 6 Crossmember replacement

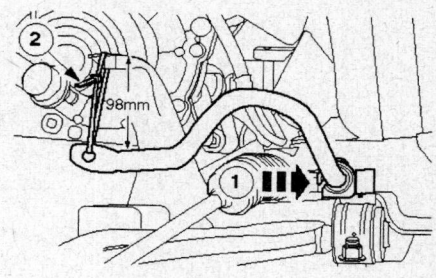

FM2020000176000X

Fig. 7 Stabilizer bar design height setting

line from cooler using coupling tool No. 310-041, or equivalent.
5. Disconnect power steering pump line.
6. Remove power steering pump lower mounting bolts.
7. Lower vehicle.
8. Remove radiator grille.
9. Remove righthand headlamp assembly.
10. Disconnect power steering pump hose.
11. Disconnect power steering line from engine and position aside.
12. Remove power steering pump.
13. Reverse procedure to install. Install new O-ring seal onto power steering pump to steering gear line union using Teflon seal installer tool No. D90P-3517-A, or equivalent.

2.0L SOHC Engine

1. Rotate tensioner in a clockwise direction using suitable ½ square drive breaker bar.
2. Disconnect serpentine drive belt from power steering pump pulley.
3. Remove power steering pump pulley mounting nut.
4. Remove power steering pump pulley mounting nut. using flange holding tool wrench tool No. T78P-4851-A, or equivalent.
5. Remove power steering pump pulley.
6. Disconnect power steering pump fluid reservoir hose. Drain fluid into suitable container.
7. Disconnect power steering high-pressure line from power steering pump. Drain fluid into suitable container.
8. Remove power steering pump.
9. Remove power steering fluid reservoir to power steering pump hose union.
10. Reverse procedure to install. Install new O-ring seal onto power steering pump to steering gear line union using Teflon seal installer tool No. D90P-3517-A, or equivalent.

POWER STEERING SYSTEM BLEED

1. Fill power steering fluid reservoir to

MAX mark with suitably, fresh power steering fluid.
2. Start engine and slowly turn wheel from lock to lock once. Ensure fluid level does not fall below MIN mark as air could enter system. **Do not hold steering wheel against lock stops for more than five seconds.**
3. Stop engine and inspect system for leaks.
4. Inspect and adjust reservoir fluid level.
5. Maintain a vacuum of 15 inches Hg. using vacuum tool No. 416-D002, or equivalent. If vacuum decreases more than 2 inches Hg in five minutes, inspect for leaks.
6. Start engine and turn wheel from lock to lock once, then turn it to righthand just off lock stop.
7. Stop engine and apply vacuum of 15 inches Hg. Maintain vacuum for five minutes until air is evacuated from system.
8. Release vacuum, then repeat previous two steps, turning wheel to left, just off stop lock.
9. Remove vacuum tool and adjust reservoir fluid level.
10. Start engine and turn wheel from lock to lock. If there is excessive noise, repeat procedure.
11. If noise level is still unacceptable, allow vehicle to stand overnight and repeat procedure.

POWER STEERING FLUID COOLER

REPLACE

1. Disconnect coolant expansion tank and position aside.
2. Remove power steering fluid reservoir hose. Drain fluid into suitable container.
3. Disconnect hose from bracket, then raise and support vehicle.
4. Remove radiator splash shield.
5. Disconnect fluid cooler hose using coupling tool No. 310-041, or equivalent. Drain fluid into suitable container.
6. Remove fluid cooler.
7. Reverse procedure to install.

TECHNICAL SERVICE BULLETINS

Front Suspension Creaking, Crunching, Grinding Or Rattle

2004

On some of these models there may be a front suspension creaking, crunching, grinding or rattle at slow speeds or while turning.

This condition may be caused by stabilizer bar and links, spring's rubber sleeve or upper strut bearing.

To correct this condition, proceed as follows:

1. Grasp stabilizer bar end links and shake them along link direction and transverse in inboard/outboard directions.
2. If there is no looseness, proceed to next step. If there is looseness, proceed as follows:
   a. Inspect link end joints.
   b. If joints are not severely corroded, **torque** nut to 36 ft. lbs.
   c. If joints are still loose or are severely corroded, replace link (P/N YS4Z-5K484-AA).
3. Inspect upper spring seat contact. If spring is positioned properly, proceed to next step. If spring is out of position, proceed as follows:
   a. Remove original sleeve.
   b. Install new rubber sleeve (P/N 1S4Z-8484-AA) starting from top of spring coil.
4. Remove strut(s) and inspect for misaligned upper strut bearing.
5. If bearing is misaligned, replace it (P/N YS4Z-18198-AAA) into existing rubber top mount on existing strut.
6. Relieve fuel system pressure as outlined under "Precautions." If clicking or popping is from front strut, install service spring end cap (P/N 4S4Z-5L302-AA) on top spring tip.

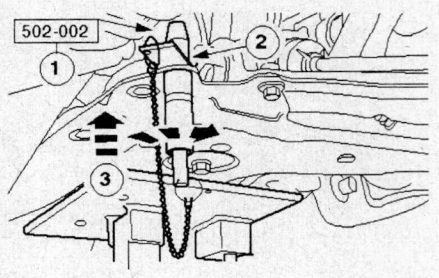

Fig. 8 Crossmember alignment

TIGHTENING SPECIFICATIONS

Year	Component	Torque Ft. Lbs.
2004–07	Caliper To Knuckle	21
	Column Shaft To Pinion	26
	Crossmember, Front	85
	Crossmember, Rear	148
	Fluid Cooler	44①
	Hose Clamps	17
	Hub Nut	233
	Knuckle To Strut Pinch Bolt	66
	Lower Arm To Knuckle Pinch Bolt	37
	Power Steering Pump	18
	Pressure Line To Pump Union	48
	Pressure Line Support Bracket	②
	PSP Switch	15
	Speed Sensor	80①
	Stabilizer Bar Link	37
	Steering Gear	59
	Steering Gear Heat Shield	53①
	Strut	18
	Strut Thrust Bearing	35
	Support Insulator Center Bolt	37
	Tie Rod End	35
	Wheel Lug Nuts	63

① — Inch lbs.
② — DOHC engine, 18 ft. lbs. SOHC engine, 44 inch lbs.

Wheel Alignment

NOTE: Prior To Performing Any Service Operations Listed In This Section, Consult The "Technical Service Bulletins" Section For Related Information.

INDEX

	Page No.
Front Wheel Alignment	6-39
Caster & Camber	6-39
Toe	6-39
Preliminary Inspection	6-39
Rear Wheel Alignment	6-39

	Page No.
Camber	6-39
Toe	6-39
Ride Height	6-39
Coupe & Sedan	6-39
Wagon	6-39

	Page No.
Technical Service Bulletins	6-39
Rear Tire Inner Edge Wear	6-39
Wheel Alignment Specifications	6-3

PRELIMINARY INSPECTION

1. Inspect suspension components for damage or wear.
2. Inflate tires to specifications.
3. Ensure vehicle is at curb weight.
4. Ensure spare tire, jack and vehicle tools are in proper locations.
5. Remove luggage and additional items.
6. Jounce vehicle to bring suspension to normal design height setting.

RIDE HEIGHT

Coupe & Sedan

1. Raise and support vehicle.
2. Fabricate .787 inch wide and 4.448 inches long spacer.
3. Remove bump stop.
4. Position spacer and raise rear control arm using suitable floor jack and wooden block.
5. Space should be between rear lower arm and crossmember in vertical plane, **Fig. 1.**

Wagon

1. Raise and support vehicle.
2. Fabricate .787 inch wide and 6.181 inches long spacer.
3. Position spacer and raise rear control arm using suitable floor jack and wooden block.
4. Space should be between rear lower arm and crossmember in vertical plane, **Fig. 2.**

FRONT WHEEL ALIGNMENT

Caster & Camber

On these models, caster and camber are not adjustable.

Toe

1. Inspect toe setting.
2. Loosen tie-rod end locknuts.
3. Remove steering gear boot outer clamps.
4. Rotate tie-rods an equal amount in either clockwise or counterclockwise direction.
5. **Torque** tie-rod end locknuts to 46 ft. lbs.
6. Install steering gear boot outer clamps.
7. Ensure toe is set to specifications.

REAR WHEEL ALIGNMENT

Camber

On these models, camber is not adjustable.

Toe

1. Inspect toe setting.
2. Raise and support vehicle.
3. Set suspension to ride height as outlined under "Ride Height."
4. Loosen rear lower arm cam bolt nut.
5. **Torque** rear lower arm cam bolt nut to 71 inch lbs.
6. Lower suspension from ride height.
7. Install coil spring as outlined under "Coil Spring, Replace" in "Rear Suspension" section.
8. Lower vehicle and bounce vehicle to ensure suspension is in its normal resting position.
9. Rotate bolt and eccentric washer until proper toe setting is reached.
10. Raise and support vehicle.
11. **Torque** rear lower arm cam bolt nut to 85 ft. lbs.
12. Lower vehicle.
13. Ensure toe setting is with specifications.

TECHNICAL SERVICE BULLETINS

Rear Tire Inner Edge Wear

On some of these models the rear tire may have inner edge wear.

This condition may be caused by rear camber beyond negative end of specifications (maximum on wagon models is -2.2°; on coupe and sedan models, -2.3°.

To correct this condition install revised +1° rear upper control arms kit (P/N 3S4Z-1A154-AA) as follows:

1. **On wagon models,** remove lower mounting bolt and position shock absorber aside.
2. **On all models,** remove inboard upper control arm mounting bolt and arm.
3. Install upper control arm and new inboard upper control arm bolt.
4. **On wagon models,** install shock absorber and lower mounting bolt.
5. **On all models,** position upper control arm in wheel knuckle and install new outboard upper control arm bolt.
6. **Final tighten of rear suspension component(s) when suspension is at load and at ride height.**
7. Inspect alignment.

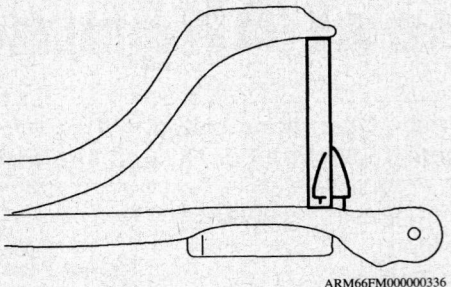

ARM66FM000000336

Fig. 1   Spacer position. Coupe & sedan

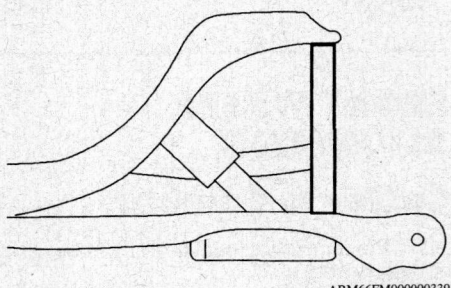

ARM66FM000000339

Fig. 2   Spacer position. Wagon

FIVE HUNDRED, FREESTYLE, MONTEGO & 2008 SABLE, TAURUS & TAURUS X

NOTE: Refer To The Rear Of This Manual For Vehicle Manufacturer's Special Service Tools.

INDEX OF SERVICE OPERATIONS

Page No.

ACTIVE SUSPENSION SYSTEMS (VOLUME 2) 7-1
AIR BAG SYSTEM PRECAUTIONS 0-18
BRAKES
  Anti-Lock Brakes (Volume 2) .. 6-1
  Disc Brakes 14-1
  Drum Brakes 15-1
  Hydraulic Brake Systems 16-1
  Power Brake Units 17-1
COMPUTER RELEARN PROCEDURE 0-31
ELECTRICAL
  Air Bag System (Volume 2) ... 4-1
  Air Conditioning 8-1
  Alternator, Replace 7-7
  Alternators 11-1
  Blower Motor, Replace 7-10
  Cabin Air Filter, Replace ... 7-10
  Cooling Fans 9-1
  Cruise Control (Volume 2) 2-1
  Dash Gauges (Volume 2) 1-1
  Dash Panel Service (Volume 2) 5-1
  Evaporator Core, Replace 7-11
  Fuel Pump Relay Location 7-7
  Fuse Panel & Flasher Location 7-7
  Headlamp Switch, Replace ... 7-7
  Heater Core, Replace 7-10
  Ignition Lock, Replace 7-7
  Ignition Switch, Replace 7-7
  Instrument Cluster, Replace ... 7-8
  Multi-Function Switch, Replace 7-8
  Neutral Safety Switch, Replace 7-7
  Passive Restraint Systems (Volume 2) 4-1
  Precautions 7-7
  Radio, Replace 7-9
  Speed Controls (Volume 2) ... 2-1
  Starter Motors 10-1
  Starter, Replace 7-7
  Steering Columns 12-1
  Steering Wheel, Replace 7-8
  Stop Light Switch, Replace ... 7-8
  Wiper Motor, Replace 7-9
  Wiper Switch, Replace 7-9
  Wiper Systems (Volume 2) 3-1
  Wiper Transmission, Replace . 7-10
ELECTRICAL SYMBOL IDENTIFICATION 0-63
FRONT SUSPENSION & STEERING
  Ball Joint, Replace 7-60
  Ball Joint Inspection 7-60
  Coil Spring & Strut Service ... 7-61

Page No.

Control Arm, Replace 7-61
Description 7-60
Power Steering 13-1
Power Steering Gear, Replace 7-61
Power Steering Pump, Replace 7-62
Stabilizer Bar, Replace 7-61
Steering Columns 12-1
Steering Knuckle, Replace 7-61
Strut, Replace 7-60
Tightening Specifications 7-64
Wheel Bearing, Replace 7-60
NON-STANDARD TIRE & WHEEL SIZE ADJUSTMENT TO RIDE HEIGHT SPECIFICATIONS & TIRE SIZE CHART 0-61
REAR DRIVE AXLE 19-1
REAR SUSPENSION
  Coil Spring, Replace 7-52
  Control Arm, Replace 7-52
  Description 7-52
  Hub & Bearing, Replace 7-52
  Knuckle, Replace 7-53
  Shock Absorber, Replace 7-52
  Stabilizer Bar, Replace 7-53
  Tightening Specifications 7-59
  Toe Link, Replace 7-54
  Trailing Arm, Replace 7-53
  Wheel Bearing, Adjust 7-52
SERVICE REMINDER & WARNING LAMP RESET PROCEDURES 0-34
SPECIFICATIONS
  Fluid Capacities & Cooling System Data 7-5
  Front Wheel Alignment Specifications 7-2
  General Engine Specifications 7-2
  Lubricant Data 7-6
  Rear Wheel Alignment Specifications 7-3
  Tune Up Specifications 7-2
  Vehicle Ride Height Specifications 7-4
VEHICLE IDENTIFICATION 0-1
VEHICLE LIFT POINTS 0-51
VEHICLE MAINTENANCE SCHEDULES 0-73
WIRE COLOR CODE IDENTIFICATION 0-63
WHEEL ALIGNMENT
  Front Wheel Alignment 7-65
  Preliminary Inspection 7-65
  Rear Wheel Alignment 7-65

Page No.

Wheel Alignment Specifications 7-2
3.0L ENGINE
  Belt Tension Data 7-19
  Camshaft, Replace 7-18
  Camshaft Lobe Lift Specifications 7-17
  Compression Pressure 7-13
  Cooling System Bleed 7-20
  Crankshaft Rear Oil Seal, Replace 7-19
  Cylinder Head, Replace 7-16
  Engine Rebuilding Specifications 21-1
  Engine, Replace 7-14
  Engine Mount, Replace 7-13
  Exhaust Manifold, Replace.... 7-15
  Front Cover, Replace 7-17
  Front Cover Seal, Replace.... 7-18
  Fuel Filter, Replace 7-21
  Fuel Pump, Replace 7-21
  Hydraulic Lifters, Replace 7-17
  Intake Manifold, Replace 7-15
  Main & Rod Bearings 7-19
  Oil Pan, Replace 7-19
  Oil Pump, Replace 7-19
  Oil Pump Service 7-19
  Piston & Rod Assembly 7-19
  Precautions 7-13
  Radiator, Replace 7-20
  Serpentine Drive Belt 7-20
  Thermostat, Replace 7-20
  Tightening Specifications 7-27
  Timing Chain, Replace 7-18
  Valve Adjustment 7-17
  Valve Cover, Replace 7-17
  Water Pump, Replace 7-20
3.5L ENGINE
  Camshaft, Replace 7-35
  Camshaft Lobe Lift Specifications 7-33
  Compression Pressure 7-28
  Cooling System Bleed 7-37
  Crankshaft Damper, Replace.. 7-33
  Cylinder Head, Replace 7-31
  Engine Rebuilding Specifications 21-1
  Engine, Replace 7-29
  Engine Mount, Replace 7-29
  Exhaust Manifold, Replace.... 7-31
  Front Cover, Replace 7-34
  Front Cover Seal, Replace.... 7-35
  Fuel Pump, Replace 7-38
  Intake Manifold, Replace 7-30
  Oil Pan, Replace 7-36
  Oil Pump, Replace 7-37
  Power Transfer Unit Seal, Replace 7-30
  Precautions 7-28

	Page No.		Page No.		Page No.
Radiator, Replace	7-38	Timing Chain, Replace	7-35	Valve Cover, Replace	7-32
Serpentine Drive Belt	7-37	Valve Adjustment	7-33	Water Pump, Replace	7-37
Thermostat, Replace	7-37	Valve Clearance			
Tightening Specifications	7-51	Specifications	7-33		

Specifications

GENERAL ENGINE SPECIFICATIONS

Year/Engine (VIN)①	Fuel System	Bore & Stroke	Comp. Ratio	Net H.P. @ RPM	Maximum Torque/Ft. Lbs. @ RPM	Normal Oil Pressure, psi
3.0L (1)	SFI	3.50 x 3.13	10:1	200 @ 5700	200 @ 4400	11②
3.5L (W)	SFI	3.64 x 3.41	10.3	250 @ 6250	240 @ 4500	—

SFI — Sequential Fuel Injection

① — The eighth digit of the VIN denotes engine code.

② — At 1500 RPM with engine hot.

TUNE UP SPECIFICATIONS

Liter (Code①)	Spark Plug Gap	Ignition Timing, °BTDC				Curb Idle Speed, RPM		Fast Idle Speed, RPM		Fuel Pump Pressure, psi	Valve Clearance
		Firing Order Fig. ②	Man. Trans.	Auto. Trans.	Mark Fig.	Man. Trans.	Auto. Trans.	Man. Trans.	Auto. Trans.		
3.0L (1)	.054	③	—	⑦	⑧	—	④	—	④	⑤	⑥
3.5L (W)	.051–.057	⑨	—	⑦	—	—	④	—	④	65	⑩

BTDC — Before Top Dead Center

① — The eighth digit of the VIN denotes engine code.

② — Before disconnecting wires from distributor cap or coil, determine location of wire, as position may have been altered from that mounting at end of this chart.

③ — Coil on plug ignition system. Cylinder numbering front to rear, **Fig. A**, righthand bank, 1, 2, 3 ; lefthand bank, 4, 5, 6. Firing order 1-4-2-5-3-6.

④ — Idle speed is controlled by an automatic idle control system.

⑤ — Key on engine off, 37–45 psi. Key on engine running, 26–45 psi.

⑥ — Equipped w/hydraulic valve lifters; no provision for adjustment.

⑦ — Non-adjustable.

⑧ — Equipped w/crankshaft position sensor.

⑨ — Firing order 1-4-2-3-5-6.

⑩ — Intake, .006–.010 inch; exhaust, .0118–.0157 inch.

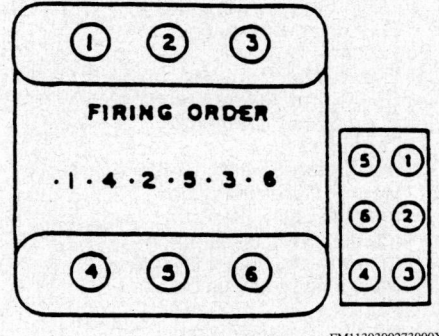

FIRING ORDER

· 1 · 4 · 2 · 5 · 3 · 6 ·

FM1139300273000X

Fig. A

FRONT WHEEL ALIGNMENT SPECIFICATIONS

Model	Caster Angle°		Camber Angle°		Total Toe°		Ball Joint Wear
	Limits	Desired	Limits	Desired	Limits	Desired	
Five Hundred & Montego (AWD)	+2.75 to +4.25	+3.50	−1.50 to +.15	−.60	0 to +.40	+.20	①
Five Hundred & Montego (FWD)	+2.55 to +4.05	+3.30	−1.50 to +.15	−.60	−.22 to +.02	−.10	①
Freestyle (AWD)	+2.25 to +3.75	+3.00	−1.07 to +1.07.	−.32	0 to +.40	+.20	①
Freestyle (FWD)	+2.35 to +3.85	+3.10	−1.03 to +1.03	−.28	−.22 to +.02	−.10	①
Sable & Taurus (AWD)	+2.55 to +4.05	+3.30	−0.35 to +1.15	−.40	0 to +.40	+.20	①
Sable & Taurus (FWD)	+2.55 to +4.05	+3.30	−1.50 to +.15	−.60	0 to +.40	+.20	①
Taurus X (AWD)	+2.25 to +3.75	+3.00	−0.35 to +1.15	−.40	0 to +.40	+.20	①

Continued

FRONT WHEEL ALIGNMENT SPECIFICATIONS—Continued

Model	Caster Angle°		Camber Angle°		Total Toe°		Ball Joint Wear
	Limits	Desired	Limits	Desired	Limits	Desired	
Taurus X (FWD)	+2.25 to +3.75	+3.00	−1.50 to +.15	−.60	0 to +.40	+.20	①

AWD — All Wheel Drive

FWD — Front Wheel Drive

① — Refer to "Ball Joint Inspection" in "Front Suspension & Steering" section.

REAR WHEEL ALIGNMENT SPECIFICATIONS

Model	Camber Angle° ①		Total Toe-In°	
	Limits	Desired	Limits	Desired
Five Hundred & Montego (AWD)	−1.05 to +1.45	+.70	−.10 to +.30	+.10
Five Hundred & Montego (FWD)	−.75 to +.75	+.75	−.10 to +.30	+.10
Freestyle (AWD)	+.75 to −.75	−.0	−.10 to +.30	+.10
Freestyle (FWD)	−.18 to +1.32	−.57	−.10 to +.30	+.10
Sable & Taurus (AWD)	−.30 to +1.20	−.45	−.10 to +.30	+.10
Sable & Taurus (FWD)	−.40 to +1.10	−.35	−.10 to +.30	+.10
Taurus X (AWD)	+.75 to −.75	0	−.10 to +.30	+.10
Taurus X (FWD)	−.48 to +1.20	−.27	−.10 to +.30	+.10

AWD — All Wheel Drive

FWD — Front Wheel Drive

① — Not adjustable.

VEHICLE RIDE HEIGHT SPECIFICATIONS

Year	Model	Manufacturer's Original Tire Size ①	Measurement Points & Specifications ②						
			Front			Rear		
			Dim.	Specification		Dim.	Specification	
				Inches	mm		Inches	mm
2005–07	Five Hundred (AWD) 17 Inch Wheel	①	③	29.33–30.11	745–765	③	29.53–30.31	750–770
	Five Hundred (FWD) 17 Inch Wheel	①	③	28.74–29.52	730–750	③	29.18–29.96	741–761
	Five Hundred (AWD) 18 Inch Wheel	①	③	29.61–30.39	752–772	③	29.78–30.56	757–777
	Five Hundred (FWD) 18 Inch Wheel	①	③	29.06–29.84	738–758	③	29.45–30.23	749–769
	Freestyle (AWD) 17 Inch Wheels	①	③	30.36–31.14	771–791	③	30.91–31.69	785–805
	Freestyle (FWD) 17 Inch Wheels	①	③	30.40–31.18	772–792	③	31.39–32.17	779–817
	Freestyle (AWD) 18 Inch Wheels	①	③	30.67–31.45	779–799	③	31.22–23.00	793–813
	Freestyle (FWD) 18 Inch Wheels	①	③	30.71–31.49	780–800	③	31.70–32.48	805–825
	Montego (AWD) 17 Inch Wheels	①	③	29.30–30.08	744–764	③	29.53–30.31	750–770
	Montego (FWD) 17 Inch Wheels	①	③	28.74–29.52	730–750	③	29.78–30.56	757–777
	Montego (AWD) 18 Inch Wheels	①	③	29.61–30.39	752–772	③	29.18–29.96	741–761
	Montego (FWD) 18 Inch Wheels	①	③	29.02–29.80	737–757	③	29.45–30.23	749–769
2008	Freestyle (AWD) 17 Inch Wheels	①	③	30.36–31.14	771–791	③	30.91–31.69	785–805
	Freestyle (FWD) 17 Inch Wheels	①	③	30.40–31.18	772–792	③	31.39–32.17	779–817
	Freestyle (AWD) 18 Inch Wheels	①	③	30.67–31.45	779–799	③	31.22–23.00	793–813
	Freestyle (FWD) 18 Inch Wheels	①	③	30.71–31.49	780–800	③	31.70–32.48	805–825
	Sable & Taurus (AWD)	①	④	—	—	⑤	—	—
	Sable & Taurus (FWD)	①	④	—	—	⑥	—	—
	Taurus X (AWD)	①	④	—	—	⑤	—	—
	Taurus X (FWD)	①	④	—	—	⑥	—	—

AWD — All Wheel Drive
Dim. — Dimension
FWD — Front Wheel Drive
① — See door sticker or inside of glove box for manufacturer's original tire size specifications. If tires on vehicle do not match manufacturer's original tire size & measurement is not within limits, it will be required to refer to the Non-Standard Tire & Wheel Size Adjustment To Ride Height Specification

& Tire Size Adjustment Charts.
② — Measurement is with fuel, radiator coolant and engine oil full, spare tire, jack, hand tools and mats in designated positions and tires properly inflated.

③ — Vehicle ride height can be checked by measuring distance between lip of fender, **Fig. A**, and ground.
④ — Refer to **Fig. B**.
⑤ — Refer to **Fig. C**.
⑥ — Refer to **Fig. D**.

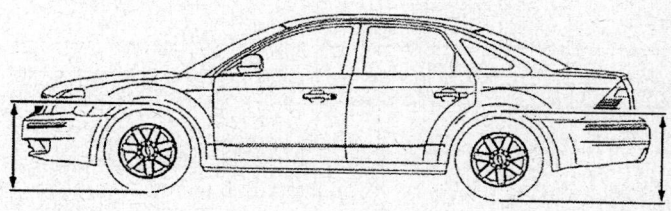

Fig. A   Front & rear ride height measurement

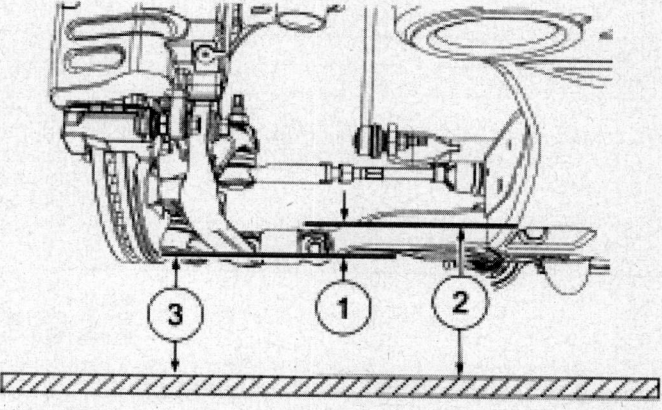

Fig. B   Front ride height measurement

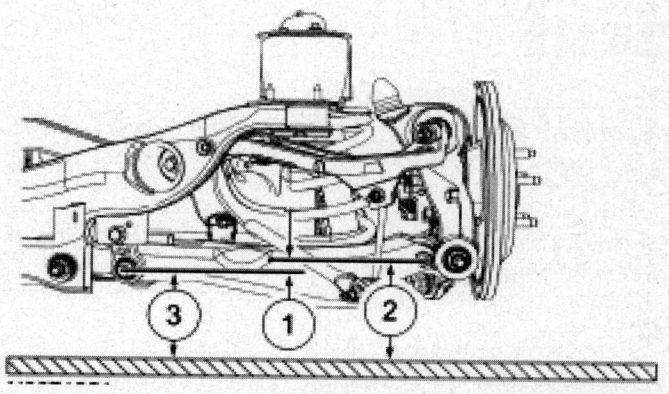

Fig. C   Rear ride height measurement. 2008 Sable, Taurus & Taurus X w/AWD

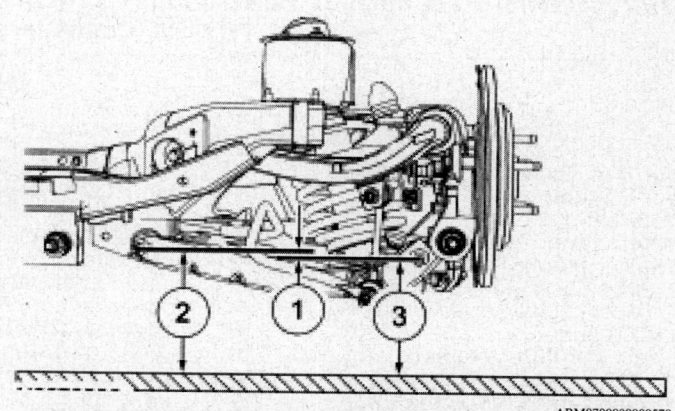

Fig. D   Rear ride height measurement. 2008 Sable, Taurus & Taurus X w/FWD

FLUID CAPACITIES & COOLING SYSTEM DATA

Engine Liter (VIN) ①	Coolant Capacity, Qts.	Coolant Type	Radiator Cap Relief Pressure, Lbs.	Thermo. Opening Temp. °F	Fuel Tank Gals.	Engine Oil Refill, Qts.②	Transaxle Capacity	
							Transfer Case., Pts.	Auto. Trans., Qts.④
3.0L (1)	⑥	⑤	13–18	180–203	19	6.0	2	③
3.5L (W)	10.0	⑦	13–18	187	⑧	5.5	2.4	10

CVT — Continuously Variable Chain Type transaxle.

① — The eighth digit of the VIN denotes engine code.
② — Includes filter.

③ — Models w/CVT transaxle, 10.0 qts.; models w/6 speed transaxle, 7.4 qts.

④ — Approximate; make final inspection w/dipstick.
⑤ — Motorcraft premium gold part No. VC-7–A, or equivalent. In California and Oregon use Motorcraft premium gold part No. VC-7–B, or equivalent.

⑥ — Less auxiliary heater 10.6 quarts; with auxiliary heater 12.7 quarts.
⑦ — Motorcraft premium gold part No. VC-7-B/WSS-M97B51-A1, or equivalent.

⑧ — Sable & Taurus, equipped w/L-shaped tank, 20 gals; w/saddle type tank, 20.5 gals; Taurus X, 19 gals.

LUBRICANT DATA

| Year | Transaxle | | Power Steering | Brake System |
	Manual/Transfer Case	Automatic		
2005–07	②	Mercon V	①	DOT 3
2008	③	④	①	DOT 3

① — Motorcraft MERCON Multi-Purpose ATF part No. XT-2-QDX, or equivalent.
② — SAE 80W-90 premium rear axle

lubricant part No. XY-80W-90–QL, or equivalent.
③ — Transfer case use Motorcraft SAE 75W-140 Synthetic rear axle lubricant XY-75W140-QL.

④ — 5 speed automatic transaxle use Motorcraft FNR5 ATF/XT-9-QMM5 or equivalent; 6 speed automatic transaxle use Motorcraft Premium ATF/XT-8-QAW.

Electrical

NOTE: On Air Bag Equipped Models, Refer To "Air Bag System Precautions" Located In The Front Of This Manual For System Disarming & Arming Procedures.

NOTE: Refer To "Computer Relearn Procedures" Located In The Front Of This Manual When Battery Power To The Computer Has Been Interrupted.

INDEX

	Page No.
Air Bag System (Volume 2)	4-1
Air Conditioning	8-1
Alternator, Replace	7-7
Alternators	11-1
Blower Motor, Replace	7-10
2008 Sable, Taurus & Taurus X	7-10
Except 2008 Sable, Taurus & Taurus X	7-10
Cabin Air Filter, Replace	7-10
Cooling Fans	9-1
Cruise Control (Volume 2)	2-1
Dash Gauges (Volume 2)	1-1
Dash Panel Service (Volume 2)	5-1
Evaporator Core, Replace	7-11
2008 Sable, Taurus & Taurus X	7-11
Except 2008 Sable, Taurus & Taurus X	7-11
Fuel Pump Relay Location	7-7
Fuse Panel & Flasher Location	7-7
Headlamp Switch, Replace	7-7
2008 Sable, Taurus & Taurus X	7-7
Except 2008 Sable, Taurus &	

	Page No.
Taurus X	7-7
Heater Core, Replace	7-10
2008 Sable, Taurus & Taurus X	7-10
Except 2008 Sable, Taurus & Taurus X	7-10
Ignition Lock, Replace	7-7
Ignition Switch, Replace	7-7
Instrument Cluster, Replace	7-8
2008 Sable, Taurus & Taurus X	7-8
Except 2008 Sable, Taurus & Taurus X	7-8
Multi-Function Switch, Replace	7-8
2008 Sable, Taurus & Taurus X	7-8
Except 2008 Sable, Taurus & Taurus X	7-8
Neutral Safety Switch, Replace	7-7
Passive Restraint Systems (Volume 2)	4-1
Precautions	7-7
Air Bag Systems	7-7
Battery Ground Cable	7-7
Radio, Replace	7-9
2008 Sable, Taurus & Taurus X	7-9

	Page No.
Except 2008 Sable, Taurus & Taurus X	7-9
Speed Controls (Volume 2)	2-1
Starter Motors	10-1
Starter, Replace	7-7
Steering Columns	12-1
Steering Wheel, Replace	7-8
Stop Light Switch, Replace	7-8
Wiper Motor, Replace	7-9
Front	7-9
2008 Sable, Taurus & Taurus X	7-9
Except 2008 Sable, Taurus & Taurus X	7-9
Rear	7-9
Wiper Switch, Replace	7-9
Front	7-9
Rear	7-10
Except Taurus X	7-10
Taurus X	7-10
Wiper Systems (Volume 2)	3-1
Wiper Transmission, Replace	7-10

PRECAUTIONS

Air Bag Systems

Refer to "Air Bag System Precautions" in the front of this manual for system disarming and arming procedures.

Battery Ground Cable

Prior to service, disconnect battery ground cable and isolate as required.

FUSE PANEL & FLASHER LOCATION

The engine compartment power distribution center is located on the front lefthand side of the engine compartment. The fuse panel is located under the instrument panel, left of the steering column. The combination turn signal/hazard flasher is located behind the lefthand side of the instrument panel reinforcement, in the Smart Junction Box (SJB).

FUEL PUMP RELAY LOCATION

The fuel pump relay is located at the front left of the engine compartment near the battery, in the power distribution center.

STARTER

REPLACE

The heavy gauge input lead connected to the starter solenoid is hot at all times. Ensure the protective cap is installed over the terminal and is replaced after service.

1. Raise and support vehicle.
2. Remove lower air deflector.
3. Remove starter solenoid safety cap.
4. Remove starter solenoid and ground stud cables.
5. Remove mounting bolts, stud and starter.
6. Reverse procedure to install.

ALTERNATOR

REPLACE

1. Remove accessory drive belt from alternator.
2. Remove mounting nut, then position engine control sensor wiring and hose bracket aside.
3. Loosen alternator pulley nut and remove inboard upper alternator mounting bolt.
4. Loosen outboard upper alternator bolt.
5. Disconnect electrical harness connector and output terminal wiring.
6. Raise and support vehicle, then remove wheel and tire assembly.
7. Remove alternator splash shield and outboard upper alternator bolt.
8. Remove lower alternator bolt.
9. Remove pulley nut and alternator.
10. Reverse procedure to install, noting the following:

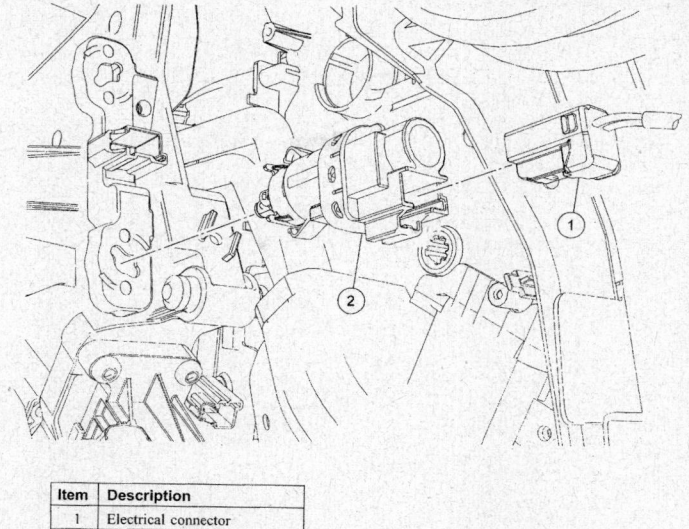

Item	Description
1	Electrical connector
2	Brake pedal position (BPP) switch

ARM0400000000457

Fig. 1   Brake light switch replacement

a. **Torque** alternator mounting bolts to 15–22 ft. lbs.
b. **Torque** alternator output nut to 80–106 inch lbs.
c. **Torque** alternator pulley nut to 60–100 ft. lbs.

IGNITION LOCK

REPLACE

1. Place ignition switch in RUN position.
2. Depress lock cylinder retaining pin with suitable ⅛ inch drill or drift punch while working through steering column lower shroud.
3. Pull ignition lock cylinder from housing.
4. Reverse procedure to install. Ensure proper installation by rotating ignition switch through it's travel range.

IGNITION SWITCH

REPLACE

1. Remove lower instrument panel steering column cover.
2. Turn ignition lock to RUN position.
3. Disconnect ignition switch electrical connector.
4. Remove mounting screws and ignition switch.
5. Reverse procedure to install, noting the following:
   a. Ensure ignition lock is in RUN position when installing ignition switch.
   b. **Torque** ignition switch mounting screws to 50–69 inch lbs.

NEUTRAL SAFETY SWITCH

REPLACE

Neutral safety switch functions are incorporated into the Transaxle Range (TR) sensor.

1. Place manual control lever in Neutral position.

2. Remove engine air cleaner and outlet tube.
3. Disconnect TR sensor electrical connector.
4. Remove manual control lever from transaxle.
5. Remove mounting bolts and TR sensor.
6. Reverse procedure to install, noting the following:
   a. Ensure manual control lever is in Neutral position.
   b. Install transaxle range sensor and mounting bolts loosely.
   c. Align position sensor using manual lever position sensor alignment tool No. T92P-70010-AH, or equivalent.
   d. **Torque** sensor mounting bolts to 84–106 inch lbs.
   e. **Torque** manual lever mounting bolts to 96–132 inch lbs.

HEADLAMP SWITCH

REPLACE

Except 2008 Sable, Taurus & Taurus X

1. Pry headlamp switch housing from instrument panel.
2. Depress release button and pull headlamp switch away from instrument panel.
3. Disconnect electrical connectors and remove headlamp switch.
4. Reverse procedure to install.

2008 Sable, Taurus & Taurus X

1. Remove instrument panel side finish panel using suitable trim stick tool.
2. Disconnect headlamp switch connector.
3. Remove switch by depressing locking

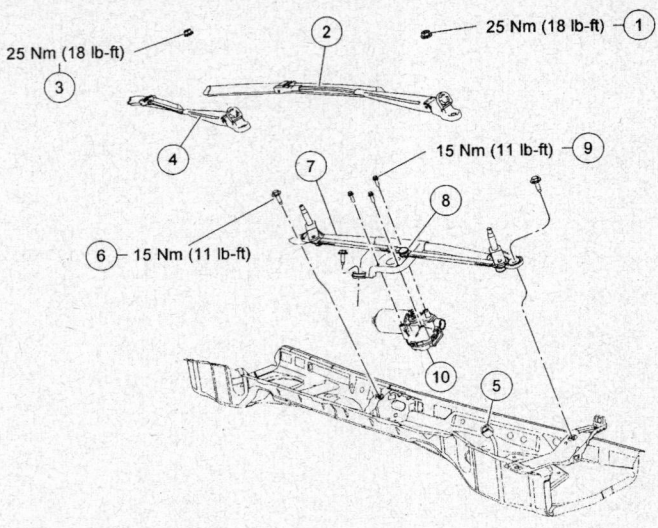

Item	Description
1	Wiper pivot arm nut
2	LH wiper arm
3	Wiper pivot arm nut
4	RH wiper arm
5	Electrical connector
6	Wiper mounting arm and pivot shaft bolts (3 required)

Item	Description
7	Wiper mounting arm and pivot shaft assembly
8	Wiper pivot arm linkage
9	Wiper motor bolt
10	Wiper motor

ARM0400000000458

Fig. 2   Front wiper motor replacement

tabs, then push switch from behind to release from panel.
4. Reverse procedure to install.
5. Pry headlamp switch housing from instrument panel.
6. Depress release button and pull headlamp switch away from instrument panel.
7. Disconnect electrical connectors and remove headlamp switch.
8. Reverse procedure to install.

STOP LIGHT SWITCH
REPLACE
1. Lift stop lamp switch harness wiring connector locking tab and remove connector, **Fig. 1.**
2. Push inward on brake light switch locking tabs, then pull switch straight back to remove from mounting bracket.
3. Reverse procedure to install.

MULTI-FUNCTION SWITCH
REPLACE

Except 2008 Sable, Taurus & Taurus X

1. **On models equipped with tilt steering column,** move column to lowest position, then remove tilt and key release levers.

2. **On all models,** place ignition switch in RUN position, then depress lock cylinder retaining pin with suitable ⅛ inch drill or drift punch while working through steering column lower shroud.
3. Pull ignition lock cylinder from housing.
4. Rotate replacement lock cylinder to RUN position, depressing retaining pin and insert lock cylinder into housing. Ensure proper installation by rotating ignition switch through travel.
5. Remove upper and lower steering column shrouds.
6. Remove multi-function switch mounting screws and disconnect switch from casting.
7. Disconnect electrical connectors and remove switch.
8. Reverse procedure to install, noting the following:
   a. **Torque** multi-function switch mounting screws to 18–27 inch lbs.
   b. **Torque** tilt lever mounting screw to 6–8 inch lbs.

2008 Sable, Taurus & Taurus X

1. Remove three steering column shroud screws.
2. Separate, then remove upper and lower steering column shrouds.
3. Disconnect multi-function switch electrical connector.
4. Remove two retaining screws, then the

multi-function switch.
5. Reverse procedure to install. **Torque** mounting screws to 27 inch lbs.

STEERING WHEEL
REPLACE
1. Place wheels in straight ahead position, then remove ignition key.
2. Disconnect speed control wire harness from steering wheel.
3. Remove driver air bag module as outlined in "Passive Restraints" chapter.
4. Remove and discard steering wheel mounting bolt.
5. Remove steering wheel using suitable steering wheel puller. Route contact assembly wire harness through steering wheel as wheel is lifted off shaft.
6. Reverse procedure to install, noting the following:
   a. Ensure front wheels are in straight ahead position.
   b. Route contact assembly wire harness through steering column opening at three o'clock position.
   c. Align steering shaft alignment marks.
   d. **Torque** new steering wheel mounting bolt to 26–35 ft. lbs.

INSTRUMENT CLUSTER
REPLACE

Except 2008 Sable, Taurus & Taurus X

1. Remove instrument finish panel mounting screws, then the finish panel.
2. Tilt steering wheel to its lowest possible position.
3. Remove instrument cluster mounting screws and pull top of cluster toward steering wheel.
4. Disconnect electrical connectors behind instrument cluster.
5. Remove instrument cluster.
6. Reverse procedure to install.

2008 Sable, Taurus & Taurus X

If installing a new instrument cluster, upload the module configuration information to a suitable scan tool.
1. Remove instrument cluster finish panel.
2. Remove four screws, then the instrument cluster. Disconnect electrical connectors as cluster is lifted from opening.
3. Reverse procedure to install. If a new cluster was installed download saved cluster configuration from scan tool.

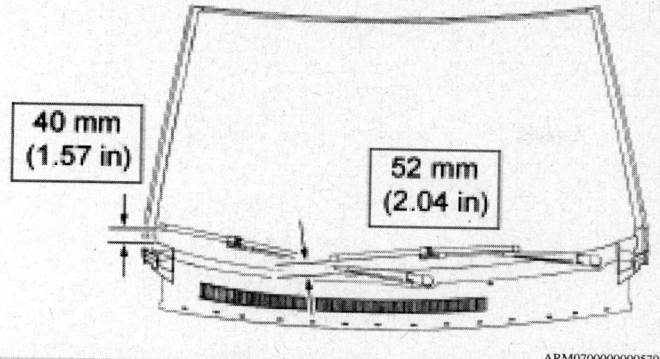

Fig. 3 Wiper arm position locations & specifications. 2008 Sable, Taurus & Taurus X

ARM0700000000579

RADIO
REPLACE

Except 2008 Sable, Taurus & Taurus X

1. Remove instrument panel center finish panel retaining screws, then the finish panel.
2. Remove two radio to instrument panel mounting screws.
3. Pull radio outward to access electrical connectors.
4. Disconnect electrical connectors and antenna lead.
5. Remove radio from instrument panel.
6. Reverse procedure to install.

2008 Sable, Taurus & Taurus X

If installing a new audio unit, upload the module configuration information to a suitable scan tool.

1. Remove floor shifter trim ring.
2. Remove instrument panel center finish panel retaining screws.
3. Disconnect electrical connectors.
4. Remove instrument panel center finish panel.
5. Remove four radio retaining screws.
6. Disconnect electrical connectors and antenna cable.
7. Remove radio from instrument panel.
8. Reverse procedure to install.

WIPER MOTOR
REPLACE

Front

EXCEPT 2008 SABLE, TAURUS & TAURUS X

The wiper mounting arm and pivot shafts are connected with non removable plastic ball joints. Except for the wiper motor, the entire wiper transmission assembly is non serviceable.

1. Note normal park position of wiper arms and blades for installation alignment.
2. Remove wiper arm mounting nuts from pivot shafts, **Fig. 2.**
3. Turn ignition switch to ON position and wiper switch to LO.
4. Turn ignition switch to OFF position when arms and blades to move to straight up-and-down position.
5. Remove wiper arms from pivot shafts.
6. Turn eight plastic cowl vent screen nuts ¼ turn counterclockwise.
7. Remove clips mounting vent screen to inner panels.
8. Remove pivot shaft assembly mounting screws and wiper assembly.
9. Reverse procedure to install, noting the following:
   a. Turn ignition switch to ON position and wiper control switch to Low or High.
   b. Turn wiper control switch to OFF position after wipers have cycled once or twice.
   c. **Torque** pivot shaft assembly to 11 ft. lbs.
   d. Install wiper arms and blades in their previously recorded park positions.
   e. **Torque** pivot arm nuts to 18 ft. lbs.

2008 SABLE, TAURUS & TAURUS X

Do not remove the wiper motor linkage arm from the wiper motor assembly. If the arm is removed, the wiper arms may not park in the correct location. A new wiper motor assembly comes with the linkage arm installed.

1. Remove wiper pivot arms, then the cowl panel grille.
2. Disconnect wiper motor electrical connector.
3. Remove three wiper motor assembly mounting bolts.

4. Remove motor and linkage arm assembly.
5. Use suitable tool to separate wiper motor linkage arm from wiper pivot arm linkage.
6. Reverse procedure to install, noting the following:
   a. **Torque** mounting bolts to 71 inch lbs.
   b. Cycle and park windshield wipers.
   c. Ensure wiper blades are located in specified position, **Fig. 3.**
   d. If wipers are not within specification, remove the wiper pivot arms and reposition to the correct location.

Rear

1. Open pivot arm nut cover, **Fig. 4,** then remove rear wiper arm pivot nut and wiper arm blade assembly.
2. Open liftgate and remove trim panel using suitable trim tool to release trim retaining clips.
3. Remove liftgate trim panel.
4. Disconnect wiper motor electrical connector, **Fig. 5.**
5. Remove three wiper motor mounting bolts, then the wiper motor.
6. Reverse procedure to install, noting the following:
   a. **Torque** wiper motor mounting bolts to 53–71 inch lbs.
   b. **Torque** wiper pivot nut to 13 ft. lbs.

WIPER SWITCH
REPLACE

Front

Refer to "Multi-Function Switch, Replace" for wiper switch replacement procedure.

Fig. 4 Rear wiper arm pivot nut replacement

ARM0400000000459

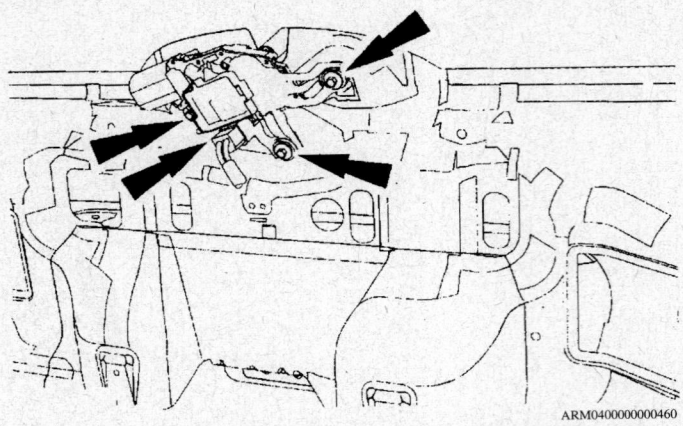

Fig. 5 Rear wiper motor replacement

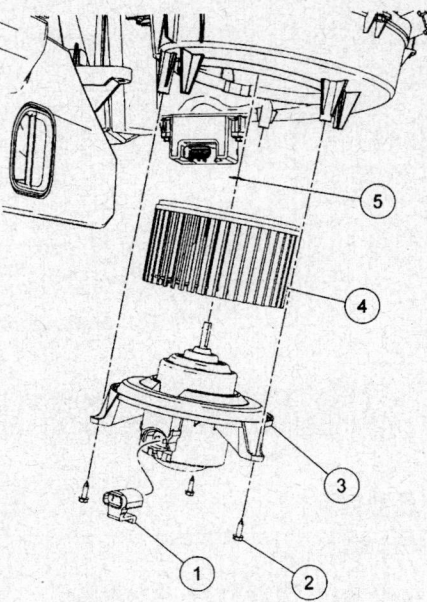

Item	Description
1	Blower motor electrical connector
2	Blower motor screws (3 required)
3	Blower motor
4	Blower motor wheel
5	Blower motor wheel clip

ARM0400000000461

Fig. 6 Blower motor replacement. Except 2008 Sable, Taurus & Taurus X

Rear

EXCEPT TAURUS X

1. Pull rear wiper/washer switch straight out of instrument panel.
2. Disconnect electrical connector and remove switch.
3. Reverse procedure to install.

TAURUS X

Refer to "Multi-Function Switch, Replace" for wiper switch replacement procedure.

WIPER TRANSMISSION
REPLACE

The wiper mounting arm and pivot shafts are connected with non removable plastic ball joints. Except for the wiper motor, the entire wiper transmission assembly is non serviceable.

Refer to "Wiper Motor, Replace" for wiper transmission replacement procedure.

BLOWER MOTOR
REPLACE

Except 2008 Sable, Taurus & Taurus X

1. Pull instrument panel insulator from lower righthand side of instrument panel reinforcement, **Fig. 6**.
2. Disconnect blower motor electrical connector.
3. Remove mounting screws and blower motor from evaporator housing.
4. Remove blower motor wheel retaining clip, then the wheel.
5. Reverse procedure to install.

2008 Sable, Taurus & Taurus X

1. Remove righthand scuff plate trim panel from righthand cowl side trim panel.
2. Remove righthand cowl side trim panel.
3. Remove two righthand lower instrument panel insulator pin type retainers, then the lower instrument panel insulator.
4. Disconnect blower motor electrical connector.
5. Release two blower motor vent tube clips and detach blower motor vent tube from heater core and evaporator core housing.
6. Rotate blower motor counterclockwise to disengage it from housing, then remove blower motor.
7. Reverse procedure to install.

CABIN AIR FILTER
REPLACE

1. Remove righthand cowl vent screen.
2. Remove water shield.
3. Remove cabin air filter.
4. Reverse procedure to install.

HEATER CORE
REPLACE

Except 2008 Sable, Taurus & Taurus X

1. Drain coolant into suitable container.
2. Remove instrument panel as outlined in "Dash Panel Service" chapter.
3. Disconnect heater hoses from core. Plug heater core tubes.
4. Remove dash panel seal from heater core.
5. Remove heater core bracket mounting screws and bracket, **Fig. 7**.
6. Remove evaporator discharge air temperature sensor electrical sensor.
7. Disconnect lefthand temperature blend door actuator electrical connector.

8. Remove lefthand temperature blend door actuator mounting screws and actuator.
9. Remove three heater core cover mounting screws and seal from evaporator housing, **Fig. 7**.
10. Remove heater core and seal by pushing on tubes.
11. Reverse procedure to install.

2008 Sable, Taurus & Taurus X

1. Drain coolant into suitable container.
2. Remove instrument panel as outlined in "Dash Panel Service" chapter.
3. Remove heater core and evaporator core housing, **Fig. 8**.
4. Disconnect heater hoses from core. Plug heater core tubes.
5. Remove dash panel seal from heater core.
6. Remove heater core bracket mounting screws and bracket, **Fig. 9**.
7. Remove evaporator discharge air temperature sensor electrical sensor.
8. Disconnect lefthand temperature

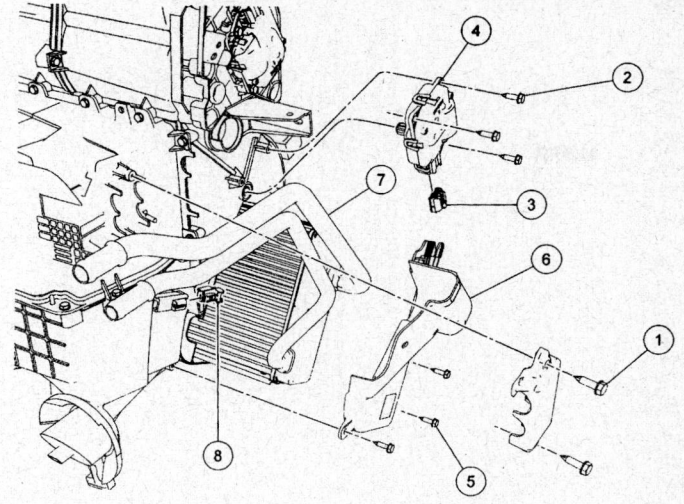

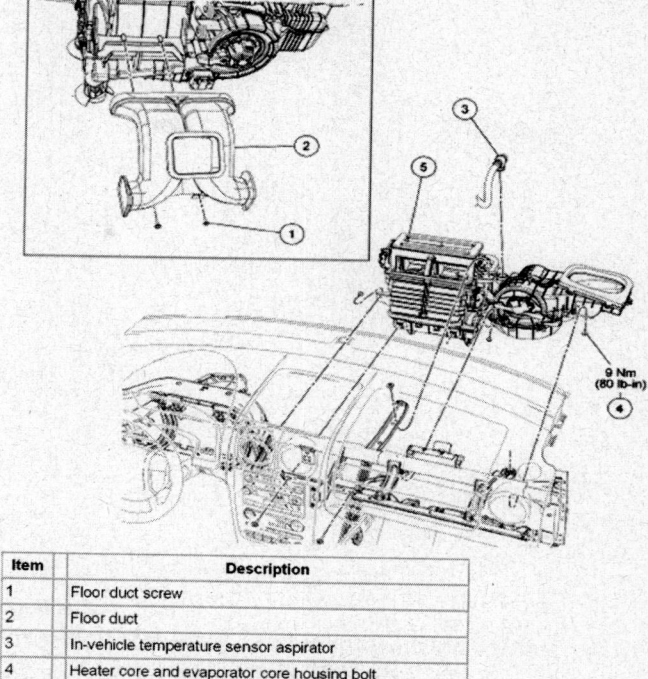

Item	Description
1	Heater tube bracket screw (2 required)
2	LH temperature blend door actuator screw (3 required)
3	LH temperature blend door actuator electrical connector
4	LH temperature blend door actuator
5	Heater core cover screw (3 required)
6	Heater core cover
7	Heater core
8	Evaporator discharge air temperature sensor electrical connector

ARM0400000000462

Fig. 7 Heater core replacement. Except 2008 Sable, Taurus & Taurus X

Item	Description
1	Floor duct screw
2	Floor duct
3	In-vehicle temperature sensor aspirator
4	Heater core and evaporator core housing bolt
5	Heater core and evaporator core housing

ARM0700000000580

Fig. 8 Heater core & evaporator core housing replacement. 2008 Sable, Taurus & Taurus X

blend door actuator electrical connector.
9. Remove lefthand temperature blend door actuator mounting screws and actuator.
10. Remove heater core cover mounting screws and seal from evaporator housing, **Fig. 9.**
11. Remove heater core and seal by pushing on tubes.
12. Reverse procedure to install.

EVAPORATOR CORE
REPLACE
Except 2008 Sable, Taurus & Taurus X

The evaporator core is serviced as a core and housing assembly. The evaporator core, internal doors, seals and door linkage are included with the housing. Transfer the blower motor and wheel assembly, heater core and cover, dash panel seals and vacuum actuators to the new housing.
1. Recover refrigerant as outlined in "Air Conditioning" chapter.
2. Drain coolant into suitable container.
3. Remove instrument panel as outlined in "Dash Panel Service" chapter.
4. Remove righthand cowl vent screen and water shield.
5. Disconnect vacuum supply hose.
6. Clamp heater hoses using suitable pinching pliers and disconnect hoses. Cap fittings.
7. Disconnect evaporator outlet spring lock coupling. Cap evaporator outlet tube and suction accumulator tube, **Fig. 10.**
8. Remove air conditioning pipe clamps' hold-down bolts.
9. Disconnect evaporator inlet spring lock coupling. Cap evaporator inlet tube and condenser to evaporator line tube.
10. Remove three evaporator housing mounting nuts.
11. Remove heater outlet floor duct.
12. Remove evaporator housing support bracket mounting nuts.
13. Remove heater/evaporator core housing and core, **Fig. 11.**
14. Reverse procedure to install. **Torque** housing mounting bolts to 80 inch lbs.

2008 Sable, Taurus & Taurus X

The evaporator core is serviced as a core and housing assembly. The evapora-

tor core, internal doors, seals and door linkage are included with the housing. Transfer the blower motor and wheel assembly, heater core and cover, dash panel seals and vacuum actuators to the new housing.
1. Recover refrigerant as outlined in "Air Conditioning" chapter.
2. Drain coolant into suitable container.
3. Remove instrument panel as outlined in "Dash Panel Service" chapter.
4. Remove righthand cowl vent screen and water shield.
5. Disconnect vacuum supply hose.
6. Clamp heater hoses using suitable pinching pliers and disconnect hoses. Cap fittings.
7. Disconnect evaporator outlet spring lock coupling. Cap evaporator outlet tube and suction accumulator tube.
8. Remove air conditioning pipe clamps' hold-down bolts.
9. Disconnect evaporator inlet spring lock coupling. Cap evaporator inlet tube and condenser to evaporator line tube.
10. Remove three evaporator housing mounting nuts.
11. Remove heater outlet floor duct.
12. Remove evaporator housing support bracket mounting nuts.
13. Remove heater/evaporator core housing and core, **Fig. 9.**
14. Reverse procedure to install. **Torque** housing mounting bolts to 80 inch lbs.

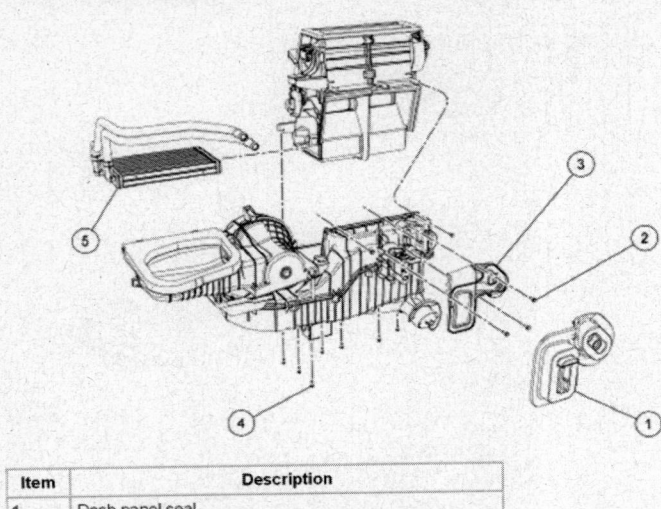

Item	Description
1	Dash panel seal
2	Heater core tube support bracket screw
3	Heater core tube support bracket
4	Plenum chamber screw
5	Heater core

ARM0700000000581

Fig. 9   Heater core replacement. 2008 Sable, Taurus & Taurus X

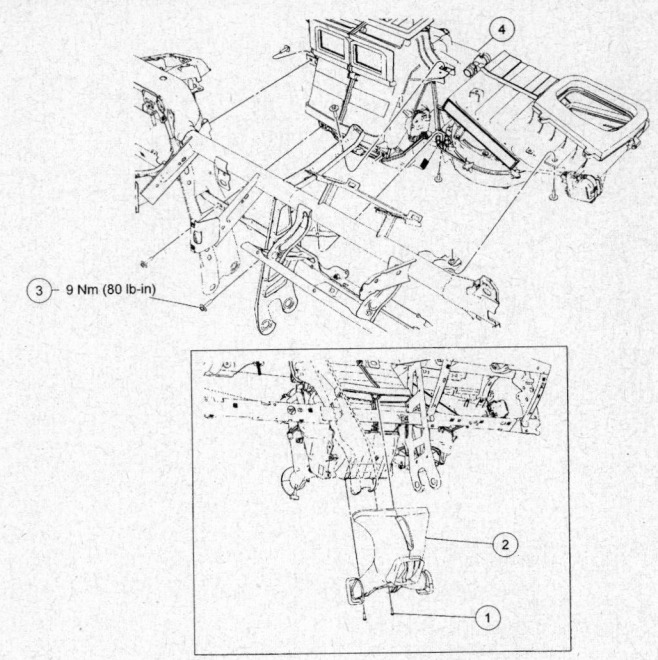

1. Floor duct screws
2. Floor duct
3. Heater core and evaporator core housing bolts
4. Heater core and evaporator core housing assembly

ARM0400000000465

Fig. 10   Evaporator core & heater core housing assembly replacement. Except 2008 Sable, Taurus & Taurus X

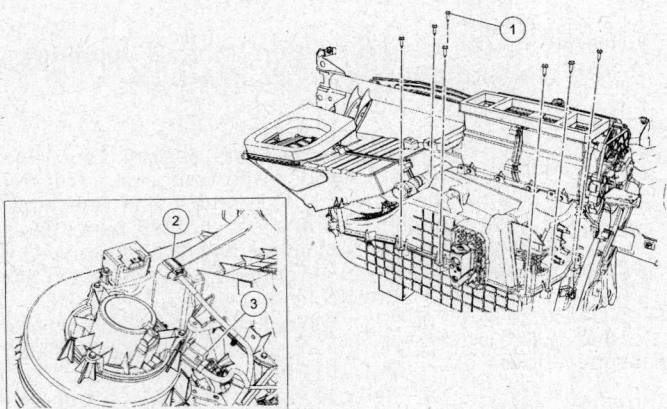

Item	Description
1	Upper evaporator core cover screw (7 required)
2	Blower motor speed control/resistor electrical connector

Item	Description
3	Blower motor electrical connector

ARM0400000000463

Fig. 11   Evaporator core replacement (Part 1 of 2). Except 2008 Sable, Taurus & Taurus X

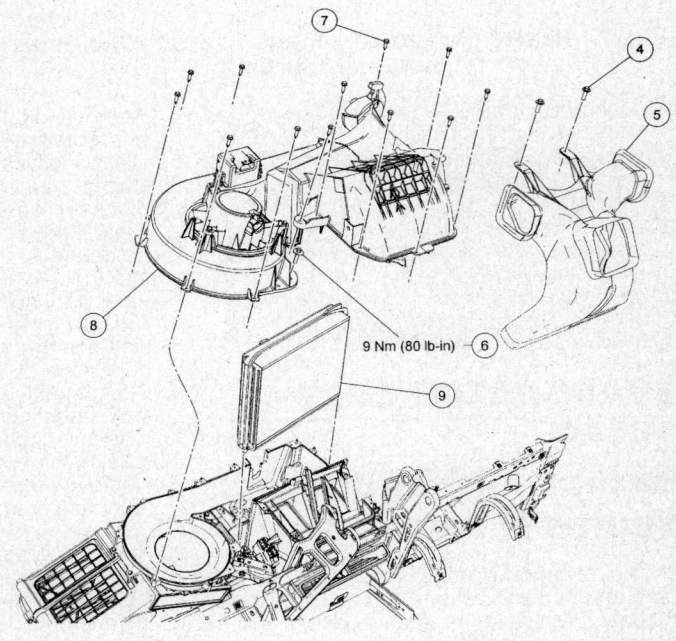

9 Nm (80 lb-in)

Item	Description
4	Floor duct screw
5	Floor duct
6	Heater core and evaporator core housing bolt

Item	Description
7	Lower evaporator core cover screw (13 required)
8	Lower evaporator core cover
9	Evaporator core

ARM0400000000464

Fig. 11   Evaporator core replacement (Part 2 of 2). Except 2008 Sable, Taurus & Taurus X

3.0L Engine

NOTE: On Air Bag Equipped Models, Refer To "Air Bag System Precautions" Located In The Front Of This Manual For System Disarming & Arming Procedures.

NOTE: Refer To "Computer Relearn Procedures" Located In The Front Of This Manual When Battery Power To The Computer Has Been Interrupted.

NOTE: Prior To Performing Any Service Operations Listed In This Section, Consult The "Technical Service Bulletins" Section For Related Information.

INDEX

	Page No.
Belt Tension Data	7-19
Camshaft, Replace	7-18
Installation	7-18
Lefthand	7-18
Righthand	7-19
Removal	7-18
Lefthand	7-18
Righthand	7-18
Camshaft Lobe Lift Specifications	7-17
Compression Pressure	7-13
Cooling System Bleed	7-20
Crankshaft Rear Oil Seal, Replace	7-19
Cylinder Head, Replace	7-16
Lefthand	7-16
Righthand	7-16
Engine Rebuilding Specifications	21-1
Engine, Replace	7-14

	Page No.
Engine Mount, Replace	7-13
Engine & Transaxle	7-13
Front	7-13
Exhaust Manifold, Replace	7-15
Lefthand	7-15
Righthand	7-16
Front Cover, Replace	7-17
Front Cover Seal, Replace	7-18
Installation	7-18
Removal	7-18
Fuel Filter, Replace	7-21
Fuel Pump, Replace	7-21
Hydraulic Lifters, Replace	7-17
Intake Manifold, Replace	7-15
Lower	7-15
Upper	7-15
Main & Rod Bearings	7-19
Oil Pan, Replace	7-19
Oil Pump, Replace	7-19
Oil Pump Service	7-19

	Page No.
Piston & Rod Assembly	7-19
Precautions	7-13
Air Bag Systems	7-13
Battery Ground Cable	7-13
Flexible Fuel Models	7-13
Fuel System Pressure Relief	7-13
Radiator, Replace	7-20
Serpentine Drive Belt	7-20
Belt Routing	7-20
Belt, Replace	7-20
Thermostat, Replace	7-20
Installation	7-20
Removal	7-20
Tightening Specifications	7-27
Timing Chain, Replace	7-18
Valve Adjustment	7-17
Valve Cover, Replace	7-17
Lefthand	7-17
Righthand	7-17
Water Pump, Replace	7-20

PRECAUTIONS

Air Bag Systems

Refer to "Air Bag System Precautions" in the front of this manual for system disarming and arming procedures.

Flexible Fuel Models

Flexible Fuel (FF) vehicles use unique methanol compatible components. Certain gasoline only components may appear identical to these FF vehicle components. Under no circumstances should these components be interchanged.

Fuel System Pressure Relief

When releasing fuel pressure on flexible fuel vehicles, use methanol resistant gloves and eye protection. Avoid prolonged skin contact with liquid or breathing of vapors.

If methanol fuel should be spilled on paint, flush immediately with cold water. **Do not wipe, or paint damage may occur. Fuel supply lines will remain pressur-** ized for long periods of time after engine shutdown. **This pressure must be relieved before any service is attempted. A valve is provided on the fuel rail assembly for this purpose.**

1. Remove air cleaner assembly.
2. Connect pressure gauge tool No. T80L-9974-A or T80L-9974-B, or equivalent, onto fuel rail assembly fuel valve.
3. Open manual valve on pressure gauge tool.
4. To pressurize fuel system, proceed as follows:
   a. Install pressure gauge tool onto fuel rail pressure fitting.
   b. Turn ignition switch to ON position for three seconds, 5–10 times until pressure gauge indicates 13 psi.

Battery Ground Cable

Prior to service, disconnect battery ground cable and isolate as required.

COMPRESSION PRESSURE

Perform compression inspection with engine at normal operating temperature, spark plugs removed and throttle wide open.

The lowest cylinder must be within 75 percent of the highest cylinder.

ENGINE MOUNT

REPLACE

Front

1. Raise and support vehicle.
2. Place suitable jack and wood block under engine block.
3. Remove lefthand and righthand front engine support insulators to subframe mounting nuts.
4. Raise jack enough to remove load from support insulators.
5. Remove mounting bolts, then the lefthand and righthand engine support insulators.
6. Reverse procedure to install.

Engine & Transaxle

1. Raise and support vehicle, then remove lefthand front tire and wheel assembly.

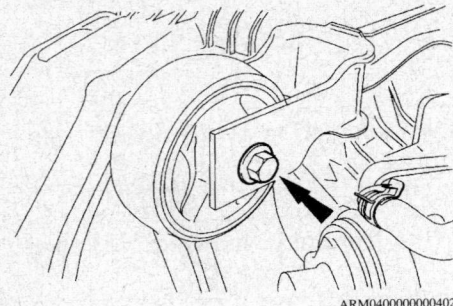

ARM0400000000402

Fig. 1   Roll restrictor bolt removal

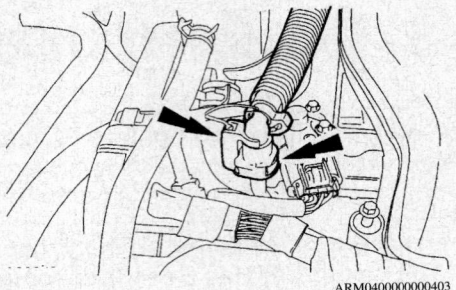

ARM0400000000403

Fig. 2   Fuel supply line removal

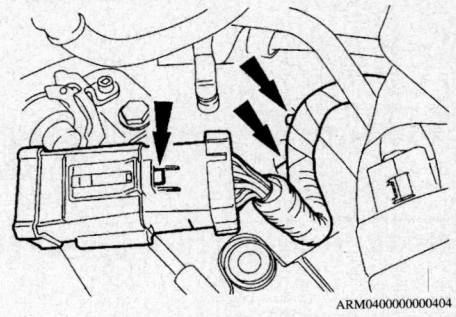

ARM0400000000404

Fig. 3   Transaxle electrical harness disconnected

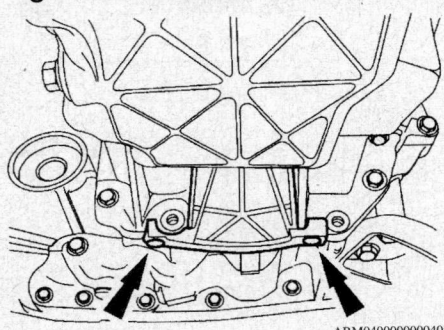

ARM0400000000405

Fig. 4   Torque converter access plug location

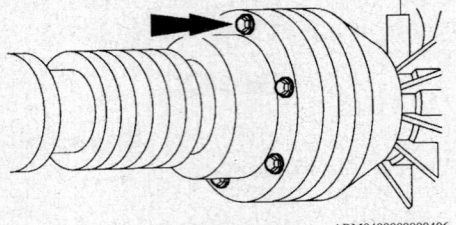

ARM0400000000406

Fig. 5   Rear drive shaft support bracket removal. AWD

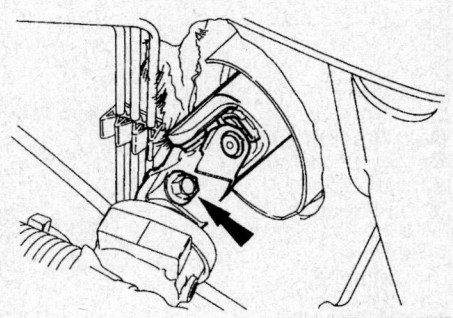

ARM0400000000407

Fig. 6   Intermediate steering shaft removal

2. Support transaxle with suitable transaxle jack.
3. Remove engine and transaxle support insulator to rear engine and transaxle bracket mounting nut.
4. Remove two engine and transaxle support insulator to subframe through bolts.
5. Raise transaxle enough to remove load from engine and transaxle support insulator.
6. Remove support insulator.
7. Reverse procedure to install.

ENGINE
REPLACE

1. Drain engine coolant and oil into suitable container.
2. Relieve fuel system pressure as outlined in "Precautions."
3. Recover refrigerant as outlined in "Air Conditioning" chapter.
4. Remove righthand and lefthand halfshafts as outlined in "Front Wheel Drive Axles" chapter.
5. Remove cowl vent screen and cowl vent extension.
6. Remove engine air cleaner and outlet tube.
7. Disconnect and position steering column input shaft coupling aside.
8. Disconnect accelerator and speed control actuator cables, then the throttle return spring from throttle body. Position accelerator cable bracket aside.
9. Remove exhaust flex pipe, then the lefthand and righthand catalytic converters.
10. Remove and discard roll restrictor cross brace bolt, **Fig. 1.**
11. Disconnect manual control lever cable

from lever and bracket, then position it bracket aside.
12. Remove and discard four roll restrictor cross brace bolts, then the cross brace.
13. Remove lefthand and righthand ground straps located on top of fenders.
14. Disconnect redundant clip, press inward on quick release coupling button, **Fig. 2,** then disconnect fuel supply line from fuel rail.
15. Disconnect fuel vapor tube from purge valve.
16. Disconnect two powertrain control module electrical connectors and position wiring conduit aside.
17. Disconnect power steering reservoir hose and hose retainer clips.
18. Disconnect shift cable from transaxle lever.
19. Disconnect transaxle 16 pin electrical connector, **Fig. 3,** then disconnect harness from shift cable bracket.
20. Remove shift cable retaining bracket and position bracket/cable assembly aside.
21. Disconnect heater and throttle body coolant hoses.
22. Disconnect upper, lower and bypass coolant hoses.
23. Remove all engine component electrical connectors, **Mark connector locations for installation.**
24. Disconnect A/C compressor manifold tube assembly.
25. Disconnect A/C tubes from condenser, position tube assembly aside.
26. Disconnect transaxle and power steering cool lines.
27. Remove two pin type retainers from torque converter access plug, **Fig. 4,** remove and four torque converter retaining nuts.
28. Remove three engine to transaxle bolts, then the lefthand catalytic converter bracket.

29. **On models equipped with AWD,** remove driveshaft support bracket.
30. Remove driveshaft to rear axle mounting bolts, **Fig. 5,** then position driveshaft aside.
31. **On all models,** disconnect outer tie rods from wheel knuckles.
32. Remove and discard steering column intermediate shaft to steering gear lock nut and bolt, **Fig. 6.** Separate intermediate shaft from steering gear.
33. Support powertrain and subframe using powertrain support/lift tool No. 014–00765, or equivalent, **Fig. 7.**
34. Remove six rear subframe bolts, then the subframe brackets.
35. Remove two front subframe bolts and washers.
36. Slowly lower powertrain and subframe far enough to access and remove the following components from subframe using powertrain support/lift tool No. 014–00765, or equivalent:
   a. Disconnect Power Steering Pressure (PSP) switch electrical connector.
   b. Remove power steering pressure tubes, **Fig. 8.**
   c. Disconnect righthand catalyst monitor sensor electrical connector and two pin type retainers from subframe.
   d. **On models equipped with CVT transaxle,** transaxle disconnect transaxle to bulkhead electrical connector, then disconnect wiring harness retainers from transaxle and subframe.
   e. Remove roll restrictor bracket, then the roll restrictor.

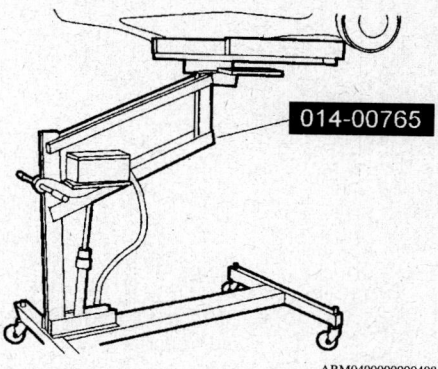

Fig. 7 Powertrain supported

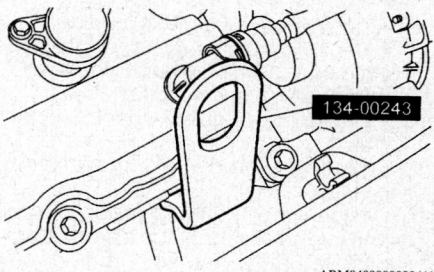

Fig. 10 Engine removal eye hook tool installation. Lefthand head

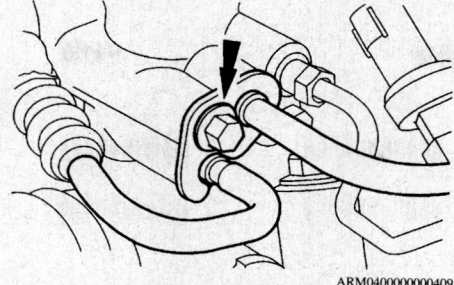

Fig. 8 Power steering pressure tubes removal

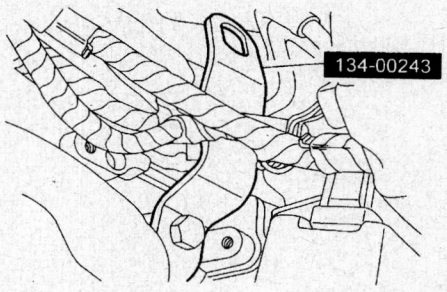

Fig. 9 Engine removal eye hook tool installation. Righthand head

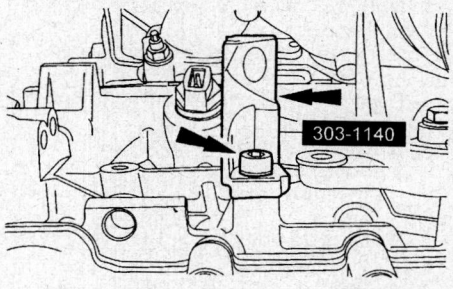

Fig. 11 Lower engine lifting bracket installed

f. Disconnect starter motor electrical connectors.
g. Remove starter motor.
h. Disconnect transaxle to frame ground cable.
i. **On models equipped with six speed transaxle,** disconnect Transaxle Control Module (TCM) electrical connector.
j. Remove four roll restrictor bracket bolts, then the roll restrictor.
k. Disconnect starter motor electrical connectors.
l. Remove starter motor.
m. Remove transaxle to frame ground cable.
37. **On all models,** install engine installation tool removal eye hooks tool No. 134–00243, or equivalent, to righthand cylinder head, **Fig. 9.**
38. Install engine installation, removal eye hooks tool No. 134–00243, or equivalent, to lefthand cylinder head, **Fig. 10.**
39. Install upper and lower engine lifting brackets tool No. 303–1140, or equivalent, **Figs. 11 and 12,** to transaxle housing.
40. Support powertrain assembly, **Fig. 13,** using suitable engine lift crane.
41. Remove front transaxle stabilizer bolt.
42. Remove exhaust heat shields.
43. Remove righthand and lefthand upper engine insulator retaining nuts.
44. **On models equipped with CVT transaxle,** remove four transaxle insulator bracket bolts, **Fig. 14.**
45. **On models equipped with six speed transaxle,** remove three transaxle insulator bracket bolts, **Fig. 15.**
46. **On all models,** use suitable engine crane, **Fig. 13,** to lift powertrain as-

sembly from subframe.
47. Lower powertrain and support transaxle using suitable wooden blocks.
48. Remove transaxle to engine mounting bolts, then separate engine from transaxle.
49. Reverse procedure to install. Replace all discarded bolts and nuts with OEM replacements.

INTAKE MANIFOLD
REPLACE

Upper

Refer to **Fig. 16** for component descriptions and locations when servicing upper intake manifold.
1. Relieve fuel system pressure as outlined in "Precautions."
2. Drain engine coolant into suitable container.
3. Remove air cleaner outlet tube.
4. Remove and discard transaxle roll restrictor cross brace bolts, then the cross brace.
5. Disconnect EVAP canister purge valve tube, then disconnect retaining clamp and position tube aside.
6. Disconnect PVC valve and brake booster vacuum harness tubes.
7. Disconnect EGR system module electrical connector and vacuum tube.
8. Disconnect and plug PCV and throttle body coolant hoses.
9. Disconnect throttle body electrical connector.
10. Remove and discard four upper manifold to lower manifold retaining screws.
11. Remove eight upper intake manifold mounting bolts.
12. Reverse procedure to install, noting the following:
    a. Replace all discarded bolts and nuts with OEM replacements.
    b. **Torque** intake mounting bolts to 89 inch lbs., in sequence, **Fig. 17.**

Lower

Refer to **Fig. 18** for component descriptions and locations when servicing upper intake manifold.
1. Relieve fuel system pressure as outlined in "Precautions."
2. Remove upper intake manifold as outlined in "Intake Manifold, Replace."
3. Disconnect fuel supply tube redundant

clip, press inward on quick release coupling button, **Fig. 2,** then disconnect fuel supply line from fuel rail.
4. Disconnect fuel injector electrical connectors.
5. Remove lower intake manifold mounting bolts.
6. Remove lower intake manifold.
7. Remove fuel rail and injectors from manifold.
8. Reverse procedure to install, noting the following:
    a. Install new gaskets and O-rings.
    b. Lubricate new O-ring seals lightly with suitable motor oil. **Do not use silicone grease.**
    c. **Torque** bolts to 89 inch lbs., in sequence, **Fig. 19.**

EXHAUST MANIFOLD
REPLACE

Lefthand

1. Drain engine coolant into suitable container.
2. Disconnect coolant hose retainers from cooling fan shroud, then position hoses aside.
3. Disconnect cooling fan electrical connector.
4. Remove lefthand exhaust manifold to exhaust pipe nuts, **Fig. 20.**
5. Remove coolant tube bracket bolt, then the bracket.
6. Disconnect heated oxygen sensor electrical connector from coolant tube.
7. Raise and support vehicle.
8. Remove front splash shield pin type retainers and mounting bolts, then the splash shield.

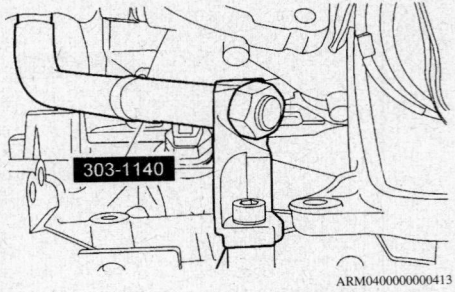

Fig. 12 Upper engine lifting bracket installed

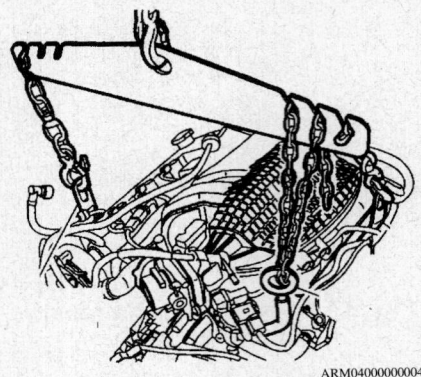

Fig. 13 Engine lifting crane installed

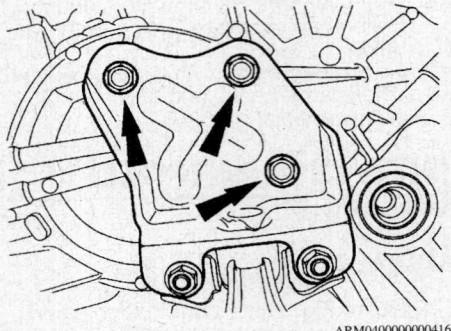

Fig. 15 Insulator bolt removal. 6 speed transaxle

Fig. 14 Insulator bolt removal. CVT transaxle

9. Remove lower exhaust manifold mounting nuts.
10. Remove coolant tube lower bracket.
11. Lower vehicle.
12. Remove upper mounting nuts and exhaust manifold.
13. Reverse procedure to install, noting the following:
   a. Install new exhaust manifold gasket.
   b. **Torque** nuts to 13–16 ft. lbs., in sequence, **Fig. 21.**
   c. **Torque** manifold to pipe nuts to 30 ft. lbs.

Righthand

1. Remove righthand catalytic converter.
2. Disconnect exhaust gas recirculation tube **Fig. 22,** from exhaust manifold.
3. Raise and support vehicle.
4. Disconnect HO2S sensor connector.
5. Remove three manifold heat shield retaining bolts, then the heat shield.
6. Remove six exhaust manifold mounting nuts, then the manifold.
7. Reverse procedure to install, noting the following:
   a. Install new exhaust manifold gasket.
   b. **Torque** exhaust manifold nuts to 15 ft. lbs., in sequence, **Fig. 23.**

CYLINDER HEAD

REPLACE

Lefthand

1. Drain engine coolant into suitable container.
2. Remove coolant bypass tube.
3. Remove oil dipstick and tube.
4. Remove exhaust manifold as outlined in "Exhaust Manifold, Replace."
5. Remove water pump as outlined in "Water Pump, Replace."
6. Remove timing chain and gears as outlined in "Timing Chain, Replace."
7. Remove air cleaner outlet tube.
8. Remove accelerator cable splash shield.
9. Disconnect throttle and cruise control cables.
10. Disconnect throttle position sensor and idle air control valve electrical connectors, then disconnect harness from throttle body and intake manifold.
11. Disconnect Exhaust Gas Recirculation

(EGR) vacuum regulator and vacuum supply hoses.
12. Disconnect PCV and EVAP vacuum hoses.
13. Remove EGR valve and vacuum regulator valve.
14. Remove upper and lower intake manifolds as outlined in "Intake Manifold, Replace."
15. Remove both valve covers as outlined in "Valve Cover, Replace."
16. Remove camshaft followers, rocker arms and hydraulic lash adjusters as outlined in "Hydraulic Liters, Replace."
17. Remove cylinder head bolts in sequence, **Fig. 24.**
18. Remove cylinder head. Discard gasket and bolts.
19. Reverse procedure to install, noting the following:
   a. Install new head gasket and bolts. **Bolts are torque to yield design and cannot be reused.**
   b. Tighten cylinder head bolts in six steps in sequence, **Fig. 25,** as follows:
   c. Step one **torque** cylinder head bolts to 30 ft. lbs.
   d. Step two tighten head bolts and additional 90° in sequence.
   e. Step three loosen all bolts one full turn.
   f. Step four **torque** cylinder head bolts to 30 ft. lbs., in sequence.
   g. Step five tighten bolts an additional 90° in sequence.
   h. Step six tighten bolts an additional 90° in sequence.

Righthand

1. Remove coolant bypass tube.
2. Remove timing chain and gears as outlined in "Timing Chain, Replace."
3. Remove air cleaner outlet tube.
4. Remove accelerator cable splash shield.
5. Disconnect throttle and cruise control cables.
6. Disconnect throttle position sensor and idle air control valve electrical connectors, then harness from throttle body and intake manifold.
7. Disconnect Exhaust Gas Recirculation (EGR) vacuum regulator and vacuum supply hoses.
8. Disconnect PCV and EVAP vacuum hoses.
9. Remove EGR valve and vacuum regulator valve.
10. Remove upper and lower intake manifolds as outlined in "Intake Manifold, Replace."
11. Remove both valve covers as outlined in "Valve Cover, Replace."
12. Remove camshafts and rocker arms. Mark rocker arms for installation alignment.
13. Raise and support vehicle.
14. Remove exhaust manifold to pipe bolts.
15. Lower vehicle.
16. Disconnect Exhaust Gas Recirculation (EGR) tube from exhaust manifold.
17. Remove camshaft followers and hydraulic lash adjusters as outlined in "Hydraulic Liters, Replace."
18. Remove exhaust manifold as outlined in "Exhaust Manifold, Replace."
19. Remove cylinder head bolts in sequence, **Fig. 26.**
20. Remove cylinder head. Discard gasket and bolts.
21. Reverse procedure to install, noting the following:
   a. Install new head gasket and bolts. **Bolts are torque to yield design and cannot be reused.**
   b. Tighten cylinder head bolts in six steps in sequence, **Fig. 27,** as follows:
   c. Step one **torque** cylinder head bolts to 30 ft. lbs.
   d. Step two tighten head bolts and additional 90° in sequence.
   e. Step three loosen bolts one full turn.
   f. Step four **torque** cylinder head

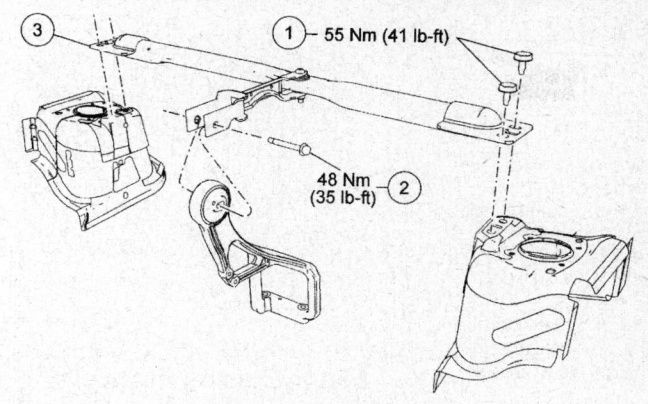

Item	Description
1	Transaxle roll restrictor cross brace bolts (4 required)
2	Transaxle roll restrictor bolt

Item	Description
3	Transaxle roll restrictor cross brace

ARM0400000000417

Fig. 16   Upper intake manifold replacement (Part 1 of 3)

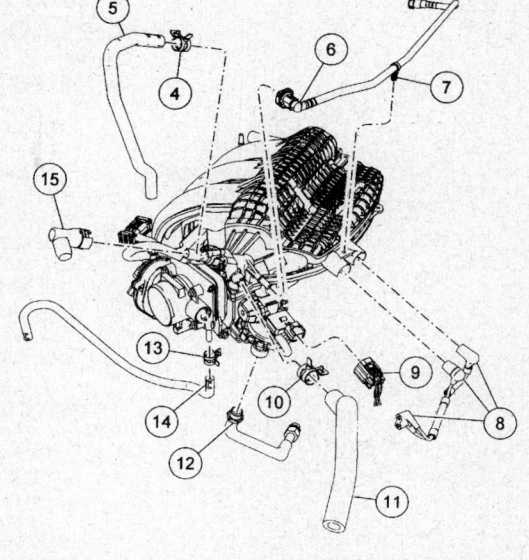

Item	Description
4	Positive crankcase ventilation (PCV) coolant hose clamp
5	PCV coolant hose
6	Evaporative emissions (EVAP) canister purge valve tube
7	EVAP canister purge valve tube retainer
8	Vacuum tube fittings (3 required)
9	Exhaust gas recirculation (EGR) system module electrical connector

Item	Description
10	Brake booster vacuum hose clamp
11	Brake booster vacuum hose
12	EGR system module tube fitting
13	Throttle body coolant hose clamp
14	Throttle body coolant hose
15	PCV tube

ARM0400000000418

Fig. 16   Upper intake manifold replacement (Part 2 of 3)

bolts to 30 ft. lbs., in sequence.
g. Step five tighten bolts an additional 90° in sequence.
h. Step six tighten bolts an additional 90° in sequence.

VALVE COVER
REPLACE
Lefthand

1. Disconnect crankcase ventilation tube from valve cover, **Fig. 28.**
2. Disconnect ignition coil electrical connector.
3. Remove ignition coil mounting bolts, then coil.
4. Remove three wiring conduit mounting nuts, then position conduit aside.
5. Remove oil dipstick.
6. Disconnect wiring harness from valve cover and position aside.
7. Remove mounting bolts, studs and valve cover.
8. Reverse procedure to install, noting the following:
   a. Install new valve cover gasket.
   b. Apply 5 mm dot of silicone gasket sealant to front cover to cylinder head joints.
   c. **Torque** valve cover mounting bolts to 89 inch lbs., in sequence, **Fig. 29.**

Righthand

1. Remove upper intake manifold as outlined in "Intake Manifold, Replace."
2. Remove ignition coil and bracket, **Fig. 30.**
3. Remove power steering pressure tube to reservoir bracket mounting bolts, then position pressure tube aside.
4. Remove power steering fluid reservoir bolts, then the reservoir.
5. Remove wiring harness nut and position harness aside.

6. Disconnect crankcase ventilation tube from valve cover.
7. Remove mounting bolts, studs and valve cover.
8. Reverse procedure to install, noting the following:
   a. Install new valve cover gasket.
   b. Apply 5 mm dot of silicone gasket and sealant to front cover cylinder head joints.
   c. **Torque** valve cover mounting bolts to 89 inch lbs., in sequence, **Fig. 31.**

CAMSHAFT LOBE LIFT SPECIFICATIONS
Exhaust.. .388 inch
Intake .... .388 inch

VALVE ADJUSTMENT

Hydraulic valve lifters are used in this engine. No adjustment is required.

HYDRAULIC LIFTERS
REPLACE

1. Remove valve covers as outlined in "Valve Cover, Replace."
2. Remove spark plugs.

3. Remove righthand splash shield.
4. Rotate crankshaft until camshaft lobe is pointing directly away from roller follower.
5. Remove hydraulic roller lifter using lifter removal tool N. 303–473, or equivalent, **Fig. 32.**
6. Reverse procedure to install. Lubricate camshaft followers using clean suitable engine oil.

FRONT COVER
REPLACE

1. Drain engine coolant and oil into suitable container.
2. Remove lefthand and righthand valve covers as outlined in "Valve Cover, Replace."
3. Remove power steering pump.
4. Raise and support vehicle.
5. Remove righthand front wheel and inner splash shield.
6. Remove dual converter Y-pipe.
7. Disconnect upper, lower, bypass and heater hoses from front of engine.
8. Remove engine to transaxle bracket.
9. Remove torque converter inspection cover.

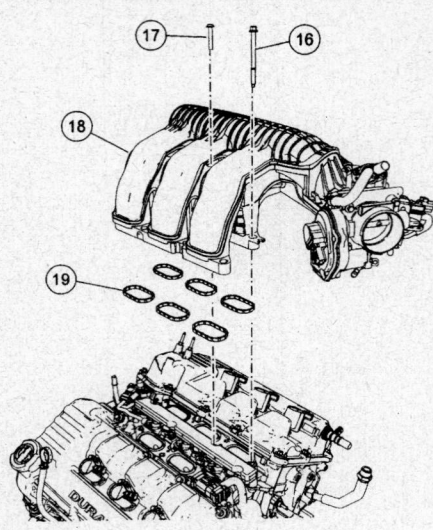

Item	Description
16	Upper intake manifold bolts (8 required)
17	Upper intake manifold-to-lower intake manifold screw (4 required)
18	Upper intake manifold
19	Upper intake manifold gaskets (6 required)

ARM0400000000419

Fig. 16 Upper intake manifold replacement (Part 3 of 3)

10. Remove oil pan as outlined in "Oil Pan, Replace."
11. Remove mounting nut, then position power steering pressure line and muffler aside.
12. Remove alternator, crankshaft pulley and Crankshaft Position (CKP) sensor.
13. Remove air conditioning compressor to front cover bracket.
14. Disconnect Camshaft Position (CMP) sensor.
15. Remove belt tensioner.
16. Disconnect cooling fan electrical connectors.
17. Remove engine cooling fan/shroud mounting bolts, then the cooling fan/shroud assembly.
18. Install suitable engine support tool.
19. Remove upper air conditioning compressor bolts and position compressor aside.
20. Lower vehicle.
21. Remove air conditioning line retaining bracket.
22. Remove front engine cover mounting bolts and studs, then the engine cover.
23. Reverse procedure to install, noting the following:
    a. Install new front cover gaskets.
    b. Apply .24 inch bead of gasket sealer to cylinder block, lower front engine block and cylinder head mating surfaces. Front cover must be installed and bolts tightened within four minutes of applying sealant.
    c. **Torque** front cover mounting bolt to 18 ft. lbs., in sequence, **Fig. 33.**

FRONT COVER SEAL
REPLACE
Removal

1. Loosen accessory drive belts and remove righthand front wheel.
2. Remove four crankshaft pulley to damper mounting bolts, then the remove accessory drive belt and pulley.
3. Remove mounting bolt, and vibration damper using suitable puller.
4. Pry seal from front timing cover using flat bladed screwdriver, or other suitable tool. **Do not damage front cover or crankshaft.**

Installation

1. Lubricate replacement seal lip with suitable, clean engine oil and install seal with suitable seal installer.
2. Lubricate inner hub surface of vibration damper with suitable clean engine oil and apply RTV sealant to keyway of inner hub surface of vibration damper.
3. Install vibration damper and tighten mounting bolt.
4. Install crankshaft pulley and tighten bolts.
5. Install accessory drive belts and righthand front wheel.

TIMING CHAIN
REPLACE

1. Remove engine front cover as outlined in "Front Cover, Replace."
2. Remove ignition pulse wheel.
3. Remove spark plugs, Install damper bolt, then rotate crankshaft clockwise to position crankshaft keyway in 11 O'clock position.
4. Ensure camshafts are correctly located in cylinder No. 1 TDC position. If not, rotate crankshaft one additional turn and inspect.
5. Rotate crankshaft clockwise 120° to 3 O'clock position to place righthand camshafts in neutral position. Ensure camshafts are correctly positioned, **Fig. 34.**
6. Remove righthand timing chain tensioner arm, timing chain guide and timing chain.
7. Rotate crankshaft clockwise two times to position crankshaft keyway in 11 O'clock position and ensure camshafts in neutral position.
8. Remove lefthand timing chain tensioner, tensioner arm and timing chain.
9. Remove crankshaft damper bolt.
10. Reverse procedure to install, noting the following:
    a. Position chain tensioner in suitable soft jawed vise.
    b. Hold chain tensioner ratchet lock mechanism away from ratchet stem with suitable small pick and slowly compress timing chain tensioner.
    c. Retain tensioner piston with .05 inch wire, or paper clip, **Fig. 35.**

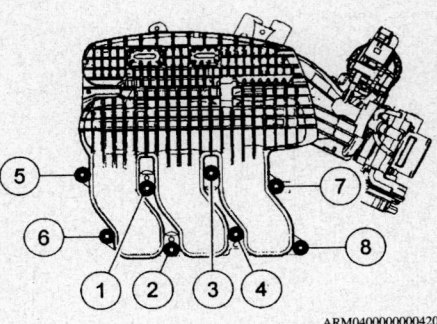

ARM0400000000420

Fig. 17 Upper intake manifold bolt tightening sequence

d. Ensure timing marks on sprockets and timing chain are aligned, **Fig. 34.**
e. Verify timing and component alignment as outlined, **Fig. 36. Failure to verify correct timing drive component alignment will result in server engine damage.**

CAMSHAFT
REPLACE

When servicing camshafts refer to **Figs. 37 and 38** for component identifications and locations.

Refer to "Cylinder Head, Replace" for camshaft replacement procedures.

Removal
LEFTHAND

1. Remove timing chain and gears as outlined in "Timing Chain, Replace."
2. Remove upper intake manifold as outlined in "Intake Manifold, Replace."
3. Remove valve covers as outlined in "Valve Cover, Replace."
4. Remove three camshaft oil seal retaining bolts, then the retaining plate and seal.
5. Press oil seal from retaining plate using suitable press.
6. Remove camshaft journal cap bolts in sequence, **Fig. 39.**
7. Remove camshafts and rocker arms. Mark rocker arms for installation alignment.

RIGHTHAND

1. Remove timing chain and gears as outlined in "Timing Chain, Replace."
2. Remove upper intake manifold as outlined in "Intake Manifold, Replace."
3. Remove both valve covers as outlined in "Valve Cover, Replace."
4. Remove camshaft journal cap bolts in sequence, **Fig. 40.**
5. Remove camshaft bearings and thrust caps.
6. Remove camshafts and rocker arms. Mark rocker arms for installation alignment.

Installation
LEFTHAND

1. Lubricate camshafts and bearings

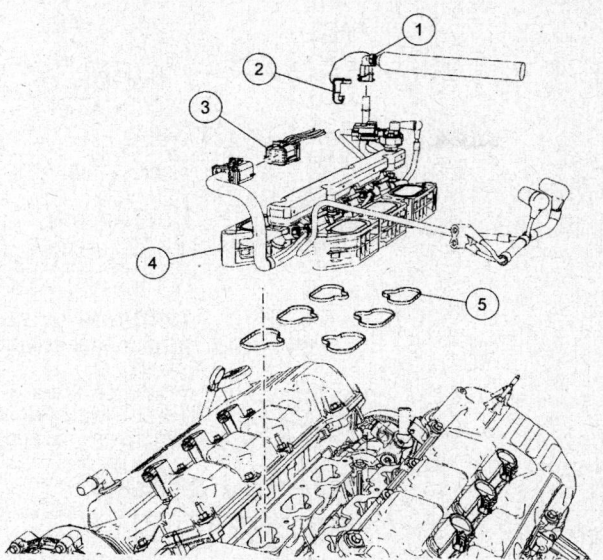

Item	Description
1	Fuel tube
2	Fuel tube redundant clip
3	Fuel charging wiring harness electrical connector

Item	Description
4	Lower intake manifold
5	Lower intake manifold gaskets (6 required)

ARM0400000000421

Fig. 18 Lower intake manifold replacement

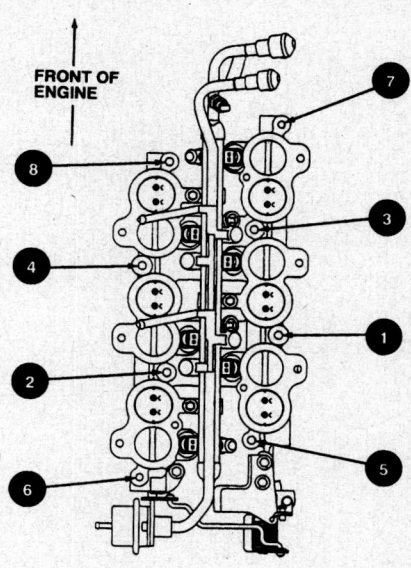

FM1069600485000X

Fig. 19 Lower intake manifold bolt tightening sequence

using suitable clean engine oil.
2. Align camshafts as outlined, **Fig. 41.**
3. Install rocker arms and thrust caps.
4. **Torque** thrust cap bolts to 89 inch lbs., in sequence, **Fig. 42.**
5. Install camshaft oil seal using seal installation tool No. 303–463, or equivalent, **Fig. 43.**
6. Install oil seal retaining plate.
7. Install timing chain and gears as outlined in "Timing Chain, Replace."
8. Install upper intake manifold as outlined in "Intake Manifold, Replace."
9. Install valve covers as outlined in "Valve Cover, Replace."

RIGHTHAND

1. Lubricate camshafts and bearings using suitable clean engine oil.
2. Align camshafts as outlined, **Fig. 44.**
3. Install rocker arms and thrust caps.
4. **Torque** thrust cap bolts to 89 inch lbs., in sequence, **Fig. 40.**
5. Install timing chain and gears as outlined in "Timing Chain, Replace."
6. Install upper intake manifold as outlined in "Intake Manifold, Replace."
7. Install both valve covers as outlined in "Valve Cover, Replace."

PISTON & ROD ASSEMBLY

The piston and rod assemblies in these engines are not serviceable, should failure occur a short block will be required.

MAIN & ROD BEARINGS

The main and rod bearings in these engines are not serviceable, should failure occur a short block will be required.

CRANKSHAFT REAR OIL SEAL
REPLACE

1. Remove transaxle as outlined in **MOTOR's "Domestic Transmission Manual, In-Vehicle Service"** manual.
2. Remove mounting bolts, then the flywheel.
3. Remove rear cover plate.
4. Punch hole into seal metal surface between lip and block using suitable tool.
5. Remove seal using slide hammer tool No. T77L-9533-B, or equivalent.
6. Coat crankshaft seal area and lip with suitable engine oil.
7. Install seal using seal replacement tool No. T82L-6701-A, or equivalent.
8. Install rear cover plate and two dowels.
9. Install flywheel.
10. Install transaxle as outlined in **MOTOR's "Domestic Transmission Manual, In-Vehicle Service"** manual.

OIL PAN
REPLACE

1. Raise and support vehicle.
2. Drain engine oil into suitable container.
3. Remove righthand front wheel and inner splash shield.
4. Remove dual converter Y-pipe.

5. Remove engine to transaxle bracket.
6. Remove torque converter inspection cover.
7. Remove oil pan mounting bolts, then the oil pan.
8. Reverse procedure to install, noting the following:
   a. Apply .40 inch diameter dot of suitable silicone gasket and sealer to areas indicated, **Fig. 45.**
   b. **Torque** oil pan mounting bolts to 18 ft. lbs., in sequence, **Fig. 46.**

OIL PUMP
REPLACE

1. Remove timing chains as outlined in "Timing Chain, Replace."
2. Remove oil pump mounting bolts in sequence, **Fig. 47.**
3. Remove oil pump and gasket.
4. Reverse procedure to install, noting the following:
   a. Install new oil pump gasket.
   b. **Torque** oil pump bolts to 89 inch lbs., in sequence, **Fig. 48.**
   c. Install timing chains as outlined in "Timing Chain, Replace."

OIL PUMP SERVICE

Oil pump is serviced as an assembly and must be replaced if failure occurs.

BELT TENSION DATA

Belt	New, Lbs.	Used, Lbs.
Five-Rib	140–160	110–130
Six-Rib	①	①

① — Automatic tensioner.

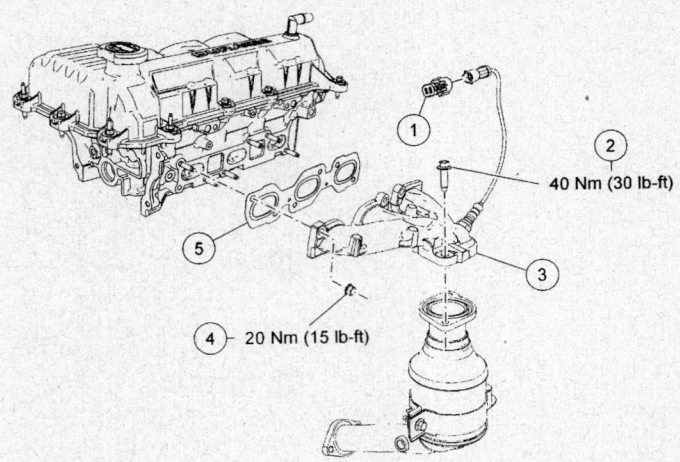

Item	Description
1	Heated oxygen sensor (HO2S) electrical connector
2	LH exhaust manifold-to-catalytic converter bolts (2 required)
3	LH exhaust manifold
4	LH exhaust manifold nut (6 required)
5	LH exhaust manifold gasket

ARM0400000000439

Fig. 20   Lefthand exhaust manifold replacement

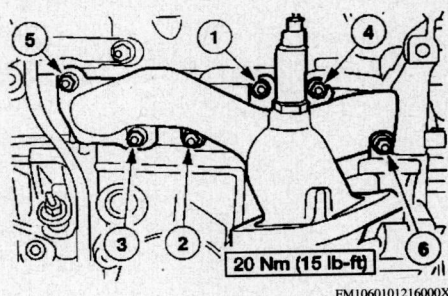

FM1060101216000X

Fig. 21   Lefthand exhaust manifold tightening sequence

5. Install upper radiator hose.
6. Fill and bleed cooling system as outlined in "Cooling System Bleed."

SERPENTINE DRIVE BELT

Belt Routing

Refer to **Fig. 49,** for serpentine drive belt routing.

Belt, Replace

1. Remove accessory drive belt splash shield, **Fig. 50.**
2. Rotate drive belt tensioner counterclockwise.
3. Remove serpentine drive belt.
4. Reverse procedure to install.

COOLING SYSTEM BLEED

1. Select maximum blower motor and heater temperature settings.
2. Set controls to discharge air through instrument panel air conditioning vents.
3. Start engine and allow to idle until operating temperature is reached.
4. Hot air should now blow through air conditioning vents, temperature gauge should rest in NORMAL range and upper radiator hose should feel hot to touch.
5. If hot air does not blow through vents or temperature gauge is not in NORMAL range, proceed as follows:
   a. Stop engine, allow to cool.
   b. Add coolant to bring level to top of Cold Fill mark on de-gas bottle.
   c. Start engine and allow it to idle. Feel for hot air at vents.
6. Stop engine and allow to cool. Inspect for leaks.
7. When engine coolant level indicator flashes, approximately one to 1 ½ quarts of coolant may now be added to de-gas bottle after proper refill.

THERMOSTAT

REPLACE

Removal

1. Drain cooling system into suitable container to below level of upper radiator hose.
2. Remove upper radiator hose.
3. Remove three thermostat housing bolts, **Fig. 51,** then separate upper and lower thermostat housings.
4. Remove thermostat from housing and discard gasket.

Installation

1. Align thermostat bridge with alignment marks in lower housing, **Fig. 52,** then install lower thermostat housing into upper housing.
2. Install gasket onto housing using bolts to hold position.
3. Install lower housing onto upper housing, **Fig. 51.**
4. Install and **torque** mounting bolts to 89 inch lbs.

WATER PUMP

REPLACE

1. Raise and support vehicle.
2. Drain engine coolant into suitable container.
3. Remove air cleaner assembly.
4. Disconnect water hose from bottom of water pump.
5. Remove radiator lower coolant tube bolt.
6. Lower vehicle.
7. Remove water pump belt.
8. Remove radiator upper front coolant tube bolt.
9. Disconnect upper radiator hose and engine vent hose.
10. Disconnect transaxle 10-pin connector.
11. Remove radiator bypass hose assembly.
12. Disconnect thermostat housing and position aside, **Fig. 53.**
13. Remove water pump mounting bolts, then the water pump.
14. Reverse procedure to install, noting the following:
    a. Tighten water pump mounting bolts in four steps as follows:
    b. Step one **torque** water pump center bolt to 35 inch lbs.
    c. Step two **torque** water pump outer mounting bolts to 89 inch lbs.
    d. Step three tighten mounting bolts an additional 90°.
    e. Step four **torque** water pump center bolt to 18 ft. lbs.

RADIATOR

REPLACE

1. Drain cooling system into suitable container.
2. Remove battery and battery tray.
3. Disconnect upper radiator hose.
4. Disconnect degas bottle return hose.
5. Disconnect upper transaxle cooler line using suitable disconnect tool.
6. Remove air conditioning condenser mounting bolts.
7. Raise and support vehicle.
8. Disconnect lower radiator hose and transaxle cooler line.
9. Remove condenser to radiator mounting bolts.

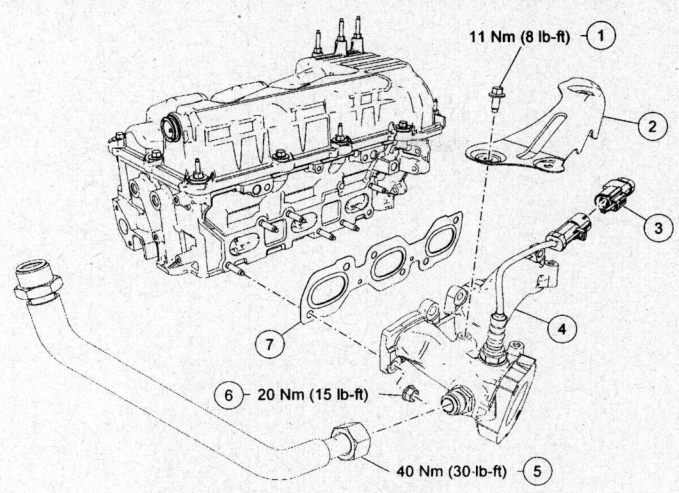

Item	Description
1	RH exhaust manifold heat shield (2 required)
2	RH exhaust manifold heat shield
3	Heated oxygen sensor (HO2S) electrical connector
4	RH exhaust manifold
5	Exhaust gas recirculation (EGR) system module tube fitting
6	RH exhaust manifold nut (6 required)
7	RH exhaust manifold gasket

ARM0400000000440

Fig. 22 Righthand exhaust manifold replacement

10. Remove power steering cooler to radiator mounting bolts.
11. Remove nuts and radiator support bracket.
12. Remove radiator.
13. Reverse procedure to install.

FUEL PUMP
REPLACE

1. Relieve fuel system pressure as outlined in "Precautions."
2. **On Five Hundred and Montego models,** release rear seat lower cushion latches, then pull upward to remove seat cushion.
3. **On Freestyle models,** position second row seat rearward. Remove seat latching bracket bolts and brackets, then the rear seat.
4. **On all models,** remove fuel pump module access cover.
5. Clean surrounding area of fuel pump module mounting flange and quick connect fittings, **Fig. 54.**
6. Disconnect fuel pump module electrical connector.
7. Disconnect fuel supply and fuel vapor tubes quick connect coupling from fuel pump module.
8. Remove fuel pump locking ring by turning it counterclockwise using lock ring tool No. ST2803-A. or equivalent.
9. Remove fuel pump, bracket and gasket assembly.
10. Reverse procedure to install. Ensure

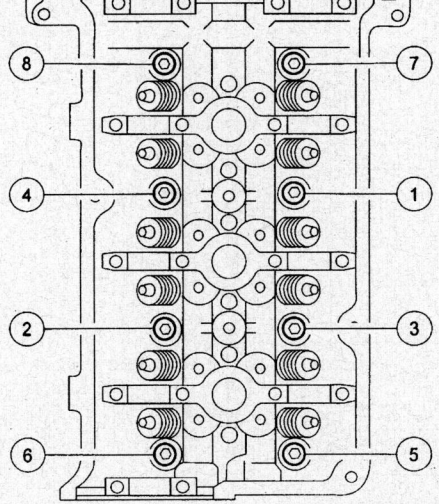

ARM0400000000442

Fig. 25 Lefthand cylinder head bolt tightening sequence

alignment arrows on fuel pump module and fuel tank meet before tightening lock ring.

FUEL FILTER
REPLACE

1. Relieve fuel system pressure as outlined in "Precautions."

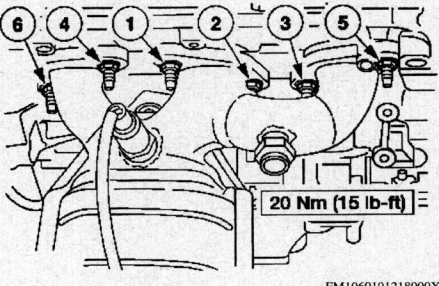

FM1060101218000X

Fig. 23 Righthand exhaust manifold bolt tightening sequence

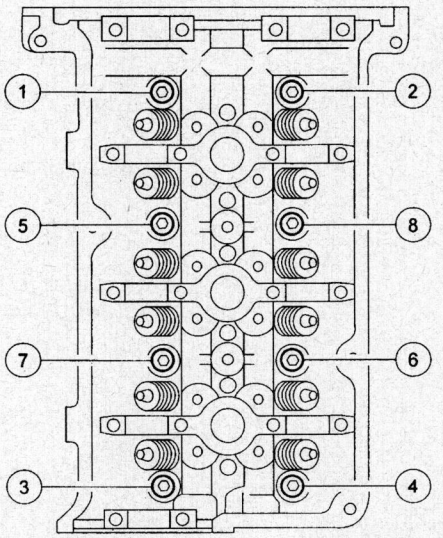

ARM0400000000441

Fig. 24 Lefthand cylinder head bolt removal sequence

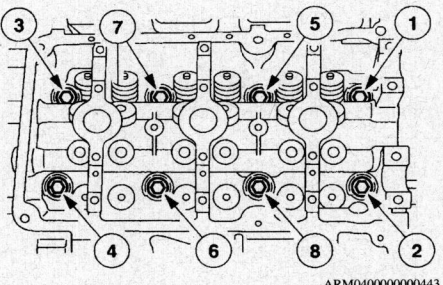

ARM0400000000443

Fig. 26 Righthand cylinder head bolt loosening sequence

2. Twist push connect fittings at each end of filter until they move freely on tube.
3. Bend and break shipping tab from hairpin clip and spread two clip legs approximately 1/8 inch.
4. Remove clip from tube and fitting by pulling gently on triangular end.
5. Separate fitting and hose assembly from fuel filter.
6. Install retainer clips in each connect fitting.
7. Loosen worm gear mounting clip and remove filter from bracket.
8. Reverse procedure to install.

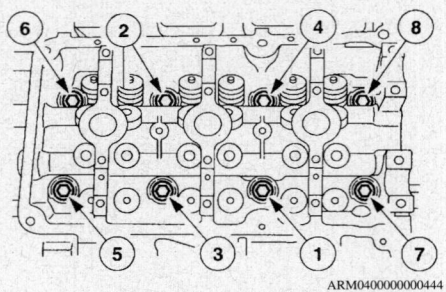

Fig. 27 Righthand cylinder head bolt tightening sequence

ARM0400000000444

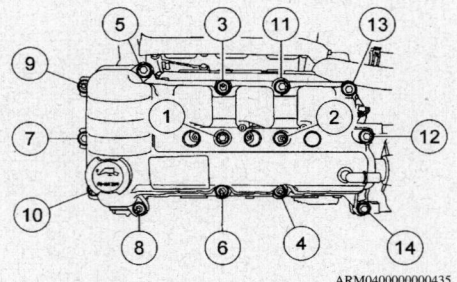

Fig. 29 Lefthand valve cover tightening sequence

ARM0400000000435

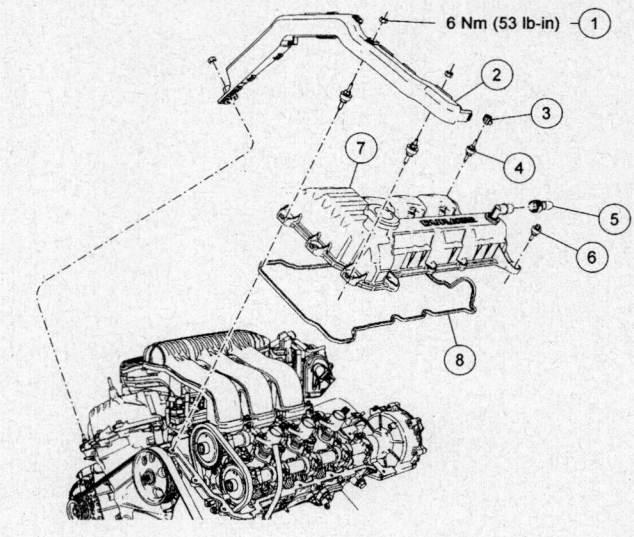

Item	Description	Item	Description
1	Wiring conduit-to-valve cover stud bolt nuts (3 required)	4	Valve cover stud bolts (8 required)
2	Wiring conduit	5	Crankcase ventilation tube
3	Wiring retainers (3 required)	6	Valve cover bolts (6 required)
		7	Valve cover
		8	Valve cover gasket

ARM0400000000434

Fig. 28 Lefthand valve cover replacement

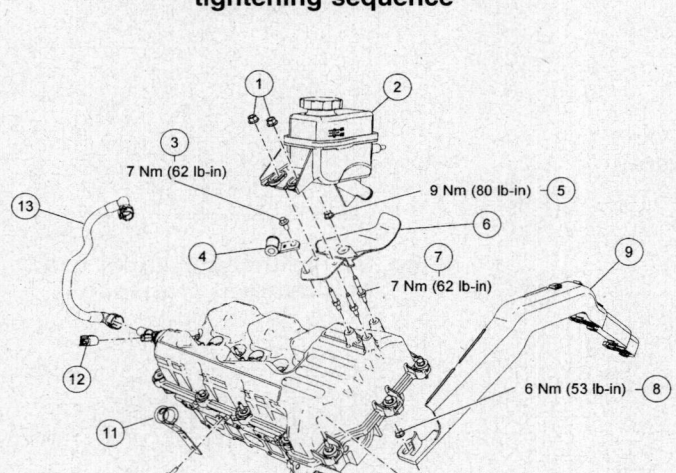

Item	Description	Item	Description
1	Power steering reservoir nuts (2 required)	8	Wiring conduit nuts (3 required)
2	Power steering fluid reservoir	9	Wiring conduit (part of
3	Power steering pressure (PSP) tube retainer bracket bolt	10	PSP tube retainer bracket bolt
4	PSP tube retainer bracket	11	PSP tube retainer bracket
5	Power steering fluid reservoir bracket nut	12	Positive crankcase ventilation (PCV) valve electrical connector
6	Power steering fluid reservoir bracket	13	PCV tube
7	Power steering fluid reservoir bracket stud bolts (3 required)		

ARM0400000000436

Fig. 30 Righthand valve cover replacement (Part 1 of 2)

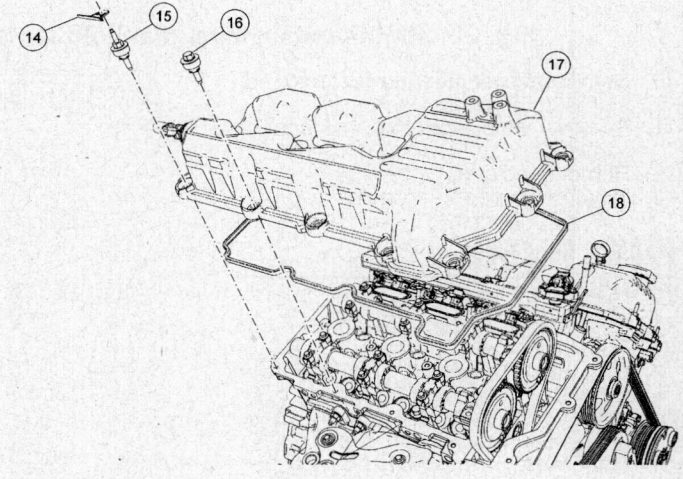

Item	Description
14	Wiring retainers (2 required)
15	Valve cover stud bolts (5 required)
16	Valve cover bolts (9 required)
17	Valve cover
18	Valve cover gasket

ARM0400000000437

Fig. 30 Righthand valve cover replacement (Part 2 of 2)

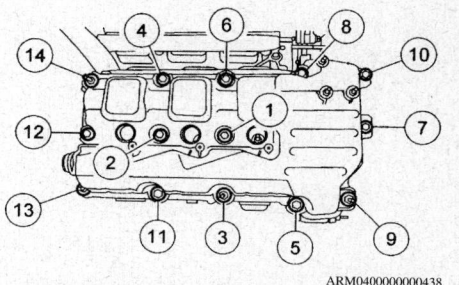

Fig. 31 Righthand valve cover tightening sequence

ARM0400000000438

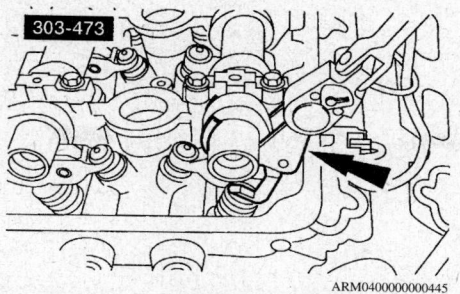

Fig. 32 Hydraulic roller lifter replacement

ARM0400000000445

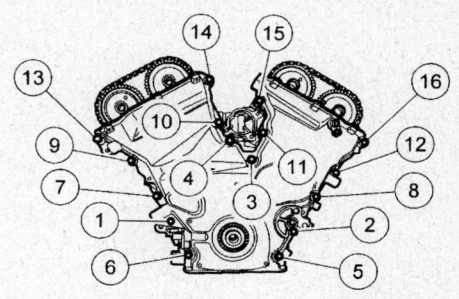

Fig. 33 Front cover bolt tightening sequence

ARM0400000000430

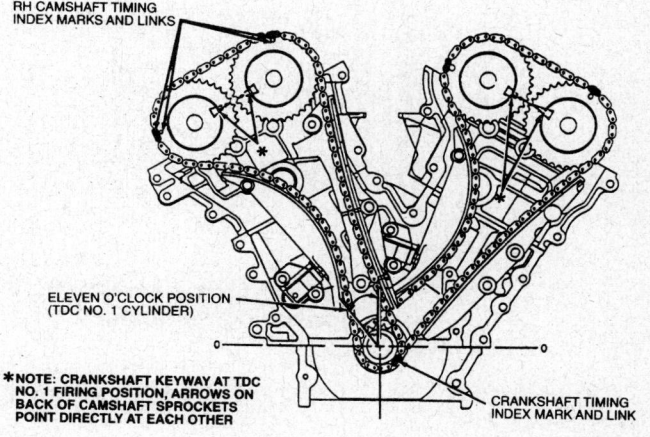

RH CAMSHAFT TIMING INDEX MARKS AND LINKS

ELEVEN O'CLOCK POSITION (TDC NO. 1 CYLINDER)

CRANKSHAFT TIMING INDEX MARK AND LINK

*NOTE: CRANKSHAFT KEYWAY AT TDC NO. 1 FIRING POSITION, ARROWS ON BACK OF CAMSHAFT SPROCKETS POINT DIRECTLY AT EACH OTHER

ARM0400000000432

Fig. 34 Timing mark alignment

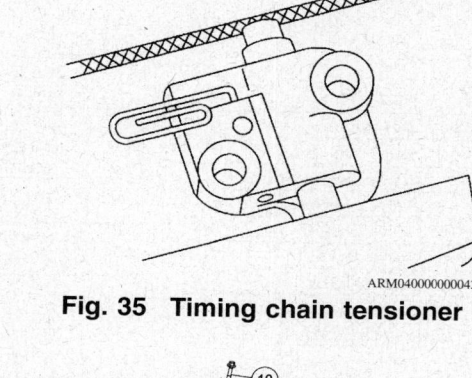

ARM0400000000431

Fig. 35 Timing chain tensioner

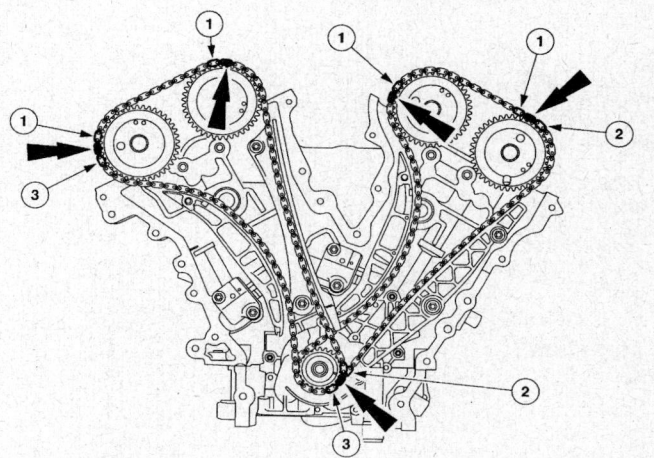

1. There should be: 12 chain links between the camshaft timing mark
2. There should be: 27 chain links between the camshaft and crankshaft timing marks
3. There should be: 30 chain links between the camshaft and crankshaft timing marks

ARM0400000000433

Fig. 36 Timing drive component alignment

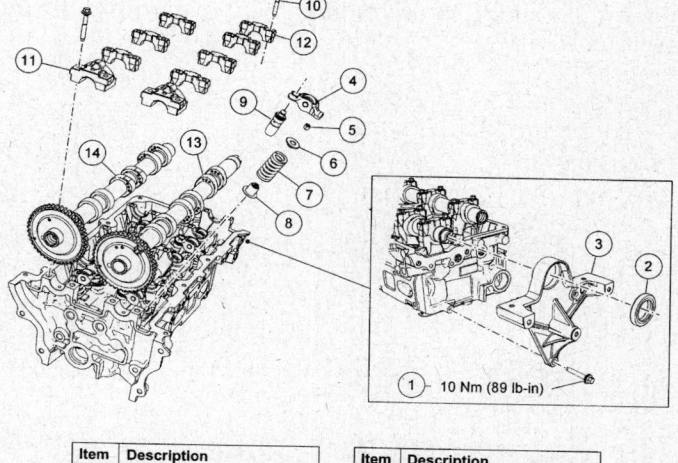

1 — 10 Nm (89 lb-in)

Item	Description	Item	Description
1	Camshaft oil seal retainer bolts (3 required)	9	Hydraulic lash adjuster
2	Camshaft oil seal	10	Camshaft bearing cap bolts (16 required)
3	Camshaft oil seal retainer	11	Camshaft bearing thrust cap (2 required)
4	Roller follower	12	Camshaft bearing cap (7 required)
5	Valve spring retainer key	13	Exhaust camshaft
6	Valve spring retainer	14	Intake camshaft
7	Valve spring		
8	Valve stem seal		

ARM0400000000428

Fig. 37 Exploded view of lefthand camshafts & rocker arms

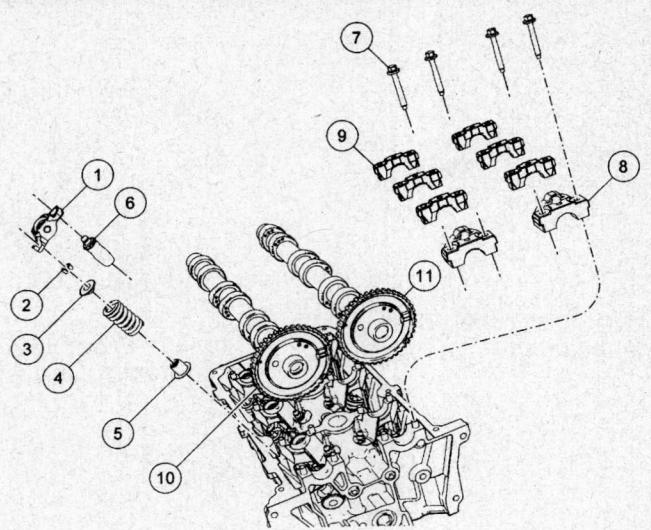

Item	Description
1	Roller follower
2	Valve spring retainer key
3	Valve spring retainer
4	Valve spring
5	Valve stem seal
6	Hydraulic lash adjuster
7	Camshaft bearing cap bolts (16 required)

Item	Description
8	Camshaft bearing thrust cap (2 required)
9	Camshaft bearing cap (6 required)
10	Exhaust camshaft
11	Intake camshaft

ARM0400000000429

Fig. 38 Exploded view of righthand camshafts & rocker arms

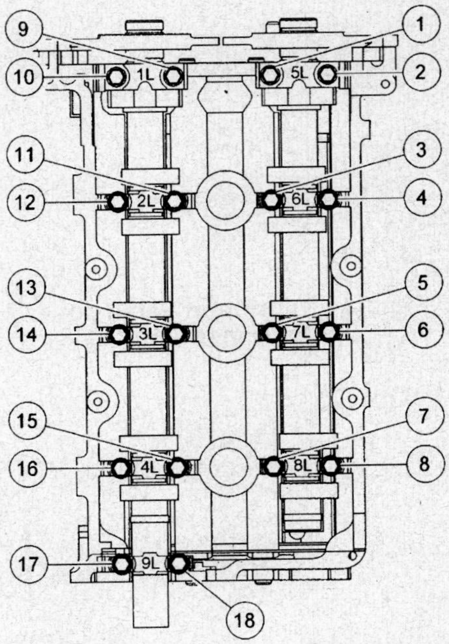

ARM0400000000424

Fig. 39 Lefthand camshaft loosening sequence

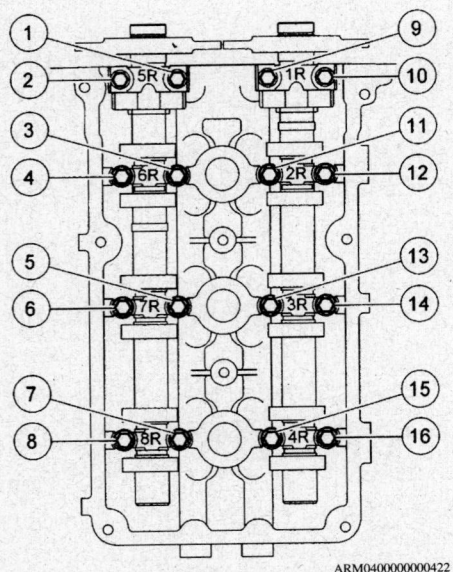

ARM0400000000422

Fig. 40 Righthand camshafts thrust cap bolt loosening & tightening sequence

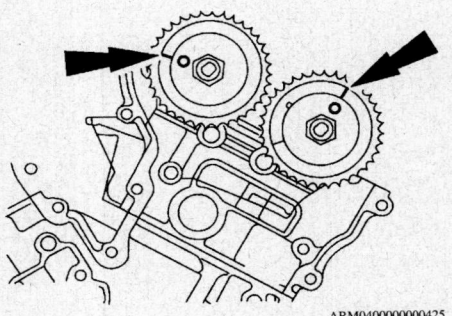

ARM0400000000425

Fig. 41 Lefthand camshafts alignment

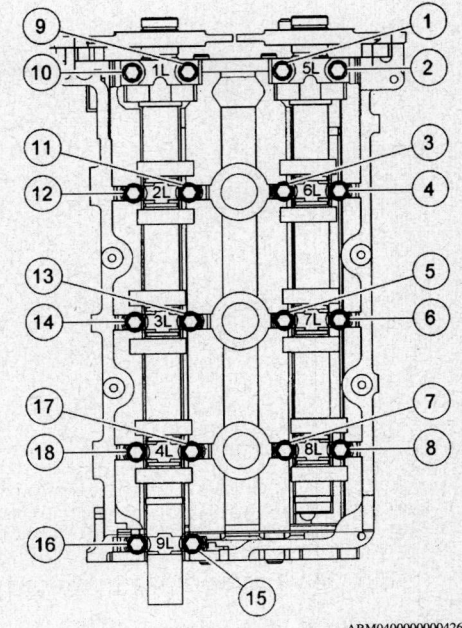

ARM0400000000426

Fig. 42 Lefthand camshafts thrust cap bolt tightening sequence

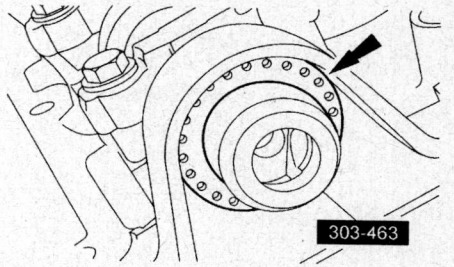

Fig. 43 Camshaft oil seal installation

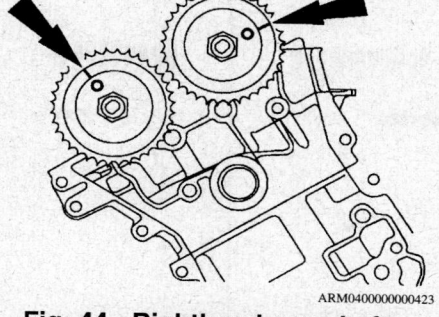

Fig. 44 Righthand camshafts alignment

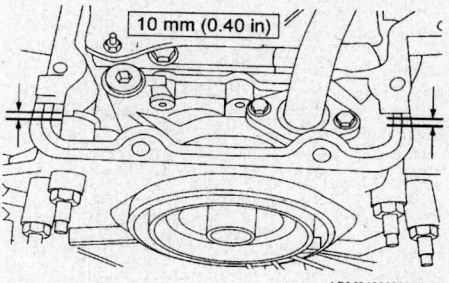

Fig. 45 Silicone gasket & sealer placement

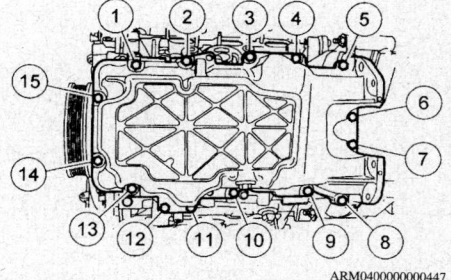

Fig. 46 Oil pan bolt tightening sequence

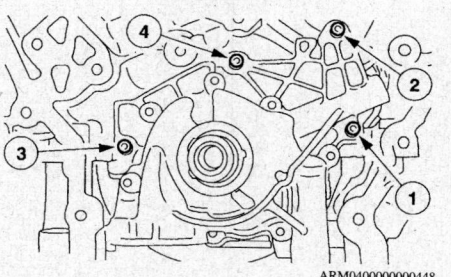

Fig. 47 Oil pump bolt loosening sequence

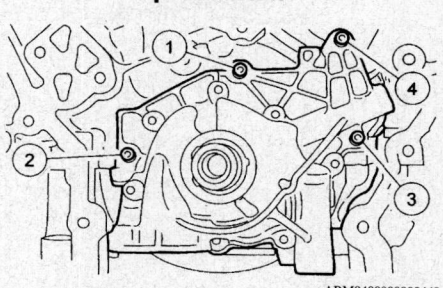

Fig. 48 Oil pump bolt tightening sequence

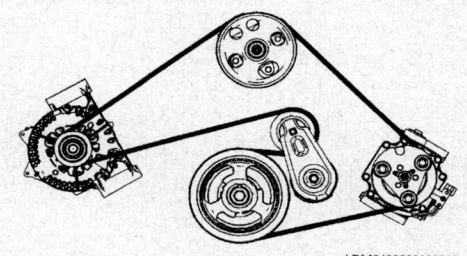

Fig. 49 Serpentine belt routing

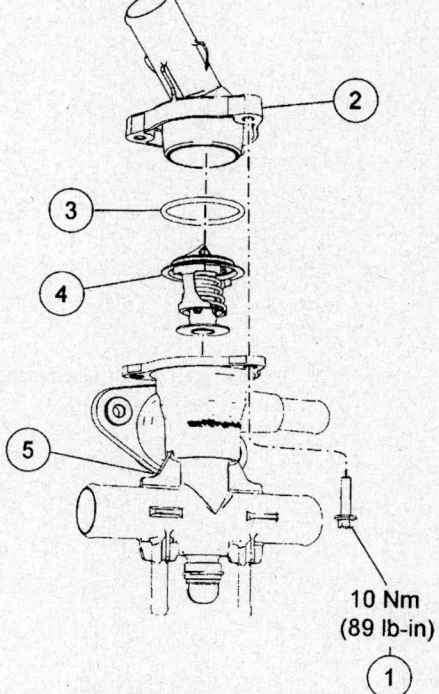

Item	Description
1	Upper-to-lower thermostat housing bolts (3 required)
2	Lower thermostat housing
3	Thermostat O-ring seal
4	Thermostat
5	Upper thermostat housing

Fig. 51 Thermostat replacement

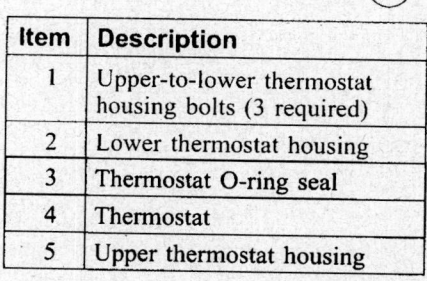

Item	Description
1	Pin-type retainer (7 required)
2	Splash shield
3	Accessory drive belt
4	Accessory drive belt tensioner bolt (part of 6B209)
5	Accessory drive belt tensioner

Fig. 50 Exploded view of serpentine drive belt system

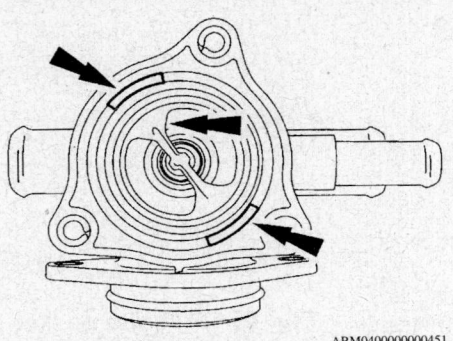

Fig. 52 Thermostat replacement

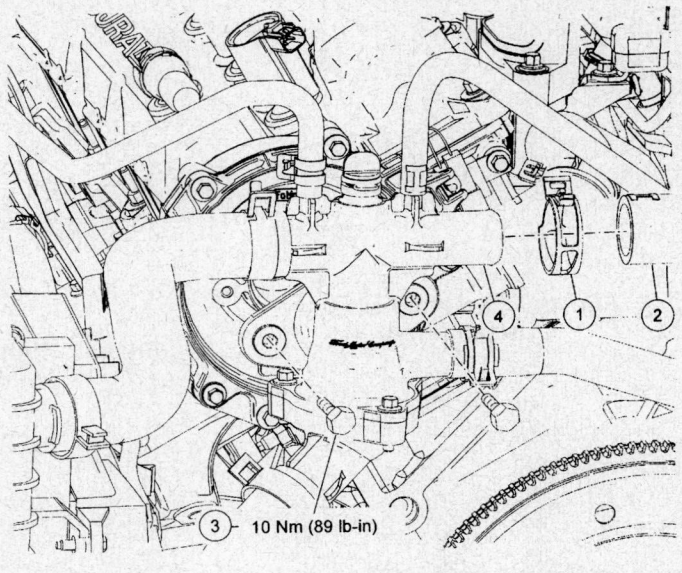

10 Nm (89 lb-in)

Item	Description	Item	Description
1	Thermostat housing-to-bypass tube hose clamp	3	Thermostat housing bolt (2 required)
2	Thermostat housing-to-bypass tube hose	4	Thermostat housing

ARM0400000000452

Fig. 53 Water pump replacement (Part 1 of 2)

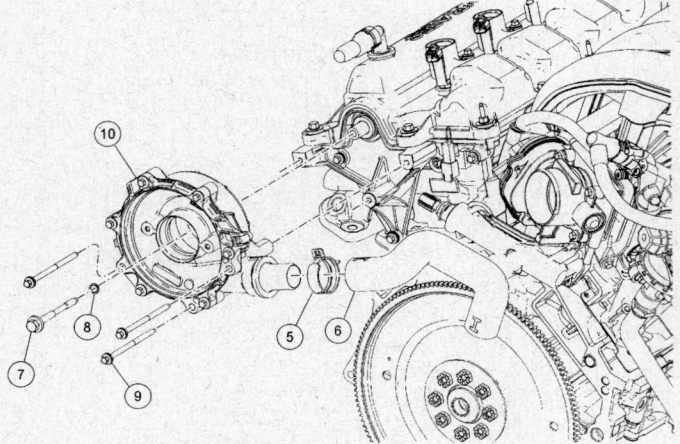

Item	Description
5	Coolant pump hose clamp
6	Coolant pump hose
7	Center coolant pump bolt
8	Center coolant pump bolt sealing washer
9	Outer coolant pump bolts (3 required)
10	Coolant pump

ARM0400000000453

Fig. 53 Water pump replacement (Part 2 of 2)

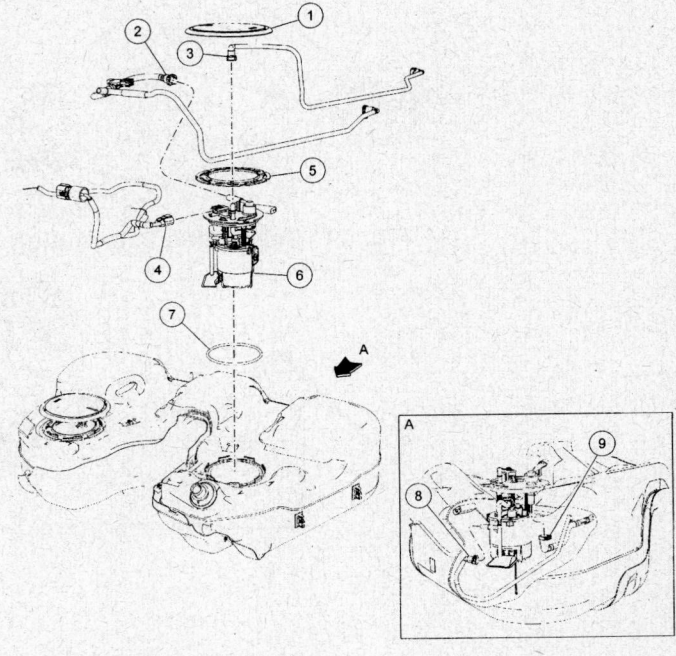

Item	Description	Item	Description
1	Fuel pump module access cover	5	Fuel pump module lock ring
2	Fuel vapor control tube assembly valve quick connect coupling	6	Fuel pump module
3	Fuel supply tube quick release coupling	7	Fuel pump module O-ring seal
4	Fuel pump module electrical connector	8	Fuel transfer supply tube quick connect coupling
		9	Fuel vapor tube quick connect coupling

ARM0400000000456

Fig. 54 Fuel pump replacement

TIGHTENING SPECIFICATIONS

Year	Component	Torque/Ft. Lbs.
2005–08	Accessory Drive Belt Tensioner Bolt	33
	Air Conditioning Compressor	18
	Alternator Mounting	18
	Ball Joint Nuts	59
	Camshaft Cap Bolt	89①
	Camshaft Oil Seal Retainer	89①
	Camshaft Position Sensor	89①
	Crankshaft Position Sensor	89①
	Cylinder Head	②
	EGR Tube	30
	EGR Valve	18
	Engine Mount	52
	Exhaust Manifold	⑤
	Flexplate	59
	Front Cover	⑧
	Fuel Rail	89①
	Halfshaft	191
	Intake Manifold	④
	Knock Sensor	13
	Lefthand Engine Support Insulator, Bolt	52
	Lefthand Engine Support Insulator, Nut	66
	Oil Pan	③
	Oil Pan To Transaxle	30
	Oil Pump	89①
	Oil Separator	89①
	Power Steering Pressure Line	27
	Power Steering Pump Nuts	18
	Righthand Engine Support Insulator, Nut	66
	Righthand Engine Support Insulator, Through Bolt	89
	Shifter Cable	13
	Spark Plugs	11
	Steering Shaft Pinch Bolt	18
	Subframe Bolts	76
	Timing Chain Guide	18
	Timing Chain Tensioner	18
	Torque Converter To Flex Plate	27
	Valve Cover	⑥
	Y-Pipe Nuts	30
	Y-Pipe To Exhaust Manifold	30
	Water Pump	⑦

① — Inch lbs.
② — Refer to "Cylinder Head, Replace" for tightening specifications and sequence.
③ — Refer to "Oil Pan, Replace" for tightening specifications and sequence.
④ — Refer to "Intake Manifold, Replace" for tightening specifications and sequence.
⑤ — Refer to "Exhaust Manifold, Replace" for tightening specifications and sequence.
⑥ — Refer to "Valve Cover, Replace" for tightening specifications and sequence.
⑦ — Refer to "Water Pump, Replace" for tightening specifications and sequence.
⑧ — Refer to "Front Cover, Replace" for tightening specifications and sequence.

3.5L Engine

NOTE: On Air Bag Equipped Models, Refer To "Air Bag System Precautions" Located In The Front Of This Manual For System Disarming & Arming Procedures.

NOTE: Refer To "Computer Relearn Procedures" Located In The Front Of This Manual When Battery Power To The Computer Has Been Interrupted.

INDEX

	Page No.
Camshaft, Replace	7-35
Installation	7-35
Removal	7-35
Camshaft Lobe Lift	
Specifications	7-33
Compression Pressure	7-28
Cooling System Bleed	7-37
Crankshaft Damper, Replace	7-33
Cylinder Head, Replace	7-31
Lefthand	7-31
Righthand	7-32
Engine Rebuilding	
Specifications	21-1
Engine, Replace	7-29
Engine Mount, Replace	7-29
Exhaust Manifold, Replace	7-31
Lefthand	7-31
Righthand	7-31
Front Cover, Replace	7-34

	Page No.
Installation	7-34
Removal	7-34
Front Cover Seal, Replace	7-35
Fuel Pump, Replace	7-38
Intake Manifold, Replace	7-30
Lower	7-31
Upper	7-30
Oil Pan, Replace	7-36
Oil Pump, Replace	7-37
Power Transfer Unit Seal,	
Replace	7-30
Installation	7-30
Removal	7-30
Precautions	7-28
Air Bag Systems	7-28
Battery Ground Cable	7-28
Fuel Pressure Relief	7-28
Quick Disconnect Hoses	7-28
R-Clip	7-28

	Page No.
Spring Lock	7-28
Vapor Tube	7-28
Radiator, Replace	7-38
Serpentine Drive Belt	7-37
Belt Routing	7-37
Belt Tensioner, Replace	7-37
Belts, Replace	7-37
Thermostat, Replace	7-37
Tightening Specifications	7-51
Timing Chain, Replace	7-35
Valve Adjustment	7-33
Valve Clearance Specifications	7-33
Valve Cover, Replace	7-32
Lefthand	7-32
Righthand	7-32
Water Pump, Replace	7-37
Installation	7-38
Removal	7-37

PRECAUTIONS

Air Bag Systems

Refer to "Air Bag System Precautions" in the front of this manual for system disarming and arming procedures.

Battery Ground Cable

Prior to service, disconnect battery ground cable and isolate as required.

Fuel Pressure Relief

1. Remove the fuel pump relay.
2. Start engine, then allow engine to idle until it stalls.
3. After engine stalls, crank engine for approximately 5 seconds to make sure fuel injection supply manifold pressure has been released.
4. When fuel system service is complete, install fuel pump relay.
5. Cycle ignition key and wait 3 seconds to pressurize fuel system. Inspect for leaks before starting engine.

Quick Disconnect Hoses

R-CLIP

When working with R-clip type connections, do not use tools to disconnect. Use of tools may deform clip components and could cause leaks.

DISCONNECT

1. Bend shipping tab downward.
2. Spread R-clip and push clip into fitting.
3. Separate fitting from tube.

CONNECT

1. Inspect fitting and tube for damage and ensure connections are clean.
2. Apply light coat of suitable, clean engine oil to male end of tube.
3. Insert R-clip into fitting.
4. Align tube and fitting, then insert tube into fitting and push together until click is heard.
5. Pull on connection to ensure it is fully engaged.

SPRING LOCK

When working with spring lock type connections, spring lock tool set No. T84L-19623-B, or equivalent, must be used to disconnect fittings.

When connecting spring lock type fittings, proceed as follows:
1. Inspect and clean both coupling ends.
2. Lubricate fuel line O-ring seals with suitable, clean engine oil.
3. When connection is made, pull on line to ensure it is fully engaged.

VAPOR TUBE

To disconnect vapor tube connections, squeeze fitting and disconnect vapor tube from fitting, proceed as follows:
1. Ensure fittings are clean and free from damage.
2. Push tube onto fitting until it snaps into place.
3. Pull on connection to verify fitting is secure.

COMPRESSION PRESSURE

1. Ensure crankcase oil is of correct viscosity and at correct level.
2. Ensure battery is fully charged and engine is at normal operating temperature.
3. Turn ignition switch to OFF position.
4. Remove spark plugs.
5. Set throttle plates to wide open position.
6. Install suitable compression gauge in cylinder No. 1.
7. Install auxiliary starter switch in starting circuit.
8. With ignition switch off, crank engine at least five compression strokes using auxiliary starter switch.
9. Record number of compression strokes required to reach highest reading, then record highest reading.
10. Repeat test on each cylinder, cranking engine same number of compression strokes.
11. Lowest cylinder reading must be within 75% of highest reading.

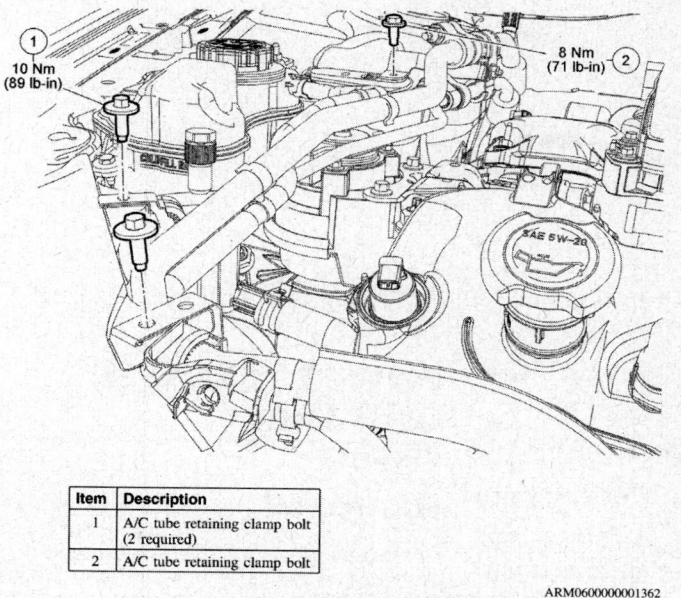

Item	Description
1	A/C tube retaining clamp bolt (2 required)
2	A/C tube retaining clamp bolt

ARM0600000001362

Fig. 1 A/C line bolt locations

ENGINE MOUNT
REPLACE

1. Raise and support vehicle.
2. Drain coolant into a suitable container, then lower vehicle.
3. Disconnect wiring harness retainer from coolant overflow bottle, then the overflow bottle vent hose.
4. Disconnect lower hose from coolant overflow bottle and position aside.
5. Remove coolant overflow bottle.
6. Remove upper intake manifold as outlined under "Intake Manifold, Replace."
7. Install engine lifting bracket tool No. 303–1245 or equivalent to lefthand cylinder head.
8. Install 3 bar engine support tool No. 303–F-072 or equivalent to support engine assembly.
9. Remove 3 A/C line retaining bolts, **Fig. 1.**
10. Disconnect power steering hose from engine mount brace, **Fig. 2.**
11. Disconnect ground wire from engine mount brace, then remove brace and engine mount, **Fig. 2.**
12. Reverse procedure to install.

ENGINE
REPLACE

1. Relieve fuel pressure as outlined under "Precautions."
2. Recover refrigerant as outlined in "Air Conditioning" chapter of this manual.
3. Remove accessory drive belts as outlined under "Serpentine Drive Belt."
4. Remove the underbody splash shield, **Fig. 3.**
5. Disconnect power steering cooler lines and drain fluid into a suitable container.
6. Disconnect wiring harness retainer from coolant overflow bottle, then the overflow bottle vent hose.

7. Disconnect lower hose from coolant overflow bottle and position aside.
8. Remove coolant overflow bottle.
9. Remove air cleaner and outlet tube, then the battery and battery tray.
10. Disconnect 2 main engine wiring harness connectors.
11. Disconnect harness retainers from transmission mount and battery tray bracket.
12. Disconnect power feed from battery terminal.
13. Disconnect ground straps as shown in **Fig. 4.**
14. Disconnect vacuum hoses and EVAP tube from upper intake manifold.
15. Raise and support vehicle.
16. Drain coolant into a suitable container, then lower vehicle.
17. Disconnect upper and lower radiator hoses, then the heater hoses from thermostat housing.
18. Disconnect transaxle control cable from control lever.
19. Remove transaxle control cable bracket and position aside.
20. **On models equipped with engine block heater,** disconnect engine block heater harness from radiator support, power steering hose, A/C tube and engine wiring harness.
21. **On all models,** disconnect coolant tube retainer clips from A/C tube.

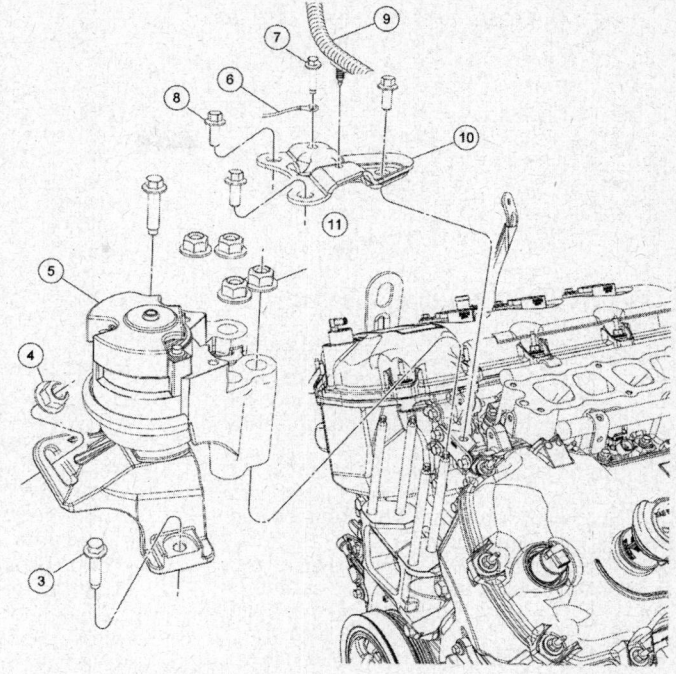

Item	Description
3	Engine mount-to-frame bolt (2 required)
4	Engine mount-to-frame nut
5	Engine mount
6	Ground wire
7	Ground wire bolt
8	Engine mount brace bolt (3 required)
9	Power steering hose retainer
10	Engine mount brace

Item	Description
11	Engine mount-to-engine nut (4 required)

ARM0600000001363

Fig. 2 Engine mount

22. Disconnect A/C tube from condenser. Discard O-ring seals.
23. Remove 2 A/C tube bracket bolts.
24. Disconnect A/C lines from evaporator, then all remaining wiring harness retainers and engine harness connectors.
25. Remove oil level indicator.
26. Disconnect hose from power steering reservoir and drain fluid into a suitable container.
27. Remove power steering reservoir from cowl.
28. Disconnect fuel supply line from fuel rail as outlined under "Precautions."
29. Remove ground strap from engine mount brace, then the brace.
30. Disconnect PCM electrical connectors and pin-type retainers.
31. Remove power steering pressure line bracket bolt.
32. Disconnect power steering pressure hose from steering gear. Power steering pressure hose bolt and seals should not be reused.
33. Ensure front wheels are in straight ahead position and that ignition key is OFF.
34. Remove steering joint cover, then place alignment marks on steering column shaft and steering gear for installation reference.
35. Disconnect steering column shaft from

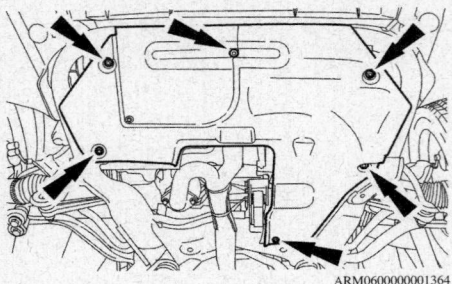

ARM0600000001364

Fig. 3   Underbody splash shield

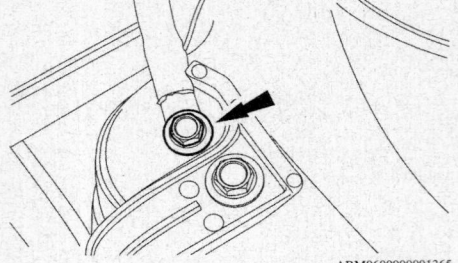

ARM0600000001365

Fig. 4   Ground strap removal (Part 1 of 2)

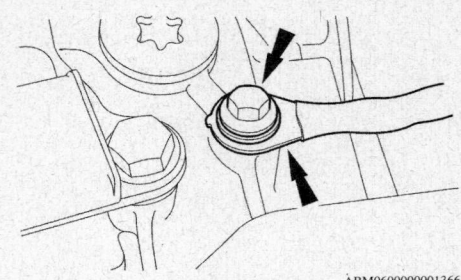

ARM0600000001366

Fig. 4   Ground strap removal (Part 2 of 2)

steering gear. Discard steering column to steering gear bolt. **Ensure that steering column shaft does not rotate or damage to clockspring may occur.**

36. Remove lefthand fender splash shield.
37. Remove steering gear-to-dash seal from steering gear and slide into passenger compartment.
38. Disconnect transaxle cooler hoses and drain fluid into a suitable container.
39. Drain engine oil into a suitable container.
40. Remove and discard engine oil filter.
41. Remove and discard 6 exhaust Y-pipe nuts, then remove Y-pipe.
42. Remove 4 oil pan to transaxle bolts, **Fig. 5.**
43. Remove flywheel inspection cover.
44. Remove and discard 4 torque converter to flywheel nuts.
45. **On models equipped with AWD,** place alignment marks on driveshaft and mounting flange for installation reference.
46. **On models equipped with AWD,** remove 4 driveshaft attaching bolts and support driveshaft with suitable mechanics wire.
47. **On all models,** remove engine roll restrictor to subframe through bolt, **Fig. 6.**
48. Remove cotter pins and attaching nuts from tie rod ends, then separate from steering knuckles using tie rod end remover tool No. 211–105 or equivalent.
49. Detach stabilizer bar links from struts, then remove 4 lower ball joint nuts.
50. Place a suitable block of wood between lower arm and outer CV joint to prevent lower arm from contacting outer CV joint.
51. Separate right and left lower ball joints from control arms using ball joint separator tool No. 205–592 or equivalent.
52. Support subframe assembly using powertrain lift tool No. 014–00765 or equivalent.
53. Remove subframe to body brackets.
54. Lower subframe assembly from vehicle enough to access halfshafts.
55. Separate lefthand halfshaft from transaxle using slide hammer tool No. 100–001, halfshaft remover tool Nos. 205–243 and 205–832 or equivalents. Support halfshaft using suitable mechanics wire.
56. Remove 2 righthand catalytic converter bracket bolts.
57. **On models equipped with FWD,** remove righthand catalytic converter

bracket, then the halfshaft carrier bearing. Support halfshaft using suitable mechanics wire.

58. **On models equipped with AWD,** proceed as follows:
    a. Remove righthand halfshaft carrier bearing bolts.
    b. Separate halfshaft from transaxle and support using suitable mechanics wire.
    c. Disconnect righthand catalyst monitor sensor.
    d. Remove righthand catalytic converter, then the power transfer unit bracket.
    e. Remove power transfer unit, **Fig. 7.**
59. **On all models,** position a suitable block of wood beneath transaxle.
60. Install engine lifting bracket set tool No. D94L-6001-A or equivalent to powertrain lift, **Fig. 8.**
61. Remove transaxle mount, then the engine mount.
62. Lower engine and transaxle assembly from vehicle.
63. Disconnect wiring harness fasteners from transaxle to engine stud bolt and starter.
64. Disconnect ground wire, **Fig. 9.**
65. Disconnect transmission control module, then remove starter.
66. Install engine lift bracket tool No. 303–1245 or equivalent to cylinder head.
67. Remove engine from powertrain lift table using a suitable floor crane.
68. Suitably support engine and transaxle assembly.
69. Remove engine to transaxle attaching bolts and separate engine from transaxle if necessary.
70. Reverse procedure to install noting the following:
    a. Replace power transfer unit seal as outlined under "Power Transfer Unit Seal, Replace."
    b. Inspect halfshaft sealing surface for wear or damage. Replace as necessary.
    c. Ensure that new torque converter nuts are used.
    d. Ensure that new A/C O-ring seals are installed where A/C lines were disconnected.
    e. Ensure that all fluids are refilled to capacity and specifications.
    f. Bleed cooling system as outlined under "Cooling System Bleed."

POWER TRANSFER UNIT SEAL
REPLACE
Removal

The seal deflector will be damaged during removal. Ensure that the seal directly behind the deflector is not damaged when removing the deflector.

1. Remove seal deflector, **Fig. 10.**
2. Remove intermediate shaft seal using a suitable slide hammer and bearing cup puller tool No. 308–047 or equivalents.
3. Remove cover seal if necessary.

Installation

Ensure that heat deflector is not overheated during installation. If damage occurs, a new seal deflector must be used.

1. Heat seal deflector using a suitable heat gun. Direct heat across the back of seal deflector near white tabs.
2. Install seal deflector immediately after heating using seal installer tool Nos. 308–430 and 308–431 or equivalents.
3. Ensure seal deflector is fully seated and that there are no cracks on face or inner diameter white tab.
4. If cover seal was removed, install a new one using seal installer tool Nos. 308–430 and 308–431 or equivalents.
5. Install a new intermediate shaft seal using bearing cup installer tool No. 204–038 and handle tool No. 205–153 or equivalents.

INTAKE MANIFOLD
REPLACE
Upper

1. Remove air cleaner outlet tube.
2. Disconnect throttle body electrical connector.
3. Disconnect EVAP tube from intake manifold as outlined under "Precautions."
4. Disconnect brake booster vacuum hose from intake manifold, then the PCV valve tube and electrical connector.
5. Detach wiring harness retainers from upper intake manifold.
6. **On models equipped with engine**

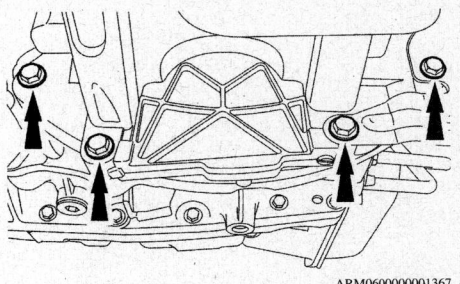

ARM0600000001367

Fig. 5 Oil pan to transaxle bolt locations

block heater, detach wiring harness retainer from upper intake manifold.

7. **On all models,** disconnect 2 support brackets from upper intake manifold, **Fig. 11.**
8. Remove six upper intake manifold attaching bolts, then the manifold.
9. Reverse procedure to install. Tighten manifold to specifications in sequence as shown in **Fig. 12.**

Lower

1. Raise and support vehicle.
2. Drain coolant into a suitable container, then lower vehicle.
3. Relieve fuel pressure as outlined under "Precautions."
4. Remove upper intake manifold as outlined under "Intake Manifold Replace," "Upper."
5. Disconnect fuel line from fuel rail as outlined under "Precautions."
6. Disconnect fuel injector electrical connectors.
7. Remove fuel rail attaching bolts.
8. Remove fuel injectors together with fuel rail.
9. Remove two thermostat housing to lower intake bolts, **Fig. 13.**
10. Remove ten lower intake manifold attaching bolts, then the lower intake manifold.
11. Reverse procedure to install noting the following:
    a. Tighten manifold to specifications in sequence as shown in **Fig. 14.**
    b. Install new fuel injector O-rings and lubricate with suitable clean engine oil.
    c. Fill all fluids to proper capacity and specifications.
    d. Bleed cooling system as outlined under "Cooling System Bleed."

EXHAUST MANIFOLD
REPLACE
Lefthand

1. Raise and support vehicle.
2. Disconnect catalyst monitor sensor.
3. Remove underbody splash shield.
4. Remove and discard two Y-pipe to resonator nuts, then the four Y-pipe to catalytic converter nuts.
5. Remove catalytic converter as follows:
    a. Remove two catalytic converter

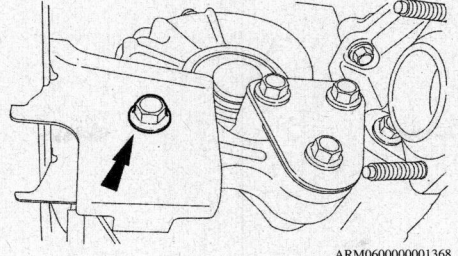

ARM0600000001368

Fig. 6 Roll restrictor removal

   support bracket to transmission bolts.
    b. Remove and discard four catalytic converter nuts and gasket.
6. Remove and discard four catalytic converter to exhaust manifold studs.
7. Disconnect HO2S sensor and remove using HO2S sensor socket tool No. 303–476 or equivalent.
8. Remove exhaust manifold heat shield.
9. Remove and discard six exhaust manifold attaching nuts.
10. Remove exhaust manifold and discard gasket.
11. Remove and discard six exhaust manifold studs.
12. Reverse procedure to install noting the following:
    a. Clean exhaust manifold mating surface of cylinder head using a suitable metal surface prep.
    b. Inspect exhaust manifold gasket surface using a suitable straight edge and feeler gauge. Warpage limit is .030.
    c. Tighten manifold to specifications in sequence as shown in **Fig. 15.**
    d. Apply a thin coating of suitable anti-seize lubricant to HO2S threads before installation.

Righthand

1. Raise and support vehicle.
2. Disconnect catalyst monitor sensor.
3. Remove underbody splash shield.
4. Remove and discard two Y-pipe to resonator nuts, then the four Y-pipe to catalytic converter nuts.
5. Remove power steering gear heat shield.
6. Remove catalytic converter as follows:
    a. Remove roll restrictor bolt and rotate engine forward.
    b. Disconnect catalyst monitor sensor.
    c. Remove two catalytic converter support bracket to engine block nuts.
    d. Remove and discard four catalytic converter nuts and gasket.
7. Remove and discard four catalytic converter to exhaust manifold studs.
8. Disconnect righthand HO2S sensor.
9. Remove and discard six exhaust manifold attaching nuts.
10. Remove exhaust manifold.
11. Remove and discard six exhaust manifold studs.
12. Reverse procedure to install noting the following:
    a. Clean exhaust manifold mating sur-

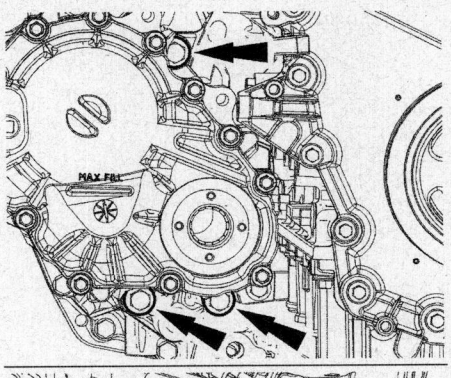

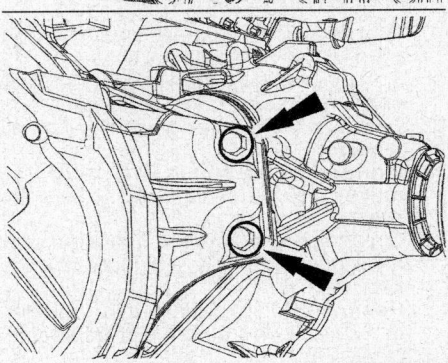

ARM0600000001369

Fig. 7 Power transfer unit removal

face of cylinder head using a suitable metal surface prep.
    b. Inspect exhaust manifold gasket surface using a suitable straight edge and feeler gauge. Warpage limit is .030.
    c. Tighten manifold to specifications in sequence as shown in **Fig. 16.**
    d. Apply a thin coating of suitable anti-seize lubricant to HO2S threads before installation.

CYLINDER HEAD
REPLACE
Lefthand

1. Remove camshafts as outlined under "Camshaft, Replace."
2. **On models equipped with engine block heater,** proceed as follows:
    a. Remove engine block heather heat shield.
    b. Disconnect engine block heater and remove harness from engine.
3. **On all models,** disconnect A/C compressor electrical connector.
4. Disconnect alternator electrical connectors.
5. Detach wiring harness from alternator.
6. Remove alternator, then disconnect oil pressure sensor and harness.
7. Disconnect fuel injector electrical connectors, then the cylinder head temperature sensor.
8. Remove radio interference capacitor and position aside.
9. Disconnect CMP sensor, then the lefthand HO2S sensor and catalyst monitor sensor.

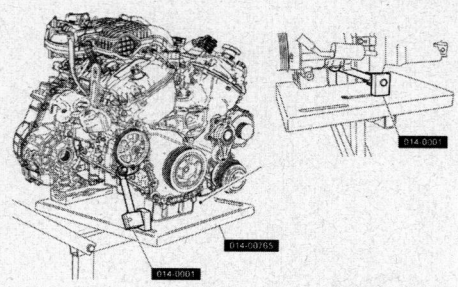

Fig. 8   Engine support bracket installation

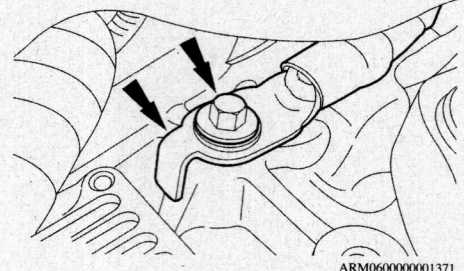

Fig. 9   Ground wire location

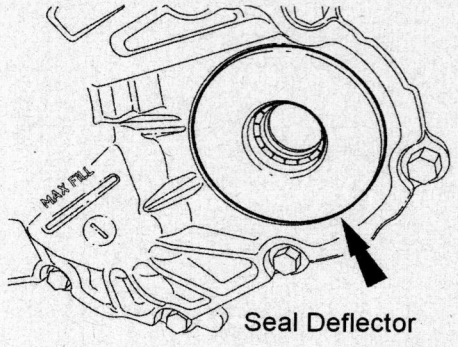

Seal Deflector

ARM0600000001372

Fig. 10   Power transfer unit seal deflector

10. Remove wiring harness retaining bolt from rear of cylinder head.
11. Remove exhaust manifold as outlined under "Exhaust Manifold, Replace."
12. Remove lefthand engine block drain plug, **Fig. 17.**
13. **On models equipped with AWD,** remove righthand catalytic converter bracket bolts.
14. **On all models,** remove righthand catalytic converter. Discard nuts and gasket.
15. Remove coolant drain plug or cylinder block heater from right side of engine block, **Fig. 18.**
16. Remove lower intake manifold as outlined under "Intake Manifold, Replace."
17. Remove lefthand CMP sensor, then the valve tappets from cylinder head. If valve tappets are to be reused, ensure that components are marked for installation reference.
18. Remove secondary timing chain tensioner.
19. Remove and discard "M6" bolt, **Fig. 19.**
20. Remove and discard 8 cylinder head bolts.
21. Remove cylinder head and gasket.
22. Reverse procedure to install noting the following:
    a. Install new gasket, cylinder head and 8 new bolts.
    b. Tighten in five stages using sequence shown in **Fig. 20,** as follows: step 1, 15 ft. lbs.; step 2, 26 ft. lbs.; step 3, tighten an additional 90°; step 4, tighten an additional 90°; step 5, tighten an additional 90°.
    c. Install "M6" cylinder head bolt and **torque** to 89 inch lbs., **Fig. 19.**
    d. Apply suitable clean engine oil to tappets prior to installation.

Righthand

1. Remove camshafts as outlined under "Camshaft, Replace."
2. **On models equipped with engine block heater,** proceed as follows:
    a. Remove engine block heather heat shield.
    b. Disconnect engine block heater and remove harness from engine.
3. **On all models,** remove radio interference capacitor and position aside.

4. Disconnect CMP sensor, then the righthand HO2S sensor and catalyst monitor sensor.
5. Remove power steering tube and bracket and position aside.
6. Disconnect fuel injector electrical connectors, then the cylinder head temperature sensor.
7. Remove lefthand catalytic converter bracket bolts.
8. Remove and discard lefthand catalytic converter nuts and gasket.
9. Remove lefthand catalytic converter.
10. Remove lefthand engine block drain plug and drain coolant into a suitable container, **Fig. 17.**
11. Remove righthand exhaust manifold as outlined under "Exhaust Manifold, Replace."
12. Remove coolant drain plug or cylinder block heater from right side of engine block and drain coolant into a suitable container, **Fig. 18.**
13. Remove lower intake manifold as outlined under "Intake Manifold, Replace."
14. Remove secondary timing chain tensioner.
15. Remove engine lift bracket and upper intake manifold bracket from cylinder head.
16. Remove lefthand CMP sensor, then the valve tappets from cylinder head. If valve tappets are to be reused, ensure that components are marked for installation reference.
17. Remove cylinder head temperature sensor jumper harness.
18. Remove and discard "M6" bolt, **Fig. 21.**
19. Remove and discard 8 cylinder head bolts.
20. Remove cylinder head and gasket.
21. Reverse procedure to install noting the following:
    a. Install new gasket, cylinder head and 8 new bolts.
    b. Tighten in five stages using sequence shown in **Fig. 22,** as follows: step 1, 15 ft. lbs.; step 2, 26 ft. lbs.; step 3, tighten an additional 90°; step 4, tighten an additional 90°; step 5, tighten an additional 90°.
    c. Install "M6" cylinder head bolt and **torque** to 89 inch lbs., **Fig. 21.**
    d. Apply suitable clean engine oil to tappets prior to installation.

VALVE COVER
REPLACE
Lefthand

1. Remove air cleaner outlet tube.
2. Disconnect crankcase vent tube from valve cover. Refer to "Precautions" for quick connect fitting procedures.
3. Disconnect coil on plug electrical connectors.
4. Remove ignition coils from spark plugs.
5. Remove dipstick, then disconnect lefthand variable cam timing solenoid.
6. Detach wiring harness retainers from hold down positions.
7. Disconnect two main engine control harness connectors, **Fig. 23.**
8. Remove wiring harness retaining bracket.
9. Detach wiring harness retainers from valve cover studs.
10. Disconnect fuel injector electrical connectors.
11. Remove valve cover attaching bolts, then the valve cover.
12. Inspect spark plug and variable cam timing solenoid seals in valve cover. If any are damaged, proceed as follows:
    a. Remove damaged seals using seal removal tool No. 303–1247/1 and handle tool No. 205–153 or equivalents.
    b. Install new seal using seal installer tool No. 303–1247/2 and handle tool No. 205–153 or equivalents.
13. Reverse procedure to install noting the following:
    a. Apply a .310 inch bead of suitable silicone gasket and sealant on engine front cover to cylinder head joints.
    b. Ensure that valve cover is installed and tightened to specifications within 5 minutes of silicone gasket application.
    c. Tighten valve cover to specifications in sequence as shown in **Fig. 24.**

Righthand

1. Remove upper intake manifold as outlined under "Intake Manifold, Replace."

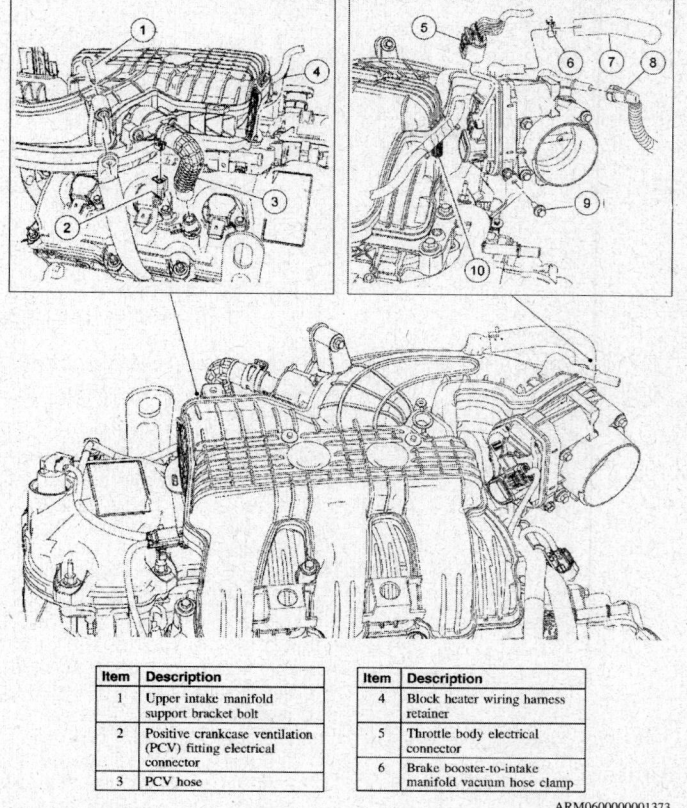

Item	Description
1	Upper intake manifold support bracket bolt
2	Positive crankcase ventilation (PCV) fitting electrical connector
3	PCV hose

Item	Description
4	Block heater wiring harness retainer
5	Throttle body electrical connector
6	Brake booster-to-intake manifold vacuum hose clamp

ARM0600000001373

Fig. 11 Upper intake manifold support brackets

2. Disconnect coil on plug electrical connectors.
3. Remove ignition coils from spark plugs.
4. Siphon fluid from power steering reservoir using a suitable suction device.
5. Disconnect return hose from power steering fluid reservoir.
6. Remove power steering fluid reservoir from bracket by using a suitable screwdriver to depress and release retaining clip.
7. Disconnect power steering pressure switch, then the righthand catalyst monitor sensor.
8. Remove power steering pressure hose bracket from valve cover and position aside.
9. Disconnect righthand HO2S sensor, then the variable cam timing solenoid.
10. Disconnect fuel injectors, then the heated PCV valve electrical connector.
11. Detach wiring harness retainers from valve cover studs.
12. Remove A/C tube clamps and position aside.
13. Remove valve cover attaching bolts, then the valve cover.
14. Inspect spark plug and variable cam timing solenoid seals in valve cover. If any are damaged, proceed as follows:
   a. Remove damaged seals using seal removal tool No. 303–1247/1 and handle tool No. 205–153 or equivalents.
   b. Install new seal using seal installer tool No. 303–1247/2 and handle tool No. 205–153 or equivalents.

15. Reverse procedure to install noting the following:
   a. Apply a .310 inch bead of suitable silicone gasket and sealant on engine front cover to cylinder head joints.
   b. Ensure that valve cover is installed and tightened to specifications within 5 minutes of silicone gasket application.
   c. Tighten valve cover to specifications in sequence as shown in **Fig. 25**.

CAMSHAFT LOBE LIFT SPECIFICATIONS

Lobe Lift, Inch	
Intake	Exhaust
.380	.380

VALVE CLEARANCE SPECIFICATIONS

Valve	Clearance, Inch
Exhaust	.012–.016
Intake	.006–.010

VALVE ADJUSTMENT

1. Remove valve covers as outlined under "Valve Cover, Replace."
2. Rotate crankshaft until base circle of camshaft lobe is resting on valve tappet, **Fig. 26**.

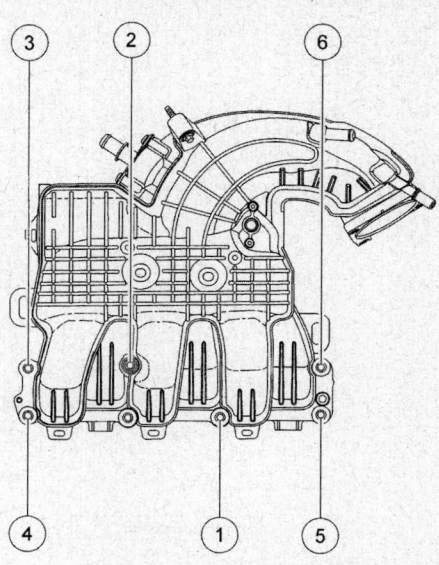

ARM0600000001374

Fig. 12 Upper intake manifold tightening sequence

3. Using a suitable feeler gauge, inspect clearance between base circle of camshaft lobe and valve tappet. For intake valves, clearance should be .006–.010 inch. For exhaust valves, clearance should be .012–.016 inch.
4. Repeat procedure for remaining valves and record results.
5. If clearance is not within specifications, install new valve tappets where necessary.
6. To calculate required thickness of new tappet, proceed as follows:
   a. Inspect valve tappet for a number. For example, a valve tappet with a number of 3.51 has a thickness of 3.51 millimeters or .138 inch.
   b. For tappets where clearance is not within specifications, select a new tappet using the following formula: "Tappet Thickness = Measured Clearance + Base Tappet Thickness – Most Desirable Thickness."
   c. Select tappets and mark installation location.
7. If new tappet installation is necessary, remove camshafts as outlined under "Camshaft, Replace."
8. Remove valve tappets to be replaced.
9. Apply suitable clean engine oil to new tappets and install to cylinder head.
10. Install camshafts as outlined under "Camshaft replace."
11. Recheck valve clearance and ensure all are within specifications.
12. Install valve covers as outlined under "Valve Cover, Replace."

CRANKSHAFT DAMPER
REPLACE

1. Raise and support vehicle.
2. Remove accessory drive belt as outlined under "Serpentine Drive Belt."
3. Hold crankshaft damper using strap

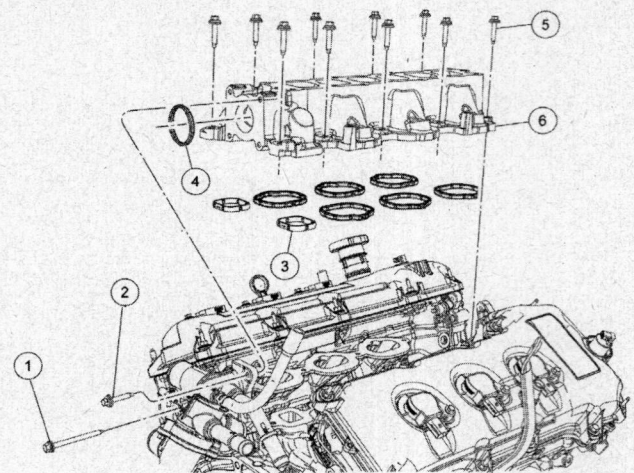

Item	Description
1	Thermostat housing-to-lower intake manifold bolt
2	Thermostat housing-to-lower intake manifold bolt
3	Lower intake manifold gasket (8 required)
4	Thermostat housing gasket
5	Lower intake manifold bolt (10 required)
6	Lower intake manifold

ARM0600000001375

Fig. 13 Lower intake manifold removal

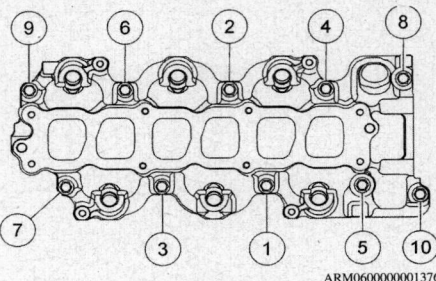

ARM0600000001376

Fig. 14 Lower intake manifold tightening sequence

wrench tool No. 303–D055 or equivalent, then remove and discard crankshaft pulley bolt.

4. Remove crankshaft pulley using puller tool No. 303–D121 or equivalent, **Fig. 27.**

5. Reverse procedure to install noting the following:
   a. Lubricate crankshaft seal inner lip and outside diameter sealing surfaces using suitable engine oil.
   b. Install crankshaft pulley using threaded installer tool No. 303–102 and seal installer tool No. 303–335 or equivalents.
   c. Hold crankshaft pulley using strap wrench tool No. 303–D055 or equivalent, then tighten new pulley bolt in 4 stages as follows: Step 1, 89 ft. lbs.; step 2, loosen bolt 360°; step 3, 37 ft. lbs.; step 4, tighten an additional 90°.

FRONT COVER
REPLACE
Removal

1. Remove engine assembly as outlined under "Engine, Replace."

2. **On models equipped with engine block heater,** detach block heater wiring harness from upper intake manifold, power steering pressure hose and power steering reservoir hose.

3. **On all models,** disconnect PCV valve electrical connector.

4. Disconnect PCV hose from PCV valve.

5. Disconnect throttle body electrical connector.

6. Detach all wiring harness retainers from upper intake manifold.

7. Remove upper intake manifold as outlined under "Intake Manifold, Replace."

8. Remove right and left valve covers as outlined under "Valve Cover, Replace."

9. Remove power steering pump and position aside.

10. Remove three belt tensioner bolts, then the tensioner.

11. Attach strap wrench tool No. 303–D055 or equivalent to crankshaft pulley

12. Hold crankshaft pulley using strap wrench tool No. 303–D055 or equivalent, then remove and discard crankshaft pulley bolt.

13. Remove crankshaft pulley using puller tool No. 303–D121 or equivalent, **Fig. 27.**

14. Remove and discard crankshaft front seal using oil seal removal tool No. 303–409 or equivalent.

15. Remove two engine mount studs shown in **Fig. 28.**

16. Remove engine mount bracket.

17. Remove 22 front cover bolts, **Fig. 29.**

18. Install bolts into four threaded holes in front cover, **Fig. 30.**

19. Tighten bolts one turn at a time using a crisscross pattern until the front cover to cylinder block seal is released, then remove front cover.

Installation

A suitable gasket and oil removing agent

must be used to ensure that all oil, gasket and foreign debris is removed from gasket surfaces.

Ensure that bolts 7, 8, 17, 18, 21, 22, 23, 24 and 25 are installed and tightened within 10 minutes of applying silicone gasket sealer to the front cover. If more than 10 minutes elapses, sealant must be removed and reapplied.

Ensure that the remainder of the front cover bolts (1, 2, 3, 4, 5, 6, 9, 10, 11, 12, 13, 14, 15, 16, 19, and 20) are installed and tightened to specifications within 60 minutes of initial sealant application. If more than 60 minutes elapses, sealant must be removed and reapplied.

1. Apply a .110 inch bead of suitable silicone gasket and sealant to front cover sealing surfaces, including the three engine mount bracket bosses, **Fig. 31.**

2. Apply a .210 inch bead of suitable silicone gasket and sealant on oil pan to engine block joints.

3. Install front cover and bolts 7, 8, 17, 18, 21 and 22, **Fig. 32. Torque** to 89 inch lbs.

4. Install engine mount bracket and three bolts. **Torque** in sequence shown in **Fig. 33,** to 11 ft. lbs.

5. **Torque** bolts 7, 8, 17, 18, 21 and 22 to 18 ft. lbs., **Fig. 34.**

6. **Torque** bolts 23, 24 and 25 to 55 ft. lbs., **Fig. 34.**

7. Install bolts 1, 2, 3, 4, 5, 6, 9, 10, 11, 12, 13, 14, 15, 16, 19, and 20 and tighten in sequence, **Fig. 35,** as follows:
   a. Step 1, 89 inch lbs.
   b. Step 2, 18 ft. lbs.

8. Install 2 engine mount studs.

9. Apply suitable clean engine oil to crankshaft seal bore in front cover.

10. Install crankshaft front cover seal using seal installer tool No. 303–1251 and threaded installer tool No. 303–102 or equivalents.

11. Apply suitable clean engine oil to sealing surfaces of crankshaft pulley.

12. Install crankshaft pulley using threaded installer tool No. 303–102 and seal installer tool No. 303–335 or equivalents.

13. Hold crankshaft pulley using strap wrench tool No. 303–D055 or equivalent, then tighten new pulley bolt in 4 stages as follows:
   a. Step 1, 89 ft. lbs.
   b. Step 2, loosen bolt 360°.
   c. Step 3, 37 ft. lbs.
   d. Step 4, tighten an additional 90°.

14. Install valve covers as outlined under

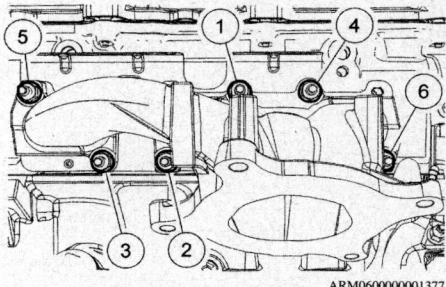

Fig. 15 Lefthand exhaust manifold tightening sequence

ARM0600000001377

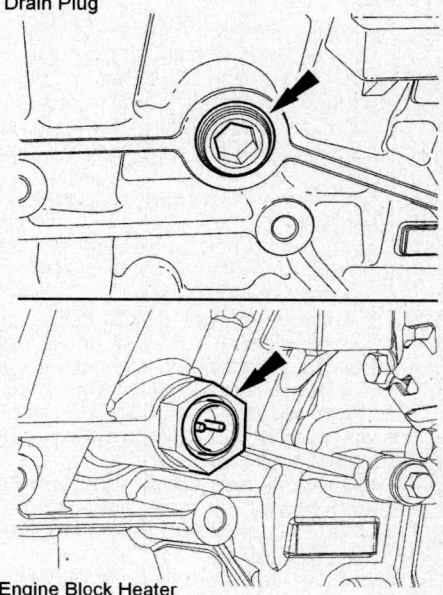

Drain Plug

Engine Block Heater

ARM0600000001409

Fig. 18 Righthand engine block drain plug & block heater

"Valve Cover, Replace."
15. Install upper intake manifold as outlined under "Intake Manifold, Replace."
16. Attach all wiring harness retainers from upper intake manifold.
17. Reconnect throttle body electrical connector.
18. Connect PCV hose from PCV valve.
19. **On models equipped with engine block heater,** attach block heater wiring harness from upper intake manifold, power steering pressure hose and power steering reservoir hose.
20. **On all models,** connect PCV valve electrical connector.
21. Install engine assembly as outlined under "Engine, Replace."

FRONT COVER SEAL
REPLACE
1. Remove crankshaft damper as outlined under "Crankshaft Damper, Replace."
2. Remove front cover seal using oil seal removal tool No. 303–409 or equivalent.

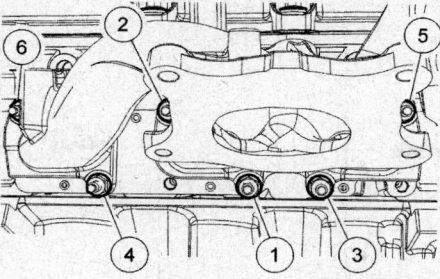

Fig. 16 Righthand exhaust manifold tightening sequence

ARM0600000001378

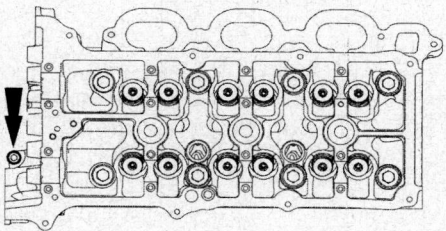

Fig. 19 Cylinder head M6 bolt location

ARM0600000001410

3. Reverse procedure to install. Apply suitable clean engine oil to new seal and install using seal installer tool No. 303–1251 or equivalent.

TIMING CHAIN
REPLACE
Refer to "Camshaft, Replace" for procedure.

CAMSHAFT
REPLACE
Removal
1. Remove front cover as outlined under "Front Cover, Replace."
2. Rotate crankshaft clockwise and align timing marks on variable cam timing assemblies as shown in **Fig. 36.**
3. Install camshaft alignment tool No. 303–1248 or equivalent to flats of camshafts, **Fig. 37.**
4. Remove variable cam timing housing from each cylinder head, **Fig. 38.**
5. Remove and discard variable cam timing housing seals.
6. Remove primary timing chain tensioner and tensioner arm, **Fig. 39.**
7. Remove lefthand lower primary timing chain guide, then the primary timing chain, **Fig. 39.**
8. Compress secondary timing chain tensioner, then install a suitable lockpin to retain tensioner in collapsed position, **Figs. 40 and 41.**
9. Remove and discard variable cam timing and exhaust camshaft sprocket bolts.
10. Remove variable cam timing sprocket, secondary timing chain and exhaust camshaft sprocket as an assembly.
11. Remove camshaft alignment tool from

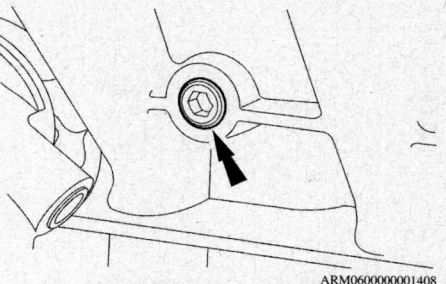

Fig. 17 Lefthand engine block drain plug

ARM0600000001408

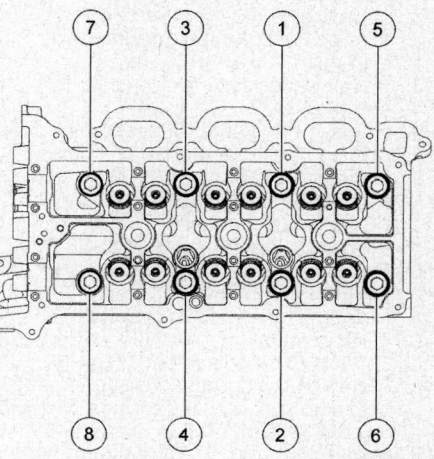

Fig. 20 Lefthand cylinder head tightening sequence

ARM0600000001411

camshafts. When alignment tool is removed, valve spring pressure will rotate camshafts approximately 3° to a neutral position.
12. Verify that camshafts are in neutral position, **Figs. 42 and 43.**
13. Remove camshaft bearing caps, then the camshafts. Note position of caps for installation reference. Caps should already be marked to verify correct installation.

Installation
Crankshaft must remain in 9 O'clock position until after camshafts are installed and valve clearance is inspected, Fig. 44. Failure to do this will result in severe engine damage.
1. Apply suitable clean engine oil to valve tappets and camshafts.
2. Position camshafts onto each cylinder head ensuring that each is in the neutral position as shown in **Figs. 42 and 43.**
3. Install camshaft bearing caps and tighten to specifications in sequence shown in **Figs. 45 and 46.**
4. Inspect valve clearance as outlined under "Valve Adjustment."
5. Install a camshaft sprocket bolt to each camshaft and finger tighten.
6. Rotate camshafts to TDC position using cam sprocket bolt, then install camshaft alignment tool No. 303–1248 or equivalent.

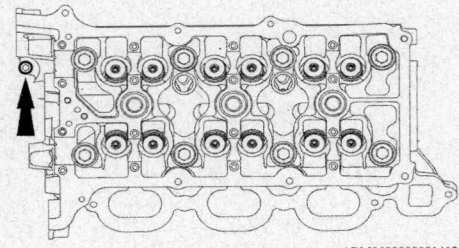

Fig. 21 Righthand cylinder head M6 bolt location

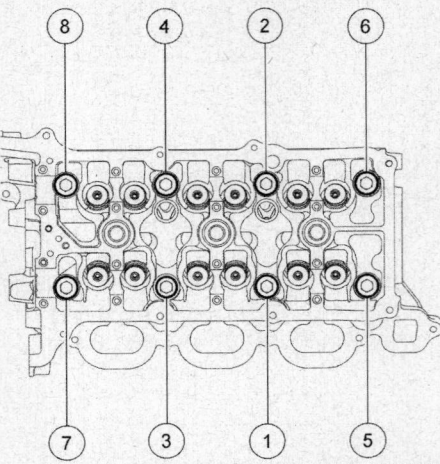

Fig. 22 Righthand cylinder head tightening sequence

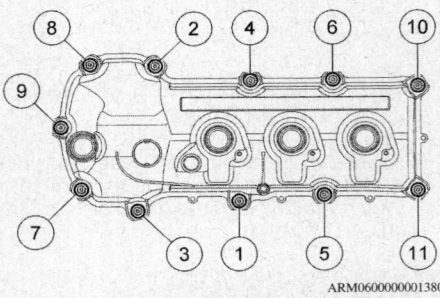

Fig. 24 Lefthand valve cover tightening sequence

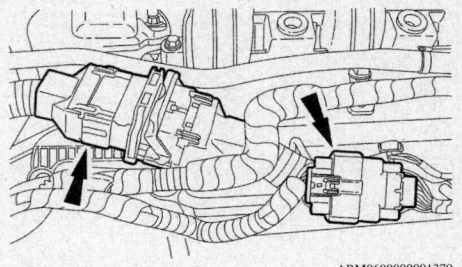

Fig. 23 Engine control main harness connectors

7. Assemble variable camshaft timing assembly ensuring that colored links are aligned with timing marks, **Figs. 47 and 48.**
8. Install secondary timing assembly to camshafts.
9. Install new camshaft sprocket bolts and tighten in sequence as follows:
   a. Step 1, 30 ft. lbs.
   b. Step 2, loosen 360°.
   c. Step 3, 89 inch lbs.
   d. Step 4, tighten an additional 90°.
10. Remove lockpin from secondary timing chain tensioner.
11. Rotate crankshaft clockwise 60° to TDC position. Crankshaft key should be at 11 O'clock position, **Fig. 49.**
12. Install primary timing chain ensuring that colored links are aligned with timing marks, **Fig. 50.**
13. Install lefthand primary timing chain guide, then the primary timing chain tensioner arm, **Fig. 39.**
14. Reset primary timing chain tensioner as follows:
   a. Rotate actuating lever counterclockwise, **Fig. 51.**
   b. Compress tensioner plunger using a suitable soft jawed vise.
   c. Align actuating lever with hole in tensioner housing and install a suitable lockpin.
15. Install primary timing chain tensioner and remove lockpin.
16. Ensure that timing marks are still aligned as shown in **Fig. 50.**
17. Install new variable cam timing control housing seals.
18. Install variable cam timing control housings and tighten in sequence, **Figs. 52 and 53. Ensure that dowels of variable cam timing control assembly housing are fully engaged into cylinder head before tightening.**
19. Install front cover as outlined under "Front Cover, Replace."

OIL PAN
REPLACE

The oil pan must be installed and aligned to cylinder block and A/C compressor within 5 minutes of sealant application. Final tightening of oil pan bolts must be carried out within 60 minutes of sealant application.
1. Remove engine as outlined under "Engine, Replace."
2. Remove flywheel, then the crankshaft sensor ring.

3. Mount engine to a suitable engine stand.
4. **On models equipped with engine block heater,** proceed as follows:
   a. Disconnect engine block heater harness retainer from upper intake manifold.
   b. Remove heat shield and disconnect harness connector from engine block heater.
5. **On all models,** disconnect PCV electrical connector, then the PCV hose from PCV valve.
6. Disconnect throttle body electrical connector.
7. Detach all wiring harness retainers from upper intake manifold.
8. Remove upper intake manifold support bracket bolts.
9. Remove six bolts, then the upper intake manifold.
10. Disconnect power steering pressure switch.
11. **On models equipped with FWD,** disconnect righthand catalyst monitor sensor.
12. **On all models,** disconnect right and left variable camshaft timing solenoids.
13. Disconnect coil on plug electrical connectors, then the lefthand catalyst monitor sensor.
14. Disconnect wire harness retainers from right and left valve covers.

15. Remove A/C compressor nut and stud, **Fig. 54.**
16. Remove accessory drive belt and power steering pump belt as outlined under "Serpentine Drive Belt."
17. Remove power steering hose retainer from engine lifting eye.
18. Remove power steering hose bracket nut.
19. Remove power steering pump and position aside.
20. Remove drive belt tensioner, then the lefthand catalytic converter. Discard converter nuts and gasket.
21. **On models equipped with FWD,** remove righthand catalytic converter. Discard converter nuts and gasket.
22. **On models less engine block heater,** remove righthand engine block drain plug and drain coolant into a suitable container, **Fig. 18.**
23. **On models equipped with engine block heater,** remove block heater and drain coolant into a suitable container, **Fig. 18.**
24. **On all models,** remove lefthand drain plug from engine block and drain coolant into a suitable container.
25. Remove valve covers as outlined under "Valve Cover, Replace."
26. Remove front cover as outlined under "Front Cover, Replace."
27. Install two oil pan bolts to locations shown in **Fig. 55.**
28. Alternately tighten bolts one turn at a time until oil pan to cylinder block seal is released, then remove oil pan.
29. Reverse procedure to install noting the following:
   a. Apply a .110 inch bead of suitable silicone gasket and sealant to sealing surface of oil pan, then apply a .210 inch bead of silicone gasket sealant to two crankshaft seal retainer plate to engine block joint areas on sealing surface of oil pan, **Fig. 56.**
   b. Install oil pan and **torque** in sequence to 27 inch lbs., **Fig. 57.**
   c. Loosen bolts 180°.
   d. Position oil pan mounting boss against A/C compressor. Align oil pan flush with rear of cylinder block using a suitable straightedge, **Fig. 58.**
   e. **Torque** bolts 1–14 to 18 ft. lbs., **Fig. 57.**
   f. **Torque** bolts 15 and 16 to 89 inch lbs.

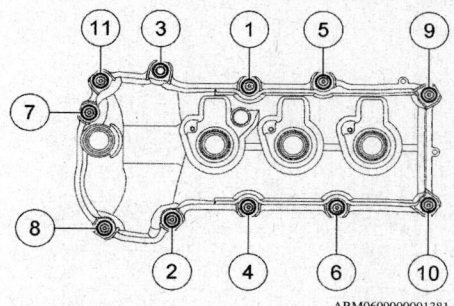

Fig. 25 Righthand valve cover tightening sequence

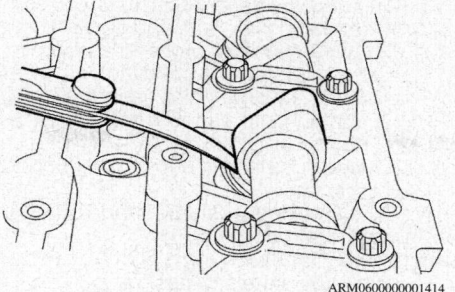

Fig. 26 Valve clearance measurement

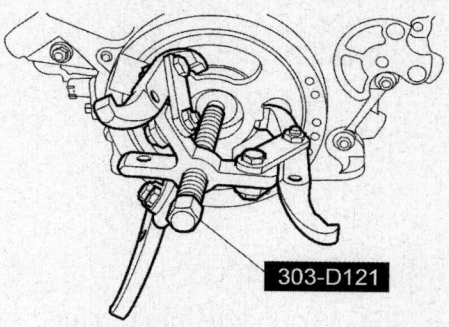

Fig. 27 Crankshaft pulley removal

OIL PUMP

REPLACE

1. Remove front cover as outlined under "Front Cover, Replace."
2. Remove primary timing chain as outlined under "Camshafts, Replace."
3. Remove crankshaft timing chain sprocket.
4. Remove oil pump screen and pickup tube bolts.
5. Remove three oil pump attaching bolts.
6. Rotate oil pump clockwise and separate oil pump from pickup screen, then remove oil pump.
7. Discard oil pump screen and pickup tube O-ring seal.
8. Reverse procedure to install. Install a new oil pump screen and pickup tube O-ring seal.

SERPENTINE DRIVE BELT

Belt Routing

Refer to **Figs. 59 through 61** for serpentine drive belt routing.

Belts, Replace

1. Rotate belt tensioner clockwise using a suitable belt tension release tool, **Fig. 59.**
2. Remove belt from alternator pulley.
3. Raise and support vehicle.
4. Remove four screws and 6 pin-type retainers, then the righthand fender splash shield.
5. Remove accessory drive belt.
6. Install power steering belt removal tool No. 303–1252/1 between power steering pump belt and pulley, **Fig. 62.**
7. Rotate crankshaft clockwise to remove power steering belt.
8. Reverse procedure to install noting the following:
   a. Install power steering belt around crankshaft pulley first, then around bottom of power steering pump pulley.
   b. Install power steering belt installation tool No. 303–1252/2 or equivalent to power steering pulley, then rotate crankshaft clockwise to install belt, **Fig. 63.**

c. Ensure accessory belt routing is as shown in **Fig. 60.**

Belt Tensioner, Replace

1. Remove accessory drive belt as outlined under "Serpentine Drive Belt", "Belts, Replace."
2. Remove three belt tensioner bolts, then the tensioner.
3. Reverse procedure to install.

COOLING SYSTEM BLEED

If engine overheats or fluid level drops below minimum fill line during this procedure, turn engine off and add fluid to degas bottle maximum fill line after the engine has cooled.

1. Open degas bottle, then the bleed valve on thermostat housing, **Fig. 64.**
2. Fill degas bottle to "MAX" line.
3. Close degas bottle cap and bleed valve.
4. Start engine and run at idle for ten minutes or until engine reaches normal operating temperature. Open thermostat housing bleed valve two full turns, **Fig. 64,** for two of the ten minutes, then close bleed valve.
5. Let engine cool and repeat procedure as necessary.
6. Start engine and turn heater to "MAX" setting.
7. Open thermostat housing bleed valve two full turns and let engine idle for two minutes, then close bleed valve.
8. Let engine idle for an additional eight minutes.
9. Operate engine at 2500 RPM for ten minutes and repeat as necessary.
10. Ensure coolant level of degas bottle is at "MAX" line.

THERMOSTAT

REPLACE

1. Release pressure in cooling system by slowly turning pressure relief cap ½ turn counterclockwise. When pressure is released, remove cap.
2. Open radiator draincock and drain coolant into a suitable container.

3. Disconnect lower radiator hose from thermostat housing and position aside, **Fig. 65.**
4. Remove thermostat housing cover, then the thermostat.
5. Reverse procedure to install. Lubricate thermostat O-ring seal with clean engine coolant before installation.

WATER PUMP

REPLACE

Removal

1. Remove front cover as outlined under "Front Cover, Replace."
2. Disconnect lefthand catalyst monitor sensor.
3. Remove lefthand catalytic converter bracket bolts, then the converter to exhaust manifold attaching nuts. Discard converter to manifold nuts.
4. Remove lefthand engine block drain plug and drain coolant into a suitable container, **Fig. 17.**
5. **On models equipped with AWD,** remove two righthand catalytic converter bracket bolts.
6. **On all models,** remove righthand catalytic converter from exhaust manifold and discard attaching nuts.
7. **On models equipped with engine block heater,** proceed as follows:
   a. Remove engine block heater heat shield.
   b. Disconnect engine block heater.
   c. Remove engine block heater and drain coolant into a suitable container, **Fig. 18.**
8. **On models less engine block heater,** remove righthand engine block drain plug and drain coolant into a suitable container, **Fig. 18.**
9. **On all models,** rotate crankshaft clockwise and align timing marks on variable cam timing assemblies as shown in **Fig. 36.**
10. Install camshaft alignment tool No. 303–1248 or equivalent to flats of camshafts, **Fig. 37.**
11. Remove variable cam timing housing from each cylinder head, **Fig. 38.**
12. Remove and discard variable cam timing housing seals.
13. Remove primary timing chain tensioner and tensioner arm, **Fig. 39.**
14. Remove lefthand lower primary timing

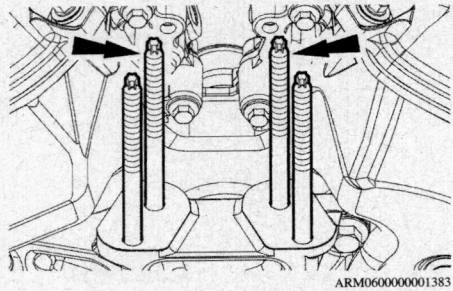

Fig. 28 Engine mount stud removal

chain guide, then the primary timing chain, **Fig. 39.**
15. Remove lefthand upper primary timing chain guide, **Fig. 39.**
16. Remove righthand timing chain guide lower bolt.
17. Loosen righthand timing chain guide upper bolt, rotate guide, then tighten bolt.
18. Remove eight water pump attaching bolts, then the water pump, **Fig. 66.**

Installation

1. Install water pump and tighten to specifications in sequence, **Fig. 66.**
2. Loosen righthand primary timing chain guide upper bolt, align guide, then reinstall lower bolt. Tighten to specifications.
3. Install primary timing chain ensuring that colored links are aligned with timing marks, **Fig. 50.**
4. Install lefthand upper and lower timing chain guides.
5. Install primary timing chain tensioner arm.
6. Reset primary timing chain tensioner as follows:
   a. Rotate actuating lever counterclockwise, **Fig. 51.**
   b. Compress tensioner plunger using a suitable soft jawed vise.
   c. Align actuating lever with hole in tensioner housing and install a suitable lockpin.
7. Install primary timing chain tensioner and remove lockpin.
8. Ensure that timing marks are still aligned as shown in **Fig. 50.**
9. Install new variable cam timing control housing seals.
10. Install variable cam timing control housings and tighten in sequence, **Figs. 52 and 53. Ensure that dowels of variable cam timing control assembly housing are fully engaged into cylinder head before tightening.**
11. **On models equipped with engine block heater,** install engine block heater, then connect wiring harness and heat shield.
12. **On models less engine block heater,** install engine block drain plug.

13. **On FWD models,** install catalytic converter using new nuts and gasket.
14. **On AWD models,** proceed as follows:
    a. Install righthand catalytic converter using new nuts and gasket. Do not tighten until support bracket is installed.
    b. Install catalytic converter support bracket
15. **On all models,** install lefthand cylinder block drain plug.
16. Install lefthand catalytic converter using new nuts and gasket.
17. Install lefthand catalytic converter bracket.
18. Connect catalyst monitor sensors.
19. Install front cover as outlined under "Front Cover, Replace."

RADIATOR
REPLACE

1. Release pressure in cooling system by slowly turning pressure relief cap ½ turn counterclockwise. When pressure is released, remove cap.
2. Open radiator draincock and drain coolant into a suitable container.
3. Disconnect MAF sensor, then remove air filter outlet tube.
4. Remove air cleaner housing assembly, then the air filter housing bracket.
5. **On models equipped with engine block heater,** disconnect three wiring harness retainers from cooling fan motor and shroud and position aside.
6. **On all models,** raise and support vehicle, then remove under vehicle splash shield.
7. Disconnect lower radiator hose from cooling fan and shroud.
8. Detach transmission cooler lines and four wiring harness retainers from cooling fan shroud and position aside.
9. Disconnect cooling fan electrical connector.
10. Lower vehicle, then release two cooling fan shroud clips and remove shroud, **Fig. 67.**
11. Detach power steering hose retainer from radiator.
12. Disconnect upper radiator hose from radiator, then the degas bottle hose.
13. Disconnect transaxle cooler lines and lower radiator hose from radiator.
14. Disengage radiator securing clips from upper radiator support.
15. Disconnect A/C condenser to radiator pushpin retainer.
16. Depress tabs, then separate A/C condenser from radiator.
17. Remove radiator from vehicle.
18. Reverse procedure to install. Bleed cooling system as outlined under "Cooling System Bleed."

FUEL PUMP
REPLACE

1. Relieve fuel pressure as outlined under "Precautions."

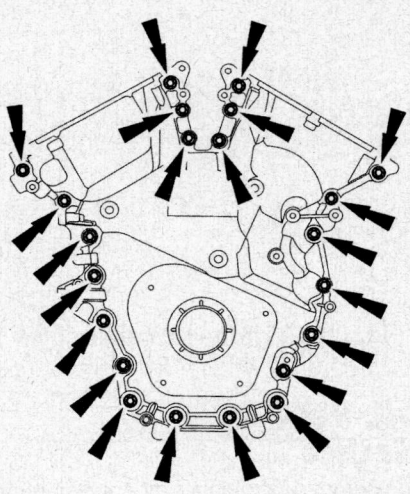

Fig. 29 Front cover bolt location

2. Remove fuel tank filler cap and position aside.
3. Insert fuel draining hose tool No. 310–102 or equivalent into fuel filler neck, then down into fuel tank.
4. Attach fuel storage tank tool No. 164–R3202 or equivalent to fuel drain hose and remove as much fuel as possible from fuel tank.
5. Push rear seat cushion rearward far enough to disengage seat retainers, then lift up on seat and remove from vehicle.
6. Lift carpet and position aside to access fuel pump access cover, **Fig. 68.**
7. **On FWD models,** remove four access cover screws, then the access cover.
8. **On AWD models,** remove 3 access cover screws, then the access cover.
9. **On all models,** disconnect fuel pump electrical connector.
10. Disconnect fuel supply tube as outlined under "Precautions", "Quick Disconnect Hoses.".
11. Remove fuel pump lockring using lock ring wrench tool No. 310–123 or equivalent.
12. **On AWD models,** lift fuel pump from fuel tank enough to access and release fuel crossover tube. Refer to "Precautions", "Quick Disconnect Hoses" for quick disconnect procedures.
13. **On all models,** remove fuel pump from tank.
14. Drain residual fuel from fuel pump into a suitable container.
15. Reverse procedure to install noting the following:
    a. Inspect fuel pump and tank sealing surfaces for damage and replace as necessary.
    b. Apply suitable clean engine oil to new O-ring seal before installation.

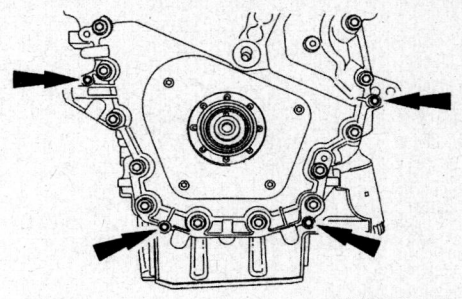

ARM0600000001385

Fig. 30 Front cover removal hole locations

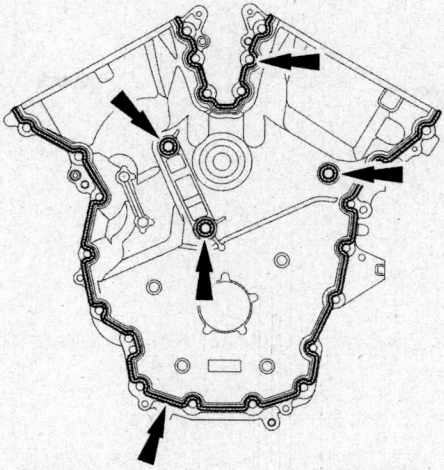

ARM0600000001386

Fig. 31 Front cover sealant application

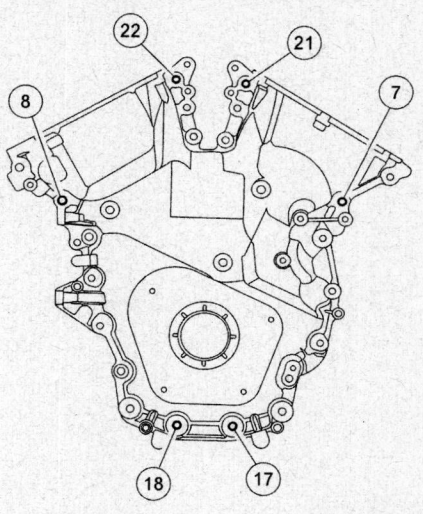

ARM0600000001387

Fig. 32 Front cover bolt installation (Sequence 1)

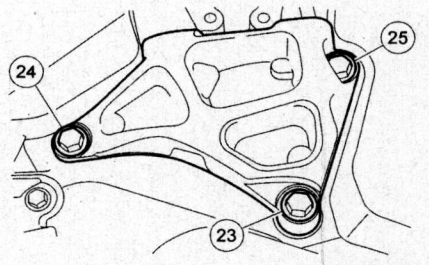

ARM0600000001388

Fig. 33 Front cover bolt installation (Sequence 2)

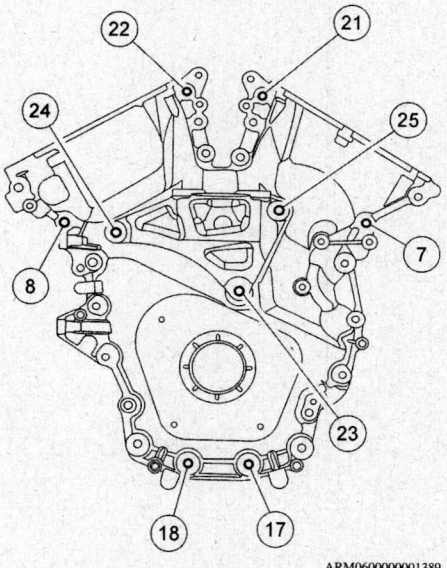

ARM0600000001389

Fig. 34 Front cover bolt installation (Sequence 3)

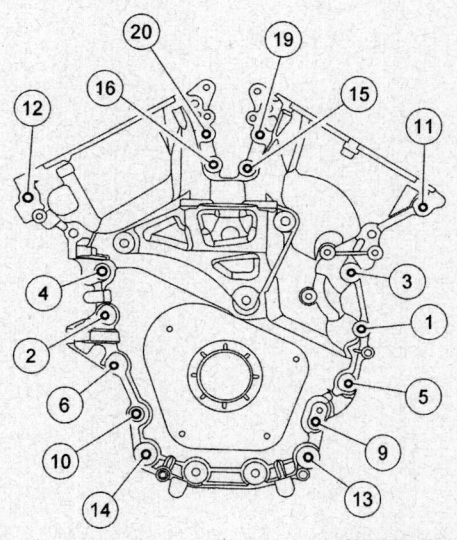

ARM0600000001390

Fig. 35 Front cover bolt installation (Sequence 4)

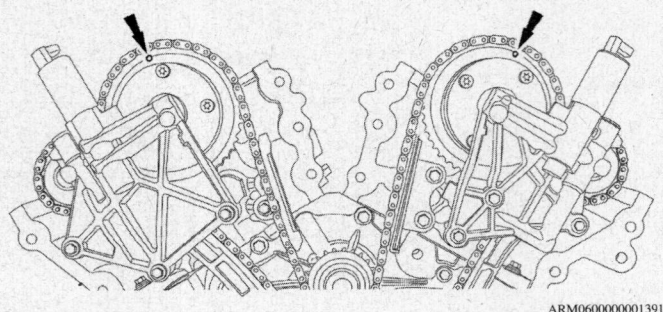

Fig. 36 Variable camshaft timing assembly timing mark alignment

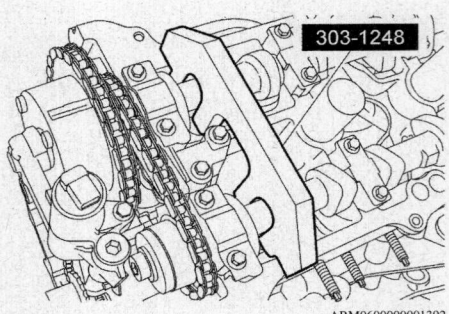

Fig. 37 Camshaft alignment tool installation

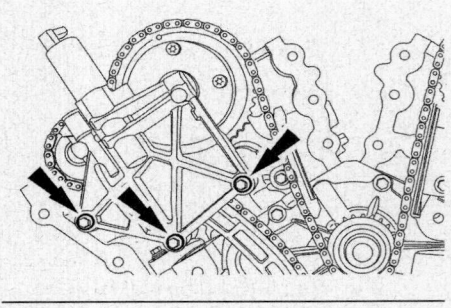

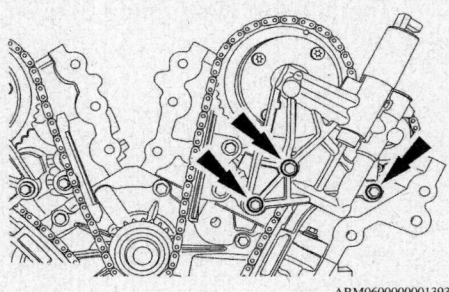

Fig. 38 Variable cam timing housing removal

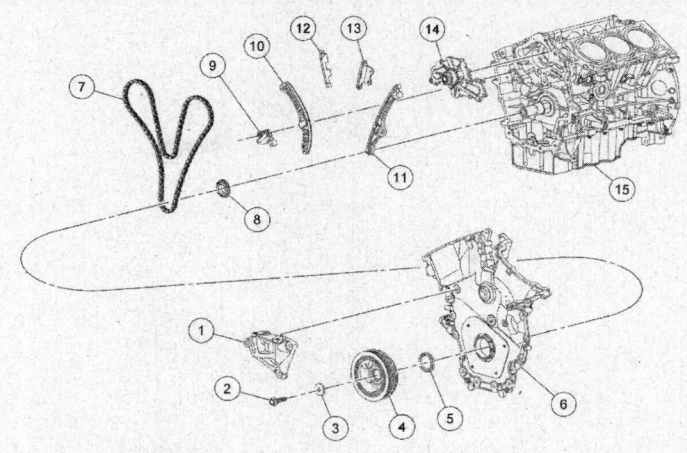

Item	Description	Item	Description
1	Engine mount bracket	10	Primary timing chain tensioner arm
2	Crankshaft pulley bolt	11	LH lower primary timing chain guide
3	Crankshaft pulley washer	12	RH primary timing chain guide
4	Crankshaft pulley	13	LH upper primary timing chain guide
5	Crankshaft front seal	14	Coolant pump
6	Engine front cover	15	Cylinder block
7	Timing chain		
8	Crankshaft timing sprocket		
9	Primary timing chain tensioner		

ARM0600000001394

Fig. 39 Exploded view of timing components. 3.5L engine

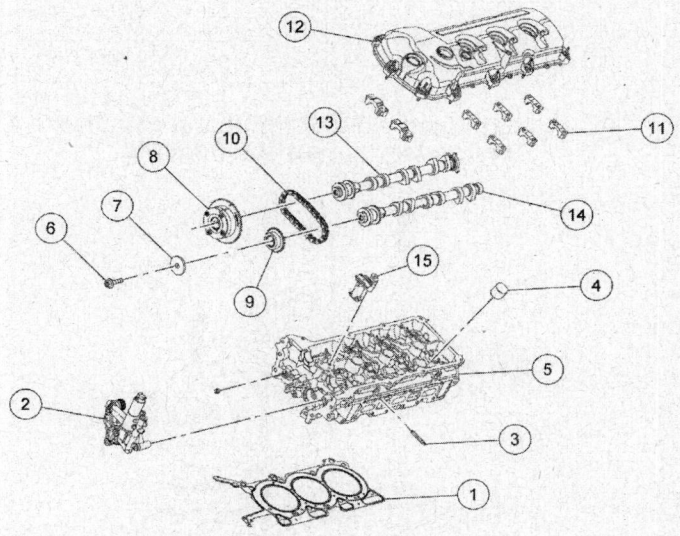

Item	Description	Item	Description
1	LH cylinder head gasket	8	LH VCT assembly
2	LH variable camshaft timing (VCT) housing	9	LH exhaust camshaft sprocket
3	LH exhaust manifold stud (6 required)	10	LH secondary timing chain
4	Valve tappet (32 required)	11	LH camshaft cap (8 required)
5	LH cylinder head	12	LH valve cover
6	LH camshaft bolt (2 required)	13	LH intake camshaft
7	LH exhaust camshaft sprocket washer	14	LH exhaust camshaft
		15	LH secondary timing chain tensioner

ARM0600000001395

Fig. 40 Exploded view of lefthand camshafts & secondary timing components

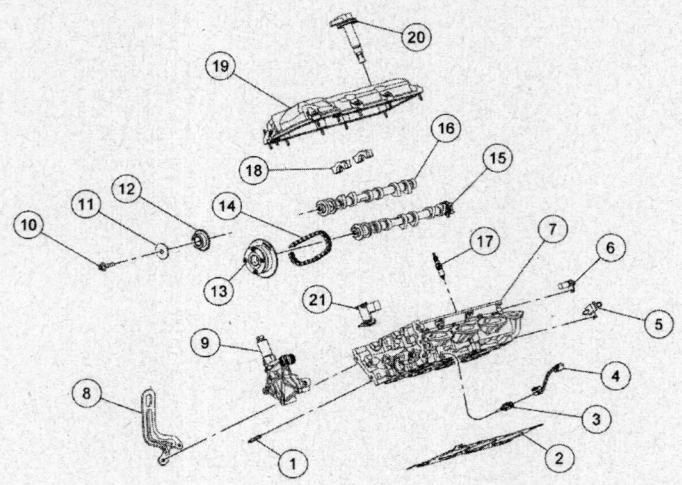

Item	Description		Item	Description
1	RH exhaust manifold stud (6 required)		10	RH camshaft bolt (2 required)
2	RH cylinder head gasket		11	RH exhaust camshaft sprocket washer
3	Cylinder head temperature (CHT) sensor		12	RH exhaust camshaft sprocket
4	CHT sensor jumper harness		13	RH VCT assembly
5	Radio interference capacitor (2 required)		14	RH secondary timing chain
6	Camshaft position sensor (2 required)		15	RH intake camshaft
			16	RH exhaust camshaft
7	RH cylinder head		17	Spark plug (6 required)
8	Engine lift eye		18	RH camshaft cap (8 required)
9	RH variable camshaft timing (VCT) housing		19	RH valve cover
			20	Coil-on-plug (6 required)
			21	RH secondary timing chain tensioner

ARM0600000001396

Fig. 41 Exploded view of righthand camshafts & secondary timing components

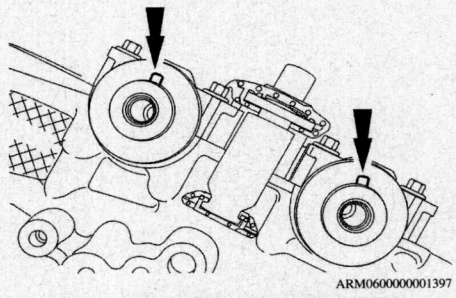

ARM0600000001397

Fig. 42 Lefthand camshaft neutral position

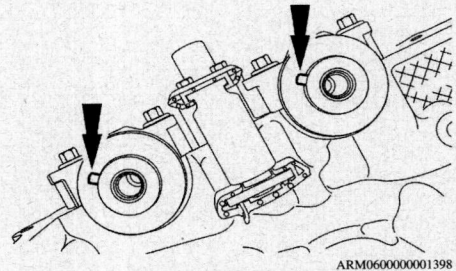

ARM0600000001398

Fig. 43 Righthand camshaft neutral position

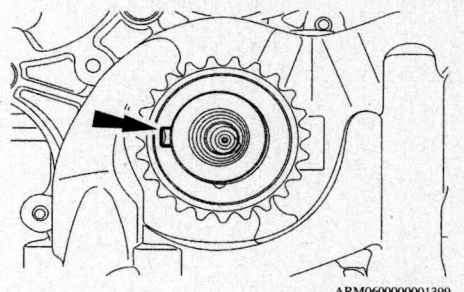

Fig. 44 Crankshaft position during camshaft installation

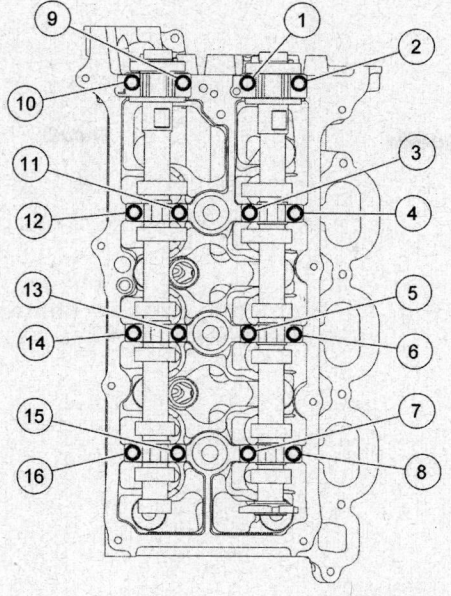

Fig. 45 Lefthand cam bearing cap tightening sequence. 3.5L engine

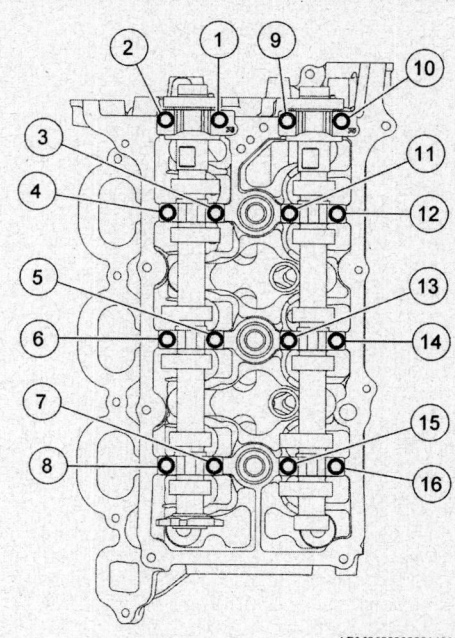

Fig. 46 Righthand cam bearing cap tightening sequence

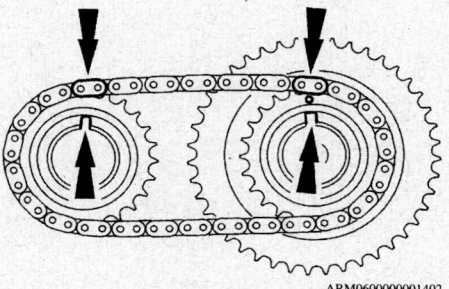

Fig. 47 Lefthand variable timing assembly timing marks

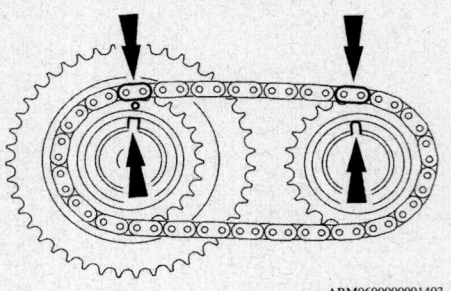

ARM0600000001403

Fig. 48 Righthand variable timing assembly timing marks

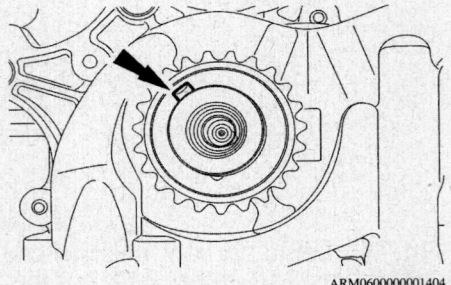

ARM0600000001404

Fig. 49 Alignment of crankshaft to TDC

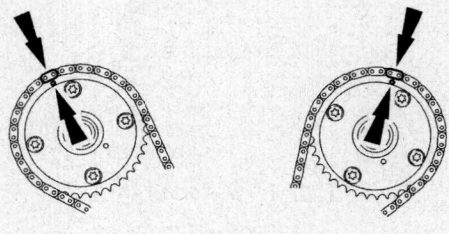

ARM0600000001423

Fig. 50 Primary timing chain alignment marks

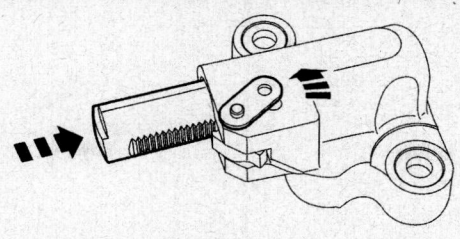

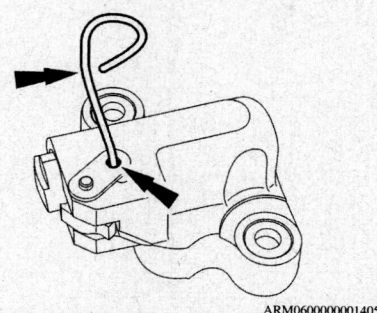

Fig. 51 Primary timing chain reset. 3.5L engine

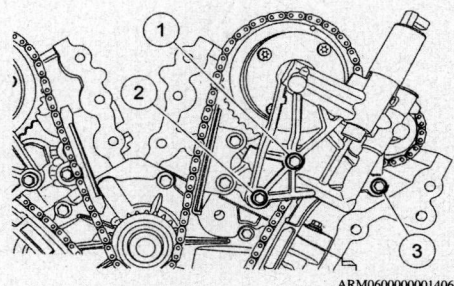

Fig. 52 Lefthand variable cam timing control housing tightening sequence

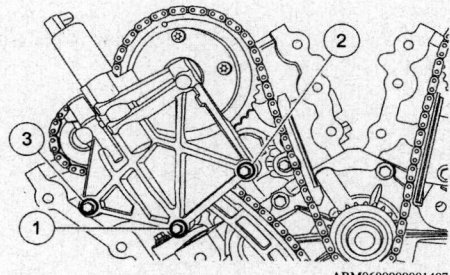

Fig. 53 Righthand variable cam timing control housing tightening sequence

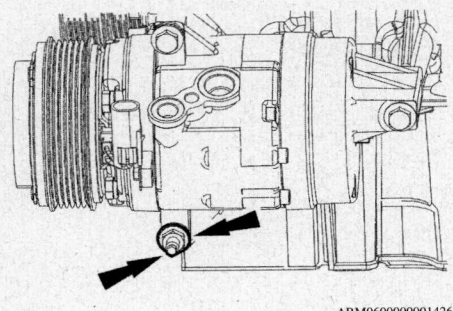

Fig. 54   A/C compressor fastener removal

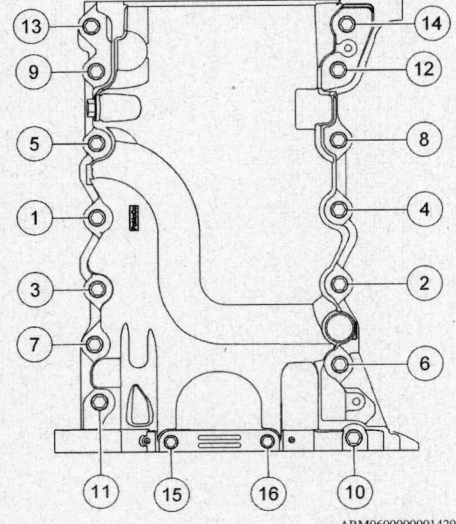

Fig. 57   Oil pan tightening sequence

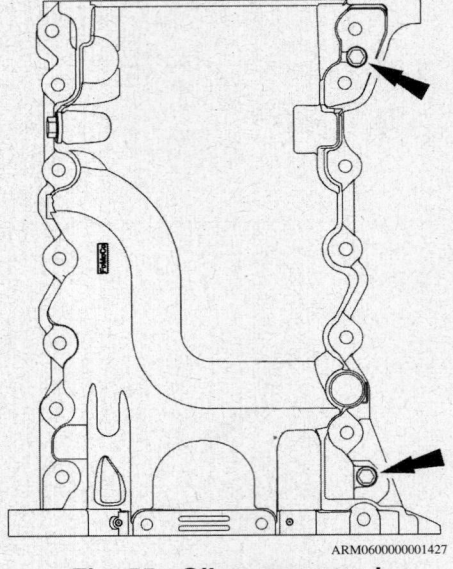

Fig. 55   Oil pan removal

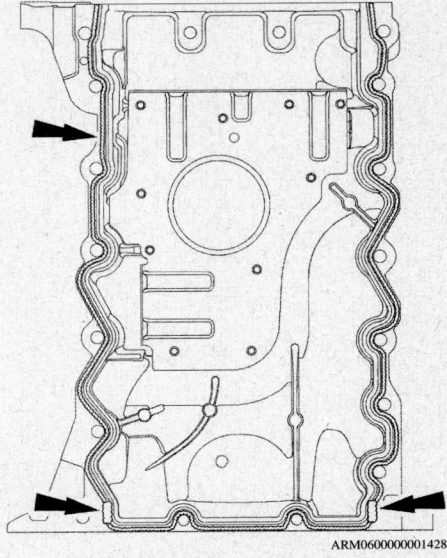

Fig. 56   Oil pan sealant application

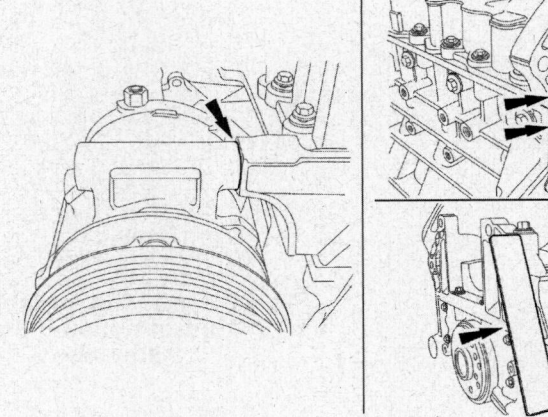

Fig. 58   Oil pan alignment. 3.5L engine

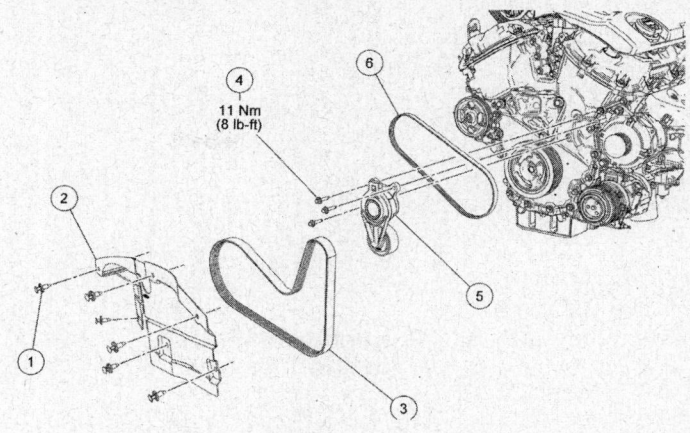

Item	Description
1	Pin-type retainer (6 required)
2	RH splash shield
3	Accessory drive belt
4	Accessory drive belt tensioner bolt (3 required)

Item	Description
5	Accessory drive belt tensioner
6	Power steering pump drive belt

ARM0600000001417

Fig. 59 Exploded view of accessory drive belt system

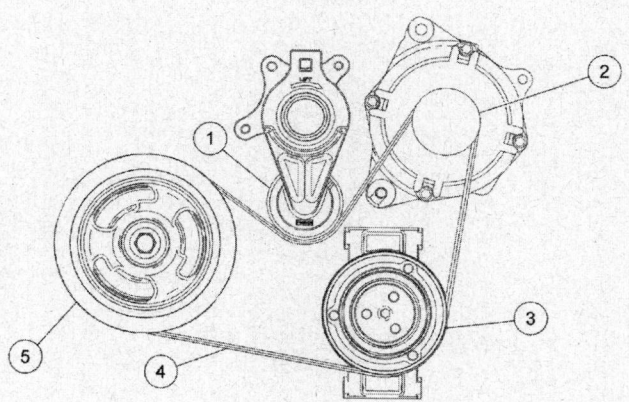

Item	Description
1	Accessory drive belt tensioner pulley
2	Generator pulley
3	A/C clutch pulley

Item	Description
4	Accessory drive belt
5	Crankshaft pulley

ARM0600000001418

Fig. 60 Accessory drive belt routing

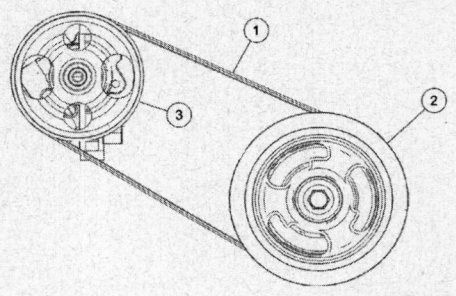

ARM0600000001419

Fig. 61   Power steering belt routing

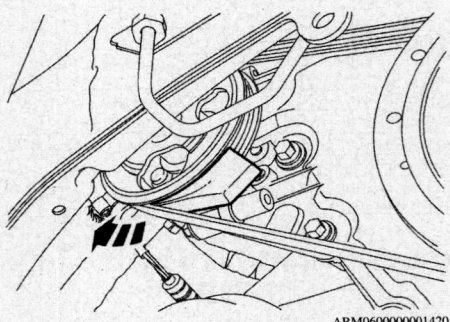

ARM0600000001420

Fig. 62   Power steering belt removal

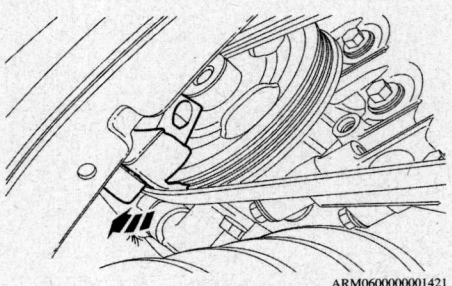

ARM0600000001421

Fig. 63   Power steering belt installation

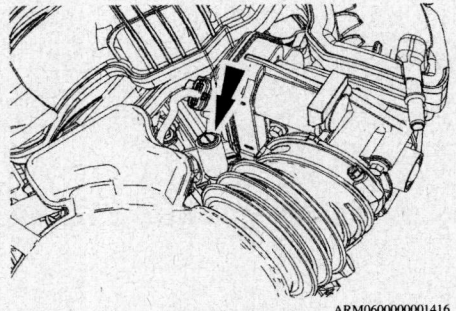

ARM0600000001416

Fig. 64   Thermostat housing bleed valve

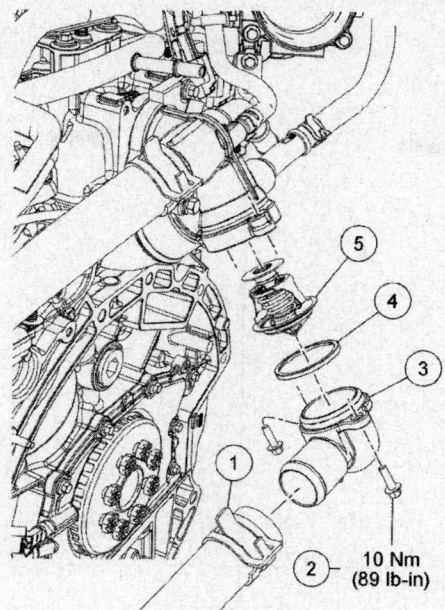

Item	Description
1	Lower radiator-to-thermostat housing cover hose
2	Thermostat housing cover bolt (2 required)
3	Thermostat housing cover
4	O-ring seal
5	Thermostat

Fig. 65 Thermostat removal

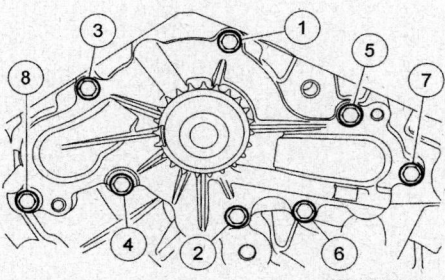

Fig. 66 Water pump bolt location & tightening sequence

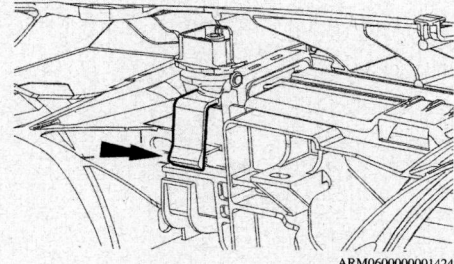

Fig. 67 Cooling fan removal

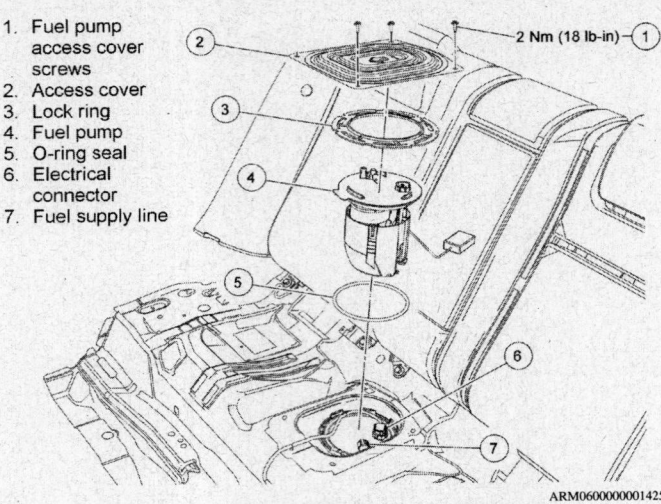

1. Fuel pump access cover screws
2. Access cover
3. Lock ring
4. Fuel pump
5. O-ring seal
6. Electrical connector
7. Fuel supply line

ARM0600000001425

Fig. 68 Fuel pump replacement

TIGHTENING SPECIFICATIONS

Component	Torque Ft. Lbs.
Accessory Drive Belt Tensioner	89①
A/C Compressor Mounting Stud	80①
A/C Compressor Mounting Nut	18
A/C Tube To Condenser	71①
Alternator	35
Alternator "B" Terminal	53①
Belt Tensioner	96①
Camshaft Bearing Cap	89①
Camshaft Position Sensor	89①
Camshaft Sprocket	⑧
Catalytic Converter Nuts	30
Catalytic Converter To Exhaust Manifold Studs	18
Catalytic Converter To Bracket Bolts	15
Cylinder Head	⑤
Driveshaft To PTU Flange	52
Engine Block Heater	30
Engine Mount	46
Engine Mount Brace	18
Engine Mount Bolts	41
Engine Mount Nuts	46
Engine Mount Studs	13
Engine To Transaxle Bolts	35
Exhaust Manifold Nuts	15
Exhaust Manifold Heat Shield	18
Exhaust Manifold Studs	108①
Exhaust Y-Pipe	30
Flexplate	59
Front Cover	④
Fuel Rail	89①
Halfshaft To Transaxle (Righthand)②	17
Halfshaft To Transaxle (Righthand)③	41
Ignition Coil	53①
Lefthand Engine Block Drain Plug	15⑥
Lower Ball Joint Nut	148
Lower Control Arm Through Bolt	76
Lower Intake Manifold	89①
Oil Pan Drain Plug	20
Oil Pan To Engine Block	⑦
Oil Pan To Transaxle	35
Oil Pump To Engine Block	89①
Oil Pump Pickup Screen To Oil Pump	89①

TIGHTENING SPECIFICATIONS—Continued

Component	Torque Ft. Lbs.
Oxygen Sensor	35
Power Feed To Battery Cable	53①
Power Steering Pressure Line To Steering Gear	27
Power Steering Pump	18
Power Transfer Unit	66
Power Transfer Unit Support Bracket	52
Radio Interference Capacitor	89①
Righthand Engine Block Drain Plug	30
Roll Restrictor Through Bolt	66
Spark Plug	11
Stabilizer Bar Link (Lower)	31
Stabilizer Bar Link (Upper)	30
Starter Motor	19
Steering Column Intermediate Shaft To Steering Gear	17
Subframe Bracket Nuts	111
Subframe To Body Bolts	76
Thermostat Housing	89①
Tie Rod To Steering Knuckle	35
Timing Chain Guide	89①
Timing Chain Tensioner	89①
Torque Converter Nuts	27
Transaxle Cooler Lines	22
Transaxle Mount Bracket	59
Transaxle Mount Through Bolt	66
Upper Intake Manifold	89①
Valve Cover	89①
Variable Cam Timing Control Assembly	89①
Water Pump	89①

PTU — Power Transfer Unit
① — Inch lbs.
② — AWD models.
③ — FWD models.
④ — Refer to "Front Cover, Replace" for tightening specifications.
⑤ — Refer to "Cylinder Head, Replace" for tightening specifications.
⑥ — Tighten an additional 180°.
⑦ — Refer to "Oil Pan, Replace" for tightening specifications.
⑧ — Refer to "Camshaft, Replace" for tightening specifications.

Rear Suspension

NOTE: On Air Bag Equipped Models, Refer To "Air Bag System Precautions" Located In The Front Of This Manual For System Disarming & Arming Procedures.

NOTE: Refer To "Computer Relearn Procedures" Located In The Front Of This Manual When Battery Power To The Computer Has Been Interrupted.

INDEX

	Page No.		Page No.		Page No.
Coil Spring, Replace	7-52	Description	7-52	FWD	7-54
Control Arm, Replace	7-52	Hub & Bearing, Replace	7-52	Tightening Specifications	7-59
Lower	7-52	Knuckle, Replace	7-53	Toe Link, Replace	7-54
Upper	7-52	Shock Absorber, Replace	7-52	Trailing Arm, Replace	7-53
Installation	7-53	Stabilizer Bar, Replace	7-53	Wheel Bearing, Adjust	7-52
Removal	7-52	AWD	7-53		

DESCRIPTION

These models utilize an independent rear suspension. Each side consists of an upper and lower control arm, a shock absorber, a two piece spindle tension control shock and a coil spring.

The top of the shock absorber is attached to the body side panel by a rubber insulated top mount and to the lower control arms by two nuts. The upper control arm attaches to the crossmember and the upper part of the spindle. The lower control arm attaches to the underbody and lower part of the spindle. The coil spring operates against the lower control arm and is located inboard of the shock absorber, **Fig. 1.**

HUB & BEARING
REPLACE

1. Remove hub cap or wheel cover.
2. Remove tire/wheel assembly.
3. Remove caliper mounting bolts, then the caliper. Position caliper aside and secure to frame using suitable wire.
4. **On models equipped with AWD,** remove and discard axle shaft nut. Using suitable hub removal tool, **Fig. 2,** press axle shaft out of hub and bearing assembly.
5. **On all models,** remove wheel bearing and hub to knuckle retaining bolts.
6. Remove wheel hub and bearing.
7. Reverse procedure to install.

WHEEL BEARING
ADJUST

The rear wheel bearings are of a sealed cartridge design and are not adjustable.

SHOCK ABSORBER
REPLACE

After removal discard all suspension component mounting bolts and nuts. Replace discarded fasteners.

1. Measure and record distance from center of hub to lip of fender with vehicle in a level static ground position (curb height), **Fig. 3.**
2. Remove interior trim panel to access upper shock absorber mounting nut, then remove nut.
3. Raise and support vehicle, then remove tire/wheel assembly.
4. Remove brake caliper mounting bolts, position caliper aside and secure to frame using suitable wire.
5. Position a V-topped transmission jack under knuckle at trailing arm attachment point.
6. Raise wheel knuckle until toe link is parallel to ground, **Fig. 4.**
7. Remove trailing arm to knuckle mounting bolt.
8. Lower transmission jack, then remove trailing arm to subframe mounting bolt.
9. Position V-topped transmission jack under lower shock absorber mount, then raise jack enough to compress shock absorber and spring.
10. Remove lower arm to knuckle mounting bolt.
11. Loosen lower arm to subframe bolt.
12. Lower and remove transmission jack.
13. Remove lower shock absorber to lower arm bolt.
14. While holding shock absorber and spring, swing lower arm downward to access and remove shock absorber and spring.
15. Reverse procedure to install, noting the following:
    a. Tape coil spring to upper rubber spring seat to ensure proper alignment of spring on seat.
    b. Before tightening suspension nuts and bolts, raise suspension with suitable floor jack to previously measured height, **Fig. 3.**

COIL SPRING
REPLACE

Refer to "Shock Absorber, Replace" for coil spring replacement procedure.

CONTROL ARM
REPLACE

After removal discard all suspension component mounting bolts and nuts. Replace discarded fasteners.

Lower

1. Measure and record distance from center of hub to lip of fender with vehicle in a level static ground position (curb height), **Fig. 3.**
2. Raise and support rear of vehicle.
3. Remove tire and wheel assembly.
4. Remove rear spring as outlined in "Coil Spring, Replace."
5. Remove lower control arm to body bracket mounting bolt and control arm.
6. Reverse procedure to install, noting the following:
    a. Tape coil spring to upper rubber spring seat to ensure proper alignment of spring on seat.
    b. Before tightening suspension nuts and bolts, raise suspension with suitable floor jack to previously measured height, **Fig. 3.**

Upper
REMOVAL

The front and rear control arm bushings must be replaced in pairs.
1. Raise and support vehicle.
2. Remove rear subframe, **Fig. 5.**
3. Raise lower control arm to normal curb height using suitable floor jack.
4. Remove wheel and tire assembly, then the brake hose bracket from body.
5. Remove front and rear upper arm to subframe mounting bolts.
6. Remove stabilizer bar link to upper arm nut, then separate link from upper arm.
7. Remove upper arm to knuckle mounting bolt.
8. Remove upper arm and upper arm

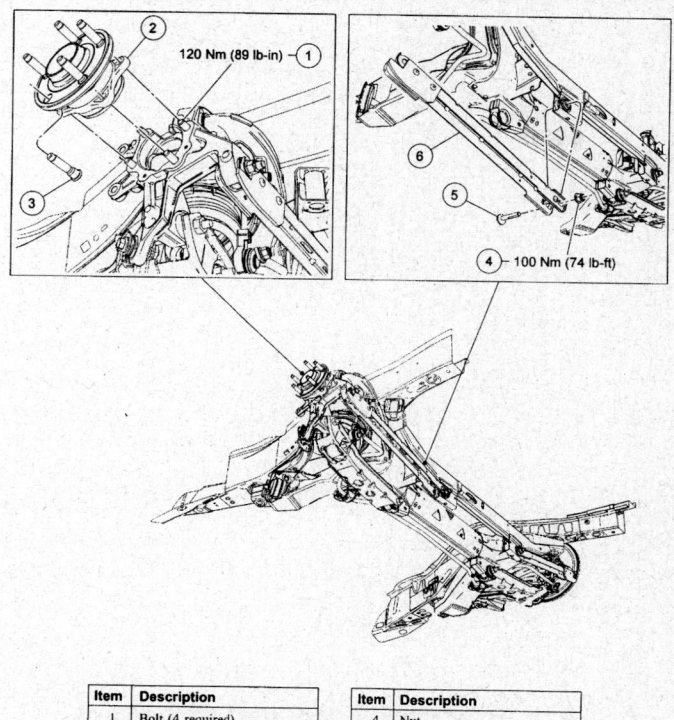

Item	Description
1	Bolt (4 required)
2	Wheel bearing and wheel hub
3	Wheel bolt (5 required)

Item	Description
4	Nut
5	Bolt
6	Toe link

ARM0400000000466

Fig. 1 Exploded view of rear suspension (Part 1 of 4)

Item	Description
7	Nut
8	Stabilizer bar link

Item	Description
9	Bolt (4 required)
10	Stabilizer bar

ARM0400000000467

Fig. 1 Exploded view of rear suspension (Part 2 of 4)

front bushing from subframe using bushing replacement tool No. 204–357, or equivalent, **Fig. 6.**
9. Remove front upper arm rear bushing from arm using jaw puller tool No. 205–D072 and 205–D064, or equivalents, **Fig. 7.**
10. Remove rear bushing from subframe using draw bar bushing tool No. 205–098, or equivalent, **Fig. 8.**
11. Remove upper arm from subframe.

INSTALLATION

1. Install rear bushing into subframe using draw bar bushing tool No. 205–098, or equivalent, **Fig. 8.** Install bushing to correct depth in subframe using opposite side bushing as a guide, **Fig. 9.**
2. Position upper arm bushing on wheel knuckle ball stud and into rear bushing, then insert forward part of upper arm into front subframe bore.
3. Loosely install rear upper arm to subframe bolt.
4. Hold upper and adjust it to correct specifications, **Fig. 10,** then tighten bolt to specifications.
5. Install rear upper arm to subframe bolt.
6. Install front upper arm bushing into subframe using bushing replacement tool No. 204–357, or equivalent, **Fig. 6,** while an assistant hold upper arm in center of bushing bore.
7. Install front bushing into subframe using draw bar bushing tool No. 205–098, or equivalent, **Fig. 8. Install bushing to correct depth in sub-**

frame using opposite side bushing as a guide.
8. Install front arm to subframe bolt.
9. Install upper arm to knuckle bolts.
10. Install stabilized bar link and nut on upper arm.
11. Install rear subframe, **Fig. 5.** Align subframe to body following alignment specification, **Fig. 11.**

KNUCKLE
REPLACE

After removal, discard all suspension component mounting bolts and nuts. Replace discarded fasteners.
1. Measure and record distance from center of hub to lip of fender with vehicle in a level static ground position (curb height), **Fig. 3.**
2. Remove tire/wheel assembly.
3. Remove hub and bearing as outlined under "Hub & Bearing, Replace."
4. Remove disc brake shield and anti-lock wheel sensor.
5. Place suitable jack stand under lower control arm and slightly raise suspension.
6. Remove trailing arm to knuckle mounting bolt.
7. Remove toe link to knuckle mounting bolt.
8. Remove shock absorber/spring assembly to lower control arm mounting bolt.
9. Remove upper and lower subframe to knuckle mounting bolts.
10. Remove wheel knuckle.

11. Reverse procedure to install, noting the following:
   a. Install new flag bolts, nuts and washers.
   b. Before tightening suspension nuts and bolts, raise suspension with suitable floor jack to previously measured height, **Fig. 3.**

TRAILING ARM
REPLACE

After removal discard all suspension component mounting bolts and nuts. Replace discarded fasteners.
1. Measure and record distance from center of hub to lip of fender with vehicle in a level static ground position (curb height), **Fig. 3.**
2. Raise and support vehicle.
3. Remove trailing arm to knuckle mounting bolt.
4. Remove trailing arm to subframe mounting bolt.
5. Remove trailing arm.
6. Reverse procedure to install. Before tightening suspension nuts and bolts, raise suspension with suitable floor jack to previously measured height, **Fig. 3.**

STABILIZER BAR
REPLACE

AWD

After removal discard all suspension component mounting bolts and nuts. Replace discarded fasteners.

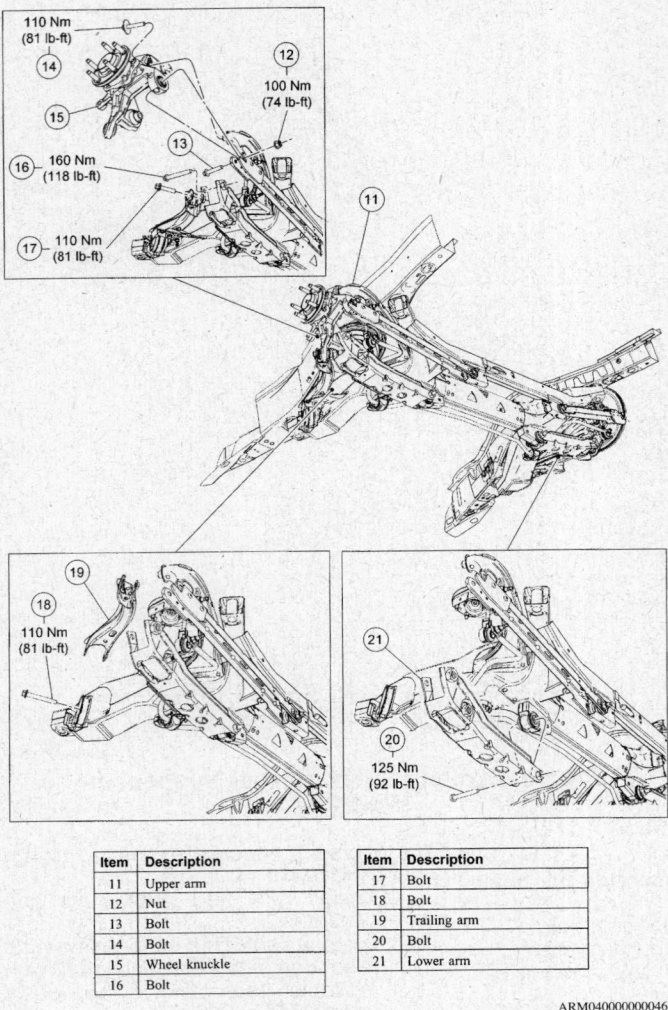

Item	Description
11	Upper arm
12	Nut
13	Bolt
14	Bolt
15	Wheel knuckle
16	Bolt

Item	Description
17	Bolt
18	Bolt
19	Trailing arm
20	Bolt
21	Lower arm

ARM0400000000468

Fig. 1 Exploded view of rear suspension (Part 3 of 4)

1. Raise and support vehicle. **Do use tension strut and bushing for support.**
2. Lower exhaust system from rear of flex pipe by disconnecting insulators.
3. Remove tire/wheel assemblies.
4. Remove lefthand and righthand brake caliper mounting bolts, then position calipers side and secure to frame using suitable wire.
5. Remove and discard lefthand and righthand axle shaft retaining nuts.
6. Press axle shafts out of hubs using suitable hub removal press.
7. Remove lefthand and righthand upper control arm to knuckle bolts.
8. Remove lefthand and righthand trailing arm to knuckle bolt, then loosen trailing arm to subframe bolt.
9. Remove lefthand and righthand lower shock to lower control arm nut, then

the lower control arm.
10. Loosen lefthand and righthand toe link to subframe bolts, allow both knuckles to hang in a downward position.
11. Remove subframe cross brace bolts, then the cross brace, **Fig. 12.**
12. Remove stabilizer bar link to stabilizer bar nuts.
13. Remove stabilizer to subframe bracket bolts.
14. Remove stabilizer bar and link assembly.
15. Reverse procedure to install.

FWD

After removal discard all suspension component mounting bolts and nuts. Replace discarded fasteners.
1. Raise and support vehicle.
2. Place jack stands under rear suspen-

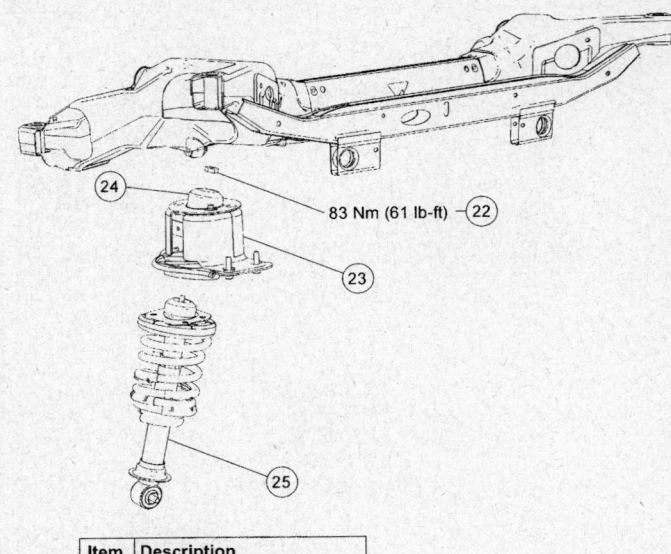

Item	Description
22	Upper shock absorber nut
23	Upper shock mount
24	Bushing
25	Shock absorber/spring

ARM0400000000469

Fig. 1 Exploded view of rear suspension (Part 4 of 4)

sion arm and bushings so bar links and bushings are neutralized.
3. Lower exhaust system from rear of flex pipe by disconnecting insulators.
4. Remove stabilizer bar link to stabilizer bar mounting nuts.
5. Remove stabilizer bar bracket to subframe mounting bolts.
6. Remove stabilizer bar and link assembly.
7. Reverse procedure to install.

TOE LINK
REPLACE

After removal discard all suspension component mounting bolts and nuts. Replace discarded fasteners.
1. Raise and support vehicle.
2. Measure and record distance from center of hub to lip of fender with vehicle in a level static ground position (curb height), **Fig. 3.**
3. Remove tire/wheel assembly.
4. Remove wheel speed sensor wire retainer and wire from toe link.
5. Remove toe link to knuckle bolt.
6. Remove toe link to subframe nut and bolt.
7. Reverse procedure to install. Before tightening suspension nuts and bolts, raise suspension with suitable floor jack to previously measured height, **Fig. 3.**

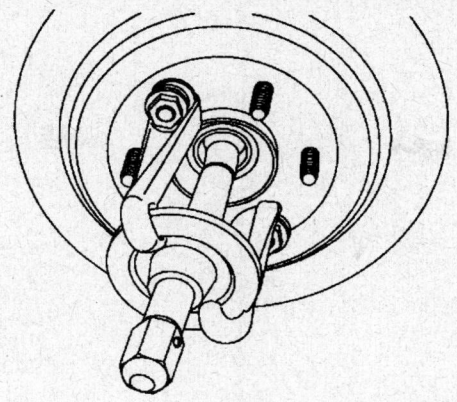

ARM0400000000471

**Fig. 2   Hub & bearing removal.
AWD models**

ARM0400000000470

**Fig. 3   Static ground position (curb height)
measurement**

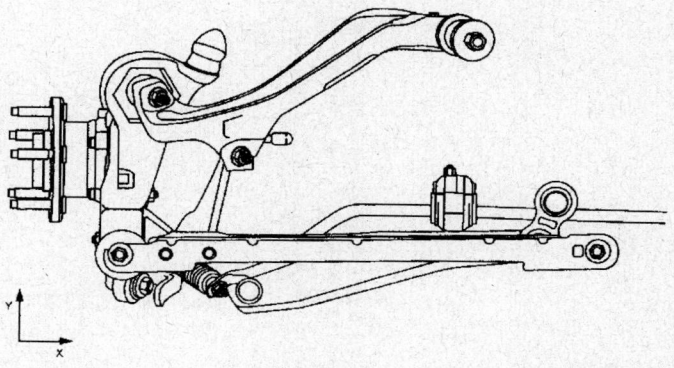

ARM0400000000472

Fig. 4   Toe link in parallel position

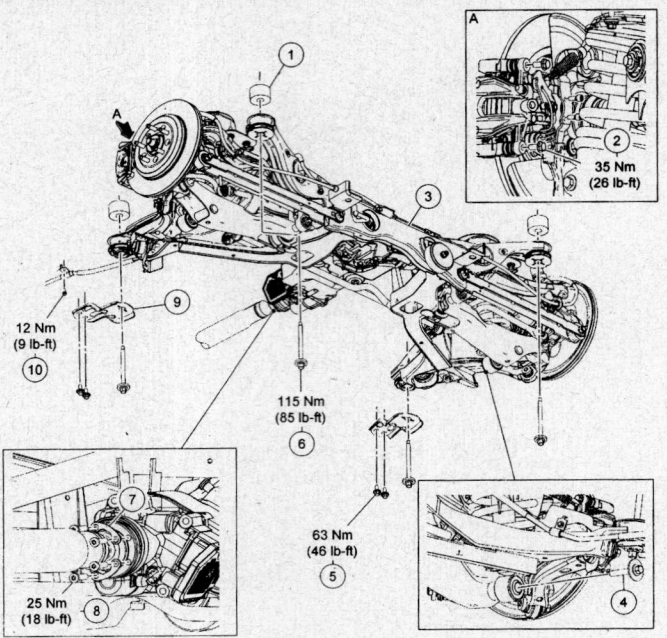

1. Rear subframe to under body spacers, FWD Freestyl only
2. Rear caliper pins
3. Rear subframe assembly
4. Rear Shock to lower control arm bolts
5. Rear subframe assembly
6. Rear subframe mounting bolts
7. Driveshaft washers, AWD only
8. Driveshaft bolts, AWD only
9. Rear subframe bracket
10. Park brake cable routing bolt

ARM0400000000473

Fig. 5   Exploded view of rear subframe

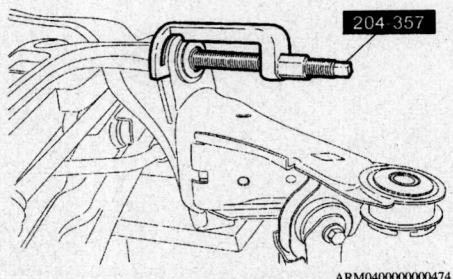

ARM0400000000474

**Fig. 6   Subframe front bushing
removal**

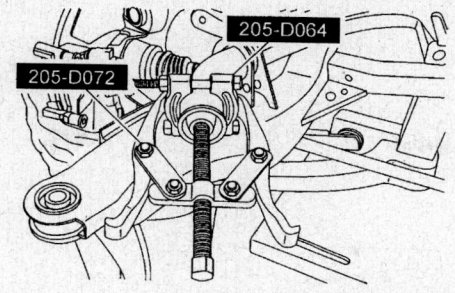

Fig. 7 Upper control arm bushing removal

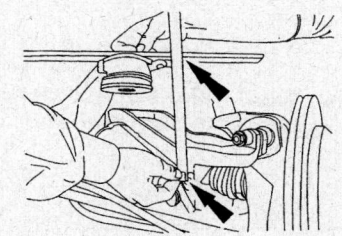

Vehicle	Ride Height Specification
Freestyle 2WD	163 mm (6.4 in)
Five Hundred/Montego 2WD	147 mm (5.7 in)
Freestyle AWD	158 mm (6.2 in)
Five Hundred/Montego AWD	138 mm (5.4 in)

Fig. 8 Subframe rear bushing replacement

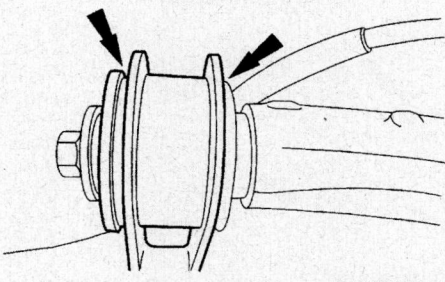

Fig. 9 Control arm bushing depth verification

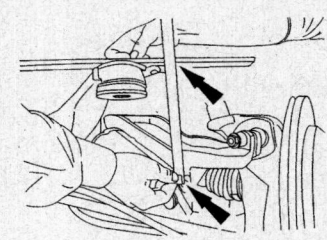

Vehicle	Ride Height Specification
Freestyle 2WD	163 mm (6.4 in)
Five Hundred/Montego 2WD	147 mm (5.7 in)
Freestyle AWD	158 mm (6.2 in)
Five Hundred/Montego AWD	138 mm (5.4 in)

ARM0400000000478

Fig. 10 Ride height specifications & measurement points

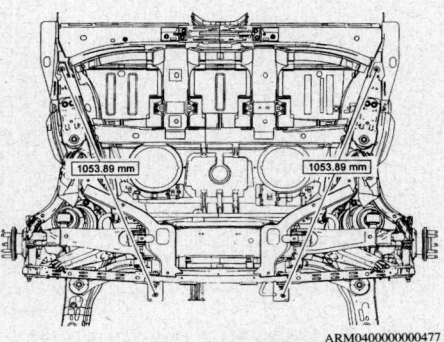

ARM0400000000477

Fig. 11 Rear subframe alignment specifications

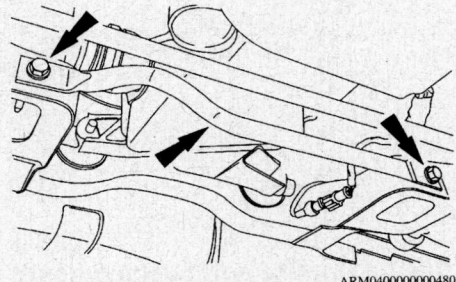

ARM0400000000480

Fig. 12 Subframe cross brace removal

TIGHTENING SPECIFICATIONS

Year	Component	Torque/Ft. Lbs.
ALL WHEEL DRIVE		
2005–08	Axle Shaft Nut	148
	Brake Hose Bracket Bolt	9–12
	Disc Brake Shield Bolt	10
	Lower Arm To Subframe Bolt	98
	Lower Arm To Wheel Knuckle Bolt	66
	Lower Shock Absorber To Mount Nut	61
	Stabilizer Bar Bracket Bolt	43
	Stabilizer Bar Link To Stabilizer Bar Bolt	41
	Subframe Cross Brace Bolts	46
	Toe Link To Subframe Bolt	74
	Toe Link To Wheel Knuckle Bolt	74
	Trailing Arm To Subframe Bolt	81
	Trailing Arm To Wheel Knuckle Bolt	77
	Upper Arm To Wheel Knuckle Nut	77
	Upper Shock Absorber To Mount Housing Bolt	22
	Upper Arm To Subframe Bolt	81
	Wheel Lug	85–105
FRONT WHEEL DRIVE		
2005–07	Axle Shaft Nut	148
	Brake Hose Bracket Bolt	9–12
	Disc Brake Shield Bolt	10
	Lower Arm To Wheel Knuckle Bolt	92
	Lower arm To Subframe Bolt	118
	Lower Shock Absorber To Mount Nut	61
	Stabilizer Bar Bracket Bolt	43
	Stabilizer Bar Link To Stabilizer Bar Bolt	41
	Toe Link To Subframe Bolt	74
	Toe Link To Wheel Knuckle Bolt	74
	Trailing Arm To Subframe Bolt	81
	Trailing Arm To Wheel Knuckle Bolt	77
	Upper Arm To Wheel Knuckle Nut	81
	Upper Shock Absorber To Mount Housing Bolt	22
	Upper Arm To Subframe Bolt	81
	Wheel Lug	85–105

Front Suspension & Steering

NOTE: On Air Bag Equipped Models, Refer To "Air Bag System Precautions" Located In The Front Of This Manual For System Disarming & Arming Procedures.

NOTE: Refer To "Computer Relearn Procedures" Located In The Front Of This Manual When Battery Power To The Computer Has Been Interrupted.

INDEX

	Page No.		Page No.		Page No.
Ball Joint, Replace	7-60	Description	7-60	Steering Knuckle, Replace	7-61
Ball Joint Inspection	7-60	Power Steering	13-1	Strut, Replace	7-60
Coil Spring & Strut Service	7-61	Power Steering Gear, Replace	7-61	Tightening Specifications	7-64
Assemble	7-61	Power Steering Pump, Replace	7-62	Wheel Bearing, Replace	7-60
Disassemble	7-61	Stabilizer Bar, Replace	7-61		
Control Arm, Replace	7-61	Steering Columns	12-1		

DESCRIPTION

This suspension is a gas filled McPherson strut type. The strut top mount consists of a rubber insulated bearing and seat and coil spring insulator. The top mount is attached to the body side apron by three bolts. The lower part of the strut is mounted in the steering knuckle and is retained by a pinch bolt. A forged lower control arm is attached to the subframe and to the steering knuckle. A tension strut is connected to the lower control arm and to the forward part of the subframe.

WHEEL BEARING

REPLACE

1. Turn ignition switch to OFF position and place steering column in unlocked position.
2. Remove wheel hub nut, then raise and support vehicle.
3. Remove cotter pin and nut from tie rod end stud. Discard cotter pin and nut.
4. Remove tie rod end from front steering knuckle using tie rod end remover tool No. 3290-D, and tie rod adapter tool No. T81P-3504-W, or equivalents. **Do not use power tools to remove nut. Avoid damaging rod boot seal.**
5. Remove stabilizer bar link from front wheel knuckle.
6. Remove disc brake caliper and support it aside.
7. Remove anti-lock brake sensor.
8. Remove and discard lower ball joint nut.
9. Compress front coil spring until lower ball joint clears front suspension lower arm using Rotunda spring compressor tool No. 164-R-3571, or equivalent.
10. Push front axle from hub using suitable service tools.
11. Remove and discard four hub and

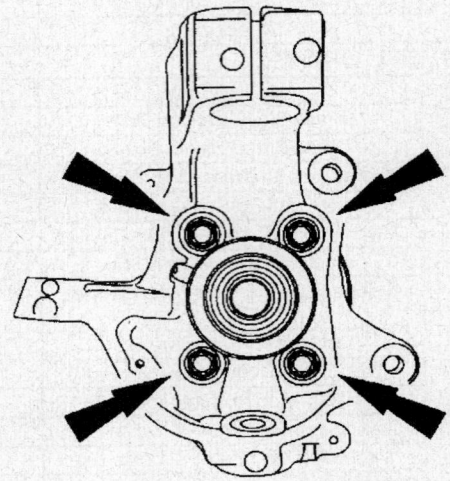

ARM0400000000481

Fig. 1 Hub & bearing removal

bearing mounting bolts, **Fig. 1**, from front steering knuckle.

12. **Wheel hub is not pressed into front wheel knuckle. Do not use slide hammer to remove stuck wheel hub. Do not strike back of inner bearing race.**
13. If bearing carrier is corroded to front steering knuckle, apply rust penetrant part No. D7AZ-19A501-AA, or equivalent, to inboard and outboard steering knuckle to hub mating surface and allow to soak. Pry wheel hub from knuckle assembly using suitable pry bar.
14. Reverse procedure to install, noting the following:
    a. If wheel hub is damaged, or if any endplay is detectable, replace wheel hub.

b. Remove any foreign material from knuckle bearing bore.
c. Lightly lubricate mating surfaces of bearing and front wheel knuckle.

BALL JOINT INSPECTION

1. Raise and support vehicle with wheels in full down position.
2. Grasp lower edge of tire, then move wheel assembly in and out.
3. As wheel is being moved, observe lower end of knuckle and lower control arm.
4. If movement is observed, replace lower control arm.

BALL JOINT

REPLACE

The ball joint must be replaced with the control arm as an assembly.

STRUT

REPLACE

1. Place ignition switch in OFF position and ensure steering wheel is not locked.
2. Remove hub nut and loosen four strut upper mounting plate retaining nuts, **Fig. 2**.
3. Raise and support vehicle. **Do not raise vehicle with lower control arm.**
4. Remove wheel and tire assembly.
5. Remove brake caliper and position it aside.
6. Remove brake rotor and tie rod end to knuckle retaining nut. **Do not use power tools to remove tie rod nut. Avoid damaging boot seal.**
7. Remove nut and stabilizer bar link from strut.

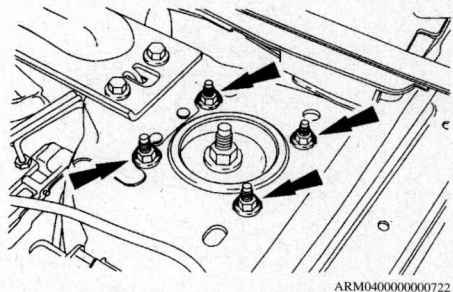

Fig. 2 Strut upper mounting plate removal

8. Remove wheel speed sensor from knuckle.
9. Remove lower strut to wheel knuckle pinch nut and bolt, **Fig. 3,** then slightly spread joint and remove lower control arm.
10. Press axle from hub using suitable hub remover/installer.
11. Wire axle shaft to body to maintain level position. **Do not allow axle shaft to move outward.**
12. Remove strut to steering knuckle pinch bolt and spread joint slightly.
13. Remove steering knuckle and hub.
14. Remove mounting nuts and strut.
15. Reverse procedure to install, noting the following:
    a. Tighten in following order: strut to wheel knuckle pinch bolt, lower control arm to steering knuckle pinch bolt, stabilizer bar assembly to strut, tie rod end mounting nut and strut mounting nuts.
    b. Tighten hub nut with vehicle on ground.

COIL SPRING & STRUT SERVICE

Disassemble

1. Compress strut spring with Rotunda coil spring compressor tool No. 164-R3571, or equivalent.
2. Hold strut shaft with suitable box wrench and remove strut mounting nut using suitable crowfoot socket. **Do not allow strut shaft to rotate.**
3. Loosen compressor tool, then remove strut top mount bracket, bearing and seat assembly, and spring.

Assemble

1. Position notch and arrow on upper strut mount outboard opposite locator on strut tab, **Fig. 4.**
2. Position notch and arrow on upper strut mount inboard aligned with locator tab on strut, **Fig. 5.**
3. Compress strut spring with Rotunda coil spring compressor tool No. 164-R3571, or equivalent.
4. Install spring over strut into lower seat, then install upper strut mounting plate with spring seat. Ensure spring is correctly seated in both upper and lower spring seats.
5. Hold strut shaft with suitable box

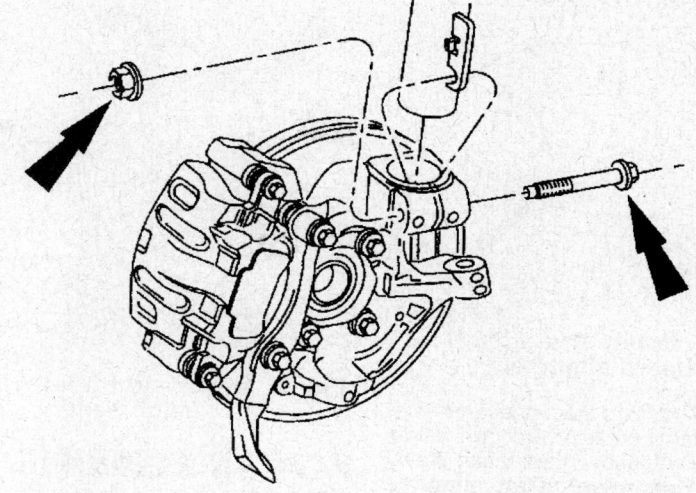

Fig. 3 Strut to wheel knuckle pinch bolt removal

wrench and install upper strut mounting plate retaining nut using suitable crowfoot socket. **Do not allow strut shaft to rotate.**
6. Install strut spring assembly with upper strut mount alignment arrow facing outward away from vehicle, **Fig. 6.**

CONTROL ARM
REPLACE

1. Turn ignition switch to OFF position and place steering column in unlocked position.
2. Raise and support vehicle.
3. Remove and discard lower ball joint nut.
4. Separate ball joint from steering knuckle using ball joint remover tool No. T96P-3010-A and tie rod end remover tool No. T81P-3504-W, or equivalents.
5. Compress front coil spring until lower ball joint clears front suspension lower arm using Rotunda spring compressor tool No. 164-R-3571, or equivalent.
6. Remove forward lower suspension arm mounting nut and bolt.
7. Remove rear lower control arm mounting nut, bolt and control arm.
8. Reverse procedure to install.

STEERING KNUCKLE
REPLACE

Wheel hub retainer is a torque prevailing design and cannot be reused. If loosened, retainer must be replaced.

1. Ensure steering wheel is in unlocked position.
2. Remove wheel cover, wheel hub retainer and washer. Discard retainer.
3. Remove steering knuckle tie rod end using suitable ball joint removal tool.
4. Remove anti-lock brake wheel speed sensor.
5. Disconnect ABS sensor wire retainer and position sensor aside.
6. Remove knuckle to shock mounting bolt and nut. Discard nut.

7. Disconnect ball joint from lower arm using suitable joint removal tool.
8. Push lower arm down until ball joint is free from arm using suitable pry bar.
9. Press halfshaft from wheel bearing and hub using front wheel hub installation tool No. T81P-1104-C, or equivalent.
10. Support halfshaft in level position.
11. Remove flag bolt and steering knuckle.
12. Reverse procedure to install.

STABILIZER BAR
REPLACE

1. Raise and support vehicle. Place safety stands behind front subframe.
2. Remove stabilizer bar link to strut and bar mounting nuts.
3. Remove mounting bolts and move steering gear off of subframe.
4. Support subframe with safety stands and remove rear subframe mounting bolts.
5. Lower rear part of subframe approximately two inches to access stabilizer bar mounting brackets, **Fig. 7.**
6. Remove mounting brackets and stabilizer bar, **Fig. 8.**
7. Reverse procedure to install.

POWER STEERING GEAR
REPLACE

1. Turn steering wheel ¼ turn and turn ignition switch to OFF position.
2. Remove both front wheel and tire assemblies.
3. Remove tie rod end jam nuts. Discard tie rod end cotter pins and nuts.
4. Record number of turns required to remove tie rod ends from steering gear for installation reference.
5. Remove tie rod ends from steering knuckle with suitable joint removal tool.
6. Remove tie rod ends.
7. Remove nuts and disconnect both stabilizer bar links from stabilizer bar.

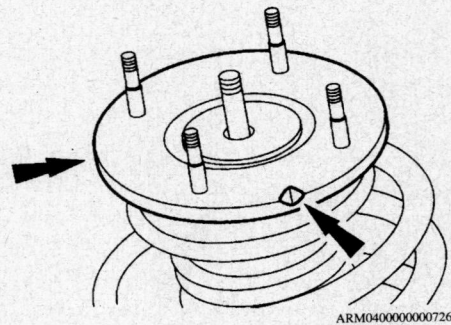

Fig. 4 Upper strut mount outboard alignment

8. Remove bolt and disconnect intermediate shaft coupling. **Do not allow steering wheel to rotate while steering column intermediate shaft is disconnected.**
9. Remove catalytic converter.
10. Remove and discard both steering gear mounting nuts.
11. Remove bolts and lower rear of front subframe approximately four inches.
12. Disconnect power steering pressure switch and remove pressure hose.
13. Remove bracket/heat shield.
14. Remove power steering lines from steering gear.
15. Remove brackets, pipes and steering gear through lefthand fender well.
16. Reverse procedure to install.

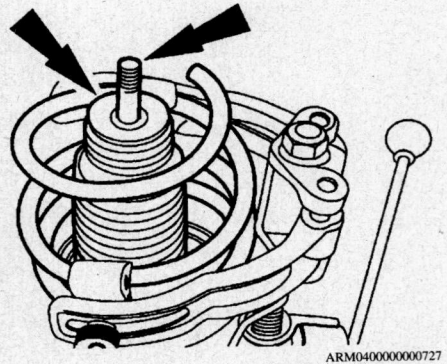

Fig. 5 Upper strut mount inboard alignment

POWER STEERING PUMP

REPLACE

The power steering pump can only be replaced as a complete assembly. The pump has no serviceable components.
1. Drain and remove coolant recovery reservoir.
2. Remove drive belt.
3. Remove power steering reservoir pump hose from between pump and reservoir. Drain fluid into suitable container.
4. Remove pulley using pump pulley remover tool No. T69L-10300-B, or equivalent.
5. Disconnect power steering lefthand turn pressure hose from pump.
6. Remove three pump mounting bolts and pump.
7. Reverse procedure to install.

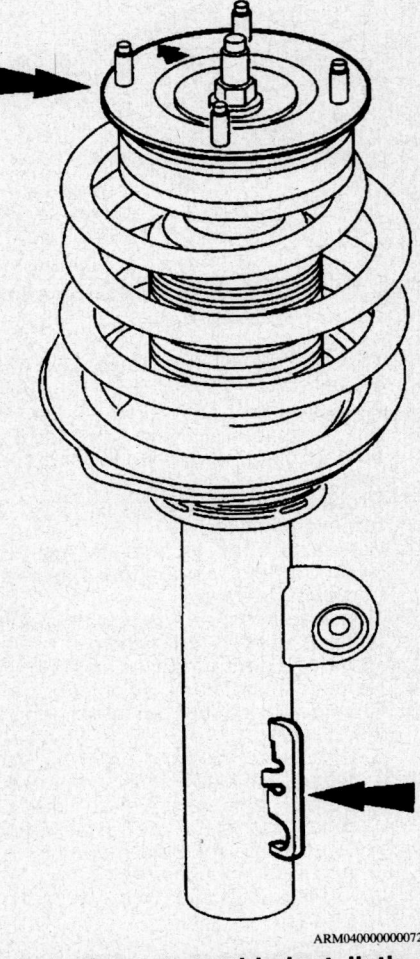

Fig. 6 Strut assembly installation alignment

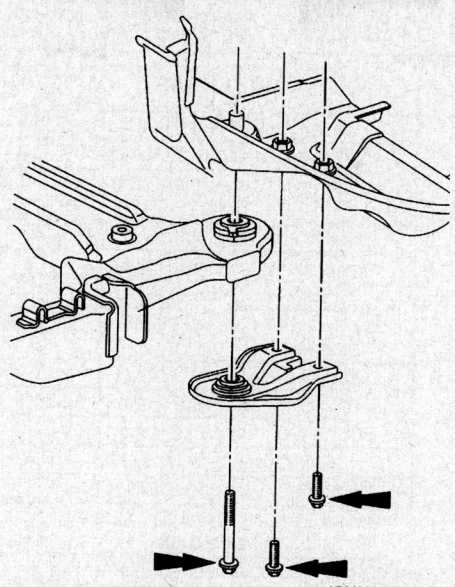

Fig. 7 Subframe lowered

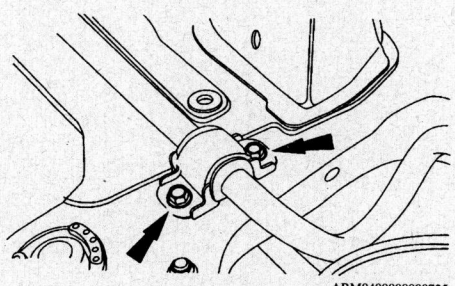

Fig. 8 Stabilizer bar mounting bracket removal

TIGHTENING SPECIFICATIONS

Year	Component	Torque/Ft. Lbs.
2005–08	Axle Shaft Wheel Hub Nut	148
	Lower Arm Ball Joint Nut	85
	Lower Arm Bushing To Subframe Bolts	73
	Lower Arm To Subframe Bolt	.111
	Rear Subframe To Body Bolts	111
	Stabilizer Bar Bracket Bolts	37
	Stabilizer Bar Link To Stabilizer Bar Nut	41
	Stabilizer Bar Link To Strut Nut	41
	Strut & Spring Mounting Bracket Bolts	37
	Strut & Spring Top Mounting Nut	59
	Subframe To Body Bolts	148
	Tie Rod To Steering Knuckle Nut	85
	Wheel Bearing & Hub To Steering Knuckle Bolts	81
	Wheel Speed Sensor Retaining Nut	10

Wheel Alignment

INDEX

	Page No.		Page No.		Page No.
Front Wheel Alignment	7-65	Preliminary Inspection	7-65	Wheel Alignment	
Camber	7-65	Rear Wheel Alignment	7-65	Specifications	7-2
Caster	7-65	Caster & Camber	7-65		
Toe-In	7-65	Toe-In	7-65		

PRELIMINARY INSPECTION

1. Ensure tires are inflated to proper pressure.
2. Inspect tires for wear patterns that may indicate improper wheel alignment, tire imbalance or damage because bulges or separations.
3. Inspect suspension for modifications such as trailer towing equipment or heavy duty handling components.
4. Inspect vehicle for signs of overloading or sagging. Ensure luggage compartment does not contain heavy objects.
5. Road test vehicle to isolate area of concern.

FRONT WHEEL ALIGNMENT

Camber

1. Raise and support vehicle.
2. Remove upper strut mount nuts. **Do not rotate strut mount to any other position than 180° from it's original position, Fig. 1.** Arrow on top of strut must be pointed to three O'clock or nine O'clock positions.
3. Push strut downward and rotate it 180°. When rotated 180° from original position, camber changes by +.05°.
4. Install strut mount nuts, **torque** nuts to 20 ft. lbs.
5. Inspect alignment for proper specifications as outlined in "Specifications."

Caster

Caster is not adjustable. If caster is not within specifications, inspect vehicle for suspension component damage, deteriorated bushings or distorted body mounting points.

Toe-In

1. Start engine and center steering wheel.
2. Turn ignition to Off position, then lock steering wheel in straight ahead position using suitable steering wheel holder.
3. Remove steering gear bellows clamps, **Fig. 2.**
4. Loosen tie rod jam nut, then adjust left-hand and righthand tie rods until each wheel has half desired total toe specification. **Do not allow steering bellows to become twisted.**
5. Tighten tie rod adjusting nuts and install clamps.
6. Remove steering wheel holding tool.

REAR WHEEL ALIGNMENT

Caster & Camber

The caster and camber angles are factory set and cannot be adjusted.

Toe-In

Loosen toe link jam nut, **Fig. 3,** approximately one full turn.

Adjust toe-in by rotating the toe link bolt from the opposite side. Rotate to link bolt to achieve the correct specifications as outlined in "Specifications." **Torque** toe link nut to 74 ft. lbs.

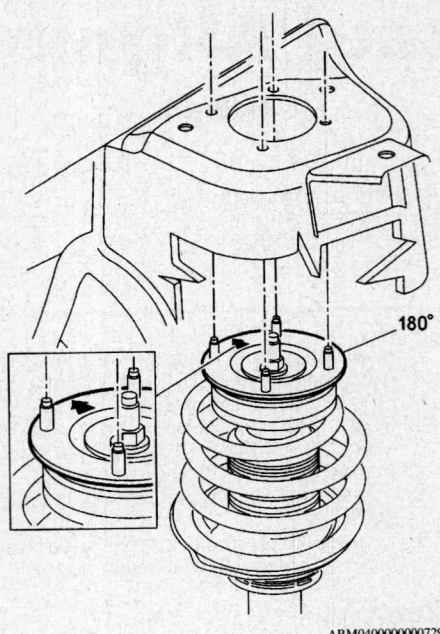

ARM0400000000729

**Fig. 1   Strut rotated 180° from
original position**

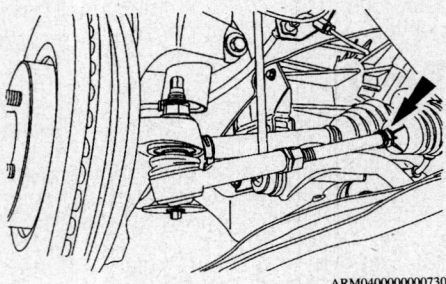

ARM0400000000730

**Fig. 2   Steering gear bellows
clamps**

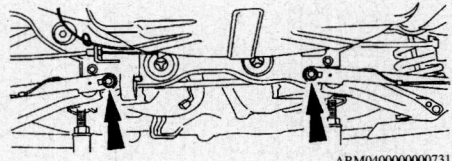

ARM0400000000731

Fig. 3   Rear toe-in adjustment

AIR CONDITIONING

TABLE OF CONTENTS

Page No.

SPECIFICATIONS 8-7
SYSTEM SERVICE 8-5

Page No.

SYSTEM TESTING 8-1

System Testing

NOTE: On Air Bag Equipped Models, Refer To "Air Bag System Precautions" Located In The Front Of This Manual For System Disarming & Arming Procedures.

NOTE: Refer To "Computer Relearn Procedures" Located In The Front Of This Manual When Battery Power To The Computer Has Been Interrupted.

INDEX

Page No.

Charging System 8-3
Discharging System 8-2
Exercise System 8-2
Leak Test 8-2
  Electronic Detectors 8-2

Page No.

Flame-Type (Halide) Detectors . . 8-2
Fluid Leak Detectors 8-2
Tracer Dye 8-2
Performance Test 8-2
Precautions 8-1

Page No.

Battery Ground Cable 8-1
Cleanliness 8-1
General Service 8-1
Safety 8-1
System Evacuation 8-3

PRECAUTIONS

Battery Ground Cable

Prior to service, disconnect battery ground cable and isolate as required.

Safety

Protective goggles should be worn when opening any refrigerant lines. A bottle of sterile mineral oil and a quantity of weak boric acid solution must always be kept nearby when servicing air conditioning system. If **liquid coolant does touch eyes, immediately use a few drops of sterile mineral oil to wash them out, then wash eyes clean with weak boric acid solution. Seek a doctor's aid immediately even though irritation may have ceased.**

Freon refrigerant used in vehicle A/C systems will usually be in a vapor state when being handled in a repair shop. But if a portion of liquid coolant should come in contact with hands or face, note that its temperature momentarily will be at least 22° below zero.

When inspecting a system for leaks with a torch type leak detector, do not breathe vapors coming from flame. Do not recover refrigerant in area of a live flame. A poisonous phosgene gas is produced when refrigerant is burned. While a small amount of this gas produced by a leak detector is not harmful unless inhaled directly at flame.

Never allow temperature of refrigerant drums to exceed 125°F. Resultant increase in temperature will cause a corresponding increase in pressure which may cause safety plug to release or drum to burst.

If it is required to heat a drum of refrigerant when charging a system, drum should be placed in water that is no hotter than 125°F. Never use a blowtorch, or other open flame. If possible, a pressure release mechanism should be attached before drum is heated.

Cleanliness

Air conditioning systems are extremely sensitive to moisture and dirt. Importance of clean working conditions is extremely important, as smallest particle of foreign matter in an air conditioning system will contaminate refrigerant, causing rust, ice or damage to compressor. For this reason, all replacement components are sold in vacuum sealed containers and should not be opened until they are to be installed in system. If, for any reason, a part has been removed from its container for any length of time, part must be completely flushed remove any dust or moisture that may have accumulated during storage. In cases of collision repairs where system has been open for any length of time, entire system must be purged completely and a new receiver-drier must be installed because element of existing unit will have become saturated and unable to remove any moisture from system once system is recharged.

When making gauge connections, purge gauge lines first by cracking charging valve and allowing a small amount of refrigerant to flow through lines, then connect lines immediately.

Cleanliness is especially important when servicing compressors because of very close tolerances used in these units. Consequently, repairs to compressor itself should not be attempted unless all proper tools are at hand and a virtually spotless work area is provided.

General Service

Use care when disconnecting or connecting refrigerant lines; always use a back-up wrench and be careful not to overtighten any connection. Overtightening may result in a line or flare seat distortion and a system leak.

When making pressure inspections on systems having service valves, ensure valve is in intermediate position. If turned in too far, hose connection will be closed, a position used for isolating compressor. When closing gauge port, do not overtighten valve or damage to seat will result.

After disconnecting gauge lines, inspect valve areas to ensure service valves are correctly seated and Schraeder valves, if used, are not leaking.

AIR CONDITIONING

EXERCISE SYSTEM

An important fact most vehicle owners ignore is that A/C system must be used periodically. Vehicle manufacturers caution that when air conditioner is not used regularly, particularly during cold months, it should be turned on for a few minutes once every two or three weeks while engine is running. This keeps system in good operating condition.

Inspecting out system for effects of disuse before onset of summer is one of most important aspects of A/C system servicing.

First clean out condenser core, mounted in most cases at front of vehicle's radiator. All obstructions, such as leaves, bugs, and dirt, must be removed, as they will reduce heat transfer and impair efficiency of system. Ensure space between condenser and radiator also is free of foreign matter.

Ensure evaporator water drain is open. Evaporator cools and dehumidifies air before it enters car.

PERFORMANCE TEST

Refrigerant system problems are diagnosed by inspecting refrigerant pressures and clutch cycle rate and times. Compare pressures and cycle time to charts, **Fig. 1.** Conditional requirements for refrigerant system tests must be satisfied to obtain accurate pressure readings. If findings do not fall between lines on respective charts, **Fig. 2,** determine specific cause of improper readings.

After required repairs have been performed, take pressure readings while meeting conditional requirements to ensure problem has been corrected.

Visual inspection of system may determine problems with refrigerant system. By making a visual inspection, some of following problems can be diagnosed: obstructed air passages, broken belts, disconnected or broken wires, loose or broken mounting brackets and refrigerant leaks.

A refrigerant leak will usually appear as an oily residue at leakage point in system.

LEAK TEST

R-134a systems require use of special service equipment designed specifically for R-134a systems. R-12 servicing equipment cannot be used on R-134a systems.

Testing refrigerant system for leaks is one of most important phases of troubleshooting. One or more of methods outlined will prove useful in detecting leaks or inspecting connections if service work is performed. Before beginning any leak test, attach a manifold gauge set and note pressure. If little or no pressure is indicated, a partial charge must be installed. Inspect all connections, compressor head gasket, oil filler plug and compressor shaft seal for leaks.

Electronic Detectors

There are a number of electronic leak detectors available to perform leak tests.

Refer to operating instructions for unit being used and observe these general procedures:

1. Move detector probe one inch per second in areas of suspected leaks.
2. Position probe below test point, as refrigerant gas is heavier than air.
3. Ensure to inspect service access gauge port valve fittings, particularly when valve caps are missing, as dirt accumulations can destroy sealing area of valve core when manifold gauge set is attached. Replace missing valve caps after cleaning valve core area. **Valve caps should only be finger tightened. Using pliers to tighten valve caps may distort sealing surface of valve.**
4. Inspect for leaks in manifold gauge set and hoses, as well as rest of system.

Flame-Type (Halide) Detectors

When using flame-type detectors, avoid inhaling fumes produced by burning refrigerant. Do not use this type detector where concentrations of combustible or explosive gases, dusts or vapors may exist.

1. Adjust detector flame as low as possible to obtain maximum sensitivity. Ensure copper element is cherry red and not burned away. Flame will be almost colorless.
2. Slowly move detector along areas of suspected leaks. A slight leak will cause flame to change to a bright yellow-green color. A significant leak will be indicated by a brilliant blue flame. Position detector under areas being tested as refrigerant gas is heavier than air. **Presence of dust in pickup hose may cause a change in color of flame. If not recognized, a false diagnosis could be made. Store leak detector in a clean place and ensure hose is free of dust before leak testing.**
3. Inspect for leaks in manifold gauge set and hoses, as well as rest of system.
4. Use a small fan to ventilate areas where leak detector indicates refrigerant constantly. These areas are contaminated with refrigerant and must be ventilated before leak can be pinpointed.

Fluid Leak Detectors

Apply leak detector solution around joints to be tested. A cluster of bubbles will form immediately if there is a leak. A white foam that forms after a short while will indicate an extremely small leak. In some confined areas such as sections of evaporator and condenser, electronic leak detectors will be more useful.

Tracer Dye

R-134a fluorescent tracer dye has been added to the A/C systems of new vehicles. Leak inspections can be performed with an ultraviolet lamp and is an acceptable alternative to using an electronic leak detector. The fluorescent lifespan of the leak tracer dye is 500 hours of A/C system use, after which another injection of dye is required. A/C system pressure must be above 80 psi for the operation. Scan all components, fittings and lines of the A/C system with Rotunda Ultraviolet Lamp 164-R0721, or equivalent, the exact location of the leak or leaks can be pinpointed by the bright yellow-green glow of the tracer dye. Since more than one leak may exist in the system, always inspect each component.

After the leak is serviced, the traces of dye can be removed from the previously leaking areas by using any general purpose oil solvent. Verify the service by operation the A/C system for a short while and reinspecting the system with the UV lamp. Rotunda Fluoro-Lite for R-134a/PAG A/C Systems 164-R3712, or equivalent, may be introduced into the A/C system using Rotunda R-134a Fluorescent Tracer Dye Injector 164-R2610, or equivalent. Inject the dye while charging the system and inspect for leaks as follows:

1. Adjust quick disconnect valve on dye injector to maximum counterclockwise (closed) position.
2. Remove plug from end of dye injector reservoir and fill reservoir with ¼ ounces of Rotunda Fluoro-Lite for R-134a/PAG A/C Systems 164-R3712, or equivalent.
3. Replace plug, then tighten securely.
4. Attach low-side quick disconnect from either the manifold gauge set or the charging station to the plug on the dye injector.
5. Install dye injector quick disconnect valve to high-pressure service port on vehicle.
6. Adjust all quick disconnect valves to maximum clockwise (open) position.
7. Charge vehicle with required amount of refrigerant , then flow of refrigerant through dye injector will inject dye into vehicle system.
8. When vehicle charging is complete, close dye injector and high-side quick disconnect valves and remove quick disconnects from vehicle.
9. Recover refrigerant from dye injector and close low-side quick disconnect valve.
10. Remove dye injector from low-side quick disconnect valve. The dye injector should only be connected to charging/recovery station when dye is to be injected. The dye injector has a one-way check valve that will prevent system refrigerant recovery and evacuation.
11. Inspect system for leaks using Rotunda Ultraviolet Lamp 164-R0721 or equivalent.

DISCHARGING SYSTEM

Use of refrigerant recovery and recycling stations allows recovery and reuse of refrigerant after contaminants and moisture have been removed.

IMPORTANT — TEST REQUIREMENTS

The following test conditions must be established to obtain accurate pressure readings:

- Run engine at 1500 rpm for 10 minutes.
- Operate A/C system on max A/C (recirculating air).
- Run blower at max speed.
- Stabilize in car temperature @ 70°F to 80°F (21°C to 22°C).

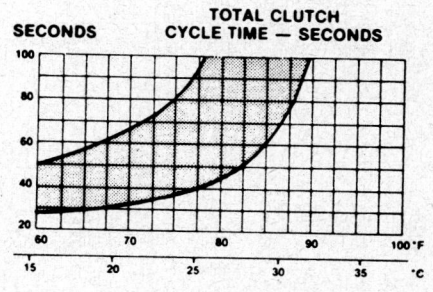

TOTAL CLUTCH CYCLE TIME — SECONDS

AMBIENT TEMPERATURES

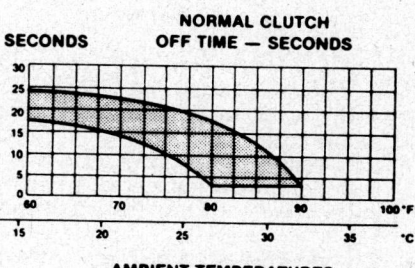

NORMAL CLUTCH OFF TIME — SECONDS

AMBIENT TEMPERATURES

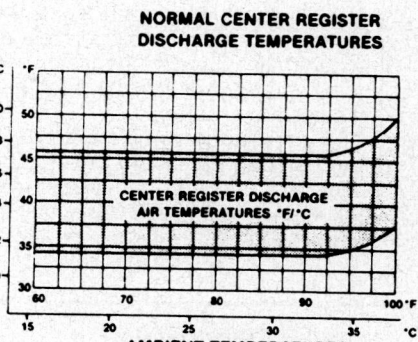

NORMAL CENTER REGISTER DISCHARGE TEMPERATURES

AMBIENT TEMPERATURES

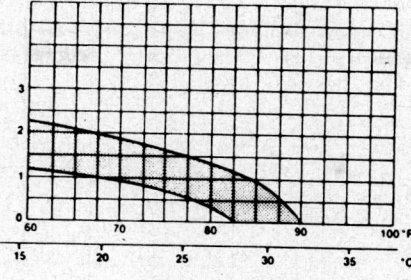

NORMAL CLUTCH CYCLE RATE PER MINUTE

CYCLES/MINUTE

AMBIENT TEMPERATURES

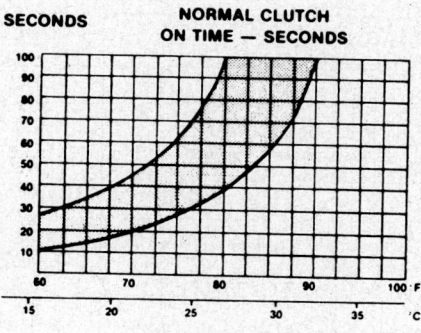

NORMAL CLUTCH ON TIME — SECONDS

AMBIENT TEMPERATURES

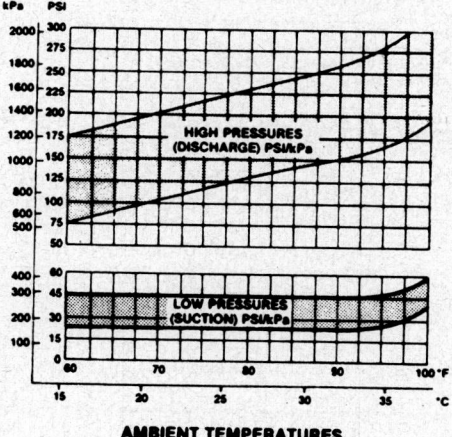

NORMAL FIXED ORIFICE TUBE CYCLING CLUTCH REFRIGERANT SYSTEM PRESSURES

AMBIENT TEMPERATURES

FM7029100026000X

Fig. 1 Refrigerant pressure & temperature charts

When using a recovery or recycling station, follow manufacturer's operating instructions, noting following:

1. **Use extreme caution and observe all safety and service precautions related to use of refrigerants.**
2. Connect refrigerant recycling station hose(s) to vehicle A/C service port(s) and recovery station inlet fitting. Hoses used should have shutoff devices or check valves within 12 inches of hose ends to minimize introduction of air into recycling station and to minimize amount of refrigerant released when hose(s) is disconnected.
3. Turn recycling station On to start recovery process. Allow recycling station to pump refrigerant from A/C system until station pressure gauge indicates vacuum.
4. After vehicle A/C system has been evacuated, close station inlet valve, if equipped.
5. Turn station Off. On some stations pump will automatically be turned Off by a low pressure switch.
6. Allow vehicle A/C system to remain closed for approximately two minutes.

Observe vacuum level indicated on gauge. If pressure does not rise, disconnect recycling station hose(s).
7. If system pressure rises, repeat steps 3 through 6 until vacuum level remains stable for two minutes.
8. Service A/C system as required, then evacuate and recharge A/C system.

SYSTEM EVACUATION

Vacuum pumps suitable for removing air and moisture from A/C systems are commercially available. A specification for system pump down used here is 28–29 ½ inches vacuum. This reading can be attained at or near sea level only. For each 1000 feet of altitude, reading will be one inch of vacuum less than standard specification given. For example, at 5000 feet elevation, only 23–24 ½ inches of vacuum can be obtained. **System must be completely discharged before it can be evacuated. Damage to vacuum pump will result if pressurized refrigerant is allowed to enter pump assembly.**

1. Connect vacuum pump to gauge manifold. With gauges connected into system, remove cap from vacuum hose connector. Install center hose from gauge manifold to vacuum pump connector. Mid position high and low side compressor service valve (if used). Open high and low side gauge manifold hand valves.
2. Operate vacuum pump a minimum of 30 minutes for air and moisture removal. Watch compound gauge to see that system pumps down into a vacuum. System will reach 28–29 ½ inches Hg. vacuum in a maximum of five minutes. If system does not pump down, inspect all connections and leak test if required.
3. Close gauge manifold hand valves and shutoff vacuum pump.
4. Inspect ability of system to hold vacuum. Watch compound gauge to see that gauge does not rise at a faster rate than one inch vacuum every four or five minutes. If compound gauge rises at too rapid a rate, install partial charge and leak test. Then discharge system as outlined above.
5. If system holds vacuum, charge system with refrigerant.

CHARGING SYSTEM

R-134a systems require use of special service equipment designed specifically for R-134a systems. R-12 servicing equipment cannot be used on R-134a systems.
Refer to "A/C Specifications" for refrigerant capacities.
When charging from small cans, do not open manifold gauge set high pressure (discharge) gauge valve, as this can cause containers to explode.

1. Connect manifold gauge set, then set valves closed to center hose, disconnect vacuum pump from manifold gauge set, **Fig. 3.**
2. Connect center hose of manifold gauge set to refrigerant supply.

NOTE: System test requirements must be met to obtain accurate test readings for evaluation. Refer to the normal refrigerant system pressure/temperature and the normal clutch cycle ratio and times charts.

High (Discharge) Pressure	Low (Suction) Pressure	Clutch Cycle Time			Component — Causes
		Rate	On	Off	
High	High				Condenser — Inadequate Airflow
High	Normal to High				Engine Overheating
Normal to High	Normal	Continuous Run			Air in Refrigerant Refrigerant Overcharge (a) Humidity or Ambient Temp Very High (b)
Normal	High				Fixed Orifice Tube — Missing O Rings Leaking/Missing
Normal	High	Slow	Long	Long	Clutch Cycling Switch — High Cut In
Normal	Normal	Slow or No Cycle	Long or Continuous	Normal or No Cycle	Moisture in Refrigerant System Excessive Refrigerant Oil
		Fast	Short	Short	Clutch Cycling Switch — Low Cut In or High Cut Out
Normal	Low	Slow	Long	Long	Clutch Cycling Switch — Low Cut Out
Normal to Low	High	Continuous Run			Compressor — Low Performance
Normal to Low	Normal to High				A/C Suction Line — Partially Restricted or Plugged (c)
Normal to Low	Normal	Fast	Short	Normal	Evaporator — Restricted Airflow
			Short to Very Short	Normal to Long	Condenser fixed orifice Tube or A/C Liquid Line — Partially Restricted or Plugged
			Short to Very Short	Short to Very Short	Low Refrigerant Charge
			Short to Very Short	Long	Evaporator Core — Partially Restricted or Plugged
Normal to Low	Low	Continuous Run			A/C Suction Line — Partially Restricted or Plugged (d) Clutch Cycling Switch — Sticking Closed
Low	Normal	Very Fast	Very Short	Very Short	Clutch Cycling Switch — Cycling Range Too Close
Erratic Operation or Compressor Not Running		—	—	—	Clutch Cycling Switch — Dirty Contacts or Sticking Open Poor Connection at A/C Clutch Connector or Clutch Cycling Switch Connector A/C Electrical Circuit Erratic

Additional Possible Cause Components Associated with Inadequate Compressor Operation

- Compressor Drive Belt — Loose
- Compressor Clutch — Slipping
- Clutch Coil Open — Shorted or Loose Mounting
- Control Assembly Switch — Dirty Contacts or Sticking Open
- Clutch Wiring Circuit — High Resistance Open or Blown Fuse

Additional Possible Cause Components Associated with a Damaged Compressor

- Compressor Clutch — Seized
- Clutch Cycling Switch — Sticking Closed
- Suction Accumulator Drier — Refrigerant Oil Bleed Hole Plugged
- Refrigerant Leaks

(a) Compressor may make noise on initial run. This is slugging condition caused by excessive liquid refrigerant.
(b) Compressor clutch may not cycle in ambient temperatures above 80°F depending on humidity conditions.
(c) Low pressure reading will be normal to high if pressure is taken at accumulator and if restriction is downstream of service access valve.
(d) Low pressure reading will be low if pressure is taken near the compressor and restriction is upstream of service access valve.

FM7029100028000X

Fig. 2   Refrigerant system pressure evaluation chart

3. Purge air from center hose by loosening hose at manifold gauge set and open refrigerant drum valve. When refrigerant escapes from hose, tighten center hose connection at manifold gauge set.
4. On vehicles so equipped, disconnect wire harness connector at clutch cycling pressure switch. Install jumper wire across terminals of connector.
5. On all models, open manifold gauge set low side valve and allow refrigerant to enter system. Refrigerant can must be kept upright if vehicle low pressure service gauge port is not on suction accumulator/drier or suction accumulator fitting.
6. When system stops drawing refrigerant in, start engine and set control lever to A/C position and blower switch to Hi position to draw remaining refrigerant into system.
7. When specified weight of refrigerant is in system, close gauge set low pressure valve and refrigerant supply valve.
8. On vehicles so equipped, remove jumper wire from clutch cycling pressure switch connector and connect connector to pressure switch.
9. On all models, operate system until pressures stabilize to inspect operation and system pressures. During high ambient temperatures, a high volume fan may be required to blow air through radiator and condenser to cool engine and prevent excessive refrigerant system pressures.
10. When charging is complete and system operating pressures are normal, disconnect manifold gauge set from vehicle and install protective caps on service gauge port valves.

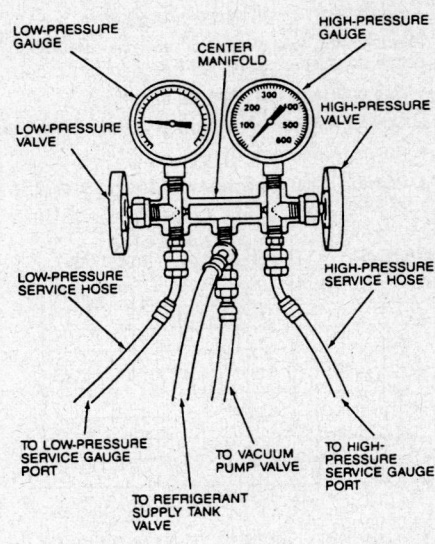

FM7029100030000X

Fig. 3   Refrigerant system service connections

System Service

NOTE: On Air Bag Equipped Models, Refer To "Air Bag System Precautions" Located In The Front Of This Manual For System Disarming & Arming Procedures.

NOTE: Refer To "Computer Relearn Procedures" Located In The Front Of This Manual When Battery Power To The Computer Has Been Interrupted.

INDEX

	Page No.
Oil Charge	8-5
Ford FS-10 Swash Plate Compressor	8-5
Ford FS-18 Fixed Scroll Compressor	8-5
Ford FS-20 Fixed Piston Compressor	8-6

	Page No.
Ford SC-100 Variable Scroll Compressor	8-5
Ford SC-105V Variable Scroll Compressor	8-6
Ford SC-115 Fixed Scroll Compressor	8-6

	Page No.
Ford SC-90V Variable Scroll Compressor	8-5
Ford SP-17 Swash Plate Compressor	8-6
Ford VS-90	8-6
Oil Level Check	8-6

OIL CHARGE

Ford FS-10 Swash Plate Compressor

A new service replacement compressor contains no refrigerant oil.
1. Drain and measure oil from old compressor.
2. Drain oil from new compressor into clean measuring device.
3. If 3–5 oz. were drained from old compressor, add equal amount plus 1 oz. of new oil to new compressor.
4. If more than 5 oz. were drained from old compressor, add equal amount of new oil to new compressor.
5. If less then 3 oz. was drained from old compressor, add 3 oz. to new compressor.
6. When other air conditioning system components are replaced, add the following quantities of refrigerant oil:
   a. Accumulator, same amount drained from old accumulator plus 2 oz.
   b. Evaporator core, 3 oz.
   c. Condenser, 1 oz.
7. Add 2 oz. of new oil after replacing other system components such as hoses, evaporator core orifice, cycling switch, compressor pressure relief valve and pressure cutoff switch, or following minor repairs such O-ring, port, compressor shaft seal and hose leaks.

Ford FS-18 Fixed Scroll Compressor

A new service replacement compressor contains no refrigerant oil.
1. Rotate compressor shaft 8 to 10 full rotations (clockwise) while collecting refrigerant oil in a clean measuring cup.

2. Add same amount plus amount collected during refrigerant recovery.
3. If an excessive amount of refrigerant oil is lost due to a hose rupture/separation or other damage, total system refrigerant oil capacity must be added.
4. When other air conditioning system components are replaced, add the following quantities of refrigerant oil:
   a. Accumulator, same amount drained from old accumulator plus 2 oz.
   b. Evaporator core, 1.5 oz.
   c. Condenser, 2 oz.
   d. Evaporator core, orifice or Thermostatic Expansion Valve (TXV) add amount collected during refrigerant recovery.
5. Add 2 oz. of new oil after replacing other system components such as hoses, evaporator core orifice, cycling switch, compressor pressure relief valve and pressure cutoff switch, or following minor repairs such O-ring, port, compressor shaft seal and hose leaks.

Ford SC-90V Variable Scroll Compressor

A new service replacement compressor contains 7 oz. of refrigerant oil.
1. Drain and measure oil from old compressor.
2. Drain oil from new compressor into clean measuring device.
3. If 3–5 oz. were drained from old compressor, add equal amount plus 1 oz. of new oil to new compressor.
4. If more than 5 oz. were drained from old compressor, add equal amount of new oil to new compressor.
5. If less then 3 oz. was drained from old compressor, add 3 oz. to new compressor.
6. When other air conditioning system

components are replaced, add the following quantities of refrigerant oil:
   a. Accumulator, same amount drained from old accumulator plus 2 oz.
   b. Evaporator core, 1 oz.
   c. Condenser, 1 oz.
7. Add .75 oz. of new oil after replacing other system components such as hoses, evaporator core orifice, cycling switch, compressor pressure relief valve and pressure cutoff switch, or following minor repairs such O-ring, port, compressor shaft seal and hose leaks.

Ford SC-100 Variable Scroll Compressor

A new service replacement compressor contains no refrigerant oil.
1. Drain and measure oil from old compressor.
2. Drain oil from new compressor into clean measuring device.
3. If 3–5 oz. were drained from old compressor, add equal amount plus 1 oz. of new oil to new compressor.
4. If more than 5 oz. were drained from old compressor, add equal amount of new oil to new compressor.
5. If less then 3 oz. was drained from old compressor, add 3 oz. to new compressor.
6. When other air conditioning system components are replaced, add the following quantities of refrigerant oil:
   a. Accumulator, same amount drained from old accumulator plus 2 oz.
   b. Condenser, same amount drained from old accumulator plus 2 oz.
   c. Expansion valve, same amount drained from old accumulator.
   d. Evaporator core, same amount drained from old accumulator plus 1.5 oz.

7. Add 2 oz. of new oil after replacing other system components such as hoses, evaporator core orifice, cycling switch, compressor pressure relief valve and pressure cutoff switch, or following minor repairs such O-ring, port, compressor shaft seal and hose leaks.

Ford SC-105V Variable Scroll Compressor

A new service replacement compressor contains no refrigerant oil.
1. Rotate compressor shaft 8 to 10 full rotations (clockwise) while collecting refrigerant oil in a clean measuring cup.
2. Add same amount plus amount collected during refrigerant recovery.
3. If an excessive amount of refrigerant oil is lost due to a hose rupture/separation or other damage, total system refrigerant oil capacity must be added.
4. When other air conditioning system components are replaced, add the following quantities of refrigerant oil:
   a. Accumulator, same amount drained from old accumulator plus 2 oz.
   b. Evaporator core, 1.5 oz.
   c. Condenser, 2 oz.
   d. Evaporator core, orifice or Thermostatic Expansion Valve (TXV) add amount collected during refrigerant recovery.
5. Add 2 oz. of new oil after replacing other system components such as hoses, evaporator core orifice, cycling switch, compressor pressure relief valve and pressure cutoff switch, or following minor repairs such O-ring, port, compressor shaft seal and hose leaks.

Ford SC-115 Fixed Scroll Compressor

Refer to "Ford FS-10 Swash Plate 10-Cylinder Compressor."

Ford SP-17 Swash Plate Compressor

A new service replacement compressor contains no refrigerant oil.
1. Rotate compressor shaft 8 to 10 full rotations (clockwise) while collecting refrigerant oil in a clean measuring cup.
2. Add same amount plus amount collected during refrigerant recovery.
3. If an excessive amount of refrigerant oil is lost due to a hose rupture/separation or other damage, total system refrigerant oil capacity must be added.
4. When other air conditioning system components are replaced, add the following quantities of refrigerant oil:
   a. Accumulator, same amount drained from old accumulator plus 2 oz.
   b. Evaporator core, 1.5 oz.
   c. Condenser, 2 oz.
5. Add 2 oz. of new oil after replacing other system components such as hoses, evaporator core orifice, cycling switch, compressor pressure relief valve and pressure cutoff switch, or following minor repairs such O-ring, port, compressor shaft seal and hose leaks.

Ford VS-90

Refer to "Ford FS-10 Swash Plate 10-Cylinder Compressor."

Ford FS-20 Fixed Piston Compressor

A new service replacement compressor contains no refrigerant oil.
1. Rotate compressor shaft 8 to 10 full rotations (clockwise) while collecting refrigerant oil in a clean measuring cup.
2. Add same amount plus amount collected during refrigerant recovery plus 1 ounce.
3. If an excessive amount of refrigerant oil is lost due to a hose rupture/separation or other damage, total system refrigerant oil capacity must be added.
4. When other air conditioning system components are replaced, add the following quantities of refrigerant oil:
   a. Drill one ½ inch hole in old accumulator, add same amount drained from old accumulator plus 2 oz.
   b. Evaporator core, 1.5 oz.
   c. Condenser, 2 oz.
   d. Evaporator core, orifice or Thermostatic Expansion Valve (TXV) add amount collected during refrigerant recovery.
5. Add 2 oz. of new oil after replacing other system components such as hoses, evaporator core orifice, cycling switch, compressor pressure relief valve and pressure cutoff switch, or following minor repairs such O-ring, port, compressor shaft seal and hose leaks.

OIL LEVEL CHECK

Oil level of these compressors should be inspected whenever refrigerant has been lost due to leakage or through normal system servicing.

Specifications

INDEX

	Page No.		Page No.		Page No.
A/C Specifications	8-7	Belt Tension	8-8	Charging Valve Location	8-8

A/C SPECIFICATIONS

Year	Compressor Model	Refrigerant Capacity, Lbs.	Refrigerant Type	Refrigerant Oil Viscosity	Refrigerant Oil Total System Capacity, Oz. ①	Compressor Clutch Air Gap, Inch
CROWN VICTORIA						
2004–05	Ford SC-115	2.38	R-134a	②	7.50	.014–.030
2006–08	Ford FS-18	2.25	R-134a	③	7.00	.014–.026
FIVE HUNDRED, FREESTYLE & MONTEGO						
2005	Ford SC-100	2.42④	R-134a	②	7.50⑤	.014–.030
2006–08	Ford SC-100	2.42④	R-134a	③	7.00⑤	.014–.030
FOCUS						
2004–05	Ford FS-10	2.20	R-134a	②	7.00	.014–.030
2006–07	Ford FS-10	2.20	R-134a	③	7.00	.014–.030
FUSION, MILAN, MKZ & ZEPHYR						
2006–08	Ford SP-17	1.75	R-134a	③	6.00	.014–.030
GRAND MARQUIS						
2004–05	Ford SC-115	2.38	R-134a	②	7.50	.014–.030
2006–08	Ford FS-18	2.25	R-134a	③	7.00	.014–.026
LS						
2004–05	Ford SC-90V	1.75	R-134a	②	7.00	.014–.030
2006	Ford SC-105V	2.33	R-134a	③	7.00	.014–.030
MARAUDER						
2004	Ford SC-115	2.38	R-134a	②	7.50	.014–.030
MUSTANG						
2004	Ford FS-10	2.13	R-134a	②	8.60	.014–.030
2005–08	Ford FS-10	2.60	R-134a	③	7.00	.014–.030
SABLE						
2004–05	Ford FS-10	2.13	R-134a	②	6.60	.014–.030
2008	Ford FS-20	⑦	R-134a	②	⑥	.014–.026
TAURUS & TAURUS X						
2004–05	Ford FS-10	2.83	R-134a	②	6.60	.014–.030
2006–07	Ford FS-10	2.83	R-134a	③	6.60	.014–.030
2008	Ford FS-20	⑦	R-134a	②	⑥	.014–.026
THUNDERBIRD						
2004–05	Ford SC-90V	1.75	R-134a	②	7.00	.014–.033
TOWN CAR						
2004	Ford SC-115	2.66	R-134a	②	8.00	.014–.030
2006–07	Ford FS-18	1.92	R-134a	③	7.00	.014–.026

① — Oil level inches cannot be inspected.

② — Motorcraft YN-12C PAG (Polyalkaline Glycol), or equivalent.

③ — Motorcraft YN-12D PAG (Polyalkaline Glycol), or equivalent.

④ — With auxiliary climate control, 3.20 lbs.

⑤ — With auxiliary climate control, 9.00 ounces.

⑥ — With auxiliary climate control 9.50 ounces; without auxiliary climate control 7 ounces.

⑦ — With auxiliary climate control 2.75 lbs.; without auxiliary climate control 2.25 lbs.

AIR CONDITIONING

CHARGING VALVE LOCATION

Model	High Pressure Fitting	Low Pressure Fitting
Crown Victoria	High Pressure Line From Compressor	Accumulator
Five Hundred, Freestyle, Montego & Taurus X	High Pressure Line From Compressor Near Condenser Fitting	Accumulator Line Near Evaporator Fitting
Focus	High Pressure Line From Compressor	Low Pressure Line From Compressor
Fusion, Milan, MKZ & Zephyr	High Pressure Condenser	Low Pressure Line From TXV Manifold And Tube Assembly
Grand Marquis	High Pressure Line From Compressor	Accumulator
LS	High Pressure Line From Compressor	Accumulator
Mustang	High Pressure Line From Compressor Near Condenser Fitting	Accumulator Line Near Evaporator Fitting
Sable	High Pressure Line From Compressor	Accumulator
Taurus	High Pressure Line From Compressor	Accumulator
Thunderbird	High Pressure Line From Compressor	Accumulator
Town Car	High Pressure Line From Compressor	Accumulator

BELT TENSION

Engine	New, Lbs.	Used, Lbs.
2.0L	①	①
2.3L	①	①
2.5L	①	①
3.0L	②	③
3.5L	④	④
3.8L	①	①
3.9L	①	①
4.0L	①	①
4.6L	①	①
5.4L	⑤	⑤

① — Drive belt tension is not adjustable. Drive belt tensioner automatically adjusts tensioner.
② — 5-rib belt, 140–160 lbs.; 6-rib belt, belt tension is not adjustable; drive belt tensioner automatically adjusts tensioner.
③ — 5-rib belt, 110–130 lbs.; 6-rib belt, belt tension is not adjustable; drive belt tensioner automatically adjusts tensioner.
④ — 5-rib belt, belt tension is not adjustable; drive belt tensioner automatically adjusts tensioner.
⑤ — 6-rib belt, belt tension is not adjustable; drive belt tensioner automatically adjusts tensioner. Supercharger 10 rib belt, belt tension is not adjustable; drive belt tensioner automatically adjusts tensione.

ALERO, GRAND AM & 2004–05 MALIBU

NOTE: Refer To Rear Of This Manual For Vehicle Manufacturer's Special Service Tool Suppliers.

NOTE: On Malibu Models In This Chapter The Fourth Digit Of The Vehicle Information Number (VIN) Is The Letter N.

NOTE: Refer To "G6 & Malibu Maxx" Chapter For Malibu Models With The Fourth Digit Of The Vehicle Information Number (VIN) The Letter Z.

INDEX OF SERVICE OPERATIONS

Page No.

AIR BAG SYSTEM PRECAUTIONS 0-18
BRAKES
Anti-Lock Brakes (Volume 2).. 6-1
Disc Brakes................... 22-1
Drum Brakes 23-1
Hydraulic Brake Systems 24-1
Power Brake Units........... 25-1
COMPUTER RELEARN PROCEDURE 0-31
ELECTRICAL
Air Bag System (Volume 2) ... 4-1
Air Conditioning............... 16-1
Alternator, Replace 1-6
Alternators................... 19-1
Blower Motor, Replace........ 1-8
Clutch Start Switch, Replace.. 1-6
Coil Pack, Replace 1-6
Cooling Fans 17-1
Cruise Control (Volume 2) 2-1
Dash Gauges (Volume 2) 1-1
Dash Panel Service (Volume 2) 5-1
Evaporator Core, Replace 1-9
Fuel Pump Relay Location 1-5
Fuse Panel & Flasher Location 1-5
Headlamp Switch, Replace ... 1-7
Heater Core, Replace......... 1-8
Ignition Lock, Replace 1-6
Ignition Switch, Replace 1-6
Instrument Cluster, Replace... 1-7
Multi-Function Switch, Replace 1-7
Neutral Safety Switch, Replace 1-6
Passive Restraint Systems (Volume 2).................... 4-1
Precautions.................. 1-5
Radio, Replace 1-7
Relay Center Location 1-5
Starter, Replace 1-5
Speed Controls (Volume 2) ... 2-1
Starter Motors 18-1
Steering Columns............. 20-1
Steering Wheel, Replace...... 1-7
Stop Light Switch, Replace ... 1-7
Turn Signal Switch, Replace .. 1-7
Wiper Motor, Replace........ 1-7
Wiper Switch, Replace........ 1-8
Wiper Systems (Volume 2).... 3-1
Wiper Transmission, Replace . 1-8

Page No.

ELECTRICAL SYMBOL IDENTIFICATION 0-63
FRONT DRIVE AXLES 26-1
FRONT SUSPENSION & STEERING
Ball Joint, Replace............ 1-32
Ball Joint Inspection 1-32
Coil Spring, Replace 1-33
Control Arm, Replace 1-34
Description 1-32
Power Steering 21-1
Power Steering Gear, Replace 1-34
Power Steering Pump, Replace 1-35
Precautions.................. 1-32
Stabilizer Bar, Replace........ 1-34
Steering Columns............. 20-1
Steering Knuckle, Replace.... 1-34
Strut, Replace 1-33
Strut Service................ 1-33
Tie Rod End, Replace 1-34
Tightening Specifications...... 1-36
Wheel Bearing, Replace 1-32
NON-STANDARD TIRE & WHEEL SIZE ADJUSTMENT TO RIDE HEIGHT SPECIFICATIONS & TIRE SIZE CHART ... 0-61
REAR AXLE & SUSPENSION
Coil Spring, Replace 1-31
Control Arm, Replace 1-31
Description 1-30
Hub & Bearing, Replace 1-30
Knuckle, Replace............. 1-31
Lateral Link, Replace 1-31
Rear Crossmember, Replace . 1-31
Shock Absorber, Replace 1-31
Stabilizer Shaft, Replace...... 1-31
Strut, Replace 1-30
Strut Service................ 1-30
Support Assembly, Replace ... 1-30
Tightening Specifications...... 1-32
Toe Link, Replace 1-31
Trailing Arm, Replace 1-31
SERVICE REMINDER & WARNING LAMP RESET PROCEDURES 0-34

Page No.

SPECIFICATIONS
Fluid Capacities & Cooling System Data................. 1-4
Front Wheel Alignment Specifications................. 1-3
General Engine Specifications................. 1-2
Lubricant Data............... 1-4
Rear Wheel Alignment Specifications................. 1-3
Tune Up Specifications 1-2
Vehicle Ride Height Specifications................. 1-3
TIRE PRESSURE MONITORING SYSTEM 20-1
VEHICLE IDENTIFICATION 0-1
VEHICLE LIFT POINTS 0-51
VEHICLE MAINTENANCE SCHEDULES 0-73
WHEEL ALIGNMENT
Front Wheel Alignment 1-37
Preliminary Inspection 1-37
Rear Wheel Alignment 1-37
Thrust Angle................. 1-37
Wheel Alignment Specifications................. 1-3
WIRE COLOR CODE IDENTIFICATION 0-63
2.2L ENGINE
Belt Tension Data............. 1-14
Camshaft, Replace 1-14
Compression Pressure........ 1-10
Cooling System Bleed 1-15
Crankshaft Damper, Replace.. 1-12
Crankshaft Rear Oil Seal, Replace 1-14
Crankshaft Seal, Replace 1-14
Cylinder Head, Replace....... 1-11
Engine Rebuilding Specifications................. 29-1
Engine, Replace 1-10
Engine Mount, Replace........ 1-10
Exhaust Manifold, Replace.... 1-11
Front Cover, Replace 1-12
Fuel Filter, Replace 1-16
Fuel Pump, Replace........... 1-16
Intake Manifold, Replace...... 1-11
Main & Rod Bearings 1-14
Oil Pan, Replace.............. 1-14
Oil Pump, Replace............ 1-14
Piston & Rod Assembly 1-14

	Page No.		Page No.		Page No.
Pistons, Pins & Rings	1-14	Precautions	1-19	Fuel Filter, Replace	1-28
Precautions	1-10	Radiator, Replace	1-20	Fuel Pump, Replace	1-28
Radiator, Replace	1-15	Tightening Specifications	1-21	Intake Manifold, Replace	1-23
Serpentine Drive Belt	1-15	**3.4L ENGINE**		Main & Rod Bearings	1-26
Thermostat, Replace	1-15	Belt Tension Data	1-27	Oil Pan, Replace	1-26
Tightening Specifications	1-18	Camshaft, Replace	1-26	Oil Pump, Replace	1-27
Timing Chain, Replace	1-12	Camshaft Lobe Lift		Oil Pump Service	1-27
Valve Adjustment	1-12	Specifications	1-24	Piston & Rod Assembly	1-26
Valve Cover, Replace	1-12	Compression Pressure	1-22	Precautions	1-22
Valve Lash Adjusters,		Cooling System Bleed	1-27	Push Rods	1-24
Replace	1-12	Crankshaft Rear Oil Seal,		Radiator, Replace	1-28
Water Pump, Replace	1-15	Replace	1-26	Serpentine Drive Belt	1-27
3.1L ENGINE		Cylinder Head, Replace	1-23	Thermostat, Replace	1-28
Compression Pressure	1-19	Engine Rebuilding		Tightening Specifications	1-29
Engine Rebuilding		Specifications	29-1	Timing Chain, Replace	1-25
Specifications	29-1	Engine, Replace	1-22	Valve Adjustment	1-24
Engine, Replace	1-19	Engine Mount, Replace	1-22	Valve Arrangement	1-24
Engine Mount, Replace	1-19	Exhaust Manifold, Replace	1-23	Valve Cover, Replace	1-24
Exhaust Manifold, Replace	1-20	Front Cover, Replace	1-25	Valve Lifters	1-24
Intake Manifold, Replace	1-20	Front Cover Seal, Replace	1-25	Water Pump, Replace	1-28

Specifications

GENERAL ENGINE SPECIFICATIONS

Engine Liter	Fuel Injection System	Bore & Stroke	Compression Ratio	Net H.P. @ RPM①	Maximum Torque Ft. Lbs. @ RPM	Normal Oil Pressure, psi
2004						
2.2L⑥⑦	SFI	3.39 x 3.73	10.0:1	140 @ 5600	150 @ 4000	50–80②
2.2L④	SFI	3.39 x 3.73	10.0:1	145 @ 5600	155 @ 4000	50–80②
3.4L⑥⑦	SFI	3.62 × 3.31	9.5:1	170 @ 4800	195 @ 4000	60⑤
3.4L③	SFI	3.62 × 3.31	9.5:1	175 @ 5200	205 @ 4000	60⑤
2005						
2.2L⑥⑦	SFI	3.39 x 3.73	10.0:1	140 @ 5600	150 @ 4000	50–80②
2.2L④	SFI	3.39 x 3.73	10.0:1	145 @ 5600	155 @ 4000	50–80②
3.4L⑦	SFI	3.62 × 3.31	9.5:1	170 @ 4800	195 @ 4000	60⑤
3.4L③	SFI	3.62 × 3.31	9.5:1	175 @ 5200	205 @ 4000	60⑤

SFI — Sequential Fuel Injection
① — Ratings are as installed in vehicle.
② — Oil Pressure @ 1000 RPM.

③ — Grand Am w/Ram Air.
④ — Malibu.
⑤ — Oil Pressure @ 1850 RPM.

⑥ — Alero.
⑦ — Grand Am less Ram Air.

TUNE UP SPECIFICATIONS

Year & Engine	Spark Plug Gap, Inch	Ignition Timing, ° BTDC				Curb Idle Speed RPM③		Fast Idle Speed RPM		Fuel Pump Pressure, psi	Valve Lash
		Firing Order	Man. Trans.	Auto. Trans.	Mark	Man. Trans.	Auto. Trans.	Man. Trans.	Auto Trans.		
2004–05											
2.2L	.042	1-3-4-2	①	①	⑤	④	④	④	④	50–60	②
3.4L	.060	1-2-3-4-5-6	—	①	⑤	—	④	—	④	52–59	②

BTDC — Before Top Dead Center
P — Park
① — Ignition timing is controlled by Powertrain Control Module (PCM).
② — Vehicle is equipped w/hydraulic valve lifters. No adjustment is required.

③ — When adjusting idle speed, set parking brake & block drive wheels.
④ — Idle speed is controlled by an Idle

Air Control (IAC) valve or an Idle Speed Control (ISC) motor.
⑤ — Equipped with crankshaft position sensor.

ALERO, GRAND AM & 2004–05 MALIBU

FRONT WHEEL ALIGNMENT SPECIFICATIONS

Model	Caster Angle, Degrees		Camber Angle, Degrees		Total Toe, Degrees	Ball Joint Wear
	Limits	Desired	Limits	Desired		
2004						
Alero & Grand Am②	+3.35 to +4.85	+4.10	-.70 to +.70	.00	-.06 to +.34	①
Alero & Grand Am③	+3.35 to +4.85	+4.10	-.70 to +.70	.00	.00 to +.40	①
Malibu	+3.35 to +4.85	+4.10	-.70 to +.70	.00	-.05 to +.35	①
2005						
All	+3.35 to +4.85	+4.10	-.70 to +.70	.00	-.05 to +.35	①

① — Refer to Front Suspension & Steering section for ball joint inspection procedure.
② — With 15 inch wheels.
③ — With 16 inch wheels.

REAR WHEEL ALIGNMENT SPECIFICATIONS

Model	Camber Angle, Degrees		Total Toe, Degrees	Thrust Angle, Degrees
	Limits	Desired		
2004				
Alero & Grand Am	-.40 to +.40	.00	-.10 to +.30	-.20 to +.20
Malibu	-.20 to +.70	.00	-.10 to +.30	-.30 to +.30
2005				
All	-.20 to +.70	.00	-.10 to +.30	-.30 to +.30

VEHICLE RIDE HEIGHT SPECIFICATIONS

Model	Year	Body Style	Manufacturer's Original Tire Size④	Rocker Arm Dim.	Rocker Arm Specification Inches	Rocker Arm Specification mm	Suspension Dim.	Suspension Specification Inches	Suspension Specification mm
Alero	2004	All②	P215/60R15	J	—	—	D	4.84	123
				K	—	—	Z	0	0
		All③	P225/50R16	J	—	—	D	4.77	120
				K	—	—	Z	-.20	-5
Grand Am	2004–05	All②	215/60R15	J	—	—	D	4.84	123
				K	—	—	Z	0	0
			P225/50R16	J	—	—	D	4.77	120
				K	—	—	Z	-.23	-6
Malibu	2004–05	All	P215/60R15	J	9.33	237	D	4.84	123

Dim. — Dimension.
J Dim. — Measurement From Ground to Rocker Panel, Inboard of Front Pinch-Weld Flange, **Fig. B.**
K Dim. — Measurement From Ground to Rocker Panel, Inboard of Rear Pinch-Weld Flange, **Fig. B.**
D Dim. — Measurement From Strut Bottom To Support Surface Forward of Mounting Bolt, **Fig. A.**
Z Dim. — Measurement From Cradle Bottom To Bottom Of Ball Joint, **Fig. C.**
① — All measurements have a tolerance of + or - 10 mm or .39 inch.
② — FE2 Suspension System, Ride Handling.
③ — FE3 Lever 3 Suspension.
④ — See door sticker or inside of glove box for manufacturers original tire size specifications. If tires on vehicle do not match manufacturers original tire size & measurement is not within limits, refer to the Non-Standard Tire & Wheel Size Adjustment To Ride Height Specification & Tire Size Adjustment Charts in the front of this manual for approximate changes in ride height specifications.

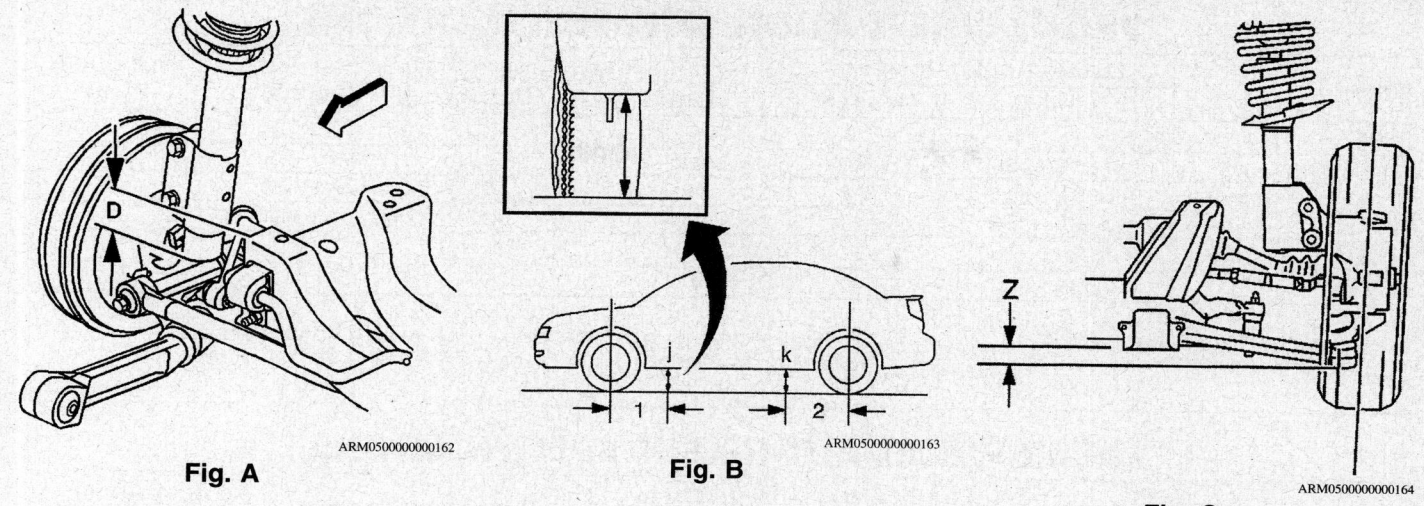

Fig. A — ARM0500000000162

Fig. B — ARM0500000000163

Fig. C — ARM0500000000164

FLUID CAPACITIES & COOLING SYSTEM DATA

Year	Engine	Coolant Capacity, Qts.	Coolant Type	Surge Tank Cap Relief Pressure, psi	Thermo. Opening Temp. Deg. F	Fuel Tank, Gals.	Engine Oil Refill, Qts.	Transaxle Oil — Manual Transaxle, Pts.	Transaxle Oil — Auto. Transaxle, Qts.①
ALERO									
2004	2.2L	8.6	Dex-Cool	15	195	14.1	5.0	3.6	②
	3.4L	13.6	Dex-Cool	15	195	14.1	4.0	3.6	②
GRAND AM									
2004–05	2.2L	8.6	Dex-Cool	15	195	14.1	5.0	3.6	②
	3.4L	13.6	Dex-Cool	15	195	14.1	4.0	3.6	②
MALIBU									
2004–05	2.2L	8.6	Dex-Cool	15	195	14.1	5.0	3.6	②

① — Approximate. Make final inspection w/dipstick.

② — Oil pan removal, 6.9 qts.; overhaul, 9.5 qts.; dry 12.9 qts.

LUBRICANT DATA

Year	Model	Lubricant Type — Transaxle Automatic	Lubricant Type — Transaxle Manual	Clutch Hydraulic System	Power Steering System	Brake System
2004–05	All	Dexron III	Dexron III	DOT 3	①	DOT 3

① — Power Steering Fluid, GM part No. 89021184, or equivalent.

Electrical

NOTE: On Air Bag Equipped Models, Refer To "Air Bag System Precautions" Located In The Front Of This Manual For System Disarming & Arming Procedures.

NOTE: Refer To "Computer Relearn Procedures" Located In The Front Of This Manual When Battery Power To The Computer Has Been Interrupted.

INDEX

	Page No.
Air Bag System (Volume 2)	4-1
Air Conditioning	16-1
Alternator, Replace	1-6
2.2L Engine	1-6
3.1L Engine	1-6
3.4L Engine	1-6
Alternators	19-1
Blower Motor, Replace	1-8
Clutch Start Switch, Replace	1-6
Coil Pack, Replace	1-6
2.2L Engine	1-6
3.1L Engine	1-6
3.4L Engine	1-6
Cooling Fans	17-1
Cruise Control (Volume 2)	2-1
Dash Gauges (Volume 2)	1-1
Dash Panel Service (Volume 2)	5-1
Evaporator Core, Replace	1-9
Alero & Grand Am	1-9
Malibu	1-10
Fuel Pump Relay Location	1-5
Fuse Panel & Flasher Location	1-5
Headlamp Switch, Replace	1-7

	Page No.
Heater Core, Replace	1-8
Alero & Grand Am	1-8
Malibu	1-9
Ignition Lock, Replace	1-6
Alero	1-6
Grand Am	1-6
Malibu	1-6
Ignition Switch, Replace	1-6
Alero	1-6
Grand Am	1-6
Malibu	1-6
Instrument Cluster, Replace	1-7
Multi-Function Switch, Replace	1-7
Alero & Grand Am	1-7
Malibu	1-7
Neutral Safety Switch, Replace	1-6
Installation	1-6
Removal	1-6
Passive Restraint Systems (Volume 2)	4-1
Precautions	1-5
Air Bag Systems	1-5
Battery Ground Cable	1-5
Radio, Replace	1-7

	Page No.
Alero & Grand Am	1-7
Malibu	1-7
Relay Center Location	1-5
Speed Controls (Volume 2)	2-1
Starter Motors	18-1
Starter, Replace	1-5
2.2L & 3.1L Engines	1-5
3.4L Engine	1-5
Installation	1-5
Removal	1-5
Steering Columns	20-1
Steering Wheel, Replace	1-7
Stop Light Switch, Replace	1-7
Installation	1-7
Removal	1-7
Turn Signal Switch, Replace	1-7
Wiper Motor, Replace	1-7
Alero & Grand Am	1-7
Malibu	1-7
Wiper Switch, Replace	1-8
Wiper Systems (Volume 2)	3-1
Wiper Transmission, Replace	1-8
Alero & Grand Am	1-8
Malibu	1-8

PRECAUTIONS

Air Bag Systems

Refer to "Air Bag System Precautions" in the front of this manual for system disarming and arming procedures.

Battery Ground Cable

Prior to service, disconnect battery ground cable and isolate as required.

FUSE PANEL & FLASHER LOCATION

The lefthand instrument panel fuse block is located behind the lefthand side of the instrument panel. The righthand instrument panel fuse block is located behind the righthand side of the instrument panel. The underhood fuse block is located on the lefthand side of the engine compartment. The turn signal and hazard flasher module is an internal component of the hazard switch located behind the center of the instrument panel.

FUEL PUMP RELAY LOCATION

The fuel pump relay is located in the engine compartment relay center on the lefthand side of the engine compartment.

RELAY CENTER LOCATION

Relays are located in all the fuse and junction blocks, refer to "Fuse Panel & Flasher Location" for relay center locations.

STARTER
REPLACE

2.2L & 3.1L Engines

1. Raise and support vehicle.
2. Remove mounting bolts and lower starter.
3. Disconnect starter electrical connectors and remove starter.
4. Reverse procedure to install, noting the following:
   a. **On models equipped with 2.2L**

engine, torque starter mounting bolts to 30 ft. lbs.
   b. **On models equipped with 3.1L engine, torque** starter mounting bolts to 37 ft. lbs.

3.4L Engine

REMOVAL

1. Raise and support vehicle.
2. Remove flywheel inspection cover.
3. Remove starter electrical connectors.
4. Remove mounting bolts and starter.

INSTALLATION

1. Tighten solenoid BAT terminal nut next to cap while starter is still on bench.
2. Connect solenoid electrical terminal.
3. **Torque** solenoid battery terminal inside nut to 84 inch lbs.
4. Install electrical connectors to starter.
5. **Torque** solenoid battery terminal outside nut to 84 inch lbs.
6. **Torque** solenoid S terminal outside nut to 22 inch lbs.
7. Install starter onto engine and **torque** mounting bolts to 32 ft. lbs.
8. Install inspection cover and **torque** bolts to 84 inch lbs.

ALERO, GRAND AM & 2004-05 MALIBU

ALTERNATOR
REPLACE

2.2L Engine

1. Remove serpentine drive belt using tool No. J37059, or equivalent, to turn tensioner.
2. Remove mounting bolts and studs.
3. Disconnect electrical leads and remove alternator.
4. Reverse procedure to install, noting the following:
   a. **Torque** alternator mounting bolts to 16 ft. lbs.
   b. **Torque** alternator electrical connector to 15 ft. lbs.

3.1L Engine

1. Remove serpentine drive belt.
2. Disconnect alternator electrical connectors and power steering line clip.
3. Remove alternator rear brace.
4. Disconnect alternator air inlet connector.
5. Remove mounting bolts, nuts and alternator.
6. Reverse procedure to install. **Torque** mounting bolts to 18 ft. lbs., and nut to 37 ft. lbs.

3.4L Engine

1. Remove cruise control module.
2. Remove engine mount.
3. Turn serpentine drive belt tensioner in clockwise direction and remove belt using suitable ⅜ inch breaker bar.
4. Disconnect alternator electrical connectors and power steering line clip.
5. Remove mounting bolts, nuts and alternator.
6. Reverse procedure to install, noting the following:
   a. **Torque** alternator mounting bolts to 37 ft. lbs.
   b. **Torque** alternator mounting nuts to 22 ft. lbs.
   c. **Torque** engine mount to body bolt to 96 ft. lbs.
   d. **Torque** engine mount to body nut to 49 ft. lbs.
   e. **Torque** engine mount bracket support bolts to 96 ft. lbs.

COIL PACK
REPLACE

2.2L Engine

1. Turn ignition to Off position.
2. Disconnect mounting screws and Ignition Control Module (ICM).
3. Reverse procedure to install. **Torque** ICM mounting screws to 13 ft. lbs.

3.1L Engine

1. Disconnect ignition control module electrical connectors.
2. Remove spark plug wires from ignition coils.

3. Remove mounting screws and ignition coils.
4. Reverse procedure to install. **Torque** mounting screws to 40 inch lbs.

3.4L Engine

1. Tag spark plug wires routing and disconnect them from ignition coils.
2. Remove mounting screws and ignition coils.
3. Reverse procedure to install. **Torque** mounting screws to 40 inch lbs.

IGNITION LOCK
REPLACE

Alero

1. Remove ignition switch bezel using suitable flat-bladed screwdriver.
2. Remove radio as outlined under "Radio, Replace."
3. Insert key and turn ignition switch lock cylinder to On position.
4. Remove ignition lock cylinder while rotating.
5. Reverse procedure to install.

Grand Am

1. Apply parking brake and place shift lever in LOW position.
2. Remove ignition switch bezel using suitable flat-bladed tool.
3. Disconnect accessory trim plate from center of instrument panel.
4. Disconnect accessory trim plate electrical connectors and remove cigar lighter from trim plate.
5. Remove accessory switch mounting plate bracket bolts and bracket.
6. Remove accessory trim plate from center of instrument panel.
7. Insert key and turn ignition switch lock cylinder to On position.
8. Depress ignition lock cylinder detent using suitable L-shaped hex wrench and pull lock cylinder out with key.
9. Reverse procedure to install.

Malibu

Refer to "Ignition Switch, Replace" for lock cylinder replacement.

IGNITION SWITCH
REPLACE

Alero

1. Remove radio as outlined under "Radio, Replace."
2. Remove instrument panel cluster as outlined under "Instrument Cluster, Replace."
3. Remove ignition switch mounting bolts.
4. Position ignition switch to cluster opening for access.
5. Remove mounting bolts and ignition switch bracket.
6. Install key and turn lock cylinder to On position.

7. Depress transaxle park lock cable retainer to release cable.
8. Remove ignition switch lock cylinder by depressing retaining tab and pulling cylinder out with key.
9. Disconnect ignition switch pass lock electrical connector.
10. Disconnect ignition switch electrical connectors.
11. Remove ignition switch through cluster opening.
12. Reverse procedure to install. **Torque** mounting bolts to 53 inch lbs.

Grand Am

1. Remove instrument cluster as outlined under "Instrument Cluster, Replace."
2. Remove mounting bolts and ignition switch.
3. Disconnect electrical connectors.
4. Disconnect ignition lock cable from switch.
5. Insert key into ignition lock cylinder and turn to Run position.
6. Depress cylinder release plunger and remove cylinder by pulling key.
7. Reverse procedure to install.

Malibu

1. Remove lefthand sound insulator, ignition switch trim ring and accessory trim plates, then the instrument cluster.
2. Remove mounting bolts, electrical connectors and console trim plate.
3. Remove ignition lock cable from shift lever and bracket at console front.
4. Remove ignition switch.
5. Reverse procedure to install. **Torque** ignition switch mounting bolts to 18 inch lbs.

CLUTCH START SWITCH
REPLACE

1. Disconnect switch electrical connector.
2. Remove mounting nuts and switch.
3. Reverse procedure to install. Inspect switch for proper operation.

NEUTRAL SAFETY SWITCH
REPLACE

Removal

1. Disconnect switch electrical connector.
2. Remove mounting nut and shift linkage.
3. Remove shift linkage lever.
4. Mark switch position for installation alignment.
5. Remove mounting screws and switch.

Installation

1. Place shift shaft in Neutral position and align flats on shaft with those on switch.
2. Loosely install switch with marks properly aligned.

3. If original switch is being installed, proceed as follows:
   a. Insert 3/32 inch drill bit into switch adjustment hole.
   b. Move switch until drill bit drops to depth of 9/64 inch.
   c. **Torque** switch mounting screws to 18 ft. lbs.
   d. Remove drill bit.
4. New switches are pinned in Neutral position. If installation is difficult, ensure shift shaft is in Neutral. **Do not turn switch.**
5. **Torque** switch mounting screws to 18 ft. lbs.

HEADLAMP SWITCH
REPLACE

Refer to "Multi-Function Switch, Replace" for replacement procedure.

STOP LIGHT SWITCH
REPLACE
Removal

1. Remove lefthand side instrument panel insulator.
2. Disconnect stop lamp switch electrical connector.
3. Remove switch retainer by grasping and turning 90° counterclockwise and pulling toward rear of vehicle.
4. Remove stop lamp switch.

Installation

1. Insert stop lamp switch into retainer until switch body has seated onto retainer.
2. Pull brake pedal upward against its internal stop.
3. Adjust switch so its plunger extends no more than .78 inch beyond threaded portion when brake pedal is fully released.
4. Turn switch 90° clockwise until it locks into position.
5. Connect switch electrical connector.

MULTI-FUNCTION SWITCH
REPLACE
Alero & Grand Am

1. Remove steering column trim panels.
2. Remove multi-function switch mounting screws.
3. Disconnect switch electrical connectors.
4. Remove switch from steering column.
5. Reverse procedure to install.

Malibu

1. Remove horn pad and steering wheel as outlined under "Steering Wheel, Replace."
2. Position spark plug boot, or other suitable device, over tilt lever and remove

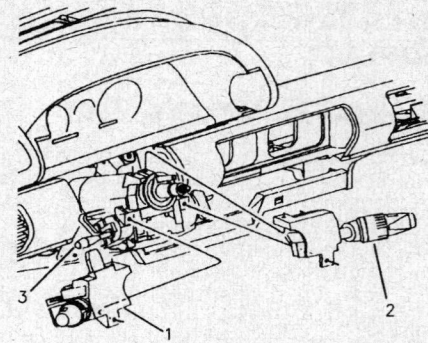

1 HEADLAMP/TURN SIGNAL/CRUISE CONTROL HAZARD SWITCH
2 WINDSHIELD WIPER/WASHER SWITCH
3 TILT LEVER (IF EQUIPPED)

GC9049200112000A

Fig. 1 Multi-function switch replacement. Malibu

steering column tilt lever using suitable locking pliers.
3. Remove steering column upper and lower covers, then the dampener.
4. Remove mounting screw and switch, **Fig. 1.**
5. Reverse procedure to install.

TURN SIGNAL SWITCH
REPLACE

Refer to "Multi-Function Switch, Replace" for replacement procedure.

STEERING WHEEL
REPLACE

1. Disarm driver's air bag module as outlined in "Air Bag System Precautions."
2. Remove mounting screws for horn pad or air bag module.
3. **On models equipped with steering wheel radio controls,** remove wire protector plate connector.
4. **On all models,** remove horn pad or air bag module and horn lead, then the steering wheel retainer and nut.
5. Remove steering wheel using puller tool No. J1859-A and legs tool No. J42120, or equivalent.
6. Reverse procedure to install, noting the following:
   a. **Torque** steering wheel nut to 27-30 ft. lbs.
   b. **Torque** air bag module screws to 89 inch lbs.

INSTRUMENT CLUSTER
REPLACE

1. Remove steering column covers.
2. Remove mounting screws and instrument panel cluster trim plate.
3. Remove instrument cluster to instrument panel mounting screws.
4. Disconnect cluster electrical connectors and remove instrument cluster.
5. Reverse procedure to install.

RADIO
REPLACE
Alero & Grand Am

1. Remove accessory trim plate.
2. Remove radio mounting screws.
3. Pull radio rearward.
4. Disconnect electrical connectors and antenna lead-in.
5. Reverse procedure to install.

Malibu

1. Remove ignition key trim cover using suitable flat-bladed pry tool.
2. Pull accessory trim plate to rear and remove.
3. Remove mounting screws and pull radio to rear.
4. Disconnect electrical connectors and antenna lead-in.
5. Remove radio.
6. Reverse procedure to install.

WIPER MOTOR
REPLACE
Alero & Grand Am

1. Remove wiper arms from shafts.
2. Remove cowl air inlet grille.
3. Disconnect wiper motor electrical connector.
4. Remove three wiper drive system mounting screws.
5. Remove wiper transmission from crank arm using separator tool No. J39232, or equivalent.
6. Remove two mounting screws and motor.
7. Reverse procedure to install, noting the following:
   a. **Torque** motor to tube frame mounting screws to 89 inch lbs.
   b. Install transmission assembly onto crank arm using installer tool No. J39529, or equivalent.
   c. **Torque** drive system module mounting screws to 89 inch lbs.

Malibu

1. Remove wiper arm and blade.
2. Remove cowl cover.
3. Disconnect drive link from crank arm using wiper transmission separator tool No. J39232, or equivalent.
4. Disconnect wiper motor electrical connectors.
5. Remove mounting screws and wiper motor.
6. Reverse procedure to install, noting the following:
   a. **Torque** motor mounting screws to 84 inch lbs.
   b. Connect drive link to crank arm using wiper transmission installer tool No. J39529, or equivalent.

WIPER SWITCH

REPLACE

Refer to "Multi-Function Switch, Replace" for replacement procedure.

WIPER TRANSMISSION

REPLACE

Alero & Grand Am

1. Remove wiper arms from transmission shafts.
2. Remove air inlet screen from cowl panel.
3. Disconnect wiper motor electrical connector.
4. Remove mounting screws and wiper transmission.
5. Disconnect motor crank arm from transmission using separator tool No. J39232, or equivalent.
6. Remove transmission cap.
7. Remove four mounting screws and transmission from tube frame.
8. Remove three grommets from tube frame and transmission.
9. Remove motor from tube frame.
10. Reverse procedure to install, noting the following:
    a. **Torque** wiper transmission to tube frame screws to 79 inch lbs.
    b. Install transmission onto crank arm using installer tool No. J39529, or equivalent.
    c. **Torque** wiper transmission mounting screws to 79 inch lbs.

Malibu

1. Remove wiper arm and blades.
2. Remove cowl cover and disconnect wiper motor connector.
3. Remove mounting screws and wiper drive system module.
4. Remove wiper motor as outlined under "Wiper Motor, Replace."
5. Remove caps, wiper motor grommets and transmission.
6. Reverse procedure to install. **Torque** mounting screws to 72 inch lbs.

BLOWER MOTOR

REPLACE

The blower motor and fan are located in the lower righthand corner of the Heating, Ventilation and Air Conditioning (HVAC) module. The fan and motor are serviced only as a complete assembly.
1. Remove righthand closeout panel and insulator.
2. **On Alero and Grand Am models,** position Body Control Module (BCM) aside.
3. **On all models,** disconnect blower motor electrical connectors.
4. Remove mounting screws, blower motor and fan.
5. Reverse procedure to install. **Torque** blower motor mounting screws to 45 inch lbs.

HEATER CORE

REPLACE

Alero & Grand Am

1. Drain coolant into suitable container.
2. Recover air conditioning refrigerant as outlined in "Air Conditioning" chapter.
3. Raise and support vehicle.
4. Remove evaporator hose assembly nut from evaporator.
5. Remove evaporator hose assembly from evaporator.
6. Remove and discard seal washers.
7. Remove inlet and outlet heater hoses from heater core.
8. Remove drain tube elbow from evaporator block heater case plate
9. Remove nuts holding heater case plate for heater pipes.
10. Remove heater case plate and seals for heater pipes.
11. Remove nuts holding heater case plate for evaporator block.
12. Remove heater case plate and seal for evaporator block.
13. Remove nut for HVAC module assembly bracket.
14. Lower vehicle.
15. Pull door weatherstrip from windshield side upper garnish molding, as required.
16. Remove windshield side upper garnish molding by disconnecting clips.
17. Remove defroster grill by disconnecting retainers using suitable small flat bladed tool.
18. Remove instrument panel endcaps by pulling outward.
19. Remove righthand sound insulator and disconnect heater hose form duct.
20. Remove mounting screws and lefthand sound insulator.
21. Remove mounting screws under glove compartment door and open door.
22. Remove pocket mounting screws and glove compartment. Disconnect compartment lamp electrical connector.
23. Remove passenger's air bag module.
24. Position front seats to most rearward position.
25. Position emergency brake lever to full up position.
26. Position gear selector to NEUTRAL position.
27. Release front floor console trim plate using suitable small flat bladed tool.
28. Remove trim plate by rotating 90° and guiding it over shift handle.
29. Position shift lever fully rearward.
30. Remove mounting screws and console cupholder.
31. Remove ignition switch bezel using suitable small flat blade tool.
32. Remove instrument panel accessory trim plate by pulling from storage compartment to release retainers.
33. Disconnect cigarette lighter and hazard warning switch electrical connectors.
34. Remove cigarette lighter fuse and element.
35. Remove cigarette lighter socket by placing one side of T portion of cigarette lighter socket remover tool No.

J42059, or equivalent, into tab window and then other should be angled into opposite tab window.
36. Pull lighter socket straight out and remove tool.
37. Disconnect cigarette lighter socket electrical connector.
38. Remove cigarette lighter retainer.
39. Remove mounting screws and hazard warning switch retainer bracket.
40. Remove flasher and switch from switch retainer bracket using suitable small flat bladed tool to depress and release flasher retainers, while pressing flasher and switch.
41. Remove flasher and switch from switch retainer bracket.
42. Remove lower steering column trim cover mounting screws.
43. Remove upper column trim cover by tilting up and unsnapping from lower column trim cover hinges.
44. Remove tilt steering wheel lever by pulling retaining pin and snapping out.
45. Remove lower column trim cover.
46. Remove lower and upper mounting screws, then the instrument panel cluster trim plate.
47. Remove mounting screws and instrument panel cluster. Disconnect electrical connector.
48. Remove mounting screws and radio. Disconnect instrument panel wiring harness and antenna cable connectors.
49. Remove steering wheel as outlined under "Steering Wheel, Replace."
50. Remove steering column as outlined in "Steering Columns" chapter.
51. Position shift lever fully rearward.
52. Remove mounting screws, then the cupholder by lifting up and rearward to clear storage compartment.
53. Disconnect storage compartment lamp from cupholder.
54. Lift up front floor console armrest and remove rubber mat from storage compartment.
55. Remove storage compartment rear mounting bolts.
56. Remove center bolts from console sides.
57. Remove covers using suitable small flat bladed tool at front edge and front mounting screws.
58. Remove bracket front mounting nuts.
59. Remove floor console by pulling up and rearward, guiding emergency brake lever boot over emergency brake lever.
60. Remove ignition switch mounting bolts. Position ignition switch for ease of removal.
61. Remove ignition switch mounting bolts and bracket.
62. Insert key and turn ignition switch lock cylinder to ACC position.
63. Depress retainer and remove transaxle park/lock cable.
64. Remove ignition switch lock cylinder by depressing retaining tab and pulling cylinder out with key.
65. Disconnect pass lock and ignition switch electrical connectors.
66. Remove ignition switch.
67. Remove fog lamp/dimmer switch/vent

trim plate using suitable small flat bladed tool. Disconnect electrical connectors.

68. Remove fog lamp switch using suitable small flat bladed tool on back side to release retainer tabs.
69. Remove instrument panel upper bolt covers.
70. Disconnect electrical junction box electrical connections.
71. Remove instrument panel to cross vehicle beam mounting screws.
72. Remove instrument panel.
73. Remove Heater-Air Conditioning (HVAC) module support bracket.
74. Remove bolts from bracket attaching cross vehicle beam to HVAC module.
75. Remove cross vehicle beam to lefthand hinge pillar mounting bolts.
76. Remove cross vehicle beam to righthand hinge pillar mounting bolts.
77. Remove cross vehicle beam.
78. Remove Daytime Running Lights (DRL) sensor wiring harness clip from HVAC module assembly.
79. Disconnect instrument panel lamp dimmer switch electrical connector.
80. Remove wiring harness clips from HVAC module assembly bracket.
81. Disconnect vacuum hose from vacuum tank.
82. Disconnect blower motor resistor and blower motor electrical connectors.
83. Disconnect temperature actuator electrical connector.
84. Remove HVAC module assembly.
85. Turn HVAC module assembly over.
86. Remove heater core case cover.
87. Remove heater core bracket and screw.
88. Remove heater core.
89. Reverse procedure to install, noting the following:
    a. **Torque** core mounting clamps to 12 inch lbs.
    b. **Torque** cover screws to 12 inch lbs.
    c. **Torque** floor air outlet screws to 12 inch lbs.
    d. Close radiator petcock, fill cooling system and inspect for leaks.

Malibu

1. Drain coolant into suitable container.
2. Remove heater hoses and drain tube.
3. Remove windshield side upper garnish molding by pulling windshield side upper garnish molding rearward to release tabs.
4. Remove defroster grille by unsnapping and lifting upward.
5. Remove end caps pulling outward in finger pull area.
6. Remove mounting screws under glove compartment door.
7. Open door and remove mounting screws inside pocket.
8. Disconnect glove compartment lamp switch electrical connection.
9. Remove glove compartment.
10. Remove push pins and lefthand half of lefthand side sound insulator.
11. Remove mounting bolts and righthand halve of lefthand side sound insulator.
12. Remove push pin and righthand side of righthand side sound insulator.

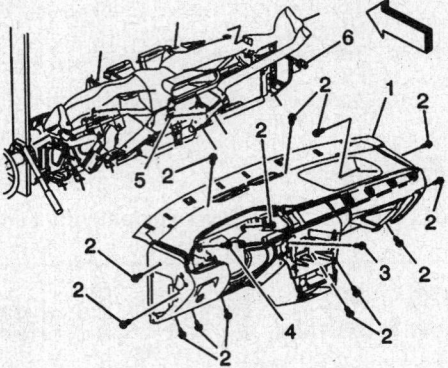

(1) Instrument Panel Assembly
(2) Screws (Tighten Last in Random Order)
(3) Screw (Tighten 1st)
(4) Screw (Tighten 2nd)
(5) Locator Pin
(6) Tie Bar Assembly

GC9149700134000X

Fig. 2   Exploded view of instrument panel. Malibu

13. Remove mounting bolts and lefthand side of righthand side sound insulator.
14. Remove passenger's air bag module.
15. Remove driver's air bag module.
16. Remove steering wheel as outlined under "Steering Wheel, Replace."
17. Disconnect electrical connectors.
18. Remove mounting screw and multifunction switch, then disconnect electrical connectors.
19. Remove steering column stalks.
20. Remove mounting screws and instrument panel cluster trim plate by gently prying out using suitable small flat bladed tool.
21. Disconnect dimmer and hazard warning switches electrical connectors.
22. Remove ignition switch trim cover by prying off with suitable small flat bladed tool.
23. Remove accessory trim plate by gently prying with suitable small flat bladed tool to disconnect retainers.
24. Disconnect cigarette lighter electrical connector.
25. Remove cigarette lighter housing from trim plate.
26. Remove mounting screws and instrument cluster by pull rearward. Disconnect electrical connector.
27. Recover air conditioning refrigerant as outlined in "Air Conditioning" chapter.
28. Raise and support vehicle.
29. Drain engine coolant into suitable container.
30. Remove righthand wheel housing splash shield.
31. Remove evaporator hose nut from accumulator using suitable back-up wrench. Discard O-ring seal.
32. Remove mounting bolt and evaporator hose from condenser. Discard O-ring seal.
33. Remove mounting nut and evaporator hose from evaporator. Discard O-ring seal.
34. Unfasten two mounting clips and evaporator hose.
35. Lower vehicle.

36. Disconnect heater hose from heater pipe by squeezing quick-connect tabs.
37. Remove heater hose with quick-connect.
38. Remove heater hose and clamps from heater core.
39. Raise and support vehicle.
40. Remove evaporator block heater case plate drain tube elbow.
41. Remove mounting nuts, heater pipes' heater case plate and seals.
42. Remove mounting nuts, evaporator block heater case plate and seal.
43. Remove HVAC module bracket mounting nut.
44. Lower vehicle.
45. Remove mounting bolts and radio.
46. Disconnect radio electrical connectors and antenna lead.
47. Remove mounting nuts and pull tape player out to access electrical connector.
48. Disconnect electrical connector and remove tape player.
49. Remove ignition switch mounting bolts and disconnect electrical connectors.
50. Insert key into ignition switch key cylinder, turn key to RUN position.
51. Depress park lock cable tab and remove cable from ignition switch housing.
52. Press cylinder release plunger located at four o'clock position on ignition switch housing.
53. Pull cylinder from ignition switch housing using key.
54. Disconnect Pass Key electrical connector.
55. Remove ignition switch.
56. Position front seat forward and remove seat adjuster mounting bolts.
57. Disconnect lefthand side seat belt wiring harness.
58. Disconnect lefthand side power seat electrical connector, as required.
59. Manually tilt forward, disconnect floor pan hooks and remove front seats.
60. Fold console compartment up.
61. Remove gear shift lever handle by pulling retainer pin and upward on handle.
62. Remove console trim plate by gently pry upward to disconnect retainers.
63. Remove rear cupholder.
64. Remove mounting screws and console.
65. Remove ashtray.
66. Remove instrument panel to tie bar mounting screws, **Fig. 2.**
67. Remove instrument panel.
68. Remove instrument panel and console as outlined in "Dash Panel Service."
69. Remove heater outlet, mounting screw and heater core cover.
70. Remove mounting clamps and heater core.
71. Reverse procedure to install.

EVAPORATOR CORE
REPLACE
Alero & Grand Am

1. Recover air conditioning refrigerant as outlined in "Air Conditioning" chapter.

2. Remove heater core as outlined under "Heater Core, Replace."
3. Remove evaporator core bracket.
4. Remove evaporator core.
5. Reverse procedure to install, noting the following:
   a. **Torque** evaporator mounting screws to 12 inch lbs.
   b. **Torque** heater core shroud and straps screws to 12 inch lbs.

c. **Torque** heater cover screws to 12 inch lbs.
d. **Torque** floor duct screws to 12 inch lbs.
e. **Torque** evaporator hose fitting bolt to 18 ft. lbs.

Malibu

1. Recover air conditioning refrigerant as

outlined in "Air Conditioning" chapter.
2. Drain coolant into suitable container.
3. Remove HVAC assembly as outlined under "Heater Core, Replace."
4. Remove mounting screw and thermal expansion valve.
5. Remove and discard sealing washers.
6. Remove evaporator core.
7. Reverse procedure to install. Install new sealing washers.

2.2L Engine

NOTE: On Air Bag Equipped Models, Refer To "Air Bag System Precautions" Located In The Front Of This Manual For System Disarming & Arming Procedures.

NOTE: Refer To "Computer Relearn Procedures" Located In The Front Of This Manual When Battery Power To The Computer Has Been Interrupted.

INDEX

	Page No.
Belt Tension Data	1-14
Camshaft, Replace	1-14
Compression Pressure	1-10
Cooling System Bleed	1-15
Crankshaft Damper, Replace	1-12
Crankshaft Rear Oil Seal, Replace	1-14
Crankshaft Seal, Replace	1-14
Cylinder Head, Replace	1-11
Engine Rebuilding Specifications	29-1
Engine, Replace	1-10
Automatic Transaxle	1-10
Manual Transaxle	1-11
Engine Mount, Replace	1-10

	Page No.
Exhaust Manifold, Replace	1-11
Front Cover, Replace	1-12
Fuel Filter, Replace	1-16
Fuel Pump, Replace	1-16
Alero & Grand Am	1-16
Malibu	1-16
Intake Manifold, Replace	1-11
Main & Rod Bearings	1-14
Oil Pan, Replace	1-14
Oil Pump, Replace	1-14
Piston & Rod Assembly	1-14
Pistons, Pins & Rings	1-14
Precautions	1-10
Air Bag Systems	1-10
Battery Ground Cable	1-10

	Page No.
Fuel System Pressure Relief	1-10
Radiator, Replace	1-15
Alero & Grand Am	1-15
Malibu	1-15
Serpentine Drive Belt	1-15
Thermostat, Replace	1-15
Tightening Specifications	1-18
Timing Chain, Replace	1-12
Installation	1-13
Removal	1-12
Valve Adjustment	1-12
Valve Cover, Replace	1-12
Valve Lash Adjusters, Replace	1-12
Water Pump, Replace	1-15

PRECAUTIONS

Air Bag Systems

Refer to "Air Bag System Precautions" in the front of this manual for system disarming and arming procedures.

Battery Ground Cable

Prior to service, disconnect battery ground cable and isolate as required.

Fuel System Pressure Relief

1. Disconnect battery ground cable and isolate as required.
2. Install fuel pressure gauge tool No. J34730-1A, or equivalent.
3. Install bleed hose into suitable container and open valve to bleed system pressure.
4. Disconnect fuel pressure gauge from fuel pressure connection.

COMPRESSION PRESSURE

When inspecting cylinder compression, the engine should be at room temperature, the throttle should be open, the spark plugs removed and the battery at full charge. The lowest reading cylinder should not be less than 70% of the highest and no cylinder reading should be less than 100 psi. Turn ignition key until engine cranks through four compression cycles per cylinder. Normal compression builds up quickly and evenly to specified compression on each cylinder.

ENGINE MOUNT

REPLACE

1. Remove cruise control module.
2. Support engine with suitable wooden block and suitable floor jack positioned below oil pan.
3. Remove engine mount mounting nuts.
4. Remove engine mount to bracket bolts.
5. Remove engine mount.
6. Reverse procedure to install.

ENGINE

REPLACE

Automatic Transaxle

1. Open and support hood. Install suitable protective covering over fenders. Mark upper hood hinge location to hood with suitable grease pencil. Remove hood with assistance.
2. Remove air cleaner resonator to accelerator bracket bolt.
3. Remove throttle body resonator, air cleaner intake duct and vent hose.
4. Remove accelerator cable and cruise control cable.
5. Disconnect brake booster hose.
6. Remove power steering pump.
7. Disconnect fuel lines.
8. Drain coolant into suitable container.
9. Remove radiator inlet hose.
10. Remove surge tank to cylinder head hose.
11. Disconnect surge tank to radiator outlet hose.
12. Remove radiator outlet hose.
13. Remove inlet and outlet heater hoses.

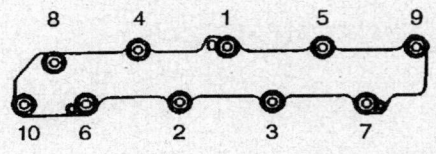

Fig. 1 Exhaust manifold tightening sequence

GC1060101226000X

14. Remove surge tank outlet hose mounting bolt to intake manifold.
15. Disconnect electrical connectors to engine components.
16. Remove engine electrical harness.
17. Remove upper transmission bellhousing mounting bolts.
18. Raise and support vehicle.
19. Remove front fender liner.
20. Turn drive belt tensioner clockwise.
21. Remove serpentine drive belt.
22. Remove air conditioning compressor.
23. Remove crankshaft balancer bolt using harmonic balancer holder tool No. J38122-A, or equivalent, to ensure crankshaft does not turn while loosening mounting bolt.
24. Remove crankshaft balancer.
25. Disconnect alternator electrical connectors.
26. Disconnect starter motor electrical connectors.
27. Drain engine oil into suitable container.
28. Disconnect front exhaust pipe from manifold.
29. Raise and support vehicle.
30. Remove mounting bolts and lower starter.
31. Disconnect starter electrical connectors and remove starter.
32. Remove flywheel to torque converter bolts.
33. Remove lower transmission bellhousing bolts.
34. Remove transmission to engine brace.
35. Lower vehicle.
36. Install engine bracket tool No. J42451, or equivalent, to righthand rear side of cylinder head.
37. Install suitable engine hoist to engine.
38. Remove cruise control module.
39. Support engine with suitable wooden block and suitable floor jack positioned below oil pan.
40. Remove engine mount mounting nuts.
41. Remove engine mount to bracket bolts.
42. Remove engine mount.
43. Remove upper transmission bellhousing bolts.
44. Separate engine from transmission.
45. Remove engine.
46. Reverse procedure to install.

Manual Transaxle

1. Open and support hood. Install suitable protective covering over fenders. Mark upper hood location to hood with suitable grease pencil. Remove hood with assistance.
2. Remove air cleaner resonator to accelerator bracket bolt.

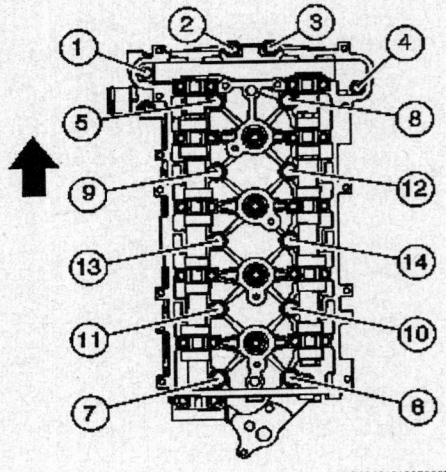

Fig. 2 Cylinder head bolt loosening

GC1060101227000X

3. Disconnect accelerator and cruise cables.
4. Disconnect brake booster hose.
5. Remove power steering pump.
6. Disconnect engine fuel lines.
7. Disconnect transmission shift control cables from bracket.
8. Disconnect clutch actuator cylinder line.
9. Drain engine coolant into suitable container.
10. Remove engine radiator inlet hose.
11. Remove cylinder head surge tank hose.
12. Disconnect surge tank outlet hose to radiator.
13. Remove surge tank outlet hose to intake manifold.
14. Remove radiator outlet hose to engine.
15. Remove inlet and outlet heater hoses.
16. Disconnect electrical connectors to engine sensors and switches.
17. Remove engine harness and set aside.
18. Raise and support vehicle.
19. Remove drive axles and front crossmember as outlined under appropriate transaxle chapter in **MOTOR's "Domestic Transmission, In-Vehicle Service" manual or "Transmission Service DVD."**
20. Remove front fender liner.
21. Turn drive belt tensioner clockwise.
22. Remove serpentine drive belt.
23. Remove air conditioning compressor.
24. Disconnect alternator and starter electrical connectors.
25. Drain engine oil into suitable container.
26. Disconnect front exhaust pipe from manifold.
27. Support front of engine using suitable block of wood at oil pan, lower vehicle onto engine support table.
28. Remove cruise control module.
29. Remove engine mount mounting nuts.
30. Remove engine mount to bracket bolts.
31. Remove engine mount.
32. Remove transmission mount mounting bolts to frame.

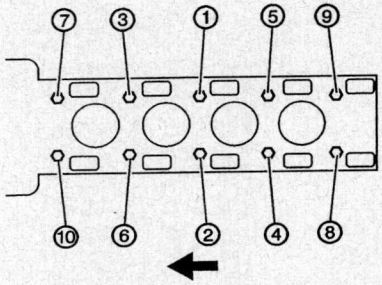

Fig. 3 Cylinder head bolt tightening sequence

GC1060101228000X

33. Raise vehicle from engine and transmission.
34. Install engine lift bracket tool No. J42451, or equivalent, to righthand rear of cylinder head.
35. Install suitable engine hoist to engine.
36. Remove transmission bellhousing mounting bolts.
37. Remove engine from transmission and mount it to suitable engine stand.
38. Reverse procedure to install.

INTAKE MANIFOLD
REPLACE

1. Remove air inlet duct and resonator.
2. Disconnect IAC, TPS and MAP sensor.
3. Disconnect EVAP and PCV hose.
4. Disconnect purge solenoid tube and brake booster hose.
5. Remove oil dipstick tube bolt.
6. Disconnect accelerator and cruise control cables.
7. Remove throttle body and fuel rail.
8. Remove KS connector from intake manifold.
9. Remove mounting nuts, bolts and intake manifold.
10. Reverse procedure to install.

EXHAUST MANIFOLD
REPLACE

1. Remove exhaust manifold heat shield.
2. Remove oxygen sensor.
3. Raise and support vehicle.
4. Remove manifold to exhaust flex decoupler mounting bolts.
5. Pull down and back on exhaust pipe in order to disconnect pipe from exhaust manifold.
6. Lower vehicle.
7. Remove exhaust manifold to cylinder head mounting nuts.
8. Remove exhaust manifold, clean sealing surfaces.
9. Reverse procedure to install. **Torque** exhaust manifold to cylinder head mounting nuts to 106 inch lbs., in sequence, **Fig. 1**.

CYLINDER HEAD
REPLACE

1. Remove air inlet duct and resonator.
2. Disconnect IAC, TPS and MAP sensor.
3. Disconnect EVAP and PCV hose.

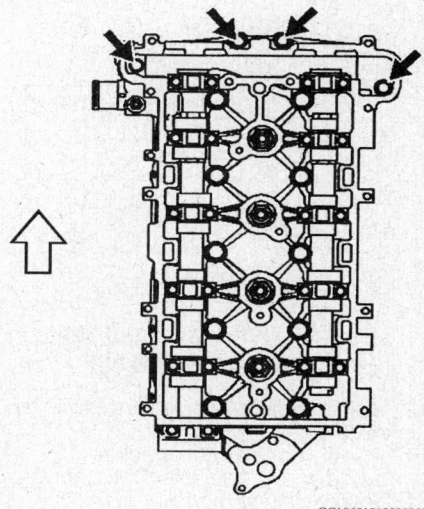

Fig. 4   Front cylinder head bolt tightening

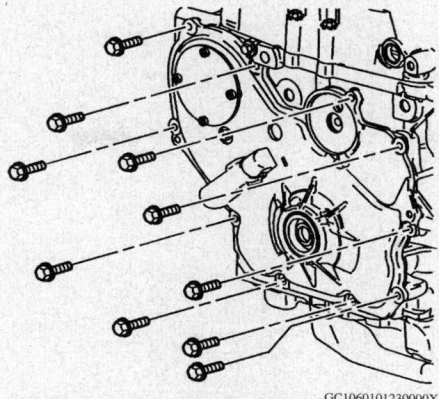

GC1060101230000X

Fig. 5   Engine front cover bolt replacement

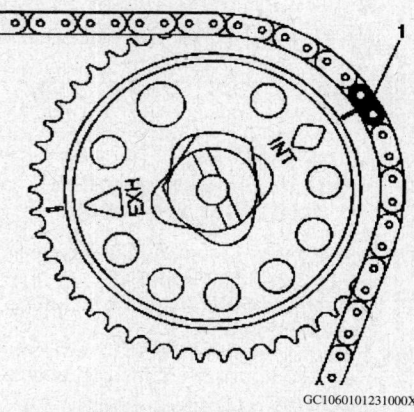

GC1060101231000X

Fig. 6   Timing chain copper link alignment

4. Disconnect purge solenoid tube and brake booster hose.
5. Remove oil dipstick tube bolt.
6. Disconnect accelerator and cruise control cables.
7. Remove throttle body and fuel rail.
8. Remove KS connector from intake manifold.
9. Remove mounting nuts, bolts and intake manifold.
10. Remove power steering pump.
11. Remove exhaust manifold heat shield.
12. Remove oxygen sensor.
13. Raise and support vehicle.
14. Remove manifold to exhaust flex decoupler mounting bolts.
15. Pull down and back on exhaust pipe in order to disconnect pipe from exhaust manifold.
16. Lower vehicle.
17. Remove exhaust manifold to cylinder head mounting nuts.
18. Remove exhaust manifold, clean sealing surfaces.
19. Remove timing chain as outlined under "Timing Chain, Replace."
20. Drain coolant system into suitable container.
21. Remove cylinder head bolts in sequence, **Fig. 2**. Discard bolts.
22. Remove cylinder head and gasket.
23. Reverse procedure to install, noting the following:
    a. Install new cylinder head bolts.
    b. **Torque** cylinder head bolts to 22 ft. lbs., in sequence, **Fig. 3**.
    c. Tighten head bolts an additional 155°.
    d. **Torque** front cylinder head bolts to 26 ft. lbs, **Fig. 4**.

VALVE COVER
REPLACE

1. Loosen vent hose clamp at air cleaner resonator, air cleaner intake duct clamp at air cleaner outlet resonator.
2. Loosen air cleaner outlet resonator to throttle body clamp, located forward of

accelerator cable bracket. Remove air cleaner resonator to accelerator bracket bolt.
3. Remove throttle body resonator, air cleaner intake duct and vent hose.
4. Disconnect accelerator and cruise control cables from throttle body, then the bracket.
5. Remove PCV valve.
6. Remove fuel line brackets and brake booster hose pipe from brackets.
7. Remove mounting screw, ignition coil and Ignition Control Module (ICM).
8. Remove ground strap.
9. Remove mounting bolts and camshaft cover.
10. Reverse procedure to install.

VALVE ADJUSTMENT

This engine is equipped with hydraulic valve lash adjusters. No adjustment is required.

VALVE LASH ADJUSTERS
REPLACE

Refer to "Camshaft, Replace" for valve lash adjuster replacement procedure.

CRANKSHAFT DAMPER
REPLACE

1. Raise and support vehicle.
2. Remove front tire and wheel assembly.
3. Remove front fender liner.
4. Turn drive belt tensioner clockwise.
5. Remove serpentine drive belt.
6. Prevent crankshaft from rotating by install harmonic balancer holder tool No. J38122A, or equivalent.
7. Remove mounting bolt and crankshaft balancer. Discard bolt.
8. Reverse procedure to install.

FRONT COVER
REPLACE

1. Raise and support vehicle.
2. Remove front fender liner.
3. Turn drive belt tensioner clockwise.
4. Remove serpentine drive belt.

5. Remove crankshaft balancer bolt using harmonic balancer holder tool No. J38122-A, or equivalent, to ensure crankshaft does not rotate while loosening mounting bolt.
6. Remove crankshaft balancer.
7. Remove engine front cover to water pump bolts, **Fig. 5**.
8. Remove remaining engine front cover mounting bolts.
9. Remove engine front cover gasket.
10. Reverse procedure to install.

TIMING CHAIN
REPLACE

Removal

1. Loosen vent hose clamp at air cleaner resonator, air cleaner intake duct clamp at air cleaner outlet resonator.
2. Loosen air cleaner outlet resonator to throttle body clamp, located forward of accelerator cable bracket. Remove air cleaner resonator to accelerator bracket bolt.
3. Remove throttle body resonator, air cleaner intake duct and vent hose.
4. Disconnect accelerator and cruise control cables from throttle body, then the bracket.
5. Remove PCV valve.
6. Remove fuel line brackets and brake booster hose pipe from brackets.
7. Remove mounting screw, ignition coil and Ignition Control Module (ICM).
8. Remove ground strap.
9. Remove mounting bolts and camshaft cover.
10. Raise and support vehicle.
11. Remove front fender liner.
12. Turn drive belt tensioner clockwise.
13. Remove serpentine drive belt.
14. Remove crankshaft balancer bolt using harmonic balancer holder tool No. J38122-A, or equivalent, to ensure crankshaft does not rotate while loosening mounting bolt.
15. Remove crankshaft balancer.
16. Remove engine front cover to water pump bolts, **Fig. 5**.
17. Remove remaining engine front cover mounting bolts.

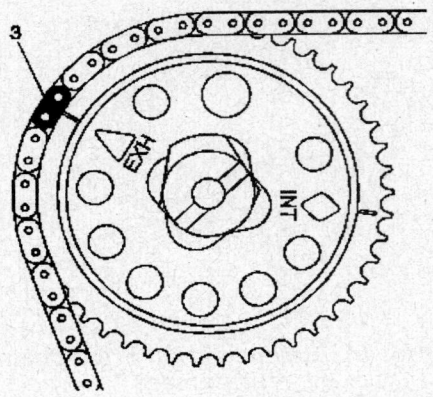

Fig. 7 **Timing chain silver link alignment**

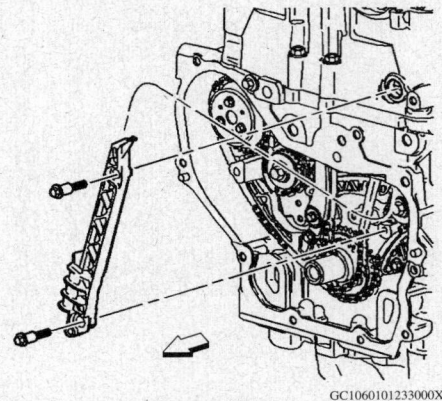

Fig. 8 **Fixed timing chain guide replacement**

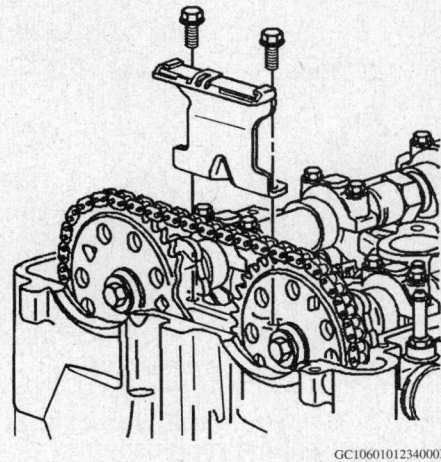

Fig. 9 **Upper timing chain guide replacement**

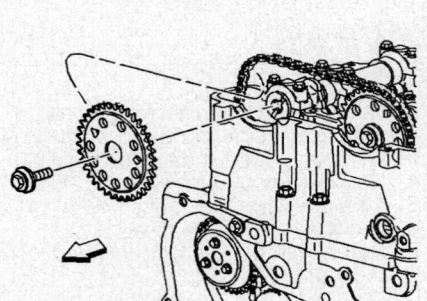

Fig. 10 **Exhaust camshaft bolt & sprocket replacement**

18. Remove engine front cover gasket.
19. Turn engine until crankshaft sprocket mark aligns with second silver link at five o'clock position.
20. Lower vehicle.
21. Ensure intake camshaft sprocket INT diamond is aligned with copper link at two o'clock position, **Fig. 6.**
22. Ensure exhaust camshaft sprocket EXH triangle is aligned with silver link at 10 o'clock position, **Fig. 7.**
23. Remove timing chain tensioner.
24. Remove fixed timing chain guide access plug.
25. Remove fixed timing chain guide, **Fig. 8.**
26. Remove upper timing chain guide, **Fig. 9.**
27. Remove exhaust camshaft sprocket bolt and camshaft sprocket using suitable 24mm wrench to hold camshafts, **Fig. 10.**
28. Remove timing chain tensioner guide, **Fig. 11.**
29. Remove intake camshaft sprocket bolt, intake camshaft sprocket and timing chain through top of cylinder head, **Fig. 12.**
30. Remove crankshaft sprocket, balance shaft drive chain tensioner and adjustable balance shaft chain guide.
31. Remove small balance shaft drive chain guide.
32. Remove upper balance shaft drive chain guide, **Fig. 13.**
33. Remove balance shaft drive chain, **Fig. 14.**

Installation

1. Install upper balance shaft chain guide.
2. Install balance shaft drive chain with colored links lined up on marks on balance shaft drive sprockets and crankshaft sprocket, **Fig. 15.**
3. Place copper link so it aligns with intake side balance shaft sprocket timing mark.
4. Move clockwise around chain, place first chrome link inline with timing mark on crankshaft drive sprocket, five o'clock position.
5. Install chain on water pump drive sprocket.
6. Align last chrome link with timing mark on exhaust side balance shaft drive sprocket.
7. Install small balance shaft chain guide.
8. Tighten balance shaft chain guide bolts.
9. Install adjustable balance shaft drive chain guide.
10. Turn tensioner plunger 90° in its bore and compress plunger until paper clip can be inserted through hole in plunger body and into hole in tensioner plunger, **Fig. 16.**
11. Install timing chain tensioner.
12. Remove paper clip from balance shaft drive chain tensioner.
13. Install crankshaft sprocket with timing mark at five o'clock position, **Fig. 17.**
14. Lower timing chain through opening in top of cylinder head and ensure chain installs around both sides of cylinder block bosses.
15. Install intake camshaft sprocket with INT diamond at two o'clock position, **Fig. 6.**
16. Hand tighten new intake camshaft sprocket bolt.
17. Install timing chain around crankshaft sprocket with second silver link aligning with timing mark.
18. Install timing chain around intake camshaft sprocket with copper link aligning with INT diamond.
19. Install timing chain tensioner guide through opening in top of cylinder head.
20. Install exhaust camshaft sprocket with

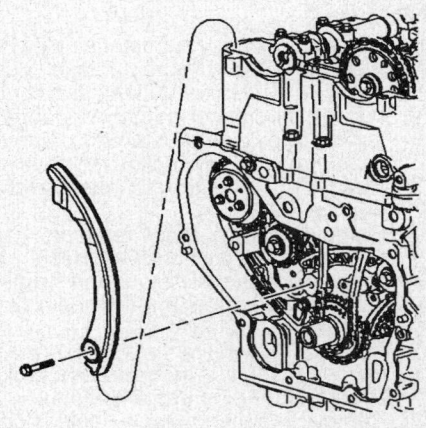

Fig. 11 **Timing chain tensioner guide replacement**

timing chain silver link at EXH triangle aligned ten o'clock position, **Fig. 7.**
21. Install suitable 24mm wrench to rotate camshaft slightly, until exhaust sprocket aligns with camshaft.
22. Hand tighten new exhaust camshaft sprocket bolt.
23. Install fixed timing chain guide.
24. Apply sealant, GM part No. 12345382, or equivalent, compound to thread and install timing chain guide bolt access hole plug.
25. Install timing chain upper guide.
26. Measure timing chain tensioner when fully compressed, tensioner will measure 2.83 inch.
27. Install timing chain tensioner.
28. Install suitable rubber tipped tool, place tool down through camshaft drive to contact timing chain, release tensioner using sharp contact downwards.
29. Install suitable 24mm wrench to hold camshaft, **Fig. 18.**
30. **Torque** mounting bolt to 63 ft. lbs.
31. Final tighten bolt an additional 30°.
32. Install valve cover.
33. Raise and support vehicle.
34. Install front engine cover.
35. Lower vehicle.

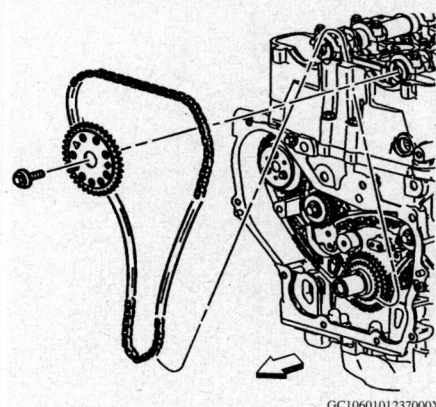

GC1060101237000X

Fig. 12 Camshaft bolt, sprocket & timing chain replacement

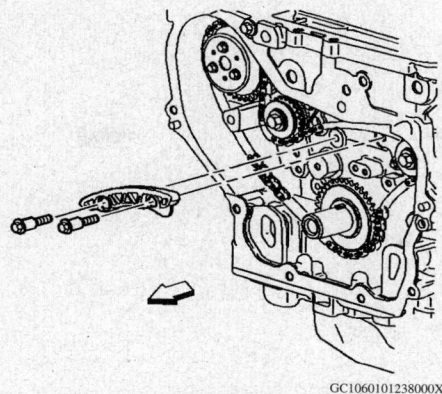

GC1060101238000X

Fig. 13 Upper balance shaft drive chain guide replacement

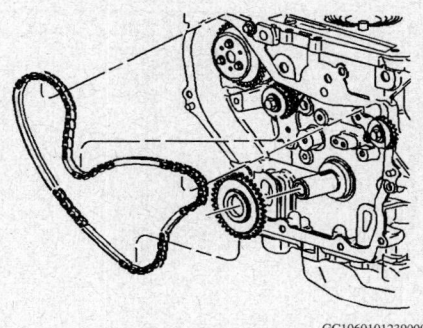

GC1060101239000X

Fig. 14 Balance shaft drive chain replacement

CAMSHAFT
REPLACE

1. Loosen vent hose clamp at air cleaner resonator, air cleaner intake duct clamp at air cleaner outlet resonator.
2. Loosen air cleaner outlet resonator to throttle body clamp, located forward of accelerator cable bracket. Remove air cleaner resonator to accelerator bracket bolt.
3. Remove throttle body resonator, air cleaner intake duct and vent hose.
4. Disconnect accelerator and cruise control cables from throttle body, then the bracket.
5. Remove PCV valve.
6. Remove fuel line brackets and brake booster hose pipe from brackets.
7. Remove mounting screw, ignition coil and Ignition Control Module (ICM).
8. Remove ground strap.
9. Remove mounting bolts and camshaft cover.
10. Remove upper timing chain guide.
11. Remove both intake and exhaust camshaft sprocket bolts using camshaft sprocket holding tool No. J43655, or equivalent.
12. Slide camshaft sprockets forward.
13. **On intake side,** remove power steering pump.
14. **On both sides,** mark bearing caps for installation reference.
15. Remove bearing caps.
16. Remove exhaust and intake camshafts.
17. Remove camshaft roller followers.
18. Remove hydraulic element lash adjusters.
19. Reverse procedure to install, noting the following:
    a. Lubricate valve tips using suitable lubricant.
    b. Ensure alignment notches are aligned with camshaft sprocket.
    c. **Torque** camshaft bearing cap bolts in three increments to 89 inch lbs.
    d. Apply anaerobic sealer bead, GM part No. 1052942, or equivalent, to rear intake camshaft bearing cap.
    e. **Torque** camshaft sprocket bolts to 63 ft. lbs.
    f. Final tighten bolts an additional 30°.

PISTON & ROD ASSEMBLY

When installing piston and rod assemblies into cylinder block, ensure arrow on top of piston faces toward front of engine. Ensure flat area on bottom of piston aligns with small dimple above connecting rod crankshaft bearing bore.

PISTONS, PINS & RINGS

Pistons and rings are available in standard size and oversize. Pistons and pins are serviced as an assembly.

MAIN & ROD BEARINGS

Main and rod bearings are available in standard size only.

CRANKSHAFT SEAL
REPLACE

1. Raise and support vehicle.
2. Remove front tire and wheel assembly.
3. Remove front fender liner.
4. Turn drive belt tensioner clockwise.
5. Remove serpentine drive belt.
6. Prevent crankshaft from rotating by install harmonic balancer holder tool No. J38122A, or equivalent.
7. Remove mounting bolt and crankshaft balancer. Discard bolt.
8. Remove front oil seal using suitable flat bladed tool.
9. Reverse procedure to install, using camshaft front main seal installer tool No. J35268A, or equivalent.

CRANKSHAFT REAR OIL SEAL
REPLACE

1. Remove transaxle as outlined in **MOTOR's "Domestic Transmission, In-Vehicle Service" manual or "Transmission Service DVD."**
2. Remove flywheel or flexplate.

3. Remove crankshaft rear oil seal using suitable flat bladed tool.
4. Reverse procedure to install.

OIL PAN
REPLACE

1. Raise and support vehicle.
2. Drain engine oil into suitable container.
3. Remove engine mount strut bracket.
4. Remove front fender liner.
5. Turn drive belt tensioner clockwise.
6. Remove serpentine drive belt.
7. Remove lower air conditioning compressor bolts.
8. Loosen upper air conditioning compressor bolts.
9. Remove oil pan bolts in sequence, **Fig. 19.**
10. Remove oil pan.
11. Reverse procedure to install. **Torque** oil pan mounting bolts to 18 ft. lbs., in reverse of loosening sequence, **Fig. 19.**

OIL PUMP
REPLACE

1. Raise and support vehicle.
2. Drain engine oil into suitable container.
3. Remove engine mount strut bracket.
4. Remove front fender liner.
5. Turn drive belt tensioner clockwise.
6. Remove serpentine drive belt.
7. Remove lower air conditioning compressor bolts.
8. Loosen upper air conditioning compressor bolts.
9. Remove oil pan bolts in sequence, **Fig. 19.**
10. Remove oil pan.
11. Remove oil pump and drive shaft extension, **Fig. 20.**
12. Reverse procedure to install.

BELT TENSION DATA

1. Turn Off accessories.
2. Bring engine to operating temperature.
3. Turn engine Off.
4. Read belt tension using belt tension gauge tool No. J23600B, or equivalent, halfway between alternator and power steering pump.
5. Start engine and allow temperature to stabilize for 15 seconds.
6. Turn engine Off.

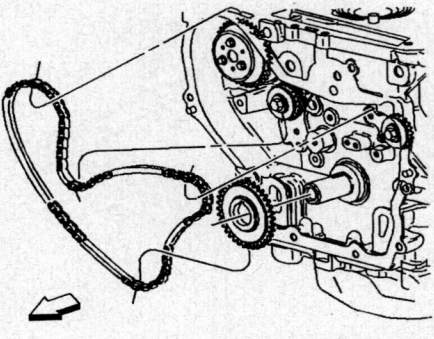

GC1060101240000X

Fig. 15 Timing chain installation

7. Install 15mm socket, apply clockwise force to tensioner pulley bolt.
8. Release force and measure belt tension without disturbing tensioner position.
9. Install 15mm socket, apply counterclockwise force to tensioner pulley bolt and raise pulley to eliminate tension.
10. Slowly lower pulley to belt and measure belt tension without disturbing tensioner position.
11. Average out readings.
12. If average is less than 30–50 lbs., replace belt tensioner.

SERPENTINE DRIVE BELT

1. Raise and support vehicle .
2. Remove front fender liner.
3. Turn drive belt tensioner clockwise.
4. Remove drive belt, **Fig. 21**.
5. Reverse procedure to install.

COOLING SYSTEM BLEED

1. Slowly add mixture of 50/50 Dex-Cool and clean water to cooling system until coolant level reaches and maintains top of surge tank label.
2. Install surge tank cap.
3. Start engine, run at 2000–2500 RPM until engine reaches normal operating temperature.
4. Allow engine to idle for three minutes.
5. Shut engine Off.
6. Top off coolant.
7. Inspect cooling system for leaks.

THERMOSTAT
REPLACE

1. **On models equipped with automatic transmission,** remove exhaust manifold as outlined under "Exhaust Manifold, Replace."
2. **On all models,** drain cooling system into suitable container.
3. Remove thermostat housing to water pump feed pipe.
4. Remove thermostat.
5. Reverse procedure to install.

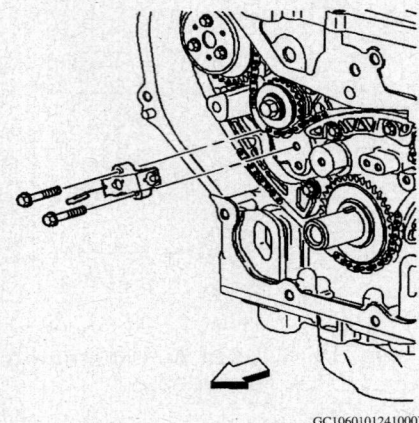

GC1060101241000X

Fig. 16 Tensioner plunger & body installation

WATER PUMP
REPLACE

1. **On models equipped with automatic transmission,** remove exhaust manifold as outlined under "Exhaust Manifold, Replace."
2. **On all models,** drain cooling system into suitable container.
3. Raise and support vehicle.
4. Remove righthand front tire and wheel.
5. Remove front fender liner.
6. Remove water pump sprocket from timing cover access plate, **Fig. 22**.
7. Remove water pump sprocket bolts by holding sprocket using water pump sprocket holding tool No. J43651, or equivalent.
8. Remove engine block to water pump and engine front cover to water pump mounting bolts, **Fig. 23**.
9. Remove feed pipes thermostat to water pump.
10. Remove mounting bolts and water pump, **Fig. 24**.
11. Reverse procedure to install.

RADIATOR
REPLACE

Alero & Grand Am

1. Remove battery and tray.
2. Recover air conditioning refrigerant as outlined in "Air Conditioning" chapter.
3. Drain engine cooling system into suitable container.
4. Remove upper radiator hose.
5. Remove upper transaxle cooler line.
6. Remove coolant surge tank hose.
7. Remove condenser inlet fitting from discharge hose.
8. Disconnect cooling fan electrical connector.
9. Raise and support vehicle.
10. Remove lower cover panel.
11. Remove lower radiator hose from radiator.
12. Remove lower transaxle cooler line.
13. Remove evaporator line to condenser outlet.

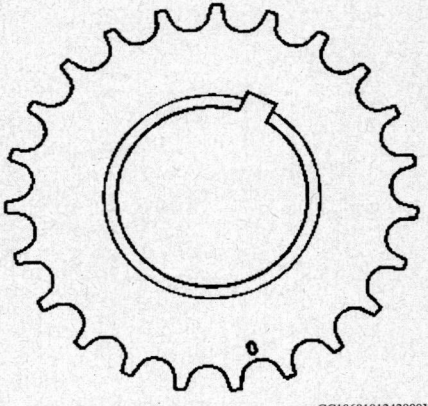

GC1060101242000X

Fig. 17 Crankshaft sprocket timing mark

14. Remove lower radiator mounting panel.
15. Remove radiator, fan and condenser as an assembly.
16. Reverse procedure to install.

Malibu

1. Drain engine coolant.
2. Remove lefthand headlamp assembly mounting bolts.
3. Lift headlamp assembly to unseat tabs on bottom edge of fender.
4. Disconnect connector and remove headlamp.
5. Remove righthand headlamp assembly mounting bolts.
6. Lift headlamp assembly to unseat tabs on bottom edge of fender.
7. Disconnect connector and remove headlamp.
8. Loop suitable rope around upper two tabs of condenser and tie rope around upper engine compartment tie bar.
9. Remove upper radiator support bracket bolts and support brackets.
10. Remove surge tank outlet hose from radiator.
11. Remove radiator inlet hose from radiator.
12. Raise and support vehicle.
13. Remove lower radiator air deflector retainers and the deflector.
14. Remove front fender liner retainers and fender liner.
15. Remove righthand and lefthand radiator air deflector retainers and deflectors.
16. Remove radiator outlet hose from radiator.
17. Place suitable drain pan under transaxle cooler lines and remove cooler lines from transaxle.
18. Remove lower radiator support bracket bolts and support brackets.
19. Remove radiator lower mounts.
20. Remove and discard condenser mounting bolts from radiator.
21. Push upward on radiator and downward on condenser to unsnap condenser mounting tabs from radiator clips.
22. Remove and discard condenser

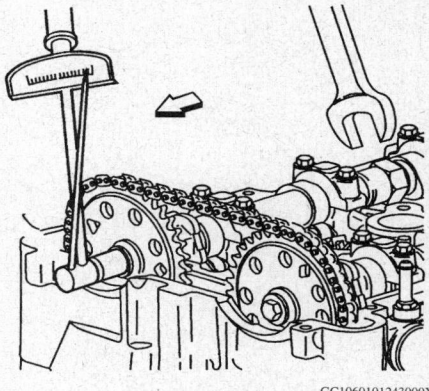

Fig. 18   Camshaft tightening

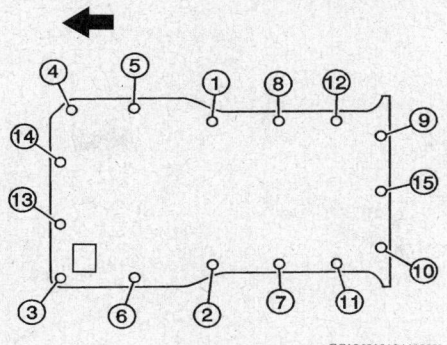

Fig. 19   Oil pan bolt loosening sequence

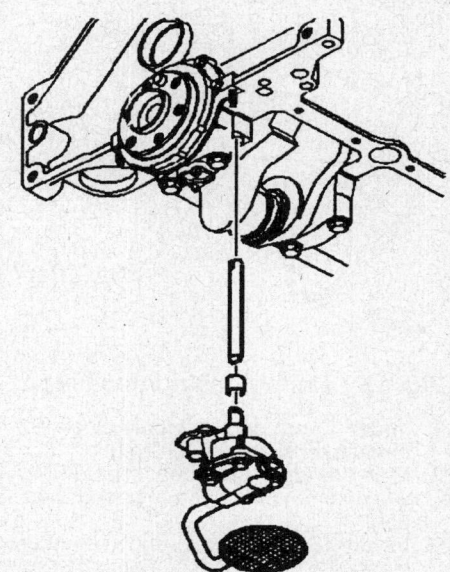

Fig. 20   Oil pump replacement

mounting nuts from radiator.
23. Remove radiator air side seals.
24. Remove radiator, cooling fan shroud and transaxle cooler line assembly.
25. Remove transaxle cooler lines from radiator.
26. Pry upward on fan shroud tabs, then remove cooling fan and shroud assembly from radiator.
27. Reverse procedure to install.

FUEL PUMP
REPLACE
Alero & Grand Am

The fuel pump is part of the fuel sender assembly and must be replaced as a complete unit.
1. Drain fuel tank into suitable container.
2. Raise and support vehicle.
3. Disconnect quick-connect fitting at fuel filter.
4. Disconnect fuel return pipe quick connect fitting.
5. Remove rubber exhaust hangers, allow exhaust system to rest on rear axle.
6. Remove exhaust heat shield.
7. Loosen clamp and disconnect fuel tank filler hose.
8. Disconnect EVAP Emission (EVAP) canister vapor pipe.
9. Disconnect electrical harness from multi-way rear body connector and fuel strap.
10. Support fuel tank with aid of an assistant, disconnect fuel tank retaining straps and lower fuel tank.
11. Disconnect wiring harness from fuel sender and fuel tank pressure sensor.
12. Turn retaining ring, press down and remove fuel sender.
13. Reverse procedure to install.

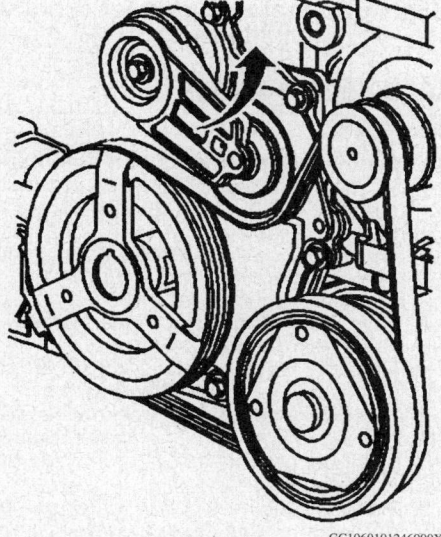

Fig. 21   Serpentine drive belt replacement

Malibu

1. Relieve fuel system pressure as outlined under "Precautions."
2. Drain fuel tank.
3. Raise and support vehicle.
4. Disconnect connector and remove fuel pump module electrical harness.
5. Disconnect EVAP vent valve solenoid harness electrical connector from underbody wiring harness.
6. Remove ABS wiring harness from retainer on EVAP canister.
7. Disconnect fuel feed and purge lines from fuel and brake line bundle on righthand side of vehicle.
8. Cap or plug fuel tank feed and vapor

lines to prevent fuel loss or contamination.
9. Disconnect fuel filler pipe jumper hose from fuel tank.
10. Disconnect vapor recirculation line runs parallel to fuel filler pipe jumper hose.
11. Remove exhaust pipe and muffler insulators from underbody hangers, then support exhaust system with suitable jackstand.
12. Support fuel tank using suitable jackstand.
13. Remove lefthand and righthand fuel tank strap bolts.
14. Lower righthand side of tank until it is clear of frame rail and remove tank toward righthand side of vehicle.
15. Remove fuel pump module assembly from fuel tank using fuel sender lock ring wrench tool No. J 45722, or equivalent.
16. Reverse procedure to install.

FUEL FILTER
REPLACE

1. Relieve fuel system pressure.
2. Raise and support vehicle.
3. Disconnect fuel filter fitting using suitable back-up wrench.
4. Disconnect fuel filter quick connect fitting.
5. Remove fuel filter.
6. Reverse procedure to install.

GC1060101247000X

Fig. 22 Water pump access plate replacement

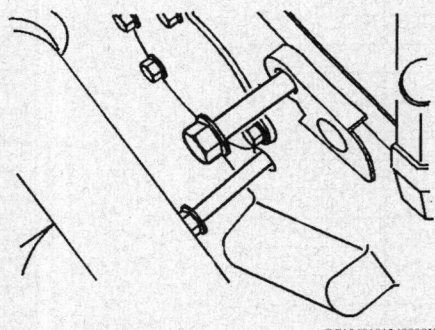

GC1060101248000X

Fig. 23 Water pump, engine block & front cover bolt replacement

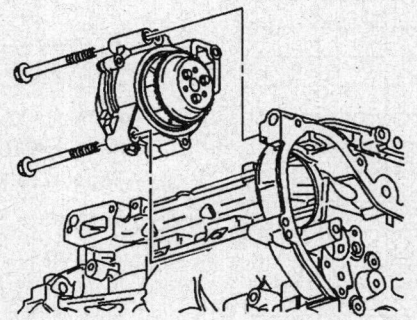

GC1060101249000X

Fig. 24 Water pump bolt replacement

TIGHTENING SPECIFICATIONS

Year	Component	Torque Ft. Lbs.
2004–05	Accelerator & Cruise Control Cable	89①
	Accelerator Pedal	22
	Access Hole Plug	30
	Access Plate	18①
	Air Cleaner Clamps	44①
	Air Cleaner Outlet Resonator	89①
	Alternator	15
	Alternator Electrical Connector	13
	Balance Shaft Chain Guide	89①
	Battery Terminal	13
	Bell Housing	66
	Blower Motor	45①
	Camshaft	③
	Camshaft Bearing Cap Bolts	89①
	Camshaft Cover	89①
	Chain Tensioner	89①
	Condenser To Inlet Discharge Hose	18
	Condenser To Radiator	44①
	Crankshaft Balancer	④
	Crankshaft Position Sensor	71①
	Cylinder Head	②
	Drive Belt Tensioner	33
	Engine Coolant Temperature Sensor	89①
	Engine Front Cover To Water Pump	15
	Engine Mount	49
	Engine To Transmission Brace	53
	Evaporator Core Bracket	9①
	EVAP Canister	89①
	EVAP Canister Purge Valve Mounting Bracket	71①
	EVAP Line	18
	Exhaust Manifold	⑥
	Exhaust Manifold Heat Shield	18
	Fixed Timing Chain Guide	89①
	Flywheel	⑤
	Front Cover	15
	Front Cover To Water Pump	15
	Fuel Filler Hose Clamp	27①
	Fuel Filler Pipe	89①
	Fuel Filter Fitting	20
	Fuel Line Bracket	89①
	Fuel Pipe	53①
	Fuel Pipe Retainer	89①
	Fuel Rail Pipe Fittings	89①
	Fuel Tank Retaining Strap	26
	Ground Strap	89①
	Heated Oxygen Sensor No. 1	22
	Heated Oxygen Sensor No. 2	30
	Heater Core Bracket	9①
	Heater Core Case	9①
	Heater Core Cover	9①

TIGHTENING SPECIFICATIONS—Continued

Year	Component	Torque Ft. Lbs.
2004–05	ICM, Bolt	89①
	ICM, Screw	13①
	Idle Air Control Valve	27①
	Ignition Switch	53①
	Ignition Switch Bracket	53①
	Intake Manifold	89①
	Knock Sensor	18
	Lower Radiator Mounting Panel	89①
	Manifold To Flex Decoupler	26
	Multi-Function Switch	35①
	Oil Pan	⑦
	Park Neutral Switch	18
	Power Steering Pump	19
	Pump To Rear Bearing Cap	30
	Radiator Drain Cock	18①
	Rear Intake Camshaft Bearing Cap	18
	Spark Plugs	15①
	Starter Motor	30
	Steering Wheel	27
	Throttle Body	89①
	Throttle Position Sensor	18①
	Timing Chain Tensioner	55
	Timing Chain Tensioner Guide	89①
	Timing Chain Upper Guide	89①
	Transaxle Oil Cooler Line	22
	Upper Air Cleaner Cover	27①
	Water Pump Drain Plug	16①
	Water Pump Feed Pipes	18①
	Water Pump Sprocket To Water Pump	89①
	Wiper Drive Module	89①
	Wiper Motor	89①

① — Inch lbs.

② — Refer to "Cylinder Head, Removal" for tightening specifications and sequence.

③ — **Torque** to 63 ft. lbs., then tighten additional 30°.

④ — **Torque** to 74 ft. lbs., then tighten additional 75°.

⑤ — **Torque** to 39 ft. lbs., then tighten additional 25°.

⑥ — Refer to "Exhaust Manifold, Removal" for tightening specifications and sequence.

⑦ — Refer to "Oil Pan, Removal" for tightening specifications and sequence.

3.1L Engine

NOTE: On Air Bag Equipped Models, Refer To "Air Bag System Precautions" Located In The Front Of This Manual For System Disarming & Arming Procedures.

NOTE: For Procedures Not Found In This Section, Refer To "3.1L Engine" Section In The "Century, Grand Prix, Impala, Intrigue, LaCrosse, Monte Carlo & Regal" Chapter.

NOTE: Refer To "Computer Relearn Procedures" Located In The Front Of This Manual When Battery Power To The Computer Has Been Interrupted.

INDEX

	Page No.		Page No.		Page No.
Compression Pressure	1-19	Lefthand	1-20	Battery Ground Cable	1-19
Engine Rebuilding		Righthand	1-20	Fuel System Pressure Relief	1-19
Specifications	29-1	Intake Manifold, Replace	1-20	Radiator, Replace	1-20
Engine, Replace	1-19	Lower	1-20	Alero & Grand Am	1-20
Engine Mount, Replace	1-19	Upper	1-20	Malibu	1-21
Strut	1-19	Precautions	1-19	Tightening Specifications	1-21
Exhaust Manifold, Replace	1-20	Air Bag Systems	1-19		

PRECAUTIONS

Air Bag Systems

Refer to "Air Bag System Precautions" in the front of this manual for system disarming and arming procedures.

Battery Ground Cable

Prior to service, disconnect battery ground cable and isolate as required.

Fuel System Pressure Relief

1. Disconnect battery ground cable and isolate as required.
2. Install fuel pressure gauge tool No. J34730-1A, or equivalent.
3. Install bleed hose into suitable container and open valve to bleed system pressure.
4. Disconnect fuel pressure gauge from fuel pressure connection.

COMPRESSION PRESSURE

When inspecting cylinder compression, the throttle should be open, the spark plugs removed and the battery at or near full charge. The lowest reading cylinder should not be less than 70% of the highest and no cylinder reading should be less than 100 psi. Turn ignition key until engine cranks through four compression cycles. Normal compression builds up quickly and evenly to specified compression on each cylinder.

ENGINE MOUNT

REPLACE

1. Support engine by oil pan and remove engine mount to engine mount bracket support bolts, **Fig. 1.**
2. Remove engine mount to body bolts and nut.
3. Remove engine mount
4. Reverse procedure to install.

Strut

1. Raise and support vehicle.
2. Remove righthand splash shield.
3. Remove mounting bolts and engine mount strut, **Fig. 2.**
4. Reverse procedure to install.

ENGINE

REPLACE

1. Relieve fuel system pressure as outlined under "Precautions."
2. Remove upper half of air cleaner and throttle body duct.
3. Drain coolant into suitable container.
4. Disconnect upper radiator hose from engine and position aside.
5. Disconnect lower radiator hose from engine and position aside.
6. Disconnect coolant inlet line from surge tank.
7. Disconnect vacuum modulator, EVAP canister purge and power brake booster vacuum hoses.
8. Disconnect heater outlet hose from water pump.
9. Remove serpentine drive belt.
10. Disconnect accelerator and cruise control cable from throttle linkage.
11. Disconnect electrical connectors at electronic ignition, heated oxygen sensor, injector harness, IAC, throttle position sensor, engine coolant temperature sensor, PNP switch, transaxle shift solenoid, TCC solenoid and EGR and battery ground cable at transaxle.
12. Remove serpentine drive belt.
13. Disconnect alternator electrical connectors and power steering line clip.
14. Remove alternator rear brace.
15. Disconnect alternator air inlet connector.
16. Remove mounting bolts, nuts and alternator.
17. Disconnect power steering lines at power steering pump.
18. Disconnect fuel lines.
19. Remove cooling fan.
20. Disconnect shift cable linkage and cable from mounting bracket. Transaxle should be in low gear for better accessibility.
21. Disconnect transaxle vent tube from transaxle.
22. Disconnect vacuum hose at vacuum reservoir.
23. Remove engine support fixture.
24. Loosen but do not remove upper two air conditioning compressor bolts.
25. Raise and support vehicle.
26. Remove front tire and wheel assemblies.
27. Remove lefthand and righthand splash shields.
28. Raise and support vehicle.
29. Remove righthand splash shield.
30. Remove mounting bolts and engine mount strut, **Fig. 2.**
31. Remove both front ABS speed sensor connectors and harness from suspension supports.
32. Remove both ball joints.
33. Remove suspension support.

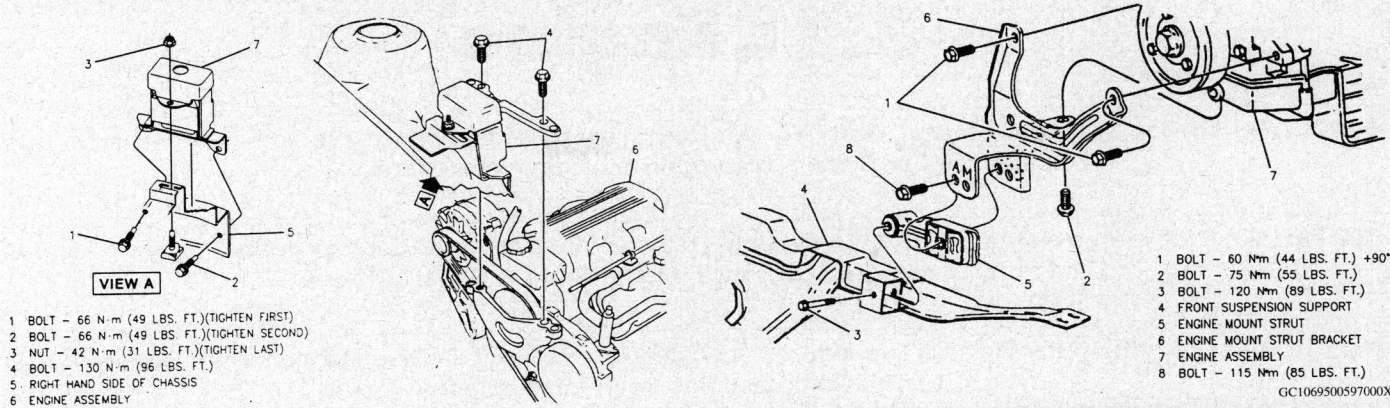

Fig. 1 Engine mount replacement

1. BOLT – 66 N·m (49 LBS. FT.)(TIGHTEN FIRST)
2. BOLT – 66 N·m (49 LBS. FT.)(TIGHTEN SECOND)
3. NUT – 42 N·m (31 LBS. FT.)(TIGHTEN LAST)
4. BOLT – 130 N·m (96 LBS. FT.)
5. RIGHT HAND SIDE OF CHASSIS
6. ENGINE ASSEMBLY
7. RIGHT ENGINE MOUNT

GC1069500596000X

Fig. 2 Engine mount strut bolt replacement

1. BOLT – 60 N·m (44 LBS. FT.) +90°
2. BOLT – 75 N·m (55 LBS. FT.)
3. BOLT – 120 N·m (89 LBS. FT.)
4. FRONT SUSPENSION SUPPORT
5. ENGINE MOUNT STRUT
6. ENGINE MOUNT STRUT BRACKET
7. ENGINE ASSEMBLY
8. BOLT – 115 N·m (85 LBS. FT.)

GC1069500597000X

34. Remove drive axles from transaxle and support.
35. Remove oil filter and adapter.
36. Remove transaxle converter cover.
37. Remove mounting bolts and lower starter.
38. Disconnect starter electrical connectors and remove starter.
39. Disconnect knock sensor, front crankshaft position sensor, side crankshaft position sensor, oil level sensor, VSS and transaxle ground cable.
40. Disconnect heater hoses.
41. Remove air conditioning compressor lower bolts and position compressor aside.
42. Remove vacuum reserve tank.
43. Remove exhaust pipe from manifold and position aside.
44. Remove engine mount strut bracket.
45. Disconnect transaxle cooling lines at radiator.
46. Remove fluid level indicator and tube.
47. Lower vehicle and engine/transaxle onto suitable table.
48. Remove transaxle mount to body bolts, **Fig. 1.**
49. Remove intermediate bracket from righthand engine mount support bracket.
50. Raise and support vehicle, leaving powertrain on table.
51. Separate engine and transaxle.
52. Reverse procedure to install. After connecting engine to transaxle, loosely install serpentine drive belt to hold components in place.

INTAKE MANIFOLD
REPLACE
Upper

1. Disconnect vacuum lines.
2. Remove electrical connector, mounting screws and MAP sensor.
3. Remove pipe, bolts, EGR valve and gaskets.
4. Remove spark plug wires.

5. Remove mounting nuts, bolts and electronic ignition control module.
6. Remove mounting nuts, studs, upper intake manifold and gasket.
7. Reverse procedure to install.

Lower

1. Remove fuel feed and return pipe mounting bolt and clip.
2. Remove mounting bolts and fuel injector rail.
3. Remove mounting nut and heater inlet pipe.
4. Remove mounting bolts and lower intake manifold.
5. Reverse procedure to install.

EXHAUST MANIFOLD
REPLACE
Lefthand

1. Remove upper half of air cleaner and throttle cable duct.
2. Partially drain coolant into suitable container and disconnect radiator hose from thermostat housing.
3. Disconnect coolant bypass pipe at coolant pump and from exhaust manifold.
4. Remove exhaust crossover heat shield.
5. Remove exhaust crossover pipe from manifold.
6. Disconnect secondary ignition wires from spark plugs.
7. Remove exhaust manifold heat shield, **Fig. 3.**
8. Remove mounting nuts and exhaust manifold.
9. Reverse procedure to install.

Righthand

1. Remove upper half of air cleaner and throttle cable duct.
2. Remove exhaust crossover heat shield.

3. Remove crossover at exhaust manifold.
4. Remove heated oxygen sensor.
5. Disconnect EGR pipe at exhaust manifold.
6. Raise and support vehicle.
7. Remove transaxle oil fill tube and level indicator.
8. Remove exhaust pipe from exhaust manifold.
9. Disconnect exhaust pipe from converter flange and support converter.
10. Remove converter heat shield from body.
11. Remove exhaust manifold heat shield.
12. Remove mounting nuts and exhaust manifold, **Fig. 3.**
13. Reverse procedure to install.

RADIATOR
REPLACE
Alero & Grand Am

1. Recover air conditioning refrigerant as outlined in "Air Conditioning" chapter.
2. Drain coolant into suitable container.
3. Remove battery and battery tray.
4. Remove upper radiator hose.
5. Remove upper transaxle cooler line.
6. Remove coolant surge tank hose.
7. Remove condenser inlet fitting from discharge hose.
8. Disconnect cooling fan electrical connector.
9. Raise and support vehicle.
10. Remove lower closeout panel.
11. Remove lower radiator hose from radiator.
12. Remove lower transaxle cooler line.
13. Remove evaporator line from condenser outlet.
14. Remove radiator lower mounting panel.
15. Remove Condenser Radiator Fan Module (CRFM).
16. Remove condenser and fan shroud from radiator.
17. Reverse procedure to install.

Malibu

1. Recover air conditioning refrigerant as outlined in "Air Conditioning" chapter.
2. Drain coolant into suitable container.
3. Remove upper radiator hose, transaxle cooler line and surge tank hose.
4. Remove condenser inlet fitting from discharge hose and lower transaxle cooler line.
5. Disconnect cooling fan electrical connector.
6. Raise and support vehicle.
7. Remove lower closeout panel, lower radiator hose and evaporator line.
8. Remove lower radiator mounting plate and condenser fan radiator module.
9. Remove condenser, fan shroud and radiator.
10. Reverse procedure to install.

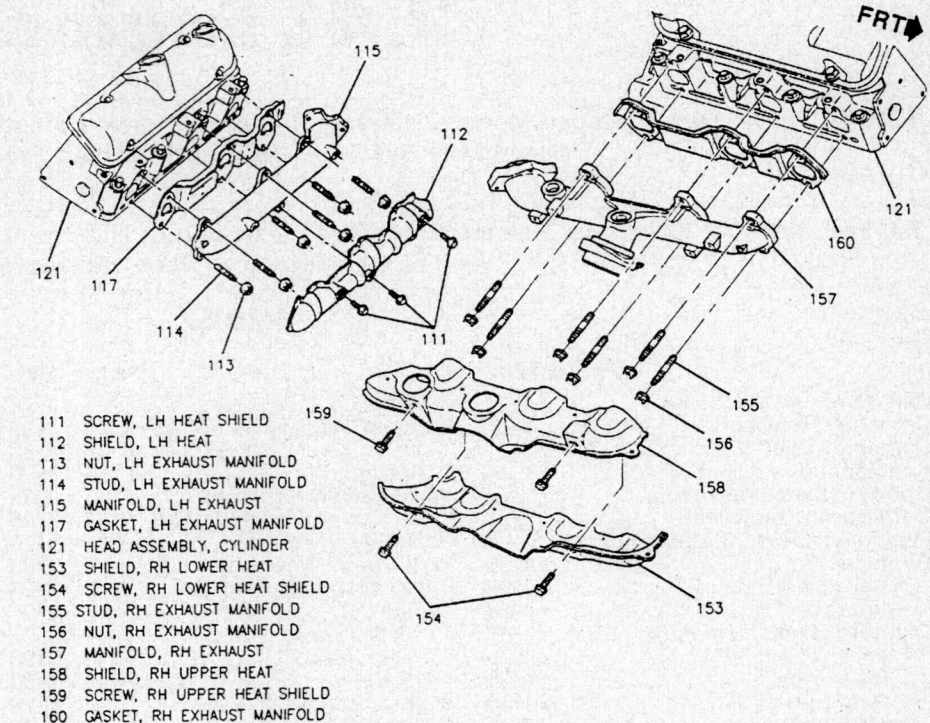

111 SCREW, LH HEAT SHIELD
112 SHIELD, LH HEAT
113 NUT, LH EXHAUST MANIFOLD
114 STUD, LH EXHAUST MANIFOLD
115 MANIFOLD, LH EXHAUST
117 GASKET, LH EXHAUST MANIFOLD
121 HEAD ASSEMBLY, CYLINDER
153 SHIELD, RH LOWER HEAT
154 SCREW, RH LOWER HEAT SHIELD
155 STUD, RH EXHAUST MANIFOLD
156 NUT, RH EXHAUST MANIFOLD
157 MANIFOLD, RH EXHAUST
158 SHIELD, RH UPPER HEAT
159 SCREW, RH UPPER HEAT SHIELD
160 GASKET, RH EXHAUST MANIFOLD

GC1069500600000X

Fig. 3 Exhaust manifold replacement

TIGHTENING SPECIFICATIONS

Year	Component	Torque Ft. Lbs.
2004–05	Accelerator Cable Bracket	89①
	Coolant Drain Plug	14
	Coolant Outlet	18
	Drive Belt Tensioner	37
	Engine Mount Strut	52
	Engine Mount To Body, Bolt	49
	Engine Mount To Body, Nut	31
	Exhaust Manifold	12
	Exhaust Manifold Heat Shield	84①
	Lower Intake Manifold	10
	Oil Filter	9–10
	Upper Intake Manifold	18
	Water Pump	89①
	Water Pump Pulley	18

① — Inch lbs.

3.4L Engine

NOTE: On Air Bag Equipped Models, Refer To "Air Bag System Precautions" Located In The Front Of This Manual For System Disarming & Arming Procedures.

NOTE: Refer To "Computer Relearn Procedures" Located In The Front Of This Manual When Battery Power To The Computer Has Been Interrupted.

INDEX

	Page No.
Belt Tension Data	1-27
Camshaft, Replace	1-26
Camshaft Lobe Lift Specifications	1-24
Compression Pressure	1-22
Cooling System Bleed	1-27
Crankshaft Rear Oil Seal, Replace	1-26
Installation	1-26
Removal	1-26
Cylinder Head, Replace	1-23
Front	1-23
Installation	1-24
Removal	1-23
Rear	1-24
Installation	1-24
Removal	1-24
Engine Rebuilding Specifications	29-1
Engine, Replace	1-22
Engine Mount, Replace	1-22

	Page No.
Strut	1-22
Exhaust Manifold, Replace	1-23
Lefthand	1-23
Righthand	1-23
Front Cover, Replace	1-25
Front Cover Seal, Replace	1-25
Fuel Filter, Replace	1-28
Fuel Pump, Replace	1-28
Intake Manifold, Replace	1-23
Lower	1-23
Installation	1-23
Removal	1-23
Upper	1-23
Main & Rod Bearings	1-26
Oil Pan, Replace	1-26
Oil Pump, Replace	1-27
Oil Pump Service	1-27
Assemble	1-27
Disassemble	1-27
Inspection	1-27
Piston & Rod Assembly	1-26

	Page No.
Precautions	1-22
Air Bag Systems	1-22
Battery Ground Cable	1-22
Fuel System Pressure Relief	1-22
Push Rods	1-24
Radiator, Replace	1-28
Serpentine Drive Belt	1-27
Thermostat, Replace	1-28
Tightening Specifications	1-29
Timing Chain, Replace	1-25
Installation	1-25
Removal	1-25
Valve Adjustment	1-24
Valve Arrangement	1-24
Front To Rear	1-24
Valve Cover, Replace	1-24
Front	1-24
Rear	1-24
Valve Lifters	1-24
Water Pump, Replace	1-28

PRECAUTIONS

Air Bag Systems

Refer to "Air Bag System Precautions" in the front of this manual for system disarming and arming procedures.

Battery Ground Cable

Prior to service, disconnect battery ground cable and isolate as required.

Fuel System Pressure Relief

1. Disconnect battery ground cable and isolate as required.
2. Install fuel pressure gauge tool No. J34730-1A, or equivalent.
3. Install bleed hose into suitable container and open valve to bleed system pressure.
4. Disconnect fuel pressure gauge from fuel pressure connection.

COMPRESSION PRESSURE

When inspecting cylinder compression, the throttle should be open, the spark plugs removed and the battery at or near full charge. The lowest reading cylinder should not be less than 70% of the highest and no cylinder reading should be less than 100 psi. Crank engine until it runs through four compression cycles. Normal compression builds up quickly and evenly to specified compression on each cylinder.

ENGINE MOUNT

REPLACE

1. Support engine with suitable wooden block and suitable floor jack positioned below oil pan.
2. Remove cruise control module.
3. Remove engine mount to bracket support bolts.
4. Remove engine mount to body bolts.
5. Remove engine mount.
6. Reverse procedure to install.

Strut

1. Raise and support vehicle.
2. Remove righthand splash shield.
3. Remove mounting bolts and engine mount strut bolts.
4. Reverse procedure to install, noting the following:
   a. **Torque** strut bolts to 74 ft. lbs.
   b. Final tighten bolts an additional 90°.

ENGINE

REPLACE

1. Relieve fuel system pressure as outlined under "Precautions."
2. Drain coolant into suitable container.
3. Remove engine air cleaner.
4. Remove hood.
5. Remove serpentine belt.
6. Remove hoses from surge tank.
7. Remove cruise control module.
8. Remove engine wiring harness from upper side of engine and position it aside.
9. Disconnect throttle and cruise control cables. **Manufacturer recommends throttle cable replacement when engine is removed and installed.**
10. Raise and support vehicle.
11. Remove starter motor.
12. Remove air conditioning compressor with lines attached and position aside.
13. Disconnect engine lower wiring harness and position it aside.
14. Disconnect catalytic converter flange from rear exhaust manifold.
15. Remove inspection cover.
16. Remove torque converter to flexplate bolts.
17. Remove engine splash shields.
18. Remove transaxle to engine brace.
19. Remove two outer transaxle mounting bolts.

20. Disconnect upper and lower radiator hoses.
21. Lower vehicle.
22. Disconnect engine fuel lines.
23. Disconnect vacuum hoses at brake booster.
24. Disconnect heater hoses.
25. Install engine support fixture tool No. J28467-360, or equivalent.
26. Raise engine.
27. Remove engine mount and adapter.
28. Remove power steering pump.
29. Install suitable engine lifting device.
30. Remove engine support fixture.
31. Remove transaxle to engine bolts.
32. Carefully remove engine.
33. If mounting engine onto suitable stand, remove flexplate mounting bolts and flexplate.
34. Reverse procedure to install.

INTAKE MANIFOLD

REPLACE

Upper

1. Drain coolant into suitable container.
2. Remove upper half of air cleaner.
3. Remove EGR valve.
4. Remove brake vacuum pipe at plenum.
5. Disconnect fuel pressure regulator vacuum hose from regulator and at PCV valve.
6. Mark and disconnect spark plug wires at plugs.
7. Remove spark plug wires from plenum harness.
8. Remove electronic ignition coil and module.
9. Remove EVAP canister purge solenoid.
10. Disconnect TP and IAC sensor electrical connectors.
11. Disconnect injector harness.
12. Disconnect ECT and CMP sensor electrical connectors.
13. Disconnect vacuum modulator.
14. Disconnect MAP sensor vacuum line and electrical connector.
15. Remove mounting bolts and MAP sensor.
16. Remove mounting bolts and upper intake manifold with gaskets.
17. Reverse procedure to install.

Lower

REMOVAL

1. Relieve fuel system pressure as outlined under "Precautions."
2. Remove upper intake manifold as outlined under "Upper."
3. Remove fuel lines at fuel rail and bracket, then the rail with injectors.
4. Support engine with suitable wooden block and suitable floor jack positioned below oil pan.
5. Remove cruise control module.
6. Remove engine mount to bracket support bolts.
7. Remove engine mount to body bolts.

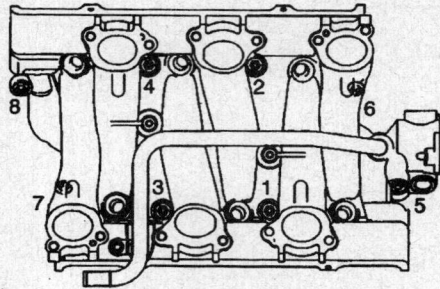

GC1059900123000X

Fig. 1 Lower intake manifold bolt tightening sequence

8. Remove engine mount.
9. Remove mounting bolts and position power steering pump aside.
10. Remove heater inlet pipe from coolant outlet housing.
11. Remove heater bypass at coolant pump and at cylinder head.
12. Remove radiator hose at heater outlet housing.
13. Remove water outlet housing.
14. Remove valve covers as outlined under "Valve Cover, Replace."
15. Remove lower intake manifold bolts. **Keep washers in original positions on center bolts.**
16. Remove lower intake manifold.
17. Loosen rocker arm bolts.
18. Remove pushrods, keeping them in order. Intakes have yellow stripes and are 5.75 inches long. Exhausts have green stripes and are six inches long.
19. Remove intake manifold gaskets.

INSTALLATION

1. Clean gasket material from mating surfaces.
2. Remove excess RTV sealer from front and rear block ridges.
3. Clean sealing surfaces using suitable degreasing compound.
4. Place .079–.118 inch bead of RTV sealer part No. 12345739, or equivalent, on each manifold-to-block contact ridge.
5. Install new manifold gaskets.
6. Coat pushrod ends with prelube part No. 1052356, or equivalent.
7. Install pushrods in proper sequence. Intake pushrods have yellow stripes and are 5.75 inches long. Exhaust pushrods have green stripes and are six inches long.
8. **Torque** rocker arm bolts to 14 ft. lbs.
9. Final tighten bolts an additional 30°.
10. Place lower intake manifold in position.
11. Apply sealant part No. 12345382, or equivalent, to lower intake manifold bolt threads.
12. **Torque** vertical bolts to 10 ft. lbs., in sequence, **Fig. 1. Always tighten vertical bolts before horizontals.**
13. **Torque** horizontal bolts to 10 ft. lbs., in sequence, **Fig. 1. Always horizontal bolts, than vertical bolts.**
14. Install valve covers.
15. Install heater outlet housing.

16. Install heater inlet pipe to thermostat housing.
17. Install fuel lines to fuel rail and bracket.
18. Install upper intake manifold as outlined under "Upper."
19. Start engine and inspect for leaks.

EXHAUST MANIFOLD

REPLACE

Lefthand

1. Partially drain coolant into suitable container.
2. Remove complete air cleaner and throttle body duct.
3. Remove exhaust crossover heat shield.
4. Remove crossover pipe at exhaust manifold.
5. Remove upper radiator hose from thermostat housing.
6. Tag, disconnect and position front spark plug wires aside.
7. Remove exhaust manifold heat shield.
8. Remove mounting nuts and exhaust manifold.
9. Reverse procedure to install. Install new gasket.

Righthand

1. Remove complete air cleaner and throttle body duct.
2. Remove O2 sensors using socket tool No. J39194-B, or equivalent.
3. Remove exhaust crossover heat shield.
4. Disconnect EGR pipe from manifold.
5. Remove exhaust crossover pipe from manifold.
6. Remove exhaust manifold heat shield.
7. Remove mounting nuts and exhaust manifold.
8. Reverse procedure to install. Install new gasket.

CYLINDER HEAD

REPLACE

Front

REMOVAL

1. Relieve fuel system pressure as outlined under "Precautions."
2. Drain coolant into suitable container.
3. Remove upper half of engine air cleaner.
4. Remove TBI unit duct.
5. Remove exhaust crossover.
6. Remove upper and lower intake manifolds as outlined under "Intake Manifold, Replace."
7. Remove valve cover as outlined under "Valve Cover, Replace."
8. Remove rocker arm bolts, pivot balls and arms.
9. Remove pushrods, keeping them in order. Intakes have yellow stripes and are 5.75 inches long. Exhausts have green stripes and are six inches long.

10. Remove front exhaust manifold as outlined under "Exhaust Manifold, Replace."
11. Remove mounting bolts and cylinder head.

INSTALLATION

1. Clean mating surfaces of head, block and intake manifold.
2. Clean cylinder head bolts and threads.
3. Place head gasket into position over dowel pins with "THIS SIDE UP" notice properly oriented.
4. Carefully place head into position.
5. Coat head bolt threads with sealer part No. 1052080, or equivalent.
6. **Torque** head bolts to 33 ft. lbs., in sequence, **Fig. 2.**
7. Tighten head bolts an additional 90°.
8. Install intake manifold gaskets.
9. Install pushrods in proper sequence. Intakes have yellow stripes and are 5.75 inches long. Exhausts have green stripes and are six inches long.
10. **Torque** rocker arms, pivot balls and bolts to 14 ft. lbs.
11. Final tighten bolts an additional 30°.
12. Install intake manifolds as outlined under "Intake Manifold, Replace."
13. Install exhaust manifold as outlined under "Exhaust Manifold, Replace."
14. Install crossover pipe and heat shield.
15. Fill cooling system.
16. Install TBI unit duct.
17. Install upper half of air cleaner.
18. Start engine and inspect for leaks.

Rear

REMOVAL

1. Relieve fuel system pressure as outlined under "Precautions."
2. Drain coolant into suitable container.
3. Remove exhaust crossover pipe.
4. Raise and support vehicle.
5. Remove rear exhaust manifold as outlined under "Exhaust Manifold, Replace."
6. Lower vehicle.
7. Support engine with suitable wooden block and suitable floor jack positioned below oil pan.
8. Remove cruise control module.
9. Remove engine mount to bracket support bolts.
10. Remove engine mount to body bolts.
11. Remove engine mount.
12. Turn belt tensioner in clockwise direction using suitable ⅜ inch breaker bar.
13. Remove serpentine belt.
14. Remove valve cover as outlined under "Valve Cover, Replace."
15. Remove rocker arm bolts, pivot balls and arms.
16. Remove pushrods, keeping them in order. Intakes have yellow stripes and are 5.75 inches long. Exhausts have green stripes and are six inches long.
17. Remove upper and lower intake manifolds as outlined under "Intake Manifold, Replace."
18. Remove mounting bolts and cylinder head.

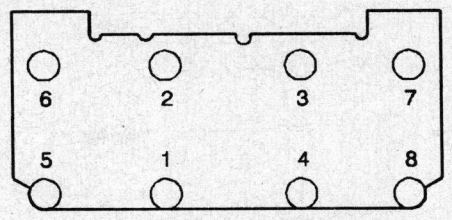

GC1059900124000X

Fig. 2   Cylinder head bolt tightening sequence

INSTALLATION

1. Clean mating surfaces of head, block and intake manifold.
2. Clean cylinder head bolts and threads.
3. Place head gasket into position over dowel pins with "THIS SIDE UP" notice properly oriented.
4. Carefully place head into position.
5. Coat head bolt threads with sealer part No. 1052080, or equivalent.
6. **Torque** head bolts to 33 ft. lbs., in sequence, **Fig. 2.**
7. Tighten head bolts an additional 90°.
8. Install intake manifold gaskets.
9. Install pushrods in proper sequence. Intakes have yellow stripes and are 5.75 inches long. Exhausts have green stripes and are six inches long.
10. **Torque** rocker arms, pivot balls and bolts to 14 ft. lbs.
11. Final tighten bolts an additional 30°.
12. Install intake manifolds as outlined under "Intake Manifold, Replace."
13. Install valve cover with new gasket.
14. Connect spark plug wires.
15. Install serpentine belt.
16. Raise and support vehicle.
17. Install exhaust manifold as outlined under "Exhaust Manifold, Replace."
18. Install crossover pipe and heat shield.
19. Fill cooling system.
20. Install TBI unit duct.
21. Install upper half of air cleaner.
22. Start engine and inspect for leaks.

VALVE COVER

REPLACE

Front

1. Partially drain coolant into suitable container.
2. Remove rear ignition wire harness and spark plug wires at spark plugs.
3. Remove heater bypass intake.
4. Disconnect PCV vacuum hose.
5. Remove mounting bolts and valve cover. If cover is stubborn, break it loose by tapping it lightly with palm of hand or suitable soft rubber mallet.
6. Reverse procedure to install, noting the following:
   a. Install new cover gasket and grommets.
   b. Apply sealer part No. 12346192, or equivalent, in cover notch.

Rear

1. Remove cruise control module.

2. Remove engine mount.
3. Turn serpentine drive belt tensioner in clockwise direction and remove belt using suitable ⅜ inch breaker bar.
4. Disconnect alternator electrical connectors and power steering line clip.
5. Remove mounting bolts, nuts and alternator.
6. Remove alternator bracket.
7. Remove rear bank spark plug wires.
8. Remove ignition coils and bracket.
9. Remove purge and vacuum canister solenoids.
10. Remove vacuum hose from rear bank valve cover grommet.
11. Remove serpentine belt tensioner.
12. Remove mounting bolts and valve cover. If cover is stubborn, break it loose by tapping it lightly with palm of hand or suitable soft rubber mallet.
13. Reverse procedure to install, noting the following:
    a. Install new cover gasket and grommets.
    b. Apply sealer part No. 12345739, or equivalent, at cylinder head to lower intake manifold joints.

VALVE ARRANGEMENT

Front To Rear

Cowl side ....E-I-E-I-I-E
Radiator side ....E-I-I-E-I-E

VALVE LIFTERS

Roller type valve lifters are must be replaced whenever the camshaft is replaced, **Fig. 3.**

Inspect the lifters and look for a bent or broken clip (1), worn pushrod socket (2), scuffed or worn sides (3), flat spots on the roller (4), a loose or damaged pin, (5) a plugged oil hole (6) or worn or damaged roller bearing. Ensure the roller can rotate freely with no binding or rough operation. If the lifter show side wear the block lifter bores should also be inspected for damage or wear. Replace any lifter which does not pass these inspections.

Valve lifters must be kept in order for installation in original positions.

CAMSHAFT LOBE LIFT SPECIFICATIONS

Intake .... .2727
Exhaust.. .2727

VALVE ADJUSTMENT

These engines are equipped with hydraulic valve lash adjusters. No adjustment is required.

PUSH RODS

1. Remove rocker arm covers and rocker arms. Identify components for installation in original positions.
2. Remove rocker arm pivot balls and rocker arms, then the pushrods, noting the following:
   a. Intakes have yellow stripes and are 5.75 inches long.

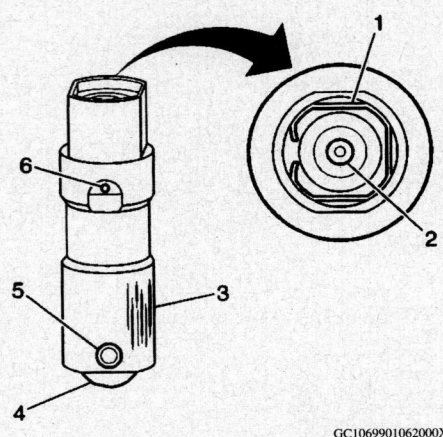

Fig. 3   Valve lifter inspection locations

b. Exhausts have green stripes and are six inches long.
3. Reverse procedure to install, noting the following:
   a. Ensure pushrods seat in lifters.
   b. Coat bearing surfaces of rocker arms and pivot balls with Molykote part No. 1052356, or equivalent lubricant.

FRONT COVER
REPLACE

1. Recover air conditioning refrigerant as outlined in "Air Conditioning" chapter.
2. Drain coolant into suitable container.
3. Install engine support tool No. J28467-360, or equivalent.
4. Support engine with suitable wooden block and suitable floor jack positioned below oil pan.
5. Remove cruise control module.
6. Remove engine mount to bracket support bolts.
7. Remove engine mount to body bolts.
8. Remove engine mount.
9. Remove engine mount bracket support.
10. Turn belt tensioner in clockwise direction using suitable ⅜ inch breaker bar.
11. Remove serpentine belt.
12. Remove complete engine air cleaner.
13. Remove TBI unit tube.
14. Disconnect power steering lines at power steering pump, allowing fluid to drain into suitable container.
15. Loosen upper two air conditioning compressor mounting bolts.
16. Disconnect alternator electrical connectors and power steering line clip.
17. Remove mounting bolts, nuts and alternator.
18. Remove alternator bracket.
19. Raise and support vehicle.
20. Drain engine oil into suitable container.
21. Remove righthand front tire and wheel.
22. Remove righthand front splash shield.
23. Remove flexplate inspection cover.
24. Remove harmonic balancer using puller tool No. J24420-C, or equivalent.
25. Remove serpentine belt tensioner.
26. Disconnect righthand front wheel

speed sensor electrical connector and wiring harness from suspension support.
27. Remove lower ball joint cotter pin and nut.
28. **On models equipped with ABS,** position wheel speed sensor wiring aside.
29. **On all models,** separate lower ball joint from steering knuckle using ball joint separator tool No. J43828, or equivalent.
30. Locate center of rivet body and mark with suitable center punch.
31. Drill pilot holes completely through rivets. **Avoid damaging CV joint boots.**
32. Drill final holes through rivets to ensure proper fitting of new ball joint.
33. Remove stabilizer shaft link mounting nut.
34. Remove ball joint from knuckle and lower control arm.
35. Remove righthand stabilizer shaft from righthand suspension support and control arm.
36. Remove righthand suspension support.
37. Separate righthand outer tie rod from knuckle.
38. Remove air conditioning compressor to oil pan bolts.
39. Remove oil filter and adapter.
40. Remove flywheel inspection cover.
41. Remove starter electrical connectors.
42. Remove mounting bolts and starter.
43. Remove lower mounting bolts and position air conditioning compressor aside.
44. Remove evaporator to accumulator air conditioning line.
45. Remove righthand front and righthand rear engine cradle bolts.
46. Remove oil pan.
47. Remove CKP sensor.
48. Remove front cover lower bolts.
49. Lower vehicle.
50. Remove coolant bypass to coolant pump and manifold.
51. Remove radiator hose to coolant outlet housing.
52. Remove front cover mounting bolts.
53. Carefully remove front cover.
54. Remove and discard front cover crankshaft oil seal using suitable flat bladed tool.
55. Reverse procedure to install, noting the following:
   a. Clean gasket mating surfaces using suitable degreaser.
   b. Lubricate new front cover crankshaft oil seal with clean engine oil.
   c. Install crankshaft oil seal with lip facing engine using crankshaft seal installer and centering tool No. J36468, or equivalent.
   d. Apply RTV sealer part No. 1052080, or equivalent, to both sides of front cover gasket's lower tabs.
   e. Fill cooling system, power steering reservoir and crankcase.
   f. Start engine and inspect for leaks.

FRONT COVER SEAL
REPLACE

1. Raise and support vehicle.

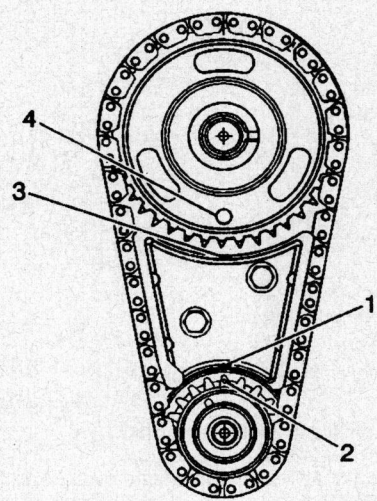

1. DAMPER LOWER TIMING MARK
2. CRANKSHAFT TIMING MARK
3. DAMPER UPPER TIMING
4. CAMSHAFT GEAR

Fig. 4   Timing mark alignment

2. Remove righthand front tire and wheel.
3. Remove righthand front splash shield.
4. Remove crankshaft balancer using torsional dampener remover tool No. J24420-C, or equivalent.
5. Remove crankshaft key.
6. Pry out seal using suitable tool, being careful not to damage crankshaft or front cover.
7. Reverse procedure to install, noting the following:
   a. Install new key if old one is damaged or worn.
   b. Lubricate new seal with clean engine oil and insert in front cover with lip facing engine.
   c. Drive seal into place using front cover alignment and oil seal installer tool No. J35468, or equivalent.

TIMING CHAIN
REPLACE

Removal

1. Remove engine front cover as outlined under "Front Cover, Replace."
2. Turn engine in normal direction of rotation until piston No. 1 reaches TDC. This is cylinder No. 4 firing position.
3. Align camshaft gear timing mark with mark on top of chain damper and crankshaft gear timing mark with damper's lower mark, **Fig. 4.**
4. Remove camshaft gear mounting bolt.
5. Remove camshaft gear and timing chain.
6. Remove crankshaft gear using puller tool No. J5825-A, or equivalent. If gear is stubborn, gently tap lower edge with suitable plastic mallet to dislodge it.

Installation

1. Apply prelube part No. 12345501, or

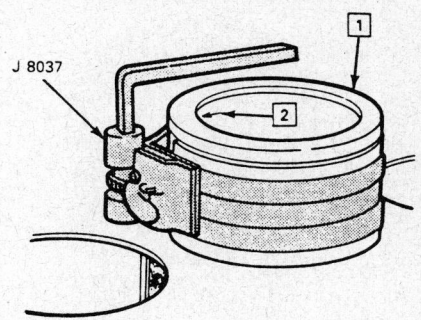

1 PISTON
2 ARROW TOWARDS FRONT OF ENGINE

GC1069100455000X

Fig. 5   Piston marking

equivalent, to crankshaft gear thrust surface.
2. Install crankshaft gear using installer tool No. J38612, or equivalent.
3. Install timing chain damper.
4. Ensure timing gear and damper marks are properly aligned.
5. Hold camshaft gear with chain hanging down.
6. Install chain to crankshaft gear.
7. Align camshaft dowel with camshaft gear dowel hole.
8. Draw camshaft gear onto camshaft by tightening mounting bolt.
9. Install front cover.
10. Fill cooling system, power steering reservoir and crankcase.
11. Start engine and inspect for leaks.

CAMSHAFT

REPLACE

1. Remove engine as outlined under "Engine, Replace."
2. Remove valve lifters.
3. Remove front cover.
4. Remove timing chain and gears.
5. Remove camshaft.
6. Reverse procedure to install, noting the following:
   a. If installing new camshaft, also install new valve lifters. **Do not install old lifters with new camshaft.**
   b. Coat camshaft lobes with engine oil supplement part No. 12345501, or equivalent.
   c. Lubricate camshaft journals with engine oil.

PISTON & ROD ASSEMBLY

When installing piston and rod assemblies into cylinder block, ensure arrow on top of piston faces toward front of engine, **Fig. 5.** Ensure flat area on bottom of piston aligns with the small dimple above the connecting rod crankshaft bearing bore.

MAIN & ROD BEARINGS

Engine bearings are of the precision insert type. They are available for service usage in standard and various undersizes.

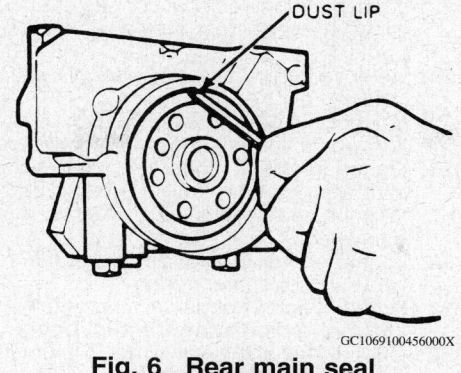

GC1069100456000X

Fig. 6   Rear main seal replacement

To determine proper replacement insert size, bearing clearance must be measured as follows:
1. Measure crankshaft journal diameter in several places, approximately 90° apart and average the measurements.
2. Measure taper and runout, which should be .0002 inch maximum.
3. Install bearing inserts, then tighten rod and main bearing cap bolts.
4. Measure connecting rod I.D. same direction as length of rod.
5. Select suitable set of inserts to provide specified clearance limits. **Do not mix inserts of different nominal size in same bearing bore.** If clearance limits cannot be met, crankshaft journal must be conditioned and undersize bearing inserts installed.

CRANKSHAFT REAR OIL SEAL

REPLACE

Removal

1. Support engine using engine support fixture tool No. J28467-360 and fixture adapters tool No. J28467-90, or equivalents.
2. Remove transaxle as outlined in **MOTOR's "Domestic Transmission, In-Vehicle Service" manual or "Transmission Service DVD."**
3. Remove flexplate.
4. Remove seal by inserting tool through dust lip at angle and prying seal out by moving tool handle toward end of crankshaft pilot, repeating around circumference of seal, **Fig. 6. Do not damage crankshaft O.D. surface or chamfer.**

Installation

1. Inspect I.D. of bore for nicks or burrs.
2. Inspect crankshaft for burrs or nicks on surface which contacts seal.
3. Apply clean engine oil to new seal I.D. and O.D.
4. Slide seal over mandrel until seal rear bottoms squarely against rear main bearing seal installer tool No. J34686, or equivalent, collar, **Fig. 7.**

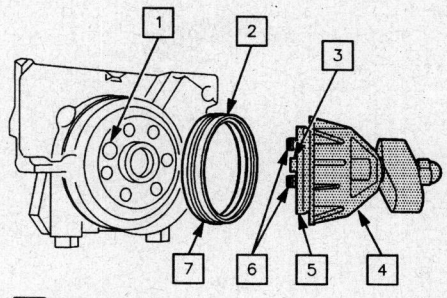

1 ALIGNMENT HOLE
2 DUST LIP
3 DOWEL PIN
4 COLLAR
5 MANDRIL
6 ATTACHING SCREWS
7 SEAL

GC1069701063000X

Fig. 7   Rear main seal installation

5. Align tool and crankshaft dowel pins by hand.
6. **Torque** mounting screws to 45 inch lbs, **Fig. 7.**
7. Push seal into bore by turning tool T handle until collar is tight against case.
8. Loosen tool T hand until it stops and remove mounting screws.
9. Ensure seal is seated squarely in bore.
10. Install flexplate and transaxle.

OIL PAN

REPLACE

1. Recover air conditioning refrigerant as outlined in "Air Conditioning" chapter.
2. Drain coolant into suitable container.
3. Support engine with suitable wooden block and suitable floor jack positioned below oil pan.
4. Remove cruise control module.
5. Remove engine mount to bracket support bolts.
6. Remove engine mount to body bolts.
7. Remove engine mount.
8. Turn belt tensioner in clockwise direction using suitable ⅜ inch breaker bar.
9. Remove serpentine belt.
10. Install engine support tool No. J28467-360, or equivalent.
11. Raise and support vehicle.
12. Drain engine oil into suitable container.
13. Remove righthand front tire and wheel.
14. Remove righthand front splash shield.
15. Remove righthand front wheel speed sensor harness from righthand front suspension support.
16. Separate righthand front ball joint from control arm.
17. Separate righthand outer tie rod end from knuckle.
18. Remove air conditioning compressor and position aside with hoses attached.
19. Remove evaporator to accumulator line.
20. Remove flexplate inspection cover.
21. Remove righthand front and rear engine cradle bolts.

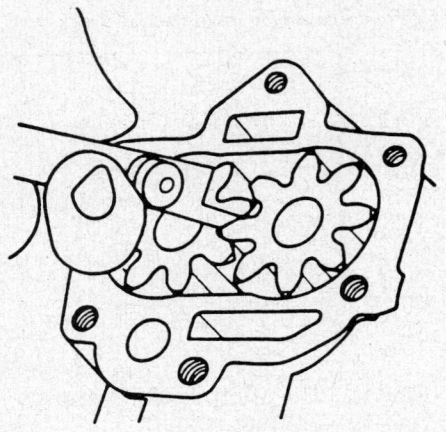

Fig. 8 Oil pump gear lash measurement

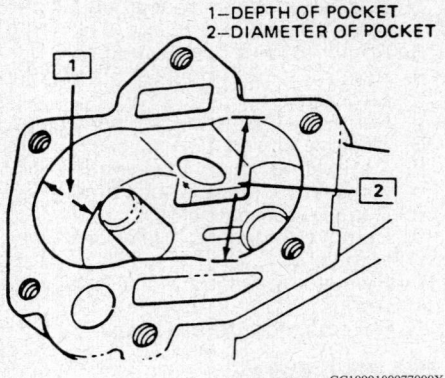

1—DEPTH OF POCKET
2—DIAMETER OF POCKET

Fig. 9 Oil pump gear pocket measurement

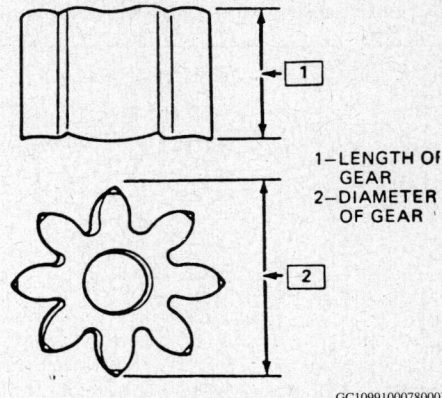

1—LENGTH OF GEAR
2—DIAMETER OF GEAR

Fig. 10 Oil pump gear measurement

22. Remove harmonic balancer using puller tool No. J24420-C, or equivalent.
23. Remove starter motor.
24. Remove mounting bolts and oil pan.
25. Reverse procedure to install, noting the following:
    a. Clean oil pan flanges and rail, front cover, rear main cap and bolt holes.
    b. Install new gasket.
    c. If installing rear main cap, install sealer part No. 1052080, or equivalent, on cap's outer gasket grooves' tabs.

OIL PUMP

REPLACE

1. Remove oil pan as outlined under "Oil Pan, Replace."
2. Remove mounting bolt, oil pump and drive shaft extension.
3. Reverse procedure to install.

OIL PUMP SERVICE

Disassemble

1. Drain pump oil into suitable container.
2. Remove pump driveshaft.
3. **Do not remove pickup tube from cover unless it is broken or loose.**
4. Remove pump cover and pump gears.
5. Remove pressure regulator valve and spring. If valve is stuck, soak pump housing in carburetor cleaning solvent. **Pressure regulator valve spring may be under pressure. Remove retaining pin carefully.**
6. Clean sludge, oil and varnish from components. Varnish may be removed by soaking in carburetor cleaning solvent.

Inspection

1. Inspect pump housing and cover for casting imperfections, cracks or damaged threads. **Do not attempt to repair pump housing.** Replace spring.
2. Inspect idler gear shaft. If loose in housing, replace pump.
3. Inspect pressure regulator valve for scoring or sticking. Burrs may be removed with fine oil stone.
4. Inspect pressure regulator valve spring for loss of tension or bending.
5. Inspect suction pipe and screen for looseness if permanently pressed into pump body. If pipe is loose or has been removed, pump body cover must be replaced. Inspect for broken wire mesh or screen.
6. Inspect gears for chipping, galling or wear.
7. Measure gear lash in several positions, **Fig. 8.** Lash should be .0037–.0077 inch.
8. Measure pump housing gear pocket depth, **Fig. 9.** Depth should be 1.202–1.204 inches.
9. Measure pump housing gear pocket diameter, **Fig. 9.** Pump housing diameter should be 1.503–1.505 inches.
10. Measure pump gear diameters, **Fig. 10.** Diameter should be 1.498–1.500 inches.
11. Measure pump gear side clearance, **Fig. 11.** Clearance should be .001–.003 inch.
12. Measure oil pump end clearance, **Fig. 12.** Clearance should be .002–.005 inch.

Assemble

1. Lubricate internal components with clean engine oil.
2. Install pump gears.
3. Install cover and gasket.
4. Install pressure spring retaining pin, ensuring it is properly secured.
5. If installing new pickup screen and tube, apply sealer part No. 1050026, or equivalent, to tube. Drive new tube into position using plastic hammer and tube installer tool No. J21882, or equivalent.

BELT TENSION DATA

Belt tension is maintained automatically by a spring tensioned idler pulley. Serpentine belt adjustment is not required.

If belt slippage is indicated and belt tensioner indicator is within normal operating range, measure belt tension as follows:

1. Bring engine to operating temperature and turn ignition switch to Off position.
2. Measure belt tension halfway between alternator and power steering pump using belt tension gauge tool No. J23600-B, or equivalent.
3. Run engine for 15 seconds with accessories turned Off.
4. Apply clockwise force to tensioner pulley arm using ⅜ inch breaker bar.
5. Release force and immediately measure belt tension without disturbing tensioner position.
6. Apply counterclockwise force to tensioner pulley arm using suitable breaker bar and raise pulley arm to release tension.
7. Slowly lower pulley to belt and measure tension without disturbing tensioner position.
8. Average out three belt tension measurements, which should be 30–50 lbs.
9. If belt tension is not as specified, replace belt tensioner.

SERPENTINE DRIVE BELT

1. Support engine with suitable wooden block and suitable floor jack positioned below oil pan.
2. Remove cruise control module.
3. Remove engine mount to bracket support bolts.
4. Remove engine mount to body bolts.
5. Remove engine mount.
6. Turn belt tensioner in clockwise direction using suitable ⅜ inch breaker bar.
7. Remove serpentine belt.
8. Reverse procedure to install. Route belt around power steering pump pulley last of all.

COOLING SYSTEM BLEED

1. Close radiator petcock.
2. If engine block drain plugs were removed, coat threads with pipe sealer part No. 12346004, or equivalent.
3. Open coolant air bleed valve located on top of thermostat bypass heater

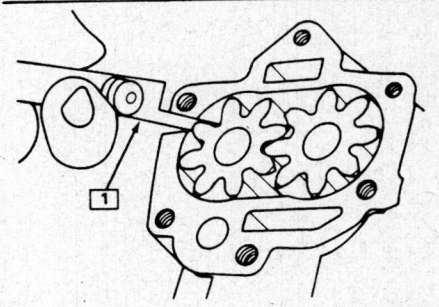

1 CHECK CLEARANCE BETWEEN GEAR TEETH AND SIDE WALL

GC1099100079000X

Fig. 11 Gear side clearance measurement

pipe. **Close this valve as soon as continuous coolant stream flows from it.**
4. Fill surge tank to base of filler neck.
5. Start engine while pressure cap is still off.
6. Operate engine until upper radiator hose starts to feel hot.
7. Adjust surge tank coolant level to Full Cold line.
8. **On models equipped with intermittent low coolant lamp,** this lamp may occasionally light during some extreme driving conditions. This might be eliminated by removing surge tank cap and adding coolant to level just at or above Full Cold line when system is cold.
9. **On all models,** install surge tank cap hand tight.

THERMOSTAT
REPLACE

1. Drain coolant into suitable container.
2. Remove complete engine air cleaner.
3. Remove surge tank line from coolant outlet.
4. Remove mounting bolts and coolant outlet.
5. Remove thermostat.
6. Reverse procedure to install.

WATER PUMP
REPLACE

1. Drain coolant into suitable container.
2. Support engine with suitable wooden block and suitable floor jack positioned below oil pan.
3. Remove cruise control module.
4. Remove engine mount to bracket support bolts.
5. Remove engine mount to body bolts.
6. Remove engine mount.
7. Turn belt tensioner in clockwise direction using suitable ⅜ inch breaker bar.
8. Remove serpentine belt.
9. Remove mounting bolts and water pump pulley.
10. Remove mounting bolts and water pump.
11. Reverse procedure to install.

RADIATOR
REPLACE

Refer to "3.1L Engine" section for radiator replacement procedure.

FUEL PUMP
REPLACE

The fuel pump is a component of the fuel sender and must be replaced as a complete unit.
1. Relieve fuel system pressure as outlined under "Precautions."
2. Drain tank into suitable container.
3. Disconnect electrical connectors.
4. Remove ground wire mounting screw from underbody.
5. Disconnect hoses from tank meter, filler and vent pipes.
6. Support fuel tank and disconnect fuel tank retaining straps.
7. Remove fuel tank.
8. Modular fuel sender might spring up from its original position. Have suitable shop towel ready to absorb spills. Tip assembly slightly to avoid float damage.
9. Remove fuel tank sending unit and pump by holding it down, then removing lockring using lockring tool No. J39765, or equivalent.
10. Reverse procedure to install, noting the following:
    a. Install new O-ring on sender tank flange.
    b. Align tab on front of fuel sender with slot on front of retainer lockring.
    c. Slowly apply pressure to top of spring loaded sender until sender aligns flush with tank retainer.
    d. Insert lockring into proper slots.

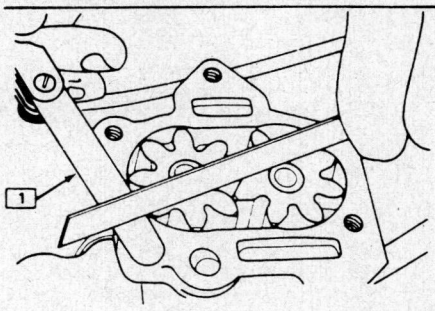

1 CHECK CLEARANCE BETWEEN STRAIGHT EDGE & GASKET

GC1099100080000X

Fig. 12 Oil pump end clearance measurement

  e. Turn ignition switch to On position for two seconds.
  f. Turn ignition switch to Off position for 10 seconds.
  g. Turn ignition On.
  h. Inspect for fuel leaks.

FUEL FILTER
REPLACE

The fuel filter is located below the rear of the vehicle, rearward of the fuel tank.
1. Relieve fuel system pressure as outlined under "Precautions."
2. Raise and support vehicle.
3. Remove fuel filter fitting.
4. Grasp filter and one nylon fuel connection line fitting, then twist quick connect fitting ¼ turn in each direction to loosen dirt in fitting.
5. Clean dirt from quick connect fitting.
6. Depress quick connect fitting plastic tabs of male end connector and pull apart.
7. Remove fuel filter.
8. Reverse procedure to install, noting the following:
    a. Apply few drops of clean engine oil to male pipe ends before connection to reduce risk of leakage and fire.
    b. Turn ignition switch to On position for two seconds.
    c. Turn ignition switch to Off position for 10 seconds.
    d. Turn ignition On.
    e. Inspect for fuel leaks.

TIGHTENING SPECIFICATIONS

Year	Component	Torque Ft. Lbs.
2004–05	Accelerator Cable Bracket	89①
	Alternator Bracket & Front Engine Lift Hook	37
	CKP Sensor To Front Cover	89①
	CKP Sensor To Block	96①
	CKP Sensor Wiring Bracket	37
	CMP Sensor	89①
	Camshaft Sprocket	103
	Camshaft Thrust Plate	89①
	Connecting Rod Bearing Cap	⑤
	Coolant Drain Plug	14
	Coolant Outlet	19
	Crankshaft Balancer	76
	Crankshaft Oil Deflector	18
	Cylinder Head	②
	ECT Sensor	17
	EGR Valve To Valve Pipe	18
	EGR Valve Adapter Pipe To Exhaust Manifold	18
	Engine Mount Bracket	43
	Engine Mount, Lower	32
	Engine Mount, Upper	35
	Engine Mount Strut	35
	Engine Mount Strut & Lift Bracket, Lefthand Rear	52
	Engine Mount Strut Bracket, Righthand	37
	Engine Mount Strut Bracket, Upper Radiator Support	21
	Exhaust Manifold Heat Shield	89①
	Exhaust Manifold, Nut	12
	Exhaust Manifold, Stud	13
	Exhaust Crossover	18
	Flexplate	52
	Front Cover, Large Bolt	41
	Front Cover, Medium Bolt	35
	Front Cover, Small Bolt	15
	Fuel Feed Pipe To Injector Rail	13
	Fuel Injector Rail	89①
	Fuel Pipe Bracket	37
	Fuel Pipe Clip	72①
	Fuel Return Pipe To Fuel Injector Rail	13
	HO2S	31
	Heater Inlet Pipe	18
	Ignition Coil Bracket	18
	Intake Manifold, Lower	⑦
	Intake Manifold, Upper	18
	Main Bearing Cap Bolts	③
	Oil Cooler Connector	37
	Oil Cooler Hose Fitting	14
	Oil Cooler Pipe Bracket	89①
	Oil Filter Fitting	29
	Oil Filter	10
	Oil Gallery Plugs, ¼ Inch	14
	Oil Gallery Plugs, ⅜ Inch	24

TIGHTENING SPECIFICATIONS—Continued

Year	Component	Torque Ft. Lbs.
2004–05	Oil Dipstick	18
	Oil Level Sensor	89①
	Oil Pan	⑥
	Oil Pan Drain Plug	18
	Oil Pressure Indicator Switch	10
	Oil Pump To Block	30
	Oil Pump Cover	89①
	Oil Pump Drive Clamp	27
	Rocker Arm	④
	Rocker Arm Cover	89①
	Serpentine Drive Belt Shield	89①
	Serpentine Drive Belt Tensioner	37
	Spark Plugs	20
	Thermostat Bypass Pipe To Cylinder Head	18
	Thermostat Bypass Pipe To Front Cover	108①
	Thermostat Bypass Pipe To Throttle Body	18
	Thermostat Housing	19
	Timing Chain Damper	15
	Valve Lifter Guide	89①
	Water Pump To Front Cover	89①
	Water Pump Pulley	18

① — Inch lbs.

② — Refer to "Cylinder Head, Replace" for tightening specifications and sequence.

③ — **Torque** to 37 ft. lbs., then tighten an additional 77°.

④ — **Torque** to 14 ft. lbs., then tighten an additional 30°.

⑤ — **Torque** to 15 ft. lbs., then tighten an additional 75°.

⑥ — **Torque** mounting bolts to 18 ft. lbs. **Torque** side bolts to 37 ft. lbs.

⑦ — Refer to "Intake Manifold, Replace" for tightening specifications and sequence.

Rear Axle & Suspension

INDEX

	Page No.		Page No.		Page No.
Coil Spring, Replace	1-31	Knuckle, Replace	1-31	Strut Service	1-30
Control Arm, Replace	1-31	Installation	1-31	Assemble	1-30
Lower	1-31	Removal	1-31	Disassemble	1-30
Upper	1-31	Lateral Link, Replace	1-31	Support Assembly, Replace	1-30
Description	1-30	Rear Crossmember, Replace	1-31	Tightening Specifications	1-32
Hub & Bearing, Replace	1-30	Shock Absorber, Replace	1-31	Toe Link, Replace	1-31
		Stabilizer Shaft, Replace	1-31	Trailing Arm, Replace	1-31
		Strut, Replace	1-30		

DESCRIPTION

The rear suspension uses coil springs over struts and lightweight aluminum knuckles, **Fig. 1.** Each wheel is mounted to a tri-link independent suspension system. The three links include the inverted U-channel trailing arms and front and rear stamped lateral links.

The knuckles are machined aluminum castings. **Do not use hammers or pry bars to loosen any components.**

HUB & BEARING

REPLACE

1. Raise and support vehicle.
2. Remove wheel and tire assembly.
3. **On models equipped with rear drum brakes,** proceed as follows:
   a. Remove brake drum. **Do not hammer on drum.**
   b. Disconnect ABS wheel sensor electrical connector.
   c. Remove mounting bolts, then the hub and bearing assembly. **Partially remove hub and bearing assembly prior to removing upper rear hub mounting bolt.**
4. **On models equipped with rear disc brakes,** proceed as follows:
   a. Remove brake rotor as outlined in "Disc Brakes" chapter.
   b. Disconnect parking brake cable from parking brake lever.
   c. Disconnect ABS wheel sensor electrical connector.
   d. Remove mounting bolts and hub assembly from knuckle.
   e. Remove rear Torx head bolts, then the hub assembly from backing plate.
5. **On all models,** reverse procedure to install.

SUPPORT ASSEMBLY

REPLACE

1. Raise and support vehicle.
2. Remove rear wheels and tires.
3. Remove exhaust system.
4. Remove lower control arms as outlined under "Control Arms, Replace."
5. Remove upper control arm to support assembly mounting bolts and nuts.

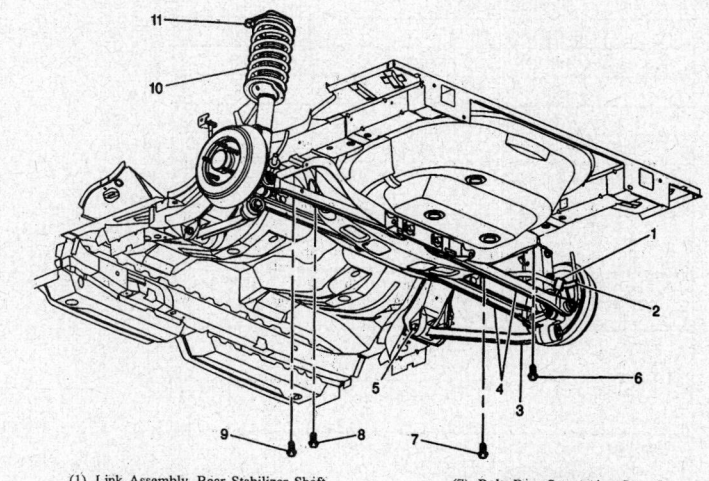

(1) Link Assembly, Rear Stabilizer Shaft
(2) Stabilizer Shaft, Rear
(3) Arm, Rear Suspension Trailing
(4) Link, Lateral
(5) Bolt, Rear Suspension Support
(6) Bolt, Rear Suspension Support
(7) Bolt, Rear Suspension Support
(8) Bolt, Rear Suspension Support
(9) Bolt, Rear Suspension Support
(10) Spring, Coil
(11) Mount, Upper Strut

GC2039700141000X

Fig. 1   Rear suspension

6. Remove toe links as outlined under "Toe Links, Replace."
7. Remove stabilizer shaft to knuckle mounting bolts.
8. Remove vehicle wiring harness from support assembly retaining clips.
9. Place suitable jack stand under support assembly.
10. Remove mounting bolts and support.
11. Reverse procedure to install.

STRUT

REPLACE

Do not hammer or pry on the machined aluminum knuckle casting or any of the components attached to it.
1. Raise and support vehicle.
2. Remove tire and wheel assembly.
3. Scribe knuckle to strut position for installation alignment.
4. Open luggage compartment and remove strut mount nut.
5. Remove mounting bolts from wheelwell.
6. Remove mounting bolts and strut knuckle.
7. Reverse procedure to install.

STRUT SERVICE

Disassemble

1. Position strut compressor tool No. J34013-B in holding fixture J3289-20 with adapter tool No. J34013-88, or equivalents.
2. Compress strut to approximately half of its height. **Do not bottom spring or damper rod.**
3. Remove nut from strut dampener shaft and position alignment rod tool No. J34013-27, or equivalent, on dampener shaft. Position dampener shaft down through bearing cap while compressing coil spring using guide rod tool.
4. Remove strut components.

Assemble

1. Install bearing cap.
2. Mount strut to strut compressor tool using bottom locking pin only.
3. Extend dampener shaft and install dampener rod clamp tool No. J34013-20, or equivalent.

4. Install spring over dampener.
5. Swing strut assembly up and install upper locking pin.
6. Install upper insulator, dust shield, bumper and upper spring seat. Flat on upper spring seat should face in same direction as centerline of strut knuckle.
7. Compress strut using guide rod tool until dampener shaft threads are visible. Remove guide rod tool and install mounting nut.
8. While holding dampener shaft in position using suitable wrench, tighten mounting nut.
9. Remove dampener rod clamp tool.

SHOCK ABSORBER
REPLACE

1. Raise and support vehicle.
2. Remove tire and wheel assembly.
3. Place suitable jack stand under knuckle assembly and raise jack to relieve spring tension.
4. Remove lower shock absorber to knuckle mounting bolt.
5. Remove upper mounting bolt and shock absorber.
6. Reverse procedure to install.

COIL SPRING
REPLACE

Refer to "Strut Service" for coil spring replacement procedures.

CONTROL ARM
REPLACE
Lower

1. Raise and support vehicle.
2. Remove wheel and tire assembly.
3. Remove coil spring as outlined under "Coil Spring, Replace."
4. Remove mounting bolt and nut, then the lower control arm.
5. Reverse procedure to install.

Upper

1. Raise and support vehicle.
2. Remove wheel and tire assembly.
3. Disconnect ABS harness connector and position aside. Record harness position for installation alignment.
4. Remove upper control arm to support assembly mounting bolt.

5. Remove mounting bolt and nut, then the upper control arm.
6. Reverse procedure to install.

KNUCKLE
REPLACE
Removal

1. Raise and support vehicle, then remove tire and wheel assembly.
2. Scribe strut to knuckle position for installation reference.
3. Remove rear lateral link nut, bolt, washer and drum or rotor.
4. Remove ABS electrical connector and rear wheel hub.
5. Remove trailing arm from knuckle.
6. Remove strut nuts and bolts.
7. Remove knuckle.

Installation

1. Install knuckle onto vehicle.
2. Install strut to knuckle nuts and bolts. Hand tighten bolts.
3. Install stabilizer shaft link.
4. Install trailing arm to knuckle bolt, washer and bushing.
5. Install hub assembly.
6. **On models equipped with rear disc brakes,** connect parking brake cable to parking brake lever.
7. **On all models,** install rotor or drum.
8. Install lateral links to knuckle nut, bolt and washer.
9. Connect wheel speed sensor harness.
10. Tighten strut to knuckle bolts.
11. Install tire and wheel.
12. Lower vehicle.
13. Inspect rear wheel alignment.

REAR CROSSMEMBER
REPLACE

1. Raise and support vehicle, then remove tire and wheel assemblies.
2. Remove tailpipe.
3. Remove brake lines and parking brake cables from crossmember.
4. Remove link bolts.
5. Remove mounting nuts and insulator brackets.
6. Remove stabilizer shaft.
7. Disconnect rear wheel speed sensor electrical connectors and position harness aside.

8. If removing front lateral line and trailing arm, remove ABS wire harness.
9. Remove knuckle bolt, nut and washer. Push bolt forward enough for removal clearance.
10. Remove crossmember nut, then the rear lateral link and trailing arm.
11. Remove bolt from EVAP canister.
12. Support crossmember using suitable jack stands.
13. Remove mounting bolts and rear crossmember.
14. Reverse procedure to install.

TRAILING ARM
REPLACE

1. Raise and support vehicle.
2. Remove trailing arm knuckle bolt, washer and bushing.
3. Remove body bolt and trailing arm.
4. Reverse procedure to install.

STABILIZER SHAFT
REPLACE

1. Raise and support vehicle, then remove tire and wheel assemblies.
2. Remove link bolts.
3. Remove mounting nuts and insulator brackets.
4. Remove stabilizer shaft.
5. Reverse procedure to install.

LATERAL LINK
REPLACE

1. Raise and support vehicle, then remove tire and wheel assembly.
2. If removing front lateral line and trailing arm, remove ABS wire harness.
3. Remove knuckle bolt, nut and washer. Push bolt forward enough for removal clearance.
4. Remove crossmember nut and rear lateral link and trailing arm.
5. Reverse procedure to install.

TOE LINK
REPLACE

1. Raise and support vehicle.
2. Remove tire and wheel assembly.
3. Remove toe link to steering knuckle mounting bolt.
4. Remove mounting bolt and nut, then the toe link.
5. Reverse procedure to install.

TIGHTENING SPECIFICATIONS

Year	Component	Torque Ft. Lbs.
2004–05	Crossmember	89
	Disc Brake Caliper To Bracket	81
	Disc Brake Caliper To Knuckle	85
	Lateral Link To Crossmember	89
	Lateral Link To Knuckle	89
	Stabilizer Shaft Bracket	39
	Stabilizer Shaft Link	51
	Strut Nut	89
	Strut To Body	18
	Strut To Knuckle	89
	Trailing Arm To Body	①
	Trailing Arm To Knuckle	51
	Wheel Hub To Knuckle	70
	Wheel Lug Nuts	100

① — **Torque** to 48 ft. lbs, then tighten an additional 120°.

Front Suspension & Steering

INDEX

	Page No.
Ball Joint, Replace	1-32
Ball Joint Inspection	1-32
Coil Spring, Replace	1-33
Control Arm, Replace	1-34
Installation	1-34
Removal	1-34
Description	1-32
Power Steering	21-1
Power Steering Gear, Replace	1-34

	Page No.
Power Steering Pump, Replace	1-35
2.2L Engine	1-35
3.1L & 3.4L Engines	1-35
Precautions	1-32
Air Bag Systems	1-32
Battery Ground Cable	1-32
Stabilizer Bar, Replace	1-34
Steering Columns	20-1
Steering Knuckle, Replace	1-34

	Page No.
Strut, Replace	1-33
Strut Service	1-33
Assemble	1-33
Disassemble	1-33
Tie Rod End, Replace	1-34
Inner	1-34
Outer	1-34
Tightening Specifications	1-36
Wheel Bearing, Replace	1-32

PRECAUTIONS

Air Bag Systems

Refer to "Air Bag System Precautions" in the front of this manual for system disarming and arming procedures.

Battery Ground Cable

Prior to service, disconnect battery ground cable and isolate as required.

DESCRIPTION

The front suspension on these vehicle is of the strut and spring design, **Fig. 1.**The lower control arms pivot from the lower side rails through rubber bushings. The upper end of the strut is isolated by a rubber mount incorporating a bearing for wheel turning. The tie rods connect to the steering arm on the strut, below the spring seat. The lower end of the steering knuckle pivots on a ball stud which is retained to the lower control arm by rivets and is secured to the steering knuckle with a nut and cotter pin. The sealed wheel bearings are integral with the hub and are serviced as an assembly.

WHEEL BEARING
REPLACE

1. Raise and support vehicle.
2. Remove wheel and tire assembly.
3. Insert suitable drift punch into caliper and rotor to prevent turning and remove axle shaft nut and washer, **Fig. 2.**
4. Remove caliper mounting bolts and brake caliper with brake hose attached. Suspend caliper from underbody using suitable wire. **Do not allow caliper to hang from brake hose.**
5. Remove brake rotor, then the hub and bearing assembly mounting bolts, **Fig. 3.**
6. Remove hub and bearing assembly.
7. Reverse procedure to install. Inspect and adjust front wheel alignment.

BALL JOINT INSPECTION

Ball joints must be replaced if any looseness is detected in the joint or the seal is cut.

To inspect the ball joints, raise the front of the vehicle allowing the suspension to hang free. Grasp the tire at the top and bottom and move the top of tire with an in-and-out motion. Look for any horizontal movement of the steering knuckle relative to the front lower control arm.

If the ball stud is disconnected from the steering knuckle and any looseness is detected or if the ball stud can be twisted in its socket using hand pressure, replace the ball joint.

Ball stud tightness in the steering knuckle boss should also be inspected when inspecting the ball joint. This may be done by shaking the wheel and feeling for movement of the stud end or castellated nut at the knuckle boss. Inspecting the torque at the castellated nut is an alternative method of inspecting for wear. A loose nut can indicate a bent stud or an opened-up hole in the knuckle boss. Worn or damaged ball joints and knuckles must be replaced.

BALL JOINT
REPLACE

1. Raise and support vehicle.
2. Remove tire and wheel assembly.
3. Remove lower ball joint cotter pin and nut.
4. **On models equipped with ABS,** position wheel speed sensor wiring aside.
5. **On all models,** separate lower ball

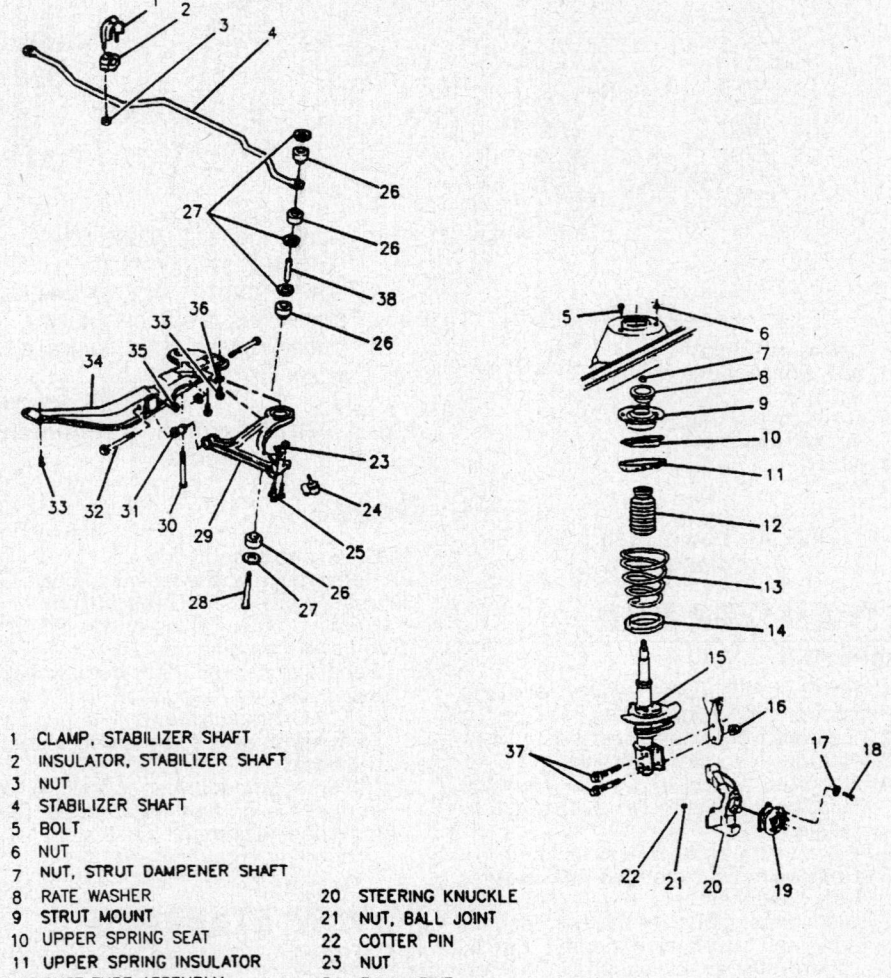

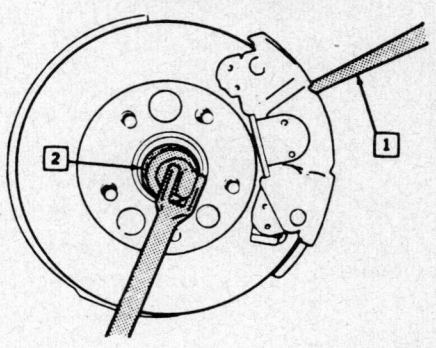

1. DRIFT PUNCH
2. 6 POINT DEEP WELL SOCKET

GC3039100240000X

Fig. 2 Drive axle shaft nut removal

Fig. 1. Do not damage spring coating.

9. Reverse procedure to install. Inspect and adjust wheel alignment.

1	CLAMP, STABILIZER SHAFT
2	INSULATOR, STABILIZER SHAFT
3	NUT
4	STABILIZER SHAFT
5	BOLT
6	NUT
7	NUT, STRUT DAMPENER SHAFT
8	RATE WASHER
9	STRUT MOUNT
10	UPPER SPRING SEAT
11	UPPER SPRING INSULATOR
12	DUST TUBE ASSEMBLY
13	SPRING
14	LOWER SPRING INSULATOR
15	STRUT
16	NUT
17	WASHER
18	BOLT
19	HUB AND BEARING ASSEMBLY

20	STEERING KNUCKLE
21	NUT, BALL JOINT
22	COTTER PIN
23	NUT
24	BALL JOINT
25	BOLT
26	INSULATOR, STABILIZER LINK
27	WASHER, STABILIZER LINK
28	BOLT, STABILIZER LINK
29	CONTROL ARM
30	BOLT
31	BUSHING, CONTROL ARM

32	BOLT
33	BOLT
34	SUSPENSION SUPPORT
35	NUT
36	WASHER
37	BOLT
38	SPACER, STABILIZER LINK

GC2029700271000X

Fig. 1 Exploded view of front suspension

joint from steering knuckle using ball joint separator tool No. J43828, or equivalent, **Fig. 4.**
6. Locate center of rivet body and mark using suitable center punch.
7. Drill pilot holes completely through rivets. **Avoid damaging CV joint boots.**
8. Drill final holes through rivets to ensure proper fitting of new ball joint.
9. Remove stabilizer shaft link mounting nut.
10. Remove ball joint from knuckle and lower control arm.
11. Reverse procedure to install using bolts provided in service package.

COIL SPRING
REPLACE

Refer to "Strut Service" for coil spring replacement.

STRUT
REPLACE

1. Remove strut body mounting nuts and bolt.
2. Raise and support vehicle.
3. Place jack stands under front crossmember and lower vehicle slightly so it rests on stands, not on control arms.
4. Remove wheel and tire. Install modified outer seal protector tool No. J34754, or equivalent.
5. Remove tie rod end cotter pin and nut, then disconnect tie rod from strut using tie rod puller tool No. J24319-01, or equivalent.
6. Remove brake line bracket.
7. Scribe alignment marks on strut flange, **Fig. 5.**
8. Remove mounting bolts and strut,

STRUT SERVICE
Disassemble

1. Position strut compressor tool No. J34013-B in holding fixture J3289-20 with adapter tool No. J34013-88, or equivalents.
2. Compress strut to approximately half of its height. **Do not bottom spring or damper rod.**
3. Remove nut from strut dampener shaft and position alignment rod tool No. J34013-27, or equivalent, on dampener shaft. Position dampener shaft down through bearing cap while compressing coil spring using guide rod tool.
4. Remove strut components, **Fig. 6.**

Assemble

1. Install bearing cap.
2. Mount strut to strut compressor tool using bottom locking pin only.
3. Extend dampener shaft and install dampener rod clamp tool No. J34013-20, or equivalent.
4. Install spring over dampener.
5. Swing strut assembly up and install upper locking pin.
6. Install upper insulator, dust shield, bumper and upper spring seat. Flat on upper spring seat should face in same direction as centerline of strut knuckle, **Fig. 7.**
7. Compress strut using guide rod tool until dampener shaft threads are visible. Remove guide rod tool and install mounting nut.
8. While holding dampener shaft in position using suitable wrench, tighten mounting nut.
9. Remove dampener rod clamp tool.

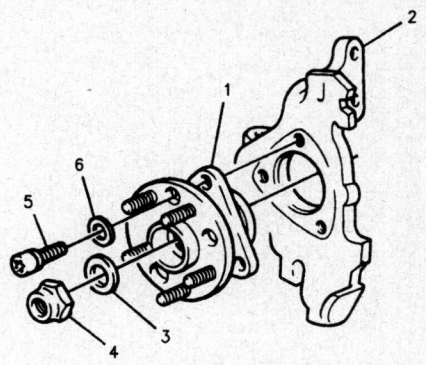

1 HUB AND BEARING ASSEMBLY
2 STEERING KNUCKLE
3 WASHER
4 DRIVE AXLE NUT
5 HUB AND BEARING RETAINING BOLT
6 WASHER

GC3039700369000X

Fig. 3   Front hub & wheel bearing replacement

CONTROL ARM
REPLACE

Removal

1. Raise and support vehicle. Remove wheel and tire assembly.
2. Disconnect stabilizer bar at lower control arm and control arm support.
3. Remove ball joint cotter pin and nut.
4. Separate ball joint from steering knuckle using ball joint separator tool No. J43828, or equivalent.
5. Remove mounting bolts, support and control arm as an assembly, **Fig. 8.**

Installation

1. Install control arm into position and hand tighten rear mounting bolt.
2. Install and hand tighten front mounting bolt.
3. Install stabilizer shaft link.
4. Install lower ball joint to knuckle.
5. Raise vehicle slightly and remove jack stands.
6. Install tire and wheel.
7. Lower vehicle to ground.
8. Tighten control arm front and rear mounting bolts, in order.
9. Inspect and adjust front wheel alignment.

STEERING KNUCKLE
REPLACE

1. Raise and support vehicle.
2. Remove wheel and tire.
3. Remove front drive shaft as outlined in "Front Wheel Drive Axles" chapter.
4. Remove mounting bolts and steering knuckle.
5. Reverse procedure to install.

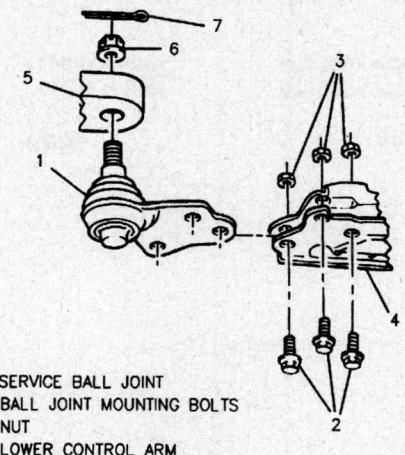

1 SERVICE BALL JOINT
2 BALL JOINT MOUNTING BOLTS
3 NUT
4 LOWER CONTROL ARM
5 STEERING KNUCKLE
6 NUT
7 PIN

GC2029700272000X

Fig. 4   Lower ball joint replacement

STABILIZER BAR
REPLACE

1. Raise and support vehicle, allowing control arms to hang free.
2. Remove front wheels and tires.
3. Remove stabilizer shaft links.
4. Separate tie rod ends from knuckles using separator tool No. J24319-01, or equivalent.
5. Remove transaxle rear mount bolt.
6. Remove power steering line bracket from crossmember.
7. Disconnect stabilizer bar from control arms and suspension support, **Fig. 9.**
8. Loosen suspension support front, then remove rear and center mounting bolts. Lower support enough to allow stabilizer bar removal.
9. Remove stabilizer bar with insulators.
10. Reverse procedure to install. Tighten lefthand rear, righthand rear, lefthand front and righthand front crossmember mounting bolts in order.

TIE ROD END
REPLACE

Inner

1. Raise and support vehicle.
2. Remove tire and wheel assembly.
3. Remove outer tie rod as outlined under "Outer."
4. Remove steering gear as outlined under "Power Steering Gear, Replace."
5. Remove steering gear boot.
6. Slide shock damper toward steering gear and remove inner tie rod from steering gear using two suitable wrenches.
7. Reverse procedure to install. Adjust front end alignment as required, refer to "Wheel Alignment" section.

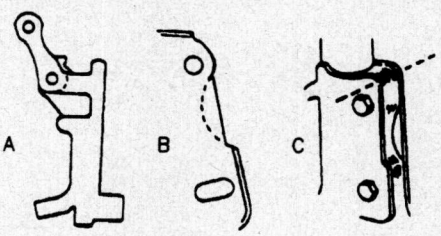

A SCRIBE KNUCKLE ALONG LOWER OUTBOARD STRUT RADIUS
B SCRIBE STRUT FLANGE ON INBOARD SIDE ALONG CURVE OF KNUCKLE
C SCRIBE ACROSS STRUT/KNUCKLE INTERFACE

GC2029700273000X

Fig. 5   Strut & knuckle alignment marks

Outer

1. Raise and support vehicle.
2. Remove tire and wheel assembly.
3. Loosen outer tie rod end jam nut.
4. Remove outer tie rod end to steering knuckle mounting nut.
5. Separate tie rod end from knuckle using tie rod separator tool No. J 24319-B, or equivalent.
6. Remove outer tie rod end from inner tie rod end.
7. Reverse procedure to install. Adjust front end alignment as required, refer to "Wheel Alignment" section.

POWER STEERING GEAR
REPLACE

1. Carefully siphon fluid from power steering reservoir.
2. Raise and support vehicle, then remove front tires and wheels.
3. Remove stabilizer shaft links from control arms.
4. Remove tie rods from knuckles using separator tool No. J24319-01, or equivalent.
5. Remove intermediate shaft lower pinch bolt.
6. Support rear of crossmember using suitable jack stands.
7. Remove stabilizer shaft.
8. Remove steering gear mounting bolts.
9. **On Malibu models,** proceed as follows:
   a. Remove transaxle mount-to-crossmember bolt.
   b. Remove rear crossmember to body bolts to provide pipe and hose removal clearance.
   c. Loosen front crossmember bolts.
10. **On all models,** remove steering gear mounting bolts.
11. Place suitable drain pan below steering gear and disconnect gear power steering fluid hoses.
12. Remove steering gear through lefthand wheel opening.
13. Reverse procedure to install.

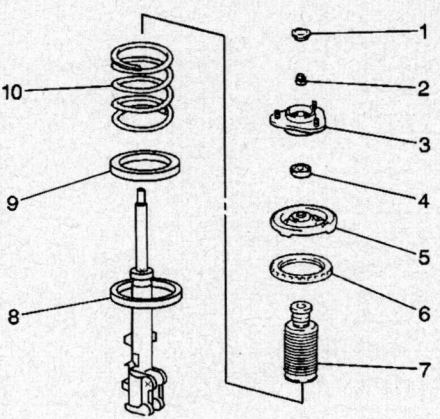

1- DUST CAP
2- STRUT ROD PISTON NUT
3- STRUT MOUNT
4- DUST SEAL
5- SPRING SEAT
6- UPPER INSULATOR
7- SPRING BUMPER
8- STRUT
9- LOWER INSULATOR
10- COIL SPRING

GC2029900274000X

Fig. 6   Exploded view of strut

POWER STEERING PUMP

REPLACE

2.2L Engine

1. Remove air cleaner outlet duct.
2. Remove relay center push in retainer.
3. Disconnect relay battery feed cable from upper air cleaner cover retaining clips.
4. Remove push in and air cleaner.
5. Disconnect Evaporative Emission (EVAP) canister purge valve harness connector and vacuum pipe from EVAP canister purge valve.
6. Disconnect purge pipe from EVAP canister purge valve.
7. Remove EVAP canister purge valve and bracket, then the EVAP canister purge valve from purge bracket.
8. Raise vehicle using suitable lift.

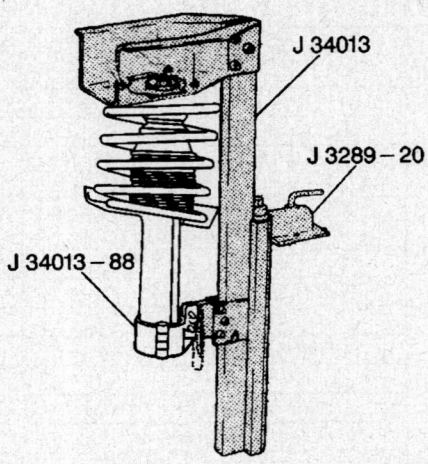

GC2029700275000X

Fig. 7   Strut replacement

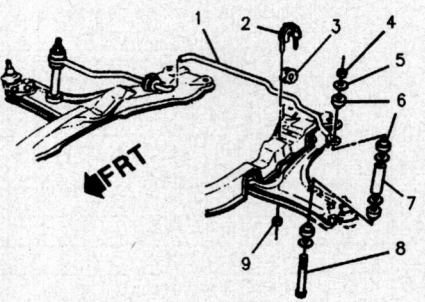

1   SHAFT, STABILIZER
2   CLAMP
3   INSULATOR, STABILIZER SHAFT
4   NUT
5   WASHER
6   INSULATOR, STABILIZER LINK
7   SPACER
8   BOLT
9   NUT

GC2029700277000X

Fig. 9   Stabilizer bar replacement

9. **On models equipped with automatic transaxles,** remove front exhaust pipe as outlined under "Exhaust Manifold, Replace" in "2.2L Engine" section.
10. **On all models,** remove power steering pressure hose from power steering

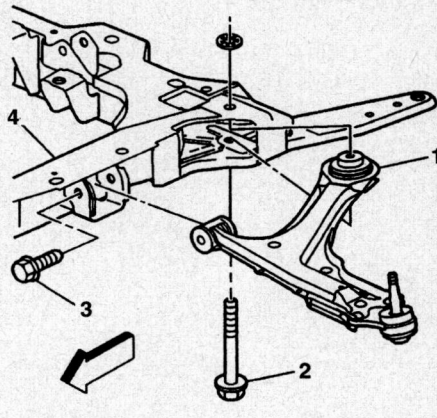

1   ARM
2   REAR MOUNTING BOLT
3   FRONT MOUNTING BOLT
4   CROSSMEMBER

GC2029700276000X

Fig. 8   Lower control arm replacement

gear and pump pipe.
11. Remove power steering hose.
12. Lower vehicle.
13. Remove upper air cleaner assembly.
14. Remove clamp and power steering return hose from power steering pump.
15. Raise vehicle using suitable lift.
16. Remove power steering return hose.
17. Remove mounting bolts and power steering pump.
18. Reverse procedure to install.

3.1L & 3.4L Engines

1. Siphon as much power steering fluid as possible from reservoir.
2. Remove engine mount as outlined under "Engine Mount, Replace" in appropriate "Engine" section.
3. Remove serpentine belt as outlined under "Serpentine Drive Belt" in appropriate "Engine" section.
4. Remove alternator bracket retaining hose nut.
5. Remove power steering pump bolts.
6. Place suitable drain pan in position and disconnect power steering pump lines at pump.
7. Remove pump.
8. Remove transfer pulley.
9. Reverse procedure to install.

TIGHTENING SPECIFICATIONS

Year	Component	Torque Ft. Lbs.
2004–05	Axle Nut	284
	Ball Joint To Knuckle (Alero)	41
	Control Arm To Frame, Front Bushing (Alero)	79
	Control Arm To Frame, Rear Bushing (Alero)	81
	Disc Brake Caliper	85
	Disc Brake Caliper To Bracket	23
	Driveshaft Nut	284
	Hub & Bearing Assembly	70
	Hub Nut	284
	Power Steering Line Fittings	20
	Power Steering Pump (2.2L Engine)	19
	Power Steering Pump (3.1L & 3.4L Engines)	25
	Stabilizer Shaft To Control Arm	13
	Stabilizer Shaft Bushing Clamp To Crossmember Support	49
	Stabilizer Shaft Link to Control Arm	13
	Steering Gear	89
	Steering Gear Mounting Clamp	22
	Steering Column Upper & Lower Pinch Bolt	16
	Steering Knuckle To Strut	133
	Strut To Body	18
	Strut Rod	52
	Tie Rod End To Steering Knuckle	15
	Tie Rod Jam Nut	50
	Transaxle Mount (Alero)	89
	Wheel Lug Nuts	100

Wheel Alignment

INDEX

	Page No.		Page No.		Page No.
Front Wheel Alignment	1-37	Toe	1-37	Thrust Angle	1-37
Camber	1-37	Preliminary Inspection	1-37	Wheel Alignment	
Caster	1-37	Rear Wheel Alignment	1-37	Specifications	1-3

PRELIMINARY INSPECTION

Ensure tires are properly inflated.

Before measuring and setting front wheel alignment, rest front wheels on turn plates.

Before setting rear toe, rest rear wheels on slider plates or turn plates.

Before setting any alignment angle, jounce vehicle three times at each end to establish trim height.

Special adapters are available for using magnetic hub gauge at rear wheels. Depending on type of equipment used, these may not be required. After removing hub cap and bearing cap, hub gauge will snap into place on brake drum. Magnetic mounting toe gauges may also be installed in same manner.

Always perform wheel alignment on level alignment rack. Before doing alignment, proceed as follows:

1. Inspect for worn suspension components.
2. Inspect standing curb height.
3. Remove heavy weights from trunk.
4. Inspect wheel bearings for excessive freeplay.
5. Ensure gas tank is full.
6. Place front seats in full rear position.
7. Inspect rear toe adjustment.
8. Road test vehicle, noting the following:
   a. If vehicle still pulls, switch front tires.
   b. If vehicle pulls in same direction, inspect alignment and rear tracking.
   c. If vehicle pulls in opposite direction, rotate tires and road test.

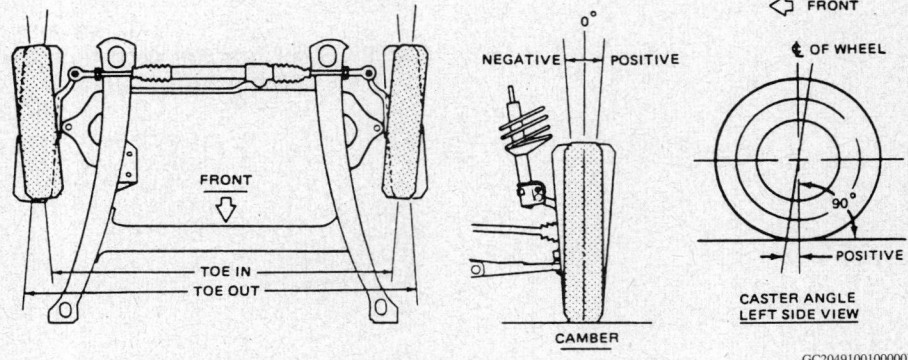

Fig. 1 Caster, camber & toe angles

GC2049100100000X

FRONT WHEEL ALIGNMENT

Caster

Caster angle is not adjustable. If caster angle is not within specifications, inspect suspension support for improper alignment and suspension components for damage.

Camber

Toe setting is the only adjustment normally required. In special circumstances such as damage because of road hazard or collision, the camber angle may be adjusted by modifying the strut, **Fig. 1.**

1. **With strut on vehicle,** disconnect strut from steering knuckle.
2. **With strut off vehicle,** secure strut bottom in suitable vise.
3. **On all models,** enlarge bottom holes in outer flanges using suitable round file, until holes in outer flanges match slots in inner flanges, **Fig. 2.**
4. Install or connect strut to steering knuckle and install bolts hand tight.
5. Grasp top of tire firmly and move tire inboard or outboard until proper camber reading is obtained. Tighten mounting bolts enough to retain camber setting.
6. Remove wheel and tire assembly, then tighten strut to steering knuckle mounting bolts.

Toe

The toe is controlled by tie rod position, **Fig. 1.**

1. Ensure front wheels are in straight-ahead position.
2. Loosen jam nut, **Fig. 3.**
3. Turn adjuster to obtain proper toe setting.
4. **Torque** jam nut to 50 ft. lbs.

REAR WHEEL ALIGNMENT

After front wheel alignment has been inspected or adjusted, rear wheel alignment angles should be inspected if vehicle still does not track properly, or if excessive rear tire wear is present. Rear wheels should be parallel to and the same distance from the vehicle centerline.

Rear wheel alignment is not adjustable. If alignment angles are not within specification, inspect for bent or damaged suspension arms, components or underbody.

THRUST ANGLE

The vehicle is steered by the front wheels. The path the rear wheels follow is the thrust angle, **Fig. 4.** In an ideal setting, the thrust angle would be aligned with the vehicle centerline.

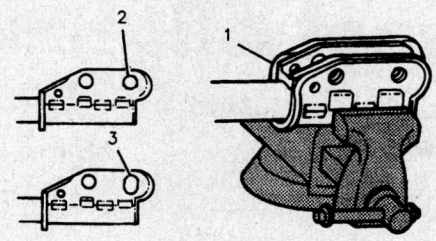

1 STRUT IN VISE
2 BEFORE FILING
3 AFTER FILING

GC2049700155000X

**Fig. 2 Strut bracket modification
for camber adjustment**

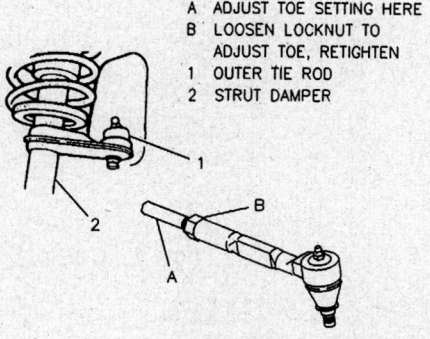

A ADJUST TOE SETTING HERE
B LOOSEN LOCKNUT TO
   ADJUST TOE, RETIGHTEN
1 OUTER TIE ROD
2 STRUT DAMPER

GC2049700145000X

Fig. 3 Toe adjustment

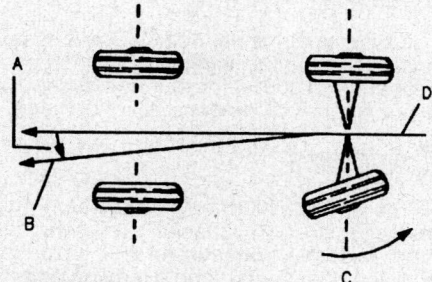

A THRUST ANGLE
B THRUST LINE – OFF CENTER
C REAR TOE–OUT CONDITION
D GEOMETRIC CENTERLINE

GC2049700156000X

Fig. 4 Thrust angle

BONNEVILLE, LESABRE & PARK AVENUE

NOTE: Refer To The Rear Of This Manual For Vehicle Manufacturer's Special Service Tool Suppliers.

INDEX OF SERVICE OPERATIONS

Page No.

AIR BAG SYSTEM
PRECAUTIONS 0-18
BRAKES
  Anti-Lock Brakes (Volume 2).. 6-1
  Disc Brakes.................. 22-1
  Drum Brakes 23-1
  Hydraulic Brake Systems 24-1
  Power Brake Units............ 25-1
COMPUTER RELEARN
PROCEDURE 0-31
ELECTRICAL
  Air Bag System (Volume 2) ... 4-1
  Air Conditioning.............. 16-1
  Alternators 19-1
  Back-Up Lamp Switch,
  Replace 2-6
  Blower Motor, Replace........ 2-7
  Cabin Air Filter, Replace 2-7
  Coil Pack, Replace 2-5
  Cooling Fans 17-1
  Cruise Control (Volume 2) 2-1
  Dash Gauges (Volume 2) 1-1
  Dash Panel Service
  (Volume 2).................. 5-1
  Dimmer Switch, Replace...... 2-6
  Evaporator Core, Replace 2-8
  Fuel Pump Relay Location.... 2-5
  Fuse Panel & Flasher
  Location 2-5
  Headlamp Switch, Replace.... 2-6
  Heater Core, Replace........ 2-8
  Ignition Lock, Replace 2-5
  Ignition Switch, Replace 2-6
  Instrument Cluster, Replace... 2-6
  Multi-Function Switch,
  Replace 2-6
  Neutral Safety Switch,
  Replace 2-6
  Passive Restraint Systems
  (Volume 2).................. 4-1
  Precautions 2-5
  Radio, Replace 2-7
  Relay Center Location 2-5
  Speed Controls (Volume 2) ... 2-1
  Starter Motors 18-1
  Starter, Replace 2-5
  Steering Columns............ 20-1
  Steering Wheel, Replace..... 2-6
  Turn Signal Switch, Replace .. 2-6
  Wiper Motor, Replace........ 2-7
  Wiper Switch, Replace....... 2-7
  Wiper Systems (Volume 2).... 3-1
  Wiper Transmission, Replace . 2-7
ELECTRICAL SYMBOL
IDENTIFICATION 0-63
FRONT DRIVE AXLES 26-1

Page No.

FRONT SUSPENSION &
STEERING
  Ball Joint, Replace............ 2-22
  Ball Joint Inspection 2-22
  Control Arm, Replace 2-23
  Description 2-22
  Hub & Bearing, Replace 2-22
  Power Steering 21-1
  Power Steering Gear,
  Replace 2-23
  Power Steering Pump,
  Replace 2-23
  Precautions 2-22
  Stabilizer Bar, Replace....... 2-23
  Steering Columns............ 20-1
  Strut, Replace 2-22
  Strut Service 2-22
  Tightening Specifications..... 2-26
NON-STANDARD TIRE &
WHEEL SIZE
ADJUSTMENT TO RIDE
HEIGHT SPECIFICATIONS
& TIRE SIZE CHART 0-61
REAR DRIVE AXLE.......... 27-1
REAR SUSPENSION
  Ball Joint, Replace............ 2-20
  Ball Joint Inspection 2-19
  Coil Spring, Replace 2-19
  Control Arm, Replace 2-20
  Description 2-19
  Hub & Bearing, Replace 2-19
  Stabilizer Bar, Replace....... 2-20
  Strut, Replace 2-19
  Tie Rod, Replace 2-20
  Tightening Specifications...... 2-21
SERVICE REMINDER &
WARNING LAMP RESET
PROCEDURES 0-34
SPECIFICATIONS
  Fluid Capacities & Cooling
  System Data................. 2-4
  Front Wheel Alignment
  Specifications................ 2-3
  General Engine
  Specifications................ 2-2
  Lubricant Data.............. 2-4
  Rear Wheel Alignment
  Specifications................ 2-3
  Tune Up Specifications 2-2
  Vehicle Ride Height
  Specifications................ 2-3
TIRE PRESSURE
MONITORING SYSTEM 20-1
VEHICLE
IDENTIFICATION 0-1
VEHICLE LIFT POINTS...... 0-51
VEHICLE MAINTENANCE
SCHEDULES 0-73

Page No.

WHEEL ALIGNMENT
  Front Wheel Alignment........ 2-27
  Precautions.................. 2-27
  Preliminary Inspection 2-27
  Rear Wheel Alignment........ 2-27
  Wheel Alignment
  Specifications 2-3
WIRE COLOR CODE
IDENTIFICATION 0-63
3.8L ENGINE
  Balance Shaft, Replace....... 2-11
  Belt Tension Data............. 2-13
  Camshaft, Replace 2-11
  Camshaft Lobe Lift
  Specifications 2-11
  Compression Pressure 2-9
  Cooling System Bleed 2-14
  Crankshaft Seal, Replace 2-13
  Cylinder Head, Replace....... 2-10
  Engine Rebuilding
  Specifications................ 29-1
  Engine, Replace 2-9
  Engine Mount, Replace....... 2-9
  Exhaust Manifold, Replace.... 2-10
  Front Cover, Replace 2-11
  Fuel Filter, Replace.......... 2-15
  Fuel Pump, Replace......... 2-15
  Intake Manifold, Replace...... 2-9
  Main & Rod Bearings 2-12
  Oil Pan, Replace............. 2-13
  Oil Pump, Replace........... 2-13
  Oil Pump Service 2-13
  Piston & Rod Assembly 2-12
  Pistons, Pins & Rings........ 2-12
  Precautions 2-9
  Radiator, Replace........... 2-15
  Rocker Arms................ 2-11
  Serpentine Drive Belt 2-14
  Supercharger, Replace 2-15
  Thermostat, Replace......... 2-14
  Tightening Specifications...... 2-16
  Timing Chain, Replace........ 2-11
  Valve Adjustment 2-11
  Valve Clearance
  Specifications 2-11
  Valve Guides 2-11
  Water Pump, Replace 2-14
4.6L ENGINE
  Engine Rebuilding
  Specifications................ 29-1
  Engine, Replace 2-17
  Engine Mount, Replace....... 2-17
  Oil Pan, Replace............. 2-18
  Precautions 2-17
  Tightening Specifications...... 2-18

Specifications

GENERAL ENGINE SPECIFICATIONS

Year/Engine	VIN Code①	Fuel System	Bore & Stroke	Compression Ratio	Net H.P. @ RPM②	Maximum Torque Ft. Lbs. @ RPM	Normal Oil Pressure, psi
2004							
3.8L	K	SFI	3.80 × 3.40	9.4:1	205 @ 5200	230 @ 4000	60③
3.8L	1	SFI	3.80 × 3.40	8.5:1	240 @ 5200	280 @ 3200	60③
2005							
3.8L	K	SFI	3.80 × 3.40	9.4:1	205 @ 5200	230 @ 4000	60③
4.6L	I	SFI	3.66 × 3.31	10.0:1	275 @ 5600	300 @ 4000	35④

MFI — Multi-Point Fuel Injection

SFI — Sequential Port Fuel Injection

① — The eighth digit denotes engine code.

② — Ratings are net as installed in vehicle.

③ — At 1850 RPM using SAE 10W-30 motor oil.

④ — At 2000 RPM.

TUNE UP SPECIFICATIONS

Engine/VIN Code①	Spark Plug Gap	Ignition Timing Firing Order, Fig.②	°BTDC	Mark	Curb Idle Speed	Fast Idle Speed	Fuel Pump Pressure	Valve Clearance, Inch
2004								
3.8L/K & 1	.060	⑥	⑦	⑧	③	③	53–59⑤	④
2005								
3.8L/K	.060	⑥	⑦	⑧	③	③	48–54⑤	④
4.6L/I	.050	⑨	⑦	⑧	③	③	41–47⑤	④

BTDC — Before Top Dead Center

① — The eighth digit of the Vehicle Identification Number (VIN) denotes engine code.

② — Before removing wires from distributor cap, determine location of No. 1 wire in cap, as distributor position may have been altered from that illustrated at end of this chart.

③ — Idle speed is controlled by an idle speed control (ISC) motor or an idle air control (IAC) valve.

④ — Equipped w/hydraulic valve lifters. There is no provision for adjustment.

⑤ — With shop towel wrapped around fuel pressure valve to prevent fuel spillage, connect a suitable fuel pressure gauge to fuel pressure valve. Measure fuel pressure w/ignition On, but engine not running.

⑥ — Cylinder numbering lefthand to righthand as viewed in Figs. A & B from front of vehicle, front bank, 1, 3, 5; rear bank, 2, 4, 6. Firing order 1-6-5-4-3-2. Two different types computer controlled coil ignition systems are used. Refer to **Figs. A and B,** for spark plug wire connections at coil unit.

⑦ — Computer controlled. No adjustment.

⑧ — Equipped w/Crankshaft Position Sensor.

⑨ — Cylinder numbering from lefthand to righthand as viewed from front of vehicle, front bank, 2, 4, 6, 8; rear bank, 1, 3, 5, 7. Firing order 1-2-7-3-4-5-6-8.

COMPUTER CONTROLLED COIL IGNITION

GC1139100129000X

Fig. A

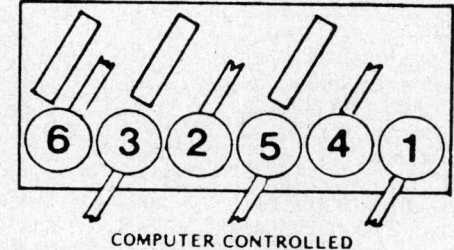

COMPUTER CONTROLLED COIL IGNITION

GC1139100130000X

Fig. B

FRONT WHEEL ALIGNMENT SPECIFICATIONS

Year	Model	Caster Angle, Degrees		Camber Angle, Degrees				Total Toe, Degrees	Ball Joint Wear
		Limits	Desired	Limits		Desired			
				Left	Right	Left	Right		
2004–05	All	+4.5 to +5.5	+5	–.7 to +.3	–.7 to +.3	–.2	–.2	+.2	①

① — Refer to Ball Joint Inspection in Front Suspension & Steering section.

REAR WHEEL ALIGNMENT SPECIFICATIONS

Year	Model	Camber Angle, Degrees		Total Toe, Degrees	Thrust Angle, Degrees	Ball Joint Wear
		Limits	Desired			
2004–05	All	–.8 to +.2	–.3	+.2	–.1 to +.1	①

① — Refer to Ball Joint Inspection in Rear Suspension section.

VEHICLE RIDE HEIGHT SPECIFICATIONS

Model	Year	Body Style	Manu-facturer's Original Tire Size	Measurement Points & Specifications①③					
				Rear			Front		
				Dim.④	Specification		Dim.④	Specification	
					Inches	mm		Inches	mm
Bonneville	2004–05	All	②	D	3.00–3.80	76.00–96.00	Z	1.20–2.00	30.00–50.00
LeSabre	2004–05	All	②	D	3.00–3.80	76.20–96.52	Z	1.20–2.00	30.48–50.80
Park Ave	2004–05	All	②	D	3.00–3.80	76.20–96.52	Z	1.20–2.00	30.48–50.80

A Dim. — Measurement From Front Wheel Center to Inspection Point On Rocker Panel

B Dim. — Measurement From Rear Wheel Center to Inspection Point On Rocker Panel

C Dim. — Ground to Rocker Panel, Front

D Dim. — Lowest Point On Ball Joint Housing Minus Grease Fitting To Centerline Of Rear Bushing

E Dim. — Ground to Front Underbody Points

F Dim. — Ground to Rear Underbody Points

Z Dim. — Pivot bolt center line down to lower corner of lower ball joint

Dim. — Dimension

① — ±.39 in (10 mm) front to rear & side to side.

② — See door sticker or inside of glove box for manufacturers original tire size specifications. If tires on vehicle do not match manufacturers original tire size & measurement is not within limits, it will be required to refer to the Non-Standard Tire & Wheel Size Adjustment To Ride Height Specification & Tire Size Adjustment Charts.

③ — Measurement is with fuel, radiator coolant and engine oil full, spare tire, jack, hand tools and mats in designated positions and tires properly inflated.

④ — Refer to **Fig. A.**

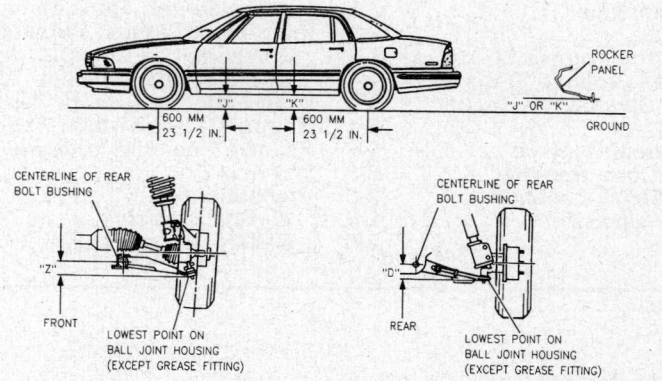

GC2049300122000X

Fig. A Ride height measurement locations

FLUID CAPACITIES & COOLING SYSTEM DATA

Year	Model	Engine	Coolant Capacity, Qts.	Coolant Type	Radiator Cap Relief Pressure, Lbs.	Thermo. Opening Temp.	Fuel Tank, Gals.	Engine Oil Refill, Qts.	Auto. Transaxle, Qts.①
2004–05	All	3.8L	10	Dex-Cool	③	188	18.5	4.5②	④

① — Approximate. Make final inspection w/dipstick.
② — With filter.
③ — Relief pressure specification is stamped on cap.
④ — Drain and refill 7.4 qts.; overhaul 10 qts.; dry 13.4 qts.

LUBRICANT DATA

Year	Model	Lubricant Type		
		Automatic Transaxle	Power Steering	Brake System
2004–05	All	Dexron III	Power Steering Fluid①	DOT 3

① — GM part No. 1052884, or equivalent.

Electrical

NOTE: On Air Bag Equipped Models, Refer To "Air Bag System Precautions" Located In The Front Of This Manual For System Disarming & Arming Procedures.

NOTE: Refer To "Computer Relearn Procedures" Located In The Front Of This Manual When Battery Power To The Computer Has Been Interrupted.

INDEX

	Page No.
Air Bag System (Volume 2)	4-1
Air Conditioning	16-1
Alternators	19-1
Back-Up Lamp Switch, Replace	2-6
Bonneville & LeSabre	2-6
Park Avenue	2-6
Blower Motor, Replace	2-7
Cabin Air Filter, Replace	2-7
Bonneville & LeSabre	2-7
Park Avenue	2-7
Coil Pack, Replace	2-5
Cooling Fans	17-1
Cruise Control (Volume 2)	2-1
Dash Gauges (Volume 2)	1-1
Dash Panel Service (Volume 2)	5-1
Dimmer Switch, Replace	2-6
Evaporator Core, Replace	2-8
Fuel Pump Relay Location	2-5
Bonneville & LeSabre	2-5
Park Avenue	2-5

	Page No.
Fuse Panel & Flasher Location	2-5
Bonneville & LeSabre	2-5
Park Avenue	2-5
Headlamp Switch, Replace	2-6
Heater Core, Replace	2-8
Ignition Lock, Replace	2-5
Bonneville	2-5
LeSabre & Park Avenue	2-5
Installation	2-5
Removal	2-5
Ignition Switch, Replace	2-6
Instrument Cluster, Replace	2-6
Bonneville	2-6
LeSabre & Park Avenue	2-6
Multi-Function Switch, Replace	2-6
Neutral Safety Switch, Replace	2-6
Passive Restraint Systems (Volume 2)	4-1
Precautions	2-5
Air Bag Systems	2-5
Battery Ground Cable	2-5

	Page No.
Radio, Replace	2-7
Relay Center Location	2-5
Speed Controls (Volume 2)	2-1
Starter Motors	18-1
Starter, Replace	2-5
4.6L	2-5
Bonneville	2-5
3.8L	2-5
Park Avenue & LeSabre	2-5
Steering Columns	20-1
Steering Wheel, Replace	2-6
Turn Signal Switch, Replace	2-6
Wiper Motor, Replace	2-7
Bonneville & LeSabre	2-7
Park Avenue	2-7
Wiper Switch, Replace	2-7
Bonneville	2-7
LeSabre & Park Avenue	2-7
Wiper Systems (Volume 2)	3-1
Wiper Transmission, Replace	2-7

PRECAUTIONS

Air Bag Systems

Refer to "Air Bag System Precautions" in the front of this manual for system disarming and arming procedures.

Battery Ground Cable

Prior to service, disconnect battery ground cable and isolate as required.

FUSE PANEL & FLASHER LOCATION

Bonneville & LeSabre

The rear fuse panel is located under the drivers side rear seat. The engine compartment fuse panel is on the righthand side of the engine compartment.

Park Avenue

The instrument panel fuse panel is located under the righthand side and near the rear of the instrument panel. The rear fuse panel is located under the passengers side rear seat. The engine compartment fuse panels are on the righthand side of the engine compartment.

The combined turn signal and hazard flasher module is attached to the lighting control module (LCM) bracket under the instrument panel.

RELAY CENTER LOCATION

The relays are located in the fuse panels. Refer to "Fuse Panel & Flasher Location" for appropriate locations.

FUEL PUMP RELAY LOCATION

Bonneville & LeSabre

The fuel pump relay is located in the rear fuse panel.

Park Avenue

The fuel pump relay is located in the engine compartment fuse panel.

STARTER

REPLACE

Park Avenue & LeSabre

When removing starter, note if any shims are used between the starter and mounting surface. If shims are used, install in their original locations.

If starter is noisy during cranking, remove one .015 inch double shim or add one

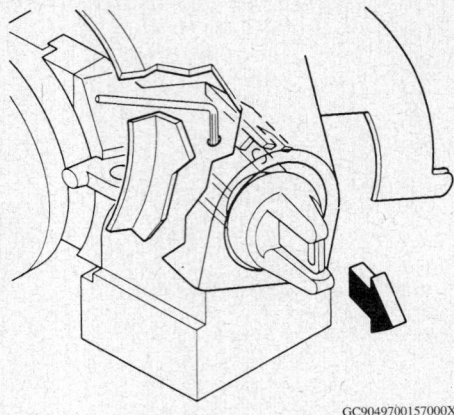

Fig. 1 Lock cylinder removal. LeSabre & Park Avenue

GC9049700157000X

.015 inch single shim to the outer bolt. If starter makes a high pitched whine after engine starts, add .015 inch double shims until noise ceases.
1. Raise and support vehicle.
2. Remove starter braces, shields or other components as required.
3. Support starter, then remove mounting bolts.
4. Lower starter, then disconnect solenoid wires and battery cable.
5. Remove starter from vehicle.
6. Reverse procedure to install, noting the following:
   a. **Torque** starter mounting bolts to 32 ft. lbs.
   b. **Torque** solenoid terminal nut to 22 inch lbs.

Bonneville

3.8L

1. Raise and support vehicle.
2. Remove torque converter cover.
3. Disconnect starter electrical connections.
4. Remove starter motor mounting bolts, then the starter.
5. Reverse procedure to install, noting the following:
   a. **Torque** starter mounting bolts to 32 ft. lbs.
   b. **Torque** solenoid electrical connection to 22 inch lbs.

4.6L

1. Disconnect knock sensor electrical connections, then remove knock sensor.
2. Remove 2 starter motor mounting bolts.
3. Remove starter by sliding forward, then disconnect starter electrical connections.
4. Reverse procedure to install, noting the following:
   a. **Torque** starter motor mounting bolts to 22 ft. lbs.
   b. **Torque** knock sensor to 15 ft. lbs.
   c. **Torque** solenoid terminal nut to 30 inch lbs.

COIL PACK

REPLACE

1. Tag electrical connectors and spark plug wires to ensure proper installation, then disconnect them from ignition control module.
2. Remove screws securing ignition coils to ignition module, then the coils.
3. Reverse procedure to install. **Torque** mounting screws to 40 inch lbs.

IGNITION LOCK

REPLACE

Bonneville

1. Apply parking brake.
2. Remove instrument cluster trim bezel.
3. Remove radio.
4. Insert key and turn ignition switch to RUN position.
5. Look through radio opening to locate release button on side of switch.
6. Depress and hold lock cylinder retaining tab using suitable flat bladed tool and pull out to remove ignition cylinder.
7. Remove theft deterrent module.
8. Reverse procedure to install.

LeSabre & Park Avenue

REMOVAL

1. Remove steering wheel as outlined under "Steering Wheel, Replace."
2. Disconnect SIR wiring harness from wiring protector and wire harness strap.
3. Lower or remove steering column from vehicle.
4. **On models equipped with tilt column,** remove tilt lever.
5. **On all models,** remove column lower and upper shrouds.
6. Insert ignition key and hold in Start position.
7. Push on lock cylinder retaining tab using a 1/16 inch hex wrench, **Fig. 1.**
8. Release key to Run position and pull lock cylinder from lock module assembly.

INSTALLATION

1. Install upper shroud. **Torque** mounting screws to 12 inch lbs.
2. Install lower shroud, ensuring slots on lower shroud engage with tabs on upper shroud.
3. Install lower shroud mounting screws. **Torque** both screws to 53 inch lbs.
4. Install shift and multi-function lever seals to column shrouds.
5. Install tilt lever.
6. Raise or install steering column into vehicle.
7. Insert key into lock cylinder.
8. Ensure sector in lock module assembly is in Run position.
9. Align locking tabs, position tab with slots in lock module assembly and push cylinder into position.

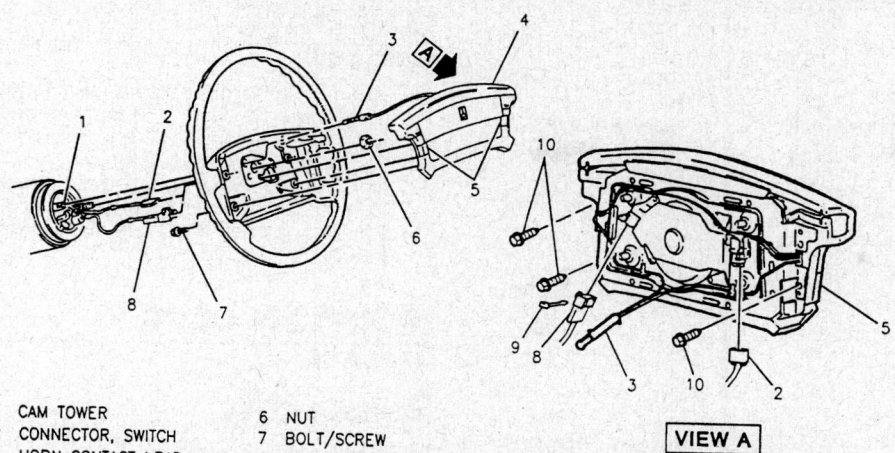

1 CAM TOWER
2 CONNECTOR, SWITCH
3 HORN CONTACT LEAD
4 INFLATOR MODULE
5 SWITCH ASM
6 NUT
7 BOLT/SCREW
8 CONNECTOR, SIR INFLATOR MODULE
9 RETAINER, CPA
10 BOLT/SCREW

VIEW A

GC6049100144000X

Fig. 2 Driver's air bag assembly

10. Install lock cylinder through upper shroud and into lock module assembly.

IGNITION SWITCH
REPLACE

1. Remove lock cylinder assembly as outlined under "Ignition Lock, Replace."
2. Remove ignition switch mounting screws.
3. Depress retaining tab on rear of ignition switch and remove switch through radio opening.
4. Disconnect electrical connectors and ignition switch bulb.
5. Disconnect shift/park lock cable.
6. Reverse procedure to install. **Torque** ignition switch mounting screws to 80 inch lbs.

NEUTRAL SAFETY SWITCH
REPLACE

The transmission Internal Mode Switch (IMS) is located within the transmission and controlled through the PCM.

BACK-UP LAMP SWITCH
REPLACE
Park Avenue

The back-up lamp switch is incorporated with the PERIM LP relay located in the I/P fuse panel and controlled by the PCM.

Bonneville & LeSabre

The back-up lamp switch is incorporated in the rear integration module (RIM) located behind the rear seat back and is controlled by the PCM.

HEADLAMP SWITCH
REPLACE

Refer to "Multi-Function Switch, Replace" for headlamp switch removal procedure.

MULTI-FUNCTION SWITCH
REPLACE

1. Remove steering wheel and tilt lever.
2. Remove two Torx screws from lower shroud, then tilt shroud down and slide back to disengage locking tabs.
3. Remove shroud protector.
4. Remove two Torx screws from upper shroud, then the shroud.
5. Remove instrument panel trim panel.
6. Remove two Torx screws from multi-function switch.
7. Disconnect multi-function switch electrical connectors, then remove switch.
8. Reverse procedure to install.

TURN SIGNAL SWITCH
REPLACE

Refer to "Multi-Function Switch, Replace" for turn signal switch removal procedure.

DIMMER SWITCH
REPLACE

Refer to "Multi-Function Switch, Replace" for dimmer switch removal procedure.

STEERING WHEEL
REPLACE

1. Remove driver's side air bag module mounting screws from back of steering wheel.
2. Remove module from steering wheel,

then disconnect horn contact by pushing slightly and twisting counterclockwise.
3. Remove connector position assurance, then disconnect coil assembly electrical connector, **Fig. 2.**
4. Remove steering wheel mounting nut.
5. Remove wheel using puller tool No. J1859-A and bolts No. J42578, or equivalents.
6. Reverse procedure to install, noting the following:
   a. **Torque** steering wheel nut to 30 ft. lbs.
   b. Ensure all wiring and electrical connectors are properly routed to avoid pinching.
   c. **Torque** driver's air bag module mounting screws to 27 inch lbs.

INSTRUMENT CLUSTER
REPLACE
Bonneville

1. Lower steering column to its lowest position.
2. Remove ignition lock cylinder bezel.
3. Remove Driver Information Center (DIC) switch.
4. Remove instrument cluster trim plate push-in fasteners.
5. Remove cluster trim plate by carefully pulling rearward and releasing clips.
6. Disconnect DIC switch electrical connector.
7. Release instrument cluster pins, then pull cluster rearward and to right.
8. Disconnect all cluster electrical connectors.
9. Reverse procedure to install, noting the following:
   a. Ensure trim plate is fully seated to instrument panel. This is critical to proper functioning of automatic A/C control in-vehicle sensor.
   b. Ensure all electrical connectors are securely connected.
   c. Push instrument cluster pins into their corresponding locations. An audible snap will be heard when cluster is fully seated.

LeSabre & Park Avenue

1. Carefully pry defroster grill away from instrument panel.
2. Disconnect sunload sensor from grill, then remove grill from instrument panel.
3. Remove righthand and lefthand windshield garnish moldings.
4. Remove instrument panel upper trim pad mounting screws, then the upper trim pad from instrument panel.
5. Lower steering column to its lowest position.
6. Remove instrument cluster trim plate bezel to instrument panel mounting screws.
7. Disengage four upper cluster trim plate bezel retaining clips, then the bottom clips.

8. Disconnect trim bezel driver information center switch electrical connector, then remove trim plate bezel from instrument panel.
9. Remove four instrument cluster pins, then pull cluster rearward to remove.
10. Reverse procedure to install.

RADIO
REPLACE

1. Remove instrument panel cluster trim plate.
2. **On Bonneville & LeSabre models,** depress spring clips on each side of radio.
3. **On Park Avenue models,** remove radio mounting screws.
4. **On all models,** pull radio rearward, then disconnect electrical connectors and antenna lead-in cable.
5. Reverse procedure to install.

WIPER MOTOR
REPLACE

Bonneville & LeSabre

1. Remove wiper arms.
2. Remove cowl cover panel.
3. Remove mounting bolts to windshield frame reinforcement, then the reinforcement.
4. Rotate wiper arm linkage from park 180° to opposite position.
5. Remove harness grommet from plenum.
6. Disconnect wiper motor harness connector.
7. Push harness and grommet through hole in plenum.
8. Remove mounting screws to wiper motor drive motor module.
9. Remove wiper drive system motor module.
10. Remove drive link from wiper motor cranks arm using tool No. J39232, or equivalent.
11. Remove wiper motor mounting screws, then the wiper motor from drive motor module.
12. Reverse procedure tom install, noting the following:
    a. **Torque** wiper drive system module screws to 71 inch lbs.
    b. **Torque** windshield reinforcement screws to 80 inch lbs.

Park Avenue

1. Disconnect electrical connectors.
2. Remove wiper motor mounting screws.
3. Place wiper arms 6–8 inches up on windshield.
4. Remove wiper motor, then disconnect drive link from crank arm.
5. Reverse procedure to install. **Torque** screws to 70 inch lbs.

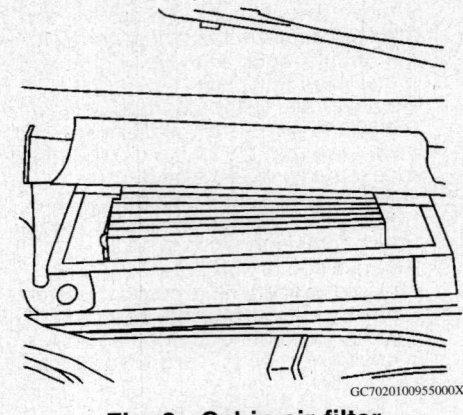

Fig. 3 Cabin air filter replacement. Bonneville & LeSabre

GC7020100955000X

WIPER SWITCH
REPLACE

Bonneville

1. **Make note of lefthand closeout and sound insulator panel fastener positions before removal. Improper installation may lead to possible accelerator or brake pedal binding.**
2. Remove instrument panel lefthand insulator.
3. Remove knee bolster and bracket.
4. Remove steering column bracket bolts. Disconnect electrical connectors from bracket.
5. Remove steering column bracket.
6. Remove steering column trim covers.
7. Remove wire harness assembly from wire restraint clips.
8. Disconnect wiper switch electrical connectors.
9. Depress switch locking tabs.
10. Pull switch assembly out of mounting bracket.
11. Reverse procedure to install, noting the following:
    a. Ensure all electrical connectors and wiring are properly routed to avoid pinching.
    b. Install new wire harness straps.
    c. Install steering column bracket and bolts. **Torque** bolts to 18 inch lbs.
    d. Install bolts and screws to knee bolster bracket at steering column support. **Torque** to 89 inch lbs.
    e. Install bolts and screws to knee bolster bracket at instrument panel. **Torque** to 18 inch lbs.
    f. Ensure lefthand closeout and insulator panel is properly positioned and fasteners are in original locations. **Torque** to 17 inch lbs.

LeSabre & Park Avenue

Refer to "Multi-Function Switch, Replace" for wiper switch removal procedure.

WIPER TRANSMISSION
REPLACE

Refer to "Wiper Motor, Replace" for wiper transmission removal procedure.

BLOWER MOTOR
REPLACE

1. Remove fasteners at rear edge of insulator to disengage from lower instrument panel.
2. Pry out retainers to release panel.
3. Turn heater temperature sensor ¼ turn to release and allow to remain connected to its wire.
4. Disconnect electrical connectors, then slide insulator panel rearward to disengage.
5. Remove Dash Integration Module (DIM) from bracket, then the bracket.
6. Disconnect blower motor electrical connector.
7. Remove blower motor mounting screws, then lower the motor and rotate counterclockwise to remove from vehicle.
8. Reverse procedure to install. **Torque** screws to 12–15 inch lbs.

CABIN AIR FILTER
REPLACE

Bonneville & LeSabre

1. Open hood.
2. Lift up cabin air filter access cover located on air inlet panel.
3. Remove cabin air filter element from filter housing, **Fig. 3.**
4. Install new cabin air filter into filter housing.
5. Close cabin air filter access cover.

Park Avenue

1. **Make note of lefthand closeout and sound insulator panel fastener positions before removal. Improper installation may lead to possible accelerator or brake pedal binding.**
2. Disconnect courtesy lamp, DSIR and heater temperature sensor electrical connectors at closeout panel.
3. Remove lefthand closeout and sound insulator panel.
4. Remove filter access cover by pushing down, then pulling out.
5. Remove tape on first filter.
6. Remove first filter by pulling filter tab.
7. Remove tape on second filter.
8. Remove second filter by pulling filter tab.
9. Remove third filter by pulling filter tab.
10. Reverse procedure to install, noting the following:
    a. Lubricate new filter guides with suitable spray silicon for ease in installation. Keep filters as straight as possible.
    b. Install first filter into HVAC assembly. Use tab or a long screwdriver to raise filter so leading edge catches on holding rib inside filter case.

c. Install second filter in first filter tab.
d. Slide second filter into remaining channels of first filter.
e. Slide third filter into remaining channels of second filter.
f. Fold second filter tab down and third filter tab up over second.
g. Install filter access cover.
h. Ensure lefthand closeout and insulator panel is properly positioned and fasteners are in original locations. **Torque** to 17 inch lbs.

HEATER CORE
REPLACE

1. Drain cooling system into suitable container.
2. Remove fuel injector sight shield.
3. **Make note of lefthand closeout and sound insulator panel fastener positions before removal. Improper installation may lead to possible accelerator or brake pedal binding.**
4. From inside of vehicle, remove righthand and lefthand side sound insulators.
5. **On models equipped with rear A/C,** remove front console assembly and auxiliary air distribution duct adapter.
6. **On all models,** remove instrument panel lower trim plate.
7. Remove air distributor duct screws (righthand side screw is difficult to remove and may be lefthand out during reassembly), then the air duct.
8. Remove heater core shield and cover.
9. Remove mounting screw and strap from heater core.
10. Remove heater core.
11. Reverse procedure to install. Ensure lefthand closeout and insulator panel is properly positioned and fasteners are in original locations. **Torque** to 17 inch lbs.

EVAPORATOR CORE
REPLACE

1. Recover A/C refrigerant as outlined in "Air Conditioning" chapter.
2. Remove evaporator hose nut, then disconnect evaporator hose connection at evaporator.
3. Remove heater hoses from heater core, then pinch off hoses to minimize leakage of coolant.
4. Raise and support vehicle.
5. Remove drain tube from A/C module.
6. Lower vehicle.
7. **Make note of lefthand closeout and sound insulator panel fastener positions before removal. Improper installation may lead to possible accelerator or brake pedal binding.**
8. Remove instrument panel assembly.
9. Remove defroster duct and air distributor duct.
10. Disconnect blower control module connection and instrument panel to HVAC module connection.
11. Remove HVAC module mounting nuts, then the module assembly.
12. Remove seal from around heater core and evaporator tubes.
13. Remove upper A/C evaporator case, then the evaporator core.
14. Reverse procedure to install. Ensure lefthand closeout and insulator panel is properly positioned and fasteners are in original locations. **Torque** to 17 inch lbs.

3.8L Engine

NOTE: On Air Bag Equipped Models, Refer To "Air Bag System Precautions" Located In The Front Of This Manual For System Disarming & Arming Procedures.

NOTE: Refer To "Computer Relearn Procedures" Located In The Front Of This Manual When Battery Power To The Computer Has Been Interrupted.

INDEX

	Page No.
Balance Shaft, Replace	2-11
Installation	2-12
Removal	2-11
Belt Tension Data	2-13
Camshaft, Replace	2-11
Camshaft Lobe Lift Specifications	2-11
Compression Pressure	2-9
Cooling System Bleed	2-14
Crankshaft Seal, Replace	2-13
Installation	2-13
Removal	2-13
Cylinder Head, Replace	2-10
Engine Rebuilding Specifications	29-1
Engine, Replace	2-9
Engine Mount, Replace	2-9
Exhaust Manifold, Replace	2-10
Lefthand	2-10
Righthand	2-10

	Page No.
Front Cover, Replace	2-11
Fuel Filter, Replace	2-15
Fuel Pump, Replace	2-15
Intake Manifold, Replace	2-9
VIN 1	2-10
VIN K	2-9
Lower	2-9
Upper	2-9
Main & Rod Bearings	2-12
Oil Pan, Replace	2-13
Oil Pump, Replace	2-13
Installation	2-13
Removal	2-13
Oil Pump Service	2-13
Assembly & Installation	2-13
Inspection	2-13
Piston & Rod Assembly	2-12
Pistons, Pins & Rings	2-12
Precautions	2-9
Air Bag Systems	2-9

	Page No.
Battery Ground Cable	2-9
Fuel System Pressure Relief	2-9
Radiator, Replace	2-15
Rocker Arms	2-11
Serpentine Drive Belt	2-14
Belt Routing	2-14
Belt Tensioner, Replace	2-14
VIN 1	2-14
VIN K	2-14
Supercharger, Replace	2-15
Thermostat, Replace	2-14
Tightening Specifications	2-16
Timing Chain, Replace	2-11
Valve Adjustment	2-11
Valve Clearance Specifications	2-11
Valve Guides	2-11
Water Pump, Replace	2-14
VIN 1 Engine	2-14
VIN K Engine	2-14

PRECAUTIONS

Air Bag Systems

Refer to "Air Bag System Precautions" in the front of this manual for system disarming and arming procedures.

Battery Ground Cable

Prior to service, disconnect battery ground cable and isolate as required.

Fuel System Pressure Relief

After relieving fuel system pressure, a small amount of fuel may be released when servicing fuel pipes or connections. In order to reduce the risk of personal injury, cover fuel pipe fittings with a suitable shop towel before disconnecting to catch any fuel that may leak.

1. Loosen fuel filler cap to relieve tank pressure.
2. Connect fuel pressure gauge tool No. J34370-1, or equivalent, to fuel pressure connection. Wrap fitting in suitable shop towel.
3. Install bleed hose to suitable container, then open valve and bleed off pressure.
4. Disconnect fuel pressure gauge, then drain gauge in suitable container.

COMPRESSION PRESSURE

When measuring compression, lowest cylinder must be within 70 percent of the highest cylinder with a minimum pressure of 100 psi. Perform compression test with engine at normal operating temperature, spark plugs removed and throttle wide open.

ENGINE MOUNT

REPLACE

1. Raise and support vehicle.
2. Support engine with suitable jack.
3. Remove righthand engine mount to engine mount bracket mounting nut.
4. Lower engine slightly.
5. Remove engine mount to frame mounting bolt.
6. Remove engine mount to frame mounting nuts, then remove the mount.
7. Reverse procedure to install, noting the following:
   a. **Torque** engine mount to frame mounting nuts to 52 ft. lbs.
   b. **Torque** engine mount to engine mount bracket mounting nut to 59 ft. lbs.

ENGINE

REPLACE

1. Scribe alignment marks on hood for installation reference, then remove hood.

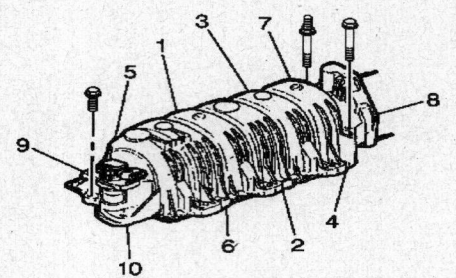

Fig. 1   Upper intake manifold. VIN K

2. Remove fuel injector sight shield.
3. Disconnect vacuum brake booster hose from connections and position aside.
4. Disconnect fuel feed and return lines and secure to air inlet grill.
5. Remove EVAP purge valve solenoid and secure hose to air inlet grill.
6. Disconnect accelerator cable and cruise cable from throttle body bracket.
7. Disconnect cruise module electrical connector.
8. Remove mounting nuts, then cruise control module.
9. Rotate drive belt tensioner counterclockwise to release belt tension, then remove belt.
10. Raise and support vehicle.
11. Remove battery ground cable and engine wire harness ground bolt from engine block.
12. Disconnect electrical connectors from A/C compressor clutch, oil level, knock, A/C pressure sensors and engine block heater.
13. Disconnect wire harness from retainer clip on back of A/C compressor.
14. Remove torque converter cover.
15. Remove starter as outlined under "Starter, Replace" in "Electrical" section.
16. Remove flywheel to torque converter bolts.
17. Disconnect electrical connectors to oil pressure, vehicle speed and knock sensors.
18. Remove transaxle brace to transaxle mounting bolts.
19. Remove mounting nuts on exhaust manifold pipe to righthand exhaust manifold, then remove pipe and position aside. Do not reuse gasket.
20. Remove righthand side front fascia extension.
21. Remove A/C compressor mounting bolts, then position compressor aside.
22. Lower vehicle.
23. Remove PCM mounting bolt from lefthand side front of cylinder head.
24. Disconnect electrical connectors on lefthand side of engine from fuel injectors, ignition harness, ECT, TP, MAF sensors and IAC valve.
25. Disconnect electrical connectors on righthand side of engine from fuel injectors, EGR valve, MAP and O2 sensors then the alternator.
26. Secure engine harness to air inlet grill.
27. Remove alternator.

28. Remove air cleaner intake duct.
29. Install suitable engine support fixture.
30. Remove front power steering pump mounting bolts.
31. Raise and support vehicle.
32. Remove remaining power steering pump mounting bolt, then position pump aside.
33. Remove righthand side engine mount bracket.
34. Remove righthand lower engine to transaxle mounting bolt.
35. Drain cooling system into suitable container.
36. Lower vehicle.
37. Remove coolant inlet hose from water pump using tool No. J38185, or equivalent, then remove coolant outlet hose from thermostat using same tool.
38. Remove heater hoses from drive belt tensioner retainers.
39. Support transaxle using suitable block of wood between floor jack and transaxle.
40. Remove engine support fixture.
41. Install suitable engine lift chain to engine lift bracket and attach to engine lift devise.
42. Remove remaining engine to transaxle mounting bolts.
43. Gently raise engine from vehicle, then drain engine oil into suitable container.
44. Remove transaxle brace to engine mounting bolts.
45. Remove exhaust manifold pipe.
46. Reverse procedure to install.

INTAKE MANIFOLD

REPLACE

VIN K

UPPER

1. Relieve fuel pressure as outlined under "Precautions."
2. Remove fuel injector sight shield and air intake duct.
3. Remove spark plug wires on righthand (rear) side of engine and position aside.
4. Remove fuel rail, then exhaust manifold heat shield.
5. Remove throttle cable bracket to cylinder head mounting bolt.
6. Remove throttle body support bracket.
7. Remove upper intake manifold mounting bolts, then the manifold, **Fig. 1.**
8. Reverse procedure to install. Tighten bolts and nuts in sequence.

LOWER

The two bolts which mount the lower intake manifold to the cylinder head are accessible only after removing the upper intake manifold. The bolts are located in the righthand front and the lefthand rear corners of the lower intake manifold.

1. Relieve fuel pressure as outlined under "Precautions."
2. Remove fuel injector sight shield and air intake duct.
3. Remove spark plug wires on righthand (rear) side of engine and position aside.

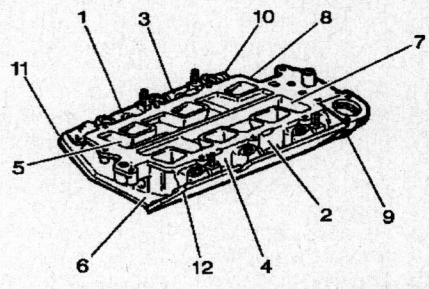

Fig. 2 Intake manifold tightening sequence. VIN K

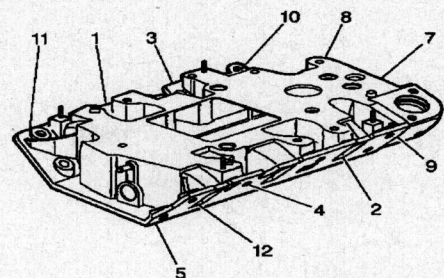

Fig. 3 Intake manifold tightening sequence. VIN 1

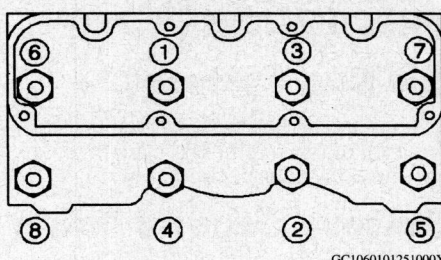

Fig. 4 Cylinder head tightening sequence

4. Remove fuel rail, then exhaust manifold heat shield.
5. Remove throttle cable bracket to cylinder head mounting bolt.
6. Remove throttle body support bracket.
7. Remove upper intake manifold mounting bolts, then the manifold, **Fig. 1.**
8. Drain cooling system into suitable container, then remove upper radiator hose from coolant outlet.
9. Remove alternator and set aside.
10. Remove drive belt tensioner.
11. Remove EGR valve outlet pipe.
12. Remove intake manifold bolts, then the manifold.
13. Reverse procedure to install, noting the following:
   a. Clean cylinder block, heads and intake manifold sealing surface of all oil using a suitable solvent.
   b. Remove adhesive compound from intake manifold bolts and bolt holes.
   c. Apply thread lock compound part No. 12345493, or equivalent, to intake manifold bolt threads prior to installation.
   d. Tighten intake manifold bolts in sequence, **Fig. 2.**

VIN 1

The two bolts which fasten the lower intake manifold to the cylinder head are accessible only after removing the upper intake manifold. The bolts are located in the righthand front and the lefthand rear corners of the lower intake manifold.
1. **On models equipped with supercharger,** remove supercharger as outlined under "Supercharger, Replace."
2. **On all models,** relieve fuel pressure as outlined under "Precautions."
3. Remove fuel injector sight shield.
4. Remove plastic engine cover and air intake duct.
5. Disconnect manifold vacuum source, then drain cooling system into suitable container.
6. Disconnect righthand spark plug wires and position aside.
7. Remove fuel rail, then exhaust manifold heat shield.
8. Disconnect upper radiator and bypass

hoses from coolant outlet.
9. Disconnect throttle position sensor and idle air control valve, then the fuel injectors and MAP sensor electrical connectors.
10. Remove EGR outlet pipe.
11. Remove throttle and cruise control cables.
12. Remove throttle bracket with power steering reservoir and set aside.
13. Mark running direction with suitable felt pen or chalk, then remove inner accessory drive belt.
14. Disconnect heater hose from intake manifold.
15. Remove tensioner bracket to supercharger retaining stud using standard double nut procedure.
16. Remove intake manifold mounting bolts, then the manifold.
17. Reverse procedure to install, noting the following:
   a. Clean cylinder block, heads and intake manifold sealing surface of all oil using a suitable solvent.
   b. Remove adhesive compound from intake manifold bolts and bolt holes.
   c. Apply thread lock compound part No. 12345493, or equivalent, to intake manifold bolt threads prior to installation.
   d. Tighten intake manifold bolts in sequence, **Fig. 3.**

EXHAUST MANIFOLD
REPLACE
Lefthand

Inspect the EGR outlet pipe for leaks whenever the pipe is removed from the righthand exhaust manifold. If a leak exists, replace the EGR adapter.
1. Disconnect spark plug wires from the spark plugs.
2. Remove oil level dipstick and tube.
3. Remove engine lift bracket.
4. Remove bolts attaching lefthand exhaust manifold to crossover pipe.
5. Remove exhaust manifold bolts, then the manifold. Do not reuse gasket.
6. Reverse procedure to instal. **Torque** exhaust manifold bolts to 22 ft. lbs.

Righthand

1. Remove fuel injector sight shield.
2. Disconnect oxygen sensor electrical connector.
3. Remove righthand side spark plugs.
4. Remove brake booster heat shield mounting nuts, then the heat shield.
5. Remove exhaust crossover to righthand side exhaust manifold bolts.
6. Remove transaxle filler tube.
7. Raise and support vehicle.
8. Remove exhaust manifold pipe.
9. Remove fuel injector sight shield bracket.
10. Remove righthand engine lift bracket.
11. Remove EGR inlet pipe to righthand side exhaust manifold mounting bolt.
12. Remove exhaust manifold bolts, then exhaust manifold. Do not reuse gasket.
13. Remove exhaust crossover pipe seal. Do not reuse seal.
14. Reverse procedure to install. **Torque** exhaust manifold bolts to 22 ft. lbs.

CYLINDER HEAD
REPLACE

1. Relieve fuel pressure as outlined under "Precautions."
2. Remove intake manifolds as outlined under "Intake Manifold, Replace."
3. Remove exhaust manifold as outlined under "Exhaust Manifold, Replace."
4. Remove appropriate valve cover.
5. Remove all wiring or brackets as required.
6. Remove rocker arm assemblies, guide plate and pushrods.
7. Remove and discard cylinder head mounting bolts, then the cylinder head.
8. Reverse procedure to install, noting the following:
   a. Clean all gasket mating surfaces and cylinder head bolt holes in block.
   b. Clean threads in block with appropriate tap.
   c. Apply suitable sealant to new bolt threads.
   d. Install new head gasket with arrow pointing towards front of engine.
   e. **Torque** cylinder head bolts to 37 ft. lbs., in sequence, **Fig. 4.**
   f. Tighten bolts an additional 120° in sequence.

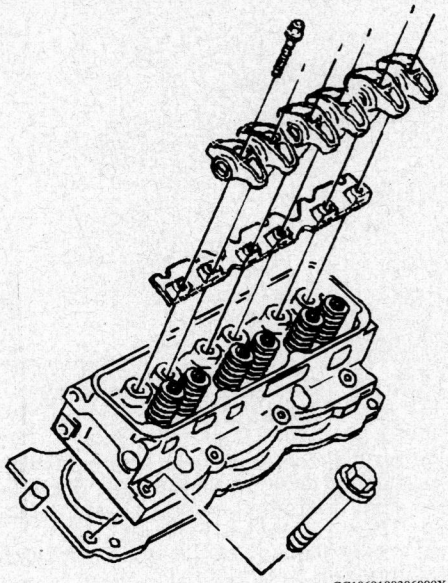

Fig. 5 Rocker arm assembly

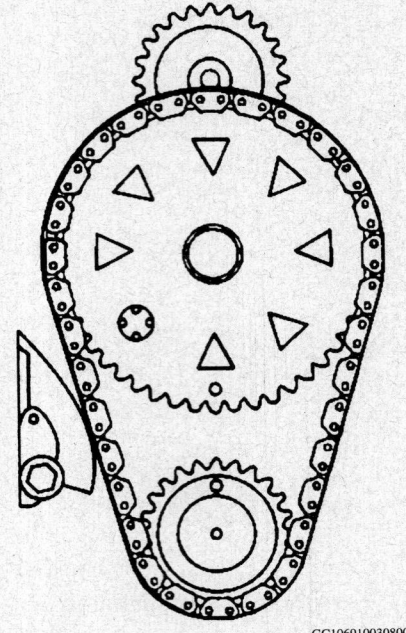

Fig. 6 Timing gear alignment marks

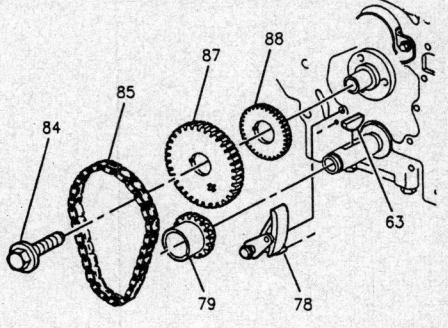

63 KEY
78 DAMPER ASSEMBLY
79 CRANKSHAFT SPROCKET
84 BOLT
85 TIMING CHAIN
87 CAMSHAFT SPROCKET
88 CAMSHAFT GEAR

Fig. 7 Timing chain & sprockets

CAMSHAFT LOBE LIFT SPECIFICATIONS

Engine	Year	Int.	Exh.
3.8L	All	.242	.234

VALVE CLEARANCE SPECIFICATIONS

These engines are equipped with hydraulic valve lifters. Valve clearance should be zero.

VALVE ADJUSTMENT

These engines are equipped with hydraulic valve lifters. There is no provision for adjustment.

ROCKER ARMS

Rocker arms are pedestal mounted over support plates, **Fig. 5.** To replace rocker arms, remove valve cover, pedestal mounting bolt(s), pedestal and the rocker arm. Replace rocker arms and pedestals as an assembly if they are damaged or excessively worn. If rocker arms are to be used again, they must be installed in original position.

VALVE GUIDES

The valve guides are an integral part of the cylinder head and cannot be replaced. If excessive valve stem clearance is noted, the valve guide must be reamed and an oversize valve guide installed. Valves are available in an oversize of .010 inch.

FRONT COVER

REPLACE

1. Remove righthand engine mount and bracket.
2. Remove drive belt tensioner as outlined under "Belt Tensioner, Replace."
3. Remove crankshaft balancer, sensor shield and crankshaft sensor.
4. Remove oil pan to front cover bolts.
5. Remove engine front cover mounting bolts, then the front cover.
6. Inspect timing chain for overall in-and-out movement, which should not exceed one inch.
7. Inspect sprockets for visible signs of wear or damage.
8. Clean gasket mating surfaces at timing chain cover and cylinder block.
9. If oil pan gasket is excessively swollen, oil pan must be removed and gasket replaced.
10. Reverse procedure to install, noting the following:
    a. Apply sealer No. 12346004, or equivalent, to bolt threads.
    b. Install engine front cover bolts.
    c. **Torque** front cover bolts to 15 ft. lbs., then tighten front cover bolts an additional 40°.
    d. Install oil pan to front engine cover bolts and **torque** to 124 inch lbs.
    e. Install crankshaft sensor and shield. **Do not adjust crankshaft sensor.**
    f. Crankshaft sensor bolt is designed to permanently stretch when installed. **Do not install a standard bolt. Components will not be tightened properly if improper bolt is used.**

TIMING CHAIN

REPLACE

1. Remove front cover as outlined under "Front Cover, Replace."
2. Align timing marks on sprockets, **Fig. 6,** so they are as close together as possible.
3. Remove timing chain dampener.
4. Remove camshaft sprocket bolts, **Fig. 7.**
5. Remove camshaft sprocket and chain, then crankshaft sprocket.
6. Reverse procedure to install, noting the following:
    a. Ensure No. 1 piston is at TDC.
    b. Assemble timing chain on sprockets with their timing marks aligned, **Fig. 6.**
    c. Tighten camshaft sprocket bolts.

CAMSHAFT

REPLACE

1. Relieve fuel pressure as outlined under "Precautions."
2. Remove intake manifold as outlined under "Intake Manifold, Replace."
3. Remove valve cover, rocker arms, pushrods and valve lifters.
4. Remove crankshaft pulley and crankshaft sensor cover.
5. Remove front cover, timing chain and sprockets.
6. Remove camshaft thrust plate and camshaft. **Avoid marring bearing surface when removing or installing camshaft.**
7. Reverse procedure to install. Coat camshaft and valve lifters with prelube part No. 1052365, or equivalent, prior to installation.

BALANCE SHAFT

REPLACE

Removal

1. Remove engine as outlined under "Engine, Replace."
2. Remove flexplate, then the intake manifold as outlined under "Intake Manifold, Replace."
3. Remove lifter guide retainer, then the front cover.
4. Remove balance shaft drive gear bolt, **Fig. 8,** then the camshaft sprocket and timing chain.

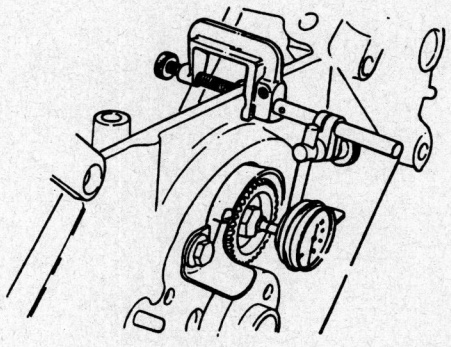

Fig. 9 Balance shaft endplay measurement

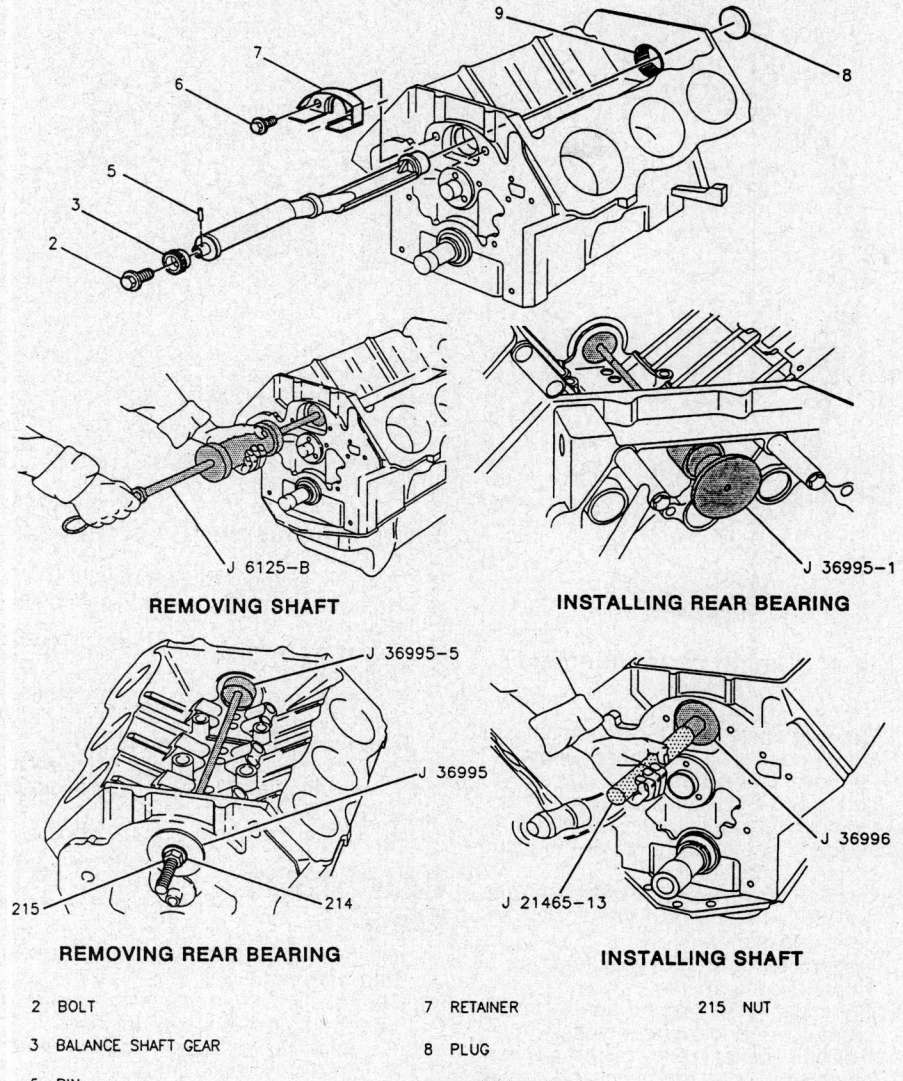

J 6125-B

REMOVING SHAFT

J 36995-1

INSTALLING REAR BEARING

J 36995-5

J 36995

215 — — 214

REMOVING REAR BEARING

J 36996

J 21465-13

INSTALLING SHAFT

2	BOLT	7	RETAINER	215	NUT
3	BALANCE SHAFT GEAR	8	PLUG		
5	PIN	9	BEARING		
6	BOLT	214	WASHER		

GC1069100311000X

Fig. 8 Balance shaft service

5. Remove balance shaft retainer bolts, retainer and gear.
6. Remove balance shaft using slide hammer tool No. J6125-1B, or equivalent. **Balance shaft and both bearings are serviced as complete package.**
7. Remove balance shaft rear plug.
8. Remove balance shaft rear bearing using replacement tool No. J36995-5, or equivalent.

Installation

1. Dip balance shaft rear bearing in clean engine oil.
2. Install bearing with rolled edge facing into engine and manufacturers markings facing flexplate side using balance shaft bearing replacement tool No. J36995-1, or equivalent.
3. Dip balance shaft front bearing into clean engine oil.

4. Install balance shaft into block using installer tool Nos. J21465-13 and J36996, or equivalent.
5. Temporarily install balance shaft bearing retainer and bolts.
6. Install balance shaft drive gear.
7. Apply suitable sealant to bolt, then install and tighten.
8. Install balance shaft rear plug.
9. Measure balance shaft endplay, **Fig. 9,** which should not exceed .008 inch.
10. Measure balance shaft radial play at rear, **Figs. 10 and 11.** Radial play should be .0005–.0047 inch.
11. With camshaft sprocket temporarily installed, turn camshaft so timing mark is straight down.
12. With camshaft sprocket and camshaft gear removed, turn balance shaft so timing mark on gear points straight down.
13. Install camshaft gear, aligning marks

on balance shaft gear and camshaft gear by turning balance shaft, **Fig. 6.**
14. Turn crankshaft so No. 1 piston is at TDC.
15. Install timing chain and camshaft sprocket.
16. Measure gear lash at four places, every ¼ turn, **Fig. 12.** Gear lash should be .002–.005 inch.
17. Install balance shaft front bearing retainer and bolts, then tighten.
18. Install front cover, then the lifter guide retainer.
19. Install intake manifold, then the flexplate. Tighten flexplate bolts.
20. Install engine in vehicle.

PISTON & ROD ASSEMBLY

1. Coat piston pin with oil.
2. Install one piston pin retainer into retainer groove.
3. Install connecting rod and piston pin, rod can be installed in either direction.
4. Push piston pin in until it bottoms against installed piston pin retainer.
5. Ensure piston moves freely.

PISTONS, PINS & RINGS

Pistons and ring are available in standard sizes and oversizes of .010. Piston pins are supplied with piston and are available in standard size only.

To inspect piston fit in bore, measure bore diameter using suitable telescoping gauges and record reading. Measure piston across skirt at a point ¾ inch below piston pin center line and record reading. Subtract piston diameter from bore diameter and compare to specified clearance.

MAIN & ROD BEARINGS

Main and rod bearings are available in standard sizes and a variety of undersizes.

1. Lubricate crankshaft to main bearing contact areas with clean engine oil or engine assembly lubricant.
2. **Torque** all bolts to 52 ft. lbs., in equal increments.
3. Loosen all bolts 360°.

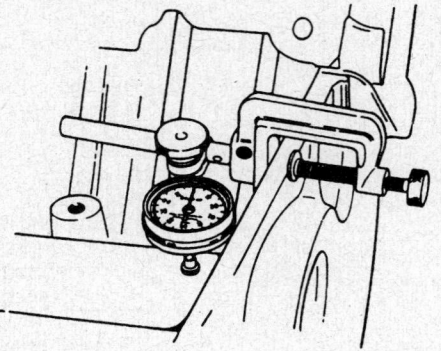

GC1069100313000X

Fig. 10   Balance shaft front radial play measurement

4. **Torque** all bolts to 15 ft. lbs.
5. **Torque** all bolts to 30 ft. lbs.
6. Tighten bolts an additional 35°.
7. Tighten bolts an additional 35°.
8. Final, tighten bolts an additional 40°.
9. Apply thread lock compound part No. 12345493, or equivalent, to side main bolts.
10. Install side main bolts and **torque** to 11 ft. lbs.
11. Tighten main bolts an additional 45°.
12. Install connecting rod bearings and bearing caps.
13. **Torque** cap bolts to 20 ft. lbs., then tighten an additional 50°.
14. Pry connecting rod back and forth, then inspect for binding.

CRANKSHAFT SEAL
REPLACE
Removal

1. Remove transaxle assembly and flexplate.
2. Pry out seal using a suitable screwdriver or other flat bladed tool.
3. Clean surfaces and inspect for visual damage or excessive wear. Repair or replace components as required.

Installation

1. Apply clean engine oil to both sides of new seal.
2. Slide seal over mandrel of rear main oil seal installer tool No. J38196, or equivalent, until back of seal bottoms squarely against collar of tool.
3. Attach main seal oil installer tool to crankshaft by hand or **torque** mounting screws to 54 inch lbs.
4. Turn tool T-handle so that collar pushes seal into bore.
5. Turn handle until collar is tight against case.
6. Loosen T-handle until it comes to a stop, then remove mounting screws.

OIL PAN
REPLACE

1. Raise vehicle and drain engine oil into suitable container.
2. Remove flexplate inspection cover.

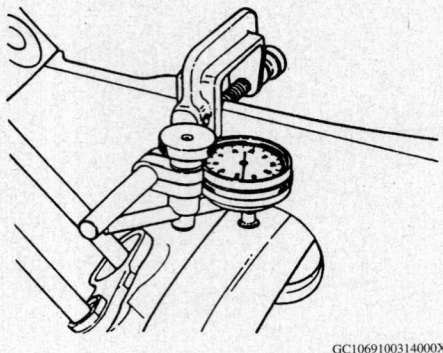

GC1069100314000X

Fig. 11   Balance shaft rear radial play measurement

59	PUMP OUTER GEAR
59	PUMP INNER GEAR
60	OIL PUMP COVER
64	SCREW
72	FRONT COVER

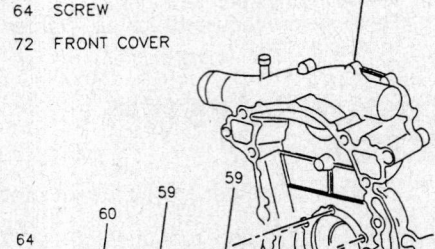

GC1089100145000X

Fig. 13   Oil pump assembly

3. Remove engine mount as outlined under "Engine Mount, Replace."
4. Remove oil level sensor located in oil pan before oil pan is removed. Damage to sensor will occur if pan is removed with sensor installed.
5. Remove oil filter.
6. Remove oil pan, then the pickup screen.
7. Remove old oil pan gasket.
8. Clean oil pan and cylinder block mating surfaces.
9. Reverse procedure to install.

OIL PUMP
REPLACE
Removal

1. Remove front cover as outlined under "Front Cover, Replace."
2. Remove oil filter adapter, pressure regulator valve and spring.
3. Remove oil pump cover and gears, **Fig. 13.**

Installation

1. Lubricate all gears with clean engine oil, then install gears in housing.

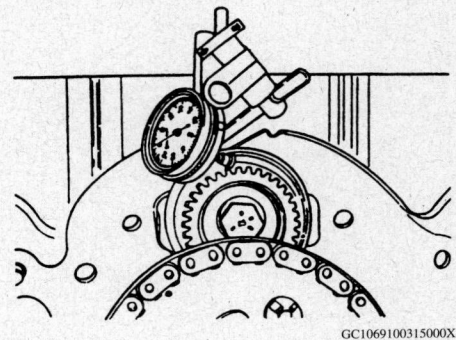

GC1069100315000X

Fig. 12   Balance shaft gear lash inspection

2. Pack pump cavity with suitable petroleum jelly.
3. Install pump cover. Tighten cover mounting screws.
4. Install pressure regulator valve and spring.
5. Install oil filter adapter using a new gasket. Tighten oil filter adapter mounting bolts.
6. Install front cover on engine. **Ensure inner pump gear is properly engaged on crankshaft sprocket during front cover installation.**

OIL PUMP SERVICE
Inspection

1. Inspect pump cover and housing for cracks, scoring, porous or damaged casting, damaged threads or excessive wear or galling. Replace as required.
2. Inspect pressure regulator valve for scoring, burrs or sticking in valve bore. Replace as required.
3. Inspect pressure regulator valve spring for tension loss or bending. Replace spring as required.
4. Inspect gears for chipping galling or excessive wear. Replace as required.

Assembly & Installation

1. Measure oil pump inner gear tip clearance, **Fig. 14.** Maximum clearance should be .006 inch.
2. Measure oil pump outer gear diameter clearance, **Fig. 15.** Clearance should be .008–.015 inch.
3. Measure oil pump gear end clearance with gear dropped in housing, **Fig. 16,** which should be .0001–.0035 inch.
4. Measure pressure regulator valve for valve to bore clearance of .0015–.0030 inch.

BELT TENSION DATA

This engine is equipped with an automatic belt tensioner.

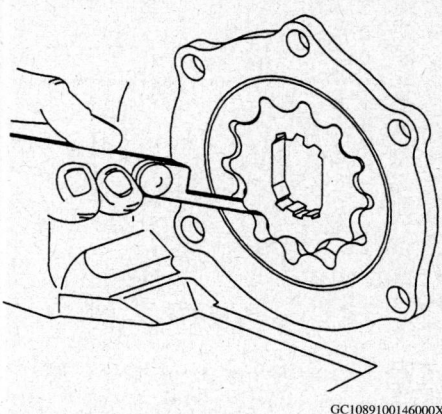

Fig. 14 Oil pump inner gear tip clearance inspection

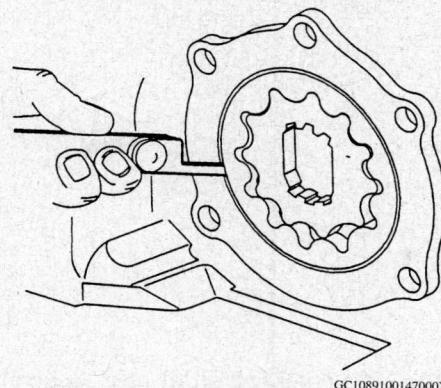

Fig. 15 Oil pump outer gear diameter clearance inspection

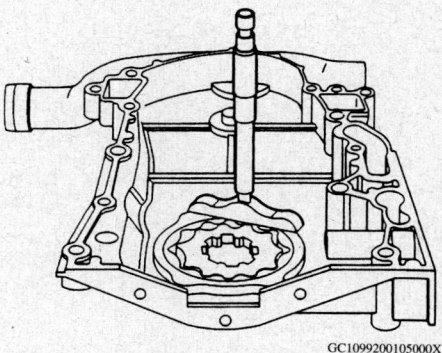

Fig. 16 Oil pump gear end clearance inspection

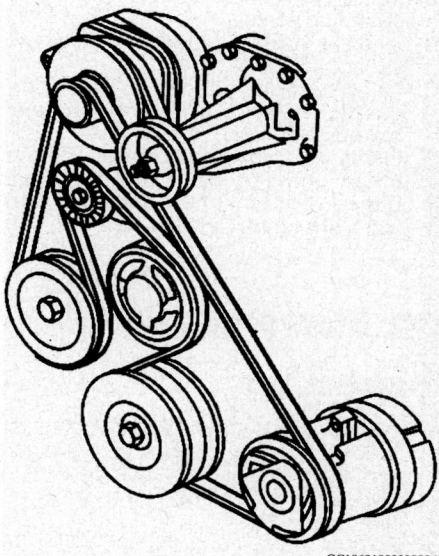

Fig. 17 Serpentine belt routing & replacement. VIN 1

SERPENTINE DRIVE BELT

Belt Routing

Refer to **Figs. 17 and 18** for serpentine drive belt routing.

Belt Tensioner, Replace

VIN 1

1. Remove supercharger belt.
2. Remove ignition module.
3. Remove tensioner bolts, then the tensioner.
4. Reverse procedure to install.

VIN K

1. Raise and support vehicle.
2. Remove lower splash shield, then drain coolant into suitable container.

3. Install front splash shield, lower vehicle.
4. Remove alternator and heater hoses.
5. Remove drive belt tensioner.
6. Reverse procedure to install. Tighten tensioner bolts.

COOLING SYSTEM BLEED

1. Fill cooling system and install radiator cap.
2. Start engine and run at 2000–2500 RPM until engine reaches operating temperature.
3. Allow engine return to idle and run for 3 minutes.
4. Shut engine off and allow to cool.
5. Inspect coolant level and top off as needed.

THERMOSTAT

REPLACE

1. Remove engine cover.
2. With engine cool, drain engine coolant below thermostat level.
3. Disconnect radiator hose from thermostat housing.
4. Remove thermostat housing, gasket and thermostat.
5. Reverse procedure to install, noting the following:
   a. Ensure thermostat gasket sealing surfaces are thoroughly clean prior to installation.
   b. Install thermostat with new gasket.
   c. Tighten thermostat housing mounting bolt(s).
   d. Fill and bleed cooling system as outlined under "Cooling System Bleed."

WATER PUMP

REPLACE

VIN K Engine

1. Drain coolant into suitable container.
2. Rotate drive belt tension counterclockwise and remove drive belt.
3. Remove water pump pulley.

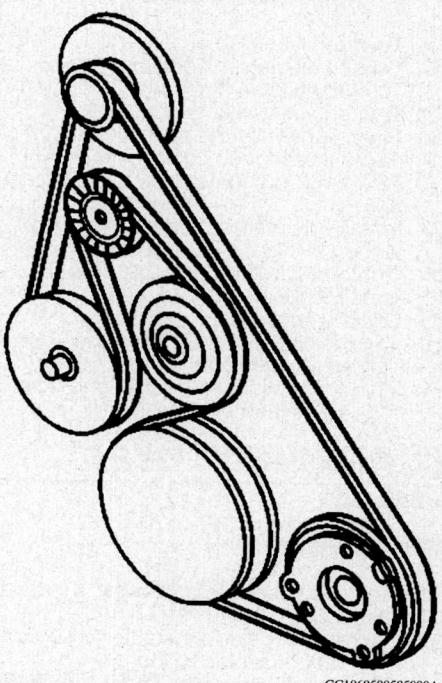

Fig. 18 Serpentine belt routing & replacement. VIN K

4. Remove water pump mounting bolts, note their locations, then remove water pump.
5. Clean gasket mating surfaces.
6. Reverse procedure to install, noting the following:
   a. **Torque** water pump short bolts to 11 ft. lbs.
   b. **Torque** water pump long bolts to 22 ft. lbs.

VIN 1 Engine

1. Drain coolant into suitable container.
2. Remove supercharger and accessory drive belts.
3. Remove supercharger belt idler pulley bolt, then the pulley.
4. Remove water pump pulley mounting bolts, then the pulley.
5. Remove water pump mounting bolts, noting their location, then the water pump.

6. Clean gasket mating surfaces.
7. Reverse procedure to install, noting the following:
   a. **Torque** short water pump bolts to 11 ft. lbs.
   b. **Torque** long water pump bolts to 22 ft. lbs.

RADIATOR

REPLACE

1. Drain engine coolant into suitable container.
2. Remove upper radiator seal.
3. **On Park Avenue models,** remove upper two bolts from hood latch support.
4. **On all models,** remove upper radiator support bar.
5. Disconnect and plug coolant overflow hose from radiator.
6. Disconnect upper and lower radiator hoses from radiator and position out of way.
7. Remove bolt from transmission oil cooler pipe clip at lower radiator tie bar.
8. Remove cooling fans.
9. Disconnect transmission fluid cooler lines from radiator using coupling tool No. J41623-B, or equivalent. Position lines aside.
10. Disconnect overflow hose from radiator.
11. **Bolt retaining condenser to radiator end tank is a special length and must be used upon installation.**
12. Remove condenser mounting bolts, then separate condenser from radiator and remove radiator from vehicle.
13. Reverse procedure to install, noting the following:
    a. **Bolt retaining condenser to radiator end tank is a special length and must be used upon installation.**
    b. Fill radiator with proper coolant.
    c. Bleed cooling system as outlined under "Cooling System Bleed."
    d. Start engine, then inspect for and correct any leakage.

FUEL PUMP

REPLACE

1. Clean fuel pipe connections, hose connections and surrounding areas to prevent fuel system contamination.

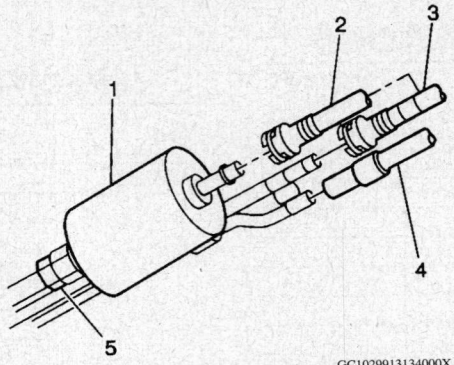

Fig. 19 Fuel filter replacement

2. Do not handle fuel sender/pump assembly by fuel pipes or damage to pipe joints could occur.
3. Relieve fuel system pressure as outlined in "Precautions."
4. Drain fuel from tank into a suitable storage unit.
5. Remove spare tire cover, jack and spare tire.
6. Remove rear compartment floor trim.
7. Remove fuel sender/pump access panel.
8. Remove quick connect fittings and electrical connector at fuel sender/pump assembly.
9. Remove electrical connector at fuel tank pressure sensor.
10. Remove fuel sender/pump retaining ring and assembly retaining cam with fuel sender locknut wrench tool No. J39765, or equivalent.
11. Remove fuel sender/pump from vehicle.
12. Reverse procedure to install, noting the following:
    a. Replace fuel sender O-rings during installation to avoid damaging sender assembly.
    b. Attach fuel lines with original type fasteners and hardware.
    c. **Do not repair sections of fuel pipe.**
    d. Upon completion of repairs, turn ignition On for two seconds, then Off for 10 seconds.
    e. Turn ignition back On and inspect for leaks.

FUEL FILTER

REPLACE

1. Relieve fuel pressure as outlined under "Precautions."
2. Raise and support vehicle using a suitable lift.
3. Remove quick-connect fitting at fuel feed line (2), **Fig. 19.**
4. Remove threaded connection (5) at inline fuel filter.
5. Inspect fuel lines and O-rings for cuts, swelling, cracks and distortion.
6. Inspect fuel return line and fuel vent pipe.
7. Drain any remaining fuel into suitable container.
8. Reverse procedure to install. Tighten fuel filter outlet nut.

SUPERCHARGER

REPLACE

1. Relieve fuel pressure as outlined under "Precautions."
2. Remove engine cover.
3. Remove injector sight shield.
4. Remove supercharger belt.
5. Disconnect vacuum brake booster hose from vacuum connections and position aside.
6. Remove evaporative emission canister purge valve, then secure hose to air inlet grille.
7. Remove alternator brace.
8. Disconnect righthand side spark plug wires from ignition module and position aside.
9. Disconnect electrical connectors from fuel injectors.
10. Remove MAP sensor bracket.
11. Remove fuel rail mounting bolts and the fuel rail with injectors.
12. Remove boost control solenoid.
13. Remove throttle body nuts.
14. Remove supercharger.
15. Reverse procedure to install, noting the following:
    a. Clean intake manifold and supercharger mating surfaces.
    b. **Do not use any sealer on supercharger gasket.**
    c. Tighten supercharger mounting bolts.

TIGHTENING SPECIFICATIONS

Year	Component	Torque Ft. Lbs.
2004–05	Accessory Drive Belt Tensioner	37
	Alternator Support Through Alternator	36
	Alternator Support To Cylinder Head	36
	Balance Shaft Gear	16①
	Balance Shaft Retainer	22
	Boost Control Solenoid Mounting Nut	71②
	Bypass Valve Actuator	18
	Camshaft Sensor To Front Cover	89②
	Camshaft Sprocket	74⑤
	Connecting Rod Bolts	20④
	Coolant Plug	13
	Coolant Temperature Sensor To Intake	15
	Crankshaft Balancer	110⑥
	Crankshaft Sensor Clamp Bolt	40②
	Crankshaft Sensor To Front Cover	22
	Cylinder Block Drain Plug	13
	Cylinder Head To Block	③
	EGR Pipe To EGR Valve	22
	EGR Pipe To Exhaust Manifold	21
	EGR Valve Adapter	37
	EGR Valve To Intake Manifold Adapter	22
	Engine Mount To Cylinder Block	70
	Engine Mount To Frame Rail	52
	Engine Mount To Mount Bracket	59
	ESC Knock Sensor	14
	Exhaust Manifold To Cylinder Head	22
	Exhaust Pipe To Exhaust Manifold	18
	Flexplate Cover To Transaxle	10
	Flexplate To Crankshaft	11④
	Front Cover To Block	22
	Fuel Rail Hold-Down	89②
	Fuel Filter Outlet Nut	22
	Fuel Injector Rail Stud	18
	Heater Hose Fitting To Intake	11
	Ignition Module To Alternator Support	18
	Intake Manifold To Cylinder Head	11
	Intake Manifold (Upper) To Lower Manifold	89②
	Main Bearing Cap Bolts	⑦
	Oil Dipstick Tube	14
	Oil Filter Adapter To Front Cover	11④
	Oil Galley Plugs	22
	Oil Level Sensor To Oil Pan	15
	Oil Pan Drain Plug	22

TIGHTENING SPECIFICATIONS—Continued

Year	Component	Torque Ft. Lbs.
2004–05	Oil Pan To Block	10
	Oil Pan To Front Cover	10
	Oil Pressure Switch	12
	Oil Pump Cover To Front Cover	98②
	Oil Screen Housing To Cylinder Block	11
	O2 Sensor	31
	Pulley Assembly To Crankshaft	111⑥
	Righthand Exhaust Manifold To Lefthand Exhaust Manifold	15
	Rocker Arm Cover	89②
	Rocker Arm Pedestal	11⑤
	Spark Plug	11
	Starter Motor	32
	Supercharger To Lower Intake Manifold	17
	Thermostat Housing	15
	Throttle Cable Bracket	35②
	Timing Chain Damper	16
	Torque Converter To Flexplate	46
	Transaxle To Engine Block	55
	Valve Lifter Guide Bolts	22
	Water Pump Pulley	116②

① — Rotate an additional 70°.

② — Inch lbs.

③ — Refer to "Cylinder Head, Replace."

④ — Rotate an additional 50°.

⑤ — Rotate an additional 90°.

⑥ — Rotate an additional 76°.

⑦ — Refer to "Crankshaft, Replace."

NOTE: Refer To "4.6L Engine" In "Deville, DTS, Seville & STS" Chapter For Procedures Not Covered In This Section.

NOTE: On Air Bag Equipped Models, Refer To "Air Bag System Precautions" Located In The Front Of This Manual For System Disarming & Arming Procedures.

NOTE: Refer To "Computer Relearn Procedures" Located In The Front Of This Manual When Battery Power To The Computer Has Been Interrupted.

INDEX

	Page No.		Page No.		Page No.
Engine Rebuilding Specifications	29-1	Front	2-17	Air Bag Systems	2-17
Engine, Replace	2-17	Righthand	2-17	Battery Ground Cable	2-17
Engine Mount, Replace	2-17	Oil Pan, Replace	2-18	Fuel System Pressure Relief	2-17
		Precautions	2-17	Tightening Specifications	2-18

PRECAUTIONS

Air Bag Systems

Refer to "Air Bag System Precautions" in the front of this manual for system disarming and arming procedures.

Battery Ground Cable

Prior to service, disconnect battery ground cable and isolate as required.

Fuel System Pressure Relief

A small amount of fuel may be released when servicing fuel connections even after pressure is released. Cover all fuel connections with shop towel before servicing.
1. Disconnect and isolate battery ground cable.
2. Remove intake manifold top cover.
3. Loosen fuel tank filler cap.
4. Install fuel pressure gauge tool No, J-34760-1A, or equivalent, to fuel pressure connection. Wrap shop towel around fitting while connecting gauge.
5. Install approved bleed hose into approved container, then open valve on gauge to relieve system pressure.

ENGINE MOUNT
REPLACE
Front

1. Install suitable engine support fixture.
2. Raise and support vehicle.
3. Remove front engine mount to engine frame mounting nut.
4. Remove engine frame.
5. Remove front engine mount to engine mount bracket mounting nut.

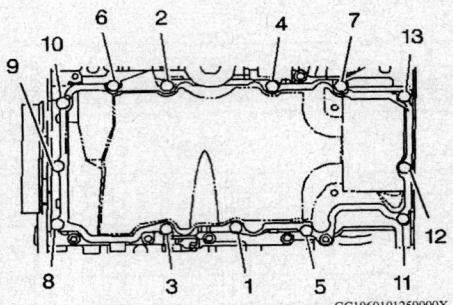

Fig. 1 Oil pan bolt tightening sequence

6. Remove engine mount.
7. Reverse procedure to install.

Righthand

1. Raise and support vehicle.
2. Remove righthand side front wheel.
3. Support engine with suitable jack stand.
4. Remove engine mount to engine mount bracket mounting nut.
5. Lower jack allowing engine to lower slightly then remove jack.
6. Remove engine mount to frame mounting bolts and nuts.
7. Lower vehicle.
8. Remove surge tank and position aside, then remove the frame rail mounting nuts.
9. Raise and support vehicle.
10. Push up on frame rail bolts to clear mount as it's tilted away from vehicle and remove mount.
11. Reverse procedure to install.

ENGINE
REPLACE

1. Recover air condition refrigerant as

outlined in "Air Conditioning" chapter.
2. Disconnect vacuum booster hose connections and position aside.
3. Disconnect fuel supply and return quick connect fittings at fuel rail and secure to air inlet grill.
4. Disconnect EVAP purge valve hose and secure to air inlet grill.
5. Remove upper filler panel and air cleaner assembly.
6. Remove fuel injector sight shield.
7. Remove positive battery cable to remote positive terminal mounting nut then secure to top of engine.
8. Remove secondary air injection relay from bracket and secure to top of engine.
9. Disconnect electrical connectors from PCM, C101 and engine electrical harness.
10. Remove battery ground cable mounting bolt from righthand frame rail.
11. Disconnect cruise control and accelerator cables from throttle body. Do not reuse accelerator cable.
12. Disconnect shift cable from manual shift lever and bracket then position aside.
13. Drain coolant into suitable container.
14. Disconnect water housing crossover to surge tank inlet hose.
15. Disconnect heater pipe to surge tank outlet hose.
16. Disconnect heater hoses from heater pipes.
17. Disconnect brake lines from master cylinder. Plug open outlet ports.
18. Remove upper transaxle oil cooler line mounting bolt, then disconnect upper and lower oil cooler lines from radiator.
19. Ensure wheels are straight then lock steering column using lockpin tool No. J-42640, or equivalent.
20. Remove lefthand and righthand strut tower bolts.
21. Raise and support vehicle.
22. Remove rear exhaust manifold pipe.

23. Disconnect electrical connectors from wheel speed and brake pad wear sensors.
24. Remove air deflector and front fascia extensions.
25. Disconnect air inlet hose from air pump.
26. Disconnect front brake lines from frame rail and rear brake lines at rear of engine frame.
27. Disconnect A/C pressure sensor.
28. Disconnect A/C suction and discharge lines from compressor and secure to cooling fan.
29. Remove intermediate shaft pinch bolt then remove steering gear from intermediate shaft.
30. Disconnect electrical connector from oxygen sensor.
31. Remove and discard engine oil cooler quick-connect fittings from oil filter adapter with oil lines still attached and position aside. **Quick-connect fittings must be replaced whenever they are removed from adapter.**
32. Remove brace between oil pan and transaxle, then remove torque converter cover.
33. Mark flywheel to torque orientation then remove mounting bolts.
34. Lower vehicle onto engine support tool No. J-39580, four suitable jack stands.
35. Remove righthand side engine mount to engine mount bracket mounting nut.
36. Remove lefthand transaxle mount to transaxle mount bracket mounting nut.
37. Secure front hoist pads to vehicle.
38. Remove six body to frame mounting bolts.
39. Slowly raise vehicle ensuring powertrain and subframe clear all wiring, hoses and lines.
40. Drain engine oil into suitable container.
41. Remove heater pipes.
42. Disconnect intermediate hose from air valve 1 and mounting nut on intermediate hose to air valve 2.
43. Remove coil ground mounting nut from righthand cylinder head.
44. Disconnect engine harness from engine.
45. Disconnect power steering lines from steering pump and reservoir.
46. Remove power steering return line mounting bolt from cylinder head.
47. Remove righthand side engine mount bracket mounting bolts then the bracket.
48. Remove front and rear transaxle braces.
49. Remove engine to transaxle center brace mounting bolts.
50. Install engine lift chain to engine lift brackets and attach to suitable engine lift devise.
51. Remove front engine mount to engine frame mounting nut.
52. remove engine to transaxle mounting bolts.
53. Raise engine from transaxle and subframe.
54. Reverse procedure to install.

OIL PAN
REPLACE

1. Raise and support vehicle.
2. Drain oil into suitable container.
3. Remove catalytic converter to exhaust manifold pipe mounting bolts. Do not reuse seal.
4. Remove exhaust manifold pipe.
5. Disconnect oil level sensor electrical connector, then remove sensor.
6. Remove oil pan mounting bolts, then the pan. Oil pan gasket is reusable unless damaged.
7. Reverse procedure to install. **Torque** oil pan mounting bolts to 89 inch lbs. in sequence, **Fig. 1.**

TIGHTENING SPECIFICATIONS

Year	Component	Torque Ft. Lbs.
2005	Engine Lefthand Bracket To Cylinder Head	35
	Engine Lift Bracket To Water Crossover	17
	Engine Mount	52
	Engine Mount Bracket	37
	Engine To Transaxle	55
	Frame Mounting Bolt	141
	Oil Pan	①
	Transaxle Mount	37

① — Refer to "Oil Pan, Replace" for tightening sequence and specification.

NOTE: On Air Bag Equipped Models, Refer To "Air Bag System Precautions" Located In The Front Of This Manual For System Disarming & Arming Procedures.

NOTE: Refer To "Computer Relearn Procedures" Located In The Front Of This Manual When Battery Power To The Computer Has Been Interrupted.

INDEX

	Page No.		Page No.		Page No.
Ball Joint, Replace	2-20	Description	2-19	Stabilizer Bar, Replace	2-20
Ball Joint Inspection	2-19	Hub & Bearing, Replace	2-19	Strut, Replace	2-19
Coil Spring, Replace	2-19	Disc Brakes	2-19	Tie Rod, Replace	2-20
Control Arm, Replace	2-20	Drum Brakes	2-19	Tightening Specifications	2-21

DESCRIPTION

The rear suspension components include independent control arms, springs, and struts for each rear wheel. This allows vertical movement of one rear wheel without any effect on the other. A suspension adjustment link on each arm provides for toe adjustment and minimal alignment variation during suspension movement. A stabilizer shaft minimizes body roll.

The bottom of each shock absorber mounts to the suspension knuckle. The top of each shock attaches to a reinforced body area. These shocks are non-adjustable and cannot be refilled. Replace any shock absorber if it suffers from loss of resistance, physical damage or fluid leakage.

Some models are equipped with Electronic Level Control (ELC) which utilizes air adjustable shocks and maintains the rear trim height under a variety of load conditions.

A single unit sealed hub and bearing is bolted to the rear knuckle and does not require wheel bearing adjustments or periodic maintenance. There is an integral speed sensor ring on the inboard side of the bearing for anti-lock brake functions. The wheel speed sensor is incorporated within the knuckle.

HUB & BEARING
REPLACE
Drum Brakes

1. Raise and support rear of vehicle.
2. Remove wheel assembly and brake drum. **Do not hammer on drum as bearing damage may occur.**
3. Disconnect ABS sensor wire.
4. Remove four hub and bearing assembly mounting bolts. **These four bolts also support brake assembly. When removing these bolts, support brake assembly with suitable wire. Do not let brake line or ABS electrical wire support weight.**

5. Remove hub and bearing assembly from axle, **Fig. 1.**
6. Reverse procedure to install. Tighten mounting bolts and wheel lug nuts.

Disc Brakes

1. Raise and support rear of vehicle.
2. Remove wheel and tire assembly.
3. Remove caliper and position aside.
4. Remove rotor, then disconnect wheel speed sensor electrical connector.
5. Remove four hub and bearing assembly mounting bolts.
6. Remove hub and bearing assembly, then the brake shield.
7. Clean control arm face and bore to remove any debris.
8. Reverse procedure to install. Tighten mounting bolts and wheel lug nuts.

STRUT
REPLACE

1. Raise and support vehicle, then remove tire and wheel.
2. Support lower control arm with suitable jack stand.
3. Disconnect air line from strut.
4. Remove strut lower mounting bolts, **Fig. 2.**
5. Remove luggage compartment trim to access strut tower mounting nuts, **Fig. 3.**
6. Remove strut tower mounting nuts and upper reinforcement, then the strut from vehicle.
7. Reverse procedure to install. Tighten mounting nuts and wheel lug nuts.

COIL SPRING
REPLACE

1. Raise and support vehicle.
2. Remove rear wheels and tires.
3. Support control arm with suitable jack stand.
4. Disconnect air line from shock.
5. Remove strut to control arm mounting bolts.

6. Remove cotter pin and slotted hex nut from tie rod.
7. Separate tie rod from lower control arm using linkage puller tool No. J24319-B, or equivalent.
8. Slowly lower control arm until it bottoms on support assembly.
9. Pry under lower spring insulator and remove spring with insulator.
10. Remove upper insulator by pulling downward.
11. Reverse procedure to install.

BALL JOINT INSPECTION

The ball joint has a visual wear indicator. Inspecting the condition of the ball joint is a simple procedure but must be followed accurately to prevent unrequired ball joint replacement.

The vehicle must be supported by the wheels during inspection to ensure vehicle weight is properly loading the ball joints.

The ball joint is inspected for wear by visual observation alone. Wear is indicated by retraction of the ½ inch diameter nipple into the ball joint cover (the ball joint grease fitting is threaded into this nipple).

The nipple protrudes .050 inch beyond the surface of the ball joint cover on a new unworn joint. Normal wear will result in the surface of this nipple retracting very slowly inward. The ball joint should be replaced if the nipple is flush or below the cover surface, **Fig. 4.**

Ball stud tightness in the knuckle boss should also be inspected when inspecting the ball joint. This may be done by shaking the wheel and feeling for movement of the stud end or castellated nut at the knuckle boss.

Inspecting the fastener tightness at the castellated nut is an alternative method of inspecting (a loose nut can indicate a bent stud or an "opened up" hole in the knuckle boss). If worn, the ball joint and knuckle must be replaced.

If the ball joint is separated from the knuckle for suspension service, the ball

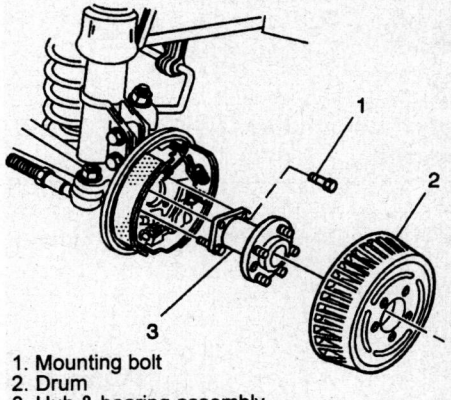

1. Mounting bolt
2. Drum
3. Hub & bearing assembly

GC2030100162000X

Fig. 1 Hub & bearing assembly

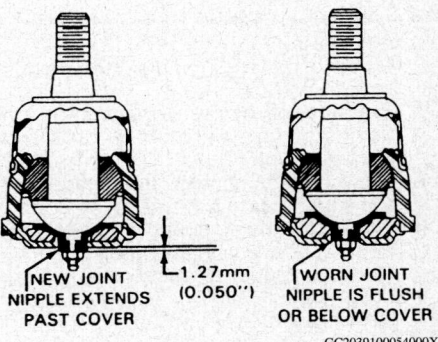

NEW JOINT NIPPLE EXTENDS PAST COVER

1.27mm (0.050")

WORN JOINT NIPPLE IS FLUSH OR BELOW COVER

GC2039100054000X

Fig. 4 Ball joint inspection

joint seal should be inspected for damage. A damaged seal will cause joint failure. If seal damage is found the ball joint should be replaced.

BALL JOINT
REPLACE

The ball joint cannot be serviced separately, refer to "Control Arm, Replace" for replacement procedure.

CONTROL ARM
REPLACE

1. Raise and support vehicle, then remove tires and wheels.
2. Remove exhaust system as required.
3. Remove coil springs as outlined under "Coil Spring, Replace."
4. Remove rear brake calipers from control arms, then parking brake cables from calipers.
5. Disconnect electrical connectors from wiring harness.
6. Disconnect Electronic Level Control (ELC) electrical connector and vent hose.

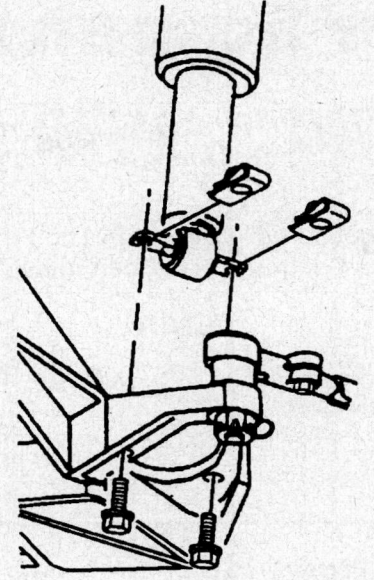

GC2030100163000X

Fig. 2 Rear strut lower mounting

7. Remove ELC air tube from compressor.
8. Support rear suspension support assembly with suitable jack.
9. Remove three bolts per side securing support assembly brackets to vehicle body, **Fig. 5.**
10. Remove front and rear suspension support assembly bolts, then support assembly.
11. On lefthand control arm, remove Electronic Level Control height sensor.
12. Remove stabilizer link bolts and nuts.
13. Remove ABS electrical connectors.
14. Remove hub and bearing as outlined under "Hub & Bearing, Replace."
15. Remove bolt and nut securing control arm to rear suspension support assembly, then the control arm.
16. Reverse procedure to install.

TIE ROD
REPLACE

1. Raise and support vehicle.
2. Remove wheel assembly, cotter key and castle nut, **Fig. 6.**
3. Disconnect outer tie rod/adjustment from lower control arm or knuckle using steering linkage puller tool No. J24319-01, or equivalent. **Do not use wedge when disconnecting tie rod/adjustment from lower control arm or knuckle.**
4. Remove rod/link assembly from lower control arm.
5. Reverse procedure to install, noting the following:
   a. Tighten link mounting nut.
   b. Tighten ball stud castellated nut.
   c. Install cotter pin retaining castellat-

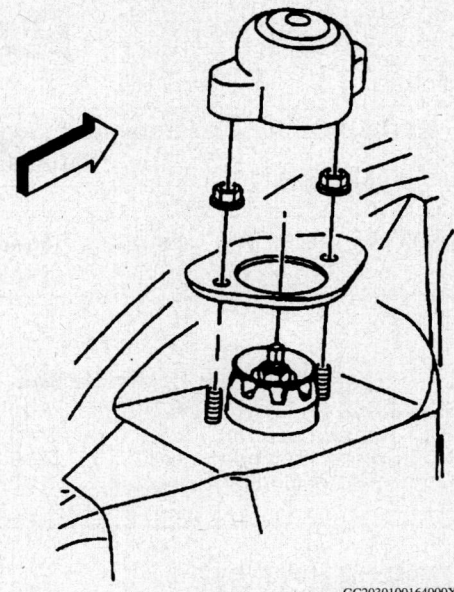

GC2030100164000X

Fig. 3 Strut tower mounting nuts

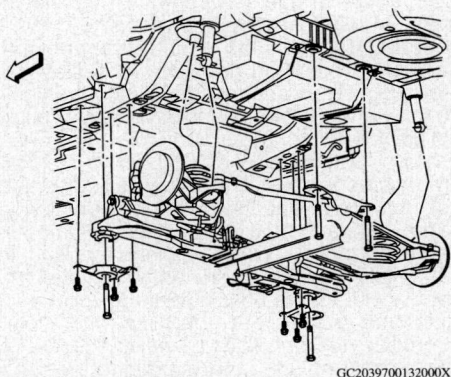

GC2039700132000X

Fig. 5 Rear suspension support assembly removal

ed nut, tightening nut to insert pin through hole in stud. **Do not loosen nut to align slots with hole.**

STABILIZER BAR
REPLACE

1. Raise and support vehicle.
2. Remove rear wheels and tires.
3. Disconnect ELC height sensor link from control arm.
4. Remove stabilizer shaft support bolt, nut, retainer, sleeve and insulators from lower control arm or knuckle bracket, **Fig. 7.**
5. Remove bushing clip bolt.
6. Bend open end of support assembly downward.
7. Remove stabilizer shaft and bushings.
8. Reverse procedure to install.

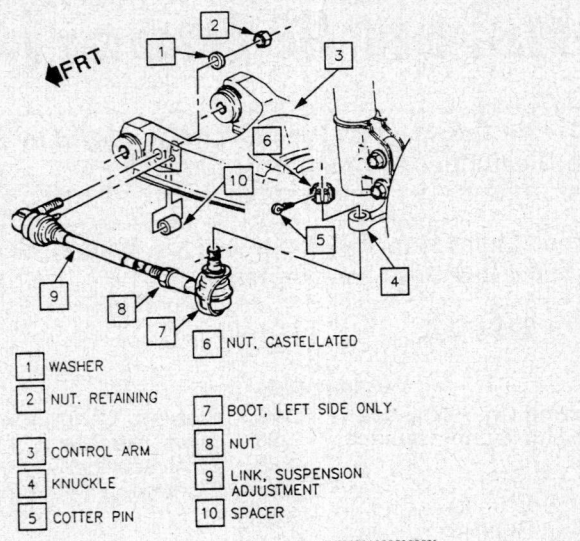

Fig. 6 Tie rod/adjustment link installation

1 WASHER
2 NUT, RETAINING
3 CONTROL ARM
4 KNUCKLE
5 COTTER PIN
6 NUT, CASTELLATED
7 BOOT, LEFT SIDE ONLY
8 NUT
9 LINK, SUSPENSION ADJUSTMENT
10 SPACER

GC2039100053000X

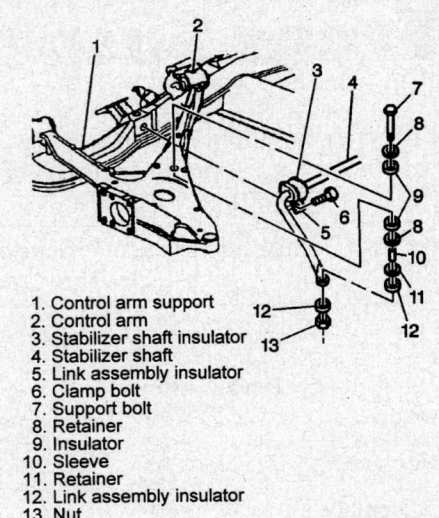

1. Control arm support
2. Control arm
3. Stabilizer shaft insulator
4. Stabilizer shaft
5. Link assembly insulator
6. Clamp bolt
7. Support bolt
8. Retainer
9. Insulator
10. Sleeve
11. Retainer
12. Link assembly insulator
13. Nut

GC2030100165000X

Fig. 7 Stabilizer bar & bushing assembly

TIGHTENING SPECIFICATIONS

Year	Component	Torque Ft. Lbs.
BONNEVILLE & LESABRE		
2004–05	Adjustment Link Pinch Bolt	38
	Adjustment Link To Suspension Support	67
	Control Arm Nuts	78
	Hub & Bearing Bolts	52
	Rear Body Mount Bolts	38
	Rear Suspension Support To Body Front Bolts	141
	Rear Suspension Support To Body Rear Bolts	191
	Stabilizer Shaft Clamp Bolt	24
	Stabilizer Shaft Link Nut	11
	Strut To Control Arm Bolts	18
	Strut Tower Mounting Nut	15
	Wheel Lug Nuts	100
PARK AVENUE		
2004–05	Adjustment Link Pinch Bolt	36
	Adjustment Link mounting bolt	67
	Body Mount Bolt	38
	Control Arm Nut	78
	Hub Mounting Bolts	52
	Shock To Control Arm Bolts	18
	Shock Tower Mounting Nut	15
	Stabilizer Shaft Clamp Bolt	24
	Stabilizer Shaft Link Bolt	10
	Suspension Support Assembly To Body Front Bolts	141
	Suspension Support Assembly To Body Rear Bolts	141
	Suspension Support Assembly To Bracket Bolts	63
	Tie Rod Pinch Bolt	36
	Wheel Lug Nuts	100

BONNEVILLE, LeSABRE & PARK AVENUE
Front Suspension & Steering

NOTE: On Air Bag Equipped Models, Refer To "Air Bag System Precautions" Located In The Front Of This Manual For System Disarming & Arming Procedures.

NOTE: Refer To "Computer Relearn Procedures" Located In The Front Of This Manual When Battery Power To The Computer Has Been Interrupted.

INDEX

	Page No.
Ball Joint, Replace	2-22
Ball Joint Inspection	2-22
Control Arm, Replace	2-23
Description	2-22
Hub & Bearing, Replace	2-22
Power Steering	21-1
Power Steering Gear, Replace	2-23
Power Steering Pump, Replace	2-23
Precautions	2-22
Air Bag Systems	2-22
Battery Ground Cable	2-22
Stabilizer Bar, Replace	2-23
Steering Columns	20-1
Strut, Replace	2-22
Strut Service	2-22
Tightening Specifications	2-26

PRECAUTIONS

Air Bag Systems

Refer to "Air Bag System Precautions" in the front of this manual for system disarming and arming procedures.

Battery Ground Cable

Prior to service, disconnect battery ground cable and isolate as required.

DESCRIPTION

The front suspension is of the McPherson design. The control arm pivots from the cradle and is mounted in rubber bushings. The upper end of the strut is isolated by a rubber mount and contains a bearing to allow for rotation. The lower end of the steering knuckle pivots on a ball joint riveted to the control arm. The ball joint is mounted to the steering knuckle with a castle nut and cotter pin. **Do not use a hammer to remove components from the steering knuckle.**

HUB & BEARING
REPLACE

1. Place transaxle selector lever in Park.
2. Raise and support vehicle, then remove tire and wheel assembly.
3. Clean and lubricate drive axle threads.
4. Insert a suitable drift into caliper and rotor to prevent assembly from rotating, then remove hub nut and washer. Discard hub nut.
5. Remove caliper bracket mounting bolts, caliper and bracket assembly and rotor. Secure assembly aside taking care not to stretch or damage brake hose.
6. Disconnect ABS front wheel speed sensor connector and unclip connector from dust shield.
7. Remove hub and bearing mounting bolts and dust shield, **Fig. 1.**
8. Separate hub and bearing from drive axle using front hub spindle removal tool No. J28733-B, or equivalent, **Fig. 2.**
9. Clean face and bore of knuckle to remove any debris before assembly.
10. Reverse procedure to install, noting the following:
    a. Fill area between seal and bearing assembly with GM lubricant part No. 12377985, or equivalent.
    b. **Do not use old hub nut. Always install a new one.**

BALL JOINT INSPECTION

Ball joints must be replaced if any looseness is detected or ball joint seal is cut or damaged.

To inspect ball joints, raise the front of the vehicle, allowing suspension to hang freely. Grasp the tire at the top and bottom, then move the top of the tire in an in-and-out motion. Inspect for any horizontal movement of the knuckle relative to the control arm. If the ball stud is disconnected from the knuckle and looseness is detected or if the ball stud can be twisted using finger pressure, replace the ball joint.

Ball stud tightness in the knuckle boss should also be inspected. This may be done by shaking the wheel and feeling for movement of the stud end or nut at the knuckle boss. Worn or damaged ball joints and knuckles must be replaced.

BALL JOINT
REPLACE

The ball joint is serviced only with the control arm and cannot be serviced separately. Refer to "Control Arm, Replace" for replacement procedure.

STRUT
REPLACE

1. **On models equipped with CCR,** disconnect CCR connector.
2. **On all models,** remove three strut mount to body bolts or nuts.
3. Raise and support vehicle.
4. Remove wheel and tire.
5. Remove ABS front wheel speed sensor connector.
6. Remove speed sensor bracket from strut.
7. Remove brake line bracket from strut.
8. Retain knuckle in position to prevent damage to ball joint and/or drive axle.
9. Remove strut to knuckle bolts.
10. Remove strut from vehicle.
11. Reverse procedure to install. Avoid cracking or chipping spring coating when handling front suspension coil spring.

STRUT SERVICE

1. Remove strut as outlined under "Strut, Replace."
2. Mount strut in compressor tool No. J34013-B and holding fixture tool No. J3289-20, or equivalents, **Fig. 3.**
3. Rotate compressor forcing screw until spring compresses slightly, **Fig. 4.**
4. Hold damper shaft from rotating and remove nut from top of strut assembly, **Fig. 5.**
5. Guide damper shaft from assembly using alignment rod tool No. J34013-38, or equivalent, **Fig. 6.**
6. Loosen compressor forcing screw while guiding damper shaft from assembly. Continue to loosen nut until strut damper and spring can be removed.
7. Reverse procedure to assemble, noting the following:
   a. When assembling spring, flat on upper spring seat must face outward 90° from centerline of vehicle or when mounted in strut compressor.

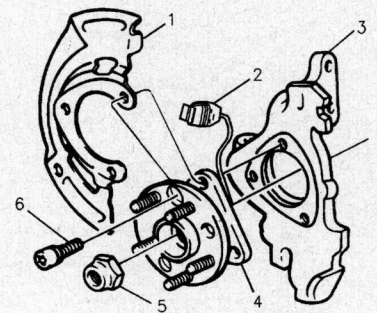

1 DUST SHIELD
2 WHEEL SPEED SENSOR CONNECTOR
3 STEERING KNUCKLE
4 HUB AND BEARING
5 NUT, DRIVE AXLE
6 RETAINING BOLT

GC2029300228000X

Fig. 1 Hub & bearing assembly

b. Seat faces in same direction as steering knuckle mounting flange.

CONTROL ARM
REPLACE

1. Raise and support vehicle.
2. Remove wheel and tire.
3. Disconnect stabilizer link to control arm bolt, **Figs. 7 and 8.**
4. Remove cotter pin and loosen nut from ball joint stud.
5. Remove ball joint from steering knuckle using a suitable ball joint separator tool.
6. Remove control arm mounting bolts, then the control arm from the frame, **Figs. 9 and 10.**
7. Reverse procedure to install, noting the following:
   a. Install control arm to frame and loosely install mounting bolts, washers and nuts. **Do not tighten control arm nuts at this time.** Weight of vehicle must be supported by control arms so that vehicle design trim heights are obtained before tightening control arm mounting bolts.
   b. Install all remaining control arm hardware, then lower vehicle to ground.
   c. Inspect trim height.
   d. Tighten control arm nuts.

STABILIZER BAR
REPLACE

1. Raise and support vehicle and place jack stands under cradle. **Vehicle weight should not be placed on control arms.**
2. Remove wheel and tire assembly.
3. Install drive axle boot protectors.
4. Remove nuts, washers, bushings and

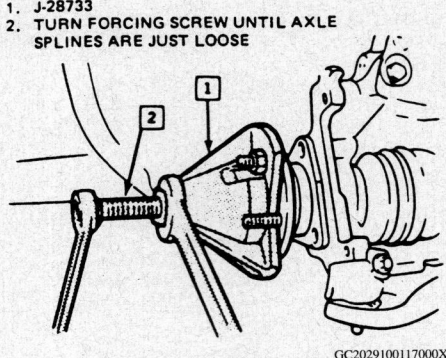

1. J-28733
2. TURN FORCING SCREW UNTIL AXLE SPLINES ARE JUST LOOSE

GC2029100117000X

Fig. 2 Separating drive axle from hub

bolt securing stabilizer shaft to each control arm, **Fig. 11.**
5. Remove stabilizer bar mounting bolts, two bolts from each side.
6. Disconnect tie rods from steering knuckles.
7. Remove exhaust pipe between exhaust manifold and catalytic converter.
8. Rotate righthand side strut assembly completely to left.
9. Slide stabilizer bar to righthand over steering knuckle and pull downward on lefthand side until stabilizer bar clears cradle, **Fig. 12.**
10. Reverse procedure to install.

POWER STEERING GEAR
REPLACE

1. Ensure front wheels are in straight-ahead position.
2. Lock steering column using lock pin tool No. J42640, or equivalent, **Fig. 13.**
3. Raise and support vehicle with weight resting on suspension.
4. Remove front tire and wheel assemblies.
5. Remove steering gear heat shield.
6. Disconnect intermediate shaft from steering gear stub shaft.
7. Disconnect both tie rod ends from steering knuckles using separator tool No. J24319-B, or equivalent.
8. Remove line retainers and disconnect hydraulic lines from steering gear.
9. Disconnect speed sensitive steering electrical connectors from steering gear.
10. Remove steering gear mounting bolts, **Fig. 14.**
11. Remove steering gear from vehicle by sliding out of side.
12. Reverse procedure to install.

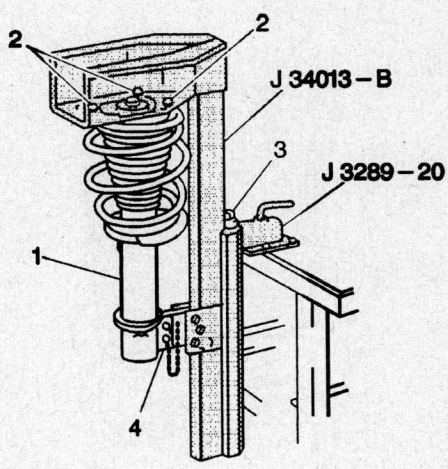

1. Strut
2. Nuts
3. Strut compressor
4. Locking pins

GC2020100304000X

Fig. 3 Strut disassembly

POWER STEERING PUMP
REPLACE

1. Remove air cleaner if required.
2. Mark running direction with suitable felt pen or chalk, then remove accessory drive belt.
3. Raise and support vehicle.
4. Position a suitable drain pan under power steering fluid lines at pump.
5. Disconnect fluid lines and electrical connectors from pump.
6. If required, disconnect righthand outer tie rod end from steering knuckle using tie rod removal tool No. J24319-B, or equivalent.
7. **On Park Avenue models,** remove pump mounting bolts, then the pump from underneath vehicle.
8. **On all models,** lower vehicle.
9. **On Bonneville and LeSabre models,** remove pump mounting bolts, then the power steering pump.
10. **On all models,** reverse procedure to install, noting the following:
    a. If new pump does not include pulley, remove pulley from old pump using removal tool No. J25034-C, or equivalent, then install onto new pump using installer tool No. J25033-C, or equivalent. Ensure axial tolerance on pump shaft meets specifications, **Fig. 15.**
    b. Ensure all electrical connectors and wiring are properly routed to avoid pinching.
    c. Fill and bleed power steering system.

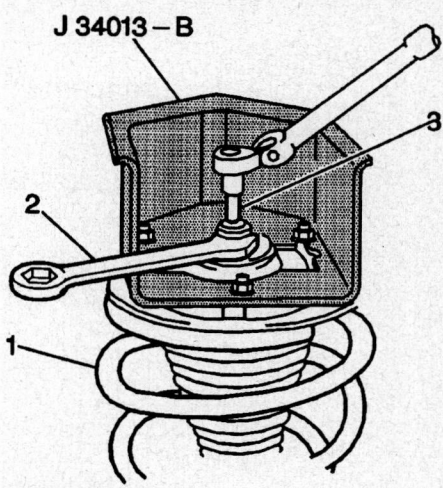

1. Coil spring
2. 24 MM wrench
3. Driver tool

GC2020100305000X

Fig. 4   Coil spring compression

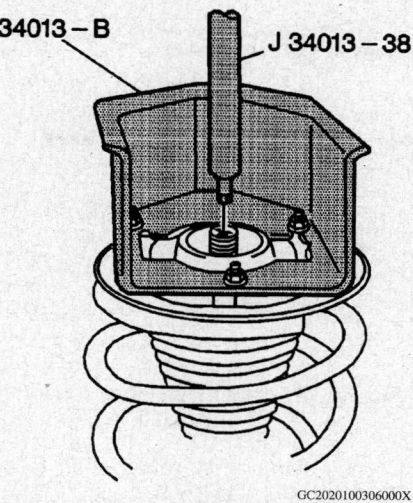

GC2020100306000X

Fig. 5   Strut shaft nut removal

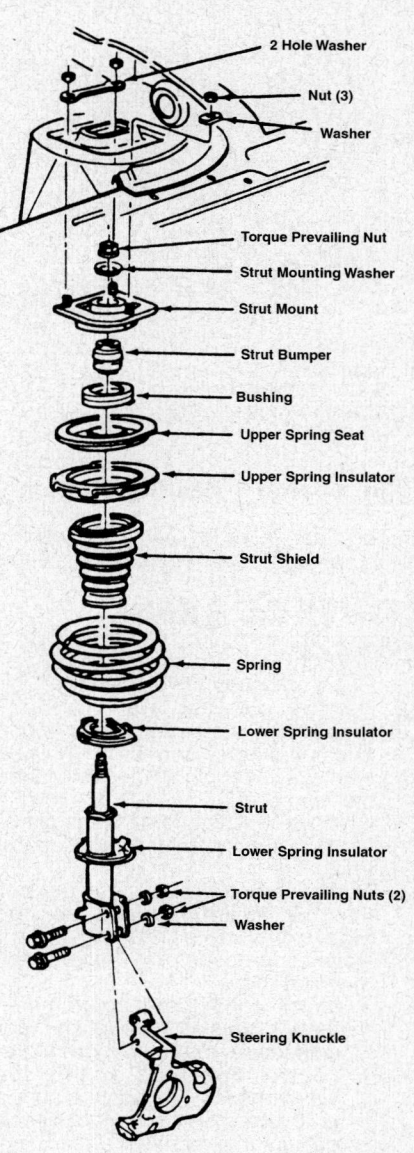

2 Hole Washer
Nut (3)
Washer
Torque Prevailing Nut
Strut Mounting Washer
Strut Mount
Strut Bumper
Bushing
Upper Spring Seat
Upper Spring Insulator
Strut Shield
Spring
Lower Spring Insulator
Strut
Lower Spring Insulator
Torque Prevailing Nuts (2)
Washer
Steering Knuckle

GC2029100127000X

Fig. 6   Exploded view of strut assembly

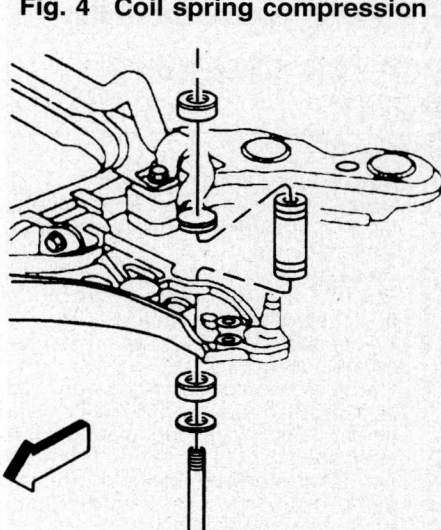

GC2029900261000X

Fig. 7   Stabilizer link to control arm bolt. Park Avenue

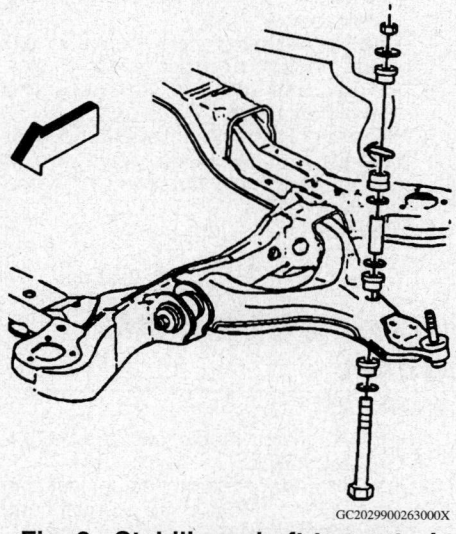

GC2029900263000X

Fig. 8   Stabilizer shaft to control arm bolt. Bonneville & LeSabre

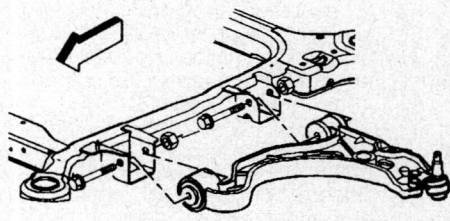

GC2029900262000X

Fig. 9   Lower control arm replacement. Park Avenue

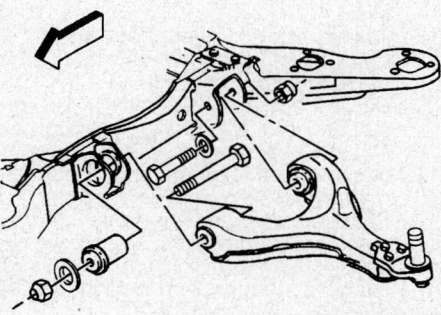

GC2029900264000X

Fig. 10   Lower control arm replacement. Bonneville & LeSabre

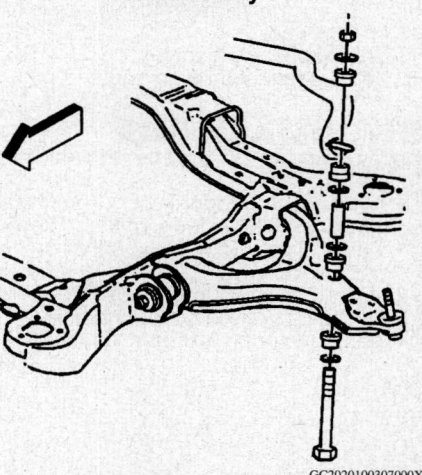

GC2020100307000X

Fig. 11   Stabilizer bar bushing assembly

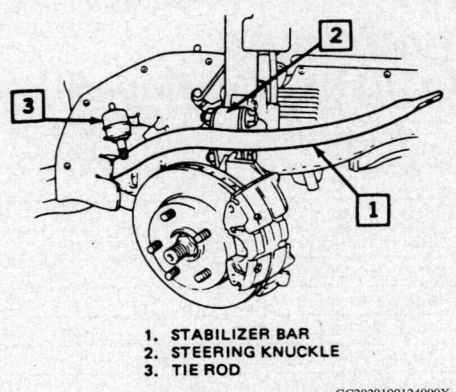

1. STABILIZER BAR
2. STEERING KNUCKLE
3. TIE ROD

GC2029100124000X

Fig. 12 Stabilizer bar replacement

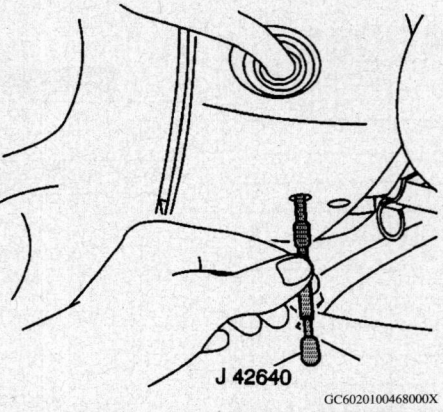

J 42640

GC6020100468000X

Fig. 13 Steering column locked in straight-ahead position

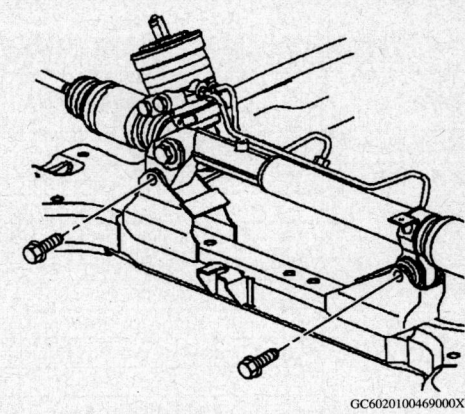

GC60201004690000X

Fig. 14 Steering gear replacement

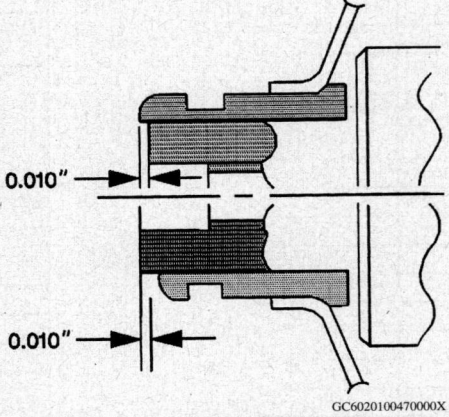

0.010"

0.010"

GC6020100470000X

Fig. 15 Power steering pump pulley axial installation

TIGHTENING SPECIFICATIONS

Year	Component	Torque Ft. Lbs.
BONNEVILLE & LESABRE		
2004–05	Ball Joint To Knuckle	50
	Brake Bracket To Strut	13
	Brake Caliper To Knuckle	38
	Brake Caliper Bracket To Knuckle	136
	Control Arm Bolts	117
	Control Arm Front Nut	93
	Cross Brace Assembly Through-Bolts	27
	Drive Axle Nut	118
	Hub And Bearing To Knuckle	70
	Inner Tie Rod	74
	Intermediate Shaft Pinch Bolt	33
	Power Steering Gear Hose Fittings To Pump And Steering Gear	20
	Power Steering Gear Mounting Bolts	48
	Power Steering Inlet/Outlet Hose Retainer Bolts	53①
	Power Steering Outer Hose Retaining Clamp Nuts	15
	Power Steering Pump Mounting Bolts	20
	Rack And Pinion Adjuster Plug Nut	50
	Rack And Pinion Cylinder End Fittings	20
	Stabilizer Shaft Bracket Bolt	35
	Stabilizer Shaft Link Nut	13
	Strut Mount Nut	55
	Strut Mount To Body Nuts	35
	Strut To Knuckle Nuts	136
	Tie Rod Locknut	50
	Tie Rod To Knuckle Castle Nut	35–52
	Wheel Speed Sensor Bracket To Strut	13
	Wheel Lug Nut	100

TIGHTENING SPECIFICATIONS—Continued

Year	Component	Torque Ft. Lbs.
PARK AVENUE		
2004–05	Ball Joint Mounting Nuts	50
	Ball Joint To Knuckle	50
	Brake Bracket To Strut	13
	Brake Caliper To Knuckle	38
	Control Arm Front Nut	93
	Control Arm Rear Bolt	117
	Cross Brace Assembly Through-Bolts	27
	Drive Axle Nut	107
	Hub & Bearing To Knuckle	70
	Intermediate Steering Shaft Pinch Bolt	35
	Outer Tie Rod mounting nut	55
	Power Steering Gear Hose Fittings To Pump & Steering Gear	20
	Power Steering Inlet/Outlet Hose Retainer Bolts	53①
	Power Steering Outer Hose Retaining Clamp Nuts	15
	Power Steering Pump Mounting Bolts	20
	Stabilizer Shaft Bracket Bolt	35
	Stabilizer Shaft Link Bolt	11
	Stabilizer Shaft Link Nut (2000)	13
	Steering Gear Mounting Bolts	48
	Strut Mount Nut	55
	Strut Mount To Body Nuts	35
	Strut To Knuckle Nuts	136
	Tie Rod End To Knuckle Nut	35
	Wheel Lug Nuts	100
	Wheel Speed Sensor Bracket To Strut	13

① — Inch lbs.

Wheel Alignment

INDEX

	Page No.		Page No.		Page No.
Front Wheel Alignment	2-27	Precautions	2-27	Camber	2-27
Camber	2-27	Air Bag Systems	2-27	Toe	2-27
Caster	2-27	Preliminary Inspection	2-27	Wheel Alignment	
Toe	2-27	Rear Wheel Alignment	2-27	Specifications	2-3

PRECAUTIONS

Air Bag Systems

Refer to "Air Bag System Precautions" in the front of this manual for system disarming and arming procedures.

PRELIMINARY INSPECTION

1. Inspect tires for proper inflation and similar tread wear.
2. Inspect hub and bearing for excessive wear. Repair as required.
3. Inspect ball joints and tie rod ends for excessive looseness.
4. Measure wheel and tire runout.
5. Inspect vehicle ride height.
6. Inspect rack and pinion for looseness at frame.
7. Ensure proper strut operation.
8. Inspect control arm bushings.
9. Inspect stabilizer shaft for loose or missing components.
10. Inspect suspension and steering components for damage. Replace as required.

FRONT WHEEL ALIGNMENT

Caster

1. Loosen cross brace assembly through-bolts, **Fig. 1.**
2. Remove inboard strut nuts, then the brace assembly.
3. Remove remaining nut over oval strut mounting hole.
4. Lift front of vehicle by body to separate strut from inner wheelhouse.

5. Remove two guide pins and file to make slotted holes.
6. File excess metal to elongate original holes, then paint exposed metal with primer.
7. Lower front of vehicle.
8. Place cross brace assembly on inboard strut studs and install strut mounting nuts.
9. Set caster to specifications by moving top of strut forward or backward. A .040 inch position change at the tower is approximately equal to a .1° caster change.
10. Tighten strut mounting nuts and cross brace bar through-bolts.

Camber

1. Loosen both strut to knuckle mounting nuts.
2. Install camber adjusting tool No. J39601, or equivalent, **Fig. 2.**
3. Inspect camber, and if it does not meet specifications, proceed as follows:
   a. Raise and support vehicle, then remove tire and wheel.
   b. Drive upper and lower bolt and nut out of strut and knuckle. **Do not turn bolts.**
   c. Separate strut from knuckle.
   d. File inner metal plate to outside plate diameter using a suitable round file or die grinder.
   e. File excess metal to create slotted holes.
   f. Paint exposed metal with suitable rust preventive paint or primer.
   g. Connect strut to knuckle. **Do not tighten bolts now.**
   h. Install camber adjusting tool No. J39601, or equivalent, to bottom strut bolt.
   i. Tighten upper strut to knuckle nut.
   j. Remove adjusting tool, then tighten

lower strut to knuckle mounting nuts.
   k. Inspect camber once again. Adjust as required.

Toe

1. Loosen locknuts on both inner tie rods, **Fig. 3.**
2. Adjust toe to specifications by rotating inner tie rod.
3. Tighten locknuts.
4. Inspect toe setting once again. Adjust as required.

REAR WHEEL ALIGNMENT

When inspecting rear wheel alignment, the electronic leveling system must have the superlift struts inflated with residual pressure only.

Place a weight in luggage compartment. Turn ignition On and move transmission selector from Park to Reverse position and back. This will activate the compressor. Turn ignition Off and remove weight from luggage compartment. Wait 30 seconds for the system to exhaust. Roll vehicle forward one complete wheel rotation. Jounce vehicle before inspecting alignment.

Camber

Rear camber is not adjustable. If rear camber does not meet specifications inspect for worn or damaged suspension components and replace as required.

Toe

Toe adjustment is made by loosening the locknut at tie rod end and turning inner tie rod to set toe to specifications.

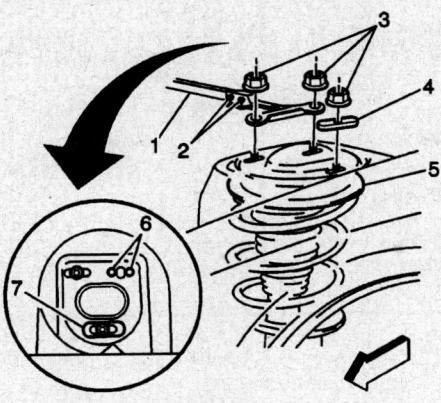

1. Strut housing tie bar
2. Through bolts
3. Nuts
4. Washers
5. Strut
6. New drilled holes
7. Washers

GC2040100169000X

Fig. 1 Cross brace removal

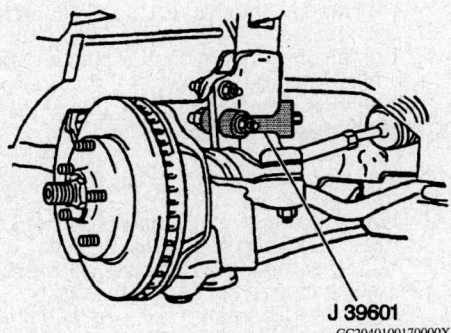

J 39601
GC2040100170000X

Fig. 2 Camber adjustment tool installation

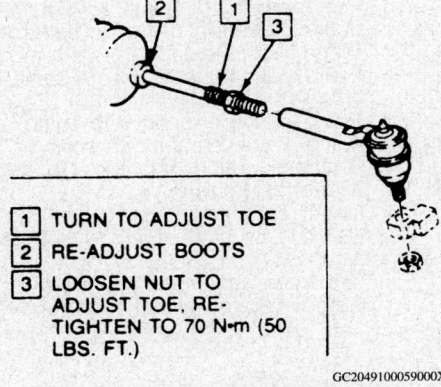

1	TURN TO ADJUST TOE
2	RE-ADJUST BOOTS
3	LOOSEN NUT TO ADJUST TOE, RE-TIGHTEN TO 70 N·m (50 LBS. FT.)

GC2049100059000X

Fig. 3 Toe adjustment

GTO

INDEX OF SERVICE OPERATIONS

Page No.

**AIR BAG SYSTEM
PRECAUTIONS** 0-18
BRAKES
  Anti-Lock Brakes (Volume 2).. 6-1
  Disc Brakes................... 22-1
  Drum Brakes 23-1
  Hydraulic Brake Systems 24-1
  Power Brake Units........... 25-1
**COMPUTER RELEARN
PROCEDURE** 0-31
ELECTRICAL
  Air Bag System (Volume 2) ... 4-1
  Air Conditioning................ 16-1
  Alternator, Replace 3-4
  Alternators.................... 19-1
  Blower Motor, Replace........ 3-8
  Clutch Start Switch, Replace.. 3-5
  Coil Pack, Replace 3-5
  Cooling Fans 17-1
  Cruise Control (Volume 2) 2-1
  Dash Gauges (Volume 2) 1-1
  Dash Panel Service
  (Volume 2)................... 5-1
  Dimmer Switch, Replace...... 3-6
  Evaporator Core, Replace 3-8
  Fuel Pump Relay Location.... 3-4
  Fuse Panel Location.......... 3-4
  Headlamp Switch, Replace ... 3-6
  Heater Core, Replace......... 3-8
  Ignition Lock, Replace 3-5
  Ignition Switch, Replace 3-5
  Instrument Cluster, Replace... 3-7
  Multi-Function Switch,
  Replace 3-6
  Neutral Safety Switch,
  Replace 3-5
  Passive Restraint Systems
  (Volume 2) 4-1
  Precautions 3-4
  Radio, Replace 3-7
  Speed Controls (Volume 2) ... 2-1
  Starter Motors 18-1
  Starter, Replace 3-4
  Steering Columns............. 20-1
  Steering Wheel, Replace...... 3-6
  Stop Light Switch, Replace ... 3-6
  Turn Signal Switch, Replace .. 3-6
  Wiper Motor, Replace......... 3-7
  Wiper Switch, Replace........ 3-7
  Wiper Systems (Volume 2).... 3-1
  Wiper Transmission, Replace . 3-8
**ELECTRICAL SYMBOL
IDENTIFICATION** 0-63

Page No.

**FRONT SUSPENSION &
STEERING**
  Coil Spring, Replace 3-29
  Control Arm, Replace 3-30
  Description 3-29
  Power Steering 21-1
  Power Steering Gear,
  Replace 3-31
  Power Steering Pump,
  Replace 3-32
  Power Steering System
  Bleed....................... 3-32
  Precautions................. 3-29
  Stabilizer Bar, Replace 3-31
  Stabilizer Link, Replace 3-31
  Steering Columns............. 20-1
  Steering Knuckle, Replace 3-30
  Strut, Replace 3-29
  Strut Service................. 3-30
  Technical Service Bulletins.... 3-32
  Tie Rod End, Replace 3-31
  Tightening Specifications...... 3-33
**NON-STANDARD TIRE &
WHEEL SIZE
ADJUSTMENT TO RIDE
HEIGHT SPECIFICATIONS
& TIRE SIZE CHART** 0-61
**REAR AXLE &
SUSPENSION**
  Adjustment Link, Replace 3-27
  Coil Spring, Replace 3-25
  Control Arm, Replace 3-26
  Description 3-22
  Differential Carrier, Replace... 3-22
  Hub & Bearing, Replace 3-24
  Precautions.................. 3-22
  Propeller Shaft, Replace 3-23
  Rear Axle Shaft, Replace 3-22
  Rear Wheel Shaft, Replace ... 3-22
  Shock Absorber, Replace 3-25
  Stabilizer Shaft, Replace 3-26
  Technical Service Bulletins.... 3-27
  Tightening Specifications...... 3-28
  U-joint, Replace.............. 3-23
REAR DRIVE AXLE 27-1
SPECIFICATIONS
  Fluid Capacities & Cooling
  System Data................. 3-3
  Front Wheel Alignment
  Specifications................ 3-2
  General Engine
  Specifications................ 3-2
  Lubricant Data............... 3-3
  Rear Wheel Alignment
  Specifications................ 3-2
  Tune Up Specifications 3-2
  Vehicle Ride Height
  Specifications................ 3-2

Page No.

**SERVICE REMINDER &
WARNING LAMP RESET
PROCEDURES** 0-34
**VEHICLE
IDENTIFICATION** 0-1
VEHICLE LIFT POINTS 0-51
**VEHICLE MAINTENANCE
SCHEDULES** 0-73
WHEEL ALIGNMENT
  Front Wheel Alignment........ 3-34
  Preliminary Inspection 3-34
  Rear Wheel Alignment 3-35
  Vehicle Ride Height........... 3-35
  Wheel Alignment
  Specifications 3-2
**WIRE COLOR CODE
IDENTIFICATION** 0-63
5.7L ENGINE
  Cooling System Bleed 3-13
  Cylinder Head, Replace 3-11
  Engine Rebuilding
  Specifications................. 29-1
  Engine, Replace 3-9
  Engine Mount, Replace 3-9
  Exhaust Manifold, Replace 3-10
  Fuel Filter, Replace 3-14
  Fuel Pump, Replace 3-13
  Precautions 3-9
  Radiator, Replace............. 3-13
  Serpentine Drive Belt 3-12
  Thermostat, Replace 3-13
  Tightening Specifications...... 3-15
  Valve Cover, Replace 3-12
  Water Pump, Replace 3-13
6.0L ENGINE
  Compression Pressure........ 3-16
  Cooling System Bleed 3-19
  Cylinder Head, Replace....... 3-18
  Engine Rebuilding
  Specifications................. 29-1
  Engine, Replace 3-16
  Engine Mount, Replace 3-16
  Exhaust Manifold, Replace.... 3-17
  Fuel Filter, Replace 3-20
  Fuel Pump, Replace 3-19
  Intake Manifold, Replace 3-17
  Precautions.................. 3-16
  Radiator, Replace............. 3-19
  Serpentine Drive Belt 3-19
  Thermostat, Replace 3-19
  Tightening Specifications...... 3-21
  Valve Cover, Replace 3-18
  Water Pump, Replace 3-19

Specifications

GENERAL ENGINE SPECIFICATIONS

Year	Engine		Fuel System	Bore & Stroke	Comp-ression Ratio	Net Brake H.P. @ RPM②	Maximum Torque, Ft. Lbs @ RPM	Normal Oil Pressure psi
	Liter	VIN Code①						
2004	5.7L	G	SFI	3.897 x 3.898	10:1	350 @ 5200	365 @ 4000	③
2005–08	6.0L	U	SFI	4.00 x 3.62	10.9	400 @ 6000	400 @ 4400	④

SFI — Sequential Fuel Injection
VIN — Vehicle Identification Number
① — The eighth digit of the VIN denotes engine code.

② — Ratings are net, as installed in vehicle.
③ — 6 psi @ 1000 RPM; 18 psi @ 2000 RPM; 24 psi @ 4000 RPM.

④ — Engine hot, minimum oil pressure @ 1000 RPM, 6 psi.; @ 2000 RPM, 18 psi.; @ 4000 RPM, 24 psi.

TUNE UP SPECIFICATIONS

Year	Engine	Spark Plug Gap	Ignition Timing, Degrees BTDC			Curb Idle Speed③		Fast Idle Speed		Fuel Pump Pressure psi	Valve Clearance Inch
			Firing Order	Manual Trans.	Automatic. Trans.	Mark	Manual Trans.	Automatic. Trans.	Manual Trans.	Automatic. Trans.		
2004	5.7L	.060	1-8-7-2-6-5-4-3	①	①	—	④	④	④	④	55–61⑤	②
2005–08	6.0L	.04	1-8-7-2-6-5-4-3	①	①	—	④	④	④	④	55–61⑤	②

BTDC — Before Top Dead Center
VIN — Vehicle Identification Number
① — Computer controlled. No adjustment.
② — Equipped w/hydraulic lifters. No adjustment is required.

③ — When inspecting idle speed, set parking brake & block drive wheels.
④ — Idle speed is controlled by an idle speed control motor.
⑤ — With shop towel wrapped around

fuel pressure fitting to prevent fuel spillage, connect a suitable fuel pressure gauge. Inspect fuel pressure with ignition On, but engine not running.

FRONT WHEEL ALIGNMENT SPECIFICATIONS

Year	Caster Angle°		Camber Angle°		Toe Per Wheel°		Steering Wheel Angle°		Ball Joint Wear
	Limits	Desired	Limits	Desired	Limits	Desired	Limits	Desired	
2004–08	+6.50 to +9.00	+7.75	-.70 to +.30	-.20	0 to +.34	.17	-3.50 to +3.50	0	—

REAR WHEEL ALIGNMENT SPECIFICATIONS

Year	Camber Angle°		Toe Per Wheel°		Thrust Angle°	
	Limits	Desired	Limits	Desired	Limits	Desired
2004–08	-.41 to -1.68	-1.05	-.06 to -.74	+.4	-.17 to +.17	0

VEHICLE RIDE HEIGHT SPECIFICATIONS

Model	Year	Body Style	Manufacturer's Original Tire Size	Measurement Points & Specifications②					
				Front			Rear		
				Dim.	Spec.		Dim.	Spec.	
					Inches	mm		Inches	mm
GTO	2004–08	Coupe	①	Z	.8–1.6	21–41	D	1.6–2.4	41–61

Dim. — Dimension
D Dim. — Measurement Of Vertical Distance From The Bottom Of The Outer Adjustment Link (2) To The Center Line Of The

Inner Adjustment Link Pivot Bolt (1), **Fig. A.**
Z Dim. — Measurement Of Vertical Distance From The Bottom Of The Control Arm (2), Below

The Ball Joint, To The Center Line Of The Control Arm Pivot Bolt (1), **Fig. B.**

① — See door sticker or inside of glove box for manufacturers original tire size specifications. If tires on vehicle do not match manufacturers original tire size & measurement is not within limits, it will be required to refer to the Non-Standard Tire & Wheel Size Adjustment To Ride Height Specification & Tire Size Adjustment Charts in the front of this manual for approximate changes in ride height specifications.

② — Measurement is with fuel, radiator coolant and engine oil full, spare tire, jack, hand tools and mats in designated positions and tires properly inflated.

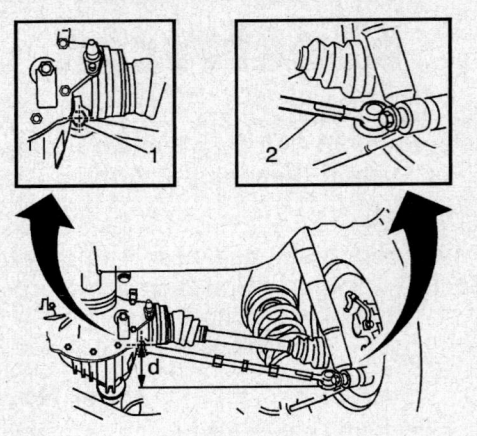

1. Center Line Of Inner Adjustment Link Pivot Bolt
2. Bottom Of Outer Adjustment Link

ARM0400000001022

Fig. A

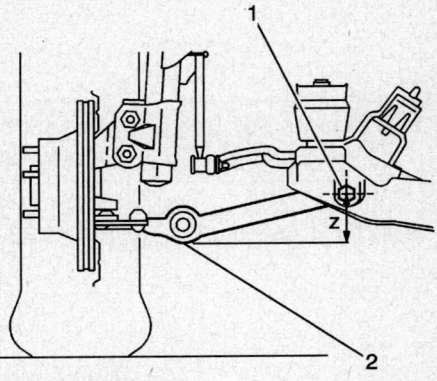

1. Center Line Of Control Arm Pivot Bolt
2. Bottom Of Control Arm

ARM0400000001021

Fig. B

FLUID CAPACITIES & COOLING SYSTEM DATA

Year	Engine (VIN) ①	Coolant Capacity, Qts.	Coolant Type	Radiator Cap Relief Pressure, psi	Thermo. Opening Temp. °F	Fuel Tank, Gals.	Engine Oil, Qts.② Less Filter Change	With Filter Change	Manual Trans., Pts.	Automatic. Trans., Qts.③ Drain & Refill	Total Capacity	Rear Axle, Pts.
2004	5.7 (G)	15.1	Dex-Cool	15	176–183	18.6	5.4	6.0	4.6	5.2	11.4	3.38④
2005–08	6.0L (U)	12.6	Dex-Cool	18	195	18.0	5.0	5.5	8.2	5.0	10.8	3.6

VIN — Vehicle Identification Number

① — The eighth digit of the VIN denotes engine code.

② — After refilling, inspect oil level again.

③ — Approximate. Make final inspection w/dipstick.

④ — Plus 1.0 oz GM part No. 89021958 Limited Slip Differential Friction Modifier 7098.

LUBRICANT DATA

Year	Lubricant Type Transmission Automatic	Manual	Rear Axle	Power Steering System	Brake System
2004–05	Dexron III	Dexron III	①	②	DOT 4
2008	Dexron VI	Dexron III	①	②	DOT 4

① — 75W-140W GL-5 final drive lubricant GM part No. 89021809 & Limited Slip Differential Friction Modifier 7098, GM part No. 89021958.

② — Power steering fluid part No. 89021184.

Electrical

NOTE: On Air Bag Equipped Models, Refer To "Air Bag System Precautions" Located In The Front Of This Manual For System Disarming & Arming Procedures.

NOTE: Refer To "Computer Relearn Procedures" Located In The Front Of This Manual When Battery Power To The Computer Has Been Interrupted.

INDEX

	Page No.		Page No.		Page No.
Air Bag System (Volume 2)	4-1	Fuse Panel Location	3-4	Radio, Replace	3-7
Air Conditioning	16-1	Headlamp Switch, Replace	3-6	Installation	3-7
Alternator, Replace	3-4	Heater Core, Replace	3-8	Removal	3-7
Alternators	19-1	Ignition Lock, Replace	3-5	Speed Controls (Volume 2)	2-1
Blower Motor, Replace	3-8	Installation	3-5	Starter Motors	18-1
Clutch Start Switch, Replace	3-5	Removal	3-5	Starter, Replace	3-4
Coil Pack, Replace	3-5	Ignition Switch, Replace	3-5	Steering Columns	20-1
Cooling Fans	17-1	Instrument Cluster, Replace	3-7	Steering Wheel, Replace	3-6
Cruise Control (Volume 2)	2-1	Multi-Function Switch, Replace	3-6	Stop Light Switch, Replace	3-6
Dash Gauges (Volume 2)	1-1	Neutral Safety Switch, Replace	3-5	Turn Signal Switch, Replace	3-6
Dash Panel Service		Passive Restraint Systems		Wiper Motor, Replace	3-7
(Volume 2)	5-1	(Volume 2)	4-1	Wiper Switch, Replace	3-7
Dimmer Switch, Replace	3-6	Precautions	3-4	Wiper Systems (Volume 2)	3-1
Evaporator Core, Replace	3-8	Air Bag Systems	3-4	Wiper Transmission, Replace	3-8
Fuel Pump Relay Location	3-4	Battery Ground Cable	3-4		

PRECAUTIONS

Air Bag Systems

Refer to "Air Bag System Precautions" in the front of this manual for system disarming and arming procedures.

Battery Ground Cable

Prior to service, disconnect battery ground cable and isolate as required.

FUSE PANEL LOCATION

The instrument panel fuse block in on the under the lefthand side of the instrument panel.

The underhood fuse block is on the righthand side of the engine compartment, mounted to the strut tower.

FUEL PUMP RELAY LOCATION

The fuel pump relay is located in the underhood fuse block.

STARTER

REPLACE

1. Raise and suitably support vehicle.
2. Remove lefthand catalytic converter.
3. Remove mounting bolts and lower starter motor.
4. Remove mounting nuts, then the wiring harness starter lead and washer.
5. Remove mounting nut and positive cable nut at starter solenoid.
6. Remove starter motor.
7. Reverse procedure to install, noting the following:
   a. **Torque** positive battery cable nut at starter solenoid to 89 inch lbs.
   b. Ensure starter lead is wrapped with heat protective tape.
   c. Ensure starter lead does not contact positive cable and/or connection.
   d. **Torque** wiring harness starter lead nut to 18 inch lbs.
   e. **Torque** starter motor mounting to 37 ft. lbs.

ALTERNATOR

REPLACE

1. Disconnect intake Air Temperature (IAT) and Mass Air Flow (MAF) sensor wiring harness connectors.
2. Loosen air intake duct to throttle body and MAF sensor to air cleaner upper body clamps.
3. Remove duct with IAT and MAF sensors installed.
4. Install suitable breaker bar with hex-head socket to drive belt tensioner bolt.
5. Relieve tension on belt by rotating drive belt tensioner clockwise.
6. Remove belt from pulleys and drive belt tensioner.
7. Slowly release tension on drive belt tensioner, then remove breaker bar and socket from drive belt tensioner bolt.
8. Place suitable drain pan below vehicle to catch power steering fluid.
9. Loosen hose clamp and remove power steering fluid reservoir outlet hose.
10. Loosen hose clamp and remove reservoir inlet hose.
11. Disconnect tab using suitable, flat-blade tool and remove power steering fluid reservoir.
12. Remove power steering gear inlet pipe and flare nut from pump.
13. Remove and discard high pressure port O-ring.
14. Loosen clamp and remove reservoir outlet hose from power steering pump.
15. Remove two mounting bolts and power steering pump.
16. Pull positive terminal cap back, then remove nut and positive cable from stud.
17. Disconnect alternator electrical connector.
18. Remove alternator rear bracket mounting bolt.
19. Remove front mounting bolts and alternator.
20. Reverse procedure to install, noting the following:
    a. **Torque** alternator front and bracket rear mounting bolts to 37 ft. lbs.
    b. **Torque** positive cable nut to 11 ft. lbs.
    c. **Torque** power steering pump mounting bolts to 21 ft. lbs.
    d. Lubricate new high pressure port O-ring with DEXRON-III, or equivalent Automatic Transmission Fluid (ATF):
    e. **Torque** high pressure port flare nut to 22 ft. lbs.
    f. **Torque** air cleaner lower housing duct clamp to 89 inch lbs.
    g. **Torque** air cleaner upper housing

mounting screws to 44 inch lbs.
h. **Torque** intake air duct clamp to 18 inch lbs.

COIL PACK
REPLACE

1. Disconnect ignition coils harness connectors.
2. Disconnect spark plug wire at ignition coils.
3. Remove mounting bolts and ignition coil.
4. Reverse procedure to install. **Torque** ignition coil mounting bolts to 106 inch lbs.

IGNITION LOCK
REPLACE
Removal

1. Disconnect three retaining clips by grabbing knee bolster panel upper and pulling it outwards.
2. Swing knee bolster panel open.
3. Disconnect knee bolster panel from instrument panel by holding each side of knee bolster panel, pulling lefthand side rearwards just enough disconnect clip.
4. Move knee bolster panel to outboard side of vehicle to disconnect retainer's pin, then remove panel.
5. Disconnect steering column position locking lever and tilt column to lowest position.
6. Remove steering column lower cover mounting screw.
7. Position steering wheel to access covers rear portion.
8. Push rear portion of lower cover in to disconnect two upper cover tabs.
9. Raise, disconnect tab and remove upper cover.
10. Push theft deterrent reader outer ring into lower cover.
11. Remove reader ignition lock illumination socket and electrical connector.
12. Slide lower cover rearward, disconnect tab and remove cover.
13. Tilt column to lowest and telescope to longest positions.
14. Disconnect theft deterrent reader connector.
15. Remove ignition lock illumination socket and bulb.
16. Remove reader from ignition lock cylinder.
17. Insert key into ignition lock cylinder and turn it to ON position.
18. Ensure steering column is not locked.
19. Insert Allen key, or equivalent .098 in diameter drift, into locking pin hole, **Fig. 1.**
20. Release ignition lock cylinder by pressing spring loaded barrel locking latch.
21. Remove ignition lock cylinder from housing by rotating key slightly.

Installation

1. Ensure steering column is not locked.

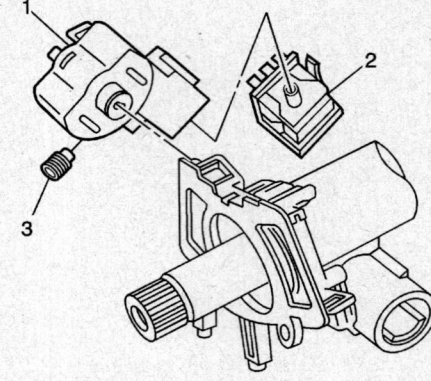

1. Ignition Switch
2. Ignition Lock Cylinder Solenoid
3. Set Screw

ARM0400000000993

Fig. 1   Exploded view of ignition switch

If steering column is locked, proceed as follows:
a. Place suitable, flat-bladed tool on steering column lock tab.
b. Rotate steering wheel slightly and push lock tab down.
2. Insert key into ignition lock cylinder.
3. Turn key to ON position.
4. Rotate key slightly and align keyed tip of ignition lock cylinder with keyed hole in ignition switch.
5. Install cylinder. Ensure latch locks into housing.
6. Remove key. Ensure ignition lock cylinder spring moves cylinder toward righthand side of vehicle.
7. Align theft deterrent reader and ignition lock cylinder flat edges.
8. Align reader indexing lug with ignition lock cylinder groove.
9. Install reader by gently pushing on reader between flat edge and indexing lug.
10. Install bulb and illumination socket to reader.
11. Connect reader connector.
12. Install steering column trim covers and knee bolster.

IGNITION SWITCH
REPLACE

1. Remove ignition lock cylinder as outlined under "Ignition Lock, Replace."
2. Insert suitable, small flat-bladed tool into ignition switch connector housing clip opening.
3. Disconnect clip by pushing.
4. Disconnect ignition switch connector.
5. Remove ignition switch mounting bolt.
6. Disconnect ignition switch from roll pin.
7. Remove ignition switch.
8. Remove ignition switch washers.
9. **On models equipped with automatic transmission,** remove ignition lock cylinder solenoid from ignition switch.
10. **On all models,** reverse procedure to install. **Torque** ignition switch mounting bolt to 11 inch lbs.

CLUTCH START SWITCH
REPLACE

1. Remove lefthand closeout panel to HVAC retainer.
2. Remove two lefthand closeout panel to instrument panel retainers.
3. Lower lefthand closeout panel and withdraw retaining lug from pedal bracket.
4. Remove step well lamp by rotating socket and removing from closeout panel.
5. Remove closeout panel.
6. Disconnect clutch pedal position switch harness electrical connector.
7. Rotate clutch pedal position switch counterclockwise quarter turn.
8. Remove switch from pedal bracket.
9. Reverse procedure to install.

NEUTRAL SAFETY SWITCH
REPLACE

The switches are incorporated into the wiring harness and cannot be serviced separately.
1. Place transmission selector lever in PARK position.
2. Raise and suitably support vehicle.
3. Remove selector lever shift linkage adjusting bolt and washers.
4. Slide trunnion, sleeve and insulator from selector linkage end.
5. Position linkage aside.
6. Remove four selector lever mounting nuts.
7. Lower vehicle.
8. Remove floor console tray insert by lifting upwards to disconnect it from console.
9. Remove console trim plate to floor console mounting screw.
10. Pull console trim plate up and disconnect six mounting tabs.
11. Disconnect power window switch and traction control switch connectors.
12. Depress six retaining tabs and remove power window switch.
13. Remove traction control switch Refer to Traction Control Switch Replacement in Antilock Brakes System.
14. Disconnect three tabs and traction control switch connector.
15. Remove selector lamp holder.
16. Remove lower housing, upper cover, gearshift lever, knob and boot from shift lever.
17. Separate lower housing from upper cover by releasing four locking tabs.
18. Remove traction control switch.
19. Remove cup holder by disconnecting retaining tab.
20. Slightly selector lever raise and disconnect Traction Control (T/C) switch connector.
21. Rotate selector lever indicator lamp counterclockwise and remove lamp assembly.
22. Remove selector lever.
23. Shift selector lever to D position using manual override lever.

24. Remove mounting screw and selector knob.
25. Disconnect selector rear wiring harness connector.
26. Disconnect selector lever housing from base by depressing four tabs.
27. Lift shift lever housing and remove insulator from base.
28. Disconnect shift lock solenoid wiring harness connector.
29. Remove mounting screws and solenoid.
30. Record micro switch wiring harness routing for installation alignment.
31. Remove mounting screws, then the park lock micro switch and wiring harness from floor shift control base plate.
32. Reverse procedure to install, noting the following:
    a. **Torque** park lock micro switch mounting screws to 4 inch lbs.
    b. **Torque** solenoid mounting screws to 18 inch lbs.
    c. **Torque** selector lever mounting nuts to 11 ft. lbs.
    d. **Torque** shift linkage adjusting bolt mounting nuts to 18 ft. lbs.
    e. **Torque** selector knob mounting screw to 18 inch lbs.
    f. **Torque** console trim plate mounting screw to 18 inch lbs.

HEADLAMP SWITCH
REPLACE

1. Release steering column adjustment lever, move column to its lowers position and lock into place with adjustment lever.
2. Remove two instrument cluster trim panel to instrument panel mounting screws.
3. Tilt cluster trim panel top away from instrument panel and disconnect retaining clips on each side.
4. Unhook each retaining lug.
5. Disconnect fuel filler door release switch wiring connector.
6. Remove cluster trim panel.
7. Remove three instrument panel outer cover to instrument panel mounting screws.
8. Remove instrument panel as outlined in "Dash Panel Service" chapter.
9. Disconnect passenger's air bag module connector.
10. Remove mounting nuts, bolts and passenger's air bag module.
11. Remove mounting screw, and separate driver side inner duct from outer duct.
12. Remove inner duct from HVAC module outlet.
13. Remove driver side inner and outer ducts.
14. Squeeze retaining clips on each side from rear and push headlamp switch part way from cavity.
15. Hold retaining clips using suitable, plastic flat-bladed tool and slowly removing switch from cavity.
16. Disconnect wiring connector and remove switch.
17. Reverse procedure to install, noting the following:

1. Turn Signal Switch Connector
2. Cruise Control Switch Connector
3. Wiper Switch Connector
4. Wiper Switch Connector
5. Tab
6. Tab

ARM0400000000996

Fig. 2 Multi-function switch replacement

a. **Torque** passenger's air bag module mounting nuts to 33 ft. lbs.
b. **Torque** passenger's air bag module mounting bolts to 84 inch lbs.
c. **Torque** driver side outer duct mounting screws to 18 inch lbs.
d. **Torque** instrument panel outer cover mounting to 18 inch lbs.
e. **Torque** instrument cluster trim panel mounting screws 18 inch lbs.

STOP LIGHT SWITCH
REPLACE

1. Disconnect three retaining clips by grabbing knee bolster panel upper and pulling it outwards.
2. Swing knee bolster panel open.
3. Disconnect knee bolster panel from instrument panel by holding each side of knee bolster panel, pulling lefthand side rearwards just enough disconnect clip.
4. Move knee bolster panel to outboard side of vehicle to disconnect retainer's pin, then remove panel.
5. Disconnect stop lamp switch electrical connector.
6. Remove stop lamp switch from brake pedal bracket.
7. Reverse procedure to install. Adjust switch as follows:
   a. With brake pedal fully released, ensure that stop lamp plunger is fully depressed against brake pedal shanks.
   b. Disconnect switch wiring harness connector.
   c. Ensure gap between switch and support bracket is .20–.23 inch.
   d. Adjust gap by rotating switch clockwise or counterclockwise to decrease or increase gap distance.

MULTI-FUNCTION SWITCH
REPLACE

1. Remove lighting fusible link from engine compartment fuse block.

2. Disconnect steering column position locking lever and tilt column to lowest position.
3. Remove steering column lower cover mounting screw.
4. Position steering wheel to access covers rear portion.
5. Push rear portion of lower cover in to disconnect two upper cover tabs.
6. Raise, disconnect tab and remove upper cover.
7. Push theft deterrent reader outer ring into lower cover.
8. Remove reader ignition lock illumination socket and electrical connector.
9. Slide lower cover rearward, disconnect tab and remove cover.
10. Press two tabs and remove switch, **Fig. 2**.
11. Disconnect cruise control and turn signal switch connectors.
12. Reverse procedure to install.

TURN SIGNAL SWITCH
REPLACE

Refer to "Multi-Function Switch, Replace" for turn signal switch replacement procedure.

DIMMER SWITCH
REPLACE

Refer to "Multi-Function Switch, Replace" for dimmer switch replacement procedure.

STEERING WHEEL
REPLACE

1. Lock steering column and ensure front wheels are in straight ahead position.
2. Disconnect steering column position locking lever and tilt column to lowest position.
3. Remove steering column lower cover mounting screw.
4. Position steering wheel to access covers rear portion.
5. Push rear portion of lower cover in to disconnect two upper cover tabs.
6. Raise, disconnect tab and remove upper cover.
7. Push theft deterrent reader outer ring into lower cover.
8. Remove reader ignition lock illumination socket and electrical connector.
9. Slide lower cover rearward, disconnect tab and remove cover.
10. Rotate steering wheel 90° exposing two of four steering wheel hub access holes.
11. Relieve tension on two spring loaded retaining clips using inflatable restraint steering wheel module removal tool No. EL-46844, or equivalent. Driver's air bag module will move slightly away from steering wheel.
12. Rotate steering wheel 180° and repeat previous step on remaining clips.
13. Disconnect steering wheel module connectors and remove driver's air bag module.
14. Remove steering wheel mounting bolt.

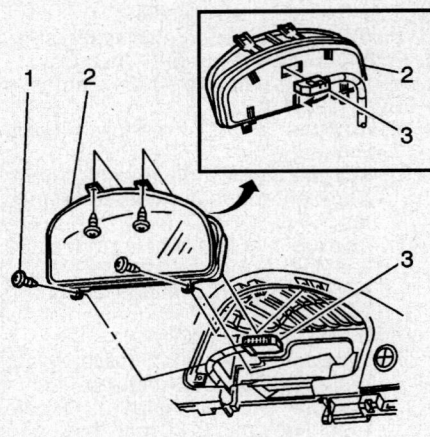

1. Mounting Screws
2. Instrument Cluster
3. Connector

ARM0400000000994

Fig. 3 Instrument cluster replacement

15. Mark steering wheel and shaft for installation alignment.
16. Remove steering wheel using steering wheel puller tool No. J-1859-A, or equivalent.
17. Reverse procedure to install, noting the following:
    a. Ensure SIR coil green indexing tab is aligned coil casing window.
    b. Apply Loctite 242, or equivalent, to steering wheel bolt.
    c. **Torque** steering wheel mounting bolt to 33 ft. lbs.

INSTRUMENT CLUSTER
REPLACE

1. Release steering column adjustment lever, move column to its lowers position and lock into place with adjustment lever.
2. Remove two instrument cluster trim panel to instrument panel mounting screws, **Fig. 3.**
3. Tilt cluster trim panel top away from instrument panel and disconnect retaining clips on each side.
4. Unhook each retaining lug.
5. Disconnect fuel filler door release switch wiring connector.
6. Remove cluster trim panel.
7. Remove four screws instrument cluster mounting screws.
8. Pull top of cluster from its cavity.
9. Open cluster wiring connector locking tab using suitable, flat-bladed tool.
10. Remove instrument cluster.
11. Reverse procedure to install, noting the following:
    a. **Torque** instrument cluster mounting screws to 18 inch lbs.
    b. **Torque** instrument cluster trim panel mounting screws 18 inch lbs.

RADIO
REPLACE
Removal

1. Insert radio removal tools No. BO-46862, or equivalent, into access holes and push service tool in to engage barbs of retaining spring clips.
2. Apply outward pressure on tools to release spring clips and pull radio out of cradle.
3. Remove tools.

Installation

1. **Do not apply pressure to radio buttons or display.**
2. Slide radio into cradle, then using finger pressure over removal tool holes, push radio in until spring clips engage.
3. If new radio head has been installed, enter new security code, as follows:
    a. Turn ignition switch to ON position.
    b. Switch radio to ON if turned OFF.
    c. Display shows CODE 1_ _ _ _.
    d. Use preset buttons to enter PIN code. Example: If PIN code belonging to radio is 3651. Press preset button 3. Display shows 3 _ _ _ . Press preset button 6. Display shows 3 6 _ _ . Press preset button 5. Display shows 3 6 5 _ Press preset button 3 6 5 1.
    e. If wrong PIN code has been entered display will show CODE ERROR WAIT.
    f. After waiting time CODE 2 _ _ _ _ will be outlined on display indicating that this is second attempt.
    g. Correct code should now be entered.
    h. After three attempts delay time will be 1 hour.
    i. Display will show LOCK OUT 1 HOUR.
    j. After delay time another three attempts at entering code will be possible.

WIPER MOTOR
REPLACE

There is a specific wiper arm for each side. The arms are identified by the letters LHD D for the drivers side and LHD P for the passengers side, located on the underside of the arm.

1. Raise hood and pry cap from front wiper arm.
2. Remove wiper arm to drive spindle nut.
3. Remove wiper arm from drive spindle. **Do not to allow wiper arm to contact rear edge of hood.**
4. Remove six air inlet grille panels retainers.
5. Pull left and righthand air inlet grille panels forward to disconnect them from windshield retainer.
6. Remove left and righthand air inlet grille panels by lifting them upwards while maneuvering them from hood hinge.

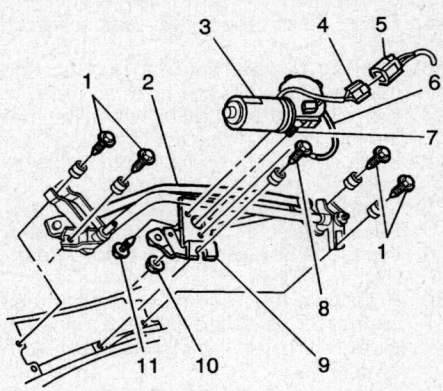

1. Mounting Bolts
2. Wiper Transmission
3. Wiper Motor
4. Main Wiper Motor Connector
5. Wiring Harness
6. Ground Strap
7. Wiper Motor Pivot
8. Mounting Bolt
9. Transmission Bracket
10. Mounting Nut
11. Mounting Bolts

ARM0400000000995

Fig. 4 Wiper motor replacement

7. Squeeze locking tab and disconnect main wiper motor harness connector, **Fig. 4.**
8. Remove four wiper transmission mounting bolts.
9. Remove wiper motor ground strap mounting bolt. Ground strap bolt is secured to strap by spacer and cannot be separated.
10. Remove wiper transmission.
11. Remove wiper transmission to wiper motor pivot mounting nut.
12. Remove three wiper motor to transmission bracket mounting bolts.
13. Remove wiper motor.
14. Reverse procedure to install, noting the following:
    a. **Torque** wiper motor mounting bolts to 71 inch lbs.
    b. **Torque** wiper motor pivot mounting nut to 13 ft. lbs.
    c. **Torque** wiper motor ground strap bolt to 44 inch lbs.
    d. **Torque** wiper transmission mounting bolts 44 inch lbs.
    e. Ensure wiper motor linkages are in parked position.
    f. Install arms so blade tip is 1.18–1.57 inches above air inlet screen edge.
    g. **Torque** wiper arm nut to 16 ft. lbs.

WIPER SWITCH
REPLACE

1. Disconnect steering column position locking lever and tilt column to lowest position.
2. Remove steering column lower cover mounting screw.
3. Position steering wheel to access covers rear portion.
4. Push rear portion of lower cover in to disconnect two upper cover tabs.

5. Raise, disconnect tab and remove upper cover.
6. Push theft deterrent reader outer ring into lower cover.
7. Remove reader ignition lock illumination socket and electrical connector.
8. Slide lower cover rearward, disconnect tab and remove cover.
9. Disconnect wiper control switch harness connector by depressing retaining tab and pulling connectors apart, **Fig. 2.**
10. Press two tabs and lift wiring harness connector retaining tabs up on each side switch, then pull connector from switch.
11. Remove wiper switch assembly.
12. Reverse procedure to install.

WIPER TRANSMISSION
REPLACE

Refer to "Wiper Motor, Replace" for wiper transmission replacement procedure.

BLOWER MOTOR
REPLACE

1. Carefully pull righthand closeout panel downwards to disconnect two retaining clips.
2. Remove righthand closeout panel from hinge pillar panel, disconnecting two lugs.
3. Lower closeout panel and remove step well lamp by rotating socket and removing from closeout panel.
4. Remove closeout panel.
5. Disconnect blower motor electrical connector.
6. Remove three mounting screws and blower motor.
7. Reverse procedure to install. **Torque** blower motor mounting screws and 15 inch lbs.

HEATER CORE
REPLACE

1. Recover refrigerant as outlined in "Air Conditioning" chapter.
2. Drain cooling system into suitable container.
3. Remove instrument panel as outlined in "Dash Panel Service" chapter.
4. Disconnect passenger's air bag module connector.
5. Remove mounting nuts, bolts and passenger's air bag module.
6. Remove righthand side duct from HVAC unit.
7. Remove lefthand inner brace to lower radio bracket mounting bolt.
8. Remove HVAC unit to lower radio bracket mounting bolt.
9. Remove instrument panel righthand end bracket to lower radio bracket mounting bolt.
10. Remove instrument panel righthand end bracket to lower radio bracket mounting screw.
11. Remove lower radio bracket mounting screws and disconnect electrical connector.
12. Remove lower radio bracket.
13. Carefully pull righthand closeout panel downwards and disconnect two retaining clips.
14. Remove righthand closeout panel from hinge pillar panel and disconnect two retaining lugs.
15. Lower righthand closeout panel and remove step well lamp by rotating socket.
16. Remove righthand closeout panel.
17. Remove mounting screw, disconnect rear retaining tab and gently remove Body Control Module (BCM) from mounting bracket.
18. Disconnect four BCM wiring harness connectors.
19. Remove righthand end bracket to lower radio bracket mounting screw.
20. Remove righthand end bracket to lower radio bracket mounting bolt.
21. Remove righthand end bracket mounting bolts.
22. Remove righthand end bracket to passenger air bag module mounting bolts.
23. Disconnect wiring harness and remove righthand end bracket.
24. Remove center support brace to lower radio bracket mounting screw and bolts.
25. Remove four mounting bolts and drivers knee bolster bracket.
26. Remove two mounting bolts and drivers inner bracket.
27. Remove bolt and center support brace.
28. Remove radio antenna lead from three HVAC unit retaining clips.
29. Mark heater hoses for install alignment.
30. Remove heater hoses from core pipes.
31. Disconnect water valve vacuum and vacuum supply hoses from check valve.
32. Recover refrigerant as outlined in "Air Conditioning" chapter.
33. Remove mounting bolt, then Thermal Expansion Valve (TXV) tube plate, inlet and outlet tubes. Remove and discard O-rings.
34. Remove mounting bolts and TXV. Remove and discard O-rings.
35. Cap or tape open evaporator inlet and outlet tubes.
36. Cap evaporator inlet and outlet tube.
37. Remove fuel line retaining bracket and nut from HVAC mounting stud.
38. Remove mounting stud and screws, then the HVAC unit.
39. Remove two heater core pipe clamp.
40. Remove mounting screws and heater core retaining strap.
41. Remove mounting screws and heater pipe bracket.
42. Remove heater core. **Do not damage foam seal on top and sides of heater core.**
43. Remove mounting screw, clamps and heater pipe. Remove and discard O-rings.
44. Reverse procedure to install, noting the following:
   a. Install O-rings on heater pipes.
   b. **Torque** heater pipes clamps and screws to 15 inch lbs.
   c. **Torque** heater pipe bracket mounting screws to 14 inch lbs.
   d. **Torque** heater core retaining strap mounting screws to 14 inch lbs.
   e. **Torque** heater core pipe clamps to 14 inch lbs.
   f. **Torque** HVAC module inside mounting nuts to 53 inch lbs.
   g. **Torque** HVAC module engine compartment mounting nuts to 89 inch lbs.
   h. **Torque** fuel line bracket nut to 89 inch lbs.
   i. **Torque** TXV mounting bolts to 40 inch lbs.
   j. Install new O-rings.
   k. **Torque** evaporator tube plate mounting bolt to 93 inch lbs.
   l. **Torque** center support brace mounting bolts to 80 inch lbs.
   m. **Torque** drivers knee bolster bracket mounting bolts to 80 inch lbs.
   n. **Torque** BCM mounting screws to 18 inch lbs.
   o. **Torque** righthand end bracket mounting bolts to 80 inch lbs.
   p. **Torque** lower radio bracket mounting screws to 18 inch lbs.
   q. **Torque** instrument panel right end bracket mounting 18 inch lbs.
   r. **Torque** lower radio bracket mounting bolt to 80 inch lbs.
   s. **Torque** HVAC unit mounting bolt to 80 inch lbs.

EVAPORATOR CORE
REPLACE

1. Remove HVAC module as outlined under "Heater Core, Replace."
2. Remove mounting screws and TXV joint bracket.
3. Remove heater core as outlined under "Heater Core, Replace."
4. Disconnect recirculation/intake actuator vacuum line.
5. Remove front HVAC module case vacuum lines and retainers.
6. Remove vacuum line and actuator rod from lever, then the mounting screws and defroster actuator.
7. Remove front HVAC module case to upper and lower cases' mounting screws.
8. Separate front HVAC module case from upper and lower cases.
9. Remove upper to lower HVAC module mounting screws and clips.
10. Separate upper from lower HVAC module case.
11. Remove evaporator core.
12. Remove mounting screw and evaporator core pipes. Remove and discard O-rings.
13. Reverse procedure to install, noting the following:
   a. Install new O-rings.
   b. **Torque** evaporator core pipes mounting screw to 44 inch lbs.
   c. **Torque** case mounting screws and 14 inch lbs.
   d. **Torque** defroster actuator mounting screws to 14 inch lbs.
   e. **Torque** TXV joint bracket mounting screws to 14 inch lbs.

5.7L Engine

NOTE: For Procedures Not Found, Refer To The "5.7L Engine" Section In The "Corvette" Chapter.

NOTE: On Air Bag Equipped Models, Refer To "Air Bag System Precautions" Located In The Front Of This Manual For System Disarming & Arming Procedures.

NOTE: Refer To "Computer Relearn Procedures" Located In The Front Of This Manual When Battery Power To The Computer Has Been Interrupted.

INDEX

	Page No.		Page No.		Page No.
Cooling System Bleed	3-13	**Exhaust Manifold, Replace**	3-10	Belt Replacement	3-12
Cylinder Head, Replace	3-11	Lefthand	3-10	Removal	3-12
Lefthand	3-11	Righthand	3-11	Belt Routing	3-12
Righthand	3-12	**Fuel Filter, Replace**	3-14	**Thermostat, Replace**	3-13
Engine Rebuilding		**Fuel Pump, Replace**	3-13	**Tightening Specifications**	3-15
Specifications	29-1	**Precautions**	3-9	**Valve Cover, Replace**	3-12
Engine, Replace	3-9	Battery Ground Cable	3-9	Lefthand	3-12
Engine Mount, Replace	3-9	Fuel System Pressure Relief	3-9	Righthand	3-12
Lefthand	3-9	**Radiator, Replace**	3-13	**Water Pump, Replace**	3-13
Righthand	3-9	**Serpentine Drive Belt**	3-12		

PRECAUTIONS

Fuel System Pressure Relief

Failure to relieve system pressure prior to disconnecting fuel system components may cause fire or personal injury.
1. Turn ignition switch to OFF position.
2. Disconnect and isolate battery ground.
3. Relieve fuel tank vapor pressure by loosening fuel filler cap.
4. Remove lefthand fuel rail cover.
5. Connect fuel pressure gauge tool No. J34730-1A, or equivalent, to fuel pressure connection.
6. Wrap shop towel around fitting while connecting gauge.
7. Install gauge bleed hose into suitable container.
8. Open gauge valve and bleed system pressure.
9. Drain remaining gauge fuel into suitable container.

Battery Ground Cable

Prior to service, disconnect battery ground cable and isolate as required.

ENGINE MOUNT
REPLACE
Lefthand

1. Remove lefthand exhaust manifold as outlined under "Exhaust Manifold, Replace."

2. Remove mounting nuts and lefthand engine mount.
3. Reverse procedure to install.

Righthand

1. Remove righthand exhaust manifold as outlined under "Exhaust Manifold, Replace."
2. Remove mounting nuts and righthand engine mount.
3. Reverse procedure to install.

ENGINE
REPLACE

1. Recover air conditioning refrigerant as outlined in "Air Conditioning" chapter.
2. Open hood.
3. Apply suitable tape to hood corners and adjacent surfaces.
4. Cut end and remove secondary latch rivet, then remove secondary latch and spring.
5. Loosen nut and remove hood latch striker bolt ensuring washer, hood pop-up spring and hood pop-up spring retainer remain on bolt.
6. **On models equipped with hood scoops,** proceed as follows:
   a. Remove hood air extractor by gently squeezing to unhook tabs.
   b. Starting at rear of hood and working toward front, remove 13 hood insulator retainers.
   c. Slide insulator from slots in hood inner panel and remove.
   d. Remove plug, retainer and scoop.
7. **On models equipped less hood scoops,** starting at rear of hood and working toward front, remove hood insulator retainers.

8. **On all models,** place suitable container under washer solvent container.
9. Reach between front bumper fascia and washer solvent container, then disconnect washer solvent hose from pump.
10. Allow washer solvent to drain from container.
11. Remove washer hose from behind fuse panel and disconnect hose adjacent to hood strut.
12. Separate and remove washer hoses from washer nozzles.
13. Squeeze retaining tabs on washer nozzle base and push nozzle out through top of hood. Remove nozzle.
14. Remove hood adjustable bumper by rotating it counterclockwise.
15. Mark upper hood hinge location to hood for installation alignment.
16. Provide alternate hood support.
17. Remove assist rod clip using suitable, small flat-bladed tool.
18. Remove assist rod to fender mounting bolts.
19. Disconnect and remove assist rod from hood strut pin.
20. Have assistant hold hood. then remove upper hood hinge mounting bolts and hood.
21. Remove four mounting nuts and front suspension support brace.
22. Remove fuel rail covers.
23. Disconnect air intake sensor connector.
24. Loosen hose clamps and remove intake duct.
25. Disconnect and isolate battery ground.
26. Relieve fuel tank vapor pressure by loosening fuel filler cap.
27. Remove lefthand fuel rail cover.
28. Connect fuel pressure gauge tool No.

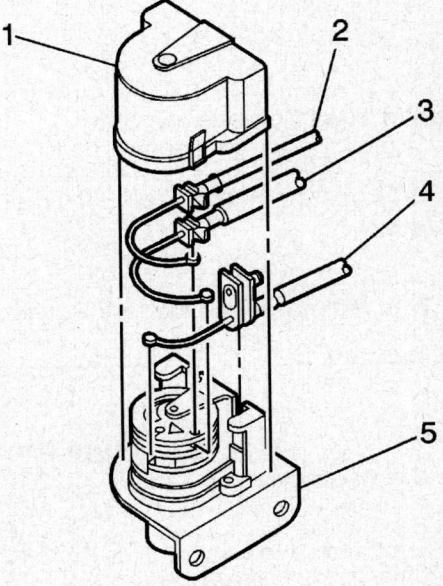

1. Throttle Relaxer Cover
2. Accelerator Cable
3. Accelerator Cable
4. Cruise Control Cable
5. Mounting Bracket

ARM0400000000999

Fig. 1 Throttle relaxer replacement

J34730-1A , or equivalent, to fuel pressure connection.

29. Wrap shop towel around fitting while connecting gauge.
30. Install gauge bleed hose into suitable container.
31. Open gauge valve and bleed system pressure.
32. Remove radiator as outlined under "Radiator, Replace."
33. Remove radiator and heater hoses from water pump.
34. Remove air conditioning compressor and condenser hose nut.
35. Separate compressor and condenser hose from compressor. Cap hoses and inlets.
36. Remove ground lead screw from engine block and lefthand engine mount.
37. Remove nut securing battery harness ground terminals to antilock brake system (ABS)/traction control system (TCS) control module bracket stud.
38. Disconnect positive lead terminal from battery. Lay harness on engine.
39. Disconnect air conditioning wiring harness connector.
40. Disconnect wiring harness retaining clips from engine compartment.
41. Disconnect theft deterrent horn connector.
42. Disconnect radiator hose from surge tank inlet fitting.
43. Disconnect surge tank vapor and overflow hoses.
44. Pivot surge tank to remove from rear anchor plate.
45. Pull tank inward toward engine and remove it from anchor plate on inner fender.

46. Disconnect coolant level switch electrical connector.
47. Remove Powertrain Control Module (PCM) harness connector cover.
48. Loosen and remove PCM connectors.
49. Disconnect PCM wiring harness retaining clip.
50. Remove engine wiring harness retaining clip from power steering pipe bracket.
51. Remove throttle relaxer cover and disconnect connector, **Fig. 1.**
52. Remove both fuel rail covers.
53. Disconnect throttle and cruise control cables form relaxer.
54. Remove mounting nuts and throttle relaxer.
55. Cut wiring harness straps and discard.
56. Disconnect powertrain to main wiring harness connector.
57. Remove harness to dash panel grommet, then feed harness and connectors out into engine bay.
58. Place powertrain wiring harness on top of engine.
59. Lift throttle cable at throttle body mounting bracket and remove it from cam lever. Set throttle cable aside.
60. Relieve vapor pressure by loosening fuel filler cap.
61. Disconnect engine compartment fuel feed pipe at fuel rail, **Fig. 2.**
62. Disconnect engine compartment EVAP pipe at EVAP canister purge solenoid.
63. Disconnect engine compartment fuel feed pipe at chassis fuel feed pipe.
64. Disconnect engine compartment EVAP pipe at chassis EVAP pipe.
65. Cap fuel pipes.
66. Disconnect line from purge valve.
67. Loosen power steering reservoir return hose clamp.
68. Place suitable container under reservoir, then remove hose and drain reservoir fluid.
69. Remove power steering pump outlet fitting high pressure line flare nut and O-ring.
70. Disconnect brake booster vacuum hose and heater control, vacuum hose from rear of intake manifold.
71. Remove four mounting bolts and undertray from crossmember.
72. Remove two power steering high pressure line brackets to oil pan mounting bolts.
73. Remove exhaust manifolds as outlined under "Exhaust Manifold, Replace."
74. Remove transmission as outlined in **MOTOR's "Domestic Transmission , In-Vehicle Service" manual or "Transmission Service DVD."**
75. Remove left and righthand engine mount to engine bracket nuts.
76. Attach suitable lifting chain and hooks to two engine lifting brackets.
77. Slightly raise engine to clear engine mount stud using suitable lifting crane.
78. Slowly lift and remove engine.
79. Reverse procedure to install.

1. Engine Compartment EVAP Pipe
2. Chassis EVAP Pipe
3. Chassis Fuel Feed Pipe
4. Engine Compartment Fuel Feed Pipe

ARM0400000001000

Fig. 2 Fuel line replacement

EXHAUST MANIFOLD
REPLACE

Lefthand

1. Remove fuel rail covers.
2. Support engine using universal engine support fixture tools Nos. J-41803 and J-28467-B, or equivalent.
3. Remove four mounting nuts and front suspension support brace.
4. Lift locking lever, then remove Mass Air Flow (MAF) and Intake Air Temperature (IAT) sensors' electrical connectors.
5. Loosen two clamps and remove intake duct.
6. Relieve fuel tank vapor pressure by loosening fuel filler cap.
7. Remove lefthand fuel rail cover.
8. Connect fuel pressure gauge tool No. J34730-1A, or equivalent, to fuel pressure connection.
9. Wrap shop towel around fitting while connecting gauge.
10. Install gauge bleed hose into suitable container.
11. Open gauge valve and bleed system pressure.
12. Partially drain cooling system into suitable container.
13. Remove coolant temperature sensor.
14. Raise and support vehicle.
15. **Do not damage oxygen sensors.**
16. Remove lefthand exhaust manifold to exhaust pipe flange nuts.
17. Lower vehicle.
18. Disconnect spark plug wire at each spark plug by twisting each ½ turn and pulling only on boot.
19. Loosen each spark plug 1–2 turns. Remove dirt from spark plugs using suitable brush or compressed air.
20. Remove spark plugs one at a time and place each plug in tray marked with corresponding cylinder numbers.
21. Remove exhaust manifold mounting bolts, working from outside to center.
22. Remove exhaust manifold and gasket.

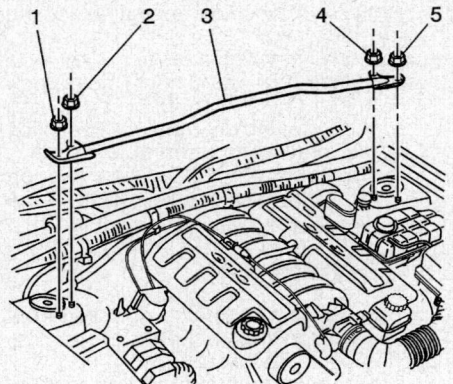

1. Mounting Nut
2. Mounting Nut
3. Front Suspension Support Brace
4. Mounting Nut
5. Mounting Nut

ARM0400000000992

Fig. 3 Front suspension support brace tightening sequence

23. Remove mounting bolts and heat shield.
24. Reverse procedure to install, noting the following:
    a. Apply .2 inch wide band of suitable threadlocker to exhaust manifold mounting bolts' threads.
    b. **Torque** exhaust manifold mounting bolts from center to outsides to 11 ft. lbs.
    c. **Torque** exhaust manifold mounting bolts from center to outsides to 18 ft. lbs.
    d. Bend over exposed edge of exhaust manifold gasket at rear of cylinder head.
    e. **Torque** front suspension support brace mounting nuts to 22 ft. lbs., in sequence, **Fig. 3.**

Righthand

1. Remove fuel rail covers.
2. Support engine using universal engine support fixture tools Nos. J-41803 and J-28467-B, or equivalent.
3. Remove four mounting nuts and front suspension support brace.
4. Lift locking lever, then remove Mass Air Flow (MAF) and Intake Air Temperature (IAT) sensors' electrical connectors.
5. Loosen two clamps and remove intake duct.
6. Relieve fuel tank vapor pressure by loosening fuel filler cap.
7. Remove lefthand fuel rail cover.
8. Connect fuel pressure gauge tool No. J34730-1A, or equivalent to fuel pressure connection.
9. Wrap shop towel around fitting while connecting gauge.
10. Install gauge bleed hose into suitable container.
11. Open gauge valve and bleed system pressure.
12. Partially drain cooling system into suitable container.
13. Remove oil dipstick from tube.

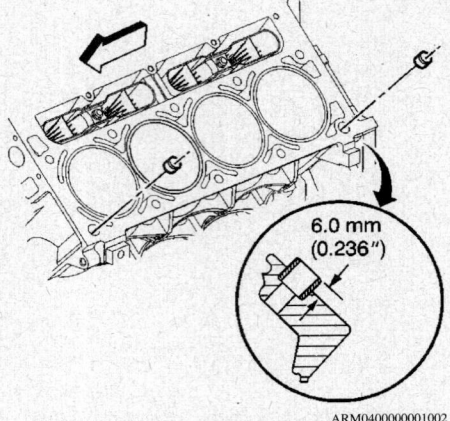

6.0 mm (0.236")

ARM0400000001002

Fig. 4 Cylinder head gasket installation

14. Remove oil dipstick tube bolt from righthand cylinder head and oil pan. Plug opening of oil dipstick tube.
15. Raise and support vehicle.
16. **Do not damage oxygen sensors.**
17. Remove righthand exhaust manifold to exhaust pipe flange nuts.
18. Lower vehicle.
19. Disconnect spark plug wire at each spark plug by twisting each ½ turn and pulling only on boot.
20. Loosen each spark plug 1–2 turns. Remove dirt from spark plugs using suitable brush or compressed air.
21. Remove spark plugs one at a time and place each plug in tray marked with corresponding cylinder numbers.
22. Remove exhaust manifold mounting bolts, working from outside to center.
23. Remove exhaust manifold and gasket.
24. Remove mounting bolts and heat shield.
25. Reverse procedure to install, noting the following:
    a. Apply .2 inch wide band of suitable threadlocker to exhaust manifold mounting bolts' threads.
    b. **Torque** exhaust manifold mounting bolts from center to outsides to 11 ft. lbs.
    c. **Torque** exhaust manifold mounting bolts from center to outsides to 18 ft. lbs.
    d. Bend over exposed edge of exhaust manifold gasket at rear of cylinder head.
    e. **Torque** front suspension support brace mounting nuts to 22 ft. lbs., in sequence, **Fig. 3.**

CYLINDER HEAD
REPLACE
Lefthand

1. Remove valve cover as outlined under "Valve Cover, Replace."
2. Remove mounting bolts, rocker arms pivot support, and pushrods. **Place rocker arms, pushrods and pivot support in suitable rack so they can be installed in original position.**
3. Remove coolant air bleed hose from

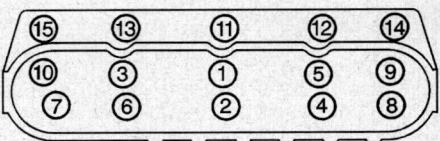

ARM0400000001003

Fig. 5 Cylinder head tightening sequence

throttle body, then the studs, coolant air bleed pipe and gaskets.

4. Remove two mounting bolts and power steering pump.
5. Remove lefthand exhaust manifold as outlined under "Exhaust Manifold Replace."
6. Remove mounting bolts and position engine wiring harness ground aside.
7. Remove and discard cylinder head bolts. **Cylinder head bolts are not reusable.**
8. Remove cylinder head and place it on two suitable wood blocks.
9. Remove and discard head gasket.
10. Reverse procedure to install, noting the following.
    a. **Do not use any type of sealant on cylinder head gasket.**
    b. Install head gasket in proper direction and position onto locating pins, **Fig. 4.** When properly installed, tab on gasket will be located left of center, or closer to front of engine and words This Side Up and engine displacement visible.
    c. Install new cylinder head bolts.
    d. **Torque** M11 cylinder head bolts 1–10 to 22 ft. lbs., in sequence, **Fig. 5.**
    e. Tighten M11 cylinder head bolts 1–10 an additional 90° in sequence.
    f. Tighten M11 cylinder head bolts 1–8 an additional 90° in sequence.
    g. Tighten M11 cylinder head bolts 9–10) and additional 50° in sequence.
    h. **Torque** M8 cylinder head bolts 11—15 to 22 ft. lbs., begin with center bolt 11 and alternating side-to-side, work outward.
    i. Lubricate rocker arms and pushrods, then rocker arm bolts and flange with suitable, clean engine oil.
    j. Ensure pushrods seat properly to rocker arms ends.
    k. After rocker arms and bolts are install, rotate crankshaft until piston No. 1 is at Top Dead Center (TDC) of compression stroke. In this position, cylinder No. 1 rocker arms will be off lobe lift and crankshaft sprocket key will be at 1:30 position.
    l. **Torque** exhaust valve rocker arm bolts Nos. 1, 2, 7 and 8 to 22 ft. lbs.
    m. **Torque** intake valve rocker arm bolts Nos. 1, 3, 4 and 5 to 22 ft. lbs.
    n. Rotate crankshaft 360°.
    o. **Torque** exhaust valve rocker arm bolts Nos. 3, 4, 5 and 6 to 22 ft. lbs.
    p. **Torque** intake valve rocker arm bolts Nos. 2, 6, 7 and 8 to 22 ft. lbs.

Righthand

1. Drain coolant into suitable container.
2. Disconnect clamp and separate inlet heater hose from heater pipe.
3. Disconnect clamp and separate heater inlet hose from water pump.
4. Remove clips and separate heater inlet hoses from water valve ports.
5. Remove inlet heater hoses.
6. Remove valve cover as outlined under "Valve Cover, Replace."
7. Remove mounting bolts, rocker arms pivot support. and pushrods. **Place rocker arms, pushrods and pivot support in suitable rack so they can be installed in original position.**
8. Remove coolant air bleed hose from throttle body, then the studs, coolant air bleed pipe and gaskets.
9. Remove righthand exhaust manifold as outlined under "Exhaust Manifold, Replace."
10. Remove engine wiring harness clip bolt.
11. Remove and discard cylinder head bolts. **Cylinder head bolts are not reusable.**
12. Remove cylinder head and place it on two suitable wood blocks.
13. Remove and discard head gasket.
14. Reverse procedure to install, noting the following.
    a. **Do not use any type of sealant on cylinder head gasket.**
    b. Install head gasket in proper direction and position onto locating pins, **Fig. 4.** When properly installed, tab on gasket will be located left of center, or closer to front of engine and words This Side Up and engine displacement visible.
    c. Install new cylinder head bolts.
    d. **Torque** M11 cylinder head bolts 1–10 to 3 22 ft. lbs., in sequence, **Fig. 5.**
    e. Tighten M11 cylinder head bolts 1–10 an additional 90° in sequence.
    f. Tighten M11 cylinder head bolts 1–8 an additional 90° in sequence.
    g. Tighten M11 cylinder head bolts 9–10) and additional 50° in sequence.
    h. **Torque** M8 cylinder head bolts 11–15 to 22 ft. lbs., begin with center bolt 11 and alternating side-to-side, work outward.
    i. Lubricate rocker arms and pushrods, then rocker arm bolts and flange with suitable, clean engine oil.
    j. Ensure pushrods seat properly to rocker arms ends.
    k. After rocker arms and bolts are install, rotate crankshaft until piston No. 1 is at Top Dead Center (TDC) of compression stroke. In this position, cylinder No. 1 rocker arms will be off lobe lift and crankshaft sprocket key will be at 1:30 position.
    l. **Torque** exhaust valve rocker arm bolts Nos. 1, 2, 7 and 8 to 22 ft. lbs.
    m. **Torque** intake valve rocker arm bolts Nos. 1, 3, 4 and 5 to 22 ft. lbs.

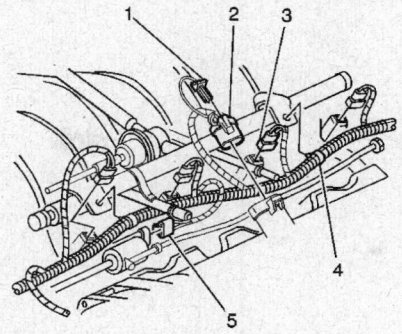

1. CPA Clip
2. Ignition Coil Wire Harness Main Electrical Connector
3. 4 & 5. Harness Clips

ARM040000001001

Fig. 6 Valve cover replacement. Lefthand

n. Rotate crankshaft 360°.
o. **Torque** exhaust valve rocker arm bolts Nos. 3, 4, 5 and 6 to 22 ft. lbs.
p. **Torque** intake valve rocker arm bolts Nos. 2, 6, 7 and 8 to 22 ft. lbs.

VALVE COVER
REPLACE
Lefthand

1. Remove four mounting nuts and front suspension support brace.
2. Remove both fuel rail covers.
3. Disconnect air intake sensor connector.
4. Loosen clamps and remove intake duct.
5. Turn ignition switch to OFF position.
6. Disconnect and isolate battery ground.
7. Relieve fuel tank vapor pressure by loosening fuel filler cap.
8. Connect fuel pressure gauge tool No. J34730-1A, or equivalent, to fuel pressure connection.
9. Wrap shop towel around fitting while connecting gauge.
10. Install gauge bleed hose into suitable container.
11. Open gauge valve and bleed system pressure.
12. Relieve vapor pressure by loosening fuel filler cap.
13. Disconnect engine compartment fuel feed pipe at fuel rail, **Fig. 2.**
14. Disconnect engine compartment EVAP pipe at EVAP canister purge solenoid.
15. Disconnect engine compartment fuel feed pipe at chassis fuel feed pipe.
16. Disconnect engine compartment EVAP pipe at chassis EVAP pipe.
17. Cap fuel pipes.
18. Disconnect line from purge valve.
19. Disconnect spark plug wires from ignition coils.
20. Remove Connector Position Assurance (CPA) Clip, **Fig. 6.**
21. Disconnect ignition coil wire harness main electrical connector.
22. Remove mounting bolts and screw, then the ignition coil bracket.
23. Remove mounting bolts and valve cover. Remove and discard gasket.

24. Reverse procedure to install, noting the following:
    a. Install new valve cover gasket.
    b. Install new valve cover bolt grommets.
    c. Apply suitable threadlock to ignition coil bracket studs' threads.
    d. **Torque** front suspension support brace mounting nuts to 22 ft. lbs., in sequence, **Fig. 3.**

Righthand

1. Remove four mounting nuts and front suspension support brace.
2. Remove both fuel rail covers.
3. Disconnect air intake sensor connector.
4. Loosen clamps and remove intake duct.
5. Remove spark plug wires from ignition coils.
6. Remove Connector Position Assurance (CPA) clip.
7. Disconnect ignition coil wire harness main electrical connector.
8. Remove mounting bolts and screw, then the ignition coil bracket.
9. Disconnect spark plug wires from ignition coils.
10. Remove Connector Position Assurance (CPA) Clip, **Fig. 7.**
11. Disconnect ignition coil wire harness main electrical connector.
12. Remove mounting bolts and screw, then the ignition coil bracket.
13. Remove mounting bolts and valve cover. Remove and discard gasket.
14. Reverse procedure to install, noting the following:
    a. Install new valve cover gasket.
    b. Install new valve cover bolt grommets.
    c. Apply suitable threadlock to ignition coil bracket studs' threads.
    d. **Torque** front suspension support brace mounting nuts to 22 ft. lbs., in sequence, **Fig. 3.**

SERPENTINE DRIVE BELT
Belt Routing

Refer to **Fig. 8** for serpentine drive belt routing.

Belt Replacement
REMOVAL

1. Install suitable breaker bar with hexhead socket to drive belt tensioner bolt.
2. Relieve tension on belt by rotating drive belt tensioner clockwise.
3. Remove belt from pulleys and drive belt tensioner.
4. Slowly release tension on drive belt tensioner. Remove breaker bar and socket from drive belt tensioner bolt.

INSTALLATION

1. Route drive belt around all pulleys, except water pump and belt tensioner.

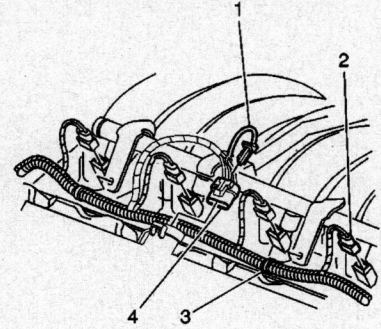

1. CPA Clip
2. Connector
3. Clip
4. Ignition Coil Wire Harness Main Electrical Connector

ARM0400000001004

Fig. 7 Valve cover replacement. Righthand

2. Install suitable breaker bar with hex-head socket to belt tensioner bolt.
3. Relieve tension on tension by rotating belt tensioner clockwise.
4. Install drive belt under water pump pulley and onto belt tensioner.
5. Slowly release tension.
6. Remove breaker bar and socket from belt tensioner bolt.
7. Inspect drive belt for proper alignment.

COOLING SYSTEM BLEED

1. Slowly fill cooling system through upper radiator hose with suitable coolant mixture until coolant comes out coolant air bleed hose.
2. Fill radiator suitable coolant through surge tank opening to full line.
3. Install coolant pressure cap.
4. Start engine and run at 2000–2500 RPM until engine reaches normal operating temperature.
5. Allow engine to idle for three minutes.
6. Shut off and allow engine to cool.
7. Adjust coolant level as required.

THERMOSTAT
REPLACE

The water pump inlet and thermostat are replaced as an assembly. The thermostat is not serviceable separately.
1. Drain cooling system into suitable container.
2. Position clamp and remove outlet hose from water pump inlet.
3. Remove mounting bolts and water pump inlet.
4. Remove thermostat housing. O-ring seal is integral to thermostat housing.
5. Reverse procedure to install.

WATER PUMP
REPLACE

1. Lift locking lever and disconnect Mass Air Flow (MAF) sensor electrical connector.
2. Lift locking lever on Intake Air Temperature (IAT) sensor electrical connector.

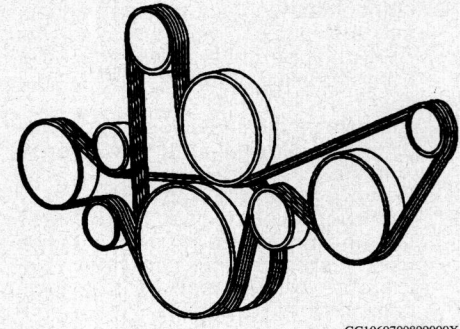

GC1069700899000X

Fig. 8 Serpentine drive belt routing

3. Loosen two clamps and remove intake duct.
4. Install suitable breaker bar with hex-head socket to drive belt tensioner bolt.
5. Relieve tension on belt by rotating drive belt tensioner clockwise.
6. Remove belt from pulleys and drive belt tensioner.
7. Slowly release tension on drive belt tensioner. Remove breaker bar and socket from drive belt tensioner bolt.
8. Drain cooling system into suitable container.
9. Disconnect two heater hoses, then the water pump inlet and outlet hoses.
10. Remove two mounting bolts and drive belt tensioner.
11. Remove six mounting bolts and water pump.
12. Remove and discard gaskets.
13. Reverse procedure to install, noting the following:
    a. **Torque** water pump mounting bolts to 11 ft. lbs.
    b. **Torque** mounting bolts to 18 ft. lbs.

RADIATOR
REPLACE

1. Lift locking levers, then disconnect Mass Air Flow (MAF) and Intake Air Temperature (IAT) sensors' electrical connectors.
2. Loosen two clamps and remove intake duct.
3. Drain cooling system into suitable container.
4. Remove vapor hose from radiator fan shroud clips and radiator clamp, then position it aside.
5. Remove vapor hose to surge tank clamp at radiator and position it aside.
6. Remove five upper shroud to radiator retainers.
7. Lift shroud on righthand side and release lefthand side locating tab.
8. Loosen and remove radiator outlet hose from radiator and thermostat housing.
9. Remove coolant vapor hose from fan shroud retaining clip.
10. Disconnect left and righthand cooling fan motor electrical connector.
11. Push shroud locking tab down, then lift fan and should assembly upwards. **Do not lift fan and shroud by fan rings.**

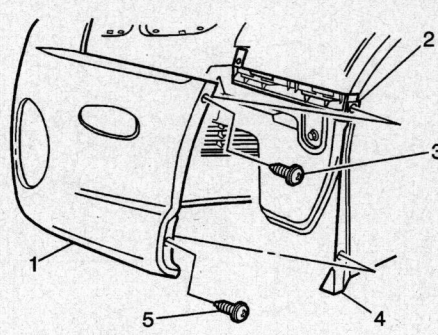

1. Fascia
2. Fascia Support
3. Mounting Screw
4. Wheelhouse Liner
5. Mounting screw

ARM0400000000997

Fig. 9 Fascia replacement (Part 1 of 2)

12. Disconnect intermediate fan motor electrical connector and remove motor wire harness from fan shroud retaining clips.
13. Remove four mounting screws, then the fan motor and wiring.
14. Remove outlet hose radiator and thermostat housing.
15. Remove inlet hose from radiator and radiator inlet pipe.
16. Release refrigerant pipe-to-receiver drier retaining clip on lefthand side of radiator.
17. Remove fascia to wheelhouse liner mounting screws on each side, **Fig. 9.**
18. Remove fascia to support mounting screws.
19. Unclip fascia from support by grabbing upper end and pulling it away.
20. Disconnect fog lamp and sidemarker lamp harness connector from lefthand side.
21. Remove three fascia to front upper panel mounting screws, then the fascia.
22. Press down on 1st locking tab while lifting on condenser.
23. Press down on 2nd locking tab lift, then slightly pull condenser assembly forward to clear radiator mounting lugs.
24. Disconnect transmission cooler lines.
25. Remove two radiator upper mounting brackets.
26. Lift radiator upwards and move it rearwards on lefthand side, then across to lefthand side to allow righthand side to clear mounting brackets.
27. Reverse procedure to install.

FUEL PUMP
REPLACE

1. Remove fuel filler cap.
2. Hold flapper door open using fuel flapper door holder tool No. J 42960-2, or equivalent.
3. Insert fuel tank drain hose tool No. J 42960-1, or equivalent, into fuel tank until hose reaches bottom of fuel tank.
4. Siphon as much fuel as possible from fuel tank using suitable air operated pump.

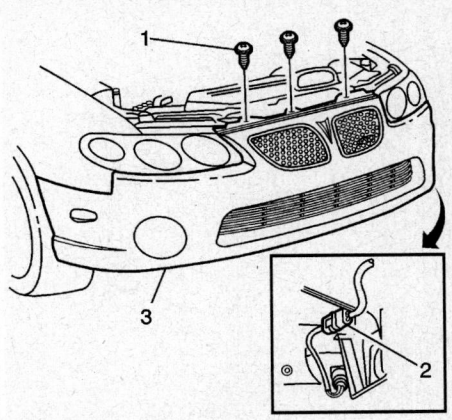

1. Mounting Screw
2. Fog Lamp Connector
3. Fascia

ARM0400000000998

**Fig. 9   Fascia replacement
(Part 2 of 2)**

5. Remove seven retainers and luggage compartment center trim panel carpet.
6. Remove two luggage compartment support brace to panel frame mounting nuts, **Fig. 10.**
7. Remove two luggage compartment support brace to underbody side rail brackets mounting nuts.
8. Remove mounting bolts, then lean support brace forward off studs and remove it.
9. Disconnect body wiring harness to fuel tank harness electrical connector.
10. Unscrew fuel filler cap from behind fuel filler door and cover end of fuel filler neck with suitable material.
11. Remove three fuel filler neck to filler pocket mounting nuts.
12. Raise and support vehicle.
13. Disconnect fuel feed line quick connect fittings and place line aside.
14. Remove fuel tank vent line quick connect fitting.
15. Remove lower fuel tank mounting strap mounting nuts.
16. Lower vehicle and remove two fuel tank upper mounting strap nuts from within luggage compartment, then the mounting straps.
17. Remove fuel tank and filler neck.

18. Disconnect fuel tank pressure sensor and fuel pump connectors, then the EVAP vapor hose quick connector from modular fuel pump and sender cover.
19. Remove modular fuel pump and sender ground terminal to fuel tank flange stud nut.
20. Remove fuel tank wiring harness.
21. Remove cover retainer lock ring by turning in counterclockwise direction using fuel sender lock ring wrench No. J 45722, or equivalent, and suitable half-inch breaker bar.
22. Partially lift modular fuel pump and sender away from fuel tank. **Do not damage fuel level sender.**
23. Disconnect fuel tank EVAP vapor line quick connector from underside of modular fuel pump and sender cover.
24. Insert hand into fuel tank opening and disconnect fuel feed line quick connector.
25. Remove modular fuel pump and sender.
26. Seal fuel tank opening using suitable plug and place suitable cover over plug.
27. Remove and discard modular fuel pump and sender to fuel tank seal.
28. Reverse procedure to install, noting the following:
    a. Only use custom sized O-rings. **Do not use off-the-shelf O-rings.**
    b. Stand assembly upright on flat surface.
    c. Ensure distance between middle of fuel sender float and flat surface is .276–.551 inch.

FUEL FILTER
REPLACE

1. Remove modular fuel sender from fuel tank as outlined under "Fuel Pump, Replace."
2. Removal of fuel level sender and fuel pump harness connectors from underneath modular fuel pump and sender cover using suitable flat blade screwdriver.
3. Press in tang and remove fuel pump connector.
4. Remove modular fuel pump and sender cover from reservoir.

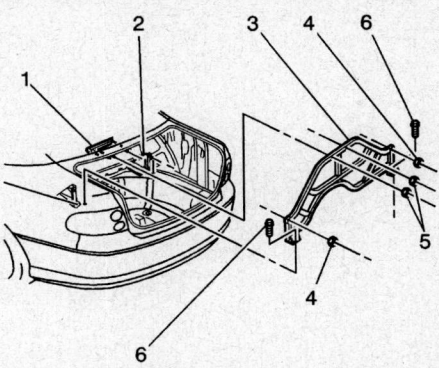

1. Rear Compartment Panel Frame
2. Underbody Side Rail Brackets
3. Rear Compartment Support Brace
4. Mounting Nuts
5. Mounting Nuts
6. Mounting Bolts

ARM0400000001005

**Fig. 10   Luggage compartment
support brace replacement**

5. Remove fuel pressure regulator.
6. Pry open both tangs securing fuel outlet connector to bottom of motor and filter.
7. Remove fuel outlet pipe from motor and filter.
8. Push motor and filter down spring shafts and remove shaft circlip (only one shaft is fitted with circlip).
9. Support fuel filter and pump by clamping protruding end of modular fuel pump in suitable soft jawed vice. **Do not over tighten vice.**
10. Insert suitable pair of medium sized flat-bladed screwdrivers through each service holes in fuel filter.
11. Firmly slide blade between fuel pump end cap and internal fuel filter clips holding fuel pump.
12. Push screwdrivers in far enough that internal fuel filter clips are deflected just free of each of fuel pump end cap retainer shoulders.
13. Hold screwdrivers in place with one hand and move fuel filter in an upward direction to separate it from fuel pump.
14. Remove fuel pump.
15. Remove black ground wiring bridge from fuel filter.
16. Reverse procedure to install.

TIGHTENING SPECIFICATIONS

Year	Component	Torque/Ft. Lbs.
2004	Air Conditioning Compressor & Condenser Hose	22
	Assist Rod	79①
	Coolant Air Bleed	106①
	Coolant Temperature Sensor	15
	Cylinder Head	④
	Engine Mount	59
	Engine Wiring Harness Ground	37
	Exhaust Manifold	②
	Exhaust Manifold Heat Shield	80①
	Exhaust Manifold To Exhaust Pipe	18
	Fan Motor	62①
	Fascia, Side & Wheel Housing	18①
	Fascia, Upper	26①
	Front Suspension Support Brace	②
	Fuel Filler Neck	44①
	Fuel Tank Flange Stud	62①
	Fuel Tank Mounting Strap, Lower	30
	Fuel Tank Mounting Strap, Upper	15
	Hood Hinge, Upper	13
	Hood Latch Striker	18
	Hood Strut Pin	13
	Ignition Coil Bracket	106①
	Luggage Compartment Support Brace	15
	Oil Dipstick Tube	18
	PCM Connector	80①
	Power Steering Pump	21
	Rocker Arms	④
	Spark Plug	③
	Undertray	22
	Valve Cover	106①
	Water Pump	⑤
	Water Pump Inlet	10

① — Inch lbs.
② — Refer to "Engine Mount, Replace" for tightening specifications and sequence.
③ — Tighten spark plug on a NEW cylinder head to 15 ft. lbs.; on subsequent installations to 11 ft. lbs.
④ — Refer to "Cylinder Head, Replace" for tightening specifications and sequence.
⑤ — Refer to "Water Pump, Replace" for tightening specifications and sequence.

6.0L Engine

NOTE: For Procedures Not Found, Refer To The "6.0L & 7.0L Engines" Section In The "Corvette" Chapter.

NOTE: On Air Bag Equipped Models, Refer To "Air Bag System Precautions" Located In The Front Of This Manual For System Disarming & Arming Procedures.

NOTE: Refer To "Computer Relearn Procedures" Located In The Front Of This Manual When Battery Power To The Computer Has Been Interrupted.

INDEX

	Page No.		Page No.		Page No.
Compression Pressure	3-16	Righthand	3-16	Belt Replacement	3-19
Cooling System Bleed	3-19	Exhaust Manifold, Replace	3-17	Removal	3-19
Cylinder Head, Replace	3-18	Fuel Filter, Replace	3-20	Belt Routing	3-19
Lefthand	3-18	Fuel Pump, Replace	3-19	Thermostat, Replace	3-19
Righthand	3-18	Intake Manifold, Replace	3-17	Tightening Specifications	3-21
Engine Rebuilding		Precautions	3-16	Valve Cover, Replace	3-18
Specifications	29-1	Battery Ground Cable	3-16	Lefthand	3-18
Engine, Replace	3-16	Fuel System Pressure Relief	3-16	Righthand	3-18
Engine Mount, Replace	3-16	Radiator, Replace	3-19	Water Pump, Replace	3-19
Lefthand	3-16	Serpentine Drive Belt	3-19		

PRECAUTIONS

Fuel System Pressure Relief

Failure to relieve system pressure prior to disconnecting fuel system components may cause fire or personal injury.
1. Turn ignition switch to OFF position.
2. Disconnect and isolate battery ground.
3. Relieve fuel tank vapor pressure by loosening fuel filler cap.
4. Remove lefthand fuel rail cover.
5. Connect fuel pressure gauge tool No. J34730-1A, or equivalent, to fuel pressure connection.
6. Wrap shop towel around fitting while connecting gauge.
7. Install gauge bleed hose into suitable container.
8. Open gauge valve and bleed system pressure.
9. Drain remaining gauge fuel into suitable container.

Battery Ground Cable

Prior to service, disconnect battery ground cable and isolate as required.

COMPRESSION PRESSURE

When measuring compression, lowest cylinder must be within 70% of the highest cylinder with a minimum pressure of 100 psi. Compression test results will fall into one of the following categories:
1. Normally, compression builds up

quickly and evenly to specifications on each cylinder.
2. If piston rings are faulty, compression will be low on first stroke, then build up on following strokes but will not reach specifications. Improvement is considerable with addition of approximately three squirts oil.
3. If valves are faulty, compression will be low on first stroke and will not tend to build up on following strokes. It will not improve much with addition of oil.
4. Ensure battery is fully charged.
5. Bring engine to operating temperature.
6. Disconnect electrical connector at crankshaft ignition timing sensor.
7. Disable fuel injection system.
8. Remove spark plugs.
9. Ensure throttle is wide open.
10. Install compression gauge tool No. J 38722, or equivalent.
11. Crank engine through four complete compression strokes, then record results for each cylinder.

ENGINE MOUNT
REPLACE
Lefthand

1. Remove lefthand exhaust manifold as outlined under "Exhaust Manifold, Replace."
2. Remove mounting nuts and lefthand engine mount.
3. Reverse procedure to install.

Righthand

1. Remove righthand exhaust manifold as outlined under "Exhaust Manifold, Replace."

2. Remove mounting nuts and righthand engine mount.
3. Reverse procedure to install.

ENGINE
REPLACE

1. Recover air conditioning refrigerant as outlined in "Air Conditioning" chapter.
2. Open hood.
3. Apply suitable tape to hood corners and adjacent surfaces.
4. Cut end and remove secondary latch rivet, then remove secondary latch and spring.
5. Loosen nut and remove hood latch striker bolt ensuring washer, hood pop-up spring and hood pop-up spring retainer remain on bolt.
6. **On models equipped with hood scoops,** proceed as follows:
   a. Remove hood air extractor by gently squeezing to unhook tabs.
   b. Starting at rear of hood and working toward front, remove 13 hood insulator retainers.
   c. Slide insulator from slots in hood inner panel and remove.
   d. Remove plug, retainer and scoop.
7. **On models equipped less hood scoops,** starting at rear of hood and working toward front, remove hood insulator retainers.
8. **On all models,** place suitable container under washer solvent container.
9. Reach between front bumper fascia and washer solvent container, then disconnect washer solvent hose from pump.
10. Allow washer solvent to drain from container.
11. Remove washer hose from behind

12. Separate and remove washer hoses from washer nozzles.
13. Squeeze retaining tabs on washer nozzle base and push nozzle out through top of hood. Remove nozzle.
14. Remove hood adjustable bumper by rotating it counterclockwise.
15. Mark upper hood hinge location to hood for installation alignment.
16. Provide alternate hood support.
17. Remove assist rod clip using suitable, small flat-bladed tool.
18. Remove assist rod to fender mounting bolts.
19. Disconnect and remove assist rod from hood strut pin.
20. Have assistant hold hood then remove upper hood hinge mounting bolts and hood.
21. Remove four mounting nuts and front suspension support brace.
22. Remove fuel rail covers.
23. Disconnect air intake sensor connector.
24. Loosen hose clamps and remove intake duct.
25. Disconnect and isolate battery ground.
26. Relieve fuel tank vapor pressure by loosening fuel filler cap.
27. Remove lefthand fuel rail cover.
28. Connect fuel pressure gauge tool No. J34730-1A, or equivalent, to fuel pressure connection.
29. Wrap shop towel around fitting while connecting gauge.
30. Install gauge bleed hose into suitable container.
31. Open gauge valve and bleed system pressure.
32. Remove radiator as outlined under "Radiator, Replace."
33. Remove radiator and heater hoses from water pump.
34. Remove air conditioning compressor and condenser hose nut.
35. Separate compressor and condenser hose from compressor. Cap hoses and inlets.
36. Remove ground lead screw from engine block and lefthand engine mount.
37. Remove nut securing battery harness ground terminals to antilock brake system (ABS)/traction control system (TCS) control module bracket stud.
38. Disconnect positive lead terminal from battery. Lay harness on engine.
39. Disconnect air conditioning wiring harness connector.
40. Disconnect wiring harness retaining clips from engine compartment.
41. Disconnect theft deterrent horn connector.
42. Disconnect radiator hose from surge tank inlet fitting.
43. Disconnect surge tank vapor and overflow hoses.
44. Pivot surge tank to remove from rear anchor plate.
45. Pull tank inward toward engine and remove it from anchor plate on inner fender.

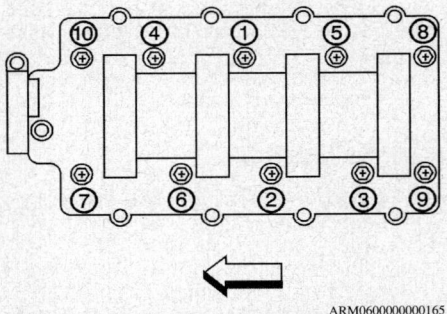

Fig. 1 Intake manifold bolt tightening sequence

ARM0600000000165

46. Disconnect coolant level switch electrical connector.
47. Remove Powertrain Control Module (PCM) harness connector cover.
48. Loosen and remove PCM connectors.
49. Disconnect PCM wiring harness retaining clip.
50. Remove engine wiring harness retaining clip from power steering pipe bracket.
51. Remove throttle relaxer cover and disconnect connector.
52. Remove both fuel rail covers.
53. Disconnect throttle and cruise control cables form relaxer.
54. Remove mounting nuts and throttle relaxer.
55. Cut wiring harness straps and discard.
56. Disconnect powertrain to main wiring harness connector.
57. Remove harness to dash panel grommet, then feed harness and connectors out into engine bay.
58. Place powertrain wiring harness on top of engine.
59. Lift throttle cable at throttle body mounting bracket and remove it from cam lever. Set throttle cable aside.
60. Relieve vapor pressure by loosening fuel filler cap.
61. Disconnect engine compartment fuel feed pipe at fuel rail.
62. Disconnect engine compartment EVAP pipe at EVAP canister purge solenoid.
63. Disconnect engine compartment fuel feed pipe at chassis fuel feed pipe.
64. Disconnect engine compartment EVAP pipe at chassis EVAP pipe.
65. Cap fuel pipes.
66. Disconnect line from purge valve.
67. Loosen power steering reservoir return hose clamp.
68. Place suitable container under reservoir, then remove hose and drain reservoir fluid.
69. Remove power steering pump outlet fitting high pressure line flare nut and O-ring.
70. Disconnect brake booster vacuum hose and heater control, vacuum hose from rear of intake manifold.
71. Remove four mounting bolts and undertray from crossmember.
72. Remove two power steering high pres-

sure line brackets to oil pan mounting bolts.
73. Remove exhaust manifolds as outlined under "Exhaust Manifold, Replace."
74. Remove transmission as outlined in **MOTOR's "Domestic Transmission, In-Vehicle Service" manual or "Transmission Service DVD."**
75. Remove left and righthand engine mount to engine bracket nuts.
76. Attach suitable lifting chain and hooks to two engine lifting brackets.
77. Slightly raise engine to clear engine mount stud using suitable lifting crane.
78. Slowly lift and remove engine.
79. Reverse procedure to install.

INTAKE MANIFOLD
REPLACE

1. Remove engine sight cover, then drain coolant into a suitable container.
2. Relieve fuel system pressure as outlined under "Precautions."
3. Disconnect electrical connector from fuel injectors and throttle body.
4. Disconnect fuel feed pipe from fuel injectors.
5. Disconnect vacuum hose from brake booster, then the electrical connector from manifold absolute pressure sensor.
6. Remove MAP sensor, then the grommet from sensor.
7. Remove EVAP clip, bolt, bracket, valve and tubes.
8. Remove bolts, fuel rail stop bracket and intake manifold.
9. Remove and discard intake manifold gaskets.
10. Reverse procedure to install.
    a. First tighten intake manifold bolts in sequence, **Fig. 1,** to 44 inch lbs.
    b. Second tighten intake manifold bolts in sequence to 89 inch lbs.

EXHAUST MANIFOLD
REPLACE

1. Remove spark plug wires from spark plugs.
2. Remove exhaust manifold mounting bolts, working from outside to center.
3. Remove exhaust manifold and gasket.
4. Remove mounting bolts and heat shield.
5. Reverse procedure to install, noting the following:
    a. Apply .2 inch wide band of suitable threadlocker to exhaust manifold mounting bolts' threads.
    b. **Torque** exhaust manifold mounting bolts from center to outsides to 11 ft. lbs.
    c. **Torque** exhaust manifold mounting bolts from center to outsides to 15 ft. lbs.
    d. Bend over exposed edge of exhaust manifold gasket at rear of cylinder head.

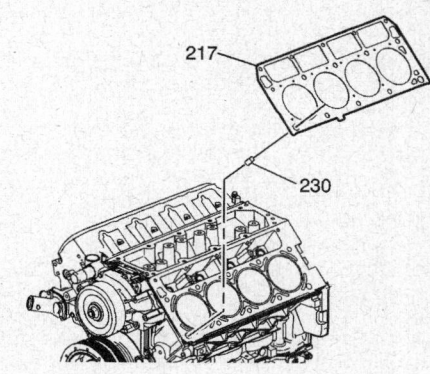

217. Cylinder head gasket
230. Locating pins

ARM0600000000162

Fig. 2 Cylinder head gasket installation

CYLINDER HEAD
REPLACE

Lefthand

1. Remove valve cover as outlined under "Valve Cover, Replace."
2. Remove mounting bolts, rocker arms pivot support. and pushrods. **Place rocker arms, pushrods and pivot support in suitable rack so they can be installed in original position.**
3. Remove coolant air bleed hose from throttle body, then the studs, coolant air bleed pipe and gaskets.
4. Remove two mounting bolts and power steering pump.
5. Remove lefthand exhaust manifold as outlined under "Exhaust Manifold Replace."
6. Remove mounting bolts and position engine wiring harness ground aside.
7. Remove and discard cylinder head bolts. **Do not reuse cylinder head bolts.**
8. Remove cylinder head and place it on two suitable wood blocks.
9. Remove and discard head gasket.
10. Reverse procedure to install, noting the following.
    a. **Do not use any type of sealant on cylinder head gasket.**
    b. Install head gasket in proper direction and position onto locating pins, **Fig. 2.** When properly installed, tab on gasket will be located left of center, or closer to front of engine and words This Side Up and engine displacement visible.
    c. Install new cylinder head bolts.
    d. **Torque** first step, **torque** M11 cylinder head bolts 1–10 to 22 ft. lbs., in sequence, **Fig. 3.**
    e. Second step, tighten M11 cylinder head bolts 1–10 an additional 90°.
    f. Third step, tighten M11 cylinder head bolts 1–10 an additional 70°.
    g. Fourth step, **torque** M8 cylinder head bolts 11–15 to 22 ft. lbs.
    h. Lubricate rocker arms and push-

rods, then rocker arm bolts and flange with suitable, clean engine oil.
    i. Ensure pushrods seat properly to rocker arms ends.

Righthand

1. Remove valve rocker arms as outlined under "Rocker Arms."
2. Remove push rods.
3. Drain engine coolant into a suitable container, then disconnect electrical connector from intake air temperature sensor.
4. Disconnect electrical connector from throttle position sensor, then the crankcase ventilation hose from throttle body.
5. Remove throttle body attaching bolts, then throttle body.
6. Remove coolant air bleed hose, then the coolant air bleed pipe mounting bolts and coolant air bleed pipe and O-rings.
7. Remove alternator as outlined under "Alternator, Replace."
8. Remove power steering pump as outlined under "Power Steering Pump, Replace" in "Front Suspension & Steering" section.
9. Remove alternator bracket bolts, then the bracket and power steering reservoir bracket.
10. Remove exhaust manifold as outlined under "Exhaust Manifold, Replace."
11. Remove oil dipstick tube bolt, then the oil dipstick tube bolt and reposition tube.
12. Remove wiring harness from clip at rear of cylinder head.
13. Remove cylinder head bolts and cylinder head. **Do not reuse cylinder head bolts.**
14. Remove cylinder head gasket and discard gasket.
15. Reverse procedure to install, noting the following.
    a. **Do not use any type of sealant on cylinder head gasket.**
    b. Install head gasket in proper direction and position onto locating pins, **Fig. 2.** When properly installed, tab on gasket will be located left of center, or closer to front of engine and words This Side Up and engine displacement visible.
    c. Install new cylinder head bolts.
    d. First step, **torque** M11 cylinder head bolts 1–10 to 22 ft. lbs.
    e. Second step, tighten M11 cylinder head bolts 1–10 an additional 90°.
    f. Third step, tighten M11 cylinder head bolts 1–10 an additional 70°.
    g. Fourth step, **torque** M8 cylinder head bolts 11–15 to 22 ft. lbs.
    h. Install engine wiring harness ground strap to rear of lefthand cylinder head.
    i. Install wiring harness to clip at rear of cylinder head.
    j. Install oil dipstick tube bolt.
    k. Install exhaust manifold as outlined under "Exhaust Manifold, Replace."
    l. Install coolant air bleed pipe and

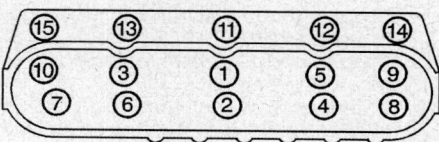

ARM0600000000163

Fig. 3 Cylinder head tightening sequence

O-rings, then the coolant air bleed hose.
    m. Install throttle body, then connect crankcase ventilation hose and electrical connector to throttle body.
    n. Connect air control valve and intake air temperature sensor electrical connectors.
    o. Install push rods as outlined under "Push Rods."
    p. Install valve rocker arms as outlined under "Rocker Arms."
    q. Fill cooling system.

VALVE COVER
REPLACE

Lefthand

1. Remove front suspension support brace.
2. Disconnect engine compartment fuel feed pipe at fuel rail.
3. Remove lefthand engine sight cover, then disconnect alternator electrical connector.
4. Remove engine wiring harness alternator lead retaining nut and lead.
5. Remove fuel rail cover, then disconnect ignition coil harness connector and spark plug wire at ignition coil.
6. Remove ignition coil mounting bolts and coils.
7. Loosen valve rocker arm cover bolts, then the valve rocker cover.
8. Remove gasket from rocker cover and discard old gasket.
9. Reverse procedure to install.

Righthand

1. Remove righthand side engine sight cover.
2. Disconnect engine vacuum pipe from EVAP canister purge solenoid valve to intake manifold EVAP pipe.
3. Disconnect engine purge pipe from EVAP canister purge valve, then disconnect electrical connector.
4. Remove EVAP canister purge valve from purge bracket.
5. Remove retaining clips, then the EVAP pipes.
6. Remove EVAP pipe from intake air temperature sensor at air intake duct valve cover, then the hose from throttle body to engine valley cover.
7. Remove fuel rail cover, then disconnect ignition coil connector and spark plug wires at ignition coils.
8. Remove mounting bolts, then the ignition coils.

9. Remove retaining bolt, then the valve rocker arm cover.
10. Remove gasket from rocker cover and discard old gasket.
11. Reverse procedure to install.

SERPENTINE DRIVE BELT

Belt Routing

Refer to **Fig. 4** for serpentine drive belt routing.

Belt Replacement

REMOVAL

1. Install suitable breaker bar with hex-head socket to drive belt tensioner bolt.
2. Relieve tension on belt by rotating drive belt tensioner clockwise.
3. Remove belt from pulleys and drive belt tensioner.
4. Slowly release tension on drive belt tensioner. Remove breaker bar and socket from drive belt tensioner bolt.

INSTALLATION

1. Route drive belt around all pulleys, except water pump and belt tensioner.
2. Install suitable breaker bar with hex-head socket to belt tensioner bolt.
3. Relieve tension on tension by rotating belt tensioner clockwise.
4. Install drive belt under water pump pulley and onto belt tensioner.
5. Slowly release tension.
6. Remove breaker bar and socket from belt tensioner bolt.
7. Inspect drive belt for proper alignment.

COOLING SYSTEM

BLEED

1. Slowly fill cooling system through upper radiator hose with suitable coolant mixture until coolant comes out coolant air bleed hose.
2. Fill radiator suitable coolant through surge tank opening to full line.
3. Install coolant pressure cap.
4. Start engine and run at 2000–2500 RPM until engine reaches normal operating temperature.
5. Allow engine to idle for three minutes.
6. Shut off and allow engine to cool.
7. Adjust coolant level as required.

THERMOSTAT

REPLACE

1. Drain engine coolant into a suitable container.
2. Remove outlet hose from water pump inlet, then the bolts and water pump inlet.
3. Remove bolts, then the thermostat housing and thermostat. **O-ring seal is integral to thermostat housing.**
4. Reverse procedure to install.

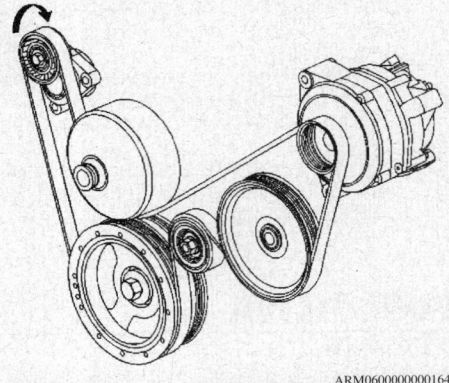

ARM0600000000164

Fig. 4 Serpentine drive belt routing

WATER PUMP

REPLACE

1. Drain engine coolant into a suitable container.
2. Remove air cleaner intake duct.
3. Remove accessory drive belts.
4. Remove inlet and outlet hoses from water pump.
5. Remove heater inlet and surge tank outlet hoses from water pump.
6. Remove retaining bolts, then the water pump and gasket.
7. Reverse procedure to install. **Torque** water pump mounting bolts to 11 ft. lbs, then to 22 ft. lbs.

RADIATOR

REPLACE

1. Lift locking levers, then disconnect Mass Air Flow (MAF) and Intake Air Temperature (IAT) sensors' electrical connectors.
2. Loosen two clamps and remove intake duct.
3. Drain cooling system into suitable container.
4. Remove vapor hose from radiator fan shroud clips and radiator clamp, then position it aside.
5. Remove vapor hose to surge tank clamp at radiator and position it aside.
6. Remove five upper shroud to radiator retainers.
7. Lift shroud on righthand side and release lefthand side locating tab.
8. Loosen and remove radiator outlet hose from radiator and thermostat housing.
9. Remove coolant vapor hose from fan shroud retaining clip.
10. Disconnect left and righthand cooling fan motor electrical connector.
11. Push shroud locking tab down, then lift fan and should assembly upwards. **Do not lift fan and shroud by fan rings.**
12. Disconnect intermediate fan motor electrical connector and remove motor wire harness from fan shroud retaining clips.
13. Remove four mounting screws, then the fan motor and wiring.

14. Remove outlet hose radiator and thermostat housing.
15. Remove inlet hose from radiator and radiator inlet pipe.
16. Release refrigerant pipe-to-receiver drier retaining clip on lefthand side of radiator.
17. Remove fascia to wheelhouse liner mounting screws on each side.
18. Remove fascia to support mounting screws.
19. Unclip fascia from support by grabbing upper end and pulling it away.
20. Disconnect fog lamp and sidemarker lamp harness connector from lefthand side.
21. Remove three fascia to front upper panel mounting screws, then the fascia.
22. Press down on 1st locking tab while lifting on condenser.
23. Press down on 2nd locking tab lift, then slightly pull condenser assembly forward to clear radiator mounting lugs.
24. Disconnect transmission cooler lines.
25. Remove two radiator upper mounting brackets.
26. Lift radiator upwards and move it rearwards on lefthand side, then across to lefthand side to allow righthand side to clear mounting brackets.
27. Reverse procedure to install.

FUEL PUMP

REPLACE

1. Remove fuel filler cap.
2. Hold flapper door open using fuel flapper door holder tool No. J 42960-2, or equivalent.
3. Insert fuel tank drain hose tool No. J 42960-1, or equivalent, into fuel tank until hose reaches bottom of fuel tank.
4. Siphon as much fuel as possible from fuel tank using suitable air operated pump.
5. Remove seven retainers and luggage compartment center trim panel carpet.
6. Remove two luggage compartment support brace to panel frame mounting nuts.
7. Remove two luggage compartment support brace to underbody side rail brackets mounting nuts.
8. Remove mounting bolts, then lean support brace forward off studs and remove it.
9. Disconnect body wiring harness to fuel tank harness electrical connector.
10. Unscrew fuel filler cap from behind fuel filler door and cover end of fuel filler neck with suitable material.
11. Remove three fuel filler neck to filler pocket mounting nuts.
12. Raise and support vehicle.
13. Disconnect fuel feed line quick connect fittings and place line aside.
14. Remove fuel tank vent line quick connect fitting.
15. Remove lower fuel tank mounting strap mounting nuts.
16. Lower vehicle and remove two fuel tank upper mounting strap nuts from within luggage compartment, then the mounting straps.
17. Remove fuel tank and filler neck.

18. Disconnect fuel tank pressure sensor and fuel pump connectors, then the EVAP vapor hose quick connector from modular fuel pump and sender cover.
19. Remove modular fuel pump and sender ground terminal to fuel tank flange stud nut.
20. Remove fuel tank wiring harness.
21. Remove cover retainer lock ring by turning in counterclockwise direction using fuel sender lock ring wrench No. J 45722, or equivalent, and suitable half-inch breaker bar.
22. Partially lift modular fuel pump and sender away from fuel tank. **Do not damage fuel level sender.**
23. Disconnect fuel tank EVAP vapor line quick connector from underside of modular fuel pump and sender cover.
24. Insert hand into fuel tank opening and disconnect fuel feed line quick connector.
25. Remove modular fuel pump and sender.
26. Seal fuel tank opening using suitable plug and place suitable cover over plug.
27. Remove and discard modular fuel pump and sender to fuel tank seal.
28. Reverse procedure to install, noting the following:
    a. Only use custom sized O-rings. **Do not use off-the-shelf O-rings.**
    b. Stand assembly upright on flat surface.
    c. Ensure distance between middle of fuel sender float and flat surface is .276–.551 inch.

FUEL FILTER
REPLACE

1. Remove modular fuel sender from fuel tank as outlined under "Fuel Pump, Replace."
2. Remove fuel level sender and fuel pump harness connectors from underneath modular fuel pump and sender cover using suitable flat blade screwdriver.
3. Press in tang and remove fuel pump connector.
4. Remove modular fuel pump and sender cover from reservoir.
5. Remove fuel pressure regulator.
6. Pry open both tangs securing fuel outlet connector to bottom of motor and filter.
7. Remove fuel outlet pipe from motor and filter.
8. Push motor and filter down spring shafts and remove shaft circlip (only one shaft is fitted with circlip).
9. Support fuel filter and pump by clamping protruding end of modular fuel pump in suitable soft jawed vice. **Do not over tighten vice.**
10. Insert suitable pair of medium sized flat-bladed screwdrivers through each service holes in fuel filter.
11. Firmly slide blade between fuel pump end cap and internal fuel filter clips holding fuel pump.
12. Push screwdrivers in far enough that internal fuel filter clips are deflected just free of each of fuel pump end cap retainer shoulders.
13. Hold screwdrivers in place with one hand and move fuel filter in an upward direction to separate it from fuel pump.
14. Remove fuel pump.
15. Remove black ground wiring bridge from fuel filter.
16. Reverse procedure to install.

TIGHTENING SPECIFICATIONS

Year	Component	Torque/Ft. Lbs.
2005–06	Alternator	37
	Camshaft Position Sensor	106①
	Camshaft Retainer	18
	Camshaft Sprocket	18
	Clutch Pressure Plate	52
	Connecting Rod	②
	Coolant Temperature Sensor	15
	Crankshaft Bearing Cap	④
	Crankshaft Damper	③
	Crankshaft Position Sensor	18
	Cylinder Head Bolts	⑤
	Cylinder Head Coolant Plug	15
	Drive Belt Pulley	37
	Drive Belt Tensioner	37
	Engine Block Coolant Heater	30
	Engine Block Oil Gallery/Coolant Plugs	44
	Engine Front Cover	18
	Engine Mount	48
	Engine Mount Bracket	37
	Engine Rear Cover	18
	Exhaust Manifold	⑦
	Flywheel	⑥
	Fuel Rail	89①
	Ignition Coil	89①
	Intake Manifold	⑧
	Knock Sensor	15
	Main Bearing Cap	④
	Oil Filter	22
	Oil Filter Fitting	40
	Oil Dipstick Tube Bolt	18
	Oil Level Sensor	15
	Oil Pan Closeout Cover	80①
	Oil Pan Cover Bolts	106①
	Oil Pan Drain Plug	18
	Oil Pan M6 Bolts Oil Pan to Rear Cover	106①
	Oil Pan M8 Bolts Oil Pan to Engine Block and Oil Pan to Front Cover	18

TIGHTENING SPECIFICATIONS—Continued

Year	Component	Torque/Ft. Lbs.
2005–06	Oil Pressure Sensor	15
	Oil Pump Cover	106①
	Oil Pump Regulator Valve Plug	106①
	Oil Pump Screen	18
	Oil Pump Screen To Oil Pump	106①
	Oil Pump to Engine Block	18
	Power Steering Pump	18
	Power Steering Reservoir Bracket to Engine	37
	Spark Plugs	⑩
	Starter Motor	37
	Throttle Body	89①
	Timing Chain Guide	18
	Valley Cover	18
	Valve Lifter Guide	89①
	Valve Rocker Arm	22
	Valve Rocker Arm Cover	106①
	Water Inlet Housing	11
	Water Pump	⑨
	Water Pump Cover	11
	Water Pump Pulley	⑨

① — Inch lbs.

② — First step, torque to 15 ft. lbs.; second step, an additional 75°.

③ — Refer to "Crankshaft Damper, Replace."

④ — Refer to "Main & Rod Bearings."

⑤ — Refer to "Cylinder Head, Replace."

⑥ — First step, torque to 15 ft. lbs.; second step, torque to 37 ft. lbs.; third step, torque to 74 ft. lbs.

⑦ — Refer to "Exhaust Manifold, Replace."

⑧ — First step, torque to 44 inch lbs.; second step, torque to 89 inch lbs.

⑨ — Refer to "Water Pump, Replace."

⑩ — New cylinder head, 15 ft. lbs.; used cylinder head 11 ft. lbs.

Rear Axle & Suspension

NOTE: On Air Bag Equipped Models, Refer To "Air Bag System Precautions" Located In The Front Of This Manual For System Disarming & Arming Procedures.

NOTE: Refer To "Computer Relearn Procedures" Located In The Front Of This Manual When Battery Power To The Computer Has Been Interrupted.

NOTE: Refer To The Rear Of This Manual For Vehicle Manufacturer's Special Tool Suppliers.

INDEX

	Page No.		Page No.		Page No.
Adjustment Link, Replace	3-27	Installation	3-24	**Shock Absorber, Replace**	3-25
Inner	3-27	Removal	3-24	**Stabilizer Shaft, Replace**	3-26
Outer	3-27	**Precautions**	3-22	**Technical Service Bulletins**	3-27
Coil Spring, Replace	3-25	Air Bag Systems	3-22	Knocking Noise From Rear,	3-27
Control Arm, Replace	3-26	Battery Ground Cable	3-22	**Tightening Specifications**	3-28
Description	3-22	**Propeller Shaft, Replace**	3-23	**U-joint, Replace**	3-23
Differential Carrier, Replace	3-22	**Rear Axle Shaft, Replace**	3-22	Installation	3-24
Hub & Bearing, Replace	3-24	**Rear Wheel Shaft, Replace**	3-22	Removal	3-23

PRECAUTIONS

Air Bag Systems

Refer to "Air Bag System Precautions" in the front of this manual for system disarming and arming procedures.

Battery Ground Cable

Prior to service, disconnect battery ground cable and isolate as required.

DESCRIPTION

The differential is a four-pinion type limited slip differential final drive assembly mounted to and independent rear suspension. The differential is mounted directly to the crossmember which is rubber mounted to the underbody. The differential case and drive pinon are mounted in opposed taper roller bearing in the carrier. Differential case side bearing preload adjustment is provided by screw adjusters in the sides of the case. Pinon bearing pre-load is provided by a collapsible spacer. Torque is transferred from the propeller shaft to the differential via the pinon flange which is splined to the hypoid pinon. The torque is then transferred from the pinon through the ring gear, differential case, differential pinon cross shafts, differential pinons, side gears, and then via splines to the inner axle shafts and the drive shafts.

The hub is retained to the wheel drive shaft flange by a nut. The hub rotates inside a sealed wheel bearing. The wheel bearing is pressed into the lower control arm.

The forward end of the lower control arm attaches to the rear suspension support with semi-rigid bushings. The adjustment link connects between the rear suspension support and the lower control arms. The inner adjustment link has a bushing. The outer adjustment link has a ball joint. The adjustment link assembly controls rear wheel camber and toe angles during suspension travel. The adjustment link also provides a means of adjusting the rear wheel toe.

The stabilizer shaft connects between the left lower control arm and the righthand lower control arm through the stabilizer shaft links. Insulators and clamps retain the stabilizer shaft to the rear suspension support. The stabilizer shaft controls the amount of independent movement of the suspension when the vehicle turns.

REAR AXLE SHAFT

REPLACE

1. Raise and support vehicle.
2. Position suitable container under axle.
3. Remove inner axle using suitable slide hammer and puller plate.
4. Reverse procedure to install, noting the following:
   a. Lubricate seal lip with suitable Lithium grease.
   b. Ensure axle shaft splines or retainer ring do not damage axle seal when installing axle.
   c. Lightly hit end of axle with suitable, soft faced hammer until retainer clip snaps into place.

REAR WHEEL SHAFT

REPLACE

1. Shift transmission into PARK or NEUTRAL position.
2. Raise and support vehicle.
3. **Support drive shaft until removed.**
4. Mark inner constant velocity joint and inner axle for installation alignment.

5. Remove mounting bolts and inner constant velocity joint retaining plates.
6. Remove mounting bolts and outer constant velocity join retaining plates.
7. Remove drive shaft.
8. Reverse procedure to install, noting the following:
   a. **Torque** inner mount and retainer plates bolts to 37 ft. lbs.
   b. Tighten bolts an additional 68°.
   c. **Torque** outer constant velocity joint mounting bolts to 37 ft. lbs.
   d. Tighten bolts an additional 68°.

DIFFERENTIAL CARRIER

REPLACE

1. Remove propeller shaft as outlined under "Propeller Shaft, Replace."
2. Pull park brake lever boot to side and loosen park brake cable adjustment nut.
3. Raise and support vehicle.
4. Remove rear cable grommet from clip and wrap cloth or tape around cable near equalizer.
5. Pull rear cable forward and up to release cable from equalizer using suitable pliers on wrapped portion of cable.
6. Pull insulation for cable rearward to release cable from bracket.
7. Wrap cloth or tape around cable near rear clevis.
8. Pull cable rearward to release clevis from park brake actuating lever using suitable pliers on wrapped portion of cable.
9. Pull insulation for cable forward to release cable from control arm retainer.
10. Remove rear parking brake cable.
11. Disconnect brake line from hose at rear suspension control arm bracket

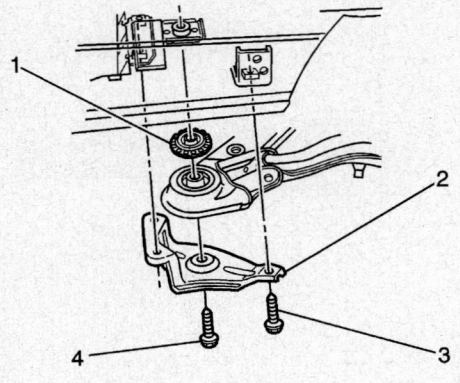

1. Isolating Rubber
2. Braces
3. Underbody Bolts
4. Mounting Bolt

ARM0400000001007

Fig. 1   Brace replacement

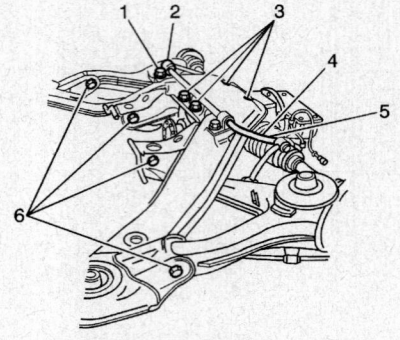

1. Stabilizer Shaft Mounting Bracket Bolts
2. Stabilizer Shaft Mounting Bracket
3. Differential Carrier To Rear Suspension Support Mounting Bolts
4. Stabilizer Shaft
5. Stabilizer Link Mounting Nuts
6. Control Arm To Rear Suspension Support Mounting Bolts & Nuts

ARM0400000001008

Fig. 2   Rear suspension support replacement

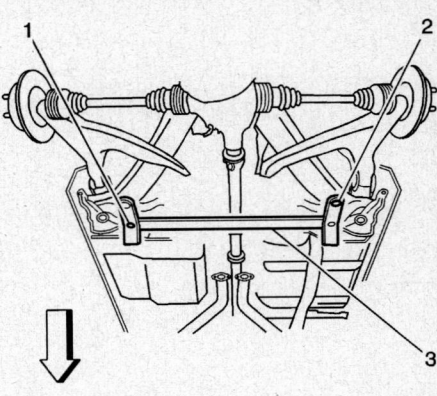

1. Body Datum Holes
2. Location Pins
3. Rear Cross-member Centering Tool

ARM0400000001009

Fig. 3   Rear suspension support centering

and remove brake hose retaining clip. Plug open ends of both pipes and hoses.

12. Pull differential carrier breather hose out of vehicle underbody rear suspension support hole.
13. Remove ABS sensor lead connectors from underbody retaining clips and disconnect them from body harness connectors.
14. Mark rear mount to vehicle under body location for installation alignment.
15. Support differential carrier with suitable floor jack.
16. Remove and discard four rear mount to vehicle underbody mountings bolts.
17. Lower differential carrier and rear suspension at least 2.36 inches.
18. Remove rear springs as outlined under, "Coil Spring, Replace."
19. Raise differential carrier and rear suspension support on floor jack until rear mount contacts vehicle underbody.
20. Remove three brace to underbody bolts from each side, **Fig. 1.**
21. Remove and discard rear suspension support to underbody mounting bolt on each side.
22. Remove braces.
23. With assistant supporting front end of rear suspension support, lower assembly and remove.
24. Remove differential carrier and rear suspension support from jack, then support rear control arms, drive shafts and differential carrier off ground.
25. Remove mounting bolts and stabilizer shaft mounting bracket, **Fig. 2.**
26. Remove and discard differential carrier to rear suspension support mounting bolts.
27. Remove rear suspension control arm to rear suspension support mounting bolts and nuts. Discard nuts.
28. Disconnect control arms from rear suspension support.
29. Loosen stabilizer link mounting nuts at each end and on each side, then swing stabilizer shaft back from rear suspension support.

30. Lift up and remove rear suspension support.
31. Mark inner constant velocity joints to axle shafts for installation alignment.
32. Remove inner drive shaft constant velocity joint bolts and retainer plates.
33. Support drive shafts so they do not hang.
34. Remove rear differential mount bolts from differential cover.
35. Remove differential carrier mounting bolts from crossmember.
36. Remove differential carrier.
37. Reverse procedure to install, noting the following:
    a. **Torque** new crossmember to differential carrier mounting bolts to 66 ft. lbs.
    b. Tighten bolts an additional 68°.
    c. **Torque** inner constant velocity joints to axle shaft bolts to 37 ft. lbs.
    d. Tighten bolts an additional 68°.
    e. Install new, self locking rear control arms mounting nuts.
    f. Install new differential carrier to rear suspension support mounting bolts.
    g. Install new rear mount to vehicle underbody mounting bolts.
    h. Fit rear crossmember centering tool No. CH-46839, or equivalent, into .74 inch diameter body datum holes forward of rear suspension support, **Fig. 3.**
    i. With an assistant, position rear suspension support until rear crossmember centering tool location pins engage alignment holes on rear suspension support.
    j. **Torque** brace to underbody bolts to 92 ft. lbs.
    k. Tighten bolts an additional 40°.
    l. **Torque** rear differential mount mounting bolts to 26 ft. lbs.
    m. Tighten bolts an additional 60°.
    n. With vehicle at curb weight, bounce rear vehicle several times to settle suspension.
    o. Tighten rear control arm mounting nuts, rear stabilizer shaft link nuts and lower rear shock absorber mounting bolts.

PROPELLER SHAFT
REPLACE

1. Raise and support vehicle rear, then remove rear tire and wheel assemblies.
2. Remove two support hangers clips and rubber hangers.
3. Loosen two ring clamp nuts and remove both rear pipes by sliding them out of muffler pipe slip joints.
4. Support catalytic converter and muffler with suitable jackstand.
5. Remove flange bolts and separate catalytic converter and muffler. Remove gasket from flange joint.
6. Remove four clips and four rubber hangers from left and righthand left muffler support hangers.
7. Remove mufflers.
8. Mark propeller shaft to pinion gear flange for installation alignment.
9. Support propeller shaft near support bearing with suitable stand.
10. Remove pinon flange coupling bolts.
11. Place an identification mark at center bearing bracket position in four places for installation alignment.
12. Remove center bearing support bolts.
13. Slide propeller shaft forward to disconnect differential pinon support pin.
14. Remove sliding yoke and two-piece propeller shaft from transmission.
15. Reverse procedure to install, noting the following:
    a. Lubricate sliding yoke with suitable transmission lubricant.
    b. Lubricate pinion support pin with molybdenum disulfide grease, or equivalent.

U-JOINT
REPLACE
Removal

1. Remove propeller shaft as outlined under "Propeller Shaft, Replace."

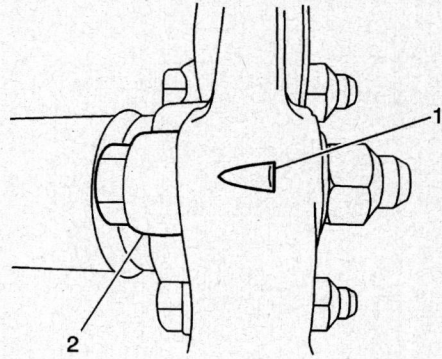

1. Coupling Arrow
2. Propeller Shaft Flange

ARM0400000001010

Fig. 4   Coupling alignment

2. Remove and discard propeller shaft sliding yoke bolts, nuts and washers.
3. Remove and discard propeller shaft coupling bolts.

Installation

1. Align coupling triangle point to face propeller shaft flange, **Fig. 4.**
2. Install new propeller shaft coupling to propeller shaft bolts, nuts and washers.
3. **Torque** bolts to 13 ft. lbs.
4. Tighten bolts an additional 55°.
5. Install new propeller shaft yoke to propeller coupling bolts, nuts and washers.
6. **Torque** bolts to 13 ft. lbs.
7. Tighten bolts an additional 55°.
8. Install propeller shaft as outlined under "Propeller Shaft, Replace."

HUB & BEARING
REPLACE
Removal

1. Remove rear suspension lower control arm as outlined under "Control Arm, Replace."
2. Align holes wheel hub remover and installer tool No. J-42094-2, or equivalent, with holes in rear wheel drive shaft flange, **Fig. 5.**
3. Align holes in wheel hub remover and installer tool J-42094-1-B, or equivalent, marked B with holes in tool No. J-42094-2 and holes in flange.
4. Retain tools to flange using outer constant velocity joint mounting bolts.
5. Unstake hub nut retainer.
6. Hold wheel hub remover and installer tool No. J-42094-1-B, or equivalent, in suitable vise.
7. Remove and discard retainer and hub nut.
8. Remove tool from vise, but leave tools on assembly.
9. Lubricate tool No. J-42094-3 threads with Extreme Press Lubricant ¼ Ounce Tub No. J 23444-A, or equivalent.
10. Install tool J-42094-3 to J-42094-4-A.

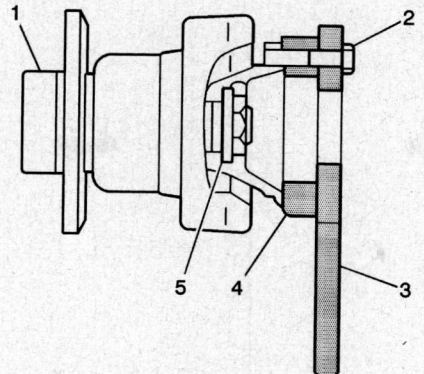

1. Rear Wheel Drive Shaft Flange
2. Outer Constant Velocity Joint Bolts
3. Tool No. J-42094-1-B
4. Tool No. J-42094-2
5. Hub Nut Retainer

ARM0400000001011

Fig. 5   Wheel & hub replacement (Part 1 of 2)

11. Lubricate ball end of tool No. J-42094-5-B with extreme press lubricant.
12. Install tool No. J-42094-5-B to end of tool No. J-42094-3.
13. Install tool No. J-42094-4-A and three mounting bolts tool No. J-42094-1-B.
14. Adjust position of tool No. J-42094-3 in tool No. J-42094-4-A to allow tool No. J-42094-4-A to be in full contact with tool No. J-42094-1-B.
15. Ensure tool No. J-42094-1-B is secure in suitable vise.
16. Have an assistant hold and support control arm.
17. Remove rear wheel drive shaft flange from hub by turning tool No. J-42094-3.
18. Remove tools.
19. Remove two Torx mounting bolts and washers from brake backing plate shield. Ensure park brake adjuster anchor bracket remains on shield.
20. Remove two park brake adjuster anchor bracket mounting bolts.
21. Clean control arm threads from inboard to outboard side using suitable M10 X 1.25 bottoming tap and suitable lubricant, **Fig. 6.**
22. Install two support tools No. J-42094-7-A , or equivalent, in two shallowest control arm to shield bolt holes, near caliper mounting holes.
23. Install support tool No. J-42094-7-AUS-2 in deepest control arm to shield bolt hole.
24. Install support tool No. J-42094-7-AUS-1 in remaining control arm to shield bolt hole.
25. Ensure four supports are in correct positions.
26. Attach tool No. J-42094-1-B to supports and install four mounting nuts to retain tool, **Fig. 7.**
27. Install tool No. J-42094-3 to tool No. J-42094-4-A.
28. Lubricate tool No. J-42094-5-B ball end with extreme press lubricant.
29. Install tool No. J-42094-5-B to tool No. J-42094-3 end.
30. Install tools Nos. J-42094-5-B and J-42094-3 through center hole in tool

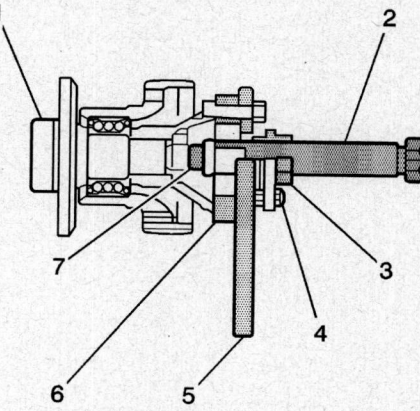

1. Rear Wheel Drive Shaft Flange
2. Tool No. J-42094-3
3. Tool No. J-42094-4-A
4. Bolt
5. Tool No. J-42094-1-B
6. Three Bolts
7. Tool No. J-42094-5-B

ARM0400000001012

Fig. 5   Wheel & hub replacement (Part 2 of 2)

No. J-42094-1-B.
31. Install tool No. J-42094-4-A and three mounting bolts to tool No. J-42094-1-B.
32. Adjust position of tool No. J-42094-3 in tool No. J-42094-4-A to allow tool No. J-42094-4-A to be in full contact with tool No. J-42094-1-B.
33. Ensure handle of tool No. J-42094-1-B is secure in vise.
34. Have assistant hold and support control arm assembly.
35. Press out ear wheel hub by turn tool No. J-42094-3.
36. Remove hub and bearing outside inner race from control arm.
37. Turn tool No. J-42094-3 away from bearing, but leave tools on assembly.
38. Remove shield and park brake anchor bracket from control arm.
39. If hub is not to be replaced, remove bearing outside inner race from using split plate bearing puller tool No. J 22912-01, or equivalent, and suitable press.
40. Remove control arm wheel bearing retainer using suitable snap ring pliers.
41. Install tool No. J-42094-6 to end of tool No. J-42094-5-B.
42. Press out control arm bearing by turning tool No. J-42094-3.
43. Discard wheel bearing.

Installation

1. Ensure control arm bearing bore is clean and free of foreign matter.
2. Apply wheel bearing lubricant No. 1051344, or equivalent lithium lubricant, to control arm bearing bore and outside of outer races of new wheel bearing.
3. Remove mounting bolts and tools Nos. J-42094-4-A and J-42094-3.
4. Apply wheel bearing lubricant No. 1051344, or equivalent lithium lubricant, to outside of outer race of tool No.

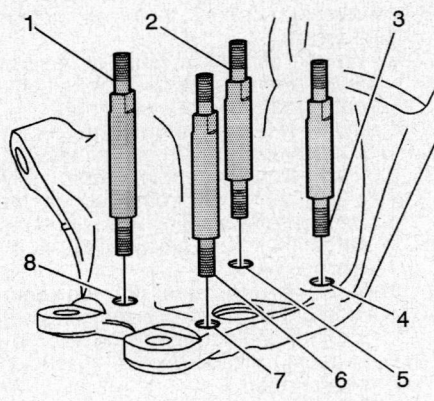

1. Support Tool No. J-42094-7-A
2. Support Tool No. J-42094-7-AUS-2
3. Support Tool No. J-42094-7-AUS-1
4. Thread
5. Thread
6. Support Tool No. J-42094-7-A
7. Thread
8. Thread

ARM0400000001013

Fig. 6 Control arm w/supports

J-42094-10 ball bearing.
5. Install tool No. J-42094-10 to flanged end of tool No. J-42094-4-A.
6. Install tools Nos. J-42094-10 and J-42094-4-A to tool No. J-42094-1-B. **Do not install tool No. J-42094-4-A to tool No. J-42094-1-B bolts**
7. Install tool No. J-42094-3 to tool No. J-42094-1-B
8. Install new wheel bearing to tool No. J-42094-8-A.
9. Position wheel bearing on control arm bearing bore.
10. Engage minimum of eight threads tool No. J-42094-3 with tool No. J-42094-8-A.
11. Hold tool No. J-42094-3 using suitable breaker bar.
12. Rotate tool No. J-42094-4-A to press wheel bearing into control arm. Ensure wheel bearing is seated properly in control arm.
13. Remove tool No. J-42094-8-A from bearing.
14. Install control arm bearing retainer using suitable snap ring pliers.
15. Remove tools from control arm.
16. Install rear disc brake backing plate shield and park brake anchor bracket.
17. Install two Torx bolts and washers to shield. Align cut edge of washers with surface of hub. Tighten bolts.
18. Apply Loctite No. 242, or equivalent, to anchor bracket bolt threads.
19. Install and tighten anchor bracket bolts.
20. Support outside end of hub on suitable hydraulic press using suitable bearing driver collar and press plates. Ensure hub weight is on outside end and not on wheel studs.
21. Position control arm and wheel bearing on hub.
22. Have assistant hold and support control arm.
23. Place tool No. J-42094-9-A on bearing inside inner race.
24. Place suitable steel pipe on tool No. J-42094-9-A.

25. Press hub to wheel bearing.
26. Remove steel pipe and tool No. J-42094-9-A.
27. Position tool No. J-42094-2 on rear wheel drive shaft flange and tool No. J-42094-1-B on tool No. J-42094-2.
28. Retain tools Nos. J-42094-2 and J-42094-1-B to flange using outer constant velocity joint bolts.
29. Apply wheel bearing lubricant No. 1051344, or equivalent lithium lubricant, to flange splines and threads on inside end of hub.
30. Align flange and hub splines.
31. Position flange on inside end of hub with outside end of hub on collar and press plates.
32. Place tool No. J-42094-9-A on flange and suitable steel pipe on tool No. J-42094-9-A.
33. Press flange to hub and bearing.
34. Remove steel pipe tool No. J-42094-9-A.
35. Remove control arm from press with tools Nos. J-42094-2 and J-42094-1-B on flange.
36. Hold tool No. J-42094-1-B using suitable vise.
37. Install and tighten new hub nut to inside end of hub.
38. Remove tool No. J-42094-1-B and control arm from vise.
39. Remove bolts from tool No. J-42094-1-B.
40. Remove tools Nos. J-42094-2 and J-42094-1-B from control arm.
41. Install and stake new hub nut retainer.
42. Install rear suspension lower control arm as outlined under "Control Arm, Replace."

SHOCK ABSORBER
REPLACE

1. Raise and support vehicle
2. Remove shock absorber lower mounting bolt and washer.
3. Separate shock absorber from control arm.
4. Lower vehicle to access luggage compartment.
5. Remove seven retainers and rear center trim panel carpet from luggage compartment.
6. **If removing righthand shock absorber,** loosen clamp and remove filler neck hose.
7. **On all models,** remove shock absorber cap.
8. Remove upper mounting nut, washer, upper mounting upper bushing and shock absorber.
9. If required, remove upper mounting lower bushing and washer.
10. Reverse procedure to install. With weight of vehicle on tire and wheel assemblies, bounce rear of vehicle several times to stabilize rear suspension, then tighten shock absorber to control arm mounting bolt.

COIL SPRING
REPLACE

1. Raise and support vehicle, then remove tire and wheel assembly.

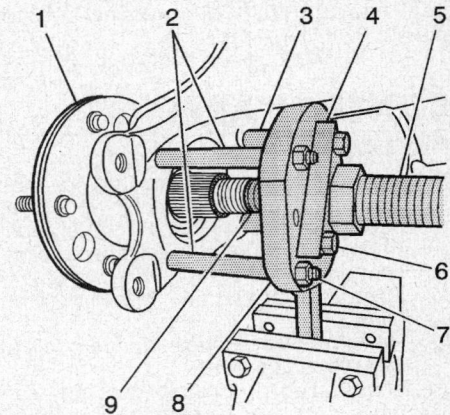

1. Hub
2. Support
3. Support
4. Tool No. J-42094-4-A
5. Tool No. J-42094-3
6. Bolts
7. Tool No. J-42094-1-B
8. Tool No. J-42094-1-B
9. Tool No. J-42094-5-B

ARM0400000001014

Fig. 7 Wheel bearing press out

2. Keep hub from turning by installing rear hub holding tool No. J 42066, or equivalent, and two wheel nuts onto two studs.
3. Support wheel drive shaft by tieing suitable wire upper shock mount and to wheel drive shaft. **Do not allow wheel drive shaft to hang freely.**
4. Remove mounting bolts and outer constant velocity joint to drive shaft flange retaining plates, **Fig. 8.**
5. Separate wheel drive shaft from drive shaft flange.
6. Loosen stabilizer shaft to shaft link nut.
7. Remove stabilizer shaft to shaft link mounting nut and bolt.
8. Loosen outer adjustment link to control arm mounting nut.
9. Position top of nut with top of outer adjustment link stud.
10. Separate stud from control arm using tie rod puller tool No. J 6627-A, or equivalent.
11. Remove and discard stud nut.
12. Position adjustment link away from control arm.
13. Support control arm with suitable jack and block of wood. Raise jack slightly to reduce spring load on control arm.
14. Remove mounting bolt and washer, then separate shock absorber from control arm.
15. Lower jack and control arm.
16. Push down gently on control arm, then remove spring and two insulators. **Do not pull on brake hose.**
17. Remove insulators.
18. Reverse procedure to install from spring, noting the following:
   a. Weight of vehicle must be on tire and wheel assemblies before tightening suspension mounting bolts and nuts.
   b. Install new outer adjustment link stud nut.
   c. **Torque** outer constant velocity joint

to drive shaft flange retainer bolts to 37 ft. lbs.

   d. Tighten bolts an additional 68°.

CONTROL ARM
REPLACE

1. Raise and support vehicle on suitable alignment rack. Ensure lift pads are positioned to minimize interference with control arms and rear suspension support.
2. Remove rear tire and wheel assemblies.
3. Remove two support hangers clips and rubber hangers.
4. Loosen two ring clamp nuts and remove both rear pipes by sliding them out of muffler pipe slip joints.
5. Support catalytic converter and muffler with suitable jackstand.
6. Remove flange bolts and separate catalytic converter and muffler. Remove gasket from flange joint.
7. Remove four clips and four rubber hangers from left and righthand left muffler support hangers.
8. Remove mufflers.
9. Loosen two rear suspension support braces to body six mounting bolts.
10. Loosen two rear suspension support to body mounting bolts.
11. Loosen stabilizer shaft to shaft link mounting nut.
12. Remove stabilizer shaft link to lower control arm mounting nut and bolt.
13. Loosen outer adjustment link to control arm mounting nut.
14. Position top of nut with top of outer adjustment link stud.
15. Separate outer adjustment link stud from control arm using tie rod puller tool No. J 6627-A, or equivalent.
16. Remove and discard outer adjustment link stud nut.
17. Position adjustment link assembly away from control arm.
18. Remove brake hose clip, then pull brake pipe and hose forward from bracket.
19. Lift brake pipe up through slot in bracket and separate brake pipe and hose from control arm.
20. Loosen brake pipe flare nut.
21. Remove backing plate bracket clip and brake pipe from brake hose. Plug brake pipe.
22. Remove brake pipe from backing plate bracket. Plug brake pipe.
23. Remove two mounting bolts and brake caliper.
24. Pull park brake lever boot to side and loosen park brake cable adjustment nut.
25. Raise and support vehicle.
26. Remove rear cable grommet from clip and wrap cloth or tape around cable near equalizer.
27. Pull rear cable forward and up to release cable from equalizer using suitable pliers on wrapped portion of cable.
28. Pull insulation for cable rearward to release cable from bracket.
29. Wrap cloth or tape around cable near rear clevis.

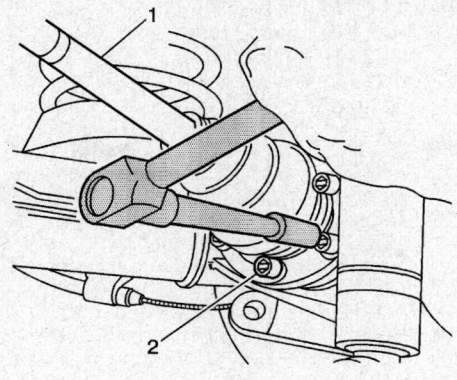

1. Wheel Drive Shaft
2. Retaining Plate Mounting Bolt

ARM0400000001006

Fig. 8 Outer constant velocity joint to drive shaft flange retaining plate replacement

30. Pull cable rearward to release clevis from park brake actuating lever using suitable pliers on wrapped portion of cable.
31. Pull insulation for cable forward to release cable from control arm retainer.
32. Remove rear parking brake cable.
33. For required access, it my be required to remove propeller shaft as outlined under "Propeller Shaft, Replace."
34. Mark brake rotor to wheel stud and to hub for installation alignment.
35. Remove brake rotor from hub. If rotor does not slide off hub easily, proceed as follows:
   a. Select block of wood longer than wheel studs.
   b. Place wood on tor between wheel studs.
   c. Tap wood with suitable hammer to loosen rotor from hub.
36. Remove spring as outlined under "Coil Spring, Replace."
37. Pull differential carrier breather hose out of hole.
38. Separate two wheel speed sensor wires from clips and disconnect connectors from body harness.
39. Mark differential carrier mount on body for installation alignment.
40. Support differential carrier mount using suitable jack.
41. Remove and discard four mount to body bolts.
42. Remove and discard two rear suspension support to body bolts.
43. Loosen six brace bolts to access control arm.
44. Lower jack with mount and rear suspension support to access control arm.
45. Remove and discard two control arm to rear suspension support mounting nuts.
46. Remove two mounting bolts and control arm.
47. If control arm is to be replaced, remove following components.
   a. Park brake components.
   b. Brake backing plate.
   c. Wheel bearing.
   d. Hub.
   e. Wheel drive shaft flange.

48. Reverse procedure to install, noting the following:
   a. Weight of vehicle must be on tire and wheel assemblies before tightening mounting bolts and nuts.
   b. Install two new control arm to rear suspension support mounting nuts.
   c. If hub was not replace, thoroughly clean corrosion from hub flange mating surface using wheel hub resurfacing kit tool No. J 42450-A, or equivalent.
   d. If brake rotor was not replaced, thoroughly clean corrosion from rotor mating surface using rotor resurfacing kit tool No. J 41013, or equivalent.
   e. If hub or wheel drive shaft flange were replaced, measure assembled lateral runout of rotor to ensure optimum performance.
   f. Bounce rear of vehicle several times in order to stabilize suspension.
   g. Tighten control arm to rear suspension support mounting nuts and bolts.
   h. Tighten stabilizer shaft link mounting nuts and bolts.
   i. Tighten shock absorber to control arm mounting bolt.
   j. Tighten outer adjustment link to control arm mounting nut.

STABILIZER SHAFT
REPLACE

1. Raise and support vehicle on suitable alignment rack. Ensure lift pads are positioned to minimize interference with control arms and rear suspension support.
2. Remove rear tire and wheel assemblies.
3. Remove two support hangers clips and rubber hangers.
4. Loosen two ring clamp nuts and remove both rear pipes by sliding them out of muffler pipe slip joints.
5. Support catalytic converter and muffler with suitable jackstand.
6. Remove flange bolts and separate catalytic converter and muffler. Remove gasket from flange joint.
7. Remove four clips and four rubber hangers from left and righthand left muffler support hangers.
8. Remove mufflers.
9. Loosen two rear suspension support braces to body six mounting bolts.
10. Loosen two rear suspension support to body mounting bolts.
11. Mark differential carrier mount on body for installation alignment.
12. Support differential carrier mount using suitable jack.
13. Remove and discard four mount to body bolts.
14. Lower jack with mount and rear suspension support to access stabilizer shaft insulator brackets to rear suspension support bolts. **Do not allow propeller shaft or wheel drive shafts to touch exhaust system.**

15. Remove mounting bolts and nuts, then the stabilizer shaft links from control arms.
16. Remove stabilizer shaft insulator brackets to rear suspension support mounting bolts.
17. Remove two brackets from rear suspension support using suitable, flat-bladed tool as lever.
18. Remove stabilizer shaft.
19. If required, remove the following:
    a. Two stabilizer shaft link nuts.
    b. Two stabilizer shaft link bolts.
    c. Two stabilizer shaft links.
    d. Two stabilizer shaft insulator brackets.
    e. Two stabilizer shaft insulators.
20. Reverse procedure to install, noting the following:
    a. Weight of vehicle must be on tire and wheel assemblies before tightening mounting bolts and nuts.
    b. Fit rear crossmember centering tool No. CH-46839, or equivalent, into .74 inch diameter body datum holes forward of rear suspension support, **Fig. 3.**
    c. With an assistant, position rear suspension support until rear crossmember centering tool location pins engage alignment holes on rear suspension support.
    d. **Torque** brace to underbody bolts to 92 ft. lbs.
    e. Tighten bolts an additional 40°.
    f. **Torque** rear differential mount mounting bolts to 26 ft. lbs.
    g. Tighten bolts an additional 60°
    h. With vehicle at curb weight, bounce rear vehicle several times to settle suspension.
    i. Tighten stabilizer shaft link mounting bolts and nuts.

ADJUSTMENT LINK
REPLACE

1. Raise and support vehicle.
2. Measure and record distance between two center adjuster lock nuts.
3. Mark two center adjuster lock nuts position to installation alignment.
4. Loosen outer adjustment link to control arm nut.
5. Position top of nut with top of outer adjustment link stud.
6. Separate stud from control arm using tie rod puller tool No. J 6627-A, or equivalent.
7. Remove and discard nut.
8. Remove inner adjustment link to rear suspension support mounting bolt and nut Discard nut.
9. Remove inner adjustment link from rear suspension support.
10. Hold center adjuster in suitable soft jaws vise, **Fig. 9.**
11. **These components have lefthand threads: inner adjustment link, inner lock nut and corresponding end of center adjuster.**
12. Loosen inner lock nut and remove inner adjustment link from center ad-

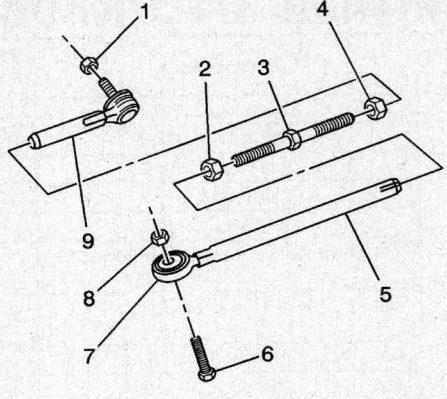

1. Nut
2. Inner Lock Nut
3. Center Adjuster
4. Nut
5. Inner Adjustment Link
6. Bolt
7. Inner Adjustment Link
8. Nut
9. Outer Adjustment Link

ARM0400000001015

Fig. 9   Adjustment link assembly

juster. **Count turns required for removal of inner adjustment link.**
13. Loosen outer lock nut and remove outer adjustment link from center adjuster. **Count turns required for removal of outer adjustment link.**
14. Reverse procedure to install, noting the following:
    a. Weight of vehicle must be on tire and wheel assemblies before tightening suspension bolts and nuts.
    b. Protruding side of bushing must be toward front of vehicle.
    c. Install new inner adjustment link to rear suspension support mounting nut and bolt.
    d. Install outer adjustment link and new nut to control arm.
    e. With weight of vehicle on tire and wheel assemblies, bounce rear of vehicle several times in order to stabilize rear suspension.
    f. Measure wheel alignment.
    g. Tighten inner adjustment link to rear suspension support and outer adjustment link to control arm mounting nuts and bolts.

Inner

1. Raise and support vehicle.
2. Mark position of inner lock nut on center adjuster for installation alignment.
3. Remove inner adjustment link to rear suspension support mounting nut and bolt. Discard nut.
4. Remove inner adjustment link from rear suspension support.
5. Following components have lefthand threads: inner adjustment link, inner lock nut and corresponding end of center adjuster.
6. Loosen inner lock nut.
7. Remove inner adjustment link from center adjuster. **Count turns required for removal of inner adjustment link.**

8. Reverse procedure to install, noting the following:
    a. Weight of vehicle must be on tire and wheel assemblies before tightening suspension bolts and nuts.
    b. Protruding side of bushing must be toward front of vehicle.
    c. Install new inner adjustment link to rear suspension support nut.
    d. With weight of vehicle on tire and wheel assemblies, bounce rear of vehicle several times in order to stabilize rear suspension.
    e. Measure wheel alignment.
    f. Adjust rear toe to specification and tighten inner lock nut.

Outer

1. Raise and support vehicle.
2. Mark outer lock nut on center adjuster for installation alignment.
3. Loosen outer adjustment link to control arm nut.
4. Position top of nut with top of outer adjustment link stud.
5. Separate stud from control arm using tie rod puller tool No. J 6627-A, or equivalent.
6. Remove and discard nut.
7. Loosen outer lock nut.
8. Remove outer adjustment link from adjuster. **Count turns required for removal of outer adjustment link.**
9. Reverse procedure to install, noting the following:
    a. Weight of vehicle must be on tire and wheel assemblies before tightening mounting nuts.
    b. Install outer adjustment link and new mounting nut to control arm.
    c. With weight of vehicle on tire and wheel assemblies, bounce rear of vehicle several times in order to stabilize rear suspension.
    d. Measure wheel alignment.
    e. Adjust rear toe to specification and tighten outer lock nut.

TECHNICAL SERVICE BULLETINS
Knocking Noise From Rear

On some of these models built prior to VIN 4L246712 there may be a knocking noise from the rear suspension during hard or aggressive acceleration.

This condition may be caused by rear cross member.

To correct this condition, proceed as follows:
1. Install two rubber insulators above rear cross member to correct a knocking noise during hard or aggressive acceleration.
2. **Torque** new mounting bolt to 92 ft. lbs.
3. Tighten mounting bolt an additional 30–40°.
4. **Torque** brace mounting bolts to 48 ft. lbs.

TIGHTENING SPECIFICATIONS

Year	Component	Torque/Ft. Lbs.
2004–06	Adjustment Link	46
	Brace To Underbody	②
	Brake Caliper	63
	Brake Line	11
	Brake Pike To Hose	12
	Brake Shield To Lower Control Arm, Lower	65
	Brake Shield To Lower Control Arm, Upper	85
	Catalytic Converter To Muffler Flange	33
	Constant Velocity Joint	③
	Cross-Member To Differential Carrier	②
	Differential Carrier	66
	Differential Mount	②
	Differential Rear Mount To Differential Cover	70
	Hub Nut	221
	Inner Adjustment Link To Rear Suspension Support	46
	Inner Constant Velocity Joints To Axle Shaft	②
	Muffler Pipe Slip	32
	Outer Adjustment Link To Control Arm	46
	Outer Constant Velocity Joint Retainer	①
	Park Brake Anchor Bracket	65
	Propeller Shaft Center Bearing	21
	Propeller Shaft Coupling	④
	Propeller Shaft Pinon Flange	85
	Rear Control Arm	74
	Rear Differential Mount	②
	Rear Control Arm	72
	Rear Suspension Brace To Body	52
	Rear Suspension Support Insulator Bracket	52
	Rear Suspension Support To Body	③
	Shield Torx Bolts	55
	Shock Absorber, Upper	10
	Shock Absorber To Control Arm	85
	Stabilizer Mounting Bracket	16
	Stabilizer Shaft Link	72
	Wheel Drive Shaft To Axle Stub Shaft	37⑤

① — Refer to "Coil Spring, Replace" for tightening specifications and sequence.
② — Refer to "Differential Carrier, Replace" for tightening specifications and sequence.
③ — Refer to "Rear Wheel Shaft, Replace" for tightening specifications and sequence.
④ — Refer to "U-Joint, Replace" for tightening specifications and sequence.
⑤ — Final tighten an additional 67°.

Front Suspension & Steering

NOTE: On Air Bag Equipped Models, Refer To "Air Bag System Precautions" Located In The Front Of This Manual For System Disarming & Arming Procedures.

NOTE: Refer To "Computer Relearn Procedures" Located In The Front Of This Manual When Battery Power To The Computer Has Been Interrupted.

NOTE: Refer To The Rear Of This Manual For Vehicle Manufacturer's Special Tool Suppliers.

INDEX

	Page No.		Page No.		Page No.
Coil Spring, Replace	3-29	Battery Ground Cable	3-29	Assemble	3-30
Control Arm, Replace	3-30	Stabilizer Bar, Replace	3-31	Disassemble	3-30
Installation	3-30	Stabilizer Link, Replace	3-31	Technical Service Bulletins	3-32
Removal	3-30	Steering Columns	20-1	Knock Noise From Front	
Description	3-29	Steering Knuckle, Replace	3-30	Suspension	3-32
Power Steering	21-1	Installation	3-31	Tie Rod End, Replace	3-31
Power Steering Gear, Replace	3-31	Removal	3-30	Outer	3-31
Power Steering Pump, Replace	3-32	Strut, Replace	3-29	Installation	3-31
Power Steering System Bleed	3-32	Installation	3-30	Removal	3-31
Precautions	3-29	Removal	3-29	Tightening Specifications	3-33
Air Bag Systems	3-29	Strut Service	3-30		

PRECAUTIONS

Air Bag Systems

Refer to "Air Bag System Precautions" in the front of this manual for system disarming and arming procedures.

Battery Ground Cable

Prior to service, disconnect battery ground cable and isolate as required.

DESCRIPTION

The steering knuckle is suspended between a lower control arm, a lower control arm rod and a strut assembly. The lower control arm attaches to the steering knuckle at the outermost point of the control arm. The attachment is through a ball and socket type joint. The ball joint allows the steering knuckle to maintain the perpendicular relationship to the road surface. The innermost end of the control arm is attached to the front frame with a semi-rigid bushing. The lower control arm is allowed to pivot at the vehicle frame in a vertical fashion. The rod is attached to the lower control arm with a semi-rigid bushing. The front of the lower control arm rod is attached to the front frame with a fluid filled insulator bushing. The upper portion of the steering knuckle is attached to a strut assembly. The strut assembly is attached to the vehicle body with an upper bearing. The steering knuckle moves up and down independent of the vehicle body structure.

This up and down motion of the steering knuckle as the vehicle travels over bumps is absorbed predominantly by the coil spring. This spring is retained under tension over the strut assembly. The strut has an absorber in order to dampen out the oscillations of the coil spring.

The front suspension has a stabilizer shaft. The stabilizer shaft connects between the left and the righthand strut through the stabilizer shaft links. Insulators and clamps retain the stabilizer shaft to the front frame.

The power steering system is a closed loop system. The system consists of the following components: power steering fluid reservoir, power steering pump, power steering gear, and power steering pipes and hoses.

The power steering fluid flows from the fluid reservoir through a hose to the power steering pump. The engine drive belt rotates the pump pulley. The pulley turns the pump drive shaft. The shaft turns the pump rotor. The vanes in the rotor pressurize the power steering fluid. The engine speed sensing type flow control valve controls the fluid pressure. This valve reduces the fluid pressure as the engine speed increases. The fluid flows, under pressure, from the pump, through the pipe and the hose, to the steering gear.

The steering gear is a rack and pinion type steering system. The steering gear has a control valve which directs the fluid to either side of the rack piston. The piston uses hydraulic pressure to move the rack to the left and to the right. The rack moves the tie rods. The tie rods move the steering knuckles. The steering knuckles rotate on ball joints and strut bearings and turn the front wheels and tires.

The power steering fluid flows from the steering gear, through the pipe and the hose, to the reservoir. If the hydraulic assist fails, the driver maintains manual steering control. Under this condition, however, the driver must use more steering effort.

COIL SPRING
REPLACE

Refer to "Strut, Replace" and "Strut Service" for coil spring replacement procedure.

STRUT
REPLACE
Removal

1. Raise and support vehicle, then remove front tire and wheel assembly.
2. Remove upper nut, washer and insulator, then the retainer. Hold stabilizer shaft link upper stud using suitable wrench.
3. Separate wheel speed sensor harness and insulator from strut bracket.
4. Turn brake hose to strut bracket sleeve and align flats with strut bracket opening.
5. Separate brake hose from strut bracket.
6. Support control arm using suitable jack and block of wood below ball joint.
7. Remove and discard two mounting nuts, washers and bolts.
8. Lift locking tab and disconnect wheel speed sensor connector from knuckle.
9. Separate knuckle from strut.
10. Remove cap and strut nut while holding end of strut rod shaft using suitable wrench.

11. Remove and discard strut nut.
12. Remove strut bumper stop.
13. Lower strut, then remove stabilizer shaft link from bracket.
14. Remove strut.
15. Reverse procedure to install.

Installation

1. Tighten strut mount nut.
2. Install top of stabilizer shaft link to strut bracket.
3. Install strut to tower.
4. Install strut bumper stop.
5. Install new strut nut. **Do not tighten strut nut now.**
6. Install two new strut to knuckle bolts, washers and nuts. Tighten nuts.
7. Tighten strut to tower mounting nut holding strut rod shaft with suitable wrench.
8. Install strut nut cap.
9. Remove jack and block of wood.
10. Align brake hose sleeve flats with strut bracket opening and install brake hose. Turn sleeve to retain brake hose to strut bracket.
11. Connect wheel speed sensor connector. ensure locking tab is secure.
12. Install wheel speed sensor harness and insulator to strut bracket.
13. Install retainer, upper insulator and upper washer.
14. Install and tighten upper nut while holding stabilizer shaft link upper stud with suitable wrench. **Do not use power tools on upper nut.**
15. Install front tire and wheel assembly, then lower vehicle onto an alignment rack to place weight of vehicle onto tires.
16. Push down on front bumper three times to stabilize suspension.
17. Measure wheel alignment.
18. Rotate camber adjustment screw to adjust front camber.
19. **Torque** two strut to knuckle nuts to 74 ft. lbs.
20. Final tighten nuts an additional 90°.

STRUT SERVICE

Disassemble

1. Compress spring using strut spring compressor tool No. J 45400, or equivalent.
2. **Do not grip strut rod with any tools below hex shaped portion.**
3. Hold end of strut rod shaft using suitable wrench.
4. Remove nut, strut mount and washers.
5. Mark strut bearing on upper spring seat orientation for assembly alignment.
6. Remove strut bearing from upper spring seat.
7. Remove and discard strut shield strap.
8. Remove upper spring seat, spring upper insulator and strut bumper,
9. Release compression and remove spring.
10. Remove and discard strut shield clamp.
11. Remove strut dust shield and filter.

Assemble

1. Hold strut rod and housing, then pull rod to maximum length. **Do not grip strut rod with any tools below hex shaped portion.**
2. Install strut dust shield. Ensure filter remains seated inside boot portion of strut dust shield.
3. Position strut dust shield on strut housing tube. Ensure distance between bottom of strut dust shield and bottom of lower spring seat is 1.182–1.379 inches.
4. Install new strut dust shield to strut housing tube clamp.
5. Install spring to strut housing.
6. Install straight projecting lower end of spring to lower spring seat.
7. Compress spring using strut spring compressor tool No. J 45400, or equivalent.
8. Install strut bumper.
9. Install upper insulator with step straight projecting upper end of spring.
10. Install upper spring seat. Ensure double notch in upper flange of is on inboard side of strut.
11. Pull strut rod to maximum length.
12. If strut rod nut is on strut rod, remove it.
13. Install strut bearing to upper spring seat in same orientation as in removal procedure. Ensure narrow outer section faces towards upper spring seat collar.
14. Install lower washer. Ensure dish shape side of lower washer faces downward.
15. Install strut mount. Ensure lower washer does not bind with lower edge of mount.
16. Install upper washer. Ensure dish shape side of upper washer faces upward.
17. Install and tighten strut mount nut while holding strut rod shaft end with suitable wrench.
18. Install strut dust shield to upper spring seat. Fit upper end of strut dust shield over lower flange of spring seat collar.
19. Install new strut dust shield to upper spring seat strap.
20. Remove strut from strut spring compressor tool.

CONTROL ARM

REPLACE

Removal

1. Raise and support vehicle, then remove front tire and wheel assembly.
2. Turn steering wheel to access control arm ball joint stud.
3. Remove and discard control arm ball joint stud to knuckle nut.
4. Separate control arm ball joint stud from knuckle using ball joint separator tool No. J 42188, or equivalent.
5. Push control arm away from knuckle using suitable block of wood.
6. Remove and discard control arm rod to control arm mounting nut. Remove washer.
7. Remove and discard control arm to front frame nut .
8. Remove mounting bolt and control arm from front frame.
9. Remove control arm from rod. **Do not remove retainer.**

Installation

1. Ensure control arm rod retainer is on properly.
2. Install control arm to rod, then the control arm and mounting bolt to front frame.
3. Install new control arm to front frame mounting nut. **Do not tighten nut now.**
4. Install washer and new nut to rod. **Do not tighten nut now.**
5. Support control arm with suitable jack and block of wood below ball joint.
6. Install control arm ball joint stud to knuckle.
7. Raise jack to seat control arm ball joint stud.
8. Install and tighten new control arm ball joint stud nut.
9. Remove jack and block of wood.
10. Lower vehicle.
11. With weight of vehicle on tire and wheel assemblies, push down on front bumper three times to stabilize suspension.
12. Tighten control arm to front frame mounting.
13. Tighten control arm rod to control arm mounting nut.

STEERING KNUCKLE

REPLACE

REMOVAL

1. Raise and support vehicle, then remove front tire and wheel assembly.
2. Remove mounting bolts, caliper and bracket from brake rotor, then support assembly with heavy mechanic's wire, or equivalent. **Do not disconnect hydraulic brake flexible hose from caliper.** Ensure there is no tension on brake hose
3. If match marks are not evident, mark brake rotor, wheel stud and hub for installation alignment.
4. Remove brake rotor, **Fig. 1.** If brake rotor does not slide off of hub easily, proceed as follows:
   a. Select block of wood longer than wheel studs.
   b. Place wood on rotor between wheel studs.
   c. Tap wood with suitable hammer to loosen rotor from hub.
5. If removing lefthand front brake shield, turn steering wheel to left. If removing righthand front brake shield, turn steering wheel to right.
6. Lift locking tab and disconnect wheel speed sensor connector from knuckle.
7. If required for access, remove and discard strut to knuckle mounting nuts and bolts.
8. Remove three Allen bolts and hub from knuckle If required, tap Allen bolts to loosen hub from knuckle.

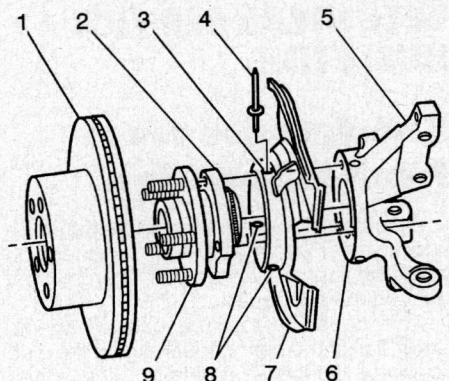

1. Rotor
2. Hub
3. Brake Shield
4. Rivets
5. Knuckle
6. Knuckle
7. Brake Shield
8. Rivets
9. Hub

ARM0400000001017

Fig. 1 Steering knuckle replacement

9. Remove three rivet heads and brake shield. Drill out rivet remains.
10. Remove cotter pin and outer tie rod nut.
11. Separate outer tie rod from knuckle using Pitman arm puller removal tool No. OTC 7314A, or equivalent.
12. Remove and discard two mounting nuts, washers and bolts.
13. If replacing knuckle, remove camber adjusting screw.
14. Remove steering knuckle from strut.
15. Remove and discard control arm ball joint stud to knuckle mounting nut.
16. Separate control arm ball joint stud from knuckle using ball joint separator tool No. J 42188, or equivalent.
17. Remove knuckle.

INSTALLATION

The weight of the vehicle must be on the tire and wheel assemblies before tightening the mounting bolts and nuts.

1. Install steering knuckle to control arm ball joint stud.
2. Align knuckle and strut bolt holes.
3. Do not use knuckle Allen bolts more than three times. If in doubt, replace 3 Allen bolts.
4. Install two knuckle to strut mounting bolts, two washes and two new nuts. **Do not tighten bolts or nuts now.**
5. Support control arm using suitable jack and block of wood below ball joint.
6. Raise jack and seat knuckle on control arm ball joint stud.
7. Install and tighten control arm ball joint stud nut.
8. Remove jack and wood.
9. Ensure plastic spacer is on ball stud for outer tie rod end.
10. Install outer tie rod to knuckle.
11. Install and tighten ball stud for outer tie rod nut.
12. Align cotter pin slot by tightening nut up to 1/6 additional turn or maximum **torque** of 63 ft. lbs. **Do not loosen nut**

to insert cotter pin.
13. Install cotter pin.
14. If camber adjusting screw was removed, install adjusting screw to knuckle.
15. Install brake shield to knuckle. Ensure brake shield position is correct to provide clearance for brake caliper.
16. Install pop-rivets.
17. Align sensor connection on hub.
18. Install hub.
19. Lower vehicle.
20. Push down on front bumper three times to stabilize suspension.
21. Measure wheel alignment. Rotate amber adjusting screw i to adjust front camber.
22. **Torque** strut to knuckle mounting nuts to 62 ft. lbs.
23. **Torque** mounting nuts to 74 ft. lbs.
24. Final tighten nuts an additional 90°.
25. **Torque** caliper mounting bolts to 63 ft. lbs.
26. Final tighten bolts an additional 45°.

STABILIZER BAR
REPLACE

1. Remove mounting nuts, insulator brackets and insulator, **Fig. 2.**
2. Remove nuts and stabilizer shaft from links. Hold link lower studs using suitable wrench.
3. Remove stabilizer shaft.
4. Reverse procedure to install, noting the following:
   a. Ensure insulators slots face forward.
   b. Ensure insulator curved portions seat in front frame curved mating surfaces.

STABILIZER LINK
REPLACE

1. Raise and support vehicle, then remove front tire and wheel assembly.
2. Hold stabilizer shaft link upper stud using suitable wrench.
3. Remove upper nut, washer and insulator.
4. Remove retainer.
5. Hold link lower stud using suitable wrench.
6. Remove mounting nut and stabilizer shaft from link lower stud.
7. Remove link, then lower insulator and washer.
8. Reverse procedure to install.

TIE ROD END
REPLACE
Outer
REMOVAL

1. Raise and support vehicle, then remove front tire and wheel assembly.
2. Remove cotter pin and outer tie rod nut
3. Separate outer tie rod from knuckle using Pitman arm puller removal tool No. OTC 7314A, or equivalent.
4. Mark inner tie rod, lock nut and outer tie rod for installation alignment.

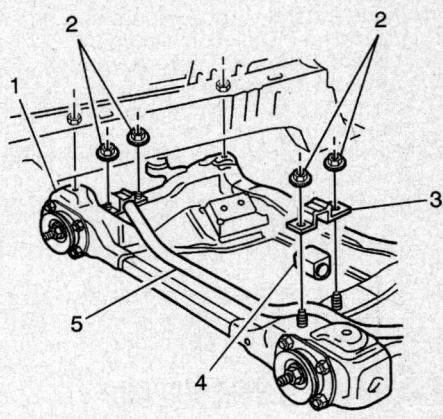

1. Front Frame
2. Nuts
3. Insulator Brackets
4. Insulators
5. Stabilizer Shaft

ARM0400000001018

Fig. 2 Stabilizer bar replacement

5. Loosen lock nut and remove outer tie rod from inner tie rod.

INSTALLATION

1. Install outer to inner tie rod.
2. Align outer tie rod with match marks. **Do not tighten lock nut.**
3. Ensure plastic spacer is on ball stud for outer tie rod end.
4. Install outer tie rod to steering knuckle.
5. Install outer tie rod nut to ball stud for outer tie rod. Tighten nut.
6. Align cotter pin slot by tightening outer tie rod nut up to 1/6 additional turn or **torque** of 63 ft. lbs., maximum. **Do not loosen nut to insert cotter pin.**
7. Install cotter pin into hole in tie rod stud.
8. Install front tire and wheel assembly.
9. Adjust front toe.
10. Tighten lock nut against outer tie rod.
11. Ensure steering gear boot is not twisted.

POWER STEERING GEAR
REPLACE

1. Lock steering column and ensure front wheels are in straight ahead position.
2. Raise and support vehicle, then remove front tire and wheel assemblies.
3. Place suitable drain pan under vehicle to collect power steering system fluid.
4. Remove pressure and return pipes from steering gear. Remove and discard two O-rings.
5. Remove and discard steering shaft coupling to steering gear pinion nut.
6. Remove bolt and separate coupling from pinion.
7. Raise and support vehicle, then remove front tire and wheel assembly.
8. Remove cotter pin and outer tie rod nut.
9. Separate outer tie rod from knuckle using Pitman arm puller removal tool No. OTC 7314A, or equivalent.

10. Mark inner tie rod, lock nut and outer tie rod for installation alignment.
11. Loosen lock nut and remove outer tie rod from inner tie rod.
12. Remove mounting nuts and bolts, then the steering gear.
13. Reverse procedure to install, noting the following:
    a. **Torque** steering gear mounting nuts to 44 ft. lbs.
    b. Tighten mounting nuts and additional 45°.
    c. Lubricate two new steering gear O-rings with suitable ATF.
    d. Install new coupling bolt.

POWER STEERING PUMP

REPLACE

1. Disconnect Intake Air Temperature (IAT) sensor and Mass Air Flow (MAF) sensor connectors.
2. Loosen air intake duct to throttle body and MAF sensor to air cleaner upper body clamp.
3. Position intake air duct away from power steering pump IAT and MAF sensors still attached.
4. Install suitable breaker bar with hex-head socket to drive belt tensioner bolt.
5. Relieve tension on belt by rotating drive belt tensioner clockwise.
6. Remove belt from pulleys and drive belt tensioner.
7. Slowly release tension on drive belt tensioner. Remove breaker bar and socket from drive belt tensioner bolt.
8. Place suitable drain pan below vehicle.
9. Loosen clamps, then remove power steering fluid reservoir outlet and inlet hoses.
10. Release bracket tab using suitable, flat-blade tool and remove reservoir.
11. Remove power steering gear inlet pipe and flare nut from pump.
12. Remove and discard O-ring from high pressure port.
13. Loosen hose clamp and remove reservoir outlet hose from pump.
14. Remove two mounting bolts and power steering pump.
15. Reverse procedure to install. Lubricate new high pressure port O-ring with suitable Automatic Transmission Fluid (ATF).

POWER STEERING SYSTEM BLEED

1. Ensure hoses do not touch any other part of vehicle.

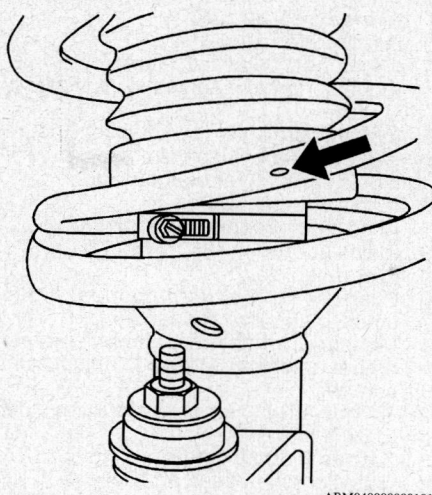

Fig. 3   Coil spring rub mark

2. Ensure all hose connections are tight. Loose connections may not leak, but could allow air into steering system.
3. Remove power steering fluid reservoir cap. Ensure fluid level is correct. Add fluid as required.
4. Attach power steering bleeder adapter tool No. J 43485 to Mity Vac tool No. J 35555, or equivalents.
5. Place adapter on or in reservoir filler neck.
6. Apply vacuum of 20 inches Hg, maximum.
7. Wait five minutes. Typical vacuum drop is 2–3 inches Hg.
8. If vacuum does not remain steady, inspect for power steering fluid leaks.
9. Remove tools and install reservoir cap.
10. Start and idle engine.
11. Turn engine off.
12. Ensure fluid level is correct and adjust as required.
13. Start and idle engine.
14. Turn steering wheel 180–360° in both directions five times. **Do not turn steering wheel to lock.**
15. Turn ignition switch to OFF position .
16. Remove reservoir cap and ensure fluid level is correct. Adjust fluid level as required.
17. Attach power steering bleeder adapter Mity Vac tools.
18. Place adapter on or in pump reservoir filler neck.
19. Apply vacuum of 20 inches Hg, maximum.
20. Wait five minutes.
21. Remove tools.
22. Ensure fluid level is correct and adjust as required.
23. Install reservoir cap.

TECHNICAL SERVICE BULLETINS

Knock Noise From Front Suspension

On some of these models there may be a knock noise from the front suspension when driving at low speeds over bumps/uneven road surfaces.

This condition may be caused by the lower coil of the spring touching on the side lip of the spring seat, **Fig. 3**. The spring coils contacting the body sheet metal within the wheelhouse area may also cause this condition.

To correct this condition, proceed as follows:

1. Inspect tightness of all front suspension nuts and bolts.
2. Inspect body sheet metal around inside of strut tower for signs of spring coil rubbing.
3. Inspect second lower coil on inboard side of spring for signs of chipped or marked paint, **Fig. 3**.
4. If marks are found, remove spring from strut assembly and install it upside down (with thin coil end resting on spring seat).
5. Carefully install upper bearing (yellow plastic housing). Ensure it is located correctly in upper spring seat.
6. While strut is removed, cycle control arm up and down.
7. If noise is heard from lower control arm rod front insulator bushing, install strut and proceed next step. If no noise is heard, proceed as follows:
    a. Install new strut-to-steering knuckle mounting bolts and nuts.
    b. Tighten nuts while applying pressure to top of brake rotor to ensure camber adjustment bolt is against strut tube, eliminating need to perform front end alignment.
    c. **Torque** nuts to 62 ft. lbs.
    d. **Torque** nuts 74 ft. lbs.
    e. Tighten nuts an additional 90°.
8. Remove front lower control arm rod nut.
9. Install new nut, but do not fully tighten.
10. Bounce front of vehicle up and down several times to stabilize suspension.
11. **Torque** control arm rod nuts to 109 ft. lbs.

TIGHTENING SPECIFICATIONS

Year	Component	Torque/Ft. Lbs.
2004–06	Brake Caliper	②
	Brake Hose Fitting	26
	Control Arm Ball Joint Stud To Knuckle	44
	Control Arm Rod Insulator Bushing To Front Frame	17
	Control Arm Rod To Control Arm Insulator Bushing	109
	Control Arm Rod To Control Arm	76
	Control Arm To Front Frame	72
	Front Suspension Support Brace To Body	22
	Hub To Knuckle	80
	Inner Tie Rod To Outer Tie Rod End	37
	Outer Tie Rod End Ball Stud To Steering Knuckle	50
	Power Steering Cooler To Body	58①
	Power Steering Cooler To Cooler Bracket	58①
	Power Steering Fluid Reservoir Bracket	37
	Power Steering Gear Inlet Pipe To Engine Bracket	18
	Power Steering Gear Inlet Pipe To Frame	58①
	Power Steering Gear Inlet Pipe To Power Steering Gear	27
	Power Steering Gear Inlet Pipe To Power Steering Pump	22
	Power Steering Gear Outlet Pipe To Power Steering Gear	27
	Power Steering Gear Outlet Pipe Clip To Front Frame	58①
	Power Steering Gear Outlet Pipe Clip To Lefthand Frame	58①
	Power Steering Pump To Cylinder Head	21
	Stabilizer Shaft Insulator Bracket To Front Frame	20
	Stabilizer Shaft Link Lower Stud To Stabilizer Shaft	37
	Stabilizer Shaft Link Upper Stud To Strut Bracket	12
	Steering Coupling To Steering Gear Pinion	21
	Steering Gear Housing To Front Frame	③
	Strut Rod Shaft To Strut Mount	58
	Strut To Body	41
	Strut To Knuckle	②

① — Inch lbs.
② — Refer to "Hub & Bearing, Replace" for tightening specifications and sequence.
③ — Refer to "Power Steering Gear, Replace" for tightening specifications and sequence.

Wheel Alignment

NOTE: On Air Bag Equipped Models, Refer To "Air Bag System Precautions" Located In The Front Of This Manual For System Disarming & Arming Procedures.

NOTE: Refer To "Computer Relearn Procedures" Located In The Front Of This Manual When Battery Power To The Computer Has Been Interrupted.

NOTE: Refer To The Rear Of This Manual For Vehicle Manufacturer's Special Tool Suppliers.

INDEX

	Page No.		Page No.		Page No.
Front Wheel Alignment	3-34	Preliminary Inspection	3-34	Front	3-35
Camber	3-34	Rear Wheel Alignment	3-35	Rear	3-35
Caster	3-34	Toe	3-35	Wheel Alignment	
Toe	3-34	Vehicle Ride Height	3-35	Specifications	3-3

PRELIMINARY INSPECTION

1. Inspect tires for proper inflation and irregular tire wear.
2. Inspect runout of wheels and tires.
3. Inspect wheel bearings for backlash and excessive play.
4. Inspect ball joints and tie rod ends for looseness or wear.
5. Inspect control arms and stabilizer shaft for looseness or wear.
6. Inspect steering gear for looseness at frame.
7. Inspect struts/shock absorbers for wear, leaks and any noticeable noises.
8. Inspect vehicle trim height.
9. Inspect steering wheel excessive drag or poor return because of stiff or rusted linkage or suspension components.
10. Inspect fuel level. Fuel tank should be full or vehicle should have compensating load added.
11. Give consideration to excess loads, such as tool boxes, sample cases, etc. If normally carried in vehicle, these items should remain in vehicle during alignment adjustments.
12. Give consideration also to condition of equipment being used for alignment.
13. Install alignment equipment according to manufacturer's instructions.
14. Jounce front and rear bumpers three times prior to inspecting wheel alignment.
15. Measure and record alignment angles.
16. When performing adjustments to vehicles requiring four-wheel alignment, set rear wheel alignment angles first to obtain proper front alignment angles.

FRONT WHEEL ALIGNMENT

Caster

1. Raise and support vehicle, then remove front tire and wheel assembly.
2. Remove and discard front lower control arm rod to front lower control arm rod insulator bushing nut.
3. Remove four insulator bushing to front frame mounting nuts.
4. Remove insulator bushing.
5. At factory, one washer is on front of lefthand control arm rod.
6. On side of vehicle with higher caster reading, install one washer to front of control arm rod. **Do not add more than one washer to control arm rod.**
7. Install insulator bushing over front of rod and to frame studs.
8. Install four insulator bushing to frame mounting nuts and **Torque** to 17 ft. lbs.
9. Install new rod to insulator bushing mounting nut. **Do not tighten nut now.**
10. Install front tire and wheel assembly, then lower vehicle.
11. With weight of vehicle on tire and wheel assemblies, push down on front bumper three times to stabilize suspension.
12. **Torque** rod to insulator bushing mounting nut to 109 ft. lbs.
13. Measure and adjust wheel alignment, as required.

Camber

1. Raise and support vehicle on suitable alignment rack.
2. If required, remove front tire and wheel assembly.
3. Remove and discard two strut to knuckle mounting nuts.
4. Remove two washers, then remove and discard two strut to knuckle mounting bolts.
5. Install two new strut to knuckle bolts. **Do not fully tighten bolts now.** Install two washers to bolts.
6. Install two new strut to knuckle mounting nuts to bolts. **Do not fully tighten nuts and bolts now.**
7. If front tire and wheel assembly were removed, install them, then lower vehicle onto alignment rack to place weight of vehicle onto tires.
8. Push down on front bumper three times to stabilize suspension.
9. Measure alignment.
10. **Camber adjustment screw has thread sealant in form of micro-encapsulation.**
11. Rotate camber adjustment screw to adjust front camber to specification.
12. **Torque** strut to knuckle mounting nuts to 63 ft. lbs.
13. **Torque** mounting nuts to 74 ft. lbs.
14. Final tighten nuts an additional 90°.

Toe

1. Ensure steering wheel and gear are in straight ahead position.
2. Measure wheel alignment.
3. Loosen steering gear boot clamp and outer tie rod end lock nut.
4. Rotate inner tie rod to adjust front toe to specification. **Do not twisted boots when rotating inner tie rods.**
5. Ensure number of threads on righthand inner tie rod is same as number on lefthand inner tie rod.
6. **Torque** lock nut to 37 ft. lbs.
7. Ensure boot is not twisted. Install boot clamp.

REAR WHEEL ALIGNMENT

Toe

The following components have lefthand threads: The inner adjustment link, inner lock nut , and the corresponding end of adjuster.

1. Measure wheel alignment.
2. Loosen two rear adjustment link lock nuts.
3. Rotate center adjuster to adjust rear toe to specification.
4. Increasing length of adjustment link will increase rear wheel toe.
5. Hold ball joint position using suitable wrench on hexagonal crimped section of outer adjustment link.
6. **Torque** lock nuts to 37 ft. lbs.

VEHICLE RIDE HEIGHT

1. Set tire pressure to specifications on tire placard.

2. Ensure tires match tire size specifications on tire placard.
3. Ensure wheels match wheel size specifications on tire placard.
4. Ensure fuel tank is full. Add additional weight in order to simulate a full tank, if required.
5. Ensure luggage compartment is empty except for spare tire and weight simulating full fuel tank.
6. Ensure vehicle is on level surface, such as alignment rack.
7. Close hood, doors and luggage compartment lid.
8. Ensure vehicle is not damaged from collision.

Front

1. Lift front bumper of vehicle up approximately 1.5 inches using hands.
2. Gently remove hands and to allow vehicle to settle.
3. Push front bumper of vehicle down approximately 1.5 inches using hands.
4. Gently remove hands to allow vehicle to settle.

5. Measure Z height dimension for lefthand righthand sides of vehicle on front lower control arms.
6. Measure vertical distance from bottom of control arm, below ball joint, to center line of control arm pivot bolt, **Fig. 1.**
7. If measurement is not within .4 inch of specification, replace front springs.

Rear

1. Lift rear bumper of vehicle up approximately 1.5 inches by hand.
2. Gently hands to allow vehicle to settle.
3. Push rear bumper of vehicle down approximately 1.5 inches using hands
4. Gently remove hands to allow vehicle to settle.
5. Measure D height dimension for left and righthand side of vehicle on rear suspension adjustment link, **Fig. 2.**
6. Measure vertical distance from bottom of outer adjustment link to center line of inner adjustment link pivot bolt.
7. If measurement is not within .4 inch of specification, replace rear springs.

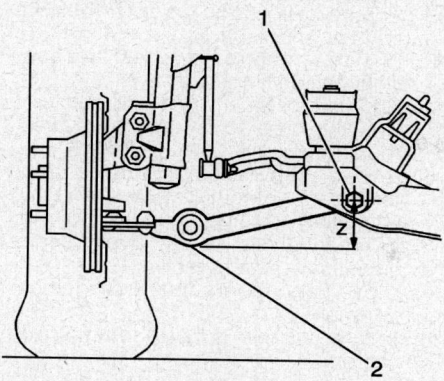

1. Center Line Of Control Arm Pivot Bolt
2. Bottom Of Control Arm

ARM0400000001023

**Fig. 1   Front ride height
measurement**

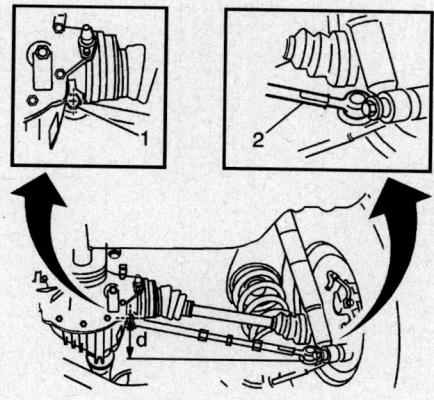

1. Center Line Of Inner Adjustment Link Pivot Bolt
2. Bottom Of Outer Adjustment Link

ARM0400000001024

**Fig. 2   Rear ride height
measurement**

SOLSTICE

NOTE: Refer To The Rear Of This Manual For Manufacturer's Special Service Tool Suppliers.

INDEX OF SERVICE OPERATIONS

Page No.

AIR BAG SYSTEM PRECAUTIONS 0-18
BRAKES
Anti-Lock Brakes (Volume 2).. 6-1
Disc Brakes.................... 22-1
Drum Brakes 23-1
Hydraulic Brake Systems 24-1
Power Brake Units 25-1
COMPUTER RELEARN PROCEDURE 0-31
ELECTRICAL
Air Bag System (Volume 2) ... 4-1
Air Conditioning............... 16-1
Alternator, Replace 4-4
Alternators 19-1
Blower Motor, Replace 4-5
Cooling Fans 17-1
Cruise Control (Volume 2) 2-1
Dash Gauges (Volume 2) 1-1
Dash Panel Service (Volume 2)................... 5-1
Evaporator Core, Replace 4-6
Fuel Pump Relay Location.... 4-4
Fuse Panel & Flasher Location 4-4
Headlamp Switch, Replace ... 4-5
Heater Core, Replace 4-5
Ignition Coil, Replace 4-4
Ignition Lock, Replace 4-4
Ignition Switch, Replace 4-4
Instrument Cluster, Replace... 4-5
Multi-Function Switch, Replace 4-5
Passive Restraint Systems (Volume 2).................. 4-1
Precautions.................. 4-4
Radio, Replace 4-5
Relay Center Location 4-4
Speed Controls (Volume 2) ... 2-1
Starter Motors 18-1
Starter, Replace 4-4
Steering Columns............. 20-1
Steering Wheel, Replace...... 4-5
Stop Light Switch, Replace ... 4-5
Turn Signal Switch, Replace .. 4-5
Wiper Motor, Replace......... 4-5
Wiper Systems (Volume 2).... 3-1
Wiper Transmission, Replace . 4-5
ELECTRICAL SYMBOL IDENTIFICATION 0-63
FRONT DRIVE AXLES 26-1
FRONT SUSPENSION & STEERING
Ball Joint, Replace............ 4-21
Ball Joint Inspection 4-21
Coil Spring, Replace 4-21
Control Arm, Replace 4-21
Hub & Bearing, Replace 21-1
Power Steering 21-1

Page No.

Power Steering Gear, Replace 4-22
Power Steering Pump, Replace 4-23
Power Steering System Bleed 4-23
Precautions................... 4-21
Stabilizer Bar, Replace........ 4-22
Stabilizer Bar Bushing, Replace 4-22
Steering Columns............. 20-1
Steering Knuckle, Replace 4-22
Strut, Replace 4-21
Strut Service.................. 4-21
Tie Rod, Replace 4-22
Tightening Specifications...... 4-23
NON-STANDARD TIRE & WHEEL SIZE ADJUSTMENT TO RIDE HEIGHT SPECIFICATIONS & TIRE SIZE CHART 0-61
REAR AXLE & SUSPENSION
Coil Spring, Replace.......... 4-19
Control Arm, Replace 4-19
Description 4-18
Differential Carrier, Replace... 4-19
Hub & Bearing, Replace 4-19
Knuckle, Replace 4-19
Propeller Shaft, Replace 4-19
Rear Axle Shaft, Replace 4-18
Shock Absorber, Replace 4-19
Stabilizer Shaft, Replace 4-20
Tightening Specifications...... 4-20
Toe Link, Replace 4-20
SERVICE REMINDER & WARNING LAMP RESET PROCEDURES 0-34
SPECIFICATIONS
Fluid Capacities & Cooling System Data.................. 4-3
Front Wheel Alignment Specifications................. 4-2
General Engine Specifications................. 4-2
Lubricant Data 4-3
Rear Wheel Alignment Specifications................. 4-2
Tune Up Specifications 4-2
Vehicle Ride Height Specifications................. 4-3
TIRE PRESSURE MONITORING SYSTEM 20-1
VEHICLE IDENTIFICATION 0-1
VEHICLE LIFT POINTS 0-51
VEHICLE MAINTENANCE SCHEDULES 0-73

Page No.

WHEEL ALIGNMENT
Front Wheel Alignment........ 4-24
Preliminary Inspection 4-24
Rear Wheel Alignment 4-24
Wheel Alignment Specifications................. 4-2
WIRE COLOR CODE IDENTIFICATION 0-63
2.0L VIN X ENGINE
Balance Shaft, Replace....... 4-12
Camshaft, Replace 4-11
Crankshaft Damper, Replace.. 4-10
Crankshaft Rear Oil Seal, Replace 4-13
Crankshaft Seal, Replace 4-13
Cylinder Head, Replace 4-9
Engine Rebuilding Specifications.................. 29-1
Engine, Replace 4-7
Engine Mount, Replace 4-7
Exhaust Manifold, Replace.... 4-8
Front Cover, Replace 4-10
Front Cover Seal, Replace 4-10
Fuel Pump, Replace 4-14
Hydraulic Lifters, Replace..... 4-9
Intake Manifold, Replace...... 4-8
Main & Rod Bearings 4-13
Oil Cooler, Replace 4-13
Oil Pan, Replace............. 4-13
Oil Pump, Replace 4-13
Oil Pump Service 4-13
Precautions.................. 4-6
Radiator, Replace 4-14
Rocker Arms................. 4-9
Serpentine Drive Belt 4-13
Thermostat, Replace 4-13
Tightening Specifications...... 4-15
Timing Chain, Replace 4-10
Turbocharger, Replace 4-14
Valve Adjustment 4-9
Valve Clearance Specifications.................. 4-9
Valve Cover, Replace 4-9
Water Pump, Replace 4-13
2.4L ENGINE
Engine Rebuilding Specifications.................. 29-1
Engine, Replace 4-16
Engine Mount, Replace 4-16
Fuel Pump, Replace 4-17
Precautions.................. 4-16
Radiator, Replace............ 4-17
Tightening Specifications...... 4-18

Specifications

GENERAL ENGINE SPECIFICATIONS

Engine Liter/VIN	Fuel System	Bore × Stroke, Inches	Comp. Ratio	Net HP @ RPM	Maximum Torque, Ft. Lbs. @ RPM	Minimum Oil Pressure, psi
2006						
2.4L/B	SFI	3.46 x 3.86	10:1	177 @ 6600	166 @ 4800	50–80
2007–08						
2.0L/X	SFI	3.38 x 3.38	9.2:1	260 @ 5300	260 @ 2500–5250	50–80
2.4L/B	SFI	3.46 x 3.86	10:1	177 @ 6600	166 @ 4800	50–80

SFI — Sequential Fuel Injection

TUNE UP SPECIFICATIONS

Engine	Spark Plug Gap, Inch	Ignition Timing		Idle Speed, RPM	Fuel Pressure, psi	Valve Clearance, Inch
		Firing Order	°BTDC			
2.0L	.35	1-3-4-2	①	③	50–60	②
2.4L	.42	1-3-4-2	①	③	50–60	②

① — Equipped w/Direct Ignition System (DIS). No adjustment.

② — Equipped w/hydraulic lifters. No adjustment is required.

③ — Idle speed is controlled by Throttle Actuator Control (TAC) motor.

FRONT WHEEL ALIGNMENT SPECIFICATIONS

Year	Caster, Degrees		Camber, Degrees②		Toe, Degrees③	Ball Joint Inspection
	Limits	Desired	Limits	Desired	Total	
2006–08	+7.4 to +8.6	+8.0	-1.1 to 0.1	-.5	-.1 to +.3	①

① — Refer to Front Steering & Suspension section for ball joint inspection procedure.

② — Camber & Caster Cross Tolerance: -.6 to +.6°.

③ — Steering Wheel Angle, -3.50 to +3.50°.

REAR WHEEL ALIGNMENT SPECIFICATIONS

Year	Camber, Degrees①		Total Toe, Degrees	Thrust, Degrees
	Limits	Desired		
2006–08	-1.0 to .0	-.5	-.1 to +.3	+.2 to +.2

① — Camber Cross Tolerance, -.5 to +.5°.

VEHICLE RIDE HEIGHT SPECIFICATIONS

Year	Body Style	Manufacturer's Original Tire Size	Measurement Points & Specifications					
			Front			Rear		
			Dim.	Specification②		Dim.	Specification②	
				Inches	mm		Inches	mm
2006–08	All	①	Z	1.45	37	D	2.44	62.2

Z — Measure between points indicated in **Fig. A.**

D — Measure between points indicated in **Fig. B.**

① — See sticker located on the driver door below the latch for manufacturers original tire size specifications.

② — Plus or minus 10 mm or .4 inch.

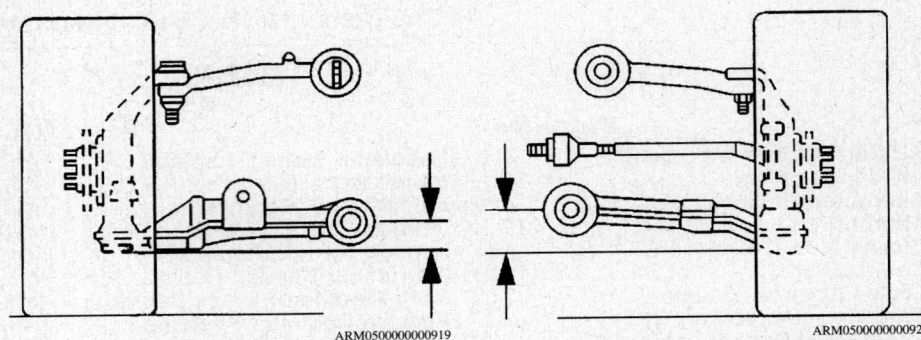

ARM0500000000919   ARM0500000000920

Fig. A   Front trim height Z measurement   **Fig. B   Rear trim height D measurement**

FLUID CAPACITIES & COOLING SYSTEM DATA

Engine	Coolant Capacity, Qts.	Coolant Type	Coolant Recovery Reservoir Cap Pressure, Lbs.	Thermo. Opening Temp., °F	Fuel Tank Capacity, Gals.	Engine Oil Refill, Qts.	Trans. Oil Refill		Rear Axle Oil, Qts.
							Automatic, Qts.	Manual, Pts.	
2006									
2.4L	7.9	①	②	190	13.8	5.0	9.0	—	1.37
2007–08									
2.0L	9.0	①	②	190	13.8	5.0	9.0	5.50	③
2.4L	8.7	①	②	190	13.8	5.0	9.0	5.50	③

① — 50/50 mixture of clean, drinkable water and use only DEX-COOL coolant.

② — Refer to pressure cap for rated pressure.

③ — Drain & fill w/cover removed, 1.27 qts., plus 3.38 oz. limited slip additive; using plug, 1.06 qts., plus 2.37 oz. limited slip additive.

LUBRICANT DATA

Year	Lubricant Type				
	Transmission		Rear Axle	Power Steering System	Brake System
	Automatic	Manual			
2006–08	DEXRON VI	①	②	③	DOT-3

① — Manual Transmission Fluid, (GM part no. 89021184) or equivalent.

② — SAE 75W-90 Synthetic Axle Lubricant (GM part no. 12378261), or equivalent, meeting GM specification 9986115.

③ — GM Power Steering Fluid, (GM part no. 89021184) or equivalent.

Electrical

NOTE: On Air Bag Equipped Models, Refer To "Air Bag System Precautions" Located In The Front Of This Manual For System Disarming & Arming Procedures.

NOTE: Refer To "Computer Relearn Procedures" Located In The Front Of This Manual When Battery Power To The Computer Has Been Interrupted.

INDEX

	Page No.
Air Bag System (Volume 2)	4-1
Air Conditioning	16-1
Alternator, Replace	4-4
Alternators	19-1
Blower Motor, Replace	4-5
Cooling Fans	17-1
Cruise Control (Volume 2)	2-1
Dash Gauges (Volume 2)	1-1
Dash Panel Service (Volume 2)	5-1
Evaporator Core, Replace	4-6
Fuel Pump Relay Location	4-4
Fuse Panel & Flasher Location	4-4

	Page No.
Headlamp Switch, Replace	4-5
Heater Core, Replace	4-5
Ignition Coil, Replace	4-4
Ignition Lock, Replace	4-4
Ignition Switch, Replace	4-4
Instrument Cluster, Replace	4-5
Multi-Function Switch, Replace	4-5
Passive Restraint Systems (Volume 2)	4-1
Precautions	4-4
Air Bag Systems	4-4
Battery Ground Cable	4-4
Radio, Replace	4-5

	Page No.
Relay Center Location	4-4
Speed Controls (Volume 2)	2-1
Starter Motors	18-1
Starter, Replace	4-4
Steering Columns	20-1
Steering Wheel, Replace	4-5
Stop Light Switch, Replace	4-5
Installation	4-5
Removal	4-5
Turn Signal Switch, Replace	4-5
Wiper Motor, Replace	4-5
Wiper Systems (Volume 2)	3-1
Wiper Transmission, Replace	4-5

PRECAUTIONS

Air Bag Systems

Refer to "Air Bag System Precautions" in the front of this manual for system disarming and arming procedures.

Battery Ground Cable

Prior to service, disconnect battery ground cable and isolate as required.

FUSE PANEL & FLASHER LOCATION

The C1, C2, C3 and C4 underhood fuse blocks are located on the rear lefthand side of the engine compartment. The Body Control Module (BCM) contains some fuses, the BCM is located behind the righthand side of the instrument panel, under the HVAC module. Flasher operation is controlled by the BCM.

FUEL PUMP RELAY LOCATION

The fuel pump relay is located in the C2 underhood fuse block.

RELAY CENTER LOCATION

Relays are located in the underhood fuse blocks and BCM.

STARTER

REPLACE

1. Remove intake manifold as outlined under "Intake Manifold, Replace" in appropriate engine section.
2. Remove starter solenoid terminal nuts and disconnect engine terminal harness.
3. Remove mounting bolts and starter.
4. Reverse procedure to install, noting the following:
   a. **Torque** starter motor mounting bolts to 30 ft. lbs.
   b. **Torque** starter solenoid terminal nut to 89 inch lbs.
   c. **Torque** starter solenoid S terminal nut to 27 inch lbs.

ALTERNATOR

REPLACE

1. Remove drive belt as outlined under "Serpentine Drive Belt."
2. Remove engine harness alternator connector.
3. Remove engine harness ground terminal boot, nut and harness.
4. Remove mounting bolts and alternator.
5. Reverse procedure to install, noting the following:
   a. **Torque** alternator bolts to 16 ft. lbs.
   b. **Torque** engine harness ground terminal nut to 15 ft. lbs.

IGNITION COIL

REPLACE

1. Pull intake manifold cover upward, disconnect studs and remove cover.
2. Disconnect ignition coil electrical connector.
3. Remove mounting bolts and coils.
4. Reverse procedure to install. **Torque** ignition coil bolts to 89 inch lbs.

IGNITION LOCK

REPLACE

1. Remove knee bolster and bracket.
2. Lower steering column, then remove steering column upper and lower trim covers.
3. Turn ignition lock cylinder to RUN position.
4. Depress first retainer through lock housing access hole with suitable small Allen wrench or pick-type tool, **Fig. 1.** Lock cylinder will back out slightly.
5. Depress second retainer through lock housing access hole and lock cylinder will back out slightly again.
6. Pull lock cylinder out enough and locate second retainer to lock housing access hole.
7. Depress retainer though access hole a second time, ignition cylinder should release from housing. If cylinder does not release, move cylinder in and out several times to locate retainer correctly in hole.
8. Remove lock cylinder from lock housing.
9. Reverse procedure to install.

IGNITION SWITCH

REPLACE

1. Remove knee bolster and bracket.
2. Lower steering column, then remove upper and lower trim covers.

3. Disconnect ignition switch harness connector.
4. Turn ignition switch to RUN position.
5. Remove mounting screws and ignition switch.
6. Reverse procedure to install.

HEADLAMP SWITCH
REPLACE

Refer to "Multi-Function Switch, Replace" for headlamp switch replacement procedure.

STOP LIGHT SWITCH
REPLACE
Removal

1. Disconnect Brake Pedal Position (BPP) sensor electrical connector.
2. Remove mounting bolt and BPP sensor.

Installation

1. Install new sensor. **Torque** mounting bolt to 18 inch lbs.
2. Connect electrical connector.
3. Apply parking brake.
4. **On models equipped with automatic transmission,** place transmission in PARK position.
5. **On models equipped with manual transmission,** place transmission in NEUTRAL position.
6. **On all models,** install a scan tool.
7. Clear all BCM DTCs.
8. Turn ignition switch to ON position with engine off.
9. Navigate to Vehicle Control System menu.
10. Select Computer/Integrating Systems menu item.
11. Select Module Setup menu item.
12. Select BCM menu item.
13. Select BPP Sensor Calibration procedure and follow directions displayed on screen.

MULTI-FUNCTION SWITCH
REPLACE

1. Remove knee bolster and bracket.
2. Lower steering column, then the upper and lower trim covers.
3. Disconnect multi-function turn signal switch harness connector.
4. Depress locking tabs and remove multi-function turn signal switch.
5. Reverse procedure to install.

TURN SIGNAL SWITCH
REPLACE

Refer to "Multi-Function Switch, Replace" for turn signal switch replacement procedure.

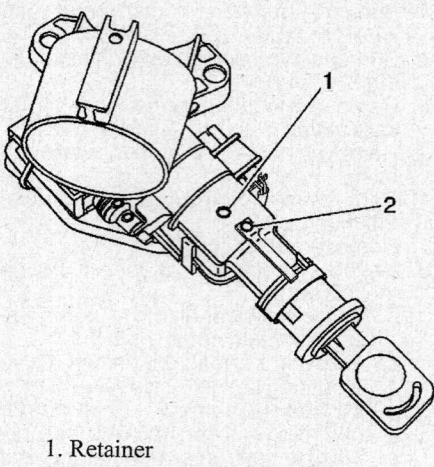

1. Retainer
2. Retainer

ARM050000000643

Fig. 1 Lock cylinder retainers

STEERING WHEEL
REPLACE

1. Remove driver's air bag module as outlined in "Passive Restraint Systems" chapter.
2. Insert suitable, small flat bladed tool through access openings, on left and righthand hand sides of steering wheel.
3. Remove nut and steering wheel.
4. Reverse procedure to install. **Torque** steering wheel nut to 27 ft. lbs.

INSTRUMENT CLUSTER
REPLACE

1. **On models equipped with manual transmission,** remove shift control lever boot ring, lever screw and lever knob.
2. **On models equipped with automatic transmission,** remove console shift lever bezel.
3. **On all models,** remove instrument panel assist handle.
4. Remove cluster trim plate and retainer clip.
5. Remove mounting screws and instrument cluster.
6. Reverse procedure to install, noting the following:
   a. **Torque** shift control lever screw and passenger assist handle mounting bolts to 89 inch lbs.
   b. **Torque** instrument panel cluster mounting screws to 18 ft. lbs.

RADIO
REPLACE

1. **On models equipped with automatic transmission,** remove console shift lever bezel.
2. **On models equipped with manual transmission,** remove shift control lever boot ring, lever screw and lever knob.
3. **On all models,** remove instrument panel assist handle.

4. Remove mounting bolt and screws, then the radio.
5. Reverse procedure to install. **Torque** radio mounting bolts and screws to 18 inch lbs.

WIPER MOTOR
REPLACE

1. Remove cap from windshield wiper arm using suitable, small flat-bladed tool.
2. Remove windshield wiper arm mounting nut.
3. Remove windshield washer nozzle hose.
4. Remove windshield wiper arm.
5. Remove air inlet grille retainers and air inlet grille.
6. Disconnect Connector Positive Assurance (CPA) cover from wiper motor electrical connector.
7. Disconnect wiper motor electrical connector.
8. Remove mounting bolts and windshield wiper system module.
9. Remove mounting bolts and separate windshield wiper motor from module.
10. Reverse procedure to install, noting the following:
    a. **Torque** windshield wiper motor mounting bolts to 40 ft. lbs.
    b. **Torque** windshield wiper module mounting bolts to 80 inch lbs.
    c. **Torque** windshield washer arm mounting nut to 24 ft. lbs.

WIPER TRANSMISSION
REPLACE

Refer to "Wiper Motor, Replace" for wiper transmission replacement procedure.

BLOWER MOTOR
REPLACE

1. Disconnect damper and remove glove compartment.
2. Remove blower motor resistor mounting screw.
3. Remove mounting screws and blower motor.
4. Reverse procedure to install. **Torque** blower motor and blower resistor mounting screws to 13 inch lbs.

HEATER CORE
REPLACE

1. Drain cooling system into suitable container.
2. Recover refrigerant as outlined in "Air Conditioning" chapter.
3. Remove air conditioning compressor tube assembly nut.
4. Remove sealing washer.
5. Remove mounting bolt, sealing washer and thermal expansion valve.
6. Remove air inlet grille panel.
7. Remove heater inlet and outlet hose.
8. Remove instrument panel cluster trim plate.
9. Remove driver knee bolster trim panel.

10. Disconnect damper and remove glove compartment.
11. Remove passenger's air bag module as outlined in "Passive Restraint Systems" chapter.
12. Remove left and righthand hand instrument panel outer trim covers.
13. Remove left and righthand hand windshield pillar garnish moldings.
14. Remove radio and cup holder.
15. Remove mounting screws and instrument panel trim pad.
16. Remove steering column as outlined in "Steering Columns" chapter.
17. Note instrument panel wiring harness routing for installation alignment.
18. Remove mounting screw, bolt and air distribution duct.
19. Remove mounting bolts and instrument panel tie bar.

20. Remove mounting nuts, bolts and HVAC module.
21. Remove mounting screw and air outlet duct.
22. Remove mounting screw and heater core cover.
23. Remove heater core pass through seal.
24. Remove mounting screws and air distribution case.
25. Remove heater core.
26. Reverse procedure to install, noting the following:
    a. **Torque** air conditioning compressor mounting nut to 12 ft. lbs.
    b. **Torque** thermal expansion valve mounting bolt to 12 ft. lbs.
    c. **Torque** instrument panel carrier mounting bolt and nut to 80 inch lbs.
    d. **Torque** instrument panel tie bar outer mounting bolts to 106 inch lbs.
    e. **Torque** instrument panel tie bar inner mounting bolts to 18 ft. lbs.

EVAPORATOR CORE
REPLACE

1. Remove HVAC module as outlined under "Heater Core, Replace."
2. Remove evaporator case seal.
3. Remove mounting bolts and thermal expansion valve.
4. Remove sealing washer.
5. Remove mounting screws and rear air outlet duct.
6. Remove mounting screw and evaporator lower case.
7. Remove evaporator.
8. Reverse procedure to install.

2.0L VIN X Engine

NOTE: On Air Bag Equipped Models, Refer To "Air Bag System Precautions" Located In The Front Of This Manual For System Disarming & Arming Procedures.

NOTE: Refer To "Computer Relearn Procedures" Located In The Front Of This Manual When Battery Power To The Computer Has Been Interrupted.

INDEX

	Page No.
Balance Shaft, Replace	4-12
Installation	4-12
Removal	4-12
Camshaft, Replace	4-11
Installation	4-12
Removal	4-11
Crankshaft Damper, Replace	4-10
Crankshaft Rear Oil Seal, Replace	4-13
Crankshaft Seal, Replace	4-13
Cylinder Head, Replace	4-9
Engine Rebuilding Specifications	29-1
Engine, Replace	4-7
Engine Mount, Replace	4-7
Lefthand	4-7
Righthand	4-7
Exhaust Manifold, Replace	4-8

	Page No.
Front Cover, Replace	4-10
Front Cover Seal, Replace	4-10
Fuel Pump, Replace	4-14
Hydraulic Lifters, Replace	4-9
Intake Manifold, Replace	4-8
Main & Rod Bearings	4-13
Connecting Rod Bearings	4-13
Main Bearings	4-13
Oil Cooler, Replace	4-13
Oil Pan, Replace	4-13
Installation	4-13
Removal	4-13
Oil Pump, Replace	4-13
Oil Pump Service	4-13
Assemble	4-13
Disassemble	4-13
Precautions	4-6
Air Bag Systems	4-6

	Page No.
Battery Ground Cable	4-6
Fuel System Pressure Relief	4-6
High Side	4-7
Low Side	4-6
Radiator, Replace	4-14
Rocker Arms	4-9
Serpentine Drive Belt	4-13
Replacement	4-13
Thermostat, Replace	4-13
Tightening Specifications	4-15
Timing Chain, Replace	4-10
Installation	4-11
Removal	4-10
Turbocharger, Replace	4-14
Valve Adjustment	4-9
Valve Clearance Specifications	4-9
Valve Cover, Replace	4-9
Water Pump, Replace	4-13

PRECAUTIONS

Air Bag Systems

Refer to "Air Bag System Precautions" in the front of this manual for system disarming and arming procedures.

Battery Ground Cable

Prior to service, disconnect battery ground cable and isolate as required.

Fuel System Pressure Relief

LOW SIDE

USING DIGITAL PRESSURE GAUGE

1. Remove engine cover.
2. Loosen fuel fill cap to relieve fuel tank vapor pressure.
3. Remove fuel rail service port cap.
4. Wrap suitable shop towel around fuel rail service port.
5. Connect digital pressure gauge tool No. CH-48027 to fuel rail service port and place hose into suitable container.
6. Open tool valve and to bleed fuel from fuel rail. Close valve.
7. Remove hose and disconnect gauge.
8. Install fuel rail service port cap and engine cover. Tighten fuel fill cap

LESS DIGITAL PRESSURE GAGE

1. Loosen fuel fill cap to relieve fuel tank vapor pressure.

2. Remove engine cover.
3. Remove fuel rail service port cap.
4. Wrap suitable shop towel around fuel rail service port and use suitable, small flat bladed tool to depress (open) fuel rail test port valve.
5. Install fuel rail service port cap and engine cover. Tighten fuel fill cap.

HIGH SIDE

1. Connect suitable programmed scan tool to vehicle and command fuel pump relay OFF.
2. Start vehicle and allow engine to idle until engine stops in approximately 20–30 seconds.
3. Turn ignition switch to OFF position.
4. Ensure there is no fuel pressure using scan tool.
5. If scan tool is not available, wait at least two hours after engine has stopped running to remove high pressure fuel line.

ENGINE MOUNT
REPLACE
Lefthand

1. Loosen clamps and remove Charge Air Cooler (CAC) outlet hose from CAC outlet pipe and throttle body.
2. Remove lefthand engine mount upper nut.
3. Raise and support vehicle.
4. Remove lefthand engine mount lower nut.
5. Remove righthand engine mount lower nut.
6. Position suitable adjustable jack below oil pan. Place suitable block of wood between oil pan and jack.
7. Raise engine and remove mount.
8. Reverse procedure to install.

Righthand

1. Raise and support vehicle, then remove tire and wheel assembly.
2. Remove upper and lower righthand engine mount nuts.
3. Remove lefthand engine mount lower nut.
4. Remove righthand brake hose bracket bolt.
5. Remove righthand brake line clip at crossmember.
6. Position suitable adjustable jack below oil pan. Place suitable block of wood between oil pan and jack.
7. Raise engine and remove engine mount.
8. Reverse procedure to install.

ENGINE
REPLACE

1. Open hood and disconnect headlamp bulb socket Connector Positive Assurance (CPA) connector.
2. Disconnect lefthand headlamp electrical harness.
3. Rotate socket a quarter turn counterclockwise and disconnect bulb.

4. Remove mounting screws and headlamp.
5. Disconnect wiring harness on both sides and mark hood for installation alignment.
6. Remove mounting nuts and hood.
7. Recover air conditioning system refrigerant as outlined in "Air Conditioning" chapter.
8. Grasp intake manifold cover and disconnect studs.
9. Remove intake manifold cover, oil fill cap and insulator. Install oil fill cap.
10. Rotate power steering pump belt tensioner pulley clockwise and remove belt.
11. Lower vehicle.
12. Remove charge air cooler inlet pipe mounting bolt at rear bracket.
13. Remove mounting nut and charge air cooler rear bracket.
14. Remove charge air cooler inlet pipe mounting bolt at front bracket.
15. Loosen charge air cooler clamp at inlet pipe. and inlet pipe clamp at pipe.
16. Remove charge air cooler inlet pipe.
17. Disconnect intake air pressure and temperature sensor engine wiring harness electrical connector.
18. Disconnect clamp and remove charge air cooler outlet pipe air bypass valve solenoid vacuum hose.
19. Remove charge air cooler outlet pipe mounting bolt, nut and rear bracket.
20. Disconnect charge air cooler outlet pipe hose clamp and remove charge air cooler outlet pipe front bracket mounting bolt.
21. Disconnect clamp and remove charge air cooler outlet pipe.
22. Disconnect air cleaner housing and turbocharger clamps and remove air cleaner outlet duct.
23. Disconnect Mass Air Flow (MAF) sensor engine wiring harness electrical connector.
24. Remove front mounting bolt and air cleaner assembly.
25. Remove drive belt.
26. Drain cooling system into suitable container.
27. Remove mounting bolts and radiator front air deflector, then the retainer and shroud air inlet.
28. Remove air cleaner outlet duct resonator and Positive Crankcase Ventilation (PCV) hose clamps.
29. Remove air cleaner outlet duct resonator.
30. Disconnect cooling fan motor electrical connector.
31. Remove mounting bolts, shroud, cooling fan and motor.
32. Remove radiator inlet and outlet hoses, then the surge tank inlet hose.
33. Remove air cleaner stud, then the mounting nuts and radiator upper bracket.
34. Remove mounting bolts, air conditioning condenser and radiator.
35. Relieve fuel system pressure as outlined under "Precautions."
36. Disconnect Evaporative Emission (EVAP) canister purge solenoid valve tube.

37. Disconnect fuel feed pipe from fuel line.
38. Remove cap and windshield wiper arm mounting nut.
39. Remove windshield washer nozzle hose and windshield wiper arm.
40. Remove retainers and air inlet grille. Disconnect washer pump hose.
41. **On models equipped with automatic transmission,** proceed as follows:
    a. Remove intake manifold as outlined under "Intake Manifold, Replace."
    b. Remove starter solenoid terminal nuts and disconnect engine terminal harness.
    c. Remove mounting bolts and starter motor.
42. **On models equipped with manual transmission,** proceed as follows:
    a. Remove transmission as outlined under **MOTOR's "Domestic Transmission, In-Vehicle Service" manual or "Transmission Service DVD."**
    b. Install differential case bracket to body mounting bolt to support rear drive module.
43. **On all models,** remove mounting bolts and turbocharger heat shield.
44. Remove mounting bolts, charge air cooler pipe and gasket from turbocharger.
45. Cap or plug turbocharger opening.
46. Disconnect clamp, then remove position radiator inlet hose from engine and position it aside.
47. Disconnect clamps, then remove radiator outlet hose from thermostat housing and oil cooler. Position hose aside.
48. Disconnect clamps, then remove surge tank outlet hose from thermostat housing and oil cooler. Position hose aside.
49. Disconnect clamp and remove surge tank outlet hose from rank.
50. Remove oil level indicator tube bracket clip and remove surge tank outlet hose.
51. Disconnect surge tank air bleed hose clamp at engine and clip at surge tank bracket. Position air bleed hose aside.
52. Disconnect clamps, then remove heater inlet and outlet hoses from thermostat housing.
53. Raise and support vehicle, then drain engine oil into suitable container.
54. Disconnect Crankshaft Position (CKP) and oil pressure sensors electrical connectors.
55. Disconnect brake booster vacuum pump electrical connector.
56. **On models equipped with manual transmission,** proceed as follows:
    a. Remove mounting nut and starter battery positive cable lead.
    b. Remove mounting nut and engine wiring harness from terminals from starter.
    c. Remove engine wiring harness clip from oil level indicator tube.
57. **On all models,** lower vehicle and cut engine harness tie straps.
58. Remove mounting bolt and battery negative cable ground terminal from

front engine lift bracket. Position cable aside.

59. Disconnect transmission oil cooler pump and alternator electrical connectors.
60. **On models equipped with manual transmission,** disconnect knock sensor electrical connector and remove engine wiring harness clip from oil level indicator tube bracket.
61. **On all models,** disconnect boot, then remove terminal nut and positive cable from alternator.
62. Disconnect air conditioning compressor and fuel injector jumper electrical connectors.
63. **On models equipped with manual transmission,** proceed as follows:
    a. Disconnect throttle actuator electrical connector.
    b. Remove engine wiring harness clip from intake manifold brace.
    c. Disconnect EVAP canister purge solenoid valve electrical connector.
    d. Disconnect Manifold Absolute Pressure (MAP) sensor electrical connector.
64. **On all models,** disconnect air conditioning refrigerant pressor sensor electrical connector.
65. Disconnect brake booster vacuum sensor and windshield wiper motor electrical connectors.
66. Remove engine harness clip from wiper motor hole.
67. Disconnect intake Camshaft Position (CMP) sensor and high pressure fuel pump electrical connectors.
68. Remove engine wiring harness clip from high pressure fuel pump bracket.
69. Disconnect intake and exhaust CMP actuator electrical connectors.
70. Remove engine harness clip from valve cover and disconnect ignition coils electrical connectors.
71. Disconnect Heated Oxygen Sensor (HO2S) and exhaust CMP sensor electrical connectors.
72. Remove bolt and position engine harness ground terminal aside.
73. Disconnect Engine Coolant Temperature (ECT) sensor electrical connector.
74. Disconnect valve cover engine harness clips.
75. Remove engine wiring harness clips from turbocharger coolant feed pipe stud and pipe tab.
76. Disconnect boost sensor electrical connector.
77. Remove mounting bolt and cylinder head ground terminal.
78. Remove engine harness clips from front studs, than gather all branches and position engine harness aside.
79. **On models equipped with manual transmission,** disconnect clamp and remove turbocharger vacuum hose.
80. **On all models,** remove vacuum hose from turbocharger coolant feed pipe clips.
81. **On models equipped with automatic transmission,** remove charge air bypass valve solenoid.
82. **On models equipped with manual transmission,** position vacuum hose aside.

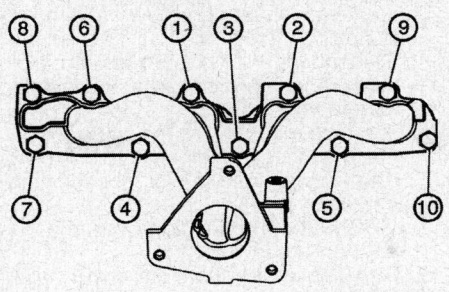

Fig. 1 Exhaust manifold tightening sequence

83. **On all models,** remove mounting bolt and turbocharger coolant feed pipe fitting from cylinder head.
84. Remove mounting bolt and turbocharger coolant feed pipe bracket from cylinder head.
85. Remove mounting bolt and position air conditioning compressor line aside.
86. Raise and support vehicle.
87. Remove mounting bolts, then position power steering pump and bracket aside.
88. **On models equipped with automatic transmission,** proceed as follows:
    a. Remove torque converter to flywheel mounting bolts.
    b. Remove four lower bellhousing mounting bolts.
89. **On all models,** lower vehicle.
90. **On models equipped with automatic transmission,** remove five upper bellhousing mounting bolts.
91. **On all models,** remove lefthand and righthand engine mount upper nuts.
92. Support engine using engine support adapter tool No. J42451-1, or equivalent, and suitable engine lifting device.
93. **On models equipped with automatic transmission,** separate engine from transmission.
94. **On all models,** remove engine.
95. **On models equipped with manual transmission,** remove mounting bolts one turn at a time, then the clutch cover and disc.
96. **On all models,** remove mounting bolts and flywheel.
97. Install engine to suitable stand.
98. Remove mounting bolts and air conditioning compressor.
99. Remove mounting bolts and nuts, then the catalytic converter and gasket.
100. Reverse procedure to install.

INTAKE MANIFOLD
REPLACE

1. Grasp cover and disconnect studs, then remove intake manifold cover.
2. Disconnect Charge Air Cooler (CAC) outlet hose clamps, then remove CAC outlet hose from outlet pipe and throttle body.
3. Remove engine wiring harness and No. 1 knock sensor clips from oil level indicator tube bracket.
4. Remove mounting bolt, then the tube and oil level indicator.

5. Relieve fuel system pressure as outlined under "Precautions."
6. Disconnect fuel rail line quick connector.
7. Disconnect line quick connect fitting from Evaporative Emission (EVAP) purge solenoid.
8. Disconnect clamp and remove brake booster hose from intake manifold.
9. Remove knock sensor electrical connector clip from intake manifold brace and oil level indicator tube bracket.
10. Disconnect EVAP canister purge solenoid, Manifold Absolute Pressure (MAP) sensor and charge air bypass vale solenoid electrical connectors.
11. Disconnect Throttle Actuator Control (TAC) module electrical connector.
12. Remove engine wiring harness clip from intake manifold brace.
13. Disconnect clamp and remove surge tank air bleed hose from engine.
14. Remove clip from tank bracket and position surge tank air bleed hose aside.
15. Disconnect clamp and remove charge air bypass valve vacuum hose from intake manifold.
16. Remove mounting bolts and position charge air bypass valve solenoid aside.
17. Remove mounting bolts and stud, then the surge tank bracket.
18. Disconnect fuel pump feed pipe fitting.
19. Remove mounting bolts and fuel feed pipe.
20. Remove mounting bolts and position power brake booster pump aside.
21. Remove mounting bolt and intake manifold brace.
22. Remove mounting bolts and nuts, then the intake manifold. Remove gasket only if damaged.
23. If replacing intake manifold, proceed as follows:
    a. Remove mounting bolts, MAP sensor and O-ring seal.
    b. Remove mounting bolts, EVAP purge solenoid and O-ring seal.
    c. Remove mounting bolts, throttle body and seal.
24. Reverse procedure to install, noting the following:
    a. Lubricate high pressure fuel pump fuel feed pipe connection threads with suitable silicon free engine oil.

EXHAUST MANIFOLD
REPLACE

1. Remove mounting bolts and exhaust manifold heat shield.
2. Remove mounting bolt and block heater.
3. Remove mounting nuts, exhaust manifold and gasket.
4. Reverse procedure to install, noting the following:
    a. Tighten new exhaust manifold nuts hand tight.
    b. **Torque** exhaust manifold nuts to 10 ft. lbs. in sequence, **Fig. 1.**
    c. **Torque** exhaust manifold nuts to 10 ft. lbs., again.

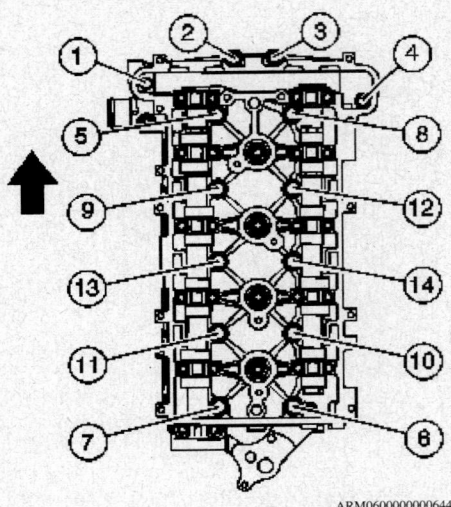

Fig. 2 Cylinder head loosening sequence

CYLINDER HEAD
REPLACE

1. Open hood and disconnect headlamp bulb socket Connector Positive Assurance (CPA) connector.
2. Disconnect lefthand headlamp electrical harness.
3. Rotate socket a quarter turn counterclockwise and disconnect bulb.
4. Remove mounting screws and headlamp.
5. Disconnect wiring harness on both sides and mark hood for installation alignment.
6. Remove mounting nuts and hood.
7. Disconnect fuel injector wiring harness electrical connector.
8. Remove intake manifold as outlined under "Intake Manifold, Replace."
9. Remove fuel injector insulator.
10. Relieve high side fuel system pressure as outlined under "Precautions."
11. Remove engine wiring harness clip from high pressure fuel pump cover.
12. Remove mounting bolts and high pressure fuel pump cover.
13. Remove high pressure fuel pump insulator.
14. Loosen and remove fuel pipe fitting from fuel pump and rail. Discard high pressure fuel pipe.
15. Disconnect fuel injectors' electrical connectors.
16. Remove mounting bolts and fuel rail. If injectors came out with fuel rail, install them.
17. Remove and discard fuel injector upper O-ring seal.
18. If replacing fuel rail, remove pressure sensor. **Do not damage sensor plastic housing with excess force.**
19. Remove exhaust manifold as outlined under "Exhaust Manifold, Replace."
20. Drain cooling system into suitable container.
21. Disconnect clamp and remove radiator surge tank hose from turbocharger coolant feed pipe fitting. Position hose aside.

22. Remove charge air bypass valve solenoid tube from turbocharger coolant feed pipe clips.
23. Remove turbocharger coolant feed pipe mounting bolt at turbocharger.
24. Remove turbocharger coolant feed pipe fitting from cylinder head.
25. Remove turbocharger coolant feed pipe bracket mounting bolt from cylinder head.
26. Remove clips and turbocharger coolant feed pipe. Remove gaskets from both banjo fittings.
27. Remove timing chain as outlined under "Timing Chain, Replace."
28. Remove fuel pump acoustic cover.
29. Remove mounting bolt and battery negative cable from engine lift bracket ground terminal.
30. Disconnect intake Camshaft Position (CMP) sensor electrical connector.
31. Disconnect chassis Evaporative Emission (EVAP) line quick connect fitting from purge solenoid.
32. Disconnect EVAP canister purge solenoid electrical connector.
33. Remove mounting bolt, EVAP canister purge solenoid and O-ring seal.
34. Disconnect exhaust CMP and Engine Coolant Temperature (ECT) sensor electrical connectors.
35. Disconnect clamp and remove radiator inlet hose from cylinder head.
36. Remove and discard cylinder head bolts in sequence, **Fig. 2.**
37. Remove cylinder head and gasket.
38. Reverse procedure to install, noting the following:
   a. **Do not use any sealing material.**
   b. Lightly apply clean engine oil to new cylinder head bolt threads and bottom side flange. Allow the oil to drain before installing.
   c. **Torque** cylinder head bolts to 22 ft. lbs. in sequence, **Fig. 3.**
   d. Final tighten head bolts an additional 155° in sequence.
   e. **Torque** new front cylinder head bolts to 26 ft. lbs., **Fig. 4.**
   f. If replacing fuel rail lubricate threads and sealing cone of new fuel rail with silicon free engine oil.
   g. Install new fuel injector upper O-ring seals, lubricate with silicon free engine oil.
   h. **Torque** fuel rail bolts to 16 ft. lbs. in sequence, **Fig. 5.**
   i. **Torque** fuel rail bolts to 16 ft. lbs. in sequence, again.
   j. Install new high pressure fuel pipe fitting

VALVE COVER
REPLACE

1. Grasp intake manifold cover and disconnect studs.
2. Remove intake manifold cover, oil fill cap and insulator. Install oil fill cap.
3. Remove intake manifold cover studs.
4. Disconnect clamps and remove air cleaner outlet duct.
5. Disconnect intake and exhaust Camshaft Position (CMP) actuator solenoid valve electrical connectors.

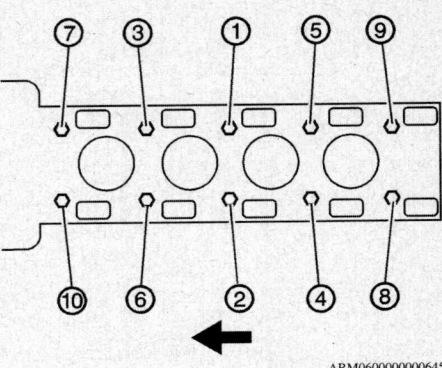

Fig. 3 Cylinder head tightening sequence

6. Remove engine wiring harness clips from valve cover.
7. Disconnect Evaporative Emission (EVAP) canister purge solenoid valve electrical connector.
8. Disconnect electrical connectors, then remove mounting bolts and ignition coils.
9. Remove Heated Oxygen Sensor (HO2S) electrical connector clip from valve cover.
10. Remove fitting mounting bolt and position Positive Crankcase Ventilation (PCV) pipe aside. **Do not disconnect PCV hose from valve cover.**
11. Remove mounting bolts and valve cover.
12. Reverse procedure to install.

VALVE CLEARANCE SPECIFICATIONS

Hydraulic valve lifters are used on this engine and no adjustment is required.

VALVE ADJUSTMENT

Hydraulic valve lifters are used on this engine and no adjustment is required.

ROCKER ARMS

Used valve rocker arms must be returned to original position on the camshaft. If the camshaft is being replaced, the rocker arms must also be replaced.
1. Remove camshaft as outlined under "Camshaft, Replace."
2. Mark roller followers and hydraulic valve lash adjusters for installation alignment in original positions.
3. Remove valve rocker arms.
4. Reverse procedure to install. Lubricate valve tips and rocket arms with suitable lubricant.

HYDRAULIC LIFTERS
REPLACE

1. Remove camshaft as outlined under "Camshaft, Replace."
2. Mark roller followers and hydraulic valve lash adjusters for installation alignment in original positions.
3. Remove valve rocker arms.

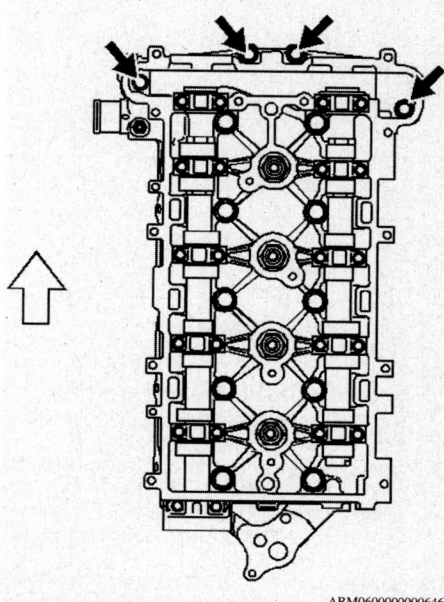

Fig. 4 Front cylinder head bolts

4. Remove hydraulic valve lash adjusters.
5. Reverse procedure to install. Lubricate hydraulic lash adjusters with suitable lubricant.

CRANKSHAFT DAMPER
REPLACE

1. Grasp intake manifold cover and disconnect studs.
2. Remove intake manifold cover, oil fill cap and insulator. Install oil fill cap.
3. Rotate power steering pump belt tensioner pulley clockwise and remove belt.
4. Lower vehicle.
5. Remove charge air cooler inlet pipe mounting bolt at rear bracket.
6. Remove mounting nut and charge air cooler rear bracket.
7. Remove charge air cooler inlet pipe mounting bolt at front bracket.
8. Loosen charge air cooler clamp at inlet pipe and inlet pipe clamp at pipe.
9. Remove charge air cooler inlet pipe.
10. Disconnect intake air pressure and temperature sensor engine wiring harness electrical connector.
11. Disconnect clamp and remove charge air cooler outlet pipe air bypass valve solenoid vacuum hose.
12. Remove charge air cooler outlet pipe mounting bolt, nut and rear bracket.
13. Disconnect charge air cooler outlet pipe hose clamp and remove charge air cooler outlet pipe front bracket mounting bolt.
14. Disconnect clamp and remove charge air cooler outlet pipe.
15. Disconnect air cleaner housing and turbocharger clamps and remove air cleaner outlet duct.
16. Disconnect Mass Air Flow (MAF) sensor engine wiring harness electrical connector.

17. Remove front mounting bolt and air cleaner assembly.
18. Remove drive belt.
19. Remove intake manifold as outlined under "Intake Manifold, Replace."
20. Remove starter solenoid terminal nuts and disconnect engine terminal harness.
21. Remove mounting bolts and starter motor.
22. Raise and support vehicle.
23. Hold flywheel using holding tool No. J43653, or equivalent.
24. Remove and discard crankshaft balancer bolt.
25. Remove balancer using suitable universal removal tool.
26. Reverse procedure to install, noting the following:
    a. Ensure proper alignment of keyway and balancer is flat on oil pump drive.
    b. Install new crankshaft balancer bolt and washer.
    c. **Torque** bolt to 74 ft. lbs.
    d. Final tighten mounting bolt an additional 125°.

FRONT COVER
REPLACE

1. Open hood and disconnect headlamp bulb socket Connector Positive Assurance (CPA) connector.
2. Disconnect lefthand headlamp electrical harness.
3. Rotate socket a quarter turn counterclockwise and disconnect bulb.
4. Remove mounting screws and headlamp.
5. Disconnect wiring harness on both sides and mark hood for installation alignment.
6. Remove mounting nuts and hood.
7. Remove crankshaft damper as outlined under "Crankshaft Damper, Replace."
8. Remove mounting bolt and drive belt tensioner.
9. Remove mounting bolts and front cover.
10. Remove and discard gasket.
11. Reverse procedure to install.

FRONT COVER SEAL
REPLACE

1. Open hood and disconnect headlamp bulb socket Connector Positive Assurance (CPA) connector.
2. Disconnect lefthand headlamp electrical harness.
3. Rotate socket a quarter turn counterclockwise and disconnect bulb.
4. Remove mounting screws and headlamp.
5. Disconnect wiring harness on both sides and mark hood for installation alignment.
6. Remove mounting nuts and hood.
7. Remove crankshaft damper as outlined under "Crankshaft Damper, Replace."
8. Remove mounting bolt and drive belt tensioner.

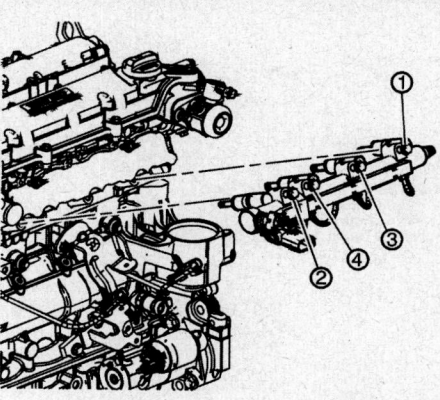

Fig. 5 Fuel rail tightening sequence

9. Remove mounting bolts and front cover.
10. Remove and discard gasket.
11. Remove crankcase front cover oil seal using suitable tool.
12. Remove and discard friction washer.
13. Reverse procedure to install. Install new seal using sprocket bearing installer tool No. J34115, or equivalent.

TIMING CHAIN
REPLACE
Removal

1. Open hood and disconnect headlamp bulb socket Connector Positive Assurance (CPA) connector.
2. Disconnect lefthand headlamp electrical harness.
3. Rotate socket a quarter turn counterclockwise and disconnect bulb.
4. Remove mounting screws and headlamp.
5. Disconnect wiring harness on both sides and mark hood for installation alignment.
6. Remove mounting nuts and hood.
7. Remove cylinder No. 1 spark plug.
8. Turn crankshaft clockwise until piston No. 1 is at Top Dead Center (TDC) on compression stroke.
9. Remove valve cover as outlined under "Valve Cover, Replace."
10. Remove front cover as outlined under "Front Cover, Replace."
11. Remove mounting bolts and upper timing chain guide.
12. Remove timing chain tensioner.
13. Hold exhaust camshaft using suitable wrench, then remove and discard exhaust camshaft actuator bolt.
14. Remove exhaust camshaft actuator.
15. Remove mounting bolt and timing chain tensioner guide.
16. Remove fixed timing chain guide access plug.
17. Remove mounting bolts and fixed timing chain guide.
18. Hold intake camshaft using suitable wrench, then remove and discard intake camshaft actuator bolt.
19. Remove intake camshaft actuator and timing chain.

Fig. 6 Crankshaft key alignment

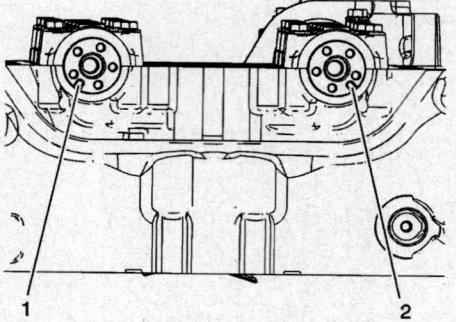

1. Exhaust camshaft notch is in the 7 o'clock position
2. Intake camshaft notch is in the 5 o'clock position

ARM0600000000649

Fig. 7 Camshaft's notch alignment

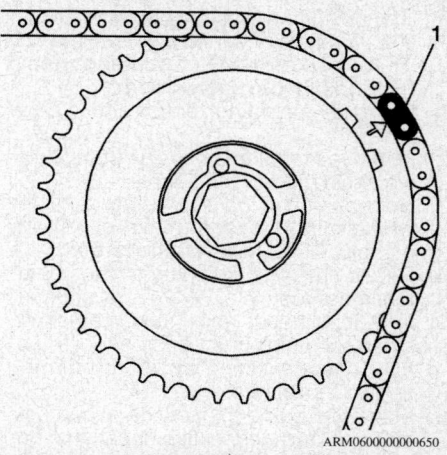

ARM0600000000650

Fig. 8 Intake actuator alignment

20. Remove timing chain crankshaft sprocket.
21. If removing balance shaft timing chain and sprocket, proceed as follows:
    a. Remove mounting bolts and balance shaft drive chain tensioner.
    b. Remove mounting bolt and adjustable balance shaft chain guide.
    c. Remove mounting bolts and upper balance shaft drive chain guide.
    d. Remove balance shaft drive chain and sprocket.

Installation

1. If installing balance shaft timing chain and sprocket, proceed as follows:
    a. Install balance shaft sprocket.
    b. Align chain cooper link to intake side of balance shaft sprocket timing mark.
    c. Work around chain clockwise.
    d. Place chrome link with balance shaft drive sprocket timing mark at approximately 6 o'clock.
    e. Place chain on water pump drive sprocket.
    f. Align last chrome link with exhaust side balance shaft drive sprocket timing mark.
    g. Install upper balance shaft drive chain guide and tighten mounting bolts.
    h. Install small balance shaft drive chain guide and tighten mounting bolts.
    i. Install adjustable balance shaft chain guide and tighten mounting bolt.
    j. Install balance shaft chain tensioner 90° in bore and compress plunger.
    k. Rotate tension back to 12 o'clock position and insert suitable paper clip through plunger body into tensioner plunger.
    l. Install tensioner and tighten mounting bolts.
    m. Remove paper clip.
2. Ensure piston No. 1 is at compression stroke TDC with crankshaft key at 12 o'clock position, **Fig. 6.**
3. Ensure intake camshaft notch at 5 o'clock position and exhaust camshaft notch at 7 o'clock position, **Fig. 7.**
4. Install timing chain drive sprocket to crankshaft with timing mark in 5 o'clock position and front of sprocket facing out.
5. Assemble intake camshaft actuator into timing chain with timing mark aligned with uniquely colored link, **Fig. 8.**
6. Lower timing chain through cylinder head opening ensuring chain goes around both sides of cylinder block bosses.
7. Install intake camshaft actuator onto intake camshaft while aligning dowel pin into the camshaft slot.
8. Hand tighten new intake camshaft actuator bolt.
9. Route timing chain around crankshaft sprocket and align first matching colored link with crankshaft sprocket, timing mark at approximately 5 o'clock position, **Fig. 9.**
10. Rotate crankshaft clockwise to remove all chain slack. **Do not rotate intake camshaft.**
11. Install adjustable timing chain guide through cylinder head opening. Tighten mounting bolt.
12. Install exhaust camshaft actuator into timing chain with timing mark aligned with second matching colored link, **Fig. 10.**
13. Install exhaust camshaft actuator onto camshaft and align dowel pin into slot.
14. Rotate exhaust camshaft approximately 45° using suitable open end wrench until camshaft actuator dowel pin goes into camshaft slot.
15. When actuator seats on cam, tighten new exhaust camshaft actuator bolt hand tight.
16. Ensure all of colored links and appropriate timing marks are still aligned.
17. Install fixed timing chain guide and tighten mounting bolts.
18. Install upper timing chain guide and tighten mounting bolts.
19. Remove snap ring and piston from timing chain tensioner body.
20. Install notch end of piston into tensioner tool No. J45027, or equivalent, in suitable vice.
21. Turn ratchet cylinder into piston, then install piston into tensioner body. Install snap ring.
22. Install and tighten timing chain tensioner.
23. Install compression timing chain .079 inch using suitable rubber end tip tool and release tensioner.
24. Feed tool down through cam drive chest to rest on cam chain.
25. Hit diagonally downward with sharp jolt to release tensioner.
26. Hold intake camshaft hex using suitable wrench.
27. **Torque** actuator bolt to 22 ft. lbs. and final tighten bolt an additional 100°.
28. Tighten exhaust camshaft actuator bolt same way.
29. Install timing chain oiling nozzle and tighten mounting bolt.
30. Apply sealant compound (GM part No. 12345382), or equivalent, to timing chain guide bolt access hole plug threads.
31. Install timing chain guide bolt and tighten.
32. Install front and valve covers, then the cylinder No. 1 spark plug and hood.

CAMSHAFT
REPLACE
Removal

1. Grasp intake manifold cover and disconnect studs.
2. Remove intake manifold cover, oil fill cap and insulator. Install oil fill cap.
3. Remove intake manifold cover studs.
4. Disconnect clamps and remove air cleaner outlet duct.
5. Disconnect intake and exhaust Camshaft Position (CMP) actuator solenoid valve electrical connectors.
6. Remove engine wiring harness clips from valve cover.
7. Disconnect Evaporative Emission (EVAP) canister purge solenoid valve electrical connector.
8. Disconnect electrical connectors, then remove mounting bolts and ignition coils.
9. Remove Heated Oxygen Sensor (HO2S) electrical connector clip from valve cover.

10. Remove fitting mounting bolt and position Positive Crankcase Ventilation (PCV) pipe aside. **Do not disconnect PCV hose from valve cover.**
11. Remove mounting bolts and valve cover.
12. Remove mounting bolts and upper timing chain guide.
13. Hold camshaft on hex using suitable wrench, then loosen intake camshaft actuator bolt. **Do not remove bolt.**
14. Retain timing chain using timing chain tensioner tools No. J44217, or equivalent, to exhaust and intake camshaft sides of timing chain. Ensure tool's tips fully engage timing chain and firmly tighten tool's nuts.
15. Mark intake and exhaust camshaft actuators, and respective locations on timing chain for installation alignment.
16. Holding camshaft with suitable wrench, remove and discard intake camshaft actuator bolt.
17. Remove intake camshaft actuator from camshaft and timing chain.
18. **If removing intake camshaft,** proceed as follows:
    a. Relieve low and high side fuel system pressure as outlined under "Precautions."
    b. Disconnect high pressure fuel pump electrical connector.
    c. Remove engine wiring harness clip from high pressure fuel pump cover.
    d. Remove mounting bolts and high pressure fuel pump cover.
    e. Remove high pressure fuel pump insulator.
    f. Loosen fuel feed pipe to pump fitting.
    g. Remove mounting bolts and fuel feed pipe from intake manifold.
    h. Loosen high pressure fuel pipe fitting at pump.
    i. Remove and discard high pressure fuel pipe.
    j. Remove and discard high pressure fuel pump mounting bolts.
    k. Remove high pressure fuel pump, then the gasket and O-ring.
19. **On all models,** mark camshaft bearing caps for installation alignment in original positions.
20. Remove each cap bolt one turn at a time until there is no spring tension pushing on camshaft.
21. Remove camshaft bearing cap bolts and caps.
22. Remove valve lifter follower.
23. Remove mounting bolts and cylinder head opening plate.
24. Remove mounting bolts and rear bearing cap.
25. Remove intake camshaft.
26. Reverse procedure to install.

Installation

1. Lubricate hydraulic lash adjusters and install into bores.
2. Lubricate valve tips.
3. Position valve rocker arms on tip of valve stem and on valve lash adjuster.

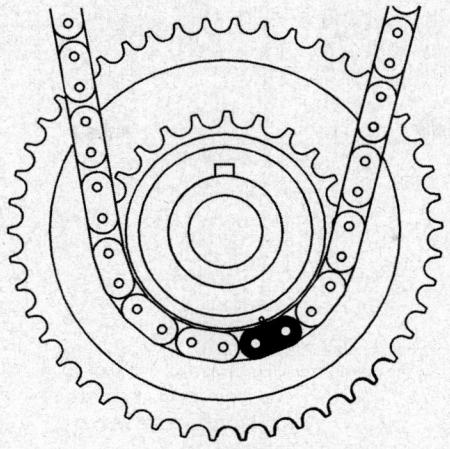

Fig. 9 Crankshaft sprocket & chain alignment

ARM0600000000651

Lubricate rocker arms.
4. Lubricate camshaft with suitable engine oil.
5. Install camshaft.
6. Apply .138 inch bead of suitable sealer to cylinder head. Were rear bearing cap ends on perimeter rail, extend sealer bead .1575 inch beyond cap edge Run sealer bead within .1575 inch of end points.
7. Install rear bearing cap and tighten mounting bolts.
8. Install cylinder head opening plate and tighten mounting bolts.
9. Install valve lifter follower.
10. Install bearing cap marked sequence.
11. Install bearing cap bolts hand tight.
12. Tighten bearing cap bolts in three-turn increments until they are seated.
13. **Torque** camshaft bearing caps to 89 inch lbs.
14. Lubricate high pressure fuel pump cylinder head bore and roller lifter with suitable silicon free engine oil.
15. **If installing intake camshaft,** proceed as follows:
    a. Install high pressure fuel pump roller lifter.
    b. Install new high pressure fuel pump O-ring.
    c. Position new high pressure fuel pump gasket to cylinder head.
    d. Ensure plastic bolt retainers are installed in high pressure fuel pump mounting holes.
    e. Push high pressure fuel pump into cylinder head bore by hand, applying force to top of pump.
    f. Install new high pressure fuel pump bolts hand tight.
    g. Ensure high pressure fuel pump and fuel rail fittings are clean.
    h. Lubricate high pressure fuel pump and fuel rail fittings with suitable silicon free engine oil.
    i. Install new high pressure fuel pipe.
    j. Tighten high pressure fuel pipe fitting to hand tight.
    k. Place fuel feed pipe onto intake manifold and install fuel feed pipe bolts hand tight.

l. Tighten fuel feed pipe bolts and fuel feed pipe to fuel pump fitting.
m. Tighten high pressure fuel pipe fittings and mounting bolts.
n. Install high pressure fuel pump insulator, then the cover and tighten mounting bolts.
o. Connect high pressure fuel pump electrical connector and install engine wiring harness clip to cover.
16. **On all models,** ensure exhaust camshaft actuator alignment mark is still aligned properly with timing chain mark .
17. Install timing chain onto intake camshaft actuator.
18. Align intake camshaft actuator alignment mark with timing chain mark and install actuator onto camshaft.
19. Install new intake camshaft actuator bolt until snug.
20. Remove timing chain tensioner tools.
21. Hold camshaft using suitable wrench onto hex.
22. **Torque** actuator bolt to 22 ft. lbs. and final tighten bolt an additional 100°.
23. Install upper timing chain guide and tighten mounting bolts.
24. Install valve cover and tighten mounting bolts.

BALANCE SHAFT
REPLACE
Removal

1. Remove timing chain, sprocket and tensioner as outlined under "Timing Chain, Replace."
2. Remove mounting bolt and lefthand (exhaust) and/or righthand (intake) balance shaft.
3. Install balance shaft bearing remover and installer tool No. J43650, or equivalent, into balance shaft hole with foot parallel to shaft.
4. Turn tool so foot is perpendicular to shaft.
5. Center tool foot on balance shaft bushing.
6. Insert centering guide into front balance shaft bore and tighten nut.
7. End of tool should be 4.6 inches from black face.
8. Tighten tool nut until tension releases.
9. Remove tool and balance shaft bushing.

Installation

1. Install balance shaft bushing using balance shaft bearing remover and installer tool No. J43650, or equivalent.
2. Seat bushing into bore and remove tool.
3. Place cylinder No. 1 at Top Dead Center (TDC).
4. Lubricate balance shaft lobes with suitable engine oil.
5. Install lefthand (exhaust) and/or righthand (intake) balance shaft.
6. Install and tighten mounting bolt.

MAIN & ROD BEARINGS

Main Bearings

1. **Torque** lower crankcase to block bedplate to 15 ft. lbs.
2. Final tighten an additional 77°.

Connecting Rod Bearings

1. **Torque** new connecting rod bolts to 18 ft. lbs.
2. Tighten bolts an additional 100°

CRANKSHAFT SEAL
REPLACE

1. Remove crankshaft balancer as outlined under "Crankshaft Damper, Replace."
2. Remove oil seal from front cover using suitable flat-bladed tool.
3. Reverse procedure to install using camshaft/front main seal installer tool No. J35268-A, or equivalent.

CRANKSHAFT REAR OIL SEAL
REPLACE

1. Remove flywheel as outlined under "Engine, Replace."
2. Remove crankshaft rear oil seal using suitable flat-bladed tool.
3. Reverse procedure to install using rear main seal installer tool No. J42067, or equivalent.

OIL PAN
REPLACE

Removal

1. Remove mounting bolts.
2. Remove oil pan at pry points.

Installation

1. Apply .138 inch beach of suitable sealant around oil pan perimeter and oil suction port opening.
2. Install oil pan.
3. **Torque** mounting bolts to 18 ft. lbs. in sequence, **Fig. 11.**

OIL PUMP
REPLACE

1. Remove front cover as outlined under "Front Cover, Replace."
2. Remove oil pump.
3. Reverse procedure to install.

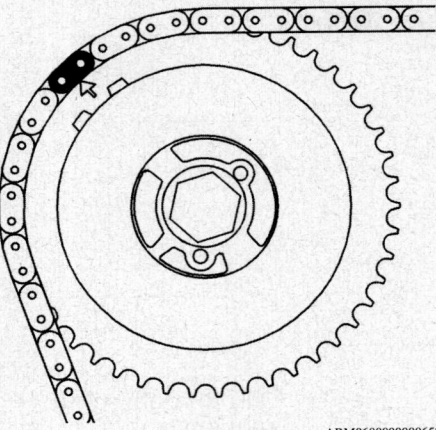

ARM0600000000652

Fig. 10 Exhaust camshaft actuator & chain alignment

OIL PUMP SERVICE

Disassemble

1. Remove pressure relief valve.
2. Remove mounting bolts and oil pump gerotor cover.

Assemble

1. Lubricate all oil pump parts with suitable engine oil.
2. Install inner into outer gear.
3. Install gears together into front cover with center gear hub facing front cover.
4. Install the oil pump gerotor cover and tighten mounting bolts bolts.
5. Install pressure relief valve piston and spring.
6. Tighten pressure relief valve plug.

OIL COOLER
REPLACE

1. Drain cooling system into suitable container.
2. Remove cap and windshield wiper arm mounting nut.
3. Remove windshield washer nozzle hose and windshield wiper arm.
4. Remove retainers and air inlet grille. Disconnect washer pump hose.
5. Remove intake Camshaft Position (CMP) sensor.
6. Remove mounting nuts and air inlet screen support.
7. Disconnect clamp and remove radiator outlet hose from thermostat housing.
8. Disconnect clamp and remove radiator outlet hose from oil cooler.
9. Remove radiator outlet hose clip from bracket.
10. Disconnect clamp and remove surge tank outlet hose from oil cooler.
11. Remove mounting bolts and oil cooler.
12. Reverse procedure to install.

SERPENTINE DRIVE BELT

Replacement

1. Grasp intake manifold cover and disconnect studs.
2. Remove intake manifold cover, oil fill cap and insulator. Install oil fill cap.
3. Rotate power steering pump belt tensioner pulley clockwise and remove belt.
4. Lower vehicle.
5. Remove charge air cooler inlet pipe mounting bolt at rear bracket.
6. Remove mounting nut and charge air cooler rear bracket.
7. Remove charge air cooler inlet pipe mounting bolt at front bracket.
8. Loosen charge air cooler clamp at inlet pipe. and inlet pipe clamp at pipe.
9. Remove charge air cooler inlet pipe.
10. Disconnect intake air pressure and temperature sensor engine wiring harness electrical connector.
11. Disconnect clamp and remove charge air cooler outlet pipe air bypass valve solenoid vacuum hose.
12. Remove charge air cooler outlet pipe mounting bolt, nut and rear bracket.
13. Disconnect charge air cooler outlet pipe hose clamp and remove charge air cooler outlet pipe front bracket mounting bolt.
14. Disconnect clamp and remove charge air cooler outlet pipe.
15. Disconnect air cleaner housing and turbocharger clamps and remove air cleaner outlet duct.
16. Disconnect Mass Air Flow (MAF) sensor engine wiring harness electrical connector.
17. Remove front mounting bolt and air cleaner assembly.
18. Remove drive belt.
19. Reverse procedure to install.

THERMOSTAT
REPLACE

1. Drain cooling system into suitable container.
2. Remove cap and windshield wiper arm mounting nut.
3. Remove windshield washer nozzle hose and windshield wiper arm.
4. Remove retainers and air inlet grille. Disconnect washer pump hose.
5. Disconnect clamp and remove radiator outlet hose from the thermostat housing.
6. Remove mounting bolts, housing and thermostat.
7. Remove and discard O-ring seal.
8. Reverse procedure to install.

WATER PUMP
REPLACE

1. Grasp intake manifold cover and disconnect studs.

2. Remove intake manifold cover, oil fill cap and insulator. Install oil fill cap.
3. Drain cooling system into suitable container.
4. Remove cap and windshield wiper arm mounting nut.
5. Remove windshield washer nozzle hose and windshield wiper arm.
6. Remove retainers and air inlet grille. Disconnect washer pump hose.
7. Disconnect clamp and remove radiator outlet hose from the thermostat housing.
8. Remove mounting bolts, housing and thermostat.
9. Remove and discard O-ring seal.
10. Remove mounting bolts and water pump access plate from the front cover.
11. Drain coolant from water pump using plug at bottom of pump.
12. Install water pump holding tool No. J43651, or equivalent. Secure tool using access cover bolts.
13. Remove three water pump inner sprocket bolts.
14. Remove four mounting bolts and water pump. Remove and discard O-ring.
15. Reverse procedure to install, noting the following:
    a. Use guide pin (M 6 m x 6 mm stud) threaded into sprocket to align with holding tool.
    b. After two inner water pump sprocket bolts are snug, remove guide pin and install third bolt.

RADIATOR
REPLACE

1. Drain cooling system into suitable container.
2. Remove mounting bolts and radiator front air deflector, then the retainer and shroud air inlet.
3. Remove air cleaner outlet duct resonator and Positive Crankcase Ventilation (PCV) hose clamps.
4. Remove air cleaner outlet duct resonator.
5. Disconnect cooling fan motor electrical connector.

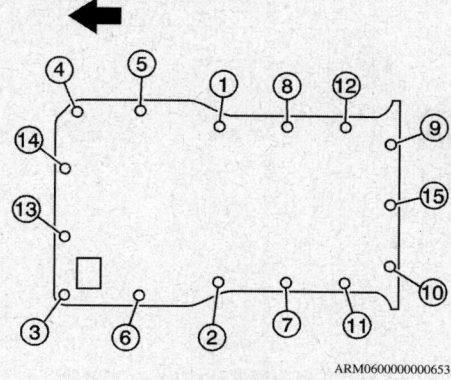

Fig. 11 Oil pan tightening sequence

ARM0600000000653

6. Remove mounting bolts, shroud, cooling fan and motor.
7. Remove radiator inlet and outlet hoses, then the surge tank inlet hose.
8. Remove air cleaner stud, then the mounting nuts and radiator upper bracket.
9. Remove mounting bolts, air conditioning condenser and radiator.
10. Reverse procedure to install.

FUEL PUMP
REPLACE

1. Relieve fuel pressure as outlined under "Precautions."
2. Remove rear compartment trim panel.
3. Remove mounting bolts and fuel sending unit access cover.
4. Disconnect fuel level sender fuel pressure sensor electrical connectors.
5. Disconnect fuel fill pipe Evaporative Emission (EVAP) pipe quick connect fitting.
6. Disconnect fuel feed pipe quick connect fitting.
7. Raise fuel sender up slightly. **Do not handle fuel sender assembly by fuel pipes.**
8. Connect large EVAP canister quick connect fitting.
9. Remove fuel sender.

10. Remove and discard fuel sender O-ring.
11. Reverse procedure to install. Install new gasket.

TURBOCHARGER
REPLACE

1. Drain cooling system into suitable container.
2. Remove charge air cooler inlet pipe mounting bolt at rear bracket.
3. Remove mounting nut and charge air cooler rear bracket.
4. Remove charge air cooler inlet pipe mounting bolt at front bracket.
5. Loosen charge air cooler clamp at inlet pipe and inlet pipe clamp at pipe.
6. Remove charge air cooler inlet pipe.
7. Remove mounting bolts and charge air cooler pipe from turbocharger.
8. Remove mounting bolts and turbocharger heat shield.
9. Remove Connector Position Assurance (CPA) retainer and disconnect Heated Oxygen Sensor (HO2S) 1 electrical connector. Remove clip from valve cover.
10. Remove HO2S using oxygen sensor wrench tool No. J39194, or equivalent.
11. Remove catalytic converter to turbocharger mounting nuts.
12. Remove CPA retainer and disconnect HO2S 2 electrical connector.
13. Raise and support vehicle.
14. Remove catalytic converter to muffler mounting nuts.
15. Separate exhaust pipe from catalytic converter studs, then position exhaust pipe aside and support.
16. Loosen driver side engine mount to frame lower nut. **Do not remove nut.**
17. Remove passenger side engine mount to frame lower nut.
18. Raise oil pan slightly using suitable adjustable jack and block of wood.
19. Remove catalytic converter to bracket bolts and position converter aside.
20. Remove mounting bolt and nut, then the catalytic converter bracket.
21. Rotate and remove catalytic converter. Remove and discard gasket.

TIGHTENING SPECIFICATIONS

Year	Component	Torque, Ft. Lbs.
2007–08	Access Hole Plug	66
	Air Cleaner	89①
	Air Cleaner Stud	89①
	Air Cleaner Outlet Duct Resonator Clamp	80①
	Air Cleaner Outlet Duct Clamp	35①
	Air Conditioning Compressor	16
	Air Conditioning Condenser	80①
	Alternator Terminal	15
	Balance Shaft	89①
	Balance Shaft Chain Guide, Adjustable	89①
	Balance Shaft Drive Chain Guide, Upper & Small	11
	Balance Shaft Drive Chain Tensioner	89①
	Bellhousing	37
	Block Heater	89①
	Brake Hose Bracket	89①
	Camshaft Actuator	⑥
	Camshaft Bearing Caps	⑦
	Catalytic Converter, Bolt	16
	Catalytic Converter, Nut	43
	Catalytic Converter Bracket	43
	Catalytic Converter To Muffler	13
	Charge Air Bypass Valve Solenoid	89①
	Charge Air Cooler Inlet And Outlet Pipe	80①
	Charge Air Cooler Pipe	16
	Cooling Fan Shroud	18
	Crankshaft Damper	⑤
	Cylinder Head	④
	Cylinder Head Opening Plate	89①
	Drive Belt Tensioner	33
	Engine Mount	41
	Engine Wiring Harness Ground	18
	EVAP Purge Solenoid	89①
	Exhaust Manifold	③
	Exhaust Manifold Heat Shield	18
	Exhaust Manifold, Stud	11
	Flywheel	39②
	Front Cover	18
	Fuel Pump Cover	89①
	Fuel Feed Fitting	22
	Fuel Feed Pipe	89①
	Fuel Injection Fuel Rail Fuel Pressure Sensor	25
	Fuel Pump Module Access Cover	89①
	Fuel Rail	④
	Heated Oxygen Sensor	31
	High Pressure Fuel Pipe Fitting	24
	High Pressure Fuel Pump	11
	Ignition Coil	89①
	Intake Manifold	16
	Intake Manifold Cover Stud	80①
	Oil Cooler	16

TIGHTENING SPECIFICATIONS—Continued

Year	Component	Torque, Ft. Lbs.
2007–08	Oil Level Indicator Tube	89①
	Oil Pump Gerotor	53①
	Power Steering Pump Bracket	43
	Pressure Relief Valve Plug	30
	Radiator Bracket	90①
	Radiator Front Air Deflector	80①
	Rear Bearing Cap⑧	89①
	Starter Motor	30
	Starter Solenoid Terminal	89①
	Starter Solenoid S Terminal	27①
	Surge Tank Bracket	80①
	Thermostat Housing Cover	89①
	Throttle Body	89①
	Timing Chain Guide, Adjustable	89①
	Timing Chain Guide, Fixed	106①
	Timing Chain Guide, Upper	89①
	Timing Chain Tensioner	55
	Timing Chain Oiling Nozzle	89①
	Torque Converter	36
	Turbocharger Coolant Feed Pipe	26
	Turbocharger Coolant Feed Pipe Bracket	89①
	Turbocharger Heat Shield	89①
	Valve Cover	89①
	Water Pump	18
	Water Pump Access Plate	89①
	Water Pump Sprocket	89①

① — Inch lbs.

② — Final tighten an additional 25°.

③ — Refer to "Exhaust Manifold, Replace" for tightening sequence and specifications.

④ — Refer to "Cylinder Head, Replace" for tightening sequence and specifications.

⑤ — Refer to "Crankshaft Damper, Replace." for tightening sequence and specifications.

⑥ — Refer to "Timing Chain, Replace." for tightening sequence and specifications.

⑦ — Refer to "Camshaft, Replace." for tightening sequence and specifications.

⑧ — Refer to "Main & Rod Bearings" for tightening sequence and specifications.

2.4L Engine

NOTE: Refer To The "2.4L Engine" Section In The "Cavalier, Cobalt & Sunfire" Chapter For Procedures Not Listed In This Section.

NOTE: On Air Bag Equipped Models, Refer To "Air Bag System Precautions" Located In The Front Of This Manual For System Disarming & Arming Procedures.

NOTE: Refer To "Computer Relearn Procedures" Located In The Front Of This Manual When Battery Power To The Computer Has Been Interrupted.

INDEX

	Page No.
Engine Rebuilding	
Specifications	29-1
Engine, Replace	4-16
Engine Mount, Replace	4-16
Lefthand	4-16
	Page No.
Righthand	4-16
Fuel Pump, Replace	4-17
Precautions	4-16
Air Bag Systems	4-16
Battery Ground Cable	4-16
	Page No.
Fuel System Pressure Relief	4-16
Less Digital Pressure Gage	4-16
Using Digital Pressure Gauge	4-16
Radiator, Replace	4-17
Tightening Specifications	4-18

PRECAUTIONS

Air Bag Systems

Refer to "Air Bag System Precautions" in the front of this manual for system disarming and arming procedures.

Battery Ground Cable

Prior to service, disconnect battery ground cable and isolate as required.

Fuel System Pressure Relief

USING DIGITAL PRESSURE GAUGE

1. Remove engine cover.
2. Loosen fuel fill cap to relieve fuel tank vapor pressure.
3. Remove fuel rail service port cap.
4. Wrap suitable shop towel around fuel rail service port.
5. Connect digital pressure gauge tool No. CH-48027 to fuel rail service port and place hose into suitable container.
6. Open tool valve and to bleed fuel from fuel rail. Close valve.
7. Remove hose and disconnect gauge.
8. Install fuel rail service port cap and engine cover. Tighten fuel fill cap

LESS DIGITAL PRESSURE GAGE

1. Loosen fuel fill cap to relieve fuel tank vapor pressure.
2. Remove engine cover.
3. Remove fuel rail service port cap.
4. Wrap suitable shop towel around fuel rail service port and use suitable, small flat bladed tool to depress (open) fuel rail test port valve.
5. Install fuel rail service port cap and engine cover. Tighten fuel fill cap.

ENGINE MOUNT

REPLACE

Lefthand

1. Loosen clamps and remove Charge Air Cooler (CAC) outlet hose from CAC outlet pipe and throttle body.
2. Remove lefthand engine mount upper nut.
3. Raise and support vehicle.
4. Remove lefthand engine mount lower nut.
5. Remove righthand engine mount lower nut.
6. Position suitable adjustable jack below oil pan. Place suitable block of wood between oil pan and jack.
7. Raise engine and remove mount.
8. Reverse procedure to install.

Righthand

1. Raise and support vehicle, then remove tire and wheel assembly.
2. Remove upper and lower righthand engine mount nuts.
3. Remove lefthand engine mount lower nut.
4. Remove righthand brake hose bracket bolt.
5. Remove righthand brake line clip at crossmember.
6. Position suitable adjustable jack below oil pan. Place suitable block of wood between oil pan and jack.
7. Raise engine and remove engine mount.
8. Reverse procedure to install.

ENGINE

REPLACE

1. Disconnect battery ground cable.
2. Open hood and disconnect headlamp bulb socket Connector Positive Assurance (CPA) connector.
3. Disconnect lefthand headlamp electrical harness.
4. Rotate socket a quarter turn counterclockwise and disconnect bulb.
5. Remove mounting screws and headlamp.
6. Disconnect wiring harness on both sides and mark hood for installation alignment.
7. Remove mounting nuts and hood.
8. Pull intake manifold cover from studs and remove cover.
9. Remove radiator as outlined under "Radiator, Replace."
10. Relieve fuel system pressure as outlined under "Precautions."
11. Disconnect Evaporative Emission (EVAP) canister purge solenoid tube from valve.
12. Disconnect fuel feed pipe from fuel rail.
13. Remove radiator inlet hose from engine.
14. Remove radiator outlet hose from thermostat housing and oil cooler.
15. Remove surge tank outlet hose from thermostat housing and oil cooler.
16. Remove surge tank clip from oil dipstick tube bracket.
17. Remove surge tank outlet hose.
18. Remove surge tank air bleed hose from engine.
19. Remove heater inlet and outlet hoses from thermostat.
20. Remove brake booster vacuum hose from intake manifold.
21. Remove fuel feed and EVAP line clip from oil dipstick tube bracket.
22. Remove engine harness clips from oil

dipstick tube and radiator outlet hose bracket.
23. Raise and support vehicle.
24. Drain engine oil into suitable container.
25. Remove catalytic converter bracket bolt.
26. Disconnect Crankshaft Position (CKP) sensor electrical connector.
27. Disconnect oil pressure sensor electrical connector.
28. Remove starter solenoid S terminal nut.
29. Remove engine harness terminal from starter.
30. Remove engine harness clip from intake manifold.
31. Remove starter solenoid terminal nut.
32. Remove positive battery cable clips from intake manifold, then the battery cable terminal from starter.
33. Lower vehicle.
34. Remove positive battery cable clip from bracket.
35. Cut engine harness tie straps.
36. Remove battery ground cable ground bolt.
37. Disconnect alternator electrical connector.
38. Reposition positive battery cable terminal boot, then remove terminal nut and cable from alternator.
39. Disconnect air conditioning compressor and knock sensor electrical connectors.
40. Position negative and positive battery cable aside.
41. Disconnect air conditioning refrigerant pressure sensor and wiper motor electrical connectors.
42. Remove engine wire harness clips from wiper motor hole and surge tank air bleed hose.
43. Disconnect fuel injector electrical connector.
44. Disconnect Throttle Actuator Control (TAC) electrical connector.
45. Disconnect electrical connectors from intake and exhaust camshaft position actuators.
46. Remove engine harness clips from camshaft cover.
47. Disconnect ignition coil electrical connectors.
48. Remove Connector Position Assurance (CPA) retainers from Heated Oxygen Sensor (HO2S) electrical connectors.
49. Disconnect front and rear HO2S electrical connectors.
50. Disconnect engine harness clips from junction block bracket.
51. Disconnect HO2S electrical connector clip from strut.
52. Disconnect intake and exhaust Camshaft Position (CMP) sensor electrical connectors.
53. Remove engine harness ground terminal bolt.
54. Disconnect Engine Coolant Temperature (ECT) sensor electrical connector.
55. Disconnect EVAP canister purge solenoid electrical connector.
56. Disconnect engine harness clip from EVAP canister purge solenoid valve bracket.
57. Disconnect evaporative emission (EVAP) canister purge valve electrical connector.
58. Disconnect EVAP canister purge valve tube.
59. Disconnect chassis EVAP vapor from EVAP canister purge valve.
60. Remove EVAP canister purge valve bracket bolt, then the EVAP canister purge valve with bracket.
61. Remove engine harness bracket bolt.
62. Disconnect engine harness clip from bracket.
63. Position engine harness aside.
64. Remove air conditioning compressor mounting bolts, then position compressor aside.
65. Remove catalytic converter mounting nuts, then the catalytic converter and gasket.
66. Raise and support vehicle.
67. Remove muffler.
68. Remove mounting bolts and starter motor.
69. **On models equipped with automatic transmission,** remove torque converter to flywheel bolts.
70. **On all models,** remove lower, then the upper bellhousing bolts.
71. Lower vehicle.
72. Remove left and righthand engine mount upper mounting nuts.
73. Support engine using suitable engine lifting device.
74. Separate engine from transmission.
75. Remove engine.
76. Reverse procedure to install.

RADIATOR

REPLACE

1. Drain cooling system into suitable container.
2. Remove mounting bolts and radiator front air deflector, then the retainer and shroud air inlet.
3. Remove air cleaner outlet duct resonator and Positive Crankcase Ventilation (PCV) hose clamps.
4. Remove air cleaner outlet duct resonator.
5. Disconnect cooling fan motor electrical connector.
6. Remove mounting bolts, shroud, cooling fan and motor.
7. Remove radiator inlet and outlet hoses, then the surge tank inlet hose.
8. Remove air cleaner stud, then the mounting nuts and radiator upper bracket.
9. Remove mounting bolts, air conditioning condenser and radiator.
10. Reverse procedure to install.

FUEL PUMP

REPLACE

1. Relieve fuel pressure as outlined under "Precautions."
2. Remove rear compartment trim panel.
3. Remove mounting bolts and fuel sending unit access cover.
4. Disconnect fuel level sender fuel pressure sensor electrical connectors.
5. Disconnect fuel fill pipe Evaporative Emission (EVAP) pipe quick connect fitting.
6. Disconnect fuel feed pipe quick connect fitting.
7. Raise fuel sender up slightly. **Do not handle fuel sender assembly by fuel pipes.**
8. Connect large EVAP canister quick connect fitting.
9. Remove fuel sender.
10. Remove and discard fuel sender O-ring.
11. Reverse procedure to install. Install new gasket.

TIGHTENING SPECIFICATIONS

Year	Component	Torque Ft. Lbs.
2006–08	Air Conditioning Compressor	16
	Air Conditioning Condenser	80①
	Air Cleaner Outlet Duct Resonator	80①
	Air Cleaner Stud	89①
	Alternator Terminal Nut	15
	Battery Ground Cable Ground	15
	Bellhousing	37
	Brake Hose Bracket	89①
	Catalytic Converter	18
	Catalytic Converter To Muffler	13
	Engine Harness Bracket	89①
	Engine Harness Ground Terminal	89①
	EVAP Canister Purge Valve Bracket	18
	Engine Mount	37
	Flywheel	②
	HO2S	30
	Hood Hinge	19
	Radiator	18
	Radiator Front Air Deflector	80①
	Radiator Upper Bracket	80①
	Starter Motor	30
	Starter Solenoid Terminal	27①
	Torque Converter	37

① — Inch lbs.
② — **Torque** to 39 ft. lbs., final tighten an additional 25°.

Rear Axle & Suspension

NOTE: On Air Bag Equipped Models, Refer To "Air Bag System Precautions" Located In The Front Of This Manual For System Disarming & Arming Procedures.

NOTE: Refer To "Computer Relearn Procedures" Located In The Front Of This Manual When Battery Power To The Computer Has Been Interrupted.

INDEX

	Page No.		Page No.		Page No.
Coil Spring, Replace	4-19	Differential Carrier, Replace	4-19	Shock Absorber, Replace	4-19
Control Arm, Replace	4-19	Hub & Bearing, Replace	4-19	Stabilizer Shaft, Replace	4-20
Lower	4-19	Knuckle, Replace	4-19	Tightening Specifications	4-20
Upper	4-19	Propeller Shaft, Replace	4-19	Toe Link, Replace	4-20
Description	4-18	Rear Axle Shaft, Replace	4-18		

DESCRIPTION

These vehicles are equipped with independent rear suspension and coil spring . The rear spring steel stabilizing bar helps minimize body roll and sway during cornering. The rear stabilizer shaft is connected to the frame through insulators and to the lower control arm through the stabilizer shaft links. The rear suspension uses the following components; rear differential, coil springs, shock absorbers, toe adjustment links, upper and lower control arms, knuckles, stabilizer shaft and stabilizer shaft links.

REAR AXLE SHAFT
REPLACE

1. Raise and support vehicle.
2. Remove propeller shaft.
3. Remove righthand rear tire and wheel assembly.
4. Prevent wheel hub and bearing from turning by inserting suitable drift or punch into brake rotor and against caliper.
5. Remove and discard drive shaft spindle nut.
6. Remove drift or punch from rotor.
7. Separate upper ball joint from rear knuckle.

SOLSTICE

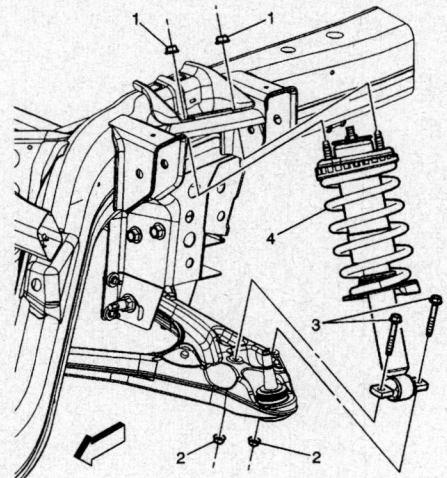

1- UPPER NUTS
2- LOWER NUTS
3- LOWER BOLTS
4- SHOCK MODULE

ARM0500000000909

Fig. 1 Shock absorber replacement

8. Carefully separate drive shaft from rear differential using suitable puller just enough to install seal protector tool No. J44394, or equivalent, into differential output seal.
9. Remove drive shaft.
10. Reverse procedure to install. If using original drive shaft, remove and discard shaft retaining ring on splined shaft of cross groove joint.

DIFFERENTIAL CARRIER
REPLACE

1. Remove drive shafts from differential as outlined under "Rear Axle, Replace."
2. Support differential carrier using suitable transmission jack.
3. Remove front differential to support mounting bolt and nut.
4. Remove lefthand rear differential to support mounting bolt as much as possible. **Rear differential support mounting bolts will not be able to be removed completely because of interference with underbody.**
5. Remove righthand rear differential to support bolt.
6. Lower jack until mounting ear at front of differential clears support attachment point.
7. Carefully release wheel drive shaft from differential enough to install seal protector tool No. J44394, or equivalent.
8. Carefully install tool No. J44394, or equivalent, over wheel drive shaft.
9. Carefully slide tool into differential output shaft seal.
10. Continue lowering jack, while simultaneously disengaging lefthand wheel drive shaft.
11. Remove differential.
12. Reverse procedure to install.

PROPELLER SHAFT
REPLACE

1. Remove driveline tunnel closeout panel.
2. Support rear drive module.
3. Remove differential case bracket assembly to body mounting bolt.
4. Remove CV joint mounting bolts and spacers.
5. Remove propeller shaft.
6. Reverse procedure to install.

HUB & BEARING
REPLACE

1. Remove tire and wheel.
2. Remove brake caliper mounting bracket.
3. Remove drive axle mounting nut.
4. Remove mounting bolt and wheel/hub.
5. Reverse procedure to install.

SHOCK ABSORBER
REPLACE

1. Raise and support vehicle, then remove tire and wheel assemblies.
2. Remove toe link as outlined under "Toe Link, Replace.".
3. Remove upper shock absorber mounting nuts, **Fig. 1.**
4. Remove lower mounting nuts and bolts, then the shock absorber
5. Reverse procedure to install.

COIL SPRING
REPLACE

1. Remove shock absorber as outlined under "Shock Absorber, Replace."
2. Install shock absorber into suitable spring compressor.
3. Mark upper control arm and insulator for installation alignment.
4. Turn spring compressor forcing screw until coil spring is compressed.
5. Remove upper mounting nut and shock absorber.

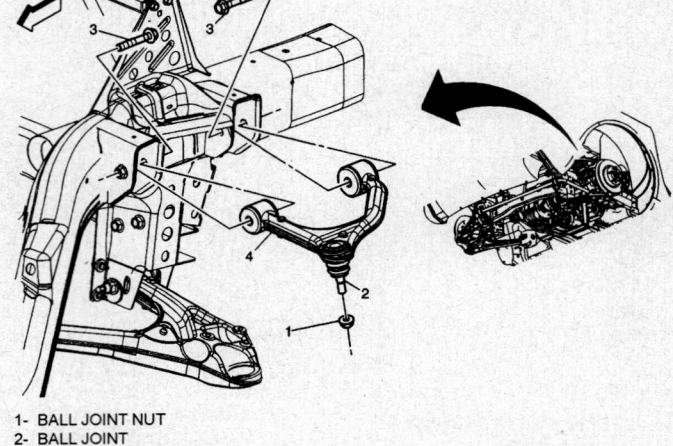

1- BALL JOINT NUT
2- BALL JOINT
3- CONTROL ARM BOLTS
4- CONTROL ARM

ARM0500000000910

Fig. 2 Upper control arm replacement

6. Loosen compressor forcing screw until upper mounting plate and coil spring may be removed.
7. Remove upper control arm bracket, insulator and coil spring.
8. Reverse procedure to install.

CONTROL ARM
REPLACE

Upper

1. Raise and support vehicle, then remove tire and wheel assembly.
2. Remove shock absorber as outlined under "Shock Absorber, Replace."
3. Loosen upper ball joint nut, **Fig. 2. Do not remove nut until ball stud has been separated from knuckle.**
4. Separate ball joint from steering knuckle using ball joint separation tool No. J42188, or equivalent.
5. Remove upper ball joint nut and upper control arm bolts, then the control arm.
6. Reverse procedure to install.

Lower

1. Remove tires and wheels.
2. Remove toe link as outlined under "Toe Link, Replace."
3. Loosen lower ball joint nut, **Fig. 3. Do not remove nut until ball stud has been separated from knuckle.**
4. Rotate knuckle forward and separate ball joint from knuckle using ball joint separation tool No. J42188, or equivalent.
5. Remove lower control arm nuts.
6. Remove lower control arm to frame bolts, and lower control arm.
7. Reverse procedure to install.

KNUCKLE
REPLACE

1. Remove toe link to knuckle mounting nut, **Fig. 4.**
2. Loosen upper ball joint nut, **Fig. 2. Do**

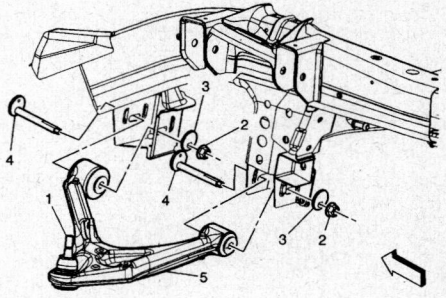

1- BALL JOINT
2- CONTROL ARM NUTS
3- ADJUSTING CAMS
4- CONTROL ARM BOLTS
5- CONTROL ARM

ARM0500000000911

Fig. 3 Lower control arm replacement

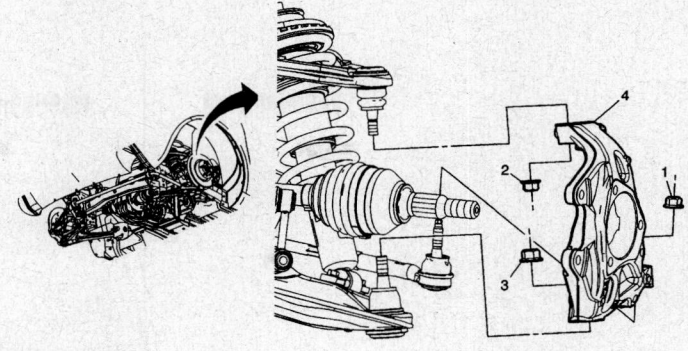

1- TOE LINK NUT
2- UPPER BALL JOINT NUT
3- LOWER BALL JOINT NUT
4- LOWER BALL JOINT NUT
5- KNUCKLE

ARM0500000000912

Fig. 4 Knuckle replacement

not remove nut until ball stud has been separated from knuckle.
5. Rotate knuckle forward and separate ball joint from knuckle using ball joint separation tool No. J42188, or equivalent.
6. Remove upper and lower ball joint to knuckle nuts.
7. Remove knuckle.
8. Reverse procedure to install.

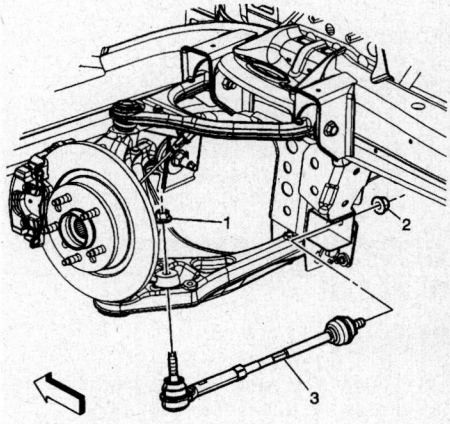

1- TOE LINK TO KNUCKLE NUT
2- TOE LINK TO FRAME NUT
3- TOE LINK

ARM0500000000913

Fig. 5 Toe link replacement

not remove nut until ball stud has been separated from knuckle.
3. Separate upper ball joint from steering knuckle using ball joint separation tool No. J42188, or equivalent, **Fig. 3.** Do
4. Loosen lower ball joint nut, **Fig. 3.** Do

TOE LINK
REPLACE

1. Remove toe link to knuckle mounting nut, **Fig. 5.**
2. Remove toe link to frame nut.
3. Remove toe link.
4. Reverse procedure to install.

STABILIZER SHAFT
REPLACE

1. Raise and support vehicle, then remove tire and wheel assemblies.
2. Remove connector position assurance retainer and disconnect HO2S electrical connector. **Do not remove pigtail from oxygen sensor.**

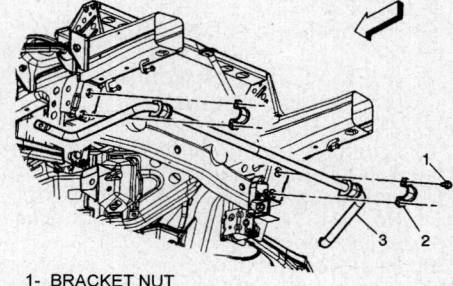

1- BRACKET NUT
2- BRACKET
3- STABILIZER

ARM0500000000914

Fig. 6 Stabilizer shaft replacement

3. Remove electrical connector clip from junction block bracket.
4. Remove HO2S and muffler.
5. Remove stabilizer shaft links from end of stabilizer shaft, **Fig. 6.**
6. Remove stabilizer shaft link and mounting bracket bolts.
7. Remove mounting brackets and stabilizer shaft.
8. Reverse procedure to install.

TIGHTENING SPECIFICATIONS

Year	Component	Torque Ft. Lbs.
2006–08	Ball Joint Nut (Lower)	30
	Ball Joint Nut (Upper)	22
	Control Arm To Frame Bolt (Upper)	81
	Control Arm To Frame Nut (Lower)	122
	Shock Absorber Top Nut	31
	Shock Absorber Lower Nut	21
	Shock Absorber Upper Nut	35
	Stabilizer Shaft Link	53
	Stabilizer Shaft Mounting Bracket	41
	Toe Link	74

Front Suspension & Steering

NOTE: On Air Bag Equipped Models, Refer To "Air Bag System Precautions" Located In The Front Of This Manual For System Disarming & Arming Procedures.

NOTE: Refer To "Computer Relearn Procedures" Located In The Front Of This Manual When Battery Power To The Computer Has Been Interrupted.

INDEX

	Page No.
Ball Joint, Replace	4-21
Ball Joint Inspection	4-21
Coil Spring, Replace	4-21
Control Arm, Replace	4-21
Lower	4-21
Upper	4-21
Hub & Bearing, Replace	4-21
Power Steering	21-1
Power Steering Gear, Replace	4-22

	Page No.
Power Steering Pump, Replace	4-23
Power Steering System Bleed	4-23
Precautions	4-21
Air Bag Systems	4-21
Battery Ground Cable	4-21
Stabilizer Bar, Replace	4-22
Stabilizer Bar Bushing, Replace	4-22
Steering Columns	20-1

	Page No.
Steering Knuckle, Replace	4-22
Strut, Replace	4-21
Strut Service	4-21
Tie Rod, Replace	4-22
Inner	4-22
Outer	4-22
Tightening Specifications	4-23

PRECAUTIONS

Air Bag Systems

Refer to "Air Bag System Precautions" in the front of this manual for system disarming and arming procedures.

Battery Ground Cable

Prior to service, disconnect battery ground cable and isolate as required.

HUB & BEARING

REPLACE

1. Raise and support vehicle, then remove tire and wheel assembly.
2. Remove brake caliper mounting bracket and brake rotor as outlined in "Disc Brakes" chapter.
3. Disconnect speed sensor electrical connector, then the wiring harness from steering knuckle retainers.
4. Remove mounting bolts and wheel hub bearing.
5. Reverse procedure to install.

BALL JOINT INSPECTION

1. Raise and support vehicle. Allow suspension to hang free.
2. Grasp tire at top and bottom.
3. Move top of tire in and out.
4. Look for any horizontal movement of knuckle relative to control arm.
5. Control arm assembly must be replaced if any of the following conditions exist:
   a. Joint is loose.
   b. Ball seal is cut.
   c. Ball stud is loose at knuckle.

BALL JOINT

REPLACE

Refer to "Control Arm, Replace" for ball joint replacement procedure.

COIL SPRING

REPLACE

Refer to "Strut Service" for coil spring replacement.

STRUT

REPLACE

1. Raise and support vehicle, then remove tire and wheel assembly.
2. Remove lower strut mounting bolt, **Fig. 1.**
3. Remove upper and lower mounting nuts, then the strut.
4. Reverse procedure to install.

STRUT SERVICE

1. Install strut into suitable spring compressor.
2. Mark upper control arm and insulator for installation alignment.
3. Compress coil spring by turning spring compressor forcing screw.
4. Remove strut upper mounting nut, then loosen compressor forcing screw until upper mounting plate and coil spring can be removed.
5. Remove shock absorber.
6. Remove upper control arm bracket, insulator and coil spring from spring compressor.
7. Reverse procedure to assemble.

CONTROL ARM

REPLACE

Upper

1. Raise and support vehicle, then remove tire and wheel assembly.
2. Remove strut as outlined under "Strut, Replace."
3. Loosen upper ball joint nut, **Fig. 2. Do not remove nut until ball stud has been separated from knuckle.**
4. Separate ball joint from steering knuckle using ball joint separation tool No. J42188, or equivalent.
5. Remove upper ball joint nut.
6. Remove mounting bolts and upper control arm.
7. Reverse procedure to install.

Lower

1. Raise vehicle and suitably support, then remove tire and wheel.
2. Loosen, outer tie rod end joint nut from outer tie rod end ball joint, **Fig. 3.**
3. Separate tie rod end ball joint from steering knuckle using ball joint separator tool No. J42188-B, or equivalent.
4. Remove tie rod end stud nut.
5. Loosen, lower ball joint nut, **Fig. 4. Do not remove nut until ball stud has been separated from knuckle.**
6. Rotate knuckle completely forward and install ball joint separator tool No. J42188-B, or equivalent.
7. Separate ball joint from steering knuckle and remove ball joint stud nut.
8. Remove alignment cam bolts and lower control arm.
9. Reverse procedure to install.

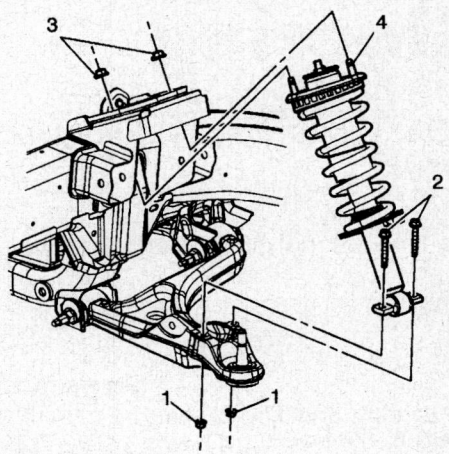

1- LOWER NUTS
2- LOWER BOLTS
3- UPPER NUTS
4- UPPER STUDS

ARM0500000000915

Fig. 1 Strut replacement

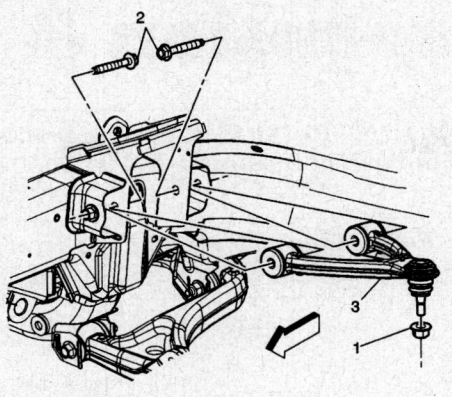

1- BALL JOINT NUT
2- CONTROL ARM TO FRAME BOLTS
3- CONTROL ARM

ARM0500000000916

Fig. 2 Upper control arm replacement

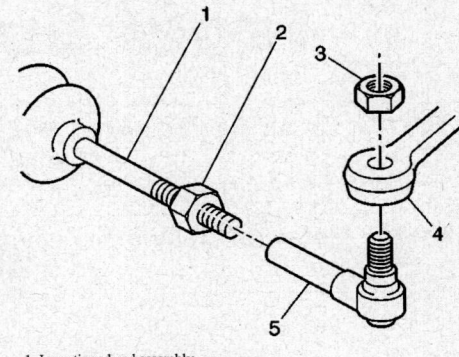

1. Inner tie rod end assembly
2. Jam nut
3. Outer tie rod end stud nut
4. Steering knuckle
5. Outer tie rod end

ARM0500000000644

Fig. 3 Outer tie rod assembly

able wrench on flats of gear teeth.

STEERING KNUCKLE

REPLACE

1. Remove wheel hub and bearing as outlined under "Hub & Bearing, Replace."
2. Remove tie rod end nut, **Fig. 5.**
3. Separate upper and lower control arm ball joints from knuckle as outlined under "Control Arm, Replace."
4. Remove steering knuckle.
5. Reverse procedure to install.

STABILIZER BAR

REPLACE

1. Raise and support vehicle, then remove tire and wheel assemblies.
2. Remove mounting nut and stabilizer shaft link.
3. Remove mounting bolt, bracket and stabilizer shaft.
4. Reverse procedure to install.

STABILIZER BAR BUSHING

REPLACE

1. Raise and support vehicle.
2. Remove mounting bolt, bracket and stabilizer shaft insulator.
3. Reverse procedure to install.

TIE ROD

REPLACE

Outer

1. Raise and support vehicle, then remove tire and wheel assembly.
2. Loosen, do not remove, outer tie rod end stud nut from outer tie rod end ball stud.

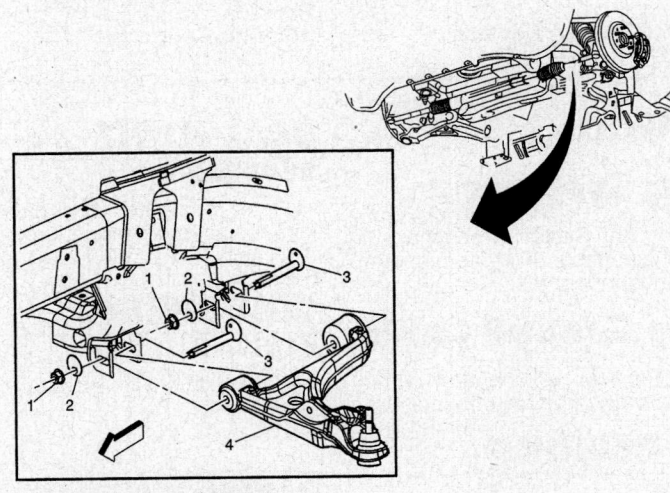

1. Lower control arm to frame nut
2. Lower control arm alignment cam
3. Lower control arm alignment bolt
4. Lower control arm

ARM0500000000645

Fig. 4 Lower control arm replacement

3. Separate tie rod end ball joint from steering knuckle using joint separator tool No. J42188-B, or equivalent.
4. Remove outer tie rod end stud nut.
5. Loosen jam nut on inner tie rod.
6. Remove outer from inner tie rod.
7. Reverse procedure to install.

Inner

1. Remove outer tie rod end as outlined under "Outer."
2. Remove inner tie rod nut, **Fig. 6.**
3. Remove tie rod clamp.
4. Remove boot clamp using suitable side cutters. Discard boot clamp.
5. Remove rack and pinion boot.
6. Remove shock dampener from inner tie rod, then slide shock dampener back onto rack.
7. Hold steering rack in place using suit-

8. Rotate inner tie rod housing counterclockwise until inner tie rod separates from rack.
9. Reverse procedure to install.

POWER STEERING GEAR

REPLACE

1. Raise and support vehicle.
2. Separate outer tie rod ends from steering knuckle.
3. Remove power steering outlet pipe hose fitting.
4. Remove and discard intermediate shaft bolt from steering gear.
5. Remove mounting nut and bolt, then the power steering gear.
6. Reverse procedure to install.

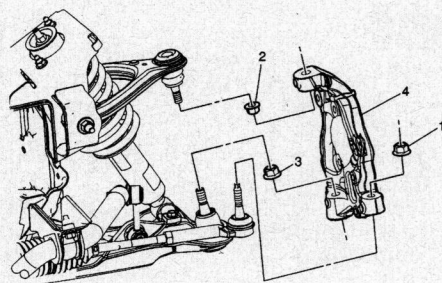

1- TIE ROD NUT
2- UPPER BALL JOINT NUT
3- LOWER BALL JOINT NUT
4- STEERING KNUCKLE

ARM0500000000917

Fig. 5 Steering knuckle replacement

POWER STEERING PUMP

REPLACE

1. Raise and support vehicle.
2. Remove power steering pump drive belt.
3. Remove power steering pump pulley using power steering pulley remover tool No. J25034-C, or equivalent.

4. Remove mounting bolt and power steering pump.
5. Reverse procedure to install.

POWER STEERING SYSTEM BLEED

1. Fill pump reservoir with fluid to minimum system level, FULL COLD level, or middle of hash mark on cap stick fluid level indicator.
2. **On models equipped with hydro-boost,** oil level will appear falsely high if hydro-boost accumulator is not fully charged. To fully charge system start engine, firmly apply brake pedal 10–15 times, then turn engine off. **Do not apply brake pedal with engine OFF. This will discharge hydro-boost accumulator.**
3. **On all models,** raise and support vehicle.
4. **On models less hydro-boost,** turn ignition key to ON position, then turn steering wheel from stop to stop 12 times.
5. **On models equipped with hydro-boost,** turn ignition key to ON position, then turn steering wheel from stop to stop 15 to 20 times.

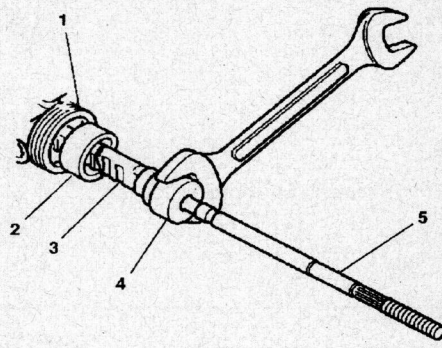

1- RACK
2- SHOCK DAMPNER
3- GEAR TEETH
4- INNER TIE ROD HOUSING
5- INNER TIE ROD

ARM0500000000918

Fig. 6 Inner tie rod replacement

6. **On all models,** verify power steering fluid level.
7. Start engine and rotate steering wheel from left to right.
8. Inspect for sign of fluid aeration (pump noise/whining).
9. Inspect fluid level. Repeat bleed procedure if required.

TIGHTENING SPECIFICATIONS

Year	Component	Torque Ft. Lbs.
2006–08	Ball Joint Nut (Lower)	①
	Ball Joint Nut (Upper)	②
	Control Arm To Frame Nut	122
	Control Arm To Frame Bolts	81
	Intermediate Shaft To Steering Column	43
	Intermediate Shaft To Steering Gear	43
	Power Steering Gear	44
	Power Steering Pump	16
	Power Steering Outlet Pipe/Hose Fitting	22
	Shock Absorber	31
	Stabilizer Shaft Link	53
	Stabilizer Shaft	41
	Strut, Lower	21
	Strut, Upper	35
	Tie Rod End Stud Nut (Outer)	③
	Upper Shock Absorber	35
	Wheel Hub/Speed Sensor	85
	Wheel Nuts	100

① — **Torque** to 30 ft. lbs.; final tighten an additional 135°.
② — **Torque** to 22 ft. lbs.; final tighten an additional 150°.
③ — **Torque** to 22 ft. lbs.; final tighten an additional 115°.

Wheel Alignment

INDEX

	Page No.		Page No.		Page No.
Front Wheel Alignment	4-24	Preliminary Inspection	4-24	Camber	4-24
Camber	4-24	Front & Rear Alignment	4-24	Toe	4-24
Caster	4-24	Level Alignment	4-24	**Wheel Alignment**	
Toe	4-24	**Rear Wheel Alignment**	4-24	**Specifications**	4-2

PRELIMINARY INSPECTION

Level Alignment

Give consideration to excess loads, such as tool boxes, sample cases, etc. If normally carried in vehicle, these items should remain in vehicle during alignment adjustments. Give consideration also to condition of equipment being used for alignment. Follow equipment manufacturers instructions.

Before performing any adjustment affecting wheel alignment, perform following inspections and adjustments in order to ensure correct alignment reading:

1. Inspect tires for proper inflation and irregular tire wear.
2. Inspect for worn suspension components.
3. Inspect vehicle trim height as outlined under "Vehicle Ride Height Specifications" in "Specifications" section.
4. Inspect steering wheel for excessive drag or poor return because of stiff or rusted linkage or suspension components.
5. Inspect fuel level. Fuel tank should be full or vehicle should have compensating load added.

Front & Rear Alignment

1. Install alignment equipment according to manufacturers instructions.
2. Jounce front and rear bumpers three times prior to inspecting wheel alignment.
3. Measure alignment angles and record readings.
4. Adjust alignment angles to vehicle specification, if required. **When performing adjustments to vehicles requiring a four wheel alignment, set rear wheel alignment angles first.**
5. Always road test vehicle after adjusting alignment, noting following:
   a. If vehicle still pulls, switch front tires.
   b. If vehicle pulls in same direction, inspect alignment and rear tracking.
   c. If vehicle pulls in opposite direction, rotate tires and road test.

FRONT WHEEL ALIGNMENT

Caster

1. Loosen control arm cam bolts nuts.
2. Rotate cam bolts to required caster specification setting, refer to "Front Wheel Alignment Specifications" in "Specifications" section. **Use correct fastener in correct location. Replacement fasteners must be correct part number for that application.**
3. Maintain caster setting while tightening cam bolt nuts.
4. Inspect caster setting after tightening.

Camber

1. Loosen control arm cam bolt nuts.
2. Rotate cam bolts to required camber specification setting, refer to "Front Wheel Alignment Specifications" in "Specifications" section. **Use correct fastener in correct location. Replacement fasteners must be correct part number for that application.**
3. Maintain camber setting while tightening cam bolt nuts.
4. Inspect camber setting after tightening.

Toe

1. Loosen jam nut on tie rod.
2. Rotate inner tie rod to required toe specification setting, refer to "Front Wheel Alignment Specifications" in "Specifications" section.
3. Tighten jam nut on tie rod. **Use correct fastener in correct location. Replacement fastener must be correct part number for that application.**
4. Inspect toe setting after tightening.
5. Adjust toe setting if required.

REAR WHEEL ALIGNMENT

Camber

1. Loosen lower control arm cam bolts.
2. Rotate cam bolts to required camber specification setting, refer to "Rear Wheel Alignment Specifications" in "Specifications" section. **Use correct fastener in correct location. Replacement fasteners must be correct part number for that application.**
3. Maintain camber setting while tightening cam bolt nuts.
4. Inspect camber setting after tightening.

Toe

1. Loosen rear suspension toe link locknut.
2. Rotate toe link to required toe specification setting, refer to "Rear Wheel Alignment Specifications" in "Specifications" section.
3. Tighten toe link locknut. **Use correct fastener in correct location. Replacement fasteners must be correct part number for that application.**
4. Inspect toe setting after tightening.

CAVALIER, COBALT, G5 & SUNFIRE

NOTE: Refer To The Rear Of This Manual For Manufacturer's Special Service Tool Suppliers.

INDEX OF SERVICE OPERATIONS

Page No.

AIR BAG SYSTEM
PRECAUTIONS 0-18
BRAKES
Anti-Lock Brakes (Volume 2).. 6-1
Disc Brakes.................. 22-1
Drum Brakes 23-1
Hydraulic Brake Systems 24-1
Power Brake Units........... 25-1
COMPUTER RELEARN
PROCEDURE 0-31
ELECTRICAL
Air Bag System (Volume 2) ... 4-1
Air Conditioning............. 16-1
Alternator, Replace 5-6
Alternators.................. 19-1
Blower Motor, Replace....... 5-8
Clutch Start Switch, Replace.. 5-7
Coil Pack, Replace 5-6
Cooling Fans 17-1
Cruise Control (Volume 2) 2-1
Dash Gauges (Volume 2) 1-1
Dash Panel Service
(Volume 2) 5-1
Dimmer Switch, Replace...... 5-7
Evaporator Core, Replace 5-9
Fuel Pump Relay Location.... 5-5
Fuse Panel & Flasher
Location 5-5
Headlamp Switch, Replace ... 5-7
Heater Core, Replace........ 5-8
Ignition Lock, Replace 5-6
Ignition Switch, Replace 5-7
Instrument Cluster, Replace... 5-8
Multi-Function Switch,
Replace 5-7
Neutral Safety Switch,
Replace 5-7
Passive Restraint Systems
(Volume 2)................. 4-1
Precautions 5-5
Relay Center Location 5-5
Speed Controls (Volume 2) ... 2-1
Starter Motors 18-1
Starter, Replace 5-5
Steering Columns............ 20-1
Steering Wheel, Replace...... 5-8
Stop Light Switch, Replace ... 5-7
Turn Signal Switch, Replace .. 5-7
Wiper Motor, Replace........ 5-8
Wiper Switch, Replace....... 5-8
Wiper Systems (Volume 2).... 3-1
Wiper Transmission, Replace . 5-8
ELECTRICAL SYMBOL
IDENTIFICATION 0-63
FRONT DRIVE AXLES 26-1
FRONT SUSPENSION &
STEERING
Ball Joint, Replace........... 5-28
Ball Joint Inspection 5-28
Control Arm, Replace........ 5-29
Description 5-28
Power Steering 21-1
Power Steering Gear,
Replace 5-30

Page No.

Power Steering Pump,
Replace 5-31
Precautions 5-28
Stabilizer Bar, Replace....... 5-30
Steering Columns............ 20-1
Steering Knuckle, Replace 5-29
Strut, Replace 5-28
Strut Service................ 5-29
Tie Rod End, Replace 5-30
Tightening Specifications...... 5-32
Wheel Bearing, Replace 5-28
NON-STANDARD TIRE &
WHEEL SIZE
ADJUSTMENT TO RIDE
HEIGHT SPECIFICATIONS
& TIRE SIZE CHART 0-61
REAR AXLE &
SUSPENSION
Coil Spring, Replace.......... 5-26
Control Arm Bushing,
Replace 5-26
Description 5-25
Hub & Bearing, Replace 5-25
Rear Axle, Replace 5-25
Shock Absorber, Replace 5-25
Tightening Specifications...... 5-27
SERVICE REMINDER &
WARNING LAMP RESET
PROCEDURES 0-34
SPECIFICATIONS
Fluid Capacities & Cooling
System Data............... 5-4
Front Wheel Alignment
Specifications.............. 5-3
General Engine
Specifications.............. 5-2
Lubricant Data.............. 5-4
Rear Wheel Alignment
Specifications.............. 5-3
Tune Up Specifications 5-2
Vehicle Ride Height
Specifications.............. 5-3
VEHICLE
IDENTIFICATION 0-1
VEHICLE LIFT POINTS....... 0-51
VEHICLE MAINTENANCE
SCHEDULES 0-73
WHEEL ALIGNMENT
Front Wheel Alignment........ 5-33
Preliminary Inspection 5-33
Wheel Alignment
Specifications.............. 5-3
WIRE COLOR CODE
IDENTIFICATION 0-63
2.0L ENGINE
Balance Shaft, Replace........ 5-12
Camshaft, Replace 5-11
Crankshaft Balancer, Replace. 5-11
Crankshaft Rear Oil Seal,
Replace 5-13

Page No.

Crankshaft Seal, Replace..... 5-12
Cylinder Head, Replace....... 5-10
Engine Rebuilding
Specifications................ 29-1
Engine, Replace 5-10
Engine Mount, Replace....... 5-10
Exhaust Manifold, Replace.... 5-10
Front Cover, Replace 5-11
Fuel Filter, Replace 5-14
Fuel Pump, Replace 5-14
Hydraulic Lash Adjusters,
Replace 5-11
Intake Manifold, Replace...... 5-10
Main & Rod Bearings 5-12
Oil Pan, Replace............. 5-13
Oil Pump, Replace........... 5-13
Oil Pump Service 5-13
Piston & Rod Assembly....... 5-12
Precautions................. 5-10
Radiator, Replace 5-14
Serpentine Drive Belt 5-13
Supercharger, Replace 5-14
Thermostat, Replace......... 5-13
Tightening Specifications...... 5-16
Timing Chain, Replace 5-11
Valve Cover, Replace 5-11
Water Pump, Replace 5-13
2.2L ENGINE
Compression Pressure........ 5-17
Engine Rebuilding
Specifications................ 29-1
Engine, Replace 5-17
Engine Mount, Replace....... 5-17
Intake Manifold, Replace...... 5-17
Precautions................. 5-17
Radiator, Replace 5-17
Tightening Specifications...... 5-18
2.4L ENGINE
Balance Shaft, Replace........ 5-21
Camshaft, Replace 5-21
Crankshaft Balancer, Replace. 5-20
Crankshaft Rear Oil Seal,
Replace 5-22
Crankshaft Seal, Replace..... 5-22
Cylinder Head, Replace....... 5-20
Engine Rebuilding
Specifications................ 29-1
Engine, Replace 5-19
Engine Mount, Replace....... 5-18
Exhaust Manifold, Replace.... 5-20
Front Cover, Replace 5-20
Fuel Filter, Replace 5-23
Fuel Pump, Replace 5-23
Hydraulic Lash Adjusters,
Replace 5-20
Intake Manifold, Replace...... 5-19
Main & Rod Bearings 5-22
Oil Pan, Replace............. 5-22
Oil Pump, Replace........... 5-22
Oil Pump Service 5-22
Piston & Rod Assembly....... 5-22
Precautions................. 5-18

Page No.		Page No.		Page No.
Radiator, Replace............. 5-23		Tightening Specifications...... 5-24		Valve Cover, Replace......... 5-20
Serpentine Drive Belt 5-23		Timing Chain, Replace........ 5-20		Water Pump, Replace 5-23
Thermostat, Replace.......... 5-23				

Specifications

GENERAL ENGINE SPECIFICATIONS

Year	Engine		Fuel System	Bore/ Stroke	Compression Ratio	Net H.P. @ RPM③	Maximum Torque Ft. Lbs. @ RPM	Normal Oil Pressure, psi
	Liter	VIN Code②						
2004	2.2L DOHC	F	SFI	3.38 x 3.72	10.00	140 @ 5600	150 @ 4000	50–80④
2005	2.0L①	P	SFI	3.40 x 3.40	9.50	205 @ 5600	200 @ 4400	50–80④
	2.2L DOHC	F	SFI	3.38 x 3.72	10.00	140 @ 5600	150 @ 4000	50–80④
2006–08	2.0L①	P	SFI	3.40 x 3.40	9.50	205 @ 5600	200 @ 4400	50–80④
	2.2L	F	SFI	3.38 x 3.72	10.00	140 @ 5600	150 @ 4000	50–80④
	2.4L	B	SFI	3.47 x 3.86	10.00	171 @ 6200	163 @ 5000	50–80④

SFI — Sequential fuel injection
① — Supercharged engine.
② — The eighth digit denotes engine code.

③ — Ratings are net as installed in vehicle.

④ — Oil pressure @ 1000 RPM.

TUNE UP SPECIFICATIONS

Year & Engine	Spark Plug Gap	Firing Order	Ignition Timing, BTDC	Timing Mark	Curb Idle Speed	Fast Idle Speed	Fuel Pump Pressure	Valve Lash
2004								
2.2L DOHC	.042	②	⑤	⑥	④	④	50–60	①
2005								
2.0L	.040	②	⑤	⑥	③	③	50–60	①
2.2L DOHC	.042	②	⑤	⑥	④	④	50–60	①
2006								
2.0L	.040	②	⑤	⑥	③	③	50–60	①
2.2L DOHC	.042	②	⑤	⑥	④	④	50–60	①
2.4L	.042	②	⑤	⑥	③	③	50–60	①
2007–08								
2.0L	.040	②	⑤	⑥	③	③	50–60	①
2.2L DOHC	.042	②	⑤	⑥	④	④	50–60	①
2.4L	.042	②	⑤	⑥	③	③	50–60	①

BTDC — Before Top Dead Center
① — Equipped w/hydraulic valve lifters. No adjustment is required.
② — Cylinder numbering from front of engine to rear of engine, 1,2,3,4.

Firing order 1-3-4-2. Coil connections are stamped on coil assemblies.
③ — Idle speeds are controlled by Throttle Actuator Control (TAC) motor.

④ — Idle speeds are controlled by Idle Air Control (IAC) valve.
⑤ — No adjustment.
⑥ — Equipped w/crankshaft sensor.

CAVALIER, COBALT, G5 & SUNFIRE

FRONT WHEEL ALIGNMENT SPECIFICATIONS

Year	Model	Caster Angle, Degree		Camber Angle, Degree		Total Toe, Degrees	Ball Joint Wear
		Limits	Desired	Limits	Desired		
2004	Cavalier & Sunfire	+3.3 to +5.3①	4.30①	−1.00 to +1.00	0	0	②
2005	Cavalier & Sunfire	+3.3 to +5.3①	4.30①	−1.00 to +1.00	0	0	②
	Cobalt③	+2.25 to +3.75	+3.00	−1.75 to −.25	−1	.2	②
	Cobalt④	+2.90 to +4.40	+3.65	−1.75 to −.25	−1	.2	②
2006	Cobalt③	+2.25 to +3.75	+3.00	−1.75 to −.25	−1	.2	②
	Cobalt④	+2.90 to +4.40	+3.65	−1.75 to −.25	−1	.2	②
2007–08	Cobalt③	+2.25 to +3.75	+3.00	−1.75 to −.25	−1	.2	②
	Cobalt④	+2.90 to +4.40	+3.65	−1.75 to −.25	−1	.2	②
	G5④	+2.90 to +4.40	+3.65	−1.75 to −.25	−1	.2	②

① — Non-adjustable. For inspection purposes only.

② — Refer to Front Suspension & Steering section for ball joint specifications and inspection procedure.

③ — Soft ride suspension.

④ — Sport suspension.

REAR WHEEL ALIGNMENT SPECIFICATIONS

Year	Model	Camber Angle, Degrees①		Thrust Angle, Degrees①		Total Toe, Degrees①	
		Limits	Desired	Limits	Desired	Limits	Desired
2004	Cavalier & Sunfire	−1.15 to +.35	−.4	−.25 to +.25	0	−.10 to +.50	+.20
2005	Cavalier & Sunfire	−1.15 to +.35	−.4	−.25 to +.25	0	−.10 to +.50	+.20
	Cobalt	—	—	−.30 to +.30	0	−.05 to +.55	+.25
2006	Cobalt	—	—	−.30 to +.30	0	−.05 to +.55	+.25
2007–08	Cobalt	—	—	−.30 to +.30	0	−.05 to +.55	+.25
	G5	—	—	−.30 to +.30	0	−.05 to +.55	+.25

① — Non-adjustable. For inspection purposes only.

VEHICLE RIDE HEIGHT SPECIFICATIONS

Model	Year	Body Style	Manufacturer's Original Tire Size	Measurement Points & Specifications①③					
				Front			Rear		
				Dim.④	Specification		Dim.④	Specification	
					Inches	mm		Inches	mm
Cavalier & Sunfire	2004–05	All	②	A	32.15	816	B	22.00	558
				C	9.17	233	D	9.45	240
Cobalt	2005–06	All	②	A	21.40	544	B	22.00	558
				C	8.82	224	D	9.17	233
	2007–08	All	②	A	21.40	544	B	22.00	558
				C	8.82	224	D	9.17	233
G5	2007–08	All	②	A	21.40	544	B	22.00	558
				C	8.82	224	D	9.17	233

A Dim. — Measurement From Front Wheel Center to Check Point On Rocker Panel

B Dim. — Measurement From Rear Wheel Center to Check Point On Rocker Panel

C Dim. — Ground to Rocker Panel, Front

D Dim. — Ground to Rocker Panel, Rear

Dim. — Dimension

① — ±.39 in (10mm) front to rear & side to side.

② — See door sticker or inside of glove box for manufacturers original tire size specifications.

③ — Measurement is with fuel, radiator coolant and engine oil full, spare tire, jack, hand tools and mats in designated positions and tires properly inflated.

④ — Refer to **Fig. A**.

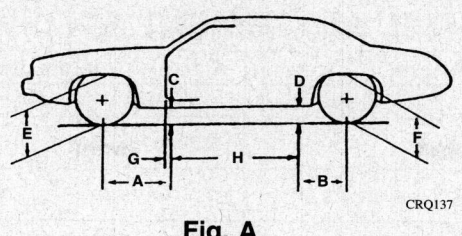

Fig. A

FLUID CAPACITIES & COOLING SYSTEM DATA

Year	Engine	Coolant Capacity, Qts.	Coolant Type	Radiator Cap Relief Pressure, Lbs.	Thermo. Opening Temp.	Fuel Tank, Gals.	Engine Oil Refill, Qts.②	Transaxle Oil	
								Manual, Pts.	Automatic, Qts.①
2004	2.2L	8.6	Dex-Cool	15	195	14.1	5.0	1.8	③
2005	2.0L	6.0	Dex-Cool	15	195	13.5	6.0	⑦	④
	2.2L⑤	8.6	Dex-Cool	15	195	14.1	5.0	1.8	③
	2.2L⑥	6.8	Dex-Cool	15	195	13.5	5.0	⑦	④
2006–08	2.0L	6.0	Dex-Cool	15	195	13.5	6.0	⑦	④
	2.2L	6.8	Dex-Cool	15	195	13.5	5.0	⑦	④
	2.4L	7.4	Dex-Cool	15	195	13.5	5.0	⑦	④

① — Approximate. Make final inspection w/dipstick.
② — When changing engine oil filter additional oil may be required.
③ — Oil pan removal, 6.9 qts.; overhaul, 9.5 qts., dry 12.9 qts.
④ — Pan only, 6.9 qts., after overhaul 9.5 qts.
⑤ — Cavalier & Sunfire.
⑥ — Cobalt & G5.
⑦ — Getrag 5-Speed, 1.8 qts.; Saab 5-Speed, 2.0 qts.

LUBRICANT DATA

Year	Model	Lubricant Type			
		Transaxle		Power Steering	Brake System
		Manual	Automatic		
2004	All	DEXRON III	DEXRON III	②	DOT-3
2005	Cavalier	DEXRON III	DEXRON III	②	DOT-3
	Cobalt③	DEXRON III	DEXRON III	②	DOT-3
	Cobalt④	①	DEXRON III	②	DOT-3
2006	Cobalt③	DEXRON III	DEXRON III	②	DOT-3
	Cobalt④	①	DEXRON III	②	DOT-3
2007–08	Cobalt③	DEXRON III	DEXRON III	②	DOT-3
	Cobalt④	①	DEXRON III	②	DOT-3
	G5③	DEXRON III	DEXRON III	②	DOT-3
	G5④	①	DEXRON III	②	DOT-3

① — Manual transmission fluid GM P/N 21018899, or equivalent.
② — Power steering fluid GM P/N 1052884, or equivalent.
③ — 2.2L & 2.4L engines.
④ — 2.0L engine.

NOTE: On Air Bag Equipped Models, Refer To "Air Bag System Precautions" Located In The Front Of This Manual For System Disarming & Arming Procedures.

NOTE: Refer To "Computer Relearn Procedures" Located In The Front Of This Manual When Battery Power To The Computer Has Been Interrupted.

NOTE: On Models Equipped With 2.2L DOHC Engine, Refer To "Alero, Grand Am & 2004-05 Malibu" Chapter For Procedures.

INDEX

	Page No.
Air Bag System (Volume 2)	4-1
Air Conditioning	16-1
Alternator, Replace	5-6
Cavalier & Sunfire	5-6
Cobalt & G5	5-6
2.0L Engine	5-6
2.2L & 2.4L Engines	5-6
Alternators	19-1
Blower Motor, Replace	5-8
Clutch Start Switch, Replace	5-7
Coil Pack, Replace	5-6
Cavalier & Sunfire	5-6
2.2L DOHC	5-6
Cobalt & G5	5-6
2.0L Engine	5-6
2.2L Engine	5-6
2.4L Engine	5-6
Cooling Fans	17-1
Cruise Control (Volume 2)	2-1
Dash Gauges (Volume 2)	1-1
Dash Panel Service (Volume 2)	5-1
Dimmer Switch, Replace	5-7
Cavalier	5-7
Sunfire	5-8

	Page No.
Evaporator Core, Replace	5-9
Cavalier & Sunfire	5-9
Cobalt & G5	5-9
Fuel Pump Relay Location	5-5
Cavalier & Sunfire	5-5
Cobalt & G5	5-5
Fuse Panel & Flasher Location	5-5
Cavalier & Sunfire	5-5
Cobalt & G5	5-5
Headlamp Switch, Replace	5-7
Heater Core, Replace	5-8
Cavalier & Sunfire	5-8
Cobalt & G5	5-8
Ignition Lock, Replace	5-6
Cavalier & Sunfire	5-6
Less Ignition Key	5-6
With Ignition Key	5-6
Cobalt & G5	5-7
Ignition Switch, Replace	5-7
Cavalier & Sunfire	5-7
Cobalt & G5	5-7
Instrument Cluster, Replace	5-8
Multi-Function Switch, Replace	5-7
Neutral Safety Switch, Replace	5-7
Cavalier & Sunfire	5-7

	Page No.
Cobalt & G5	5-7
Passive Restraint Systems (Volume 2)	4-1
Precautions	5-5
Air Bag Systems	5-5
Battery Ground Cable	5-5
Relay Center Location	5-5
Speed Controls (Volume 2)	2-1
Starter Motors	18-1
Starter, Replace	5-5
Cavalier & Sunfire	5-5
2.2L Engine	5-5
2.4L Engine	5-6
Cobalt & G5	5-6
2.0L Engine	5-6
2.2L & 2.4L Engines	5-6
Steering Columns	20-1
Steering Wheel, Replace	5-8
Stop Light Switch, Replace	5-7
Turn Signal Switch, Replace	5-7
Wiper Motor, Replace	5-8
Wiper Switch, Replace	5-8
Wiper Systems (Volume 2)	3-1
Wiper Transmission, Replace	5-8

PRECAUTIONS
Air Bag Systems

Refer to "Air Bag System Precautions" in the front of this manual for system disarming and arming procedures.

Battery Ground Cable

Prior to service, disconnect battery ground cable and isolate as required.

FUSE PANEL & FLASHER LOCATION
Cavalier & Sunfire

The instrument panel fuse panel is located behind the lefthand side of the instrument panel. The underhood fuse panel is located on the lefthand side of the engine compartment.

The turn signal/hazard flasher module is located under the instrument panel on the righthand side of steering column.

Cobalt & G5

The interior fuse panel is part of the Body Control Module (BCM) which is located behind the center of the instrument panel, under the radio. The underhood fuse block is located on the lefthand side of the engine compartment, near the strut tower.

Turn signal and hazard flasher operation is controlled by the Body Control Module (BCM). The BCM is located behind the center of the instrument panel, under the radio.

FUEL PUMP RELAY LOCATION
Cavalier & Sunfire

The fuel pump relay is located in the front lefthand corner of the engine compartment, in the engine compartment fuse block.

Cobalt & G5

The fuel pump relay is located is located on the lefthand side of the engine compartment, in the underhood fuse block.

RELAY CENTER LOCATION

The relay center is located in the fuse panels, see "Fuse Panel & Flasher Location" for appropriate locations.

STARTER
REPLACE
Cavalier & Sunfire

2.2L ENGINE

1. Remove wiring harness bracket nut from starter bolt.
2. Raise and support vehicle using suitable lift.

3. Remove flywheel inspection shield.
4. Remove electrical connectors.
5. Remove starter bolts, then the starter.
6. Reverse procedure to install, noting the following:
   a. **On models equipped with 2.2L DOHC engines, torque** starter bolts to 30 ft. lbs.
   b. **On models equipped with 2.2L DOHC engines, torque** electrical attaching nuts to 13 inch lbs.

2.4L ENGINE

1. Remove air inlet duct to throttle body.
2. Remove top starter bolt.
3. Raise and support vehicle.
4. Remove lower starter bolt and position starter aside.
5. Disconnect electrical wiring and remove starter.
6. Reverse procedure to install.

Cobalt & G5

2.0L ENGINE

1. Raise and support vehicle.
2. Remove charge air cooler pump.
3. Remove terminal nuts, then disconnect starter motor electrical connectors.
4. Remove starter motor mounting bolts, then the starter motor.
5. Reverse procedure to install. **Torque** mounting bolts to 37 ft. lbs.

2.2L & 2.4L ENGINES

1. Raise and support vehicle.
2. Remove terminal nuts, then disconnect starter motor electrical connectors.
3. Remove starter motor mounting bolts, then the starter motor.
4. Reverse procedure to install. **Torque** mounting bolts to 30 ft. lbs.

ALTERNATOR
REPLACE

Cavalier & Sunfire

1. Disconnect alternator electrical connectors.
2. Rotate tensioner counterclockwise with suitable wrench and slide belt from alternator pulley.
3. Release tensioner and remove belt.
4. Remove alternator through bolts, then the alternator.
5. Reverse procedure to install, noting the following:
   a. **On models equipped with 2.2L DOHC engine, torque** alternator bolts to 15 ft. lbs.
   b. **On models equipped with 2.2L DOHC engine, torque** alternator electrical connector bolts to 13 ft. lbs.
   c. **On models equipped with 2.4L engine, torque** alternator mounting bolts to 37 ft. lbs.

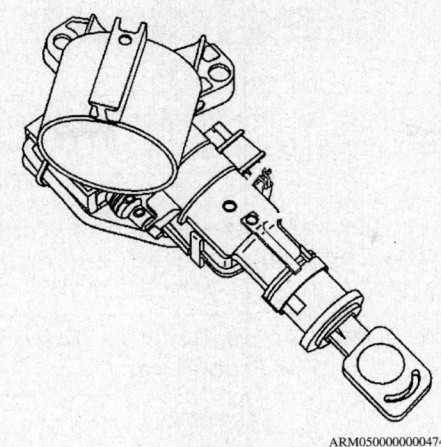

Fig. 1   Lock cylinder replacement. Cobalt & G5

Cobalt & G5

2.0L ENGINE

1. Remove supercharger as outlined under "Supercharger, Replace" in "2.0L Engine" section.
2. Position starter solenoid wire boot aside and remove alternator harness nut.
3. Remove starter solenoid wire terminal from alternator.
4. Disconnect engine harness wire connector from alternator.
5. Remove alternator mounting bolts, then the alternator.
6. Reverse procedure to install. **Torque** mounting bolts to 18 ft. lbs.

2.2L & 2.4L ENGINES

1. Remove drive belt.
2. Remove air cleaner outlet duct.
3. Disconnect engine harness electrical connector.
4. Position starter solenoid wire boot aside, then remove terminal nut.
5. Remove starter solenoid wire terminal.
6. Remove alternator mounting bolts, then the alternator.
7. Reverse procedure to install. **Torque** mounting bolts to 16 ft. lbs.

COIL PACK
REPLACE

Cavalier & Sunfire

2.2L DOHC

1. Remove accelerator and cruise control cables from brackets, then the brackets as required.
2. Remove ignition control module (ICM).
3. Remove ignition coil housing attaching bolts.
4. Remove ignition coils and ICM assembly.
5. Reverse procedure to install, torque ignition coil retaining bolts to 89 inch lbs.

Cobalt & G5

2.0L ENGINE

1. Disconnect electrical connectors from ignition coils.
2. Remove ignition coil retaining bolts.
3. Remove ignition coils.
4. Reverse procedure to install. **Torque** retaining bolts to 89 inch lbs.

2.2L ENGINE

1. Remove accelerator cable from bracket.
2. Remove accelerator cable bracket bolt, then the bracket.
3. Disconnect ignition control module electrical connector.
4. Remove ignition control module retaining bolts, then the module.
5. Reverse procedure to install. **Torque** ignition control module retaining bolts to 13 inch lbs. and cable bracket bolt to 18 inch lbs.

2.4L ENGINE

1. Remove intake manifold cover.
2. Disconnect ignition coil electrical connectors.
3. Remove ignition coil retaining bolts, then the coils.
4. Reverse procedure to install. **Torque** coil retaining bolts to 89 inch lbs.

IGNITION LOCK
REPLACE

Cavalier & Sunfire

LESS IGNITION KEY

1. Remove steering column upper and lower trim covers.
2. Drill out lock button on back of steering column housing.
3. Remove lock cylinder by pulling out from column housing.
4. Disconnect ignition switch electrical connector.
5. Remove metal shavings from lock cylinder steering column housing.
6. Reverse procedure to install.

WITH IGNITION KEY

1. **On models equipped with tilt column,** remove tilt lever.
2. **On all models,** remove steering column upper and lower trim covers.
3. Turn lock cylinder to Run.
4. Push against locking button on rear side of bearing and housing, then remove lock cylinder by pulling it out of column.
5. Disconnect lock cylinder electrical connector.
6. Reverse procedure to install, noting the following:
   a. Turn lock cylinder to Run position and depress locking button.
   b. Gently push cylinder into place while rotating key approximately 5° counterclockwise.
   c. Inspect for proper operation.

Cobalt & G5

1. Lower steering column to lowest position.
2. Remove steering column upper and lower trim covers.
3. Remove theft deterrent control module.
4. Depress first retainer through lock housing access hole "2" with a small allen wrench or similar tool, **Fig. 1.**
5. Lock cylinder will back out slightly, then depress second retainer through lock housing access hole "1" until lock cylinder backs out slightly again.
6. Pull lock cylinder out enough to locate second retainer to lock housing access hole "2."
7. Depress retainer though access hole "2" a second time.
8. Ignition cylinder should release from housing. If cylinder does not release, it may need to be moved in and out several times to locate retainer correctly in hole.
9. Remove lock cylinder from lock housing.
10. Reverse procedure to install.

IGNITION SWITCH
REPLACE
Cavalier & Sunfire

1. Remove steering column trim covers.
2. Remove ignition lock as outlined under "Ignition Lock, Replace."
3. Remove Torx head screws, then the ignition switch from steering column.
4. Reverse procedure to install. **Torque** screws to 36 inch lbs.

Cobalt & G5

1. Remove steering column trim covers.
2. Disconnect the ignition switch harness connector.
3. Turn ignition switch to Run position.
4. Remove ignition switch screws, then the ignition switch from steering column, **Fig. 2.**
5. Reverse procedure to install.

CLUTCH START SWITCH
REPLACE

1. Remove driver's instrument panel knee bolster.
2. Disconnect clutch start switch electrical connector.
3. Remove clutch start switch from pedal bracket.
4. Reverse procedure to install. Ensure starter cranks only when clutch pedal is fully depressed.

NEUTRAL SAFETY SWITCH
REPLACE
Cavalier & Sunfire

On models equipped with automatic transmission, the neutral start and back-up

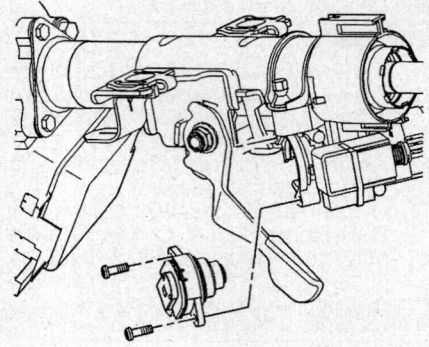

ARM0500000000475

Fig. 2   Ignition switch replacement. Cobalt & G5

lamp switches are combined into one unit and must be replaced as an assembly.
1. Disconnect shift linkage.
2. Disconnect electrical connector from switch.
3. Remove mounting bolts and switch.
4. If same switch is to be installed again, proceed as follows:
   a. Place shift shaft in Neutral position.
   b. Align flats of shift shaft with switch and install switch.
   c. Loosely install mounting bolts.
   d. Insert gauge pin or 3/32 inch drill bit in service adjustment hole and rotate switch until pin drops to depth of 9/64 inch.
   e. **Torque** mounting bolts to 15 ft. lbs.
5. If new switch is to be installed, proceed as follows:
   a. Place shift shaft in Neutral position.
   b. Align flats of shift shaft with switch and install switch.
   c. If bolt holes do not align with mounting boss on transaxle, ensure shift shaft is in Neutral position and do not rotate switch. Switch is pinned in Neutral position. If switch has been rotated and pin has broken, replace as required.
   d. **Torque** mounting bolts to 15 ft. lbs.
6. Ensure engine will start only in Park or Neutral positions.

Cobalt & G5

1. Apply parking brake and place control assembly in Neutral. Transaxle manual shaft must be in Neutral position prior to installing range switch.
2. Remove shift control cable from transaxle range switch lever.
3. Disconnect electrical connectors from transaxle range switch.
4. Remove transaxle range switch lever nut and lever.
5. Remove transaxle range switch bolts, then the switch.
6. Reverse procedure to install, noting the following:
   a. Install transaxle range switch alignment tool No. J41545, or equivalent over shaft and switch.
   b. Rotate switch until alignment tool drops into position.
   c. **Torque** switch bolts to 15 ft. lbs.

HEADLAMP SWITCH
REPLACE

Refer to "Multi-Function Switch, Replace" for replacement procedure.

STOP LIGHT SWITCH
REPLACE

1. Remove driver's side sound insulator.
2. Disconnect and remove electrical connectors.
3. Disconnect brake switch by grasping switch and turning it one quarter turn counterclockwise while pulling toward rear of vehicle.
4. Reverse procedure to install, adjust switch as follows:
   a. Ensure brake pedal is fully released.
   b. Ensure that stoplamp plunger is fully depressed against brake pedal shanks.
   c. Hold brake pedal forward and ensure stoplamp switch and cruise control switch are fully seated into brake pedal bracket.
   d. Pull brake pedal to rear, against internal stop.
   e. Stoplamp switch and cruise control switch will be adjusted.
   f. Inspect stoplamps for proper operation.

MULTI-FUNCTION SWITCH
REPLACE

1. Remove steering column trim covers.
2. Remove multi-function switch retaining screws.
3. Disconnect muti-function switch electrical connector, then remove switch from column.
4. Reverse procedure to install.

TURN SIGNAL SWITCH
REPLACE

Refer to "Multi-Function Switch, Replace" for turn signal switch replacement procedure.

DIMMER SWITCH
REPLACE
Cavalier

1. Remove instrument panel accessory trim plate to access fog lamp switch.
2. Release retainers on fog lamp/dimmer switch housing using suitable flat bladed tool.
3. Remove fog lamp/dimmer switch housing from instrument panel.
4. Release retainers on dimmer switch using a flat bladed tool.
5. Remove dimmer lamp switch from fog lamp/dimmer switch housing.
6. Reverse procedure to install.

CAVALIER, COBALT, G5 & SUNFIRE

Sunfire

1. Remove fog lamp/dimmer switch trim plate from instrument panel using suitable flat bladed tool.
2. Disconnect electrical connectors from fog lamp/dimmer switch.
3. Release retainer tabs on dimmer lamp switch using suitable flat bladed tool on reverse side.
4. Remove dimmer lamp switch from trim plate.
5. Reverse procedure to install.

STEERING WHEEL
REPLACE

1. Remove steering wheel center pad and mounting screws as required.
2. Disable driver's air bag module as outlined in "Air Bag System Precautions" in front of this manual.
3. Remove covers and two driver's air bag module mounting bolts from steering wheel rear.
4. Disconnect driver's air bag module electrical connector.
5. Remove air bag module.
6. Disconnect horn electrical connector.
7. Remove steering wheel nut.
8. Remove steering wheel using steering wheel puller No. J1859A, or equivalent.
9. Disconnect electrical connectors from steering wheel.
10. Remove steering wheel from column.
11. Reverse procedure to install, **torque** steering wheel nut to 30 ft. lbs.

INSTRUMENT CLUSTER
REPLACE

1. Remove instrument panel trim plate.
2. Remove screws from top of cluster.
3. Pull cluster rearward.
4. Remove cluster assembly.
5. Reverse procedure to install.

WIPER MOTOR
REPLACE

1. Remove wiper arm assemblies.
2. Disconnect washer tubing from air inlet screen.
3. Remove air inlet grille panel push-in retainers from panel using door trim pad and garnish clip remover tool No. J38778, or equivalent.
4. Remove air inlet grille panel from vehicle.
5. Disconnect electrical connector from wiper motor.
6. Remove screws and wiper drive system module from vehicle.
7. Remove wiper transmission from wiper motor crank arm using wiper transmission separator tool No. J39232, or equivalent.
8. Remove screws, then the wiper motor from frame.
9. Reverse procedure to install. **Torque** mounting screws to 88 inch lbs.

WIPER SWITCH
REPLACE

1. Remove steering column trim covers.
2. Remove multi-function switch as outlined in "Multi-Function Switch, Replace."
3. Remove retaining screws, then the wiper switch from column.
4. Disconnect electrical connector.
5. Reverse procedure to install. **Torque** attaching screws to 36 inch lbs.

WIPER TRANSMISSION
REPLACE

1. Remove wiper arm assemblies.
2. Disconnect the washer tubing from the air inlet screen.
3. Remove air inlet grille panel push-in retainers from panel using door trim pad and garnish clip remover tool No. J38778, or equivalent.
4. Remove air inlet grille panel from vehicle.
5. Remove wiper drive module.
6. Disconnect electrical connector from wiper motor.
7. Remove wiper transmission from wiper motor crank arm using wiper transmission separator tool No. J39232, or equivalent.
8. Remove cap from wiper transmission.
9. Remove screws and wiper transmission from tube frame.
10. Reverse procedure to install, noting the following:
    a. **Torque** wiper transmission screws to 79 inch lbs.
    b. **Torque** wiper drive system module screws to 88 inch lbs.

BLOWER MOTOR
REPLACE

1. Disconnect blower motor electrical connectors.
2. Remove sound insulator panels as required.
3. Remove mounting screws, then the blower motor assembly.
4. Reverse procedure to install, **torque** attaching screws to 44 inch lbs.

HEATER CORE
REPLACE
Cavalier & Sunfire

1. Drain cooling system into suitable container.
2. Recover refrigerant as outlined in "Air Conditioning" chapter.
3. Remove evaporator lines to evaporator.
4. Raise and support vehicle.
5. Disconnect heater hoses from heater core.
6. Lower vehicle.
7. Remove evaporator case drain tube.
8. Remove instrument panel carrier as outlined in "Dash Panel Service" chapter.

9. Disconnect wiring harness from cross beam.
10. Remove attaching bolts to righthand and lefthand HVAC module.
11. Remove two cross vehicle beam bolts.
12. Remove cross beam.
13. Remove floor console.
14. Reposition floor carpet aside in order to access floor outlet duct connections.
15. Remove floor outlet ducts from heater outlet cover, then the floor outlet ducts.
16. Disconnect wiring harness from HVAC module.
17. Disconnect electrical connections to blower motor and resistor.
18. Remove HVAC module assembly.
19. Remove heater core case cover attaching screws and cover.
20. Remove heater core bracket screws and brackets.
21. Remove heater core from HVAC module assembly.
22. Reverse procedure to install, noting the following:
    a. **Torque** bracket and cover screws to 9 inch lbs.
    b. **Torque** HVAC module mounting bracket bolts and screws to 18 inch lbs.
    c. **Torque** cross vehicle beam bolts and studs to 89 inch lbs.
    d. **Torque** righthand and lefthand side HVAC module support bolts to 18 inch lbs.
    e. **Torque** evaporator tube to evaporator fittings to 18 ft. lbs.

Cobalt & G5

1. Drain cooling system.
2. Raise and support vehicle.
3. Place a drain pan under water pump drain port, then loosen water pump drain bolt and drain coolant from water pump, **Fig. 3.**
4. Tighten water pump drain bolt, then lower vehicle.
5. Reposition heater outlet hose clamp at heater core.
6. Remove heater outlet hose from heater core, then reposition heater inlet hose clamp at heater core.
7. Remove heater inlet hose from heater core.
8. Pull bottom of front floor console extension to release lower clips, then tilt extension upward to release upper clips and hooks.
9. Remove front floor console left side extension panel.
10. Pull back carpet at bottom of left instrument panel center support bracket and remove left instrument panel center support bracket nuts.
11. Remove left instrument panel center support bracket.
12. Remove accelerator control pedal from front of dash and position aside.
13. Raise center floor outlet duct while pushing floor ducts down to disengage ducts.
14. Rotate center floor outlet duct forward and pull down to disengage it from HVAC module.
15. Remove heater core cover heat stakes with a small chisel.

16. Loosen nut that is behind fuel line bracket and remove stud from dash panel at heater hoses.
17. Pull heater core cover down just enough to clear locating pins from HVAC module.
18. Slide heater core cover rearward until drain tube clears front of dash.
19. Slide heater core cover down, rearward and then to the right.
20. Remove heater core cover, then the heater core.
21. Reverse procedure to install.

EVAPORATOR CORE
REPLACE

Cavalier & Sunfire

1. Remove HVAC module as outlined in "Heater Core, Replace."
2. Remove heater core as outlined in "Heater Core, Replace."
3. Remove attaching screws and evaporator core brackets.
4. Remove evaporator core assembly.
5. Reverse procedure to install, **torque** evaporator core bracket screws to 9 inch lbs.

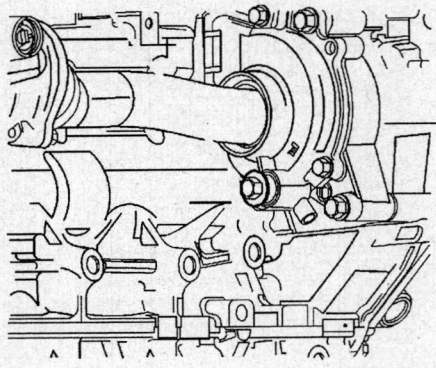

ARM0500000000476

Fig. 3 Water pump drain port location

Cobalt & G5

1. Recover refrigerant as outlined in "Air Conditioning" chapter.
2. Drain cooling system, then reposition heater outlet hose clamp at heater core.
3. Remove heater outlet hose from heater core, then position hose upright against front of dash.
4. Reposition heater inlet hose clamp at heater core.

5. Remove heater inlet hose from heater core, then position hose upright against front of dash.
6. Remove condenser tube and evaporator hose from the thermal expansion valve.
7. Remove and discard seal washers.
8. Remove HVAC module nuts from front of dash, then disconnect blower motor connector.
9. Disconnect blower motor resistor electrical connector.
10. Remove instrument panel as outlined in "Dash Panel Service" chapter.
11. Raise center floor outlet duct while pushing the floor ducts down to disengage ducts.
12. Rotate center floor outlet duct forward in vehicle and pull down to disengage duct from HVAC module.
13. Disconnect recirculation actuator electrical connector.
14. Remove heater core as outlined under "Heater Core, Replace."
15. Remove HVAC module from vehicle.
16. Unsnap and open passenger compartment filter door.
17. Remove lower HVAC case screws, then the lower HVAC case.
18. Remove evaporator core.
19. Reverse procedure to install.

2.0L Engine

NOTE: On Air Bag Equipped Models, Refer To "Air Bag System Precautions" Located In The Front Of This Manual For System Disarming & Arming Procedures.

NOTE: Refer To "Computer Relearn Procedures" Located In The Front Of This Manual When Battery Power To The Computer Has Been Interrupted.

INDEX

	Page No.
Balance Shaft, Replace	5-12
Camshaft, Replace	5-11
Crankshaft Balancer, Replace	5-11
Crankshaft Rear Oil Seal, Replace	5-13
Crankshaft Seal, Replace	5-12
Cylinder Head, Replace	5-10
Engine Rebuilding Specifications	29-1
Engine, Replace	5-10
Engine Mount, Replace	5-10
Exhaust Manifold, Replace	5-10
Front Cover, Replace	5-11

	Page No.
Fuel Filter, Replace	5-14
Fuel Pump, Replace	5-14
Hydraulic Lash Adjusters, Replace	5-11
Intake Manifold, Replace	5-10
Main & Rod Bearings	5-12
Oil Pan, Replace	5-13
Oil Pump, Replace	5-13
Oil Pump Service	5-13
Assemble	5-13
Disassemble	5-13
Piston & Rod Assembly	5-12
Precautions	5-10

	Page No.
Air Bag Systems	5-10
Battery Ground Cable	5-10
Fuel System Pressure Relief	5-10
Radiator, Replace	5-14
Serpentine Drive Belt	5-13
Supercharger, Replace	5-14
Thermostat, Replace	5-13
Tightening Specifications	5-16
Timing Chain, Replace	5-11
Valve Cover, Replace	5-11
Water Pump, Replace	5-13

PRECAUTIONS

Air Bag Systems

Refer to "Air Bag System Precautions" in the front of this manual for system disarming and arming procedures.

Battery Ground Cable

Prior to service, disconnect battery ground cable and isolate as required.

Fuel System Pressure Relief

1. Turn ignition OFF and loosen fuel filler cap to relieve fuel tank vapor pressure.
2. Remove cap from fuel pressure service port.
3. Remove engine identification cover nuts and cover.
4. Install fuel pressure gauge tool No. J34730-1A, or equivalent, into fuel pressure service port.
5. Install bleed hose into suitable container, then open valve to bleed system pressure.
6. Disconnect fuel pressure gauge from fuel pressure connection.

ENGINE MOUNT
REPLACE

1. Raise and support vehicle.
2. Support engine with a suitable hydraulic floor jack. Place a piece of wood between jack and oil pan.
3. Remove engine mount to intermediate bracket bolts.
4. Remove engine mount to midrail nuts.
5. Remove engine mount from engine compartment.
6. Reverse procedure to install.

ENGINE
REPLACE

1. Place front wheels in straight forward position.
2. Remove air outlet duct.
3. Secure cooling module to upper body structure.
4. Relieve fuel system pressure as outlined under "Precautions."
5. Disconnect fuel line from fuel rail.
6. Drain cooling system.
7. Remove radiator inlet hose and surge tank to cylinder head pipe.
8. Remove radiator outlet hose, then the inlet and outlet heater hoses.
9. Disconnect the following harness connectors:
   a. Electronic Temperature Control (ETC) sensor.
   b. Manifold Absolute Pressure (MAP) sensor.
   c. Barometric Pressure (BARO) sensor.
   d. Crankshaft (CKP) sensor.
   e. Oil pressure sensor.
   f. Purge solenoid.

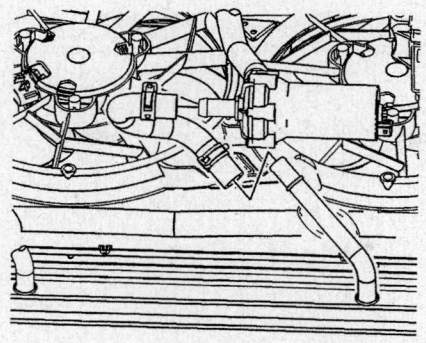

ARM0500000000477

Fig. 1 Charge air cooler reservoir

   g. Ignition coils.
   h. Oxygen (O2) sensor.
   i. Vehicle speed sensor.
   j. Engine temperature sensor.
   k. Boost solenoid.
   l. Back-up lamp switch.
10. Remove drive belt as outlined under "Serpentine Drive Belt."
11. Recover A/C system refrigerant as outlined in "Air Conditioning" chapter.
12. Raise and support vehicle.
13. Disconnect compressor and condenser hose assembly from A/C compressor.
14. Remove A/C compressor mounting bolts and set compressor aside.
15. Disconnect starter motor harness connectors.
16. Disconnect alternator harness connectors.
17. Drain engine oil and disconnect front exhaust pipe from exhaust manifold.
18. Disconnect transmission shift cable from transmission.
19. Place blocks of wood to support powertrain assembly between frame and powertrain.
20. Remove engine mount.
21. Remove left transmission mount.
22. Disconnect stabilizer links from stabilizer bar.
23. Disconnect intermediate shaft from steering gear.
24. Disconnect lower control arms from steering knuckles.
25. Remove drive axles from steering knuckle.
26. Lower vehicle to approximately 3 feet off the ground in order to position lift table under frame.
27. Place wood blocks as necessary between lift table and frame to support assembly.
28. Remove front frame bolts, then partially unscrew rear frame bolts until 1.5 inches (38mm) of bolt shank is exposed.
29. Slowly lower the table to the floor.
30. Attach engine lift hoist to engine lift hooks.
31. Remove starter.
32. Remove transmission to engine bolts, then separate engine from transmission.
33. Remove clutch pressure plate and disk.

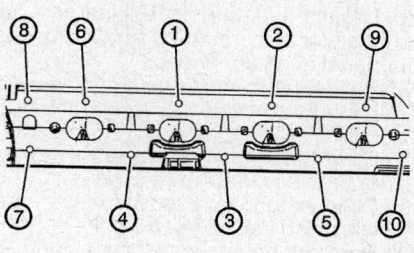

ARM0500000000478

Fig. 2 Exhaust manifold tightening sequence

34. Remove exhaust manifold and exhaust manifold studs.
35. Remove engine mount bracket and fuel rail.
36. Remove thermostat housing and feed pipe, then the alternator.
37. Remove engine.
38. Reverse procedure to install.

INTAKE MANIFOLD
REPLACE

1. Remove supercharger as outlined under "Supercharger, Replace."
2. Remove alternator.
3. Remove cap from charge air cooler reservoir, **Fig. 1**.
4. Raise and support vehicle, then place a suitable drain pan under charge air cooler radiator.
5. Remove inlet hose from auxiliary water pump and drain charged air cooling system.
6. Disconnect charged air cooling system inlet and outlet hoses from charged air coolant pump, then remove the pump.
7. Remove cooling fan assembly.
8. Remove oil level indicator tube bolt, then disconnect electrical connector from intake manifold.
9. Remove coolant hoses from intake manifold.
10. Remove intake manifold nuts and bolts, then the intake manifold.
11. Reverse procedure to install. Intake manifold gasket is reusable, only replace gasket if damage has occurred.

EXHAUST MANIFOLD
REPLACE

1. Remove exhaust manifold heat shield.
2. Remove oxygen sensor.
3. Remove and discard exhaust manifold to cylinder head retaining nuts.
4. Remove exhaust manifold.
5. Reverse procedure to install. Using sequence shown in **Fig. 2**, **torque** new exhaust manifold to cylinder head retaining nuts 10 ft. lbs.

CYLINDER HEAD
REPLACE

1. Drain cooling system.
2. Remove supercharger as outlined under "Supercharger Replace."
3. Remove intake manifold as outlined under "Intake Manifold, Replace."

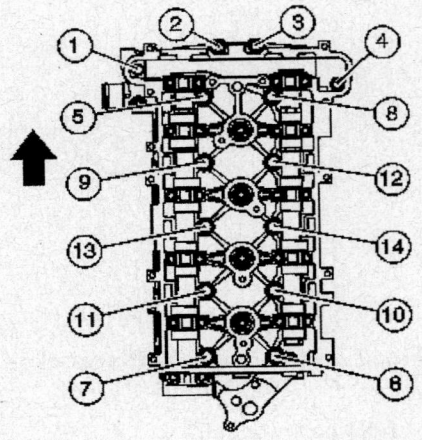

Fig. 3 Cylinder head bolt loosening sequence

ARM0500000000479

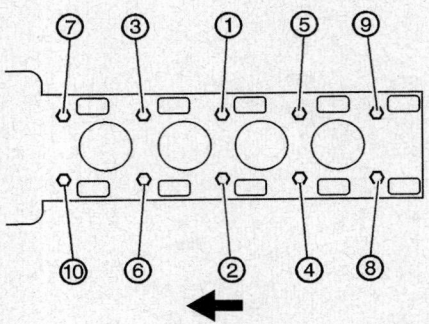

Fig. 4 Rear cylinder head bolt tightening sequence

ARM0500000000480

4. Remove exhaust manifold as outlined under "Exhaust Manifold, Replace."
5. Remove timing chain as outlined under "Timing Chain, Replace."
6. Remove cylinder head bolts in sequence, **Fig. 3**. Discard bolts.
7. Remove cylinder head and gasket.
8. Reverse procedure to install, noting the following:
   a. Clean all gasket surfaces.
   b. Using sequence shown in **Fig. 4**, tighten rear cylinder head bolts in two steps: First step, **torque** bolts 22 ft. lbs.; second step, tighten an additional 155.°
   c. **Torque** front cylinder head bolts to 26 ft. lbs., **Fig. 5**.

VALVE COVER
REPLACE

1. Remove ignition coils.
2. Remove ground strap and stud.
3. Disconnect PCV hose from valve cover.
4. Disconnect fuel feed pipe from fuel rail.
5. Remove camshaft cover bolts, then the camshaft cover.
6. Reverse procedure to install.

HYDRAULIC LASH ADJUSTERS
REPLACE

1. Remove camshafts as outlined under "Camshaft, Replace."
2. Remove camshaft roller followers.
3. Remove hydraulic lash adjusters.
4. Reverse procedure to install.

CRANKSHAFT BALANCER
REPLACE

1. Remove engine drive belt.
2. Hold crankshaft with holding tool No. 38122, or equivalent, then remove crankshaft balancer bolt. Discard bolt.
3. Remove crankshaft balancer.
4. Reverse procedure to install.

FRONT COVER
REPLACE

1. Remove crankcase balancer as outlined under "Crankshaft Balancer, Replace."
2. Raise and support vehicle.
3. Remove drive belt tensioner, then the idler pulley, **Fig. 6**.
4. Remove engine front cover to water pump bolt.
5. Remove remaining engine front cover bolts.
6. Remove engine front cover.
7. Reverse procedure to install.

TIMING CHAIN
REPLACE

1. Remove camshaft cover as outlined under "Valve Cover, Replace."
2. Remove engine front cover as outlined under "Front Cover, Replace."
3. Lower vehicle and remove spark plugs.
4. Place a 24mm open-end wrench on camshaft flats and rotate camshaft in a clockwise direction until diamond shaped hole on intake camshaft sprocket is at the 12 o'clock position (No. 1 piston is approximately at 60° before top dead center), **Fig. 7**.
5. Remove timing chain tensioner, **Fig. 8**.
6. Remove fixed timing chain guide access plug, **Fig. 9**.
7. Remove fixed timing chain guide and upper timing chain guide.
8. Hold exhaust camshaft with a suitable 24mm open end wrench, then remove exhaust camshaft sprocket bolt and sprocket. Discard bolt.
9. Remove timing chain tensioner guide.
10. Hold intake camshaft with a suitable 24mm open end wrench, then remove intake camshaft sprocket bolt and sprocket. Discard bolt.
11. Remove timing chain through the top of cylinder head.
12. Remove crankshaft sprocket.
13. Remove oil nozzle and bolt.
14. Remove balance shaft drive chain tensioner.
15. Remove adjustable balance shaft chain guide, then the small balance shaft drive chain guide.

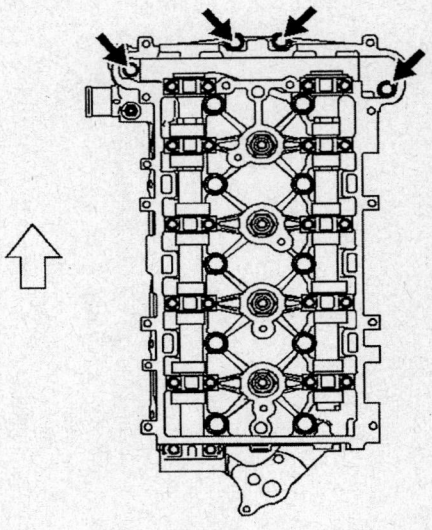

Fig. 5 Front cylinder head bolt location

ARM0500000000481

16. Remove upper balance shaft drive chain guide.
17. Remove all slack from balance shaft drive chain between crankshaft and water pump sprockets.
18. Remove balance shaft drive chain.
19. Reverse procedure to install, noting the following:
   a. Install balance shaft drive chain with colored links aligned with marks on balance shaft drive sprockets and crankshaft sprocket as follows: Align colored link (1) with timing mark on intake side balance shaft sprocket, **Fig. 10**, align first matching colored link (2) with timing mark on crankshaft drive sprocket (approximately 5 o'clock position on the crank sprocket); place chain link (3) on water pump drive sprocket (alignment is not critical); align matching colored link (4) with timing mark on exhaust side balance shaft drive sprocket.
   b. Lower timing chain through the opening in the top of the cylinder head. Ensure chain goes around both sides of the cylinder block bosses (1 & 2), **Fig. 11**.
   c. Install intake camshaft sprocket with the INT diamond at 2 o'clock position, **Fig. 12**.
   d. Route timing chain around crankshaft sprocket with matching colored link aligned with timing mark.
   e. Install exhaust camshaft sprocket with timing chain matching colored link at EXH triangle aligned at the 10 o'clock position, **Fig. 13**.

CAMSHAFT
REPLACE

1. Remove camshaft cover as outlined under "Valve Cover, Replace."
2. Remove upper timing chain guide, **Fig. 6**.

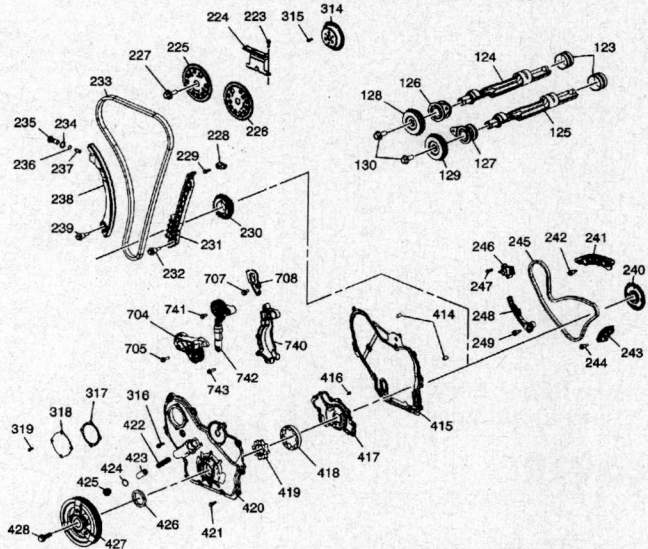

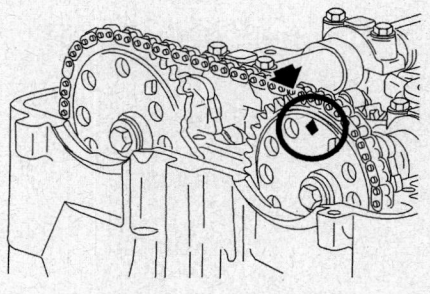

ARM0500000000885

Fig. 7 Intake camshaft sprocket alignment

(123) Balance Shaft Rear Bearing
(124) Exhaust Balance Shaft
(125) Intake Balance Shaft
(126) Exhaust Balance Shaft Bearing Carrier
(127) Intake Balance Shaft Bearing Carrier
(128) Exhaust Balance Shaft Drive Sprocket
(129) Intake Balance Shaft Drive Sprocket
(130) Balance Shaft Drive Sprocket Bolts
(223) Upper Timing Chain Guide Bolt
(224) Upper Timing Chain Guide
(225) Exhaust Camshaft Sprocket
(226) Intake Camshaft Sprocket
(227) Camshaft Sprocket to Camshaft Bolt
(228) Timing Chain Oil Nozzle
(229) Timing Chain Oil Nozzle Bolt
(230) Timing Chain Drive Sprocket
(231) Fixed Timing Chain Guide
(232) Fixed Timing Chain Guide Bolt
(233) Timing Chain
(234) Timing Chain Tensioner Washer
(235) Timing Chain Tensioner Body
(236) Timing Chain Tensioner O-ring Seal
(237) Timing Chain Tensioner Plunger
(238) Adjustable Timing Chain Guide
(239) Adjustable Timing Chain Guide Bolt
(240) Balance Shaft Drive Sprocket
(241) Balance Shaft Drive Chain Guide
(242) Balance Shaft Drive Chain Guide Bolt
(243) Balance Shaft Drive Chain Guide
(244) Balance Shaft Drive Chain Guide Bolt
(245) Balance Shaft Drive Chain
(246) Balance Shaft Drive Chain Tensioner Assembly
(247) Balance Shaft Drive Chain Tensioner Assembly Bolt

(248) Balance Shaft Drive Chain Tensioner Assembly Bolt
(249) Adjustable Balance Shaft Drive Chain Guide
(314) Water Pump Drive Sprocket
(315) Water Pump Drive Sprocket Bolt
(316) Water Pump Bolt
(317) Engine Front Cover Access Plate Gasket
(318) Engine Front Cover Access Plate
(319) Engine Front Cover Access Plate Bolt
(414) Engine Front Cover Alignment Pins
(415) Engine Front Cover Gasket
(416) Oil Pump Cover Bolt
(417) Oil Pump Cover
(418) Oil Pump Outer Gerotor
(419) Oil Pump Inner Gerotor
(420) Engine Front Cover
(421) Engine Front Cover Bolt
(422) Oil Pressure Relief Valve Spring
(423) Oil Pressure Relief Valve Plunger
(424) Oil Pressure Relief Valve O-ring Seal
(425) Oil Pressure Relief Valve Plug
(426) Crankshaft Front Seal
(427) Crankshaft Dampener
(428) Crankshaft Dampener Bolt
(704) Belt Tensioner
(705) Belt Tensioner Bolt
(707) Front Lift Bracket Bolt
(708) Front Lift Bracket
(740) Generator Bracket
(741) Belt Tensioner Bolt
(742) Belt Tensioner
(743) Generator Bracket Bolt

ARM0500000000884

Fig. 6 Front cover & timing chain components

3. Install camshaft sprocket holding tool No. J43655, or equivalent.
4. Remove both intake and exhaust camshaft sprocket bolts and discard.
5. Slide camshaft sprockets forward.
6. Mark camshaft caps to ensure they are installed in their original position.
7. Remove camshaft caps, then the camshaft.
8. Reverse procedure to install.

BALANCE SHAFT
REPLACE

1. Remove hydraulic lash adjusters as outlined under "Hydraulic Lash Adjusters, Replace."
2. Remove timing chain as outlined under "Timing Chain, Replace."
3. Remove balance shaft bearing carrier bolts, **Fig. 6. Do not remove bolt**

holding sprocket.
4. Remove balance shaft assemblies.
5. Reverse procedure to install, noting the following:
   a. It is possible to install intake side balance shaft into exhaust side and exhaust balance shaft into intake side. Ensure correct balance shaft is installed into correct bore.
   b. Install balancer shaft bearing remover and installer tool No. J43650, or equivalent, into balance shaft hole with foot parallel to shaft.
   c. When balancer shaft bearing remover and installer tool No. J43650, or equivalent, is inserted in block turn tool so foot becomes perpendicular to shaft.
   d. Center foot of tool on balance shaft bushing, then insert centering guide into front balance shaft bore and tighten nut with an appropriate wrench.
   e. When tool is properly installed, before removing bushing, end of tool should be 4.6 inches from block face. If tool is less than 4.6 inches from block face, recheck tool alignment.

PISTON & ROD ASSEMBLY

The piston must be installed so that the mark on the top of the piston faces the front of the engine, **Fig. 14.**

MAIN & ROD BEARINGS

Using sequence **Fig. 15,** tighten crankshaft bearing bolts in two steps. First step **torque** to 15 ft. lbs.; second step, tighten an additional 70.° Using sequence **Fig. 16,** **torque** the lower crankcase perimeter bolts to 18 ft. lbs.

CRANKSHAFT SEAL
REPLACE

1. Remove crankshaft balancer as outlined under "Crankshaft Balancer, Replace."

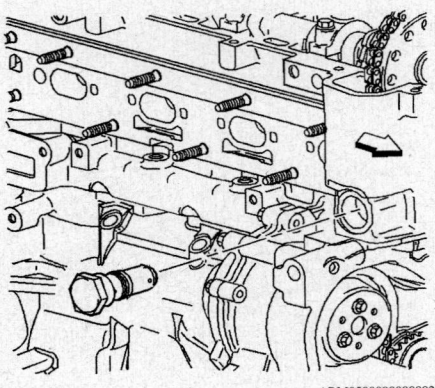

Fig. 8   Timing chain tensioner

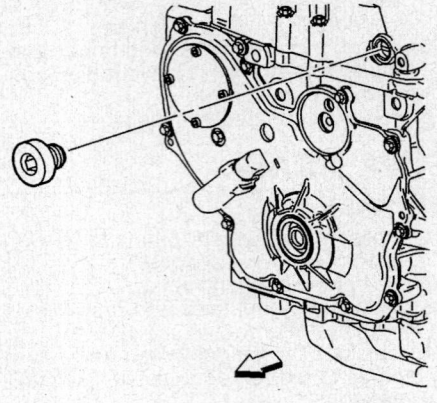

Fig. 9   Timing chain access plug

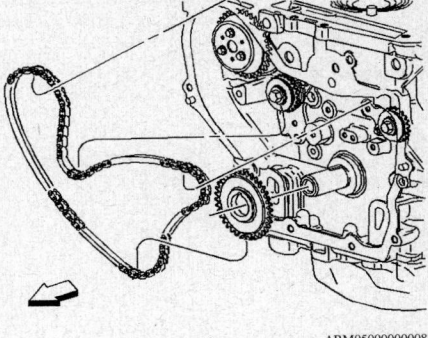

Fig. 10   Balance shaft drive chain installation

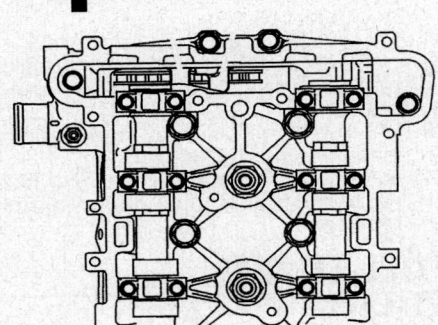

Fig. 11   Cylinder block bosses

2. Remove crankshaft seal from front cover using a suitable flat-bladed tool.
3. Reverse procedure to install.

CRANKSHAFT REAR OIL SEAL
REPLACE
1. Remove transaxle.
2. Remove flywheel.
3. Remove crankshaft rear oil seal from cylinder block with a suitable flat-bladed tool.
4. Reverse procedure to install.

OIL PAN
REPLACE
1. Raise and support vehicle.
2. Drain engine oil and remove engine drive belt as outlined under "Serpentine Drive Belt."
3. Remove intercooler pump bracket bolts and lower A/C compressor bolt from oil pan.
4. Remove oil pan bolts, then the oil pan.
5. Reverse procedure to install, noting the following:
   a. Ensure oil pan and mounting surface on lower crankcase are free of all oil and debris.
   b. Apply a 2mm bead of General Motors part No. 123785251, or equivalent sealant, around perimeter of oil pan and oil suction port opening.

Do not over apply the RTV, more than a 2mm bead is not required.

OIL PUMP
REPLACE
1. Remove drive belt tensioner bolts, then the drive belt tensioner and idler pulley.
2. Remove alternator bracket and lift hook assembly.
3. Remove engine front cover bolts as outlined under "Front Cover, Replace."
4. Remove crankshaft front cover oil seal with a suitable flat-bladed tool.
5. Remove oil pump from front cover.
6. Reverse procedure to install.

OIL PUMP SERVICE
Disassemble
1. Disassemble pressure relief valve.
2. Remove oil pump gerotor cover and bolts.
3. Remove outer gear and inner gear from front cover.
4. Replace front cover and oil pump assembly if it is out of specification or damaged.

Assemble
1. Lubricate all oil pump parts with engine oil.
2. Install inner gear into outer gear.
3. Install gears together into front cover with hub of center gear facing front cover.
4. Install oil pump gerotor cover and bolts.
5. Install pressure relief valve piston and pressure relief valve spring.

SERPENTINE DRIVE BELT
1. Install a suitable tight fitting 15mm open end wrench to drive belt tensioner lug on rear of tensioner.
2. Very slowly push down and towards back of vehicle to slowly compress drive belt tensioner.

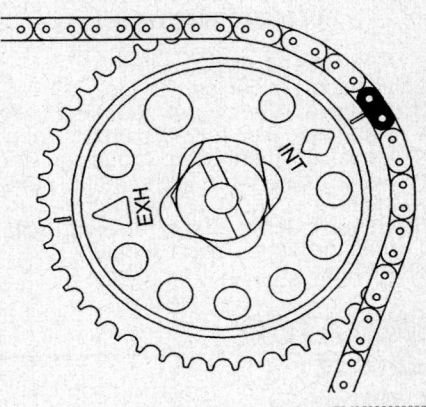

Fig. 12   Intake camshaft sprocket alignment

3. Remove drive belt from drive belt tensioner.
4. Very slowly, allow drive belt tensioner to return to extended position.
5. Remove drive belt from around supercharger and alternator pulleys.
6. Remove right front fender liner.
7. Remove drive belt from under idler pulley and around the air conditioning (A/C) compressor and crankshaft balancer.
8. Remove drive belt through wheelhouse opening.
9. Reverse procedure to install.

THERMOSTAT
REPLACE
1. Drain cooling system.
2. Loosen radiator surge tank outlet hose clamp at thermostat cover, then remove hose.
3. Loosen oil cooler inlet and outlet hose clamps at thermostat cover, then remove hoses.
4. Remove thermostat cover bolts and cover.
5. Remove thermostat and O-ring seal. Discard seal.
6. Reverse procedure to install.

WATER PUMP
REPLACE
1. Remove thermostat as outlined under

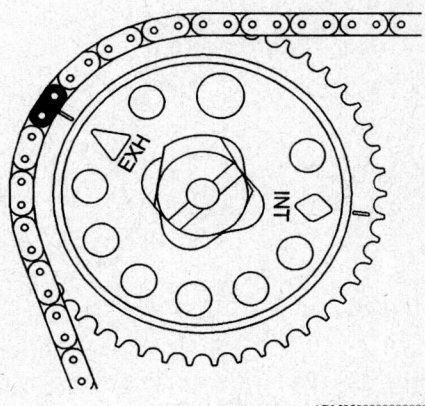

Fig. 13 Exhaust camshaft sprocket alignment

"Thermostat, Replace."
2. Remove oxygen sensor clip.
3. Remove thermostat housing and water feed pipe retaining bolts.
4. Remove thermostat housing and water feed pipe from water pump cover.
5. Remove water pump retaining bolts, then the water pump assembly.
6. Reverse procedure to install.

RADIATOR
REPLACE

1. Drain cooling system.
2. Remove air cleaner outlet resonator.
3. Loosen radiator inlet hose clamp at radiator, then remove hose.
4. Loosen radiator outlet hose clamp at radiator, then remove hose.
5. **On models equipped with VTi or automatic transaxle,** proceed as follows:
   a. Clean upper transmission oil cooler line connection point and remove line from radiator.
   b. Remove left front wheelhouse liner.
   c. Remove left engine splash shield.
6. **On all models,** remove cooling fan assembly from radiator by pushing up on fan shroud to unsnap retainers.
7. Position cooling fan assembly away from radiator and support.
8. Remove air dam push-in retainer, then the air dam.
9. **On models equipped with A/C,** remove condenser bolts, then slide condenser down to disengage upper mounting tabs from radiator. Position condenser away from radiator and support condenser.
10. **On all models,** remove right and left radiator side baffles.
11. Remove right engine splash shield to radiator mount push-in retainer.
12. **On models equipped with manual transaxle,** remove left engine splash shield to radiator mount push-in retainer.
13. **On all models,** remove lower radiator mounts, brackets and bolts.

14. **On models equipped with A/C,** tilt condenser forward in vehicle.
15. **On all models,** tilt cooling fan assembly rearward, then remove radiator assembly from vehicle.
16. Reverse procedure to install.

FUEL PUMP
REPLACE

1. Relieve fuel system pressure as outlined under "Precautions."
2. Raise and support vehicle.
3. Disconnect fuel feed and return lines from fuel filter.
4. Cap or plug fuel tank feed and return pipes to prevent fuel loss or contamination.
5. Disconnect EVAP purge pipe and fuel tank EVAP vapor pipe from EVAP canister. Cap or plug pipes to prevent contamination.
6. Loosen fuel filler hose clamp at fuel tank, then disconnect hose.
7. Disconnect fuel pump module harness electrical connector from vehicle underbody connector.
8. Remove exhaust extension pipe insulators from underbody hangers.
9. Remove muffler insulator from underbody hanger and slowly lower exhaust, then rest exhaust on rear axle beam.
10. Support fuel tank with a suitable jack, then remove left and right fuel tank strap bolts and straps.
11. Slowly lower righthand side of fuel tank. Use care in feeding fuel feed and return pipes, EVAP vapor pipe and fuel pump module electrical harness to clear axle.
12. Once tank is clear of righthand frame rail, remove tank by pulling tank down and toward righthand side of vehicle. For installation reference, note position of fuel tank rear shield before releasing pump module retainer.
13. Release retaining tab on fuel tank retainer used to secure fuel pump module pipes in position on tank.
14. Release fuel pump module electrical harness from retaining slot on tank.
15. Disconnect fuel pump module harness electrical connector from fuel tank pressure sensor.
16. Carefully rotate fuel pump module retaining lock ring using lock ring removal tool No. J39765, or equivalent.
17. Remove fuel pump module retaining lock ring, by sliding ring over module pipes and electrical harness.
18. Slowly raise fuel pump module assembly until fuel level sensor float arm is visible.
19. Ensure fuel level sensor harness connector clears tank opening. **Be aware that when removing fuel pump module assembly from fuel tank, the pump module reservoir bowl is full of fuel. The reservoir must be tipped slightly during removal to avoid bending the fuel level sensor float arm.**
20. Tilt pump module toward rear of fuel

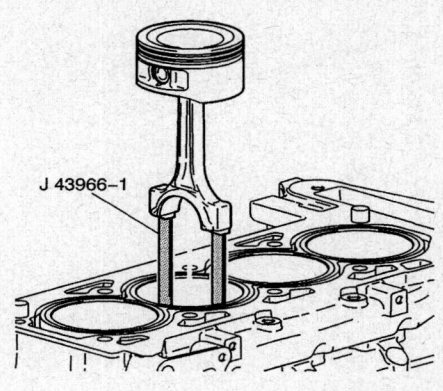

Fig. 14 Piston & connecting rod installation

tank to enable level sensor float arm to clear tank opening.
21. Remove pump module from the tank.
22. Carefully discard fuel in pump module reservoir bowl into a suitable container.
23. Remove and discard fuel pump module-to-fuel tank seal.
24. Reverse procedure to install. **Do not reuse old fuel pump module-to-fuel tank seal.**

FUEL FILTER
REPLACE

1. Relieve fuel system pressure as outlined under "Precautions."
2. Disconnect fuel filter from engine feed fuel pipe, **Fig. 17.**
3. Tilt fuel filter downward and drain off fuel into a suitable container.
4. Disconnect fuel tank feed and return hose fittings from filter.
5. Drain any remaining fuel and discard fuel filter.
6. Reverse procedure to install.

SUPERCHARGER
REPLACE

1. Remove drive belt as outlined under "Serpentine Drive Belt."
2. Remove evaporative emission tube from EVAP valve.
3. Remove the air cleaner outlet duct, then disconnect evaporative emission purge line.
4. Disconnect throttle body control harness connector.
5. Remove throttle body attaching bolts, then the throttle body and gasket from supercharger.
6. Remove Supercharger Inlet Pressure (SCIP) sensor.
7. Disconnect vacuum brake booster hose.
8. Remove intercooler fill neck bracket bolts.
9. Remove vacuum line from supercharger.
10. Remove supercharger and gasket.
11. Reverse procedure to install.

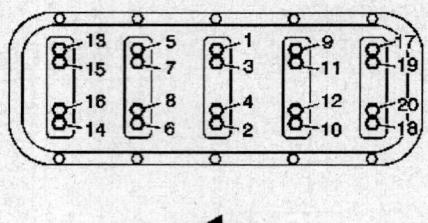

ARM0500000000891

Fig. 15 Crankshaft bearing bolt tightening sequence

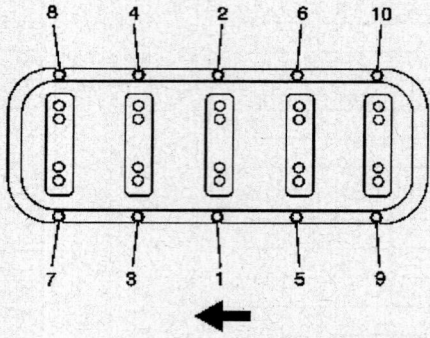

ARM0500000000892

Fig. 16 Lower crankcase bolt tightening sequence

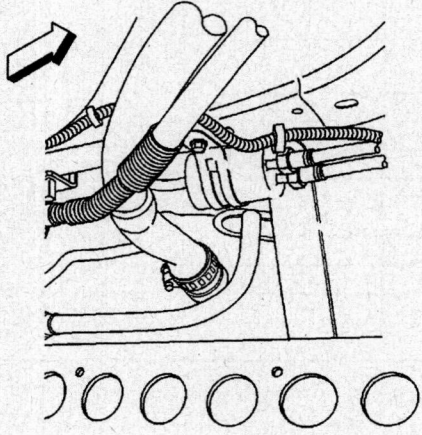

ARM0500000000893

Fig. 17 Fuel filter replacement

TIGHTENING SPECIFICATIONS

Year	Component	Ft. Lbs.
2004–08	A/C Compressor to Block	15
	Alternator Bracket	31
	Alternator To Block	15
	Balance Shaft Adjustable Chain Guide Bolt	11
	Balance Shaft Bearing Carrier To Block	89①
	Balance Shaft Fixed Chain Guide Bolt	11
	Balance Shaft Sprocket Bolt	37
	Cam Sensor	71①
	Camshaft Position Sensor Housing Stud	16
	Camshaft Bearing Cap Bolt	89①
	Camshaft Sprocket Bolt	②
	Camshaft Timing Chain Tensioner	55
	Chain Guide Access Hole Plug	59
	Connecting Rod Bolts	③
	Crankshaft Bearing Lower Crankcase To Block	④
	Crankshaft Position Sensor	71①
	Crankshaft Pulley	⑤
	Cylinder Head	⑥
	Cylinder Head Oil Gallery Plug	26
	Drive Belt Tensioner	24
	Engine Coolant Temperature Sensor	16
	Engine Lift Bracket	18
	Engine Mount Intermediate Bracket	74
	Engine Mount To Intermediate Bracket	37
	Exhaust Manifold To Cylinder Head Nut	106①
	Exhaust Manifold To Cylinder Head Stud	89①
	Exhaust Manifold Pipe Flange To Stud	12
	Flywheel	⑦
	Front Cover To Block	18
	Fuel Feed Line	10
	Fuel Line Bracket	89①
	ICM Cover	71①
	Idler Pulley	16
	Intake Camshaft Rear Cap Bolt	18

TIGHTENING SPECIFICATIONS—Continued

Year	Component	Ft. Lbs.
2004–08	Intake Manifold To Cylinder Head	16
	Knock Sensor Bolt	18
	Lower Crankcase To Block	18
	Oil Cooler	18
	Oil Filter Housing Cover	18
	Oil Gallery Plug	26
	Oil Gallery Plug (Rear)	44
	Oil Pan Drain Plug	18
	Oil Pan To Block	18
	Oil Pressure Sensor	13
	Oil Pump Gerotor Cover Bolt	53①
	Oil Pump Pressure Relief Valve Plug	30
	Oxygen Sensor	31
	Power Steering Pump	18
	Spark Plug	15
	Starter Motor To Block	30
	Supercharger Bolts	18
	Thermostat Housing	89①
	Throttle Body	89①
	Timing Chain Adjustable Chain Guide	89①
	Timing Chain Fixed Guide Bolt	11
	Timing Chain Oil Nozzle Bolt	89①
	Timing Chain Upper Guide Bolt	89①
	Torque Converter Bolts	46
	Transaxle To Engine	55
	Valve (Cam) Cover To Cylinder Head	71①
	Water Pump Balance Shaft Chain Tensioner	89①
	Water Pump Bolts	18
	Water Pump Drain Plug	15
	Water Pump Sprocket Bolt	89①

① — Inch lbs.
② — First step, 63 ft. lbs.; second step, an additional 30.°
③ — First step, 18 ft. lbs.; second step, an additional 100.°
④ — Refer to "Main & Rod Bearings."
⑤ — First step, 74 ft. lbs.; second step, an additional 75.°
⑥ — Refer to "Cylinder Head, Replace" procedure.
⑦ — First step, 39 ft. lbs.; second step, an additional 25.°

NOTE: Refer To "2.2L Engine" In "Alero, Grand Am & 2004-05 Malibu" Chapter For Procedures Not Covered In This Section.

NOTE: On Air Bag Equipped Models, Refer To "Air Bag System Precautions" Located In The Front Of This Manual For System Disarming & Arming Procedures.

NOTE: Refer To "Computer Relearn Procedures" Located In The Front Of This Manual When Battery Power To The Computer Has Been Interrupted.

INDEX

	Page No.
Compression Pressure	5-17
Engine Rebuilding Specifications	29-1
Engine, Replace	5-17

	Page No.
Engine Mount, Replace	5-17
Intake Manifold, Replace	5-17
Precautions	5-17
Air Bag Systems	5-17

	Page No.
Battery Ground Cable	5-17
Fuel System Pressure Relief	5-17
Radiator, Replace	5-17
Tightening Specifications	5-18

PRECAUTIONS

Air Bag Systems

Refer to "Air Bag System Precautions" in the front of this manual for system disarming and arming procedures.

Battery Ground Cable

Prior to service, disconnect battery ground cable and isolate as required.

Fuel System Pressure Relief

1. Disconnect battery ground cable, isolate as required.
2. Install fuel pressure gauge tool No. J34730-1A, or equivalent.
3. Install bleed hose into suitable container, then open valve to bleed system pressure.
4. Disconnect fuel pressure gauge from fuel pressure connection.

COMPRESSION PRESSURE

Refer to "2.2L Engine" in "Alero, Grand Am & 2004-05 Malibu" chapter for procedure.

ENGINE MOUNT
REPLACE

Refer to "2.2L Engine" in "Alero, Grand Am & 2004-05 Malibu" chapter for engine mount replacement procedure.

ENGINE
REPLACE

Refer to "2.2L Engine" in "Alero, Grand Am & 2004-05 Malibu" chapter for engine replacement procedure.

INTAKE MANIFOLD
REPLACE

Refer to "2.2L Engine" in "Alero, Grand Am & 2004-05 Malibu" chapter for intake manifold replacement procedure.

RADIATOR
REPLACE

1. Drain cooling system into suitable container.
2. Remove hood latch assembly.
3. Remove righthand and lefthand headlamp assemblies.
4. Remove radiator upper mount attaching bolts, then the mounts.
5. Raise vehicle using suitable lift.
6. Remove cooling fan mounting bolts, disconnect electrical connectors, then the cooling fan.
7. Remove radiator outlet hose clamp from radiator using tool No. J38185, or equivalent, then the radiator outlet hose.
8. Remove lower transmission oil cooler line, then lower vehicle.
9. Remove hood latch support bracket and forward sensors with harness.
10. Remove upper transmission oil cooler line from radiator.
11. Remove surge tank hose and clamp from radiator.
12. Remove condenser from radiator.
13. Remove radiator assembly.
14. Reverse procedure to install.

TIGHTENING SPECIFICATIONS

Year	Component	Torque, Ft. Lbs.
2004–08	Accelerator & Cruise Control Cable	89②
	Air Cleaner Clamps	44②
	Air Cleaner Outlet Resonator Mounting Bolt	89②
	Alternator	15
	Engine Mount Strut	74①
	Engine To Transmission Bolts	55
	Power Steering Pump	19
	Radiator Drain Cock	18②
	Righthand Engine Mount Bolts	44①
	Righthand Engine Mount To Body Nuts	55
	Torque Converter Bolts	46
	Upper Air Cleaner Cover Screws	27②

① — Plus 90°.
② — Inch lbs.

2.4L Engine

NOTE: On Air Bag Equipped Models, Refer To "Air Bag System Precautions" Located In The Front Of This Manual For System Disarming & Arming Procedures.

NOTE: Refer To "Computer Relearn Procedures" Located In The Front Of This Manual When Battery Power To The Computer Has Been Interrupted.

INDEX

	Page No.
Balance Shaft, Replace	5-21
Camshaft, Replace	5-21
Exhaust	5-21
Intake	5-21
Crankshaft Balancer, Replace	5-20
Crankshaft Rear Oil Seal, Replace	5-22
Crankshaft Seal, Replace	5-22
Cylinder Head, Replace	5-20
Engine Rebuilding Specifications	29-1
Engine, Replace	5-19
Engine Mount, Replace	5-18

	Page No.
Exhaust Manifold, Replace	5-20
Front Cover, Replace	5-20
Fuel Filter, Replace	5-23
Fuel Pump, Replace	5-23
Hydraulic Lash Adjusters, Replace	5-20
Intake Manifold, Replace	5-19
Main & Rod Bearings	5-22
Oil Pan, Replace	5-22
Oil Pump, Replace	5-22
Oil Pump Service	5-22
Assemble	5-22
Disassemble	5-22

	Page No.
Piston & Rod Assembly	5-22
Precautions	5-18
Air Bag Systems	5-18
Battery Ground Cable	5-18
Fuel System Pressure Relief	5-18
Radiator, Replace	5-23
Serpentine Drive Belt	5-23
Thermostat, Replace	5-23
Tightening Specifications	5-24
Timing Chain, Replace	5-20
Valve Cover, Replace	5-20
Water Pump, Replace	5-23

PRECAUTIONS

Air Bag Systems

Refer to "Air Bag System Precautions" in the front of this manual for system disarming and arming procedures.

Battery Ground Cable

Prior to service, disconnect battery ground cable and isolate as required.

Fuel System Pressure Relief

1. Turn ignition OFF and loosen fuel filler cap to relieve fuel tank vapor pressure.
2. Remove cap from fuel pressure service port.
3. Remove engine identification cover nuts and cover.
4. Install fuel pressure gauge tool No. J34730-1A, or equivalent, into fuel pressure service port.
5. Install bleed hose into suitable container, then open valve to bleed system pressure.
6. Disconnect fuel pressure gauge from fuel pressure connection.

ENGINE MOUNT
REPLACE

1. Remove air cleaner assembly.
2. Support engine with a suitable hydraulic floor jack. Place a piece of wood between jack and oil pan.

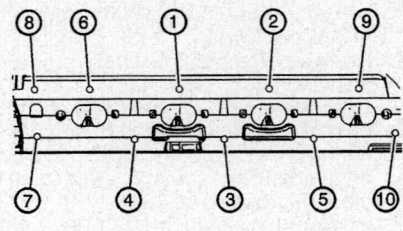

ARM0500000000894

Fig. 1 Exhaust manifold tightening sequence

3. Remove engine mount to bracket bolts.
4. Remove engine mount to side rail nuts.
5. Remove engine mount from engine compartment.
6. Reverse procedure to install.

ENGINE
REPLACE

1. Place front wheels in straight forward position.
2. Remove air outlet duct.
3. Secure cooling module to upper body structure.
4. Relieve fuel system pressure as outlined under "Precautions."
5. Disconnect fuel line from fuel rail.
6. Disconnect EVAP line from EVAP purge solenoid.
7. Remove fuel line clips from engine brackets.
8. Drain cooling system, then secure cooling module to upper body.
9. Remove engine drive belt.
10. Disconnect cooling fan electrical connector.
11. Remove radiator inlet hose from engine, then the radiator outlet hose from water outlet and oil cooler.
12. Remove inlet and outlet heater hoses from thermostat housing.
13. Remove brake booster vacuum hose from intake manifold.
14. Disconnect the following harness connectors:
    a. Throttle Actuator Control (TAC).
    b. Fuel injector harness.
    c. Alternator.
    d. Oil level indicator.
    e. Intake and exhaust camshaft position actuator connectors.
    f. Engine harness ground terminal.
    g. Manifold Absolute Pressure (MAP) sensor.
    h. Crankshaft (CKP) sensor.
    i. Oil pressure sensor.
    j. EVAP purge solenoid.
    k. Ignition coils.
    l. A/C pressure sensor.
15. Recover A/C system refrigerant as outlined in "Air Conditioning" chapter.
16. Remove A/C compressor mounting bolts and set compressor aside.
17. Raise and support vehicle, then drain engine oil.
18. Remove transaxle fluid cooler bracket nut, then the transaxle fluid cooler lines from transaxle.
19. **On models equipped with automat-**

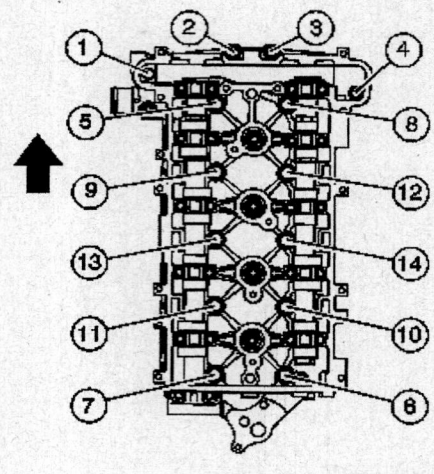

ARM0500000000895

Fig. 2 Cylinder head bolt loosening sequence

ic transaxle, disconnect vehicle speed sensor electrical connector.
20. **On all models,** disconnect starter motor harness connectors and lower vehicle.
21. **On models equipped with automatic transaxle,** disconnect the following electrical connectors:
    a. Engine harness at transaxle.
    b. Disconnect alternator harness connectors.
    c. Disconnect Heated Oxygen (HO2S) connectors.
    d. Disconnect Park/Neutral switch connector.
    e. Transaxle range switch connector.
22. **On models equipped with manual transaxle,** disconnect the following electrical connectors:
    a. Engine harness at back-up lamp switch.
    b. Disconnect Heated Oxygen (HO2S) connectors.
    c. Disconnect vehicle speed sensor connector.
23. **On all models,** remove shift lever and range selector lever cables from transaxle.
24. Disconnect front exhaust pipe from exhaust manifold.
25. Disconnect transmission shift cable from transmission.
26. Lower vehicle.
27. Place blocks of wood to support powertrain assembly between frame and powertrain.
28. Remove engine mount.
29. Remove transaxle mount.
30. Raise and support vehicle.
31. Disconnect stabilizer links from stabilizer bar.
32. Disconnect outer tie rod ends from steering knuckles.
33. Disconnect intermediate shaft from steering gear.
34. Disconnect lower control arms from steering knuckles.
35. Remove drive axles from steering knuckle.
36. Lower vehicle to approximately 3 feet off the ground in order to position lift

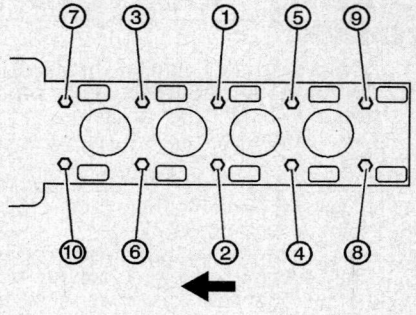

ARM0500000000896

Fig. 3 Rear cylinder head bolt tightening sequence

table under frame.
37. Place wood blocks as necessary between lift table and frame to support assembly.
38. Remove front frame bolts, then partially unscrew rear frame bolts until 1.5 inches (38mm) of bolt shank is exposed.
39. Slowly lower the table to the floor.
40. Attach engine lift hoist to engine lift hooks.
41. Remove starter.
42. **On models equipped with automatic transaxle,** remove torque converter housing access plug, then the torque converter bolts.
43. **On all models,** remove transaxle to engine bolts, then separate engine from transaxle.
44. **On models equipped with manual transaxle,** remove clutch pressure plate and disk.
45. Remove exhaust manifold and exhaust manifold studs.
46. Remove engine mount bracket and fuel rail.
47. Remove engine.
48. Reverse procedure to install.

INTAKE MANIFOLD
REPLACE

1. Relieve fuel system pressure as outlined under "Precautions."
2. Remove engine oil fill cap, then the cover from intake manifold.
3. Remove air cleaner outlet duct.
4. Disconnect the following electrical connectors:
    a. Throttle Actuator Control (TAC).
    b. Fuel injector harness.
    c. Manifold Absolute Pressure (MAP) sensor.
5. Remove brake booster vacuum hose from intake manifold.
6. Remove throttle body attaching bolts, then the throttle body and seal.
7. Disconnect EVAP canister purge tube from intake manifold and EVAP solenoid.
8. Remove oil level indicator tube.
9. Remove fuel rail.
10. Remove intake manifold nuts and bolts, then the intake manifold.
11. Reverse procedure to install. Intake manifold gasket is reusable, only replace gasket if damage has occurred.

EXHAUST MANIFOLD
REPLACE

1. Remove exhaust manifold heat shield.
2. **On models equipped with block heater,** remove block heater.
3. **On all models,** remove oxygen sensor.
4. Remove and discard exhaust manifold to cylinder head retaining nuts.
5. Remove exhaust manifold.
6. Reverse procedure to install. Using sequence shown in **Fig. 1, torque** new exhaust manifold to cylinder head retaining nuts 10 ft. lbs.

CYLINDER HEAD
REPLACE

1. Drain cooling system.
2. Remove intake manifold as outlined under "Intake Manifold, Replace."
3. Remove exhaust manifold as outlined under "Exhaust Manifold, Replace."
4. Remove radiator surge tank air bleed hose and radiator inlet hose from cylinder head.
5. Remove timing chain as outlined under "Timing Chain, Replace."
6. Remove cylinder head bolts in sequence, **Fig. 2.** Discard bolts.
7. Remove cylinder head and gasket.
8. Reverse procedure to install, noting the following:
    a. Clean all gasket surfaces.
    b. Using sequence shown in **Fig. 3,** tighten rear cylinder head bolts in two steps: First step, **torque** bolts 22 ft. lbs.; second step, tighten an additional 155.°
    c. **Torque** front cylinder head bolts to 26 ft. lbs., **Fig. 4.**

VALVE COVER
REPLACE

1. Remove intake manifold cover.
2. Relieve fuel system pressure as outlined under "Precautions."
3. Remove air cleaner outlet duct.
4. Disconnect intake and exhaust camshaft position actuator solenoid valve electrical connectors.
5. Remove ignition coils.
6. Disconnect fuel feed pipe from fuel rail.
7. Remove camshaft cover bolts, then the camshaft cover.
8. Reverse procedure to install.

HYDRAULIC LASH ADJUSTERS
REPLACE

1. Remove camshafts as outlined under "Camshaft, Replace."
2. Remove camshaft roller followers.
3. Remove hydraulic lash adjusters.
4. Reverse procedure to install.

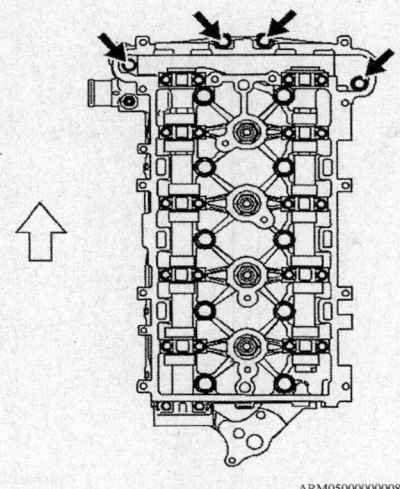

Fig. 4 Front cylinder head bolt location

ARM050000000897

CRANKSHAFT BALANCER
REPLACE

1. Remove engine drive belt.
2. Hold crankshaft with holding tool No. 38122, or equivalent, then remove crankshaft balancer bolt. Discard bolt.
3. Remove crankshaft balancer.
4. Reverse procedure to install.

FRONT COVER
REPLACE

1. Remove crankcase balancer as outlined under "Crankshaft Balancer, Replace."
2. Raise and support vehicle.
3. Remove drive belt tensioner, then the idler pulley, **Fig. 5.**
4. Remove engine front cover to water pump bolt.
5. Remove remaining engine front cover bolts.
6. Remove engine front cover and gasket. Discard gasket.
7. Reverse procedure to install.

TIMING CHAIN
REPLACE

1. Remove No. 1 park plug and rotate engine until No. 1 piston is at TDC of compression stroke.
2. Remove camshaft cover as outlined under "Valve Cover, Replace."
3. Remove engine front cover as outlined under "Front Cover, Replace."
4. Remove upper timing chain guide, then the timing chain tensioner, **Fig. 5.**
5. Place a 24mm open-end wrench on exhaust camshaft and hold camshaft, then remove exhaust camshaft actuator bolt and actuator from camshaft and timing chain.
6. Remove fixed timing chain guide bolts and guide.
7. Place a 24mm wrench on intake camshaft flats, then remove and discard in-

take camshaft actuator bolt, then the actuator and timing chain through top of cylinder head.
8. Remove fixed timing chain guide access plug.
9. Remove timing chain sprocket. If it is not necessary to replace balance shaft timing chain, proceed to step 10. If balance shaft timing chain needs to be replaced, proceed as follows:
    a. Remove balance shaft drive chain tensioner.
    b. Remove adjustable balance shaft chain guide, then the small balance shaft drive chain guide.
    c. Remove upper balance shaft drive chain guide.
    d. Remove all slack from balance shaft drive chain between crankshaft and water pump sprockets.
    e. Remove balance shaft drive chain.
10. Reverse procedure to install, noting the following:
    a. If installing balance shaft drive chain: Align balance shaft drive chain colored links with marks on balance shaft drive sprockets and crankshaft sprocket as follows: Align colored link with timing mark on intake side balance shaft sprocket, **Fig. 6,** align chrome link with timing mark on balance shaft drive sprocket (approximately 6 o'clock position on sprocket); place chain link on water pump drive sprocket (alignment is not critical); align last chrome link with timing mark on exhaust side balance shaft drive sprocket.
    b. Rotate balance shaft drive chain tensioner plunger 90° in its bore and compress plunger, then rotate tensioner back to original 12 O'clock position and insert a paper clip through hole in plunger body and into hole in tensioner plunger.
    c. Install balance shaft drive chain tensioner, then remove paper clip.
    d. Install timing chain crankshaft sprocket and position timing mark at 5 O'clock position.
    e. Timing chain has three colored links (2 pink and 1 blue).
    f. Assemble intake camshaft actuator to timing chain and align timing mark with blue link on chain, then install and hand tighten new actuator retaining bolt.
    g. Lower timing chain through opening in cylinder head and ensure chain goes around both sides of cylinder block bosses, **Fig. 7.**
    h. Route timing chain around crankshaft sprocket and align pink colored chain link to timing mark on sprocket, **Fig. 8.**
    i. Install exhaust camshaft actuator, then install actuator bolt hand tight. Align actuator with last pink colored link on chain, **Fig. 9.**
    j. **Do not rotate either camshaft more than half turn in either direction with crankshaft at TDC. Turning camshaft more than half turn may result in piston to valve contact.**

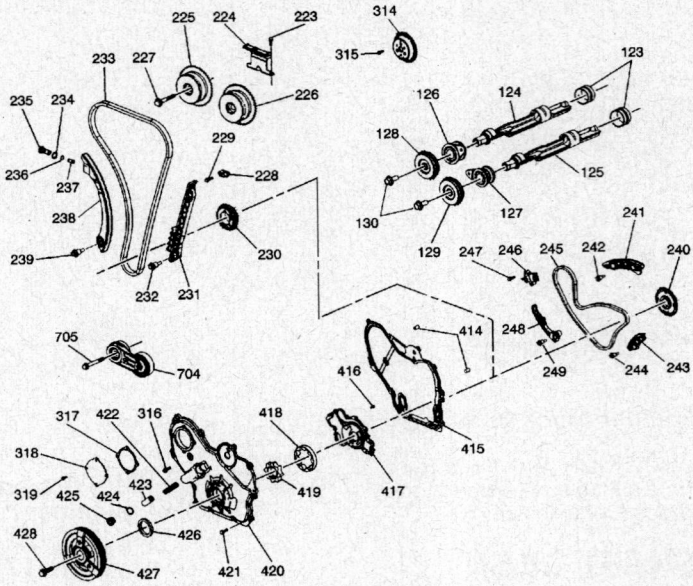

Fig. 5 Front cover & timing chain components

(123) Balance Shaft Rear Bearing
(124) Exhaust Balance Shaft
(125) Intake Balance Shaft
(126) Exhaust Balance Shaft Bearing Carrier
(127) Intake Balance Shaft Bearing Carrier
(128) Exhaust Balance Shaft Drive Sprocket
(129) Intake Balance Shaft Drive Sprocket
(130) Balance Shaft Drive Sprocket Bolts
(223) Upper Timing Chain Guide Bolt
(224) Upper Timing Chain Guide
(225) Exhaust Camshaft Position Actuator
(226) Intake Camshaft Position Actuator
(227) Camshaft Position Actuator Bolt
(228) Timing Chain Oil Nozzle
(229) Timing Chain Oil Nozzle Bolt
(230) Timing Chain Drive Sprocket
(231) Fixed Timing Chain Guide
(232) Fixed Timing Chain Guide Bolt
(233) Timing Chain
(234) Timing Chain Tensioner Washer
(235) Timing Chain Tensioner Body
(236) Timing Chain Tensioner O-ring Seal
(237) Timing Chain Tensioner Plunger
(238) Adjustable Timing Chain Guide
(239) Adjustable Timing Chain Guide Bolt
(240) Balance Shaft Drive Sprocket
(241) Balance Shaft Drive Chain Guide
(242) Balance Shaft Drive Chain Guide Bolt
(243) Balance Shaft Drive Chain Guide

(244) Balance Shaft Drive Chain Guide Bolt
(245) Balance Shaft Drive Chain
(246) Balance Shaft Drive Chain Tensioner Assembly
(247) Balance Shaft Drive Chain Tensioner Assembly Bolt
(248) Adjustable Balance Shaft Drive Chain Guide
(249) Adjustable Balance Shaft Drive Chain Guide Bolt
(314) Water Pump Drive Sprocket
(315) Water Pump Drive Sprocket Bolt
(316) Water Pump Bolt
(317) Engine Front Cover Access Plate Gasket
(318) Engine Front Cover Access Plate
(319) Engine Front Cover Access Plate Bolt
(414) Engine Front Cover Alignment Pins
(415) Engine Front Cover Gasket
(416) Oil Pump Cover Bolt
(417) Oil Pump Cover
(418) Oil Pump Outer Gerotor
(419) Oil Pump Inner Gerotor
(420) Engine Front Cover
(421) Engine Front Cover Bolt
(422) Oil Pressure Relief Valve Spring
(423) Oil Pressure Relief Valve Plunger
(424) Oil Pressure Relief Valve O-ring Seal
(425) Oil Pressure Relief Valve Plug
(426) Crankshaft Front Seal
(427) Crankshaft Damper
(428) Crankshaft Damper Bolt
(704) Belt Tensioner
(705) Belt Tensioner Bolt

ARM0500000000898

k. **If camshaft is 180° out of time,** turn intake camshaft until alignment feature on back of camshaft actuator seats in notch in front of intake camshaft. Turn crankshaft 45° in either direction and turn intake camshaft to appropriate location, then crankshaft back to TDC.
l. Ensure timing marks are aligned.

CAMSHAFT
REPLACE
Exhaust

1. Remove camshaft cover as outlined under "Valve Cover, Replace."
2. Remove upper timing chain guide, **Fig. 5.**

3. Remove timing chain tensioner.
4. Hold exhaust camshaft with a suitable wrench and loosen camshaft actuator bolt. **Do not remove bolt.**
5. Install timing chain tensioner tool No. J44217, or equivalent, into timing chain, **Fig. 10.**
6. Mark intake and exhaust camshaft actuators locations on timing chain.
7. Remove and discard exhaust camshaft actuator attaching bolt, then the actuator from camshaft and timing chain.
8. Mark camshaft caps to ensure they are installed in their original position.
9. Remove camshaft caps, then the camshaft.
10. Reverse procedure to install.

Intake

1. Remove camshaft cover as outlined under "Valve Cover, Replace."
2. Remove upper timing chain guide, **Fig. 5.**
3. Remove timing chain tensioner.
4. Hold intake camshaft with a suitable wrench and loosen camshaft actuator bolt. **Do not remove bolt.**
5. Install timing chain tensioner tool No. J44217, or equivalent, into timing chain, **Fig. 10.**
6. Mark intake and exhaust camshaft actuators locations on timing chain.
7. Remove and discard intake camshaft actuator attaching bolt, then the actuator from camshaft and timing chain.
8. Mark camshaft caps to ensure they are installed in their original position.
9. Remove camshaft caps, then the camshaft.
10. Reverse procedure to install.

BALANCE SHAFT
REPLACE

1. Remove hydraulic lash adjusters as outlined under "Hydraulic Lash Adjusters, Replace."
2. Remove timing chain and balance shaft timing chain as outlined under "Timing Chain, Replace."
3. Remove balance shaft bearing carrier bolts, **Fig. 5. Do not remove bolt holding sprocket.**
4. Remove balance shaft assemblies.
5. Reverse procedure to install, noting the following:
   a. Install balancer shaft bearing remover and installer tool No. J43650, or equivalent, into balance shaft hole with foot parallel to shaft.
   b. When balancer shaft bearing remover and installer tool No. J43650, or equivalent, is inserted in block turn tool so foot becomes perpendicular to shaft.
   c. Center foot of tool on balance shaft bushing, then insert centering guide into front balance shaft bore and tighten nut with an appropriate wrench.

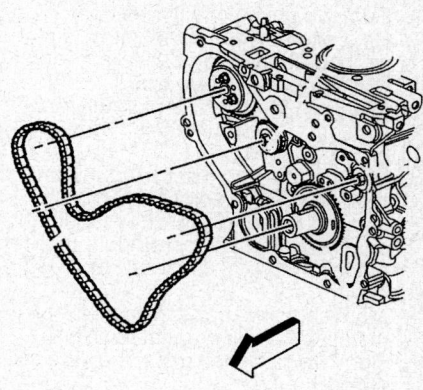

Fig. 6 Balance shaft drive chain installation

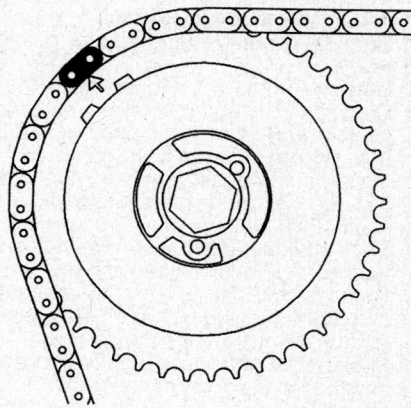

Fig. 9 Exhaust camshaft actuator & chain alignment

d. When tool is properly installed, before removing bushing, end of tool should be 4.6 inches from block face. If tool is less than 4.5 inches from block face, recheck tool alignment.

PISTON & ROD ASSEMBLY

The piston must be installed so that the mark on the top of the piston faces the front of the engine, **Fig. 11.**

MAIN & ROD BEARINGS

Using sequence **Fig. 12,** tighten crankshaft bearing bolts in two steps. First step, **torque** to 15 ft. lbs.; second step, tighten an additional 70.° Using sequence, **Fig. 13, torque** the lower crankcase perimeter bolts to 18 ft. lbs.

CRANKSHAFT SEAL

REPLACE

1. Remove crankshaft balancer as outlined under "Crankshaft Balancer, Replace."

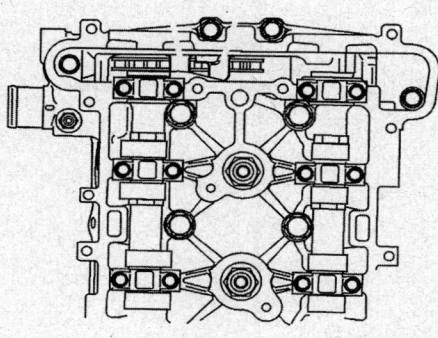

Fig. 7 Cylinder block bosses

2. Remove crankshaft seal from front cover using a suitable flat-bladed tool.
3. Reverse procedure to install.

CRANKSHAFT REAR OIL SEAL

REPLACE

1. Remove transaxle.
2. Remove flywheel.
3. Remove crankshaft rear oil seal from cylinder block using a suitable flat-bladed tool.
4. Reverse procedure to install.

OIL PAN

REPLACE

1. Raise and support vehicle.
2. Drain engine oil and remove engine drive belt as outlined under "Serpentine Drive Belt."
3. Remove lower A/C compressor mounting bolt.
4. Remove oil pan to transaxle bolts.
5. Remove oil pan to crankcase bolts, then the oil pan.
6. Reverse procedure to install, noting the following:
   a. Ensure oil pan and mounting surface on lower crankcase are free of all oil and debris.
   b. Apply a 2mm bead of General Motors part No. 123785251, or equivalent sealant, around perimeter of oil pan and oil suction port opening. **Do not over apply the RTV, more than a 2mm bead is not required.**
   c. Using sequence, **Fig. 14,** torque oil pan bolts to 18 ft. lbs.

OIL PUMP

REPLACE

1. Remove drive belt tensioner bolts, then the drive belt tensioner and idler pulley.
2. Remove alternator bracket and lift hook assembly.
3. Remove engine front cover bolts as outlined under "Front Cover, Replace."
4. Remove crankshaft front cover oil seal with a suitable flat-bladed tool.

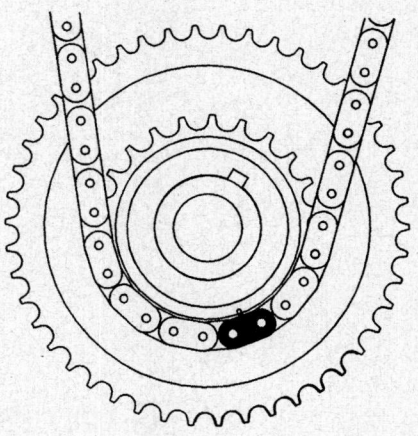

Fig. 8 Timing chain & crankshaft sprocket alignment

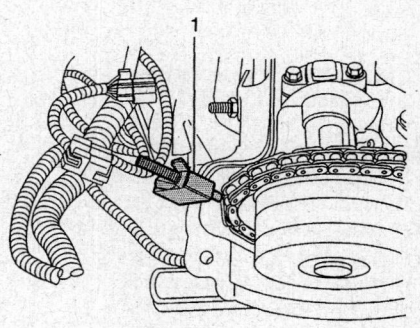

Fig. 10 Timing chain tensioner tool installation

5. Remove oil pump from front cover.
6. Reverse procedure to install.

OIL PUMP SERVICE

Disassemble

1. Disassemble pressure relief valve.
2. Remove oil pump gerotor cover and bolts.
3. Remove outer gear and inner gear from front cover.
4. Replace front cover and oil pump assembly if it is out of specification or damaged.

Assemble

1. Lubricate all oil pump parts with engine oil.
2. Install inner gear into outer gear.
3. Install gears together into front cover with hub of center gear facing front cover.
4. Install oil pump gerotor cover and bolts.
5. Install pressure relief valve piston and pressure relief valve spring.

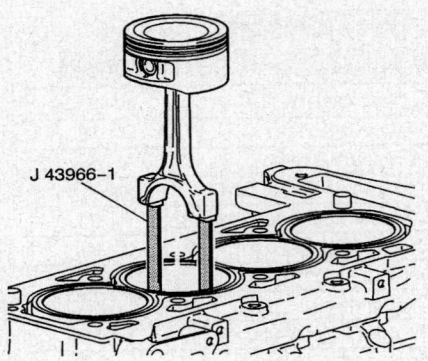

Fig. 11 Piston & connecting rod installation

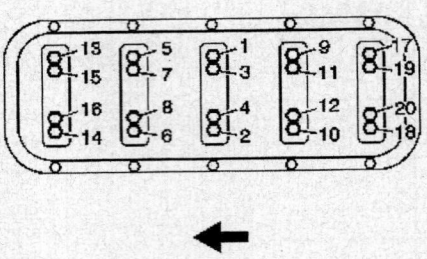

Fig. 12 Crankshaft bearing bolt tightening sequence

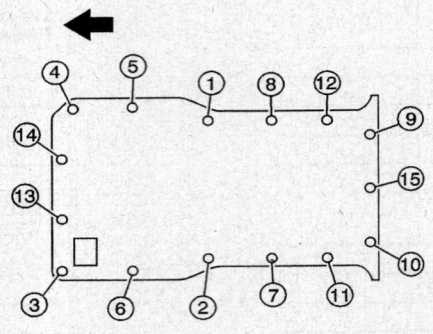

Fig. 14 Oil pan bolt tightening sequence

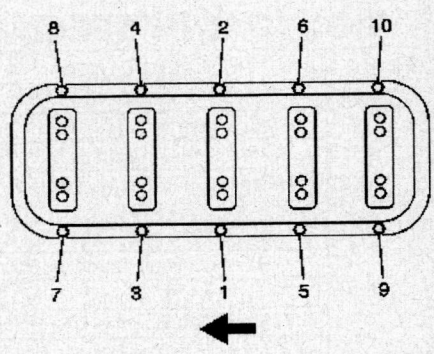

Fig. 13 Lower crankcase bolt tightening sequence

SERPENTINE DRIVE BELT

1. Raise and support vehicle.
2. Remove lefthand front tire and wheel assembly.
3. Remove front fender inner lining and engine splash shield.
4. Install accessory belt tensioner unloader tool No. J44811, or equivalent, to drive belt tensioner.
5. Rotate tensioner counterclockwise to release tension.
6. Remove drive belt from drive belt tensioner.
7. Reverse procedure to install.

THERMOSTAT
REPLACE

1. Drain cooling system.
2. Loosen radiator surge tank outlet hose clamp at thermostat cover, then remove hose.
3. Loosen oil cooler inlet and outlet hose clamps at thermostat cover, then remove hoses.

4. Remove thermostat cover bolts and cover.
5. Remove thermostat and O-ring seal. Discard seal.
6. Reverse procedure to install.

WATER PUMP
REPLACE

1. Remove thermostat as outlined under "Thermostat, Replace."
2. Remove oxygen sensor clip.

3. Remove thermostat housing and water feed pipe retaining bolts.
4. Remove thermostat housing and water feed pipe from water pump cover.
5. Remove water pump retaining bolts, then the water pump assembly.
6. Reverse procedure to install.

RADIATOR
REPLACE

Refer to "2.0L Engine" section for radiator replacement procedure.

FUEL PUMP
REPLACE

Refer to "2.0L Engine" section for fuel pump replacement procedure.

FUEL FILTER
REPLACE

Refer to "2.0L Engine" section for fuel filter replacement procedure.

TIGHTENING SPECIFICATIONS

Year	Component	Ft. Lbs.
2006–08	A/C Compressor To Block	15
	Alternator To Block	17
	Balance Shaft Adjustable Chain Guide	11
	Balance Shaft Bearing Carrier To Block	89①
	Balance Shaft Fixed Chain Guide Bolt	11
	Balance Shaft Sprocket Bolt	37
	Cam Sensor	71①
	Camshaft Bearing Cap Bolt	89①
	Camshaft Position Sensor Housing Stud	16
	Camshaft Position Actuator Solenoid Valve Bolt	89①
	Camshaft Position Sensor	89①
	Camshaft Timing Chain Tensioner	55
	Chain Guide Access Hole Plug	59
	Connecting Rod Bolts	②
	Crankshaft Balancer	③
	Crankshaft Bearing Lower Crankcase To Block	④
	Crankshaft Position Sensor	71①
	Cylinder Head	⑤
	Cylinder Head Oil Gallery Plug	26
	Drive Belt Tensioner	33
	Engine Coolant Temperature Sensor	15
	Engine Lift Bracket	18
	Exhaust Camshaft Position Actuator	⑥
	Exhaust Manifold Pipe Flange To Stud	12
	Exhaust Manifold To Cylinder Head Nut	10
	Exhaust Manifold To Cylinder Head Stud	89①
	Flywheel	⑦
	Front Cover To Block	18
	Fuel Line Bracket	89①
	ICM Cover	71①
	Idler Pulley	16
	Intake Camshaft Position Actuator	⑥
	Intake Camshaft Rear Cap Bolt	18
	Intake Manifold To Cylinder Head	89①
	Knock Sensor Bolt	18
	Lower Crankcase To Block	18
	Oil Cooler	16
	Oil Filter Housing Cover	16
	Oil Gallery Plug	26
	Oil Gallery Plug (Rear)	44
	Oil Pan Drain Plug	18

TIGHTENING SPECIFICATIONS—Continued

Year	Component	Ft. Lbs.
2006–08	Oil Pan To Block	18
	Oil Pressure Switch	16
	Oil Pump Gerotor Cover Bolt	53①
	Oil Pump Pressure Relief Valve Plug	30
	Oxygen Sensor	31
	Power Steering Pump	18
	Spark Plug	15
	Starter Motor To Block	39
	Thermostat Housing	89①
	Throttle Body	89①
	Timing Chain Adjustable Chain Guide	89①
	Timing Chain Fixed Guide Bolt	11
	Timing Chain Oil Nozzle Bolt	89①
	Timing Chain Upper Guide Bolt	89①
	Torque Converter Bolts	46
	Transaxle To Engine	55
	Valve (Cam) Cover To Cylinder Head	89①
	Water Pump Balance Shaft Chain Tensioner	89①
	Water Pump Bolts	18
	Water Pump Sprocket Bolt	89①

① — Inch lbs.

② — First step, 18 ft. lbs.; second step, an additional 100.°

③ — First step, 74 ft. lbs.; second step, an additional 125.°

④ — Refer to "Main & Rod Bearings."

⑤ — Refer to "Cylinder Head, Replace" procedure.

⑥ — First step, 22 ft. lbs.; second step, an additional 100.°

⑦ — First step, 39 ft. lbs.; second step, an additional 25.°

Rear Axle & Suspension

INDEX

	Page No.		Page No.		Page No.
Coil Spring, Replace	5-26	Cavalier & Sunfire	5-25	Drum Brakes	5-25
Cavalier & Sunfire	5-26	Cobalt & G5	5-25	**Rear Axle, Replace**	5-25
Cobalt & G5	5-26	**Hub & Bearing, Replace**	5-25	**Shock Absorber, Replace**	5-25
Control Arm Bushing, Replace	5-26	Cavalier & Sunfire	5-25	Cavalier & Sunfire	5-25
Cavalier & Sunfire	5-26	Cobalt & G5	5-25	Cobalt & G5	5-26
Description	5-25	Disc Brakes	5-25	**Tightening Specifications**	5-27

DESCRIPTION

Cavalier & Sunfire

The rear suspension is a semi-independent type consisting of an axle assembly with trailing arms and twisting cross beam, coil springs and coil-over shock absorbers. A stabilizer bar is available and is attached to the inside of the axle beam and to the lower end of the control arms. A single unit hub and bearing assembly is bolted to each end of the axle assembly. The hub and bearing assembly is a sealed, non-serviceable unit and must be replaced as an assembly.

Cobalt & G5

This vehicle is equipped with a semi-independent twist-beam rear suspension system. The suspension consists of the following components: An axle with integral trailing arms, a V-shaped twisting cross beam, coil springs and standard shock absorbers and an optional integrated stabilizer bar.

REAR AXLE

REPLACE

1. Raise and support vehicle using suitable lift.
2. Remove rear wheels and tires.
3. Remove brake drums. **Do not hammer on drums.**
4. Remove brake fluid pipe retainer bolts from axle, **Fig. 1.**
5. Disconnect brake pipe at brake hose.
6. Disconnect wheel speed sensor harnesses at sensors.
7. Remove wheel speed sensor harness from retainers on axle.
8. Disconnect parking brake cables from equalizers.
9. Remove parking brake cables from axle.
10. Support rear suspension with suitable jack.
11. Remove shock absorber lower mounting bolts, **Fig. 2.**
12. Remove mounting bolts, washers and nuts from axle.
13. Carefully lower rear axle.
14. Remove control arm to underbody bracket bolts, lower rear axle and remove.
15. Remove hub to rear axle mounting

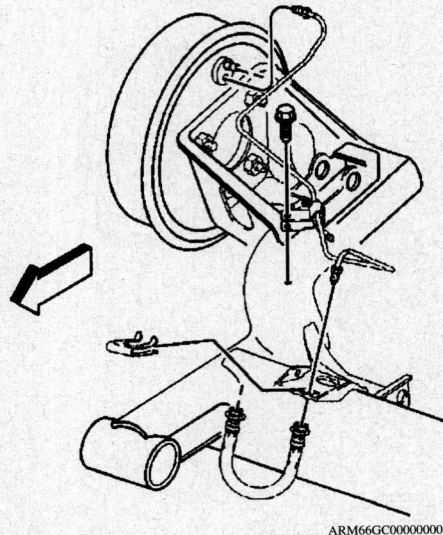

ARM66GC000000002

Fig. 1   Brake pipe retainer removal

bolts, hubs, bearings and backing plates from rear axle, **Fig. 3.**
16. Reverse procedure to install. Bleed brake system.

HUB & BEARING

REPLACE

Cavalier & Sunfire

1. Raise and support vehicle using suitable lift, then remove wheel and tire assembly.
2. Remove brake drum. **Do not hammer brake drum.**
3. Disconnect wheel speed sensor electrical connector.
4. Remove mounting bolts and hub/bearing, **Fig. 4. Upper rear hub mounting bolt may not clear brake shoe when removing hub and bearing. Partially remove hub and bearing prior to removing this bolt.**
5. Reverse procedure to install. **Do not drop hub/bearing assembly.**

Cobalt & G5

DISC BRAKES

1. Raise and support vehicle, then the tire

and wheel assembly.
2. Without disconnecting the hydraulic brake flex hose, remove and support rear brake caliper and bracket as an assembly.
3. Mark position of brake rotor to wheel studs, then remove brake rotor.
4. Disconnect electrical connector from wheel speed sensor.
5. Remove wheel bearing/hub assembly mounting nuts.
6. Remove wheel bearing/hub assembly and disc brake backing plate from rear axle assembly.
7. Reverse procedure to install.

DRUM BRAKES

1. Raise and support vehicle.
2. Remove tire and wheel assembly.
3. Remove brake drum.
4. Remove plug from drum brake actuator access hole in backing plate, **Fig. 5.**
5. Install a support for brake backing plate through access hole.
6. Disconnect electrical connector from wheel speed sensor.
7. Remove wheel bearing/hub assembly mounting nuts, then the wheel bearing/hub assembly from rear axle and brake backing plate.
8. Reverse procedure to install.

SHOCK ABSORBER

REPLACE

Cavalier & Sunfire

1. Position rear compartment carpet aside to access shock absorber upper mounting nut, **Fig. 6.**
2. Remove shock absorber upper mounting nut.
3. Raise and support vehicle, then remove tire and wheel assembly.
4. Place a jackstand under rear axle to maintain tension on shock absorber.
5. Remove shock absorber upper mounting bolts, then lower jackstand to relieve tension on shock absorber.
6. Remove shock absorber lower mounting bolt, then the shock absorber from vehicle.
7. Reverse procedure to install.

ARM66GC000000003

Fig. 2 Lower shock absorber bolt removal

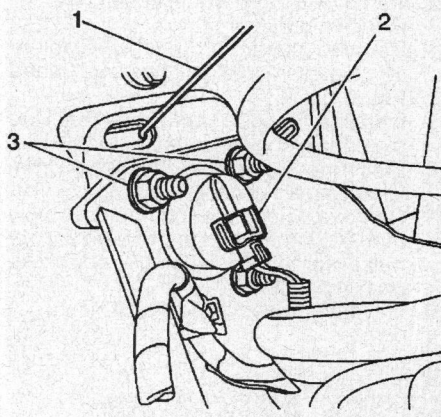

1- SUPPORT
2- CONNECTOR
3- MOUNTING NUTS

ARM0500000000908

Fig. 5 Backing plate support installation. Cobalt & G5

Cobalt & G5

1. Raise and support vehicle, then remove tire and wheel assembly.
2. Support rear axle with a suitable jack stand.
3. Remove upper and lower shock absorber mounting bolts, then the shock absorber.
4. Reverse procedure to install.

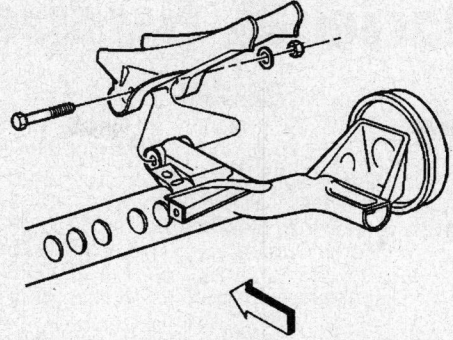

ARM66GC000000004

Fig. 3 Rear axle assembly removal

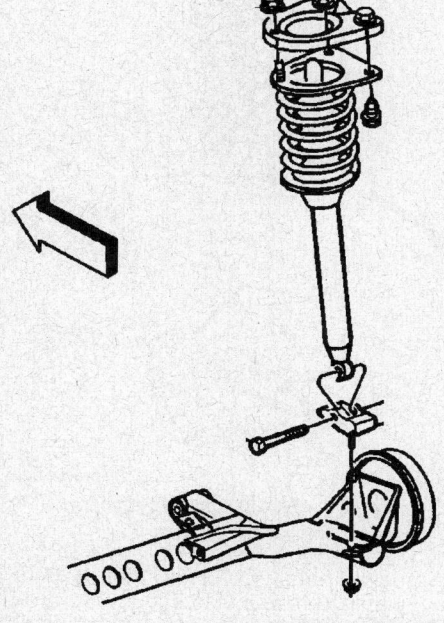

ARM66GC000000006

Fig. 6 Shock absorber removal. Cavalier & Sunfire

COIL SPRING
REPLACE

Cavalier & Sunfire

1. Remove shock absorber as outlined under "Shock Absorber, Replace."
2. Install shock absorber assembly into spring compressor tool No. J45400, or equivalent.
3. Turn spring compressor forcing screw until coil spring is compressed.
4. Remove shock absorber shaft nut from shock mount.
5. Remove shock bumper and shield from shock absorber.
6. Loosen compressor forcing screw until upper strut mount and coil spring can be removed.

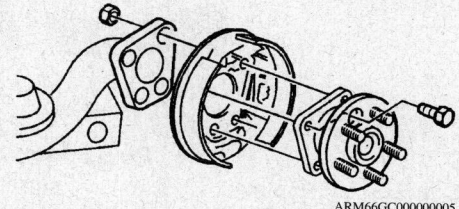

ARM66GC000000005

Fig. 4 Hub & bearing removal. Cavalier & Sunfire

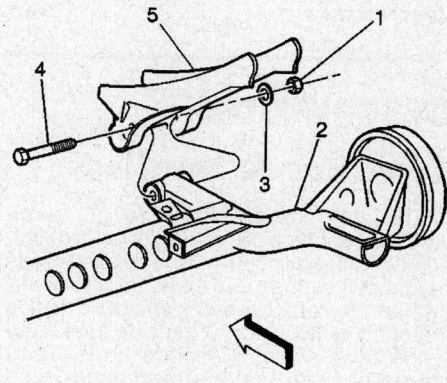

1- NUT
2- AXLE
3- WASHER
4- BOLT
5- CONTROL ARM

ARM0500000000921

Fig. 7 Control arm. Cavalier & Sunfire

7. Remove upper strut mount and coil spring.
8. Reverse procedure to install.

Cobalt & G5

1. Raise and support vehicle.
2. Support rear axle with suitable jack stands near each shock absorber.
3. Remove U-clips from rear axle brake hose brackets.
4. Remove lower shock bolts.
5. Slowly lower rear axle to remove tension from springs.
6. Remove spring.
7. Remove upper spring seat/jounce bumper from spring.
8. Reverse procedure to install.

CONTROL ARM BUSHING
REPLACE

Cavalier & Sunfire

Remove and install one control arm bushing at a time.
1. Raise and support vehicle, then remove tire and wheel assemblies.
2. Disconnect brake hoses from axle.
3. Remove wheel speed sensor harness from retainers on axle.

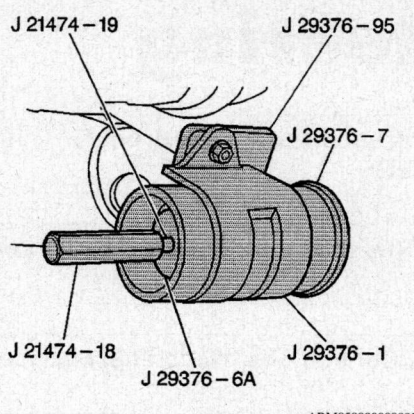

Fig. 8 Control arm bushing replacement. Cavalier & Sunfire

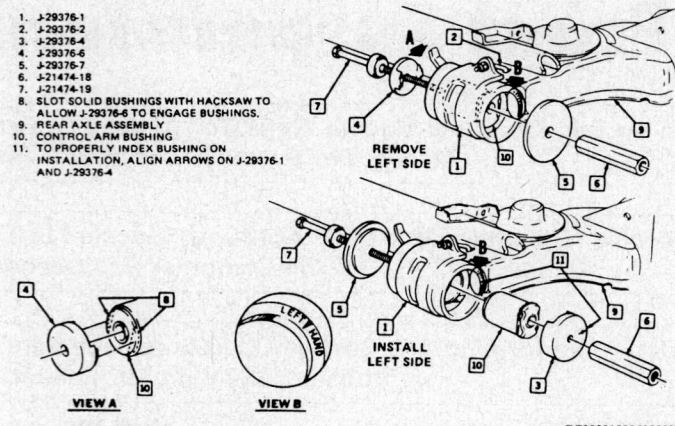

1. J-29376-1
2. J-29376-2
3. J-29376-4
4. J-29376-6
5. J-29376-7
6. J-21474-18
7. J-21474-19
8. SLOT SOLID BUSHINGS WITH HACKSAW TO ALLOW J-29376-6 TO ENGAGE BUSHINGS.
9. REAR AXLE ASSEMBLY
10. CONTROL ARM BUSHING
11. TO PROPERLY INDEX BUSHING ON INSTALLATION, ALIGN ARROWS ON J-29376-1 AND J-29376-4

REMOVE LEFT SIDE

INSTALL LEFT SIDE

VIEW A   VIEW B

GC2039100069000X

Fig. 9 Control arm bushing replacement. Cavalier & Sunfire

4. Remove bolts, washers and nuts from control arm, **Fig. 7.**
5. Rotate control arm downward to gain access to bushings.
6. Install rear control arm bushing adapter tool No. J29376-95, or equivalent, on rear control arm, **Fig. 8.**
7. Install coupling from rear control arm bushing service set J29376-A, or equivalent, on rear control arm.
8. Assemble removal tools J21474-19 and J21474-18 on to control arm, **Fig. 8.**
9. Tighten tool No. J21474-19 until bushing is removed from control arm.
10. Reverse procedure to install, noting the following:
   a. Arrow on installer must align with arrow on receiver, **Fig. 9.**
   b. Apply high pressure lubricant No. J23444-A, or equivalent, as required.
   c. When bushing reaches its proper position end flange will sit flush against control arm face.
   d. Ensure bushing washer and nut are installed on outboard side.
   e. **Control arm mounting bolt must be tightened after vehicle is lowered to floor and is in its standing height position.**

TIGHTENING SPECIFICATIONS

Year	Component	Torque/Ft. Lbs.
CAVALIER & SUNFIRE		
2004–05	Brake Pipe Retainer Bolts To Rear Axle	50①
	Brake Pipe To Bracket Hose	20
	Control Arm Nuts	52
	Hub & Bearing Axle Bolts	44
	Rear Axle Mounting Bolts	88
	Shock Absorber Lower Mounting Bolt	52
	Shock Absorber Upper Mounting Nut	18
	Wheel Lug Nuts	100
COBALT & G5		
2005–08	Bracket To Body Bolts	②
	Brake Hose Fittings	14
	Bushing Through Bolts	③
	Shock Bolt (Lower)	81
	Shock Bolt (Upper)	66
	Wheel Bearing/Hub Assembly Mounting Nuts	④
	Wheel Lug Nuts	100

① — Inch lbs.
② — First step, 66 ft. lbs.; second step, tighten an additional 45°.
③ — First step, 66 ft. lbs.; second step, tighten an additional 60°.
④ — First step, 33 ft. lbs.; second step, tighten an additional 30°.

Front Suspension & Steering

NOTE: On Air Bag Equipped Models, Refer To "Air Bag System Precautions" Located In The Front Of This Manual For System Disarming & Arming Procedures.

NOTE: Refer To "Computer Relearn Procedures" Located In The Front Of This Manual When Battery Power To The Computer Has Been Interrupted.

NOTE: Prior To Performing Any Service Operations Listed In This Section, Consult The "Technical Service Bulletins" Section For Related Information.

INDEX

	Page No.		Page No.		Page No.
Ball Joint, Replace	5-28	Manual Transaxle	5-30	Steering Knuckle, Replace	5-29
Ball Joint Inspection	5-28	Cobalt & G5	5-31	Strut, Replace	5-28
Control Arm, Replace	5-29	Power Steering Pump, Replace	5-31	Cavalier & Sunfire	5-28
Cavalier & Sunfire	5-29	Precautions	5-28	Cobalt & G5	5-28
Cobalt & G5	5-29	Air Bag Systems	5-28	Strut Service	5-29
Description	5-28	Battery Ground Cable	5-28	Tie Rod End, Replace	5-30
Power Steering	21-1	Stabilizer Bar, Replace	5-30	Inner	5-30
Power Steering Gear, Replace	5-30	Cavalier & Sunfire	5-30	Outer	5-30
Cavalier & Sunfire	5-30	Cobalt & G5	5-30	Tightening Specifications	5-32
Automatic Transaxle	5-30	Steering Column	20-1	Wheel Bearing, Replace	5-28

PRECAUTIONS

Air Bag Systems

Refer to "Air Bag System Precautions" in the front of this manual for system disarming and arming procedures.

Battery Ground Cable

Prior to service, disconnect battery ground cable and isolate as required.

DESCRIPTION

The front suspension on these models is a combination strut and spring design. The control arms pivot from the crossmember, **Fig. 1.** The upper end of the strut is isolated by a rubber mount incorporating a non-serviceable bearing for wheel turning. The tie rods connect to the steering arm on the strut, below the spring seat. The lower end of the steering knuckle pivots on a ball stud which is retained to the lower control arm by rivets and is secured to the steering knuckle with a nut and cotter pin. The sealed wheel bearings are integral with the hub and are serviced as an assembly.

WHEEL BEARING

REPLACE

1. Raise and support vehicle using suitable lift.
2. Remove tire and wheel assemblies.
3. Remove drive axle nut, **Fig. 2.**
4. Remove brake caliper and rotor assembly.

5. Remove hub and bearing assembly, **Figs. 3 and 4.**
6. Reverse procedure to install.

BALL JOINT INSPECTION

1. Raise and support vehicle so suspension is allowed to hang free.
2. Grasp wheel and tire assembly at top and bottom, then rock top of wheel and tire assembly inward and outward.
3. While rocking wheel and tire assembly, observe movement between steering knuckle and control arm. If any horizontal movement is present, replace ball joint.
4. If ball joint is disconnected from steering knuckle, use hand to try to twist ball joint in its socket. If ball joint can be twisted in its socket, replace ball joint.

BALL JOINT

REPLACE

1. Remove control arm as outlined under "Control Arm, Replace."
2. Secure control arm in a suitable vise.
3. Drill out three rivets retaining ball joint to lower control arm. Install a 1/8 inch bit in order to make a pilot hole through rivets. Complete drilling rivets using suitable 1/2 drill bit, **Fig. 5.**
4. Remove ball joint from control arm, **Fig. 5.**
5. Reverse procedure to install.

STRUT

REPLACE

Cavalier & Sunfire

1. Remove strut assembly attaching nuts and bolts to body, **Fig. 6.**
2. Raise and support vehicle using suitable lift, install suitable jackstand under crossmember, then lower vehicle for weight to rest slightly on jackstand.
3. Remove tire and wheel assembly.
4. Remove brake line bracket.
5. Scribe strut flange using suitable sharp tool.
6. Remove strut assembly to steering knuckle attaching nuts and bolts, **Fig. 7.**
7. Remove strut assembly.
8. Reverse procedure to install. Inspect alignment.

Cobalt & G5

1. Remove strut assembly upper mounting nuts.
2. Raise and support vehicle, then remove tire and wheel assembly.
3. Remove stabilizer shaft link to strut assembly retaining nut, then separate shaft link from strut.
4. Remove lower strut to steering knuckle attaching nuts and bolts.
5. Remove strut from vehicle.
6. Reverse procedure to install. Adjust front wheel alignment as outlined in "Wheel Alignment" section.

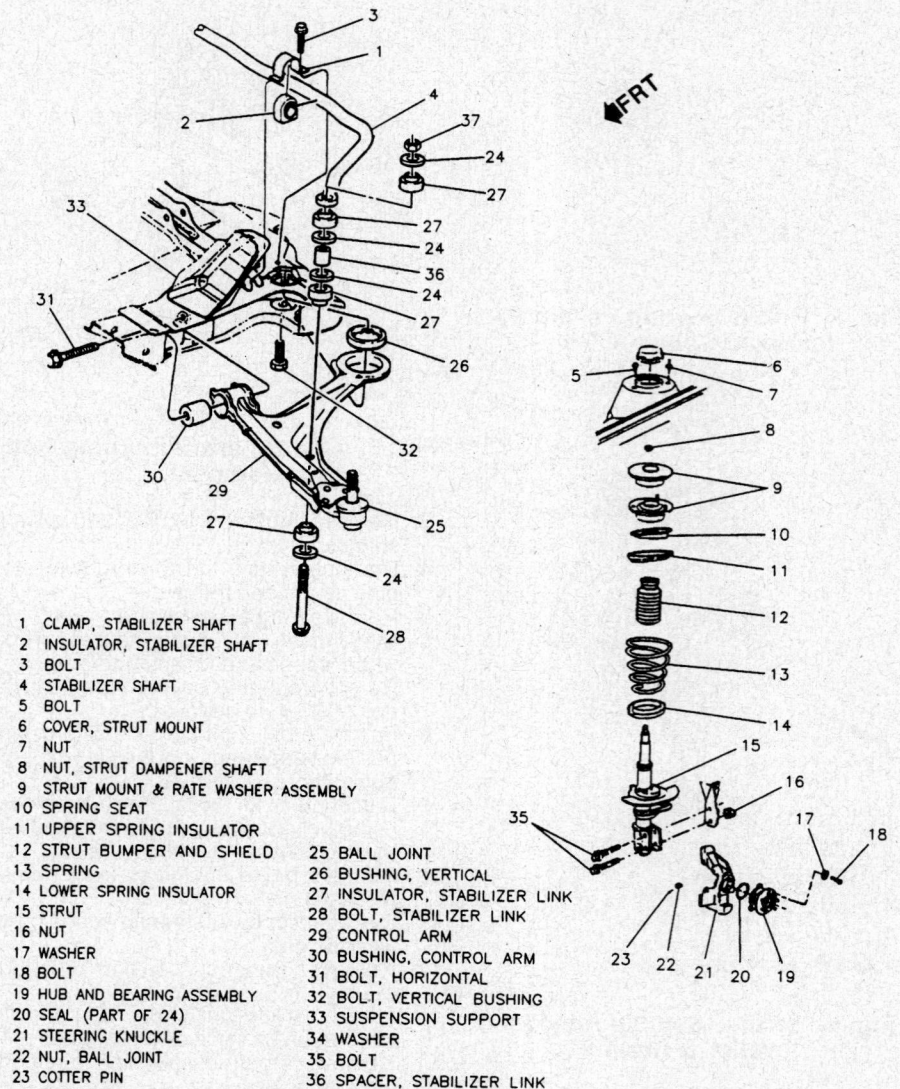

1 CLAMP, STABILIZER SHAFT
2 INSULATOR, STABILIZER SHAFT
3 BOLT
4 STABILIZER SHAFT
5 BOLT
6 COVER, STRUT MOUNT
7 NUT
8 NUT, STRUT DAMPENER SHAFT
9 STRUT MOUNT & RATE WASHER ASSEMBLY
10 SPRING SEAT
11 UPPER SPRING INSULATOR
12 STRUT BUMPER AND SHIELD
13 SPRING
14 LOWER SPRING INSULATOR
15 STRUT
16 NUT
17 WASHER
18 BOLT
19 HUB AND BEARING ASSEMBLY
20 SEAL (PART OF 24)
21 STEERING KNUCKLE
22 NUT, BALL JOINT
23 COTTER PIN
24 WASHER

25 BALL JOINT
26 BUSHING, VERTICAL
27 INSULATOR, STABILIZER LINK
28 BOLT, STABILIZER LINK
29 CONTROL ARM
30 BUSHING, CONTROL ARM
31 BOLT, HORIZONTAL
32 BOLT, VERTICAL BUSHING
33 SUSPENSION SUPPORT
34 WASHER
35 BOLT
36 SPACER, STABILIZER LINK
37 NUT, STABILIZER LINK

GC2029600214000A

Fig. 1   Exploded view of front suspension

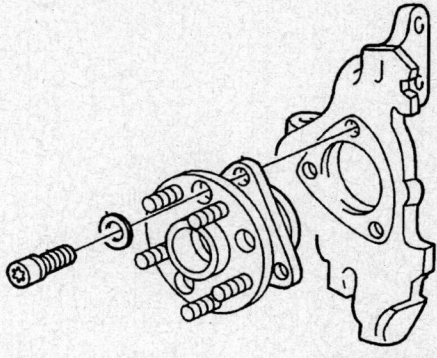

ARM66GC000000007

Fig. 2   Drive axle nut removal

front suspension support brace bolts, then the brace, **Fig. 9.**
6. Remove ball joint from steering knuckle as outlined in "Ball Joint, Replace."
7. Remove wiring harness.
8. Remove lower control arm mounting bolts.
9. Remove lower control arm from suspension crossmember, **Fig. 10.**
10. Reverse procedure to install.

Cobalt & G5

1. Raise and support vehicle, then remove tire and wheel assembly.
2. Remove ball stud to steering knuckle pinch bolt, then separate ball stud from steering knuckle.
3. Remove control arm to rear frame bolt.
4. Remove remaining control arm to frame bolts, then the control arm from vehicle.
5. Reverse procedure to install, tighten ball joint to steering knuckle nut in four steps as follows:
   a. First step, **torque** nut to 37 ft. lbs.
   b. Second step, loosen nut ¾ turn.
   c. Third step, **torque** nut to 37 ft. lbs.
   d. Fourth step, tighten nut an additional 30°.

STEERING KNUCKLE
REPLACE

1. Raise and support vehicle using suitable lift.
2. Remove tire and wheel assemblies.
3. Separate outer tie rod end from steering knuckle as outlined under "Tie Rod End, Replace."
4. Disconnect ABS wiring harness connector.
5. Remove hub and bearing assembly as outlined in "Wheel Bearing, Replace."
6. Remove steering knuckle to strut bolts and nuts, **Figs. 11 and 12.**
7. Remove lower ball joint from steering knuckle.
8. Remove steering knuckle assembly.
9. Reverse procedure to install.

STRUT SERVICE

1. Remove strut assembly from vehicle as outlined under "Strut, Replace."
2. Install strut assembly into spring compressor tool No. J45400, or equivalent.
3. Turn spring compressor forcing screw until coil spring is compressed.
4. Loosen compressor forcing screw until upper strut mount and coil spring can be removed.
5. Hold strut shaft with a suitable 45 Torx socket, then remove upper strut mount nut with a suitable socket.
6. Remove upper strut mount and coil spring.

7. Reverse procedure to assemble.

CONTROL ARM
REPLACE
Cavalier & Sunfire

1. Raise and support vehicle using suitable lift.
2. Remove tire and wheel assemblies.
3. Remove stabilizer shaft link bolt, insulator and spacer.
4. On righthand lower control arm, remove engine mount strut bolts, then the engine mount, **Fig. 8.**
5. On lefthand lower control arm, remove

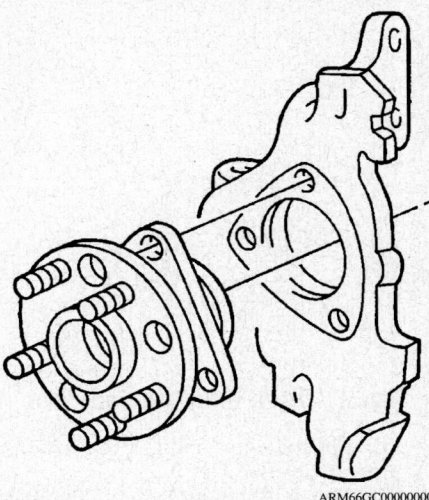

Fig. 3 Hub & bearing assembly removal. Cavalier & Sunfire

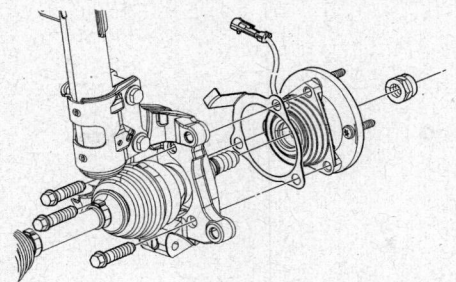

ARM0500000000923

Fig. 4 Hub & bearing assembly removal. Cobalt & G5

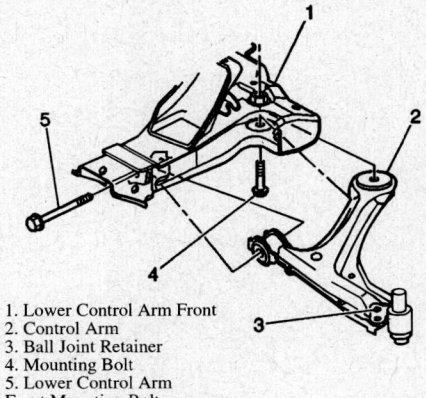

1. Lower Control Arm Front
2. Control Arm
3. Ball Joint Retainer
4. Mounting Bolt
5. Lower Control Arm Front Mounting Bolt

GC2020100293000X

Fig. 5 Control arm mounting bolt removal

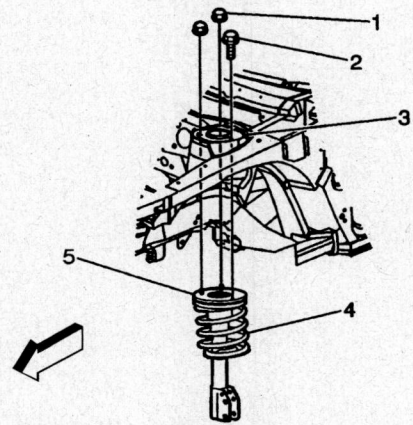

1. Attaching Nuts
2. Attaching Bolts
3. Body
4. Strut Spring
5. Strut Assembly

GC2020100297000X

Fig. 6 Strut assembly removal. Cavalier & Sunfire

STABILIZER BAR

REPLACE

Cavalier & Sunfire

1. Raise and support vehicle using suitable lift.
2. Remove front tire and wheel assemblies.
3. Reposition intermediate steering shaft seal in order to gain access to lower pinch bolt, then remove lower pinch bolt.
4. Remove stabilizer link nut from stabilizer link bolt, then the stabilizer link bolt, insulator and spacer.
5. Support front suspension crossmember using suitable jack stand.
6. Remove suspension crossmember attaching bolts, then lower crossmember six inches using support jack stands.
7. Remove stabilizer shaft insulator brackets and retaining bolts.
8. Remove stabilizer shaft assembly.
9. Reverse procedure to install.

Cobalt & G5

1. Raise and support vehicle, then remove tire and wheel assemblies.
2. Remove rear transaxle mount.
3. **On models equipped with soft or sport suspensions,** remove steering gear as outlined under "Power Steering Gear, Replace."
4. **On all models,** remove lower stabilizer shaft link retaining nuts.
5. Remove front stabilizer shaft clamps, then the shaft insulators.
6. Remove stabilizer shaft from vehicle.
7. Reverse procedure to install.

TIE ROD END

REPLACE

Inner

Refer to "Power Steering" chapter for inner tie rod replacement procedure.

Outer

1. Raise and support vehicle using suitable lift.
2. Remove tire and wheel assemblies.
3. Remove attaching nut from outer tie rod ball stud, loosen jam nut.
4. Remove outer tie rod ball stud from steering knuckle using ball joint seperator tool No. J24319-B, or equivalent.
5. Remove tie rod end from shaft, then inspect inner tie rod shaft for bending or damaged threads.
6. Reverse procedure to install.

POWER STEERING GEAR

REPLACE

Cavalier & Sunfire

AUTOMATIC TRANSAXLE

1. Raise and support vehicle.
2. Remove front tires and wheels.

3. Remove righthand and lefthand splash shields.
4. Remove engine strut from lower engine mount and frame.
5. Remove front exhaust pipe.
6. Disconnect ABS wiring harness from wheel speed sensor and body.
7. Remove steering column lower pinch bolt at steering gear.
8. Separate ball joint from knuckle using ball joint separator tool No. J43828, or equivalent.
9. Disconnect tie rods from knuckles using universal steering linkage puller tool No. J24319-01, or equivalent.
10. Remove brake fluid lines from frame retainers.
11. Disconnect power steering hoses from steering gear.
12. Remove front suspension support brace.
13. Lower vehicle until front suspension support brace rests on jack stands.
14. Remove front suspension support mounting bolts.
15. Raise vehicle up from front suspension support.
16. Remove steering gear to suspension support mounting bolts and gear.
17. Reverse procedure to install.

MANUAL TRANSAXLE

1. Raise and support vehicle.
2. Remove front tires and wheels.
3. Remove power steering hoses from steering gear.
4. Disconnect tie rods from knuckles using universal steering linkage puller tool No. J24319-01, or equivalent.
5. Remove brake fluid lines from frame retainers.
6. Remove steering column lower pinch bolt at steering gear.
7. Support front suspension support with suitable jack stand.
8. Remove front suspension crossmember mounting bolts.
9. Lower suspension enough to access steering gear mounting bolts.
10. Remove mounting bolts and steering gear.
11. Reverse procedure to install.

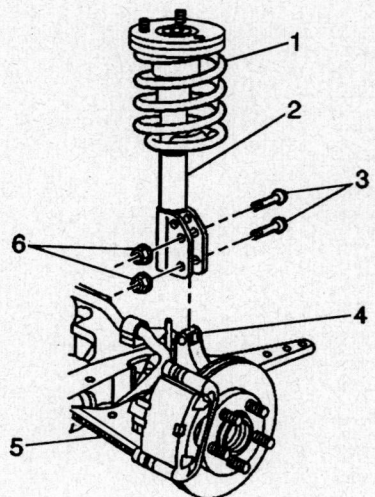

1. Strut Assebly
2. Strut Shaft
3. Strut Attaching Bolts
4. Steering Knuckle
5. Brake Line
6. Strut Attaching Nuts

GC2020100298000X

Fig. 7 Strut to steering knuckle removal. Cavalier & Sunfire

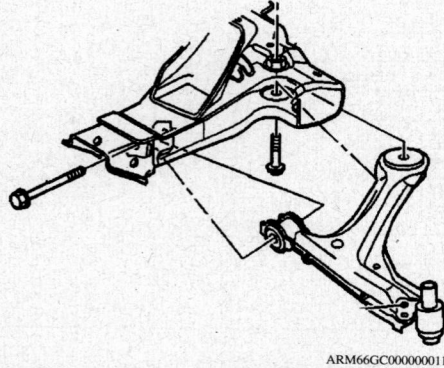

ARM66GC000000011

Fig. 10 Lower control arm to front suspension crossmember. Cavalier & Sunfire

Cobalt & G5

1. Ensure front wheels are in straight ahead position, then secure steering wheel to prevent rotation.
2. Raise and support vehicle, then re-

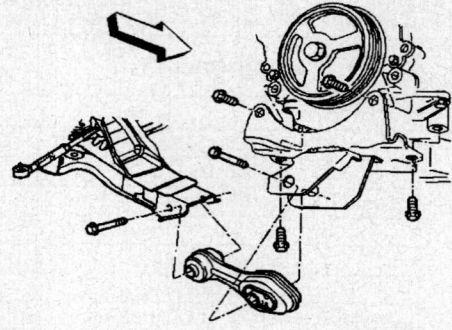

ARM66GC000000009

Fig. 8 Righthand lower control arm removal. Cavalier & Sunfire

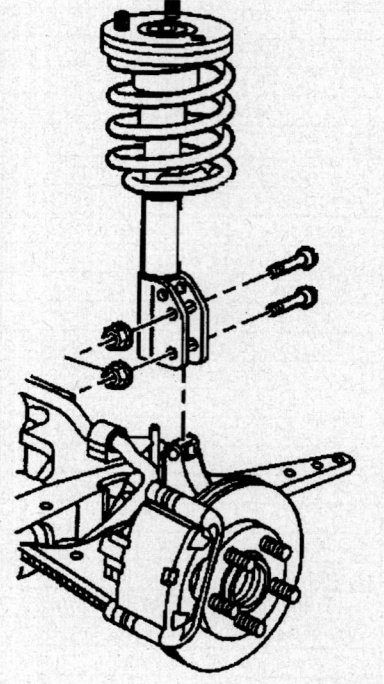

ARM66GC000000012

Fig. 11 Steering knuckle to strut removal. Cavalier & Sunfire

move wheel and tire assemblies.
3. Remove steering gear to intermediate shaft pinch bolt. Discard bolt.
4. Separate steering gear from intermediate shaft.
5. Remove attaching nut from outer tie rod ball stud.
6. Remove outer tie rod ball stud from steering knuckle using ball joint separator tool No. J24319-B, or equivalent.
7. Remove steering gear mounting bolts.

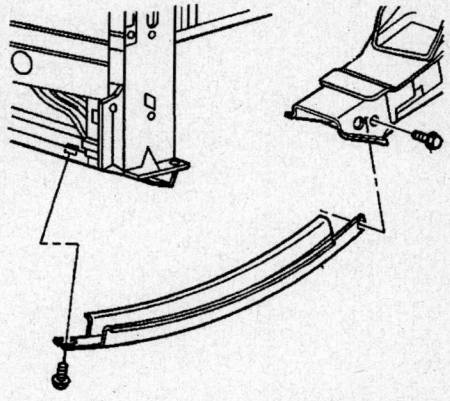

ARM66GC000000010

Fig. 9 Lefthand lower control arm & support brace removal. Cavalier & Sunfire

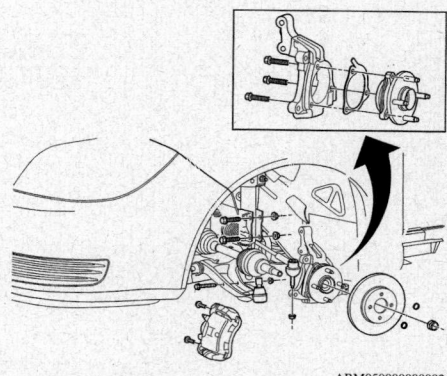

ARM0500000000924

Fig. 12 Steering knuckle removal. Cobalt & G5

8. Remove rear transaxle mount.
9. Remove steering gear from frame, then from vehicle through lefthand wheel opening.
10. Reverse procedure to install.

POWER STEERING PUMP

REPLACE

1. **On models equipped with 2.2L engine,** remove EVAP purge valve.
2. **On all models,** remove power steering fluid lines.
3. Remove power steering pump mounting bolts.
4. Remove pump and transfer pulley, if required.
5. Reverse procedure to install.

CAVALIER, COBALT, G5 & SUNFIRE

TIGHTENING SPECIFICATIONS

Year	Component	Torque/Ft. Lbs.
CAVALIER & SUNFIRE		
2004–05	Ball Joint To Knuckle	41–50
	Caliper	38
	Control Arm To Crossmember, Front	79
	Control Arm To Crossmember, Rear	125
	Hub & Bearing	70
	Hub Nut	185
	Stabilizer Shaft To Control Arm	13
	Stabilizer To Support	49
	Steering Column Pinch Bolt	16
	Steering Knuckle To Strut	133
	Strut To Body	18
	Strut Piston	34
	Tie Rod Jam Nuts	50
	Tie Rod Stud Nuts	33
	Wheel Lug Nuts	100
COBALT & G5		
2005–08	Ball Joint To Control Arm	50
	Ball Joint To Steering Knuckle Nut	①
	Control Arm To Front Frame Bolts	41
	Control Arm To Rear Frame Bolts	②
	Frame To Chassis Bolts	②
	Intermediate Shaft Pinch Bolt	25
	Power Steering Gear Mounting Bolts	81
	Stabilizer Link To Strut	48
	Stabilizer Shaft Clamp	37
	Stabilizer Shaft Link To Stabilizer Bar	59
	Srut To Body Nut	15
	Strut To Steering Knuckle	89
	Strut Shaft Nut	52
	Tie Rod End To Steering Knuckle Nut	44
	Transmission Mount Through Bolt	74
	Transmission Mount To Frame	37
	Wheel Bearing & Hub Mounting Bolts	85
	Wheel Lug Nuts	100

① — Refer to "Control Arm, Replace" for tightening procedure.
② — First step, 74 ft. lbs.; second step, an additional 180°.

Wheel Alignment

INDEX

	Page No.		Page No.		Page No.
Front Wheel Alignment	5-33	Cobalt & G5	5-33	**Preliminary Inspection**	5-33
Camber	5-33	Caster	5-33	**Wheel Alignment**	
Cavalier & Sunfire	5-33	Toe	5-33	**Specifications**	5-3

PRELIMINARY INSPECTION

1. Ensure all tires are of recommended size and are inflated to proper pressure.
2. Inspect all tires for damage and uneven tread wear.
3. Ensure wheel bearings, control arm ball studs and bushings, relay rods and tie rod ends are in satisfactory condition. Looseness must be corrected before wheels can be aligned.
4. Inspect wheel and tire radial and lateral runout, as follows:
   a. With wheel and tire assembly off vehicle, runout should be approximately .050 inch.
   b. When on vehicle, runout should be approximately .060 inch.
5. If wheel and tire assembly runout specifications cannot be met, separate tire from wheel and measure wheel runout. Wheel runout should be approximately .030 inch.
6. Inspect vehicle ride height as outlined in "Vehicle Ride Height" in "Specifications." If corrections are required, complete them prior to setting wheel alignment.
7. Ensure steering gear is not loose at frame mounting.
8. Inspect stabilizer shafts for loose or missing components.
9. Ensure struts and shocks are not leaking or excessively worn and strut upper mounts are in satisfactory condition.
10. Inspect all remaining suspension and steering components for damage and repair or replace prior to setting wheel alignment.
11. Ensure fuel tank is full or compensating ballast is added for proper weight distribution.
12. Ensure vehicle is on level surface and all loads that are normally carried inside vehicle are present.
13. Bounce front and rear of vehicle three times before beginning wheel alignment procedures.

FRONT WHEEL ALIGNMENT

Caster

Caster is not adjustable. If caster angle is not within specifications, inspect for suspension support misalignment or front suspension damage.

Camber

CAVALIER & SUNFIRE

Toe setting is the only adjustment normally required. However, in special circumstances, such as damage because of road hazard or collision, camber may be adjusted by modifying the strut. Proceed as follows:
1. Mount strut bottom in suitable vise.
2. Enlarge bottom holes in outer flanges with round file until holes in outer flanges match slots in inner flanges, **Fig. 1.**
3. Connect strut to steering knuckle and install bolts hand tight.
4. Grasp top of tire firmly and move tire inboard or outboard until proper camber reading is obtained. Tighten mounting bolts enough to secure camber setting.
5. Remove wheel and tire. **Torque** strut to steering knuckle mounting bolt to 133 ft. lbs.

COBALT & G5

1. Loosen both strut to knuckle nuts just enough to allow for movement.
2. If strut has not been modified previously, proceed as follows:
   a. Remove strut from knuckle as outlined under "Strut, Replace."
   b. File lower hole until groove of stamped ring around hole, **Fig. 2.**
   c. Install strut.
3. Adjust camber to specification by moving top of wheel in or out.

Toe

Toe-out is controlled by tie rod position. Adjustment is made by loosening the clamp bolts or jam nuts at the steering knuckle end of the tie rods and rotating the rods to obtain proper toe setting, **Fig. 3.** After proper toe setting is obtained, **torque** mounting nuts and bolts to 50 ft. lbs.

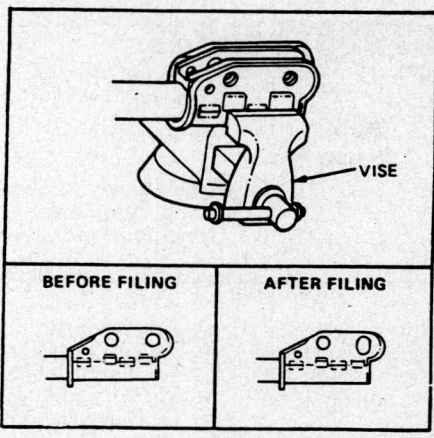

GC2049100070000X

Fig. 1 Strut bracket modification for camber adjustment. Cavalier & Sunfire

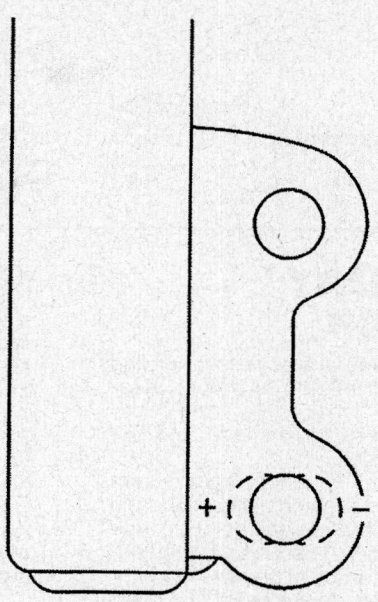

ARM0500000000925

Fig. 2 Strut modification for camber adjustment. Cobalt & G5

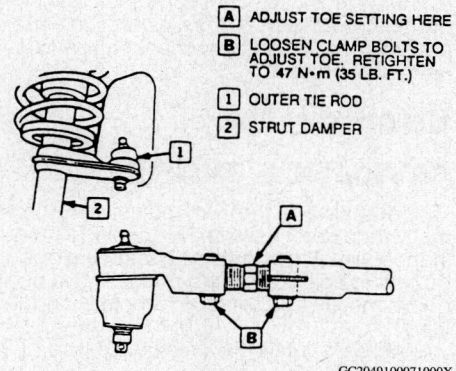

A ADJUST TOE SETTING HERE
B LOOSEN CLAMP BOLTS TO ADJUST TOE. RETIGHTEN TO 47 N·m (35 LB. FT.)
1 OUTER TIE ROD
2 STRUT DAMPER

GC2049100071000X

Fig. 3 Toe adjustment

CENTURY, GRAND PRIX, IMPALA, LACROSSE, MONTE CARLO & REGAL

NOTE: Refer To Rear Of This Manual For Vehicle Manufacturer's Special Service Tool Suppliers.

INDEX OF SERVICE OPERATIONS

Page No.

AIR BAG SYSTEM
PRECAUTIONS 0-18
BRAKES
    Anti-Lock Brakes (Volume 2).. 6-1
    Disc Brakes.................. 22-1
    Drum Brakes 23-1
    Hydraulic Brake Systems 24-1
    Power Brake Units........... 25-1
COMPUTER RELEARN
PROCEDURE 0-31
ELECTRICAL
    Air Bag System (Volume 2)... 4-1
    Air Conditioning.............. 16-1
    Alternator, Replace.......... 6-11
    Alternators.................. 19-1
    Blower Motor, Replace........ 6-16
    Cabin Air Filter, Replace 6-16
    Coil Pack, Replace 6-11
    Cooling Fans 17-1
    Cruise Control (Volume 2) ... 2-1
    Dash Gauges (Volume 2) 1-1
    Dash Panel Service
    (Volume 2)................... 5-1
    Evaporator Core, Replace 6-18
    Fuel Pump Relay Location.... 6-10
    Fuse Panel & Flasher
    Location 6-10
    Headlamp Switch, Replace ... 6-13
    Heater Core, Replace......... 6-16
    Ignition Lock, Replace 6-11
    Ignition Switch, Replace 6-12
    Instrument Cluster, Replace... 6-14
    Multi-Function Switch,
    Replace 6-13
    Passive Restraint Systems
    (Volume 2) 4-1
    Precautions.................. 6-10
    Radio, Replace 6-15
    Speed Controls (Volume 2) ... 2-1
    Starter Motors 18-1
    Starter, Replace 6-10
    Steering Columns............ 20-1
    Steering Wheel, Replace...... 6-14
    Stop Light Switch, Replace ... 6-13
    Transmission Range (TR)
    Switch, Replace 6-13
    Turn Signal Switch, Replace .. 6-14
    Wiper Module, Replace....... 6-16
    Wiper Motor, Replace........ 6-16
    Wiper Switch, Replace........ 6-16
    Wiper Systems (Volume 2)... 3-1
    Wiper Transmission, Replace . 6-16
ELECTRICAL SYMBOL
IDENTIFICATION 0-63
FRONT SUSPENSION &
STEERING
    Ball Joint, Replace........... 6-59
    Ball Joint Inspection 6-59
    Control Arm, Replace 6-60

Page No.

Description 6-59
Hub & Bearing, Replace 6-59
Power Steering 21-1
Power Steering Gear,
Replace 6-61
Power Steering Pump,
Replace 6-61
Power Steering System
Bleed 6-62
Precautions................. 6-59
Stabilizer Bar, Replace........ 6-60
Steering Columns............ 20-1
Steering Knuckle, Replace.... 6-60
Strut, Replace 6-59
Strut Service................. 6-59
Tie Rod End, Replace........ 6-60
Tightening Specifications...... 6-63
NON-STANDARD TIRE &
WHEEL SIZE
ADJUSTMENT TO RIDE
HEIGHT SPECIFICATIONS
& TIRE SIZE CHART 0-61
REAR DRIVE AXLE 27-1
REAR AXLE &
SUSPENSION
    Coil Spring, Replace.......... 6-57
    Description 6-57
    Hub & Bearing, Replace 6-57
    Knuckle, Replace............. 6-57
    Lateral Link, Replace 6-57
    Stabilizer Bar, Replace........ 6-57
    Strut, Replace 6-57
    Strut Service................. 6-57
    Tightening Specifications...... 6-58
    Trailing Arm, Replace......... 6-57
SERVICE REMINDER &
WARNING LAMP RESET
PROCEDURES 0-34
SPECIFICATIONS
    Fluid Capacities & Cooling
    System Data................. 6-8
    Front Wheel Alignment
    Specifications............... 6-4
    General Engine
    Specifications............... 6-3
    Lubricant Data 6-9
    Rear Wheel Alignment
    Specifications............... 6-5
    Tune Up Specifications....... 6-3
    Vehicle Ride Height
    Specifications............... 6-6
TIRE PRESSURE
MONITORING SYSTEM 28-1
VEHICLE
IDENTIFICATION 0-1
VEHICLE LIFT POINTS 0-51
VEHICLE MAINTENANCE
SCHEDULES 0-73

Page No.

WHEEL ALIGNMENT
    Front Wheel Alignment........ 6-64
    Precautions.................. 6-64
    Preliminary Inspection 6-64
    Rear Wheel Alignment 6-64
    Wheel Alignment
    Specifications................ 6-4
WIRE COLOR CODE
IDENTIFICATION 0-63
3.1L ENGINE
    Belt Tension Data............ 6-24
    Camshaft, Replace 6-22
    Camshaft Lobe Lift
    Specifications................ 6-21
    Compression Pressure........ 6-19
    Cooling System Bleed 6-24
    Crankshaft Rear Oil Seal,
    Replace 6-23
    Cylinder Head, Replace....... 6-21
    Engine Rebuilding
    Specifications................ 29-1
    Engine, Replace 6-20
    Engine Mount, Replace 6-19
    Exhaust Manifold, Replace.... 6-20
    Front Cover, Replace 6-22
    Front Cover Seal, Replace.... 6-22
    Fuel Filter, Replace 6-24
    Fuel Pump, Replace 6-24
    Hydraulic Lifters, Replace..... 6-22
    Intake Manifold, Replace...... 6-20
    Main & Rod Bearings 6-22
    Oil Pan, Replace.............. 6-23
    Oil Pump, Replace........... 6-23
    Oil Pump Service 6-23
    Piston & Rod Assembly 6-22
    Precautions................. 6-19
    Push Rods 6-21
    Radiator, Replace............. 6-24
    Rocker Arms, Replace 6-21
    Serpentine Drive Belt 6-24
    Technical Service Bulletins.... 6-24
    Thermostat, Replace......... 6-24
    Tightening Specifications...... 6-27
    Timing Chain, Replace........ 6-22
    Valve Adjustment 6-21
    Valve Arrangement........... 6-21
    Valve Clearance
    Specifications................ 6-21
    Valve Cover, Replace 6-21
    Valve Lifters 6-21
    Water Pump, Replace 6-24
3.4L ENGINE
    Belt Tension Data............ 6-32
    Camshaft, Replace 6-31
    Camshaft Lobe Lift
    Specifications................ 6-31
    Compression Pressure........ 6-28
    Cooling System Bleed 6-32
    Crankshaft Damper, Replace.. 6-31

Page No.

Crankshaft Rear Oil Seal,
Replace 6-31
Cylinder Head, Replace....... 6-30
Engine Rebuilding
Specifications................. 29-1
Engine, Replace 6-29
Engine Mount, Replace....... 6-28
Exhaust Manifold, Replace.... 6-30
Front Cover, Replace 6-31
Front Cover Seal, Replace.... 6-31
Fuel Filter, Replace 6-32
Fuel Pump, Replace 6-32
Intake Manifold, Replace...... 6-29
Main & Rod Bearings 6-31
Oil Pan, Replace.............. 6-31
Oil Pump, Replace............ 6-32
Piston & Rod Assembly 6-31
Precautions................... 6-28
Radiator, Replace............. 6-32
Rocker Arms, Replace 6-31
Serpentine Drive Belt 6-32
Technical Service Bulletins.... 6-33
Thermostat, Replace.......... 6-32
Tightening Specifications...... 6-34
Timing Chain, Replace........ 6-31
Valve Cover, Replace 6-30
Valve Lifters 6-31
Water Pump, Replace 6-32

3.5L & 3.9L ENGINES

Camshaft, Replace 6-39
Camshaft Lobe Lift
Specifications................. 6-38
Compression Pressure........ 6-35
Cooling System Bleed 6-40
Crankshaft Damper, Replace.. 6-38
Crankshaft Rear Oil Seal,
Replace 6-39
Crankshaft Seal, Replace..... 6-39
Cylinder Head, Replace....... 6-37
Engine Rebuilding
Specifications................. 29-1

Page No.

Engine, Replace 6-35
Engine Mount, Replace....... 6-35
Engine Mount Strut, Replace . 6-35
Exhaust Manifold, Replace.... 6-37
Front Cover, Replace 6-38
Fuel Pump, Replace 6-41
Hydraulic Lifters, Replace..... 6-38
Intake Manifold, Replace...... 6-36
Main & Rod Bearings 6-39
Oil Pan, Replace.............. 6-39
Oil Pump, Replace............ 6-40
Oil Pump Service 6-40
Piston & Rod Assembly 6-39
Precautions................... 6-35
Push Rods 6-38
Radiator, Replace............. 6-41
Rocker Arms, Replace 6-38
Serpentine Drive Belt 6-40
Thermostat, Replace.......... 6-40
Tightening Specifications...... 6-42
Timing Chain, Replace........ 6-39
Valve Adjustment 6-38
Valve Cover, Replace 6-37
Water Pump, Replace 6-40

3.6L ENGINE

Compression Pressure........ 6-43
Engine Rebuilding
Specifications................. 29-1
Engine, Replace 6-43
Engine Mount, Replace....... 6-43
Engine Mount Strut, Replace . 6-43
Fuel Pump, Replace 6-44
Precautions................... 6-43
Radiator, Replace............. 6-44
Tightening Specifications...... 6-45

3.8L ENGINE

Compression Pressure........ 6-46
Engine Rebuilding
Specifications................. 29-1
Engine, Replace 6-46
Engine Mount, Replace....... 6-46

Page No.

Fuel Filter, Replace 6-47
Fuel Pump, Replace 6-46
Precautions................... 6-46
Technical Service Bulletins.... 6-47
Tightening Specifications...... 6-47

5.3L ENGINE

Camshaft, Replace 6-53
Compression Pressure........ 6-48
Cooling System Bleed 6-54
Crankshaft Damper, Replace.. 6-52
Crankshaft Rear Oil Seal,
Replace 6-53
Crankshaft Seal, Replace..... 6-53
Cylinder Head, Replace....... 6-50
Engine Rebuilding
Specifications................. 29-1
Engine, Replace 6-49
Engine Mount, Replace....... 6-48
Exhaust Manifold, Replace.... 6-50
Front Cover, Replace 6-52
Fuel Pump, Replace 6-55
Hydraulic Lifters, Replace..... 6-52
Intake Manifold, Replace...... 6-49
Main & Rod Bearings 6-53
Oil Pan, Replace.............. 6-53
Oil Pump, Replace............ 6-54
Oil Pump Service 6-54
Piston & Rod Assembly 6-53
Precautions................... 6-48
Push Rods 6-51
Radiator, Replace............. 6-54
Rocker Arms.................. 6-51
Serpentine Drive Belt 6-54
Thermostat, Replace.......... 6-54
Tightening Specifications...... 6-56
Timing Chain, Replace........ 6-53
Valve Adjustment 6-51
Valve Arrangement............ 6-51
Valve Cover, Replace 6-51
Water Pump, Replace 6-54

Specifications

GENERAL ENGINE SPECIFICATIONS

Year	Engine Displacement	Engine VIN Code[2]	Fuel System	Bore & Stroke	Compression Ratio	Net H.P. @ RPM[3]	Maximum Torque Ft. Lbs. @ RPM	Normal Oil Pressure, psi
2004	3.1L	J	SFI	3.51 × 3.31	9.6	175 @ 5200	195 @ 4000	60[4]
	3.4L	E	SFI	3.62 × 3.31	9.6	180 @ 5200	205 @ 4000	60[4]
	3.8L	K	SFI	3.80 × 3.40	9.4	200 @ 5200	225 @ 4000	60[4]
	3.8L[1]	1	SFI	3.80 × 3.40	8.5	240 @ 5200	280 @ 3200	60[4]
	3.8L	2	SFI	3.80 × 3.40	9.4	200 @ 5200	225 @ 4000	60[4]
	3.8L[1]	4	SFI	3.80 × 3.40	8.5	240 @ 5200	280 @ 3200	60[4]
2005	3.1L	J	SFI	3.51 × 3.31	9.6	175 @ 5200	195 @ 4000	60[4]
	3.4L	E	SFI	3.62 × 3.31	9.6	180 @ 5200	205 @ 4000	60[4]
	3.6L	7	SFI	3.70 x 3.37	10.2	240 @ 6000	230 @ 3200	20[5]
	3.8L	K	SFI	3.80 × 3.40	9.4	200 @ 5200	225 @ 4000	60[4]
	3.8L[1]	1	SFI	3.80 × 3.40	8.5	240 @ 5200	280 @ 3200	60[4]
	3.8L	2	SFI	3.80 × 3.40	9.4	200 @ 5200	225 @ 4000	60[4]
	3.8L[1]	4	SFI	3.80 × 3.40	8.5	240 @ 5200	280 @ 3200	60[4]
2006	3.5L	N	SFI	3.90 x 2.99	9.8	211 @ 5800	214 @ 4000	30–45[4]
	3.6L	7	SFI	3.70 x 3.37	10.2	240 @ 6000	225 @ 2000	20[5]
	3.8L	2	SFI	3.80 × 3.40	9.4	200 @ 5200	230 @ 4000	60[4]
	3.8L[1]	4	SFI	3.80 × 3.40	8.5	260 @ 5200	280 @ 3600	60[4]
	3.9L	1	SFI	3.90 x 3.31	9.8	242 @ 6000	242 @ 4800	30–45[4]
	5.3L	C	SFI	3.78 x 3.62	9.9	303 @ 5600	323 @ 4400	18[5]
2007–08	3.5L	N	SFI	3.90 x 2.99	9.8	211 @ 5800	214 @ 4000	30–45[4]
	3.6L	7	SFI	3.70 x 3.37	10.2	240 @ 6000	225 @ 2000	20[5]
	3.8L	2	SFI	3.80 × 3.40	9.4	200 @ 5200	230 @ 4000	60[4]
	3.8L[1]	4	SFI	3.80 × 3.40	8.5	260 @ 5200	280 @ 3600	60[4]
	3.9L	1	SFI	3.90 x 3.31	9.8	242 @ 6000	242 @ 4800	30–45[4]
	5.3L	C	SFI	3.78 x 3.62	9.9	303 @ 5600	323 @ 4400	18[5]

SFI — Sequential-Port Fuel Injection
[1] — Supercharged engine.
[2] — The eighth digit of the VIN denotes engine code.
[3] — Ratings are net as installed in vehicle.
[4] — @ 1850 RPM.
[5] — @ 2000 RPM.

TUNE UP SPECIFICATIONS

Year, Engine & VIN Code[1]	Spark Plug Gap, Inch	Ignition Timing Firing Order[3]	Ignition Timing °BTDC	Ignition Timing Mark	Curb Idle Speed[2]	Fast Idle Speed	Fuel Pump Pressure, Psi	Valve Clearance, Inch
2004								
3.1L	.060	[9]	[4]	[5]	[6]	[6]	52–59	[10]
3.4L	.060	[9]	[4]	[5]	[6]	[5]	52–59	[10]
3.8L (K)	.060	[7]	[4]	[5]	[6]	[6]	53–59	[10]
3.8L (1)	.060	[7]	[4]	[5]	[6]	[6]	48–54	[10]
3.8L (2)	.060	[7]	[4]	[5]	[6]	[6]	55–60	[10]
3.8L (4)	.060	[7]	[4]	[5]	[6]	[6]	55–60	[10]
2005								
3.1L	.060	[9]	[4]	[5]	[6]	[6]	52–59	[10]
3.4L	.060	[9]	[4]	[5]	[6]	[5]	52–59	[10]
3.6L	.043	[9]	[4]	[5]	[6]	[6]	55–60	[10]
3.8L (K)	.060	[7]	[4]	[5]	[6]	[6]	53–59	[10]
3.8L (1)	.060	[7]	[4]	[5]	[6]	[6]	48–54	[10]
3.8L (2)	.060	[7]	[4]	[5]	[6]	[6]	56–62	[10]
3.8L (4)	.060	[7]	[4]	[5]	[6]	[6]	56–62	[10]

Continued

TUNE UP SPECIFICATIONS—Continued

| Year, Engine & VIN Code① | Spark Plug Gap, Inch | Ignition Timing | | | Curb Idle Speed② | Fast Idle Speed | Fuel Pump Pressure, Psi | Valve Clearance, Inch |
		Firing Order③	°BTDC	Mark				
2006								
3.5L	.040	⑨	④	⑤	⑥	⑥	50–60	⑩
3.6L	.043	⑨	④	⑤	⑥	⑥	55–60	⑩
3.8L (2)	.060	⑦	④	⑤	⑥	⑥	56–62	⑩
3.8L (4)	.060	⑦	④	⑤	⑥	⑥	56–62	⑩
3.9L	.040	⑨	④	⑤	⑥	⑥	50–60	⑩
5.3L	.040	⑧	④	⑤	⑥	⑥	55–62	⑩
2007–08								
3.5L	.040	⑨	④	⑤	⑥	⑥	50–60	⑩
3.6L	.043	⑨	④	⑤	⑥	⑥	55–60	⑩
3.8L (2)	.060	⑦	④	⑤	⑥	⑥	56–62	⑩
3.8L (4)	.060	⑦	④	⑤	⑥	⑥	56–62	⑩
3.9L	.040	⑨	④	⑤	⑥	⑥	50–60	⑩
5.3L	.040	⑧	④	⑤	⑥	⑥	55–62	⑩

BTDC — Before Top Dead Center
① — The eighth digit of Vehicle Identification Number (VIN) denotes engine code.
② — Idle speed is adjusted in Drive. When adjusting idle speed, set parking brake & block drive wheels. Where two idle speeds are listed, the higher speed is w/idle or air conditioning solenoid energized.

③ — Note ignition wire locations before disconnecting from ignition coil.
④ — Computer controlled, no adjustment.
⑤ — Equipped w/crankshaft position sensor.
⑥ — Idle speed is controlled by an Idle Air Control (IAC) valve or Idle Speed Control (ISC) motor.
⑦ — 1-6-5-4-3-2.

⑧ — 1-8-7-2-6-5-4-3.
⑨ — 1-2-3-4-5-6.
⑩ — Equipped w/hydraulic valve lash adjusters. There is no provision for valve lash adjustment. If valve lash exists, inspect for excessive pushrod & rocker arm wear & for an inoperative lifter.

FRONT WHEEL ALIGNMENT SPECIFICATIONS

| Year | Model | Caster Angle, Degrees① | | Camber Angle, Degrees | | Toe-In, Degrees | Steering Angle, Degrees | | Ball Joint Wear |
		Limits	Desired	Limits	Desired		Limits	Desired	
2004	Century	+2.49 to +3.49	+2.99	-1.32 to -.32	-.82	-.10 to +.30	-.10 to +.30	+.10	.125 inch⑤
	Grand Prix	+2.57 to +3.57	+3.07	-1.44 to -.44	-.94	-.10 to +.30	-3.50 to +3.50	0	.125 Inch⑤
	Impala	+2.70 to +3.50	+3.10	-1.28 to -.28	-.78	-.10 to +.30	-3.50 to +3.50	0	.125 Inch⑤
	Monte Carlo	+2.70 to +3.50	+3.10	-1.35 to -.35	-.85	-.10 to +.30	-3.50 to +3.50	0	.125 Inch⑤
	Regal	+2.54 to +3.54	+3.04	-1.40 to -.40	-.90	-.10 to +.30	-3.50 to +3.50	0	.125 Inch⑤
2005	Century	+2.25 to +3.75	+3.00	-1.05 to -.15	-.90	-.10 to +.30	-.10 to +.30	+.10	.125 inch⑤
	Grand Prix (GT & GTP)	+2.40 to +3.90	+3.15	-1.55 to -.05	-.80	-.10 to +.30	-3.50 to +3.50	0	.125 Inch⑤
	Grand Prix (GXP)	+2.45 to +3.95	+3.20	-1.75 to -.25	-1.00	-.10 to +.30	-3.50 to +3.50	0	.125 Inch⑤
	Impala②③	+2.25 to +3.75	+3.00	-1.50 to 0	-.75	-.10 to +.30	-3.50 to +3.50	0	.125 Inch⑤
	Impala④	+2.75 to +4.25	+3.50	-1.45 to +.05	-.70	-.10 to +.30	-3.50 to +3.50	0	.125 Inch⑤
	Impala⑥⑧	+2.75 to +4.25	+3.50	-1.35 to +.15	-.60	-.10 to +.30	-3.50 to +3.50	0	.125 Inch⑤
	LaCrosse	+2.75 to +4.15	+3.40	-1.55 to -.05	-.80	-.10 to +.30	-3.50 to +3.50	0	.125 Inch⑤
	Monte Carlo	+2.70 to +3.70	+3.10	-1.35 to -.35	-.85	-.10 to +.30	-3.50 to +3.50	0	.125 Inch⑤

FRONT WHEEL ALIGNMENT SPECIFICATIONS—Continued

Year	Model	Caster Angle, Degrees①		Camber Angle, Degrees		Toe-In, Degrees	Steering Angle, Degrees		Ball Joint Wear
		Limits	Desired	Limits	Desired		Limits	Desired	
2006	Grand Prix (GT & GTP)	+2.40 to +3.90	+3.15	−1.55 to −.05	−.80	−.10 to +.30	−3.50 to +3.50	0	.125 Inch⑤
	Grand Prix (GXP)	+2.45 to +3.95	+3.20	−1.75 to −.25	−1.00	−.10 to +.30	−3.50 to +3.50	0	.125 Inch⑤
	Impala②	+2.40 to +3.40	+2.90	-1.30 to -.30	−.80	−.10 to +.30	−3.50 to +3.50	0	.125 inch⑤
	Impala⑦	+2.65 to +3.65	+3.15	-1.20 to -.20	−.70	−.10 to +.30	−3.50 to +3.50	0	.125 inch⑤
	Impala⑥	+2.70 to +3.70	+3.20	-1.00 to 0	−.50	−.10 to +.30	−3.50 to +3.50	0	.125 inch⑤
	Impala⑧	+2.55 to +3.55	+3.05	-1.15 to -.15	−.65	−.10 to +.30	−3.50 to +3.50	0	.125 inch⑤
	LaCrosse	+2.75 to +4.15	+3.40	−1.55 to −.05	−.80	−.10 to +.30	−3.50 to +3.50	0	.125 Inch⑤
	Monte Carlo③	+2.00 to +4.00	+3.00	-1.15 to -.15	−.65	−.10 to +.30	−3.50 to +3.50	0	.125 inch⑤
	Monte Carlo④	+2.65 to +3.65	+3.15	-1.30 to -.30	−.80	−.10 to +.30	−3.50 to +3.50	0	.125 inch⑤
2007–08	Grand Prix (GT & GTP)	+2.40 to +3.90	+3.15	−1.55 to −.05	−.80	−.10 to +.30	−3.50 to +3.50	0	.125 Inch⑤
	Grand Prix (GXP)	+2.45 to +3.95	+3.20	−1.75 to −.25	−1.00	−.10 to +.30	−3.50 to +3.50	0	.125 Inch⑤
	Impala②	+2.40 to +3.40	+2.90	-1.30 to -.30	−.80	−.10 to +.30	−3.50 to +3.50	0	.125 inch⑤
	Impala⑦	+2.65 to +3.65	+3.15	-1.20 to -.20	−.70	−.10 to +.30	−3.50 to +3.50	0	.125 inch⑤
	Impala⑥	+2.70 to +3.70	+3.20	-1.00 to 0	−.50	−.10 to +.30	−3.50 to +3.50	0	.125 inch⑤
	Impala⑧	+2.55 to +3.55	+3.05	-1.15 to -.15	−.65	−.10 to +.30	−3.50 to +3.50	0	.125 inch⑤
	LaCrosse	+4.15 to +2.75	+3.40	−1.55 to −.05	−.80	−.10 to +.30	−3.50 to +3.50	0	.125 Inch⑤
	Monte Carlo③	+2.00 to +4.00	+3.00	-1.15 to -.15	−.65	−.10 to +.30	−3.50 to +3.50	0	.125 inch⑤
	Monte Carlo④	+3.65 to +2.65	+3.15	-1.30 to -.30	−.80	−.10 to +.30	−3.50 to +3.50	0	.125 inch⑤

① — Not Adjustable.
② — Soft Ride Suspension System.
③ — Ride & Handling Suspension System.
④ — Special Ride & Handling Suspension System.

⑤ — Remove tension from ball joints. To measure horizontal looseness rock wheel in and out while reading suitable dial indicator. To measure vertical looseness move ball joint up and down while reading suitable dial indicator.

⑥ — SEO Vehicle Police Car.
⑦ — Sport Suspension System.
⑧ — SEO Vehicle Police Car, Limited Content.

REAR WHEEL ALIGNMENT SPECIFICATIONS

Year	Model	Camber Angle, Degrees		Total Toe, Degrees		Thrust Angle, Degrees	
		Limits	Desired	Limits	Desired	Limits	Desired
2004	Century	−.70 to +.70	0	−.10 to +.30	+.10	−.15 to +.15	0
	Grand Prix	−1.37 to −.37	−.87	−.10 to +.30	+.06	−.25 to + .15	0
	Impala	-1.00 to 0	−.50	−.10 to +.30	+.10	−.15 to +.15	0
	Monte Carlo	-1.20 to -.20	−.70	−.10 to +.30	+.10	−.15 to +.15	0
	Regal	-1.10 to -.10	−.60	−.10 to +.30	+.10	−.15 to +.15	0

Continued

REAR WHEEL ALIGNMENT SPECIFICATIONS—Continued

Year	Model	Camber Angle, Degrees		Total Toe, Degrees		Thrust Angle, Degrees	
		Limits	Desired	Limits	Desired	Limits	Desired
2005	Century	-1.30 To -.30	-.80	-.10 to +.30	+.10	-.20 to +.20	0
	Grand Prix (GT & GTP)	–1.45 to –.45	–.95	-.10 to +.30	+.10	–.20 to +.20	0
	Grand Prix (GXP)	–1.85 to –.40	–1.15	-.10 to +.30	+.10	–.20 to +.20	0
	Impala②③	-1.15 to -.15	-.65	-.30 to +.10	-.10	-.20 to +.20	0
	Impala③	-1.40 to -.40	-.90	-.30 to +.10	-.10	-.20 to +.20	0
	Impala①⑤	-1.20 to -.20	-.70	-.30 to +.10	-.10	-.20 to +.20	0
	LaCrosse	–1.30 to –.30	–.80	-.10 to +.30	+.10	–.20 to +.20	0
	Monte Carlo	-1.35 to -.35	-.85	-.30 to +.10	-.10	-.20 to +.20	0
2006	Grand Prix (GT & GTP)	–1.45 to –.45	–.95	-.10 to +.30	+.10	–.20 to +.20	0
	Grand Prix (GXP)	–1.85 to –.40	–1.15	-.10 to +.30	+.10	–.20 to +.20	0
	Impala②	-1.15 to -.15	-.65	-.10 to +.30	+.10	-.15 to +.15	0
	Impala⑥	-1.40 to -.40	-.90	-.10 to +.30	+.10	-.15 to +.15	0
	Impala①⑤	-1.20 to -.20	-.70	-.10 to +.30	+.10	-.15 to +.15	0
	LaCrosse	–1.30 to –.30	–.80	-.10 to +.30	+.10	–.20 to +.20	0
	Monte Carlo③	-1.35 to -.35	-.85	-.10 to +.30	+.10	-.15 to +.15	0
	Monte Carlo④	-1.40 to -.40	-.90	-.10 to +.30	+.10	-.15 to +.15	0
2007–08	Grand Prix (GT & GTP)	–1.45 to –.45	–.95	-.10 to +.30	+.10	–.20 to +.20	0
	Grand Prix (GXP)	–1.85 to –.40	–1.15	-.10 to +.30	+.10	–.20 to +.20	0
	Impala②	-1.15 to -.15	-.65	-.10 to +.30	+.10	-.15 to +.15	0
	Impala⑥	-1.40 to -.40	-.90	-.10 to +.30	+.10	-.15 to +.15	0
	Impala①⑤	-1.20 to -.20	-.70	-.10 to +.30	+.10	-.15 to +.15	0
	LaCrosse	–1.30 to –.30	–.80	-.10 to +.30	+.10	–.20 to +.20	0
	Monte Carlo③	-1.35 to -.35	-.85	-.10 to +.30	+.10	-.15 to +.15	0
	Monte Carlo④	-1.40 to -.40	-.90	-.10 to +.30	+.10	-.15 to +.15	0

① — SEO Vehicle Police Car.
② — Soft Ride Suspension System.
③ — Ride & Handling Suspension System.
④ — Special Ride & Handling Suspension System.
⑤ — SEO Vehicle Police Car, Limited Content.
⑥ — Sport Suspension System.

VEHICLE RIDE HEIGHT SPECIFICATIONS

Model	Year	Body Style	Manufacturer's Original Tire Size①	Measurement Points & Specifications②					
				Front			Rear		
				Dim.	Specification		Dim.	Specification	
					Inches	mm		Inches	mm
Century	2004–05	Four-Door	P205/70R15	J	8.6	218	D	10.7	273
				Z	1.8	45	K	8.6	223
Grand Prix	2004	Four-Door, GT w/3.8L Engine	P225/60R16	J	8.4	213	D	10.0	255
				Z	1.4	35	K	8.4	213
		Four-Door, GTP w/3.8L SC Engine	P225/60R16	J	8.4	213	D	10.1	256
				Z	1.4	36	K	8.4	213
	2005	Four-Door, GT w/3.8L Engine	P225/60R16	J	8.4	213	D	10.0	255
				Z	1.4	35	K	8.4	213
		Four-Door, GTP w/3.8L SC Engine	P225/60R16	J	8.4	213	D	10.1	256
				Z	1.4	36	K	8.4	213
		Four-Door, GXP w/3.8L SC Engine	Front, P255/45R18 & Rear P225/50R18	J	9.0	228	D	10.0	254
				Z	1.1	28	K	8.7	221

VEHICLE RIDE HEIGHT SPECIFICATIONS—Continued

Model	Year	Body Style	Manufacturer's Original Tire Size①	Measurement Points & Specifications②					
				Front			Rear		
				Dim.	Specification		Dim.	Specification	
					Inches	mm		Inches	mm
Grand Prix	2006–08	GT	P225/60R16	J	6.9	176	D	10.5	266
				Z	1.2	41	K	8.2	209
		GT	P225/55R17	J	7.0	179	D	10.5	266
				Z	1.6	41	K	8.3	212
		GTP	P225/55R17	J	7.2	183	D	10.5	267
				Z	1.8	45	K	8.4	214
		GXP	Front, P255/45R18 & Rear P225/50R18	J	9.0	228	D	10.0	254
				Z	1.1	28	K	8.7	221
Impala	2004–05	Four-Door Base w/3.4L Engine	P225/60R16	J	9.4	240	D	11.0	279
				Z	2.4	61	K	9.4	240
		Four-Door Base/LS w/3.8L Engine	P225/60R16	J	9.4	240	D	10.9	278
				Z	2.4	61	K	9.4	240
		Police (RPO Code 9C1)	P225/60R16	J	10.1	256	D	10.9	278
				X	3.1	79	K	9.6	244
		Police (RPO Code 9C3)	P225/60R16	J	9.8	248	D	10.9	278
				Z	2.7	69	K	9.5	242
		Taxi (RPO Code 9C6)	P60R1225/6	J	9.8	248	D	10.9	278
				Z	2.7	69	K	9.5	242
	2006–08	Four-Door LS/LT (RPO FE1 QPX)	P225/60R16	J	9.2	233	D	11.0	279
				Z	1.9	48	K	9.4	238
		Four-Door LT/LTZ (RPO FE1 QVS)	P225/55R17	J	9.3	236	D	11.0	279
				Z	1.9	48	K	9.5	241
		Four-Door SS (RPO FE3 QDG)	P235/50R18	J	9.6	244	D	10.6	268
				Z	1.9	48	K	9.6	243
		Four-Door Police (RPO PC1)	P225/60R16	J	9.8	249	D	10.9	277
				Z	2.6	66	K	9.6	244
		Four-Door Police (RPO PC3)	P225/60R16	J	9.5	242	D	10.9	277
				Z	2.2	56	K	9.5	241
LaCrossse	2005–08	Four-Door (RPO Code FE1)	—	J	9.4	238	D	10.7	273
				Z	1.9	48	K	9.10	232
		Four-Door (RPO Code FE2)	—	J	9.3	237	D	10.7	273
				Z	1.9	48	K	9.3	235
Monte Carlo	2004–05	Two-Door	P225/60R16	J	9.2	234	D	10.7	271
				Z	2.2	55	K	9.1	233
	2006–07	Two-Door LS/LT (RPO FE2 QPX)	P225/60R16	J	9.0	228	D	10.7	271
				Z	1.7	43	K	9.1	232
		Two-Door LT/LTZ (RPO FE1 QVS)	P225/55R17	J	9.1	231	D	10.7	271
				Z	1.7	43	K	9.5	241
		Four-Door SS (RPO FE4 QDG)	P235/50R18	J	9.6	246	D	10.6	268
				Z	1.9	48	K	9.6	244
Regal	2004	Two-Door	215/70R15 & P225/60R16 &	J	8.8	223	D	10.5	267
				Z	1.8	45	K	8.9	225

Dim. — Dimension.

D Dim. — Measurement At Point 1.18 inches 30 mm Outboard Of Rear Brake Hose Bracket Bolt Centerline To Knuckle Arm Training Arm Bolt Centerline, **Fig. A.**

J Dim. — Measurement From Ground to Rocker Panel, Inboard of Front Pinch-Weld Flange, **Fig. C.**

K Dim. — Measurement From Ground to Rocker Panel, Inboard of Rear Pinch-Weld Flange, **Fig. C.**

Z Dim. — Measurement In Line W/Wheel Center, **Fig. B.**

① — See door sticker or inside of glove box for manufacturers original tire size specifications. If tires on vehicle do not match manufacturers original tire size & measurement is not within limits, refer to the "Non-Standard Tire & Wheel Size Adjustment To Ride Height Specification & Tire Size Adjustment Charts" in the front of this manual for approximate changes in ride height specifications.

② — Measurement is with fuel, radiator coolant & engine oil full, spare tire, jack, hand tools & mats in designated positions & tires properly inflated.

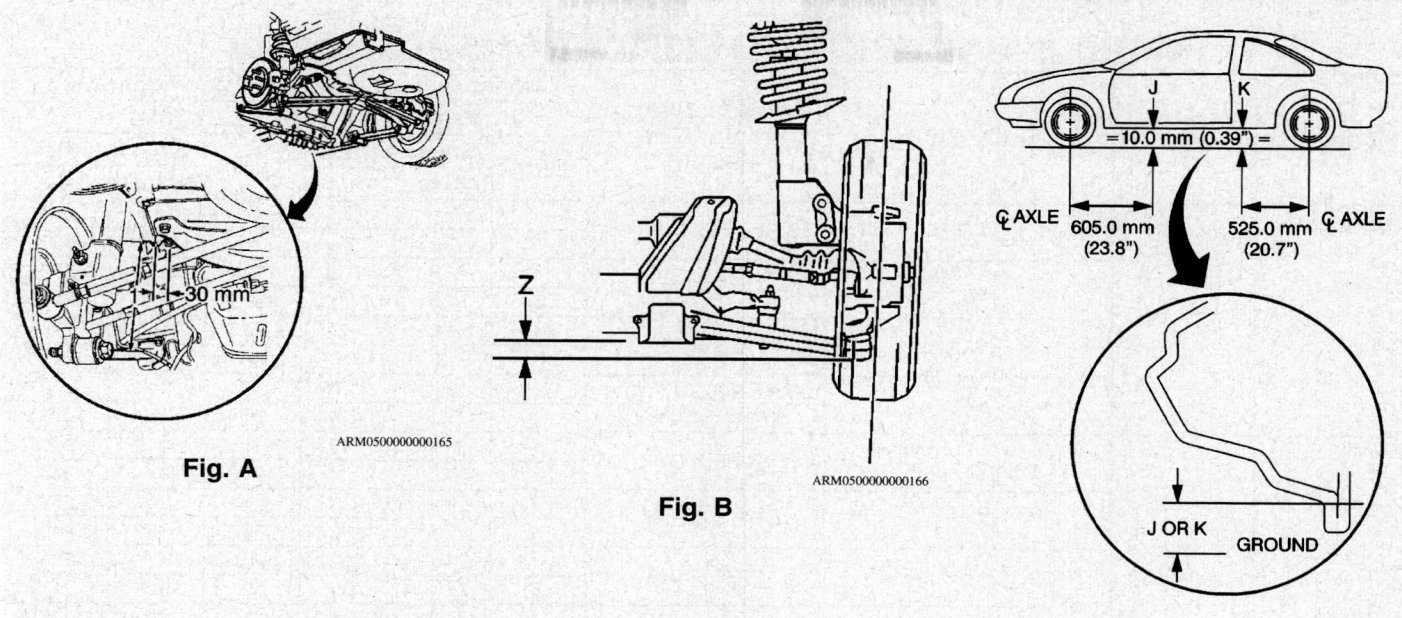

Fig. A

Fig. B

Fig. C

FLUID CAPACITIES & COOLING SYSTEM DATA

Year	Model	Engine	Coolant Capacity, Qts.	Coolant Type	Radiator Cap Relief Pressure, psi	Thermostat Opening Temp. °F	Fuel Tank, Gals.	Engine Oil Refill, Qts.①	Transaxle, Qts.②	
									Pan, Drain & Refill	Total Capacity
2004	Century	3.1L	11.7	Dex-Cool	15	195	17.0	4.5	7.4	③
	Grand Prix	3.8L	11.2	Dex-Cool	15	195	17.0	4.5	7.4	③
	Impala & Monte Carlo	3.4L	11.3	Dex-Cool	15	195	17.0	4.5	7.4	③
		3.8L	11.7	Dex-Cool	15	195	17.0	4.5	7.4	③
	Regal	3.8L	11.7	Dex-Cool	15	195	17.0	4.5	7.4	③
2005	Century	3.1L	11.7	Dex-Cool	15	195	17.0	4.5	7.4	③
	Grand Prix	3.8L	11.2	Dex-Cool	15	195	17.5	4.5	7.4	③
	Impala & Monte Carlo	3.4L	11.3	Dex-Cool	15	195	17.0	4.5	7.4	③
		3.8L	11.7	Dex-Cool	15	195	17.0	4.5	7.4	③
	LaCrosse	3.6L	11.0	Dex-Cool	15	195	17.5	5.5	7.4	③
		3.8L	11.7	Dex-Cool	15	195	17.5	4.5	7.4	③
2006	Grand Prix	3.8L	11.2	Dex-Cool	15	195	17.5	4.5	7.4	③
		5.3L	13.0	Dex-Cool	15	195	17.5	6.0	7.4	③
	Impala & Monte Carlo	3.5L	12.2	Dex-Cool	15	195	17.5	4.5	7.4	③
		3.9L	12.2	Dex-Cool	15	195	17.5	4.0	7.4	③
		5.3L	12.8	Dex-Cool	15	195	17.5	6.0	7.4	③
	LaCrosse	3.6L	11.0	Dex-Cool	15	195	17.5	5.5	7.4	③
		3.8L	11.7	Dex-Cool	15	195	17.5	4.5	7.4	③
2007–08	Grand Prix	3.8L	11.2	Dex-Cool	15	195	17.5	4.5	7.4	③
		5.3L	13.0	Dex-Cool	15	195	17.5	6.0	7.4	③
	Impala & Monte Carlo	3.5L	12.2	Dex-Cool	15	195	17.5	4.0	7.4	③
		3.9L	12.2	Dex-Cool	15	195	17.5	4.0	7.4	③
		5.3L	12.8	Dex-Cool	15	195	17.5	6.0	7.4	③
	LaCrosse	3.6L	11.0	Dex-Cool	15	195	17.5	5.5	7.4	③
		3.8L	11.7	Dex-Cool	15	195	17.5	4.5	7.4	③
		5.3L	13.3	Dex-Cool	15	195	17.5	6.0	7.4	③

① — Additional oil may be required to bring oil level to full mark when changing oil filter.

② — Capacity approximate. Make final inspection w/dipstick & add fluid as required.

③ — Overhaul, 10.0 Qts.; Dry, 13.4 Qts.

LUBRICANT DATA

Year	Model	Lubricant Type		
		Transaxle	Power Steering	Brake System
2004–05	All	Dexron III	①	DOT 3
2006–08	All	Dexron VI	①	DOT 3

① — GM Power Steering Fluid part No. 89021184, or equivalent.

Electrical

NOTE: On Air Bag Equipped Models, Refer To "Air Bag System Precautions" Located In The Front Of This Manual For System Disarming & Arming Procedures.

NOTE: Refer To "Computer Relearn Procedures" Located In The Front Of This Manual When Battery Power To The Computer Has Been Interrupted.

NOTE: Prior To Performing Any Service Operations Listed In This Section, Consult The "Technical Service Bulletins" Section For Related Information.

INDEX

	Page No.
Air Bag System (Volume 2)	4-1
Air Conditioning	16-1
Alternator, Replace	6-11
3.5L & 3.9L Engines	6-11
3.6L Engine	6-11
3.8L Engine	6-11
5.3L Engine	6-11
Alternators	19-1
Blower Motor, Replace	6-16
Cabin Air Filter, Replace	6-16
Coil Pack, Replace	6-11
3.5L & 3.9L Engines	6-11
3.6L Engine	6-11
3.8L Engine	6-11
5.3L Engine	6-11
Cooling Fans	17-1
Cruise Control (Volume 2)	2-1
Dash Gauges (Volume 2)	1-1
Dash Panel Service (Volume 2)	5-1
Evaporator Core, Replace	6-18
Century, Grand Prix, LaCrosse & Regal	6-18
Impala & Monte Carlo	6-18
Fuel Pump Relay Location	6-10
Fuse Panel & Flasher Location	6-10
Century & Regal	6-10
Grand Prix	6-10
Impala & Monte Carlo	
2004–05	6-10
2006–08	6-10
LaCrosse	6-10
Headlamp Switch, Replace	6-13

	Page No.
Century & Regal	6-13
Grand Prix	6-13
Impala	6-13
2004–05	6-13
2006–08	6-13
LaCrosse	6-13
Monte Carlo	6-13
Heater Core, Replace	6-16
Century & Impala	6-16
Grand Prix, LaCrosse, Monte Carlo & Regal	6-17
Ignition Lock, Replace	6-11
Century, LaCrosse & Regal	6-11
Grand Prix	6-12
Impala	6-12
Monte Carlo	6-12
Ignition Switch, Replace	6-12
Century, LaCrosse & Regal	6-12
Grand Prix	6-13
Impala & Monte Carlo	6-13
Instrument Cluster, Replace	6-14
Century & Regal	6-14
Grand Prix	6-14
Impala	6-14
2004–05	6-14
2006–08	6-14
LaCrosse	6-15
Monte Carlo	6-14
Multi-Function Switch, Replace	6-13
Passive Restraint Systems (Volume 2)	4-1
Precautions	6-10
Air Bag Systems	6-10

	Page No.
Battery Ground Cable	6-10
Radio Theft Deterrent System	6-10
Radio, Replace	6-15
Century & Regal	6-15
Grand Prix	6-15
Impala	6-15
2004–05	6-15
2006–08	6-15
LaCrosse	6-15
Monte Carlo	6-15
Speed Controls (Volume 2)	2-1
Starter Motors	18-1
Starter, Replace	6-10
3.1L Engine	6-10
3.4L Engine	6-10
3.5L & 3.9L Engines	6-10
3.6L Engine	6-10
3.8L Engine	6-10
5.3L Engine	6-11
Steering Columns	20-1
Steering Wheel, Replace	6-14
Stop Light Switch, Replace	6-13
Transmission Range (TR) Switch, Replace	6-13
Turn Signal Switch, Replace	6-14
Wiper Module, Replace	6-16
Wiper Motor, Replace	6-16
Wiper Switch, Replace	6-16
Wiper Systems (Volume 2)	3-1
Wiper Transmission, Replace	6-16
Installation	6-16
Removal	6-16

PRECAUTIONS

Air Bag Systems

Refer to "Air Bag System Precautions" in the front of this manual for system disarming and arming procedures.

Radio Theft Deterrent System

Anti-theft radios have a coded theft deterrent circuit. **The security code number must be obtained before disconnecting the battery, removing the radio fuse or the radio.**

After service procedure has been performed, connect the radio power supply and turn it On. When "LOC" is displayed, enter security code to activate the radio.

Battery Ground Cable

Prior to service, disconnect battery ground cable and isolate as required.

FUSE PANEL & FLASHER LOCATION

Century & Regal

The fuse panel is located behind the righthand side instrument panel, in front of the door opening. The underhood accessory wiring junction block is located on the righthand side of the engine compartment, mounted on the strut tower. The hazard and turn signal flasher module is located behind the lefthand side of the instrument panel, mounted on the multi-purpose bracket, near the Body Control Module (BCM).

Grand Prix

The fuse panel is located behind the righthand side instrument panel, behind the access panel. The underhood accessory wiring junction block is located on the righthand side of the engine compartment, mounted on the strut tower. The hazard and turn signal flasher function is controlled by the Body Control Module (BCM). The BCM is located behind the lefthand side of the instrument panel, left of the steering column.

Impala & Monte Carlo

2004-05

The lefthand instrument panel junction block is located behind the lefthand side of the instrument panel, behind an access panel. The righthand instrument panel junction block is located behind the righthand side of the instrument panel, behind an access panel. The rear junction block is located in the luggage compartment, behind the righthand rear wheelhouse. The underhood junction blocks are located on the righthand side of the engine compart-

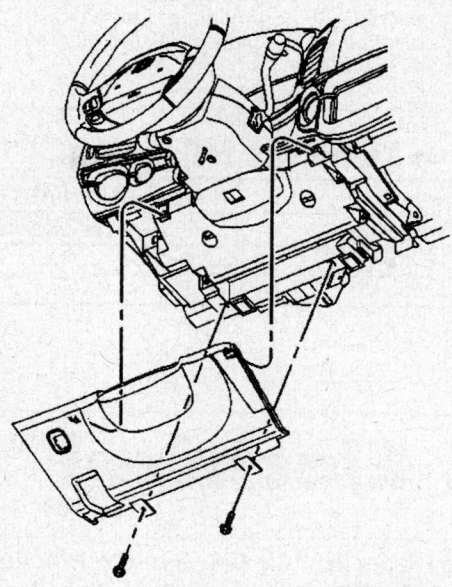

ARM66GC000000301

Fig. 1   Steering column filler replacement. Monte Carlo

ment, forward of the strut tower. The Special Equipment (SEO) fuse block is located behind the lefthand side of the instrument panel, right of the steering column. The hazard and turn signal flasher is part of the hazard switch assembly. The hazard switch assembly is located behind the righthand side of the instrument panel, in the instrument panel fuse block.

2006-08

The instrument panel fuse block is located behind the righthand front kick panel. The rear junction block is located in the luggage compartment, behind the righthand rear wheelhouse. The underhood junction blocks are located on the righthand side of the engine compartment, forward of the strut tower. The special equipment fuse block is located behind the instrument, right of the steering column, above the accelerator pedal. Hazard and turn signal flasher operation is controlled by the Body Control Module (BCM). The BCM is located behind the lefthand side of the instrument panel, left of the steering column.

LaCrosse

The fuse panel is located behind the righthand side of the instrument panel, behind the access panel. The underhood fuse block is located on the righthand side of the engine compartment, mounted on the strut tower. The hazard and turn signals are controlled by the Body Control Module (BCM). The BCM is located behind the lefthand side of the instrument panel, left of the steering column.

FUEL PUMP RELAY LOCATION

The fuel pump relay is located in the underhood junction block, on the righthand side of the engine compartment.

STARTER

REPLACE

3.1L Engine

1. Remove air cleaner assembly.
2. Raise and support vehicle.
3. Remove mounting bolts and torque converter cover.
4. Remove mounting bolts, lower starter motor and disconnect starter wiring.
5. Remove starter motor and shims.
6. Reverse procedure to install, noting the following:
   a. Install shims removed in their original locations.
   b. **Torque** starter motor mounting bolts to 32 ft. lbs.

3.4L Engine

1. Raise and support vehicle.
2. Remove front lower air deflector panel.
3. Remove torque converter covers.
4. Remove mounting nuts and disconnect starter motor electrical connectors.
5. Remove mounting bolts and starter motor.
6. Reverse procedure to install. **Torque** starter motor mounting bolts to 32 ft. lbs.

3.5L & 3.9L Engines

1. Raise and support vehicle.
2. Remove radiator air deflector attaching screws and retainers, then the air deflector.
3. Remove torque converter cover attaching bolts and the cover.
4. Disconnect starter electrical connectors.
5. Remove mounting bolts and starter.
6. Reverse procedure to install, noting the following:
   a. **Torque** solenoid battery terminal inside nut to 13 ft. lbs.
   b. **Torque** solenoid battery terminal outside nut to 89 inch lbs.
   c. **Torque** solenoid S terminal outside nut to 27 inch lbs.
   d. **Torque** mounting bolts to 32 ft. lbs.

3.6L Engine

1. Raise and support vehicle.
2. Disconnect starter motor electrical connectors.
3. Remove mounting bolts and starter motor.
4. Reverse procedure to install. **Torque** starter motor mounting bolts to 37 ft. lbs.

3.8L Engine

1. Raise and support vehicle.
2. Remove lower air deflector fog lamp access panels.
3. Remove lower air deflector retainers.
4. Remove lower air deflector attaching bolts and screws.
5. Remove right and left side lower front

fender liner screws from lower air deflector.
6. Remove lower air deflector.
7. Remove mounting bolts and torque
converter cover.
8. Disconnect starter motor electrical
connectors.
9. Remove mounting bolts and starter
motor.
10. Reverse procedure to install. **Torque**
starter motor mounting bolts to 32 ft.
lbs.

5.3L Engine

1. Remove starter solenoid BAT terminal
nut and positive battery cable from
starter motor.
2. Remove engine harness terminal from
starter motor.
3. Disconnect starter motor electrical
connector.
4. Remove air cleaner.
5. Remove mounting bolts and starter
motor.
6. Reverse procedure to install, noting
the following:
a. **Torque** starter motor mounting
bolts to 37 ft. lbs.
b. **Torque** BAT terminal nut to 89 inch
lbs.

ALTERNATOR
REPLACE

3.5L & 3.9L Engines

1. Remove engine oil fill cap and intake
manifold cover.
2. Remove mounting bolts and lefthand
inner fender brace.
3. Loosen clamp and remove air cleaner
outlet duct from throttle body.
4. Disconnect PCV tube from air inlet
duct.
5. Disconnect Mass Air Flow (MAF) sensor electrical connector.
6. Remove upper from lower air cleaner
housing.
7. Remove Powertrain Control Module
(PCM) and harness from lower air
cleaner housing. **Do not disconnect
connectors.**
8. Remove Transmission Control Module
(TCM) and harness from lower air
cleaner housing. **Do not disconnect
connectors.**
9. Loosen clamp and remove air cleaner
outlet duct from air cleaner.
10. Remove engine mount strut from front
of engine and radiator support.
11. Rotate tensioner clockwise and remove serpentine drive belt.
12. Remove alternator mounting bolts and
nuts.
13. Disconnect electrical connectors and
remove alternator.
14. Reverse procedure to install. **Torque**
mounting bolts to 37 ft. lbs., and nuts to
22 ft. lbs.

3.6L Engine

1. Remove drive belt from alternator.
2. Raise and support vehicle.

Fig. 2 Fuse/relay panel access
cover & instrument cluster trim
plate replacement. Monte Carlo

3. Disconnect alternator electrical connector.
4. Position alternator output BAT terminal
protective boot aside.
5. Remove alternator output BAT terminal nut and disconnect battery positive
lead from alternator.
6. Remove alternator lower mounting
bolts.
7. Lower vehicle and remove upper
mounting bolt.
8. Remove alternator.
9. Reverse procedure to install. **Torque**
alternator bolts 37 ft. lbs.

3.8L Engine

1. Remove serpentine drive belt.
2. Disconnect alternator electrical connectors.
3. Remove mounting bolts and alternator.
4. Reverse procedure to install.

5.3L Engine

1. Remove engine cover.
2. Remove fender brace from righthand
side of engine compartment.
3. Rotate drive belt tensioner clockwise
using serpentine belt tension unloader
tool No. EN-47988, or equivalent.
4. Remove drive belt.
5. Disconnect alternator electrical connector.
6. Position output BAT terminal boot
aside, then remove terminal nut and
positive battery lead.

7. Remove mounting bolts and alternator.
8. Reverse procedure to install, noting
the following:
a. **Torque** alternator mounting bolts to
37 ft. lbs.
b. **Torque** BAT terminal nut to 15 ft.
lbs.

COIL PACK
REPLACE

3.5L & 3.9L Engines

1. Remove engine oil fill cap and intake
manifold cover.
2. Disconnect Manifold Absolute Pressure (MAP) sensor electrical connector.
3. Disconnect ignition coil electrical connector.
4. Disconnect spark plug wires from ignition coil.
5. Remove mounting bolts and ignition
coil.
6. Reverse procedure to install. **Torque**
mounting bolts to 15 ft. lbs.

3.6L Engine

1. Remove engine cover.
2. **If removing coil for cylinder Nos. 2
or 5,** remove upper intake manifold as
outlined under "Intake Manifold, Replace" in "3.6L Engine" section.
3. **When removing all coils,** remove coil
retaining bolts, then the coil.
4. Reverse procedure to install. **Torque**
coil retaining bolts to 89 inch lbs.

3.8L Engine

1. Remove spark plug wires from ignition
coils. Note spark plug wire position for
installation reference.
2. Remove mounting screws and ignition
coils.
3. Reverse procedure to install. **Torque**
mounting screws to 40 inch lbs.

5.3L Engine

1. Remove engine cover.
2. Disconnect Connector Position Assurance (CPA) retainer.
3. Disconnect ignition coil main electrical
connector.
4. Disconnect spark plug wires from ignition coil.
5. Remove mounting bolts and ignition
coil.
6. Reverse procedure to install. **Torque**
mounting bolts to 71 inch lbs.

IGNITION LOCK
REPLACE

Century, LaCrosse &
Regal

1. Remove steering wheel as outlined
under "Steering Wheel, Replace."
2. Pull tilt lever out of steering column.

3. Remove pan head tapping screws from steering column lower trim cover.
4. Remove lower trim cover.
5. Remove upper trim cover attaching screw, then the cover.
6. Push lock cylinder retaining pin with suitable ¹⁄₁₆ inch Allen wrench.
7. Release key to RUN position and pull lock cylinder set from lock module.
8. Reverse procedure to install.

Grand Prix

1. Remove ignition switch bezel.
2. Pull instrument panel accessory trim plate rearward and disconnect electrical connector from driver information display assembly.
3. Remove driver information display retaining screws, then the driver information display from instrument panel.
4. Remove instrument panel center air outlet attaching screws and the air outlet.
5. Remove instrument panel accessory trim plate.
6. Remove lefthand instrument panel insulator fasteners.
7. Rotate courtesy lamp and remove lamp from lefthand insulator.
8. Remove insulator panel from under lefthand side of instrument panel.
9. Remove left instrument panel fuse block access hole cover.
10. Disengage Data Link Connector (DLC) retainers, then remove DLC from instrument panel.
11. Remove steering column opening filler panel attaching screws, then pull filler panel rearward to disengage retainers.
12. Remove steering column opening filler panel.
13. Remove lefthand knee bolster attaching screws.
14. Remove knee bolster attaching bolts at instrument panel carrier cross car beam.
15. Remove harness retainer from knee bolster, then the knee bolster from under lefthand side of instrument panel.
16. Remove ignition switch attaching bolts, then lower the ignition switch away from instrument panel trim pad.
17. Insert key into ignition lock cylinder and turn to ON/RUN position.
18. Depress and hold detent on bottom of ignition switch in order to release ignition lock cylinder.
19. Remove ignition lock cylinder with key.
20. Remove key from lock cylinder and disengage theft deterrent reader/exciter module retainers.
21. Remove theft deterrent reader/exciter module from the lock cylinder housing.
22. Reverse procedure to install.

Impala

1. Apply parking brake and remove ignition switch cylinder bezel.
2. **On models equipped with column shift,** place transaxle shift control indicator to No. 1 position. Keep key in ignition switch cylinder.
3. **On all models,** remove instrument

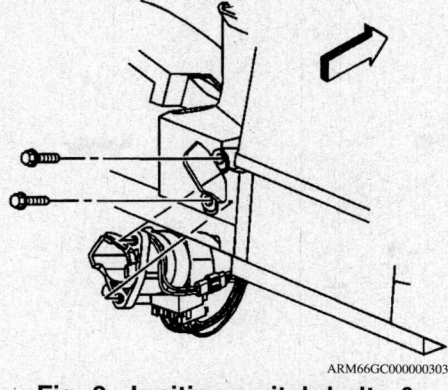

Fig. 3   Ignition switch bolts & switch replacement. Monte Carlo

panel fuse block access hole cover.
4. Disengage left instrument panel insulator retainers from lower trim pad.
5. Remove steering column filler panel bolts.
6. Pull steering column filler panel rearward to disengage retainers.
7. Lower filler panel away from lower trim panel.
8. Disconnect rear compartment release switch electrical connector.
9. Remove rear compartment release switch.
10. Remove steering column filler panel.
11. Remove instrument cluster trim plate attaching screws.
12. Starting at right end of cluster trim plate, grasp trim plate and pull rearward.
13. Continue working around cluster trim plate until all retainers are released.
14. Disconnect hazard and traction control switch electrical connectors, then remove cluster trim plate.
15. Insert key and turn ignition lock cylinder to ON/RUN position.
16. Depress and hold detent on ignition lock cylinder using a small curved tool or an L-shaped hex wrench.
17. Access detent by placing tool through instrument panel opening to right of ignition switch. If you cannot locate detent with tool, lower ignition switch away from instrument panel.
18. Using key as an aid, pull lock cylinder from switch.
19. Remove key from lock cylinder. If cylinder does not rotate or is seized, refer to "Ignition Switch, Replace."
20. Reverse procedure to install.

Monte Carlo

1. Remove knee bolster and bracket from under steering column.
2. Remove steering column filler panel mounting screws, **Fig. 1.**
3. Carefully lower filler panel, then disconnect trunk release switch electrical connector and remove panel.
4. Apply parking brake.
5. Remove ignition switch cylinder bezel from cylinder using suitable flat-bladed tool.
6. **On models equipped with column**

shift, place gear selector lever in D 1 position.
7. **On all models,** remove lefthand and righthand fuse/relay instrument panel access covers, **Fig. 2.**
8. Starting at righthand end of trim panel, remove instrument cluster trim plate bezel mounting screws, then pull cluster trim plate bezel away from instrument panel trim pad.
9. Remove mounting bolts and lower ignition switch away from instrument panel.
10. Disconnect electrical connector from hazard and traction control switches.
11. Remove mounting bolts, then lower ignition switch away form instrument carrier, **Fig. 3.**
12. Insert key into ignition lock cylinder and turn it to RUN position.
13. Depress ignition switch housing to release lock cylinder.
14. If ignition switch lock cylinder is seized or will not rotate, proceed as follows:
    a. Protect surrounding area with suitable shop towels or clean fender cover.
    b. Locate release button on ignition lock cylinder plastic switch housing, then center punch a location mark on rib approximately ³⁄₈ inch reward, toward key entry end, from cylinder release button.
    c. Carefully drill pilot hole through plastic housing using suitable ¹⁄₈ inch drill bit, then larger hole with suitable ⁹⁄₃₂ inch bit at pilot location and slightly into surface of lock cylinder, **Fig. 4.**
    d. Remove lock cylinder from switch housing, using compressed air blow out ignition switch.
    e. Depress retainer and remove transaxle park/lock cable by pulling outward.
    f. **Passlock electrical connector cannot be removed until lock cylinder is removed.**
    g. Depress detent and remove ignition lock cylinder with key.
15. Reverse procedure to install.

IGNITION SWITCH
REPLACE

Century, LaCrosse & Regal

1. Remove steering wheel as outlined under "Steering Wheel, Replace."
2. Pull tilt lever out of steering column.
3. Remove pan head tapping screws from steering column lower trim cover.
4. Remove lower trim cover.
5. Remove upper trim cover attaching screw, then the cover.
6. Remove turn signal and multi-function wire harness retaining straps from steering column and wire harness.
7. Slide turn signal and multi-function switch assembly connectors out of bulkhead connector.
8. Rotate key alarm connector 90° and

pull key alarm connector out of lock module, **Fig. 5.**

9. Remove mounting screws, then the ignition and key alarm switch, **Fig. 6.**
10. Reverse procedure to install.

Grand Prix

Refer to "Ignition Lock, Replace" for ignition switch replacement.

Impala & Monte Carlo

Refer to "Ignition Lock, Replace" for ignition switch replacement procedure.

TRANSMISSION RANGE (TR) SWITCH
REPLACE

1. Apply parking brake and block drive wheels.
2. Place selector lever in Neutral position.
3. Remove throttle body air inlet duct.
4. Remove automatic transaxle range selector cable from switch.
5. Disconnect switch electrical connectors.
6. Remove range selector lever from switch.
7. Remove mounting screws and switch.
8. Reverse procedure to install, noting the following:
   a. **Do not rotate new switch. New switch is pinned to Neutral position.**
   b. **If bolts do not align with mounting boss on transaxle, ensure transaxle shaft is in Neutral position.**
   c. Align flats of shift shaft to flats of switch.
   d. **Torque** switch mounting bolts to 18 ft. lbs.

HEADLAMP SWITCH
REPLACE

Century & Regal

1. Pull rear edge of access opening cover away from lefthand side of instrument panel to release retainers.
2. Release forward edge of access opening cover from behind hinge pillar and remove cover.
3. Remove headlamp switch retaining screws.
4. Carefully pull headlamp switch away from instrument panel to disconnect electrical connector.
5. Remove headlamp switch.
6. Reverse procedure to install.

Grand Prix

Refer to "Multi-Function Switch, Replace."

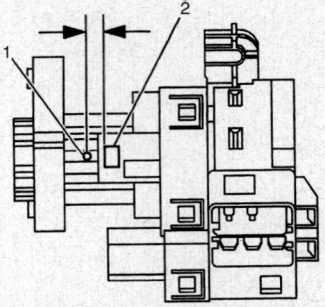

1- CENTER PUNCH LOCATION APPROXIMATELY 3/8 INCH REWARD
2- INGNITION LOCK CYLINDER RELEASE BUTTON

ARM66GC000000304

Fig. 4 Ignition switch lock & switch removal. Monte Carlo

Impala
2004-05

1. Apply parking brake and remove ignition switch cylinder bezel.
2. **On models equipped with column shift,** place transaxle shift control indicator to No. 1 position. Keep key in ignition switch cylinder.
3. **On all models,** remove instrument panel fuse block access hole cover.
4. Disengage left instrument panel insulator retainers from lower trim pad.
5. Remove steering column filler panel bolts.
6. Pull steering column filler panel rearward to disengage retainers.
7. Lower filler panel away from lower trim panel.
8. Disconnect rear compartment release switch electrical connector.
9. Remove rear compartment release switch.
10. Remove steering column filler panel.
11. Remove instrument cluster trim plate attaching screws.
12. Starting at right end of cluster trim plate, grasp trim plate and pull rearward.
13. Continue working around cluster trim plate until all retainers are released.
14. Disconnect hazard and traction control switch electrical connectors, then remove cluster trim plate.
15. Remove headlamp switch housing attaching screws, then the switch housing from instrument panel.
16. Disconnect electrical connector from headlamp switch and foglamp switch.
17. Remove foglamp switch from headlamp switch housing.
18. Reverse procedure to install.

2006-08

1. Pull headlamp/dimmer switch assembly from instrument panel.
2. Disconnect switch electrical connector.
3. Reverse procedure to install.

Monte Carlo

1. Remove knee bolster and bracket from under steering column.

2. Remove steering column filler panel mounting screws, **Fig. 1.**
3. Carefully lower filler panel, then disconnect trunk release switch electrical connector and remove panel.
4. Apply parking brake.
5. Remove ignition switch cylinder bezel from cylinder using suitable flat-bladed tool.
6. **On models equipped with column shift,** place gear selector lever in D 1 position.
7. **On all models,** remove lefthand and righthand fuse/relay instrument panel access covers, **Fig. 2.**
8. Starting at righthand end of trim panel, remove instrument cluster trim plate bezel mounting screws, then pull cluster trim plate bezel away from instrument panel trim pad.
9. Remove mounting screws, and headlamp switch.
10. Disconnect headlamp switch housing and fog lamp switch electrical connector.
11. Remove headlamp switch from instrument panel using suitable flat-bladed tool.
12. Reverse procedure to install.

LaCrosse

1. Open glove compartment and remove instrument panel cluster trim plate attaching screw, **Fig. 7.**
2. Pull trim plate away from instrument panel and disconnect fog lamp and headlamp switch electrical connectors.
3. Remove trim plate retaining nut and clips, then the trim plate from instrument panel.
4. Remove fog lamp and headlamp switch assembly from vehicle.
5. Reverse procedure to install.

STOP LIGHT SWITCH
REPLACE

1. Remove push-in retainers and lefthand instrument panel sound insulator.
2. Remove mounting screws and brake lamp switch.
3. Reverse procedure to install, adjust brake switch as follows:
   a. Push brake pedal as far forward as possible to set brake push rod into booster.
   b. Pull brake pedal rearward, against internal stop.
   c. Brake lamp switch is adjusted.

MULTI-FUNCTION SWITCH
REPLACE

1. Remove steering wheel as outlined under "Steering Wheel, Replace."
2. Remove upper and lower steering column trim covers.
3. Remove wire harness straps from wiring harness and upper tilt head.
4. Remove mounting screws and multi-function switch.

5. Reverse procedure to install, noting the following:
   a. **Torque** multi-function switch mounting screws to 62 inch lbs.
   b. **Torque** steering shaft nut to 30 ft. lbs.

TURN SIGNAL SWITCH

REPLACE

Refer to "Multi-Function Switch, Replace" for turn signal switch replacement.

STEERING WHEEL

REPLACE

1. Turn ignition Off.
2. Remove air bag module as outlined in "Passive Restraint Systems" chapter.
3. Scribe alignment mark on steering wheel hub in line with slash mark on steering shaft.
4. Loosen and position steering wheel nut flush with shift end.
5. Loosen steering wheel using suitable puller. **When removing a steering wheel with accessory controls in hub, avoid damaging electronic circuits. Steering wheel puller bolts should be turned in no more than 4–6 threads to avoid contact with electrical circuits.**
6. Remove steering shaft nut and steering wheel.
7. Reverse procedure to install. **Torque** steering shaft nut to 30 ft. lbs.

INSTRUMENT CLUSTER

REPLACE

Century & Regal

1. Remove push-in retainers and left-hand side instrument panel sound insulator.
2. Remove steering column opening filler panel from under steering column.
3. Remove knee bolster bracket from under lefthand side of instrument panel.
4. Remove support mounting bolts and lower steering column.
5. Pull bottom edge of instrument cluster trim plate away from instrument panel to release retainer clips.
6. Disconnect fog lamp switch electrical connector and remove instrument cluster trim plate from instrument panel.
7. Remove instrument cluster mounting screws.
8. Pull instrument cluster towards rear and upward to Disconnect retaining clips.
9. Disconnect cluster electrical connectors and remove cluster.
10. Reverse procedure to install.

Grand Prix

1. Remove ignition switch bezel.
2. Pull instrument panel accessory trim plate rearward and disconnect driver

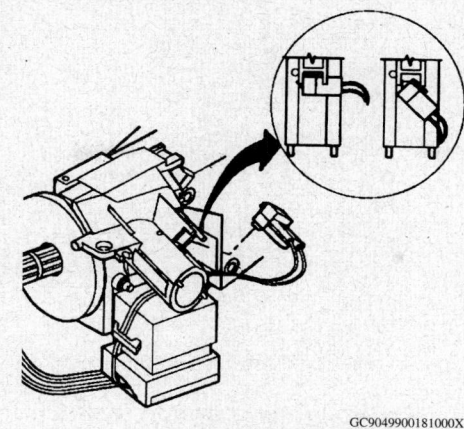

GC9049900181000X

Fig. 5   Key alarm connector. Century, LaCrosse & Regal

information display assembly electrical connector.
3. Remove driver information display screws and the display from instrument panel.
4. Remove instrument panel center air outlet retaining screws, then the center air outlet.
5. Remove instrument panel accessory trim plate.
6. Remove left instrument panel fuse block access hole cover.
7. Disengage Data Link Connector (DLC) retainers, then remove DLC from trim pad.
8. Remove steering column opening filler screws, then pull filler panel rearward to disengage retainers.
9. Remove steering column opening filler panel.
10. Tilt steering wheel to lowest position.
11. Grasp edge of instrument panel cluster trim plate.
12. Pull trim plate rearward to disengage retainers and disconnect headlamp dimmer switch electrical connector.
13. Remove headlamp dimmer switch retaining screws, then the switch and cluster trim plate.
14. Remove instrument cluster retaining screws.
15. Pull instrument cluster away from instrument panel and disconnect electrical connector.
16. Remove instrument cluster.
17. Reverse procedure to install.

Impala

2004–05

1. Apply parking brake and remove ignition switch cylinder bezel.
2. **On models equipped with column shift,** place transaxle shift control indicator to No. 1 position. Keep key in ignition switch cylinder.
3. **On all models,** remove instrument panel fuse block access hole cover.
4. Disengage left instrument panel insulator retainers from lower trim pad.
5. Remove steering column filler panel bolts.
6. Pull steering column filler panel rear-

ward to disengage retainers.
7. Lower filler panel away from lower trim panel.
8. Disconnect rear compartment release switch electrical connector.
9. Remove the rear compartment release switch.
10. Remove steering column filler panel.
11. Remove instrument panel fuse block access hole covers.
12. Remove instrument cluster trim plate attaching screws.
13. Starting at right end of cluster trim plate, grasp trim plate and pull rearward.
14. Continue working around cluster trim plate until all retainers are released.
15. Disconnect hazard and traction control switch electrical connectors, then remove cluster trim plate.
16. Remove instrument cluster retaining screws.
17. Pull instrument cluster away from instrument panel and disconnect electrical connector.
18. Remove instrument cluster.
19. Reverse procedure to install.

2006–08

1. Remove left and right outer trim covers from instrument panel.
2. Remove instrument panel trim plate attaching screws, **Fig. 8.**
3. Pull trim panel away from instrument panel and disconnect electrical connectors.
4. Tilt steering column to lowest position and remove driver information center switch.
5. Remove instrument cluster retaining screws.
6. Pull instrument cluster away from instrument panel and disconnect electrical connector.
7. Remove instrument cluster.
8. Reverse procedure to install.

Monte Carlo

1. Remove instrument panel fuse block access hole cover.
2. Disengage lefthand instrument panel insulator retainers from instrument panel trim pad.
3. Remove steering column filler panel bolts.
4. Pull steering column filler panel rearward to disengage retainers.
5. Lower steering column filler panel away from lower trim panel.
6. Disconnect rear compartment release switch electrical connector.
7. Remove rear compartment release switch and steering column filler panel.
8. Remove instrument cluster trim plate retaining screws.
9. Starting at right end of cluster, grasp trim plate and pull rearward.
10. Continue working around cluster trim plate until all retainers are released from trim pad.
11. Disconnect hazard and traction control switch electrical connectors.
12. Remove cluster trim plate.
13. Remove instrument cluster retaining screws.

14. Pull instrument cluster away from instrument panel and disconnect electrical connector.
15. Remove instrument cluster.
16. Reverse procedure to install.

LaCrosse

1. Open glove compartment and remove instrument panel cluster trim plate attaching screw, **Fig. 7.**
2. Pull trim plate away from instrument panel and disconnect fog lamp and headlamp switch electrical connectors.
3. Remove trim plate retaining nut and clips, then the trim plate from instrument panel.
4. Remove instrument cluster retaining screws.
5. Pull instrument cluster away from instrument panel and disconnect electrical connector.
6. Remove instrument cluster.
7. Reverse procedure to install.

RADIO
REPLACE

Century & Regal

1. Remove push-in retainers and lefthand side instrument panel sound insulator.
2. Remove steering column opening filler panel from under steering column.
3. Remove instrument panel accessory trim panel mounting screws.
4. Pull accessory trim plate rearward and release two retaining tabs.
5. Remove accessory trim plate.
6. Remove radio mounting screws and pull radio away from instrument panel.
7. Disconnect electrical connectors and antenna lead-in cable.
8. Remove radio.
9. Reverse procedure to install.

Grand Prix

1. Remove ignition switch bezel.
2. Pull instrument panel accessory trim plate rearward and disconnect driver information display assembly electrical connector.
3. Remove driver information display screws and the display from instrument panel.
4. Remove instrument panel center air outlet retaining screws, then the center air outlet.
5. Remove instrument panel accessory trim plate.
6. Apply park brake and shift transaxle to No. 1 position.
7. Remove instrument panel center compartment retaining screws, then the center compartment.
8. Remove HVAC control module retaining screws, then pull HVAC control module out of instrument panel.
9. Disconnect HVAC module electrical connectors, then remove control module.
10. Remove radio mounting screws.

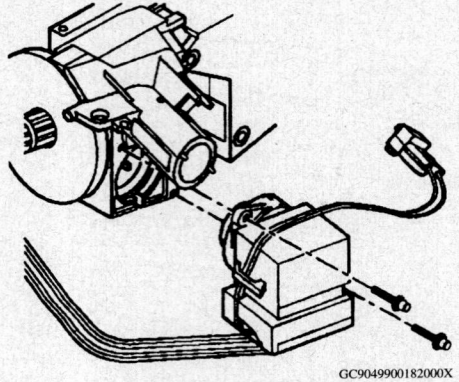

GC9049900182000X

Fig. 6 Ignition & alarm switch replacement. Century, LaCrosse & Regal

11. Pull radio away from instrument panel, then disconnect electrical connectors and antenna lead-in cable.
12. Remove radio.
13. Reverse procedure to install.

Impala
2004–05

1. Apply parking brake and remove ignition switch cylinder bezel.
2. **On models equipped with column shift,** place transaxle shift control indicator to No. 1 position. Keep key in ignition switch cylinder.
3. **On all models,** remove instrument panel fuse block access hole cover.
4. Disengage left instrument panel insulator retainers from lower trim pad.
5. Remove steering column filler panel bolts.
6. Pull steering column filler panel rearward to disengage retainers.
7. Lower filler panel away from lower trim panel.
8. Disconnect rear compartment release switch electrical connector.
9. Remove the rear compartment release switch.
10. Remove steering column filler panel.
11. Remove instrument panel fuse block access hole covers.
12. Remove instrument cluster trim plate attaching screws.
13. Starting at right end of cluster trim plate, grasp trim plate and pull rearward.
14. Continue working around cluster trim plate until all retainers are released.
15. Disconnect hazard and traction control switch electrical connectors, then remove cluster trim plate.
16. Remove radio mounting screws.
17. Pull radio away from instrument panel, then disconnect electrical connectors and antenna lead-in cable.
18. Remove radio.
19. Reverse procedure to install.

2006–08

1. Remove instrument panel accessory trim plate from center of instrument panel.
2. Remove heater and A/C control assembly retaining screws and pull assembly away from instrument panel.
3. Disconnect heater and A/C control assembly electrical connector and remove from instrument panel.
4. Slightly push antenna lead toward radio to relieve tension on internal fingers, then pull back on spring-loaded locking ring and remove connector from radio.
5. Remove radio mounting screws, then pull radio away from instrument panel.
6. Disconnect electrical connectors and remove radio.
7. Reverse procedure to install.

LaCrosse

1. Pull instrument panel lower trim plate assembly from under center of instrument panel.
2. Disconnect trim plate electrical connector and remove from vehicle.
3. Remove HVAC control assembly mounting screws and pull control assembly away from instrument panel.
4. Disconnect HVAC control assembly electrical connectors and remove assembly from instrument panel.
5. Pull driver information display bezel away from instrument panel, disconnect electrical connectors and remove bezel.
6. Remove inflatable restraint indicator assembly and driver information display switch assembly from instrument panel.
7. Remove radio mounting screws, then pull radio away from instrument panel.
8. Disconnect electrical connectors and remove radio.
9. Reverse procedure to install.

Monte Carlo

1. Remove knee bolster and bracket from under steering column.
2. Remove steering column filler panel mounting screws, **Fig. 1.**
3. Carefully lower filler panel, then disconnect trunk release switch electrical connector and remove panel.
4. Apply parking brake.
5. Remove ignition switch cylinder bezel from cylinder using suitable flat-bladed tool.
6. **On models equipped with column shift,** place gear selector lever in D 1 position.
7. **On all models,** remove lefthand and righthand fuse/relay instrument panel access covers, **Fig. 2.**
8. Starting at righthand end of trim panel, remove instrument cluster trim plate bezel mounting screws, then pull cluster trim plate bezel away from instrument panel trim pad.
9. Remove radio mounting screws.
10. Pull radio away from instrument panel, then disconnect electrical connectors and antenna lead-in cable.
11. Remove radio.
12. Reverse procedure to install.

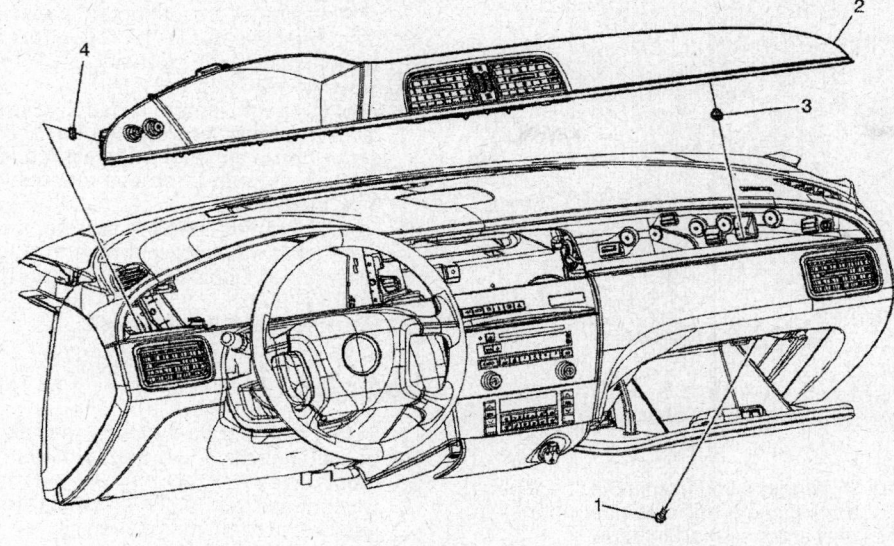

1-Screw
2-Instrument panel cluster trim plate
3-Nut
4-Clip

ARM0700000000210

Fig. 7 Instrument cluster trim plate removal. LaCrosse

WIPER MOTOR
REPLACE

1. Remove wiper module as outlined under "Wiper Module, Replace."
2. Remove wiper motor crank arm from wiper transmission using wiper transmission separator tool No. J39232, or equivalent.
3. Remove wiper motor crank arm to wiper motor mounting nut.
4. Remove bracket mounting screws and wiper motor.
5. Reverse procedure to install.

WIPER SWITCH
REPLACE

Refer to "Multi-Function Switch, Replace" for wiper switch replacement procedure.

WIPER TRANSMISSION
REPLACE

The windshield wiper module consists of both the wiper motor and the wiper transmission.

Removal

1. Turn ignition to Accessory position and set wiper switch to Pulse/Delay position.
2. Wait until wiper arms are in inner wipe position and are not moving, then turn ignition switch to OFF position.
3. Remove hose from nozzle on wiper arm driveshaft.
4. Remove covers, mounting nuts and wiper arms from wiper transmission driveshaft.
5. Remove mounting bolts and inlet shroud.
6. Disconnect wiper motor electrical connectors.
7. Remove mounting bolts and wiper module.
8. Remove two mounting screws and transmission socket from link ball.
9. Remove bellcrank mounting screws, and transmission.

Installation

1. Connect new transmission to module.
2. Ensure wiper motor is in inner wipe position.
3. Align holes in module and bellcrank, then install transmission socket screws.
4. Ensure body seal is in proper place on righthand side of module and install wiper module.
5. Install passenger side wiper arm and blade.
6. Measure from tip of blade to bottom edge of glass. Ensure distance is approximately 9 1/8 inches, then tighten nut.
7. Install protective cap and connect washer hose.
8. Install driver side wiper arm and blade.
9. Measure from tip of blade to bottom edge of glass. Ensure distance is ap-

proximately two inches, then tighten nut.
10. Install protective cap and connect washer hose.

WIPER MODULE
REPLACE

The windshield wiper module consists of both the wiper motor and the wiper transmission.

1. Turn ignition to Accessory position and set wiper switch to Pulse/Delay position.
2. Wait until wiper arms are in inner wipe position and are not moving, then turn ignition switch to OFF position.
3. Remove hose from nozzle on wiper arm driveshaft.
4. Remove covers, mounting nuts and wiper arms from wiper transmission driveshaft.
5. Remove air inlet grille push-in retainers, then the grille.
6. Disconnect wiper motor electrical connectors.
7. Remove mounting bolts and wiper module.
8. Reverse procedure to install.

BLOWER MOTOR
REPLACE

1. Remove sound insulator panel from under righthand side of instrument panel.
2. **On models equipped with convenience center,** remove convenience center mounting screws, then slide convenience center out.
3. **On all models,** disconnect blower motor electrical connector and remove harness from clip.
4. Disconnect blower motor cooling hose.
5. Remove mounting screws and blower motor.
6. Reverse procedure to install.

CABIN AIR FILTER
REPLACE

1. Operate windshield wipers until blades are in up position, then turn ignition switch to OFF position.
2. Open hood.
3. Lift rear hood seal from righthand air inlet grille area flange.
4. Disconnect retaining clips and remove righthand air inlet grille.
5. Remove cabin air filter, **Fig. 9.**
6. Reverse procedure to install.

HEATER CORE
REPLACE

Century & Impala

1. Remove oil filler cap, mounting nut and fuel injector cover.
2. Drain cooling system into suitable container, then disconnect heater hoses from heater core.

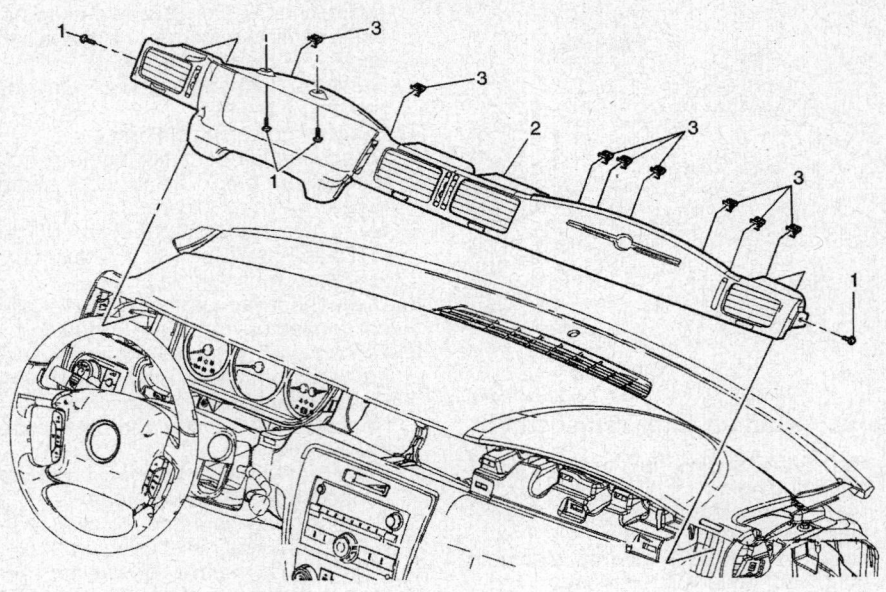

1-Screws
2-Instrument panel trim plate
3-Retainers

ARM0700000000211

Fig. 8   Instrument panel trim plate. 2006-08 Impala

Grand Prix, LaCrosse, Monte Carlo & Regal

1. Remove oil filler cap, mounting nut and fuel injector cover.
2. Drain cooling system into suitable container, then disconnect heater hoses from heater core.
3. Disconnect heater hoses from heater core.
4. Remove sound insulator panels from under lefthand and righthand sides of instrument panel.
5. Remove covers from front end of seat adjuster tracks by spreading two rear feet and pulling forward.
6. Spread track cover arms and pull rearward to remove.
7. Position seats forward and in full up position.
8. Remove seat belt nuts from door sides of front seats.
9. Remove seat adjuster to floor pan bolts at rear of seats.
10. Disengage seat hook attachments from floor pan.
11. Tip seat forward and disconnect power, seat heater and driver side air bag electrical connectors.
12. Remove front bucket seats.
13. Position transaxle shift lever in LOW position.
14. Remove floor console storage compartment rubber mat and front mounting bolts.
15. Remove floor console rear mounting bracket bolts from behind transaxle shift lever.
16. Remove floor console lefthand and righthand mounting bolts.
17. Disconnect console electrical connectors.
18. Pull console rearward and remove.
19. Remove rear seat cushion by lifting up and pulling out of retainer.
20. Remove rear seat back nuts from child seat latch bracket.
21. Grasp bottom of rear seat back and lift upward to disengage offsets on upper frame bar from hangers.
22. Remove rear seat back from vehicle.
23. Remove seat belt from rear upper quarter trim panel.
24. Remove coat hook from rear upper trim panel, then the upper trim panel by disengaging push-in retainers.
25. Reposition front door carpet retainer, then remove seat belt from rear lower quarter trim panel.
26. Remove rear quarter lower trim panel from vehicle.
27. Remove push-in retainers that secure carpet on top of rocker panels.
28. Remove carpet from vehicle.
29. Remove rear floor air outlet duct from holes in floor reinforcement.
30. Disconnect rear floor air outlet duct from heater air outlet cover and remove duct from vehicle.
31. Remove heater air outlet cover attaching screws.
32. Remove heater air outlet cover heat stakes with a small chisel.
33. Remove heater air outlet cover from HVAC module assembly.

3. Disconnect heater hoses from heater core.
4. Remove sound insulator panels from under lefthand and righthand sides of instrument panel.
5. Move front seat back and disconnect seat air bag electrical connector (located under seat, yellow in color).
6. Remove covers from front end of seat adjuster track by spreading two rear feet and pulling forward.
7. Spread track cover arms and pull rearward to remove.
8. Position front seat forward to between mid-forward position and full-forward position.
9. Raise seat to full-up position, then remove bolts which secure front seat adjuster to floor pan.
10. Move seat to a center position over adjuster.
11. Remove harness from between electrical connector and power motor.
12. Remove seat belt nut from door side of seats.
13. Tip seat forward to remove from front hook attachments.
14. Remove front seat from vehicle.
15. Remove trim plate from front floor console.
16. Remove front floor console attaching bolts.
17. Pull console rearward to disengage retaining clips from instrument panel.
18. Disconnect floor console electrical connectors and remove floor console.
19. Remove rear seat cushion by lifting up and pulling out of retainer.
20. Remove rear seat back nuts from child seat latch bracket.

21. Grasp bottom of rear seat back and lift upward to disengage offsets on upper frame bar from hangers.
22. Remove rear seat back from vehicle.
23. Pull down on rear quarter upper trim panels to disengage clip retainers on roof side rails.
24. Pull trim panel out to disengage clips located at bottom of triangular window.
25. Slide roof leg out from under upper trim panel of center pillar.
26. Remove rear quarter upper trim panel.
27. Pull up disengage carpet retainer leg clip and out to disengage lower quarter trim panel clips.
28. Slide lower quarter trim panel down and out from under quarter upper panel.
29. Remove rear quarter lower trim panel from vehicle.
30. Remove push-in retainers that secure carpet on top of rocker panels.
31. Remove carpet from vehicle.
32. Remove rear floor air outlet duct from holes in floor reinforcement.
33. Disconnect rear floor air outlet duct from heater air outlet cover and remove duct from vehicle.
34. Remove heater air outlet cover attaching screws.
35. Remove heater air outlet cover heat stakes with a small chisel.
36. Remove heater air outlet cover from HVAC module assembly.
37. Remove heater core from HVAC lower case.
38. Reverse procedure to install. Install all new seals.

34. Remove heater core from HVAC lower case.
35. Reverse procedure to install. Install all new seals.

EVAPORATOR CORE
REPLACE

Century, Grand Prix, LaCrosse & Regal

1. Recover refrigerant as outlined in "Air Conditioning" chapter.
2. Remove air cleaner and duct.
3. Drain engine coolant into suitable container.
4. Remove instrument panel as outlined in "Dash Panel Service" chapter.
5. Remove passenger's side air bag module as outlined in "Passive Restraints Systems" chapter.
6. Disconnect and position fuse block aside.
7. Remove brake pedal bracket and reinforcement.
8. Remove mounting bolts and position Body Control Module (BCM) bracket aside.
9. Disconnect clips and position instrument panel wiring harness aside.
10. Remove mounting bolts and HVAC module center support bracket.
11. Remove upper support bracket mounting bolts, then the HVAC module from cross vehicle beam support.
12. Remove support braces from top of engine compartment.
13. Disconnect refrigerant lines from evaporator block fitting.
14. Disconnect heater hoses at heater core.

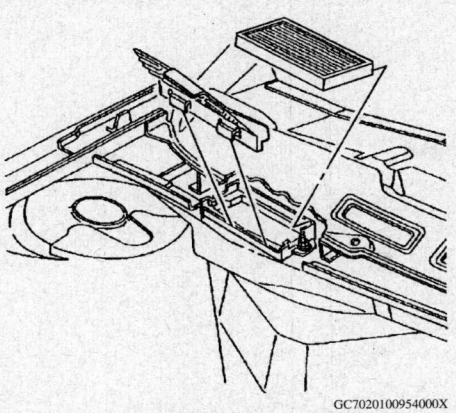

GC7020100954000X

Fig. 9 Cabin air filter replacement

15. Remove HVAC module to dash panel mounting nuts.
16. Mark connectors and hoses for installation alignment.
17. Disconnect HVAC module electrical connectors and vacuum hoses.
18. Remove HVAC module outer seals and air inlet housing.
19. Disconnect and remove heater/defrost valve vacuum actuator.
20. Remove upper mounting screws and separate HVAC module case.
21. Remove module seal and evaporator core from lower case.
22. Remove and discard evaporator core seals and water core filter.
23. Reverse procedure to install. **Torque** HVAC case screws to 13 inch lbs.

Impala & Monte Carlo

1. Recover air conditioning refrigerant as

outlined in "Air Conditioning" chapter.
2. Drain cooling system into suitable container.
3. Remove lefthand fender diagonal brace.
4. Remove cross vehicle brace.
5. Disconnect air conditioning lines from evaporator block fitting and heater hoses from heater core.
6. Remove instrument panel as outlined in "Dash Panel Service" chapter.
7. Remove cross vehicle beam.
8. Disconnect vacuum hoses and electrical connectors from HVAC module.
9. Disconnect instrument panel wiring harness from HVAC module retainers.
10. Remove evaporator drain elbow.
11. Remove HVAC module to dash panel mounting nuts.
12. Pull HVAC module rearward and disconnect from mounting studs.
13. Position dash insulator pad away from HVAC module air inlet opening.
14. Roll HVAC module downward and rearward, then remove heater outlet cover from rear floor air outlet duct.
15. Remove outer HVAC module seals.
16. Remove air inlet housing and heater/defroster valve vacuum actuator from HVAC module.
17. Remove HVAC module case upper screws.
18. Separate module upper from lower case.
19. Remove seal from module lower case.
20. Remove evaporator core from case.
21. Reverse procedure to install.

3.1L Engine

NOTE: On Air Bag Equipped Models, Refer To "Air Bag System Precautions" Located In The Front Of This Manual For System Disarming & Arming Procedures.

NOTE: Refer To "Computer Relearn Procedures" Located In The Front Of This Manual When Battery Power To The Computer Has Been Interrupted.

NOTE: Prior To Performing Any Service Operations Listed In This Section, Consult The "Technical Service Bulletins" Section For Related Information.

INDEX

	Page No.		Page No.		Page No.
Belt Tension Data	6-24	Front Cover Seal, Replace	6-22	Radiator, Replace	6-24
Camshaft, Replace	6-22	Fuel Filter, Replace	6-24	Rocker Arms, Replace	6-21
Camshaft Lobe Lift		Fuel Pump, Replace	6-24	Serpentine Drive Belt	6-24
Specifications	6-21	Hydraulic Lifters, Replace	6-22	Adjustment	6-24
Compression Pressure	6-19	Intake Manifold, Replace	6-20	Replacement	6-24
Cooling System Bleed	6-24	Lower	6-20	Routing	6-24
Crankshaft Rear Oil Seal,		Upper	6-20	Technical Service Bulletins	6-24
Replace	6-23	Main & Rod Bearings	6-22	Crankshaft Rear Main Oil Leak	6-24
Installation	6-23	Connecting Rod	6-22	Thermostat, Replace	6-24
Removal	6-23	Main Bearings	6-22	Tightening Specifications	6-27
Cylinder Head, Replace	6-21	Oil Pan, Replace	6-23	Timing Chain, Replace	6-22
Engine Rebuilding		Oil Pump, Replace	6-23	Installation	6-22
Specifications	29-1	Oil Pump Service	6-23	Removal	6-22
Engine, Replace	6-20	Assemble	6-23	Valve Adjustment	6-21
Engine Mount, Replace	6-19	Disassemble	6-23	Valve Arrangement	6-21
Engine Mount	6-19	Inspection	6-23	Front To Rear	6-21
Engine Strut	6-19	Piston & Rod Assembly	6-22	Valve Clearance Specifications	6-21
Transaxle Mount	6-19	Precautions	6-19	Valve Cover, Replace	6-21
Exhaust Manifold, Replace	6-20	Air Bag Systems	6-19	Lefthand	6-21
Lefthand	6-20	Battery Ground Cable	6-19	Righthand	6-21
Righthand	6-21	Fuel System Pressure Relief	6-19	Valve Lifters	6-21
Front Cover, Replace	6-22	Push Rods	6-21	Water Pump, Replace	6-24

PRECAUTIONS

Air Bag Systems

Refer to "Air Bag System Precautions" in the front of this manual for system disarming and arming procedures.

Battery Ground Cable

Prior to service, disconnect battery ground cable and isolate as required.

Fuel System Pressure Relief

To reduce the risk of fire and personal injury, relieve the fuel system pressure before servicing fuel system components.
1. Loosen fuel tank filler cap to relieve tank pressure.
2. Connect fuel pressure gauge tool No. J34730-1, or equivalent, to fuel pressure valve. Wrap a shop towel around fitting while connecting gauge to avoid spillage.

3. Install bleed hose into suitable container and open valve to bleed system pressure.

COMPRESSION PRESSURE

When inspecting compression, lowest cylinder must be within 70% of the highest cylinder with a minimum pressure of 100 psi. Perform compression test with engine at normal operating temperature, spark plugs removed and throttle wide open.

ENGINE MOUNT
REPLACE

Engine Mount

1. Remove throttle body air inlet duct, and engine mount struts.
2. Raise and support vehicle, then remove righthand front tire and wheel assembly.
3. Remove catalytic converter pipe from rear exhaust manifold.

4. Remove righthand engine splash shield and engine mount lower nuts.
5. Place suitable wood block under oil pan and raise engine using suitable floor jack stand.
6. Remove engine mount bracket to oil pan bolts, then engine mount and bracket.
7. Remove upper mount nuts and engine mount from bracket.
8. Reverse procedure to install.

Engine Strut

1. Remove bolt from engine mount strut bracket, then bolt from bracket.
2. Remove strut.
3. Reverse procedure to install.

Transaxle Mount

1. Support transaxle using suitable jack.
2. Remove cross member to mount mounting nuts, **Fig. 1.**
3. Remove bracket to transaxle mounting bolts.
4. Remove mount and bracket.
5. Separate mount from bracket.
6. Reverse procedure to install.

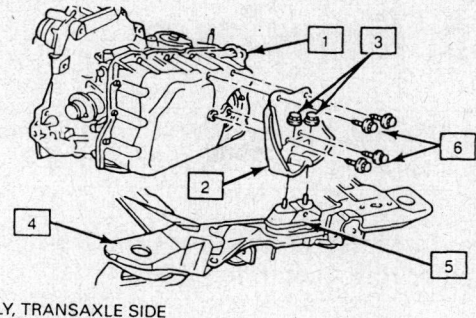

1	COVER ASSEMBLY, TRANSAXLE SIDE
2	BRACKET, TRANSAXLE MOUNT TRANSAXLE SIDE
3	NUT, TRANSAXLE MOUNT TRANSAXLE SIDE BRACKET
4	FRAME ASSEMBLY, DRIVETRAIN AND FRONT SUSPENSION
5	MOUNT ASSEMBLY, TRANSAXLE
6	BOLT/SCREW, TRANSAXLE MOUNT TRANSAXLE SIDE BRACKET

GC1069400816000X

Fig. 1 Transaxle mount

ENGINE

REPLACE

1. Drain engine coolant into suitable container.
2. Drain engine oil into suitable container.
3. Relieve fuel system pressure as outlined under "Precautions."
4. Scribe alignment marks and remove hood.
5. Remove air flow tube from air cleaner and throttle valve, then the air cleaner assembly.
6. Remove transaxle filler tube.
7. Disconnect required electrical wiring, then the throttle and TV cables.
8. Remove engine mount strut bracket.
9. Disconnect fuel lines.
10. Remove AIR pump belt, then serpentine drive belt cover and belt.
11. Disconnect radiator hoses at engine.
12. Remove air conditioning compressor bolts from front bracket.
13. Remove power steering pump and position aside.
14. Disconnect heater hoses from engine.
15. Disconnect brake booster vacuum supply line.
16. Disconnect EGR from exhaust.
17. Raise and support vehicle.
18. Remove mounting bolts and torque converter cover.
19. Remove mounting bolts, lower starter motor and disconnect starter wiring.
20. Remove starter motor and shims.
21. Remove rear bracket mounting bolts and position air conditioning compressor aside.
22. Remove flywheel cover, then disconnect starter and position aside.
23. Remove torque converter bolts and transaxle mount bracket.
24. Remove engine front mount mounting nuts.
25. Disconnect exhaust pipe at crossover and lower vehicle.
26. Remove coolant recovery bottle.
27. Disconnect bracket and position accelerator control cable aside.
28. Disconnect crossover pipe at lefthand manifold.
29. Remove serpentine belt and alternator.
30. Remove power steering pump.
31. Remove front shock tower plastic cover and remove automatic transaxle modulator pipe.
32. Pull engine forward and support in position.
33. Disconnect crossover pipe at righthand manifold.
34. Disconnect bulkhead connector.
35. Remove engine support and allow engine to roll to normal position.
36. Remove engine to transaxle mounting bolts.
37. Support engine and transaxle with suitable lifting device.
38. Remove engine.
39. Reverse procedure to install.

INTAKE MANIFOLD

REPLACE

Upper

1. Disconnect vacuum hose from throttle body air inlet duct and wiring harness from intake air temperature sensor.
2. Remove throttle body air inlet duct.
3. Drain engine coolant into suitable container.
4. Remove accelerator control and cruise control cables with bracket from throttle body.
5. Disconnect wiring harness connectors from throttle body.
6. Disconnect front spark plug wires.
7. Disconnect wiring harness attachment clips from camshaft position sensor, front spark plug wire harness and engine wiring harness.
8. Disconnect thermostat bypass pipe coolant hoses from throttle body.
9. Remove ignition coil bracket with coils, purge solenoid and vacuum canister solenoid.
10. Disconnect vacuum hose and remove MAP sensor and bracket.
11. Disconnect emission control vacuum harness and upper intake manifold to vacuum booster vacuum hose.
12. Disconnect automatic transaxle vacuum modulator hose.
13. Disconnect heater/air conditioning vacuum source and fuel pressure regulator vacuum hoses.
14. Remove front and rear braces, then the alternator bracket.
15. Remove EGR valve, then upper intake manifold mounting bolts and studs.
16. Remove upper intake manifold and gaskets.
17. Reverse procedure to install.

Lower

1. Remove upper intake manifold as outlined under "Intake Manifold, Replace."
2. Remove valve covers and disconnect ECT wiring harness.
3. Remove mounting bolt and fuel pipe clip.
4. Disconnect fuel feed and fuel return pipes from fuel injector rail.
5. Remove fuel injector rail.
6. Remove and position power steering pump aside.
7. Disconnect and position heater inlet pipe with heater hose aside.
8. Disconnect radiator inlet hose from engine, then the thermostat bypass hose from thermostat bypass pipe and lower intake manifold pipe.
9. Remove manifold bolts lower intake manifold. Discard mounting bolts.
10. Remove pushrods, then the lower intake manifold gaskets and seals.
11. Reverse procedure to install, noting the following:
    a. Install new intake manifold gaskets.
    b. Apply .31–.39 inch drops of suitable RTV sealant to four corners of manifold to block joints, **Fig. 2.**
    c. Connect sealant drops with sealant beads .31–.39 inch wide and .12–.20 inch thick.
    d. **Install new manifold mounting bolts.**
    e. **Vertical bolts must be tightened before diagonal bolts.**
    f. **Torque** bolts to 62 inch lbs., in sequence, **Fig. 3.**
    g. **Torque** bolts 1, 2, 3 and 4 to 115 inch lbs., in sequence.
    h. **Torque** bolts 5, 6, 7 and 8 to 18 ft. lbs., in sequence.

EXHAUST MANIFOLD

REPLACE

Lefthand

1. Remove throttle body air inlet duct, then drain engine coolant into suitable container.
2. Remove righthand engine mount strut bracket, then disconnect radiator inlet hose from engine.
3. Remove automatic transaxle vacuum modulator and thermostat bypass pipes.

4. Remove exhaust crossover pipe heat shield and exhaust crossover mounting bolts.
5. Remove mounting bolts and exhaust manifold heat shield.
6. Remove mounting nuts, exhaust manifold and gasket.
7. Reverse procedure to install.

Righthand

1. Remove throttle body air inlet duct, then drain engine coolant into suitable container.
2. Remove righthand engine mount strut bracket, then disconnect radiator inlet hose from engine.
3. Remove automatic transaxle vacuum modulator and thermostat bypass pipes.
4. Remove exhaust crossover pipe heat shield and exhaust crossover mounting bolts.
5. Remove mounting bolts and exhaust manifold heat shield.
6. Disconnect heated oxygen sensor wiring harness connector, then raise and support vehicle.
7. Remove EGR tube, then the mounting bolts and exhaust manifold upper heat shield.
8. Remove mounting bolts exhaust lower heat shield.
9. Remove mounting nuts, exhaust manifold and gasket.
10. Reverse procedure to install.

CYLINDER HEAD
REPLACE

1. Drain engine coolant into suitable container.
2. Drain engine oil into suitable container.
3. Remove upper and lower intake manifolds as outlined under "Intake Manifold, Replace."
4. Remove valve cover as outlined under "Valve Cover, Replace."
5. Remove exhaust crossover and oil lever indicator bracket.
6. Remove lefthand exhaust manifold as outlined under "Exhaust Manifold, Replace."
7. Disconnect plug wires and remove pushrods.
8. Remove mounting bolts and cylinder head.
9. Reverse procedure to install, noting following:
   a. Coat cylinder head bolt threads with suitable sealant.
   b. Refer to sequence, **Fig. 4,** tighten cylinder head bolts in two steps: First step, **torque** bolts to 44 ft. lbs.; second step, tighten an additional 95.°
   c. Intake pushrods are marked orange and are 5.68 inches long. Exhaust pushrods are marked blue and are six inches long.

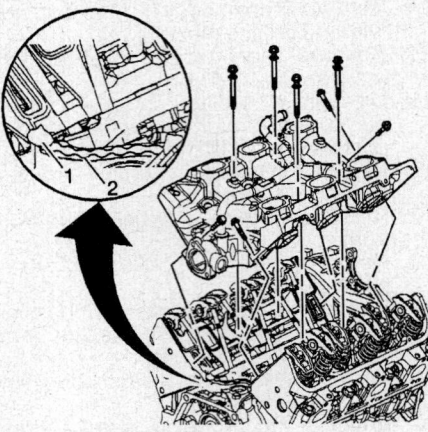

1. Corner sealant
2. Manifold to block sealant

ARM0400000000164

Fig. 2   Lower intake manifold replacement

VALVE COVER
REPLACE

Lefthand

1. Remove lefthand side spark plug wires.
2. Remove automatic transaxle vacuum modulator pipe.
3. Remove PCV valve.
4. remove mounting bolts, cover and gasket.
5. Reverse procedure to install, noting the following:
   a. Install new gasket and ensure gasket is seated properly in rocker cover groove.
   b. Apply suitable sealer into cylinder head notch.

Righthand

1. Remove serpentine drive belt, then the braces and alternator.
2. Remove spark plug wires.
3. Remove ignition coil bracket with coils.
4. Remove purge and vacuum canister solenoids.
5. Remove vacuum hose from grommet in valve cover.
6. Remove mounting bolts, valve cover and gasket.
7. Reverse procedure to install, noting the following:
   a. Install new gasket and ensure gasket is seated properly in rocker cover groove.
   b. Apply suitable sealer into cylinder head notch.

VALVE ARRANGEMENT
Front To Rear

Cowl side ....E-I-E-I-I-E
Radiator side ....E-I-I-E-I-E

VALVE LIFTERS

Roller type valve lifters used in this en-

gine must be replaced whenever the camshaft is replaced, **Fig. 5.**

Valve lifters should be kept in order so they will be installed in their original positions. Some engines will have both standard and .010 inch oversize valve lifters. Where oversize lifters are used, crankcase will be marked ".25 OS" with white paint on lifter boss, **Fig. 6.**

If replacement is required, use lifters with a narrow flat ground along the lower ¾ of the lifter. These flats provide additional oil to the cam lobe and lifter surfaces.

CAMSHAFT LOBE LIFT SPECIFICATIONS
Intake .... .2500
Exhaust .... .2550

VALVE CLEARANCE SPECIFICATIONS

This engine is equipped with hydraulic lifters. Valve lash should always be zero. If valve lash exists, inspect pushrod and rocker arm for excessive wear and inspect for inoperative lifters.

VALVE ADJUSTMENT

There is no valve adjustment for these engines.

ROCKER ARMS
REPLACE

1. Remove valve covers as outlined under "Valve Cover, Replace."
2. Remove rocker arms. Mark components so they can be installed in original location.
3. Remove pivot balls and rocker arms, then the pushrods.
4. Reverse procedure to install. **Exhaust pushrods are longer than intakes. Exhaust pushrods have blue marks. Intake pushrods are marked with orange.**

PUSH RODS

1. Remove valve covers as outlined under "Valve Cover, Replace."
2. Remove rocker arms. Mark components so they can be installed in original location.
3. Remove rocker arm pivot balls and rocker arms, then the pushrods. **Exhaust pushrods are longer than intakes. Exhaust pushrods have blue marks. Intake pushrods are marked with orange.**
4. Reverse procedure to install, noting the following:
   a. Ensure pushrods seat in lifters.
   b. Coat bearing surfaces of rocker arms and pivot balls with Molykote, or equivalent lubricant.

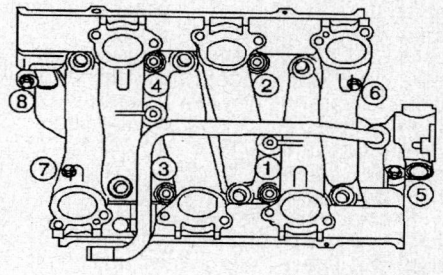

Fig. 3 Lower intake manifold bolt tightening sequence

HYDRAULIC LIFTERS
REPLACE

1. Remove upper and lower intake manifolds as outlined under "Intake Manifold, Replace."
2. Remove valve covers as outlined under "Valve Cover, Replace."
3. Remove rocker arms. Mark components so they can be installed in original location.
4. Remove pivot balls and rocker arms, then the pushrods.
5. Remove intake manifold oil splash shield.
6. Remove mounting bolts and lifter guides, then the lifters. **Keep lifters in order for installation alignment.**
7. Reverse procedure to install, noting the following:
   a. Clean all gasket surfaces and valve train components.
   b. Coat lifters with suitable pre-lube.
   c. Install lifters in their original position.
   d. Ensure pushrods seat in lifter.
   e. Coat bearing surfaces of rocker arms and pivot balls with Molykote, or equivalent lubricant.

FRONT COVER
REPLACE

1. Drain engine coolant into suitable container.
2. Remove cover and serpentine drive belt.
3. Remove serpentine drive belt tensioner and alternator.
4. Remove and position power steering pump aside.
5. Remove mounting bolts and cross vehicle brace.
6. Remove coolant overflow hose from radiator neck.
7. Remove mounting nuts and coolant reservoir.
8. Raise and support vehicle, then drain engine oil into suitable container.
9. Remove inner splash shield and flywheel cover.
10. Remove starter motor.
11. Remove crankshaft balancer using torsional damper remover tool No. J24420, or equivalent.
12. Remove serpentine drive belt idler pulley.
13. Remove lower timing cover mounting bolts and lower vehicle.

14. Remove throttle body air inlet duct and lefthand engine mount strut.
15. Remove spark plug wires from lefthand bank.
16. Disconnect radiator hose at water pump and heater coolant hose from cooling system fill pipe.
17. Disconnect bypass, overflow and canister purge hoses.
18. Remove thermostat bypass pipe from front cover.
19. Remove mounting bolts and water pump pulley.
20. Remove lower crankshaft position sensor wiring harness bracket from engine front cover.
21. Remove mounting bolts and upper timing cover.
22. Reverse procedure to install, noting the following:
    a. Install new gasket.
    b. Apply suitable sealant, **Fig. 7.**
    c. Crankshaft damper mounting bolt to 52 ft. lbs., then final tighten an additional 72°.

FRONT COVER SEAL
REPLACE

1. Remove inner splash shield.
2. Remove crankshaft balancer using torsional damper remover tool No. J24420, or equivalent.
3. Pry out seal using suitable flat-bladed tool. **Do not damage crankshaft.**
4. Reverse procedure to install, noting the following:
   a. Lubricate new seal with clean engine oil and insert in front cover with lip facing engine.
   b. Drive seal into place with front cover alignment and oil seal installer tool No. J35468, or equivalent.

TIMING CHAIN
REPLACE
Removal

1. Remove front cover as outlined under "Front Cover, Replace."
2. Rotate crankshaft until timing marks align, **Fig. 8.**
3. Remove mounting bolt, camshaft sprocket and timing chain.
4. Remove mounting bolts and timing chain damper.
5. Remove crankshaft sprocket using sprocket removal tool No. J5825-A, or equivalent.

Installation

1. Install crankshaft sprocket until it is fully seated on flange of crankshaft, using sprocket installer tool No. J38612, or equivalent.
2. Coat camshaft and crankshaft sprockets with suitable engine oil.
3. Hold camshaft sprocket with chain hanging down and align camshaft and crankshaft sprockets marks with engine block cast timing marks, **Fig. 9.**
4. Install front cover as outlined under "Front Cover, Replace."

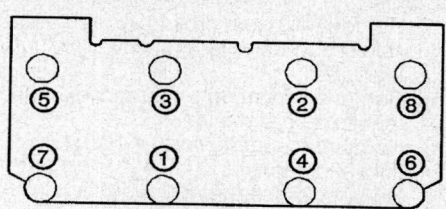

ARM0400000000163

Fig. 4 Cylinder head bolt tightening sequence

CAMSHAFT
REPLACE

1. Remove engine as outlined under "Engine, Replace."
2. Remove upper and lower intake manifolds as outlined under "Intake Manifold, Replace."
3. Remove valve covers as outlined under "Valve Cover, Replace."
4. Remove rocker arms. Mark components so they can be installed in original location.
5. Remove pivot balls and rocker arms, then the pushrods.
6. Remove intake manifold oil splash shield.
7. Remove mounting bolts and lifter guides, then the lifters. **Keep lifters in order for installation alignment.**
8. Remove timing chain and sprocket as outlined under "Timing Chain, Replace."
9. Remove mounting bolts and camshaft thrust plate.
10. Carefully rotate and remove camshaft using suitable large screwdriver into camshaft bolt hole. **Do not damage threads.**
11. Reverse procedure to install, noting the following:
    a. If installing new camshaft, coat camshaft lobes with GM E.O.S. part No. 1052367, or equivalent.
    b. Lubricate camshaft journals with suitable engine oil.

PISTON & ROD ASSEMBLY

When installing piston and rod assemblies, ensure arrow on top of piston faces toward front of engine, **Fig. 10.**

MAIN & ROD BEARINGS
Connecting Rod

1. **Torque** connecting rod bolts to 18 ft. lbs.
2. Final tighten bolts and addition 100°.

Main Bearings

Engine bearings are of the precision insert type. They are available for service use in standard and various undersizes, **Fig. 11.**

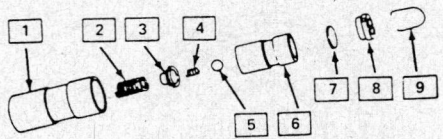

1–LIFTER BODY
2–PLUNGER SPRING
3–BALL CHECK RETAINER
4–BALL CHECK SPRING
5–BALL CHECK
6–PLUNGER
7–OIL METERING VALVE
8–PUSH ROD SEAT
9–RETAINER RING

GC1069100448000X

Fig. 5 Exploded view of valve lifter

To determine proper replacement insert size, bearing clearance must be measured as follows:

1. Measure crankshaft journal diameter in several places, approximately 90° apart and average measurements.
2. Measure taper and runout. Taper and runout should be .0002 inch maximum.
3. Install bearing inserts, then tighten rod and main bearing cap bolts.
4. Measure connecting rod I.D. in same direction as length of rod.
5. Select suitable set of inserts to provide specified clearance limits. **Do not mix inserts of different nominal size in same bearing bore.**
6. If clearance limits cannot be met, crankshaft journal must be reconditioned and undersized bearing inserts installed.
7. **Torque** main bearing cap bolts to 37 ft. lbs.
8. Final tighten caps bolts an additional 77°.

CRANKSHAFT REAR OIL SEAL
REPLACE
Removal

1. Support engine with engine support fixture tool No. J28467, or equivalent, and an extra support leg.
2. Remove transaxle as outlined in MOTOR's "Domestic Transmission, InVehicle Service" manual or "Transmission Service DVD.""
3. Remove flywheel.
4. Remove seal using suitable tool through dust lip at an angle, **Fig. 12. Do not damage crankshaft outer surface.**

Installation

1. Apply suitable engine oil to inner and outer diameters of new seal.
2. Slide seal over mandrel until back of seal bottoms squarely against collar of rear main bearing seal installer tool No. J34686, or equivalent, **Fig. 13.**
3. Align tool dowel pin with crankshaft dowel pin by hand and **torque** mounting screws to 45 inch lbs., **Fig. 13.**
4. Turn tool handle so collar pushes seal

into bore, continue turning handle until collar is tight against case.
5. Loosen handle until it comes to a stop and remove mounting screws.
6. Ensure seal is seated squarely in bore.
7. Install flywheel and transaxle.

OIL PAN
REPLACE

1. Remove engine mount struts from engine.
2. Remove mounting bolts and position air conditioning compressor aside.
3. Support engine using engine support fixture tool No. J28467-A, engine support fixture adapter tool No. J28467-90 and engine support adapter leg tool No. J36462, or equivalents.
4. Raise and support vehicle, then disconnect three-way catalytic converter pipe from rear exhaust manifold.
5. Drain engine oil into suitable container and remove oil level sensor harness connector.
6. Remove air cleaner assembly.
7. Remove mounting bolts and torque converter cover.
8. Remove mounting bolts, lower starter motor and disconnect starter wiring.
9. Remove starter motor and shims.
10. Remove transaxle brace from oil pan.
11. Remove transaxle mount and engine mount lower nuts.
12. Raise engine.
13. Remove engine mount bracket with engine mount from oil pan.
14. Remove rear and front oil pan side bolts.
15. Remove mounting bolts, oil pan and gasket.
16. Reverse procedure to install using new gasket.

OIL PUMP
REPLACE

1. Remove oil pan as outlined under "Oil Pan, Replace."
2. Remove mounting nuts and crankshaft oil deflector.
3. Remove mounting bolt, oil pump and drive rod.
4. Reverse procedure to install.

OIL PUMP SERVICE
Disassemble

1. Drain pump oil into suitable container.
2. Remove pump cover and pump gears, **Fig. 14.**
3. Remove pressure regulator valve. If valve is stuck, soak pump housing in suitable carburetor cleaning solvent.
4. Carefully remove pressure regulator valve spring retaining pin. **Spring may be under pressure.**
5. Clean sludge, oil and/or varnish from all components.

Inspection

1. Inspect pump housing and cover for

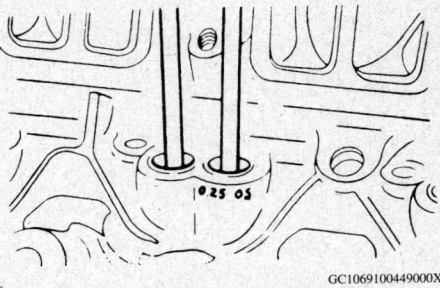

GC1069100449000X

Fig. 6 Oversize lifter marking

cracks or damaged threads. **Do not repair pump housing.**
2. Inspect idler gear shaft. If loose in housing, replace pump.
3. Inspect pressure regulator valve for scoring or sticking. Burrs may be removed with a fine oil stone.
4. Inspect pressure regulator valve spring for loss of tension or bending.
5. Inspect suction pipe and screen for looseness, if permanently pressed into pump body. If pipe is loose or has been removed, pump body cover must be replaced. Inspect for broken wire mesh or screen.
6. Inspect gears for chipping, galling or wear.
7. Measure gear lash in several positions, **Fig. 15.** Gear lash should be .004–.008 inch.
8. Measure pump housing gear pocket depth, **Fig. 16.** Note the following:
   a. **On models equipped with aluminum pump body,** pump depth should be 1.195–1.198 inches.
   b. **On models equipped with cast pump body,** pump depth should be 1.202–1.204 inches.
9. **On all models,** measure pump housing gear pocket diameter, **Fig. 16.** Pump housing gear pocket diameter should be 1.5 inch.
10. Measure pump gear diameters, **Fig. 17.** Pump gear diameters should be 1.5 inch.
11. Measure pump gear side clearance, **Fig. 18.** Pump gear side clearance should be .001–.003 inch.
12. Measure oil pump end clearance, **Fig. 19.** Note the following:
   a. **On models equipped with aluminum pump body,** end clearance should be .002–.006 inch.
   b. **On models equipped with cast pump body,** end clearance should be .002–.005 inch.

Assemble

1. Lubricate all internal components with suitable engine oil.
2. Install pump gears.
3. Prime engine oil galleries by removing engine oil pump drive unit and rotating oil pump, using drill motor, appropriate socket and extension.
4. Install cover and gasket.
5. Install and ensure pin is properly secured.
6. Install cover bolts.

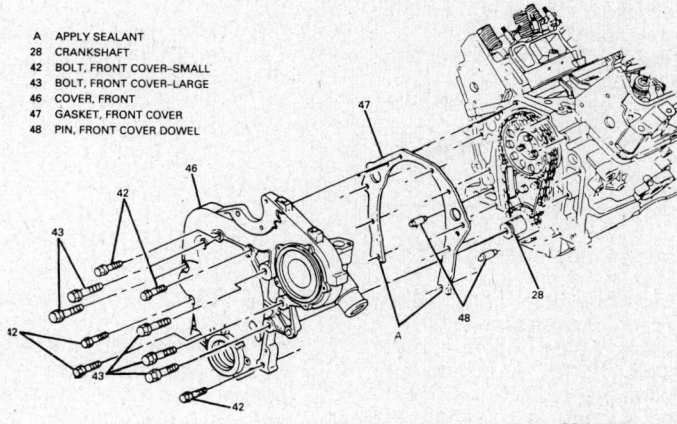

A   APPLY SEALANT
28 CRANKSHAFT
42 BOLT, FRONT COVER-SMALL
43 BOLT, FRONT COVER-LARGE
46 COVER, FRONT
47 GASKET, FRONT COVER
48 PIN, FRONT COVER DOWEL

GC1069400817000X

Fig. 7   Front cover replacement

BELT TENSION DATA

Belt tension is maintained automatically by a spring tensioned idler pulley. Adjustment of serpentine belt is not required.

If belt slippage is indicated and belt tensioner indicator is within normal operating range, measure belt tension as follows:
1. Run engine for 10 minutes, then shut off and measure belt tension between any two pulleys using V-belt tension gauge tool No. J23600-B, or equivalent.
2. Run engine for 30 seconds and repeat measurement.
3. Repeat preceding step, then average all three belt tension measurements.
4. Replace serpentine drive belt if tension is not 30–50 lbs.

SERPENTINE DRIVE BELT

Replacement

1. Lift or rotate tensioner using suitable ½ inch breaker bar.
2. Remove serpentine belt.
3. Reverse procedure to install.

Routing

Refer to **Fig. 20** for serpentine belt routing.

Adjustment

There is no provision for serpentine belt adjustment. Refer to "Belt Tension Data" for belt tension measurement procedures and to determine whether belt requires replacement.

COOLING SYSTEM BLEED

1. Open vent valves located on thermostat housing and throttle body return pipe above water pump, **Fig. 21.** Turn both vents screws 2–3 turns.
2. Fill cooling system to base of radiator neck.

3. Close both vent valves. **Do not overtighten vent valves.**
4. Install radiator cap.
5. Add sufficient coolant to recovery tank.
6. Start engine and observe low coolant warning lamp.
7. If lamp remains illuminated, repeat bleed procedure.

THERMOSTAT
REPLACE

1. Drain engine coolant into suitable container.
2. Disconnect radiator hose from thermostat housing.
3. Remove mounting bolts, thermostat housing and thermostat.
4. Reverse procedure to install.

WATER PUMP
REPLACE

1. Drain engine coolant into suitable container.
2. Remove serpentine drive belt, then disconnect radiator and heater hose.
3. Remove mounting bolts water pump, **Fig. 22.**
4. Reverse procedure to install.

RADIATOR
REPLACE

1. Remove battery and cooling system into suitable container.
2. Remove air cleaner.
3. Remove mounting bolts, then rotate engine strut and upper brace rearward.
4. Disconnect upper radiator mounting panel bolts and clamps.
5. Disconnect mounting bolts and cooling fan electrical connector.
6. Remove cooling fan and upper radiator bracket.
7. Remove upper and lower radiator hoses at radiator.
8. Disconnect low coolant sensor wiring.
9. Disconnect oil cooler lines and remove radiator.
10. Reverse procedure to install.

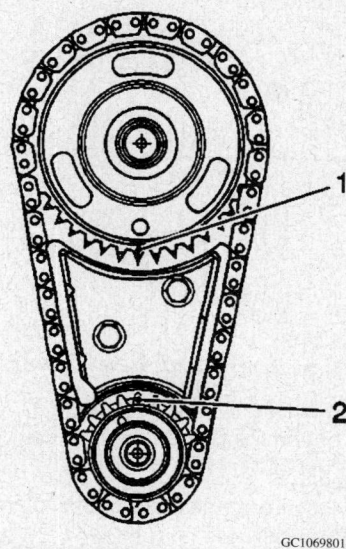

GC1069801252000X

Fig. 8   Timing mark alignment

FUEL PUMP
REPLACE

1. Relieve fuel system pressure as outlined under "Precautions."
2. Remove cover, jack, spare tire and trunk liner.
3. Remove seven mounting nuts and fuel pump access panel.
4. Disconnect fuel tank pressure sensor electrical connector.
5. Disconnect quick connect fittings and remove fuel pump retaining snap ring.
6. Remove modular fuel pump.
7. Reverse procedure to install.

FUEL FILTER
REPLACE

1. Relieve fuel system pressure as outlined under "Precautions."
2. Raise and support vehicle.
3. Remove mounting screw and filter bracket, **Fig. 23.**
4. Grasp filter and fuel line fitting. Twist quick-connect fitting ¼ turn in each direction to loosen any dirt within fitting.
5. Blow out dirt from quick-connect fitting.
6. Remove feed pipe nut from fuel filter and drain any remaining fuel into suitable container.
7. Remove fuel filter.
8. Reverse procedure to install.

TECHNICAL SERVICE BULLETINS

Crankshaft Rear Main Oil Leak

On some of these models there may be an engine oil leak at crankshaft rear main oil seal.

This condition may be caused by the rear main oil seal design.

To correct this condition, install revised rear main oil seal (part No. 12592195).

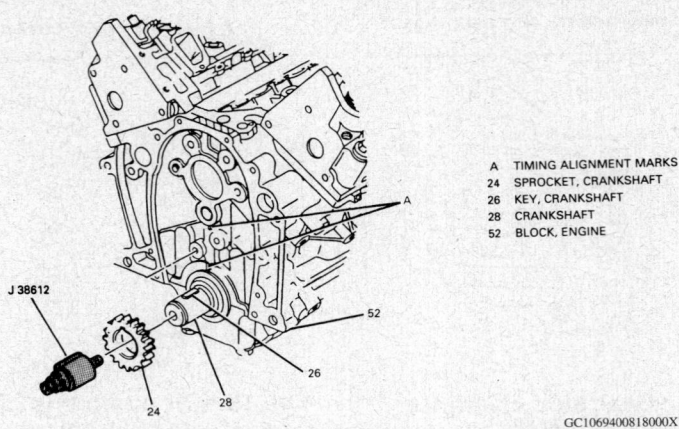

A TIMING ALIGNMENT MARKS
24 SPROCKET, CRANKSHAFT
26 KEY, CRANKSHAFT
28 CRANKSHAFT
52 BLOCK, ENGINE

GC1069400818000X

Fig. 9   Timing chain installation

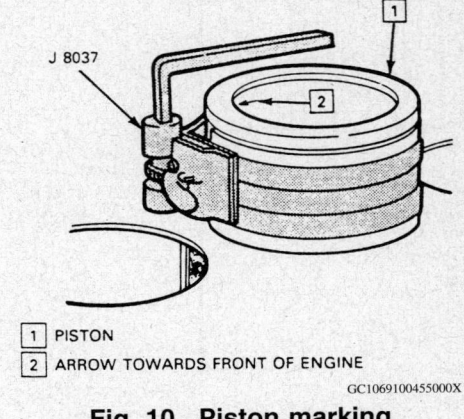

1 PISTON
2 ARROW TOWARDS FRONT OF ENGINE

GC1069100455000X

Fig. 10   Piston marking

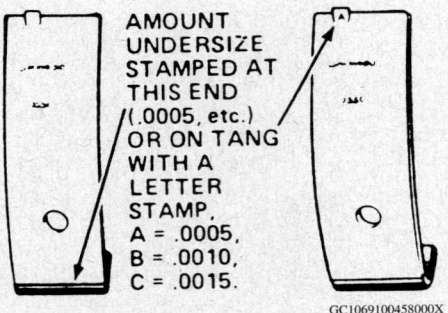

AMOUNT UNDERSIZE STAMPED AT THIS END (.0005, etc.) OR ON TANG WITH A LETTER STAMP. A = .0005, B = .0010, C = .0015.

GC1069100458000X

Fig. 11   Main bearing insert markings

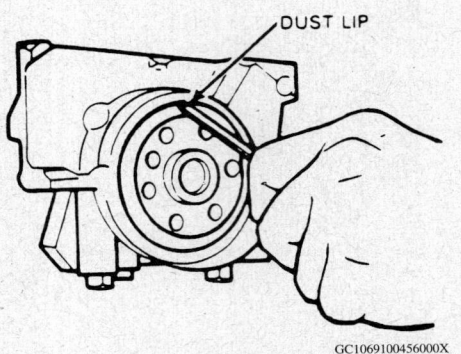

DUST LIP

GC1069100456000X

Fig. 12   Rear main seal removal

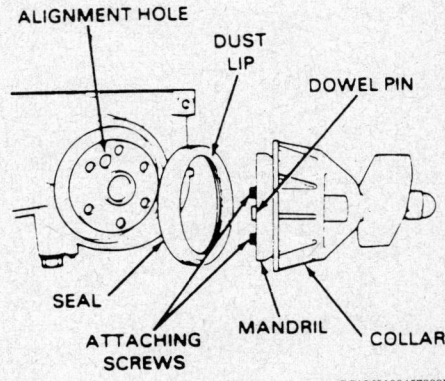

ALIGNMENT HOLE
DUST LIP
DOWEL PIN
SEAL
ATTACHING SCREWS
MANDRIL
COLLAR

GC1069100457000X

Fig. 13   Rear main seal installation

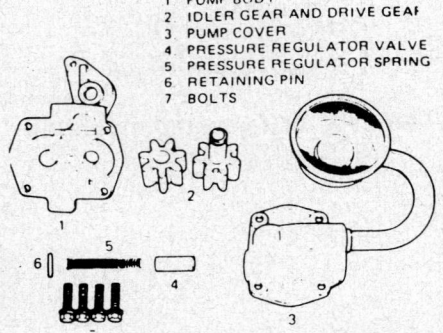

1 PUMP BODY
2 IDLER GEAR AND DRIVE GEAR
3 PUMP COVER
4 PRESSURE REGULATOR VALVE
5 PRESSURE REGULATOR SPRING
6 RETAINING PIN
7 BOLTS

GC1099100075000X

Fig. 14   Exploded view of oil pump

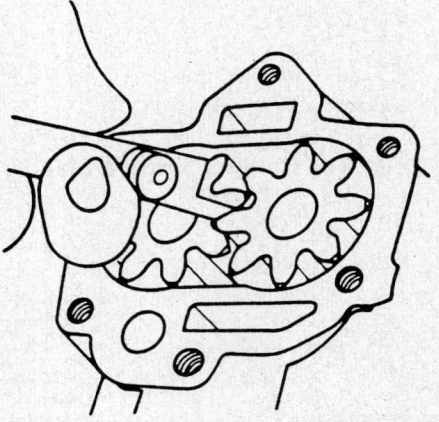

GC1099100076000X

Fig. 15   Oil pump gear lash measurement

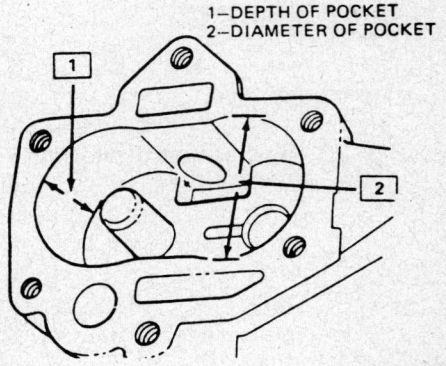

1—DEPTH OF POCKET
2—DIAMETER OF POCKET

GC1099100077000X

Fig. 16   Oil pump gear pocket measurement

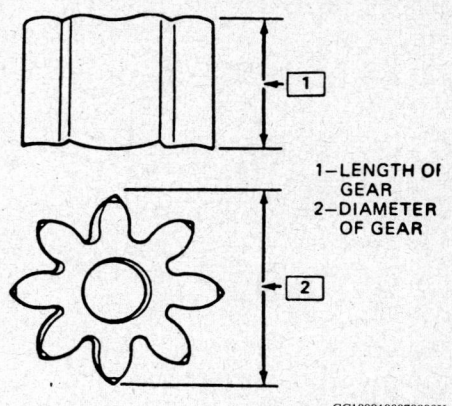

1—LENGTH OF GEAR
2—DIAMETER OF GEAR

GC1099100078000X

Fig. 17 Oil pump gear measurement

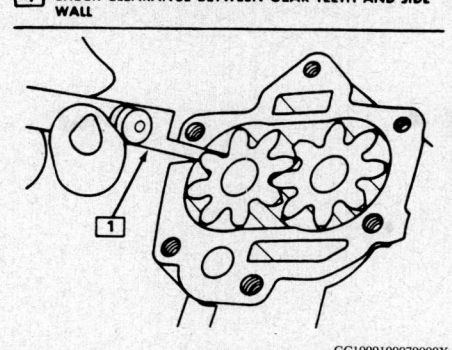

① CHECK CLEARANCE BETWEEN GEAR TEETH AND SIDE WALL

GC1099100079000X

Fig. 18 Gear side clearance measurement

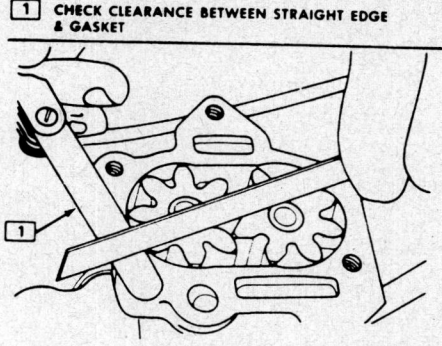

① CHECK CLEARANCE BETWEEN STRAIGHT EDGE & GASKET

GC1099100080000X

Fig. 19 Oil pump end clearance measurement

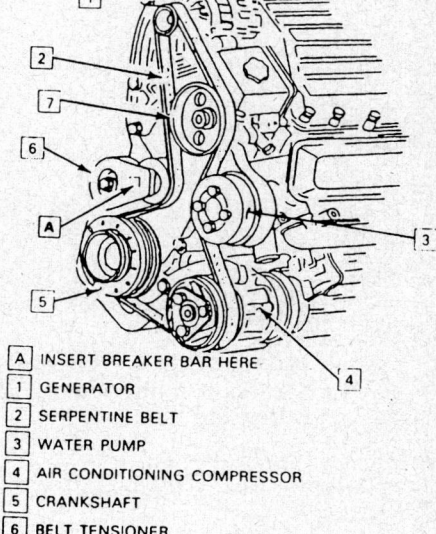

A INSERT BREAKER BAR HERE
1 GENERATOR
2 SERPENTINE BELT
3 WATER PUMP
4 AIR CONDITIONING COMPRESSOR
5 CRANKSHAFT
6 BELT TENSIONER
7 POWER STEERING PUMP

GC1069100459000X

Fig. 20 Serpentine drive belt routing

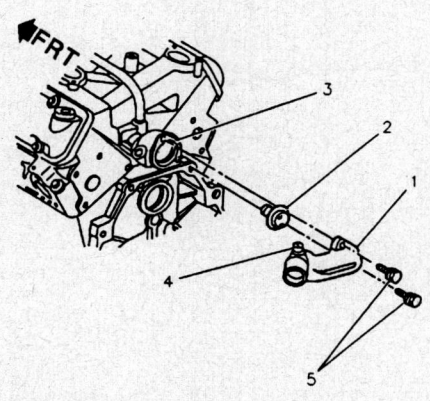

1 WATER OUTLET
2 THERMOSTAT
3 INLET
4 BLEEDER
5 BOLT/SCREW 25 N•m (18 LB. FT.)

GC1089100172000X

Fig. 21 Cooling system bleed vent

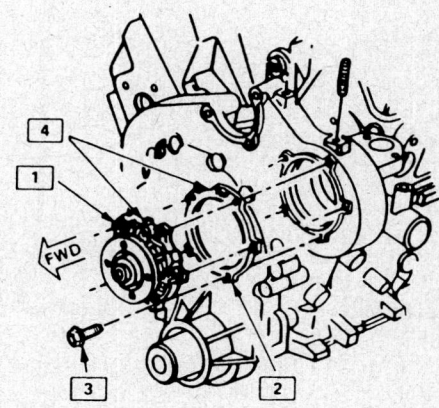

1. WATER PUMP
2. GASKET
3. 10 N•m (89 LB. IN.)
4. LOCATOR – MUST BE VERTICAL

GC1089100171000X

Fig. 22 Water pump mounting

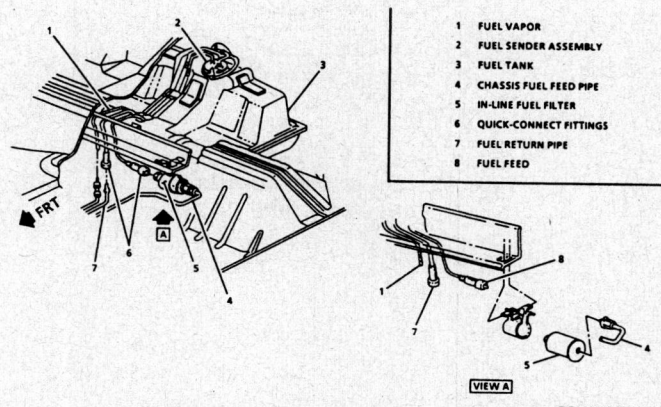

1 FUEL VAPOR
2 FUEL SENDER ASSEMBLY
3 FUEL TANK
4 CHASSIS FUEL FEED PIPE
5 IN-LINE FUEL FILTER
6 QUICK-CONNECT FITTINGS
7 FUEL RETURN PIPE
8 FUEL FEED

VIEW A

GC1029102741000X

Fig. 23 Fuel filter replacement

TIGHTENING SPECIFICATIONS

Year	Component	Torque/Ft. Lbs.
2004–05	Camshaft Position Sensor	89①
	Camshaft Sprocket	103
	Camshaft Thrust Plate	89①
	Connecting Rod Bearing	④
	Coolant Drain Plug	14
	Coolant Temperature Sensor	17
	Crankshaft Balancer	③
	Cylinder Head	②
	Drive Belt Idler Pulley	37
	Drive Belt Shield	89①
	Drive Belt Tensioner	37
	Engine Mount	35
	Engine Mount Bracket	43
	Engine Mount Strut Bracket To Engine	35
	Engine Mount Strut Bracket To Radiator	21
	Exhaust Manifold Heat Shield	96①
	Exhaust Manifold Nut	12
	Exhaust Manifold Stud	12
	Flywheel	52
	Front Cover (Large)	41
	Front Cover (Small)	20
	Intake Manifold (Lower)	⑤
	Intake Manifold (Upper)	18
	Intake Manifold Stud (Upper)	18
	Main Bearing Cap	④
	Oil Cooler Connector	50
	Oil Dipstick Retainer	18
	Oil Filter	10
	Oil Filter Adapter	29
	Oil Level Sensor	96①
	Oil Pan Drain Plug	18
	Oil Pan (Lower)	18
	Oil Pan (Side)	35
	Oil Pump	30
	Oil Pump Cover	96①
	Oil Pump Drive Assembly	27
	Rocker Arm	14①
	Serpentine Drive Belt Tensioner	40
	Spark Plugs	15
	Timing Chain Damper	15
	Valve Cover	89①
	Valve Lifter Guide	89①
	Water Pump	96①
	Water Pump Pulley	18

① — Inch lbs.
② — Refer to "Cylinder Head, Replace" for tightening specifications and sequence.
③ — Refer to "Front Cover, Replace" for tightening specifications and sequence.
④ — Refer to "Main & Rod Bearings" for tightening specifications and sequence.
⑤ — Refer to "Intake Manifold, Replace" for tightening specifications and sequence.

3.4L Engine

NOTE: On Air Bag Equipped Models, Refer To "Air Bag System Precautions" Located In The Front Of This Manual For System Disarming & Arming Procedures.

NOTE: Refer To "Computer Relearn Procedures" Located In The Front Of This Manual When Battery Power To The Computer Has Been Interrupted.

NOTE: Prior To Performing Any Service Operations Listed In This Section, Consult The "Technical Service Bulletins" Section For Related Information.

INDEX

	Page No.		Page No.		Page No.
Belt Tension Data	6-32	Upper	6-29	Fuel System Pressure Relief	6-28
Camshaft, Replace	6-31	Exhaust Manifold, Replace	6-30	Radiator, Replace	6-32
Camshaft Lobe Lift		Lefthand	6-30	Rocker Arms, Replace	6-31
Specifications	6-31	Righthand	6-30	Serpentine Drive Belt	6-32
Compression Pressure	6-28	Front Cover, Replace	6-31	Replacement	6-32
Cooling System Bleed	6-32	Front Cover Seal, Replace	6-31	Routing	6-32
Crankshaft Damper, Replace	6-31	Fuel Filter, Replace	6-32	Technical Service Bulletins	6-33
Crankshaft Rear Oil Seal,		Fuel Pump, Replace	6-32	Crankshaft Rear Main Oil Leak	6-33
Replace	6-31	Intake Manifold, Replace	6-29	Whistle Noise on Light	
Cylinder Head, Replace	6-30	Lower	6-29	Acceleration	6-33
Lefthand	6-30	Upper	6-29	Impala & Monte Carlo	6-33
Righthand	6-30	Main & Rod Bearings	6-31	Thermostat, Replace	6-32
Engine Rebuilding		Connecting Rod	6-31	Tightening Specifications	6-34
Specifications	29-1	Main Bearings	6-31	Timing Chain, Replace	6-31
Engine, Replace	6-29	Oil Pan, Replace	6-31	Valve Cover, Replace	6-30
Engine Mount, Replace	6-28	Oil Pump, Replace	6-32	Lefthand	6-30
Front	6-28	Piston & Rod Assembly	6-31	Righthand	6-30
Lefthand	6-28	Precautions	6-28	Valve Lifters	6-31
Righthand	6-29	Air Bag Systems	6-28	Replace	6-31
Lower	6-29	Battery Ground Cable	6-28	Water Pump, Replace	6-32

PRECAUTIONS

Air Bag Systems

Refer to "Air Bag System Precautions" in the front of this manual for system disarming and arming procedures.

Battery Ground Cable

Prior to service, disconnect battery ground cable and isolate as required.

Fuel System Pressure Relief

To reduce the risk of fire and personal injury, it is required to relieve the fuel system pressure before servicing fuel system components.
1. Loosen fuel tank filler cap to relieve tank pressure.
2. Remove fuel injection sight shield.
3. Connect fuel pressure gauge tool No. J34730-1, or equivalent, to fuel pressure valve. Wrap a shop towel around fitting while connecting gauge to avoid spillage.

4. Install bleed hose into suitable container and open valve to bleed system pressure.

COMPRESSION PRESSURE

When inspecting compression, lowest cylinder must be within 70 percent of the highest cylinder with a minimum pressure of 100 psi. Perform compression test with engine at normal operating temperature, spark plugs removed and throttle wide open.

ENGINE MOUNT

REPLACE

Front

1. Disconnect air inlet duct from throttle body.
2. Remove lefthand and righthand engine mount struts.
3. Raise and support vehicle.
4. Disconnect catalytic converter pipe from righthand exhaust manifold.
5. Remove righthand front tire and wheel assembly.

6. Remove righthand side engine splash shield.
7. Remove engine mount to subframe nuts.
8. Lower vehicle and support engine using lifting tool No. J28467-B, or equivalent.
9. Raise engine until mount is clear of subframe.
10. Raise and support vehicle.
11. Remove engine mount mounting bolts, **Fig. 1.**
12. Reverse procedure to install.

Lefthand

1. Remove engine mount strut from engine mount strut bracket.
2. Remove engine exhaust crossover pipe.
3. Remove throttle body air inlet duct.
4. Partially drain cooling system into suitable container.
5. Remove radiator hose from thermostat housing.
6. Remove mounting bolts, housing and thermostat.
7. Remove engine mount strut bracket mounting bolts.
8. Remove engine mount strut bracket.
9. Reverse procedure to install.

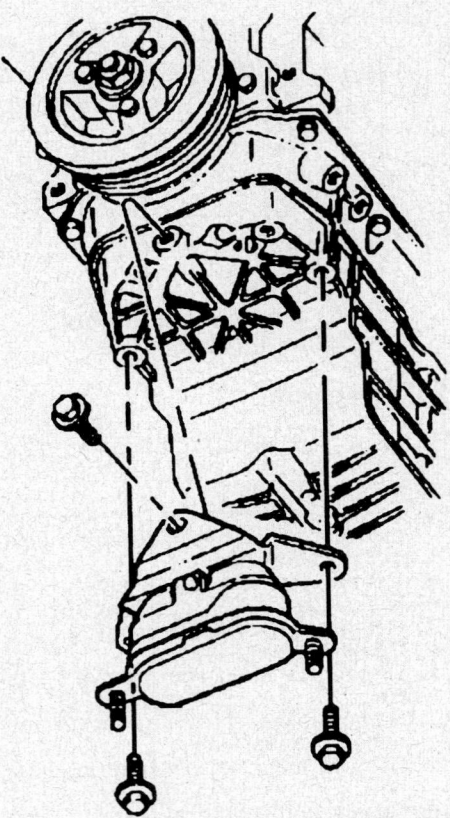

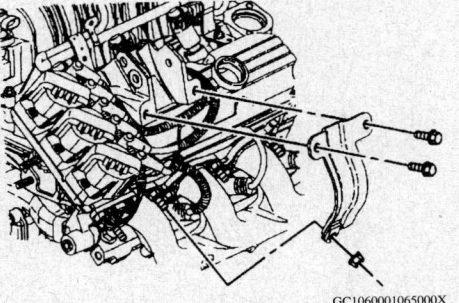

GC1060001065000X

Fig. 2   Righthand lower engine mount replacement

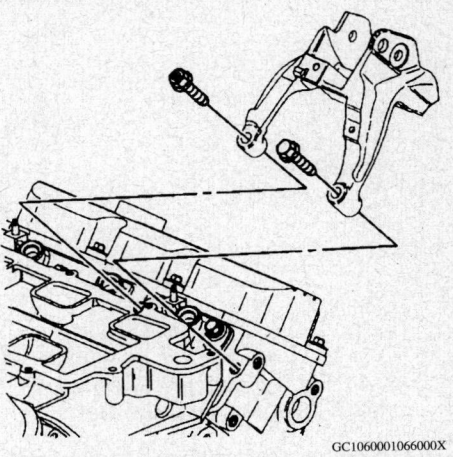

GC1060001066000X

Fig. 3   Righthand upper engine mount bracket replacement

GC1060001068000X

Fig. 1   Front engine mount replacement

Righthand
LOWER

1. Remove righthand lower engine mount strut bracket mounting bolts, **Fig. 2.**
2. Remove engine mount mounting nut, then the engine mount.
3. Reverse procedure to install.

UPPER

1. Remove righthand engine mount strut from upper engine strut mount bracket.
2. Remove fuel injector sight shield.
3. Remove EVAP emissions canister purge valve.
4. Remove mounting bolts and righthand upper engine mount strut bracket, **Fig. 3.**
5. **On models equipped with oil cooler,** remove oil cooler pipe bracket bolt from righthand engine mount strut bracket.
6. **On all models,** remove mounting bolts and position air conditioning compressor aside.
7. Remove vertical bolt from righthand engine mount strut bracket, **Fig. 4.**
8. Remove righthand engine mount bracket.
9. Reverse procedure to install.

ENGINE
REPLACE

1. Relieve fuel system pressure as out-

lined under "Precautions."
2. Remove hood and cross vehicle brace.
3. Remove throttle body air inlet duct and Mass Air Flow (MAF) sensor from air cleaner.
4. Remove engine mount struts and accessory drive belt.
5. Disconnect brake booster hose from upper intake manifold.
6. Mark electrical connectors for install alignment.
7. Disconnect heated oxygen sensor and AIR check valve solenoid, then the EGR and EVAP valves connectors.
8. Disconnect TP sensor and IAC valve, then the alternator and ignition coil connectors.
9. Remove harness ground connectors and body to engine wiring harnesses.
10. Raise and support vehicle.
11. Remove lower radiator air baffle, then righthand side engine splash shield.
12. Drain engine cooling system and oil.
13. Remove oil filter.
14. Disconnect vehicle speed and oil lever sensors, then the oil pressure switch and engine block heater electrical connectors:
15. Disconnect knock and heated oxygen sensors, then the crankshaft position sensor and air conditioning compressor electrical connectors:
16. Disconnect wiring harness grounds.
17. Remove catalytic converter from righthand exhaust manifold.
18. Remove engine mount lower mounting nuts.
19. Remove torque converter cover and starter motor.
20. Remove mounting bolts and position air conditioning compressor aside.
21. Remove torque converter mounting bolts.
22. Remove transaxle brace, then lower transaxle to engine bolt and stud.
23. Disconnect lower radiator outlet hose from engine.
24. Lower vehicle.
25. Disconnect accelerator and cruise control cables from throttle body and cable bracket.
26. Disconnect upper intake manifold and EVAP vacuum hoses.
27. Disconnect fuel feed and return hoses.
28. Disconnect AIR check valve hose.
29. Remove and position power steering pump aside.
30. Disconnect heater inlet and outlet

hoses from engine.
31. Disconnect upper radiator hose from engine.
32. Support transaxle using suitable floor stands.
33. Support engine using suitable lifting device.
34. Remove upper engine to transaxle bolts.
35. Remove engine.
36. Reverse procedure to install.

INTAKE MANIFOLD
REPLACE
Upper

1. Disconnect vacuum hose from throttle body air inlet duct.
2. Disconnect IAT sensor electrical connector and air inlet duct.
3. Drain engine coolant into suitable container.
4. Disconnect accelerator and cruise control cables from throttle body.
5. Disconnect TP sensor and IAC valve electrical connectors.
6. Disconnect wiring harness attachment clips for CMP sensor and lefthand side spark plug wires.
7. Disconnect thermostat bypass hose from throttle body and remove rear alternator brace.
8. Disconnect vacuum lines from upper intake manifold.
9. Remove MAP sensor, EGR valve, spark plug wires and ignition control module.
10. Remove mounting bolts and upper intake manifold.
11. Reverse procedure to install.

Lower

1. Relieve fuel system pressure as outlined under "Precautions."
2. Remove upper intake manifold.
3. Remove lefthand and righthand valve covers as outlined under "Valve Cover, Replace."
4. Disconnect ECT sensor electrical connector.

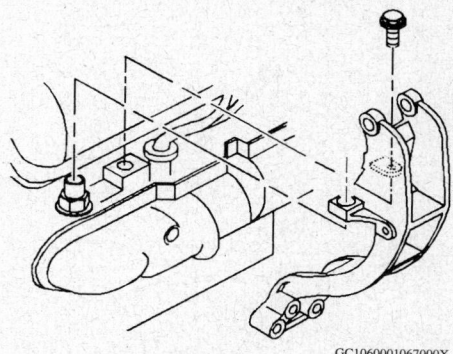

GC1060001067000X

Fig. 4 Righthand engine mount strut bracket replacement

5. Disconnect fuel injector and MAP sensor electrical connectors.
6. Remove mounting bolt and fuel pipe clip.
7. Disconnect fuel feed and return pipes from fuel rail.
8. Remove fuel injector rail.
9. Remove and position power steering pump aside.
10. Disconnect heater inlet pipe with heater hose from lower intake manifold and position aside.
11. Disconnect upper radiator hose from engine.
12. Disconnect thermostat bypass hose from bypass and lower intake manifold pipes.
13. Remove mounting bolts, lower manifold and gaskets.
14. Reverse procedure to install, noting the following:
    a. Install new intake manifold gaskets.
    b. Apply .31–.39 inch drops of suitable RTV sealant to four corners of manifold to block joints, **Fig. 5.**
    c. Connect sealant drops with sealant beads .31–.39 inch wide and .12–.20 inch thick.
    d. **Install new mounting bolts.**
    e. **Vertical bolts must be tightened before diagonal bolts.**
    f. Refer to sequence, **Fig. 6,** and tighten intake manifold mounting bolts in three steps: First step, **torque** all bolts to 62 inch lbs.; second step, **torque** bolts 1, 2, 3 and 4 to 115 inch lbs.; third step, **torque** bolts 5, 6, 7 and 8 to 18 ft. lbs.

EXHAUST MANIFOLD
REPLACE
Righthand

1. Disconnect throttle body air inlet duct.
2. Remove righthand engine mount strut bracket and AIR pipe.
3. Remove thermostat bypass pipe.
4. Remove heat shield and exhaust crossover pipe.
5. Remove mounting bolts exhaust manifold heat shield.
6. Remove mounting nuts and exhaust manifold.
7. Reverse procedure to install.

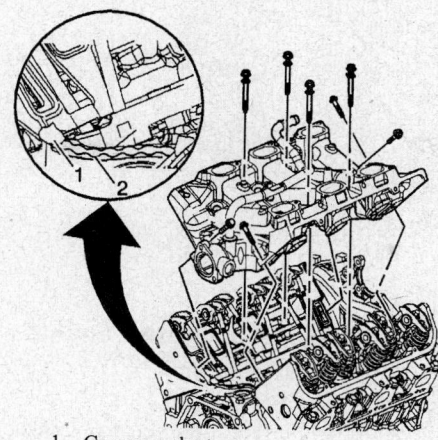

1. Corner sealant
2. Manifold to block sealant

ARM0400000000167

Fig. 5 Lower intake manifold replacement

Lefthand

1. Disconnect throttle body air inlet duct.
2. Remove AIR check valve.
3. Remove heat shield and exhaust crossover pipe.
4. Disconnect oxygen sensor electrical connector.
5. Raise and support vehicle, then remove catalytic converter from exhaust manifold.
6. Remove EGR valve from lower intake manifold.
7. Remove mounting bolts and exhaust manifold head shield.
8. Remove mounting nuts, exhaust manifold and gasket.
9. Reverse procedure to install.

CYLINDER HEAD
REPLACE
Righthand

1. Raise and support vehicle, then drain engine coolant and oil into suitable containers.
2. Lower vehicle, then remove lower intake manifold as outlined under "Intake Manifold, Replace."
3. Remove righthand valve cover as outlined under "Valve Cover, Replace."
4. Remove exhaust crossover pipe and righthand engine mount strut bracket.
5. Remove oil dipstick tube.
6. Remove spark plugs and righthand exhaust manifold as outlined under "Exhaust Manifold, Replace."
7. Remove mounting bolts, cylinder head and gasket.
8. Reverse procedure to install, noting the following:
    a. Install new gasket.
    b. Refer to sequence, **Fig. 7,** and tighten cylinder head bolts in two steps: First step, **torque** bolts to 44 ft. lbs.; second step, tighten bolts an additional 95.°

ARM0400000000168

Fig. 6 Intake manifold bolt tightening sequence

Lefthand

1. Raise and support vehicle, then drain engine coolant and oil into suitable containers.
2. Lower vehicle and remove lower intake manifold as outlined under "Intake Manifold, Replace."
3. Remove lefthand valve cover as outlined under "Valve Cover, Replace."
4. Remove exhaust crossover pipe.
5. Remove fuel line bracket.
6. Disconnect wires and remove spark plugs.
7. Remove exhaust manifold as outlined under "Exhaust Manifold, Replace."
8. Remove mounting bolts and cylinder head.
9. Reverse procedure to install, noting the following:
    a. Install new gasket.
    b. Refer to sequence, **Fig. 7,** and tighten cylinder head bolts in two steps: First step, **torque** bolts to 44 ft. lbs.; second step, tighten bolts an additional 95.°

VALVE COVER
REPLACE
Lefthand

1. Rotate tensioner clockwise using suitable box end wrench and remove serpentine belt.
2. Remove mounting bolts and position coolant recovery reservoir aside.
3. Remove alternator mounting bolts and disconnect electrical connector.
4. Remove mounting nut and disconnect battery lead.
5. Remove alternator and bracket.
6. Disconnect righthand spark plug wires and EVAP vacuum hoses from EVAP valve.
7. Remove EVAP and AIR check valves.
8. Remove ignition coils and bracket.
9. Remove vacuum hose from valve cover grommet.
10. Remove mounting bolts and valve cover.
11. Reverse procedure to install.

Righthand

1. Drain engine coolant into suitable container.

2. Disconnect spark plug wires and n remove engine mount strut from engine.
3. Remove AIR check valve.
4. Remove thermostat bypass hose and pipe.
5. Remove PCV valve.
6. Remove mounting bolts and valve cover.
7. Reverse procedure to install.

VALVE LIFTERS
Replace

1. Remove both valve covers as outlined under "Valve Cover, Replace."
2. Remove lower intake manifold as outlined under "Intake Manifold, Replace."
3. Remove rocker arm mounting bolts, rocker arms and push rods. Keep valve train components in order.
4. Remove bolts, lifter guides and valve lifters.
5. Reverse procedure to install. Ensure valve train components are installed in original positions.

CAMSHAFT LOBE LIFT SPECIFICATIONS

Intake ....2727 inch
Exhaust ....2727 inch

ROCKER ARMS
REPLACE

1. Remove both valve covers as outlined under "Valve Cover, Replace."
2. Remove rocker arm mounting bolts, rocker arms and push rods. Keep valve train components in order.
3. Reverse procedure to install, noting the following:
   a. Ensure valve train components are installed in original position.
   b. **Torque** mounting bolts to 14 ft. lbs.
   c. Tighten bolts an additional 30.°

CRANKSHAFT DAMPER
REPLACE

1. Rotate belt tensioner clockwise using suitable box end wrench and remove serpentine belt.
2. Raise and support vehicle.
3. Remove righthand tire and wheel assembly, then the engine splash shield.
4. Support frame with suitable jack, then remove bolts and lower frame.
5. Remove front lower air deflector panel.
6. Remove torque converter covers.
7. Remove mounting nuts and disconnect starter motor electrical connectors from solenoid.
8. Remove mounting bolts and starter motor.
9. Lock flywheel using holding tool No. J37096, or equivalent.
10. Remove crankshaft pulley bolt and pulley.
11. Remove crankshaft damper/balancer using crankshaft damper removal tool No. J24430, or equivalent.

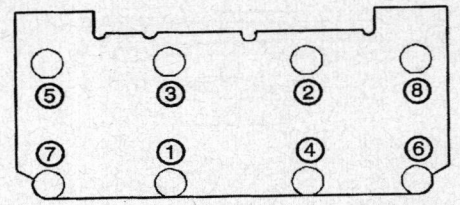

Fig. 7 Cylinder head bolt tightening sequence

ARM0400000000166

12. Reverse procedure to install, noting the following:
   a. Coat front cover oil seal with engine oil.
   b. Install suitable sealant to keyway of damper before installation.
   c. Install damper using crankshaft damper installer tool No. J29113, or equivalent.

FRONT COVER
REPLACE

1. Raise and support vehicle, then drain engine coolant and oil into suitable containers.
2. Remove crankshaft balancer as outlined under "Crankshaft Damper, Replace."
3. Remove mounting bolt and drive belt tensioner.
4. Remove and position power steering pump aside with lines.
5. Disconnect thermostat bypass pipe from front cover and radiator outlet hose from water pump.
6. Remove mounting bolts and water pump pulley.
7. Disconnect CKP sensor wiring harness bracket from front cover.
8. Remove mounting bolts, front cover and gasket.
9. Remove drive belt shield, CKP sensor and water pump from front cover.
10. Reverse procedure to install.

FRONT COVER SEAL
REPLACE

1. Remove crankshaft pulley and damper as outlined under "Crankshaft Damper, Replace."
2. Pry out seal using suitable pry tool.
3. Reverse procedure to install, noting the following:
   a. Lubricate seal with oil.
   b. Install seal using seal installer tool No. J34995, or equivalent.

TIMING CHAIN
REPLACE

1. Remove engine front cover as outlined under "Front Cover, Replace."
2. Align crankshaft until timing marks, **Fig. 8.**
3. Remove mounting bolt and camshaft sprocket with timing chain.
4. Reverse procedure to install. Coat crankshaft and camshaft sprockets with suitable oil before installing front cover.

CAMSHAFT
REPLACE

1. Remove timing chain as outlined under "Timing Chain, Replace."
2. Remove mounting bolts and camshaft thrust plate.
3. Carefully rotate and pull camshaft out of camshaft bearings using suitable large screwdriver.
4. Reverse procedure to install, noting the following:
   a. Coat camshaft journals with suitable, clean engine oil.
   b. Coat camshaft lobes with suitable pre-lube.

PISTON & ROD ASSEMBLY

When installing piston and rod assemblies, ensure arrow on top of piston faces toward the front of the engine, **Fig. 9.**

MAIN & ROD BEARINGS

Connecting rod and main bearing are of the precision insert type. They are available for service use in standard and two undersizes of .016 and .032 inch. Bearing undersize amount is stamped at either end of the bearing, **Fig. 10.**

Connecting Rod

Tighten connecting rod bolts in two steps: First step, **torque** bolts to 15 ft. lbs.; second step, tighten bolts an additional 75.°

Main Bearings

Tighten main bearing cap bolts in two steps: First step, **torque** bolts to 37 ft. lbs.; second step, tighten bolts an additional 77.°

CRANKSHAFT REAR OIL SEAL
REPLACE

1. Remove transaxle as outlined in **MOTOR's** "Domestic Transmission, In-Vehicle Service" manual or "Transmission Service DVD.""
2. Remove flywheel.
3. Remove oil seal using suitable pry tool, **Fig. 11.**
4. Reverse procedure to install using seal installer tool No. J34686, or equivalent.

OIL PAN
REPLACE

1. Remove engine mount struts from engine.
2. Remove mounting bolts and position air conditioning compressor aside.
3. Support engine using support fixture tool No. J28467-360, or equivalent.
4. Raise and support vehicle.

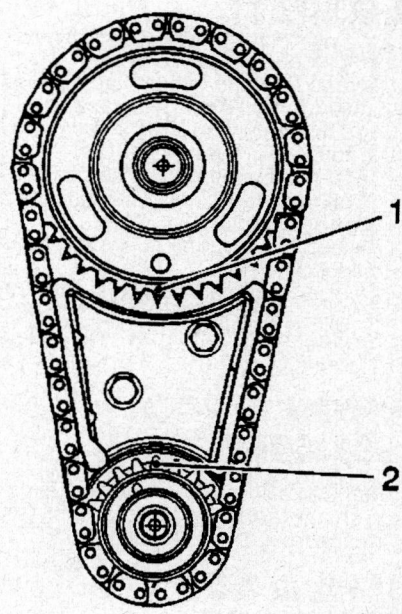

Fig. 8   Timing chain alignment

5. Remove catalytic converter from exhaust manifold.
6. Drain engine oil into suitable container, then disconnect oil level sensor electrical connector.
7. Remove starter motor and transaxle brace from oil pan.
8. Remove transaxle lower mount mounting nuts.
9. Remove engine mount lower mounting nuts.
10. Raise engine slightly, then remove engine mount bracket and engine mount from oil pan.
11. Remove lefthand and righthand side oil pan mounting bolts.
12. Remove mounting bolts and oil pan.
13. Reverse procedure to install. Apply suitable sealant to main bearing cap and engine block, **Fig. 12.**

OIL PUMP
REPLACE

1. Remove oil pan as outlined under "Oil Pan, Replace."
2. Remove mounting bolt and oil pump.
3. Reverse procedure to install.

BELT TENSION DATA

Belt tension is maintained automatically by a spring tensioned idler pulley. No adjustment of serpentine belt is required.

If belt slippage is indicated and belt tensioner indicator is within normal operating range, measure belt tension as follows:
1. Run engine for 10 minutes, then shut off and measure belt tension between any two pulleys using V-belt tension gauge tool No. J23600-B, or equivalent.
2. Run engine for 30 seconds and repeat measurement.

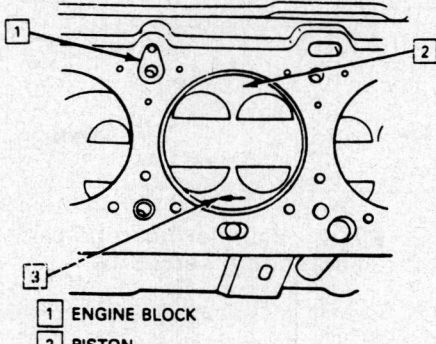

1 ENGINE BLOCK
2 PISTON
3 ARROW FACES TOWARDS FRONT OF ENGINE

Fig. 9   Piston marking

3. Repeat preceding step, then average all three belt tension measurements.
4. Replace drive belt if tension is not 35–55 lbs.

SERPENTINE DRIVE BELT
Replacement

1. Rotate tensioner clockwise using suitable box end wrench.
2. Remove serpentine belt.
3. Reverse procedure to install.

Routing

Refer to **Fig. 13** for belt routing.

COOLING SYSTEM BLEED

1. Open air bleed vents on thermostat housing and heater water inlet pipe.
2. Fill system with suitable coolant until level of coolant has reached base of radiator neck.
3. Close bleed vents and adjust coolant level to base of radiator neck.

THERMOSTAT
REPLACE

1. Remove throttle body air inlet duct.
2. Partially drain cooling system into suitable container.
3. Remove radiator hose from thermostat housing.
4. Remove exhaust crossover pipe.
5. Remove mounting bolts, housing and thermostat.
6. Reverse procedure to install.

WATER PUMP
REPLACE

1. Remove air cleaner.
2. Drain engine coolant into suitable container.
3. Remove serpentine belt.
4. Remove water pump pulley.

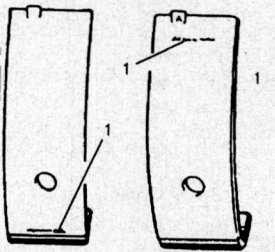

1 AMOUNT UNDERSIZE STAMPED AT EITHER END (.016, .032)

Fig. 10   Bearing marking

5. Remove mounting bolts, water pump and gasket, **Fig. 14.**
6. Reverse procedure to install.

RADIATOR
REPLACE

1. Remove air cleaner assembly, then drain engine coolant into suitable container.
2. Remove mounting bolts, then the engine strut and upper brace rearward.
3. Disconnect upper radiator mounting panel bolts and clamps.
4. Disconnect cooling fan electrical connector.
5. Remove mounting bolts and cooling fan, then the upper radiator bracket.
6. Remove upper and lower radiator hoses at radiator.
7. Disconnect low coolant sensor wiring.
8. Disconnect oil cooler lines and remove radiator.
9. Reverse procedure to install.

FUEL PUMP
REPLACE

1. Relieve fuel system pressure as outlined under "Precautions."
2. Remove fuel pump/sender luggage compartment access cover.
3. Remove mounting bolts, pull assembly upward and disconnect electrical connector.
4. Remove pump/sender.
5. Reverse procedure to install.

FUEL FILTER
REPLACE

1. Relieve fuel system pressure as outlined under "Precautions."
2. Raise and support vehicle.
3. Remove mounting screw and filter bracket, **Fig. 15.**
4. Grasp filter and fuel line fitting. Twist quick-connect fitting ¼ turn in each direction to loosen any dirt within fitting.
5. Remove feed pipe nut and drain fuel into suitable container.
6. Remove fuel filter.
7. Reverse procedure to install.

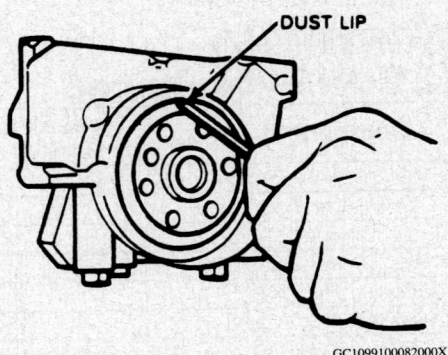

Fig. 11 **Rear main seal replacement**

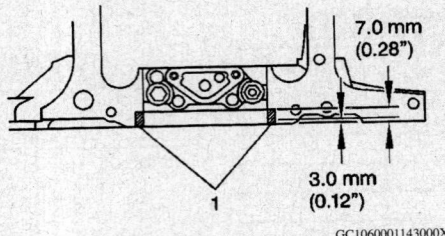

Fig. 12 **Oil pan sealant application**

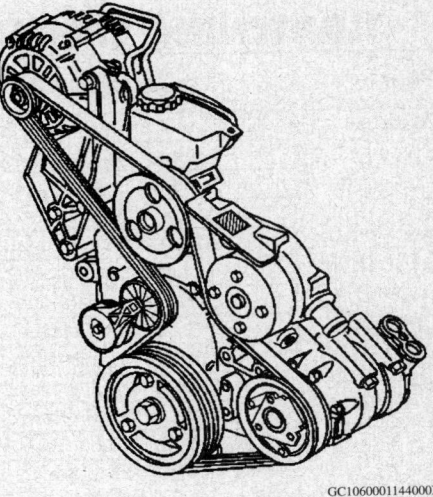

Fig. 13 **Serpentine drive belt routing**

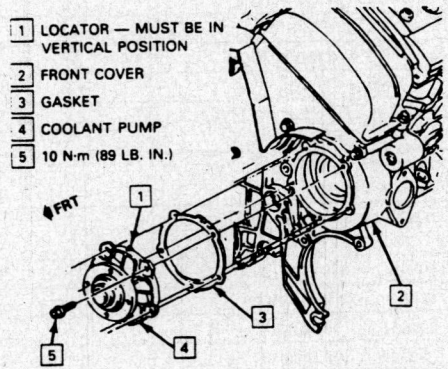

1 LOCATOR — MUST BE IN VERTICAL POSITION
2 FRONT COVER
3 GASKET
4 COOLANT PUMP
5 10 N·m (89 LB. IN.)

Fig. 14 **Water pump replacement**

TECHNICAL SERVICE BULLETINS

Crankshaft Rear Main Oil Leak

On some of these models there may be an engine oil leak at crankshaft rear main oil seal.

This condition may be caused by the rear main oil seal design.

To correct this condition, install revised rear main oil seal (part No. 12592195).

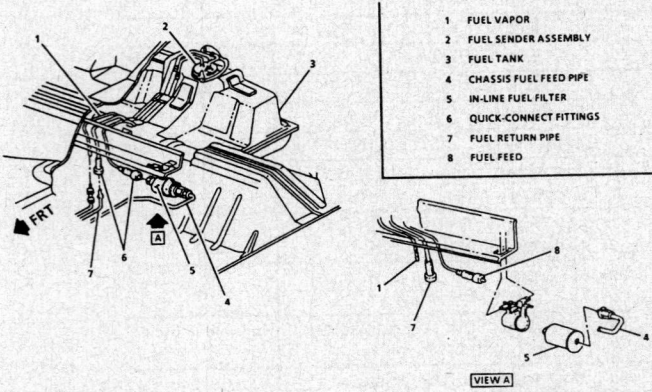

1 FUEL VAPOR
2 FUEL SENDER ASSEMBLY
3 FUEL TANK
4 CHASSIS FUEL FEED PIPE
5 IN-LINE FUEL FILTER
6 QUICK-CONNECT FITTINGS
7 FUEL RETURN PIPE
8 FUEL FEED

Fig. 15 **Fuel filter replacement**

Whistle Noise on Light Acceleration

IMPALA & MONTE CARLO

On some of these models there may be a whistle type noise on light acceleration.

This condition may be caused by a throttle body casting porosity.

To correct this condition, replace the throttle body and gasket.

TIGHTENING SPECIFICATIONS

Year	Component	Torque/Ft. Lbs.
2002–05	Accelerator Control Cable Bracket	89
	Alternator Brace Bracket	37
	Camshaft Position Sensor	89①
	Camshaft Sprocket	103
	Camshaft Thrust Plate	89①
	Connecting Rod Cap	②
	Coolant Drain Plug	14
	Crankshaft Balancer	76
	Crankshaft Main Bearing Cap	②
	Crankshaft Oil Deflector	18
	Crankshaft Position Sensor Bolt	89①
	Crankshaft Position Sensor Stud	98①
	Crankshaft Position Sensor Wiring Bracket	20
	Cylinder Head	③
	Drive Belt Tensioner	37
	EGR Valve Adapter Pipe	18
	EGR Valve To EGR Valve Pipe	18
	Engine Flywheel	52
	Engine Mount Bracket	43
	Engine Mount Lower Nut	32
	Engine Mount Strut Bolt/Nut	35
	Engine Mount Strut Bracket Bolt (Upper Radiator Support)	21
	Engine Mount Strut Bracket Bolt (Vehicle Righthand Side)	37
	Engine Mount Strut & Lift Bracket (Lefthand Side)	52
	Engine Mount Strut & Lift Bracket (Righthand Side)	37
	Engine Mount Upper Nut	35
	Engine Oil Pressure Indicator Switch	12
	Exhaust Crossover	18
	Exhaust Crossover Heat Shield	89①
	Exhaust Manifold Heat Shield	89①
	Exhaust Manifold Nut	12
	Exhaust Manifold Pipe Stud	13
	Front Cover (Large & Medium Bolts)	41
	Front Cover (Small Bolts)	20
	Fuel Injector Rail Nut	89①
	Fuel Pipe Clip Bolt	71①
	Fuel Return Pipe To Fuel Injector Rail Nut	13
	Heated Oxygen Sensor	31
	Ignition Coil Bracket	18
	Intake Manifold Coolant Pipe Bolt	89①
	Intake Manifold, Lower	⑥
	Intake Manifold, Upper	18
	Main Bearing Cap	②
	MAP Sensor	44①
	Oil Cooler Connector	37

TIGHTENING SPECIFICATIONS—Continued

Year	Component	Torque/Ft. Lbs.
2002–05	Oil Cooler Hose Fitting	14
	Oil Dipstick Tube	18
	Oil Filter	22
	Oil Filter Bypass Hole Plug	14
	Oil Gallery Plug ¼ Inch	14
	Oil Gallery Plug ⅜ Inch	24
	Oil Level Sensor	89①
	Oil Pan	18
	Oil Pan Drain Plug	18
	Oil Pump Cover	89①
	Oil Pump Drive Clamp Bolt	27
	Oil Pump Mounting Bolt	30
	Spark Plug	④
	Thermostat Bypass Pipe To Cylinder Head Nut	18
	Thermostat Bypass Pipe To Front Cover	106①
	Thermostat Bypass Pipe To Throttle Body	18
	Throttle Body Bolt/Nut	18
	Timing Chain Damper	15
	Transaxle To Engine	55
	Valve Lifter Guide	89①
	Valve Rocker Arm	⑤
	Valve Rocker Arm Cover	89①
	Water Outlet	18
	Water Pump	98①
	Water Pump Pulley	18

① — Inch lbs.

② — Refer to "Main & Rod Bearings" for tightening specifications and sequence.

③ — Refer to "Cylinder Head, Replace" for tightening specifications and sequence.

④ — Initial installation, 15 ft. lbs. Later installation, 13 ft. lbs.

⑤ — Refer to "Rocker Arms, Replace" for tightening specifications and sequence.

⑥ — Refer to "Intake Manifold, Replace" for tightening specifications and sequence.

3.5L & 3.9L Engines

NOTE: On Air Bag Equipped Models, Refer To "Air Bag System Precautions" Located In The Front Of This Manual For System Disarming & Arming Procedures.

NOTE: Refer To "Computer Relearn Procedures" Located In The Front Of This Manual When Battery Power To The Computer Has Been Interrupted.

INDEX

	Page No.			Page No.			Page No.
Camshaft, Replace	6-39		Front Cover, Replace	6-38		Battery Ground Cable	6-35
Camshaft Lobe Lift			Fuel Pump, Replace	6-41		Fuel System Pressure Relief	6-35
Specifications	6-38		Hydraulic Lifters, Replace	6-38		Push Rods	6-38
Compression Pressure	6-35		Intake Manifold, Replace	6-36		Radiator, Replace	6-41
Cooling System Bleed	6-40		Lower	6-36		Rocker Arms, Replace	6-38
Crankshaft Damper, Replace	6-38		Upper	6-36		Serpentine Drive Belt	6-40
Crankshaft Rear Oil Seal,			Main & Rod Bearings	6-39		Replacement	6-40
Replace	6-39		Connecting Rod	6-39		Routing	6-40
Crankshaft Seal, Replace	6-39		Main Bearing Caps	6-39		Thermostat, Replace	6-40
Cylinder Head, Replace	6-37		Oil Pan, Replace	6-39		Tightening Specifications	6-42
Engine Rebuilding			Oil Pump, Replace	6-40		Timing Chain, Replace	6-39
Specifications	29-1		Oil Pump Service	6-40		Installation	6-39
Engine, Replace	6-35		Assemble	6-40		Removal	6-39
Engine Mount, Replace	6-35		Disassemble	6-40		Valve Adjustment	6-38
Engine Mount Strut, Replace	6-35		Inspection	6-40		Valve Cover, Replace	6-37
Exhaust Manifold, Replace	6-37		Piston & Rod Assembly	6-39		Lefthand	6-37
Lefthand	6-37		Precautions	6-35		Righthand	6-38
Righthand	6-37		Air Bag Systems	6-35		Water Pump, Replace	6-40

PRECAUTIONS

Air Bag Systems

Refer to "Air Bag System Precautions" in the front of this manual for system disarming and arming procedures.

Battery Ground Cable

Prior to service, disconnect battery ground cable and isolate as required.

Fuel System Pressure Relief

Failure to relieve system pressure prior to disconnecting fuel system components may cause fire or personal injury.
1. Remove engine oil fill cap and intake manifold cover.
2. Remove fuel rail pressure fitting cap and connect suitable fuel pressure gauge to fuel pressure valve.
3. Place fuel gauge bleed hose into suitable container.
4. Relieve fuel tank vapor pressure by loosening fuel fill cap.
5. Relieve fuel pressure by opening fuel gauge bleed valve.

COMPRESSION PRESSURE

1. Disable ignition and fuel systems.
2. Remove all spark plugs.
3. Remove air duct from throttle body and block throttle plate in open position.
4. Firmly install suitable compression gauge to spark plug hole and crank engine through at least four compression strokes in testing cylinder.
5. Record readings at each stroke.
6. Disconnect and repeat compression test for each cylinder.
7. Record compression readings from all of cylinders.
8. Lowest reading should not be less than 70% of highest reading.
9. No cylinder reading should be less than 100 psi.

ENGINE MOUNT

REPLACE

1. Raise and support vehicle, then remove righthand tire and wheel assembly.
2. Remove ABS lead retainers and engine splash shield
3. Remove engine mount to frame nuts.
4. Support engine using suitable jackstand. Place a wood block under oil pan.
5. Remove engine mount bracket bolts.
6. Raise engine and remove engine mount/bracket.
7. Reverse procedure to install. **Torque** mounting bolts to 37 ft. lbs., in sequence, **Fig. 1.**

ENGINE MOUNT STRUT

REPLACE

1. Remove engine mount strut to radiator support mounting bolts.
2. Remove engine mount strut to bracket mounting bolts and nuts.
3. Remove engine mount strut.
4. Reverse procedure to install. Ensure righthand engine harness clamp is sandwiched between bolt and strut bracket.

ENGINE

REPLACE

1. Remove mounting bolts and hood.
2. Remove engine oil fill cap and intake manifold cover.
3. Relieve fuel system pressure as outlined under "Precautions."
4. Remove mounting bolts and lefthand inner fender brace.
5. Remove air cleaner outlet duct from throttle body.
6. Disconnect PCV tube from air inlet duct.

7. Disconnect Mass Air Flow (MAF) sensor electrical connector.
8. Remove upper from lower air cleaner housing.
9. Remove Powertrain Control Module (PCM) and harness from lower air cleaner housing. **Do not disconnect connectors.**
10. Remove Transmission Control Module (TCM) and harness from lower air cleaner housing. **Do not disconnect connectors.**
11. Remove air cleaner outlet duct from air cleaner.
12. Remove lower air cleaner housing.
13. Remove engine mount strut to radiator support and bracket mounting bolts and nuts.
14. Remove engine mount strut.
15. Remove drive belt as outlined under "Serpentine Drive Belt."
16. Drain cooling system and engine oil into suitable containers.
17. Remove mounting nuts and oil pressure sensor heat shield.
18. Disconnect oil pressure and knock sensor electrical connectors.
19. Disconnect starter motor and air conditioning compressor electrical connectors.
20. Disconnect oil level sensor electrical connector.
21. Remove engine harness clips from transaxle brace and oil pan.
22. Lower vehicle.
23. Disconnect EVAP canister purge solenoid, Electronic Throttle Control (ETC) and Manifold Absolute Pressure (MAP) sensor electrical connectors.
24. Position alternator terminal boot aside, then remove nut and disconnect alternator connector.
25. Disconnect ignition coil and fuel injector electrical connectors.
26. Remove engine harness clips from brackets.
27. Disconnect camshaft position (CMP) sensor electrical connector.
28. Remove mounting bolt and engine harness clip from transaxle bracket.
29. Disconnect rear upper Heated Oxygen Sensor (HO2S) and knock sensor electrical connectors.
30. Remove engine harness clips from transaxle bracket.
31. Remove mounting bolt and engine harness ground terminals from transaxle.
32. Remove engine harness clip bolt from transaxle.
33. Position engine harness branches aside.
34. Remove mounting bolts and exhaust manifold heat shield.
35. Remove upper catalytic converter to exhaust manifold mounting nut.
36. Raise and support vehicle.
37. Disconnect electrical connectors and remove HO2Ss.
38. Remove catalytic converter to muffler mounting nuts and insulators.
39. Remove catalytic converter lower mounting nut and position muffler aside.
40. Remove catalytic converter and gasket.

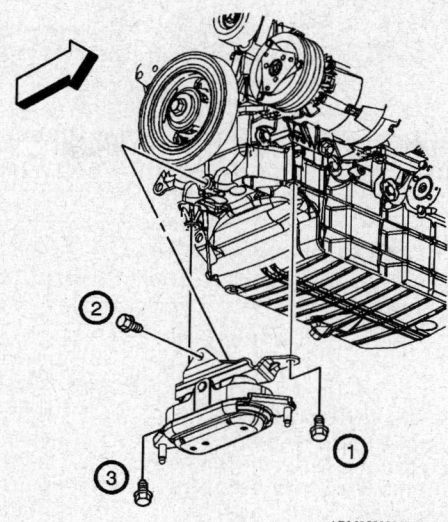

Fig. 1 Engine mount bolt tightening sequence

41. Remove engine mount lower nuts.
42. Remove mounting bolts and torque converter cover.
43. Disconnect connector, then remove mounting bolts and starter motor.
44. Remove torque converter mounting bolts.
45. Remove front mounting bolt and nut, then the rear bolt and position air conditioning compressor aside. **Do not discharge air conditioning system.**
46. Remove mounting bolts and transaxle brace.
47. Remove engine lower transaxle to engine lower rear mounting bolt.
48. Remove radiator outlet hose from thermostat housing.
49. Lower vehicle and support transaxle with suitable jack.
50. Remove brake booster vacuum hose from intake manifold.
51. Remove heater inlet and outlet hoses from engine pipes.
52. Remove mounting bolts and exhaust crossover pipe heat shield.
53. Remove mounting nuts, exhaust crossover pipe and seals.
54. Disconnect fuel feed line from rail.
55. Disconnect EVAP purge line from canister purge solenoid.
56. Remove radiator inlet hose from engine.
57. Remove mounting bolts and position power steering pump aside.
58. Remove transaxle to engine mounting bolts/studs.
59. Remove engine.
60. Reverse procedure to install.

INTAKE MANIFOLD
REPLACE

Upper

1. Remove engine oil fill cap and intake manifold cover.
2. Drain cooling system into suitable container.
3. Remove PCV fresh and foul air tubes.

4. Remove intake manifold vacuum hoses.
5. Remove heater inlet and outlet hose/pipe clamps at engine pipes.
6. Remove heater inlet and outlet hose/pipe clamp nuts from throttle body studs.
7. Remove heater inlet and outlet hoses/pipes from engine pipes and throttle body studs. Position hoses/pipes aside.
8. Disconnect Manifold Absolute Pressure (MAP) sensor and EVAP canister purge solenoid electrical connectors
9. Disconnect chassis EVAP line quick connect fitting from purge solenoid.
10. Disconnect Electronic Throttle Control (ETC) electrical connector.
11. Remove mounting bolts and lefthand inner fender brace.
12. Remove air cleaner outlet duct from throttle body.
13. Disconnect PCV tube from air inlet duct.
14. Disconnect Mass Air Flow (MAF) sensor electrical connector.
15. Remove upper from lower air cleaner housing.
16. Remove Powertrain Control Module (PCM) and harness from lower air cleaner housing. **Do not disconnect connectors.**
17. Remove Transmission Control Module (TCM) and harness from lower air cleaner housing. **Do not disconnect connectors.**
18. Remove air cleaner outlet duct from air cleaner.
19. Disconnect and remove lefthand spark plug wires from plugs, ignition coil and brackets.
20. Remove mounting bolts and nuts, then the throttle body and gasket.
21. Remove mounting bolt and EVAP canister purge solenoid valve.
22. Remove mounting bolt, then the MAP sensor bracket and sensor.
23. Remove ignition coil bracket to intake manifold mounting bolts.
24. Remove intake manifold cover ball stud nut.
25. Remove upper intake manifold to lower intake manifold mounting bolts.
26. Remove upper intake manifold and gasket. Discard gasket.
27. Reverse procedure to install, noting the following:
    a. Install new gasket.
    b. Apply suitable threadlock to intake manifold and throttle body mounting bolt/stud threads.

Lower

1. Remove upper intake manifold as outlined under "Upper."
2. Remove valve covers as outlined under "Valve Cover, Replace."
3. Disconnect fuel feed line from rail.
4. Disconnect fuel injector connector.
5. Remove fuel injector harness connect bracket.
6. Disconnect Engine Coolant Temperature (ECT) and Camshaft Position (CMP) sensors electrical connectors.
7. Remove mounting bolts and fuel rail.

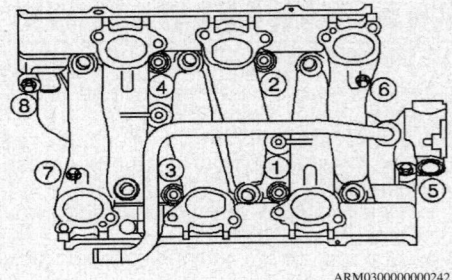

ARM0300000000242

Fig. 2 Lower intake manifold bolt tightening sequence

8. Remove mounting bolts and lower intake manifold.
9. Loosen mounting bolts, then remove rocker arms. **Ensure valve train components are kept in order for correct installation.**
10. Remove push rods.
11. Remove lower intake manifold gaskets and seals.
12. Reverse procedure to install, noting the following:
    a. Clean gasket and seal surface with suitable de-greaser.
    b. Remove loose RTV sealer.
    c. **Do not apply RTV sealer under lower intake manifold gaskets.**
    d. Coat push rod ends with suitable pre-lube.
    e. Intake valve push rods are 5.75 inches and exhausts are 6.0 inches long.
    f. Coat rocker arm friction surfaces with suitable pre-lube.
    g. Install new gaskets and seals.
    h. Apply small .31–.39 inch drop of suitable RTV sealant to four corners of intake manifold block joints.
    i. Install new intake manifold bolts using suitable sealer on threads.
    j. Refer to sequence, **Fig. 2,** and **torque** lower intake manifold mounting bolts 1–4 to 12 ft. lbs. and bolts 5–8 to 18 ft. lbs.

EXHAUST MANIFOLD
REPLACE
Lefthand

1. Remove engine mount strut as outlined under "Engine Mount Strut, Replace."
2. Remove engine harness clip from strut bracket.
3. Raise and support vehicle.
4. Remove air conditioning compressor mounting bolts and nut, then position compressor aside.
5. Remove lefthand engine mount strut bracket to engine lower bolts.
6. Lower vehicle.
7. Remove upper mounting bolt and lefthand engine mount strut bracket.
8. Remove exhaust manifold and crossover pipe heat shields.
9. Remove exhaust crossover pipe to lefthand exhaust manifold retaining nuts.

10. Remove exhaust manifold mounting bolts and manifold. Discard gasket.
11. Reverse procedure to install.

Righthand

1. Remove alternator as outlined under "Alternator, Replace" in "Electrical" section.
2. Remove Connector Position Assurance (CPA) retainer HO2S electrical connector, then disconnect Heated Oxygen Sensor (HO2S) electrical connector and remove clip from ignition coil bracket.
3. Remove HO2S using oxygen sensor wrench tool No. J39194-B, or equivalent.
4. Remove exhaust manifold heat shield.
5. Remove spark plug wires and spark plugs.
6. Remove EGR pipe and EGR valve mounting bolts, then the EGR pipe.
7. Remove crossover pipe heat shield.
8. Remove exhaust crossover pipe to righthand exhaust manifold retaining nuts.
9. Remove exhaust manifold upper mounting bolts.
10. Remove upper catalytic converter to exhaust manifold attaching nut.
11. Raise and support vehicle.
12. Disconnect HO2S electrical connectors, then remove sensors.
13. Remove catalytic converter to muffler mounting nuts and insulators.
14. Remove catalytic converter lower mounting nut and position muffler aside.
15. Remove catalytic converter and gasket.
16. Remove lower mounting bolts and lefthand exhaust manifold. Discard gasket.
17. Reverse procedure to install.

CYLINDER HEAD
REPLACE

1. Raise and support vehicle, then drain cooling system and engine oil.
2. Lower vehicle.
3. Remove lower intake manifold as outlined under "Intake Manifold, Replace."
4. Remove exhaust manifold as outlined under "Exhaust Manifold, Replace."
5. Remove dip stick, then the mounting bolt and oil level tube.
6. Remove spark plugs.
7. Remove and discard cylinder head bolts.
8. Remove cylinder head. Discard gasket.
9. Reverse procedure to install, noting the following:
    a. Install new cylinder head gasket.
    b. Refer to sequence, **Fig. 3,** and tighten cylinder head bolts in two steps: First step, **torque** cylinder head bolts to 44 ft. lbs.; second step, tighten head bolts an additional 140.°

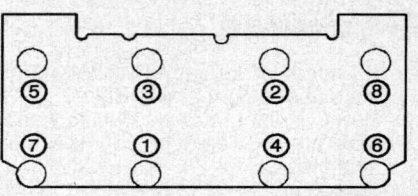

ARM0300000000243

Fig. 3 Cylinder head bolt tightening sequence

VALVE COVER
REPLACE
Lefthand

1. Partially drain cooling system into suitable container.
2. Remove engine oil fill cap and intake manifold cover.
3. Remove dipstick, then the mounting bolts and oil level tube.
4. Disconnect lefthand spark plug wires.
5. Remove spark plug wire harness clip from heater inlet and outlet front pipe bracket. Position spark plug harness aside.
6. Remove PCV foul air tube.
7. Remove engine mount strut as outlined under "Engine Mount Strut, Replace."
8. Remove engine harness clip from strut bracket.
9. Raise and support vehicle.
10. Remove air conditioning compressor mounting bolts and nut, then position compressor aside.
11. Remove lefthand engine mount strut bracket to engine lower bolts.
12. Lower vehicle.
13. Remove upper mounting bolt and lefthand engine mount strut bracket.
14. Disconnect clamps and clip nuts at throttle body, then remove heater inlet and outer hoses/pipes from engine inlet and outlet pipes.
15. Remove throttle body stud clips and position hose/pipe aside.
16. Remove front heater outlet hose from outlet heater pipe.
17. Remove bolt and stud, then the heater inlet and outlet pipe.
18. Loosen mounting bolts and remove lefthand valve cover. **Ensure gasket stays attached to cylinder head.**
19. Cut RTV in channel where intake, cylinder head and valve rocker arm cover meet using suitable tool.
20. Remove valve cover gasket.
21. Reverse procedure to install, noting the following:
    a. Remove old gasket material and sealer from cylinder head and valve cover mating surfaces.
    b. Clean mating surfaces with suitable cleaner.
    c. Install new gasket and ensure it is properly seated in cover groove.
    d. Apply suitable sealant to surfaces where cylinder head and intake manifold meet.
    e. Apply sealer part No. 12378521, or equivalent, into groove on valve cover.

Righthand

1. Remove serpentine drive belt as outlined under "Serpentine Belt."
2. Remove alternator as outlined under "Alternator, Replace" in "Electrical" section.
3. Disconnect PCV fresh air tube from air cleaner outlet duct and valve cover.
4. Disconnect righthand spark plug wires from plugs, ignition coil and bracket. Remove spark plug harness.
5. Disconnect Manifold Absolute Pressure (MAP) sensor and ignition coil electrical connectors.
6. Remove engine harness and HO2S electrical connector clips from ignition coil bracket.
7. Remove ignition coil mounting nuts, then the coil and bracket.
8. Loosen lefthand valve cover mounting bolts and valve cover. **Ensure gasket stays attached to cylinder head.**
9. Cut RTV in channel where intake, cylinder head and valve rocker arm cover meet using suitable tool.
10. Remove valve cover gasket.
11. Reverse procedure to install, noting the following:
    a. Remove old gasket material and sealer from cylinder head and valve cover mating surfaces.
    b. Clean mating surfaces with suitable cleaner.
    c. Install new gasket, ensure it is seated in cover groove.
    d. Apply sealer part No. 12378521, or equivalent, into groove on valve cover.
    e. Apply suitable sealant to surfaces where cylinder head and intake manifold meet.

CAMSHAFT LOBE LIFT SPECIFICATIONS

Intake .... .2727
Exhaust .... .2727

VALVE ADJUSTMENT

These engines are equipped with hydraulic valve lash adjusters. No adjustment is required.

ROCKER ARMS
REPLACE

1. Remove valve cover as outlined under "Valve Cover, Replace."
2. Loosen mounting bolts, then remove rocker arms. **Ensure valve train components are kept in order for correct installation.**
3. Reverse procedure to install. Coat rocker arm friction surfaces with suitable pre-lube.

PUSH RODS

1. Remove valve cover as outlined under "Valve Cover, Replace."

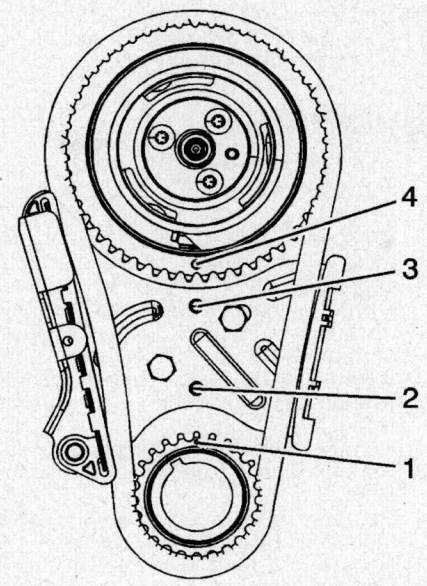

ARM0500000000172

Fig. 4   Timing mark alignment

2. Loosen mounting bolts, then remove rocker arms. **Ensure valve train components are kept in order for correct installation.**
3. Remove push rods.
4. Reverse procedure to install, noting the following:
    a. Coat push rod ends with suitable pre-lube.
    b. Intake valve push rods are 5.75 inches and exhausts are 6.0 inches long.
    c. Coat rocker arm friction surfaces with suitable pre-lube.

HYDRAULIC LIFTERS
REPLACE

1. Remove lower intake manifold as outlined under "Intake Manifold, Replace."
2. Remove valve cover as outlined under "Valve Cover, Replace."
3. Loosen mounting bolts, then remove rocker arms. **Ensure valve train components are keep in order to ensure install in original positions.**
4. Remove push rods.
5. Loosen mounting bolts and remove valve lifter guides. **Valve lifter guide bolts are not removable.**
6. Remove lifters from guides.
7. Reverse procedure to install, noting the following:
    a. Coast valve lifts with suitable pre-lube.
    b. Apply suitable threadlock to valve lifter guide bolt threads.
    c. Coat push rod ends with suitable pre-lube.
    d. Intake valve push rods are 5.75 inches and exhausts are 6.0 inches long.
    e. Coat rocker arm friction surfaces with suitable pre-lube.

CRANKSHAFT DAMPER
REPLACE

1. Remove drive belt as outlined under "Serpentine Drive Belt."
2. Raise and support vehicle, then remove righthand front tire and wheel assembly.
3. Remove ABS wire retainers and engine splash shield.
4. Support frame using suitable jack stands.
5. Loosen lefthand frame mounting bolts, then remove righthand frame mounting bolts, lower righthand side of frame.
6. Remove torque converter covers and hold flywheel in place using flywheel holder tool No. J37096, or equivalent.
7. Remove crankshaft balancer bolt and washer.
8. Remove crankshaft balancer with harmonic balancer remover tool No. J41816 and puller end protector tool No. EN46359, or equivalents. **Do not use power assisted tool to remove balancer.**
9. Reverse procedure to install, noting the following:
    a. Apply suitable sealer to crankshaft balancer keyway.
    b. Install balancer using balancer and crank sprocket installer tool No. J29113, or equivalent.

FRONT COVER
REPLACE

1. Drain cooling system.
2. Remove drive belt as outlined under "Serpentine Drive Belt."
3. Remove belt tensioner mounting bolt and tensioner.
4. Remove oil pan as outlined under "Oil Pan, Replace."
5. Remove torque converter covers.
6. Hold flywheel in place using flywheel holder tool No. J37096, or equivalent, then remove crankshaft balancer bolt and washer.
7. Remove crankshaft balancer with harmonic balancer remover tool No. J41816 and puller end protector tool No. EN46359, or equivalents. **Do not use power assisted tool to remove balancer.**
8. Disconnect crankshaft position actuator connector.
9. Remove crankshaft position actuator mounting bolt.
10. Remove thermostat housing as outlined under "Thermostat, Replace."
11. Remove water pump pulley mounting bolts and pulley.
12. Remove water pump mounting bolts, then the water pump and gasket.
13. Remove front cover mounting bolts, then the front cover and gasket.
14. Reverse procedure to install.

TIMING CHAIN
REPLACE
Removal

1. Remove engine front cover as outlined under "Front Cover, Replace."
2. Align timing marks, **Fig. 4.**
3. Remove camshaft gear mounting bolt.
4. Remove timing chain, camshaft and gear.
5. Remove mounting bolts and chain tensioner.

Installation

1. Apply suitable pre-lube to crankshaft gear thrust surface.
2. Install tensioner and tighten mounting bolts.
3. Collapse tensioner using tensioner clamping tool No. EN-47719, or equivalent, install suitable pin into tensioner retaining hole.
4. Align timing marks, **Fig. 4.**
5. Hold camshaft gear with chain hanging down, then install chain to crankshaft gear.
6. Align camshaft gear timing marks and dowel with camshaft gear dowel hole.
7. Draw camshaft gear onto camshaft by tightening mounting bolt.
8. Coat crankshaft and camshaft gears with suitable, clean engine oil.
9. Install engine front cover as outlined under "Front Cover, Replace."

CAMSHAFT
REPLACE

1. Remove engine assembly as outlined under "Engine, Replace."
2. Remove mounting bolt and Camshaft Position (CMP) sensor .
3. Remove mounting screws and camshaft thrust plate.
4. Install sprocket bolt into camshaft hand tight, then carefully rotate and remove camshaft.
5. Reverse procedure to install, noting the following:
   a. Coat camshaft journals with suitable clean engine oil.
   b. Coast camshaft lobes with suitable pre-lube.

PISTON & ROD ASSEMBLY

Pistons are specific to lefthand and righthand cylinder bank applications. Ensure alignment marks face front of engine, **Figs. 5 and 6.**

MAIN & ROD BEARINGS

Connecting Rod

Tighten connecting rod bearing cap bolts in two steps. First step **torque** bolts to 18 ft. lbs.; second step, tighten bolts an additional 110.°

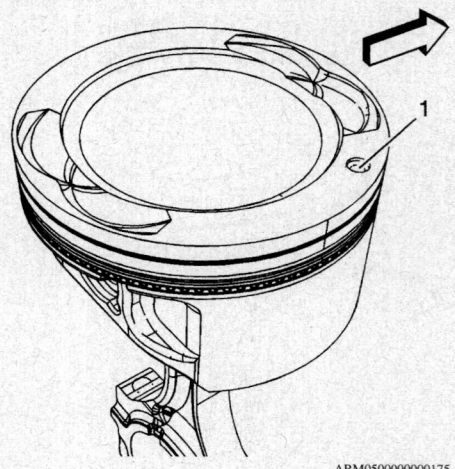

Fig. 5 Lefthand cylinder bank piston alignment

ARM0500000000175

Main Bearing Caps

1. Dip crankshaft bearing cap bolts in suitable clean engine oil.
2. **Upper and lower inserts may be different. Do not obstruct any oil passages.**
3. Place crankshaft bearing inserts into crankshaft bearing cap and into engine block.
4. **Ensure bearing inserts project an equal distance on both sides.**
5. **Ensure insert tangs are engaged.**
6. Lubricate crankshaft main bearing surface with suitable clean engine oil.
7. Install crankshaft.
8. Install crankshaft main bearing caps. **Tap caps into cylinder block cavity using suitable brass, lead, or a leather mallet. Do not use mounting bolts to pull crankshaft bearing caps into seats.**
9. Apply small amount of suitable sealer to rear of crankshaft main bearing cap No. 4 sealing surface.
10. Tighten crankshaft main bearing cap bolts in four steps: First step, **torque** bolts to 37 ft. lbs.; second step, loosen bolts one full turn; third step, **torque** bolts to 37 ft. lbs.; fourth step, tighten bolts an addition 77.°
11. Thrust crankshaft forward or rearward, then measure clearance between crankshaft bearing No. 3 and crankshaft bearing surface.
12. If bearing clearance is not 002–.008 inch, inspect thrust surfaces for nicks, gouges or raised metal. Minor imperfections may be removed with fine stone.

CRANKSHAFT SEAL
REPLACE

1. Remove crankshaft balancer as outlined under "Crankshaft Damper, Replace."
2. Remove crankshaft key.
3. Pry out crankshaft front oil seal using suitable tool. **Do not damage engine front cover or crankshaft.**

4. Lubricate new oil seal with suitable clean engine oil.
5. Install seal using cover aligner and seal installer tool No. J35468, or equivalent.

CRANKSHAFT REAR OIL SEAL
REPLACE

1. Remove transaxle as outlined in **MO-TOR's "MOTOR's "Domestic Transmission, In-Vehicle Service" manual or "Transmission Service DVD."**
2. Hold flywheel using flywheel holder tool No. J37096, or equivalent, then loosen flywheel mounting bolts.
3. Remove five of six mounting bolts. Leaving one bolt at top of crankshaft.
4. Secure flywheel and remove final mounting bolt. Remove flywheel.
5. Remove seal using suitable flatbladed tool through dust lip at an angle. **Do not nick crankshaft sealing surface.**
6. Reverse procedure to install. Install new seal using rear main seal installer tool No. J34686, or equivalent.

OIL PAN
REPLACE

1. Remove engine mount strut as outlined under "Engine Mount Strut, Replace."
2. Support engine using engine support fixture tool No. J28467-B, or equivalent.
3. Remove mounting bolts, then the exhaust manifold and crossover pipe heat shields.
4. Remove exhaust crossover pipe to righthand exhaust manifold mounting nuts.
5. Remove exhaust manifold upper mounting bolts.
6. Remove upper catalytic converter to exhaust manifold mounting nut.
7. Raise and support vehicle.
8. Disconnect electrical connectors and remove HO2Ss.
9. Remove catalytic converter to muffler mounting nuts and insulators.
10. Remove catalytic converter lower mounting nut and position muffler aside.
11. Remove catalytic converter and gasket.
12. Drain engine oil, then remove oil filter.
13. Remove flywheel inspection cover.
14. Remove starter electrical connectors.
15. Remove mounting bolts and starter.
16. Remove air conditioning mounting bolts and nut, then position compressor aside.
17. Disconnect oil level sensor electrical connector.
18. Remove engine harness clips from oil pan and transaxle brace.
19. Remove mounting bolts and front transaxle brace.
20. Remove engine mounting lower nuts and loosen transaxle mount lower nuts.

21. Remove rear transaxle brace to engine/oil pan bolts.
22. Lower vehicle and raise engine.
23. Hold steering column using steering column anti-rotation pin tool No. J42640, or equivalent.
24. Remove steering shaft intermediate lower pinch bolt, then separate shaft from steering gear.
25. Remove mounting bolts, engine mount and bracket.
26. Remove righthand lower ball joint from steering knuckle using ball joint/stud separator tool No. J41820, or equivalent.
27. Remove righthand outer tie rod from steering knuckle using ball joint/stud separator tool No. J41820, or equivalent.
28. Remove mounting bolt and nut, then the righthand stabilizer link.
29. Support frame using suitable jack stands.
30. Loosen lefthand frame bolts and remove righthand frame bolts, then lower righthand side of frame.
31. Remove mounting bolts, oil pan and gasket.
32. Reverse procedure to install, noting the following:
    a. Clean oil pan flanges and rail, front cover, rear main cap and bolt holes.
    b. Apply suitable sealer to both side of crankshaft rear main bearing cap.
    c. Press suitable sealer into crankshaft rear main bearing gap using suitable putty knife.
    d. Install new gasket.

OIL PUMP
REPLACE
1. Remove oil pan as outlined under "Oil Pan, Replace."
2. Remove mounting bolt, oil pump and drive shaft extension.
3. Reverse procedure to install.

OIL PUMP SERVICE
Disassemble
1. Remove pump driveshaft and retainer.
2. Remove oil pump screen. **Do not remove oil pump screen from pipe.**
3. Remove mounting bolts and pump cover.
4. Remove pump gears.
5. Place match marks on gear teeth for assembly reference.

Inspection
1. Inspect pump housing and cover for casting imperfections, cracks, scoring or damaged threads. **Replace, do not repair pump housing.**
2. Inspect gears for scoring and excessive wear.
3. Inspect idler gear shaft. If loose or damaged, replace pump.
4. Inspect drive gear shaft for looseness or scoring.

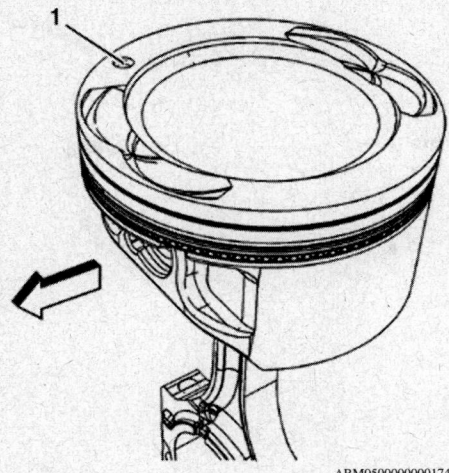

1

ARM0500000000174

Fig. 6 Righthand cylinder bank piston alignment

5. Inspect pressure regulator valve for scoring or sticking. Remove burrs with fine oil stone.
6. Inspect pressure regulator valve spring for loss of tension or bending.
7. Inspect suction pipe and screen for looseness. If pipe is loose, bent or has been removed, replace pump body cover and suction pipe.
8. Inspect for broken wire mesh or screen.

Assemble
1. Lubricate internal components with suitable clean engine oil.
2. Install pump gears and cover.
3. Install cover and gasket.
4. Install pressure regulator valve and spring. Ensure cotter pin is properly installed.
5. Apply suitable sealer and tape new suction pipe in place using suitable plastic hammer and oil suction pipe installer tool No. J22144, or equivalent.

SERPENTINE DRIVE BELT
Replacement
1. Remove intake manifold cover.
2. Remove mounting bolts and lefthand inner fender brace.
3. Remove air cleaner outlet duct from throttle body.
4. Disconnect PCV tube from air inlet duct.
5. Disconnect Mass Air Flow (MAF) sensor electrical connector.
6. Remove upper from lower air cleaner housing.
7. Remove Powertrain Control Module (PCM) and harness from lower air cleaner housing. **Do not disconnect connectors.**
8. Remove Transmission Control Module (TCM) and harness from lower air cleaner housing. **Do not disconnect connectors.**

9. Remove air cleaner outlet duct from air cleaner.
10. Disconnect two rubber grommets on inner rail, then remove lower air cleaner housing.
11. Release spring tension by turning belt tensioner clockwise.
12. Remove belt from pulleys.
13. Reverse procedure to install.

Routing
Refer to **Fig. 7** for serpentine drive belt routing.

COOLING SYSTEM BLEED
These engines do not require a specified bleed procedure. After filling cooling system, run engine to operating temperature with radiator/pressure cap off. Air will then be automatically bled through cap opening.

THERMOSTAT
REPLACE
1. Drain cooling system.
2. Remove lefthand inner fender brace mounting bolts and the fender brace.
3. Remove air cleaner outlet duct from throttle body.
4. Disconnect PCV tube from air inlet duct.
5. Disconnect Mass Air Flow (MAF) sensor electrical connector.
6. Remove upper from lower air cleaner housing.
7. Remove Powertrain Control Module (PCM) and harness from lower air cleaner housing. **Do not disconnect connectors.**
8. Remove Transmission Control Module (TCM) and harness from lower air cleaner housing. **Do not disconnect connectors.**
9. Remove air cleaner outlet duct from air cleaner.
10. Disconnect clamp and remove radiator outlet hose from thermostat housing.
11. Remove mounting bolts and thermostat housing.
12. Reverse procedure to install. Install new gasket.

WATER PUMP
REPLACE
1. Drain coolant.
2. Loosen water pump pulley mounting bolts.
3. Remove serpentine belt as outlined under "Serpentine Belt."
4. Remove mounting bolts and water pump pulley.
5. Remove mounting bolts, water pump and gasket.
6. Reverse procedure to install. Install new gasket

RADIATOR
REPLACE

1. Remove intake manifold cover.
2. Remove lefthand inner fender brace.
3. Remove air cleaner outlet duct from throttle body.
4. Disconnect PCV tube from air inlet duct.
5. Disconnect Mass Air Flow (MAF) sensor electrical connector.
6. Remove upper air cleaner housing.
7. Remove Powertrain Control Module (PCM) and harness from lower air cleaner housing. **Do not disconnect connectors.**
8. Remove Transmission Control Module (TCM) and harness from lower air cleaner housing. **Do not disconnect connectors.**
9. Loosen clamp and remove air cleaner outlet duct from air cleaner.
10. Disconnect two rubber grommets on inner rail and remove lower air cleaner housing.
11. Drain cooling system.
12. Remove engine mount strut as outlined under "Engine Strut Mount, Replace."
13. Remove upper radiator hose from radiator.
14. Remove PCM harness clip from fan shroud.
15. Remove condenser tubes bracket mounting bolt from fan shroud.
16. Remove mounting bolt, then the condenser hold down bracket from radiator and condenser.
17. Remove cooling fan shroud mounting bolts.
18. Remove radiator upper support brackets and bolts from fan shroud.

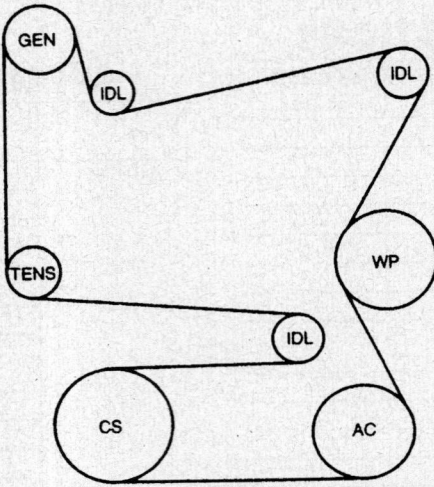

Fig. 7 Serpentine drive belt routing

19. Disconnect electrical connectors and remove cooling fan motors' harness from shroud clips.
20. Remove cooling fan shroud.
21. Remove lower radiator hose from radiator.
22. Disconnect transaxle oil cooler pipes from radiator.
23. Tilt radiator top rearward and list condenser from radiator mounting tabs. Position condenser aside.
24. Reverse procedure to install.

FUEL PUMP
REPLACE

1. Relieve fuel system pressure as outlined under "Precautions."
2. Drain fuel tank.
3. Raise and support vehicle.
4. Loosen clamp and remove fuel tank fill hose from tank.
5. Disconnect EVAP vent pipe quick connect fitting from fill pipe EVAP vent pipe quick connect fitting.
6. Disconnect EVAP vent solenoid hose on tank from vent valve solenoid hose.
7. Disconnect fuel feed and EVAP lines from fuel tank lines.
8. Support exhaust system.
9. Remove retainers and fuel tank shield.
10. Support fuel tank with suitable adjustable jack.
11. Remove strap bolts mounting bolts and lower fuel tank. **Do not bend fuel tank straps.**
12. Disconnect fuel sender jumper harness electrical connector.
13. Remove fuel tank.
14. Disconnect EVAP and fuel feed lines from sender. Position lines aside.
15. Turn fuel sender lock ring counterclockwise using fuel sender lock ring wrench No. J45722, or equivalent, and suitable long breaker-bar.
16. Remove lock ring and fuel sender. Discard O-ring seal.
17. Reverse procedure to install, noting the following
    a. Replace lock ring if warpage is more than .016 inch.
    b. Install new O-ring seal.
    c. Ensure tab is properly aligned.

TIGHTENING SPECIFICATIONS

Year	Component	Torque/Ft. Lbs.
2006–08	Air Cleaner Outlet Duct Clamp	27①
	Air Conditioning Compressor	37
	Alternator Terminal	18
	Belt Tensioner	37
	Camshaft End Plate	89①
	Camshaft Gear	12
	Catalytic Converter, Lower	26
	Catalytic Converter To Exhaust Manifold	26
	Catalytic Converter To Muffler	44
	Radiator Upper Support Bracket	53①
	Condenser Tubes Bracket	89①
	Connecting Rod	⑤
	Cooling Fan Shroud	89①
	Crankshaft Damper	118
	Cylinder Head	④
	Exhaust Crossover Pipe	15
	Exhaust Crossover Pipe Heat Shield	89①
	Exhaust Manifold	15
	Exhaust Manifold Heat Shield	89①
	Engine Mount	②
	Engine Mount Strut	37
	EVAP Canister Purge Solenoid Valve	12
	Flywheel	52
	Frame, Front	107
	Frame, Rail	119
	Front Cover	18
	Fuel Injector Harness Connector Bracket	71①
	Fuel Injector Rail	89①
	Fuel Tank Hose Clamp	22①
	Fuel Tank Strap	35
	Ground	18
	Heated Oxygen Sensor	31
	Heater Hose Clamps	89①
	Heater Inlet And Outlet Pipe, Bolt	18
	Heater Inlet And Outlet Pipe, Stud	89①
	Hood	19
	Ignition Coil	18
	Inner Fender Brace	89①
	Intake Manifold, Upper	18
	Intake Manifold Cover Ball Stud	44①
	Main Bearings	⑤
	MAP Sensor	18
	Oil Level Tube	18
	Oil Pan	③
	Oil Pump	30
	Oil Pump Cove	89①

TIGHTENING SPECIFICATIONS—Continued

Year	Component	Torque/Ft. Lbs.
2006–08	Oil Pressure Sensor Heat Shield	89①
	Power Steering Pump	18
	Radiator Upper Support Bracket	53①
	Rocker Arm	25
	Solenoid Battery Terminal, Inside	13
	Solenoid Battery Terminal, Outside	89①
	Solenoid S Terminal	27
	Starter Motor	32
	Thermostat Housing	18
	Throttle Body	89①
	Timing Chain Tensioner	15
	Torque Converter	46
	Torque Converter Cover	89①
	Transaxle Brace	46
	Transaxle-To-Engine	55
	Valve Cover	89①
	Water Pump	89①
	Water Pump Pulley	18
	Valve Lifter Guide	89①
	Wiring Harness Clip	18

① — Inch lbs.

② — Refer to "Engine Mount, Replace" for tightening specifications and sequence.

③ — Bottom bolts to 18 ft. lbs.,; side bolts to 37 ft. lbs.

④ — Refer to "Cylinder Head, Replace" for tightening specifications and sequence.

⑤ — Refer to "Main & Rod Bearings" for tightening specifications and sequence.

3.6L Engine

NOTE: Refer To "3.6L Engine" Located In The "CTS" Chapter For Procedures Not Covered In This Section.

NOTE: On Air Bag Equipped Models, Refer To "Air Bag System Precautions" Located In The Front Of This Manual For System Disarming & Arming Procedures.

NOTE: Refer To "Computer Relearn Procedures" Located In The Front Of This Manual When Battery Power To The Computer Has Been Interrupted.

INDEX

	Page No.
Compression Pressure	6-43
Engine Rebuilding Specifications	29-1
Engine, Replace	6-43
Engine Mount, Replace	6-43
Engine Mount Strut, Replace	6-43
Fuel Pump, Replace	6-44
Precautions	6-43
Air Bag Systems	6-43
Battery Ground Cable	6-43
Fuel System Pressure Relief	6-43
Radiator, Replace	6-44
Tightening Specifications	6-45

PRECAUTIONS

Air Bag Systems

Refer to "Air Bag System Precautions" in the front of this manual for system disarming and arming procedures.

Battery Ground Cable

Prior to service, disconnect battery ground cable and isolate as required.

Fuel System Pressure Relief

To reduce the risk of fire and personal injury, relieve the fuel system pressure before servicing fuel system components.
1. Turn ignition Off.
2. Remove fuel pump fuse and fuel pump relay.
3. Loosen fuel filler cap to relieve fuel tank vapor pressure.
4. Attempt to start engine and allow engine to run until it stops.
5. Loosen fuel tank filler cap to relieve tank pressure.
6. Connect fuel pressure gauge tool No. J34730-1, or equivalent, to fuel pressure valve. Wrap a shop towel around fitting while connecting gauge to avoid spillage.
7. Install bleed hose into suitable container and open valve to bleed system pressure.

COMPRESSION PRESSURE

1. Ensure battery is at full charge.
2. Start and run engine until it reaches normal operating temperature.

3. Turn engine Off, then remove Powertrain Control Module (PCM) and ignition fuse from instrument panel fuse block.
4. Remove spark plugs from all cylinders.
5. Remove air duct from throttle body and block throttle plate in open position.
6. Thread compression gauge into spark plug hole.
7. Crank engine through at least four compression strokes.
8. Record readings on gauge at each stroke.
9. Repeat test on each cylinder.
10. Lowest reading should not be less than 70 percent of the highest reading. No cylinder reading should be less than 140 psi.

ENGINE MOUNT
REPLACE

1. Remove throttle body air inlet duct.
2. Remove mounting bolt and nut from engine mount strut at engine mount strut bracket on engine.
3. Remove mounting bolt and nut from engine mount strut at engine mount strut bracket on upper radiator support.
4. Remove engine mount strut.
5. Raise and support vehicle.
6. Remove three-way catalytic converter pipe from engine righthand exhaust manifold.
7. Remove righthand front tire and wheel, then the engine splash shield.
8. Remove engine mount lower nuts.
9. Support engine using suitable adjustable jack stand with suitable wood block.
10. Remove engine mount bracket to oil pan bolts.
11. Remove engine mount bracket to engine bolts.
12. Remove engine mount and bracket.
13. Reverse procedure to install.

ENGINE MOUNT STRUT
REPLACE

1. Remove engine mount strut mounting bolt and nut from engine strut mounting bracket on engine.
2. Remove mounting bolt and nut from engine mount strut at engine mount strut bracket on upper radiator support.
3. Remove engine mount strut.
4. Reverse procedure to install.

ENGINE
REPLACE

1. Remove fuel injector sight shield and throttle body air inlet duct.
2. Remove engine mount strut as outlined under "Engine Mount Strut, Replace."
3. Relieve fuel system pressure as outlined under "Precautions."
4. Disconnect fuel lines and position aside.
5. Disconnect cooling fan electrical connectors.
6. Remove fan shroud cooling fan wiring harnesses and secure aside.
7. Drain cooling system.
8. Remove throttle and cruise control cables with mounting brackets from throttle body.
9. Disconnect surge tank outlet hose from surge tank. Position hose aside.
10. Disconnect surge tank inlet (vent) hose from water outlet housing and radiator. Position hose aside.
11. Disconnect heater hoses from heater core.
12. Disconnect purge line from purge solenoid.
13. Disconnect fuel pipe from fuel rail.
14. Plug fuel pipe and cap fuel rail to prevent fuel loss and/or contamination.

15. Recover air conditioning refrigerant as outlined in "Air Conditioning" chapter.
16. Remove wiper module.
17. Disconnect air conditioning suction hose from evaporator and remove suction hose bracket from shock tower. Position hose aside. **Do not disconnect suction hose from air conditioning compressor.**
18. Disconnect air conditioning pressure switch electrical connector and remove liquid line from compressor. **Do not disconnect liquid line from condenser.**
19. Remove radiator support brackets.
20. Disconnect brake booster check valve and vacuum hose from brake booster. Position hose aside.
21. Disconnect brake fluid level switch electrical connector from master cylinder.
22. Disconnect Mass Air Flow (MAF) sensor electrical connector.
23. Disconnect instrument panel electrical connector from engine located at rear of lefthand bank cylinder head. Position harness aside.
24. Disconnect engine module wiring harness connectors from underhood electrical center.
25. Disconnect wiring harness from Transmission Control Module (TCM).
26. Remove ground bolt and wire from longitudinal rail.
27. Disconnect engine harness electrical connector at longitudinal rail. Position ground wire, engine harness and TCM harness aside.
28. Remove master cylinder mounting nuts, then position master cylinder aside. **Do not disconnect brake pipes from master cylinder.**
29. Raise and support vehicle, then remove muffler.
30. Remove propeller shaft and air deflector.
31. Remove washer bottle bracket. **Do not remove water bottle.**
32. Disconnect radiator side air baffles.
33. Disconnect lefthand front brake pipe retainer with brake pipe from longitudinal rail.
34. Remove righthand front brake pipe from brake pipe bundle retainer.
35. Disconnect two center rear brake pipes from Brake Modulator Valve (BPVM). Cap or plug brake pipes and BPMV.
36. Remove front tire and wheel assemblies.
37. Remove intermediate steering shaft.
38. Remove lower engine mount nuts.
39. Disconnect shift linkage from transaxle.
40. Disconnect low oil level sensor electrical connector. Secure connector and harness to engine mount bracket.
41. Remove headlamp leveling sensors.
42. Secure shock modules to lower control arms with suitable strap.
43. Remove lefthand and righthand shock module upper mounting bolts.
44. Raise vehicle and support engine using suitable lift table.
45. Remove transaxle brace to underbody and front frame mounting bolts.
46. Lower table and remove engine, transaxle, front frame and suspension.
47. Separate front frame and suspension from engine.
48. Reverse procedure to install.

RADIATOR
REPLACE

1. Remove air cleaner
2. Drain cooling system into suitable container.
3. Remove lefthand and righthand engine mount struts.
4. Remove inlet hose from radiator and PCM harness clip from fan shroud.
5. Remove transaxle oil cooler lines from retainer clip at bottom of cooling fan shroud.
6. Remove fan shroud clip from condenser tubes.
7. Remove fan shroud to condenser hold down bracket bolt.
8. Remove air deflectors from top of radiator.
9. Remove cooling fan shroud bolts and coolant reservoir hose from radiator overflow neck.
10. Remove radiator upper support brackets and fan shroud mounting bolts.
11. Disconnect engine cooling fan motors electrical connectors.
12. Remove cooling fan motors electrical harness from fan shroud clips.
13. Remove cooling fan shroud.
14. Remove outlet hose from radiator.
15. Disconnect transaxle oil cooler pipes from radiator.
16. Tilt top of radiator rearward.
17. Remove condenser hold down bracket from radiator.
18. Lift condenser from mounting tabs on radiator.
19. Position condenser aside and remove radiator.
20. Reverse procedure to install.

FUEL PUMP
REPLACE

1. Relieve fuel system pressure as outlined under "Precautions."
2. Raise and support vehicle.
3. Remove fuel tank filler hose from fuel tank.
4. Disconnect fuel feed and fuel return pipe from tank.
5. Disconnect EVAP pipes located at fuel filter area.
6. Support exhaust system, then remove rubber exhaust pipe hangers and allow exhaust system to drop slightly.
7. Separate two halves of EVAP fresh air hose at splice.
8. Remove push pins and fuel tank shield.
9. Support fuel tank with suitable adjustable jack.
10. Remove fuel tank strap bolts.
11. Lower fuel tank and disconnect fuel sender electrical connectors.
12. Remove fuel tank.
13. Record pipe and retaining clips routing for installation alignment.
14. Disconnect and remove fuel feed, fuel return and EVAP pipe assemblies from fuel tank.
15. Remove EVAP canister from fuel tank and insulator pads from fuel tank. Record insulator pads locations for installation alignment.
16. Disconnect fuel sender module electrical connectors.
17. Disconnect fuel pipes from fuel sender.
18. Remove fuel sender lock ring with lock ring removal tool No. J45722, or equivalent, and a suitable long breaker-bar.
19. Remove fuel sender.
20. Remove and discard fuel sender seal.
21. Remove fuel level sensor from fuel sender module.
22. Reverse procedure to install.

TIGHTENING SPECIFICATIONS

Year	Component	Torque Ft. Lbs.
2005–08	Air Conditioning Compressor Bracket, Front Bolt	37
	Air Conditioning Compressor Bracket, Rear Bolt	17
	Air Conditioning Compressor Hose	80①
	Alternator	37
	Catalytic Converter To Exhaust Manifold	10
	Coolant Outlet	89①
	Drive Belt Idler Pulley	37
	Drive Belt Tensioner	37
	ECM	89①
	Engine Mount Bracket To Cylinder Block (M8 Bolt)	28
	Engine Mount Bracket To Cylinder Block (M11 Bolt)	45
	Engine Mount To Bracket	59
	Heater Inlet/Outlet Pipe	89①
	Power Steering Pump Bracket To Engine	37
	Power Steering Pump Reservoir	18

① — Inch lbs.

3.8L Engine

NOTE: Refer To The "3.8L Engine" Section In the "Bonneville, LeSabre & Park Avenue" Chapter For Procedures Not Found In This Section.

NOTE: On Air Bag Equipped Models, Refer To "Air Bag System Precautions" Located In The Front Of This Manual For System Disarming & Arming Procedures.

NOTE: Refer To "Computer Relearn Procedures" Located In The Front Of This Manual When Battery Power To The Computer Has Been Interrupted.

NOTE: Prior To Performing Any Service Operations Listed In This Section, Consult The "Technical Service Bulletins" Section For Related Information.

INDEX

	Page No.
Compression Pressure	6-46
Engine Rebuilding Specifications	29-1
Engine, Replace	6-46
Engine Mount, Replace	6-46
Engine Block	6-46
Strut	6-46
Transaxle	6-46

	Page No.
Fuel Filter, Replace	6-47
Fuel Pump, Replace	6-46
Precautions	6-46
Air Bag Systems	6-46
Battery Ground Cable	6-46
Fuel System Pressure Relief	6-46
Technical Service Bulletins	6-47
Engine Compartment Rattling,	

	Page No.
Ticking or Scraping Noise	6-47
2005 Grand Prix, Impala, LaCrosse & Monte Carlo	6-47
Engine/Accessory Drive Noisy, Lack of Power, Supercharger Not Functioning Properly	6-47
2004 Pontiac Grand Prix	6-47
Tightening Specifications	6-47

PRECAUTIONS

Air Bag Systems

Refer to "Air Bag System Precautions" in the front of this manual for system disarming and arming procedures.

Battery Ground Cable

Prior to service, disconnect battery ground cable and isolate as required.

Fuel System Pressure Relief

To reduce the risk of fire and personal injury, it is required to relieve the fuel system pressure before servicing fuel system components.
1. Loosen fuel tank filler cap to relieve tank pressure.
2. Connect fuel pressure gauge tool No. J34730-1, or equivalent, to fuel pressure valve. Wrap a shop towel around fitting while connecting gauge to avoid spillage.
3. Install bleed hose into suitable container, then open valve to bleed system pressure.

COMPRESSION PRESSURE

When inspecting compression, lowest cylinder must be within 70 percent of the highest cylinder with a minimum pressure of 100 psi. Perform compression test with engine at normal operating temperature, spark plugs removed and throttle wide open.

ENGINE MOUNT
REPLACE

Engine Block

1. Remove lefthand and righthand mounting bolts and nuts from bracket on engine.
2. Remove lefthand and righthand mounting bolts and nuts from bracket on upper radiator support.
3. Remove lefthand and righthand engine mount struts.
4. Install engine support fixture tool No. J28467-A, engine support fixture adapter tool No. J28467-90 and engine support adapter leg tool No. J36462, or equivalents.
5. Raise and support vehicle, then remove righthand front tire and wheel assembly.
6. Remove righthand engine splash shield.
7. Remove engine mount lower mounting nuts from frame.
8. Raise engine, then remove conditioning compressor mounting bolts. Position compressor aside.
9. Remove front engine mount bracket

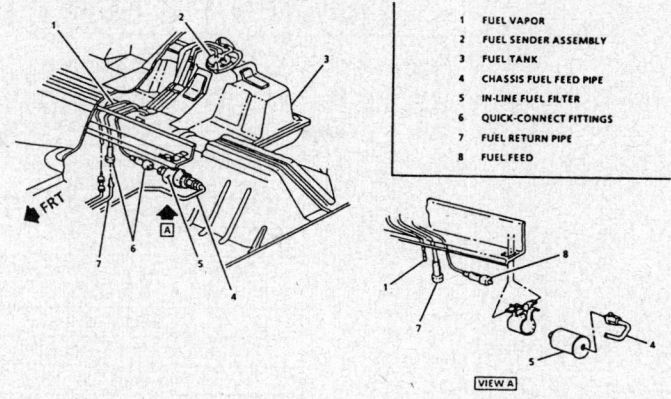

1	FUEL VAPOR
2	FUEL SENDER ASSEMBLY
3	FUEL TANK
4	CHASSIS FUEL FEED PIPE
5	IN-LINE FUEL FILTER
6	QUICK-CONNECT FITTINGS
7	FUEL RETURN PIPE
8	FUEL FEED

GC1029102743000X

Fig. 1 Fuel filter replacement

bolts, then the engine mount with bracket from engine.
10. Remove rear engine mount upper mounting nuts, then the rear engine mount and bracket from engine.
11. Reverse procedure to install.

Transaxle

1. Remove lefthand and righthand mounting bolts and nuts from bracket on engine.
2. Remove lefthand and righthand mounting bolts and nuts from bracket on upper radiator support.
3. Remove lefthand and righthand engine mount struts.
4. Raise and support vehicle.
5. Remove lefthand tire and wheel assembly, then the lower splash shield.
6. Support transaxle using suitable jack.
7. Remove mounting nuts and mount.
8. Reverse procedure to install.

Strut

1. Remove mounting bolt and nut from bracket on engine.
2. Remove mounting bolt and nut from bracket on upper radiator support.
3. Remove engine mount strut.
4. Reverse procedure to install.

ENGINE
REPLACE

1. Mark hood for installation reference, then remove hood.
2. Remove air cleaner.
3. Relieve fuel system pressure as outlined under "Precautions."
4. Remove fuel lines from rail and mounting bracket.
5. Remove coolant bottle and inner fender electrical cover.
6. Remove fuel injector sight cover.
7. Remove throttle cables, bracket and vacuum line from throttle body.
8. Remove heat shield and exhaust crossover pipe.
9. Remove engine torque strut from engine.
10. Remove engine cooling fan.

11. Remove vacuum line from transaxle module.
12. Remove serpentine drive belt.
13. Remove power steering pump and alternator.
14. Disconnect electrical connectors.
15. Remove upper and lower radiator, then the heater hoses.
16. Remove transaxle to engine bolts and ground wire harness with bolt.
17. Raise and support vehicle.
18. Remove righthand tire and wheel assembly, then the inner splash shield.
19. Remove flywheel cover and mark torque converter to flywheel for installation alignment.
20. Remove flywheel mounting bolts.
21. Disconnect wire harness clamps from frame near radiator.
22. Remove and position air conditioning compressor aside.
23. Remove starter motor.
24. Remove transaxle to engine bolt through wheelwell using suitable extension.
25. Disconnect engine mount to frame nuts.
26. Remove oil filter.
27. Disconnect front exhaust pipe from manifold.
28. Disconnect oil cooler piper from hose connections.
29. Lower vehicle.
30. Support and remove engine using suitable lifting device,
31. Reverse procedure to install.

FUEL PUMP
REPLACE

1. Relieve fuel system pressure as outlined under "Precautions."
2. Remove cover, jack, spare tire and trunk liner.
3. Remove seven mounting nuts and fuel pump access panel.
4. Disconnect fuel tank pressure sensor electrical connector.
5. Disconnect quick connect fittings and remove fuel pump retaining snap ring.
6. Remove modular fuel pump.
7. Reverse procedure to install.

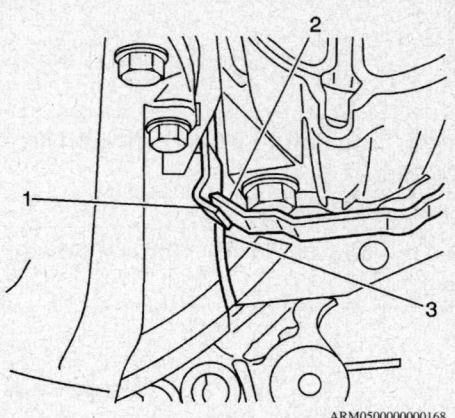

ARM0500000000168

Fig. 2   Cover tab positioning

FUEL FILTER
REPLACE

1. Relieve fuel system pressure as outlined under "Precautions."
2. Raise and support vehicle.
3. Remove mounting screw and filter bracket, **Fig. 1.**
4. Grasp filter and fuel line fitting. Twist quick-connect fitting ¼ turn in each direction to loosen any dirt within fitting.
5. Remove feed pipe nut from fuel filter and drain fuel into suitable container.
6. Remove fuel filter.
7. Reverse procedure to install.

TECHNICAL SERVICE BULLETINS

Engine Compartment Rattling, Ticking or Scraping Noise
2005 GRAND PRIX, IMPALA, LACROSSE & MONTE CARLO

On some of these models there may be a rattling, ticking or scraping noise coming from the engine compartment.

This condition may be caused by the transaxle rear (flywheel/flexplate) dust cover contacting the flexplate.

To correct this condition, proceed as follows:
1. Install front dust cover.
2. Position rear cover so front cover tab is behind rear cover, **Fig. 2.**
3. Ensure alignment features position with tab, **Fig. 3.**

Engine/Accessory Drive Noisy, Lack of Power, Supercharger Not Functioning Properly
2004 PONTIAC GRAND PRIX

On some of these models the engine or

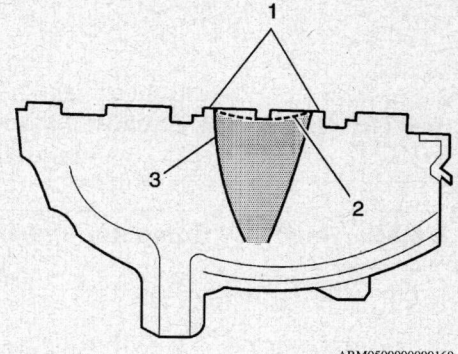

ARM0500000000169

Fig. 3   Tab alignment

accessory drive may be noisy. In addition, there may be a lack of power or the supercharger not functioning correctly.

This condition may be cause by incorrect belt installed, idler pulley bearing damaged or an out of round idler strut bracket.

To correct this condition, proceed as follows:
1. Inspect idler pulley for bearing damage, out of round condition, backwards installation or missing ferule.
2. If bearing is damaged, replace pulley, pulley bolt and ferule.
3. Idler pulley is out of round, install new engine mount strut bracket.
4. Ensure supercharger accessory belt is correct.

TIGHTENING SPECIFICATIONS

Year	Component	Torque/Ft. Lbs.
2004–08	Air Conditioning Compressor	22
	Air Conditioning Compressor Bracket	37
	Battery Cable	11
	Engine Mount	32
	Engine Mount Bracket	75
	Engine Mount Strut	35
	Exhaust Manifold Pipe Stud	22
	Fan Shroud	53①
	Frame, Front	133
	Oil Level Sensor	89①
	Power Steering Pump	25
	Torque Converter	47
	Torque Converter Cover	89①
	Transaxle Brace To Transaxle	32
	Transaxle Brace To Engine	46
	Transaxle To Engine	55
	Water Pump Pulley	116①

① — Inch lbs.

5.3L Engine

NOTE: On Air Bag Equipped Models, Refer To "Air Bag System Precautions" Located In The Front Of This Manual For System Disarming & Arming Procedures.

NOTE: Refer To "Computer Relearn Procedures" Located In The Front Of This Manual When Battery Power To The Computer Has Been Interrupted.

INDEX

	Page No.
Camshaft, Replace	6-53
Compression Pressure	6-48
Cooling System Bleed	6-54
Crankshaft Damper, Replace	6-52
Crankshaft Rear Oil Seal, Replace	6-53
Installation	6-53
Removal	6-53
Crankshaft Seal, Replace	6-53
Cylinder Head, Replace	6-50
Lefthand	6-50
Righthand	6-51
Engine Rebuilding Specifications	29-1
Engine, Replace	6-49
Engine Mount, Replace	6-48
Lefthand	6-48
Righthand	6-48
Strut	6-48

	Page No.
Exhaust Manifold, Replace	6-50
Lefthand	6-50
Righthand	6-50
Front Cover, Replace	6-52
Fuel Pump, Replace	6-55
Hydraulic Lifters, Replace	6-52
Intake Manifold, Replace	6-49
Main & Rod Bearings	6-53
Connecting Rod	6-53
Main	6-53
Oil Pan, Replace	6-53
Oil Pump, Replace	6-54
Oil Pump Service	6-54
Assemble	6-54
Disassemble	6-54
Inspection	6-54
Piston & Rod Assembly	6-53
Precautions	6-48
Air Bag Systems	6-48

	Page No.
Battery Ground Cable	6-48
Fuel System Pressure Relief	6-48
Push Rods	6-51
Installation	6-52
Removal	6-51
Radiator, Replace	6-54
Rocker Arms	6-51
Serpentine Drive Belt	6-54
Replacement	6-54
Routing	6-54
Thermostat, Replace	6-54
Tightening Specifications	6-56
Timing Chain, Replace	6-53
Valve Adjustment	6-51
Valve Arrangement	6-51
Front To Rear	6-51
Valve Cover, Replace	6-51
Water Pump, Replace	6-54

PRECAUTIONS

Air Bag Systems

Refer to "Air Bag System Precautions" in the front of this manual for system disarming and arming procedures.

Battery Ground Cable

Prior to service disconnect battery ground cable and isolate as required.

Fuel System Pressure Relief

Failure to relieve system pressure prior to disconnecting fuel system components may cause fire or personal injury.

1. Remove fuel rail pressure fitting cap and connect suitable fuel pressure gauge to fuel pressure valve.
2. Place fuel gauge bleed hose into suitable container.
3. Relieve fuel tank vapor pressure by loosening fuel fill cap.
4. Relieve fuel pressure by opening fuel gauge bleed valve.

COMPRESSION PRESSURE

1. Disable ignition and fuel systems.
2. Remove all spark plugs.
3. Turn ignition switch to ON position and hold accelerator pedal in wide open position.
4. Firmly install suitable compression gauge to spark plug hole and crank engine through at least four compression strokes in testing cylinder.
5. Record readings at each stroke.
6. Disconnect and repeat compression test for each cylinder.
7. Record compression readings from all of cylinders.
8. Lowest reading should not be less than 70% of highest reading.
9. No cylinder reading should be less than 100 psi.

ENGINE MOUNT

REPLACE

Strut

1. Remove front and rear engine mount strut mounting bolts and nuts.
2. Remove engine mount strut.
3. Reverse procedure to install.

Lefthand

1. Remove front and rear engine mount strut mounting bolts and nuts.
2. Remove engine mount strut.
3. Remove lefthand exhaust manifold as outlined under "Exhaust Manifold, Replace."
4. Remove upper engine mount nuts.
5. Support and raise engine using universal engine support fixture tool No. J28467-B, fixture adapters tool No. J28467-501 and support adapter tool No. J42451-1, or equivalents.
6. Remove mounting bolts and engine mount bracket.
7. Raise and support vehicle.
8. Remove lower mounting nut and engine mount.
9. Reverse procedure to install.

Righthand

1. Remove front and rear engine mount strut mounting bolts and nuts.
2. Remove engine mount strut.
3. Remove righthand exhaust manifold as outlined under "Exhaust Manifold, Replace."
4. Remove upper engine mount nuts.
5. Support and raise engine using universal engine support fixture tool No. J28467-B, fixture adapters tool No. J28467-501 and support adapter tool No. J42451-1, or equivalents.

6. Remove mounting bolts and engine mount bracket.
7. Raise and support vehicle.
8. Remove lower mounting nut and engine mount.
9. Reverse procedure to install.

ENGINE
REPLACE

1. Disconnect clips and remove engine cover.
2. Recover air conditioning refrigerant as outlined in "Air Conditioning" chapter.
3. Raise and support vehicle, then remove front tire and wheel assemblies.
4. Drain cooling system and engine oil into suitable containers.
5. Lower vehicle.
6. Disconnect clamps, then remove inlet and hoses from radiator.
7. Remove air conditioning receiver/dehydrator tube and condenser hose nuts, then the compressor hose.
8. Remove brake booster vacuum hose from booster and intake manifold.
9. Disconnect engine harness electrical connectors from instrument panel harness electrical connectors.
10. Disconnect brake fluid level switch electrical connector and remove fluid from master cylinder.
11. Disconnect brake pipe fittings from master cylinder and Antilock Brake (ABS) module.
12. Remove mounting nuts and secure master cylinder aside.
13. Relieve fuel system pressure as outlined under "Precautions."
14. Disconnect fuel feed line from rail.
15. Disconnect Evaporative Emission (EVAP) line from purge solenoid.
16. Remove mounting bolts and righthand front fender diagonal brace.
17. Remove underhood electrical center cover, then loosen four integral bolts and position fuse block aside.
18. Loosen mounting bolt and remove engine harness connector from bracket.
19. Disconnect Camshaft Position (CMP) sensor lead.
20. Disconnect engine harness electrical connectors from ABS module and Electronic Brake Control Module (EBCM).
21. Disconnect Positive Crankcase Ventilation (PCV) tube from air inlet duct.
22. Loosen clamp and remove air inlet duct from throttle body.
23. Loosen clamp and remove air inlet duct from Mass Air Flow/Intake Air Temperature (MAF/IAT) sensor.
24. Disconnect clamps, remove cover and air filter element.
25. Disconnect Transmission Control Module (TCM) and Engine Control Module (ECM) electrical connectors.
26. Disconnect air conditioning pressure sensor connector.
27. Disconnect engine harness electrical connector from Crankshaft Position (CKP) sensor harness and power steering gear harness.
28. Remove power steering gear harness bracket clip.
29. Remove clip and disconnect shift

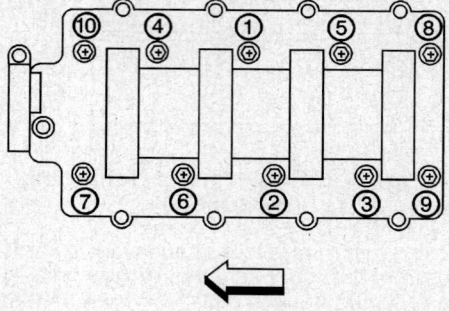

Fig. 1 Intake manifold tightening sequence

ARM0500000000173

cable from transaxle selector lever stud. Remove cable from bracket.
30. Remove mounting nut and bolt, then the Vehicle Speed Sensor (VSS) shield.
31. Disconnect engine harness electrical connector from VSS.
32. Position all engine wiring harness branches on top of engine.
33. Position boot aside and remove intermediate shaft to steering gear bolt.
34. Separate intermediate shaft from steering gear.
35. Disconnect front wheels' speed sensors' connectors.
36. Disconnect ABS wire harness from lower control arm.
37. Disconnect clamps, then remove inlet and outlet hoses from heater inlet/outlet pipe.
38. Raise and support vehicle.
39. Disconnect links from stabilizer shaft.
40. Disconnect steering knuckles' ball joints using suitable ball joint/stud separator tool.
41. Disconnect power steering pressure hose from steering gear.
42. Disconnect steering knuckles' outer tie rod ends using suitable ball joint/stud separator tool.
43. Loosen clamp and remove power steering hose from inlet pipe.
44. Remove front wheel drive shaft nut. Prevent rotor from turning by insert suitable drift or flat-bladed tool into caliper and rotor.
45. Separate front wheel drive axle from front wheel drive shaft bearing using hub spindle remover tool No. J42129, or equivalent. Partially install nut to protect threads.
46. Remove lefthand and righthand front wheel drive axles from transaxle using axle shaft remover tool No. J42129, axle shaft remover extension tool No. J29794 and slide hammer tool No. J2619-01, or equivalent.
47. Support drive shafts aside.
48. Remove transaxle oil cooler line bracket bolt/stud and oil cooler lines from transaxle.
49. Remove positive battery cable nut and cable terminal from starter.
50. Remove battery cable ground nut and terminal from stud.
51. Remove battery cable retainers from engine frame.
52. Disconnect Heated Oxygen Sensor

(HO2S) electrical connector.
53. Remove catalytic converter pipe stud nuts and mounting nuts.
54. Support exhaust system using suitable adjustable jack.
55. Remove catalytic converter hangers and disconnect exhaust system. Discard catalytic converter gaskets.
56. Disconnect O2 sensor harness pigtail.
57. Remove bolt/stud and transaxle converter cover.
58. Remove flywheel bolts.
59. Remove retainers and front air deflectors.
60. Support engine, frame and front suspension using universal engine support table tool No. J39580, or equivalent. Preload weight.
61. Support rear of vehicle with suitable jack stand.
62. Remove radiator to frame brackets.
63. Remove engine frame front bolts.
64. Remove engine and frame. **Ensure hoses, wires and pipes clear vehicle.**
65. Support engine using suitable lift.
66. Remove front and rear engine mount and frame nuts.
67. Remove transaxle to engine bolts and stud, then separate engine from transaxle.
68. Remove engine from frame.
69. Reverse procedure to install, noting the following:
   a. Install new catalytic converter gaskets.
   b. Install new front wheel drive shaft nut.

INTAKE MANIFOLD
REPLACE

1. Remove engine cover.
2. Disconnect PCV tube from air inlet duct.
3. Loosen clamp and remove air inlet duct from throttle body.
4. Loosen clamp and remove air inlet duct from Mass Air Flow/Intake Air Temperature (MAF/IAT) sensor.
5. Disconnect throttle actuator control motor electrical connector.
6. Disconnect EVAP canister purge tube from throttle body.
7. Remove mounting bolts and throttle body. Discard gasket.
8. Relieve fuel system pressure as outlined under "Precautions."
9. Disconnect EVAP purge solenoid and Manifold Absolute Pressure (MAP) sensor electrical connectors.
10. Disconnect Electronic Throttle Control (ETC) and oil pressure sensor electrical connectors.
11. Disconnect valve lifter oil manifold and alternator electrical connectors.
12. Remove Connector Position Assurance (CPA) retainer.
13. Disconnect main ignition coil harness electrical connector.
14. Mark connectors and injectors for installation alignment.
15. Disconnect fuel injector electrical connectors.
16. Remove CPA retainer.

17. Disconnect main ignition coil harness electrical connector.
18. Mark connectors and ignition connectors for installation alignment.
19. Disconnect ignition electrical connectors.
20. Remove fuel rail retainers and position engine wiring harness aside.
21. Disconnect fuel feed and EVAP lines.
22. Remove intake manifold bolt and ground strap, then the fuel rail mounting bolts.
23. Remove fuel rail with injectors. **Do not separate fuel injectors from rail.**
24. Remove brake booster vacuum hose from intake manifold and booster check valve.
25. Remove PCV clean and foul air tubes from air intake duct and valve cover.
26. Remove EVAP purge solenoid tube from solenoid. Position tube aside.
27. Disconnect oil pressure sensor electrical connector.
28. Remove MAP sensor, then the EVAP purge solenoid valve and bracket.
29. Remove mounting bolts and intake manifold. Discard gasket.
30. Reverse procedure to install, noting the following:
    a. Install new intake manifold gaskets.
    b. Apply suitable threadlock to intake manifold bolts' threads.
    c. Refer to sequence, **Fig. 1** and tighten intake manifold bolts in two steps: First step, **torque** bolts to 44 inch lbs.; second step, **torque** bolts to 89 inch lbs.
    d. Install new fuel injector O-ring seals lubricate with suitable clean engine oil.
    e. Apply .2 inch band of suitable to fuel rail mounting bolt threads.
    f. Install new throttle body gasket.

EXHAUST MANIFOLD
REPLACE
Lefthand

1. Remove engine sight shield.
2. Remove mounting bolts and exhaust crossover pipe heat shield.
3. Remove exhaust crossover pipe mounting nuts from lefthand exhaust manifold.
4. Disconnect wires and remove lefthand spark plugs.
5. Remove dipstick, then the mounting bolt and oil dipstick tube.
6. Remove mounting bolts and exhaust manifold heat shield.
7. Remove heater hose mounting bolts.
8. Remove mounting bolts and exhaust manifold. Discard gasket.
9. Reverse procedure to install, noting the following
    a. Apply .2 inch wide band of suitable threadlock to exhaust manifold bolts' threads. **Do not apply threadlock to first three thread.**
    b. Install new exhaust manifold gasket.
    c. Tighten manifold mounting bolts in two steps as follows: Begin with center two bolts, then alternate

Fig. 2 Cylinder head tightening sequence

from side to side and work towards outside. First step, **torque** bolts to 11 ft. lbs.; second step, **torque** bolts to 15 ft. lbs.

Righthand

1. Raise and support vehicle.
2. Disconnect wires and remove righthand spark plugs.
3. Remove exhaust crossover pipe nuts from righthand exhaust manifold
4. Disconnect Heated Oxygen Sensor (HO2S) electrical connector.
5. Remove catalytic converter pipe stud nuts and mounting nuts.
6. Support exhaust system using suitable adjustable jack.
7. Remove catalytic converter hangers and disconnect exhaust system. Discard catalytic converter gaskets.
8. Support catalytic convertor and exhaust system aside.
9. Lower vehicle.
10. Remove Connector Position Assurance (CPA) retainer.
11. Disconnect ignition coil main electrical connector and spark plug wire from ignition coils.
12. Remove mounting bolts and ignition coils.
13. Disconnect connectors and remove O2 sensors.
14. Remove mounting bolts and exhaust manifold heat shield.
15. Remove exhaust manifold, bolts and gasket. Discard gasket.
16. Reverse procedure to install, noting the following:
    a. Apply .2 inch wide band of suitable threadlock to exhaust manifold bolts' threads. **Do not apply threadlock to first three thread.**
    b. Install new exhaust manifold gasket.
    c. Tighten manifold mounting bolts in two steps as follows: Begin with center two bolts, then alternate from side to side and work towards outside. First step, **torque** bolts to 11 ft. lbs.; second step, **torque** bolts to 15 ft. lbs.
    d. Apply suitable threadlock to ignition coil bolts' threads.

CYLINDER HEAD
REPLACE
Lefthand

1. Remove intake manifold as outlined under "Intake Manifold, Replace."
2. Pull up on front and rear, then remove engine cover.

3. Relieve belt tension by turning tensioner clockwise using suitable wrench.
4. Remove drive belt.
5. Disconnect alternator electrical connector.
6. Position output BAT terminal boot aside, then remove terminal nut and positive battery lead.
7. Remove mounting bolts and alternator.
8. Drain cooling system into suitable container.
9. Disconnect clamp and coolant fill neck hose.
10. Remove mounting bolts and coolant air bleed pipe with hose and seals.
11. Remove lefthand exhaust manifold as outlined under "Exhaust Manifold, Replace."
12. Remove engine sight shield.
13. Remove Connector Position Assurance (CPA) retainer.
14. Disconnect ignition coil electrical connector and position engine harness aside.
15. Remove spark plug wires from ignition coils, then the mounting bolts, ignition coils and bracket.
16. **On lefthand valve cover,** remove Positive Crankcase Ventilation (PCV) clean air tube from valve cover.
17. **On righthand valve cover,** remove Positive Crankcase Ventilation (PCV) foul air tube from valve cover.
18. **On all valve covers,** remove mounting bolts and valve cover. Discard gasket.
19. Remove mounting bolts and rocker arms.
20. Remove rocker arm pivot support.
21. Remove pushrods.
22. Relieve belt tension by rotate tensioner clockwise.
23. Remove drive belt and release tensioner tension.
24. Remove power steering pump pulley using pulley remover tool No. J25034-C, or equivalent.
25. Remove three coolant manifold to cylinder head mounting bolts.
26. Remove front and rear engine mount strut mounting bolts and nuts.
27. Remove engine mount strut, then the mounting bolts and brackets.
28. Remove mounting bolts and cylinder head. Discard cylinder head bolts and gaskets.
29. Remove cylinder head bolts and discard M11 bolts.
30. Remove cylinder head and gasket. Discard gasket.
31. Reverse procedure to install, noting the following:
    a. Install new gasket onto locating pins.
    b. Refer to sequence, **Fig. 2,** and tighten M11 cylinder head bolts in five steps: First step, **torque** bolts to 22 ft. lbs.; second step, tighten bolts an additional 90°; third step, tighten bolts an additional 70°; fourth step, tighten bolts 1–8 an additional 90°; fifth step, tighten bolts 9 and 10 an additional 50.°
    c. **Torque** M8 cylinder head bolts to

22 ft. lbs., beginning with center bolts and working outward.

Righthand

1. Remove intake manifold as outlined under "Intake Manifold, Replace."
2. Remove alternator and mounting bracket as outlined under "Alternator, Replace" in "Electrical" section.
3. Drain cooling system into suitable container.
4. Disconnect clamp and coolant fill neck hose.
5. Remove mounting bolts and coolant air bleed pipe with hose and seals.
6. Pull up on front and rear, then remove engine cover.
7. Relieve belt tension by turning tensioner clockwise using suitable wrench.
8. Remove drive belt.
9. Disconnect alternator electrical connector.
10. Position output BAT terminal boot aside, then remove terminal nut and positive battery lead.
11. Remove mounting bolts and alternator.
12. Relieve belt tension by rotate tensioner clockwise.
13. Remove drive belt and release tensioner tension.
14. Remove mounting bolt and idle pulley.
15. Raise and support vehicle.
16. Remove lower bolt and turn tensioner to access alternator bracket mounting bolt.
17. Lower vehicle, then remove mounting bolt and alternator bracket.
18. Remove righthand exhaust manifold as outlined under "Exhaust Manifold, Replace."
19. Remove engine sight shield.
20. Remove Connector Position Assurance (CPA) retainer.
21. Disconnect ignition coil electrical connector and position engine harness aside.
22. Remove spark plug wires from ignition coils, then the mounting bolts, ignition coils and bracket.
23. **On lefthand valve cover,** remove Positive Crankcase Ventilation (PCV) clean air tube from valve cover.
24. **On righthand valve cover,** remove Positive Crankcase Ventilation (PCV) foul air tube from valve cover.
25. **On all valve covers,** remove mounting bolts and valve cover. Discard gasket.
26. Remove mounting bolts and rocker arms.
27. Remove rocker arm pivot support.
28. Remove pushrods.
29. Relieve belt tension by rotate tensioner clockwise.
30. Remove drive belt and release tensioner tension.
31. Remove power steering pump pulley using pulley remover tool No. J25034-C, or equivalent.
32. Remove three coolant manifold to cylinder head mounting bolts.
33. Remove front and rear engine mount strut mounting bolts and nuts.
34. Remove engine mount strut, then the

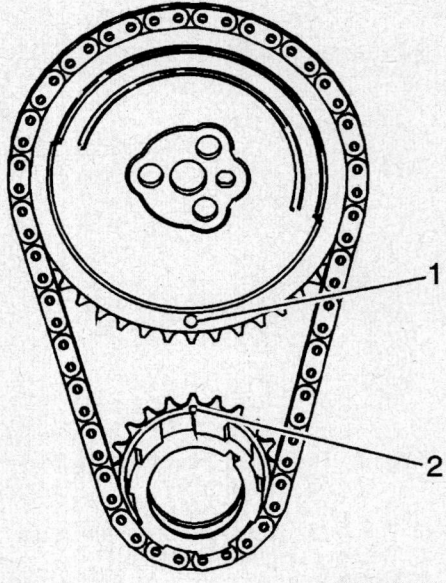

Fig. 3 Crankshaft & camshaft gear alignment

mounting bolts and brackets.
35. Remove mounting bolts and cylinder head. Discard cylinder head bolts and gaskets.
36. Remove cylinder head bolts and discard M11 bolts.
37. Remove cylinder head and gasket. Discard gasket.
38. Reverse procedure to install, noting the following:
   a. Install new gasket onto locating pins.
   b. Refer to sequence, **Fig. 2,** and tighten M11cylinder head bolts in five steps: First step, **torque** bolts to 22 ft. lbs.; second step, tighten bolts an additional 90°; third step, tighten bolts an additional 70°; fourth step, tighten bolts 1–8 an additional 90°; fifth step, tighten bolts 9 and 10 an additional 50.°
   c. **Torque** M8 bolts to 22 ft. lbs., beginning with center bolts and working outward.

VALVE COVER
REPLACE

1. Remove engine sight shield.
2. Remove Connector Position Assurance (CPA) retainer.
3. Disconnect ignition coil electrical connector and position engine harness aside.
4. Remove spark plug wires from ignition coils, then the mounting bolts, ignition coils and bracket.
5. **On lefthand valve cover,** remove PCV clean air tube from valve cover.
6. **On righthand valve cover,** remove PCV foul air tube from valve cover.
7. **On all valve covers,** remove mounting bolts and valve cover. Discard gasket.
8. Reverse procedure to install.

VALVE ARRANGEMENT
Front To Rear
Left Side ....I-E-I-E-I-E-I-E
Right Side ....E-I-E-I-E-I-E-I

VALVE ADJUSTMENT

Valve lash is net build and no valve adjustment is required on these models.

ROCKER ARMS

1. Remove engine sight shield.
2. Remove Connector Position Assurance (CPA) retainer.
3. Disconnect ignition coil electrical connector and position engine harness aside.
4. Remove spark plug wires from ignition coils, then the mounting bolts, ignition coils and bracket.
5. **On lefthand valve cover,** remove PCV clean air tube from valve cover.
6. **On righthand valve cover,** remove PCV foul air tube from valve cover.
7. **On all valve covers,** remove mounting bolts and valve cover. Discard gasket.
8. Mark rocker arms for installation in original positions.
9. Remove mounting bolt and rocker arm.
10. Remove rocker arm pivot support.
11. Reverse procedure to install, noting the following:
   a. Lubricate valve rocker arm and pushrod with suitable clean engine oil.
   b. **Do not tighten mounting bolt.** Turn crankshaft until piston No. 1 is at compressor stroke Top Dead Center (TDC). Cylinder number one rocker arms will be off lobe lift, and crankshaft sprocket key will be at 1:30 position.
   c. Tighten cylinder Nos. 1, 2, 7 and 8 exhaust valve rocker arm bolts.
   d. Tighten cylinder Nos. 1, 3, 4 and 5 intake valve rocker arm bolts.
   e. Turn crankshaft 360°.
   f. Tighten cylinder Nos. 3, 4, 5 and 6 exhaust valve rocker arm bolts.
   g. Tighten cylinder Nos. 2, 6, 7 and 8 intake valve rocker arm bolts.

PUSH RODS

Place the valve rocker arm, pushrod and pivot support, in suitable rack so they can be installed in the original location.

Removal

1. Remove engine sight shield.
2. Remove Connector Position Assurance (CPA) retainer.
3. Disconnect ignition coil electrical connector and position engine harness aside.
4. Remove spark plug wires from ignition coils, then the mounting bolts, ignition coils and bracket.
5. **On lefthand valve cover,** remove PCV clean air tube from valve cover.

6. **On righthand valve cover,** remove PCV foul air tube from valve cover.
7. **On all valve covers,** remove mounting bolts and valve cover. Discard gasket.
8. Mark rocker arms for installation in original positions.
9. Remove mounting bolt and rocker arm.
10. Remove rocker arm pivot support.
11. Remove pushrods.

Installation

1. Lubricate rocker arms and pushrods with suitable clean engine oil.
2. Lubricate flange of rocker arm bolts with suitable clean engine oil.
3. Install valve rocker arm pivot support.
4. Install pushrods. Ensure pushrods are seated properly in valve lifter sockets.
5. Install rocker arms and bolts. **Do not tighten bolts now.** Ensure pushrods seat properly to ends of rocker arms.
6. Turn crankshaft until piston No. 1 is at compressor stroke Top Dead Center (TDC). Cylinder number one rocker arms will be off lobe lift, and crankshaft sprocket key will be at 1:30 position.
7. Tighten cylinder Nos. 1, 2, 7 and 8 exhaust valve rocker arm bolts.
8. Tighten cylinder Nos. 1, 3, 4 and 5 intake valve rocker arm bolts.
9. Turn crankshaft 360°.
10. Tighten cylinder Nos. 3, 4, 5 and 6 exhaust valve rocker arm bolts.
11. Tighten cylinder Nos. 2, 6, 7 and 8 intake valve rocker arm bolts.

HYDRAULIC LIFTERS
REPLACE

1. Remove cylinder head and gasket as outlined under "Cylinder Head, Replace."
2. Remove mounting bolts and guide with valve lifters using valve lifter remover tool No. J3049-A, or equivalent.
3. Remove valve lifters from guide.
4. Reverse procedure to install, noting the following:
   a. Install lifters in original locations.
   b. Lubricate valve lifters and engine block valve lifter bores with suitable clean engine oil.
   c. Align lifter and lifter guide bore flat areas.

CRANKSHAFT DAMPER
REPLACE

1. Lock steering column by inserting steering column lock pin No. J42640, or equivalent, into the steering column access hole.
2. Remove drive belt as outlined under "Serpentine Drive Belt."
3. Disconnect PCV tube from air inlet duct.
4. Remove air inlet duct from throttle body.
5. Loosen clamp and remove air inlet duct from Mass Air Flow/Intake Air Temperature (MAF/IAT) sensor.

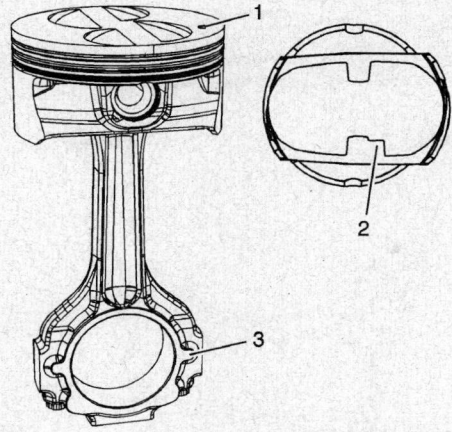

ARM050000000178

Fig. 4 Piston & connecting rod assembly

6. Remove cover and air filter element.
7. Remove engine mount strut.
8. Raise and support vehicle, then remove front tire and wheel assemblies.
9. Remove starter motor as outlined under "Starter, Replace" in "Electrical" section.
10. Remove front lefthand fender splash shield.
11. Remove transaxle bellhousing bolt that is located at approximately the 10 o'clock position when looking from rear of engine.
12. Disconnect cooler lines from transaxle.
13. Disconnect links from stabilizer shaft.
14. Remove intermediate shaft to steering gear bolt, then separate intermediate shaft from steering gear.
15. Remove front fascia lower retainers.
16. Remove retainers, braces and front lower air deflector.
17. Remove radiator to frame braces.
18. Support engine and frame using universal engine support table tool No. J39580, or equivalent.
19. Raise and support vehicle, then remove frame to body bolts.
20. Lock flywheel using flywheel holding tool No. EN47699, or equivalent.
21. Lower engine approximately four inches.
22. Remove crankshaft balancer bolt. **Do not discard bolt.**
23. Remove crankshaft balancer using crankshaft balancer remover tool No. J41816 and crankshaft end protector tool No. J41816-2, or equivalents.
24. Reverse procedure to install, noting the following:
   a. **Torque** used crankshaft balancer mounting bolt to 240 ft. lbs. Remove and discard used bolt.
   b. Ensure crankshaft nose is recessed .09–.18 inch.
   c. Tighten new crankshaft balancer mounting bolt in two steps: First step, **torque** to 37 ft. lbs.; second step, tighten bolt an additional 140.°

FRONT COVER
REPLACE

1. Remove engine cover.
2. Remove drive belt as outlined under "Serpentine Drive Belt.".
3. Remove alternator as outlined under "Alternator, Replace" in "Electrical" section.
4. Remove power steering pump pulley using pulley remover tool No. J25034-C, or equivalent.
5. Clamp power steering pump hose and remove fluid from reservoir.
6. Disconnect and plug power steering high pressure hose.
7. Remove mounting bolts and power steering pump.
8. Drain cooling system into suitable container.
9. Remove water pump mounting bolts and disconnect hose from coolant reservoir.
10. Remove pressure pipe clip mounting bolt on engine front.
11. Remove mounting bolts and water pump. Discard gasket.
12. Remove Camshaft Position (CMP) sensor.
13. Disconnect engine front wiring harness.
14. Disconnect clamp and coolant fill neck hose.
15. Remove mounting bolts and coolant air bleed pipe with hose and seals.
16. Remove three coolant pump manifold to cylinder head mounting bolts.
17. Disconnect clamps and coolant pump manifold heater hoses.
18. Disconnect clamps and coolant pump manifold radiator hoses.
19. Remove mounting bolts and coolant pump manifold. Discard gaskets.
20. Remove crankshaft balancer as outlined under "Crankshaft Damper, Replace."
21. Remove mounting bolt and position tensioner aside.
22. Remove mounting bolts and front cover. Discard gasket.
23. Reverse procedure to install, noting the following:
   a. Install new front cover gasket.
   b. Apply .2 inch bead of suitable sealant .8 inches long to oil pan to engine block junction.
   c. Tighten front cover mounting bolts. **Do not overtighten.**
   d. Align tapered legs of front and rear cover alignment tool No. J41476, or equivalent, with machined alignment surfaces on front cover.
   e. Install crankshaft balancer bolt. **Do not overtighten.**
   f. Tighten oil pan to front cover mounting bolts to specification.
   g. Tighten front cover mounting bolts to specification. Remove alignment tool.
   h. Install new water pump and manifold gaskets.

TIMING CHAIN
REPLACE

1. Remove oil pan as outlined under "Oil Pan, Replace."
2. Remove engine front cover as outlined under "Front Cover, Replace."
3. Remove mounting bolts and nuts, then the oil pump screen. Discard O-ring seal.
4. Remove mounting nuts and crankshaft oil deflector.
5. Remove mounting bolts and oil pump.
6. Turn crankshaft, then align crankshaft gear and camshaft gear timing marks, **Fig. 3.**
7. Remove mounting bolts, camshaft gear and timing chain.
8. Remove mounting bolts and timing chain dampener.
9. Reverse procedure to install.

CAMSHAFT
REPLACE

1. Remove engine as outlined under "Engine, Replace."
2. Remove crankshaft balancer as outlined under "Crankshaft Damper, Replace."
3. Remove oil level dipstick.
4. Remove exhaust manifolds as outlined under "Exhaust Manifold, Replace."
5. Drain cooling system into suitable container.
6. Remove battery and tray.
7. Remove drive belt as outlined under "Serpentine Drive Belt."
8. Remove mounting bolts and water pump. Discard gasket.
9. Remove mounting bolts and coolant air bleed pipe.
10. Remove three coolant pump manifold to cylinder head mounting bolts.
11. Disconnect clamps and coolant pump manifold heater radiator hoses.
12. Remove mounting bolts and coolant pump manifold. Discard gaskets.
13. Remove intake manifold as outlined under "Intake Manifold, Replace."
14. Remove mounting bolts and valve lifter oil manifold. **Do not lift manifold by electrical lead frame.**
15. Remove rocker arms as outlined under "Rocker Arms."
16. Remove pushrods as outlined under "Pushrod, Replace."
17. Remove mounting bolts and front cover.
18. Turn crankshaft, then align crankshaft gear and camshaft gears timing marks, **Fig. 3.**
19. Remove camshaft gear mounting bolts, then the camshaft gear and timing chain.
20. Remove mounting bolts and camshaft retainer.
21. Remove camshaft using three 125 x 100 mm (M8) bolts in front holes as a handle.
22. Reverse procedure to install, noting the following:
    a. Lubricate camshaft journals and bearings with suitable clean engine oil.

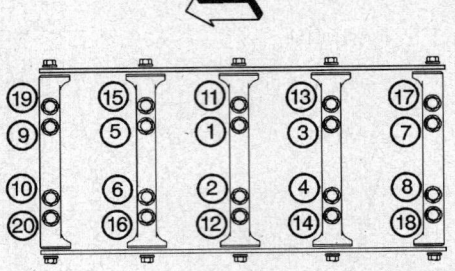

Fig. 5   Main bearing cap bolt tightening sequence

b. Install retainer plate with sealing gasket facing engine block.

PISTON & ROD ASSEMBLY

Assemble the piston and connecting rod with the lug on the bottom of the piston and tab on the side of connecting rod facing the same direction, **Fig. 4.** Install the piston and connecting rod assembly, the mark on the top of the piston and the tab on the side of the connecting rod should face the front of the engine.

MAIN & ROD BEARINGS
Connecting Rod

Tighten connecting rod bolts in two steps: First step, **torque** bolts to 15 ft. lbs.; second step, tighten bolts an additional 75.°

Main

1. Install crankshaft bearing to block and bearing caps.
2. Thrust bearings are installed into center journal.
3. Lubricate bearing surfaces and crankshaft journals with suitable clean engine oil.
4. Install crankshaft.
5. Install crankshaft bearing caps with bearings into block.
6. Install M10 bolts and studs.
7. Tap bearing caps into place using suitable plastic-faced hammer.
8. Install new M8 bearing cap side bolts.
9. Refer to sequence, **Fig. 5,** and tighten inner M10 bearing cap bolts 1–10 in two steps: First step, **torque** bolts to 15 ft. lbs.; second step, tap crankshaft rearward and then forward to align thrust bearings using suitable plastic faced hammer, then tighten bolts an additional 80.°
10. Refer to sequence, **Fig. 5,** and tighten outer M10 studs 11–20 in two steps: First step, **torque** studs to 15 ft. lbs.; second step, tighten studs an additional 51.°
11. **Torque** bearing cap M8 bolts to 18 ft. lbs.

CRANKSHAFT SEAL
REPLACE

1. Remove crankshaft balancer as outlined under "Crankshaft Damper, Replace."
2. Remove and discard crankshaft oil seal.
3. Install seal using crankshaft front oil seal installer tool No. J41478, or equivalent.

CRANKSHAFT REAR OIL SEAL
REPLACE

Removal

1. Raise and support vehicle.
2. Remove transaxle as outlined in **MOTOR's "Domestic Transmission, In-Vehicle Service" manual or "Transmission Service DVD.""**
3. Remove mounting bolts and flywheel.
4. Remove rear oil seal using suitable tool.

Installation

1. Lubricate outside diameter OD of oil seal with suitable clean engine oil. **Do not allow oil or any other lubricants to contact seal lip surface of rear oil seal.**
2. Lubricate rear cover oil seal bore with suitable clean engine oil.
3. Install crankshaft rear oil seal installer tool No. J41479, or equivalent, onto rear of crankshaft.
4. Tighten bolts until snug. Do not overtighten.
5. Install rear oil seal onto tapered cone and push seal to rear cover bore.
6. Thread tool threaded rod into tapered cone until tool contacts oil seal.
7. Align oil seal into tool, then rotate handle of the tool clockwise until seal enters rear cover and bottoms into cover bore.

OIL PAN
REPLACE

1. Support engine and frame using universal engine support table tool No. J39580, or equivalent.
2. Raise and support vehicle, then remove front tire and wheel assemblies.
3. Remove and discard two radiator lower air deflector plastic braces below front cradle mounting bolts.
4. Position cover aside, then loosen positive battery terminal nut and remove terminal.
5. Disconnect battery cable connector from instrument panel harness electrical connector.
6. Disconnect instrument panel harness electrical connector from battery current sensor.
7. Remove cover and positive battery cable junction block lead nut, then the Bussed Electrical Center (BEC) positive battery lead terminal.

8. Disconnect and remove BEC from strut tower.
9. Remove ground wire to top rail attaching bolt, position ground wire aside.
10. Remove battery cable harness clips from front rail and fan shroud.
11. Remove battery cable harness retainers from engine cradle.
12. Remove transaxle stud nut and engine ground cable, then the starter positive battery cable.
13. Remove battery cable.
14. Disconnect power steering return hose from frame. Secure hose aside.
15. Remove links and turn stabilizer shaft upward.
16. Disconnect straps and remove power steering gear heat shield.
17. Remove power steering gear mounting bolts, secure gear.
18. Remove engine to frame mounting nuts.
19. Disconnect front wheel speed sensor connectors, then the harness from frame and lower control arms.
20. Disconnect steering knuckles' ball joints using suitable ball joint separator tool.
21. Remove support brace mounting bolts, front frame mounting stud mounting nut and drivetrain reinforcement.
22. Lower vehicle until frame contacts fixture and remove radiator to front frame brackets.
23. Remove front and rear frame mounting bolts.
24. Raise vehicle and separate frame from body.
25. Drain engine oil into suitable container and remove oil filter.
26. Remove mounting bolt and stud, then the transaxle converter cover.
27. Disconnect oil level sensor electrical connector and remove engines harness retainer from oil pan.
28. Remove mounting bolts and oil pan.
29. Drill out rivets and remove gasket. Discard rivets and gasket.
30. Reverse procedure to install, noting the following:
    a. Ensure black and oil pan rears are flush. **Oil pan must not protrude beyond engine block and transaxle housing plane.**
    b. Install new gasket.
    c. Apply .2 inch bead of suitable sealant .8 inches long to engine block. Apply sealant directly onto tabs of front cover gasket that protrudes into oil pan surface.

OIL PUMP
REPLACE

1. Remove oil pan as outlined under "Oil Pan, Replace."
2. Remove engine front cover as outlined under "Front Cover, Replace."
3. Remove mounting bolts and nuts, then the oil pump screen. Discard O-ring seal.
4. Remove mounting nuts and crankshaft oil deflector.
5. Remove mounting bolts and oil pump.

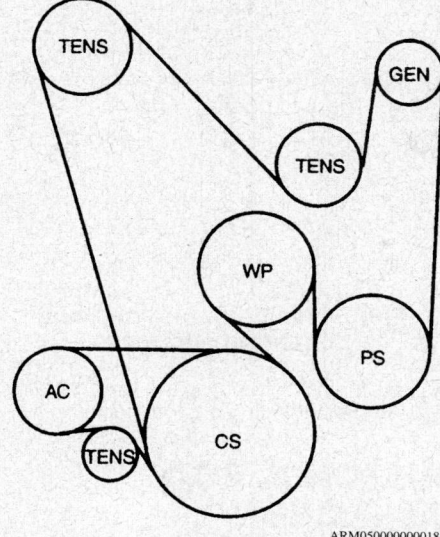

Fig. 6 Serpentine drive belt routing

ARM0500000000181

6. Reverse procedure to install, noting the following:
   a. Install and lubricate new oil pump screen O-ring seal with suitable clean engine oil.
   b. Push screen tube complete into oil pump. **Do not pull tube into pump using bolt.**

OIL PUMP SERVICE
Disassemble

1. Remove mounting bolts and pump cover.
2. Mark gear for assembly alignment.
3. Remove drive and driven gear.
4. Remove pressure relief valve plug, spring and valve.

Inspection

1. Wash components in cleaning solvent and dry with compressed air.
2. Inspect pump housing and cover for cracks, excessive wear, scoring or casting imperfections.
3. Inspect oil pump housing-to-engine block oil gallery surface for scratches, gouging or damaged bolt hole threads.
4. Inspect relief valve plug and plug bore for damaged threads.
5. Inspect oil pump internal oil passages for restrictions.
6. Inspect pump gears for chipping, galling or wear. **Minor burrs or imperfections may be removed with fine oil stone.**
7. Inspect drive gear splines for excessive wear.
8. Inspect pressure relief valve and bore for scoring or wear.
9. Inspect oil pump screen for debris or restrictions, then for broken or loose wire mesh.

Assemble

Coat all wear or internal surfaces with suitable clean engine oil.
1. Install driven gear into pump housing.
2. Install driven gear with orientation mark facing pump cover.
3. Install drive gear into pump housing.
4. Install oil pump cover.
5. Tighten oil pump cover mounting bolts.
6. Install new relief valve spring.
7. Tighten pressure relief valve plug.

SERPENTINE DRIVE BELT
Replacement

1. Rotate tensioner clockwise.
2. Remove drive belt.
3. Reverse procedure to install.

Routing

Refer to **Fig. 6** for serpentine drive belt routing.

COOLING SYSTEM BLEED

These engines do not require a specified bleed procedure. After filling cooling system, run engine to operating temperature with radiator/pressure cap off. Air will then be automatically bled through cap opening.

THERMOSTAT
REPLACE

1. Partially drain cooling system into suitable container.
2. Disconnect clamp and remove radiator inlet hose from water outlet housing.
3. Remove mounting bolts, water outlet housing and O-ring seal.
4. Remove thermostat.
5. Reverse procedure to install.

WATER PUMP
REPLACE

1. Drain cooling system into suitable container.
2. Remove battery and tray.
3. Remove drive belt as outlined under "Serpentine Drive Belt."
4. Remove mounting bolts and water pump. Discard gasket.
5. Reverse procedure to install.

RADIATOR
REPLACE

1. Disconnect Positive Crankcase Ventilation (PCV) tube from air inlet duct.
2. Remove air inlet duct from throttle body.
3. Remove air inlet duct from Mass Air Flow/Intake Air Temperature (MAF/IAT) sensor.
4. Remove cover and air filter element.

5. Drain cooling system into suitable container, then disconnect coolant reservoir hose.
6. Remove coolant recovery reservoir mounting screws, then the reservoir.
7. Remove engine mount strut.
8. Remove Powertrain Control Module (PCM) harness clip from fan shroud.
9. Remove condenser tubes bracket bolt from fan shroud.
10. Remove mounting bolt, then the condenser hold down bracket from radiator and condenser.
11. Remove cooling fan shroud mounting bolts.
12. Remove radiator vent hose from right-hand upper radiator tank.
13. Remove radiator upper support brackets and fan shroud bolts.
14. Disconnect engine cooling fan motor electrical connectors.
15. Remove cooling fan motor electrical harness from fan shroud clips.
16. Disconnect transaxle oil cooler pipes from radiator.

17. Remove cooling fan shroud.
18. Remove upper and lower radiator hoses from radiator.
19. Tilt radiator rearward, then lift and position condenser aside.
20. Remove radiator.
21. Reverse procedure to install.

FUEL PUMP
REPLACE

1. Relieve fuel system pressure as outlined under "Precautions."
2. Drain fuel tank into suitable container.
3. Raise and support vehicle.
4. Loosen clamp and remove fuel tank fill hose from tank.
5. Disconnect EVAP vent pipe quick connect fitting from fill pipe EVAP vent pipe quick connect fitting.
6. Disconnect EVAP vent solenoid hose on tank from vent valve solenoid hose.
7. Disconnect fuel feed and EVAP lines from fuel tank lines.

8. Support exhaust system.
9. Remove retainers and fuel tank shield.
10. Support fuel tank with suitable adjustable jack.
11. Remove strap bolts mounting bolts and lower fuel tank. **Do not bend fuel tank straps.**
12. Disconnect fuel sender jumper harness electrical connector and EVAP and fuel feed lines from sender.
13. Remove fuel tank.
14. Turn fuel sender lock ring counterclockwise using fuel sender lock ring wrench tool No. J45722, or equivalent, and suitable long breaker-bar.
15. Remove fuel sender. Discard O-ring seal.
16. Reverse procedure to install, noting the following
    a. Replace lock ring if warpage is more than .016 inch.
    b. Install new O-ring seal.
    c. Ensure tab is properly aligned.

TIGHTENING SPECIFICATIONS

Year	Component	Torque/Ft. Lbs.
2006–08	ABS Module Brake Pipe Fittings	11
	Air Conditioning Compressor Hose	12
	Air Inlet Duct	27①
	Alternator Bracket	37
	Battery Cable Ground	22
	Camshaft Gear	18
	Camshaft Retainer	18
	Catalytic Converter	44
	Catalytic Converter Pipe Stud	26
	CMP Sensor	106①
	Cooling Fan Shroud	89①
	Condenser Tubes Bracket	89①
	Connecting Rod	④
	Crankshaft Gear	18
	Cylinder Head	⑤
	Engine Coolant Air Bleed Cover	106①
	Engine Frame, Front	107
	Engine Frame, Rear	118
	Engine Harness Connector	89①
	Engine Mount	37
	Engine Mount Strut	35
	Exhaust Crossover Pipe	18
	Exhaust Manifold	③
	Exhaust Manifold Heat Shield	80①
	Flywheel	47
	Front Cover	18
	Front Fender Diagonal Brace, Lefthand	89①
	Front Fender Diagonal Brace, Righthand	35
	Front Wheel Drive Shaft	118
	Fuse Block	89①
	Heater Pipe Bracket	12
	Hood	19
	Ignition Coil	71①
	Intake Manifold	②
	Intermediate Shaft To Steering Gear	35
	Main Bearings	④
	Master Cylinder	24
	Master Cylinder Brake Pipe Fittings	22
	Oil Dipstick Tube	18
	Oil Pan	18
	Oil Pump	18
	Oil Pump Cover	106①
	Oil Pump Pressure Relief Valve Plug	106①

TIGHTENING SPECIFICATIONS—Continued

Year	Component	Torque/Ft. Lbs.
2006–08	Oil Pump Screen, Bolt	106①
	Oil Pump Screen, Nut	18
	Oxygen Sensor	31
	Positive Battery Cable	89①
	Power Steering High Pressure Hose	20
	Power Steering Hose	53①
	Power Steering Pump	18
	Radiator Upper Support Bracket	53①
	Rocker Arm	22
	Thermostat Housing	11
	Timing Chain Guide	18
	Transaxle Converter Cover	89①
	Transaxle Oil Cooler Line Bracket	18
	Transaxle To Engine	55
	Valve Cover	106①
	VSS Shield	18
	Water Outlet Housing	11
	Water Pump	89①
	Water Pump Manifold, M8	33
	Water Pump Manifold, M10	44

① — Inch lbs.

② — Refer to "Intake Manifold, Replace" for tightening specifications and sequence.

③ — Refer to "Exhaust Manifold, Replace" for tightening specifications and sequence.

④ — Refer to "Main & Rod Bearings" for tightening specifications and sequence.

⑤ — Refer to "Cylinder Head, Replace" for tightening specifications and sequence.

Rear Axle & Suspension

NOTE: On Air Bag Equipped Models, Refer To "Air Bag System Precautions" Located In The Front Of This Manual For System Disarming & Arming Procedures.

NOTE: Refer To "Computer Relearn Procedures" Located In The Front Of This Manual When Battery Power To The Computer Has Been Interrupted.

INDEX

	Page No.		Page No.		Page No.
Coil Spring, Replace	6-57	Lateral Link, Replace	6-57	Strut, Replace	6-57
Description	6-57	Front	6-57	Strut Service	6-57
Hub & Bearing, Replace	6-57	Rear	6-57	Tightening Specifications	6-58
Knuckle, Replace	6-57	Stabilizer Bar, Replace	6-57	Trailing Arm, Replace	6-57

DESCRIPTION

These vehicles use a Tri-Link independent rear suspension system with a transverse leaf spring and tubular struts with large lateral links attached to the body crossmember. The three mounting points are the crossmember, strut tower and trailing arm. The crossmember is stamped steel and the composite fiberglass mono leaf spring is transversely mounted to the under side of the crossmember, with its padded ends free riding on the cast knuckle assembly.

HUB & BEARING
REPLACE

The rear hub and bearing assembly is not serviceable. If the hub and/or bearing is damaged, the complete assembly must be replaced.
1. Raise and support vehicle, then remove tire and wheel assembly.
2. Remove brake caliper with hose attached and suspend aside.
3. Remove brake rotor.
4. Disconnect anti-lock brake system electrical harness connector.
5. Remove hub and bearing to knuckle bolts.
6. Remove parking brake lever bracket and actuator.
7. Remove hub and bearing assembly.
8. Reverse procedure to install.

STRUT
REPLACE

1. Remove three strut to body mount mounting nuts.
2. Raise and support vehicle, then remove rear tire and wheel assembly.
3. Disconnect stabilizer shaft link from strut.
4. Mark strut and knuckle for installation alignment.
5. Remove strut to knuckle bolts and strut.
6. Reverse procedure to install.

STRUT SERVICE

1. Position strut into strut spring compressor tool No. J34013-B, or equivalent.
2. Compress spring approximately ½ inch.
3. Hold shaft with suitable bit, then remove and discard shaft nut.
4. Release spring tension then remove upper mount plate, spring, baffle and lower mount plate.
5. Reverse procedure to assemble.

COIL SPRING
REPLACE

1. Position strut into strut spring compressor tool No. J34013-B, or equivalent.
2. Compress spring assembly approximately ½ inch.
3. Hold shaft with suitable bit, then remove and discard shaft nut.
4. Release spring tension and remove upper mount plate, spring, baffle and lower mount plate.
5. Reverse procedure to assemble.

KNUCKLE
REPLACE

1. Raise and support vehicle, then remove tire and wheel assembly.
2. Mark strut and knuckle for installation alignment.
3. Disconnect rear spindle rods from knuckle.
4. Remove brake caliper and bracket, then the brake rotor.
5. Disconnect ABS electrical connector.
6. Remove wheel hub and bearing.
7. Disconnect trailing arm from knuckle.
8. Remove rear suspension strut to knuckle mounting bolts.
9. Remove knuckle.
10. Reverse procedure to install.

TRAILING ARM
REPLACE

1. Raise and support vehicle.

2. Disconnect ABS electrical harness connector.
3. Remove trailing arm to knuckle mounting nut and bolt, **Fig. 1.**
4. Remove trailing rod to body mounting nut and bolt.
5. Remove trailing arm.
6. Reverse procedure to install.

STABILIZER BAR
REPLACE

1. Raise and support vehicle, then remove rear tire and wheel assemblies.
2. Remove lefthand and righthand stabilizer shaft link bolts, then open brackets and remove insulator.
3. Remove lefthand and righthand strut to knuckle to stabilizer shaft nuts, **Fig. 2. Do not remove strut to knuckle bolts.**
4. Remove insulator brackets from bolts and from stabilizer shaft, then the stabilizer shaft.
5. Reverse procedure to install.

LATERAL LINK
REPLACE
Front

1. Raise and support vehicle, then remove tire and wheel assembly.
2. Remove rod to knuckle bolt and exhaust pipe heat shield.
3. Lower fuel tank .
4. Remove lateral link to knuckle mounting bolt.
5. Remover crossmember mounting nut and bolt, then the lateral link.
6. Reverse procedure to install.

Rear

1. Raise and support vehicle, then remove tire and wheel assembly.
2. Remove transverse spring as outlined under "Coil Spring, Replace."
3. Remove lower auxiliary spring bracket from rod.

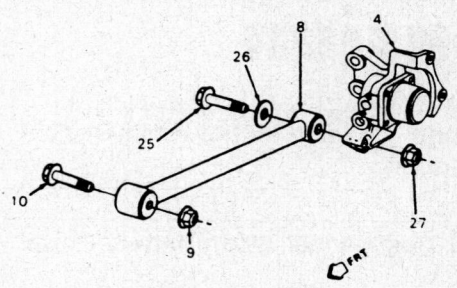

4 KNUCKLE ASSEMBLY
8 TRAILING LINK
9 65 N•m (48 lbs ft.)
10 BOLT
25 BOLT
26 WASHER
27 NUT 260 N•m (192 lbs ft.)

GC2039100085000X

Fig. 1 Trailing arm replacement

4. Remove rear lateral link mounting nut from crossmember.
5. Push bolt forward and remove rear lateral link.
6. Reverse procedure to install.

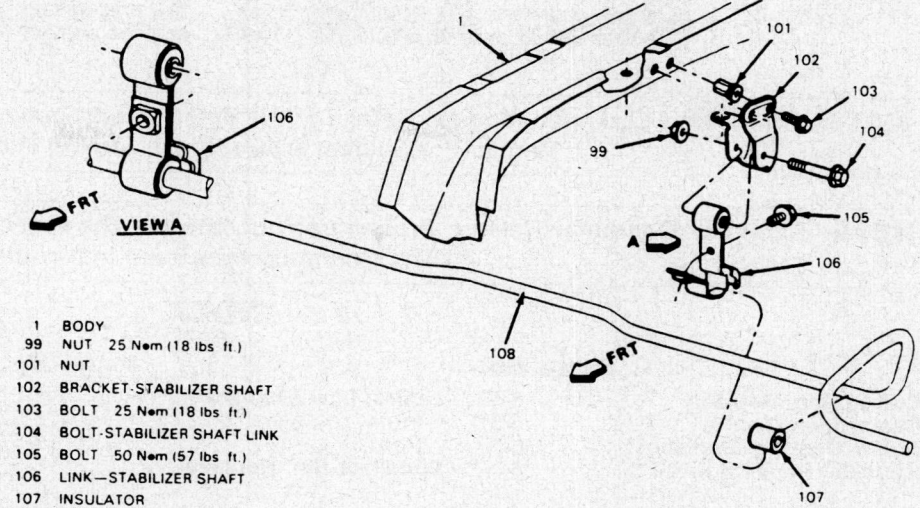

VIEW A

1   BODY
99   NUT   25 N•m (18 lbs ft.)
101 NUT
102 BRACKET-STABILIZER SHAFT
103 BOLT 25 N•m (18 lbs ft.)
104 BOLT-STABILIZER SHAFT LINK
105 BOLT 50 N•m (57 lbs ft.)
106 LINK—STABILIZER SHAFT
107 INSULATOR
108 STABILIZER SHAFT

GC2039100083000X

Fig. 2 Stabilizer shaft assembly replacement

TIGHTENING SPECIFICATIONS

Year	Component	Torque/Ft. Lbs.
2004–08	Brake Hose Bracket	20
	Brake Hose To Brake Caliper	40
	Caliper	32
	Caliper Bracket	85
	Spindle Rods To Knuckle	110
	Spindle Rods To Rear Suspension Support	103
	Stabilizer Shaft Insulator Bracket	35
	Stabilizer Shaft Link	38
	Strut Mount To Body	33
	Strut Shaft	55
	Strut To Knuckle	90
	Suspension Support	81
	Trailing Arm Bolt To Body Bracket	37
	Trailing Arm To Knuckle	52①
	Wheel Hub To Knuckle	55
	Wheel Lug Nuts	100

① — Final tighten an additional 65°.

Front Suspension & Steering

NOTE: On Air Bag Equipped Models, Refer To "Air Bag System Precautions" Located In The Front Of This Manual For System Disarming & Arming Procedures.

NOTE: Refer To "Computer Relearn Procedures" Located In The Front Of This Manual When Battery Power To The Computer Has Been Interrupted.

INDEX

	Page No.
Ball Joint, Replace	6-59
Ball Joint Inspection	6-59
Control Arm, Replace	6-60
Description	6-59
Hub & Bearing, Replace	6-59
Power Steering Gear, Replace	6-61
Power Steering Pump, Replace	6-61
Century, LaCrosse & Regal	6-61
Grand Prix	6-61
3.1L Engine	6-61
3.8L Engine	6-62
5.3L Engine	6-62

	Page No.
Impala & Monte Carlo	6-62
3.4L Engine	6-62
3.5L, 3.9L & 5.3L Engines	6-62
3.8L Engine	6-62
Power Steering	21-1
Power Steering System Bleed	6-62
Precautions	6-59
Air Bag Systems	6-59
Stabilizer Bar, Replace	6-60
Installation	6-60
Removal	6-60
Steering Columns	20-1

	Page No.
Steering Knuckle, Replace	6-60
Strut, Replace	6-59
Strut Service	6-59
Assemble	6-59
Disassemble	6-59
Tie Rod End, Replace	6-60
Inner	6-60
Installation	6-61
Removal	6-60
Outer	6-61
Tightening Specifications	6-63

PRECAUTIONS

Air Bag Systems

Refer to "Air Bag System Precautions" in the front of this manual for system disarming and arming procedures.

DESCRIPTION

The front suspension system on these vehicles is of the McPherson strut design. This design incorporates McPherson struts with coil springs and a one piece configuration with lower control arms. The use of tapered top coil springs on top of the struts provides a well controlled ride and allows a lower hood profile.

HUB & BEARING

REPLACE

1. Raise and support vehicle, then remove tire and wheel assembly.
2. Disconnect ABS wheel speed sensor electrical connector.
3. Remove wheel speed sensor electrical connector from bracket.
4. Remove and support brake caliper aside.
5. Remove caliper bracket and brake rotor.
6. Remove and discard driveshaft nut.
7. Push driveshaft out of wheel hub and bearing using front hub spindle remover tool No. J28733-B, or equivalent.
8. Remove mounting bolts, then the hub and bearing assembly from steering knuckle.
9. Reverse procedure to install. **Install new mounting bolts.**

BALL JOINT INSPECTION

With vehicle raised and supported to allow front suspension to hang freely, grasp wheel at top and bottom and attempt to move bottom of wheel inward and outward. **Ball joints must be replaced if looseness is observed between knuckle and control arm.**

BALL JOINT

REPLACE

1. Raise and support vehicle, then remove tire and wheel assembly.
2. Remove steering gear outer tie rod from steering knuckle.
3. Remove stabilizer shaft to lower control arm insulator bracket bolts.
4. Disconnect ABS speed sensor and remove control arm mounting bolts.
5. Remove cotter pin and loosen nut from ball joint.
6. Separate front lower control arm ball joint from steering knuckle using ball joint separator tool No. J41820, or equivalent.
7. Remove control arm from frame.
8. Drill out three rivets holding ball joint to control arm and remove ball joint from control arm.
9. Reverse procedure to install.

STRUT

REPLACE

1. Remove three strut to body nuts, **Fig. 1.**
2. Raise and support vehicle, then remove tire and wheel assembly.
3. Remove strut to knuckle mounting bolts. **After removing bolts, retain knuckle in its original position.**
4. Remove strut.
5. Reverse procedure to install.

STRUT SERVICE

Disassemble

1. Mount strut and knuckle assembly into strut spring compressor tool No. J34013-A and strut compressor adapter tool No. J34013-88, or equivalents.
2. Compress spring with compressor forcing screw just enough to release tension from upper spring insulator.
3. Remove strut shaft nut using suitable bit and strut rod nut remover/installer tool No. J35669, or equivalents.
4. Relieve spring tension, then remove spring and strut components.

Assemble

1. Install spring seat and bearing.
2. Install lower spring insulator. Lower spring coil end must be visible between step and first retention tab of insulator.
3. Install front suspension spring.
4. Install dust shield to lower spring seat.
5. Install jounce bumper.
6. Install upper spring insulator. Upper spring coil end must be between step and location mark on insulator.
7. Install jounce bumper retainer to strut mount using strut mount plate wrench tool No. J35670, or equivalent.
8. Install strut mount and upper strut mount bushing.
9. Compress strut assembly using strut spring compressor and strut compressor adapter tools No. J34013-A and

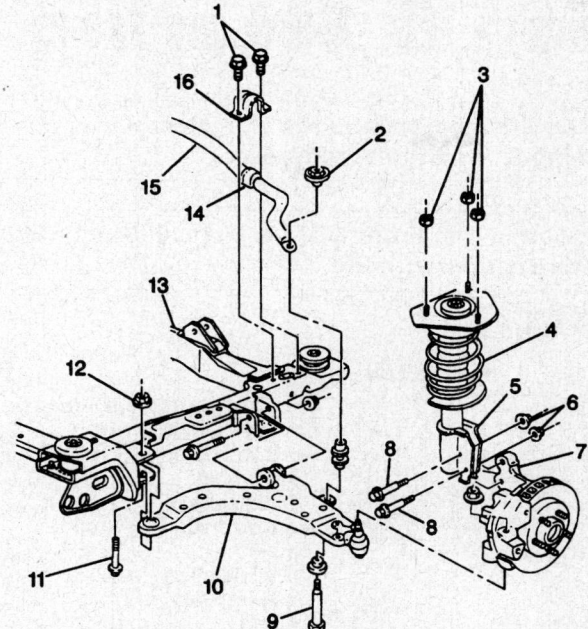

(1) Front Stabilizer Shaft Insulator Clamp Bolt/screw
(2) Front Stabilizer Shaft Link Nut
(3) Front Suspension Strut Mount Nut
(4) Front Suspension Spring
(5) Front Suspension Strut
(6) Strut To Knuckle Nut
(7) Front Steering Knuckle
(8) Strut To Knuckle Bolt/screw

(9) Front Stabilizer Shaft Link]
(10) Front Lower Control Arm
(11) Front Lower Control Arm Bolt/screw
(12) Front Lower Cotrol Arm Nut
(13) Frame
(14) Front Stabilizer Shaft Insulator
(15) Front Stabilizer Shaft
(16) Front Stabilizer Shaft Clamp

GC2029700266000X

Fig. 1 Front suspension

J34013-38, or equivalents.
10. Align strut cartridge shaft with strut extension rod tool No. J35668, or equivalent.
11. Install strut shaft nut using strut rod nut remover/installer tool No. J35669, or equivalent, and suitable bit.

CONTROL ARM
REPLACE

1. Raise and support vehicle, then remove tire and wheel assembly.
2. Remove steering gear outer tie rod from steering knuckle.
3. Remove stabilizer shaft to lower control arm insulator bracket bolts.
4. Disconnect ABS speed sensor and remove control arm mounting bolts.
5. Remove cotter pin and loosen nut from ball joint.
6. Separate front lower control arm ball joint from steering knuckle using ball joint separator tool No. J41820, or equivalent.
7. Remove control arm from frame.
8. Reverse procedure to install, noting the following:
   a. Lower control arm to frame bolts, **Fig. 2.**
   b. **Torque** lower ball joint nut 40 ft. lbs. Rotate to align next slot in nut with cotter pin hole in stud. **Do not rotate more than 60° to align with hole. Do not loosen nut at any time during installation.**

STEERING KNUCKLE
REPLACE

1. Raise and support vehicle, then remove tire and wheel assembly.
2. Remove front wheel driveshaft bearing as outlined in "Front Wheel Drive Axles" chapter.
3. Disconnect ABS wheel speed sensor electrical connector.
4. Remove wheel speed sensor electrical connector from bracket.
5. Remove and support brake caliper aside.
6. Remove caliper bracket and brake rotor.
7. Remove driveshaft nut and discard.
8. Push driveshaft out of wheel hub and bearing using front hub spindle remover tool No. J28733-B, or equivalent.
9. Remove mounting bolts, then the hub and bearing assembly from steering knuckle.
10. Remove lower control arm ball joint cotter pin and mounting nut.
11. Separate ball joint from control arm using ball joint stud separator tool No. J41820, or equivalent.
12. Separate outer tie rod end from steering knuckle using universal steering linkage puller tool No. J24319-B, or equivalent.
13. Mark strut and steering knuckle for installation alignment.
14. Remove strut to knuckle mounting bolts and steering knuckle.
15. Reverse procedure to install.

STABILIZER BAR
REPLACE
Removal

1. Raise and support vehicle, then remove tire and wheel assembly.
2. Move steering shaft dust seal and remove lower intermediate shaft pinch bolt.
3. Loosen insulator clamp mounting nuts and bolts, **Fig. 3.**
4. Support rear frame crossmember using suitable jack stand.
5. Loosen two front frame to body mounting bolts four turns.
6. Remove two rear frame to body mounting bolts and lower rear of frame. Discard frame to body bolts.
7. Remove insulators and clamps from frame.
8. Remove stabilizer bar links from control arms.
9. Pull stabilizer shaft rearward, swing shaft downward and remove from lefthand side of vehicle.

Installation

Weight of vehicle must be supported by the control arms so that trim height is obtained before tightening link nut.
1. Install stabilizer shaft from lefthand side of vehicle.
2. Loosely install stabilizer shaft link to control arm. **Do not tighten stabilizer link mounting nut now.**
3. Install insulator clamps onto frame, then raise frame into position while guiding steering shaft onto steering gear.
4. Install new frame to body mounting bolts and remove jack stand.
5. Install intermediate shaft pinch bolt.
6. Install dust seal onto steering gear.
7. Support vehicle weight with control arms and tighten stabilizer link nut.
8. Install tire and wheel assembly.

TIE ROD END
REPLACE
Inner
REMOVAL

1. Remove steering gear as outlined under "Power Steering Gear, Replace."
2. Loosen outer tie rod end to inner tie rod jam nut.
3. Turn outer tie rod counterclockwise to remove from inner tie rod end using suitable pipe wrench to hold inner tie rod.
4. Loosen rack and pinion boot inner and outer clamps, then remove boot and breather tube.
5. Slide shock damper boot back on rack and place suitable pipe wrench on rack next to inner tie rod housing.
6. Place suitable wrench on flats of inner

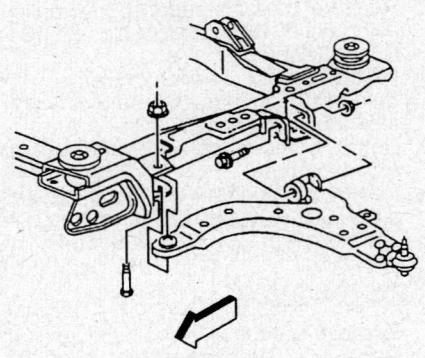

GC2029800225000X

Fig. 2 Lower control arm installation

tie rod housing and turn outer tie rod counterclockwise to remove from inner tie rod end.

INSTALLATION

1. Apply Loctite 262, or equivalent, to inner tie rod threads.
2. Place suitable pipe wrench on rack next to inner tie rod housing and **torque** tie rod to 74 ft. lbs.
3. Place tie rod assembly in suitable vise and stake both sides of female inner tie rod assembly housing to male rack.
4. Insert suitable .25 mm gage between male rack and female inner tie rod housing. Feeler gauge must not pass between rack and housing stake.
5. Slide shock damper over inner tie rod housing until front lip of damper bottoms against inner tie rod housing.
6. Install rack and pinion boot, then the breather tube using new boot clamps.
7. Install outer tie rod end to inner tie rod and loosely install jam nut.
8. Install steering gear as outlined under "Power Steering Gear, Replace."
9. Set front wheel toe as outlined under "Front Wheel Alignment" in "Wheel Alignment" section.
10. **Torque** jam nut to 50 ft. lbs.

Outer

1. Raise and support vehicle, then remove tire and wheel assembly.
2. Remove and discard hex torque prevailing nut, then loosen jam nut, **Fig. 4.**
3. Separate tie rod end from steering knuckle using universal steering linkage puller tool No. J24319-01, or equivalent.
4. Loosen outer tie rod end to inner tie rod jam nut.
5. Turn outer tie rod counterclockwise to remove from inner tie rod end using suitable pipe wrench to hold inner tie rod.
6. Reverse procedure to install. **Torque** jam nut to 50 ft. lbs.

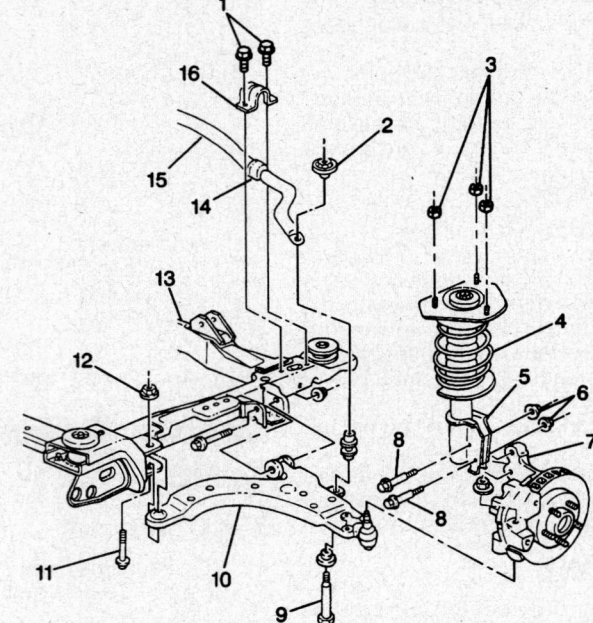

(1) Front Stabilizer Shaft Insulator Clamp Bolt/Screw
(2) Front Stabilizer Shaft Link Nut
(3) Front Suspension Strut Mount Nut
(4) Front Suspension Spring
(5) Front Suspension Strut
(6) Strut-to-Knuckle Nut
(7) Front Steering Knuckle
(8) Strut-to-Knuckle Bolt/Screw
(9) Front Stabilizer Shaft Link
(10) Front Lower Control Arm
(11) Front Lower Control Arm Bolt/Screw
(12) Front Lower Control Arm Nut
(13) Frame
(14) Front Stabilizer Shaft Insulator
(15) Front Stabilizer Shaft
(16) Front Stabilizer Shaft Clamp

GC2029800226000X

Fig. 3 Stabilizer shaft & insulators replacement

POWER STEERING GEAR

REPLACE

1. Position front wheels straight ahead and turn ignition switch to LOCK position.
2. Raise and support vehicle, then remove lefthand tire and wheel assembly.
3. Separate lower bolt and steering shaft from power steering gear.
4. Remove hex torque prevailing nuts and separate both outer tie rod ends from steering knuckle using tie rod end puller/ball joint remover tool No. J35917, or equivalent.
5. Support frame with suitable jack stands.
6. Remove mounting bolts and lower rear of frame. **Do not lower frame too far.**
7. Remove pipe retaining clip from steering gear.
8. Place suitable drain pan under steering rack fluid pipes, then remove inlet pipes and outlet line from steering gear.
9. Remove "S" mounting bolts and nuts, then the power steering gear through wheel opening.
10. Reverse procedure to install. Bleed power steering system as outlined under "Power Steering System Bleed."

POWER STEERING PUMP

REPLACE

Century, LaCrosse & Regal

1. **On models equipped with 3.1L engine,** place suitable drain pan under engine, then remove coolant recovery reservoir and position aside.
2. **On all models,** remove drive belt from pump.
3. **On models equipped with 3.1L engine,** disconnect ignition control wiring harness near pump and position aside.
4. **On all models,** place suitable drain pan under engine, then disconnect inlet and outlet hoses from pump.
5. Remove mounting bolts and pump.
6. Reverse procedure to install. Bleed power steering system as outlined under "Power Steering System Bleed."

Grand Prix

3.1L ENGINE

1. Place suitable drain pan under engine, then remove coolant recovery reservoir and position aside.
2. Remove drive belt from pump.
3. Disconnect ignition control wiring harness near pump and position aside.

4. Place suitable drain pan under engine, then disconnect inlet and outlet hoses from pump.
5. Remove mounting bolts and pump.
6. Reverse procedure to install. Bleed power steering system as outlined under "Power Steering System Bleed."

3.8L ENGINE

1. Remove accessory drive belt.
2. Raise and support vehicle, then remove tire and wheel assembly.
3. Place suitable drain pan under vehicle, then disconnect pressure and return lines from power steering pump.
4. Remove mounting bolts and power steering pump.
5. Remove fluid reservoir and pump pulley.
6. Reverse procedure to install. Bleed power steering system as outlined under "Power Steering System Bleed."

5.3L ENGINE

1. Remove drive belt as outlined in appropriate engine section.
2. Remove power steering pump pulley using pulley remover tool No. J25034-C, or equivalent.
3. Remove intake manifold cover.
4. Disconnect clamps and remove power steering pump hoses.
5. Remove mounting bolt and power steering pump.
6. Reverse procedure to install. Install pulley using power steering pump pulley installer tool No.J25033-C, or equivalent.

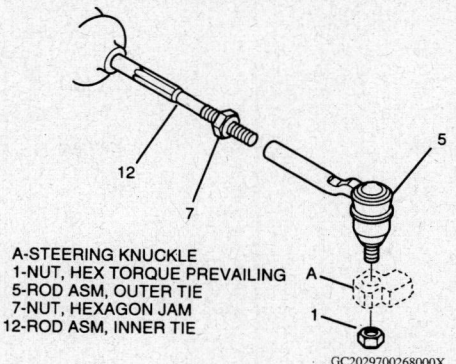

A-STEERING KNUCKLE
1-NUT, HEX TORQUE PREVAILING
5-ROD ASM, OUTER TIE
7-NUT, HEXAGON JAM
12-ROD ASM, INNER TIE

GC2029700268000X

Fig. 4 Tie rod end replacement

Impala & Monte Carlo

3.4L ENGINE

1. Place suitable drain pan under vehicle and remove coolant recovery reservoir.
2. Remove drive belt from power steering pump pulley.
3. Remove ignition wiring harness from retainer near power steering pump.
4. Disconnect power steering pressure and return hoses.
5. Remove mounting bolts and power steering pump.
6. Reverse procedure to install.

3.5L, 3.9L & 5.3L ENGINES

1. Remove drive belt as outlined in appropriate engine section.

2. Remove power steering pump pulley using pulley remover tool No. J25034-C, or equivalent.
3. Remove intake manifold cover.
4. Disconnect clamps and remove power steering pump hoses.
5. Remove mounting bolt and power steering pump.
6. Reverse procedure to install. Install pulley using power steering pump pulley installer tool No. J25033-C, or equivalent.

3.8L ENGINE

1. Remove accessory drive belt.
2. Raise and support vehicle, then remove tire and wheel assembly.
3. Place suitable drain pan under vehicle, then disconnect pressure and return lines from power steering pump.
4. Remove mounting bolts and power steering pump.
5. Remove fluid reservoir and pump pulley.
6. Reverse procedure to install. Bleed power steering system as outlined under "Power Steering System Bleed."

POWER STEERING SYSTEM BLEED

1. Turn wheels all way to left.
2. Add power steering to Cold mark on fluid level indicator.
3. Start engine and run at fast idle.
4. Adjust fluid level to Cold mark.
5. Bleed system by turning wheels from side to side without hitting stops. Keep fluid level at Cold mark.
6. Return wheels to center position and continue running engine for 2–3 minutes.

TIGHTENING SPECIFICATIONS

Year	Component	Torque/Ft. Lbs.
2004–08	Ball Joint To Control Arm	50
	Ball Joint To Knuckle	15②
	Frame To Body	122
	Hub & Bearing	96
	Inner Tie Rod	74
	Lower Control Arm	92
	O-Ring Union Fitting	55
	Outer Tie Rod End	34
	Rack Bearing Preload Lock	50
	Stabilizer Shaft Bracket	38
	Stabilizer Shaft Link	17
	Steering Cooler Pipe/Hose	89①
	Steering Cooler Retainer	11
	Steering Gear Cylinder Line Fittings	13
	Steering Gear	59
	Steering Gear Valve End Fittings	20
	Steering Gear Pipe Fittings	20
	Steering Pump Flow Control Valve Union Fitting	55
	Steering Pump	25
	Strut Mount	63
	Strut To Body Mount	24
	Strut To Knuckle	90
	Tie Rod End Jam Nut	50
	Wheel Lug Nuts	100

① — Inch lbs.
② — Tighten an additional 120.°

Wheel Alignment

INDEX

	Page No.
Front Wheel Alignment	6-64
Camber	6-64
Toe	6-64
Precautions	6-64

	Page No.
Preliminary Inspection	6-64
Rear Wheel Alignment	6-64
Camber	6-64
Toe	6-64

	Page No.
Wheel Alignment Specifications	6-4

PRECAUTIONS

When adjusting wheel alignment, always adjust both front and rear alignment. Begin with rear wheel camber, then proceed to rear wheel toe, tracking and final adjustment of front wheel camber and toe.

PRELIMINARY INSPECTION

1. Ensure tires are inflated to proper pressure and inspect for uneven wear.
2. Inspect front wheel bearings and related suspension components for damage.
3. Inspect ball joints and tie rods.
4. Inspect vehicle trim heights.
5. Inspect steering gear for looseness at frame.
6. Inspect struts for improper operation.
7. Inspect for loose control arms.
8. Inspect for loose or missing stabilizer shaft attachments.

FRONT WHEEL ALIGNMENT

Camber

1. Remove three strut to body nuts.
2. Raise and support vehicle, then remove tire and wheel assembly.
3. Remove strut to knuckle mounting bolts. **After removing bolts, retain knuckle in its original position.**
4. Remove strut.
5. Place strut in suitable vise.
6. File lower strut to knuckle mounting hole oblong as outlined, **Fig. 1.**
7. Install strut and adjust camber as required.
8. **Torque** strut to knuckle bolts to 90 ft. lbs.

Toe

1. Remove power steering gear seal clamps.

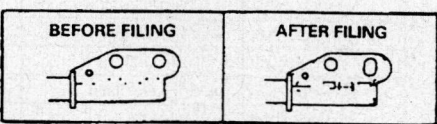
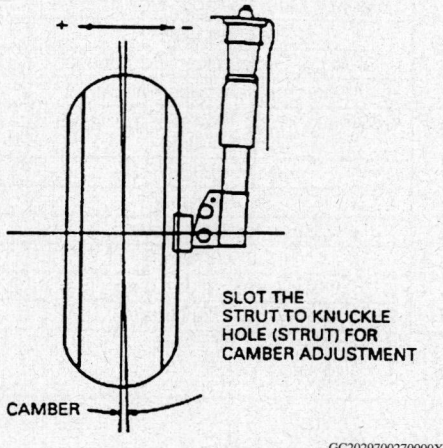

Fig. 1   Front camber adjustment

GC2029700270000X

2. With steering wheel in straight ahead position, loosen jam nuts on tie rods.
3. Rotate inner tie rod to obtain proper toe angle, then ensure number of threads showing on each tie rod is approximately equal.
4. Ensure tie rod ends are square, then **torque** jam nuts to 50 ft. lbs.
5. Ensure seals are not twisted, then install seal clamps.

REAR WHEEL ALIGNMENT

Camber

1. Remove three strut to body mount mounting nuts.
2. Raise and support vehicle, then remove rear tire and wheel assembly.

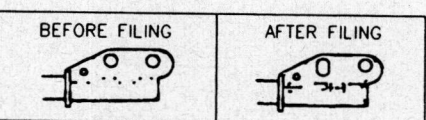
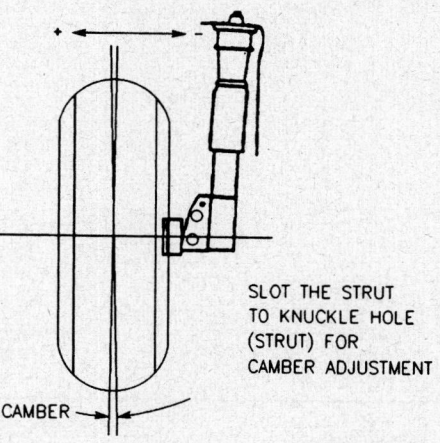

Fig. 2   Rear camber adjustment

GC2039700149000X

3. Disconnect stabilizer shaft link from strut.
4. Mark strut and knuckle for installation alignment.
5. Remove strut to knuckle bolts and strut.
6. Place strut in suitable vise.
7. File upper strut to knuckle mounting hole oblong, **Fig. 2.**
8. Install strut and adjust camber as required.
9. **Torque** strut to knuckle bolts to 88 ft. lbs.

Toe

1. Loosen hex nuts at rear wheel spindle rod.
2. Adjust toe to specifications.
3. **Torque** hex nuts to 50 ft. lbs.

CORVETTE

INDEX OF SERVICE OPERATIONS

Page No.

**ACTIVE SUSPENSION
SYSTEM (VOLUME 2)** 7-1
**AIR BAG SYSTEM
PRECAUTIONS** 0-18
BRAKES
   Anti-Lock Brakes (Volume 2).. 6-1
   Disc Brakes.................... 22-1
   Drum Brakes 23-1
   Hydraulic Brake Systems 24-1
   Power Brake Units........... 25-1
**COMPUTER RELEARN
PROCEDURE** 0-31
ELECTRICAL
   Air Bag System (Volume 2) ... 4-1
   Air Conditioning............... 16-1
   Alternator, Replace 7-5
   Alternators 19-1
   Blower Motor, Replace........ 7-6
   Cooling Fans 17-1
   Cruise Control (Volume 2) 2-1
   Dash Gauges (Volume 2) 1-1
   Dash Panel Service
   (Volume 2) 5-1
   Dimmer Switch, Replace...... 7-6
   Evaporator Core, Replace 7-7
   Fuel Pump Relay Location.... 7-5
   Fuse Panel & Flasher
   Location 7-5
   Headlamp Switch, Replace ... 7-5
   Heater Core, Replace........ 7-6
   Instrument Cluster, Replace... 7-6
   Multi-Function Switch,
   Replace 7-5
   Passive Restraint Systems
   (Volume 2).................... 4-1
   Precautions................... 7-5
   Radio, Replace 7-6
   Relay Center Location 7-5
   Speed Controls (Volume 2) ... 2-1
   Starter Motors 18-1
   Starter, Replace 7-5
   Steering Columns............. 20-1
   Steering Wheel, Replace...... 7-6
   Turn Signal Switch, Replace .. 7-6
   Wiper Motor, Replace......... 7-6
   Wiper Switch, Replace........ 7-6
   Wiper Systems (Volume 2).... 3-1
**ELECTRICAL SYMBOL
IDENTIFICATION** 0-63
**FRONT SUSPENSION &
STEERING**
   Ball Joint, Replace............ 7-34
   Ball Joint Inspection 7-34
   Control Arm, Replace 7-35
   Hub & Bearing, Replace 7-34
   Power Steering 21-1
   Power Steering Gear,
   Replace 7-35
   Power Steering Pump,
   Replace 7-36
   Shock Absorber, Replace 7-34
   Stabilizer Bar, Replace 7-35
   Steering Columns............. 20-1
   Steering Knuckle, Replace.... 7-35

Page No.

   Tightening Specifications...... 7-36
   Transverse Leaf Spring,
   Replace 7-35
**NON-STANDARD TIRE &
WHEEL SIZE
ADJUSTMENT TO RIDE
HEIGHT SPECIFICATIONS
& TIRE SIZE CHART** 0-61
**REAR AXLE &
SUSPENSION**
   Control Arm, Replace 7-31
   Hub & Bearing, Replace 7-30
   Propeller Shaft, Replace 7-30
   Rear Axle, Replace 7-30
   Rear Wheel Shaft, Replace ... 7-30
   Rear Wheel Spindle, Replace . 7-30
   Shock Absorber, Replace 7-30
   Spindle Knuckle, Replace..... 7-30
   Stabilizer Shaft, Replace 7-32
   Tie Rod, Replace 7-32
   Tightening Specifications...... 7-33
   Transverse Leaf Spring,
   Replace 7-31
REAR DRIVE AXLES 27-1
**SERVICE REMINDER &
WARNING LAMP RESET
PROCEDURES** 0-34
SPECIFICATIONS
   Fluid Capacities & Cooling
   System Data.................. 7-4
   Front Wheel Alignment
   Specifications................. 7-3
   General Engine
   Specifications................. 7-2
   Lubricant Data................ 7-4
   Rear Wheel Alignment
   Specifications................. 7-3
   Tune Up Specifications 7-2
   Vehicle Ride Height
   Specifications................. 7-3
**TIRE PRESSURE
MONITORING SYSTEM** 20-1
**VEHICLE
IDENTIFICATION** 0-1
VEHICLE LIFT POINTS 0-51
**VEHICLE MAINTENANCE
SCHEDULES** 0-73
WHEEL ALIGNMENT
   Front Wheel Alignment........ 7-37
   Preliminary Inspection 7-37
   Rear Wheel Alignment 7-37
   Thrust Angle................. 7-37
   Wheel Alignment
   Specifications................. 7-3
**WIRE COLOR CODE
IDENTIFICATION** 0-63
5.7L ENGINE
   Camshaft, Replace 7-14
   Compression Pressure........ 7-8
   Cooling System Bleed 7-15
   Crankshaft Damper, Replace.. 7-13
   Crankshaft Rear Oil Seal,
   Replace 7-14

Page No.

   Crankshaft Seal, Replace 7-14
   Cylinder Head, Replace....... 7-11
   Engine Rebuilding
   Specifications................. 29-1
   Engine, Replace 7-9
   Engine Mount, Replace 7-8
   Exhaust Manifold, Replace.... 7-10
   Front Cover, Replace 7-13
   Fuel Filter, Replace 7-15
   Fuel Pump, Replace.......... 7-15
   Hydraulic Lifters, Replace 7-13
   Intake Manifold, Replace...... 7-10
   Main & Rod Bearings 7-14
   Oil Pan, Replace............. 7-14
   Oil Pump, Replace........... 7-14
   Piston & Rod Assembly 7-14
   Pistons, Pins & Rings 7-14
   Precautions.................. 7-8
   Push Rods 7-12
   Radiator, Replace............. 7-15
   Rear Cover, Replace.......... 7-13
   Rocker Arms.................. 7-12
   Serpentine Drive Belt 7-15
   Thermostat, Replace 7-15
   Tightening Specifications...... 7-16
   Timing Chain, Replace 7-13
   Valve Adjustment 7-12
   Valve Clearance
   Specifications................. 7-12
   Valve Cover, Replace......... 7-12
   Water Pump, Replace 7-15
**6.0L, 6.2L & 7.0L
ENGINES**
   Camshaft, Replace 7-22
   Compression Pressure........ 7-17
   Cooling System Bleed 7-23
   Crankshaft Damper, Replace.. 7-21
   Crankshaft Seal, Replace 7-22
   Cylinder Head, Replace....... 7-19
   Engine Rebuilding
   Specifications................. 29-1
   Engine, Replace 7-18
   Engine Mount, Replace 7-18
   Exhaust Manifold, Replace.... 7-19
   Front Cover, Replace 7-21
   Fuel Filter, Replace 7-26
   Fuel Pump, Replace.......... 7-24
   Hydraulic Lifters, Replace 7-21
   Intake Manifold, Replace...... 7-19
   Main & Rod Bearings 7-22
   Oil Pan, Replace............. 7-22
   Oil Pump, Replace........... 7-23
   Piston & Rod Assembly 7-22
   Pistons, Pins & Rings 7-22
   Precautions.................. 7-17
   Radiator, Replace............. 7-23
   Rocker Arms, Replace 7-20
   Serpentine Drive Belt 7-23
   Thermostat, Replace 7-23
   Tightening Specifications...... 7-27
   Timing Chain, Replace 7-21
   Valve Adjustment 7-20
   Valve Cover, Replace......... 7-20
   Water Pump, Replace 7-23

Specifications

GENERAL ENGINE SPECIFICATIONS

Year	Engine Liter	Engine VIN Code①	Fuel System	Bore & Stroke	Compression Ratio	Net Brake H.P. @ RPM②	Maximum Torque	Normal Oil Pressure, psi
2004	5.7L	G	SFI	3.90 × 3.62	10.1	345 @ 5200	④	③
	5.7L	S	SFI	3.90 × 3.62	10.5	405 @ 6000	400 @ 4800	③
2005	6.0L	U	SFI	4.00 × 3.62	10.9	400 @ 6000	400 @ 4400	③
2006	6.0L	U	SFI	4.00 × 3.62	10.9	400 @ 6000	400 @ 4400	③
	7.0L	Y/E	SFI	4.13 × 4.00	11:1	500 @ 6200	475 @ 4800	③
2007	6.0L	U	SFI	4.00 × 3.62	10.9	400 @ 6000	400 @ 4400	③
	7.0L	Y/E	SFI	4.13 × 4.00	11:1	505 @ 6300	470 @ 4800	③
2008	6.2L	W	SFI	4.06 × 3.62	10.7	430 @ 6000	424 @ 4400	③
	7.0L	Y/E	SFI	4.13 × 4.00	11:1	505 @ 6300	470 @ 4800	③

SFI — Sequential Fuel Injection
VIN — Vehicle Identification Number
① — The eighth digit of the VIN denotes engine code.
② — Ratings are net, as installed in vehicle.

③ — Engine hot, minimum oil pressure @ 1000 RPM, 6 psi.; @ 2000 RPM, 18 psi.; @ 4000 RPM, 24 psi.

④ — Manual transmission, 375 ft. lbs., @ 4400 RPM; automatic transmission, 360 ft. lbs., @ 4000 RPM.

TUNE UP SPECIFICATIONS

Year	Engine	Spark Plug Gap	Ignition Timing, Deg. BTDC Firing Order	Ignition Timing Man. Trans.	Ignition Timing Auto. Trans.	Ignition Timing Mark	Curb Idle Speed③ Man. Trans.	Curb Idle Speed③ Auto. Trans.	Fast Idle Speed Man. Trans.	Fast Idle Speed Auto. Trans.	Fuel Pump Pressure, psi	Valve Clearance, Inch
2004	5.7L	.060	1-8-7-2-6-5-4-3	①	①	—	④	④	④	④	55–61⑤	②
2005	6.0L	.04	1-8-7-2-6-5-4-3	①	①	—	④	④	④	④	55–61⑤	②
2006	6.0L	.04	1-8-7-2-6-5-4-3	①	①	—	④	④	④	④	55–61⑤	②
	7.0L	.04	1-8-7-2-6-5-4-3	①	①	—	④	④	④	④	55–61⑤	②
2007	6.0L	.04	1-8-7-2-6-5-4-3	①	①	—	④	④	④	④	55–62⑤	②
	7.0L	.04	1-8-7-2-6-5-4-3	①	①	—	④	④	④	④	55–62⑤	②
2008	6.2L	.04	1-8-7-2-6-5-4-3	①	①	—	④	④	④	④	55–62⑤	②
	7.0L	.04	1-8-7-2-6-5-4-3	①	①	—	④	④	④	④	55–62⑤	②

BTDC — Before Top Dead Center
VIN — Vehicle Identification Number
① — Computer controlled. No adjustment.
② — Equipped w/hydraulic lifters. No adjustment is required.

③ — When inspecting idle speed, set parking brake & block drive wheels.
④ — Idle speed is controlled by an idle speed control motor.
⑤ — With shop towel wrapped around

fuel pressure fitting to prevent fuel spillage, connect a suitable fuel pressure gauge. Inspect fuel pressure with ignition On, but engine not running.

FRONT WHEEL ALIGNMENT SPECIFICATIONS

Year	Models	Caster Angle, Degrees		Camber Angle, Degrees		Toe Per Wheel, Degrees		Steering Wheel Angle, Degrees	Ball Joint Wear	
		Limits	Desired	Limits	Desired	Limits	Desired		Upper	Lower
2004	FE1 & FE3	+7.9 to +6.9	7.4	.3 to -.7	-.2	.28 to -.12	.08	1.0 to -1.0	①	①
	FE4 (Z06)	+7.4 to +6.4	6.9	.3 to -.7	-.2	.14 to -.06	.08	1.0 to -1.0	①	①
2005	All	8.5 to 7.3	7.9	.15 to -1.05	-.45	.30 to -.10	.10	-3.5 to 3.5	①	①
2006–08	FE1/FE2/FE3	7.3 to 8.5	7.9	.15 to -1.05	-.45	.30 to -.20	.10	-3.5 to 3.5	①	①
	FE4	7.4 to 8.6	8.0	.5 to -1.6	-1	.300 to -.20	.10	-3.5 to 3.5	①	①

① — Refer to Front Suspension & Steering for proper wear.

REAR WHEEL ALIGNMENT SPECIFICATIONS

Year	Models	Camber Angle, Degrees		Toe Per Wheel, Degrees		Thrust Angle, Degrees	
		Limits	Desired	Limits	Desired	Limits	Desired
2004	①	-.68 to .32	-.18	-.22 to +.18	-.02	-.1 to +.1	0
	②	-1.18 to -.18	-.68	-.22 to +.18	-.02	-.1 to +.1	0
2005	All	-.95 to .05	-.45	-.2 to +.2	0	-.2 to +.1	0
2006	①	-.95 to .05	-.45	-.2 to +.2	0	-.2 to +.2	0
	②	-1.5 to -.5	-1	-.2 to +.2	0	-.2 to +.2	0
2007–08	FE1/FE2/FE3	-.95 to .05	-.45	-.2 to +.2	0	-.2 to +.2	0
	FE4	-1.5 to -.5	-1	-.2 to +.2	0	-.2 to +.2	0

① — Except Special Ride & Handling suspension.

② — Special Ride & Handling suspension.

VEHICLE RIDE HEIGHT SPECIFICATIONS

Model	Year	Body Style	Manufacturer's Original Tire Size	Measurement Points & Specifications①③					
				Front			Rear		
				Dim.④	Spec.		Dim.④	Spec.	
					Inches	mm		Inches	mm
Corvette	2004–08	All	②	C	5.9	150	D	5.31	135

A Dim. — Measurement From Front Wheel Center to Check Point On Rocker Panel

B Dim. — Measurement From Rear Wheel Center to Check Point On Rocker Panel

C Dim. — Ground to Rocker Panel, Front

D Dim. — Ground to Rocker Panel, Rear

Dim. — Dimension

① — ± .39 inch (10 mm) front to rear & side to side.

② — See door sticker or inside of glove box for manufacturers original tire size specifications. If tires on vehicle do not match manufacturers original tire size & measurement is not within limits, it will be required to refer to the Non-Standard Tire & Wheel Size Adjustment To Ride Height Specification & Tire Size Adjustment Charts in the front of this manual for approximate changes in ride height specifications.

③ — Measurement is with fuel, radiator coolant and engine oil full, spare tire, jack, hand tools and mats in designated positions and tires properly inflated.

④ — Refer to **Fig. A**.

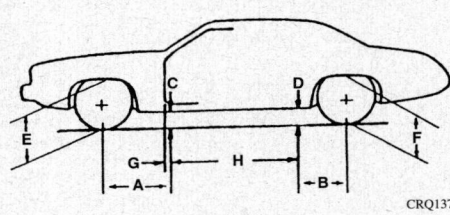

CRQ137

Fig. A

FLUID CAPACITIES & COOLING SYSTEM DATA

Year	Model Or Engine (VIN) ①	Coolant Capacity, Qts.	Coolant Type	Radiator Cap-Relief Pressure, psi	Thermo. Opening Temp. °F	Fuel Tank, Gals.	Engine Oil, Qts.② Less Filter Change	Engine Oil, Qts.② With Filter Change	Man Trans., Pts.	Auto. Trans., Qts.③ Drain & Refill	Auto. Trans., Qts.③ Total Capacity	Rear Axle, Pts.
2004	5.7L (G)	⑤	Dex-Cool	15	187	18.5	6.0④	6.5④	8.2	5.0	10.8	3.4
	5.7L (S)	⑤	Dex-Cool	15	187	18.5	6.0④	6.5④	8.2	5.0	10.8	3.4
2005	6.0L (U)	12.6	Dex-Cool	18	195	18.0	5.0	5.5	8.2	5.0	10.8	3.6
2006	6.0L (U)	12.6	Dex-Cool	18	195	18.0	5.0	5.5	8.2	6.5	12.5	3.6
	7.0L(Y/E)	12.6	Dex-Cool	⑥	188	18.0	7.5	8.0	8.2	6.5	12.5	—
2007	6.0L (U)⑦	12.6	Dex-Cool	⑥	188	18.0	5.0	5.5	7.2	6.5	12.5	3.4
	6.0L (U)⑧	12.6	Dex-Cool	⑥	188	18.0	—	6.0	8.4	6.5	12.5	3.4
	7.0L(Y/E)	12.6	Dex-Cool	⑥	188	18.0	7.5	8.0	9.0	6.5	12.5	5.4
2008	6.2L (W)⑦	12.6	Dex-Cool	⑥	188	18.0	5.0	5.5	7.2	6.5	12.5	3.4
	6.2L (W)⑧	12.6	Dex-Cool	⑥	188	18.0	—	6.0	8.4	6.5	12.5	3.4
	7.0L(Y/E)	12.6	Dex-Cool	⑥	188	18.0	7.5	8.0	9.0	6.5	12.5	5.4

VIN — Vehicle Identification Number
① — The eighth digit of the VIN denotes engine code.
② — After refilling, inspect oil level again.
③ — Approximate. Make final inspection w/dipstick.
④ — Recommended engine oil SG SAE 5W-30 synthetic engine oil meeting GM specification GM4718M.
⑤ — On models w/A/T, 11.5 qts.; w/M/T, 11.8 qts.
⑥ — Refer to radiator cap for pressure specification.
⑦ — Except Engine Performance Package Z51.
⑧ — Engine Performance Package Z51.

LUBRICANT DATA

Year	Lubricant Type — Transmission Automatic	Lubricant Type — Transmission Manual	Rear Axle	Power Steering System	Brake System
2004–05	Dexron III	Dexron III	①	②	DOT 3
2006	Dexron VI	Dexron III	①	②	DOT 3
2007–08	Dexron VI	③	④	②	DOT 3

① — 75W-90 synthetic axle lubricant P/N 12378261, or an equivalent meeting GM specification 9986115. When completely draining & filling add 4 ounces of lubricant additive P/N 1052358, or equivalent.
② — Power steering fluid P/N 89021184 or equivalents.
③ — GM Manual Transmission Fluid P/N 88861800.
④ — SAE 75W-90 Synthetic Axle Lubricant GM Part No. U.S. 89021677.

Electrical

NOTE: On Air Bag Equipped Models, Refer To "Air Bag System Precautions" Located In The Front Of This Manual For System Disarming & Arming Procedures.

NOTE: Refer To "Computer Relearn Procedures" Located In The Front Of This Manual When Battery Power To The Computer Has Been Interrupted.

NOTE: Prior To Performing Any Service Operations Listed In This Section, Consult The "Technical Service Bulletins" Section For Related Information.

INDEX

	Page No.		Page No.		Page No.
Air Bag System (Volume 2)	4-1	Fuse Panel & Flasher Location	7-5	Starter Motors	18-1
Air Conditioning	16-1	Headlamp Switch, Replace	7-5	Starter, Replace	7-5
Alternator, Replace	7-5	Heater Core, Replace	7-6	Steering Columns	20-1
Alternators	19-1	Instrument Cluster, Replace	7-6	Steering Wheel, Replace	7-6
Blower Motor, Replace	7-6	2004	7-6	Installation	7-6
Cooling Fans	17-1	2005–08	7-6	2004–06	7-6
Cruise Control (Volume 2)	2-1	Multi-Function Switch, Replace	7-5	2007–08	7-6
Dash Gauges (Volume 2)	1-1	Passive Restraint Systems		Removal	7-6
Dash Panel Service		(Volume 2)	4-1	2004–06	7-6
(Volume 2)	5-1	Precautions	7-5	2007–08	7-6
Dimmer Switch, Replace	7-6	Air Bag Systems	7-5	Turn Signal Switch, Replace	7-6
2004–06	7-6	Battery Ground Cable	7-5	Wiper Motor, Replace	7-6
2007–08	7-6	Radio, Replace	7-6	Wiper Switch, Replace	7-6
Evaporator Core, Replace	7-7	Relay Center Location	7-5	Wiper Systems (Volume 2)	3-1
Fuel Pump Relay Location	7-5	Speed Controls (Volume 2)	2-1		

PRECAUTIONS

Air Bag Systems

Refer to "Air Bag System Precautions" in the front of this manual for system disarming and arming procedures.

Battery Ground Cable

Prior to service, record radio presets, then disconnect battery ground cable and isolate as required.

FUSE PANEL & FLASHER LOCATION

The fuse panel is located behind the far righthand corner of the instrument panel. The turn signal and hazard flasher is incorporated into the hazard warning switch, which is located behind the center air vent.

FUEL PUMP RELAY LOCATION

The fuel pump relay is located in the underhood electrical center.

RELAY CENTER LOCATION

The relay center, or underhood electrical center, is located on the righthand side of the engine compartment.

STARTER
REPLACE

1. Disconnect battery ground cable.
2. Remove righthand catalytic converter.
3. Remove positive battery cable nut.
4. Remove positive battery cable terminal and engine harness leads from solenoid.
5. Remove S terminal nut.
6. Remove purple wire lead and washer from solenoid.
7. Remove starter motor mounting bolts, then the starter motor.
8. Reverse procedure to install.

ALTERNATOR
REPLACE

1. Mark running direction, then remove drive belt.
2. Disconnect alternator electrical connector.

3. Remove battery feed terminal nut, then the battery feed cable.
4. Remove alternator mounting bolts, then the alternator.
5. Reverse procedure to install.

HEADLAMP SWITCH
REPLACE

Refer to "Multi-Function Switch, Replace" for headlamp switch replacement procedure.

MULTI-FUNCTION SWITCH
REPLACE

1. Remove steering column upper and lower trim covers.
2. Remove wire harness straps from steering column tilt head assembly and column.
3. Remove wire harness assembly from wire harness strap.
4. Remove two pan head tapping screws.
5. Remove multi-function turn signal switch assembly.
6. Reverse procedure to install.

TURN SIGNAL SWITCH
REPLACE

Refer to "Multi-Function Switch, Replace" for turn signal switch procedure.

DIMMER SWITCH
REPLACE

2004-06

1. Remove instrument panel cluster as outlined under "Instrument Cluster, Replace."
2. Disconnect electrical connectors at instrument panel dimmer switch and driver information center switch.
3. Remove mounting screws and instrument panel dimmer switch.
4. Reverse procedure to install.

2007-08

1. Remove righthand side front floor console side trim panel.
2. Remove center console accessory trim plate.
3. Remove instrument panel dimmer switch using a flat-bladed tool in order to release the switch from trim plate.
4. Disconnect electrical connectors, then remove dimmer switch from vehicle.
5. Reverse procedure to install.

STEERING WHEEL
REPLACE

Removal

2004-06

1. Remove driver's air bag module as outlined in "Passive Restraint Systems."
2. Remove horn electrical connector.
3. Install steering column lock pin tool No. J42640 or equivalent, to steering column.
4. Remove steering wheel set nut. Discard nut.
5. Remove steering wheel using a suitable puller.
6. Remove steering wheel.

2007-08

1. Remove driver's air bag module as outlined in "Passive Restraint Systems."
2. Remove and discard steering wheel retaining nut.
3. Mark steering wheel mounting to column shaft orientation.
4. Remove steering wheel using puller tool No. J 1859-A with puller legs tool No. J 36541-A, or equivalent.

Installation

2004-06

1. Install steering wheel to steering column observing alignment marks.
2. Install new steering wheel set nut.

3. Remove steering column lock pin tool No. J 42640 or equivalent, from steering column.
4. Connect horn electrical connector.
5. Install driver's side air bag module as outlined in "Passive Restraint Systems."

2007-08

1. Ensure steering wheel is properly aligned to column.
2. Install steering wheel with a new retaining nut. **Do not use old nut. Always install a new one.**
3. Install driver's side air bag module as outlined in "Passive Restraint Systems."

INSTRUMENT CLUSTER
REPLACE

2004

1. Remove instrument panel upper trim pad.
2. **On models equipped with Head Up Display (HUD),** carefully lift HUD electrical harness from between cluster and display, then disconnect electrical connector.
3. **On all models,** remove Instrument Panel Cluster (IPC) to steering column bracket mounting screws.
4. Lift rear of IPC slightly to release locator tab, then lift IPC to access and disconnect electrical connectors.
5. Remove IPC.
6. Reverse procedure to install, ensuring cluster retaining tab is properly positioned to steering column bracket.

2005-08

1. Lower the steering column to its lowest position.
2. Pull outward on lower edge of trim panel and release lower clips.
3. Disconnect electrical connectors, then remove instrument panel cluster trim plate.
4. Remove retaining bolts, then the instrument panel cluster.
5. Reverse procedure to install.

RADIO
REPLACE

1. Remove cover from instrument panel electrical center.
2. Remove Radio/CD minifuse No. 5 from instrument panel electrical center.
3. Remove I/P accessory trim plate.
4. Remove HVAC control module.
5. Remove radio to instrument panel center support bracket retaining screws.
6. Pull radio control from center support bracket, then disconnect electrical connectors and antenna cable connector from radio.
7. Remove radio.
8. Reverse procedure to install.

WIPER MOTOR
REPLACE

1. Remove wiper arm assemblies.
2. Remove air inlet screen.
3. Remove wiper motor module.
4. Disconnect wiper transmission linkage from crank arm using linkage separator tool No. J 39232, or equivalent.
5. Remove three wiper motor to wiper motor module mounting screws.
6. Remove wiper motor.
7. Reverse procedure to install, noting the following:
   a. Install motor into module.
   b. Connect linkage to crank arm using linkage installer tool No. J 39529, or equivalent.

WIPER SWITCH
REPLACE

1. Remove tilt wheel lever as outlined in "Steering Columns" chapter.
2. Remove driver's side knee bolster trim panel.
3. Remove steering column upper and lower covers.
4. Disconnect wiring harness electrical connector.
5. Release upper and lower mounting clips, then slide wiper washer switch from steering column lock module.
6. Reverse procedure to install.

BLOWER MOTOR
REPLACE

1. Remove righthand insulator panel.
2. Disconnect blower motor electrical connector.
3. Remove blower motor retaining screws.
4. Remove blower motor from HVAC module.
5. Reverse procedure to install.

HEATER CORE
REPLACE

1. Evacuate and recover air conditioning system refrigerant as outlined in "Air Conditioning" chapter.
2. Raise and support vehicle.
3. Drain cooling system.
4. Lower vehicle.
5. Disconnect front evaporator inlet line from body retaining clip.
6. Disconnect refrigerant pressure sensor electrical connector.
7. Locate the A/C coupling assembly locking tab access slots.
8. Carefully insert a small flat-bladed screwdriver into first locking tab access slot and gently lift locking tab to release lock.
9. Carefully insert a small flat-bladed screwdriver into second locking tab access slot and gently lift locking tab to release lock.
10. Open and remove the A/C coupling assembly from the A/C refrigerant component.
11. Disconnect front evaporator inlet line from the evaporator rear line assembly.

12. Remove and discard O-rings.
13. Cap or tape front evaporate inlet line.
14. Disconnect A/C compressor line from evaporator rear line assembly.
15. Remove and discard O-rings.
16. Cap or tape front evaporator line and A/C compressor line.
17. Remove heater pipe bracket retaining nut from cowl stud.
18. Remove thermal expansion valve (TXV) block fitting but.
19. Disconnect evaporator rear line assembly from TXV.
20. Disconnect evaporator rear line assembly from retainer bracket stud.
21. Remove rear evaporator line assembly from vehicle.
22. Remove and discard seal washers.
23. Cap or tape TXV.
24. Release and reposition heater inlet and outlet hose clamps using tool no. J 38185 or equivalent.
25. Separate heater hoses from heater pipes.
26. Cap or plug open heater hoses.
27. Remove heater pipe assembly to heater core retaining bolt.
28. Disconnect heater pipe assembly from heater pipe bracket retainer.
29. Disconnect heater pipe assembly from heater core.
30. Remove heater pipe assembly from vehicle.
31. Remove and discard sealing washers.
32. Cap or plug heater core.
33. Remove evaporator drain tube from HVAC module.
34. Remove instrument panel as outlined in "Dash Panel Service" chapter.
35. Remove air distribution duct.
36. Remove Discharge Temperature Management (DTM) sensors from air distribution duct.
37. Remove retainers from upper defogger on left side window.
38. Disconnect and remove upper defogger outlet duct.
39. Disconnect Head-Up Display (HUD) electrical connector.
40. Remove HUD retaining nuts.
41. Remove screw that secures HUD to steering column bracket.
42. Remove retainer from lower defogger outlet duct.
43. Disconnect and remove outlet duct from defroster duct.
44. Remove retaining screws from floor air outlet duct, then the outlet duct.

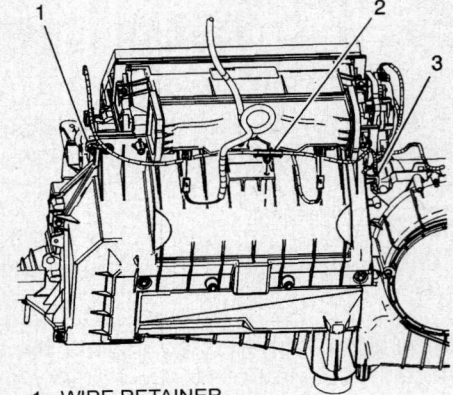

1- WIRE RETAINER
2- RETAINER PIN
3- WIRE RETAINER

ARM0500000000041

Fig. 1 Heater core cover wiring location

45. Remove retainers from upper outlet duct on right side window defogger.
46. Disconnect and remove defogger upper outlet from defogger lower outlet duct.
47. Disconnect defogger lower outlet duct from knee bolster bracket.
48. Disconnect defogger lower outlet duct from defroster duct.
49. Remove SIR bracket as outlined in "Passive Restraint Systems" chapter.
50. Remove retaining screws from floor air outlet duct, then the air outlet duct.
51. Remove defroster duct retaining screws, then the defroster duct.
52. Disconnect blower motor electrical connector.
53. Remove blower motor retaining screws, then the blower motor from HVAC module.
54. Remove retaining and sealing nuts from cowl.
55. Remove retaining bolts from upper instrument panel cross vehicle beam.
56. Completely loosen studs on HVAC module.
57. Loosen front lefthand recirculation housing retaining screw. **Reposition HVAC module rearward to access front lefthand screw. Front lefthand retaining tab of recirculation housing is slotted.**
58. Disconnect recirculation actuator electrical connector.

59. Disconnect HVAC module wiring harness from recirculation housing.
60. Remove remaining recirculation housing retaining screws.
61. Remove recirculation housing from HVAC module.
62. Reposition center console wiring harness and corresponding electrical connectors to sides of HVAC module and forward of lower tie bar. **Reposition center console wiring harness that runs beneath HVAC module to aide in HVAC module removal.**
63. Carefully remove HVAC module from vehicle.
64. Remove and discard air inlet, drain and plumbing seals from HVAC module.
65. Remove and discard HVAC module assembly foam seal.
66. Disconnect discharge temperature management (DTM) sensor electrical connectors.
67. Disconnect HVAC module wiring harness wiring pin from HVAC module, **Fig. 1.**
68. Disconnect wiring harness from heater core cover wire harness retainer and reposition wiring harness aside, **Fig. 1.**
69. Disconnect wiring harness from heater core cover wire harness retainer and position aside, **Fig. 1.**
70. Remove heater cover screws, then the cover from HVAC module.
71. Remove heater core from HVAC module.
72. Reverse procedure to install.

EVAPORATOR CORE
REPLACE

1. Remove HVAC module as outlined in "Heater Core, Replace."
2. Remove and discard HVAC module assembly foam seal.
3. Remove thermal expansion valve (TXV) mounting bolts.
4. Remove TXV from evaporator core.
5. Remove and discard sealing washers.
6. Disconnect discharge temperature management sensor electrical connectors.
7. Separate HVAC module upper case from HVAC module lower case.
8. Remove evaporator core from HVAC module.
9. Reverse procedure to install.

5.7L Engine

NOTE: On Air Bag Equipped Models, Refer To "Air Bag System Precautions" Located In The Front Of This Manual For System Disarming & Arming Procedures.

NOTE: Refer To "Computer Relearn Procedures" Located In The Front Of This Manual When Battery Power To The Computer Has Been Interrupted.

NOTE: Prior To Performing Any Service Operations Listed In This Section, Consult The "Technical Service Bulletins" Section For Related Information.

INDEX

	Page No.		Page No.		Page No.
Camshaft, Replace	7-14	Righthand	7-11	Rear Cover, Replace	7-13
Compression Pressure	7-8	Front Cover, Replace	7-13	Installation	7-13
Cooling System Bleed	7-15	Installation	7-13	Removal	7-13
Crankshaft Damper, Replace	7-13	Removal	7-13	Rocker Arms	7-12
Crankshaft Rear Oil Seal,		Fuel Filter, Replace	7-15	Installation	7-12
Replace	7-14	Fuel Pump, Replace	7-15	Removal	7-12
Crankshaft Seal, Replace	7-14	Hydraulic Lifters, Replace	7-13	Serpentine Drive Belt	7-15
Cylinder Head, Replace	7-11	Intake Manifold, Replace	7-10	Belt Replacement	7-15
Lefthand	7-11	Main & Rod Bearings	7-14	Belt Routing	7-15
Installation	7-11	Oil Pan, Replace	7-14	Thermostat, Replace	7-15
Removal	7-11	Oil Pump, Replace	7-14	Tightening Specifications	7-16
Righthand	7-11	Piston & Rod Assembly	7-14	Timing Chain, Replace	7-13
Installation	7-11	Pistons, Pins & Rings	7-14	Installation	7-14
Removal	7-11	Precautions	7-8	Removal	7-13
Engine Rebuilding		Battery Ground Cable	7-8	Valve Adjustment	7-12
Specifications	29-1	Fuel System Pressure Relief	7-8	Valve Clearance Specifications	7-12
Engine, Replace	7-9	Push Rods	7-12	Valve Cover, Replace	7-12
Engine Mount, Replace	7-8	Installation	7-12	Lefthand	7-12
Exhaust Manifold, Replace	7-10	Removal	7-12	Righthand	7-12
Lefthand	7-10	Radiator, Replace	7-15	Water Pump, Replace	7-15

PRECAUTIONS

Fuel System Pressure Relief

Failure to relieve system pressure prior to disconnecting fuel system components may cause fire or personal injury.
1. Record radio presets, then disconnect and isolate battery ground cable.
2. Remove fuel tank filler cap to release fuel tank pressure.
3. Remove lefthand fuel rail cover.
4. Prior to disconnecting fuel line, position shop towel over fitting.
5. Connect pressure gauge tool No. J 34730-1A, or equivalent, to pressure tap on fuel rail.
6. Position bleed hose into suitable container.
7. Slowly relieve fuel system pressure.

Battery Ground Cable

Prior to service, record radio presets, then disconnect battery ground cable and isolate as required.

COMPRESSION PRESSURE

When measuring compression, lowest cylinder must be within 70% of the highest cylinder with a minimum pressure of 100 psi. Compression test results will fall into one of the following categories:
1. Normally, compression builds up quickly and evenly to specifications on each cylinder.
2. If piston rings are faulty, compression will be low on first stroke, then build up on following strokes but will not reach specifications. Improvement is considerable with addition of approximately three squirts oil.
3. If valves are faulty, compression will be low on first stroke and will not tend to build up on following strokes. It will not improve much with addition of oil.
4. Ensure battery is fully charged.
5. Bring engine to operating temperature.
6. Disconnect electrical connector at crankshaft ignition timing sensor.
7. Disable fuel injection system.
8. Remove spark plugs.
9. Ensure throttle is wide open.
10. Install compression gauge tool No. J 38722, or equivalent.
11. Crank engine through four complete compression strokes, then record results for each cylinder.

ENGINE MOUNT
REPLACE

1. Remove alternator from accessory mount bracket.
2. Remove windshield washer reservoir.
3. Disconnect coolant switch electrical connector and position wiring aside.
4. Disconnect headlamp electrical connector and position wiring aside.
5. Support engine using engine support tool Nos. J 41803 and J 28467-B, or equivalent.
6. Raise and support vehicle.
7. Remove front wheels.
8. Remove tie rod end nuts.
9. Remove tie rod ends from steering knuckles using separator tool No. J 42188, or equivalent.
10. Remove stabilizer bar bolts and straps.
11. Disconnect stabilizer from cradle.
12. Remove power steering cooler bolts.
13. Disconnect power steering cooler from cradle and position it upward.
14. Remove power steering gear from cradle and position it upward.

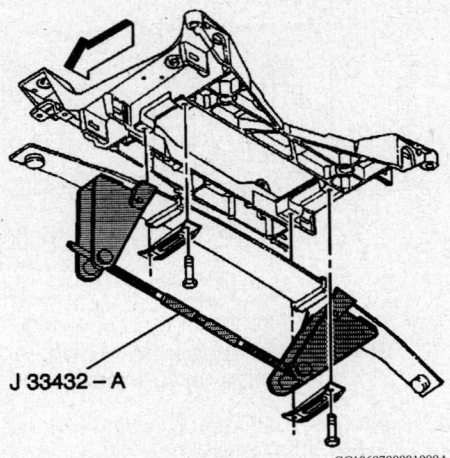

Fig. 1   Transverse leaf spring compression

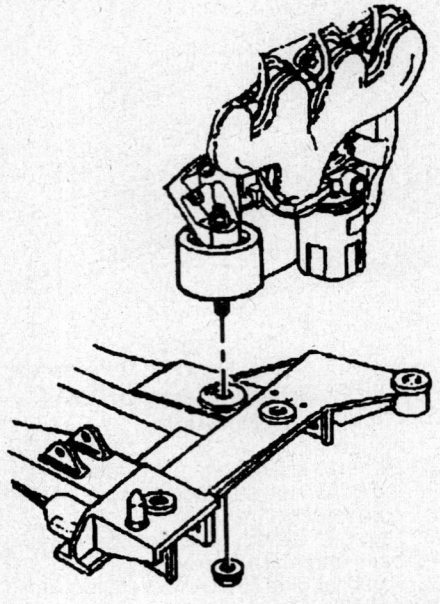

GC1069700889000X

Fig. 2   Engine mount to cradle removal

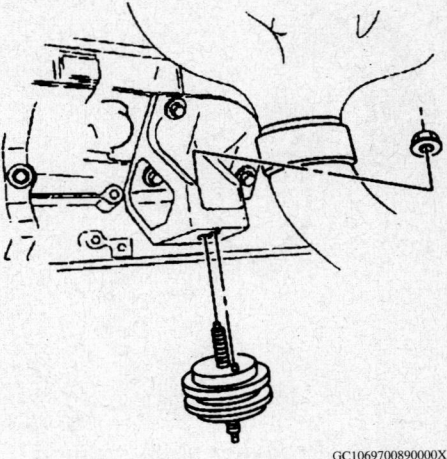

GC1069700890000X

Fig. 3   Upper engine mount removal

15. Compress spring using transverse leaf spring compressor tool No. J 33432-A, or equivalent, **Fig. 1.**
16. Remove shock absorber lower mounting bolts.
17. Loosen, but do not remove, lower ball joint nuts.
18. Separate lower ball joints using separator tool No. J 42188, or equivalent.
19. Remove tool and ball joint nuts.
20. Disconnect crossmember electrical connectors.
21. Disconnect cradle electrical harnesses.
22. Remove brake pressure valve modulator valve bracket bolts, then position valve and bracket away from crossmember.
23. Remove motor mount to cradle nuts, **Fig. 2.**
24. Support cradle using suitable transmission jack, or equivalent.
25. Remove mounting nuts and cradle.
26. Remove upper engine mount nut, **Fig. 3.**
27. Remove engine mount.
28. Remove engine block bolts and motor mount bracket.
29. Reverse procedure to install.

ENGINE

REPLACE

1. Raise and support vehicle.
2. Drain coolant into suitable container.
3. Lower vehicle.
4. Recover air conditioning refrigerant charge.
5. Disconnect electrical connectors at IAT and MAF sensors.
6. Disconnect air intake duct fuel pressure regulator purge tube.
7. Position air intake duct and air cleaner forward.
8. Remove radiator as outlined in "Radiator, Replace."
9. Remove EBTCM/BPMV and bracket, then position brake pipes aside, cap and plug lines.
10. Remove serpentine belt as outlined in "Serpentine Drive Belt."
11. Remove lefthand fuel line from con-

nector at front of firewall. Cap and plug fittings and openings.
12. Remove engine appearance covers.
13. Disconnect fuel lines at fuel rail. Cap and plug fittings and openings.
14. Disconnect radiator hoses and heater hoses at water pump.
15. Disconnect the following electrical connectors:
    a. Fuel injectors.
    b. Ignition coil main connectors.
    c. EVAP solenoid.
    d. Electric throttle motor.
    e. Throttle position sensor.
    f. ECT sensor.
    g. Air conditioning compressor.
    h. Alternator.
16. Remove alternator rear bracket bolts and bracket.
17. Remove alternator mounting bolts then the alternator as outlined in "Alternator, Replace" in "Electrical" section.
18. Disconnect brake booster vacuum hose.
19. Remove steering intermediate shaft to steering gear bolt.
20. Disconnect steering intermediate shaft from steering gear and position it to lefthand onto frame rail.
21. Disconnect lefthand exhaust manifold AIR hose.
22. Raise and support vehicle, then remove front tires and wheels.
23. Disconnect and unclip intermediate exhaust pipes HO2S electrical connectors.
24. Remove intermediate exhaust pipes.
25. Remove mounting bolts and closeout panel.
26. Disconnect starter electrical connectors and wiring.
27. Remove starter mounting bolts, then the starter as outlined in "Starter, Replace" in "Electrical" section.
28. Disconnect righthand and rear engine

block wiring harness clips.
29. Disconnect oil level, CKP and righthand HO2S sensors electrical connectors.
30. Remove mounting bolt and air conditioning compressor hose.
31. Disconnect engine oil temperature and lefthand HO2S sensors electrical connectors.
32. Remove mounting bolts and straps, then disconnect front stabilizer bar from cradle.
33. Disconnect electric cooling fans' electrical connectors and harness.
34. Slide up and remove electric cooling fans.
35. Loosen nuts and remove tie rod ends from steering knuckles using ball joint separator tool No. J 42188, or equivalent.
36. Disconnect ABS electrical, EVO and RTD connectors clips from cradle.
37. Remove lower shock absorber mounting bolts.
38. Compress and remove front transverse spring using transverse spring compressor tool No. J33432-A, or equivalent, **Fig. 1.**
39. **On models equipped with automatic transmission,** proceed as follows:
    a. Disconnect fluid cooler lines at bellhousing junction.
    b. Disconnect cooler pipe clamps from front and rear of engine oil pan.
    c. Disconnect cooler pipes from radiator.
    d. Remove two plugs in driveline support.
    e. Install M10 1.5 × 2.166 inches, or longer bolt, in each plug location, **Fig. 4,** and **torque** to 26 ft. lbs.
    f. Remove bellhousing lower inspection cover.
    g. Position transmission flexplate hub collar downward to access and loosen mounting bolt.
    h. Unclip wiring harness from engine and position it to driveline.
40. **On models equipped with manual transmission,** proceed as follows:
    a. Unclip hydraulic clutch actuator

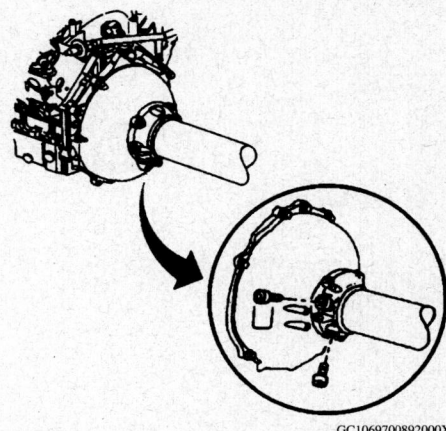

Fig. 4 Propeller shaft support bolt installation

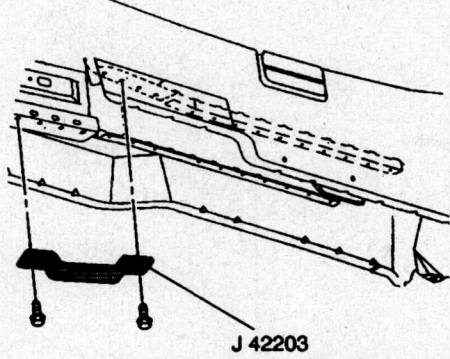

J 42203

GC1069700893000X

Fig. 5 Driveline support tool installation

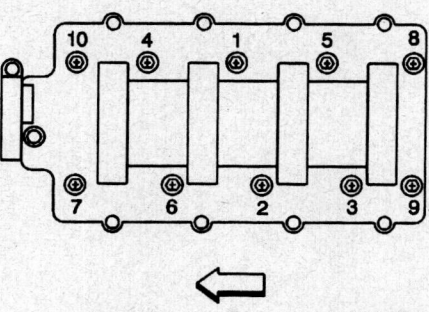

GC1069700894000A

Fig. 6 Intake manifold bolt tightening sequence

hose from bellhousing clip.
b. Depress white circular release ring on actuator hose using hydraulic clutch line separator tool No. J 36221, or equivalent, while pulling lightly on master cylinder hose. This will separate two portions.
c. Plug both open hydraulic hose ends.
d. Remove driveline support bellhousing bolts.
41. **On all models,** install driveline support tool No. J 42203, or equivalent, to closeout panel flange, **Fig. 5. Do not support engine weight with driveline line support tool.**
42. Slowly lower vehicle on to engine support table tools Nos. J 39580 and No. J 39580-500, or equivalents.
43. Remove front and rear cradle nuts by hand.
44. Partially raise vehicle.
45. Remove and position AIR tube bracket bolt to access and remove lefthand rear ground strap at cylinder head.
46. Disconnect following electrical connectors:
a. Engine oil pressure sensor.
b. Camshaft position sensor.
c. MAP sensor.
d. Knock sensor.
e. Ground on rear of lefthand head.
f. All remaining electrical connections.
47. Remove front driveline support bolts.
48. Pry engine loose from driveline using suitable flat-bladed screwdriver, between edge of driveline support and bellhousing.
49. Slowly and carefully pull engine away from driveshaft.
50. Slowly raise vehicle as soon as input shaft clears bellhousing.
51. Slide engine and cradle forward to clear driveshaft spline.
52. **Ensure wiring harnesses are free and clear,** then carefully raise vehicle completely off engine and cradle.
53. Remove power steering pump using pulley removal tool No. J 25034-B, or equivalent.
54. Remove mounting bolts, then position power steering pump and reservoir aside.

55. Remove air conditioning belt, mounting bolts, nut, stud and air conditioning compressor.
56. Remove exhaust manifolds' mounting bolts and AIR tube.
57. Install engine lifting brackets tool No. J 41798, or equivalent.
58. Install suitable lifting device to lifting brackets.
59. Mark locations, disconnect wires and remove spark plugs.
60. Remove cradle mount nuts and engine.
61. Reverse procedure to install, noting the following:
a. **Only use hand tools to install new engine cradle nuts.**
b. **On models equipped with automatic transmission,** tighten flexplate hub collar bolt by hand after bellhousing to driveline support bolts have been tightened.
c. After running engine to operating temperature and allowing to cool to room temperature.

INTAKE MANIFOLD
REPLACE

1. Raise and support vehicle.
2. Drain cooling system into suitable container and lower vehicle.
3. Disconnect IAT and MAF sensors electrical connectors.
4. Disconnect air intake duct fuel regulator purge line.
5. Remove air intake duct and air cleaner.
6. Remove fuel rail covers.
7. Disconnect fuel rail lines. Cap and plug open fittings.
8. Remove vacuum and PCV hoses.
9. Remove throttle body coolant outlet hose.
10. Disconnect fuel injector and knock sensor electrical connectors.
11. Disconnect remaining intake manifold electrical connectors.
12. Remove intake manifold bolts and fuel rail stop bracket.
13. Remove lefthand and righthand valve covers' PCV valve pipe.
14. Remove throttle body coolant air bleed hose.
15. Remove throttle body heater outlet hose.
16. Remove intake manifold and gaskets.

17. Remove manifold to cylinder head gaskets from intake manifold.
18. Reverse procedure to install, noting the following:
a. Install new intake manifold to cylinder head gaskets.
b. Apply threadlocker P/N 12345383, or equivalent, to intake manifold bolt threads.
c. **Torque** intake manifold bolts to 44 inch lbs., in sequence, **Fig. 6.**
d. Final **torque** bolts to 89 inch lbs., in sequence.
e. Lubricate MAP sensor grommet with suitable clean engine oil before installing.
f. Install new fuel injector O-rings lubricated with suitable clean engine oil.

EXHAUST MANIFOLD
REPLACE
Lefthand

1. Raise and support vehicle.
2. Remove lefthand intermediate exhaust pipe flange nuts from exhaust manifold studs.
3. Disconnect HO2S electrical connector and remove HO2S.
4. Lower vehicle and remove lefthand fuel rail cover.
5. Remove accessory drive belt as outlined in "Serpentine Drive Belt."
6. Remove alternator as outlined in "Alternator, Replace" in "Electrical" section.
7. Remove Secondary Air Injection (SAI) hoses.
8. Remove SAI pipe, bolts and gasket, then position aside.
9. Remove spark plug wires.
10. Remove spark plugs.
11. Remove No. 5 coil bolts and position aside.
12. Remove exhaust manifold and mounting bolts.
13. Reverse procedure to install, noting the following:
a. Install new exhaust manifold gasket.
b. Apply threadlocker P/N 12345493, or equivalent, to exhaust manifold bolt threads.
c. **Torque** exhaust manifold bolts to 11 ft. lbs., beginning with center two

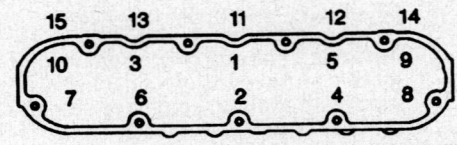

Fig. 7 Cylinder head bolt tightening sequence

bolts, then alternate from side to side and work toward outside bolts.

d. Final **Torque** to 18 ft. lbs., in sequence.

e. Bend over exposed edge of exhaust manifold gasket at rear of lefthand cylinder head using suitable flat punch.

f. Install AIR pipe and gasket and **torque** to 15 ft. lbs.

Righthand

1. Raise and support vehicle.
2. Remove intermediate exhaust pipe nuts from exhaust manifold studs.
3. Remove HO2S.
4. Lower vehicle.
5. Remove righthand exhaust manifold AIR pipe, bolts and gasket.
6. Remove spark plug wires from spark plugs.
7. Remove engine oil dipstick.
8. Remove mounting bolt and dipstick tube.
9. Remove exhaust manifold and mounting bolts.
10. Reverse procedure to install, noting the following:
    a. Install new exhaust manifold gasket.
    b. Apply threadlocker P/N 12345493, or equivalent, to exhaust manifold bolt threads.
    c. **Torque** exhaust manifold bolts to 11 ft. lbs., beginning with center two bolts, then alternate from side to side and work toward outside bolts.
    d. Final **torque** to 18 ft. lbs., in sequence.
    e. Bend over exposed edge of exhaust manifold gasket at front of righthand cylinder head using suitable flat punch.
    f. Install AIR pipe and gasket and **torque** to 15 ft. lbs.

CYLINDER HEAD

REPLACE

This procedure has been revised by a Technical Service Bulletin.

Lefthand

REMOVAL

1. Remove valve cover, rocker arms, pedestal and pushrods.
2. Remove lefthand exhaust manifold as outlined in "Exhaust Manifold, Replace."
3. Remove intake manifold as outlined in "Intake Manifold, Replace."
4. Remove vapor vent pipe.

5. Remove power steering pump pulley using pulley puller tool No. J 25034-B, or equivalent.
6. Remove power steering pump mounting bolts.
7. Remove power steering reservoir bracket bolts, then position pump and reservoir aside.
8. Remove mounting bolts and lower accessory mounting bracket.
9. Remove cylinder head rear ground wire bolt.
10. Remove spark plugs.
11. Remove and discard cylinder head bolts.
12. Remove cylinder head.

INSTALLATION

1. Clean cylinder head bolt holes using compressed air.
2. Inspect cylinder head locating pins for proper installation.
3. Install new lefthand cylinder head gasket onto locating pins. When properly installed, tab on lefthand cylinder head gasket will be located lefthand side of center or closer to front of engine.
4. Ensure THIS SIDE UP and engine displacement are visible.
5. Install cylinder head onto locating pins and gasket.
6. Install M11 cylinder head bolts.
7. Apply threadlocker P/N 12345382, or equivalent, to threads of M8 cylinder head bolts.
8. Install M8 cylinder head bolts.
9. Tighten cylinder head bolts as follows:
   a. **Torque** M11 cylinder head bolts 1–10 to 22 ft. lbs., in sequence, **Fig. 7.**
   b. Tighten M11 cylinder head bolts 1–10 an additional 90° in sequence.
   c. Final tighten M11 cylinder head bolts 1–8 an additional 90° in sequence.
   d. Final tighten M11 medium length cylinder head bolts 9 and 10 at front and rear of each head an additional 50° in sequence.
   e. **Torque** M8 inner cylinder head bolts 11–15 to 22 ft. lbs., beginning with center bolt 11, then alternating side to side while working outward.
10. Install spark plugs into cylinder head.
11. Install ground wire bolt into rear of cylinder head.
12. Install accessory mounting bracket.
13. Install lower accessory mounting bracket bolts.
14. Install power steering reservoir bracket bolts.
15. Install power steering pump mounting bolts.
16. Install power steering pump pulley.
17. Install vapor vent pipe.
18. Install intake manifold as outlined in "Intake Manifold, Replace."
19. Install lefthand exhaust manifold to cylinder head as outlined in "Exhaust Manifold, Replace."
20. Install valve rocker arms, pedestal and pushrods.

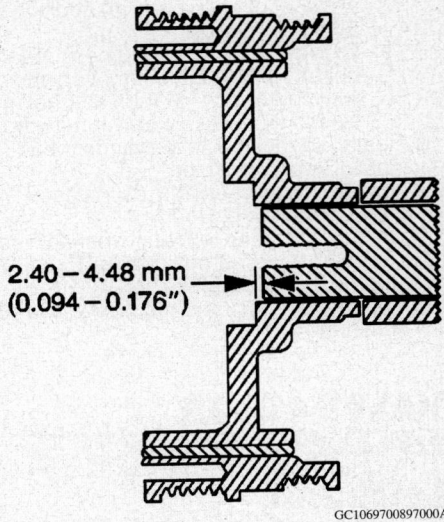

2.40 – 4.48 mm (0.094 – 0.176")

Fig. 8 Dampner installed measurement

Righthand

REMOVAL

1. Remove valve rocker arms, pedestal and pushrods.
2. Remove righthand exhaust manifold as outlined in "Exhaust Manifold, Replace."
3. Remove intake manifold as outlined in "Intake Manifold, Replace."
4. Remove vapor vent pipe.
5. Remove spark plugs.
6. Remove and discard cylinder head bolts.
7. Remove cylinder head.

INSTALLATION

1. Clean cylinder head bolt holes using compressed air.
2. Inspect cylinder head locating pins for proper installation.
3. Install new righthand cylinder head gasket onto locating pins. When properly installed, tab on righthand cylinder head gasket will be located lefthand side of center or closer to front of engine.
4. Ensure THIS SIDE UP and engine displacement are visible.
5. Install cylinder head onto locating pins and gasket.
6. Install M11 cylinder head bolts.
7. Apply threadlocker P/N 12345382, or equivalent, to threads of M8 cylinder head bolts.
8. Install M8 cylinder head bolts.
9. Tighten cylinder head bolts as follows:
   a. **Torque** M11 cylinder head bolts 1–10 to 22 ft. lbs., in sequence, **Fig. 7.**
   b. Tighten M11 cylinder head bolts 1–10 an additional 90° in sequence.
   c. Final tighten M11 cylinder head bolts 1–8 an additional 90° in sequence.
   d. Final tighten M11 medium length cylinder head bolts 9 and 10 at front

and rear of each head an additional 50° in sequence.
  e. **Torque** M8 inner cylinder head bolts 11–15 to 22 ft. lbs., beginning with center bolt 11, then alternating side to side while working outward.
10. Install spark plugs into cylinder head.
11. Install vapor vent pipe.
12. Install intake manifold as outlined in "Intake Manifold, Replace."
13. Install righthand exhaust manifold to cylinder head as outlined in "Exhaust Manifold, Replace."
14. Install valve rocker arms, pedestal and pushrods.

VALVE COVER
REPLACE
Lefthand

1. Remove lefthand fuel rail cover.
2. Disconnect fuel rail lines.
3. Disconnect electrical connectors at alternator and coolant temperature sensors.
4. Disconnect check valve secondary AIR hose.
5. Remove lefthand valve cover PCV valve pipe.
6. Disconnect ignition coils' spark plug wires.
7. Disconnect ignition coil main harness electrical connector.
8. Disconnect EVAP purge solenoid valve hoses.
9. Remove intake manifold EVAP purge solenoid.
10. Remove crankcase vent vacuum tube.
11. Remove valve rocker arm cover bolts and cover.
12. Remove and discard lefthand cover crankcase vent valve grommet.
13. Remove ignition coil wire harness.
14. Remove ignition coils and bolts.
15. Remove cover gasket and bolt grommets.
16. Discard gasket. Bolt grommets may be used again if not damaged.
17. Reverse procedure to install, noting the following:
    a. Install new cover gasket and PCV valve grommet.
    b. **Torque** valve cover mounting bolts to 106 inch lbs.
    c. **Torque** ignition coil mounting bolts to 106 inch lbs.

Righthand

1. Remove righthand fuel rail cover.
2. Remove exhaust manifold secondary AIR hose.
3. Disconnect check valve AIR hose.
4. Remove valve cover breather pipes PCV hoses.
5. Remove ignition coils' spark plug wires.
6. Disconnect ignition coil main harness electrical connector.
7. Remove ignition coil, bracket and bolts.
8. Remove valve rocker arm cover bolts and cover.

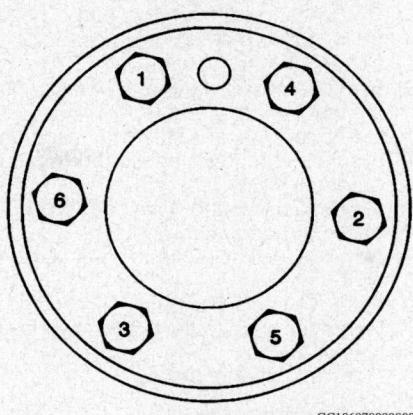

GC1069700898000X

Fig. 9   Flywheel tightening sequence

9. Remove oil fill cap and tube, if required. Discard tube.
10. Remove gasket and bolt grommets.
11. Discard gasket. Bolt grommets may be used again if not damaged.
12. Remove ignition coil bolts, wire harness and coils.
13. Reverse procedure to install, noting the following:
    a. Install new cover gasket.
    b. Install new oil fill tube, as required.
    c. **Torque** valve cover mounting bolts to 106 inch lbs.
    d. **Torque** ignition coil mounting bolts to 106 inch lbs.

VALVE CLEARANCE SPECIFICATIONS

This engine is equipped with hydraulic valve lash adjusters. No adjustment is required.

VALVE ADJUSTMENT

This engine is equipped with hydraulic valve lash adjusters. No adjustment is required.

ROCKER ARMS
Removal

It is required to keep components in original order if they will be installed again.
1. Remove valve rocker arm bolts and arms.
2. Remove valve rocker arm pedestals.

Installation

When using valve train components over again, always install them into original location and position. Valve lash is net build. No valve adjustment is required.
1. Lubricate valve rocker arms with suitable clean engine oil.
2. Lubricate flange of valve rocker arm bolts with suitable clean engine oil.
3. Lubricate flange or washer surface of bolt that will contact valve rocker arm.

4. Install valve rocker arm pedestals.
5. Install rocker arms and bolts. Ensure pushrods seat properly to valve lifter sockets and in ends of rocker arms.
6. Turn crankshaft until number one piston is at top dead center of compression stroke. Cylinders 1, 3, 5 and 7 are lefthand in bank. Cylinders 2, 4, 6 and 8 are in righthand bank. In this position sprocket marks on crankshaft and camshaft will be aligned.
7. With engine in number one firing position, proceed as follows:
    a. **Torque** exhaust valve rocker arm bolts 1, 2, 7 and 8 to 22 ft. lbs.
    b. **Torque** intake valve rocker arm bolts 1, 3, 4 and 5 to 22 ft. lbs.
8. Rotate crankshaft 360° and proceed as follows:
    a. **Torque** exhaust valve rocker arm bolts 3, 4, 5 and 6 to 22 ft. lbs.
    b. **Torque** intake valve rocker arm bolts 2, 6, 7 and 8 to 22 ft. lbs.

PUSH RODS
Removal

It is required to keep components in original order if they will be installed again.
1. Remove valve rocker arm bolts, arms and pedestals as outlined in "Rocker Arms."
2. Remove pushrods.

Installation

When using valve train components over again, always install them into original location and position. Valve lash is net build. No valve adjustment is required.
1. Lubricate valve rocker arms and pushrods with suitable clean engine oil.
2. Lubricate flange of valve rocker arm bolts with suitable clean engine oil.
3. Lubricate flange or washer surface of bolt that will contact valve rocker arm.
4. Install valve rocker arm pedestal.
5. Install rocker arms and bolts.
6. Install pushrods. Ensure pushrods seat properly to valve lifter sockets and in ends of rocker arms.
7. Turn crankshaft until number one piston is at top dead center of compression stroke. Cylinders 1, 3, 5 and 7 are lefthand in bank. Cylinders 2, 4, 6 and 8 are in righthand bank. In this position sprocket marks on crankshaft and camshaft will be aligned.
8. With engine in number one firing position, proceed as follows:
    a. **Torque** exhaust valve rocker arm bolts 1, 2, 7 and 8 to 22 ft. lbs.
    b. **Torque** intake valve rocker arm bolts 1, 3, 4 and 5 to 22 ft. lbs.
9. Rotate crankshaft 360° and proceed as follows:
    a. **Torque** exhaust valve rocker arm bolts 3, 4, 5 and 6 to 22 ft. lbs.
    b. **Torque** intake valve rocker arm bolts 2, 6, 7 and 8 to 22 ft. lbs.

HYDRAULIC LIFTERS
REPLACE

1. Remove cylinder head as outlined in "Cylinder Head, Replace."
2. Remove valve lifter guide bolts.
3. Remove valve lifters and guide. If lifters stick in bores use valve lifter removal tool No. J 3049-A, or equivalent, to remove them.
4. Remove guide valve lifters.
5. Organize or mark components so that they can be installed in original positions.
6. Reverse procedure to install, noting the following:
   a. Lubricate valve lifters and bores with suitable clean engine oil.
   b. Align lifters' and bores' flat sides.

CRANKSHAFT DAMPER
REPLACE

1. Release accessory drive belt tensioner and remove drive belt as outlined in "Serpentine Drive Belt."
2. Remove electronic brake control module from its bracket and position aside. Cap and plug open lines.
3. Remove power steering gear as outlined in "Power Steering Gear, Replace" in "Front Suspension & Steering."
4. Remove starter motor as outlined in "Starter, Replace" in "Electrical" section.
5. Remove power steering cooler mounting bolts and cooler from front crossmember, then position aside.
6. Release tensioner and remove air conditioning drive belt.
7. Install flywheel holding tool No. J 42386, or equivalent, and flywheel mounting bolts. **Torque** mounting bolts to 37 ft. lbs.
8. Remove crankshaft dampner bolt.
9. Mark crankshaft dampner and end of crankshaft. Record dampner installed position on crankshaft for installation. Also record location of any weights, which must return to original positions.
10. Remove crankshaft dampner using crankshaft end protector and dampner removal tool Nos. J 41816 and J 41816-2, or equivalents.
11. Reverse procedure to install, noting the following:
    a. Install dampner using crankshaft balancer and sprocket installer tool No. J 41665, or equivalent.
    b. **Torque** used crankshaft dampner bolt to 240 ft. lbs.
    c. Remove bolt and measure for properly installed dampner, **Fig. 8.**
    d. **Torque** new crankshaft dampner bolt to 37 ft. lbs.
    e. Tighten bolt an additional 140°.

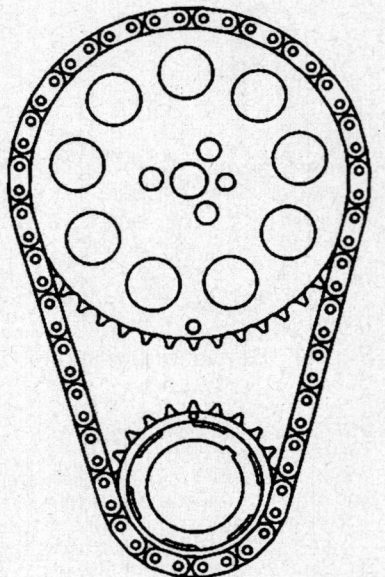

Fig. 10 Camshaft & crankshaft sprocket alignment

GC1069700896000A

FRONT COVER
REPLACE

Removal

1. Drain coolant into suitable container.
2. Disconnect air intake duct fuel regulator purge line.
3. Remove air intake duct and air cleaner.
4. Remove crankshaft dampner as outlined in "Crankshaft Dampner, Replace."
5. Remove water pump radiator and heater hoses.
6. Remove water pump mounting bolts, pump and gaskets.
7. Remove front cover bolts.
8. Remove front cover and gasket. **Avoid sliding front cover or gasket across oil pan gasket.**
9. Remove and discard crankshaft oil seal.

Installation

1. Apply .20 inch bead of GM silicone gasket P/N 12378190, or equivalent, to corner where oil pan meets engine block.
2. Install new gasket, front cover and mounting bolts to engine block. Tighten bolts hand tight.
3. Align cover alignment tool No. J 41476, or equivalent, on front of crankshaft.
4. Install crankshaft dampner bolt and hand tighten.
5. Hand tighten oil pan to cover bolts so cover properly positions itself at pan rail.
6. **Torque** front cover bolts to 18 ft. lbs.
7. Remove alignment tool.
8. Install crankshaft oil seal using oil seal installer tool No. J 41478, or equiva-

lent. **Do not lubricate oil seal sealing surface.**
9. Install water pump, gaskets and mounting bolts.
10. Install radiator and heater hoses to water pump.
11. Fill cooling system.
12. Install crankshaft dampner as outlined in "Crankshaft Damper, Replace."
13. Install air intake duct and air cleaner.
14. Connect fuel regulator purge line to air intake duct.

REAR COVER
REPLACE

Removal

1. Mark crankshaft end and flywheel for installation, then remove flywheel.
2. Remove engine rear cover mounting bolts and cover. Discard gasket.
3. Remove and discard crankshaft rear cover oil seal.

Installation

1. Apply .20 inch bead of GM silicone gasket P/N 12378190, or equivalent, to corner were oil pan meets engine block.
2. Install rear cover, gasket and bolts onto engine, hand tighten bolts.
3. Rotate crankshaft until two opposing flywheel bolt holes are parallel to oil pan surface.
4. Install cover alignment tool No. J 41476, or equivalent, and bolts onto rear of crankshaft. Hand tighten tool mounting bolts.
5. Hand tighten oil pan to cover bolts so cover properly positions itself at pan rail.
6. **Torque** oil pan to cover bolts to 106 inch lbs.
7. **Torque** rear cover mounting bolts to 18 ft. lbs.
8. Remove alignment tool.
9. Install crankshaft rear oil seal using rear oil seal installer tool No. J 41479, or equivalent.
10. Install flywheel as follows:
    a. Align alignment mark made during removal and install mounting bolts hand tight.
    b. **Torque** flywheel mounting bolts to 15 ft. lbs., in sequence, **Fig. 9.**
    c. **Torque** flywheel mounting bolts to 37 ft. lbs., in sequence.
    d. **Torque** flywheel mounting bolts to 74 ft. lbs., in sequence.

TIMING CHAIN
REPLACE

Removal

1. Remove oil pump as outlined in "Oil Pump, Replace."
2. Rotate crankshaft until crankshaft and camshaft sprocket timing marks are aligned.
3. Remove camshaft sprocket bolts.

4. Remove camshaft sprocket and timing chain.
5. Remove crankshaft sprocket using puller tool Nos. J 8433, J 21427-01, J 41816-2 and J 41558, or equivalents.
6. Remove crankshaft sprocket key, if required.

Installation

1. Install key into crankshaft keyway.
2. Install crankshaft sprocket onto front of crankshaft, aligning key with keyway.
3. Install crankshaft sprocket using sprocket installation tool No. J 41665, or equivalent. Ensure sprocket fully seats against crankshaft flange.
4. Rotate crankshaft sprocket until alignment mark is in 12 o'clock position.
5. Install camshaft sprocket and timing chain.
6. Properly locate camshaft sprocket locating pin with camshaft sprocket alignment hole.
7. Sprocket teeth and timing chain must mesh properly.
8. Camshaft and crankshaft sprocket alignment marks must be aligned properly, **Fig. 10.** Locate camshaft sprocket alignment mark in 6 o'clock position.
9. Install camshaft sprocket bolts.
10. Install oil pump as outlined in "Oil Pump, Replace."

CAMSHAFT
REPLACE

1. Remove valve lifters as outlined in "Hydraulic Lifters, Replace."
2. Remove radiator as outlined in "Radiator, Replace."
3. Remove timing chain and sprockets as outlined in "Timing Chain, Replace."
4. Remove camshaft sensor bolt and sensor.
5. Remove camshaft retainer plate bolts and retainer.
6. Install three M8 1.25 × 3.937 inches bolts in camshaft front bolt holes.
7. Carefully rotate and pull camshaft out of engine block using bolts as handle.
8. Remove camshaft bolts.
9. Reverse procedure to install, noting the following:
   a. Ensure camshaft journals are lubricated with suitable clean engine oil before installation.
   b. Install camshaft retainer plate with sealing gasket facing engine block.
   c. Lubricate camshaft sensor O-ring with suitable clean engine oil.

PISTON & ROD ASSEMBLY

1. Insert piston onto piston pin press tool No. J 24086-C, or equivalent. Record location of alignment mark on top of piston.
2. Apply mild heat to pin end of connecting rod using torch. This will ease piston and pin assembly.
3. Position connecting rod so bolt flange flat area faces engine block front.

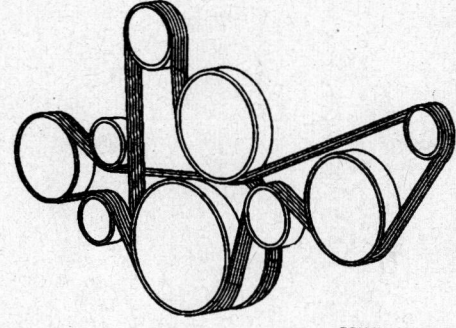

GC1069700899000X

Fig. 11   Serpentine drive belt routing

4. Press pin into connecting rod using piston pin press tool.
5. Measure piston, pin and connecting rod for proper assembly as follows:
   a. Place piston and connecting rod with flat top of piston on flat surface.
   b. Slide connecting rod and pin to one side and hold firmly against inside of piston.
   c. Measure pin for proper installation. Properly installed piston pin should protrude .05 inch from piston side.
6. Install piston ring assembly onto piston as follows:
   a. Install oil control ring spacer in groove. Ends of oil control ring spacer should not overlap.
   b. Install upper and lower control rings. Oil control rings do not have dimple or orientation mark and may be installed in either direction.
   c. Stagger three oil control ring end gaps minimum of 90°.
   d. Install upper and lower compression rings. Upper compression ring does not have dimple or orientation mark and may be installed in either direction.
   e. Stagger compression ring end gaps minimum of 1 inch.

PISTONS, PINS & RINGS

Pistons are available in standard and .010 inch oversize.
Piston rings are available in standard and .010 inch oversize.

MAIN & ROD BEARINGS

Connecting rod bearings are available in standard size only.
Main bearings are available in standard size only.

CRANKSHAFT SEAL
REPLACE

Refer to "Front Cover, Replace" for crankshaft front seal replacement.

CRANKSHAFT REAR OIL SEAL
REPLACE

Refer to "Rear Cover, Replace" for crankshaft rear seal replacement.

OIL PAN
REPLACE

1. Drain engine oil into suitable container and remove oil filter.
2. Remove engine cradle as outlined in "Engine Mount, Replace."
3. **On models equipped with automatic transmission,** remove fluid cooler line front and rear mounting clamp bolts.
4. **On all models,** remove engine flywheel housing to oil pan bolts.
5. Remove engine flywheel housing cover bolts.
6. Remove lefthand and righthand close-out cover bolts and covers.
7. Disconnect electrical connector and remove engine oil level sensor.
8. Disconnect engine oil temperature sensor electrical connector.
9. Remove oil pan mounting bolts and oil pan.
10. Remove and discard oil pan gasket and pan rivets.
11. Remove oil pan baffle bolt and baffle.
12. Reverse procedure to install, noting the following:
   a. Ensure block and oil pan rears are flush or even. **Rear of pan must never protrude beyond block and bellhousing plane.**
   b. Apply .20 inch wide by .80 inch long beads of GM silicone gasket sealer P/N 12378190, or equivalent, to front and rear cover gasket surfaces where covers attach to oil pan mating surface.
   c. Install mounting bolts through oil pan and gasket before installation.

OIL PUMP
REPLACE

1. Remove engine front cover as outlined in "Front Cover, Replace."
2. Remove oil pan as outlined in "Oil Pan, Replace."
3. Remove oil pump screen bolt and nuts.
4. Remove oil pump screen.
5. Remove and discard O-ring seal.
6. Remove remaining crankshaft oil deflector nuts.
7. Remove crankshaft oil deflector.
8. Remove oil pump bolts.
9. Reverse procedure to install, noting the following:
   a. Ensure pump and oil gallery passages are clean and free of obstructions.
   b. Align crankshaft sprocket's and oil pump's splined surfaces.
   c. Install oil pump onto crankshaft sprocket until pump housing contacts engine block face.

SERPENTINE DRIVE BELT

Belt Routing

Refer to **Fig. 11** for serpentine drive belt routing.

Belt Replacement

1. Reduce tension by rotating tensioner away from belts using suitable hex-head socket.
2. Remove accessory drive belts.
3. Clean accessory drive belt surfaces.
4. Install accessory drive belts. Record running direction or arrow markings.
5. Tighten accessory drive belt tensioners to increase tension on accessory drive belts.
6. Ensure accessory drive belts are aligned in proper pulley grooves.

COOLING SYSTEM BLEED

1. Park vehicle on level surface.
2. Fill cooling system.
3. Start engine and let idle for one minute.
4. Install radiator surge tank cap.
5. Cycle RPM from idle to 3000 RPM in 30 second intervals until engine coolant reaches 210°F.
6. Shut off engine and carefully remove radiator surge tank cap.
7. Start engine and idle for one minute.
8. Fill surge tank to ½ inch above COLD FULL mark.
9. Install radiator surge tank cap and cycle RPM as stated.
10. Shut off engine and remove radiator surge tank cap.
11. Fill surge tank to ½ inch above cold full line.
12. Rinse any excess coolant piston from engine and compartment.

THERMOSTAT

REPLACE

1. Drain cooling system into suitable container.
2. Remove radiator outlet hose clamp at thermostat housing using clamp pliers tool No. J 38185, or equivalent.
3. Disconnect thermostat housing radiator outlet hose.
4. Record position of thermostat before removing.
5. Remove mounting bolts and thermostat housing.
6. Remove and discard gasket.
7. Reverse procedure to install.

WATER PUMP

REPLACE

1. Drain cooling system into suitable container.
2. Disconnect IAT and MAF sensor electrical connectors.

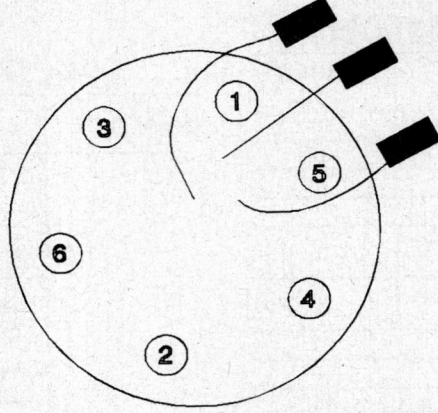

GC1019700417000X

Fig. 12   Fuel sender bolt tightening sequence

3. Remove air intake duct fuel regulator purge line.
4. Remove air intake duct cleaner.
5. Remove drive belts as outlined in "Serpentine Drive Belt."
6. Remove radiator inlet and outlet hose clamps, then the water pump hoses using clamp pliers tool No. J 38185, or equivalent.
7. Remove heater hose clamps and water pump hoses.
8. Remove water pump pulley bolts and pulley.
9. Remove mounting bolts and water pump.
10. Reverse procedure to install, noting the following:
    a. **Torque** water pump mounting bolts to 11 ft. lbs., then to 22 ft. lbs.
    b. **Torque** water pump pulley bolts to 90 inch lbs., then to 18 ft. lbs.

RADIATOR

REPLACE

1. Disconnect Intake Air Temperature (IAT) and Mass Air Flow (MAF) sensor connectors.
2. Remove air intake duct/cleaner.
3. Remove mounting bolts and radiator upper support. Record upper radiator support position in relation to fan shroud for installation.
4. Raise and support vehicle, then drain coolant into suitable container.
5. Remove fan shroud electrical connectors and harness.
6. Remove fan shroud.
7. Remove radiator hoses.
8. **On models equipped with automatic transmission,** remove radiator cooler lines.
9. **On all models,** remove condenser and position forward. **Disconnecting condenser air conditioning lines is not required.**
10. Lower and remove radiator.
11. Reverse procedure to install. Tighten mounting bolts.

FUEL PUMP

REPLACE

1. Raise and support vehicle.
2. Remove lefthand rear wheel and tire.
3. Clean fuel line connections before disconnecting.
4. Drain lefthand fuel tank into suitable container, then mark and disconnect fuel lines.
5. Cap fuel lines.
6. Disconnect fuel sender electrical connector.
7. Remove fuel tank strap and shield.
8. Support fuel tank.
9. Remove mounting bolts and fuel sender.
10. Record positioning of fuel pump strainer before discarding.
11. Reverse procedure to install, noting the following:
    a. Install new fuel pump strainer, ensuring it is properly positioned as noted during removal.
    b. Align sender cover and tank marks.
    c. Look through tank opening to ensure long side of strainer is visible. It should be approximately one inch from tank opening. Rotate sender counterclockwise approximately 90°, as required.
    d. Hand tighten new breakaway head sender mounting bolts, then tighten using suitable wrench until upper heads break off in sequence, **Fig. 12.**

FUEL FILTER

REPLACE

1. Raise and support vehicle.
2. Clean fuel filter connections before disconnecting.
3. **On models equipped with automatic transmission,** proceed as follows:
    a. Disconnect stabilizer bar from rear cradle.
    b. Remove exhaust intermediate pipe to muffler bolts.
    c. Lower lefthand muffler.
4. **On all models,** remove fuel filter bracket nut from mounting stud.
5. Disconnect fuel filter quick-connect fittings and cap fuel lines.
6. Disconnect filter mounting stud ground strap.
7. Remove fuel filter and bracket, then filter from bracket.
8. Reverse procedure to install. Ensure mounting bracket anti-rotation tab is securely seated into tunnel reinforcement hole.

TIGHTENING SPECIFICATIONS

Year	Component	Torque Ft. Lbs.
2004	Air Conditioning Compressor Bracket	37
	Air Conditioning Idler Pulley	37
	Air Conditioning Tensioner	18
	AIR Pipe To Exhaust Manifold	15
	AIR Righthand Side Pipe Bracket To Cylinder Head	15
	Alternator & Power Steering Pump Bracket	37
	Alternator Rear Bracket	37
	Camshaft Retainer	18
	Camshaft Sensor	18
	Camshaft Sprocket	26
	Connecting Rod Bolts	15⑩
	Coolant Temperature Gauge Sensor	15
	Crankshaft Bearing Cap Bolts	③
	Crankshaft Bearing Cap Side Bolts	18
	Crankshaft Bearing Cap Studs	④
	Crankshaft Dampner	②
	Crankshaft Oil Deflector	18
	Crankshaft Position Sensor	18
	Cylinder Head Bolts	⑤
	Cylinder Head Coolant Plug	15
	Cylinder Head Core Hole Plug	15
	Drive Belt Idler Pulley	37
	Drive Belt Tensioner	37
	Engine Block Coolant Drain Plugs	44
	Engine Block Heater	30
	Engine Block Oil Gallery Plugs	44
	Engine Flywheel Hub Collar Bolt (Automatic Transmission)	96
	Engine Front Cover	18
	Engine Mount Bracket To Engine Block	37
	Engine Rear Cover	18
	Engine Service Lift Bracket (M8 Bolts)	18
	Engine Service Lift Bracket (M10 Bolts)	37
	Engine Valley Cover	18
	Exhaust Manifold	⑦
	Flywheel	⑥
	Fuel Injection Fuel Rail	90①
	Ignition Coil	106①
	Ignition Coil Wire Harness Connector	106①
	Intake Manifold Bolts	⑧
	Knock Sensors	15
	Oil Dipstick Tube	12
	Oil Filter	22
	Oil Filter Fitting	40

TIGHTENING SPECIFICATIONS—Continued

Year	Component	Torque Ft. Lbs.
2004	Oil Level Sensor	115①
	Oil Pan Baffle	106①
	Oil Pan Cover	106①
	Oil Pan Drain Plug	18
	Oil Pan M8 Bolts (Oil Pan To Engine Block & Oil Pan To Front Cover)	18
	Oil Pan M6 Bolts (Oil Pan To Rear Cover)	106①
	Oil Pressure Sensor	15
	Oil Pump Cover	106①
	Oil Pump Relief Valve Plug	106①
	Oil Pump Screen	18
	Oil Pump Screen To Oil Pump	106①
	Oil Pump To Engine Block	18
	Oil Temperature Sensor	15
	Oil Transfer Cover Bolts	106①
	Oxygen Sensor	30
	Power Steering Pump	18
	Power Steering Pump & Alternator Bracket	37
	Power Steering Reservoir Bracket	37
	Spark Plugs	⑪
	Starter Motor	37
	Throttle Body	106①
	Valve Lifter Guide	106①
	Valve Rocker Arm	22
	Valve Rocker Arm Cover	106①
	Vapor Vent Pipe	106①
	Water Inlet Housing	11
	Water Pump	⑨
	Water Pump Cover	11
	Water Pump Pulley	⑨

① — Inch lbs.
② — Refer to Crankshaft Damper, Replace.
③ — First pass, 15 ft. lbs.; second pass, tighten an additional 80°.
④ — First pass, 15 ft. lbs.; second pass, tighten an additional 53°.
⑤ — Refer to Cylinder Head, Replace.
⑥ — Refer to Rear Cover, Replace.
⑦ — Refer to Exhaust Manifold, Replace.
⑧ — Refer to Intake Manifold, Replace.
⑨ — Refer to Water Pump, Replace.
⑩ — First design (single dimple/mark on bolt head), then tighten an additional 60°; Second design (two dimples/marks on bolt head), then tighten an additional 75°.
⑪ — New cylinder head, 15 ft. lbs.; Used cylinder head, 11 ft. lbs.

6.0L, 6.2L & 7.0L Engines

NOTE: On Air Bag Equipped Models, Refer To "Air Bag System Precautions" Located In The Front Of This Manual For System Disarming & Arming Procedures.

NOTE: Refer To "Computer Relearn Procedures" Located In The Front Of This Manual When Battery Power To The Computer Has Been Interrupted.

NOTE: Prior To Performing Any Service Operations Listed In This Section, Consult The "Technical Service Bulletins" Section For Related Information.

INDEX

	Page No.
Camshaft, Replace	7-22
Installation	7-22
Removal	7-22
Compression Pressure	7-17
Cooling System Bleed	7-23
Crankshaft Damper, Replace	7-21
Crankshaft Seal, Replace	7-22
Cylinder Head, Replace	7-19
Lefthand	7-19
Installation	7-19
Removal	7-19
Righthand	7-19
Installation	7-20
Removal	7-19
Engine Rebuilding Specifications	29-1
Engine, Replace	7-18
Engine Mount, Replace	7-18
Exhaust Manifold, Replace	7-19
Lefthand	7-19
Righthand	7-19
Front Cover, Replace	7-21

	Page No.
Installation	7-21
Removal	7-21
Fuel Filter, Replace	7-26
All Models w/In-Tank Filter	7-26
Fuel Pump, Replace	7-24
Lefthand	7-24
2004	7-24
2005–08	7-25
Righthand	7-25
2004	7-25
2005–08	7-25
Hydraulic Lifters, Replace	7-21
Intake Manifold, Replace	7-19
Main & Rod Bearings	7-22
Oil Pan, Replace	7-22
Oil Pump, Replace	7-23
Piston & Rod Assembly	7-22
Pistons, Pins & Rings	7-22
Precautions	7-17
Battery Ground Cable	7-17
Fuel System Pressure Relief	7-17
2004–06	7-17

	Page No.
2007–08	7-17
Radiator, Replace	7-23
2004	7-23
2005–08	7-23
Rocker Arms, Replace	7-20
Installation	7-20
Removal	7-20
Serpentine Drive Belt	7-23
Belt Replacement	7-23
Belt Routing	7-23
Thermostat, Replace	7-23
Tightening Specifications	7-27
Timing Chain, Replace	7-21
Installation	7-21
Removal	7-21
Valve Adjustment	7-20
Valve Cover, Replace	7-20
Lefthand	7-20
Righthand	7-20
Water Pump, Replace	7-23

PRECAUTIONS

Fuel System Pressure Relief

2004–06

1. Record radio presets, then disconnect and isolate battery ground cable.
2. Remove fuel tank filler cap to release fuel tank pressure.
3. Remove lefthand fuel rail cover.
4. Prior to disconnecting fuel line, position shop towel over fitting.
5. Connect pressure gauge tool No. J 34730-1A, or equivalent, to pressure tap on fuel rail.
6. Position bleed hose into suitable container.
7. Slowly relieve fuel system pressure.

2007–08

LESS GAUGE TOOL

1. Loosen fuel tank filler cap to release fuel tank pressure.
2. Remove engine cover if required.
3. Remove service port cap from fuel rail.
4. Wrap a suitable shop towel around fuel rail service port.
5. Depress fuel rail test port valve using a small flat bladed tool.

WITH GAUGE TOOL

1. Loosen fuel tank filler cap to release fuel tank pressure.
2. Remove engine cover if required.
3. Remove service port cap from fuel rail.
4. Wrap a suitable shop towel around fuel rail service port.
5. Connect gauge tool No. CH-48027, or equivalent and fittings to service port.
6. Route hose into an approved gasoline container.
7. Open valve and bleed any fuel from fuel rail.
8. Close valve, then remove hose from gasoline container.

Battery Ground Cable

Prior to service, record radio presets, then disconnect battery ground cable and isolate as required.

COMPRESSION PRESSURE

When measuring compression, lowest cylinder must be within 70% of the highest cylinder with a minimum pressure of 100 psi. Compression test results will fall into one of the following categories:

1. Normally, compression builds up quickly and evenly to specifications on each cylinder.
2. If piston rings are faulty, compression will be low on first stroke, then build up on following strokes but will not reach specifications. Improvement is considerable with addition of approximately three squirts of oil.
3. If valves are faulty, compression will be low on first stroke and will not tend to build up on following strokes. It will not improve much with addition of oil.
4. Ensure battery is fully charged.
5. Bring engine to operating temperature.
6. Disconnect electrical connector at crankshaft ignition timing sensor.
7. Disable fuel injection system.

8. Remove spark plugs.
9. Ensure throttle is wide open.
10. Install compression gauge tool No. J 38722, or equivalent.
11. Crank engine through four complete compression strokes, then record results for each cylinder.

ENGINE MOUNT
REPLACE

1. Remove front suspension crossmember.
2. Remove engine mount to bracket nut, then the mount, **Fig. 1.**
3. Remove engine mount heat shield from mount.
4. Reverse procedure to install.

ENGINE
REPLACE

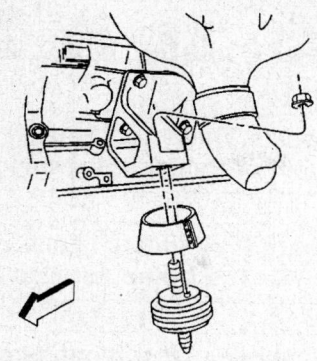

1. Remove the front suspension crossmember.
2. Remove the engine mount-to-engine mount bracket nut.
3. Remove the engine mount.
4. Remove the engine mount heat shield from the engine mount, if necessary.

ARM0400000000082

Fig. 1   Engine mount replacement

1. Recover air conditioning refrigerant as outlined in "Air Conditioning" chapter.
2. Drain engine coolant into a suitable container.
3. Remove radiator as outlined under "Radiator, Replace."
4. Remove brake pressure modulator valve assembly and bracket as outlined in "Anti-Lock Brakes" chapter. Position brake pipes aside, cap and plug lines.
5. Remove serpentine belt as outlined under "Serpentine Drive Belt."
6. Relieve fuel system pressure as outlined under "Precautions."
7. Disconnect EVAP canister purge hose at fuel line.
8. Remove fuel feed hose, then the radiator hoses from water pump.
9. Remove heater hoses from water pump, then disconnect the following connectors:
   a. Fuel injectors.
   b. Ignition coil main harness connectors.
   c. EVAP solenoid and air conditioning compressor.
   d. Electric throttle motor and throttle position sensor.
   e. Engine coolant temperature sensor.
10. Remove alternator as outlined under "Alternator, Replace" in "Electrical" section.
11. Remove power brake booster vacuum hose, then the intermediate steering shaft to steering gear bolt.
12. Raise and support vehicle, then remove front tires and wheels.
13. Remove intermediate steering shaft from steering gear, then position it to lefthand side frame rail.
14. Install adjustable jack stands under front and rear of intermediate pipe.
15. Loosen exhaust muffler band clamps, then separate lefthand side and righthand side mufflers from intermediate pipe.
16. Remove exhaust pipe hanger lower bolts, then the exhaust manifold nuts and seal.
17. Lower jack stands, then remove intermediate pipe.

18. Remove oxygen sensors from catalytic convertor, then the mounting nuts and gasket from exhaust manifold.
19. Remove catalytic convertor from vehicle.
20. Remove driveline tunnel close-out panel bolts, then the close-out panel.
21. Remove starter as outlined under "Starter, Replace" in "Electrical" section.
22. Disconnect electrical connectors from crankshaft position, oil level and righthand side heated oxygen sensors.
23. Remove air conditioning compressor and condenser hose bolt at compressor, then separate hoses from compressor.
24. Disconnect electrical connectors from oil temperature sensor and lefthand side heated oxygen sensor.
25. Remove ground strap bolt, then the ground straps from engine block.
26. Disconnect wheel speed sensor electrical connectors.
27. **On models equipped with real time damping system,** disconnect electrical connectors from shock absorber dampner and position sensor pigtail.
28. **On all models,** unclip transmission wire harness, then disconnect electronic variable orifice control connector clips from crossmember.
29. Remove transmission harness clip bolts from engine block, then the transmission wire harness from engine wire harness.
30. Remove stabilizer shaft link nuts from stabilizer shaft, then the stabilizer shaft insulator clamps from front crossmember.
31. Remove stabilizer shaft from vehicle.
32. Loosen steering knuckle nut from lower control arm ball stud, then separate steering knuckle and lower control arm ball stud using joint remover tool No. J 42188, or equivalent.
33. Disconnect anti-lock brake system electrical connector clips from crossmember.
34. Remove front transverse leaf spring as outlined under "Transverse Leaf Spring, Replace."
35. **On models equipped with automat-**

ic transmission, proceed as follows:
   a. Disconnect fluid cooler pipe clip from front of engine oil pan.
   b. Disconnect front fluid cooler pipes from rear pipes.
   c. Disconnect automatic transmission cooler pipe clip at righthand side transmission cover.
   d. Remove driveline support hole plug bolts.
   e. Install a M10.0 - 1.5 × 55 mm bolt or longer in each plug location. **Torque** M10 bearing support bolts to 26 ft. lbs.
   f. Remove flywheel housing plug, then orientate prop shaft hub clamp for access to bolt.
   g. Position clamp bolt facing downward, then loosen prop shaft hub clamp bolt.
   h. Remove bolts attaching transmission wire harness bracket to flywheel housing, then the transmission wire harness from mounting location, rearward toward driveline support.
36. **On models equipped with manual transmission,** proceed as follows:
   a. Unclip clutch actuator hose from clutch actuator hose clip.
   b. Depress white circular release ring on actuator hose and simultaneously pull lightly on master cylinder hose to disconnect using tool No. J 36221.
   c. Protect both ends from dirt and damage.
37. **On all models,** install drive line support tool No. J 42203, or equivalent, to close-out panel flange, then slowly lower vehicle onto engine support table tool No. J 39580, or equivalent.
38. Remove front and rear crossmember nuts.
39. Remove AIR pipe bracket bolt at rear of cylinder head, then AIR pipe with check valve and gasket.
40. Remove ground strap bolt, then the ground strap from lefthand side cylinder head.
41. Disconnect electrical connectors from engine oil pressure sensor, manifold

absolute pressure sensor and camshaft position sensor and knock sensors.

42. Disconnect vacuum hose from MAP sensor.
43. Remove driveline support bolts, then insert a flat-bladed screwdriver between edge of driveline support and flywheel housing and separate.
44. Slowly pull engine away from propeller shaft, as soon as propeller input shaft clears flywheel housing, slowly raise vehicle.
45. Slide engine and crossmember forward to clear propeller shaft spline.
46. Raise vehicle completely off of engine and crossmember, remove power steering pump pulley hub cap.
47. Remove power steering pump pulley using puller tool No. J 24034-C, or equivalent.
48. Remove power steering pump bolts, then the power steering pump brace.
49. Remove power steering pump with reservoir from engine, then attach to crossmember.
50. Remove A/C compressor bracket, then the alternator bracket bolts.
51. Remove alternator bracket and power steering pump bracket.
52. Install engine lifting brackets tool No. J 41798, or equivalent, to engine, then remove spark plugs.
53. Remove engine mount nuts, then attach a suitable engine lifting device to engine lifting brackets and slowly raise engine.
54. Remove engine from crossmember.
55. Reverse procedure to install.

INTAKE MANIFOLD
REPLACE

1. Remove engine sight cover, then drain coolant into a suitable container.
2. Relieve fuel system pressure as outlined under "Precautions."
3. Disconnect electrical connector from fuel injectors and throttle body.
4. Disconnect fuel feed pipe from fuel injectors.
5. Disconnect vacuum hose from brake booster, then the electrical connector from manifold absolute pressure sensor.
6. Remove MAP sensor, then the grommet from sensor.
7. Remove EVAP clip, bolt, bracket, valve and tubes.
8. **On models equipped with 6.2L engine,** remove positive crankcase ventilation (PCV) hose.
9. **On all models,** remove bolts, fuel rail stop bracket and intake manifold **Fig. 2.**
10. Remove and discard intake manifold gaskets.
11. Reverse procedure to install.

EXHAUST MANIFOLD
REPLACE
Lefthand

1. Remove engine sight cover, then raise and support vehicle.

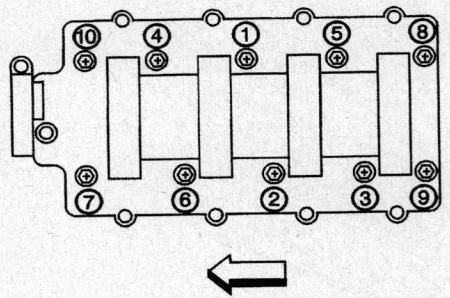

ARM0500000004242

Fig. 2 Intake manifold removal

2. Disconnect bank one oxygen sensor electrical connector and remove sensor. Lower vehicle.
3. Remove spark plugs from engine, then the alternator as outlined under "Alternator, Replace."
4. Remove catalytic convertor to exhaust manifold mounting nuts, then the catalytic convertor from vehicle.
5. Remove exhaust manifold heat shield, then the exhaust manifold.
6. Reverse procedure to install, noting the following:
   a. Apply threadlock GM part No. 12345493, or equivalent, to exhaust manifold bolt threads.
   b. Tighten exhaust manifold bolts in two steps beginning with two center bolts, then alternating from side to side and working toward outside bolts. First step, **torque** bolts to 11 ft. lbs.; second step, **torque** bolts to 18 ft. lbs.

Righthand

1. Remove engine sight cover, then the spark plugs from engine.
2. Raise vehicle, then disconnect bank two oxygen sensor electrical connectors and remove sensor.
3. Lower vehicle, then remove oil dipstick tube bolt and tube.
4. Remove catalytic convertor to exhaust manifold mounting nuts, then the catalytic convertor from vehicle.
5. Remove exhaust manifold heat shield, then the exhaust manifold.
6. Reverse procedure to install, noting the following:
   a. Apply threadlock GM part No. 12345493, or equivalent, to exhaust manifold bolt threads.
   b. Tighten exhaust manifold bolts in two steps beginning with two center bolts, then alternating from side to side and working toward outside bolts. First step, **torque** bolts to 11 ft. lbs.; second step, **torque** bolts to 18 ft. lbs.

CYLINDER HEAD
REPLACE
Lefthand
REMOVAL

1. Remove valve rocker arms as outlined

under "Rocker Arms, Replace."
2. Remove push rods.
3. Remove exhaust manifold as outlined under "Exhaust Manifold, Replace."
4. Remove engine wiring harness ground bolt from rear of lefthand side cylinder head, then move engine wire harness ground strap away from cylinder head.
5. Remove cylinder head bolts and cylinder head, **Fig. 3. Do not reuse cylinder head bolts.**
6. Remove cylinder head gasket and discard gasket.

INSTALLATION

1. Clean engine block cylinder head bolt holes using tool No. J 42385-107, or equivalent.
2. Spray cleaner GM P/N 12346139, GM P/N 12377981, or equivalent into bolt holes.
3. Clean cylinder head bolt holes with compressed air, then install cylinder head locating pins.
4. Inspect locating pins for proper installation and displacement markings on gasket for proper usage.
5. Install new cylinder head gasket onto locating pins, then the cylinder head onto locating pins and gasket.
6. Install new cylinder head bolts, then using sequence in **Fig. 4,** tighten bolts as follows:
   a. First step, **torque** M11 cylinder head bolts 1–10 to 22 ft. lbs.
   b. Second step, tighten M11 cylinder head bolts 1–10 an additional 90°.
   c. Third step, tighten M11 cylinder head bolts 1–10 an additional 70°.
   d. Fourth step, **torque** M8 cylinder head bolts 11–15 to 22 ft. lbs.
7. Install engine wiring harness ground strap to rear of lefthand side cylinder head.
8. Install exhaust manifold as outlined under "Exhaust Manifold, Replace."
9. Install power steering reservoir bracket, then the alternator bracket and bolts.
10. Install alternator as outlined under "Alternator, Replace."
11. Install coolant air bleed pipe and O-rings, then the coolant air bleed hose.
12. Install throttle body, then connect crankcase ventilation hose and electrical connector to throttle body.
13. Connect air control valve and intake air temperature sensor electrical connectors.
14. Install push rods as outlined under "Push Rods."
15. Install valve rocker arms as outlined under "Rocker Arms."
16. Refill cooling system.

Righthand
REMOVAL

1. Remove valve rocker arms as outlined under "Rocker Arms."
2. Remove push rods.
3. Drain engine coolant into a suitable container, then disconnect electrical

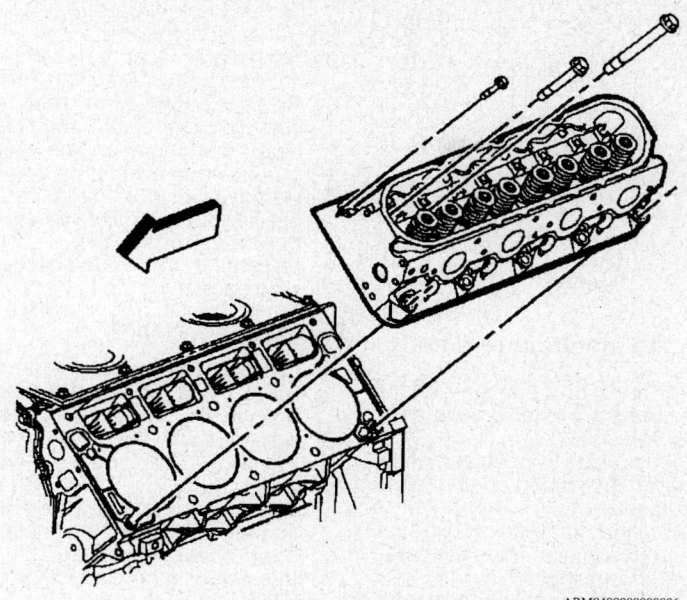

ARM0400000000086

Fig. 3 Cylinder head removal

connector from intake air temperature sensor.

4. Disconnect electrical connector from throttle position sensor, then the crankcase ventilation hose from throttle body.
5. Remove throttle body attaching bolts, then throttle body.
6. Remove coolant air bleed hose, then the coolant air bleed pipe mounting bolts and coolant air bleed pipe and O-rings.
7. Remove alternator as outlined under "Alternator, Replace."
8. Remove power steering pump as outlined under "Power Steering Pump, Replace" in "Front Suspension & Steering" section.
9. Remove alternator bracket bolts, then the bracket and power steering reservoir bracket.
10. Remove exhaust manifold as outlined under "Exhaust Manifold, Replace."
11. Remove oil dipstick tube bolt, then the oil dipstick tube bolt and reposition tube.
12. Remove wiring harness from clip at rear of cylinder head.
13. Remove cylinder head bolts and cylinder head. **Do not reuse cylinder head bolts.**
14. Remove cylinder head gasket and discard gasket.

INSTALLATION

1. Clean engine block cylinder head bolt holes using tool No. J 42385-107 or equivalent.
2. Spray cleaner GM P/N 12346139, GM P/N 12377981, or equivalent into bolt holes.
3. Clean cylinder head bolt holes with compressed air, then install cylinder head locating pins.
4. Inspect locating pins for proper installation and displacement markings on gasket for proper usage.

5. Install new cylinder head gasket onto locating pins, then the cylinder head onto locating pins and gasket.
6. Install new cylinder head bolts, then using sequence shown in **Fig. 4,** tighten bolts as follows:
   a. First step, **torque** M11 cylinder head bolts 1–10 to 22 ft. lbs.
   b. Second step, tighten M11 cylinder head bolts 1–10 an additional 90°.
   c. Third step, tighten M11 cylinder head bolts 1–10 an additional 70°.
   d. Fourth step, **torque** M8 cylinder head bolts 11–15 to 22 ft. lbs.
7. Install engine wiring harness ground strap to rear of lefthand cylinder head.
8. Install wiring harness to clip at rear of cylinder head.
9. Install oil dipstick tube bolt.
10. Install exhaust manifold as outlined under "Exhaust Manifold, Replace."
11. Install coolant air bleed pipe and O-rings, then the coolant air bleed hose.
12. Install throttle body, then connect crankcase ventilation hose and electrical connector to throttle body.
13. Connect air control valve and intake air temperature sensor electrical connectors.
14. Install push rods as outlined under "Push Rods."
15. Install valve rocker arms as outlined under "Rocker Arms."
16. Fill cooling system.

VALVE COVER
REPLACE
Lefthand

1. Remove lefthand engine sight cover, then disconnect alternator electrical connector.
2. Remove engine wiring harness alternator lead retaining nut and lead.

3. Remove fuel rail cover, then disconnect ignition coil harness connector and spark plug wire at ignition coil.
4. Remove ignition coil mounting bolts and coils.
5. Loosen valve rocker arm cover bolts, then the valve rocker cover.
6. Remove gasket from rocker cover and discard old gasket.
7. Reverse procedure to install.

Righthand

1. Remove righthand side engine sight cover.
2. Disconnect engine vacuum pipe from EVAP canister purge solenoid valve to intake manifold EVAP pipe.
3. Disconnect engine purge pipe from EVAP canister purge valve, then disconnect electrical connector.
4. Remove EVAP canister purge valve from purge bracket.
5. Remove retaining clips, then the EVAP pipes.
6. Remove EVAP pipe from intake air temperature sensor at air intake duct valve cover, then the hose from throttle body to engine valley cover.
7. Remove fuel rail cover, then disconnect ignition coil connector and spark plug wires at ignition coils.
8. Remove mounting bolts, then the ignition coils.
9. Remove retaining bolt, then the valve rocker arm cover.
10. Remove gasket from rocker cover and discard old gasket.
11. Reverse procedure to install.

VALVE ADJUSTMENT

This engine is equipped with hydraulic valve lash adjusters. No adjustment is required.

ROCKER ARMS
REPLACE
Removal

Place components in a rack so that they can be installed in same location from which they were removed.

1. Remove valve rocker arm cover as outlined under "Valve Cover, Replace."
2. Remove valve rocker arm bolts, then the valve rocker arms.
3. Remove valve rocker arm pivot support, then the pushrods.
4. Clean and inspect valve rocker arms and pushrods.

Installation

When using valve train components over again, always install them into original location and position. Valve lash is net build. No valve adjustment is required.

1. Lubricate valve rocker arms and flange of rocker arm bolts with suitable clean engine oil.
2. Install valve rocker arm pivot support. **Ensure pushrods seat properly to valve lifter socket.**

3. Install pushrods, ensure pushrods seat properly to ends of rocker arms. **Do not tighten rocker arm bolts at this time.**
4. Install rocker arms and bolts.
5. Turn crankshaft until number one piston is at top dead center of compression stroke. Cylinders 1, 3, 5 and 7 are in lefthand bank. Cylinders 2, 4, 6 and 8 are in righthand bank. In this position sprocket marks on crankshaft and camshaft will be aligned.
6. With engine in number one firing position, proceed as follows:
   a. **Torque** exhaust valve rocker arm bolts 1, 2, 7 and 8 to 22 ft. lbs.
   b. **Torque** intake valve rocker arm bolts 1, 3, 4 and 5 to 22 ft. lbs.
7. Rotate crankshaft 360° and proceed as follows:
   a. **Torque** exhaust valve rocker arm bolts 3, 4, 5 and 6 to 22 ft. lbs.
   b. **Torque** intake valve rocker arm bolts 2, 6, 7 and 8 to 22 ft. lbs.
8. Install valve rocker arm cover as outlined under "Valve Cover, Replace."

HYDRAULIC LIFTERS
REPLACE

1. Remove cylinder head as outlined under "Cylinder Head, Replace."
2. Remove guide bolts, then the guides with lifters.
3. Note installed position of guides. Notched area of guide should align with locating tab on block.
4. Remove valve lifters from guide.
5. Mark components so they are installed in their original position.
6. Reverse procedure to install, noting the following:
   a. Lubricate valve lifters and bores with suitable clean engine oil.
   b. Align flat sides of lifters and bores.

CRANKSHAFT DAMPER
REPLACE

1. Remove drive belt as outlined in "Serpentine Drive Belt."
2. Remove power steering gear as outlined under "Power Steering Gear, Replace" in "Front Suspension & Steering" section.
3. Remove starter motor as outlined in "Starter, Replace."
4. Remove power steering cooler mounting bolts, then the cooler from front crossmember. Position cooler aside.
5. Remove air conditioning drive belt.
6. Install flywheel holding tool No. J 42386-A, or equivalent.
7. Remove crankshaft dampner bolt.
8. Mark crankshaft dampner and end of crankshaft. Note dampner installed position on crankshaft for installation reference. Also note location of any weights, which must return to their original position.
9. Remove crankshaft dampner using crankshaft end protector and dampner removal tool Nos. J 41816 and J 41816-2, or equivalents. Use one M10

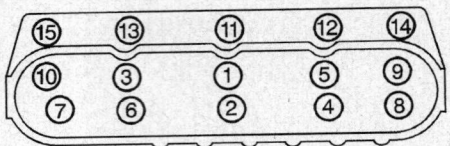

Fig. 4 Cylinder head bolt tightening sequence

- 1.5 ×120 mm and one M10 - 1.5 × 45 mm bolt for proper tool operation.
10. Reverse procedure to install, noting the following:
    a. **On models equipped with 6.0L engine,** a thin washer (part No. 12598247) has been added. If this washer is present it does not need to be replaced. If there is no washer present, one should be added.
    b. **On all models,** install dampner using crankshaft balancer and sprocket installer tool No. J 41665, or equivalent.
    c. **Torque** used crankshaft dampner bolt to 240 ft. lbs.
    d. Remove bolt and measure for properly installed dampner, **Fig. 5.**
    e. **Torque** new crankshaft dampner bolt to 37 ft. lbs., then rotate an additional 140°.

FRONT COVER
REPLACE
Removal

1. Remove crankshaft dampner as outlined under "Crankshaft Damper, Replace."
2. Remove water pump as outlined under "Water Pump, Replace."
3. Remove front cover bolts, then the front cover and gasket. Discard front cover gasket and oil seal.

Installation

1. Apply .20 inch bead of GM silicone gasket P/N 12378521, or equivalent, to corner where oil pan meets engine block.
2. Install new gasket, front cover and mounting bolts to engine block. Tighten bolts hand tight.
3. Install cover alignment tool No. J 41480, or equivalent. **Torque** tool to block bolts to 18 ft. lbs.
4. Install alignment tool No. J 41476, or equivalent.
5. Install crankshaft dampner bolt and hand tighten.
6. Tighten tool No. J 41480.
7. Hand tighten oil pan to cover bolts so cover properly positions itself at pan rail.
8. **Torque** front cover bolts to 18 ft. lbs.
9. Remove alignment tools.
10. Measure the oil pan surface flatness, front cover-to-engine block as follows:
    a. Place a straight edge across engine block and front cover oil pan sealing surfaces. Avoid contact with

gasket section that protrudes into oil pan surface.
    b. Insert a feeler gage between front cover and straight edge tool. Cover must be flush with oil pan surface, or no greater than .02 inch below flush.
    c. If front cover to engine block oil pan surface alignment is not within specifications, repeat cover alignment procedure.
    d. If proper front cover to engine block alignment cannot be obtained, install a new front cover.
11. Install water pump as outlined under "Water Pump, Replace."
12. Install crankshaft dampner as outlined under "Crankshaft Damper, Replace."

TIMING CHAIN
REPLACE
Removal

1. Remove oil pump as outlined in "Oil Pump, Replace."
2. Rotate crankshaft until crankshaft and camshaft sprocket timing marks are aligned.
3. Remove camshaft sprocket bolts.
4. Remove camshaft sprocket and timing chain.
5. Remove chain dampener bolts, then chain dampener.
6. Remove crankshaft sprocket using puller tool Nos. J 8433, J 41816-2 and J 41558, or equivalents.

Installation

1. Install crankshaft sprocket onto front of crankshaft, aligning key with keyway.
2. Install crankshaft sprocket using sprocket installation tool No. J 41665, or equivalent. Ensure sprocket fully seats against crankshaft flange.
3. Rotate crankshaft sprocket until alignment mark is in 12 o'clock position.
4. **On models equipped with 6.2L engine,** compress timing chain tensioner guide, using installation tool No. EN 46330, or equivalent.
5. Install timing chain tensioner and bolts.
6. **On models equipped with 6.0L & 7.0L engines,** install timing chain tensioner and bolts.
7. **On all models, torque** timing chain tensioner bolts to 18 ft. lbs.
8. Install camshaft sprocket and timing chain.
9. Properly locate camshaft sprocket locating pin with camshaft sprocket alignment hole.
10. Sprocket teeth and timing chain must mesh properly.
11. Camshaft and crankshaft sprocket alignment marks must be aligned properly, **Fig. 6.** Locate camshaft sprocket alignment mark in 6 o'clock position.
12. Install camshaft sprocket bolts.
13. **On models equipped with 6.2L engine,** remove installation tool No. EN 46330, or equivalent.
14. **On all models,** install oil pump as outlined in "Oil Pump, Replace."

CAMSHAFT
REPLACE
Removal

1. Remove engine assembly as outlined under "Engine, Replace."
2. Remove crankshaft dampner as outlined under "Crankshaft Damper, Replace."
3. Remove oil dipstick tube.
4. Remove exhaust manifolds as outlined under "Exhaust Manifold, Replace."
5. Remove water pump as outlined under "Water Pump, Replace."
6. Remove intake manifold as outlined under "Intake Manifold, Replace."
7. Remove engine valley cover, then the coolant air bleed pipe.
8. Remove lefthand side and righthand side valve rocker arm covers as outlined under "Valve Cover, Replace."
9. Remove valve rocker arms and push rods as outlined under "Rocker Arms."
10. Remove lefthand side and righthand side cylinder heads as outlined under "Cylinder Head, Replace."
11. Remove valve lifters as outlined under "Hydraulic Lifters."
12. Remove oil pan to front cover bolts, then the front cover bolts.
13. Remove front cover and gasket, then discard old gasket.
14. Rotate engine in order to align timing marks, **Fig. 6.**
15. Remove camshaft sprocket bolts, then the timing chain from camshaft sprocket. Allow timing chain to rest on crankshaft sprocket.
16. Remove camshaft retainer bolts and retainer.
17. **On models equipped with 6.0L & 7.0L engines,** install three M8 - 1.25 × 4.0 inch bolts in camshaft front bolt holes.
18. Carefully rotate and pull camshaft out of engine block using bolts handle.
19. Remove bolts from front of camshaft.
20. **On models equipped with 6.2L engine,** install camshaft sprocket bolt into camshaft front bolt hole.
21. Using bolt as a handle, carefully rotate and pull camshaft out of engine block.
22. Remove bolt from the front of camshaft.

Installation

If camshaft replacement is required, valve lifters must also be replaced.
1. Lubricate camshaft journals and bearings with clean engine oil.
2. **On models equipped with 6.0L & 7.0L engines,** Install three M8 1.25 × 4.0 inch bolts into camshaft front bolt holes.
3. Carefully install camshaft into engine block using bolts handle, then remove three bolts from front of camshaft.
4. **On models equipped with 6.2L engine,** Install camshaft sprocket bolt into camshaft front bolt hole.
5. Using bolt as a handle, carefully install camshaft into engine block, then re-

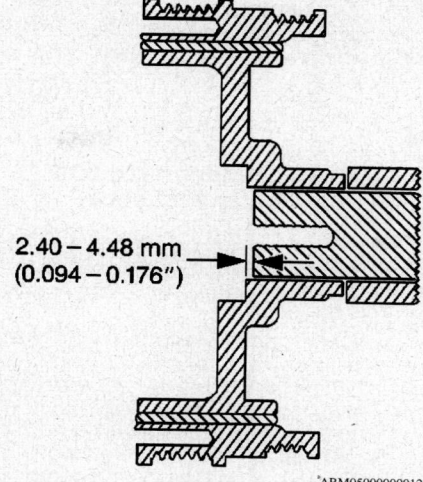

2.40 – 4.48 mm
(0.094 – 0.176")

ARM0500000001211

Fig. 5 Dampner installed measurement

move bolt from front of camshaft.
6. **On all models,** Install camshaft retainer and bolts.
7. Align camshaft sprocket alignment mark in 6 o'clock position, then install camshaft sprocket and timing chain.
8. Install camshaft sprocket bolts.
9. Apply a .2 inch bead of sealant GM P/N 12378190, or equivalent .8 inch long at oil pan to engine block junction.
10. Install front cover and a new gasket, then the cover bolts until snug.
11. Install oil pan to front cover bolts until snug.
12. Install front and rear cover alignment tool No. J 41476, or equivalent, then the crankshaft balancer bolt to front cover.
13. Align tapered legs of front and rear cover alignment tool No. J 41476, or equivalent, with machined alignment surfaces on front cover.
14. Install crankshaft balancer bolt until snug, then tighten oil pan and front cover bolts to specifications and remove tool.
15. Install a new crankshaft front oil seal, then install valve lifters as outlined under "Hydraulic Lifters."
16. Install righthand side and lefthand side cylinder heads, as outlined under "Cylinder Head, Replace."
17. Install valve rocker arms and push rods as outlined under "Rocker Arms."
18. Install righthand side and lefthand side valve rocker arm covers as outlined under "Valve Cover, Replace."
19. Install coolant air bleed pipe.
20. Install intake manifold as outlined under "Intake Manifold, Replace."
21. Install water pump as outlined under "Water Pump, Replace."
22. Install lefthand side and righthand side exhaust manifolds as outlined under "Exhaust Manifold, Replace."
23. Install oil dipstick tube.
24. Install crankshaft dampner as outlined under "Crankshaft Damper, Replace."
25. Install engine assembly as outlined under "Engine, Replace."

PISTON & ROD ASSEMBLY

1. Install retaining clip. Clip should be seated in groove of pin bore.
2. Install piston pin to piston and connecting rod.
3. Install retaining clip. Clip should be seated in groove of pin bore.
4. Identify compression and oil control rings for proper installation. Upper compression ring can be identified by a paint mark located 180° from end gap.
5. Lower compression ring can be identified by a paint mark located 90° from end gap, then install upper and lower with orientation marks facing top of piston.
6. Install piston rings onto piston using piston ring pliers, then position oil control ring end gaps a minimum 1 inch from each other.
7. Position compression ring end gaps 180° opposite each other.
8. Install connecting rod bearings to rod and cap.

PISTONS, PINS & RINGS

Pistons are available in standard and .002 inch oversize.
Piston rings are available in standard and .002 inch oversize.

MAIN & ROD BEARINGS

Refer to sequence in **Fig. 7,** then tighten the main bearing cap bolts using the following procedure.
1. **Torque** M10 bolts 1–10 to 15 ft. lbs.
2. Tap crankshaft rearward using a plastic faced hammer, then forward to align thrust bearings.
3. Rotate M10 bolts 1–10 an additional 80°.
4. **Torque** M10 bolts 11–20 to 15 ft. lbs., then rotate an additional 50°.
5. **Torque** M8 bearing cap side bolts to 18 ft. lbs. Tighten bolt on one side of bearing cap and then tighten bolt on the opposite side of same bearing cap.

CRANKSHAFT SEAL
REPLACE

Refer to "Front Cover, Replace" for crankshaft front seal replacement.

OIL PAN
REPLACE

1. Drain engine oil into a suitable container, then remove oil filter.
2. Remove front suspension crossmember.
3. Remove lefthand side and righthand side rear transmission covers.
4. Remove starter motor assembly as

outlined under "Starter, Replace" in "Electrical" section.

5. Disconnect electrical connectors from engine oil level and engine oil temperature sensors.
6. Remove transmission lines from rear and front of oil pan.
7. Remove two oil cooler bolts, separate oil cooler from oil pan, discard oil cooler seal.
8. Remove oil pan mounting bolts, then the oil pan from engine block.
9. Remove oil pan gasket from engine block.
10. Reverse procedure to install.

OIL PUMP
REPLACE

1. Remove engine front cover as outlined in "Front Cover, Replace."
2. Remove oil pan as outlined in "Oil Pan, Replace."
3. Remove oil pump screen bolt and nuts.
4. Remove oil pump screen.
5. Remove and discard O-ring seal.
6. Remove remaining crankshaft oil deflector nuts.
7. Remove crankshaft oil deflector.
8. Remove oil pump bolts.
9. Reverse procedure to install, noting the following:
   a. Ensure pump and oil gallery passages are clean and free of obstructions.
   b. Align crankshaft sprocket and oil pump splined surfaces.
   c. Install oil pump onto crankshaft sprocket until pump housing contacts engine block face.

SERPENTINE DRIVE BELT

Belt Routing

Refer to **Fig. 8** for serpentine drive belt routing.

Belt Replacement

1. Mark belt running directions.
2. Reduce tension by rotating tensioner away from belts using suitable hex-head socket.
3. Remove accessory drive belts.
4. Clean accessory drive belt surfaces.
5. Install accessory drive belts.
6. Ensure accessory drive belts are aligned in proper pulley grooves.

COOLING SYSTEM BLEED

1. Fill cooling system.
2. Start engine and let idle for approximately four minutes.
3. Slowly fill coolant mixture until level stabilizes at base of surge tank fill neck.
4. Run engine between 2000–2500 RPM for approximately two minutes.
5. Allow engine to idle, then add approximately 1 quart of coolant to surge tank.

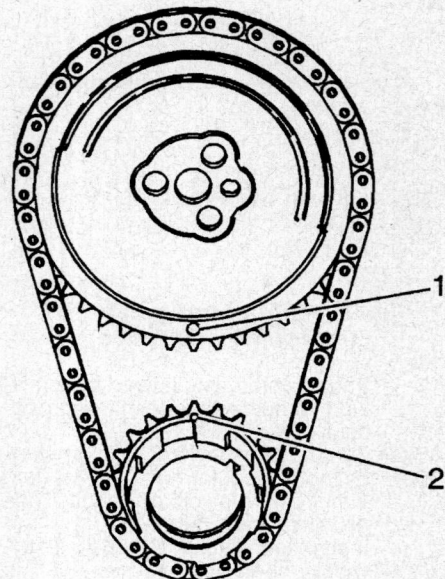

ARM0500000001213

Fig. 6 Camshaft & crankshaft sprocket alignment.

6. Install coolant pressure cap, then turn ignition Off.
7. Allow engine to cool, then top off coolant as required.

THERMOSTAT
REPLACE

1. Drain engine coolant into a suitable container.
2. Remove outlet hose from water pump inlet, then the bolts and water pump inlet.
3. Remove bolts, then the thermostat housing and thermostat. **O-ring seal is integral to thermostat housing.**
4. Reverse procedure to install.

WATER PUMP
REPLACE

1. Drain engine coolant into a suitable container.
2. Remove air cleaner intake duct.
3. Mark running directions, then remove accessory drive belts.
4. Remove inlet and outlet hoses from water pump.
5. Remove heater inlet and surge tank outlet hoses from water pump.
6. Remove retaining bolts, then the water pump and gasket.
7. Reverse procedure to install, noting the following:
   a. **Torque** water pump mounting bolts in two passes: first, to 11 ft. lbs, second, to 22 ft. lbs.
   b. Install drive belts in proper running directions.
   c. Fill and bleed cooling system, then inspect for leaks.

RADIATOR
REPLACE

2004

1. Recover air conditioning refrigerant as outlined in "Air Conditioning" chapter.
2. Drain engine coolant into a suitable container.
3. Remove splash shield from vehicle, then disconnect electrical connector from mass air flow/intake air temperature sensor.
4. Remove connector from IAT sensor, then air intake duct, MAF/IAT sensor and air cleaner assembly.
5. Disconnect surge tank inlet hose assembly from radiator support tabs, then remove bolts and radiator support.
6. Disconnect A/C compressor hose assembly from A/C condenser fitting, then remove and discard seal washer.
7. Cap or tape A/C compressor hose assembly.
8. Raise and support vehicle, then disconnect front evaporator inlet line from A/C condenser, then remove and discard seal washer.
9. Cap or tape A/C compressor hose assembly, then lower vehicle.
10. Remove lefthand side and righthand side radiator air baffle upper retainer pins.
11. Gently tilt air baffle forward for additional clearance.
12. Raise A/C condenser along radiator to release A/C condenser tabs from radiator slots and remove from vehicle.
13. Disengage tension on radiator inlet hose clamp at radiator using tool No. J 38185 or equivalent.
14. Disconnect radiator inlet hose from radiator, then the engine wiring harness from cooling fan shroud.
15. Disconnect surge tank outlet hose from retaining clips on cooling fan shroud and position aside.
16. Raise and support vehicle, then remove tire and wheel assemblies.
17. Remove nuts and insulator clamps, then the stabilizer shaft from vehicle.
18. Disconnect cooling fan electrical connector.
19. **On models equipped with transmission fluid cooler,** disconnect transmission oil cooler lines from radiator, using tool Nos. J 41623-B, DT 47624 and DT-47731 or equivalents.
20. **On models equipped with engine oil cooler,** disconnect engine oil cooler pipes from radiator using tool No. DT-47731 or equivalent.
21. Remove retaining bolts, then the cooling fan and shroud.
22. Disconnect surge tank hoses from radiator, then radiator outlet hose.
23. Remove radiator from vehicle.
24. Reverse procedure to install.

2005-08

1. Recover air conditioning refrigerant as outlined in "Air Conditioning" chapter.

2. Drain engine coolant into a suitable container.
3. Remove A/C condenser.
4. Disconnect radiator inlet hose from radiator.
5. Remove cooling fan and shroud assembly from radiator.
6. Disconnect surge tank inlet hose from radiator.
7. **On models equipped with transmission fluid cooler,** disconnect upper cooler line from radiator.
8. **On models equipped with engine oil cooler,** disconnect upper cooler line from radiator.
9. **On all models,** raise and safely support vehicle.
10. Disconnect radiator outlet hose from radiator.
11. **On models equipped with transmission fluid cooler,** disconnect lower cooler line from radiator.
12. **On models equipped with engine oil cooler,** disconnect lower cooler line from radiator.
13. **On all models,** remove radiator from vehicle.
14. Reverse procedure to install.

FUEL PUMP

REPLACE

Lefthand

2004

1. Relieve fuel system pressure as outlined under "Precautions."
2. Remove fuel tank filler pipe cap, then drain fuel through fuel tank filler pipe using a hand or air operated fuel pump device and fuel tank drain hose tool No. J 45004, or equivalent.
3. Remove lefthand rear wheel and tire, then the lefthand side rear wheelhouse panel.
4. Install adjustable jack stands under front and rear of intermediate pipe, then loosen exhaust muffler band clamps.
5. Separate lefthand side and righthand side mufflers from intermediate pipe, then remove exhaust pipe hanger lower bolts exhaust manifold nuts and exhaust seals.
6. Lower jack stands, then remove intermediate pipe from jack stands.
7. Remove mufflers from hangers, then mufflers from vehicle.
8. Remove oxygen sensors from catalytic convertors, then the catalytic convertors from vehicle.
9. Remove driveline tunnel closeout panel bolts and panel.
10. **On models equipped with automatic transmission,** proceed as follows:
    a. Remove rear bellhousing access plug, then matchmark transmission flexplate to transmission torque converter through access hole in rear bellhousing.
    b. Remove starter motor as outlined under "Starter, Replace."
    c. Remove access plug from driveline support assembly, then matchmark

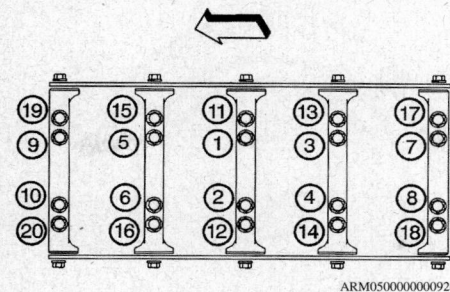

Fig. 7 Main bearing cap bolt tightening sequence

transmission flexplate to transmission torque converter through access hole.
d. Turn engine flywheel through starter motor opening until one of flexplate to torque converter bolts lines up with access hole.
e. Install tool No. J 42386-A to flywheel, then remove flexplate to torque converter bolts.
f. Remove two plastic plugs from front of driveline support assembly.
g. Install two bolts, M10 - 1.5 × 55 mm or longer in place of plastic plugs. **Long bolts are used to maintain propeller input shaft front bearing in original position during removal and installation.**
h. Tighten propeller input shaft front bearing positioning bolts to 26 ft. lbs.
i. Remove engine flywheel housing access plug, then loosen propeller shaft hub clamp bolt.
j. Remove nuts retaining transmission shift cable bracket to transmission.
k. Disconnect transmission shift control cable from transmission shift lever.
l. Reposition transmission shift cable and bracket.
11. **On models equipped with manual transmission,**
    a. Remove instrument panel accessory trim plate, then the center console trim plate.
    b. Remove bolts, nuts and floor console. Disconnect electrical connector.
    c. Pry off shift control knob button, then the shift control knob retainer and remove retainer.
    d. Unscrew shift control knob, release shift boot retaining tabs from instrument panel accessory trim plate.
    e. Lift boot away from trim plate and remove boot.
    f. Remove shift control closeout boot, then place shiftier into neutral.
    g. Press down to engage shift control neutral lock pin, then remove transmission shift rod clamp bolt and shift control mounting bolts.
    h. Raise shift control to release locator from shiftier bracket on side of driveline support assembly.
    i. Release shift control from transmission shift rod clamp and remove shift control assembly.

j. Remove lefthand side I/P lower insulator panel, then the clutch master cylinder pushrod retainer.
k. Disconnect clutch master cylinder pushrod from clutch pedal,
l. Raise and support vehicle, then remove clutch actuator cylinder hose from hose retaining clip at rear of engine.
m. Depress white circular release ring on actuator cylinder hose and simultaneously pull lightly on master cylinder hose to disconnect using tool No. J 36221 or equivalent.
12. **On all models,** using spring compressor tool No. J 33432-A, or equivalent, compress transverse spring.
13. Disconnect shock absorber from lower control arm, then loosen but do not remove upper ball joint stud nut.
14. Separate upper joint stud from suspension knuckle using tool No. J 42188 or equivalent, then remove upper ball joint stud nut from suspension knuckle.
15. Remove nut from wheel drive shaft on suspension knuckle.
16. Loosen but do not remove lower ball joint stud nut, then separate lower ball joint stud from suspension knuckle using ball join separator tool No. J 42188, or equivalent.
17. Remove lower ball joint stud nut from suspension knuckle.
18. Remove stabilizer shaft link from lower control arm.
19. Mark position of, then remove cam bolts, washers and nuts retaining control arm to crossmember.
20. Remove lower control arms from vehicle.
21. Remove transverse spring bolts and retainers, discard old transverse spring bolts.
22. Remove transverse spring from vehicle.
23. Install tool No. J 42055 or equivalent to a transmission jack, then position and firmly secure tool with transmission jack to transmission.
24. Disconnect wiring harness and brake pipe clip retainers from rear suspension crossmember.
25. Remove transaxle mount to rear crossmember nuts, then position a transmission jack under rear suspension crossmember and firmly secure crossmember to jack.
26. Remove rear suspension crossmember retaining nuts using only hand tools.
27. With aid of an assistant, slowly lower rear suspension crossmember away from vehicle frame rails and remove crossmember.
28. Remove transaxle mount with bracket, then using a pry bar release wheel drive shafts from differential.
29. Tie off wheel drive shafts to underbody to support shafts out of way.
30. Release retainer securing wiring harness to L shaped brackets along driveline support assembly, then slide harness up out of brackets and position out of way.
31. Slowly lower driveline approximately

two inches, while simultaneously adjusting angle of tilt to access electrical connectors.

32. Disconnect vehicle speed sensor electrical connector, then wiring harness retainer from stud at differential rear cover.

33. Disconnect wiring harness retainer clip from top of differential then the transmission harness 20-way connector

34. Disconnect park/neutral position switch electrical connectors, then remove bolt retaining transmission wiring harness to lefthand side of transmission case.

35. Slowly lower driveline, observe relationship between top rear of differential and lowest part of rear compartment panel floor.

36. Differential should not be lowered more than approximately even with specified body point of reference. Engine positive crankcase ventilation pipes which route along rear of engine intake manifold.

37. Release wiring harness from harness retainer along top of transmission, ensure wiring harness is free from driveline being removed.

38. Disconnect transmission oil cooler rear pipes from junction fittings at engine flywheel housing, then cap pipes and plug junction fittings to prevent contamination.

39. Place a jack under rear of engine oil pan for support and prevent contact with composite dash panel using a block of wood to protect engine oil pan.

40. Remove five driveline support assembly to engine flywheel housing bolts.

41. Bend wiring harness bracket away from driveline and toward driveline tunnel wall to make a clear removal path for driveline.

42. Have an assistant insert a flat bladed tool between edge of driveline support assembly and engine flywheel housing, then begin to pry driveline loose from engine.

43. Have assistant guide front of driveline during removal, then slowly lower driveline completely out of vehicle.

44. Disconnect fuel fill hose and recirculation line from fill pipe, then the fuel pump jumper harness connector.

45. Disconnect fuel feed pipe at rear of lefthand side fuel tank, then cap fuel pipes to prevent fuel system contamination.

46. Loosen fuel tank strap to drop tank approximately one inch.

47. Disengage crossover tube connector position assurance retainer, then rotate crossover tube collar counterclockwise to disengage.

48. Disconnect crossover tube from lefthand side fuel tank by pulling straight out.

49. Disconnect evaporative emission crossover pipe quick connect fitting at lefthand side fuel tank. Cap EVAP pipe to prevent system contamination.

50. Remove fuel tank strap mounting bolts, then the fuel tank strap from the vehicle.

51. Remove fuel tank, then place tank on a suitable work surface.

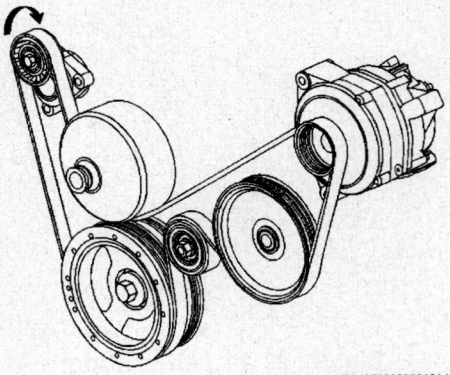

ARM0500000001214

**Fig. 8 Drive belt routing
(Part 1 of 2)**

52. Disconnect fuel pump jumper harness from fuel pump module, then the jet line insert connector from crossover tube to fuel tank opening.

53. Disconnect fuel feed line from welded clip on side of fuel tank. **Fuel pump module is spring loaded and will spring upward when locking ring is removed.**

54. Remove fuel pump module locking ring using lock ring removal tool No. J 39765-A, or equivalent.

55. Remove fuel pump module from fuel tank with jet lines connected, then disconnect jet line quick-connect connectors from fuel pump module inner port.

56. Remove jet line from module retainer cup, then the fuel pump module O-ring from fuel tank opening.

57. Remove jet line insert through crossover tube to fuel tank opening.

58. Reverse procedure to install.

2005-08

1. Remove lefthand fuel tank from vehicle, then move to a suitable workbench.

2. Disconnect fuel pump jumper harness from fuel pump module.

3. Disconnect jet line insert connector from crossover tube to fuel tank opening.

4. Disconnect fuel feed line at welded clip on side of fuel tank.

5. Remove fuel pump module lock ring using wrench tool No. J 39765-A, or equivalent.

6. Remove fuel pump module from fuel tank with jet lines connected. Avoid damaging fuel sender float arm.

7. Remove and discard fuel pump module O-ring.

8. Reverse procedure to install, noting the following:
   a. Inspect jet line insert for damage and replace if necessary.
   b. Install a new fuel pump module O-ring into fuel tank opening.
   c. Place tape around jet line with connector to permit line access after module is inserted into tank.
   d. Turn fuel tank upside down and measure fuel tank sender resistance, which should be 40 Ohms at empty position or 250 Ohms at full.

Righthand
2004

1. Relieve fuel system pressure as outlined under "Fuel System Pressure Relief."

2. Remove fuel tank filler pipe cap, then drain fuel through fuel tank filler pipe using a hand or air operated fuel pump device and fuel tank drain hose tool no. J 45004, or equivalent.

3. Raise and support vehicle, then remove righthand side rear tire.

4. Remove righthand side rear wheelhouse panel, then the evaporative emission canister access cover.

5. Disconnect fill limit vent valve hose at EVAP canister, then the fuel pump module harness connector.

6. Remove crossover tube from clamp located above transmission.

7. Disengage crossover tube connector position assurance retainer by pulling tab outward and rotate.

8. Rotate crossover tube collar counterclockwise and disengage.

9. Disconnect crossover tube from righthand side fuel tank by pulling the tube straight out of fuel tank connection.

10. Disconnect EVAP crossover pipe quick connect fitting at righthand side fuel tank. Cap EVAP pipe to prevent system contamination.

11. Remove fuel tank strap from vehicle, then the fuel tank.

12. Place fuel tank on a suitable work surface, then disconnect evaporative emission purge line from fuel pump module.

13. Disconnect fuel pump module harness connector, then the fuel tank pressure sensor harness connector.

14. Pry fuel tank pressure sensor out of fuel tank with a screwdriver.

15. Disconnect jet line insert connector from crossover tube to fuel tank opening.

16. Remove fuel pump module locking ring using tool No. J 39765-A, or equivalent.

17. Remove fuel pump module from fuel tank with jet lines connected. Do not damage fuel sender float arm.

18. Disconnect jet line quick-connect connectors from fuel pump module, noting location of lines for installation.

19. Remove fuel pump module O-ring from fuel tank opening.

20. Remove jet line insert through crossover tube to fuel tank opening.

21. Reverse procedure to install.

2005-08

1. Remove lefthand fuel tank from vehicle, then move to a suitable workbench.

2. Disconnect EVAP purge line from fuel pump module.

3. Disconnect fuel pump module harness and fuel tank pressure (FTP) sensor harness electrical connectors.

4. If replacing fuel pump module, remove FTP sensor.

5. Disconnect fuel pump jumper harness from fuel pump module.

6. Note locations, then disconnect jet line quick-connect connectors from fuel pump module.
7. Remove fuel pump module lock ring using wrench tool No. J 39765-A, or equivalent.
8. Remove fuel pump module from fuel tank with jet lines connected. Avoid damaging fuel sender float arm.
9. Remove and discard fuel pump module O-ring.
10. Reverse procedure to install, noting the following:
   a. Inspect jet line insert for damage and replace if necessary.
   b. Install a new fuel pump module O-ring into fuel tank opening.
   c. Pull jet line quick-connectors up

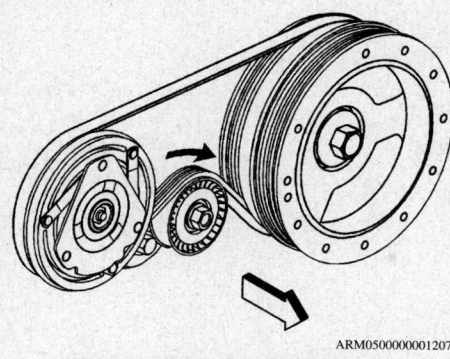

ARM0500000001207

Fig. 8   Drive belt routing (Part 2 of 2)

through pump module opening, connecting lines to pump module as noted.
   d. Turn fuel tank upside down and measure fuel tank sender resistance, which should be 40 Ohms at empty position or 250 Ohms at full.

FUEL FILTER

REPLACE

All Models w/In-Tank Filter

On these models, the fuel filter is combined with the fuel tank sender and pump unit and is not serviced separately.

TIGHTENING SPECIFICATIONS

Year	Component	Torque Ft. Lbs.
2005–06		
	Alternator	37
	Camshaft Position Sensor	106①
	Camshaft Retainer	18
	Camshaft Sprocket	18
	Clutch Pressure Plate	52
	Connecting Rod	②
	Coolant Temperature Sensor	15
	Crankshaft Bearing Cap	④
	Crankshaft Dampner	③
	Crankshaft Position Sensor	18
	Cylinder Head Bolts	⑤
	Cylinder Head Coolant Plug	15
	Drive Belt Pulley	37
	Drive Belt Tensioner	37
	Engine Block Coolant Heater	30
	Engine Block Oil Gallery/Coolant Plugs	44
	Engine Front Cover	18
	Engine Mount	48
	Engine Mount Bracket	37
	Engine Rear Cover	18
	Exhaust Manifold	⑦
	Flywheel	⑥
	Fuel Rail	89①
	Ignition Coil	89①
	Intake Manifold	⑧
	Knock Sensor	15
	Main Bearing Cap	④
	Oil Dipstick Tube Bolt	18
	Oil Filter	22
	Oil Filter Fitting	40
	Oil Level Sensor	15
	Oil Pan Closeout Cover	80①
	Oil Pan Cover Bolts	106①
	Oil Pan Drain Plug	18
	Oil Pan M6 Bolts Oil Pan to Rear Cover	106①
	Oil Pan M8 Bolts Oil Pan to Engine Block and Oil Pan to Front Cover	18
	Oil Pressure Sensor	15
	Oil Pump Cover	106①
	Oil Pump Regulator Valve Plug	106①
	Oil Pump Screen	18
	Oil Pump Screen To Oil Pump	106①
	Oil Pump to Engine Block	18
	Power Steering Pump	18
	Power Steering Reservoir Bracket to Engine	37
	Spark Plugs	⑩
	Starter Motor	37
	Throttle Body	89①
	Timing Chain Guide	18
	Valley Cover	18
	Valve Lifter Guide	89①
	Valve Rocker Arm	22

TIGHTENING SPECIFICATIONS—Continued

Year	Component	Torque Ft. Lbs.
2005–06		
	Valve Rocker Arm Cover	106①
	Water Inlet Housing	11
	Water Pump	⑨
	Water Pump Cover	11
	Water Pump Pulley	⑨
2007 (6.0L)		
	Alternator	37
	Camshaft Position Sensor	106①
	Camshaft Retainer (Hex Bolts)	18
	Camshaft Retainer (Torx Bolts)	11
	Camshaft Sprocket	⑪
	Clutch Pressure Plate	52
	Connecting Rod	②
	Coolant Temperature Sensor	15
	Crankshaft Bearing Cap	④
	Crankshaft Dampner	③
	Crankshaft Position Sensor	18
	Cylinder Head Bolts	⑤
	Cylinder Head Coolant Plug	15
	Drive Belt Pulley	37
	Drive Belt Tensioner	37
	Engine Block Coolant Heater	30
	Engine Block Oil Gallery/Coolant Plugs	44
	Engine Front Cover	18
	Engine Mount	48
	Engine Mount Bracket	37
	Exhaust Manifold	⑦
	Flywheel	⑥
	Fuel Rail	89①
	Ignition Coil	89①
	Intake Manifold	⑧
	Knock Sensor	15
	Main Bearing Cap	④
	Oil Dipstick Tube Bolt	18
	Oil Filter	22
	Oil Filter Fitting	40
	Oil Level Sensor	15
	Oil Pan Closeout Cover	80①
	Oil Pan Cover Bolts	106①
	Oil Pan Drain Plug	18
	Oil Pan M6 Bolts Oil Pan to Rear Cover	106①
	Oil Pan M8 Bolts Oil Pan to Engine Block and Oil Pan to Front Cover	18
	Oil Pressure Sensor	26
	Oil Pump Cover	106①
	Oil Pump Relief Valve Plug	106①
	Oil Pump Screen	18
	Oil Pump Screen To Oil Pump	106①
	Oil Pump to Engine Block	18
	Power Steering Pump	18

Continued

TIGHTENING SPECIFICATIONS—Continued

Year	Component	Torque Ft. Lbs.
2007 (6.0L)		
	Power Steering Reservoir Bracket to Engine	37
	Spark Plugs	11
	Starter Motor	37
	Throttle Body	89①
	Timing Chain Guide	18
	Valley Cover	18
	Valve Lifter Guide	106①
	Valve Rocker Arm	22
	Valve Rocker Arm Cover	106①
	Water Inlet Housing	11
	Water Pump	⑨
	Water Pump Pulley	⑨
2007–08 (7.0L)		
	Alternator	37
	Camshaft Position Sensor	106①
	Camshaft Retainer (Hex Bolts)	18
	Camshaft Retainer (Torx Bolts)	11
	Camshaft Sprocket	18
	Clutch Pressure Plate	52
	Connecting Rod	⑫
	Coolant Temperature Sensor	15
	Crankshaft Bearing Cap	④
	Crankshaft Dampner	③
	Crankshaft Position Sensor	18
	Cylinder Head Bolts	⑤
	Cylinder Head Coolant Plug	15
	Drive Belt Pulley	37
	Drive Belt Tensioner	37
	Engine Block Coolant Heater	37
	Engine Block Oil Gallery/Coolant Plugs	44
	Engine Front Cover	18
	Engine Mount	48
	Engine Mount Bracket	37
	Engine Rear Cover	18
	Exhaust Manifold	⑦
	Flywheel	⑬
	Fuel Rail	89①
	Ignition Coil	89①
	Intake Manifold	⑧
	Knock Sensor	18
	Main Bearing Cap	④
	Oil Filter	22
	Oil Filter Fitting	40 (7.0L)
	Oil Pan Closeout Cover	80①
	Oil Pan Cover Bolts	106①
	Oil Pan Drain Plugs	18
	Oil Pan M6 Bolts Oil Pan to Rear Cover	106①
	Oil Pan M8 Bolts Oil Pan to Engine Block and Oil Pan to Front Cover	18
	Oil Pressure Sensor	26
	Oil Pump Cover	106①

TIGHTENING SPECIFICATIONS—Continued

Year	Component	Torque Ft. Lbs.
2007–08 (7.0L)		
	Oil Pump Relief Valve Plug	106①
	Oil Pump Screen	18
	Oil Pump Screen To Oil Pump	106①
	Oil Pump to Engine Block	18
	Power Steering Pump	18
	Power Steering Reservoir Bracket to Engine	37
	Spark Plugs	11
	Starter Motor	37
	Throttle Body	89①
	Timing Chain Dampner	18
	Valley Cover	18
	Valve Lifter Guide	106①
	Valve Rocker Arm	22
	Valve Rocker Arm Cover	106①
	Water Inlet Housing	11
	Water Pump	⑨
	Water Pump Cover	11
	Water Pump Pulley	⑨
2008 (6.2L)		
	Alternator	37
	Camshaft Position Sensor	106①
	Camshaft Retainer (Hex Bolts)	18
	Camshaft Retainer (Torx Bolts)	11
	Camshaft Sprocket	18
	Clutch Pressure Plate	52
	Connecting Rod	⑭
	Coolant Temperature Sensor	15
	Crankshaft Bearing Cap	④
	Crankshaft Dampner	③
	Crankshaft Position Sensor	18
	Cylinder Head Bolts	⑤
	Cylinder Head Coolant Plug	15
	Drive Belt Pulley	37
	Drive Belt Tensioner	37
	Engine Block Coolant Heater	37
	Engine Block Oil Gallery/Coolant Plugs	44
	Engine Front Cover	18
	Engine Mount	48
	Engine Mount Bracket	37
	Engine Rear Cover	22
	Exhaust Manifold	⑦
	Flywheel	⑮
	Fuel Rail	89①
	Ignition Coil	106①
	Intake Manifold	⑧
	Knock Sensor	15
	Main Bearing Cap	④
	Oil Filter	22
	Oil Filter Fitting	40
	Oil Pan Closeout Cover	80①
	Oil Pan Cover Bolts	106①

Continued

TIGHTENING
SPECIFICATIONS—Continued

Year	Component	Torque Ft. Lbs.
2008 (6.2L)		
	Oil Pan Drain Plugs	18
	Oil Pan M6 Bolts Oil Pan to Rear Cover	106①
	Oil Pan M8 Bolts Oil Pan to Engine Block and Oil Pan to Front Cover	18
	Oil Pressure Sensor	26
	Oil Pump Relief Valve Plug	106①
	Oil Pump Screen	18
	Oil Pump Screen To Oil Pump	106①
	Oil Pump to Engine Block	18
	Power Steering Pump	18
	Power Steering Reservoir Bracket to Engine	37
	Spark Plugs	11
	Starter Motor	37
	Throttle Body	89①
	Timing Chain Dampner	18
	Valley Cover	18
	Valve Lifter Guide	106①
	Valve Rocker Arm	22
	Valve Rocker Arm Cover	106①
	Water Inlet Housing	11
	Water Pump	⑨
	Water Pump Cover	11
	Water Pump Pulley	⑨

① — Inch lbs.

② — First step, torque to 15 ft. lbs.; second step, an additional 75°.

③ — Refer to Crankshaft Damper, Replace.

④ — Refer to Main & Rod Bearings.

⑤ — Refer to Cylinder Head, Replace.

⑥ — First step, torque to 15 ft. lbs.; second step, torque to 37 ft. lbs.; third step, torque to 74 ft. lbs.

⑦ — Refer to Exhaust Manifold, Replace.

⑧ — First step, torque to 44 inch lbs.; second step, torque to 89 inch lbs.

⑨ — Refer to Water Pump, Replace.

⑩ — New cylinder head, 15 ft. lbs.; used cylinder head 11 ft. lbs.

⑪ — First step, torque to 55 ft. lbs.; second step, additional 50°.

⑫ — First step, torque to 15 ft. lbs.; second step, additional 110°.

⑬ — First step, torque to 22 ft. lbs.; second step, additional 40°.

⑭ — First step, torque to 15 ft. lbs.; second step , additional 85°.

⑮ — First step in sequence, torque to 15 ft. lbs.; second pass in sequence, torque to 37 ft. lbs.; final pass in sequence, torque to 74 ft. lbs.

Rear Axle & Suspension

NOTE: On Air Bag Equipped Models, Refer To "Air Bag System Precautions" Located In The Front Of This Manual For System Disarming & Arming Procedures.

NOTE: Refer To "Computer Relearn Procedures" Located In The Front Of This Manual When Battery Power To The Computer Has Been Interrupted.

INDEX

	Page No.
Control Arm, Replace	7-31
Lower	7-31
2004	7-31
2005–08	7-31
Upper	7-31
2004–05	7-31
2006–08	7-32
Hub & Bearing, Replace	7-30

	Page No.
Propeller Shaft, Replace	7-30
Rear Axle, Replace	7-30
Rear Wheel Shaft, Replace	7-30
Rear Wheel Spindle, Replace	7-30
Shock Absorber, Replace	7-30
Spindle Knuckle, Replace	7-30
Stabilizer Shaft, Replace	7-32
Tie Rod, Replace	7-32

	Page No.
Inner Tie Rod & Suspension Adjustment Link	7-32
Outer Tie Rod End	7-32
Tightening Specifications	7-33
Transverse Leaf Spring, Replace	7-31
2004	7-31
2005–08	7-31

REAR AXLE

REPLACE

Refer to **MOTOR's "Domestic Transmission, In-Vehicle Service" manual** or **"Transmission Service DVD"** for rear axle replacement.

REAR WHEEL SHAFT

REPLACE

1. Apply parking brake and shift transmission into park or neutral.
2. Raise and support vehicle and remove rear wheel and tire.
3. Prevent wheel hub and bearing turning by insert suitable drift or punch into brake rotor cooling fins and against brake caliper.
4. Remove spindle nut mounting rear wheel driveshaft to hub.
5. Remove drift or punch.
6. Release parking brake.
7. Remove rear transverse spring as outlined in "Transverse Leaf Spring, Replace."
8. Separate outer tie rod end from knuckle and position tie rod toward rear of vehicle. **Do not loosen outer tie rod jam nut.**
9. Disconnect wheel speed sensor electrical connector.
10. Disconnect parking brake cable from parking brake lever at rear hub.
11. Remove parking brake cable from bracket and position toward vehicle rear.
12. Install rear hub spindle remover tool No. J 42129, or equivalent, onto wheel hub and secure with lug nuts.
13. Begin to disengage driveshaft from wheel hub and bearing. This will give additional clearance to lower ball joint nut.
14. Separate lower ball joint from suspension knuckle.

15. Disengage driveshaft completely from wheel hub and bearing.
16. Support driveshaft, suspension knuckle and upper control arm, then position knuckle toward front.
17. Remove driveshaft using axle shaft remover, extension and slide hammer tool Nos. J 42128, J 29794 & J 2619-01, or equivalents.
18. Remove rear hub spindle remover tool.
19. Reverse procedure to install.

PROPELLER SHAFT

REPLACE

Refer to **MOTOR's "Domestic Transmission, In-Vehicle Service" manual,** for propeller shaft replacement.

HUB & BEARING

REPLACE

1. Raise and support vehicle, then remove tire and wheel.
2. Disconnect wheel speed sensor electrical connector.
3. Disconnect ESC rear position sensor link.
4. **On models equipped with Real Time Damping (RTD) suspension,** disconnect RTD position sensor link.
5. **On all models,** remove brake caliper and disc rotor.
6. Remove shock absorber solenoid electrical connector.
7. Separate outer tie rod end from suspension knuckle.
8. Remove spindle nut retainer, nut and washer.
9. Separate suspension knuckle from upper control arm.
10. Separate suspension knuckle from lower control arm ball joint stud.
11. Remove suspension knuckle.
12. Remove wheel hub mounting bolts.

13. Remove hub and bearing from suspension knuckle.
14. Reverse procedure to install.

SPINDLE KNUCKLE

REPLACE

1. Raise and support vehicle, then remove tire and wheel assembly.
2. Disconnect wheel speed sensor electrical connector.
3. Disconnect the ESC position sensor link.
4. **On models equipped with Real Time Damping (RTD) suspension,** disconnect RTD position sensor link.
5. **On all models,** disconnect shock absorber electrical connector.
6. Remove brake caliper and disc rotor.
7. Separate outer tie rod end from suspension knuckle.
8. Remove spindle nut retainer, nut and washer.
9. Separate suspension knuckle from upper control arm.
10. Separate suspension knuckle from lower control arm ball joint stud.
11. Remove suspension knuckle.
12. Reverse procedure to install.

REAR WHEEL SPINDLE

REPLACE

Refer to "Hub & Bearing, Replace" for rear wheel spindle replacement.

SHOCK ABSORBER

REPLACE

1. Raise and support vehicle, then remove tire and wheel.
2. Disconnect shock absorber solenoid electrical connector.
3. Remove upper mounting bolts.
4. Remove lower shock absorber to lower control arm mounting bolt.

5. Remove shock absorber from lower control arm and shock tower.
6. Remove upper insulator retainer and insulator.
7. Reverse procedure to install.

TRANSVERSE LEAF SPRING
REPLACE

2004

1. Raise and support vehicle, then remove both rear tires and wheels.
2. Measure transverse spring stud height, **Fig. 1.**
3. Install transverse leaf spring compressor and adapters, tool Nos. J 33432-A and J 33432-97, or equivalents, **Fig. 2.**
4. Compress spring.
5. Remove spring to control arm mounting nuts, bolts and insulators.
6. Remove spring to crossmember retainer bolts, retainer, spring spacers and insulators.
7. Remove transverse leaf spring.
8. Reverse procedure to install, noting the following:
   a. Set spring stud height to that noted during removal.
   b. Ensure spring stud bolt has minimum of two threads showing above nut.
   c. Tighten mounting bolts, nuts and screws.

2005-08

1. Raise and support vehicle, then remove both rear tires and wheels.
2. Compress the transverse spring using spring compressor tool No. J 33432-A, or equivalent.
3. Remove a lower control arm as outlined under "Control Arm, Replace."
4. Remove transverse spring mounting bolts and retainers. Discard bolts.
5. Remove transverse spring from vehicle.
6. Remove compressor tool from spring if spring will be discarded.
7. Reverse procedure to install, noting the following:
   a. If installing a new transverse spring, compress the new spring with the compressor tool.
   b. Do not remove compressor tool until after shock absorber has been installed. The leaf spring bolt pad could move out of position, leading to pad damage or a suspension rattle.
   c. **Do not use old spring mounting bolts. Always install new ones.**
   d. Tighten all fasteners to specifications.

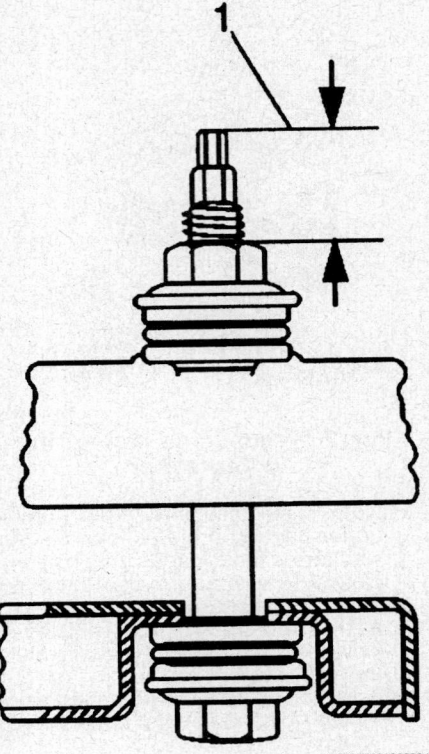

Fig. 1 Spring stud height measurement. 2004

GC2039700138000A

CONTROL ARM
REPLACE

Lower

2004

1. Raise and support vehicle, then remove tire and wheel.
2. Remove transverse leaf spring as outlined under "Transverse Leaf Spring, Replace."
3. Support lower control arm using suitable jack stand and remove shock absorber to lower control arm mounting bolt.
4. Loosen lower ball joint stud nut.
5. Separate lower ball joint stud from suspension knuckle using separator tool No. J 42188, or equivalent.
6. Remove separator tool and lower ball joint stud nut from suspension knuckle.
7. Remove stabilizer bar link from lower control arm.
8. Mark position of control arm to crossmember cam bolts, washers and nuts, then remove bolts, washers and nuts.
9. Remove jack stand and control arm.
10. Reverse procedure to install, noting the following:
    a. Use hex-head wrench to hold ball joint stud in place when installing stud nut as required.

b. **Torque** stud nut to 15 ft. lbs. in order to seat stud.
c. Turn nut an additional 3½ flats.
d. Inspect stud nut for minimum final **torque** of 41 ft. lbs.

2005-08

1. Raise and support vehicle, then remove tire and wheel.
2. Disconnect suspension position sensor link from control arm link stud.
3. Compress the transverse spring using spring compressor tool No. J 33432-A, or equivalent.
4. Disconnect shock absorber from lower control arm.
5. Insert an Allen wrench in end of ball stud to prevent stud rotation.
6. Loosen, but do not remove, lower ball joint stud nut. **Do not use power tools. Use hand tools only.**
7. Support suspension knuckle.
8. Separate lower ball joint stud from suspension knuckle using separator tool No. J 42188, or equivalent.
9. Remove stabilizer shaft link from lower control arm.
10. Support lower control arm with jack stand.
11. Mark their positions, then remove cam bolts, washers, and nuts from control arm to crossmember.
12. Remove jack stand from under lower control arm, then the control arm from vehicle.
13. Reverse procedure to install, noting the following:
    a. If installing a new transverse spring, compress the new spring with the compressor tool.
    b. Do not remove compressor tool until after shock absorber has been installed. The leaf spring bolt pad could move out of position, leading to pad damage or a suspension rattle.
    c. **Do not use old spring mounting bolts. Always install new ones.**
    d. Install cam bolts, washers, and nuts at positions marked during removal. Tighten cam bolts, but not to final specification just yet.
    e. Inspect wheel alignment and adjust as required.
    f. Tighten cam bolts to specifications.

Upper

2004-05

1. Raise and support vehicle, then remove tire and wheel.
2. Disconnect electronic suspension control sensor link.
3. Support lower control arm using suitable jack stand.
4. **On models equipped with Real Time Damping (RTD) suspension,** disconnect RTD position sensor link at upper control arm.
5. **On all models,** loosen upper ball joint

stud nut, but do not remove it.

6. Separate upper ball joint stud from upper control arm using separator tool No. J 42188, or equivalent.
7. Remove separator tool and stud nut.
8. Remove mounting bolts and upper control arm.
9. Reverse procedure to install, noting the following:
   a. Use hex-head wrench to hold ball joint stud in place when installing stud nut, as required.
   b. **On 2004 models, torque** stud nut to 15 ft. lbs. to seat stud, then rotate nut an additional 250°.
   c. **On 2005 models, torque** stud nut to 22 ft. lbs. to seat stud, then rotate nut an additional 195°.

2006–08

LESS FE4 SUSPENSION

1. Raise and support vehicle, then remove tire and wheel.
2. Disconnect wheel speed sensor electrical connector.
3. Disconnect the electronic suspension control sensor link.
4. Disconnect suspension knuckle from upper control arm using separator tool No. J 42188, or equivalent.
5. Support lower control arm with a suitable jack stand.
6. Loosen, but do not remove, upper ball joint stud nut.
7. Remove separator tool and ball joint stud nut from ball joint stud.
8. Remove upper control arm to frame mounting bolts, then the control arm from vehicle.
9. Reverse procedure to install, noting the following:
   a. Install suspension knuckle upper ball joint stud into upper control arm. Use an Allen wrench to prevent ball joint stud from spinning while tightening stud nut.
   b. **Torque** suspension knuckle ball joint stud nut to 22 ft. lbs., then rotate an additional 195°.
   c. Inspect wheel alignment and adjust as required.

WITH FE4 (Z06) SUSPENSION

1. Raise and support vehicle, then remove tire and wheel.
2. Separate ball joint stud from upper control arm using separator tool No. J 42188, or equivalent.
3. Note their locations, then remove upper control arm to frame mounting bolts.

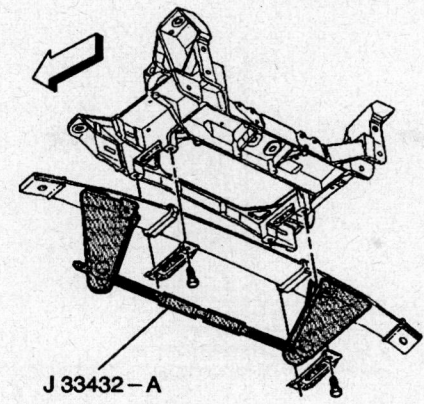

J 33432 – A

GC2039700139000A

Fig. 2 Transverse leaf spring compressor

4. Note their locations, then remove upper control arm washers. Be sure washers without inserts are positioned closest to control arm and those with inserts are closest to frame.
5. Remove control arm from vehicle.
6. Reverse procedure to install, noting the following:
   a. Install suspension knuckle upper ball joint stud into upper control arm.
   b. **Torque** suspension knuckle ball joint stud nut to 15 ft. lbs., then rotate an additional 195°.
   c. Inspect wheel alignment and adjust as required.

TIE ROD

REPLACE

Inner Tie Rod & Suspension Adjustment Link

1. Raise and support vehicle, then remove tire and wheel.
2. Loosen outer tie rod end stud nut, but do not remove it.
3. Separate tie rod end from suspension knuckle using ball joint separator tool No. J 42188, or equivalent.
4. Remove rear suspension adjustment link to crossmember mounting nut.
5. Remove rear suspension adjustment link.
6. Reverse procedure to install, noting the following:

a. Install rear suspension adjustment link nut to rear side of crossmember.
b. **Torque** adjustment link nut to 44 ft. lbs.
c. **On 2004 models,** inspect outer tie rod end nut for a minimum **torque** of 33 ft. lbs.
d. **On 2005–08 models,** inspect outer tie rod end nut for a minimum **torque** of 45 ft. lbs.
e. **On all models,** adjust rear wheel toe as required and tighten suspension adjustment link locknut.

Outer Tie Rod End

1. Raise and support vehicle, then remove tire and wheel.
2. Loosen outer tie rod end stud nut, but do not remove it.
3. Separate tie rod end from suspension knuckle using ball joint separator tool No. J 42188, or equivalent.
4. Loosen jam nut on rear suspension adjustment link.
5. Remove outer tie rod end from adjustment link.
6. Reverse procedure to install, noting the following:
   a. Install outer tie rod end to rear suspension adjustment link, then the outer tie rod end into knuckle.
   b. **Torque** outer tie rod end nut to 15 ft. lbs., then rotate an additional 160°.
   c. **On 2004 models,** inspect outer tie rod end nut for a minimum **torque** of 33 ft. lbs.
   d. **On 2005–08 models,** inspect outer tie rod end nut for a minimum **torque** of 45 ft. lbs.
   e. **On all models,** adjust rear wheel toe as required and tighten suspension adjustment link locknut.

STABILIZER SHAFT

REPLACE

1. Raise and support vehicle, then remove tires and wheels.
2. Remove stabilizer bar link mounting nuts from lower control arms.
3. Remove stabilizer bar to crossmember bracket mounting bolts and bracket.
4. Remove stabilizer bar.
5. Remove stabilizer bar link mounting nuts and shaft links.
6. Reverse procedure to install.

TIGHTENING SPECIFICATIONS

Year	Component	Torque/Ft. Lbs.
2004–08	Clutch Actuator Cylinder	106①
	Driveline Support To Engine Flywheel Housing	37
	Driveline Tunnel Closeout Panel	80①
	EBTCM Lefthand Mounting Bracket	37
	Flexplate To Propeller Shaft Rear Bearing	37
	Input Shaft To Front Propeller Shaft Coupler	41
	Lower Control Arm Ball Joint	②
	Lower Control Arm Cam, Front	107
	Lower Control Arm Cam, Rear	70
	Outer Tie Rod	④
	Outer Tie Rod End Jam	44
	Propeller Input Shaft Front Bearing	26
	Propeller Shaft Hub Clamp	96
	Rear Bearing To Driveline Support Tube	48
	Rear Bearing To Rear Propeller Shaft Coupler	52
	Rear Crossmember	81③
	Rear Drive Axle Spindle	118
	Rear Exhaust Hanger	37
	Rear Shock Absorber, Lower (2004)	162
	Rear Shock Absorber, Lower (2005–08)	107
	Rear Shock Absorber, Upper	22
	Rear Spring Anchor Plate	46
	Shift Control	22
	Shift Control Closeout Boot	106①
	Stabilizer Bar Insulator, Lower	70
	Stabilizer Bar Insulator, Upper	49
	Stabilizer Bar Link	53
	Tie Rod	④
	Upper Control Arm	81
	Upper Control Arm Ball Joint	②
	Wheel Hub	96

① — Inch lbs.
② — Refer to "Control Arm, Replace" for tightening specifications & procedure.
③ — Always install new nuts & tighten them using hand tools only.
④ — Refer to "Tie Rod, Replace" for tightening specifications & procedure.

Front Suspension & Steering

NOTE: On Air Bag Equipped Models, Refer To "Air Bag System Precautions" Located In The Front Of This Manual For System Disarming & Arming Procedures.

NOTE: Refer To "Computer Relearn Procedures" Located In The Front Of This Manual When Battery Power To The Computer Has Been Interrupted.

INDEX

	Page No.
Ball Joint, Replace	7-34
Lower	7-34
Upper	7-34
Ball Joint Inspection	7-34
Control Arm, Replace	7-35
Lower	7-35
Upper	7-35
Hub & Bearing, Replace	7-34

	Page No.
Power Steering	21-1
Power Steering Gear, Replace	7-35
2004	7-35
2005–08	7-35
Power Steering Pump, Replace	7-36
Shock Absorber, Replace	7-34
Installation	7-35
Removal	7-34

	Page No.
Stabilizer Bar, Replace	7-35
Steering Columns	20-1
Steering Knuckle, Replace	7-35
Tightening Specifications	7-36
Transverse Leaf Spring, Replace	7-35

HUB & BEARING

REPLACE

1. Raise and support vehicle, then remove tire and wheel.
2. Remove brake caliper and rotor.
3. Remove stabilizer shaft link from lower control arm.
4. Disconnect wheel speed sensor electrical connector.
5. Support lower control arm using suitable jack stand.
6. Disconnect steering linkage outer tie rod from steering knuckle using separator tool No. J 42188, or equivalent.
7. Loosen upper and lower ball joint stud nuts.
8. Separate steering knuckle from upper and lower control arm using ball joint separator tool No. J 42188, or equivalent.
9. Remove upper and lower ball joint stud nuts.
10. Remove steering knuckle from upper and lower control arms.
11. Remove wheel hub mounting bolts.
12. Remove hub and bearing from steering knuckle.
13. Reverse procedure to install, noting the following:
    a. **Front and rear hub and bearing are not interchangeable. Ensure proper replacement component is being installed.**
    b. Tighten mounting bolts, nuts and screws.

BALL JOINT INSPECTION

1. Raise and support vehicle with jack stands positioned as far outboard as possible near lower ball joint.
2. Wipe ball joints clean. Inspect seals for cuts or tears. Replace ball joint if seals are cut or torn.

3. Inspect and adjust wheel bearings as required.
4. Position dial indicator tool No. J 8001, or equivalent against lowest outboard point on wheel rim.
5. Rock wheel in and out and observe dial indicator reading. This shows horizontal looseness in both joints.
6. Dial indicator reading should not exceed .125 inch. If reading exceeds specifications, inspect lower ball joints for wear and for vertical looseness as follows:
    a. Visually inspect lower ball joint for wear. The retraction of grease fitting into threaded housing indicates wear. On a new ball joint, this round housing projects .050 inch beyond lower ball joint cover surface. Under normal wear, the lower ball joint housing surface retreats inward very slowly.
    b. Visually observe, then scrape a fingernail, scale or screwdriver, across the cover. If housing is flush with or inside cover surface, install a new lower control arm.
    c. Position dial indicator tool against spindle to show vertical movement.
    d. Pry between lower control arm and outer bearing race while observing dial indicator reading. This shows vertical looseness in ball joints. Lower ball joint is not preloaded and may show some looseness.
    e. If dial indicator reading exceeds .125 inch, install a new lower control arm.
    f. If lower ball joint is within specifications but there is excessive horizontal looseness, inspect upper ball joint for wear by disconnecting upper joint from knuckle. Install a new upper ball joint if there is any looseness or stud can be twisted with fingers.

BALL JOINT

REPLACE

Upper

1. Remove steering knuckle as outlined in "Steering Knuckle, Replace."
2. Remove ball joint from knuckle using ball joint remover kit tool Nos. J 9519-E and J 21474-5, or equivalents.
3. Install new ball joint into knuckle using ball joint removal tool kit No. J 9519-E and installer tool No. J 28685, or equivalents.
4. **On 2004 models, torque** ball stud nut to 15 ft. lbs., then rotate an additional 250°.
5. **On 2005–08 models, torque** ball stud nut to 22 ft. lbs., then rotate an additional 225°.
6. **On all models,** install knuckle onto vehicle.

Lower

1. Remove lower control arm as outlined in "Transverse Leaf Spring, Replace."
2. Remove ball joint from control arm using ball joint tool Nos. J 9519-98 and J 9519-E, or equivalents.
3. Install new ball joint into control arm using ball joint tool Nos. J 9519-99 and J 9519-E, or equivalents.
4. **Torque** ball stud nut to 20 ft. lbs., then rotate an additional 180°.
5. Install lower control arm onto vehicle.

SHOCK ABSORBER

REPLACE

Removal

1. Raise and support vehicle, then remove tire and wheel.

2. Remove shock absorber upper mounting nut, insulator retainer and insulator.
3. Remove shock absorber lower mounting nuts.
4. **On models equipped with heavy duty shock option (FE3),** proceed as follows:
   a. Compress shock absorber from bottom upward using suitable pry bar.
   b. Install shock support tool No. J 43822, or equivalent, onto shock to keep it compressed.
5. **On all models,** remove shock absorber from lower control arm and shock tower.
6. Remove shock support tool.
7. Remove insulator and retainer.

Installation

1. **On models less heavy duty shock option (FE3),** proceed as follows:
   a. Install retainer and insulator to new shock absorber.
   b. Install absorber to upper tower.
   c. Install upper insulator, retainer and nut.
   d. Install absorber lower mounting bolts and nuts.
2. **On models equipped with heavy duty shock option (FE3),** proceed as follows:
   a. Install shock support tool No. J 43822, or equivalent, onto new shock absorber.
   b. Install absorber onto vehicle.
   c. Install upper insulator, retainer and nut.
   d. Remove shock support tool.
   e. Compress transverse spring using spring compressor tool No. J 33432-A, or equivalent.
   f. Raise lower control arm, then install absorber lower mounting bolts and nuts.
   g. Tighten mounting bolts and nuts.
   h. Remove spring compressor tool.
3. **On all models,** install tire and wheel, then lower vehicle.

TRANSVERSE LEAF SPRING
REPLACE

1. Raise and support vehicle, then remove tires and wheels.
2. Measure and record front spring adjuster bolt gap, **Fig. 1.**
3. Install transverse spring compressor tool No. J 33432-A and adapters, or equivalents.
4. Compress transverse spring.
5. Remove lower shock absorber mounting bolts from one lower control arm.
6. Disconnect stabilizer bar link from lower control arm.
7. Loosen lower ball joint nut on control arm, but do not remove it.
8. Separate lower ball joint from steering knuckle using ball joint separator tool No. J 42188, or equivalent.
9. Remove separator tool, ball joint nut and ball joint from steering knuckle. Discard ball joint stud nut.

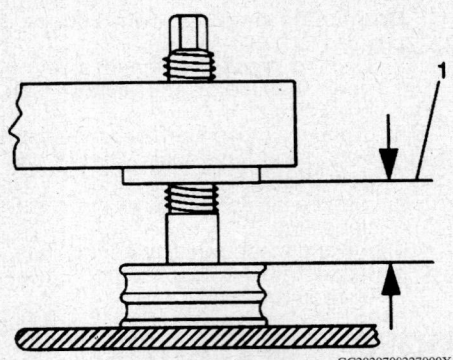

Fig. 1 Transverse spring adjuster gap

10. Support lower control arms using suitable jack stands.
11. Mark position of cam bolts for reference.
12. Remove cam bolts from lower control arm.
13. Remove lower control arm.
14. Remove transverse spring retainers.
15. Remove and discard transverse spring bolts.
16. Remove transverse leaf spring.
17. Remove compressor tool.
18. Reverse procedure to install, noting the following:
    a. Install spring adjuster bolts to height measured.
    b. Install cam bolts to position marked.
    c. Align front wheels.

CONTROL ARM
REPLACE

Upper

1. Raise and support vehicle, then remove tire and wheel.
2. Support lower control arm using suitable jack stand.
3. **On models equipped with Real Time Damping (RTD) suspension,** disconnect RTD sensor link.
4. **On all models,** loosen ball joint stud nut, but do not remove it.
5. Separate upper ball joint stud from upper control arm using ball joint separator tool No. J 42188, or equivalent.
6. Remove tool, nut and ball joint.
7. Remove upper control arm mounting bolts and shims. Record number and position of shims.
8. Remove upper control arm.
9. Reverse procedure to install. **Torque** ball stud nut to 15 ft. lbs., tighten an additional 250° and inspect nut for final **torque** of 41 ft. lbs.

Lower

Refer to "Transverse Leaf Spring, Replace" for lower control arm replacement procedure.

STEERING KNUCKLE
REPLACE

1. Raise and support vehicle, then remove tire and wheel.
2. Remove brake caliper and rotor.
3. Disconnect stabilizer shaft link from lower control arm.
4. Disconnect wheel speed sensor electrical connector.
5. Support lower control arm using suitable jack stand.
6. Separate outer tie rod ball stud from steering knuckle using ball joint separator tool No. J 42188, or equivalent.
7. Separate upper ball joint stud from upper control arm using separator tool.
8. Separate lower ball joint stud from steering knuckle using separator tool.
9. Remove steering knuckle.
10. Reverse procedure to install.

STABILIZER BAR
REPLACE

1. Raise and support vehicle, then remove tire and wheel.
2. Remove stabilizer bar link nuts and link from stabilizer bar and lower control arm.
3. Remove stabilizer bar insulator clamps from front crossmember.
4. Remove stabilizer bar.
5. Reverse procedure to install.

POWER STEERING GEAR
REPLACE
2004

Refer to "Engine Mount, Replace" in "5.7L Engine" section for power steering gear replacement procedure.

2005-08

1. Raise and support vehicle, then remove tires and wheels.
2. Disconnect tie rod ends from steering knuckles.
3. Turn steering wheel far to lefthand side to gain access, then remove upper coupling bolt.
4. Insert tool No. J 42640 or equivalent into steering column access hole to maintain orientation.
5. Remove lower coupling shield, then the lower coupling retaining bolt.
6. Remove stabilizer shaft as outlined under "Stabilizer Bar, Replace."
7. Remove power steering pressure and return hoses from power steering gear.
8. Remove power steering line holddowns from crossmember, then the brake pressure modulator valve bracket.
9. Remove two front crossmember mounting nuts, then using hand tools loosen two rear crossmember mounting nuts .394 inch.

10. Disconnect height sensor arm to control arm then support front of crossmember.
11. Compress coil spring tool allow crossmember lower enough to remove gear using tool No. J 33432-A or equivalent.
12. Remove lower shock mounting bolts, then the brake pipe bracket for lefthand side front brake caliper from crossmember.
13. Remove plastic brake pipe hold down for righthand side front brake pipe.
14. Remove power steering gear mounting bolts and nuts.
15. Move steering gear around brake lines, then remove from vehicle through lefthand side wheelhouse opening.
16. Reverse procedure to install, noting the following:

17. **On models equipped with Z06,** proceed as follows:
   a. Discard crossmember to steering gear insulators and install new ones.
   b. Tighten crossmember mounting nuts using hand tools. Do not use power tools.
   c. Tighten all fasteners to specifications.
   d. Fill and bleed power steering lines.
   e. Inspect front wheel toe and adjust as required.

POWER STEERING PUMP
REPLACE

1. Remove EBTCM/BPMV and bracket.

Position brake pipes aside as required. Cap and plug open lines.
2. Drain power steering fluid into suitable container.
3. Remove power steering fluid reservoir.
4. Remove accessory drive belt.
5. Remove power steering pump pulley using pulley removal tool No. J 25034-B, or equivalent.
6. Disconnect power steering gear inlet hose.
7. Remove power steering pump mounting bolts.
8. Remove power steering pump and bracket.
9. Reverse procedure to install.

TIGHTENING SPECIFICATIONS

Year	Component	Torque/Ft. Lbs.
2004–08	Crossmember	81①
	Lower Control Arm	125
	Lower Control Arm Ball Stud	②
	Power Steering Line End Fittings	20
	Power Steering Pump	18
	Power Steering Reservoir Bracket	37
	Shock Absorber, Lower	21
	Shock Absorber, Upper	19
	Steering Link Outer Tie Rod End Stud	③
	Stabilizer Bar Insulator Clamp	43
	Stabilizer Bar Link	53
	Transverse Leaf Spring	46①
	Upper Control Arm	48
	Upper Control Arm Ball Stud	②
	Wheel Hub Bearing	96

① — Always install new bolts & nuts. Do not use old bolts & nuts.
② — Refer "Ball Joint, Replace" for tightening specifications & procedure.
③ — **Torque** outer tie rod end nut to 15 ft. lbs., to seat outer tie rod stud. Turn the nut an additional 160°. Inspect outer tie rod end nut for a minimum **torque** of 33 ft. lbs.

Wheel Alignment

INDEX

	Page No.		Page No.		Page No.
Front Wheel Alignment	7-37	Preliminary Inspection	7-37	Thrust Angle	7-37
Camber	7-37	Rear Wheel Alignment	7-37	Wheel Alignment	
Caster	7-37	Camber	7-37	Specifications	7-3
Toe-In	7-37	Toe-In	7-37		

PRELIMINARY INSPECTION

Prior to inspecting or adjusting front suspension alignment, inspect suspension components and wheel bearings for damage or excessive wear and replace as required. Ensure tire pressure is properly adjusted, then raise and release front bumper several times to allow vehicle to assume normal ride height. The following items should be inspected prior to performing wheel alignment procedures:

1. Inspect tires for proper inflation pressure.
2. Inspect hubs and bearings for excessive wear.
3. Inspect ball joints and tie rod ends for looseness and wear.
4. Inspect for bent wheel rims, wheel runout and faulty tires (belt shifts).
5. Inspect suspension and steering components for looseness and wear.
6. Inspect for excessive cargo loads.
7. Measure vehicle trim height.

FRONT WHEEL ALIGNMENT

Caster

1. Loosen lower control arm cam bolt nuts.
2. Rotate cam bolts to caster specification setting.
3. Maintain caster setting, then **torque** cam bolt nuts to 125 ft. lbs.
4. Inspect caster and camber settings after tightening. Adjust as required.

Camber

1. Loosen lower control arm cam bolt nuts.
2. Rotate cam bolts to required camber specification setting.
3. Maintain camber setting, then **torque** cam bolt nuts to 125 ft. lbs.
4. Inspect caster and camber settings after tightening. Adjust as required.
5. To obtain additional negative camber beyond cam adjustment capability, remove shims from upper control arms.

Toe-In

1. Loosen jam nut on tie rod.
2. Rotate inner tie rod to toe specification setting.
3. **Torque** jam nut on tie rod end to 50 ft. lbs.
4. Inspect toe setting after tightening. Adjust as required.

REAR WHEEL ALIGNMENT

Camber

1. Loosen lower control arm cam bolt nuts.
2. Rotate cam bolts to required camber specification setting.
3. Maintain camber setting, then **torque** front cam bolt nut to 107 ft. lbs. and **torque** rear cam bolt nut to 70 ft. lbs.
4. Inspect caster and camber settings after tightening. Adjust as required.

Toe-In

1. Loosen rear suspension adjustment link locknut.
2. Rotate inner tie rod to toe specification setting.
3. **Torque** rear suspension adjustment link lock nut to 44 ft. lbs.
4. Inspect toe setting after tightening. Adjust as required.

THRUST ANGLE

The vehicle is steered by the front wheels. The path the rear wheels follow is the thrust angle, **Fig. 1.** Thrust angle should be aligned with the vehicle centerline.

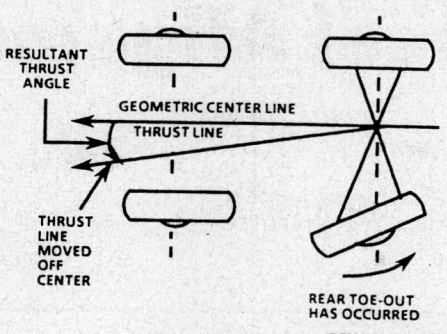

RESULTANT
THRUST
ANGLE

GEOMETRIC CENTER LINE

THRUST LINE

THRUST
LINE
MOVED
OFF
CENTER

REAR TOE-OUT
HAS OCCURRED

GC2049100055000X

Fig. 1   Vehicle thrust angle

CTS

INDEX OF SERVICE OPERATIONS

Page No.

AIR BAG SYSTEM PRECAUTIONS 0-18
BRAKES
Anti-Lock Brakes (Volume 2).. 6-1
Disc Brakes.................... 22-1
Drum Brakes 23-1
Hydraulic Brake Systems 24-1
Power Brake Units 25-1
COMPUTER RELEARN PROCEDURE 0-31
ELECTRICAL
Air Bag System (Volume 2) ... 4-1
Air Conditioning............... 16-1
Alternator, Replace 8-6
Alternators.................. 19-1
Blower Motor, Replace 8-9
Cabin Air Filter, Replace 8-9
Clutch Start Switch, Replace.. 8-7
Coil Pack, Replace 8-7
Cooling Fans 17-1
Cruise Control (Volume 2) 2-1
Dash Gauges (Volume 2) 1-1
Dash Panel Service
(Volume 2)..................... 5-1
Evaporator Core, Replace 8-10
Fuel Pump Relay Location.... 8-5
Fuse Panel & Flasher
Location 8-5
Headlamp Switch, Replace ... 8-8
Heater Core, Replace......... 8-9
Ignition Lock, Replace 8-7
Ignition Switch, Replace 8-7
Instrument Cluster, Replace... 8-8
Multi-Function Switch,
Replace 8-8
Neutral Safety Switch,
Replace 8-8
Passive Restraint Systems
(Volume 2) 4-1
Precautions.................. 8-5
Radio, Replace 8-8
Relay Center Location 8-5
Speed Controls (Volume 2) ... 2-1
Starter Motors 18-1
Starter, Replace 8-6
Steering Columns.............. 20-1
Steering Wheel, Replace...... 8-8
Turn Signal Switch, Replace .. 8-8
Wiper Motor, Replace......... 8-8
Wiper Switch, Replace........ 8-9
Wiper Systems (Volume 2).... 3-1
Wiper Transmission, Replace . 8-9
ELECTRICAL SYMBOL IDENTIFICATION 0-63
FRONT SUSPENSION & STEERING
Ball Joint, Replace 8-58
Ball Joint Inspection 8-58
Coil Spring, Replace 8-58
Control Arm, Replace 8-58
Hub & Bearing, Replace 8-58
Power Steering 21-1
Power Steering Gear,
Replace 8-58

Page No.

Power Steering Pump,
Replace 8-59
Precautions................... 8-58
Stabilizer Bar, Replace........ 8-58
Steering Columns............. 20-1
Steering Knuckle, Replace 8-58
Strut, Replace 8-58
Strut Service................. 8-58
Tie Rod, Replace 8-58
Tightening Specifications...... 8-62
NON-STANDARD TIRE & WHEEL SIZE ADJUSTMENT TO RIDE HEIGHT SPECIFICATIONS & TIRE SIZE CHART 0-61
REAR DRIVE AXLES 27-1
REAR SUSPENSION
Adjustment Link, Replace 8-55
Coil Spring, Replace 8-54
Control Arm, Replace 8-54
Hub & Bearing, Replace 8-54
Knuckle, Replace 8-54
Precautions.................. 8-54
Shock Absorber, Replace 8-54
Stabilizer Shaft, Replace...... 8-55
Tightening Specifications...... 8-57
SERVICE REMINDER & WARNING LAMP RESET PROCEDURES 0-34
SPECIFICATIONS
Fluid Capacities & Cooling
System Data.................. 8-4
Front Wheel Alignment
Specifications.................. 8-3
General Engine
Specifications.................. 8-2
Lubricant Data................ 8-5
Rear Wheel Alignment
Specifications.................. 8-3
Tune Up Specifications 8-3
Vehicle Ride Height
Specifications.................. 8-4
TIRE PRESSURE MONITORING SYSTEM 28-1
VEHICLE IDENTIFICATION 0-1
VEHICLE LIFT POINTS 0-51
VEHICLE MAINTENANCE SCHEDULES 0-73
WHEEL ALIGNMENT
Front Wheel Alignment........ 8-63
Preliminary Inspection 8-63
Rear Wheel Alignment 8-63
Wheel Alignment
Specifications.................. 8-3
WIRE COLOR CODE IDENTIFICATION 0-63
2.8L ENGINE
Camshaft, Replace 8-15
Compression Pressure........ 8-11
Cooling System Bleed......... 8-16
Crankshaft Balancer, Replace. 8-13

Page No.

Crankshaft Front Oil Seal,
Replace 8-16
Crankshaft Rear Oil Seal,
Replace 8-16
Cylinder Head, Replace....... 8-13
Engine Rebuilding
Specifications.................. 29-1
Engine, Replace 8-11
Engine Mount, Replace 8-11
Exhaust Manifold, Replace.... 8-13
Front Cover, Replace 8-14
Fuel Filter, Replace 8-16
Fuel Pump, Replace 8-16
Intake Manifold, Replace...... 8-12
Main & Rod Bearings 8-15
Oil Pan, Replace.............. 8-16
Oil Pump, Replace........... 8-16
Oil Pump Service 8-16
Piston & Rod Assembly 8-15
Pistons, Pins & Rings......... 8-15
Precautions.................. 8-11
Radiator, Replace............. 8-16
Serpentine Drive Belt,
Replace 8-16
Thermostat, Replace.......... 8-16
Tightening Specifications...... 8-17
Timing Chain, Replace........ 8-14
Valve Adjustment 8-13
Water Pump, Replace 8-16
3.2L ENGINE
Camshaft, Replace 8-21
Compression Pressure........ 8-18
Cooling System Bleed......... 8-23
Crankshaft Balancer, Replace. 8-22
Crankshaft Front Oil Seal,
Replace 8-22
Crankshaft Rear Oil Seal,
Replace 8-22
Cylinder Head, Replace....... 8-20
Engine Rebuilding
Specifications.................. 29-1
Engine, Replace 8-18
Engine Mount, Replace 8-18
Exhaust Manifold, Replace.... 8-20
Front Cover, Replace 8-20
Fuel Filter, Replace 8-23
Fuel Pump, Replace 8-23
Intake Manifold, Replace...... 8-19
Intake Plenum, Replace 8-19
Main & Rod Bearings 8-22
Oil Pan, Replace.............. 8-22
Oil Pump, Replace........... 8-22
Piston & Rod Assembly 8-21
Pistons, Pins & Rings......... 8-21
Precautions.................. 8-18
Radiator, Replace............. 8-23
Serpentine Drive Belt 8-23
Thermostat, Replace.......... 8-23
Tightening Specifications...... 8-27
Timing Belt, Replace.......... 8-20
Valve Adjustment 8-20
Valve Cover, Replace 8-20
Water Pump, Replace 8-23

3.6L ENGINE | Page No.

Camshaft, Replace 8-33
Compression Pressure........ 8-29
Cooling System Bleed 8-34
Crankshaft Balancer, Replace. 8-31
Crankshaft Front Oil Seal,
Replace 8-33
Crankshaft Rear Oil Seal,
Replace 8-34
Cylinder Head, Replace....... 8-30
Engine Rebuilding
Specifications................. 29-1
Engine, Replace 8-29
Engine Mount, Replace 8-29
Exhaust Manifold, Replace.... 8-30
Front Cover, Replace 8-31
Fuel Filter, Replace 8-35
Fuel Pump, Replace 8-35
Intake Manifold, Replace...... 8-30
Main & Rod Bearings 8-33
Oil Pan, Replace.............. 8-34
Oil Pump, Replace............ 8-34
Oil Pump Service 8-34
Piston & Rod Assembly 8-33
Pistons, Pins & Rings 8-33
Precautions................... 8-29
Radiator, Replace............. 8-35
Serpentine Drive Belt,
Replace 8-34
Thermostat, Replace.......... 8-35
Tightening Specifications...... 8-41
Timing Chain, Replace........ 8-31
Valve Adjustment 8-31
Valve Cover, Replace 8-31
Water Pump, Replace 8-35

5.7L Engine | Page No.

Camshaft, Replace 8-45
Compression Pressure........ 8-42
Cooling System Bleed 8-46
Crankshaft Balancer, Replace. 8-45
Crankshaft Rear Oil Seal,
Replace 8-45
Crankshaft Seal, Replace..... 8-45
Cylinder Head, Replace....... 8-44
Engine Rebuilding
Specifications................. 29-1
Engine, Replace 8-42
Engine Mount, Replace 8-42
Exhaust Manifold, Replace.... 8-44
Front Cover, Replace 8-45
Fuel Filter, Replace 8-46
Fuel Pump, Replace 8-46
Intake Manifold, Replace...... 8-43
Main & Rod Bearings 8-45
Oil Pan, Replace.............. 8-46
Oil Pump, Replace............ 8-46
Oil Pump Service 8-46
Piston & Rod Assembly 8-45
Pistons, Pins & Rings 8-45
Precautions................... 8-42
Radiator 8-46
Serpentine Drive Belt 8-46
Thermostat, Replace.......... 8-46
Tightening Specifications...... 8-47
Timing Chain, Replace........ 8-45
Valve Adjustment 8-45
Valve Cover, Replace 8-44
Water Pump, Replace 8-46

6.0L Engine | Page No.

Camshaft, Replace 8-51
Compression Pressure........ 8-48
Cooling System Bleed 8-51
Crankshaft Balancer, Replace. 8-50
Crankshaft Rear Oil Seal,
Replace 8-51
Crankshaft Seal, Replace 8-51
Cylinder Head, Replace....... 8-50
Engine Rebuilding
Specifications................. 29-1
Engine, Replace 8-49
Engine Mount, Replace 8-48
Exhaust Manifold, Replace.... 8-50
Front Cover, Replace 8-51
Fuel Filter, Replace 8-52
Fuel Pump, Replace 8-52
Intake Manifold, Replace...... 8-49
Main & Rod Bearings 8-51
Oil Pan, Replace.............. 8-51
Oil Pump, Replace............ 8-51
Oil Pump Service 8-51
Piston & Rod Assembly 8-51
Pistons, Pins & Rings 8-51
Precautions................... 8-48
Radiator, Replace............. 8-52
Serpentine Drive Belt 8-51
Thermostat, Replace.......... 8-52
Tightening Specifications...... 8-53
Timing Chain, Replace........ 8-51
Valve Adjustment 8-50
Valve Cover, Replace 8-50
Water Pump, Replace 8-52

Specifications

GENERAL ENGINE SPECIFICATIONS

Year	Engine		Fuel Injection System	Bore & Stroke	Compression Ratio	Net H.P. @ RPM	Maximum Torque Ft. Lbs. @ RPM	Normal Oil Pressure, Pounds
	Liter	VIN Code①						
2004	3.2L	N	SMFI	3.45 × 3.47	10.0:1	220 @ 6000	220 @ 3400	21.7
	3.6L	7	SMFI	3.70 × 3.37	10.2:1	255 @ 6500	252 @ 2800	②
	5.7L	S	SMFI	3.90 × 3.62	10.5:1	400 @ 6000	395 @ 4800	②
2005	3.6L	7	SMFI	3.70 × 3.37	10.2:1	255 @ 6500	252 @ 2800	②
	5.7L	S	SMFI	3.90 × 3.62	10.5:1	400 @ 6000	395 @ 4800	②
2006–07	2.8L	T	SMFI	3.50 × 2.94	10:0:1	210 @ 6500	194 @ 3300	③
	3.6L	7	SMFI	3.70 × 3.37	10.2:1	255 @ 6500	252 @ 3400	②
	6.0L	U	SMFI	4.00 × 3.62	10:9:1	400 @ 6000	395 @ 4800	②
2008	2.8L	T	SFI	3.50 × 2.94	10:0:1	210 @ 6500	194 @ 3300	③
	3.6L	V	SIDI	3.70 × 3.37	10.2:1	255 @ 6500	252 @ 3400	②
	3.6L	7	SFI	3.70 × 3.37	10.2:1	255 @ 6500	252 @ 3400	②

① — The eight digit denotes engine code.

② — Engine hot, minimum oil pressure 6 psi @ 1000 RPM; 18 psi @ 2000 RPM; 24 psi @ 4000 RPM.

③ — Engine hot, minimum oil pressure 10 psi @ 1000 RPM; 20 psi @ 2000 RPM.

TUNE UP SPECIFICATIONS

| Year & Engine, VIN① | Spark Plug Gap | Ignition Timing | | | Curb Idle Speed | Fast Idle Speed | Fuel Pump Pressure, psi | Valve Lash |
		Firing Order	Degrees BTDC	Mark				
2004								
3.2L/N	.053	②	③	—	③	③	49–55	④
3.6L/7	.043	②	③	—	③	③	55–60	④
5.7L/S	.040	1-8-7-2-6-5-4-3	③	—	③	③	55–62	④
2005								
3.6L/7	.043	②	③	—	③	③	55–60	④
5.7L/S	.040	1-8-7-2-6-5-4-3	③	—	③	③	55–62	④
2006								
2.8L/T	.043	②	③	—	③	③	55–60	④
3.6L/7	.043	②	③	—	③	③	55–60	④
6.0L/U	.040	1-8-7-2-6-5-4-3	③	—	③	③	55–62	④
2007								
2.8L/T	.043	②	③	—	③	③	55–60	④
3.6L/7	.043	②	③	—	③	③	55–60	④
6.0L/U	.040	1-8-7-2-6-5-4-3	③	—	③	③	55–62	④
2008								
2.8L/T	.043	②	③	—	③	③	55–60	④
3.6L/V	.043	②	③	—	③	③	55–60	④
3.6L/7	.043	②	③	—	③	③	55–60	④

① — The eight digit denotes engine code.

② — Cylinder numbering from front to rear: righthand bank, 1, 3, 5; lefthand bank, 2, 4, 6. Firing order 1-2-3-4-5-6.

③ — Computer controlled, not adjustable.

④ — Equipped w/hydraulic lash adjusters.

FRONT WHEEL ALIGNMENT SPECIFICATIONS

| Year | Caster Angle, Degrees | | Camber Angle, Degrees | | Total Toe, Degrees | | Ball Joint Inspection |
	Limits	Desired	Limits	Desired	Limits	Desired	
2004	+4.6 to +5.6②	+5.1②	–1 to 0②	–.5②	0 to +.4	+.2	①
2005–08	+4.5 to +5.7③	+5.1③	–1.1 to +1③	–.5③	0 to +.4	+.2	①

① — Refer to Front Suspension & Steering section for ball joint inspection procedure.

② — Cross caster or camber (LH-RH) 0 (+/-.5°).

③ — Cross caster or camber (LH-RH) 0 (+/-.6°).

REAR WHEEL ALIGNMENT SPECIFICATIONS

| Year | Model | Camber Angle, Degrees | | Total Toe, Degrees | | Thrust Angle, Degrees | |
		Limits	Desired	Limits	Desired	Limits	Desired
2004	①	–1.4 to –.6③	–1.0③	+.08 to +.40	+.24	–.15 to +.15	0
	②	–1.8 to –1.0③	–1.4③	+.08 to +.40	+.24	–.15 to +.15	0
2005–08	①	–1.5 to –.5	–.5	0 to +.40	+.20⑤	–.20 to +.20	0
	④	–1.5 to –.5	–.5	0 to +.40	+.20⑥	–.20 to +.20	0

① — Soft ride suspension FE1.

② — Sport suspension FE3.

③ — Cross camber (LH-RH) 0 (+/-.75°).

④ — Optional suspensions FE2, FE3 & FE4.

⑤ — Individual toe to be greater than or equal to –.05°.

⑥ — Individual toe to be greater than or equal to –.00°.

VEHICLE RIDE HEIGHT SPECIFICATIONS

Model	Year	Body Style	Manu-facturer's Original Tire Size	Front Dim.	Front Specification Inches	Front Specification mm	Rear Dim.	Rear Specification Inches	Rear Specification mm
All	2004–08	All	①	Z②	1.7–2.5	43.6–63.6	D③	2.0–2.7	49.7–69.7
FE2	2005–08	All	①	Z②	1.7–2.5	43.6–63.6	D③	2.4	59.7
FE3	2005–08	All	①	Z②	1.7–2.5	43.6–63.6	D③	2.3	59.5
FE4	2005–08	All	①	Z②	1.7–2.5	33.2–53.2	D③	1.9	48.7

D-Dimension — Vertical distance between centerline of inboard rear lower control arm bolt and centerline of outboard rear lower control arm bolt.

Z-Dimension — From pivot bolt center line down to lower corner of lower ball joint.

FE2 — Suspension System Ride, Handling

FE3 — Suspension System Soft Ride

FE4 — Suspension System Special Ride and Handling

① — See door sticker or inside of glove compartment for manufacturers original tire size specifications. If tires on vehicle do not match original tire size and measurement is not within limits, it will be required you refer to the Non-Standard Tire & Wheel Size Adjustment To Ride Height Specification & Tire Size Adjustment Charts.

② — Refer to **Fig. 1** for measurement location.

③ — Refer to **Fig. 2** for measurement location.

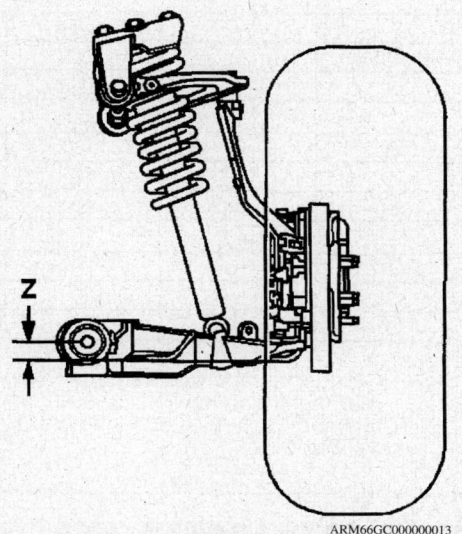

ARM66GC000000013

Fig. 1 Front suspension measurement

ARM66GC000000014

Fig. 2 Rear suspension measurement

FLUID CAPACITIES & COOLING SYSTEM DATA

Year	Engine/Liter	Coolant Capacity, Qts.	Coolant Type	Radiator Cap Relief Pressure, Lbs.	Thermo-stat Opening Temp., F°	Fuel Tank, Gals	Engine Oil Refill, Qts.	Transmission Oil Manual, Pts.	Transmission Oil Auto-matic, Qts.	Rear Axle Oil, Pts.
2004	3.2L	10.4	Dex-Cool	—	194	17.5	5.0	2.6	9.0	2.74
	3.6L	10.4	Dex-Cool	—	194	17.5	6.0	2.6	9.0	2.74
	5.7L	13.2	Dex-Cool	—	194	17.5	6.0	①	9.0	2.74
2005	3.6L	10.4	Dex-Cool	—	194	17.5	6.0	2.6	9.0	2.74
	5.7L	13.2	Dex-Cool	—	194	17.5	6.0	①	9.0	2.74
2006	2.8L	10.6	Dex-Cool	—	194	17.5	6.0	①	9.0	2.74
	3.6L	12.0	Dex-Cool	—	194	17.5	6.0	2.6	9.0	2.74
	6.0L	13.4	Dex-Cool	—	194	17.5	5.5	①	9.0	2.74
2007	2.8L	11.7	Dex-Cool	—	194	17.5	6.0	①	9.0	2.74
	3.6L	12.1	Dex-Cool	—	194	17.5	6.0	2.6	9.0	2.74
	6.0L	13.4	Dex-Cool	—	194	17.5	6.0	①	9.0	2.74
2008	2.8L/T	10.6	Dex-Cool	—	194	17.5	6.0	①	9.0	2.74
	3.6L/V	12.0	Dex-Cool	—	194	17.5	6.0	2.6	9.0	2.74
	3.6L/7	12.0	Dex-Cool	—	194	17.5	6.0	2.6	9.0	2.74

① — CTS, 3.8 pts. CTS-V, 7.4 pts.

LUBRICANT DATA

Year	Model	Lubricant Type		
		Automatic Transaxle	Power Steering	Brake System
2004–05	All	Dexron III	①	DOT 3
2006–08	All	Dexron VI	①	DOT 3

① — Power steering fluid GM part No. 89021184, or equivalent.

Electrical

NOTE: On Air Bag Equipped Models, Refer To "Air Bag System Precautions" Located In The Front Of This Manual For System Disarming & Arming Procedures.

NOTE: Refer To "Computer Relearn Procedures" Located In The Front Of This Manual When Battery Power To The Computer Has Been Interrupted.

INDEX

	Page No.
Air Bag System (Volume 2)	4-1
Air Conditioning	16-1
Alternator, Replace	8-6
3.2L Engine	8-6
3.6L Engine	8-6
5.7L & 6.0L Engines	8-6
Alternators	19-1
Blower Motor, Replace	8-9
Cabin Air Filter, Replace	8-9
Clutch Start Switch, Replace	8-7
Coil Pack, Replace	8-7
3.2L Engine	8-7
Lefthand	8-7
Righthand	8-7
3.6L Engine	8-7
5.7L & 6.0L Engines	8-7
Cooling Fans	17-1
Cruise Control (Volume 2)	2-1

	Page No.
Dash Gauges (Volume 2)	1-1
Dash Panel Service (Volume 2)	5-1
Evaporator Core, Replace	8-10
Fuel Pump Relay Location	8-5
Fuse Panel & Flasher Location	8-5
Headlamp Switch, Replace	8-8
Heater Core, Replace	8-9
Ignition Lock, Replace	8-7
Ignition Switch, Replace	8-7
Instrument Cluster, Replace	8-8
Multi-Function Switch, Replace	8-8
Neutral Safety Switch, Replace	8-8
Passive Restraint Systems (Volume 2)	4-1
Precautions	8-5
Air Bag Systems	8-5
Battery Ground Cable	8-5

	Page No.
Fuel Pressure Relief	8-5
Radio, Replace	8-8
Relay Center Location	8-5
Speed Controls (Volume 2)	2-1
Starter Motors	18-1
Starter, Replace	8-6
2.8L Engine	8-6
3.2L Engine	8-6
3.6L Engine	8-6
5.7L & 6.0L Engines	8-6
Steering Columns	20-1
Steering Wheel, Replace	8-8
Turn Signal Switch, Replace	8-8
Wiper Motor, Replace	8-8
Wiper Switch, Replace	8-9
Wiper Systems (Volume 2)	3-1
Wiper Transmission, Replace	8-9

PRECAUTIONS

Air Bag Systems

Refer to "Air Bag System Precautions" in the front of this manual for system disarming and arming procedures.

Battery Ground Cable

Prior to service, record radio presets, then disconnect battery ground cable and isolate as required.

Fuel Pressure Relief

1. Record radio presets.
2. Turn ignition Off.
3. Disconnect battery ground cable and isolate as required.
4. Loosen fuel filler cap to relieve fuel tank vapor pressure.
5. Remove cap to fuel pressure service connection.
6. Install tool Nos. J 34730-1A and J 42242, or equivalents, to fuel pressure service connection.
7. Place bleed hose into suitable container, then open bleed valve to relieve fuel system.
8. Place a suitable shop towel under connections to protect fuel spillage.
9. Remove tools from service connections.
10. Install cap to fuel pressure service connection.

FUSE PANEL & FLASHER LOCATION

The lefthand side rear passenger compartment fuse block is located under the lefthand side of the rear seat. The righthand side rear passenger compartment fuse block is located under the righthand side of the rear seat. The steering column fuse block is located behind the driver knee bolster, at the base of the steering column. The underhood fuse block is located on the righthand side front corner of the engine compartment.

The turn signal/hazard lamp control flasher module is located behind the lefthand side of the instrument panel.

FUEL PUMP RELAY LOCATION

The fuel pump relay is located in the fuse block under the righthand side of the rear seat.

RELAY CENTER LOCATION

Relays are located in the rear and underhood fuse blocks. Refer to "Fuse Panel & Flasher Location."

STARTER
REPLACE

2.8L Engine

1. Raise and support vehicle.
2. Disconnect starter solenoid electrical connector.
3. Remove starter terminal nut, then the positive battery cable from starter.
4. Remove starter motor mounting bolts, then the starter.
5. Reverse procedure to install, noting the following:
   a. **Torque** starter motor mounting bolts to 37 ft. lbs.
   b. **Torque** starter terminal nut to 115 inch lbs.

3.2L Engine

1. Raise and support vehicle using suitable lift.
2. Disconnect HO2S electrical connector at sensor.
3. Remove exhaust pipe to lefthand and righthand catalytic converter attaching nuts.
4. Lower exhaust and allow to rest on floor panel brace.
5. Remove lefthand and righthand converter seal and gasket.
6. Remove converter to hanger and then the converter to exhaust manifold attaching nuts.
7. Remove righthand catalytic converter.
8. Remove starter heat shield bolt and nut, then the starter heat shield.
9. Remove starter solenoid S terminal and disconnect lead from starter.
10. Remove starter terminal nut, then the battery positive from starter.
11. Remove starter mounting bolts, then the starter assembly.
12. Reverse procedure to install, noting the following:
    a. **Torque** starter motor bolts to 30 ft. lbs.
    b. **Torque** battery positive cable to 10 ft. lbs.
    c. **Torque** starter S terminal nut to 44 inch lbs.
    d. **Torque** starter heat shield nuts to 71 inch lbs.
    e. **Torque** exhaust manifold pipe nuts to 18 ft. lbs.
    f. **Torque** converter hanger nuts to 18 ft. lbs.
    g. **Torque** catalytic converter nuts to 11 ft. lbs.

3.6L Engine

1. Raise and support vehicle.
2. Disconnect starter solenoid electrical connector.
3. Remove starter terminal nut, then the positive battery cable from starter.
4. Remove starter motor mounting bolts, then the starter.
5. Reverse procedure to install, noting the following:
   a. **Torque** starter motor mounting bolts to 37 ft. lbs.

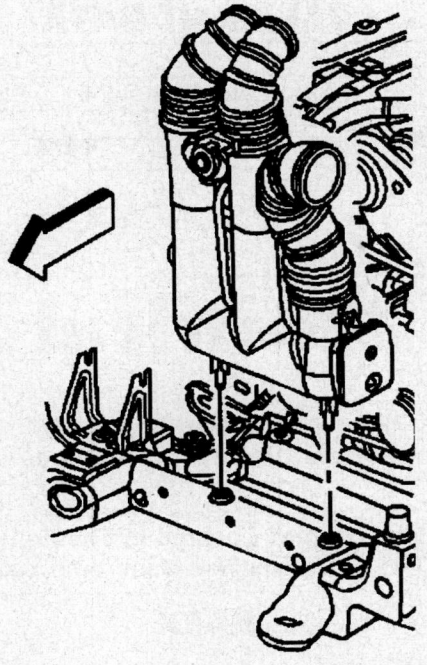

ARM66GC000000031

Fig. 1   Air resonator removal. 3.2L engine

   b. **Torque** starter terminal nut to 115 inch lbs.

5.7L & 6.0L Engines

1. Raise and support vehicle.
2. Support exhaust system with suitable jack.
3. Disconnect exhaust system from lefthand and righthand catalytic converters.
4. Disconnect oxygen sensor electrical connector.
5. Remove righthand catalytic converter to exhaust manifold retaining nuts.
6. Remove catalytic converter. Discard seal.
7. Remove positive battery cable retaining nut.
8. Remove starter motor mounting bolts, then the starter.
9. Reverse procedure to install. **Torque** starter motor mounting bolts to 37 ft. lbs.

ALTERNATOR
REPLACE

3.2L Engine

1. Disconnect air intake duct hose from Mass Air Flow (MAF) and Intake Air Temperature (IAT) sensor.
2. Remove intake air resonator to cooling fan attaching bolts.
3. Disconnect air intake duct hoses from throttle body then lift intake air resonator from frame, **Fig. 1.**
4. Rotate drive belt tensioner clockwise to release tension.
5. Slide drive belt from water pump pul-

ley, allowing tensioner to return and then remove drive belt from accessory pulleys.
6. Loosen drive belt tensioner bolts, then remove tensioner bolts and tensioner from engine.
7. Remove alternator mounting bolts.
8. Disconnect electrical connector wiring harness, then the battery positive cable.
9. Remove alternator assembly.
10. Reverse procedure to install, noting the following:
    a. **Torque** battery terminal nut to 111 inch lbs.
    b. **Torque** alternator mounting nuts to 26 ft. lbs.
    c. Route drive belt as outlined in "Serpentine Drive Belt" in "3.2L Engine" section.
    d. **Torque** drive belt tension bolts to 26 ft. lbs.

3.6L Engine

1. Remove drive belt as outlined in "Serpentine Drive Belt" in "3.6L Engine" section.
2. Install suitable engine support tool.
3. Raise and support vehicle.
4. Disconnect alternator electrical connector.
5. Position alternator output BAT terminal boot aside, then remove terminal nut and disconnect battery positive lead from alternator.
6. Disconnect electronic brake control module electrical connector.
7. Remove engine mount lower retaining nuts.
8. Remove lower alternator mounting bolts.
9. Lower vehicle.
10. Raise engine using suitable engine support tool.
11. Remove upper alternator mounting bolts, then the alternator.
12. Reverse procedure to install, noting the following:
    a. **Torque** alternator mounting bolts to 37 ft. lbs.
    b. **Torque** "BAT" terminal nut to 89 inch lbs.

5.7L & 6.0L Engines

1. Remove air cleaner assembly.
2. Drain coolant into suitable container.
3. Disconnect surge tank hose.
4. Remove fan shroud to radiator mounting bolts.
5. Disconnect upper radiator hose at radiator.
6. Remove A/C line retaining clip retaining screw.
7. Disconnect fan motor electrical connector.
8. Pull upward to remove fan assembly.
9. Remove accessory drive belt.
10. Remove alternator mounting bolts.
11. Remove alternator from mounting bracket.
12. Disconnect alternator electrical connectors.
13. Reverse procedure to install. **Torque** alternator mounting bolts to 37 ft. lbs.

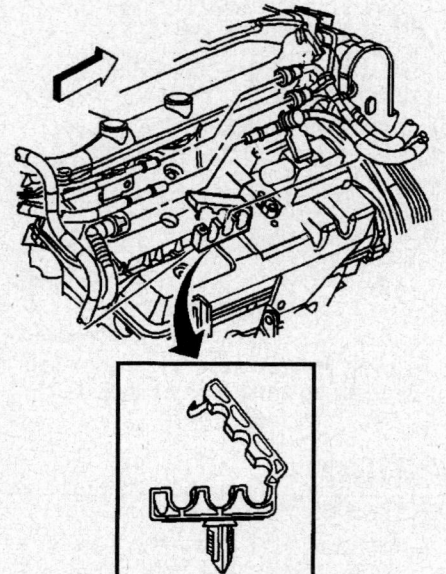

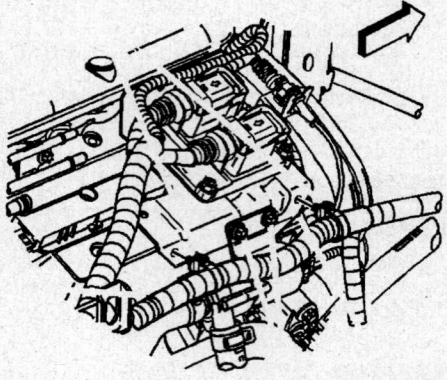

ARM66GC000000019

Fig. 3 EVAP & retainer connect fitting removal. 3.2L engine

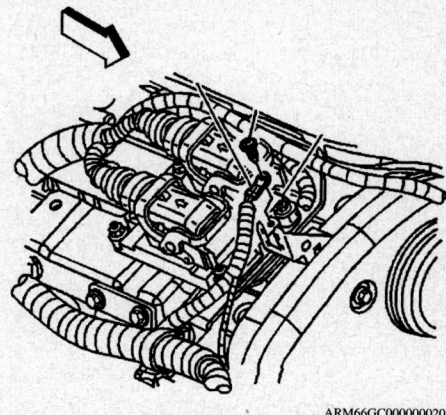

ARM66GC000000020

Fig. 4 ECM wire removal. 3.2L engine

ARM66GC000000018

Fig. 2 Quick connect fitting removal. 3.2L engine

COIL PACK
REPLACE

3.2L Engine
LEFTHAND

1. Relieve fuel pressure as outlined in "Precautions."
2. Disconnect return hose/pipe and feed hose/pipe quick connect fittings from fuel rail, **Fig. 2.**
3. Disconnect EVAP quick connect fitting, then open retainer at engine control module (ECM) bracket to remove chassis hose/pipes, **Fig. 3.**
4. Disconnect electrical wiring harness at ECM bracket.
5. Remove coolant pump attaching bolts to ECM bracket.
6. Remove ECM ground wire at ECM, **Fig. 4.**
7. Disconnect ECM connectors from ECM.
8. Remove coolant inlet pipe to ECM bracket attaching bolt.
9. Remove ECM bracket bolts from intake plenum and cylinder head.
10. Remove ECM bracket from engine with ECM attached.
11. Disconnect electrical connectors from righthand knock sensor.
12. Disconnect electrical connectors from coil pack.
13. Remove coil pack attaching bolts, then install tool No. J 43301, or equivalent, into coil pack and pull coil pack evenly from camshaft cover, **Fig. 5.**
14. Reverse procedure to install, noting the following:
    a. **Torque** coil pack bolts to 71 inch lbs.
    b. **Torque** ECM bracket to cylinder head bolt to 15 ft. lbs.
    c. **Torque** ECM bracket to intake ple-

num bolts to 71 ft. lbs.
    d. **Torque** coolant pipe support bolt to 15 ft. lbs.
    e. **Torque** ECM screw to 40 inch lbs.
    f. **Torque** coolant pump to ECM bracket to 89 inch lbs.

RIGHTHAND

1. Remove oil filler spout.
2. Disconnect vacuum brake booster hose and wiring harness from remote power steering fluid reservoir.
3. Disconnect vacuum brake booster hose from vacuum.
4. Remove remote power steering fluid reservoir mounting bolts Nos. 1 and 3, **Fig. 6.**
5. Disconnect coil pack electrical connector.
6. Remove coil pack attaching bolts, install tool No. J 43301, or equivalent, into coil pack and remove coil pack pulling evenly off from camshaft cover, **Fig. 5.**
7. Reverse procedure to install, noting the following:
    a. **Torque** coil pack bolts to 71 inch lbs.
    b. **Torque** intake plenum mounting bolts to 80 inch lbs.
    c. **Torque** cylinder head mounting bolts to 18 ft. lbs.

3.6L Engine

1. Remove engine cover.
2. Disconnect air cleaner duct from throttle body.
3. **On cylinders 1, 2 and 3,** reposition intake manifold as follows:
    a. Disconnect PCV hose from camshaft cover.
    b. Remove intake manifold attaching bolts.
    c. Remove intake manifold brace bolts, then the brace.
    d. Reposition upper and lower intake manifolds to gain access to ignition coils.
4. **On all cylinders,** disconnect ignition coil electrical connector.
5. Remove ignition coil retaining bolts, then the coil.
6. Reverse procedure to install.

5.7L & 6.0L Engines

1. Remove fuel injector sight shield.
2. Disconnect coil assembly electrical connector.
3. Disconnect spark plug wire at ignition coils.
4. Remove ignition coil bracket mounting bolts.
5. Remove ignition coil assembly.
6. Reverse procedure to install. Torque ignition coil bracket mounting bolts to 106 inch lbs.

IGNITION LOCK
REPLACE

1. Ensure ignition is in Start position.
2. Press in release button using suitable awl tool.
3. Turn ignition to Run, then remove ignition lock cylinder.
4. Reverse procedure to install.

IGNITION SWITCH
REPLACE

1. Remove upper and lower steering column trim covers.
2. Remove ignition lock cylinder as outlined in "Ignition Lock, Replace."
3. Disconnect electrical connector from theft deterrent control module.
4. Remove theft deterrent control module.
5. Rotate key alarm 90°, then remove key alarm electrical connector from ignition lock cylinder, **Fig. 7.**
6. Disconnect electrical connector from ignition switch.
7. Remove wires located within ignition switch clip.
8. Remove ignition switch assembly, **Fig. 8.**
9. Reverse procedure to install.

CLUTCH START SWITCH
REPLACE

1. Remove driver's side lower instrument panel.
2. Disconnect clutch pedal position switch electrical connector.

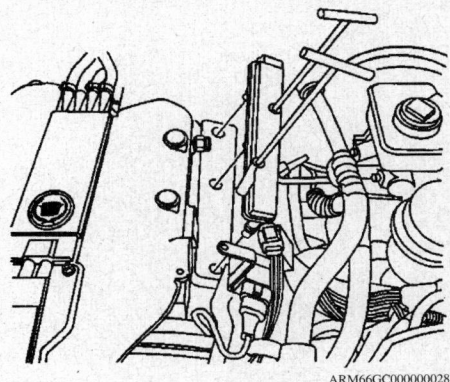

Fig. 5 Coil pack removal. 3.2L engine

3. Remove retaining plate from clutch pedal position switch, then the switch from cylinder push rod.
4. Reverse procedure to install.

NEUTRAL SAFETY SWITCH
REPLACE

1. Raise and support vehicle.
2. Remove transmission manual shift shaft attaching nut.
3. Disconnect transmission manual shift shaft shift linkage.
4. Remove floor panel tunnel brace to floor panel attaching bolts, then the tunnel brace from floor panel, **Fig. 9.**
5. Remove exhaust pipe to catalytic converter nuts.
6. Disconnect propeller shaft coupler from transmission flange.
7. Push front propeller shaft toward rear of vehicle to release coupler from transmission flange.
8. Secure front propeller shaft to shift control lever using suitable wire.
9. Remove and discard shaft seal and cup plug using suitable screwdriver.
10. Remove transmission oil pan and filter as outlined in **MOTOR's "Domestic Transmission, In-Vehicle Service" manual or "Transmission Service DVD."**
11. Disconnect electrical connector from manual shift shaft position switch.
12. Remove manual shift shaft position switch retaining pin.
13. Remove manual shaft spring and bolts.
14. Support transmission using a suitable transmission jack.
15. Lower transmission jack to access manual shift shaft.
16. Remove manual shift shaft position assembly from transmission, **Fig. 10.**
17. Reverse procedure to install, noting the following:
    a. Install a .8 mm spacer between lever and spring, **Fig. 11.**
    b. **Torque** detent spring bolts to 97 inch lbs.
    c. **Torque** manual shift shaft nut to 11 ft. lbs.
    d. **Torque** catalytic converter nuts to 11 ft. lbs.

e. **Torque** floor panel tunnel brace bolts to 18 ft. lbs.
f. **Torque** propeller shaft bolts to 63 ft. lbs.
g. **Torque** support bearing nuts to 37 ft. lbs.

HEADLAMP SWITCH
REPLACE

Refer to "Multi-Function Switch, Replace" for headlamp switch replacement procedure.

MULTI-FUNCTION SWITCH
REPLACE

1. Remove upper and lower steering column trim covers.
2. Place tilt column in center position.
3. Disconnect multi-function switch assembly electrical connectors, then remove assembly mounting screws, **Fig. 12.**
4. Remove multi-function switch assembly.
5. Reverse procedure to install, noting the following:
    a. **Torque** multi-function switch top of column screw to 27 inch lbs.
    b. **Torque** multi-function switch front face screw to 62 inch lbs.

TURN SIGNAL SWITCH
REPLACE

Refer to "Multi-Function Switch, Replace" for turn signal switch replacement procedure.

STEERING WHEEL
REPLACE

1. Remove driver's side air bag module from steering wheel as outlined in "Passive Restraint Systems" chapter.
2. Disconnect steering column electrical connector.
3. Remove steering wheel retaining nut.
4. Remove steering wheel using steering wheel puller tool Nos. J 42578 and J 1859-A, or equivalent.
5. Reverse procedure to install. **Torque** steering wheel nut to 30 ft. lbs.

INSTRUMENT CLUSTER
REPLACE

1. Tilt steering wheel to lowest position.
2. Remove instrument panel cluster trim panel using suitable flat bladed tool.
3. Remove instrument panel to cluster attaching screws.
4. Install suitable flat bladed tool between cluster and instrument panel, release cluster retainers, then remove cluster and disconnect electrical connectors.
5. Reverse procedure to install. **Torque** screws to 18 inch lbs.

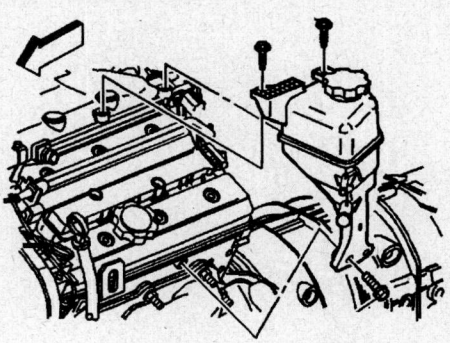

Fig. 6 Power steering reservoir mounting bolt Nos. 1 & 3. 3.2L engine

RADIO
REPLACE

1. Remove center instrument panel air vents.
2. Remove screw behind ashtray.
3. Remove HVAC control module trim plate.
4. Disconnect HVAC control module and ash tray electrical connectors.
5. Remove HVAC control module.
6. Remove radio to instrument panel attaching screws.
7. Disconnect electrical connectors, then remove radio.
8. Reverse procedure to install, noting the following:
    a. **Torque** ashtray attaching screw to 18 inch lbs.
    b. **Torque** HVAC control module screws to 18 inch lbs.
    c. **Torque** radio assembly screws to 80 inch lbs.

WIPER MOTOR
REPLACE

1. Remove wiper motor fuses from underhood fuse block.
2. Remove wiper arm assemblies.
3. Remove air inlet grille attaching screws, then the inlet grille.
4. Push or pull on wiper transmission linkage to rotate wiper motor crank arm from park position to area opposite park position.
5. Remove wiper motor module mounting bolts.
6. Disconnect module electrical connector, then remove module, **Fig. 13.**
7. Remove drive links from wiper motor crank arm using wiper linkage separator tool No. J 39232, or equivalent.
8. Remove wiper motor to wiper motor module retaining screws.
9. Remove wiper motor.
10. Reverse procedure to install, noting the following:
    a. **Torque** attaching bolts and screws to 89 inch lbs.
    b. Install drive links onto crank arm and wiper transmission drive shafts using wiper linkage installer tool No. J 39529, or equivalent.

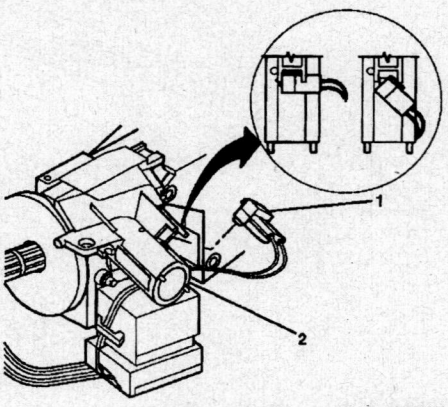

Fig. 7 Key alarm electrical connector

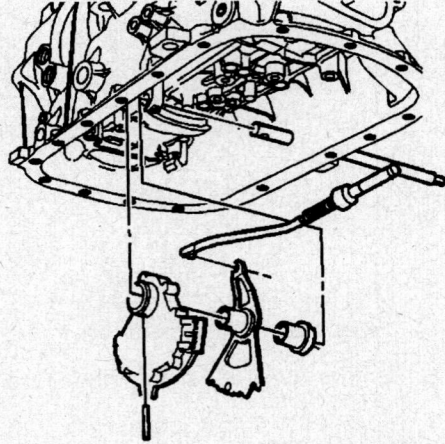

Fig. 10 Manual shift shaft assembly

WIPER SWITCH

REPLACE

Refer to "Multi-Function Switch, Replace" for wiper switch replacement procedure.

WIPER TRANSMISSION

REPLACE

1. Remove drive links from wiper crank arm and wiper transmission shafts as outlined in "Wiper Motor, Replace."
2. Remove transmission links from module.
3. Reverse procedure to install.

BLOWER MOTOR

REPLACE

1. Remove righthand side lower instrument panel trim panel.
2. Release locking tabs, then disconnect instrument panel trim panel electrical connector.
3. Release glove compartment door tabs.
4. Lower door and remove glove compartment door attaching screws.

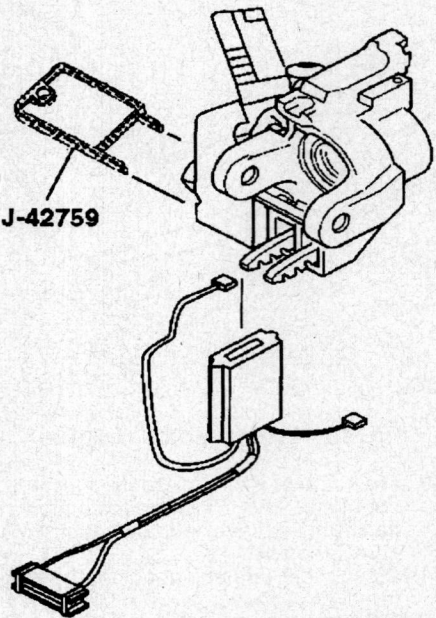

Fig. 8 Ignition switch

5. Remove instrument panel compartment screws, then the compartment.
6. Disconnect blower motor electrical connector.
7. Disconnect blower motor processor electrical connector.
8. Remove blower motor attaching screws, then the blower motor.
9. Reverse procedure to install, noting the following:
   a. **Torque** lower instrument panel and glove compartment screws to 18 inch lbs.
   b. **Torque** blower motor screws to 13 inch lbs.
   c. **Torque** air inlet housing bolts to 53 inch lbs.

CABIN AIR FILTER

REPLACE

1. Remove air inlet grille as outlined in "Wiper Motor, Replace."
2. Remove access cover by releasing tabs on either side.
3. Lift filter cover, then remove cabin air filter, **Fig. 14**.
4. Reverse procedure to install.

HEATER CORE

REPLACE

1. Recover refrigerant as outlined in "Air Conditioning" chapter.
2. Remove battery, then drain engine coolant into suitable container.
3. Disconnect heater inlet and heater outlet hoses.
4. Disconnect both A/C lines at cowl panel.
5. Install probe tool No. J 45689 or equivalent, into two small openings of plastic quick joint, then remove quick joint clamps, **Fig. 15**.
6. Disconnect both A/C lines.

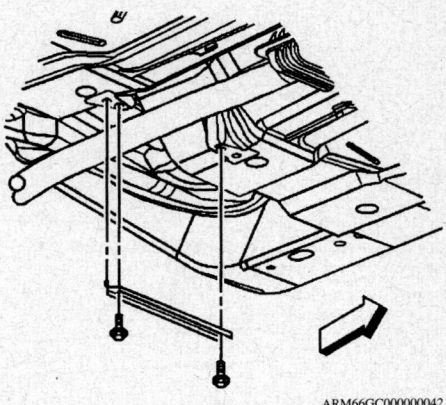

Fig. 9 Floor panel removal

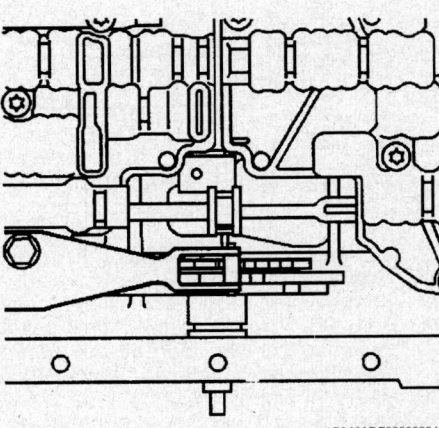

Fig. 11 Spacer installation

7. Remove gearshift trim cover and disconnect electrical connector.
8. Remove console lefthand side and righthand trim panels.
9. Remove six mounting screws, then the console.
10. Remove upper A/C vents.
11. Remove mounting screws and radio, then disconnect electrical connectors and antenna lead.
12. Remove glove compartment.
13. Tilt steering column to lowest position.
14. Remove cluster trim cover by prying upward using a suitable small flat bladed tool.
15. Remove cluster mounting screws.
16. Pry cluster upward at top to release retainers, then pull out and disconnect electrical connectors.
17. Pry upward on defroster grille using suitable flat bladed tool to release retainers.
18. Disconnect sun load sensor connector, then remove defroster grille.
19. Remove lefthand insulator panel mounting screws. Disconnect courtesy lamp electrical connector.
20. Remove righthand insulator panel mounting screws and pull downward to release retainers. Disconnect courtesy lamp electrical connector.
21. Remove driver's side air bag module as outlined in "Passive Restraint Systems" chapter.

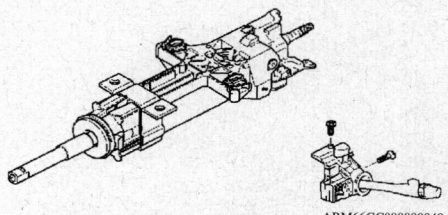

Fig. 12 Multi-function switch assembly

ARM66GC000000049

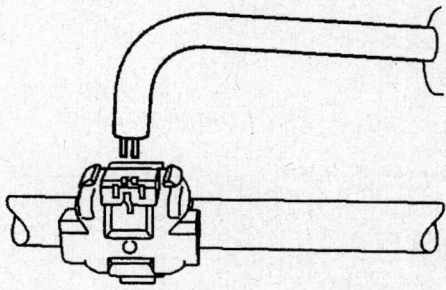

Fig. 15 Quick joint clamp removal

ARM66GC000000066

22. Remove steering wheel as outlined in "Steering Wheel, Replace."
23. Remove steering column tilt lever.
24. Remove lower column trim cover mounting screws, then tilt downward and slide back to release retainers.
25. Remove upper column trim cover mounting screws, then the trim cover.
26. Remove mounting nuts, then lower steering column.
27. Remove lower retainer support bracket mounting bolts.
28. Remove mounting screws from side of instrument panel to carrier.
29. Remove mounting screws from lower center trim panel.
30. Remove instrument panel mounting screws from behind glove compartment.
31. Remove mounting screws and instrument panel.
32. Remove air inlet assemblies.

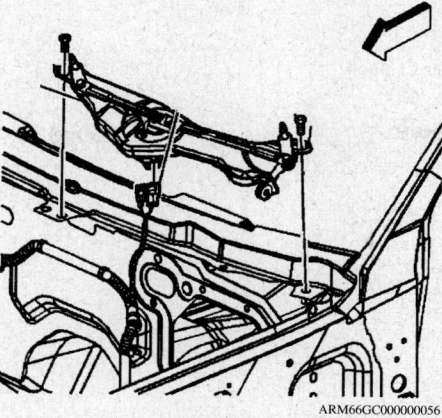

ARM66GC000000056

Fig. 13 Wiper motor module

33. Disconnect HVAC module electrical connector, HVAC module drain tube at floor and release lefthand duct from HVAC module.
34. Disconnect lefthand rear heater duct from HVAC module.
35. Release tab to righthand rear duct from HVAC module.
36. Disconnect righthand rear heater ducts from HVAC module.
37. Remove lower lefthand HVAC module mounting nut.
38. Remove upper lefthand HVAC module nut.
39. Remove HVAC module from vehicle.
40. Remove heater hose bracket screw, then the heater hose bracket.
41. Remove heater core from HVAC module.
42. Reverse procedure to install, noting the following:
   a. **Torque** heater hose bracket screws to 9 inch lbs.
   b. **Torque** HVAC mounting nuts to 80 inch lbs.

EVAPORATOR CORE
REPLACE

1. Remove HVAC module as outlined in "Heater Core, Replace."
2. Remove TXV insulation, **Fig. 16.**

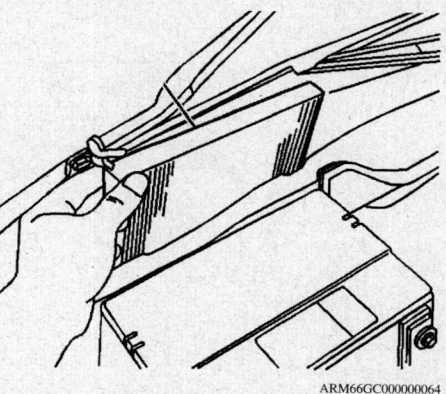

ARM66GC000000064

Fig. 14 Cabin air filter removal

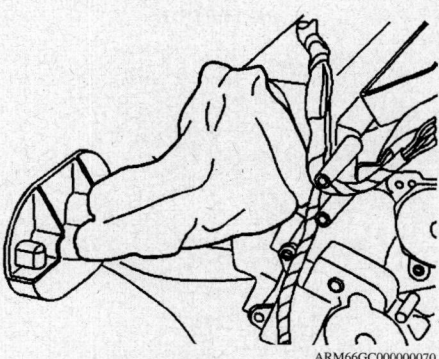

ARM66GC000000070

Fig. 16 TXV insulation

3. Remove HVAC line clamp screw, then the line clamp.
4. Remove TXV to evaporator bolts.
5. Remove TXV line bracket, then the TXV from evaporator core.
6. Separate lines from A/C, then remove TXV.
7. Remove case attaching screws, clips then disconnect thermistor electrical connector.
8. Separate HVAC module, then remove thermistor from evaporator core.
9. Remove evaporator core assembly.
10. Reverse procedure to install.

2.8L Engine

NOTE: On Air Bag Equipped Models, Refer To "Air Bag System Precautions" Located In The Front Of This Manual For System Disarming & Arming Procedures.

NOTE: Refer To "Computer Relearn Procedures" Located In The Front Of This Manual When Battery Power To The Computer Has Been Interrupted.

NOTE: Prior To Performing Any Service Operations Listed In This Section, Consult The "Technical Service Bulletins" Section For Related Information.

NOTE: Refer To "3.2L Engine" Section For Procedures Not Found In This Section.

INDEX

	Page No.
Camshaft, Replace	8-15
Lefthand	8-15
Righthand	8-15
Compression Pressure	8-11
Cooling System Bleed	8-16
Crankshaft Balancer, Replace	8-13
Crankshaft Front Oil Seal, Replace	8-16
Crankshaft Rear Oil Seal, Replace	8-16
Cylinder Head, Replace	8-13
Lefthand	8-13
Righthand	8-13
Engine Rebuilding Specifications	29-1
Engine, Replace	8-11
Engine Mount, Replace	8-11
Exhaust Manifold, Replace	8-13
Lefthand	8-13
Righthand	8-13

	Page No.
Front Cover, Replace	8-14
Installation	8-14
Removal	8-14
Fuel Filter, Replace	8-16
Fuel Pump, Replace	8-16
Intake Manifold, Replace	8-12
Lower	8-13
Upper	8-12
Main & Rod Bearings	8-15
Oil Pan, Replace	8-16
Oil Pump, Replace	8-16
Oil Pump Service	8-16
Piston & Rod Assembly	8-15
Pistons, Pins & Rings	8-15
Precautions	8-11
Air Bag Systems	8-11
Battery Ground Cable	8-11
Fuel Pressure Relief	8-11
Radiator, Replace	8-16
Serpentine Drive Belt, Replace	8-16

	Page No.
Air Conditioning & Power Steering	8-16
Alternator & Water Pump	8-16
Thermostat, Replace	8-16
Tightening Specifications	8-17
Timing Chain, Replace	8-14
Lefthand Secondary Drive Chain	8-14
Installation	8-15
Removal	8-14
Primary Drive Chain	8-14
Installation	8-14
Removal	8-14
Righthand Secondary Drive Chain	8-14
Installation	8-14
Removal	8-14
Valve Adjustment	8-13
Water Pump, Replace	8-16

PRECAUTIONS

Air Bag Systems

Refer to "Air Bag System Precautions" in the front of this manual for system disarming and arming procedures.

Battery Ground Cable

Prior to service, record radio presets, then disconnect battery ground cable and isolate as required.

Fuel Pressure Relief

1. Record radio presets.
2. Turn ignition Off.
3. Disconnect battery ground cable and isolate as required.
4. Loosen fuel filler cap to relieve fuel tank vapor pressure.
5. Remove cap to fuel pressure service connection.
6. Install tool Nos. J34730-1A and J42242, or equivalents, to fuel pressure service connection.
7. Place bleed hose into suitable container, then open bleed valve to relieve fuel system.
8. Place a suitable shop towel under connections to protect fuel spillage.
9. Remove tool Nos. J34730-1A and J42242, or equivalents, from service connections.
10. Install cap to fuel pressure service connection.

COMPRESSION PRESSURE

The minimum compression in any one cylinder should not be less than 70 percent of the highest cylinder. No cylinder should read less than 140 psi.

ENGINE MOUNT

REPLACE

1. Raise and support vehicle.
2. Place a suitable adjustable jack stand with a block of wood under engine oil pan.
3. Remove upper engine mount retaining nut.
4. Remove lefthand engine mount bracket retaining nut, then the bracket.
5. Remove lower engine mount retaining nut, then the engine mount.
6. Reverse procedure to install.

ENGINE

REPLACE

1. Turn front wheels to straight ahead position.
2. Turn ignition lock cylinder to Lock position and remove key.
3. Lock steering column by inserting steering column anti-rotation pin tool No. J 42640, or equivalent, through access hole in lower steering column trim cover.
4. Relieve fuel system pressure as outlined in "Precautions."
5. Raise and support vehicle.
6. Mark relationship of center intermediate shaft to lower intermediate shaft for installation reference.

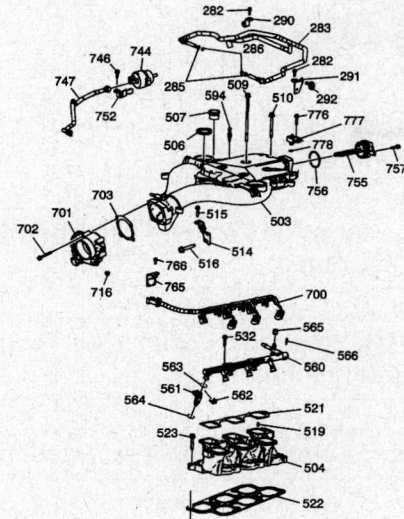

(282) PCV Hose Bolt
(282) PCV Hose Bolt
(283) Dirty PCV Hose
(285) PCV Hose O-Ring Outer/Larger
(286) PCV Hose O-Ring Inner/Smaller
(290) PCV Hose Right Bracket
(291) PCV Hose Left Bracket
(292) PCV Hose Clip
(503) Upper Intake Manifold
(504) Lower Intake Manifold
(506) Expansion Plug
(507) Sight Plug
(509) Upper Intake Manifold Bolt - Long
(510) Upper Intake Manifold Bolt - Short
(514) Intake Manifold Brace
(515) Intake Manifold Brace Small Bolt
(516) Intake Manifold Brace Large Bolt
(519) Lower Intake Manifold to Upper Intake Manifold
(521) Upper Intake Manifold Gasket
(522) Lower Intake Manifold Gasket
(523) Lower Intake Manifold Bolt
(532) Fuel Rail Bolt
(560) Fuel Rail
(561) Fuel Injector

(562) Fuel Injector Retainer
(563) Fuel Injector Upper Seal
(564) Fuel Injector Lower Seal
(565) Fuel Pressure Service Valve Cap
(566) Fuel Pressure Service Valve
(594) Fuel Injector Sight Shield Cover Ball Stud
(700) Fuel Injector Wiring Harness
(701) Throttle Body
(702) Throttle Body Bolt
(703) Throttle Body Gasket
(716) Throttle Body Engine Wiring Harness Clip
(744) EVAP Purge Solenoid
(746) EVAP Purge Solenoid Bolt
(747) EVAP Purge Solenoid Tube
(752) EVAP Purge Solenoid Bracket
(755) Intake Manifold Tuning Valve
(756) Intake Manifold Tuning Valve O-Ring
(757) Intake Manifold Tuning Valve Bolt
(765) Fuel Injector Wiring Harness Bracket
(766) Fuel Injector Wiring Harness Bracket Bolt
(776) BARO Sensor Bolt
(777) BARO Sensor
(778) BARO Sensor O-Ring

ARM0300000000251

Fig. 1 Exploded view of intake manifold

7. Remove center intermediate shaft to lower intermediate shaft retaining bolt.
8. Remove lower intermediate shaft to power steering gear retaining bolt.
9. Mark relationship of lower intermediate shaft to power steering gear for installation reference.
10. Disconnect lower intermediate shaft from power steering gear.
11. Remove lower intermediate shaft from center intermediate shaft.
12. Remove battery and fuel injector sight shield.
13. Remove air cleaner duct, then disconnect cooling fan electrical connectors.
14. Remove cooling fan wiring harness from shroud, then secure harnesses aside.
15. Drain cooling system into suitable container.
16. Disconnect outlet hose from surge tank. Secure hose aside.
17. Disconnect surge tank inlet hose from water outlet housing and radiator. Se-cure hose aside.
18. Disconnect hoses from heater core.
19. Disconnect purge line from purge sole-noid.
20. Recover A/C system refrigerant as out-lined in "Air Condition" chapter.
21. Remove wiper module assembly as outlined in electrical section.
22. Disconnect suction hose from evapo-rator and remove suction hose bracket from shock tower. Secure suction hose to engine.
23. Disconnect A/C pressure switch elec-trical connector, then remove liquid line.
24. Remove radiator support brackets.
25. Disconnect brake booster check valve, then brake booster vacuum hose. Se-cure booster hose to engine.
26. Disconnect brake fluid level switch electrical connector.
27. Disconnect Mass Air Flow (MAF) sen-sor electrical connector.
28. Disconnect instrument cluster electri-

cal connector from rear of lefthand cyl-inder head. Secure electrical harness aside.
29. Disconnect engine module wiring har-ness connectors from underhood elec-trical center.
30. Disconnect Transmission Control Module (TCM) electrical connector.
31. Remove ground wire to rail retaining bolt, then position ground wire aside.
32. Disconnect engine harness electrical connector. Harness connector is locat-ed on engine compartment longitudi-nal rail. Position TCM harness aside.
33. Secure ground wire, engine harness and TCM harness to engine.
34. Remove master cylinder retaining nuts, then secure master cylinder to engine.
35. Raise and support engine.
36. Remove exhaust system and propeller shaft.
37. Remove air deflector and washer bot-tle bracket.
38. Disconnect side air baffles from radia-tor.
39. Remove lefthand front brake pipe re-tainer and brake pipe rail.
40. Remove righthand front brake pipe from pipe retainer.
41. Disconnect rear brake pipes from BPMV.
42. Remove front tire and wheel assem-blies.
43. Remove intermediate steering shaft from steering gear.
44. Remove lower engine mount retaining nut.
45. Disconnect transmission shift linkage from transmission.
46. Disconnect low oil level sensor electri-cal connector, then secure sensor har-ness and connector to engine.
47. Remove headlamp leveling sensors.
48. Secure shock modules to lower control arms with a suitable strap in order to prevent damage to front brake hoses.
49. Remove righthand side and lefthand side shock modules upper mounting bolts.
50. Place a suitable lift platform in engine and transmission assembly.
51. Remove transmission brace to under-body attaching bolts.
52. Remove front frame bolts.
53. Lower lift platform and remove engine transmission assembly from vehicle.
54. Separate transmission assembly from engine.
55. Reverse procedure to install.

INTAKE MANIFOLD
REPLACE
Upper

1. Remove fuel injector sight shield from top of engine.
2. Remove air inlet duct, then disconnect brake booster vacuum hose from in-take manifold.
3. Disconnect electrical connector and purge line from purge solenoid valve, **Fig. 1.**

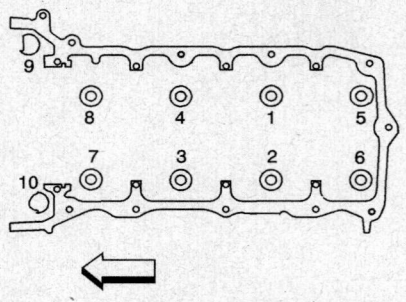

Fig. 2 Lefthand cylinder head bolt tightening sequence

4. Remove wiring harness retainer from front of intake manifold.
5. Disconnect throttle body electrical connector.
6. Remove upper intake manifold brake bolts, then the brace.
7. Disconnect PCV hose from righthand camshaft cover.
8. Disconnect barometric pressure sensor and intake manifold runner control solenoid electrical connectors.
9. Remove injector harness bracket attaching bolt, then the lefthand ignition coil wiring harness from bracket.
10. Remove upper intake manifold attaching bolts, then the manifold with throttle body from engine.
11. Reverse procedure to install.

Lower

1. Remove upper intake manifold as outlined under "Upper."
2. Remove lower intake manifold attaching bolts.
3. Position intake manifold to gain access to fuel pipe connector.
4. Remove fuel feed pipe retainer, then disconnect fuel feed pipe from fuel rail.
5. Remove lower intake manifold.
6. Reverse procedure to install.

EXHAUST MANIFOLD
REPLACE
Lefthand

1. Remove heat shield attaching bolts, then the heat shield.
2. Remove exhaust manifold upper and lower insulators from oil dipstick tube.
3. Remove lefthand catalytic converter.
4. Remove lefthand exhaust manifold retaining nuts, then the exhaust manifold.
5. Reverse procedure to install.

Righthand

1. Remove exhaust manifold heat shield attaching bolts, then the heat shield.
2. Remove Engine Coolant Temperature (ECT) sensor.
3. Remove exhaust manifold to cylinder head attaching bolts, then the exhaust manifold.
4. Reverse procedure to install.

CYLINDER HEAD
REPLACE
Lefthand

1. Remove lefthand secondary timing chain as outlined under "Timing Chain, Replace."
2. Remove oil dipstick.
3. Remove heat shield from coolant temperature sensor and disconnect sensor electrical connector.
4. Remove wiring harness ground from cylinder head.
5. Disconnect wiring harness electrical connector from side of cylinder head.
6. Remove wiring harness connector bracket from cylinder head.
7. Remove power steering pump mounting bolts. **Do not disconnect power steering pipes or hoses.**
8. Remove surge tank hose from cylinder head bracket.
9. Remove wiring harness bracket from rear of cylinder head.
10. Remove lefthand catalytic converter.
11. Remove oil dipstick and oil filter adapter upper bolt. **Do not remove oil filter adapter.**
12. Remove cylinder head attaching bolts, then the cylinder head along with exhaust manifold. **Discard cylinder head M11 bolts.**
13. If required, remove exhaust manifold mounting bolts, then the manifold from cylinder head.
14. Reverse procedure to install, noting the following:
    a. If required, **torque** exhaust manifold mounting bolts to 18 ft. lbs.
    b. Ensure crankshaft is in timing drive assembly position using crankshaft rotation socket tool No. EN 46111, or equivalent.
    c. Install new M11 cylinder head bolts.
    d. **Torque** M11 bolts to 33 ft. lbs., **Fig. 2,** then tighten an additional 120°.
    e. **Torque** M8 bolts to 10 ft. lbs., then tighten an additional 60°.

Righthand

1. Remove righthand secondary timing chain as outlined under "Timing Chain, Replace."
2. Remove coolant inlet pipe.
3. Remove wiring harness ground from cylinder head.
4. Disconnect wiring harness electrical connector from side of cylinder head.
5. Remove wiring harness conduit upper bolt from cylinder head, then position conduit aside.
6. Remove battery cable from cylinder head.
7. Remove righthand catalytic converter.
8. Remove cylinder head attaching bolts, then the cylinder head along with exhaust manifold. **Discard cylinder head M11 bolts.**
9. If required, remove exhaust manifold mounting bolts, then the manifold from cylinder head.

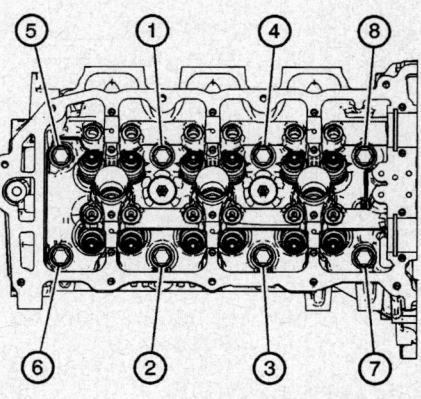

Fig. 3 Righthand cylinder head bolt tightening sequence

10. Reverse procedure to install, noting the following:
    a. If required, **torque** exhaust manifold mounting bolts to 18 ft. lbs.
    b. Ensure crankshaft is in timing drive assembly position using crankshaft rotation socket tool No. EN 46111, or equivalent.
    c. Install new M11 cylinder head bolts.
    d. **Torque** M11 bolts to 33 ft. lbs., **Fig. 3,** then tighten an additional 120°.
    e. **Torque** M8 bolts to 10 ft. lbs., then tighten an additional 60°.

VALVE ADJUSTMENT

This engine is equipped with hydraulic valve lash adjusters. No adjustment is required.

CRANKSHAFT BALANCER
REPLACE

1. Remove alternator and water pump drive belt.
2. Raise and support vehicle.
3. Remove transmission bell housing inspection hole cover.
4. Install tool No. 48018, or equivalent flywheel holding tool as illustrated, **Fig. 4.**
5. Remove front air deflector.
6. Remove crankshaft balancer using tool No. J 24420-C, or equivalent. **Fig. 5.**
7. Install crankshaft balancer using tool No. J 41998-B, or equivalent, **Fig. 5.**
8. Install front air deflector.
9. Remove flywheel holding tool, **Fig. 4.**
10. Install transmission bell housing inspection hole cover.
11. Lower vehicle.
12. Install A/C compressor and power steering pump drive belt.

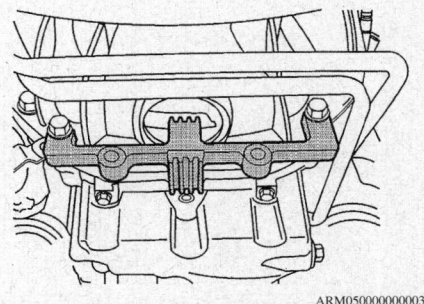

ARM0500000000034

Fig. 4 Flywheel holding tool No. 48018

FRONT COVER

REPLACE

Removal

1. Remove camshaft position actuator valve bolts.
2. Remove camshaft position actuator valves from front cover.
3. Remove engine front cover bolts.
4. Loosely install a 10 ×1.5 mm bolt into jackscrew hole (1), **Fig. 6. Do not pry between engine cover and camshaft position sensors or camshaft position actuators in order to shear RTV. Use pry points and a bolt in the jackscrew hole in order to remove engine front cover. Damage to camshaft position sensors or the camshaft position actuators may occur if camshaft position sensors or camshaft position actuators are used to pry against in order to remove engine front cover.**
5. Shear room temperature vulcanizer (RTV) sealant using pry points (2) located at edge of front cover and jackscrew, **Fig. 6.**
6. Remove engine front cover.
7. Rotate crankshaft until lefthand cylinder head camshafts align with tool No. 46105-2 and righthand cylinder head camshafts align with tool No. 46105-1, or equivalents.
8. Install tool No. 46105-1, or equivalent to righthand camshafts.
9. Install tool No. 46105-2, or equivalent to lefthand camshafts.

Installation

1. Install .315 in. guide from tool No. 46109, or equivalent into cylinder block positions as outlined, **Fig. 7.**
2. Install new engine front cover to cylinder block seal.
3. Place a .118 in. bead of RTV sealant, GM P/N 12378521 or equivalent, on engine front cover.
4. Place engine front cover onto tool No. 46109, or equivalent and slide into position.
5. Remove tool No. 46109, or equivalent from cylinder block.
6. Hand start all engine front cover bolts.
7. Tighten engine front cover bolts in sequence as outlined, **Fig. 8.** Tighten to specifications.

8. Install new O-rings on camshaft position sensor.
9. Place camshaft position sensors in position on front cover.
10. Install camshaft position sensor bolts. Tighten to specifications.
11. Place camshaft position.
12. Place camshaft position actuator valves in position on front cover.
13. Install camshaft position actuator valve bolts. Tighten to specifications.

TIMING CHAIN

REPLACE

Primary Drive Chain

REMOVAL

1. Remove spark plugs.
2. Remove front cover as outlined under "Front Cover, Replace."
3. Remove righthand side secondary camshaft drive chain tensioner attaching bolts, then the drive chain tensioner.
4. Remove righthand side secondary timing chain shoe, then the righthand side secondary drive chain.
5. Remove primary camshaft drive chain tensioner.
6. Remove primary camshaft drive chain upper guide, then the primary chain.

INSTALLATION

Ensure that crankshaft is in stage one timing drive assembly position.

1. Install primary camshaft drive chain.
2. Wrap primary camshaft drive chain around large sprockets of each camshaft intermediate drive chain idler and crankshaft sprocket.
3. Lefthand side camshaft intermediate drive chain idler timing mark (3) will align with a timing camshaft drive chain link (4), **Fig. 9.**
4. Righthand camshaft intermediate drive chain idler timing mark (2) will align with a timing camshaft drive chain link (1), **Fig. 9.**
5. Crankshaft sprocket timing mark (6) will align with a timing camshaft drive chain link (5), **Fig. 9.**
6. Ensure all timing marks are properly aligned with timing camshaft drive chain links.

Righthand Secondary Drive Chain

REMOVAL

1. Remove spark plugs.
2. Remove engine front cover.
3. Remove righthand side secondary camshaft drive chain tensioner attaching bolts, then the drive chain tensioner.
4. Remove righthand side secondary timing chain shoe.
5. Remove righthand bank secondary camshaft drive chain guide.
6. Remove righthand bank secondary camshaft drive chain.

ARM0500000000035

Fig. 5 Harmonic balancer puller tool No. J 24420-C

INSTALLATION

1. Install righthand bank secondary camshaft drive chain.
2. Install righthand bank secondary camshaft drive chain guide.
3. Install righthand bank secondary camshaft drive chain shoe.
4. Install righthand bank secondary camshaft drive chain tensioner.
5. Install spark plugs.
6. Install engine front cover.

Lefthand Secondary Drive Chain

REMOVAL

1. Remove spark plugs in order to ease crankshaft / engine rotation.
2. Remove engine front cover.
3. Remove righthand bank secondary camshaft drive chain tensioner.
4. Remove righthand bank secondary camshaft drive chain shoe.
5. Remove righthand bank secondary camshaft drive chain guide.
6. Remove righthand bank secondary camshaft drive chain.
7. Remove primary camshaft drive chain tensioner.
8. Remove primary upper camshaft drive chain guide.
9. Remove primary camshaft drive chain.
10. Remove righthand bank camshaft intermediate drive chain idler.
11. Remove lefthand bank secondary camshaft drive tensioner.
12. Remove lefthand bank secondary camshaft drive chain shoe.
13. Remove lefthand bank secondary camshaft drive chain guide.
14. Remove lefthand bank camshaft intermediate drive chain idler.
15. Remove lefthand bank secondary camshaft drive chain.
16. Clean and inspect all of camshaft timing drive components. Replace components as required.

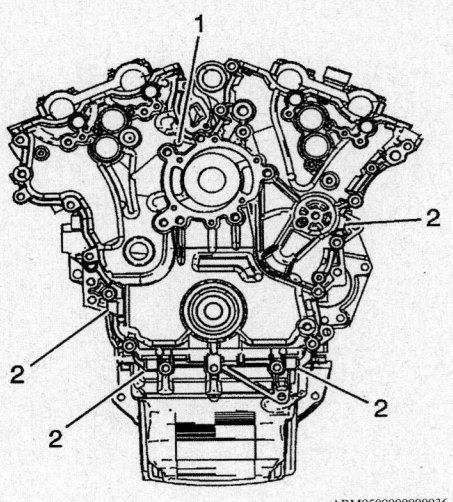

Fig. 6 Pry point location including jackscrew

INSTALLATION

1. Install lefthand bank secondary camshaft drive chain.
2. Install lefthand bank camshaft intermediate drive chain idler.
3. Install lefthand bank secondary camshaft drive chain guide.
4. Install lefthand bank secondary camshaft drive chain shoe.
5. Install lefthand bank secondary camshaft drive chain tensioner.
6. Install righthand bank camshaft intermediate drive chain idler.
7. Install primary camshaft drive chain.
8. Install primary upper camshaft drive chain guide.
9. Install primary camshaft drive chain tensioner.
10. Install righthand bank secondary camshaft drive chain.
11. Install righthand bank secondary camshaft drive chain guide.
12. Install righthand bank secondary camshaft drive chain shoe.
13. Install righthand bank secondary camshaft drive chain tensioner.
14. Install spark plugs.
15. Install engine front cover.

CAMSHAFT
REPLACE
Righthand

1. Remove upper intake manifold with lower intake manifold.
2. Remove camshaft cover.
3. Remove camshaft position.
4. Remove intake camshaft position actuator solenoid.
5. Remove crankshaft balancer.
6. Rotate crankshaft with tool No. 46111, or equivalent until camshafts are in a neutral (low tension) position. Camshaft flats will be parallel with camshaft cover rail. **Use an open-end wrench at the camshaft hex to prevent camshaft / engine rotation. DO NOT re-**

move camshaft position actuator bolt at this time.
7. Loosen camshaft position actuator bolt. **Ensure that tips of tool No. 46108, or equivalent are fully engaged into timing chain.**
8. Install tool No. 46108, or equivalent in order to retain timing chain. Firmly tighten tool No. 46108, or equivalent nuts.
9. Mark timing chain and respective locations on camshaft position actuators. **Ensure that camshaft timing chain and camshaft position actuators are marked for proper assembly.**
10. Remove camshaft position actuator bolt.
11. Remove camshaft bearing caps and camshaft. **Ensure that marks on camshaft position actuators and timing chain are aligned. DO NOT tighten camshaft position actuator bolts at this time.**
12. Locate camshafts on cylinder head and assemble camshaft actuators to camshafts.
13. Install camshafts and camshaft bearing caps.
14. Remove tool No. 46108, or equivalent.
15. Install crankshaft balancer. **Use an open-end wrench at camshaft hex to prevent camshaft / engine rotation.**
16. Install and tighten camshaft position actuators.
17. Install intake camshaft position actuator solenoid.
18. Install CMP sensors.
19. Install camshaft cover.
20. Install upper intake manifold with lower intake manifold.

Lefthand

1. Remove upper intake manifold with lower intake manifold.
2. Remove lefthand bank camshaft cover.
3. Remove camshaft position (CMP) sensors.
4. Remove CMP actuator solenoid.
5. Remove crankshaft balancer.
6. Rotate crankshaft with tool No. 46111, or equivalent until camshafts are in a neutral (low tension) position. Camshaft flats will be parallel with camshaft cover rail. **Use an open-end wrench at camshaft hex to prevent camshaft / engine rotation. DO NOT remove camshaft position actuator bolt at this time.**
7. Loosen camshaft position actuator bolt. **Ensure that tips of tool No. 46108, or equivalent are fully engaged into timing chain.**
8. Install tool No. 46108, or equivalent in order to retain timing chain. Firmly tighten tool No. 46108, or equivalent.
9. Mark timing chain and respective locations on camshaft position actuators. **Ensure that camshaft timing chain and camshaft position actuators are marked for proper assembly.**
10. Remove camshaft position actuator bolt.
11. Remove camshaft.

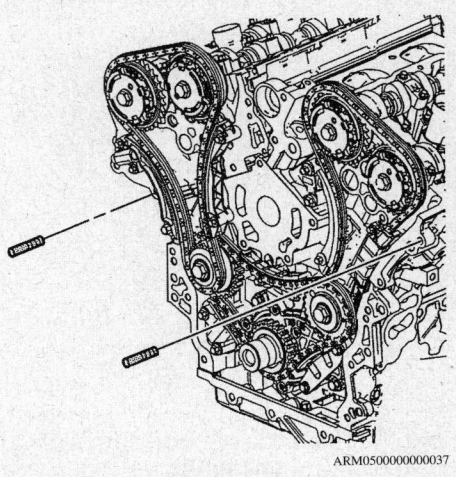

ARM0500000000037

Fig. 7 Guide pin installation

12. Locate camshafts to cylinder head and assemble camshaft actuators to camshafts. **Ensure that marks on camshaft position actuator and timing chain are aligned. DO NOT tighten camshaft position actuator bolt at this time.**
13. Install camshafts and camshaft bearing caps.
14. Remove tool No. 46108, or equivalent.
15. Install and tighten camshaft position actuators. **Use an open-end wrench at camshaft hex to prevent camshaft / engine rotation.**
16. Install intake camshaft position actuator solenoid.
17. Install CMP sensors.
18. Install crankshaft balancer.
19. Install camshaft cover.
20. Install upper intake manifold with lower intake manifold.

PISTON & ROD ASSEMBLY

When installing piston and rod assemblies into cylinder block, ensure dot on top of piston faces toward front of engine.

Tighten connecting rod bolts in four steps as follows: First step, **torque** bolts to 22 ft. lbs.; second step, loosen bolts; third step, **torque** bolts to 18 ft. lbs.; fourth step, tighten bolts an additional 110°.

PISTONS, PINS & RINGS

Pistons and rings are available in standard size and oversize. Pistons and their pins are serviced as an assembly.

MAIN & ROD BEARINGS

Main and rod bearings are available in standard size only. Tighten main bearing cap bolts as follows: **Torque** inboard bolts to 15 ft. lbs., then tighten an additional 80°; **torque** outboard bolts to 11 ft. lbs., then tighten an additional 110°; **torque** short inner and long outer bolts to 22 ft. lbs.

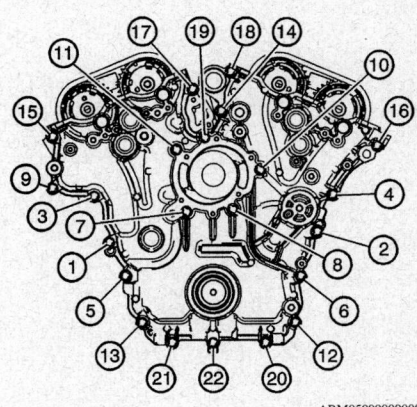

Fig. 8 Front cover bolt tightening sequence

CRANKSHAFT FRONT OIL SEAL

REPLACE

1. Remove crankshaft balancer as outlined under "Crankshaft Balancer, Replace."
2. Remove seal using a suitable flat-bladed tool.
3. Reverse procedure to install.

CRANKSHAFT REAR OIL SEAL

REPLACE

1. Remove transmission as outlined in **MOTOR's "Domestic Transmission, In-Vehicle Service" manual or "Transmission Service DVD."**
2. Remove flywheel bolts, then the flywheel from crankshaft.
3. Remove oil pan as outlined under "Oil Pan, Replace."
4. Remove crankshaft rear oil seal housing bolts.
5. Pry oil seal housing from cylinder block using pry points located at edge of housing.
6. Remove oil seal from housing.
7. Reverse procedure to install.

OIL PAN

REPLACE

1. Remove front cover as outlined under "Front Cover, Replace."
2. Remove power steering hose retainer from A/C compressor bracket.
3. Disconnect intermediate steering shaft from steering gear.
4. Remove engine mount lower nuts.
5. Remove A/C compressor bracket bolts and position compressor and bracket aside.
6. Drain engine oil.
7. Remove transmission oil cooler pipe retainer from engine righthand side.
8. Install suitable engine support fixture, then raise engine enough to access oil pan.

9. Remove oil pan bolts, then pry oil pan from engine block using suitable flat bladed tool.
10. Reverse procedure to install, noting the following:
    a. Apply a suitable bead of silicone sealing compound part No. 12378521, or equivalent, to oil pan surface.
    b. Tighten oil pan to engine block bolts to specification.

OIL PUMP

REPLACE

1. Remove primary timing chain as outlined under "Timing Chain, Replace."
2. Remove crankshaft sprocket.
3. Remove oil pump bolts and oil pump.
4. Reverse procedure to install.

OIL PUMP SERVICE

There are no serviceable components inside the oil pump. If pump is not working properly, it must be replaced.

SERPENTINE DRIVE BELT

REPLACE

Alternator & Water Pump

1. Rotate drive belt tensioner clockwise to release drive belt tension.
2. Slide drive belt off of water pump pulley.
3. Slowly release drive belt tensioner and remove drive belt from accessory drive pulleys.
4. Reverse procedure to install.

Air Conditioning & Power Steering

1. Remove alternator and water pump drive belt as outlined under "Alternator & Water Pump."
2. Rotate drive belt tensioner clockwise to release drive belt tension.
3. Remove drive belt from power steering pulley.
4. Slowly release drive belt tensioner and remove drive belt from accessory drive pulleys.
5. Reverse procedure to install.

COOLING SYSTEM BLEED

1. Place transmission in Park or Neutral position.
2. Engage park brake.
3. Run engine until thermostat opens.
4. Stop engine.
5. Fill system using only clean drinkable water.
6. Repeat procedure if required, until fluid is nearly colorless.

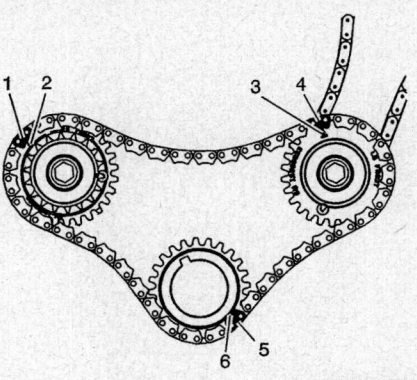

Fig. 9 Timing mark alignment

7. Fill coolant reservoir to FULL HOT mark.

THERMOSTAT

REPLACE

1. Remove lower intake manifold as outlined under "Intake Manifold, Replace."
2. Disconnect surge tank hose from thermostat.
3. Remove coolant pipe/thermostat housing bolt.
4. Remove coolant pipe upper bolt, then the coolant inlet pipe from thermostat.
5. Remove thermostat housing bolts, then the thermostat housing.
6. Remove thermostat and discard seal.
7. Reverse procedure to install.

WATER PUMP

REPLACE

1. Drain cooling system into suitable container.
2. Remove alternator drive belt as outlined under "Serpentine Drive Belt."
3. Hold water pump pulley with pulley holding tool No. 46104, or equivalent.
4. Remove water pump pulley bolts, then the pulley.
5. Remove water pump attaching bolts, then the pump. Discard water pump seal.
6. Reverse procedure to install.

RADIATOR

REPLACE

Refer to "Radiator, Replace" in the "3.2L Engine" section.

FUEL PUMP

REPLACE

Refer to "Fuel Pump, Replace" in the "3.2L Engine" section.

FUEL FILTER

REPLACE

Refer to "Fuel Filter, Replace" in the "3.2L Engine" section.

TIGHTENING SPECIFICATIONS

Year	Component	Torque Ft. Lbs.
2006–08	A/C Compressor Bracket Front Bolt	37
	A/C Compressor Bracket Rear Bolt	17
	A/C Compressor Hose Assembly	80①
	Alternator Bolt	37
	Camshaft Cap Bolts	89①
	Camshaft Intermediate Drive Idler Sprocket Bolt	48
	Camshaft Position Actuator Bolt	43
	Camshaft Position Sensor Bolt	89①
	Camshaft (Valve) Cover	89①
	Catalytic Converter To Exhaust Manifold	37
	Close Out Cover Bolt	89①
	Connecting Rod Bolts	②
	Coolant Manifold Pipe	89①
	Coolant Outlet Bolt	89①
	Crankshaft Balancer Bolt	③
	Crankshaft Main Bearing (Inner) Bolts	④
	Crankshaft Main Bearing (Outer) Bolts	⑤
	Crankshaft Main Bearing (Side) Bolts	⑨
	Crankshaft Position Sensor	89①
	Cylinder Head Bolt (M8 Bolt)	⑥
	Cylinder Head Bolt (M11 Bolt)	⑦
	Drive Belt Idler Pulley Bolt	37
	Drive Belt Tensioner Bolt	37
	ECM Bolt	89①
	ECT Sensor	18
	Engine Mount Bracket To Cylinder Block (M8 Bolt)	28
	Engine Mount Bracket To Cylinder Block (M11 Bolt)	45
	Engine Mount To Bracket	59
	EVAP Purge Valve Bolt	89①
	Exhaust Manifold Bolt	15
	Exhaust Manifold Heat Shield Bolt	89①
	Flywheel Bolts	⑧
	Front Cover Bolts	17
	Fuel Rail Bolt	89①
	Ground Cable Bolt	37
	Heater Inlet/Outlet Pipe Assembly Bolt	89①
	Ignition Coil Bolt	89①
	Intake Manifold (Upper) To Cylinder Head Bolts	17
	Intake Manifold (Upper) To Intake Manifold (Lower) Bolts	17
	Knock Sensor Bolt	17
	Main Bearing (Inner) Bolts	④
	Main Bearing (Outer) Bolts	⑤
	Main Bearing (Side) Bolts	⑨
	MAP Sensor Bolt	89①
	Oil Dipstick Tube Bolt	89①
	Oil Drain Plug	18
	Oil Filter Cap	18
	Oil Filter Housing Adapter To Cylinder Block	17
	Oil Filter Housing Adapter To Cylinder Head	48

TIGHTENING SPECIFICATIONS—Continued

Year	Component	Torque Ft. Lbs.
2006–08	Oil Gallery Plug	23
	Oil Level Sensor	89①
	Oil Pan To Cylinder Block Bolts	17
	Oil Pressure Sender	15
	Oil Pump Bolt	17
	Oil Pump Cover Bolts	115①
	Oxygen Sensor	30
	Power Steering Pump Bracket To Engine Bolt	37
	Power Steering Pump Reservoir Lower Bolt	18
	Power Steering Pump Reservoir Upper Bolt	80①
	Power Steering Pump To Bracket Bolt	16
	Primary Camshaft Drive Chain Guide Bolt	17
	Primary Camshaft Drive Chain Lefthand Guide Bolt – Oil Pump (1st Design)	115①
	Primary Camshaft Drive Chain Lefthand Guide Bolt – Oil Pump (2nd Design)	17
	Primary Camshaft Drive Chain Tensioner Bolt	17
	Secondary Camshaft Drive Chain Guide Bolt	17
	Secondary Camshaft Drive Chain Shoe Bolt	17
	Secondary Camshaft Drive Chain Tensioner Bolt	17
	Starter Motor Bolts	37
	Suction Screen Bolt	89①
	Thermostat Housing Bolt	89①
	Throttle Body Bolt	89①
	Torque Converter Bolts	44
	Transmission Mount To Transmission Bolt	45
	Transmission To Engine Bolts	37
	Water Pump Bolts	89①
	Water Pump Pulley Bolts	89①

① — Inch lbs.

② — Refer to "Piston & Rod Assembly" for tightening procedure.

③ — First pass, 74 ft. lbs.; final pass, 150°.

④ — First pass, 15 ft. lbs.; final pass, 80°.

⑤ — First pass, 10 ft. lbs.; final pass, 110°.

⑥ — First pass, 10 ft. lbs.; final pass, 60°.

⑦ — First pass, 33 ft. lbs.; final pass, 120°.

⑧ — First pass, 22 ft. lbs.; final pass, 45°.

⑨ — First pass, 22 ft. lbs.; final pass, 60°.

3.2L Engine

NOTE: On Air Bag Equipped Models, Refer To "Air Bag System Precautions" Located In The Front Of This Manual For System Disarming & Arming Procedures.

NOTE: Refer To "Computer Relearn Procedures" Located In The Front Of This Manual When Battery Power To The Computer Has Been Interrupted.

NOTE: Prior To Performing Any Service Operations Listed In This Section, Consult The "Technical Service Bulletins" Section For Related Information.

INDEX

	Page No.
Camshaft, Replace	8-21
Compression Pressure	8-18
Cooling System Bleed	8-23
Crankshaft Balancer, Replace	8-22
Crankshaft Front Oil Seal, Replace	8-22
Crankshaft Rear Oil Seal, Replace	8-22
Cylinder Head, Replace	8-20
Engine Rebuilding Specifications	29-1
Engine, Replace	8-18
Engine Mount, Replace	8-18
Exhaust Manifold, Replace	8-20

	Page No.
Lefthand	8-20
Righthand	8-20
Front Cover, Replace	8-20
Fuel Filter, Replace	8-23
Fuel Pump, Replace	8-23
Intake Manifold, Replace	8-19
Intake Plenum, Replace	8-19
Main & Rod Bearings	8-22
Oil Pan, Replace	8-22
Oil Pump, Replace	8-22
Piston & Rod Assembly	8-21
Pistons, Pins & Rings	8-21
Precautions	8-18
Air Bag Systems	8-18

	Page No.
Battery Ground Cable	8-18
Fuel Pressure Relief	8-18
Radiator, Replace	8-23
Serpentine Drive Belt	8-23
Replace	8-23
Thermostat, Replace	8-23
Tightening Specifications	8-27
Timing Belt, Replace	8-20
Installation	8-21
Removal	8-20
Valve Adjustment	8-20
Valve Cover, Replace	8-20
Water Pump, Replace	8-23

PRECAUTIONS

Air Bag Systems

Refer to "Air Bag System Precautions" in the front of this manual for system disarming and arming procedures.

Battery Ground Cable

Prior to service, record radio presets, then disconnect battery ground cable and isolate as required.

Fuel Pressure Relief

1. Record radio presets.
2. Turn ignition Off.
3. Disconnect battery ground cable and isolate as required.
4. Loosen fuel filler cap to relieve fuel tank vapor pressure.
5. Remove cap to fuel pressure service connection.
6. Install tool Nos. J34730-1A and J42242, or equivalents, to fuel pressure service connection.
7. Place bleed hose into suitable container, then open bleed valve to relieve fuel system.
8. Place a suitable shop towel under connections to protect fuel spillage.
9. Remove tool Nos. J34730-1A and J42242, or equivalents, from service connections.
10. Install cap to fuel pressure service connection.

COMPRESSION PRESSURE

The minimum compression in any one cylinder should not be less than 70 percent of the highest cylinder. No cylinder should read less than 100 psi.

ENGINE MOUNT
REPLACE

1. Raise and support vehicle.
2. Remove starter as outlined in "Starter, Replace" in "Electrical" section.
3. Disconnect HO2S at sensor, then remove HO2S.
4. Remove catalytic converter attaching nuts, position exhaust system rearward to allow rear of catalytic converters to clear exhaust pipe flange.
5. Rest exhaust system on floor panel tunnel brace.
6. Remove catalytic converter seal, then the catalytic converter gasket.
7. Remove catalytic converter to catalytic converter hanger bracket attaching nuts.
8. Remove catalytic converter to exhaust manifold attaching nuts, then the catalytic converter and seal.
9. Install a suitable adjustable jack with a block of wood under engine oil pan.
10. Remove upper engine mount retaining nut.
11. Remove engine mount bracket retaining bolts, then the engine mount bracket.
12. Remove lower engine mount retaining nut, then the engine mount.
13. Reverse procedure to install.

ENGINE
REPLACE

1. Open and support hood.
2. Mark upper hoof hinge location using suitable grease pencil, remove hood.
3. Remove front clips to air inlet panel and battery tray/cowl assembly.
4. Remove front air inlet panel.
5. Remove battery ground cable to side rail attaching bolt and disconnect body electrical harness from battery ground cable.
6. Remove underhood fuse block cover.
7. Remove battery positive cable from underhood fuse block.
8. Disconnect engine wiring harness from underhood fuse block and righthand shock tower, then secure to engine.
9. Disconnect electrical connectors from transmission control module, then secure harness to engine.
10. Remove MAF/IAT sensor.
11. Remove air cleaner assembly.
12. Remove intake air resonator to cooling fan assembly attaching bolt.
13. Disconnect air intake duct hoses from

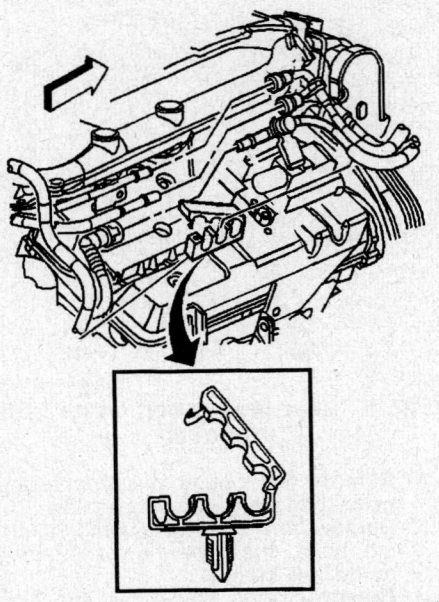

Fig. 1 Quick connect fitting removal

throttle body and lift intake air resonator from front frame.

14. Disconnect electrical connectors, vacuum hoses, upper radiator hose and surge tank inlet hose.
15. Remove air intake resonator assembly.
16. Disconnect coolant bypass solenoid electrical connector, then remove bolt securing engine wiring harness ground lead to righthand body rail.
17. Drain cooling system into suitable container.
18. Remove surge tank inlet hose, inlet radiator hose and outlet radiator hose using suitable hose clamp pliers.
19. Remove coolant bypass outlet hose from coolant inlet pipe using suitable hose clamp pliers.
20. Disconnect quick connect fittings to return hose and feed hose from fuel rail, plug ports to prevent fuel loss and contamination, **Fig. 1.**
21. Disconnect EVAP quick connect fitting, then open retainer at ECM bracket to release chassis hose.
22. Remove outlet heater hose from coolant pump using suitable clamp pliers.
23. Remove inlet hose from heater core.
24. Remove surge tank outlet hose from tank and then secure hose to engine.
25. Disconnect electrical connector from air conditioning refrigerant pressure sensor.
26. Disconnect engine wiring harness from lefthand side body rail connectors.
27. Remove power steering hose nut from air conditioning compressor stud.
28. Disconnect engine wiring harness to A/C pressure hose and secure to engine.
29. Remove drive belt as outlined in "Serpentine Drive Belt."
30. Remove power steering pump mounting bolts, then position pump aside.

31. Disconnect vacuum brake booster and wiring harness from power steering fluid reservoir.
32. Disconnect vacuum brake booster hose from vacuum source.
33. Remove power steering fluid reservoir mounting bolts, then position reservoir aside.
34. Disconnect A/C compressor electrical connector.
35. Remove A/C compressor mounting bolts and place compressor aside.
36. Raise and support vehicle.
37. Remove bolts securing floor panel tunnel brace to floor panel, then the floor panel tunnel brace from floor panel.
38. Remove nuts securing exhaust pipe to catalytic converter, and suitable support exhaust system.
39. Pry front exhaust hanger free from rear suspension hanger rod, then lower exhaust system.
40. Remove catalytic converter seal. Do not reuse seal.
41. Disconnect oxygen sensor retainers from catalytic converter hanger bracket.
42. Remove bolts securing catalytic converter hanger bracket to transmission, then the catalytic converter hanger bracket from catalytic converters.
43. Disconnect Electronic Brake Control Module (EBCM) electrical connector.
44. Disconnect Anti-Lock Brake System (ABS) electrical connectors from speed sensors.
45. Remove ABS wiring harness retainers from lower control arms, engine frame and cooling fan.
46. Remove transmission fluid cooler pipes.
47. Drain engine oil into suitable container.
48. Remove engine mount retaining nut.
49. Remove transmission shift shaft nut, then disconnect linkage from transmission.
50. Remove propeller shaft as outlined in "Neutral Safety Switch, Replace" in "Electrical" section.
51. **On models equipped with manual transmission,** remove retaining pin from transmission and disconnect shift reaction and control arm.
52. **On all models,** remove transmission inner mounting nuts, then lower vehicle using a jack to support rear of transmission.
53. Remove transmission outer support mounting nuts, then the transmission support from vehicle.
54. Install engine lift chain to lift brackets, carefully raise engine assembly using suitable lifting devise.
55. Reverse procedure to install, noting the following:
    a. With engine ignition in Off position, crank engine several times listening for unusual noises/binding components.
    b. Inspect oil pressure gauge and confirm engine has acceptable oil pressure.
    c. Idle engine at 1000 RPM until engine reaches normal operating temperature.

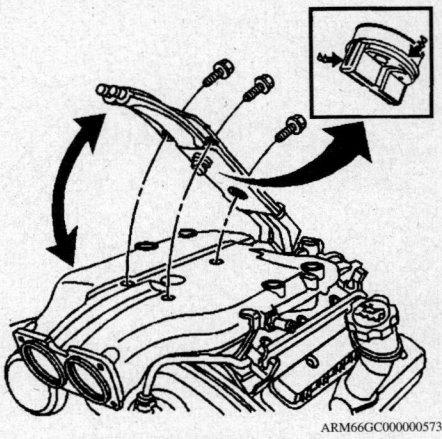

Fig. 2 Crankshaft vent bolt

    d. Inspect for oil, coolant and exhaust leaks.
    e. Perform idle relearn procedure as outlined in "Computer Relearn Procedures" in front of this manual.

INTAKE PLENUM
REPLACE

1. Remove intake plenum clamps and hoses from throttle body, then disconnect fuel pressure regulator.
2. Remove throttle body to intake plenum attaching bolts, then the throttle body from intake plenum.
3. Remove throttle body O-rings.
4. Remove crankcase adapter to intake plenum attaching bolts, then lift adapter from intake plenum and place aside, **Fig. 2.**
5. Disconnect crankcase vent air hose retainer from fuel pipe.
6. Remove power steering fluid reservoir mounting bolts.
7. Disconnect electrical connector and vacuum hose from valve at rear of plenum.
8. Remove throttle body to heater hose attaching bolt, then disconnect vacuum brake booster hose.
9. Remove ECM bracket to intake plenum attaching bolts, then the bracket, **Fig. 3.**
10. Remove intake plenum bolts, then the intake plenum from intake manifold.
11. Reverse procedure to install, noting the following:
    a. Lightly coat plenum O-rings with suitable engine oil.
    b. Apply suitable engine oil to crankcase vent seal.

INTAKE MANIFOLD
REPLACE

1. Remove intake plenum as outlined in "Intake Plenum, Replace."
2. Remove and disconnect quick connect fittings from return hose/pipe, then plug outlet ports to prevent fuel loss and contamination.
3. Disconnect fuel injector electrical harness connector from engine wiring harness.

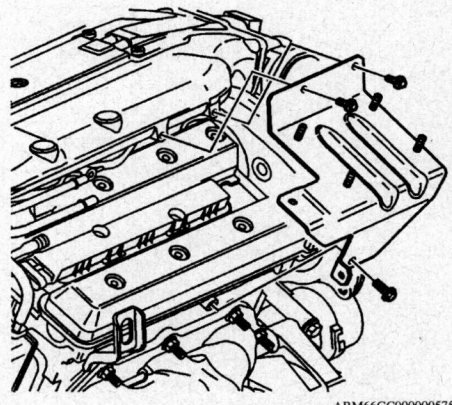

Fig. 3 ECM bracket

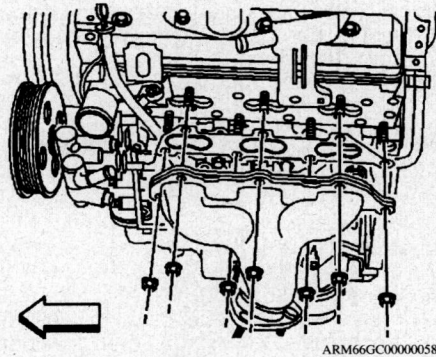

Fig. 4 Exhaust manifold

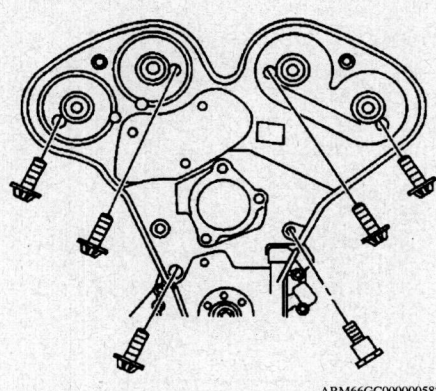

Fig. 5 Rear timing belt cover bolt removal

4. Disconnect fuel pressure regulator, then the fuel rail assembly.
5. Remove intake manifold bolts, then the intake manifold and seals.
6. Remove intake manifold flange bolts, then the intake manifold flange from cylinder heads.
7. Reverse procedure to install.

EXHAUST MANIFOLD
REPLACE
Lefthand

1. Remove air cleaner and intake air resonator.
2. Disconnect HO2S sensor from wiring harness.
3. Remove lefthand catalytic converter.
4. Remove lefthand exhaust manifold retaining nuts, then the exhaust manifold, **Fig. 4.**
5. Reverse procedure to install.

Righthand

1. Remove drive belt tensioner.
2. Disconnect engine wiring harness to ECM bracket.
3. Remove coolant pump to ECM bracket bolts, then the coolant pump.
4. Disconnect HO2S sensor from wiring harness connector.
5. Remove righthand exhaust manifold nuts, then the exhaust manifold.
6. Reverse procedure to install.

CYLINDER HEAD
REPLACE

1. Drain coolant into suitable container.
2. Remove intake manifold flange as outlined in "Intake Manifold, Replace."
3. Disconnect electrical connector from engine coolant temperature (ECT) sensor, then the throttle body heater hose from fitting.
4. Remove following from cylinder heads with heater hose still attached: water crossover fittings, upper and lower seals, water crossover.
5. Remove camshafts as outlined in "Camshaft, Replace."

6. Remove timing belt tensioner as outlined in "Timing Belt, Replace."
7. Remove rear timing belt cover to cylinder head attaching bolts, **Fig. 5.**
8. Remove cylinder head bolts in sequence, **Fig. 6.** Discard bolts.
9. Remove cylinder head and gasket.
10. Reverse procedure to install, noting the following:
    a. Remove gaskets material from cylinder head and cylinder block.
    b. Install new righthand gasket, **Fig. 7.**
    c. Install new lefthand gasket, **Fig. 8.**
    d. Tighten new cylinder head bolts in five steps using sequence, **Fig. 9.** First step, **torque** bolts to 18 ft. lbs.; second step, tighten bolts an additional 30°; third step, tighten bolts an additional 30°; fourth step, tighten bolts an additional 30°; fifth step, tighten bolts an additional 15°.

VALVE COVER
REPLACE

1. Remove intake manifold as outlined in "Intake Manifold, Replace."
2. Remove ignition coil as outlined in "Ignition Coil, Replace" in "Electrical" section.
3. Remove knock sensor wire harness bolt and bracket, then disconnect front throttle body heater inlet hose bracket.
4. Disconnect HO2S from rear of throttle body heater inlet hose, then remove throttle body heater inlet hose to engine bracket attaching bolt.
5. Remove camshaft cover attaching bolts, then the camshaft cover.
6. Reverse procedure to install.

VALVE ADJUSTMENT

This engine is equipped with hydraulic valve lash adjusters. No adjustment is required.

FRONT COVER
REPLACE

1. Remove intake air resonator as outlined in "Engine, Replace."
2. Remove intake plenum as outlined in "Intake Plenum, Replace."
3. Remove drive belt tensioner.

4. Remove water pump pulley attaching bolts, then the water pump pulley.
5. Remove power steering pump attaching bolts, then the power steering pump from bracket.
6. Remove timing belt cover attaching bolts, then the cover.
7. Reverse procedure to install.

TIMING BELT
REPLACE
Removal

1. Remove timing belt cover as outlined in "Front Cover, Replace."
2. Remove intake air resonator as outlined in "Engine, Replace."
3. Remove drive belt as outlined in "Alternator, Replace" in "Electrical" section.
4. Remove crankshaft balancer bolts, then the crankshaft balancer from crankshaft sprocket.
5. Rotate crankshaft clockwise using crank hub tool No. J 42098 or equivalent to top dead center (TDC) on compression stroke, **Fig. 10.** Reference marks on camshaft gears should be aligned with notches on rear timing belt cover, crankshaft sprocket and oil pump housing.
6. Rotate crankshaft counterclockwise using crank hub tool No. J 42098 or equivalent, to 60° before TDC to index mark on oil pump cover, **Fig. 11.**
7. Install timing belt alignment tool No. J 42069-10, or equivalent, to crankshaft sprocket, **Fig. 12,** rotate crankshaft clockwise using crank hub tool No. J 42098 or equivalent, until lever of tool No. J 42069-10, or equivalent, contacts water pump pulley flange. No. 1 cylinder is at TDC.
8. Ensure that reference marks on camshaft gears should be aligned with notches on rear timing belt cover. If not aligned, engine is 180° off.
9. Install tool Nos. J 42069-1 and J 42069-2, or equivalents, to camshaft gears, **Fig. 13.**
10. Loosen timing belt tensioner nut, upper idler pulley bolt, then remove lower idler pulley bolt and pulley with spacer.

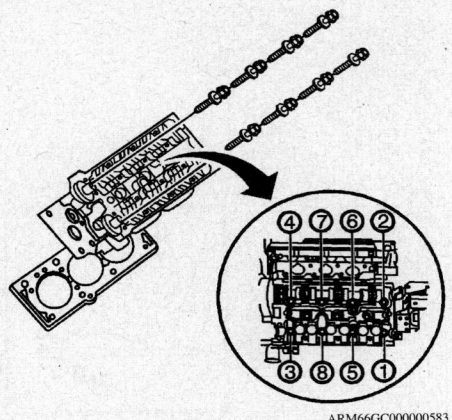

Fig. 6 Cylinder head bolt removal sequence

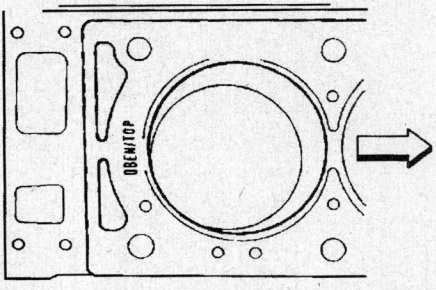
ARM66GC000000584

Fig. 7 Righthand cylinder head gasket installation

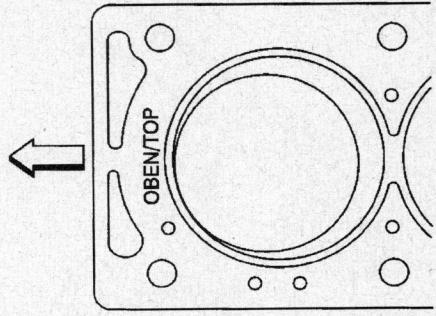
ARM66GC000000585

Fig. 8 Lefthand cylinder head gasket installation

11. Remove timing belt alignment tool No. J 42069-10, or equivalent, then the timing belt.

Installation

Arrows are printed on timing belt indicating required direction of travel and installation. Ensure that arrows are installed in correct clockwise direction. Inspect timing belt for wear or damage and replace as required.

1. Install timing belt starting at crankshaft sprocket, aligning double dash TDC mark on timing belt with marks on oil pump housing and on crankshaft sprocket, **Fig. 14.** Secure tool No. J 42069-30, or equivalent, in between oil pump housing and timing belt to prevent belt from moving.
2. Install timing belt through numbered sequence, **Fig. 15,** slide timing belt over camshaft gears simultaneously, ensuring that dash marks on timing belt align with marks on camshaft gears and notches on rear timing belt cover.
3. Rotate crankshaft counterclockwise to 3° BTDC using crank hub tool No. J 42098 or equivalent, allowing timing belt to slide on tool No. J 42069-30, or equivalent, **Fig. 16.**
4. Install lower idler pulley and spacer, then tighten.
5. Rotate crankshaft back to TDC using crank hub tool No. J 42098 or equivalent.
6. Tighten idler pulley locking bolt, while holding eccentric using tool No. J 42069-40, or equivalent, **Fig. 17.**
7. Rotate tensioner eccentric counterclockwise to full stop, turn eccentric back until reference mark is .03 inch over flange, **Fig. 18.**
8. Tighten timing belt tensioner locking nut, lock nut will be tightened after final adjustments.
9. Inspect and ensure that alignment marks on timing belt and reference points, **Fig. 19.**
10. Remove tool Nos. J 42069-30, J 42069-1 and J 42069-2, or equivalents.
11. Rotate crankshaft clockwise two revolutions using tool No. J 42098 or equivalent, until No. 1 cylinder is 60° BTDC, **Fig. 11.**
12. Install timing belt alignment tool No. J 42069-10, or equivalent, to crankshaft sprocket, **Fig. 12,** secure lever of tool to water pump pulley flange.
13. Inspect alignment of reference marks on camshaft gears with notches on rear timing belt cover and crankshaft sprocket and oil pump housing. **Alignment marks on timing belt will no longer align with marks on camshaft gears after one or more engine revolutions.**
14. Inspect alignment of camshaft gears 1 and 2, then 3 and 4 using tool No. J 42069-20, **Fig. 20.**
15. Loosen timing belt eccentric locking nut, then turn eccentric counterclockwise to full stop, then back to .118–.157 inch for new belt and reference mark alignment with datum line for used belt, **Fig. 21.** Tighten belt tensioner locking nut.
16. Secure upper idler pulley using tool No. J 42069-40, or equivalent, **Fig. 22,** and tighten.
17. Remove tool No. J 42069-20, or equivalent, from camshaft gears.
18. Remove tool No. J 42069-10, or equivalent from engine.
19. Rotate crankshaft in clockwise direction two revolutions using tool No. J 42098 or equivalent, reaching 60° BTDC.
20. Install timing belt alignment tool No. J 42069-10, or equivalent.
21. Rotate crankshaft in clockwise direction using tool No. J 42098 or equivalent, until lever contacts water pump pulley flange. Secure lever tool to water pump pulley flange.
22. Inspect alignment of reference marks on camshaft gears with notches on rear timing belt cover. Alignment marks will no longer align with marks on camshaft gears after one or more revolutions.
23. Install tool No. J 42069-20, or equivalent, to inspect alignment of camshaft gears.
24. Remove crankshaft balancer bolts, then the crankshaft balancer from crankshaft sprocket.
25. Remove drive belt as outlined in "Alternator, Replace" in "Electrical" section.
26. Remove intake air resonator as outlined in "Engine, Replace."
27. Remove timing belt cover as outlined in "Front Cover, Replace."

CAMSHAFT
REPLACE

1. Remove camshaft cover(s) as outlined in "Valve Cover, Replace."
2. Remove timing belt as outlined in "Timing Belt, Replace."
3. Install tool Nos. J 42069-1 and J 42069-2 or equivalents, then remove camshaft drive sprocket bolts, **Fig. 23.** Discard bolts.
4. Remove tool Nos. J 42069-1 and J 42069-2 or equivalents, then the camshaft sprockets.
5. Alternately loosen camshaft bearing bolts in numbered sequence, **Figs. 24 and 25.**
6. Remove camshaft bearing caps, then the camshafts, **Figs. 26 and 27.**
7. Reverse procedure to install, noting the following:
   a. Intake camshaft is stamped with a "G" next to bearing 1.
   b. Exhaust camshaft is stamped with a "J" next to bearing 1.
   c. Lubricate camshaft bearing and lobe surfaces using suitable engine oil.
   d. Apply small amount of GM part No. 1052942, or equivalent, to forward edge of front bearing caps.
   e. Install camshaft bearing caps by identification mark.
   f. Tighten camshaft bearing cap bolts in sequence, **Figs. 28 and 29.**

PISTON & ROD ASSEMBLY

When installing piston and rod assemblies into cylinder block, ensure that arrow on top of piston faces toward front of engine. Ensure flat area on bottom of piston aligns with small dimple above connecting rod crankshaft bearing bore.

PISTONS, PINS & RINGS

Pistons and rings are available in standard size and oversize. Pistons and their pins are serviced as an assembly.

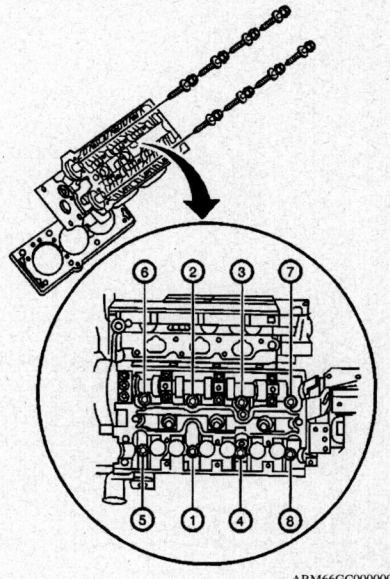

Fig. 9   Cylinder head bolt tightening sequence

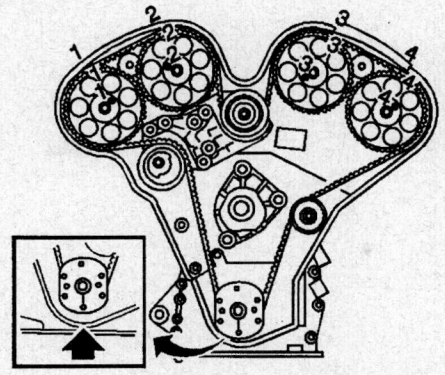

Fig. 10   No. 1 cylinder TDC rotation & alignment

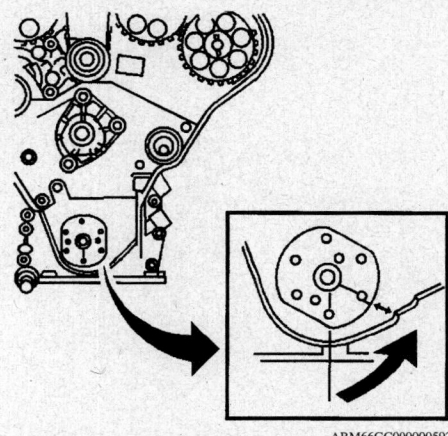

Fig. 11   Crankshaft 60° indication mark

MAIN & ROD BEARINGS

Main and rod bearings are available in standard size only. Tighten main bearing cap bolts in three steps: First step, **torque** bolts to ft. lbs.; second step, tighten bolts an additional 60°; third step, tighten bolts an additional 15°.

CRANKSHAFT FRONT OIL SEAL
REPLACE

1. Remove timing belt as outlined in "Timing Belt, Replace."
2. Install tool No. J 42065 or equivalent, to crankshaft gear.
3. Counterhold crankshaft gear using tool No. J 42065 or equivalent, remove crankshaft gear bolt using tool No. J 42098 or equivalent. Discard crankshaft gear bolt.
4. Remove crankshaft gear, then the oil pump collar.
5. Drill a small pilot hole into steel ring of crankshaft front oil seal, **Fig. 30,** screw a self-tapping screw, then using suitable pliers, remove crankshaft front oil seal.
6. Reverse procedure to install.

CRANKSHAFT BALANCER
REPLACE

1. Remove intake air resonator as outlined in "Engine, Replace."
2. Remove drive belt as outlined in "Serpentine Drive Belt."
3. Remove crankshaft balancer bolts, then the crankshaft balancer, **Fig. 31.**
4. Reverse procedure to install.

CRANKSHAFT REAR OIL SEAL
REPLACE

1. Remove transmission as outlined in **MOTOR's "Domestic Transmission, In-Vehicle Service"** manual.
2. Counterhold crankshaft using tool No. J 42098 and remove flywheel bolts. Discard flywheel bolts as required.
3. Remove engine flywheel and retainer from crankshaft.
4. Center punch steel ring of rear main oil seal, then drill small pilot hole into steel ring of rear main oil seal.
5. Screw a self-tapping screw into seal, then using suitable pliers, remove seal, **Fig. 32.**
6. Reverse procedure to install.

OIL PAN
REPLACE

1. Drain engine oil into suitable container.
2. Install suitable engine lifting device.
3. Remove front tire and wheel assemblies.
4. Remove front air deflector.
5. Disconnect electrical wiring harness, secure harness to frame.
6. Disconnect rearward retainer and anti-lock brake wiring harness from lower control arms.
7. Remove brake lines and brake line bracket from frame.
8. Support radiator and condenser assembly using suitable wire to front absorber bracket bolt.
9. Remove washer bottle bracket, then loosen brake pressure modulator valve nuts to separate brake pressure valve from bracket.
10. Loosen stabilizer shaft mounting bolts, then remove lower stabilizer shaft link retaining nut and link from lower control arm.
11. Remove power steering pressure hose retaining nut from air conditioning compressor.
12. Remove power steering gear mounting bolts, support gear using suitable wire.
13. Remove outer tie rod retaining nut, then separate outer tie rod from steering knuckle using tool No. J 42319-B or equivalent.
14. Remove lower shock bolts, then disconnect lower ball joint from steering knuckle as outlined in "Control Arm, Replace." in "Front Suspension & Steering" section.
15. Remove engine mount lower retaining nuts.
16. Install tool No. J 39580 or equivalent, then lower engine to frame support table and remove frame bolts.
17. Raise engine from frame.
18. Remove transmission fluid cooler pipes brace to engine, then the three lower transmission mounting bolts.
19. Remove oil pan bolts, then pry oil pan from engine block using suitable flat bladed tool.
20. Reverse procedure to install, noting the following:
    a. Apply a suitable bead of silicone sealing compound part No. 12346286, or equivalent, to oil pan surface.
    b. Tighten oil pan to engine block bolts in sequence, **Fig. 33.**

OIL PUMP
REPLACE

1. Remove oil pan as outlined in "Oil Pan, Replace."
2. Remove oil pump pipe screen brace bolts, screen bolts, then the oil pump pipe screen from engine.
3. Remove crankshaft drive gear as outlined in "Crankshaft Front Oil Seal, Replace."
4. Remove engine oil pressure switch.
5. Remove alternator and position aside.
6. Remove oil pump bolts, pump and gasket, **Fig. 34.**
7. Reverse procedure to install, noting the following:
    a. Clean and inspect oil pump gasket surfaces.
    b. Install oil pump bolts in numbered sequence, **Fig. 35.**

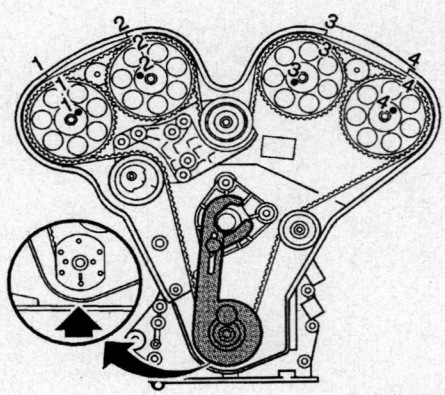

Fig. 12 Timing belt alignment tool installation

SERPENTINE DRIVE BELT
Replace

1. Rotate drive belt tensioner clockwise to release tension.
2. Slide drive belt from water pump pulley, allowing tensioner to return.
3. Remove drive belt from accessory pulleys.
4. Reverse procedure to install. Refer to **Fig. 36** for serpentine drive belt routing.

COOLING SYSTEM
BLEED

1. Place transmission in Park or Neutral position.
2. Engage park brake.
3. Run engine until thermostat opens.
4. Stop engine.
5. Fill system using only clean drinkable water.
6. Repeat procedure if required, until fluid is nearly colorless.
7. Fill coolant reservoir to FULL HOT mark.

THERMOSTAT
REPLACE

1. Drain cooling system into suitable container. Position J 38185 to clamp in order to remove O-ring seals from coolant outlet pipe. Discard O-rings.
2. Remove radiator inlet hose from coolant outlet pipe.
3. Remove bolts securing oil dipstick tube, coolant outlet pipe, engine front lift bracket and coolant outlet pipe from thermostat housing.
4. Remove intake manifold as outlined in "Intake Manifold, Replace."
5. Remove thermostat housing bolts, then the thermostat housing.
6. Remove thermostat.
7. Reverse procedure to install.

WATER PUMP
REPLACE

1. Drain cooling system into suitable container.
2. Remove timing belt cover as outlined in "Front Cover, Replace."
3. Remove water pump bolts, then the water pump, **Fig. 37**.
4. Reverse procedure to install, noting the following:
   a. Clean and inspect surfaces as required.
   b. Apply seal ring silicone grease part No. 12345579, or equivalent.

RADIATOR
REPLACE

1. Drain engine coolant into suitable container.
2. Remove condenser seal, radiator attaching bolts, then the support brackets.
3. Disconnect surge tank hose, then remove fan shroud attaching bolts.
4. Disconnect upper radiator hose to radiator using tool No. J 38185, or equivalent.
5. Remove coolant bypass valve, placing aside, then release solenoid from fan shroud.
6. Remove air cleaner assembly.
7. Rotate, then remove A/C retaining clip and disconnect fan motor electrical connectors.
8. Remove coolant bypass hose from radiator using suitable pliers.
9. Remove fan shroud attaching bolts, then the fan assembly.
10. Remove upper condenser attaching bolts, raise and support vehicle using suitable lift.
11. Disconnect lower transaxle oil cooler line and lower radiator hose from radiator using suitable pliers.
12. Remove lower condenser bolts, then the radiator seal push pins.
13. Lower vehicle, then remove radiator assembly.
14. Reverse procedure to install.

FUEL PUMP
REPLACE

1. Drain fuel tank into suitable container.
2. Raise and support vehicle.
3. Remove catalytic converter attaching nuts, support exhaust system.
4. Remove exhaust system from front and rear hanger rods.
5. Remove floor panel brace, then the exhaust system.
6. Disconnect propeller shaft coupler from transmission flange.
7. Push front propeller shaft toward rear of vehicle to release coupler from transmission flange.
8. Secure front propeller shaft to shift control lever using suitable wire.

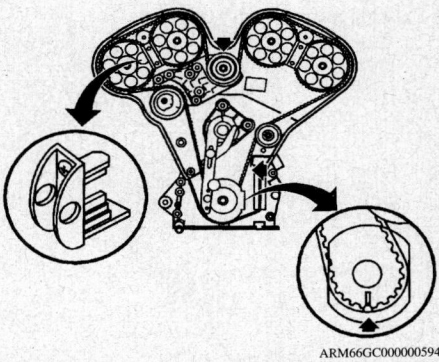

Fig. 13 Camshaft tool installation

9. Disconnect filler hose and vent tube from fuel tank.
10. Disconnect fuel feed, fuel return and fuel EVAP hoses, then the fuel tank electrical connector.
11. Disconnect EVAP hoses and retainer from underside of vehicle.
12. Support shock absorber using a suitable jack, then the remove lower shock absorber bolts.
13. Install a suitable jack under rear tie bar, to support front of rear frame, remove two rear frame attaching bolts.
14. Lower jack until there is two inches of clearance between front surface and chassis.
15. Remove fuel tank strap bolts, then pull straps downward and position aside.
16. Lower tank and disconnect pressure and return hose from primary fuel tank module.
17. Disconnect primary fuel tank module electrical connector.
18. Remove fuel tank from vehicle.
19. Turn cam lock counterclockwise using lock ring tool No. J 45747, or equivalent.
20. Remove primary fuel tank module from tank.
21. Reverse procedure to install.

FUEL FILTER
REPLACE

1. Disconnect fuel filter bracket release tabs.
2. Twist quick-connect fitting ¼ turn in each direction to loosen dirt within fitting.
3. Clean quick-connect fitting at ends of filter.
4. Disconnect quick-connect fittings by squeezing plastic tabs of male end connector and pulling apart.
5. Disconnect threaded fitting at fuel filter outlet.
6. Remove fuel filter.
7. Reverse procedure to install, noting the following:
   a. Turn ignition On for two seconds, then Off for ten seconds.
   b. Turn ignition On and inspect for fuel leakage.

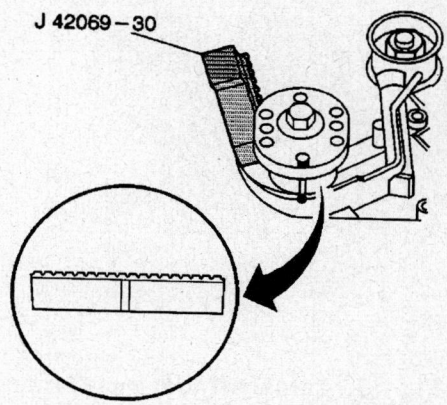

Fig. 14 Timing belt starting installation starting point

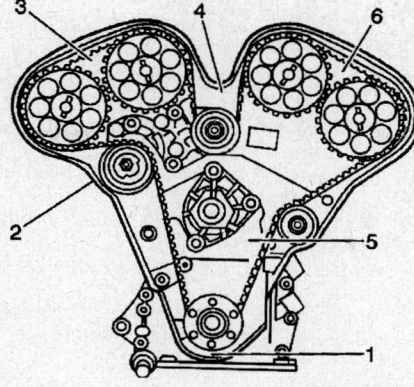

Fig. 15 Timing belt installation

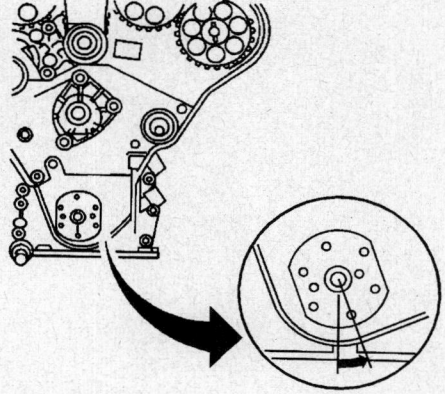

Fig. 16 Crankshaft counterclockwise timing belt installation

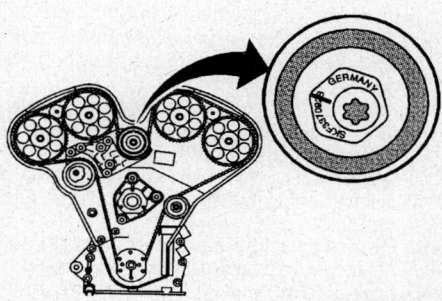

Fig. 17 Idler pulley bolt tightening

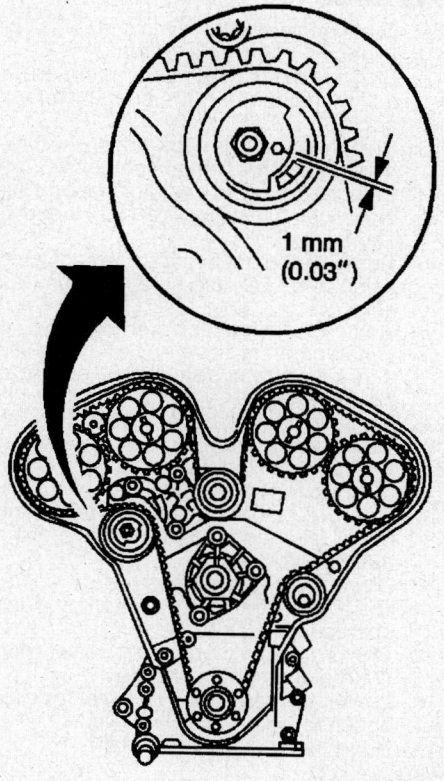

Fig. 18 Initial timing belt tension

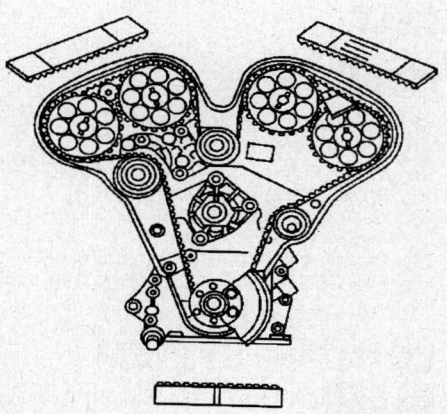

Fig. 19 Alignment marks & reference points

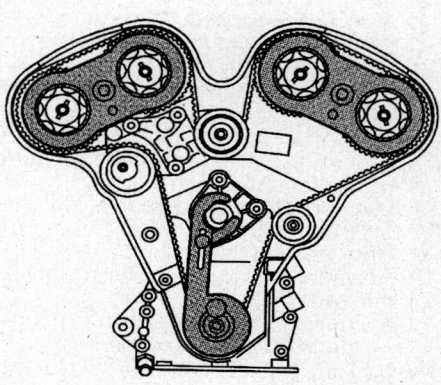

Fig. 20 Camshaft gear alignment inspections

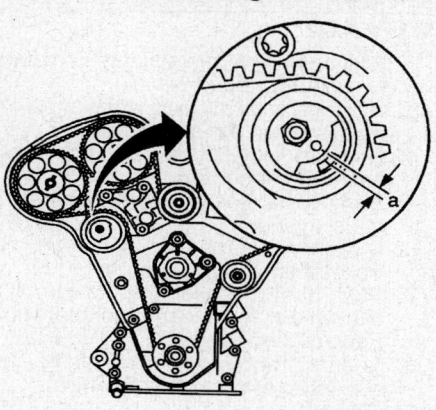

Fig. 21 Timing belt tension adjustment

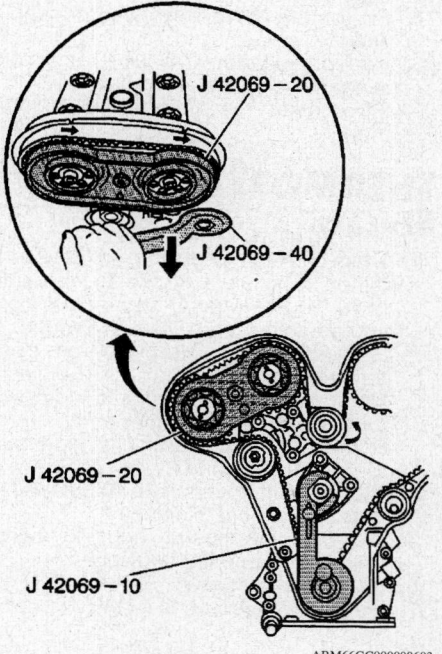

Fig. 22 Upper idler pulley

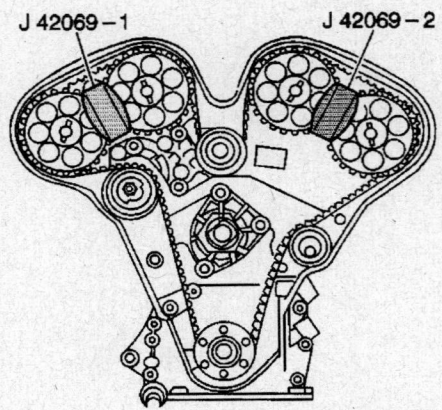

Fig. 23 Camshaft drive sprocket bolt removal

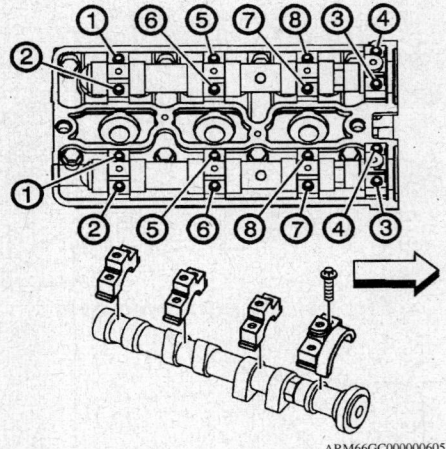

ARM66GC000000605

Fig. 24 Righthand camshaft bearing cap removal

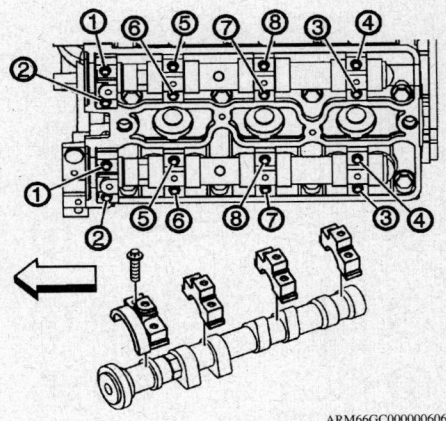

ARM66GC000000606

Fig. 25 Lefthand camshaft bearing cap removal

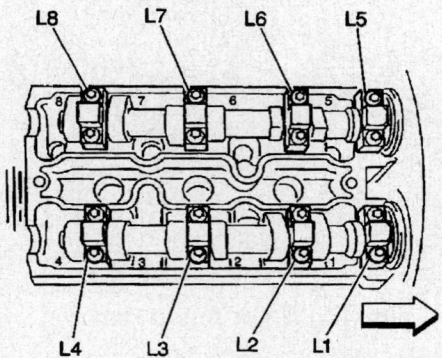

ARM66GC000000607

Fig. 26 Lefthand bearing cap identification

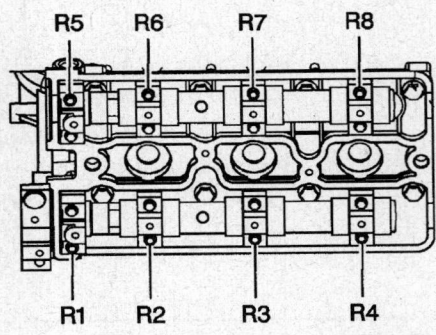

ARM66GC000000608

Fig. 27 Righthand bearing cap identification

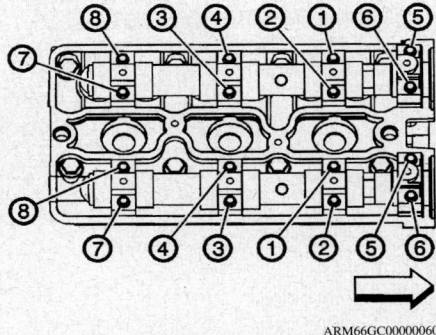

ARM66GC000000609

Fig. 28 Righthand camshaft bearing cap tightening sequence

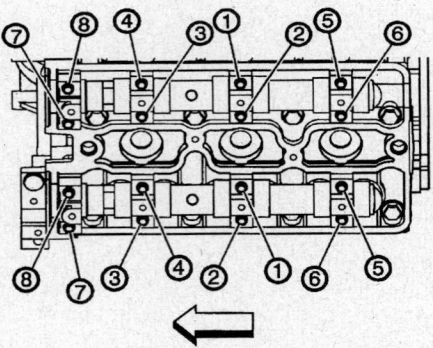

ARM66GC000000610

Fig. 29 Lefthand camshaft bearing cap tightening sequence

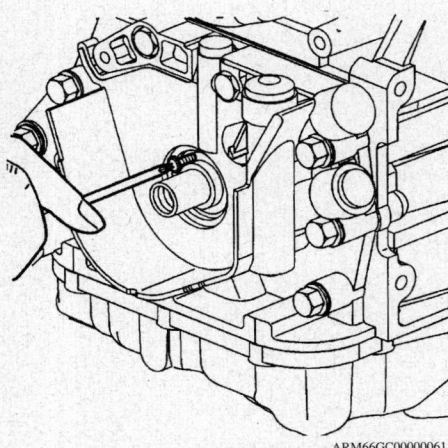

ARM66GC000000611

Fig. 30 Crankshaft front oil seal removal

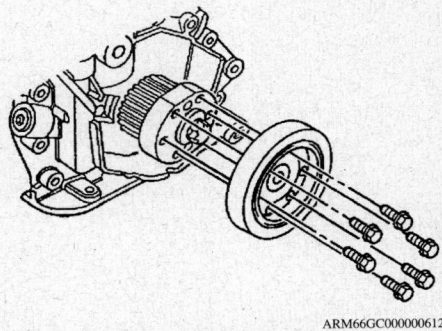

ARM66GC000000612

Fig. 31 Crankshaft balancer removal

ARM66GC000000613

Fig. 32 Crankshaft rear oil seal removal

16
12
14
7
10
3
6
1
2
5
4
9
8
15
13
11
17
ARM66GC000000621

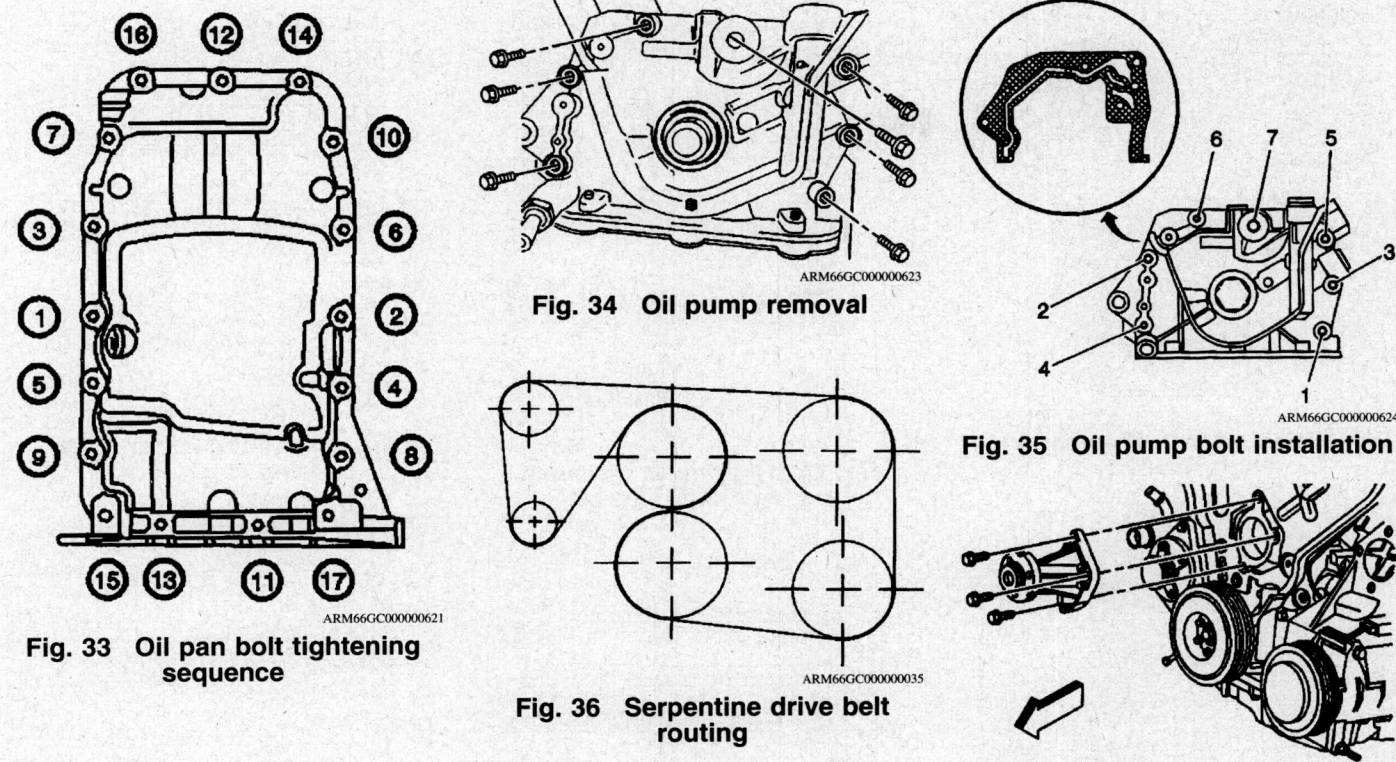

Fig. 33 Oil pan bolt tightening sequence

ARM66GC000000623

Fig. 34 Oil pump removal

ARM66GC000000035

Fig. 36 Serpentine drive belt routing

6
7
5
3
2
4
1
ARM66GC000000624

Fig. 35 Oil pump bolt installation

ARM66GC000000625

Fig. 37 Water pump removal

TIGHTENING SPECIFICATIONS

Year	Component	Torque Ft. Lbs.
2004	Accessory Mounting Bracket Bolt	26
	A/C Compressor Mounting Bolt	15
	A/C Condenser Mounting Bolt	58①
	A/C Line Clip To Fan Shroud Screw	40①
	Afterboil Coolant Pump Bolt	89①
	Alternator Mounting Bolt	26
	Auxiliary Cooling Fan Mounting Bolt	58①
	Battery Cable To Battery Bolt	13
	Battery Ground To Side Rail Bolt	27
	Battery Positive To Underhood Fuse Block Nut	11
	Blow-By Plate To Cylinder Block Bolt	71①
	Bumper Nut	18
	Camshaft Bearing Cap Bolt	71①
	Camshaft Cover Bolt	71
	Camshaft Position Sensor Bolt	71
	Camshaft Sprocket Bolt	②
	Catalytic Converter Hanger Bracket Bolt	37
	Catalytic Converter Hanger Bracket Nut	18
	Catalytic Converter Nut	11
	Center Bearing Heat Shield Bolt	71①
	Coil Ground To Lefthand Cylinder Head Bolt	37
	Connecting Rod	③
	Coolant Bypass Inlet Hose/Pipe Bolt	80①
	Coolant Bypass Valve Bolt	58①
	Coolant Heater	44
	Coolant Heater Ground Lead Bolt	80①
	Coolant Inlet Pipe Bolt	15
	Coolant Inlet Pipe Support Bolt	15
	Coolant Jacket Plug	48
	Coolant Jacket Support Plug	48
	Crankcase Vent Housing Bolt	71①
	Crankcase Ventilation Tube Adapter Bolt	71①
	Crankshaft Balancer Bolt	15
	Crankshaft Bearing Bridge Adjusting Sleeve	15
	Crankshaft Bearing Bridge Bolt	15
	Crankshaft Bearing Cap	④
	Crankshaft Drive Gear Bolt	⑤
	Crankshaft Position Sensor Bolt	71①
	Crankshaft Reluctor Ring Screw	11
	Cylinder Head Bolts	⑥
	Drive Belt Tensioner Bolt	26
	ECM Bracket To Cylinder Head Bolt	15
	ECM Bracket To Intake Plenum Bolt	71①
	ECM To Bracket Nut	71①
	Electric Cooling Fan Blade Retaining Nut	62①
	Electric Cooling Fan Motor Mounting Screw	44①
	Electric Cooling Fan To Plenum Mounting Bolt	58①
	Electric Cooling Fan To Radiator Mounting Bolt	58①

TIGHTENING SPECIFICATIONS—Continued

Year	Component	Torque Ft. Lbs.
2004	Engine Coolant Temperature Sensor	13
	Engine Ground Lead To Lefthand Cylinder Head Bolt	22
	Engine Mount Bracket Bolt	44
	Engine Mount Nut	59
	Engine Rear Lift Bracket Bolt	15
	Engine Wiring Harness Ground Lead Bolt	80①
	Engine Wiring Harness Retainer To Oil Pan Bolt	37
	EVAP Canister Purge Valve Bracket Bolt	71①
	Exhaust Manifold Nut	15
	Exhaust Manifold Pipe Nut	18
	Exhaust Manifold Stud	22
	Floor Panel Tunnel Brace Bolt	18
	Front Air Inlet Panel	53①
	Fuel Rail Bolt	71①
	Ignition Coil Cassette Bolt	71①
	Intake Manifold Bolt	15
	Intake Manifold Flange Bolt	15
	Intake Plenum Bolt	15
	Intake Plenum Tuning Solenoid Bolt	71①
	Intake Plenum Tuning Valve Bolt	71①
	Knock Sensor Bolt	15
	Knock Sensor Wire Harness Bracket Bolt	71①
	Oil Baffle Bolt	71①
	Oil Cooler Cover Bolt	15
	Oil Cooler Feed & Return Lines To Engine Block	22
	Oil Cooler Inlet & Outlet Nut	22
	Oil Cooler Pipe Fitting To Oil Cooler	22
	Oil Filter Adapter Bolt	15
	Oil Filter Adapter Female Screw	18
	Oil Filter Adapter Plug	18
	Oil Filter Cartridge Housing Drain Plug	89①
	Oil Filter Cartridge Plastic Cap To Adapter	18
	Oil Intake Pipe Bolt	71①
	Oil Intake Pipe Brace Bolt	71①
	Oil Dipstick Tube Bolt	15
	Oil Pan Bolt	11
	Oil Pan Drain Plug	89①
	Oil Pressure Sender	26
	Oil Pump Bolt	15
	Oil Pump Cover Bolt	71①
	Power Steering Hose Retaining Nut	71①
	Power Steering Pump Mounting Bolt	26
	Radiator Support Bracket Bolt	80①
	Remote Power Steering Fluid Reservoir To Cylinder Head Mounting Bolt	18
	Remote Power Steering Fluid Reservoir To Intake Plenum Mounting Bolt	80①
	Spark Plug	18

Continued

TIGHTENING SPECIFICATIONS—Continued

Year	Component	Torque Ft. Lbs.
2004	Surge Tank Outlet Pipe To Vent Housing Bolt	80①
	Thermostat Housing Bolt	15
	Threaded Block Heater	44
	Throttle Body Bolt	71①
	Throttle Body Heater Inlet Hose/Pipe Bolt	80①
	Throttle Body Inlet Heater Hose Fitting	15
	Timing Belt Front Cover Bolt	71①
	Timing Belt Idler Pulley Bolt	30
	Timing Belt Rear Cover Bolt	71①
	Timing Belt Rear Cover Threaded Pin	89①
	Timing Belt Tensioner Bracket Bolt	30
	Timing Belt Tensioner Pulley Nut	15
	Torque Converter Bolt	46
	Transmission Fluid Cooler Pipes Retaining Bolt	18
	Transmission Manual Shift Shaft Nut	80①
	Transmission Mounting Bolt (M10)	37
	Transmission Mounting Bolt (M12)	55
	Transmission Mount Nut	44
	Transmission Support Mounting Bolt	44
	Vacuum Brake Booster Fitting	18
	Water Crossover Bolt	22
	Water Crossover Fitting	15
	Water Crossover Pipe Plug	44①
	Water Pump Bolt	18
	Water Pump Pulley Bolt	71①

① — Inch lbs.

② — First pass, 37 ft. lbs.; second pass, 60°; third pass, 15°.

③ — First pass, 26 ft. lbs.; second pass, 45°; third pass, 15°.

④ — First pass, 37 ft. lbs.; second pass, 60°; third pass, 15°.

⑤ — First pass, 184 ft. lbs.; second pass, 45°; third pass, 15°.

⑥ — Refer to "Cylinder Head, Replace" for tightening sequence.

3.6L Engine

NOTE: On Air Bag Equipped Models, Refer To "Air Bag System Precautions" Located In The Front Of This Manual For System Disarming & Arming Procedures.

NOTE: Refer To "Computer Relearn Procedures" Located In The Front Of This Manual When Battery Power To The Computer Has Been Interrupted.

NOTE: Prior To Performing Any Service Operations Listed In This Section, Consult The "Technical Service Bulletins" Section For Related Information.

NOTE: Refer To "3.2L Engine" Section For Procedures Not Found In This Section.

INDEX

	Page No.		Page No.		Page No.
Camshaft, Replace	8-33	Fuel Filter, Replace	8-35	Alternator & Water Pump	8-34
Compression Pressure	8-29	Fuel Pump, Replace	8-35	Thermostat, Replace	8-35
Cooling System Bleed	8-34	Intake Manifold, Replace	8-30	Tightening Specifications	8-41
Crankshaft Balancer, Replace	8-31	Lower	8-30	Timing Chain, Replace	8-31
Crankshaft Front Oil Seal,		Upper	8-30	Lefthand Secondary Drive	
Replace	8-33	Main & Rod Bearings	8-33	Chain	8-33
Crankshaft Rear Oil Seal,		Oil Pan, Replace	8-34	Installation	8-33
Replace	8-34	Oil Pump, Replace	8-34	Removal	8-33
Cylinder Head, Replace	8-30	Oil Pump Service	8-34	Primary Drive Chain	8-31
Lefthand	8-30	Piston & Rod Assembly	8-33	Installation	8-31
Righthand	8-30	Pistons, Pins & Rings	8-33	Removal	8-31
Engine Rebuilding		Precautions	8-29	Righthand Secondary Drive	
Specifications	29-1	Air Bag Systems	8-29	Chain	8-32
Engine, Replace	8-29	Battery Ground Cable	8-29	Installation	8-32
Engine Mount, Replace	8-29	Fuel Pressure Relief	8-29	Removal	8-32
Exhaust Manifold, Replace	8-30	Radiator, Replace	8-35	Valve Adjustment	8-31
Lefthand	8-30	Serpentine Drive Belt, Replace	8-34	Valve Cover, Replace	8-31
Righthand	8-30	Air Conditioning & Power		Water Pump, Replace	8-35
Front Cover, Replace	8-31	Steering	8-34		

PRECAUTIONS

Air Bag Systems

Refer to "Air Bag System Precautions" in the front of this manual for system disarming and arming procedures.

Battery Ground Cable

Prior to service, record radio presets, then disconnect battery ground cable and isolate as required.

Fuel Pressure Relief

1. Record radio presets.
2. Turn ignition Off.
3. Disconnect battery ground cable and isolate as required.
4. Loosen fuel filler cap to relieve fuel tank vapor pressure.
5. Remove cap to fuel pressure service connection.
6. Install tool Nos. J34730-1A and J42242, or equivalents, to fuel pressure service connection.
7. Place bleed hose into suitable container, then open bleed valve to relieve fuel system.
8. Place a suitable shop towel under connections to protect fuel spillage.
9. Remove tool Nos. J34730-1A and J42242, or equivalents, from service connections.
10. Install cap to fuel pressure service connection.

COMPRESSION PRESSURE

The minimum compression in any one cylinder should not be less than 70 percent of the highest cylinder. No cylinder should read less than 140 psi.

ENGINE MOUNT
REPLACE

1. Raise and support vehicle.
2. Place a suitable adjustable jack stand with a block of wood under engine oil pan.
3. Remove upper engine mount retaining nut.
4. Remove lefthand engine mount bracket retaining nut, then the bracket.
5. Remove lower engine mount retaining nut, then the engine mount.
6. Reverse procedure to install.

ENGINE
REPLACE

1. Turn front wheels to straight ahead position.
2. Turn ignition lock cylinder to Lock position and remove key.
3. Lock steering column by inserting steering column anti-rotation pin tool No. J 42640, or equivalent, through access hole in lower steering column trim cover.
4. Relieve fuel system pressure as outlined in "Precautions."
5. Raise and support vehicle.
6. Mark relationship of center intermediate shaft to lower intermediate shaft for installation reference.
7. Remove center intermediate shaft to lower intermediate shaft retaining bolt.

8. Remove lower intermediate shaft to power steering gear retaining bolt.
9. Mark relationship of lower intermediate shaft to power steering gear for installation reference.
10. Disconnect lower intermediate shaft from power steering gear.
11. Remove lower intermediate shaft from center intermediate shaft.
12. Remove battery and fuel injector sight shield.
13. Remove air cleaner duct, then disconnect cooling fan electrical connectors.
14. Remove cooling fan wiring harness from shroud, then secure harnesses aside.
15. Drain cooling system.
16. Disconnect outlet hose from surge tank. Secure hose aside.
17. Disconnect surge tank inlet hose from water outlet housing and radiator. Secure hose aside.
18. Disconnect hoses from heater core.
19. Disconnect purge line from purge solenoid.
20. Recover A/C system refrigerant as outlined in "Air Condition" chapter.
21. Remove wiper module assembly as outlined in electrical section.
22. Disconnect suction hose from evaporator and remove suction hose bracket from shock tower. Secure suction hose to engine.
23. Disconnect A/C pressure switch electrical connector, then remove liquid line.
24. Remove radiator support brackets.
25. Disconnect brake booster check valve, then brake booster vacuum hose. Secure booster hose to engine.
26. Disconnect brake fluid level switch electrical connector.
27. Disconnect Mass Air Flow (MAF) sensor electrical connector.
28. Disconnect instrument cluster electrical connector from rear of lefthand cylinder head. Secure electrical harness aside.
29. Disconnect engine module wiring harness connectors from underhood electrical center.
30. Disconnect Transmission Control Module (TCM) electrical connector.
31. Remove ground wire to rail retaining bolt, then position ground wire aside.
32. Disconnect engine harness electrical connector. Harness connector is located on engine compartment longitudinal rail. Position TCM harness aside.
33. Secure ground wire, engine harness and TCM harness to engine.
34. Remove master cylinder retaining nuts, then secure master cylinder to engine.
35. Raise and support engine.
36. Remove exhaust system and propeller shaft.
37. Remove air deflector and washer bottle bracket.
38. Disconnect side air baffles from radiator.
39. Remove lefthand front brake pipe retainer and brake pipe rail.
40. Remove righthand front brake pipe from pipe retainer.

41. Disconnect rear brake pipes from BPVM valve.
42. Remove front tire and wheel assemblies.
43. Remove intermediate steering shaft from steering gear.
44. Remove lower engine mount retaining nut.
45. Disconnect transmission shift linkage from transmission.
46. Disconnect low oil level sensor electrical connector, then secure sensor harness and connector to engine.
47. Remove headlamp leveling sensors.
48. Secure shock modules to lower control arms with a suitable strap in order to prevent damage to front brake hoses.
49. Remove righthand side and lefthand side shock modules upper mounting bolts.
50. Place a suitable lift platform in engine and transmission assembly.
51. Remove transmission brace to underbody attaching bolts.
52. Remove front frame bolts.
53. Lower lift platform and remove engine transmission assembly from vehicle.
54. Separate transmission assembly from engine.
55. Reverse procedure to install.

INTAKE MANIFOLD
REPLACE
Upper

1. Remove fuel injector sight shield from top of engine.
2. Remove air inlet duct, then disconnect brake booster vacuum hose from intake manifold.
3. Disconnect electrical connector and purge line from purge solenoid valve.
4. Remove wiring harness retainer from front of intake manifold.
5. Disconnect throttle body electrical connector.
6. Remove upper intake manifold brake bolts, then the brace.
7. Disconnect PCV hose from righthand camshaft cover.
8. Disconnect barometric pressure sensor and intake manifold runner control solenoid electrical connectors.
9. Remove injector harness bracket attaching bolt, then the lefthand ignition coil wiring harness from bracket.
10. Remove upper intake manifold attaching bolts, then the manifold with throttle body from engine.
11. Reverse procedure to install.

Lower

1. Remove upper intake manifold as outlined under "Upper."
2. Remove lower intake manifold attaching bolts.
3. Position intake manifold to gain access to fuel pipe connector.
4. Remove fuel feed pipe retainer, then disconnect fuel feed pipe from fuel rail.
5. Remove lower intake manifold.
6. Reverse procedure to install.

EXHAUST MANIFOLD
REPLACE
Lefthand

1. Remove heat shield attaching bolts, then the heat shield.
2. Remove exhaust manifold upper and lower insulators from oil dipstick tube.
3. Remove lefthand catalytic converter.
4. Remove lefthand exhaust manifold retaining nuts, then the exhaust manifold.
5. Reverse procedure to install.

Righthand

1. Remove exhaust manifold heat shield attaching bolts, then the heat shield.
2. Remove Engine Coolant Temperature (ECT) sensor.
3. Remove exhaust manifold to cylinder head attaching bolts, then the exhaust manifold.
4. Reverse procedure to install.

CYLINDER HEAD
REPLACE
Lefthand

1. Remove lefthand secondary timing chain as outlined under "Timing Chain, Replace."
2. Remove oil dipstick.
3. Remove heat shield from coolant temperature sensor and disconnect sensor electrical connector.
4. Remove wiring harness ground from cylinder head.
5. Disconnect wiring harness electrical connector from side of cylinder head.
6. Remove wiring harness connector bracket from cylinder head.
7. Remove power steering pump mounting bolts. **Do not disconnect power steering pipes or hoses.**
8. Remove surge tank hose from cylinder head bracket.
9. Remove wiring harness bracket from rear of cylinder head.
10. Remove lefthand catalytic converter.
11. Remove oil dipstick and oil filter adapter upper bolt.
12. Remove exhaust manifold attaching bolts, then the exhaust manifold.
13. Remove cylinder head attaching bolts, then the cylinder head. **Discard cylinder head M11 bolts.**
14. Reverse procedure to install, noting the following:
    a. Install new M11 bolts.
    b. **Torque** M11 bolts to 33 ft. lbs., **Fig. 1,** then tighten an additional 120°.
    c. **Torque** M8 bolts to 10 ft. lbs., then tighten an additional 60°.

Righthand

1. Remove righthand secondary timing chain as outlined under "Timing Chain, Replace."
2. Remove coolant inlet pipe.

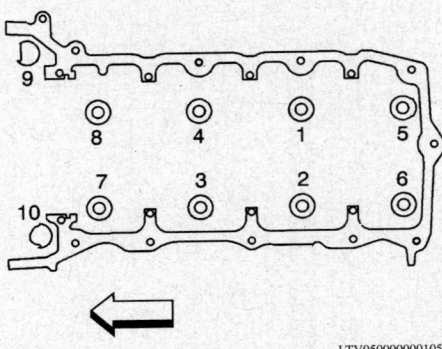

Fig. 1 Lefthand cylinder head bolt tightening sequence

3. Remove wiring harness ground from cylinder head.
4. Disconnect wiring harness electrical connector from side of cylinder head.
5. Remove wiring harness conduit upper bolt from cylinder head, then position conduit aside.
6. Remove battery cable from cylinder head.
7. Remove righthand catalytic converter.
8. Remove exhaust manifold attaching bolts, then the exhaust manifold.
9. Remove cylinder head attaching bolts, then the cylinder head. **Discard cylinder head M11 bolts.**
10. Reverse procedure to install, noting the following:
    a. Install new M11 bolts.
    b. **Torque** M11 bolts to 33 ft. lbs., **Fig. 2,** then tighten an additional 120°.
    c. **Torque** M8 bolts to 10 ft. lbs., then tighten an additional 60°.

VALVE COVER
REPLACE

1. Remove intake manifold as outlined under "Intake Manifold, Replace."
2. Remove wiring harness from side of camshaft cover.
3. Remove wiring harness conduit retainers from camshaft cover by rotating counterclockwise.
4. Remove wiring harness from front of camshaft cover. Position harness aside.
5. Remove ignition coil as outlined under "Ignition Coil, Replace" in "Electrical" section.
6. Remove camshaft cover attaching bolts, then the camshaft cover, **Fig. 3.**
7. Reverse procedure to install, noting the following:
   a. Install spark plug guide seal tools No. EN 46101, or equivalent, onto spark plug tubes.
   b. Ensure new grommets are installed before cover mounting bolts.
   c. Apply .3150 inch diameter by .1575 inch high bead of suitable RTV sealant on engine front cover split lines, **Fig. 4.**
   d. **Torque** valve cover mounting bolts to 89 inch lbs. in sequence, **Figs. 5 and 6.**

e. Remove tube seal guide tools, then install spark plugs.

VALVE ADJUSTMENT

This engine is equipped with hydraulic valve lash adjusters. No adjustment is required.

CRANKSHAFT BALANCER
REPLACE

1. Remove drive belts as outlined under "Serpentine Drive Belt."
2. Raise and support vehicle.
3. Remove crankshaft balancer retaining bolt.
4. Remove crankshaft balancer using harmonic balancer pulling tool No. J 24420-C, or equivalent.
5. Reverse procedure to install.

FRONT COVER
REPLACE

1. Remove fuel injector sight shield.
2. Remove upper and lower intake manifolds as outlined under "Intake Manifold, Replace."
3. Remove camshaft covers as outlined under "Valve Cover, Replace."
4. Drain engine coolant and disconnect purge vent hose from water outlet.
5. Remove water outlet with radiator hose and position aside.
6. Remove accessory drive belts as outlined under "Serpentine Drive Belt."
7. Remove idler pulley and drive belt tensioners.
8. Remove alternator and alternator bracket.
9. Remove power steering fluid reservoir and position aside.
10. Remove power steering pump pulley.
11. Remove power steering pump upper front bolt, then loosen two remaining bolts.
12. Remove crankshaft balancer as outlined under "Crankshaft Balancer, Replace."
13. Remove camshafts as outlined under "Camshaft, Replace."
14. Remove camshaft position actuator solenoid valves, **Fig. 7.**
15. Remove front cover attaching bolts, then the cover and cover deadener.
16. Reverse procedure to install, noting the following:
    a. Install .315 inch guides from guide pin tool set No. EN 46109 into cylinder block, **Fig. 8.**
    b. Install new engine front cover to cylinder block seal.
    c. Place a .118 inch bead of RTV sealant part No. 12378521, or equivalent on front cover, **Fig. 9.**
    d. Install front cover and deadener, then remove guide pins. Start mounting bolts by hand.
    e. **Torque** front cover mounting bolts to 17 ft. lbs. in sequence, **Fig. 10.**
    f. Install new CMP sensor O-rings.

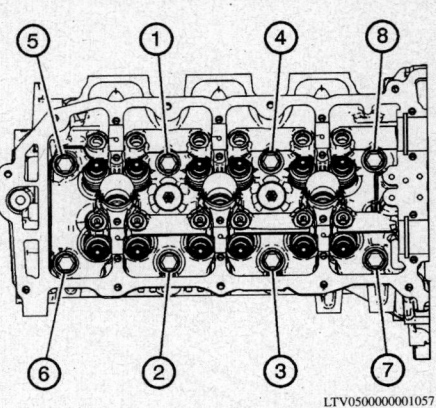

Fig. 2 Righthand cylinder head bolt tightening sequence

   g. **Torque** alternator bracket mounting bolts Nos. 1 and 2 to 37 ft. lbs., **Fig. 11.**
   h. **Torque** alternator bracket mounting bolts Nos. 3 to 17 ft. lbs.

TIMING CHAIN
REPLACE
Primary Drive Chain
REMOVAL

1. Remove spark plugs.
2. Remove front cover as outlined under "Front Cover, Replace."
3. Remove righthand side secondary camshaft drive chain tensioner attaching bolts, then the drive chain tensioner, **Fig. 12.**
4. Remove righthand side secondary timing chain shoe, then the righthand side secondary drive chain.
5. Remove primary camshaft drive chain tensioner.
6. Remove primary camshaft drive chain upper guide, then the primary chain.

INSTALLATION

1. Hold righthand camshafts in place by installing camshaft holding tool No. 46105, or equivalent, onto camshafts.
2. Wrap primary camshaft drive chain around large sprockets of each camshaft intermediate chain idler and crankshaft sprocket.
3. Align lefthand side camshaft intermediate drive chain idler timing mark with bright plated camshaft drive chain link, **Fig. 13.**
4. Align righthand side camshaft intermediate drive chain idler timing mark with bright plated camshaft drive chain link, **Fig. 13.**
5. Align crankshaft sprocket timing mark with bright plated camshaft drive chain link, **Fig. 13.**
6. Compress primary drive chain tensioner plunger into tensioner body using tensioner tool No. J 45027, or equivalent.
7. Install tensioner retraction pins tool No. 46112, or equivalent, into tensioner body to hold plunger in place.

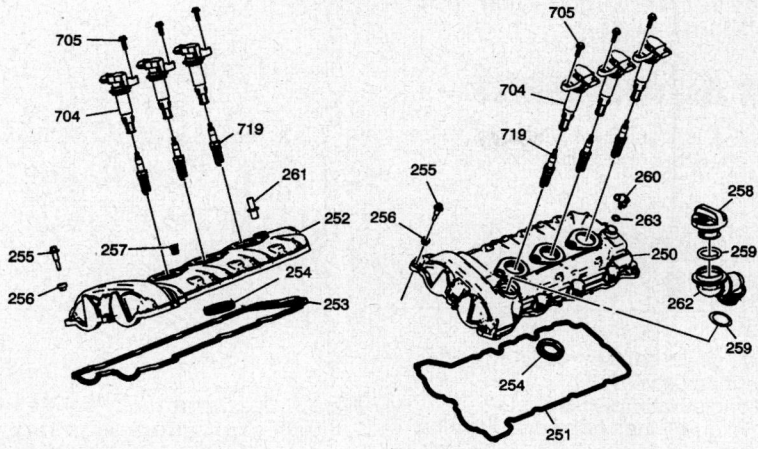

Fig. 4   Front cover sealant application

(250) Left Camshaft Cover
(251) Left Camshaft Cover Gasket
(252) Right Camshaft Cover
(253) Right Camshaft Cover Gasket
(254) Camshaft Cover Spark Plug Port Seal
(254) Camshaft Cover Spark Plug Port Seal
(255) Camshaft Cover Bolt
(255) Camshaft Cover Bolt
(256) Camshaft Cover Bolt Insulator
(256) Camshaft Cover Bolt Insulator
(257) Ignition Coil Bolt Thread Insert
(258) Oil Fill Cap

(259) Oil Fill O-Ring
(259) Oil Fill O-Ring
(260) Left Camshaft Cover PCV Fitting
(261) Right Camshaft Cover PCV Fitting Orifice
(262) Oil Fill Tube
(263) Left Camshaft Cover PCV Fitting O-Ring
(704) Ignition Coil
(704) Ignition Coil
(705) Ignition Coil Bolt
(705) Ignition Coil Bolt
(719) Spark Plug
(719) Spark Plug

ARM0300000000252

Fig. 3   Exploded view of camshaft covers

8. Install a new primary camshaft drive chain tensioner gasket to primary camshaft drive chain tensioner.
9. Install primary camshaft drive chain tensioner bolts through primary camshaft drive chain tensioner and gasket.
10. Install drive tensioner, then tighten bolts loosely.
11. Ensure tensioner gasket is in place, then tighten tensioner bolts to specification.
12. Remove tensioner retraction pins and release tensioner plunger.
13. Place righthand side secondary camshaft drive chain around righthand side camshaft intermediate drive chain idler outer sprocket, align bright plated camshaft drive link with alignment access hole in camshaft drive chain idler inner sprocket, **Fig. 14**.
14. Wrap secondary camshaft drive chain around both righthand side actuator drive sprockets, ensure there are seven darkened links between bright plated camshaft drive chain links for camshaft position actuator sprockets, **Fig. 15**.
15. Align righthand side exhaust camshaft position actuator sprocket alignment triangle mark with bright plated camshaft drive chain link, **Fig. 16**.
16. Align righthand side intake camshaft position actuator sprocket alignment triangle mark with bright plated camshaft drive chain link, **Fig. 17**.
17. Install chain guide.
18. Compress righthand side secondary camshaft drive chain tensioner plung-

er into tensioner body using tensioner tool No. J 45027, or equivalent.
19. Install tensioner retraction pins tool No. 46112, or equivalent, into tensioner body to hold plunger in place.
20. Install a new righthand side secondary camshaft drive chain tensioner gasket to drive chain tensioner.
21. Install righthand side secondary camshaft drive chain tensioner bolts through drive chain tensioner and gasket.
22. Install drive tensioner, then tighten bolts loosely.
23. Ensure tensioner gasket is in place, then tighten tensioner bolts to specification.
24. Remove tensioner retraction pins and release tensioner plunger.
25. Ensure all timing marks are aligned, **Fig. 18**.
26. Install front cover as outlined under "Front Cover, Replace."
27. Install spark plugs.

Righthand Secondary Drive Chain

REMOVAL

1. Remove spark plugs.
2. Remove front cover as outlined under "Front Cover, Replace."
3. Remove righthand side secondary camshaft drive chain tensioner attaching bolts, then the drive chain tensioner, **Fig. 12**.

4. Remove righthand side secondary timing chain shoe, then the righthand side secondary drive chain.

INSTALLATION

1. Hold righthand camshafts in place by installing camshaft holding tool No. 46105, or equivalent, onto camshafts.
2. Place righthand side secondary camshaft drive chain around righthand side camshaft intermediate drive chain idler outer sprocket, align bright plated camshaft drive link with alignment access hole in camshaft drive chain idler inner sprocket, **Fig. 14**.
3. Wrap secondary camshaft drive chain around both righthand side actuator drive sprockets, ensure there are seven darkened links between bright plated camshaft drive chain links for camshaft position actuator sprockets, **Fig. 15**.
4. Align righthand side exhaust camshaft position actuator sprocket alignment triangle mark with bright plated camshaft drive chain link, **Fig. 16**.
5. Align righthand side intake camshaft position actuator sprocket alignment triangle mark with bright plated camshaft drive chain link, **Fig. 17**.
6. Compress righthand side secondary camshaft drive chain tensioner plunger into tensioner body using tensioner tool No. J 45027, or equivalent.
7. Install tensioner retraction pins tool No. 46112, or equivalent, into tensioner body to hold plunger in place.
8. Install a new righthand side secondary camshaft drive chain tensioner gasket to drive chain tensioner.
9. Install righthand side secondary camshaft drive chain tensioner bolts through drive chain tensioner and gasket.
10. Install drive tensioner, then tighten bolts loosely.
11. Ensure tensioner gasket is in place, then tighten tensioner bolts to specification.
12. Remove tensioner retraction pins and release tensioner plunger.

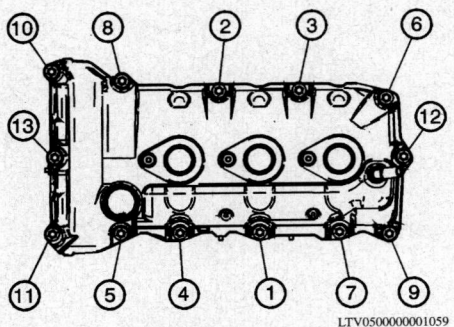

Fig. 5 Lefthand valve cover bolt tightening sequence

13. Ensure all timing marks are aligned, **Fig. 18.**
14. Install front cover as outlined under "Front Cover, Replace."
15. Install spark plugs.

Lefthand Secondary Drive Chain

REMOVAL

1. Remove primary drive chain as outlined under "Primary Drive Chain."
2. Remove lefthand side secondary camshaft drive chain tensioner and chain guide.
3. Remove lefthand side secondary camshaft drive chain idler.
4. Remove lefthand side secondary camshaft drive chain.

INSTALLATION

1. Hold lefthand camshafts in place by installing camshaft holding tool No. 46105, or equivalent, onto camshafts.
2. Ensure crankshaft is in "Stage 1" timing drive assembly position, **Fig. 19.**
3. Place lefthand side secondary camshaft drive chain around inner sprocket of camshaft intermediate drive chain idler with bright plated drive chain link aligned to access hole in idler outer sprocket, **Fig. 20.**
4. Wrap secondary camshaft drive chain around both lefthand side actuator drive sprockets.
5. Ensure there are seven darkened links between bright plated camshaft drive chain links for camshaft position actuator sprockets, **Fig. 21.**
6. Align lefthand side exhaust camshaft position actuator sprocket alignment circle mark with bright plated camshaft drive chain link, **Fig. 22.**
7. Align lefthand side intake camshaft position actuator sprocket alignment circle mark with bright plated camshaft drive chain link, **Fig. 23.**
8. Install chain guide.
9. Compress lefthand side secondary camshaft drive chain tensioner plunger into tensioner body using tensioner tool No. J 45027, or equivalent.
10. Install tensioner retraction pins tool No. 46112, or equivalent, into tensioner body to hold plunger in place.
11. Install a new lefthand side secondary camshaft drive chain tensioner gasket to drive chain tensioner.
12. Install lefthand side secondary camshaft drive chain tensioner bolts through drive chain tensioner and gasket.
13. Install drive tensioner, then tighten bolts loosely.
14. Ensure tensioner gasket is in place, then tighten tensioner bolts to specification.
15. Remove tensioner retraction pins and release tensioner plunger.
16. Install righthand side camshaft secondary and primary timing chains.
17. Ensure all timing marks are aligned, **Fig. 18.**
18. Install front cover as outlined under "Front Cover, Replace."

CAMSHAFT

REPLACE

1. Remove camshaft cover as outlined under "Valve Cover, Replace."
2. Remove camshaft position actuator solenoid.
3. Remove crankshaft balancer as outlined under "Crankshaft Balancer, Replace."
4. Rotate crankshaft until camshafts are in a neutral (low tension) position. Camshaft flats will be parallel with camshaft cover rail.
5. Hold camshafts in place with a suitable open end wrench, then loosen camshaft position actuator (sprocket) bolts.
6. Install timing chain retention tool No. 46108, or equivalent, over lefthand side secondary timing chain.
7. Mark timing chain and actuators (sprockets) for installation reference.
8. Remove camshaft actuator (sprocket) attaching bolts.
9. Prior to removing camshafts, observe markings on camshaft bearing caps as follows:
   a. Each bearing cap is marked in order to identify its location.
   b. Raised feature on cap must always be oriented toward center of cylinder head.
   c. Stamped letter "I" indicates intake camshaft and stamped letter "E" indicates exhaust camshaft.
   d. Stamped number indicates journal position from front of engine.
10. Remove camshafts from cylinder head.
11. Reverse procedure to install, noting the following:
   a. Apply a liberal amount of lubricant GM part No. 12345501, or equivalent, to camshaft journals and lefthand side cylinder head camshaft carriers.
   b. Position camshaft lobes in a neutral position with flats on back of camshafts up and parallel with cylinder head camshaft cover rail.
   c. Apply a liberal amount of lubricant GM part No. 12345501, or equivalent, to camshaft bearing caps.
   d. **Torque** camshaft bearing cap bolts to 89 inch lbs., using sequence, **Fig. 24.**

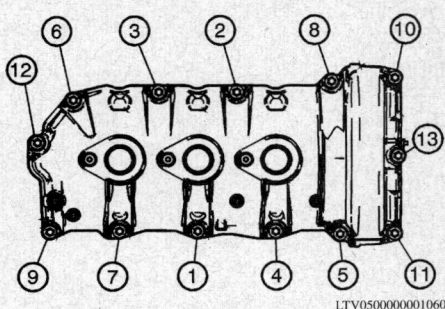

Fig. 6 Righthand valve cover bolt tightening sequence

   e. Loosen center intake camshaft bearing cap bolts (1 and 2) and center exhaust camshaft bearing cap bolts (3 and 4), then **torque** camshaft bearing cap bolts 1, 2, 3 and 4 to 89 inch lbs.

PISTON & ROD ASSEMBLY

When installing piston and rod assemblies into cylinder block, ensure dot on top of piston faces toward front of engine.

Tighten connecting rod bolts in four steps as follows: First step, **torque** bolts to 22 ft. lbs.; second step, loosen bolts; third step, **torque** bolts to 18 ft. lbs.; fourth step, tighten bolts an additional 110°.

PISTONS, PINS & RINGS

Pistons and rings are available in standard size and oversize. Pistons and their pins are serviced as an assembly.

MAIN & ROD BEARINGS

Main and rod bearings are available in standard size only. Tighten main bearing cap bolts as follows: **Torque** inboard bolts to 15 ft. lbs., then tighten an additional 80°, **Fig. 25. Torque** outboard bolts to 11 ft. lbs., then tighten an additional 110°, **Fig. 26. Torque** short inner and long outer bolts to 22 ft. lbs., **Fig. 27.**

CRANKSHAFT FRONT OIL SEAL

REPLACE

1. Remove crankshaft balancer as outlined under "Crankshaft Balancer, Replace."
2. Remove seal using a suitable flat-bladed tool.
3. Reverse procedure to install.

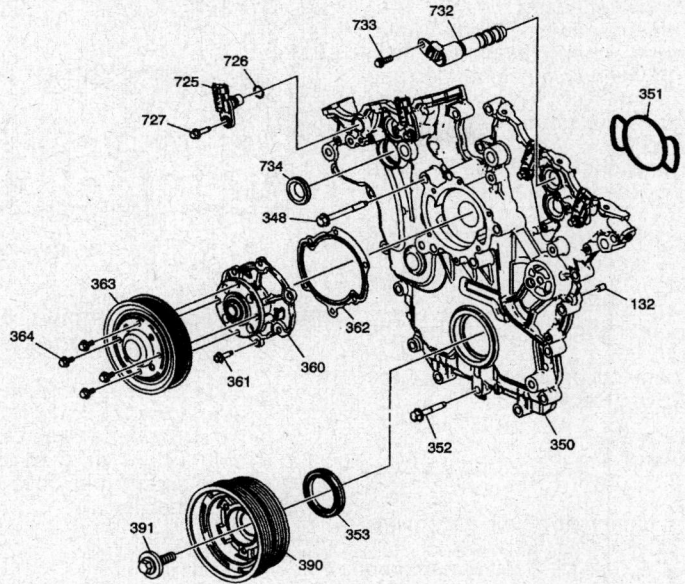

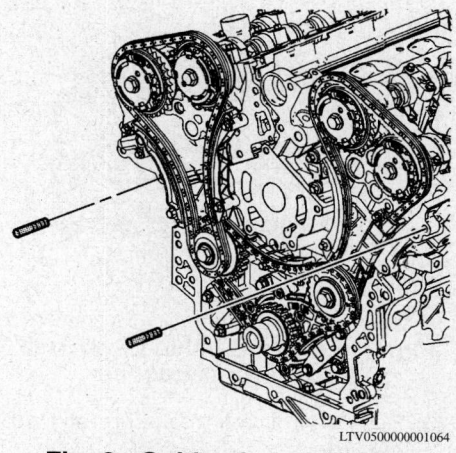

LTV0500000001064

Fig. 8 Guide pin installation

(132) Engine Front Cover Locating Pin
(348) Engine Front Cover Bolt - M10
(350) Engine Front Cover
(351) Engine Front Cover Gasket
(352) Engine Front Cover Bolt - M8
(353) Engine Front Cover Seal
(360) Water Pump Assembly
(361) Water Pump Bolt
(362) Water Pump Gasket
(363) Water Pump Pulley

(364) Water Pump Pulley Bolt
(390) Crankshaft Balancer
(391) Crankshaft Balancer Bolt
(725) Camshaft Position Sensor
(726) Camshaft Position Sensor O-Ring
(727) Camshaft Position Sensor Bolt
(732) Camshaft Position Actuator Solenoid Valve
(733) Camshaft Position Actuator Solenoid Valve Bolt
(734) Camshaft Position Actuator Solenoid Valve Seal

ARM0300000000253

Fig. 7 Exploded view of front cover

CRANKSHAFT REAR OIL SEAL
REPLACE

1. Remove transmission as outlined in **MOTOR's "Domestic Transmission, In-Vehicle Service"** manual.
2. Remove flywheel bolts, then the flywheel from crankshaft
3. Remove oil pan as outlined under "Oil Pan, Replace."
4. Remove crankshaft rear oil seal housing bolts.
5. Pry oil seal housing from cylinder block using pry points located at edge of housing.
6. Remove oil seal from housing.
7. Reverse procedure to install.

OIL PAN
REPLACE

1. Remove front cover as outlined under "Front Cover, Replace."
2. Remove power steering hose retainer from A/C compressor bracket.
3. Disconnect intermediate steering shaft from steering gear.
4. Remove engine mount lower nuts.
5. Remove A/C compressor bracket bolts and position compressor and bracket aside.
6. Drain engine oil.

7. Remove transmission oil cooler pipe retainer from engine righthand side.
8. Install suitable engine support fixture, then raise engine enough to access oil pan.
9. Remove oil pan bolts, then pry oil pan from engine block using suitable flat bladed tool.
10. Reverse procedure to install, noting the following:
    a. Apply a suitable bead of silicone sealing compound GM part No. 12346286, or equivalent, to oil pan surface.
    b. Tighten oil pan to engine block bolts to specifications in sequence, **Fig. 28.**

OIL PUMP
REPLACE

1. Remove primary timing chain as outlined under "Timing Chain, Replace."
2. Remove crankshaft sprocket.
3. Remove oil pump bolts and oil pump, **Fig. 29.**
4. Reverse procedure to install.

OIL PUMP SERVICE

There are no serviceable components inside the oil pump. If pump is not working properly, it must be replaced.

SERPENTINE DRIVE BELT
REPLACE

Alternator & Water Pump

1. Rotate drive belt tensioner clockwise to release drive belt tension.
2. Slide drive belt off of water pump pulley.
3. Slowly release drive belt tensioner and remove drive belt from accessory drive pulleys.
4. Reverse procedure to install.

Air Conditioning & Power Steering

1. Remove alternator and water pump drive belt as outlined under "Alternator & Water Pump."
2. Rotate drive belt tensioner clockwise to release drive belt tension.
3. Remove drive belt from power steering pulley.
4. Slowly release drive belt tensioner and remove drive belt from accessory drive pulleys.
5. Reverse procedure to install.

COOLING SYSTEM BLEED

1. Place transmission in Park or Neutral position.
2. Engage park brake.
3. Run engine until thermostat opens.
4. Stop engine.
5. Fill system using only clean drinkable water.
6. Repeat procedure if required, until fluid is nearly colorless.
7. Fill coolant reservoir to FULL HOT mark.

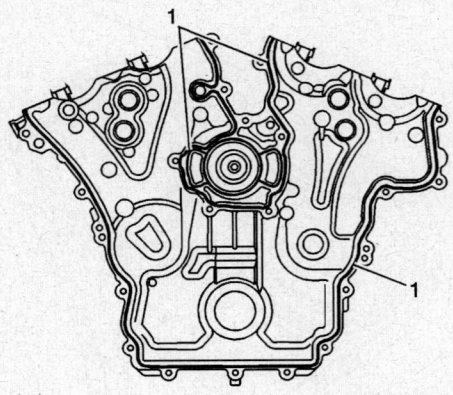

Fig. 9 Front cover RTV sealant application

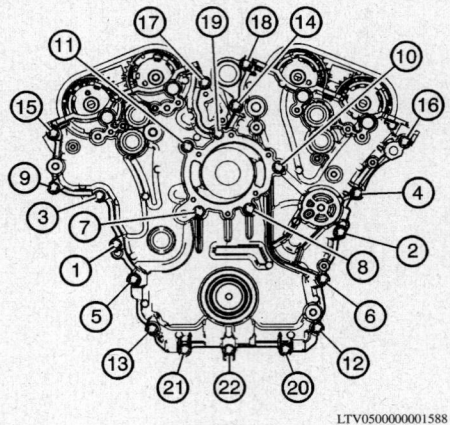

Fig. 10 Front cover bolt tightening sequence

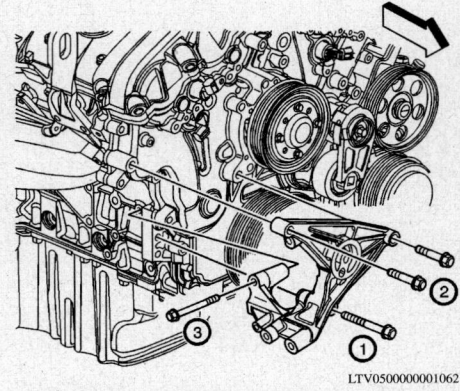

Fig. 11 Alternator bracket bolt tightening sequence

THERMOSTAT

REPLACE

1. Remove lower intake manifold as outlined under "Intake Manifold, Replace."
2. Disconnect surge tank hose from thermostat.
3. Remove coolant pipe/thermostat housing bolt.
4. Remove coolant pipe upper bolt, then the coolant inlet pipe from thermostat.
5. Remove thermostat housing bolts, then the thermostat housing.
6. Remove thermostat and discard seal.
7. Reverse procedure to install.

WATER PUMP

REPLACE

1. Drain cooling system into suitable container.
2. Remove alternator drive belt as outlined under "Serpentine Drive Belt."
3. Hold water pump pulley with pulley holding tool No. 46104, or equivalent.
4. Remove water pump pulley bolts, then the pulley.
5. Remove water pump attaching bolts, then the pump. Discard water pump seal.
6. Reverse procedure to install.

RADIATOR

REPLACE

Refer to "Radiator, Replace" in the "3.2L Engine" section.

FUEL PUMP

REPLACE

Refer to "Fuel Pump, Replace" in the "3.2L Engine" section.

FUEL FILTER

REPLACE

Refer to "Fuel Filter, Replace" in the "3.2L Engine" section.

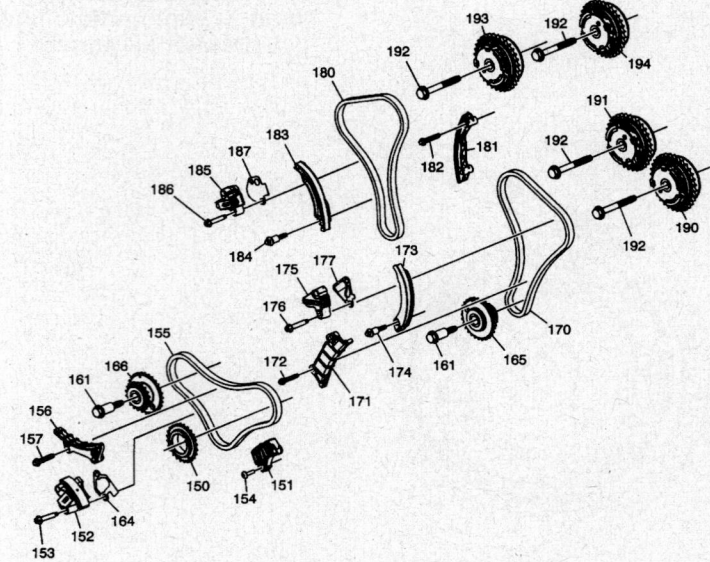

(150) Crankshaft Sprocket
(151) Lower Primary Timing Chain Guide
(152) Primary Timing Chain Tensioner
(153) Primary Timing Chain Tensioner Bolt
(154) Lower Primary Timing Chain Guide Bolt
(155) Primary Timing Chain
(156) Upper Primary Timing Chain Guide
(157) Upper Primary Timing Chain Guide Bolt
(161) Camshaft Intermediate Drive Shaft Sprocket Bolt
(164) Primary Timing Chain Tensioner Gasket
(165) Left Camshaft Intermediate Drive Shaft Sprocket
(166) Right Camshaft Intermediate Drive Shaft Sprocket
(170) Left Secondary Timing Chain
(171) Left Secondary Timing Chain Guide
(172) Left Secondary Timing Chain Guide Bolt
(173) Left Secondary Timing Chain Shoe
(174) Left Secondary Timing Chain Shoe Bolt
(175) Left Secondary Timing Chain Tensioner

(176) Left Secondary Timing Chain Tensioner Bolt
(177) Left Secondary Timing Chain Tensioner Gasket
(180) Right Secondary Timing Chain
(181) Right Secondary Timing Chain Guide
(182) Right Secondary Timing Chain Guide Bolt
(183) Right Secondary Timing Chain Shoe
(184) Right Secondary Timing Chain Shoe Bolt
(185) Right Secondary Timing Chain Tensioner
(186) Right Secondary Timing Chain Tensioner Bolt
(187) Right Secondary Timing Chain Tensioner Gasket
(190) Left Exhaust Camshaft Position Actuator
(191) Left Intake Camshaft Position Actuator
(192) Camshaft Position Actuator Bolt
(192) Camshaft Position Actuator Bolt
(192) Camshaft Position Actuator Bolt
(192) Camshaft Position Actuator Bolt
(193) Right Exhaust Camshaft Position Actuator
(194) Right Intake Camshaft Position Actuator

Fig. 12 Primary & secondary timing chains

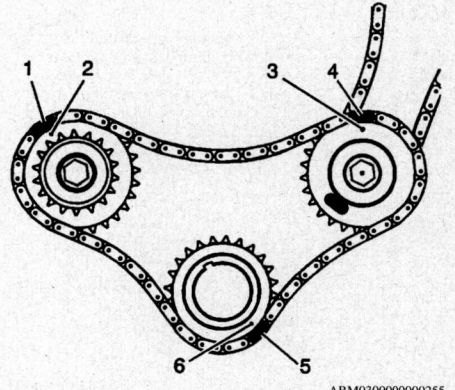

Fig. 13   Primary timing chain
alignment marks

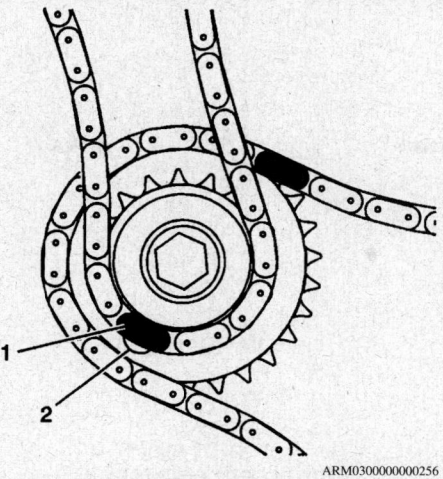

Fig. 14   Righthand camshaft drive
chain & intermediate idler
sprocket alignment

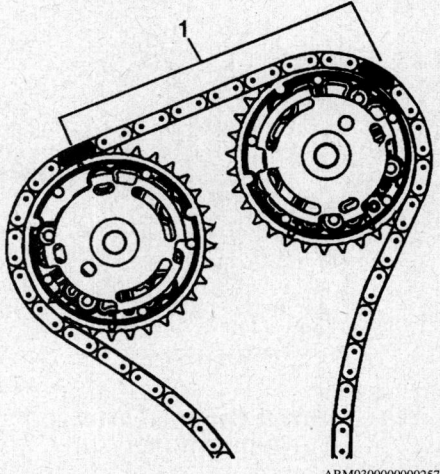

Fig. 15   Righthand camshaft drive
chain installation

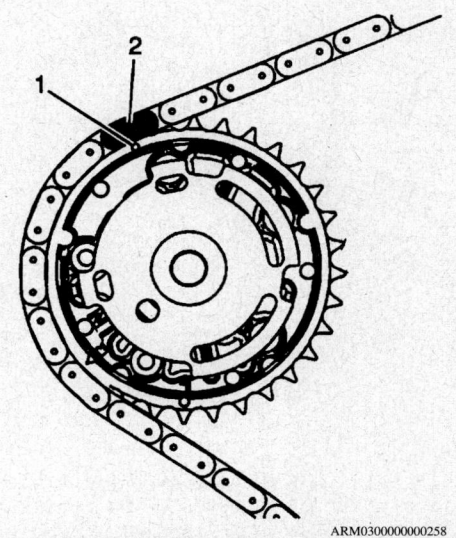

Fig. 16   Righthand camshaft drive
chain & exhaust camshaft
sprocket alignment

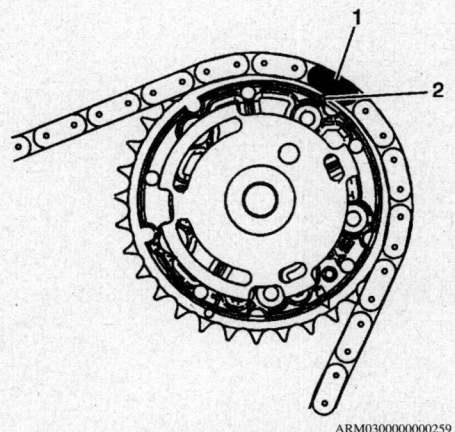

Fig. 17   Righthand camshaft drive
chain & intake camshaft sprocket
alignment

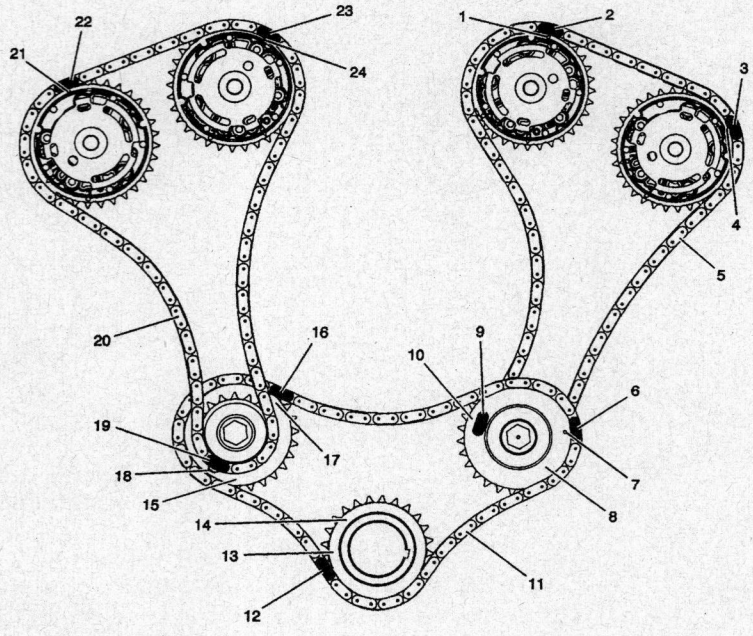

(1) Left Intake Camshaft Position Actuator (CMP) Timing Mark
(2) Left Intake Secondary Camshaft Timing Drive Chain Bright Plated Link
(3) Left Exhaust Secondary Camshaft Timing Drive Chain Bright Plated Link
(4) Left Exhaust Camshaft Position Actuator (CMP) Timing Mark
(5) Left Secondary Camshaft Timing Drive Chain
(6) Primary Camshaft Drive Chain Bright Plated Link for the Left Primary Camshaft Intermediate Drive Chain Sprocket
(7) Left Primary Camshaft Intermediate Drive Chain Sprocket Timing Mark for the Primary Camshaft Drive Chain
(8) Left Primary Camshaft Intermediate Drive Chain Sprocket
(9) Left Secondary Camshaft Timing Drive Chain Bright Plated Link for the Left Primary Camshaft Intermediate Drive Chain Sprocket
(10) Left Primary Camshaft Intermediate Drive Chain Sprocket Timing Window
(11) Primary Camshaft Drive Chain
(12) Primary Camshaft Drive Chain Bright Plated Link for the Crankshaft Sprocket
(13) Crankshaft Sprocket Timing Mark
(14) Crankshaft Sprocket
(15) Right Primary Camshaft Intermediate Drive Chain Sprocket
(16) Primary Camshaft Drive Chain Bright Plated Link for the Right Primary Camshaft Intermediate Drive Chain Sprocket
(17) Right Primary Camshaft Intermediate Drive Chain Sprocket Timing Mark for the Primary Camshaft Drive Chain
(18) Right Primary Camshaft Intermediate Drive Chain Sprocket Timing Mark/Window for the Right Secondary Camshaft Timing Drive Chain
(19) Right Secondary Camshaft Timing Drive Chain Bright Plated Link for the Right Primary Camshaft Intermediate Drive Chain Sprocket
(20) Right Secondary Camshaft Timing Drive Chain
(21) Right Exhaust Camshaft Position Actuator (CMP) Timing Mark
(22) Right Exhaust Secondary Camshaft Timing Drive Chain Bright Plated Link
(23) Right Intake Camshaft Position Actuator (CMP) Timing Mark
(24) Right Intake Camshaft Position Actuator (CMP) Timing Mark

ARM0300000000261

Fig. 18   Timing chain alignment

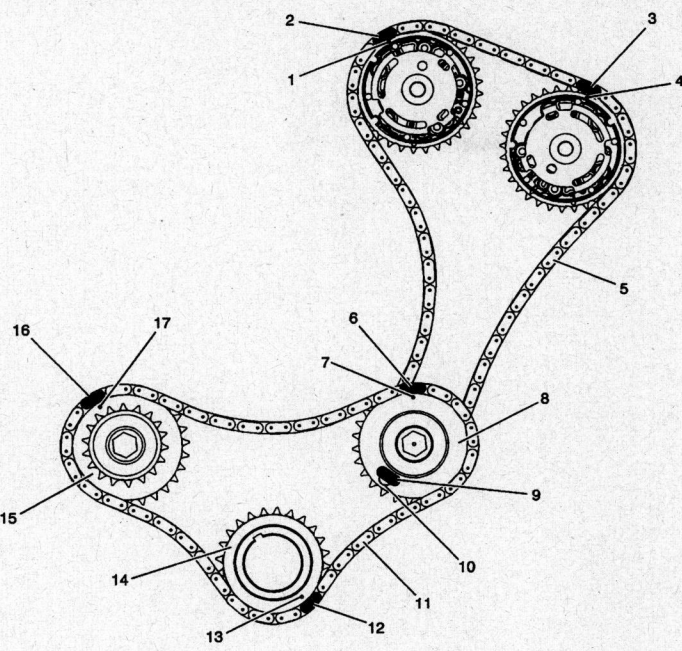

(1) Left Intake Camshaft Position Actuator (CMP) Timing Mark
(2) Left Intake Secondary Camshaft Timing Drive Chain Bright Plated Link
(3) Left Exhaust Secondary Camshaft Timing Drive Chain Bright Plated Link
(4) Left Exhaust Camshaft Position Actuator (CMP) Timing Mark
(5) Left Secondary Camshaft Timing Drive Chain
(6) Primary Camshaft Drive Chain Bright Plated Link for the Left Primary Camshaft Intermediate Drive Chain Sprocket
(7) Left Primary Camshaft Intermediate Drive Chain Sprocket Timing Mark for the Primary Camshaft Drive Chain
(8) Left Primary Camshaft Intermediate Drive Chain Sprocket
(9) Left Secondary Camshaft Timing Drive Chain Bright Plated Link for the Left Primary Camshaft Intermediate Drive Chain Sprocket
(10) Left Primary Camshaft Intermediate Drive Chain Sprocket Timing Window for the Left Secondary Camshaft Timing Drive Chain Bright Plated Link
(11) Primary Camshaft Drive Chain
(12) Primary Camshaft Drive Chain Bright Plated Link for the Crankshaft Sprocket
(13) Crankshaft Sprocket Timing Mark
(14) Crankshaft Sprocket
(15) Right Primary Camshaft Intermediate Drive Chain Sprocket
(16) Primary Camshaft Drive Chain Bright Plated Link for the Right Primary Camshaft Intermediate Drive Chain Sprocket
(17) Right Primary Camshaft Intermediate Drive Chain Sprocket Timing Mark

ARM0300000000260

Fig. 19   Camshaft timing drive chain alignment (stage 1)

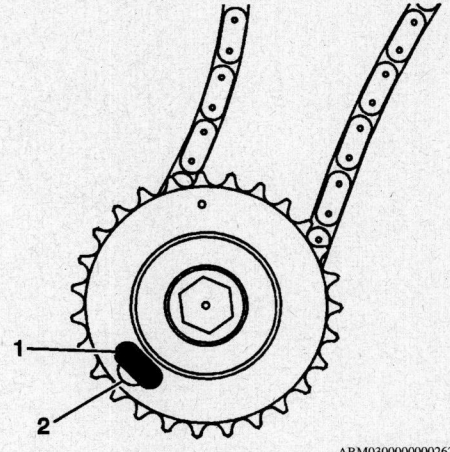

ARM0300000000262

Fig. 20   Lefthand camshaft drive chain idler sprocket alignment

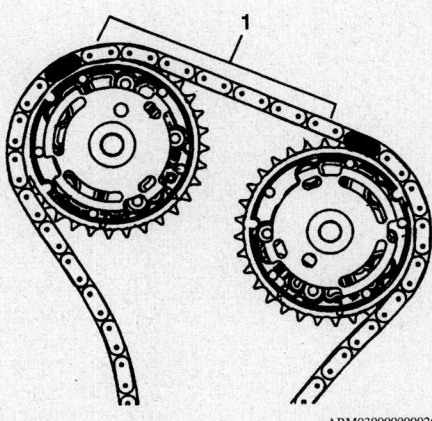

ARM0300000000263

Fig. 21   Lefthand camshaft drive chain installation

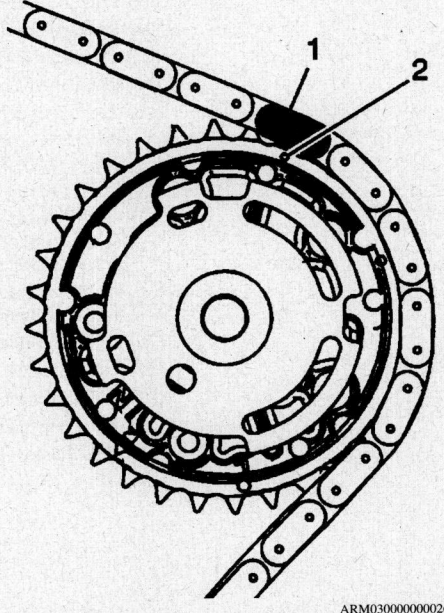

ARM0300000000264

Fig. 22   Lefthand camshaft drive chain & exhaust camshaft sprocket alignment

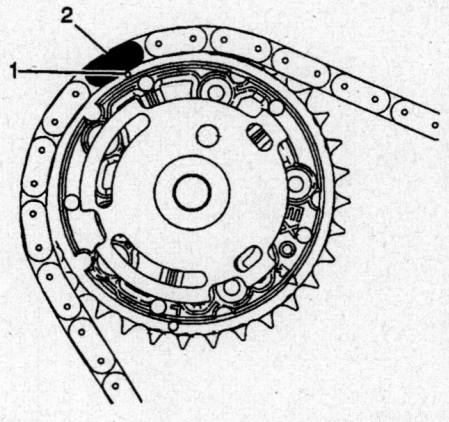

ARM030000000265

Fig. 23 Lefthand camshaft drive chain & intake camshaft sprocket alignment

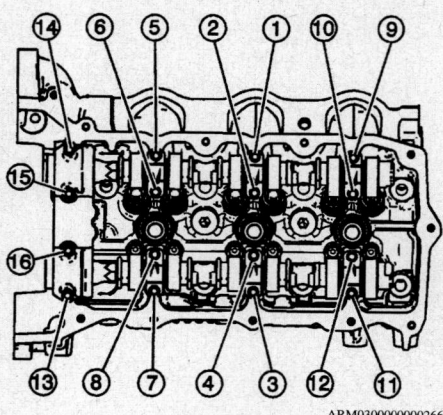

ARM030000000266

Fig. 24 Camshaft bearing cap bolt tightening sequence

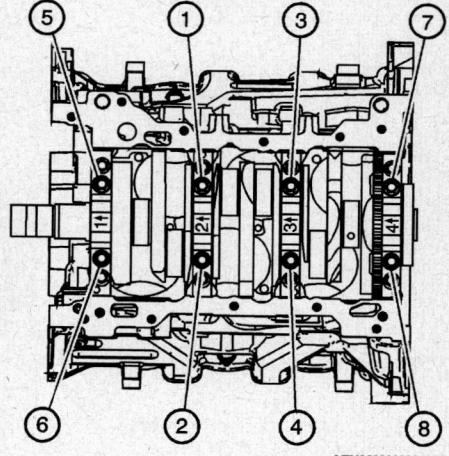

LTV0500000001078

Fig. 25 Inboard main bearing cap tightening sequence

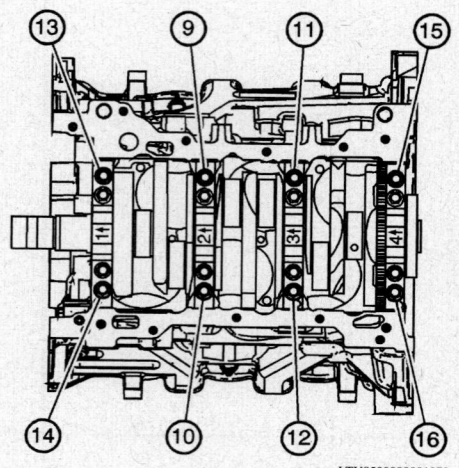

LTV0500000001079

Fig. 26 Outboard main bearing cap tightening sequence

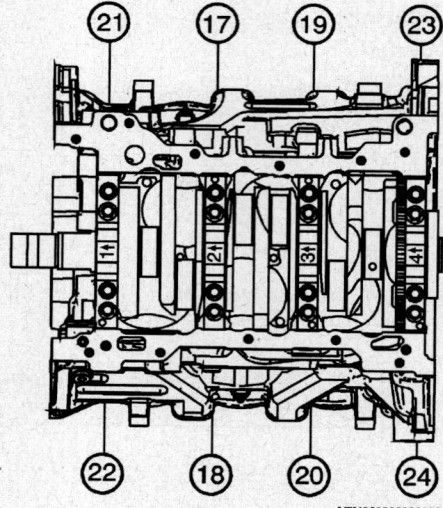

LTV0500000001080

Fig. 27 Short & long/inner bolt tightening sequence

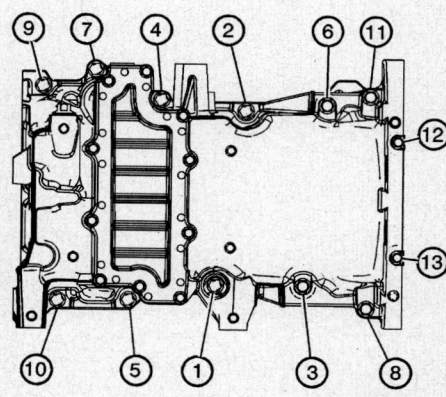

LTV0500000001083

Fig. 28 Oil pan bolt tightening sequence

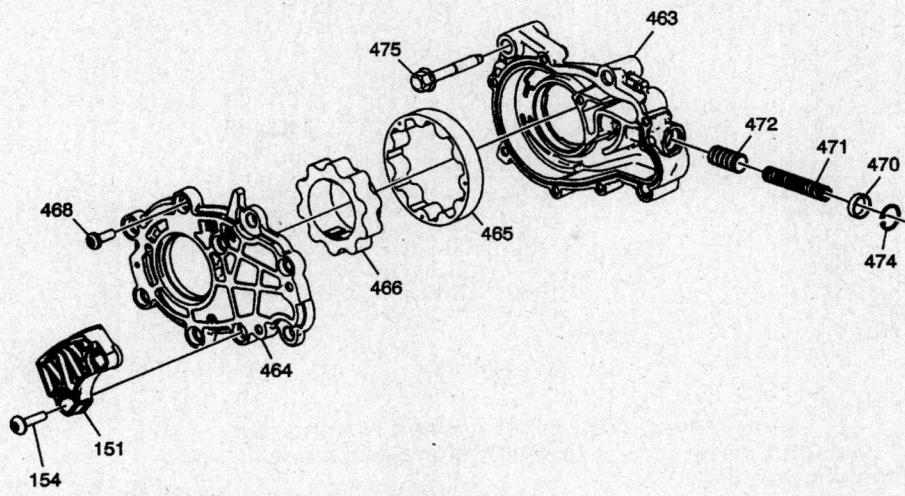

(151) Lower Primary Timing Chain Guide
(154) Lower Primary Timing Chain Guide Bolt
(463) Oil Pump Housing
(464) Oil Pump Cover
(465) Oil Pump Driven Gear
(466) Oil Pump Drive Gear
(468) Oil Pump Cover Bolt
(470) Oil Pressure Relief Valve Bore Plug
(471) Oil Pressure Relief Valve Spring
(472) Oil Pressure Relief Valve
(474) Oil Pressure Relief Valve Bore Plug Retainer Clip
(475) Oil Pump Bolt

ARM0300000000267

Fig. 29   Exploded view of oil pump

TIGHTENING SPECIFICATIONS

Year	Component	Torque Ft. Lbs.
2004–08	A/C Compressor Bracket Front Bolt	37
	A/C Compressor Bracket Rear Bolt	17
	A/C Compressor Hose Assembly	80①
	Alternator Bolt	37
	Camshaft Cap Bolts	89①
	Camshaft Intermediate Drive Idler Sprocket Bolt	48
	Camshaft Position Actuator Bolt	43
	Camshaft Position Sensor Bolt	89①
	Camshaft (Valve) Cover	89①
	Catalytic Converter To Exhaust Manifold	37
	Close Out Cover Bolt	89①
	Connecting Rod Bolts	②
	Coolant Manifold Pipe	89①
	Coolant Outlet Bolt	89①
	Crankshaft Balancer Bolt	③
	Crankshaft Main Bearing (Inner) Bolts	④
	Crankshaft Main Bearing (Outer) Bolts	⑤
	Crankshaft Main Bearing (Side) Bolts	⑨
	Crankshaft Position Sensor	89①
	Cylinder Head Bolt (M8 Bolt)	⑥
	Cylinder Head Bolt (M11 Bolt)	⑦
	Drive Belt Idler Pulley Bolt	37
	Drive Belt Tensioner Bolt	37
	ECM Bolt	89①
	ECT Sensor	18
	Engine Mount Bracket To Cylinder Block (M8 Bolt)	28
	Engine Mount Bracket To Cylinder Block (M11 Bolt)	45
	Engine Mount To Bracket	59
	EVAP Purge Valve Bolt	89①
	Exhaust Manifold Bolt	15
	Exhaust Manifold Heat Shield Bolt	89①
	Flywheel Bolts	⑧
	Front Cover Bolts	17
	Fuel Rail Bolt	89①
	Ground Cable Bolt	37
	Heater Inlet/Outlet Pipe Assembly Bolt	89①
	Ignition Coil Bolt	89①
	Intake Manifold (Upper) To Cylinder Head Bolts	17
	Intake Manifold (Upper) To Intake Manifold (Lower) Bolts	17
	Knock Sensor Bolt	17
	Main Bearing (Inner) Bolts	④
	Main Bearing (Outer) Bolts	⑤
	Main Bearing (Side) Bolts	⑨
	MAP Sensor Bolt	89①
	Oil Dipstick Tube Bolt	89①
	Oil Drain Plug	18
	Oil Filter Cap	18
	Oil Filter Housing Adapter To Cylinder Block	17
	Oil Filter Housing Adapter To Cylinder Head	48

TIGHTENING SPECIFICATIONS—Continued

Year	Component	Torque Ft. Lbs.
2004–08	Oil Gallery Plug	23
	Oil Level Sensor	89①
	Oil Pan To Cylinder Block Bolts	17
	Oil Pressure Sender	15
	Oil Pump Bolt	17
	Oil Pump Cover Bolts	115①
	Oxygen Sensor	30
	Power Steering Pump Bracket To Engine Bolt	37
	Power Steering Pump Reservoir Lower Bolt	18
	Power Steering Pump Reservoir Upper Bolt	80①
	Power Steering Pump To Bracket Bolt	16
	Primary Camshaft Drive Chain Guide Bolt	17
	Primary Camshaft Drive Chain Lefthand Guide Bolt – Oil Pump (1st Design)	115①
	Primary Camshaft Drive Chain Lefthand Guide Bolt – Oil Pump (2nd Design)	17
	Primary Camshaft Drive Chain Tensioner Bolt	17
	Secondary Camshaft Drive Chain Guide Bolt	17
	Secondary Camshaft Drive Chain Shoe Bolt	17
	Secondary Camshaft Drive Chain Tensioner Bolt	17
	Starter Motor Bolts	37
	Suction Screen Bolt	89①
	Thermostat Housing Bolt	89①
	Throttle Body Bolt	89①
	Torque Converter Bolts	44
	Transmission Mount To Transmission Bolt	45
	Transmission To Engine Bolts	37
	Water Pump Bolts	89①
	Water Pump Pulley Bolts	89①

① — Inch lbs.

② — Refer to "Piston & Rod Assembly" for tightening procedure.

③ — First pass, 74 ft. lbs.; final pass, 150°.

④ — First pass, 15 ft. lbs.; final pass, 80°.

⑤ — First pass, 10 ft. lbs.; final pass, 110°.

⑥ — First pass, 10 ft. lbs.; final pass, 60°.

⑦ — First pass, 33 ft. lbs.; final pass, 120°.

⑧ — First pass, 22 ft. lbs.; final pass, 45°.

⑨ — First pass, 22 ft. lbs.; final pass, 60°.

5.7L Engine

NOTE: On Air Bag Equipped Models, Refer to "Air Bag System Precautions" Located In The Front Of This Manual For System Disarming & Arming Procedures.

NOTE: Refer To "Computer Relearn Procedures" Located In The Front Of This Manual When Battery Power To The Computer Has Been Interrupted.

NOTE: Prior To Performing Any Service Operations Listed In This Section, Consult The "Technical Service Bulletins" Section For Related Information.

NOTE: Refer To The "5.7L Engine" In The "Corvette" Chapter For Procedures Not Found In This Section.

INDEX

	Page No.			Page No.			Page No.
Camshaft, Replace	8-45		Righthand	8-42		Air Bag Systems	8-42
Compression Pressure	8-42		Exhaust Manifold, Replace	8-44		Battery Ground Cable	8-42
Cooling System Bleed	8-46		Lefthand	8-44		Fuel Pressure Relief	8-42
Crankshaft Balancer, Replace	8-45		Righthand	8-44		Radiator	8-46
Crankshaft Rear Oil Seal,			Front Cover, Replace	8-45		Serpentine Drive Belt	8-46
Replace	8-45		Fuel Filter, Replace	8-46		Accessory	8-46
Crankshaft Seal, Replace	8-45		Fuel Pump, Replace	8-46		Air Conditioning	8-46
Cylinder Head, Replace	8-44		Intake Manifold, Replace	8-43		Thermostat, Replace	8-46
Lefthand	8-44		Main & Rod Bearings	8-45		Tightening Specifications	8-47
Righthand	8-44		Oil Pan, Replace	8-46		Timing Chain, Replace	8-45
Engine Rebuilding			Oil Pump, Replace	8-46		Valve Adjustment	8-45
Specifications	29-1		Oil Pump Service	8-46		Valve Cover, Replace	8-44
Engine, Replace	8-42		Piston & Rod Assembly	8-45		Lefthand	8-44
Engine Mount, Replace	8-42		Pistons, Pins & Rings	8-45		Righthand	8-45
Lefthand	8-42		Precautions	8-42		Water Pump, Replace	8-46

PRECAUTIONS

Air Bag Systems

Refer to "Air Bag System Precautions" in the front of this manual for system disarming and arming procedures.

Battery Ground Cable

Prior to service, record radio presets, then disconnect battery ground cable and isolate as required.

Fuel Pressure Relief

1. Record radio presets.
2. Turn ignition Off.
3. Disconnect battery ground cable and isolate as required.
4. Loosen fuel filler cap to relieve fuel tank vapor pressure.
5. Remove cap to fuel pressure service connection.
6. Install tool Nos. J34730-1A and J42242, or equivalents, to fuel pressure service connection.
7. Place bleed hose into suitable container, then open bleed valve to relieve fuel system.
8. Place a suitable shop towel under connections to protect fuel spillage.
9. Remove tool Nos. J34730-1A and J42242, or equivalents, from service connections.
10. Install cap to fuel pressure service connection.

COMPRESSION PRESSURE

The minimum compression in any one cylinder should not be less than 70 percent of the highest cylinder. No cylinder should read less than 100 psi.

ENGINE MOUNT
REPLACE
Lefthand

1. Raise and support vehicle.
2. Place suitable adjustable jack stand with a block of wood under engine oil pan.
3. Remove engine mount bracket to engine retaining bolts.
4. Remove engine mount bracket to frame mounting bolts.
5. Remove lower engine mount bracket retaining nuts.
6. Remove lefthand engine mount bracket to frame bolt, then the bracket.
7. Remove engine mount from engine mount bracket.
8. Reverse procedure to install.

Righthand

1. Raise and support vehicle.
2. Remove starter motor as outlined under "Starter Motor, Replace" in the "Electrical" section.
3. Place suitable adjustable jack stand with a block of wood under engine oil pan.
4. Remove righthand engine mount upper retaining nut.
5. Remove righthand engine mount bracket mounting bolts, then the bracket.
6. Remove engine mount retaining nut, then the mount.
7. Reverse procedure to install.

ENGINE
REPLACE

1. Turn front wheels to straight ahead position.
2. Turn ignition lock cylinder to Lock position and remove key.
3. Lock steering column by inserting

steering column anti-rotation pin tool No. J 42640, or equivalent, through access hole in lower steering column trim cover.

4. Remove shifter assembly mounting bolts.
5. Raise and support vehicle.
6. Disconnect exhaust system from catalytic converters, then remove exhaust. Do not reuse catalytic converter seals.
7. Remove propeller shaft.
8. Support transmission with suitable jack and block of wood.
9. Remove transmission lower mount retaining nuts, inner and outer transmission mounting bolts, then remove transmission support from vehicle.
10. Lower transmission assembly for access to top of transmission.
11. Remove shift control rods from shift control assembly using a suitable flat bladed tool, then remove shift control assembly.
12. Lower vehicle.
13. Remove underhood cross vehicle brace.
14. Remove fuel injector sight shield and air cleaner assembly.
15. Disconnect throttle body heater outlet hose from throttle body and secure to radiator.
16. Recover A/C refrigerant as outlined in "Air Conditioning" chapter.
17. Disconnect A/C suction hose from evaporator, then remove from shock tower retainer and secure to engine.
18. Disconnect A/C liquid line and remove from vehicle.
19. Disconnect brake booster vacuum hose from brake booster and secure to engine.
20. Remove electrical connector from brake fluid level switch.
21. Remove master cylinder retaining nuts.
22. Disconnect master cylinder brake lines from shock tower retainers, then secure master cylinder to engine.
23. Disconnect electrical connectors from C105 and C107 at lefthand shock tower.
24. Disconnect body fuel line from engine fuel line at righthand side rear of engine.
25. Disconnect engine to chassis EVAP pipe at righthand side rear of engine.
26. Disconnect electrical connector to C102 at front of dash.
27. Remove underhood fuse block electrical connector.
28. Remove battery ground cable retaining bolt from inner fender and secure to engine.
29. Disconnect battery positive cable from fuse block and secure to engine.
30. Disconnect electrical connectors from throttle actuator control (TAC) module, then remove (TAC) module.
31. Disconnect ground strap from righthand frame rail.
32. Drain coolant into suitable container.
33. Remove fan shroud to radiator attaching bolts.
34. Disconnect upper radiator hose at radiator.
35. Disconnect cooling fan motor electrical

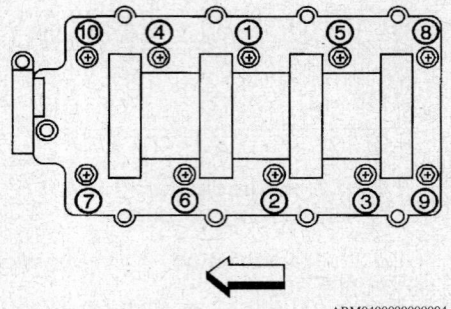

Fig. 1 Intake manifold bolt tightening sequence

connector, then remove cooling fan.
36. Remove condenser seal.
37. Remove radiator support bracket mounting bolts, then the brackets.
38. Remove upper condenser mounting bolts.
39. Disconnect surge tank hose from radiator.
40. Raise and support vehicle, then remove air deflector.
41. Disconnect lower radiator hose from radiator.
42. Disconnect lower transmission oil cooler line from radiator.
43. Remove lower condenser mounting bolts.
44. Separate side seals from radiator.
45. Disconnect A/C discharge hose mounting bolt, then remove hose.
46. Remove condenser tube mounting bolt, then tube.
47. Lower vehicle and remove radiator and condenser.
48. Remove power steering oil cooler retaining nuts from frame, then secure to engine.
49. Raise and support vehicle.
50. Remove front tire and wheel assemblies.
51. Remove righthand front wheel well liner, then remove windshield washer reservoir to frame brace.
52. Remove upper intermediate shaft to center intermediate shaft attaching bolt, then separate shafts.
53. Lower vehicle.
54. Disconnect heater hoses from engine.
55. Disconnect rear brake lines from brake pressure modulator valve.
56. Secure brake lines away from wire harness
57. Raise and support vehicle.
58. Disconnect electrical connectors to back-up lamp switch, reverse lockout solenoid, gear select/skip shift solenoid, VSS and transmission fluid temperature sensor.
59. Remove transmission as outlined in **MOTOR's "Domestic Transmission, In-Vehicle Service" manual or "Transmission Service DVD."**
60. Remove brake bundle retainer clips from righthand and lefthand frame rails, then remove rear brake lines from retainer clip on righthand frame rail.
61. Remove PCM wire harness attaching screws, then remove PCM. Secure

wire harness to engine.
62. Lower vehicle.
63. Remove righthand and lefthand shock module mounting bolts, then secure modules to frame.
64. Raise engine enough to install suitable lift under engine, front frame and front suspension.
65. Support rear of vehicle.
66. Raise lift to remove weight of engine from front frame.
67. Remove front frame mounting bolts.
68. Raise vehicle on suitable lift to clear engine assembly.
69. Reverse procedure to install.

INTAKE MANIFOLD
REPLACE

1. Drain coolant into suitable container.
2. Remove fuel injector sight shield.
3. Remove air cleaner outlet duct.
4. Disconnect air control valve electrical connector.
5. Disconnect TPS electrical connector.
6. Disconnect crankcase ventilation hose from throttle body.
7. Disconnect coolant hose from throttle body.
8. Remove throttle body mounting bolts, then the throttle body. Do not reuse gasket.
9. Disconnect fuel rail quick-connect fitting from fuel line.
10. Disconnect EVAP line from purge valve.
11. Disconnect fuel injector electrical connectors, noting their locations for installation reference.
12. Remove fuel rail mounting bolts, then the fuel rail, noting location of fuel rail ground strap.
13. Disconnect EVAP canister purge tube from purge solenoid valve, then from fuel line.
14. Disconnect TPS electrical connector.
15. Remove coolant air bleed hose.
16. Disconnect electrical connectors from EVAP canister purge valve and electronic throttle control.
17. Remove EVAP canister valve from bracket.
18. Disconnect power brake booster vacuum hose from booster.
19. Remove TPS harness retainer from PCV tube.
20. Remove PCV tube from righthand valve cover.
21. Remove intake manifold bolts, then fuel rail stop bracket.
22. Disconnect MAP sensor electrical connector and vacuum hose.
23. Remove intake manifold. Do not reuse gasket.
24. Reverse procedure to install, noting the following:
   a. Apply thread lock No. 12345382, or equivalent, to threads of intake manifold mounting bolts.
   b. **Torque** intake manifold bolts to 44 inch lbs., in sequence, **Fig. 1** .
   c. **Torque** intake manifold bolts to 89 inch lbs., in sequence.

EXHAUST MANIFOLD
REPLACE
Lefthand

1. Turn front wheels to straight ahead position.
2. Lock steering column by inserting steering column anti-rotation pin tool No. J 42640, or equivalent, through access hole in lower steering column trim cover.
3. Remove fuel injector sight shield.
4. Disconnect ignition wires at ignition coils.
5. Disconnect ignition coil bank electrical connector.
6. Remove ignition coil assembly mounting bolts, then ignition coil assembly.
7. Remove spark plugs.
8. Raise and support vehicle.
9. Support exhaust system with suitable jack, then disconnect exhaust pipes from lefthand and righthand catalytic converters.
10. Disconnect oxygen sensor electrical connector.
11. Remove lefthand catalytic converter to exhaust manifold attaching nuts.
12. Remove catalytic converter from exhaust manifold.
13. Remove transmission as outlined in MOTOR's "Domestic Transmission, In-Vehicle Service" manual.
14. Remove center steering shaft to lower steering shaft attaching bolt, then separate shafts.
15. Remove exhaust manifold mounting bolts, then the manifold. Do not reuse gasket.
16. Reverse procedure to install, noting the following:
    a. **Torque** exhaust manifold bolts to 12 ft. lbs., beginning with center two bolts, then alternate from side to side and work toward outside bolts.
    b. Final **Torque** to 18 ft. lbs., in sequence.
    c. Bend over exposed edge of exhaust manifold gasket at rear of lefthand cylinder head using suitable flat punch.

Righthand

1. Remove fuel injector sight shield.
2. Remove ignition wires at ignition coils.
3. Remove ignition coil bank electrical connector.
4. Remove ignition coil assembly mounting bolts, then the ignition coil assembly.
5. Remove spark plugs.
6. Remove oil level dip stick tube.
7. Raise and support vehicle.
8. Support exhaust system using suitable jack, then disconnect lefthand and righthand exhaust pipes from catalytic converters.
9. Disconnect oxygen sensor electrical connector.
10. Remove righthand catalytic converter to exhaust manifold attaching nuts.
11. Remove transmission and clutch housing as outlined in MOTOR's "Domes-

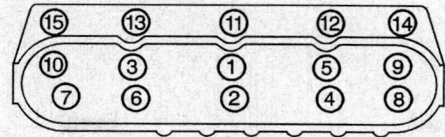

Fig. 2   Cylinder head bolt tightening sequence

tic Transmission, In-Vehicle Service" manual.
12. Remove starter motor, then lower vehicle.
13. Remove exhaust manifold mounting bolts.
14. Raise and support vehicle.
15. Remove exhaust manifold. Do not reuse gasket.
16. Reverse procedure to install, noting the following:
    a. **Torque** exhaust manifold bolts to 12 ft. lbs., beginning with center two bolts, then alternate from side to side and work toward outside bolts.
    b. Final **Torque** to 18 ft. lbs., in sequence.
    c. Bend over exposed edge of exhaust manifold gasket at rear of lefthand cylinder head using suitable flat punch.

CYLINDER HEAD
REPLACE
Lefthand

1. Remove fuel injector sight shield and air cleaner assembly.
2. Disconnect spark plug wires from ignition coils.
3. Disconnect ignition coil wire harness electrical connector.
4. Disconnect EVAP canister purge tube connections from intake manifold, EVAP canister purge solenoid valve, fuel supply line then at rear of righthand cylinder head.
5. Disconnect EVAP purge valve electrical connector, then remove valve from bracket.
6. Remove ignition coil bracket mounting bolts, then the bracket.
7. Remove valve cover mounting bolts, then valve cover.
8. Remove rocker arm mounting bolts, rocker arms and pushrods.
9. Remove intake manifold as outlined under "Intake Manifold, Replace."
10. Raise and support vehicle.
11. Remove front air deflector.
12. Remove drive belt as outlined under "Serpentine Drive Belt."
13. Remove power steering pulley.
14. Remove power steering pump and bracket.
15. Remove exhaust manifold as outlined under "Exhaust Manifold, Replace."
16. Remove engine wire harness ground mounting bolt from rear of lefthand cylinder head, then secure ground away from cylinder head.
17. Remove cylinder head mounting bolts,

then cylinder head. **Discard cylinder head M11 bolts.**
18. Reverse procedure to install, noting the following:
    a. **Torque** new M11 cylinder head bolts 1–10 to 22 ft. lbs., in sequence, **Fig. 2.**
    b. Tighten M11 cylinder head bolts 1–10 an additional 90° in sequence.
    c. Final tighten M11 cylinder head bolts 1–10 an additional 70° in sequence.
    d. **Torque** M8 inner cylinder head bolts 11–15 to 22 ft. lbs., beginning with center bolt 11, then alternating side to side while working outward.

Righthand

1. Remove fuel injector sight shield and air cleaner assembly.
2. Remove PCV hose from throttle body and valve cover.
3. Disconnect spark plug wires from ignition coils.
4. Disconnect ignition coil wire harness electrical connector.
5. Remove ignition coil bracket mounting bolts, then the bracket.
6. Remove valve cover mounting bolts, then valve cover.
7. Remove rocker arm mounting bolts, rocker arms and pushrods.
8. Remove intake manifold as outlined under "Intake Manifold, Replace."
9. Remove exhaust manifold as outlined under "Exhaust Manifold, Replace."
10. Remove oil level dip stick tube.
11. Remove battery ground cable from righthand cylinder head.
12. Remove cylinder head mounting bolts, then cylinder head. **Discard cylinder head M11 bolts.**
13. Reverse procedure to install, noting the following:
    a. **Torque** M11 cylinder head bolts 1–10 to 22 ft. lbs., in sequence, **Fig. 2.**
    b. Tighten M11 cylinder head bolts 1–10 an additional 90° in sequence.
    c. Final tighten M11 cylinder head bolts 1–10 an additional 70° in sequence.
    d. Torque M8 inner cylinder head bolts 11–15 to 22 ft. lbs., beginning with center bolt 11, then alternating side to side while working outward.

VALVE COVER
REPLACE
Lefthand

1. Remove fuel injector sight shield.
2. Disconnect spark plug wires from ignition coils.
3. Disconnect ignition coil wire harness electrical connector.
4. Disconnect EVAP canister purge tube connections from intake manifold, purge solenoid valve, fuel supply line, then at rear of righthand cylinder head.
5. Disconnect EVAP canister purge valve

electrical connector, then remove valve from bracket.

6. Remove ignition coil bracket mounting bolts, then the bracket.
7. Remove valve cover mounting bolts, then valve cover. Do not reuse gasket.
8. Reverse procedure to install. **Torque** valve cover mounting bolts to 106 inch lbs.

Righthand

1. Remove fuel injector sight shield.
2. Remove PCV hose from throttle body and valve cover.
3. Disconnect spark plug wires from ignition coils.
4. Disconnect ignition coil wire harness electrical connector.
5. Remove ignition coil bracket mounting bolts, then the bracket.
6. Remove valve cover mounting bolts, then valve cover. Discard gasket.
7. Reverse procedure to install. **Torque** valve cover mounting bolts to 106 inch lbs.

VALVE ADJUSTMENT

This engine is equipped with hydraulic valve lash adjusters. No adjustment is required.

CRANKSHAFT BALANCER
REPLACE

1. Drain coolant into suitable container.
2. Recover A/C system refrigerant as outlined in "Air Conditioning" chapter.
3. Remove radiator as outlined under "Radiator, Replace."
4. Disconnect A/C discharge hose from condenser, then remove condenser.
5. Remove starter motor as outlined under "Starter Motor, Replace" in "Electrical" section.
6. Remove crankshaft balancer bolt, noting the following:
   a. Crankshaft balancer weights must be installed in same location on new balancer as old balancer.
   b. Crankshaft balancer must be installed in original position on crankshaft.
7. Remove crankshaft balancer using balancer removal tool No. J 41816, or equivalent.
8. Reverse procedure to install.

FRONT COVER
REPLACE

1. Remove crankshaft balancer as outlined under "Crankshaft Balancer, Replace."
2. Remove water pump as outlined under "Water Pump, Replace."
3. Remove fan shroud to radiator mounting bolts.
4. Disconnect upper radiator hose at radiator.
5. Remove A/C line retaining clip mounting screw.

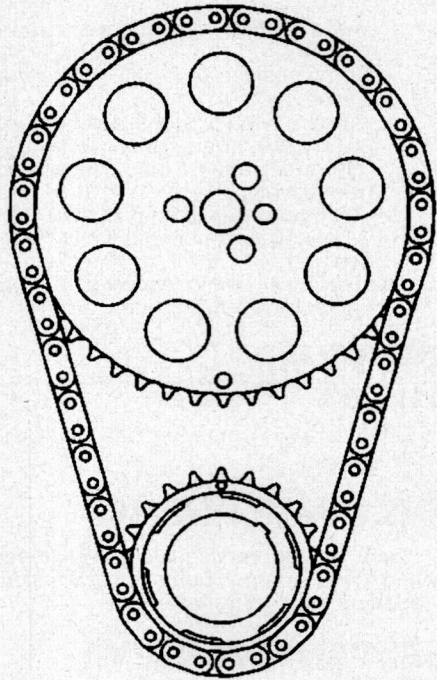

Fig. 3 Camshaft & crankshaft sprocket alignment

ARM0400000000006

6. Disconnect fan motor electrical connectors.
7. Pull upward to remove electric cooling fan.
8. Remove A/C drive belt tensioner bolt, then the tensioner.
9. Remove drive belt idler pulley.
10. Remove alternator as outlined under "Alternator, Replace" in "Electrical" section, then remove alternator bracket.
11. Remove oil pan to front cover mounting bolts.
12. Remove front cover mounting bolts.
13. Remove front cover. Discard gasket.
14. Reverse procedure to install.

TIMING CHAIN
REPLACE

Refer to "Timing Chain, Replace" in "Corvette" chapter.

CAMSHAFT
REPLACE

1. Remove engine as outlined under "Engine, Replace."
2. Remove intake manifold as outlined under "Intake Manifold, Replace."
3. Remove lefthand and righthand cylinder heads as outlined under "Cylinder Head, Replace."
4. Remove camshaft sensor.
5. Remove engine front cover as outlined under "Front Cover, Replace."
6. Remove valve lifter guide mounting bolts.
7. Remove lifters and guides.
8. Rotate engine to align timing marks, **Fig. 3.**

9. Remove camshaft sprocket mounting bolts.
10. Remove timing chain from camshaft sprocket allowing it to rest on crankshaft sprocket.
11. Remove camshaft retainer bolts, then the retainer.
12. Install three M8 1.25 × 100 mm bolts in camshaft front bolt holes.
13. Carefully rotate and pull camshaft out of engine using bolts as handle.
14. Reverse procedure to install, noting the following:
   a. Lubricate camshaft journals with clean engine oil before installation.
   b. Install camshaft retainer plate with sealing gasket facing engine block.
   c. Lubricate camshaft sensor O-ring with clean engine oil.

PISTON & ROD ASSEMBLY

1. Install retaining clip into groove inside of pin bore.
2. Install piston pin to piston and connecting rod.
3. Install retaining clip into groove inside of pin bore.

PISTONS, PINS & RINGS

Pistons and rings are available in standard size and oversize. Pistons and their pins are serviced as an assembly.

MAIN & ROD BEARINGS

Main and rod bearings are available in standard size only. Tighten main bearing cap bolts as follows: **Torque** inboard bolts to 15 ft. lbs., then tighten an additional 80°; **torque** outboard bolts to 15 ft. lbs., then tighten an additional 51°; **torque** short inner and long outer bolts to 18 ft. lbs.

CRANKSHAFT SEAL
REPLACE

1. Remove crankshaft balancer as outlined under "Crankshaft Balancer, Replace."
2. Pry crankshaft oil seal from front cover using suitable flat bladed tool.
3. Reverse procedure to install.

CRANKSHAFT REAR OIL SEAL
REPLACE

1. Remove transmission as outlined in **MOTOR's "Domestic Transmission, In-Vehicle Service"** manual.
2. Mark end of crankshaft and flywheel.
3. Remove flywheel mounting bolts, then the flywheel noting position and location of flywheel balance weights.
4. Pry crankshaft rear oil seal from housing using suitable flat bladed tool.
5. Reverse procedure to install.

OIL PAN

REPLACE

1. Install suitable engine support fixture.
2. Raise and support vehicle.
3. Drain engine oil into suitable container.
4. Remove lefthand closeout cover.
5. Remove starter motor as outlined under "Starter Motor, Replace" in "Electrical" section.
6. Remove righthand transmission closeout cover.
7. Remove two bottom transmission housing to oil pan mounting bolts.
8. Disconnect oil temperature sensor electrical connector.
9. Remove front wheels and air deflector.
10. Disconnect engine harness to frame wire harness retainers.
11. Disconnect righthand and lefthand rearward wire harness retainers.
12. Disconnect ABS wire harness from lower control arms.
13. Disconnect brake lines from frame.
14. Support radiator and A/C condenser using suitable mechanics wire, or equivalent to front inner energy absorber bracket.
15. Remove washer bottle bracket retaining nuts, then the bracket.
16. Loosen brake pressure modulator retaining nuts, then separate brake pressure modulator from bracket.
17. Mark position of stabilizer shaft to ease installation , then loosen stabilizer shaft mounting bolts.
18. Remove stabilizer shaft link retaining nut, then remove link from control arm.
19. Remove power steering hose to A/C compressor retaining nut and position steering hose aside.
20. Remove power steering gear mounting bolts.
21. Support power steering gear to bolt bracket on oil pan using suitable mechanics wire, or equivalent.
22. Remove outer tie rod retaining nut, then separate outer tie rod from steering knuckle using tie rod pulling tool No. J 24319-B or equivalent.
23. Remove lower shock mounting bolts.
24. Remove engine mount lower retaining nuts.
25. Install suitable engine support stand, or equivalent, then lower vehicle.
26. Remove frame mounting bolts.
27. Carefully raise body from frame with aid of an assistant.
28. Remove power steering and A/C line retainers from front of oil pan and position aside.
29. Reposition power steering gear to gain access to oil pan.
30. Remove oil level sensor from oil pan.
31. Remove oil pan mounting bolts, then the oil pan.
32. Reverse position to install, noting the following:
    a. Apply a bead of sealer part number 12378190, or equivalent along engine block and on tabs of front and rear cover gaskets.
    b. **Torque** oil pan to engine block and front cover mounting bolts to 18 ft. lbs.
    c. **Torque** oil pan to rear cover mounting bolts to 106 inch lbs.

OIL PUMP

REPLACE

Refer to "Oil Pump, Replace" in "Corvette" chapter.

OIL PUMP SERVICE

There are no serviceable components inside the oil pump. If pump is not working properly, it must be replaced.

SERPENTINE DRIVE BELT

Accessory

1. Rotate drive belt tensioner clockwise to release drive belt tension.
2. Slide drive belt off of water pump pulley.
3. Slowly release drive belt tensioner and remove drive belt from accessory drive pulleys.
4. Reverse procedure to install.

Air Conditioning

1. Remove accessory drive belt as outlined under "Serpentine Drive Belt."
2. Disconnect surge tank hose.
3. Remove fan shroud to radiator mounting bolts.
4. Disconnect upper radiator hose at radiator.
5. Remove air cleaner assembly.
6. Remove A/C line retaining clip mounting screw.
7. Disconnect fan motor electrical connectors.
8. Pull upward on fan assembly to remove from vehicle.
9. Rotate A/C drive belt tensioner clockwise to release tension from belt.
10. Remove A/C drive belt from pulleys.
11. Slowly release drive belt tensioner.
12. Reverse procedure to install.

COOLING SYSTEM BLEED

1. Start engine and let idle for two minutes intermittently raising idle to 3000 RPM.
2. Inspect surge tank for consistent flow.
3. Allow engine to cool.
4. Remove surge tank cap and fill to FULL COLD level.

THERMOSTAT

REPLACE

Thermostat is serviced as an assembly with the thermostat housing.

1. Drain cooling system into suitable container.
2. Disconnect surge tank hose.
3. Remove fan shroud to radiator mounting bolts.
4. Disconnect upper radiator hose.
5. Remove A/C line retaining clip attaching screw.
6. Disconnect fan motor electrical connector.
7. Pull upward to remove fan assembly from vehicle.
8. Remove outlet hose from water pump.
9. Remove thermostat housing mounting bolts, then the thermostat.
10. Reverse procedure to install. **Torque** thermostat housing bolts to 11 ft. lbs.

WATER PUMP

REPLACE

Refer to "Water Pump, Replace" in "Corvette" chapter.

RADIATOR

Refer to "Radiator, Replace" in "Corvette" chapter.

FUEL PUMP

REPLACE

Refer to "Fuel Pump, Replace" in "3.2L Engine" section.

FUEL FILTER

REPLACE

1. Remove fuel injector sight shield.
2. Raise and support vehicle.
3. Disconnect fuel filter inlet quick-connect fittings.
4. Disconnect fuel filter outlet threaded fitting.
5. Remove fuel pipe O-ring, then fuel filter.
6. Reverse procedure to install.

TIGHTENING SPECIFICATIONS

Year	Component	Torque/Ft. Lbs.
2004–05	Air Conditioning Compressor Bracket	37
	Air Conditioning Idler Pulley	37
	Air Conditioning Tensioner	18
	AIR Pipe To Exhaust Manifold	15
	AIR Righthand Side Pipe Bracket To Cylinder Head	15
	Alternator & Power Steering Pump Bracket	37
	Alternator Rear Bracket	37
	Camshaft Retainer	18
	Camshaft Sensor	18
	Camshaft Sprocket	26
	Connecting Rod Bolts	15⑩
	Coolant Temperature Gauge Sensor	15
	Crankshaft Bearing Cap Bolts	③
	Crankshaft Bearing Cap Side Bolts	18
	Crankshaft Bearing Cap Studs	④
	Crankshaft Damper	②
	Crankshaft Oil Deflector	18
	Crankshaft Position Sensor	18
	Cylinder Head Bolts	⑤
	Cylinder Head Coolant Plug	15
	Cylinder Head Core Hole Plug	15
	Drive Belt Idler Pulley	37
	Drive Belt Tensioner	37
	Engine Block Coolant Drain Plugs	44
	Engine Block Heater	30
	Engine Block Oil Galley Plugs	44
	Engine Flywheel Hub Collar Bolt (Automatic Transmission)	96
	Engine Front Cover	18
	Engine Mount Bracket To Engine Block	44
	Engine Rear Cover	18
	Engine Service Lift Bracket (M8 Bolts)	18
	Engine Service Lift Bracket (M10 Bolts)	37
	Engine Valley Cover	18
	Exhaust Manifold	⑦
	Flywheel	⑥
	Fuel Injection Fuel Rail	90①
	Ignition Coil	106①
	Ignition Coil Wire Harness Connector	106①
	Intake Manifold Bolts	⑧
	Knock Sensors	15
	Oil Filter	22
	Oil Filter Fitting	40
	Oil Dipstick Tube	37
	Oil Level Sensor	115①
	Oil Pan Baffle	106①
	Oil Pan Cover	106①
	Oil Pan Drain Plug	18
	Oil Pan M8 Bolts (Oil Pan To Engine Block & Oil Pan To Front Cover)	18

TIGHTENING SPECIFICATIONS—Continued

Year	Component	Torque/Ft. Lbs.
2004–05	Oil Pan M6 Bolts (Oil Pan To Rear Cover)	106①
	Oil Pressure Sensor	15
	Oil Pump Cover	106①
	Oil Pump Relief Valve Plug	106①
	Oil Pump Screen	18
	Oil Pump Screen To Oil Pump	106①
	Oil Pump To Engine Block	18
	Oil Temperature Sensor	15
	Oil Transfer Cover Bolts	106①
	Oxygen Sensor	30
	Power Steering Pump	18
	Power Steering Pump & Alternator Bracket	37
	Power Steering Reservoir Bracket	37
	Spark Plugs	⑪
	Starter Motor	37
	Throttle Body	106①
	Valve Lifter Guide	106①
	Valve Rocker Arm	22
	Valve Rocker Arm Cover	106①
	Vapor Vent Pipe	106①
	Water Inlet Housing	11
	Water Pump	⑨
	Water Pump Cover	11
	Water Pump Pulley	⑨

① — Inch lbs.
② — Refer to "Crankshaft Damper, Replace."
③ — First pass, torque to 15 ft. lbs.; second pass, tighten an additional 80°.
④ — First pass, torque to 15 ft. lbs.; second pass, tighten an additional 51°.
⑤ — Refer to "Cylinder Head, Replace."
⑥ — Refer to "Rear Cover, Replace."
⑦ — Refer to "Exhaust Manifold, Replace."
⑧ — Refer to "Intake Manifold, Replace."
⑨ — Refer to "Water Pump, Replace."
⑩ — First design (single dimple/mark on head bolt), then tighten an additional 60°; Second design (two dimples/marks on bolt head), then tighten an additional 75°.
⑪ — New cylinder head, 15 ft. lbs.; Used cylinder head, 11 ft. lbs.

6.0L Engine

NOTE: On Air Bag Equipped Models, Refer to "Air Bag System Precautions" Located In The Front Of This Manual For System Disarming & Arming Procedures.

NOTE: Refer To "Computer Relearn Procedures" Located In The Front Of This Manual When Battery Power To The Computer Has Been Interrupted.

NOTE: Prior To Performing Any Service Operations Listed In This Section, Consult The "Technical Service Bulletins" Section For Related Information.

NOTE: Refer To The "6.0L Engine" In The "Corvette" Chapter For Procedures Not Found In This Section.

INDEX

	Page No.		Page No.		Page No.
Camshaft, Replace	8-51	Engine Mount, Replace	8-48	Air Bag Systems	8-48
Compression Pressure	8-48	Lefthand	8-48	Battery Ground Cable	8-48
Cooling System Bleed	8-51	Righthand	8-48	Fuel Pressure Relief	8-48
Crankshaft Balancer, Replace	8-50	Exhaust Manifold, Replace	8-50	Radiator, Replace	8-52
Crankshaft Rear Oil Seal,		Lefthand	8-50	Serpentine Drive Belt	8-51
Replace	8-51	Righthand	8-50	Accessory	8-51
Crankshaft Seal, Replace	8-51	Front Cover, Replace	8-51	Air Conditioning	8-51
Cylinder Head, Replace	8-50	Fuel Filter, Replace	8-52	Thermostat, Replace	8-52
Lefthand	8-50	Fuel Pump, Replace	8-52	Tightening Specifications	8-53
Installation	8-50	Intake Manifold, Replace	8-49	Timing Chain, Replace	8-51
Removal	8-50	Main & Rod Bearings	8-51	Valve Adjustment	8-50
Righthand	8-50	Oil Pan, Replace	8-51	Valve Cover, Replace	8-50
Installation	8-50	Oil Pump, Replace	8-51	Lefthand	8-50
Removal	8-50	Oil Pump Service	8-51	Righthand	8-50
Engine Rebuilding		Piston & Rod Assembly	8-51	Water Pump, Replace	8-52
Specifications	29-1	Pistons, Pins & Rings	8-51		
Engine, Replace	8-49	Precautions	8-48		

PRECAUTIONS

Air Bag Systems

Refer to "Air Bag System Precautions" in the front of this manual for system disarming and arming procedures.

Battery Ground Cable

Prior to service, record radio presets, then disconnect battery ground cable and isolate as required.

Fuel Pressure Relief

1. Record radio presets.
2. Turn ignition Off.
3. Disconnect battery ground cable and isolate as required.
4. Loosen fuel filler cap to relieve fuel tank vapor pressure.
5. Remove cap to fuel pressure service connection.
6. Install tool Nos. J34730-1A and J42242, or equivalents, to fuel pressure service connection.
7. Place bleed hose into suitable contain-er, then open bleed valve to relieve fuel system.
8. Place a suitable shop towel under connections to protect fuel spillage.
9. Remove tool Nos. J34730-1A and J42242, or equivalents, from service connections.
10. Install cap to fuel pressure service connection.

COMPRESSION PRESSURE

The minimum compression in any one cylinder should not be less than 70 percent of the highest cylinder. No cylinder should read less than 100 psi.

ENGINE MOUNT

REPLACE

Lefthand

1. Raise and support vehicle.
2. Place suitable adjustable jack stand with a block of wood under engine oil pan.
3. Remove engine mount bracket to engine retaining bolts.
4. Remove engine mount bracket to frame mounting bolts.
5. Remove lower engine mount bracket retaining nuts.
6. Remove lefthand engine mount bracket to frame bolt, then the bracket.
7. Remove engine mount from engine mount bracket.
8. Reverse procedure to install.

Righthand

1. Raise and support vehicle.
2. Remove starter motor as outlined under "Starter Motor, Replace" in the "Electrical" section.
3. Place suitable adjustable jack stand with a block of wood under engine oil pan.
4. Remove righthand engine mount upper retaining nut.
5. Remove righthand engine mount bracket mounting bolts, then the bracket.
6. Remove engine mount retaining nut, then the mount.
7. Reverse procedure to install.

ENGINE
REPLACE

1. Turn front wheels to straight ahead position.
2. Turn ignition lock cylinder to Lock position and remove key.
3. Lock steering column by inserting steering column anti-rotation pin tool No. J 42640, or equivalent, through access hole in lower steering column trim cover.
4. Remove shifter assembly mounting bolts.
5. Disconnect positive and battery ground from the battery.
6. Remove cross vehicle brace.
7. Remove engine sight shield.
8. Remove air cleaner assembly.
9. Disconnect throttle body heater outlet hose from throttle body and position hose to radiator.
10. Evacuate air conditioning system.
11. Release retainer and disconnect air conditioning suction hose from evaporator.
12. Remove suction hose from retaining feature on shock tower and position hose to engine.
13. Release retainer and disconnect air conditioning liquid from connector at front of dash. Disconnect line from connector at radiator fan shroud. Remove liquid line from vehicle.
14. Disconnect brake booster vacuum hose from brake booster. Position hose to engine.
15. Disconnect brake fluid level switch electrical connector from master cylinder.
16. Remove master cylinder mounting nuts.
17. Remove master cylinder brake lines from retainers located on lefthand shock tower.
18. Position master cylinder to engine. Hold master cylinder in place using mechanic's wire. Do not disconnect brake lines from master cylinder.
19. Disconnect two electrical connectors, C105 and C107, at lefthand shock tower.
20. Relieve fuel system pressure.
21. Disconnect chassis fuel line from engine fuel line at righthand rear of engine.
22. Disconnect quick connect fitting service (Metal Collar.)
23. Disconnect chassis-to-engine evaporative emission (EVAP) pipe at righthand rear of engine.
24. Disconnect wiring harness connector C102 at front of dash.
25. Disconnect underhood fuse block connector C103 located between righthand shock tower and cam cover.
26. Remove underhood electrical center cover.
27. Remove battery ground bolt from fender flange near hood shock.
28. Remove battery ground from retaining feature on righthand shock tower and position cable to engine.
29. Remove battery from vehicle.
30. Remove positive battery cable nut from inside underhood electrical center. Remove cable from electrical center and position cable from electrical center and position cable to engine.
31. Disconnect chassis electrical connector at top of righthand shock tower. Position wire to engine.
32. Disconnect engine wiring harness C5 connector from inside of underhood electrical center.
33. Remove ground strap bolt and strap from righthand frame rail.
34. Drain cooling system.
35. Remove electrical cooling fan assembly.
36. Remove radiator assembly.
37. Remove air conditioning condenser assembly.
38. Remove power steering oil cooler counting nuts from front frame assembly. Do not disconnect lines from cooler.
39. Position power steering hose and air conditioning suction hose to engine and hold in place with mechanic's wire.
40. Remove front tire and wheel assemblies.
41. Remove righthand front wheelhouse liner.
42. Working through righthand wheelhouse opening, remove windshield washer reservoir-to-frame brace.
43. Remove upper intermediate shaft to center intermediate shaft bolt.
44. Separate upper intermediate shaft from center intermediate shaft.
45. Lower vehicle.
46. Disconnect heater hoses from engine.
47. Remove two rear brake lines from brake pressure modulator valve (BPMV).
48. Pull brake lines out from behind wiring harness and secure lines to chassis with mechanic's wire.
49. Raise vehicle.
50. Remove transmission assembly.
51. Remove concentric slave cylinder.
52. Remove brake bundle clips from righthand and lefthand frame rails. Remove rear brake lines from clip on righthand frame rail.
53. Remove engine control module (ECM) from ECM housing.
54. Remove (ECM) wiring harness screws.
55. Remove ECM. Secure ECM wiring harness to engine.
56. Lower vehicle.
57. Remove righthand and lefthand shock module upper mounting bolts.
58. Secure chock modules to front frame to avoid stretching front brake hoses.
59. Raise vehicle enough to place a suitable lift table under engine, front frame and front suspension assembly. **To avoid any vehicle damage, serious personal injury or death when major components are removed from the vehicle and the vehicle is supported by a hoist, support the vehicle with jack stands at the opposite end from which components are being removed.**
60. Support rear of vehicle with suitable jack stands.
61. Raise lift table, lower vehicle to preload weight of engines, front frame and front suspension assembly.
62. Remove front frame bolts.
63. With aid of an assistant, lower table and/or raise vehicle to remove engine, front frame and suspension assembly from vehicle.
64. Ensure that all hoses, wires, pipes, and shock modules clear vehicle during removal process.
65. Install engine mount brackets tool No. J 41798, or equivalent, to engine.
66. Remove engine from front frame assembly.
67. Reverse procedure to install.

INTAKE MANIFOLD
REPLACE

1. Remove engine sight shield.
2. Remove air cleaner outlet duct.
3. Disconnect fuel injector electrical connectors.
4. Disconnect throttle body electrical connectors.
5. Relieve fuel system pressure .
6. Remove engine compartment fuel feed pipe.
7. Remove fuel rail if required.
8. Remove vacuum hose from intake manifold.
9. Disconnect electrical connector from manifold absolute pressure (MAP) sensor.
10. Remove MAP sensor.
11. Remove grommet from sensor, as required.
12. Remove evaporative emission (EVAP) clip, bolt, bracket, valve, and tubes.
13. Remove intake manifold bolts and fuel rail stop bracket.
14. Remove intake manifold.
15. Remove and discard intake manifold gaskets.
16. Disassemble intake manifold as required.
17. Clean and inspect intake manifold if it is not being replaced.
18. Install intake manifold-to-cylinder head gaskets.
19. Install intake manifold.
20. Apply a .20 in. band of threadlocker GM P/N 12345382, or equivalent to threads of intake manifold bolts.
21. Install fuel rail stop bracket.
22. Install intake manifold bolts.
23. Lubricate MAP sensor grommet with clean engine oil.
24. Install MAP sensor and grommet.
25. Install EVAP valve, bracket and bolt.
26. Install EVAP tubes.
27. Install fuel rail.
28. Connect MAP sensor electrical connector.
29. Install brake booster vacuum hose to intake manifold.
30. Connect throttle body electrical connector.
31. Connect fuel injector electrical connectors.
32. Install air cleaner outlet duct.
33. Install engine sight shield.

EXHAUST MANIFOLD

REPLACE

Lefthand

1. Remove spark plug wires from spark plugs.
2. Remove exhaust manifold, bolts and gasket. Discard gasket.
3. Remove heat shield and bolts from manifold, as required.
4. Reverse procedure to install, noting the following:
   a. **Torque** exhaust manifold bolts to 11 ft. lbs., beginning with center two bolts, then alternate from side to side and work toward outside bolts.
   b. Final **torque** to 15 ft. lbs., in sequence.
   c. Bend over exposed edge of exhaust manifold gasket at rear of lefthand cylinder head using suitable flat punch.

Righthand

1. Remove spark plug wires from the spark plugs.
2. Remove exhaust manifold, bolts and gasket.
3. Discard gasket.
4. Remove heat shield and bolts from manifold.
5. Reverse procedure to install, noting the following:
   a. **Torque** exhaust manifold bolts to 11 ft. lbs., beginning with center two bolts, then alternate from side to side and work toward outside bolts.
   b. Final **torque** to 15 ft. lbs., in sequence.
   c. Bend over exposed edge of exhaust manifold gasket at rear of lefthand cylinder head using suitable flat punch.

CYLINDER HEAD

REPLACE

Lefthand

REMOVAL

1. Remove valve rocker arms and push-rods.
2. Remove intake manifold.
3. Remove engine coolant air bleed pipe.
4. Remove power steering pipe.
5. Remove exhaust manifold.
6. Remove engine wiring harness ground bolt from rear of lefthand cylinder head.
7. Reposition engine wire harness ground strap away from cylinder head.
8. Remove cylinder head bolts.
9. Remove cylinder head. **After removal, place cylinder head on two wood blocks in order to prevent damage to the sealing surfaces.**
10. Remove cylinder head gasket.
11. Discard gasket.
12. Discard cylinder head bolts.
13. Disassemble cylinder head, if required.
14. Clean and inspect cylinder head.
15. Assemble cylinder head, if required.

INSTALLATION

1. Install cylinder head.
2. Position engine wire harness ground strap to cylinder head.
3. Install engine wiring harness ground bolt to rear of lefthand cylinder head.
4. Install exhaust manifold.
5. Install power steering pump.
6. Install engine coolant air bleed pipe.
7. Install intake manifold.
8. Install valve rocker arms and push-rods.

Righthand

REMOVAL

1. Remove valve rocker arms and push-rods.
2. Remove intake manifold.
3. Remove engine coolant air bleed pipe and covers.
4. Remove exhaust manifold.
5. Remove oil dipstick tube.
6. Remove battery ground from righthand cylinder head.
7. Remove cylinder head bolts.
8. Remove cylinder head.
9. Remove cylinder head gasket.
10. Discard gasket.
11. Discard cylinder head bolts.
12. Disassemble cylinder head, if required.
13. Clean and inspect cylinder head.
14. Assemble cylinder head, if required.

INSTALLATION

1. Install righthand cylinder head.
2. Install battery ground to righthand cylinder head.
3. Install oil dipstick tube.
4. Install exhaust manifold.
5. Install engine coolant air bleed pipe.
6. Install intake manifold.
7. Install valve rocker arms and push-rods.

VALVE COVER

REPLACE

Lefthand

1. Remove fuel injector sight shield.
2. Disconnect spark plug wires from ignition coils.
3. Disconnect ignition coil wire harness electrical connector.
4. Disconnect EVAP canister purge tube connections from intake manifold, purge solenoid valve, fuel supply line, then at rear of righthand cylinder head.
5. Disconnect EVAP canister purge valve electrical connector, then remove valve from bracket.
6. Remove ignition coil bracket mounting bolts, then the bracket.
7. Remove valve cover mounting bolts, then valve cover. Do not reuse gasket.
8. Reverse procedure to install. **Torque** valve cover mounting bolts to 106 inch lbs.

Righthand

1. Remove fuel injector sight shield.
2. Remove PCV hose from throttle body and valve cover.
3. Disconnect spark plug wires from ignition coils.
4. Disconnect ignition coil wire harness electrical connector.
5. Remove ignition coil bracket mounting bolts, then the bracket.
6. Remove valve cover mounting bolts, then valve cover. Discard gasket.
7. Reverse procedure to install. **Torque** valve cover mounting bolts to 106 inch lbs.

VALVE ADJUSTMENT

This engine is equipped with hydraulic valve lash adjusters. No adjustment is required.

CRANKSHAFT BALANCER

REPLACE

For manual transmission applications, note the position of the crankshaft balancer before removal. The balancer does not use a key or keyway for positioning. Mark or scribe the end of the crankshaft and the balancer before component removal. The crankshaft balancer must be installed to the original position. If replacing the crankshaft balancer, note the location of any existing balance weights, if applicable. Install new balance weights into the new crankshaft balancer, if applicable. Crankshaft balancer weights must be installed into the new balancer in the same location as the old balancer. A properly installed balance weight will be either flush or below flush with the face of the balancer. The crankshaft balancer installation and bolt tightening involves a 4 stage tightening process. The first pass ensures that the balancer is installed completely onto the crankshaft. The second, third and fourth passes tighten the new bolt to the proper torque. The used crankshaft balancer bolt will be used only during the first pass of the balancer installation procedure. Install a new crankshaft balancer bolt and tighten as outlined in the second, third and fourth passes of the balancer bolt tightening procedure.

Ensure that the teeth of the flywheel holding tool mesh with the teeth of the engine flywheel.

1. Remove radiator assembly.
2. Remove air conditioning condenser.
3. Remove air conditioner (A/C) drive belt.
4. Raise vehicle.
5. Remove starter motor to gain access to engine flywheel.
6. Remove crankshaft balancer.
7. Reverse procedure to install. Tighten to specifications.

FRONT COVER

REPLACE

1. Remove crankshaft balancer as outlined under "Crankshaft Balancer, Replace."
2. Remove water pump as outlined under "Water Pump, Replace."
3. Remove fan shroud to radiator mounting bolts.
4. Disconnect upper radiator hose at radiator.
5. Remove A/C line retaining clip mounting screw.
6. Disconnect fan motor electrical connectors.
7. Pull upward to remove electric cooling fan.
8. Remove A/C drive belt tensioner bolt, then the tensioner.
9. Remove drive belt idler pulley.
10. Remove alternator as outlined under "Alternator, Replace" in the "Electrical" section, then remove alternator bracket.
11. Remove oil pan to front cover mounting bolts.
12. Remove front cover mounting bolts.
13. Remove front cover. Discard gasket.
14. Reverse procedure to install.

TIMING CHAIN

REPLACE

Refer to "Timing Chain, Replace" in "Corvette" chapter.

CAMSHAFT

REPLACE

1. Remove engine cover assembly.
2. Remove intake manifold.
3. Remove lefthand cylinder head.
4. Remove righthand cylinder head.
5. Remove engine front cover.
6. Remove valve lifter guide bolts.
7. Remove valve lifters and guides.
8. Rotate engine in order to align timing marks.
9. Remove camshaft sprocket bolts.
10. Remove timing chain from camshaft sprocket, and allow chain to rest on crankshaft sprocket.
11. Remove camshaft retainer bolts and retainer.
12. Remove camshaft. **Rear cover removal is not required, if camshaft bearing are not being replaced.**
13. Reverse procedure to install, tighten to specifications.

PISTON & ROD ASSEMBLY

1. Install retaining clip into groove inside of pin bore.
2. Install piston pin to piston and connecting rod.
3. Install retaining clip into groove inside of pin bore.

PISTONS, PINS & RINGS

Pistons and rings are available in standard size and oversize. Pistons and their pins are serviced as an assembly.

MAIN & ROD BEARINGS

Main and rod bearings are available in standard size only. Tighten main bearing cap bolts as follows: **Torque** inboard bolts to 15 ft. lbs., then tighten an additional 80°; **torque** outboard bolts to 15 ft. lbs., then tighten an additional 51°; **torque** short inner and long outer bolts to 18 ft. lbs.

CRANKSHAFT SEAL

REPLACE

1. Remove crankshaft balancer as outlined under "Crankshaft Balancer, Replace."
2. Pry crankshaft oil seal from front cover using suitable flat bladed tool.
3. Reverse procedure to install.

CRANKSHAFT REAR OIL SEAL

REPLACE

1. Remove transmission as outlined in **MOTOR's "Domestic Transmission, In-Vehicle Service"** manual.
2. Mark end of crankshaft and flywheel.
3. Remove flywheel mounting bolts, then the flywheel noting position and location of flywheel balance weights.
4. Pry crankshaft rear oil seal from housing using suitable flat bladed tool.
5. Reverse procedure to install.

OIL PAN

REPLACE

The alignment of the structural oil pan is critical. The rear bolt hole locations of the oil pan provide mounting points for the transmission housing. To ensure the rigidity of the powertrain and correct transmission alignment, it is important that the rear of the block and the rear of the oil pan are flush or even. The rear of the oil pan must never protrude beyond the engine block and transmission housing plane.

Do not use oil pan gasket again. It is not required to rivet new gasket to oil pan.

1. Disconnect battery ground cable.
2. Install engine support fixture.
3. Raise vehicle.
4. Drain engine oil.
5. Install engine oil drain plug until snug.
6. Remove lefthand closeout cover and bolt.
7. Remove starter motor.
8. Remove righthand transmission closeout cover and bolt.
9. Remove and drain engine oil filter.
10. Install engine oil filter until snug.
11. Remove bottom two transmission housing-to-oil pan bolts.
12. Disconnect engine oil temperature sensor electrical connector.
13. Remove front frame assembly.
14. Remove power steering and air conditioning line retainers from front of oil pan and position aside.
15. Reposition power steering rack in order to gain access to oil pan bolts and to provide clearance while removing oil pan.
16. Remove oil level sensor from oil pan.
17. Remove oil pan bolts.
18. Remove oil pan and gasket.
19. Reverse procedure to install, tighten to specifications.

OIL PUMP

REPLACE

Refer to "Oil Pump, Replace" in "Corvette" chapter.

OIL PUMP SERVICE

There are no serviceable components inside the oil pump. If pump is not working properly, it must be replaced.

SERPENTINE DRIVE BELT

Accessory

1. Rotate drive belt tensioner clockwise to release drive belt tension.
2. Slide drive belt off of water pump pulley.
3. Slowly release drive belt tensioner and remove drive belt from accessory drive pulleys.
4. Reverse procedure to install.

Air Conditioning

1. Remove accessory drive belt as outlined under "Serpentine Drive Belt."
2. Disconnect surge tank hose.
3. Remove fan shroud to radiator mounting bolts.
4. Disconnect upper radiator hose at radiator.
5. Remove air cleaner assembly.
6. Remove A/C line retaining clip mounting screw.
7. Disconnect fan motor electrical connectors.
8. Pull upward on fan assembly to remove from vehicle.
9. Rotate A/C drive belt tensioner clockwise to release tension from belt.
10. Remove A/C drive belt from pulleys.
11. Slowly release drive belt tensioner.
12. Reverse procedure to install.

COOLING SYSTEM BLEED

1. Start engine and let idle for two minutes intermittently raising idle to 3000 RPM.
2. Inspect surge tank for consistent flow.
3. Allow engine to cool.

4. Remove surge tank cap and fill to FULL COLD level.

THERMOSTAT

REPLACE

Thermostat is serviced as an assembly with thermostat housing.

1. Drain cooling system into suitable container.
2. Disconnect surge tank hose.
3. Remove fan shroud to radiator mounting bolts.
4. Disconnect upper radiator hose.
5. Remove A/C line retaining clip attaching screw.
6. Disconnect fan motor electrical connector.

7. Pull upward to remove fan assembly from vehicle.
8. Remove outlet hose from water pump.
9. Remove thermostat housing mounting bolts, then the thermostat.
10. Reverse procedure to install. **Torque** thermostat housing bolts to 11 ft. lbs.

WATER PUMP

REPLACE

Refer to "Water Pump, Replace" in "Corvette" chapter.

RADIATOR

REPLACE

Refer to "Radiator, Replace" in "Corvette" chapter.

FUEL PUMP

REPLACE

Refer to "Fuel Pump, Replace" in "3.2L Engine" section.

FUEL FILTER

REPLACE

1. Remove fuel injector sight shield.
2. Raise and support vehicle.
3. Disconnect fuel filter inlet quick-connect fittings.
4. Disconnect fuel filter outlet threaded fitting.
5. Remove fuel pipe O-ring, then fuel filter.
6. Reverse procedure to install.

TIGHTENING SPECIFICATIONS

Year	Component	Torque/Ft. Lbs.
2006–08	Air Conditioning Compressor Bracket	37
	Air Conditioning Idler Pulley	37
	Air Conditioning Tensioner	18
	AIR Pipe To Exhaust Manifold	15
	AIR Righthand Side Pipe Bracket To Cylinder Head	15
	Alternator & Power Steering Pump Bracket	37
	Alternator Rear Bracket	37
	Camshaft Retainer (2006)	18
	Camshaft Retainer Hex Bolts (2007)	18
	Camshaft Retainer Torx Bolts (2007)	11
	Camshaft Sensor	18
	Camshaft Sprocket (2006)	26
	Camshaft Sprocket (2007)	⑪
	Connecting Rod Bolts	⑩
	Coolant Temperature Gauge Sensor	15
	Crankshaft Bearing Cap Bolts	③
	Crankshaft Bearing Cap Side Bolts	18
	Crankshaft Bearing Cap Studs	④
	Crankshaft Damper	②
	Crankshaft Oil Deflector	18
	Crankshaft Position Sensor	18
	Cylinder Head Bolts	⑤
	Cylinder Head Coolant Plug	15
	Cylinder Head Core Hole Plug	15
	Drive Belt Idler Pulley	37
	Drive Belt Tensioner	37
	Engine Block Coolant Drain Plugs	44
	Engine Block Heater	30
	Engine Block Oil Galley Plugs	44
	Engine Flywheel Hub Collar Bolt (Automatic Transmission)	96
	Engine Front Cover	18
	Engine Mount Bracket To Engine Block	44
	Engine Rear Cover	18
	Engine Service Lift Bracket (M8 Bolts)	18
	Engine Service Lift Bracket (M10 Bolts)	37
	Engine Valley Cover	18
	Exhaust Manifold	⑦
	Flywheel	⑥
	Fuel Injection Fuel Rail	90①
	Ignition Coil	106①
	Ignition Coil Wire Harness Connector	106①
	Intake Manifold Bolts	⑧
	Knock Sensors	15
	Oil Filter	22
	Oil Filter Fitting	40

TIGHTENING SPECIFICATIONS—Continued

Year	Component	Torque/Ft. Lbs.
2006–08	Oil Dipstick Tube	37
	Oil Level Sensor	115①
	Oil Pan Baffle	106①
	Oil Pan Cover	106①
	Oil Pan Drain Plug	18
	Oil Pan M8 Bolts (Oil Pan To Engine Block & Oil Pan To Front Cover)	18
	Oil Pan M6 Bolts (Oil Pan To Rear Cover)	106①
	Oil Pressure Sensor	15
	Oil Pump Cover	106①
	Oil Pump Relief Valve Plug	106①
	Oil Pump Screen	18
	Oil Pump Screen To Oil Pump	106①
	Oil Pump To Engine Block	18
	Oil Temperature Sensor	15
	Oil Transfer Cover Bolts	106①
	Oxygen Sensor	30
	Power Steering Pump	18
	Power Steering Pump & Alternator Bracket	37
	Power Steering Reservoir Bracket	37
	Spark Plugs	11
	Starter Motor	37
	Throttle Body	106①
	Valve Lifter Guide	106①
	Valve Rocker Arm	22
	Valve Rocker Arm Cover	106①
	Vapor Vent Pipe	106①
	Water Inlet Housing	11
	Water Pump	⑨
	Water Pump Cover	11
	Water Pump Pulley	⑨

① — Inch lbs.
② — Refer to "Crankshaft Damper, Replace."
③ — First pass, torque to 15 ft. lbs.; second pass, tighten an additional 80°.
④ — First pass, torque to 15 ft. lbs.; second pass, tighten an additional 51°.
⑤ — Refer to "Cylinder Head, Replace."
⑥ — Refer to "Rear Cover, Replace."
⑦ — Refer to "Exhaust Manifold, Replace."
⑧ — Refer to "Intake Manifold, Replace."
⑨ — Refer to "Water Pump, Replace."
⑩ — First design (single dimple/mark on head bolt), torque to 15 ft. lbs., then tighten an additional 60°; Second design (two dimples/marks on bolt head), torque to 15 ft. lbs., then tighten an additional 75°.
⑪ — First pass, torque to 55 ft. lbs.; second pass, rotate an additional 50°.

Rear Suspension

NOTE: On Air Bag Equipped Models, Refer To "Air Bag System Precautions" Located In The Front Of This Manual For System Disarming & Arming Procedures.

NOTE: Refer To "Computer Relearn Procedures" Located In The Front Of This Manual When Battery Power To The Computer Has Been Interrupted.

NOTE: Prior To Performing Any Service Operations Listed In This Section, Consult The "Technical Service Bulletins" Section For Related Information.

INDEX

	Page No.		Page No.		Page No.
Adjustment Link, Replace	8-55	Hub & Bearing, Replace	8-54	Shock Absorber, Replace	8-54
Coil Spring, Replace	8-54	Knuckle, Replace	8-54	Stabilizer Shaft, Replace	8-55
Control Arm, Replace	8-54	Precautions	8-54	Tightening Specifications	8-57
Lower	8-54	Air Bag Systems	8-54		
Upper	8-54	Battery Ground Cable	8-54		

PRECAUTIONS

Air Bag Systems

Refer to "Air Bag System Precautions" in the front of this manual for system disarming and arming procedures.

Battery Ground Cable

Prior to service, record radio presets, then disconnect battery ground cable and isolate as required.

HUB & BEARING

REPLACE

1. Raise and support vehicle.
2. Remove tire and wheel assembly.
3. Remove rear brake caliper and caliper mounting bracket as an assembly.
4. Remove brake rotor mounting screw, then the brake rotor.
5. Remove and discard drive shaft nut.
6. Disconnect ABS connector from backing plate.
7. Remove parking brake cable mounting bolts, then the parking brake cable from knuckle, **Fig. 1.**
8. Remove hub and bearing using tool No. J 42129, or equivalent, **Fig. 2.**
9. Reverse procedure to install. Install new wheel drive shaft nut.

SHOCK ABSORBER

REPLACE

1. Remove sill plate retainers, then the sill plate, **Fig. 3.**
2. Remove rear compartment floor trim panel and side trim retainers, then the trim panels, **Fig. 4.**

3. Remove seat upper retaining nuts from rear of back seat, then the rear seat cushion.
4. Remove shock upper mounting nuts.
5. Raise and support vehicle.
6. Remove lower shock bolt, then the shock absorber, **Fig. 5.**
7. Reverse procedure to install.

COIL SPRING

REPLACE

1. Raise and support vehicle.
2. Remove tire and wheel assemblies.
3. Remove brake pipe bracket nuts and bracket from mounts, **Fig. 6.**
4. Support lower control arm using suitable jack.
5. Remove lower shock bolt, then lower control arm and jack.
6. Support engine cradle using suitable jack.
7. Remove engine cradle bolts and washers.
8. Lower engine cradle and remove coil spring from vehicle.
9. Reverse procedure to install.

CONTROL ARM

REPLACE

Upper

1. Raise and support vehicle.
2. Remove tire and wheel assemblies.
3. Remove shock absorber as outlined under "Shock Absorber, Replace."
4. Remove brake rotor as outlined under "Hub & Bearing, Replace."
5. Remove upper control arm nuts and bolts, **Fig. 7.**
6. Remove upper ball joint nut, then separate ball joint from knuckle using tool No. J 43631 or equivalent, **Fig. 8.**
7. Remove upper control arm assembly.

8. Reverse procedure to install.

Lower

1. Raise and support vehicle.
2. Remove tire and wheel assemblies.
3. Remove stabilizer shaft link nut, then disconnect link from lower control arm, **Fig. 9.**
4. Remove rear drive shaft nut.
5. Remove shock lower mounting bolt.
6. Remove lower control arm to knuckle bolt.
7. Remove lower control arm frame attaching nut and bolt.
8. Separate lower control arm from knuckle, then lower jack and remove rear coil spring and lower control arm.
9. Reverse procedure to install.

KNUCKLE

REPLACE

1. Raise and support vehicle.
2. Remove tire and wheel assemblies.
3. Remove brake caliper and caliper mounting bracket as an assembly from suspension knuckle, support caliper assembly with suitable wire.
4. Remove driveshaft nut, then disconnect ABS electrical connector.
5. Remove parking brake cable bracket from knuckle.
6. Remove upper ball joint mounting nut, then the ball stud from knuckle as outlined under "Lower Control Arm, Replace."
7. Remove lower control arm and trailing arm to knuckle bolts, **Fig. 10.**
8. Remove adjustment link to knuckle mounting bolt, **Fig. 11.**
9. Separate drive shaft from hub as outlined under "Hub & Bearing, Replace."
10. Remove knuckle.
11. Reverse procedure to install.

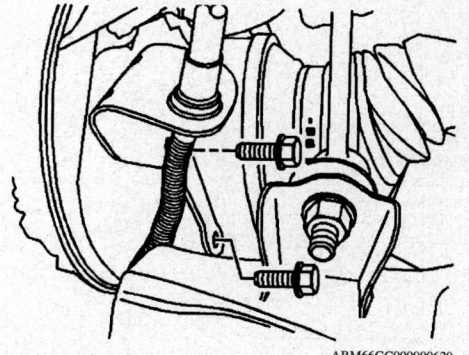

Fig. 1 Parking brake cable removal

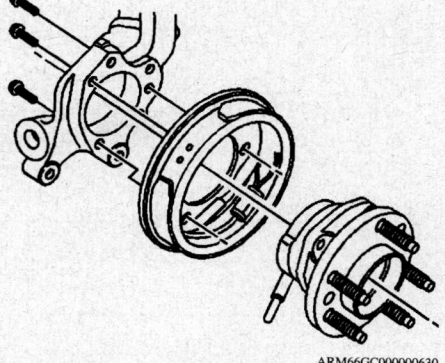

Fig. 2 Hub & bearing removal

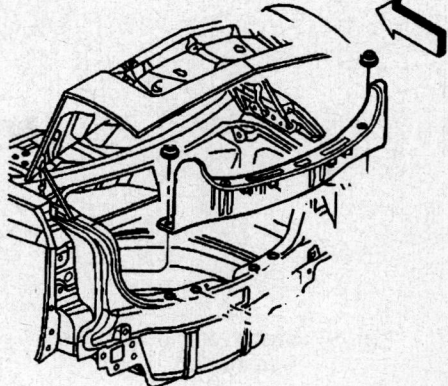

Fig. 3 Sill plate removal

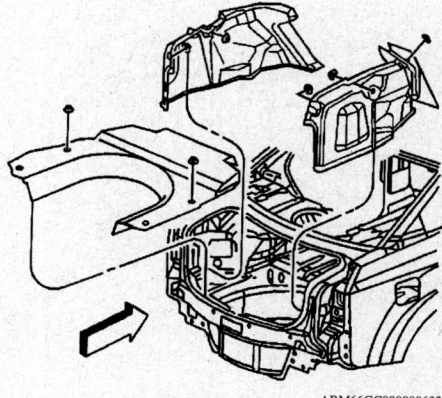

Fig. 4 Floor & side trim panel removal

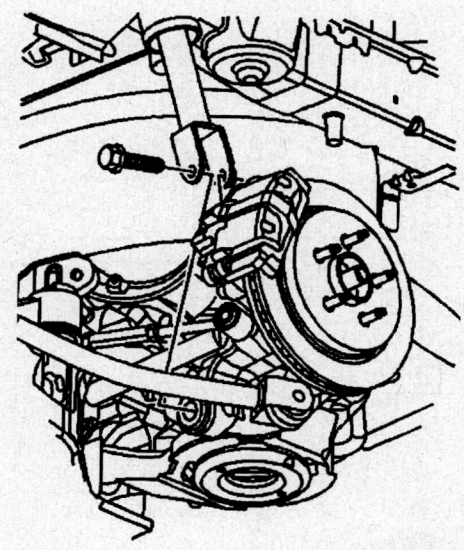

Fig. 5 Lower shock bolt removal

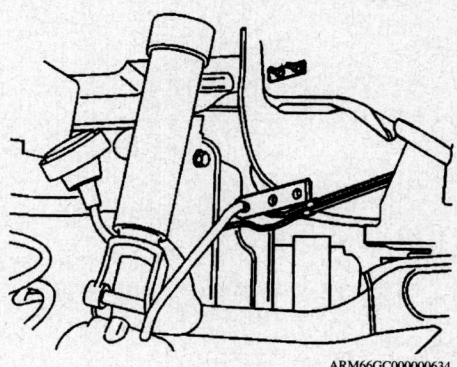

Fig. 6 Brake pipe bracket removal

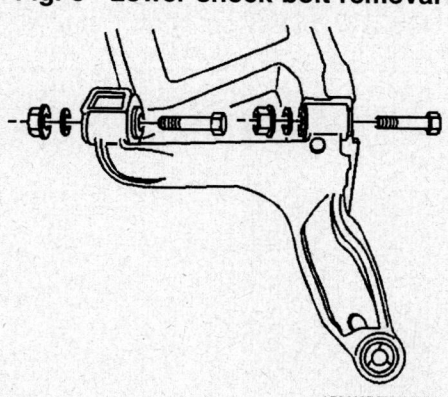

Fig. 7 Upper control arm removal

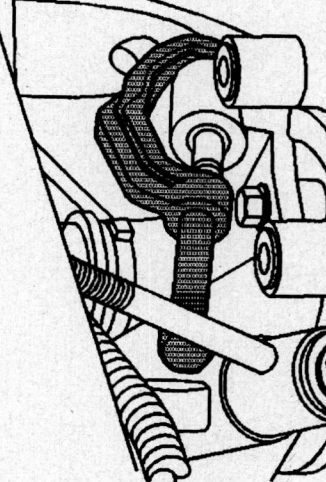

Fig. 8 Upper ball joint removal

STABILIZER SHAFT

REPLACE

1. Raise and support vehicle.
2. Remove tire and wheel assemblies.
3. Remove stabilizer links from shafts, **Fig. 12.**
4. Remove stabilizer shaft attaching bolts and brackets, then the shaft from vehicle, **Fig. 13.**
5. Reverse procedure to install.

ADJUSTMENT LINK

REPLACE

1. Raise and support vehicle.
2. Remove tire and wheel assemblies.
3. Remove adjustment link to knuckle bolt, then the link, **Fig. 14.**
4. Reverse procedure to install.

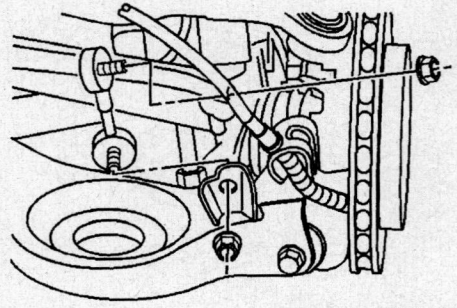

ARM66GC000000638

Fig. 9 Stabilizer shaft link removal

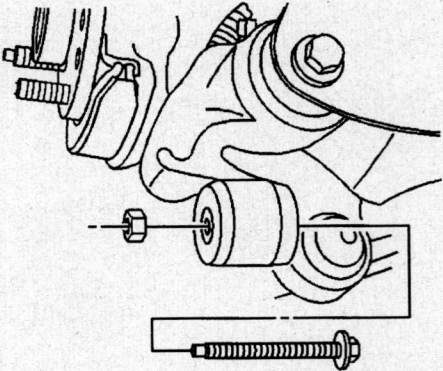

ARM66GC000000640

Fig. 10 Trailing arm removal

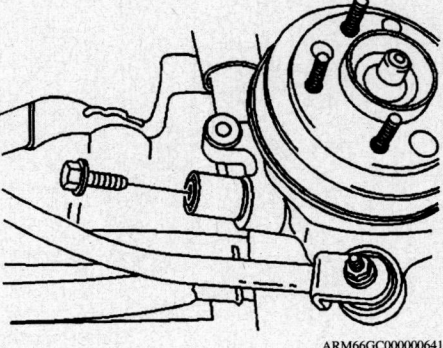

ARM66GC000000641

Fig. 11 Adjustment link removal

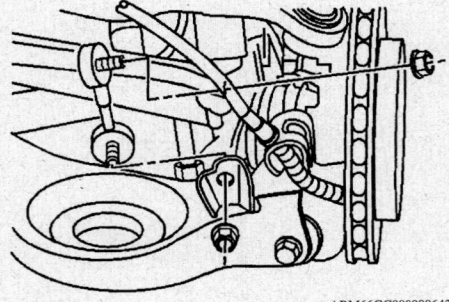

ARM66GC000000642

Fig. 12 Stabilizer shaft link removal

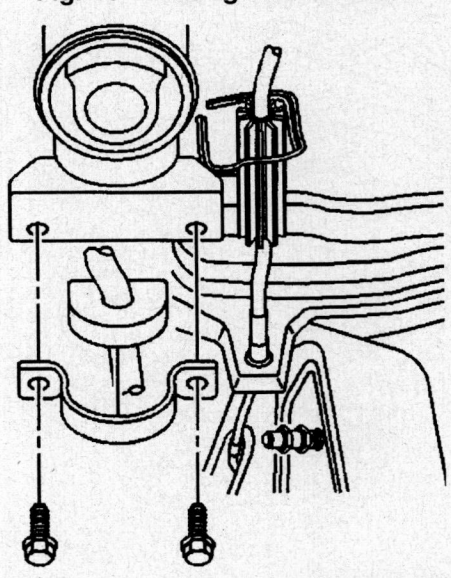

ARM66GC000000643

Fig. 13 Stabilizer shaft removal

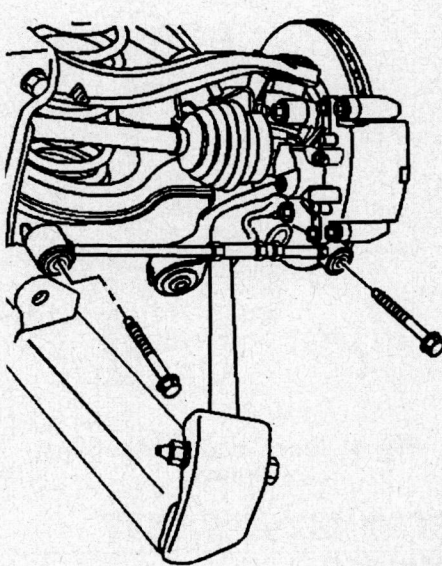

ARM66GC000000644

Fig. 14 Adjustment link removal

TIGHTENING SPECIFICATIONS

Year	Component	Torque Ft. Lbs.
2004–08	Adjustment Link To Frame Retaining Nut & Bolt	129
	Brake Pipe Bracket Retaining Nuts	89①
	Differential To Frame Mounting Bolts	129
	Drive Shaft Nut	118
	Frame To Body Bolts (Front)	195
	Frame To Body Bolts (Rear)	141
	Lower Control Arm To Frame Retaining Nut	111
	Lower Control Arm To Knuckle Bolts	129
	Parking Brake Cable Bracket Bolts	44
	Shock Absorber To Body Retaining Nuts	18
	Shock Absorber To Knuckle Retaining Bolt	111
	Stabilizer Shaft Bracket Bolts	44
	Stabilizer Shaft Link Nuts	37
	Trailing Link To Frame Retaining Nut	66
	Trailing Link To Knuckle Retaining Bolt	129
	Upper Control Arm Ball Stud To Retaining Nut	②
	Upper Control Arm To Frame Retaining Bolt	129
	Wheel Bearing & Hub Assembly Retaining Bolts	92

① — Inch lbs.
② — Torque to 15 ft. lbs., plus additional 210° rotation.

Front Suspension & Steering

NOTE: On Air Bag Equipped Models, Refer To "Air Bag System Precautions" Located In The Front Of This Manual For System Disarming & Arming Procedures.

NOTE: Refer To "Computer Relearn Procedures" Located In The Front Of This Manual When Battery Power To The Computer Has Been Interrupted.

NOTE: Prior To Performing Any Service Operations Listed In This Section, Consult The "Technical Service Bulletins" Section For Related Information.

INDEX

	Page No.
Ball Joint, Replace	8-58
Ball Joint Inspection	8-58
Coil Spring, Replace	8-58
Control Arm, Replace	8-58
Hub & Bearing, Replace	8-58
Power Steering	21-1
Power Steering Gear, Replace	8-58

	Page No.
Power Steering Pump, Replace	8-59
Precautions	8-58
Air Bag Systems	8-58
Battery Ground Cable	8-58
Stabilizer Bar, Replace	8-58
Steering Columns	20-1
Steering Knuckle, Replace	8-58

	Page No.
Strut, Replace	8-58
Strut Service	8-58
Tie Rod, Replace	8-58
Inner	8-58
Outer	8-58
Tightening Specifications	8-62

PRECAUTIONS

Air Bag Systems

Refer to "Air Bag System Precautions" in the front of this manual for system disarming and arming procedures.

Battery Ground Cable

Prior to service, record radio presets, then disconnect battery ground cable and isolate as required.

HUB & BEARING
REPLACE

1. Raise and support vehicle.
2. Remove tire and wheel assembly.
3. Remove brake caliper and caliper mounting bracket as an assembly.
4. Disconnect ABS electrical connector, then remove connector from splash shield, **Fig. 1**.
5. Remove hub and bearing mounting bolts, then the hub and bearing, **Fig. 2**.
6. Reverse procedure to install.

BALL JOINT INSPECTION

Refer to **Figs. 3 and 4** for ball joint and bearing inspections.
1. Inspect any aftermarket devices which could affect operation of suspension systems.
2. Inspect system components for damage or conditions which could cause symptoms.
3. Inspect proper tire size and inflation pressure.

BALL JOINT
REPLACE

Refer to "Control Arm, Replace" for ball joint replacement procedure.

COIL SPRING
REPLACE

Refer to "Strut Service" for coil spring replacement.

STRUT
REPLACE

1. Raise and support vehicle.
2. Remove tire and wheel assemblies.
3. Remove upper control arm to steering knuckle bolt and nut, **Fig. 5**.
4. Remove strut lower mounting bolts, **Fig. 6**.
5. Lower vehicle, then remove air conditioning line and bracket, position and secure line and bracket aside.
6. Remove strut upper bolts, then the strut assembly, **Fig. 7**.
7. Reverse procedure to install.

STRUT SERVICE

1. Install strut in suitable spring compres-

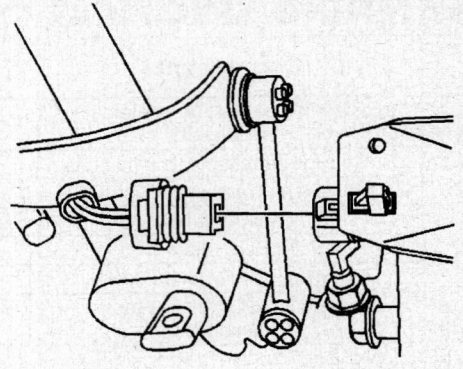

ARM66GC000000626

Fig. 1   ABS connector removal

sion tool. Mark upper control arm and insulator for assembly alignment.
2. Compress spring, then remove upper retaining nut and strut absorber.
3. Loosen compressor screw, then remove upper control arm bracket and coil spring.
4. Reverse procedure to assemble.

CONTROL ARM
REPLACE

1. Raise and support vehicle.
2. Remove tire and wheel assemblies.
3. Remove stabilizer shaft link lower retaining nut, then the link from lower control arm, **Fig. 8**.
4. Remove strut lower bolts.
5. Remove outer tie rod to steering knuckle nut, then separate tie rod end from knuckle using tool No. J 42319-B or equivalent, **Fig. 9**.
6. Remove upper control arm to steering knuckle bolt, then separate upper control arm from knuckle.
7. Remove lower ball joint nut and discard, **Fig. 10**.
8. Remove lower ball joint from steering knuckle using tool No. J 43631 or equivalent.
9. Remove ABS electrical harness.
10. Remove lower control arm, **Fig. 11**.
11. Reverse procedure to install.

STEERING KNUCKLE
REPLACE

1. Raise and support vehicle.
2. Remove tire and wheel assemblies.
3. Remove hub and bearing as outlined under "Hub & Bearing, Replace."
4. Separate steering knuckle from control arm as outlined under "Control Arm, Replace."
5. Remove steering knuckle from lower ball joint stud.
6. Reverse procedure to install.

STABILIZER BAR
REPLACE

1. Raise and support vehicle.
2. Remove tire and wheel assemblies.
3. Disconnect ABS wiring harness.
4. Remove stabilizer shaft link to shaft nuts, **Fig. 12**.

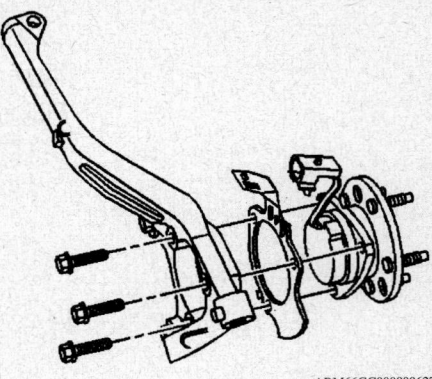

ARM66GC000000627

Fig. 2   Hub & bearing removal

5. Remove stabilizer shaft bolts and brackets, then the stabilizer shaft, **Fig. 13**.
6. Reverse procedure to install.

TIE ROD
REPLACE

Inner

Refer to the "Power Steering" chapter for inner tie rod end replacement.

Outer

1. Raise and support vehicle.
2. Remove tire and wheel assembly.
3. Loosen tie rod end jam nut.
4. Remove tie rod end ball joint to steering knuckle retaining nut.
5. Separate tie rod end ball joint from steering knuckle using ball joint separator tool No. J 42319-B or equivalent.
6. Remove tie rod end from steering gear.
7. Reverse procedure to install. Adjust front end alignment as outlined in "Wheel Alignment" section.

POWER STEERING GEAR
REPLACE

1. Install steering column anti-rotation pin No. J 42640, or equivalent, to steering column, **Fig. 14**.
2. Raise and support vehicle.
3. Remove tire and wheel assemblies.
4. Remove front lower air deflector.
5. Remove intermediate shaft lower pinch bolt, then disconnect intermediate shaft from power steering gear, **Fig. 15**.
6. Remove outer tie rod as outlined under "Tie Rod End, Replace."
7. Disconnect variable effort steering electrical connector from steering gear.
8. Remove stabilizer bar a outlined under "Stabilizer Bar, Replace."
9. Disconnect and remove power steering gear pressure and return hoses from gear.
10. Remove power steering pressure hose retaining bolt from gear.

Step	Action	Values	Yes	No
1	Did you review the General Description and perform the necessary inspections?	--	Go to Step 2	Symptoms
2	1. Raise and support the vehicle. 2. Clean the ball joint and inspect the seal for damage. Is the ball joint seal damaged?	--	Go to Step 6	Go to Step 3
3	Check the wheel bearing for looseness. Did you find and correct the condition?	--	Go to Step 7	Go to Step 4
4	**Important** Remove tension from the ball joints. Check the ball joint for horizontal looseness using the following procedure: 1. Position the J 8001 Dial Indicator against the lowest outboard point of the wheel rim. 2. Rock the wheel in and out while reading the dial indicator. Does the dial indicator measure greater than the specified value?	3.18 mm (0.125 in)	Go to Step 6	Go to Step 5

ARM66GC000000646

Fig. 3 Ball joint inspection (Part 1 of 2)

Step	Action	Values	Yes	No
1	Did you review the General Description and perform the necessary inspections?	--		Symptoms
2	Road test the vehicle in order to verify the customer's complaint. Does the vehicle operate normally?	--	System OK	Go to Step 3
3	1. Raise and support the vehicle. 2. Inspect for tire or wheel damage. Did you find and correct the condition?	--	Go to Step 7	Go to Step 4
4	1. Install the J 39570 Chassis Ear. 2. Road test the vehicle to verify the location of the wheel bearing noise. Did you locate the source of the wheel bearing noise?	--	Go to Step 6	Go to Step 5

ARM66GC000000648

Fig. 4 Wheel bearing inspection (Part 1 of 2)

11. Remove power steering gear mounting bolts.
12. Remove gear through lefthand wheel opening.
13. Reverse procedure to install, noting the following:
    a. Bleed power steering system as outlined in "Power Steering" chapter.
    b. Adjust front toe outlined in "Wheel Alignment" section.

Step	Action	Values	Yes	No
5	**Important** Remove tension from the ball joints. Check the ball joint for vertical looseness using the following procedure: 1. Install the J 8001. 2. Move the ball joint up and down while reading the dial indicator. Does the dial indicator measure greater than the specified value?	3.18 mm (0.125 in)	Go to Step 6	Go to Step 7
6	Replace the ball joint. Did you complete the repair?	--	Go to Step 7	--
7	Operate the system in order to verify the repair. Did you correct the condition?	--	System OK	Go to Step 2

ARM66GC000000647

Fig. 3 Ball joint inspection (Part 2 of 2)

Step	Action	Values	Yes	No
5	**Important** Support the vehicle by the lower control arms or the rear axle to prevent movement during wheel bearing/hub inspection. 1. Mount and secure the J 8001 Dial Indicator. 2. Ensure that the dial indicator contacts the vertical surface of the wheel as close as possible to the top wheel stud. 3. Push and pull on the top of the tire in order to inspect the total travel indicated by the dial indicator. Is the measurement greater then the specified value?	0.27 mm (0.005 in)	Go to Step 6	System OK
6	Replace the wheel bearing. Did you complete the repair?	--	Go to Step 7	--
7	Road test the vehicle to verify the repair. Does the vehicle operate normally?	--	System OK	Go to Step 3

ARM66GC000000649

Fig. 4 Wheel bearing inspection (Part 2 of 2)

POWER STEERING PUMP

REPLACE

1. Remove air cleaner assembly, then the drive belt as outlined under "Alternator, Replace" in "Electrical" section.
2. Remove power steering pulley pump using tool No. J 25034-C, or equivalent.
3. Disconnect power steering reservoir outlet hose from pump, then the power steering pressure hose from pump, **Fig. 16**.
4. Remove power steering pump bolts, then the pump, **Fig. 17**.
5. Reverse procedure to install. Bleed power steering system as outlined in "Power Steering" chapter.

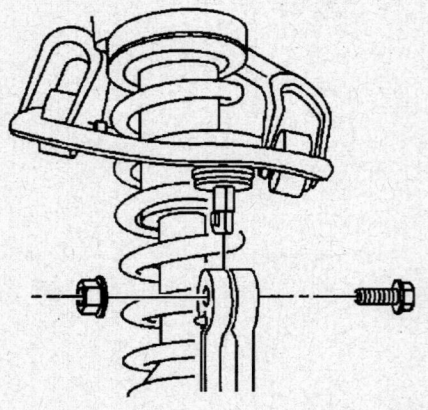

ARM66GC000000650

Fig. 5 Upper control arm to strut bolt removal

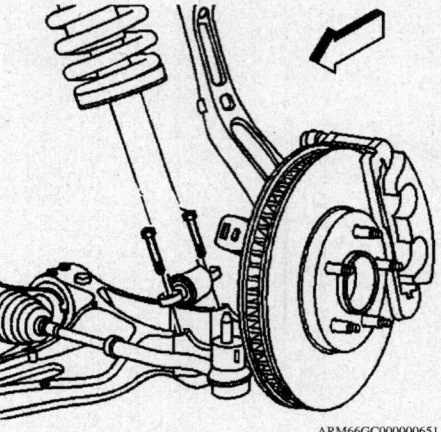

ARM66GC000000651

Fig. 6 Lower strut bolt removal

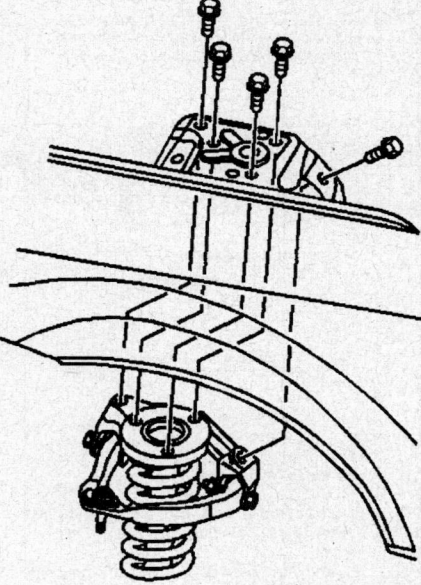

ARM66GC000000652

Fig. 7 Upper strut bolt removal

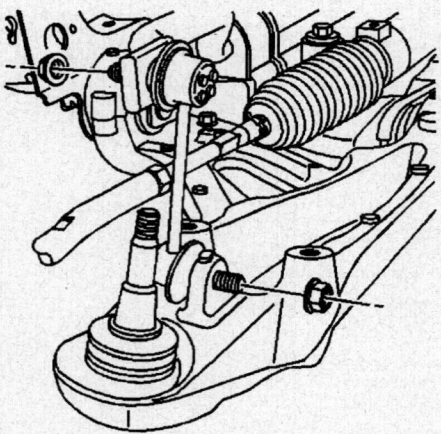

ARM66GC000000653

Fig. 8 Stabilizer shaft link removal

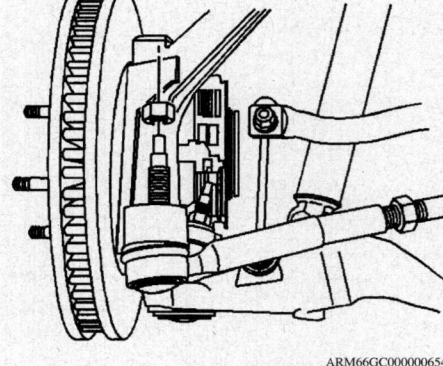

ARM66GC000000654

Fig. 9 Outer tie rod removal

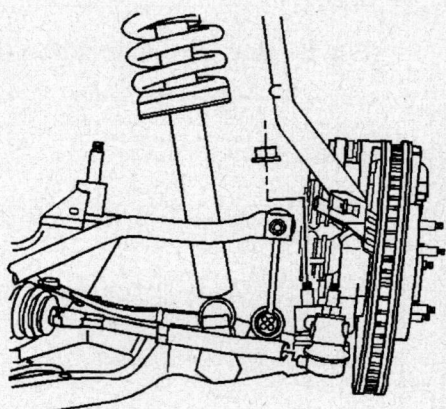

ARM66GC000000655

Fig. 10 Lower ball joint removal

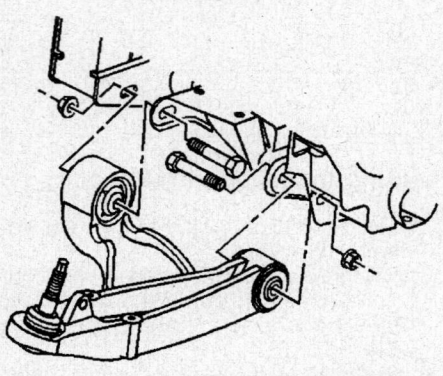

ARM66GC000000656

Fig. 11 Lower control arm removal

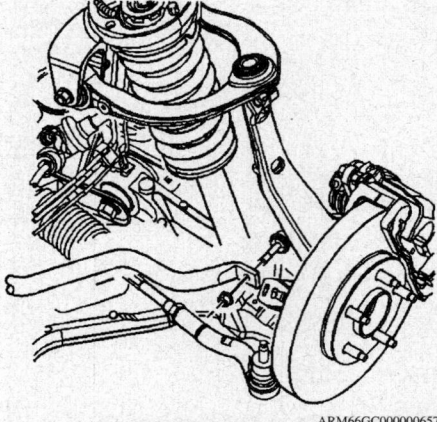

ARM66GC000000657

Fig. 12 Stabilizer shaft link attaching bolt removal

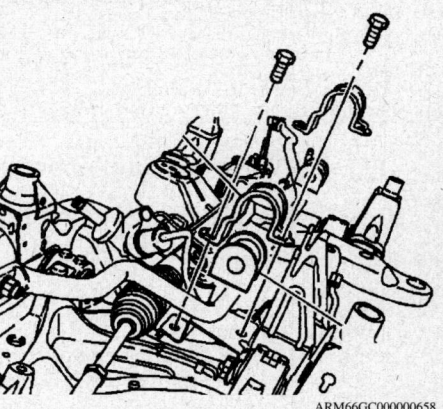

ARM66GC000000658

Fig. 13 Stabilizer shaft removal

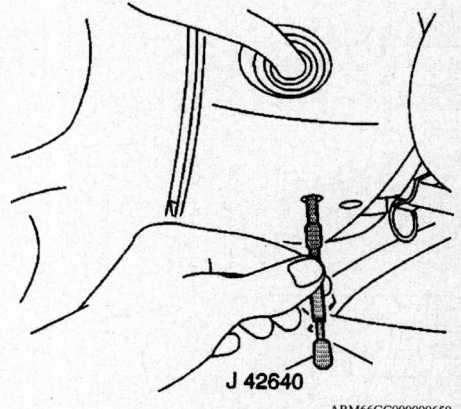

J 42640

Fig. 14   Steering column anti-rotation pin installation

ARM66GC000000659

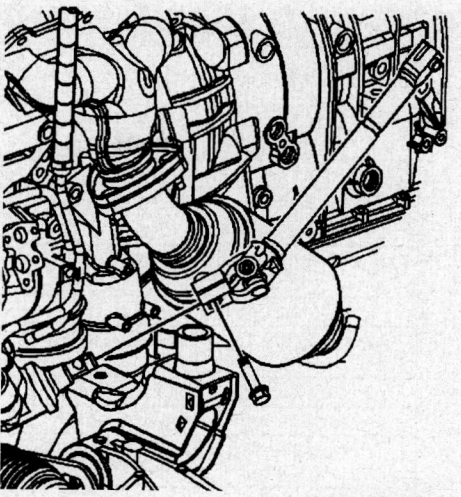

ARM66GC000000660

Fig. 15   Intermediate shaft removal

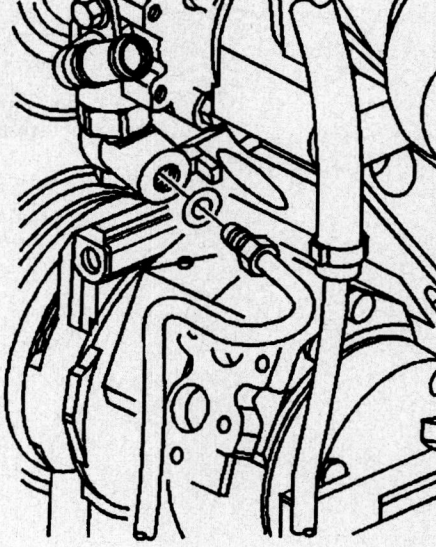

ARM66GC000000662

Fig. 16   Power steering reservoir hose removal

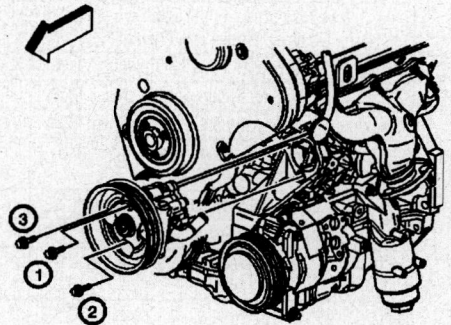

ARM66GC000000663

Fig. 17   Power steering pump removal

TIGHTENING SPECIFICATIONS

Year	Components	Torque Ft. Lbs.
2004–08	A/C Line Bracket To Shock Tower Stud Retaining Nut	80①
	Intermediate Steering Shaft Pinch Bolt	37
	Lower Ball Joint To Knuckle Nut	②
	Lower Control Arm To Cradle Nut	100
	Lower Strut Module To Lower Control Arm Bolts	18
	Outer Tie Rod Jam Nut	55
	Outer Tie Rod To Knuckle Retaining Nut	52
	Power Steering Cooler Screws	48①
	Power Steering Cooler To Frame	80①
	Power Steering Lines To Power Steering Gear	22
	Power Steering Pressure Hose To Frame	80①
	Power Steering Pressure Hose To Power Steering Gear Retainer Bolt	80①
	Power Steering Pressure Line To Power Steering Pump	30
	Power Steering Pump Mounting Bolts	26
	Power Steering Reservoir Lower Bolt	18
	Power Steering Reservoir Upper Bolt	80①
	Power Steering Return & Pressure Hose Nuts	71①
	Stabilizer Shaft Bracket Bolt	44
	Stabilizer Shaft Link Nut	37
	Steering Gear Mounting Bolts (2003–05)	70
	Steering Gear Mounting Bolts (2006–07)	30
	Tie Rod To Knuckle Nut	55
	Upper Control Arm To Steering Knuckle Bolt	44
	Upper Strut Module To Body Bolts	83
	Wheel Bearing/Hub To Knuckle Bolts	100

① — Inch lbs.
② — Torque to 30 ft. lbs., then rotate an additional 120°.

Wheel Alignment

INDEX

	Page No.		Page No.		Page No.
Front Wheel Alignment	8-63	Preliminary Inspection	8-63	Wheel Alignment Specifications	8-3
Camber	8-63	Rear Wheel Alignment	8-63		
Caster	8-63	Camber	8-63		
Toe	8-63	Toe	8-63		

PRELIMINARY INSPECTION

1. Inspect tires for proper inflation and irregular tire wear.
2. Inspect runout of wheels and tires.
3. Inspect wheel bearings for backlash and excessive play.
4. Inspect ball joints and tie rod ends for looseness or wear.
5. Inspect control arms and stabilizer shaft for looseness or wear.
6. Inspect steering gear for looseness at frame.
7. Inspect shock absorbers for wear, leaks, and any noticeable noises.
8. Inspect vehicle trim height.
9. Inspect steering wheel for excessive drag or poor return due to stiff or rusted linkage or suspension components.
10. Inspect fuel level.

FRONT WHEEL ALIGNMENT

Caster

1. Jounce vehicle three times, then allow vehicle to return to normal ride height.
2. Avoid pushing or pulling on tires during alignment process.
3. Ensure trim height is as specified in "Specifications."
4. Identify caster and camber angles, **Figs. 1 and 2.**
5. Install caster and camber adjusting tool No. J 45845, or equivalent, to lower control arm and frame, **Fig. 3.**
6. Loosen control arm adjustment nuts, then adjust caster and camber as required.
7. **Torque** lower control arm adjustment bolts to 100 ft. lbs., then ensure alignment is within specifications as outlined under "Specifications."

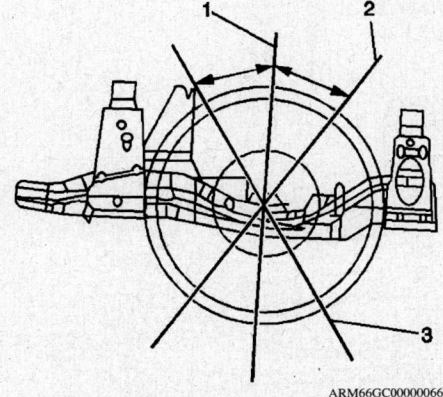

Fig. 1 Caster angle locations

Camber

Refer to "Caster" in this section for alignment procedure.

Toe

1. Loosen outer tie rod nut, **Fig. 4.**
2. Rotate inner tie rod to set required toe adjustment within "Specifications."
3. **Torque** outer tie rod nut to 55 ft. lbs.
4. Inspect toe setting after tightening.

REAR WHEEL ALIGNMENT

Camber

1. Install caster and camber adjusting tool No. J 45845, or equivalent to lower control arm and frame.
2. Loosen lower control arm to frame bolt, then adjust angle as required.
3. **Torque** bolt to 111 ft. lbs., and ensure alignment is within specifications as outlined under "Specifications."

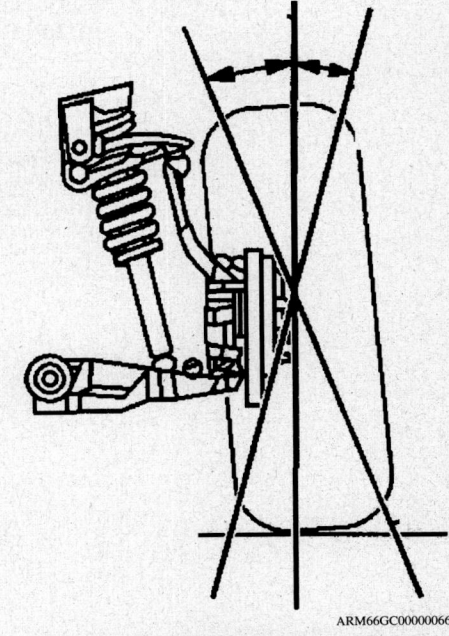

Fig. 2 Camber angle locations

Toe

1. Loosen adjustment link nuts, **Fig. 5.**
2. Rotate turnbuckle to adjust toe as required.
3. **Torque** adjustment nuts to 55 ft. lbs., then inspect toe. Ensure alignment is within specifications as outlined under "Specifications."

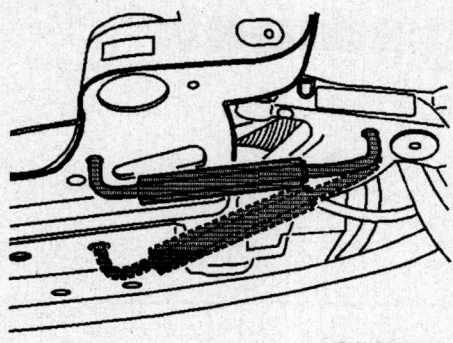

ARM66GC000000667

Fig. 3 Caster/camber tool installation

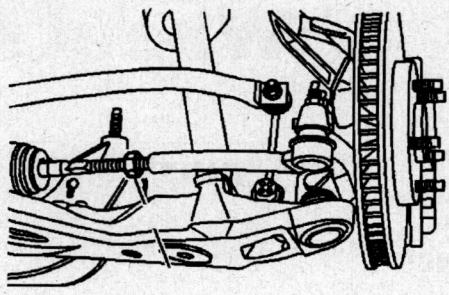

ARM66GC000000668

Fig. 4 Tie rod nut adjustment

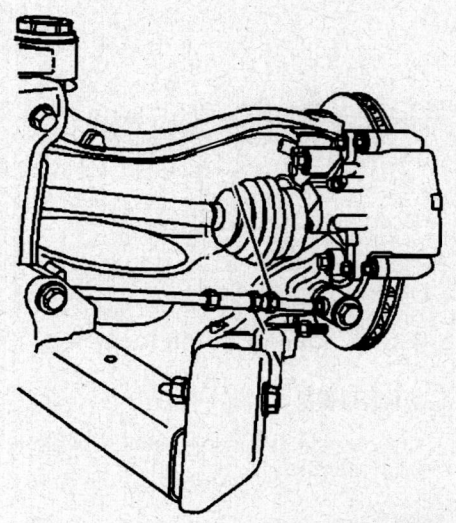

ARM66GC000000669

Fig. 5 Adjustment link nut locations

DEVILLE, DTS, SEVILLE & STS

NOTE: Refer To Rear Of This Manual For Vehicle Manufacturer's Special Service Tool Suppliers.

INDEX OF SERVICE OPERATIONS

Page No.

**ACTIVE SUSPENSION
SYSTEM** 7-1
**AIR BAG SYSTEM
PRECAUTIONS** 0-18
BRAKES
Anti-Lock Brakes (Volume 2).. 6-1
Disc Brakes................. 22-1
Drum Brakes 23-1
Hydraulic Brake Systems 24-1
Power Brake Units......... 25-1
**COMPUTER RELEARN
PROCEDURE**................. 0-31
ELECTRICAL
Air Bag System (Volume 2) ... 4-1
Air Conditioning.............. 16-1
Alternator, Replace 9-7
Alternators.................. 19-1
Blower Motor, Replace........ 9-12
Cabin Air Filter, Replace 9-12
Cooling Fans 17-1
Cruise Control (Volume 2) 2-1
Dash Gauges (Volume 2) 1-1
Dash Panel Service
(Volume 2)................ 5-1
Dimmer Switch, Replace..... 9-10
Evaporator Core, Replace 9-13
Fuel Pump Relay Location.... 9-7
Fuse Panel & Flasher
Location 9-6
Headlamp Switch, Replace ... 9-10
Heater Core, Replace......... 9-13
Ignition Coils, Replace 9-8
Ignition Lock, Replace 9-9
Ignition Switch, Replace 9-9
Instrument Cluster, Replace... 9-10
Multi-Function Switch,
Replace 9-10
Passive Restraint Systems
(Volume 2).................. 4-1
Precautions.................. 9-6
Radio, Replace 9-11
Relay Center Location 9-7
Speed Controls (Volume 2) ... 2-1
Starter Motors 18-1
Starter, Replace 9-7
Steering Columns............. 20-1
Steering Wheel, Replace...... 9-10
Technical Service Bulletins.... 9-14
Wiper Motor, Replace........ 9-11
Wiper Switch, Replace........ 9-12
Wiper Systems (Volume 2).... 3-1
Wiper Transmission, Replace . 9-12
**ELECTRICAL SYMBOL
IDENTIFICATION** 0-63
**FRONT SUSPENSION &
STEERING**
Ball Joint, Replace 9-62
Ball Joint Inspection 9-62
Coil Spring, Replace.......... 9-62
Control Arm, Replace 9-63
Hub & Bearing, Replace 9-61
Power Steering 21-1
Power Steering Gear,
Replace 9-65

Page No.

Power Steering Pump,
Replace 9-65
Precautions................. 9-61
Shock Absorber, Replace 9-63
Stabilizer Bar, Replace........ 9-64
Steering Columns............. 20-1
Steering Knuckle, Replace 9-64
Strut, Replace 9-62
Strut Service................. 9-63
Technical Service Bulletins.... 9-65
Tie Rod, Replace 9-64
Tightening Specifications...... 9-67
**NON-STANDARD TIRE &
WHEEL SIZE
ADJUSTMENT TO RIDE
HEIGHT SPECIFICATIONS
& TIRE SIZE CHART** 0-61
REAR DRIVE AXLE 27-1
REAR SUSPENSION
Adjustment Link, Replace 9-58
Coil Spring, Replace.......... 9-57
Control Arm, Replace 9-57
Hub & Bearing, Replace 9-56
Precautions................. 9-56
Shock Absorber, Replace 9-57
Stabilizer Shaft, Replace...... 9-57
Technical Service Bulletins.... 9-58
Tightening Specifications...... 9-60
**SERVICE REMINDER &
WARNING LAMP RESET
PROCEDURES** 0-34
SPECIFICATIONS
Fluid Capacities & Cooling
System Data................ 9-5
Front Wheel Alignment
Specifications............... 9-3
General Engine
Specifications............... 9-2
Lubricant Data.............. 9-5
Rear Wheel Alignment
Specifications............... 9-3
Tune Up Specifications 9-2
Vehicle Ride Height
Specifications............... 9-4
**TIRE PRESSURE
MONITORING SYSTEM** 28-1
**VEHICLE
IDENTIFICATION** 0-1
VEHICLE LIFT POINTS 0-51
**VEHICLE MAINTENANCE
SCHEDULES** 0-73
WHEEL ALIGNMENT
Front Wheel Alignment........ 9-69
Preliminary Inspection 9-69
Rear Wheel Alignment 9-69
Vehicle Ride Height 9-70
Wheel Alignment
Specifications............... 9-3
**WIRE COLOR CODE
IDENTIFICATION** 0-63
3.6L ENGINE
Compression Pressure........ 9-16
Engine Rebuilding

Page No.

Specifications................. 29-1
Engine, Replace 9-17
Engine Mount, Replace 9-16
Precautions................. 9-16
Tightening Specifications..... 9-18
Valve Adjustment 9-17
4.4L ENGINE
Camshaft, Replace 9-25
Camshaft Lobe Lift
Specifications................ 9-22
Compression Pressure........ 9-19
Cooling System Bleed 9-29
Crankshaft Damper, Replace.. 9-22
Crankshaft Rear Oil Seal,
Replace 9-27
Cylinder Head, Replace....... 9-21
Drive Belt, Replace 9-29
Engine Rebuilding
Specifications................ 29-1
Engine, Replace 9-19
Engine Mount, Replace 9-19
Exhaust Manifold, Replace.... 9-20
Front Cover, Replace 9-22
Fuel Filter, Replace 9-30
Fuel Pump, Replace 9-30
Hydraulic Lifters, Replace..... 9-22
Intake Manifold, Replace...... 9-20
Main & Rod Bearings 9-26
Oil Cooler, Replace 9-29
Oil Pan, Replace............. 9-28
Oil Pump, Replace........... 9-28
Oil Pump Service 9-28
Piston & Rod Assembly 9-25
Pistons, Pins & Rings 9-25
Precautions................. 9-19
Radiator, Replace............ 9-30
Rocker Arms................ 9-22
Supercharger, Replace 9-30
Technical Service Bulletins.... 9-30
Thermostat, Replace.......... 9-29
Tightening Specifications...... 9-32
Timing Chain, Replace........ 9-23
Timing Chain Tensioner,
Replace 9-25
Valve Adjustment 9-22
Valve Clearance
Specifications................ 9-22
Valve Cover, Replace 9-22
Water Outlet Housing,
Replace 9-29
Water Pump, Replace 9-29
4.6L ENGINE
Camshaft, Replace 9-46
Compression Pressure........ 9-35
Cooling System Bleed 9-51
Crankshaft Damper, Replace.. 9-42
Crankshaft Rear Oil Seal,
Replace 9-48
Cylinder Head, Replace....... 9-40
Engine Rebuilding
Specifications................ 29-1
Engine, Replace 9-36
Engine Mount, Replace 9-35
Exhaust Manifold, Replace.... 9-39
Front Cover, Replace 9-42

	Page No.		Page No.		Page No.
Fuel Filter, Replace	9-53	Pistons, Pins & Rings	9-48	Valve Adjustment	9-42
Fuel Pump, Replace	9-53	Precautions	9-35	Valve Clearance	
Intake Manifold, Replace	9-38	Radiator, Replace	9-52	Specifications	9-42
Main & Rod Bearings	9-48	Serpentine Drive Belt	9-51	Valve Cover, Replace	9-41
Oil Pan, Replace	9-49	Technical Service Bulletins	9-53	Water Crossover, Replace	9-51
Oil Pump, Replace	9-50	Thermostat, Replace	9-51	Water Pump, Replace	9-51
Oil Pump Service	9-51	Tightening Specifications	9-54		
Piston & Rod Assembly	9-48	Timing Chain, Replace	9-43		

Specifications

GENERAL ENGINE SPECIFICATIONS

Year	Engine		Fuel Injection System	Bore & Stroke	Compression Ratio	Net H.P. @ RPM③	Maximum Torque Ft. Lbs. @ RPM	Normal Oil Pressure Pounds①
	Liter	VIN Code②						
2004	4.6L	Y	TPFI	3.66 × 3.31	10.0	275 @ 5600	300 @ 4400	35
	4.6L	9	TPFI	3.66 × 3.31	10.0	300 @ 6000	295 @ 4400	35
2005–06	3.6L	7	SMFI	3.70 × 3.37	10.2	255 @ 6500	252 @ 3400	20
	4.6L	A	TPFI	3.66 × 3.31	10.0	300 @ 6000	295 @ 4400	35
	4.6L	Y	TPFI	3.66 × 3.31	10.0	275 @ 5600	300 @ 4400	35
	4.6L	9	TPFI	3.66 × 3.31	10.0	300 @ 6000	295 @ 4400	35
2007	3.6L	7	SMFI	3.70 × 3.37	10.2	254 @ 6500	252 @ 3400	18
	4.4L	D	TPFI	3.58 × 3.31	9.0	469 @ 6400	439 @ 3800	35
	4.6L	A	TPFI	3.66 × 3.31	10.0	300 @ 6000	295 @ 4400	35
	4.6L	Y	TPFI	3.66 × 3.31	10.0	275 @ 6000	295 @ 4400	35
	4.6L	9	TPFI	3.66 × 3.31	10.0	292 @ 6300	288 @ 4500	35
2008	3.6L	7	SMFI	3.70 × 3.37	11.3	302 @ 6300	272 @ 5200	18
	4.4L	D	TPFI	3.58 × 3.31	9.0	469 @ 6400	439 @ 3800	35
	4.6L	A	TPFI	3.66 × 3.31	10.0	300 @ 6000	295 @ 4400	35
	4.6L	Y	TPFI	3.66 × 3.31	10.0	275 @ 6000	295 @ 4400	35
	4.6L	9	TPFI	3.66 × 3.31	10.0	292 @ 6300	288 @ 4500	35

TPFI — Tuned Port Fuel Injection
① — At 2000 RPM.

② — The eighth digit denotes engine code.

③ — Ratings are net as installed in vehicle.

TUNE UP SPECIFICATIONS

Year & Engine, VIN①	Spark Plug Gap	Ignition Timing			Curb Idle Speed③	Fast Idle Speed	Fuel Pump Pressure, psi	Valve Lash
		Firing Order Fig.④	Degrees BTDC	Mark				
2004								
4.6L/Y	.050	②	⑤	⑨	⑥	⑥	41–47⑦	⑧
4.6L/9	.050	②	⑤	⑨	⑥	⑥	41–47⑦	⑧
2005–06								
3.6L/7	.043	⑩	⑤	⑨	—	⑨	55–60	⑧
4.6L/A	.050	②	⑤	⑨	⑥	⑥	41–47⑦	⑧
4.6L/Y	.050	②	⑤	⑨	⑥	⑥	41–47⑦	⑧
4.6L/9	.050	②	⑤	⑨	⑥	⑥	41–47⑦	⑧
2007–08								
3.6L/7	.044	⑩	⑤	⑨	—	⑨	55–60	⑧
4.4L/D	.040	②	⑤	⑨	650	⑥	55–60	⑧
4.6L/A	.050	②	⑤	⑨	650	⑥	55–60	⑧
4.6L/Y	.050	②	⑤	⑨	⑥	⑥	41–47⑦	⑧
4.6L/9	.050	②	⑤	⑨	⑥	⑥	41–47⑦	⑧

BTDC — Before top dead center
① — The eighth digit denotes engine code.
② — Cylinder numbering from lefthand to righthand as viewed from front of vehicle. Front bank, 2, 4, 6, 8; rear bank, 1, 3, 5, 7. Firing order 1-2-7-3-4-5-6-8. Refer to **Fig. A** for spark plug wire connections at coil unit.
③ — On auto. trans. models, idle speed is adjusted in Drive. When adjusting idle speed, set parking brake & block drive wheels.
④ — Before disconnecting wires from distributor cap or coil pack , determine location of No. 1 wire, as position may have been altered from that illustrated at end of this chart.

⑤ — Computer controlled. No adjustment.
⑥ — Idle speed is controlled by an Idle Speed Control (ISC) motor or an Idle Air Control (IAC) valve.
⑦ — With shop towel wrapped around fuel pressure valve to prevent fuel spillage, connect suitable fuel pressure gauge to fuel pressure valve. Measure fuel pressure w/ignition On, engine not running.
⑧ — Equipped hydraulic valve lifters.
⑨ — Equipped w/crankshaft position sensor.
⑩ — Cylinder numbering from front to rear: righthand bank, 1, 3, 5; lefthand bank, 2, 4, 6. Firing order, 1-2-3-4-5-6.

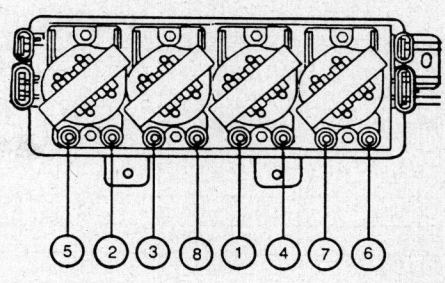

GC1139100136000X

Fig. A

FRONT WHEEL ALIGNMENT SPECIFICATIONS

Year	Model	Caster Angle, Degrees		Camber Angle, Degrees		Total Toe, Degrees①		Ball Joint Inspection
		Limits	Desired	Limits	Desired	Limits	Desired	
2004	DeVille	+4.50 to +5.50④	+5.00④	−.70 to +.30④	−.2④	0 to +.4	+.2	②
	Seville	+4.50 to +5.50④	+5.00④	−.70 to +.30④	−.2④	0 to +.4	+.2	②
2005	DeVille	+4.50 to +5.50④	+5.00④	−.70 to +.30④	−.2④	0 to +.4	+.2	②
	STS (AWD)	+4.90 to +6.10③	+5.50③	-1.10 to +.10③	−.5③	0 to +.4	+.2	②
	STS (RWD)	+5.25 to +6.45③	+5.85③	-1.10 to +.10③	−.5③	0 to +.4	+.2	②
2006–08	DTS	+5.05 to +6.55⑤	+5.80⑤	−.75 to +.75⑤	0⑤	0 to +.4	+.2	②
	STS (AWD)	+4.90 to +6.10③	+5.50③	-1.10 to +.10③	−.5③	0 to +.4	+.2	②
	STS (RWD)	+5.25 to +6.45③	+5.85③	-1.10 to +.10③	−.5③	0 to +.4	+.2	②

① — Toe-In (+). Toe-Out (−).
② — Refer to "Ball Joint Inspection" in "Front Suspension & Steering."
③ — Cross caster or camber within .6°.
④ — Cross caster or camber within .5°.
⑤ — Cross caster or camber within .75°.

REAR WHEEL ALIGNMENT SPECIFICATIONS

Year	Model	Camber Angle, Degrees		Total Toe, Degrees①		Thrust Angle, Degrees	
		Limits	Desired	Limits	Desired	Limits	Desired
2004	DeVille	−.80 to +.20	−.30	0 to +.4	+.2	−.1 to +.1	0
	Seville	−.80 to +.20	−.30	0 to +.4	+.2	−.1 to +.1	0
2005	DeVille	−.80 to +.20	−.30	0 to +.4	+.2	−.1 to +.1	0
	STS	−1.40 to −.40	−.90	0 to +.4	+.2	−.2 to +.2	0
2006–08	DTS	−.80 to +.70	−..05	−.1 to +.3	+.1	−.1 to +.1	0
	STS	−1.40 to −.40	−.90	0 to +.4	+.2	−.2 to +.2	0

① — Toe-In (+). Toe-Out (−).

VEHICLE RIDE HEIGHT SPECIFICATIONS

Model	Year	Body Style	Manu- facturer's Original Tire Size	Measurement Points & Specifications①②					
				Front			Rear		
				Dim.	Specification		Dim.	Specification	
					Inches	mm		Inches	mm
DeVille	2004–05	All	③	Z⑨	1.6	40	D⑥	3.4	86
DTS	2006–08	All	③	Z⑨	1.2–2.0	30–50	D⑥	3.0–3.8	76–96
Seville	2004	SLS④	③	Z⑨	1.2–2.0	30–50	D⑥	3.0–3.8	76–96
		SLS⑤	③	Z⑨	.8–1.6	20–40	D⑥	2.6–3.4	66–86
		STS	③	Z⑨	.8–1.6	20–40	D⑥	2.6–3.4	66–86
STS	2005	All⑩	③	Z⑦	3.11–3.88	79–99	D⑧	2.52–3.31	64–86
		All⑪	③	Z⑦	1.14–1.93	29–49	D⑧	2.13–2.91	54–74
	2006–08	All④⑩	③	Z⑦	2.68–3.46	68–88	D⑧	2.13–2.91	54–74
		All④⑪	③	Z⑦	1.14–1.93	29–49	D⑧	2.05–2.83	52–72
		All⑫	③	Z⑦	.71–1.50	18–38	D⑧	2.05–2.83	52–72

Dim. — Dimension

① — ±.39 inch (10 mm) front to rear & side to side.

② — Measurement is with fuel, radiator coolant and engine oil full, spare tire, jack, hand tools & mats in designated positions and tires properly inflated.

③ — See door sticker or inside of glove box for manufacturers original tire size specifications. If tires on vehicle do not match manufacturers original tire size & measurement is not within limits, refer to the "Non-Standard Tire & Wheel Size Adjustment To Ride Height Specification & Tire Size Adjustment Charts" in the front of this manual for approximate changes in ride height specifications.

④ — Soft Ride Suspension System.

⑤ — Sport Suspension System.

⑥ — Refer to **Fig. A**.

⑦ — Refer to **Fig. D**.

⑧ — Refer to **Fig. B**.

⑨ — Refer to **Fig. C**.

⑩ — Five-speed automatic transmission.

⑪ — Six-speed automatic transmission.

⑫ — Special Ride & Handling.

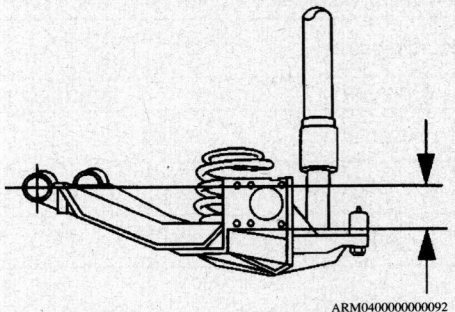

ARM0400000000092

Fig. A Dimension D. DeVille, DTS & Seville

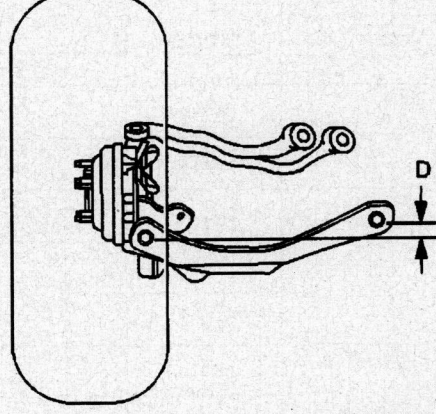

ARM0500000000928

Fig. B Dimension D. STS

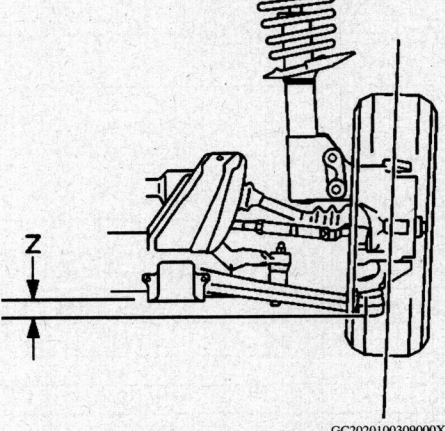

GC2020100309000X

Fig. C Dimension Z. DeVille, DTS & Seville

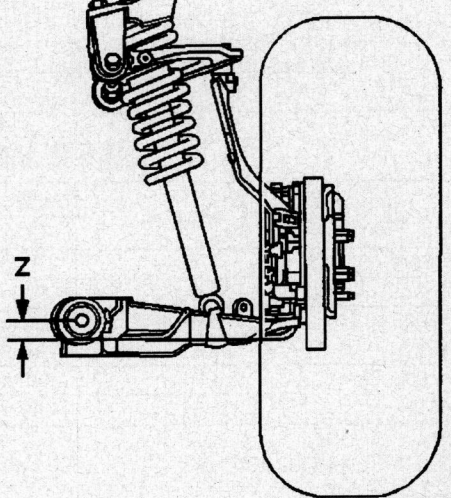

ARM0500000000929

Fig. D Dimension Z. STS

FLUID CAPACITIES & COOLING SYSTEM DATA

Model/ Year	Engine/ Liter	Coolant Capacity, Qts.	Coolant Type	Radiator Cap Relief Pressure, Lbs.	Thermostat Opening Temp., °F	Fuel Tank Gals	Engine Oil Refill, Qts. ①	ATF, Qts.②
DEVILLE								
2004–05	4.6L	13.0	Dex-Cool	18	197	19.0	7.5	③
DTS								
2006–08	4.6L	13.0	Dex-Cool	—	185	18.5	7.5	⑦
SEVILLE								
2004	4.6L	12.5	Dex-Cool	18	197	19.0	7.5	③
STS								
2005	3.6L	9.7	Dex-Cool	18	194	17.5	6.0	⑤
	4.6L	10.4	Dex-Cool	18	185	17.5	8.0	⑤
2006–08	3.6L	11.7	Dex-Cool	—	194	17.5	6.0	⑤
	4.4L	12.7④	Dex-Cool	—	185	17.5	9.0	⑥
	4.6L	12.5	Dex-Cool	—	185	17.5	8.0	⑥

① — Includes filter.

② — Approximate. Make final inspection w/dipstick.

③ — Drain & refill 11 qts.; after overhaul 12.6 qts.; dry refill 15 qts.

④ — Intercooler system capacity 2.6 qts.

⑤ — Pan removal 7.4 qts., overhaul 9.5 qts.

⑥ — Pan removal 6.5 qts., overhaul 10 qts.

⑦ — Pan removal, 7.4 qts.; overhaul (2WD), 13.1 qts.; overhaul (AWD), 15 qts.

LUBRICANT DATA

Year	Model	Lubricant Type		
		Automatic Transaxle	**Power Steering**	**Brake System**
2004–05	All	Dexron III	GM Power Steering Fluid①	DOT 3
2006–08	All	Dexron VI	GM Power Steering Fluid①	DOT 3

① — GM part No. 89021184, or equivalent.

Electrical

NOTE: Refer To "Air Bag System Precautions" Located In The Front Of This Manual For System Disarming & Arming Procedures.

NOTE: Refer To "Computer Relearn Procedures" Located In The Front Of This Manual When Battery Power To The Computer Has Been Interrupted.

NOTE: Prior To Performing Any Service Operations Listed In This Section, Consult The "Technical Service Bulletins" Section For Related Information.

INDEX

	Page No.		Page No.		Page No.
Air Bag System (Volume 2)	4-1	Fuse Panel & Flasher Location	9-6	Precautions	9-6
Air Conditioning	16-1	DTS	9-6	Air Bag Systems	9-6
Alternator, Replace	9-7	DeVille & Seville	9-6	Battery Ground Cable	9-6
3.6L Engine	9-7	STS	9-7	Radio, Replace	9-11
4.4L Engine	9-7	Headlamp Switch, Replace	9-10	DTS & STS	9-11
4.6L Engine	9-8	DeVille, DTS & Seville	9-10	DeVille & Seville	9-11
DTS	9-8	STS	9-10	Column Shift	9-11
DeVille & Seville	9-8	Heater Core, Replace	9-13	Console Shift	9-11
STS	9-8	DTS	9-13	Relay Center Location	9-7
Alternators	19-1	DeVille	9-13	DTS	9-7
Blower Motor, Replace	9-12	STS	9-13	DeVille & Seville	9-7
DTS & STS	9-12	Seville	9-13	STS	9-7
DeVille & Seville	9-12	Ignition Coils, Replace	9-8	Speed Controls (Volume 2)	2-1
Cabin Air Filter, Replace	9-12	3.6L Engine	9-8	Starter Motors	18-1
DTS	9-12	4.4L Engine	9-8	Starter, Replace	9-7
DeVille	9-12	4.6L Engine	9-9	3.6L Engine	9-7
STS	9-13	DTS	9-9	4.4L Engine	9-7
Seville	9-12	DeVille & Seville	9-9	4.6L Engine	9-7
Installation	9-12	STS	9-9	Steering Columns	20-1
Removal	9-12	Ignition Lock, Replace	9-9	Steering Wheel, Replace	9-10
Cooling Fans	17-1	DeVille & DTS	9-9	Technical Service Bulletins	9-14
Cruise Control (Volume 2)	2-1	STS	9-9	Charging System Lamp	
Dash Gauges (Volume 2)	1-1	Seville	9-9	Illuminated	9-14
Dash Panel Service		Ignition Switch, Replace	9-9	2006 DTS	9-14
(Volume 2)	5-1	DeVille & DTS	9-9	Wiper Motor, Replace	9-11
Dimmer Switch, Replace	9-10	STS	9-10	DeVille & DTS	9-11
DeVille, DTS & Seville	9-10	Seville	9-10	STS	9-11
STS	9-10	Instrument Cluster, Replace	9-10	Seville	9-11
Evaporator Core, Replace	9-13	DTS	9-11	Wiper Switch, Replace	9-12
DTS	9-13	DeVille & Seville	9-10	DeVille, DTS & Seville	9-12
DeVille	9-13	STS	9-11	STS	9-12
STS	9-14	Multi-Function Switch, Replace	9-10	Wiper Systems (Volume 2)	3-1
Seville	9-13	DeVille, DTS & Seville	9-10	Wiper Transmission, Replace	9-12
Fuel Pump Relay Location	9-7	STS	9-10	DeVille, DTS & STS	9-12
DeVille, DTS & Seville	9-7	Passive Restraint Systems		Seville	9-12
STS	9-7	(Volume 2)	4-1		

PRECAUTIONS

Air Bag Systems

Refer to "Air Bag System Precautions" in the front of this manual for system disarming and arming procedures.

Battery Ground Cable

Prior to service, disconnect battery ground cable and isolate as required.

FUSE PANEL & FLASHER LOCATION

DeVille & Seville

The engine compartment fuse/relay center is located on the rear righthand side of the engine compartment, near the power steering pump.

The rear fuse block is located under the lefthand side of the rear seat.

The hazard/turn flasher is located at the lefthand side of the instrument panel behind the knee bolster.

DTS

The engine compartment fuse/relay center is located on the rear righthand side of the engine compartment, near the power steering pump.

The rear fuse block is located under the lefthand side of the rear seat.

Hazard and turn signal operation is controlled by the Body Control Module (BCM). The BCM is located behind the righthand side of the instrument panel, near the blower motor.

STS

The engine compartment fuse/relay center is located on the righthand side of the engine compartment.

The instrument panel fuse block is located behind the lefthand side of the instrument panel, near the steering column. The lefthand rear fuse block is located under the lefthand side of the rear seat. The righthand rear fuse block is located under the righthand side of the rear seat.

Hazard and turn signal operation is controlled by the Rear Integration Module (RIM). The RIM is located in the luggage compartment, under the lefthand side trim panel.

FUEL PUMP RELAY LOCATION

DeVille, DTS & Seville

The fuel pump relay is located in the rear fuse block, under the lefthand side of the rear seat.

STS

The fuel pump relay is located in the rear fuse block, under the righthand side of rear seat.

RELAY CENTER LOCATION

DeVille & Seville

The rear compartment relay center is located under the lefthand side of rear seat.

DTS

The engine compartment fuse/relay center is located on the rear righthand side of the engine compartment, near the power steering pump.

STS

The engine compartment fuse/relay center is located on the righthand side of the engine compartment.

STARTER

REPLACE

3.6L Engine

1. Remove left bank exhaust manifold heat shield.
2. Remove left bank catalytic converter to manifold attaching nuts.
3. Raise and support vehicle.

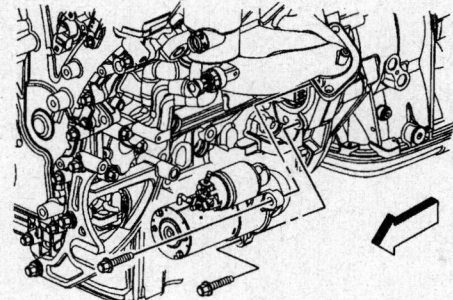

ARM0400000000093

Fig. 1   Starter motor replacement. 3.6L engine

4. Disconnect oxygen sensor electrical connector.
5. Disconnect muffler pipe from left side catalytic converter.
6. Remove left side catalytic converter with heat shield and oxygen sensor from exhaust manifold.
7. Disconnect starter S terminal wire and battery cable, **Fig. 1.**
8. Remove mounting bolts and starter.
9. Remove solenoid and battery cable terminal nuts.
10. Reverse procedure to install, noting the following:
    a. **Torque** starter mounting bolts to 37 ft. lbs.
    b. **Torque** battery cable lead to 115 inch lbs.

4.4L Engine

1. Remove supercharger as outlined under "Supercharger, Replace" in "4.4L Engine" section.
2. Disconnect the battery positive cable from starter.
3. Disconnect wire from the starter S terminal.
4. Remove mounting bolts and starter.
5. Reverse procedure to install, noting the following:
    a. **Torque** starter motor mounting bolts to 22 ft. lbs.
    b. **Torque** starter S terminal nut to 35 inch lbs.
    c. **Torque** battery positive cable to starter nut to 89 inch lbs.

4.6L Engine

1. Remove intake manifold as outlined in "Intake Manifold, Replace" in "4.6L Engine" section.
2. Disconnect starter S terminal wire and battery cable, **Fig. 2.**
3. Remove mounting bolts and starter.
4. Remove solenoid and battery cable terminal nuts.
5. Reverse procedure to install, noting the following:
    a. **Torque** starter mounting bolts to 22 ft. lbs.
    b. **Torque** battery cable lead to 89 inch lbs.
    c. **Torque** S terminal nuts to 35 inch lbs.

ALTERNATOR

REPLACE

3.6L Engine

1. Rotate drive belt tensioner clockwise to release drive belt tension.
2. Slide drive belt off water pump pulley.
3. Slowly release drive belt tensioner and remove drive belt from accessory drive pulleys.
4. Raise and support vehicle.
5. Disconnect alternator electrical connector.
6. Position alternator output BAT terminal boot aside, then remove terminal nut and disconnect battery positive lead from alternator.
7. Remove lower alternator mounting bolts.
8. Lower vehicle.
9. Remove upper mounting bolts and alternator.
10. Reverse procedure to install, noting the following:
    a. **Torque** alternator mounting bolts to 37 ft. lbs.
    b. **Torque** BAT terminal nut to 89 inch lbs.

4.4L Engine

1. Remove six plastic retainers, then the left and righthand front compartment sight shields.
2. Remove mounting bolts and cross-vehicle brace.
3. Remove power steering reservoir and engine oil fill caps, then the intake manifold sight shield.
4. Disconnect air cleaner duct vacuum hose.
5. Loosen air duct clamps at supercharger inlet duct and air cleaner housing cover.
6. Remove air cleaner duct.
7. Disconnect inlet duct PCV hose fitting.
8. Loosen rear screw clamps between front and rear section of inlet duct.
9. Remove six inlet duct to the supercharger ball studs.
10. Remove supercharger inlet duct front section.
11. Remove hinge bolts and hood.
12. Remove covers and wiper arm mounting nuts.
13. Remove upper hood assist rods from ball studs.
14. Remove wiper arm from drive spindle using wiper arm puller tool No. J39822, or equivalent.
15. Remove rear hood seal.
16. Remove three mounting screws and air inlet grille.
17. Remove mounting nut and air inlet grille panel.
18. Remove wiper motor module mounting bolts and disconnect electrical connector. Remove wiper motor module.
19. Remove mounting nuts, bolts and air inlet housing panel.
20. Disconnect Evaporative Emission (EVAP) line fittings from EVAP valve and chassis bundle. Remove EVAP line.

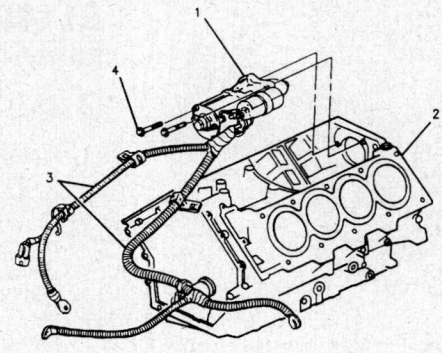

1 STARTER MOTOR ASSEMBLY
2 ENGINE BLOCK ASSEMBLY
3 STARTER SOLENOID
  CABLE ASSEMBLY
4 BOLT, 30 N·m (22 LB. FT.)

GC1129600079000X

Fig. 2 Starter motor replacement. 4.6L engine

21. Remove brake booster hose from supercharger rear port.
22. Loosen rear screw clamp and remove supercharger inlet duct rear section.
23. Rotate tensioner in clockwise using serpentine belt tool No. EN47913, or equivalent, and remove supercharger drive belt.
24. Rotate tensioner clockwise and remove belt from water pump pulley.
25. Remove drive belt from behind tensioner.
26. Allow tensioner to return to relaxed position and remove belt.
27. Remove charge air cooling system pressure and coolant caps.
28. Raise and support vehicle.
29. Remove six plastic retainers and front air deflector.
30. Remove charge air coolant radiator drain plug and drain coolant into suitable container.
31. Disconnect tension clamps using hose clamp pliers tool. No. J38185, or equivalent, then the charge air coolant pump outlet and inlet hoses.
32. Disconnect electrical connector and pump mounting nuts.
33. Open clamps and remove pump.
34. Rotate tensioner clockwise and remove alternator drive belt.
35. Remove upper mounting bolts and cut alternator wiring harness strap.
36. Remove lower mounting bolt, then lift alternator and disconnect electrical connector.
37. Position output battery terminal protective boot aside.
38. Remove terminal nut and disconnect alternator battery positive lead.
39. Remove alternator.
40. Reverse procedure to install, noting the following:
    a. **Torque** output battery terminal nut to 89 inch lbs.
    b. **Torque** alternator mounting bolts to 37 ft. lbs in sequence, **Fig. 3.**

4.6L Engine

DEVILLE & SEVILLE

1. Mark belt running direction.
2. Rotate drive belt tensioner mechanism

upward and away from drive belt using suitable ½ inch breaker bar.
3. Remove serpentine drive belt.
4. Disconnect alternator electrical connector and position protective boot away from output BAT terminal.
5. Remove alternator output BAT terminal nut and disconnect positive lead.
6. Remove mounting bolts and alternator.
7. Reverse procedure to install.

DTS

1. Remove radiator as outlined under "Radiator, Replace."
2. Raise and support vehicle, then remove righthand front tire and wheel.
3. Remove 10 retainers and front wheel housing liner.
4. Release belt tensioner using suitable ½ inch drive breaker.
5. Remove drive belt from power steering pump and release tensioner to original position.
6. Remove belt from lower pulley and idlers.
7. Disconnect alternator engine wiring harness electrical connector.
8. Position alternator starter solenoid cable protective boot aside, then remove alternator terminal nut and starter solenoid cable terminal.
9. Remove mounting bolt and position ground cable aside, then remove alternator.
10. Reverse procedure to install, noting the following:
    a. **Torque** alternator mounting bolts to 37 ft. lbs.
    b. **Torque** alternator terminal nut to 106 inch lbs.

STS

ALL WHEEL DRIVE

1. Mark belt running direction.
2. Rotate drive belt tensioner mechanism upward and away from drive belt using suitable ½ inch breaker bar.
3. Remove serpentine drive belt.
4. Remove upper alternator mounting bolts, then raise and support vehicle.
5. Remove front air deflector.
6. Remove front wheels and righthand side wheelhouse liner.

7. Remove stabilizer shaft link upper and lower mounting nuts.
8. Remove stabilizer shaft link.
9. Rotate stabilizer shaft downward.
10. Lift alternator off of mounting bracket, disconnect electrical connector and position protective boot away from alternator output battery terminal.
11. Remove alternator output battery terminal nut and disconnect battery positive lead.
12. Remove alternator.
13. Reverse procedure to install.

TWO WHEEL DRIVE

1. Mark belt running direction.
2. Rotate drive belt tensioner mechanism upward and away from drive belt using suitable ½ inch breaker bar.
3. Remove serpentine drive belt.
4. Remove upper alternator mounting bolts, then raise and support vehicle.
5. Remove front air deflector.
6. Cut wiring harness tie strap and remove alternator lower mounting bolt.
7. Lift alternator off of mounting bracket, disconnect electrical connector and position protective boot away from alternator output battery terminal.
8. Remove alternator output battery terminal nut and disconnect battery positive lead.
9. Remove alternator.
10. Reverse procedure to install.

IGNITION COILS

REPLACE

3.6L Engine

1. Remove engine cover.
2. Disconnect air cleaner duct from throttle body.
3. **On cylinder Nos. 1 and 3,** remove intake manifold as outlined under "Intake Manifold, Replace" in "3.6L Engine" section.
4. **On all cylinders,** disconnect ignition coil electrical connector.
5. Remove mounting bolts and ignition coil.
6. Reverse procedure to install.

4.4L Engine

1. Remove mounting bolts and cross vehicle brace.
2. Remove engine oil filler and power steering fluid filler caps, then the engine sight shield.
3. Disconnect vacuum hose from air cleaner duct.
4. Remove air cleaner duct.
5. Disconnect PCV hose fitting from underside of inlet duct.
6. Loosen supercharger inlet duct front and rear section screw clamps.
7. Remove six ball studs retaining inlet duct to supercharger.
8. Remove supercharger inlet duct front section.
9. Remove ignition coil cover.
10. Remove mounting bolts and disconnect main electrical connectors required.

11. Remove ignition coil.
12. Reverse procedure to install, noting the following:
    a. Ensure spark plug seals are intact.
    b. **Torque** coil mounting bolts to 89 inch lbs.
    c. **Torque** cross vehicle brace mounting bolts to 83 ft. lbs.

4.6L Engine

DEVILLE & SEVILLE

LEFTHAND

1. Remove mounting bolts and engine sight shield.
2. Disconnect ignition control module electrical connector.
3. Remove engine oil dipstick.
4. Remove ignition mounting bolts in sequence, **Fig. 4**.
5. Remove ignition assembly.
6. Remove mounting screws and ignition control module.
7. Reverse procedure to install, noting the following:
    a. **Torque** ignition control module mounting screws to 7 inch lbs.
    b. **Torque** ignition mounting bolts to 80 inch lbs. in reverse of removal sequence, **Fig. 4**.
    c. **Torque** engine sight shield mounting bolts to 70 inch lbs.

RIGHTHAND

1. Remove mounting bolts and engine sight shield, then disconnect ignition control module electrical connector.
2. **On models equipped with Secondary Air Injection (AIR),** proceed as follows:
    a. Disconnect AIR vent solenoid.
    b. Remove AIR pipe to exhaust manifold mounting bolts.
    c. Mark for installation alignment and disconnect AIR vacuum hoses.
    d. Remove AIR assembly.
3. **On all models,** remove ignition mounting bolts in sequence, **Fig. 4**.
4. Remove ignition assembly.
5. Remove mounting screws and ignition control module.
6. Reverse procedure to install, noting the following:
    a. **Torque** ignition control module mounting screws to 7 inch lbs.
    b. **Torque** ignition assembly mounting bolts to 80 inch lbs., in reverse of removal sequence, **Fig. 4**.
    c. **Torque** engine sight shield mounting bolts to 70 inch lbs.

DTS

1. Remove power steering and engine oil fill caps, then the engine sight shield.
2. Disconnect ignition coil electrical connector.
3. Remove mounting bolts and ignition coils.
4. Reverse procedure to install. **Torque** mounting bolts to 89 inch lbs.

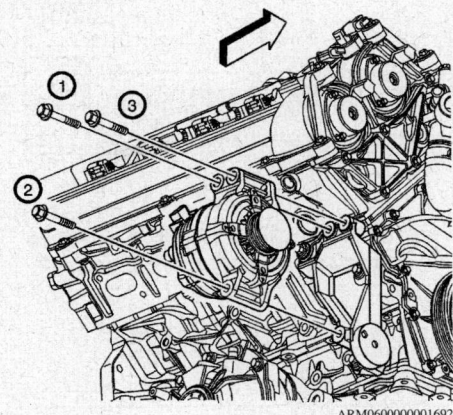

ARM0600000001692

Fig. 3 Alternator tightening sequence

STS

1. Remove mounting bolts and cross vehicle brace.
2. Remove power steering and engine oil fill caps, then the sight shield.
3. Remove ignition coil cover.
4. Disconnect electrical connector, then remove mounting bolt and ignition coil.
5. Reverse procedure to install, nothing the following:
    a. **Torque** coil mounting bolt to 89 inch lbs.
    b. **Torque** cross vehicle brace mounting bolts to 83 ft. lbs.

IGNITION LOCK

REPLACE

DeVille & DTS

1. Remove lefthand knee bolster.
2. Turn ignition switch to OFF position.
3. Remove air bag module as outlined in "Passive Restraint Systems" chapter.
4. Remove horn contact by pushing slightly and twisting counterclockwise.
5. Insert steering column lock pin tool No. J42640, or equivalent.
6. Disconnect Connector Position Assurance (CPA) and coil electrical connector from air bag module.
7. Remove steering column shaft nut.
8. Remove steering wheel using puller tool No. J1859-A and legs tool No. J42578, or equivalents. **Do not thread puller bolts too far into steering wheel.**
9. Remove steering column upper shroud.
10. Remove one screw from upper shroud to access lock cylinder access hole.
11. Turn ignition to START position and push down on ignition lock cylinder retaining pin through access hole using suitable bent tip awl.
12. Release lock cylinder to RUN position and remove it by pulling away from steering column.
13. Reverse procedure to install. **Torque** steering wheel mounting nut to 30 ft. lbs.

Seville

1. Apply parking brake.
2. Remove radio as outlined in "Radio, Replace."
3. Remove HVAC control head.
4. Turn ignition to RUN position.
5. Depress lock cylinder retaining tab through radio opening located on right-hand lower side of ignition switch using suitable flat-headed tool.
6. Remove ignition cylinder.
7. Reverse procedure to install, noting the following:
    a. Insert ignition key into lock cylinder, then turn to RUN position.
    b. Install lock cylinder into instrument panel opening.
    c. Cylinder release button will produce an audible click when fully engaged.
    d. Pull lightly on lock cylinder to ensure secure engagement.

STS

1. Remove steering wheel as outlined under "Steering Wheel Replace."
2. Remove self closeout insulator panel to instrument panel attaching screws, then disconnect electrical connector and pull insulator panel from instrument panel.
3. Release clips and remove lefthand knee bolster trim panel.
4. Remove lower steering column trim cover attaching screws, then separate closeout shroud from lower trim cover.
5. Disconnect power tilt and telescopic switch electrical connector and remove from lower trim cover.
6. Remove upper steering column trim cover mounting screw, then lift trim cover to gain access to lock cylinder access hole.
7. Turn ignition lock cylinder to START position using suitable bent tip awl through access hole.
8. Push ignition lock cylinder retaining pin down using bent tip awl.
9. Release to RUN position and remove ignition lock cylinder.
10. Reverse procedure to install.

IGNITION SWITCH

REPLACE

DeVille & DTS

1. Remove lefthand knee bolster.
2. Remove steering wheel as outlined in "Steering Wheel, Replace."
3. Remove upper and lower steering column trim covers.
4. Remove theft deterrent module from ignition lock cylinder case.
5. Disconnect ignition switch electrical connector.
6. Remove key alarm connector from ignition lock cylinder case.
7. Remove mounting screws and ignition switch.
8. Reverse procedure to install.

Seville

1. Apply parking brake and ensure ignition switch is in OFF or LOCK position.
2. Remove radio as outlined in "Radio, Replace."
3. Remove HVAC control head and knee bolster.
4. Lock steering column using lock pin tool No. J42640, or equivalent, in underside of column.
5. Disconnect electrical connectors.
6. Remove ignition switch lamp socket .
7. Disconnect ignition switch park lock cable.
8. Turn ignition switch to RUN position.
9. Depress park lock cable release button located on bottom of ignition switch at 6 o'clock position, then pull cable to disconnect from ignition switch.
10. Depress lock cylinder retaining tab through radio opening located on righthand lower side of ignition switch using suitable flat-headed tool.
11. Remove ignition cylinder.
12. Remove mounting screws located at access hole in steering column opening and through radio opening, then the ignition switch.
13. Reverse procedure to install, noting the following:
    a. **Torque** ignition switch mounting screws to 18 inch lbs.
    b. Insert ignition key into lock cylinder, then turn to RUN position.
    c. Install lock cylinder into instrument panel opening.
    d. Cylinder release button will produce an audible click when fully engaged.
    e. Pull lightly on lock cylinder to ensure secure engagement.

STS

1. Pull outward to release center trim panel to instrument panel clip retainers, then remove trim panel from instrument panel.
2. Pull outward on instrument cluster trim panel to release clips.
3. Pull cluster trim panel away from instrument panel, then disconnect electrical connector and aspirator tube.
4. Release ignition switch retaining tabs and remove switch.
5. Reverse procedure to install.

HEADLAMP SWITCH
REPLACE

DeVille, DTS & Seville

1. Remove lefthand instrument panel end cap.
2. Remove air outlet duct.
3. Remove switch and disconnect electrical connector.
4. Reverse procedure to install.

STS

Refer to "Multi-Function Switch, Replace" for replacement procedure.

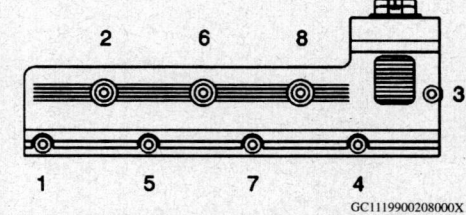

Fig. 4 Ignition control module removal sequence. DeVille & Seville

MULTI-FUNCTION SWITCH
REPLACE

DeVille, DTS & Seville

1. Remove steering wheel as outlined under "Steering Wheel, Replace."
2. Remove steering column trim covers and wiring tie straps.
3. Depress shaft lock using pressing tool No. J23653-SIR, or equivalent, in upper steering shaft.
4. Remove bearing retainer from upper steering shaft and pressing tool from steering shaft.
5. Mark steering column wiring harness routing in lower harness shield for installation alignment.
6. Remove shaft lock, turn signal cancel cam and upper bearing spring.
7. Remove tilt lever handle.
8. Remove multi-function switch mounting screws.
9. Disconnect electrical connectors and remove multi-function switch.
10. Reverse procedure to install. **Torque** multi-function switch mounting screws to 62 inch lbs.

STS

1. Remove steering wheel as outlined under "Steering Wheel Replace."
2. Remove lefthand closeout insulator panel retaining screws, then disconnect electrical connector and pull insulator panel out of instrument panel.
3. Release clips and remove lefthand knee bolster trim panel.
4. Remove lower steering column trim cover mounting screws and disconnect closeout shroud from lower trim cover.
5. Disconnect electrical connector, then remove power tilt and telescopic switch.
6. Remove mounting screw and lift upper steering column trim cover to access to lock cylinder access hole.
7. Turn ignition lock cylinder to START position with bent tip awl in access hole.
8. Push ignition lock cylinder retaining pin with bent tip awl.
9. Release to RUN position and remove ignition lock cylinder.
10. Remove upper trim cover and closeout shroud.
11. Remove multifunction switch mounting

screws and disconnect electrical connector.
12. Remove multifunction switch.
13. Reverse procedure to install.

DIMMER SWITCH
REPLACE

DeVille, DTS & Seville

1. **On models equipped with floor shift,** place transaxle selector in Park and turn ignition switch to RUN position.
2. **On all models,** remove lefthand hush panel, steering column lower cover, toe plate insulator and steering column lower mounting screws.
3. Remove upper steering column bracket to instrument panel mounting nuts and lower column. Prior to lowering column disconnect shift indicator cable and electrical connectors. **Do not force column down.**
4. Remove mounting nut, screw and dimmer switch. Tape actuator rod to steering column.
5. Reverse procedure to install.

STS

1. Pull center trim panel outward to release clip retainers, then remove center trim from instrument panel.
2. Pull outward on cluster trim panel to release retaining clips, then disconnect cluster trim panel electrical connector and aspirator tube.
3. Release dimmer switch retaining tabs, then disconnect electrical connector and remove dimmer switch.
4. Reverse procedure to install.

STEERING WHEEL
REPLACE

1. Turn ignition switch to OFF position.
2. Remove air bag module as outlined in "Passive Restraint Systems" chapter.
3. Remove horn contact by pushing slightly and twisting counterclockwise.
4. Lock steering column using steering column lock pin tool No. J42640, or equivalent.
5. Disconnect Connector Position Assurance (CPA) and coil assembly electrical connector from air bag module.
6. Remove steering column shaft nut.
7. Remove steering wheel using puller tool No. J1859-A and legs tool No. J42578, or equivalents. **Do not thread puller bolts too far into steering wheel.**
8. Reverse procedure to install. **Torque** steering wheel mounting nut to 30 ft. lbs.

INSTRUMENT CLUSTER
REPLACE

DeVille & Seville

1. Remove left and righthand windshield pillar garnish moldings.

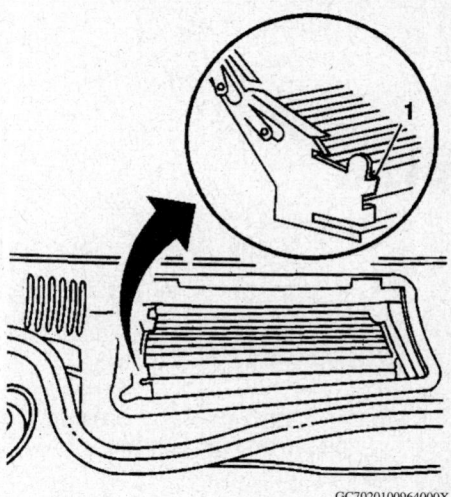

Fig. 7   Cabin air filter replacement. DeVille

GC7020100964000X

module. Ensure leading edge of filter engages filter case holding rib.
4. Engage third new cabin air filter in tab of second filter. Slide third filter into remaining channels of second filter.
5. Fold tab of second filter down.
6. Fold tab of third filter up and over second filter.
7. Install air conditioning and heater module filter cover. Ensure cover is properly seated.
8. Position shift cable grommet, **Fig. 11.**
9. Position lefthand sound insulator to instrument panel and connect electrical connectors.
10. Install lefthand sound insulator fasteners and **Torque** to 18 inch lbs.

STS

1. Remove air inlet grille panel and with both hands release tabs on each side of access cover.
2. Lift up filter access cover and filter from filter housing.
3. Reverse procedure to install.

HEATER CORE
REPLACE
DeVille

1. Drain coolant into suitable container.
2. Disconnect heater hoses from heater core using clamp tool No. J37097-A, or equivalent.
3. Remove instrument panel as outlined in "Dash Panel Service" chapter.
4. Remove heat shield.
5. Remove heater core cover retainers, straps and cover.
6. Remove heater core. Discard case side seals.
7. Reverse procedure to install.

DTS

1. Drain cooling system.
2. Recover air condition refrigerant as outlined in "Air Conditioning" chapter.
3. Remove evaporator tube from thermal expansion valve.
4. Remove heater hoses from heater core.
5. Remove brake pedal bracket, then pull back and position carpet aside.
6. Remove lower instrument panel support brace.
7. Position auxiliary air distribution duct aside.
8. Remove instrument panel as outlined in "Dash Panel Service" chapter.
9. Disconnect HVAC module electrical connectors.
10. Remove lefthand floor duct.
11. Remove TXV pass through seal, then the heater and air condition pipe cover from HVAC module, **Fig. 12.**
12. Remove tube clamp and heater core.
13. Reverse procedure to install.

Seville

1. Drain coolant into suitable container.
2. Disconnect heater hoses from heater core using clamp tool No. J37097-A, or equivalent.
3. Remove instrument panel as outlined in "Dash Panel Service" chapter.
4. Remove heat shield.
5. Remove retainers, straps and heater core cover.
6. Remove heater core. Discard case side seals.
7. Reverse procedure to install.

STS

1. Recover air conditioning refrigerant as outlined in "Air Conditioning" chapter.
2. Disconnect both battery cables, then remove heat shield and battery.
3. Drain coolant into suitable container.
4. Disconnect heater inlet and outlet hoses using tool No. J38185, or equivalent.
5. Disconnect both air condition lines at cowl using tool No. J45689, or equivalent.
6. Remove instrument panel as outlined in "Dash Panel Service" chapter.
7. Remove air inlet assembly and disconnect HVAC module electrical connector.
8. Disconnect HVAC module drain tube from floor, then press tab and release lefthand rear duct from HVAC module.
9. Disconnect lefthand rear heater duct from HVAC module, then press tab and release righthand rear duct from HVAC module.
10. Disconnect righthand rear heater ducts from HVAC module and remove lower lefthand HVAC module mounting nut.
11. Remove upper lefthand mounting nut and HVAC module.
12. Remove heater hose bracket and slide heater core out of HVAC module.
13. Reverse procedure to install.

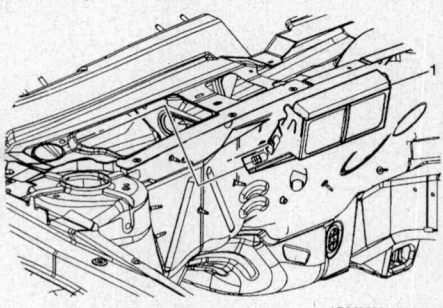

ARM0500000000930

Fig. 8   Cabin air filter replacement. DTS

EVAPORATOR CORE
REPLACE
DeVille

1. Recover refrigerant as outlined in "Air Conditioning" chapter.
2. Disconnect evaporator lines.
3. Disconnect heater hoses using clamp tool No. J37097-A, or equivalent.
4. Remove center console.
5. Remove instrument panel as outlined in "Dash Panel Service" chapter.
6. Remove evaporator drain, defroster and heater duct.
7. Remove heater and evaporator module.
8. Remove heater and evaporator tube seal, then the upper evaporator case.
9. Remove evaporator core and case seals.
10. Reverse procedure to install, noting the following:
    a. **Torque** HVAC module mounting nuts to 80 inch lbs.
    b. **Torque** evaporator nut to 18 ft. lbs.

DTS

1. Remove heater core as outlined under "Heater Core, Replace."
2. Remove evaporator tube and thermal expansion valve mounting bolts, **Fig. 13.**
3. Remove thermal expansion valve and evaporator tube O-rings. Discard O-rings.
4. Remove evaporator tube and bracket, then the thermal expansion valve.
5. Remove air inlet housing.
6. Remove blower motor resistor.
7. Remove mounting screws and upper evaporator case, **Fig. 14.**
8. Remove evaporator core.
9. Reverse procedure to install.

Seville

1. Recover refrigerant as outlined in "Air Conditioning" chapter.
2. Disconnect evaporator lines.
3. Disconnect heater hoses using clamp tool No. J37097-A, or equivalent.
4. Remove center console.
5. Remove instrument panel as outlined in "Dash Panel Service" chapter.
6. Remove evaporator drain, defroster

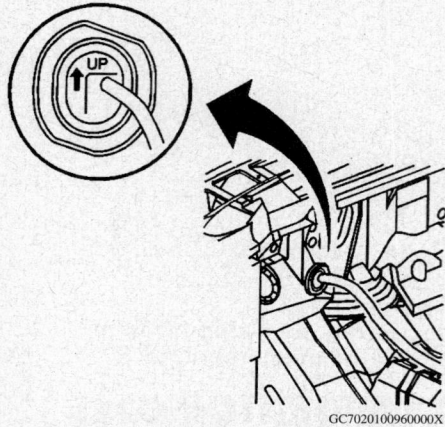

GC7020100960000X

Fig. 9 Cabin air filter access cover replacement. Seville

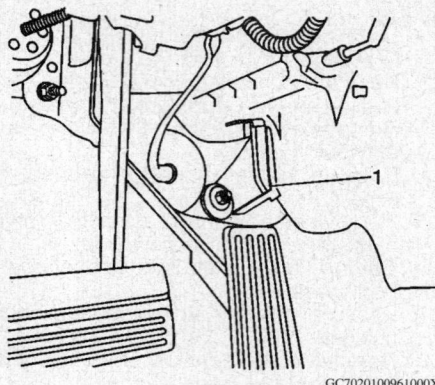

GC7020100961000X

Fig. 10 Cabin air filter replacement. Seville

GC7020100962000X

Fig. 11 Shift cable grommet positioning. Seville

and heater duct assembly.

7. Remove heater and evaporator module.
8. Remove heater and evaporator tube seal, then the upper evaporator case.
9. Remove evaporator core and case seals.
10. Reverse procedure to install, noting the following:
    a. **Torque** HVAC module mounting nuts to 80 inch lbs.
    b. **Torque** evaporator nut to 18 ft. lbs.

STS

1. Recover air conditioning refrigerant as outlined in "Air Conditioning" chapter.
2. Disconnect both battery cables, then remove heat shield and battery.
3. Drain coolant into suitable container.
4. Disconnect heater inlet and outlet hoses using clamp tool No. J38185 or equivalent.
5. Disconnect both air condition lines at cowl using removal tool No. J45689 or equivalent.
6. Remove instrument panel as outlined in "Dash Panel Service" chapter.
7. Remove air inlet and disconnect HVAC module electrical connector.
8. Disconnect HVAC module drain tube from floor, then press tab and release lefthand rear duct from HVAC module.
9. Disconnect lefthand rear heater duct from HVAC module, then press tab and release righthand rear duct from the HVAC module.
10. Disconnect righthand rear heater ducts from HVAC module, then remove lower lefthand HVAC module mounting nut.
11. Remove upper lefthand mounting nut and HVAC module.
12. Remove insulation from thermal expansion valve, then the HVAC line clamp screw and clamp.
13. Remove TXV to evaporator bolts and TXV line bracket.
14. Remove TXV from evaporator core, then separate TXV from air condition lines by pulling straight out.

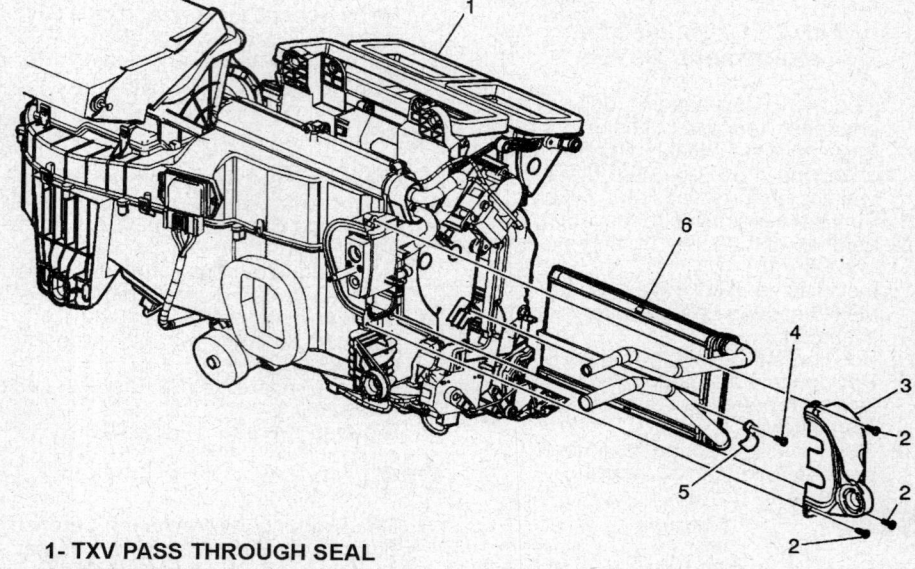

1- TXV PASS THROUGH SEAL
2- SCREWS
3- HEATER & A/C PIPE COVER
4- SCREW
5- HEATER CORE TUBE CLAMP
6- HEATER CORE

ARM0500000000931

Fig. 12 Heater core replacement. DTS

15. Remove screws and clips that hold case together.
16. Disconnect thermistor electrical connector and separate HVAC module.
17. Remove thermistor and evaporator core.
18. Reverse procedure to install.

TECHNICAL SERVICE BULLETINS

Charging System Lamp Illuminated

2006 DTS

On some of these models, the charging system light may be illuminated in the instrument panel cluster and the "Service Battery Charging System" message may be displayed on the Driver Information Center. Diagnostic Trouble Codes (DTCs) B1405 and/or B1516 may be set.

This condition may be caused by Body Control Model (BCM) resetting while cranking the engine under low voltage conditions. The battery current sensor may draw excessive current during the BCM reset

To correct this condition program the BCM with the latest software. **Do not replace the battery current sensor or the BCM.**

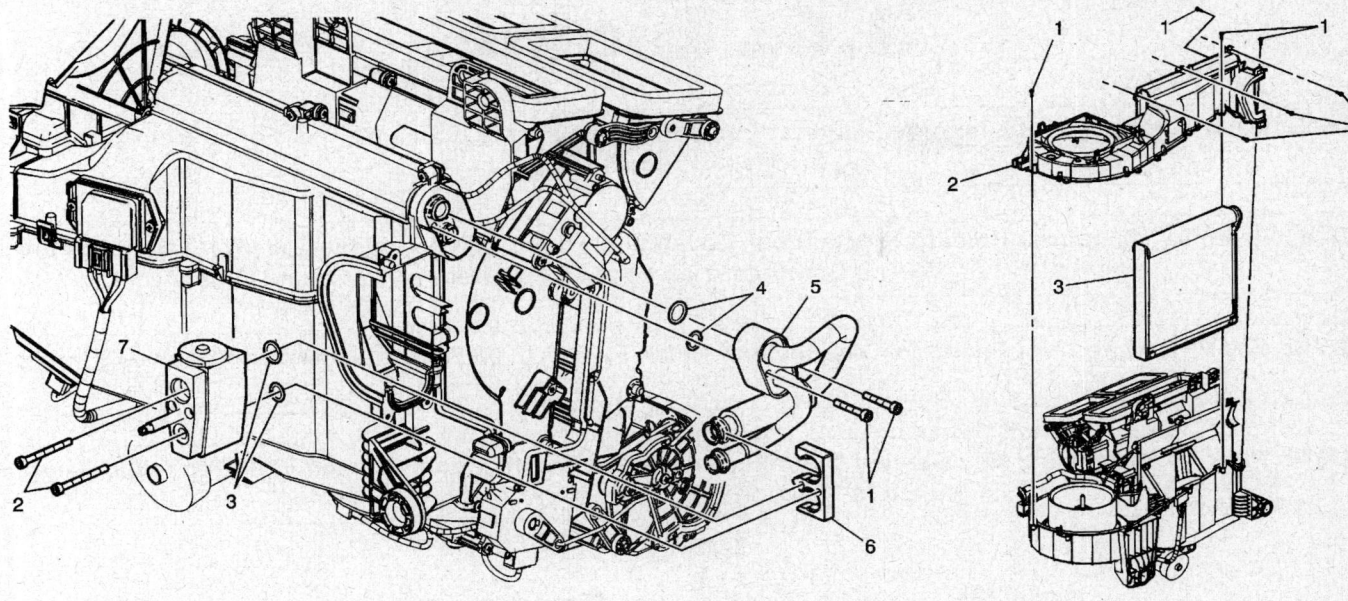

1- A/C EVAPORATOR TUBE BOLTS
2- THERMAL EXPANSION VALVE BOLTS
3- THERMAL EXPANSION VALVE O-RING
4- EVAPORATOR TUBE O-RING
5- EVAPORATOR TUBE
6- EVAPORATOR TUBE BRACKET
7- THERMAL EXPANSION VALVE

ARM0500000000939

Fig. 13 Thermal expansion valve replacement. DTS

1- CASE SCREWS
2- EVAPORATOR CASE
3- EVAPORATOR CORE

ARM0500000000938

Fig. 14 Evaporator core
replacement DTS

3.6L Engine

NOTE: Refer To "Air Bag System Precautions" Located In The Front Of This Manual For System Disarming & Arming Procedures.

NOTE: Refer To "Computer Relearn Procedures" Located In The Front Of This Manual When Battery Power To The Computer Has Been Interrupted.

NOTE: For Procedures Not Found In This Section, Refer To The "3.6L Engine" Section In The "CTS" chapter.

NOTE: Prior To Performing Any Service Operations Listed In This Section, Consult The "Technical Service Bulletins" Section For Related Information.

INDEX

	Page No.
Compression Pressure	9-16
Engine Rebuilding Specifications	29-1
Engine, Replace	9-17
Engine Mount, Replace	9-16

	Page No.
Lefthand	9-16
Righthand	9-16
All Wheel Drive	9-16
Two-Wheel Drive	9-17
Precautions	9-16

	Page No.
Air Bag Systems	9-16
Battery Ground Cable	9-16
Fuel Pressure Relief	9-16
Tightening Specifications	9-18
Valve Adjustment	9-17

PRECAUTIONS

Air Bag Systems

Refer to "Air Bag System Precautions" in the front of this manual for system disarming and arming procedures.

Battery Ground Cable

Prior to service, disconnect battery ground cable and isolate as required.

Fuel Pressure Relief

1. Turn ignition switch to OFF position.
2. Disconnect battery ground cable and isolate as required.
3. Remove mounting bolts and cross-vehicle brace.
4. Remove oil fill cap.
5. Disconnect ball studs and remove engine cover/sight shield.
6. Loosen fuel filler cap to relieve fuel tank vapor pressure.
7. Remove fuel pressure service connection cap.
8. Install tool Nos. J34730-1A and J42242, or equivalents, to fuel pressure service connection.
9. Place bleed hose into suitable container, then open bleed valve to relieve fuel system.
10. Place suitable shop towel under connections to protect fuel spillage.
11. Remove tool Nos. J34730-1A and J42242, or equivalents, from service connections.
12. Install cap to fuel pressure service connection.

13. Remove six plastic retainers and three engine compartment sight shields.
14. Remove air cleaner duct resonator Positive Crankcase Ventilation (PCV) hose.
15. Loosen clamps and remove air cleaner duct.
16. Disconnect intake manifold brake booster vacuum hose.
17. Disconnect purge solenoid valve electrical connector and purge line.
18. Remove wiring harness retainer and disconnect throttle body electrical connector.
19. Remove stud, mounting bolt and upper intake manifold brace.
20. Disconnect righthand bank valve cover Positive Crankcase Ventilation (PCV) hose.
21. Disconnect barometric pressure sensor and intake manifold runner control solenoid electrical connectors.
22. Remove injector harness bracket mounting bolt.
23. Remove lefthand bank ignition coil wiring harness from bracket.
24. Remove mounting bolts and upper intake manifold with throttle body.
25. Wrap suitable shop towel around fitting and connect suitable fuel pressure gauge to fuel pressure valve.
26. Install bleed hose into suitable container.
27. Open valve and bleed system pressure.

COMPRESSION PRESSURE

The minimum compression in any one cylinder should not be less than 70 percent of the highest cylinder. No cylinder should read less than 140 psi.

ENGINE MOUNT
REPLACE

Lefthand

1. Raise and support vehicle, then support oil pan using suitable jack with block of wood.
2. Remove lower engine mount mounting nut and remove mount by raising engine using jack.
3. Remove upper mounting nut and engine mount.
4. Reverse procedure to install.

Righthand

ALL WHEEL DRIVE

1. Raise and support vehicle.
2. Remove mounting bolts and exhaust manifold heat shield.
3. Remove Engine Coolant Temperature (ECT) sensor.
4. Remove mounting bolts and exhaust manifold.
5. Support oil pan using suitable jack with block of wood.
6. Remove righthand engine mount upper mounting nut, **Do not distort or bend engine mount heat shield.**
7. Remove mounting bolts and engine mount bracket.
8. Remove mounting nut and engine mount.
9. Reverse procedure to install.

TWO-WHEEL DRIVE

1. Raise and support vehicle, then support oil pan using suitable jack with block of wood.
2. Remove lower engine mount mounting nut, and remove mount by raising engine using jack.
3. Remove upper mounting nut and engine mount.
4. Reverse procedure to install.

ENGINE

REPLACE

1. Turn front wheels to straight ahead position.
2. Turn ignition switch to LOCK position and remove key.
3. Lock steering column by inserting steering column anti-rotation pin tool No. J42640, or equivalent, through access hole in lower steering column trim cover.
4. Recover air conditioning refrigerant as outlined in "Air Conditioning" chapter.
5. Relieve fuel system pressure as outlined in "Precautions."
6. Remove fuel injector sight shield and PCV hose from air cleaner duct resonator.
7. Loosen clamps and remove air cleaner duct.
8. Disconnect cooling fan electrical connectors and remove cooling fan wiring harnesses from fan shroud.
9. Secure wiring harnesses to vehicle, then drain cooling system into suitable container. **Do not disconnect surge hoses from engine or radiator.**
10. Disconnect surge tank outlet hose from surge tank, then position and secure surge hose to engine.
11. Disconnect surge tank inlet hose from water outlet housing and radiator, then position and secure surge tank inlet hose.
12. Remove cowl panel and inlet heater hose from heater core.
13. Disconnect purge line from purge solenoid, then fuel pipe from fuel rail.
14. Plug fuel pipe and cap fuel rail.
15. Remove wipers arms and air inlet grille panel.
16. Remove mounting bolts and nuts, then the windshield frame reinforcement.
17. Rotate wiper motor crank arm to opposite of park position by pushing or pulling on transmission linkage.
18. Disconnect wiper motor electrical connector, then push harness and grommet through hole in plenum.
19. Remove mounting bolts and wiper transmission.
20. Disconnect air conditioning suction hose from evaporator and remove bracket from shock tower. **Do not disconnect suction hose from air condition compressor or liquid line from condenser.**
21. Position and secure suction hose to engine, then disconnect air conditioning pressure switch electrical connector and remove liquid line.
22. Remove mounting bolts and radiator support brackets.
23. Disconnect brake booster check valve and vacuum hose from brake booster and secure hose to engine.
24. Disconnect brake fluid level switch electrical connector from master cylinder.
25. Disconnect electrical connector from Mass Air Flow (MAF) sensor.
26. Unlock and disconnect instrument electrical connector from engine located at rear of lefthand bank two cylinder head. Position and secure harness to vehicle.
27. Disconnect engine module wiring harness connectors from underhood electrical center and wiring harness from transmission control module.
28. Remove ground bolt and wire from longitudinal rail, then disconnect engine harness electrical connector at longitudinal rail.
29. Position and secure ground wire, engine harness and TCM harness to engine.
30. Remove master cylinder nuts, **Do not disconnect brake pipes from master cylinder.** Remove and secure master cylinder to engine.
31. Raise and support vehicle, then remove heated oxygen sensors from exhaust pipes.
32. Remove mounting bolts and floor panel tunnel brace from floor panel.
33. Support exhaust system with suitable jack and remove exhaust pipes to exhaust manifolds nuts.
34. Pry front exhaust hangers free from rear suspension hanger rods and tail pipe hangers free from tail pipe hanger rods.
35. Lower exhaust system with assistant's aid and remove exhaust manifold seals.
36. Support propeller shaft close to support bearing using suitable jack.
37. Mark location of propeller shaft consent velocity joint to transfer case flange for installation alignment.
38. Remove retainers, then push front propeller shaft toward rear and out of vehicle.
39. Remove air deflector and washer bottle bracket. **Do not remove water bottle.**
40. Disconnect side air baffles from radiator and lefthand front brake pipe retainer along with brake pipe from longitudinal rail.
41. Remove righthand front brake pipe from brake pipe bundle retainer and disconnect rear brake pipes from brake pressure modulator valve. Plug brake pipes and brake modulator valve.
42. Remove front tire and wheel assemblies.
43. Mark shafts for installation alignment.
44. Remove center intermediate shaft to lower intermediate shaft mounting bolt and lower intermediate shaft to power steering gear mounting bolt.
45. Remove lower intermediate shaft from center intermediate shaft.
46. Remove lower engine mount nuts and disconnect transmission shift linkage from transmission.
47. Disconnect low oil level sensor electrical connector and remove headlamp leveling sensors.
48. Secure shock modules to lower control arms with suitable strap.
49. Remove shock to yoke mounting nut and bolt by pulling up slightly on lower control arm.
50. Remove yoke to lower control arm mounting nut and separate yoke from lower control arm using separation tool No. J24319-B, or equivalent.
51. Remove yoke.
52. **On models equipped with Magnaride or headlamp sensors,** disconnect sensor link from the upper control arm.
53. **On all models,** hold upper control arm to steering knuckle using suitable hex head tool.
54. Remove upper control arm to steering knuckle nut and separate upper control arm from steering knuckle.
55. Lower vehicle and remove shock module.
56. Raise vehicle and position suitable powertrain or engine lift table below frame, engine and transmission.
57. Remove transmission brace to underbody and front frame mounting bolts.
58. Lower table or raise vehicle then remove engine, transmission, front frame and front suspension assembly. **Ensure all hoses, wires, pipes and shock modules clear vehicle during removal.**
59. Reverse procedure to install.

VALVE ADJUSTMENT

This engine is equipped with hydraulic valve lash adjusters. No adjustment is required.

TIGHTENING SPECIFICATIONS

Year	Component	Torque Ft. Lbs.
2005–08	Air Cleaner Outlet Duct Clamp	27①
	Air Condition Compressor Bracket, Front	37
	Air Condition Compressor Bracket, Rear	17
	Air Condition Compressor Hose Assembly	80①
	Alternator	37
	Catalytic Converter To Exhaust Manifold	37
	Close Out Cover	89①
	Coolant Outlet	89①
	Crankshaft Position Sensor	89①
	Drive Belt Idler Pulley	37
	Drive Belt Tensioner	37
	Engine Control Module	89①
	Engine Coolant Temperature Sensor	18
	Engine Mount	59
	Engine Mount Bracket To Cylinder Block (M8 Bolt)	28
	Engine Mount Bracket To Cylinder Block (M11 Bolt)	45
	Engine Mount To Bracket	59
	Engine Mount Bracket	44
	EVAP Purge Valve Bolt	89①
	Exhaust Manifold Heat Shield	89①
	Ground Cable	37
	Heater Inlet/Outlet Pipe	89①
	Ignition Coil	89①
	Knock Sensor	17
	MAP Sensor	89①
	Oil Dipstick Tube	89①
	Oil Drain Plug	18
	Oil Gallery Plug	23
	Oil Level Sensor	89①
	Oil Pressure Sender	15
	Oxygen Sensor	30
	Power Steering Pump Bracket To Engine	37
	Power Steering Pump Reservoir, Lower	18
	Power Steering Pump Reservoir, Upper	80①
	Power Steering Pump To Bracket	16
	Starter Motor	37
	Suction Screen	89①
	Thermostat Housing	89①
	Transmission Mount To Transmission	45
	Transmission To Engine	37

① — Inch lbs.

4.4L Engine

NOTE: Refer To "Air Bag System Precautions" Located In The Front Of This Manual For System Disarming & Arming Procedures.

NOTE: Refer To "Computer Relearn Procedures" Located In The Front Of This Manual When Battery Power To The Computer Has Been Interrupted.

NOTE: Prior To Performing Any Service Operations Listed In This Section, Consult The "Technical Service Bulletins" Section For Related Information.

INDEX

	Page No.
Camshaft, Replace	9-25
Installation	9-25
Removal	9-25
Camshaft Lobe Lift Specifications	9-22
Compression Pressure	9-19
Cooling System Bleed	9-29
Crankshaft Damper, Replace	9-22
Crankshaft Rear Oil Seal, Replace	9-27
Installation	9-27
Removal	9-27
Cylinder Head, Replace	9-21
Drive Belt, Replace	9-29
Air Conditioning, Power Steering & Water Pump	9-29
Alternator	9-29
Supercharger	9-29
Engine Rebuilding Specifications	29-1
Engine, Replace	9-19
Engine Mount, Replace	9-19
Exhaust Manifold, Replace	9-20
Lefthand	9-20
Righthand	9-21
Front Cover, Replace	9-22
Fuel Filter, Replace	9-30

	Page No.
Fuel Pump, Replace	9-30
Hydraulic Lifters, Replace	9-22
Intake Manifold, Replace	9-20
Main & Rod Bearings	9-26
Connecting Rod	9-26
Crankshaft	9-27
Oil Cooler, Replace	9-29
Oil Pan, Replace	9-28
Oil Pump, Replace	9-28
Installation	9-28
Removal	9-28
Oil Pump Service	9-28
Assembly	9-29
Disassemble	9-28
Piston & Rod Assembly	9-25
Pistons, Pins & Rings	9-25
Precautions	9-19
Air Bag Systems	9-19
Battery Ground Cable	9-19
Fuel System Pressure Relief	9-19
Radiator, Replace	9-30
Rocker Arms	9-22
Supercharger, Replace	9-30
Technical Service Bulletins	9-30
Very Faint Engine Whine Noise At Speeds Of 0-30 mph At 1000-2500 RPM	9-31

	Page No.
2005–07 STS	9-31
Muffler, Tailpipes, Exhaust Tips Do Not Appear Centered In Rear Fascia Cut Outs	9-30
2005–07 STS	9-30
Whine, Whistle, Ringing Type Noise Heard From Front of Engine	9-31
2005 STS w/3.6L Engine	9-31
Thermostat, Replace	9-29
Tightening Specifications	9-32
Timing Chain, Replace	9-23
Primary	9-23
Installation	9-23
Removal	9-23
Secondary	9-23
Lefthand	9-23
Righthand	9-24
Timing Chain Tensioner, Replace	9-25
Valve Adjustment	9-22
Valve Clearance Specifications	9-22
Valve Cover, Replace	9-22
Lefthand	9-22
Righthand	9-22
Water Outlet Housing, Replace	9-29
Water Pump, Replace	9-29

PRECAUTIONS

Air Bag Systems

Refer to "Air Bag System Precautions" in the front of this manual for system disarming and arming procedures.

Battery Ground Cable

Prior to service, disconnect battery ground cable and isolate as required.

Fuel System Pressure Relief

A small amount of fuel may be released when servicing fuel connections even after pressure is released. Cover all fuel connections with shop towel before servicing.
1. Remove fuel pump fuse.
2. Relieve fuel tank vapor pressure by loosen fuel filler cap.
3. Remove fuel rail service port cap.
4. Wrap shop towel around fitting and depress (open) fuel rail test port valve using suitable, small flat-bladed tool.
5. Remove shop towel and place in suitable container.
6. Install fuel rail service port cap.

COMPRESSION PRESSURE

Perform compression test with engine at normal operating temperature, spark plugs removed and throttle wide open. Disable the ignition and fuel systems. Lowest cylinder must be within 70% of highest cylinder with a minimum pressure of 140 psi.

ENGINE MOUNT

REPLACE

1. Raise and support vehicle.
2. Remove mounting bolts and cross-vehicle brace.
3. Remove power steering and engine oil fill caps, then the sight shield.
4. Remove exhaust manifold as outlined under "Exhaust Manifold, Replace."
5. Support engine with suitable screw jack and block of wood under oil pan.
6. Remove upper engine mount mounting nut.
7. Remove mounting bolts and engine mount bracket. **Do not distort or bend engine mount heat shield.**
8. Remove lower mounting nut and engine mount.

ENGINE

REPLACE

1. Lock steering using steering column anti-rotation pin tool No. J42640, or equivalent.
2. Remove supercharger front and rear inlet duct assemblies as outlined under "Supercharger, Replace."

3. Drain coolant system into suitable container.
4. Rotate tensioner clockwise and remove belt from water pump pulley.
5. Remove drive belt from behind tensioner.
6. Allow tensioner to return to relaxed position and remove belt.
7. Remove charge air cooling system pressure and coolant caps.
8. Raise and support vehicle.
9. Remove six plastic retainers and front air deflector.
10. Remove charge air coolant radiator drain plug and drain coolant into suitable container.
11. Disconnect water outlet housing surge tank inlet hose fitting.
12. Disconnect and position radiator inlet hose aside.
13. Recover air conditioning refrigerant as outlined in "Air Conditioning" chapter.
14. Disconnect condenser tube quick connect fitting and liquid line from strut tower clip.
15. Disconnect quick connect fitting and liquid line from evaporator core. Remove liquid line and discard O-ring seals.
16. Remove lefthand tire and wheel assembly, then three plastic retainers and engine splash shield.
17. Remove compressor suction hose mounting bolt and lower vehicle.
18. Remove suction hose clamp screw and separate line from bracket.
19. Remove bulk head quick connect fitting and disconnect suction hose from evaporator core.
20. Remove hose hose. Discard O-ring seals.
21. Remove from lefthand shock tower retainer and position suction hose to engine.
22. Disconnect brake fluid level switch electrical connector and remove master cylinder mounting nuts.
23. Position master cylinder to engine and hold in place with suitable mechanics wire. **Do not disconnect brake lines from master cylinder.**
24. Remove fuel pump fuse.
25. Relieve tank vapor pressure by loosen fuel filler cap.
26. Remove fuel rail service port cap.
27. Wrap shop towel around fitting and depress (open) fuel rail test port valve using suitable, small flat-bladed tool.
28. Remove shop towel and place in suitable container.
29. Install fuel rail service port cap.
30. Disconnect fuel line from fuel rail and position line aside.
31. Disconnect charge air cooler reservoir hose from reservoir and position line aside.
32. Disconnect engine wiring harness connector C102 at front of firewall, then the underhood fuse block connector C5 between righthand shock tower and camshaft cover.
33. Remove underhood fuse and relay center cover, then disconnect battery current sensor electrical connector.
34. Remove battery ground cable bolt from righthand shock tower.

35. Remove ground cable retainer from righthand shock tower stud and position cable aside.
36. Disconnect both of chassis electrical connectors at righthand shock tower top and position wires to engine.
37. Disconnect engine wire harness C5 connector from inside of underhood electrical center.
38. Loosen crank adapter shaft fan nut using fan clutch remove and installer tool No. J41240, or equivalent. **Do not completely remove fan from crank adapter shaft.**
39. Disconnect condenser tube from retainer clip, then remove mounting bolts and cooling fan shroud.
40. Remove nut and fan.
41. Raise and support vehicle, then remove lefthand front tire and wheel assembly.
42. Remove three plastic retainers and lefthand engine splash shield.
43. Remove plastic retainers, then the left and righthand wheel housing liners.
44. Remove windshield washer reservoir brace from frame and disconnect chassis wire harness electrical connector through righthand wheel housing opening.
45. Disconnect transmission oil cooler lines near air conditioning compressor through lefthand wheel housing opening.
46. Remove bolt and separate center from lower intermediate shaft.
47. Remove power steering cooler lines to radiator mounting bolts.
48. Disconnect clamp tension using suitable hose clamp pliers, then disconnect radiator inlet hose from radiator and pipe. Remove hose.
49. Disconnect clamp tension using suitable hose clamp pliers and radiator outlet hose from pipe.
50. Remove mounting bolts and supercharger charge air cooler radiator.
51. Remove upper and lower condenser mounting bolts, then disconnect radiator side air baffle lower retaining pins.
52. Position condenser aside.
53. Remove transmission oil cooler mount bolts and lower vehicle.
54. Disconnect clamp tension using suitable hose clamp pliers and radiator outlet hose.
55. Disconnect clamp tension using suitable hose clamp pliers and remove surge tank inlet hose from radiator.
56. Remove mounting bolts and radiator support bracket.
57. Disconnect upper air baffle retaining pins, then remove radiator, condenser and transmission oil cooler.
58. Raise and support vehicle.
59. Remove mounting bracket bolts, then position power steering oil cooler to engine and secure with suitable mechanics wire.
60. Disconnect heater hose from water outlet housing and position to vehicle.
61. Remove transmission as outlined in **MOTOR's "Domestic Transmission, In-Vehicle Service" manual or "Transmission Service DVD."**
62. Remove front frame rails brake bundle

clips. **Do not remove lines from clips.**
63. Disconnect fuel filter feed line and EVAP hose connection from filter rear.
64. Disconnect rear brake lines from bracket above righthand side of rear axle.
65. Remove fuel and brake line bundle retainers from frame rail along length of vehicle. **Do not remove retainers from lines.**
66. Remove fuel and brake line bundle bracket from righthand wheel housing.
67. Disconnect outlet hose from righthand frame rail heater outlet pipe. Position hose aside.
68. Disconnect water housing inlet hose, Position hose aside.
69. **On models equipped with Magnaride,** disconnect shock modules' top electrical connectors.
70. **On all models,** remove left and righthand shock modules' upper mounting bolts. Secure modules to front frame with suitable mechanics wire.
71. Raise vehicle, then place suitable lift table under engine, subframe and front suspension.
72. **Support rear of vehicle with suitable jack stands.**
73. Preload weight of engine, subframe and front suspension by raising lift table or lowering vehicle.
74. Remove front frame bolts.
75. Lower table and/or raise vehicle to remove engine, front frame, fuel/brake bundle and front suspension with assistant's aid. **Ensure hoses, wires, pipes and shock modules clear vehicle during removal.**
76. Install engine lift bracket tool No. J28467-86, or equivalent, to lefthand cylinder head and engine lift bracket tool No. J28467-87, or equivalent, to righthand cylinder head.
77. Remove engine from front frame using hoist
78. Reverse procedure to install.

INTAKE MANIFOLD
REPLACE

The intake manifold is an integral part of the Roots-style supercharger. A forward section to the induction system consists of a central intake port that splits into twin thin wall cast aluminum induction tubes.

Refer to "Supercharger, Replace" for intake manifold replacement procedure.

EXHAUST MANIFOLD
REPLACE

Lefthand

1. Remove mounting bolts and cross vehicle brace.
2. Remove power steering and engine oil fill caps, then the sight shield.
3. Disconnect PCV tube from air cleaner duct.
4. Loosen air duct clamp at throttle body Mass Air Flow/Intake Air Temperature (MAF/IAT) sensor.
5. Remove air cleaner duct.

6. Disconnect electrical connector, then remove mounting screws and MAF/IAT sensor.
7. Remove coolant hose from top of air cleaner assembly. Position hose aside.
8. Remove mounting screws and air cleaner.
9. Remove nut attaching air conditioning lines to lefthand shock tower, position lines aside.
10. Remove exhaust manifold heat shield front upper mounting bolt.
11. Disconnect master cylinder electrical connector.
12. Remove master cylinder mounting nuts, then position master cylinder toward engine.
13. Remove exhaust heat shield rear upper mounting bolt.
14. Disconnect both heated oxygen sensor pigtail connectors from wiring harness connector.
15. Remove power steering gear as outlined in "Front Suspension & Steering" section.
16. Mark position of steering column center intermediate shaft to lower intermediate shaft installation reference.
17. Remove steering column center intermediate shaft to lower intermediate shaft retaining bolts.
18. Disconnect steering column lower intermediate shaft from center intermediate shaft.
19. Disconnect electrical connectors and remove oxygen sensors from exhaust pipes.
20. Remove floor panel tunnel brace from floor panel.
21. Support exhaust system
22. Remove exhaust pipe to manifold attaching nuts.
23. Pry front exhaust hangers free from rear suspension hanger rods.
24. Apply suitable lubricant to tail pipe hanger rods and pry tail pipe hangers free from the tail pipe hanger rods.
25. Lower and remove exhaust system. Discard exhaust manifold seals.
26. Disconnect electrical connectors and remove oxygen sensors from exhaust manifolds.
27. Remove remaining bolts from exhaust manifold heat shield.
28. Remove exhaust manifold mounting bolts and nuts. Discard mounting bolts.
29. Remove studs and exhaust manifold. Discard gasket.
30. Reverse procedure to install.

Righthand

1. Remove supercharger front and rear inlet duct assemblies as outlined under "Supercharger, Replace."
2. Rotate tensioner in clockwise using serpentine belt tool No. EN47913, or equivalent, and remove supercharger drive belt.
3. Rotate tensioner clockwise and remove belt from water pump pulley.
4. Remove drive belt from behind tensioner.
5. Allow tensioner to return to relaxed position and remove belt.

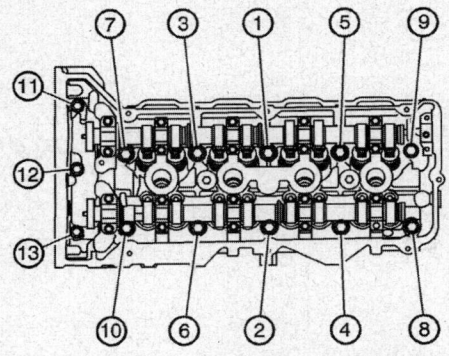

Fig. 1 Lefthand cylinder head bolt tightening sequence

ARM0700000000003

6. Remove charge air cooling system pressure and coolant caps.
7. Raise and support vehicle.
8. Remove six plastic retainers and front air deflector.
9. Remove charge air coolant radiator drain plug and drain coolant into suitable container.
10. Disconnect tension clamps using hose clamp pliers tool. No. J38185, or equivalent, then the charge air coolant pump outlet and inlet hoses.
11. Disconnect charge air coolant pump electrical connector.
12. Remove pump mounting nuts and clamps, then the pump.
13. Rotate tensioner clockwise and remove alternator drive belt.
14. Remove upper mounting bolts and cut alternator wiring harness strap.
15. Remove lower mounting bolt, then lift alternator and disconnect electrical connector.
16. Position output battery terminal protective boot aside.
17. Remove terminal nut and disconnect alternator battery positive lead.
18. Remove alternator.
19. Disconnect electrical connector and remove oxygen sensors from exhaust pipes.
20. Remove floor panel tunnel brace from floor panel.
21. Support exhaust system
22. Remove exhaust pipe to manifold mounting nuts.
23. Pry front exhaust hangers free from rear suspension hanger rods.
24. Apply suitable lubricant to tail pipe hanger rods and pry tail pipe hangers free from the tail pipe hanger rods.
25. Lower and remove exhaust system. Discard exhaust manifold seals.
26. Remove oxygen sensors from exhaust manifolds.
27. Remove exhaust manifold heat shield.
28. Remove exhaust manifold mounting bolts and nuts. Discard bolts.
29. Remove mounting studs and exhaust manifold. Discard gasket.
30. Disconnect bank 1, sensor 1 Heated Oxygen Sensor (HO2S) pigtail from wiring harness connector.
31. **On models equipped with AWD,** proceed as follows:

a. Remove tire and wheel assembly.
b. Loosen steering linkage inner tie rod nut.
c. Remove rack and pinion outer tie rod end nut.
d. Disconnect rack and pinion outer tie rod end from steering knuckle using steering linkage and tie rod puller tool No. J24319-B, or equivalent. **Record number of complete turns tie rod end makes during removal for installation alignment.**
e. Remove rack and pinion outer tie rod end from steering linkage inner tie rod.
32. **On all models,** remove mounting bolt and position engine wiring harness bracket aside.
33. Remove mounting bolts and position exhaust manifold heat shield near alternator.
34. Remove exhaust manifold mounting nuts and bolts. Discard bolts.
35. Remove studs and exhaust manifold. Discard gasket.
36. Reverse procedure to install.

CYLINDER HEAD
REPLACE

The thread pitch on the M11 cylinder head bolts and the engine block cylinder head bolt holes have been revised. The thread length of cylinder head bolts with a pitch of 1.5 mm is approximately 1.89 inches. The thread length of cylinder head bolts with a pitch of 2 mm is approximately 2.64 inches.

1. Remove exhaust manifold as outlined under "Exhaust Manifold, Replace."
2. Remove supercharger as outlined under "Supercharger, Replace."
3. Remove water crossover as outlined under "Water Outlet Housing, Replace."
4. Remove lefthand secondary camshaft drive chain as outlined under "Timing Chain, Replace."
5. Remove lefthand camshaft as outlined under "Camshaft, Replace."
6. Remove power steering reservoir return hose mounting bolts from cylinder head.
7. Remove three M6 external drive bolts from cylinder head front portion.
8. Remove and discard internal drive cylinder head bolts.
9. Remove cylinder head and discard gasket. Ensure no dowel guide pins are stuck in cylinder head.
10. Remove any remaining bolt thread sealant material from threaded cylinder block holes.
11. Remove remaining gasket material from cylinder head and cylinder block.
12. Reverse procedure to install, noting the following:

a. Refer to sequence, **Figs. 1 and 2,** and tighten M11 cylinder head bolts in five steps: First step, **torque** bolts to 22 ft. lbs.; second step, tighten bolts an additional 60°; third step, tighten bolts an additional 60°;

fourth step, tighten bolts an additional 60°; fifth step, tighten bolts an additional 40.°
  b. **Torque** front M6 bolts to 106 inch lbs.

VALVE COVER
REPLACE

Lefthand

1. Remove supercharger front and rear inlet duct assemblies as outlined under "Supercharger, Replace"
2. Remove PCV fresh air tube from camshaft cover.
3. Remove cover and two mounting bolts, then two studs and ignition coil.
4. Remove valve cover ground strap bolt.
5. Remove oil level dipstick tube mounting bolts. Position tube aside.
6. Remove valve cover attaching bolts and the valve cover. Discard cover gasket and spark plug port seals.
7. Reverse procedure to install, noting the following:
   a. Install new cover gasket.
   b. Place small amount of suitable sealant on head and camshaft position actuator housing split line.
   c. Work cover into position by pivoting it down and aligning bolt holes.

Righthand

1. Remove supercharger front and rear inlet duct assemblies as outlined under "Supercharger, Replace"
2. Relieve fuel system pressure as outlined under "Precautions."
3. Disconnect fuel rail fuel line and position it aside.
4. Remove PCV fresh air tube from camshaft cover.
5. Remove battery, then the mounting bolts and tray.
6. Remove ignition coil.
7. Remove valve cover ground strap bolt and wiring harness clips.
8. Remove mounting bolts and valve cover. Discard cover gasket and spark plug port seals.
9. Reverse procedure to install, noting the following:
   a. Install new cover gasket.
   b. Place small amount of suitable sealant on head and camshaft position actuator housing split line.
   c. Work cover into position by pivoting it down and aligning bolt holes.

CAMSHAFT LOBE LIFT SPECIFICATIONS

Camshaft	Lobe Lift, Inch
Exhaust	.2339
Intake	.2428

VALVE CLEARANCE SPECIFICATIONS

This engine is equipped with hydraulic lifters. Valve adjustment is not required.

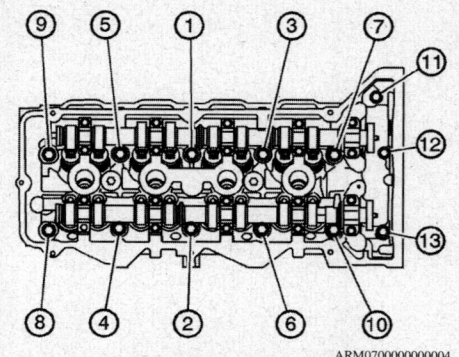

Fig. 2   Righthand cylinder head bolt tightening sequence

VALVE ADJUSTMENT

This engine is equipped with hydraulic lifters. Valve adjustment is not required.

ROCKER ARMS

1. Remove camshaft as outlined under "Camshaft, Replace."
2. Mark position of each follower and Stationary Hydraulic Lash Adjuster (SHLAs) for installation reference.
3. Remove followers.
4. Reverse procedure to install, noting the following:
   a. Liberally lubricate roller pivot pocket and valve slot areas,
   b. Follower must be positioned squarely on valve tip so full width of roller will completely contact camshaft lobe.
   c. Rounded head of follower goes on SHLA, while flat end goes on valve tip.

HYDRAULIC LIFTERS
REPLACE

1. Remove camshaft as outlined under "Camshaft, Replace."
2. Mark position of each follower and Stationary Hydraulic Lash Adjuster (SHLA)s for installation reference.
3. Remove followers.
4. Reverse procedure to install, noting the following:
   a. Ensure crankshaft is Top Dead Center (TDC) position for cylinder No. 1.
   b. Fill SHLA with suitable, clean engine oil.
   c. **Do not scratch pivot sphere area.**
   d. Lubricate SHLA cylinder head bores with suitable, clean engine oil.
   e. Liberally lubricate roller pivot pocket and valve slot areas.
   f. Follower must be positioned squarely on valve tip so full width of roller will completely contact camshaft lobe.
   g. Rounded head of follower goes on SHLA, while flat end goes on valve tip.

CRANKSHAFT DAMPER
REPLACE

1. Remove mounting bolts and hood.
2. Remove mounting bolts and cross vehicle brace.
3. Remove power steering reservoir and engine oil fill caps, then the intake manifold sight shield.
4. Remove wiper motor module as outlined under "Wiper Motor, Replace" in "Electrical" section.
5. Remove mounting nuts, bolts and air inlet housing front panel.
6. Disconnect air cleaner duct vacuum hose.
7. Loosen air cleaner duct.
8. Disconnect PCV hose fitting from underside of inlet duct.
9. Remove supercharger inlet duct front section.
10. Remove drive belts as outlined under "Drive Belt, Replace."
11. Remove charge air cooling system pressure and coolant caps.
12. Raise and support vehicle.
13. Remove six plastic retainers and front air deflector.
14. Remove charge air coolant radiator drain plug and drain coolant.
15. Remove charge air coolant pump outlet and inlet hoses.
16. Disconnect charge air coolant pump electrical connector.
17. Remove charge air coolant pump mounting nuts and pump.
18. Disconnect cooling fan electrical connectors, then the auxiliary water pump and hoses.
19. Disconnect condenser tube from cooling fan shroud retainer clip.
20. Disengage surge tank inlet hose from cooling fan shroud retainer and position aside.
21. Raise and support vehicle, then remove transmission bell housing inspection hole cover.
22. Hold flywheel using flywheel locking tool No. EN48018, or equivalent.
23. Remove crankshaft balancer bolt.
24. Remove crankshaft balancer using crankshaft balancer remover tool No. J41816, or equivalent. **Do not lose oil pump drive to crankshaft dampner friction washer.**
25. Reverse procedure to install, noting the following:
    a. Ensure oil pump drive to damper friction washer is intact.
    b. Press crankshaft dampner into place using balancer installer tool No. J41998-B, or equivalent.
    c. Clean and apply engine oil to dampner bolt threads.
    d. Tighten crankshaft balancer bolt in two steps: First step, **torque** bolt to 74 ft. lbs.; second step, tighten an additional 150.°

FRONT COVER
REPLACE

1. Raise and support vehicle.
2. Remove six plastic retainers and front air deflector.

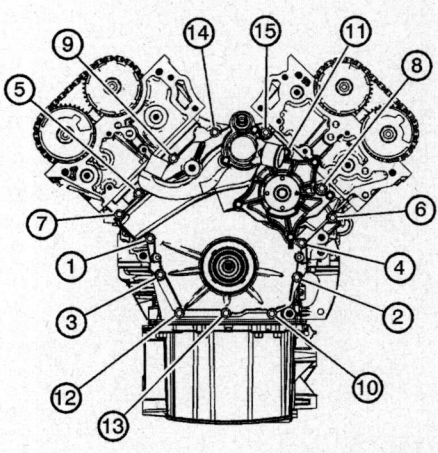

Fig. 3 Front cover bolt tightening sequence

3. Remove charge air coolant radiator drain plug and drain coolant into suitable container.
4. Remove supercharger as outlined under "Supercharger, Replace."
5. Remove water outlet housing as outlined under "Water Outlet Housing, Replace."
6. Rotate tensioner clockwise and remove belt from water pump pulley.
7. Remove drive belt from behind tensioner.
8. Allow tensioner to return to relaxed position and remove belt.
9. Remove mounting bolts, then the drive belt tensioner and pulley.
10. Remove mounting bolts, then the supercharger drive belt tensioner and pulley.
11. Disconnect the cooling fan electrical connectors, then the auxiliary water pump and hoses.
12. Disconnect condenser tube from cooling fan shroud retainer clip.
13. Disengage surge tank inlet hose from cooling fan shroud retainer and position aside.
14. Disconnect tension clamps using hose clamp pliers tool. No. J38185, or equivalent, then the charge air coolant pump outlet and inlet hoses.
15. Disconnect electrical connector and pump mounting nuts.
16. Open clamps and remove pump.
17. Disconnect clamps, then remove charge air cooler radiator inlet and outlet hoses.
18. Disconnect clamps, then remove heater and radiator hoses from thermostat housing.
19. Disconnect electrical connector and charge air cooler coolant pump mounting nuts.
20. Open clamps and remove pump.
21. Rotate tensioner clockwise and remove alternator drive belt.
22. Remove mounting bolt and alternator drive belt tensioner.
23. Remove mounting bolts and water pump pulley.
24. Raise and support vehicle, then remove transmission bell housing inspection hole cover.
25. Hold flywheel using flywheel locking tool No. EN48018, or equivalent.
26. Remove crankshaft balancer bolt.
27. Remove crankshaft balancer using crankshaft balancer remover tool No. J41816, or equivalent. **Do not lose oil pump drive to crankshaft dampner friction washer.**
28. Remove mounting bolts and engine front cover. Discard gaskets.
29. Reverse procedure to install, noting the following:
    a. Apply small amount of suitable sealant at upper and lower crankcase split lines and at front cover gasket pad area on top of split lines.
    b. Apply suitable thread locking compound to front cover bolt threads.
    c. **Torque** front cover bolts to 11 ft. lbs. in sequence, **Fig. 3.**
    d. Clean and apply engine oil to dampner bolt threads.
    e. Tighten crankshaft balancer bolt in two steps: First step, **torque** bolt to 74 ft. lbs.; second step, tighten an additional 150.°

TIMING CHAIN
REPLACE
Primary
REMOVAL

1. Remove front cover as outlined under "Front Cover, Replace."
2. Remove oil pump drive to crankshaft balancer friction washer.
3. Remove three oil pump mounting bolts identified by larger head size.
4. Slide oil pump off crankshaft nose with drive collar in place.
5. Remove crankshaft sprocket to oil pump drive friction washer.
6. Align primary timing marks using crankshaft socket tool No. J39946, or equivalent, **Fig. 4.**
7. Remove secondary camshaft drive chains as outlined under "Secondary."
8. Remove two mounting bolts and primary camshaft drive chain tensioner, allow tensioner to expand.

INSTALLATION

1. Rotate primary camshaft drive chain tensioner ratchet release lever clockwise and hold.
2. Collapse tensioner shoe and hold.
3. Release ratchet lever.
4. Slowly release shoe pressure until ratchet lever moves to first detent.
5. Collapse tensioner shoe and hold.
6. Lock shoe in collapsed position by inserting suitable pin through release lever hole.
7. Install primary camshaft drive chain tensioner with release lever facing outward and tighten mounting bolts.
8. Remove pin holding tensioner to tighten any slack in timing chain.
9. Ensure primary timing marks are aligned vertically, **Fig. 4.**
10. Install suitable crankshaft sprocket to oil pump drive friction washer.

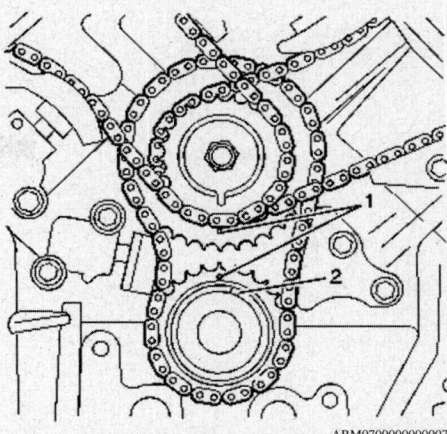

Fig. 4 Primary timing chain alignment

11. Install space into oil pump so drive flat engages rotor.
12. Install oil pump alignment tool No. EN48036, or equivalent, over crankshaft nose and up to oil pump.
13. Loosely install mounting bolts and apply hand force to alignment tool against oil pump to align I pump to drive.
14. Keeping hand force against alignment tool, refer to sequence, **Fig. 5,** and tighten mounting bolts in two steps: First step, **torque** bolts to 89 inch lbs.; second step, tighten bolts an additional 35.°
15. Remove special tool and install oil pump drive to crankshaft balancer friction washer.
16. Install front cover outlined under "Front Cover, Replace."

Secondary

The secondary timing chains have three black links that aid in timing the camshaft position actuators to the intermediate sprocket. One black link is aligned with the intermediate sprocket; the second black link is aligned with the bank 1 exhaust actuator timing mark, and the third black link is aligned with bank 1 intake actuator timing mark. The intermediate sprocket right righthand bank timing mark is labeled RB and lefthand bank LB.

It is not required that the black chain links be aligned with the camshaft actuator timing marks when the secondary chain and gear components are being serviced separately.

LEFTHAND
REMOVAL

1. Remove righthand secondary timing chain as outlined under "Righthand."
2. Align primary timing marks using crankshaft socket tool No. J39946, or equivalent, **Fig. 4.**
3. Remove mounting bolts and cross vehicle brace.
4. Remove power steering reservoir and engine oil fill caps, then the intake

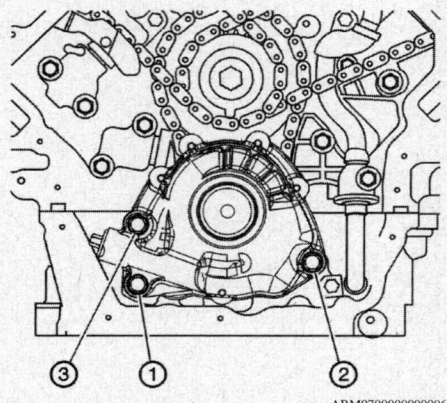

Fig. 5   Oil pump tightening sequence

manifold sight shield.
5. Remove front and rear supercharger inlet ducts outlined under "Supercharger, Replace."
6. Remove mounting bolt and exhaust Camshaft Position (CMP) sensor.
7. Remove mounting bolt and intake CMP sensor.
8. Raise and support vehicle.
9. Remove six plastic retainers and front air deflector.
10. Disconnect cooler and outlet hoses from power steering reservoir and drain into suitable container.
11. Remove mounting nuts and power steering reservoir.
12. Remove lefthand camshaft cover as outlined under "Valve Cover, Replace."
13. Remove air conditioning, power steering and water pump drive belt tensioner.
14. Remove mounting bolts and lefthand camshaft position actuator housing. **Do not remove actuator solenoids from housing.**
15. Hold righthand camshafts using camshaft holding tool No. EN46328, or equivalent.
16. Remove mounting bolts and lefthand secondary timing chain tensioner.
17. Hold exhaust camshaft with a suitable open-end wrench and remove camshaft oil control valve.
18. Slide exhaust camshaft position actuator off of camshaft and remove secondary timing chain from teeth.
19. Hold intake camshaft with a suitable open-end wrench and remove intake camshaft oil control valve.
20. Slide intake camshaft position actuator off of camshaft and remove secondary timing chain from teeth.
21. Remove lefthand secondary timing chain.

INSTALLATION.

1. Align LB intake camshaft position actuator timing mark with timing chain black link and install actuator on camshaft with actuator timing mark perpendicular (90°) to cylinder head deck surface near top of rotation.

2. Secure intake actuator by loosely installing oil control valve.
3. Prevent camshaft form using suitable open-end wrench on hex cast and tighten oil control valve.
4. Align left bank exhaust camshaft position actuator timing mark (labeled LB) with timing chain black link, install actuator on camshaft with actuator timing mark perpendicular (90°) to cylinder head deck surface near top of rotation.
5. Secure exhaust actuator by loosely installing oil control valve.
6. Hold camshaft with a suitable open-end wrench and tighten oil control valve.
7. Rotate lefthand secondary timing chain tensioner ratchet release lever counterclockwise and hold.
8. Collapse tensioner shoe and hold, then release ratchet lever.
9. Slowly release shoe pressure until ratchet lever moves to first detent. Detent should be felt and heard.
10. Collapse and hold tensioner shoe.
11. Lock tensioner shoe in collapsed position by inserting a pin through release lever hole.
12. Install lefthand secondary camshaft drive chain tensioner with release lever facing outward. Tighten mounting bolts.
13. Remove pin to tighten chain slack.
14. Ensure actuator and chain timing marks remain aligned, **Fig. 6.**
15. Install righthand secondary timing chain as outlined under "Righthand.".
16. Install new gasket and righthand camshaft position actuator housing. Tighten mounting bolts and stud.

RIGHTHAND

REMOVAL

1. Remove front cover as outlined under "Front Cover, Replace."
2. Remove oil pump drive to crankshaft balancer friction washer.
3. Remove three oil pump mounting bolts identified by larger head size.
4. Slide oil pump off crankshaft nose with drive collar in place.
5. Remove crankshaft sprocket to oil pump drive friction washer.
6. Align primary timing marks using crankshaft socket tool No. J39946, or equivalent, **Fig. 4.**
7. Remove supercharger as outlined under "Supercharger, Replace."
8. Remove water outlet housing as outlined under "Water Outlet Housing, Replace."
9. Remove mounting bolt and supercharger drive belt tensioner.
10. Remove righthand exhaust and intake Camshaft Position (CMP) sensors.
11. Remove righthand valve cover as outlined under "Valve Cover, Replace."
12. Remove cam sensor harness from retainers.
13. Remove mounting bolts and righthand camshaft position actuator housings. **Do not remove actuator solenoids from housing.**
14. Hold righthand camshafts using cam-

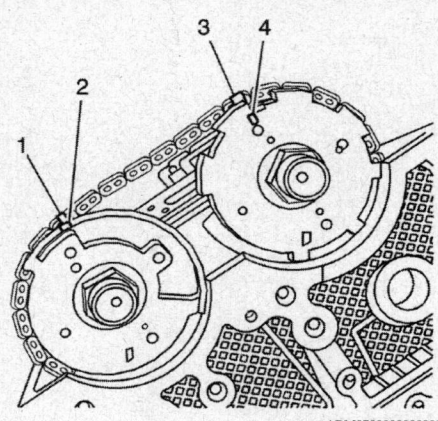

Fig. 6   Actuator & timing chain alignment

shaft holding tool No. EN46328, or equivalent.
15. Remove mounting bolts and righthand secondary timing chain tensioner.
16. Mark chain link adjacent to each actuator timing mark.
17. Install engine front cover bolt into engine front.
18. Wrap suitable mechanics wire tightly around both righthand secondary camshaft drive chain shoe and front cover bolt.
19. Remove two secondary camshaft drive chain tensioner mounting bolts.
20. Remove righthand secondary camshaft drive chain tensioner allowing tensioner to expand.
21. Prevent camshaft from rotating by holding using suitable open-end wrench on camshaft hex cast.
22. Remove righthand exhaust camshaft position oil control valve.
23. Slide righthand exhaust camshaft position actuator off camshaft and remove secondary timing chain from actuator teeth.
24. Prevent camshaft from rotating by holding using suitable open-end wrench on camshaft hex cast.
25. Remove righthand intake camshaft position oil control valve.
26. Slide righthand intake camshaft position actuator off camshaft and remove secondary timing chain from actuator teeth.
27. Remove secondary timing chain.

INSTALLATION

1. Align intake camshaft position actuator timing mark (labeled RB) with timing chain black link and install actuator on camshaft with actuator timing mark perpendicular (90°) to cylinder head deck surface near top of rotation.
2. Install secondary timing chain to intermediate sprocket, align sprocket timing mark (labeled RB) to timing chain black link.
3. Secure intake actuator by loosely installing oil control valve.
4. Hold camshaft with a suitable open

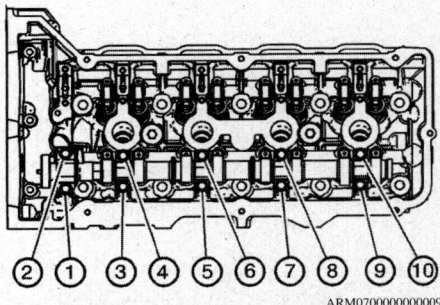

Fig. 7 Camshaft bearing cap tightening sequence (lefthand exhaust)

end wrench and tighten oil control valve.

5. Align exhaust camshaft position actuator timing mark (labeled RB) with timing chain black link, install actuator on camshaft with actuator timing mark perpendicular (90°) to cylinder head deck surface near top of rotation.
6. Secure exhaust actuator by loosely installing oil control valve.
7. Hold camshaft with a suitable open-end wrench and tighten oil control valve.
8. Rotate righthand secondary timing chain tensioner ratchet release lever counterclockwise and hold.
9. Collapse tensioner shoe and hold, then release ratchet lever.
10. Slowly release shoe pressure until ratchet lever moves to first detent. Detent should be felt and heard.
11. Collapse and hold tensioner shoe.
12. Lock tensioner shoe in collapsed position by inserting pin through release lever hole.
13. Install righthand secondary camshaft drive chain tensioner with release lever facing outward. Tighten mounting bolts.
14. Remove pin to tighten chain slack.
15. Ensure actuator and chain timing marks remain aligned, **Fig. 6.**
16. Remove righthand secondary camshaft drive chain support wire and engine front cover bolt.
17. Install new gasket and righthand camshaft position actuator housing. Tighten mounting bolts and stud.
18. Install camshaft cover as outlined under "Valve Cover, Replace."
19. Lubricate O-rings with suitable engine oil, then install righthand intake and exhaust CMP sensors.
20. Install CMP sensor harness to retainers.
21. Install supercharger drive belt tensioner and mounting bolts.
22. Install water outlet housing as outlined under "Water Outlet Housing, Replace."
23. Install suitable crankshaft sprocket to oil pump drive friction washer.
24. Install space into oil pump so drive flat engages rotor.
25. Install oil pump alignment tool No.

EN48036, or equivalent, over crankshaft nose and up to oil pump.

26. Loosely install mounting bolts and apply hand force to alignment tool against oil pump to align oil pump to drive.
27. Keeping hand force against alignment tool, refer to sequence, **Fig. 5,** and tighten mounting bolts in two steps: First step, **torque** bolts to 89 inch lbs.; second step, tighten bolts an additional 35.°
28. Remove special tool and install oil pump drive to crankshaft balancer friction washer.
29. Install front cover as outlined under "Front Cover, Replace."

TIMING CHAIN TENSIONER
REPLACE

Refer to "Timing Chain, Replace."

CAMSHAFT
REPLACE

The secondary timing chain has black links that are used for alignment when the primary and secondary timing gear and chain assemblies are being installed together. It is not required that the black chain links be aligned with the camshaft actuator timing marks when the secondary chain and gear components are being serviced separately.

Removal

1. Remove camshaft position actuator oil control valve as outlined in "Secondary" under "Timing Chain, Replace."
2. Bearing caps are marked with an arrow pointing toward front of engine. Each cap is marked with either an "I" indicating intake camshaft or an "E" indicating exhaust camshaft. Each cap is numbered to indicate its journal position from front of engine. **Do not mix bearing caps.**
3. Remove bolts, camshaft bearing caps and camshafts.

Installation

1. Clean journals, camshaft and caps with suitable lint-free cloth.
2. Apply liberal amount of suitable camshaft prelube to camshaft bearing journals.
3. Apply liberal amount of suitable camshaft prelube to camshaft lobes and journals.
4. Ensure each valve rocker arm is properly aligned to valve tip, lifter and camshaft lobe. Inspect alignment prior to and after camshaft caps are tightened.
5. Install camshaft in journals with drive pins near top of rotation and lobes in neutral position. Camshaft can be identified by stamping near rear journal. For example: L-EXH is Left Bank Exhaust.

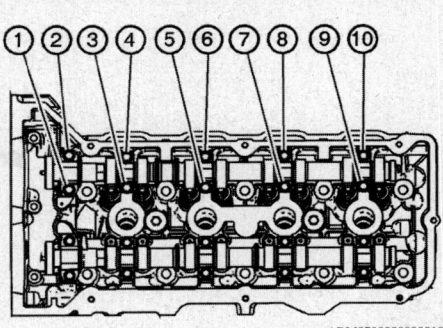

Fig. 8 Camshaft bearing cap tightening sequence (lefthand intake)

6. Apply liberal amount of suitable camshaft prelube to camshaft bearing cap journals. **Ensure caps are installed in original positions.**
7. Hand start all camshaft bearing cap bolts.
8. Refer to sequences, **Figs. 7 through 10,** and tighten camshaft bearing cap bolts in two steps: First step, **torque** bolts to 44 inch lbs.; second step, tighten bolts an additional 30.°

PISTON & ROD ASSEMBLY

Ensure the locating mark cast into the underside of the piston faces towards the front of the engine and locating notch on the connecting rod cap points towards the rear of the engine on odd-numbered cylinders and towards the front of the engine on even-numbered cylinders, **Fig. 11.**

PISTONS, PINS & RINGS

1. Lubricate piston pin bores with suitable crankshaft prelube.
2. Install new piston pin retainers using piston pin clip remover/installer tool No. EN46745, or equivalent.
3. Ensure oil control ring expander ends face toward piston top and install oil control piston ring spacer.
4. Install oil control piston ring spacer
5. Install lower and upper oil control piston rings using suitable piston ring expander tool.
6. Space oil control piston ring end gaps at least 90° apart.
7. Install lower compression piston ring using suitable piston ring expander tool. with mark ring side facing piston top.
8. Install upper compression piston ring using suitable piston ring expander tool. Top compression ring may be installed with either side up.
9. Oil control ring expander and second compression ring gaps set centerline position 1, **Fig. 12.**

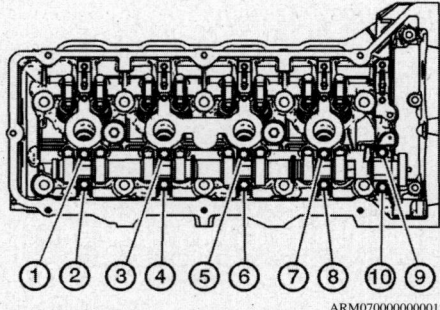

Fig. 9 Camshaft bearing cap tightening sequence (righthand exhaust)

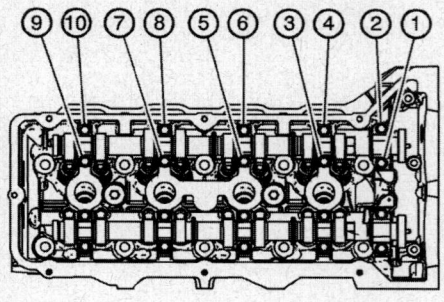

Fig. 10 Camshaft bearing cap tightening sequence (righthand intake)

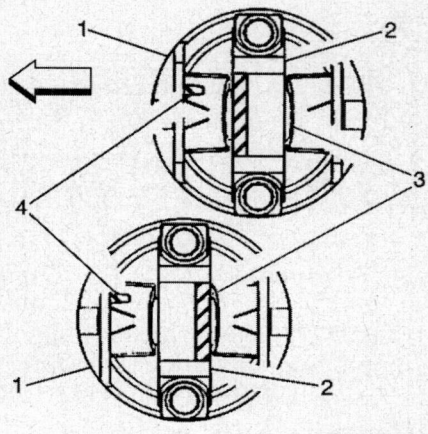

Fig. 11 Piston & rod installation position

10. Top compressing ring gap 180° opposite oil control ring expander and second compression ring gaps.
11. Upper oil control ring gap position 2 should be 30° clockwise from top compression ring gap.
12. Lower oil control ring gap position 4 should be 30° counterclockwise from top compression ring gap.

MAIN & ROD BEARINGS

Connecting Rod

1. Clean connecting rod and cap bearing bore with suitable, lint-free cloth.
2. Clean oil from behind connecting rod bearing halves.
3. Roll new upper connecting rod bearings into position so lock tang engages alignment slot. Bearing must fit flush in connecting rod.
4. Roll new lower connecting rod bearings into position so lock tang engages alignment slot. Bearing must fit flush in connecting rod cap.
5. Rotate crankshaft using crankshaft socket tool No. J39946, or equivalent, and align crankshaft connecting rod journal being serviced to Bottom Dead Center (BDC).
6. Liberally lubricate cylinder walls, piston rings and piston skirts with suitable, clean engine oil.
7. Select correctly numbered piston/connecting rod assembly for cylinder.
8. Ensure connecting rod bearing bore tang notches are aligned to same side.
9. Ensure locator lugs on bottom of piston are oriented towards front of engine.
10. Ensure lefthand piston assembly connecting rod cap notch is oriented towards front of engine.
11. Ensure lefthand piston locator lugs and connecting rod cap notch are in same orientation.
12. Ensure righthand piston assembly connecting rod cap notch is oriented towards rear of engine.
13. Ensure righthand piston locator lugs and connecting rod cap notch is in opposing orientation.

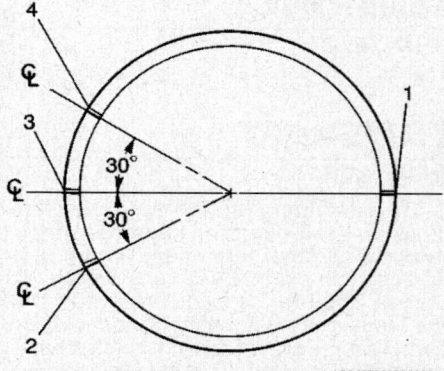

Fig. 12 Piston ring gap set positions

14. Install new bearings into connecting rod.
15. Install connecting rod guide pin set tool EN46121, or equivalent, into connecting rod bolt holes.
16. Compress piston rings using ring compressor tool No. J8037, or equivalent.
17. **Ensure connecting rod does not scrape or nick cylinder bore or crankshaft journal surfaces.**
18. Slowly guide piston and connecting rod assembly into cylinder from top and bottom. **Do not allow connecting rod to contact cylinder wall.**
19. When ring compressor tool contacts deck surface, gently tap piston into cylinder using handle end of dead-blow hammer
20. Guide connecting rod onto crankshaft bearing journal using connecting rod guide pin set tool while taping piston into cylinder. Remove connecting rod guide pin set tool.
21. Place length of fresh, room temperature plastic gaging material all the way across entire connecting rod bearing journal.
22. Install connecting rod end cap on original connecting rod ensuring bearing lock tangs are aligned on same side of rod.
23. Ensure connecting rod bearing cap

notches are paired on the crankpin, **Fig. 13.**
24. Lubricate old connecting rod bolts with suitable engine oil and install.
25. Tighten connecting rod bolts in four steps: First step, **torque** bolts to 22 ft. lbs.; second step, loosen bolts to zero; third step, **torque** bolts to 18 ft. lbs.; fourth step, tighten bolts an additional 110.°
26. Let sit for at least two minutes.
27. Remove bolts and connecting rod cap.
28. Measure flattened plastic gaging material at widest point. Clearance should be .001–.003 inch.
29. Clean plastic gaging material from connecting rod bearing and crankshaft connecting rod journal using suitable, soft lint-free cloth.
30. Install connecting rod guide pin set tool into connecting rod bolt holes.
31. Back connecting rod away from crankshaft, then coat crankshaft connecting rod bearing journal and installed connecting rod bearings with suitable crankshaft prelube.
32. Guide connecting rod onto journal and remove guide pin set tool.
33. Install connecting rod end cap on its original connecting rod making sure bearing lock tangs are aligned on same side of rod, **Fig. 13.**
34. Lubricate new bolts with suitable engine oil and install in connecting rod.
35. Tighten connecting rod bolts in four steps: First step, **torque** bolts to 22 ft. lbs.; second step, loosen bolts to zero; third step, **torque** bolts to 18 ft. lbs.; fourth step, tighten bolts an additional 110.°
36. Ensure each piston is positioned properly in the correct cylinder.
37. Repeat these steps to install piston/connecting rod assembly on common crankshaft connecting rod journal.
38. Measure and ensure connecting rod side clearance is .008–.020 inch.
39. Repeat steps to install remaining piston/connecting rod assemblies.

Fig. 13 Connecting rod bearing cap notch alignment

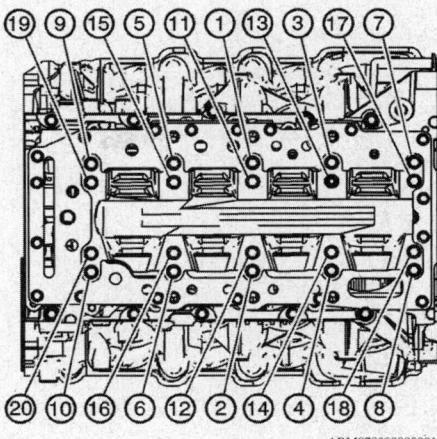

Fig. 14 Lower crankcase tightening sequence

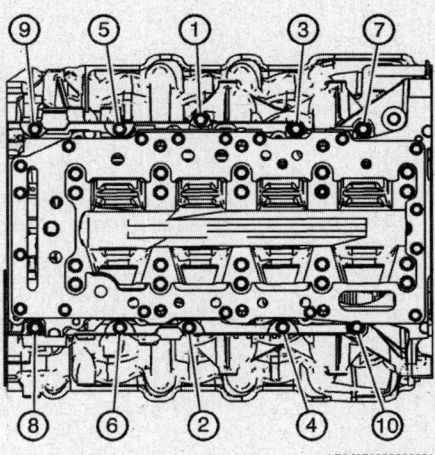

Fig. 15 Upper to lower crankcase tightening sequence

Crankshaft

1. Clean upper and lower crankcase crank bore with suitable lint-free cloth
2. Clean oil from backside of new bearing halves.
3. Install new upper crankshaft bearings into position. Thrust bearing belongs in No. 3 journal.
4. Ensure upper bearing insert contains oil transfer hole and groove. Roll bearing into position so lock tang engages crank slot. Bearing must fit flush with upper crankcase.
5. Install new lower crankshaft bearings into position. Lower crankcase crankshaft bearings are identified by no grooves or holes. Bearings must fit flush with lower crankcase.
6. Apply liberal amount of suitable crankshaft prelube or engine oil to upper and lower bearing surfaces.
7. If old crankshaft sprocket drive pin was damaged, install new pin with height of 0689-.1280 inch.
8. Gently lower crankshaft into position in cylinder block. Ensure crankshaft turns without binding or noise.
9. Place length of fresh, room temperature plastic gaging material all the way across all crankshaft bearing journals.
10. Align lower crankcase with upper dowel pins.
11. Install lower crankcase onto upper slowly until feeling positive stop.
12. Inspect upper to lower crankcase joint to ensure lower crankcase is fully seated on cylinder block.

13. Install old oil manifold and scraper plates, then tighten mounting bolts.
14. Loosely install main bearing bolts. Single stud-end bolt used to attach oil pump pipe and screen support bracket is installed in inboard position in second set of main bearing bolts from front and lefthand bank side of engine.
15. Install left and righthand side upper-to-lower crankcase perimeter bolts.
16. Refer to sequence, **Fig. 14,** and tighten lower crankcase mounting bolts in two steps: First step, **torque** bolts to 15 ft. lbs.; second step, tighten bolts an additional 65.°
17. Refer to sequence, **Fig. 15,** torque upper to lower crankcase perimeter bolts to 22 ft. lbs.
18. Let assembly sit for at least two minutes.
19. Remove main bearing and stud-head bolts.
20. Remove mounting bolts, old oil manifold and oil scraper plate.
21. Working on either side of lower crankcase, separate crankcase halves by alternately prying in grooves using suitable plastic pry tool until lower crankcase is free of dowel pins. **Do not continue to push pry tool in crankcase as the upper and lower crankcase halves separate.**
22. Remove lower crankcase.
23. Measure flattened plastic gaging material at widest point. Bearing clearance should be .0006-.0025 inch.
24. Clean plastic gaging material from crankshaft bearings and journals using suitable, soft lint-free cloth.
25. Apply liberal amount of suitable crankshaft prelube or engine oil to upper and lower bearing surfaces.
26. Gently lower crankshaft into position in cylinder block. Ensure crankshaft turns without binding or noise.
27. Align lower crankcase with upper dowel pins.
28. Install lower crankcase onto upper slowly until feeling positive stop.
29. Inspect upper to lower crankcase joint to ensure lower crankcase is fully seat-

ed on cylinder block.
30. Install oil manifold and scraper plates, then tighten mounting bolts.
31. Loosely install main bearing bolts. Single stud-end bolt used to attach oil pump pipe and screen support bracket is installed in inboard position in second set of main bearing bolts from front and lefthand bank side of engine.
32. Install left and righthand side upper-to-lower crankcase perimeter bolts.
33. Refer to sequence, **Fig. 14,** and tighten lower crankcase mounting bolts in two steps: First step, **torque** bolts to 15 ft. lbs.; second step, tighten bolts an additional 65.°
34. **Torque** upper to lower crankcase perimeter bolts to 22 ft. lbs. in sequence, **Fig. 15.**

CRANKSHAFT REAR OIL SEAL
REPLACE
Removal

1. Remove transmission as outlined in **MOTOR's "Domestic Transmission, In-Vehicle Service" manual or "Transmission Service DVD."**
2. Prevent engine from turning using Snap-On flywheel turner tool No. A144A, or equivalent.
3. Remove mounting bolts and flywheel.
4. Remove rear oil seal using rear oil seal remover tool No. J42841-A, or equivalent.

Installation

1. Ensure oil drain back hole is clear of debris using suitable wire.
2. Clean bore with suitable cleaner solvent.
3. Install sealant installer tool No. EN48072, or equivalent, onto crankshaft. Crankshaft hub will fit into inboard tool recess.
4. Install tool applicator housing over pilot

base. Ensure applicator housing bottoms in block bore.

5. Apply suitable RTV sealant to block bore outer diameter evenly using tool applicator housing. **Ensure sealant does not block drain hole.**

6. Spread sealant within bore to ensure an even coating.

7. **Ensure components sealed with RTV sealant are assembled within 20 minutes.**

8. Slowly and evenly, pull applicator housing out of bore and remove it from pilot base. **Do not twist or turn tool applicator housing as it is pulled away from bottom of the bore.**

9. Remove bolts and tool pilot base. **Ensure that sealant is evenly spread across bore and drain block hole is clear.**

10. **Do not use any lubricant to install crankshaft rear oil seal. Do not use any lubricant on coating pre-applied to inner diameter of crankshaft rear oil seal.**

11. Turn center nut of crankshaft rear oil seal installer tool J45930-A until center hub protrudes approximately .6 inch beyond outer plate.

12. **Do not use any lubricant on crankshaft rear oil seal outer diameter. Do not lubricate any part of new cassette style crankshaft rear oil seal.**

13. Install new cassette style crankshaft rear oil seal using crankshaft rear oil seal installer tool until drive bottoms against crankcase.

14. Remove tool and wipe excessive sealant from block.

15. Seal outer surface should be .02–.03 inch below engine block surface.

16. Sleeve inner surface should be .02–.03 inch below seal outer surface.

17. Installed seal and sleeve need to be parallel to block within .02 inch.

18. Apply suitable sealant to flywheel mounting bolts.

19. Tighten flywheel mounting bolts in a diagonal pattern in two steps: First step, **torque** bolts to 22 ft. lbs.; second step, tighten bolts an additional 50.°

OIL PAN

REPLACE

1. Remove mounting bolts and cross-vehicle brace.

2. Remove power steering reservoir and engine oil fill caps, then the intake manifold sight shield.

3. Support engine using universal engine support fixture kit tools No. J28467-B, or equivalent.

4. **Ensure rear portion of rail support is resting on fender flange reinforced section.**

5. Install front support assemblies tools No. J28467-4A, or equivalent, to tube assembly using quick release pins tools No. J28467-9, or equivalent. Ensure J28467-16 are as level as possible by selecting the appropriate hole for the quick release pins.

6. Raise and support vehicle, then remove front tires and wheels.

7. Drain engine oil into suitable container.

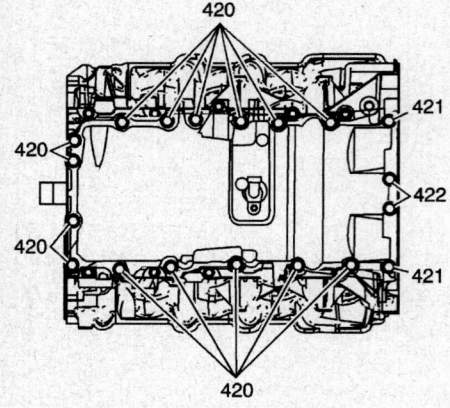

420 – Short bolts
421 – Medium bolts
422 – Long bolts

ARM0600000001690

Fig. 16 Oil pan bolt locations

8. Remove six plastic retainers and front air deflector.

9. Disconnect engine harness to frame retainers.

10. Disconnect left and righthand rearward retainer, then the antilock brake wiring harness from lower control arm.

11. Loose bracket nut and disconnect brakes lines from frame.

12. Support radiator and air conditioning condenser to front inner energy absorber bracket bolt using suitable mechanics wire.

13. Remove mounting nuts and washer bottle bracket.

14. Loosening mounting nuts and separate Brake Pressure Modulator Valve (BPMV) from bracket.

15. Mark stabilizer shaft for installation alignment.

16. Loosen shaft mounting bolts, then remove link lower mounting nut and stabilizer shaft link from lower control arm.

17. Remove mounting nut from air conditioning compressor and position power steering pressure hose aside.

18. Remove mounting bolts and support power steering gear to oil pan bolt bracket using suitable mechanics wire.

19. Remove mounting nut and outer tie rod using steering linkage and tie rod puller tool No. J24319-B, or equivalent.

20. Remove lower shock mounting bolts.

21. **Do not remove brake calipers from knuckle.**

22. Remove mounting nut and separate lower ball joint from steering knuckle (joint stub on AWD models) using ball joint separator tool. No. J42188, or equivalent. Position knuckle away from lower control arm.

23. Remove engine mounts lower mounting nuts.

24. Lower vehicle to engine support stand tool No. J39580, or equivalent.

25. Remove front frame mounting bolts.

26. Raise body from frame ensuring brake pipes, steering knuckle and wheel

speed sensor electrical harness are clear.

27. Disconnect electrical connector and remove engine oil level sensor from oil pan.

28. Remove mounting bolts and oil pan.

29. Drill rivets, then remove and discard gasket.

30. Reverse procedure to install, noting the following:

    a. New oil pan gasket does not require riveting.

    b. Oil pan must be held flush to .020 inch forward of rear face of engine block.

    c. Ensure oil pan mounting bolts are correctly located, **Fig. 16.**

    d. **Torque** oil pan mounting bolts to 11 ft. lbs. in sequence, **Fig. 17.**

    e. Final **torque** mounting bolts to 18 ft. lbs.

OIL PUMP

REPLACE

Removal

1. Remove front cover as outlined under "Front Cover, Replace."

2. Remove oil pump drive to crankshaft balancer friction washer.

3. Remove three oil pump mounting bolts identified by larger head size.

4. Slide oil pump off crankshaft nose with drive collar in place.

5. Remove crankshaft sprocket to oil pump drive friction washer.

Installation

1. Install suitable crankshaft sprocket to oil pump drive friction washer.

2. Install space into oil pump so drive flat engages rotor.

3. Install oil pump alignment tool No. EN48036, or equivalent, over crankshaft nose and up to oil pump.

4. Loosely install mounting bolts and apply hand force to alignment tool against oil pump to align oil pump to drive.

5. Keeping hand force against alignment tool, refer to sequence, **Fig. 5,** and tighten bolts in two steps: First step, **torque** bolts to 89 inch lbs.; second step, tighten bolts an additional 35.°

6. Remove special tool and install oil pump drive to crankshaft balancer friction washer.

7. Install front cover as outlined under "Front Cover, Replace."

OIL PUMP SERVICE

Disassemble

1. Remove driver spacer.

2. Remove mounting bolts and cover.

3. Remove drive and driven gears.

4. Remove relief valve plug, spring and plunger.

5. Remove body to cover alignment dowels.

Assembly

1. Install alignment dowels.
2. Install oil pump relief valve plunger and spring, then tighten plug.
3. Install driven and drive gears. Outer driven gear chamfered edge must facedown into pump body.
4. Ensure pump priming by packing body housing with suitable, clean white petroleum jelly.
5. Install cover and tighten mounting bolts.
6. Install oil pump drive spacer.

OIL COOLER

REPLACE

The engine oil cooler is the top part of a combined engine oil and transmission fluid cooling system.

It is not necessary to recover air conditioning refrigerant during oil cooler replacement.

1. Remove mounting bolts and position air conditioning condenser aside.
2. Disconnect lines from Transmission Oil Cooler (TOC) using cooler quick connect tool No. J41623-B, or equivalent.
3. Disconnect TOC lines from clip.
4. Disconnect Engine Oil Cooler (EOC) lines from cooler using ½ inch quick connect release tool No. DT-47731, or equivalent.
5. Remove mounting bolts and cooler.
6. Reverse procedure to install.

DRIVE BELT

REPLACE

Alternator

1. Remove supercharger drive belt as outlined under "Supercharger."
2. Remove air conditioning, power steering and water pump belt as outlined under "Air Conditioning, Power Steering & Water Pump."
3. Drain charge air cooler cooling system into suitable container.
4. Remove outlet and inlet hoses from charge air cooler coolant pump.
5. Disconnect charge air cooler coolant pump electrical connector.
6. Remove mounting nuts and open clamps, then remove charge air cooler coolant pump.
7. Rotate belt tensioner clockwise and remove alternator drive belt.
8. Reverse procedure to install.

Air Conditioning, Power Steering & Water Pump

1. Remove supercharger drive belt as outlined under "Supercharger."
2. Rotate belt tensioner clockwise and remove belt from water pump pulley.
3. Remove belt from behind tensioner.
4. Allow tensioner to return to a relaxed

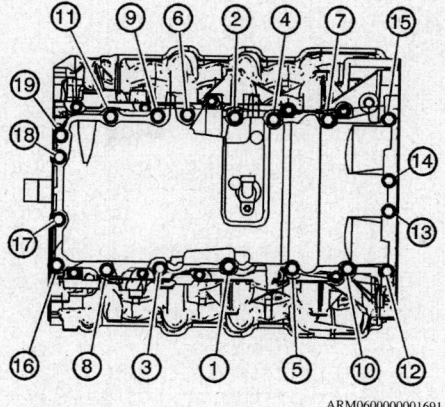

Fig. 17   Oil pan tightening sequence

position, then remove belt from side of tensioner pulley in area of lower power steering reservoir mounting nut.
5. Reverse procedure to install.

Supercharger

1. Remove supercharger inlet duct front section as outlined under "Supercharger, Replace."
2. Rotate belt tensioner in a clockwise direction using belt tool No. EN47913, or equivalent.
3. Remove supercharger drive belt.
4. Reverse procedure to install.

COOLING SYSTEM BLEED

1. Slowly fill cooling system until coolant stabilizes at one inch above surge tank FULL COLD mark. Install surge tank cap.
2. Start and run engine at 2000–2500 RPM until it reaches normal operating temperature.
3. Idle engine for three minutes, then turn ignition switch to OFF position.
4. Allow engine to cool.
5. Add or remove coolant at surge tank until level is at FULL COLD mark.

THERMOSTAT

REPLACE

1. Drain coolant into suitable container.
2. Remove six plastic retainers and two front engine compartment sight shields.
3. Disconnect air cleaner duct vacuum hose, then loosen air duct clamp at supercharger inlet duct and air cleaner housing cover.
4. Remove air cleaner duct.
5. Disconnect radiator and heater hoses from thermostat housing.
6. Remove mounting bolts and thermostat housing. Discard seal ring.
7. Separate thermostat from housing.
8. Reverse procedure to install.

WATER PUMP

REPLACE

1. Remove auxiliary cooling fan to condenser upper mounting bolts.
2. Raise and support vehicle, then remove retainers and front air deflector.
3. Drain coolant into suitable container.
4. Disconnect auxiliary cooling fan electrical connectors.
5. Remove mounting bolts and auxiliary cooling fan.
6. Loosen water pump pulley bolts.
7. Remove supercharger inlet duct front section as outlined under "Supercharger, Replace."
8. Remove supercharger drive belt, then the air conditioning, power steering and water pump drive belt as outlined under "Drive Belt, Replace."
9. Remove air conditioning, power steering and water pump drive belt tensioner.
10. Remove mounting bolts and water pump pulley.
11. Position suitable drain pan below water pump.
12. Remove mounting bolts and water pump. Discard seal.
13. Reverse procedure to install.

WATER OUTLET HOUSING

REPLACE

1. Drain engine cooling system into suitable containers.
2. Remove charge air cooling system pressure and coolant caps.
3. Raise and support vehicle.
4. Remove six plastic retainers and front air deflector.
5. Remove charge air coolant radiator drain plug and drain coolant into suitable container.
6. Remove supercharger as outlined under "Supercharger, Replace."
7. Remove mounting bolts and cross-vehicle brace.
8. Remove power steering and engine oil fill caps, then the sight shield.
9. Remove wiper motor module as outlined under "Wiper Motor, Replace" in "Electrical" section.
10. Remove mounting nuts, bolts and air inlet housing front panel.
11. Disconnect air cleaner duct vacuum hose.
12. Loosen supercharger inlet duct and air cleaner housing cover air duct clamps, then remove air cleaner duct.
13. Disconnect PCV hose fitting from underside of inlet duct.
14. Loosen inlet duct front and rear section screw clamps.
15. Remove six ball studs retaining inlet duct to supercharger.
16. Remove supercharger drive belt as outlined under "Drive Belt, Replace."
17. Remove bolt and supercharger drive belt tensioner, then the mounting bolt and inboard idler pulley.
18. Remove two coolant hoses from water outlet housing.

19. Remove radiator hose from water outlet housing.
20. Remove two mounting bolts, then the water outlet housing with bypass hose. Discard gaskets.
21. Reverse procedure to install.

RADIATOR

REPLACE

1. Remove auxiliary cooling fan to condenser upper mounting bolts.
2. Raise and support vehicle, then remove retainers and front air deflector.
3. Drain coolant into suitable container.
4. Disconnect auxiliary cooling fan electrical connectors.
5. Remove mounting bolts and auxiliary cooling fan.
6. Remove condenser upper and lower mounting bolts.
7. Disconnect side air baffle lower retaining pins from radiator.
8. Position condenser aside and remove ATF cooler mounting bolts.
9. Lower vehicle and disconnect condenser tube from fan shroud clip.
10. Remove mounting bolts and fan shroud.
11. Remove radiator outlet and inlet hoses from radiator.
12. Remove surge tank inlet hose from radiator.
13. Remove mounting bolts and radiator support brackets.
14. Disconnect upper air baffle retaining pins and remove radiator.
15. Reverse procedure to install.

FUEL PUMP

REPLACE

Refer to "4.6L Engine" section for fuel pump replacement procedure.

FUEL FILTER

REPLACE

1. Relieve fuel system pressure as outlined under "Precautions."
2. Raise and safely support vehicle.
3. Disconnect fuel filter inlet and outlet quick-connect fittings.
4. Drain remaining fuel into suitable container.
5. Slide fuel filter out of mounting bracket.
6. Reverse procedure to install.

SUPERCHARGER

REPLACE

1. Relieve fuel system pressure as outlined under "Precautions."
2. Remove mounting bolts and hood.
3. Remove mounting bolts and cross vehicle brace.
4. Remove power steering reservoir and engine oil fill caps, then remove intake manifold sight shield.
5. Remove wiper motor module as outlined under "Wiper Motor, Replace" in "Electrical" section.
6. Remove air inlet housing front panel mounting bolts and nuts.

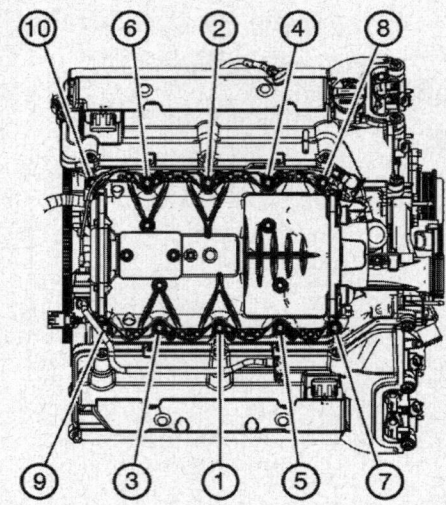

Fig. 18 Supercharger tightening sequence. 4.4L engine

ARM0700000000002

7. Disconnect air cleaner duct vacuum hose.
8. Loosen supercharger inlet duct clamp, then remove air cleaner duct.
9. Disconnect PCV hose fitting from underside of supercharger inlet duct.
10. Loosen inlet duct front and rear section screw clamps.
11. Remove six ball studs retaining inlet duct to supercharger.
12. Remove front section of supercharger inlet duct.
13. Disconnect line fitting from EVAP valve and chassis bundle, then remove EVAP line.
14. Remove brake booster hose from supercharger rear port.
15. Remove rear section of supercharger inlet duct.
16. Remove charge air cooling system pressure and coolant caps.
17. Raise and support vehicle.
18. Remove front air deflector from under engine.
19. Remove plug and drain charge air coolant radiator.
20. Remove supercharger front manifold mounting bolts. **Do remove manifold hoses. Discard O-ring seals.** Position hoses and manifold aside.
21. Disconnect electrical connectors from Supercharger Inlet Absolute Pressure (SCIAP), Barometric Pressure (BARO) and Manifold Absolute Pressure (MAP) sensors.
22. Disconnect vacuum lines from MAP and SCIAP, then remove SCIAP, BARO and MAP sensors with bracket.
23. Disconnect Inlet Air Temperature (IAT) sensor electrical connector, position sensor aside.
24. Disconnect supercharger bypass solenoid valve harness electrical connector, position harness aside.
25. Disconnect supercharger actuator valve vacuum line and position line aside.
26. Disconnect engine compartment fuel line fitting from fuel rail using fuel line

disconnect tool No. J44581, or equivalent.
27. Disconnect fuel injector electrical connectors from left and righthand side of engine.
28. Open fuel rail jumper clip at front of supercharger.
29. Remove mounting studs and fuel rail. **Do not damage injector electrical connector terminals and injector spray tips. Support fuel rail after removal. Cap fuel system fittings and plug holes.**
30. Disconnect throttle body, EVAP canister purge solenoid valve and supercharger bypass regulator solenoid valve electrical connectors.
31. Disconnect MAP sensor vacuum line and supercharger IAT sensor electrical connector.
32. Disconnect IAT sensor vacuum line fitting.
33. Position sensors, vacuum lines and wire harness aside.
34. Disconnect PCV tube fitting from righthand camshaft cover.
35. Remove supercharger drive belt.
36. Remove supercharger using supercharger lift bracket tool No. EN47748, or equivalent, and asuitable engine hoist.
37. Reverse procedure to install, noting the following:
   a. Refer to sequence, **Fig. 18,** and **torque** supercharger mounting bolts to 18 ft. lbs.
   b. Lubricate new fuel injector O-ring seals with suitable clean engine oil.
   c. Ensure injectors are aligned by positioning electrical connectors perpendicular to crankshaft centerline.
   d. Lubricate injector spray tip end O-ring seals.

TECHNICAL SERVICE BULLETINS

Muffler, Tailpipes, Exhaust Tips Do Not Appear Centered In Rear Fascia Cut Outs

2005–07 STS

On some of these models the muffler, tailpipes or exhaust tips do not appear centered in the rear fascia cut outs.

This condition may be caused by the muffler hanger rod moving inside the rubber isolator mounts causing incorrect positioning of the exhaust pipes.

To correct this condition install washers and retaining fasteners over the muffler hanger rods at the front and rear positions of the muffler as follows:
1. Raise and support vehicle.
2. Remove mounting nut and lefthand front muffler hanger.
3. Install washer and new retainer fastener to lefthand front muffler hanger, leaving .2 inch gap from flat rod end to retainer.

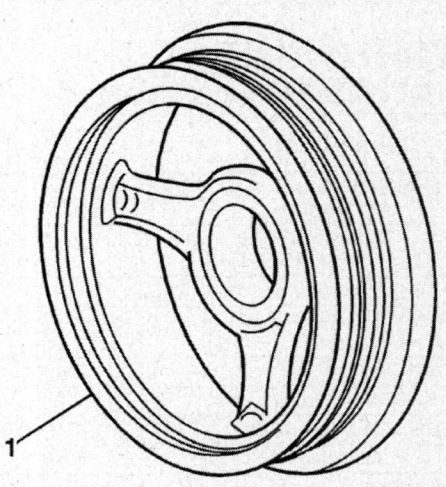

Fig. 19   Three-spoke crankshaft harmonic balance. 2005 STS w/3.6L engine

4. Remove mounting nuts and lefthand rear muffler hangers.
5. Install lefthand rear washers and new retainer fasteners while aligning muffler to cut out in rear fascia exit.
6. Install washer and new retainer fastener to righthand front muffler hanger, leaving .2 inch gap from flat rod end to retainer.
7. Remove righthand rear retainer nuts from muffler hangers.
8. Install righthand rear washers and new retainer while aligning muffler to cut out in rear fascia exit.
9. Lower vehicle.

Very Faint Engine Whine Noise At Speeds Of 0-30 mph At 1000-2500 RPM

2005-07 STS

On some of these mounting there may be a very faint engine whine-type noise heard at speeds of 0-30 mph at 1000-2500 RPM. This type of noise may be amplified by the vehicle's body structure. The noise may be present at idle (hot or cold) and, in some vehicles, this noise may be louder.

This condition may be caused by may be caused by the primary camshaft drive chain.

This type of noise is characteristic and/or normal for this engine. No abnormal engine wear or internal damage will result due to this noise condition. An engine noise primarily around 1600 RPM that can be described as a howl will typically be coming from the exhaust system. This is also considered a characteristic and/or normal type of noise

Whine, Whistle, Ringing Type Noise Heard From Front of Engine

2005 STS w/3.6L ENGINE

On some of these models not equipped with heavy duty cooling, there may be a whine, whistle or ringing type noise from

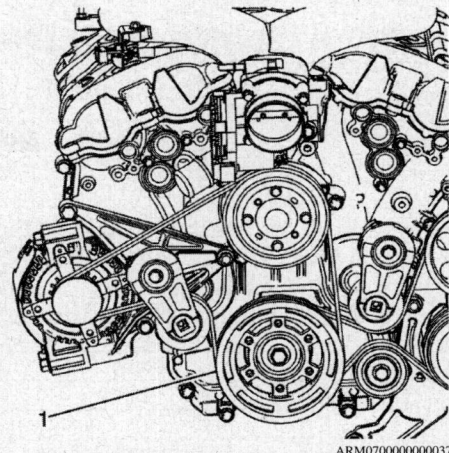

Fig. 20   Six-spoke crankshaft harmonic balance. 2005 STS w/3.6L engine

the front of the engine that increases in intensity as engine RPM increases. This noise is most audible standing in front of the vehicle with the hood opened.

This condition may be caused may by the harmonic balancer.

To correct this condition replace three-spoke design crankshaft harmonic balancer with part No. 12597654, **Fig. 19.**

Do not replace the six-spoke design crankshaft harmonic balancer, Fig. 20.

If the vehicle is equipped with the heavy duty cooling package, do not replace the six-spoke design crankshaft harmonic balancer.

TIGHTENING SPECIFICATIONS

Year	Component	Torque Ft. Lbs.
2007–08	Air Cleaner	89①
	Air Cleaner Outlet Duct Clamp	27①
	Air Condition Compressor	18
	Air Condition Compressor Bracket	37
	Air Inlet Front Housing	53①
	Air Inlet Grille	26①
	Air Inlet Grille Panel	53①
	Auxiliary Cooling Fan	48①
	Battery Tray	53①
	BPMV	89①
	Brake Pipe Connection	89①
	Camshaft Bearing	②
	Camshaft Cover Ground Strap, Cam Cover	89①
	Camshaft Cover Ground Strap. Cylinder Head	18
	Camshaft Drive Chain Guide	18
	Camshaft Drive Chain Shoe	18
	Camshaft Drive Chain Tensioner	18
	Camshaft Intermediate Drive Shaft	11
	Camshaft Intermediate Drive Sprocket	44
	Camshaft Position Actuator	89
	Camshaft Position Actuator Housing	89①
	Camshaft Position Actuator Magnet	71①
	Camshaft Position Actuator Solenoid	71①
	Charge Air Bypass Regulator Solenoid Valve Bracket	89①
	Charge Air Coolant Pump	12
	Charge Air Coolant Radiator Drain Plug	89①
	Charge Air Cooler	89
	Charge Air Cooler Coolant Front Manifold	89①
	Charge Air Cooler Cooling Fill Cap	89①
	Charge Air Cooler Front & Rear Manifold	89①
	CKP & KS Wiring Harness Bracket	89①
	CKP Sensor	89①
	CMP Sensor	89①
	Cooling Fan Shroud	48①
	Coolant Pump	12
	Connecting Rod	③
	Crankcase	③
	Crankshaft Balancer	④
	Cross-Vehicle Brace	83
	Cylinder Head	⑤
	Drive Belt Idler	37
	Drive Belt Tensioner	37
	ECT Sensor	15
	Energy Absorber Bracket	18
	Engine Block Coolant Drain Plug	15
	Engine Front Cover	11
	Engine Front Cover Fitting	18
	Engine Oil Level Switch/Temperature Sensor	89①
	Engine Mount	59
	Engine Mount Bracket	44

TIGHTENING SPECIFICATIONS—Continued

Year	Component	Torque Ft. Lbs.
2007–08	Engine Oil and Transmission Fluid Cooler	44①
	Engine Wiring Harness LH Rear Bracket	89①
	Engine Wiring Harness Rear Bracket	18
	Engine Wiring Harness RH Side Bracket	33
	EVAP Canister Purge Valve	89①
	Exhaust Manifold	18
	Exhaust Manifold Stud	53①
	Exhaust Manifold Heat Shield	89①
	Exhaust Pipe To Manifold Flange	22
	Floor Panel Tunnel Brace	18
	Flywheel	⑥
	Front Frame	141
	Fuel Filter	80①
	Fuel Injector Sight Shield Ball Stud	89①
	Fuel Rail	v
	Fuel Tank Strap	37
	Hood	80①
	Ignition Coil	89①
	Intermediate Shaft, Center To Lower	23
	Intermediate Shaft, Lower To Power Steering Gear	57
	Lower Control Arm Ball Joint	15
	MAF/IAT Sensor	35①
	Main Bearings	③
	Oil Control Valve	89①
	Oil Cooler Pipe Fitting	18
	Oil Filter	24
	Oil Filter Adapter Hole Plug	48
	Oil Filter Adapter	18
	Oil Filter Fitting	21
	Oil Level Indicator Tube	37
	Oil Manifold Plate	89①
	Oil Pan	⑧
	Oil Pan Drain Plug	18
	Oil Pressure Switch	15
	Oil Pressure Switch Heat Shield	89①
	Oil Pump	⑨
	Oil Pump Cover	106①
	Oil Pump Relief Valve Plug	106①
	Oil Suction Tube, Bolt	89①
	Oil Suction Tube, Nut	18
	Outer Tie Rod To Steering Knuckle	52
	Oxygen Sensor	31
	Piston Oil Nozzle	89①
	Plenum Duct Clamp	29①
	Power Steering Gear	70
	Power Steering Pump	37
	Power Steering Pump Reservoir Bracket	89①
	Propeller Shaft Coupler To Differential	63

Continued

TIGHTENING SPECIFICATIONS—Continued

Year	Component	Torque Ft. Lbs.
2007–08	Propeller Shaft Coupler To Transmission	63
	Propeller Shaft Coupler To Transfer Case	29
	Radiator Support Bracket	80①
	Shock Absorber, Lower	18
	Spark Plugs	11
	Stabilizer Shaft	44
	Stabilizer Shaft 44	37
	Starter Motor	22
	Starter Nut - Large	89①
	Starter Nut - Small	35①
	Supercharger	⑦
	Supercharger Bypass Valve Actuator & Cable Bolt	89①
	Supercharger Charge Air Cooler Radiator	48①
	Supercharger IAT Sensor 2	15
	Supercharger Inlet Duct Ball Stud	89①
	Supercharger Inlet Seal Screw Clamp	20①
	Rack And Pinion Outer Tie Rod End	41
	Thermostat Housing	89①
	Throttle Body	89①
	Transmission Oil Cooler	44①
	Valve Cover	89①
	Washer Bottle Bracket	89①
	Water Outlet Housing	18
	Water Pump	89①
	Water Pump Pulley	106①
	Wiper Arm	26
	Wiper Motor	89①

① — Inch pounds.

② — Refer to "Camshaft, Replace" for tightening specifications and sequence.

③ — Refer to "Main & Rod Bearings" for tightening specifications and sequence.

④ — Refer to "Crankshaft Damper, Replace" for tightening specifications and sequence.

⑤ — Refer to "Cylinder Head, Replace" for tightening specifications and sequence.

⑥ — Refer to "Crankshaft Rear Oil Seal, Replace" for tightening specifications and sequence.

⑦ — Refer to "Supercharger, Replace" for tightening specifications and sequence.

⑧ — Refer to "Oil Pan, Replace" for tightening specifications and sequence.

⑨ — Refer to "Oil Pump, Replace" for tightening specifications and sequence.

4.6L Engine

NOTE: Refer To "Air Bag System Precautions" Located In The Front Of This Manual For System Disarming & Arming Procedures.

NOTE: Refer To "Computer Relearn Procedures" Located In The Front Of This Manual When Battery Power To The Computer Has Been Interrupted.

NOTE: Prior To Performing Any Service Operations Listed In This Section, Consult The "Technical Service Bulletins" Section For Related Information.

INDEX

Page No.

Camshaft, Replace	9-46
DTS	9-47
Installation	9-47
Removal	9-47
DeVille & Seville	9-46
Camshaft Timing	9-46
Installation	9-46
Removal	9-46
STS	9-47
Installation	9-47
Removal	9-47
Compression Pressure	9-35
Cooling System Bleed	9-51
Crankshaft Damper, Replace	9-42
DTS	9-42
DeVille & Seville	9-42
STS	9-42
Crankshaft Rear Oil Seal, Replace	9-48
Installation	9-48
Removal	9-48
Cylinder Head, Replace	9-40
DTS	9-40
Lefthand	9-40
Righthand	9-40
DeVille & Seville	9-40
STS	9-41
Engine Rebuilding Specifications	29-1
Engine, Replace	9-36
DTS	9-36
DeVille & Seville	9-36
STS	9-37
Engine Mount, Replace	9-35
DTS	9-35
Front	9-35
Righthand	9-35
Strut	9-35
DeVille & Seville	9-35
Front	9-35
Righthand	9-35
STS	9-36
Lefthand	9-36

Page No.

Righthand	9-36
Exhaust Manifold, Replace	9-39
DTS	9-39
Lefthand	9-39
Righthand	9-39
DeVille & Seville	9-39
Lefthand	9-39
Righthand	9-39
STS	9-39
Lefthand	9-39
Righthand	9-40
Front Cover, Replace	9-42
DTS	9-43
DeVille & Seville	9-42
STS	9-43
Fuel Filter, Replace	9-53
DTS & STS	9-53
DeVille & Seville	9-53
Fuel Pump, Replace	9-53
DTS	9-53
DeVille & Seville	9-53
STS	9-53
Intake Manifold, Replace	9-38
DTS & STS	9-39
DeVille & Seville	9-38
Main & Rod Bearings	9-48
Connecting Rod	9-48
Crankshaft	9-48
Oil Pan, Replace	9-49
DTS	9-49
DeVille & Seville	9-49
STS	9-49
Oil Pump, Replace	9-50
Installation	9-50
Removal	9-50
Oil Pump Service	9-51
Assembly	9-51
Disassemble	9-51
Piston & Rod Assembly	9-48
Pistons, Pins & Rings	9-48
Precautions	9-35
Air Bag Systems	9-35
Battery Ground Cable	9-35

Page No.

Fuel System Pressure Relief	9-35
2004–06	9-35
2007–08	9-35
Radiator, Replace	9-52
DTS	9-52
DeVille & Seville	9-52
STS	9-52
Serpentine Drive Belt	9-51
Technical Service Bulletins	9-53
Coolant Leak At Upper Radiator Hose	9-53
2006 DTS	9-53
Engine Oil Leak From Front Of Vehicle	9-53
2005 STS	9-53
Thermostat, Replace	9-51
Tightening Specifications	9-54
Timing Chain, Replace	9-43
Primary	9-43
DTS & STS	9-43
DeVille & Seville	9-43
Secondary	9-44
DTS	9-44
DeVille & Seville	9-44
STS	9-45
Valve Adjustment	9-42
Valve Clearance Specifications	9-42
Valve Cover, Replace	9-41
DTS	9-41
Lefthand	9-41
Righthand	9-41
DeVille & Seville	9-41
Lefthand	9-41
Righthand	9-41
STS	9-42
Lefthand	9-42
Righthand	9-42
Water Crossover, Replace	9-51
DeVille, DTS & Seville	9-51
Water Pump, Replace	9-51
DTS	9-51
DeVille & Seville	9-51
STS	9-51

PRECAUTIONS

Air Bag Systems

Refer to "Air Bag System Precautions" in the front of this manual for system disarming and arming procedures.

Battery Ground Cable

Prior to service, disconnect battery ground cable and isolate as required.

Fuel System Pressure Relief

2004-06

1. Disconnect ball studs and remove intake manifold top sight shield cover.
2. Remove fuel rail pressure fitting cap and connect suitable fuel pressure gauge wrapping fitting with suitable towel.
3. Install bleed hose into suitable container.
4. Relieve fuel tank vapor pressure by loosening fuel filler cap.
5. Open valve and bleed system pressure.

2007-08

1. Remove fuel pump fuse.
2. Relieve fuel tank vapor pressure by loosen fuel filler cap.
3. Remove fuel rail service port cap.
4. Wrap shop towel around fitting and depress (open) fuel rail test port valve using suitable, small flat-bladed tool.
5. Remove shop towel and place in suitable container.
6. Install fuel rail service port cap.

COMPRESSION PRESSURE

Perform compression test with engine at normal operating temperature, spark plugs removed and throttle wide open. Disable the ignition and fuel systems. Lowest cylinder must be within 70% of highest cylinder with a minimum pressure of 140 psi.

ENGINE MOUNT

REPLACE

DeVille & Seville

FRONT

1. Raise and support vehicle.
2. Remove retainers and front air deflector.
3. Support engine and transmission with suitable adjustable support.
4. Support frame front with suitable adjustable support.
5. Remove mounting nuts and bolts, then lower front frame.
6. Remove two lower engine mount bracket nuts, then the mounting nut and support bracket.

7. Remove two upper mounting bolts, then the front engine mount and bracket, rotating the mount and bracket counterclockwise.
8. Remove nut and mount from bracket.
9. Reverse procedure to install, tightening nuts and bolts in following sequence:
   a. **Torque** front engine mount to bracket nut to 84 ft. lbs.
   b. **Torque** two lower engine mount bracket nuts to 30 ft. lbs.
   c. **Torque** transaxle support brace bolt to 37 ft. lbs.
   d. **Torque** two upper engine mount bracket bolts to 37 ft. lbs.
   e. **Torque** two front mount to frame bolts to 141 ft. lbs.
   f. **Torque** front engine mount to frame nut to 52 ft. lbs.

RIGHTHAND

1. Raise and support vehicle, then remove righthand front tire and wheel.
2. Support engine with suitable jack.
3. Remove mount to bracket mounting nut and lower engine slightly. Remove jack.
4. Remove righthand engine mount to frame mounting nuts and bolt.
5. Lower vehicle, the remove mounting bolt and position surge tank aside.
6. Remove frame rail bolts' mounting screws, then raise and support vehicle.
7. Push frame rail bolts and remove righthand engine mount.
8. Reverse procedure to install, tightening nuts and bolts in following sequence:
   a. **Torque** frame rail bolt retaining screws to 35 inch lbs.
   b. **Torque** righthand engine mount to body rail nuts to 52 ft. lbs.
   c. **Torque** righthand engine mount nut to 59 ft. lbs.

DTS

FRONT

1. Support engine using suitable engine support fixture tool and adapters.
2. Raise and support vehicle, then remove front tires and wheels.
3. Remove mounting bolt and nut, then the washers, insulators, spacer and stabilizer link.
4. Remove stabilizer shaft as outlined under "Stabilizer Shaft, Replace" in "Front Suspension & Steering" section.
5. Remove steering gear to engine frame mounting bolts.
6. **On models equipped with soft ride and sport suspension,** separate ball joint from lower control arm using ball joint separator tool No. J36226, or equivalent.
7. **On all models,** remove retainers and front air deflector.
8. Remove retainers and lefthand front wheelhouse liner.
9. Disconnect Electronic Brake Control Module (EBCM) electrical connector.
10. Remove two brake pipes and three fit-

tings, then the mounting bracket bolt and Brake Pressure Modulator Valve (BPMV). **Do not separate BPMV from EBCM.**
11. Disconnect electronic suspension control sensor links from lower control arm ball studs.
12. Disconnect secondary air injection pump electrical connector.
13. Disconnect secondary air injection pump inlet and outlet hose quick connect fittings.
14. Remove mounting bolt and nuts, then secondary air injection pump from cradle bracket.
15. Remove mounting bolts and steering gear heat shield, then disconnect electrical harness from shield.
16. Remove mounting bolts and bracket, then the retainer and position power steering line aside.
17. Support power steering gear to body using suitable mechanics wire.
18. Lower vehicle until engine frame rests on engine support stand tool No. J39580, or suitable jack stands.
19. Remove front engine mount to frame mounting nuts.
20. Remove rear transaxle mount to engine frame bolts and nuts.
21. Remove engine frame mounting bolts and raise vehicle away.
22. Remove steering gear to engine frame mounting bolts.
23. Disconnect ESC sensor links from lower control arm ball studs.
24. Remove fasteners and steering gear heat shield, then disconnect retainer and electrical harness from shield.
25. Remove brackets and power steering line along lefthand side of engine frame.
26. Support steering gear to body using suitable mechanics wire.
27. Lower vehicle until engine frame rests on suitable jack stands.
28. Remove front engine mount to frame nuts.
29. Remove rear transaxle mount nuts and bolts.
30. Remove engine frame mounting bolts, then raise vehicle away from frame.
31. Remove engine mount bracket to cylinder head bolts.
32. Remove bracket to lower engine mount bracket nuts and upper engine mount bracket.
33. Remove transaxle brace bolt.
34. Remove lower engine mount bracket to engine stud nuts and transaxle brace.
35. Remove lower engine mount bracket.
36. Remove mount to bracket nut and front engine mount.
37. Reverse procedure to install.

RIGHTHAND

1. Remove front frame as outlined under "Front."
2. Remove bracket nut and righthand engine mount.
3. Reverse procedure to install.

STRUT

1. Remove surge tank mounting nuts and

retainer, then position surge tank aside.
2. Remove engine mount strut mounting bolts and strut.
3. Reverse procedure to install.

STS

LEFTHAND

1. Raise and support vehicle.
2. Remove lefthand exhaust manifold as outlined under "Exhaust Manifold, Replace."
3. Support engine at oil pan using suitable adjustable jack and wood block.
4. Remove upper engine mounting nut, then the mounting bolts and lefthand engine mounting bracket.
5. Remove lower mounting nut and engine mount.
6. Reverse procedure to install.

RIGHTHAND

1. Raise and support vehicle.
2. Remove righthand exhaust manifold as outlined under "Exhaust Manifold, Replace."
3. Place a suitable adjustable jack and wood block under oil pan.
4. Remove righthand engine mount upper nut.
5. Remove mounting bolts and righthand engine mount bracket. **Do not distort or bend engine mount heat shield.**
6. Remove mounting nut and engine mount.
7. Reverse procedure to install.

ENGINE
REPLACE

DeVille & Seville

1. Drain coolant into suitable container.
2. Recover air conditioning refrigerant as outlined in "Air Conditioning" chapter.
3. Remove upper filler panel.
4. Disconnect PCM electrical connectors.
5. Remove air cleaner.
6. Drain engine oil into suitable container.
7. Remove intake manifold sight shield.
8. Remove lower radiator hose using clamp tool No. J37097-A, or equivalent.
9. Remove upper radiator hose from thermostat housing clamp tool No. J38185, or equivalent.
10. Disconnect upper and lower transaxle fluid cooler lines from radiator.
11. Disconnect surge tank inlet hose.
12. Disconnect surge tank outlet hose from heater pipe.
13. **Always replace accelerator cable with new one whenever engine is removed. Position cruise control cable aside during engine removal or installation. Do not pry on, lean against or kink cruise control cable.**
14. Disconnect accelerator and cruise control cables from TBI unit.
15. Disconnect heater hoses.
16. Disconnect two brake fluid lines from

master cylinder. Cap open lines and ports to prevent entry of dirt and debris.
17. Remove bracket and shift cable from manual shift lever, then position aside.
18. Disconnect vacuum hose from brake booster.
19. Disconnect hose from EVAP purge valve.
20. Disconnect secondary AIR relay from relay bracket and secure to top of engine.
21. Disconnect fuel inlet and return fittings at fuel rail.
22. Disconnect engine ground wire from body frame rail.
23. Disconnect main engine harness.
24. Disconnect wiring harness from underhood fuse block.
25. Remove strut tower bolts.
26. Raise and support vehicle.
27. Remove front tires and wheels.
28. Disconnect dampening sensor links from lower control arms.
29. Disconnect wheel speed and road sensing suspension sensor electrical connectors.
30. Disconnect two brake lines from both front subframe brackets and at rear of engine subframe. Cap open lines to prevent system contamination.
31. Remove air deflector.
32. Remove front fascia extensions.
33. Remove and discard engine oil cooler quick-connect fittings from oil filter adapter with oil lines still attached, then position lines aside. **Quick-connect fittings must be replaced whenever they are removed from adapter.**
34. Remove dust cover from quick connect joint.
35. Remove internal spring clip from engine oil cooler fittings.
36. Remove engine oil cooler lines from cooler fittings.
37. Disconnect secondary AIR inlet hose from secondary AIR pump.
38. Disconnect air conditioning suction and discharge hoses from compressor. Cap open lines and fittings to prevent system contamination.
39. Ensure front wheels are in straight-ahead position.
40. Lock steering column using lock pin tool No. J42640, or equivalent, in underside of column.
41. Remove steering intermediate shaft pinch bolt.
42. Disconnect steering gear from intermediate shaft.
43. Disconnect wheel speed and brake wear sensors at strut towers.
44. Disconnect downstream heated oxygen sensor electrical connector.
45. Remove front exhaust pipe.
46. Remove engine oil pan to transaxle case brace.
47. Remove flexplate inspection cover.
48. Mark flexplate to torque converter orientation, then remove mounting bolts.
49. Lower vehicle.
50. Position powertrain support dolly tool No. J39580, or equivalent, under engine assembly. Four suitable jack stands may be substituted if dolly is not available.

51. Remove engine mount to engine mount bracket nuts.
52. Secure front hoist pads to vehicle.
53. Remove subframe mount bolts.
54. Slowly raise vehicle. **Ensure powertrain and subframe assembly clear all wiring, hoses and fluid lines.**
55. Attach suitable lifting crane to engine.
56. Remove heater pipes.
57. Disconnect coil pack ground wire from cylinder head.
58. Remove crossover pipe from cylinder head.
59. Remove power steering pump.
60. Remove front and rear transaxle brace bolt and nuts, then braces.
61. Remove front engine mount to engine subframe nut.
62. Remove transaxle to engine mounting bolts.
63. Raise engine from subframe and transaxle assembly.
64. Reverse procedure to install.

DTS

1. Remove mounting bolts and cross vehicle brace.
2. Remove power steering and engine oil fill caps, then the fuel injector sight shield.
3. Recover air conditioning refrigerant as outlined in "Air Conditioning" chapter.
4. Disconnect engine port and booster clamp, then reposition booster vacuum hose aside.
5. Disconnect fuel feed and EVAP line quick-connect fittings.
6. Disconnect eight retainers and remove front compartment sight shield.
7. Disconnect Mass Air Flow/Intake Air Temperature (MAF/IAT) sensor electrical connector.
8. Disconnect PCV fresh air tube quick connect fitting from air cleaner outlet duct.
9. Disconnect Secondary Air Injection (AIR) pump inlet hose quick connect fitting from air cleaner.
10. Loosen clamp and remove air cleaner outlet duct from throttle body.
11. Disconnect three lower housing integral clips and remove air cleaner upper housing.
12. Disconnect locking tabs and remove junction block cover.
13. Remove nut, clip and starter cable from Bussed Electrical Center (BEC), then position BEC aside on top of engine.
14. Disconnect lever lock and Transaxle Control Module (TCM) engine harness electrical connector.
15. Disconnect lever lock and engine harness electrical connector from body harness electrical connector.
16. Secure engine harness wiring branches to engine.
17. Disconnect lever lock and Engine Control Module (ECM) engine harness electrical connector.
18. Remove mounting bolts and junction block.
19. Remove engine harness from BEC.
20. Remove righthand frame rail bolt and secure engine ground strap to engine.

21. Remove bracket clip and retainer, then disconnect transaxle shift cable from range selector lever.
22. Remove transaxle shift cable from bracket and position cable aside.
23. Drain cooling system into suitable container.
24. Remove radiator inlet and outlet hoses from water pump housing. Position hoses aside.
25. Remove surge tank inlet hose.
26. Remove heater inlet and outlet hoses from pipes.
27. Remove master cylinder mounting nuts, then secure master cylinder to engine.
28. Loosen upper transaxle oil cooler pipe to fan shroud bolt, then slide plastic caps off transaxle oil cooler pipe quick connect fittings.
29. Remove righthand front engine mount strut bolt and disconnect transaxle oil cooler pipes from radiator.
30. Ensure wheels and in straight ahead position.
31. Lock steering column by installing steering column lock pin tool No. J42640, or equivalent, into underside of steering column.
32. Remove left and righthand side strut tower bolts.
33. Raise and support vehicle.
34. Drain engine oil into suitable container.
35. Remove catalytic converter to rear exhaust manifold pipe nuts.
36. Position exhaust system rearward to allow catalytic converter studs to clear rear exhaust manifold pipe. **Do not over-flex or damage flex joint.** Discard catalytic converter gasket.
37. Remove rear exhaust manifold pipe, discard gasket and seal.
38. Remove front tires and wheels.
39. Remove engine harness grommet from frame rail bracket, then the engine harness clip from ride lever sensor bracket.
40. Disconnect electronic suspension front position sensor link from lower control arms ball stud.
41. Loosen mounting nut and remove lefthand front brake pipe bracket from body frame rail.
42. Loosen mounting nut and remove righthand front brake pipe bracket from body frame rail.
43. Disconnect rear from the brake pipes. Plug open brake lines.
44. Remove mounting bolt and air conditioning compressor discharge hose from engine. Secure hose to engine, then plug discharge port and condenser.
45. Remove mounting nut and air conditioning compressor suction hose from condenser. Secure hose to engine, then plug condenser suction and discharge ports.
46. Remove cover and pinch bolt, then disconnect intermediate steering shaft from steering gear.
47. Drill out rivets, then disconnect HO2S clips and remove heat shield.
48. Disconnect HO2S electrical connector.
49. Remove transaxle brace and torque converter cover mounting bolts.
50. Mark flywheel to toque converter position for installation reference.
51. Remove flywheel to torque converter mounting bolts.
52. Place universal engine support table tool No. J39580, or equivalent, under frame and lower vehicle onto table. If suitable table is not available, support powertrain with four suitable jack stands with 2 x 4 inch wood blocks between front of engine oil pan and engine frame.
53. Secure front hoist pads to vehicle and support rear of vehicle with suitable jack stands.
54. Disengage front fascia cover retainers, then remove mounting bolt and front fascia.
55. Remove frame to body mounting bolts.
56. Ensure there is clearance between engine/transmission assembly and air conditioning components, brake pipes, heater hoses, radiator hoses, wheel speed sensor lead and wiring harness.
57. Raise vehicle to clear support engine/transmission assembly.
58. Remove heater outlet pipe to transaxle stud nut.
59. Disconnect clamp and remove heater outlet pipe from water pump housing.
60. Remove Secondary Air Injection (AIR) to transaxle stud inlet hose retainer, the disconnect pump quick connect fitting and remove inlet hose.
61. Disconnect clamp and separate AIR outlet hose from pipe.
62. Remove AIR pipe outlet pipe nuts transaxle and inspect valve bracket studs.
63. Disconnect quick connect fitting and remove AIR outlet pipe.
64. Remove mounting bolt and Ignition Control Module (ICM) ground strap from righthand cylinder head.
65. Disconnect EVAP solenoid, EGR valve, fuel injectors and ICM electrical connectors from rear of engine.
66. Disconnect fuel injectors, Manifold Absolute Pressure (MAP) sensor and throttle actuator electrical connectors from front of engine.
67. Remove engine harness clip from fuel rail stud.
68. Disconnect starter inline and AIR check valve electrical connectors from top of engine.
69. Disconnect engine harness electrical connector from engine valley jumper harness electrical connector.
70. Disconnect engine harness electrical connector from power steering sensor and harness clip from steering gear shield.
71. Remove mounting nut and engine harness ground.
72. Disconnect engine harness electrical connectors from Engine Coolant Temperature (ECT) sensor and Vehicle Speed Sensor (VSS).
73. Remove engine harness clips from rear engine mount bracket and steering gear shield.
74. Disconnect engine harness electrical connector from air conditioning pressure sensor and remove harness clip from engine boss.
75. Disconnect oil pressure sensor, oil level sensor, air conditioning compressor and alternator electrical connectors.
76. Disconnect AIR pump and brake modulator engine harness electrical connectors.
77. Remove engine bracket harness clip.
78. Disconnect engine harness electrical connector from HO2S and transaxle.
79. Remove ground bolts and engine harness with all branches.
80. Disconnect clamp and remove power steering outlet hose from reservoir.
81. Remove power steering outlet pipe bolt from engine mount strut bracket.
82. Remove power steering pump inlet pipe fitting and rear engine mount bracket stud power steering inlet pipe nut.
83. Remove power steering inlet pipe bracket from stud.
84. Remove compressor nut and disconnect discharge hose from engine. Remove hose and plug compressor discharge port.
85. Remove compressor nut and disconnect suction hose from engine. Remove hose and plug compressor suction port.
86. Remove mounting bolt and nuts, then the transaxle brace.
87. Remove mounting bolts, bolt/stud and transaxle brace.
88. Loosen front engine mount bracket nut in front to transaxle brace.
89. Remove mounting bolt and transaxle brace.
90. Support engine with suitable lifting device with chain to lift brackets.
91. Remove rear engine mount to frame nut.
92. Remove mounting bolts, stud and rear engine mount bracket.
93. Remove front engine mount to frame nut and rear transaxle bolt.
94. Remove upper transaxle bolts and separate engine from transaxle.
95. Raise engine from supported frame and transaxle.
96. Remove mounting bolts, nuts and front engine mount bracket.
97. Reverse procedure to install.

STS

1. Lock front wheels and steering column in straight ahead position by installing steering column anti-rotation pin tool No. J42640, or equivalent, to steering column.
2. Remove mounting bolts and cross-vehicle brace.
3. Remove power steering and engine oil fill caps, then the sight shield.
4. Disconnect PCV tube from air cleaner duct.
5. Loosen clamps at throttle body and Mass Air Flow (MAF/Intake Air Temperature (IAT) sensor, then remove air cleaner duct.
6. Disconnect electrical MAF/IAT sensor connector and remove.

7. Remove from top of air cleaner and position coolant hose aside.
8. Remove mounting screws and air cleaner.
9. Disconnect and position surge tank inlet hose to engine.
10. Recover air conditioning refrigerant as outlined in "Air Conditioning" chapter.
11. Disconnect air conditioning suction hose fitting at top of lefthand shock tower.
12. Disconnect retainer and position suction hose to engine.
13. Disconnect conditioning liquid line from condenser and fan shroud.
14. Disconnect from brake booster and position vacuum line to engine.
15. Disconnect master cylinder brake fluid level switch electrical connector.
16. Remove mounting nuts and secure master cylinder to engine using suitable mechanics wire. **Do not disconnect brake lines.**
17. Relieve fuel system pressure as outlined in "Precautions."
18. Remove fuel line retainer from heater lines bracket on front of dash.
19. Disconnect engine wiring harness connector C102 on front of dash.
20. Disconnect underhood fuse block connector C5 between righthand shock tower and valve cover.
21. Remove underhood electrical center cover.
22. Remove battery ground cable bolt and retainer from righthand shock tower, then position cable to engine.
23. Remove mounting nut and battery cable from inside underhood electrical center, then position cable to engine.
24. Disconnect chassis electrical connector at top of righthand shock tower and position wire to engine.
25. Disconnect engine wiring harness C5 connector from inside of underhood electrical center and C113 from righthand frame rail.
26. Loosen fan nut from crank adapter shaft using tool No. J41240-5A or equivalent, then raise and support vehicle.
27. Remove fan from crank adapter shaft, then the front tire and wheel assemblies.
28. **On models equipped with standard cooling,** proceed as follows:
    a. Disconnect cooling fan electrical connectors.
    b. Remove auxiliary water pump and hoses.
    c. Disconnect condenser tube from cooling fan shroud clip.
    d. Disconnect from fan shroud and position surge tank inlet hose aside.
    e. Remove mounting bolts and shroud, then the cooling fan.
29. **On models equipped with heavy duty cooling,** proceed as follows:
    a. Loosen fan nut from crank adapter shaft using fan clutch remove and installer tool No. J41240, or equivalent.
    b. Disconnect condenser tube from fan shroud clip.
    c. Remove mounting bolts and cool-

ing fan shroud.
    d. Remove fan. **Do not completely remove fan from crank adapter shaft.**
30. **On all models,** raise and support vehicle, then remove front tires and wheels.
31. Remove three push-in retainers and splash shields from both wheel housings.
32. Remove six push-in retainers and wheel housing liners.
33. Remove windshield washer reservoir brace from front frame through righthand wheel housing.
34. Disconnect transmission oil cooler lines through lefthand wheelhouse and drain into suitable container.
35. Remove bolt, then separate center from lower intermediate shaft.
36. Drain cooling system into suitable container.
37. Remove power steering cooler lines radiator bolt and lower vehicle.
38. Remove condenser upper and lower mounting bolts.
39. Disconnect side air baffle to radiator lower pins and transmission oil cooler mounting bolts.
40. Lower vehicle.
41. Disconnect clamps, then remove radiator outlet and inlet hoses.
42. Disconnect clamp, then remove surge tank inlet hose.
43. Remove mounting bolts and radiator support brackets.
44. Disconnect air baffle to radiator upper pins and remove radiator.
45. Raise and support vehicle.
46. Remove bracket mounting bolts and secure power steering oil cooler to engine using suitable mechanics wire.
47. **On models equipped with AWD,** remove transfer case as outlined in **MOTOR's "Domestic Transmission, In-Vehicle Service" manual or "Transmission Service DVD."**
48. **On all models,** remove transmission as outlined in **MOTOR's "Domestic Transmission, In-Vehicle Service" manual or "Transmission Service DVD."**
49. Remove brake bundle clips from left and righthand rails. **Do not remove clips from brake lines.**
50. Disconnect fuel line from fuel filter and evaporative emission hose connection at rear of fuel filter.
51. Disconnect rear brake lines from bracket above rear axle.
52. Remove fuel and brake line bundle retainers from frame rail along length of vehicle. **Do not remove retainers from lines.**
53. Remove fuel filter bracket for access path for fuel and brake line bundle.
54. Remove fuel and brake line bundle bracket from righthand wheel house.
55. Lower vehicle.
56. Disconnect heater outlet hose from pipe and position hose to engine, then inlet hose from water housing and position hose to vehicle.
57. **On models equipped with Magnaride,** disconnect left and righthand

shock module top electrical connectors.
58. **On all models,** remove upper mounting bolts and secure shock modules to front frame using suitable mechanics wire.
59. Raise vehicle, then support under engine, front frame and suspension using suitable lift table. **Support vehicle with suitable jack stands.**
60. Raise lift table and or lower vehicle to preload engine, front frame, and front suspension weight .
61. Remove front frame bolts.
62. Lower table or raise vehicle to remove engine, front frame, fuel/brake bundle and front suspension. **Ensure hoses, wires, pipes and shock modules clear vehicle.**
63. Install engine lift bracket No. J28467-86, or equivalent, to lefthand cylinder head and J28467-87, or equivalent, to righthand cylinder head.
64. Remove engine from frame using suitable engine lift.
65. Reverse procedure to install.

INTAKE MANIFOLD
REPLACE

DeVille & Seville

1. Drain coolant into suitable container.
2. Remove intake manifold sight shield.
3. Disconnect ball studs and remove intake manifold top sight shield cover.
4. Remove fuel rail pressure fitting cap and connect suitable fuel pressure gauge wrapping fitting with suitable towel.
5. Install bleed hose into suitable container.
6. Relieve fuel tank vapor pressure by loosening fuel filler cap.
7. Open valve and bleed system pressure.
8. Remove TBI air intake duct.
9. Remove transaxle vent hose and shift cable at bracket.
10. Disconnect TP sensor and IAC valve electrical connectors.
11. Disconnect TBI accelerator and cruise control cables.
12. Mark location for installation alignment, then disconnect front bank spark plug wires or coil units. Position wires or coils aside.
13. Disconnect TBI unit coolant hoses at TBI unit and surge tank pipe.
14. Disconnect TBI unit spacer. EGR and crankcase ventilation pipes.
15. Disconnect vacuum lines, PCV hoses and electrical connectors.
16. Disconnect brake booster vacuum hose at intake manifold vacuum fitting.
17. Remove fuel rail ground wire at rear cylinder head.
18. Twist fuel rail fuel line female quick-connector fittings ¼ turn in each direction to loosen any dirt within fitting. Blow dirt out of fitting using compressed air.
19. Disconnect fuel line quick-connect fittings using separator tool No. J37088-A, or equivalent.

20. Disconnect fuel rail bracket at EGR valve.
21. Disconnect PCV hose at intake manifold.
22. Disconnect injector harness main electrical connector.
23. Remove mounting bolts and studs, then the intake manifold. Carrier gaskets remain attached to manifold.
24. Reverse procedure to install. **Torque** manifold mounting bolts and nuts to 89 inch lbs. in sequence, **Fig. 1.**

DTS & STS

1. **On STS models,** remove mounting bolts and cross-vehicle brace.
2. **On all models,** remove power steering and engine oil fill caps, then the sight shield.
3. Remove PCV dirty air tube from valve cover.
4. Remove PCV fresh air tube.
5. Remove mounting nuts and sight shield bracket.
6. Disconnect left and righthand fuel injector electrical connectors, then the EVAP purge valve line and connector.
7. Remove EVAP line from righthand cylinder head and position line aside.
8. Relieve fuel system pressure as outlined under "Precautions."
9. Disconnect fuel line from fuel rail remove line from righthand cylinder head.
10. Remove mounting bolts, then the fuel rail and injector assembly.
11. Loosen plenum duct clamp at front of intake manifold
12. Remove mounting bolts and intake manifold.
13. Reverse procedure to install, noting the following:
    a. Lightly grease inside edge of rubber plenum duct.
    b. Install new intake manifold gaskets.
    c. **Torque,** intake manifold bolts to 89 inch lbs. in sequence **Fig. 1.**
    d. Lubricate fuel injector bores with suitable, light mineral or clean engine oil.

EXHAUST MANIFOLD
REPLACE

DeVille & Seville
LEFTHAND

1. Disconnect AIR pipe from manifold.
2. Remove engine mount as outlined in "Engine Mount, Replace."
3. Remove manifold outlet flange mounting bolts.
4. Disconnect oxygen sensor electrical connector.
5. Remove mounting bolts, exhaust manifold and oxygen sensor.
6. Reverse procedure to install. Coat oxygen sensor threads with suitable high temperature anti-seize compound.

RIGHTHAND

1. Disconnect both battery cables, then

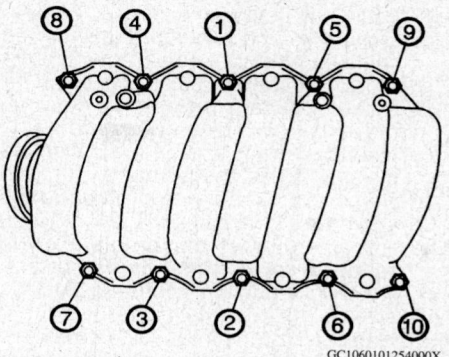

Fig. 1 Intake manifold tightening sequence

GC1060101254000X

rear oxygen sensor electrical connector and harness clip.
2. Lock steering column in straight-ahead position using lock pin tool No. J42640, or equivalent, in underside of column.
3. Raise and support vehicle.
4. Disconnect exhaust pipe from catalytic converter.
5. Disconnect AIR pipe from manifold.
6. Disconnect suspension position sensor at both lower control arms.
7. Remove heat shields from power steering gear, VSS and transaxle.
8. Remove steering intermediate shaft pinch bolt.
9. Disconnect intermediate shaft from steering gear.
10. Remove righthand engine mount to mount bracket nut.
11. Remove lefthand transaxle mount to mount bracket nut.
12. Support engine cradle rear crossmember using suitable screw jack and remove cradle to body mounting bolts.
13. Lower rear of engine cradle.
14. Remove pipe to exhaust manifold and crossover exhaust pipe mounting bolts.
15. Remove righthand side cylinder head to transaxle brace.
16. Remove mounting nuts and exhaust manifold.
17. Reverse procedure to install. Coat oxygen sensor threads with high temperature anti-seize compound.

DTS
LEFTHAND

1. Remove front engine mount bracket as outlined under "Engine Mount, Replace."
2. Remove Connector Position Assurance (CPA) retainer.
3. Disconnect electrical connector and remove Heated Oxygen Sensor (HO2S).
4. Remove front pipe mounting bolts.
5. Remove exhaust manifold bolts mounting bolts and manifold.
6. Reverse procedure to install, noting the following:
    a. Install new front exhaust manifold pipe flange seal and exhaust manifold gasket.

    b. Coat HO2S thread with suitable anti-seize compound.

RIGHTHAND

1. Remove Connector Position Assurance (CPA) retainer.
2. Disconnect HO2S electrical connector.
3. Remove Secondary Air Injection (AIR) valve hose bracket HO2S clip.
4. Lock front wheels and steering column in straight ahead position using steering column lock pin tool No. J42640, or equivalent.
5. Raise and support vehicle.
6. Remove catalytic converter to rear exhaust manifold pipe nuts.
7. Pull exhaust system rearward to allow catalytic converter studs to clear rear exhaust manifold pipe. **Do not over-flex or damage flex joint.** Discard catalytic converter gasket.
8. Remove rear exhaust manifold pipe.
9. Disconnect AIR check valve electrical connector.
10. Pinch constant tension clamp and remove pipe from AIR check valve.
11. Remove mount nuts, bolts and AIR check valve. Discard gasket.
12. Disconnect steering gear heat shield engine harness clip.
13. Remove mounting bolts and steering gear heat shield.
14. Disconnect electronic suspension position sensor link ball studs from lower control arms.
15. Disconnect and remove intermediate shaft seal.
16. Remove pinch bolt and separate intermediate shaft from steering gear.
17. Support rear of frame using suitable adjustable jack.
18. Remove four rearward engine frame to body bolts, then lower rear engine frame approximately 1.5 inches.
19. Remove HO2S.
20. Remove mounting nuts and exhaust manifold. Discard gasket.
21. Reverse procedure to install.

STS
LEFTHAND

1. Remove mounting bolts and cross-vehicle brace.
2. Remove power steering and engine oil fill caps, then the fuel injector sight shield.
3. Disconnect PCV tube from air cleaner duct.
4. Loosen throttle body and Mass Air Flow/Intake Air Temperature (MAF/IAT) sensor clamps, remove air cleaner duct.
5. Disconnect MAF/IAT sensor electrical connector.
6. Remove MAF/IAT sensor mounting screws and sensor. Discard gasket.
7. Remove coolant hose from air cleaner top and position hose aside.
8. Remove air cleaner.
9. Remove air conditioning lines to lefthand shock tower attaching nut, position lines aside.
10. Remove exhaust manifold heat shield

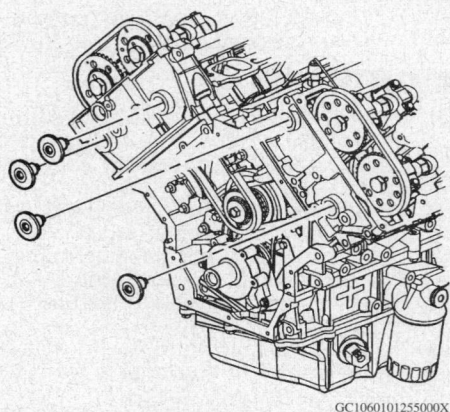

Fig. 2 Chain guide access plug replacement. DeVille & Seville

upper front mounting bolt.

11. Disconnect electrical connector, the remove mounting bolt and position master cylinder toward engine.
12. Remove exhaust manifold heat shield upper rear mounting bolt.
13. Disconnect both heated oxygen sensor pigtail connectors from wiring harness connector.
14. Remove power steering gear as outlined under "Power Steering Gear, Replace" in "Front Suspension & Steering" section.
15. Remove bolt and intermediate from center steering shaft.
16. Remove HO2Ss.
17. Remove two mounting bolts and floor panel tunnel brace.
18. Support exhaust system.
19. Remove exhaust pipes to manifold mounting nuts.
20. Pry front exhaust hangers free from rear suspension hanger rods.
21. Apply suitable lubricant and pry tail pipe hangers from tail pipe hanger rods.
22. Lower exhaust system. Discard seals.
23. Remove mounting bolts and exhaust manifold heat shield.
24. Remove mounting bolts, nuts and studs, then the exhaust manifold. Discard mounting bolts and gasket.
25. Reverse procedure to install.

RIGHTHAND

1. Remove alternator as outlined under "Alternator, Replace" in "Electrical" section.
2. Raise and support vehicle, then remove right front tire and wheel.
3. Remove bolt and intermediate from center steering shaft.
4. Disconnect connectors and remove HO2Ss.
5. Remove two mounting bolts and floor panel tunnel brace.
6. Support exhaust system.
7. Remove exhaust pipes to manifold mounting nuts.
8. Pry front exhaust hangers free from rear suspension hanger rods.
9. Apply suitable lubricant and pry tail pipe hangers from tail pipe hanger rods.
10. Lower exhaust system. Discard ex-

haust manifold seals.
11. Loosen steering linkage inner tie rod nut, then remove rack and pinion outer tie rod end nut.
12. Disconnect rack and pinion outer tie rod end from steering knuckle using steering linkage and tie rod puller tool No. J24319-B, or equivalent.
13. Remove rack and pinion outer tie rod end from steering linkage inner tie rod. **Record number of complete turns required for installation alignment.**
14. Remove mounting bolts and position wire harness bracket aside.
15. Remove exhaust manifold heat shield mounting bolts, then position shield forward near alternator mounts.
16. Remove mounting bolts, nuts and studs, then the righthand exhaust manifold. Discard mounting bolts and gasket.
17. Reverse procedure to install.

CYLINDER HEAD
REPLACE

DeVille & Seville

1. Remove exhaust manifolds as outlined under "Exhaust Manifold, Replace."
2. Remove intake manifold as outlined under "Intake Manifold, Replace."
3. Remove valve covers as outlined under "Valve Cover, Replace."
4. Remove crankshaft dampner as outlined under "Crankshaft dampner, Replace."
5. Remove front cover as outlined under "Front Cover, Replace."
6. Remove timing chain tensioner from cylinder head.
7. Remove camshaft sprockets. **Timing chains should remain in chain case.**
8. Remove timing chain guide mounting screws through access plugs at cylinder head front, **Fig. 2.**
9. Remove water crossover and exhaust manifold as outlined under "Exhaust Manifold, Replace."
10. Remove cylinder head mounting bolts. **Discard M11 bolts.** M6 bolts can be used again.
11. Remove cylinder head and gasket. **Do not rest cylinder head on a flat surface with head face down.**
12. Reverse procedure to install, noting the following:
    a. Install new M11 bolts. M6 bolts can be used again.
    b. Refer to sequences, **Figs. 3 and 4,** and tighten M11 cylinder head bolts in four steps: First step, **torque** bolts to 30 ft. lbs.; second step, tighten bolts an additional 70°; third step, tighten bolts an additional 60°; fourth step, tighten bolts an additional 45.°
    c. **Torque** M6 cylinder head bolts to 106 inch lbs.

DTS
LEFTHAND

1. Remove lefthand exhaust manifolds

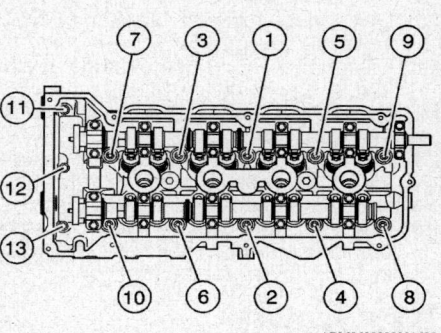

Fig. 3 Cylinder head bolt tightening sequence. Lefthand

as outlined under "Exhaust Manifold, Replace."
2. Remove mounting nuts and retainer, then position surge tank aside.
3. Remove mounting bolts and engine mount strut, then the righthand front tire and wheel.
4. Remove alternator as outlined under "Alternator, Replace" in "Electrical" section.
5. Remove intake manifold as outlined under "Intake Manifold, Replace."
6. Remove camshaft cover as outlined under "Valve Cover, Replace."
7. Recover air conditioning refrigerant as outlined in "Air Conditioning" chapter.
8. Disconnect air conditioning compressor suction hose from evaporator hose. Position hose aside and discard seal.
9. Remove mounting bolt and drive belt tensioner.
10. Loosen mounting bolt and remove drive belt idler pulley.
11. Remove Crankshaft Balancer as outlined under "Crankshaft Damper, Replace."
12. Remove mounting bolts, front cover and gasket.
13. Remove lefthand secondary camshaft drive chain as outlined under "Timing Chain, Replace."
14. Remove M6 and M11 cylinder head bolts. **Discard M11 cylinder head bolts.**
15. Remove lefthand cylinder head. Ensure no locating puns are stuck in head. Discard gasket.
16. Reverse procedure to install, noting the following:
    a. Install new M11 bolts. M6 bolts can be used again.
    b. Refer to sequences, **Figs. 3 and 4,** and tighten M11 cylinder head bolts in four steps: First step, **torque** bolts to 22 ft. lbs.; second step, tighten bolts an additional 60°; third step, tighten bolts an additional 60°; fourth step, tighten bolts an additional 60.°
    c. **Torque** M6 bolts to 106 inch lbs.

RIGHTHAND

1. Remove righthand exhaust manifolds as outlined under "Exhaust Manifold, Replace."
2. Remove water crossover as outlined under "Water Crossover, Replace."

3. Remove intake manifold as outlined under "Intake Manifold, Replace."
4. Remove camshaft cover as outlined under "Valve Cover, Replace."
5. Recover air conditioning refrigerant as outlined in "Air Conditioning" chapter.
6. Disconnect air conditioning compressor suction hose from evaporator hose. Position hose aside and discard seal.
7. Remove mounting bolt and drive belt tensioner.
8. Loosen mounting bolt and remove drive belt idler pulley.
9. Remove Crankshaft Balancer as outlined under "Crankshaft Damper, Replace."
10. Remove mounting bolts, front cover and gasket.
11. Remove righthand secondary camshaft drive chain as outlined under "Timing Chain, Replace."
12. Disconnect Engine Coolant Temperature (ECT) sensor electrical connector.
13. Remove nut and engine harness ground terminal.
14. Remove exhaust manifold front pipe to cylinder head stud.
15. Raise and support vehicle.
16. Remove right engine mount bracket to cylinder head mounting stud.
17. Loosen engine mount bracket to transaxle mounting bolts.
18. Remove transaxle brace to the transaxle mounting bolt.
19. Lower vehicle.
20. Remove transaxle brace to the lift bracket studs and transaxle brace.
21. Remove studs and rear lift bracket.
22. Remove M6 and M11 cylinder head bolts. **Discard M11 cylinder head bolts.**
23. Remove lefthand cylinder head. Ensure no locating puns are stuck in head. Discard gasket
24. Reverse procedure to install, noting the following:
    a. Install new M11 bolts. M6 bolts can be used again.
    b. Refer to sequences, **Figs. 3 and 4,** and tighten M11 cylinder head bolts in four steps: First step, **torque** bolts to 22 ft. lbs.; second step, tighten bolts an additional 60°; third step, tighten bolts an additional 60°; fourth step, tighten bolts an additional 60.°
    c. **Torque** M6 bolts to 106 inch lbs.

STS

1. Remove exhaust manifolds as outlined under "Exhaust Manifold, Replace."
2. Remove water crossover as outlined under "Water Crossover, Replace."
3. Remove intake manifold as outlined under "Intake Manifold Replace."
4. Remove secondary camshaft drive chain as outlined under "Timing Chain Replace."
5. Remove camshafts as outlined under "Camshaft Replace."
6. Remove cylinder head power steering reservoir return hose mounting bolts.
7. Remove M6 and M11 cylinder head

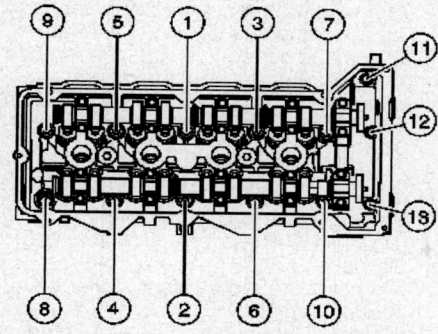

ARM0600000001686

Fig. 4 Cylinder head bolt tightening sequence. Righthand

bolts. **Discard M11 cylinder head bolts.**
8. Remove lefthand cylinder head. Ensure no locating puns are stuck in head. Discard gasket
9. Reverse procedure to install, noting the following:
    a. Install new M11 bolts. M6 bolts can be used again.
    b. Refer to sequences, **Figs. 3 and 4,** and tighten M11 cylinder head bolts in four steps: First step, **torque** bolts to 22 ft. lbs.; second step, tighten bolts an additional 60°; third step, tighten bolts an additional 60°; fourth step, tighten bolts an additional 60.°
    c. **Torque** M6 bolts to 106 inch lbs.

VALVE COVER
REPLACE
DeVille & Seville
LEFTHAND

1. Remove intake manifold sight shield and upper filler panel.
2. Partially drain coolant into suitable container.
3. Remove radiator hose from water crossover and position aside.
4. Disconnect PCV fresh air tube.
5. Tag their locations, then remove ignition coils and spark plug boots.
6. Remove engine coolant heater wire and position aside.
7. Disconnect alternator cooler outlet hose from pipe and position pipe aside.
8. Remove shield and water pump drive belt.
9. Remove water pump belt tensioner and dust cap from end of camshaft.
10. Remove water pump drive pulley using pulley removal tool No. J38825, or equivalent.
11. Remove camshaft seal and discard.
12. Remove valve cover mounting bolts.
13. Lift valve cover drive end and remove reward to clear water pump driveshaft.
14. Reverse procedure install, noting the following:
    a. Install new camshaft seal. Apply sealer part No. 1052080, or equivalent, to retainer bolt threads.

b. Install water pump pulley using pulley installer tool No. J38823, or equivalent.

RIGHTHAND

1. Remove intake manifold sight shield.
2. Disconnect PCV valve and oxygen sensor wire.
3. Disconnect AIR vent solenoid vacuum tubes and electrical connector, then remove AIR bracket and tube.
4. Tag their locations, then disconnect and remove ignition coils and spark plug boots.
5. Remove mounting bolts and valve cover.
6. Reverse procedure to install.

DTS
LEFTHAND

1. Remove power steering and engine oil fill caps, then the sight shield.
2. Remove two front latch support and four upper tie bar mounting two bolts, then two radiator upper support bracket mounting bolts and upper tie bar.
3. Drain cooling system into suitable container.
4. Disconnect clamp and remove water pump radiator inlet hose.
5. Disconnect Positive Crankcase Ventilation (PCV) fresh air tube quick connect fitting.
6. Disconnect ignition coil electrical connector, then remove mounting bolts and ignition coils.
7. Remove valve cover clip and position engine harness aside.
8. Loosen Ignition Control Module (ICM) wiring harness ground bolt and from ground wire terminal/bolt from valve cover.
9. Remove mounting bolts and nuts, then the water pump drive belt shield.
10. Remove water pump belt from pulleys.
11. Remove stud and water pump belt tensioner.
12. Remove intake camshaft plastic dust cap.
13. Remove water pump pulley from intake camshaft using water pump drive pulley remover tool No. J38825, or equivalent.
14. Remove mounting bolts and camshaft seal. Discard seal.
15. Loosen mounting bolts and lift valve cover drive end up.
16. Remove valve cover rearward clearing water pump drive shaft. Disconnect valve cover perimeter and spark plug.
17. Reverse procedure to install, noting the following:
    a. Lubricate new camshaft seal lip with suitable engine oil and push into position using protective sleeve provided with new seal.
    b. Coat camshaft seal bolts' threads with suitable sealant.

RIGHTHAND

1. Remove power steering and engine oil fill caps, then the sight shield.
2. Disconnect Secondary Air Injection (AIR) check valve electrical connector.

3. Pinch constant tension clamp and remove pipe from AIR check valve.
4. Remove mount nuts, bolts and AIR check valve. Discard gasket.
5. Disconnect Positive Crankcase Ventilation (PCV) foul air tube quick connect fitting.
6. Disconnect ignition coil electrical connector, then remove mounting bolts and ignition coils.
7. Loosen mounting bolts and remove valve cover. . Disconnect valve cover perimeter and spark plug.
8. Reverse procedure to install, noting the following:
   a. Lubricate new camshaft seal lip with suitable engine oil and push into position using protective sleeve provided with new seal.
   b. Coat camshaft seal bolts' threads with suitable sealant.

STS

LEFTHAND

1. Remove mounting bolts and cross vehicle brace.
2. Remove power steering and engine oil fill caps, then the sight shield.
3. Disconnect PCV fresh air tube from valve cover.
4. Remove ignition coil cover.
5. Disconnect electrical connector, then remove mounting bolt and ignition coil.
6. Remove ground strap to valve cover mounting bolt.
7. Remove mounting bolt and position oil level indicator tube aside.
8. Remove mounting bolts, and remove valve cover.
9. Reverse procedure install, noting the following:
   a. Install new cover gasket.
   b. Apply small amount of suitable sealer to split line of lefthand cylinder head and camshaft position actuator.

RIGHTHAND

1. Remove mounting bolts and cross-vehicle brace.
2. Remove power steering and engine oil fill caps, then the sight shield.
3. Disconnect PCV dirty air tube from valve cover.
4. Remove covers wiper arm mounting nuts from spindles.
5. Remove upper assist rods and ball studs, then the driver's side wiper arm. **Apply pressure only at assist rod end.**
6. Remove passenger side wiper arm using wiper arm puller tool No. J39822, or equivalent.
7. Remove rear hood seal, then three mounting screws and air inlet grille.
8. Remove mounting nut and air inlet grille panel.
9. Remove wiper motor mini 10 and 30 amp fuses from underhood fuse block.
10. Remove wiper motor module mounting bolts and disconnect electrical connector. Remove wiper motor module.
11. Remove mounting bolts, and remove valve cover.

12. Remove battery, then the mounting bolts and battery tray.
13. Raise and support vehicle, the remove 16 retainers and front air deflector.
14. Remove cylinder head wire harness bracket mounting bolts and lower vehicle.
15. Remove ignition coil cover.
16. Disconnect electrical connector, then remove mounting bolt and ignition coil.
17. Disconnect clips and position cable harness aside.
18. Remove ground strap to valve cover mounting bolt.
19. Remove mounting bolts, and remove valve cover.
20. Reverse procedure install, noting the following:
    a. Install new cover gasket.
    b. Apply small amount of suitable sealer to split line of righthand cylinder head and camshaft position actuator.

VALVE CLEARANCE SPECIFICATIONS

This engine is equipped with hydraulic lifters. Valve adjustment is not required.

VALVE ADJUSTMENT

This engine is equipped with hydraulic lifters. Valve adjustment is not required.

CRANKSHAFT DAMPER
REPLACE

DeVille & Seville

1. Mark running direction and remove serpentine belt.
2. Raise and support vehicle.
3. Remove righthand front wheel and splash shields.
4. Remove brace between engine oil pan and transaxle case.
5. Remove flexplate inspection cover.
6. Install flexplate holder tool No. J44214, or equivalent.
7. Remove balancer mounting bolt.
8. Support engine cradle with suitable screw jack.
9. Remove engine mount to mount bracket nut.
10. Lower engine to allow clearance for puller tool below body rail.
11. Install pilot into end of crankshaft.
12. Remove crankshaft dampner using puller tool No. J41816, or equivalent.
13. Reverse procedure to install using crankshaft balancer installer tool No. J41998-B, or equivalent.

DTS

1. Remove mounting bolts and transaxle to engine brace.
2. Remove mounting bolt and torque converter cover.
3. Lock engine using flywheel holder tool No. J44214, or equivalent.
4. Remove crankshaft balancer bolt.

5. Remove eight retainers and radiator support sight shield.
6. Remove retainers and front air deflector.
7. Remove 12 retainers and two mounting bolts, then two mounting nuts and front fascia cover. Disconnect electrical connector.
8. Support engine frame with suitable adjustable jack, then remove righthand side mounting bolts and lower frame for body rail working clearance.
9. Remove crankshaft balancer using crankshaft balancer remover tool No. J41816, or equivalent.
10. Reverse procedure to install using crankshaft balancer installer tool No. J41998-B, or equivalent.

STS

1. Remove mounting bolts and cross-vehicle brace.
2. Remove power steering and engine oil fill caps, then the sight shield.
3. Disconnect air cleaner duct Positive Crankcase Ventilation (PCV) tube.
4. Loosen throttle body and Mass Air Flow (MAF/Intake Air Temperature (IAT) sensor clamps, then remove air cleaner duct.
5. Release drive belt tension by turning tensioner clockwise.
6. Remove belt from water pump pulley and slide it from behind drive tensioner.
7. Allow tensioner to return to relaxed position and remove belt from remaining pulley.
8. Release alternator drive belt tension by turning tensioner clockwise.
9. Remove belt from alternator pulley and allow tensioner to return to relaxed position.
10. Remove alternator drive belt from pulleys.
11. **On models equipped with crankshaft driven cooling fan,** remove mounting bolts and fan bracket.
12. **On all models,** raise and support vehicle, then remove transmission bell housing inspection hole cover.
13. Lock engine using flywheel holding tool No. EN48018, or equivalent.
14. Remove crankshaft balancer bolt.
15. Remove crankshaft balancer using crankshaft button tool No. J38416-2 and crankshaft balancer remover tool No. J24420-C, or equivalents.
16. Reverse procedure to install using crankshaft balancer installer tool No. J41998-B, or equivalent.

FRONT COVER
REPLACE

DeVille & Seville

1. Remove serpentine drive belt.
2. Remove crankshaft dampner as outlined under "Crankshaft dampner, Replace."
3. Remove belt tensioner and idler pulley.

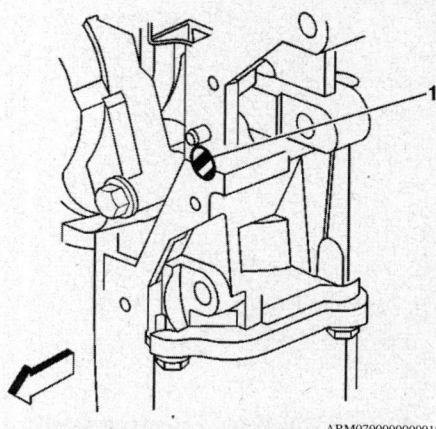

Fig. 5 Front cover sealant application. DeVille, DTS & Seville

4. Raise and support vehicle, then support engine assembly using suitable jack.
5. Remove engine mount to mount bracket and bracket to engine mounting nuts.
6. Remove mounting bolts and front cover. **Do not discard gasket unless it is damaged.**
7. Reverse procedure to install, noting the following:
   a. Apply small amount of sealant part No. 12345739, or equivalent, at split line of upper and lower crankcases, **Fig. 5.**
   b. **Torque** front cover bolts to 89 inch lbs. in sequence, **Fig. 6.**

DTS

1. Remove mounting bolt and drive belt tensioner.
2. Loosen mounting bolt and remove drive belt idler pulley.
3. Remove crankshaft balancer as outlined under "Crankshaft Damper, Replace."
4. Remove mounting bolts, front cover and gasket.
5. Reverse procedure to install, noting the following:
   a. Apply small amount of sealant part No. 12345739, or equivalent, at split line of upper and lower crankcases, **Fig. 5.**
   b. **Torque** front cover bolts to 89 inch lbs. in sequence, **Fig. 6.**

STS

1. Drain engine coolant into suitable container.
2. Disconnect Positive Crankcase Ventilation (PCV) tube from air cleaner duct.
3. Disconnect air duct clamp at throttle body and Mass Air Flow (MAF/Intake Air Temperature (IAT) sensor.
4. Disconnect heater outlet hose from thermostat housing using suitable hose clamp pliers.
5. Disconnect clamp and remove bypass

hose water outlet housing and front cover.
6. **On models equipped with auxiliary water pump,** proceed as follows:
   a. Disconnect clamps and remove auxiliary water pump hoses.
   b. Disconnect electrical connector.
   c. Remove mounting nuts and auxiliary water pump.
7. **On all models,** remove mounting bolts and cross-vehicle brace.
8. Remove power steering and engine oil fill caps, then the sight shield.
9. Disconnect air cleaner duct Positive Crankcase Ventilation (PCV) tube.
10. Loosen throttle body and Mass Air Flow (MAF/Intake Air Temperature (IAT) sensor clamps, then remove air cleaner duct.
11. Remove mounting bolts and fan bracket.
12. Release drive belt tension by turning tensioner clockwise.
13. Remove belt from water pump pulley and slide it from behind drive tensioner.
14. Allow tensioner to return to relaxed position and remove belt from remaining pulley.
15. Remove mounting bolt and belt tensioner.
16. Release alternator drive belt tension by turning tensioner clockwise.
17. Remove belt from alternator pulley and allow tensioner to return to relaxed position.
18. Remove alternator drive belt from pulleys.
19. Remove mounting bolt and belt tensioner.
20. Remove mounting bolts, then the drive belt idler and water pump pulleys.
21. Raise and support vehicle, then remove crankshaft balancer as outlined under "Crankshaft Damper, Replace."
22. Remove mounting bolts and engine front cover. Discard gasket.
23. Reverse procedure to install, noting the following:
   a. Apply small amount of sealant part No. 12345739, or equivalent, at split line of upper and lower crankcases, **Fig. 7.**
   b. Place gasket evenly over dowel pins.
   c. **Torque** front cover bolts to 11 ft. lbs. in sequence, **Fig. 8.**

TIMING CHAIN
REPLACE
Primary

DEVILLE & SEVILLE

1. Remove engine as outlined under "Engine, Replace" and mount on suitable stand.
2. Mark running direction and remove serpentine belt.
3. Remove idler pulley and belt tensioner.
4. Remove front cover as outlined under "Front Cover, Replace."
5. Remove oil pump as outlined under "Oil Pump, Replace."

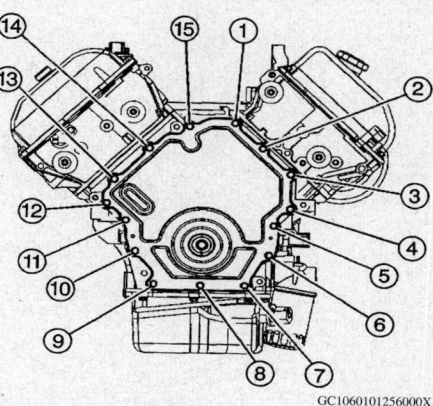

Fig. 6 Front cover bolt tightening sequence. DeVille, DTS & Seville

6. Remove valve covers as outlined under "Valve Cover, Replace."
7. Remove timing chain tensioners and camshaft sprockets.
8. Remove secondary drive chains from intermediate shaft sprocket.
9. Remove one intermediate shaft sprocket bolt, then slide gears and primary drive chain off crankshaft and intermediate shaft.
10. Reverse procedure to install. Time camshafts as outlined under "Camshaft, Replace."

DTS & STS
REMOVAL

1. Remove front cover as outlined under "Front Cover, Replace."
2. Remove three larger head mounting bolts.
3. Slide oil pump off crankshaft nose with drive collar in place, **Fig. 9.**
4. Align primary timing marks using crankshaft socket tool No. J39946, or equivalent, **Fig. 10.**
5. Remove secondary camshaft drive chains as outlined under "Secondary."
6. Remove two mounting bolts and primary camshaft drive chain tensioner.
7. Remove oil outlet tube, then the mounting bolts and primary camshaft drive chain guide.
8. Remove camshaft intermediate sprocket mounting bolt, then the primary camshaft drive chain, crankshaft and camshaft intermediate sprockets as an assembly.

Installation

1. Align camshaft intermediate and crankshaft sprockets timing marks in vertical position, **Fig. 10.**
2. Install primary camshaft drive chain on sprockets.
3. Turn crankshaft using crankshaft sprocket tool until crankshaft keyway is at approximately 1 o'clock position.
4. Install primary camshaft drive chain, crankshaft and camshaft intermediate sprockets as an assembly.
5. Tighten camshaft intermediate sprocket mounting bolt.
6. Install primary drive chain guide and tighten mounting bolts.

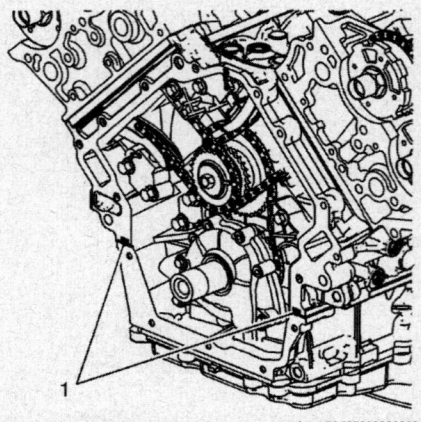

Fig. 7 Front cover sealant application. STS

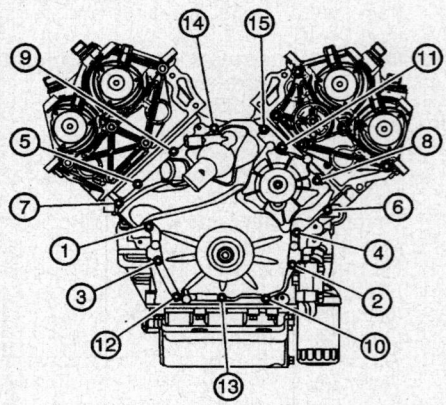

Fig. 8 Front cover bolt tightening sequence. STS

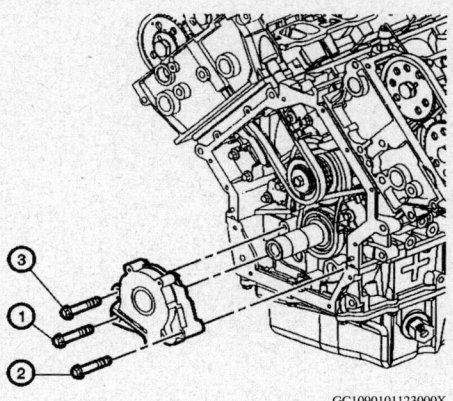

Fig. 9 Oil pump replacement

7. Rotate ratchet release lever clockwise and hold, collapse tensioner shoe and hold, then release ratchet lever.
8. Slowly release pressure on shoe until ratchet lever moves to first detent with click. Collapse tensioner shoe and hold.
9. Lock tensioner, by inserting suitable pin through release lever hole.
10. Ensure tensioner release lever is facing outward, then install primary camshaft drive chain tensioner and tighten mounting bolts.
11. Remove holding pin.
12. Install oil outlet tube and tighten mounting bolts.
13. Ensure timing marks are aligned vertically.
14. Refer to sequence, **Fig. 9,** and tighten pump mounting bolts in two steps: First step, **torque** bolts to 89 inch lbs.; second step, tighten bolts an additional 35.°

Secondary

DEVILLE & SEVILLE

1. Remove front cover as outlined under "Front Cover, Replace."
2. Remove lefthand valve cover as outlined under "Valve Cover, Replace."
3. Align timing marks.
4. Remove lefthand secondary chain tensioner.
5. Remove lefthand chain guide as outlined under "Cylinder Head, Replace."
6. Remove lefthand cam sprocket bolts and sprockets.
7. Remove lefthand secondary drive chain, **Fig. 11.**
8. Remove righthand secondary chain tensioner.
9. Remove righthand chain guide as outlined under "Cylinder Head, Replace."
10. Remove righthand cam sprocket bolts and sprockets.
11. Remove righthand secondary drive chain, **Fig. 11.**
12. Reverse procedure to install. Time camshafts as outlined under "Camshaft, Replace."

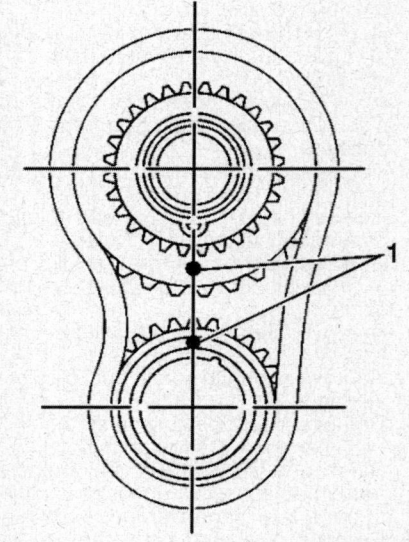

Fig. 10 Primary timing chain alignment mark alignment

DTS

REMOVAL

1. Remove front cover as outlined under "Front Cover, Replace."
2. Align primary timing marks, **Fig. 10.**
3. Install front cover bolt into engine, then wrap suitable mechanics wire tightly around both righthand secondary camshaft drive chain shoe and front cover bolt .
4. Remove two mounting bolts and righthand secondary camshaft drive chain tensioner.
5. Disconnect mounting bolt and remove Camshaft Position (CMP) sensor
6. Remove righthand camshaft cover as outlined under "Valve Cover, Replace."
7. Ensure both camshaft sprocket drive pins are at top of their rotation, **Fig. 12.**
8. Hold camshaft in position using camshaft holding tool No. J44212, or equivalent.
9. Remove mechanics wire and cover

bolt support righthand secondary camshaft drive chain shoe.
10. Prevent camshaft rotation by holding hex cast with suitable open end wrench.
11. Remove mounting bolt and righthand exhaust camshaft sprocket, then the drive chain.
12. Lift and remove chain from camshaft intermediate drive shaft sprocket teeth.
13. Install front cover bolt into engine, then wrap suitable mechanics wire tightly around both lefthand secondary camshaft drive chain shoe and front cover bolt .
14. Remove two mounting bolts and lefthand secondary camshaft drive chain tensioner.
15. Disconnect mounting bolt and remove Camshaft Position (CMP) sensor
16. Remove lefthand camshaft cover as outlined under "Valve Cover, Replace."
17. Ensure both camshaft sprocket drive pins are at top of their rotation, **Fig. 12.**
18. Hold camshaft in position using camshaft holding tool No. J44212, or equivalent.
19. Remove mechanics wire and cover bolt support lefthand secondary camshaft drive chain shoe.
20. Prevent camshaft rotation by holding hex cast with suitable open end wrench.
21. Remove mounting bolt and righthand exhaust camshaft sprocket, then the drive chain.
22. Lift and remove chain from camshaft intermediate drive shaft sprocket teeth.

INSTALLATION

1. Slide lefthand secondary camshaft drive chain down through lefthand cylinder head and place it on lefthand exhaust camshaft sprocket.
2. Route chain around camshaft intermediate drive shaft sprocket teeth inner row.
3. Install lefthand intake camshaft sprocket into the secondary camshaft drive chain.
4. Install lefthand intake camshaft sprocket onto camshaft ensuring sprocket notch marked LI (left intake) engages intake camshaft pin.

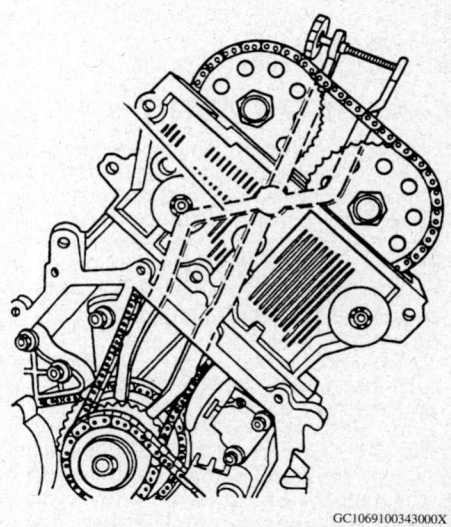

Fig. 11 Drive chain tensioning

5. Prevent camshaft rotation by holding hex cast with suitable open end wrench.
6. Tighten camshaft sprocket bolts.
7. Remove holding tool.
8. Slide righthand secondary camshaft drive chain down through righthand cylinder head and place it on righthand exhaust camshaft sprocket.
9. Route chain around camshaft intermediate drive shaft sprocket teeth inner row.
10. Install righthand intake camshaft sprocket into the secondary camshaft drive chain.
11. Install righthand intake camshaft sprocket onto camshaft ensuring sprocket notch marked LI (left intake) engages intake camshaft pin.
12. Prevent camshaft rotation by holding hex cast with suitable open end wrench.
13. Tighten camshaft sprocket bolts.
14. Remove holding tool.
15. Install camshaft coves as outlined under "Valve Cover, Replace."
16. Rotate lefthand secondary timing chain tensioner ratchet release lever counterclockwise and hold.
17. Collapse tensioner shoe and hold, then release ratchet lever.
18. Slowly release shoe pressure until ratchet lever moves to first detent with felt and heard click.
19. Collapse and hold tensioner shoe.
20. Lock tensioner shoe in collapsed position by insert pin through release lever hole.
21. Install lefthand secondary camshaft drive chain tensioner with release lever is facing outward. Tighten mounting bolts.
22. Remove pin to tighten chain slack.
23. Rotate righthand secondary timing chain tensioner ratchet release lever counterclockwise and hold.
24. Collapse tensioner shoe and hold, then release ratchet lever.
25. Slowly release shoe pressure until ratchet lever moves to first detent with felt and heard click.

26. Collapse and hold tensioner shoe.
27. Lock tensioner shoe in collapsed position by insert pin through release lever hole.
28. Install righthand secondary camshaft drive chain tensioner with release lever is facing outward. Tighten mounting bolts.
29. Remove pin to tighten chain slack.
30. Install CMP sensor and tighten mounting bolts.
31. Remove mechanics wire and cover bolt supporting secondary camshaft drive chain shoes.
32. Install engine front cover as outlined under "Front Cover, Replace."

STS

The secondary timing chains have three black links that aid in timing the camshaft position actuators to the intermediate sprocket. One black link is aligned with the intermediate sprocket; the second black link is aligned with bank 1 exhaust actuator timing mark, and the third black link is aligned with bank 1 intake actuator timing mark. The intermediate sprocket right righthand bank timing mark is labeled RB and lefthand bank LB.

It is not required that the black chain links be aligned with the camshaft actuator timing marks when the secondary chain and gear components are being serviced separately.

REMOVAL

1. Remove front cover as outlined under "Front Cover, Replace."
2. Remove three larger head mounting bolts.
3. Slide oil pump off crankshaft nose with drive collar in place, **Fig. 9.**
4. Align primary timing marks, **Fig. 10.**
5. Disconnect electrical connectors, then remove mounting bolts, then the righthand exhaust and intake Camshaft Position (CMP) sensors.
6. Remove cam sensor harness from retainers.
7. Remove righthand camshaft cover as outlined under "Valve Cover, Replace."
8. Remove mounting bolts and camshaft position actuator housings. **Do not remove actuator solenoids from housing.**
9. Hold righthand camshafts using camshaft holding tool No. EN46328, or equivalent.
10. Prevent camshaft rotation by holding hex cast with suitable open end wrench.
11. Loosen and remove exhaust and intake camshaft position oil control valves.
12. Slide intake camshaft position actuator off of camshaft and remove secondary timing chain from actuator teeth.
13. Remove timing chain.
14. Disconnect electrical connectors, then remove mounting bolts, then the lefthand exhaust and intake Camshaft Position (CMP) sensors.
15. Remove cam sensor harness from retainers.
16. Disconnect power steering reservoir cooler and outlet hoses, draining fluid

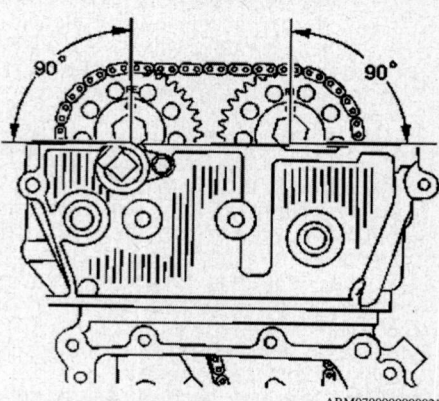

Fig. 12 Camshaft positioning. DTS & STS

into suitable container.
17. Remove mounting nuts and power steering reservoir.
18. Remove lefthand camshaft cover as outlined under "Valve Cover, Replace."
19. Remove mounting bolts and fan bracket.
20. Release drive belt tension by turning tensioner clockwise.
21. Remove belt from water pump pulley and slide it from behind drive tensioner.
22. Allow tensioner to return to relaxed position and remove belt from remaining pulley.
23. Remove mounting bolt and belt tensioner.
24. Remove mounting bolts and camshaft position actuator housings. **Do not remove actuator solenoids from housing.**
25. Hold righthand camshafts using camshaft holding tool No. EN46328, or equivalent.
26. Remove mounting bolts and secondary timing chain tensioner.
27. Prevent camshaft rotation by holding hex cast with suitable open end wrench.
28. Loosen and remove exhaust and intake camshaft position oil control valves.
29. Slide intake camshaft position actuator off of camshaft and remove secondary timing chain from actuator teeth.
30. Remove timing chain.

INSTALLATION

1. Assemble secondary timing chain to intermediate sprocket aligning sprocket LB (lefthand bank) timing mark to timing chain black link.
2. Align LB intake camshaft position actuator timing mark with timing chain black link and install actuator on camshaft with actuator timing mark perpendicular (90°) to cylinder head deck surface near top of rotation.
3. Secure intake actuator by loosely installing oil control valve.
4. Prevent camshaft form using suitable open-end wrench on hex cast and tighten oil control valve.

5. Align LB exhaust camshaft position actuator timing mark with timing chain black link and install actuator on camshaft with actuator timing mark perpendicular (90°) to cylinder head deck surface near top of rotation.
6. Secure exhaust actuator by loosely installing oil control valve.
7. Prevent camshaft form using suitable open-end wrench on hex cast and tighten oil control valve.
8. Rotate lefthand secondary timing chain tensioner ratchet release lever counterclockwise and hold.
9. Collapse tensioner shoe and hold, then release ratchet lever.
10. Slowly release shoe pressure until ratchet lever moves to first detent with felt and heard click.
11. Collapse and hold tensioner shoe.
12. Lock tensioner shoe in collapsed position by insert pin through release lever hole.
13. Install lefthand secondary camshaft drive chain tensioner with release lever is facing outward. Tighten mounting bolts.
14. Remove pin to tighten chain slack.
15. Align RB intake camshaft position actuator timing mark with timing chain black link and install actuator on camshaft with actuator timing mark perpendicular (90°) to cylinder head deck surface near top of rotation.
16. Install secondary timing chain to intermediate sprocket aligning sprocket RB timing mark to timing chain black link.
17. Secure intake actuator by loosely installing oil control valve.
18. Prevent camshaft form using suitable open-end wrench on hex cast and tighten oil control valve.
19. Align RB exhaust camshaft position actuator timing mark with timing chain black link and install actuator on camshaft with actuator timing mark perpendicular (90°) to cylinder head deck surface near top of rotation.
20. Secure exhaust actuator by loosely installing oil control valve.
21. Prevent camshaft form using suitable open-end wrench on hex cast and tighten oil control valve.
22. Rotate righthand secondary timing chain tensioner ratchet release lever counterclockwise and hold.
23. Collapse tensioner shoe and hold, then release ratchet lever.
24. Slowly release shoe pressure until ratchet lever moves to first detent with felt and heard click.
25. Collapse and hold tensioner shoe.
26. Lock tensioner shoe in collapsed position by insert pin through release lever hole.
27. Install righthand secondary camshaft drive chain tensioner with release lever is facing outward. Tighten mounting bolts.
28. Remove pin to tighten chain slack.
29. Ensure actuator and chain timing marks remain aligned.
30. Remove righthand secondary camshaft drive chain show support wire and engine front cover bolt.
31. Remove camshaft holding tool.

32. Install new gasket and righthand camshaft position actuator housing. Tighten mounting bolts and stud.
33. Install camshaft cover as outlined under "Valve Cover, Replace."
34. Lubricate O-rings with suitable engine oil, then install righthand bank intake and exhaust CMP sensors.
35. Tighten CMP sensors' mounting bolts and connect electrical connectors.
36. Install CMP sensor harness to retainers.
37. Install oil pump alignment tool No. EN48036, or equivalent, over crankshaft nose and up to oil pump.
38. Loosely install mounting bolts and apply hand force to alignment tool against oil pump to align oil pump to drive.
39. Install front cover as outlined under "Front Cover, Replace."

CAMSHAFT
REPLACE
DeVille & Seville
REMOVAL

1. Remove valve cover as outlined under "Valve Cover, Replace."
2. Secure cam sprocket to timing chain by installing four tie wraps per sprocket through sprocket holes.
3. Install cam chain holder tool No. J38822, or equivalent, behind camshaft sprockets, positioned between chain tensioner and chain guide, **Fig. 11.**
4. Apply tension to tool by tightening tension adjusting screw.
5. Remove camshaft sprocket bolts. **Record cam drive pins location in camshafts end for installation alignment.**
6. Work sprockets off cams using play in chain.
7. Loosen cam bearing cap bolts a few turns at time until all valve spring pressure has been released.
8. Remove bolts, bearing caps and camshaft.

INSTALLATION

1. Apply camshaft prelube part No. 1052365, or equivalent, to face of each cam lobe.
2. Install camshaft and position cam bearing caps to cylinder head.
3. Arrow on top of bearing cap points towards front of engine.
4. "E" mark on top of bearing cap indicates cap for exhaust cam.
5. "I" mark on top of bearing cap indicates cap for intake cam.
6. "No. 1" mark on top of bearing cap should be towards front of engine.
7. Loosely install cam bearing cap bolts.
8. Alternately tighten each bearing cap bolt few turns at time against valve spring pressure until all bolts are snug.
9. Tighten bearing cap bolts.
10. Rotate camshaft until drive pins are in position to engage cam sprockets over cams and install mounting bolts.

11. Remove chain holder tool and tie wraps.
12. Install cam cover.

CAMSHAFT TIMING

Setting camshaft timing is required whenever the camshaft drive system has been disturbed, such that the relationship between any chain and sprocket has been lost. Even when only one sprocket is involved, the following procedure should be observed since one crankshaft rotation will not provide conditions where proper timing can be confirmed.

1. Remove valve covers as outlined under "Valve Cover, Replace."
2. Remove front cover as outlined under "Front Cover, Replace."
3. Remove or retract three chain tensioners. **Tensioners may be in installed positions but must be fully retracted as outlined under "Timing Chain, Replace."**
4. Remove oil pump assembly as outlined under "Oil Pump, Replace."
5. Primary and secondary chain guides should be installed if previously removed.
6. Rotate crankshaft until sprocket drive key is at approximately 1 o'clock position using crankshaft rotation socket tool No. J39946, or equivalent.
7. Install crankshaft and intermediate shaft sprockets to primary drive chain with timing marks aligned, **Fig. 13.**
8. Install crank and intermediate shaft sprockets over their respective shafts.
9. Rotate crankshaft so crankshaft key engages sprocket without changing timing mark position using crankshaft rotation socket tool.
10. Tighten intermediate sprocket mounting bolt.
11. Install primary chain tensioner and release tensioner shoe. Tighten tensioner mounting bolts.
12. Lock crankshaft in position using flexplate holder tool No. J39411, or equivalent.
13. Route lefthand cylinder head secondary drive chain over intermediate shaft inner row teeth.
14. **Righthand exhaust camshaft sprocket (marked RE) must contain camshaft position sensor pickup.**
15. Route secondary drive chain over chain guide and install exhaust camshaft sprocket to chain so that camshaft drive pin engages lefthand head exhaust sprocket notch (marked LE). There should be no slack in lower section of chain and camshaft drive pin must be perpendicular to cylinder head face, **Fig. 13.**
16. Install intake camshaft sprocket into chain so notch on lefthand head intake sprocket (marked LI) engages cam drive pin while pin remains perpendicular to cylinder head face.
17. A hex is cast into camshafts behind cylinders Nos. 1 and 2 so an open end wrench can be used to provide minor positioning of camshafts.
18. Loosely install exhaust and intake cam sprocket bolts.

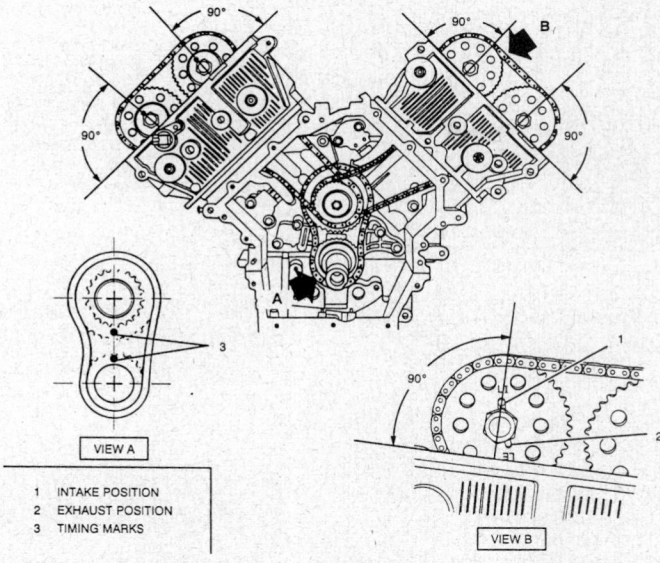

VIEW A

1 INTAKE POSITION
2 EXHAUST POSITION
3 TIMING MARKS

VIEW B

GC1069100347000X

Fig. 13 Camshaft timing procedure

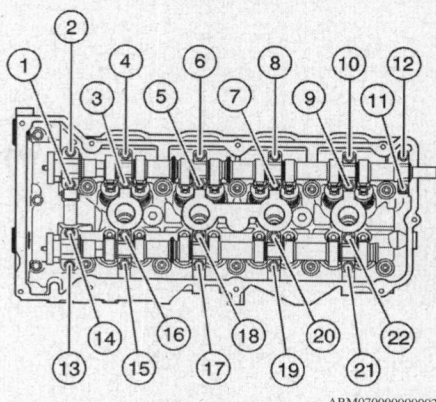

ARM0700000000022

Fig. 14 Lefthand camshaft tightening sequence. DTS

19. Install chain tensioner and release tension on shoe. Tighten tensioner mounting bolts.
20. Tighten camshaft sprocket bolts.
21. **Righthand exhaust camshaft sprocket (marked RE) must contain camshaft position sensor pickup.**
22. Route righthand cylinder head secondary drive chain over intermediate shaft outer row of teeth, then repeat procedure for righthand cams.

DTS

REMOVAL

1. Remove camshaft cover as outlined under "Valve Cover, Replace."
2. Turn crankshaft to cylinder No. 1 is at compression stroke Top Dead Center (TDC) and both camshaft sprocket drive pins are at top of their rotation, **Fig. 12.**
3. Hold camshaft in position using camshaft holding tool No. J44212, or equivalent.
4. Mark timing chain link adjacent to each camshaft sprocket timing mark for installation alignment.
5. Hold timing chain alignment by installing both timing chain retention tool No, EN46327, or equivalent.
6. Prevent camshaft rotation by holding hex cast with suitable open end wrench.
7. Remove mounting bolts and camshaft sprockets.
8. Alternately loosen camshaft bearing cap bolts a few turns at a time until all valve spring pressure has been released.
9. Remove camshaft bearing caps and camshaft holding tool.
10. Remove camshafts and followers.

INSTALLATION

1. Apply liberal amount of suitable lubricant to camshaft followers roller pivot pocket and valve slot areas.
2. Place camshaft followers in original position on valve tip and Follower must be positioned squarely on valve tip so full width of roller will completely contact camshaft lobe. Stationary Hydraulic Lash Adjusters (SHLA). Rounded head of follower goes on SHLA, while flat end goes on valve tip.
3. Apply suitable liberal amount of lubricant to camshaft carriers, camshaft lobes and camshaft journals (2).
4. Place camshaft in carriers with sprocket drive pins near top of rotation and camshaft lobes in neutral position. Camshafts can be identified by stamping near rear journal. For example: L-EXH is defined as Left bank Exhaust.
5. Arrow should point to front of engine and number indicates position from front of engine.
6. Apply liberal amount of suitable lubricant to camshaft bearing caps.
7. Install camshaft bearing caps according to identification marks and alternately hand tighten bolts a few turns at a time until all caps are fully seated.
8. Refer to sequences, **Figs. 14 and 15,** and tighten camshaft bearing cap bolts in two steps: First step, **torque** bolts to 44 inch lbs.; second step, tighten bolts an additional 30.°
9. Align camshafts and hold in position using camshaft holding tool No. J44212, or equivalent.
10. Install intake and exhaust camshaft sprockets aligning marks made during disassembly. Ensure that camshaft sprockets align with camshaft pins.
11. Prevent camshaft rotation by holding hex cast with suitable open end wrench.
12. Install and tighten camshaft sprocket bolts.
13. Remove tools and ensure camshaft sprocket alignment.
14. Install lefthand camshaft cover as outlined under "Valve Cover, Replace."

STS

The secondary timing chain has black links that are used for alignment when the primary and secondary timing gear and chain assemblies are being installed together. It is not required that the black chain links be aligned with the camshaft actuator timing marks when the secondary chain and gear components are being serviced separately.

REMOVAL

1. Remove camshaft position actuator oil control valve as outlined in "Secondary" under "Timing Chain, Replace."
2. Each bearing cap is marked with an arrow pointing toward front of engine, an "I" mark indicates intake camshaft, an "E" mark indicates exhaust camshaft, the number reference mark indicates journal position from front of engine. **Do not mix bearing caps.**
3. Remove bolts and camshaft bearing caps. Store bearing caps in suitable, clean shop towel.
4. Remove camshafts and store covered with an oil soaked towel.

INSTALLATION

1. Clean journals, camshaft and caps with suitable, clean, lint-free cloth.
2. Apply liberal amount of suitable camshaft prelube to camshaft bearing journals.
3. Apply liberal amount of suitable camshaft prelube to camshaft lobes and journals.
4. Ensure each valve rocker arm is properly aligned to valve tip, lifter and camshaft lobe. Inspect alignment prior to and after camshaft caps are tightened.
5. Install camshaft in journals with drive pins near top of rotation and lobes in neutral position. Camshaft can be identified by stamping near rear journal. For example: L-EXH is Left Bank Exhaust.
6. Apply liberal amount of suitable camshaft prelube to camshaft bearing cap journals. **Ensure caps are installed**

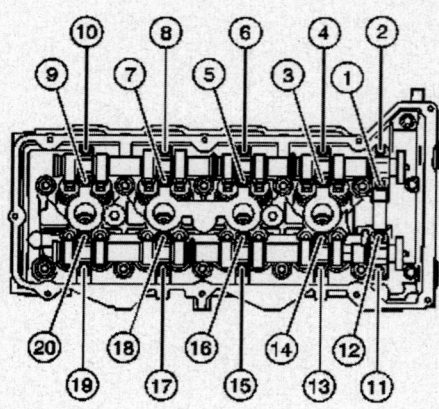

Fig. 15 Righthand camshaft tightening sequence. DTS

ARM0700000000023

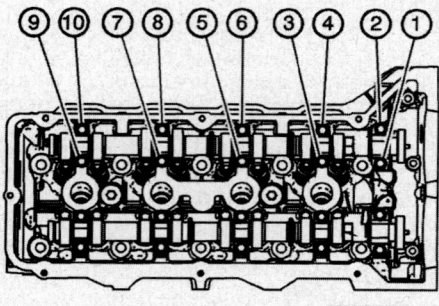

Fig. 18 Righthand intake camshaft tightening sequence. STS

ARM0700000000026

in original positions.
7. Hand start all camshaft bearing cap bolts.
8. Refer to sequences, **Figs. 16 through 19**, tighten bearing cap bolts in two steps: First step, **torque** bolts to 44 inch lbs.; tighten bolts an additional 30.°
9. Install camshaft position actuator oil control valve as outlined in "Secondary" under "Timing Chain, Replace."

PISTON & ROD ASSEMBLY

Ensure the locating mark cast into the underside of the piston faces towards the front of the engine and locating notch on the connecting rod cap points towards the rear of the engine on odd-numbered cylinders and towards the front of the engine on even-numbered cylinders, **Figs. 20 and 21.**

PISTONS, PINS & RINGS

1. Lubricate piston pin bores with suitable crankshaft prelube.
2. Install new piston pin retainers using

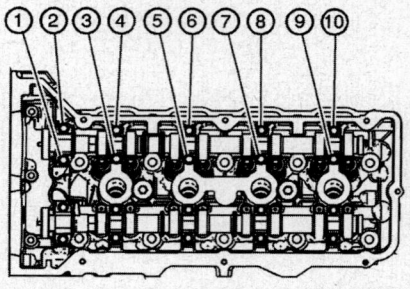

ARM0700000000024

Fig. 16 Lefthand Intake camshaft tightening sequence. STS

piston pin clip remover/installer tool No. EN46745, or equivalent.
3. Ensure oil control ring expander ends face toward piston top and install oil control piston ring spacer.
4. Install oil control piston ring spacer
5. Install lower and upper oil control pris-on rings using suitable piston ring expander tool.
6. Space oil control piston ring end gaps at least 90° apart.
7. Install lower compression piston ring using suitable piston ring expander tool. with mark ring side facing piston top.
8. Install upper compression piston ring using suitable piston ring expander tool. Top compression ring may be installed with either side up.
9. Oil control ring expander and second compression ring gaps set centerline position 1, **Fig. 22.**
10. Top compressing ring gap 180° opposite oil control ring expander and second compression ring gaps.
11. Upper oil control ring gap position 2 should be 30° clockwise from top compression ring gap.
12. Lower oil control ring gap position 4 should be 30° counterclockwise from top compression ring gap.

MAIN & ROD BEARINGS

Connecting Rod

Lubricate new connecting bolts with suitable engine oil. Tighten connecting rod bolts in four steps: First step, **torque** bolts to 22 ft. lbs.; second step, loosen bolts to zero; third step, **torque** bolts to 18 ft. lbs.; fourth step, tighten bolts an additional 110.°

Crankshaft

Refer to sequence, **Figs. 23 and 24,** and tighten lower crankcase mounting bolts in two steps: First step, **torque** bolts to 15 ft. lbs.; second step, tighten bolts an additional 65.°
Refer to sequences, **Figs. 25 and 26,** **torque** upper to lower crankcase perimeter bolts to 22 ft. lbs.

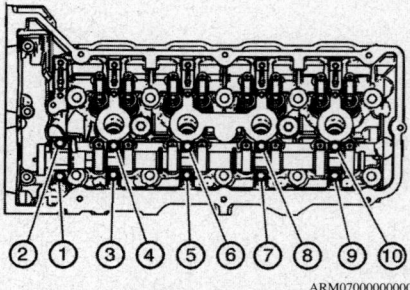

ARM0700000000025

Fig. 17 Lefthand exhaust camshaft tightening sequence. STS

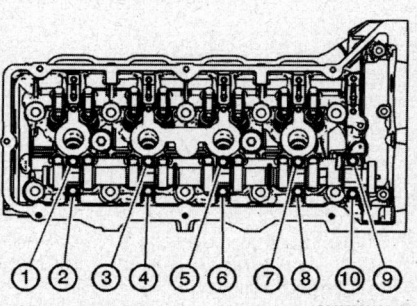

ARM0700000000027

Fig. 19 Righthand exhaust camshaft tightening sequence. STS

CRANKSHAFT REAR OIL SEAL

REPLACE

The flexplate bolt hole threads in the crankshaft were revised from 8 ×1.25 mm to 11 ×1.5 mm beginning with the 2006 model year. Rear oil seal removal tool No. J42841-A will service the cassette seals installed on engines from March 1, 1996 and later. If the older J42841 is to be used on a 2006 or later engine the update kit, J42841-10, must be used to convert the J42841 to a J42841-A .

Removal

1. Remove transaxle as outlined in **MO-TOR's "Domestic Transmission, In-Vehicle Service" manual or "Transmission Service DVD."'**
2. Prevent engine from turning using Snap-On flywheel turner tool No. A144A, or equivalent.
3. Remove mounting bolts and flywheel.
4. Remove rear oil seal using rear oil seal remover tool No. J42841-A, or equivalent.

Installation

1. Ensure oil drain back hole is clear of debris using suitable wire or unbound plastic tie wrap.
2. Clean bore with suitable cleaner solvent.

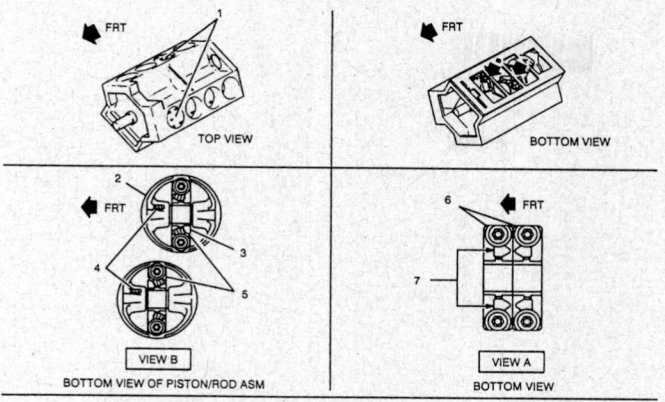

1 PISTON ARROW TOWARD CHAIN CASE ON BOTH SIDES
2 PISTON
3 ROD CAP
4 LOCATER LUGS INDICATE PISTON FRONT TOWARDS ENGINE FRONT
5 BEARING CAP ARROWS POINT TOWARD EACH OTHER ON PAIRED RODS
6 ROD CAPS
7 BEARING CAP ARROWS POINT TOWARD EACH OTHER ON PAIRED RODS

GC1069100349000X

Fig. 20 Piston & rod assembly. DeVille & Seville

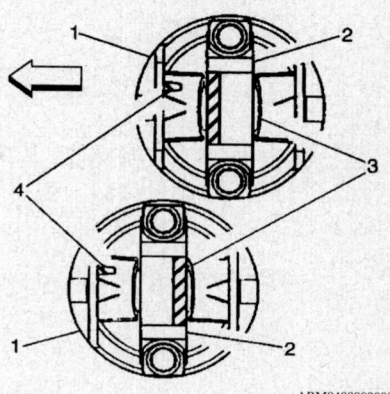

ARM0400000000095

Fig. 21 Piston & rod assembly. DTS & STS

3. Install sealer installer tool No. EN48072 pilot base, or equivalent, onto crankshaft. Crankshaft hub will fit into inboard tool recess.
4. Install tool applicator housing over pilot base. Ensure applicator housing bottoms in block bore.
5. Apply suitable RTV sealant to block bore outer diameter evenly using tool applicator housing. **Ensure sealant does not block drain hole.**
6. Spread sealant within bore to ensure an even coating.
7. **Ensure components sealed with RTV sealant are assembled within 20 minutes.**
8. Slowly and evenly, pull applicator housing out of bore and remove it from pilot base. **Do not twist or turn tool applicator housing as it is pulled away from bottom of the bore.**
9. Remove bolts and tool pilot base. **Ensure that sealant is evenly spread across bore and drain block hole is clear.**
10. **Do not use any lubricant to install crankshaft rear oil seal. Do not use any lubricant on coating pre-applied to inner diameter of crankshaft rear oil seal.**
11. Turn center nut of crankshaft rear oil seal installer tool J45930-A until center hub protrudes approximately .591 inch beyond outer plate.
12. **Do not use any lubricant on crankshaft rear oil seal outer diameter. Do not lubricate any part of new cassette style crankshaft rear oil seal.**
13. Install new cassette style crankshaft rear oil seal using crankshaft rear oil seal installer tool until drive bottoms against crankcase. Remove tool and wipe excessive sealant from block.
14. Seal outer surface should be .02–.03 inch below engine block surface.
15. Sleeve inner surface should be 0.02–.03 inch below seal outer surface.
16. Installed seal and sleeve need to be parallel to block by .02 inch.
17. Apply suitable sealant to flywheel

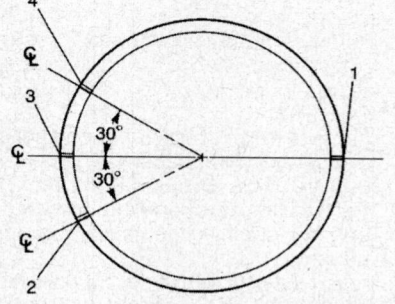

ARM0700000000028

Fig. 22 Piston ring gap set positions

mounting bolts.
18. Tighten flywheel mounting bolts in two steps: First step, **torque** bolts to 22 ft. lbs.; second step, tighten bolts an additional 50.°

OIL PAN
REPLACE

DeVille & Seville

1. Drain engine oil into suitable container.
2. Remove exhaust crossover pipe. Discard flange gaskets.
3. Remove mounting bolts and oil pan. **Do not remove gasket from pan groove unless replacement is required.**
4. Reverse procedure to install, noting the following:
   a. . **Torque** mounting bolts to 71 inch lbs. in sequence, **Fig. 27.**
   b. **Torque** bolts to 106 inch lbs in sequence.

DTS

1. Raise and support vehicle, then drain engine oil into suitable container.

2. Remove catalytic converter to rear exhaust manifold pipe nuts.
3. Position exhaust system rearward, allowing catalytic converter studs to clear rear exhaust manifold pipe. **Do not over-flex or damage flex joint.** Discard catalytic converter gasket.
4. Remove rear exhaust manifold pipe to righthand and front exhaust manifold pipe bolts. Discard rear exhaust manifold pipe gasket. and seal.
5. Remove rear exhaust manifold pipe flange.
6. Remove transaxle as outlined in **MOTOR's "Domestic Transmission, In-Vehicle Service" manual or "Transmission Service DVD.""**
7. Remove front exhaust pipe to exhaust manifold bolts.
8. Disconnect EGR inlet pipe nut from front exhaust manifold pipe.
9. Remove front exhaust manifold pipe to lower crankcase bolt and to cylinder head stud bolt.
10. Remove front exhaust manifold pipe seal from lefthand exhaust manifold and discard seal.
11. Remove exhaust manifold flange retainer.
12. Disconnect oil level sensor electrical connector.
13. Remove mounting bolts an oil pan. Discard gasket.
14. Reverse procedure to install, noting the following:
   a. Completely fill and slightly overfill oil pan seal groove with continuous bead of suitable RTV sealant.
   b. Install one engine front cover installation guide pin No. EN46109, or equivalent, into bolt hole in each side of lower crankcase.
   c. Ensure RTV sealant is higher than oil pan sealing surface by .118 inch.
   d. . **Torque** mounting bolts to 71 inch lbs. in sequence, **Fig. 27.**
   e. **Torque** bolts to 106 inch lbs in sequence.

STS

1. Support engine using suitable universal engine support fixture.
2. Raise and support vehicle, then remove front tires and wheels.

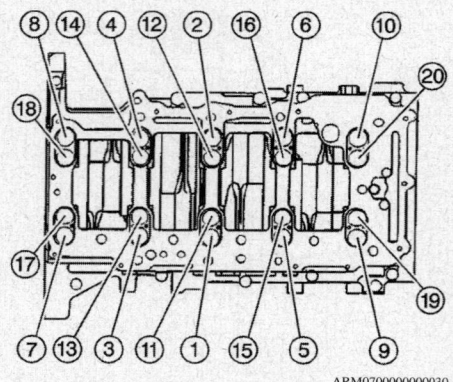

Fig. 23 Lower crankcase tightening sequence. DeVille, DTS & Seville

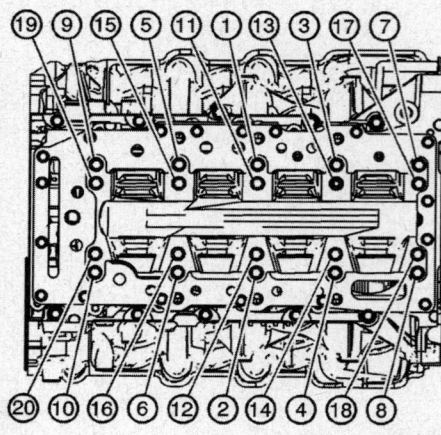

Fig. 24 Lower crankcase tightening sequence. STS

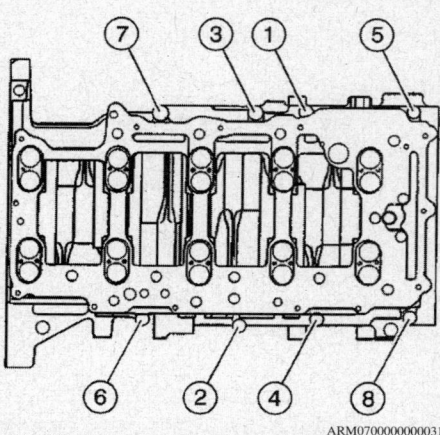

Fig. 25 Upper-to-lower crankcase tightening sequence. DeVille, DTS & Seville

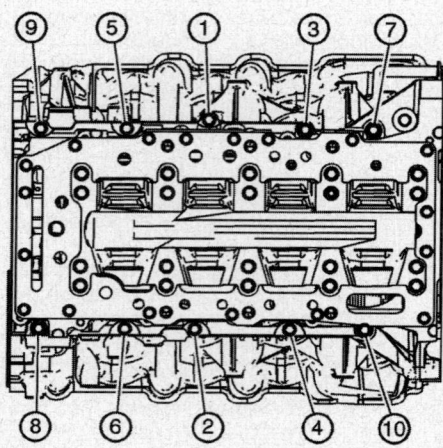

Fig. 26 Upper-to-lower crankcase tightening sequence. STS

3. Remove front air deflector, then disconnect electrical harness retainers securing engine harness to frame.
4. Disconnect left and righthand rearward frame retainer, then the anti-lock brake wiring harness from lower control arms.
5. Loosen nut and disconnect brake lines from frame.
6. Support radiator and air conditioning condenser to front inner energy absorber bracket bolt using mechanics wire.
7. Remove mounting nuts and washer bottle bracket.
8. Loosen brake pressure modulator valve nuts and separate brake pressure modulator valve (BPMV) from bracket.
9. **Mark stabilizer shaft for installation alignment.** and loosen stabilizer shaft mounting bolts.
10. Remove lower mounting nut and stabilizer shaft link from lower control arm.
11. Remove mounting nut from air conditioning compressor, and position power steering pressure hose aside.

12. Remove mounting bolts and support power steering gear to bolt bracket installed in oil pan using suitable mechanics wire.
13. Remove mounting nut and remove outer tie rod using steering linkage and tie rod puller tool No. J24319-B, or equivalent.
14. Remove lower shock mounting bolts.
15. Disconnect lower ball joint and position knuckle aside. **Brake calipers do not need to be removed from knuckle.**
16. Remove engine mounts lower mounting nuts.
17. Lower vehicle to frame support table No. J39580, or equivalent.
18. Remove frame mounting bolts and raise body from frame. **Ensure brake pipes, steering knuckle and wheel speed sensor electrical harness clear frame.**
19. Remove mounting nuts, bolts and lower control arm by lowering arm at frame and moving ball stud upwards.
20. Remove stabilizer shaft and frame from support fixture.
21. Remove differential carrier as outlined in "Front Drive Axle" chapter.
22. **On all models,** disconnect electrical connector and remove engine oil level sensor.
23. Remove mounting bolts and oil pan.
24. If gasket is damaged, drill out rivets and remove oil pan gasket.
25. to be replace
26. Reverse procedure to install, noting the following:
    a. If installing new gasket it must be held flus to .02 inch forward of rear engine block face.
    b. Install short 420, medium 421 and long 422 bolts in correct positions, **Fig. 28.**
    c. **Torque** oil pan mounting bolts to 11 ft. lbs. in sequence, **Fig. 29.**
    d. . **Torque** mounting bolts to 18 ft. lbs. in sequence.

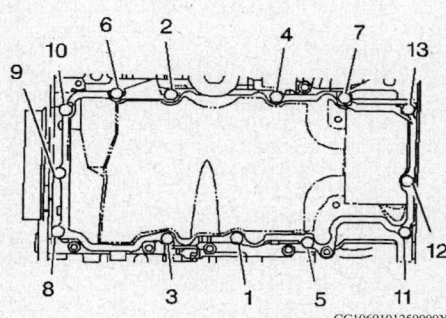

Fig. 27 Oil pan bolt tightening sequence. DeVille, DTS & Seville

OIL PUMP

REPLACE

Removal

1. Remove front cover as outlined under "Front Cover, Replace."
2. Remove oil pump drive to crankshaft balancer friction washer.
3. Remove three oil pump mounting bolts identified by larger head size.
4. Slide oil pump off crankshaft nose with drive collar in place.
5. Remove crankshaft sprocket to oil pump drive friction washer.

Installation

1. Install suitable crankshaft sprocket to oil pump drive friction washer.
2. Install space into oil pump so drive flat engages rotor.
3. Install oil pump alignment tool No. EN48036, or equivalent, over crankshaft nose and up to oil pump.
4. Loosely install mounting bolts and apply hand force to alignment tool against oil pump to align oil pump to drive.
5. Keeping hand force against alignment tool, tighten mounting bolts in two

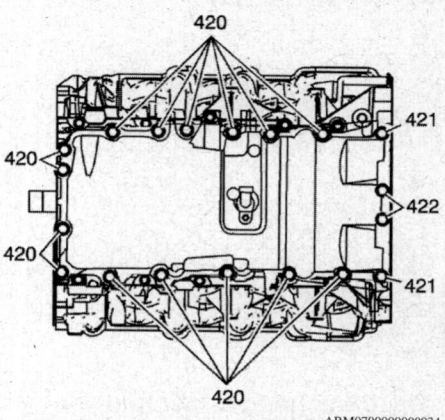

Fig. 28 Oil pan bolt positioning. STS w/4.6L engine

steps: First step, **torque** bolts to 89 inch lbs.; second step, tighten bolts an additional 35.°

6. Remove special tool and install oil pump drive to crankshaft balancer friction washer.
7. Install front cover as outlined under "Front Cover, Replace."

OIL PUMP SERVICE
Disassemble

1. Remove driver spacer.
2. Remove mounting bolts and cover.
3. Remove drive and driven gears.
4. Remove relief valve plug, spring and plunger.
5. Remove body to cover alignment dowels.

Assembly

1. Install alignment dowels.
2. Install oil pump relief valve plunger and spring, then tighten plug.
3. Install driven and drive gears. Outer driven gear chamfered edge must facedown into pump body.
4. Ensure pump priming by packing body housing with suitable, clean white petroleum jelly.
5. Install cover and tighten mounting bolts.
6. Install oil pump drive spacer.

SERPENTINE DRIVE BELT

1. Rotate drive belt tensioner mechanism upward and away from drive belt using suitable ½ inch breaker bar.
2. Remove serpentine drive belt.
3. Reverse procedure to install. Refer to **Figs. 30 and 31** for serpentine drive belt routing.

COOLING SYSTEM BLEED

1. Fill radiator with proper antifreeze solution.

2. Install radiator cap.
3. Start and idle engine.
4. Place HVAC controls in any air conditioning mode except Max and temperature at highest setting.
5. Idle engine until lower radiator to water pump hose is hot.
6. Turn ignition Off.
7. Allow engine to cool to ambient temperature.
8. Ensure coolant in surge tank is at proper level.

THERMOSTAT
REPLACE

1. Drain coolant into suitable container.
2. Remove engine sight shields and air cleaner.
3. Disconnect thermostat housing radiator and heater hoses.
4. Remove mounting bolts and thermostat housing, **Fig. 32.**
5. Remove thermostat and discard O-ring seal.
6. Reverse procedure to install.

WATER PUMP
REPLACE
DeVille & Seville

1. Drain coolant into suitable container.
2. Remove air cleaner.
3. Remove engine cover and front end filler panel.
4. **On models equipped with AIR,** remove check valve.
5. **On all models,** remove water pump belt shield.
6. Remove water pump drive belt.
7. Disconnect radiator outlet hose from thermostat housing clamp tool No. J38185, or equivalent.
8. Remove mounting bolts and water pump cover.
9. Disconnect heater return hose.
10. Rotate pump clockwise to remove from housing coolant pump remover/installer tool No. J38816-1A, or equivalent.
11. Remove support plate from water housing crossover.
12. Remove water pump
13. Remove discard water crossover seal.
14. Reverse procedure to install.

DTS

1. Remove water crossover as outlined under "Water Crossover, Replace."
2. Remove mounting bolts and water pump cover.
3. Remove mounting bolts and water pump. Discard seal.
4. Reverse procedure to install.

STS

1. Drain engine coolant into suitable container.
2. **On models equipped with standard cooling,** proceed as follows:
   a. Disconnect Positive Crankcase

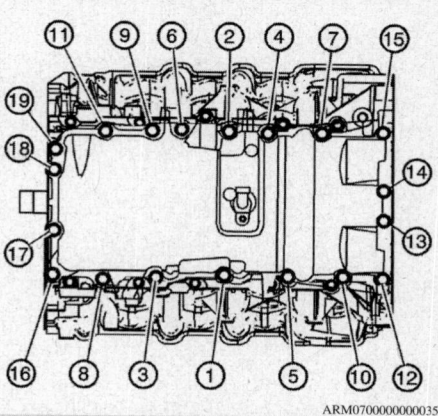

Fig. 29 Oil pan tightening sequence. STS w/4.6L engine

   Ventilation (PCV) tube from air cleaner duct.
   b. Disconnect air duct clamps at throttle body and Mass Air Flow/Intake Air Temperature (MAF/IAT) sensor.
   c. Remove air cleaner duct.
   d. Disconnect and position surge tank inlet hose aside.
   e. Remove cooling fan shroud upper radiator upper and lefthand lower mounting bolts.
   f. Disconnect cooling fan electrical connectors, then raise and support vehicle.
   g. Remove 16 retainers and front air deflector.
   h. Remove cooling fan shroud to radiator righthand lower mounting bolt.
   i. Disconnect and position engine wiring harness aside.
   j. Remove power steering line and transmission oil cooler lines mounting bolts from fan shroud.
   k. Lower vehicle and remove cooling fan.
3. **On models equipped with heavy duty cooling,** proceed as follows:
   a. Remove auxiliary cooling fan to condenser upper mounting bolts.
   b. Raise and support vehicle, then remove 16 retainers and front air deflector.
   c. Disconnect electrical connectors, then remove mounting bolts and auxiliary cooling fan.
4. **On all models** remove water pump drive belt and tensioner.
5. Remove mounting bolt and water pump pulley.
6. Remove mounting bolts and water pump. Discard seal.
7. Reverse procedure to install.

WATER CROSSOVER
REPLACE
DEVILLE, DTS & SEVILLE

1. Drain cooling system into suitable container.
2. Remove air cleaner and fuel injector sight shield.

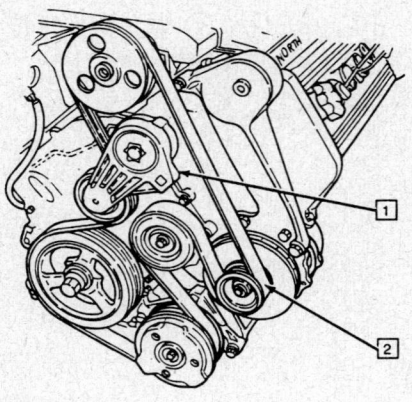

| 1 | DRIVE BELT TENSIONER |
| 2 | SERPENTINE DRIVE BELT |

GC1069100351000X

Fig. 30 Serpentine drive belt routing. DeVille, DTS & Seville

3. Disconnect brake booster, fuel regulator, and Secondary Air Injection (AIR) solenoid vacuum tubes.
4. Disconnect ball studs and remove intake manifold top sight shield cover.
5. Remove fuel rail pressure fitting cap and connect suitable fuel pressure gauge wrapping fitting with suitable towel.
6. Install bleed hose into suitable container.
7. Relieve fuel tank vapor pressure by loosening fuel filler cap.
8. Open valve and bleed system pressure.
9. Remove air cleaner intake duct and PCV valve fresh air tube.
10. Remove cruise control and accelerator cables from cable bracket, then from throttle body lever.
11. Disconnect IAC valve and TP sensor electrical connectors.
12. Remove fuel feed and return lines from accelerator controls cable bracket retainer.
13. Remove transaxle shift cable clip from accelerator controls cable bracket.
14. Remove mounting bolts and throttle body.
15. Disconnect fuel rail bracket nut at rear lift bracket.
16. Disconnect surge tank inlet hose and remove inlet fitting.
17. Remove mounting bolt and rear lift bracket.
18. Disconnect Exhaust Gas Recirculation (EGR) electrical connector.
19. Remove mounting nuts and heat shield
20. Remove mounting nuts and bolts, then the EGR valve.
21. Disconnect exhaust crossover EGR inlet pipe mounting nut.
22. Remove mounting bolt and flange, then the EGR inlet pipe from water crossover. Discard EGR inlet pipe.
23. Disconnect Evaporative Emission (EVAP) canister purge valve electrical connector.

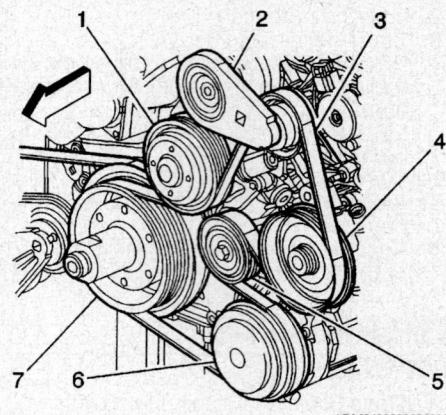

ARM0400000000098

Fig. 31 Serpentine drive belt routing. STS

24. Disconnect the EVAP canister purge valve purge pipe and partially open the throttle.
25. Remove mounting bolt and EVAP canister purge valve from intake manifold.
26. Disconnect electrical connector and remove Manifold Absolute Pressure (MAP) sensor.
27. Remove radiator inlet hose from water crossover and outlet hose from thermostat using suitable hose clamp pliers.
28. Remove water pump as outlined under "Water Pump, Replace."
29. Remove two mounting bolts and water pump tensioner.
30. Disconnect and position cable harness clip aside.
31. Disconnect water hose and remove water housing crossover.
32. Reverse procedure to install.

RADIATOR
REPLACE
DeVille & Seville

1. Drain coolant into suitable container.
2. Remove radiator outlet hose using clamp tool No. J38185, or equivalent.
3. Remove cooling fans as outlined in "Engine Cooling Fans" chapter.
4. Disconnect lower transaxle fluid cooler line.
5. Disconnect lower engine oil cooler line.
6. Remove alternator cooler inlet hose.
7. Remove mounting bolts and lift condenser up slightly to release radiator lower mounting feet. **Do not damage radiator and condenser lower attachment points.**
8. Remove radiator by lifting up and out.
9. Reverse procedure to install.

DTS

1. Recover air conditioning refrigerant as outlined in "Air Conditioning" chapter.
2. Remove eight retainers and front compartment sight shield.
3. Remove mounting bolts and upper tie bar.

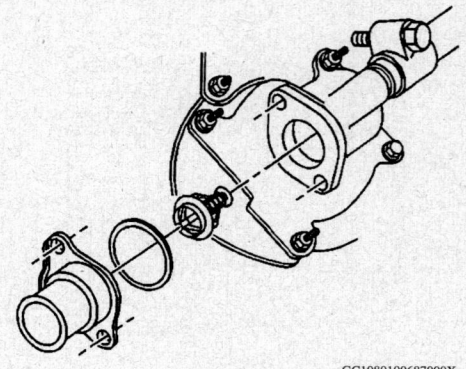

GC1080100687000X

Fig. 32 Thermostat replacement

4. Remove 16 retainers and front air deflector.
5. Remove 12 retainers, two mounting bolts, two mounting nuts and front fascia cover. Disconnect electrical connector.
6. Remove six mounting bolts and front impact bar.
7. Loosen mount bolts, disconnect electrical connector and remove distance sensing cruise control module.
8. Remove four mounting bolts and front fascia bumper support.
9. Remove three mounting bolts and hood latch. Disconnect cable and electrical connector.
10. Remove four mounting bolts and hood latch support.
11. Disconnect nuts, then the condenser discharge and suction hoses. Discard sealing washers.
12. Remove condenser line to radiator mounting bolt.
13. Remove engine oil cooler lines from radiator.
14. Remove mounting bolts and condenser.
15. Disconnect clamp and radiator inlet hose.
16. Remove fan shroud transmission oil cooler pipe mounting bolts and transmission lines from radiator.
17. Disconnect cooling fan electrical connectors and fan shroud harness clips.
18. Remove mounting bolts and electric cooling fan.
19. Remove radiator.
20. Reverse procedure to install.

STS

1. Drain coolant into suitable container.
2. **On models equipped with standard cooling,** proceed as follows:
   a. Disconnect Positive Crankcase Ventilation (PCV) tube from air cleaner duct.
   b. Disconnect air duct clamps at throttle body and Mass Air Flow/Intake Air Temperature (MAF/IAT) sensor.
   c. Remove air cleaner duct.
   d. Disconnect and position surge tank inlet hose aside.
   e. Remove cooling fan shroud upper radiator upper and lefthand lower mounting bolts.
   f. Disconnect cooling fan electrical

connectors, then raise and support vehicle.

g. Remove 16 retainers and front air deflector.

h. Remove cooling fan shroud to radiator righthand lower mounting bolt.

i. Disconnect and position engine wiring harness aside.

j. Remove power steering line and transmission oil cooler lines mounting bolts from fan shroud.

k. Lower vehicle and remove cooling fan.

3. **On models equipped with heavy duty cooling,** proceed as follows:

a. Remove auxiliary cooling fan to condenser upper mounting bolts.

b. Raise and support vehicle, then remove 16 retainers and front air deflector.

c. Disconnect electrical connectors, then remove mounting bolts and auxiliary cooling fan.

4. **On all models,** remove condenser upper and lower mounting bolts.

5. Disconnect radiator side air baffle retaining pins and position condenser aside.

6. Remove transmission oil cooler (TOC) mounting bolts.

7. Lower vehicle.

8. **On models equipped with heavy duty cooling,** disconnect condenser tube, then remove mounting bolts and cooling fan shroud.

9. **On all models,** disconnect clamps, then remove radiator outlet and inlet hoses.

10. Disconnect clamps and remove surge tank inlet hose from radiator.

11. Remove mount bolts and radiator support brackets.

12. Disconnect upper air baffle pins and remove radiator.

13. Reverse procedure to install.

FUEL PUMP
REPLACE

The fuel pump is combined with the tank level sending unit and cannot be serviced separately.

DeVille & Seville

1. Adjust tank fuel level to ¾ full by draining fuel into suitable container.

2. Remove spare tire cover, jack, spare tire and rear compartment floor trim.

3. Remove fuel sender access panel.

4. Disconnect quick-connect fittings at fuel sender.

5. Disconnect fuel sender and fuel tank pressure sensor electrical connectors.

6. Remove fuel sender mounting ring using fuel sender locknut wrench tool No. J39765, or equivalent.

7. Remove fuel sending unit by pulling straight up while pumping fuel from reservoir.

8. Reverse procedure to install using new fuel sender O-ring.

DTS

1. Remove fuel pump fuse.

2. Relieve fuel tank vapor pressure by loosen fuel filler cap.

3. Remove fuel rail service port cap.

4. Wrap shop towel around fitting and depress (open) fuel rail test port valve using suitable, small flat-bladed tool.

5. Remove shop towel and place in suitable container.

6. Install fuel rail service port cap.

7. Remove retaining clips and luggage compartment sill plate.

8. Remove retaining clips, then the left and righthand rear compartment side trim panels.

9. Remove retaining clips and luggage compartment front trim panel.

10. Remove push-in retainers and rear compartment liner.

11. Remove mounting bolts and fuel sender access hole cover.

12. Disconnect, then position aside the fuel feed rear pip quick connect fitting and electrical connectors.

13. Unlock locking ring counterclockwise using fuel sender lock ring wrench tool No. J45722, or equivalent, and suitable, long breaker bar. **Do not use impact tools.**

14. **Fuel module may spring up.**

15. Remove tool and lock ring.

16. Raise module until fuel level sensor float arm is just visible. **Do not handle fuel sender by pipes.**

17. Tilt module to rear allowing float arm to clear opening.

18. Remove module and discard fuel module reservoir bucket fuel into suitable container. Discard O-ring seal.

19. Reverse procedure to install.

STS

1. Remove tank fuel, then disconnect hoses and electrical connector.

2. Remove cam lock ring counterclockwise using fuel sender lock ring wrench tool No. J45747, or equivalent.

3. Lift fuel tank model and disconnect transfer tube.

4. Remove fuel tank module. Discard seal.

5. Reverse procedure to install.

FUEL FILTER
REPLACE

DeVille & Seville

1. Disconnect fuel filter bracket release tabs.

2. Disconnect quick-connect and threaded fittings.

3. Remove fuel filter.

4. Reverse procedure to install

DTS & STS

1. Remove fuel pump fuse.

2. Relieve fuel tank vapor pressure by loosen fuel filler cap.

3. Remove fuel rail service port cap.

4. Wrap shop towel around fitting and depress (open) fuel rail test port valve using suitable, small flat-bladed tool.

5. Remove shop towel and place in suitable container.

6. Install fuel rail service port cap.

7. Raise and support vehicle.

8. Disconnect fuel filter inlet and outlet quick connect fittings, draining fuel into suitable container.

9. Slide filter out of bracket.

10. Reverse procedure to install

TECHNICAL SERVICE BULLETINS

Coolant Leak At Upper Radiator Hose

2006 DTS

On some of these models there may be a coolant leak at the radiator inlet hose.

This condition may be caused by a nylon tracer thread inside the hose that may cut through the inner layer of the hose.

To correct this condition, replace the radiator inlet hose. **Do not replace or reposition the radiator hose clamps.**

Engine Oil Leak From Front Of Vehicle

2005 STS

On some of these models there may be a engine oil leak coming from the front of the vehicle.

This condition may be caused by the front cover or gasket.

To correct this condition, proceed as follows:

1. **On model built be before engine No. L050460029,** replace engine front cover and gasket

2. **On models built with engine No. L050460029, or after,** replace engine front cover gasket, only, as outlined under "Front Cover, Replace."

3. **On all models,** thoroughly clean mating surface of engine block and front cover.

4. Apply .25 inch diameter bead (chocolate chip size) of suitable gray engine sealer to left and righthand sides of front side of gasket at area of upper and lower crankcase split line.

5. Apply suitable thread sealer to all bolts.

TIGHTENING SPECIFICATIONS

Year	Component	Torque/Ft. Lbs.
DEVILLE & SEVILLE		
2004–05	Alternator Upper	37
	Belt Tensioner	37
	Camshaft Bearing Cap	44⑨
	Camshaft Cover	89①
	Camshaft Drive Chain Tensioner	18
	Camshaft Seal Retainer To Cover	27①
	Camshaft Sprocket	89
	Camshaft Intermediate Sprocket	44
	Catalytic Converter To Exhaust Inlet Pipe	18
	Cooling Fan	53①
	Connecting Rod	⑥
	Crankshaft Balancer	37④
	Cylinder Head	③
	Engine Mount	⑧
	Exhaust Manifold To Cylinder Head	18
	Flexplate	11⑤
	Flexplate Inspection Cover	80①
	Front Cover	⑭
	Fuel Filter	22
	Ignition Module	80①
	Intake Manifold	⑦
	Lefthand Strut Bracket To Water Crossover	17
	Main Bearing Cap	⑥
	Oil Filter Adapter	12
	Oil Pan	⑫
	Oil Pan Drain Plug	15
	Oil Pump	②
	Oil Pump To Suction Pipe	89①
	O2 Sensor	30
	Power Steering Return Hose	115①
	Righthand Strut Bracket	37
	Secondary AIR Pipe	80①
	TBI Unit	106①
	Thermostat Housing	89①
	Torque Strut Bracket To Water Manifold	18
	Transaxle Brace	35
	Water Pump (2004–05)	74
	Water Pump Cover	89①
DTS		
2006–08	AIR Check Valve	80①
	Air Cleaner Intake Duct Clamp	27①
	AIR Pipe Outlet Pipe	80①
	AIR Pump, Bolt	106①
	AIR Pump, Nut	89①
	Alternator	37
	Ball Joint	22
	Ball Joint	22
	BPMV	89①
	Brake Caliper	27
	Brake Fitting	13
	Brake Pipe	20
	Brake Rotor	106①
	Cable Bracket	106①
	Camshaft	⑪

TIGHTENING SPECIFICATIONS—Continued

Year	Component	Torque/Ft. Lbs.
DTS		
2006–08	Camshaft Intermediate Drive Shaft Sprocket	44
	Camshaft Seal	27①
	Camshaft Sprocket	89
	Camshaft Tensioner	18
	Compressor Hose	12
	Connecting Rod	⑥
	Crankshaft Balancer	37④
	Cylinder Head	③
	Drive Belt Tensioner	37
	EGR Valve	18
	EGR Valve Heat Shield	80①
	EGR Valve Inlet Pipe	18
	EGR Inlet Pipe-To-Crossover Pipe	44
	Engine Frame	141
	Engine Mount	59
	Engine Mount, Front To Engine Frame	52
	Engine Mount Bracket	37
	Engine Mount, Rear Bracket	54
	Engine Mount Strut	52
	Engine To Transaxle	55
	Exhaust Manifold	18
	Front Cover	⑭
	Front Fascia	68①
	Front Latch Support	89①
	Fuel Rail Bracket	35①
	Ground	12
	Heater Pipe	18
	Ignition Coil	89①
	Junction Block	58①
	Main Bearing Cap	⑥
	Master Cylinder	22
	Oil Pan	⑫
	Oil Pump	②
	Power Steering Inlet Pipe	80①
	Rear Lift Bracket	18
	Rear Transaxle Mount	37
	Stabilizer Link	17
	Stabilizer Shaft Bracket	24
	Stabilizer Shaft Insulator Bracket	24
	Stater Cable	11
	Steering Gear	70
	Steering Gear Intermediate Shaft	33
	Steering Gear Heat Shield	80①
	Strut Tower	30
	Surge Tank Inlet Fitting	35
	Throttle Body	106①
	Torque Converter	44
	Torque Converter Cover	106①
	Transaxle Brace	37
	Transaxle Oil Cooler Pipe	53①
	Upper Tie Bar	37
	Valve Cover	89①

Continued

TIGHTENING SPECIFICATIONS—Continued

Year	Component	Torque/Ft. Lbs.
DTS		
2006–08	Water Crossover Housing	18
	Water Pump Tensioner	89①
STS		
2005–08	Air Cleaner	89①
	Air Duct	27①
	Alternator	37
	Battery Cable	11
	Belt Tensioner	37
	Brake Line Bracket	80①
	Brake Master Cylinder	18
	Camshaft	⑪
	Camshaft Cover	89①
	Camshaft Drive Shaft	89①
	Camshaft Intermediate Drive Shaft Sprocket	44
	Camshaft Sprocket	89
	Camshaft Tensioner	18
	Catalytic Converter To Exhaust Manifold	37
	Chain Guide, Primary	18
	Condenser	48①
	Cooling Fan	74
	Cooling Fan Shroud	48①
	Cross Vehicle Brace	53
	Crankshaft Balancer	37⑩
	Cylinder Head	③
	Engine Mount	59
	Engine Mount Bracket	44
	Exhaust Manifold	18
	Exhaust Manifold Heat Shield	89①
	Exhaust Manifold Stud	53①
	Front Cover	⑭
	Fuel & Brake Line Bundle Bracket	80①
	Fuel Filter	22
	Fuel Filter Bracket	80①
	Fuel Rail	89①
	Ignition Module	89①
	Intake Manifold	⑦
	MAF/IAT Sensor	35①
	Main Bearing Cap	⑥
	Oil Filter	18
	Oil Outlet Tube	89①
	Oil Pan	⑫
	Oil Pan Drain Plug	18
	Oil Pump	②
	Oil Pump To Suction Pipe	89①
	Outer Tie Rod End To Steering Knuckle	22⑬
	O2 Sensor	31
	Power Steering Line	80①
	Power Steering Pump	18
	Radiator Support Bracket	80①
	Steering Shaft, Intermediate to Center	23

TIGHTENING SPECIFICATIONS—Continued

Year	Component	Torque/Ft. Lbs.
STS		
2005–08	Thermostat Housing	89①
	Throttle Body Bolts	89①
	Transmission Oil Cooler	48①
	Washer Fluid Reservoir	53①
	Water Outlet Housing	18
	Water Pump	89①
	Water Pump, Auxiliary	80①
	Water Pump Pulley	89①

① — Inch pounds.

② — Refer to "Oil Pump, Replace" for tightening specifications & sequence.

③ — Refer to "Cylinder Head, Replace" for tightening specifications & sequence.

④ — Tighten an additional 120°.

⑤ — Tighten an additional 50°.

⑥ — Refer to "Main & Rod Bearings" for tightening specifications & sequence.

⑦ — Refer to "Intake Manifold, Replace" for tightening specifications & sequence.

⑧ — Refer to "Engine Mount, Replace" for tightening specifications & sequence.

⑨ — Tighten an additional 30°.

⑩ — Tighten an additional 150°.

⑪ — Refer to "Camshaft, Replace" for tightening specifications & sequence.

⑫ — Refer to "Oil Pan, Replace" for tightening specifications & sequence.

⑬ — Final tighten an additional 210°.

⑭ — Refer to "Front Cover, Replace" for tightening specifications & sequence.

Rear Suspension

NOTE: Refer To "Air Bag System Precautions" Located In The Front Of This Manual For System Disarming & Arming Procedures.

NOTE: Refer To "Computer Relearn Procedures" Located In The Front Of This Manual When Battery Power To The Computer Has Been Interrupted.

NOTE: Prior To Performing Any Service Operations Listed In This Section, Consult The "Technical Service Bulletins" Section For Related Information.

INDEX

	Page No.
Adjustment Link, Replace	9-58
DeVille & DTS	9-58
STS	9-58
Seville	9-58
Inner	9-58
Outer	9-58
Coil Spring, Replace	9-57
DeVille, DTS & Seville	9-57
Installation	9-57
Removal	9-57
STS	9-57
Control Arm, Replace	9-57
DeVille, DTS & Seville	9-57
STS	9-57

	Page No.
Lower	9-57
Upper	9-57
Hub & Bearing, Replace	9-56
DeVille, DTS & Seville	9-56
Heavy Duty Suspension	9-56
Soft Ride & Sport Suspension	9-56
STS	9-56
Precautions	9-56
Air Bag Systems	9-56
Battery Ground Cable	9-56
Shock Absorber, Replace	9-57
DeVille, DTS & Seville	9-57
STS	9-57

	Page No.
Stabilizer Shaft, Replace	9-57
Technical Service Bulletins	9-58
Creak/Squeak Type Noise From Rear of Vehicle During Slow Speed Turns	9-59
2004 DeVille	9-59
Firm/Harsh Rear Seat Ride	9-58
2004 DeVille	9-58
Groaning or Shuddering Noise at Low Speeds When Driving Over Low Profile Bumps	9-58
2005–06 STS	9-58
Tightening Specifications	9-60

PRECAUTIONS
Air Bag Systems

Refer to "Air Bag System Precautions" in the front of this manual for system disarming and arming procedures.

Battery Ground Cable

Prior to service, disconnect battery ground cable and isolate as required.

HUB & BEARING
REPLACE
DeVille, DTS & Seville
SOFT RIDE & SPORT SUSPENSION

1. Raise and support vehicle.
2. Remove tire and wheel.
3. Remove brake caliper mounting bolts, then position caliper aside using suitable wire or rope. **Do not disconnecting fluid line from caliper.**
4. Remove brake rotor and ABS sensor wire connector.
5. Remove mounting bolts, hub and bearing, **Fig. 1.**
6. Remove brake shield from control arm.
7. Reverse procedure to install.

HEAVY DUTY SUSPENSION

1. Raise and support vehicle, then remove tire and wheel assembly.
2. Remove brake caliper mounting bolts, then position caliper aside using suitable wire or rope. **Do not suspend caliper by brake line.**
3. Remove brake rotor.
4. Disconnect ABS sensor electrical connector.
5. Disconnect parking brake cable from lower control arm.
6. Remove wheel speed sensor.
7. Remove hub and bearing mounting bolts, **Fig. 2.**
8. Remove and discard wheel speed sensor reluctor ring. **Do not use reluctor ring again after it has been removed.**
9. Remove bearing nut and washer from hub.
10. Remove brake shield.
11. Remove bearing from hub.
12. Reverse procedure to install, noting the following:
    a. Install a new ABS wheel speed sensor reluctor ring using reluctor installer tool No. J44253, or equivalent. Turn installer to thread reluctor until it just touches ring.
    b. Install a new ABS sensor using installer tool No. J44252, or equivalent.
    c. Measure wheel speed sensor signal AC voltage using suitable multimeter. Voltage should be greater than 100 mV while wheel is revolving.

STS

1. Raise and support vehicle.
2. Remove tire and wheel.
3. Remove brake caliper mounting bolts, then position caliper aside using suitable wire or rope. **Do not disconnecting fluid line from caliper.**
4. Disconnect wheel speed sensor electrical connector, then remove wheel drive shaft mounting nut and discard.
5. Remove upper control arm to knuckle mounting nut, then separate upper control arm from knuckle using ball joint removal tool No. J43631 or equivalent.
6. **Avoid tool contact to outer constant velocity boot seal,** then remove wheel bearing/hub mounting bolts **Fig. 3.**
7. Using tool No. J45859 or equivalent, separate wheel driveshaft from wheel bearing/hub.
8. Remove wheel bearing/hub.
9. Reverse procedure to install noting the following:
    a. **Torque,** bearing/hub mounting bolts to 92 ft. lbs.
    b. **Torque,** upper ball joint nut to 15 ft. lbs. plus additional 210°.
    c. **Torque,** new wheel drive shaft mounting nut to 118 ft. lbs.

SHOCK ABSORBER
REPLACE

DeVille, DTS & Seville

1. Raise and support vehicle, then remove tire and wheel assembly.
2. Place suitable jack under lower control arm.
3. Disconnect electronic level control air tube from shock.
4. Disconnect shock electrical connector and remove wiring from control arm.
5. Remove shock to control arm mounting bolts.
6. Pull trunk trim back to gain access to upper shock.
7. Remove upper shock dust cover.
8. Remove shock upper mounting nuts and reinforcement.
9. Remove shock.
10. Reverse procedure to install.

STS

1. Remove trim panel, then move sound insulator away from shock tower.
2. Disconnect electrical connector, then remove upper shock mounting nuts.
3. Raise and support vehicle, then disconnect automatic level control from shock.
4. Remove lower mounting bolt and shock, **Fig. 4.**
5. Reverse procedure to install.

COIL SPRING
REPLACE

DeVille, DTS & Seville
REMOVAL

1. Raise and support vehicle, then remove tire and wheel assembly.
2. Support control arm using suitable jack.
3. Disconnect electronic level control air tube from shock.
4. Remove shock to control arm mounting bolts.
5. Remove cotter pin and hex nut.
6. Separate adjustment link from knuckle using universal steering linkage puller tool No. J24319-B, or equivalent.
7. **On DeVille and DTS models equipped with heavy duty suspension,** install coil spring compressor tool No. J4425, or equivalent.
8. **On all models,** lower control arm until it bottoms on support assembly.
9. Pry under lower spring insulator using suitable pry bar and remove spring with insulator, **Fig. 5.**
10. Remove upper insulator by pulling downward.

INSTALLATION

1. **On DeVille and DTS models equipped with heavy duty front and rear suspension,** install coil spring into compressor tool No. J4425, or equivalent.

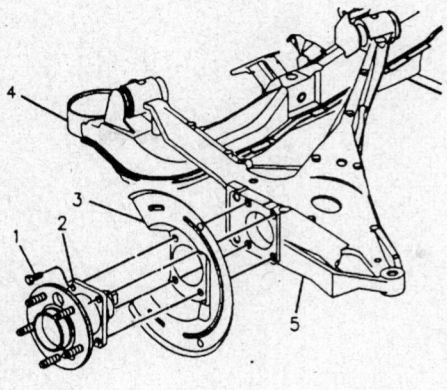

1 BOLT
2 HUB & BEARING
3 BRAKE SHIELD
4 REAR SUSPENSION SUPPORT ASSEMBLY
5 CONTROL ARM

GC2039500108000X

Fig. 1 Hub & bearing replacement. DeVille, DTS & Seville w/soft ride & sport suspension

2. **On all models,** install upper spring insulator in body.
3. Install lower spring insulator in control arm.
4. Install spring, ensuring insulator is seated in control arm.
5. Raise lower control arm and install shock to control arm mounting bolts.
6. Install adjustment link to control arm.
7. **Torque** adjustment link nut to 22 ft. lbs., then Tighten an additional 180°.
8. **On Seville models, torque** adjustment link nut to 55 ft. lbs.
9. **On all models,** connect electronic level control air tube to shock absorber.
10. Install tire and wheel, then tighten lug nuts.

STS

Refer to "Lower Control Arm, Replace" for coil spring replacement procedures.

CONTROL ARM
REPLACE

DeVille, DTS & Seville

1. Remove rear suspension support assembly as outlined under "Rear Suspension, Replace."
2. If lefthand control arm is being replaced, disconnect Electronic Level Control (ELC) height sensor link.
3. Remove stabilizer link bolt and nut, then disconnect ABS electrical connector.
4. Remove hub and bearing, if required, as outlined under "Hub & Bearing, Replace."
5. **On DeVille and DTS models equipped with heavy duty front and**

rear suspension, remove center support bracket bolts.
6. **On all models,** remove control arm to rear suspension support mounting bolt and nut.
7. Reverse procedure to install, noting the following:
   a. Tighten control arm nuts with vehicle weight resting on rear wheels.
   b. Install tires and wheels, then tighten lug nuts.

STS
LOWER

1. Raise and support vehicle, then remove tire and wheel assembly.
2. Remove stabilizer shaft link lower mounting nut, then disconnect stabilizer shaft link from lower control arm.
3. Disconnect and remove automatic level control sensor link from upper control arm.
4. Support and raise lower control arm using suitable jack, then remove shock absorber lower mounting bolt.
5. Lower control arm, then remove support.
6. Support rear frame with suitable jack, then remove frame bolts from side that coil spring is to replaced.
7. Lower frame enough, then remove coil spring without going past guide pins.
8. Remove lower control arm to knuckle mounting bolt
9. Remove mounting bolt, nut and lower control arm.
10. Reverse procedure to install.

UPPER

1. Raise and support vehicle, then remove tire and wheel assembly.
2. Remove upper control arm to knuckle mounting nut, **Do not free ball stud by using a pickle fork or a wedge-type tool.**
3. Disconnect upper control arm from knuckle using tool No. J43631 or equivalent.
4. Remove mounting nuts and upper control arm. **Discard nuts.**
5. Reverse procedure to install noting the following:
   a. Tighten upper control arm to knuckle nut to 15 ft. lbs. plus an additional 210°.
   b. Tighten new upper control arm to frame bolts and nuts to 111 ft. lbs.

STABILIZER SHAFT
REPLACE

1. Raise and support vehicle, then remove tires and wheels.
2. Remove stabilizer shaft link mounting bolt, nut, retainer and insulators from control arm, **Fig. 6.**
3. Remove clamp bolt, then bend open end of clamp upward.
4. Remove stabilizer shaft and insulators.
5. Reverse procedure to install, noting the following:

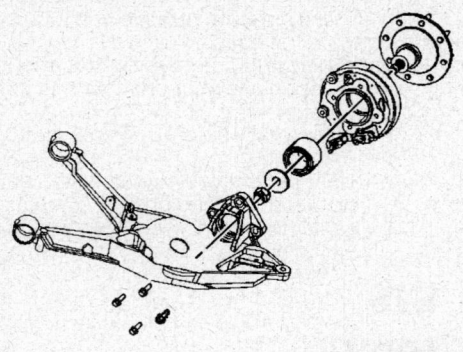

GC20301001660000X

Fig. 2 Hub & bearing replacement. DeVille & DTS w/heavy duty suspension

a. Install stabilizer shaft insulator to shaft with slit facing forward.
b. Ensure stabilizer shaft is centered before tightening clamp bolt.

ADJUSTMENT LINK
REPLACE
DeVille & DTS

1. Raise and support vehicle.
2. Remove adjustment link nut.
3. Separate adjustment link from control arm using universal steering linkage puller tool No. J24319-B, or equivalent.
4. Support exhaust and rear support assembly using suitable block of wood.
5. Remove exhaust hangers and rear support mounting bolts.
6. Lower support assembly and exhaust together.
7. Remove cam nut, bolt and adjustment link from rear support.
8. Reverse procedure to install. Inspect and adjust rear toe as outlined in "Wheel Alignment" section.

Seville
INNER

1. Raise and support vehicle, then remove tire and wheel assembly.
2. Loosen pinch bolt.
3. Support exhaust and rear suspension support with suitable wood block at least seven inches long.
4. Remove exhaust hangers and rear suspension support mounting bolts.
5. Lower support and exhaust together.
6. Remove cam bolt, nut and adjustment link.
7. Remove inner link from outer link. **Note number of turns for installation alignment.**
8. Reverse procedure to install. Inspect and adjust rear toe as outlined in "Wheel Alignment" section.

OUTER

1. Raise and support vehicle, then remove tire and wheel assembly.
2. Loosen pinch bolt.

3. Remove cotter pin and clotted hex nut.
4. Separate adjustment link from knuckle using universal steering linkage puller tool No. J24319-B, or equivalent. **Do not drive wedge between joint and attached part.**
5. Remove outer link from inner link. **Note number of turns for installation.**
6. Reverse procedure to install. Inspect and adjust rear toe as outlined in "Wheel Alignment" section.

STS

1. Raise and support vehicle, then remove tire and wheel assembly.
2. Remove mounting bolt, nut and adjustment link.
3. Reverse procedure to install.

TECHNICAL SERVICE BULLETINS

Groaning or Shuddering Noise at Low Speeds When Driving Over Low Profile Bumps

2005–06 STS

On some of these models equipped with electronic suspension control there may be a groaning or shuddering noise at low speeds when driving over low profile bumps.

This condition may be caused by the Electronic Suspension Control (ESC) system overcompensating at slow speeds due to road inputs. The groaning noise occurs in the ESC shock absorbers due to excessive fluctuating commands.

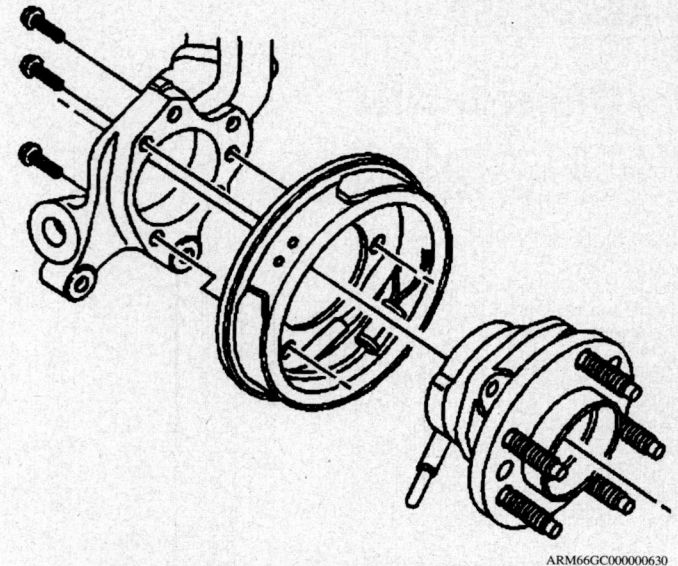

ARM66GC000000630

Fig. 3 Hub & bearing replacement. STS

To correct the condition, update the ESC module software with the latest version. **Do not replace the ESC module or shock absorbers.**

Firm/Harsh Rear Seat Ride

2004 DEVILLE

On some of these models with limo package built before VIN break 4U550590 there may be a firm, harsh or rough rear seat ride condition that is most pronounced when the vehicle is operated on irregular type road surfaces.

This condition may be caused by front and rear suspension components.

Prior to performing repairs, it is important to determine vehicle curb weight to make proper front spring selection. Contact the GM Cadillac Coachbuilder Representative at 800-528-5515 or 810-469-8400 and provide the VIN for vehicle weight information.

To correct this condition proceed as follows:

1. Raise and support vehicle, then remove tires and wheels.
2. Remove and discard rear stabilizer shaft, link and associated components as outlined under "Stabilizer Shaft, Replace.".
3. Remove left and righthand rear leveling shock absorbers as outlined under "Shock Absorber, Replace."
4. Replace rear spring upper jounce bumper (part No. 25768036) and lower insulator (part No. 25768035).
5. Replace leveling shock absorber (kit part Nos. 88964541 (righthand) and 88964542 (lefthand)) as outlined under "Shock Absorber, Replace."
6. Remove left and righthand front strut assemblies as outlined under "Strut Replace." in "Front Suspension & Steering" section.
7. Replace lefthand and righthand No. 3

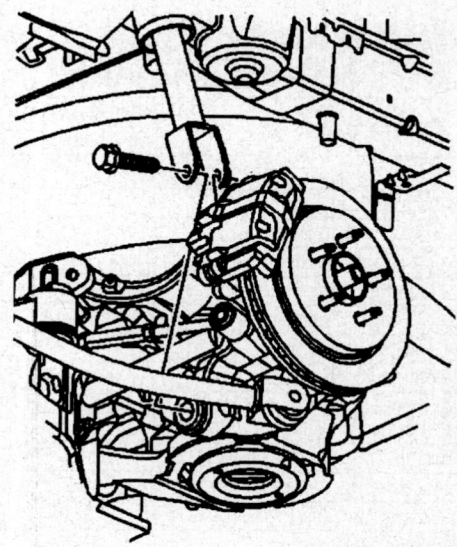

Fig. 4 Shock absorber replacement. STS

position, blue front suspension frame upper insulators (Part No. 25757176.)
8. Install left and righthand front struts (part No. 88964312).
9. Install tires and wheels, then lower vehicle.
10. Inspect and adjust front and rear wheel alignment.

Creak/Squeak Type Noise From Rear of Vehicle During Slow Speed Turns
2004 DEVILLE

On some of these models there may be a

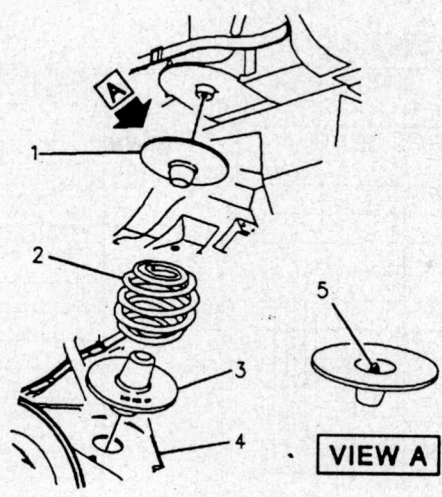

1 JOUNCE BUMPER
2 SPRING
3 LOWER SPRING INSULATOR
4 CONTROL ARM
5 RETAINER

GC2039500111000X

Fig. 5 Coil spring replacement. DeVille, DTS & Seville w/soft ride & sport suspension

creak/squeak type noise from the rear of the vehicle during slow speeds and slow turns.

This condition may be caused by insufficient lubrication on the ball stud on the automatic level control sensor assembly.

To correct this condition lubricate automatic level control sensor link sockets as follows:
1. Raise and support vehicle.
2. Remove automatic level control sensor link from ball studs.

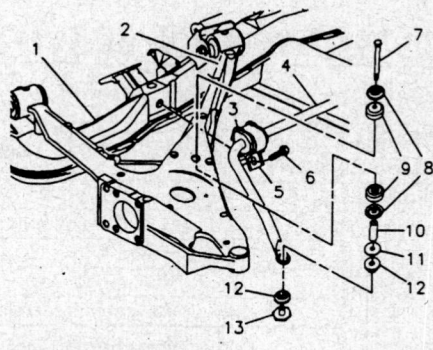

1	REAR SUSPENSION SUPPORT ASSEMBLY	7	BOLT, 13 N•m (115 LB. IN.)
2	CONTROL ARM	8	RETAINER, UPPER
3	INSULATOR, STABILIZER SHAFT	9	INSULATOR, UPPER
		10	SLEEVE
4	SHAFT, STABILIZER	11	RETAINER, LOWER
5	CLAMP, STABILIZER SHAFT	12	INSULATOR, LOWER
6	BOLT, 33 N•m (24 LB. IN.)	13	NUT

GC2039500113000X

Fig. 6 Stabilizer shaft replacement

3. Clean ball studs and sensor link sockets of dirt and debris.
4. Apply suitable lubricant to both sensor link sockets.
5. Install automatic level control sensor link to ball studs.

TIGHTENING SPECIFICATIONS

Year	Component	Torque Ft. Lbs.
DEVILLE & DTS w/HEAVY DUTY FRONT & REAR SUSPENSION		
2004–08	Adjustment Link Cam	77
	Adjustment Link To Control Arm	②
	Control Arm	110
	Front Insulator To Body	63
	Front Support Assembly To Body	138
	Hub & Bearing	87
	Rear Insulator To Body	57
	Rear Support Assembly To Body	153
	Shock Absorber To Control Arm	27
	Shock Absorber Upper	21
	Stabilizer Link	11
	Stabilizer Shaft Bracket	38
	Suspension Support Insulator Bracket	94
	Wheel Bearing	147
	Wheel Lug Nuts	80
DEVILLE & DTS w/SOFT RIDE & SPORT SUSPENSION		
2004–08	Adjustment Link Cam	59
	Adjustment Link To Control Arm	②
	Control Arm	78
	ELC Height Sensor	60①
	Hub & Bearing	50
	Rear Insulator To Body	63
	Rear Suspension Support Assembly To Body Rear	141
	Shock Absorber To Control Arm	18
	Shock Absorber Upper	18
	Stabilizer Link	11
	Stabilizer Shaft Clamp	24
	Stabilizer Shaft Link	11
	Wheel Lug Nuts	80

TIGHTENING SPECIFICATIONS—Continued

Year	Component	Torque Ft. Lbs.
SEVILLE		
2004	Adjustment Link Cam	55
	Adjustment Link To Control Arm	②
	Body Bracket Front	63
	Control Arm	78
	ELC Height Sensor	60①
	Hub & Bearing	50
	Rear Body Mount	38
	Rear Suspension Support Assembly To Body Rear	141
	Shock Absorber To Control Arm	18
	Shock Absorber Upper	18
	Stabilizer Link	108①
	Stabilizer Shaft Clamp	24
	Wheel Lug Nuts	100
STS		
2005–08	Adjustment Link To Frame	125
	Adjustment Link To Knuckle	118
	Hub & Bearing	92
	Lower Control Arm To Frame	100
	Lower Control Arm To Knuckle	118
	Shock Absorber Lower	111
	Shock Absorber Upper	18
	Stabilizer Shaft Bracket Bolt	44
	Stabilizer Shaft Link Nuts	49
	Upper Control Arm Ball Stud To Knuckle	③
	Upper Control Arm To Frame	89
	Wheel Driveshaft To Wheel Bearing	118
	Wheel Lug Nuts	100

① — Inch lbs.
② — Refer to "Coil Spring, Replace" for tightening specifications.
③ — Refer to "Control Arm, Replace" for tightening specifications.

Front Suspension & Steering

NOTE: Refer To "Air Bag System Precautions" Located In The Front Of This Manual For System Disarming & Arming Procedures.

NOTE: Refer To "Computer Relearn Procedures" Located In The Front Of This Manual When Battery Power To The Computer Has Been Interrupted.

NOTE: Prior To Performing Any Service Operations Listed In This Section, Consult The "Technical Service Bulletins" Section For Related Information.

INDEX

	Page No.
Ball Joint, Replace	9-62
DeVille & DTS	9-62
Heavy Duty Suspension	9-62
Soft Ride & Sport Suspension	9-62
STS	9-62
Seville	9-62
Ball Joint Inspection	9-62
Coil Spring, Replace	9-62
STS	9-62
Control Arm, Replace	9-63
DeVille & DTS	9-63
Heavy Duty Suspension	9-63
Soft Ride & Sport Suspension	9-63
STS	9-63
Seville	9-63
Hub & Bearing, Replace	9-61
DeVille, DTS & Seville	9-61
STS	9-61
Power Steering	21-1
Power Steering Gear, Replace	9-65
DeVille, DTS & Seville	9-65
Installation	9-65
Removal	9-65
STS	9-65
Power Steering Pump, Replace	9-65

	Page No.
DeVille, DTS & Seville	9-65
STS	9-65
Precautions	9-61
Air Bag Systems	9-61
Battery Ground Cable	9-61
Shock Absorber, Replace	9-63
STS	9-63
Stabilizer Bar, Replace	9-64
DeVille & DTS	9-64
STS	9-64
Seville	9-64
Steering Columns	20-1
Steering Knuckle, Replace	9-64
DeVille, DTS & Seville	9-64
STS	9-64
Strut, Replace	9-62
DeVille, DTS & Seville	9-62
Strut Service	9-63
Assembly	9-63
Disassembly	9-63
Technical Service Bulletins	9-65
Clunk Felt/Noise Heard From Steering Column, Steering Gear and/or Front of Vehicle During Maneuver and/or Steering Wheel Rotation	9-66
2004 Seville	9-66

	Page No.
Firm/Harsh Rear Seat Ride	9-66
2004 DeVille	9-66
Groaning or Shuddering Noise at Low Speeds When Driving Over Low Profile Bumps	9-66
2005–06 STS	9-66
Moan Type Noise During Low Speed Turning Maneuvers	9-66
2006 STS	9-66
Moan/Squawk Noise During Low Speed Turning Maneuvers	9-66
2004–05 DeVille & 2004 Seville	9-66
Rattle or Chatter Noise Heard from Front of Vehicle at Slow Speeds Over Bumps w/Light Braking	9-66
2005 STS	9-66
Snap/Pop Type Noise During Steering Wheel Rotation	9-65
2004–05 DeVille, 2004 Seville & 2006 DTS	9-65
Tie Rod, Replace	9-64
Inner	9-64
Outer	9-65
Tightening Specifications	9-67

PRECAUTIONS

Air Bag Systems

Refer to "Air Bag System Precautions" in the front of this manual for system disarming and arming procedures.

Battery Ground Cable

Prior to service, disconnect battery ground cable and isolate as required.

HUB & BEARING

REPLACE

DeVille, DTS & Seville

1. Raise and support vehicle, then remove tire and wheel assembly.

2. Remove hub nut and washer using suitable punch to keep rotor stationary. Discard hub nut.
3. Remove caliper, support and rotor.
4. Separate drive axle from hub using drive axle separator tool No. J28733-B, or equivalent, **Fig. 1.**
5. Remove hub and bearing mounting bolts.
6. Disconnect speed sensor connector.
7. Remove hub and bearing assembly.
8. Reverse procedure to install, noting the following:
   a. Clean rust and dirt from knuckle bore, chamber and mounting face allow proper seating of bearing and knuckle.
   b. Apply a light coating of grease to steering knuckle bore.
   c. **Do not use old hub nut.**
   d. Draw hub and bearing onto axle with hub nut.

STS

1. Raise and support vehicle, then remove tire and wheel assembly.
2. Remove wheel driveshaft mounting nut and discard.
3. Remove brake caliper and caliper mounting bracket as an assembly from suspension knuckle. Support caliper assembly aside, ensure there is no tension on hydraulic brake flexible hose.
4. Mark position of brake rotor to wheel studs, then remove brake rotor.
5. Disconnect ABS electrical connector, then remove connector from splash shield.
6. **On AWD models,** proceed as follows:
   a. **Avoid tool contact to outer constant velocity boot seal,** then remove wheel bearing and hub assembly mounting bolts.

b. Disengage wheel driveshaft from wheel bearing and hub using puller tool No. J45859, or equivalent, **Fig. 2.**
7. **On all models,** remove wheel bearing and hub.
8. Reverse procedure to install.

BALL JOINT INSPECTION

Replace ball joints if any looseness is detected in the joint or ball joint seal is cut. Complete the following steps in order to inspect ball joint.
1. Raise and support front of vehicle.
2. Support lower control arm with suitable jack stand as far outboard as possible near lower ball joint.
3. Wipe ball joint clean. Inspect seals for tears or cuts.
4. Mount dial indicator kit tool No. J8001, or equivalent, against lowest outboard point on wheel rim.
5. Grasp tire at top and bottom and rock it in and out.
6. Dial indicator reading should not exceed .125 inch. If reading is too high, inspect lower ball joint for vertical looseness as follows:
   a. Wear in ball joints is indicated by a .50 inch diameter nipple which retracts into joint cover as joint wears.
   b. Replace ball joint if nipple is flush with or below joint cover, **Fig. 3.**
7. Replace ball joint if ball stud is disconnected from knuckle and looseness is detected or ball stud twists in its socket while using hand pressure.
8. Inspect for ball stud tightness in knuckle boss. Shake wheel and feel for movement of stud end or nut at knuckle boss.
9. Replace all worn or damaged ball joints and knuckles.

BALL JOINT
REPLACE
DeVille & DTS
SOFT RIDE & SPORT SUSPENSION

On these models the lower ball joint is combined with the lower control arm and is not serviced separately.

HEAVY DUTY SUSPENSION

1. Raise and support vehicle, then remove tire and wheel.
2. Remove and discard axle nut.
3. Remove brake caliper and rotor. Position caliper aside using suitable wire or rope.
4. Disconnect wheel speed sensor electrical connector.
5. Separate tie rod from knuckle using separator tool No. J24319-B, or equivalent.
6. Remove cotter pin and loosen nut from ball stud.

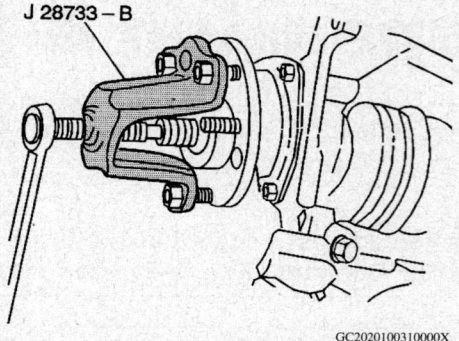

J 28733 – B

GC2020100310000X

Fig. 1   Drive axle separation. DeVille, DTS & Seville

7. Separate ball joint from knuckle using separator tool No. J39549, or equivalent.
8. Remove mounting nuts, bolts and knuckle.
9. Remove snap ring from steering knuckle, then mount knuckle in suitable vise.
10. Press ball joint out of knuckle using ball joint replacement tool No. J44254, or equivalent.
11. Reverse procedure to install, noting the following:
    a. Inspect tapered hole in lower control arm and remove any dirt or debris. Install a new control arm if hole is deformed, rounded out or damaged.
    b. Clean steering knuckle and new ball joint mounting surfaces. Do not apply solvent to ball joint seal.
    c. Apply an even .236 inch bead of Loctite 680, or equivalent to ball joint.
    d. Press in the new ball joint using replacement tool until joint bottoms in knuckle. Ensure notch in tool aligns with grease fitting.
    e. **Torque** strut to knuckle nuts to 131 ft. lbs.
    f. **On DeVille models, torque** ball joint nut to 22 ft. lbs., then tighten an additional 190°.
    g. **On DTS models, torque** ball joint nut to 22 ft. lbs., then tighten an additional 210°.
    h. **On all models, torque** tie rod to knuckle nut to 22 ft. lbs., then tighten an additional 200°. **Do not loosen nut to align cotter pin.**

Seville

1. Raise and support vehicle with control arms hanging free. Remove tire and wheel.
2. Disconnect stabilizer link to control arm bolt.
3. Remove cotter pin and loosen nut from ball stud.
4. Separate ball joint from knuckle using separator tool No. J35315, or equivalent.
5. Remove mounting bolts and control arm.
6. Reverse procedure to install, noting the following:

a. **Torque** ball joint mounting nut to 88 inch lbs., then tighten an additional 180–300°, or three to five flats.
b. **On all models, continue rotating for cotter pin installation if required, but do not exceed 60° additional rotation. Do not back off ball joint nut for cotter pin alignment.**

STS

On these models the lower ball joint is combined with the lower control arm and is not serviced separately.

COIL SPRING
REPLACE
STS

1. Raise and support vehicle, then remove tire and wheel.
2. Remove shock yoke retainers, then using tool No. J24319-B, or equivalent, separate yoke from lower control arm.
3. Remove yoke.
4. Disconnect sensor links from upper control arm.
5. **Ball stud must not rotate during disassembly or assembly.** Hold upper control arm to steering knuckle and remove mounting nut.
6. Separate upper control arm from steering knuckle, then lower vehicle.
7. Disconnect electrical connector from sensor, then remove mounting bolts and shock module.
8. Install shock module into spring compressor, then mark upper control arm assembly and insulator for proper installation.
9. Turn spring compressor forcing screw until coil spring is compressed, then remove Magnaride sensor nut.
10. Remove upper mounting nut and shock absorber from shock.
11. Loosen compressor forcing screw until upper mounting plate and coil spring may be removed.
12. Remove upper control arm bracket assembly, insulator and coil spring from spring compressor.
13. Reverse procedure to install.

STRUT
REPLACE
DeVille, DTS & Seville

1. Remove strut to body mounting bolts.
2. Raise and support vehicle, then remove tire and wheel assembly.
3. Disconnect ABS front wheel speed sensor electrical connector.
4. Remove speed sensor bracket from strut.
5. Remove brake line bracket from strut.
6. Remove strut to knuckle bolts. **Knuckle must be retained after strut to knuckle bolts have been removed.**
7. Remove strut.
8. Reverse procedure to install.

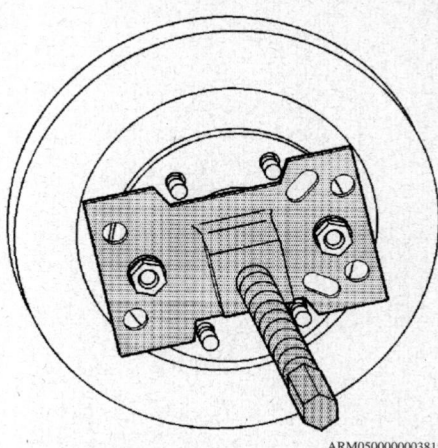

Fig. 2 Wheel driveshaft separation. STS w/AWD

STRUT SERVICE

Disassembly

1. Compress spring slightly using strut compressor tool No. J34013, **Fig. 4.**
2. Remove dampner shaft top nut. Prevent shaft from turning by using a T-50 Torx bit.
3. Guide dampner shaft out of assembly using rod tool No. J34013-38, or equivalent.
4. Loosen compressor screw while guiding dampner shaft out of assembly.
5. Continue loosening compressor screw until strut dampner and spring can be removed. **Do not chip or crack spring coating.**

Assembly

1. Install strut dampner in strut compressor tool No. J34013 with clamp tool No. J34013-20, or equivalents, **Fig. 5.**
2. Install spring over strut in proper position.
3. Move assembly upright in strut compressor and install upper lock pin. **Flat on upper spring seat must face out from centerline of vehicle. If mounted in strut compressor, spring seat faces same direction as steering knuckle mounting flange.**
4. Guide dampner shaft onto strut using installer rod tool No. J34013-38, or equivalent.
5. Center dampner shaft by turning compressor tool screw clockwise while guiding rod.
6. Continue turning compressor screw until dampner shaft threads are visible through top of strut assembly.
7. Install washer and nut. Remove clamp tool.
8. Hold dampner shaft with socket, then tighten dampner shaft nut.

SHOCK ABSORBER

REPLACE

STS

Refer to "Coil Spring Replace," for replacement procedure.

CONTROL ARM

REPLACE

Do not overextend driveshaft tri-pot joints when replacing suspension components.

DeVille & DTS

SOFT RIDE & SPORT SUSPENSION

1. Raise and support vehicle, then remove tire and wheel.
2. Disconnect stabilizer link to control arm bolt.
3. Remove cotter pin and loosen nut from ball stud.
4. Separate ball joint from knuckle using separator tool No. J36226, or equivalent.
5. Remove mounting bolts and control arm.
6. Reverse procedure to install, noting the following:
   a. **On DeVille models, torque** ball joint nut to 22 ft. lbs., then tighten an additional 190°.
   b. **On DTS models, torque** ball joint nut to 22 ft. lbs., then tighten an additional 210°.
   c. **On all models, torque** tie rod to knuckle nut to 22 ft. lbs., then tighten an additional 200°. **Do not loosen nut to align cotter pin.**

HEAVY DUTY SUSPENSION

1. Raise and support vehicle, then remove tire and wheel.
2. Remove stabilizer shaft link.
3. Remove cotter pin and nut from ball stud. Discard nut.
4. Separate ball joint from control arm using separator tool No. J39549, or equivalent.
5. Remove control arm rear mounting nut and bolt.
6. Remove control arm front mounting nut and bolt.
7. Remove control arm.
8. Reverse procedure to install, noting the following:
   a. **On DeVille models, torque** ball joint nut to 22 ft. lbs., then tighten an additional 190°.
   b. **On DTS models, torque** ball joint nut to 22 ft. lbs., then tighten an additional 210°.
   c. **On all models, torque** tie rod to knuckle nut to 22 ft. lbs., then tighten an additional 200°. **Do not loosen nut to align cotter pin.**
   d. Tighten control arm nuts after vehicle is sitting back on the ground at normal ride height.

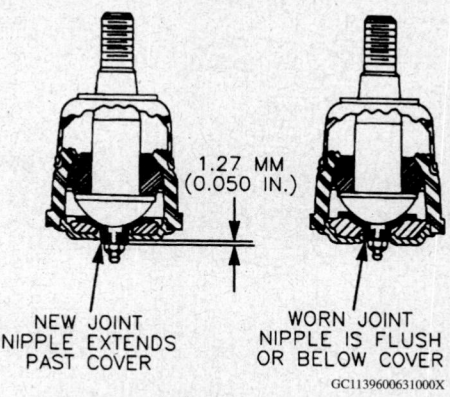

Fig. 3 Ball joint vertical wear inspection

Seville

1. Raise and support vehicle with control arms hanging free. Remove tire and wheel.
2. Disconnect stabilizer link to control arm bolt.
3. Remove cotter pin and loosen nut from ball stud.
4. Separate ball joint from knuckle using separator tool No. J35315, or equivalent.
5. Remove mounting bolts and control arm.
6. Reverse procedure to install, noting the following:
   a. **Torque** ball joint mounting nut to 88 inch lbs., then tighten an additional 180–300°, or three to five flats.
   b. **On all models, continue rotating for cotter pin installation if required, but do not exceed 60° additional rotation. Do not back off ball joint nut for cotter pin alignment.**

STS

1. Raise and support vehicle, then remove tire and wheel.
2. Remove shock yoke retainers, then using tool No. J24319-B or equivalent separate yoke from lower control arm.
3. Remove yoke.
4. Remove lower mounting nut and stabilizer shaft link from lower control arm.
5. Remove ABS wire harness and lower control arm to steering knuckle nut.
6. Separate lower control arm from steering knuckle using separator tool No. J43631, or equivalent.
7. Loosen power steering gear mounting bolts and raise power steering gear.
8. Remove lower control arm to cradle nuts and bolts, then the lower control arm by lowering it at frame and moving ball stud upwards.
9. Reverse procedure to install noting the following:
   a. **Torque** lower control arm ball stud mounting nut to 15 ft. lbs. then tighten an additional 180°.

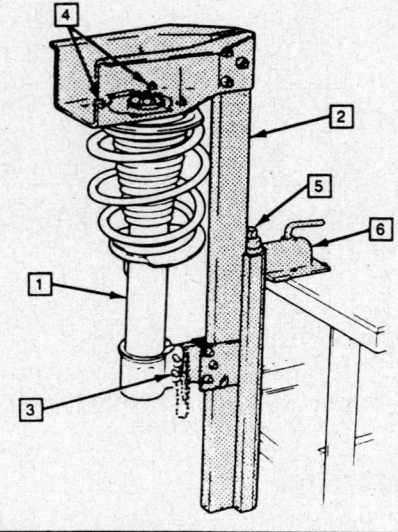

1	STRUT ASSEMBLY
2	STRUT COMPRESSOR J-34013
3	INSTALL LOCKING PINS THROUGH STRUT ASSEMBLY
4	TIGHTEN NUTS TILL FLUSH WITH STRUT COMPRESSOR
5	COMPRESSOR FORCING SCREW
6	HOLDING FIXTURE J3289-20

GC2029100135000X

Fig. 4 Strut spring compression

b. Install ABS wire harness to lower control arm.
c. Tighten all fasteners to specifications.

STEERING KNUCKLE
REPLACE

DeVille, DTS & Seville

1. Raise and support vehicle, then remove tire and wheel assembly.
2. Remove hub nut and washer using suitable punch to keep rotor stationary. Discard hub nut.
3. Remove caliper, support and rotor.
4. Separate drive axle from hub using drive axle separator tool No. J28733-B, or equivalent, **Fig. 1.**
5. Remove hub and bearing mounting bolts.
6. Disconnect speed sensor connector.
7. Remove hub and bearing assembly.
8. Disconnect wheel speed sensor electrical connector.
9. Remove tie rod mounting nut.
10. Separate tie rod from knuckle using tie rod separator tool No. J24319-B, or equivalent.
11. Remove cotter pin and lower ball joint mounting nut.
12. Separate ball joint from steering knuckle using ball joint separator tool No. J43828, or equivalent.
13. Remove strut mounting bolts and steering knuckle.
14. Reverse procedure to install. Refer to "Control Arm, Replace" for ball joint nut tightening specifications.

STS

1. Raise and support vehicle, then remove tire and wheel.
2. Remove wheel bearing/hub as outlined under "Hub & Bearing Replace."
3. Remove outer tie rod to steering knuckle mounting nut, then disconnect tie rod from steering knuckle using separator tool No. J24319-B, or equivalent.
4. Remove brake hose bracket to steering knuckle mounting bolts, then upper control arm ball stud to steering knuckle mounting nut.
5. Separate upper control arm ball stud from steering knuckle, then remove lower control arm ball stud to steering knuckle mounting nut.
6. Separate lower control arm ball stud from steering knuckle using separator tool No. J43631, or equivalent.
7. Remove steering knuckle.
8. Reverse procedure to install.

STABILIZER BAR
REPLACE

DeVille & DTS

1. Raise and support vehicle with control arms hanging free. Remove front tires and wheels.
2. Remove lefthand and righthand stabilizer link bolts.
3. Remove lefthand and righthand stabilizer bar brackets.
4. Remove lefthand tie rod end from knuckle using linkage puller tool No. J24319-B, or equivalent.
5. Separate ball joint from steering knuckle using ball joint separator tool No. J36226, or equivalent.
6. **On DTS models,** remove exhaust manifold pipe.
7. **On all models,** turn steering knuckle to left or right as required, then guide stabilizer shaft out between axle and lower control arm.
8. Remove stabilizer shaft out from under vehicle.
9. Reverse procedure to install.

Seville

1. Raise and support vehicle with control arms hanging free. Remove front tires and wheels.
2. Remove lefthand and righthand stabilizer link bolts.
3. Remove lefthand and righthand stabilizer bar brackets.
4. Remove lefthand tie rod end from knuckle using linkage puller tool No. J24319-B, or equivalent.
5. Separate ball joint from steering knuckle using ball joint separator tool No. J36226, or equivalent.
6. Turn righthand steering knuckle to lefthand, then guide stabilizer shaft out righthand side in an upward direction.
7. Remove stabilizer shaft out of bottom center.
8. Reverse procedure to install.

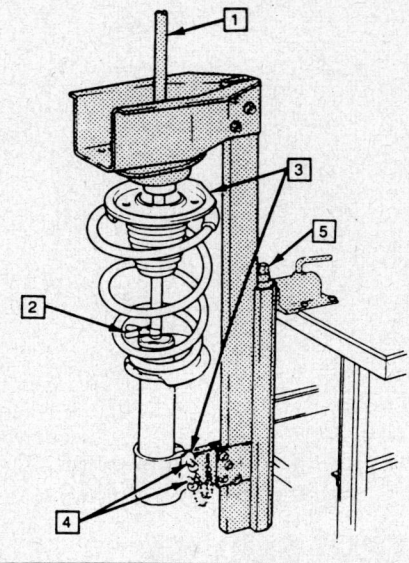

1	ROD J-34013-38 INSTALLED
2	CLAMP J-34013-20 INSTALLED
3	FLAT ON SPRING SEAT MUST FACE SAME DIRECTION AS STEERING KNUCKLE FLANGE
4	BOTH LOCKING PINS INSTALLED
5	COMPRESSOR FORCING SCREW

GC2029100136000X

Fig. 5 Strut assembly

STS

1. Raise and support vehicle.
2. **Hold shaft link studs with hex tool to prevent damage to link seal.**
3. Remove stabilizer shaft link upper and lower mounting nuts.
4. Remove stabilizer shaft link.
5. Reverse procedure to install.

TIE ROD
REPLACE

Inner

1. Remove steering gear as outlined under "Power Steering Gear, Replace."
2. Remove outer tie rod jam nut.
3. Remove inner tie rod assembly jam nut and end clamp.
4. Remove boot clamp using suitable side cutters.
5. Mark breather tube location on steering gear for installation.
6. Remove rack and pinion boot, then the breather tube.
7. Loosen inner tie rod assembly shock dampner and slide back on rack.
8. Hold rack in suitable vise.
9. Turn inner tie rod housing counterclockwise and remove using one wrench on rack assembly flats and another on inner tire rod housing flats.
10. Reverse procedure to install. Gap between rack and housing stakes should be .01 inch.

Outer

1. Remove cotter pin and hex slotted nut.
2. Loosen jam nut.
3. Remove outer tie rod from steering knuckle using universal steering linkage puller tool No. J24319-01, or equivalent.
4. Remove outer tie rod from inner tie rod.
5. Reverse procedure to install.

POWER STEERING GEAR

REPLACE

DeVille, DTS & Seville

REMOVAL

1. Ensure front wheels are in straight-ahead position.
2. Lock steering column using lock pin tool No. J42640, or equivalent, in underside of steering column.
3. Disconnect intermediate shaft lower coupling.
4. Disconnect Magnasteer electrical connector and remove heat shield.
5. Separate outer tie rod ends from steering knuckles using separator tool No. J24319-B, or equivalent.
6. **On DeVille models,** remove righthand transaxle mount. **Frame must be properly supported before partially lowering and should not be lowered any further than required to access steering gear.**
7. **On DTS models,** remove rear transmission mount upper mounting nuts.
8. **On all models,** position suitable drain pan below steering gear fluid pipe fittings.
9. Disconnect steering gear pressure and return pipes or hoses from steering gear.
10. Remove steering gear mounting bolts.
11. Position suitable floor jack below rear side of frame.
12. Remove rear mounting bolts from frame.
13. Lower the rear portion of frame.
14. Remove steering gear assembly.

INSTALLATION

1. Install steering gear onto frame.
2. Raise rear portion of frame and install mounting bolts.
3. Install transaxle mount nuts.
4. Install steering gear mounting bolts.
5. Install power steering pressure and return hoses.
6. Connect Magnasteer electrical connector and install heat shield.
7. Connect outer tie rod ends to knuckles.
8. Connect intermediate shaft to steering gear.
9. Install tires and wheels, then tighten lug nuts.
10. Fill and bleed power steering fluid system as outlined under "Power Steering System Bleed" in "Power Steering" chapter.

STS

1. Ensure front wheels are in straight-ahead position.
2. Lock steering column using lock pin tool No. J42640, or equivalent, in underside of steering column.
3. Remove front tires and wheels, then the front air deflector.
4. Remove intermediate shaft lower pinch bolt, then disconnect intermediate shaft from power steering gear.
5. Disconnect electrical connector variable effort steering, then remove outer tie rod mounting nuts.
6. Separate outer tie rod from steering knuckles using separator tool No. J24319-B, or equivalent.
7. Place a drain pan under vehicle, then remove power steering hoses to power steering gear mounting bolt.
8. Disconnect power steering hoses from power steering gear and lefthand brake line from brake hose. Plug brake line.
9. Position brake line aside.
10. **On AWD models,** support bottom of front differential housing, loosen right engine mount nut and raise differential housing to clear steering rack bolt.
11. **On all models,** remove power steering gear mounting bolts.
12. **On models equipped with 4.6L engine,** remove lefthand rearward lower control arm to frame mounting nut and bolt.
13. **On all models,** remove power steering gear through left wheel opening.
14. Reverse procedure to install, noting the following:
    a. Tighten all fasteners to specifications.
    b. Inspect and adjust front wheel toe as required.
    c. Fill and bleed power steering fluid system as outlined under "Power Steering System Bleed" in "Power Steering" chapter.

POWER STEERING PUMP

REPLACE

DeVille, DTS & Seville

1. Mark running direction, then remove serpentine belt.
2. Drain power steering fluid from reservoir into suitable container.
3. Position suitable drain pan below steering pump fluid pipe fittings.
4. Disconnect steering pump fluid lines.
5. Remove mounting bolt and power steering pump assembly.
6. If replacement pump arrived without pulley and reservoir, proceed as follows:
    a. Place pump assembly in suitable soft jawed vise.
    b. Remove power steering pump and reservoir from bracket.
    c. Remove pump pulley using pulley removal tool No. J25034-C, or equivalent.

d. Remove mounting bolts and pump bracket.
    e. Remove retaining clips from reservoir using clip removal tool No. J42649, or equivalent.
    f. Remove reservoir from pump. Discard O-rings.
7. Reverse procedure to install, noting the following:
    a. Lubricate new O-ring seals with fresh power steering fluid, then install O-rings onto reservoir.
    b. Ensure retaining clip is fully seated on reservoir assembly so reservoir assembly and pump housing are securely installed.
    c. Install power steering pump pulley using pulley installation tool No. J25033-C, or equivalent.

STS

1. Remove front air deflector and front compartment sight shields.
2. Remove PCV hose, MAF/IAT sensor from air cleaner duct resonator and air cleaner duct.
3. Rotate drive belt tensioner clockwise to release drive belt tension, then remove drive belts.
4. Remove power steering pump pulley from power steering pump using puller tool No. J25034-C, or equivalent.
5. Place a drain pan under vehicle, then remove air cleaner assembly.
6. Disconnect power steering reservoir outlet hose and power steering pressure hose from power steering pump.
7. Remove power steering bracket to engine mounting bolts.
8. Remove power steering pump with bracket.
9. Remove power steering pump bracket from power steering pump.
10. Reverse procedure to install, noting the following:
    a. **On models equipped with 3.6L engine, torque** power steering pump bracket to engine mounting bolts to 37 ft. lbs. in sequence, **Fig. 6.**
    b. Fill and bleed power steering fluid system as outlined under "Power Steering System Bleed" in "Power Steering" chapter.
    c. Inspect for and correct leakage as required.

TECHNICAL SERVICE BULLETINS

Snap/Pop Type Noise During Steering Wheel Rotation

2004-05 DEVILLE, 2004 SEVILLE & 2006 DTS

On some of these models there may be a snap or pop type noise coming from the front of the vehicle. This noise usually occurs during steering wheel rotation.

This condition may be due to the inner tie rod boot collapsing unevenly, allowing for contact between the inner tie rod and the boot.

To correct this condition replace the inner tie rod boot. **Do not replace the steering gear.**

Groaning or Shuddering Noise at Low Speeds When Driving Over Low Profile Bumps

2005–06 STS

On some of these models equipped with electronic suspension control there may be a groaning or shuddering noise at low speeds when driving over low profile bumps.

This condition may be caused by the Electronic Suspension Control (ESC) system overcompensating at slow speeds due to road inputs. The groaning noise occurs in the ESC shock absorbers due to excessive fluctuating commands.

To correct the condition update the ESC module software with the latest version. **Do not replace the ESC module or shock absorbers.**

Moan Type Noise During Low Speed Turning Maneuvers

2006 STS

On some of these models with 4.6L engine built before Aug. 8, 2005, there may be an audible moan type noise that is heard during low speed turning maneuvers, such as in parking lots.

This condition may be caused by power steering system vibration caused by the accessory drive belt.

To correct this condition, install new belt may with a different cord material (Part No. 12593189).

Rattle or Chatter Noise Heard from Front of Vehicle at Slow Speeds Over Bumps w/Light Braking

2005 STS

On some of these models there may be a rattle or chatter noise coming from the front of the vehicle. The noise can be heard while driving over bumps with light brake apply.

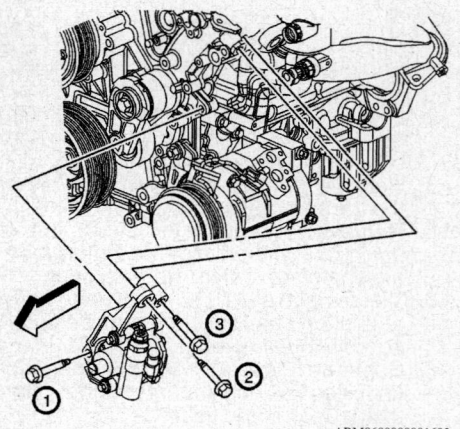

Fig. 6   Power steering pump bracket to engine mounting bolt tightening sequence. 3.6L engine

ARM0600000001693

This condition may be caused by the front suspension lower control arm hydraulic bushing.

To correct this condition, replace the front lower control arm using chassis ears to help determine which front lower control arm is causing the noise.

Moan/Squawk Noise During Low Speed Turning Maneuvers

2004–05 DEVILLE & 2004 SEVILLE

On some of these models there may be an audible moan/squawk type noise that is heard during low speed turning maneuvers.

This condition may be caused by power steering gear valve instability resulting in a pressure disturbance which creates an audible noise that is transferred through the vehicle structure.

To correct this condition replace the power steering gear outlet (return) hose assembly.

Firm/Harsh Rear Seat Ride

2004 DEVILLE

On some of these models with limo package built before VIN break 4U550590 there may be a firm, harsh or rough rear seat ride condition that is most pronounced when the vehicle is operated on irregular type road surfaces.

This condition may be caused by front and rear suspension components.

Prior to performing repairs, it is important to determine vehicle curb weight to make proper front spring selection. Contact the GM Cadillac Coachbuilder Representative at 800-528-5515

or 810-469-8400 and provide the VIN for vehicle weight information.

To correct this condition proceed as follows:
1. Raise and support vehicle, then remove tires and wheels.
2. Remove and discard rear stabilizer shaft, link and associated components as outlined under "Stabilizer Shaft, Replace" in "Rear Suspension" section.
3. Remove left and righthand rear leveling shock absorbers as outlined under "Shock Absorber, Replace" in "Rear Suspension" section.
4. Replace rear spring upper jounce bumper (part No. 25768036) and lower insulator (part No. 25768035).
5. Replace leveling shock absorber (kit part Nos. 88964541 (righthand) and 88964542 (lefthand)) as outlined under "Shock Absorber, Replace" in "Rear Suspension" section.
6. Remove left and righthand front strut assemblies as outlined under "Strut Replace."
7. Replace lefthand and righthand No. 3 position, blue front suspension frame upper insulators (Part No. 25757176.)
8. Install left and righthand front struts (part No. 88964312).
9. Install tires and wheels, then lower vehicle.
10. Inspect and adjust front and rear wheel alignment.

Clunk Felt/Noise Heard From Steering Column, Steering Gear and/or Front of Vehicle During Maneuver and/or Steering Wheel Rotation

2004 SEVILLE

On some of these models there may be a clunk type noise coming from the front of the vehicle while driving during a turning maneuver. This condition may also be felt through the steering wheel when the vehicle is stationary and the wheel is rotated from steering stop to steering stop. Some vehicles may only exhibit the noise once for every 360° of wheel rotation. On all other vehicles, this clunk noise will be noticed during low speed acceleration or deceleration, typically in light turns of the steering wheel.

This condition may be caused by inadequate lubrication of the steering intermediate shaft which results in a slip stick condition possibly resulting in the clunk noise.

To correct this condition replace original concentric style steering shaft with double D design, part No. 26068295.

TIGHTENING SPECIFICATIONS

Year	Component	Torque/Ft. Lbs.
DEVILLE & DTS w/HEAVY DUTY SUSPENSION		
2004–08	Ball Joint To Control Arm	①
	Brake Line & Speed Sensor Bracket	13
	Caliper Pin (DeVille)	②
	Caliper Pin (DTS)	③
	Control Arm	108
	Drive Axle Nut	170
	Hub & Bearing	112
	Power Steering Gear	70
	Power Steering Gear Hose	22
	Power Steering Pump	37
	Power Steering Pump Reservoir Torx Bolt	18
	Power Steering Pump Reservoir Valve Bore Plug	44
	Stabilizer Shaft Bracket	49
	Stabilizer Shaft Link	17
	Steering Shaft Pinch Bolt	33
	Strut Mount	55
	Strut To Body	49
	Strut To Knuckle	131
	Subframe Mount Nut	142
	Tie Rod End To Knuckle	①
	Transmission Mount Nut	30
	Wheel Lug Nuts (DeVille)	80
	Wheel Lug Nuts (DTS)	100
DEVILLE & DTS w/SOFT RIDE & SPORT SUSPENSION		
2004–08	Ball Joint To Control Arm Nut	①
	Brake Line & Speed Sensor Bracket	13
	Caliper Pin (DeVille)	②
	Caliper Pin (DTS)	③
	Control Arm Bolts	111
	Control Arm Nuts	116
	Drive Axle Nut	118
	Hub & Bearing	96
	Power Steering Gear	70
	Power Steering Gear Hose	22
	Power Steering Pump	37
	Power Steering Pump Reservoir Torx Bolt	18
	Power Steering Pump Reservoir Valve Bore Plug	44
	Stabilizer Shaft Bracket	24
	Stabilizer Shaft Link	13
	Steering Shaft Pinch Bolt	33
	Strut Mount	55
	Strut To Body	44
	Strut To Knuckle	131
	Subframe Mount Nut	142
	Tie Rod End To Knuckle	①
	Transmission Mount Nut	30
	Wheel Lug Nuts (DeVille)	80
	Wheel Lug Nuts (DTS)	100

TIGHTENING SPECIFICATIONS—Continued

Year	Component	Torque/Ft. Lbs.
SEVILLE		
2004	Adjuster Plug Nut	55
	Ball Joint	①
	Brake Line & Speed Sensor Bracket	13
	Caliper Bracket	137
	Caliper Pin	63
	Control Arm	117
	Drive Axle	118
	Hub & Bearing	96
	Inner Tie Rod	74
	Power Steering Gear	89
	Power Steering Gear Hose	20
	Power Steering Pump	37
	Stabilizer Bracket	24
	Stabilizer Shaft Link	13
	Strut Mount	55
	Strut Tower	33
	Strut To Knuckle	108
	Tie Rod End To Knuckle	35
	Wheel Lug Nuts	100
STS		
2005–08	Alternator	37
	Drive Axle Nut	118
	Engine Wiring Harness Bracket to Cylinder Head	33
	Engine Mount	59
	Engine Mount Bracket	44
	Exhaust Pipes To Exhaust Manifold	22
	Floor Panel Tunnel Brace	18
	Hub & Bearing	100
	Lower Control Arm Ball Stud	①
	Lower Control Arm To Cradle	96
	Power Steering Bracket To Engine Bolt (3.6L)	④
	Power Steering Bracket To Engine Bolt (4.6L)	37
	Power Steering Gear To Cradle	89
	Power Steering Pump To Engine Bolt (4.6L)	37
	Power Steering Hoses To Gear Bolt	17
	Rack & Pinion Outer Tie Rod End	41
	Shock Absorber Nut	18
	Shock Module To Body	83
	Shock To Yoke Nut	66
	Shock Yoke To Lower Control Arm (AWD)	133
	Shock Yoke To Lower Control Arm (RWD)	184
	Stabilizer Shaft Bracket	81
	Stabilizer Shaft Link Upper mounting nut	95
	Stabilizer Shaft Link To Stabilizer Shaft mounting nut	81
	Steering Shaft, Lower Intermediate to Center	23

Continued

TIGHTENING SPECIFICATIONS—Continued

Year	Component	Torque/Ft. Lbs.
2005–08	Steering Shaft, Lower Intermediate to Power Steering Gear	37
	Tie Rod End To Knuckle	52
	Upper Control Arm To Knuckle Nut	59
	Wheel Lug Nuts	100

① — Refer to "Ball Joint, Replace" for tightening specifications & procedure.

② — With standard brakes, 63 ft. lbs.; w/J55 heavy duty brakes, 83 ft. lbs.

③ — With JL9 brakes, 27 ft. lbs.; w/J55 brakes, 83 ft. lbs.

④ — Refer to "Power Steering Pump, Replace" for tightening specifications & procedure.

Wheel Alignment

INDEX

	Page No.
Front Wheel Alignment	9-69
DeVille, DTS & Seville	9-69
Camber	9-69
Caster	9-69
Toe	9-69
STS	9-69

	Page No.
Caster & Camber	9-69
Toe	9-69
Preliminary Inspection	9-69
Rear Wheel Alignment	9-69
DeVille, DTS & Seville	9-69
STS	9-69

	Page No.
Caster & Camber	9-69
Toe	9-70
Vehicle Ride Height	9-70
Wheel Alignment	
Specifications	9-3

PRELIMINARY INSPECTION

1. Inspect all tires for proper inflation pressures and approximately equal tread wear.
2. Inspect hub and bearing assemblies for excessive wear, correcting as required.
3. Inspect ball joints and tie rod ends. If they are excessively loose, correct before making adjustment.
4. Measure runout of wheels and tires.
5. Inspect vehicle trim height, correcting as required before adjusting alignment.
6. Inspect for proper operation of Electronic Level Control system.
7. Inspect strut dampners for proper operation.
8. Inspect control arms for loose bushings.
9. Inspect stabilizer bar for loose or missing components.

FRONT WHEEL ALIGNMENT

1. Install alignment equipment following manufacturers instructions.
2. Jounce front and rear bumpers three times to normalize suspension prior to measuring angles.
3. Measure alignment angles and record the readings.
4. If adjustments are required, they must be made in order:
   a. Caster.
   b. Camber.
   c. Toe.

DeVille, DTS & Seville

CASTER

1. Remove top strut mounting bolts.
2. Raise and support front of vehicle to separate strut from inner wheel housing.
3. Enlarge bolt hole opening in strut tower at front and rear of strut mounting holes using suitable round file. File excess metal to create slotted holes. **Paint exposed metal with rust resistant paint or primer.**
4. Lower the front of vehicle.
5. Install strut mounting bolts. **Do not tighten just yet.**

6. Adjust caster by moving top of strut forward or rearward. A .040 inch position change at tower is approximately .1° change in caster.
7. **On models equipped with soft ride and sport suspension, torque** strut mounting bolts to 30 ft. lbs. when caster is within specifications.
8. **On models equipped with heavy duty suspension, torque** strut mounting bolts to 49 ft. lbs. when caster is within specifications.

CAMBER

1. Raise and support vehicle, then remove both front tires and wheels.
2. Tap out upper and lower strut to knuckle bolts, then separate strut from knuckle.
3. Grind lower bolt hole on strut inner metal plates to match outside plate diameters.
4. File excess metal to make slotted holes, then paint exposed metal with rust resistant paint or primer.
5. Replace strut to knuckle and install bolts. **Do not tighten just yet.**
6. Set camber to specifications using camber adjustment tool No. J39601, or equivalent.
7. **On models equipped with soft ride or sport suspension, torque** strut to knuckle mounting nuts to 108 ft. lbs.
8. **On models equipped with heavy duty suspension, torque** strut to knuckle mounting nuts to 131 ft. lbs.

TOE

1. Loosen locknuts on tie rod ends. **Ensure boots are not twisted or damaged during adjustment.**
2. Rotate inner tie rod to adjust toe to specifications.
3. **Torque** locknuts to 47 ft. lbs.

STS

CASTER & CAMBER

1. Install caster and camber adjustment tool No. J45845 or equivalent, to lower control arm and frame, then loosen lower control arm to frame bolt.
2. Adjust camber angle by turning tool turnbuckle until specifications have been met. **Torque** bolt to 96 ft. lbs.
3. Ensure camber is still within specifications.

TOE

1. Loosen jam nut on outer tie rod.
2. Rotate inner tie rod to set toe to specifications.
3. **Torque** jam nut to outer tie rod to 41 ft. lbs.

REAR WHEEL ALIGNMENT

DeVille, DTS & Seville

Adjust lefthand and righthand toe separately.

1. Loosen inner adjustment link cam nut, **Fig. 1.**
2. Rotate cam bolt using suitable wrench or socket and adjust toe to specifications.
3. **On models equipped with soft ride or sport suspension, torque** cam nut to 55 ft. lbs.
4. **On models equipped with heavy duty suspension, torque** cam nut to 77 ft. lbs.

STS

The caster and camber adjustments are made by loosening the lower control arm adjustment bolts and repositioning the lower control arm.

CASTER & CAMBER

1. For an accurate reading, do not push or pull on tires during alignment process.
2. Determine caster angle, **Fig. 2.**
3. Determine the camber angle, **Fig. 3.**
4. Install adjustment tool No. J45845, or equivalent, to lower control arm and frame.
5. Loosen lower control arm adjustment nuts.
6. Adjust caster and camber angle by repositioning lower control arm until specifications have been met.
7. When adjustments are complete, hold lower control arm in position to ensure specifications do not change while tightening lower control arm adjustment bolts.
8. **Torque** lower control arm adjustment bolts to 96 ft. lbs.

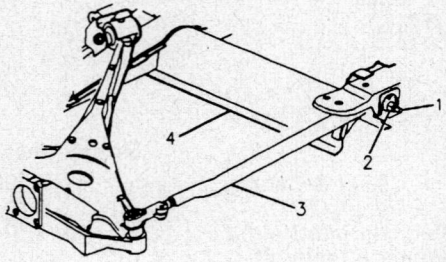

1 CAM BOLT
2 NUT, 75 N·m (55 LB. FT.)
3 INNER ADJUSTMENT LINK
4 REAR SUSPENSION SUPPORT
   ASSEMBLY

GC2049500110000X

**Fig. 1 Rear toe adjustment.
DeVille, DTS & Seville**

TOE

Complete the left and right rear toe adjustments separately.
1. Loosen adjustment link jam nuts, then rotate turnbuckle.
2. Hold turnbuckle while tightening jam nuts.
3. **Torque** jam nuts to 30 ft. lbs.

VEHICLE RIDE HEIGHT

Refer to "Vehicle Ride Height Specifications" in "Specifications" section. When inspecting ride height measurements, note the following:
1. Fuel tank should be full.
2. Tires should be at proper pressure.
3. Front seat should be in rearmost position.
4. Luggage compartment should be empty except for spare tire and jack.
5. Vehicle should be on level ground.
6. If fuel tank is not full, add weight to

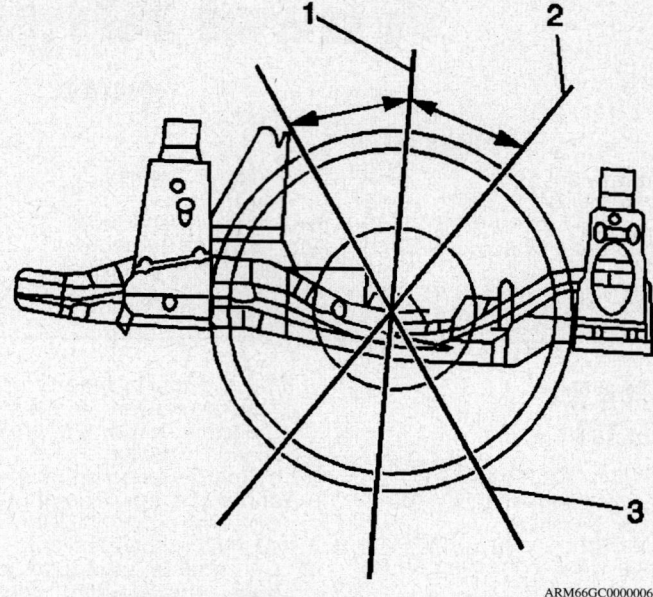

ARM66GC000000664

Fig. 2 Rear caster angle. STS

trunk to compensate for amount fuel vehicle is below the full level.
7. Prior to inspecting ride height, lift front bumper upward approximately 1 ½ inches and release three times.
8. Inspect front ride height.
9. Push front bumper downward approximately 1 ½ inches and release three times.
10. Inspect front ride height.
11. Average out both readings to determine vehicle ride height.
12. Inspect rear ride height in same manner, lifting and pushing rear bumper.

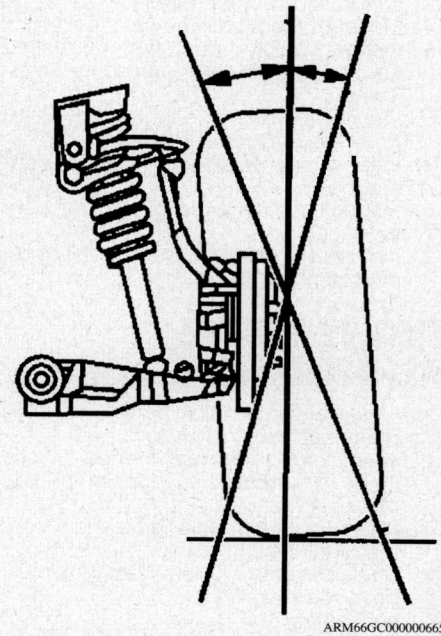

ARM66GC000000665

Fig. 3 Rear camber angle. STS

LUCERNE

NOTE: Refer To Rear Of This Manual For Vehicle Manufacturer's Special Service Tool Suppliers.

INDEX OF SERVICE OPERATIONS

Page No.

**AIR BAG SYSTEM
PRECAUTIONS** 0-18
BRAKES
   Anti-Lock Brakes (Volume 2).. 6-1
   Disc Brakes.................. 22-1
   Drum Brakes 23-1
   Hydraulic Brake Systems 24-1
   Power Brake Units........... 25-1
**COMPUTER RELEARN
PROCEDURE** 0-31
ELECTRICAL
   Air Bag System (Volume 2) ... 4-1
   Air Conditioning............. 16-1
   Alternator, Replace 10-4
   Alternators.................. 19-1
   Blower Motor, Replace........ 10-7
   Coil Pack, Replace 10-5
   Cooling Fans 17-1
   Cruise Control (Volume 2) 2-1
   Dash Gauges (Volume 2) 1-1
   Dash Panel Service
   (Volume 2).................. 5-1
   Dimmer Switch, Replace...... 10-6
   Evaporator Core, Replace 10-8
   Fuel Pump Relay Location 10-4
   Fuse Panel & Flasher
   Location 10-4
   Headlamp Switch, Replace ... 10-5
   Heater Core, Replace......... 10-7
   Ignition Lock, Replace 10-5
   Ignition Switch, Replace 10-5
   Instrument Cluster, Replace... 10-6
   Multi-Function Switch,
   Replace 10-6
   Neutral Safety Switch,
   Replace 10-5
   Precautions................. 10-4
   Radio, Replace 10-6
   Passive Restraint Systems
   (Volume 2)................. 4-1
   Speed Controls (Volume 2) ... 2-1
   Starter Motors 18-1
   Starter, Replace 10-4
   Steering Columns............ 20-1
   Steering Wheel, Replace...... 10-6
   Stop Light Switch, Replace ... 10-5
   Turn Signal Switch, Replace .. 10-6
   Wiper Motor, Replace........ 10-6
   Wiper Switch, Replace........ 10-6
   Wiper Systems (Volume 2).... 3-1
   Wiper Transmission, Replace . 10-7

Page No.

**ELECTRICAL SYMBOL
IDENTIFICATION** 0-63
FRONT DRIVE AXLES 26-1
**FRONT SUSPENSION &
STEERING**
   Ball Joint, Replace............ 10-17
   Ball Joint Inspection 10-16
   Coil Spring, Replace.......... 10-17
   Control Arm, Replace 10-17
   Hub & Bearing, Replace 10-16
   Power Steering 21-1
   Power Steering Gear,
   Replace 10-18
   Power Steering Pump,
   Replace 10-18
   Power Steering System
   Bleed...................... 10-18
   Precautions................. 10-16
   Stabilizer Bar, Replace....... 10-17
   Steering Columns............ 20-1
   Steering Knuckle, Replace.... 10-17
   Strut, Replace 10-17
   Strut Service................ 10-17
   Tie Rod End, Replace 10-18
   Tightening Specifications...... 10-19
**NON-STANDARD TIRE &
WHEEL SIZE
ADJUSTMENT TO RIDE
HEIGHT SPECIFICATIONS
& TIRE SIZE CHART** 0-61
**REAR AXLE &
SUSPENSION**
   Adjustment Link, Replace..... 10-15
   Coil Spring, Replace.......... 10-14
   Control Arm, Replace 10-14
   Description 10-14
   Hub & Bearing, Replace 10-14
   Precautions................. 10-14
   Shock Absorber, Replace 10-14
   Stabilizer Shaft, Replace...... 10-15
   Tightening Specifications...... 10-16
**SERVICE REMINDER &
WARNING LAMP RESET
PROCEDURES** 0-34
SPECIFICATIONS
   Fluid Capacities & Cooling
   System Data................. 10-3
   Front Wheel Alignment
   Specifications................ 10-2

Page No.

   General Engine
   Specifications................ 10-2
   Lubricant Data 10-3
   Rear Wheel Alignment
   Specifications................ 10-2
   Tune Up Specifications 10-2
   Vehicle Ride Height
   Specifications................ 10-2
**TIRE PRESSURE
MONITORING SYSTEM** 28-1
**VEHICLE
IDENTIFICATION** 0-1
VEHICLE LIFT POINTS...... 0-51
**VEHICLE MAINTENANCE
SCHEDULES** 0-73
**WIRE COLOR CODE
IDENTIFICATION** 0-63
WHEEL ALIGNMENT
   Front Wheel Alignment........ 10-20
   Preliminary Inspection 10-20
   Rear Wheel Alignment 10-21
   Vehicle Ride Height 10-21
   Wheel Alignment
   Specifications................ 10-2
3.8L ENGINE
   Engine Rebuilding
   Specifications................ 29-1
   Engine, Replace 10-9
   Engine Mount, Replace 10-9
   Fuel Pump, Replace 10-10
   Precautions................. 10-9
   Radiator, Replace........... 10-10
   Tightening Specifications...... 10-10
4.6L ENGINE
   Engine Rebuilding
   Specifications................ 29-1
   Engine, Replace 10-11
   Engine Mount, Replace 10-11
   Fuel Pump, Replace 10-13
   Precautions................. 10-11
   Radiator, Replace........... 10-13
   Tightening Specifications...... 10-13

Specifications

GENERAL ENGINE SPECIFICATIONS

Year	Engine		Fuel System	Bore & Stroke	Comp- ression Ratio	Net Brake H.P. @ RPM②	Maximum Torque, Ft. Lbs @ RPM	Normal Oil Pressure psi
	Liter	VIN Code①						
2006–08	3.8L	K	SFI	3.90 x 3.40	9.4	197 @ 5200	227 @ 3800	60③
	4.6L	Y	SFI	3.66 x 3.31	10.0	275 @ 6000	295 @ 4400	④

SFI — Sequential Fuel Injection
VIN — Vehicle Identification Number
① — The eighth digit of the VIN denotes engine code.

② — Ratings are net, as installed in vehicle.
③ — At 1850 RPM.

④ — 5 psi @ idle; 35 psi @ 2000 RPM.

TUNE UP SPECIFICATIONS

Year	Engine	Spark Plug Gap	Firing Order	Ignition Timing, Degrees BTDC	Curb Idle Speed	Fast Idle Speed	Fuel Pump Pressure psi	Valve Clear- ance Inch
2006–08	3.8L	.060	1-6-5-4-3-2	①	④	④	56–62③	②
	4.6L	.050	1-2-7-3-4-5-6-8	①	④	④	55–61③	②

BTDC — Before Top Dead Center
VIN — Vehicle Identification Number
① — Computer controlled. No adjustment.
② — Equipped w/hydraulic lifters. No adjustment is required.

③ — With shop towel wrapped around fuel pressure fitting to prevent fuel spillage, connect a suitable fuel pressure gauge. Inspect fuel pressure with ignition On, but engine not running.

④ — Idle speed is controlled by the Throttle Actuator Control (TAC) module.

FRONT WHEEL ALIGNMENT SPECIFICATIONS

Year	Caster Angle°		Camber Angle°		Toe Per Wheel°		Steering Wheel Angle°		Ball Joint Wear
	Limits	Desired	Limits	Desired	Limits	Desired	Limits	Desired	
2006–08	+5.05 to +6.55	+5.8	-.75 to +.75	0	0 to +.40	.2	-3.50 to +3.50	0	①

① — Refer to Front Suspension & Steering section for ball joint inspection.

REAR WHEEL ALIGNMENT SPECIFICATIONS

Year	Camber Angle°		Toe Per Wheel°		Thrust Angle°	
	Limits	Desired	Limits	Desired	Limits	Desired
2006–08	-.8 to +.7	-.05	-.10 to -.30	+.1	-.2 to +.2	0

VEHICLE RIDE HEIGHT SPECIFICATIONS

Model	Year	Body Style	Manu- facturer's Original Tire Size	Measurement Points & Specifications②					
				Front			Rear		
				Dim.	Spec.		Dim.	Spec.	
					Inches	mm		Inches	mm
Lucerne③	2006–08	Sedan	①	Z	1.5–2.4	40–60	D	3.4–4.2	87–107
Lucerne④	2006–08	Sedan	①	Z	1.2–2.0	30–50	D	3.0–3.8	76–96

Dim. — Dimension
D Dim. — Measurement from front outboard control arm bolt center line to bottom of control arm wheel bearing and hub face, **Fig. A.**

Z Dim. — Measure from pivot bolt center line down to lower corner of lower ball joint, **Fig. B.**
① — See door sticker or inside of glove box for manufacturers original tire size specifications. If tires on

vehicle do not match manufacturers original tire size & measurement is not within limits, it will be required to refer to the Non-Standard Tire & Wheel Size Adjustment To Ride Height Specification & Tire Size

Adjustment Charts in the front of this manual for approximate changes in ride height specifications.

② — Measurement is with fuel, radiator coolant and engine oil full, spare tire, jack, hand tools and mats in designated positions and tires properly inflated.

③ — Soft ride suspension.

④ — Firm ride & sport suspensions.

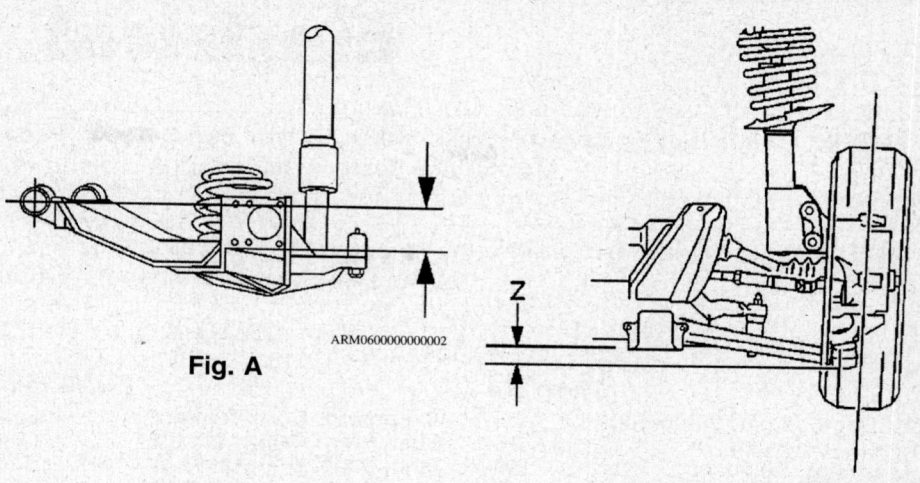

ARM0600000000002

Fig. A

ARM0600000000003

Fig. B

FLUID CAPACITIES & COOLING SYSTEM DATA

Year	Engine (VIN)①	Coolant Capacity, Qts.	Coolant Type	Radiator Cap Relief Pressure, psi	Thermo. Opening Temp. °F	Fuel Tank, Gals.	Engine Oil, Qts.②		Transmission Oil③	
							Less Filter Change	With Filter Change	Drain & Refill	Total Capacity
2006–08	3.8L (K)	11.1	Dex-cool	15	176–183	18.5	4.0	4.5	7.4	10.0
	4.6L (U)	12.7	Dex-Cool	15	195	18.5	7.0	7.5	7.4	12.6

VIN — Vehicle Identification Number
① — The eighth digit of the VIN denotes engine code.

② — After refilling, inspect oil level again.

③ — Approximate. Make final inspection w/dipstick.

LUBRICANT DATA

Year	Lubricant Type		
	Transaxle	Power Steering	Brake System
2006–08	Dexron VI	①	Dot 3

① — Power steering fluid part No. 89021184.

Electrical

NOTE: On Air Bag Equipped Models, Refer To "Air Bag System Precautions" Located In The Front Of This Manual For System Disarming & Arming Procedures.

NOTE: Refer To "Computer Relearn Procedures" Located In The Front Of This Manual When Battery Power To The Computer Has Been Interrupted.

INDEX

	Page No.
Air Bag System (Volume 2)	4-1
Air Conditioning	16-1
Alternator, Replace	10-4
3.8L Engine	10-4
4.6L Engine	10-5
Alternators	19-1
Blower Motor, Replace	10-7
Coil Pack, Replace	10-5
3.8L Engine	10-5
4.6L Engine	10-5
Cooling Fans	17-1
Cruise Control (Volume 2)	2-1
Dash Gauges (Volume 2)	1-1
Dash Panel Service (Volume 2)	5-1
Dimmer Switch, Replace	10-6

	Page No.
Evaporator Core, Replace	10-8
Fuel Pump Relay Location	10-4
Fuse Panel & Flasher Location	10-4
Headlamp Switch, Replace	10-5
Heater Core, Replace	10-7
Ignition Lock, Replace	10-5
Ignition Switch, Replace	10-5
Instrument Cluster, Replace	10-6
Multi-Function Switch, Replace	10-6
Neutral Safety Switch, Replace	
3.8L Engine	10-5
4.6L Engine	10-5
Passive Restraint Systems (Volume 2)	4-1
Precautions	10-4
Air Bag Systems	10-4

	Page No.
Battery Ground Cable	10-4
Radio, Replace	10-6
Speed Controls (Volume 2)	2-1
Starter Motors	18-1
Starter, Replace	10-4
3.8L Engine	10-4
4.6L Engine	10-4
Steering Columns	20-1
Steering Wheel, Replace	10-6
Stop Light Switch, Replace	10-5
Turn Signal Switch, Replace	10-6
Wiper Motor, Replace	10-6
Wiper Switch, Replace	10-6
Wiper Systems (Volume 2)	3-1
Wiper Transmission, Replace	10-7

PRECAUTIONS

Air Bag Systems

Refer to "Air Bag System Precautions" in the front of this manual for system disarming and arming procedures.

Battery Ground Cable

Prior to service, disconnect battery ground cable and isolate as required.

FUSE PANEL & FLASHER LOCATION

The rear fuse block is located under the lefthand side of the rear seat. The underhood fuse block is located on the front righthand side of the engine compartment.

Turn signal and hazard flasher operation are controlled by the Body Control Module (BCM). The BCM is located behind the righthand side of the instrument panel.

FUEL PUMP RELAY LOCATION

The fuel pump relay is located in the rear fuse block.

STARTER

REPLACE

3.8L Engine

1. Raise and support vehicle.

2. Disconnect cooler line retainer from bracket.
3. Remove transaxle brace bolts, then the transaxle brace from torque converter housing.
4. Remove right front tire and wheel.
5. Remove transaxle brace bolts, then the transaxle brace from extension housing.
6. Remove transaxle converter cover bolt, then the converter cover.
7. Remove starter solenoid "S" terminal nut, then the engine harness terminal from starter.
8. Remove starter solenoid "BAT" terminal nut, then the starter cable terminal from starter.
9. Remove starter motor bolts, then the starter motor.
10. Reverse procedure to install, noting the following:
    a. **Torque** starter motor bolts to 32 ft. lbs.
    b. **Torque** starter solenoid "BAT" terminal nut to 89 inch lbs.
    c. **Torque** starter solenoid "S" terminal nut to 21 inch lbs.
    d. **Torque** converter cover bolt to 66 inch lbs.
    e. **Torque** transaxle brace bolts to 37 ft. lbs.

4.6L Engine

1. Remove intake manifold as outlined under "Intake Manifold, Replace" in "4.6L Engine" section of the "DeVille, DTS, Seville & STS" chapter.

2. Remove "BAT" terminal nut from starter.
3. Remove "S" terminal nut from starter.
4. Remove starter solenoid cable from starter.
5. Remove starter motor bolts, then the starter motor.
6. Reverse procedure to install, noting the following:
    a. **Torque** starter motor bolts to 18 ft. lbs.
    b. **Torque** "S" terminal nut to 35 inch lbs.
    c. **Torque** "BAT" terminal nut to 89 inch lbs.

ALTERNATOR

REPLACE

3.8L Engine

1. Twist oil fill tube counterclockwise to unlock tube from valve rocker cover.
2. Lift front of intake manifold cover up and slide tab out of engine bracket.
3. Replace oil fill tube into valve rocker cover.
4. Remove drive belt.
5. Remove alternator brace bolt and nut, then the brace.
6. Disconnect engine harness electrical connector from alternator.
7. Reposition starter cable boot, then remove alternator terminal nut and starter cable.
8. Remove alternator front bolt, rear bolt and stud, then the alternator.

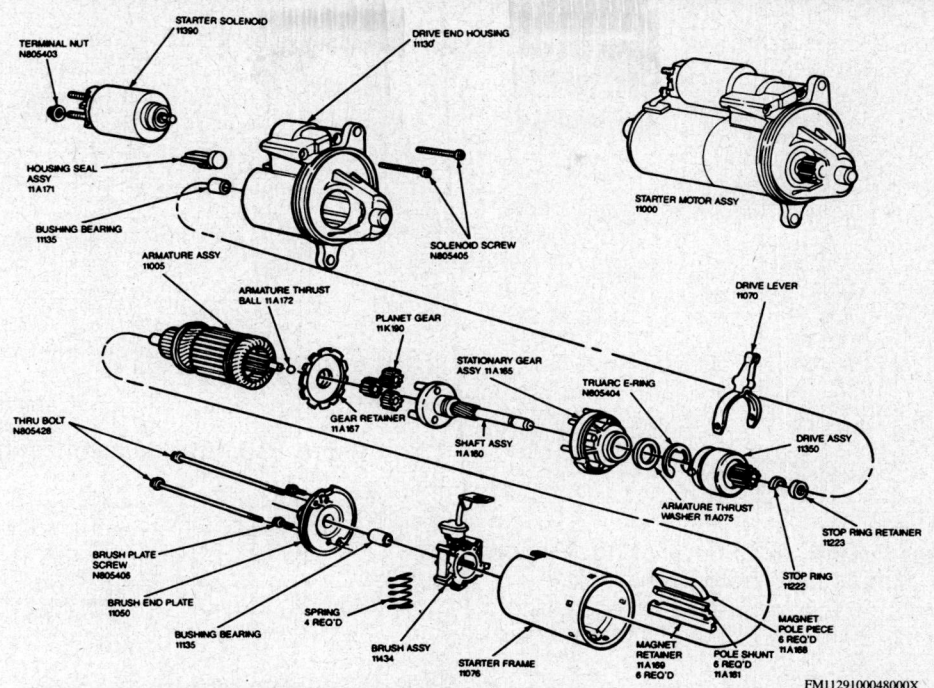

Fig. 1   Exploded view of Ford Motorcraft gear reduced permanent magnet starter motor

Condition	Possible Source	Action
• The Engine Does Not Crank	• Battery. • Starter motor. • Starter motor solenoid relay switch. • Starter motor relay. • Ignition switch (11572). • Damaged fuse. • Anti-theft system. • Circuitry.	• GO to Pinpoint Test A.
• The Engine Cranks in Reverse and Other Forward Gears	• Shift linkage (Adjustment). • Digital Transmission Range (TR) Sensor.	
• The Engine Cranks Slowly	• Battery. • Starter motor. • Circuitry.	• PERFORM the Starter Motor—Voltage Drop Test REFER to Starter Motor—Voltage Drop

FM1120100612010X

Fig. 2   Starting system troubleshooting (Part 1 of 2). Crown Victoria, Grand Marquis & Marauder

Condition	Possible Sources	Action
• Engine does not crank but relay clicks	• Battery. • Starter motor • Relay. • Circuit.	• GO to Pinpoint Test A.
• Engine does not crank and relay does not click	• PATS. • Battery. • Fuse. • Relay. • Circuit. • Starter motor. • Ignition switch. • Ignition switch (manual transaxle only)	• GO to Pinpoint Test B.
• Engine cranks slowly	• Battery. • Circuit. • Starter motor.	• GO to Pinpoint Test C.
• Unusual starter motor noise	• Starter motor. • Flywheel ring gear.	• CHECK flywheel ring gear. • INSPECT starter motor for alignment, cracked case. Make sure the mounting bolts are tightened. If necessary, INSTALL a new starter motor.

FM1120100685010X

Fig. 3   Starting system troubleshooting (Part 1 of 2). 2004–07 Focus

Condition	Possible Source	Action
• Unusual Starter Noise	• Starter mounting. • Flywheel/ring gear. • Starter motor.	• GO to Pinpoint Test B.
• The Starter Spins But the Engine Does Not Crank	• Starter motor. • Damaged flywheel/ring gear teeth.	• INSPECT the starter motor mounting and engagement. REPAIR as required. • INSPECT the flywheel/ring gear for damaged, missing or worn teeth. REPAIR as required.

FM1120100612020X

Fig. 2   Starting system troubleshooting (Part 2 of 2). Crown Victoria, Grand Marquis & Marauder

Condition	Possible Sources	Action
• The starter spins but the engine does not crank	• Starter motor.	• INSPECT the flywheel ring gear for missing teeth. CHECK starter motor for correct mounting. If concern persists, INSTALL a new starter motor.

FM1120100685020X

Fig. 3   Starting system troubleshooting (Part 2 of 2). 2004–07 Focus

Condition	Possible Source	Action
• The engine cranks slowly	• Battery. • Ignition switch. • Starter motor. • Circuitry.	• CARRY OUT the starter motor-motor feed circuit and/or the starter motor-ground circuit test.
• The engine does not crank	• Battery. • Central junction box (CJB) fuse F201 (5A). • Auxiliary junction box (AJB) fuse F121 (30A). • Battery junction box (BJB) fuse F422 (20A). • Ignition switch. • Starter relay. • Anti-theft system. • Circuitry.	• GO to Pinpoint Test A.
• Unusual starter noise	• Starter motor. • Starter motor mounting. • Incorrect starter motor drive engagements.	• GO to Pinpoint Test B.
• The starter spins but the engine does not crank	• Starter motor. • Broken flywheel/ring gear teeth.	• INSPECT the starter motor mounting and engagement. • INSPECT the flywheel/ring gear for broke, missing or worn teeth. REPAIR as necessary.
• Engine cranks with clutch pedal not applied (manual transmission)	• Starter clutch pedal position (CPP) switch.	• INSTALL a new clutch pedal position (CPP) switch.

FM1120100652000X

Fig. 4   Starting system troubleshooting. LS & Thunderbird

Condition	Possible Sources	Action
• The engine does not crank	• Battery • Battery junction box (BJB) fuse(s): — 23 (60A) — 14 (15A) • Smart junction box (SJB) fuse(s): — 10 (30A) — 22 (7.5A) - 3.0L vehicles • Starter motor • Circuitry • Starter motor relay - part of SJB • Anti-theft system • Transmission range (TR) sensor - automatic transmission • Clutch cutoff switch - manual transmission only	• GO to Pinpoint Test A.
• The engine cranks slowly	• Battery • Starter motor • Circuitry	• CARRY OUT the Starter Motor Component Test.
• Unusual starter noise	• Starter motor mounting • Starter motor • Incorrect starter drive engagement	• GO to Pinpoint Test B.
• The starter spins but the engine does not crank	• Starter motor • Damaged flywheel/flexplate ring gear teeth	• INSPECT the starter motor mounting and engagement. REPAIR as necessary. • INSPECT the flywheel/flexplate ring gear for damaged, missing or worn teeth. REPAIR as necessary.

ARM0500000000508

Fig. 5   Starter system troubleshooting. Fusion, Milan, MKZ & Zephyr

Condition	Possible Source	Action
• The engine does not crank	• Battery. • Open fuse. • Starter motor. • Ignition switch. • Digital transmission range (TR) sensor. • Circuitry. • Starter motor relay. • Anti-theft system.	• GO to Pinpoint Test A.
• The engine cranks slowly	• Battery. • Starter motor. • Ignition switch. • Circuitry.	• CARRY OUT the starter motor component test.
• Unusual starter noise	• Starter motor mounting. • Starter motor. • Incorrect starter drive engagement.	• GO to Pinpoint Test B.
• The starter spins but the engine does not crank	• Starter motor. • Damaged flywheel/ring gear teeth.	• INSPECT the starter motor mounting and engagement. • INSPECT the flywheel/ring gear for damaged, missing or worn teeth. REPAIR as necessary.

FM1120100672000X

Fig. 7   Starting system troubleshooting. Five Hundred, Freestyle, Montego, 2005–07 Sable & Taurus

Condition	Possible Source	Action
• The Engine Does Not Crank	• Battery. • Starter motor. • Starter motor solenoid relay switch. • Starter motor relay. • Ignition switch (11572). • Damaged fuse. • Anti-theft system. • Circuitry.	• GO to Pinpoint Test A.
• The Engine Cranks in Reverse and Other Forward Gears	• Shift linkage (Adjustment). • Digital Transmission Range (TR) Sensor.	• Diagnose transmission shift linkage & digital sensor
• The Engine Cranks Slowly	• Battery. • Starter motor. • Circuitry.	• PERFORM the Starter Motor—Voltage Drop Test Component Test.

FM1120100682010X

Fig. 9   Starting system troubleshooting (Part 1 of 2). Town Car

Condition	Possible Source	Action
• Unusual Starter Noise	• Starter mounting. • Flywheel/ring gear. • Starter motor.	• GO to Pinpoint Test B.
• The Starter Spins But the Engine Does Not Crank	• Starter motor. • Damaged flywheel/ring gear teeth.	• INSPECT the starter motor mounting and engagement. REPAIR as required. • INSPECT the flywheel/ring gear for damaged, missing or worn teeth. REPAIR as required.

FM1120100682020X

Fig. 9   Starting system troubleshooting (Part 2 of 2). Town Car

Condition	Possible Source	Action
• The engine does not crank	• Battery. • BJB fuse ignition switch (40A). • CJB Fuse 6 (20A). • Starter motor (11002). • Ignition switch (11572). • Circuitry. • Starter motor relay. • Clutch pedal position (CPP) switch.	• GO to Pinpoint Test A.
• The engine cranks slowly	• Battery. • Starter motor. • Ignition switch. • Circuitry.	• CARRY OUT The Starter Motor-Voltage Drop Test Component Test.
• Unusual starter noise	• Starter motor mounting. • Starter motor. • Incorrect starter drive engagement.	• GO to Pinpoint Test B.
• The starter spins but the engine does not crank	• Starter Motor • Damaged flywheel/ring gear teeth.	• INSPECT the starter motor mounting and engagement. REPAIR as necessary. • INSPECT the flywheel/ring gear for damaged, missing or worn teeth. REPAIR as necessary.

FM1120100659000X

Fig. 6   Starting system troubleshooting. Mustang

Condition	Possible Sources	Action
• The engine does not crank	• Battery • Fuse(s) • Starter motor • Circuitry • PCM • Starter motor relay • Anti-theft system • Ignition switch • Start diode	• Go To Pinpoint Test A .
• One-touch integrated start (OTIS) does not operate correctly	• Circuitry • PCM	• Go To Pinpoint Test B .
• The engine cranks slowly	• Battery • Starter motor • Circuitry	• CARRY OUT the Starter Motor Component Test.
• Unusual starter noise	• Starter motor mounting • Starter motor • Incorrect starter drive engagement	• Go To Pinpoint Test C .
• The starter spins but the engine does not crank	• Starter motor • Damaged flywheel/ring gear teeth	• INSPECT the starter motor mounting and engagement. • INSPECT the flexplate/ring gear for damaged, missing or worn teeth. REPAIR as necessary.

ARM0700000000419

Fig. 8   Starting system troubleshooting. 2008 Sable, Taurus & Taurus X

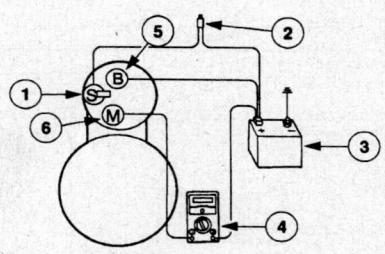

Item	Part Number	Description
1	—	S-Terminal
2	—	Remote Starter Switch
3	10653	Battery
4	—	Rotunda 73 Digital Multimeter
5	—	B-Terminal
6	—	M-Terminal

FM1120100598000X

Fig. 10   Starter motor feed circuit voltage drop test

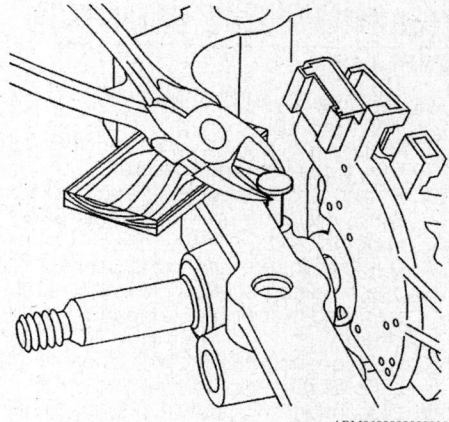

Fig. 1   Manual shift shaft pin removal

9. Reverse procedure to install, noting the following:
   a. **Torque** alternator bolts and stud to 37 ft. lbs.
   b. **Torque** starter cable terminal nut to 15 ft. lbs.
   c. **Torque** alternator brace bolt and nut to 18 ft. lbs.

4.6L Engine

1. Remove radiator assembly as outlined under "Radiator, Replace" in "4.6L Engine" section.
2. Remove drive belt.
3. Disconnect engine wiring harness electrical connector from alternator.
4. Reposition starter solenoid cable protective boot at alternator.
5. Remove alternator terminal nut, then the starter solenoid cable terminal from alternator.
6. Remove alternator mounting bolts.
7. Position engine ground cable aside and remove alternator.
8. Reverse procedure to install, noting the following:
   a. **Torque** alternator mounting bolts to 37 ft. lbs.
   b. **Torque** starter solenoid cable terminal nut to 106 inch lbs.

COIL PACK
REPLACE
3.8L Engine

1. Remove intake manifold cover.
2. Disconnect spark plug wire at ignition coils.
3. Remove mounting bolts and ignition coil.
4. Reverse procedure to install. **Torque** ignition coil mounting bolts to 40 inch lbs.

4.6L Engine

1. Remove both fuel injector sight shields.
2. Disconnect engine harness electrical connector from ignition coil assembly.

---

3. Remove fuel injector sight shield studs.
4. Remove ignition coil assembly retaining bolts, then the ignition coil assembly.
5. Disconnect individual ignition coil electrical connector, as required.
6. Remove individual ignition coil bolt, as required then the individual ignition coil, as required.
7. Reverse procedure to install, noting the following:
   a. **Torque** individual ignition coil to ignition coil assembly bolts to 89 inch lbs.
   b. **Torque** ignition coil assembly bolts to 89 inch lbs.

IGNITION LOCK
REPLACE

1. Remove steering wheel as outlined under "Steering Wheel, Replace."
2. Remove retaining screw from lower steering column trim covers.
3. Tilt trim cover down and slide rearward to disengage locking tabs.
4. Remove lower steering column trim covers.
5. Remove retaining screws from upper steering column trim cover.
6. Lift trim cover to gain access to lock cylinder access hole.
7. Insert bent-tip awl tool No. A173A, or equivalent, into ignition lock cylinder access hole.
8. Turn ignition lock cylinder to Start position.
9. Push down on awl tool and release ignition lock cylinder to RUN position.
10. Remove ignition lock cylinder from lock cylinder case.
11. Reverse procedure to install.

IGNITION SWITCH
REPLACE

1. Remove ignition lock cylinder as outlined under "Ignition Lock, Replace."
2. Disconnect theft deterrent control module and fused jumper assembly connectors.
3. Slide theft deterrent control module from ignition lock cylinder case.
4. Remove key alarm connector from ignition lock cylinder case.
5. Remove tapping screws from ignition switch assembly.
6. Reverse procedure to install. **Torque** ignition switch tapping screws to 13 inch lbs.

NEUTRAL SAFETY SWITCH
REPLACE
3.8L Engine

Transaxle position is sent to the Powertrain Control Module (PCM) by the Internal Mode Switch (IMS). Use the following procedure to replace the IMS.

1. Place transmission selector lever in PARK position.

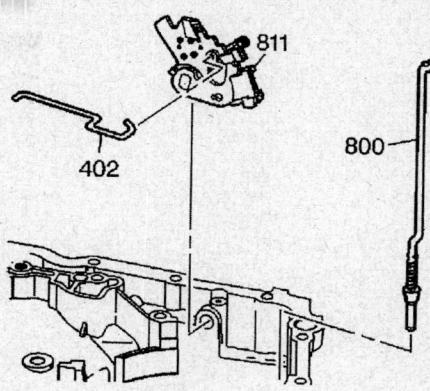

402-Manual valve link

800-Park pawl assembly

811-IMS/detent lever assembly

Fig. 2   Internal mode switch removal

2. Raise and support vehicle.
3. Remove manual shift shaft pin using suitable side cutting pliers, **Fig. 1**.
4. Disconnect manual valve link from IMS detent lever assembly, **Fig. 2**.
5. Remove IMS switch/detent lever and park pawl actuator assembly.
6. Reverse procedure to install.

4.6L Engine

Transaxle position is sent to the Powertrain Control Module (PCM) by the Internal Mode Switch (IMS). On these transaxles, the IMS switch is located inside the transaxle assembly, mounted on the valve body assembly.

HEADLAMP SWITCH
REPLACE

1. Release headlamp bezel assembly from instrument panel using a suitable flat-bladed tool.
2. Disconnect headlamp switch electrical connector.
3. Release air outlet from headlamp bezel using a suitable flat-bladed tool.
4. Remove headlamp switch from instrument panel.
5. Reverse procedure to install.

STOP LIGHT SWITCH
REPLACE

1. Remove knee bolster assembly retaining screws, then pull knee bolster assembly away from instrument panel to release retaining clips.
2. Remove knee bolster from under steering column.
3. Remove instrument panel insulator panel from under lefthand side of instrument panel.
4. Remove courtesy lamp from insulator panel.
5. Disconnect electrical connector from stoplamp/ABS/shift lock switch.

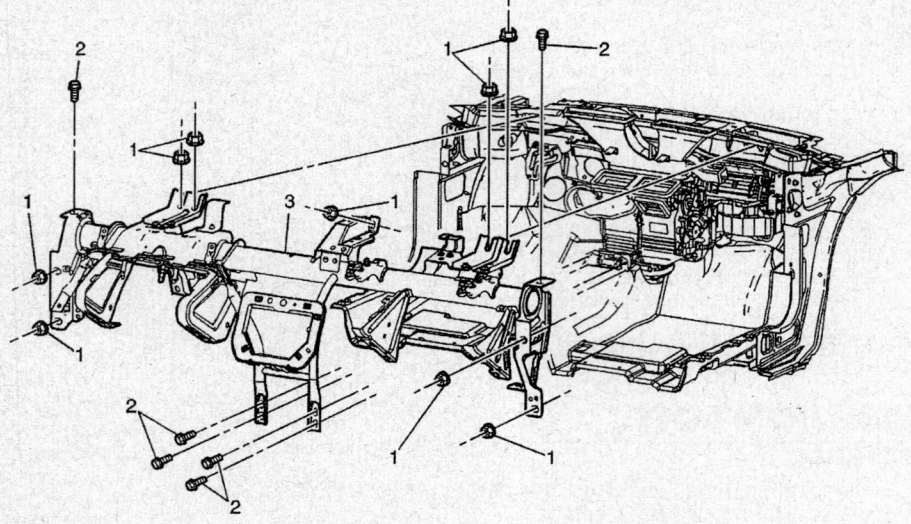

1-Nuts

2-Bolts

3-Carrier

ARM0600000000049

Fig. 3 Instrument panel carrier removal

6. Rotate switch counterclockwise, then pull to remove the switch.
7. Reverse procedure to install.

MULTI-FUNCTION SWITCH
REPLACE

1. Remove steering wheel as outlined under "Steering Wheel, Replace."
2. Remove knee bolster panel from under steering column.
3. Remove gap hider trim from steering column.
4. Place steering column in CENTER position, then remove tilt lever.
5. Remove lower steering column trim cover retaining screws.
6. Separate closeout trim cover from lower steering column trim cover.
7. Remove upper steering column trim cover retaining screw.
8. Lift upper trim cover to gain access to lock cylinder access hole.
9. Insert tip of a suitable bent tip awl into access hole in ignition lock cylinder.
10. Turn ignition lock cylinder to START position.
11. Push down on awl to release ignition lock cylinder retaining pin, then turn key to RUN position and remove lock cylinder.
12. Remove upper trim cover, then the closeout trim cover from upper trim cover.
13. Remove wire harness assembly from wire harness strap.
14. Disconnect multifunction switch assembly connector from SIR system coil connector.
15. Slide two connectors of multifunction switch assembly out of bulkhead connector.
16. Remove two pan head tapping screws from multifunction switch assembly.
17. Remove multifunction switch assembly from the steering column tilt head assembly.
18. Reverse procedure to install.

TURN SIGNAL SWITCH
REPLACE

Refer to "Multi-Function Switch, Replace" for turn signal switch replacement procedure.

DIMMER SWITCH
REPLACE

Refer to "Headlamp Switch, Replace" for dimmer switch replacement procedure.

STEERING WHEEL
REPLACE

1. Disconnect steering wheel electrical connector.
2. Remove weight block from steering wheel base.
3. Remove steering wheel retaining nut.
4. Place a reference mark on steering shaft and steering wheel for installation reference.
5. Install pulling tools J42578 and J1859-A, or equivalent, on steering wheel.
6. Separate and remove steering wheel from steering column.
7. Reverse procedure to install.

INSTRUMENT CLUSTER
REPLACE

1. Remove left and right windshield garnish moldings.
2. Remove outer trim covers from left and right sides of instrument panel.
3. Remove defroster grill and hazard lamp switch from instrument panel upper trim pad.
4. Remove instrument panel upper trim pad retaining screws, then the upper trim pad assembly from instrument panel.
5. Release instrument panel cluster trim plate bezel retaining clips.
6. Disconnect trim plate bezel electrical connectors, then remove trim plate bezel from cluster.
7. Remove instrument cluster retaining screws.
8. Disconnect cluster electrical connectors, then remove cluster from instrument panel.
9. Reverse procedure to install.

RADIO
REPLACE

1. Pry instrument panel center trim plate away from instrument panel using a suitable flat-bladed plastic trim tool to release retainer clips.
2. Remove HVAC control assembly retaining screws.
3. Disconnect HVAC control assembly electrical connectors, then remove control assembly from instrument panel.
4. Remove radio assembly retaining screws.
5. Pull radio away from instrument panel and disconnect electrical connectors and antenna, then remove radio assembly from instrument panel.
6. Reverse procedure to install. If new radio is installed, a VIN Relearn procedure must completed using a suitable scan tool.

WIPER MOTOR
REPLACE

1. Remove wiper module and motor assembly as outlined under "Wiper Transmission, Replace."
2. Separate motor from module assembly.
3. Reverse procedure to install.

WIPER SWITCH
REPLACE

Refer to "Multi-Function Switch, Replace" for wiper switch replacement procedure.

WIPER TRANSMISSION
REPLACE

1. Remove caps from windshield wiper arms.
2. Remove wiper arm assembly retaining nuts.
3. Slightly rock arms on pivot shaft and remove from shafts.
4. Remove wiper arm hose. Note correct hose routing around wiper arm for installation reference.
5. Remove air inlet grille.
6. Remove windshield frame reinforcement.
7. Disconnect wiper transmission electrical connector from main engine harness.
8. Remove windshield washer system module retaining bolt.
9. Raise rearward edge of module assembly out, then remove module and wiper motor assembly from plenum panel.
10. Reverse procedure to install.

BLOWER MOTOR
REPLACE

1. Carefully pull righthand closeout panel downward to disengage two retaining clips.
2. Disconnect courtesy lamp connector, then remove closeout panel from instrument panel.
3. Disconnect blower motor electrical connector.
4. Remove three blower motor mounting screws, then the motor.
5. Reverse procedure to install.

HEATER CORE
REPLACE

1. Drain cooling system.
2. Recover A/C refrigerant as outlined in "Air Conditioning."
3. Remove evaporator tube from thermal expansion valve.
4. Remove heater hoses from heater core.
5. Remove instrument panel cluster as outlined under "Instrument Cluster, Replace."
6. Insert steering column lock pin tool No. J42640, or equivalent, into steering column access hole to lock the steering column.
7. Raise and support vehicle.
8. Remove intermediate shaft lower pinch bolt, then separate intermediate shaft from steering gear.
9. Lower vehicle, then remove knee bolster from under steering column.
10. Disconnect steering column wiring harness connector from main body wiring harness.
11. Disconnect shift lever cable from linear shift assembly.
12. Remove shift cable retaining clip, then press shift cable tabs together and remove shift cable from steering column.

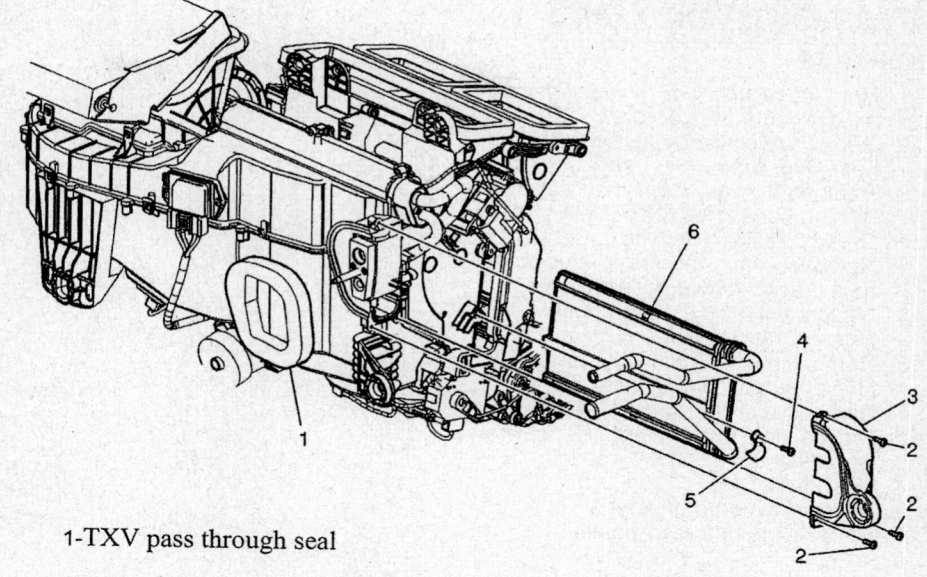

1-TXV pass through seal

2-Screws

3-Heater & A/C pipe cover

4-Screw

5-Heater core tube clamp

6-Heater core

ARM0600000000037

Fig. 4 Heater core replacement

13. Support steering column.
14. Remove lower and upper steering column retaining nuts, then the steering column.
15. Remove instrument panel compartment and ashtray assembly.
16. Remove trim panels from left and right sides of floor console.
17. Remove floor console retaining bolts and screws.
18. Disconnect console assembly electrical connectors, then remove floor console.
19. Remove radio as outlined under "Radio, Replace."
20. Remove instrument panel left and right air outlets.
21. Remove right and left side window air outlet ducts.
22. Remove left and right body hinge pillar trim panels.
23. Remove lower instrument trim panel assembly attaching bolts.
24. Disconnect lower instrument trim panel electrical harness connectors. Note routing of electrical harness prior to removal of lower instrument trim panel assembly for installation reference.
25. Remove lower instrument trim panel assembly.
26. Remove left and right upper air distribution ducts.
27. Remove center and floor air outlet ducts.
28. Remove left and right window defroster outlet ducts.
29. Remove windshield defroster nozzle duct to instrument panel carrier attaching screws.
30. Remove instrument panel carrier assembly attaching nuts and bolts, **Fig. 3**.
31. Disconnect instrument panel carrier assembly electrical harness connectors. Note routing of electric harness prior to removal of carrier for installation reference.
32. Remove carrier from vehicle.
33. Disconnect HVAC module assembly electrical connectors.
34. Remove HVAC module assembly mounting bolts, then the HVAC assembly.
35. Remove left hand floor duct from HVAC assembly.
36. Remove heater and A/C pipe retaining screws, **Fig. 4**.
37. Remove TXV pass through seal.
38. Remove heater and A/C pipe cover attaching screws, then the cover.
39. Remove heater core tube clamp retaining screw, heater core tube clamp and heater core.
40. Reverse procedure to install.

EVAPORATOR CORE

REPLACE

1. Remove heater core as outlined under "Heater Core, Replace."
2. Remove A/C evaporator tube retaining bolts, **Fig. 5.**
3. Remove thermal expansion valve attaching bolts, then the valve and tube O-rings. Discard O-rings.
4. Remove evaporator tube, evaporator tube bracket and expansion valve.
5. Disconnect recirculation actuator electrical connector, **Fig. 6**
6. Remove recirculation actuator screws , then the recirculation actuator.
7. Remove air inlet housing door lever, screws, door and housing.
8. Separate upper HVAC module case from lower case.
9. Remove evaporator core.
10. Reverse procedure to install.

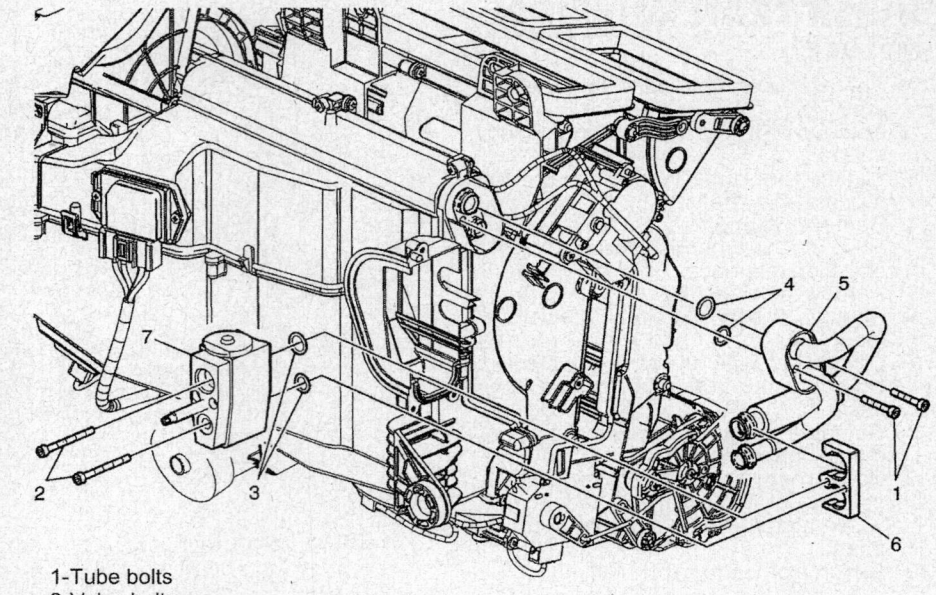

1-Tube bolts
2-Valve bolts
3-O-rings
4-O-rings
5-EVAP tube
6-EVAP tube bracket
7-Thermal expansion valve

ARM0600000000039

Fig. 5   Thermal expansion valve replacement

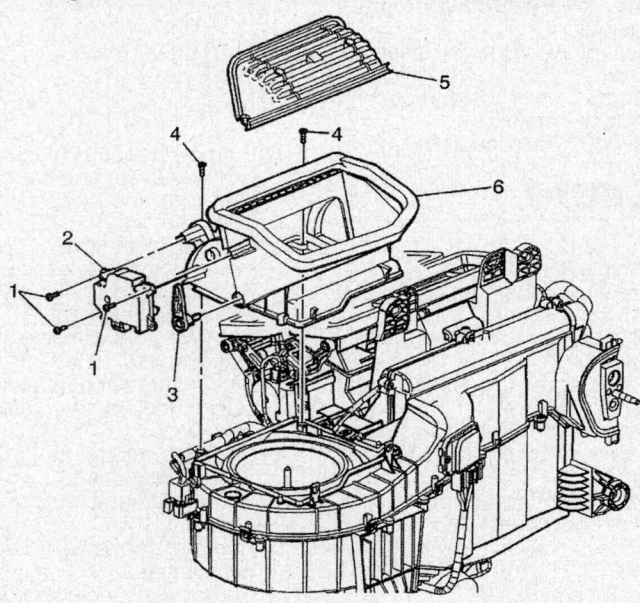

1-Screws

2-Recirculation actuator

3-Air inlet housing door lever

4-Screw

5-Air inlet housing door

6-Air inlet housing

ARM0600000000038

Fig. 6   Air inlet housing removal

3.8L Engine

NOTE: For Procedures Not Found In This Section, Refer To The "3.8L Engine" Section In The "Bonneville, LeSabre & Park Avenue" Chapter.

NOTE: On Air Bag Equipped Models, Refer To "Air Bag System Precautions" Located In The Front Of This Manual For System Disarming & Arming Procedures.

NOTE: Refer To "Computer Relearn Procedures" Located In The Front Of This Manual When Battery Power To The Computer Has Been Interrupted.

INDEX

	Page No.		Page No.		Page No.
Engine Rebuilding Specifications	29-1	Front	10-9	Battery Ground Cable	10-9
		Rear	10-9	Fuel System Pressure Relief	10-9
Engine, Replace	10-9	Fuel Pump, Replace	10-10	Radiator, Replace	10-10
Engine Mount, Replace	10-9	Precautions	10-9	Tightening Specifications	10-10

PRECAUTIONS

Fuel System Pressure Relief

Failure to relieve system pressure prior to disconnecting fuel system components may cause fire or personal injury.
1. Turn ignition switch to OFF position.
2. Disconnect and isolate battery ground.
3. Relieve fuel tank vapor pressure by loosening fuel filler cap.
4. Remove lefthand fuel rail cover.
5. Connect fuel pressure gauge tool No. J34730-1A, or equivalent, to fuel pressure connection.
6. Wrap shop towel around fitting while connecting gauge.
7. Install gauge bleed hose into suitable container.
8. Open gauge valve and bleed system pressure.
9. Drain remaining gauge fuel into suitable container.

Battery Ground Cable

Prior to service, disconnect battery ground cable and isolate as required.

ENGINE MOUNT
REPLACE

Front

1. Raise and support vehicle.
2. Remove front air deflector from under engine.
3. Place a suitable adjustable jack and a block of wood under oil pan.
4. Remove engine mount bracket bolts, then the engine mount to frame nut.
5. Remove engine mount to bracket nut.
6. Using adjustable jack and block of wood, raise engine enough to remove engine mount.
7. Reverse procedure to install.

Rear

1. Raise and support vehicle.
2. Remove right front wheel and tire.
3. Place a suitable adjustable jack under transaxle oil pan.
4. Remove engine mount to frame nut and engine mount to bracket nut.
5. Using adjustable jack and block of wood, raise engine enough to remove engine mount.
6. Reverse procedure to install.

ENGINE
REPLACE

1. Remove hood.
2. Clean area around oil fill tube, then twist oil fill tube counterclockwise to unlock tube from valve rocker cover.
3. Lift front of manifold cover up and slide tab out of engine bracket.
4. Replace oil fill tube into valve rocker cover.
5. Raise and support the vehicle.
6. Drain engine oil and cooling system.
7. Remove transaxle brace to transaxle and oil pan bolts, then the brace.
8. Remove front transaxle converter cover bolts and the cover.
9. Remove rear transaxle converter cover bolts and the cover.
10. Remove starter motor as outlined under "Starter, Replace" in "Electrical" section.
11. Remove torque converter bolts.
12. Mark relationship of torque converter to flywheel for installation reference.
13. Remove front engine mount to frame nut.
14. Remove rear engine mount to frame nut.
15. Remove exhaust manifold to catalytic converter nuts.
16. Disconnect engine harness to oil pressure sensor and Vehicle Speed Sensor (VSS) connectors.
17. Remove engine harness clip from engine bracket.
18. Remove engine harness clip from steering gear bracket.
19. Disconnect engine harness electrical connector from rear knock sensor jumper harness.
20. Disconnect engine harness electrical connector from front knock sensor.
21. Disconnect engine harness from oil level sensor, A/C pressure sensor and A/C compressor electrical connectors.
22. Remove starter cable ground bolt and reposition starter cable terminal away from engine.
23. Remove right wheel drive shaft as outlined under "Driveshaft, Replace" in "Front Drive Axle" chapter.
24. Remove oil filter adapter mounting bolts, adapter and gasket.
25. Remove lower rear and lower front transaxle bolts.
26. Lower vehicle while supporting transaxle.
27. Remove air cleaner assembly.
28. Remove alternator terminal nut, then starter cable from alternator.
29. Disconnect fuel feed line quick connect fitting from fuel rail.
30. Disconnect EVAP line quick connect fitting from purge solenoid.
31. Loosen water pump pulley bolts and remove drive belt.
32. Remove water pump pulley bolts and water pump pulley.
33. Remove engine mount strut and fan shroud.
34. Remove brake booster vacuum hose from intake manifold.
35. Remove power steering pump bolts position pump aside.
36. Disconnect engine harness electrical

37. Remove engine harness electrical connector retainers (2) from fuel rail.
38. Disconnect engine harness to rear heated oxygen sensor and alternator electrical connectors.
39. Disconnect engine harness from throttle actuator and ECT sensor electrical connectors.
40. Disconnect engine harness clips from heat shield.
41. Disconnect engine harness to EGR valve electrical connector.
42. Disconnect engine harness to front fuel injectors electrical connectors.
43. Remove engine harness retainers from fuel rail.
44. Disconnect engine harness ignition control module harness electrical connector.
45. Disconnect engine harness to MAP sensor electrical connector.
46. Gather all branches of engine wiring harness and position harness aside.
47. Remove radiator inlet hose from thermostat housing.
48. Remove radiator outlet hose from front cover.
49. Remove heater inlet and outlet hose adapter bolts, then the heater inlet and outlet adapters from drive belt tensioner.
50. Remove A/C compressor bolts and nut. **Do not discharge A/C system.**
51. Secure A/C compressor to frame.
52. Install a suitable engine lifting device to engine lift brackets.
53. Remove upper transaxle bolts.
54. Remove engine from vehicle.
55. Reverse procedure to install.

RADIATOR
REPLACE

1. Partially drain the cooling system, then remove cooling fan shroud assembly.
2. Remove condenser line to radiator retaining bolt.
3. Remove radiator outlet hose from radiator.
4. Remove condenser mounting bolts, then lift condenser upward slightly to release lower feet from lower mounting features located at front of radiator.
5. Lift radiator up and out vehicle.
6. Reverse procedure to install.

FUEL PUMP
REPLACE

1. Relieve fuel system pressure as outlined under "Precautions."
2. Open rear luggage compartment and remove rear seat back trim panel retainers. Access retainers through seat back opening.
3. Remove rear seat back trim panel assembly.
4. Tuck edges of floor panel trim panel into side panel trim channel. Press down to secure.
5. Remove rear compartment liner.
6. Remove fuel sender access hole cover bolts, then the access hole cover.
7. Disconnect fuel feed rear pipe quick connect fitting from sender.
8. Disconnect fuel level sensor wiring harness electrical connectors from pressure sensor and sender.
9. Position fuel feed pipe and harness connectors aside.
10. Install lock ring removal tool No. J45722 onto lock ring.
11. Attach a suitable long breaker bar to lock ring removal tool and rotate lock fuel sender lock ring in a counterclockwise direction.
12. Remove fuel sender lock ring.
13. Slowly raise sender until fuel level sensor float arm is just visible. **When removing sender from fuel tank, be aware that sender reservoir bucket is full of fuel.**
14. Remove sender from tank. Tilt sender toward rear of fuel tank to allow level sensor float arm to clear tank opening.
15. Carefully discard fuel in sender reservoir bucket into an approved fuel container. **Do not reuse old fuel pump sender seal.**
16. Remove and discard fuel pump sender O-ring seal.
17. Reverse procedure to install.

TIGHTENING SPECIFICATIONS

Year	Component	Torque/Ft. Lbs.
2006–08	A/C Compressor Mounting Bolt	37
	Alternator Brace Bracket Bolt	37
	Alternator Bracket Bolt	37
	Drive Belt Tensioner	37
	Engine Mount Bracket To Engine	44
	Engine Mount To Bracket Nut	59
	Engine Mount To Frame Rail Nuts	52
	Engine To Transaxle Mounting Bolt	55
	Flywheel To Torque Converter Bolt	46
	Fuel Injector Rail Assembly Nut	89①
	Oil Pan Drain Plug	22
	Oil Filter Adapter Bolt	22
	Right Engine Mount Bracket Stud	71①
	Water Pump Pulley Bolt	10

① — Inch lbs.

4.6L Engine

NOTE: For Procedures Not Found In This Section, Refer To The "4.6L Engine" Section In The "DeVille, DTS, Seville & STS" Chapter.

NOTE: On Air Bag Equipped Models, Refer To "Air Bag System Precautions" Located In The Front Of This Manual For System Disarming & Arming Procedures.

NOTE: Refer To "Computer Relearn Procedures" Located In The Front Of This Manual When Battery Power To The Computer Has Been Interrupted.

INDEX

	Page No.		Page No.		Page No.
Engine Rebuilding Specifications	29-1	Front	10-11	Battery Ground Cable	10-11
Engine, Replace	10-11	Right	10-11	Fuel System Pressure Relief	10-11
Engine Mount, Replace	10-11	Fuel Pump, Replace	10-13	Radiator, Replace	10-13
		Precautions	10-11	Tightening Specifications	10-13

PRECAUTIONS

Fuel System Pressure Relief

Failure to relieve system pressure prior to disconnecting fuel system components may cause fire or personal injury.
1. Turn ignition switch to OFF position.
2. Disconnect and isolate battery ground.
3. Relieve fuel tank vapor pressure by loosening fuel filler cap.
4. Remove lefthand fuel rail cover.
5. Connect fuel pressure gauge tool No. J34730-1A, or equivalent, to fuel pressure connection.
6. Wrap shop towel around fitting while connecting gauge.
7. Install gauge bleed hose into suitable container.
8. Open gauge valve and bleed system pressure.
9. Drain remaining gauge fuel into suitable container.

Battery Ground Cable

Prior to service, disconnect battery ground cable and isolate as required.

ENGINE MOUNT
REPLACE
Front

1. Support engine with support fixture tool No. J28467-A, or equivalent.
2. Raise and support vehicle, then remove front tires and wheels.
3. Remove stabilizer shaft.
4. Remove steering gear to engine frame mounting bolts.
5. Separate ball joints from steering knuckle as outlined under "Ball Joint, Replace" in "Front Suspension & Steering" section.
6. Remove air deflector from under engine.
7. Remove brake pressure modulator valve and bracket from frame.
8. Disconnect Electronic Suspension Control (ESC) sensor links from lower control arm ball studs.
9. Remove secondary air injection pump assembly.
10. Remove steering gear heat shield fasteners and heat shield.
11. Disconnect electrical harness retainer mounted on heat shield, then separate harness from heat shield.
12. Remove power steering line to frame brackets.
13. Remove power steering line retainer along left side of engine frame.
14. Retain steering gear to body using suitable mechanics wire.
15. Lower vehicle until engine frame rests on Engine Support Stand tool No. J39580, or suitable jack stands.
16. Remove fastener retaining front engine mount to engine frame.
17. Remove fasteners retaining rear transaxle mount to engine frame.
18. Remove engine frame insulator bolts retaining engine frame to vehicle.
19. Raise vehicle away from engine frame, then remove control arms as outlined under "Control Arm, Replace" in "Front Suspension & Steering" section.
20. Remove engine mount bracket to cylinder head bolts.
21. Remove upper engine mount bracket to lower engine mount bracket nuts.
22. Remove upper engine mount bracket.
23. Remove transaxle brace bolt, then the lower engine mount bracket to engine stud nuts.
24. Remove transaxle brace and remove lower engine mount bracket.
25. Remove front engine mount to engine mount bracket nut, then the engine mount.
26. Reverse procedure to install.

Right

1. Remove engine frame as outlined under "Front" in "Engine Mount, Replace."
2. Remove right engine mount to engine mount bracket nut, then the engine mount.
3. Reverse procedure to install.

ENGINE
REPLACE

1. Remove fuel injector sight shield.
2. Recover A/C refrigerant as outlined in "Air Conditioning" chapter.
3. Relieve fuel system pressure as outlined.
4. Disconnect brake booster vacuum hose from vacuum connection and position aside.
5. Disconnect fuel feed and EVAP line quick-connect fittings.
6. Remove front compartment sight shield, then the air cleaner.
7. Disengage junction block cover lock tabs, then remove junction block cover.
8. Remove nut securing starter cable to Bussed Electrical Center (BEC).
9. Remove starter cable clip and cable from BEC terminal, secure cable to top of engine.
10. Disengage lever lock, then disconnect engine harness electrical connector from Transaxle Control Module (TCM).
11. Disengage lever lock, then disconnect engine harness electrical connector from body harness electrical connector. Secure TCM and engine harness wiring branches to engine.

12. Disengage lever locks, then disconnect engine harness electrical connectors from Engine Control Module (ECM).
13. Remove junction block bolts and the junction block.
14. Remove engine harness from BEC.
15. Remove engine ground strap bolt from right side frame rail. Secure ground strap to engine.
16. Remove transaxle shift cable clip from cable bracket.
17. Remove transaxle shift cable retainer, then disconnect transaxle shift cable end from range selector lever.
18. Remove transaxle shift cable from bracket and position cable aside.
19. Drain cooling system.
20. Remove radiator inlet hose from water pump housing and position aside.
21. Remove radiator outlet hose from thermostat housing and position aside.
22. Remove surge tank inlet hose from surge tank.
23. Remove heater inlet and outlet hoses from heater pipes.
24. Remove master cylinder nuts and master cylinder from brake booster. Reposition master cylinder and secure master cylinder to engine.
25. Loosen upper transaxle oil cooler pipe bolt from fan shroud.
26. Slide plastic caps off transaxle oil cooler pipe quick connect fittings.
27. Remove right front engine mount strut bolt.
28. Disconnect transaxle oil cooler pipes from radiator.
29. Lock steering column by installing locking pin tool No. J42640, or equivalent, to underside of steering column.
30. Remove left and right side strut tower bolts.
31. Raise and support vehicle, then drain engine oil.
32. Remove rear exhaust manifold pipe, then the front wheels.
33. Remove engine harness grommet from frame rail bracket.
34. Remove engine harness clip from ride lever sensor bracket.
35. Disconnect electronic suspension front position sensor link from lower control arms ball stud.
36. Loosen nut securing left front brake pipe bracket to body frame rail.
37. Remove front brake pipe bracket from body frame rail.
38. Loosen nut securing right front brake pipe bracket to body frame rail.
39. Remove front brake pipe bracket from body frame rail.
40. Disconnect rear brake pipes from front brake pipes.
41. Plug open brake lines in order to prevent fluid loss and/or system contamination.
42. Remove A/C compressor discharge hose from condenser and secure to engine. Plug A/C condenser discharge port.
43. Remove A/C compressor suction hose from condenser and secure to engine. Plug A/C condenser suction port.
44. Remove intermediate steering shaft cover.

45. Remove intermediate shaft pinch bolt, then separate intermediate shaft from steering gear.
46. Remove oxygen sensor wiring harness heat shield.
47. Disconnect engine harness electrical connector from heated oxygen sensor.
48. Remove transaxle brace bolts and the brace.
49. Remove torque converter cover bolt, then the cover.
50. Remove flywheel to torque converter bolts.
51. Position universal engine support table tool No. J39580, or equivalent, under frame.
52. Lower vehicle onto support table.
53. If a support table is not available, support powertrain with four suitable jackstands. Place a 2 x 4 inch block of wood between front of engine oil pan and engine frame.
54. Secure front hoist pads to vehicle.
55. Remove front retainer from wheelhouse liner.
56. Remove air deflector from under engine.
57. Remove front fascia bolts, nuts and retainers, then the front fascia.
58. Remove frame to body attaching bolts. Ensure clearance is maintained between engine/transaxle assembly and A/C compressor components, brake pipes, heater hoses, radiator hoses, wheel speed sensor leads and wiring harnesses.
59. Carefully raise vehicle to clear supported engine/transaxle assembly.
60. Remove heater outlet pipe nut from transaxle stud.
61. Remove heater outlet pipe.
62. Remove secondary air injection inlet hose retainer from transaxle stud.
63. Disconnect AIR inlet hose quick connect fitting from AIR pump, then remove AIR inlet hose.
64. Separate AIR outlet hose from outlet pipe.
65. Remove AIR pipe outlet pipe nut from transaxle stud.
66. Remove AIR pipe outlet pipe nut from check valve bracket stud.
67. Disconnect AIR outlet pipe quick connect fitting from check valve, then remove AIR outlet pipe from studs.
68. Remove ignition control module ground strap bolt and ground strap from right cylinder head.
69. Disconnect EVAP solenoid, EGR valve, fuel injectors and ignition control module electrical connectors from rear of engine.
70. Disconnect fuel injectors, ignition control module, MAP sensor and throttle actuator electrical connectors from front of engine.
71. Remove engine harness clip from fuel rail stud.
72. Disconnect starter inline and AIR check valve electrical connectors from top of engine.
73. Disconnect engine harness electrical connector from engine valley jumper harness electrical connector.
74. Disconnect power steering sensor

from engine harness electrical connector.
75. Remove engine harness clip from steering gear shield.
76. Remove engine harness ground nut, then the ground.
77. Disconnect ECT and VSS sensors from engine harness electrical connectors.
78. Remove engine harness clips from rear engine mount bracket and steering gear shield.
79. Disconnect A/C pressure sensor from engine harness electrical connector.
80. Remove engine harness clip from boss on engine block.
81. Disconnect oil pressure sensor, oil level sensor, A/C compressor, alternator, AIR pump and brake modulator electrical connectors.
82. Remove engine harness clip from engine bracket.
83. Remove Connector Position Assurance (CPA) retainer, then disconnect HO2S electrical connector.
84. Disconnect engine harness electrical connector from transaxle.
85. Remove engine harness ground bolts.
86. Gather all branches of engine harness and remove harness from engine.
87. Remove power steering outlet hose from reservoir.
88. Remove power steering outlet pipe bolt from engine mount strut bracket.
89. Remove power steering inlet pipe fitting from power steering pump.
90. Remove power steering inlet pipe nut from rear engine mount bracket stud, then the inlet pipe bracket from stud.
91. Remove A/C compressor discharge hose nut at compressor.
92. Separate hose from engine, then remove discharge hose from A/C compressor. Plug compressor discharge port.
93. Remove A/C compressor suction hose nut at compressor.
94. Separate hose from engine, then remove suction hose from A/C compressor. Plug compressor suction port.
95. Remove transaxle brace to transaxle bolt, nuts and the brace.
96. Remove transaxle brace to transaxle bolt/stud.
97. Remove transaxle brace to engine bolts.
98. Loosen front engine mount bracket nut with transaxle brace behind it.
99. Remove transaxle brace bolt, then the brace.
100. Install a suitable engine lift chain to engine lift brackets, then attach chain to a suitable lifting device.
101. Remove rear engine mount to frame nut.
102. Remove rear engine mount bracket bolts and stud, then the engine mount bracket.
103. Remove front engine mount to frame nut.
104. Remove rear and upper transaxle bolts, then separate engine from transaxle.
105. Raise engine from supported frame and transaxle assembly.
106. Reverse procedure to install.

RADIATOR

REPLACE

1. Partially drain cooling system, then remove cooling fan shroud assembly.
2. Remove condenser line to radiator retaining bolt.
3. Remove radiator outlet hose from radiator.
4. Remove condenser mounting bolts, then lift condenser upward slightly to release lower feet from lower mounting features located at front of radiator.
5. Lift radiator up and out vehicle.
6. Reverse procedure to install.

FUEL PUMP

REPLACE

Refer to "Fuel Pump, Replace" in "3.8L Engine" section for fuel pump replacement on these models.

TIGHTENING SPECIFICATIONS

Year	Component	Torque/Ft. Lbs.
2006–08	A/C Compressor Discharge Hose Nut	15
	A/C Compressor Mounting Bolt	37
	A/C Compressor Suction Hose Nut	15
	Alternator Brace Bracket Bolt	37
	Alternator Bracket Bolt	37
	Brake Pipe	11
	Drive Belt Tensioner	37
	EGR Tube Bolt	18
	EGR Tube Nut	44
	Engine Mount Bracket To Engine	84
	Engine Mount To Bracket Nut	59
	Engine Mount To Frame Rail Nuts	52
	Engine To Transaxle Mounting Bolt	55
	Flywheel To Torque Converter Bolt	46
	Fuel Injector Rail Assembly Nut	89①
	Intermediate Shaft Pinch Bolt	33
	Oil Pan Drain Plug	15
	Oil Filter Adapter Bolt	22
	Power Steering Pressure Hose	22
	Right Engine Mount Bracket Stud	71①
	Transaxle Support Brace	37
	Water Pump Pulley Bolt	10

① — Inch lbs.

Rear Axle & Suspension

NOTE: On Air Bag Equipped Models, Refer To "Air Bag System Precautions" Located In The Front Of This Manual For System Disarming & Arming Procedures.

NOTE: Refer To "Computer Relearn Procedures" Located In The Front Of This Manual When Battery Power To The Computer Has Been Interrupted.

NOTE: Refer To The Rear Of This Manual For Vehicle Manufacturer's Special Tool Suppliers.

INDEX

	Page No.
Adjustment Link, Replace	10-15
Coil Spring, Replace	10-14
Control Arm, Replace	10-14
Description	10-14
Hub & Bearing, Replace	10-14
Precautions	10-14
Air Bag Systems	10-14
Battery Ground Cable	10-14
Shock Absorber, Replace	10-14
Stabilizer Shaft, Replace	10-15
Tightening Specifications	10-16

PRECAUTIONS

Air Bag Systems

Refer to "Air Bag System Precautions" in the front of this manual for system disarming and arming procedures.

Battery Ground Cable

Prior to service, disconnect battery ground cable and isolate as required.

DESCRIPTION

The rear suspension consists of independent control arms, springs, and struts for each rear wheel. This enables the vertical movement of one rear wheel without affecting the other. A suspension adjustment link on each arm provides for toe adjustment and minimal alignment variation during suspension movement. A stabilizer shaft minimizes body roll.

The bottom of each shock attaches to the suspension knuckle, and the top of each shock attaches to the reinforced body area. Some vehicles are equipped with Electronic Level Control (ELC), which utilizes air adjustable shocks. ELC maintains the rear trim height under a wide range of loads.

A single unit hub and bearing is bolted to the rear knuckle. The hub and bearing has an integral speed sensor ring on the inboard side of the bearing for anti-lock brake functions.

HUB & BEARING

REPLACE

1. Raise and support vehicle, then remove tire and wheel.
2. Remove brake rotor as outlined in "Disc Brakes" chapter.
3. Disconnect wheel bearing and hub electrical connector.
4. Remove wheel bearing and hub retaining bolts, then the bearing and hub assembly.
5. Remove brake shield from lower control arm.
6. Reverse procedure to install. Clean control arm face and bore before installing hub and bearing assembly.

SHOCK ABSORBER

REPLACE

1. Raise and support vehicle, then remove tire and wheel assembly.
2. Support control arm with a suitable jack stand.
3. **On models equipped with Electronic Level Control (ELC),** disconnect air tube from shock.
4. **On all models,** remove lower shock absorber retaining bolts.
5. Remove trunk trim to gain access to shock absorber upper mounting nuts.
6. Remove upper shock absorber cover, then the upper retaining nuts and upper shock absorber reinforcement.
7. Remove shock from vehicle.
8. Reverse procedure to install.

COIL SPRING

REPLACE

1. Raise and support vehicle, then remove tire and wheel assembly.
2. Support control arm with a suitable jack.
3. **On models equipped with Electronic Level Control (ELC),** remove control sensor link from control arm.
4. **On all models,** remove lower shock absorber retaining bolts.
5. Disconnect stabilizer link from control arm.
6. Remove rear caliper pin bolts. Suspend brake caliper aside using heavy wire.
7. Remove adjustment link retaining nut, then separate adjustment link from lower control arm using ball joint separation tool No. J24319-B, or equivalent.
8. Slowly lower control arm until it bottoms on support assembly.
9. Pry under lower coil spring insulator and remove coil spring with insulator.
10. Remove upper coil spring insulator by pulling downward.
11. Separate lower control arm insulator from coil spring.
12. Reverse procedure to install.

CONTROL ARM

REPLACE

1. Raise and support vehicle, then remove tire and wheel assembly.
2. Remove wheel bearing and hub as outlined under "Hub & Bearing, Replace."
3. **On models equipped with Electronic Level Control (ELC),** remove control sensor link from control arm.
4. **On all models,** remove stabilizer shaft link.
5. Remove exhaust system.
6. Remove coil springs as outlined under "Coil Spring, Replace."
7. Disconnect electrical connector from each wheel speed sensor and remove wire from rear support.
8. **On models equipped with Electronic Level Control (ELC),** remove electronic level control link from ball stud on lower control arm.
9. **On all models,** disconnect park brake cables from both calipers and remove cables from suspension support assembly.
10. Remove brake calipers and support from vehicle underbody. **Do not disconnect brake hydraulic lines.**
11. Support rear suspension support assembly with a suitable transmission jack.
12. Remove suspension support reinforcement brace bolts, **Fig. 1.**

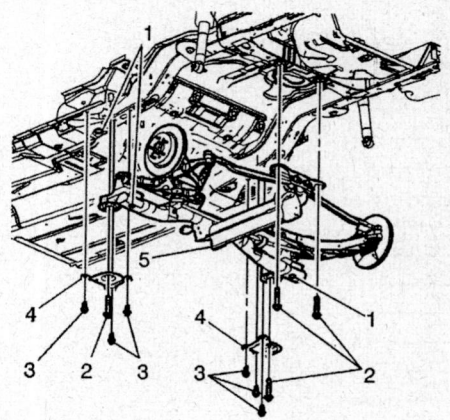

1-Ball stud

2-Suspension support assembly bolts

3-Support reinforcement brace bolts

4-Support reinforcement braces

5-Suspension support

ARM0600000000040

Fig. 1 Suspension support assembly

13. Remove suspension support assembly bolts.
14. Remove suspension support reinforcement braces.
15. Lower transmission jack and remove suspension support assembly.
16. If replacing suspension support assembly, transfer all necessary parts from old support to new support.
17. Remove adjustment link retaining nut, then separate adjustment link from lower control arm using ball joint separation tool No. J24319-B, or equivalent, **Fig. 2.**
18. Remove rear control arm nuts and bolts, then the control arm.
19. Reverse procedure to install.

STABILIZER SHAFT
REPLACE

1. Raise and support vehicle.
2. Remove stabilizer shaft links.
3. Remove stabilizer shaft insulator bracket bolt.
4. Bend open end of clamp upward, then remove stabilizer shaft insulators.
5. Remove stabilizer shaft.
6. Reverse procedure to install.

ADJUSTMENT LINK
REPLACE

1. Remove adjustment link retaining nut, then separate adjustment link from lower control arm using ball joint separation tool No. J24319-B, or equivalent, **Fig. 2.**

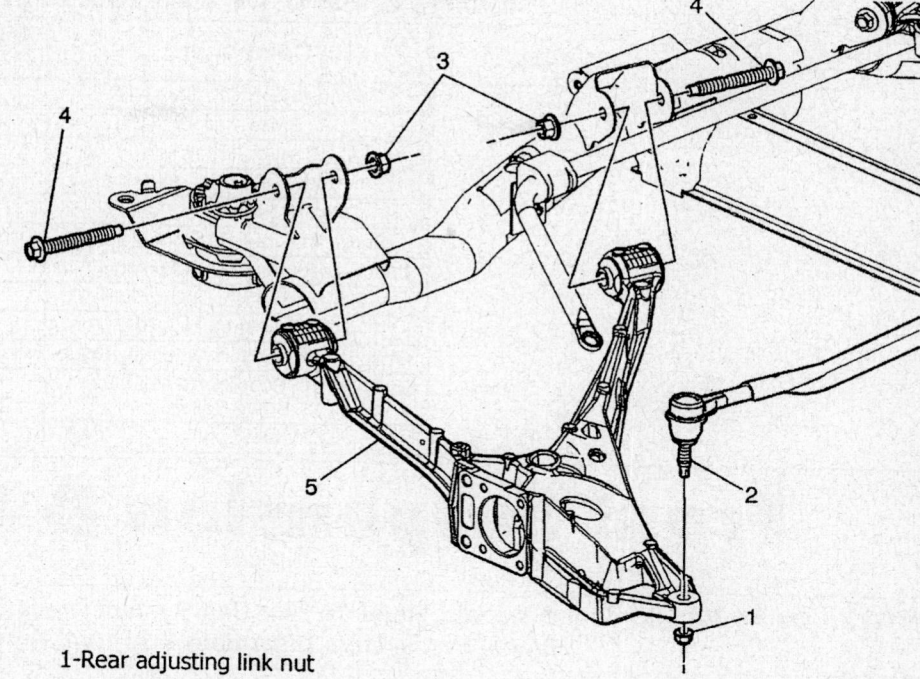

1-Rear adjusting link nut

2-Rear adjusting link

3-Rear control arm nut

4-Rear control arm bolt

5-Rear control arm

ARM0600000000041

Fig. 2 Control arm replacement

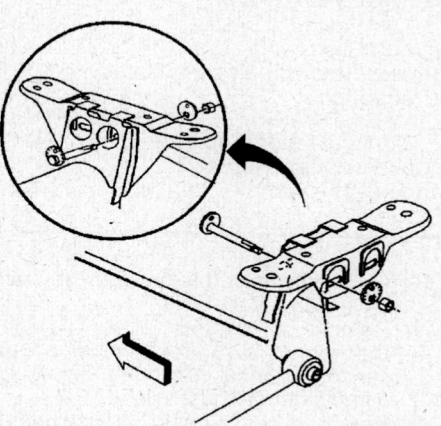

ARM0600000000042

Fig. 3 Adjustment link removal

2. **On models equipped with Electronic Level Control (ELC),** remove control sensor link from control arm.
3. **On all models,** remove stabilizer shaft link.
4. Remove exhaust system.
5. Remove coil springs as outlined under "Coil Spring, Replace."
6. Disconnect electrical connector from each wheel speed sensor and remove wire from rear support.
7. **On models equipped with Electronic Level Control (ELC),** remove electronic level control link from ball stud on lower control arm.
8. **On all models,** disconnect park brake cables from both calipers and remove cables from suspension support assembly.
9. Remove brake calipers and support from vehicle underbody. **Do not disconnect brake hydraulic lines.**
10. Support rear suspension support assembly with a suitable transmission jack.
11. Remove suspension support reinforcement brace bolts, **Fig. 1.**
12. Remove cam lock nut and bolt, then the adjustment link from support assembly, **Fig. 3.**
13. Reverse procedure to install.

TIGHTENING SPECIFICATIONS

Year	Component	Torque/Ft. Lbs.
2006–08	Adjustment Link Cam Nut	67
	Brake Caliper	25
	Control Arm Nuts	78
	Hub & Bearing Bolts	50
	Rear Body Mount Bolts	38
	Shock Absorber To Control Arm	18
	Shock Absorber Tower Mounting Nut	15
	Stabilizer Shaft Clamp Bolt	24
	Stabilizer Shaft Link Bolt	10
	Suspension Support Assembly Bolts	141
	Suspension Support Reinforcement Brace Bolts	63
	Wheel Lug Nut	100

Front Suspension & Steering

NOTE: On Air Bag Equipped Models, Refer To "Air Bag System Precautions" Located In The Front Of This Manual For System Disarming & Arming Procedures.

NOTE: Refer To "Computer Relearn Procedures" Located In The Front Of This Manual When Battery Power To The Computer Has Been Interrupted.

NOTE: Refer To The Rear Of This Manual For Vehicle Manufacturer's Special Tool Suppliers.

INDEX

	Page No.
Ball Joint, Replace	10-17
Ball Joint Inspection	10-16
Coil Spring, Replace	10-17
Control Arm, Replace	10-17
Hub & Bearing, Replace	10-16
Power Steering	21-1
Power Steering Gear, Replace	10-18
Power Steering Pump, Replace	10-18

	Page No.
3.8L Engine	10-18
4.6L Engine	10-18
Power Steering System Bleed	10-18
Precautions	10-16
Air Bag Systems	10-16
Battery Ground Cable	10-16
Stabilizer Bar, Replace	10-17
Steering Columns	20-1

	Page No.
Steering Knuckle, Replace	10-17
Strut, Replace	10-17
Strut Service	10-17
Tie Rod End, Replace	10-18
Inner	10-18
Outer	10-18
Tightening Specifications	10-19

PRECAUTIONS
Air Bag Systems

Refer to "Air Bag System Precautions" in the front of this manual for system disarming and arming procedures.

Battery Ground Cable

Prior to service, disconnect battery ground cable and isolate as required.

HUB & BEARING
REPLACE

1. Raise and support vehicle, then remove tire and wheel assembly. Clean drive axle threads of all dirt.
2. Insert a drift punch or a screwdriver into caliper and rotor in order to pre- vent rotor from turning, then remove drive axle nut.
3. Remove brake rotor.
4. Disconnect ABS front wheel speed sensor electrical connector and unclip connector from dust shield.
5. Remove wheel bearing and hub retain- ing bolts, then the bearing and hub as- sembly from steering knuckle.
6. Remove dust shield, then separate hub and bearing from drive axle using front hub spindle remover tool No. J28733-B, or equivalent.
7. Reverse procedure to install. Clean rust and foreign material from knuckle mounting face, bore and chamber.

BALL JOINT INSPECTION

1. Raise and support vehicle.
2. Clean ball joint and inspect seal for damage.
3. Check wheel bearing for looseness.
4. Remove tension from ball joints.
5. Position dial indicator tool J8001, or equivalent, against lowest outboard point of wheel rim, then check ball joint for horizontal looseness by rocking wheel in and out while reading dial indi- cator. If measurement is greater than .125 inch, replace ball joint.
6. Position dial indicator tool J8001, or equivalent, against ball joint, then check ball joint for vertical looseness by moving ball joint up and down while reading dial indicator. If measurement is greater than .125 inch, replace ball joint.

BALL JOINT
REPLACE

The ball joint is an integral part of the control arm, refer to "Control Arm, Replace" for ball joint replacement.

COIL SPRING
REPLACE

Refer to "Strut, Replace" and "Strut Service" for coil spring replacement procedure.

STRUT
REPLACE

1. Remove upper strut mount retaining bolts.
2. Raise and support vehicle, then remove tire and wheel assembly.
3. Disconnect ABS front wheel speed sensor harness connector.
4. Remove speed sensor bracket from strut.
5. Remove brake line bracket from strut.
6. Remove strut to knuckle bolts and nuts, then the strut from vehicle. **Knuckle must be retained after strut to knuckle bolts have been removed. Failure to retain knuckle may cause ball joint or wheel drive shaft damage.**
7. Reverse procedure to install.

STRUT SERVICE

1. Mount strut assembly in strut spring compressor tool No. J45400, or equivalent, then compress spring.
2. **Do not grip strut rod with any tools below hex shaped portion.**
3. Hold end of strut rod shaft using suitable wrench.
4. Remove upper strut mount nut using a suitable 45 Torx socket.
5. Remove upper strut mount and coil spring.
6. Reverse procedure to assemble.

CONTROL ARM
REPLACE

1. Raise and support vehicle, then remove front tire and wheel assembly.
2. Remove front stabilizer shaft link.
3. Remove lower ball joint to steering knuckle nut, **Fig. 1.**
4. Separate ball joint from steering knuckle using ball joint separator tool No. J39549, or equivalent.
5. Remove control arm front nuts and bolts.
6. Remove bolts from control arm bracket.
7. Remove control arm rear nut and bolt.
8. Remove bolt from control arm, then the control arm from vehicle.
9. Reverse procedure to install, noting the following:
   a. Always replace ball joint to steering knuckle nut after it has been used.
   b. Do not tighten control arm nut until weight of vehicle is supported by control arm. Vehicle needs to be sitting at normal trim height.

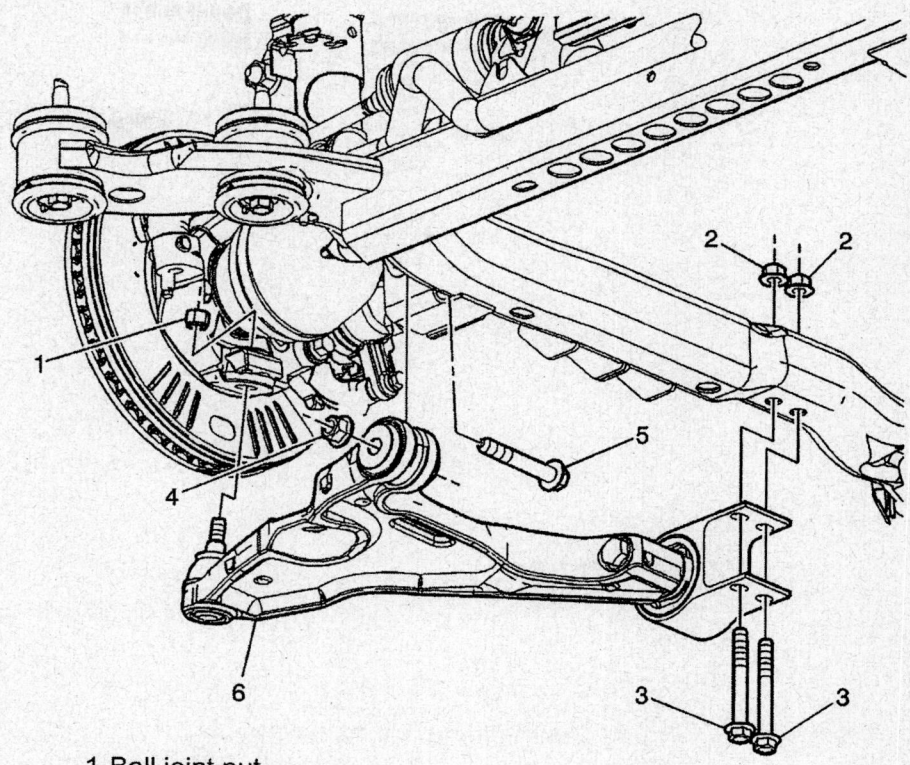

1-Ball joint nut

2-Control arm front nuts

3-Control arm front bolts

4-Control arm rear nut

5-Control arm rear bolt

6-Control arm

ARM0600000000043

Fig. 1 Control arm replacement

STEERING KNUCKLE
REPLACE

1. Raise and support vehicle, then remove front tire and wheel assembly.
2. Remove mounting bolts, caliper and bracket from brake rotor, then support assembly with heavy mechanic's wire, or equivalent. **Do not disconnect hydraulic brake flexible hose from caliper.**
3. Remove brake rotor as outlined in "Disc Brakes" chapter.
4. Remove hub and bearing assembly as outlined under "Hub & Bearing, Replace."
5. Remove outer tie rod end to steering knuckle nut, **Fig. 2.**
6. Separate tie rod end from steering knuckle using ball joint separator tool No. J39549, or equivalent.
7. Remove ball joint to steering knuckle nut.
8. Separate ball joint from steering knuckle using ball joint separator tool No. J39549, or equivalent.
9. Remove steering knuckle.
10. Reverse procedure to install. **Always replace ball joint and tie rod end nuts after they have been used.**

STABILIZER BAR
REPLACE

1. Raise and support vehicle, then remove front tires and wheels.
2. Remove stabilizer shaft links and shaft insulators.
3. Remove left outer tie rod retaining nut.
4. Separate left outer tie rod end from steering knuckle using ball joint separator tool No. J24319-B, or equivalent.
5. Remove exhaust manifold pipe.
6. Turn left strut completely to left, then remove stabilizer shaft.
7. Reverse procedure to install. **Always replace tie rod end nut after it has been used.**

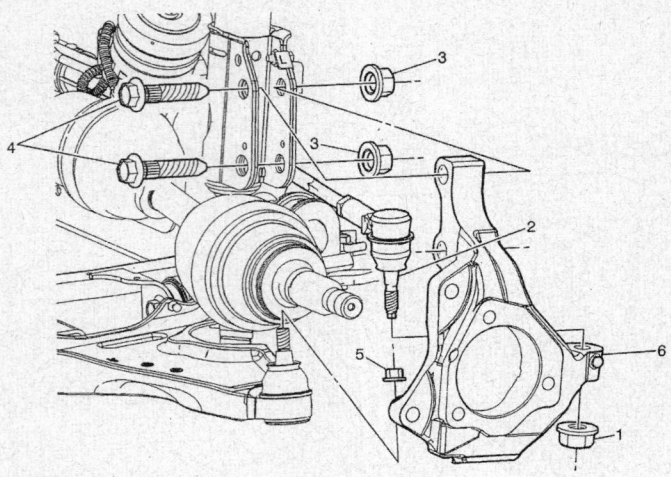

1-Tie rod end nut

2-Tie rod end

3-Strut to steering knuckle nuts

4-Strut to steering knuckle bolts

5-Ball joint nut

6-Steering knuckle

ARM0600000000044

Fig. 2   Steering knuckle replacement

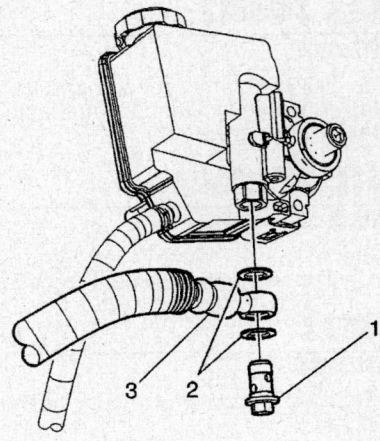

1-Banjo bolt

2-Washers

3-Pressure hose

ARM0600000000045

Fig. 3   Power steering pump replacement. 3.8L engine

TIE ROD END
REPLACE
Outer

1. Raise and support vehicle, then remove tire and wheel assembly.
2. Remove lock nut from outer tie rod to steering knuckle ball stud.
3. Loosen jam nut on inner tie rod.
4. Separate outer tie rod from steering knuckle using ball joint separator tool No. J24319-B, or equivalent.
5. Remove outer tie rod from inner tie rod.
6. Reverse procedure to install. **Always replace tie rod end nut after it has been used.**

Inner

Refer to "Power Steering" chapter for inner tie rod end replacement.

POWER STEERING GEAR
REPLACE

1. Lock steering column by installing steering column anti-rotation pin tool No. J42640, or equivalent, into underside of steering column.
2. Raise and support vehicle, then remove tire and wheel assemblies.
3. Remove power steering gear heat shield.
4. Remove steering column intermediate shaft lower pinch bolt.
5. Separate steering column intermediate shaft from power steering gear.

6. Remove outer tie rods to steering knuckle retaining nuts.
7. Separate outer tie rods from steering knuckles using ball joint separator tool No. J24319-B, or equivalent.
8. Remove power steering pressure and return hoses from power steering gear.
9. **On models equipped with variable effort steering,** disconnect electrical connector.
10. **On all models,** remove left stabilizer shaft insulator.
11. Remove power steering gear mounting bolts.
12. Remove power steering gear through left wheel opening.
13. Reverse procedure to install. Bleed power steering system as outlined under "Power Steering System Bleed" in this section.

POWER STEERING PUMP
REPLACE
3.8L Engine

1. Remove drive belt.
2. Raise and support vehicle, then place a suitable drain pan under vehicle.
3. Disconnect power steering pressure hose banjo bolt, then remove washers and position hose aside, **Fig. 3.**
4. Disconnect power steering return hose from power steering pump.
5. Disconnect wiring harness from power steering pump.
6. Lower vehicle and remove coolant recovery reservoir.

7. Remove power steering pump retaining bolts, then the pump.
8. Reverse procedure to install. Bleed power steering system as outlined under "Power Steering System Bleed" in this section.

4.6L Engine

1. Remove drive belt.
2. Place a suitable drain pan under vehicle.
3. Disconnect power steering return hose from reservoir.
4. Remove power steering pressure hose from pump.
5. Remove power steering pump mounting bolt.
6. Remove power steering pump from vehicle.
7. Reverse procedure to install. Bleed power steering system as outlined under "Power Steering System Bleed" in this section.

POWER STEERING SYSTEM BLEED

1. Fill pump reservoir with fluid to minimum system level, FULL COLD level, or middle of hash mark on cap stick fluid level indicator.
2. Raise vehicle until front wheels are off the ground.
3. Key on engine OFF, turn the steering wheel from stop to stop 12 times.
4. Verify power steering fluid level.
5. Start engine and rotate steering wheel from left to right.
6. Check for sign of cavitation or fluid aeration (pump noise/whining).
7. Verify fluid level.

TIGHTENING SPECIFICATIONS

Year	Component	Torque/Ft. Lbs.
2006–08	Adjuster Plug Locknut	50
	Ball Joint Nut	③
	Ball Stud	106①
	Brake Line Bracket	17
	Front Insulator Bolts	144
	Front Lower Control Arm Bolt	116
	Hub Bearing Bolts	96
	Intermediate Steering Shaft Pinch Bolt	37
	Power Steering Flow Control Valve	55
	Power Steering Gear Heat Shield	80①
	Power Steering Hose Fittings	22
	Power Steering Pressure Hose Banjo Bolt	41
	Power Steering Pressure Hose Bracket Nut	80①
	Power Steering Pump Bracket Bolt (4.6L Engine)	37
	Power Steering Pump Mounting Bolts (3.8L Engine)	18
	Power Steering Return Hose Bracket Bolt	80①
	Rear Lower Control Arm Bolts	108
	Stabilizer Shaft Bracket Bolts	37
	Stabilizer Shaft Link Nut	17
	Steering Gear Mounting Bolts	70
	Strut To Knuckle Nuts	131
	Strut Mount Nut	37
	Strut Tower Bolts	44
	Tie Rod End To Knuckle Nut	②
	Wheel Drive Shaft Axle Nut	118
	Wheel Lug Nut	100

① — Inch lbs.

② — First pass, 22 ft. lbs.; second pass, 55 ft. lbs.

② — First pass, 22 ft. lbs.; second pass, an additional 210°.

Wheel Alignment

NOTE: On Air Bag Equipped Models, Refer To "Air Bag System Precautions" Located In The Front Of This Manual For System Disarming & Arming Procedures.

NOTE: Refer To "Computer Relearn Procedures" Located In The Front Of This Manual When Battery Power To The Computer Has Been Interrupted.

NOTE: Refer To The Rear Of This Manual For Vehicle Manufacturer's Special Tool Suppliers.

INDEX

	Page No.		Page No.		Page No.
Front Wheel Alignment	10-20	Preliminary Inspection	10-20	Front	10-21
Camber	10-20	Rear Wheel Alignment	10-21	Rear	10-21
Caster	10-20	Toe	10-21	Wheel Alignment	
Toe	10-20	Vehicle Ride Height	10-21	Specifications	10-2

PRELIMINARY INSPECTION

1. Inspect tires for proper inflation and irregular tire wear.
2. Inspect runout of wheels and tires.
3. Inspect wheel bearings for backlash and excessive play.
4. Inspect ball joints and tie rod ends for looseness or wear.
5. Inspect control arms and stabilizer shaft for looseness or wear.
6. Inspect steering gear for looseness at frame.
7. Inspect struts/shock absorbers for wear, leaks and any noticeable noises.
8. Inspect vehicle trim height.
9. Inspect steering wheel excessive drag or poor return because of stiff or rusted linkage or suspension components.
10. Inspect fuel level. The fuel tank should be full or vehicle should have compensating load added.
11. Give consideration to excess loads, such as tool boxes, sample cases, etc. If normally carried in vehicle, these items should remain in vehicle during alignment adjustments.
12. Give consideration also to condition of equipment being used for alignment.
13. Install alignment equipment according to manufacturers instructions.
14. Jounce front and rear bumpers three times prior to inspecting wheel alignment.
15. Measure and record alignment angles.
16. When performing adjustments to vehicles requiring four-wheel alignment, set rear wheel alignment angles first to obtain proper front alignment angles.

FRONT WHEEL ALIGNMENT

Caster

1. Remove top strut mounting bolts at strut tower.
2. Lift front of vehicle by the body to separate strut from inner wheelhouse.
3. Pop out two guide pins out of strut tower, **Fig. 1.**
4. Hand file excess metal to make slotted holes.
5. Lower front of vehicle and install strut attaching fasteners. Do not tighten the fasteners at this time.
6. Move top of strut forward or rearward to adjust caster. A .04 inch in position change at tower is about equal to a 0.1 degree change in caster.
7. Adjust to specified measurement, refer to "Front Wheel Alignment Specifications" in "Specifications" section.
8. **Torque** strut tower bolts to 44 ft. lbs.
9. Perform a complete wheel alignment.

Camber

1. Raise and support vehicle, then remove tire and wheel assembly.
2. Remove nut and tap upper and lower bolt from strut and knuckle. **Do not allow bolts to turn. This will ruin serrated shoulder.**
3. Separate strut from knuckle. It will be necessary to grind lower bolt hole on strut to achieve proper camber setting.
4. If camber specification is not achieved by this procedure check for bent or worn parts.
5. Using a round file or a die grinder, file inner metal plate to outside plates diameter.
6. File excess metal to make slotted holes.
7. Install strut to knuckle, then both upper and lower bolts. Do not tighten at this time.
8. Install camber adjustment tool No. J39601, or equivalent, to bottom strut bolt, **Fig. 2.**
9. Set camber, refer to "Front Wheel Alignment Specifications" in "Specifications" section.
10. **Torque** upper strut to knuckle nut to 108 ft. lbs. and remove adjustment tool.
11. **Torque** lower strut to knuckle nut to 108 ft. lbs.
12. Perform a complete wheel alignment.

Toe

1. Ensure steering wheel and gear are in straight ahead position.
2. Measure wheel alignment.
3. Loosen outer tie rod end lock nut.
4. Rotate inner tie rod to adjust front toe to specification, refer to "Front Wheel Alignment Specifications" in "Specifications" section. **Do not twisted boots when rotating inner tie rods.**
5. **Torque** locknut to 47 ft. lbs.

REAR WHEEL ALIGNMENT

Toe

1. Loosen the inner adjustment link cam nut, **Fig. 3.**
2. To adjust toe, rotate cam bolt. Refer to "Front Wheel Alignment Specifications" in "Specifications" section.
3. **Torque** cam nut to 67 ft. lbs.
4. Recheck toe setting after tightening.

VEHICLE RIDE HEIGHT

1. Set tire pressure to specifications on tire placard.
2. Ensure tires match tire size specifications on tire placard.
3. Ensure wheels match wheel size specifications on tire placard.
4. Ensure fuel tank is full. Add additional weight in order to simulate a full tank, if required.
5. Ensure luggage compartment is empty except for spare tire and weight simulating full fuel tank.

6. Ensure vehicle is on level surface, such as alignment rack.
7. Close hood, doors and luggage compartment lid.
8. Ensure vehicle is not damaged from collision.

Front

The "Z height" dimension measurement determines the proper ride height for the front end of the vehicle. There is no adjustment procedure. Repair may require replacement of suspension components.

1. Lift front bumper of vehicle up about 1.5 inches, then gently remove hands and allow vehicle to settle. Repeat this operation a total of three times.
2. Refer to "Vehicle Ride Height Specifications" under "Specifications" for correct vehicle ride height measurement.
3. Push front bumper of vehicle down about 1.5 inches, then gently remove hands and allow vehicle to settle. Repeat jouncing operation two more times.
4. Measure Z dimension again.
5. True Z height dimension number is av-

erage of high and low measurements.
6. Refer to "Vehicle Ride Height Specifications" under "Specifications" for correct vehicle ride height.
7. There is no adjustment procedure for ride height. If ride height is not within specifications, repair or replace components as required.

Rear

1. Lift rear bumper of vehicle up approximately 1.5 inches by hand.
2. Gently hands to allow vehicle to settle.
3. Push rear bumper of vehicle down approximately 1.5 inches using hands
4. Gently remove hands to allow vehicle to settle.
5. Refer to "Vehicle Ride Height Specifications" under "Specifications" for correct vehicle ride height measurement and specification.
6. There is no adjustment procedure for ride height. If ride height is not within specifications, repair or replace components as required.

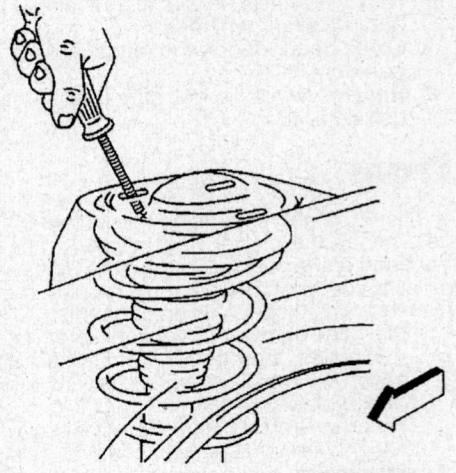

ARM0600000000046

Fig. 1   Guide pin removal

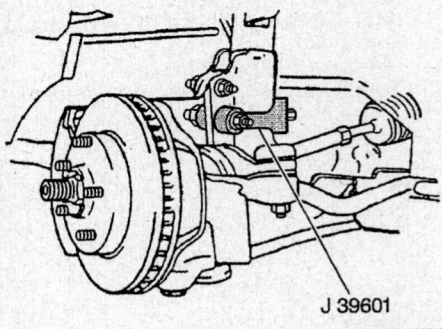

J 39601

ARM0600000000047

**Fig. 2   Camber adjustment tool
installation**

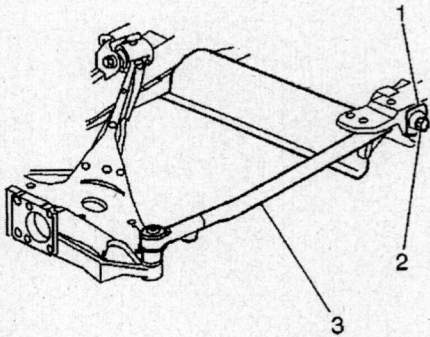

1-Inner adjustment link cam nut

2-Cam bolt

3-Adjustment link

ARM0600000000048

Fig. 3   Rear toe adjustment

VIBE

INDEX OF SERVICE OPERATIONS

Page No.

AIR BAG SYSTEM
PRECAUTIONS 0-18
BRAKES
   Anti-Lock Brakes (Volume 2) .. 6-1
   Disc Brakes 22-1
   Drum Brakes 23-1
   Hydraulic Brake Systems 24-1
   Power Brake Units 25-1
COMPUTER RELEARN
PROCEDURE 0-31
CLUTCH & MANUAL
TRANSAXLE
   Adjustments 11-14
   Clutch, Replace 11-14
   Hydraulic System Service 11-14
   Tightening Specifications 11-20
   Transaxle, Replace 11-14
ELECTRICAL
   Air Bag System (Volume 2) ... 4-1
   Air Conditioning 16-1
   Alternator, Replace 11-4
   Alternators 19-1
   Blower Motor, Replace 11-5
   Cabin Air Filter, Replace 11-5
   Combination Switch, Replace . 11-5
   Cooling Fans 17-1
   Cruise Control (Volume 2) 2-1
   Dash Gauges (Volume 2) 1-1
   Dash Panel Service
   (Volume 2) 5-1
   Evaporator Core, Replace 11-6
   Fuel Pump Relay Location 11-4
   Fuse Panel & Flasher
   Location 11-4
   Headlamp Switch, Replace ... 11-5
   Heater Core, Replace 11-5
   Ignition Coil, Replace 11-4
   Ignition Lock, Replace 11-4
   Ignition Switch, Replace 11-5
   Instrument Cluster, Replace... 11-5
   Passive Restraint Systems
   (Volume 2) 4-1
   Speed Controls (Volume 2) ... 2-1
   Starter Motors 18-1
   Precautions 11-4
   Radio, Replace 11-5
   Relay Center Location 11-4
   Starter, Replace 11-4
   Steering Columns 20-1
   Steering Wheel, Replace 11-5
   Turn Signal Switch, Replace .. 11-5
   Wiper Motor, Replace 11-5
   Wiper Switch, Replace 11-5
   Wiper Systems (Volume 2) 3-1

Page No.

ELECTRICAL SYMBOL
IDENTIFICATION 0-63
FRONT DRIVE AXLES 26-1
FRONT SUSPENSION &
STEERING
   Ball Joint, Replace 11-24
   Ball Joint Inspection 11-24
   Coil Spring, Replace 11-24
   Control Arm, Replace 11-24
   Power Steering 21-1
   Power Steering Gear,
   Replace 11-25
   Power Steering Pump,
   Replace 11-25
   Precautions 11-24
   Stabilizer Bar, Replace 11-25
   Steering Columns 20-1
   Steering Knuckle, Replace 11-24
   Strut, Replace 11-24
   Strut Service 11-24
   Tie Rod End, Replace 11-25
   Tightening Specifications 11-26
   Wheel Hub, Replace 11-24
NON-STANDARD TIRE &
WHEEL SIZE
ADJUSTMENT TO RIDE
HEIGHT SPECIFICATIONS
& TIRE SIZE CHART 0-61
REAR AXLE &
SUSPENSION
   Coil Spring, Replace 11-21
   Control Arm, Replace 11-22
   Differential Carrier, Replace... 11-21
   Hub & Bearing, Replace 11-21
   Knuckle, Replace 11-22
   Propeller Shaft, Replace 11-21
   Rear Axle Shaft, Replace 11-21
   Shock Absorber, Replace 11-21
   Stabilizer Bar, Replace 11-22
   Tightening Specifications 11-23
SERVICE REMINDER &
WARNING LAMP RESET
PROCEDURES 0-34
SPECIFICATIONS
   Fluid Capacities & Cooling
   System Data 11-3
   Front Wheel Alignment
   Specifications 11-2
   General Engine
   Specifications 11-2
   Lubricant Data 11-3
   Rear Wheel Alignment
   Specifications 11-3

Page No.

   Tune Up Specifications 11-2
   Vehicle Ride Height
   Specifications 11-3
TIRE PRESSURE
MONITORING SYSTEM 20-1
VEHICLE
IDENTIFICATION 0-1
VEHICLE LIFT POINTS 0-51
VEHICLE MAINTENANCE
SCHEDULES 0-73
WHEEL ALIGNMENT
   Front Wheel Alignment 11-27
   Precautions 11-27
   Preliminary Inspection 11-27
   Rear Wheel Alignment 11-27
   Wheel Alignment
   Specifications 11-2
WIRE COLOR CODE
IDENTIFICATION 0-63
1.8L ENGINE
   Belt Tension Data 11-11
   Camshaft, Replace 11-10
   Compression Pressure 11-7
   Cooling System Bleed 11-11
   Crankshaft Rear Oil Seal,
   Replace 11-11
   Cylinder Head, Replace 11-9
   Engine Rebuilding
   Specifications 29-1
   Engine, Replace 11-7
   Engine Mount, Replace 11-7
   Exhaust Manifold, Replace 11-9
   Fuel Filter, Replace 11-11
   Fuel Pump, Replace 11-11
   Intake Manifold, Replace 11-8
   Main & Rod Bearings 11-10
   Oil Pan, Replace 11-11
   Oil Pump, Replace 11-11
   Piston & Rod Assembly 11-10
   Precautions 11-7
   Radiator, Replace 11-11
   Serpentine Drive Belt 11-11
   Thermostat, Replace 11-11
   Tightening Specifications 11-13
   Timing Chain, Replace 11-10
   Valve Adjustment 11-10
   Valve Clearance
   Specifications 11-10
   Valve Lifters, Replace 11-10
   Water Pump, Replace 11-11

Specifications

GENERAL ENGINE SPECIFICATIONS

Year	Engine Liter	Fuel System	Bore & Stroke, Inch	Compression Ratio	Net H.P. @ RPM	Maximum Torque, Ft. Lbs. @ RPM	Normal Oil Pressure, psi
2004–06	1.8L①	SFI	3.11 X 3.60	10.0	123 @ 6000	118 @ 4400	43–78 @ 3000
	1.8L②	SFI	3.11 X 3.60	10.0	130 @ 6000	125 @ 4400	43–78 @ 3000
	1.8L HO	SFI	3.23 X 3.35	11.5	170 @ 7600	127 @ 4400	43–78 @ 3000
2007–08	1.8L	SFI	3.11 X 3.60	10.0	126 @ 6000	122 @ 4200	43–79 @ 3000

SFI — Sequential Fuel Injection   ① — All wheel drive (AWD).   ② — Two wheel drive (2WD).

TUNE UP SPECIFICATIONS

Engine	Spark Plug Gap, Inch	Ignition Timing BTDC				Curb Idle Speed		Fast Idle Speed		Fuel Pump Pressure, psi	Valve Clearance, Inch
		Firing Order Fig.	Man. Trans.	Auto. Trans.	Mark Fig.	Man. Trans.	Auto. Trans.	Man. Trans.	Auto Trans.		
1.8L⑤	.043	1-3-4-2	10–18①	10–18①	A	700	750N	②	②	44–50	③
1.8L HO	.043	1-3-4-2	8–12①	8–12①	A	800	750N	②	②	44–50	④
1.8L⑥	.040–.048	1-3-4-2	10–18②	10–18②	A	700	700N	②	②	44–50	③

BTDC — Before Top Dead Center

N — Neutral

① — With check connector terminals T & E shorted.

② — Electronically controlled.

③ — Intake, .006–.010; exhaust, .010–.014.

④ — Intake, .006–.010; exhaust, .014–.018.

⑤ — 2004–06.

⑥ — 2007–08.

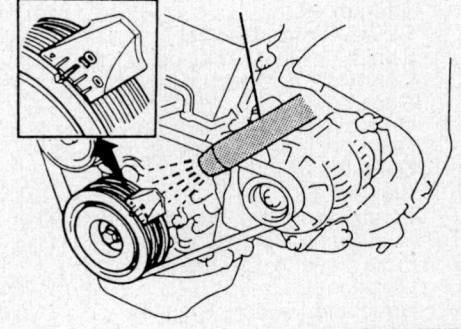

GC11391100157000X

Fig. A

FRONT WHEEL ALIGNMENT SPECIFICATIONS

Year	Model	Caster Angle, Degrees		Camber Angle, Degrees				Toe-In, Inch	Toe Out On Turns, Degrees		Ball Joint Wear
		Limits	Desired	Limits		Desired			Outer Wheel	Inner Wheel	
				Left	Right	Left	Right				
2004–06	AWD	+2.02 to +3.52	+2.77	−1.23 to +.27	−1.23 to +.27	−.48	−.48	−.02 to +.02	—	—	①
	FWD	+2.03 to +3.53	+2.78	−1.32 to +.18	−1.32 to +.18	−.57	−.57	−.20 to +.02	—	—	①
2007–08	All	+2.03 to +3.53	+2.78	−1.32 to +.18	−1.32 to +.18	−.57	−.57	−.20 to +.02	—	—	①

① — Refer to "Ball Joint Inspection" for proper resting procedure.

REAR WHEEL ALIGNMENT SPECIFICATIONS

| Year | Model | Camber Angle, Degrees | | | | Toe-In, Inch | Ball Joint Wear |
| | | Limits | | Desired | | | |
		Left	Right	Left	Right		
2004–06	AWD	−1.48 to +.02	−1.48 to +.02	−.73	−.73	+.20	①
	FWD	−1.95 to −.95	−1.95 to −.95	−1.45	−1.45	+.26	①
2007–08	All	−1.95 to −.95	−1.95 to −.95	−1.45	−1.45	+.26	①

① — Replace ball joint if any looseness is detected or if ball joint seal is cut.

VEHICLE RIDE HEIGHT SPECIFICATIONS

Year	Model	Body Style	Manufacturer's Original Tire Size②	Measurement Points & Specifications①③					
				Front			Rear		
				Dim.	Specification		Dim.	Specification	
					Inches	mm		Inches	mm
2004–06	AWD	All	205	Z	2.2	57	D	1.5	38
	FWD	All	215	Z	2.0	51	D	1.6	41
2007–08	All	All	215	Z	2.0	51	D	1.6	41

Z Dim. — Center line of control arm pivot bolt to the lower edge of steering knuckle ball joint, Front

D Dim. — 2WD, center line of the rear wheel to the center line of the rear axle pivot bolt; 4WD, center line of the rear wheel to the lower control arm pivot bolt, Rear

Dim. — Dimension
① — ± .40 in (10 MM) front to rear & side to side.
② — See door sticker or inside of glove box for manufacturer's original tire size specifications. If tires on vehicle do not match manufacturer's original tire size & measurement is not within limits, refer to the "Non-Standard Tire & Wheel Size Adjustment To Ride Height Specification & Tire Size Adjustment Charts" in the front of this manual for approximate changes in ride height specifications.
③ — Measurement is with fuel, radiator coolant and engine oil full, spare tire, jack, hand tools & mats in designated positions & tires properly inflated.

FLUID CAPACITIES & COOLING SYSTEM DATA

| Year | Engine | Coolant Capacity, Qts. | | Coolant Type | Radiator Cap Relief Pressure, Lbs. | Thermo. Opening Temp., Deg. F | Fuel Tank, Gals. | Engine Oil Refill, Qts. | Transaxle Oil | |
		Manual Trans.	Auto. Trans.						Man. Transaxle, Qts.	Auto. Transaxle, Qts.①
2004–06	1.8L	6.9	6.9	⑤	13.0	183	④	3.9	②	③
	1.8L HO	7.1	7.1	⑤	13.0	183	13	4.8	②	3.3
2007–08	1.8L	6.9	6.9	⑤	11–15	176–183	13.2	4.4	2	3.2

① — Approximate. Make final inspection w/dipstick.
② — 5-speed transaxle, 2.0 qts.; 6-speed transaxle, 2.4 qts.
③ — AWD drive, 3.3 qts.; 2WD, 3.0 qts.

④ — AWD, 12 gals.; 2WD, 13 gals.
⑤ — Use a 50/50 mixture of distilled water & GM coolant P/N 12378560, or equivalent conforming to GM Specification 1825M. An

approved recycled coolant conforming to GM Specification 1825M may also be used.

LUBRICANT DATA

| Year | Model | Lubricant Type | | | |
| | | Transaxle | | Power Steering | Brake System |
		Manual	Automatic		
2004–06	All	②	ATF Type T-IV	①	DOT-3
2007–08	AlII	②	ATF Type T-IV	③	DOT-3

① — Dexron III Revision "H."
② — Synthetic Manual Transmission

Fluid GM P/N 12346190, or an equivalent SAE 75W-90 GL-4 gear oil.

③ — DEXRON-VI Automatic Transmission Fluid.

Electrical

NOTE: On Air Bag Equipped Models, Refer To "Air Bag System Precautions" For System Disarming & Arming Procedures.

NOTE: Refer To "Computer Relearn Procedures" When Battery Power To The Computer Has Been Interrupted.

INDEX

	Page No.
Air Bag System (Volume 2)	4-1
Air Conditioning	16-1
Alternator, Replace	11-4
Alternators	19-1
Blower Motor, Replace	11-5
Cabin Air Filter, Replace	11-5
Combination Switch, Replace	11-5
Cooling Fans	17-1
Cruise Control (Volume 2)	2-1
Dash Gauges (Volume 2)	1-1
Dash Panel Service (Volume 2)	5-1
Evaporator Core, Replace	11-6

	Page No.
Fuel Pump Relay Location	11-4
Fuse Panel & Flasher Location	11-4
Headlamp Switch, Replace	11-5
Heater Core, Replace	11-5
Ignition Coil, Replace	11-4
Ignition Lock, Replace	11-4
Ignition Switch, Replace	11-5
Instrument Cluster, Replace	11-5
Passive Restraint Systems (Volume 2)	4-1
Precautions	11-4
Air Bag Systems	11-4
Battery Ground Cable	11-4

	Page No.
Radio, Replace	11-5
Relay Center Location	11-4
Speed Controls (Volume 2)	2-1
Starter Motors	18-1
Starter, Replace	11-4
Steering Columns	20-1
Steering Wheel, Replace	11-5
Turn Signal Switch, Replace	11-5
Wiper Motor, Replace	11-5
Wiper Switch, Replace	11-5
Wiper Systems (Volume 2)	3-1

PRECAUTIONS

Air Bag Systems

Refer to "Air Bag System Precautions" for system disarming and arming procedures.

Battery Ground Cable

Prior to service, record radio presets, then disconnect battery ground cable and isolate as required.

FUSE PANEL & FLASHER LOCATION

The instrument panel fuse block is located behind the lefthand side of the instrument panel, lefthand side of the steering column. The lefthand instrument panel junction block is located behind the lefthand side of the instrument panel, above the instrument panel fuse block. The righthand instrument panel junction block is located behind the righthand side of the instrument panel, above the instrument panel storage compartment. The underhood fuse block is located on the lefthand side of the engine compartment. The flasher relay is located behind the lefthand side of the instrument panel, in the instrument panel fuse block.

RELAY CENTER LOCATION

Refer to "Fuse Panel & Flasher Location" for relay center location.

FUEL PUMP RELAY LOCATION

The circuit opening/fuel pump relay is located behind the lefthand side of the instrument panel, in the instrument panel fuse block. The EFI relay is located on the lefthand side of the engine compartment, in the underhood fuse block.

STARTER
REPLACE

1. Disconnect starter motor electrical connectors and positive battery cable.
2. Remove starter motor upper and lower mounting bolts, then the starter motor from vehicle.
3. Reverse procedure to install, noting the following:
   a. **Torque** starter mounting bolts to 27 ft. lbs.
   b. **Torque** positive battery cable to starter mounting nut to 84 inch lbs.

ALTERNATOR
REPLACE

1. Rotate drive belt tensioner clockwise and remove drive belt.

2. Disconnect wire harness clamp from retaining clip.
3. Remove wire terminal cap and retaining nut.
4. Disconnect alternator connector.
5. Remove alternator mounting bolts, then the alternator.
6. Reverse procedure to install, noting the following:
   a. **Torque** upper mounting bolt to 18 ft. lbs.
   b. **On models equipped w/HO engine, torque** lower mounting bolts to 43 ft. lbs.
   c. **On models less HO engine, torque** lower mounting bolts to 40 ft. lbs.

IGNITION COIL
REPLACE

1. Remove retainers, then the engine cover.
2. Disconnect electrical connectors from ignition coils.
3. Remove bolts from ignition coils, then the electrical harness.
4. Remove electrical harness package, then the ignition coils from cylinder head.
5. Reverse procedure to install. **Torque** coil mounting bolts to 80 inch lbs.

IGNITION LOCK
REPLACE

1. Remove lower and upper steering column covers.

2. Insert key into ignition lock cylinder, then turn key to Accessory.
3. Push down stop pin, then remove cylinder using a suitable screwdriver, **Fig. 1.**
4. Reverse procedure to install.

IGNITION SWITCH

REPLACE

1. Remove lower and upper steering column covers.
2. Disconnect ignition switch electrical connector.
3. Remove screws, then the ignition switch.
4. Reverse procedure to install.

HEADLAMP SWITCH

REPLACE

Refer to "Combination Switch, Replace" for headlamp switch replacement.

COMBINATION SWITCH

REPLACE

1. Remove lower and upper steering column covers.
2. Disconnect turn signal/headlamp switch electrical connector.
3. Remove turn signal/headlamp switch from steering column by depressing tab.
4. Reverse procedure to install.

TURN SIGNAL SWITCH

REPLACE

Refer to "Combination Switch, Replace" for turn signal switch replacement.

STEERING WHEEL

REPLACE

1. Remove air bag module as outlined in "Passive Restraint Systems" chapter.
2. Disconnect horn electrical connector, then remove cruise control switch.
3. Remove steering wheel mounting nut.
4. Place match marks on steering wheel and on steering shaft.
5. Remove steering using steering wheel puller tool No. J 1859-A or equivalent.
6. Reverse procedure to install. **Torque** steering wheel nut to 37 ft. lbs.

INSTRUMENT CLUSTER

REPLACE

1. Remove instrument cluster bezel screws, then the bezel by disengaging two lower clips.
2. Remove instrument cluster mounting screws, then disconnect electrical connectors.
3. Carefully remove instrument cluster.
4. Reverse procedure to install.

RADIO

REPLACE

1. Remove instrument panel accessory center trim plate.

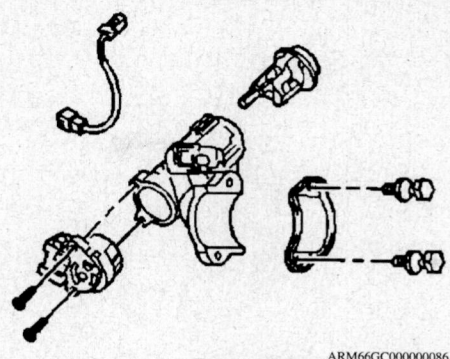

ARM66GC000000086

Fig. 1 Ignition lock replacement

2. Remove screws, then the clamp from radio receiver bracket.
3. Pull radio from instrument panel, then disconnect electrical connector and antenna lead in cable.
4. Reverse procedure to install.

WIPER MOTOR

REPLACE

1. Remove plastic nut cover from wiper arm, then the retaining nut and wiper arm.
2. Remove air inlet grille panel, then disconnect wiper motor electrical connector.
3. Remove wiper motor assembly bolts, then the wiper motor assembly.
4. Disengage meshing of inner rod from crank arm pivot using a flat bladed tool, then remove wiper transmission from wiper motor.
5. Reverse procedure to install.

WIPER SWITCH

REPLACE

1. Remove lower and upper steering column covers.
2. Disconnect wiper/washer switch electrical connector.
3. Remove wiper/washer switch from steering column by depressing tab.
4. Reverse procedure to install.

BLOWER MOTOR

REPLACE

1. Remove two retainers from PCM close out panel below instrument panel compartment door.
2. Swing PCM close out panel down, then open instrument panel compartment door.
3. Push in on both sides of instrument panel compartment door to release safety catches, then remove door.
4. Remove PCM bracket retainers.
5. Pull PCM with brackets outward and swing both components down away from under instrument panel.
6. Disconnect blower motor electrical connector, then remove blower motor cooling tube.
7. Remove bolts, then blower motor and fan from vehicle.
8. Reverse procedure to install.

CABIN AIR FILTER

REPLACE

1. Open instrument panel compartment.
2. Remove screw from righthand side of compartment door.
3. Push in on each side of compartment door, then lower the door.
4. Push down on tabs and open filter door.
5. Remove filter from vehicle.
6. Reverse procedure to install.

HEATER CORE

REPLACE

1. Drain coolant into suitable container.
2. Recover refrigerant charge as outlined in "Air Conditioning" chapter.
3. Disconnect heater hoses at heater core.
4. Remove evaporator inlet and outlet tubes from evaporator.
5. Remove center instrument panel trim plate using a suitable taped flat bladed tool.
6. Disconnect A/C, hazard warning, rear defogger and passenger's side seat belt indicator electrical connectors.
7. Remove mounting screws and disconnect bracket clamp to pull radio out.
8. Disconnect radio electrical connector and antenna lead.
9. **On models equipped with manual transaxle,** remove gearshift knob.
10. **On all models,** remove center A/C control knob and screw.
11. Remove front floor console trim plate using a suitable taped flat bladed tool.
12. Disconnect two cigarette lighters and accessory power receptacle electrical connectors.
13. Disconnect HVAC control electrical connector, then the mode, temperature and A/C cables.
14. Remove HVAC control.
15. Remove driver's air bag module as outlined in "Passive Restraint Systems" chapter.
16. Remove steering wheel as outlined under "Steering Wheel, Replace."
17. Remove three attaching screws, then the steering column lower and upper trim covers.
18. Disconnect electrical connectors, then remove turn signal/headlamp and wiper/washer switches.
19. Disconnect electrical connector and remove clockspring.
20. Remove passenger's air bag module as outlined in "Passive Restraint Systems" chapter.
21. Remove cluster trim plate using a suitable flat bladed tool.
22. **Ensure ignition is turned Off,** then remove mounting screw.
23. Release two lower retainers, then disconnect electrical connector.
24. Remove lefthand and righthand windshield garnish moldings.
25. Remove lefthand instrument panel trim plate using a suitable taped flat bladed tool.
26. Disconnect power mirror and dimmer switch electrical connectors.

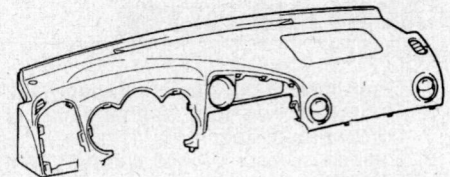

Fig. 2 Upper trim panel replacement

27. Remove mounting screws and upper instrument panel by pulling rearward, **Fig. 2.**
28. **On models equipped with automatic transaxle,** proceed as follows:
    a. Insert and turn ignition key to Accessory.
    b. Disconnect park lock cable by pushing release button.
    c. Remove ignition key and lock steering column in original position.
29. **On all models,** position insulator pad away from steering column.
30. Mark steering shaft coupling and shaft for installation alignment, **Fig. 3.**
31. Loosen upper coupling pinch bolt.
32. Remove lower pinch bolt and position coupling on to steering column shaft.
33. Disconnect steering column connectors and release wire harness retainers.
34. Remove mounting bolts and steering column.
35. Remove lefthand and righthand door sill and kick panel trim plates.
36. Remove front floor console compartment door.
37. Remove mounting screws, then pull front floor console rearward and up.
38. Open door and remove glove compartment mounting screw.
39. Release upper tabs and remove glove compartment by pulling it out.
40. **On models equipped with automatic transaxle,** remove manual selector as follows:
    a. Disconnect cable from gearshift by pushing retainer clip in.

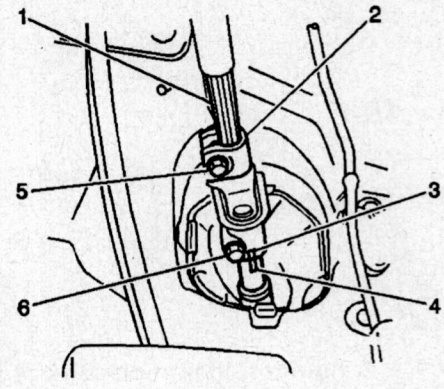

1. Steering Column Shaft
2. Upper Coupling
3. Lower Coupling
4. Lower Shaft
5 & 6. Pinch Bolts

Fig. 3 Steering column removal

Fig. 5 Evaporator core replacement

b. Disconnect park lock cable from bracket using a suitable flat bladed tool.
c. Disconnect shift cable from gear-

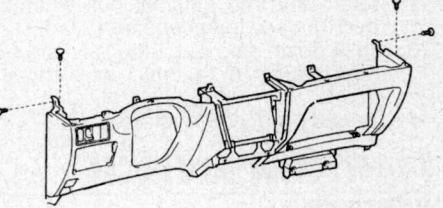

Fig. 4 Lower trim panel replacement

shift lever and plate.
d. Disconnect electrical connectors and wire harness clip.
e. Remove four mounting nuts and manual selector.
41. **On all models,** gently pry hood release handle from knee bolster trim.
42. Disconnect cable and remove hood release handle.
43. Remove eight mounting bolts and four retainers, then the wire harness clamps.
44. Remove lower instrument panel by pulling it rearward, **Fig. 4.**
45. Remove instrument panel reinforcement.
46. Disconnect blower motor electrical connector.
47. Separate rear heater ducts from HVAC module.
48. Remove HVAC module mounting nuts.
49. Carefully pull HVAC module out.
50. Remove brackets and heater core.
51. Reverse procedure to install.

EVAPORATOR CORE
REPLACE

1. Remove heater core as outlined under "Heater Core, Replace."
2. Remove blower motor cover, **Fig. 5.**
3. Remove all HVAC module case half mounting screws.
4. Separate case halves.
5. Remove evaporator core.
6. Reverse procedure to install.

1.8L Engine

NOTE: On Air Bag Equipped Models, Refer To "Air Bag System Precautions" For System Disarming & Arming Procedures.

NOTE: Refer To "Computer Relearn Procedures" When Battery Power To The Computer Has Been Interrupted.

INDEX

	Page No.		Page No.		Page No.
Belt Tension Data	11-11	Engine, Replace	11-7	Battery Ground Cable	11-7
Camshaft, Replace	11-10	Except HO Engine	11-7	Fuel System Pressure Relief	11-7
Compression Pressure	11-7	HO Engine	11-8	Radiator, Replace	11-11
Cooling System Bleed	11-11	Engine Mount, Replace	11-7	Serpentine Drive Belt	11-11
Crankshaft Rear Oil Seal,		Exhaust Manifold, Replace	11-9	Installation	11-11
Replace	11-11	Fuel Filter, Replace	11-11	Removal	11-11
Installation	11-11	Fuel Pump, Replace	11-11	Routing	11-11
Removal	11-11	Intake Manifold, Replace	11-8	Thermostat, Replace	11-11
Cylinder Head, Replace	11-9	Main & Rod Bearings	11-10	Tightening Specifications	11-13
Except High Output (HO)		Oil Pan, Replace	11-11	Timing Chain, Replace	11-10
Engine	11-9	Oil Pump, Replace	11-11	Valve Adjustment	11-10
High Output (HO) Engine	11-9	Piston & Rod Assembly	11-10	Valve Clearance Specifications	11-10
Engine Rebuilding		Precautions	11-7	Valve Lifters, Replace	11-10
Specifications	29-1	Air Bag Systems	11-7	Water Pump, Replace	11-11

PRECAUTIONS

Air Bag Systems

Refer to "Air Bag System Precautions" in the front of this manual for system disarming and arming procedures.

Battery Ground Cable

Prior to service, record radio presets, then disconnect battery ground cable and isolate as required.

Fuel System Pressure Relief

1. Loosen fuel filler cap to relieve fuel tank pressure.
2. Remove instrument panel compartment door.
3. Reach through compartment opening and remove fuel pump (circuit opening) relay from instrument panel fuse block, **Fig. 1.**
4. Start engine and allow it to run until it stalls from lack of fuel.
5. Crank engine for an additional three seconds to relieve remaining fuel pressure, then turn ignition Off.
6. Install relay, then install instrument panel compartment door.
7. Tighten fuel filler cap.

COMPRESSION PRESSURE

Compression readings should be 218 psi, with a minimum of 145 psi. Maximum difference between cylinders should be 15 psi.

ENGINE MOUNT
REPLACE

1. Remove windshield wiper arms.
2. Remove air inlet grille panel.
3. Raise and support engine using engine support tool Nos. J 28467-B and J 28467–VIBE, or equivalent.
4. Remove three righthand side engine mount to frame bracket bolts.
5. Remove righthand side engine mount to engine bracket bolts.
6. Raise engine slightly to provide clearance for engine mount removal.
7. Remove righthand side engine mount.
8. Remove righthand side engine mount to frame bracket.
9. Remove righthand side engine mount to engine bracket.
10. Reverse procedure to install.

ENGINE
REPLACE

Except HO Engine

1. From inside vehicle, disconnect ECM connectors and cowl wire electrical connectors from connector mounting bracket.
2. Remove engine harness wire from passenger compartment.
3. Remove engine cover, then relieve fuel pressure as outlined under "Precautions."
4. Raise and support vehicle, then drain coolant into a suitable container and remove engine undercovers.
5. Drain engine oil into a suitable container, then lower vehicle, release tensioner and remove accessory drive belt.
6. **On models equipped with air conditioning,** recover A/C refrigerant as outlined in "Air Conditioning" chapter.
7. **On models equipped with manual transaxle,** remove crankshaft pulley retaining bolt using tool No. J 8614-01 or equivalent, then the bolt, nut and drive belt tensioner.
8. **On all models,** remove accelerator cable and cable bracket from throttle body.
9. Disconnect IAT and MAF sensor electrical connectors, then the vacuum hoses from air cleaner.
10. Disconnect air intake hoses from throttle body, then unclip and remove air cleaner cap.
11. Remove air filter, disconnect wire harness retaining clip from air cleaner lower case.
12. Remove bolt, then the vacuum switching valve bracket.
13. Remove retaining bolts, then air cleaner lower box.
14. Disconnect cruise control actuator electrical connector, then remove fuel line hose clamp.
15. Disconnect fuel hose from fuel line, then the heater hose from water bypass pipe.
16. Disconnect heater hose from water hose union on cylinder head, then the brake booster vacuum hose from brake booster.
17. Remove radiator inlet and outlet hoses from radiator.

18. Disconnect electrical connectors, then remove retaining bolts and alternator from vehicle.
19. Disconnect transmission oil cooler lines, then the fan motor electrical connector and fan motor electrical harness clamps from fan shroud.
20. Remove radiator mounting bolts, then the radiator fan with motor and radiator.
21. Remove engine relay box cover, then disconnect engine compartment relay box connectors.
22. Disconnect ground cables from front lefthand side of engine compartment, then the wire harness clamps.
23. **On models equipped with manual transaxle,** proceed as follows:
    a. Remove clutch actuator cylinder fluid line.
    b. Remove clutch actuator cylinder from transaxle.
    c. Unclip cable from mounting bracket and disconnect transaxle control cables from transaxle.
24. **On models equipped with automatic transaxle,** proceed as follows:
    a. Unclip cable from mounting bracket and remove shift cable nut.
    b. Unclip wire harness then remove shift cable mounting bracket bolt and disconnect oil cooler hoses.
25. **On all models,** remove driveshaft as outlined under "Driveshaft, Replace" in "Front Wheel Drive Axles" chapter.
26. **On models equipped w/AWD,** remove propeller shaft as outlined under "Propeller Shaft, Replace" in "Rear Axle & Suspension" section.
27. **On all models,** disconnect power steering lines and drain power steering fluid into a suitable container.
28. Remove oxygen sensors, then the floor panel brace.
29. Remove bolts, then springs and front exhaust pipe from vehicle.
30. Disconnect front stabilizer link assembly from strut.
31. Support front suspension crossmember.
32. Remove lower control arm from ball joint, then the cotter pin and nut from ball joint stud.
33. Remove ball joint from knuckle.
34. Set engine lift, then remove lefthand side mounting insulator bolt and nut.
35. Remove bolts and nuts from righthand side engine mount, then crossmember bolts.
36. Lower engine and transaxle assembly.
37. Reverse procedure to install.

HO Engine

1. From inside vehicle, disconnect ECM connectors and cowl wire electrical connectors from connector mounting bracket.
2. Pull engine harness wire from passenger compartment.
3. Lock steering column, then ensure front wheels are in straight ahead position.
4. Move silencer pad away from steering column, then place match marks on steering shaft coupling and on shaft.

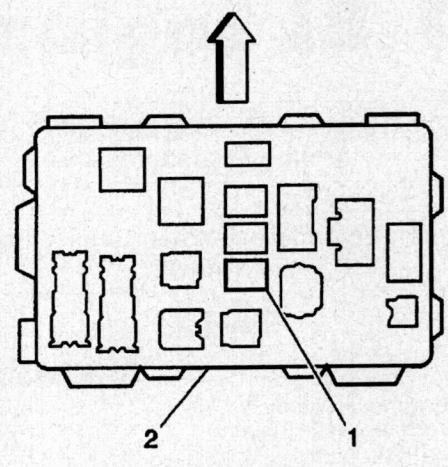

1. Circuit opening relay
2. I/P fuse block

ARM0400000000175

Fig. 1 Fuel pump (circuit opening) relay location

5. Remove upper bolt, then the lower bolt from couplings and move coupling onto steering column shaft.
6. Remove coupling from steering column shaft.
7. Remove engine cover, then relieve fuel pressure as outlined under "Precautions."
8. Drain coolant into a suitable container, then disconnect accelerator cable.
9. Remove air cleaner cover, then the air filter, air cleaner case bolts and air cleaner.
10. Remove fuel tube clamp, then disconnect fuel tube from fuel pipe using tool No. J 43178, or equivalent.
11. Disconnect heater hose from water by pass pipe, then heater hose from water hose union on cylinder head.
12. Disconnect brake booster vacuum hose from brake booster.
13. Disconnect radiator inlet and outlet hoses.
14. Mark running direction, then release tensioner and remove accessory drive belt.
15. Disconnect electrical connectors, then remove retaining bolts and alternator from vehicle.
16. Disconnect ATF cooler lines, then the fan motor electrical connector and fan motor electrical harness clamps from fan shroud.
17. Remove radiator mounting bolts, then the radiator fan with motor and radiator.
18. Remove clutch slave cylinder bolts, then the cylinder line bolt and cylinder line bracket bolt.
19. Remove engine relay box cover, then disconnect engine compartment relay box connector.
20. Disconnect wire harness clamps, then the ground cables from transaxle and engine.
21. **On models equipped with manual transaxle,** proceed as follows:

a. Remove clutch actuator cylinder fluid line.
b. Remove clutch actuator cylinder from transaxle.
c. Unclip cable from mounting bracket and disconnect transaxle control cables from transaxle.
22. **On models equipped with automatic transaxle,** unclip cable from mounting bracket and remove shift cable nut.
23. **On all models,** raise and support vehicle, then remove lefthand and righthand engine splash shields.
24. Drain engine oil into a suitable container.
25. Place reference mark on pinion flange yoke and differential pinion flange.
26. Remove retaining bolts and nuts, then the mid shaft bearing support bolts.
27. Remove sliding yoke and two piece propeller shaft assembly from transaxle.
28. Disconnect power steering lines and drain power steering fluid into a suitable container.
29. Remove oxygen sensors, then the floor panel brace.
30. Remove bolts, then springs and front exhaust pipe from vehicle.
31. Remove righthand and lefthand driveshaft locknut, then separate lefthand and righthand tie rod ends.
32. Disconnect front stabilizer link assembly from strut.
33. Support front suspension crossmember.
34. Remove lower control arm from ball joint, then the cotter pin and nut from ball joint stud.
35. Remove ball joint from knuckle.
36. Set engine lift, then remove lefthand side mounting insulator bolt and nut.
37. Remove bolts and nuts from righthand side engine mount, then crossmember bolts.
38. Lower engine and transaxle assembly.
39. Reverse procedure to install.

INTAKE MANIFOLD
REPLACE

1. Remove engine cover attaching nuts and retainers, then the cover.
2. Remove air inlet duct from throttle body assembly.
3. Remove PCV breather hose.
4. Disconnect TP sensor electrical connectors.
5. Rotate throttle lever, then disconnect accelerator cable and throttle valve cable.
6. Disconnect IAC valve electrical connector.
7. Drain cooling system, then remove coolant hoses from throttle body.
8. Remove accelerator control cable and throttle body brackets.
9. Remove manifold support bracket attaching bolts.
10. Remove throttle body bolts and position the throttle body aside.
11. Disconnect ECT and CMP sensor connectors.
12. Disconnect camshaft position actuator and rocker arm control solenoid valve connectors.

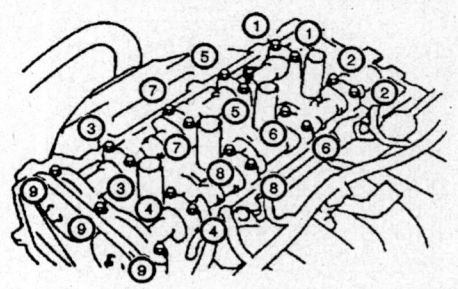

Fig. 2 Camshaft bearing cap bolt loosening sequence. Except HO engine

ARM66GC000000092

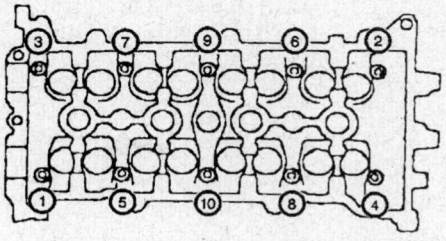

ARM66GC000000089

Fig. 3 Cylinder head bolt loosening sequence

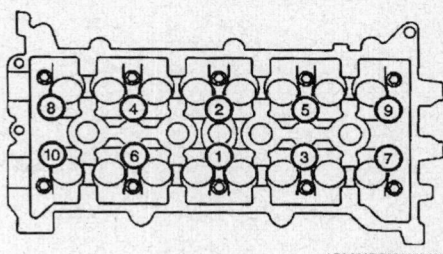

ARM66GC000000090

Fig. 4 Cylinder head tightening bolt sequence

13. Disconnect oil pressure switch and ground connectors.
14. Release clamps and remove engine harness wire protector from intake manifold.
15. Disconnect EVAP and brake booster vacuum hoses.
16. Remove oil dipstick guide.
17. Remove intake manifold attaching bolts and nuts, then the intake manifold, gasket and insulator.
18. Reverse procedure to install.

EXHAUST MANIFOLD
REPLACE

1. **On models equipped w/AWD,** disconnect secondary AIR pump hose clamp and remove AIR pipe retaining bolt.
2. **On all models,** raise and support vehicle.
3. Remove HO2S.
4. Remove exhaust pipe hanger.
5. Remove front exhaust pipe to manifold flange attaching bolts, then the exhaust pipe and flange gasket.
6. Remove exhaust manifold brace to manifold attaching bolt.
7. Lower vehicle and remove upper heat insulator attaching bolts, then the heat insulator.
8. Remove exhaust manifold attaching bolts and nuts.
9. Remove exhaust manifold and gasket.
10. Reverse procedure to install.

CYLINDER HEAD
REPLACE
EXCEPT HIGH OUTPUT (HO) ENGINE

1. Relieve fuel pressure as outlined under "Precautions."
2. Drain engine coolant, then engine oil into suitable containers.
3. Mark drive belt running direction.
4. Release drive belt tensioner and remove accessory drive belt.
5. Remove alternator as outlined under "Alternator, Replace" in "Electrical" section.
6. Remove intake manifold as outlined under "Intake Manifold, Replace."
7. Disconnect fuel injector connectors, then remove radiator inlet hose.

8. Remove bolts, then the fuel injector harness.
9. Remove exhaust manifold as outlined under "Exhaust Manifold, Replace."
10. Install engine support fixture tool No. J 28467-A, or equivalent.
11. Remove righthand side engine mount, then disconnect ignition coil electrical connectors.
12. Disconnect fuel line at fuel rail, then remove fuel injector fuel rail hold down clamp and ignition coils.
13. Remove fuel rail and ground wires from cylinder head.
14. Position injector harness aside, then remove heater hose at cylinder head.
15. Remove water bypass pipe from cylinder head.
16. Remove camshaft and engine coolant temperature sensors.
17. Remove PCV hoses and valve from cylinder head cover, then the cylinder head cover.
18. Set number 1 piston to top dead center, then align camshaft timing sprockets.
19. Disconnect power steering oil pressure switch connector.
20. Remove both engine splash shields, then the power steering through bolts and nut.
21. Remove power steering pump and position aside.
22. Remove crankshaft pulley retaining bolt using tool No. J 8614-01 or equivalent.
23. Remove CKP sensor, then the drive belt tensioner.
24. Remove righthand side engine mounting bracket, then the timing chain tensioner.
25. Remove timing chain cover, then the CKP sensor reluctor.
26. Remove timing chain slipper, then the crankshaft sprocket and timing chain.
27. Remove camshaft sprockets.
28. Remove camshaft bearing cap bolts in sequence, **Fig. 2,** then the camshafts and lifters. Keep lifters in order to ensure installation in original locations.
29. Raise engine, then reposition holding fixture.
30. Disconnect EVAP hose for on-board refueling vapor recovery, then the brake booster vacuum hose.
31. Remove oil dipstick guide bolt, then the intake manifold bolts and nuts.
32. Remove intake manifold, gasket and intake manifold insulator.
33. Remove upper heat insulator, then exhaust manifold nuts and bolts.

34. Remove exhaust manifold, gasket and lower heat insulator.
35. Remove cylinder head bolts and washers in sequence, **Fig. 3. Discard the bolts.**
36. Remove cylinder head, then the gasket.
37. Reverse procedure to install, noting the following:
    a. **Do not use old cylinder head bolts. Always install new ones.**
    b. **Torque** cylinder head bolts in three steps in sequence, **Fig. 4.** First step, to 18 ft. lbs.; second step, to 36 ft. lbs.; third step, rotate bolts an additional 90°.
    c. **Torque** camshaft bearing cap bolts to 10 ft. lbs., then **torque** front bearing cap bolts to 17 ft. lbs., in sequence, **Fig. 5.**

HIGH OUTPUT (HO) ENGINE

1. Remove engine undercovers, then drain engine oil into a suitable container.
2. Remove engine sight shield, then the air cleaner assembly.
3. Disconnect accelerator cable, then relieve fuel pressure as outlined under "Precautions."
4. Release tensioner and remove accessory drive belt.
5. Remove alternator as outlined under "Alternator, Replace" in "Electrical" section.
6. Remove timing chain dampner bolts, then the dampner.
7. Remove timing chain shoe bolts, then the shoe.
8. Remove crankshaft sprocket with timing chain.
9. Remove exhaust pipe, then the exhaust manifold bracket nut and bolts.
10. Remove ignition coils as outlined under "Ignition Coil, Replace" in "Electrical" section.
11. Remove spark plugs, then disconnect PCV hoses from cylinder head cover and throttle body.
12. Remove intake manifold as outlined under "Intake Manifold, Replace."
13. Disconnect coupling for fuel feed hose from fuel feed pipe of fuel rail using tool No. J 43178, or equivalent.
14. Disconnect electrical connectors to four fuel injectors.
15. Remove retainers from fuel supply pipe bracket, then the fuel rail and spacers from engine.
16. Remove fuel injectors with O-rings and

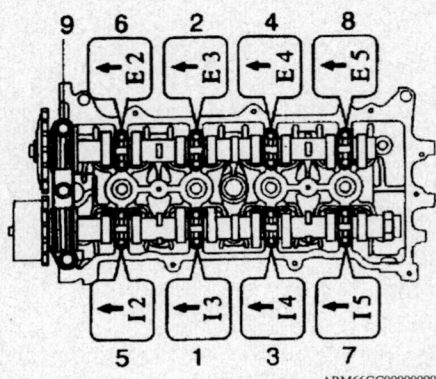

Fig. 5 Camshaft bearing cap bolt tightening sequence. Except HO engine

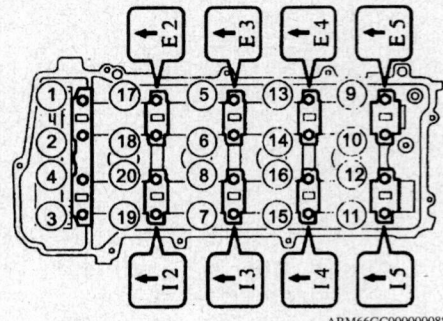

Fig. 6 Camshaft bearing cap bolt loosening sequence. HO engine

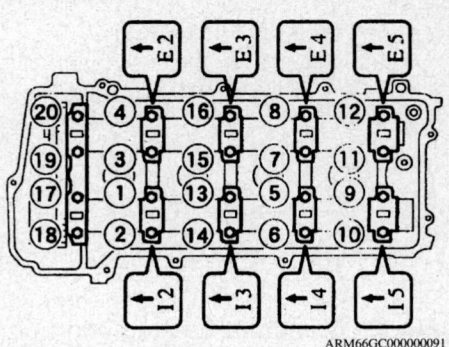

Fig. 7 Camshaft bearing cap bolt tightening sequence. HO engine

grommets from cylinder head.
17. Remove both intake and exhaust camshaft bearing cap bolts in sequence, **Fig. 6.**
18. Remove bolt, then gasket and oil control valve filter.
19. Disconnect upper radiator hose, then the heater hose from water hose union.
20. Remove cylinder head bolts in sequence, **Fig. 3.**
21. Remove water bypass to cylinder block bolt.
22. Remove cylinder head from engine.
23. Reverse procedure to install, noting the following:
   a. **Torque** cylinder head bolts to 26 ft. lbs., in sequence, **Fig. 4.**
   b. Mark front of cylinder head bolts with paint, then rotate an additional 180° using torque angle meter tool No. J 36660-A, or equivalent.
   c. **Torque** camshaft bearing cap bolts to 14 ft. lbs., in sequence, **Fig. 7.**

VALVE CLEARANCE SPECIFICATIONS

Refer to "Specifications" in this chapter.

VALVE ADJUSTMENT

Measure and adjust valve clearance while the engine is cold.
1. Remove cylinder head cover.
2. Set No. 1 cylinder at TDC on compression stroke.
3. Turn crankshaft to align groove in crankshaft pulley with 0 mark on No. 1 front cover. **Ensure valve lifters on No. 1 cylinder have freeplay. If not, rotate crankshaft pulley 360° and align 0 mark on front cover.**
4. Measure and record valve lash clearance between intake cam lobes and lifters on cylinder Nos. 1 and 2. Record any clearances which do not meet specifications.
5. Measure and record valve lash clearance between exhaust cam lobes and lifters on cylinder Nos. 1 and 3. Record any clearances which do not meet specifications.

6. Rotate crankshaft pulley 360° and align 0 mark on front cover.
7. Measure and record valve lash clearance between intake cam lobes and lifters on cylinder Nos. 3 and 4. Record any clearances which do not meet specifications.
8. Measure and record valve lash clearance between exhaust cam lobes and lifters on cylinder Nos. 2 and 4. Record any clearances which do not meet specifications.
9. If clearance is not within specifications, refer to "Hydraulic Lifters, Replace."

VALVE LIFTERS
REPLACE

1. Remove timing chain as outlined under "Timing Chain, Replace."
2. Remove intake camshaft as outlined under "Cylinder Head, Replace."
3. Remove valve lifters as required.
4. Reverse procedure to install.

TIMING CHAIN
REPLACE

1. Release tensioner and remove accessory drive belt.
2. Remove alternator as outlined under "Alternator, Replace" in "Electrical" section.
3. Drain engine coolant into a suitable container.
4. Install a suitable engine support fixture to engine.
5. **On models equipped with air conditioning,** loosen A/C receiver pinch clamps and lift receiver for access.
6. **On all models,** remove righthand side engine mount, then the cylinder head cover as outlined under "Cylinder Head, Replace."
7. Rotate No. 1 piston to TDC and align camshaft timing sprockets.
8. Disconnect power steering oil pressure switch connector.
9. Raise and support vehicle, then remove engine splash shields.
10. Remove power steering pump through bolts and nut, then move pump aside from mounting surface.
11. Remove crankshaft pulley retaining bolt using tool No. J 8614-01 or equivalent, **Fig. 8.**
12. Remove crankshaft pulley.

13. Remove CKP sensor, then lower the vehicle.
14. Remove drive belt tensioner mounting bolt and nut, then the tensioner.
15. Remove timing chain tensioner bolt, then the tensioner.
16. Remove timing chain cover bolt, then the nut and timing chain cover.
17. Remove crankshaft sensor reluctor.
18. Remove timing chain dampner bolt, then the dampner.
19. Remove timing chain shoe bolt and shoe.
20. Remove crankshaft sprocket and timing chain.
21. Reverse procedure to install, noting the following:
   a. Align camshaft and crankshaft timing marks, **Figs. 9 and 10.**
   b. Turn crankshaft until crankshaft keyway faces upward.

CAMSHAFT
REPLACE

Refer to "Cylinder Head, Replace" for replacement procedure.

PISTON & ROD ASSEMBLY

Refer to **Fig. 11** for piston and rod assembly.
The connecting rod bearings are available in standard and various undersizes. If replacing a bearing, replace with one having the same number as marked on the connecting rod.
Torque connecting rod bearing cap bolts to 22 ft. lbs., then rotate an additional 90°.

MAIN & ROD BEARINGS

Main bearings are available in standard and various undersizes. If using a standard bearing, replace it with one having the same number. If the number of the bearing cannot be determined, select the proper bearing by determining the numbers imprinted on the cylinder block 1–5.
Torque main bearing cap bolts in sequence, **Fig. 12,** in three steps: first step, to 16 ft. lbs.; second step, to 32 ft. lbs.; third step, rotate an additional 90°.

CRANKSHAFT REAR OIL SEAL
REPLACE
Removal

1. Remove transaxle as outlined in **MO-TOR's "Domestic Transmission, In-Vehicle Service" manual or "Transmission Service DVD."**
2. Mark flywheel to crankshaft position and remove flywheel.
3. Remove rear end plate.
4. Pry out old seal using suitable screwdriver with tape-wrapped tip.

Installation

1. Apply suitable multi-purpose grease to lip of new seal.
2. Carefully tap new seal into place until its surface is flush with retainer edge.
3. Install flywheel, ensure marks are properly aligned.
4. Apply sealant P/N 12345493, or equivalent, to bolt threads.
5. Install transaxle.

OIL PAN
REPLACE

1. Raise and support vehicle.
2. Drain engine oil into a suitable container.
3. Remove lefthand side engine splash shield.
4. **On models equipped with manual transaxle,** remove flywheel inspection cover.
5. **On all models,** remove oil pan mounting bolts, nuts and oil pan.
6. Reverse procedure to install. Apply continuous bead of silicone sealant P/N 12346240, or equivalent to engine oil pan mating surface.

OIL PUMP
REPLACE

1. Remove timing chain as outlined under "Timing Chain, Replace."
2. Remove mounting bolts and pump. Discard gasket.
3. Reverse procedure to install.

BELT TENSION DATA

This engine is equipped with a serpentine drive belt. Tension is controlled by an automatic tensioner.

SERPENTINE DRIVE BELT
Routing

Refer to **Fig. 13** for serpentine drive belt routing.

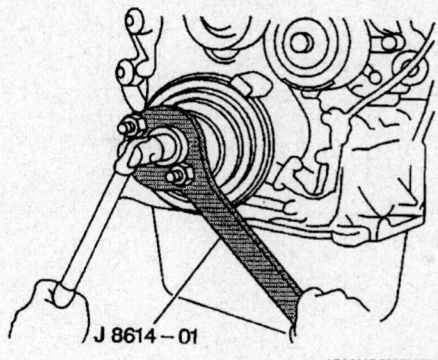

J 8614 – 01

ARM66GC000000096

Fig. 8 Crankshaft pulley bolt removal

Removal

1. Rotate belt tensioner clockwise using a suitable wrench.
2. Continue to apply pressure to tensioner, then remove belt.

Installation

1. Raise and support vehicle.
2. Remove righthand side lower engine splash shield.
3. Rotate belt tensioner clockwise using suitable wrench.
4. Route and install drive belt onto drive pulleys with pressure applied to tensioner.
5. Release belt tensioner.
6. Install righthand side lower engine splash shield.

COOLING SYSTEM BLEED

This engine does not require a specific bleeding procedure. After filling cooling system, bring engine to operating temperature with radiator/pressure cap off. Air will then be automatically bled through cap opening.

THERMOSTAT
REPLACE

1. Drain engine coolant into a suitable container.
2. Remove alternator as outlined under "Alternator, Replace" in "Electrical" section.
3. Remove thermostat housing mounting nuts, then the housing, thermostat and O-ring.
4. Reverse procedure to install. Ensure O-ring contact surfaces are clean and free of debris.

WATER PUMP
REPLACE

1. Drain coolant into suitable container.

2. Remove serpentine drive belt.
3. Raise and support vehicle.
4. Remove engine splash shields.
5. Remove alternator as outlined under "Alternator, Replace" in "Electrical" section.
6. **On models less HO engine,** remove water pump pulley.
7. **On all models,** remove mounting bolts, water pump and O-ring.
8. Reverse procedure to install.

RADIATOR
REPLACE

1. Drain engine coolant into a suitable container.
2. Remove radiator inlet hose, then the outlet hose.
3. **On models equipped with automatic transaxle,** disconnect ATF cooler hoses at radiator.
4. **On all models,** disconnect fan motor electrical connectors, then the electrical harness clamps from shroud.
5. Remove radiator mounting bolts, then the radiator and cooling fan.
6. Reverse procedure to install.

FUEL PUMP
REPLACE

1. Remove rear seat cushion, then the lefthand side door opening sill plate.
2. Fold back carpet, then remove floor service hole cover mounting screws and cover.
3. Disconnect fuel sender and fuel tank pressure sensor electrical connectors.
4. Remove fuel feed and return hoses, then disconnect fuel tank vapor line.
5. Remove mounting bolts and fuel sender.
6. Remove bottom cap, then the lower cushion from fuel sender.
7. Remove fuel pressure regulator.
8. Disconnect fuel level sensor connector and remove sensor.
9. Disconnect fuel pump electrical connector.
10. Remove fuel pump from fuel filter, then the retaining ring from fuel pump.
11. Reverse procedure to install.

FUEL FILTER
REPLACE

On 2004–06 FWD models and 2007-08 models, the fuel pump and fuel filter are combined into the fuel sender assembly and are not serviced separately. Replace the fuel sender assembly in order to replace the fuel pump or filter.

1. Remove fuel sender assembly as outlined under "Fuel Pump, Replace."
2. Remove fuel filter and pump assembly.
3. Separate fuel filter from fuel pump.
4. Reverse procedure to install.

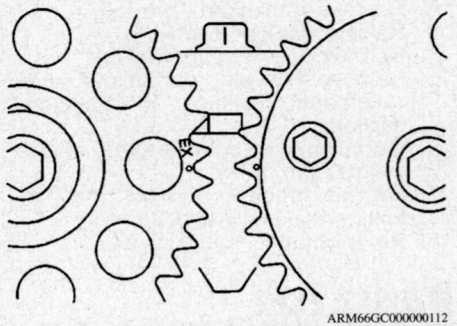

Fig. 9 Camshaft alignment marks

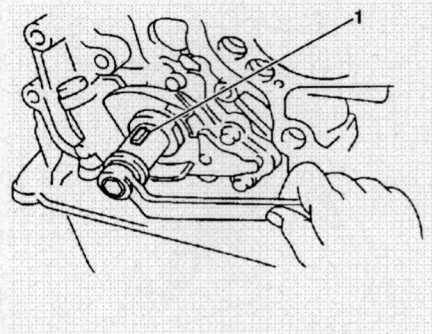

1. Keyway facing upward

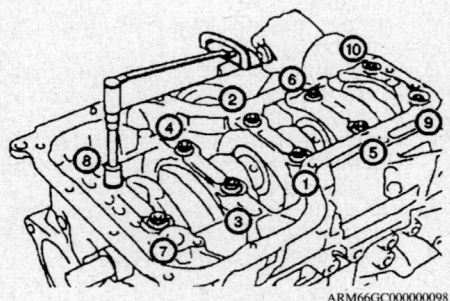

Fig. 12 Main bearing cap tightening sequence

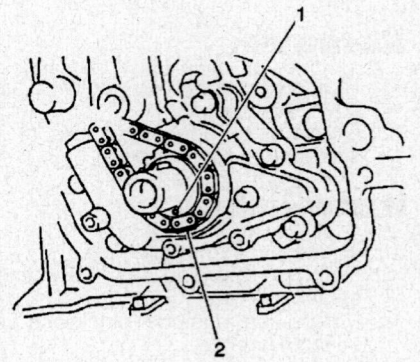

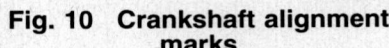

1. Sprocket mark
2. Yellow chain link

Fig. 10 Crankshaft alignment marks

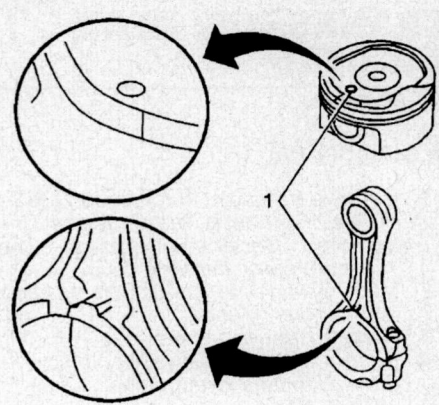

Fig. 11 Piston & rod assembly

Fig. 13 Serpentine drive belt routing

TIGHTENING SPECIFICATIONS

Year	Component	Torque Ft. Lbs.
EXCEPT HIGH OUTPUT (HO) ENGINE		
2004–08	Air Cleaner	89①
	Alternator	17
	Camshaft Bearing	②
	Camshaft Sprocket	40
	Connecting Rod Cap Bolts	15④
	Crankshaft Main Bearing Cap Bolts	③
	Crankshaft Position Sensor	106①
	Crankshaft Pulley	105
	Cylinder Head	②
	Drive Belt Tensioner Bolt	74
	Drive Belt Tensioner Nut	21
	Engine Crossmember To Body	29
	Engine Mount Lefthand Side	60
	Engine Mount Righthand Side	38
	Engine Mount Insulator Righthand Side	38
	Exhaust Manifold Bracket	26
	Exhaust Manifold Heat Shield	11
	Exhaust Manifold	36
	Exhaust Pipe	32
	Flywheel, Automatic Transaxle	61
	Flywheel, Manual Transaxle	36④
	Front Engine Mount	40
	Fuel Injector Wiring Harness	106①
	Heat Insulator	106①
	Heated Oxygen Sensor	32
	Ignition Coil Bracket	10
	Intake Manifold Nuts & Bolts	13
	Intake Manifold Support Bracket	37
	Lower Transmission To Engine	47
	Oil Drain Plug	26
	Oil Pan	97①
	Oil Pump	97①
	Oil Strainer	97①
	Power Steering Pump	27
	Radiator Upper Support Bracket	14
	Starter	22
	Thermostat Housing	84①
	Timing Chain Cover (10 MM)	89①
	Timing Chain Cover (12 MM)	14
	Timing Chain Tensioner	89①
	Torque Converter	26
	Water Bypass Pipe To Cylinder Head Bolt	11
	Water Bypass Pipe To Cylinder Head Nut	84①
	Water Pump	80①
HIGH OUTPUT (HO) ENGINE		
2004–08	A/C Compressor Hose	89①
	A/C Mounting Bolts	18
	Air Cleaner Mounting	89①
	Alternator	17
	Axle Shaft Heat Shield	13
	Camshaft Bearing Cap	②
	Camshaft Sensor	11

TIGHTENING SPECIFICATIONS—Continued

Year	Component	Torque Ft. Lbs.
HIGH OUTPUT (HO) ENGINE		
2004–08	Camshaft Sprocket	40
	Connecting Rod Cap Bolts	22④
	Coolant Inlet Pipe	11
	Crankshaft Main Bearing Cap Bolts	③
	Crankshaft Position Sensor	106①
	Crankshaft Pulley	105
	Cylinder Head	②
	Drive Belt Tensioner Bolt	51
	Drive Belt Tensioner, Nut	21
	Engine Ground Wire	11
	Engine Mounting Bracket	40
	Exhaust Manifold	36
	Exhaust Manifold Bracket	26
	Exhaust Manifold Heat Shield	11
	Exhaust Pipe	46
	Flywheel, Auto Transaxle	61
	Flywheel, Manual Transaxle	36④
	Fuel Injector Wiring Harness	106①
	Heat Insulator	106①
	Heated Oxygen Sensor	30
	Ignition Coil Bracket	10
	Intake Manifold	13
	Intake Manifold Support Bracket	37
	Lower Transmission To Engine	47
	Mounting Insulator, Bolt	47
	Mounting Insulator, Nut	38
	Oil Drain Plug	26
	Oil Pan	97①
	Oil Pump	97①
	Oil Strainer	97①
	Oxygen Sensor	31
	Power Steering Pump	27
	Radiator Upper Support Bracket	14
	Starter	27
	Thermostat Housing	84①
	Timing Chain Cover (10 MM)	89①
	Timing Chain Cover (12 MM)	14
	Timing Chain Dampner	14
	Timing Chain Shoe	89①
	Timing Chain Tensioner	89①
	Torque Converter	26
	Washer Fluid Tank	80①
	Water Bypass Pipe To Cylinder Head	80①
	Water Pump	80①

① — Inch lbs.

② — Refer to "Cylinder Head, Replace" for tightening specifications and sequence.

③ — Refer to "Main & Rod Bearings" for tightening specifications.

④ — Rotate an additional 90°.

Clutch & Manual Transaxle

INDEX

	Page No.
Adjustments	11-14
Clutch Pedal Height	11-14
Clutch, Replace	11-14
Hydraulic System Service	11-14
Clutch Release Cylinder, Replace	11-14

	Page No.
Clutch Slave Cylinder, Replace	11-14
Clutch System Bleed	11-14
Tightening Specifications	11-20
Transaxle, Replace	11-14
MK5 Transaxle	11-14
Installation	11-15

	Page No.
Removal	11-14
MTN Transaxle	11-15
Installation	11-16
Removal	11-15

ADJUSTMENTS

Clutch Pedal Height

1. Measure clutch pedal height as outlined, **Fig. 1.**
2. Clutch pedal height should be 5.45–5.84 inches.
3. If clutch pedal height is not as specified, remove lower instrument panel finish panel and air duct.
4. Loosen clutch pedal locknut, then rotate stopper bolt until specified height is achieved.
5. Tighten locknut.
6. Inspect clutch pedal freeplay by depressing clutch pedal until resistance is felt. Freeplay should be .039–.197 inch. pushrod play at top of pedal should be .197–.591 inch.
7. If required to adjust freeplay, loosen locknut and rotate pushrod until freeplay is as specified.
8. Tighten locknut.
9. Ensure clutch pedal height and freeplay are as specified, then reinstall air duct and finish panel.

HYDRAULIC SYSTEM SERVICE

Clutch Slave Cylinder, Replace

1. **On models equipped with audio coded anti-theft system,** obtain three digit anti-theft code.
2. **On all models,** remove brake booster.
3. Remove clutch tube from clutch hose.
4. Remove clip, clevis pin and return spring.
5. Remove clutch slave cylinder, then if required, clutch tube from cylinder.
6. Reverse procedure to install. Tighten to specifications, then bleed and adjust system. Reset audio anti-theft system, if equipped, as outlined under "Precautions."

Clutch Release Cylinder, Replace

1. **On models equipped with audio coded anti-theft system,** obtain three digit anti-theft code.

2. **On all models,** using suitable tool, disconnect clutch line tube, using suitable container to catch fluid.
3. Remove release cylinder attaching bolts, then remove cylinder.
4. Reverse procedure to install. Tighten attaching bolts to specifications, then bleed clutch system as outlined under "Clutch System Bleed."

Clutch System Bleed

If any service is performed on the clutch system or air is suspected in the clutch lines, bleed the system.
1. Fill clutch reservoir with suitable brake fluid. **Do not allow fluid to come in contact with painted surfaces.**
2. Inspect reservoir frequently and add fluid as required.
3. Connect vinyl tube to bleeder plug, then insert other tube end in half full container of brake fluid.
4. Slowly pump clutch pedal several times.
5. While depressing, pedal, loosen bleeder plug until fluid runs out, then close bleeder plug.
6. Repeat procedure until air bubbles are no longer evident in fluid. **Do not reuse fluid.**

CLUTCH
REPLACE

1. **On models with audio coded anti-theft system,** obtain three digit anti-theft code.
2. **On all models,** remove transaxle assembly as outlined under "Transaxle, Replace."
3. Place installation alignment marks on clutch cover and flywheel.
4. Loosen each set bolt one turn at a time until spring tension is released.
5. Remove clutch cover attaching bolts, then remove cover and disc.
6. Remove release bearing, fork and boot.
7. Measure clutch disc rivet head depth using suitable calipers. Minimum rivet depth should be .012 inch. If not as indicated, replace clutch disc.
8. Measure flywheel runout using suitable dial indicator. Maximum runout should be .004 inch. If not as indicated, replace flywheel.

9. Measure clutch disc runout. Maximum runout is .031 inch. If not as indicated, replace disc.
10. Reverse to install, noting the following:
    a. Install clutch disc using suitable tool.
    b. Match clutch cover and flywheel alignment marks, then **torque** cover bolts to 14 ft. lbs., one turn at a time in a criss-cross pattern, ensuring clutch disc and pressure plate remain aligned.

TRANSAXLE
REPLACE

MK5 Transaxle
REMOVAL

CAUTION: Before servicing any electrical component, the ignition key must be OFF or LOCK position and all electrical loads must be OFF, unless instructed otherwise in these procedures. If a tool or equipment could easily come in contact with a live exposed electrical terminal, also disconnect the battery ground. Failure to follow these precautions may cause personal injury and/or damage to the vehicle or its components.
1. Remove battery.
2. Remove four bolts that secure battery tray, then remove battery tray from vehicle.
3. Remove air cleaner case assembly.
4. Remove cruise control servo from vehicle.
5. Remove cylinder head cover from engine.
6. Disconnect wire harness (2) from transaxle, **Fig. 2.**
7. Remove two bolts, then disconnect two wire harness brackets (1), **Fig. 2.**
8. Remove two bolts and ground cables from transaxle, **Fig. 3.**
9. Disconnect backup lamp connector, **Fig. 4.**
10. Disconnect vehicle speed sensor connector, **Fig. 5.**
11. Remove clutch actuator cylinder and piping from transaxle assembly.
12. Remove clip and washer (1), then disconnect shift cable from transaxle, **Fig. 6.**
13. Remove clip (2), then disconnect shift cable from bracket, **Fig. 6.**

14. Remove clip and washer (1), then disconnect shift cable from transaxle, **Fig. 7.**
15. Remove clip (2), then disconnect shift cable from bracket, **Fig. 7.**
16. Remove starter assembly from vehicle.
17. Install engine support fixture.
18. Raise vehicle.
19. Remove front wheels.
20. Remove left and right lower splash shields.
21. Remove exhaust pipe from the vehicle, **Fig. 8.**
22. Remove transaxle drain plug and drain oil into a suitable container.
23. Remove left and right drive shafts.
24. Remove front suspension crossmember.
25. Support transaxle with a suitable jack.
26. Remove five bolts from left engine mount, then remove mount from vehicle.
27. Remove three bolts from lefthand engine mount bracket, then remove bracket from vehicle, **Fig. 9.**
28. Remove six bolts that secure transaxle to engine, **Fig. 10.**
29. Slightly lower transaxle.
30. Remove transaxle from engine.

INSTALLATION

CAUTION: Before servicing any electrical component, the ignition key must be OFF or LOCK position and all electrical loads must be OFF, unless instructed otherwise in these procedures. If a tool or equipment could easily come in contact with a live exposed electrical terminal, also disconnect the battery ground. Failure to follow these precautions may cause personal injury and/or damage to the vehicle or its components.

NOTICE: Use the correct fastener in the correct location. Replacement fasteners must be the correct part number for that application. Fasteners requiring replacement or fasteners requiring the use of thread locking compound or sealant are identified in the service procedure. Do not use paints, lubricants, or corrosion inhibitors on fasteners or fastener joint surfaces unless specified. These coatings affect fastener torque and joint clamping force and may damage the fastener. Use the correct tightening sequence and specifications when installing fasteners in order to avoid damage to components and systems.

1. Align input shaft with clutch disc and install transaxle to engine.
2. Install six bolts that secure transaxle to engine, **Fig. 11.** Tighten to specifications.
3. Install left engine mounting bracket to transaxle with three bolts. Tighten to specifications.
4. Install lefthand engine mount with five bolts and nuts. Tighten to specifications.
5. Lower jack from the transaxle.

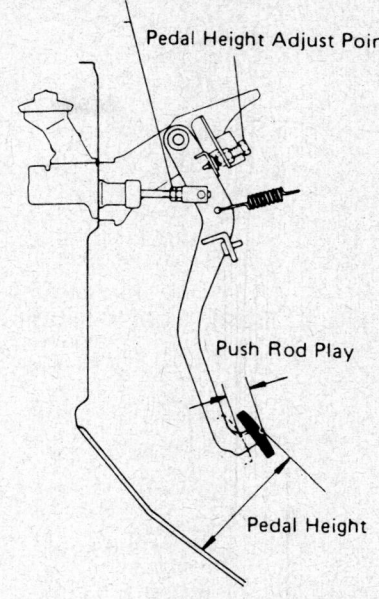

Fig. 1 Push Rod Play and Freeplay Adjust Point
Pedal Height Adjust Point
Push Rod Play
Pedal Height

TY5049100013000X

Fig. 1 Clutch pedal height adjustment

6. Install front suspension crossmember.
7. Install lefthand and righthand drive shafts.
8. Install lefthand and righthand lower splash shields.
9. Install exhaust pipe.
10. Install front wheels.
11. Install drain plug with a new gasket. Tighten to specifications.
12. Fill transaxle to specifications.
13. Install fill plug with a new gasket. Tighten to specifications.
14. Lower vehicle.
15. Remove engine support fixture.
16. Install starter assembly.
17. Connect shift cable to transaxle, then install clip and the washer (1), **Fig. 12.**
18. Connect shift cable to the bracket, then install clip (2). **Fig. 12.**
19. Connect shift cable to transaxle, then install clip and washer (1), **Fig. 13.**
20. Connect shift cable to bracket, then install clip (2), **Fig. 13.**
21. Install clutch actuator cylinder and piping.
22. Connect backup lamp connector, **Fig. 14.**
23. Connect vehicle speed sensor connector, **Fig. 15.**
24. Connect wire harness (2) to transaxle, **Fig. 16.**
25. Connect two wire harness brackets (1), then install two bolts. Tighten to specifications.
26. Install two bolts and ground cables to transaxle. Tighten to specification, **Fig. 17.**
27. Install cruise control servo.
28. Install battery tray and four bolts. Tighten to specifications.
29. Install battery.
30. Install air cleaner case assembly.
31. Install cylinder head cover.

MTN Transaxle

REMOVAL

CAUTION: Before servicing any electrical component, the ignition key must be OFF or LOCK position and all electrical loads must be OFF, unless instructed otherwise in these procedures. If a tool or equipment could easily come in contact with a live exposed electrical terminal, also disconnect the battery ground. Failure to follow these precautions may cause personal injury and/or damage to the vehicle or its components.

1. Remove battery.
2. Remove four battery tray retaining bolts, then remove battery tray from vehicle.
3. Remove air cleaner assembly.
4. Remove cruise control servo from vehicle.
5. Remove cylinder head cover from engine.
6. Disconnect wire harness (2) from transaxle, **Fig. 18.**
7. Remove two bolts, then disconnect two wire harness brackets (1). **Fig. 18.**
8. Remove two bolts and ground cables from transaxle, **Fig. 19.**
9. Disconnect backup lamp connector, **Fig. 20.**
10. Disconnect vehicle speed sensor connector, **Fig. 21.**
11. Remove clutch actuator cylinder and piping from transaxle assembly.
12. Remove clip and washer (1), then disconnect shift cable from transaxle, **Fig. 22.**
13. Remove clip (2), then disconnect shift cable from the bracket, **Fig. 22.**
14. Remove clip and washer (1), then disconnect shift cable from transaxle, **Fig. 23.**
15. Remove clip (2), then disconnect shift cable from bracket, **Fig. 23.**
16. Remove starter assembly.
17. Install engine support fixture.
18. Raise vehicle.
19. Remove front wheels.
20. Remove left and right lower splash shields.
21. Remove exhaust pipe from vehicle, **Fig. 24.**
22. Remove transaxle drain plug and the oil.
23. Support transaxle with a suitable jack.
24. Remove five bolts from left engine mount, then remove mount from vehicle.
25. Remove left and right drive shafts.
26. Remove front suspension crossmember.
27. Remove three bolts from left engine mount bracket, then remove bracket from vehicle. **Fig. 25.**
28. Remove six bolts that secure transaxle to engine mounting, **Fig. 26.**
29. Slightly lower transaxle.
30. Remove transaxle from engine.

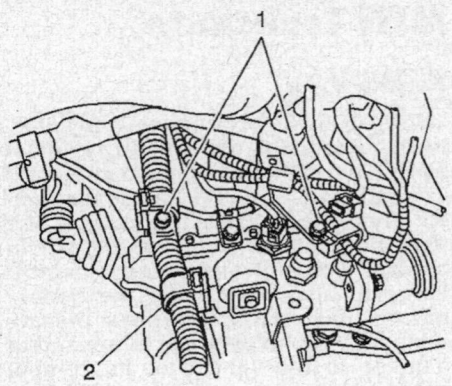

Fig. 2 Wire harness & brackets location

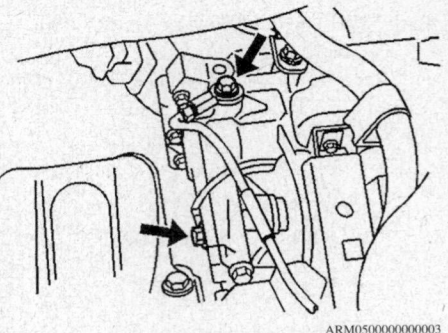

ARM0500000000003

Fig. 3 Ground cable locations

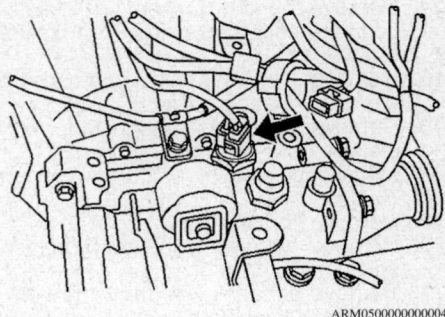

ARM0500000000004

Fig. 4 Backup lamp connector

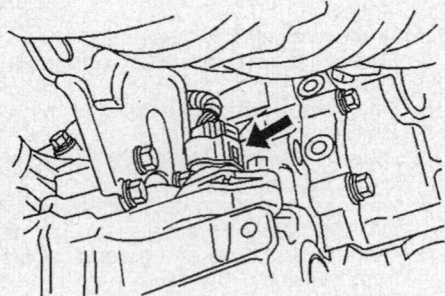

ARM0500000000002

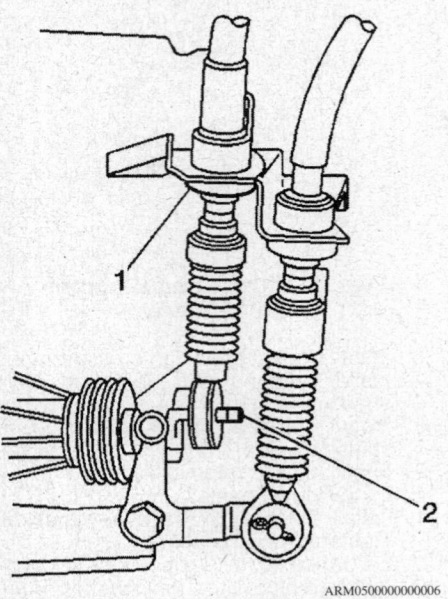

ARM0500000000005

Fig. 5 Vehicle speed sensor connector

INSTALLATION

CAUTION: Before servicing any electrical component, the ignition key must be OFF or LOCK position and all electrical loads must be OFF, unless instructed otherwise in these procedures. If a tool or equipment could easily come in contact with a live exposed electrical terminal, also disconnect the battery ground. Failure to follow these precautions may cause personal injury and/or damage to the vehicle or its components.

NOTICE: Use the correct fastener in the correct location. Replacement fasteners must be the correct part number for that application. Fasteners requiring replacement or fasteners requiring the use of thread locking compound or sealant are identified in the service procedure. Do not use paints, lubricants, or corrosion inhibitors on fasteners or fastener joint surfaces unless specified. These coatings affect fastener torque and joint clamping force and may damage the fastener. Use the correct tightening sequence and specifications when installing fasteners in order to avoid damage to components and systems.

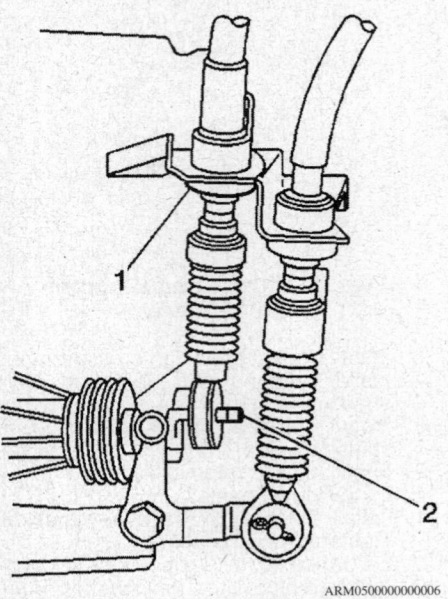

ARM0500000000006

Fig. 6 Shift cable removal

1. Align input shaft with clutch disc and install transaxle to engine.
2. Install six bolts that secure transaxle to engine retaining, **Fig. 27**. Tighten to specifications.
3. Install left engine mounting bracket to transaxle with three bolts. Tighten to specifications.
4. Install left engine mount with five bolts and nuts. Tighten to specifications.
5. Lower jack from transaxle.
6. Install front suspension crossmember.
7. Install left and right drive shafts.
8. Install left and right lower splash shields.
9. Install exhaust pipe in vehicle.
10. Install front wheels.
11. Install drain plug with a new gasket.
12. Install fill plug with a new gasket.
13. Fill transaxle to specifications.
14. Lower vehicle.
15. Remove engine support fixture.
16. Install starter assembly.
17. Connect shift cable to transaxle, then

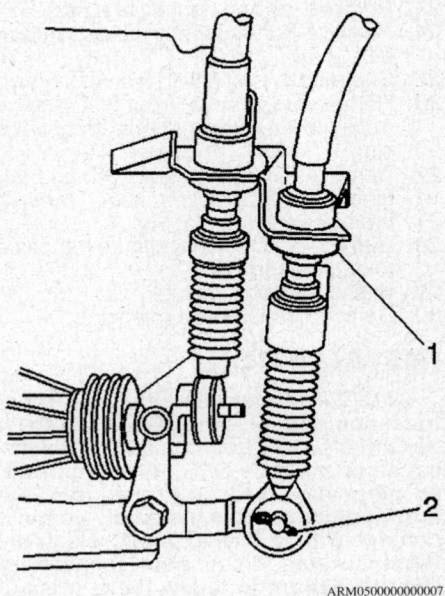

ARM0500000000007

Fig. 7 Shift cable removal

install clip and washer (1), **Fig. 28**.
18. Connect shift cable to bracket, then install clip (2), **Fig. 28**.
19. Connect shift cable to transaxle, then install clip and washer (1), **Fig. 29**.
20. Connect shift cable to bracket, then install clip (2), **Fig. 28**.
21. Install clutch actuator cylinder and piping.
22. Connect backup lamp connector, **Fig. 30**.
23. Connect vehicle speed sensor connector, **Fig. 31**.
24. Connect wire harness (2) from the transaxle, **Fig. 32**.
25. Connect two wire harness brackets (1), then install two bolts, **Fig. 32**.
26. Install two bolts and ground cables to transaxle, **Fig. 33**.
27. Install cruise control servo in vehicle.
28. Install battery tray and four bolts.
29. Install battery.
30. Install air cleaner case assembly.
31. Install cylinder head cover on engine.

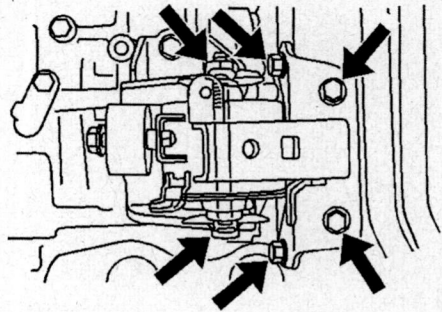

Fig. 8 Exhaust pipe removal

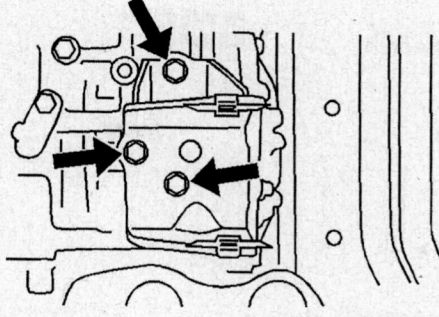

Fig. 9 Left engine mount bracket bolt location

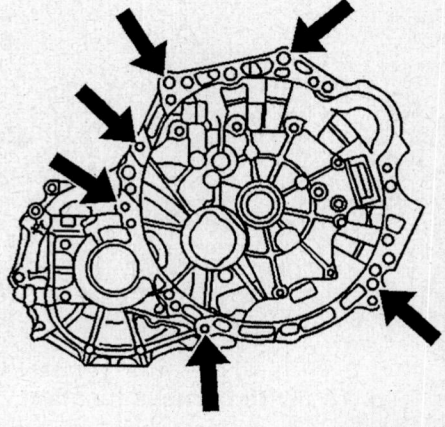

Fig. 10 Transaxle to engine secure bolt locations

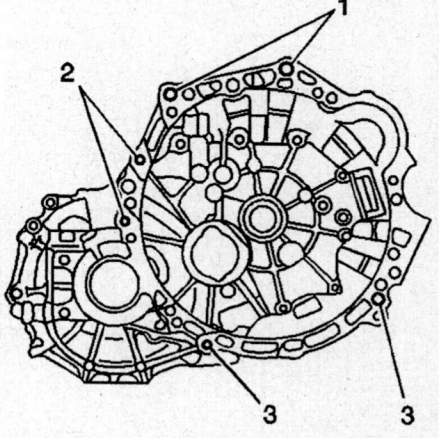

Fig. 11 Transaxle to engine attaching bolts

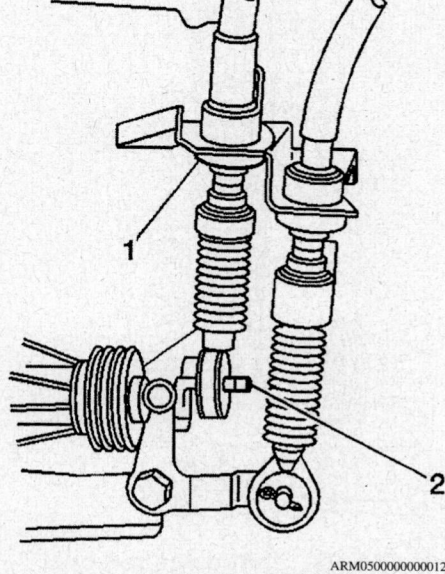

Fig. 12 Shift cable installation

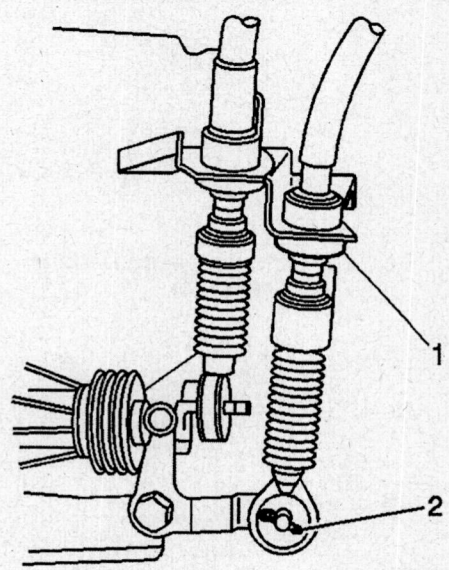

Fig. 13 Shift cable installation

Fig. 14 Backup lamp connector

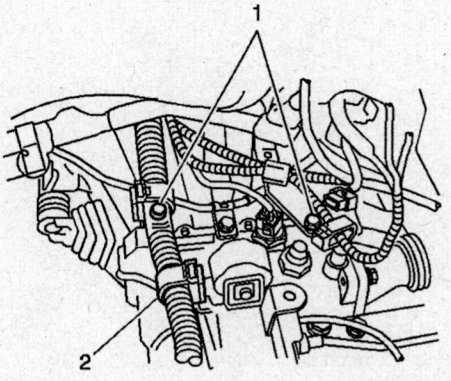

Fig. 16 Wire harness installation

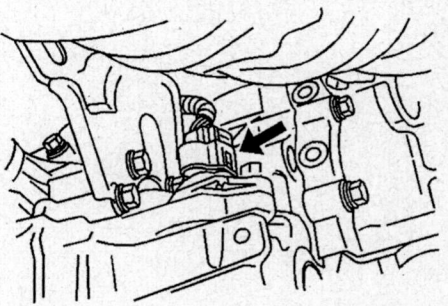

Fig. 15 Vehicle speed sensor connector

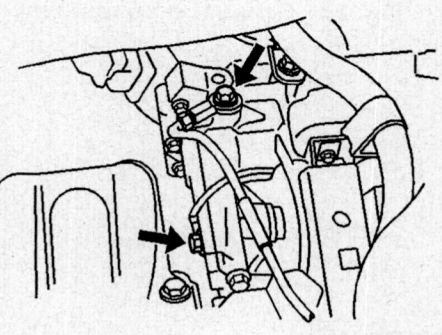

Fig. 17 Ground cable installation

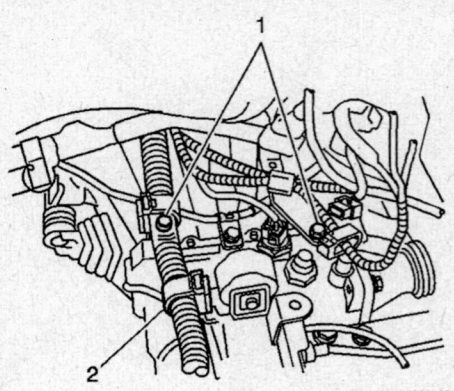

Fig. 18   Wire harness location

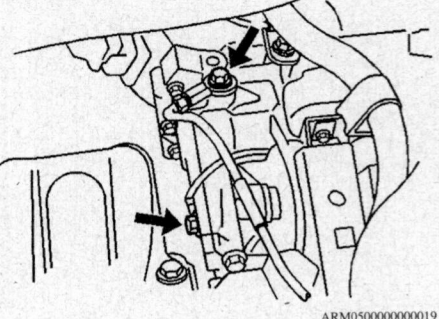

Fig. 19   Ground cable removal

Fig. 20   Backup lamp removal

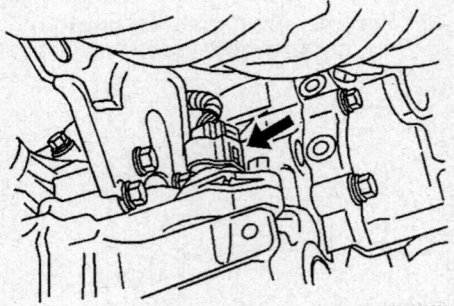

Fig. 21   Vehicle speed sensor removal

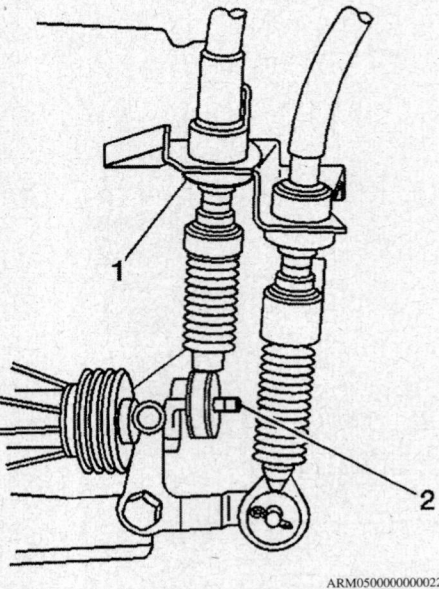

Fig. 22   Shift cable removal

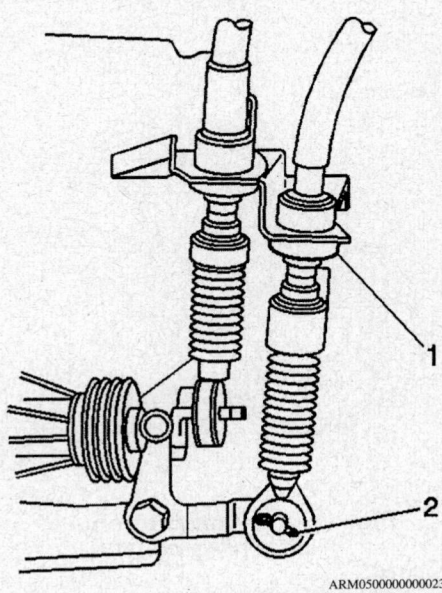

Fig. 23   Shift cable removal

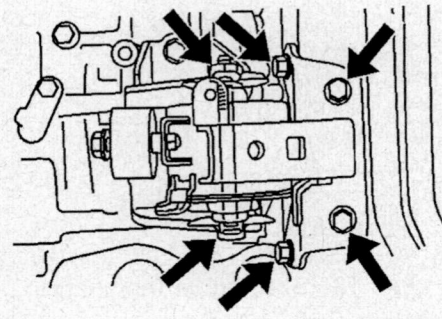

Fig. 24   Exhaust pipe removal

Fig. 25   Engine mount bracket removal

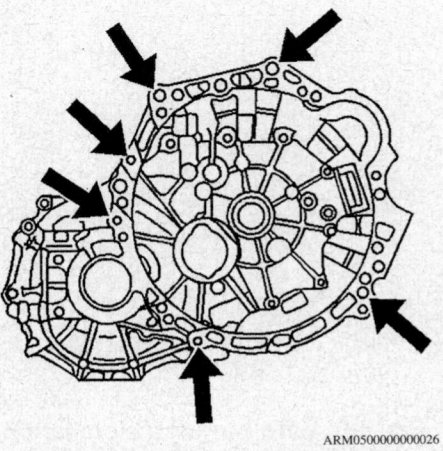

Fig. 26   Transaxle removal

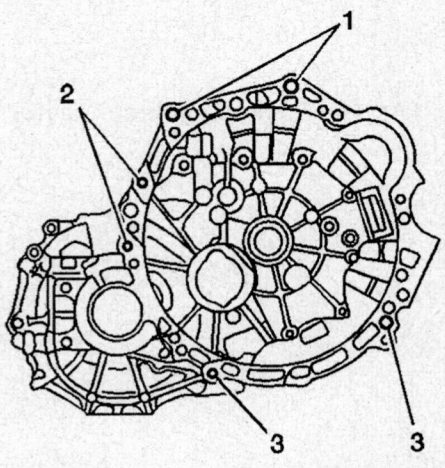

Fig. 27   Transaxle to engine tightening sequence

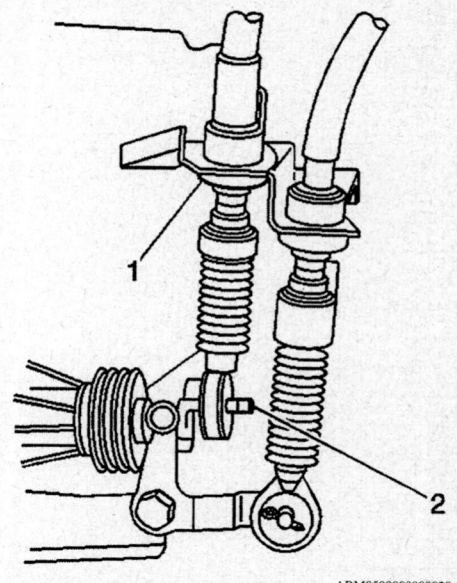

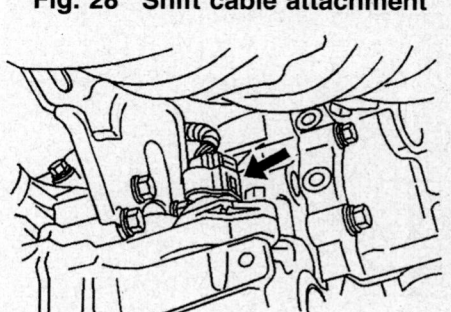

Fig. 28   Shift cable attachment

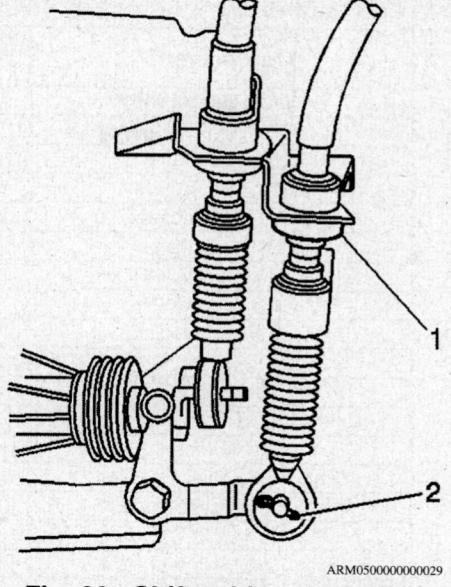

Fig. 29   Shift cable attachment

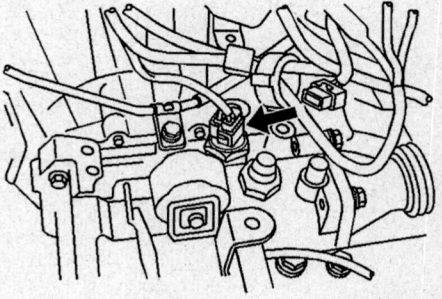

Fig. 30   Backup lamp connector

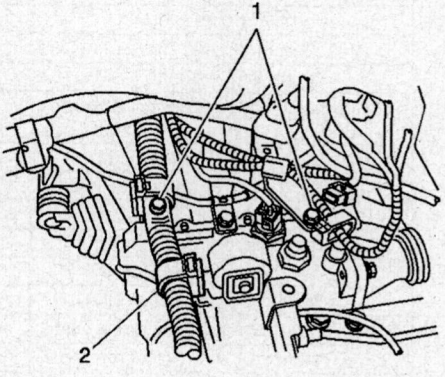

Fig. 32   Wire harness connection

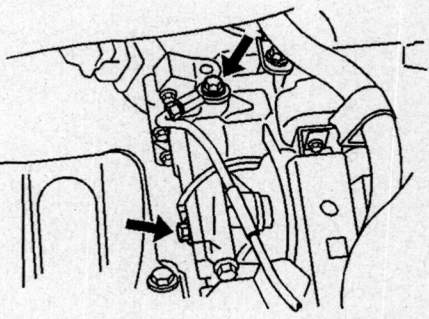

Fig. 33   Ground cable installation

Fig. 31   Vehicle speed sensor
          installation

TIGHTENING SPECIFICATIONS

Year	Component	Torque Ft. Lbs.
2004–08	Back-Up Lamp Switch	30
	Battery Tray	10
	Bleeder Plug	96①
	Bond Cable To Body	14
	Clutch Accumulator	15
	Clutch Cover	14
	Clutch Line Bracket Bolts	18
	Clutch Line Union	11
	Clutch Master Cylinder	108①
	Control Shaft Cover	14
	Drain Plug	29
	Driveshaft To Side Gear Shaft	27
	Engine Mount	59
	Engine Mounting Bracket	38
	Exhaust Pipe Clamp Bolt	14
	Exhaust Pipe To Converter	32
	Exhaust Pipe To Manifold	46
	Filler Plug	29
	Front Bearing Retainer	96①
	Front Engine Mount	64
	Ground Cable Bolts	10
	Lock Ball Assembly	22
	Lower Ball Joint to Steering Knuckle Nut	76
	Master Cylinder Reservoir Tank	18
	Output Shaft Bearing Lock Plate	96①
	Rear Endplate To Transaxle	17
	Release Cylinder To Transaxle	108①
	Shift Fork To Set Bolt	12
	Shift Lever Shaft Assembly	14
	Speedometer Driven Gear Lock Plate	96①
	Transaxle Case Protector	108①
	Transaxle Case To Case Cover	13
	Transaxle Case To Transaxle Case	22
	Transaxle To Engine (MK5)	②
	Transaxle To Engine (MTN)	③
	Transaxle To Starter	28
	Wire Harness Bracket Bolts	11

① — Inch lbs.
② — **Torque** bolts (1) to 47 ft. lbs., bolts (2) to 35 ft. lbs., and bolts (3) to 17 ft. lbs., refer to **Fig. 11,** for tightening sequence.
③ — **Torque** bolts (1) to 47 ft. lbs., bolts (2) to 35 ft. lbs., and bolts (3) to 17 ft. lbs., refer to **Fig. 27,** for tightening sequence.

Rear Axle & Suspension

NOTE: On Air Bag Equipped Models, Refer To "Air Bag System Precautions" Located In The Front Of This Manual For System Disarming & Arming Procedures.

NOTE: Refer To "Computer Relearn Procedures" Located In The Front Of This Manual When Battery Power To The Computer Has Been Interrupted.

INDEX

	Page No.
Coil Spring, Replace	11-21
Control Arm, Replace	11-22
Lower	11-22
Upper	11-22
Differential Carrier, Replace	11-21

	Page No.
Hub & Bearing, Replace	11-21
AWD	11-21
FWD	11-21
Knuckle, Replace	11-22
Propeller Shaft, Replace	11-21

	Page No.
Rear Axle Shaft, Replace	11-21
Shock Absorber, Replace	11-21
Stabilizer Bar, Replace	11-22
Tightening Specifications	11-23

REAR AXLE SHAFT
REPLACE

1. Raise and support vehicle.
2. Remove tire and wheel assembly.
3. Remove cotter pin and lock cap.
4. Apply parking brake, then remove and discard drive shaft nut.
5. Release parking brake.
6. Remove suspension knuckle as outlined under "Knuckle, Replace."
7. Remove rear wheel driveshaft from vehicle using slide hammer tool No. J 2619-01 and axle shaft remover tool No. J 45341, or equivalents.
8. Reverse procedure to install.

DIFFERENTIAL CARRIER
REPLACE

1. Raise and support vehicle.
2. Place drain pan under differential carrier.
3. Remove differential carrier drain plug and drain differential carrier.
4. Remove propeller shaft as outlined under "Propeller Shaft, Replace."
5. Remove rear tire and wheel assemblies.
6. Remove lefthand and righthand knuckles as outlined under "Knuckle, Replace."
7. Remove lefthand and righthand drive shafts from vehicle as outlined under "Rear Axle Shaft, Replace."
8. Remove catalytic converter.
9. Place a suitable jack under differential assembly.
10. Remove rear differential support bracket bolts.
11. Remove lower differential support bolts.
12. Carefully lower differential assembly with differential support from vehicle.
13. Remove bolts and nuts from differential, then the differential support from differential carrier.
14. Reverse procedure to install.

PROPELLER SHAFT
REPLACE

1. Raise and support vehicle.
2. Place a reference mark on pinion flange yoke and differential pinion flange.
3. Remove pinion flange yoke to differential pinion flange attaching bolts and nuts.
4. Remove mid shaft bearing support bolts.
5. Remove sliding yoke and two piece propeller shaft assembly from transaxle.
6. Reverse procedure to install.

HUB & BEARING
REPLACE

AWD

1. Remove rear knuckle as outlined under "Knuckle, Replace."
2. Remove dust deflector.
3. Remove retaining bolts, then the wheel bearing and hub assembly.
4. Reverse procedure to install.

FWD

1. Release parking brake, then raise and support vehicle.
2. Remove tire and wheel assembly.
3. **On models equipped with rear disc brakes,** remove brake caliper and pads as an assembly from suspension knuckle. Support assembly with heavy mechanic's wire, then remove brake rotor.
4. **On models equipped with rear drum brakes,** remove rear brake drum.
5. **On all models,** disconnect rear wheel speed sensor.
6. Remove retaining bolts, then the wheel bearing and hub assembly.
7. Reverse procedure to install.

SHOCK ABSORBER
REPLACE

1. Unlock rear compartment front side panel by turning knob, then lift up and remove rear compartment from vehicle.
2. Remove tool storage access panel, then the bolt and panel.
3. Remove spare tire retainer, then the rear storage compartment.
4. Remove shock absorber fastener access panel.
5. **On models equipped with 2WD,** remove shock absorber retaining nuts.
6. **On all models,** raise and support vehicle.
7. **On models equipped with 2WD,** proceed as follows:
   a. Support rear axle and lower control arm.
   b. Remove nut, then the stabilizer shaft link stud from lower control arm.
8. **On all models,** remove all retaining nuts and bolt.
9. Remove shock absorber with coil spring.
10. Reverse procedure to install.

COIL SPRING
REPLACE

1. Remove shock absorber with coil spring as outlined under "Shock Absorber, Replace."
2. Compress coil spring using spring compressor tool No. J 45400, or equivalent.

3. Disassemble components using a suitable wrench.
4. Carefully release compressed spring and remove it from shock absorber.
5. Reverse procedure to install.

CONTROL ARM
REPLACE
Lower

1. Raise and support vehicle, then remove rear tire and wheel assembly.
2. Remove bolts, then separate parking brake cable from lower control arm.
3. Remove nut, then the stabilizer shaft link stud from lower control arm.
4. Support lower control arm with a suitable jack.
5. Place match marks on cams and on lower control arm, then remove cam and bolt.
6. Remove nut and bolt, then separate shock absorber from lower control arm.
7. Remove bolts and nuts, then the lower control arm from vehicle.
8. Reverse procedure to install.

Upper

1. Raise and support vehicle, then remove rear tire and wheel assemblies.
2. Remove heated oxygen sensor, then bolts retaining front pipe to catalytic converter.
3. Remove three-way catalytic converter to muffler/tail pipe assembly bolt and clamp.
4. Remove hangers from rear of three-way catalytic converter, then the converter from vehicle.
5. Place match mark on pinion flange yoke and differential pinion flange.
6. Remove mid shaft bearing support bolts, then sliding yoke and two piece propeller shaft assembly from transaxle.
7. Remove rear wheel speed sensor and pigtail.
8. Remove brake drum, then the brake shoes and brake hardware.

9. Place a suitable container below backing plate, then remove brake pipe from back of wheel cylinder.
10. Remove bleeder valve, then the wheel cylinder.
11. Remove lefthand, then the righthand rear park brake cables from equalizers.
12. Remove bolts and nuts, then separate rear shocks from lower control arms.
13. Remove bolts and nuts, then separate rear lower control arms from body.
14. Place match marks on camber adjust cams and on upper control arm.
15. Remove nut and bolt then separate upper control arm from knuckle.
16. Remove nut from cam bolt, then the rear cam from cam bolt.
17. Remove cam bolt and upper control arm from crossmember.
18. Reverse procedure to install.

KNUCKLE
REPLACE

1. Apply parking brake, then raise and support vehicle.
2. Remove tire and wheel assembly.
3. Remove nut, then separate stabilizer shaft link stud from knuckle.
4. Remove and discard cotter pin from wheel drive shaft nut.
5. Remove and discard wheel drive shaft nut, then release parking brake.
6. Remove rear wheel speed sensor and pigtail.
7. Remove brake drum, then the brake shoes and brake hardware.
8. Place a suitable container below backing plate, then remove brake pipe from back of wheel cylinder.
9. Remove bleeder valve, then the wheel cylinder.
10. Place match marks on camber adjust cams, then remove cam.
11. Remove nut and bolt, then separate lower control arm from knuckle.
12. Remove nut and bolt, then separate upper control arm from knuckle.
13. Support wheel drive shaft with a suitable jack.
14. Remove the knuckle from the wheel drive shaft, then the wheel bearing and

hub assembly and drum brake backing plate from knuckle.
15. Reverse procedure to install.

STABILIZER BAR
REPLACE

1. Raise and support vehicle, then remove rear tire and wheel assemblies.
2. Remove heated oxygen sensor, then the bolts retaining front pipe to catalytic converter.
3. Remove three-way catalytic converter to muffler/tail pipe assembly bolt and clamp.
4. Remove hangers from rear of three-way catalytic converter, then the converter from vehicle.
5. Place match mark on pinion flange yoke and differential pinion flange.
6. Remove mid shaft bearing support bolts, then sliding yoke and two piece propeller shaft assembly from transaxle.
7. Remove rear wheel speed sensor and pigtail.
8. Remove brake drum, then the brake shoes and brake hardware.
9. Place a suitable container below backing plate, then remove brake pipe from back of wheel cylinder.
10. Remove bleeder valve, then the wheel cylinder.
11. Remove lefthand, then the righthand rear park brake cables from equalizers.
12. Remove bolts and nuts, then separate rear shocks from lower control arms.
13. Remove bolts and nuts, then separate rear lower control arms from body.
14. Place a jack under differential support.
15. Remove bolts, then nuts and separate rear suspension crossmember and rear drive module from body.
16. Lower rear drive module, then remove stabilizer link from knuckle and shaft.
17. Place match marks on stabilizer shaft insulators and on stabilizer shaft.
18. Remove stabilizer shaft insulators, then the stabilizer shaft from rear suspension crossmember.
19. Reverse procedure to install.

TIGHTENING SPECIFICATIONS

Year	Component	Torque Ft. Lbs.
2004–08	Axle Hub To Knuckle FWD	45
	Axle Hub To Knuckle (AWD)	41
	Axle Shaft Nut	159
	Brake Pipe Fittings	11
	Crossmember To Body	77
	Differential Carrier Drain Plug	29
	Differential Carrier Fill Plug	29
	Differential Carrier To Differential Support	76
	Differential Carrier To Rear Differential Support	123
	Differential Support To Rear Suspension Crossmember	87
	Driveshaft Nut	159
	Lower Control Arm To Body Front Bolt (AWD)	48
	Lower Control Arm To Crossmember (AWD)	55
	Lower Control Arm To Knuckle (AWD)	55
	Mid Shaft Bearing Support Bolts	27
	Parking Brake Cable Bracket	48①
	Propeller Shaft Flange To Pinion Flange	54
	Rear Axle To Body FWD	63
	Rear Differential Support To Rear Suspension Crossmember	101
	Rear Wheel Drive Shaft Spindle Nut	159
	Shock Absorber Piston Rod Nut	41
	Shock Absorber To Lower Control Arm (AWD)	103
	Shock Absorber To Rear Axle FWD	59
	Spring Mount	59
	Stabilizer Shaft Insulator Bracket (AWD)	13
	Stabilizer Shaft Link Nut	33
	Stabilizer Shaft To Rear Axle FWD	144
	Upper Control Arm To Crossmember (AWD)	55
	Upper Control Arm To Knuckle (AWD)	55
	Wheel Lug Nuts	76

① — Inch lbs.

Front Suspension & Steering

NOTE: On Air Bag Equipped Models, Refer To "Air Bag System Precautions" Located In The Front Of This Manual For System Disarming & Arming Procedures.

NOTE: Refer To "Computer Relearn Procedures" Located In The Front Of This Manual When Battery Power To The Computer Has Been Interrupted.

INDEX

	Page No.
Ball Joint, Replace	11-24
Ball Joint Inspection	11-24
Coil Spring, Replace	11-24
Control Arm, Replace	11-24
Power Steering	21-1
Power Steering Gear, Replace	11-25
Power Steering Pump, Replace	11-25
Precautions	11-24
Air Bag Systems	11-24
Battery Ground Cable	11-24
Stabilizer Bar, Replace	11-25
Steering Columns	20-1
Steering Knuckle, Replace	11-24
Strut, Replace	11-24
Strut Service	11-24
Tie Rod End, Replace	11-25
Tightening Specifications	11-26
Wheel Hub, Replace	11-24

PRECAUTIONS

Air Bag Systems

Refer to "Air Bag System Precautions" in the front of this manual for system disarming and arming procedures.

Battery Ground Cable

Prior to service, record radio presets, then disconnect battery ground cable and isolate as required.

WHEEL HUB

REPLACE

1. Remove steering knuckle as outlined under "Steering Knuckle, Replace."
2. Remove wheel bearing retainer using snap ring pliers, **Fig. 1.**
3. Place a bearing driver collar on inside end of hub.
4. Remove hub from wheel bearing using a press. Press from inside end of hub toward outside of hub.
5. Remove brake shield from knuckle, then using a press and a split plate remove bearing outside inner race from hub.
6. Place a bearing driver collar on bearing outside outer race.
7. Remove bearing from knuckle using suitable press. Press from outside of knuckle toward inside of knuckle.
8. Reverse procedure to install.

BALL JOINT INSPECTION

1. Remove steering knuckle w/hub, then clamp knuckle into suitable soft-jawed vise.
2. Flip ball stud back & forth five times, then install castle nut onto ball joint stud.
3. Rotate nut continuously for one turn every 3–5 seconds, then note torque reading on fifth turn.
4. Replace ball joint if reading is not 9–43 inch lbs.

BALL JOINT

REPLACE

1. Raise and support vehicle, then support front suspension crossmember.
2. Remove retainers, then the lower control arm from ball joint.
3. Remove cotter pin, then the nut from ball joint stud.
4. Remove ball joint from knuckle using a suitable ball joint remover.
5. Reverse procedure to install, noting the following:
   a. Install new self-locking nut and cotter pin.
   b. Adjust wheel alignment.

COIL SPRING

REPLACE

Refer to "Strut Service" for coil spring replacement procedure.

STRUT

REPLACE

1. Raise and support vehicle, then remove front tire and wheel assembly.
2. Remove nut and stud from bracket and separate link from strut using a wrench hold front stabilizer shaft link stud.
3. Remove wheel speed sensor from steering knuckle, then position sensor aside.
4. Remove front brake hose bolt and hose from bracket on strut, then position hose and bolt aside.
5. Loosen nuts on lower side of strut assembly, do not remove bolts.
6. Partially lower vehicle, then remove nuts and bolts from top of strut.
7. Remove nuts and bolts from lower side of strut.
8. Remove strut assembly from vehicle.
9. Reverse procedure to install.

STRUT SERVICE

1. Remove strut as outlined under "Strut, Replace."
2. Compress spring slightly using strut holding/spring compression tool No. J 45400, or equivalent.
3. Remove strut mount cover, then the strut mount nuts.
4. Remove seal, then the spring seat and strut shield.
5. Remove spring, then the strut bumper and spring lower insulator.
6. Remove the absorber portion of the strut.
7. Reverse procedure to install.

CONTROL ARM

REPLACE

1. Install engine support fixture.
2. Raise and support vehicle, then remove tire and wheel assembly.
3. Remove nuts from studs, then separate links from front struts.
4. Remove engine splash shields.
5. Remove lower control arm mounting nuts and bolts.
6. Use wire to suspend steering gear.
7. Remove mounting bolts, nuts and support crossmember with a jack.
8. Lower jack and crossmember.
9. Remove mounting bolts, nuts and control arm.
10. Reverse procedure to install.

STEERING KNUCKLE

REPLACE

1. Raise and support vehicle, then remove tire and wheel assembly.
2. Remove wheel speed sensor from steering knuckle, then position sensor aside.
3. Remove drive shaft nut from drive axle with an assistant holding brake pedal.

4. Remove nuts and bolt from lower control arm.
5. Remove caliper housing and bracket. Suspend them with suitable wire or rope.
6. Carefully remove brake rotor. Avoid damaging speed sensor rotor, boot and inner oil seal.
7. Loosen nuts on lower side of strut. Do not remove bolts.
8. Remove outer tie rod cotter pin and nut, then separate tie rod using separator tool No. J 6627-A, or equivalent.
9. Remove strut lower nuts and bolts.
10. Remove steering knuckle from strut.
11. Remove front wheel bearing and disc brake shield as outlined under "Wheel Hub, Replace."
12. Remove steering knuckle cotter pin and ball stud nut.
13. Remove ball joint from steering knuckle using tool No. J 24319-B or equivalent.
14. Reverse procedure to install.

STABILIZER BAR
REPLACE

1. Install engine support fixture.
2. Raise and support vehicle, then remove tire and wheel assembly.
3. Remove nuts from studs, then separate links from front struts.
4. Remove engine splash shields.
5. Remove lower control arm mounting nuts and bolts.
6. Use wire to suspend steering gear.
7. Remove mounting bolts, nuts and support crossmember with a jack.
8. Lower jack and crossmember.
9. Remove nuts, then the stabilizer shaft links from stabilizer shaft.
10. Remove stabilizer shaft clamps, then the stabilizer shaft insulators.
11. Remove stabilizer shaft from crossmember.
12. Reverse procedure to install.

TIE ROD END
REPLACE

1. Raise and support vehicle, then remove tire and wheel assembly.
2. Remove cotter pin from outer tie rod nut, then the outer tie rod nut.

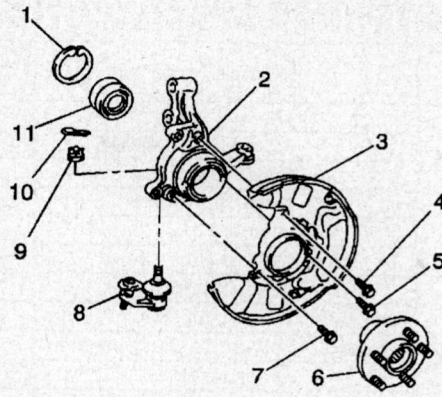

1. Bearing retainer
2. Steering knuckle
3. Brake shield
4. Bolt
5. Bolt
6. Axle hub
7. Bolt
8. Ball stub
9. Ball stud castle nut
10. Cotter pin
11. Hub bearing

ARM66GC000000100

Fig. 1   Exploded view of hub & bearing assembly

3. Separate outer tie rod from knuckle using tool No. J 6627-A or equivalent.
4. Place match marks on inner tie rod, lock nut and outer tie rod.
5. Loosen lock nut, then remove outer tie rod from inner tie rod.
6. Reverse procedure to install.

POWER STEERING GEAR
REPLACE

1. Ensure front wheels are in a straight ahead position and remove ignition key.
2. Move silencer pad away from steering column.
3. Place match marks on steering shaft coupling and on intermediate shaft.
4. Loosen upper coupling bolt, then remove lower coupling bolt.

5. Remove steering column hole cover from bulkhead.
6. Install a suitable engine support fixture tool, then raise and support vehicle.
7. Remove front tire and wheel assemblies, then the engine splash shields.
8. Remove tie rod ends as outlined under "Tie Rod End, Replace."
9. Place a drain pan under vehicle, then remove pressure and return pipes from steering gear.
10. Remove bolt and pipe bracket from steering gear.
11. Remove nuts from studs, then separate link from front struts.
12. Remove front suspension brace.
13. Remove suspension crossmember, transaxle support, control arms and stabilizer shaft as unit.
14. Remove engine rear mount insulator, then the bracket from crossmember.
15. Place match marks on intermediate shaft and steering gear.
16. Remove retaining bolt and intermediate shaft.
17. Remove retaining bolts, then the steering gear from crossmember.
18. Reverse procedure to install.

POWER STEERING PUMP
REPLACE

1. Siphon as much power steering fluid from reservoir as possible.
2. Raise and support vehicle, then remove tire and wheel assemblies.
3. Remove engine splash shields, then release tensioner and remove drive belt.
4. Loosen hose clamp on power steering pump inlet hose and remove hose from pump.
5. Remove bolt from power steering pump outlet pipe bracket, then the outlet pipe fitting from pump.
6. Disconnect power steering pressure switch connector.
7. Remove nuts and bolt from power steering pump front bracket, then power steering pump.
8. Remove rear bracket from pump.
9. **On AWD models,** remove heat shield from pump.
10. **On all models,** reverse procedure to install.

TIGHTENING SPECIFICATIONS

Year	Component	Torque Ft. Lbs.
2004–08	Brake Hose Clamp	21
	Brake Shield	73①
	Control Arm To Lower Ball Joint	66
	Crossmember Center	38
	Crossmember Front Corner	83
	Crossmember Rear Corner	116
	Driveshaft Nut	159
	Lower Ball Joint To Steering Knuckle	76
	Lower Control Arm To Crossmember	101
	Outer Tie Rod	36
	Power Steering Gear FWD	43
	Power Steering Gear AWD	94
	Stabilizer Shaft Insulator Clamp	14
	Stabilizer Shaft Link Nut	55
	Steering Column Intermediate Shaft	26
	Steering Shaft Coupling	26
	Strut Mount To Absorber Shaft Nut	35
	Strut To Strut Tower	29
	Strut To Steering Knuckle	162
	Trans Support Bolts	38
	Wheel Lug Nuts	76

① — Inch lbs.

Wheel Alignment

INDEX

	Page No.
Front Wheel Alignment	11-27
Camber	11-27
Caster	11-27
Toe-In	11-27

	Page No.
Precautions	11-27
Air Bag Systems	11-27
Preliminary Inspection	11-27
Rear Wheel Alignment	11-27

	Page No.
Camber & Toe Adjustment	11-27
AWD	11-27
Wheel Alignment Specifications	11-2

PRECAUTIONS

Air Bag Systems

Refer to "Air Bag System Precautions" in the front of this manual for system disarming and arming procedures.

PRELIMINARY INSPECTION

Steering and vibration problems are not always caused by improper alignment. They may also be caused by wheel and tire imbalance or other factors. To ensure proper alignment readings, the following inspections should be done and corrections made before inspecting caster, camber or toe:

1. Inspect tires for proper inflation pressures and even tread wear.
2. Inspect wheel bearings for looseness.
3. Inspect ball joints and tie rod ends for excessive looseness.
4. Inspect steering gear operation and mounting.
5. Inspect operation of struts.
6. Inspect control arms.
7. Inspect hub and bearing assemblies for excessive wear.

FRONT WHEEL ALIGNMENT

Caster

Caster cannot be adjusted. Should caster be out of specification, locate the cause

first. If components are damaged, bent, loose, dented or worn, they should be replaced. To prevent an improper caster reading, jounce the bumper three times before inspection.

Camber

1. Estimate amount camber must be adjusted.
2. Select proper combination of bolts, **Fig. 1.**
3. To move camber .25°, install bolt No. 1 in upper position and bolt No. 2 in lower position.
4. To move camber .50°, install bolt No. 1 in upper position and bolt No. 3 in lower position.
5. To move camber .75°, install bolt No. 1 in upper position and bolt No. 4 in lower position.
6. To move camber 1.00°, install bolt No. 2 in upper position and bolt No. 4 in lower position.
7. To move camber 1.25°, install bolt No. 3 in upper position and bolt No. 4 in lower position.
8. To move camber 1.50°, install bolt No. 4 in upper position and bolt No. 4 in lower position.
9. Install bolts, inspect alignment and adjust as required.

Toe-In

1. Ensure steering wheel is in straight-ahead position.
2. Remove clamp from steering gear boot.
3. Rotate inner tie rod to adjust toe to

specifications, **Fig. 2.**
4. Ensure number of threads visible on righthand inner tie rod is same as number of threads on lefthand inner tie rod.
5. Tighten nut to the outer tie rod.
6. **Torque** tie rod locking nut to 55 ft. lbs.
7. Measure alignment and adjust toe if required.
8. Ensure boots are not twisted, then install clamps to steering gear boots.

REAR WHEEL ALIGNMENT

Camber & Toe Adjustment

AWD

1. Loosen nut on upper control arm cam bolt.
2. Loosen nut on lower control arm cam bolt.
3. Rotate cam bolts to adjust camber and toe to specification.
4. Measure distance from lower lefthand control arm bracket to righthand rear crossmember bolt.
5. Measure distance from lower righthand control arm bracket to lefthand rear crossmember bolt, **Fig. 3.**
6. Ensure difference between measurements "a" and "b" is within specifications.
7. Tighten nuts on control arm cam bolts, then **torque** to 55 ft. lbs.
8. Inspect alignment, then adjust rear camber and toe if required.

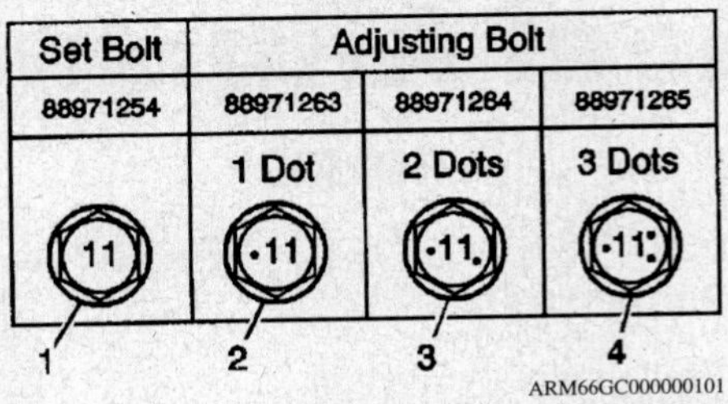

Set Bolt	Adjusting Bolt		
88971254	88971263	88971264	88971265
	1 Dot	2 Dots	3 Dots
(11)	(·11)	(·11·)	(·11·)
1	2	3	4

ARM66GC000000101

Fig. 1   Front camber adjustment bolts

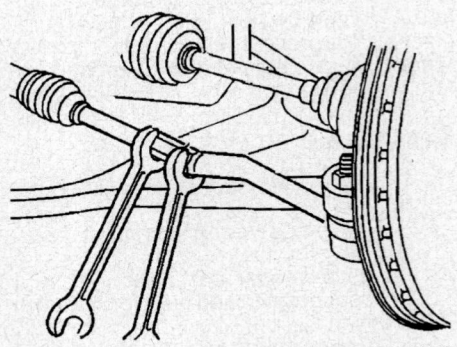

ARM66GC000000102

Fig. 2   Front toe adjustment

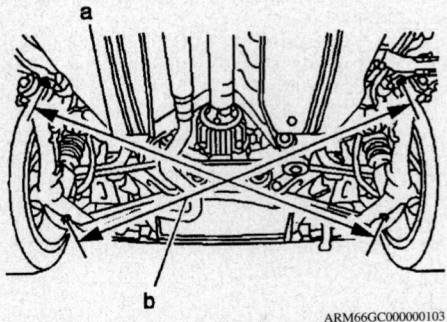

ARM66GC000000103

Fig. 3   Rear camber & toe adjustment

SATURN

NOTE: Refer To The Rear Of This Manual For Vehicle Manufacturer's Special Tool Suppliers.

INDEX OF SERVICE OPERATIONS

Page No.

AIR BAG SYSTEM
PRECAUTIONS 0-18
BRAKES
  Anti-Lock Brakes (Volume 2).. 6-1
  Disc Brakes.................. 22-1
  Drum Brakes 23-1
  Hydraulic Brake Systems 24-1
  Power Brake Units........... 25-1
COMPUTER RELEARN
PROCEDURE 0-31
ELECTRICAL
  Air Bag System (Volume 2) ... 4-1
  Air Conditioning.............. 16-1
  Alternator, Replace 12-11
  Alternators 19-1
  Blower Motor, Replace........ 12-17
  Cabin Air Filter, Replace 12-19
  Clutch Start Switch, Replace . 12-14
  Coil Pack, Replace 12-13
  Cooling Fans 17-1
  Cruise Control (Volume 2) ... 2-1
  Dash Gauges (Volume 2) 1-1
  Dash Panel Service
  (Volume 2).................. 5-1
  Evaporator Core, Replace 12-19
  Fuel Pump Relay Location.... 12-9
  Fuse Panel & Flasher
  Location 12-9
  Generator With Starter,
  Replace 12-12
  Headlamp Switch, Replace ... 12-15
  Heater Core, Replace......... 12-18
  Ignition Coil, Replace 12-13
  Ignition Lock, Replace 12-13
  Ignition Switch, Replace 12-14
  Instrument Cluster, Replace... 12-15
  Multi-Function Switch,
  Replace 12-15
  Neutral Safety Switch,
  Replace 12-14
  Passive Restraint Systems
  (Volume 2).................. 4-1
  Precautions 12-9
  Radio, Replace 12-16
  Relay Center Location 12-9
  Speed Controls (Volume 2) ... 2-1
  Starter Motors 18-1
  Starter, Replace 12-10
  Steering Columns............ 20-1
  Steering Wheel, Replace 12-15
  Stop Light Switch, Replace ... 12-15
  Technical Service Bulletins.... 12-20
  Turn Signal Switch, Replace .. 12-15
  Wiper Motor, Replace........ 12-16
  Wiper Switch, Replace 12-17
  Wiper Systems (Volume 2).... 3-1
  Wiper Transmission, Replace . 12-17
ELECTRICAL SYMBOL
IDENTIFICATION 0-63
FRONT DRIVE AXLES 26-1
FRONT SUSPENSION &
STEERING
  Ball Joint, Replace...........12-101
  Ball Joint Inspection 12-101

Page No.

  Coil Spring, Replace.........12-101
  Control Arm, Replace 12-102
  Control Arm Bushing,
  Replace 12-103
  Hub & Bearing, Replace 12-100
  Hub & Bearing Service........12-101
  Power Steering 21-1
  Power Steering Gear,
  Replace 12-104
  Power Steering Pump,
  Replace 12-105
  Power Steering System
  Bleed 12-106
  Precautions 12-99
  Stabilizer Bar, Replace.......12-103
  Steering Columns............ 20-1
  Steering Knuckle, Replace 12-103
  Strut, Replace 12-101
  Strut Service................12-102
  Technical Service Bulletins....12-106
  Tension Strut, Replace.......12-103
  Tie Rod, Replace 12-104
  Tightening Specifications......12-108
  Wheel Hub & Steering
  Knuckle, Replace............12-100
NON-STANDARD TIRE &
WHEEL SIZE
ADJUSTMENT TO RIDE
HEIGHT SPECIFICATIONS
& TIRE SIZE CHART 0-61
REAR AXLE &
SUSPENSION
  Adjustment Link, Replace 12-95
  Ball Joint, Replace............ 12-94
  Coil Spring, Replace.......... 12-93
  Control Arm, Replace 12-94
  Differential Carrier, Replace ... 12-92
  Hub & Bearing, Replace 12-92
  Knuckle, Replace 12-95
  Precautions 12-91
  Propeller Shaft, Replace 12-92
  Rear Axle Shaft, Replace 12-92
  Shock Absorber, Replace 12-93
  Stabilizer Bar, Replace........ 12-95
  Strut, Replace 12-93
  Strut Service................ 12-93
  Suspension Insulator,
  Replace 12-94
  Suspension Support, Replace. 12-94
  Tightening Specifications...... 12-98
  Toe Link, Replace 12-95
  Trailing Arm, Replace 12-95
SERVICE REMINDER &
WARNING LAMP RESET
PROCEDURES 0-34
SPECIFICATIONS
  Fluid Capacities & Cooling
  System Data................. 12-7
  Front Wheel Alignment
  Specifications................ 12-4
  General Engine
  Specifications................ 12-3
  Lubricant Data............... 12-7

Page No.

  Rear Wheel Alignment
  Specifications................ 12-5
  Tune Up Specifications 12-3
  Vehicle Ride Height
  Specifications................ 12-5
TIRE PRESSURE
MONITORING SYSTEM 20-1
VEHICLE
IDENTIFICATION 0-1
VEHICLE LIFT POINTS 0-51
VEHICLE MAINTENANCE
SCHEDULES 0-73
WHEEL ALIGNMENT
  Front Wheel Alignment........12-109
  Preliminary Inspection 12-109
  Rear Wheel Alignment 12-110
  Wheel Alignment
  Specifications................ 12-4
WIRE COLOR CODE
IDENTIFICATION 0-63
2.0L VIN P ENGINE
  Camshaft, Replace 12-23
  Compression Pressure....... 12-21
  Cooling System Bleed 12-25
  Crankshaft Rear Oil Seal,
  Replace 12-25
  Cylinder Head, Replace....... 12-22
  Engine Rebuilding
  Specifications................ 29-1
  Engine, Replace 12-21
  Engine Mount, Replace 12-21
  Exhaust Manifold, Replace.... 12-22
  Front Cover, Replace 12-22
  Fuel Filter, Replace 12-26
  Fuel Pump, Replace 12-26
  Intake Manifold, Replace...... 12-22
  Main & Rod Bearings 12-24
  Oil Pan, Replace............. 12-25
  Oil Pump, Replace........... 12-25
  Oil Pump Service............ 12-25
  Piston & Rod Assembly 12-24
  Pistons, Pins & Rings........ 12-24
  Precautions 12-21
  Radiator, Replace............ 12-26
  Serpentine Drive Belt 12-25
  Supercharger, Replace 12-26
  Thermostat, Replace.......... 12-25
  Tightening Specifications...... 12-27
  Timing Chain, Replace........ 12-23
  Valve Adjustment 12-22
2.0L VIN X ENGINE
  Balance Shaft, Replace 12-35
  Camshaft, Replace 12-34
  Crankshaft Damper, Replace.. 12-32
  Crankshaft Rear Oil Seal,
  Replace 12-35
  Crankshaft Seal, Replace 12-35
  Cylinder Head, Replace....... 12-31
  Engine Rebuilding
  Specifications................ 29-1
  Engine, Replace 12-29
  Engine Mount, Replace 12-29
  Exhaust Manifold, Replace.... 12-31
  Front Cover, Replace 12-33

	Page No.
Front Cover Seal, Replace....	12-33
Fuel Pump, Replace	12-36
Hydraulic Lifters, Replace.....	12-32
Intake Manifold, Replace......	12-31
Main & Rod Bearings	12-35
Oil Cooler, Replace	12-35
Oil Pan, Replace..............	12-35
Oil Pump, Replace.............	12-35
Oil Pump Service	12-35
Precautions..................	12-29
Radiator, Replace.............	12-36
Rocker Arms.................	12-32
Serpentine Drive Belt	12-36
Thermostat, Replace..........	12-36
Tightening Specifications......	12-38
Timing Chain, Replace........	12-33
Turbocharger, Replace........	12-36
Valve Adjustment	12-32
Valve Clearance Specifications	12-32
Valve Cover, Replace..........	12-32
Water Pump, Replace	12-36

2.2L ENGINE
Camshaft, Replace	12-43
Compression Pressure	12-39
Cooling System Bleed	12-44
Crankshaft Damper, Replace..	12-42
Crankshaft Rear Oil Seal, Replace	12-43
Crankshaft Seal, Replace	12-43
Cylinder Head, Replace.......	12-41
Engine Rebuilding Specifications	29-1
Engine, Replace	12-40
Engine Mount, Replace	12-39
Exhaust Manifold, Replace....	12-41
Front Cover, Replace	12-43
Fuel Filter, Replace	12-47
Fuel Pump, Replace	12-45
Intake Manifold, Replace......	12-41
Main & Rod Bearings	12-43
Oil Pan, Replace..............	12-43
Oil Pump, Replace.............	12-44
Oil Pump Service	12-44
Piston & Rod Assembly	12-43
Pistons, Pins & Rings	12-43
Precautions..................	12-39
Radiator, Replace.............	12-45
Serpentine Drive Belt	12-44
Technical Service Bulletins....	12-47
Thermostat, Replace..........	12-45
Tightening Specifications......	12-50
Timing Chain, Replace........	12-43
Valve Adjustment	12-42
Valve Guides	12-42
Water Pump, Replace	12-45

2.4L ENGINE
Balance Shaft, Replace.......	12-58
Camshaft, Replace	12-58
Crankshaft Balancer, Replace.	12-57
Crankshaft Rear Oil Seal, Replace	12-58
Crankshaft Seal, Replace	12-58
Cylinder Head, Replace.......	12-56
Engine Rebuilding	

	Page No.
Specifications.................	29-1
Engine, Replace	12-52
Engine Mount, Replace	12-52
Exhaust Manifold, Replace....	12-56
Front Cover, Replace	12-57
Fuel Filter, Replace	12-61
Fuel Pump, Replace	12-60
Hydraulic Lash Adjusters, Replace	12-57
Intake Manifold, Replace.....	12-55
Main & Rod Bearings	12-58
Oil Pan, Replace..............	12-58
Oil Pump, Replace.............	12-59
Oil Pump Service	12-59
Piston & Rod Assembly	12-58
Precautions..................	12-51
Radiator, Replace.............	12-60
Serpentine Drive Belt	12-59
Thermostat, Replace..........	12-59
Tightening Specifications......	12-62
Timing Chain, Replace........	12-57
Valve Cover, Replace..........	12-57
Water Pump, Replace	12-60

3.0L ENGINE
Belt Tension Data.............	12-68
Camshaft, Replace	12-66
Camshaft Lobe Lift Specifications	12-65
Compression Pressure	12-63
Cooling System Bleed	12-68
Crankshaft Rear Oil Seal, Replace	12-67
Cylinder Head, Replace.......	12-64
Engine Rebuilding Specifications	29-1
Engine, Replace	12-63
Engine Mount, Replace	12-63
Exhaust Manifold, Replace....	12-64
Front Cover, Replace	12-65
Fuel Filter, Replace	12-69
Fuel Pump, Replace	12-68
Intake Manifold, Replace.....	12-64
Main & Rod Bearings	12-67
Oil Pan, Replace..............	12-67
Oil Pump, Replace.............	12-67
Piston & Rod Assembly	12-67
Pistons, Pins & Rings	12-67
Precautions..................	12-63
Radiator, Replace.............	12-68
Serpentine Drive Belt	12-68
Technical Service Bulletins....	12-69
Thermostat, Replace..........	12-68
Tightening Specifications......	12-70
Timing Belt, Replace..........	12-65
Valve Adjustment	12-65
Valve Cover, Replace..........	12-65
Water Pump, Replace	12-68

3.5L ENGINE
Camshaft, Replace	12-74
Camshaft Lobe Lift Specifications	12-74
Compression Pressure	12-71
Cooling System Bleed	12-76
Crankshaft Damper, Replace..	12-74
Crankshaft Rear Oil Seal,	

	Page No.
Replace	12-75
Crankshaft Seal, Replace	12-75
Cylinder Head, Replace.......	12-73
Engine Rebuilding Specifications.................	29-1
Engine, Replace	12-71
Engine Mount, Replace	12-71
Engine Mount Strut, Replace .	12-71
Exhaust Manifold, Replace....	12-72
Front Cover, Replace	12-74
Fuel Pump, Replace	12-76
Hydraulic Lifters, Replace.....	12-74
Intake Manifold, Replace......	12-72
Main & Rod Bearings	12-75
Oil Pan, Replace..............	12-75
Oil Pump, Replace.............	12-75
Oil Pump Service	12-76
Piston & Rod Assembly	12-75
Precautions..................	12-71
Push Rods	12-74
Radiator, Replace.............	12-76
Rocker Arms, Replace	12-74
Serpentine Drive Belt	12-76
Technical Service Bulletins....	12-76
Thermostat, Replace..........	12-76
Tightening Specifications......	12-78
Timing Chain, Replace........	12-74
Valve Adjustment	12-74
Valve Cover, Replace..........	12-73
Water Pump, Replace	12-76

3.6L ENGINE
Camshaft, Replace	12-83
Compression Pressure	12-79
Cooling System Bleed	12-84
Crankshaft Damper, Replace..	12-81
Crankshaft Front Oil Seal, Replace	12-83
Crankshaft Rear Oil Seal, Replace	12-83
Cylinder Head, Replace.......	12-80
Engine Rebuilding Specifications.................	29-1
Engine, Replace	12-80
Engine Mount, Replace	12-79
Engine Mount Strut, Replace .	12-79
Exhaust Manifold, Replace....	12-80
Front Cover, Replace	12-81
Fuel Pump, Replace	12-85
Intake Manifold, Replace......	12-80
Main & Rod Bearings	12-83
Oil Pan, Replace..............	12-84
Oil Pump, Replace.............	12-84
Oil Pump Service	12-84
Piston & Rod Assembly	12-83
Pistons, Pins & Rings	12-83
Precautions..................	12-79
Radiator, Replace.............	12-85
Serpentine Drive Belt	12-84
Thermostat, Replace..........	12-84
Tightening Specifications......	12-90
Timing Chain, Replace........	12-81
Valve Adjustment	12-81
Valve Cover, Replace..........	12-80
Water Pump, Replace	12-84

Specifications

GENERAL ENGINE SPECIFICATIONS

Engine/Liter (VIN)①	Fuel Injection System	Bore & Stoke	Compression Ratio	Net H.P. @ RPM	Maximum Torque, Ft. Lbs. @ RPM	Normal Oil Pressure, psi
2004						
2.0L (P)	SPFI	3.39 × 3.39	9.5	205 @ 5,600	200 @ 4,400	50–80③
2.2L (F)	SPFI	3.39 × 3.72	10.0	135 @ 5200	142 @ 4400	65.0③
3.0L (R)	SPFI	3.39 × 3.34	10.0	182 @ 6000	190 @ 3600	21.7②
2005						
2.0L (P)	SPFI	3.39 × 3.39	9.5	205 @ 5600	200 @ 4400	50–80③
2.2L (F)	SPFI	3.39 × 3.72	10.0	140 @ 5800	145 @ 4400	50–80③
3.0L (R)	SPFI	3.39 × 3.34	10.0	182 @ 5600	190 @ 3600	16②
2006						
2.0L (P)	SPFI	3.39 x 3.39	9.5	205 @ 5600	200 @ 4400	50–80③
2.2L (F)	SPFI	3.39 × 3.72	10.0	140 @ 5800	145 @ 4400	50–80③
2.4L (B)	SPFI	3.46 x 3.85	10.5	170 @ 6200	162 @ 5000	50–80③
2007						
2.0L (P)⑥	SPFI	3.39 x 3.39	9.5	205 @ 5600	200 @ 4400	50–80③
2.0L (X)⑦	SPFI	3.38 x 3.38	9.2	260 @ 5300	260 @ 2500–5250	50–80
2.2L (F)	SPFI	3.39 × 3.72	10.0	145 @ 5800	150 @ 4200	50–80③
2.4L (B)	SPFI	3.46 x 3.85	10.5	170 @ 6200	164 @ 4800	50–80③
3.5L (N)	SPFI	3.70 x 3.37	10.2	224 @ 5800	220 @ 4000	20④
3.6L (7)	SPFI	3.90 x 3.31	9.8	252 @ 6400	251 @ 3200	30–45⑤
2008						
2.0L (X)	SPFI	3.38 x 3.38	9.2	260 @ 5300	260 @ 2500–5250	50–80
2.4L (B)	SPFI	3.46 x 3.85	10.0	170 @ 6200	164 @ 4800	50–80③
3.5L (N)	SPFI	3.70 x 3.37	10.2	224 @ 5800	220 @ 4000	20④
3.6L (7)	SPFI	3.90 x 3.31	9.8	252 @ 6400	251 @ 3200	30–45⑤

SPFI — Sequential-Point Fuel Injection
① — Eighth digit of Vehicle Identification Number (VIN) denotes engine code.
② — At idle.
③ — At 1000 RPM
④ — At 2000 RPM
⑤ — 1850 RPM w/engine at operating temperature.
⑥ — ION.
⑦ — SKY.

TUNE UP SPECIFICATIONS

Year & Engine/ Liter (VIN) ①	Spark Plug Gap	Ignition Timing, Degrees, BTDC				Curb Idle Speed②		Fast Idle Speed②		Fuel Pump Press- ure, psi.	Valve Lash, Inch
		Firing Order	Man. Trans.	Auto. Trans.	Mark	Man. Trans.	Auto. Trans.	Man. Trans.	Auto. Trans.		
2004–05											
2.0L (P)	.039	⑪	⑤	⑤	⑥	⑦	⑦	⑦	⑦	50–60⑨	③
2.2L (F)	.042	④	⑤	⑤	⑥	850–875⑦	750–775N⑦	⑦	⑦	50–80⑨	③
3.0L (R)	.040	⑩	—	⑤	⑥	—	750–775N⑦	—	⑦	39–49⑨	③
2006											
2.0L (P)	.040	⑪	⑤	⑤	⑥	⑦	⑦	⑦	⑦	50–60⑨	③
2.2L (F)	.042	④	⑤	⑤	⑥	850–875⑦	750–775N⑦	⑦	⑦	50–80⑨	③
2.4L (B)	.042	⑪	⑤	⑤	⑥	⑧	⑧	⑧	⑧	50–60⑨	③
2007											
2.0L (P)	.040	⑪	⑤	⑤	⑥	⑦	⑦	⑦	⑦	50–60⑨	③
2.0L (X)	.35	⑪	⑤	⑤	⑥	⑬	⑬	⑬	⑬	50–60	③
2.2L (F)	.042	④	⑤	⑤	⑥	850–875⑦	750–775N⑦	⑦	⑦	50–80⑨	③

Continued

TUNE UP SPECIFICATIONS—Continued

Year & Engine/ Liter (VIN) ①	Spark Plug Gap	Ignition Timing, Degrees, BTDC				Curb Idle Speed②		Fast Idle Speed②		Fuel Pump Pressure, psi.	Valve Lash, Inch
		Firing Order	Man. Trans.	Auto. Trans.	Mark	Man. Trans.	Auto. Trans.	Man. Trans.	Auto. Trans.		
2007											
2.4L (B)	.042	⑪	⑤	⑤	⑥	⑧	⑧	⑧	⑧	50–60⑨	③
3.5L (N)	.0431	1-2-3-4-5-6	—	⑫	⑥	—	⑦	—	⑦	50–60	③
3.6L (7)	.040	1-2-3-4-5-6	⑫	⑫	⑥	⑦	⑦	⑦	⑦	50–60	③
2008											
2.0L (X)	.35	⑪	⑤	⑤	⑥	⑬	⑬	⑬	⑬	50–60	③
2.4L (B)	.042	⑪	⑤	⑤	⑥	⑧	⑧	⑧	⑧	50–60⑨	③
3.5L (N)	.0431	1-2-3-4-5-6	—	⑫	⑥	—	⑦	—	⑦	50–60	③
3.6L (7)	.040	1-2-3-4-5-6	⑫	⑫	⑥	⑦	⑦	⑦	⑦	50–60	③

BTDC — Before Top Dead Center
D — Drive
N — Neutral
① — Eighth digit of Vehicle Identification Number (VIN) denotes engine code.
② — When adjusting idle speed, set parking brake & block drive wheels. Where two idle speeds are listed, higher speed is w/idle or air conditioning solenoid energized.
③ — Equipped w/hydraulic valve lifters.
④ — Cylinder numbering from front of engine to rear 1, 2, 3, 4. Firing order 1-3-4-2. Refer to **Fig. A** for spark plug wire connections at coil unit.
⑤ — Equipped w/Distributorless Ignition System (DIS). No adjustment.
⑥ — Equipped w/crankshaft position sensor.

⑦ — Idle speed is controlled by Idle Air Control (IAC) valve or Idle Speed Control (ISC).
⑧ — Idle speed is controlled through Engine Control Module (ECM).
⑨ — Wrap shop towel around fuel pressure test port to prevent fuel spillage. Connect suitable fuel pressure gauge to fuel pressure test port. Energize fuel pump using a suitably programmed scan tool & inspect fuel pressure.
⑩ — 1-2-3-4-5-6.
⑪ — Cylinder numbering from front of engine to rear 1, 2, 3, 4. Firing order 1-3-4-2.
⑫ — Ignition timing is controlled by Powertrain Control Module (PCM).
⑬ — Idle speed is controlled by Throttle Actuator Control (TAC) motor.

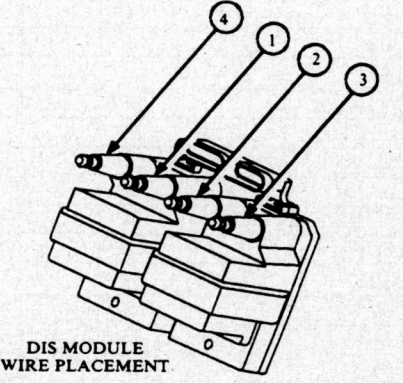

DIS MODULE WIRE PLACEMENT

G31139100019000X

Fig. A

FRONT WHEEL ALIGNMENT SPECIFICATIONS

Model	Caster Angle, Degrees①		Camber Angle, Degrees①		Total Toe, Degrees②		Ball Joint Wear
	Limits	Desired	Limits	Desired	Limits	Desired	
AURA	+2.35 to +3.85	+3.10	⑦	⑧	−.10 to +.30	+.20	③
ION⑤	+2.50 to +4.00④	+3.25④	−1.75 to −.25	−1.00	−.10 to +.30	+.20	③
ION ⑥	+2.85 to +4.35	+3.60④	−1.65 to −.15	−.90	−.10 to +.30	+.20	③
L-Series	+3.20 to +4.20④	+3.70④	−1.75 to −.50	−1.00	+.04 to +.36	+.20	③
SKY	+7.40 to +8.60	+ 8.00	-1.10 to + .10	-.50	−.10 to +.30	+.10	③

① — Cross camber, 0° (±1°).
② — Toe-In (+). Toe-Out (−).
③ — Refer to "Ball Joint Inspection" in "Front Suspension & Steering" section.
④ — Caster is not adjustable.
⑤ — Soft ride & handling ride suspensions.
⑥ — Sport & Tuner suspensions.
⑦ — Lefthand, -1.65° to -.15°; Righthand, -1.45° to +.05°
⑧ — Lefthand, -.90°; Righthand, -.70°.

REAR WHEEL ALIGNMENT SPECIFICATIONS

Model	Year	Camber Angle, Degrees		Total Toe, Degrees[1]	
		Limits	Desired	Limits	Desired
AURA	2007–08	-1.30 to -.30	-.80	0 to +.40	+.20
ION	2004	-.15 to -65	-1.4	0 to .50	+.20
	2005[2]	-.90 to -40	-1.15	-.30 to +.30	0
	2005[3]	-.55 to -05	-.80	-.05 to +.55	+.25
	2006–07	-.55 to -.05	-.80	-.05 to +.55	+.25
L-Series	2004–05	-1.50 to -.50	-1.0	+.13 to +.47	+.30
SKY	2007–08	-1.00 to 0	-.50	-.10 to +.10	+.10

① — Toe-In (+). Toe-Out (–).

② — Soft ride & handling ride suspensions.

③ — Sport & Tuner suspensions.

VEHICLE RIDE HEIGHT SPECIFICATIONS

Model	Year	Body Style	Manufacturer's Original Tire Size[3]	Front			Rear		
				Dim.	Specification		Dim.	Specification	
					Inches	mm		Inches	mm
AURA	2007–08	All	All	Z[12]	—	—	D[13]	—	—
ION	2004–05	Two-Door	P195/60R15[4]	J[8]	8.90	225	K[8]	9.20	234
				Z[9]	-.40	-10	D[10]	8.70	222
			P205/55R16[5]	J[8]	8.90	225	K[8]	9.20	234
				Z[9]	-.90	-22	D[10]	9.10	232
			P215/45R17[6]	J[8]	8.50	215	K[8]	8.80	224
				Z[9]	-1.10	-28	D[10]	9.00	230
		Four-Door	P185/70R14[4]	J[8]	8.90	225	K[8]	9.20	234
				Z[9]	-.30	-7	D[10]	8.60	220
			P195/60R15[4]	J[8]	8.90	225	K[8]	9.20	234
				Z[9]	-.40	-10	D[10]	8.70	222
			P205/55R16[4]	J[8]	8.90	225	K[8]	9.20	234
				Z[9]	-.90	-22	D[10]	9.10	232
	2006–07	Two-Door	P195/60R15[4]	J[8]	8.90	225	K[8]	9.20	234
				Z[9]	-.40	-10	D[10]	9.00	228
			P205/55R16[4]	J[8]	8.90	225	K[8]	9.20	234
				Z[9]	-.90	-22	D[10]	8.50	216
			P205/55R16[5]	J[8]	8.90	225	K[8]	9.20	234
				Z[9]	-.90	-22	D[10]	8.50	216
			P215/45R17[6]	J[8]	8.50	215	K[8]	8.80	224
				Z[9]	-1.10	-28	D[10]	8.90	226
		Four-Door	P195/60R15[4]	J[8]	8.90	225	K[8]	9.20	234
				Z[9]	-.40	-10	D[10]	9.00	228
			P205/55R16[4]	J[8]	8.90	225	K[8]	9.20	234
				Z[9]	-.90	-22	D[10]	8.50	216
			P205/55R16[5]	J[8]	8.90	225	K[8]	9.20	234
				Z[9]	-.90	-22	D[10]	8.50	216
L-Series[7]	2004–05	Sedan	—	E	20.80	529	F	24.40	620
		Wagon	—	E	20.80	529	F	16.00	407
SKY	2007–08	ALL	—	Z[14]	1.45	37	D[11]	2.44	62

A Dim. — Measurement From Front Wheel Opening to Inspection Point On Rocker Panel Flange

B Dim. — Measurement From Rear Wheel Opening to Inspection Point On Rocker Panel Flange

C Dim. — Distance from Front Rocker Flange Panel to Ground

D Dim. — ION: Distance from Bottom Edge Upper Spring Seat to Notch In Lower Spring Seat

D Dim. — SKY: Measure from Bottom of Strut to Support Surface Forward of Mounting Bolt

E Dim. — Measure from Bottom Center of Front Bumper

F Dim. — Measure from Bottom Center of Rear Bumper

J Dim. — Measure from Front Inboard Pinch-Weld Flange to Ground

K Dim. — Measure from Rear Inboard Pinch-Weld Flange to Ground

Z Dim. — ION & SKY: Measure from Cradle to Bottom of Front Ball Joint

Z Dim. — AURA: Measure from Bottom Edge of Support Flat to

Ground, then subtract Measurement from Bottom Edge of Lowest Point on Ball Stud to Ground.

Dim. Dimension

① — Measurement is with fuel, radiator coolant & engine oil full, spare tire, jack, hand tools & mats in designated positions & tires properly inflated.

② — L-Series, ± .98 inch (25 mm); ION & SKY, ± .39 inch (10 mm).

③ — See door sticker or inside of glove box for manufacturers original tire size specifications. If tires on vehicle do not match manufacturers original tire size & measurement is not within limits, refer to the "Non-Standard Tire & Wheel Size Adjustment To Ride Height Specification & Tire Size Adjustment Charts" in the front of this manual for approximate changes in ride height specifications.

④ — Soft Ride Suspension System.
⑤ — Handling Suspension System.
⑥ — Sport Suspension System.
⑦ — Refer to **Fig. A**
⑧ — Refer to **Fig. B**
⑨ — Refer to **Fig. C**
⑩ — Refer to **Fig. D**
⑪ — Refer to **Fig. F**
⑫ — Refer to **Fig. G**
⑬ — Refer to **Fig. H**
⑭ — Refer to **Fig. E**

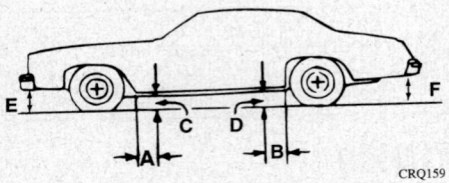

CRQ159

Fig. A

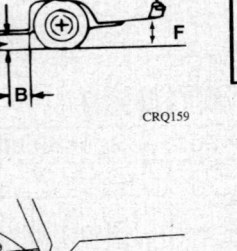

ARM66GC000000104

Fig. B   Dimensions J & K

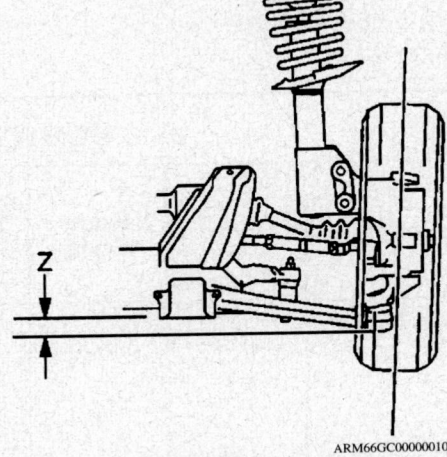

ARM66GC000000105

Fig. C   Dimension Z. ION

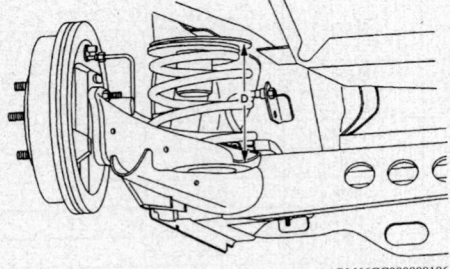

ARM66GC000000106

Fig. D   Dimension D. ION

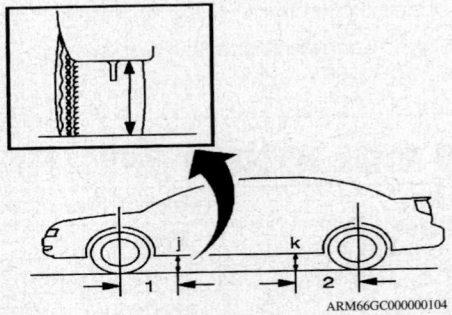

ARM0500000000919

Fig. E   Dimension Z. SKY

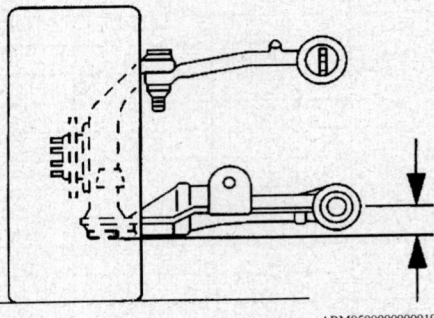

ARM0500000000920

Fig. F   Dimension D. SKY

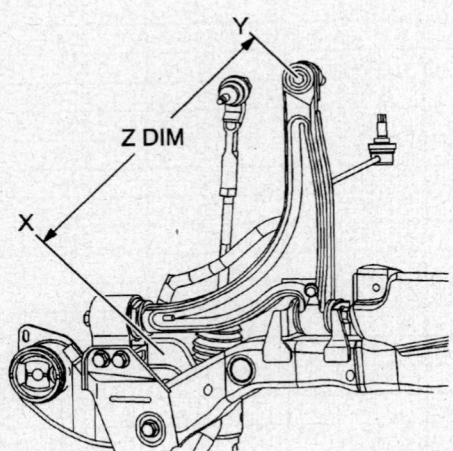

ARM0600000000654

Fig. G   Dimension Z. AURA

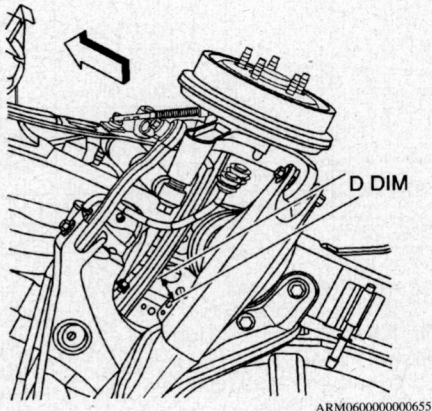

ARM0600000000655

Fig. H   Dimension D. AURA

FLUID CAPACITIES & COOLING SYSTEM DATA

Engine/ Liter ①	Cooling Capacity, Qts.	Coolant Type	Radiator Cap Relief Pressure, Lbs.	Thermo. Opening Temp., Deg. F	Fuel Tank, Gals.	Engine Oil Refill, Qts.③	Transaxle Oil		Rear Axle Oil, Qts.
							Manual, Pts.	Automatic, Qts.②	
2004–05									
2.0L	7.9⑥	DEX-COOL	13–17	194	13.5	6.0	3.6	⑤	—
2.2L	9.0	DEX-COOL	13–17	194	15.7	5.0	4.0	⑤	—
3.0L	10.2	DEX-COOL	20–21	188–196	15.7	5.0	—	⑤	—
2006									
2.0L	6.9⑥	DEX-COOL	13–17	194	13.5	6.0	④	⑤	—
2.2L	6.9	DEX-COOL	13–17	194	13.5	5.0	④	⑤	—
2.4L	9.3	DEX-COOL	—	190	13.5	5.0	④	⑤	—
2007									
2.0L (P)⑩	9.25⑪	DEX-COOL	13–17	194	13.0	6.0	④	⑤	—
2.0L (X)⑨	9.0	DEX-COOL	⑧	190	13.8	5.0	5.50	5.50	⑦
2.2L (F)	6.9	DEX-COOL	13–17	194	13.0	5.0	④	⑤	—
2.4L (B)	6.9	DEX-COOL	13–17	190	13.0	5.0	④	⑤	⑦
3.5L (N)	9.3	DEX-COOL	15	195	16.3	4.0	—	⑫	—
3.6L (7)	9.3	DEX-COOL	15	203	16.3	5.2	—	⑫	—
2008									
2.0L (X)⑨	9.0	DEX-COOL	⑧	190	13.8	5.0	5.50	5.50	⑦
2.4L (B)	6.9	DEX-COOL	13–17	190	13.0	5.0	④	⑤	⑦
3.5L (N)	9.3	DEX-COOL	15	195	16.3	4.0	—	⑫	—
3.6L (7)	9.3	DEX-COOL	15	203	16.3	5.2	—	⑫	—

① — Eighth digit of Vehicle Identification Number (VIN) denotes engine code.

② — Approximate, make final inspection w/dipstick.

③ — Additional oil may be required to bring oil level to full mark when changing oil filter.

④ — Getrag 5-Speed 1.8 qts.; MU3 2.0 qts.

⑤ — Bottom pan removal, 6.9 qts.; complete overhaul, 9.5 qts.; total capacity, 12.9 qts.

⑥ — Intercooler system, 2.0 qts.

⑦ — Drain & fill w/cover removed, 1.3 qts., plus 3.4 oz. limited slip addi-tive; using plug, 1.2 qts., plus 2.4 oz. limited slip additive.

⑧ — Refer to pressure cap for rated pressure.

⑨ — SKY.

⑩ — ION.

⑪ — Include intercooler circuit.

⑫ — Four-speed, 7.0 qts.; six-speed, 9.5 qts.

LUBRICANT DATA

Year	Model	Lubricant Type				
		Transaxle		Power Steering	Brake System	Hydraulic Clutch
		Manual	Automatic			
2004–08	All	①	③	②	DOT 3	DOT 3

① — DEXRON® III ATF meeting GM H Revision specification.

② — Must meet GM specification 9985010.

③ — DEXRON® VI ATF.

Electrical

NOTE: On Air Bag Equipped Models, Refer To "Air Bag System Precautions" Located In The Front Of This Manual For System Disarming & Arming Procedures.

NOTE: Refer To "Computer Relearn Procedures" Located In The Front Of This Manual When Battery Power To The Computer Has Been Interrupted.

NOTE: Prior To Performing Any Service Operations Listed In This Section, Consult The "Technical Service Bulletins" Section For Related Information.

INDEX

	Page No.
Air Bag System (Volume 2)	4-1
Air Conditioning	16-1
Alternator, Replace	12-11
AURA	12-11
3.5L Engine	12-11
3.6L Engine	12-11
ION	12-11
2.0L Engine	12-11
2.2L & 2.4L Engines	12-11
L-Series	12-11
2.2L Engine	12-11
3.0L Engine	12-11
SKY	12-12
Alternators	19-1
Blower Motor, Replace	12-17
AURA	12-17
ION	12-18
L-Series	12-18
SKY	12-18
Cabin Air Filter, Replace	12-19
ION	12-19
L-Series	12-19
Clutch Start Switch, Replace	12-14
Coil Pack, Replace	12-13
AURA	12-13
3.5L Engine	12-13
ION	12-13
2.2L Engine	12-13
L-Series	12-13
3.0L Engine	12-13
Cooling Fans	17-1
Cruise Control (Volume 2)	2-1
Dash Gauges (Volume 2)	1-1
Dash Panel Service (Volume 2)	5-1
Evaporator Core, Replace	12-19
AURA	12-19
ION	12-19
L-Series	12-19
SKY	12-19
Fuel Pump Relay Location	12-9
AURA	12-9
ION	12-9
L-Series	12-9
SKY	12-9
Fuse Panel & Flasher Location	12-9
AURA	12-9
ION	12-9
L-Series	12-9
SKY	12-9
Generator With Starter, Replace	12-12
AURA Hybrid	12-12
Headlamp Switch, Replace	12-15

	Page No.
Heater Core, Replace	12-18
AURA	12-18
ION	12-18
L-Series	12-18
SKY	12-19
Ignition Coil, Replace	12-13
AURA & L-Series	12-13
2.4L & 3.6L Engines	12-13
ION	12-13
2.0L Engine	12-13
2.4L Engine	12-13
SKY	12-13
Ignition Lock, Replace	12-13
AURA	12-13
ION	12-13
L-Series	12-13
SKY	12-13
Ignition Switch, Replace	12-14
AURA	12-14
ION	12-14
L-Series	12-14
SKY	12-14
Instrument Cluster, Replace	12-15
AURA	12-15
ION	12-16
L-Series	12-16
SKY	12-16
Multi-Function Switch, Replace	12-15
AURA	12-15
ION & L-Series	12-15
SKY	12-15
Neutral Safety Switch, Replace	12-14
AURA	12-14
Installation	12-14
Removal	12-14
ION	12-14
L-Series	12-14
Installation	12-14
Removal	12-14
Passive Restraint Systems (Volume 2)	4-1
Precautions	12-9
Air Bag Systems	12-9
Battery Ground Cable	12-9
Hybrid Battery Service	12-9
Connect	12-9
Disconnect	12-9
Radio, Replace	12-16
AURA	12-16
ION	12-16
L-Series	12-16
SKY	12-16
Relay Center Location	12-9
AURA	12-9

	Page No.
ION	12-10
L-Series	12-10
SKY	12-10
Speed Controls (Volume 2)	2-1
Starter Motors	18-1
Starter, Replace	12-10
AURA	12-10
2.4L Engine	12-10
3.5L Engine	12-10
3.6L Engine	12-10
ION	12-10
2.0L Engine	12-10
2.2L & 2.4L Engines	12-10
L-Series	12-10
2.2L Engine	12-10
3.0L Engine	12-11
SKY	12-11
Steering Columns	20-1
Steering Wheel, Replace	12-15
AURA	12-15
ION	12-15
L-Series	12-15
SKY	12-15
Stop Light Switch, Replace	12-15
AURA	12-15
ION & L-Series	12-15
SKY	12-15
Installation	12-15
Removal	12-15
Technical Service Bulletins	12-20
Intermittent No Crank/No Start	12-20
2004–06 ION	12-20
2006–07 ION	12-20
All Models w/Side-Mounted Battery Terminals	12-20
Key Sticks, Binds, Is Hard To Insert, Or Will Not Rotate	12-20
2004–05 ION	12-20
Turn Signal Switch, Replace	12-15
Wiper Motor, Replace	12-16
AURA	12-16
ION	12-17
L-Series	12-17
SKY	12-17
Wiper Switch, Replace	12-17
AURA & SKY	12-17
ION	12-17
L-Series	12-17
Wiper Systems (Volume 2)	3-1
Wiper Transmission, Replace	12-17
AURA	12-17
ION	12-17
L-Series & SKY	12-17

PRECAUTIONS

Air Bag Systems

Refer to "Air Bag System Precautions" in the front of this manual for system disarming and arming procedures.

Battery Ground Cable

Prior to service, disconnect battery ground cable and isolate as required.

Hybrid Battery Service

DISCONNECT

To help avoid personal injury, always ensure the ignition switch is in the OFF position and the ignition key has been removed prior to working on any 36V components. After the key has been removed, disconnect the battery ground cable and then open the generator battery disconnect control module cover. After waiting for at least 5 minutes, measure the voltage potential using a DMM between the following: 36V positive and battery ground cables; 36V positive battery cable and vehicle ground; 36V battery ground cable and vehicle ground. All measured voltage levels must be below 3 volts.

1. Remove ignition key from ignition switch.
2. Secure ignition key to ensure that key CANNOT be installed without your knowledge.
3. Disconnect 12 volt battery ground cable.
4. Fold down both rear seat backs, then carefully lift up on load floor rear compartment cover at retaining clip locations, **Fig. 1.**
5. Tilt load floor rear compartment cover towards rear of vehicle slightly, disengage tabs and remove load floor rear compartment cover. **To avoid personal injury, be careful when working in vicinity of generator battery disconnect control module. Internal components will still be live, 36V potential, even when cover has been opened or removed.**
6. Remove generator battery disconnect control module cover bolt, **Fig. 2.**
7. Open and slide generator battery disconnect control module cover to right, removing cover. **Wait at least 5 minutes in order to allow generator control module capacitors to discharge.**
8. **Never assume battery pack is disabled when generator battery disconnect control module cover is opened. Generator battery will have to be checked for voltage potential using a voltmeter first**
9. Set voltmeter to DC voltage and measure vehicle 12-volt battery voltage (at 12-volt positive jumper location and battery ground cable).

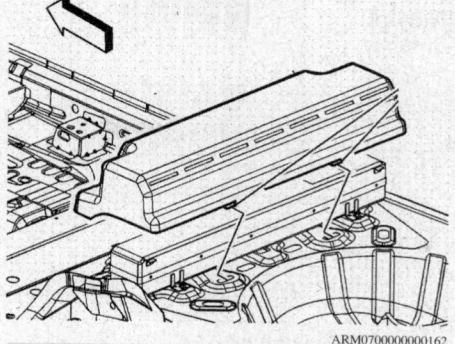

Fig. 1   Rear hybrid battery compartment. AURA

ARM0700000000162

10. Meter should read greater than 12 volts DC.
11. To ensure generator battery has been disabled, inspect generator battery for voltage potential as follows:
    a. Refer to **Fig. 3** for voltage measurement locations.
    b. Measure from positive stud to negative stud, voltage should be less than 3 volts.
    c. Measure from positive stud to vehicle chassis ground, voltage should be less than 3 volts.
    d. Measure from negative stud to vehicle chassis ground, voltage should be less than 3 volts.
12. After verifying there is no voltage present, vehicle is now safe to work on.

CONNECT

1. Install and close generator battery disconnect control module cover.
2. Install generator battery cover bolt and **torque** to 89 inch lbs.
3. Tilt load floor rear compartment cover towards rear of vehicle slightly in order to insert tabs into battery tray rear support.
4. Set load floor rear compartment cover down, ensure retaining clips align to proper locations, carefully push down to secure cover.
5. Place rear seats backs to their proper positions.
6. Connect 12 volt battery ground cable.

FUSE PANEL & FLASHER LOCATION

AURA

The underhood fuse block is located on the lefthand side of the engine compartment. The rear fuse block is located on the rear lefthand side of the passenger compartment, behind the lefthand rear wheelwell.

Turn signal and hazard flasher operation is controlled by the Body Control Module (BCM). The BCM is located under the righthand side of the center console, near the instrument panel.

ION

The interior fuse panel is part of the Body Control Module (BCM) which is located behind the center of the instrument panel, under the radio. The underhood fuse block is located on the lefthand side of the engine compartment, near the strut tower.

Turn signal and hazard flasher operation is controlled by the BCM. The BCM is located behind the center of the instrument panel, under the radio.

L-Series

The underhood fuse block is located on the rear lefthand side of the engine compartment. The lefthand instrument panel fuse block is located behind the lefthand side kick panel. The righthand instrument panel fuse block is located behind the righthand side kick panel.

The hazard switch, located in the center of the instrument panel, controls turn signal and hazard lamp flashing.

SKY

The underhood fuse block is located in the righthand rear corner of the engine compartment.

Turn signal and hazard flasher operation is controlled by the BCM. The BCM is located behind the righthand side of the instrument panel, under the footwell carpet area.

FUEL PUMP RELAY LOCATION

AURA

The fuel pump relay is located on the rear lefthand side of the passenger compartment, in the rear fuse block.

ION

The fuel pump relay is located in the instrument panel fuse block, which is part of the Body Control Module (BCM) which is located behind the center of the instrument panel, under the radio.

L-Series

The fuel pump relay is located behind the lefthand side kick panel, on the lefthand instrument panel fuse block.

SKY

The fuel pump relay is located in the underhood fuse block.

RELAY CENTER LOCATION

AURA

Relays are located in all the fuse and junction blocks, refer to "Fuse Panel & Flasher Location" for relay center locations.

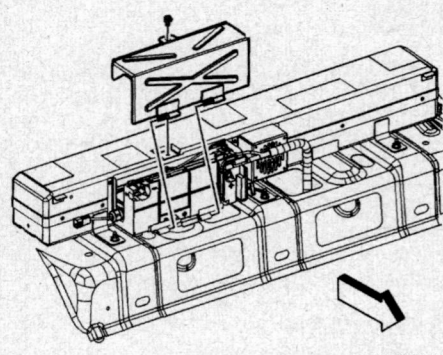

ARM0700000000163

Fig. 2 Disconnect control module cover. AURA Hybrid

ION

Relays are in the located in both the underhood junction block and the instrument panel junction block. Refer to "Fuse Panel & Flasher Location" for junction block locations.

L-Series

Relays are located in three fuse panels. Refer to "Fuse Panel & Flasher Location" for fuse block locations.

SKY

Relays are located in the underhood fuse blocks and BCM. Refer to "Fuse Panel & Flasher Location" for fuse block locations.

STARTER
REPLACE
AURA
2.4L ENGINE

1. Raise and support vehicle.
2. Disconnect engine wiring harness electrical connector from generator control module coolant pump.
3. Remove generator control module coolant pump bolt.
4. Remove generator control module coolant pump (with the hoses attached) from oil pan. Reposition and secure control module coolant pump aside.
5. Disconnect engine wiring harness electrical connector from starter.
6. Remove positive battery cable to starter motor retaining nut, then the cable lead from starter motor.
7. Remove starter motor mounting bolts and starter.
8. Reverse procedure to install, noting the following:
   a. **Torque** starter motor mounting bolts to 39 ft. lbs.
   b. **Torque** positive battery cable to starter motor nut to 89 inch lbs.

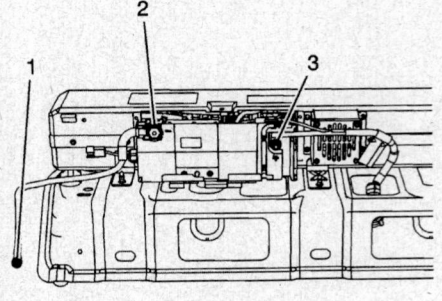

1-Chassis ground
2-Negative stud
3-Positive stud

ARM0700000000164

Fig. 3 Battery disconnect control module voltage measurement locations. AURA Hybrid

   c. **Torque** generator control module coolant pump bolts to 16 ft. lbs.

3.5L ENGINE

1. Raise and support vehicle.
2. Remove flywheel inspection cover.
3. Remove starter solenoid electrical connector retaining nuts.
4. Disconnect starter solenoid electrical connectors.
5. Remove mounting bolts and starter.
6. Reverse procedure to install, noting the following:
   a. **Torque** solenoid battery terminal inside nut to 13 ft. lbs.
   b. **Torque** solenoid battery terminal outside nut to 89 inch lbs.
   c. **Torque** solenoid S terminal outside nut to 27 inch lbs.
   d. **Torque** starter mounting bolts to 32 ft. lbs.
   e. **Torque** inspection cover bolts to 84 inch lbs.

3.6L ENGINE

1. Remove air cleaner assembly.
2. Remove exhaust manifold heat shield bolts and shield.
3. Remove left catalytic converter nuts at exhaust manifold.
4. Remove Connector Position Assurance (CPA) retainer from rear left HO2S electrical connector, then disconnect HO2S electrical connector.
5. Remove front catalytic converter to rear catalytic converter nuts.
6. Remove left catalytic converter. Remove and discard gaskets.
7. Disconnect wiring harness electrical connector from left bank knock sensor.
8. Remove knock sensor retaining bolt, then the knock sensor.
9. Remove starter solenoid BAT terminal nut, then disconnect electrical connector.
10. Remove starter motor mounting bolts, then the starter.
11. Reverse procedure to install, noting the following:
   a. **Torque** starter motor mounting bolts to 37 ft. lbs.

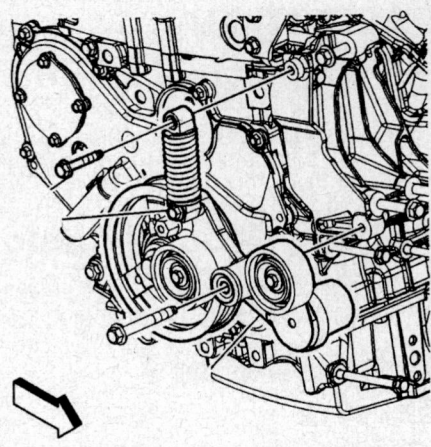

ARM0700000000165

Fig. 4 Drive belt spring tensioner. AURA Hybrid

   b. **Torque** solenoid BAT terminal nut to 10 ft. lbs.
   c. **Torque** knock sensor retaining bolt to 17 ft. lbs.
   d. **Torque** catalytic converter nuts to 18 ft. lbs.

ION

2.0L ENGINE

1. Raise and support vehicle.
2. Remove mounting bolts and intercooler pump outer bracket.
3. Disconnect electrical connectors and position aside.
4. Remove mounting bolts and starter motor.
5. Reverse procedure to install, noting the following:
   a. **Torque** starter mounting bolts to 37 ft. lbs.
   b. **Torque** intercooler pump outer bracket mounting bolts to 15 ft. lbs.

2.2L & 2.4L ENGINES

1. Raise and support vehicle.
2. Disconnect and position electrical connectors aside.
3. Remove mounting bolts and starter motor.
4. Reverse procedure to install, noting the following:
   a. **Torque** starter mounting bolts to 30 ft. lbs.
   b. **Torque** starter solenoid S terminal nut to 27 inch lbs.
   c. **Torque** starter solenoid terminal nut to 13 ft. lbs.

L-Series

2.2L ENGINE

1. Raise and support vehicle.
2. Disconnect and position electrical connectors aside.
3. Remove mounting bolts and starter motor.
4. Reverse procedure to install, noting the following:

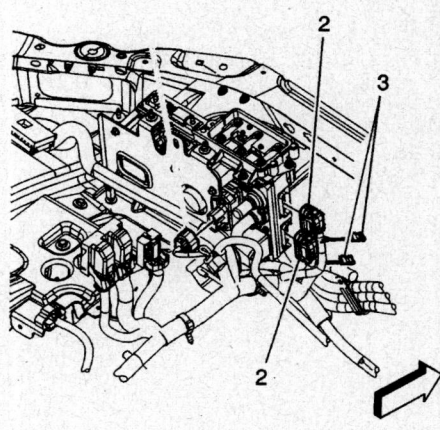

2-Electrical connectors
3-CPA retainers

ARM0700000000166

Fig. 5   Generator control module electrical connectors. AURA Hybrid

a. **Torque** starter mounting bolts to 30 ft. lbs.
b. **Torque** starter solenoid S terminal nut to 27 inch lbs.
c. **Torque** starter solenoid terminal nut to 13 ft. lbs.

3.0L ENGINE

1. Raise and support vehicle.
2. Remove righthand front wheel and disconnect starter electrical connectors.
3. Loosen electrical harness bracket to engine block mounting bolt.
4. Remove starter motor lower mounting bolt. Lower vehicle.
5. Remove starter upper mounting bolt.
6. Move starter to righthand side to clear engine block, then to lefthand side and out of flywheel housing.
7. Reverse procedure to install. **Torque** starter mounting bolts to 30 ft. lbs.

SKY

1. Remove intake manifold as outlined under "Intake Manifold, Replace" in either "2.0L Engine" or "2.4L Engine" sections.
2. Remove starter solenoid terminal nuts and disconnect engine terminal harness.
3. Remove mounting bolts and starter.
4. Reverse procedure to install, noting the following:
   a. **Torque** starter motor mounting bolts to 30 ft. lbs.
   b. **Torque** starter solenoid terminal nut to 89 inch lbs.
   c. **Torque** starter solenoid S terminal nut to 27 inch lbs.

ALTERNATOR
REPLACE
AURA
3.5L ENGINE

1. Remove air cleaner.
2. Remove engine mount strut from front of engine and radiator support.
3. Turn drive belt tensioner using tool No. J37059, or equivalent, then remove serpentine drive belt.
4. Remove alternator mounting bolts and nuts.
5. Disconnect electrical connectors and remove alternator.
6. Reverse procedure to install. **Torque** mounting bolts to 37 ft. lbs., and nuts to 22 ft. lbs.

3.6L ENGINE

1. Reposition positive battery cable boot at alternator terminal.
2. Remove positive battery cable nut at alternator, then the positive battery cable terminal from alternator.
3. Disconnect engine harness connector from alternator.
4. Remove air cleaner assembly.
5. Remove engine mount strut to engine mount strut bracket bolts.
6. Rotate engine mount strut to vertical position.
7. Remove engine mount strut bracket bolts, then the engine mount strut bracket.
8. Rotate drive belt tensioner clockwise to release drive belt tension.
9. Slide drive belt off of belt idler pulley and slowly release drive belt tensioner.
10. Remove drive belt from accessory drive pulleys.
11. Completely loosen idler pulley bolt.
12. Reposition battery cable boot, then disconnect battery cable from alternator.
13. Remove alternator bolts and position aside.
14. Remove drive belt idler pulley bolt.
15. Remove alternator mounting bolts. When removing alternator from vehicle, it may be necessary to maneuver alternator from vehicle.
16. Reverse procedure to install, noting the following:
   a. **Torque** drive belt idler pulley bolt to 43 ft. lbs.
   b. **Torque** alternator mounting bolts to 37 ft. lbs.
   c. **Torque** positive battery cable nut to 15 ft. lbs.

ION
2.0L ENGINE

1. Remove supercharger as outlined under "Supercharger, Replace" in "2.0L Engine" section.
2. Disconnect alternator electrical connectors.

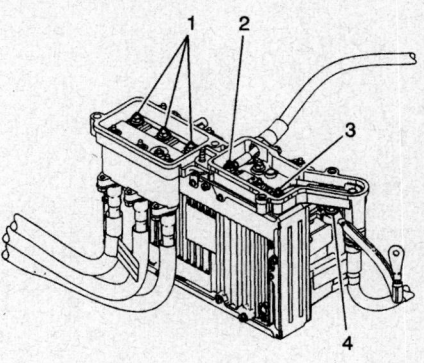

1-Control module phase terminals
2-12 volt positive terminal
3-36 volt positive terminal
4-Ground terminal

ARM0700000000167

Fig. 6   Generator control module terminal locations. AURA Hybrid

3. Remove mounting bolts and alternator,
4. Reverse procedure to install, noting the following:
   a. **Torque** alternator mounting bolts to 18 ft. lbs.
   b. **Torque** alternator terminal nut to 15 ft. lbs.

2.2L & 2.4L ENGINES

1. Remove throttle body air duct and accessory drive belt.
2. Disconnect alternator electrical connectors.
3. Remove mounting bolts and alternator.
4. Reverse procedure to install, noting the following:
   a. **Torque** alternator mounting bolts to 16 ft. lbs.
   b. **Torque** alternator terminal nut to 15 ft. lbs.

L-Series
2.2L ENGINE

1. Remove throttle body air duct and accessory drive belt.
2. Disconnect alternator electrical connectors.
3. Remove mounting bolts and alternator.
4. Reverse procedure to install, noting the following:
   a. **Torque** alternator mounting bolts to 16 ft. lbs.
   b. **Torque** alternator terminal nut to 15 ft. lbs.

3.0L ENGINE

1. Turn steering wheel toward righthand side.
2. Mark running direction, then remove

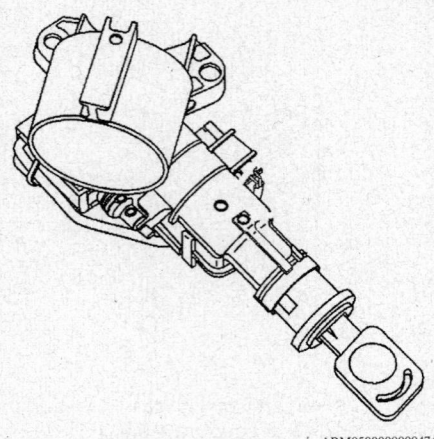

ARM0500000000474

Fig. 7 Lock cylinder replacement. ION

accessory drive belt and belt tensioner.
3. Remove alternator upper mounting bolts.
4. Raise and support vehicle.
5. Remove alternator lower mounting bolt. Lower vehicle.
6. Separate alternator from engine block.
7. Disconnect electrical connectors and remove alternator.
8. Reverse procedure to install. **Torque** alternator mounting bolts to 30 ft. lbs.

SKY

1. Remove air cleaner outlet duct.
2. Pull intake manifold cover in middle of right side to disengage cover from studs.
3. Pull intake manifold cover in middle of left side to disengage cover from studs.
4. Disconnect ignition coils and remove electrical harness from stud.
5. Disconnect cam phaser electrical connector and remove intake manifold cover.
6. Rotate power steering pump drive belt tensioner, then remove drive belt from pulley.
7. Rotate accessory drive belt tensioner, then remove drive belt.
8. Remove engine harness alternator connector.
9. Remove engine harness ground terminal boot, nut and harness.
10. Remove mounting bolts and alternator.
11. Reverse procedure to install, noting the following:
   a. **Torque** alternator mounting bolts to 16 ft. lbs.
   b. **Torque** engine harness ground terminal nut to 15 ft. lbs.

GENERATOR w/ STARTER
REPLACE

AURA Hybrid

Disable hybrid battery as outlined under "Hybrid Battery Service" in "Precautions."
1. Remove air cleaner assembly.
2. Install hydraulic belt tensioner compressor tool No. EN-48079, or equivalent to drive belt tensioner spring.
3. Compress drive belt tensioner spring fully, then rotate drive belt tensioner clockwise in to release tension from drive belt, **Fig. 4.**
4. With tensioner released, remove drive belt from under middle idler pulley.
5. Slowly rotate tensioner clockwise to allow tensioner to rest, remove drive belt from vehicle.
6. Raise and support vehicle.
7. Remove engine splash shield plastic retainers and attaching screw, then the splash shield from under engine.
8. Lower vehicle.
9. Recover A/C system refrigerant as outlined in "Air Conditioning."
10. Disconnect A/C refrigerant lines from A/C compressor.
11. Remove belt tensioner spring bolts from tensioner, then the tensioner spring from tensioner.
12. Loosen engine mount to bracket bolts.
13. Insert a suitable tool between engine mount bracket and frame to reposition engine.
14. Loosen drive belt tensioner attaching bolt.
15. Raise and support vehicle and remove drive belt tensioner
16. Drain cooling system and remove radiator inlet hose.
17. Remove power brake booster vacuum hose from intake manifold.
18. Remove power brake booster vacuum hose from clamp on generator control module coolant outlet hose. Position vacuum hose aside.
19. Remove Connector Position Assurance (CPA) retainers from generator control module electrical connectors, **Fig. 5.**
20. Disconnect engine wiring harness electrical connectors from generator control module. **Wait at least 5 minutes in order to allow the voltage stored in the generator control module to discharge.**
21. Remove coolant inlet hose from generator control module.
22. Remove generator control module bracket mounting bolt and nuts.
23. Loosen generator control module cover integral bolts and remove cover.
24. To ensure module has been disabled, inspect generator control module for voltage potential as follows:

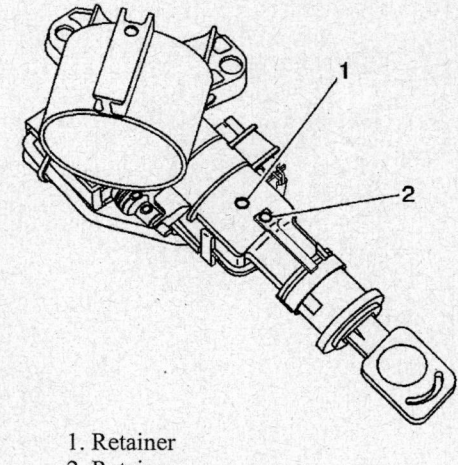

1. Retainer
2. Retainer

ARM0500000000643

Fig. 8 Lock cylinder retainers. SKY

   a. Refer to **Fig. 6** for generator control module terminal locations.
   b. Measure from 36-volt positive terminal to a known good chassis ground, voltage should be less than 3 volts.
   c. Measure from 12-volt positive terminal to a known good chassis ground, voltage should be less than 3 volts.
   d. Measure from ground terminal to a known good chassis ground, continuity should exist.
25. Verify generator control module 3-phase cables are disabled as follows:
   a. Measure from each phase 1, 2, and 3 connection to a known good chassis ground, voltage should be less than 3 volts.
   b. After verifying that there is no voltage present, generator control module 3-phase cables can now be removed from generator control module.
26. Disconnect engine wiring harness electrical connectors from generator starter. Position wiring harness out of the way.
27. Remove 36-volt terminal block nuts from generator control module.
28. Lift up and reposition 36-volt terminal block, secure block out of the way. Discard terminal block seal.
29. Remove generator control module 3-phase cable terminal block nuts from generator control module.
30. Lift up and reposition generator control module 3-phase cable terminal block from generator control module. Discard terminal block seal.
31. Remove A/C condenser/evaporator tube clip from front end upper tie bar reinforcement. Position A/C condenser/evaporator tube aside.

32. Remove starter 3-phase cable clip bolt from oil level indicator tube bracket.
33. Remove upper generator starter bolt.
34. Raise and support vehicle.
35. Remove lower generator starter bolts.
36. Lower vehicle.
37. Remove generator starter (with generator control module 3-phase cables attached) from vehicle.
38. Reverse procedure to install, noting the following:
    a. **Torque** generator control module 3-phase cable retaining nuts to 71 inch lbs.
    b. **Torque** generator control module 3-phase cable bracket bolts to 71 inch lbs.
    c. **Torque** generator starter cover bolts to 44 inch lbs.
    d. **Torque** rear generator control module 3-phase cable bolts to 71 inch lbs.
    e. **Torque** generator starter bolts to 43 ft. lbs.
    f. **Torque** 36-volt terminal block to generator control module retaining nuts to 89 inch lbs.
    g. **Torque** generator control module bracket retaining nuts to 89 inch lbs.
    h. **Torque** tensioner spring to tensioner bolts 16 ft. lbs.
    i. **Torque** lower tensioner bolt to 43 ft. lbs.

COIL PACK
REPLACE
AURA
3.5L ENGINE

1. Remove engine oil fill cap, then pull up on intake manifold cover to disengage cover from studs.
2. Disconnect engine wiring harness electrical connector MAP sensor.
3. Disconnect engine wiring harness electrical connector from ignition coil.
4. Reposition brake booster vacuum hose clamp at upper intake manifold.
5. Remove brake booster vacuum hose from upper intake manifold.
6. Remove HO2S electrical connector rosebud clip from ignition coil bracket.
7. Mark spark plug wires for installation reference.
8. Disconnect ignition coil wires.
9. Remove mounting bolts, then the ignition coil.
10. Reverse procedure to install. **Torque** mounting bolts to 18 ft. lbs.

ION
2.2L ENGINE

1. Turn ignition switch to OFF.
2. Remove accelerator cable and bracket.
3. Disconnect ignition module electrical connector.
4. Remove mounting screws and electronic ignition module.
5. Remove mounting bolts and coil pack.

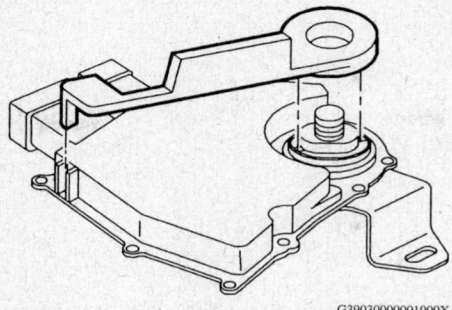

G39030000001000X

Fig. 9 Transaxle range switch alignment. L-Series

6. Reverse procedure to install, noting the following:
    a. **Torque** coil pack bolts to 84 inch lbs.
    b. **Torque** ignition module mounting screws to 13 inch lbs.

L-Series
3.0L ENGINE

1. Turn ignition switch to OFF.
2. Remove upper intake manifold runner as outlined under "Intake Manifold, Replace" in "3.0L Engine" section.
3. Disconnect electrical connector, then remove ignition coil and gasket.
4. Reverse procedure to install.

IGNITION COIL
REPLACE
ION
2.0L ENGINE

1. Disconnect ignition coil electrical connector.
2. Remove mounting bolt and coil,
3. Reverse procedure to install. **Torque** coil mounting bolt to 89 inch lbs.

2.4L ENGINE

1. Ensure ignition key is in OFF position.
2. Remove engine oil fill cap.
3. Remove intake manifold cover.
4. Disconnect ignition coil electrical connector.
5. Remove mounting bolt and ignition coil.
6. Reverse procedure to install. **Torque** ignition coil mounting bolts to 89 inch lbs.

AURA & L-Series
2.4L & 3.6L ENGINES

1. Ensure ignition key is in OFF position.
2. Remove engine oil fill cap.
3. Remove intake manifold cover.
4. Disconnect ignition coil electrical connector.
5. Remove mounting bolt and ignition coil.
6. Reverse procedure to install. **Torque** ignition coil mounting bolts to 89 inch lbs.

SKY

1. Pull intake manifold cover upward, disconnect studs and remove cover.
2. Disconnect ignition coil electrical connector.
3. Remove mounting bolts and coils.
4. Reverse procedure to install. **Torque** ignition coil bolts to 89 inch lbs.

IGNITION LOCK
REPLACE
AURA

1. Remove outer trim cover from lefthand side of instrument panel.
2. Remove lower trim panels from lower lefthand closeout panel.
3. Remove lower lefthand closeout panel from lefthand knee bolster.
4. Turn ignition switch to RUN position.
5. Depress retaining tab, and remove lock cylinder.
6. Reverse procedure to install.

ION

1. Lower steering column to lowest position.
2. Remove steering column upper and lower trim covers.
3. Remove theft deterrent control module.
4. Depress first retainer through lock housing access hole 2 using suitable, small Allen wrench or similar tool, **Fig. 7.**
5. Back lock cylinder out slightly, then depress second retainer through lock housing access hole 1 until lock cylinder backs out slightly again.
6. Pull lock cylinder out enough to locate second retainer to lock housing access hole 2.
7. Depress retainer though access hole 2 second time.
8. Ignition cylinder should release from housing. If cylinder does not release, it may need to be moved in and out several times to locate retainer correctly in hole.
9. Remove lock cylinder from lock housing.
10. Reverse procedure to install.

L-Series

1. Remove ignition lock bezel.
2. Remove upper steering column shroud panel.
3. Insert ignition key in switch.
4. Turn key to START, then back to RUN.
5. Depress locking button at top and remove lock cylinder.
6. Reverse procedure to install.

SKY

1. Remove knee bolster and bracket.
2. Lower steering column, then remove steering column upper and lower trim covers.

3. Turn ignition lock cylinder to RUN position.
4. Depress first retainer through lock housing access hole with suitable small Allen wrench or pick-type tool, **Fig. 8.** Lock cylinder will back out slightly.
5. Depress second retainer through lock housing access hole and lock cylinder will back out slightly again.
6. Pull lock cylinder out enough and locate second retainer to lock housing access hole.
7. Depress retainer though access hole a second time, ignition cylinder should release from housing. If cylinder does not release, move cylinder in and out several times to locate retainer correctly in hole.
8. Remove lock cylinder from lock housing.
9. Reverse procedure to install.

IGNITION SWITCH
REPLACE
AURA

1. Tilt steering column upper trim cover upward and remove nuts from instrument panel seal.
2. Remove steering column upper trim cover.
3. Remove steering column lower trim cover mounting screws.
4. Lower rake lever and lower steering column, then fully telescope column toward driver and remove lower trim cover.
5. Remove mounting screws and instrument panel cluster trim plate bezel.
6. Remove fog lamp and adjustable pedal switch.
7. Remove instrument panel dimmer switch and lefthand center instrument panel trim panel.
8. Remove righthand instrument panel trim panel.
9. Remove righthand closeout panel and glove compartment.
10. Remove instrument panel center trim bezel.
11. Remove outer trim cover from lefthand side of instrument panel.
12. Remove lower trim panels from lower lefthand closeout panel.
13. Remove lower lefthand closeout panel from lefthand knee bolster.
14. Remove knee bolster from under lefthand side of instrument panel.
15. Disconnect ignition switch and theft deterrent control module harness connectors.
16. Turn ignition switch to RUN position.
17. Disconnect park lock cable from ignition switch.
18. Remove mounting screws and ignition switch.
19. Reverse procedure to install.

ION

1. Remove steering column upper and lower shrouds.

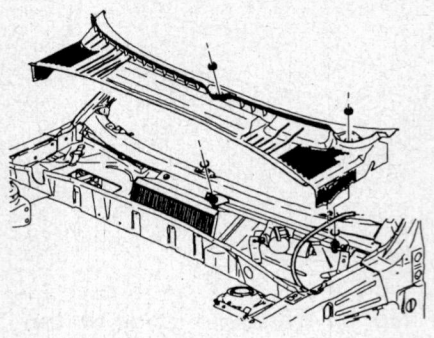

Fig. 10 Windshield cowl screen replacement. L-Series

2. Disconnect ignition switch electrical connector.
3. Turn ignition to RUN position.
4. Remove mounting screws and ignition switch.
5. Reverse procedure to install. **Torque** switch mounting screws to 17 inch lbs.

L-Series

1. Remove ignition lock cylinder bezel from steering column shroud.
2. Remove steering column upper and lower shrouds.
3. Remove mounting screws and disconnect electrical connector, then remove ignition switch.
4. Reverse procedure to install. **Torque** switch mounting screws to 13 inch lbs.

SKY

1. Remove knee bolster and bracket.
2. Lower steering column, then remove upper and lower trim covers.
3. Disconnect ignition switch harness connector.
4. Turn ignition switch to RUN position.
5. Remove mounting screws and ignition switch.
6. Reverse procedure to install.

CLUTCH START SWITCH
REPLACE

1. Disconnect clutch switch electrical connector.
2. Remove mounting bolt and switch.
3. Reverse procedure to install. **Torque** clutch switch mounting bolt to 96 inch lbs.

NEUTRAL SAFETY SWITCH
REPLACE
AURA

REMOVAL

1. Apply parking brake and place shift lever in Neutral position.
2. Remove shift control cable from switch lever.

3. Disconnect switch electrical connectors.
4. Remove mounting nut and switch lever.
5. Remove mounting bolts and switch.

INSTALLATION

1. Place shift shaft in Neutral position, then align shaft and switch flats.
2. Loosely install switch.
3. Insert Park/Neutral Switch Aligner tool No. J41545, or equivalent, and turn switch until tool drops into position.
4. **Torque** switch bolts to 15 ft. lbs.

ION

The neutral safety switch functions are part of the transaxle range switch.
1. Apply parking brake and place control assembly in Neutral.
2. Remove shift control cable from transaxle range switch lever.
3. Disconnect electrical connectors from transaxle range switch.
4. Remove mounting nut and transaxle range switch lever.
5. Remove mounting bolts and transaxle range switch.
6. Reverse procedure to install, noting the following:
   a. Install transaxle range switch alignment tool No. J41545, or equivalent, over shaft and switch.
   b. Turn switch until alignment tool drops into position.
   c. **Torque** switch bolts to 15 ft. lbs.

L-Series

The neutral safety switch functions are part of the transaxle range switch.

REMOVAL

1. Apply parking brake and place control lever in Neutral position.
2. Remove shift control cable from transaxle range switch lever.
3. Disconnect transaxle range switch electrical connectors.
4. Remove mounting nut and range switch lever.
5. Remove mounting bolts and transaxle range switch.

INSTALLATION

1. Ensure transaxle manual shaft is in Neutral position.
2. Align transaxle shift shaft and transaxle range switch flats.
3. Install switch and loosely install mounting bolts.
4. Insert transaxle range switch alignment tool No. J41545, or equivalent, over manual shaft, **Fig. 9.**
5. Turn switch until alignment tool drops into position.
6. **Torque** switch mounting bolts to 15 ft. lbs.
7. **Torque** switch lever mounting nut to 26 ft. lbs.
8. Connect switch electrical connectors.
9. Install control cable.

HEADLAMP SWITCH
REPLACE

Refer to "Multi-Function Switch, Replace" for replacement procedure.

STOP LIGHT SWITCH
REPLACE
AURA

1. Remove closeout panel from under lefthand side of instrument panel.
2. Remove mounting bolt and position steering column stub shaft aside.
3. Disconnect electrical connector, then remove mounting bolt and brake pedal position sensor.
4. Reverse procedure to install.

ION & L-Series

1. Remove driver's side sound insulator.
2. Disconnect and remove electrical connectors.
3. Disconnect brake switch by grasping switch and turning it one quarter turn counterclockwise while pulling toward rear of vehicle.
4. Reverse procedure to install, adjust switch as follows:
   a. Ensure brake pedal is fully released.
   b. Ensure stoplamp plunger is fully depressed against brake pedal shanks.
   c. Hold brake pedal forward, then ensure stoplamp switch and cruise control switch are fully seated into brake pedal bracket.
   d. Pull brake pedal to rear, against internal stop.

SKY
REMOVAL

1. Disconnect Brake Pedal Position (BPP) sensor electrical connector.
2. Remove mounting bolt and BPP sensor.

INSTALLATION

1. Install new sensor. **Torque** mounting bolt to 18 inch lbs.
2. Connect electrical connector.
3. Apply parking brake.
4. **On models equipped with automatic transmission,** place transmission in PARK position.
5. **On models equipped with manual transmission,** place transmission in NEUTRAL position.
6. **On all models,** install a scan tool.
7. Clear all BCM DTCs.
8. Turn ignition switch to ON position with engine off.
9. Navigate to Vehicle Control System menu.
10. Select Computer/Integrating Systems menu item.
11. Select Module Setup menu item.
12. Select BCM menu item.

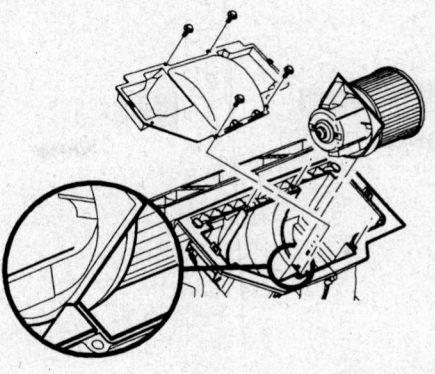

G37029900003400X

Fig. 11 Blower motor replacement. L-Series

13. Select BPP Sensor Calibration procedure and follow directions displayed on screen.

MULTI-FUNCTION SWITCH
REPLACE
AURA

1. Tilt steering column upper trim cover upward and remove nuts from instrument panel seal.
2. Remove steering column upper trim cover.
3. Remove steering column lower trim cover mounting screws.
4. Lower rake lever and steering column, then fully telescope column toward driver and remove lower trim cover from column.
5. Remove mounting screw and switch.
6. Reverse procedure to install.

ION & L-Series

1. Remove steering column upper and lower shrouds.
2. Disconnect multi-function switch electrical connector.
3. Remove mounting screws multi-function switch.
4. Reverse procedure to install.

SKY

1. Remove knee bolster and bracket.
2. Lower steering column, then the upper and lower trim covers.
3. Disconnect multi-function turn signal switch harness connector.
4. Depress locking tabs and remove multi-function turn signal switch.
5. Reverse procedure to install.

TURN SIGNAL SWITCH
REPLACE

Refer to "Multi-Function Switch, Replace" for turn signal switch replacement procedure.

STEERING WHEEL
REPLACE
AURA

1. Remove driver's air bag module as outlined in "Passive Restraint Systems" chapter.
2. Remove steering wheel using puller tool No. J1859-A and legs tool No. J42120, or equivalent.
3. Reverse procedure to install. **Torque** steering wheel nut to 27–30 ft. lbs.

ION

1. Remove driver's air bag module as outlined in "Passive Restraint Systems" chapter.
2. Disconnect horn electrical connector.
3. Remove steering wheel nut.
4. Remove steering wheel using steering wheel puller No. J1859A, or equivalent.
5. Disconnect electrical connectors and remove steering wheel.
6. Reverse procedure to install. **Torque** steering wheel nut to 30 ft. lbs.

L-Series

1. Remove driver's air bag module as outlined in "Passive Restraint Systems" chapter.
2. Disconnect horn and cruise control switch electrical connectors.
3. Remove and discard steering wheel mounting nut.
4. Remove steering wheel using suitable steering wheel puller tool.
5. Feed electrical wiring through steering wheel and remove steering wheel.
6. Prevent SIR coil rotation by inserting yellow tab into SIR coil or using tape.
7. Reverse procedure to install. **Torque** new steering wheel mounting nut to 31 ft. lbs.

SKY

1. Remove driver's air bag module as outlined in "Passive Restraint Systems" chapter.
2. Insert suitable, small flat bladed tool through access openings, on left and righthand hand sides of steering wheel.
3. Remove nut and steering wheel.
4. Reverse procedure to install. **Torque** steering wheel nut to 27 ft. lbs.

INSTRUMENT CLUSTER
REPLACE
AURA

1. Tilt steering column upper trim cover upward and remove nuts from instrument panel seal.
2. Remove steering column upper trim cover.
3. Remove steering column lower trim cover mounting screws.

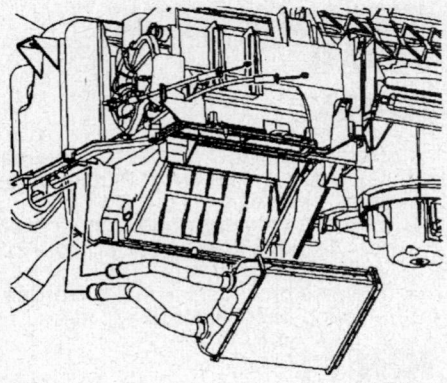

ARM66GC000000109

Fig. 12 Heater core replacement. ION

4. Lower rake lever and lower steering column, then fully telescope column toward driver and remove lower trim cover from column.
5. Remove mounting screws and instrument panel cluster trim plate bezel.
6. Remove instrument cluster mounting screws.
7. Disconnect cluster electrical connectors and remove instrument cluster.
8. Reverse procedure to install.

ION

1. Remove accessory trim panel and disconnect electrical connectors.
2. Remove cluster trim plate to center trim panel mounting screw.
3. Lift cluster trim plate up to disconnect fasteners and remove cluster trim plate.
4. Remove mounting screws and pull cluster out.
5. Disconnect electrical connector and remove cluster.
6. Reverse procedure to install.

L-Series

1. Remove steering wheel as outlined under "Steering Wheel, Replace."
2. Remove hush panel from under left-hand side of instrument panel.
3. Remove knee bolster panel from under steering column.
4. Remove upper and lower steering column covers.
5. Lower steering column to its lowest position.
6. Remove mounting screws and instrument cluster trim plate.
7. Remove mounting screws and instrument cluster.
8. Reverse procedure to install.

SKY

1. **On models equipped with manual transmission,** remove shift control lever boot ring, lever screw and lever knob.
2. **On models equipped with automatic transmission,** remove console shift lever bezel.
3. **On all models,** remove instrument

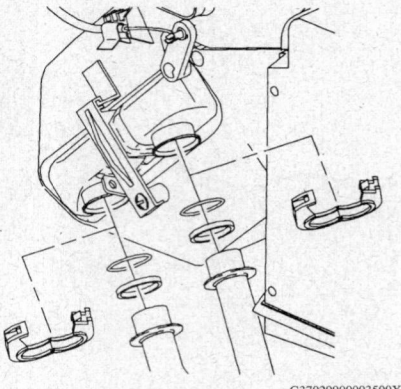

G37029900003500X

Fig. 13 Heater core pipe replacement. L-Series

panel assist handle.
4. Remove cluster trim plate and retainer clip.
5. Remove mounting screws and instrument cluster.
6. Reverse procedure to install, noting the following:
   a. **Torque** shift control lever screw and passenger assist handle mounting bolts to 89 inch lbs.
   b. **Torque** instrument panel cluster mounting screws to 18 ft. lbs.

RADIO
REPLACE
AURA

1. Remove fog lamp, dimmer and adjustable pedal switches from lower left-hand trim panel.
2. Remove trim panels from under left and righthand sides of instrument panel.
3. Remove closeout panel from under righthand side of instrument panel.
4. Remove glove compartment from front of center console.
5. Remove knee bolster from under left-hand side of instrument panel.
6. Remove instrument panel center trim bezel.
7. Remove hazard warning switch.
8. Remove heater-air conditioning control head from center of instrument panel.
9. Remove mounting screws and radio.
10. Reverse procedure to install.

ION

1. Remove accessory trim panel and disconnect electrical connectors.
2. Remove mounting screws and pull radio out.
3. Disconnect radio electrical connectors and remove radio.
4. Reverse procedure to install.

L-Series

1. Remove control cover push pin fasteners, then pull radio, and heater and air conditioning control cover rearward.

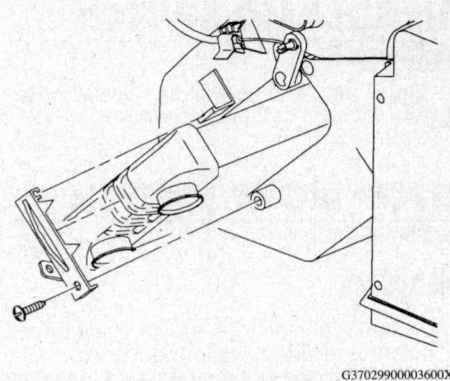

G37029900003600X

Fig. 14 Heater core replacement. L-Series

2. Disconnect single traction control, fog lamp and rear defroster electrical connectors.
3. Remove radio mounting screws.
4. Depress both radio side spring clips and pull out slightly.
5. Disconnect antenna and electrical connectors.
6. **On models equipped with base radio,** remove storage tray by pulling out toward front of radio.
7. **On all models,** remove radio.
8. Reverse procedure to install.

SKY

1. **On models equipped with automatic transmission,** remove console shift lever bezel.
2. **On models equipped with manual transmission,** remove shift control lever boot ring, lever screw and lever knob.
3. **On all models,** remove instrument panel assist handle.
4. Remove mounting bolt and screws, then the radio.
5. Reverse procedure to install. **Torque** radio mounting bolts and screws to 18 inch lbs.

WIPER MOTOR
REPLACE
AURA

1. Remove wiper arm and blade.
2. Remove cowl cover.
3. Disconnect drive link from crank arm using wiper transmission separator tool No. J39232, or equivalent.
4. Disconnect wiper motor electrical connectors.
5. Remove mounting screws and wiper motor.
6. Reverse procedure to install, noting the following:
   a. **Torque** motor mounting screws to 84 inch lbs.
   b. Connect drive link to crank arm using wiper transmission installer tool No. J39529, or equivalent.

Fig. 15 Evaporator core replacement. ION

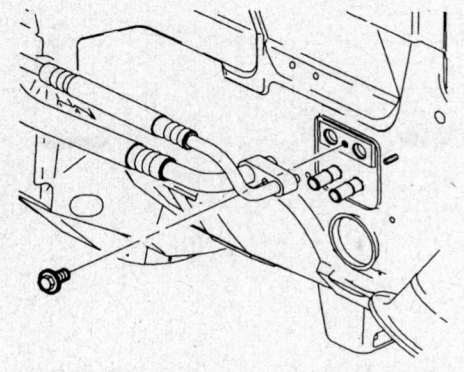

Fig. 16 Suction/liquid line replacement. L-Series

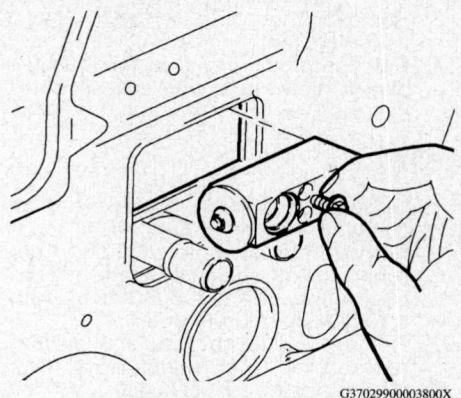

Fig. 17 TXV replacement. L-Series

ION

1. Remove wiper arm finish cap and mounting screw.
2. Remove wiper arm from pivot using tool No. J39637, or equivalent.
3. Remove cowl trim panel.
4. Disconnect wiper motor electrical connector.
5. Remove retainers, and wiper motor.
6. Reverse procedure to install.

L-Series

1. Remove wiper arm finish cap.
2. Mark wiper arm positions on windshield for installation alignment.
3. Remove mounting nuts and wiper arms.
4. Remove weatherstrip from rear of hood.
5. Remove mounting nuts and cowl screen, **Fig. 10.**
6. Disconnect wiper motor electrical connector.
7. Remove mounting bolts and wiper motor.
8. Separate wiper motor from transmission.
9. Reverse procedure to install. **Torque** wiper motor mounting bolts to 44 inch lbs., and wiper arm mounting nuts to 21 ft. lbs.

SKY

1. Remove cap from windshield wiper arm using suitable, small flat-bladed tool.
2. Remove windshield wiper arm mounting nut.
3. Remove windshield washer nozzle hose.
4. Remove windshield wiper arm.
5. Remove air inlet grille retainers and air inlet grille.
6. Disconnect Connector Positive Assurance (CPA) cover from wiper motor electrical connector.
7. Disconnect wiper motor electrical connector.
8. Remove mounting bolts and windshield wiper system module.
9. Remove mounting bolts and separate windshield wiper motor from module.
10. Reverse procedure to install, noting the following:
    a. **Torque** windshield wiper motor mounting bolts to 40 ft. lbs.

b. **Torque** windshield wiper module mounting bolts to 80 inch lbs.
c. **Torque** windshield washer arm mounting nut to 24 ft. lbs.

WIPER SWITCH
REPLACE
AURA & SKY

Refer to "Multi-Function Switch, Replace" for replacement procedure.

ION

1. Remove steering column upper and lower shrouds.
2. Disconnect wiper switch electrical connector.
3. Remove mounting screws and wiper switch.
4. Reverse procedure to install.

L-Series

1. Remove steering wheel as outlined under "Steering Wheel, Replace."
2. Remove ignition switch bezel, then the upper and lower steering column covers.
3. Remove wiper/washer switch.
4. Reverse procedure to install.

WIPER TRANSMISSION
REPLACE
AURA

1. Remove wiper arm and blades.
2. Remove cowl cover and disconnect wiper motor connector.
3. Remove mounting screws and wiper drive system module.
4. Remove wiper arm and blade.
5. Remove cowl cover.
6. Disconnect drive link from crank arm using wiper transmission separator tool No. J39232, or equivalent.
7. Disconnect wiper motor electrical connectors.
8. Remove mounting screws and wiper motor.

9. Remove caps, wiper motor grommets and transmission.
10. Reverse procedure to install, noting the following:
    a. **Torque** transmission mounting screws to 72 inch lbs.
    b. **Torque** motor mounting screws to 84 inch lbs.
    c. Connect drive link to crank arm using wiper transmission installer tool No. J39529, or equivalent.

ION

1. Remove wiper arms.
2. Disconnect washer tubing from air inlet screen.
3. Remove air inlet grille panel push-in retainers from panel using door trim pad and garnish clip remover tool No. J38778, or equivalent.
4. Remove air inlet grille panel.
5. Remove wiper drive module.
6. Disconnect wiper motor electrical connector.
7. Remove wiper transmission from wiper motor crank arm using wiper transmission separator tool No. J39232, or equivalent.
8. Remove wiper transmission cap.
9. Remove screws and wiper transmission.
10. Reverse procedure to install, noting the following:
    a. **Torque** wiper transmission screws to 79 inch lbs.
    b. **Torque** wiper drive system module screws to 88 inch lbs.

L-Series & SKY

Refer to "Wiper Motor, Replace" for wiper transmission replacement procedure.

BLOWER MOTOR
REPLACE
AURA

1. Remove righthand closeout panel and insulator.
2. Disconnect blower motor electrical connectors.

3. Remove mounting screws, blower motor and fan.
4. Reverse procedure to install. **Torque** blower motor mounting screws to 45 inch lbs.

ION

1. Disconnect blower motor electrical connector.
2. Remove blower motor and cup from lower case by cutting through case between circular ribs around motor with suitable, sharp utility knife.
3. Remove mounting nuts and disconnect tab. then remove motor from cup.
4. Reverse procedure to install.

L-Series

1. Turn ignition to ON position and select control head Outside Air position.
2. Remove wiper arm finish cap.
3. Mark wiper arm positions on windshield for installation alignment.
4. Remove mounting nuts and wiper arms.
5. Remove weatherstrip from rear of hood.
6. Remove mounting nuts and cowl screen, **Fig. 10.**
7. Remove filter by rotating locking tabs outward.
8. Remove mounting bolts and filter housing.
9. Remove mounting screws and blower motor housing, **Fig. 11.**
10. Disconnect electrical connector and remove blower motor.
11. Reverse procedure to install. **Torque** blower motor housing screws to 9 inch lbs., and filter housing bolts to 31 inch lbs.

SKY

1. Disconnect damper and remove glove compartment.
2. Remove blower motor resistor mounting screw.
3. Remove mounting screws and blower motor.
4. Reverse procedure to install. **Torque** blower motor and blower resistor mounting screws to 13 inch lbs.

HEATER CORE

REPLACE

AURA

1. Drain coolant into suitable container
2. Remove inlet and outlet heater core hoses.
3. Recover air conditioning system refrigerant as outlined in "Air Conditioning" chapter.
4. Remove thermostatic expansion valve suction hose.
5. Remove and discard sealing washers.
6. Disconnect HVAC module to front of dash plate mounting bolts.
7. Remove left and righthand console trim panels.

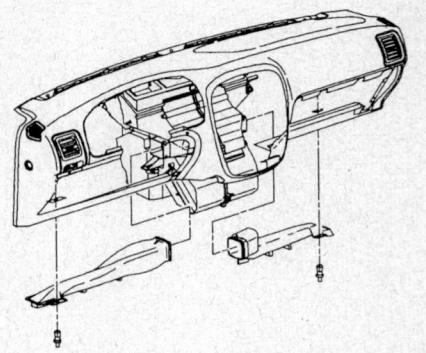

G39149900002500X

Fig. 18 Heater duct replacement. L-Series

8. Remove front console screw covers from behind console.
9. Remove front console mounting screws and position front seats to full forward position.
10. Remove rear console mounting bolts and place shifter in drive.
11. Remove lefthand closeout panel and both instrument panel outer trim panels.
12. Disconnect instrument panel to body wire harness and antenna connectors.
13. Disconnect instrument panel to wire harness righthand connectors.
14. Remove knee bolster from under lefthand side of instrument panel.
15. Remove accelerator pedal and disconnect steering column to instrument panel wire harness connector.
16. Remove crush bracket to front of dash plate mounting nuts.
17. Remove upper steering column shroud from lower shroud.
18. Remove stalk switches and SIR coil connectors.
19. Position steering wheel in full forward telescoping position, and front seat in full rearward position.
20. Remove steering column mounting bolts.
21. Remove brake pedal.
22. Remove Body Control Module (BCM).
23. Remove center support bracket floor bolts and shifter assembly.
24. Remove both windshield pillar garnish moldings.
25. Remove instrument panel upper trim panel.
26. Remove left and righthand instrument panel to body bolts.
27. Remove left and righthand floor heater ducts from center floor heater duct.
28. Remove instrument panel.
29. Remove and discard HVAC module drain and dash seals.
30. Remove lower center floor air outlet duct.
31. Remove mounting screws and upper center floor air outlet duct.
32. Drill out heater core cover heat stakes.
33. Remove mounting screws and heater core cover.
34. Remove heater core.
35. Reverse procedure to install.

ION

1. Park vehicle on a level surface and remove surge tank cap.
2. Raise and support vehicle, then place suitable drain pan under water pump drain port.
3. Loosen water pump drain bolt and drain coolant from water pump. Lower vehicle.
4. Disconnect clamps, then remove heater outlet and inlet hoses from heater core.
5. Apply parking brake.
6. **On models equipped with automatic transaxle,** shift transaxle into Neutral and remove console shift lever bezel.
7. **On models equipped with manual transaxle,** disconnect shift boot from front console cupholder.
8. **On all models,** lift front console cupholder to disconnect retainers.
9. Disconnect cigarette lighter electrical connector and remove front console cupholder..
10. **On models equipped with manual transaxle,** slide shift boot through front console cupholder.
11. **On all models,** turn and remove retainer counterclockwise, then remove left and righthand console extensions.
12. Remove mounting screws and console center extension.
13. Remove wiring harness rosebud from righthand side center support bracket.
14. Pull back carpet at bottom of righthand side center support bracket and remove lower nuts.
15. Remove mounting nuts and center support bracket.
16. Disconnect harness connectors, then remove mounting nuts and Body Control Module (BCM),
17. Remove and position accelerator control pedal aside.
18. Raise center floor outlet duct while pushing floor ducts down to disconnect ducts.
19. Turn center floor outlet duct forward and disconnect duct from HVAC module.
20. Remove retainers and pull heater core cover down enough to clear HVAC module locating pins .
21. Slide heater core cover rearward until drain tube clears front of dash.
22. Slide heater core cover down, rearward and to righthand side to remove, **Fig. 12.**
23. Reverse procedure to install.

L-Series

1. Drain engine coolant into suitable container.
2. Remove heater inlet and return hoses.
3. Place heater return hose end in suitable container, apply low air pressure to inlet hose and blow coolant out of heater core.
4. Remove righthand console extension.
5. Remove heater core pipe to heater core clamps and pipe from core end tank, **Fig. 13.**

6. Remove core mounting screw and strap.
7. Pull center console forward edge outward for access.
8. Pull heater core out of module into passenger foot area, **Fig. 14.**
9. Reverse procedure to install.

SKY

1. Drain cooling system into suitable container.
2. Recover refrigerant as outlined in "Air Conditioning" chapter.
3. Remove air conditioning compressor tube assembly nut.
4. Remove sealing washer.
5. Remove mounting bolt, sealing washer and thermal expansion valve.
6. Remove air inlet grille panel.
7. Remove heater inlet and outlet hose.
8. Remove instrument panel cluster trim plate.
9. Remove driver knee bolster trim panel.
10. Disconnect damper and remove glove compartment.
11. Remove passenger's air bag module as outlined in "Passive Restraint Systems" chapter.
12. Remove left and righthand hand instrument panel outer trim covers.
13. Remove left and righthand hand windshield pillar garnish moldings.
14. Remove radio and cup holder.
15. Remove mounting screws and instrument panel trim pad.
16. Remove steering column as outlined in "Steering Columns" chapter.
17. Note instrument panel wiring harness routing for installation alignment.
18. Remove mounting screw, bolt and air distribution duct.
19. Remove mounting bolts and instrument panel tie bar.
20. Remove mounting nuts, bolts and HVAC module.
21. Remove mounting screw and air outlet duct.
22. Remove mounting screw and heater core cover.
23. Remove heater core pass through seal.
24. Remove mounting screws and air distribution case.
25. Remove heater core.
26. Reverse procedure to install, noting the following:
    a. **Torque** air conditioning compressor tube assembly nut to 12 ft. lbs.
    b. **Torque** thermal expansion valve mounting bolt to 12 ft. lbs.
    c. **Torque** instrument panel carrier mounting bolt and nut to 80 inch lbs.
    d. **Torque** instrument panel tie bar outer mounting bolts to 106 inch lbs.
    e. **Torque** instrument panel tie bar inner mounting bolts to 18 ft. lbs.

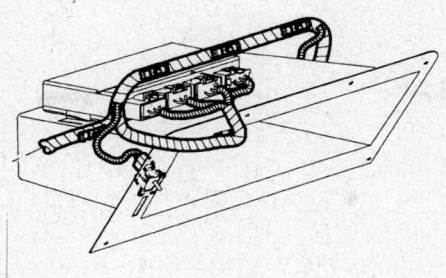

G39149900002600X

Fig. 19 BCM replacement. L-Series

EVAPORATOR CORE
REPLACE
AURA

1. Recover air conditioning refrigerant as outlined in "Air Conditioning" chapter.
2. Drain coolant into suitable container.
3. Remove HVAC assembly as outlined under "Heater Core, Replace."
4. Remove mounting screw and thermal expansion valve.
5. Remove and discard sealing washers.
6. Remove evaporator core.
7. Reverse procedure to install.

ION

1. Remove heater core as outlined under "Heat Core, Replace."
2. Unsnap and open passenger compartment filter door.
3. Remove mounting screws and lower HVAC case.
4. Remove evaporator core, **Fig. 15.**
5. Reverse procedure to install.

L-Series

1. Remove blower motor as outlined under "Blower Motor, Replace."
2. Recover refrigerant as outlined in "Air Conditioning" chapter.
3. Remove mounting bolts and suction/liquid line from Thermo Expansion Valve (TXV), **Fig. 16.** Cap suction/liquid line hose.
4. Remove TXV mounting bolts.
5. Install suction/liquid line bolt hand tight.
6. Remove TXV from evaporator by gently pulling forward using bolt as handle, **Fig. 17.**
7. Open glove box door and remove lamp by pulling on plunger.
8. Disconnect glove box lamp electrical connector.
9. Remove righthand side instrument panel lower dash insulator retainers.
10. Pull insulator rearward to disconnect from forward insulator retainers.

11. Remove retainer and righthand side heater duct, **Fig. 18.**
12. Remove glove box door and bin fasteners.
13. Slowly tilt glove box bin downward to expose Body Control Module (BCM), **Fig. 19.**
14. Slide BCM out of mounting slots and remove glove box bin.
15. Remove hush panel support from front of dash.
16. Cut evaporator access door through module wall following inside of raised bead as guide using suitable, sharp utility knife, **Fig. 20. Several passes may be required.**
17. Slide evaporator core out through access door opening. Cap pipes.
18. Reverse procedure to install, noting the following:
    a. Add 2.4 ounces of PAG oil to new evaporator.
    b. **Torque** TXV and suction/liquid mounting bolts to 62 inch lbs.
    c. Lubricate O-rings using clean mineral oil.
    d. Apply provided sealant to service door at tongue and groove locations.

SKY

1. Remove HVAC module as outlined under "Heater Core, Replace."
2. Remove evaporator case seal.
3. Remove mounting bolts and thermal expansion valve.
4. Remove sealing washer.
5. Remove mounting screws and rear air outlet duct.
6. Remove mounting screw and evaporator lower case.
7. Remove evaporator.
8. Reverse procedure to install.

CABIN AIR FILTER
REPLACE
ION

1. Open glove compartment door.
2. Tilt door down, then squeeze in on each side of bin until door stops can be removed from tracks.
3. Lower glove compartment completely.
4. Open cabin air filter door through opening in rear of instrument panel compartment, raising tab until door can be opened downward.
5. Slide filter out of housing.
6. Reverse procedure to install.

L-Series

This procedure has been revised by a Technical Service Bulletin.
1. Open hood and filter access door in cowl leaf screen using suitable screwdriver.

2. Turn locking tabs outward to release filter assembly.
3. Remove filter by pulling straight out.
4. Reverse procedure to install. Ensure air flow direction indicator is pointed in correct direction.

TECHNICAL SERVICE BULLETINS

Intermittent No Crank/No Start

ALL MODELS w/ SIDE-MOUNTED BATTERY TERMINALS

On some of these models there may be an intermittent no crank, no start condition.

This condition may be caused by poor battery cable connections. Cross-threaded/stripped battery cable bolts inside the battery side post terminals may cause poor battery cable connections

To correct the is condition clean the threads in the battery side post terminals using a ⅜ inch (#16) NC bottom tap. and replace battery cable bolt.

2004-06 ION

On some of these models built through VIN 6Z147837, there may be intermittent no start conditions. There may be a clicking noise may when the key is first turned to the START position, but no noise is heard after

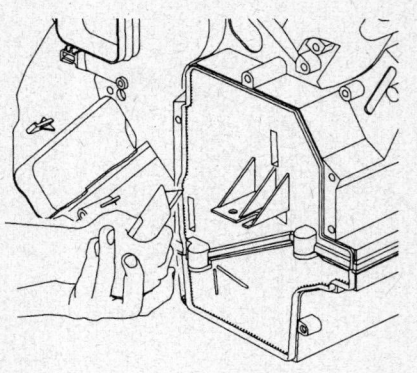

G37029900003900X

Fig. 20　Evaporator core replacement. L-Series

the initial start attempt. The Security lamp may flash immediately after trying to start the vehicle along with the message Driver Information Center Service Vehicle signal. The vehicle may not start for at least 10 minutes after the first attempt.

This condition may be caused and early ignition switch bounce voltage signal from RUN to START with the Body Control Module (BCM) interprets as a PASSLOCK system failure. Then the BCM disables the starting circuit.

To correct this condition, proceed as follows:
1. Ensure the ignition switch has been replaced at least once using part No. 10392423.
2. Replace the BCM.

2006-07 ION

On some of these models built between VINs 6Z161624 and 7Z119036, there may be a intermittent no start condition. There may be a clicking noise when the key is first turned to the START position, but no noise is heard after the initial start attempt. The Security lamp may flash immediately after trying to start the vehicle along with the message Driver Information Center Service Vehicle signal. The vehicle may not start for at least 10 minutes after the first attempt.

This condition may be caused by an inconsistent contact inside the ignition switch between the printed circuit board and the contact finger.

To correct this condition, replace the ignition switch.

Key Sticks, Binds, Is Hard To Insert, Or Will Not Rotate

2004-05 ION

On some of these models the key sticks, binds, is hard to insert or will not rotate in the ignition cylinder.

This condition may be caused by lack of material to stake ignition lock cylinder tumbler retainer plate.

Replace the ignition lock cylinder, tumblers and retainer plate using new components. **Do not use any original components.**

2.0L VIN P Engine

NOTE: On Air Bag Equipped Models, Refer To "Air Bag System Precautions" Located In The Front Of This Manual For System Disarming & Arming Procedures.

NOTE: Refer To "Computer Relearn Procedures" Located In The Front Of This Manual When Battery Power To The Computer Has Been Interrupted.

INDEX

	Page No.
Camshaft, Replace	12-23
Exhaust	12-24
Installation	12-24
Removal	12-24
Intake	12-23
Installation	12-24
Removal	12-23
Compression Pressure	12-21
Cooling System Bleed	12-25
Crankshaft Rear Oil Seal, Replace	12-25
Cylinder Head, Replace	12-22
Engine Rebuilding Specifications	29-1
Engine, Replace	12-21
Engine Mount, Replace	12-21

	Page No.
Exhaust Manifold, Replace	12-22
Front Cover, Replace	12-22
Fuel Filter, Replace	12-26
Fuel Pump, Replace	12-26
Intake Manifold, Replace	12-22
Main & Rod Bearings	12-24
Connecting Rod Bearings	12-25
Main Bearings	12-24
Oil Pan, Replace	12-25
Oil Pump, Replace	12-25
Oil Pump Service	12-25
Assemble	12-25
Disassemble	12-25
Piston & Rod Assembly	12-24
Pistons, Pins & Rings	12-24
Precautions	12-21

	Page No.
Air Bag Systems	12-21
Battery Ground Cable	12-21
Fuel System Pressure Relief	12-21
Radiator, Replace	12-26
Serpentine Drive Belt	12-25
Belt, Replace	12-25
Tensioner, Replace	12-25
Supercharger, Replace	12-26
Thermostat, Replace	12-25
Tightening Specifications	12-27
Timing Chain, Replace	12-23
Installation	12-23
Removal	12-23
Valve Adjustment	12-22

PRECAUTIONS

Air Bag Systems

Refer to "Air Bag System Precautions" in the front of this manual for system disarming and arming procedures.

Battery Ground Cable

Prior to service, disconnect battery ground cable and isolate as required.

Fuel System Pressure Relief

1. Loosen fuel filler cap to relieve fuel tank vapor pressure.
2. Remove fuel pressure service port cap.
3. Remove nuts and engine identification cover.
4. Connect pressure test kit tool No. SA9127-E, or equivalent to fuel pressure service port connection. Wrap shop towel around port during connection to prevent spillage.
5. Place end of bleed hose in suitable container and open valve to bleed system pressure.
6. Remove gauge after pressure has dissipated and replace cap.
7. Install engine identification cover.
8. Tighten fuel filler cap.

COMPRESSION PRESSURE

1. Start and run engine until it reaches normal operating temperature.
2. Turn ignition switch to OFF position and disconnect ignition module electrical connectors.
3. Ensure battery is fully charged.
4. Remove ignition coils and spark plugs.
5. Install suitable compression gauge tool in spark plug hole.
6. Ensure throttle is wide open.
7. Crank engine through four compression strokes for each cylinder.
8. Lowest reading cylinder should be within 70% of highest.
9. No cylinder should read less than 100 psi.

ENGINE MOUNT
REPLACE

1. Support engine with suitable floor jack and wooden block under oil pan.
2. Remove engine mount to intermediate bracket bolts.
3. Remove mount to mid-rail nuts and engine mount.
4. Reverse procedure to install, noting the following:
   a. Hand start mounting nuts and bolts, then tighten.
   b. **Do not pry engine mount to align holes.**

ENGINE
REPLACE

1. Ensure front wheels are in straight ahead position.
2. Remove air outlet duct.
3. Secure cooling module to upper body structure.
4. Drain coolant and engine oil into an suitable containers.
5. Relieve fuel system pressure as outlined under "Precautions."
6. Disconnect fuel line from fuel rail.
7. Remove radiator inlet hose.
8. Remove surge tank to cylinder head pipe.
9. Remove radiator outlet hose.
10. Remove heater inlet and outlet hoses.
11. Disconnect MAP sensor and Electronic Temperature Control (ETC) electrical connectors.
12. Disconnect BARO and CKP sensors electrical connectors:
13. Disconnect oil pressure sensor and EVAP purge solenoid electrical connectors,
14. Disconnect ignition coils and O2 sensor electrical connectors.
15. Disconnect VSS and ECT sensor electrical connectors.
16. Disconnect boost solenoid and .back-up lamp switch electrical connectors.
17. Remove righthand front fender liner.
18. Mark serpentine belt running direction.
19. Slowly tensioner counterclockwise to relieve tension, then remove serpentine belt.
20. Raise and support vehicle.

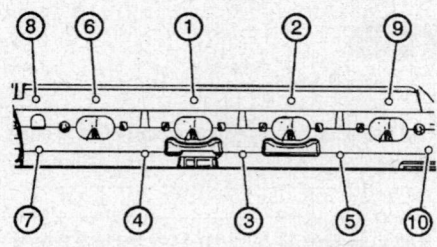

Fig. 1 Exhaust manifold nut tightening sequence

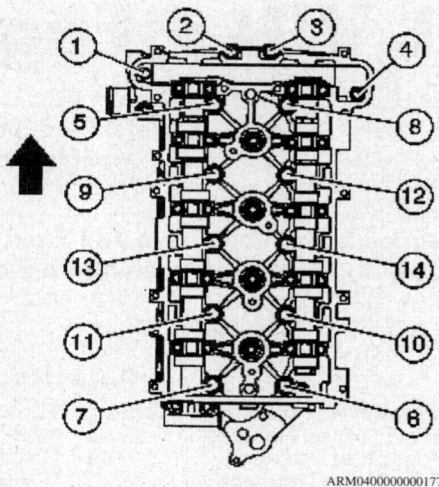

Fig. 2 Cylinder head bolt loosening sequence

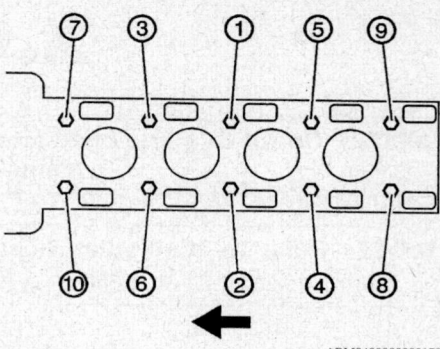

Fig. 3 Cylinder head bolt tightening sequence

21. Recover refrigerant as outlined in "Air Conditioning" chapter.
22. Disconnect air conditioning suction discharge hose assembly from compressor.
23. Remove mounting bolts, and position air conditioning compressor aside.
24. Disconnect starter and alternator electrical connectors.
25. Disconnect front exhaust pipe from manifold.
26. Disconnect shift cable from transaxle.
27. Support powertrain assembly between frame and powertrain using suitable wooden blocks.
28. Remove engine mount to intermediate bracket bolts.
29. Remove mount to mid-rail nuts and engine mount.
30. Remove transaxle lefthand mount.
31. Disconnect stabilizer links from stabilizer bar.
32. Disconnect outer tie rod ends from steering knuckles.
33. Remove lefthand front tire and wheel assembly.
34. Remove and discard intermediate shaft to steering gear pinch bolt. **Do turn steering shaft.**
35. Disconnect intermediate shaft from steering gear.
36. Disconnect lower control arms from steering knuckles. **Do not separate ball joint using pickle fork or wedge type tool.**
37. Remove wheel driveshaft nut. Insert drift or flat bladed tool into caliper and rotor to prevent rotor from turning.
38. Carefully loosen wheel driveshaft splines from wheel bearing/hub using wooden block and hammer. Temporarily install nut to protect threads.
39. Disconnect outer tie rod assembly from steering knuckle. **Do not loosen tie rod adjustment jamb nut.**
40. Loosen outer to inner tie rod jam nut.
41. Remove and discard tie rod to steering knuckle nut.
42. Separate outer tie rod from steering knuckle using tool tie rod separator tool No. SA91100C, or equivalent.
43. Mark frame to body position for installation alignment.
44. Lower vehicle to approximately three feet off ground.
45. Position wooden blocks as required between lift table and frame.
46. Slowly remove front frame bolts.
47. Partially remove rear frame bolts until 1½ inches of bolt shank is exposed.
48. Slowly lower table to floor.

49. Support engine using suitable crane or hoist at lift hooks.
50. Remove mounting bolts and starter.
51. Remove mounting bolts and separate engine from transaxle.
52. **On models equipped with manual transaxle,** remove clutch pressure plate and disk.
53. **On all models,** reverse procedure to install.

INTAKE MANIFOLD
REPLACE

1. Remove supercharger as outlined under "Supercharger, Replace."
2. Disconnect alternator electrical connectors.
3. Remove mounting bolts and alternator,
4. Drain coolant into suitable container.
5. Disconnect charged air cooling system inlet and outlet hoses.
6. Remove charged air coolant pump.
7. Remove cooling fan.
8. Remove mounting bolts and position air conditioning compressor aside.
9. Remove oil level dipstick tube bolt.
10. Remove mounting nuts and bolts, then the intake manifold,
11. Reverse procedure to install.

EXHAUST MANIFOLD
REPLACE

1. Remove exhaust manifold heat shield.
2. Disconnect oxygen sensor electrical connector.
3. Remove oxygen sensor using wrench tool No. J39194-C, or equivalent.
4. Raise and support vehicle.
5. Remove exhaust pipe to manifold nuts.
6. Pull down and back on exhaust pipe to disconnect pipe from manifold. **Do not bend exhaust flex decoupler more than 3° in any direction.**
7. Lower vehicle.
8. Remove mounting nuts, exhaust manifold and gasket, Discard nuts and gasket.

9. Reverse procedure to install. **Torque** new exhaust manifold mounting nuts to 115 inch lbs. in sequence, **Fig. 1.**

CYLINDER HEAD
REPLACE

1. Remove supercharger as outlined under "Supercharger, Replace."
2. Remove intake manifold as outlined under "Intake Manifold, Replace."
3. Remove exhaust manifold as outlined under "Exhaust Manifold, Replace."
4. Remove timing chain as outlined under "Timing Chain, Replace."
5. Loosen cylinder head bolts in sequence, **Fig. 2.**
6. Remove and discard bolts.
7. Remove cylinder head and discard gasket.
8. Reverse procedure to install, noting the following:
   a. Refer to sequence, **Fig. 3,** and tighten cylinder head bolts in two steps: First step, **torque** bolts to 22 ft. lbs.; second step, tighten bolts an additional 155.°
   b. **Torque** new cylinder head front bolts to 26 ft. lbs.

VALVE ADJUSTMENT

This engine is equipped with hydraulic lifters and no adjustment is required.

FRONT COVER
REPLACE

1. Remove righthand front fender liner.
2. Relieve tension by slowly turn belt tensioner counterclockwise and remove serpentine belt.
3. Prevent crankshaft rotation using holder tool No. J38122-A, or equivalent.
4. Remove mounting bolt and crankshaft balance. Discard bolt.
5. Remove mounting bolts and belt tensioner.
6. Remove mounting bolts and idler pulley.
7. Remove front cover to water pump bolt.
8. Remove mounting bolts and front cover.
9. Remove engine mount to intermediate bracket bolts.

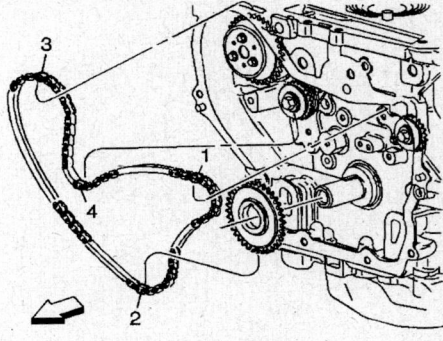

1. Uniquely colored link
2. First matching colored link
3. Balancer shaft chain
4. Last matching colored link

ARM0400000000179

Fig. 4 Balance shaft chain mark alignment

10. Remove mount to mid-rail nuts and engine mount.
11. Remove front engine mount bracket.
12. Discard front cover gasket.
13. Reverse procedure to install.

TIMING CHAIN
REPLACE
Removal

1. Disconnect ignition coil electrical connectors.
2. Remove mounting bolts and ignition coils,
3. Remove ground strap and stud.
4. Disconnect PCV hose from valve cover.
5. Disconnect fuel feed pipe from fuel rail.
6. Remove mounting bolts and valve cover.
7. Raise and support vehicle.
8. Remove engine front cover as outlined under "Front Cover, Replace."
9. Lower vehicle and remove spark plugs.
10. Hold camshaft flats using suitable open end wrench.
11. Position piston No. 1 at approximately 60° before TDC by turning intake camshaft sprocket until diamond shaped hole on sprocket reaches 12 o'clock position. **Turn in clockwise direction only.**
12. Remove timing chain tensioner.
13. Remove access plug and fixed timing chain guide.
14. Remove upper timing chain guide.
15. Remove mounting bolt and exhaust camshaft sprocket. Discard bolt.
16. Remove timing chain tensioner guide.
17. Remove mounting bolt and intake camshaft sprocket. Discard bolt
18. Remove timing chain through top of cylinder head.
19. Remove crankshaft sprocket.
20. Remove oil nozzle and bolt.
21. Remove balance shaft drive chain tensioner.
22. Remove adjustable balance shaft chain guide.

23. Remove small balance shaft drive chain guide.
24. Remove upper balance shaft drive chain guide.
25. Remove balance shaft drive chain by gathering all chain slack between crankshaft and water pump sprockets.

Installation

1. Install upper balance shaft chain guide.
2. Align uniquely colored link with timing mark on intake side balance shaft sprocket, **Fig. 4.**
3. Work clockwise around chain and align first matching colored link with crankshaft drive sprocket timing mark.
4. Place chain on water pump drive sprocket.
5. Align last matching colored link with exhaust side balance shaft drive sprocket timing mark.
6. Install small balance shaft chain guide.
7. Install adjustable balance shaft drive chain guide.
8. Turn tensioner plunger 90° in its bore and compress plunger until paper clip can be inserted through plunger body hole and into hole in plunger.
9. Install timing chain tensioner.
10. Remove paper clip from tensioner.
11. Install oil nozzle and bolt.
12. Install crankshaft sprocket with timing mark at 5 o'clock position.
13. Lower new timing chain through opening in top of cylinder head, ensure chain goes around both sides of cylinder block bosses, **Fig. 5.**
14. Install intake camshaft sprocket with INT diamond at 2 o'clock position.
15. Install new intake camshaft sprocket bolt hand tight.
16. Route timing chain around crankshaft sprocket with matching colored link aligning with timing mark.
17. Route timing chain around intake camshaft sprocket with uniquely colored link aligned with INT diamond.
18. Install timing chain tensioner guide through opening in top of cylinder head.
19. Install exhaust camshaft sprocket with timing chain matching colored link at EXH triangle aligned at 10 o'clock position.
20. Turn camshaft slightly using suitable wrench until exhaust sprocket aligns with camshaft.
21. Install new exhaust camshaft sprocket bolt hand tight.
22. Install fixed timing chain guide.
23. Apply Saturn sealant compound part No. 21485277, or equivalent, to threads, then install timing chain guide bolt access hole plug.
24. Install timing chain upper guide.
25. Measure timing chain tensioner assembly from end to end. New tensioner under compression should measure 2.83 inches. In active state it should measure 3.35 inches.
26. If tensioner is not in compressed state, proceed as follows:
    a. Pull piston out of tensioner body.
    b. Install tension tool No. J45027-2, or

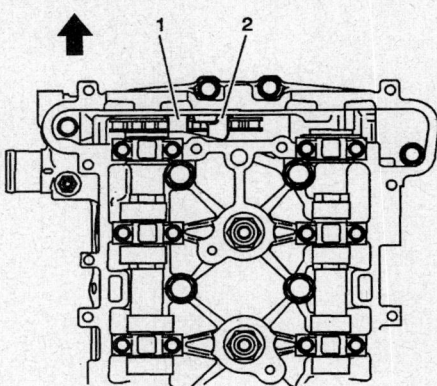

1. Boss
2. Boss

ARM0400000000180

Fig. 5 Timing chain routing around block bosses

   equivalent, into suitable vise, **Fig. 6.**
    c. Install notch end of piston assembly into tool.
    d. Turn ratchet cylinder into piston.
27. Install compressed piston back into tensioner body until it stops at bottom of bore.
28. Tensioner should measure approximately 2.83 inches from end to end. Repeat compression procedure if tensioner does not measure as specified.
29. Install timing chain tensioner.
30. Turn tool down through camshaft drive chain to rest on timing chain using suitable rubber end tip tool, then give sharp downward diagonal jolt to release tensioner.
31. Hold camshaft using suitable wrench.
32. Install valve cover.
33. Install ground strap to valve cover.
34. Install spark plugs and ignition coils.
35. Connect fuel feed pipe to fuel rail.
36. Install fuel pipe bracket.
37. Connect PCV hose to valve cover.
38. Install new engine front cover gasket.
39. Install front engine mount bracket and engine mount.
40. Install engine front cover and water pump.
41. Install idler pulley.
42. Install serpentine belt tensioner.
43. Install crankshaft balancer using new bolt.
44. Install serpentine belt.
45. Install fender liner, then the tire and wheel.

CAMSHAFT
REPLACE
Intake
REMOVAL

1. Disconnect ignition coil electrical connectors.
2. Remove mounting bolts and coils,
3. Remove ground strap and stud.
4. Disconnect PCV hose from valve cover.

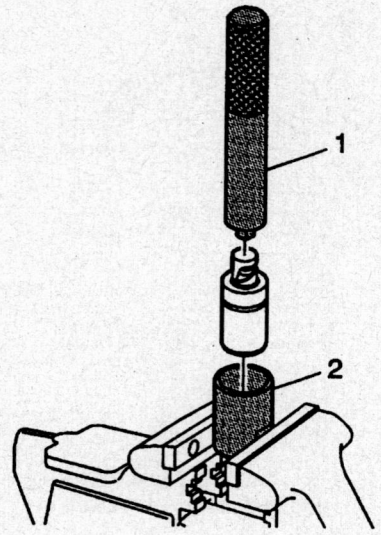

1. J 45027-1
2. J45027-2

ARM0400000000181

Fig. 6 Timing chain tensioner compression

5. Disconnect fuel feed pipe from fuel rail.
6. Remove mounting bolts and valve cover.
7. Remove mounting bolts and timing chain upper guide.
8. Install sprocket holding tool No. J43655, or equivalent, **Fig. 7.**
9. Remove and discard both intake and exhaust camshaft sprocket bolts, **Fig. 8.**
10. Move camshaft sprockets forward.
11. Mark intake camshaft bearing caps for installation alignment in original locations.
12. Remove each bearing cap bolt one turn at a time until spring tension is removed.
13. Remove bearing caps and intake camshaft.
14. Remove camshaft roller followers and lash adjusters.

INSTALLATION

1. Lubricate valve tips.
2. Install lash adjusters and roller followers.
3. Ensure alignment notches are aligned with camshaft sprocket, **Fig. 9.**
4. Install intake camshaft and camshaft bearing caps.
5. Tighten cap bolts in three steps until they are seated, then tighten.
6. Apply .197 inch bead of Permatex Anaerobic Gasket Maker part No. 51813, or equivalent, to rear camshaft bearing cap.
7. Install rear bearing cap bolts.
8. Install sprockets onto camshafts using new bolts.
9. Remove sprocket holding tool.
10. **Torque** sprocket bolts to 63 ft. lbs.
11. Final tighten bolts an additional 30°.
12. Install timing chain upper guide and tighten mounting bolts.

ARM0400000000182

Fig. 7 Holding tool No. J43655

13. Install valve cover. and tighten mounting bolts.
14. Install ground strap to valve cover and tighten stud.
15. Install ignition coils and tighten mounting bolts. Connect electrical connectors.
16. Install fuel feed pipe to fuel rail and tighten.
17. Install fuel pipe bracket and tighten mounting bolts.
18. Connect PCV hose to valve cover.

Exhaust
REMOVAL

1. Disconnect ignition coil electrical connectors.
2. Remove mounting bolts and coils.
3. Remove ground strap and stud.
4. Disconnect PCV hose from valve cover.
5. Disconnect fuel feed pipe from fuel rail.
6. Remove mounting bolts and valve cover.
7. Remove mounting bolts and timing chain upper guide.
8. Install sprocket holding tool No. J43655, or equivalent, **Fig. 7.**
9. Remove and discard both intake and exhaust camshaft sprocket bolts, **Fig. 8.**
10. Move camshaft sprockets forward.
11. Mark exhaust camshaft bearing caps to ensure installation in original locations.
12. Remove each bearing cap bolt one turn at a time until spring tension disappears.
13. Remove bearing caps and exhaust camshaft.
14. Remove camshaft roller followers and lash adjusters.

INSTALLATION

1. Lubricate valve tips.
2. Install lash adjusters and roller followers.
3. Ensure alignment notches are aligned with camshaft sprocket, **Fig. 9.**
4. Install exhaust camshaft and camshaft bearing caps.
5. Tighten cap bolts in three steps until they are seated, then tighten.
6. Apply .197 inch bead of Permatex Anaerobic Gasket Maker part No. 51813, or equivalent, to rear camshaft bearing cap.

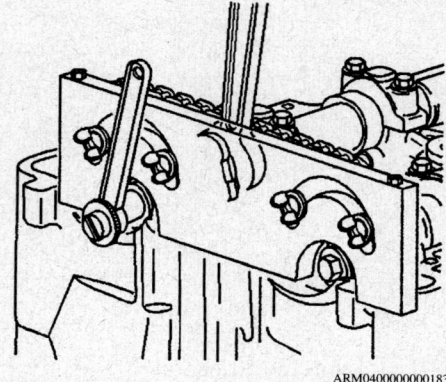

ARM0400000000183

Fig. 8 Camshaft sprocket bolt replacement

7. Install rear bearing cap bolts and tighten.
8. Install sprockets onto camshafts. Tighten new camshaft sprocket bolts hand tight.
9. Remove sprocket holding tool.
10. **Torque** sprocket bolts to 63 ft. lbs., then tighten an additional 30°.
11. Install timing chain upper guide.
12. Install valve cover.
13. Install ground strap to valve cover.
14. Install ignition coils, then connect electrical connectors.
15. Install fuel feed pipe to fuel rail.
16. Install fuel pipe bracket.
17. Connect PCV hose to valve cover.

PISTON & ROD ASSEMBLY

Install the piston onto the connecting rod with the arrow pointed toward the front of the engine.

PISTONS, PINS & RINGS

Replace any pistons that show signs of damage or excessive wear. Piston pin bores and pins must be free of varnish or scuffing. Use an outside micrometer to measure the piston contact areas and piston pin bore. Subtract the measurement of the piston pin bore from the piston pin.

MAIN & ROD BEARINGS
Main Bearings

1. Install crankshaft bearing caps using suitable brass, lead, leather, or equivalent soft faced mallet. **Do not use lower crankcase bolts to pull bearing caps into seats.**
2. Refer to sequence, **Fig. 10,** and tighten lower crankcase inner bolts in two steps: First step, **torque** bolts to 15 ft. lbs.; second step, tighten and additional 70°.
3. Refer to sequence, **Fig. 11,** and tighten lower crankcase outer bolts in two

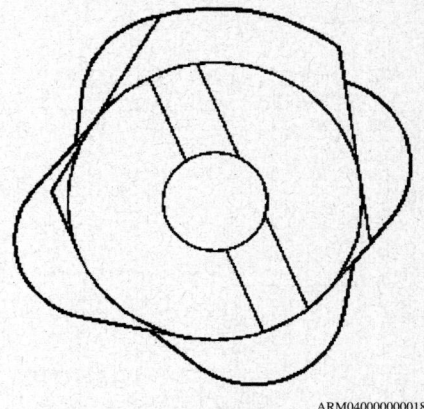

Fig. 9 Camshaft sprocket alignment notches

steps: First step, **torque** bolts to 18 ft. lbs.; second step, tighten bolts an additional 70.°

Connecting Rod Bearings

Tighten connecting rod bearing cap bolts in two steps. First step, **torque,** bolts to 18 ft. lbs.; second step, tighten bolts an additional 100.°

CRANKSHAFT REAR OIL SEAL

REPLACE

1. Remove transaxle as outlined in **MOTOR's "Domestic Transmission, In-Vehicle Service" manual or "Transmission Service DVD."**
2. Remove flywheel and cover.
3. remove seal using suitable screwdriver in seal carrier pry tangs.
4. Apply suitable clean engine oil to seal lip and inside diameter of seal carrier.
5. Install seal using seal installer tool No. J42067, or equivalent.
6. Install transaxle and flywheel, noting the following:
   a. **Torque** flywheel mounting bolts to 39 ft. lbs.
   b. Final tighten mounting bolts an additional 25°.

OIL PAN

REPLACE

1. Raise and support vehicle.
2. Drain engine oil into suitable container and remove front exhaust pipe.
3. Remove righthand front tire/wheel, splash shield and vibration dampener.
4. Remove mounting bolts and oil pan.
5. Reverse procedure to install, noting the following:
   a. Apply .08 inch bead of RTV part No. 21019581, or equivalent, around perimeter of oil pan and oil suction port opening. **Do not apply an excessive amount of RTV.**
   b. **Torque** oil pan mounting bolts to 18 ft. lbs. in sequence, **Fig. 12.**

OIL PUMP

REPLACE

1. Remove air cleaner, then raise and support vehicle.
2. Drain engine oil into suitable container.
3. Remove righthand front tire/wheel assembly and splash shield.
4. Mark running direction and remove accessory drive belt.
5. Remove crankshaft pulley using pulley holding tool No. J38122, or equivalent.
6. Remove righthand front fender liner.
7. Mark serpentine belt running direction.
8. Slowly turn belt tensioner counterclockwise to relieve tension, then remove serpentine belt.
9. Remove mounting bolts and tensioner.
10. Install engine support fixture tool No. SA9150-E, or equivalent.
11. Support engine with suitable floor jack and wooden block under oil pan.
12. Remove engine mount to intermediate bracket bolts.
13. Remove mount to mid-rail nuts and engine mount.
14. Remove front cover mounting and bolts under water pump cover.
15. Remove front cover and gasket.
16. Reverse procedure to install. **Torque** crankshaft pulley mounting bolt to 74 ft. lbs., then tighten an additional 75.°

OIL PUMP SERVICE

Disassemble

1. Remove pressure relief valve.
2. Remove cover plate mounting bolts.
3. Mark drive and driven rotors for installation alignment.
4. Remove drive and driven rotors.

Assemble

1. Remove front cover oil seal using suitable screwdriver or punch.
2. Install new oil seal using oil seal installer tool No. J35268-A, or equivalent, and suitable press.
3. Install pressure relief valve, valve spring and oil pump pressure relief valve plug.
4. Lubricate drive and driven rotors with clean engine oil.
5. Align and Install drive and driven rotors into pump body.
6. Fill oil pump with petroleum jelly to prime oil pump.
7. Install oil pump gear cover plate screws.

SERPENTINE DRIVE BELT

Belt, Replace

1. Remove righthand front fender liner.
2. Mark serpentine belt running direction.
3. Relieve tension by slowly turn belt tensioner counterclockwise and remove serpentine belt.
4. Reverse procedure to install.

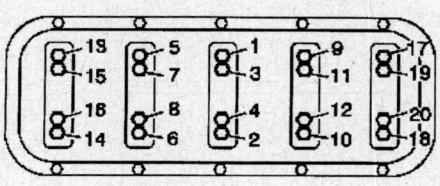

Fig. 10 Lower crankcase inner bolt tightening sequence

Tensioner, Replace

1. Remove righthand front fender liner.
2. Mark serpentine belt running direction.
3. Relieve tension by slowly turn belt tensioner counterclockwise and remove serpentine belt.
4. Remove belt tensioner bolts, then the tensioner.
5. Reverse procedure to install.

COOLING SYSTEM BLEED

1. Remove surge tank cap.
2. Raise and support vehicle.
3. Place suitable drain pan below righthand side of radiator lower mount.
4. Open petcock and drain coolant into container.
5. After all coolant has drained, close petcock hand tight.
6. Lower vehicle and disconnect radiator upper hose from righthand side of radiator.
7. Slowly add 50/50 mixture of Dex-Cool antifreeze and deionized water to engine through upper hose.
8. Connect upper hose to radiator.
9. Slowly add antifreeze and water mixture to surge tank to just above Cold Fill line.
10. Install surge tank cap and start engine.
11. Run engine at 2000–2500 RPM for three minutes.
12. Idle engine for 30 seconds and turn ignition switch to OFF.
13. Inspect and adjust coolant level as required.

THERMOSTAT

REPLACE

1. Drain engine coolant into suitable container.
2. Remove mounting bolts and feed pipe from thermostat housing to water pump.
3. Record orientation, then remove thermostat and retaining sleeve. Discard O-ring.
4. Reverse procedure to install, noting the following:
   a. Install new thermostat and retaining sleeve with dimple placed into housing slot.
   b. Lubricate new O-ring with soapy water or coolant before installation into water pump.

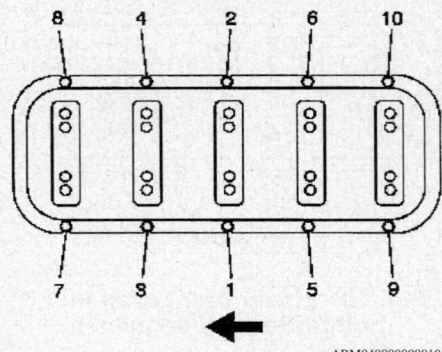

Fig. 11 Lower crankcase outer bolt tightening sequence

RADIATOR

REPLACE

1. Remove surge tank cap.
2. Raise and support vehicle.
3. Place suitable drain pan below righthand side of radiator lower mount.
4. Open petcock and drain coolant into suitable container.
5. Place drain pan below water pump drain plug.
6. Open drain plug and drain coolant into suitable container.
7. After all coolant has drained, close petcock hand tight.
8. **Torque** water pump drain plug to 16 ft. lbs.
9. Lower vehicle and remove air cleaner outlet resonator.
10. Disconnect radiator inlet and outlet hoses from radiator.
11. **On models equipped with automatic or VTi transaxle,** proceed as follows:
    a. Disconnect transaxle upper oil cooler line from radiator.
    b. Remove lefthand front wheelhouse liner.
    c. Remove engine lefthand splash shield.
    d. Disconnect transaxle lower oil cooler line from radiator.
12. **On all models,** remove cooling fan from radiator by pushing up on fan shroud and unsnapping retainers.
13. Position and support cooling fan aside.
14. Remove push-in retainer and air dam.
15. Remove air conditioning condenser mounting bolts.
16. Slide condenser down to disconnect upper mounting tabs from radiator.
17. Position and support condenser aside.
18. Remove left and righthand radiator side baffles.
19. Remove engine righthand splash shield to radiator mount push-in retainer.
20. **On models equipped with manual transaxle,** remove engine lefthand splash shield to radiator mount push-in retainer.
21. **On all models,** remove radiator lower mounts, brackets and bolts.
22. Tilt air conditioning condenser forward

and cooling fan rearward.
23. Remove radiator,
24. Remove upper air baffle from radiator.
25. Reverse procedure to install.

FUEL PUMP

REPLACE

1. Connect suitably programmed scan tool to Diagnostic Link Connector (DLC) and turn ignition switch to ON position.
2. Raise and support vehicle, keeping scan tool accessible outside of vehicle.
3. Disconnect fuel feed line at outlet to filter.
4. Install $\frac{3}{8} \times \frac{1}{4}$ inch adapter onto flow/pressure adapter tool No. SA9127E-7, or equivalent, and insert adapter into fuel feed line.
5. Connect one end of suitable drain hose to other end of adapter. Connect other end of drain hose to suitable fuel handling cart.
6. Turn fuel pump on using scan tool and pump fuel into suitable container.
7. If fuel pump is inoperative, proceed as follows:
    a. Insert siphon hose guide/funnel into fuel filler pipe.
    b. Insert siphon hose J43290, or equivalent, into guide funnel and fuel filler pipe. Some resistance may be encountered when tip of siphon hose reaches inlet check valve. Repeated probing may be required to slide hose tip through check valve.
    c. Siphon fuel into suitable container.
8. Ensure fuel tank is less than quarter full.
9. Remove exhaust system intermediate pipe and rear heat shield mounting bolts.
10. Remove fuel filler pipe lower bracket mounting screw and disconnect EVAP canister vent hose.
11. Loosen fuel filler pipe hose clamp closest to fuel tank and remove tank ground strap mounting screw near fuel filter.
12. Disconnect fuel feed line after fuel filter.
13. Disconnect fuel return and EVAP canister purge lines between tank and chassis fuel bundle.
14. Disconnect fuel tank electrical connectors.
15. Loosen, but do not remove, front tank strap bolt.
16. Remove rear tank mounting strap bolts with assistance.
17. Remove tank by lowering at rear, then sliding downward and rearward.
18. Disconnect fuel lines from fuel pump module cover.
19. Remove fuel pump module retainer ring using lock ring service tool No. J43827, or equivalent.
20. Remove sending unit first by pulling retaining clip toward float arm and lifting upward. **Do not bend sending unit float arm.**

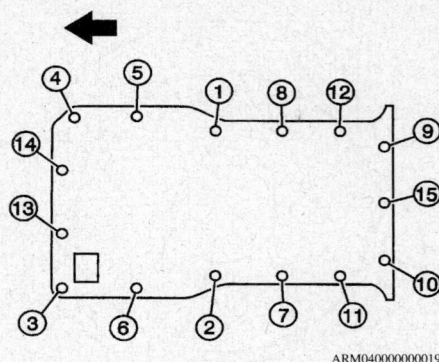

Fig. 12 Oil pan bolt tightening sequence

21. Carefully lift fuel pump straight up from fuel tank. Clips must be disconnected at same time to disconnect fuel pump from housing.
22. Discard fuel pump module to tank seal and remove fuel feed line from bottom of fuel pump cover using removal tool No. J44078, or equivalent.
23. Disconnect fuel pump electrical connector from fuel pump cover.
24. Reverse procedure to install, noting the following:
    a. Replace plastic fuel line retainers.
    b. Install new module to tank seal lubricated with suitable clean engine oil.

FUEL FILTER

REPLACE

1. Raise and support vehicle.
2. Remove bracket screw, then disconnect fuel lines from inlet and outlet sides of fuel filter.
3. Slide fuel filter out of bracket.
4. Reverse procedure.

SUPERCHARGER

REPLACE

1. Remove righthand front fender liner.
2. Mark serpentine belt running direction.
3. Relieve tension by slowly turn belt tensioner counterclockwise and remove serpentine belt.
4. Remove EVAP tube and valve.
5. Remove air cleaner outlet duct.
6. Disconnect EVAP purge line.
7. Disconnect Throttle Body Injection (TBI) control harness electrical connector.
8. Remove mounting bolts and TBI unit from supercharger. Discard gasket.
9. Remove Supercharger Inlet Pressure (SCIP) sensor.
10. Disconnect vacuum brake booster hose.
11. Remove intercooler fill neck bracket bolts.
12. Remove supercharger.
13. Reverse procedure to install. Install new TBI gasket.

TIGHTENING SPECIFICATIONS

Year	Component	Torque/Ft. Lbs.
2004–07	Air Conditioning Compressor	15
	Air Conditioning Condenser	88①
	Alternator	15
	Alternator Bracket	31
	Alternator Connector	15
	ATF Cooler Lines To Radiator	15
	Axle Shaft Nut	81
	Balance Shaft Bearing Carrier	89①
	Balance Shaft Chain Guides	89①
	Balance Shaft Sprocket	37
	BARO Sensor & Coolant Return Line Assembly	71①
	Boost Solenoid Bracket	89①
	Camshaft Bearing Cap	⑩
	Camshaft Sprocket	②
	CMP Sensor	71①
	CMP Sensor Housing	16
	Chain Guide Access Hole Plug	59
	Connecting Rod	④
	Crankshaft Bearing Lower Crankcase To Block	④
	Crankshaft Damper	⑤
	CKP Sensor	89①
	Crankshaft Pulley	⑤
	Cylinder Head	⑥
	Cylinder Head Oil Gallery Plug	26
	Dipstick Guide	89①
	Driveshaft Nut	81
	Electronic ICM Cover	71①
	ECT Sensor	16
	Engine Lift Bracket	18
	Engine Mount Intermediate Bracket	74
	Engine Mount To Intermediate Bracket	37
	Engine Mount To Mid-Rail	74
	Exhaust Manifold, Nut	③
	Exhaust Manifold, Stud	89①
	Exhaust Manifold Heat Shield	15
	Exhaust Manifold Pipe Flange, Nut	37
	Exhaust Manifold Pipe Flange, Stud	12
	Exhaust Pipe	22
	Flywheel	⑦
	Frame Bolt, Rear	148
	Frame To Body	74⑧
	Front Cover	18
	Fuel Feed Line	10
	Fuel Feed Line & Injector Harness Bracket	89①
	Fuel Rail Bracket	89①
	Fuel Supply Line Fitting	10
	Fuel Tank Strap	18
	Idler Pulley	16
	Ignition Coil	71①
	Intake Camshaft Rear Cap	18
	Intake Manifold, Nut	106①
	Intake Manifold, Stud	89①

TIGHTENING SPECIFICATIONS—Continued

Year	Component	Torque/Ft. Lbs.
2004–07	Intercooler Fill Neck Bracket	89①
	Knock Sensor	18
	Lift Bracket, Rear	16
	Main Bearings	④
	MAF Sensor	18①
	Oil Bypass Tube	16
	Oil Cooler	16
	Oil Filter Housing Cover	18
	Oil Gallery Plug	26
	Oil Gallery Plug, Rear	44
	Oil Dipstick Tube	89①
	Oil Pan	⑨
	Oil Pan Drain Plug	18
	Oil Pressure Sensor	13
	Oil Pump Gerotor Cover	53①
	Oil Pump Pressure Relief Valve Plug	30
	Oxygen Sensor	31
	Power Steering Pump	18
	Radiator, Lower	18
	Serpentine Belt Tensioner	33
	Spark Plugs	15
	Starter Motor	30
	Starter Terminal	13
	SCIP Sensor	89①
	Supercharger	18
	Thermostat Housing	89①
	Throttle Body	89①
	Timing Chain Guides	89①
	Timing Chain Nozzle	89①
	Timing Chain Tensioner	55
	Torque Converter	46
	Transaxle	55
	Transaxle Mount, Front	37
	Transaxle Mount, Through Bolt	74
	Transaxle Mount Bracket To Transmission Bolts, Rear	44
	Transaxle Mount to Frame Bolts, Rear	44
	Transaxle Mount To Mid-Rail Bolts, Side	25
	Transaxle To Engine	55
	Transaxle Mount, Side	33
	Transaxle Mount To Mid-Rail Bolts	20
	Valve Cover	71①
	Valve Cover Ground Cable	89①
	Vent Tube To Cylinder Head	11
	Water Pipe Support Bracket	89①
	Water Pump	18
	Water Pump Access Cover	62①
	Water Pump/Balance Shaft Chain Tensioner	89①
	Water Pump Feed Pipe	18①
	Water Pump Sprocket	89①
	Wheel Lug Nuts	100

① — Inch lbs.
② — Refer to "Camshaft, Replace" for tightening specifications & sequence.

③ — Refer to "Exhaust, Replace" for tightening specifications & sequence.

④ — Refer to "Main & Rod Bearings" for tightening specifications & sequence.

⑤ — Refer to "Oil Pump, Replace" for tightening specifications & sequence.

⑥ — Refer to "Cylinder Head, Replace" for tightening specifications & sequence.

⑦ — Refer to "Crankshaft Rear Oil Seal, Replace" for tightening specifications & sequence.

⑧ — Final tighten an additional 180°.

⑨ — Refer to "Oil Pan, Replace" for tightening specifications & sequence.

⑩ — Torque to 89 inch lbs. in three steps.

2.0L VIN X Engine

NOTE: On Air Bag Equipped Models, Refer To "Air Bag System Precautions" Located In The Front Of This Manual For System Disarming & Arming Procedures.

NOTE: Refer To "Computer Relearn Procedures" Located In The Front Of This Manual When Battery Power To The Computer Has Been Interrupted.

INDEX

	Page No.
Balance Shaft, Replace	12-35
Installation	12-35
Removal	12-35
Camshaft, Replace	12-34
Installation	12-34
Removal	12-34
Crankshaft Damper, Replace	12-32
Crankshaft Rear Oil Seal, Replace	12-35
Crankshaft Seal, Replace	12-35
Cylinder Head, Replace	12-31
Engine Rebuilding Specifications	29-1
Engine, Replace	12-29
Engine Mount, Replace	12-29
Lefthand	12-29
Righthand	12-29
Exhaust Manifold, Replace	12-31

	Page No.
Front Cover, Replace	12-33
Front Cover Seal, Replace	12-33
Fuel Pump, Replace	12-36
Hydraulic Lifters, Replace	12-32
Intake Manifold, Replace	12-31
Main & Rod Bearings	12-35
Connecting Rod Bearings	12-35
Main Bearings	12-35
Oil Cooler, Replace	12-35
Oil Pan, Replace	12-35
Oil Pump, Replace	12-35
Oil Pump Service	12-35
Assemble	12-35
Disassemble	12-35
Precautions	12-29
Air Bag Systems	12-29
Battery Ground Cable	12-29
Fuel System Pressure Relief	12-29

	Page No.
High Side	12-29
Low Side	12-29
Radiator, Replace	12-36
Rocker Arms	12-32
Serpentine Drive Belt	12-36
Replace	12-36
Thermostat, Replace	12-36
Tightening Specifications	12-38
Timing Chain, Replace	12-33
Installation	12-33
Removal	12-33
Turbocharger, Replace	12-36
Valve Adjustment	12-32
Valve Clearance Specifications	12-32
Valve Cover, Replace	12-32
Water Pump, Replace	12-36

PRECAUTIONS

Air Bag Systems

Refer to "Air Bag System Precautions" in the front of this manual for system disarming and arming procedures.

Battery Ground Cable

Prior to service, disconnect battery ground cable and isolate as required.

Fuel System Pressure Relief

LOW SIDE

USING DIGITAL PRESSURE GAUGE

1. Remove engine cover.
2. Loosen fuel fill cap to relieve fuel tank vapor pressure.
3. Remove fuel rail service port cap.
4. Wrap suitable shop towel around fuel rail service port.
5. Connect digital pressure gauge tool No. CH-48027 to fuel rail service port and place hose into suitable container.
6. Open tool valve and to bleed fuel from fuel rail. Close valve.
7. Remove hose and disconnect gauge.
8. Install fuel rail service port cap and engine cover. Tighten fuel fill cap

LESS DIGITAL PRESSURE GAGE

1. Loosen fuel fill cap to relieve fuel tank vapor pressure.
2. Remove engine cover.
3. Remove fuel rail service port cap.
4. Wrap suitable shop towel around fuel rail service port and use suitable, small flat bladed tool to depress (open) fuel rail test port valve.
5. Install fuel rail service port cap and engine cover. Tighten fuel fill cap.

HIGH SIDE

1. Connect suitable programmed scan tool to vehicle and command fuel pump relay OFF.
2. Start vehicle and allow engine to idle until engine stops in approximately 20–30 seconds.
3. Turn ignition switch to OFF position.
4. Ensure there is no fuel pressure using scan tool.
5. If scan tool is not available, what at least two hours after engine has stopped running to remove high pressure fuel line.

ENGINE MOUNT

REPLACE

Lefthand

1. Loosen clamps and remove Charge Air Cooler (CAC) outlet hose from CAC outlet pipe and throttle body.

2. Remove lefthand engine mount upper nut.
3. Raise and support vehicle.
4. Remove lefthand engine mount lower nut.
5. Remove righthand engine mount lower nut.
6. Position suitable adjustable jack below oil pan. Place suitable block of wood between oil pan and jack.
7. Raise engine and remove mount.
8. Reverse procedure to install.

Righthand

1. Raise and support vehicle, then remove tire and wheel assembly.
2. Remove upper and lower righthand engine mount nuts.
3. Remove lefthand engine mount lower nut.
4. Remove righthand brake hose bracket bolt.
5. Remove righthand brake line clip at crossmember.
6. Position suitable adjustable jack below oil pan. Place suitable block of wood between oil pan and jack.
7. Raise engine and remove engine mount.
8. Reverse procedure to install.

ENGINE

REPLACE

1. Open hood and remove headlamp

bulb socket Connector Positive Assurance (CPA) retainer, then disconnect connector.
2. Disconnect lefthand headlamp electrical harness.
3. Turn socket a quarter turn counterclockwise and disconnect bulb.
4. Remove mounting screws and headlamp.
5. Disconnect wiring harness on both sides and mark hood for installation alignment.
6. Remove mounting nuts and hood.
7. Relieve fuel system pressure as outlined under "Precautions."
8. Recover air conditioning system refrigerant as outlined in "Air Conditioning" chapter.
9. Grasp intake manifold cover and remove from studs.
10. Remove intake manifold cover, oil fill cap and insulator.
11. Turn power steering pump belt tensioner pulley clockwise and remove belt.
12. Lower vehicle.
13. Remove charge air cooler inlet pipe mounting bolt at rear bracket.
14. Remove mounting nut and charge air cooler rear bracket.
15. Remove charge air cooler inlet pipe mounting bolt at front bracket.
16. Loosen charge air cooler clamp at inlet pipe. and inlet pipe clamp at pipe.
17. Remove charge air cooler inlet pipe.
18. Disconnect intake air pressure and temperature sensor engine wiring harness electrical connector.
19. Disconnect clamp and remove charge air cooler outlet pipe air bypass valve solenoid vacuum hose.
20. Remove charge air cooler outlet pipe mounting bolt, nut and rear bracket.
21. Disconnect charge air cooler outlet pipe hose clamp and remove charge air cooler outlet pipe front bracket mounting bolt.
22. Disconnect clamp and remove charge air cooler outlet pipe.
23. Disconnect air cleaner housing and turbocharger clamps and remove air cleaner outlet duct.
24. Disconnect Mass Air Flow (MAF) sensor engine wiring harness electrical connector.
25. Remove front mounting bolt and air cleaner.
26. Remove drive belt.
27. Drain cooling system into suitable container.
28. Remove mounting bolts and radiator front air deflector.
29. Remove shroud air inlet, air cleaner outlet duct resonator and PCV hose clamps.
30. Remove air cleaner outlet duct resonator.
31. Disconnect cooling fan motor electrical connector.
32. Remove mounting bolts, shroud, cooling fan and motor.
33. Remove radiator inlet and outlet hoses, then the surge tank inlet hose.
34. Remove air cleaner stud, then the mounting nuts and radiator upper bracket.

35. Remove mounting bolts, air conditioning condenser and radiator.
36. Disconnect Evaporative Emission (EVAP) canister purge solenoid valve tube.
37. Disconnect fuel feed pipe from fuel line.
38. Remove cap and windshield wiper arm mounting nut.
39. Remove windshield washer nozzle hose and windshield wiper arm.
40. Remove retainers and air inlet grille. Disconnect washer pump hose.
41. **On models equipped with automatic transmission,** proceed as follows:
    a. Remove intake manifold as outlined under "Intake Manifold, Replace."
    b. Remove starter solenoid terminal nuts and disconnect engine terminal harness.
    c. Remove mounting bolts and starter motor.
42. **On models equipped with manual transmission,** proceed as follows:
    a. Remove transmission as outlined in **MOTOR's "Domestic Transmission, In-Vehicle Service" manual or "Transmission Service DVD."**
    b. Install differential case bracket to body mounting bolt to support rear drive module.
43. **On all models,** remove mounting bolts and turbocharger heat shield.
44. Remove mounting bolts, charge air cooler pipe and gasket from turbocharger.
45. Cap or plug turbocharger opening.
46. Disconnect clamp, then remove position radiator inlet hose from engine and position it aside.
47. Disconnect clamps, then remove radiator outlet hose from thermostat housing and oil cooler. Position hose aside.
48. Disconnect clamps, then remove surge tank outlet hose from thermostat housing and oil cooler. Position hose aside.
49. Disconnect clamp and remove surge tank outlet hose from rank.
50. Remove oil dipstick tube bracket clip and remove surge tank outlet hose.
51. Disconnect surge tank air bleed hose clamp at engine and clip at surge tank bracket. Position air bleed hose aside.
52. Disconnect clamps, then remove heater inlet and outlet hoses from thermostat housing.
53. Raise and support vehicle, then drain engine oil into suitable container.
54. Disconnect Crankshaft Position (CKP) and oil pressure sensors electrical connectors.
55. Disconnect brake booster vacuum pump electrical connector.
56. **On models equipped with manual transmission,** proceed as follows:
    a. Remove mounting nut and starter battery positive cable lead.
    b. Remove mounting nut and engine wiring harness from terminals from starter.
    c. Remove engine wiring harness clip from oil dipstick tube.
57. **On all models,** lower vehicle and cut

engine harness tie straps.
58. Remove mounting bolt and battery ground cable ground terminal from front engine lift bracket. Position cable aside.
59. Disconnect transmission oil cooler pump and alternator electrical connectors.
60. **On models equipped with manual transmission,** disconnect knock sensor electrical connector and remove engine wiring harness clip from oil dipstick tube bracket.
61. **On all models,** disconnect boot, then remove terminal nut and positive cable from alternator.
62. Disconnect air conditioning compressor and fuel injector jumper electrical connectors.
63. **On models equipped with manual transmission,** proceed as follows:
    a. Disconnect throttle actuator electrical connector.
    b. Remove engine wiring harness clip from intake manifold brace.
    c. Disconnect EVAP canister purge solenoid valve electrical connector.
    d. Disconnect Manifold Absolute Pressure (MAP) sensor electrical connector.
64. **On all models,** disconnect air conditioning refrigerant pressor sensor electrical connector.
65. Disconnect brake booster vacuum sensor and windshield wiper motor electrical connectors.
66. Remove engine harness clip from wiper motor hole.
67. Disconnect intake Camshaft Position (CMP) sensor and high pressure fuel pump electrical connectors.
68. Remove engine wiring harness clip from high pressure fuel pump bracket.
69. Disconnect intake and exhaust CMP actuator electrical connectors.
70. Remove engine harness clip from valve cover and disconnect ignition coils electrical connectors.
71. Disconnect Heated Oxygen Sensor (HO2S) and exhaust CMP sensor electrical connectors.
72. Remove bolt and position engine harness ground terminal aside.
73. Disconnect Engine Coolant Temperature (ECT) sensor electrical connector.
74. Disconnect valve cover engine harness clips.
75. Remove engine wiring harness clips from turbocharger coolant feed pipe stud and pipe tab.
76. Disconnect boost sensor electrical connector.
77. Remove mounting bolt and cylinder head ground terminal.
78. Remove engine harness clips from front studs, than gather all branches and position engine harness aside.
79. **On models equipped with manual transmission,** disconnect clamp and remove turbocharger vacuum hose.
80. **On all models,** remove vacuum hose from turbocharger coolant feed pipe clips.
81. **On models equipped with automatic transmission,** remove charge air bypass valve solenoid.

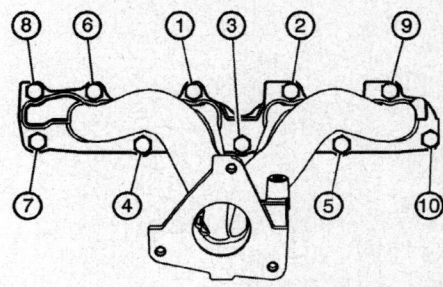

Fig. 1   Exhaust manifold tightening sequence

82. **On models equipped with manual transmission,** position vacuum hose aside.
83. **On all models,** remove mounting bolt and turbocharger coolant feed pipe fitting from cylinder head.
84. Remove mounting bolt and turbocharger coolant feed pipe bracket from cylinder head.
85. Remove mounting bolt and position air conditioning compressor line aside.
86. Raise and support vehicle.
87. Remove mounting bolts, then position power steering pump and bracket aside.
88. **On models equipped with automatic transmission,** proceed as follows:
    a. Remove torque converter to flywheel mounting bolts.
    b. Remove four lower bellhousing mounting bolts.
89. **On all models,** lower vehicle.
90. **On models equipped with automatic transmission,** remove five upper bellhousing mounting bolts.
91. **On all models,** remove lefthand righthand engine mount upper nuts.
92. Support engine using engine support adapter tool No. J42451-1, or equivalent, and suitable engine lifting device.
93. **On models equipped with automatic transmission,** separate engine from transmission.
94. **On all models,** remove engine.
95. **On models equipped with manual transmission,** remove mounting bolts one turn at a time, then the clutch cover and disc.
96. **On all models,** remove mounting bolts and flywheel.
97. Install engine to suitable stand.
98. Remove mounting bolts and air conditioning compressor.
99. Remove mounting bolts and nuts, then the catalytic converter and gasket.
100. Reverse procedure to install.

INTAKE MANIFOLD
REPLACE

1. Grasp cover and disconnect studs, then remove intake manifold cover.
2. Disconnect Charge Air Cooler (CAC) outlet hose clamps, then remove CAC outlet hose from outlet pipe and throttle body.
3. Remove engine wiring harness and No. 1 knock sensor clips from oil dipstick tube bracket.

4. Remove mounting bolt, then the tube and oil dipstick.
5. Relieve fuel system pressure as outlined under "Precautions."
6. Disconnect fuel rail line quick connector.
7. Disconnect line quick connect fitting from Evaporative Emission (EVAP) purge solenoid.
8. Disconnect clamp and remove brake booster hose from intake manifold.
9. Remove knock sensor electrical connector clip from intake manifold brace and oil dipstick tube bracket.
10. Disconnect EVAP canister purge solenoid, Manifold Absolute Pressure (MAP) sensor and charge air bypass vale solenoid electrical connectors.
11. Disconnect Throttle Actuator Control (TAC) module electrical connector.
12. Remove engine wiring harness clip from intake manifold brace.
13. Disconnect clamp and remove surge tank air bleed hose from engine.
14. Remove clip from tank bracket and position surge tank air bleed hose aside.
15. Disconnect clamp and remove charge air bypass valve vacuum hose from intake manifold.
16. Remove mounting bolts and position charge air bypass valve solenoid aside.
17. Remove mounting bolts and stud, then the surge tank bracket.
18. Disconnect fuel pump feed pipe fitting.
19. Remove mounting bolts and fuel feed pipe.
20. Remove mounting bolts and position power brake booster pump aside.
21. Remove mounting bolt and intake manifold brace.
22. Remove mounting bolts and nuts, then the intake manifold. Remove gasket only if damaged.
23. If replacing intake manifold, proceed as follows:
    a. Remove mounting bolts, MAP sensor and O-ring seal.
    b. Remove mounting bolts, EVAP purge solenoid and O-ring seal.
    c. Remove mounting bolts, throttle body and seal.
24. Reverse procedure to install, noting the following:
    a. Lubricate high pressure fuel pump fuel feed pipe connection threads with suitable silicon free engine oil.

EXHAUST MANIFOLD
REPLACE

1. Remove mounting bolts and exhaust manifold heat shield.
2. Remove mounting bolt and block heater.
3. Remove mounting nuts, exhaust manifold and gasket.
4. Reverse procedure to install, noting the following:
    a. Tighten new exhaust manifold nuts hand tight.
    b. **Torque** exhaust manifold nuts to 10 ft. lbs. in sequence, **Fig. 1.**
    c. **Torque** exhaust manifold nuts to 10 ft. lbs., again.

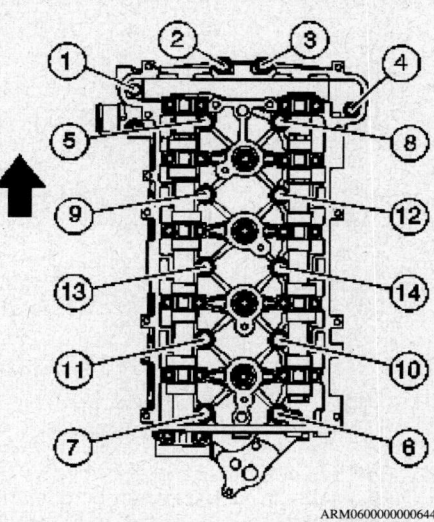

Fig. 2   Cylinder head loosening sequence

CYLINDER HEAD
REPLACE

1. Open hood and disconnect headlamp bulb socket Connector Positive Assurance (CPA) connector.
2. Disconnect lefthand headlamp electrical harness.
3. Turn socket a quarter turn counterclockwise and disconnect bulb.
4. Remove mounting screws and headlamp.
5. Disconnect wiring harness on both sides and mark hood for installation alignment.
6. Remove mounting nuts and hood.
7. Disconnect fuel injector wiring harness electrical connector.
8. Remove intake manifold as outlined under "Intake Manifold, Replace."
9. Remove fuel injector insulator.
10. Relieve high side fuel system pressure as outlined under "Precautions."
11. Remove engine wiring harness clip from high pressure fuel pump cover.
12. Remove mounting bolts and high pressure fuel pump cover.
13. Remove high pressure fuel pump insulator.
14. Loosen and remove fuel pipe fitting from fuel pump and rail. Discard high pressure fuel pipe.
15. Disconnect fuel injectors' electrical connectors.
16. Remove mounting bolts and fuel rail. If injectors came out with fuel rail, install them.
17. Remove and discard fuel injector upper O-ring seal.
18. If replacing fuel rail, remove pressure sensor. **Do not damage sensor plastic housing with excess force.**
19. Remove exhaust manifold as outlined under "Exhaust Manifold, Replace."
20. Drain cooling system into suitable container.
21. Disconnect clamp and remove radiator surge tank hose from turbocharger coolant feed pipe fitting. Position hose aside.

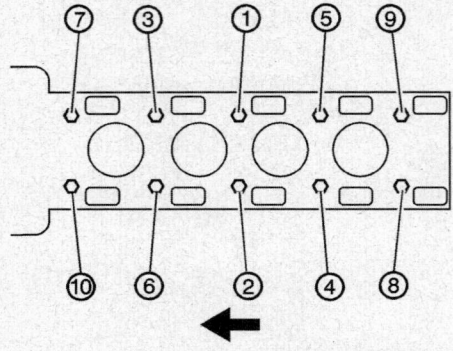

Fig. 3 Cylinder head bolt tightening sequence

22. Remove charge air bypass valve solenoid tube from turbocharger coolant feed pipe clips.
23. Remove turbocharger coolant feed pipe mounting bolt at turbocharger.
24. Remove turbocharger coolant feed pipe fitting from cylinder head.
25. Remove turbocharger coolant feed pipe bracket mounting bolt from cylinder head.
26. Remove clips and turbocharger coolant feed pipe. Remove gaskets from both banjo fittings.
27. Remove timing chain as outlined under "Timing Chain, Replace."
28. Remove fuel pump acoustic cover.
29. Remove mounting bolt and battery ground cable from engine lift bracket ground terminal.
30. Disconnect intake Camshaft Position (CMP) sensor electrical connector.
31. Disconnect chassis Evaporative Emission (EVAP) line quick connect fitting from purge solenoid.
32. Disconnect EVAP canister purge solenoid electrical connector.
33. Remove mounting bolt, EVAP canister purge solenoid and O-ring seal.
34. Disconnect exhaust CMP and Engine Coolant Temperature (ECT) sensor electrical connectors.
35. Disconnect clamp and remove radiator inlet hose from cylinder head.
36. Remove and discard cylinder head bolts in sequence, **Fig. 2**.
37. Remove cylinder head and gasket.
38. Reverse procedure to install, noting the following:
    a. **Do not use any sealing material.**
    b. Lightly apply clean engine oil to new cylinder head bolt threads and bottom side flange. Allow the oil to drain before installing.
    c. Refer to sequence, **Fig. 3,** and tighten cylinder head bolts in two steps. First step, **torque** bolts to 22 ft. lbs.; second step, tighten an additional 155°.
    d. **Torque** new front cylinder head bolts to 26 ft. lbs., **Fig. 4.**
    e. If replacing fuel rail, lubricate threads and sealing cone of new fuel rail with silicon free engine oil.
    f. Install new fuel injector upper O-ring seals, lubricate seals with silicon free engine oil.

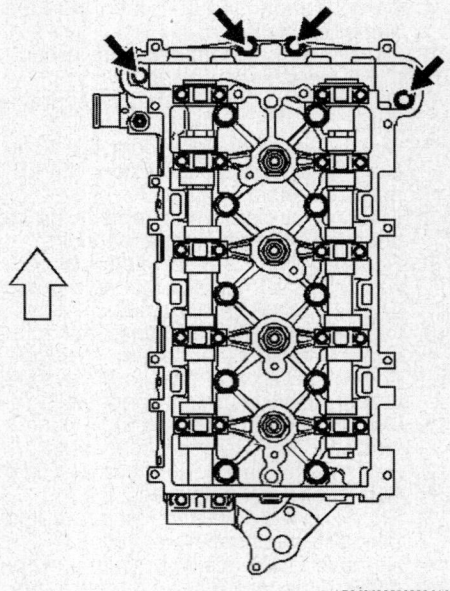

Fig. 4 Front cylinder head bolts

    g. Refer to sequence, **Fig. 5, torque** fuel rail bolts to 16 ft. lbs.
    h. Install new high pressure fuel pipe fitting

VALVE COVER
REPLACE

1. Grasp intake manifold cover and remove from studs.
2. Remove intake manifold cover, oil fill cap and insulator.
3. Remove intake manifold cover studs.
4. Disconnect clamps and remove air cleaner outlet duct.
5. Disconnect intake and exhaust Camshaft Position (CMP) actuator solenoid valve electrical connectors.
6. Remove engine wiring harness clips from valve cover.
7. Disconnect Evaporative Emission (EVAP) canister purge solenoid valve electrical connector.
8. Disconnect electrical connectors, then remove mounting bolts and ignition coils.
9. Remove Heated Oxygen Sensor (HO2S) electrical connector clip from valve cover.
10. Remove fitting mounting bolt and position PCV pipe aside. **Do not disconnect PCV hose from valve cover.**
11. Remove mounting bolts and valve cover.
12. Reverse procedure to install.

VALVE CLEARANCE SPECIFICATIONS

Hydraulic valve lifters are used on this engine and no adjustment is required.

VALVE ADJUSTMENT

Hydraulic valve lifters are used on this engine and no adjustment is required.

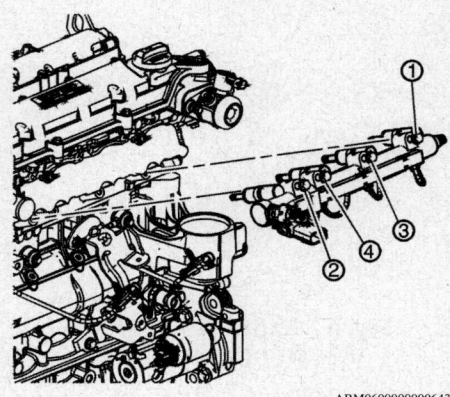

Fig. 5 Fuel rail bolt tightening sequence

ROCKER ARMS

Used valve rocker arms must be returned to original position on the camshaft. If the camshaft is being replaced, the rocker arms must also be replaced.

1. Remove camshaft as outlined under "Camshaft, Replace."
2. Mark roller followers and hydraulic valve lash adjusters for installation reference.
3. Remove valve rocker arms.
4. Reverse procedure to install. Lubricate valve tips and rocket arms with suitable lubricant.

HYDRAULIC LIFTERS
REPLACE

1. Remove camshaft as outlined under "Camshaft, Replace."
2. Mark roller followers and hydraulic valve lash adjusters for installation reference.
3. Remove valve rocker arms.
4. Remove hydraulic valve lash adjusters.
5. Reverse procedure to install. Lubricate hydraulic lash adjusters with suitable lubricant.

CRANKSHAFT DAMPER
REPLACE

1. Grasp intake manifold cover and disconnect studs.
2. Remove intake manifold cover, oil fill cap and insulator.
3. Turn power steering pump belt tensioner pulley clockwise and remove belt.
4. Remove charge air cooler inlet pipe mounting bolt at rear bracket.
5. Remove mounting nut and charge air cooler rear bracket.
6. Remove charge air cooler inlet pipe mounting bolt at front bracket.
7. Loosen charge air cooler clamp at inlet pipe. and inlet pipe clamp at pipe.
8. Remove charge air cooler inlet pipe.
9. Disconnect intake air pressure and temperature sensor engine wiring harness electrical connector.
10. Disconnect clamp and remove charge

Fig. 6 Crankshaft key alignment

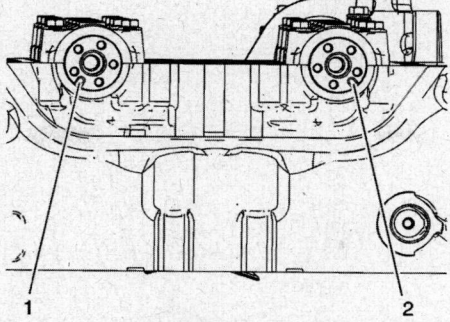

1. Exhaust camshaft notch is in the 7 o'clock position
2. Intake camshaft notch is in the 5 o'clock position

ARM0600000000649

Fig. 7 Camshaft's notch alignment

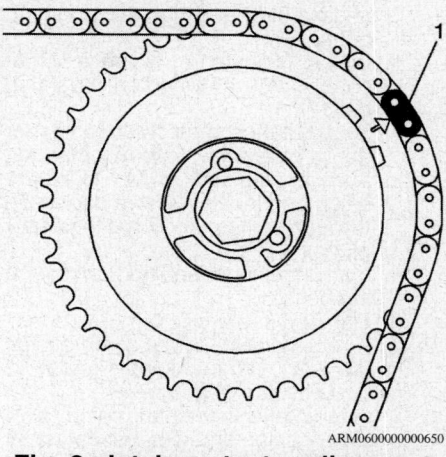

ARM0600000000650

Fig. 8 Intake actuator alignment

air cooler outlet pipe air bypass valve solenoid vacuum hose.
11. Remove charge air cooler outlet pipe mounting bolt, nut and rear bracket.
12. Disconnect charge air cooler outlet pipe hose clamp and remove charge air cooler outlet pipe front bracket mounting bolt.
13. Disconnect clamp and remove charge air cooler outlet pipe.
14. Disconnect air cleaner housing and turbocharger clamps and remove air cleaner outlet duct.
15. Disconnect Mass Air Flow (MAF) sensor engine wiring harness electrical connector.
16. Remove front mounting bolt and air cleaner.
17. Remove drive belt.
18. Remove intake manifold as outlined under "Intake Manifold, Replace."
19. Remove starter solenoid terminal nuts and disconnect engine terminal harness.
20. Remove mounting bolts and starter motor.
21. Raise and support vehicle.
22. Hold flywheel using holding tool No. J43653, or equivalent.
23. Remove and discard crankshaft balancer bolt.
24. Remove balancer using suitable universal removal tool.
25. Reverse procedure to install, noting the following:
   a. Ensure properly align of keyway and balance flats on with oil pump drive.
   b. Install new crankshaft balancer bolt and washer.
   c. **Torque** bolt to 74 ft. lbs.
   d. Final tighten mounting bolt an additional 125°.

FRONT COVER
REPLACE

1. Open hood and remove Connector Positive Assurance (CPA) retainer from headlamp bulb socket connector.
2. Disconnect lefthand headlamp electrical harness.
3. Turn socket a quarter turn counterclockwise and disconnect bulb.

4. Remove mounting screws and headlamp.
5. Disconnect wiring harness on both sides and mark hood for installation alignment.
6. Remove mounting nuts and hood.
7. Remove crankshaft damper as outlined under "Crankshaft Damper, Replace."
8. Remove mounting bolt and drive belt tensioner.
9. Remove mounting bolts and front cover.
10. Remove and discard gasket.
11. Reverse procedure to install.

FRONT COVER SEAL
REPLACE

1. Remove front cover as outlined under "Front Cover, Replace."
2. Remove and discard gasket.
3. Remove crankcase front cover oil seal using suitable tool.
4. Remove and discard friction washer.
5. Reverse procedure to install. Install new seal using sprocket bearing installer tool No. J34115, or equivalent.

TIMING CHAIN
REPLACE
Removal

1. Open hood and remove Connector Positive Assurance (CPA) retainer from headlamp bulb socket connector.
2. Disconnect lefthand headlamp electrical harness.
3. Turn socket a quarter turn counterclockwise and disconnect bulb.
4. Remove mounting screws and headlamp.
5. Disconnect wiring harness on both sides and mark hood for installation alignment.
6. Remove mounting nuts and hood.
7. Remove cylinder No. 1 spark plug.
8. Turn crankshaft clockwise until piston No. 1 is at Top Dead Center (TDC) on compression stroke.
9. Remove valve cover as outlined under "Valve Cover, Replace."

10. Remove front cover as outlined under "Front Cover, Replace."
11. Remove mounting bolts and upper timing chain guide.
12. Remove timing chain tensioner.
13. Hold exhaust camshaft using suitable wrench, then remove and discard exhaust camshaft actuator bolt.
14. Remove exhaust camshaft actuator.
15. Remove mounting bolt and timing chain tensioner guide.
16. Remove fixed timing chain guide access plug.
17. Remove mounting bolts and fixed timing chain guide.
18. Hold intake camshaft using suitable wrench, then remove and discard intake camshaft actuator bolt.
19. Remove intake camshaft actuator and timing chain.
20. Remove timing chain crankshaft sprocket.
21. If removing balance shaft timing chain and sprocket, proceed as follows:
   a. Remove mounting bolts and balance shaft drive chain tensioner.
   b. Remove mounting bolt and adjustable balance shaft chain guide.
   c. Remove mounting bolts and upper balance shaft drive chain guide.
   d. Remove balance shaft drive chain and sprocket.

Installation

1. If installing balance shaft timing chain and sprocket, proceed as follows:
   a. Install balance shaft sprocket.
   b. Align chain cooper link to intake side balance shaft sprocket timing mark.
   c. Work chain around clockwise.
   d. Place chrome link with balance shaft drive sprocket timing mark at approximately 6 o'clock.
   e. Place chain on water pump drive sprocket.
   f. Align last chrome link with exhaust side balance shaft drive sprocket timing mark.
   g. Install upper balance shaft drive chain guide and tighten mounting bolts.
   h. Install small balance shaft drive

chain guide and tighten mounting bolts.

i. Install adjustable balance shaft chain guide and tighten mounting bolt.

j. Total balance shaft chain tensioner 90° in bore and compress plunger.

k. Turn tension back to 12 o'clock position and insert suitable paper clip through plunger body into tensioner plunger.

l. Install tensioner and tighten mounting bolts.

m. Remove paper clip.

2. Ensure piston No. 1 is at compression stroke TDC with crankshaft key at 12 o'clock position, **Fig. 6.**

3. Ensure intake camshaft notch at 5 o'clock position and exhaust camshaft notch at 7 o'clock position, **Fig. 7.**

4. Install timing chain drive sprocket to crankshaft with timing mark in 5 o'clock position and front of sprocket facing out.

5. Assemble intake camshaft actuator into timing chain with timing mark aligned with uniquely colored link, **Fig. 8.**

6. Lower timing chain through cylinder head opening ensuring chain goes around both sides of cylinder block bosses.

7. Install intake camshaft actuator onto intake camshaft while aligning dowel pin into the camshaft slot.

8. Hand tighten new intake camshaft actuator bolt.

9. Route timing chain around crankshaft sprocket and align first matching colored link with crankshaft sprocket, timing mark at approximately 5 o'clock position, **Fig. 9.**

10. Turn crankshaft clockwise to remove all chain slack. **Do not turn intake camshaft.**

11. Install adjustable timing chain guide through cylinder head opening. Tighten mounting bolt.

12. Install exhaust camshaft actuator into timing chain with timing mark aligned with second matching colored link, **Fig. 10.**

13. Install exhaust camshaft actuator onto camshaft and align dowel pin into slot.

14. Turn exhaust camshaft approximately 45° using suitable open end wrench until camshaft actuator dowel pin goes into camshaft slot.

15. When actuator seats on cam, tighten new exhaust camshaft actuator bolt hand tight.

16. Ensure all of colored links and appropriate timing marks are still aligned.

17. Install fixed timing chain guide and tighten mounting bolts.

18. Install upper timing chain guide and tighten mounting bolts.

19. Remove snap ring and piston from timing chain tensioner body.

20. Install notch end of piston into tensioner tool No. J45027, or equivalent, in suitable vice.

21. Turn ratchet cylinder into piston, then install piston into tensioner body. Install snap ring.

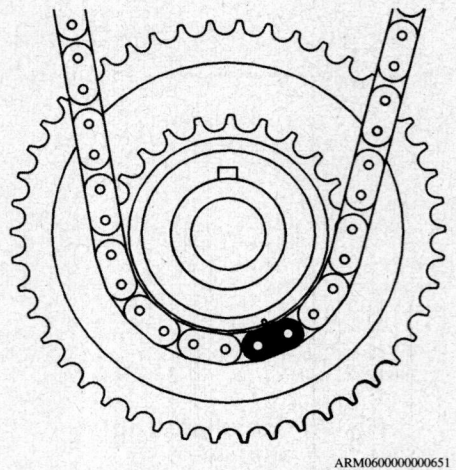

Fig. 9 Crankshaft sprocket & chain alignment

ARM0600000000651

22. Install and tighten timing chain tensioner.

23. Compress timing chain .079 inch using suitable rubber end tip tool and release tensioner.

24. Feed tool down through cam drive chest to rest on cam chain.

25. Hit downward with sharp jolt to release tensioner.

26. Hold intake camshaft hex using suitable wrench, **torque** actuator bolt to 22 ft. lbs., then tighten bolt an additional 100°.

27. Hold exhaust camshaft hex using suitable wrench, **torque** actuator bolt to 22 ft. lbs., then tighten bolt an additional 100°.

28. Install timing chain oiling nozzle and tighten mounting bolt.

29. Apply sealant compound (GM part No. 12345382), or equivalent, to timing chain guide bolt access hole plug threads.

30. Install timing chain guide bolt and tighten.

31. Install front and valve covers, then the cylinder No. 1 spark plug and hood.

CAMSHAFT
REPLACE
Removal

1. Relieve low and high side fuel system pressure as outlined under "Precautions."

2. Remove valve cover as outlined under "Valve Cover, Replace."

3. Remove mounting bolts and upper timing chain guide.

4. Hold camshaft on hex using suitable wrench, then loosen intake camshaft actuator bolt. **Do not remove bolt.**

5. Retain timing chain by attaching timing chain tensioner tool No. J44217, or equivalent, to exhaust and intake camshaft sides of timing chain. Ensure tips of tool fully engage timing chain, firmly tighten tool nuts.

6. Mark intake and exhaust camshaft ac-

tuators locations on timing chain for installation reference.

7. Holding camshaft with suitable wrench, remove and discard intake camshaft actuator bolt.

8. Remove intake camshaft actuator from camshaft and timing chain.

9. Disconnect high pressure fuel pump electrical connector.

10. Remove engine wiring harness clip from high pressure fuel pump cover.

11. Remove mounting bolts and high pressure fuel pump cover.

12. Remove high pressure fuel pump insulator.

13. Loosen fuel feed pipe to pump fitting.

14. Remove mounting bolts and fuel feed pipe from intake manifold.

15. Loosen high pressure fuel pipe fitting at pump.

16. Remove and discard high pressure fuel pipe.

17. Remove and discard high pressure fuel pump mounting bolts.

18. Remove high pressure fuel pump, then the gasket and O-ring.

19. Mark camshaft bearing caps for installation reference.

20. Remove each cap bolt one turn at a time until there is no spring tension pushing on camshaft.

21. Remove camshaft bearing cap bolts and caps.

22. Remove valve lifter follower.

23. Remove mounting bolts and cylinder head opening plate.

24. Remove mounting bolts and rear bearing cap.

25. Remove intake camshaft.

26. Reverse procedure to install.

Installation

1. Lubricate hydraulic lash adjusters and install into bores.

2. Lubricate valve tips.

3. Position valve rocker arms on tip of valve stem and on valve lash adjuster. Lubricate rocker arms.

4. Lubricate camshaft with suitable engine oil.

5. Install camshaft.

6. Apply .14 inch bead of suitable sealer to cylinder head. Where rear bearing cap ends on perimeter rail, extend sealer bead .16 inch beyond cap edge.

7. Install rear bearing cap and tighten mounting bolts.

8. Install cylinder head opening plate and tighten mounting bolts.

9. Install valve lifter follower.

10. Install bearing caps, then the cap bolts, hand tighten.

11. Tighten bearing cap bolts in three-turn increments until they are seated.

12. **Torque** camshaft bearing cap bolts to 89 inch lbs.

13. Lubricate high pressure fuel pump cylinder head bore and roller lifter with suitable silicon free engine oil.

14. Install high pressure fuel pump roller lifter.

15. Install new high pressure fuel pump O-ring.

16. Position new high pressure fuel pump gasket to cylinder head.

17. Ensure plastic bolt retainers are installed in high pressure fuel pump mounting holes.
18. Push high pressure fuel pump into cylinder head bore by hand.
19. Install new high pressure fuel pump bolts hand tight.
20. Lubricate high pressure fuel pump and fuel rail fittings with suitable silicon free engine oil.
21. Install new high pressure fuel pipe and tighten fitting hand tight.
22. Place fuel feed pipe onto intake manifold, tighten feed pipe bolts hand tight.
23. Tighten fuel feed pipe bolts and fuel feed pipe to fuel pump fitting.
24. Tighten high pressure fuel pipe fittings and mounting bolts.
25. Install high pressure fuel pump insulator, then the cover.
26. Connect high pressure fuel pump electrical connector and install engine wiring harness clip to cover.
27. Ensure exhaust camshaft actuator alignment mark is still aligned properly with timing chain mark.
28. Install timing chain onto intake camshaft actuator.
29. Align intake camshaft actuator alignment mark with timing chain mark, then install actuator onto camshaft.
30. Install new intake camshaft actuator bolt until snug.
31. Remove timing chain tensioner tools.
32. Hold camshaft using suitable wrench, **torque** actuator bolt to 22 ft. lbs. then tighten an additional 100°.
33. Install upper timing chain guide and tighten mounting bolts.
34. Install valve cover.

BALANCE SHAFT
REPLACE
Removal

1. Remove timing chain, sprocket and tensioner as outlined under "Timing Chain, Replace."
2. Remove mounting bolt and lefthand (exhaust) and/or righthand (intake) balance shaft.
3. Install balance shaft bearing remover and installer tool No. J43650, or equivalent, into balance shaft hole with foot parallel to shaft.
4. Turn tool so foot is perpendicular to shaft.
5. Center tool foot on balance shaft bushing.
6. Insert centering guide into front balance shaft bore and tighten nut.
7. End of tool should be 4.6 inches from block face.
8. Tighten tool nut until tension releases.
9. Remove tool and balance shaft bushing.

Installation

1. Install balance shaft bushing using balance shaft bearing remover and installer tool No. J43650, or equivalent.
2. Seat bushing into bore and remove tool.

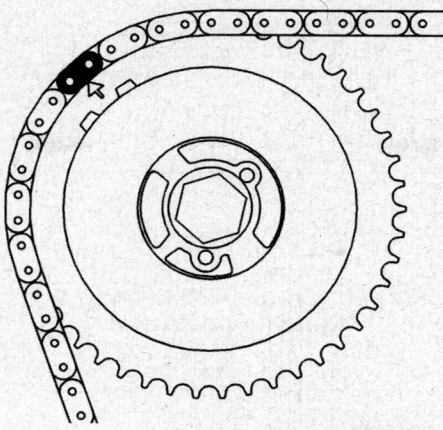

ARM0600000000652

Fig. 10 Exhaust camshaft actuator & chain alignment

3. Place cylinder No. 1 at Top Dead Center (TDC).
4. Lubricate balance shaft lobes with suitable engine oil.
5. Install lefthand (exhaust) and/or righthand (intake) balance shaft.
6. Install and tighten mounting bolt.

MAIN & ROD BEARINGS
Main Bearings

1. Refer to sequence, **Fig. 11,** and tighten crankshaft bearing bolts in two steps: First step, **torque** to 15 ft. lbs.; second step, tighten an additional 77°.
2. Refer to sequence, **Fig. 12,** torque lower crankcase perimeter bolts to 18 ft. lbs.

Connecting Rod Bearings

Torque new connecting rod bolts to 18 ft. lbs., then tighten an additional 100°.

CRANKSHAFT SEAL
REPLACE

1. Remove crankshaft balancer as outlined under "Crankshaft Damper, Replace."
2. Remove oil seal from front cover using suitable flat-bladed tool.
3. Reverse procedure to install. Use camshaft/front main seal installer tool No. J35268-A, or equivalent, to install seal.

CRANKSHAFT REAR OIL SEAL
REPLACE

1. Remove engine and flywheel as outlined under "Engine, Replace."
2. Remove crankshaft rear oil seal using suitable flat-bladed tool.
3. Reverse procedure to install. Use rear

main seal installer tool No. J42067, or equivalent, to install seal.

OIL PAN
REPLACE

1. Remove engine as outlined under "Engine Replace."
2. Remove oil pan mounting bolts.
3. Pry oil pan away from engine.
4. Reverse procedure to install, noting the following:
   a. Apply .14 inch beach of suitable sealant around oil pan perimeter and oil suction port opening.
   b. **Torque** mounting bolts to 18 ft. lbs. in sequence, **Fig. 13.**

OIL PUMP
REPLACE

Refer to "Front Cover, Replace" for oil pump replacement.

OIL PUMP SERVICE
Disassemble

1. Remove pressure relief valve from front cover/oil pump assembly.
2. Remove mounting bolts and oil pump gerotor cover.

Assemble

1. Lubricate all oil pump parts with suitable engine oil.
2. Install inner into outer gear.
3. Install gears together into front cover with center gear hub facing front cover.
4. Install oil pump gerotor cover and tighten mounting bolts.
5. Install pressure relief valve piston and spring.

OIL COOLER
REPLACE

1. Drain cooling system into suitable container.
2. Remove cap, then the windshield wiper arm mounting nut.
3. Remove windshield washer nozzle hose and windshield wiper arm.
4. Remove air inlet grille, then disconnect washer pump hose.
5. Remove intake Camshaft Position (CMP) sensor.
6. Remove mounting nuts and air inlet screen support.
7. Remove radiator outlet hoses from thermostat housing and oil cooler.
8. Remove radiator outlet hose clip from bracket.
9. Remove surge tank outlet hose from oil cooler.
10. Remove mounting bolts and oil cooler.
11. Reverse procedure to install.

SERPENTINE DRIVE BELT

Replace

1. Remove intake manifold cover from studs.
2. Raise and support vehicle.
3. Turn power steering pump belt tensioner pulley clockwise and remove belt.
4. Lower vehicle.
5. Remove charge air cooler inlet pipe mounting bolt at rear bracket.
6. Remove mounting nut and charge air cooler rear bracket.
7. Remove charge air cooler inlet pipe mounting bolt at front bracket.
8. Loosen charge air cooler clamp at inlet pipe. and inlet pipe clamp at pipe.
9. Remove charge air cooler inlet pipe.
10. Disconnect intake air pressure and temperature sensor electrical connector.
11. Remove charge air cooler outlet pipe air bypass valve solenoid vacuum hose.
12. Remove charge air cooler outlet pipe mounting bolt, nut and rear bracket.
13. Disconnect charge air cooler outlet pipe hose clamp and remove charge air cooler outlet pipe front bracket mounting bolt.
14. Disconnect clamp and remove charge air cooler outlet pipe.
15. Disconnect air cleaner housing and turbocharger clamps and remove air cleaner outlet duct.
16. Disconnect Mass Air Flow (MAF) sensor electrical connector.
17. Remove front mounting bolt and air cleaner.
18. Remove drive belt.
19. Reverse procedure to install.

THERMOSTAT

REPLACE

1. Drain cooling system into suitable container.
2. Remove cap and windshield wiper arm mounting nut.
3. Remove windshield washer nozzle hose and windshield wiper arm.
4. Remove retainers and air inlet grille, then disconnect washer pump hose.
5. Remove radiator outlet hose from thermostat housing.
6. Remove mounting bolts, housing and thermostat.
7. Remove and discard O-ring seal.
8. Reverse procedure to install.

WATER PUMP

REPLACE

1. Remove intake manifold cover from studs.
2. Drain cooling system into suitable container.
3. Remove cap and windshield wiper arm mounting nut.

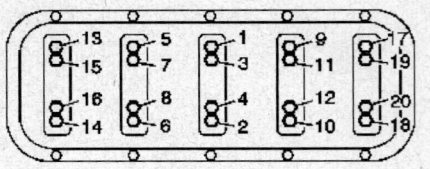

ARM0700000000168

Fig. 11 Crankshaft bearing bolt tightening sequence

4. Remove windshield washer nozzle hose and windshield wiper arm.
5. Remove retainers and air inlet grille. Disconnect washer pump hose.
6. Disconnect clamp and remove radiator outlet hose from the thermostat housing.
7. Remove mounting bolts, housing and thermostat.
8. Remove and discard O-ring seal.
9. Remove mounting bolts and water pump access plate from the front cover.
10. Drain coolant from water pump using plug at bottom of pump.
11. Install water pump holding tool No. J43651, or equivalent. Secure tool using access cover bolts.
12. Remove three water pump inner sprocket bolts.
13. Remove four mounting bolts and water pump. Discard O-ring.
14. Reverse procedure to install, noting the following:
    a. Thread guide pin (M 6 m x 6 mm stud) into sprocket to align with holding tool.
    b. After two inner water pump sprocket bolts are snug, remove guide pin and install third bolt.

RADIATOR

REPLACE

1. Drain cooling system into suitable container.
2. Remove mounting bolts and radiator front air deflector.
3. Remove retainer and shroud air inlet.
4. Remove air cleaner outlet duct resonator and PCV hose clamps.
5. Remove air cleaner outlet duct resonator.
6. Disconnect cooling fan motor electrical connector.
7. Remove mounting bolts, shroud, cooling fan and motor.
8. Remove radiator inlet and outlet hoses, then the surge tank inlet hose.
9. Remove air cleaner stud, then the mounting nuts and radiator upper bracket.
10. Remove mounting bolts, air conditioning condenser and radiator.
11. Reverse procedure to install.

FUEL PUMP

REPLACE

1. Relieve fuel pressure as outlined under "Precautions."
2. Remove courtesy lamp from luggage compartment trim panel.
3. Remove tire inflator.
4. Disconnect right and left water management tubes from rear floor panel.
5. Remove luggage compartment trim panel.
6. Remove mounting bolts and fuel sending unit access cover.
7. Disconnect fuel level sender fuel pressure sensor electrical connectors.
8. Disconnect fuel fill pipe EVAP pipe quick connect fitting.
9. Disconnect fuel feed pipe quick connect fitting.
10. Raise fuel sender up slightly. **Do not handle fuel sender assembly by fuel pipes.**
11. Connect large EVAP canister quick connect fitting.
12. Remove fuel sender.
13. Remove and discard O-ring.
14. Reverse procedure to install.

TURBOCHARGER

REPLACE

1. Drain cooling system into suitable container.
2. Remove charge air cooler inlet pipe mounting bolt at rear bracket.
3. Remove mounting nut and charge air cooler rear bracket.
4. Remove charge air cooler inlet pipe mounting bolt at front bracket.
5. Loosen charge air cooler clamp at inlet pipe. and inlet pipe clamp at pipe.
6. Remove charge air cooler inlet pipe.
7. Remove mounting bolts and charge air cooler pipe from turbocharger.
8. Remove mounting bolts and turbocharger heat shield.
9. Remove Connector Position Assurance (CPA) retainer and disconnect Heated Oxygen Sensor (HO2S) 1 electrical connector. Remove clip from valve cover.
10. Remove HO2S using oxygen sensor wrench tool No. J39194, or equivalent.
11. Remove catalytic converter to turbocharger mounting nuts.
12. Remove CPA retainer and disconnect HO2S 2 electrical connector.
13. Raise and support vehicle.
14. Remove catalytic converter to muffler mounting nuts.
15. Separate exhaust pipe from catalytic converter studs, then position exhaust pipe aside and support.
16. Loosen driver side engine mount to frame lower nut. **Do not remove nut.**
17. Remove passenger side engine mount to frame lower nut.
18. Raise oil pan slightly using suitable adjustable jack and block of wood.
19. Remove catalytic converter to bracket bolts and position converter aside.
20. Remove mounting bolt and nut, then the catalytic converter bracket.
21. Turn and remove catalytic converter. Remove and discard gasket.

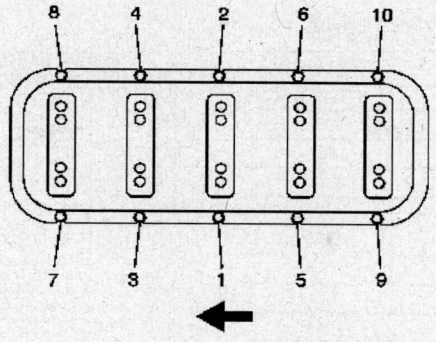

ARM0700000000169

Fig. 12   Crankshaft perimeter bolt tightening sequence

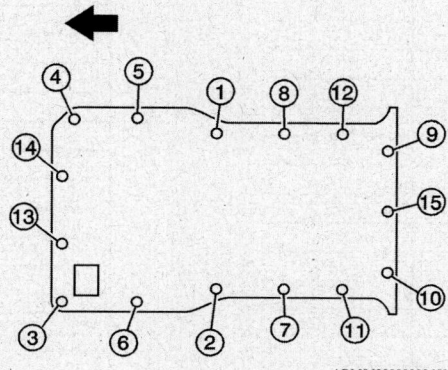

ARM0600000000653

Fig. 13   Oil pan tightening sequence

SATURN

TIGHTENING SPECIFICATIONS

Year	Component	Torque, Ft. Lbs.
2007–08	Access Hole Plug	66
	Air Cleaner	89①
	Air Cleaner Stud	89①
	Air Cleaner Outlet Duct Resonator Clamp	80①
	Air Cleaner Outlet Duct Clamp	35①
	Air Conditioning Compressor	16
	Air Conditioning Condenser	80①
	Alternator Terminal	15
	Balance Shaft	89①
	Balance Shaft Chain Guide, Adjustable	89①
	Balance Shaft Drive Chain Guide, Upper & Small	11
	Balance Shaft Drive Chain Tensioner	89①
	Bellhousing	37
	Block Heater	89①
	Brake Hose Bracket	89①
	Camshaft Actuator	⑥
	Camshaft Bearing Caps	⑦
	Catalytic Converter, Bolt	16
	Catalytic Converter, Nut	43
	Catalytic Converter Bracket	43
	Catalytic Converter To Muffler	13
	Charge Air Bypass Valve Solenoid	89①
	Charge Air Cooler Inlet And Outlet Pipe	80①
	Charge Air Cooler Pipe	16
	Cooling Fan Shroud	18
	Crankshaft Damper	⑤
	Cylinder Head	④
	Cylinder Head Opening Plate	89①
	Drive Belt Tensioner	33
	Engine Mount	41
	Engine Wiring Harness Ground	18
	EVAP Purge Solenoid	89①
	Exhaust Manifold	③
	Exhaust Manifold Heat Shield	18
	Exhaust Manifold, Stud	11
	Flywheel	39②
	Front Cover	18
	Fuel Pump Cover	89①
	Fuel Feed Fitting	22
	Fuel Feed Pipe	89①
	Fuel Injection Fuel Rail Fuel Pressure Sensor	25
	Fuel Pump Module Access Cover	89①
	Fuel Rail	④
	Heated Oxygen Sensor	31
	High Pressure Fuel Pipe Fitting	24
	High Pressure Fuel Pump	11
	Ignition Coil	89①
	Intake Manifold	16

TIGHTENING SPECIFICATIONS—Continued

Year	Component	Torque, Ft. Lbs.
2007–08	Intake Manifold Cover Stud	80①
	Oil Cooler	16
	Oil dipstick Tube	89①
	Oil Pump Gerotor	53①
	Power Steering Pump Bracket	43
	Pressure Relief Valve Plug	30
	Radiator Bracket	90①
	Radiator Front Air Deflector	80①
	Rear Bearing Cap	89①
	Starter Motor	30
	Starter Solenoid Terminal	89①
	Starter Solenoid S Terminal	27①
	Surge Tank Bracket	80①
	Thermostat Housing Cover	89①
	Throttle Body	89①
	Timing Chain Guide, Adjustable	89①
	Timing Chain Guide, Fixed	106①
	Timing Chain Guide, Upper	89①
	Timing Chain Tensioner	55
	Timing Chain Oiling Nozzle	89①
	Torque Converter	36
	Turbocharger Coolant Feed Pipe	26
	Turbocharger Coolant Feed Pipe Bracket	89①
	Turbocharger Heat Shield	89①
	Valve Cover	89①
	Water Pump	18
	Water Pump Access Plate	89①
	Water Pump Sprocket	89①

① — Inch lbs.

② — Tighten an additional 25°.

③ — Refer to "Exhaust Manifold, Replace" for tightening sequence and specifications.

④ — Refer to "Cylinder Head, Replace" for tightening sequence and specifications.

⑤ — Refer to "Crankshaft Damper, Replace." for tightening sequence and specifications.

⑥ — Refer to "Timing Chain, Replace." for tightening sequence and specifications.

⑦ — Refer to "Camshaft, Replace." for tightening sequence and specifications.

2.2L Engine

NOTE: On Air Bag Equipped Models, Refer To "Air Bag System Precautions" Located In The Front Of This Manual For System Disarming & Arming Procedures.

NOTE: Refer To "Computer Relearn Procedures" Located In The Front Of This Manual When Battery Power To The Computer Has Been Interrupted.

NOTE: Prior To Performing Any Service Operations Listed In This Section, Consult The "Technical Service Bulletins" Section For Related Information.

INDEX

	Page No.
Camshaft, Replace	12-43
Compression Pressure	12-39
Cooling System Bleed	12-44
ION	12-44
L-Series	12-44
Crankshaft Damper, Replace	12-42
Crankshaft Rear Oil Seal, Replace	12-43
Crankshaft Seal, Replace	12-43
Cylinder Head, Replace	12-41
Installation	12-42
Removal	12-41
Engine Rebuilding Specifications	29-1
Engine, Replace	12-40
ION	12-40
L-Series	12-40
Automatic Transaxle	12-40
Manual Transaxle	12-40
Engine Mount, Replace	12-39
ION	12-39
L-Series	12-39
Exhaust Manifold, Replace	12-41
Front Cover, Replace	12-43
Fuel Filter, Replace	12-47

	Page No.
ION	12-47
L-Series	12-47
Fuel Pump, Replace	12-45
ION	12-45
L-Series	12-46
Intake Manifold, Replace	12-41
Main & Rod Bearings	12-43
Connecting Rod Bearings	12-43
Main Bearings	12-43
Oil Pan, Replace	12-43
Oil Pump, Replace	12-44
Oil Pump Service	12-44
Assemble	12-44
Disassemble	12-44
Inspection	12-44
Piston & Rod Assembly	12-43
Pistons, Pins & Rings	12-43
Precautions	12-39
Air Bag Systems	12-39
Battery Ground Cable	12-39
Fuel System Pressure Relief	12-39
Radiator, Replace	12-45
ION	12-45
L-Series	12-45
Serpentine Drive Belt	12-44

	Page No.
Belt Routing	12-44
Belt, Replace	12-44
Installation	12-44
Removal	12-44
Tensioner, Replace	12-44
Technical Service Bulletins	12-47
Engine Oil Leak	12-47
2006 ION	12-47
Excessive Oil Consumption, Blue Smoke on Acceleration	12-47
2004–05 ION & L-Series	12-47
Front Cover Crankshaft Oil Seal Leak	12-47
2004–05 ION & L-Series	12-47
Slight Coolant Loss	12-47
2004 ION & L-Series	12-47
Thermostat, Replace	12-45
Tightening Specifications	12-50
Timing Chain, Replace	12-43
Valve Adjustment	12-42
Valve Guides	12-42
Water Pump, Replace	12-45
ION	12-45
L-Series	12-45

PRECAUTIONS

Air Bag Systems

Refer to "Air Bag System Precautions" in the front of this manual for system disarming and arming procedures.

Battery Ground Cable

Prior to service, disconnect battery ground cable and isolate as required.

Fuel System Pressure Relief

1. Connect gauge bar tool No. 53476, or equivalent, to fuel gauge pressure adapter tool No. 309725, or equivalent, using flexible hose from pressure test kit tool No. SA9127-E, or equivalent.
2. Ensure needle valve on pressure kit is closed and connect pressure adapter to fuel line test port, **Fig. 1.**
3. Place end of bleed hose in suitable container and open valve to bleed system pressure.
4. Remove gauge and replace cap.

COMPRESSION PRESSURE

1. Start and run engine until it reaches normal operating temperature.
2. Turn ignition switch to OFF position, then disconnect ignition module wiring and remove spark plugs.
3. Install suitable compression gauge tool in spark plug hole.
4. Ensure battery is charged and throttle is fully open.
5. Crank engine through four compression strokes for each cylinder.
6. Lowest reading cylinder should be within 70% of highest.
7. No cylinder should read less than 100 psi.
8. Place shop towel over spark plug holes and crank engine a few seconds without compression gauge or spark plugs installed.
9. Repeat compression measuring steps on all cylinders.

ENGINE MOUNT

REPLACE

ION

1. Remove air cleaner.
2. Support engine using suitable hydraulic floor jack with piece of wood between jack and oil pan.
3. Remove mounting bolts and discard engine mount to intermediate bracket bolts, **Fig. 2.**
4. Remove mounting nuts and engine mount.
5. Reverse procedure to install.

L-Series

1. Remove air cleaner.

2. Support engine using engine support fixture tool No. SA9150-E, or equivalent.
3. Remove mounting bolts and engine mount, **Fig. 3.**
4. Reverse procedure to install.

ENGINE
REPLACE
ION

1. Position tires in straight ahead and remove key from ignition switch.
2. Disconnect IAT sensor harness connector and loosen air cleaner fresh air duct to resonator clamp.
3. Remove push pin from air outlet resonator/duct assembly to support bracket.
4. Loosen resonator to throttle body clamp, then disconnect air cleaner fresh air duct from resonator and remove from throttle body.
5. Secure cooling module to upper body structure and n disconnect accelerator cable from throttle body.
6. Relieve fuel system pressure as outlined under "Precautions."
7. Disconnect fuel lines from fuel rail and drain coolant into suitable container.
8. Remove radiator inlet and outlet hoses from radiator, then the surge tank to cylinder head hose.
9. Remove inlet and outlet heater hoses.
10. Disconnect IAC motor and throttle position sensor connectors:
11. Disconnect manifold absolute pressure (MAP), Crankshaft Position (CKP) and oil pressure sensors connectors:
12. Disconnect purge solenoid and ignition coil connectors:
13. Disconnect oxygen and vehicle speed sensors connectors:
14. Disconnect engine temperature sensor and back-up lamp switch connectors:
15. Raise and support vehicle, then remove front tire and wheel assemblies.
16. Remove righthand side fender liner, then release tensioner and remove drive belt.
17. Remove mounting bolts and position air conditioning compressor aside.
18. Disconnect stater and alternator electrical connectors , then drain engine oil into suitable container.
19. Disconnect front exhaust pipe from exhaust manifold.
20. Disconnect transaxle electrical connectors and transaxle shift cable.
21. Support powertrain assembly between frame and powertrain, using suitable wood blocks.
22. Remove engine mount to intermediate bracket bolts, then the engine mount to mid-rail nuts and engine mount from engine compartment.
23. Remove transaxle mount to transaxle bolts, and transaxle mount to mid rail bolts.
24. Remove transaxle mount,
25. Remove bolts and separate tie rod

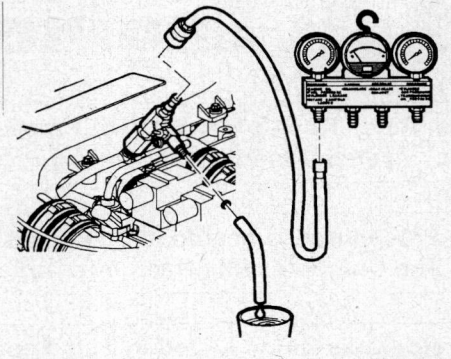

G31029900155000X

Fig. 1   Fuel pressure bleed

from steering knuckle using tool No. SA91100-C, or equivalent. Discard tie rod bolts.
26. Remove stabilizer bar links from strut.
27. Remove and discard pinch bolt, then disconnect intermediate shaft from steering gear.
28. Remove pinch bolt and nut, then separate ball stud from steering knuckle.
29. Remove nut, then separate front wheel drive axle from front wheel hub using suitable hammer and wood
30. Match mark frame to body position for installation reference.
31. Lower vehicle to approximately three feet off ground to position lift table under frame.
32. Slowly remove front frame bolts, then partially unscrew rear bolts until 1.5 inches of bolt shank is exposed.
33. Slowly lower table to floor and attach suitable engine lift hoist to lift hooks.
34. Remove starter motor and torque converter to flywheel bolts.
35. Remove mounting bolts and separate engine from transaxle.
36. Reverse procedure to install.

L-Series
AUTOMATIC TRANSAXLE

1. Remove battery and disconnect fuse block main wire feed.
2. Disconnect lefthand fenderwell main ground and intake air temperature electrical connector.
3. Remove air cleaner lid and inlet duct.
4. Remove air box and disconnect purge hose from throttle body and position aside.
5. Disconnect EVAP purge solenoid and rear oxygen sensor electrical connectors, then the main master cylinder wiring harness.
6. Remove cowl cover and PCM boot from cowl.
7. Disconnect PCM electrical connector and secure to engine.
8. Remove fuse block lid and disconnect engine harness main connector from bottom of fuse block.
9. Remove battery and fuse block trays.
10. Disconnect cruise control and throttle cables.
11. Disconnect brake assist vacuum line from throttle body and position aside.

12. Remove coolant reservoir cap.
13. Disconnect fuel lines and EVAP purge hose at EVAP purge solenoid.
14. Raise and support vehicle.
15. Drain engine coolant into suitable container.
16. Disconnect heater hoses at lower cowl and remove starter.
17. Remove torque converter bolts.
18. Remove exhaust system from catalytic converter forward.
19. Disconnect transaxle nose bracket, remove mounting bolts and secure air conditioning compressor to frame rail. **Do not disconnect air conditioning lines.**
20. Disconnect lower engine to transaxle bell housing bolts. **Do not remove upper bolts now.**
21. Lower vehicle and remove main hose to coolant reservoir from engine inlet adapter.
22. Remove engine lower and upper radiator hoses.
23. Drain power steering fluid into suitable container by removing smaller hose from under reservoir.
24. Disconnect metal power steering line.
25. Support engine using suitable engine lift hoist to engine lift hooks, **Fig. 4.**
26. Support transaxle weight using suitable floor jack or jack stand.
27. Remove righthand front engine mount from wheel housing and engine mount bracket from engine.
28. Remove upper bell housing bolts and remove engine.
29. Reverse procedure to install.

MANUAL TRANSAXLE

1. Remove steering gear to intermediate shaft pinch bolt.
2. Remove battery and disconnect fuse block main wire feed.
3. Disconnect lefthand fenderwell main ground and intake air temperature electrical connector.
4. Remove air cleaner lid and inlet duct.
5. Remove air box, disconnect purge hose from throttle body and position aside.
6. Disconnect EVAP purge solenoid, rear oxygen sensor and transaxle back-up lamp switch electrical connectors, then the master cylinder main harness connector.
7. Remove dash cover front and PCM boot.
8. Disconnect PCM electrical connector and secure to engine.
9. Remove fuse block lid and disconnect engine harness main connector from bottom of fuse block.
10. Remove battery and fuse block trays.
11. Disconnect cruise control and throttle cables.
12. Disconnect brake assist vacuum line from throttle body and lay aside.
13. Loosen control rod to lever pinch bolt. **Control shaft lever retaining pin has spring loaded locking feature securing pin in place.**
14. Remove control shaft lever to shaft retaining pin.

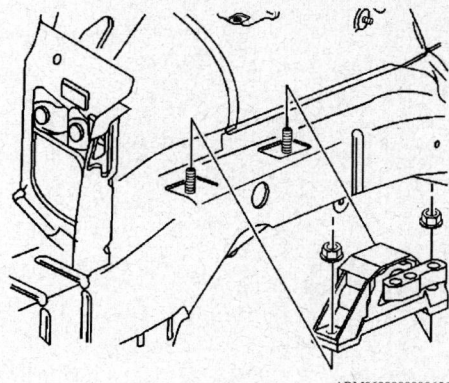

ARM0600000000656

Fig. 2 Engine mount replacement. ION

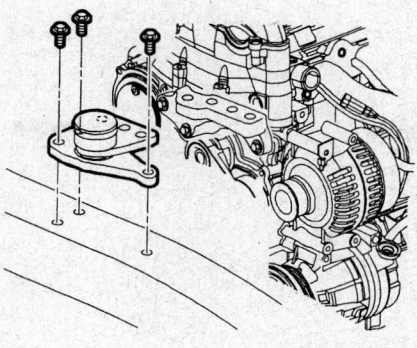

G31069900036000X

Fig. 3 Engine mount replacement. L-Series

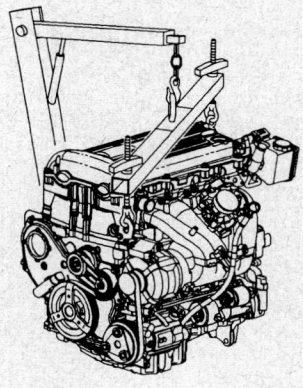

G31069900037000X

Fig. 4 Engine lift hoist attachment

15. Remove control shaft lever to transaxle and frame brackets retaining clips.
16. Remove control shaft lever by pulling straight up from pivot pins.
17. Drain coolant into suitable container.
18. Remove dash front heater hoses, then the radiator upper and lower hoses.
19. Disconnect fuel lines and secure radiator to upper radiator support.
20. Raise and support vehicle, then remove righthand front tire/wheel assembly.
21. Remove righthand front splash shield and lefthand front wheel liner push pin from frame.
22. Install suitable wood blocks between transaxle case and frame, and between crank pulley and frame.
23. Lower vehicle.
24. Disconnect righthand engine and lefthand transaxle mounts by removing mount to engine/transaxle bolts. Mount brackets will remain on engine and transaxle.
25. Disconnect rear oxygen sensor harness from frame at two attachment points.
26. Remove exhaust manifold pipe from catalytic converter forward.
27. Remove air conditioning line to frame attachment clip at front of frame. **Do not disconnect air conditioning lines.**
28. Remove air conditioning compressor from engine and secure to cooling module.
29. Remove tie rod to steering knuckle bolts and separate tie rod from steering knuckle using No. SA91100-C, or equivalent. Discard tie rod bolts.
30. Remove stabilizer bar links from strut.
31. Remove lower ball stud bolt and separate ball from steering knuckle using suitable tool. **Do not separate ball studs using pickle fork or wedge type separator tool.**
32. Remove suspension support assemblies and suspension support cage nuts from body. Discard cage nuts.
33. Support powertrain and frame with powertrain lifting table and service tool No. J43628, or equivalent, **Fig. 5.**
34. Remove remaining frame to body mounting bolts.

35. Carefully lower powertrain and frame.
36. Remove remaining cage nuts and discard.
37. Attach engine lift hoist to engine lift hooks, **Fig. 4.**
38. Place suitable 1¾ × 2 × 4 inch and 1¼ × 2 × 4 inch long wood blocks under transaxle housing support. **Engine must be moved approximately four inches forward in cradle to disconnect input shaft.**
39. Remove transaxle bell housing mounting bolts.
40. Carefully lift engine from cradle and mount on suitable engine stand or transportation pallet.
41. Reverse procedure to install.

INTAKE MANIFOLD
REPLACE

Intake manifold is made of a composite plastic and can be damaged if removed when engine is hot. Do not remove the manifold from a hot engine. Allow engine to cool to ambient temperature.

1. Remove air inlet tube and air cleaner.
2. Disconnect fuel lines using fuel line disconnection tools Nos. J37088-1A and J37088-2A, or equivalents.
3. Disconnect throttle position sensor, IAC and MAP sensor electrical connectors.
4. Disconnect throttle and cruise control cables.
5. Disconnect fuel pressure regulator hose from throttle body and fuel rail.
6. Remove mounting bolts and throttle body.
7. Remove fuel rail.
8. Remove mounting bolts, nuts and intake manifold, **Fig. 6.**
9. Remove intake manifold gasket.
10. If intake manifold needs to be replaced, transfer throttle body and gasket.
11. Reverse procedure to install.

EXHAUST MANIFOLD
REPLACE

1. Remove oxygen sensor from exhaust manifold.
2. Remove exhaust manifold heat shield.

3. Remove mounting nuts and exhaust manifold, **Fig. 7.**
4. Reverse procedure to install, noting the following:
   a. Install new exhaust manifold studs.
   b. Coat oxygen sensor threads with anti seize compound, Saturn No. 21485279, or equivalent.

CYLINDER HEAD
REPLACE
Removal

1. Remove exhaust and intake manifolds as outlined under "Exhaust Manifold, Replace" and "Intake Manifold, Replace."
2. Remove mounting bolt and crankshaft pulley using crankshaft pulley holder tool No. J38122, or equivalent, **Fig. 8.**
3. Remove valve cover grounding strap, ignition module and coil.
4. Remove valve cover, **Fig. 9.**
5. Depress tensioner arm and remove accessory drive belt.
6. Remove mounting bolts and tensioner.
7. Remove mounting bolts and engine front cover.
8. Remove upper timing chain guide.
9. Remove timing chain tensioner plunger. **Do not allow any tension on timing chain when loosening camshaft sprocket bolt.**
10. Remove exhaust cam sprocket using suitable open end wrench to hold camshaft while loosening camshaft sprocket bolt. Discard bolt.
11. Remove adjustable timing chain guide and fixed timing chain guide bolt access plug.
12. Remove fixed timing guide.
13. Remove intake cam sprocket timing chain through top of cylinder head, **Fig. 10.**
14. Remove crankshaft sprocket and oiling nozzle.
15. Remove each cap one turn at a time until there is no spring tension on camshaft.
16. Mark bearing caps for installation alignment. Keep roller finger followers

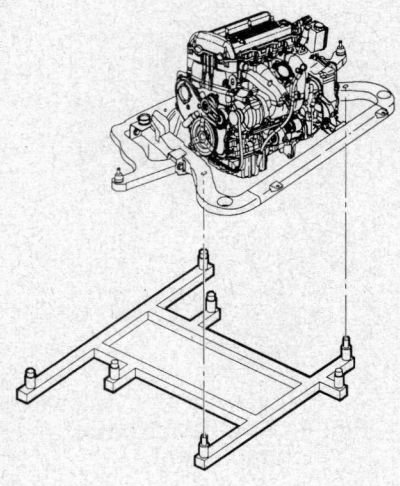

G31069900038000X

Fig. 5 Frame alignment tool

and hydraulic element adjusters in order so they can be installed in original positions.

17. Remove mounting bolts, intake camshaft bearing caps and camshaft, **Fig. 11.**
18. Remove intake camshaft roller finger followers and hydraulic adjusters.
19. Remove exhaust camshaft bearing cap bolts, bearing caps and camshaft, **Fig. 12.**
20. Remove balance shaft drive chain tensioner and adjustable balance shaft chain guide.
21. Remove small balance shaft drive chain guide and upper balance shaft chain guide.
22. Remove balance shaft drive chain and crankshaft drive sprocket.
23. Remove bearing carrier bolts and balance shafts, **Fig. 13.**
24. Keep each balance shaft separate. **Do not remove front balance shaft bearing bolts.**
25. Remove thermostat and water feed pipe mounting bolts.
26. Remove thermostat housing and water feed pipe from water pump cover. Ensure bolt through front of engine block is removed.
27. Remove mounting bolts and water pump.
28. Remove cylinder head bolts in sequence, **Fig. 14.**
29. Remove cylinder head and gasket.

Installation

1. Install new gasket and cylinder head. **Do not use any sealing material.**
2. Lightly apply clean engine oil to threads and bottom side of flange of head bolt. Allow oil to drain before installation.
3. Refer to sequence, **Fig. 15,** and tighten cylinder head bolts in two steps: First step, **torque** bolts to 22 ft. lbs.; second step, tighten bolts an additional 155.°
4. **Torque** front cylinder head bolts to 18 ft. lbs., **Fig. 16.**

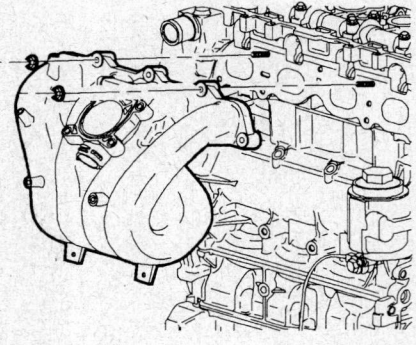

G31059900004000X

Fig. 6 Intake manifold replacement

5. Lubricate and install hydraulic element lash adjusters into cylinder head bores.
6. Lubricate valve tips with suitable engine oil supplement, then position roller followers on tip of valve stem and lash adjuster. Ensure roller followers are lubricated.
7. Set intake and exhaust camshaft on top of roller followers in camshaft bearing journals. Lubricate with engine oil supplement.
8. Install camshaft bearing caps and hand start camshaft cap bolts.
9. Timing chain sprocket alignment notch should be oriented to 11 o'clock position, **Fig. 17.**
10. Tighten camshaft bearing cap bolts in increments of three turns until seated.
11. Apply $^{13}/_{64}$ inch bead of Loctite Anerobic Gasket Maker 578, or equivalent, to rear intake camshaft bearing cap.
12. Place piston No. 1 to top dead center and install balance shaft drive chain sprocket on crankshaft.
13. Install balance shafts in bores.
14. Install water pump, feed tube and thermostat housing.
15. Position chain so copper colored and chrome links are visible, **Fig. 18.**
16. Align copper colored link with intake side balance shaft sprocket timing mark.
17. Working clockwise around chain, align first chrome link with crankshaft drive sprocket timing mark (approximately 5 o'clock position).
18. Align last chrome link with exhaust side balance shaft drive sprocket timing mark and install balance shaft chain guides.
19. Turn tensioner plunger 30° in bore and compress plunger until paper clip can be inserted through hole in plunger body and tensioner plunger.
20. Install timing chain tensioner. Remove paper clip from balance shaft drive chain tensioner.
21. Install timing chain drive sprocket to crankshaft with timing mark in 5 o'clock position.
22. Assemble intake camshaft sprocket to timing chain. Align timing mark with copper colored link.
23. Lower timing chain through opening in cylinder head.

G31079900002000X

Fig. 7 Exhaust manifold replacement

24. Route timing chain around crankshaft sprocket and align second link with timing mark on crankshaft sprocket (approximately 5 o'clock position).
25. Install intake camshaft sprocket onto intake camshaft. Hand tighten new sprocket mounting bolt. Sprocket to camshaft offset notch alignment is not required now.
26. Install adjustable timing chain guide through opening in cylinder head.
27. Install exhaust camshaft sprocket onto exhaust camshaft. Hand tighten new sprocket mounting bolt. Align sprocket timing mark with silver link.
28. Ensure colored links and timing marks are aligned.
29. Install fixed and upper timing chain guides.
30. Tighten intake and exhaust camshafts' hex using suitable wrench, **Fig. 19.**
31. Install new sealing washer and timing chain tensioner.
32. Install timing chain oiling nozzle.
33. Apply Loctite 242 thread locker compound, or equivalent, and install timing chain guide bolt access hole plug.
34. Install engine front cover and new gasket.
35. Install accessory drive belt tensioner, valve cover and gasket.
36. Install crankshaft pulley.
37. Install intake and exhaust manifolds.

VALVE ADJUSTMENT

This engine is equipped with hydraulic lifters and no adjustment is required.

VALVE GUIDES

Valve guides are an integral part of the cylinder head and are pressed in. If valve stem clearance becomes excessive, the valve guides must be hand reamed to the oversize using valve guide reamer tool J42096, or equivalent. Service valves are available in standard and .003 inch oversize.

CRANKSHAFT DAMPER
REPLACE

1. Raise and support vehicle.
2. Remove front tire/wheel assembly.
3. Remove front fender liner.

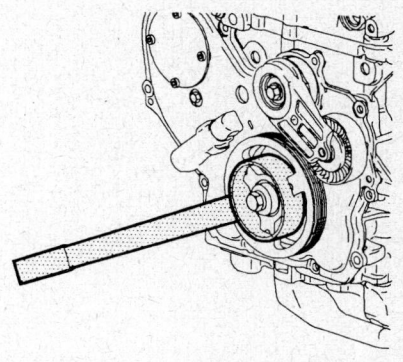

Fig. 8   Crankshaft pulley replacement

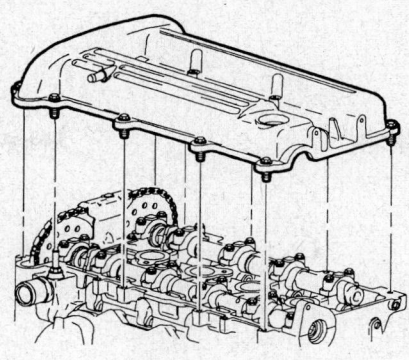

Fig. 9   Valve cover replacement

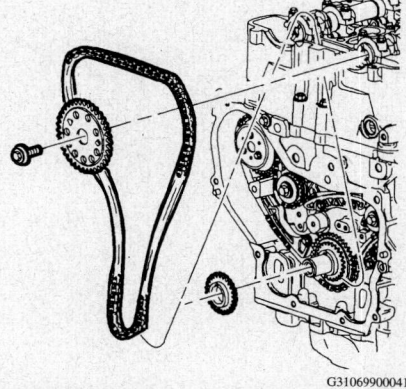

Fig. 10   Intake camshaft sprocket timing chain replacement

4. Turn drive belt tensioner clockwise.
5. Remove serpentine drive belt.
6. Prevent crankshaft from rotating by install harmonic balancer holder tool No. J38122A, or equivalent.
7. Remove mounting bolt and crankshaft balancer. Discard bolt.
8. Reverse procedure to install.

FRONT COVER
REPLACE

1. Remove air cleaner, then raise and support vehicle.
2. Drain engine oil into suitable container, then remove righthand front tire/wheel and splash shield.
3. Remove righthand front fender liner.
4. Mark serpentine belt running direction.
5. Relieve tension by slowly turn belt tensioner counterclockwise and remove serpentine belt.
6. Install crankshaft holder tool J38122, or equivalent, onto crankshaft pulley.
7. Remove crankshaft pulley and discard bolt.
8. Depress tensioner arm and remove accessory drive belt.
9. Remove mounting bolts and tensioner.
10. Remove righthand engine mount as outlined under "Engine Mount, Replace.".
11. Remove front cover and gasket.
12. Reverse procedure to install.

TIMING CHAIN
REPLACE

Refer to "Cylinder Head, Replace" for timing chain replacement.

CAMSHAFT
REPLACE

1. Remove ignition coil, accessory drive belt, PCV fresh air hose and valve cover.
2. Position cylinder No. 1 piston at Top Dead Center (TDC) with intake and exhaust valves closed.
3. Remove upper timing chain guide and timing chain tensioner.
4. Install camshaft sprocket holding tool No. J43655, or equivalent, onto cylinder head, **Fig. 20. Torque** holding tool to 108 inch lbs.
5. Remove camshaft timing sprockets mounting bolts and washers while holding each camshaft in place using suitable open end wrench.
6. Remove remaining camshaft bearing cap bolts in several passes.
7. Slide camshaft sprockets away from camshafts.
8. Carefully pull camshafts straight up to avoid damaging cylinder head thrust surface, **Fig. 21.**
9. Reverse procedure to install.

PISTON & ROD ASSEMBLY

Install the piston onto the connecting rod with the arrow pointed toward the front of the engine.

PISTONS, PINS & RINGS

Replace any pistons that show signs of damage or excessive wear. Piston pin bores and pins must be free of varnish or scuffing. Use an outside micrometer to measure the piston contact areas and piston pin bore. Subtract the measurement of the piston pin bore from the piston pin.

MAIN & ROD BEARINGS
Main Bearings

1. Install crankshaft bearing caps using suitable brass, lead, leather, or equivalent soft faced mallet. **Do not use lower crankcase bolts to pull bearing caps into seats.**
2. Refer to sequence, **Fig. 22,** and tighten lower crankcase inner bolts in two steps: First step, **torque** bolts to 15 ft. lbs.; second step, tighten bolts an additional 70.°
3. Refer to sequence, **Fig. 23.** and tighten lower crankcase outer bolts in two steps: First step, **torque** bolts to 18 ft. lbs.; second step, tighten bolts an additional 70.°

Connecting Rod Bearings

Torque connecting rod bear caps to 18 ft. lbs., then tighten an additional 70.°

CRANKSHAFT SEAL
REPLACE

1. Raise and support vehicle, then remove front tire/wheel assembly.
2. Remove front fender liner.
3. Turn drive belt tensioner clockwise.
4. Remove serpentine drive belt.
5. Prevent crankshaft from rotating by install harmonic balancer holder tool No. J38122A, or equivalent.
6. Remove mounting bolt and crankshaft balancer. Discard bolt.
7. Remove front oil seal using suitable flat bladed tool.
8. Reverse procedure to install, using camshaft front main seal installer tool No. J35268A, or equivalent.

CRANKSHAFT REAR OIL SEAL
REPLACE

1. Remove transaxle as outlined in **MOTOR's "Domestic Transmission, In-Vehicle Service" manual or "Transmission Service DVD."**
2. Remove flywheel and cover.
3. Insert suitable screwdriver into pry tangs of seal carrier and remove seal.
4. Apply suitable clean engine oil to seal lip and inside diameter of seal carrier.
5. Install seal using seal installer tool No. J42067, or equivalent.
6. Install transaxle and flywheel.

OIL PAN
REPLACE

1. Raise and support vehicle.
2. Drain engine oil into suitable container and remove front exhaust pipe.
3. Remove righthand front wheel, splash shield and vibration dampner.
4. Remove mounting bolts and oil pan.

Fig. 11 Intake camshaft & bearing caps replacement

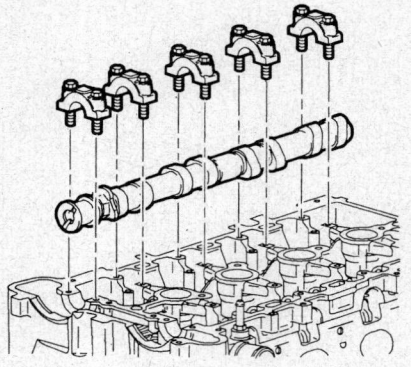

Fig. 12 Exhaust camshaft & bearing caps replacement

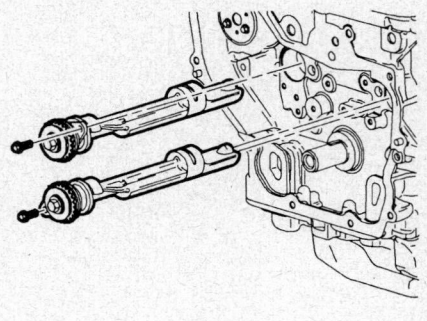

Fig. 13 Balance shaft replacement

5. Reverse procedure to install, noting the following:
   a. Apply .08 inch bead of suitable around perimeter of oil pan and oil suction port opening. **Do not apply excessive RTV.**
   b. **Torque** oil pan mounting bolts to 18 ft. lbs. in sequence, **Fig. 24.**

OIL PUMP

REPLACE

1. Remove air cleaner, then raise and support vehicle.
2. Drain engine oil into suitable container, then remove righthand front wheel and splash shield.
3. Mark running direction, then remove accessory drive belt.
4. Remove crankshaft pulley using pulley holding tool No. J38122, or equivalent.
5. Remove righthand front fender liner.
6. Mark serpentine belt running direction.
7. Relieve tension by slowly turn belt tensioner counterclockwise and remove serpentine belt.
8. Install engine support fixture tool No. SA9150-E, or equivalent.
9. Remove engine mount as outlined under "Engine Mount, Replace."
10. Remove front cover bolts and bolts under water pump cover.
11. Remove front cover and gasket.
12. Reverse procedure to install.

OIL PUMP SERVICE

Disassemble

1. Remove cover plate mounting bolts.
2. Mark drive and driven rotors for installation alignment.
3. Remove drive and driven rotors, then the pressure relief valve.

Inspection

1. Measure clearance between driven rotor and pump body, **Fig. 25,** which should not exceed .012 inch.
2. Inspect clearance between both tips, **Fig. 26,** which should not exceed .006 inch.
3. Measure clearance between side of drive and driven rotors, and oil pump cover plate, **Fig. 27,** which should not exceed .003 inch.

Assemble

1. Remove front cover oil seal using suitable screwdriver or punch.
2. Install new oil seal using oil seal installer tool No. J35268-A, or equivalent, and suitable press.
3. Install pressure relief valve, valve spring and oil pump pressure relief valve plug.
4. Lubricate drive and driven rotors with clean engine oil, then align marks on drive and driven rotors.
5. Install drive and driven rotors into pump body.
6. Fill oil pump with petroleum jelly to prime oil pump.
7. Install oil pump gear cover plate screws.

SERPENTINE DRIVE BELT

Belt Routing

Refer to **Fig. 28** for serpentine belt routing.

Belt, Replace

REMOVAL

1. Mark belt running direction.
2. Depress tensioner arm using suitable ⅜ inch drive breaker bar, **Fig. 28.**
3. Remove belt from idler or air conditioning compressor pulley and accessory pulleys.

INSTALLATION

1. Route belt around pulleys, except for idler pulley.
2. Depress tensioner arm using ⅜ inch drive breaker bar.
3. Ensure belt is properly aligned on pulleys and slip belt over idler pulley.

Tensioner, Replace

Do not disassemble tensioner. Internal components are not serviceable.
1. Depress tensioner arm and remove accessory drive belt.
2. Remove mounting bolts and tensioner, **Fig. 29.**
3. Reverse procedure to install.

COOLING SYSTEM BLEED

ION

1. Remove surge tank cap.
2. Raise and support vehicle.
3. Place suitable drain pan below righthand side of radiator lower mount.
4. Open petcock and drain coolant into container.
5. **On models equipped with water pump drain plug,** place drain pan below drain plug, **Fig. 30,** then open plug and drain coolant into container.
6. **On all models,** after all coolant has drained, close petcock hand tight.
7. **On models equipped with water pump drain plug,** install drain plug, then **torque** to 16 ft. lbs.
8. **On all models,** lower the vehicle, then disconnect radiator upper hose from righthand side of radiator.
9. Slowly add a 50/50 mixture of Dex-Cool antifreeze and deionized water to engine through upper hose.
10. Connect upper hose to radiator.
11. Slowly add antifreeze and water mixture to surge tank to just above Cold Fill line.
12. Install surge tank cap, then start engine.
13. Run engine at 2000–2500 RPM for three minutes.
14. Idle engine for 30 seconds, then turn ignition Off.
15. Inspect coolant level and add if required.

L-Series

1. Slowly add mixture of 50/50 Dex-Cool and clean water to cooling system until

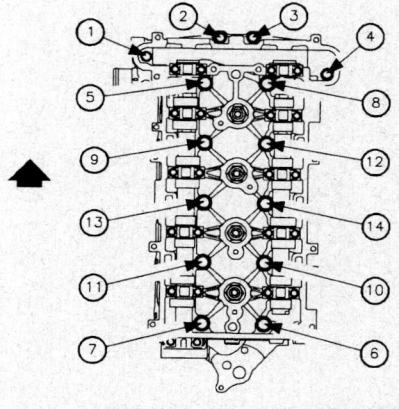

Fig. 14 Cylinder head bolt loosening sequence

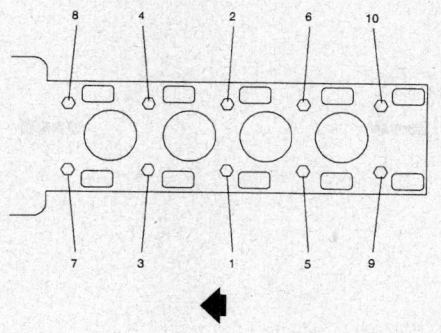

Fig. 15 Cylinder head bolt tightening sequence

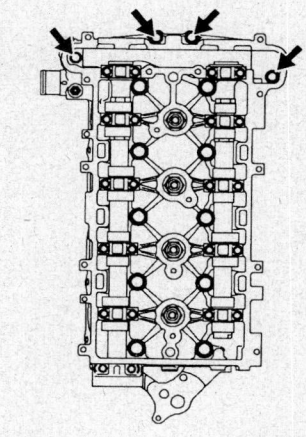

Fig. 16 Front cylinder head bolt locations

coolant level reaches and maintains top of surge tank label.
2. Install surge tank cap.
3. Start engine, run at 2000–2500 RPM until engine reaches normal operating temperature.
4. Allow engine to idle for three minutes.
5. Shut engine Off.
6. Top off coolant.
7. Inspect cooling system for leaks.

THERMOSTAT
REPLACE

1. Drain engine coolant into suitable container.
2. Disconnect lower radiator hose at thermostat housing using Snap-On hose removal tool HCP10, or equivalent. Twist water feed pipe and remove from water pump.
3. Remove thermostat, water feed and housing mounting bolts.
4. Remove thermostat housing and element.
5. Inspect thermostat components for damage and seat deterioration.
6. Reverse procedure to install. Install new O-ring.

WATER PUMP
REPLACE
ION

1. **On models equipped with automatic transmission,** remove exhaust manifold as outlined under "Exhaust Manifold, Replace."
2. **On all models,** drain cooling system into suitable container.
3. Raise and support vehicle.
4. Remove righthand front tire/wheel.
5. Remove front fender liner.
6. Remove water pump sprocket from timing cover access plate, **Fig. 31.**
7. Remove water pump sprocket bolts by holding sprocket using water pump sprocket holding tool No. J43651, or equivalent.
8. Remove engine block to water pump and engine front cover to water pump mounting bolts, **Fig. 32.**

9. Remove feed pipes thermostat to water pump.
10. Remove mounting bolts and water pump, **Fig. 33.**
11. Reverse procedure to install.

L-Series

1. Remove air inlet tube and air cleaner.
2. Drain coolant into suitable container and remove exhaust manifold heat shield.
3. Remove thermostat and water feed mounting bolts.
4. Remove water pump sprocket access plate from front cover and install water pump sprocket holding tool J43651, or equivalent.
5. Remove water pump mounting bolts accessed from front of engine block, then the water pump.
6. Reverse procedure to install.

RADIATOR
REPLACE

ION

1. Drain cooling system into suitable container.
2. Remove hood latch assembly.
3. Remove left and righthand headlamp assemblies.
4. Remove mounting bolts and radiator upper mounts.
5. Raise and support vehicle.
6. Remove mounting bolts and disconnect electrical connectors, then remove cooling fan.
7. Disconnect clamp and remove radiator outlet hose.
8. Remove lower transmission oil cooler line and lower vehicle.
9. Remove hood latch support bracket and forward sensors with harness.
10. Remove upper transmission oil cooler line from radiator.
11. Remove surge tank hose and clamp from radiator.
12. Remove condenser from radiator.
13. Remove radiator.
14. Reverse procedure to install.

L-Series

1. Remove battery and drain coolant into suitable container.
2. Disconnect cooling fans electrical connectors and slide electrical connectors out of retainers.
3. Remove pusher fan electrical harness from fan shroud retaining tabs.
4. Remove wiring harness from clamp on fan shroud.
5. **On models equipped with automatic transaxle,** disconnect upper transaxle cooler lines from radiator end tank. Cap line.
6. **On all models,** disconnect upper radiator hose from radiator.
7. Remove mounting bolts and fan shroud.
8. Remove forward wiring harness from retaining clips and lower radiator hose from radiator.
9. **On models equipped with automatic transaxle,** remove lower transaxle cooler line. Cap line.
10. **On all models,** remove mounting bolts, upper bracket and rubber mounts.
11. Secure condenser away from upper rail using suitable tie strap.
12. Raise and support vehicle.
13. Remove condenser mounting bolts.
14. Pull condenser and pusher fan down slightly to disconnect radiator tabs.
15. Lower vehicle.
16. Remove radiator.
17. Remove upper radiator to condenser gaskets.
18. Reverse procedure to install.

FUEL PUMP
REPLACE

ION

1. Relieve fuel system pressure as outlined under "Precautions."
2. Raise and support vehicle.
3. Disconnect fuel feed and return lines from fuel filter.

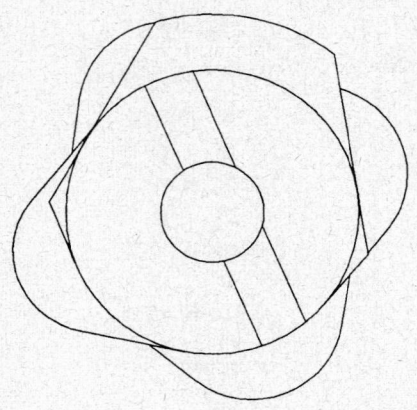

Fig. 17 Timing chain sprocket notch alignment

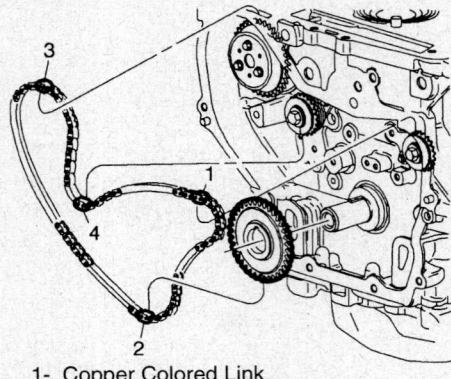

1- Copper Colored Link
2- First Chrome Link
3- Last Chrome Link

Fig. 18 Balance shaft drive chain installation

Fig. 19 Camshaft sprocket bolts installation

4. Cap or plug fuel tank feed and return pipes to prevent fuel loss or contamination.
5. Disconnect EVAP purge pipe and fuel tank EVAP vapor pipe from EVAP canister. Cap or plug pipes to prevent contamination.
6. Loosen fuel filler hose clamp at fuel tank, then disconnect hose.
7. Disconnect fuel pump module harness electrical connector from vehicle underbody connector.
8. Remove exhaust extension pipe insulators from underbody hangers.
9. Remove muffler insulator from underbody hanger and slowly lower exhaust, then rest exhaust on rear axle beam.
10. Support fuel tank with a suitable jack, then remove left and right fuel tank strap bolts and straps.
11. Slowly lower righthand side of fuel tank. Use care in feeding fuel feed and return pipes, EVAP vapor pipe and fuel pump module electrical harness to clear axle.
12. Once tank is clear of righthand frame rail, remove tank by pulling tank down and toward righthand side of vehicle. For installation reference, note position of fuel tank rear shield before releasing pump module retainer.
13. Release retaining tab on fuel tank retainer used to secure fuel pump module pipes in position on tank.
14. Release fuel pump module electrical harness from retaining slot on tank.
15. Disconnect fuel pump module harness electrical connector from fuel tank pressure sensor.
16. Carefully rotate fuel pump module retaining lock ring using lock ring removal tool No. J 39765, or equivalent.
17. Remove fuel pump module retaining lock ring, by sliding ring over module pipes and electrical harness.
18. Slowly raise fuel pump module assembly until fuel level sensor float arm is visible.
19. Ensure fuel level sensor harness connector clears tank opening.
20. Tilt pump module toward rear of fuel tank to enable level sensor float arm to clear tank opening.

21. Remove pump module from the tank.
22. Carefully discard fuel in pump module reservoir bowl into a suitable container.
23. Remove and discard fuel pump module-to-fuel tank seal.
24. Reverse procedure to install. **Do not use old fuel pump module-to-fuel tank seal.**

L-Series

This procedure has been revised by a Technical Service Bulletin.

Whenever fuel line fittings are loosened or removed, wrap a shop cloth around the fitting and have suitable container available to collect any fuel spillage.
1. Connect suitably programmed scan tool to Diagnostic Link Connector (DLC) and turn ignition On.
2. Raise and support vehicle, keeping scan tool outside of vehicle and accessible.
3. Disconnect fuel feed line at outlet to filter.
4. Install ⅜ × ¼ inch adapter onto flow/pressure adapter tool No. SA9127E-7, or equivalent, and insert adapter into fuel feed line.
5. Connect one end of suitable drain hose to other end of adapter. Connect other end of drain hose to suitable fuel handling cart.
6. Turn fuel pump on using scan tool and pump fuel into suitable container.
7. If fuel pump is inoperative, proceed as follows:
   a. Insert siphon hose guide/funnel into fuel filler pipe.
   b. Insert siphon hose J43290, or equivalent, into guide funnel and fuel filler pipe. Some resistance may be encountered when tip of siphon hose reaches inlet check valve. Repeated probing may be required to slide hose tip through check valve.
   c. Begin siphon process and collect fuel in suitable container.
8. Ensure fuel tank is less than quarter full.
9. Remove exhaust system intermediate

pipe and rear heat shield mounting bolts.
10. Remove fuel filler pipe lower bracket mounting screw and disconnect EVAP canister vent hose.
11. Loosen fuel filler pipe hose clamp closest to fuel tank and remove tank ground strap mounting screw near fuel filter.
12. Disconnect fuel feed line after fuel filter.
13. Disconnect fuel return and EVAP canister purge lines between tank and chassis fuel bundle.
14. Disconnect fuel tank electrical connectors.
15. Loosen, but do not remove, front tank strap bolt.
16. Remove rear tank mounting strap bolts with assistance.
17. Remove tank by lowering at the rear, then sliding downward and rearward.
18. Disconnect fuel lines from fuel pump module cover. **Do not remove retainer using 12-inch or shorter ratchet or breaker bar.**
19. Remove fuel pump module retainer ring using lock ring service tool No. J43827, or equivalent.
20. To prevent bending of sending unit float arm, remove sending unit first by pulling retaining clip toward float arm and lifting upward.
21. Carefully lift fuel pump straight up from fuel tank. Clips must be disconnected at same time to disconnect fuel pump from housing.
22. Discard fuel pump module to tank seal and remove fuel feed line from bottom of fuel pump cover using removal tool No. J44078, or equivalent.
23. Disconnect fuel pump electrical connector from fuel pump cover.
24. Inspect fuel tank for metal chips or debris. Remove contaminants and replace inline fuel filter before installing new pump.
25. Reverse procedure to install, noting the following:
   a. Replace plastic fuel line retainers.
   b. Install new module to tank seal lubricated with suitable clean engine oil.

G31069900051000X

Fig. 20 Camshaft sprocket holding tool installation

G31069900052000X

Fig. 21 Camshaft replacement

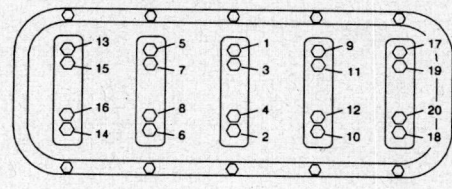

G31069900077000X

Fig. 22 Lower crankcase inner bolt tightening sequence

FUEL FILTER

REPLACE

ION

1. Relieve fuel system pressure.
2. Raise and support vehicle.
3. Disconnect fuel filter fitting using suitable back-up wrench.
4. Disconnect fuel filter quick connect fitting.
5. Remove fuel filter.
6. Reverse procedure to install.

L-Series

1. Raise and support vehicle.
2. Remove fuel filter bracket screw, then disconnect fuel lines from inlet and outlet sides of fuel filter.
3. Slide fuel filter out of bracket.
4. Reverse procedure, noting the following:
   a. Turn ignition On for two seconds, then Off for 10 seconds.
   b. Turn ignition On.
   c. Inspect fuel system for leaks.

TECHNICAL SERVICE BULLETINS

Excessive Oil Consumption, Blue Smoke on Acceleration

2004–05 ION & L-SERIES

On some of these models there may be excessive oil consumption (more than one quart with 2000 miles) or blue smoke on acceleration.

This condition may be caused by PCV orifice sizing and/or misalignment of the cam cover oil baffle.

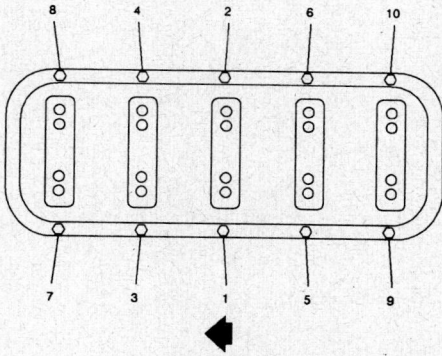

G31069900078000X

Fig. 23 Lower crankcase outer bolt tightening sequence

To correct this condition, proceed as follows:

1. Remove valve cover and inspect for heat stakes marks, **Fig. 34.**
2. If heat stake marks are not present, install new valve cover. **On ION models,** oil fill tube must be replaced.
3. **On all models,** if heat stake marks are present, install existing valve cover.
4. Remove intake manifold.
5. Attempt to install chuck end of 5/64 inch drill bit into PCV orifice slightly below surface, **Fig. 35.**
6. If chuck end can be inserted, install new intake manifold.
7. If chuck end cannot be inserted, install original intake manifold.

Front Cover Crankshaft Oil Seal Leak

2004–05 ION & L-SERIES

On some of these models the front engine cover crankshaft oil seal may leak during extremely cold weather.

This condition may be caused by a seal torn when moisture at the engine crankshaft balancer froze.

To correct this condition, install new seal

built with improved sealing compound (part No. 12584041) as outlined under "Crankshaft Seal, Replace."

Slight Coolant Loss

2004 ION & L-SERIES

On some of these mounts the low coolant lamp my light and/or the coolant level may be low with no external leaks visible. In addition, then engine may be difficult to start or misfire for several seconds, or there may be white smoke or coolant odor from tailpipe.

This condition may be caused by aluminum cylinder head casting porosity.

To correct this condition, proceed as follows:

1. Pressurize cooling system to 25 psi and monitor gauge for pressure leak. If there is no sign of external leakage, proceed to next step.
2. If coolant is present on any spark plug thread or visible in combustion chamber, replace cylinder head.
3. If pressure gauge shows loss and there are no external leaks, remove cylinder head and inspect cylinder liner height to block deck surface for flushness, noting the following:
   a. If cylinder liner is not flush with block (lower than block surface), replace cylinder block.
   b. If all cylinder liners are flush with block surface, replace cylinder head.

Engine Oil Leak

2006 ION

On some of these models there may be an engine oil leak that appears to be rear main seal seepage.

This condition may be caused by damaged oil galley plug(s).

To correct this condition, proceed as follows:

1. Remove flywheel and leaking plugs, **Fig. 36.**
2. Replacement plugs have pre-applied thread sealant.
3. Apply suitable sealant if installing old plugs.
4. **Torque** plugs to 44 ft. lbs.

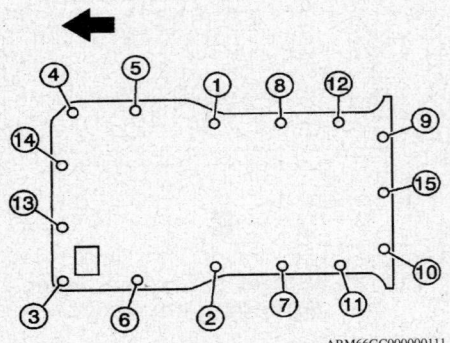

Fig. 24 Oil pan bolt tightening sequence

ARM66GC000000111

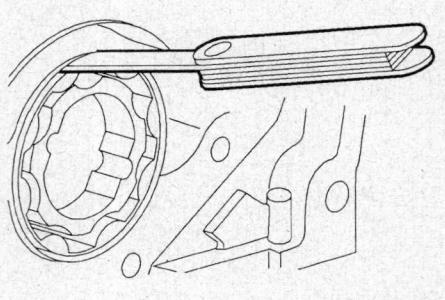

Fig. 25 Oil pump body clearance measurement

G31099900005000X

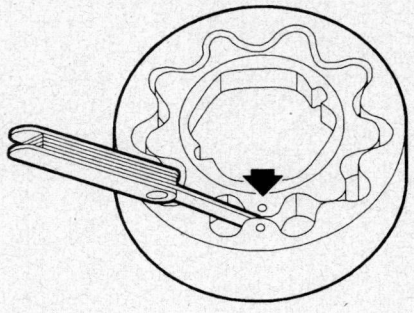

Fig. 26 Oil pump tip clearance measurement

G31099900006000X

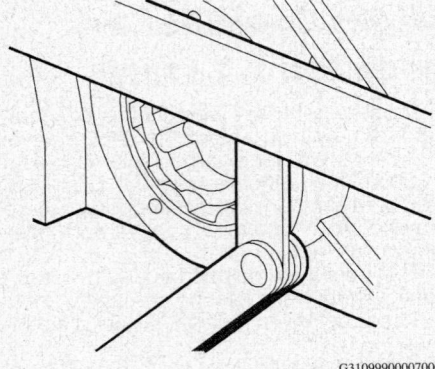

Fig. 27 Oil pump end to end clearance measurement

G31099900007000X

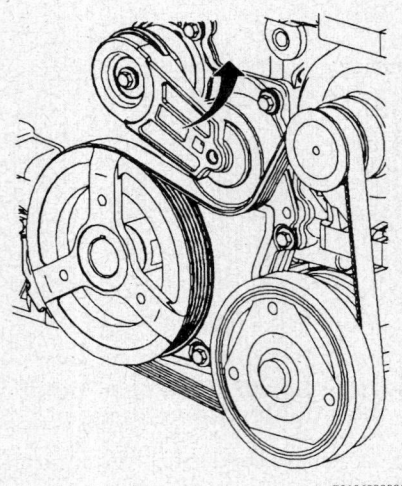

Fig. 28 Serpentine belt routing

G31069900054000X

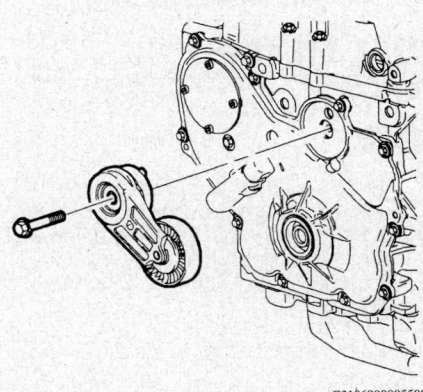

Fig. 29 Belt tensioner replacement

G31069900055000X

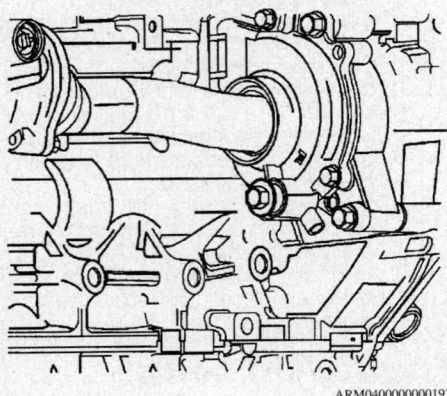

Fig. 30 Water pump drain plug

ARM0400000000193

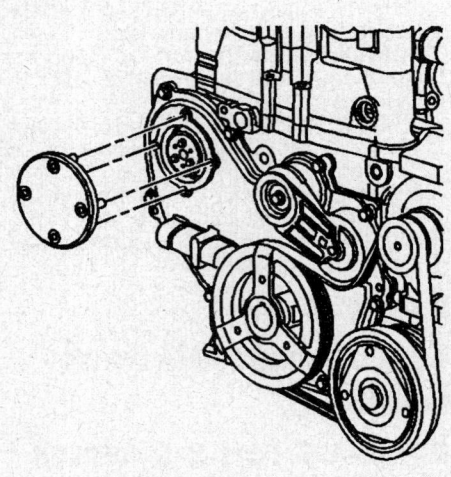

Fig. 31 Water pump access plate replacement. ION

GC1060101247000X

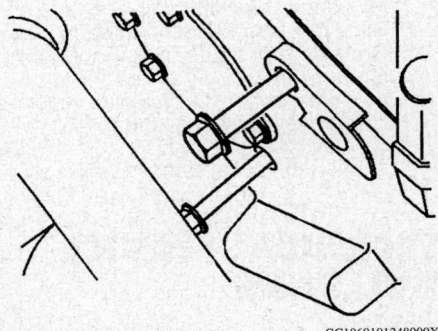

Fig. 32 Water pump cover replacement. ION

GC1060101248000X

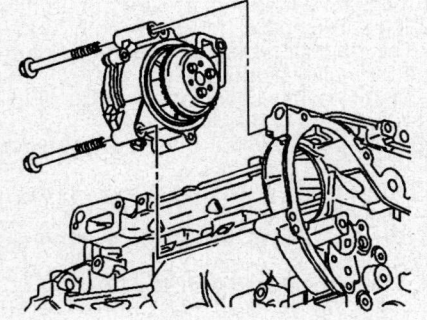

Fig. 33 Water pump replacement, ION

GC1060101249000X

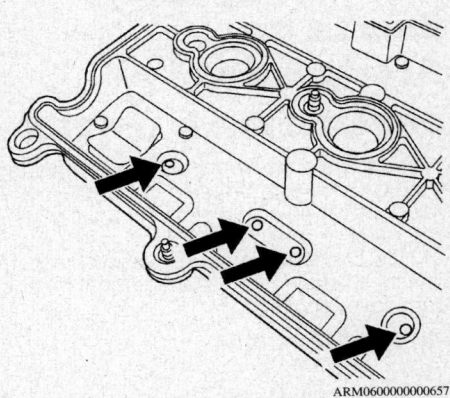

Fig. 34 Heat stake marks

ARM0600000000657

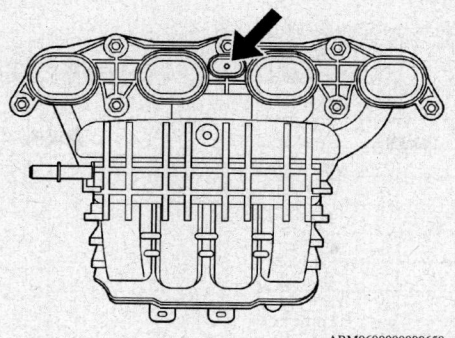

ARM0600000000658

Fig. 35 Intake manifold PCV orifice inspection

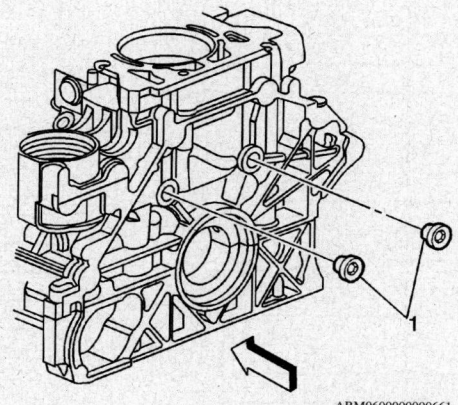

ARM0600000000661

Fig. 36 Oil galley plug locations

SATURN

TIGHTENING SPECIFICATIONS

Year	Component	Torque/Ft. Lbs.
2004–07	Air Conditioning Compressor	15
	Alternator	⑬
	Balance Shaft Bearing Carrier	89①
	Balance Shaft Chain Guide Plug	59
	Balance Shaft Sprocket	37
	Battery Hold-Down Bracket	15
	Battery Terminal	13
	Battery Tray	11
	Block Heater	89①
	Camshaft Bearing Cap	89①
	Camshaft Sprocket	②
	Camshaft Timing Chain Tensioner	55
	Chain Guide Plug	59
	Connecting Rod	⑤
	Crankshaft Position Sensor	89①
	Crankshaft Pulley	⑧
	Crankshaft Rear Oil Seal Carrier To Block	96①
	Cylinder Head	③
	Cylinder Head Vent Tube	11
	Dipstick Guide Tube	89①
	Drive Belt Tensioner	33
	ECT Sensor	16
	EGR Cover	18
	Electric ICM Cover	89①
	Engine Lift Bracket	18
	Engine Mount Bracket (L-Series)	66
	Engine Mount Intermediate Bracket (ION)	74
	Engine Mount To Body (L-Series)	41
	Engine Mount To Intermediate Bracket (ION)	37
	Engine Mount To Mid-Rail (ION)	74
	EVAP Emission Canister Valve	16
	Exhaust Manifold, Nut (ION)	⑪
	Exhaust Manifold, Nut (L-Series)	13
	Exhaust Manifold, Stud	89①
	Exhaust Manifold Heat Shield (ION)	17
	Exhaust Manifold Heat Shield (L-Series)	89①
	Exhaust Manifold Pipe Flange	12
	Exhaust Takedown Pipe	12
	Flexplate (Automatic Transaxle)	⑥
	Flywheel (Manual Transaxle)	⑥
	Frame	74⑫
	Front Cover	18
	Fuel Fill Neck To Fuel Tank Clamp	44①
	Fuel Filter Bracket	35①
	Fuel Pipe Bracket	89①
	Fuel Pressure Regulator	44①
	Fuel Rail Bracket	96①
	Fuel Tank Ground Strap	40①
	Fuel Tank Strap	15
	Idle Air Control Motor	27①

TIGHTENING SPECIFICATIONS—Continued

Year	Component	Torque/Ft. Lbs.
2004–07	Ignition Coil	89①
	Intake Camshaft Rear Cap	18
	Intake Manifold, Bolt or Nut	89①
	Intake Manifold, Stud	53①
	Knock Sensor	18
	Main Bearings	⑤
	Oil Drain Plug	18
	Oil Filter Housing Cover	18
	Oil Gallery Plug	26
	Oil Gallery Plug, Rear	44
	Oil Pan	⑦
	Oil Pump Gerotor Cover	53①
	Oil Pump Pressure Relief Valve Plug	30
	Oil Pressure Switch	89①
	Oxygen Sensor	31
	Power Steering Pump	18
	Radiator Upper Bracket	53①
	Spark Plug	15
	Starter Motor	⑩
	Starter Terminal	⑨
	Thermostat Housing	89①
	Throttle Body, Bolt Or Nut	89①
	Throttle Body, Stud	53①
	Throttle Position Sensor	18①
	Timing Chain Guide	89①
	Timing Chain Oil Nozzle	89①
	Timing Chain Tensioner	55
	Transaxle Mount	41
	Transaxle Range Switch	18
	Transaxle Range Switch Lever	26
	Valve Cover	89①
	Water Pump	④
	Water Pump Access Cover	62①
	Water Pump Drain Plug	15
	Water Pump/Balance Shaft Chain Tensioner	89①
	Water Pump Sprocket	89①

① — Inch lbs.
② — **Torque** to 63 ft. lbs, then final tighten an additional 30°.
③ — Refer to "Cylinder Head, Replace" for tightening specifications & sequence.
④ — 2004–05, 15 ft. lbs.; 2006–07, 18 ft. lbs.
⑤ — Refer to "Main & Rod Bearings" for tightening specifications & sequence.
⑥ — **Torque** to 39 ft. lbs., then final tighten an additional 25°.
⑦ — Refer to "Oil Pan, Replace" for tightening specifications & sequence.
⑧ — **Torque** to 74 ft. lbs, then final tighten an additional 75°.
⑨ — 2004–05, 89 inch lbs.; 2006–07, 13 ft. lbs.
⑩ — 2004–05, 39 ft. lbs.; 2006–07, 30 ft. lbs.
⑪ — 124 inch lbs. in two passes.
⑫ — Tighten an additional 180°.
⑬ — 2004–05, 15 ft. lbs.; 2006–07, 17 ft. lbs.

2.4L Engine

NOTE: On Air Bag Equipped Models, Refer To "Air Bag System Precautions" Located In The Front Of This Manual For System Disarming & Arming Procedures.

NOTE: Refer To "Computer Relearn Procedures" Located In The Front Of This Manual When Battery Power To The Computer Has Been Interrupted.

INDEX

	Page No.
Balance Shaft, Replace	12-58
Camshaft, Replace	12-58
Exhaust	12-58
Intake	12-58
Crankshaft Balancer, Replace	12-57
Crankshaft Rear Oil Seal, Replace	12-58
Crankshaft Seal, Replace	12-58
Cylinder Head, Replace	12-56
Engine Rebuilding Specifications	29-1
Engine, Replace	12-52
AURA	12-52
ION	12-53
SKY	12-54
Engine Mount, Replace	12-52
AURA & ION	12-52
SKY	12-52
Lefthand	12-52
Righthand	12-52
Exhaust Manifold, Replace	12-56
Front Cover, Replace	12-57
Fuel Filter, Replace	12-61
AURA & Sky	12-61

	Page No.
ION	12-61
Fuel Pump, Replace	12-60
AURA	12-60
ION	12-61
SKY	12-61
Hydraulic Lash Adjusters, Replace	12-57
Intake Manifold, Replace	12-55
Main & Rod Bearings	12-58
Oil Pan, Replace	12-58
AURA	12-58
Ion	12-59
Oil Pump, Replace	12-59
Oil Pump Service	12-59
Assemble	12-59
Disassemble	12-59
Piston & Rod Assembly	12-58
Precautions	12-51
Air Bag Systems	12-51
Battery Ground Cable	12-51
Fuel System Pressure Relief	12-51
Less Digital Gauge Tool	12-51
With Digital Gauge Tool	12-51
Hybrid Battery Service	12-51

	Page No.
Connect	12-52
Disconnect	12-51
Radiator, Replace	12-60
AURA	12-60
ION	12-60
Sky	12-60
Serpentine Drive Belt	12-59
AURA	12-59
Installation	12-59
Removal	12-59
Ion	12-59
Sky	12-59
Thermostat, Replace	12-59
AURA	12-59
Ion	12-60
Sky	12-60
Tightening Specifications	12-62
Timing Chain, Replace	12-57
Installation	12-57
Removal	12-57
Valve Cover, Replace	12-57
Water Pump, Replace	12-60

PRECAUTIONS

Air Bag Systems

Refer to "Air Bag System Precautions" in the front of this manual for system disarming and arming procedures.

Battery Ground Cable

Prior to service, disconnect battery ground cable and isolate as required.

Fuel System Pressure Relief

LESS DIGITAL GAUGE TOOL

1. Loosen fuel fill cap to relieve fuel tank vapor pressure.
2. Remove engine cover.
3. Remove fuel rail service port cap. Wrap a shop towel around service port.
4. Depress (open) fuel rail test port valve using a small flat bladed tool.
5. Remove shop towel from around fuel rail service port, and place in an approved container.
6. Install fuel rail service port cap.
7. Install engine cover and tighten fuel fill cap.

WITH DIGITAL GAUGE TOOL

1. Turn ignition OFF.
2. Disconnect battery ground cable as outlined in "Precautions."
3. Loosen fuel filler cap to relieve fuel tank vapor pressure.
4. Remove cap from fuel pressure service port.
5. Remove engine identification cover nuts and cover.
6. Connect digital pressure gauge tool No. J34730-1A, or equivalent, to fuel pressure service port connection.
7. Wrap a shop towel around port while connecting gauge in order to avoid spillage.
8. Install bleed hose of gauge tool into an suitable container.
9. Open bleed valve on gauge tool to bleed fuel system pressure.
10. Fuel connections are now safe for servicing.
11. Place a shop towel under fuel pressure service port to catch any remaining fuel spillage.
12. Disconnect gauge tool from fuel pressure service port connection.
13. Drain any fuel remaining in gauge into an approved container.
14. Install fuel pressure service port cap.

Hybrid Battery Service

DISCONNECT

To help avoid personal injury, always ensure the ignition switch is in the OFF position and the ignition key has been removed prior to working on any 36V components. After the key has been removed, disconnect the battery ground cable and then open the generator battery disconnect control module cover. After waiting for at least 5 minutes, measure the voltage potential using a Digital Multi-Meter (DMM) between the following: 36V positive and battery ground cables; 36V positive battery cable and vehicle ground; 36V battery ground cable and vehicle ground. All measured voltage levels must be below 3 volts.

1. Remove ignition key from ignition switch.
2. Secure ignition key to ensure that key CANNOT be installed without your knowledge.

3. Disconnect 12 volt battery ground cable.
4. Fold down both rear seat backs, then carefully lift up on load floor rear compartment cover at retaining clip locations, **Fig. 1.**
5. Tilt load floor rear compartment cover towards rear of vehicle slightly, disengage tabs and remove load floor rear compartment cover. **To avoid personal injury, be careful when working in vicinity of generator battery disconnect control module. Internal components will still be live, 36V potential, even when cover has been opened or removed.**
6. Remove generator battery disconnect control module cover bolt, **Fig. 2.**
7. Open and slide generator battery disconnect control module cover to right, removing cover. **Wait at least 5 minutes in order to allow generator control module capacitors to discharge.**
8. **Never assume battery pack is disabled when generator battery disconnect control module cover is opened. Generator battery will have to be checked for voltage potential using a voltmeter first**
9. Set voltmeter to DC voltage and measure vehicle 12-volt battery voltage (at 12-volt positive jumper location and battery ground cable).
10. Meter should read greater than 12 volts DC.
11. To ensure generator battery has been disabled, check generator battery for voltage potential as follows:
    a. Refer to **Fig. 3** for voltage measurement locations.
    b. Measure from positive stud to negative stud, voltage should be less than 3 volts.
    c. Measure from positive stud to vehicle chassis ground, voltage should be less than 3 volts.
    d. Measure from negative stud to vehicle chassis ground, voltage should be less than 3 volts.
12. After verifying there is no voltage present, vehicle is now safe to work on.

CONNECT

1. Install and close generator battery disconnect control module cover.
2. Install generator battery cover bolt and **torque** to 89 inch lbs.
3. Tilt load floor rear compartment cover towards rear of vehicle slightly in order to insert tabs into battery tray rear support.
4. Set load floor rear compartment cover down, ensure retaining clips align to proper locations, carefully push down to secure cover.
5. Place rear seats backs to their proper positions.
6. Connect 12 volt battery ground cable.

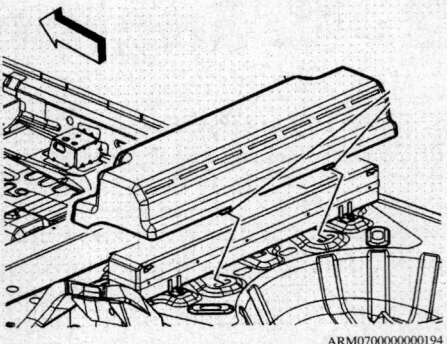

Fig. 1 Rear hybrid battery compartment. AURA

ARM0700000000194

ENGINE MOUNT
REPLACE
AURA & ION

1. Remove air cleaner.
2. Support engine using suitable hydraulic floor jack. Place a piece of wood between floor jack and oil pan.
3. Remove engine mount to bracket bolts.
4. Remove engine mount to side rail nuts.
5. Remove engine mount from engine compartment.
6. Reverse procedure to install.

SKY
LEFTHAND

1. Loosen clamps and remove Charge Air Cooler (CAC) outlet hose from CAC outlet pipe and throttle body.
2. Remove lefthand engine mount upper nut.
3. Raise and support vehicle.
4. Remove lefthand engine mount lower nut.
5. Remove righthand engine mount lower nut.
6. Position suitable adjustable jack below oil pan. Place suitable block of wood between oil pan and jack.
7. Raise engine and remove mount.
8. Reverse procedure to install.

RIGHTHAND

1. Raise and support vehicle, then remove tire and wheel assembly.
2. Remove upper and lower righthand engine mount nuts.
3. Remove lefthand engine mount lower nut.
4. Remove righthand brake hose bracket bolt.
5. Remove righthand brake line clip at crossmember.
6. Position suitable adjustable jack below

oil pan. Place suitable block of wood between oil pan and jack.
7. Raise engine and remove engine mount.
8. Reverse procedure to install.

ENGINE
REPLACE
AURA

1. Relieve fuel system pressure as outlined under "Precautions."
2. **Disable hybrid battery as outlined under "Hybrid Battery Service" in "Precautions."**
3. Remove air cleaner assembly.
4. Disconnect fuel feed pipe quick connect fitting at fuel rail.
5. Disconnect EVAP line quick connect fitting from EVAP purge solenoid.
6. Remove fuel feed pipe clips from fuel line bracket.
7. Remove transaxle shift cable clip from fuel line bracket.
8. Remove battery, then the underhood bussed electrical center cover.
9. Loosen integral bolt on positive battery cable lead and remove lead from electrical center.
10. Position positive battery cable aside.
11. Loosen integral bolt on steering column harness package lead and remove lead from bussed electrical center.
12. Loosen junction block bolts, then tap bolts once to disengage from electrical connectors.
13. Remove junction block.
14. Remove engine wiring harness underhood bussed electrical center connector from electrical center bracket and secure out of way.
15. Remove forward lamp and body wiring harness electrical connectors from electrical center bracket and secure out of way.
16. Disconnect body wiring harness electrical connector from ECM.
17. Disconnect engine wiring harness electrical connectors from ECM.
18. Remove engine wiring harness clips from ECM/Transmission Control Module (TCM) bracket.
19. Disconnect engine wiring harness electrical connector from TCM.
20. Remove ECM/TCM bracket bolt.
21. Slide ECM/TCM bracket up and remove bracket with ECM and TCM still attached from battery tray.
22. Remove battery tray.
23. Remove generator starter as outlined under "Generator With Starter, Replace" in "Electrical" section.
24. Remove vacuum brake booster hose from intake manifold. Position hose aside.
25. Drain cooling system.

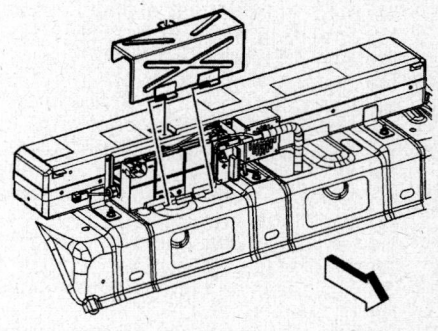

Fig. 2 Disconnect control module cover. AURA Hybrid

26. Remove coolant recovery inlet hose clamp at cylinder head, then the inlet pipe clip from fuel rail.
27. Remove coolant recovery inlet hose from cylinder head. Position hose aside.
28. Remove radiator inlet hose from cylinder head, then the radiator outlet hose.
29. Remove generator control module coolant hose from generator control module.
30. Disconnect engine wiring harness electrical connector from transaxle auxiliary pump module.
31. Remove heater inlet hose and coolant recovery reservoir/heater inlet hose from thermostat housing.
32. Raise and support vehicle, then drain engine oil.
33. Disconnect engine wiring harness electrical connector from generator control module coolant pump.
34. Disconnect engine wiring harness electrical connector from A/C compressor.
35. Remove generator control module coolant pump bolt and pump.
36. Remove A/C compressor mounting bolts, position compressor aside.
37. Remove positive battery cable to starter motor nut, then the cable lead from starter motor.
38. Remove positive battery cable from between starter and engine. Position cable aside.
39. Disconnect engine wiring harness electrical connector from auxiliary heater water pump.
40. Remove auxiliary heater water pump bolt and pump.
41. Lower vehicle.
42. Remove transaxle shift cable from range select lever.
43. Release shift control cable retaining clip and remove cable from shift control cable bracket.
44. Secure radiator/condenser/fan assembly to radiator support using long tie straps.
45. Raise and support vehicle, then remove front wheels and tires.
46. Remove front fender liners.
47. Install a suitable piece of hardwood (1 x 2 x 4 inch) between transaxle and engine cradle.

48. Install a suitable piece of hardwood (1 x 2 x 4 inch) between engine oil pan and engine cradle.
49. Drain transaxle fluid, then remove transaxle oil cooler lines from transaxle.
50. Remove Heated Oxygen Sensor (HO2S) from exhaust manifold pipe.
51. Remove exhaust manifold pipe to muffler attaching nuts.
52. Remove exhaust manifold/catalytic converter to exhaust manifold pipe nuts.
53. Remove exhaust manifold/catalytic converter.
54. Remove intermediate shaft to steering gear pinch bolt, then disconnect shaft from steering gear. Discard pinch bolt.
55. Remove both outer tie rod to steering knuckle nuts. Discard nuts.
56. Separate tie rods from steering knuckles using ball joint separation tool No. SA91100C, or equivalent.
57. Remove stabilizer link to stabilizer shaft nuts, then disconnect links from shafts.
58. Remove both of the lower control arm ball stud cotter pins.
59. Loosen ball stud nuts until nuts are level with top of ball stud.
60. Separate lower control arms from steering knuckles using ball joint separation tool No. J 43828, or equivalent. Remove ball stud nuts.
61. Remove front drive axles as outlined in "Front Drive Axle" chapter.
62. Lower vehicle.
63. Remove engine mount to bracket bolts.
64. Remove transaxle mount to transaxle bolts.
65. Raise and support vehicle.
66. Position a suitable engine support table under engine and transaxle assembly. Blocks of wood can be used between front of cradle and oil pan to table to level engine and transaxle assembly during removal.
67. Fully raise table to contact with engine and transaxle assembly.
68. Remove cradle to body bolts. Discard bolts.
69. When lowering engine/transaxle assembly, ensure all brake lines, shifter cables and other components are free.
70. Lower engine table and raise body on hoist until engine, transaxle and cradle are free from vehicle.
71. Disconnect engine wiring harness electrical connector from throttle actuator.
72. Disconnect engine wiring harness electrical connector from fuel injector wiring harness electrical connector.
73. Remove engine wiring harness clip from oil level indicator tube bracket.
74. Disconnect engine wiring harness electrical connectors from ignition coils and camshaft actuators.
75. Disconnect engine wiring harness electrical connectors from Crankshaft Position (CKP) sensor, oil pressure sensor and knock sensor.
76. Disconnect engine wiring harness electrical connector from intake and

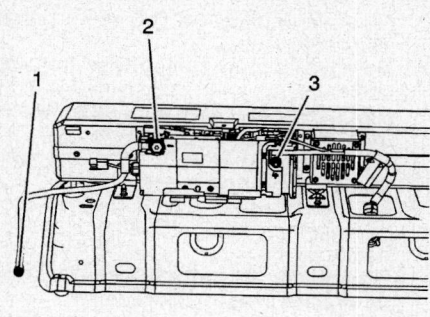

1-Chassis ground
2-Negative stud
3-Positive stud

Fig. 3 Battery disconnect control module voltage measurement locations. AURA Hybrid

exhaust Camshaft Position (CMP) sensors, EVAP emission canister purge solenoid valve and Engine Coolant Temperature (ECT) sensor.
77. Remove engine wiring harness clip from stud.
78. Remove engine wiring harness ground bolt and position ground terminal away from engine.
79. Gather all branches of engine wiring harness and position harness aside.
80. Remove starter motor mounting bolts and starter.
81. Remove torque converter to flexplate bolts.
82. Attach a suitable lifting devise to engine.
83. Remove transaxle to engine bolts, then separate engine from transaxle.
84. Reverse procedure to install.

ION

1. Relieve fuel pressure as outlined in "Precautions."
2. Disconnect fuel feed line quick connect from fuel rail.
3. Disconnect EVAP line quick connect from EVAP purge solenoid.
4. Remove fuel line clips from engine brackets.
5. Drain cooling system into suitable container.
6. Secure cooling module to upper body structure.
7. Remove righthand front fender liner.
8. Mark serpentine belt running direction.
9. Relieve tension by slowly turn belt tensioner counterclockwise and remove serpentine belt.
10. Disconnect cooling fan electrical connector.
11. Position radiator inlet hose clamp at engine.
12. Disconnect clamp and remove radiator inlet hose from engine.

13. Remove radiator outlet hose clamp from water outlet.
14. Remove radiator outlet hose from oil cooler.
15. Remove heater inlet and outlet hoses from thermostat housing.
16. Remove brake booster vacuum hose from intake manifold.
17. Disconnect TAC, MAP, fuel injector harness and alternator electrical connectors.
18. Disconnect engine harness clip from oil dipstick tube.
19. Disconnect engine harness clips from intake manifold.
20. Disconnect ignition coils electrical connectors.
21. Disconnect intake and exhaust camshaft position actuator electrical connectors.
22. Remove engine harness clips from valve cover.
23. Remove battery ground cable nut from engine ground connection.
24. Remove engine harness ground terminal from stud, battery cable ground terminal and stud connections.
25. Remove engine harness ground terminals.
26. Disconnect oil pressure sensor, CKP and knock sensor engine harness electrical connectors.
27. Disconnect EVAP purge solenoid electrical connector.
28. Remove engine harness clip from purge solenoid bracket.
29. Remove engine harness ground bolt and reposition engine harness ground terminal.
30. Disconnect engine harness electrical connector from air conditioning pressure switch.
31. Disconnect engine harness electrical connector from air conditioning compressor.
32. Unbolt and reposition air conditioning compressor aside using suitable wire for support.
33. Raise and support vehicle using suitable lift or jack.
34. Drain engine oil into suitable container.
35. Remove transaxle fluid cooler bracket nut and fluid cooler lines from transaxle.
36. Remove engine harness clip nut, then the clip from engine stud.
37. **On models equipped with automatic transaxle,** disconnect VSS engine harness electrical connector and remove engine harness clip from speed sensor.
38. **On all models,** remove positive battery cable lead nut from starter solenoid.
39. Remove positive battery cable terminal from starter.
40. Remove engine harness to starter solenoid S terminal nut.
41. Remove engine harness lead terminals from starter solenoid.
42. Lower vehicle.
43. Reposition engine harness boot.
44. Remove alternator nut and engine harness lead terminal from alternator.
45. **On models equipped with automat-**

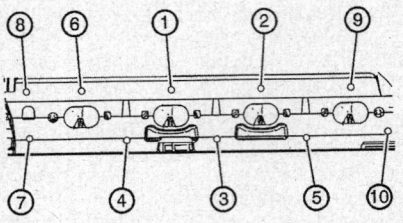

Fig. 4 Exhaust manifold tightening sequence

ic transaxle, proceed as follows:
  a. Disconnect engine harness from transaxle.
  b. Disconnect engine harness electrical connector from ECT sensor.
  c. Remove HO2S CPA retainers.
  d. Disconnect engine harness electrical connectors from HO2S.
  e. Remove HO2S connector clips from thermostat housing and engine bracket.
  f. Disconnect engine harness electrical connector from PNP switch.
46. **On models equipped with manual transaxle,** disconnect engine harness electrical connector from VSS.
47. **On all models,** disconnect engine harness electrical connector from back-up lamp switch.
48. Remove HO2S CPA retainers.
49. Disconnect engine harness electrical connectors from HO2S.
50. Remove HO2S clips from engine brackets.
51. Place all engine harness branches out of way using suitable wire.
52. **On models equipped with automatic transaxle,** disconnect range selector lever cable from transaxle lever and remove range selector lever cable from transaxle bracket.
53. **On models equipped with manual transaxle,** disconnect range selector and shift lever cables from transaxle levers, then remove range selector and shift lever cables from transaxle bracket.
54. **On all models,** remove catalytic converter.
55. Lower vehicle.
56. Insert blocks of wood between powertrain and frame to support powertrain.
57. Remove engine mount as outlined in "Engine Mount, Replace."
58. Remove transaxle mount to transaxle bolts, raise vehicle using suitable lift or jack.
59. Remove stabilizer links from stabilizer bar as outlined under "Stabilizer Bar, Replace" in "Front Suspension & Steering" section.
60. Remove outer tie rod ends from steering knuckles as outlined under "Tie Rod, Replace" in "Front Suspension & Steering" section.
61. Remove intermediate shaft from steering gear as outlined under "Power Steering Gear, Replace" in "Front Suspension & Steering" section.
62. Disconnect lower control arms from

steering knuckle as outlined under "Control Arm, Replace" in "Front Suspension & Steering" section.
63. Place matching marks on frame to body for correct installation alignment.
64. Lower vehicle to 3 feet above ground.
65. Position suitable engine lift table under frame.
66. Place wood blocks on top of lift table between table and frame.
67. Lower vehicle until frame is resting on blocks of wood.
68. Slowly loosen and remove frame bolts as follows:
  a. Loosen and remove front frame bolts.
  b. Loosen and remove rear frame bolts.
69. Slowly raise vehicle away from powertrain assembly.
70. Slide lift table out from under vehicle.
71. Attach engine lift hoist to engine lift hooks.
72. Remove starter as outlined under "Starter, Replace" in "Electrical" section.
73. **On models equipped with automatic transaxle,** remove torque converter housing access plug, then the torque converter bolts.
74. **On all models,** remove transaxle brace bolts and brace.
75. Remove transaxle to engine bolts and stud, then separate transaxle from engine.
76. **On models equipped with manual transaxle,** remove clutch pressure plate and disc.
77. **On all models,** remove engine mount bracket, engine block heater and alternator.
78. Reverse procedure to install.

SKY

1. Disconnect battery ground cable.
2. Open hood and disconnect headlamp bulb socket Connector Positive Assurance (CPA) connector.
3. Disconnect lefthand headlamp electrical harness.
4. Rotate socket a quarter turn counterclockwise and disconnect bulb.
5. Remove mounting screws and headlamp.
6. Disconnect wiring harness on both sides and mark hood for installation alignment.
7. Remove mounting nuts and hood.
8. Pull intake manifold cover from studs and remove cover.
9. Remove radiator as outlined under "Radiator, Replace."
10. Relieve fuel system pressure as outlined under "Precautions."
11. Disconnect Evaporative Emission (EVAP) canister purge solenoid tube from valve.
12. Disconnect fuel feed pipe from fuel rail.
13. Remove radiator inlet hose from engine.
14. Remove radiator outlet hose from thermostat housing and oil cooler.
15. Remove surge tank outlet hose from thermostat housing and oil cooler.

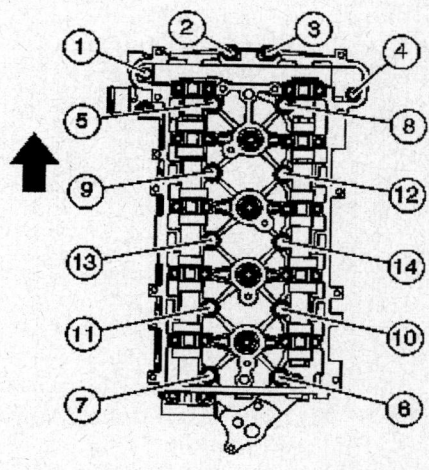

Fig. 5 Cylinder head bolt loosening sequence

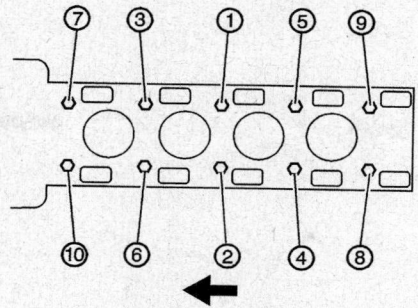

ARM0500000000896

Fig. 6 Rear cylinder head bolt tightening sequence

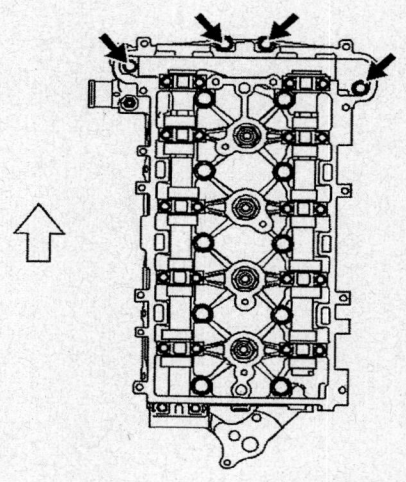

ARM0500000000897

Fig. 7 Front cylinder head bolt location

16. Remove surge tank clip from oil dipstick tube bracket.
17. Remove surge tank outlet hose.
18. Remove surge tank air bleed hose from engine.
19. Remove heater inlet and outlet hoses from thermostat.
20. Remove brake booster vacuum hose from intake manifold.
21. Remove fuel feed and EVAP line clip from oil dipstick tube bracket.
22. Remove engine harness clips from oil dipstick tube and radiator outlet hose bracket.
23. Raise and support vehicle.
24. Drain engine oil into suitable container.
25. Remove catalytic converter bracket bolt.
26. Disconnect Crankshaft Position (CKP) sensor electrical connector.
27. Disconnect oil pressure sensor electrical connector.
28. Remove starter solenoid S terminal nut.
29. Remove engine harness terminal from starter.
30. Remove engine harness clip from intake manifold.
31. Remove starter solenoid terminal nut.
32. Remove positive battery cable clips from intake manifold, then the battery cable terminal from starter.
33. Lower vehicle.
34. Remove positive battery cable clip from bracket.
35. Cut engine harness tie straps.
36. Remove battery ground cable ground bolt.
37. Disconnect alternator electrical connector.
38. Reposition positive battery cable terminal boot, then remove terminal nut and cable from alternator.
39. Disconnect air conditioning compressor and knock sensor electrical connectors.
40. Position negative and positive battery cable aside.
41. Disconnect air conditioning refrigerant pressure sensor and wiper motor electrical connectors.

42. Remove engine wire harness clips from wiper motor hole and surge tank air bleed hose.
43. Disconnect fuel injector electrical connector.
44. Disconnect Throttle Actuator Control (TAC) electrical connector.
45. Disconnect electrical connectors from intake and exhaust camshaft position actuators.
46. Remove engine harness clips from camshaft cover.
47. Disconnect ignition coil electrical connectors.
48. Remove Connector Position Assurance (CPA) retainers from Heated Oxygen Sensor (HO2S) electrical connectors.
49. Disconnect front and rear HO2S electrical connectors.
50. Disconnect engine harness clips from junction block bracket.
51. Disconnect HO2S electrical connector clip from strut.
52. Disconnect intake and exhaust Camshaft Position (CMP) sensor electrical connectors.
53. Remove engine harness ground terminal bolt.
54. Disconnect Engine Coolant Temperature (ECT) sensor electrical connector.
55. Disconnect EVAP canister purge solenoid electrical connector.
56. Disconnect engine harness clip from EVAP canister purge solenoid valve bracket.
57. Disconnect evaporative emission (EVAP) canister purge valve electrical connector.
58. Disconnect EVAP canister purge valve tube.
59. Disconnect chassis EVAP vapor from EVAP canister purge valve.
60. Remove EVAP canister purge valve bracket bolt, then the EVAP canister purge valve with bracket.
61. Remove engine harness bracket bolt.
62. Disconnect engine harness clip from bracket.
63. Position engine harness aside.
64. Remove air conditioning compressor mounting bolts, then position compressor aside.
65. Remove catalytic converter mounting nuts, then the catalytic converter and gasket.
66. Raise and support vehicle.

67. Remove muffler.
68. Remove mounting bolts and starter motor.
69. **On models equipped with automatic transmission,** remove torque converter to flywheel bolts.
70. **On all models,** remove lower and upper bellhousing bolts.
71. Lower vehicle.
72. Remove left and righthand engine mount upper mounting nuts.
73. Support engine using suitable engine lifting device.
74. Separate engine from transmission.
75. Remove engine.
76. Reverse procedure to install.

INTAKE MANIFOLD
REPLACE

1. Relieve fuel system pressure as outlined under "Precautions."
2. **On AURA models, disable hybrid battery as outlined under "Hybrid Battery Service" in "Precautions."**
3. **On all models,** remove engine oil fill cap, then the cover from intake manifold.
4. Remove air cleaner outlet duct.
5. **On AURA models,** proceed as follows:
   a. Drain engine cooling system and remove radiator inlet hose.
   b. Disconnect engine wiring harness electrical connectors from generator starter.
   c. Remove fuel injector wiring harness electrical connector retainer from generator starter.
   d. Disconnect fuel injector wiring harness electrical connector from engine wiring harness electrical connector.
   e. Remove engine wiring harness clips from intake manifold.
6. **On all models,** disconnect the following electrical connectors:
   a. Throttle Actuator Control (TAC).
   b. Fuel injector harness.

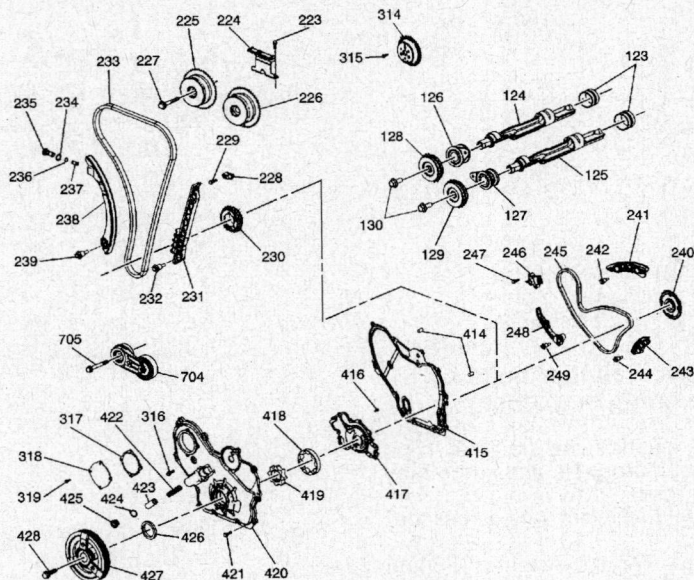

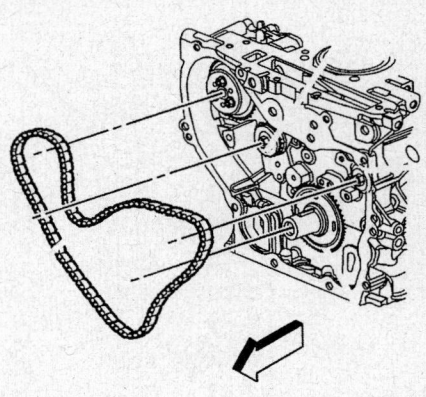

ARM0500000000899

Fig. 9   Balance shaft drive chain installation

(123) Balance Shaft Rear Bearing
(124) Exhaust Balance Shaft
(125) Intake Balance Shaft
(126) Exhaust Balance Shaft Bearing Carrier
(127) Intake Balance Shaft Bearing Carrier
(128) Exhaust Balance Shaft Drive Sprocket
(129) Intake Balance Shaft Drive Sprocket
(130) Balance Shaft Drive Sprocket Bolts
(223) Upper Timing Chain Guide Bolt
(224) Upper Timing Chain Guide
(225) Exhaust Camshaft Position Actuator
(226) Intake Camshaft Position Actuator
(227) Camshaft Position Actuator Bolt
(228) Timing Chain Oil Nozzle
(229) Timing Chain Oil Nozzle Bolt
(230) Timing Chain Drive Sprocket
(231) Fixed Timing Chain Guide
(232) Fixed Timing Chain Guide Bolt
(233) Timing Chain
(234) Timing Chain Tensioner Washer
(235) Timing Chain Tensioner Body
(236) Timing Chain Tensioner O-ring Seal
(237) Timing Chain Tensioner Plunger
(238) Adjustable Timing Chain Guide
(239) Adjustable Timing Chain Guide Bolt
(240) Balance Shaft Drive Sprocket
(241) Balance Shaft Drive Chain Guide
(242) Balance Shaft Drive Chain Guide Bolt
(243) Balance Shaft Drive Chain Guide

(244) Balance Shaft Drive Chain Guide Bolt
(245) Balance Shaft Drive Chain
(246) Balance Shaft Drive Chain Tensioner Assembly
(247) Balance Shaft Drive Chain Tensioner Assembly Bolt
(248) Adjustable Balance Shaft Drive Chain Guide
(249) Adjustable Balance Shaft Drive Chain Guide Bolt
(314) Water Pump Drive Sprocket
(315) Water Pump Drive Sprocket Bolt
(316) Water Pump Bolt
(317) Engine Front Cover Access Plate Gasket
(318) Engine Front Cover Access Plate
(319) Engine Front Cover Access Plate Bolt
(414) Engine Front Cover Alignment Pins
(415) Engine Front Cover Gasket
(416) Oil Pump Cover Bolt
(417) Oil Pump Cover
(418) Oil Pump Outer Gerotor
(419) Oil Pump Inner Gerotor
(420) Engine Front Cover
(421) Engine Front Cover Bolt
(422) Oil Pressure Relief Valve Spring
(423) Oil Pressure Relief Valve Plunger
(424) Oil Pressure Relief Valve O-ring Seal
(425) Oil Pressure Relief Valve Plug
(426) Crankshaft Front Seal
(427) Crankshaft Damper
(428) Crankshaft Damper Bolt
(704) Belt Tensioner
(705) Belt Tensioner Bolt

ARM0500000000898

Fig. 8   Front cover & timing chain components

   c. Manifold Absolute Pressure (MAP) sensor.
7. Remove brake booster vacuum hose from intake manifold.
8. Remove throttle body attaching bolts, then the throttle body and seal.
9. Disconnect EVAP canister purge tube from intake manifold and EVAP solenoid.
10. Remove oil level indicator tube.
11. Disconnect fuel feed line quick connect fitting from fuel rail.
12. Remove fuel rail mounting bolts, then pull fuel rail back and upward to fuel in-

jectors from cylinder head.
13. **On AURA models,** proceed as follows:
   a. Remove 3-phase voltage cable bracket bolt at tie bar.
   b. Remove generator starter bolts, then position and secure generator starter aside.
14. **On all models,** remove intake manifold nuts and bolts, then the intake manifold.
15. Reverse procedure to install. Intake manifold gasket is reusable, only replace gasket if damage has occurred.

EXHAUST MANIFOLD
REPLACE

1. Remove exhaust manifold heat shield.
2. **On models equipped with block heater,** remove block heater.
3. **On all models,** remove oxygen sensor.
4. Raise and support vehicle.
5. Remove catalytic converter to front exhaust pipe to muffler attaching nuts.
6. Remove front muffler hanger insulator, then the front exhaust pipe from converter.
7. Lower vehicle.
8. Remove upper exhaust manifold brace bolt.
9. Remove and discard exhaust manifold to cylinder head retaining nuts.
10. Remove exhaust manifold.
11. Reverse procedure to install. Using sequence shown in **Fig. 4, torque** new exhaust manifold to cylinder head retaining nuts 10 ft. lbs.

CYLINDER HEAD
REPLACE

1. Drain cooling system.
2. Remove intake manifold as outlined under "Intake Manifold, Replace."
3. Remove exhaust manifold as outlined under "Exhaust Manifold, Replace."
4. Remove radiator surge tank air bleed hose and radiator inlet hose from cylinder head.
5. Remove timing chain as outlined under "Timing Chain, Replace."
6. Remove cylinder head bolts in sequence, **Fig. 5.** Discard bolts.
7. Remove cylinder head and gasket.
8. Reverse procedure to install, noting the following:
   a. Clean all gasket surfaces.
   b. Refer to sequence, **Fig. 6,** and tighten rear cylinder head bolts in two steps: First step, **torque** bolts 22 ft. lbs.; second step, tighten an additional 155.°
   c. **Torque** front cylinder head bolts to 26 ft. lbs., **Fig. 7.**

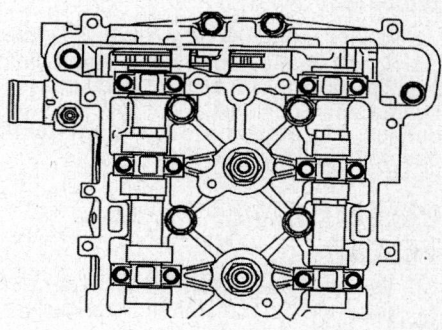

Fig. 10 Cylinder block bosses

VALVE COVER
REPLACE

1. Remove intake manifold cover.
2. Relieve fuel system pressure as outlined under "Precautions."
3. Remove air cleaner outlet duct.
4. Disconnect intake and exhaust camshaft position actuator solenoid valve electrical connectors.
5. Remove ignition coils.
6. Disconnect fuel feed pipe from fuel rail.
7. Remove camshaft cover bolts, then the camshaft cover.
8. Reverse procedure to install.

HYDRAULIC LASH ADJUSTERS
REPLACE

1. Remove camshafts as outlined under "Camshaft, Replace."
2. Remove camshaft roller followers.
3. Remove hydraulic lash adjusters.
4. Reverse procedure to install.

CRANKSHAFT BALANCER
REPLACE

1. Remove engine drive belt.
2. Hold crankshaft with holding tool No. 38122, or equivalent, then remove crankshaft balancer bolt. Discard bolt.
3. Remove crankshaft balancer.
4. Reverse procedure to install.

FRONT COVER
REPLACE

1. Remove crankcase balancer as outlined under "Crankshaft Balancer, Replace."
2. Raise and support vehicle.
3. Remove drive belt tensioner, then the idler pulley, **Fig. 8.**
4. Remove engine front cover to water pump bolt.
5. Remove remaining engine front cover bolts.
6. Remove engine front cover and gasket. Discard gasket.
7. Reverse procedure to install.

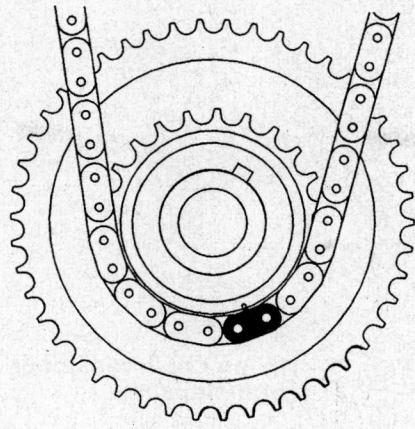

Fig. 11 Timing chain & crankshaft sprocket alignment

TIMING CHAIN
REPLACE

Removal

1. Remove No. 1 park plug and rotate engine until No. 1 piston is at TDC of compression stroke.
2. Remove camshaft cover as outlined under "Valve Cover, Replace."
3. Remove engine front cover as outlined under "Front Cover, Replace."
4. Remove upper timing chain guide, then the timing chain tensioner, **Fig. 8.**
5. Place a 24 mm open-end wrench on exhaust camshaft and hold camshaft, then remove exhaust camshaft actuator bolt and actuator from camshaft and timing chain.
6. Remove fixed timing chain guide bolts and guide.
7. Place a 24 mm wrench on intake camshaft flats, then remove and discard intake camshaft actuator bolt, then the actuator and timing chain through top of cylinder head.
8. Remove fixed timing chain guide access plug.
9. Remove timing chain sprocket. If replacing balance shaft timing chain is not required, proceed to "Installation." If balance shaft timing chain needs to be replaced, proceed as follows:
   a. Remove balance shaft drive chain tensioner.
   b. Remove adjustable balance shaft chain guide, then the small balance shaft drive chain guide.
   c. Remove upper balance shaft drive chain guide.
   d. Remove all slack from balance shaft drive chain between crankshaft and water pump sprockets.
   e. Remove balance shaft drive chain.

Installation

1. If installing balance shaft timing chain, proceed as follows:
   a. Align colored link of balance shaft drive chain with timing mark on in-

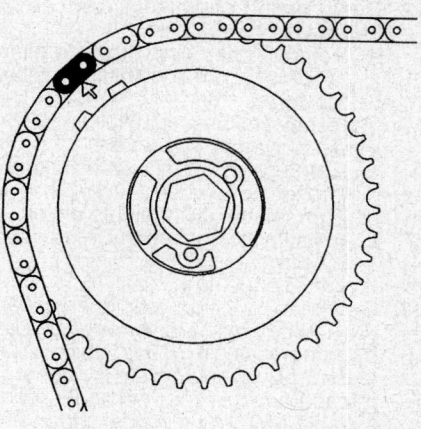

Fig. 12 Exhaust camshaft actuator & chain alignment

   take side balance shaft sprocket, **Fig. 9.**
   b. Align chrome link with timing mark on balance shaft drive sprocket (approximately 6 o'clock position).
   c. Place chain link on water pump drive sprocket, then align last chrome link with timing mark on exhaust side balance shaft drive sprocket.
   d. Rotate balance shaft drive chain tensioner plunger 90° in its bore and compress plunger, then rotate tensioner back to original 12 O'clock position and insert a paper clip through hole in plunger body and into hole in tensioner plunger.
   e. Install balance shaft drive chain tensioner, then remove paper clip.
2. Install timing chain crankshaft sprocket and position timing mark at 5 O'clock position.
3. Timing chain has three colored links (2 pink and 1 blue).
4. Assemble intake camshaft actuator to timing chain and align timing mark with blue link on chain, then install and hand tighten new actuator retaining bolt.
5. Lower timing chain through opening in cylinder head and ensure chain goes around both sides of cylinder block bosses, **Fig. 10.**
6. Route timing chain around crankshaft sprocket and align pink colored chain link to timing mark on sprocket, **Fig. 11.**
7. Install exhaust camshaft actuator, rotate exhaust camshaft approximately 45 degrees until dowel pin in actuator goes into camshaft slot. **Do not rotate either camshaft more than half turn in either direction with crankshaft at TDC. Turning camshaft more than half turn may result in piston to valve contact.**
8. Install actuator bolt hand tight.
9. Ensure timing marks are aligned, **Fig. 12.**
10. Install fixed timing chain guide and bolts.
11. Install upper timing chain guide and bolts.

12. Reset timing chain tensioner as follows:
  a. Remove snap ring, then the piston assembly from body of timing chain tensioner.
  b. Install tensioner tool No. J 45027-2, or equivalent, into a vise.
  c. Install notch end of piston assembly into tensioner tool.
  d. Turn ratchet cylinder into piston.
  e. Install piston assembly into body of tensioner.
  f. Install snap ring.
13. Install timing chain tensioner assembly. Timing chain tensioner is released by compressing it .079 in, which will release locking mechanism in ratchet. To release timing chain tensioner, use a suitable tool with a rubber tip on end. Feed tool down through cam drive chest to rest on cam chain. Then give a sharp jolt diagonally downwards to release tensioner.
14. Tighten intake and exhaust camshaft position actuator bolts to specification.
15. Install timing chain oiling nozzle.
16. Apply sealant compound part No. 12345382, or equivalent, to thread of timing chain guide bolt access hole plug.
17. Install timing chain guide bolt access hole plug.
18. Install engine front cover as outlined under "Front Cover, Replace."
19. Install camshaft cover as outlined under "Valve Cover Replace."

CAMSHAFT

REPLACE

Exhaust

1. Remove camshaft cover as outlined under "Valve Cover, Replace."
2. Remove upper timing chain guide, **Fig. 8.**
3. Remove timing chain tensioner.
4. Hold exhaust camshaft with a suitable wrench and loosen camshaft actuator bolt. **Do not remove bolt.**
5. Install timing chain tensioner tool No. J 44217, or equivalent, into timing chain, **Fig. 13.**
6. Mark intake and exhaust camshaft actuators locations on timing chain.
7. Remove and discard exhaust camshaft actuator attaching bolt, then the actuator from camshaft and timing chain.
8. Mark camshaft caps to ensure they are installed in their original position.
9. Remove camshaft caps, then the camshaft.
10. Reverse procedure to install.

Intake

1. Remove camshaft cover as outlined under "Valve Cover, Replace."
2. Remove upper timing chain guide, **Fig. 8.**
3. Remove timing chain tensioner.
4. Hold intake camshaft with a suitable wrench and loosen camshaft actuator bolt. **Do not remove bolt.**

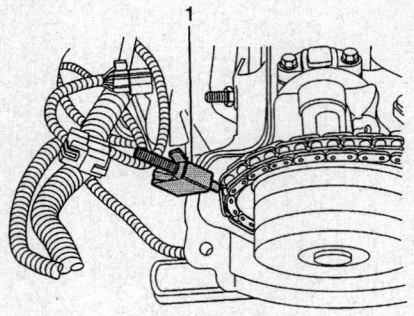

ARM0500000000903

Fig. 13 Timing chain tensioner tool installation

5. Install timing chain tensioner tool No. J 44217, or equivalent, into timing chain, **Fig. 13.**
6. Mark intake and exhaust camshaft actuators locations on timing chain.
7. Remove and discard intake camshaft actuator attaching bolt, then the actuator from camshaft and timing chain.
8. Mark camshaft caps to ensure they are installed in their original position.
9. Remove camshaft caps, then the camshaft.
10. Reverse procedure to install.

BALANCE SHAFT

REPLACE

1. Remove hydraulic lash adjusters as outlined under "Hydraulic Lash Adjusters, Replace."
2. Remove timing chain and balance shaft timing chain as outlined under "Timing Chain, Replace."
3. Remove balance shaft bearing carrier bolts, **Fig. 8. Do not remove bolt holding sprocket.**
4. Remove balance shaft assemblies.
5. Reverse procedure to install, noting the following:
  a. Install balancer shaft bearing remover and installer tool No. J 43650, or equivalent, into balance shaft hole with foot parallel to shaft.
  b. When balancer shaft bearing remover and installer tool No. J 43650, or equivalent, is inserted in block turn tool so foot becomes perpendicular to shaft.
  c. Center foot of tool on balance shaft bushing, then insert centering guide into front balance shaft bore and tighten nut with an appropriate wrench.
  d. When tool is properly installed, before removing bushing, end of tool should be 4.6 inches from block face. If tool is less than 4.5 inches from block face, recheck tool alignment.

PISTON & ROD ASSEMBLY

Ensure mark on top of the piston faces the front of the engine, **Fig. 14.**

MAIN & ROD BEARINGS

Refer to sequence, **Fig. 15,** and tighten crankshaft bearing bolts in two steps. First step, **torque** to 15 ft. lbs.; second step, tighten an additional 70.° Refer to sequence, **Fig. 16, torque** lower crankcase perimeter bolts to 18 ft. lbs.

CRANKSHAFT SEAL

REPLACE

1. Remove crankshaft balancer as outlined under "Crankshaft Balancer, Replace."
2. Remove crankshaft seal from front cover using a suitable flat-bladed tool.
3. Reverse procedure to install.

CRANKSHAFT REAR OIL SEAL

REPLACE

1. Remove engine and transaxle assembly as outlined under "Engine, Replace."
2. Remove transaxle from engine.
3. Remove flywheel.
4. Remove crankshaft rear oil seal from cylinder block using a suitable flat-bladed tool.
5. Reverse procedure to install.

OIL PAN

REPLACE

AURA

1. Remove drive belt as outlined under "Serpentine Drive Belt."
2. Remove oil level indicator tube.
3. Install suitable engine support and lifting device.
4. Remove engine mount as outlined under "Engine Mount, Replace."
5. Raise engine assembly approximately three inches.
6. Raise and support vehicle.
7. Loosen upper air A/C compressor bolts, then remove lower A/C compressor bolt.
8. Drain engine oil.
9. Disconnect engine wiring harness electrical connector from generator control module coolant pump.
10. Remove generator control module coolant pump bolt, then the coolant pump from oil pan.
11. Remove oil pan to transaxle bolts, then the oil pan bolts and oil pan.
12. Reverse procedure to install, noting the following:
  a. Apply a .08 inch (2 mm) bead of sealant around perimeter of oil pan and oil suction port opening. **Do not over apply sealant.**
  b. Refer to sequence, **Fig. 17, torque** oil pan bolts to 18 ft. lbs.
  c. Ensure anti-rotation tab of generator control module coolant pump is inserted into hole in oil pan.

Ion

1. Raise and support vehicle.
2. Drain engine oil and remove engine drive belt as outlined under "Serpentine Drive Belt."
3. Remove lower A/C compressor mounting bolt.
4. Remove oil pan to transaxle bolts.
5. Remove oil pan to crankcase bolts, then the oil pan.
6. Reverse procedure to install, noting the following:
   a. Ensure oil pan and mounting surface on lower crankcase are free of all oil and debris.
   b. Apply a .08 inch (2 mm) bead of sealant part No. 123785251, or equivalent, around perimeter of oil pan and oil suction port opening. **Do not over apply sealant.**
   c. Refer to sequence, **Fig. 17**, torque oil pan bolts to 18 ft. lbs.

OIL PUMP

REPLACE

1. Remove engine front cover bolts as outlined under "Front Cover, Replace."
2. Remove crankshaft front cover oil seal with a suitable flat-bladed tool.
3. Remove oil pump from front cover.
4. Reverse procedure to install.

OIL PUMP SERVICE

Disassemble

1. Disassemble pressure relief valve.
2. Remove oil pump gerotor cover and bolts.
3. Remove outer gear and inner gear from front cover.

Assemble

1. Lubricate all oil pump parts with engine oil.
2. Install inner gear into outer gear.
3. Install gears together into front cover with hub of center gear facing front cover.
4. Install oil pump gerotor cover and bolts.
5. Install pressure relief valve piston and pressure relief valve spring.

SERPENTINE DRIVE BELT

AURA

REMOVAL

1. Remove air cleaner assembly.
2. Remove front fender inner lining and engine splash shield.
3. Install hydraulic belt tensioner compressor tool No. EN-48079, or equivalent, to drive belt tensioner spring, **Fig. 18.**

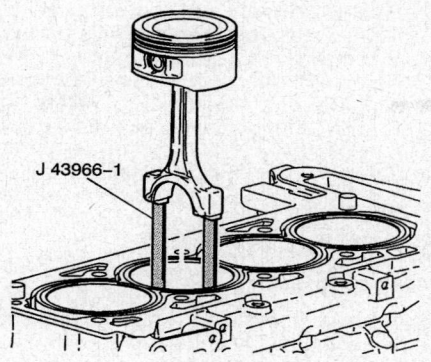

J 43966-1

ARM0500000000904

Fig. 14 Piston & connecting rod installation

4. Rotate tensioner clockwise to release tension from drive belt.
5. With tensioner released, remove drive belt from under middle idler pulley.
6. Slowly rotate tensioner clockwise to allow tensioner to rest.
7. Remove drive belt from drive belt tensioner.

INSTALLATION

1. Install drive belt around all pulleys except middle idler pulley.
2. Rotate tensioner counterclockwise to release tensioner.
3. Install drive belt under middle idler pulley.
4. Slowly rotate tensioner counterclockwise to allow tensioner to rest against drive belt.
5. Loosen forcing bolt on hydraulic belt tensioner compressor tool No. EN-48079, or equivalent, remove from drive belt tensioner spring.
6. Ensure drive belt tensioner idler is fully seated against drive belt.
7. Install air cleaner assembly.

Ion

1. Raise and support vehicle.
2. Remove lefthand front tire and wheel assembly.
3. Remove front fender inner lining and engine splash shield.
4. Install accessory belt tensioner unloader tool No. J44811, or equivalent, to drive belt tensioner.
5. Rotate tensioner counterclockwise to release tension.
6. Remove drive belt from drive belt tensioner.
7. Reverse procedure to install.

Sky

1. Remove intake manifold cover.
2. Raise and support vehicle.
3. Rotate power steering pump belt tensioner clockwise and remove belt.
4. Lower vehicle.
5. Remove air cleaner assembly.
6. Rotate drive belt tensioner clockwise and remove belt.
7. Reverse procedure to install.

THERMOSTAT

REPLACE

AURA

1. Raise and support vehicle.
2. Drain cooling system at radiator and water pump drains.
3. Lower vehicle.
4. **Disable hybrid battery as outlined under "Hybrid Battery Service" in "Precautions."**
5. Remove air cleaner assembly.
6. Disconnect fuel feed pipe quick connect fitting at fuel rail.
7. Disconnect EVAP line quick connect fitting from EVAP purge solenoid.
8. Remove fuel feed pipe clips from fuel line bracket.
9. Remove transaxle shift cable clip from fuel line bracket.
10. Remove battery, then the underhood bussed electrical center cover.
11. Loosen integral bolt on positive battery cable lead and remove lead from electrical center.
12. Position positive battery cable aside.
13. Loosen integral bolt on steering column harness package lead and remove lead from bussed electrical center.
14. Loosen junction block bolts, then tap bolts once to disengage from electrical connectors.
15. Remove junction block.
16. Remove engine wiring harness underhood bussed electrical center connector from electrical center bracket and secure out of way.
17. Remove forward lamp and body wiring harness electrical connectors from electrical center bracket and secure out of way.
18. Disconnect body wiring harness electrical connector from ECM.
19. Disconnect engine wiring harness electrical connectors from ECM.
20. Remove engine wiring harness clips from ECM/Transmission Control Module (TCM) bracket.
21. Disconnect engine wiring harness electrical connector from TCM.
22. Remove ECM/TCM bracket bolt.
23. Slide ECM/TCM bracket up and remove bracket with ECM and TCM still attached from battery tray.
24. Remove battery tray.
25. Disconnect engine wiring harness electrical connector from Engine Coolant Temperature (ECT) sensor.
26. Remove HO2S electrical connector rosebud clip from thermostat housing.
27. Remove the radiator outlet hose from the thermostat cover.
28. Remove the exhaust heat shield.
29. Remove auxiliary heater water pump hose clip from heater outlet hose.
30. Remove auxiliary heater water pump hose from thermostat housing.
31. Remove heater inlet hose from thermostat housing.
32. Raise and support vehicle.
33. Remove thermostat housing bolts. Twist water transfer pipe while pulling to remove it from water pump.

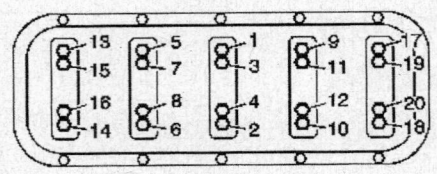

ARM0500000000905

Fig. 15 Crankshaft bearing bolt tightening sequence

34. Remove thermostat housing from engine.
35. Remove thermostat cover bolts and thermostat. Discard thermostat cover O-ring seal.
36. Reverse procedure to install.

Ion

1. Remove intake manifold cover.
2. Raise and support vehicle and drain cooling system from radiator and water pump drains.
3. Lower vehicle.
4. To access thermostat housing, position underhood electrical center/junction block bracket aside.
5. **On models equipped with automatic transaxle,** disconnect HO2S electrical connector clip from thermostat housing.
6. **On all models,** disconnect Engine Coolant Temperature (ECT) sensor connector.
7. Remove radiator surge tank outlet hose from thermostat cover and oil cooler.
8. Remove radiator hoses from thermostat housing.
9. Remove exhaust manifold heat shield.
10. Remove heater inlet and outlet hoses from thermostat housing.
11. Remove thermostat housing bolts. Twist water transfer pipe while pulling to remove it from water pump.
12. Remove thermostat housing from engine. Discard O-ring seal.
13. Remove thermostat cover and thermostat.
14. Reverse procedure to install.

Sky

1. Remove cap and nut from windshield wiper arms.
2. Remove windshield washer nozzle hose assembly from wiper arms.
3. Remove wiper arms from air inlet grill panel.
4. Remove air inlet grill panel retainers, then the panel.
5. Disconnect Engine Coolant Temperature (ECT) sensor connector.
6. Remove radiator outlet hose from thermostat housing.
7. Remove radiator outlet hose clip from outlet hose bracket.
8. Remove exhaust heat shield.
9. Disconnect heater inlet and outlet

hoses from thermostat housing pipes.
10. Remove thermostat housing bolts. Twist water transfer pipe while pulling to remove it from water pump.
11. Remove thermostat housing from engine. Discard O-ring seal.
12. Remove thermostat cover and thermostat.
13. Reverse procedure to install.

WATER PUMP
REPLACE

1. Remove thermostat housing as outlined under "Thermostat, Replace."
2. Remove water pump access plate from engine front cover.
3. **On ION models,** remove righthand fender liner.
4. **On all models,** install water pump holding tool No. J 43651, or equivalent, onto water pump sprocket.
5. Install water pump access cover bolts to secure pump holding tool to front cover.
6. Remove inner water pump sprocket to water pump bolts.
7. Remove water pump retaining bolts, then the water pump.
8. Reverse procedure to install.

RADIATOR
REPLACE
AURA

1. Drain the coolant.
2. Loop a rope around each of upper two tabs of condenser and tie rope around upper tie bar.
3. Remove bolt holding air cleaner outlet duct to upper front bumper fascia grille.
4. Remove both front fender liners.
5. Raise and support vehicle, then remove engine splash shields.
6. Remove front bumper fascia bracket bolts. Access bolts through front fender liner openings.
7. Remove front bumper fascia to tie bar bolts and retaining clips.
8. Remove front bumper fascia to headlamp bolts.
9. Disconnect any electrical connectors, then pull gently on fascia at fenders to disengage fascia from bumper brackets, remove fascia.
10. Lower vehicle.
11. Release retainers, then remove upper center grill from center grill.
12. Radiator upper bracket mounting bolts, then the upper bracket.
13. Remove inlet hose from radiator.
14. Remove front air dam metal retainers, then the front air dam.
15. Remove outlet hose from radiator.
16. Remove oil cooler pipes from transaxle.
17. Remove lower radiator support bracket attaching bolts, then the support brackets and radiator lower mounts.
18. Remove and discard condenser mounting bolts from radiator.
19. Push upward on radiator and down-

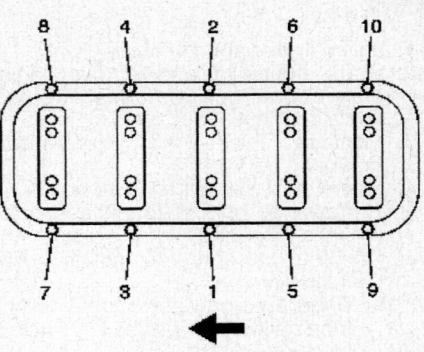

ARM0500000000906

Fig. 16 Lower crankcase bolt tightening sequence

ward on condenser to unsnap condenser mounting tabs from radiator clips.
20. Remove and discard condenser mounting nuts from radiator.
21. Remove radiator air side seals.
22. Remove radiator and cooling fan shroud assembly from vehicle.
23. Reverse procedure to install. Ensure alignment tabs on fascia slide into place under headlamps during installation.

ION

Refer to "2.0L VIN P Engine" for radiator replacement procedure.

Sky

Refer to "2.0L VIN X Engine" for radiator replacement procedure.

FUEL PUMP
REPLACE
AURA

1. Relieve fuel system pressure as outlined under "Precautions."
2. **Disable hybrid battery as outlined under "Hybrid Battery Service" in "Precautions."**
3. Drain fuel tank.
4. Raise and support vehicle.
5. Disconnect fuel pump module electrical harness connector from vehicle underbody wiring harness.
6. Disconnect EVAP vent valve solenoid harness electrical connector from vehicle underbody wiring harness.
7. Remove ABS wiring harness from retainer on EVAP canister.
8. Disconnect fuel feed and purge lines from fuel and brake line bundle on righthand side of vehicle.
9. Cap or plug fuel tank feed and vapor lines to prevent fuel loss or contamination.
10. Disconnect fuel filler pipe jumper hose from fuel tank.
11. Disconnect vapor recirculation line that runs parallel to fuel filler pipe jumper hose.

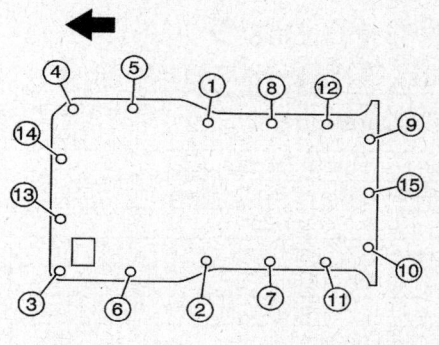

Fig. 17   Oil pan bolt tightening sequence

12. Remove exhaust pipe and muffler insulators from underbody hangers, then support exhaust system with suitable jackstand.
13. Support fuel tank with a suitable jackstand.
14. Remove left and right fuel tank strap bolts.
15. Carefully lower righthand side of tank until is clear of frame rail, then remove tank toward righthand side of vehicle.
16. Disconnect fuel tank fuel pump module wiring harness electrical connectors from fuel pressure sensor and module.
17. Disconnect fuel tank vent pipe quick connect fittings from module.
18. Install fuel sender lock ring wrench tool No. J 45722, or equivalent, onto fuel pump module lock ring.
19. Rotate lock ring in a counterclockwise direction to unlock lock ring.
20. Lift fuel pump module up slightly to disconnect fuel tank vent pipe quick connect fitting from module cover.
21. Raise fuel pump module up from fuel tank.
22. Tilt module to allow fuel level sensor arm and float to clear module opening.
23. Remove fuel pump module. Discard fuel pump module seal.
24. Reverse procedure to install.

ION

1. Remove fuel tank as outlined under "Fuel Pump, Replace" in "2.2L Engine" section.

2. Release retaining tab on fuel tank retainer used to secure fuel pump module pipes in position on tank.
3. Release fuel pump module electrical harness from retaining slot on tank.
4. Disconnect fuel pump module harness electrical connector from fuel tank pressure sensor.
5. Disengage fuel pump module lock ring.
6. Remove fuel pump module lock ring by sliding ring over module pipes and electrical harness.
7. Lift fuel pump module assembly until fuel level sensor float arm is visible. Ensure that fuel level sensor harness connector clears tank opening.
8. Tilt fuel pump module toward rear of fuel tank to enable level sensor float arm to clear tank opening.
9. Remove fuel pump module from tank.
10. Remove and discard fuel pump module seal.
11. Reverse procedure to install, noting the following:
    a. Install new fuel pump module seal.
    b. Ensure that fuel pump module lock ring is fully seated within fuel tank retaining slots.

SKY

1. Relieve fuel pressure as outlined under "Precautions."
2. Remove rear compartment trim panel.
3. Remove mounting bolts and fuel sending unit access cover.
4. Disconnect fuel level sender fuel pressure sensor electrical connectors.
5. Disconnect fuel fill pipe Evaporative Emission (EVAP) pipe quick connect fitting.
6. Disconnect fuel feed pipe quick connect fitting.
7. Raise fuel sender up slightly. **Do not handle fuel sender assembly by fuel pipes.**
8. Connect large EVAP canister quick connect fitting.
9. Remove fuel sender.
10. Remove and discard fuel sender O-ring.
11. Reverse procedure to install. Install new gasket.

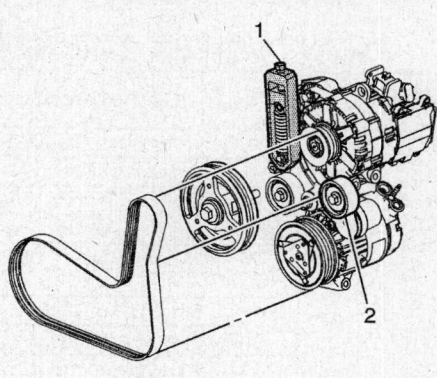

1-Hydraulic belt tensioner compressor
2-Drive belt tensioner

Fig. 18   Drive belt removal. AURA

FUEL FILTER
REPLACE
AURA & Sky

The fuel filter is part of the fuel pump module/sender assembly, refer to "Fuel Pump, Replace" for filter replacement procedure.

ION

1. Relieve fuel pressure as outlined in "Precautions."
2. Raise and support vehicle using suitable lift or jack.
3. Remove fuel filter bracket bolt.
4. Disconnect fuel filter from engine fuel feed pipe.
5. Tilt fuel filter downward and drain off fuel into suitable container.
6. Disconnect fuel tank feed and return hose fittings from fuel filter.
7. Drain remaining fuel into suitable container.
8. Discard fuel filter into suitable container.
9. Reverse procedure to install, noting the following:
    a. Install new fuel filter.
    b. Inspect fuel system for leaks.

SATURN

TIGHTENING SPECIFICATIONS

Year	Component	Torque Ft. Lbs.
2006–08	Air Conditioning Compressor Bolts	16
	Alternator Mounting Nut	27
	Alternator Terminal Nut	15
	Balance Shaft Adjustable Chain Guide	11
	Balance Shaft Bearing Carrier To Block	89①
	Balance Shaft Fixed Chain Guide Bolt	11
	Balance Shaft Sprocket Bolt	37
	Battery Cable Ground Nut (ION)	89①
	Battery Cable Ground Nut (SKY)	15
	Battery Cable Lead Nut To Starter Solenoid	13
	Block Core Plug	30
	Block Heater Bolt	89①
	Brake Hose Bracket	89①
	Cam Sensor	71①
	Camshaft Bearing Cap Bolt	89①
	Camshaft Position Sensor Housing Stud	16
	Camshaft Position Actuator Solenoid Valve Bolt	89①
	Camshaft Position Sensor	89①
	Camshaft Timing Chain Tensioner	55
	Catalytic Converter	18
	Chain Guide Access Hole Plug	59
	Connecting Rod Bolts	②
	Crankshaft Balancer	③
	Crankshaft Bearing Lower Crankcase To Block	④
	Crankshaft Position Sensor	89①
	Cylinder Head	⑤
	Cylinder Head Oil Gallery Plug	26
	Drive Belt Tensioner	33
	Engine Coolant Temperature Sensor	15
	Engine Harness Clip Nut To Engine Stud	37
	Engine Harness Ground Bolt	18
	Engine Harness Ground Terminals To Stud	18
	Engine Lift Bracket	18
	Engine Mount Side Rail Nuts	74
	Engine Mount To Bracket Bolts	37
	Exhaust Camshaft Position Actuator	⑥
	Exhaust Manifold Pipe Flange To Stud	12
	Exhaust Manifold To Cylinder Head Nut	10
	Exhaust Manifold To Cylinder Head Stud	89①
	Flywheel	⑦
	Frame Bolts	74⑧
	Front Cover To Block	18
	Fuel Filter Bracket Bolt	89①
	Fuel Line Bracket	89①
	ICM Cover	71①
	Idler Pulley	16
	Intake Camshaft Position Actuator	⑥

TIGHTENING SPECIFICATIONS—Continued

Year	Component	Torque Ft. Lbs.
2006–08	Intake Camshaft Rear Cap Bolt	18
	Intake Manifold To Cylinder Head	89①
	Knock Sensor Bolt	18
	Lower Crankcase To Block	18
	Oil Cooler	16
	Oil Filter Housing Cover	16
	Oil Gallery Plug	26
	Oil Gallery Plug (Rear)	44
	Oil Pan Drain Plug	18
	Oil Pan To Block	18
	Oil Pressure Switch	16
	Oil Pump Gerotor Cover Bolt	53①
	Oil Pump Pressure Relief Valve Plug	30
	Oxygen Sensor	31
	Power Steering Pump	18
	S Terminal Nut	27①
	Spark Plug	15
	Starter Bolts	30
	Thermostat Housing	89①
	Throttle Body	89①
	Timing Chain Adjustable Chain Guide	89①
	Timing Chain Fixed Guide Bolt	11
	Timing Chain Oil Nozzle Bolt	89①
	Timing Chain Upper Guide Bolt	89①
	Torque Converter Bolts	46
	Transaxle Brace Bolts	37
	Transaxle Fluid Cooler Bracket Nut	62①
	Transaxle Mount To Transaxle Bolts	33
	Transaxle To Engine Bolts/Stud	55
	Valve (Cam) Cover To Cylinder Head	89①
	Water Pump Balance Shaft Chain Tensioner	89①
	Water Pump Bolts	18
	Water Pump Sprocket Bolt	89①

① — Inch lbs.

② — First step, 18 ft. lbs.; second step, an additional 100.°

③ — First step, 74 ft. lbs.; second step, an additional 125.°

④ — Refer to "Main & Rod Bearings."

⑤ — Refer to "Cylinder Head, Replace" procedure.

⑥ — First step, 22 ft. lbs.; second step, an additional 100.°

⑦ — First step, 39 ft. lbs.; second step, an additional 25.°

⑧ — First step, 74 ft. lbs.; second step, an additional 25.°

3.0L Engine

NOTE: On Air Bag Equipped Models, Refer To "Air Bag System Precautions" Located In The Front Of This Manual For System Disarming & Arming Procedures.

NOTE: Refer To "Computer Relearn Procedures" Located In The Front Of This Manual When Battery Power To The Computer Has Been Interrupted.

NOTE: Prior To Performing Any Service Operations Listed In This Section, Consult The "Technical Service Bulletins" Section For Related Information.

INDEX

	Page No.		Page No.		Page No.
Belt Tension Data	12-68	Fuel Filter, Replace	12-69	Serpentine Drive Belt	12-68
Camshaft, Replace	12-66	Fuel Pump, Replace	12-68	Belt Replacement	12-68
Installation	12-66	Intake Manifold, Replace	12-64	Belt Routing	12-68
Removal	12-66	Lower	12-64	Technical Service Bulletins	12-69
Camshaft Lobe Lift		Upper	12-64	Blue Smoke At Engine Start-Up	12-69
Specifications	12-65	Main & Rod Bearings	12-67	2004 L-Series	12-69
Compression Pressure	12-63	Oil Pan, Replace	12-67	Front Bank Chirp Nose	12-69
Cooling System Bleed	12-68	Oil Pump, Replace	12-67	2005 L-Series	12-69
Crankshaft Rear Oil Seal,		Piston & Rod Assembly	12-67	Thermostat, Replace	12-68
Replace	12-67	Pistons, Pins & Rings	12-67	Tightening Specifications	12-70
Cylinder Head, Replace	12-64	Precautions	12-63	Timing Belt, Replace	12-65
Engine Rebuilding		Air Bag Systems	12-63	Installation	12-65
Specifications	29-1	Battery Ground Cable	12-63	Removal	12-65
Engine, Replace	12-63	Fuel System Pressure Relief	12-63	Valve Adjustment	12-65
Engine Mount, Replace	12-63	Less Scan Tool	12-63	Valve Cover, Replace	12-65
Exhaust Manifold, Replace	12-64	With Scan Tool	12-63	Water Pump, Replace	12-68
Front Cover, Replace	12-65	Radiator, Replace	12-68		

PRECAUTIONS

Air Bag Systems

Refer to "Air Bag System Precautions" in the front of this manual for system disarming and arming procedures.

Battery Ground Cable

Prior to service, disconnect battery ground cable and isolate as required.

Fuel System Pressure Relief

WITH SCAN TOOL

Start vehicle and locate SPECIAL TESTS, select ECM, then select fuel delivery. Select FUEL PUMP, then command fuel pump off.

LESS SCAN TOOL

Remove Schraeder valve cap and install fuel pressure gauge tool No. SA9127-E, or equivalent. Open valve on pressure gauge and drain fuel into suitable container.

COMPRESSION PRESSURE

1. Start and run engine until it reaches normal operating temperature. Turn engine off.
2. Remove ignition modules and spark plugs.
3. Connect compression gauge tool No. SA9127-E, or equivalent, into spark plug hole.
4. Open throttle fully.
5. Crank engine at not less than 250 RPM.
6. Measure compression while cranking engine. Prior to reading compression gauge needle should bounce at least 10 times.
7. Repeat previous steps for each cylinder.
8. Minimum compression on any one cylinder should not be less than 70% of highest cylinder. No cylinder should read less than 100 psi.
9. Place shop towel over spark plug holes and crank engine over a few seconds without compression gauge or spark plugs installed.
10. Repeat compression measuring steps on each cylinder.

ENGINE MOUNT
REPLACE

1. Disconnect MAF sensor and remove air box.
2. Remove EVAP purge assembly and position aside.
3. Loosen hose clamp at throttle body, then slide off MAF hose to throttle body hose.
4. Remove air box mount bolt and box.
5. Install engine support fixture and adapter tools Nos. SA9150E and J43405, or equivalents.
6. Remove engine mount and bracket.
7. Reverse procedure to install.

ENGINE
REPLACE

1. Disconnect MAF sensor, then remove air cleaner and battery.
2. Remove positive main feed cable at fuse block.
3. Disconnect main TCM connector under cowl cover and position aside.
4. Disconnect inline TCM connector near brake master cylinder.
5. Disconnect air conditioning pressure connector.
6. Disconnect black engine harness connector from under fuse block and lower weather pack connector inside fuse block.

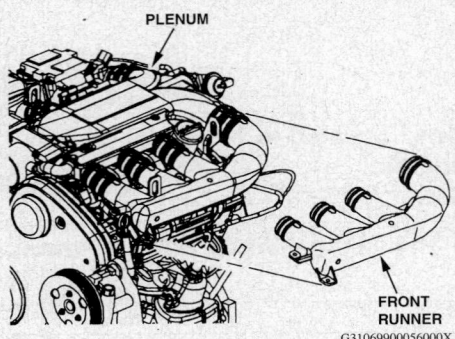

Fig. 1 Upper intake manifold front runner & plenum replacement

7. Remove fuse block and position aside.
8. Secure engine harness to top of engine.
9. Remove battery tray.
10. Disconnect EVAP purge connector.
11. Disconnect righthand front speed sensor and secure to engine.
12. Disconnect front oxygen sensor.
13. Disconnect transaxle ground, main connector, shift control and rear ECM connectors.
14. Remove brake booster vacuum hose.
15. Disconnect fuel lines and position aside.
16. Disconnect EVAP purge hose at EVAP purge solenoid.
17. Remove starter and torque converter mounting bolts.
18. Remove exhaust system from catalytic convertor forward.
19. Disconnect transaxle nose bracket.
20. Remove air conditioning compressor and position aside.
21. Drain engine coolant into suitable container and disconnect heater hoses at cowl.
22. Remove lower engine to transaxle bell housing bolts. **Do not remove upper bolts now.**
23. Remove main coolant reservoir hose from engine inlet adapter.
24. Remove upper and lower radiator hoses from engine.
25. Remove small hose under power steering fluid reservoir and drain fluid into suitable container.
26. Disconnect metal power steering line.
27. Remove power steering reservoir and secure to engine.
28. Support engine using suitable engine lift hoist.
29. Remove righthand front engine mount and bracket.
30. Remove upper bell housing bolts.
31. Remove engine.
32. Reverse procedure to install. Ensure engine aligns with dowel pins on transaxle.

INTAKE MANIFOLD
REPLACE

Upper

1. Remove front runner rubber boot hose

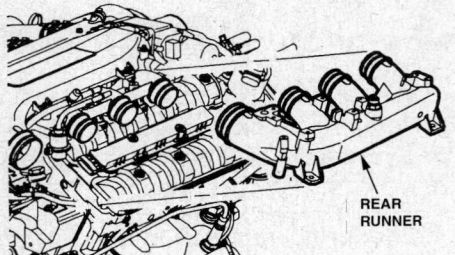

Fig. 2 Upper intake manifold rear runner replacement

clamps using hose clamp pliers tool No. J43914, or equivalent.
2. Remove front runner, **Fig. 1.**
3. Remove ECM.
4. Remove rear runner rubber boot hose clams using hose clamp pliers tool No. J43914, or equivalent.
5. Disconnect brake vacuum hose.
6. Disconnect intake plenum switch over valve vacuum hose from switch over valve. Mark hose routing for installation.
7. Disconnect throttle body vent hose. Mark hose routing for installation.
8. Remove rear runner, **Fig. 2.**
9. Disconnect throttle body electrical connectors.
10. Remove electrical connector and vacuum hoses from plenum switch over valve solenoid.
11. Remove fuel pressure regulator vacuum and throttle body heater hoses.
12. Remove plenum.
13. Mask off ports to lower intake.
14. Remove upper intake manifold.
15. Reverse procedure to install.

Lower

1. Remove upper intake as outlined under "Intake Manifold Replace," "Upper."
2. Remove fuel supply and return hoses from fuel rail using fuel line separator tool No. SA9805-E, or equivalent.
3. Disconnect and remove fuel injector harness.
4. Remove fuel rail.
5. Remove lower intake manifold, **Fig. 3.**
6. Remove lower intake manifold spacer.
7. Mask off ports to lower intake manifold spacer.
8. Remove sealing rings.
9. Clean manifold sealing surfaces with nonabrasive cleaner.
10. Reverse procedure to install. Apply Loctite 242, or equivalent, to lower intake manifold spacer and lower intake manifold mounting bolts.

EXHAUST MANIFOLD
REPLACE

1. Remove front oxygen sensor using oxygen sensor socket tool No. J39194-C, or equivalent.
2. Remove front exhaust manifold and gasket.
3. Remove rear oxygen sensor using oxygen sensor socket tool.

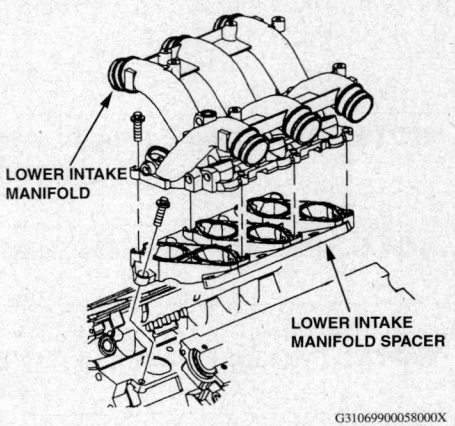

Fig. 3 Lower intake manifold & spacer replacement

4. Disconnect EGR pipe.
5. Remove rear exhaust manifold and gasket.
6. Reverse procedure to install.

CYLINDER HEAD
REPLACE

1. Remove air cleaner.
2. Remove upper and lower intake manifolds as outlined under "Intake Manifold, Replace."
3. Remove coolant intake and heater hoses.
4. Remove coolant bridge and seals, **Fig. 4.**
5. Remove engine ventilation chamber, **Fig. 5.**
6. Drain coolant into suitable container.
7. Remove upper radiator hose.
8. Remove exhaust manifold heat shield.
9. Remove exhaust pipe to exhaust manifold mounting nuts.
10. Remove front exhaust pipes from exhaust manifolds.
11. Support powertrain using suitable floor jack under oil pan.
12. Remove front transaxle mount bolt.
13. Raise powertrain using floor jack to gain access to coolant extension housing.
14. Remove oil dipstick tube.
15. Twist and remove coolant extension housing.
16. Remove grounds from front lift bracket.
17. Disconnect oxygen sensor connector.
18. Remove EGR to exhaust manifold pipe.
19. Remove valve cover.
20. Remove front timing belt cover as outlined under "Front Cover, Replace."
21. Remove timing belt as outlined under "Timing Belt, Replace."
22. Remove timing belt tensioner bracket.
23. Remove rear timing belt cover as outlined under "Front Cover, Replace."
24. Disconnect camshaft sensor connector.
25. Remove exhaust camshaft as outlined under "Camshaft, Replace."
26. Loosen and remove cylinder head bolts in several steps in sequence, **Fig. 6.**

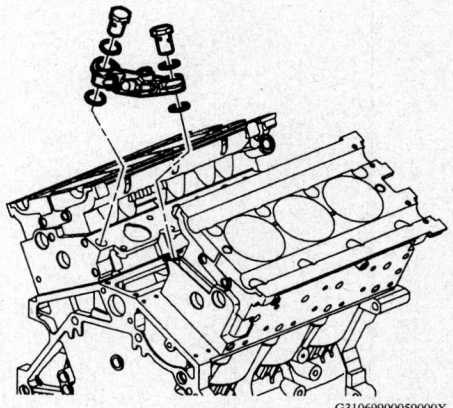

Fig. 4 Coolant bridge replacement

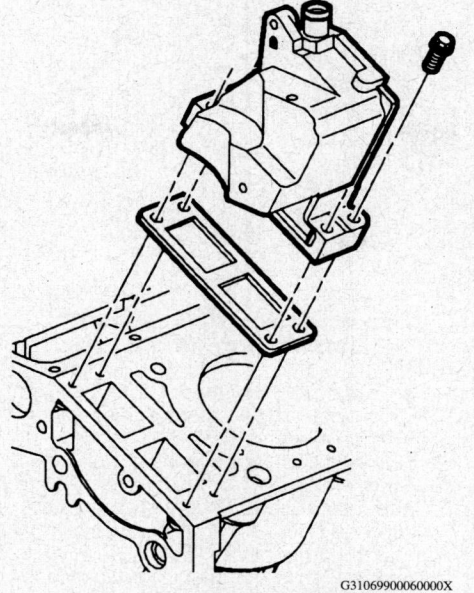

G31069900060000X

Fig. 5 Engine ventilation chamber replacement

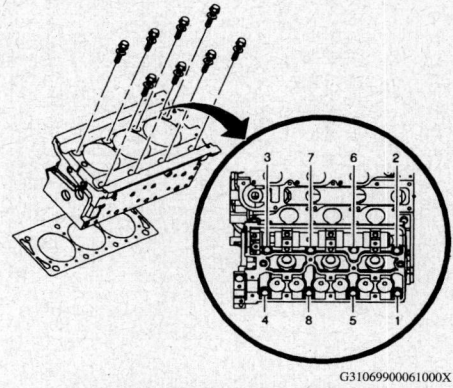

G31069900061000X

Fig. 6 Cylinder head bolt loosening sequence

27. Remove cylinder head and gasket.
28. Remove exhaust manifold.
29. Clean and inspect cylinder head and sealing surfaces.
30. Reverse procedure to install, noting the following:
    a. Ensure new cylinder head gasket part number imprint is facing toward top of engine.
    b. **Torque** cylinder head bolts to 18 ft. lbs. in sequence, **Fig. 7.**
    c. Turn cylinder head bolts an additional 90° in sequence.
    d. Turn head bolts an additional 90° in sequence.
    e. Turn bolts an additional 90° in sequence.
    f. Finally, turn cylinder head bolts an additional 15° in sequence.
    g. Replace sealing rings on coolant pipe and lubricate with coolant.

VALVE COVER
REPLACE

1. Remove upper and lower intake manifolds as outlined under "Intake Manifold, Replace."
2. Remove ignition coils and lift bracket.
3. Remove rear cover knock sensor wire harness and disconnect CMP sensor.
4. Remove cover and O-ring seals. Ensure O-rings are accounted for.
5. Clean cover and sealing surfaces.
6. Reverse procedure to install. Apply thin coat of Loctite 5900, or equivalent to front and rear of cover, **Fig. 8.**

CAMSHAFT LOBE LIFT SPECIFICATIONS

Exhaust cam lobe lift is .3409–.3441 inch. Minimum service limit is .339 inch.

VALVE ADJUSTMENT

This engine is equipped with hydraulic lifters. No adjustment is required.

FRONT COVER
REPLACE

1. Remove air cleaner.
2. Raise and support vehicle, then remove righthand front wheel and splash shield.
3. Lower vehicle, then loosen, but do not remove, water pump pulley bolts.
4. Install engine support fixture and adapters tools Nos. SA9150-E and J43405, or equivalents.
5. Remove serpentine belt as outlined under "Serpentine Drive Belt."
6. Remove water pump and power steering pulleys.
7. Remove serpentine belt tensioner and crankshaft balancer.
8. Disconnect air conditioning pressure connector to allow additional slack in harness, remove wiring harness channel from front cover and position away from front of engine.
9. Remove timing belt front cover.
10. Inspect outer edge sealing strip on front timing cover for cracks or tears and replace as required.
11. Remove timing belt as outlined under "Timing Belt, Replace."
12. To prevent valve to piston contact, turn crankshaft counterclockwise to 60° BTDC, **Fig. 9.**
13. Remove camshaft gears using camshaft lock tools Nos. J42069-1 and J42069-2, or equivalents, when initially loosening camshaft bolts, **Fig. 10.**
14. Remove timing belt tensioner bracket.
15. Remove timing belt idler pulley for camshaft Nos. 3 and 4, **Fig. 11.**
16. Remove mounting bolts, threaded pin and rear timing belt cover.
17. Reverse procedure to install, noting the following:
    a. Install threaded pin with Loctite 242, or equivalent.
    b. Tighten timing belt idler pulley until

snug. After final timing belt adjustments are made, tighten to specifications.
    c. Adjust timing belt as outlined under "Timing Belt, Replace."
    d. Install new camshaft gear bolts.

TIMING BELT
REPLACE
Removal

1. Remove timing belt front cover as outlined under "Front Cover, Replace."
2. Turn crankshaft using crank hub Torx socket tool No. J42098, or equivalent, until cylinder No. 1 is at 60° BTDC, **Fig. 9.**
3. Install crankshaft locking tool No. J42069-10, or equivalent.
4. Turn crankshaft clockwise using crank hub Torx socket tool No. J42098, or equivalent, until cylinder No. 1 is at TDC and tighten lever arm to water pump pulley flange.
5. **Ensure alignment of crankshaft is not 180° off. Alignment marks must align with corresponding notches on rear timing belt cover.**
6. Install camshaft gear locking tools Nos. J42069-1 and J42069-2, or equivalents, **Fig. 10.**
7. Remove upper and lower idler pulleys.
8. Remove timing belt tensioner.
9. Remove timing belt.
10. **Do not turn crankshaft if camshaft locking tools are not in place.**
11. **Do not turn camshafts unless crankshaft is at 60° BTDC.**

Installation

1. Remove crankshaft locking tool.
2. Mark furthest point from Torx head bolt on upper and lower idler pulleys, **Fig. 12.**
3. Idler pulleys provide adjustment by rotating eccentric circle around mounting bolt.
4. Install lower idler pulley allowing pulley to turn with slight resistance using idler pulley wrench tool No. J42069-40, or equivalent.

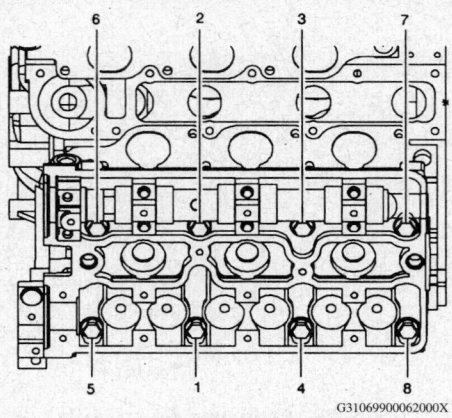

Fig. 7 Cylinder head bolt tightening sequence

G31069900062000X

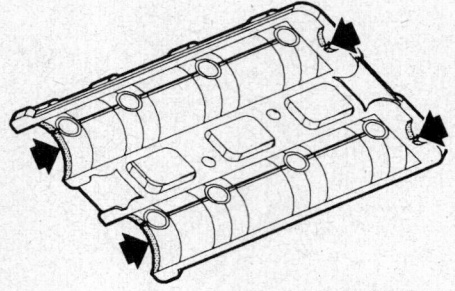

G31069900072000X

Fig. 8 Valve cover sealant application points

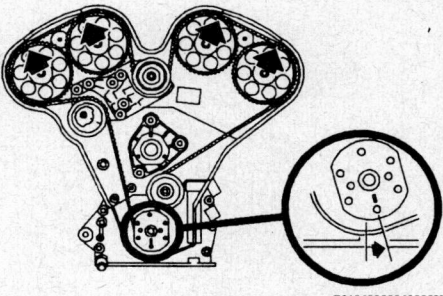

G31069900063000X

Fig. 9 Crankshaft aligned at 60° BTDC

5. Align marks on timing belt with marks on camshaft sprockets Nos. 3 and 4, **Fig. 13.**
6. Route timing belt around lower idler pulley and crankshaft sprocket. Ensure timing belt and crankshaft sprocket marks align.
7. Lock timing belt to crankshaft sprocket using plastic wedge tool No. J42069-30, or equivalent.
8. Route belt around timing belt tensioner, then around Nos. 1 and 2 camshaft sprockets. Ensure timing belt and sprockets' marks align.
9. Install upper idler pulley using idler pulley wrench tool No. J42069-40, or equivalent. Allow pulley to turn.
10. Install crankshaft locking tool No. J42069-10, or equivalent, and tighten lever arm to water pump pulley flange.
11. Adjust timing belt tensioner alignment mark ⅛ inch above mark on spring loaded idler, **Fig. 14.**
12. Adjust mark on upper idler pulley to 10 o'clock position to align Nos. 1 and 2 timing marks close to settings. Snug the pulley, but do not fully tighten.
13. Adjust mark on lower idler pulley to 11 o'clock position to align Nos. 3 and 4 timing marks close to settings. Snug the pulley, but do not fully tighten.
14. Remove camshaft locking tools and install inspecting gauge tool No. J42069-20, or equivalent.
15. Pull timing belt between tensioner and crankshaft sprocket to remove slack between camshaft Nos. 3 and 4 and lower idler pulley. Ensure timing marks on camshaft Nos. 3 and 4 are .0394 inch on retard side, **Fig. 15.** If timing marks are not .0394 inch on retard side, turn lower idler clockwise and repeat procedure.
16. Remove camshaft locking tool.
17. Turn crankshaft 1¾ turns clockwise and install crankshaft locking tool at TDC.
18. Tighten lever arm to water pump pulley flange.
19. If TDC is passed, do not turn counterclockwise, turn crankshaft an additional two turns.
20. Turn lower idler pulley counterclockwise until timing marks on camshaft sprocket Nos. 3 and 4 align with marks

on inspecting gauge tool.
21. Hold idler pulley using idler pulley wrench tool and tighten.
22. Remove crankshaft locking tool.
23. Turn crankshaft 1¾ turns clockwise and install crankshaft locking tool. Stop at TDC and tighten lever arm to water pump pulley flange. If TDC is passed, do not turn counterclockwise, turn crankshaft an additional two turns.
24. Inspect alignment marks on camshaft Nos. 3 and 4, realign if required.
25. Install inspecting gauge tool on camshaft Nos. 1 and 2, then install camshaft locking tool on camshaft Nos. 2 and 4.
26. Turn upper idler pulley counterclockwise until timing marks on camshaft sprocket Nos. 1 and 2 align with marks on inspecting gauge tool.
27. Hold idler pulley and tighten using idler pulley wrench tool.
28. Remove camshaft and crankshaft locking tools.
29. Turn crankshaft 1¾ turns clockwise and install crankshaft locking tool. Stop at TDC and tighten lever arm to water pump pulley flange. If TDC is passed, do not turn counterclockwise, turn crankshaft an additional two turns.
30. Inspect both pairs of camshaft timing marks using inspecting gauge tool. Adjust as required.
31. Adjust timing belt tensioner mark ⅛ inch above alignment mark on spring loaded idler, **Fig. 14.**
32. Remove crankshaft locking tool and inspecting gauge tool.
33. Install timing belt front cover.

CAMSHAFT
REPLACE
Removal

1. Remove upper and lower intake manifold as outlined under "Intake Manifold, Replace."
2. Remove air cleaner.
3. Remove timing belt cover as outlined under "Front Cover, Replace."
4. Remove timing belt as outlined under "Timing Belt, Replace."
5. Turn crankshaft counterclockwise to 60° BTDC to prevent valve to piston contact, **Fig. 9.**
6. Remove gear bolt and gear using cam-

shaft locking tools Nos. J42069-1 and J42069-2, or equivalents.
7. Ensure camshaft is not under load from lifters.
8. Remove bearing cap bolts, starting in center and moving outward in spiral direction, in stages of ½–1 turn.
9. Code marks on bearing caps are as follows:
   a. Rear cylinder head cylinders Nos. 1, 3 and 5 bearing caps are marked with L followed by a number.
   b. Front cylinder head cylinders Nos. 2, 4 and 6 bearing caps are marked with R followed by a number.
10. Remove camshaft with seal, then clean bearing and sealing surfaces.

Installation

1. Lubricate camshaft bearing surfaces with oil.
2. Install camshafts as follows:
   a. **When installing rear exhaust camshaft,** ensure pin points toward 1 o'clock position.
   b. **When installing rear intake camshaft,** ensure pin points toward 11 o'clock position.
   c. **When installing front exhaust camshaft,** ensure pin points toward 12 o'clock position.
   d. **When installing front intake camshaft,** ensure pin points toward 7 o'clock position.
3. Apply sealant Loctite 573, or equivalent, to forward edge of front bearing cap, ensure sealant does not enter oil journal.
4. Install bearing caps in appropriate positions, **Figs. 16 and 17.**
5. Tighten bearing caps, starting in center and moving outward in spiral direction.
6. Coat lip of camshaft seal with engine oil and tap into place using camshaft front seal installer tool No. J35268-A, or equivalent, ensure seal is fully seated.
7. Install camshaft gear with new bolts and camshaft locking tool.
8. Install new camshaft gear mounting bolts.
9. Install and adjust timing belt.
10. Install valve cover.
11. Install upper and lower intake manifold.
12. Install air cleaner.

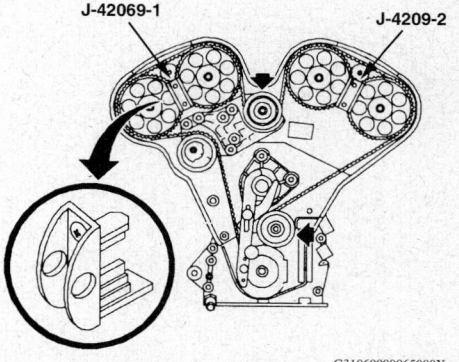

Fig. 10 Camshaft gear locking tool installation

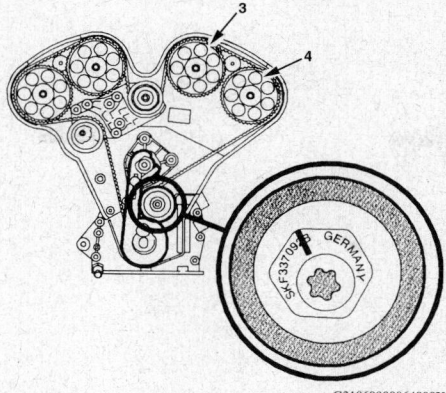

Fig. 11 Camshaft Nos. 3 & 4 idler pulley replacement

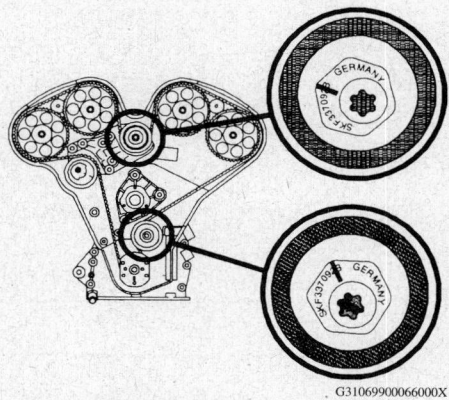

Fig. 12 Upper & lower idler pulleys alignment

PISTON & ROD ASSEMBLY

Ensure arrow on piston head faces toward front of engine and bump on connecting rod face toward rear of engine.

Tighten connecting rod cap bolts in three steps: first step, **torque** bolts to 26 ft. lbs.; second step, Tighten an additional 45°; third step, Tighten an additional 15°.

PISTONS, PINS & RINGS

1. If cylinders have been honed, proper size piston must be selected for each bore from chart, **Fig. 18.**
2. If piston must be separated from connecting rod.
3. Remove and install piston pin clips using piston pin clip replacement tool No. J43654, or equivalent.
4. Remove or install piston from connecting rod using piston pin remover/installer tool No. SA9101-E, or equivalent.
5. Ensure arrow on top of piston and bump on connecting rod face in opposite directions when assembling piston and rod. Arrow on piston will face front of engine block, bump on connecting rod will face rear of engine block.
6. Measure piston pin bore to piston pin clearance. Replace piston and piston pin if clearance is not .0001–.0003 inch.
7. Hone cylinders.
8. Install 1st and 2nd compression rings in cylinder bore. Gap should be .0118–.0196 inch.
9. Install oil control ring in cylinder bore. Gap should be .0157–.0551 inch.
10. Replace rings if end gap clearance is more than specified.
11. First and 2nd compression ring groove clearance should be .0008–.0015 inch.
12. Oil control ring groove clearance should be .0004–.0012 inch.
13. Replace piston if ring groove clearance is more than specified.
14. Refer to **Fig. 19** for piston ring orientation.

MAIN & ROD BEARINGS

The crankshaft main bearing caps are numbered 1, 2 and 3 from the front of the engine. The rear bearing cap is not numbered and contains the thrust bearings. The Nos. 2 and 3 bearing shells do not have oil grooves on the cap sides.

There is a 0 or a 1 stamped on the cylinder block oil pan mating flange near the end of each main bearing cap. This is the Determining Number. The Determining Number corresponds to each crankshaft main bearing size and color to be installed. The main journal diameter for a determining Number 0 is 2.8368–2.8371 inches. The main journal diameter for a determining Number 1 is 2.8371–2.8373 inches.

To select the proper main bearing, measure crankshaft main bearing journal diameter and refer to main bearing selective fits chart, **Fig. 20.**

Tighten main bearing cap bolts in three steps: first step, **torque** bolts to 37 ft. lbs.; second step, turn bolts an additional 60°; third step, turn bolts an additional 15°.

CRANKSHAFT REAR OIL SEAL
REPLACE

1. Remove transaxle as outlined in **MOTOR's "Domestic Transmission, In-Vehicle Service" manual or "Transmission Service DVD."**
2. Counterhold crankshaft using crank hub Torx socket tool No. J42098, or equivalent, and remove flexplate.
3. Center punch steel ring in rear oil seal, then drill small, shallow pilot hole in steel ring.
4. Screw self tapping screw into steel ring and remove rear oil seal using suitable pliers.
5. Reverse procedure to install, noting the following:
   a. Coat lip of rear oil seal with suitable clean engine oil.
   b. Install rear oil seal using rear main oil seal installer tool No. J42067, or equivalent.

OIL PAN
REPLACE

1. Raise and support vehicle.
2. Remove nose cone bracket bolts from oil pan.
3. Remove lower transaxle flange to oil pan bolts.
4. Remove oil pan using RTV cutter tool No. SA9123-E, or equivalent, to break pan loose from engine block.
5. Reverse procedure to install using Loctite 5900, or equivalent, .118 inch from inside edge of oil pan.

OIL PUMP
REPLACE

1. Drain coolant into suitable container.
2. Remove air cleaner.
3. Remove timing belt front and rear covers as outlined under "Front Cover, Replace."
4. Remove timing belt as outlined under "Timing Belt, Replace."
5. Remove and position air conditioning compressor and power steering pump aside.
6. Pivot alternator aside.
7. Remove oil pan as outlined under "Oil Pan, Replace."
8. Remove oil pump pickup tube.
9. Hold crankshaft drive gear using crank hub holding tool No. J42065, or equivalent.
10. Remove drive gear using crank hub Torx socket tool No. J42098, or equivalent.
11. Remove oil pan housing bolts and oil pump.
12. Remove front main oil seal and collar from oil pump.
13. Reverse procedure to install, noting the following:
    a. Coat pump side of new oil pump gasket with anaerobic sealant Loctite 518, or equivalent.
    b. Install oil pump and align using guide pins. Apply thread sealant Loctite 242, or equivalent, to bolts.
    c. Coat lip of front main oil seal with suitable clean engine oil, then install using front main seal installer

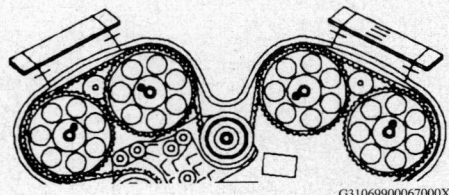

Fig. 13 Timing belt alignment

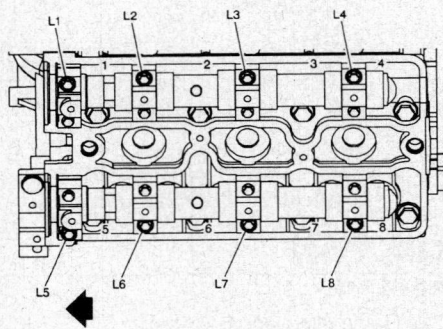

Fig. 16 Rear cylinder head bearing cap locations

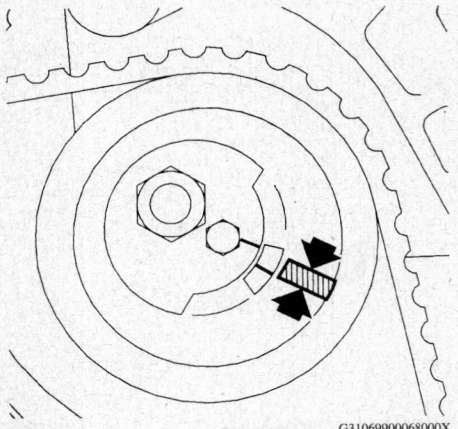

Fig. 14 Timing belt tensioner alignment

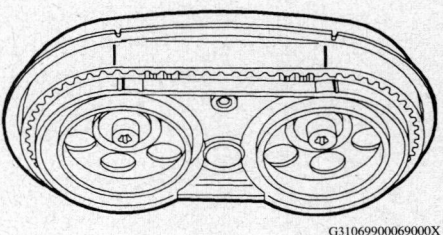

Fig. 15 Timing belt alignment retarded .0394 inch

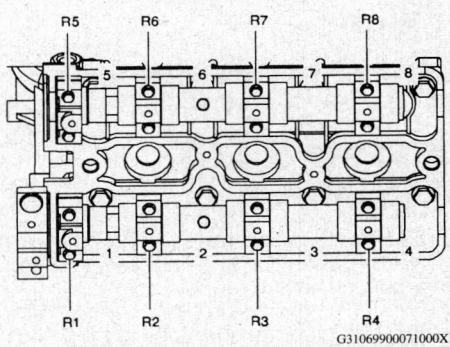

Fig. 17 Front cylinder head bearing cap locations

tool No. J35268-A, or equivalent. Ensure seal is fully and evenly seated.

d. Install new crankshaft drive gear bolt.

e. Tighten oil pump after alternator and drive belt idler pulley for camshafts Nos. 3 and 4 have been tightened.

f. Fill and bleed cooling system as required.

BELT TENSION DATA

1. Allow engine to run for approximately 10 minutes with accessories turned on to ensure engine is warmed up.
2. Turn tensioner arm clockwise until belt becomes loose and slowly apply tension back on belt.
3. Marking on tensioner arm must fall within two marks on tensioner body. Replace drive belt if tensioner marks fall outside operating range.
4. Record belt tension at mid span using calibrated belt tension gauge tool No. SA9181-NE, or equivalent. This inspection can be performed with engine removed. If engine is in vehicle, upper engine mount must be removed.
5. Repeat previous steps three times. Determine average belt tension.
6. New belt tension should be 50–65 lbs. Used belt tension should be at least 45 lbs.

SERPENTINE DRIVE BELT

Belt Routing

Refer to **Fig. 21** for serpentine belt routing.

Belt Replacement

1. Remove righthand front engine mount as outlined under "Engine Mount, Replace."
2. Remove belt by rotating tensioner pulley clockwise and sliding drive belt off tensioner.
3. Reverse procedure to install.

COOLING SYSTEM BLEED

Run engine until thermostat opens, then cycle engine speed from idle to 3000 RPM in 30 second intervals. Add coolant as required to bring level to cold line on reservoir after engine has cooled.

THERMOSTAT
REPLACE

1. Remove thermostat housing extension bolt.
2. Remove extension by pulling it out from thermostat housing.
3. Remove thermostat housing and thermostat.
4. Reverse procedure to install.

WATER PUMP
REPLACE

1. Remove air cleaner inlet duct from throttle body, then raise and support vehicle.
2. Remove lefthand front wheel and splash shield.
3. Loosen but do not remove water pump and power steering pump pulley bolts.
4. Remove accessory drive belt as outlined under "Serpentine Drive Belt."
5. Remove water pump and power steering pump pulleys, then the drive belt tensioner.
6. Remove front timing belt cover as outlined under "Front Cover, Replace."
7. Remove water pump and O-ring.
8. Reverse procedure to install.

RADIATOR
REPLACE

1. Slide fan control module up and off bracket, then position aside.
2. Remove battery.
3. Drain coolant into suitable container.
4. Remove power steering fluid reservoir and position to rear of vehicle.
5. Disconnect both cooling fans and auxiliary water pump, then remove fan shroud harnesses.
6. Remove upper transaxle cooler line and unsnap front end tank retainer.
7. Remove upper radiator hose and auxiliary water pump outlet and inlet hoses.
8. Remove fan shroud and forward wiring harness.
9. Remove lower radiator hose and lower transaxle cooler line from radiator.
10. Remove upper radiator bracket and mounts, then the upper hose.
11. Support condenser from upper rail and remove condenser block bolt from radiator end tank.
12. Remove condenser bolts, then disconnect radiator tabs by pulling condenser and pusher fan down.
13. Remove radiator leaving condenser and pusher fan, then the upper and lower radiator to condenser gaskets.
14. Reverse procedure to install.

FUEL PUMP
REPLACE

1. Drain fuel tank into suitable container using suitable hand operated pump.
2. Remove exhaust system intermediate pipe with muffler and heat shield.
3. Remove fuel filler pipe lower bracket

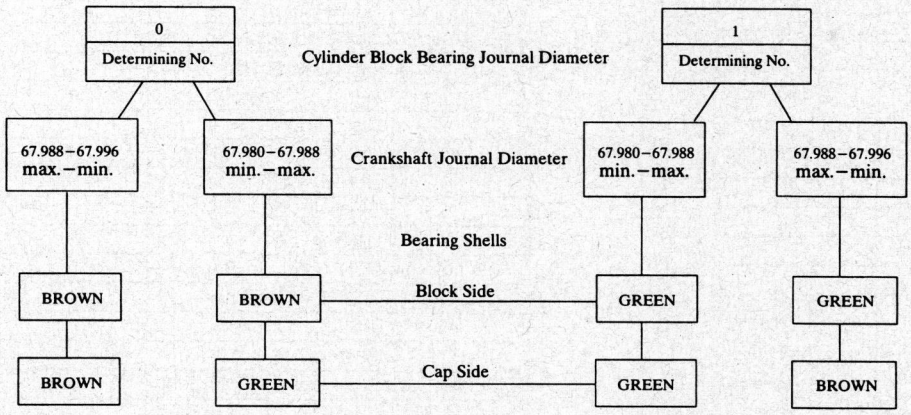

CYLINDER BORE	PISTON SIZE
(8) 85.976 - 85.985 mm (3.3848 - 3.3852 inch)	(8) 85.940 - 85.950 mm (3.3834 - 3.3838 inch)
(99) 85.985 - 85.995 mm (3.3852 - 3.3856 inch)	(99) 85.950 - 85.960 mm (3.3838 - 3.3842 inch)
(00) 85.995 - 86.005 mm (3.3856 - 3.3860 inch)	(00) 85.960 - 85.970 mm (3.3842 - 3.3846 inch)
(01) 86.005 - 86.015 mm (3.3860 - 3.3864 inch)	(01) 85.970 - 85.980 mm (3.3846 - 3.3850 inch)
(02) 86.015 - 86.025 mm (3.3864 - 3.3868 inch)	(02) 85.980 - 85.990 mm (3.3850 - 3.3854 inch)
† (7 + 0.5) 86.465 - 86.475 mm (3.4041 - 3.4045 inch)	† (7 + 0.5) 86.430 - 86.440 mm (3.4027 - 3.4031 inch)

GC1069700845000X

Fig. 18   Piston selection chart

Note: Brown Bearing Thickness 1.989–1.995 mm.   Green Bearing Thickness 1.995–2.001 mm.

G31069900079000X

Fig. 20   Main bearing selective fits chart

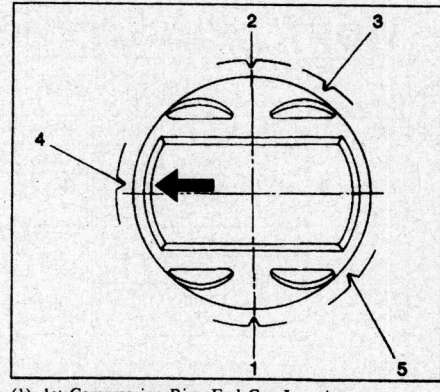

(1) 1st Compression Ring End Gap Location
(2) 2nd Compression Ring End Gap Location
(3) Oil Control Ring Upper Ring End Gap Location
(4) Oil Control Ring Spacer End Gap Location
(5) Oil Control Ring Lower Ring End Gap Location

GC1069700848000X

Fig. 19   Piston ring orientation

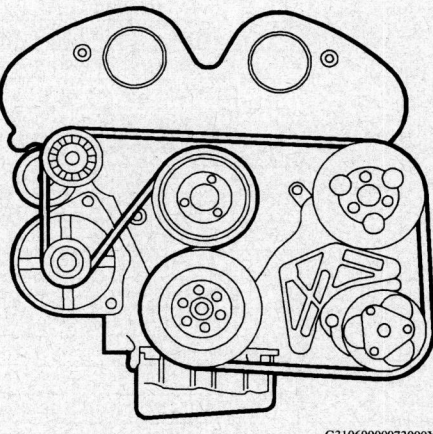

G31069900073000X

Fig. 21   Serpentine drive belt routing

and disconnect filler pipe hose from tank.

4. Disconnect EVAP canister vent hose and quick connect at recirc line.
5. Remove fuel tank grounding strap.
6. Disconnect fuel feed line after fuel filter, then the fuel return and EVAP canister purge lines between tank and chassis fuel bundle.
7. Disconnect fuel tank electrical connections.
8. Support fuel tank.
9. Remove rear mounting strap bolts and fuel tank.
10. Remove fuel lines from fuel pump module cover.
11. Remove fuel pump module retaining ring using suitable ½ inch breaker bar and lock ring service tool No. J43827, or equivalent.
12. Disconnect fuel pump housing clips and remove fuel pump from fuel tank.
13. Remove fuel feed line from bottom of fuel pump using fuel clamp pliers tool No. J44078, or equivalent.
14. Disconnect fuel pump connector from fuel pump cover.
15. Reverse procedure to install, noting the following:
    a. Install new fuel pump seal.
    b. Install pump cover lock ring with bumps facing away from tank using lock ring service tool.
    c. Install new retainers into female

portion of quick connect fitting on fuel and EVAP canister purge lines.

FUEL FILTER

REPLACE

1. Disconnect fuel feed lines.
2. Remove fuel filter.
3. Reverse procedure to install. Install new fuel line retainers into fuel line fittings' female portion.

TECHNICAL SERVICE BULLETINS

Front Bank Chirp Nose

2005 L-SERIES

On some of these models built between VINs 5Y501038 and 5Y505543, there may be squawk, chirp or cricket noise from the engine. This noise is most noticeable around timing belt cover at 600–3500 RPM.

This condition may be caused by either of the front bank timing belt camshaft sprockets being cracked near the base of the tooth area.

To correct this condition, replace the front bank timing belt camshaft sprockets.

Blue Smoke At Engine Start-Up

2004 L-SERIES

On some of these models there may be blue smoke from exhaust during engine start-up after vehicle has been parked for several hours.

This condition may be caused by leaking valve seal or excessive stem and guide clearance.

To correct this condition, proceed as follows:

1. **On models equipped with brown valve seals,** replace seals.
2. **On models equipped with green valve seals,** replace valve guides or cylinder head as required.

TIGHTENING SPECIFICATIONS

Year	Component	Torque/Ft. Lbs.
2004–05	Accelerator Pedal Bracket	89①
	Accelerator Pedal Position Sensor	53①
	Accessory Bracket, Air Conditioning & Power Steering	30
	Accessory Drive Belt Tensioner	30
	Air Conditioning Compressor Bracket	30
	Air Conditioning Compressor Hose Support Strap	71①
	Alternator	30
	Battery Hold Down Bracket	15
	Battery Terminal	13
	Battery Tray	11
	Bell Housing	48
	Belt Tensioner	30
	Camshaft Bearing	71①
	valve cover	71①
	Camshaft Gear	37⑤
	Camshaft Position Sensor	71①
	Catalytic Converter	15
	Catalytic Converter Hanger	15
	Connecting Rod Cap	⑦
	Coolant Bridge	22
	Crankshaft Balancer	15
	Crankshaft Main Bearing	②
	Crankshaft Torsional Bearing Bridge	15
	Crankshaft Drive Gear	184⑥
	Crankshaft Position Sensor	71①
	Crankshaft Reluctor Ring	11
	Crankshaft Sensor	71①
	Cylinder Head	④
	Drive Belt Tensioner	30
	Engine Control Module	71①
	Engine Coolant Temperature Sensor	13
	Engine Mount	41
	Engine Mount Bracket	41
	Engine Oil Cooler Cover	22
	Engine Oil Cooler Inlet & Outlet	15
	Engine Rear Cover	71①
	Engine Rear Cover Threaded Pin	89①
	Engine Ventilation Chamber	71①
	Exhaust Gas Recirculation Pipe	19
	Exhaust Gas Recirculation Valve	15
	Exhaust Manifold	15
	Flexplate	65
	Front Timing Belt Cover	48③
	Fuel Fill Neck To Fuel Tank Clamp	71①
	Fuel Fill Pipe To Body, Lower	114①
	Fuel Fill Pipe To Body, Upper	35①
	Fuel Filter Bracket	35①
	Fuel Line Stone Chip Guard	106①
	Fuel Rail	71①
	Fuel Tank Mounting Strap	15

TIGHTENING SPECIFICATIONS—Continued

Year	Component	Torque/Ft. Lbs.
2004–05	Fuel Tank Pressure Sensor	18①
	Heated Oxygen Sensor	37
	Ignition Coil	71①
	Ignition Module	71①
	Intake Manifold	15
	Intake Manifold Spacer	15
	Intake Plenum	71①
	Intake Plenum Switchover Valve	71①
	Intake Runner	71①
	Knock Sensors	15
	Main Bearing	②
	Manifold Absolute Pressure Sensor	44①
	Battery Ground To Chassis	114①
	Oil Cooler Inlet & Outlet	15
	Oil Filter Cap	19
	Oil Filter Cartridge Housing Drain Plug	89①
	Oil Filter Cartridge Housing To Engine Block	33
	Oil Intake Pipe	71①
	Oil Pan Baffle	71①
	Oil Pan	11
	Oil Pan Drain Plug	19
	Oil Pressure Switch	30
	Oil Pump	80①
	Oxygen Sensors, Exhaust Manifold	37
	Oxygen Sensors, Lower Exhaust Pipe	33
	Power Steering Pump Pulley	15
	Rear Timing Belt Cover Threaded Pin	89①
	Rear Timing Cover	71①
	Resonance Chamber	27①
	Spark Plug	19
	Starter	30
	Thermostat Housing	15
	Throttle Boot	71①
	Timing Belt Idler Pulley	30
	Timing Belt Tensioner Bracket	30
	Timing Belt Tensioner	15
	Torque Convertor Bolts	48
	Transaxle Cooler Line, Lower	36①
	Transaxle Cooler Line, Upper	18
	Transaxle Range Switch	18
	Transaxle Range Switch Lever	26
	Water Pump	19
	Water Pump Pulley	71①
	Water Pump	19
	Wheel Bolt	92
	Wiring Channel	71①

① — Inch lbs.
② — Refer to "Main & Rod Bearings" for tightening specifications & sequence.
③ — Tighten an additional 30°, then an additional 15°.
④ — Refer to "Cylinder Head, Replace" for tightening specifications & sequence.
⑤ — Tighten an additional 60°, then an additional 15°.
⑥ — Tighten an additional 45°, then an additional 15°.
⑦ — Refer to "Piston & Rod Assembly" for tightening specifications & sequence.

3.5L Engine

NOTE: On Air Bag Equipped Models, Refer To "Air Bag System Precautions" Located In The Front Of This Manual For System Disarming & Arming Procedures.

NOTE: Refer To "Computer Relearn Procedures" Located In The Front Of This Manual When Battery Power To The Computer Has Been Interrupted.

NOTE: Prior To Performing Any Service Operations Listed In This Section, Consult The "Technical Service Bulletins" Section For Related Information.

INDEX

	Page No.		Page No.		Page No.
Camshaft, Replace	12-74	Fuel Pump, Replace	12-76	Push Rods	12-74
Camshaft Lobe Lift		Hydraulic Lifters, Replace	12-74	Radiator, Replace	12-76
Specifications	12-74	Intake Manifold, Replace	12-72	Rocker Arms, Replace	12-74
Compression Pressure	12-71	Lower	12-72	Serpentine Drive Belt	12-76
Cooling System Bleed	12-76	Upper	12-72	Replacement	12-76
Crankshaft Damper, Replace	12-74	Main & Rod Bearings	12-75	Routing	12-76
Crankshaft Rear Oil Seal,		Connecting Rod	12-75	Technical Service Bulletins	12-76
Replace	12-75	Main Bearing Caps	12-75	Crankshaft Rear Main Oil Seal	
Crankshaft Seal, Replace	12-75	Oil Pan, Replace	12-75	Leak	12-76
Cylinder Head, Replace	12-73	Oil Pump, Replace	12-75	Thermostat, Replace	12-76
Engine Rebuilding		Oil Pump Service	12-76	Tightening Specifications	12-78
Specifications	29-1	Assemble	12-76	Timing Chain, Replace	12-74
Engine, Replace	12-71	Disassemble	12-76	Installation	12-74
Engine Mount, Replace	12-71	Inspection	12-76	Removal	12-74
Engine Mount Strut, Replace	12-71	Piston & Rod Assembly	12-75	Valve Adjustment	12-74
Exhaust Manifold, Replace	12-72	Precautions	12-71	Valve Cover, Replace	12-73
Lefthand	12-72	Air Bag Systems	12-71	Lefthand	12-73
Righthand	12-73	Battery Ground Cable	12-71	Righthand	12-73
Front Cover, Replace	12-74	Fuel System Pressure Relief	12-71	Water Pump, Replace	12-76

PRECAUTIONS

Air Bag Systems

Refer to "Air Bag System Precautions" in the front of this manual for system disarming and arming procedures.

Battery Ground Cable

Prior to service, disconnect battery ground cable and isolate as required.

Fuel System Pressure Relief

Failure to relieve system pressure prior to disconnecting fuel system components may cause fire or personal injury.
1. Loosen fuel tank filler cap to relieve tank pressure.
2. Raise and support vehicle.
3. Disconnect fuel pump electrical connector.
4. Lower vehicle.
5. Start and operate engine until fuel supply is consumed.
6. Crank engine for approximately three seconds to relieve remaining pressure.
7. Disconnect and isolate battery ground cable, then connect fuel pump electrical connector.

COMPRESSION PRESSURE

1. Disable ignition and fuel systems.
2. Remove all spark plugs.
3. Remove air duct from throttle body and block throttle plate in open position.
4. Firmly install suitable compression gauge to spark plug hole and crank engine through at least four compression strokes in testing cylinder.
5. Record readings at each stroke.
6. Disconnect and repeat compression test for each cylinder.
7. Record compression readings from all of cylinders.
8. Lowest reading should not be less than 70% of highest reading.
9. No cylinder reading should be less than 100 psi.

ENGINE MOUNT

REPLACE

1. Raise and support vehicle.
2. Remove righthand tire and wheel assembly.
3. Remove splash shield from under engine.
4. Remove engine mount to engine mount bracket nuts.
5. Remove engine mount to frame nuts.
6. Raise engine with a suitable jackstand.
7. Remove motor mount from vehicle.
8. Reverse procedure to install.

ENGINE MOUNT STRUT

REPLACE

1. Remove air cleaner.
2. Remove engine mount strut to engine mounting bolts.
3. Rotate engine mount strut to a vertical position.
4. Remove engine mount strut to body mounting bolts, then the strut from vehicle.
5. Reverse procedure to install.

ENGINE

REPLACE

1. Relieve fuel system pressure as outlined under "Precautions."
2. Drain coolant into suitable container.
3. Drain engine oil.

4. Remove engine air cleaner.
5. Mark engine hinge locations for installation reference, then remove hood.
6. Remove serpentine belt.
7. Remove engine mount strut as outlined under "Engine Mount Strut, Replace."
8. Disconnect the following electrical connectors:
   a. Knock sensor.
   b. Camshaft Position (CMP) sensor.
   c. Crankshaft Position (CKP) sensor.
   d. Oxygen sensor.
   e. Manifold Absolute Pressure (MAP) sensor.
   f. EGR valve.
   g. EVAP emission canister purge solenoid.
   h. Electronic throttle control.
   i. Ignition coil.
   j. Body wiring harness to engine harness.
9. Raise and support vehicle.
10. Remove exhaust crossover pipe mounting nuts, then the pipe.
11. Remove engine wiring harness grounds from transaxle.
12. Remove engine mount lower nuts.
13. Remove torque converter covers and starter motor.
14. Remove A/C compressor from mount. **Do not discharge A/C system refrigerant.**
15. Remove torque converter mounting bolts.
16. Remove transaxle support brace.
17. Remove lower transaxle to engine mounting bolts.
18. Remove radiator outlet hose from engine.
19. Lower vehicle and support transaxle with a suitable lifting device.
20. Remove heater inlet and outlet hoses from engine.
21. Remove vacuum and brake booster hoses from upper intake manifold.
22. Remove fuel lines from fuel rail.
23. Remove radiator inlet hose from engine.
24. Install a suitable engine lifting device to engine.
25. Remove upper transaxle to engine mounting bolts.
26. Remove engine from vehicle.
27. Reverse procedure to install.

INTAKE MANIFOLD
REPLACE
Upper

1. Remove engine oil fill cap and intake manifold cover.
2. Relieve fuel system pressure as outlined under "Precautions."
3. Disconnect fuel feed pipe quick connect fitting from fuel rail.
4. Disconnect EVAP pipe quick connect fitting from purge solenoid.
5. Remove fuel line clip from Manifold Absolute Pressure (MAP) sensor bracket. Position fuel and EVAP lines aside.
6. Drain cooling system.
7. Remove air cleaner outlet duct.

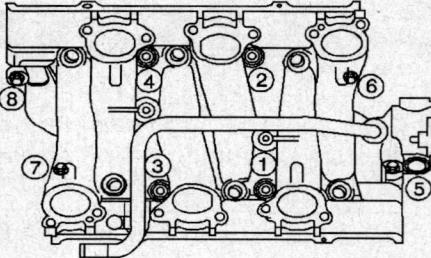

Fig. 1   Lower intake manifold bolt tightening sequence

8. Remove PCV fresh an foul air tubes from rocker cover.
9. Remove brake booster vacuum hose from intake manifold.
10. Remove radiator surge tank inlet hose from inlet pipe.
11. Remove radiator surge tank inlet pipe attaching bolts, then the inlet pipe. Discard O-ring seal.
12. Disconnect MAP sensor and EVAP canister purge solenoid electrical connectors
13. Disconnect chassis EVAP line quick connect fitting from purge solenoid.
14. Disconnect Electronic Throttle Control (ETC) electrical connector.
15. Disconnect left side spark plug wires from spark plugs and ignition coil.
16. Disengage spark plug wire retainer clips from heater inlet and outlet pipe bracket and MAP sensor bracket.
17. Remove left side spark plug wires.
18. Remove heater inlet and outlet hose/pipe clamp nuts from throttle body studs.
19. Remove heater inlet and outlet hoses from pipes.
20. Remove heater inlet and outlet pipe bracket from throttle body studs. Position inlet and outlet pipe aside.
21. Remove ignition coil bracket bolts.
22. Remove alternator rear brace upper nut, alternator through bolt, then the alternator rear brace.
23. Remove mounting bolts and nuts, then the throttle body and gasket.
24. Remove mounting bolt and EVAP canister purge solenoid valve. Discard O-ring.
25. Remove mounting bolt, then the MAP sensor bracket and sensor.
26. Remove intake manifold cover ball stud nut.
27. Remove mounting bolts and stud, and remove upper from lower intake manifold.
28. Remove upper to lower intake manifold gasket.
29. Reverse procedure to install, noting the following:
    a. Install new gasket.
    b. Apply suitable threadlock to intake manifold and throttle body mounting bolt/stud threads.

Lower

1. Remove upper intake manifold as outlined under "Upper."
2. Remove valve covers as outlined

under "Valve Cover, Replace."
3. Remove alternator as outlined under "Alternator, Replace" in "Electrical" section.
4. Remove drive belt as outlined under "Serpentine Drive Belt."
5. Loosen drive belt idler pulley attaching bolt and drive belt idler pulley.
6. Remove power steering pump pulley.
7. Remove much power steering fluid from fluid reservoir as possible.
8. Remove engine lift bracket bolts and lift brackets.
9. Remove power steering gear inlet hose. Discard hose O-ring.
10. Remove power steering pump mounting bolts, then the pump.
11. Remove the radiator surge tank pipe from the crossover pipe.
12. Remove radiator inlet hose from engine coolant crossover pipe.
13. Remove thermal bypass hose from engine coolant crossover pipe.
14. Remove coolant crossover pipe mounting bolts, then the crossover pipe.
15. Disconnect Engine Coolant Temperature (ECT) and Camshaft Position (CMP) sensors electrical connectors.
16. Remove mounting bolts and fuel rail.
17. Remove mounting bolts and lower intake manifold.
18. Loosen mounting bolts, then remove rocker arms. **Ensure valve train components are kept in order for correct installation.**
19. Remove push rods.
20. Remove lower intake manifold gaskets and seals.
21. Reverse procedure to install, noting the following:
    a. Clean gasket and seal surface with suitable de-greaser.
    b. **Do not apply RTV sealer under lower intake manifold gaskets.**
    c. Coat push rod ends with suitable pre-lube.
    d. Intake valve push rods are 5.75 inches and exhausts are 6.0 inches long.
    e. Coat rocker arm friction surfaces with suitable pre-lube.
    f. Install new gaskets and seals.
    g. Apply small 1/3 inch drop of suitable RTV sealant to four corners of intake manifold block joints.
    h. Install new intake manifold bolts using suitable sealer on threads.
    i. Refer to sequence, **Fig. 1, torque** lower intake manifold mounting bolts 1–4 to 12 ft. lbs.
    j. Refer to sequence, **Fig. 1, torque** lower intake manifold mounting bolts 5–8 to 18 ft. lbs.

EXHAUST MANIFOLD
REPLACE
Lefthand

1. Remove engine mount strut to radiator support mounting bolts.
2. Remove engine mount strut to bracket mounting bolts and nuts.
3. Remove engine mount strut.

4. Remove engine harness clip from strut bracket.
5. Raise and support vehicle.
6. Remove front mounting bolt and nut, then the rear mounting bolt and position air conditioning compressor aside.
7. Remove lefthand engine mount strut bracket to engine lower bolts.
8. Lower vehicle.
9. Remove upper mounting bolt and lefthand engine mount strut bracket.
10. Remove mounting bolts, then the exhaust manifold and crossover pipe heat shields.
11. Remove exhaust crossover pipe to lefthand exhaust manifold mounting nuts.
12. Remove mounting bolts and lefthand exhaust manifold. Discard gasket.
13. Reverse procedure to install.

Righthand

1. Remove alternator as outlined under "Alternator" in "Electrical" section.
2. Remove Connector Position Assurance (CPA) retainer.
3. Disconnect Heated Oxygen Sensor (HO2S) electrical connector and remove clip from ignition coil bracket.
4. Remove HO2S using oxygen sensor wrench tool No. J39194-B, or equivalent.
5. Remove mounting bolts and exhaust manifold shield.
6. Remove spark plug wires and spark plugs.
7. Remove EGR pipe to manifold and EGR valve mounting bolts, then the EGR pipe.
8. Remove mounting bolts, then the exhaust manifold and crossover pipe heat shields.
9. Remove exhaust crossover pipe to righthand exhaust manifold mounting nuts.
10. Remove exhaust manifold upper mounting bolts.
11. Remove upper catalytic converter to exhaust manifold mounting nut.
12. Raise and support vehicle.
13. Disconnect electrical connectors and remove HO2Ss.
14. Remove catalytic converter to muffler mounting nuts and insulators.
15. Remove catalytic converter lower mounting nut and position muffler aside.
16. Remove catalytic converter and gasket.
17. Remove lower mounting bolts and lefthand exhaust manifold. Discard gasket.
18. Reverse procedure to install.

CYLINDER HEAD
REPLACE

1. Raise and support vehicle, then drain cooling system and engine oil into suitable containers.
2. Lower vehicle.
3. Remove lower intake manifold as outlined under "Intake Manifold, Replace."
4. Remove exhaust manifold as outlined under "Exhaust Manifold, Replace."

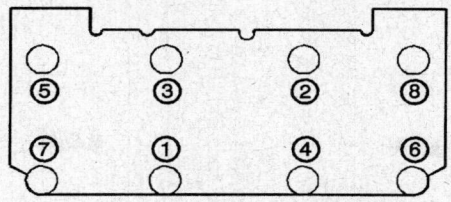

-ARM0300000000243

Fig. 2 Cylinder head bolt tightening sequence

5. Remove dip stick, then the mounting bolt and oil level tube.
6. Remove spark plugs.
7. Remove and discard cylinder head bolts.
8. Remove cylinder head. Discard gasket.
9. Reverse procedure to install, noting the following:
   a. Install new cylinder head gasket.
   b. Refer to sequence, **Fig. 2,** and tighten new cylinder head bolts in two steps: First step, **torque** bolts to 44 ft. lbs.; second step, tighten bolts an additional 140.°

VALVE COVER
REPLACE
Lefthand

1. Partially drain cooling system into suitable container.
2. Remove engine oil fill cap and intake manifold cover.
3. Remove dipstick, then the mounting bolts and oil level tube.
4. Disconnect lefthand spark plug wires.
5. Remove spark plug wire harness clip from heater inlet and outlet front pipe bracket. Position spark plug harness aside.
6. Remove Positive Crankcase Ventilation (PCV) foul air tube.
7. Remove engine mount strut to radiator support mounting bolts.
8. Remove engine mount strut to bracket mounting bolts and nuts.
9. Remove engine mount strut.
10. Remove engine harness clip from strut bracket.
11. Raise and support vehicle.
12. Remove front mounting bolt and nut, then the rear mounting bolt and position air conditioning compressor aside.
13. Remove lefthand engine mount strut bracket to engine lower bolts.
14. Lower vehicle.
15. Remove upper mounting bolt and lefthand engine mount strut bracket.
16. Disconnect clamps and clip nuts at throttle body, then remove heater inlet and outer hoses/pipes from engine inlet and outlet pipes.
17. Remove throttle body stud clips and position hose/pipe aside.
18. Remove front heater outlet hose from outlet heater pipe.
19. Remove bolt and stud, then the heater inlet and outlet pipe.
20. Loosen mounting bolts and remove

lefthand valve cover. **Ensure gasket stays attached to cylinder head.**
21. Cut RTV in channel where intake, cylinder head and valve rocker arm cover meet using suitable tool.
22. Remove valve cover gasket.
23. Reverse procedure to install, noting the following:
   a. Remove old gasket material and sealer from cylinder head and valve cover mating surfaces.
   b. Clean mating surfaces with suitable cleaner.
   c. Install new gasket and ensure it is properly seated in cover groove.
   d. Apply suitable sealant to surfaces where cylinder head and intake manifold meet.
   e. Apply sealer part No. 12378521, or equivalent, into groove on valve cover.
   f. **Torque** valve cover mounting bolts to 89 inch lbs., in alternating crisscross pattern.

Righthand

1. Remove serpentine drive belt as outlined under "Serpentine Belt."
2. Remove alternator as outlined under "Alternator, Replace" in "Electrical" section.
3. Disconnect Positive Crankcase Ventilation (PCV) fresh air tube from air cleaner outlet duct.
4. Remove PCV fresh air tube from righthand valve cover.
5. Disconnect righthand spark plug wires from plugs, ignition coil and bracket. Remove spark plug harness.
6. Disconnect Manifold Absolute Pressure (MAP) sensor and ignition coil electrical connectors.
7. Remove engine harness and Heated Oxygen Sensor (HO2S) electrical connector clips from ignition coil bracket.
8. Remove mounting nuts, bracket and ignition coil.
9. Loosen mounting bolts and remove lefthand valve cover. **Ensure gasket stays attached to cylinder head.**
10. Cut RTV in channel where intake, cylinder head and valve rocker arm cover meet using suitable tool.
11. Remove valve cover gasket.
12. Reverse procedure to install, noting the following:
   a. Remove old gasket material and sealer from cylinder head and valve cover mating surfaces.
   b. Clean mating surfaces with suitable cleaner.
   c. Install new gasket and ensure it is properly seated in cover groove.
   d. Apply suitable sealant to surfaces where cylinder head and intake manifold meet.
   e. Apply sealer part No. 12378521, or equivalent, into groove on valve cover.
   f. **Torque** valve cover mounting bolts to 89 inch lbs., in a alternating crisscross pattern.

CAMSHAFT LOBE LIFT SPECIFICATIONS

Intake .... .2727
Exhaust .... .2727

VALVE ADJUSTMENT

These engines are equipped with hydraulic valve lash adjusters. No adjustment is required.

ROCKER ARMS

REPLACE

1. Remove valve cover as outlined under "Valve Cover, Replace."
2. Loosen mounting bolts, then remove rocker arms. **Ensure valve train components are kept in order for correct installation.**
3. Reverse procedure to install. Coat rocker arm friction surfaces with suitable pre-lube.

PUSH RODS

1. Remove valve cover as outlined under "Valve Cover, Replace."
2. Loosen mounting bolts, then remove rocker arms. **Ensure valve train components are kept in order for correct installation.**
3. Remove push rods.
4. Reverse procedure to install, noting the following:
   a. Coat push rod ends with suitable pre-lube.
   b. Intake push rods are 5.75 inches and exhaust push rods are 6.0 inches long.
   c. Coat rocker arm friction surfaces with suitable pre-lube.

HYDRAULIC LIFTERS

REPLACE

1. Remove lower intake manifold as outlined under "Intake Manifold, Replace."
2. Remove valve cover as outlined under "Valve Cover, Replace."
3. Loosen mounting bolts, then remove rocker arms. **Ensure valve train components are keep in order to ensure install in original positions.**
4. Remove push rods.
5. Loosen mounting bolts and remove valve lifter guides. **Valve lifter guide bolts are not removable.**
6. Remove lifters from guides.
7. Reverse procedure to install, noting the following:
   a. Coast valve lifts with suitable pre-lube.
   b. Apply suitable threadlock to valve lifter guide bolt threads.
   c. Coat push rod ends with suitable pre-lube.
   d. Intake push rods are 5.75 inches and exhaust push rods are 6.0 inches long.
   e. Coat rocker arm friction surfaces with suitable pre-lube.

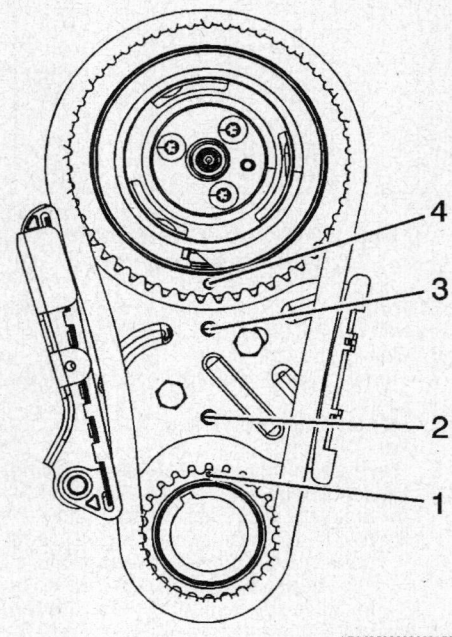

ARM0500000000172

Fig. 3 Timing mark alignment

CRANKSHAFT DAMPER

REPLACE

1. Remove drive belt as outlined under "Serpentine Drive Belt."
2. Raise and support vehicle, then remove righthand front tire and wheel assembly.
3. Remove ABS lead retainers and engine splash shield
4. Support frame using suitable jack stands.
5. Loosen lefthand and remove righthand mounting bolts, then lower righthand side of frame.
6. Remove torque converter covers and hold flywheel in place using flywheel holder tool No. J37096, or equivalent.
7. Remove crankshaft balancer bolt and washer.
8. Remove crankshaft balancer with harmonic balancer remover tool No. J41816 and puller end protector tool No. EN46359, or equivalents. **Do not use power-assisted tool to remove balancer.**
9. Reverse procedure to install, noting the following:
   a. Apply suitable sealer to crankshaft balancer keyway.
   b. Install balancer using balancer and crank sprocket installer tool No. J29113, or equivalent.
   c. **Torque** frame mounting bolts to 74 ft. lbs.
   d. Tighten frame bolts and additional 90°.

FRONT COVER

REPLACE

1. Drain cooling system into suitable container.
2. Remove drive belt as outlined under "Serpentine Drive Belt."

3. Remove mounting bolt and tensioner.
4. Remove oil pan as outlined under "Oil Pan, Replace."
5. Remove torque converter covers and hold flywheel in place using flywheel holder tool No. J37096, or equivalent.
6. Remove crankshaft balancer bolt and washer.
7. Remove crankshaft balancer with harmonic balancer remover tool No. J41816 and puller end protector tool No. EN46359, or equivalents. **Do not use power-assisted tool to remove balancer.**
8. Disconnect connector, then remove mounting bolt crankshaft position actuator magnet.
9. Remove thermostat housing as outlined under "Thermostat, Replace."
10. Remove mounting bolts and water pump pulley.
11. Remove mounting bolts, water pump and gasket.
12. Remove mounting bolts, front cover and gasket.
13. Reverse procedure to install.

TIMING CHAIN

REPLACE

Removal

1. Remove engine front cover as outlined under "Front Cover, Replace."
2. Align timing marks, **Fig. 3.**
3. Remove camshaft gear mounting bolt.
4. Remove timing chain, camshaft and gear.
5. Remove mounting bolts and chain tensioner.

Installation

1. Apply suitable pre-lube to crankshaft gear thrust surface.
2. Install tensioner and tighten mounting bolts.
3. Collapse tensioner using tensioner clamping tool No. EN-47719, or equivalent, and install suitable pin in retaining hole.
4. Align timing marks, **Fig. 3.**
5. Hold camshaft gear with chain hanging down and install chain to crankshaft gear.
6. Align camshaft gear timing marks and dowel with camshaft gear dowel hole.
7. Draw camshaft gear onto camshaft by tightening mounting bolt.
8. Coat crankshaft and camshaft gears with suitable, clean engine oil.
9. Install engine front cover as outlined under "Front Cover, Replace."

CAMSHAFT

REPLACE

1. Remove mounting bolt and Camshaft Position (CMP) sensor .
2. Remove mounting screws and camshaft thrust plate.
3. Install sprocket bolt into camshaft hand tight, then carefully rotate and remove camshaft.

4. Reverse procedure to install, noting the following:
   a. Coat camshaft journals with suitable clean engine oil.
   b. Coast camshaft lobes with suitable pre-lube.

PISTON & ROD ASSEMBLY

Pistons are specific to left and right cylinder bank applications. Ensure alignment marks face front of engine, **Figs. 4 and 5.**

MAIN & ROD BEARINGS

Connecting Rod

Torque connecting rod bearing cap to 18 ft. lbs., then tighten an additional 110.°

Main Bearing Caps

1. Dip crankshaft bearing cap bolts in suitable clean engine oil.
2. **Upper and lower inserts may be different. Do not obstruct any oil passages.**
3. Place crankshaft bearing inserts into crankshaft bearing cap and into engine block.
4. **Ensure bearing inserts project an equal distance on both sides.**
5. **Ensure insert tangs are engaged.**
6. Lubricate crankshaft main bearing surface with suitable clean engine oil.
7. Install crankshaft.
8. Install crankshaft main bearing caps. **Tap caps into cylinder block cavity using suitable brass, lead, or a leather mallet. Do not use mounting bolts to pull crankshaft bearing caps into seats.**
9. Apply small amount of suitable sealer to rear of crankshaft main bearing cap No. 4 sealing surface.
10. Tighten crankshaft main bearing cap bolts in two steps: First step, **torque** bolts to 37 ft. lbs.; second step, tighten bolts an additional 77.°
11. Thrust crankshaft forward or rearward, then measure clearance between crankshaft bearing No. 3 and crankshaft bearing surface.
12. If bearing clearance is not 002–.008 inch, inspect thrust surfaces for nicks, gouges or raised metal. Minor imperfections may be removed with fine stone.

CRANKSHAFT SEAL

REPLACE

1. Remove crankshaft balancer as outlined under "Crankshaft Damper, Replace."
2. Remove crankshaft key.
3. Pry out crankshaft front oil seal using suitable tool. **Do not damage engine front cover or crankshaft.**
4. Lubricate new oil seal with suitable clean engine oil.

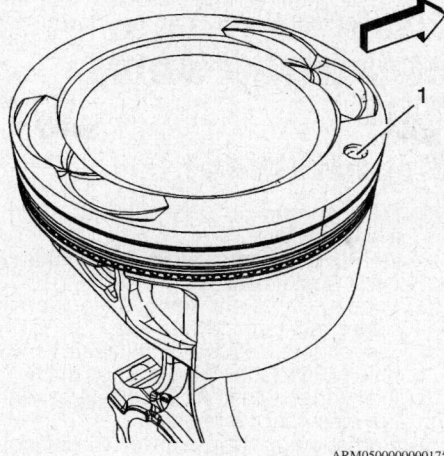

ARM0500000000175

Fig. 4   Left piston alignment

5. Install seal using cover aligner and seal installer tool No. J35468, or equivalent.

CRANKSHAFT REAR OIL SEAL

REPLACE

This procedure has been revised by a Technical Service Bulletin.

1. Separate transaxle from engine as outlined under "Engine, Replace."
2. Hold flywheel using flywheel holder tool No. J37096, or equivalent, then loosen flywheel mounting bolts.
3. Remove five of six mounting bolts. Leaving one bolt at top of crankshaft.
4. Secure flywheel and remove final mounting bolt. Remove flywheel.
5. Remove seal noting the following:
   a. Remove new style seal with protective nylon sleeve install, **Fig. 6.**
   b. Remove old style seal using suitable flat-bladed tool through dust lip at an angle, **Fig. 7.**
   c. **Do not nick crankshaft sealing surface.**
6. Install new seal with protective nylon sleeve attached using new rear main seal installer tool No. EN-48108, or equivalent.

OIL PAN

REPLACE

1. Remove engine mount strut to radiator support mounting bolts.
2. Remove engine mount strut to bracket mounting bolts and nuts.
3. Remove engine mount strut.
4. Support engine using engine support fixture tool No. J28467-B, or equivalent.
5. Remove mounting bolts, then the exhaust manifold and crossover pipe heat shields.
6. Remove exhaust crossover pipe to righthand exhaust manifold mounting nuts.
7. Remove exhaust manifold upper mounting bolts.

8. Remove upper catalytic converter to exhaust manifold mounting nut.
9. Raise and support vehicle.
10. Disconnect electrical connectors and remove HO2Ss.
11. Remove catalytic converter to muffler mounting nuts and insulators.
12. Remove catalytic converter lower mounting nut and position muffler aside.
13. Remove catalytic converter and gasket.
14. Drain engine oil into suitable container.
15. Remove oil filter.
16. Remove flywheel inspection cover.
17. Remove starter electrical connectors.
18. Remove mounting bolts and starter.
19. Remove front mounting bolt and nut, then the rear mounting bolt and position air conditioning compressor aside.
20. Disconnect oil level sensor electrical connector.
21. Remove engine harness clips from oil pan and transaxle brace.
22. Remove mounting bolts and front transaxle brace.
23. Remove engine mounting lower nuts and loosen transaxle mount lower nuts.
24. Remove rear transaxle brace to engine/oil pan bolts.
25. Lower vehicle and raise engine.
26. Hold steering column using steering column anti-rotation pin tool No. J42640, or equivalent.
27. Remove steering shaft intermediate lower pinch bolt.
28. Remove mounting bolts, engine mount and bracket.
29. Remove righthand lower ball joint from steering knuckle using ball joint/stud separator tool No. J41820, or equivalent.
30. Remove righthand outer tie rod from steering knuckle using ball joint/stud separator tool No. J41820, or equivalent.
31. Remove mounting bolt and nut, then the righthand stabilizer link.
32. Support frame using suitable jack stands.
33. Loosen lefthand bolts, then remove righthand bolts and lower righthand side of frame.
34. Remove mounting bolts, oil pan and gasket.
35. Reverse procedure to install, noting the following:
   a. Clean oil pan flanges and rail, front cover, rear main cap and bolt holes.
   b. Apply suitable sealer to both side of crankshaft rear main bearing cap.
   c. Press suitable sealer into crankshaft rear main bearing gap using suitable putty knife.
   d. Install new gasket.

OIL PUMP

REPLACE

1. Remove oil pan as outlined under "Oil Pan, Replace."
2. Remove mounting bolt, oil pump and drive shaft extension.
3. Reverse procedure to install.

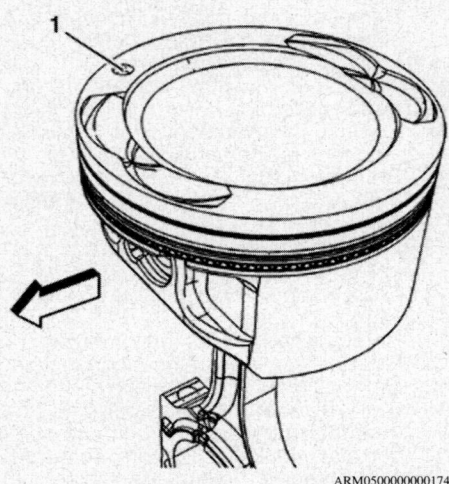

Fig. 5   Right piston alignment

OIL PUMP SERVICE
Disassemble

1. Remove pump driveshaft and retainer.
2. Remove oil pump screen. **Do not remove oil pump screen from pipe.**
3. Remove mounting bolts and pump cover.
4. Remove pump gears.
5. Match mark gear teeth for assembly alignment

Inspection

1. Inspect pump housing and cover for casting imperfections, cracks, scoring or damaged threads. **Replace, do not repair pump housing.**
2. Inspect gears for scoring and excessive wear.
3. Inspect idler gear shaft. If loose or damaged, replace pump.
4. Inspect drive gear shaft for looseness or scoring.
5. Inspect pressure regulator valve for scoring or sticking. Remove burrs with fine oil stone.
6. Inspect pressure regulator valve spring for loss of tension or bending.
7. Inspect suction pipe and screen for looseness. If pipe is loose, bent or has been removed, replace pump body cover and suction pipe.
8. Inspect for broken wire mesh or screen.
9. Measure gear lash, oil pump housing gear pocket and gears.

Assemble

1. Lubricate internal components with suitable clean engine oil.
2. Install pump gears and cover.
3. Install cover and gasket.
4. Install the pressure regulator valve and spring. Ensure cotter pin is properly secured.
5. Apply suitable sealer and tape new suction pipe in place using suitable plastic hammer and oil suction pipe installer tool No. J22144, or equivalent.

SERPENTINE DRIVE BELT
Replacement

1. Remove engine oil fill cap and intake manifold cover.
2. Remove mounting bolts and lefthand inner fender brace.
3. Loosen clamp and remove air cleaner outlet duct from throttle body.
4. Disconnect Positive Crankcase Ventilation (PCV) tube from air inlet duct.
5. Disconnect Mass Air Flow (MAF) sensor electrical connector.
6. Remove upper from lower air cleaner housing.
7. Remove Powertrain Control Module (PCM) and harness from lower air cleaner housing. **Do not disconnect connectors.**
8. Remove Transmission Control Module (TCM) and harness from lower air cleaner housing. **Do not disconnect connectors.**
9. Loosen clamp and remove air cleaner outlet duct from air cleaner.
10. Disconnect two rubber grommets on inner rail and remove lower air cleaner housing.
11. Release spring tension by turning belt tensioner clockwise.
12. Remove belt from pulleys.
13. Reverse procedure to install.

Routing

Refer to **Fig. 8** for serpentine drive belt routing.

COOLING SYSTEM BLEED

These engines do not require a specified bleed procedure. After filling cooling system, run engine to operating temperature with radiator/pressure cap off. Air will then be automatically bled through cap opening.

THERMOSTAT
REPLACE

1. Drain cooling system into suitable container.
2. Remove mounting bolts and lefthand inner fender brace.
3. Loosen clamp and remove air cleaner outlet duct from throttle body.
4. Disconnect Positive Crankcase Ventilation (PCV) tube from air inlet duct.
5. Disconnect Mass Air Flow (MAF) sensor electrical connector.
6. Remove upper from lower air cleaner housing.
7. Remove Powertrain Control Module (PCM) and harness from lower air cleaner housing. **Do not disconnect connectors.**
8. Remove Transmission Control Module

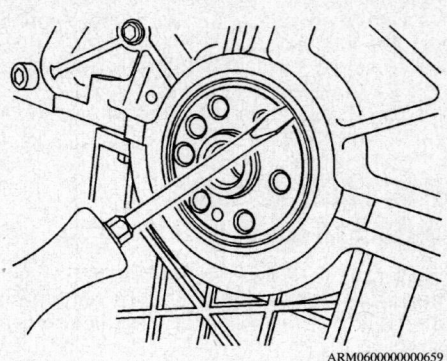

ARM0600000000659

Fig. 6   Removing new style rear main seal

(TCM) and harness from lower air cleaner housing. **Do not disconnect connectors.**
9. Loosen clamp and remove air cleaner outlet duct from air cleaner.
10. Disconnect clamp and remove radiator outlet hose from thermostat housing.
11. Remove mounting bolts and thermostat housing.
12. Reverse procedure to install. Install new gasket.

WATER PUMP
REPLACE

1. Drain coolant into suitable container.
2. Loosen water pump pulley mounting bolts.
3. Remove serpentine belt as outlined under "Serpentine Drive Belt."
4. Remove mounting bolts and water pump pulley.
5. Remove mounting bolts, water pump and gasket.
6. Reverse procedure to install. Install new gasket

RADIATOR
REPLACE

Refer to "Radiator, Replace" in the "2.4L Engine" section.

FUEL PUMP
REPLACE

Refer to "Fuel Pump, Replace" in "2.4L Engine" section

TECHNICAL SERVICE BULLETINS
Crankshaft Rear Main Oil Seal Leak

On some of these models there may be an external oil leakage. This condition may be caused by a leaking rear main oil seal.

To correct this condition, install new style rear main oil seal as outlined under "Crankshaft Rear Oil Seal, Replace."

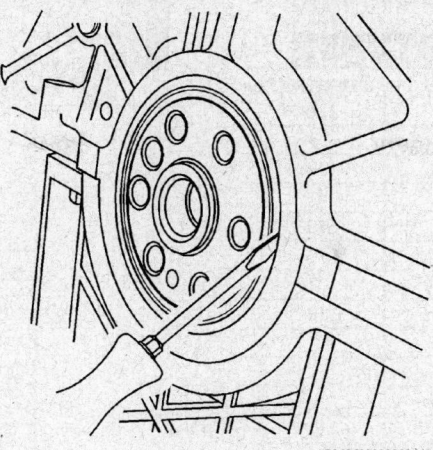

ARM0600000000660

Fig. 7   Removing old style rear main seal

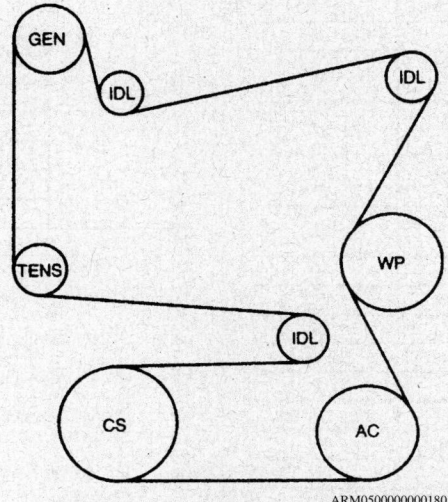

ARM0500000000180

Fig. 8   Serpentine drive belt routing

SATURN

TIGHTENING SPECIFICATIONS

Year	Component	Torque/Ft. Lbs.
2007–08	A/C Compressor Bracket	37
	Camshaft Position Sensor Bolt	89①
	Camshaft Sprocket Bolt	103
	Camshaft Thrust Plate	89①
	Connecting Rod Bearing Cap Bolt	②
	Coolant Crossover Pipe (Front)	37
	Coolant Crossover Pipe (Side)	89①
	Coolant Drain Plug	14
	Coolant Temperature Sensor	17
	Crankshaft Balancer Bolt	③
	Crankshaft Main Bearing Cap Bolt	④
	Cylinder Head Bolts	⑤
	Drive Belt Tensioner Bolt	37
	EGR Valve Assembly Bolt	22
	EGR Valve Pipe Bolt (Exhaust Manifold)	89①
	EGR Valve Pipe Bolt (EGR)	18
	Engine Mount Strut To A/C Bracket Bolt	37
	Engine Mount Strut To Alternator Bracket	37
	Engine Mount Strut To Lift Bracket Bolt	52
	Engine Mount Strut To Support Bracket Bolt	18
	Engine Oil Pressure Switch	12
	Engine Wiring Harness Bracket	115①
	EVAP Purge Valve Bolt	12
	Exhaust Manifold Heat Shield Bolt	89①
	Exhaust Manifold Nut	12
	Flywheel Bolt	52
	Front Cover (Large & Medium Bolts)	41
	Front Cover (Small Bolts)	20
	Fuel Feed Pipe To Injector Rail Bolt	89①
	Fuel Injector Rail Bolt	89①
	Heater Inlet Pipe Nut	18
	Ignition Coil Bracket Bolt	18
	Intake Manifold Coolant Pipe Bolt	89①
	Intake Manifold (Lower)	⑥
	Intake Manifold (Upper)	18
	Knock Sensor	18
	Main Bearing Cap Bolt	④
	MAP Sensor	89①
	Oil Dipstick Tube Bolt	18
	Oil Filter	22
	Oil Filter Adapter Bolt	18
	Oil Filter Bypass Hole Plug	14
	Oil Filter Fitting	29

TIGHTENING SPECIFICATIONS—Continued

Year	Component	Torque/Ft. Lbs.
2007–08	Oil Pan Bolt	18
	Oil Pan Drain Plug	18
	Oil Pan Side Bolt	37
	Oil Pump Cover Bolt	89①
	Oil Pump Drive Clamp Bolt	27
	Oil Pump Mounting Bolt	30
	Oxygen Sensor	31
	PCV Tube Clip Bolt	89①
	Rocker Arm Bolt	24
	Spark Plug	15
	Thermostat Bypass Pipe To Front Cover	89①
	Thermostat Bypass Pipe To Throttle Body	89①
	Throttle Body Bolt	89①
	Timing Chain Dampener Bolt	15
	Valve Lifter Guide Bolt	89①
	Valve Rocker Arm Bolt	24
	Valve Cover Bolts	89①
	Water Outlet Bolt	18
	Water Pump Bolt	89①
	Water Pump Pulley Bolt	18

① — Inch lbs.

② — 18 ft. lbs., plus an additional 110.°

③ — 92 ft. lbs., plus an additional 130.°

④ — 37 ft. lbs., plus an additional 77.°

⑤ — Refer to "Cylinder Head, Replace" for tightening procedure.

⑥ — Refer to "Intake Manifold, Replace" for tightening procedure.

3.5L ENGINE

3.6L Engine

NOTE: On Air Bag Equipped Models, Refer To "Air Bag System Precautions" Located In The Front Of This Manual For System Disarming & Arming Procedures.

NOTE: Refer To "Computer Relearn Procedures" Located In The Front Of This Manual When Battery Power To The Computer Has Been Interrupted.

INDEX

	Page No.		Page No.		Page No.
Camshaft, Replace	12-83	Righthand	12-80	Replacement	12-84
Compression Pressure	12-79	Front Cover, Replace	12-81	Thermostat, Replace	12-84
Cooling System Bleed	12-84	Fuel Pump, Replace	12-85	Tightening Specifications	12-90
Crankshaft Damper, Replace	12-81	Intake Manifold, Replace	12-80	Timing Chain, Replace	12-81
Crankshaft Front Oil Seal,		Lower	12-80	Lefthand Secondary Drive	
Replace	12-83	Upper	12-80	Chain	12-82
Crankshaft Rear Oil Seal,		Main & Rod Bearings	12-83	Installation	12-82
Replace	12-83	Oil Pan, Replace	12-84	Removal	12-82
Cylinder Head, Replace	12-80	Oil Pump, Replace	12-84	Primary Drive Chain	12-81
Lefthand	12-80	Oil Pump Service	12-84	Installation	12-81
Righthand	12-80	Piston & Rod Assembly	12-83	Removal	12-81
Engine Rebuilding		Pistons, Pins & Rings	12-83	Righthand Secondary Drive	
Specifications	29-1	Precautions	12-79	Chain	12-81
Engine, Replace	12-80	Air Bag Systems	12-79	Installation	12-82
Engine Mount, Replace	12-79	Battery Ground Cable	12-79	Removal	12-81
Engine Mount Strut, Replace	12-79	Fuel System Pressure Relief	12-79	Valve Adjustment	12-81
Exhaust Manifold, Replace	12-80	Radiator, Replace	12-85	Valve Cover, Replace	12-80
Lefthand	12-80	Serpentine Drive Belt	12-84	Water Pump, Replace	12-84

PRECAUTIONS

Air Bag Systems

Refer to "Air Bag System Precautions" in the front of this manual for system disarming and arming procedures.

Battery Ground Cable

Prior to service, disconnect battery ground cable and isolate as required.

Fuel System Pressure Relief

To reduce the risk of fire and personal injury, relieve the fuel system pressure before servicing fuel system components.
1. Turn ignition Off.
2. Remove fuel pump fuse and fuel pump relay.
3. Loosen fuel filler cap to relieve fuel tank vapor pressure.
4. Attempt to start engine and allow engine to run until it stops.
5. Loosen fuel tank filler cap to relieve tank pressure.
6. Connect fuel pressure gauge tool No. J34730-1, or equivalent, to fuel pressure valve. Wrap a shop towel around fitting while connecting gauge to avoid spillage.
7. Install bleed hose into suitable container and open valve to bleed system pressure.

COMPRESSION PRESSURE

1. Ensure battery is at full charge.
2. Start and run engine until it reaches normal operating temperature.
3. Turn engine Off, then remove Powertrain Control Module (PCM) and ignition fuse from instrument panel fuse block.
4. Remove spark plugs from all cylinders.
5. Remove air duct from throttle body and block throttle plate in open position.
6. Thread compression gauge into spark plug hole.
7. Crank engine through at least four compression strokes.
8. Record readings on gauge at each stroke.
9. Repeat test on each cylinder.
10. Lowest reading should not be less than 70 percent of the highest reading. No cylinder reading should be less than 140 psi.

ENGINE MOUNT
REPLACE

1. Remove air cleaner assembly.
2. Remove engine mount strut to engine mount strut bracket bolts.
3. Rotate engine mount strut to vertical position.
4. Remove engine mount strut bracket bolts and engine mount strut bracket.
5. Rotate drive belt tensioner clockwise to release drive belt tension using a long breaker bar, then slide drive belt off of belt idler pulley.
6. Slowly release drive belt tensioner and remove drive belt from accessory drive pulleys.
7. Support engine using engine support fixture tool No. J 28467-B, or equivalent.
8. Raise and support vehicle.
9. Remove three upper engine mount bracket bolts, **Fig. 1.**
10. Loosen right upper front engine mount bracket bolt.
11. Remove upper engine mount bracket nuts, **Fig. 2.**
12. Remove lower bracket bolts, mount and lower bracket from vehicle.
13. Remove upper bracket bolt from bracket.
14. Remove upper bracket and engine mount from lower bracket.
15. Reverse procedure to install.

ENGINE MOUNT STRUT
REPLACE

1. Remove mounting bolt and nut from engine mount strut at engine mount strut bracket on engine.
2. Remove mounting bolt and nut from engine mount strut at engine mount strut bracket on upper radiator support.

3. Remove engine mount strut.
4. Reverse procedure to install.

ENGINE

REPLACE

Refer to "Engine, Replace" in the "3.5L Engine" section for procedure.

INTAKE MANIFOLD

REPLACE

Upper

1. Remove fuel injector sight shield from top of engine.
2. Remove air inlet duct, then disconnect brake booster vacuum hose from intake manifold.
3. Relieve fuel system pressure as outlined under "Precautions."
4. Disconnect fuel feed line quick connect fitting from fuel rail.
5. Remove fuel feed pipe line nut and fuel feed line clip from stud. Position fuel feed line aside.
6. Remove coolant air bleed hose/pipe clip bolt from upper intake manifold.
7. Remove coolant air bleed hose from water outlet.
8. Remove coolant air bleed hose/pipe clip from upper intake manifold stud and position aside.
9. Remove brake booster vacuum hose from upper intake manifold.
10. Disconnect engine wiring harness electrical connectors from Manifold Absolute Pressure (MAP) sensor and Electronic Throttle Control (ETC).
11. Disconnect electrical connector and purge line from canister purge solenoid valve.
12. Remove wiring harness retainer from front of intake manifold.
13. Disconnect PCV tube from upper intake manifold and position aside.
14. Disconnect EVAP canister purge solenoid tube quick connect fitting at upper intake manifold and position aside.
15. Remove fuel rail to bracket bolt.
16. Remove fuel rail wiring harness electrical connector bolt and position harness aside.
17. Remove upper intake manifold mounting bolts, then the manifold with throttle body from engine.
18. Reverse procedure to install.

Lower

1. Remove upper intake manifold as outlined under "Upper."
2. Remove fuel rail with fuel injectors from lower intake manifold.
3. Remove lower intake manifold mounting bolts.
4. Remove lower intake manifold.
5. Reverse procedure to install.

EXHAUST MANIFOLD

REPLACE

Lefthand

1. Remove heat shield mounting bolts,

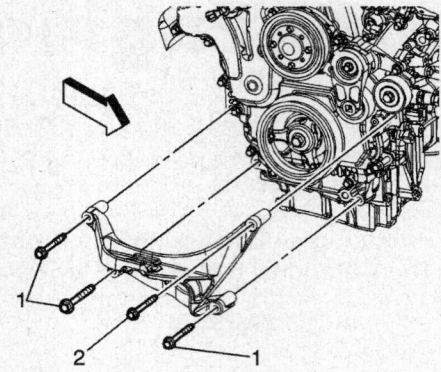

1-Upper engine mount bracket bolts
2-Right upper front engine mount bracket bolt

ARM0600000000052

Fig. 1   Upper engine mount bracket bolts

then the heat shield.
2. Remove exhaust manifold upper and lower insulators from oil dipstick tube.
3. Remove oil level indicator tube bolt, then pull tube up through exhaust manifold.
4. Remove lefthand catalytic converter.
5. Remove lefthand exhaust manifold mounting nuts, then the exhaust manifold.
6. Reverse procedure to install.

Righthand

1. Remove exhaust manifold heat shield.
2. Remove catalytic converter to exhaust manifold nuts.
3. Remove bank 1 sensor 2 HO2S.
4. Remove left catalytic converter to right catalytic converter attaching nuts.
5. Remove exhaust pipe to right catalytic converter nuts.
6. Remove catalytic converter from vehicle.
7. Remove exhaust manifold lower bolts and lower vehicle half way.
8. Remove exhaust manifold to cylinder head mounting bolts, then the exhaust manifold.
9. Reverse procedure to install.

CYLINDER HEAD

REPLACE

Lefthand

1. Remove lefthand secondary timing chain as outlined under "Timing Chain, Replace."
2. Remove oil level indicator tube bolt, then pull tube up through exhaust manifold.
3. Remove heat shield from coolant temperature sensor and disconnect sensor electrical connector.
4. Remove wiring harness ground from cylinder head.
5. Remove exhaust manifold heat shield.
6. Remove left catalytic converter to exhaust manifold nuts.
7. Remove bank 2 HO2S sensor 2 con-

nector position assurance retainer, then disconnect HO2S electrical connector from engine wiring harness connector.
8. Remove lefthand catalytic converter to righthand catalytic converter nuts.
9. Remove lefthand catalytic converter.
10. Remove cylinder head bolts, then the cylinder head with exhaust manifold.
11. Reverse procedure to install, noting the following:
   a. Install new M11 bolts.
   b. Refer to sequence, **Fig. 3,** and tighten M11 bolts in two steps: First step, **torque** bolts to 22 ft. lbs.; second step, tighten bolts an additional 150.°
   c. Refer to sequence, **Fig. 3,** tighten M8 bolts in two steps: First step, **torque** bolts to 11 ft. lbs.; second step, tighten bolts an additional 75.°

Righthand

1. Remove righthand secondary timing chain as outlined under "Timing Chain, Replace."
2. Remove coolant inlet pipe.
3. Remove wiring harness ground from cylinder head.
4. Disconnect wiring harness electrical connector from side of cylinder head.
5. Remove wiring harness conduit upper bolt from cylinder head, then position conduit aside.
6. Remove battery cable from cylinder head.
7. Remove righthand catalytic converter.
8. Remove exhaust manifold mounting bolts, then the exhaust manifold.
9. Remove cylinder head mounting bolts, then the cylinder head. **Discard cylinder head bolts.**
10. Reverse procedure to install, noting the following:
   a. Install new M11 bolts.
   b. Refer to sequence, **Fig. 4,** and tighten bolts in two steps: First step, **torque** bolts to 22 ft. lbs.; second step, tighten bolts an additional 150.°

VALVE COVER

REPLACE

1. Remove upper intake manifold as outlined under "Intake Manifold, Replace."
2. Remove wiring harness from side of camshaft cover.
3. Remove wiring harness conduit retainers from camshaft cover by rotating counterclockwise.
4. Remove wiring harness from front of camshaft cover and position aside.
5. Remove ignition coil as outlined under "Ignition Coil, Replace" in "Electrical" section.
6. Remove camshaft cover mounting bolts, then the camshaft cover, **Fig. 5.**
7. Reverse procedure to install.

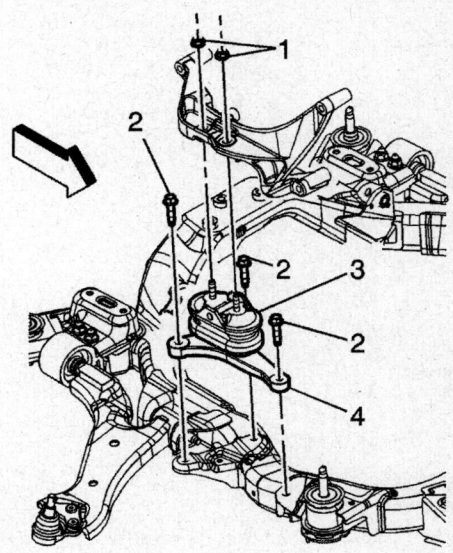

1-Upper engine mount bracket nuts
2-Lower bracket bolts
3-Enging mount
4-Lower bracket

ARM0600000000053

Fig. 2 Engine mount replacement

VALVE ADJUSTMENT

This engine is equipped with hydraulic valve lash adjusters. No adjustment is required.

CRANKSHAFT DAMPER

REPLACE

1. Remove drive belts as outlined under "Serpentine Drive Belt."
2. Raise and support vehicle.
3. Remove crankshaft balancer mounting bolt.
4. Remove crankshaft balancer using harmonic balancer pulling tool No. J 24420-C, or equivalent.
5. Reverse procedure to install.

FRONT COVER

REPLACE

1. Remove fuel injector sight shield.
2. Remove upper and lower intake manifolds as outlined under "Intake Manifold, Replace."
3. Remove camshaft covers as outlined under "Valve Cover, Replace."
4. Drain engine coolant and disconnect purge vent hose from water outlet.
5. Remove water outlet with radiator hose and position aside.
6. Remove drive belts as outlined under "Serpentine Drive Belt."
7. Remove idler pulley and drive belt tensioners.
8. Remove alternator and alternator bracket.
9. Remove power steering fluid reservoir and position aside.
10. Remove power steering pump pulley.

11. Remove power steering pump upper front bolt, then loosen two remaining bolts.
12. Remove crankshaft balancer as outlined under "Crankshaft Damper, Replace."
13. Remove camshafts as outlined under "Camshaft, Replace."
14. Remove camshaft position actuator solenoid valves, **Fig. 6.**
15. Remove front cover mounting bolts, then the cover.
16. Reverse procedure to install.

TIMING CHAIN

REPLACE

Primary Drive Chain

REMOVAL

1. Remove spark plugs.
2. Remove front cover as outlined under "Front Cover, Replace."
3. Remove righthand side secondary camshaft drive chain tensioner mounting bolts, then the drive chain tensioner, **Fig. 7.**
4. Remove righthand side secondary timing chain shoe, then the righthand side secondary drive chain.
5. Remove primary camshaft drive chain tensioner.
6. Remove primary camshaft drive chain upper guide, then the primary chain.

INSTALLATION

1. Install camshaft holding tool No. 46105, or equivalent, onto camshafts.
2. Wrap primary camshaft drive chain around large sprockets of each camshaft intermediate chain idler and crankshaft sprocket.
3. Align lefthand side camshaft intermediate drive chain idler timing mark with bright plated camshaft drive chain link, **Fig. 8.**
4. Align righthand side camshaft intermediate drive chain idler timing mark with bright plated camshaft drive chain link, **Fig. 8.**
5. Align crankshaft sprocket timing mark with bright plated camshaft drive chain link, **Fig. 8.**
6. Compress primary drive chain tensioner plunger into tensioner body using tensioner tool No. J 45027, or equivalent.
7. Install tensioner retraction pins tool No. 46112, or equivalent, into tensioner body to hold plunger in place.
8. Install a new primary camshaft drive chain tensioner gasket to primary camshaft drive chain tensioner.
9. Install primary camshaft drive chain tensioner bolts through primary camshaft drive chain tensioner and gasket.
10. Install drive tensioner, then tighten bolts loosely.
11. Ensure tensioner gasket is in place, then tighten tensioner bolts to specification.
12. Remove tensioner retraction pins and release tensioner plunger.
13. Place righthand side secondary cam-

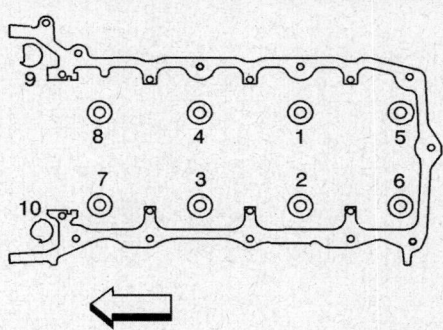

ARM0600000000054

Fig. 3 Lefthand cylinder head bolt tightening sequence

shaft drive chain around righthand side camshaft intermediate drive chain idler outer sprocket, align bright plated camshaft drive link with alignment access hole in camshaft drive chain idler inner sprocket, **Fig. 9.**
14. Wrap secondary camshaft drive chain around both righthand side actuator drive sprockets, ensure there are seven darkened links between bright plated camshaft drive chain links for camshaft position actuator sprockets, **Fig. 10.**
15. Align righthand side exhaust camshaft position actuator sprocket alignment triangle mark with bright plated camshaft drive chain link, **Fig. 11.**
16. Align righthand side intake camshaft position actuator sprocket alignment triangle mark with bright plated camshaft drive chain link, **Fig. 12.**
17. Install chain guide.
18. Compress righthand side secondary camshaft drive chain tensioner plunger into tensioner body using tensioner tool No. J 45027, or equivalent.
19. Install tensioner retraction pins tool No. 46112, or equivalent, into tensioner body to hold plunger in place.
20. Install a new righthand side secondary camshaft drive chain tensioner gasket to drive chain tensioner.
21. Install righthand side secondary camshaft drive chain tensioner bolts through drive chain tensioner and gasket.
22. Install drive tensioner, then tighten bolts loosely.
23. Ensure tensioner gasket is in place, then tighten tensioner bolts to specification.
24. Remove tensioner retraction pins and release tensioner plunger.
25. Ensure all timing marks are aligned, **Fig. 13.**
26. Install front cover as outlined under "Front Cover, Replace."
27. Install spark plugs.

Righthand Secondary Drive Chain

REMOVAL

1. Remove spark plugs.
2. Remove front cover as outlined under "Front Cover, Replace."

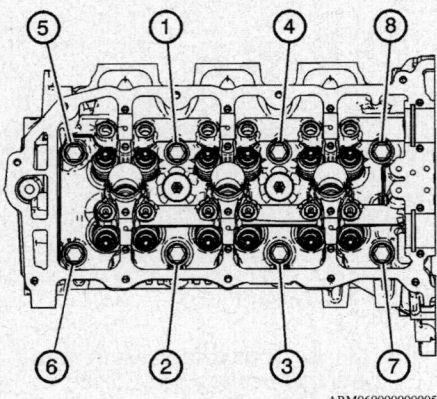

Fig. 4 Righthand cylinder head bolt tightening sequence

3. Remove righthand side secondary camshaft drive chain tensioner mounting bolts, then the drive chain tensioner, **Fig. 7.**
4. Remove righthand side secondary timing chain shoe, then the righthand side secondary drive chain.

INSTALLATION

1. Hold righthand camshafts in place by installing camshaft holding tool No. 46105, or equivalent, onto camshafts.
2. Place righthand side secondary camshaft drive chain around righthand side camshaft intermediate drive chain idler outer sprocket, align bright plated camshaft drive link with alignment access hole in camshaft drive chain idler inner sprocket, **Fig. 9.**
3. Wrap secondary camshaft drive chain around both righthand side actuator drive sprockets, ensure there are seven darkened links between bright plated camshaft drive chain links for camshaft position actuator sprockets, **Fig. 10.**
4. Align righthand side exhaust camshaft position actuator sprocket alignment triangle mark with bright plated camshaft drive chain link, **Fig. 11.**
5. Align righthand side intake camshaft position actuator sprocket alignment triangle mark with bright plated camshaft drive chain link, **Fig. 12.**
6. Compress righthand side secondary camshaft drive chain tensioner plunger into tensioner body using tensioner tool No. J 45027, or equivalent.
7. Install tensioner retraction pins tool No. 46112, or equivalent, into tensioner body to hold plunger in place.
8. Install a new righthand side secondary camshaft drive chain tensioner gasket to drive chain tensioner.
9. Install righthand side secondary camshaft drive chain tensioner bolts through drive chain tensioner and gasket.
10. Install drive tensioner, then tighten bolts loosely.
11. Ensure tensioner gasket is in place, then tighten tensioner bolts to specification.
12. Remove tensioner retraction pins and

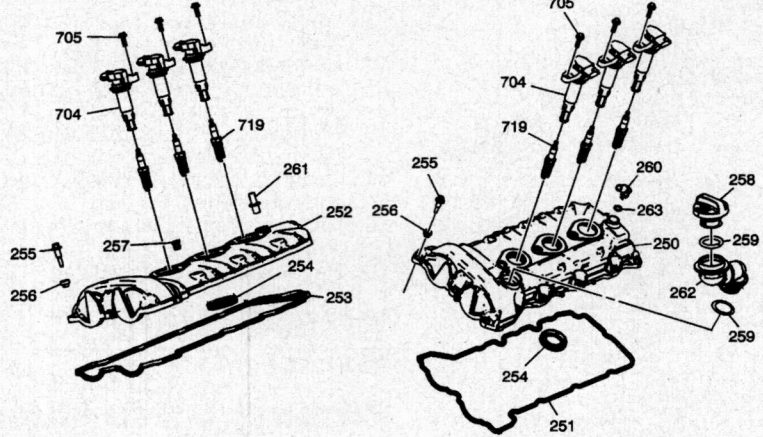

(250) Left Camshaft Cover
(251) Left Camshaft Cover Gasket
(252) Right Camshaft Cover
(253) Right Camshaft Cover Gasket
(254) Camshaft Cover Spark Plug Port Seal
(254) Camshaft Cover Spark Plug Port Seal
(255) Camshaft Cover Bolt
(255) Camshaft Cover Bolt
(256) Camshaft Cover Bolt Insulator
(256) Camshaft Cover Bolt Insulator
(257) Ignition Coil Bolt Thread Insert
(258) Oil Fill Cap

(259) Oil Fill O-Ring
(259) Oil Fill O-Ring
(260) Left Camshaft Cover PCV Fitting
(261) Right Camshaft Cover PCV Fitting Orifice
(262) Oil Fill Tube
(263) Left Camshaft Cover PCV Fitting O-Ring
(704) Ignition Coil
(704) Ignition Coil
(705) Ignition Coil Bolt
(705) Ignition Coil Bolt
(719) Spark Plug
(719) Spark Plug

Fig. 5 Camshaft covers

release tensioner plunger.
13. Ensure all timing marks are aligned, **Fig. 13.**
14. Install front cover as outlined under "Front Cover, Replace."
15. Install spark plugs.

Lefthand Secondary Drive Chain

REMOVAL

1. Remove primary drive chain as outlined under "Primary Drive Chain."
2. Remove lefthand side secondary camshaft drive chain tensioner and chain guide.
3. Remove lefthand side secondary camshaft drive chain idler.
4. Remove lefthand side secondary camshaft drive chain.

INSTALLATION

1. Hold lefthand camshafts in place by installing camshaft holding tool No. 46105, or equivalent, onto camshafts.
2. Ensure crankshaft is in "Stage 1" timing drive assembly position, **Fig. 14.**
3. Place lefthand side secondary camshaft drive chain around inner sprocket of camshaft intermediate drive chain idler with bright plated drive chain link aligned to access hole in idler outer sprocket, **Fig. 15.**
4. Wrap secondary camshaft drive chain around both lefthand side actuator drive sprockets.

5. Ensure there are seven darkened links between bright plated camshaft drive chain links for camshaft position actuator sprockets, **Fig. 16.**
6. Align lefthand side exhaust camshaft position actuator sprocket alignment circle mark with bright plated camshaft drive chain link, **Fig. 17.**
7. Align lefthand side intake camshaft position actuator sprocket alignment circle mark with bright plated camshaft drive chain link, **Fig. 18.**
8. Install chain guide.
9. Compress lefthand side secondary camshaft drive chain tensioner plunger into tensioner body using tensioner tool No. J 45027, or equivalent.
10. Install tensioner retraction pins tool No. 46112, or equivalent, into tensioner body to hold plunger in place.
11. Install a new lefthand side secondary camshaft drive chain tensioner gasket to drive chain tensioner.
12. Install lefthand side secondary camshaft drive chain tensioner bolts through drive chain tensioner and gasket.
13. Install drive tensioner, then tighten bolts loosely.
14. Ensure tensioner gasket is in place, then tighten tensioner bolts to specification.
15. Remove tensioner retraction pins and release tensioner plunger.
16. Install righthand side camshaft secondary and primary timing chains.
17. Ensure all timing marks are aligned, **Fig. 13.**

18. Install front cover as outlined under "Front Cover, Replace."

CAMSHAFT
REPLACE

1. Remove camshaft cover as outlined under "Valve Cover, Replace."
2. Remove camshaft position actuator solenoid.
3. Remove crankshaft balancer as outlined under "Crankshaft Damper, Replace."
4. Rotate crankshaft until camshafts are in a neutral (low tension) position. Camshaft flats will be parallel with camshaft cover rail.
5. Hold camshafts in place with a suitable open end wrench, then loosen camshaft position actuator (sprocket) bolts.
6. Install timing chain retention tool No. 46108, or equivalent, over lefthand side secondary timing chain.
7. Mark timing chain and actuators (sprockets) for installation reference.
8. Remove camshaft actuator (sprocket) mounting bolts.
9. Prior to removing camshafts, observe markings on camshaft bearing caps as follows:
    a. Each bearing cap is marked in order to identify its location.
    b. Raised feature on cap must always be oriented toward center of cylinder head.
    c. Stamped letter "I" indicates intake camshaft and stamped letter "E" indicates exhaust camshaft.
    d. Stamped number indicates journal position from front of engine.
10. Remove camshafts from cylinder head.
11. Reverse procedure to install, noting the following:
    a. Apply a liberal amount of lubricant GM part No. 12345501, or equivalent, to camshaft journals and lefthand side cylinder head camshaft carriers.
    b. Position camshaft lobes in a neutral position with flats on back of camshafts up and parallel with cylinder head camshaft cover rail.
    c. Apply a liberal amount of lubricant GM part No. 12345501, or equivalent, to camshaft bearing caps.
    d. Refer to sequence, **Fig. 19**, **torque** camshaft bearing cap bolts to 89 inch lbs.
    e. Loosen center intake camshaft bearing cap bolts (1 and 2) and center exhaust camshaft bearing cap bolts (3 and 4), then **torque** camshaft bearing cap bolts 1, 2, 3 and 4 to 89 inch lbs.

PISTON & ROD ASSEMBLY

When installing piston and rod assemblies into cylinder block, ensure dot on top of piston faces toward front of engine.

Tighten connecting rod bolts in four steps as follows: First step, **torque** bolts to

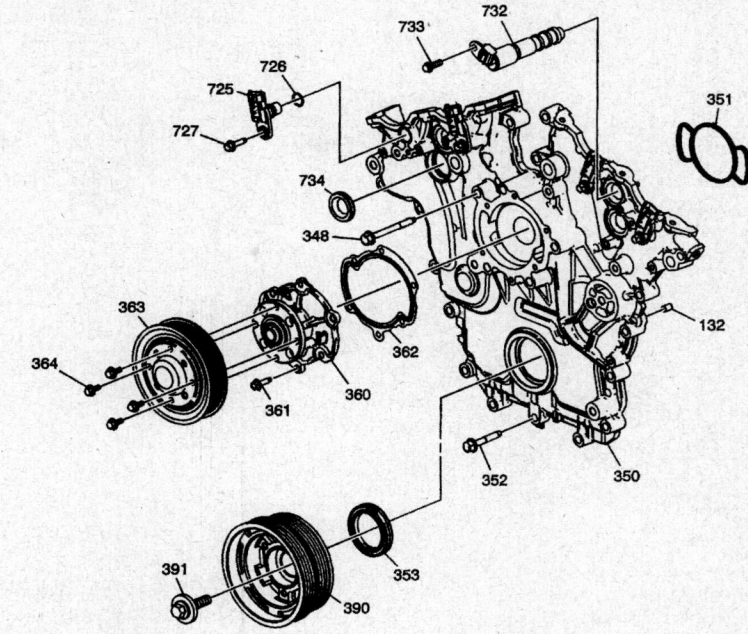

(132) Engine Front Cover Locating Pin
(348) Engine Front Cover Bolt - M10
(350) Engine Front Cover
(351) Engine Front Cover Gasket
(352) Engine Front Cover Bolt - M8
(353) Engine Front Cover Seal
(360) Water Pump Assembly
(361) Water Pump Bolt
(362) Water Pump Gasket
(363) Water Pump Pulley

(364) Water Pump Pulley Bolt
(390) Crankshaft Balancer
(391) Crankshaft Balancer Bolt
(725) Camshaft Position Sensor
(726) Camshaft Position Sensor O-Ring
(727) Camshaft Position Sensor Bolt
(732) Camshaft Position Actuator Solenoid Valve
(733) Camshaft Position Actuator Solenoid Valve Bolt
(734) Camshaft Position Actuator Solenoid Valve Seal

ARM0300000000253

Fig. 6 Exploded view of front cover

22 ft. lbs.; second step, loosen bolts; third step, **torque** bolts to 18 ft. lbs.; fourth step, tighten bolts an additional 110°.

PISTONS, PINS & RINGS

Pistons and rings are available in standard size and oversize. Pistons and their pins are serviced as an assembly.

MAIN & ROD BEARINGS

Main and rod bearings are available in standard size only. Refer to **Figs. 20 through 22** for main bearing bolt identification and tightening sequence. Tighten main bearing cap bolts as follows: **Torque** inboard bolts 1–8 to 15 ft. lbs., then tighten an additional 80°; **torque** outboard bolts 9–16 to 11 ft. lbs., then tighten an additional 110°; **torque** side short bolts 17–20 to 22 ft. lbs., then an additional 60°.; **torque** side longer bolts 21–24 to 22 ft. lbs., then an additional 60°.

CRANKSHAFT FRONT OIL SEAL
REPLACE

1. Remove crankshaft balancer as outlined under "Crankshaft Damper, Replace."
2. Remove seal using a suitable flat-bladed tool.
3. Reverse procedure to install.

CRANKSHAFT REAR OIL SEAL
REPLACE

1. Remove transmission as outlined in MOTOR's "Domestic Transmission, In-Vehicle Service" manual or "Transmission Service DVD."
2. Remove flywheel bolts, then the flywheel from crankshaft
3. Remove oil pan as outlined under "Oil Pan, Replace."
4. Remove crankshaft rear oil seal housing bolts.
5. Pry oil seal housing from cylinder block using pry points located at edge of housing.
6. Remove oil seal from housing.
7. Reverse procedure to install.

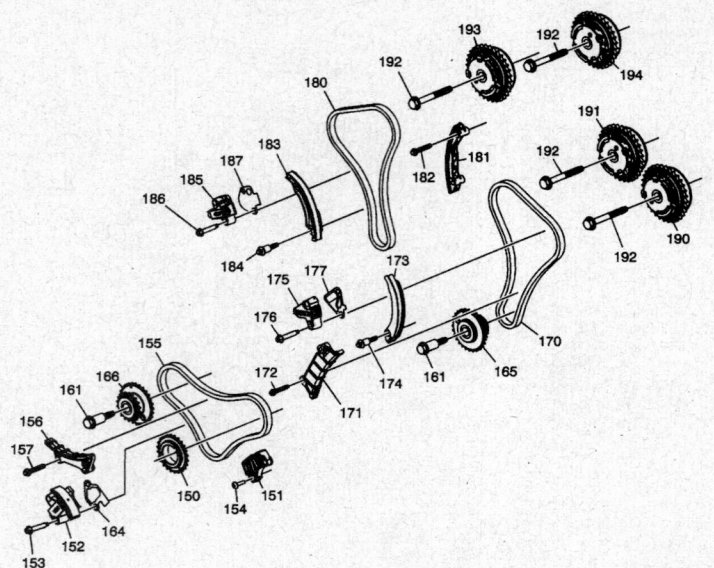

(150) Crankshaft Sprocket
(151) Lower Primary Timing Chain Guide
(152) Primary Timing Chain Tensioner
(153) Primary Timing Chain Tensioner Bolt
(154) Lower Primary Timing Chain Guide Bolt
(155) Primary Timing Chain
(156) Upper Primary Timing Chain Guide
(157) Upper Primary Timing Chain Guide Bolt
(161) Camshaft Intermediate Drive Shaft Sprocket Bolt
(164) Primary Timing Chain Tensioner Gasket
(165) Left Camshaft Intermediate Drive Shaft Sprocket
(166) Right Camshaft Intermediate Drive Shaft Sprocket
(170) Left Secondary Timing Chain
(171) Left Secondary Timing Chain Guide
(172) Left Secondary Timing Chain Guide Bolt
(173) Left Secondary Timing Chain Shoe
(174) Left Secondary Timing Chain Shoe Bolt
(175) Left Secondary Timing Chain Tensioner

(176) Left Secondary Timing Chain Tensioner Bolt
(177) Left Secondary Timing Chain Tensioner Gasket
(180) Right Secondary Timing Chain
(181) Right Secondary Timing Chain Guide
(182) Right Secondary Timing Chain Guide Bolt
(183) Right Secondary Timing Chain Shoe
(184) Right Secondary Timing Chain Shoe Bolt
(185) Right Secondary Timing Chain Tensioner
(186) Right Secondary Timing Chain Tensioner Bolt
(187) Right Secondary Timing Chain Tensioner Gasket
(190) Left Exhaust Camshaft Position Actuator
(191) Left Intake Camshaft Position Actuator
(192) Camshaft Position Actuator Bolt
(192) Camshaft Position Actuator Bolt
(192) Camshaft Position Actuator Bolt
(192) Camshaft Position Actuator Bolt
(193) Right Exhaust Camshaft Position Actuator
(194) Right Intake Camshaft Position Actuator

ARM0300000000254

Fig. 7 Primary & secondary timing chains

OIL PAN

REPLACE

1. Remove engine mount as outlined under "Engine Mount, Replace."
2. Remove drive belt as outlined under "Serpentine Drive Belt."
3. Recover A/C system refrigerant as outlined in "Air Conditioning" chapter.
4. Raise and support vehicle, then drain engine oil.
5. Lower vehicle.
6. Remove exhaust manifold heat shield, then the left catalytic converter to exhaust manifold nuts.
7. Disconnect bank 2 sensor 2 Heated Oxygen Sensor (HO2S) electrical connector from engine wiring harness electrical connector.
8. Raise and support vehicle.
9. Remove left catalytic converter to right catalytic converter nuts.
10. Remove left catalytic converter from vehicle.
11. Remove right front fender liner and disconnect A/C compressor electrical connector.
12. Remove A/C compressor hose from A/C compressor. Cap hose.
13. Remove and discard compressor sealing washers.
14. Remove A/C compressor mounting nut and bolt, then the compressor.
15. Remove oil pan bolts, then pry oil pan from engine block using suitable flat bladed tool.
16. Reverse procedure to install, noting the following:
    a. Apply a suitable bead of silicone sealing compound GM part No. 12346286, or equivalent, to oil pan surface.
    b. Refer to sequence, **Fig. 23, torque** oil pan 8 mm bolts to 17 ft. lbs., and **torque** 6 mm bolts to 89 inch lbs.

OIL PUMP

REPLACE

1. Remove primary timing chain as outlined under "Timing Chain, Replace."
2. Remove crankshaft sprocket.
3. Remove oil pump bolts and the oil pump, **Fig. 24.**
4. Reverse procedure to install.

OIL PUMP SERVICE

There are no serviceable components inside the oil pump. If pump is not working properly, it must be replaced.

SERPENTINE DRIVE BELT

Replacement

1. Remove air cleaner assembly.
2. Remove engine mount strut to engine mount strut bracket bolts.
3. Rotate engine mount strut to vertical position.
4. Remove engine mount strut bracket bolts and strut bracket.
5. Rotate drive belt tensioner clockwise to release drive belt tension.
6. Slide drive belt off of belt idler pulley.
7. Slowly release drive belt tensioner and remove drive belt from accessory drive pulleys.
8. Reverse procedure to install.

COOLING SYSTEM BLEED

1. Place transmission in Park or Neutral position.
2. Engage park brake.
3. Run engine until thermostat opens.
4. Stop engine.
5. Fill system using only clean drinkable water.
6. Repeat procedure if required, until fluid is nearly colorless.
7. Fill coolant reservoir to FULL HOT mark.

THERMOSTAT

REPLACE

1. Drain cooling system.
2. Remove radiator outlet hose from thermostat housing.
3. Remove heater inlet and outlet hoses.
4. Remove surge tank outlet hose from thermostat.
5. Remove thermostat housing bolts, then the thermostat housing.
6. Remove thermostat and discard seal.
7. Reverse procedure to install.

WATER PUMP

REPLACE

1. Drain cooling system into suitable container.
2. Remove drive belt as outlined under "Serpentine Drive Belt."
3. Hold water pump pulley with pulley holding tool No. 46104, or equivalent.
4. Remove water pump pulley bolts, then the pulley.
5. Remove water pump mounting bolts, then the pump. Discard water pump seal.
6. Reverse procedure to install.

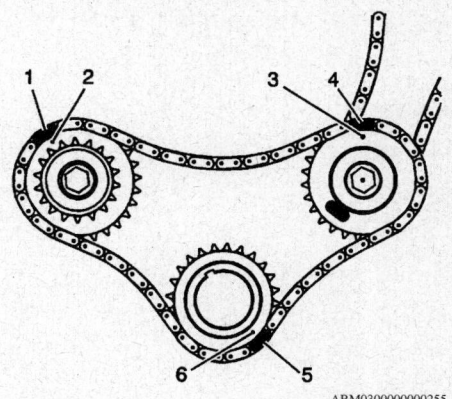

Fig. 8 Primary timing chain alignment marks

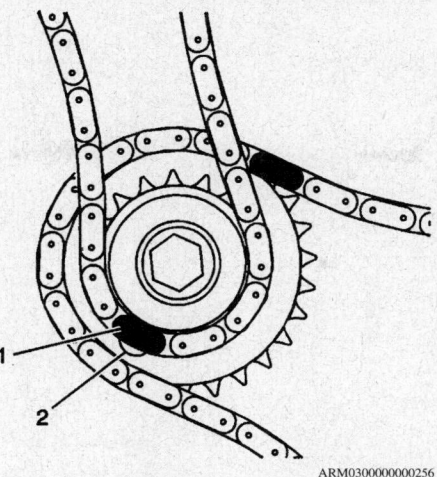

Fig. 9 Righthand camshaft drive chain & intermediate idler sprocket alignment

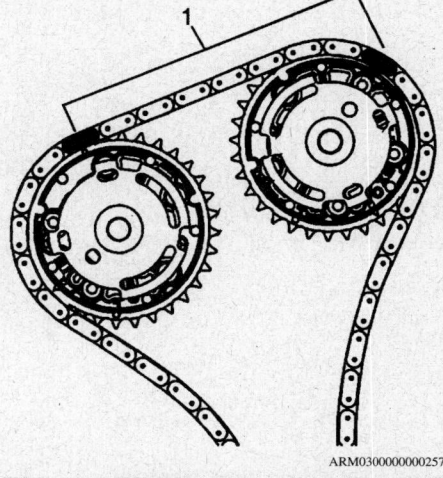

Fig. 10 Righthand camshaft drive chain installation

RADIATOR

REPLACE

Refer to "Radiator, Replace" in "2.4L Engine" section.

FUEL PUMP

REPLACE

Refer to "Fuel Pump, Replace" in "2.4L Engine" section.

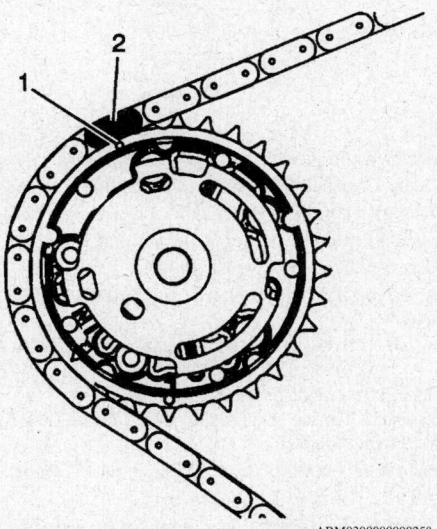

Fig. 11 Righthand camshaft drive chain & exhaust camshaft sprocket alignment

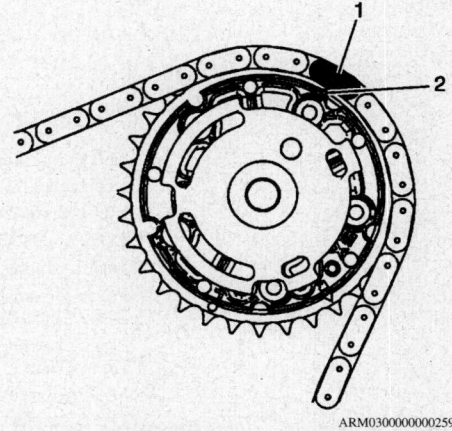

Fig. 12 Righthand camshaft drive chain & intake camshaft sprocket alignment

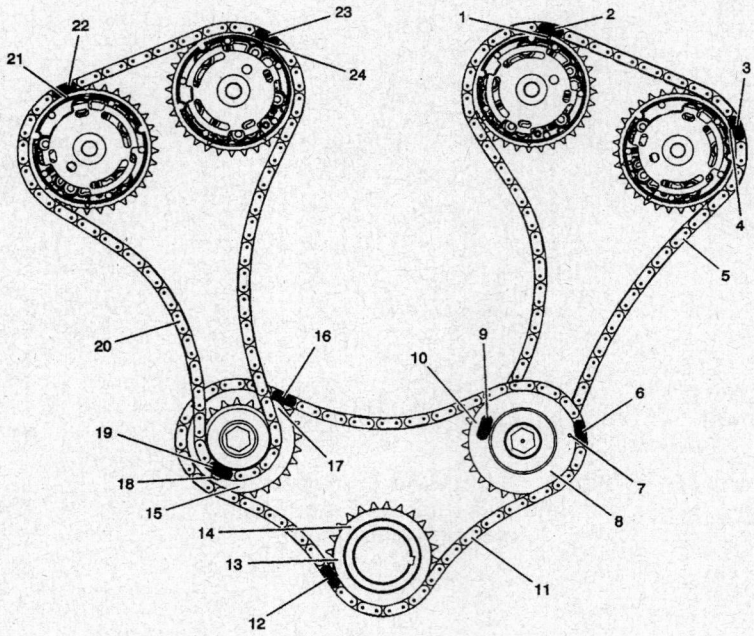

(1) Left Intake Camshaft Position Actuator (CMP) Timing Mark
(2) Left Intake Secondary Camshaft Timing Drive Chain Bright Plated Link
(3) Left Exhaust Secondary Camshaft Timing Drive Chain Bright Plated Link
(4) Left Exhaust Camshaft Position Actuator (CMP) Timing Mark
(5) Left Secondary Camshaft Timing Drive Chain
(6) Primary Camshaft Drive Chain Bright Plated Link for the Left Primary Camshaft Intermediate Drive Chain Sprocket
(7) Left Primary Camshaft Intermediate Drive Chain Sprocket Timing Mark for the Primary Camshaft Drive Chain
(8) Left Primary Camshaft Intermediate Drive Chain Sprocket
(9) Left Secondary Camshaft Timing Drive Chain Bright Plated Link for the Left Primary Camshaft Intermediate Drive Chain Sprocket
(10) Left Primary Camshaft Intermediate Drive Chain Sprocket Timing Window
(11) Primary Camshaft Drive Chain
(12) Primary Camshaft Drive Chain Bright Plated Link for the Crankshaft Sprocket
(13) Crankshaft Sprocket Timing Mark
(14) Crankshaft Sprocket
(15) Right Primary Camshaft Intermediate Drive Chain Sprocket
(16) Primary Camshaft Drive Chain Bright Plated Link for the Right Primary Camshaft Intermediate Drive Chain Sprocket
(17) Right Primary Camshaft Intermediate Drive Chain Sprocket Timing Mark for the Primary Camshaft Drive Chain
(18) Right Primary Camshaft Intermediate Drive Chain Sprocket Timing Mark/Window for the Right Secondary Camshaft Timing Drive Chain
(19) Right Secondary Camshaft Timing Drive Chain Bright Plated Link for the Right Primary Camshaft Intermediate Drive Chain Sprocket
(20) Right Secondary Camshaft Timing Drive Chain
(21) Right Exhaust Camshaft Position Actuator (CMP) Timing Mark
(22) Right Exhaust Secondary Camshaft Timing Drive Chain Bright Plated Link
(23) Right Intake Camshaft Position Actuator (CMP) Timing Mark
(24) Right Intake Camshaft Position Actuator (CMP) Timing Mark

ARM0300000000261

Fig. 13 Timing chain alignment

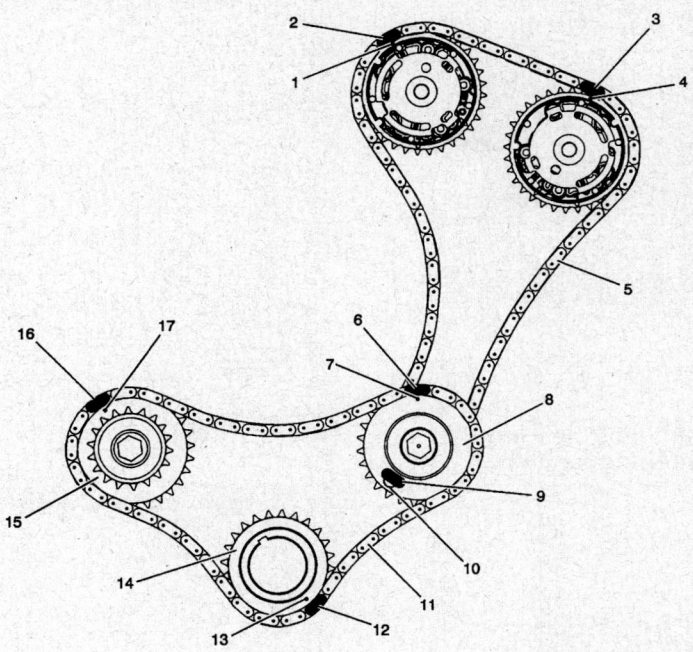

(1) Left Intake Camshaft Position Actuator (CMP) Timing Mark
(2) Left Intake Secondary Camshaft Timing Drive Chain Bright Plated Link
(3) Left Exhaust Secondary Camshaft Timing Drive Chain Bright Plated Link
(4) Left Exhaust Camshaft Position Actuator (CMP) Timing Mark
(5) Left Secondary Camshaft Timing Drive Chain
(6) Primary Camshaft Drive Chain Bright Plated Link for the Left Primary Camshaft Intermediate Drive Chain Sprocket
(7) Left Primary Camshaft Intermediate Drive Chain Sprocket Timing Mark for the Primary Camshaft Drive Chain
(8) Left Primary Camshaft Intermediate Drive Chain Sprocket
(9) Left Secondary Camshaft Timing Drive Chain Bright Plated Link for the Left Primary Camshaft Intermediate Drive Chain Sprocket
(10) Left Primary Camshaft Intermediate Drive Chain Sprocket Timing Window for the Left Secondary Camshaft Timing Drive Chain Bright Plated Link
(11) Primary Camshaft Drive Chain
(12) Primary Camshaft Drive Chain Bright Plated Link for the Crankshaft Sprocket
(13) Crankshaft Sprocket Timing Mark
(14) Crankshaft Sprocket
(15) Right Primary Camshaft Intermediate Drive Chain Sprocket
(16) Primary Camshaft Drive Chain Bright Plated Link for the Right Primary Camshaft Intermediate Drive Chain Sprocket
(17) Right Primary Camshaft Intermediate Drive Chain Sprocket Timing Mark

ARM0300000000260

Fig. 14 Camshaft timing drive chain alignment (stage 1)

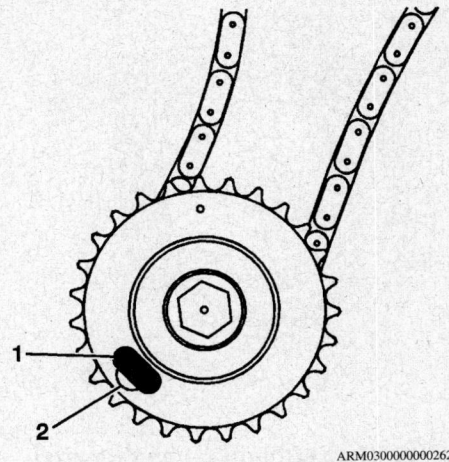

ARM0300000000262

Fig. 15 Lefthand camshaft drive chain idler sprocket alignment

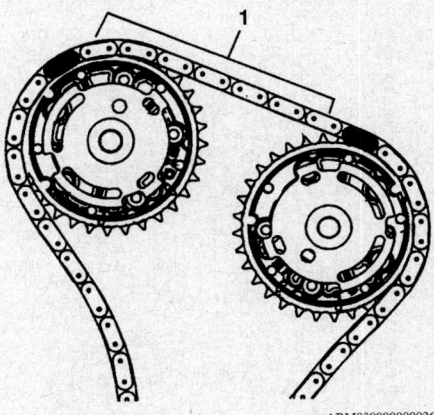

ARM0300000000263

Fig. 16 Lefthand camshaft drive chain installation

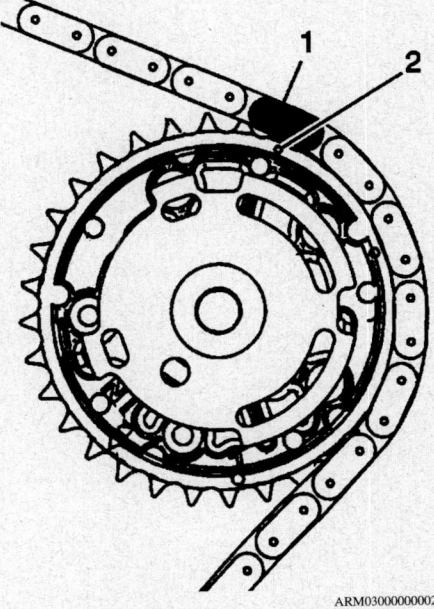

ARM0300000000264

Fig. 17 Lefthand camshaft drive chain & exhaust camshaft sprocket alignment

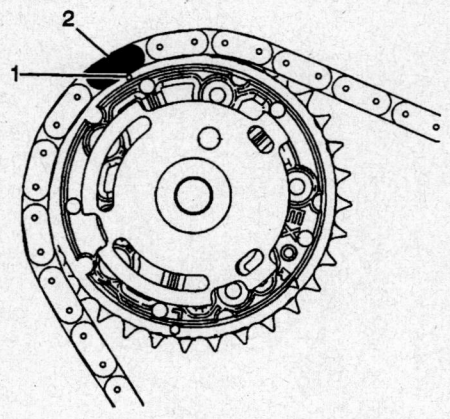

ARM0300000000265

Fig. 18 Lefthand camshaft drive chain & intake camshaft sprocket alignment

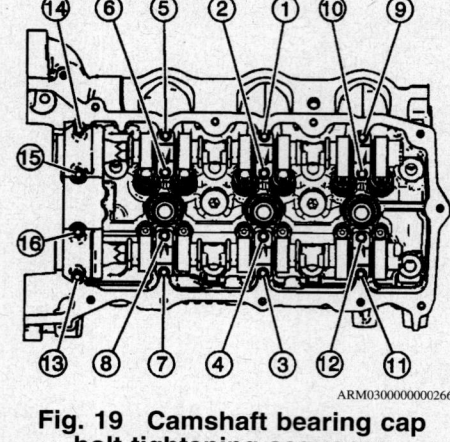

ARM0300000000266

Fig. 19 Camshaft bearing cap bolt tightening sequence

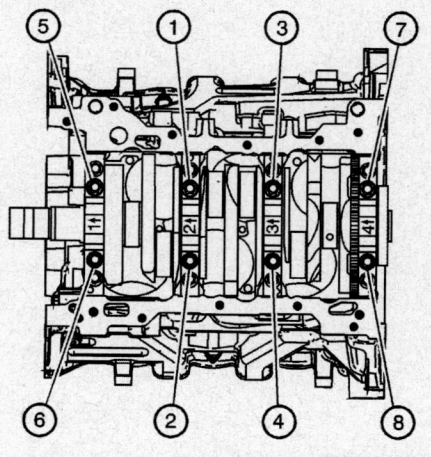

ARM0700000000199

Fig. 20 Main bearing bolts (1–8)

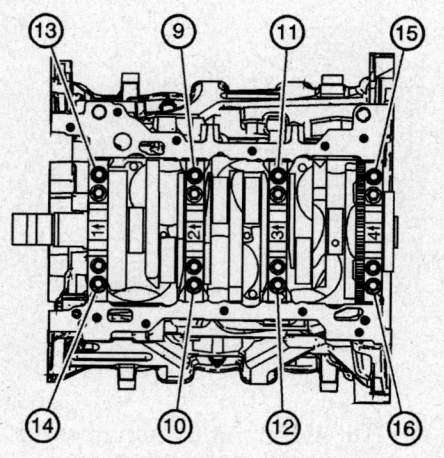

ARM0700000000200

Fig. 21 Main bearing bolts (9–16)

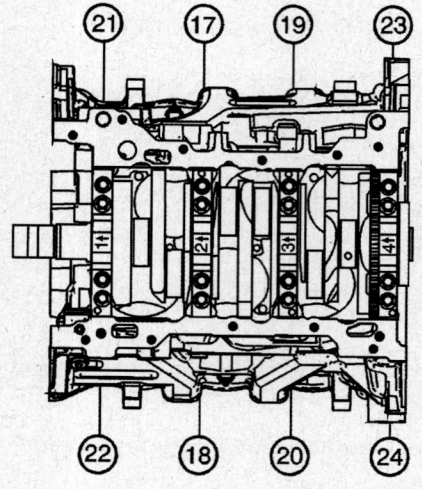

ARM0700000000201

Fig. 22 Main bearing bolts (17–24)

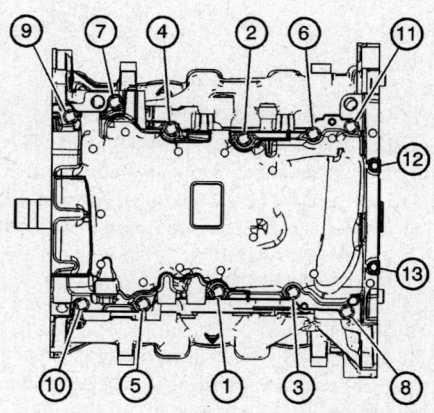

ARM0700000000198

Fig. 23 Oil pan bolt tightening sequence

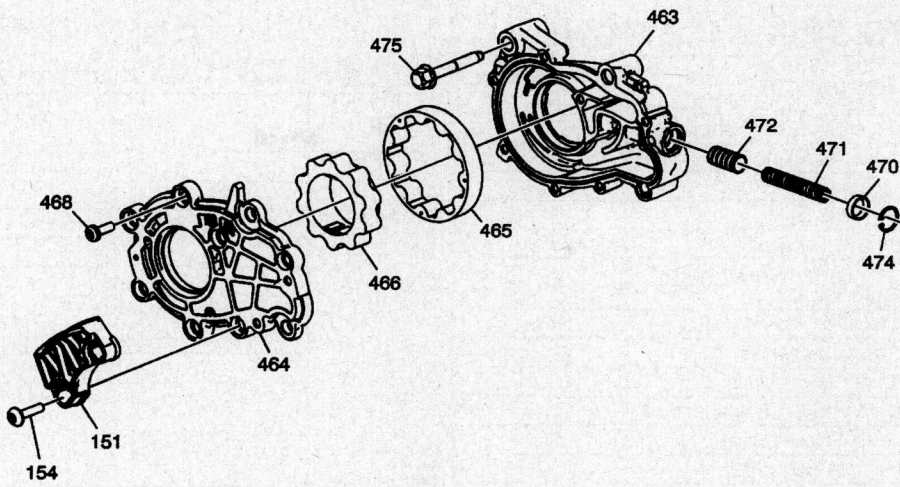

(151) Lower Primary Timing Chain Guide

(154) Lower Primary Timing Chain Guide Bolt

(463) Oil Pump Housing

(464) Oil Pump Cover

(465) Oil Pump Driven Gear

(466) Oil Pump Drive Gear

(468) Oil Pump Cover Bolt

(470) Oil Pressure Relief Valve Bore Plug

(471) Oil Pressure Relief Valve Spring

(472) Oil Pressure Relief Valve

(474) Oil Pressure Relief Valve Bore Plug Retainer Clip

(475) Oil Pump Bolt

ARM0300000000267

Fig. 24 Exploded view of oil pump

TIGHTENING SPECIFICATIONS

Year	Component	Torque Ft. Lbs.
2007–08	A/C Compressor Bracket, Front Bolt	37
	A/C Compressor Bracket, Rear Bolt	17
	A/C Compressor Hose	80①
	Alternator	37
	Camshaft Cap Bolts	89①
	Camshaft Intermediate Drive Idler Sprocket Bolt	48
	Camshaft Position Actuator Bolt	48
	Camshaft Position Sensor Bolt	89①
	Camshaft (Valve) Cover	89①
	Catalytic Converter To Exhaust Manifold	10
	Close Out Cover Bolt	89①
	Connecting Rod Bolts	②
	Coolant Manifold Pipe	89①
	Coolant Outlet	89①
	Crankshaft Balancer Bolt	③
	Crankshaft Main Bearing Bolts	④
	Crankshaft Position Sensor	89①
	Cylinder Head Bolts	⑥
	Drive Belt Idler Pulley	37
	Drive Belt Tensioner	37
	ECM	89①
	ECT Sensor	18
	Engine Mount Bracket To Cylinder Block (M8 Bolt)	28
	Engine Mount Bracket To Cylinder Block (M11 Bolt)	45
	Engine Mount To Bracket	59
	EVAP Purge Valve Bolt	89①
	Exhaust Manifold Bolt	15
	Exhaust Manifold Heat Shield Bolt	89①
	Flywheel Bolts	⑤
	Front Cover Bolts	17
	Fuel Rail Bolt	89①
	Ground Cable Bolt	37
	Heater Inlet/Outlet Pipe	89①
	Ignition Coil Bolt	89①
	Intake Manifold (Upper) To Cylinder Head Bolts	17
	Intake Manifold (Upper) To Intake Manifold (Lower) Bolts	17
	Knock Sensor Bolt	17
	Main Bearing Bolts	④
	MAP Sensor Bolt	89①
	Oil Dipstick Tube Bolt	89①
	Oil Drain Plug	18
	Oil Filter Cap	18
	Oil Filter Housing Adapter To Cylinder Block	17
	Oil Filter Housing Adapter To Cylinder Head	48
	Oil Gallery Plug	23

TIGHTENING SPECIFICATIONS—Continued

Year	Component	Torque Ft. Lbs.
2007–08	Oil Level Sensor	89①
	Oil Pan To Cylinder Block Bolts	17
	Oil Pressure Sender	15
	Oil Pump Bolt	17
	Oxygen Sensor	30
	Power Steering Pump Bracket To Engine	37
	Power Steering Pump Reservoir	18
	Primary Camshaft Drive Chain Guide Bolt	17
	Primary Camshaft Drive Chain Tensioner Bolt	17
	Secondary Camshaft Drive Chain Guide Bolt	17
	Secondary Camshaft Drive Chain Tensioner Bolt	17
	Starter Motor Bolts	37
	Suction Screen Bolt	89①
	Thermostat Housing Bolt	89①
	Throttle Body Bolt	89①
	Torque Converter Bolts	47
	Transmission Mount To Transmission Bolt	45
	Transmission To Engine Bolts	37
	Water Pump Bolts	89①
	Water Pump Pulley Bolts	106①

① — Inch lbs.

② — Refer to "Piston & Rod Assembly" for tightening procedure.

③ — First pass, 74 ft. lbs.; final pass, 150°.

④ — Refer to "Main & Rod Bearings" for tightening sequence & specification.

⑤ — First pass, 22 ft. lbs.; final pass, 45°.

⑥ — Refer to "Cylinder Head, Replace" for tightening sequence & specification.

Rear Axle & Suspension

NOTE: On Air Bag Equipped Models, Refer To "Air Bag System Precautions" Located In The Front Of This Manual For System Disarming & Arming Procedures.

NOTE: Refer To "Computer Relearn Procedures" Located In The Front Of This Manual When Battery Power To The Computer Has Been Interrupted.

INDEX

	Page No.
Adjustment Link, Replace	12-95
SKY	12-95
Ball Joint, Replace	12-94
SKY	12-94
Coil Spring, Replace	12-93
AURA	12-93
ION	12-93
L-Series	12-94
SKY	12-94
Control Arm, Replace	12-94
AURA	12-94
Lower	12-94
Upper	12-94
SKY	12-94
Lower	12-94
Upper	12-94
Differential Carrier, Replace	12-92
SKY	12-92
Hub & Bearing, Replace	12-92
AURA	12-92
ION	12-92

	Page No.
L-Series	12-92
SKY	12-93
Knuckle, Replace	12-95
AURA	12-95
SKY	12-95
Precautions	12-91
Air Bag Systems	12-91
Battery Ground Cable	12-91
Hybrid Battery Service	12-91
Connect	12-92
Disconnect	12-91
Propeller Shaft, Replace	12-92
SKY	12-92
Rear Axle Shaft, Replace	12-92
SKY	12-92
Shock Absorber, Replace	12-93
AURA	12-93
ION	12-93
L-Series	12-93
SKY	12-93
Stabilizer Bar, Replace	12-95

	Page No.
AURA	12-95
L-Series	12-95
SKY	12-95
Strut, Replace	12-93
L-Series	12-93
SKY	12-93
Strut Service	12-93
L-Series	12-93
SKY	12-93
Suspension Insulator, Replace	12-94
ION	12-94
Suspension Support, Replace	12-94
AURA	12-94
L-Series	12-94
Tightening Specifications	12-98
Toe Link, Replace	12-95
AURA	12-95
Trailing Arm, Replace	12-95
AURA	12-95

PRECAUTIONS

Air Bag Systems

Refer to "Air Bag System Precautions" in the front of this manual for system disarming and arming procedures.

Battery Ground Cable

Prior to service, disconnect battery ground cable and isolate as required.

Hybrid Battery Service

DISCONNECT

To help avoid personal injury, always ensure the ignition switch is in the OFF position and the ignition key has been removed prior to working on any 36V components. After the key has been removed, disconnect the battery ground cable and then open the generator battery disconnect control module cover. After waiting for at least 5 minutes, measure the voltage potential using a DMM between the following: 36V positive and battery ground cables; 36V positive bat-

tery cable and vehicle ground; 36V battery ground cable and vehicle ground. All measured voltage levels must be below 3 volts.

1. Remove ignition key from ignition switch.
2. Secure ignition key to ensure that key CANNOT be installed without your knowledge.
3. Disconnect 12 volt battery ground cable.
4. Fold down both rear seat backs, then carefully lift up on load floor rear compartment cover at retaining clip locations, **Fig. 1**.
5. Tilt load floor rear compartment cover towards rear of vehicle slightly, disengage tabs and remove load floor rear compartment cover. **To avoid personal injury, be careful when working in vicinity of generator battery disconnect control module. Internal components will still be live, 36V potential, even when cover has been opened or removed.**
6. Remove generator battery disconnect control module cover bolt, **Fig. 2**.
7. Open and slide generator battery disconnect control module cover to right, removing cover. **Wait at least 5 minutes in order to allow generator con-**

trol module capacitors to discharge.
8. **Never assume battery pack is disabled when generator battery disconnect control module cover is opened. Generator battery will have to be checked for voltage potential using a voltmeter first**
9. Set voltmeter to DC voltage and measure vehicle 12-volt battery voltage (at 12-volt positive jumper location and battery ground cable).
10. Meter should read greater than 12 volts DC.
11. To ensure generator battery has been disabled, inspect generator battery for voltage potential as follows:
    a. Refer to **Fig. 3** for voltage measurement locations.
    b. Measure from positive stud to negative stud, voltage should be less than 3 volts.
    c. Measure from positive stud to vehicle chassis ground, voltage should be less than 3 volts.
    d. Measure from negative stud to vehicle chassis ground, voltage should be less than 3 volts.
12. After verifying there is no voltage present, vehicle is now safe to work on.

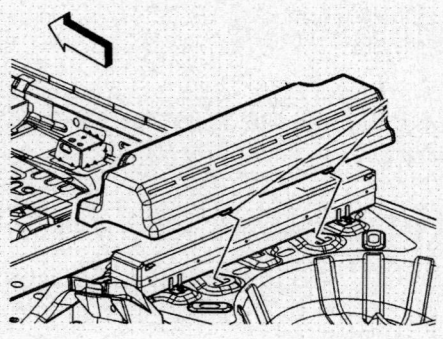

ARM0700000000202

Fig. 1   Rear hybrid battery compartment. AURA

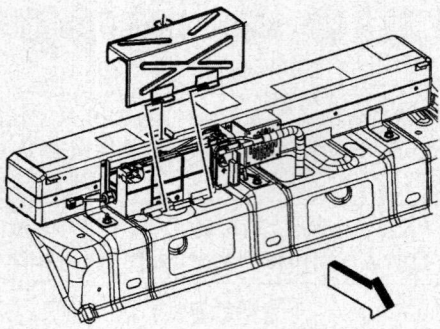

ARM0700000000203

Fig. 2   Disconnect control module cover. AURA

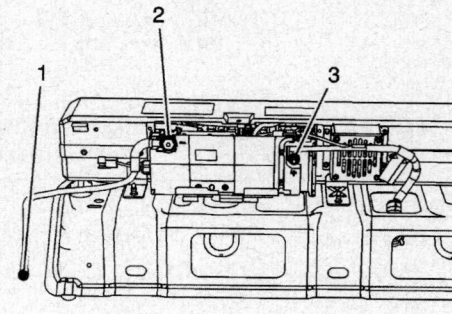

1-Chassis ground
2-Negative stud
3-Positive stud

ARM0700000000204

Fig. 3   Battery disconnect control module voltage measurement locations. AURA

CONNECT

1. Install and close generator battery disconnect control module cover.
2. Install generator battery cover bolt and **torque** to 89 inch lbs.
3. Tilt load floor rear compartment cover towards rear of vehicle slightly in order to insert tabs into battery tray rear support.
4. Set load floor rear compartment cover down, ensure retaining clips align to proper locations, carefully push down to secure cover.
5. Place rear seats backs to their proper positions.
6. Connect 12 volt battery ground cable.

REAR AXLE SHAFT
REPLACE
SKY

1. Raise and support vehicle.
2. Remove propeller shaft as outlined under "Propeller Shaft, Replace."
3. Remove righthand rear tire and wheel assembly.
4. Prevent wheel hub and bearing from turning by inserting suitable drift or punch into brake rotor and against caliper.
5. Remove and discard drive shaft spindle nut.
6. Remove drift or punch from rotor.
7. Separate upper ball joint from rear knuckle.
8. Carefully separate drive shaft from rear differential just enough to install seal protector tool No. J44394, or equivalent, into differential output seal.
9. Remove drive shaft using a suitable puller.
10. Reverse procedure to install. If using original drive shaft, remove and discard shaft retaining ring on splined shaft of cross groove joint.

DIFFERENTIAL CARRIER
REPLACE
SKY

1. Remove drive shafts from differential

as outlined under "Rear Axle, Replace."
2. Support differential carrier using suitable transmission jack.
3. Remove front differential to support mounting bolt and nut.
4. Remove lefthand rear differential to support mounting bolt as much as possible. **Rear differential support mounting bolts will not be able to be removed completely because of interference with underbody.**
5. Remove righthand rear differential to support bolt.
6. Lower jack until mounting ear at front of differential clears support attachment point.
7. Carefully separate wheel drive shaft from differential enough to install seal protector tool No. J44394, or equivalent, over wheel drive shaft.
8. Carefully slide tool into differential output shaft seal.
9. Continue lowering jack, while simultaneously disengaging lefthand wheel drive shaft.
10. Remove differential.
11. Reverse procedure to install.

PROPELLER SHAFT
REPLACE
SKY

1. Raise and support vehicle.
2. Remove exhaust pipe and muffler.
3. Remove driveline tunnel closeout panel.
4. Support rear differential with a suitable adjustable jack stand.
5. Remove left and right rear differential support bolts.
6. Remove front differential support bolt.
7. Remove propeller shaft bolts from transmission output flange.
8. Remove propeller shaft nut and bolts from differential drive flange.
9. Lower rear differential assembly enough to remove propeller shaft from vehicle.
10. Reverse procedure to install.

HUB & BEARING
REPLACE
AURA

1. Raise and support vehicle.
2. Remove tire and wheel assembly.
3. Remove brake rotor as outlined in "Disc Brakes" chapter.
4. Disconnect wheel speed sensor electrical connector.
5. Remove wheel bearing and hub assembly retaining nuts, then the assembly from knuckle.
6. Reverse procedure to install.

ION

1. Raise and support vehicle, then remove the tire and wheel assembly.
2. Remove brake drum.
3. Remove plug from drum brake actuator access hole in backing plate.
4. Install support for brake backing plate through actuator access hole.
5. Disconnect wheel speed sensor electrical connector.
6. Remove wheel bearing and hub mounting nuts.
7. Remove wheel hub and bearing from rear axle assembly and brake backing plate.
8. Reverse procedure to install.

L-Series

1. Raise and support vehicle, then remove tire and wheel assembly.
2. Remove brake rotor as outlined under "Disc Brake" chapter.
3. Disconnect electrical connector from ABS wheel speed sensor.
4. Remove wheel hub to control arm retaining nuts. Discard nuts.

5. Remove wheel bearing and hub as-sembly from vehicle.
6. Reverse procedure to install.

SKY

1. Remove tire and wheel.
2. Remove brake rotor as outlined in "Disc Brakes" chapter.
3. Remove drive axle retaining nut. Dis-card nut.
4. Remove hub and bearing assembly mounting bolts, then the hub and bear-ing assembly.
5. Reverse procedure to install.

STRUT
REPLACE
L-Series

1. Raise and support vehicle, then re-move tire and wheel assembly.
2. Remove inner wheel liner.
3. Remove lower shock mounting bolt. Discard bolt.
4. Remove upper carrier assembly to body bolts.
5. Loosen lower carrier to body bolts, then lift carrier and remove strut from vehicle.
6. Reverse procedure to install.

SKY

1. Raise and support vehicle, then re-move tire and wheel.
2. Separate rear adjustment link from suspension knuckle, refer to "Rear Ad-justment Link, Replace." **Do not loos-en adjustment jam nut.**
3. Remove upper mounting nuts, **Fig. 4.**
4. Remove lower mounting nuts and bolts, then the shock module (strut) to-ward rear of vehicle.
5. Reverse procedure to install.

STRUT SERVICE
L-Series

1. Position strut in strut spring compres-sor tool No. SA9155-S, or equivalent, mounted in suitable holding device.
2. Fasten strut to tool using one strut to knuckle bolt and nut in lower strut mounting hole.
3. Compress spring until upper spring supports are unloaded.
4. Remove strut shaft nut while holding strut shaft in position using suitable Torx wrench.
5. Release spring compressor and tilt strut outward, then remove upper spring support and spring.
6. Remove dust shield and strut from compressor tool.
7. Reverse procedure to assemble, not-ing the following:
   a. Compress spring only enough to in-stall upper washer and shaft nut. **Do not compress spring beyond this point.**

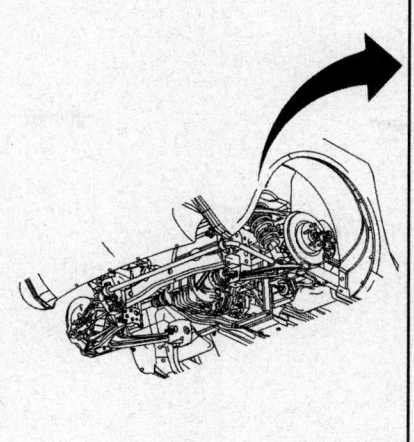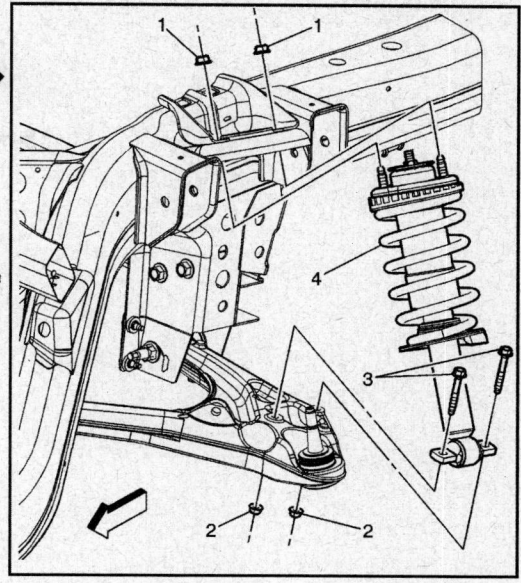

1-Upper Mounting Nuts
2-Lower Mounting Nuts
3-Lower Mounting Bolts
4-Shock module

ARM0600000000062

Fig. 4   Shock module (strut) replacement. SKY

   b. Ensure spring is properly seated in spring supports.

SKY

1. Install shock module (strut) into spring compressor tool No. J 45400, or equiv-alent.
2. Mark upper control arm assembly and insulator for installation reference.
3. Remove shock absorber upper retain-ing nut.
4. Remove shock absorber from strut.
5. Loosen compressor forcing screw until upper mounting plate and coil spring can be removed.
6. Remove upper control arm bracket as-sembly, insulator and coil spring from spring compressor.
7. Reverse procedure to assemble.

SHOCK ABSORBER
REPLACE
AURA

1. Raise and support vehicle.
2. Remove tire and wheel assembly.
3. Place a suitable jack stand under knuckle assembly, then raise jack to relieve spring tension.
4. Remove lower shock absorber to knuckle attaching bolt.
5. Remove upper shock absorber to sup-port assembly attaching nuts, then the shock absorber from vehicle.
6. Reverse procedure to install.

ION

1. Raise and support vehicle, then re-move tire and wheel assembly.
2. Support rear axle with suitable jack stand near shock absorber.
3. Remove upper and lower mounting bolts, then the shock absorber,
4. Reverse procedure to install.

L-Series

Refer to "Strut, Replace" and "Srut Ser-vice" for shock absorber replacement.

SKY

Refer to "Strut, Replace" and "Srut Ser-vice" for shock absorber replacement.

COIL SPRING
REPLACE
AURA

1. Raise and support vehicle.
2. Remove tire and wheel assembly.
3. Place a suitable jack stand under lower control arm.
4. Remove lower control arm to knuckle attaching bolt and nut.
5. Lower control arm with coil spring at-tached.
6. Remove coil spring from lower control arm.
7. Reverse procedure to install.

ION

1. Raise and support vehicle.

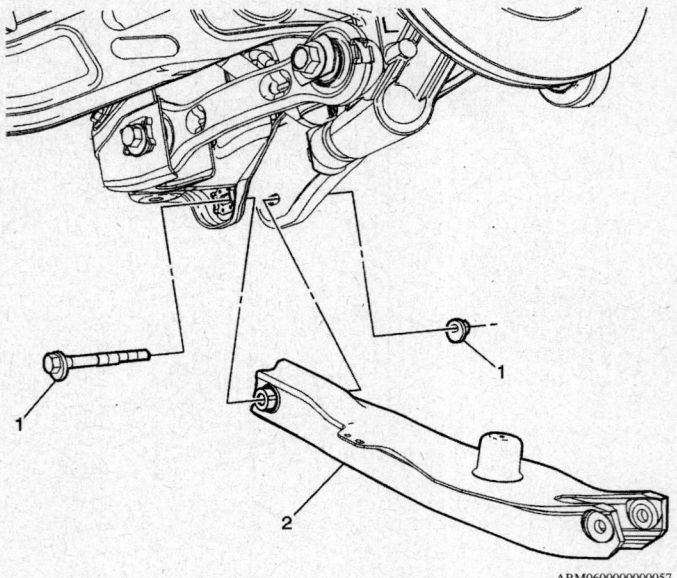

Fig. 5 Lower control arm replacement. AURA

2. Support rear axle with suitable jack stands near each rear shock absorber.
3. Remove U-clips from rear brake hose brackets at rear axle.
4. Remove lower shock bolts and slowly lower rear axle to relieve tension from rear springs.
5. Remove spring and upper spring seat/jounce bumper from spring while leaving lower spring seat on axle.
6. Reverse procedure to install.

L-Series

Refer to "Strut, Replace" and "Srut Service" for coil spring replacement.

SKY

Refer to "Strut, Replace" and "Srut Service" for coil spring replacement.

BALL JOINT

REPLACE

SKY

The ball joints are integral with the lower and upper control arm assemblies. Refer to "Control Arm, Replace" for ball joint replacement.

CONTROL ARM

REPLACE

AURA

LOWER

1. Raise and support vehicle.
2. Remove wheel and tire assembly.
3. Remove coil spring as outlined under "Coil Spring, Replace."
4. Remove lower control arm to support assembly attaching bolt and nut, **Fig. 5.**

5. Remove lower control arm from vehicle.
6. Reverse procedure to install.

UPPER

1. Raise and support vehicle.
2. Remove wheel and tire assembly.
3. Disconnect ABS harness connector and position aside. Note position of harness for installation reference.
4. Remove upper control arm to support assembly attaching bolt.
5. Remove upper control arm to knuckle bolt and nut.
6. Remove upper control arm from vehicle through wheelwell opening.
7. Reverse procedure to install.

SKY

LOWER

1. Disconnect stabilizer link from lower control arm.
2. Disconnect shock module (strut) from lower control arm.
3. Separate rear adjustment link from suspension knuckle, refer to "Rear Adjustment Link, Replace." **Do not loosen adjustment jam nut.**
4. Loosen but do not remove lower control arm ball joint to knuckle nut, **Fig. 6.**
5. Rotate forward edge of knuckle outboard to gain access for ball joint separator tool No. J-42188-B, or equivalent.
6. Separate ball stud from knuckle using ball joint separator tool No. J-42188-B, or equivalent, then remove ball stud nut.
7. Mark adjusting cam position for installation reference.
8. Remove lower control arm nuts.
9. Remove lower control arm to frame bolts, then the control arm assembly.
10. Reverse procedure to install. Inspect alignment as outlined in "Wheel Alignment" section.

UPPER

1. Remove shock module (strut) as outlined under "Strut, Replace."
2. Loosen upper ball joint nut, **Fig. 7.**
3. Separate ball stud from knuckle assembly with ball joint separator tool No. J-42188-B, or equivalent.
4. Remove upper ball joint nut.
5. Remove upper control arm bolts, then the upper control arm.
6. Reverse procedure to install.

SUSPENSION INSULATOR

REPLACE

ION

1. Raise and support vehicle, then remove rear tire and wheel assemblies.
2. Place two screw type jack stands under both ends of rear axle.
3. Remove U-clips from rear brake hose brackets at rear axle and lower shock bolts.
4. Lower jacks and remove coil springs. **Avoid kinking brake pipes while lowering axle.**
5. Support axle by temporarily installing lower shock bolts.
6. Remove bushing bracket to body bolts from both ends of rear axle.
7. Raise rear of axle until bushing brackets pivot away from body.
8. Remove through bolts and bushing brackets.
9. Note depth and orientation of old bushing before removal.
10. Remove bushing using rear axle bushing remover/installer tool No. J44570, or equivalent
11. Reverse procedure to install.

SUSPENSION SUPPORT

REPLACE

AURA

1. Raise and support vehicle.
2. Remove rear wheels and tires.
3. Remove exhaust system.
4. Remove lower control arms as outlined under "Control Arm, Replace."
5. Remove upper control arm to support assembly attaching bolts and nuts.
6. Remove toe links as outlined under "Toe Links, Replace."
7. Remove stabilizer shaft to knuckle attaching bolts.
8. Remove vehicle wiring harness from support assembly retaining clips.
9. Place a suitable jack stand under support assembly.
10. Remove support assembly to body attaching bolts, **Fig. 8.**
11. Remove support assembly from vehicle.
12. Reverse procedure to install.

L-Series

1. Raise and support vehicle, then remove tire and wheel assemblies.

2. Remove rear exhaust system from resonator back and heat shield from rear suspension support.
3. Remove upper and lower control arm to rear axle control arm mounting bolts and nuts.
4. Remove both stabilizer bar links from rear axle control arms.
5. Support rear suspension using suitable jack stand.
6. Remove four rear suspension support to body bolts. Discard bolts.
7. Remove rear suspension support.
8. Reverse procedure to install.

KNUCKLE
REPLACE
AURA

1. Raise and support vehicle.
2. Remove tire and wheel assembly.
3. Remove rear wheel bearing as outlined under "Wheel Bearing & Hub, Replace."
4. Place a suitable jack stand under steering knuckle, then raise knuckle to relieve tension from shock absorber.
5. Remove lower shock absorber to steering knuckle attaching bolt.
6. Remove coil spring as outlined under "Coil Spring, Replace."
7. Remove toe link as outlined under "Toe Link, Replace."
8. Remove upper control arm to knuckle attaching bolt and nut, **Fig. 9.**
9. Remove trailing arm to knuckle bolts.
10. Remove stabilizer shaft link to knuckle attaching bolt, then the knuckle from vehicle.
11. Reverse procedure to install.

SKY

1. Remove hub and bearing assembly as outlined under "Hub & Bearing, Replace."
2. Remove rear adjustment link retaining nut, **Fig. 10.**
3. Loosen, but do not remove upper ball joint nut.
4. Separate ball stud from knuckle assembly with ball joint separator tool No. J-42188-B, or equivalent.
5. Remove upper ball joint nut.
6. Loosen but do not remove lower control arm ball joint to knuckle nut.
7. Rotate forward edge of knuckle outboard to gain access for ball joint separator tool No. J-42188-B, or equivalent.
8. Separate ball stud from knuckle using ball joint separator tool No. J-42188-B, or equivalent, then remove ball stud nut and knuckle.
9. Reverse procedure to install.

TRAILING ARM
REPLACE
AURA

1. Raise and support vehicle.
2. Remove wheel and tire assembly.

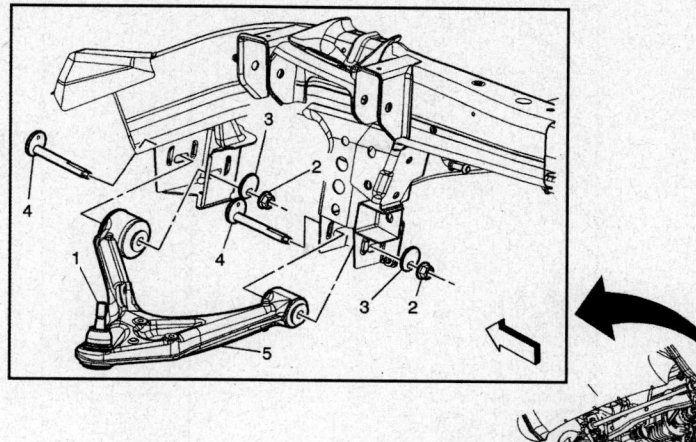

1-Ball joint stud
2-Control arm nut
3-Adjusting cams
4-Control arm to frame bolts
5-Lower control arm

ARM0600000000064

Fig. 6   Lower control arm replacement. SKY

3. Remove trailing arm bracket to body attaching bolts.
4. Remove trailing arm to knuckle through bolts, **Fig. 11.**
5. Disconnect parking brake cable from trailing arm.
6. Remove trailing arm to bracket bolt and nut.
7. Remove trailing arm from bracket.
8. Reverse procedure to install.

STABILIZER BAR
REPLACE
AURA

1. Raise and support vehicle, then remove tire and wheel assemblies.
2. Remove link bolts.
3. Remove mounting nuts and insulator brackets.
4. Remove stabilizer shaft.
5. Reverse procedure to install.

L-Series

1. Raise and support vehicle, then remove tire and wheel assemblies.
2. Remove heat shield from rear suspension.
3. Remove left and righthand rear stabilizer bar links to rear axle control arm bolts.
4. Remove mounting bolts and stabilizer bar.
5. Reverse procedure to install.

SKY

1. Raise and support vehicle, then remove tires and wheels.
2. Remove muffler.

3. Remove stabilizer shaft links from end of stabilizer shaft.
4. Remove stabilizer shaft mounting brackets, then the stabilizer shaft.
5. Remove insulators from stabilizer shaft.
6. Reverse procedure to install.

TOE LINK
REPLACE
AURA

1. Raise and support vehicle.
2. Remove tire and wheel assembly.
3. Remove toe link to steering knuckle attaching bolt, **Fig. 12.**
4. Remove toe link to support assembly attaching bolt and nut, then the toe link from vehicle.
5. Reverse procedure to install.

ADJUSTMENT LINK
REPLACE
SKY

1. Raise and support vehicle, then remove tire and wheel assembly.
2. Loosen adjustment link to knuckle nut, **Fig. 13. Do not loosen adjustment jam nut.**
3. Separate adjustment link ball stud from knuckle using Ball Joint Separator tool No. J-42188-B, or equivalent, then remove adjustment link to knuckle nut.
4. Remove adjustment link to frame nut, then the adjustment link.
5. Reverse procedure to install. Adjust rear toe as outlined in "Wheel Alignment" section.

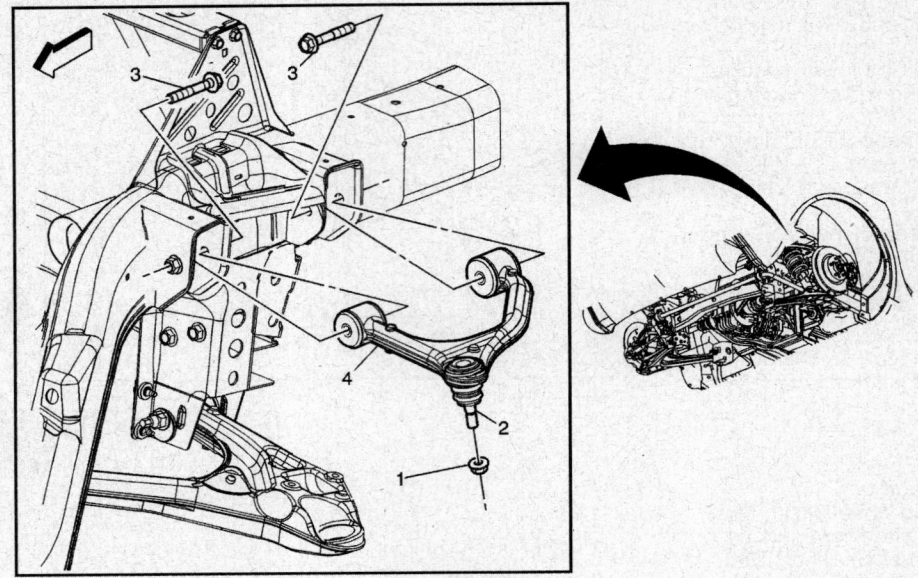

1-Ball joint nut

2-Ball joint stud

3-Upper control arm bolts

4-Upper control arm

ARM0600000000063

Fig. 7   Upper control arm replacement. SKY

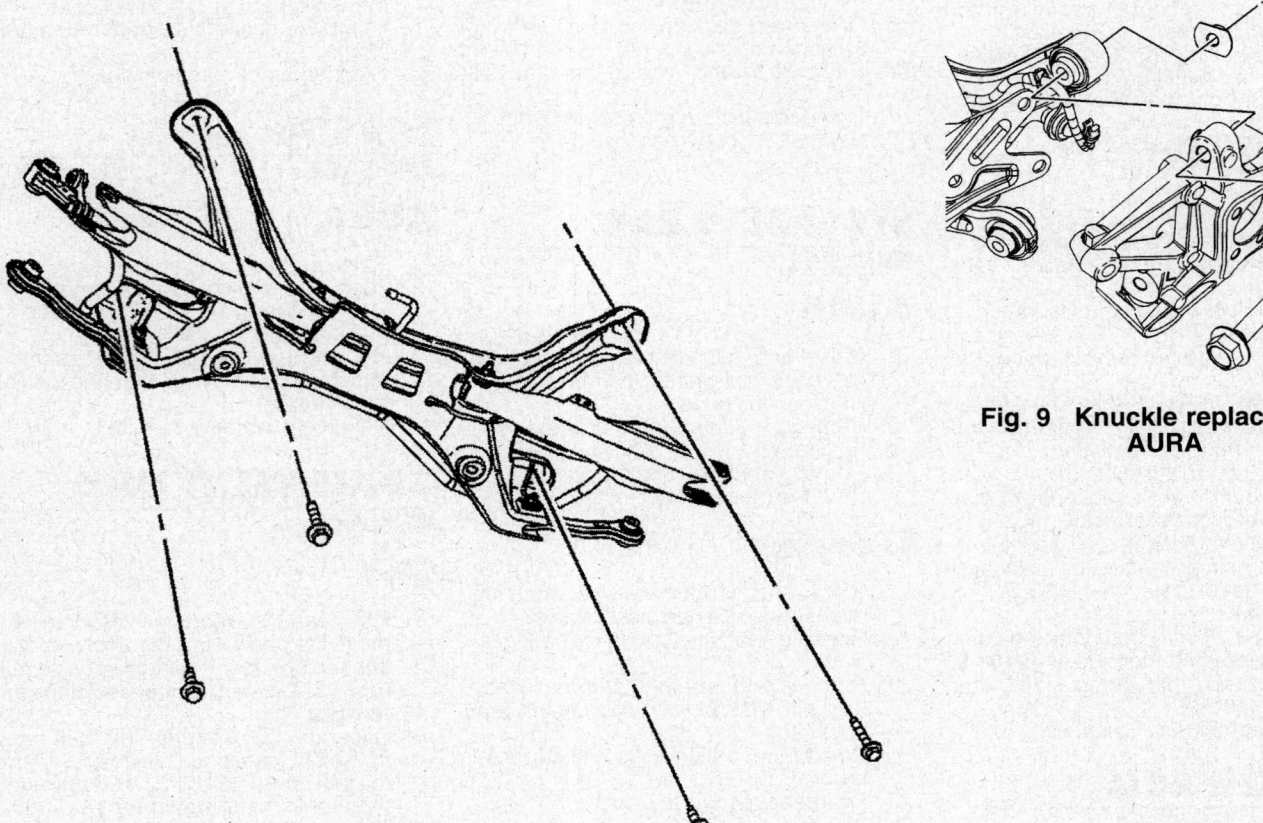

ARM0600000000059

Fig. 9   Knuckle replacement. AURA

ARM0600000000058

Fig. 8   Suspension support assembly replacement. AURA

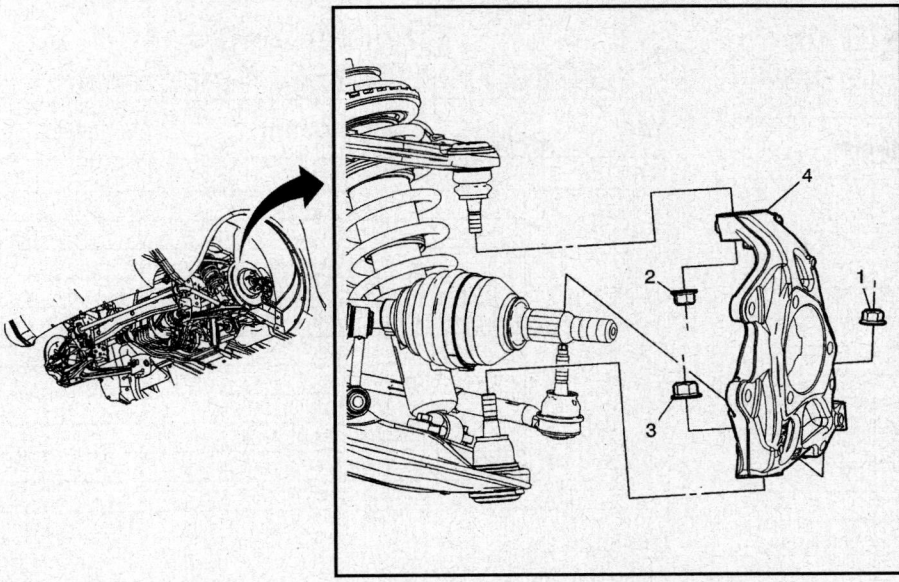

Fig. 11 Trailing arm to knuckle through bolts

1-Adjustment link nut

2-Upper ball joint nut

3-Lower ball joint nut

4-Knuckle

Fig. 10 Knuckle replacement. SKY

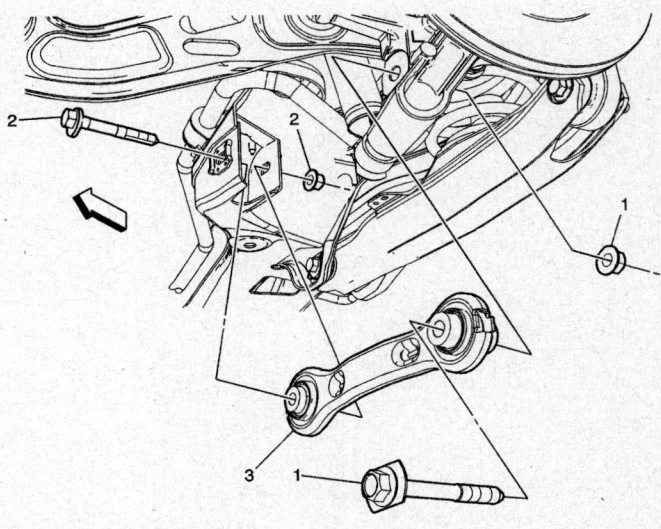

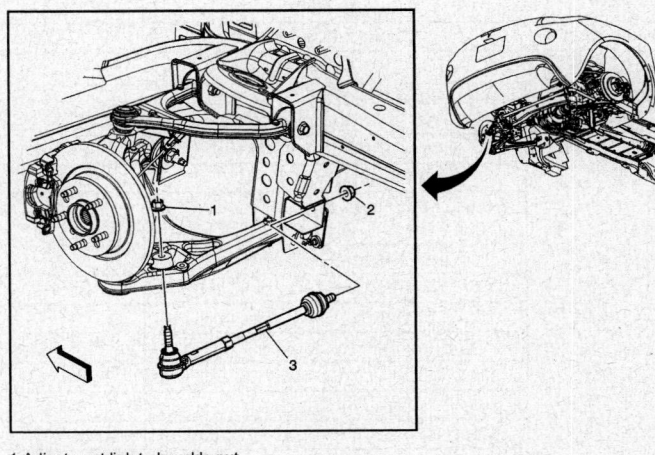

1-Adjustment link to knuckle nut

2-Adjustment link to frame nut

3-Adjustment link

Fig. 13 Adjustment link replacement. SKY

1-Toe link to knuckle bolt & nut

2-Toe link to support bolt & nut

3-Toe link

Fig. 12 Toe link replacement. AURA

SATURN

TIGHTENING SPECIFICATIONS

Year	Component	Torque/Ft. Lbs.
AURA		
2007–08	Lower Control Arm To Knuckle	81⑥
	Lower Control Arm To Support Assembly	81
	Shock Absorber To Body	66
	Shock Absorber To Knuckle	133
	Stabilizer Shaft Insulator Bracket	26
	Stabilizer Shaft Link To Knuckle	37
	Support Assembly To Body	44②
	Toe Link To Steering Knuckle	133
	Trailing Arm To Body	66③
	Trailing Arm To Bracket Through Bolt	44②
	Trailing Arm To Knuckle	133
	Upper Control Arm To Knuckle	81⑥
	Upper Control Arm To Support Assembly	44②
	Wheel Bearing & Hub Assembly	47
	Wheel Lug Nut	100
ION		
2004–07	Bearing Hub	37
	Bracket To Body	66
	Brake Hose Fittings	14
	Lower Shock	81
	Through Bushing	66②
	Upper Shock	66
	Wheel Lug Nut	100
L-SERIES		
2004–05	Heat Shield To Rear Suspension Support	72①
	Rear Axle Control Bracket	65②
	Rear Brake Drum To Hub	35①
	Rear Brake Hose Bracket To Control Arm	72①
	Rear Caliper To Back Plate	59
	Rear Hub To Knuckle	35③
	Stabilizer Bar Clamp	41
	Stabilizer To Control Arm	41
	Strut Carrier To Body	41
	Strut To Knuckle	110③
	Suspension Control Arm To Knuckle	66④
	Suspension Control Arm To Suspension Support	90④
	Suspension Support To Body	66⑤

TIGHTENING SPECIFICATIONS—Continued

Year	Component	Torque/Ft. Lbs.
SKY		
2007–08	Adjustment Link	74
	Ball Joint Nut (Lower)	30
	Ball Joint Nut (Upper)	22
	Control Arm To Frame Bolt (Upper)	81
	Control Arm To Frame Nut (Lower)	122
	Shock Absorber Top Nut	31
	Shock Absorber Lower Nut	21
	Shock Absorber Upper Nut	35
	Stabilizer Shaft Link	53
	Stabilizer Shaft Mounting Bracket	41
	Wheel Lug Nut	100

① — Inch lbs.

② — Tighten an additional 60°.

③ — Tighten an additional 30°.

④ — Tighten an additional 60–75°.

⑤ — Tighten an additional 90–115°.

⑥ — Tighten an additional 70°.

Front Suspension & Steering

NOTE: On Air Bag Equipped Models, Refer To "Air Bag System Precautions" Located In The Front Of This Manual For System Disarming & Arming Procedures.

NOTE: Refer To "Computer Relearn Procedures" Located In The Front Of This Manual When Battery Power To The Computer Has Been Interrupted.

NOTE: Prior To Performing Any Service Operations Listed In This Section, Consult The "Technical Service Bulletins" Section For Related Information.

INDEX

	Page No.
Ball Joint, Replace	12-101
AURA, L-Series & SKY	12-101
Lower	12-101
ION	12-101
Lower	12-101
Ball Joint Inspection	12-101
Coil Spring, Replace	12-101
Control Arm, Replace	12-102
AURA	12-102
ION	12-102
L-Series	12-102
SKY	12-102
Lower	12-102
Upper	12-102
Control Arm Bushing, Replace	12-103
ION	12-103
Hub & Bearing, Replace	12-100
AURA	12-100
SKY	12-100
Hub & Bearing Service	12-101
L-Series	12-101
Power Steering	21-1
Power Steering Gear, Replace	12-104
AURA	12-104
2.4L Engine	12-104
3.5L Engine	12-104
3.6L Engine	12-104
ION	12-105
L-Series	12-105
SKY	12-105
Power Steering Pump, Replace	12-105
AURA	12-105

	Page No.
3.5L Engine	12-105
3.6L Engine	12-105
ION	12-105
L-Series	12-106
2.2L Engine	12-106
3.0L Engine	12-106
SKY	12-106
Power Steering System Bleed	12-106
Precautions	12-99
Air Bag Systems	12-99
Battery Ground Cable	12-99
Hybrid Battery Service	12-99
Connect	12-100
Disconnect	12-99
Stabilizer Bar, Replace	12-103
AURA	12-103
ION & L-Series	12-103
SKY	12-103
Steering Columns	20-1
Steering Knuckle, Replace	12-103
AURA	12-103
SKY	12-103
Strut, Replace	12-101
AURA	12-101
ION	12-101
L-Series	12-101
Installation	12-101
Removal	12-101
SKY	12-102
Strut Service	12-102
Assemble	12-102
Disassemble	12-102

	Page No.
Technical Service Bulletins	12-106
Clunk Noise During Turning	12-106
2004–06 ION	12-106
L-Series	12-107
Front Suspension Creaking/ Squeaking Noise When Turning	12-107
2004 ION	12-107
Low Speed Steering Moan Or Groan	12-107
2004 L-Series	12-107
Power Steering Inoperative/ Steering Wheel Hard to Turn	12-107
ION	12-107
Premature Or Irregular Tire Wear	12-106
2004–06 ION	12-106
Steering Rattle Noise	12-107
2004 ION	12-107
Steering Wheel Shake or Vibration at Highway Speed	12-106
L-Series	12-106
Tension Strut, Replace	12-103
Tie Rod, Replace	12-104
Inner	12-104
Outer	12-104
Tightening Specifications	12-108
Wheel Hub & Steering Knuckle, Replace	12-100
ION	12-100
L-Series	12-100

PRECAUTIONS

Air Bag Systems

Refer to "Air Bag System Precautions" in the front of this manual for system disarming and arming procedures.

Battery Ground Cable

Prior to service, disconnect battery ground cable and isolate as required.

Hybrid Battery Service

DISCONNECT

To help avoid personal injury, always ensure the ignition switch is in the OFF position and the ignition key has been removed prior to working on any 36V components. After the key has been removed, disconnect the battery ground cable and then open the generator battery disconnect control module cover. After waiting for at least 5 minutes, mea-

sure the voltage potential using a DMM between the following: 36V positive and battery ground cables; 36V positive battery cable and vehicle ground; 36V battery ground cable and vehicle ground. All measured voltage levels must be below 3 volts.

1. Remove ignition key from ignition switch.
2. Secure ignition key to ensure that key CANNOT be installed without your knowledge.
3. Disconnect 12 volt battery ground cable.

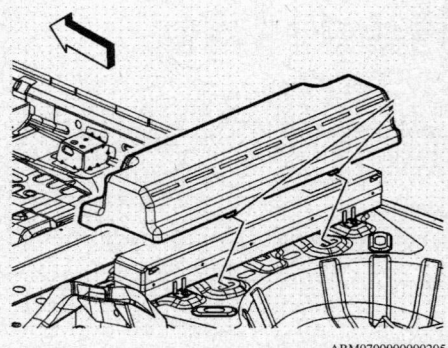

Fig. 1   Rear hybrid battery compartment. AURA

ARM0700000000205

4. Fold down both rear seat backs, then carefully lift up on load floor rear compartment cover at retaining clip locations, **Fig. 1.**
5. Tilt load floor rear compartment cover towards rear of vehicle slightly, disengage tabs and remove load floor rear compartment cover. **To avoid personal injury, be careful when working in vicinity of generator battery disconnect control module. Internal components will still be live, 36V potential, even when cover has been opened or removed.**
6. Remove generator battery disconnect control module cover bolt, **Fig. 2.**
7. Open and slide generator battery disconnect control module cover to right, removing cover. **Wait at least 5 minutes in order to allow generator control module capacitors to discharge.**
8. **Never assume battery pack is disabled when generator battery disconnect control module cover is opened. Generator battery will have to be checked for voltage potential using a voltmeter first**
9. Set voltmeter to DC voltage and measure vehicle 12-volt battery voltage (at 12-volt positive jumper location and battery ground cable).
10. Meter should read greater than 12 volts DC.
11. To ensure generator battery has been disabled, inspect generator battery for voltage potential as follows:
   a. Refer to **Fig. 3** for voltage measurement locations.
   b. Measure from positive stud to negative stud, voltage should be less than 3 volts.
   c. Measure from positive stud to vehicle chassis ground, voltage should be less than 3 volts.
   d. Measure from negative stud to vehicle chassis ground, voltage should be less than 3 volts.
12. After verifying there is no voltage present, vehicle is now safe to work on.

CONNECT

1. Install and close generator battery disconnect control module cover.
2. Install generator battery cover bolt and **torque** to 89 inch lbs.
3. Tilt load floor rear compartment cover towards rear of vehicle slightly in order to insert tabs into battery tray rear support.
4. Set load floor rear compartment cover down, ensure retaining clips align to proper locations, carefully push down to secure cover.
5. Place rear seats backs to their proper positions.
6. Connect 12 volt battery ground cable.

HUB & BEARING
REPLACE
AURA

1. Raise and support vehicle.
2. Remove tire and wheel assembly.
3. Insert suitable drift punch into caliper and rotor to prevent turning, then remove axle shaft nut.
4. Remove brake rotor as outlined in "Disc Brakes."
5. Disconnect wheel speed sensor electrical connector.
6. Remove wheel speed sensor connector from bracket.
7. Remove hub and bearing assembly attaching bolts.
8. Remove hub and bearing assembly from drive shaft using hub and bearing removal tool No. J 42129, or equivalent.
9. Reverse procedure to install.

SKY

1. Raise and support vehicle, then remove tire and wheel assembly.
2. Remove brake caliper mounting bracket and brake rotor as outlined in "Disc Brakes" chapter.
3. Disconnect speed sensor electrical connector, then the wiring harness from steering knuckle retainers.
4. Remove mounting bolts and wheel hub bearing.
5. Reverse procedure to install.

WHEEL HUB & STEERING KNUCKLE
REPLACE
ION

1. Raise and support vehicle, then remove tire and wheel assembly.
2. Remove wheel drive shaft nut, insert suitable flat bladed tool into caliper and rotor to prevent rotor from turning.
3. Remove and support front brake caliper and bracket, then the front brake rotor.
4. **On models equipped with ABS,** disconnect electrical connector from

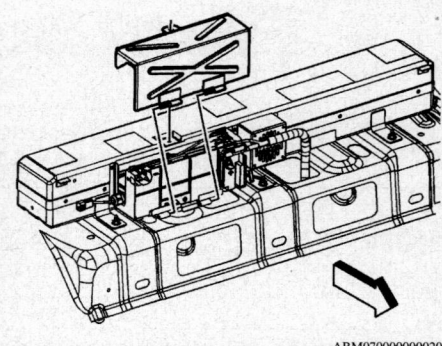

Fig. 2   Disconnect control module cover. AURA

ARM0700000000206

wheel speed sensor and wheel speed sensor jumper connector from bracket on strut.
5. **On all models,** remove wheel bearing mounting bolts from behind steering knuckle.
6. Remove wheel bearing/hub and spacer from steering knuckle and wheel drive shaft.
7. Remove outer tie rod to knuckle nut, then separate tie rod from steering knuckle, using tool tie rod separator tool No. SA91100C, or equivalent.
8. Remove lower control arm ball stud to steering knuckle pinch bolt and nut.
9. Separate ball stud from steering knuckle by lowering control arm.
10. Remove strut to steering knuckle nuts and bolts, then the steering knuckle,
11. Reverse procedure to install.

L-Series

1. Depress brake pedal and loosen axle to hub nut.
2. Raise and support vehicle, then remove tire and wheel assembly.
3. Remove caliper to knuckle mounting bolts. Support caliper with mechanics wire.
4. Loosen but do not remove knuckle to strut mounting bolts.
5. If rotor is difficult to remove, use two M8 × 1.25 self tapping bolts, **Fig. 4.**
6. Remove axle nut and washer. Discard lower control arm ball stud cotter pin.
7. Loosen castle nut until level with top of ball stud.
8. Remove and discard tie rod cotter pin.
9. Remove tie rod and castle nut.
10. Separate lower control arm from knuckle using lower control arm ball stud separator tool No. SA9132-S, or equivalent. **Do not use pickle fork or wedge type tool to separate.**
11. Remove lower ball joint castle nut, **Fig. 5.**
12. Separate tie rod end from steering knuckle using tie rod separator tool No. SA91100-C, or equivalent.
13. **On models equipped with Anti-Lock Brakes (ABS),** disconnect wheel speed sensor electrical connector.
14. **On all models,** support drive axle.
15. Remove strut to knuckle mounting

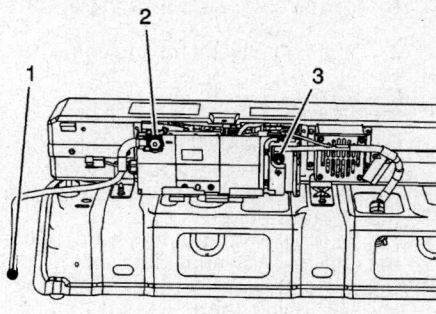

1-Chassis ground
2-Negative stud
3-Positive stud

ARM0700000000207

Fig. 3   Battery disconnect control module voltage measurement locations. AURA

bolts, then knuckle and hub. If it is difficult to separate axle from hub, tap end of drive axle shaft using suitable wood block wood and hammer. **Do not hammer end of axle.**

16. Reverse procedure to install, noting the following:
   a. **Torque** strut to knuckle mounting bolts to 37 ft. lbs.
   b. **Torque** mounting bolts to 73 ft. lbs.
   c. Final tighten bolts an additional 30–40°.

HUB & BEARING SERVICE

L-Series

1. Remove steering knuckle as outlined under "Wheel Hub & Steering Knuckle, Replace."
2. Remove splash shields and ABS wheel speed sensor.
3. Install wheel bearing/hub removal tool No. SA9159-S, or equivalent, **Fig. 6.**
4. Place assembly in suitable soft jawed vise.
5. Hold hub drive using suitable wrench. Tighten driver screw to remove hub.
6. Remove inner bearing race using inner race puller, **Fig. 7.**
7. Remove steering knuckle from vise, then the retainer and bridge.
8. Remove bridge snap ring using suitable snap ring pliers.
9. Press out bearing using knuckle support tube and small driver, **Fig. 8.**
10. Reverse procedure to assemble.

BALL JOINT INSPECTION

1. Raise and support front of vehicle. Allow suspension to hang free.

2. Grasp tire at top and bottom, then move bottom of tire in and out.
3. While moving bottom of tire in and out, observe ball joint for any side to side movement.
4. If any side to side movement is noticed, replace lower control arm.

BALL JOINT

REPLACE

AURA, L-Series & SKY

LOWER

The ball joint and the lower control arm are serviced as an assembly. Refer to "Control Arm, Replace" for replacement procedure.

ION

LOWER

This procedure has been revised by a Technical Service Bulletin.
1. Raise and support vehicle, then remove tire and wheel assembly.
2. Remove ball stud to steering knuckle pinch bolt and nut, then separate ball stud from steering knuckle.
3. Remove rear frame and control arm to frame bolts.
4. Remove control arm from frame, then place lower control arm in suitable vise.
5. Drill pilot hole through rivets using 1/8 inch drill bit.
6. Complete drilling rivets using 31/64 inch drill bit.
7. Remove ball joint from lower control arm.
8. Reverse procedure to install, noting the following:
   a. Follow instructions in ball joint kit.
   b. **Torque** ball joint to steering knuckle to 37 ft. lbs.
   c. Loosen nut 3/4 turn.
   d. **Torque** ball joint to steering knuckle to 37 ft. lbs.
   e. Final tighten joint an additional 30°.

COIL SPRING

REPLACE

Refer to "Strut Service" for coil spring replacement procedure.

STRUT

REPLACE

AURA

1. Raise and support vehicle.
2. Remove wheel and tire assembly.
3. Disconnect stabilizer link from strut.
4. Remove strut to steering knuckle nuts.
5. Position wheel speed sensor harness aside.
6. Remove strut to steering knuckle attaching bolts.
7. Remove upper strut cap to body retaining nuts.
8. Remove strut assembly from vehicle.

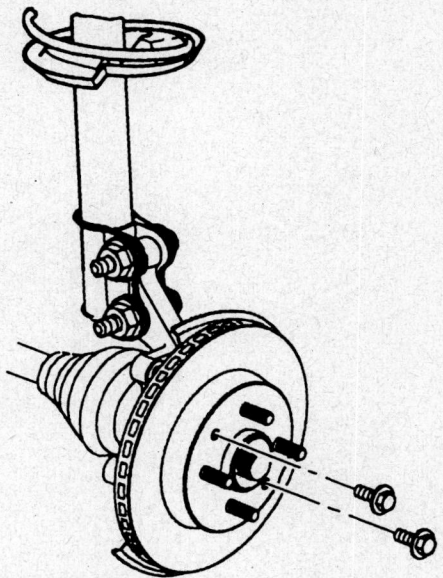

G32029100001000X

Fig. 4   Brake rotor replacement. L-Series

9. Reverse procedure to install. Adjust front end alignment as required, refer to "Wheel Alignment" section.

ION

1. Raise and support vehicle, then remove front tire and wheel assembly.
2. Disconnect stabilizer link from strut.
3. Remove strut to steering knuckle nuts, then position wheel speed sensor harness and bracket aside.
4. Remove strut to steering knuckle bolts, then the upper strut cap to body nut.
5. **Place shop towel over CV joint to prevent joint boot damage.**
6. Remove strut,
7. Reverse procedure to install.

L-Series

REMOVAL

1. Raise and support vehicle, then remove tire and wheel assembly.
2. **On models equipped with ABS,** disconnect wheel speed sensor electrical connector bracket.
3. **On all models,** loosen, but do not remove steering knuckle to strut housing mounting bolts.
4. Support lower control arm using suitable floor jack.
5. Remove and discard upper strut mounting nuts.
6. Slowly raise vehicle and lower strut.
7. Remove knuckle to housing mounting bolts, **Fig. 5.** Place cloth over CV joint seal.
8. Remove strut.

INSTALLATION

1. Install new upper strut mounting nuts.
2. Install new strut to steering knuckle mounting bolts.

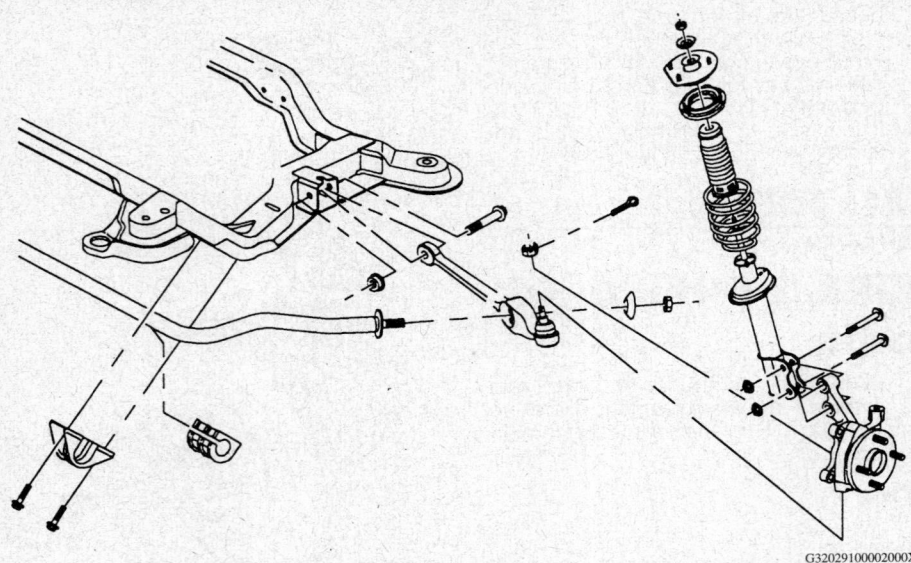

G32029100002000X

Fig. 5 Exploded view of front suspension. L-Series

3. **Torque** strut to knuckle mounting bolts to 37 ft. lbs.
4. **Torque** mounting bolts to 73 ft. lbs.
5. Final tighten bolts an additional 30–40°.
6. **On models equipped with ABS,** install sensor electrical connector bracket.

SKY

1. Raise and support vehicle, then remove tire and wheel assembly.
2. Remove brake caliper and caliper bracket as outlined in "Disc Brakes" chapter. Do not disconnect brake hydraulic line.
3. Loosen lower control arm ball joint to steering knuckle nut.
4. Rotate forward edge of knuckle outward to provide access for ball joint separator tool No. J-42188-B, or equivalent.
5. Separate ball joint from steering knuckle using separator tool No. J-42188-B, or equivalent, then remove control arm to steering knuckle nut.
6. Remove lower strut mounting bolts, **Fig. 9.**
7. Remove upper and lower mounting nuts, then the strut.
8. Reverse procedure to install.

STRUT SERVICE
Disassemble

1. Compress spring to unload upper strut mount using spring compressor tool No. SA9155-C, or equivalent, and suitable holding fixture.
2. While holding strut shaft, remove strut shaft nut.
3. Release spring compressor and tilt strut outward.
4. Remove upper strut.
5. Remove strut spring and dust shield.
6. Remove strut from holding fixture.

Assemble

1. Place strut in compressor tool and attach with strut to knuckle bolt through lower mounting hole.
2. Extend strut shaft to travel limit.
3. Install dust shield, spring isolator and mount, ensure spring is properly seated in seat and isolator.
4. Compress spring and install strut shaft mounting nut.

CONTROL ARM
REPLACE
AURA

1. Raise and support vehicle.
2. Remove wheel and tire assembly.
3. Remove front control arm bushing to frame attaching bolt and nut.
4. Remove rear control arm bushing to frame attaching bolts and nuts.
5. Note position of lower control ball stud to steering knuckle pinch bolt for installation reference.
6. Remove control arm ball stud to steering knuckle pinch bolt. Discard bolt.
7. Separate ball stud from steering knuckle, then remove knuckle from vehicle.
8. Reverse procedure to install.

ION

1. Raise and support vehicle, then remove tire and wheel assembly.
2. Remove ball stud to steering knuckle pinch bolt and nut, then separate ball stud from steering knuckle.
3. Remove rear frame and control arm to frame bolts.
4. Remove control arm from frame.
5. Reverse procedure to install, noting the following:
   a. **Torque** ball joint to steering knuckle to 37 ft. lbs.
   b. Loosen nut ¾ turn.
   c. **Torque** ball joint to steering knuckle to 37 ft. lbs.
   d. Final tighten joint an additional 30°.

L-Series

1. Raise and support vehicle, then remove tire and wheel assembly.
2. Remove and discard lower control arm ball stud cotter pin.
3. Loosen lower control ball stud castle nut until level with top of ball stud.
4. Separate lower control arm from knuckle using lower control arm ball stud separator tool No. SA9132-S, or equivalent. **Do not use pickle fork or a wedge type tool.**
5. Remove lower control arm ball stud castle nut.
6. Remove inner front fender splash shield.
7. Remove lower control arm to cradle mounting nut and bolt, **Fig. 5.**
8. Remove lower control arm to tension strut mounting nut, and arm.
9. Reverse procedure to install.

SKY
LOWER

1. Raise vehicle and suitably support, then remove tire and wheel.
2. Disconnect stabilizer link from lower control arm.
3. Remove brake caliper and caliper bracket as outlined in "Disc Brakes" chapter. Do not disconnect brake hydraulic line.
4. Remove lower strut mounting bolts.
5. Loosen, outer tie rod end joint nut from outer tie rod end ball joint, **Fig. 10. Do not loosen adjustment jam nut.**
6. Separate tie rod end ball joint from steering knuckle using ball joint separator tool No. J42188-B, or equivalent.
7. Remove tie rod end stud nut.
8. Loosen, lower ball joint nut, **Fig. 11. Do not remove nut until ball stud has been separated from knuckle.**
9. Rotate knuckle completely forward and install ball joint separator tool No. J42188-B, or equivalent.
10. Separate ball joint from steering knuckle and remove ball joint stud nut.
11. Remove alignment cam bolts and lower control arm.
12. Reverse procedure to install. Inspect front end alignment as outlined in "Wheel Alignment" section.

UPPER

1. Raise and support vehicle, then remove tire and wheel assembly.
2. Remove strut as outlined under "Strut, Replace."
3. Loosen upper ball joint nut, **Fig. 12. Do not remove nut until ball stud has been separated from knuckle.**
4. Separate ball joint from steering knuckle using ball joint separation tool No. J42188, or equivalent.
5. Remove upper ball joint nut.
6. Remove mounting bolts and upper control arm.
7. Reverse procedure to install.

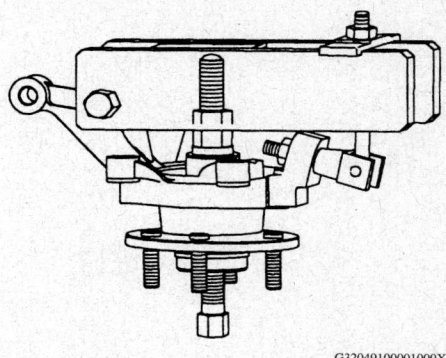

Fig. 6   Wheel bearing/hub removal. L-Series

CONTROL ARM BUSHING
REPLACE
ION

1. Raise and support vehicle, then remove tire and wheel assembly.
2. Remove ball stud to steering knuckle pinch bolt and nut, then separate ball stud from steering knuckle.
3. Remove rear frame and control arm to frame bolts.
4. Remove control arm from frame.
5. Wrap control arm with shop towel and place it in suitable vise.
6. **Note depth and orientation of old bushing.**
7. Remove bushing using bushing removes/installer kit tool No. KM906-B, or equivalent.
8. Reverse procedure to install noting the following:
   a. Place new bushing onto tapered side of control arm.
   b. Pull new bushing through opposite direction of control arm.
   c. Install control arm.
   d. **Torque** ball joint to steering knuckle to 37 ft. lbs.
   e. Loosen nut ¾ turn.
   f. **Torque** ball joint to steering knuckle to 37 ft. lbs.
   g. Final tighten joint an additional 30°.

STEERING KNUCKLE
REPLACE
AURA

1. Raise and support vehicle.
2. Remove wheel and tire assembly.
3. Remove wheel bearing and hub assembly as outlined under "Wheel Hub & Bearing, Replace."
4. Remove outer tie rod to steering knuckle retaining nut, then separate steering knuckle from tie rod.
5. Remove strut to steering knuckle attaching bolts and nuts.
6. Remove steering knuckle from vehicle.

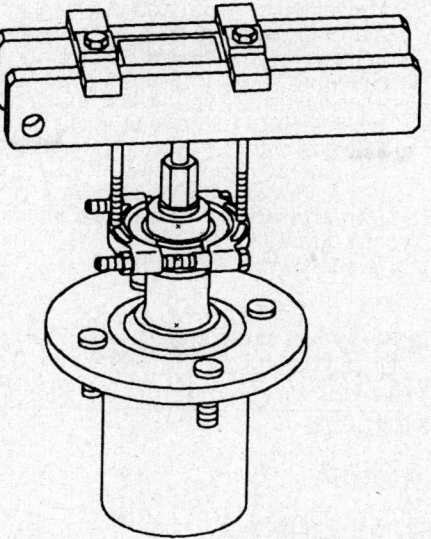

Fig. 7   Inner bearing race removal. L-Series

7. Reverse procedure to install. Adjust front end alignment as required, refer to "Wheel Alignment" section.

SKY

1. Remove wheel hub and bearing as outlined under "Hub & Bearing, Replace."
2. Remove tie rod end nut, **Fig. 13.**
3. Separate upper and lower control arm ball joints from knuckle as outlined under "Control Arm, Replace."
4. Remove steering knuckle.
5. Reverse procedure to install.

STABILIZER BAR
REPLACE
AURA

1. Raise and support vehicle.
2. Remove tire and wheel assemblies.
3. Disconnect stabilizer links from stabilizer shaft.
4. Place a suitable jack stand under rear of frame assembly.
5. Remove frame support to body attaching bolts.
6. Remove rear frame assembly mounting bolts.
7. Lower rear of cradle to access stabilizer shaft.
8. Remove stabilizer bar clamps and insulators.
9. Remove stabilizer shaft through frame and body opening.
10. Reverse procedure to install.

ION & L-Series

1. Raise and support vehicle.
2. Remove rear transaxle mount through bolt and heat shield.
3. Remove mounting bolts and rear transaxle mount.

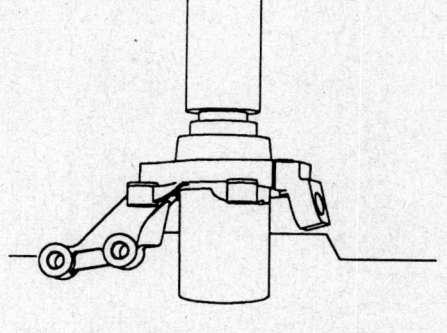

Fig. 8   Bearing removal. L-Series

4. Remove front tire and wheel assemblies.
5. Remove steering gear to intermediate shaft pinch bolt and discard.
6. Disconnect intermediate shaft from steering gear.
7. Remove both steering gear outer tie rod to knuckle nuts. Discard nuts.
8. Separate outer tie rods from steering knuckles using tool tie rod separator tool No. SA91100C, or equivalent.
9. Remove mounting bolts and steering gear through lefthand wheel opening.
10. Disconnect stabilizer link from stabilizer shaft.
11. Remove mounting bolts and stabilizer bar mounting clamps.
12. Remove bushings from stabilizer bar, then lift and turn stabilizer bar up and to right.
13. Remove stabilizer bar from righthand side.
14. Reverse procedure to install.

SKY

1. Raise and support vehicle, then remove tire and wheel assemblies.
2. Remove mounting nut and stabilizer shaft link.
3. Remove mounting bolt, bracket and stabilizer shaft.
4. Reverse procedure to install.

TENSION STRUT
REPLACE

1. Raise and support vehicle, then remove tire and wheel assembly.
2. Remove and discard lower control arm ball stud cotter pin.
3. Loosen, but do not remove, lefthand lower control arm ball stud castle nut.
4. **On lefthand side of vehicle,** proceed as follows:
   a. Separate lower control arm from steering knuckle using lower control arm ball stud separator tool No. SA9132-S, or equivalent. **Do not use pickle fork or wedge type tool.**
   b. Remove lower control arm ball joint castle nut.
   c. Remove lefthand front inner fender splash shield.
   d. Remove lower control arm to cradle mounting nut and bolt.

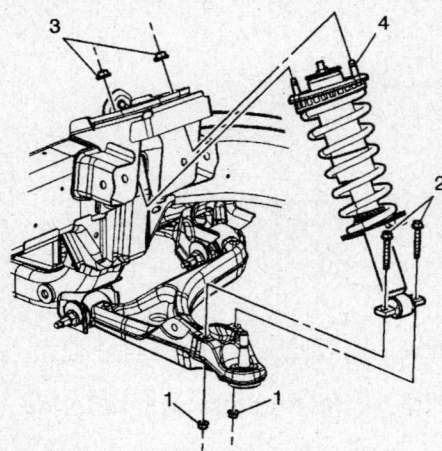

1- LOWER NUTS
2- LOWER BOLTS
3- UPPER NUTS
4- UPPER STUDS

ARM0500000000915

Fig. 9   Strut replacement. SKY

5. **On righthand side of vehicle,** turn wheel to left, then remove tension strut to lower control arm mounting nut and washer.
6. **On both sides of vehicle,** remove tension strut to cradle bracket mounting bolts.
7. Remove tension strut and lefthand control arm.
8. Remove control arm to tension strut mounting nut and washer, then separate.
9. Reverse procedure to install.

TIE ROD
REPLACE
Inner

1. Raise and support vehicle, then remove tire and wheel assemblies.
2. Remove outer tie rod to inner tie rod locknut.
3. Remove steering gear as outlined under "Steering Gear, Replace."
4. Remove outer tie rod from inner tie rod.
5. Remove outer tie rod locknut.
6. Remove steering gear boot.
7. Slide shock dampner toward steering gear and remove from inner tie rod.
8. **Hold steering gear rack using suitable wrench on rack teeth. Protect teeth with suitable shop cloth.**
9. When removing righthand inner tie rod it may be required to remove lefthand side boot to access teeth.
10. Remove inner tie rod.
11. Reverse procedure to install, noting the following:
    a. Apply Loctite No. 262, or equivalent, evenly to inner tie rod threads.
    b. Install inner tie rod using tool No. SA9209-C, or equivalent.

Outer

1. Raise and support vehicle, then remove front tire and wheel assemblies.

2. Loosen outer tie rod to inner tie rod jam nut, then remove tie rod to steering knuckle nut and discard.
3. Separate outer tie rod from steering knuckle using tool tie rod separator tool No. SA91100C, or equivalent.
4. Remove outer tie rod from inner tie rod. Record number of turns used in removal for installation alignment.
5. Remove outer to inner tie rod jam nut and discard.
6. Reverse procedure to install.

POWER STEERING GEAR
REPLACE
AURA

2.4L ENGINE

1. Turn front wheels to straight forward position, secure steering wheel to keep wheel from moving.
2. Raise and support vehicle, then remove tire and wheel assemblies.
3. Separate outer tie rod ends from steering knuckles as outlined under "Tie Rod, Replace."
4. Remove pinch bolt and separate intermediate steering shaft from steering gear. **Do not rotate intermediate shaft after separating from steering gear.**
5. Remove transmission rear mount bolt.
6. Remove steering gear mounting bolts and nuts.
7. Remove steering gear through left front wheel opening.
8. Reverse procedure to install. Adjust front end alignment as required, refer to "Wheel Alignment" section.

3.5L ENGINE

1. Place steering wheel in straight forward position.
2. Raise and support vehicle.
3. Remove as much power steering fluid from remote fluid reservoir as possible.
4. Raise and support vehicle.
5. Remove wheel and tire assemblies.
6. Disconnect outer tie rod ends from steering knuckles as outlined under "Tie Rod End, Replace."
7. Remove and discard intermediate shaft to steering gear pinch bolt.
8. Separate intermediate shaft from steering gear. **Do not rotate intermediate shaft after separating from steering gear.**
9. Loosen rear transaxle mount bracket bolt.
10. Disconnect HO2S sensor electrical connector, then remove HO2S sensor harness from rear transmission mount bracket.
11. Remove transmission mount to frame bolts and nuts. Position transmission rear mount and bracket aside.
12. Remove steering gear inlet hose retaining bolt, then disconnect inlet and outlet hoses from steering gear. Cap hoses and position aside.

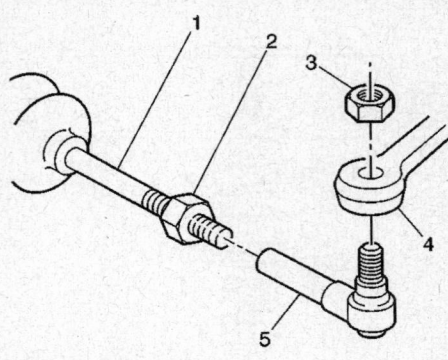

1. Inner tie rod end assembly
2. Jam nut
3. Outer tie rod end stud nut
4. Steering knuckle
5. Outer tie rod end

ARM0500000000644

Fig. 10   Outer tie rod assembly. SKY

13. Remove steering gear outlet hose retainer from rear righthand side of frame.
14. **On models equipped with convertible top,** support rear side of front frame with a suitable jack stand, then remove front frame rear bolts.
15. **On all models,** remove steering gear mounting bolts, then the steering gear through lefthand side wheelwell.
16. Reverse procedure to install. Adjust front end alignment as required, refer to "Wheel Alignment" section.

3.6L ENGINE

1. Place steering wheel in straight forward position.
2. Raise and support vehicle.
3. Remove as much power steering fluid from remote fluid reservoir as possible.
4. Remove wheel and tire assemblies.
5. Disconnect outer tie rod ends from steering knuckles as outlined under "Tie Rod End, Replace."
6. Remove intermediate shaft to steering gear pinch bolt. Discard bolt.
7. Separate intermediate shaft from steering gear. **Do not rotate intermediate shaft after separating from steering gear.**
8. Remove steering gear heat shield from steering gear.
9. Remove transmission brace bolt.
10. Remove transmission rear mount bolt. Position transmission brace aside.
11. Loosen rear transmission mount bracket through bolt, then remove remaining rear transmission mount bolts.
12. Remove transmission mount bracket to frame nuts and bolts, position mount and bracket aside.
13. Remove steering gear inlet hose bolt, then disconnect inlet and outlet hoses from steering gear. Cap off hoses and position aside.
14. Remove steering gear to frame mounting bolts, then the steering gear through lefthand side wheelwell.
15. Reverse procedure to install. Adjust front end alignment as required, refer to "Wheel Alignment" section.

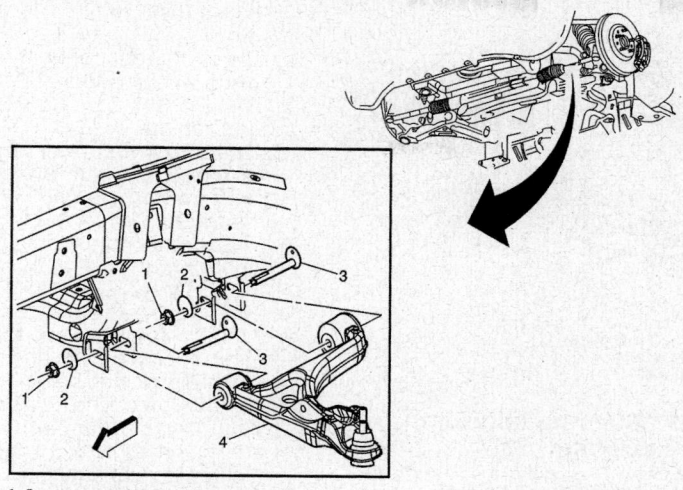

1. Lower control arm to frame nut
2. Lower control arm alignment cam
3. Lower control arm alignment bolt
4. Lower control arm

ARM0500000000645

Fig. 11   Lower control arm replacement. SKY

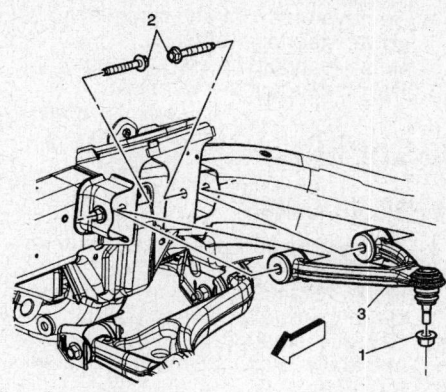

1- BALL JOINT NUT
2- CONTROL ARM TO FRAME BOLTS
3- CONTROL ARM

ARM0500000000916

Fig. 12   Upper control arm replacement. SKY

ION

1. Turn steering wheel to straight ahead position and lock steering column in place.
2. Raise and support vehicle, then remove front tire and wheel assemblies.
3. Remove steering gear to intermediate shaft pinch bolt and discard.
4. Disconnect intermediate shaft from steering gear.
5. Remove and discard both steering gear outer tie rod to knuckle nuts.
6. Separate outer tie rods from steering knuckles using tool tie rod separator tool No. SA91100C, or equivalent.
7. Remove mounting bolts and steering gear through lefthand wheel opening.
8. Reverse procedure to install, noting the following:
   a. **Torque** ball joint to steering knuckle to 37 ft. lbs.
   b. Loosen nut ¾ turn.
   c. **Torque** ball joint to steering knuckle to 37 ft. lbs.
   d. Final tighten joint an additional 30°.

L-Series

1. Remove pinch bolt and disconnect intermediate shaft from steering gear.
2. **On models equipped with 3.0L engine,** remove rear exhaust manifold heat shield.
3. **On all models,** remove through bolt and transaxle mount to frame bolt.
4. Place suitable drain container under steering gear pressure and return hoses.
5. Remove power steering gear hoses and allow fluid to drain.
6. Raise and support vehicle, then remove tire and wheel assemblies.
7. Remove righthand front lower splash shield.
8. **On models equipped with 3.0L engine,** remove exhaust manifold pipe

and remaining transaxle mount to frame bolts.
9. **On all models,** remove and discard tie rod end torque prevailing nuts.
10. Separate tie rod end from steering knuckle using tie rod end separator tool No. SA91100-C, or equivalent.
11. Remove steering gear to frame mounting bolts and steering gear heat shield.
12. Remove stabilizer bar links from strut and front suspension supports.
13. Loosen remaining mounting bolts until there is enough clearance to remove gear through lefthand side wheel opening.
14. Remove steering gear.
15. Reverse procedure to install.

SKY

1. Raise and support vehicle, then remove tire and wheel assembly.
2. Loosen, do not remove, outer tie rod end stud nuts from outer tie rod end ball studs.
3. Separate right and left tie rod end ball joints from steering knuckle using joint separator tool No. J42188-B, or equivalent.
4. Remove outer tie rod end stud nuts.
5. Remove power steering outlet pipe hose fitting.
6. Remove and discard intermediate shaft bolt from steering gear.
7. Remove mounting nut and bolt, then the power steering gear.
8. Reverse procedure to install.

POWER STEERING PUMP

REPLACE

AURA

3.5L ENGINE

1. Remove intake manifold cover.

2. Remove air cleaner assembly and engine mount strut.
3. Remove drive belt, then the drive belt idler pulley.
4. Remove power steering pump pulley.
5. Drain as much fluid as possible from power steering fluid reservoir.
6. Remove engine lift bracket.
7. Remove steering gear inlet hose fitting and O-ring. Discard O-ring.
8. Remove power steering reservoir inlet hose.
9. Remove power steering pump mounting bolts, then the pump.
10. Reverse procedure to install. Bleed power steering system as outlined under "Power Steering System Bleed."

3.6L ENGINE

1. Remove air cleaner assembly and engine mount strut bracket.
2. Remove drive belt.
3. Raise and support vehicle, then remove righthand front tire and wheel assembly.
4. Drain as much fluid as possible from remote power steering fluid reservoir.
5. Remove outlet hose from power steering fluid reservoir.
6. Remove power steering gear inlet hose fitting and O-ring seal. Discard O-ring seal.
7. Remove engine mount adapter bolt.
8. Remove power steering pump mounting bolt, then the pump.
9. Remove power steering pump pulley using power steering pump pulley remover/replacer tool No. SA9162C, or equivalent.
10. Remove engine mount adapter bracket bolts, then the bracket.
11. Reverse procedure to install.

ION

1. Remove power steering pump reservoir fill cap.
2. Place suitable container under power steering hoses at steering gear.
3. Remove steering gear power hoses and allow to drain. **Do not turn steering wheel.**

4. Remove pressure and return hoses at power steering pump.
5. Remove mounting bolts and pump.
6. Reverse procedure to install.

L-Series

2.2L ENGINE

1. Remove power steering pump reservoir fill cap.
2. Place suitable container under power steering hoses at steering gear.
3. Remove steering gear power hoses and allow to drain. **Do not turn steering wheel.**
4. Remove pressure and return hoses at power steering pump.
5. Remove mounting bolts and pump.
6. Reverse procedure to install.

3.0L ENGINE

1. Remove air cleaner and power steering pulley bolts.
2. Remove accessory drive belt and power steering pump pulley.
3. Place suitable container under power steering pump.
4. Remove power steering pump pressure and return hoses, allow to drain.
5. Remove bracket mounting bolts and power steering pump.
6. Reverse procedure to install.

SKY

1. Remove intake manifold cover.
2. Remove air cleaner assembly.
3. Remove as much power steering fluid as possible from remote power steering fluid reservoir.
4. Remove power steering fluid reservoir outlet and inlet hoses from pump, **Fig. 14.**
5. Remove power steering pump mounting bolts, then the pump.
6. Reverse procedure to install. Fill and bleed system as outlined under "Power Steering System Bleed."

POWER STEERING SYSTEM BLEED

1. Fill pump reservoir with fluid to minimum system level, FULL COLD level, or middle of hash mark on cap stick fluid level indicator.
2. Raise vehicle until front wheels are off ground.
3. Key on engine OFF, turn steering wheel from stop to stop 12 times.
4. Verify power steering fluid level.
5. Start engine and rotate steering wheel from left to right.
6. Inspect for sign of cavitation or fluid aeration pump noise.
7. Verify fluid level.

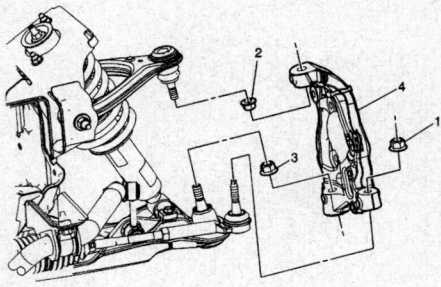

1- TIE ROD NUT
2- UPPER BALL JOINT NUT
3- LOWER BALL JOINT NUT
4- STEERING KNUCKLE

ARM0500000000917

Fig. 13 Steering knuckle replacement. SKY

TECHNICAL SERVICE BULLETINS

Premature Or Irregular Tire Wear

2004-06 ION

On some of these models there may be premature and/or irregular tire wear on the inside edge of the tire.

This condition may be caused by a negative front total toe (sum toe) that is outside of wheel alignment specifications. Correction

To correct this condition set total toe to +.20°, plus or minus .20°.

Steering Wheel Shake or Vibration at Highway Speed

L-SERIES

On some of these models there may be a steering week choke or vibration at highway speeds. This condition is most noticeable on smooth roads at more than 65 mph.

This condition may be caused by vehicle sensitivity to out-of-balance tire/wheel assemblies.

To correct this condition, proceed as follows:

1. Balance all four tire/wheel assemblies, then ensure balance by repeating balance with assembly shifted 90°.
2. **On models built before and including VIN YY697118,** replace front lower control arm rear bushing is not previously replaced, as follows:
   a. Remove righthand lower splash shield.
   b. Remove ball stud bolt and nut.
   c. Separate ball stud from steering knuckle using suitable pry bar. **Do not damage ABS speed sensor ring.**
   d. Remove and discard mounting

bolts, then remove lower control arm.
   e. Press out rear control arm bushing using bushing tools Nos. LM-907-21, LM-907-22 and KM-671, or equivalents.
   f. **Bushings must be installed with notched cut-out areas aligned with front lower control arm weld flanges .**
   g. Press new control arm bushing into control arm using bushing tools Nos. KM-907-23, KM-907-24 and KM-671, or equivalents.
   h. Install control arm and hand tighten new mounting bolts and nuts.
   i. **Torque** ball stud nut to 75 ft. lbs.
   j. **Torque** mounting bolts only when front lower control arm are at normal ride height to 65 ft. lbs. and final tighten an additional 75°.
3. **On models built before and including VIN 2Y525531,**
   a. Ensure steering wheel is centered and wheels are straight ahead.
   b. Raise and support vehicle.
   c. Mark adjust plug for installation alignment.
   d. Loosen steering gear adjuster lock nut using steering gear adjuster lock nut socket tool No. J45874, or equivalent.
   e. Remove plug and yellow, 40 lb. steering gear preload spring.
   f. Install purple, 110 lb. steering gear preload spring (part No. 26030764).
   g. Turn plug clockwise until it bottoms in housing.
   h. **Torque** plug to 89 inch lbs, then back adjuster plug off to original alignment position.
   i. If install new adjuster plug, back it off 30–40°, approximately ½ nut flat.
   j. **Torque** lock using steering gear adjuster locknut socket tool No. J45874, or equivalent, to 52 ft. lbs.
   k. Hand tighten wheel bolts, then **torque** bolts to 46 ft. lbs. using star pattern.
   l. **Torque** wheel bolts to 92 ft. lbs. using star pattern.

Clunk Noise During Turning

2004-06 ION

On some of these models there may be clunk during turning maneuvers. This condition may be felt in steering wheel when vehicle is stationary and wheel is turned stop-to-stop. Typically, clunk is heard every 900° of steering wheel rotation. Noise is noticed during low speed acceleration or deceleration, in tight turns.

This condition may be caused by inadequate steering intermediate shaft lubrication.

To correct this condition, replace the steering intermediate shaft.

L-SERIES

On some of these models there may be clunk during turning maneuvers. This condition may be felt in steering wheel when vehicle is stationary and wheel is turned stop-to-stop. Typically, clunk is heard every 180° of steering wheel rotation. Noise is noticed during low speed acceleration or deceleration, in tight turns.

This condition may be caused by inadequate steering intermediate shaft lubrication.

To correct this condition, proceed as follows:

1. Remove steering intermediate shaft.
2. Mark shaft to ensure proper installation indexing.
3. Fully extend shaft.
4. Apply grease kit lubrication (part No. 26098237) in yoke opening aluminum end, place syringe tip as deep as possible and fully dispense contents.
5. Install kit supplied rubber stop plug.
6. Distribute grease by extending and collapsing slip joint fully 16 time.
7. Extend intermediate shaft and ensure grease is at least .2 inch past splines.
8. Remove rubber stopper and install shaft.

Low Speed Steering Moan Or Groan

2004 L-SERIES

On some of these models equipped with 2.2L engine and automatic transmission, there may be a moan or groan noise from the power steering system while turning the steering wheel at low vehicle speeds.

This condition may be caused by power steering pump pressure pulses creating resonance throughout the system.

To correct this condition, install new tuned power steering pressure hose (part No. 227141740, then flush fluid and vacuum bleed steering system.

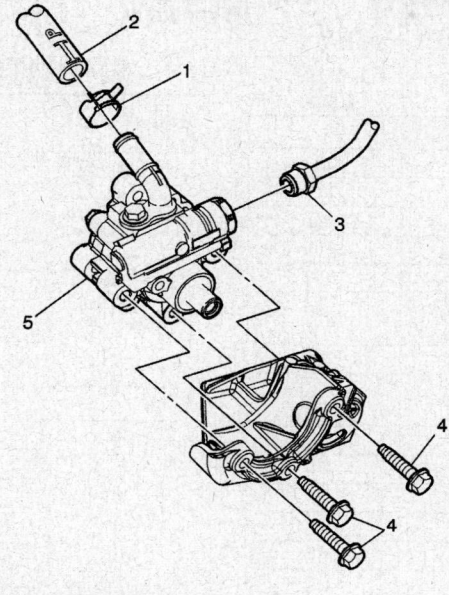

1-Outlet hose clamp
2-Outlet hose
3-Inlet hose
4-Pump mounting bolts
5-Pump

ARM0600000000067

Fig. 14 Power steering pump replacement. SKY

Power Steering Inoperative/Steering Wheel Hard to Turn

ION

On some of these models, the steering wheel may be hard to turn and Driver Information Center (DIC) displays PWR STR.

This condition may be caused by improper jump starting vehicle. This happens when the Underhood Junction Block (UHJB) is mistaken from the battery. When jumper cables are connected to the UHJB posts, the power steering fuses will blow.

To correct this condition, replace the blown fuses.

Front Suspension Creaking/Squeaking Noise When Turning

2004 ION

On some of these models there may be a creaking or squeaking noise from the front suspension when turning the steering wheel.

This condition may be caused by the fit between front suspension strut bumper and shaft.

To correct this condition replace the front suspension strut bumpers.

Steering Rattle Noise

2004 ION

On some of these models there may be a rattle noise when changing direction or hitting bumps.

This condition may be caused by excessive clearance between the steering column assist motor gear teeth.

To correct this condition, replace the steering column as outlined in "Steering Columns" chapter.

SATURN

TIGHTENING SPECIFICATIONS

Year	Component	Torque/Ft. Lbs.
AURA		
2007–08	Ball Stud Pinch Bolt	32
	Control Arm Bushing To Frame	37
	Drive Shaft Nut	159
	Frame Support Bracket To Body	⑥
	Hub & Bearing Assembly	85
	Intermediate Shaft To Steering Gear Pinch Bolt	36
	Lower Control Arm To Bushing	32
	Outer Tie Rod End To Steering Knuckle	⑦
	Power Steering Gear To Frame	⑧
	Rear Frame To Body	⑥
	Stabilizer Link Nut	48
	Stabilizer Shaft Clamp	18
	Steering Knuckle To Strut	89
	Upper Strut Cap To Body	18
	Upper Strut Shaft	52
	Wheel Lug Nut	100
ION		
2004–07	Ball Joint To Control Arm	50
	Ball Joint To Steering Knuckle	④
	Control Arm To Front Frame	49
	Control Arm To Rear Frame	⑤
	Intermediate Shaft Pinch	25
	Outer Tie Rod	②
	Stabilizer Link To Strut	48
	Stabilizer Shaft Clamp	37
	Stabilizer Shaft Link To Bar	81
	Steering Gear	81
	Strut Cap To Body	81
	Strut Shaft	52
	Strut To Steering Knuckle	89
	Transaxle Mount To Frame	37
	Transaxle Through Bolt	74
	Wheel Bearing/Hub To Knuckle	85
	Wheel Driveshaft Nut	81
	Wheel Lug Nuts	100
L-SERIES		
2004–05	ABS Sensor Bracket To Knuckle	72
	Caliper Bracket To Knuckle	70
	Control Arm To Frame	65
	Frame To Body	66
	Inner Tie Rod To Steering Gear	70
	Intermediate Shaft To Steering Column	20
	Intermediate Shaft To Steering Gear	20
	Power Steering High Pressure Line	20
	Power Steering Pump Pulley	15
	Power Steering Pump To Bracket	15

TIGHTENING SPECIFICATIONS—Continued

Year	Component	Torque/Ft. Lbs.
L-SERIES		
2004–05	Power Steering Pump To Engine	18
	Stabilizer Bar To Link	50
	Steering Wheel Nut	26
	Strut Shaft To Body	40
	Strut Shaft To Mount	40
	Strut To Steering Knuckle	①
	Wheel Lug Nut	③
SKY		
2007–08	Ball Joint Nut (Lower)	⑨
	Ball Joint Nut (Upper)	⑩
	Control Arm To Frame Nut	122
	Control Arm To Frame Bolts	81
	Intermediate Shaft To Steering Column	43
	Intermediate Shaft To Steering Gear	43
	Power Steering Gear	44
	Power Steering Pump	16
	Power Steering Outlet Pipe/Hose Fitting	22
	Shock Absorber	31
	Stabilizer Shaft Link	53
	Stabilizer Shaft	41
	Strut, Lower	21
	Strut, Upper	35
	Tie Rod End Stud Nut (Outer)	⑪
	Upper Shock Absorber	35
	Wheel Hub/Speed Sensor	85
	Wheel Nuts	100

① — Refer to "Wheel Hub & Steering Knuckle, Replace" for tightening specifications and sequence.

② — First pass, torque to 15 ft. lbs.; 2nd pass, tighten an additional 180.°

③ — First pass, torque to 46 ft. lbs.; 2nd pass, torque to 92 ft. lbs.

④ — Refer to "Ball Joint, Replace" for tightening specifications and sequence.

⑤ — First pass, torque to 74 ft. lbs.; 2nd pass, tighten an additional 180.°

⑥ — First pass, torque to 74 ft. lbs.; 2nd pass, tighten an additional 90.°

⑦ — First pass, torque to 15 ft. lbs.; 2nd pass, tighten an additional 180.°

⑧ — First pass, torque to 52 ft. lbs.; 2nd pass, tighten an additional 90.°

⑨ — First pass, torque to 30 ft. lbs.; 2nd pass, tighten an additional 135°.

⑩ — First pass, torque to 22 ft. lbs.; 2nd pass, tighten an additional 150°.

⑪ — First pass, torque to 22 ft. lbs.; 2nd pass, tighten an additional 115.°

Wheel Alignment

INDEX

	Page No.
Front Wheel Alignment	12-109
AURA	12-109
Camber	12-109
Caster	12-109
Toe	12-109
ION	12-109
Camber	12-109
Caster	12-109
Toe-In	12-109
L-Series	12-109

	Page No.
Camber	12-109
Caster	12-109
Toe-In	12-109
SKY	12-109
Camber	12-109
Caster	12-109
Toe	12-110
Preliminary Inspection	12-109
Rear Wheel Alignment	12-110
AURA	12-110

	Page No.
Camber	12-110
Toe	12-110
L-Series	12-110
Toe-In	12-110
SKY	12-110
Camber & Caster	12-110
Toe	12-110
Wheel Alignment Specifications	12-4

PRELIMINARY INSPECTION

1. Inspect tires for proper inflation, wear pattern or out of round condition.
2. Inspect suspension and steering components for wear and damage.
3. Inspect strut bushings for wear or damage.
4. Inspect vehicle ride height as outlined under "Vehicle Ride Height."
5. Road test vehicle.
6. Wheel alignment should be performed in the following order:
   a. Rear camber.
   b. Rear toe.
   c. Righthand front camber and caster.
   d. Lefthand front camber and caster.
   e. Front toe.

FRONT WHEEL ALIGNMENT

AURA

CASTER

Front wheel caster is not adjustable on these vehicles. These angles can be measured but are set by design of the front suspension. If caster angle is not within specifications, inspect front suspension.

CAMBER

1. Disconnect strut from steering knuckle, refer to "Strut, Replace" procedure in "Front Suspension & Steering" section.
2. Enlarge bottom holes in outer flanges with suitable round file, until holes in outer flanges match slots in inner flanges, **Fig. 1.**
3. Install or connect strut to steering knuckle and install bolts hand tight.
4. Grasp top of tire firmly and move tire inboard or outboard until proper camber reading is obtained. Tighten mounting bolts enough to retain camber setting.
5. Remove wheel and tire assembly, then tighten strut to steering knuckle mounting bolts to specification. Refer to "Tightening Specifications" in "Front Suspension & Steering" section.

TOE

1. Ensure front wheels are in straight-ahead position.
2. Loosen jam nut, **Fig. 2.**
3. Turn adjuster to obtain proper toe setting.
4. **Torque** jam nut to 50 ft. lbs.

L-Series

Rear wheel alignment must be set to specifications before front wheel alignment adjustment.

CASTER

Front wheel caster is not adjustable on these vehicles. These angles can be measured but are set by design of the front suspension. If caster angle is not within specifications, inspect front suspension.

CAMBER

1. Raise and support vehicle, then remove tire and wheel assemblies.
2. Remove strut to knuckle mounting bolts and discard.
3. Remove material from strut bracket lower hole using suitable file or grinder, **Fig. 3.**
4. To increase negative camber, remove from outside hole. To increase positive camber, remove from inside hole.
5. Tighten strut to knuckle mounting bolts in three steps: First step, **torque** bolts to 37 ft. lbs.; second step, **torque** bolts to 73 ft. lbs.; third step, tighten bolts an additional 30–40°.
6. **Torque** wheel lug nuts to 46 ft. lbs., then to 92 ft. lbs.
7. Lower vehicle, then inspect camber angle.

TOE-IN

1. Lock steering wheel in straight ahead position.
2. Loosen both inner tie rod jam nuts and inner tie rod seal to boot surface. **Ensure tie rods turn freely from boot seal surface. Do not allow boot to turn.**
3. Adjust toe angle using suitable wrench.

4. **Torque** inner tie rod end jam nuts to 44 ft. lbs.
5. Inspect toe angle.

ION

CASTER

Front wheel caster is not adjustable on these vehicles. These angles can be measured but are set by design of the front suspension. If caster angle is not within specifications, inspect front suspension.

CAMBER

1. Loosen both strut to knuckle nuts just enough to allow movement.
2. Disconnect strut from knuckle.
3. File lower hole out to groove of stamped ring around hole.
4. Connect strut to knuckle.
5. Adjust camber by moving top of wheel in or out.

TOE-IN

1. Lock steering wheel in straight ahead position.
2. Loosen tie rod jam nut.
3. Adjust toe by turning adjuster.
4. **Torque** tie rod jam nut to 50 ft. lbs.

SKY

CASTER

1. Loosen control arm caster adjustment bolt nut, **Fig. 4.**
2. Rotate bolts to required caster specification setting, refer to "Front Wheel Alignment Specifications" in "Specifications" section.
3. Maintain caster setting, then **torque** bolt to 122 ft. lbs.
4. Inspect caster setting after tightening.

CAMBER

1. Loosen control arm camber adjustment bolt nut, **Fig. 4.**
2. Rotate bolts to required camber specification setting, refer to "Front Wheel Alignment Specifications" in "Specifications" section.
3. Maintain camber setting, then **torque** bolt to 122 ft. lbs.
4. Inspect camber setting.

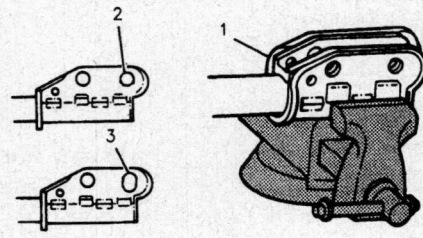

1 STRUT IN VISE
2 BEFORE FILING
3 AFTER FILING

GC2049700155000X

Fig. 1 Strut bracket modification for camber adjustment. AURA

TOE

1. Loosen jam nut on tie rod.
2. Rotate inner tie rod to required toe specification setting, refer to "Front Wheel Alignment Specifications" in "Specifications" section.
3. **Torque** jam nut on tie rod to 50 ft. lbs.
4. Inspect toe setting after tightening.

REAR WHEEL ALIGNMENT

AURA

CAMBER

1. Loosen inner lower control arm cam bolt nuts.
2. Rotate cam bolts to required camber specification setting, **Fig. 5.** Refer to "Rear Wheel Alignment Specifications" in "Specifications" section.
3. Maintain camber setting while tightening cam bolt nuts. **Torque** inner lower control arm (front) bolt nut to 81 ft. lbs. Recheck setting after tightening.
4. Inspect toe setting after changing camber.

TOE

1. Loosen inner toe link cam bolt and nuts.
2. Rotate cam bolt to specification. Refer to "Rear Wheel Alignment Specifications" in "Specifications" section.

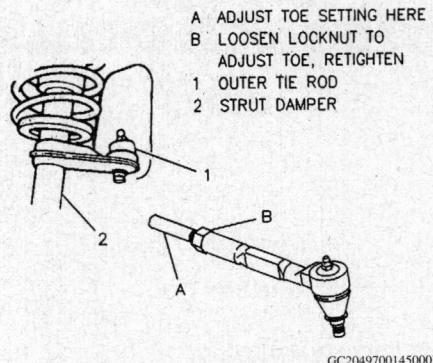

A ADJUST TOE SETTING HERE
B LOOSEN LOCKNUT TO ADJUST TOE, RETIGHTEN
1 OUTER TIE ROD
2 STRUT DAMPER

GC2049700145000X

Fig. 2 Toe adjustment

3. Maintain toe setting and **torque** rear suspension adjustment link lock nut to 81 ft. lbs.
4. Inspect toe setting after tightening.

L-Series

Rear wheel alignment involves setting the toe angle. Rear wheel camber is not adjustable.

TOE-IN

1. Remove and discard rear axle control arm bolts.
2. Install new bolts. **Do not tighten now.** Leave inside forward bolt out.
3. Move rear axle control arm in direction of required toe correction using rear toe adjusting tool No. KM-900, or equivalent.
4. Snug rear axle control arm bolts. **Do not tighten now.**
5. Inspect toe. Adjust as required.
6. **Torque** rear axle control arm bolts to 65 ft. lbs., then tighten an additional 30–45°.
7. Repeat procedure for other rear wheel.

SKY

CAMBER & CASTER

Camber must be set before adjusting caster.
1. Choose either driver or passenger side.
2. Turn Digital Angle Gage unit tool No. CH-47960, or equivalent, on.
3. Choose zero setting on key pad and push enter, then program in required

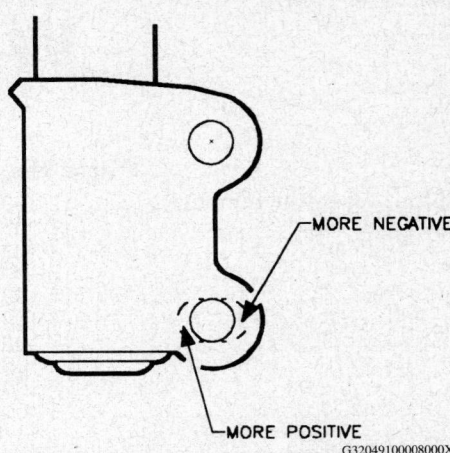

—MORE NEGATIVE

—MORE POSITIVE

G32049100008000X

Fig. 3 Front & rear camber adjustment

offset of +3.7 degrees.
4. Before installing sensor to knuckle, use a soft nylon bristle brush to clean debris from the gauge holes. **Do not use power tools or abrasives.**
5. Verify locating pins are installed into back of sensor.
6. Loosen and adjust locator pins, then install gage tool to rear knuckle gage holes, **Fig. 6.**
7. Loosen lower control arm cam bolt nuts, **Fig. 7.**
8. Rotate cam bolts to required camber setting.
9. Maintain camber settings while tightening cam bolt nuts. **Torque** cam bolt nuts to 122 ft. lbs.
10. Rotate cam bolts to required caster setting.
11. Maintain caster settings while tightening cam bolt nuts. **Torque** cam bolt nuts to 122 ft. lbs.

TOE

1. Loosen rear suspension toe link locknut.
2. Rotate toe link to required toe specification setting, refer to "Rear Wheel Alignment Specifications" in "Specifications" section.
3. Tighten toe link locknut. **Use correct fastener in correct location. Replacement fasteners must be correct part number for that application.**
4. Inspect toe setting after tightening.

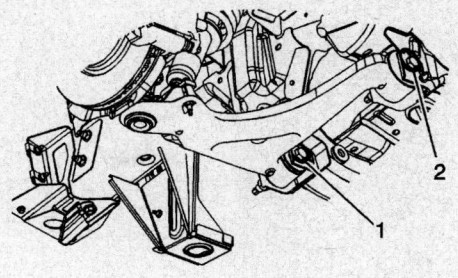

1-Camber adjustment bolt
2-Caster adjustment bolt

ARM0600000000069

**Fig. 4   Front camber & caster
adjustment bolts. SKY**

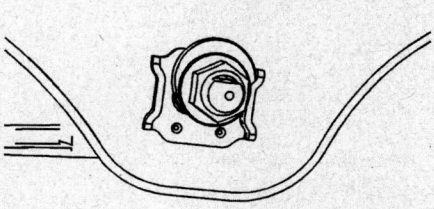

ARM0600000000068

**Fig. 5   Rear camber adjustment
bolt. AURA**

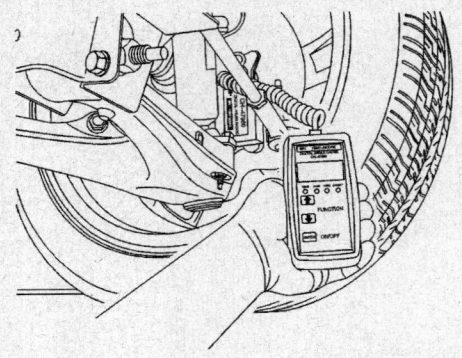

ARM0600000000070

**Fig. 6   Alignment gage tool
installation. SKY**

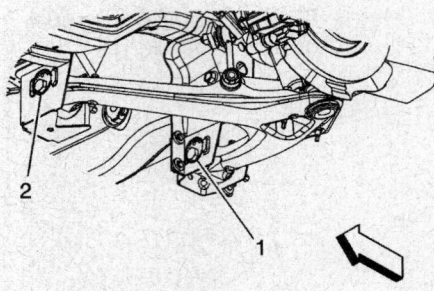

2

1

1-Camber adjustment bolt

2-Caster adjustment bolt

ARM0600000000071

**Fig. 7   Camber & caster cam bolt
locations. SKY**

XLR

NOTE: Refer To The Rear Of This Manual For Manufacturer's Special Service Tool Supplies.

INDEX OF SERVICE OPERATIONS

Page No.

AIR BAG SYSTEM
PRECAUTIONS 0-18
BRAKES
    Anti-Lock Brakes (Volume 2).. 6-1
    Disc Brakes.................. 22-1
    Drum Brakes................. 23-1
    Hydraulic Brake Systems 24-1
    Power Brake Units........... 25-1
COMPUTER RELEARN
PROCEDURE 0-31
ELECTRICAL
    Air Bag System (Volume 2) ... 4-1
    Air Conditioning.............. 16-1
    Alternator, Replace 13-4
    Alternators.................... 19-1
    Blower Motor, Replace........ 13-7
    Cabin Air Filter, Replace 13-7
    Cooling Fans 17-1
    Cruise Control (Volume 2) 2-1
    Dash Gauges (Volume 2) 1-1
    Dash Panel Service
    (Volume 2).................... 5-1
    Evaporator Core, Replace 13-8
    Fuel Pump Relay Location.... 13-4
    Fuse Panel & Flasher
    Location 13-4
    Heater Core, Replace........ 13-7
    Ignition Coils, Replace 13-5
    Ignition Lock, Replace 13-5
    Ignition Switch, Replace 13-5
    Instrument Cluster, Replace... 13-6
    Multi-Function Switch,
    Replace 13-5
    Neutral Safety Switch,
    Replace 13-5
    Passive Restraint Systems
    (Volume 2).................... 4-1
    Precautions.................. 13-4
    Radio, Replace 13-6
    Relay Center Location 13-4
    Speed Controls (Volume 2) ... 2-1
    Starter Motors 18-1
    Starter, Replace 13-4
    Steering Columns............ 20-1
    Steering Wheel, Replace...... 13-6
    Stop Light Switch, Replace ... 13-5
    Wiper Motor, Replace......... 13-6
    Wiper Switch, Replace........ 13-7
    Wiper Systems (Volume 2).... 3-1

Page No.

ELECTRICAL SYMBOL
IDENTIFICATION 0-63
FRONT DRIVE AXLES 26-1
FRONT SUSPENSION &
STEERING
    Ball Joint, Replace........... 13-21
    Ball Joint Inspection 13-21
    Control Arm, Replace 13-22
    Crossmember, Replace 13-22
    Hub & Bearing, Replace 13-21
    Power Steering 21-1
    Power Steering Gear,
    Replace 13-23
    Power Steering Pump,
    Replace 13-23
    Power Steering System
    Bleed........................ 13-23
    Shock Absorber, Replace 13-21
    Stabilizer Bar, Replace....... 13-22
    Steering Columns............ 20-1
    Steering Knuckle, Replace.... 13-22
    Tie Rod, Replace 13-22
    Tightening Specifications...... 13-24
    Transverse Spring, Replace... 13-21
NON-STANDARD TIRE &
WHEEL SIZE
ADJUSTMENT TO RIDE
HEIGHT SPECIFICATIONS
& TIRE SIZE CHART 0-61
REAR AXLE &
SUSPENSION
    Ball Joint, Replace........... 13-19
    Control Arm, Replace 13-19
    Description 13-17
    Differential Carrier, Replace... 13-18
    Hub & Bearing, Replace 13-18
    Rear Axle Shaft, Replace 13-17
    Rear Crossmember, Replace . 13-20
    Shock Absorber, Replace 13-19
    Stabilizer Shaft, Replace..... 13-20
    Suspension Knuckle,
    Replace 13-20
    Tie Rod, Replace 13-19
    Tightening Specifications...... 13-20
    Transverse Spring, Replace... 13-19
SERVICE REMINDER &
WARNING LAMP RESET
PROCEDURES 0-34
SPECIFICATIONS
    Fluid Capacities & Cooling
    System Data................. 13-3

Page No.

Front Wheel Alignment
Specifications.................. 13-2
General Engine
Specifications.................. 13-2
Lubricant Data................. 13-3
Rear Wheel Alignment
Specifications.................. 13-2
Tune Up Specifications 13-2
Vehicle Ride Height
Specifications.................. 13-2
TIRE PRESSURE
MONITORING SYSTEM 28-1
VEHICLE
IDENTIFICATION 0-1
VEHICLE LIFT POINTS 0-51
VEHICLE MAINTENANCE
SCHEDULES 0-73
WHEEL ALIGNMENT
    Front Wheel Alignment........ 13-25
    Preliminary Inspection 13-25
    Rear Wheel Alignment 13-25
    Vehicle Ride Height 13-25
    Wheel Alignment
    Specifications................ 13-2
WIRE COLOR CODE
IDENTIFICATION 0-63
4.4L ENGINE
    Engine Rebuilding
    Specifications................ 29-1
    Engine, Replace 13-9
    Engine Mount, Replace 13-9
    Fuel Filter, Replace 13-11
    Fuel Pump, Replace 13-11
    Oil Pan, Replace............. 13-10
    Precautions.................. 13-9
    Radiator, Replace............ 13-11
    Serpentine Drive Belt 13-10
    Supercharger, Replace 13-11
    Tightening Specifications...... 13-12
4.6L ENGINE
    Engine Rebuilding
    Specifications................ 29-1
    Engine, Replace 13-13
    Engine Mount, Replace 13-13
    Fuel Filter, Replace 13-16
    Fuel Pump, Replace 13-15
    Oil Pan, Replace............. 13-14
    Precautions.................. 13-13
    Radiator, Replace............ 13-15
    Serpentine Drive Belt 13-15
    Tightening Specifications...... 13-16

Specifications

GENERAL ENGINE SPECIFICATIONS

Engine Liter/VIN Code①	Fuel System	Bore & Stroke	Compression Ratio	Net H.P. @ RPM②	Maximum Torque Ft. Lbs. @ RPM	Normal Oil Pressure, psi
4.4L/A	SFI	3.58 x 3.31	9.0	443 @ 6400	414 @ 3900	③
4.6L/A	SFI	3.66 x 3.31	10.5	320 @ 6400	310 @ 4400	③

① — Eighth digit of VIN denotes engine code.

② — Ratings are net-as installed in vehicle.

③ — 5 psi @ idle speed, 35 psi @ 2000 RPM.

TUNE UP SPECIFICATIONS

| Engine Liter/VIN Code① | Spark Plug Gap | Ignition Timing | | Idle Speed | Fuel Pump Pressure, psi④ | Valve Clearance, Inch |
		Firing Order	Wire Connections			
4.4L/A	.040	②	—	⑤	55–60	③
4.6L/A	.050	②	—	⑤	55–62	③

① — Eighth digit of VIN denotes engine code.

② — Cylinder numbering from lefthand side to righthand side as viewed from front of vehicle, front bank 2, 4, 6, 8; rear bank 1, 3, 5, 7. Firing order, 1-2-7-3-4-5-6-8.

③ — Equipped w/hydraulic valve lifters; no adjustment required.

④ — With shop towel wrapped around fuel pressure gauge & fuel pressure test port to prevent spillage, connect fuel pressure gauge to fuel pressure test port. Inspect fuel pressure w/ignition key in On position and engine not running.

⑤ — Idle speed is controlled by a throttle actuator motor.

FRONT WHEEL ALIGNMENT SPECIFICATIONS

| Year | Model | Caster Angle, Degrees | | Camber Angle, Degrees | | Total Toe, Degree | Steering Angle, Degrees | Ball Joint Wear |
		Limits	Desired	Limits	Desired			
2004–05	All	+7.50 to +8.50	+8.00	-1.0 to 0	-.5	-.10 to +.30	-1.0 to +1.0	①
2006	All	+6.47 to +7.67	+7.07	-1.0 to 0	-.5	.10 to .20	-3.5 to +3.5	①
2007–08	All	+8.30 to +7.10	+7.70	-.105 to .15	-.45	-.10 to +.30	-3.5 to +3.5	①

① — Refer to "Ball Joint Inspection" in "Front Suspension & Steering" section.

REAR WHEEL ALIGNMENT SPECIFICATIONS

| Year | Model | Camber Angle, Degrees | | Total Toe, Degrees | Thrust Angle, Degrees |
		Limits	Desired		
2004–05	All	-1.00 to 0	-.50	-.20 to +.20	-.10 to +.10
2006–08	All	-.95 to +.05	-.45	-.25 to +.15	-.20 to +.20

VEHICLE RIDE HEIGHT SPECIFICATIONS

Model	Year	Body Style	Manufacturer's Original Tire Size	Measurement Points & Specifications①②					
				Front			Rear		
				Dim.	Specification		Dim.	Specification	
					Inches	mm		Inches	mm
XLR	2004–05	All	②	Z	1.48–1.98	37.6–50.4	D	4.0–4.5	101.6–114.4

Continued

VEHICLE RIDE HEIGHT SPECIFICATIONS—Continued

Model	Year	Body Style	Manu-facturer's Origi-nal Tire Size	Measurement Points & Specifications①②					
				Front			Rear		
				Dim.	Specification		Dim.	Specification	
					Inches	mm		Inches	mm
XLR	2006–08	FE2 (Base W/RPO LC3)	②	Z	1.72–2.22	43.6–56.4	D	4.83–5.33	122.6–135.4
		FE2 (Base W/RPO LH2)	②	Z	1.52–2.06	37.6–50.4	D	4.55–5.05	113.6–126.4

Dim. — Dimension

D Dim. — Rear suspension measurement from front outboard control arm bolt center line to bottom of control arm ball joint, **Fig. A.**

Z Dim. — Front suspension measurement from front pivot bolt center line to lowest point of ball joint, **Fig. B.**

① — Measurement is with fuel, radiator coolant and engine oil full, spare tire, jack, hand tools and mats in designated positions and tires properly inflated.

② — See door sticker or inside of glove compartment for manufacturers original tire size specifications.

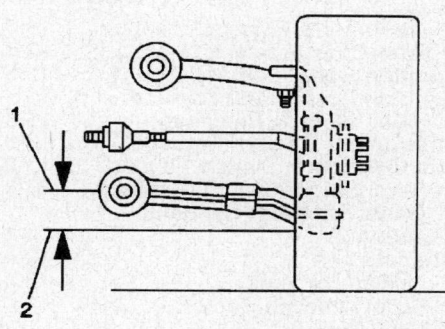

ARM0300000000268

Fig. A Rear "D" dimension trim height inspection

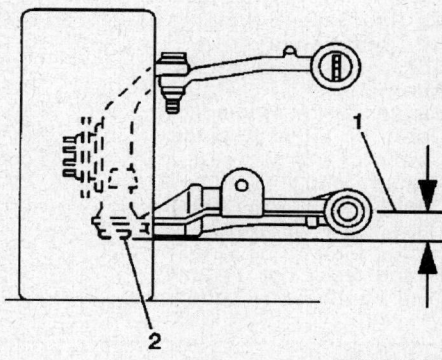

ARM0300000000269

Fig. B Front "Z" dimension trim height inspection

FLUID CAPACITIES & COOLING SYSTEM DATA

Model	Engine Liter/VIN Code①	Coolant Capacity, Qts.	Coolant Type	Radiator Cap Relief Pressure, Lbs.	Thermo Opening Temp.	Fuel Tank, Gallons	Engine Oil Refill, Qts. ③	Auto Transaxle, Qts.
XLR	4.6L/A	14.8	DEX-COOL②	15	188	18	8.0	④
	4.4L/A	14.8	DEX-COOL②	18	195	18	8.0	④

① — Eighth digit of VIN denotes engine code.

② — DEX-COOL, or equivalent, silicant-free antifreeze conforming to GM specification No. 6277M.

③ — With filter change.

④ — Pan removal, 6.5 qts.; complete overhaul, 9.0 qts.

LUBRICANT DATA

Year	Model	Lubricant Type			
		Automatic Transaxle	Power Steering System	Rear Differential	Brake System
2004–05	All	Dexron III	GM Part No. 89021184	75W-90 Synthetic GM Part No. 12378261	DOT 3
2006	All	Dexron VI	GM Part No. 89021184	75W-90 Synthetic GM Part No. 12378261	DOT 3
2007–08	All	Dexron VI	GM Part No. 89021184	75W-90 Synthetic GM Part No. 89021677①	DOT 3

① — Complete drain and refill add 4 ounces of Limited-Slip Axle Lubricant Additive GM Part No. 1052358.

Electrical

NOTE: On Air Bag Equipped Models, Refer To "Air Bag System Precautions" Located In The Front Of This Manual For System Disarming & Arming Procedures.

NOTE: Refer To "Computer Relearn Procedures" Located In The Front Of This Manual When Battery Power To The Computer Has Been Interrupted.

INDEX

	Page No.		Page No.		Page No.
Air Bag System (Volume 2)	4-1	Fuse Panel & Flasher Location	13-4	Radio, Replace	13-6
Air Conditioning	16-1	Heater Core, Replace	13-7	Relay Center Location	13-4
Alternator, Replace	13-4	Ignition Coils, Replace	13-5	Speed Controls (Volume 2)	2-1
Alternators	19-1	Ignition Lock, Replace	13-5	Starter Motors	18-1
Blower Motor, Replace	13-7	Ignition Switch, Replace	13-5	Starter, Replace	13-4
Cabin Air Filter, Replace	13-7	Instrument Cluster, Replace	13-6	Steering Columns	20-1
Cooling Fans	17-1	Multi-Function Switch, Replace	13-5	Steering Wheel, Replace	13-6
Cruise Control (Volume 2)	2-1	Neutral Safety Switch, Replace	13-5	Stop Light Switch, Replace	13-5
Dash Gauges (Volume 2)	1-1	Passive Restraint Systems		Wiper Motor, Replace	13-6
Dash Panel Service		(Volume 2)	4-1	Wiper Switch, Replace	13-7
(Volume 2)	5-1	Precautions	13-4	Wiper Systems (Volume 2)	3-1
Evaporator Core, Replace	13-8	Air Bag Systems	13-4		
Fuel Pump Relay Location	13-4	Battery Ground Cable	13-4		

PRECAUTIONS

Air Bag Systems

Refer to "Air Bag System Precautions" in the front of this manual for system disarming and arming procedures.

Battery Ground Cable

Prior to service, disconnect battery ground cable and isolate as required.

FUSE PANEL & FLASHER LOCATION

The instrument panel fuse block is located in the righthand foot well, mounted on the toe board, behind the carpet. The underhood fuse block is located on the righthand side of the engine compartment. The turn signal and hazard flasher operation is controlled by the Body Control Module (BCM), the BCM is located in the righthand foot well, mounted on the toe board, behind the carpet.

FUEL PUMP RELAY LOCATION

Fuel pump operation is controlled by the fuel pump control module. The module is mounted on a brace in the lefthand side rear quarter panel, on the side of the fuel filler neck.

RELAY CENTER LOCATION

The instrument panel righthand relay block is located in the righthand foot well, mounted on the toe board, behind the carpet.

STARTER

REPLACE

1. **On models equipped with a 4.6L engine,** remove intake manifold as outlined under "Intake Manifold, Replace" in "4.6L Engine" section.
2. **On models equipped with a 4.4L engine,** remove supercharger assembly as outlined under "Supercharger, Replace"
3. **On all models,** disconnect starter solenoid "S" and battery terminals electrical connectors.
4. Remove mounting bolts and starter.
5. Reverse procedure to install, noting the following:
   a. **Torque** starter mounting bolts to 22 ft. lbs.
   b. **Torque** "S" terminal nut to 35 inch lbs.
   c. **Torque** battery terminal nut to 9 ft. lbs.

ALTERNATOR

REPLACE

1. Rotate drive belt tensioner and remove drive belt.
2. Raise and support vehicle, then drain cooling system.
3. Remove tire and wheel assemblies.
4. Loosen, do not remove, outer tie rod end stud nut from outer tie rod end ball stud.
5. Loosen outer tie rod end stud to steering knuckle connection using tie rod remover tool No. J 42188, or equivalent.
6. Remove outer tie rod end stud nut and separate tie rod from steering knuckle.
7. Loosen jam nut on inner tie rod assembly, then remove outer tie rod end from inner tie rod assembly.
8. Disconnect Electronic Suspension Control (ESC) sensor links.
9. Remove stabilizer shaft link nuts from stabilizer shaft.
10. Remove stabilizer shaft insulator clamps from front crossmember, then stabilizer shaft from vehicle.
11. Turn steering wheel far enough to left-hand side to gain access to intermediate shaft bolts, then place ignition in locked position.
12. Remove upper to lower intermediate shaft bolts, then lower coupling shield.
13. Remove lower coupling pinch bolt, then lower coupling from steering gear.
14. Slide lower intermediate shaft from upper intermediate shaft and remove lower intermediate shaft from vehicle.
15. Remove bolts from Electronic Brake Control Module/Brake Pressure Modulator Valve (EBCM/BPMV) bracket.
16. Support and reposition EBCM/BPMV and bracket away from crossmember.
17. Remove power steering gear mounting bolts.
18. Remove power steering fluid cooler from crossmember.
19. Lift power steering gear off of crossmember and support.
20. Remove transverse spring from vehicle.
21. Remove lower shock absorber bolts from lower control arms.
22. Remove lower control arm bolts from crossmember.
23. Place a transmission jack under crossmember, then remove engine mount lower nuts.

24. Disconnect wheel speed sensor wiring harness from crossmember.
25. Disconnect electrical harness and brake pipe from clips on crossmember.
26. Remove crossmember mounting nuts, then lower crossmember from vehicle.
27. Remove bolt from alternator coolant hose assembly on alternator.
28. Disconnect alternator coolant hose assembly from alternator port.
29. Slide boot back along cable, then remove starter cable nut.
30. Remove starter cable terminal from stud.
31. Remove upper alternator mounting bolt.
32. Remove idler pulley thru-bolt and nut.
33. Remove idler pulley assembly, then alternator.
34. Reverse procedure to install.

IGNITION COILS
REPLACE

1. Remove fuel injector sight shield from top of engine.
2. **On models equipped with a 4.4L engine,** remove Supercharger Inlet Duct Assembly as outlined under "Supercharger, Replace".
3. **On all models,** disconnect ignition coil wiring harness connector.
4. Remove ignition coil retaining bolt, then coil.
5. Reverse procedure to install.

IGNITION LOCK
REPLACE

1. Remove steering wheel as outlined under "Steering Wheel, Replace."
2. Pry fuel door and rear compartment lid release switch from knee bolster, then disconnect switch electrical connectors.
3. Remove driver knee bolster trim panel lower retaining screws, **Fig. 1.**
4. Grasp knee bolster trim panel at side edges, then remove trim panel by pulling firmly to release locking tabs.
5. Remove lower steering column trim cover retaining screws.
6. Disconnect closeout shroud from steering column lower trim cover.
7. Disconnect steering column power tilt and telescopic switch electrical connectors.
8. Remove lower trim cover from steering column.
9. Remove steering column upper trim cover retaining screw.
10. Lift upper trim cover to gain access to lock cylinder access hole.
11. Insert tip of a suitable bent tip awl into ignition lock cylinder access hole.
12. Turn ignition lock cylinder to START position, then push bent tip awl down on lock cylinder retaining pin.
13. Turn ignition lock cylinder to RUN position and remove from steering column.
14. Reverse procedure to install.

IGNITION SWITCH
REPLACE

1. Pry fuel door and rear compartment lid

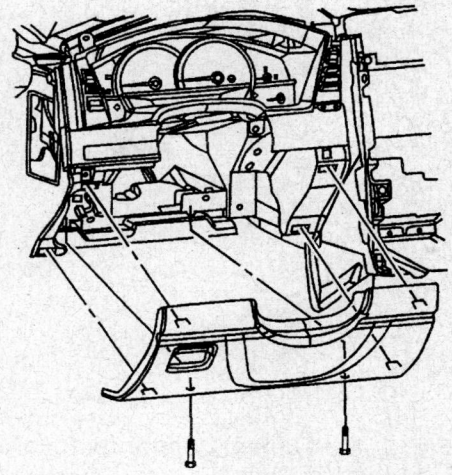

ARM0300000000292

Fig. 1   Driver knee bolster removal

release switch from knee bolster, then disconnect switch electrical connectors.
2. Remove driver knee bolster trim panel lower retaining screws, **Fig. 1.**
3. Grasp knee bolster trim panel at side edges, then remove trim panel by pulling firmly to release locking tabs.
4. Carefully pry instrument panel courtesy lamp assembly from lefthand side lower closeout panel using a suitable flat-bladed tool.
5. Insert instrument panel courtesy lamp assembly up through opening in closeout panel.
6. Release notch in righthand side forward edge of closeout panel from tab on accelerator pedal bracket, then remove closeout panel.
7. Remove retaining screws from bottom of Driver Information Center (DIC) switch pad.
8. Pull outward on DIC switch pad to disengage retaining clip, then disconnect switch pad electrical connectors.
9. Remove DIC switch retaining screws, then the switch.
10. Disconnect ignition switch electrical connector, then remove ignition switch from DIC pod.
11. Reverse procedure to install.

NEUTRAL SAFETY SWITCH
REPLACE

On these models, the transmission range function is controlled by the transmission manual shift shaft switch. The switch, which is mounted on the side of the transmission case, inputs the Park/Neutral position to the Transmission Control Module (TCM). The TCM will then input this signal to the Powertrain Control Module (PCM). The PCM based on this signal will allow the engine to start.

STOP LIGHT SWITCH
REPLACE

Brake lamp operation is controlled by the Body Control Module (BCM). The BCM uses an input signal from the brake pedal position sensor to determine when the brake lamps should operate. Use the following procedure to replace the brake pedal position sensor.

1. Carefully pry instrument panel courtesy lamp assembly from lefthand side lower closeout panel using a suitable flat-bladed tool.
2. Remove push-on retaining nut from steering column bracket stud.
3. Release lefthand side lower closeout panel to instrument panel lower support beam push-in retainers.
4. Insert instrument panel courtesy lamp assembly up through opening in closeout panel.
5. Release notch in righthand side forward edge of closeout panel from tab on accelerator pedal bracket, then lower and remove closeout panel.
6. Disengage but do not remove Connector Position Assurance (CPA) from brake pedal position sensor connector.
7. Disconnect brake pedal position sensor electrical connector.
8. Remove brake pedal position sensor retaining screw, then sensor from bracket.
9. Reverse procedure to install.

MULTI-FUNCTION SWITCH
REPLACE

1. Remove steering wheel as outlined under "Steering Wheel, Replace."
2. Pry fuel door and rear compartment lid release switch from knee bolster, then disconnect switch electrical connectors.
3. Remove driver knee bolster trim panel lower retaining screws, **Fig. 1.**
4. Grasp knee bolster trim panel at side edges, then remove trim panel by pulling firmly to release locking tabs.
5. Remove lower steering column trim cover retaining screws.
6. Disconnect closeout shroud from steering column lower trim cover.
7. Disconnect steering column power tilt and telescopic switch electrical connectors.
8. Remove lower trim cover from steering column.
9. Remove steering column upper trim cover retaining screw.
10. Remove lock cylinder from steering column as outlined under "Ignition Lock, Replace."
11. Remove upper trim cover from steering column.
12. Remove multi-function switch retaining screws.
13. Disconnect multi-function switch electrical connectors, then remove switch from steering column.
14. Reverse procedure to install.

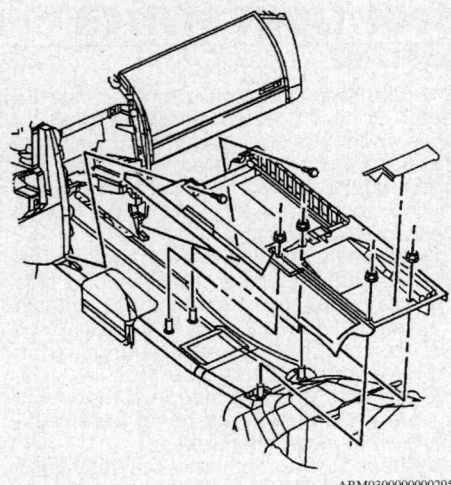

Fig. 2   Console removal

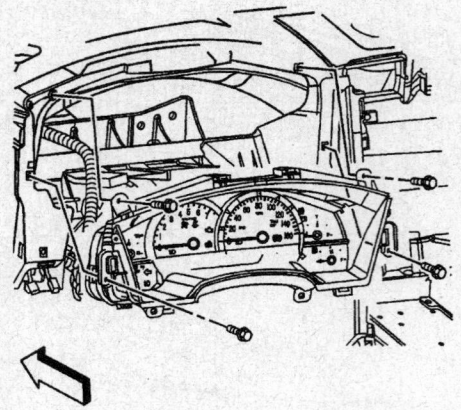

Fig. 3   Instrument cluster removal

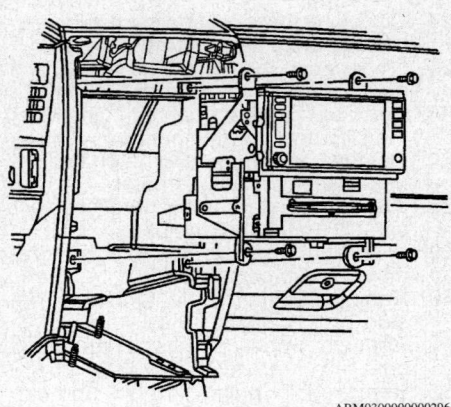

Fig. 4   Radio removal

STEERING WHEEL

REPLACE

1. Remove air bag module from steering wheel.
2. Disconnect horn electrical connector.
3. Insert steering column lock pin tool No. J 42640, or equivalent, into steering column.
4. Remove and discard steering wheel retaining nut.
5. Remove steering wheel from steering column using steering wheel puller tool No. J 1859-A, or equivalent.
6. Reverse procedure to install. **Torque** new steering wheel retaining nut to 30 ft. lbs.

INSTRUMENT CLUSTER

REPLACE

1. Remove shifter knob, then open center console door.
2. Remove hinge cover from console bin, then pull at rear of cover to disengage retainer.
3. Remove console cupholder, ashtray and trim plate.
4. Remove console retaining nuts, **Fig. 2.**
5. Remove front of console to instrument panel carrier retaining bolts.
6. Lift rear of console slightly and pull rearward to release front of console from under instrument panel carrier.
7. Disconnect accessory plug electrical connector.
8. Remove accessory plug retainer from housing, then housing from console.
9. Disengage lamp from retainer using a suitable flat-bladed tool.
10. Push lamp through hole in console bin, then remove console from vehicle.
11. Pry fuel door and rear compartment lid release switch from knee bolster, then disconnect switch electrical connectors.
12. Remove driver knee bolster trim panel lower retaining screws, **Fig. 1.**
13. Grasp knee bolster trim panel at side edges, then remove trim panel by pulling firmly to release locking tabs.

14. Carefully pry instrument panel courtesy lamp assembly from lefthand side lower closeout panel using a suitable flat-bladed tool.
15. Insert instrument panel courtesy lamp assembly up through opening in closeout panel.
16. Release notch in righthand side forward edge of closeout panel from tab on accelerator pedal bracket, then remove closeout panel.
17. Remove retaining screws from bottom of Driver Information Center (DIC) switch pad.
18. Pull outward on DIC switch pad to disengage retaining clip, then disconnect switch pad electrical connectors.
19. Remove DIC switch retaining screws, then switch.
20. Remove retaining screw from instrument panel dimmer/Head-Up Display (HUD) switch assembly.
21. Disconnect HUD switch electrical connector.
22. Remove HUD switch to bezel retaining screws, then switch from bezel.
23. Manually open folding top.
24. Pull windshield side garnish molding with its retainers from windshield frame.
25. Remove instrument panel side trim panels.
26. Remove instrument panel trim pad retaining screws. Screws are located at each end of instrument panel, in center of instrument panel and behind DIC switch.
27. Pull up carefully on instrument panel trim pad to disengage retaining clips.
28. Disconnect sunload/twilight sensor from trim pad, then remove trim pad from vehicle.
29. Carefully lift HUD electrical harness from between instrument panel cluster and HUD.
30. Disconnect HUD electrical connector from cluster.
31. Remove cluster to steering column bracket retaining screws, **Fig. 3.**
32. Raise rear of cluster slightly, then disconnect cluster electrical connector.
33. Remove cluster from vehicle.
34. Reverse procedure to install.

RADIO

REPLACE

1. Remove cover from instrument panel electrical center.
2. Remove RDO/CD MiniFuse from electrical center.
3. Remove center console trim plate.
4. Pull top edge of instrument panel accessory trim plate rearward to disengage retaining clips.
5. Disconnect hazard flasher switch electrical connector.
6. Remove hazard flasher switch from trim plate.
7. Remove radio control to instrument panel center support bracket retaining screws, **Fig. 4.**
8. Pull radio rearward and disconnect electrical/audio and coaxial cable connectors from radio.
9. Remove radio from instrument panel.
10. Reverse procedure to install.

WIPER MOTOR

REPLACE

1. Turn ignition switch to ACCY position and wiper switch to DELAY position.
2. Turn ignition switch OFF when wiper arms are in mid-wipe position.
3. Place a piece of masking tape onto windshield at tip of each wiper blade for installation reference.
4. Disconnect washer hose from air inlet grille panel.
5. Remove wiper arm nut cover, then wiper arm nut.
6. Grasp wiper arm at hinged joint, then remove arm from shaft by applying a rocking motion toward windshield to loosen arm.
7. Remove air inlet grille panel push-in retainers.
8. Disconnect washer hose connector.
9. Remove air inlet grille panel to fender retainers, then grille panel from vehicle.
10. Separate wiper transmission from wiper motor crank arm using wiper linkage separator tool No. J 39232, or equivalent.
11. Remove wiper drive system module mounting screws, then wiper drive system module from plenum, **Fig. 5.**

12. Disconnect wiper motor electrical connector.
13. Remove wiper drive system module from vehicle.
14. Remove wiper motor mounting screws, then wiper motor from wiper motor module.
15. Reverse procedure to install.

WIPER SWITCH
REPLACE

1. Remove steering wheel as outlined under "Steering Wheel, Replace."
2. Pry fuel door and rear compartment lid release switch from knee bolster, then disconnect switch electrical connectors.
3. Remove driver knee bolster trim panel lower retaining screws, **Fig. 1.**
4. Grasp knee bolster trim panel at side edges, then remove trim panel by pulling firmly to release locking tabs.
5. Remove lower steering column trim cover retaining screws.
6. Disconnect closeout shroud from steering column lower trim cover.
7. Disconnect steering column power tilt and telescopic switch electrical connectors.
8. Remove lower trim cover from steering column.
9. Disconnect windshield wiper and washer switch assembly.
10. Press on switch locking tabs, then pull switch assembly out of switch mounting bracket.
11. Reverse procedure to install.

BLOWER MOTOR
REPLACE

1. Carefully pry instrument panel courtesy lamp assembly from righthand side lower closeout panel.
2. Remove righthand side lower closeout panel to instrument panel lower support beam push-in retainers.
3. Lower righthand side lower closeout panel slightly, then carefully maneuver lefthand side of closeout panel from above driveline tunnel.
4. Insert courtesy lamp assembly up through closeout panel opening.
5. Remove closeout panel from instrument panel.
6. Disconnect blower motor electrical connector.
7. Remove blower motor retaining screws, then blower motor from HVAC module.
8. Reverse procedure to install.

CABIN AIR FILTER
REPLACE

Under normal operating conditions the cabin air filter should be replaced every 12 months or 15,000 miles. In dusty areas change the cabin air filter more often.
1. Open hood.
2. Lift up cabin air filter access cover located on air inlet panel.
3. Remove cabin air filter element from housing.

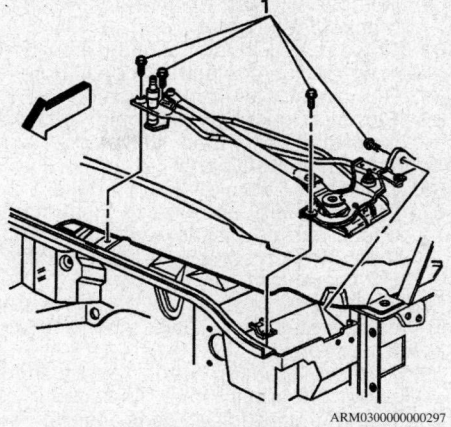

Fig. 5 Wiper drive system module removal

4. Install new cabin air filter into filter housing.
5. Close cabin air filter access cover.
6. Close hood.

HEATER CORE
REPLACE

1. Recover air conditioning refrigerant as outlined in "Air Conditioning" chapter.
2. Drain cooling system.
3. Remove intake manifold as outlined under "Intake Manifold, Replace."
4. Disconnect front evaporator inlet line from body retaining clip.
5. Disconnect refrigerant pressure sensor electrical connector.
6. Disconnect and remove A/C tube connectors from evaporator rear line assembly. Cap lines to prevent contamination.
7. Disconnect front evaporator inlet line from evaporator rear line assembly. Remove and discard O-rings.
8. Disconnect A/C compressor line from evaporator rear line assembly. Remove and discard O-rings.
9. Remove heater pipe bracket retaining nut from cowl stud.
10. Remove TXV block fitting nut and disconnect evaporator rear line assembly from TXV.
11. Disconnect evaporator rear line assembly from retainer bracket.
12. Remove rear evaporator line assembly from vehicle. Remove and discard seal washers.
13. Release and reposition heater inlet and outlet hose clamps.
14. Separate heater hoses from heater pipes. Cap or plug open heater hoses.
15. Remove heater pipe assembly to heater core retaining bolt. **Do not apply excessive force on heater core pipes during hose removal.**
16. Disconnect heater pipe assembly from heater pipe bracket retainer.
17. Disconnect heater pipe assembly from heater core.
18. Remove heater pipe assembly from vehicle. Remove and discard sealing washers. Cap or plug heater core.

19. Remove evaporator drain tube from HVAC module.
20. Remove shifter knob, then open center console door.
21. Remove hinge cover from console bin, then pull at rear of cover to disengage retainer.
22. Remove console cupholder, ashtray and trim plate.
23. Remove console retaining nuts, **Fig. 2.**
24. Remove front of console to instrument panel carrier retaining bolts.
25. Lift rear of console slightly and pull rearward to release front of console from under instrument panel carrier.
26. Disconnect accessory plug electrical connector.
27. Remove accessory plug retainer from housing, then housing from console.
28. Disengage lamp from retainer using a suitable flat-bladed tool.
29. Push lamp through hole in console bin, then remove console from vehicle.
30. Remove radio as outlined under "Radio, Replace."
31. Carefully pry instrument panel courtesy lamp assembly from righthand side lower closeout panel.
32. Remove righthand side lower closeout panel to instrument panel lower support beam push-in retainers.
33. Lower righthand side lower closeout panel slightly, then carefully maneuver lefthand side of closeout panel from above driveline tunnel.
34. Insert courtesy lamp assembly up through closeout panel opening.
35. Remove righthand closeout panel from instrument panel.
36. Pry fuel door and rear compartment lid release switch from knee bolster, then disconnect switch electrical connectors.
37. Remove driver knee bolster trim panel lower retaining screws, **Fig. 1.**
38. Grasp knee bolster trim panel at side edges, then remove trim panel by pulling firmly to release locking tabs.
39. Carefully pry instrument panel courtesy lamp assembly from lefthand side lower closeout panel using a suitable flat-bladed tool.
40. Insert instrument panel courtesy lamp assembly up through opening in closeout panel.
41. Release notch in righthand side forward edge of closeout panel from tab on accelerator pedal bracket, then remove lefthand closeout panel.
42. Open door on instrument panel compartment, then disconnect door dampener.
43. Disconnect instrument panel compartment lamp switch electrical connector.
44. With compartment open, depress both rear corners of compartment and swing compartment down towards floor.
45. Starting at outboard side, release compartment hinge from pin at bottom of door.
46. Slowly pull compartment far enough out of instrument panel to disconnect wiring harness connector from inflatable restraint module switch.

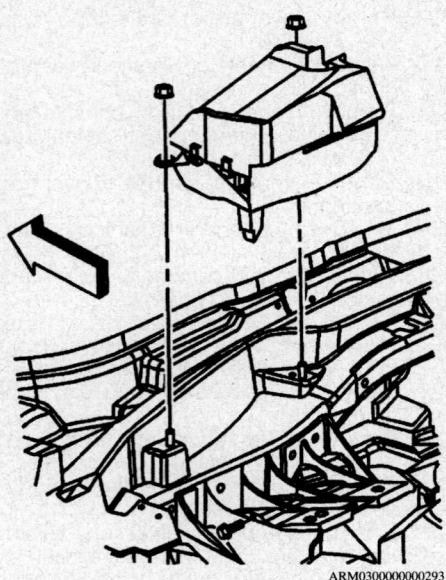

Fig. 6 Head-Up Display (HUD) unit removal

47. Remove instrument panel compartment.
48. Mark location of driver knee bolster bracket for installation reference.
49. Remove driver knee bolster bracket to steering column bracket retaining screws, then driver knee bolster bracket from instrument panel.
50. Remove retaining screw from bottom of lefthand side trim panel.
51. Pull lefthand side trim panel outward to disengage retaining clips, then disconnect electrical connectors.
52. Remove fastener attaching top of upper trim panel and windshield side garnish molding to hinge pillar.
53. Unsnap hinge pillar upper trim from hinge pillar.
54. Remove lower hinge pillar trim.
55. Manually open folding top.
56. Pull windshield side garnish molding with its retainers from windshield frame.
57. Remove instrument panel trim pad retaining screws. Screws are located at each end of instrument panel, in center of instrument panel and behind DIC switch.
58. Pull up carefully on instrument panel trim pad to disengage retaining clips.
59. Disconnect sunload/twilight sensor from trim pad, then remove trim pad from vehicle.
60. Carefully lift HUD electrical harness from between instrument panel cluster and HUD.
61. Disconnect HUD electrical connector from cluster.

62. Remove cluster to steering column bracket retaining screws.
63. Raise rear of cluster slightly, then disconnect cluster electrical connector.
64. Remove cluster from vehicle.
65. Remove speaker retaining screws from speakers, then lift speaker out from instrument panel carrier.
66. Disconnect speaker wire harness.
67. Remove GPS antenna to instrument panel carrier plastic rivet retainers, then GPS antenna with antenna lead from carrier.
68. Remove remote control door lock receiver retaining screws, then receiver from carrier.
69. Remove steering wheel as outlined under "Steering Wheel, Replace."
70. Remove instrument panel carrier retaining bolts and nuts.
71. Remove carrier retaining bolts from lower beam behind compartment door.
72. Remove compartment striker from carrier.
73. Remove instrument panel carrier from mounting, then slowly route all wiring from carrier.
74. Remove instrument panel carrier from vehicle.
75. Remove retainers from upper defogger duct on lefthand side window, then upper defogger outlet duct.
76. Disconnect Head Up Display (HUD) electrical connector.
77. Remove HUD retaining nuts, then screw that secures HUD to steering column bracket, **Fig. 6.**
78. Remove lower defogger outlet duct retainer, then outlet duct from defroster duct.
79. Remove floor air outlet duct to lower instrument panel beam retainer.
80. Disconnect floor air outlet duct from rear floor air outlet duct.
81. Remove upper defogger duct to righthand side window defogger retainers, then upper outlet duct from defogger.
82. Disconnect defogger lower outlet duct from knee bolster bracket and defroster duct.
83. Remove righthand side knee bolster bracket to passenger SIR bracket attaching bolts, then knee bolster bracket.
84. Remove sealing nuts from cowl, then upper instrument pane cross vehicle beam retaining bolts.
85. Loosen front lefthand recirculation housing retaining screw.
86. Disconnect recirculation actuator electrical connector and HVAC module wiring harness from recirculation housing.
87. Remove remaining recirculation housing retaining screws, then housing from HVAC module.
88. Carefully remove HVAC module from

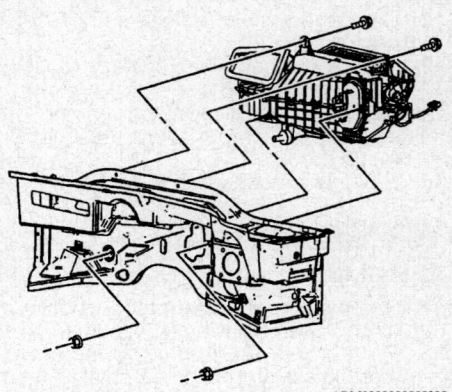

Fig. 7 HVAC module removal

vehicle, **Fig. 7.**
89. Remove and discard HVAC module assembly foam seal.
90. Disconnect discharge temperature management (DTM) sensor electrical connectors.
91. Disconnect HVAC module wiring harness retainer pin from HVAC module.
92. Disconnect wiring harness from heater core cover wire harness retainer and position harness aside.
93. Remove heater cover retaining screws, then heater cover from HVAC module.
94. Remove heater core from HVAC module.
95. Reverse procedure to install.

EVAPORATOR CORE
REPLACE

1. Recover air conditioning refrigerant as outlined in "Air Conditioning" chapter.
2. Remove HVAC module as outlined under "Heater Core, Replace."
3. Remove and discard HVAC module assembly foam seal.
4. Remove TXV mounting bolts, then TXV from evaporator core. Remove and discard sealing washers.
5. Disconnect Discharge Temperature Management (DTM) sensor electrical connectors.
6. Disconnect HVAC module wiring harness retainer pin from HVAC module.
7. Disconnect wiring harness from heater core cover wire harness retainers and position harness aside.
8. Remove heater cover screws, then heater cover from HVAC module.
9. Remove HVAC module case retaining screws and separate HVAC module upper case from lower case.
10. Remove evaporator core from HVAC module.
11. Reverse procedure to install.

4.4L Engine

NOTE: On Air Bag Equipped Models, Refer To "Air Bag System Precautions" Located In The Front Of This Manual For System Disarming & Arming Procedures.

NOTE: Refer To "Computer Relearn Procedures" Located In The Front Of This Manual When Battery Power To The Computer Has Been Interrupted.

INDEX

	Page No.
Engine Rebuilding	
Specifications	29-1
Engine, Replace	13-9
Engine Mount, Replace	13-9
Fuel Filter, Replace	13-11
Fuel Pump, Replace	13-11
Oil Pan, Replace	13-10

	Page No.
Precautions	13-9
Air Bag Systems	13-9
Battery Ground Cable	13-9
Fuel Pressure Relief	13-9
Radiator, Replace	13-11
Serpentine Drive Belt	13-10
Accessory Drive Belt, Replace	13-10

	Page No.
Alternator and Water Pump	
Drive Belt, Replace	13-10
Routing	13-10
Supercharger Drive Belt,	
Replace	13-10
Supercharger, Replace	13-11
Tightening Specifications	13-12

PRECAUTIONS

Air Bag Systems

Refer to "Air Bag System Precautions" in the front of this manual for system disarming and arming procedures.

Battery Ground Cable

Prior to service, disconnect battery ground cable and isolate as required.

Fuel Pressure Relief

1. Turn ignition off and remove fuel pump relay.
2. Loosen fuel filler cap.
3. Remove mounting nuts and fuel injector sight shield.
4. Connect suitable fuel pressure gauge to fuel pressure connection located on fuel rail assembly. Wrap connection with a suitable shop towel to prevent fuel leakage.
5. Install suitable bleed hose to gauge and into a suitable container, then open pressure valve to bleed system pressure.

ENGINE MOUNT

REPLACE

For engine mount replacement, refer to "Engine Mount, Replace" under "4.6L Engine."

ENGINE

REPLACE

1. Relieve fuel system pressure as outlined under "Precautions."
2. Disconnect Electronic Suspension Control (ESC) control module electri-

cal connectors. ESC control module is located in luggage compartment.
3. Recover A/C system refrigerant as outlined in "Air Conditioning" chapter.
4. Remove fuel injector sight shield.
5. Disconnect EVAP emission canister purge pipe from chassis purge pipe. Cap open pipes to prevent contamination.
6. Disconnect fuel inlet quick-connect fitting at fuel line.
7. Remove air cleaner assembly.
8. Remove charge air cooler radiator.
9. Remove radiator as outlined under "Radiator, Replace."
10. Remove surge tank.
11. Remove air conditioning condenser.
12. Remove front portion of supercharger front manifold and position hoses aside.
13. Disconnect vacuum brake booster hose from brake booster.
14. Disconnect electrical connector from brake fluid level sensor.
15. Remove brake master cylinder nuts from brake booster studs, then pull master cylinder forward. Secure master cylinder to engine.
16. Remove bolts from intermediate steering shaft, then disconnect steering shaft from steering gear. Tie-wrap steering shaft to engine.
17. Remove battery, then battery tray.
18. Remove engine ground strap nut and terminal from stud on frame.
19. Disconnect A/C electrical connector from pressure sensor.
20. Remove hydraulic junction block from wheelhouse, then disconnect wiring harness connector from junction block. Secure wiring harness to engine.
21. Raise and support vehicle, then remove front wheels and tires.
22. Remove righthand side front wheelhouse panel.
23. Disconnect and secure Engine Control

Module (ECM) electrical harness, engine electrical harness.
24. Disconnect A/C lines from front of dash connections.
25. Disconnect heater hoses from heater pipes.
26. Disconnect wheel speed sensor electrical connectors.
27. Disconnect road sensing suspension position sensor links from front lower control arms.
28. Support righthand lower control arm with a suitable straight jack.
29. Remove righthand shock absorber lower mounting bolts.
30. Disconnect upper righthand ball joint from suspension knuckle.
31. Remove straight jack from under control arm.
32. Support lefthand lower control arm with a straight jack.
33. Remove lefthand shock absorber lower mounting bolts.
34. Disconnect upper lefthand ball joint from suspension knuckle.
35. Remove straight jack from under control arm.
36. Disconnect rear wheel speed sensor electrical connectors.
37. Disconnect road sensing suspension position sensor links from rear lower control arms.
38. Support rear lefthand lower control arm with a suitable straight jack.
39. Remove rear lefthand shock absorber lower mounting bolt.
40. Disconnect lefthand upper ball joint from suspension knuckle.
41. Remove straight jack from control arm.
42. Support rear righthand lower control arm with a straight jack.
43. Remove rear righthand shock absorber lower mounting bolt.
44. Disconnect righthand upper ball joint from suspension knuckle.
45. Remove straight jack from control arm.

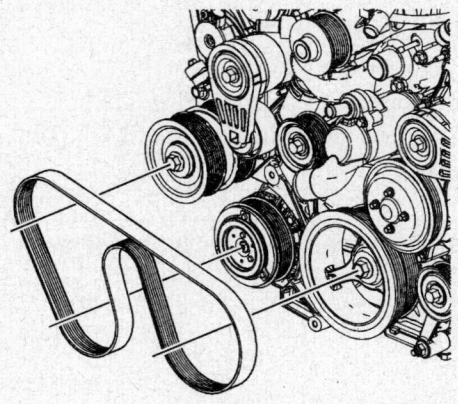

Fig. 1 Accessory Drive belt routing

ARM0600000000803

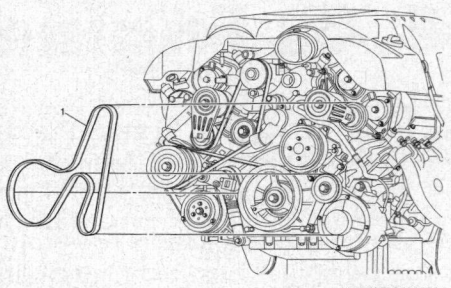

ARM0600000000804

Fig. 2 Alternator and water pump drive belt

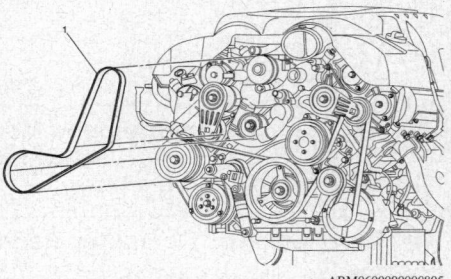

ARM0600000000805

Fig. 3 Supercharger drive belt routing

46. Remove righthand and lefthand muffler assemblies.
47. Remove bolts from driveline tunnel closeout panel, then closeout panel from under vehicle.
48. Remove retaining transmission shift cable bracket to transmission retaining nuts.
49. Disconnect transmission shift control cable from transmission shift lever. Position shift cable and bracket aside.
50. Position a suitable powertrain table under front cradle.
51. Position a suitable powertrain table under rear cradle.
52. Slowly lower vehicle on to a suitable powertrain table.
53. Remove front and rear crossmember nuts.
54. Carefully raise vehicle to clear supported powertrain assembly.
55. Remove lefthand side exhaust manifold assembly, then lefthand side engine mount bracket.
56. Remove water pump and generator drive belt tensioner.
57. Remove supercharger drive belt tensioner.
58. Remove drive belt tensioner.
59. Remove bolt securing starter/alternator harness clip to front of engine.
60. Remove bolts and nut securing engine wiring harness to lefthand side of engine.
61. Remove righthand side exhaust manifold assembly, then righthand side engine mount bracket.
62. Disconnect engine oil level sensor electrical connector.
63. Remove power steering reservoir bracket.
64. Remove A/C compressor and bracket.
65. Remove transmission cooler lines, then Engine Coolant Temperature (ECT) sensor.
66. Remove wiring harness to engine attaching bolts and nut.
67. Remove supercharger assembly as outlined under "Supercharger, Replace"

68. Remove lefthand side and righthand side ignition module assemblies.
69. Remove starter motor from engine.
70. Disconnect lefthand and righthand knock sensor electrical connectors.
71. Disconnect crank sensor electrical connector.
72. Remove driveline support bolts.
73. Insert a suitable flat-headed screwdriver between driveline support and flywheel housing, then separate driveline assembly from engine.
74. Slowly pull driveline support assembly away from engine.
75. Install engine lift brackets tool Nos. J 28467-86 and J 28467-87, or equivalent to engine.
76. Install engine hoist tool No. J 41798, or equivalent, to lift brackets.
77. Remove flywheel housing bolts, then separate flywheel housing from engine.
78. Remove engine from lift table.
79. Reverse procedure to install.

OIL PAN

REPLACE

For oil pan replacement, refer to "Oil Pan, Replace" under "4.6L Engine."

SERPENTINE DRIVE BELT

Routing

Refer to **Figs. 1 through 3** for alternator and water pump drive belt, supercharger drive belt and accessory drive belt routings.

Supercharger Drive Belt, Replace

1. Remove fluid from power steering reservoir into a suitable container.
2. Remove power steering reservoir hose.
3. Remove power steering reservoir bracket nuts and power steering reservoir.
4. Insert a suitable 1/2 inch drive breaker

bar into supercharger drive belt tensioner.
5. Rotate breaker bar clockwise to release tension.
6. Remove supercharger drive belt from supercharger pulley.
7. Slowly return supercharger drive belt tensioner to original position.
8. Remove supercharger drive belt.
9. Reverse procedure to install.

Alternator and Water Pump Drive Belt, Replace

1. Insert a suitable 1/2 inch drive breaker bar into alternator and water pump drive belt tensioner.
2. Rotate breaker bar clockwise to release tension.
3. Remove generator and water pump drive belt from alternator pulley.
4. Slowly return generator and water pump drive belt tensioner to original position.
5. Remove generator and water pump drive belt.
6. Reverse procedure to install.

Accessory Drive Belt, Replace

1. Insert a suitable 1/2 inch drive breaker bar into A/C compressor and power steering pump drive belt tensioner.
2. Rotate breaker bar clockwise to release tension.
3. Remove A/C compressor and power steering pump drive belt from A/C compressor pulley.
4. Slowly return A/C compressor and power steering pump drive belt tensioner to original position.
5. Remove A/C compressor and power steering pump tensioner lower and upper bolt.
6. Remove A/C compressor and power steering pump tensioner.
7. Remove A/C compressor and power steering pump drive belt.

RADIATOR

REPLACE

1. Recover refrigerant from A/C system as outlined in "Air Conditioning" chapter.
2. Drain cooling system into a suitable container.
3. Remove upper radiator support.
4. Remove A/C compressor hose assembly to A/C condenser fitting bolt and disconnect A/C condenser fitting.
5. Remove and discard seal washer.
6. Cap or tape A/C compressor hose assembly.
7. Raise and suitably support vehicle.
8. Remove front evaporator inlet line bolt from A/C condenser and disconnect inlet line.
9. Remove and discard seal washer.
10. Cap or tape front evaporator inlet line.
11. Lower vehicle.
12. Remove LH and RH radiator air baffle upper retainer pin.
13. Raise A/C condenser along radiator to release A/C condenser tabs from radiator slots.
14. Remove A/C condenser from vehicle.
15. Disengage tension on radiator inlet hose clamp at radiator using Clamp Pliers, tool No.J 38185 or equivalent and disconnect hose from radiator.
16. Disconnect cooling fan and shroud assembly from radiator.
17. Disengage tension and reposition surge tank inlet hose clamp at radiator using clamp pliers and disconnect hose from radiator.
18. Disconnect upper transmission oil cooler line from radiator.
19. Raise and suitably support vehicle.
20. Disengage tension on radiator outlet hose clamp at radiator using clamp pliers and disconnect surge tank inlet hose from radiator.
21. Disconnect lower transmission oil cooler line from radiator.
22. Disengage generator cooling hose clamp at radiator and disconnect hose from radiator.
23. Lower vehicle.
24. Remove radiator from vehicle.
25. Reverse procedure to install.

FUEL PUMP

REPLACE

For fuel pump replacement, refer to "Fuel Pump, Replace" under "4.6L Engine."

FUEL FILTER

REPLACE

The fuel filter is contained within the fuel sender assembly, inside the lefthand side fuel tank. Refer to "Fuel Pump, Replace" for fuel filter replacement.

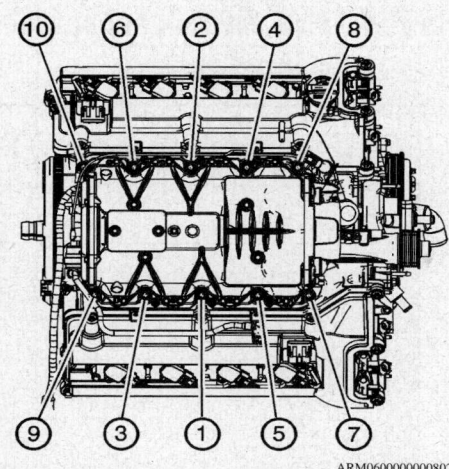

ARM0600000000802

Fig. 4 Supercharger Tightening Sequence

SUPERCHARGER

REPLACE

1. Disconnect underhood lamp connector.
2. Remove hood assist rod from hood side, remove hood bolts and remove hood.
3. Remove engine oil fill cap and engine sight shield.
4. Remove front supercharger inlet duct assembly.
5. Remove air cleaner outlet duct.
6. Disconnect (PCV) hose fitting from underside of inlet duct assembly.
7. Loosen rear screw clamps located between front and rear section of inlet duct assembly.
8. Remove 6 ball studs that retain inlet duct to supercharger.
9. Remove front section of supercharger inlet duct.
10. Loosen rear screw clamps on inlet duct seal.
11. Remove rear section of supercharger inlet duct from supercharger.
12. Drain charge air cooling system into a suitable container.
13. Remove front portion of supercharger front manifold, discard manifold O-ring seals, position hoses with manifold aside.
14. Disconnect throttle body electrical connector.
15. Disconnect supercharger inlet absolute pressure (SCIAP) sensor, barometric pressure (BARO) sensor and manifold absolute pressure (MAP) sensor.
16. Disconnect vacuum lines from MAP and SCIAP sensors.
17. Remove SCIAP, BARO and MAP sensors with bracket.

18. Disconnect electrical connector from air inlet temperature 2 sensor and supercharger bypass solenoid valve electrical connector and position aside.
19. Disconnect vacuum line from supercharger actuator valve and position aside.
20. Disconnect engine compartment fuel line fitting from fuel rail.
21. Disconnect fuel injector electrical connectors from left and right side of engine.
22. Remove ground wire from right rear injector rail bolt and remove oxygen sensor electrical connector assemblies from right and left side fuel rail brackets.
23. Open clip that secures fuel rail to front of supercharger.
24. Remove fuel rail attaching studs and reposition rear inlet duct as necessary.
25. Remove fuel rail assembly from supercharger.
26. Disconnect evaporative emission (EVAP) canister purge solenoid valve hose from EVAP valve and position aside.
27. Disconnect EVAP canister purge solenoid valve electrical connector and disconnect brake booster vacuum hose from fitting on supercharger and position aside.
28. Disconnect supercharger bypass regulator solenoid valve connector.
29. Disconnect manifold absolute pressure (MAP) sensor vacuum line from supercharger.
30. Disconnect supercharger intake air temperature (IAT) sensor connector.
31. Disconnect supercharger inlet absolute pressure (SIAP) sensor vacuum line fitting from rear of supercharger and position aside.
32. Disconnect positive crankcase ventilation (PCV) tube fitting from right camshaft cover.
33. Remove supercharger drive belt.
34. Install a suitable lift bracket, No. EN-47748 or equivalent to supercharger.
35. Install a suitable engine hoist to lift bracket.
36. Remove and discard supercharger bolts.
37. Remove supercharger.
38. Reverse procedure to install. **Torque** new supercharger bolts in sequence to 30 ft. lbs., **Fig. 4.**

TIGHTENING SPECIFICATIONS

Year	Component	Torque Ft. Lbs.
2006–08	A/C Compressor, Mounting Bolt	37
	A/C Compressor & Power Steering Bracket Bolt	37
	A/C Drive Belt Tensioner	18
	Alternator	37
	Alternator Coolant Inlet Hose Fitting	18
	Alternator Rear Brace Bolt	37
	Alternator Stud	106①
	Bell Housing Bolt	37
	Block Coolant Drain Hole Plug	15
	Camshaft Position Sensor	89①
	Charge Air Cooler Rear Manifold Bolts	89①
	Charge Air Cooler Front Manifold Bolts	89①
	Crossmember	81
	Cylinder Head Coolant Plug	60
	Drive Belt Idler Bolt	37
	Drive Belt Idler Nut	37
	Drive Belt Tensioner Bolt	37
	ECT Sensor	15
	Engine Mount Bracket Bolt	43
	Engine Mount Nut	43
	Flywheel To Torque Converter	②
	Fuel Rail Attaching Studs	89①
	Intermediate Shaft Pinch Bolt	25
	Lower Control Arm Cam Bolt	125
	Oil Filter Bypass Hole Plug	22
	Oil Filter Fitting	21
	Oil Filter Mounting Bolt	18
	Oil Level Sensor	15
	Oil Pan	18
	Oil Pan Drain Plug	18
	Oil Pressure Switch	15
	Oxygen Sensor	31
	Power Steering Pump	18
	Power Steering Pump Reservoir Bracket Nut	89①
	Starter Motor Bolt	22
	Steering Rack	74
	Supercharger Bypass Valve Actuator Bolt	89①
	Supercharger Bypass Valve Cable Bolt	89①
	Supercharger Inlet Duct Ball Studs	89①
	Supercharger Inlet Seal Screw Clamps	20①
	Supercharger Intake Air Temperature (IAT) Sensor 2	15
	Supercharger Bolts	18
	Throttle Body	89①
	Tie Rod	33

① — Inch lbs.
② — First pass, 11 ft. lbs. second pass, tighten an additional 50°.

4.6L Engine

NOTE: On Air Bag Equipped Models, Refer To "Air Bag System Precautions" Located In The Front Of This Manual For System Disarming & Arming Procedures.

NOTE: Refer To "Computer Relearn Procedures" Located In The Front Of This Manual When Battery Power To The Computer Has Been Interrupted.

NOTE: Refer To "4.6L Engine" Section In The "DeVille, DTS, Seville & STS" Chapter For Procedures Not Covered In This Section.

INDEX

	Page No.
Engine Rebuilding Specifications	29-1
Engine, Replace	13-13
Engine Mount, Replace	13-13
Fuel Filter, Replace	13-16
Fuel Pump, Replace	13-15
Lefthand	13-15

	Page No.
Righthand	13-15
Oil Pan, Replace	13-14
Precautions	13-13
Air Bag Systems	13-13
Battery Ground Cable	13-13
Fuel Pressure Relief	13-13
Radiator, Replace	13-15

	Page No.
Serpentine Drive Belt	13-15
Accessory Drive Belt, Replace	13-15
Drive Belt, Replace	13-15
Routing	13-15
Tightening Specifications	13-16

PRECAUTIONS
Air Bag Systems

Refer to "Air Bag System Precautions" in the front of this manual for system disarming and arming procedures.

Battery Ground Cable

Prior to service, disconnect battery ground cable and isolate as required.

Fuel Pressure Relief

1. Turn ignition off and remove fuel pump relay.
2. Loosen fuel filler cap.
3. Remove mounting nuts and fuel injector sight shield.
4. Connect suitable fuel pressure gauge to fuel pressure connection located on fuel rail assembly. Wrap connection with a suitable shop towel to prevent fuel leakage.
5. Install suitable bleed hose to gauge and into a suitable container, then open pressure valve to bleed system pressure.

ENGINE MOUNT
REPLACE

1. Support engine with a suitable engine support fixture.
2. Raise vehicle and suitably support.
3. Remove tire and wheel assemblies.
4. Loosen, do not remove, outer tie rod end stud nut from outer tie rod end ball stud.
5. Loosen outer tie rod end stud to steer-ing knuckle connection using a Ball Joint Separator tool No. J 42188, or equivalent.
6. Remove outer tie rod end stud nut in order to separate tie rod from steering knuckle.
7. Loosen jam nut on inner tie rod assembly.
8. Remove outer tie rod end from inner tie rod assembly.
9. Disconnect ESC position sensor harness connector.
10. Remove position sensor link from control arm link stud.
11. Remove position sensor mounting bolts and sensor from vehicle.
12. Remove stabilizer shaft link nuts from shaft and shaft insulator clamps from front crossmember.
13. Remove stabilizer shaft from vehicle.
14. Turn steering wheel far enough to left to gain access to upper to lower intermediate shaft bolts. **Wheels of vehicle must be straight ahead to avoid damage to SIR coil assembly.**
15. Insert Steering Column Lock Pin tool No. J 42640, or equivalent into steering column access hole in order to lock steering column. This will maintain correct orientation.
16. Remove upper to lower intermediate shaft bolts.
17. Remove lower coupling shield and lower coupling pinch bolt.
18. Remove lower coupling from steering gear.
19. Slide lower intermediate shaft from upper intermediate shaft and lower intermediate shaft from vehicle.
20. Remove BPMV bracket bolts.
21. Remove steering gear nut and bolt.
22. Remove BPMV bracket.
23. Support and reposition EBCM/BPMV and bracket away from crossmember.
24. Remove power steering gear mounting bolts and power steering fluid cooler from crossmember.
25. Lift power steering gear off of crossmember and support.
26. Remove transverse spring from vehicle using a Transverse Spring Compressor tool No. J 33432-A, or equivalent.
27. Disconnect lower shock absorber bolts from lower control arms.
28. Remove lower control arm bolts from crossmember.
29. Place a suitable transmission jack under crossmember.
30. Remove engine mount lower nuts.
31. Disconnect wheel speed sensor wiring harness from crossmember and electrical harness from clips on crossmember.
32. Disconnect brake pipe from clips on crossmember.
33. Remove crossmember mounting nuts.
34. Lower crossmember out of vehicle by removing transmission jack from under crossmember.
35. Remove engine mount-to-engine mount bracket nut.
36. Remove engine mount from engine mount bracket.
37. Remove engine mount heat shield from engine mount.
38. Reverse procedure to install. Tighten to specifications.

ENGINE
REPLACE

1. Relieve fuel system pressure as outlined under "Precautions."
2. Disconnect Electronic Suspension Control (ESC) control module electrical connectors. ESC control module is located in luggage compartment.

3. Recover A/C system refrigerant as outlined in "Air Conditioning" chapter.
4. Remove fuel injector sight shield.
5. Disconnect EVAP emission canister purge pipe from chassis purge pipe. Cap open pipes to prevent contamination.
6. Disconnect fuel inlet quick-connect fitting at fuel line.
7. Remove air cleaner assembly.
8. Remove radiator as outlined under "Radiator, Replace."
9. Remove surge tank.
10. Remove air conditioning condenser.
11. Disconnect vacuum brake booster hose from brake booster.
12. Disconnect electrical connector from brake fluid level sensor.
13. Remove brake master cylinder nuts from brake booster studs, then pull master cylinder forward. Secure master cylinder to engine.
14. Remove bolts from intermediate steering shaft, then disconnect steering shaft from steering gear. Tie-wrap steering shaft to engine.
15. Remove battery, then battery tray.
16. Remove engine ground strap nut and terminal from stud on frame.
17. Disconnect A/C electrical connector from pressure sensor.
18. Remove hydraulic junction block from wheelhouse, then disconnect wiring harness connector from junction block. Secure wiring harness to engine.
19. Raise and support vehicle, then remove front wheels and tires.
20. Remove righthand side front wheelhouse panel.
21. Disconnect and secure Engine Control Module (ECM) electrical harness, engine electrical harness.
22. Disconnect A/C lines from front of dash connections.
23. Disconnect heater hoses from heater pipes.
24. Disconnect wheel speed sensor electrical connectors.
25. Disconnect road sensing suspension position sensor links from front lower control arms.
26. Support righthand lower control arm with a straight jack.
27. Remove righthand shock absorber lower mounting bolts.
28. Disconnect upper righthand ball joint from suspension knuckle.
29. Remove straight jack from under control arm.
30. Support lefthand lower control arm with a straight jack.
31. Remove lefthand shock absorber lower mounting bolts.
32. Disconnect upper lefthand ball joint from suspension knuckle.
33. Remove straight jack from under control arm.
34. Disconnect rear wheel speed sensor electrical connectors.
35. Disconnect road sensing suspension position sensor links from rear lower control arms.
36. Support rear lefthand lower control arm with a straight jack.
37. Remove rear lefthand shock absorber lower mounting bolt.

38. Disconnect lefthand upper ball joint from suspension knuckle.
39. Remove straight jack from control arm.
40. Support rear righthand lower control arm with a straight jack.
41. Remove rear righthand shock absorber lower mounting bolt.
42. Disconnect righthand upper ball joint from suspension knuckle.
43. Remove straight jack from control arm.
44. Remove righthand and lefthand muffler assemblies.
45. Remove bolts from driveline tunnel closeout panel, then closeout panel from under vehicle.
46. Remove retaining transmission shift cable bracket to transmission retaining nuts.
47. Disconnect transmission shift control cable from transmission shift lever. Position shift cable and bracket aside.
48. Position a suitable powertrain table under front cradle.
49. Position a suitable powertrain table under rear cradle.
50. Slowly lower vehicle on to powertrain tables.
51. Remove front and rear crossmember nuts.
52. Carefully raise vehicle to clear supported powertrain assembly.
53. Remove lefthand side exhaust manifold assembly, then lefthand side engine mount bracket.
54. Remove drive belt tensioner.
55. Remove bolt securing starter/alternator harness clip to front of engine.
56. Remove bolts and nut securing engine wiring harness to lefthand side of engine.
57. Remove righthand side exhaust manifold assembly, then righthand side engine mount bracket.
58. Disconnect engine oil level sensor electrical connector.
59. Remove power steering reservoir bracket.
60. Remove A/C compressor and bracket.
61. Remove transmission cooler lines, then Engine Coolant Temperature (ECT) sensor.
62. Remove wiring harness to engine attaching bolts and nut.
63. Disconnect throttle body assembly electrical connector.
64. Remove throttle body attaching bolts, then throttle body and gasket. Discard gasket.
65. Remove lefthand side and righthand side ignition module assemblies.
66. Remove starter motor from engine.
67. Disconnect lefthand and righthand knock sensor electrical connectors.
68. Disconnect crank sensor electrical connector.
69. Remove driveline support bolts.
70. Insert a suitable flat-headed screwdriver between driveline support and flywheel housing, then separate driveline assembly from engine.
71. Slowly pull driveline support assembly away from engine.
72. Install engine lift brackets tool Nos. J 28467-86 and J 28467-87, or equivalent to engine.

73. Install engine hoist tool No. J 41798, or equivalent, to lift brackets.
74. Remove flywheel housing bolts, then separate flywheel housing from engine.
75. Remove engine from lift table.
76. Reverse procedure to install.

OIL PAN
REPLACE

1. Rotate drive belt tensioner and remove drive belt.
2. Raise and support vehicle, then drain cooling system.
3. Remove tire and wheel assemblies.
4. Loosen, do not remove, outer tie rod end stud nut from outer tie rod end ball stud.
5. Loosen outer tie rod end stud to steering knuckle connection using tie rod remover tool No. J 42188, or equivalent.
6. Remove outer tie rod end stud nut and separate tie rod from steering knuckle.
7. Loosen jam nut on inner tie rod assembly, then remove outer tie rod end from inner tie rod assembly.
8. Disconnect Electronic Suspension Control (ESC) sensor links.
9. Remove stabilizer shaft link nuts from stabilizer shaft.
10. Remove stabilizer shaft insulator clamps from front crossmember, then stabilizer shaft from vehicle.
11. Turn steering wheel far enough to lefthand side to gain access to intermediate shaft bolts, then place ignition in locked position.
12. Remove upper to lower intermediate shaft bolts, then lower coupling shield.
13. Remove lower coupling pinch bolt, then lower coupling from steering gear.
14. Slide lower intermediate shaft from upper intermediate shaft and remove lower intermediate shaft from vehicle.
15. Remove bolts from Electronic Brake Control Module/Brake Pressure Modulator Valve (EBCM/BPMV) bracket.
16. Support and reposition EBCM/BPMV and bracket away from crossmember.
17. Remove power steering gear mounting bolts.
18. Remove power steering fluid cooler from crossmember.
19. Lift power steering gear off of crossmember and support.
20. Remove transverse spring from vehicle.
21. Remove lower shock absorber bolts from lower control arms.
22. Remove lower control arm bolts from crossmember.
23. Place a transmission jack under crossmember, then remove engine mount lower nuts.
24. Disconnect wheel speed sensor wiring harness from crossmember.
25. Disconnect electrical harness and brake pipe from clips on crossmember.
26. Remove crossmember mounting nuts, then lower crossmember from vehicle.
27. Drain engine oil, then remove oil filter and allow to drain.
28. Remove transmission fluid cooler lines.

29. Disconnect engine oil level sensor electrical connector.
30. Remove oil level sensor.
31. Remove oil pan bolts, then oil pan.
32. Reverse procedure to install. **Torque** oil pan bolts to 18 ft. lbs..

SERPENTINE DRIVE BELT

Routing

Refer to **Figs. 1 and 2** for drive belt and accessory drive belt routings.

Drive Belt, Replace

1. Install a suitable 1/2 inch drive breaker bar into belt drive tensioner.
2. Push down on breaker bar to release tension.
3. Remove drive belt from tensioner pulley.
4. Slowly return tensioner to original position.
5. Raise and support vehicle, then remove belt.
6. Reverse procedure to install.

Accessory Drive Belt, Replace

1. Remove drive belt as outlined under "Drive Belt, Replace."
2. Place a suitable drain pan under vehicle.
3. Remove capstick from power steering fluid reservoir.
4. Remove power steering fluid reservoir from bracket.
5. Install a suitable wrench on accessory drive belt tensioner, then rotate tensioner to release tension.
6. With tension applied, remove belt from power steering pulley.
7. Reverse procedure to install.

RADIATOR

REPLACE

1. Recover refrigerant from A/C system as outlined in "Air Conditioning" chapter.
2. Drain cooling system into a suitable container.
3. Remove upper radiator support.
4. Remove A/C compressor hose assembly to A/C condenser fitting bolt and disconnect A/C condenser fitting.
5. Remove and discard seal washer.
6. Cap or tape A/C compressor hose assembly.
7. Raise and suitably support vehicle.
8. Remove front evaporator inlet line bolt from A/C condenser and disconnect inlet line.
9. Remove and discard seal washer.
10. Cap or tape front evaporator inlet line.
11. Lower vehicle.
12. Remove LH and RH radiator air baffle upper retainer pin.

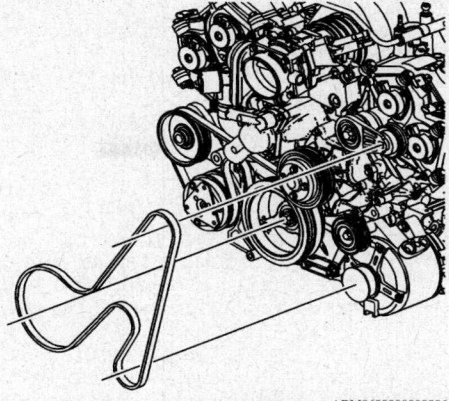

Fig. 1 Drive belt routing

ARM0600000000806

13. Raise A/C condenser along radiator to release A/C condenser tabs from radiator slots.
14. Remove A/C condenser from vehicle.
15. Disengage tension on radiator inlet hose clamp at radiator using Clamp Pliers, tool No. J 38185 or equivalent and disconnect hose from radiator.
16. Disconnect cooling fan and shroud assembly from radiator.
17. Disengage tension and reposition surge tank inlet hose clamp at radiator using clamp pliers and disconnect hose from radiator.
18. Disconnect upper transmission oil cooler line from radiator.
19. Raise and suitably support vehicle.
20. Disengage tension on radiator outlet hose clamp at radiator using clamp pliers and disconnect surge tank inlet hose from radiator.
21. Disconnect lower transmission oil cooler line from radiator.
22. Disengage generator cooling hose clamp at radiator and disconnect hose from radiator.
23. Lower vehicle.
24. Remove radiator from vehicle.
25. Reverse procedure to install.

FUEL PUMP

REPLACE

Lefthand

1. Relieve fuel system pressure as outlined under "Precautions."
2. Drain fuel tank.
3. Raise and support vehicle.
4. Remove rear tire and wheel assemblies.
5. Remove lefthand rear wheelhouse liner panel.
6. Loosen lefthand side and righthand side exhaust muffler clamps, then slide mufflers from hangers.
7. Remove intermediate exhaust pipe.
8. Remove driveline tunnel closeout panel bolts, then closeout panel.
9. Disconnect fuel fill hose and recirculation line from fill pipe.
10. Disconnect fuel pump jumper harness connector.

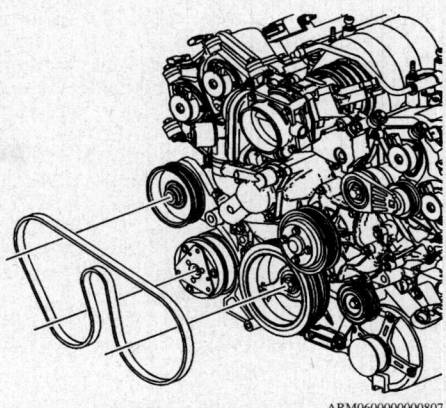

Fig. 2 Accessory drive belt routing

ARM0600000000807

11. Disconnect fuel feed pipe from rear of lefthand side fuel tank. Cap fuel pipes to prevent contamination.
12. Loosen fuel tank strap and lower tank approximately one inch.
13. Disengage crossover tube CPA retainer by pulling tab outward and rotate.
14. Disengage crossover tube collar by rotating counterclockwise.
15. Disconnect crossover tube from lefthand side fuel tank by pulling straight out.
16. Disconnect EVAP crossover pipe quick connect fitting from lefthand side fuel tank. Cap EVAP pipe to prevent system contamination.
17. Remove fuel tank strap mounting bolts, then fuel tank from vehicle.
18. Disconnect fuel pump jumper harness from fuel pump module.
19. Disconnect jet line insert connector from fuel tank opening crossover tube.
20. Disconnect fuel feed line from welded clip on side of fuel tank.
21. Remove fuel pump module locking ring using lock ring removal tool No. J39765-A, or equivalent. **Fuel pump module is spring loaded and will spring upward when locking ring is removed.**
22. Carefully remove fuel pump module from fuel tank, with jet lines connected. **Ensure not to damage fuel sender float arm.**
23. Disconnect jet line quick-connect connectors from fuel pump module inner port.
24. Remove jet line from module retainer cup.
25. Remove fuel pump module O-ring from fuel tank opening.
26. Remove jet line insert through crossover tube to fuel tank opening.
27. Reverse procedure to install.

Righthand

1. Relieve fuel system pressure as outlined under "Precautions."
2. Drain fuel tank.
3. Raise and support vehicle, then remove righthand side rear tire and wheel assembly.

4. Remove righthand side rear wheel-house liner panel.
5. Remove EVAP canister access cover.
6. Disconnect FLVV hose at EVAP Canister.
7. Disconnect fuel pump module harness connector, then remove crossover tube from clamp located above transmission.
8. Disengage crossover tube CPA retainer by pulling tab outward and rotate.
9. Disengage crossover tube collar by rotating counterclockwise.
10. Disconnect crossover tube from fuel tank by pulling tube straight out of fuel tank connection.
11. Disconnect EVAP crossover pipe quick connect fitting at righthand side fuel tank. Cap EVAP pipe to prevent system contamination.
12. Remove fuel tank strap mounting bolts, then fuel tank strap and fuel tank from vehicle.
13. Disconnect EVAP purge line from fuel pump module.
14. Disconnect fuel pump module harness and Fuel Tank Pressure (FTP) sensor connectors.
15. Remove FTP sensor.
16. Remove fuel pump module locking ring using lock ring removal tool No. J39765-A, or equivalent. **Fuel pump module is spring loaded and will spring upward when locking ring is removed.**
17. Carefully remove fuel pump module from fuel tank, with jet lines connected. **Ensure not to damage fuel sender float arm.**
18. Disconnect jet line quick-connect connectors from fuel pump module inner port.
19. Remove jet line from module retainer cup.
20. Remove fuel pump module O-ring from fuel tank opening.
21. Remove jet line insert through crossover tube to fuel tank opening.
22. Reverse procedure to install.

FUEL FILTER

REPLACE

The fuel filter is contained within the fuel sender assembly, inside the lefthand side fuel tank. Refer to "Fuel Pump, Replace" for fuel filter replacement.

TIGHTENING SPECIFICATIONS

Year	Component	Torque Ft. Lbs.
2006–08	A/C Compressor, Mounting Bolt	37
	A/C Compressor & Power Steering Bracket Bolt	37
	A/C Drive Belt Tensioner	18
	Alternator	37
	Alternator Coolant Inlet Hose Fitting	18
	Alternator Coolant Line Bolt	19
	Alternator Rear Brace Bolt	37
	Alternator Stud	106①
	Bell Housing Bolt	37
	Block Coolant Drain Hole Plug	15
	Camshaft Position Sensor	89①
	Charge Air Cooler Rear Manifold Bolts	89①
	Charge Air Cooler Front Manifold Bolts	89①
	Crossmember	81
	Cylinder Head Coolant Plug	60
	Drive Belt Idler Bolt	37
	Drive Belt Idler Nut	37
	Drive Belt Tensioner Bolt	37
	ECT Sensor	15
	Engine Mount Bracket Bolt	43
	Engine Mount Nut	43
	Flywheel To Torque Converter	②
	Fuel Injector Sight Shield	89①
	Fuel Rail Attaching Studs	89①
	Intermediate Shaft Pinch Bolt	25
	Lower Control Arm Cam Bolt	125
	Oil Dipstick Tube Bolt	37
	Oil Filter Bypass Hole Plug	22
	Oil Filter Fitting	21
	Oil Filter Mounting Bolt	18
	Oil Level Sensor	15
	Oil Pan	18
	Oil Pan Drain Plug	18
	Oil Pressure Switch	15
	Oxygen Sensor	31
	Power Steering Pump	18

Continued

4.6L ENGINE

TIGHTENING
SPECIFICATIONS—Continued

Year	Component	Torque Ft. Lbs.
2006–08	Power Steering Pump Reservoir Bracket Nut	89①
	Starter Motor Bolt	22
	Starter Motor Wiring Harness - Large	89①
	Starter Motor Wiring Harness - Small	35①
	Steering Rack	74
	Throttle Body	89①
	Tie Rod	33
	Wheel Lug Nuts	100

① — Inch lbs.
② — First pass, 11 ft. lbs. second pass, tighten an additional 50°.

Rear Axle & Suspension

NOTE: On Air Bag Equipped Models, Refer To "Air Bag System Precautions" Located In The Front Of This Manual For System Disarming & Arming Procedures.

NOTE: Refer To "Computer Relearn Procedures" Located In The Front Of This Manual When Battery Power To The Computer Has Been Interrupted.

INDEX

	Page No.
Ball Joint, Replace	13-19
Control Arm, Replace	13-19
Lower	13-19
Upper	13-19
Description	13-17
Differential Carrier, Replace	13-18
Hub & Bearing, Replace	13-18

	Page No.
Rear Axle Shaft, Replace	13-17
Installation	13-18
Removal	13-17
Rear Crossmember, Replace	13-20
Shock Absorber, Replace	13-19
Stabilizer Shaft, Replace	13-20
Suspension Knuckle, Replace	13-20

	Page No.
Tie Rod, Replace	13-19
Inner	13-19
Outer	13-19
Tightening Specifications	13-20
Transverse Spring, Replace	13-19

DESCRIPTION

The rear suspension uses a single lightweight fiberglass transverse spring mounted to the crossmember and lower control arms. The rear suspension uses the following lightweight aluminum components; rear suspension knuckles, upper control arms, lower control arms, rear suspension toe links, crossmember and drive shaft support tube. The shock absorbers are attached to the frame and the lower control arm. Shock absorbers reduce crash-through at full jounce and rebound. The electronically controlled shock absorbers are gas charged to reduce aeration (foaming) of the shock fluid.

REAR AXLE SHAFT
REPLACE
Removal

1. Shift transmission into PARK, then apply parking brake.

2. Raise and support vehicle.
3. Remove tire and wheel assembly.
4. Insert a suitable drift or punch into brake rotor cooling fins and against brake caliper to prevent wheel hub and bearing from turning.
5. Remove spindle nut retaining rear wheel drive shaft to hub.
6. Remove drift or punch, then release parking brake.
7. Loosen, do not remove, outer tie rod end stud nut from outer tie rod end ball stud.
8. Install ball joint separator tool No. J 42188, or equivalent, between suspension knuckle and outer tie rod end stud, then tighten bolt on separator tool until knuckle and outer tie rod end stud separate.
9. Separate outer tie rod end from knuckle and reposition tie rod toward rear of vehicle.
10. Disconnect wheel speed sensor electrical connector.
11. Disconnect parking brake cable from parking brake lever.

12. Remove parking brake cable from bracket and reposition toward rear of vehicle.
13. Install rear hub spindle remover tool No. J 42129, or equivalent, onto wheel hub and secure with wheel nuts, **Fig. 1.**
14. Begin to separate drive shaft from wheel hub and bearing to provide additional clearance to lower ball joint nut.
15. Loosen, but do not remove upper ball joint stud nut. **Do not allow ball joint to rotate.** Use a suitable Torx wrench inserted into top of ball stud while removing ball stud nut, **Fig. 2.**
16. Separate lower ball joint from suspension knuckle.
17. Separate drive shaft completely from wheel hub and bearing.
18. Support drive shaft, suspension knuckle and upper control arm. Reposition knuckle toward front of vehicle.
19. Assemble axle shaft remover tool No. J 42128 , extension tool No. J 29794 and slide hammer tool No. J 2619-O1,

or equivalents, onto rear beveled surface of drive shaft inner joint housing, **Fig. 3.**

20. Separate drive shaft from rear axle differential, then remove tool assembly.
21. Remove drive shaft from vehicle, then spindle remover tool from wheel hub.

Installation

1. Support drive shaft until it is completely installed.
2. Position drive shaft to rear axle differential output shaft. **Do not damage rear axle differential output shaft seal.**
3. Carefully align and guide drive shaft onto differential output shaft.
4. Engage drive shaft fully onto differential output shaft using light force.
5. Align and guide drive shaft into wheel hub and bearing, but do not seat fully.
6. Install lower ball joint to suspension knuckle.
7. Install parking brake cable into bracket.
8. Connect parking brake cable to parking brake lever.
9. Connect wheel speed sensor electrical connector.
10. Install outer tie rod end on to suspension knuckle.
11. Apply parking brake, then insert a drift or punch into brake rotor cooling fins and against caliper to prevent wheel hub and bearing from turning.
12. Begin to install drive shaft retaining nut onto drive shaft by hand.
13. Slowly tighten nut to draw drive shaft into wheel hub and bearing.
14. Tighten drive axle spindle nut to specifications, then remove drift or punch and release parking brake.
15. Install tire and wheel assembly, then lower vehicle.

DIFFERENTIAL CARRIER
REPLACE

1. Raise and suitably support vehicle.
2. Remove rear tire and wheel assemblies.
3. Remove bolts securing brake hydraulic line and hose bracket to suspension crossmember.
4. Remove bolts securing rear brake calipers to rear knuckles and support caliper.
5. Slide caliper forward, away from knuckle and rotor.
6. Disconnect wheel speed sensor electrical wire harness from wheel speed sensor.
7. Disconnect retainers securing wheel speed sensor harness to park brake cables.
8. Remove wheel speed sensor harness from suspension crossmember.
9. Route sensor harnesses away from suspension crossmember.
10. Disconnect park brake cables from actuator levers.
11. Pull park brake cable housing out of park brake cable brackets attached to knuckle.

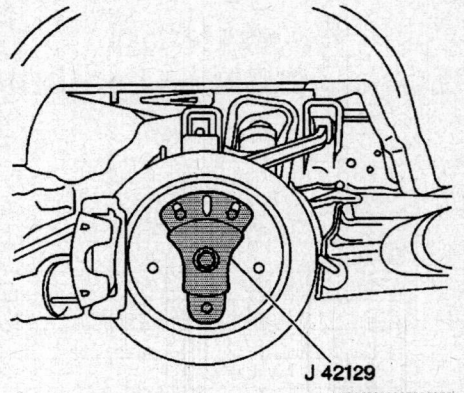

Fig. 1   Spindle remover tool installation

J 42129
ARM0300000000275

12. Remove push pins retaining right and left park brake cables to suspension crossmember.
13. Route park brake cables away from suspension crossmember.
14. Remove rear suspension position sensors if equipped.
15. Position a suitable adjustable tall jack stand under lower control arm near ball joint location.
16. Raise jack stand to reduce transverse spring load on lower control arm.
17. Remove nut from upper ball joint stud.
18. Separate upper ball joint stud from suspension knuckle using Ball Joint Separator, tool No. J 42188, or equivalent.
19. Remove lower shock absorber bolt and nut.
20. Lower tall jack stand supporting lower control arm.
21. Position knuckle away from upper control arm.
22. Disconnect inner axle joints from differential.
23. Position knuckle away from upper control arm.
24. Position a suitable tall jack stand under front cradle to support weight of front of vehicle on hoist.
25. Position a suitable tall jack stand under front of transmission.
26. Position a suitable transmission jack under suspension crossmember.
27. Route a suitable safety strap over suspension crossmember, under brake pipe to secure rear suspension crossmember to transmission jack.
28. Using HAND TOOLS ONLY, remove lower nuts securing rear mounts to crossmember.
29. Using HAND TOOLS ONLY, remove nuts from rear crossmember bolts.
30. Lower rear crossmember approximately 1.3 inches.
31. Disconnect plastic brake pipe retainers from crossmember.
32. Lower rear suspension crossmember from vehicle. This assembly includes suspension crossmember, lower control arms, transverse leaf spring, rear stabilizer bar and links, knuckles, outer and inner tie rod ends, rotors, hubs, and drive axle assemblies.
33. Disconnect vacuum lines from rear

muffler valves, if equipped.
34. Disconnect muffler/tailpipe assemblies from rubber isolators at rear of mufflers.
35. Remove intermediate pipe.
36. Remove left muffler/tailpipe assembly.
37. Using a hoist, raise vehicle approximately 2 inches and suitably support.
38. Remove right muffler/tailpipe assembly.
39. Disconnect vehicle speed sensor (VSS) connector from top of differential.
40. Disconnect VSS wiring harness retainers from differential studs at top of differential.
41. Remove nuts securing rear mounts to differential.
42. Remove mounts from differential.
43. Reposition hydraulic brake line forward and away from differential.
44. Assemble a Drivetrain Support Fixture, tool No. J 42055, or equivalent.
45. Install drivetrain support fixture to a suitable transmission jack.
46. Position and firmly secure drivetrain support fixture with transmission jack to differential.
47. Remove fasteners securing differential to the transmission.
48. Using transmission jack, carefully slide differential rearward from transmission.
49. After differential has cleared output shaft of transmission, differential can be lowered using transmission jack.
50. Reverse procedure to install.

HUB & BEARING
REPLACE

1. Shift transmission into PARK, then apply parking brake.
2. Raise and support vehicle.
3. Remove tire and wheel assembly.
4. Disconnect wheel speed sensor harness connector.
5. Disconnect Electronic Suspension Control (ESC) rear position sensor link.
6. Remove brake caliper and rotor as outlined in "Disc Brakes" chapter.
7. Disconnect shock absorber ESC harness connector.
8. Loosen, do not remove, outer tie rod end stud nut from outer tie rod end ball stud.
9. Install ball joint separator tool No. J 42188, or equivalent, between suspension knuckle and outer tie rod end stud, then tighten bolt on separator tool until knuckle and outer tie rod end stud separate.
10. Separate outer tie rod end from suspension knuckle.
11. Insert a drift or punch into brake rotor cooling fins and against brake caliper to prevent wheel hub and bearing from turning.
12. Remove spindle nut retaining rear wheel drive shaft to hub.
13. Remove drift or punch, then release parking brake.
14. Separate upper control arm from suspension knuckle, **Fig. 2.**

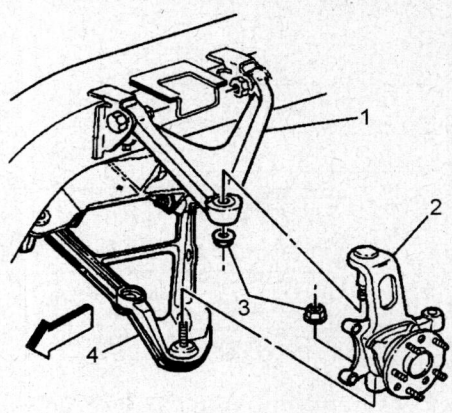

1 Upper control arm
2 SUspension knuckle
3 Ball stud nuts
4 Lower control arm

ARM0300000000271

Fig. 2   Suspension knuckle & control arms

15. Separate suspension knuckle from lower control arm ball joint stud.
16. Remove suspension knuckle from vehicle.
17. Remove wheel hub mounting bolts, then hub and bearing assembly from suspension knuckle.
18. Reverse procedure to install.

SHOCK ABSORBER
REPLACE

1. Raise and support vehicle.
2. Remove tire and wheel assembly.
3. Disconnect rear shock electronic suspension control (ESC) harness connector, **Fig. 4.**
4. Disconnect harness pigtail from upper shock tower clip.
5. Remove lower shock absorber to lower control arm retaining bolt.
6. Remove upper shock absorber mounting bolts.
7. Loosen, do not remove, outer tie rod end stud nut from outer tie rod end ball stud.
8. Install ball joint separator tool No. J 42188, or equivalent, between suspension knuckle and outer tie rod end stud, then tighten bolt on separator tool until knuckle and outer tie rod end stud separate.
9. Separate outer tie rod end from suspension knuckle.
10. Remove shock absorber from vehicle. **Use caution when routing ESC pigtail and connector through upper shock tower.**
11. Remove upper insulator retainer and insulator from shock absorber.
12. Reverse procedure to install.

BALL JOINT
REPLACE

Refer to "Control Arm, Replace" for ball joint replacement.

TRANSVERSE SPRING
REPLACE

1. Raise and support vehicle.
2. Remove tire and wheel assemblies.
3. Measure rear spring adjuster bolt gap, **Fig. 5.** This measurement should be used in installation procedure to setup vehicle trim height.
4. Remove one lower control arm as outlined under "Control Arms, Replace."
5. Compress transverse spring using spring compressor tool No. J 33432-A, or equivalent. Do not scratch transverse spring.
6. Remove transverse spring bolts and retainers. Discard old transverse spring bolts.
7. Remove transverse spring from vehicle.
8. Remove transverse spring compressor from transverse spring.
9. Reverse procedure to install.

CONTROL ARM
REPLACE
Lower

1. Raise and support vehicle.
2. Remove tire and wheel assembly.
3. Compress transverse spring using transverse spring compressor tool No. J 33432-A, or equivalent.
4. Disconnect suspension position sensor link, if equipped from control arm link stud.
5. Place a suitable jack stand under lower control arm.
6. Disconnect shock absorber from lower control arm.
7. Loosen, but do not remove upper ball joint stud nut. **Do not allow ball joint to rotate.** Use a suitable Torx wrench inserted into top of ball stud while removing ball stud nut.
8. Remove upper ball joint stud nut from suspension knuckle.
9. Separate upper ball joint stud from suspension knuckle using ball joint separator tool No. J 42188, or equivalent.
10. Insert a drift or punch into brake rotor cooling fins and against brake caliper to prevent wheel hub and bearing from turning.
11. Remove spindle nut retaining rear wheel drive shaft to hub.
12. Remove drift or punch, then release parking brake.
13. Loosen, but do not remove lower ball joint stud nut. Separate lower ball joint stud from suspension knuckle using J 42188 . Remove J 42188 and lower ball joint stud nut from suspension knuckle.
14. Remove stabilizer shaft link from lower control arm.
15. Mark position of lower control arm cam bolts, then remove cam bolts, washers and nuts. retaining control arm to crossmember.
16. Remove jack stand, then lower control arm from vehicle.
17. Reverse procedure to install.

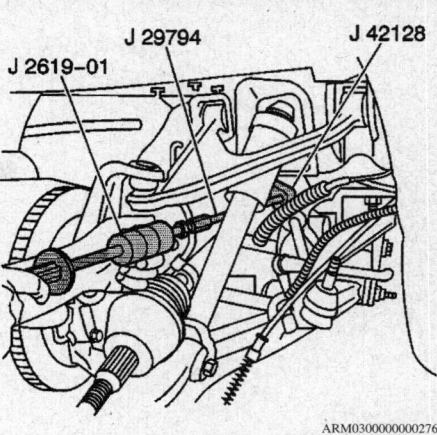

J 2619–01   J 29794   J 42128

ARM0300000000276

Fig. 3   Axle shaft removal

Upper

1. Raise and support vehicle.
2. Remove tire and wheel assembly.
3. Disconnect wheel speed sensor electrical connector.
4. Disconnect Electronic Suspension Control (ESC) sensor link.
5. Separate suspension knuckle from upper control arm using ball joint separator tool No. J 42188, or equivalent.
6. Support lower control arm with a suitable jack stand.
7. Loosen upper ball joint stud nut, but do not remove nut.
8. Remove ball joint stud nut from ball joint stud.
9. Remove upper control arm to frame attaching bolts.
10. Remove upper control arm from vehicle.
11. Reverse procedure to install.

TIE ROD
REPLACE
Inner

1. Raise and support vehicle.
2. Remove tire and wheel assembly.
3. Loosen, do not remove, outer tie rod end stud nut from outer tie rod end ball stud.
4. Install ball joint separator tool No. J 42188, or equivalent, between suspension knuckle and outer tie rod end stud, then tighten bolt on separator tool until knuckle and outer tie rod end stud separate.
5. Separate outer tie rod end from suspension knuckle.
6. Remove nut retaining rear suspension adjustment link (inner tie rod) to crossmember.
7. Remove rear suspension adjustment link (inner tie rod) from vehicle.
8. Reverse procedure to install.

Outer

1. Raise and support vehicle.
2. Remove tire and wheel assembly.
3. Loosen, do not remove, outer tie rod

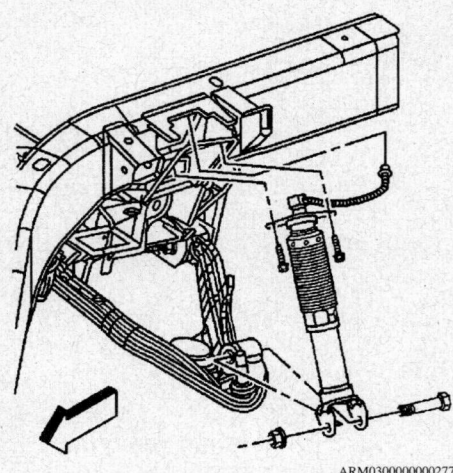

Fig. 4 Shock absorber removal

end stud nut from outer tie rod end ball stud.

4. Install ball joint separator tool No. J 42188, or equivalent, between suspension knuckle and outer tie rod end stud, then tighten bolt on separator tool until knuckle and outer tie rod end stud separate.
5. Separate outer tie rod end from suspension knuckle.
6. Loosen jam nut on rear suspension adjustment link.
7. Remove outer tie rod end from rear suspension adjustment link.
8. Reverse procedure to install.

REAR CROSSMEMBER
REPLACE

1. Raise and support vehicle.
2. Remove tire and wheel assemblies.
3. Disconnect wheel speed sensors harness connectors.
4. Disconnect park brake cables from actuator levers.
5. Disconnect electrical connectors from electronic suspension control (ESC) shock absorbers harnesses, if equipped.
6. Remove rear suspension position sensors.
7. Disconnect rear suspension adjustment link (inner tie rod end) studs from rear crossmember.
8. Disconnect lower control arms from crossmember as outlined under "Control Arms, Replace."
9. Support rear drive shafts and rear suspension knuckles.
10. Remove transverse spring as outlined under "Transverse Spring, Replace."
11. Remove transmission mount lower nuts.
12. Disconnect all electrical harness and connectors from crossmember.
13. Disconnect brake pipes from crossmember.
14. Support transmission with a suitable transmission jack.
15. Remove rear crossmember mounting nuts. **Using hand tools only.**
16. Remove crossmember from vehicle. Discard crossmember mounting nuts.
17. Reverse procedure to install.

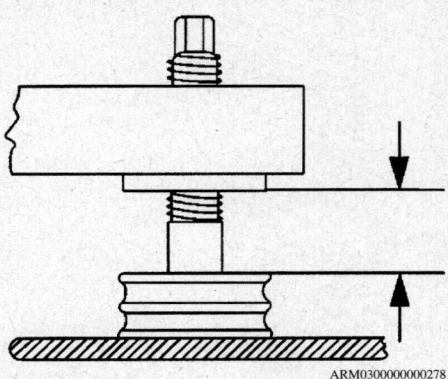

Fig. 5 Spring adjuster bolt gap measurement

SUSPENSION KNUCKLE
REPLACE

Refer to "Hub & Bearing, Replace" for rear wheel suspension knuckle replacement.

STABILIZER SHAFT
REPLACE

1. Raise and support vehicle.
2. Remove tire and wheel assemblies.
3. Remove stabilizer shaft link nuts from stabilizer shaft.
4. Remove stabilizer shaft clamps, bolts and nuts retaining shaft to crossmember.
5. Remove stabilizer shaft from vehicle.
6. Reverse procedure to install.

TIGHTENING SPECIFICATIONS

Year	Component	Torque Ft. Lbs.
2004–08	Carrier Assembly - Differential-to-Transmission Bolts and Nuts	37
	Crossmember Mounting Nuts	81
	Differential Drain Plug	26
	Differential Fill Plug	26
	Lower Control Arm Ball Joint Stud Nut	①
	Lower Control Arm Front Cam Bolt Nut	107
	Lower Control Arm Rear Cam Bolt Nut	70
	Outer Tie Rod End Stud Nut	②
	Rear Suspension Adjustment Link To Crossmember Nut	44
	Shock Absorber Lower Mounting Bolt	162
	Shock Absorber Upper Mounting Bolts	22
	Stabilizer Shaft Insulator Clamp Bolt	49
	Stabilizer Shaft Insulator Clamp Nut	70
	Stabilizer Shaft Link Nuts	53
	Transverse Spring Mounting Bracket Bolts	46
	Upper Control Arm Ball Joint Stud Nut	③
	Wheel Hub Mounting Bolts	96
	Wheel Lug Nuts	100

① — First step, 15 ft. lbs.; second step, 3½ flats; third step, 52 ft. lbs.

② — First step, 15 ft. lbs.; second step, an additional 160°; third step, 33 ft. lbs.

③ — First step, 15 ft. lbs.; second step, an additional 250°; third step, 41 ft. lbs.

Front Suspension & Steering

NOTE: On Air Bag Equipped Models, Refer To "Air Bag System Precautions" Located In The Front Of This Manual For System Disarming & Arming Procedures.

NOTE: Refer To "Computer Relearn Procedures" Located In The Front Of This Manual When Battery Power To The Computer Has Been Interrupted.

INDEX

	Page No.
Ball Joint, Replace	13-21
Lower	13-21
Upper	13-21
Ball Joint Inspection	13-21
Control Arm, Replace	13-22
Lower	13-22
Upper	13-22
Crossmember, Replace	13-22

	Page No.
Hub & Bearing, Replace	13-21
Power Steering	21-1
Power Steering Gear, Replace	13-23
Power Steering Pump, Replace	13-23
4.4L Engine	13-23
4.6L Engine	13-23
Power Steering System Bleed	13-23
Shock Absorber, Replace	13-21

	Page No.
Stabilizer Bar, Replace	13-22
Steering Columns	20-1
Steering Knuckle, Replace	13-22
Tie Rod, Replace	13-22
Inner	13-22
Outer	13-23
Tightening Specifications	13-24
Transverse Spring, Replace	13-21

HUB & BEARING

REPLACE

1. Raise and support vehicle.
2. Remove tire and wheel assembly.
3. Disconnect wheel speed sensor harness connector.
4. Remove brake caliper and rotor as outlined in "Disc Brakes" chapter.
5. Remove stabilizer shaft link from lower control arm.
6. Support lower control arm using a suitable jackstand.
7. Remove outer tie rod end ball stud to steering knuckle retaining nut.
8. Separate outer tie rod ball stud from steering knuckle using ball joint separator tool No. J 42188, or equivalent.
9. Remove lower ball joint stud to steering knuckle retaining nut.
10. Separate lower ball joint stud from steering knuckle using ball joint separator tool No. J 42188, or equivalent.
11. Remove wheel hub mounting bolts, then hub and bearing assembly from steering knuckle.
12. Reverse procedure to install.

BALL JOINT INSPECTION

1. Raise and support vehicle.
2. Support lower control arm with a jack stand, as far outboard as possible, near lower ball joint.
3. Wipe ball joints clean, then inspect seal for cuts and tears. If ball joint seal is cut or torn, replace ball joint.
4. Position dial indicator tool No. J 8001, or equivalent, against lowest outboard point on wheel rim.

5. Rock wheel in and out while reading dial indicator. Dial indicator reading should be no more than .125 inch. If reading is too high, proceed to next step.
6. Inspect lower ball joints for wear and for vertical looseness as follows:
   a. Position of housing into which grease fitting is threaded indicates wear. This round housing projects .050 inch beyond surface of lower ball joint cover on a new ball joint.
   b. Under normal wear, surface of lower ball joint housing retreats inward very slowly.
   c. Remove any dirt from housing, if housing is flush with or inside of cover, replace lower control arm.
7. Position dial indicator tool No. J 8001, or equivalent, against spindle.
8. Pry between lower control arm and outer bearing race with a suitable pry bar while reading dial indicator. If dial indicator reading is more than .125 inch, replace lower control arm.
9. Inspect upper ball joint for wear.
10. Disconnect upper ball joint from steering knuckle as outlined under "Ball Joint, Replace." If there is any looseness or stud can be twisted with your fingers, replace upper ball joint.

BALL JOINT

REPLACE

Lower

The ball joint is a component of the lower control arm and cannot be serviced separately. Refer to "Control Arm, Replace" for replacement procedure.

Upper

The upper ball joint is a component of the steering knuckle and cannot be serviced separately. Refer to "Steering Knuckle, Replace" for replacement procedure.

SHOCK ABSORBER

REPLACE

1. Disconnect shock Electronic Suspension Control (ESC) harness connector.
2. Raise and support vehicle.
3. Remove tire and wheel assembly.
4. Remove upper mounting nut, insulator retainer and insulator. **Use hand tools only.**
5. Remove shock absorber lower mounting bolts and nuts, **Fig. 1.**
6. Compress shock absorber from bottom upward using a suitable pry bar.
7. With shock in compressed position, install shock support tool No. J 43822, or equivalent.
8. Remove shock absorber from vehicle, then support tool from shock.
9. Remove insulator and insulator retainer from shock absorber.
10. Reverse procedure to install.

TRANSVERSE SPRING

REPLACE

1. Raise and support vehicle.
2. Remove tire and wheel assemblies.
3. If transverse spring is to be replaced, measure front spring adjuster bolt gap, **Fig. 2.** This measurement will be used during installation to setup vehicle trim height.
4. Compress transverse spring with

spring compressor tool No. J 33432-A, or equivalent, **Fig. 3.**

5. Remove lower shock absorber mounting bolts from lower control arm.
6. Disconnect stabilizer shaft link from lower control arm.
7. Loosen lower ball joint stud nut on lower control arm. **Do not remove nut.**
8. Separate lower ball joint from steering knuckle using ball joint separator tool No. J 42188, or equivalent.
9. Remove lower ball joint stud nut and discard.
10. Support lower control arms with jackstands.
11. Mark position of cam bolts for installation reference.
12. Remove cam bolts from lower control arm.
13. Remove lower control arm.
14. Remove transverse spring bolts and retainers, then transverse spring and spring compressor from vehicle. Discard transverse spring bolts transverse spring compressor from transverse spring.
15. Reverse procedure to install.

CONTROL ARM
REPLACE

Lower

1. Raise and support vehicle.
2. Remove tire and wheel assembly.
3. Remove transverse spring as outlined under "Transverse Spring, Replace."
4. Disconnect wheel speed sensor electrical connector.
5. Remove shock absorber from lower control arm.
6. Remove stabilizer shaft link from lower control arm.
7. Loosen ball joint stud nut. **Do not remove nut.**
8. Separate lower ball joint stud from steering knuckle using ball joint separator tool No. J 42188, or equivalent.
9. Remove ball joint stud nut, then ball joint stud from steering knuckle.
10. Mark position of cam bolts for installation reference.
11. Remove cam bolts, washers and nuts attaching control arm to crossmember, **Fig. 4.**
12. Remove lower control arm from vehicle.
13. Reverse procedure to install.

Upper

1. Raise and support vehicle.
2. Remove tire and wheel assembly.
3. Disconnect Electronic Suspension Control (ESC) sensor links.
4. Support lower control arm with a jackstand.
5. Loosen ball joint stud nut. **Do not remove nut.**
6. Separate upper ball joint stud from upper control arm using ball joint separator tool No. J 42188, or equivalent.
7. Remove ball joint stud nut from ball joint stud.
8. Remove upper control arm bolts and

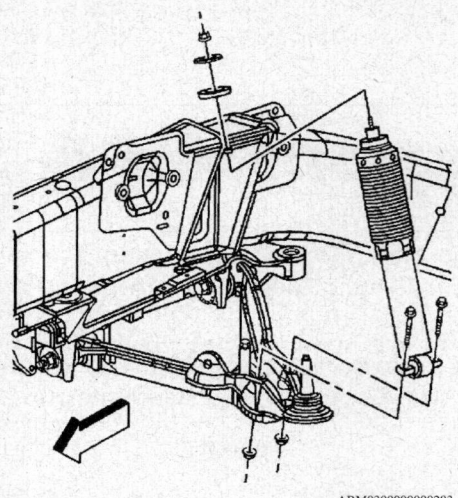

ARM0300000000283

Fig. 1   Shock absorber removal

shims, **Fig. 5.** Upper control arm shims will have an effect on camber and caster, be sure to use an equal thickness of shims on both sides of each individual upper control arm bushing. Note number and position of shims for installation reference.

9. Remove upper control arm from vehicle.
10. Reverse procedure to install.

STEERING KNUCKLE
REPLACE

1. Raise and support vehicle.
2. Remove brake caliper and rotor as outlined in "Disc Brakes" chapter.
3. Remove stabilizer shaft link from lower control arm.
4. Disconnect wheel speed sensor electrical connector.
5. Support lower control arm with a suitable jackstand.
6. Remove outer tie rod end to steering knuckle retaining nut.
7. Separate outer tie rod ball stud from steering knuckle using ball joint separator tool No. J 42188, or equivalent.
8. Loosen ball joint stud nut. **Do not remove nut.**
9. Separate upper ball joint stud from upper control arm using ball joint separator tool No. J 42188, or equivalent.
10. Remove ball joint stud nut from ball joint stud.
11. Loosen ball joint stud nut. **Do not remove nut.**
12. Separate lower ball joint stud from steering knuckle using ball joint separator tool No. J 42188, or equivalent.
13. Remove lower ball joint stud nut, then ball joint stud from steering knuckle.
14. Remove steering knuckle from vehicle.
15. Reverse procedure to install.

STABILIZER BAR
REPLACE

1. Raise and support vehicle.
2. Remove tire and wheel assemblies.

3. Remove stabilizer shaft link nuts from stabilizer shaft, **Fig. 6.**
4. Remove stabilizer shaft insulator clamps from front crossmember.
5. Remove stabilizer shaft from vehicle.
6. Reverse procedure to install.

CROSSMEMBER
REPLACE

1. Attach engine support fixture tool No. J 28467-B, or equivalent, to engine.
2. Raise and support vehicle.
3. Remove tire and wheel assemblies.
4. Remove steering linkage outer tie rod end stud nuts as outlined under "Tie Rod End, Replace."
5. Disconnect Electronic suspension control (ESC) sensor links.
6. Remove stabilizer shaft from vehicle as outlined under "Stabilizer Bar, Replace."
7. Disconnect intermediate shaft lower coupling from steering gear.
8. Remove bolts from Electronic Brake Control Module/Brake Pressure Modulator Valve (EBCM/BPMV) bracket. Support and position EBCM/BPMV and bracket away from crossmember.
9. Remove power steering gear mounting bolts, then power steering fluid cooler from crossmember.
10. Lift power steering gear off of crossmember and support.
11. Remove transverse spring as outlined under "Transverse Spring, Replace."
12. Remove lower shock absorber to lower control arms attaching bolts.
13. Remove lower control arm to crossmember mounting bolts.
14. Place a suitable transmission jack under crossmember.
15. Remove engine mount lower retaining nuts.
16. Disconnect wheel speed sensor wiring harness from crossmember.
17. Disconnect electrical harness from clips on crossmember.
18. Disconnect brake pipe from clips on crossmember.
19. Remove crossmember mounting nuts, then lower crossmember out of vehicle, **Fig. 7.**
20. Reverse procedure to install.

TIE ROD
REPLACE

Inner

1. Raise and support vehicle.
2. Remove tire and wheel assembly.
3. Remove rack and pinion boot. **Do not change rack bearing preload adjustment before removing inner tie rod from steering rack. This could cause damage to pinion or steering rack or both.**
4. Remove shock dampener from inner tie rod.
5. Slide shock dampener back onto rack. **Do not hold steering rack while removing inner tie rod.**
6. Place a wrench on flats of inner tie rod

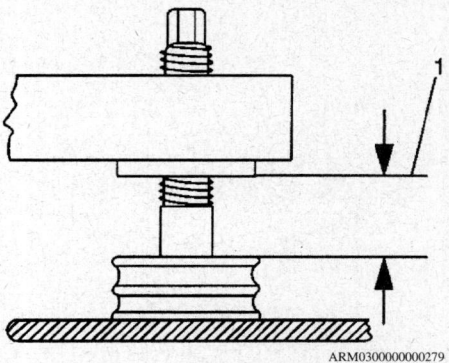

Fig. 2   Transverse spring adjuster bolt gap measurement

housing, then rotate inner tie rod housing counterclockwise until inner tie rod separates from rack.

7. Remove inner tie rod from rack assembly.
8. Reverse procedure to install, noting the following:
   a. Remove old Loctite from threads of rack and inner tie rod.
   b. Apply Loctite 262, or equivalent, to inner tie rod threads.

Outer

1. Raise and suitable support vehicle.
2. Remove tire and wheel assemblies.
3. Loosen, but do not remove outer tie rod end stud nut from outer tie rod end ball stud.
4. Loosen outer tie rod end stud to steering knuckle connection using ball joint separator tool No. J 42188.
5. Remove outer tie rod end stud nut in order to separate tie rod from steering knuckle.
6. Loosen jam nut on inner tie rod assembly.
7. Remove outer tie rod end from inner tie rod assembly.
8. Reverse procedure to install.

POWER STEERING GEAR

REPLACE

1. Remove Brake Pressure Modulator Valve (BPMV) bracket.
2. Raise and support vehicle.
3. Remove tires and wheels.
4. Disconnect tie rod ends from steering knuckles.
5. Remove lower shock mounting bolts.
6. Disconnect intermediate shaft from power steering gear.
7. Remove stabilizer shaft as outlined under "Stabilizer Bar, Replace."
8. Remove power steering pressure and return hoses.
9. Remove brake pipes from crossmember.

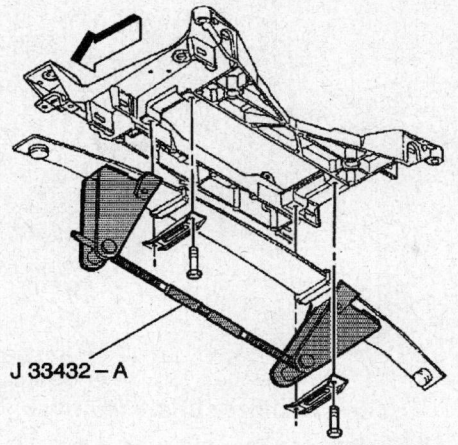

Fig. 3   Transverse spring removal

10. Remove power steering gear mounting bolts and nuts. **Use hand tools only.**
11. Remove four crossmember mounting nuts, then power steering gear from vehicle through lefthand side wheelhouse opening.
12. Reverse procedure to install. Bleed power steering.

POWER STEERING PUMP

REPLACE

4.4L Engine

1. Remove air cleaner assembly.
2. Use a suitable tool to remove fluid from power steering pump reservoir.
3. Remove supercharger drive belt. Refer to "Supercharger Drive Belt, Replace" under "4.4L Engine" section.
4. Remove air conditioner belt tensioner.
5. Remove power steering pump pulley.
6. Remove power steering pump inlet hose clamp.
7. Place a suitable drain pan under vehicle. Release hose clamp and pull inlet hose off of power steering pump inlet tube.
8. Remove power steering pump pressure hose fitting bolt.
9. Remove power steering pump bolts and power steering pump.
10. Reverse procedure to install, noting the following:
   a. Fill and bleed power steering system after repair has been completed. "Power Steering System Bleed".
   b. Apply a suitable grease to splines on power steering pump shaft.

4.6L Engine

1. Remove power steering fluid reservoir.
2. Remove accessory drive belt. Refer to

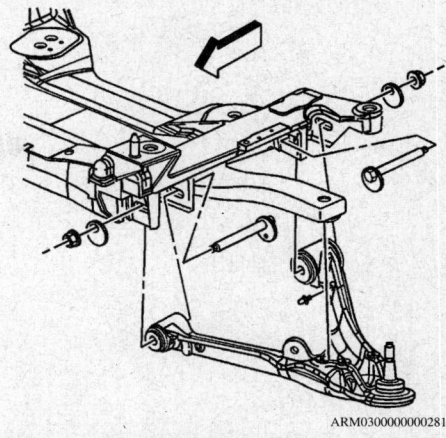

Fig. 4   Lower control arm removal

"Accessory Drive Belt, Replace" under "4.6L Engine" section

3. Remove pulley from power steering pump using a Power Steering Pump Pulley Remover, tool No. J 25034-C, or equivalent.
4. Remove power steering reservoir outlet pipe/hose.
5. Remove power steering gear inlet pipe/hose.
6. Remove power steering pump mounting bolts from power steering pump.
7. Reverse procedure to install. Install power steering pump using a Power Steering Pump Pulley Installer, tool No. J 25033-C, or equivalent.

POWER STEERING SYSTEM BLEED

1. Fill pump reservoir with fluid to minimum system level, FULL COLD level, or middle of hash mark on cap stick fluid level indicator. With hydro-boost only, oil level will appear falsely high if hydro-boost accumulator is not fully charged.
2. **On models equipped with hydro-boost,** fully charge hydro-boost accumulator using the following procedure:
   a. Start engine.
   b. Firmly apply brake pedal 10-15 times.
   c. Turn engine OFF.
3. **On all models,** raise vehicle until front wheels are off ground and suitably support.
4. Key on engine OFF, turn steering wheel from stop to stop 12 times.
5. **On models equipped with hydro-boost,** may require turns up to 15 to 20 stop to stops.
6. **On all models,** verify power steering fluid level is at operating specification.
7. Start engine. Rotate steering wheel from left to right. Inspect for sign of cavitation or fluid aeration (pump noise/whining).
8. Verify fluid level. Repeat bleed procedure, if required.

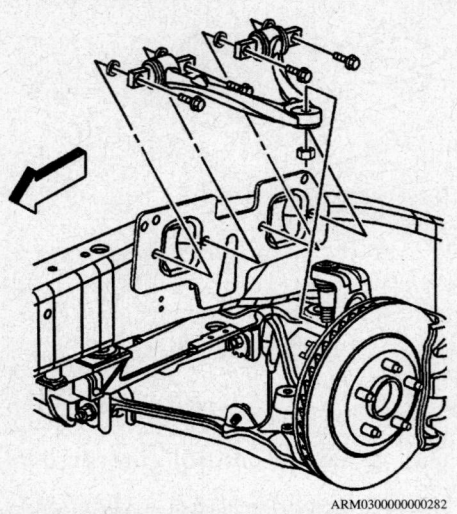

ARM0300000000282

Fig. 5 Upper control arm removal

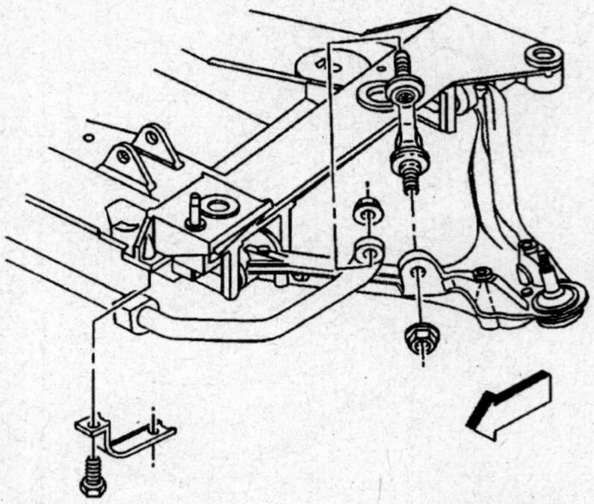

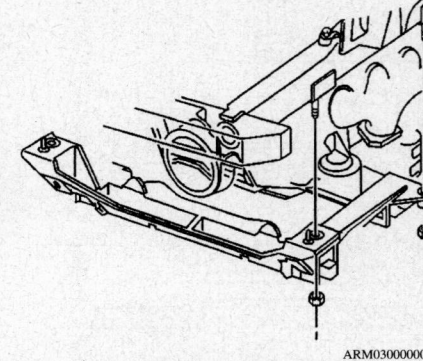

ARM0300000000284

Fig. 6 Stabilizer shaft removal

ARM0300000000285

Fig. 7 Crossmember removal

TIGHTENING SPECIFICATIONS

Year	Component	Torque Ft. Lbs.
2004–08	Adjuster Plug Lock Nut	50
	Crossmember Mounting Nuts	81
	Cylinder Line End Fittings	20
	Cylinder Line Valve End Fittings	13③
	Inner Tie Rod	74
	Lower Control Arm Ball Joint Stud Nut	①
	Lower Control Arm Mounting Bolt Nuts	125
	Outer Tie Rod End Stud Nut To Knuckle	④
	Power Steering Cooler To Crossmember Mounting Bolts	97③
	Power Steering Gear Mounting Bolts & Nuts	74
	Power Steering Hose Fittings	20
	Power Steering Pump Mounting Bolts	18
	Power Steering Reservoir Bracket Bolts	84③
	Shock Absorber Lower Mounting Nuts	21
	Shock Absorber Upper Mounting Nut	19
	Stabilizer Shaft Insulator Clamp Bolts	43
	Stabilizer Shaft Link Nuts	53
	Transverse Spring Retainer Bolts	46
	Upper Control Arm Ball Joint Stud Nut	②
	Upper Control Arm Mounting Bolts	48
	Wheel Hub/Bearing Mounting Bolts	96
	Wheel Lug Nuts	100

① — First step, 15 ft. lbs.; second step, an additional 210°; third step, 41 ft. lbs.
② — First step, 15 ft. lbs.; second step, an additional 250°; third step, 41 ft. lbs.
③ — Inch lbs.
④ — First step, 15 ft. lbs.; second step, an additional 160°; third step, 33 ft. lbs.

Wheel Alignment

INDEX

Page No.

Front Wheel Alignment.......... 13-25
  Caster & Camber 13-25
  Toe 13-25
Preliminary Inspection 13-25
Rear Wheel Alignment........... 13-25
  Camber....................... 13-25

Page No.

Toe 13-25
Vehicle Ride Height............. 13-25
  Adjustment 13-25
    Front 13-25
    Rear........................ 13-25
  Measurement.................. 13-25

Page No.

Front 13-25
Rear......................... 13-25
Wheel Alignment
Specifications 13-2

PRELIMINARY INSPECTION

Inspect tires for proper inflation.

Inspect tie rods for lateral end motion relative to the steering knuckle and tie rod end seals for any visible signs of damage. Replace tie rod end if either of these conditions exist.

Inspect runout of wheels and tires.

Inspect trim height. If out of specifications, correct before alignment. Inspect shocks, rack and pinion and control arms for looseness and proper operation. Replace any damaged steering/suspension components.

If any excess weight is normally carried in the trunk of vehicle, alignment is recommended with load in place.

Ensure vehicle is level.

FRONT WHEEL ALIGNMENT

Caster & Camber

1. Loosen lower control arm cam bolt nuts.
2. Rotate cam bolts to specification setting. Refer to "Front Wheel Alignment Specifications" in "Specifications" section.
3. Maintain caster or camber setting while tightening cam bolt nuts. **Torque** cam bolt nuts to 125 ft. lbs.
4. Inspect toe setting after changing camber or caster.

Toe

1. Loosen jam nut on tie rod.
2. Rotate inner tie rod to specification. Refer to "Front Wheel Alignment Specifications" in "Specifications" section.
3. **Torque** jam nut on tie rod 50 ft. lbs.

REAR WHEEL ALIGNMENT

Camber

1. Loosen lower control arm cam bolt nuts.
2. Rotate cam bolts to specification. Refer to "Rear Wheel Alignment Specifications" in "Specifications" section.
3. Maintain camber setting and **torque** lower control arm front bolt nut to 107 ft. lbs.
4. **Torque** lower control arm rear bolt nut to 71 ft. lbs.
5. Inspect toe setting after changing camber.

Toe

1. Loosen rear suspension adjustment link lock nut, **Fig. 1.**
2. Rotate inner tie rod to specification. Refer to "Rear Wheel Alignment Specifications" in "Specifications" section.
3. **Torque** rear suspension adjustment link lock nut to 44 ft. lbs.

VEHICLE RIDE HEIGHT

Measurement

FRONT

1. With vehicle on a flat surface, lift upward on rear bumper approximately 1.5 inches.
2. Allow vehicle to settle into position, then repeat jouncing operation two more times for a total of three times.
3. Measure distance between lowest point of ball joint and center of front side of lower control arm mounting bolt, **Fig. 2.**
4. Refer to "Vehicle Ride Height Specifications" in "Specifications" section for correct vehicle ride height.

REAR

1. Manually push rear of vehicle down approximately 1.5 inches, then let vehicle settle.
2. Repeat jouncing operation two more times for a total of three times.
3. Raise and support vehicle.
4. Measure distance between lowest point of ball joint and center of front side of lower control arm mounting bolt, **Fig. 3.**
5. Refer to "Vehicle Ride Height Specifications" in "Specifications" section for correct vehicle ride height.

Adjustment

FRONT

1. Adjust trim height using trim height adjustment tool J 42743, or equivalent, to turn spring adjuster bolt, **Fig. 4.**
2. Lower transverse spring back onto lower control arm and remove trim height adjustment tool.

REAR

1. Remove retainers on top of transverse spring bolts, **Fig. 5.**
2. Adjust trim height by turning spring bolt, **Fig. 6.**
3. Measure trim height again.
4. Measure rear spring stud heights, maximum difference between lefthand and righthand sides should be .196 inches.
5. Install retainers to bolts and lower vehicle.

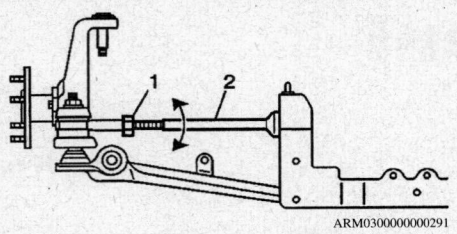

Fig. 1   Rear toe adjustment

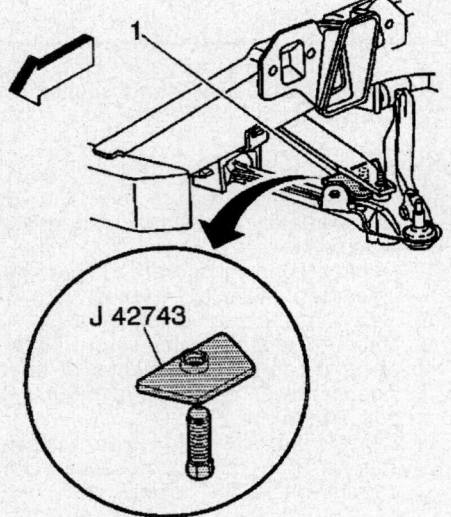

Fig. 4   Front trim height adjustment

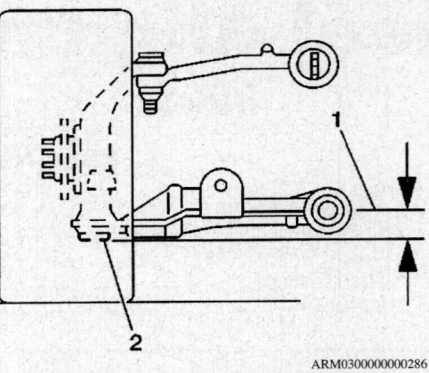

Fig. 2   Front vehicle ride height measurement

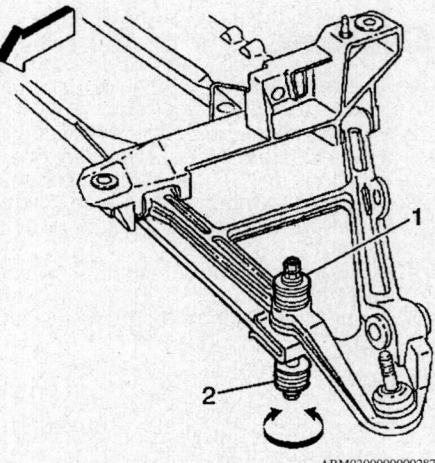

Fig. 5   Transverse spring bolt retainers

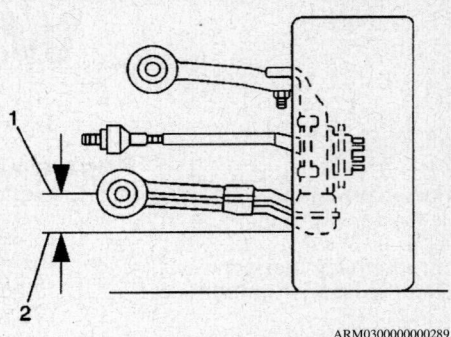

Fig. 3   Rear vehicle ride height measurement

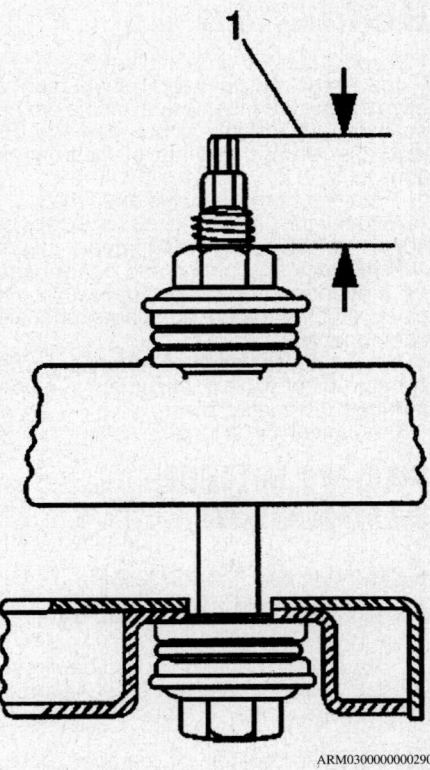

Fig. 6   Rear trim height adjustment

G6, MALIBU MAXX & 2006-08 MALIBU

NOTE: Refer To Rear Of This Manual For Vehicle Manufacturer's Special Service Tool Suppliers.

INDEX OF SERVICE OPERATIONS

Page No.

AIR BAG SYSTEM
PRECAUTIONS 0-18
BRAKES
Anti-Lock Brakes (Volume 2).. 6-1
Disc Brakes.................. 22-1
Drum Brakes................. 23-1
Hydraulic Brake Systems 24-1
Power Brake Units........... 25-1
COMPUTER RELEARN
PROCEDURE 0-31
ELECTRICAL
Air Bag System (Volume 2) ... 4-1
Air Conditioning.............. 16-1
Alternator, Replace 14-5
Alternators 19-1
Blower Motor, Replace 14-7
Coil Pack, Replace 14-6
Cooling Fans 17-1
Cruise Control (Volume 2) 2-1
Dash Gauges (Volume 2) 1-1
Dash Panel Service
(Volume 2) 5-1
Evaporator Core, Replace 14-7
Fuel Pump Relay Location.... 14-5
Fuse Panel & Flasher
Location 14-5
Headlamp Switch, Replace ... 14-6
Heater Core, Replace......... 14-7
Ignition Lock, Replace 14-6
Ignition Switch, Replace 14-6
Instrument Cluster, Replace... 14-6
Multi-Function Switch,
Replace 14-6
Neutral Safety Switch,
Replace 14-6
Passive Restraint Systems
(Volume 2)................. 4-1
Precautions................. 14-5
Radio, Replace 14-6
Relay Center Location 14-5
Speed Controls (Volume 2) ... 2-1
Starter Motors 18-1
Starter, Replace 14-5
Steering Columns............ 20-1
Steering Wheel, Replace...... 14-6
Stop Light Switch, Replace ... 14-6
Turn Signal Switch, Replace .. 14-6
Wiper Motor, Replace........ 14-7
Wiper Switch, Replace....... 14-7
Wiper Systems (Volume 2).... 3-1
Wiper Transmission, Replace . 14-7
ELECTRICAL SYMBOL
IDENTIFICATION 0-63
FRONT DRIVE AXLES 26-1
FRONT SUSPENSION &
STEERING
Ball Joint, Replace........... 14-18

Page No.

Ball Joint Inspection 14-18
Coil Spring, Replace.......... 14-18
Control Arm, Replace 14-19
Description 14-18
Power Assist Motor, Replace.. 14-20
Power Steering 21-1
Power Steering Gear,
Replace 14-20
Power Steering Pump,
Replace 14-20
Precautions................. 14-18
Stabilizer Bar, Replace....... 14-19
Steering Columns........... 20-1
Steering Knuckle, Replace.... 14-19
Strut, Replace 14-18
Strut Service............... 14-18
Tie Rod End, Replace 14-19
Tightening Specifications...... 14-20
Wheel Bearing, Replace 14-18
NON-STANDARD TIRE &
WHEEL SIZE
ADJUSTMENT TO RIDE
HEIGHT SPECIFICATIONS
& TIRE SIZE CHART 0-61
REAR AXLE &
SUSPENSION
Coil Spring, Replace 14-16
Control Arm, Replace 14-17
Description 14-16
Hub & Bearing, Replace 14-16
Knuckle, Replace 14-17
Shock Absorber, Replace 14-16
Stabilizer Shaft, Replace...... 14-17
Support Assembly, Replace ... 14-16
Tightening Specifications...... 14-17
Toe Link, Replace 14-17
Trailing Arm, Replace 14-17
SERVICE REMINDER &
WARNING LAMP RESET
PROCEDURES 0-34
SPECIFICATIONS
Fluid Capacities & Cooling
System Data................ 14-4
Front Wheel Alignment
Specifications 14-2
General Engine
Specifications 14-2
Lubricant Data 14-4
Rear Wheel Alignment
Specifications 14-3
Tune Up Specifications....... 14-2
Vehicle Ride Height
Specifications 14-3
TIRE PRESSURE
MONITORING SYSTEM 28-1

Page No.

VEHICLE
IDENTIFICATION 0-1
VEHICLE LIFT POINTS 0-51
VEHICLE MAINTENANCE
SCHEDULES 0-73
WHEEL ALIGNMENT
Front Wheel Alignment........ 14-21
Preliminary Inspection 14-21
Rear Wheel Alignment 14-21
Thrust Angle 14-21
Wheel Alignment
Specifications 14-2
WIRE COLOR CODE
IDENTIFICATION 0-63
2.2L DOHC ENGINE
Compression Pressure........ 14-8
Engine Rebuilding
Specifications 29-1
Engine, Replace ....: 14-8
Engine Mount, Replace 14-8
Intake Manifold, Replace...... 14-8
Precautions................. 14-8
Radiator, Replace........... 14-8
Tightening Specifications...... 14-9
2.4L ENGINE
Cylinder Head, Replace....... 14-10
Engine Rebuilding
Specifications 29-1
Engine, Replace 14-9
Engine Mount, Replace 14-9
Exhaust Manifold, Replace.... 14-10
Intake Manifold, Replace...... 14-9
Precautions................. 14-9
Radiator, Replace............ 14-10
Tightening Specifications..... 14-10
3.5L & 3.9L ENGINES
Compression Pressure........ 14-12
Engine Rebuilding
Specifications 29-1
Engine, Replace 14-12
Engine Mount, Replace 14-12
Engine Mount Strut, Replace . 14-12
Fuel Pump, Replace 14-12
Precautions................. 14-12
Radiator, Replace............ 14-12
Tightening Specifications...... 14-13
3.6L ENGINE
Compression Pressure........ 14-15
Engine Rebuilding
Specifications 29-1
Engine, Replace 14-15
Engine Mount, Replace 14-15
Engine Mount Strut, Replace . 14-15
Fuel Pump, Replace 14-15
Precautions................. 14-15
Radiator, Replace............ 14-15
Tightening Specifications...... 14-16

Specifications

GENERAL ENGINE SPECIFICATIONS

Engine Liter	VIN	Fuel Injection System	Bore & Stroke	Compression Ratio	Net H.P. @ RPM[2]	Maximum Torque Ft. Lbs. @ RPM	Normal Oil Pressure, psi
2004–05							
2.2L	F	SFI	3.39 x 3.72	10.0:1	144 @ 5600	155 @ 4000	50–80[3]
3.5L	8	SFI	3.90 x 2.99	9.8	201 @ 5400	222 @ 3200	30–45[1]
2006							
2.2L	F	SFI	3.39 x 3.72	10.0:1	144 @ 5600	155 @ 4000	50–80[3]
2.4L	B	SFI	3.47 x 3.81	10.0:1	167 @ 6300	162 @ 4500	50–80[3]
3.5L	8	SFI	3.90 x 2.99	9.8	201 @ 5400	222 @ 3200	30–45[1]
3.9L	1	SFI	3.90 x 3.31	9.8	240 @ 6000	241 @ 2800	30–45[1]
2007–08							
2.2L	F	SFI	3.39 x 3.72	10.0:1	144 @ 5600	155 @ 4000	50–80[3]
2.4L	B	SFI	3.47 x 3.81	10.0:1	167 @ 6300	162 @ 4500	50–80[3]
3.5L	8	SFI	3.90 x 2.99	9.8	201 @ 5400	222 @ 3200	30–45[1]
3.6L	7	SFI	3.70 x 3.37	10.2	255 @ 6500	252 @ 2800	20[4]
3.9L	1	SFI	3.90 x 3.31	9.8	240 @ 6000	241 @ 2800	30–45[1]

SFI — Sequential Fuel Injection
[1] — 1850 RPM w/engine at operating temperature.
[2] — Ratings are as installed in vehicle.
[3] — 1000 RPM w/engine at operating temperature.
[4] — @ 2000 RPM

TUNE UP SPECIFICATIONS

Engine	Spark Plug Gap, Inch	Ignition Timing, ° BTDC			Curb Idle Speed, RPM[3]		Fast Idle Speed, RPM		Fuel Pump Pressure, psi	Valve Lash
		Firing Order	Man. Trans.	Auto. Trans.	Mark	Man. Trans.	Auto. Trans.	Man. Trans.	Auto Trans.		
2.2L	042	1-3-4-2	—	[1]	[5]	—	[4]	—	[4]	50–60	[2]
2.4L	042	1-3-4-2	—	[1]	[5]	—	[4]	—	[4]	50–60	[2]
3.5L	.060	1-2-3-4-5-6	—	[1]	[5]	—	[4]	—	[4]	50–60	[2]
3.6L	.0431	1-2-3-4-5-6	—	[1]	[5]	—	[4]	—	[4]	50–60	[6]
3.9L	.040	1-2-3-4-5-6	[1]	[1]	[5]	[4]	[4]	[4]	[4]	50–60	[2]

BTDC — Before Top Dead Center
[1] — Ignition timing is controlled by Powertrain Control Module (PCM).
[2] — Vehicle is equipped w/hydraulic valve lifters. No adjustment is required.
[3] — P: Park. When adjusting idle speed, set parking brake & block drive wheels.
[4] — Idle speed is controlled by an Idle Air Control (IAC) valve or an Idle Speed Control (ISC) motor.
[5] — Equipped with crankshaft position sensor.
[6] — Engine hot, minimum oil pressure 10 psi @ 1000 RPM; 20 psi @ 2000 RPM

FRONT WHEEL ALIGNMENT SPECIFICATIONS

Model	Caster Angle, Degrees		Camber Angle, Degrees		Total Toe, Degrees	Ball Joint Wear
	Limits	Desired	Limits	Desired		
2004						
Malibu Maxx	+2.50 to +4.00	+3.25	-1.50 to -.50	-1.00	0 to +.40	[1]
2005–08						
G6	+2.35 to +3.85	+3.10	[2]	[3]	0 to +.40	[1]
Malibu Maxx & 2005–08 Malibu	+2.25 to +3.75	+3.00	[4]	[5]	0 to +.40	[1]

[1] — Refer to "Front Suspension & Steering" section for ball joint inspection procedure.
[2] — Lefthand wheel, -1.65 to -.15; righthand wheel, -1.45 to +.05.
[3] — Lefthand wheel, -.90; righthand wheel, -.70.
[4] — Lefthand wheel, -1.75 to -.05; righthand wheel, -1.15 to +.35.
[5] — Lefthand wheel, -.80; righthand wheel, -.40.

REAR WHEEL ALIGNMENT SPECIFICATIONS

Year	Camber Angle, Degrees		Total Toe, Degrees	Thrust Angle, Degrees
	Limits	Desired		
2004-08	-1.3 to -.3	-.8	.0 to +.4	-.30 to +.30

VEHICLE RIDE HEIGHT SPECIFICATIONS

Model	Year	Body Style	Manufacturer's Original Tire Size①	Measurement Points & Specifications②					
				Front			Rear		
				Dim.	Specification		Dim.	Specification	
					Inches	mm		Inches	mm
G6	2005	All④	P215/60R15	J	9.1	230	D	6.7	171
				Z	2.7	68	K	9.8	248
	2006-08	All⑤	P225/50R17	J	8.6	219	D	6.6	168
				Z	2.3	58	K	9.5	242
		Coupe	P225/50R17	J	8.9	225	D	7.2	184
				Z	2.2	56	K	9.6	243
			P225/50R18	J	9.7	247	D	7.2	184
				Z	2.6	66	K	10.4	264
		Convertible	P225/50R18	J	9.7	247	D	7.2	184
				Z	2.6	66	K	10.4	264
		Sedan	P215/60R15	J	9.0	230	D	7.2	184
				Z	2.6	66	K	9.8	248
			P225/50R17	J	8.9	225	D	7.2	184
				Z	2.2	56	K	9.6	243
			P225/50R18	J	9.7	247	D	7.2	184
				Z	2.6	66	K	10.4	264
Malibu MAXX & 2004-08 Malibu	2004	Base, LS & LT	P215/60R15	J	9.3	235	D	.7	18
				Z	-.2	-6	K	9.6	245
	2005	Base, LS & LT	P215/60R15	J	8.9	226	D	6.8	174
				Z	2.8	70	K	9.2	234
	2006-08	Base, LS & LT④	P215/60R15	J	9.1	230	D	6.7	171
				Z	2.7	68	K	9.5	241
		LT③	P215/60R15	J	9.1	230	D	6.7	171
				Z	2.7	68	K	9.5	241
		SS	P225/50R18	J	9.2	235	D	7.2	184
				Z	2.6	67	K	9.6	245

Dim. — Dimension

D Dim. — Measurement At Point 1.18 inches 30 mm Outboard Of Rear Brake Hose Bracket Bolt Centerline To Knuckle Arm Training Arm Bolt Centerline, **Fig. A.**

J Dim. — Measurement From Ground to Rocker Panel, Inboard of Front Pinch-Weld Flange, **Fig. B.**

K Dim. — Measurement From Ground to Rocker Panel, Inboard of Rear Pinch-Weld Flange

Z Dim. — Measurement In Line With Wheel Center, **Fig. C.**

① — See door sticker or inside of glove box for manufacturers original tire size specifications. If tires on vehicle do not match manufacturers original tire size & measurement is not within limits, refer to the "Non-Standard Tire & Wheel Size Adjustment To Ride Height Specification & Tire Size Adjustment Charts" in the front of this manual for approximate changes in ride height specifications.

② — Measurement is with fuel, radiator coolant & engine oil full, spare tire, jack, hand tools & mats in designated positions & tires properly inflated. All measurements are plus or minus .39 inch (10 mm).

③ — Less active suspension.

④ — With active suspension. (RPO Code FE0).

⑤ — With ride & handling suspension (RP) Code FE2).

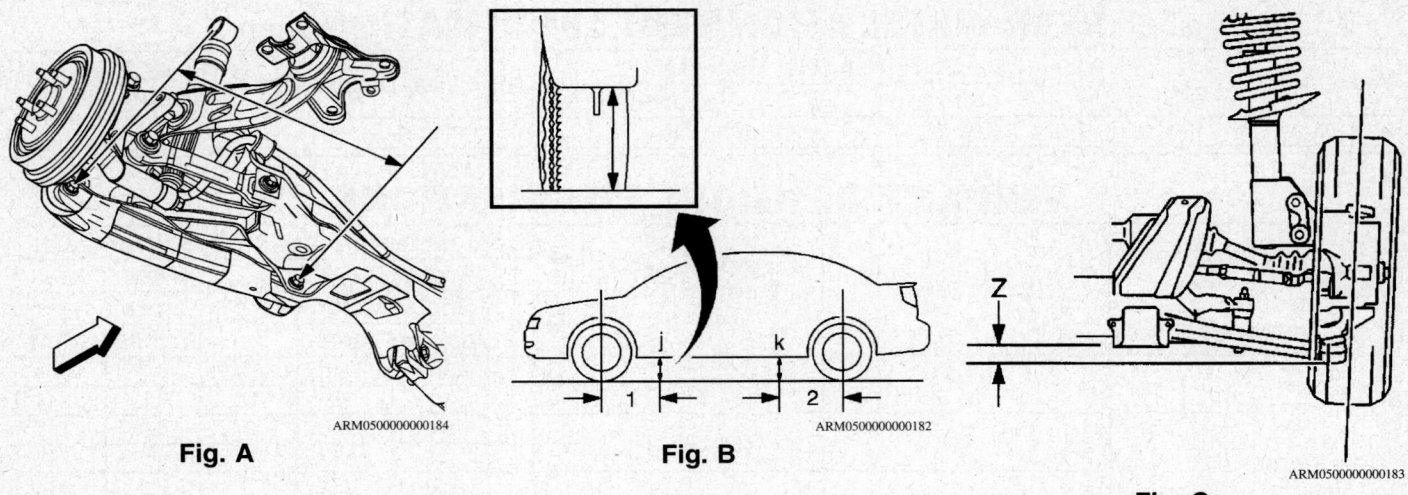

Fig. A   ARM0500000000184

Fig. B   ARM0500000000182

Fig. C   ARM0500000000183

FLUID CAPACITIES & COOLING SYSTEM DATA

Year	Engine	Coolant Capacity, Qts.	Coolant Type	Surge Tank Cap Relief Pressure, psi	Thermo. Opening Temp. Deg. F	Fuel Tank Gals.	Engine Oil Refill Qts.	Transaxle Oil 5 Speed Manual Transaxle Pts.	Auto. Transaxle Qts.①
G6									
2005	3.5L	9.6	Dex-Cool	15	195	16.3	4.0	—	②
2006	2.4L	7.3	Dex-Cool	15	195	16.3	5.0	—	②
	3.5L	9.7	Dex-Cool	15	195	16.3	4.0	—	②
	3.9L	9.7	Dex-Cool	15	195	16.3	4.0	6.2	②
2007–08	2.4L	7.3	Dex-Cool	15	195	16.3	5.0	—	②
	3.5L	9.7	Dex-Cool	15	195	16.3	4.0	—	②
	3.6L	9.7	Dex-Cool	15	203	16.3	5.5	—	②
	3.9L	9.7	Dex-Cool	15	195	16.3	4.0	6.2	②
MALIBU & MALIBU MAXX									
2004	2.2L	9.6	Dex-Cool	15	195	16.5	5.0	—	②
	3.5L	10.1	Dex-Cool	15	195	16.5	4.0	—	②
2005	2.2L	9.6	Dex-Cool	15	195	16.1	5.0	—	②
	3.5L	10.1	Dex-Cool	15	195	16.1	4.0	—	②
2006–08	2.2L	9.6	Dex-Cool	15	195	16.1	5.0	—	②
	3.5L	10.1	Dex-Cool	15	195	16.1	4.0	—	②
	3.9L	13.1	Dex-Cool	15	195	16.1	4.0	—	②

① — Approximate. Make final inspection w/dipstick.

② — FWD: Oil pan removal, 6.9 qts.; overhaul, 9.5 qts.; dry 12.9 qts.;

AWD: Oil pan removal, 10.0 qts.; overhaul, 9.5 qts.; dry 13.4 qts.

LUBRICANT DATA

Year	Model	Lubricant Type				
		Transaxle		Clutch Hydraulic System	Power Steering System	Brake System
		Automatic	Manual			
2004–05	All	Dexron III	Dexron III	DOT 3	①	DOT 3
2006–08	All	Dexron VI	Dexron III	DOT 3	①	DOT 3

① — GM part No. 1052884, or equivalent.

Electrical

NOTE: On Air Bag Equipped Models, Refer To "Air Bag System Precautions" Located In The Front Of This Manual For System Disarming & Arming Procedures.

NOTE: Refer To "Computer Relearn Procedures" Located In The Front Of This Manual When Battery Power To The Computer Has Been Interrupted.

NOTE: On Malibu Models Equipped With 2.2L Engine, Refer To "Alero, Grand Am & 2004–05 Malibu" Chapter.

NOTE: On Malibu Models Equipped With 2.4L Engine, Refer To "Cavalier, Cobalt, G5 & Sunfire" Chapter.

NOTE: On Malibu Models Equipped With 3.6L Engine, Refer To "Century, Grand Prix, Impala, LaCrosse, Monte Carlo & Regal" Chapter.

INDEX

	Page No.
Air Bag System (Volume 2)	4-1
Air Conditioning	16-1
Alternator, Replace	14-5
Alternators	19-1
Blower Motor, Replace	14-7
Coil Pack, Replace	14-6
Cooling Fans	17-1
Cruise Control (Volume 2)	2-1
Dash Gauges (Volume 2)	1-1
Dash Panel Service (Volume 2)	5-1
Evaporator Core, Replace	14-7
Fuel Pump Relay Location	14-5
Fuse Panel & Flasher Location	14-5
Headlamp Switch, Replace	14-6

	Page No.
Heater Core, Replace	14-7
Ignition Lock, Replace	14-6
Ignition Switch, Replace	14-6
Instrument Cluster, Replace	14-6
Multi-Function Switch, Replace	14-6
Neutral Safety Switch, Replace	14-6
Installation	14-6
Removal	14-6
Passive Restraint Systems (Volume 2)	4-1
Precautions	14-5
Air Bag Systems	14-5
Battery Ground Cable	14-5
Radio, Replace	14-6
Relay Center Location	14-5

	Page No.
Speed Controls (Volume 2)	2-1
Starter Motors	18-1
Starter, Replace	14-5
Installation	14-5
Removal	14-5
Steering Columns	20-1
Steering Wheel, Replace	14-6
Stop Light Switch, Replace	14-6
Turn Signal Switch, Replace	14-6
Wiper Motor, Replace	14-7
Wiper Switch, Replace	14-7
Wiper Systems (Volume 2)	3-1
Wiper Transmission, Replace	14-7

PRECAUTIONS
Air Bag Systems

Refer to "Air Bag System Precautions" in the front of this manual for system disarming and arming procedures.

Battery Ground Cable

Prior to service, disconnect battery ground cable and isolate as required.

FUSE PANEL & FLASHER LOCATION

The rear fuse block is located on the rear lefthand side of the passenger compartment, behind the wheelwell. The underhood fuse block is located on the lefthand side of the engine compartment. The turn signal and hazard flasher module is an internal component of the hazard switch located behind the center of the instrument panel.

FUEL PUMP RELAY LOCATION

The fuel pump relay is located on the rear lefthand side of the passenger compartment, in the rear fuse block.

RELAY CENTER LOCATION

Relays are located in all the fuse and junction blocks, refer to "Fuse Panel & Flasher Location" for relay center locations.

STARTER
REPLACE
Removal

1. Raise and support vehicle.
2. Remove flywheel inspection cover.
3. Remove starter electrical connectors.
4. Remove mounting bolts and starter.

Installation

1. Tighten solenoid BAT terminal nut next to cap while starter is still on bench.
2. Connect solenoid electrical terminal.
3. **Torque** solenoid battery terminal inside nut to 13 ft. lbs.
4. Install electrical connectors to starter.
5. **Torque** solenoid battery terminal outside nut to 89 inch lbs.
6. **Torque** solenoid S terminal outside nut to 27 inch lbs.
7. Install starter onto engine and **torque** mounting bolts to 32 ft. lbs.
8. Install inspection cover and **torque** bolts to 84 inch lbs.

ALTERNATOR
REPLACE

1. Remove air cleaner assembly.
2. Remove engine mount strut from front of engine and radiator support.
3. Rotate drive belt tensioner using tool No. J 37059 or equivalent, then remove serpentine drive belt.

4. Remove alternator mounting bolts and nuts.
5. Disconnect electrical connectors and remove alternator.
6. Reverse procedure to install. **Torque** mounting bolts to 37 ft. lbs., and nuts to 22 ft. lbs.

COIL PACK
REPLACE

1. Note position of spark plug wires for installation reference, then disconnect wires from ignition coil and module assembly.
2. Remove ignition coil and module assembly mounting screws, then separate assembly from bracket.
3. Reverse procedure to install. **Torque** mounting screws to 40 inch lbs.

IGNITION LOCK
REPLACE

1. Remove outer trim cover from lefthand side of instrument panel.
2. Remove lower trim panels from lower lefthand closeout panel.
3. Remove lower lefthand closeout panel from lefthand knee bolster.
4. Turn ignition switch to the RUN position.
5. Depress lock cylinder retaining tab, then remove lock cylinder.
6. Reverse procedure to install.

IGNITION SWITCH
REPLACE

1. Tilt steering column upper trim cover upward and remove nuts from instrument panel seal.
2. Remove steering column upper trim cover.
3. Remove steering column lower trim cover attaching screws.
4. Lower steering column rake lever and lower steering column, then fully telescope column toward driver and remove lower trim cover from column.
5. Remove instrument panel cluster trim plate bezel attaching screws, then the bezel from cluster.
6. Remove fog lamp and adjustable pedal switch.
7. Remove instrument panel dimmer switch, then the lefthand center instrument panel trim panel.
8. Remove righthand instrument panel trim panel.
9. Remove righthand closeout panel and glove compartment from instrument panel.
10. Remove instrument panel center trim bezel.
11. Remove outer trim cover from lefthand side of instrument panel.
12. Remove lower trim panels from lower lefthand closeout panel.
13. Remove lower lefthand closeout panel from lefthand knee bolster.
14. Remove knee bolster from under lefthand side of instrument panel.
15. Disconnect ignition switch and theft deterrent control module harness connectors.
16. Turn ignition switch to the RUN position.
17. Disconnect park lock cable from ignition switch.
18. Remove ignition switch to instrument panel attaching screws.
19. Remove ignition switch from instrument panel.
20. Reverse procedure to install.

NEUTRAL SAFETY SWITCH
REPLACE

Removal

1. Apply parking brake and place shift lever in Neutral.
2. Remove shift control cable from switch lever.
3. Disconnect switch electrical connectors.
4. Remove switch lever nut and lever.
5. Remove switch attaching bolts and the switch.

Installation

1. Place shift shaft in Neutral position and align flats on shaft with flats on switch.
2. Loosely install switch with marks properly aligned.
3. Insert Park/Neutral Switch Aligner tool No. J 41545 as outlined and rotate switch until tool drops into position.
4. **Torque** switch bolts to 15 ft. lbs., and remove alignment tool.

HEADLAMP SWITCH
REPLACE

Refer to "Multi-Function Switch, Replace" for replacement procedure.

STOP LIGHT SWITCH
REPLACE

1. Remove closeout panel from under lefthand side of instrument panel.
2. Remove steering column stub shaft bolt, then position steering column stub shaft aside.
3. Disconnect brake pedal position sensor electrical connector.
4. Remove brake pedal position sensor retaining bolt, then the sensor.
5. Reverse procedure to install.

MULTI-FUNCTION SWITCH
REPLACE

1. Tilt steering column upper trim cover upward and remove nuts from instrument panel seal.
2. Remove steering column upper trim cover.
3. Remove steering column lower trim cover attaching screws.
4. Lower steering column rake lever and lower steering column, then fully telescope column toward driver and remove lower trim cover from column.
5. Remove mounting screw and switch.
6. Reverse procedure to install.

TURN SIGNAL SWITCH
REPLACE

Refer to "Multi-Function Switch, Replace" for replacement procedure.

STEERING WHEEL
REPLACE

1. Remove mounting screws for horn pad or air bag module.
2. **On models equipped with radio controls,** remove wire protector plate connector.
3. **On all models,** remove horn pad or air bag module and horn lead, then the steering wheel retainer and nut.
4. Remove steering wheel using puller tool No. J 1859-A and legs tool No. J 42120 or equivalent.
5. Reverse procedure to install, noting the following:
   a. **Torque** steering wheel nut to 27–30 ft. lbs.
   b. **Torque** air bag module screws to 89 inch lbs.

INSTRUMENT CLUSTER
REPLACE

1. Tilt steering column upper trim cover upward and remove nuts from instrument panel seal.
2. Remove steering column upper trim cover.
3. Remove steering column lower trim cover attaching screws.
4. Lower steering column rake lever and lower steering column, then fully telescope column toward driver and remove lower trim cover from column.
5. Remove instrument panel cluster trim plate bezel attaching screws, then the bezel from cluster.
6. Remove instrument cluster to instrument panel mounting screws.
7. Disconnect cluster electrical connectors and remove instrument cluster.
8. Reverse procedure to install.

RADIO
REPLACE

1. Remove fog lamp, dimmer and adjustable pedal switches from lower lefthand trim panel.
2. Remove trim panels from under lefthand and righthand sides of instrument panel.
3. Remove closeout panel from under righthand side of instrument panel.
4. Remove instrument panel compartment from front of center console.
5. Remove knee bolster from under lefthand side of instrument panel.
6. Remove instrument panel center trim bezel.
7. Remove hazard warning switch.

8. Remove heater-A/C control head from center of instrument panel.
9. Remove radio retaining screws, then the radio.
10. Reverse procedure to install.

WIPER MOTOR
REPLACE

1. Remove wiper arm and blade.
2. Remove cowl cover.
3. Disconnect drive link from crank arm using wiper transmission separator tool No. J 39232 or equivalent.
4. Disconnect wiper motor electrical connectors.
5. Remove mounting screws and wiper motor.
6. Reverse procedure to install, noting the following:
   a. **Torque** motor mounting screws to 84 inch lbs.
   b. Connect drive link to crank arm using wiper transmission installer tool No. J 39529 or equivalent.

WIPER SWITCH
REPLACE

Refer to "Multi-Function Switch, Replace" for replacement procedure.

WIPER TRANSMISSION
REPLACE

1. Remove wiper arm and blades.
2. Remove cowl cover and disconnect wiper motor connector.
3. Remove mounting screws and wiper drive system module.
4. Remove wiper motor as outlined under "Wiper Motor, Replace."
5. Remove caps, wiper motor grommets and transmission.
6. Reverse procedure to install. **Torque** mounting screws to 72 inch lbs.

BLOWER MOTOR
REPLACE

The blower motor and fan are located in the lower righthand corner of the Heating, Ventilation and Air Conditioning (HVAC) module. The fan and motor are serviced only as a complete assembly.
1. Remove righthand closeout panel and insulator.
2. Disconnect blower motor electrical connectors.
3. Remove mounting screws, blower motor and fan.
4. Reverse procedure to install. **Torque** blower motor mounting screws to 45 inch lbs.

HEATER CORE
REPLACE

1. Drain coolant.
2. Remove inlet and outlet heater hoses from heater core.
3. Recover A/C system refrigerant.
4. Remove suction hose from thermostatic expansion valve.
5. Remove and discard sealing washers.
6. Disconnect the HVAC module to front of dash plate bolts.
7. Remove righthand and lefthand console trim panels.
8. Remove front console screw covers from behind console.
9. Remove front console screws, then position front seats to full forward position.
10. Remove rear console bolts, then place shifter in drive.
11. Remove lefthand closeout panel and both instrument panel outer trim panels.
12. Disconnect instrument panel to body wire harness and antenna connectors.
13. Disconnect instrument panel to wire harness righthand connectors.
14. Remove knee bolster from under lefthand side of instrument panel.
15. Remove accelerator pedal, then disconnect steering column to instrument panel wire harness connector.
16. Remove crush bracket to front of dash plate nuts.
17. Remove upper steering column shroud from lower shroud.
18. Remove stalk switches and SIR coil connectors.
19. Position steering wheel in full forward telescoping position, then place front seat in full rearward position.
20. Remove steering column mounting bolts.
21. Remove brake pedal assembly.
22. Remove Body Control Module (BCM).
23. Remove center support bracket floor bolts, then the shifter assembly.
24. Remove both windshield pillar garnish moldings.
25. Remove instrument panel upper trim panel.
26. Remove lefthand and righthand instrument panel to body bolts.
27. Remove righthand and lefthand floor heater ducts from center floor heater duct.
28. Remove instrument panel.
29. Remove and discard HVAC module drain seal and dash seal.
30. Remove lower center floor air outlet duct.
31. Remove upper center floor air outlet duct screws, then the upper center floor air outlet duct.
32. Drill out heater core cover heat stakes.
33. Remove heater core cover screws, then the cover.
34. Remove heater core from module.
35. Reverse procedure to install.

EVAPORATOR CORE
REPLACE

1. Recover air conditioning refrigerant as outlined in "Air Conditioning" chapter.
2. Drain coolant into suitable container.
3. Remove HVAC assembly as outlined under "Heater Core, Replace."
4. Remove thermal expansion valve screw, then the thermal expansion valve.
5. Remove and discard sealing washers.
6. Remove evaporator core.
7. Reverse procedure to install. Use new sealing washers.

2.2L DOHC Engine

NOTE: Refer To "2.2L Engine" In "Alero, Grand Am & 2004–08 Malibu" Chapter For Procedures Not Covered In This Section.

NOTE: On Air Bag Equipped Models, Refer To "Air Bag System Precautions" Located In The Front Of This Manual For System Disarming & Arming Procedures.

NOTE: Refer To "Computer Relearn Procedures" Located In The Front Of This Manual When Battery Power To The Computer Has Been Interrupted.

INDEX

	Page No.		Page No.		Page No.
Compression Pressure	14-8	Engine Mount, Replace	14-8	Battery Ground Cable	14-8
Engine Rebuilding		Intake Manifold, Replace	14-8	Fuel System Pressure Relief	14-8
Specifications	29-1	Precautions	14-8	Radiator, Replace	14-8
Engine, Replace	14-8	Air Bag Systems	14-8	Tightening Specifications	14-9

PRECAUTIONS

Air Bag Systems

Refer to "Air Bag System Precautions" in the front of this manual for system disarming and arming procedures.

Battery Ground Cable

Prior to service, disconnect battery ground cable and isolate as required.

Fuel System Pressure Relief

Failure to relieve system pressure prior to disconnecting fuel system components may cause fire or personal injury.
1. Loosen fuel tank filler cap to relieve tank pressure.
2. Raise and support vehicle.
3. Disconnect fuel pump electrical connector.
4. Lower vehicle.
5. Start and operate engine until fuel supply is consumed.
6. Crank engine for approximately three seconds to relieve remaining pressure.
7. Disconnect and isolate battery ground cable, then connect fuel pump electrical connector.

COMPRESSION PRESSURE

Refer to "2.2L Engine" in "Alero, Grand Am & 2004–08 Malibu" chapter for procedure.

ENGINE MOUNT

REPLACE

1. Remove air cleaner assembly.
2. Support engine with suitable wooden block and suitable floor jack positioned below oil pan.
3. Remove engine mount mounting nuts.
4. Remove engine mount to bracket bolts.
5. Remove engine mount.
6. Reverse procedure to install.

ENGINE

REPLACE

Refer to "2.2L Engine" in "Alero, Grand Am & 2004–08 Malibu" chapter for engine replacement procedure.

INTAKE MANIFOLD

REPLACE

Refer to "2.2L Engine" in "Alero, Grand Am & 2004–08 Malibu" chapter for intake manifold replacement procedure.

RADIATOR

REPLACE

1. Drain cooling system into suitable container.
2. Remove hood latch assembly.
3. Remove righthand and lefthand headlamp assemblies.
4. Remove radiator upper mount attaching bolts, then the mounts.
5. Raise vehicle using suitable lift.
6. Remove cooling fan mounting bolts, disconnect electrical connectors, then the cooling fan.
7. Remove radiator outlet hose clamp from radiator using tool No. J38185, or equivalent, then the radiator outlet hose.
8. Remove lower transmission oil cooler line, then lower vehicle.
9. Remove hood latch support bracket and forward sensors with harness.
10. Remove upper transmission oil cooler line from radiator.
11. Remove surge tank hose and clamp from radiator.
12. Remove condenser from radiator.
13. Remove radiator assembly.
14. Reverse procedure to install.

TIGHTENING SPECIFICATIONS

Year	Component	Torque, Ft. Lbs.
2004-08	Accelerator & Cruise Control Cable	89②
	Air Cleaner Clamps	44②
	Air Cleaner Outlet Resonator Mounting Bolt	89②
	Alternator	15
	Engine Mount Strut	74①
	Engine To Transmission Bolts	55
	Power Steering Pump	19
	Radiator Drain Cock	18②
	Righthand Engine Mount Bolts	44①
	Righthand Engine Mount To Body Nuts	55
	Torque Converter Bolts	46
	Upper Air Cleaner Cover Screws	27②

① — Plus 90°.
② — Inch lbs.

2.4L Engine

NOTE: Refer To "2.4L Engine" In "Cavalier, Cobalt, G5 & Sunfire" Chapter For Procedures Not Covered In This Section.

NOTE: On Air Bag Equipped Models, Refer To "Air Bag System Precautions" Located In The Front Of This Manual For System Disarming & Arming Procedures.

NOTE: Refer To "Computer Relearn Procedures" Located In The Front Of This Manual When Battery Power To The Computer Has Been Interrupted.

INDEX

	Page No.
Cylinder Head, Replace	14-10
Engine Rebuilding Specifications	29-1
Engine, Replace	14-9
Engine Mount, Replace	14-9
Exhaust Manifold, Replace	14-10
Intake Manifold, Replace	14-9
Precautions	14-9
Air Bag Systems	14-9
Battery Ground Cable	14-9
Fuel System Pressure Relief	14-9
Radiator, Replace	14-10
Tightening Specifications	14-10

PRECAUTIONS

Air Bag Systems

Refer to "Air Bag System Precautions" in the front of this manual for system disarming and arming procedures.

Battery Ground Cable

Prior to service, disconnect battery ground cable and isolate as required.

Fuel System Pressure Relief

Failure to relieve system pressure prior to disconnecting fuel system components may cause fire or personal injury.

1. Loosen fuel tank filler cap to relieve tank pressure.
2. Raise and support vehicle.
3. Disconnect fuel pump electrical connector.
4. Lower vehicle.
5. Start and operate engine until fuel supply is consumed.
6. Crank engine for approximately three seconds to relieve remaining pressure.
7. Disconnect and isolate battery ground cable, then connect fuel pump electrical connector.

ENGINE MOUNT
REPLACE

1. Remove air cleaner assembly.
2. Support engine with a suitable hydraulic floor jack. Place a piece of wood between jack and oil pan.
3. Remove engine mount to bracket bolts.
4. Remove engine mount to side rail nuts.
5. Remove engine mount from engine compartment.
6. Reverse procedure to install.

ENGINE
REPLACE

Refer to "2.4L Engine" in "Cavalier, Cobalt, G5 & Sunfire" chapter for engine replacement procedure.

INTAKE MANIFOLD
REPLACE

Refer to "2.4L Engine" in "Cavalier, Cobalt, G5 & Sunfire" chapter for intake manifold replacement procedure.

EXHAUST MANIFOLD

REPLACE

Refer to "2.4L Engine" in "Cavalier, Cobalt, G5 & Sunfire" chapter for exhaust manifold replacement procedure.

CYLINDER HEAD

REPLACE

Refer to "2.4L Engine" in "Cavalier, Cobalt, G5 & Sunfire" chapter for cylinder head replacement procedure.

RADIATOR

REPLACE

1. Drain cooling system.
2. Remove air cleaner outlet resonator.
3. Loosen radiator inlet hose clamp at radiator, then remove hose.
4. Loosen radiator outlet hose clamp at radiator, then remove hose.
5. Remove cooling fan assembly from radiator by pushing up on fan shroud to unsnap retainers.
6. Position cooling fan assembly away from radiator and support.
7. Remove air dam push-in retainer, then the air dam.
8. **On models equipped with A/C,** remove condenser bolts, then slide condenser down to disengage upper mounting tabs from radiator. Position condenser away from radiator and support condenser.
9. **On all models,** remove right and left radiator side baffles.
10. Remove right engine splash shield to radiator mount push-in retainer.
11. **On models equipped with manual transaxle,** remove left engine splash shield to radiator mount push-in retainer.
12. **On all models,** remove lower radiator mounts, brackets and bolts.
13. **On models equipped with A/C,** tilt condenser forward in vehicle.
14. **On all models,** tilt cooling fan assembly rearward, then remove radiator assembly from vehicle.
15. Reverse procedure to install.

TIGHTENING SPECIFICATIONS

Year	Component	Ft. Lbs.
2006–08	A/C Compressor To Block	15
	Alternator To Block	17
	Balance Shaft Adjustable Chain Guide	11
	Balance Shaft Bearing Carrier To Block	89①
	Balance Shaft Fixed Chain Guide Bolt	11
	Balance Shaft Sprocket Bolt	37
	Cam Sensor	71①
	Camshaft Bearing Cap Bolt	89①
	Camshaft Position Sensor Housing Stud	16
	Camshaft Position Actuator Solenoid Valve Bolt	89①
	Camshaft Position Sensor	89①
	Camshaft Timing Chain Tensioner	55
	Chain Guide Access Hole Plug	59
	Connecting Rod Bolts	②
	Crankshaft Balancer	③
	Crankshaft Bearing Lower Crankcase To Block	④
	Crankshaft Position Sensor	71①
	Cylinder Head	⑤
	Cylinder Head Oil Gallery Plug	26
	Drive Belt Tensioner	33
	Engine Coolant Temperature Sensor	15
	Engine Lift Bracket	18
	Exhaust Camshaft Position Actuator	⑥
	Exhaust Manifold Pipe Flange To Stud	12
	Exhaust Manifold To Cylinder Head Nut	10
	Exhaust Manifold To Cylinder Head Stud	89①
	Flywheel	⑦
	Front Cover To Block	18
	Fuel Line Bracket	89①
	ICM Cover	71①
	Idler Pulley	16
	Intake Camshaft Position Actuator	⑥
	Intake Camshaft Rear Cap Bolt	18
	Intake Manifold To Cylinder Head	89①
	Knock Sensor Bolt	18
	Lower Crankcase To Block	18
	Oil Cooler	16
	Oil Filter Housing Cover	16
	Oil Gallery Plug	26
	Oil Gallery Plug (Rear)	44
	Oil Pan Drain Plug	18

Continued

TIGHTENING
SPECIFICATIONS—Continued

Year	Component	Ft. Lbs.
2006–08	Oil Pan To Block	18
	Oil Pressure Switch	16
	Oil Pump Gerotor Cover Bolt	53①
	Oil Pump Pressure Relief Valve Plug	30
	Oxygen Sensor	31
	Power Steering Pump	18
	Spark Plug	15
	Starter Motor To Block	39
	Thermostat Housing	89①
	Throttle Body	89①
	Timing Chain Adjustable Chain Guide	89①
	Timing Chain Fixed Guide Bolt	11
	Timing Chain Oil Nozzle Bolt	89①
	Timing Chain Upper Guide Bolt	89①
	Torque Converter Bolts	46
	Transaxle To Engine	55
	Valve (Cam) Cover To Cylinder Head	89①
	Water Pump Balance Shaft Chain Tensioner	89①
	Water Pump Bolts	18
	Water Pump Sprocket Bolt	89①

① — Inch lbs.
② — First step, 18 ft. lbs.; second step, an additional 100.°
③ — First step, 74 ft. lbs.; second step, an additional 125.°
④ — Refer to "Main & Rod Bearings."
⑤ — Refer to "Cylinder Head, Replace" procedure.
⑥ — First step, 22 ft. lbs.; second step, an additional 100.°
⑦ — First step, 39 ft. lbs.; second step, an additional 25.°

3.5L & 3.9L Engines

NOTE: On Air Bag Equipped Models, Refer To "Air Bag System Precautions" Located In The Front Of This Manual For System Disarming & Arming Procedures.

NOTE: Refer To "Computer Relearn Procedures" Located In The Front Of This Manual When Battery Power To The Computer Has Been Interrupted.

NOTE: For Procedures Not Found In This Section, Refer To "3.5L (VIN 8) & 3.9L Engines" Section In The "Century, Grand Prix, Impala, Intrigue, LaCrosse, Monte Carlo & Regal" Chapter.

INDEX

	Page No.		Page No.		Page No.
Compression Pressure	14-12	Engine Mount Strut, Replace	14-12	Fuel System Pressure Relief	14-12
Engine Rebuilding Specifications	29-1	Fuel Pump, Replace	14-12	Radiator, Replace	14-12
Engine, Replace	14-12	Precautions	14-12	Tightening Specifications	14-13
Engine Mount, Replace	14-12	Air Bag Systems	14-12		
		Battery Ground Cable	14-12		

PRECAUTIONS

Air Bag Systems

Refer to "Air Bag System Precautions" in the front of this manual for system disarming and arming procedures.

Battery Ground Cable

Prior to service, disconnect battery ground cable and isolate as required.

Fuel System Pressure Relief

Failure to relieve system pressure prior to disconnecting fuel system components may cause fire or personal injury.

1. Loosen fuel tank filler cap to relieve tank pressure.
2. Raise and support vehicle.
3. Disconnect fuel pump electrical connector.
4. Lower vehicle.
5. Start and operate engine until fuel supply is consumed.
6. Crank engine for approximately three seconds to relieve remaining pressure.
7. Disconnect and isolate battery ground cable, then connect fuel pump electrical connector.

COMPRESSION PRESSURE

When inspecting cylinder compression, the throttle should be open, the spark plugs removed and the battery at or near full charge. The lowest reading cylinder should not be less than 70% of the highest and no cylinder reading should be less than 100 psi. Crank engine until it runs through four compression cycles. Normal compression builds up quickly and evenly to specified compression on each cylinder.

ENGINE MOUNT

REPLACE

1. Raise and support vehicle.
2. Remove righthand tire and wheel assembly.
3. Remove splash shield from under engine.
4. Remove engine mount to engine mount bracket nuts.
5. Remove engine mount to frame nuts.
6. Raise engine with a suitable jackstand.
7. Remove motor mount from vehicle.
8. Reverse procedure to install.

ENGINE MOUNT STRUT

REPLACE

1. Remove air cleaner assembly.
2. Remove engine mount strut to engine attaching bolts.
3. Rotate engine mount strut to a vertical position.

4. Remove engine mount strut to body attaching bolts, then the strut from vehicle.
5. Reverse procedure to install.

ENGINE

REPLACE

1. Relieve fuel system pressure as outlined under "Precautions."
2. Drain coolant into suitable container.
3. Drain engine oil.
4. Remove engine air cleaner assembly.
5. Mark engine hinge locations for installation reference, then remove hood.
6. Remove serpentine belt.
7. Remove engine mount strut as outlined under "Engine Mount Strut, Replace."
8. Disconnect the following electrical connectors:
   a. Knock sensor.
   b. Camshaft Position (CMP) sensor.
   c. Crankshaft Position (CKP) sensor.
   d. Oxygen sensor.
   e. Manifold Absolute Pressure (MAP) sensor.
   f. EGR valve.
   g. Evaporative (EVAP) emission canister purge solenoid.
   h. Electronic throttle control.
   i. Ignition coil.
   j. Body wiring harness to engine harness.
9. Raise and support vehicle.
10. Remove exhaust crossover pipe retaining nuts, then the pipe.
11. Remove engine wiring harness grounds from transaxle.
12. Remove engine mount lower nuts.
13. Remove torque converter covers and starter motor.
14. Remove A/C compressor from mount. **Do not discharge A/C system refrigerant.**
15. Remove torque converter attaching bolts.
16. Remove transaxle support brace.
17. Remove lower transaxle to engine attaching bolts.
18. Remove radiator outlet hose from engine.
19. Lower vehicle and support transaxle with a suitable lifting device.
20. Remove heater inlet and outlet hoses from engine.
21. Remove vacuum and brake booster hoses from upper intake manifold.
22. Remove fuel lines from fuel rail.
23. Remove radiator inlet hose from engine.
24. Install a suitable engine lifting device to engine.
25. Remove upper transaxle to engine attaching bolts.
26. Remove engine from vehicle.
27. Reverse procedure to install.

RADIATOR

REPLACE

1. Drain engine coolant.
2. Remove lefthand headlamp assembly attaching bolts.

3. Lift headlamp assembly to unseat tabs on bottom edge of fender.
4. Disconnect headlamp assembly electrical connector and remove assembly from vehicle.
5. Remove righthand headlamp assembly attaching bolts.
6. Lift headlamp assembly to unseat tabs on bottom edge of fender.
7. Disconnect headlamp assembly electrical connector and remove assembly from vehicle.
8. Loop a suitable rope around upper two tabs of condenser, then tie rope around upper engine compartment tie bar.
9. Remove upper radiator support bracket bolts and support brackets.
10. Remove surge tank outlet hose from radiator.
11. Remove radiator inlet hose from radiator.
12. Raise and support vehicle.
13. Remove lower radiator air deflector retainers and the deflector.
14. Remove front fender liner retainers and fender liner.
15. Remove righthand and lefthand radiator air deflector retainers and deflectors.
16. Remove radiator outlet hose from radiator.
17. Place a suitable drain pan under transaxle cooler lines, then remove cooler lines from transaxle.
18. Remove lower radiator support bracket bolts and support brackets.
19. Remove radiator lower mounts.
20. Remove and discard condenser mounting bolts from radiator.
21. Push upward on radiator and downward on condenser to unsnap condenser mounting tabs from radiator clips.
22. Remove and discard condenser mounting nuts from radiator.
23. Remove radiator air side seals.
24. Remove radiator, cooling fan shroud and transaxle cooler line assembly.
25. Remove transaxle cooler lines from radiator.
26. Pry upward on fan shroud tabs, then remove cooling fan and shroud assembly from radiator.
27. Reverse procedure to install.

FUEL PUMP

REPLACE

1. Relieve fuel system pressure as outlined under "Precautions."
2. Drain fuel tank.
3. Raise and support vehicle.
4. Disconnect fuel pump module electrical harness connector from vehicle underbody wiring harness.
5. Disconnect EVAP vent valve solenoid harness electrical connector from vehicle underbody wiring harness.
6. Remove ABS wiring harness from retainer on EVAP canister.
7. Disconnect fuel feed and purge lines from fuel and brake line bundle on righthand side of vehicle.

8. Cap or plug fuel tank feed and vapor lines to prevent fuel loss or contamination.
9. Disconnect fuel filler pipe jumper hose from fuel tank.
10. Disconnect vapor recirculation line that runs parallel to fuel filler pipe jumper hose.
11. Remove exhaust pipe and muffler insulators from underbody hangers, then support exhaust system with suitable jackstand.
12. Support fuel tank with a suitable jackstand.
13. Remove lefthand and righthand fuel tank strap bolts.
14. Carefully lower righthand side of tank until is clear of frame rail, then remove tank toward righthand side of vehicle.
15. Remove fuel pump module assembly from fuel tank using fuel sender lock ring wrench tool No. J 45722 or equivalent.
16. Reverse procedure to install.

TIGHTENING SPECIFICATIONS

Year	Component	Torque/Ft. Lbs.
2004–08	Camshaft Position Sensor Bolt	89①
	Camshaft Sprocket Bolt	103
	Camshaft Thrust Plate	89①
	Connecting Rod Bearing Cap Bolt	②
	Coolant Drain Plug	14
	Coolant Temperature Sensor	17
	Crankshaft Balancer Bolt	③
	Crankshaft Main Bearing Cap Bolt	④
	Cylinder Head Bolts	⑤
	Drive Belt Tensioner Bolt	37
	EGR Valve Assembly Bolt	22
	EGR Valve Pipe Bolt (Exhaust Manifold)	89①
	EGR Valve Pipe Bolt (EGR)	18
	Engine Mount Strut To A/C Bracket Bolt	37
	Engine Mount Strut To Alternator Bracket	37
	Engine Mount Strut To Lift Bracket Bolt	52
	Engine Mount Strut To Support Bracket Bolt	18
	Engine Oil Pressure Switch	12
	Engine Wiring Harness Bracket	115①
	EVAP Purge Valve Bolt	12
	Exhaust Manifold Heat Shield Bolt	89①
	Exhaust Manifold Nut	12
	Flywheel Bolt	52
	Front Cover (Large & Medium Bolts)	41
	Front Cover (Small Bolts)	20
	Fuel Feed Pipe To Injector Rail Bolt	89①
	Fuel Injector Rail Bolt	89①
	Heater Inlet Pipe Nut	18
	Ignition Coil Bracket Bolt	18
	Intake Manifold Coolant Pipe Bolt	89①
	Intake Manifold (Lower)	⑥
	Intake Manifold (Upper)	18
	Knock Sensor	18
	Main Bearing Cap Bolt	④
	MAP Sensor	89①
	Oil Dipstick Tube Bolt	18
	Oil Filter	22
	Oil Filter Adapter Bolt	18
	Oil Filter Bypass Hole Plug	14
	Oil Filter Fitting	29
	Oil Pan Bolt	18
	Oil Pan Drain Plug	18
	Oil Pan Side Bolt	37
	Oil Pump Cover Bolt	89①

TIGHTENING
SPECIFICATIONS—Continued

Year	Component	Torque/Ft. Lbs.
2004–08	Oil Pump Drive Clamp Bolt	27
	Oil Pump Mounting Bolt	30
	Oxygen Sensor	31
	PCV Tube Clip Bolt	89①
	Rocker Arm Bolt	24
	Spark Plug	15
	Thermostat Bypass Pipe To Front Cover	89①
	Thermostat Bypass Pipe To Throttle Body	89①
	Throttle Body Bolt	89①
	Timing Chain Dampener Bolt	15
	Valve Lifter Guide Bolt	89①
	Valve Rocker Arm Bolt	24
	Valve Cover Bolts	89①
	Water Outlet Bolt	18
	Water Pump Bolt	89①
	Water Pump Pulley Bolt	18

① — Inch lbs.
② — 18 ft. lbs., plus an additional 110.°
③ — 52 ft. lbs., plus an additional 70.°
④ — 37 ft. lbs., plus an additional 77.°
⑤ — Refer to "Cylinder Head, Replace" in "Alero, Grand Am & 2004–08 Malibu" chapter for tightening procedure.
⑥ — Refer to "Intake Manifold, Replace" in "Alero, Grand Am & 2004–08 Malibu" chapter for tightening procedure.

3.6L Engine

NOTE: Refer To "3.6L Engine" Located In The "CTS" Chapter For Procedures Not Covered In This Section.

NOTE: On Air Bag Equipped Models, Refer To "Air Bag System Precautions" Located In The Front Of This Manual For System Disarming & Arming Procedures.

NOTE: Refer To "Computer Relearn Procedures" Located In The Front Of This Manual When Battery Power To The Computer Has Been Interrupted.

INDEX

	Page No.		Page No.		Page No.
Compression Pressure	14-15	Engine Mount Strut, Replace	14-15	Fuel System Pressure Relief	14-15
Engine Rebuilding Specifications	29-1	Fuel Pump, Replace	14-15	Radiator, Replace	14-15
Engine, Replace	14-15	Precautions	14-15	Tightening Specifications	14-16
Engine Mount, Replace	14-15	Air Bag Systems	14-15		
		Battery Ground Cable	14-15		

PRECAUTIONS

Air Bag Systems

Refer to "Air Bag System Precautions" in the front of this manual for system disarming and arming procedures.

Battery Ground Cable

Prior to service, disconnect battery ground cable and isolate as required.

Fuel System Pressure Relief

To reduce the risk of fire and personal injury, relieve the fuel system pressure before servicing fuel system components.

1. Turn ignition Off.
2. Remove fuel pump fuse and fuel pump relay.
3. Loosen fuel filler cap to relieve fuel tank vapor pressure.
4. Attempt to start engine and allow engine to run until it stops.
5. Loosen fuel tank filler cap to relieve tank pressure.
6. Connect fuel pressure gauge tool No. J34730-1, or equivalent, to fuel pressure valve. Wrap a shop towel around fitting while connecting gauge to avoid spillage.
7. Install bleed hose into suitable container and open valve to bleed system pressure.

COMPRESSION PRESSURE

1. Ensure battery is at full charge.
2. Start and run engine until it reaches normal operating temperature.
3. Turn engine Off, then remove Powertrain Control Module (PCM) and ignition fuse from instrument panel fuse block.
4. Remove spark plugs from all cylinders.
5. Remove air duct from throttle body and block throttle plate in open position.
6. Thread compression gauge into spark plug hole.
7. Crank engine through at least four compression strokes.
8. Record readings on gauge at each stroke.
9. Repeat test on each cylinder.
10. Lowest reading should not be less than 70 percent of the highest reading. No cylinder reading should be less than 140 psi.

ENGINE MOUNT
REPLACE

1. Remove throttle body air inlet duct.
2. Remove mounting bolt and nut from engine mount strut at engine mount strut bracket on engine.
3. Remove mounting bolt and nut from engine mount strut at engine mount strut bracket on upper radiator support.
4. Remove engine mount strut.
5. Raise and support vehicle.
6. Remove three-way catalytic converter pipe from engine righthand exhaust manifold.
7. Remove righthand front tire and wheel, then the engine splash shield.
8. Remove engine mount lower nuts.
9. Support engine using suitable adjustable jack stand with suitable wood block.
10. Remove engine mount bracket to oil pan bolts.
11. Remove engine mount bracket to engine bolts.
12. Remove engine mount and bracket.
13. Reverse procedure to install.

ENGINE MOUNT STRUT
REPLACE

1. Remove mounting bolt and nut from engine mount strut at engine mount strut bracket on engine.
2. Remove mounting bolt and nut from engine mount strut at engine mount strut bracket on upper radiator support.
3. Remove engine mount strut.
4. Reverse procedure to install.

ENGINE
REPLACE

Refer to "3.5L & 3.9L Engines" in this chapter for engine replacement procedure.

RADIATOR
REPLACE

1. Remove air cleaner
2. Drain cooling system into suitable container.
3. Remove lefthand and righthand engine mount struts.
4. Remove inlet hose from radiator and PCM harness clip from fan shroud.
5. Remove transaxle oil cooler lines from retainer clip at bottom of cooling fan shroud.
6. Remove fan shroud clip from condenser tubes.
7. Remove fan shroud to condenser hold down bracket bolt.
8. Remove air deflectors from top of radiator.
9. Remove cooling fan shroud bolts and coolant reservoir hose from radiator overflow neck.
10. Remove radiator upper support brackets and fan shroud mounting bolts.
11. Disconnect engine cooling fan motors electrical connectors.
12. Remove cooling fan motors electrical harness from fan shroud clips.
13. Remove cooling fan shroud.
14. Remove outlet hose from radiator.
15. Disconnect transaxle oil cooler pipes from radiator.
16. Tilt top of radiator rearward.
17. Remove condenser hold down bracket from radiator.
18. Lift condenser from mounting tabs on radiator.
19. Position condenser aside and remove radiator.
20. Reverse procedure to install.

FUEL PUMP
REPLACE

1. Relieve fuel system pressure as outlined under "Precautions."
2. Raise and support vehicle.
3. Remove fuel tank filler hose from fuel tank.
4. Disconnect fuel feed and fuel return pipe from tank.
5. Disconnect EVAP pipes located at fuel filter area.
6. Support exhaust system, then remove rubber exhaust pipe hangers and allow exhaust system to drop slightly.
7. Separate two halves of EVAP fresh air hose at splice.
8. Remove push pins and fuel tank shield.
9. Support fuel tank with suitable adjustable jack.
10. Remove fuel tank strap bolts.
11. Lower fuel tank and disconnect fuel sender electrical connectors.
12. Remove fuel tank.
13. Record pipe and retaining clips routing for installation alignment.
14. Disconnect and remove fuel feed, fuel return and EVAP pipe assemblies from fuel tank.
15. Remove EVAP canister from fuel tank and insulator pads from fuel tank. Record insulator pads locations for installation alignment.
16. Disconnect fuel sender module electrical connectors.
17. Disconnect fuel pipes from fuel sender.
18. Remove fuel sender lock ring with lock ring removal tool No. J45722, or equivalent, and suitable, long breaker-bar.
19. Remove fuel sender.
20. Remove and discard fuel sender seal.
21. Remove fuel level sensor from fuel sender module.
22. Reverse procedure to install.

TIGHTENING SPECIFICATIONS

Year	Component	Torque Ft. Lbs.
2007–08	Air Conditioning Compressor Bracket, Front Bolt	37
	Air Conditioning Compressor Bracket, Rear Bolt	17
	Air Conditioning Compressor Hose	80①
	Alternator	37
	Catalytic Converter To Exhaust Manifold	10
	Coolant Outlet	89①
	Drive Belt Idler Pulley	37
	Drive Belt Tensioner	37
	ECM	89①
	Engine Mount Bracket To Cylinder Block (M8 Bolt)	28
	Engine Mount Bracket To Cylinder Block (M11 Bolt)	45
	Engine Mount To Bracket	59
	Heater Inlet/Outlet Pipe	89①
	Power Steering Pump Bracket To Engine	37
	Power Steering Pump Reservoir	18

① — Inch lbs.

Rear Axle & Suspension

INDEX

	Page No.		Page No.		Page No.
Coil Spring, Replace	14-16	Hub & Bearing, Replace	14-16	Tightening Specifications	14-17
Control Arm, Replace	14-17	Knuckle, Replace	14-17	Toe Link, Replace	14-17
Lower	14-17	Shock Absorber, Replace	14-16	Trailing Arm, Replace	14-17
Upper	14-16	Stabilizer Shaft, Replace	14-17		
Description	14-16	Support Assembly, Replace	14-16		

DESCRIPTION

The rear suspension used on these vehicles is an independent link type. Coil springs are mounted between the body and lower control arms. The coil springs are controlled by shock absorbers attached to the knuckles and body.

HUB & BEARING
REPLACE

1. Raise and support vehicle.
2. Remove tire and wheel assembly.
3. Remove brake rotor as outlined in "Disc Brakes" chapter.
4. Disconnect wheel speed sensor electrical connector.
5. Remove stabilizer from wheel bearing and hub assembly, then loosen stabilizer shaft insulator bolts enough to position stabilizer shaft aside.
6. Remove wheel bearing and hub assembly retaining nuts, then the assembly from knuckle.
7. Reverse procedure to install.

SUPPORT ASSEMBLY
REPLACE

1. Raise and support vehicle.
2. Remove rear wheels and tires.
3. Remove exhaust system.
4. Remove lower control arms as outlined under "Control Arms, Replace."
5. Remove upper control arm to support assembly attaching bolts and nuts.
6. Remove toe links as outlined under "Toe Links, Replace."
7. Remove stabilizer shaft to knuckle attaching bolts.
8. Remove vehicle wiring harness from support assembly retaining clips.
9. Place a suitable jack stand under support assembly.
10. Remove support assembly to body attaching bolts.
11. Remove support assembly from vehicle.
12. Reverse procedure to install.

SHOCK ABSORBER
REPLACE

1. Raise and support vehicle.
2. Remove tire and wheel assembly.
3. Place a suitable jack stand under knuckle assembly, then raise jack to relieve spring tension.
4. Remove lower shock absorber to knuckle attaching bolt.
5. Remove upper shock absorber to support assembly attaching bolt, then the shock absorber from vehicle.
6. Reverse procedure to install.

COIL SPRING
REPLACE

1. Raise and support vehicle.
2. Remove tire and wheel assembly.
3. Remove rear splash shield to inner fender fasteners, then the splash shield from inner fender.
4. Compress coil spring with spring compressor tool No. OTC 204-167 or equivalent.
5. Place a suitable adjustable jack stand under lower control arm.
6. Remove lower control arm to knuckle attaching bolt and nut.
7. Lower control arm with coil spring attached.

8. Remove coil spring from lower control arm.
9. Reverse procedure to install.

CONTROL ARM
REPLACE

Lower

1. Raise and support vehicle.
2. Remove wheel and tire assembly.
3. Remove coil spring as outlined under "Coil Spring, Replace."
4. Remove lower control arm to support assembly attaching bolt and nut.
5. Remove lower control arm from vehicle.
6. Reverse procedure to install.

Upper

1. Raise and support vehicle.
2. Remove wheel and tire assembly.
3. Disconnect ABS harness connector and position aside. Note position of harness for installation reference.
4. Remove upper control arm to support assembly attaching bolt.
5. Remove upper control arm to knuckle bolt and nut.
6. Remove upper control arm from vehicle through wheelwell opening.
7. Reverse procedure to install.

KNUCKLE
REPLACE

1. Raise and support vehicle.
2. Remove tire and wheel assembly.
3. Remove rear wheel bearing as outlined under "Wheel Bearing & Hub, Replace."
4. Place a suitable jack stand under steering knuckle, then raise knuckle to relieve tension from shock absorber.
5. Remove lower shock absorber to steering knuckle attaching bolt.
6. Remove coil spring as outlined under "Coil Spring, Replace."
7. Remove toe link as outlined under "Toe Link, Replace."
8. Remove upper control arm to knuckle attaching bolt and nut.
9. Remove trailing arm to knuckle bolts.
10. Remove stabilizer shaft link to knuckle attaching bolt, then the knuckle from vehicle.
11. Reverse procedure to install.

TRAILING ARM
REPLACE

1. Raise and support vehicle.
2. Remove wheel and tire assembly.
3. Remove trailing arm bracket to body attaching bolts.

4. Remove trailing arm to knuckle through bolt.
5. Disconnect parking brake cable from trailing arm.
6. Remove trailing arm to bracket bolt and nut.
7. Remove trailing arm from bracket.
8. Reverse procedure to install.

STABILIZER SHAFT
REPLACE

1. Raise and support vehicle, then remove tire and wheel assemblies.
2. Remove link bolts.
3. Remove mounting nuts and insulator brackets.
4. Remove stabilizer shaft.
5. Reverse procedure to install.

TOE LINK
REPLACE

1. Raise and support vehicle.
2. Remove tire and wheel assembly.
3. Remove toe link to steering knuckle attaching bolt.
4. Remove toe link to support assembly attaching bolt and nut, then the toe link from vehicle.
5. Reverse procedure to install.

TIGHTENING SPECIFICATIONS

Year	Component	Torque/Ft. Lbs.
2004–08	Lower Control Arm To Knuckle	②
	Lower Control Arm To Support Assembly	81
	Shock Absorber To Body	66
	Shock Absorber To Knuckle	133
	Stabilizer Shaft Insulator Bracket	26
	Stabilizer Shaft Link To Knuckle	37
	Support Assembly To Body	③
	Toe Link To Steering Knuckle	133
	Trailing Arm To Body	③
	Trailing Arm To Bracket Through Bolt	②
	Trailing Arm To Knuckle	133
	Upper Control Arm To Knuckle	①
	Upper Control Arm To Support Assembly	②
	Wheel Bearing & Hub Assembly	47
	Wheel Lug Nut	100

① — **Torque** to 81 ft. lbs, then tighten an additional 70°.
② — **Torque** to 44 ft. lbs, then tighten an additional 60°.
③ — **Torque** to 66 ft. lbs, then tighten an additional 30°.

Front Suspension & Steering

INDEX

	Page No.		Page No.		Page No.
Ball Joint, Replace	14-18	Power Steering Pump, Replace	14-20	Strut Service	14-18
Ball Joint Inspection	14-18	Precautions	14-18	Assemble	14-18
Coil Spring, Replace	14-18	Air Bag Systems	14-18	Disassemble	14-18
Control Arm, Replace	14-19	Battery Ground Cable	14-18	Tie Rod End, Replace	14-19
Description	14-18	Stabilizer Bar, Replace	14-19	Inner	14-19
Power Assist Motor, Replace	14-20	Steering Columns	20-1	Outer	14-19
Power Steering	21-1	Steering Knuckle, Replace	14-19	Tightening Specifications	14-20
Power Steering Gear, Replace	14-20	Strut, Replace	14-18	Wheel Bearing, Replace	14-18

PRECAUTIONS

Air Bag Systems

Refer to "Air Bag System Precautions" in the front of this manual for system disarming and arming procedures.

Battery Ground Cable

Prior to service, disconnect battery ground cable and isolate as required.

DESCRIPTION

The front suspension on these vehicles, **Fig. 1,** is of the strut and spring design. The lower control arms pivot from the lower side rails through rubber bushings. The upper end of the strut is isolated by a rubber mount incorporating a bearing for wheel turning. The tie rods connect to the steering arm on the strut, below the spring seat. The lower end of the steering knuckle pivots on a ball stud which is retained to the lower control arm by rivets and is secured to the steering knuckle with a nut and cotter pin. The sealed wheel bearings are integral with the hub and are serviced as an assembly.

WHEEL BEARING

REPLACE

1. Raise and support vehicle.
2. Remove tire and wheel assembly.
3. Insert suitable drift punch into caliper and rotor to prevent turning, then remove axle shaft nut.
4. Remove brake rotor as outlined in "Disc Brakes."
5. Disconnect wheel speed sensor electrical connector.
6. Remove wheel speed sensor connector from bracket.
7. Remove hub and bearing assembly attaching bolts.
8. Remove hub and bearing assembly from drive shaft using hub and bearing removal tool No. J 42129 or equivalent.
9. Reverse procedure to install.

BALL JOINT INSPECTION

Ball joints must be replaced if any looseness is detected in the joint or the seal is cut.

To inspect the ball joints, raise the front of the vehicle allowing the suspension to hang free. Grasp the tire at the top and bottom and move the top of tire with an in-and-out motion. Look for any horizontal movement of the steering knuckle relative to the front lower control arm.

If the ball stud is disconnected from the steering knuckle and any looseness is detected or if the ball stud can be twisted in its socket using hand pressure, replace the ball joint.

Ball stud tightness in the steering knuckle boss should also be inspected when inspecting the ball joint. This may be done by shaking the wheel and feeling for movement of the stud end or castellated nut at the knuckle boss. Inspecting the torque at the castellated nut is an alternative method of inspecting for wear. A loose nut can indicate a bent stud or an opened-up hole in the knuckle boss. Worn or damaged ball joints and knuckles must be replaced.

BALL JOINT

REPLACE

To replace the lower ball joint on these vehicles, the lower control arm must be replaced. Refer to "Control Arm, Replace" for procedure.

COIL SPRING

REPLACE

Refer to "Strut Service" for coil spring replacement.

STRUT

REPLACE

1. Raise and support vehicle.
2. Remove wheel and tire assembly.
3. Disconnect stabilizer link from strut.
4. Remove strut to steering knuckle nuts.

5. Position wheel speed sensor harness aside.
6. Remove strut to steering knuckle attaching bolts.
7. Remove upper strut cap to body retaining nuts.
8. Remove strut assembly from vehicle.
9. Reverse procedure to install. Adjust front end alignment as required, refer to "Wheel Alignment" section.

STRUT SERVICE

Disassemble

1. Position strut compressor tool No. J 34013-B in holding fixture J 3289-20 with adapter tool No. J 34013-88 or equivalents, **Fig. 2.**
2. Compress strut to approximately half of its height. **Do not bottom spring or damper rod.**
3. Remove nut from strut dampener shaft and position alignment rod tool No. J 34013-27 or equivalent, on dampener shaft. Position dampener shaft down through bearing cap while compressing coil spring using guide rod tool.
4. Remove strut components

Assemble

1. Install bearing cap.
2. Mount strut to strut compressor tool using bottom locking pin only.
3. Extend dampener shaft and install dampener rod clamp tool No. J 34013-20 or equivalent.
4. Install spring over dampener.
5. Swing strut assembly up and install upper locking pin.
6. Install upper insulator, dust shield, bumper and upper spring seat. Flat on upper spring seat should face in same direction as centerline of strut knuckle.
7. Compress strut using guide rod tool until dampener shaft threads are visible. Remove guide rod tool and install mounting nut.
8. While holding dampener shaft in position with suitable wrench, tighten mounting nut.
9. Remove dampener rod clamp tool.

CONTROL ARM
REPLACE

1. Raise and support vehicle.
2. Remove wheel and tire assembly.
3. **On lefthand control arm,** remove transaxle mount.
4. **On righthand control arm,** remove engine mount.
5. **On lefthand and righthand control arms,** remove front control arm bushing to frame attaching bolt and nut.
6. Remove rear control arm bushing to frame attaching bolts and nuts.
7. Remove control arm ball stud to steering knuckle pinch bolt.
8. Separate ball stud from steering knuckle, then remove knuckle from vehicle.
9. Reverse procedure to install.

STEERING KNUCKLE
REPLACE

1. Raise and support vehicle.
2. Remove wheel and tire assembly.
3. Remove wheel bearing and hub assembly as outlined under "Wheel Hub & Bearing, Replace."
4. Remove outer tie rod to steering knuckle retaining nut, then separate steering knuckle from tie rod.
5. Remove strut to steering knuckle attaching bolts and nuts.
6. Remove steering knuckle from vehicle.
7. Reverse procedure to install. Adjust front end alignment as required, refer to "Wheel Alignment" section.

STABILIZER BAR
REPLACE

1. Raise and support vehicle.
2. Remove tire and wheel assemblies.
3. Disconnect stabilizer links from stabilizer shaft.
4. Place a suitable jack stand under rear of frame assembly.
5. Remove frame support to body attaching bolts.
6. Remove rear frame assembly mounting bolts.
7. Lower rear of cradle to access stabilizer shaft.
8. Remove stabilizer bar clamps and insulators.
9. Remove stabilizer shaft through frame and body opening.
10. Reverse procedure to install.

TIE ROD END
REPLACE

Inner

1. Raise and support vehicle.
2. Remove tire and wheel assembly.
3. Remove outer tie rod as outlined under "Outer."

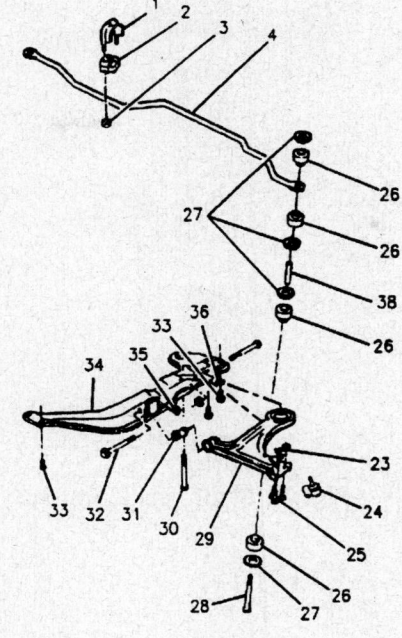

1	CLAMP, STABILIZER SHAFT
2	INSULATOR, STABILIZER SHAFT
3	NUT
4	STABILIZER SHAFT
5	BOLT
6	NUT
7	NUT, STRUT DAMPENER SHAFT
8	RATE WASHER
9	STRUT MOUNT
10	UPPER SPRING SEAT
11	UPPER SPRING INSULATOR
12	DUST TUBE ASSEMBLY
13	SPRING
14	LOWER SPRING INSULATOR
15	STRUT
16	NUT
17	WASHER
18	BOLT
19	HUB AND BEARING ASSEMBLY

20	STEERING KNUCKLE
21	NUT, BALL JOINT
22	COTTER PIN
23	NUT
24	BALL JOINT
25	BOLT
26	INSULATOR, STABILIZER LINK
27	WASHER, STABILIZER LINK
28	BOLT, STABILIZER LINK
29	CONTROL ARM
30	BOLT
31	BUSHING, CONTROL ARM

32	BOLT
33	BOLT
34	SUSPENSION SUPPORT
35	NUT
36	WASHER
37	BOLT
38	SPACER, STABILIZER LINK

GC2029700271000X

Fig. 1   Exploded view of front suspension

4. Remove steering gear as outlined under "Power Steering Gear, Replace."
5. Remove steering gear boot.
6. Slide shock damper toward steering gear, then remove inner tie rod from steering gear using two suitable wrenches.
7. Reverse procedure to install. Adjust front end alignment as required, refer to "Wheel Alignment" section.

Outer

1. Raise and support vehicle.
2. Remove tire and wheel assembly.
3. Loosen outer tie rod end jam nut.
4. Remove outer tie rod end to steering knuckle retaining nut.
5. Separate tie rod end from knuckle with tie rod separator tool No. J 24319-B or equivalent.
6. Remove outer tie rod end from inner tie rod end.
7. Reverse procedure to install. Adjust front end alignment as required, refer to "Wheel Alignment" section.

POWER STEERING GEAR

REPLACE

1. Place steering wheel in straight forward position.
2. Raise and support vehicle.
3. Remove wheel and tire assemblies.
4. Disconnect outer tie rod ends from steering knuckles as outlined under "Tie Rod End, Replace."
5. Remove and discard intermediate shaft to steering gear pinch bolt.
6. Separate intermediate shaft from steering gear. **Do not rotate intermediate shaft after separating from steering gear.**
7. Remove steering gear to frame mounting bolts, then remove steering gear through lefthand side wheelwell.
8. Reverse procedure to install. Adjust front end alignment as required, refer to "Wheel Alignment" section.

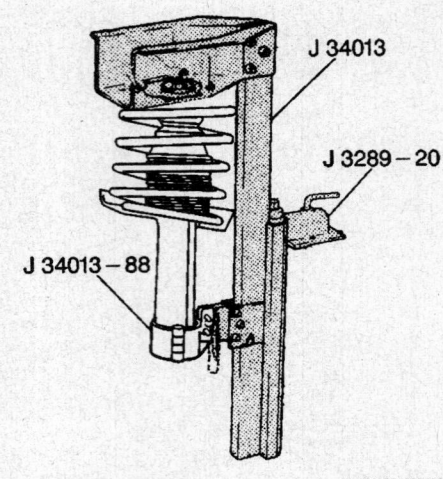

GC2029700275000X

Fig. 2   Strut replacement

POWER STEERING PUMP

REPLACE

These models use a power steering assist motor, Power Steering Control Module (PSCM), Powertrain Control Module (PCM) and the Body Control Module (BCM) to control the power steering function. Refer to "Power Steering Assist Motor, Replace" for motor replacement procedure.

POWER ASSIST MOTOR

REPLACE

The power assist motor is located on the steering column.

1. Disconnect sensor wire harness from power assist motor assembly.
2. Remove wire strap clip using suitable needle nose pliers.
3. Remove power assist motor mounting screws with a suitable TORX wrench.
4. Remove power assist motor from steering column.
5. Reverse procedure to install.

TIGHTENING SPECIFICATIONS

Year	Component	Torque/Ft. Lbs.
2004–08	Ball Stud Pinch Bolt	32
	Control Arm Bushing To Frame	37
	Drive Shaft Nut	159
	Frame Support Bracket To Body	①
	Hub & Bearing Assembly	85
	Intermediate Shaft To Steering Gear Pinch Bolt	36
	Lower Control Arm To Bushing	32
	Outer Tie Rod End To Steering Knuckle	②
	Power Steering Gear To Frame	③
	Rear Frame To Body	①
	Stabilizer Link Nut	48
	Stabilizer Shaft Clamp	18
	Steering Knuckle To Strut	89
	Upper Strut Cap To Body	18
	Upper Strut Shaft	52
	Wheel Lug Nut	100

① — **Torque** to 74 ft. lbs., then tighten an additional 90°.
② — **Torque** to 15 ft. lbs., then tighten an additional 180°.
③ — **Torque** to 52 ft. lbs., then tighten an additional 90°.

Wheel Alignment

INDEX

	Page No.		Page No.		Page No.
Front Wheel Alignment	14-21	Toe	14-21	Thrust Angle	14-21
Camber	14-21	Preliminary Inspection	14-21	Wheel Alignment	
Caster	14-21	Rear Wheel Alignment	14-21	Specifications	14-2

PRELIMINARY INSPECTION

Ensure tires are properly inflated.

Before measuring and setting front wheel alignment, rest front wheels on turn plates.

Before setting rear toe, rest rear wheels on slider plates or turn plates.

Before setting any alignment angle, jounce the vehicle three times at each end to establish trim height.

Special adapters are available for using magnetic hub gauge at rear wheels. Depending on type of equipment used, these may not be required. After removing hub cap and bearing cap, hub gauge will snap into place on brake drum. Magnetic mounting toe gauges may also be installed in the same manner.

Always perform wheel alignment on level alignment rack. Before doing alignment, proceed as follows:

1. Inspect for worn suspension components.
2. Inspect standing curb height.
3. Remove heavy weights from trunk.
4. Inspect wheel bearings for excessive freeplay.
5. Ensure gas tank is full.
6. Place front seats in full rear position.
7. Inspect rear toe adjustment.
8. Always road test vehicle after adjusting alignment, noting the following:
   a. If vehicle still pulls, switch front tires.
   b. If vehicle pulls in same direction, inspect alignment and rear tracking.
   c. If vehicle pulls in opposite direction, rotate tires and road test.

FRONT WHEEL ALIGNMENT

Caster

Caster angle is not adjustable. If caster angle is not within specifications, **Fig. 1,** inspect suspension support for improper alignment and suspension components for damage.

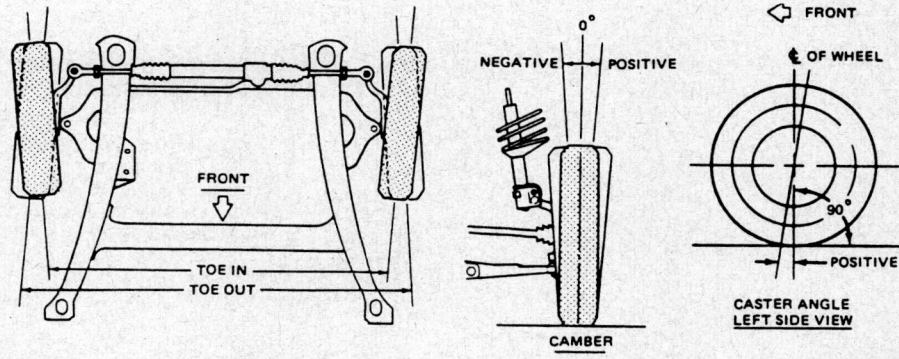

Fig. 1   Caster, camber & toe angles

GC2049100100000X

Camber

Toe setting is the only adjustment normally required. In special circumstances such as damage because of road hazard or collision, the camber angle may be adjusted by modifying the strut, **Fig. 1.**

1. **With strut on vehicle,** disconnect strut from steering knuckle.
2. **With strut off vehicle,** secure strut bottom in suitable vise.
3. **On all models,** enlarge bottom holes in outer flanges with suitable round file, until holes in outer flanges match slots in inner flanges, **Fig. 2.**
4. Install or connect strut to steering knuckle and install bolts hand tight.
5. Grasp top of tire firmly and move tire inboard or outboard until proper camber reading is obtained. Tighten mounting bolts enough to retain camber setting.
6. Remove wheel and tire assembly, then tighten strut to steering knuckle mounting bolts.

Toe

The toe is controlled by tie rod position, **Fig. 1.**
1. Ensure front wheels are in straight-ahead position.
2. Loosen jam nut, **Fig. 3.**

3. Turn adjuster to obtain proper toe setting.
4. **Torque** jam nut to 50 ft. lbs.

REAR WHEEL ALIGNMENT

After front wheel alignment has been inspected or adjusted, rear wheel alignment angles should be inspected if vehicle still does not track properly or if excessive rear tire wear is present. Rear wheels should be parallel to and the same distance from the vehicle centerline.

Rear wheel alignment is not adjustable. If alignment angles are not within specification, inspect for bent or damaged suspension arms, components or underbody.

THRUST ANGLE

The vehicle is steered by the front wheels. The path the rear wheels follow is the thrust angle, **Fig. 4.** In an ideal setting, the thrust angle would be aligned with the vehicle centerline.

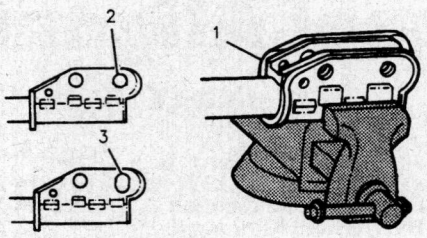

1 STRUT IN VISE
2 BEFORE FILING
3 AFTER FILING

GC2049700155000X

**Fig. 2 Strut bracket modification
for camber adjustment**

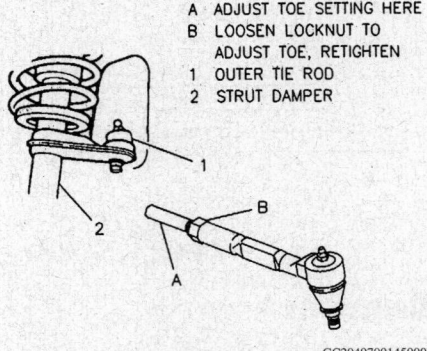

A ADJUST TOE SETTING HERE
B LOOSEN LOCKNUT TO
  ADJUST TOE, RETIGHTEN
1 OUTER TIE ROD
2 STRUT DAMPER

GC2049700145000X

Fig. 3 Toe adjustment

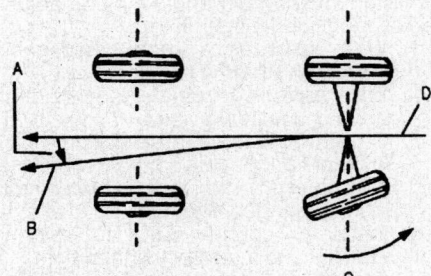

A THRUST ANGLE
B THRUST LINE — OFF CENTER
C REAR TOE—OUT CONDITION
D GEOMETRIC CENTERLINE

GC2049700156000X

Fig. 4 Thrust angle

AVEO

INDEX OF SERVICE OPERATIONS

Page No.

AIR BAG SYSTEM
PRECAUTIONS 0-18
BRAKES
Anti-Lock Brakes (Volume 2).. 6-1
Disc Brakes.................. 22-1
Drum Brakes................. 23-1
Hydraulic Brake Systems 24-1
Power Brake Units........... 25-1

COMPUTER RELEARN
PROCEDURE 0-31
ELECTRICAL
Air Bag System (Volume 2) ... 4-1
Air Conditioning.............. 16-1
Alternator, Replace 15-3
Alternators.................. 19-1
Blower Motor, Replace........ 15-4
Coil Pack, Replace 15-3
Cooling Fans 17-1
Cruise Control (Volume 2) 2-1
Dash Gauges (Volume 2) 1-1
Dash Panel Service
(Volume 2)................... 5-1
Evaporator Core, Replace 15-5
Fuel Pump Relay Location.... 15-3
Fuse Panel & Flasher
Location 15-3
Headlamp Switch, Replace ... 15-4
Heater Core, Replace......... 15-4
Ignition Lock, Replace 15-4
Ignition Switch, Replace 15-4
Instrument Cluster, Replace... 15-4
Multi-Function Switch,
Replace 15-4
Neutral Safety Switch,
Replace 15-4
Passive Restraint Systems
(Volume 2).................. 4-1
Precautions.................. 15-3
Relay Center Location 15-3
Speed Controls (Volume 2) ... 2-1
Starter Motors 18-1
Steering Columns............. 20-1
Starter, Replace 15-3
Steering Wheel, Replace...... 15-4
Stop Light Switch, Replace ... 15-4
Turn Signal Switch, Replace .. 15-4
Wiper Motor, Replace......... 15-4

Page No.

Wiper Switch, Replace........ 15-4
Wiper Systems (Volume 2).... 3-1
ELECTRICAL SYMBOL
IDENTIFICATION 0-63
FRONT DRIVE AXLES 26-1
FRONT SUSPENSION &
STEERING
Ball Joint, Replace........... 15-11
Ball Joint Inspection 15-11
Coil Spring, Replace 15-11
Control Arm, Replace 15-12
Description 15-11
Power Steering 21-1
Power Steering Gear,
Replace 15-12
Power Steering Pump,
Replace 15-13
Precautions.................. 15-11
Steering Columns............. 20-1
Steering Knuckle, Replace 15-12
Strut, Replace 15-11
Strut Service................. 15-11
Tie Rod End, Replace 15-12
Tightening Specifications...... 15-13
Wheel Bearing, Replace 15-11

NON-STANDARD TIRE &
WHEEL SIZE
ADJUSTMENT TO RIDE
HEIGHT SPECIFICATIONS
& TIRE SIZE CHART 0-61
REAR AXLE &
SUSPENSION
Coil Spring, Replace 15-10
Hub & Bearing, Replace 15-10
Rear Axle, Replace 15-10
Shock Absorber, Replace 15-10
Tightening Specifications...... 15-11

SERVICE REMINDER &
WARNING LAMP RESET
PROCEDURES 0-34
SPECIFICATIONS
Fluid Capacities & Cooling
System Data.................. 15-2
Front Wheel Alignment
Specifications................. 15-2

Page No.

General Engine
Specifications.................. 15-2
Lubricant Data................ 15-3
Rear Wheel Alignment
Specifications................. 15-2
Tune Up Specifications 15-2

VEHICLE
IDENTIFICATION 0-1
VEHICLE LIFT POINTS...... 0-51
VEHICLE MAINTENANCE
SCHEDULES 0-73
WIRE COLOR CODE
IDENTIFICATION 0-63
WHEEL ALIGNMENT
Front Wheel Alignment........ 15-14
Preliminary Inspection 15-14
Rear Wheel Alignment 15-14
Wheel Alignment
Specificatons 15-2

1.6L ENGINE
Camshaft, Replace 15-7
Compression Pressure........ 15-5
Cooling System Bleed 15-8
Cylinder Head, Replace....... 15-6
Engine, Replace 15-5
Engine Rebuilding
Specifications................. 29-1
Engine Mount, Replace 15-5
Exhaust Manifold, Replace.... 15-6
Fuel Filter, Replace 15-8
Fuel Pump, Replace 15-8
Intake Manifold, Replace...... 15-6
Main & Rod Bearings 15-8
Oil Pan, Replace.............. 15-8
Oil Pump, Replace........... 15-8
Precautions.................. 15-5
Radiator, Replace 15-8
Thermostat, Replace.......... 15-8
Tightening Specifications...... 15-9
Timing Belt, Replace.......... 15-7
Valve Cover, Replace 15-7
Water Pump, Replace 15-8

Specifications

GENERAL ENGINE SPECIFICATIONS

Engine Liter	Fuel Injection System	Bore & Stroke	Compression Ratio	Net H.P. @ RPM②	Maximum Torque Ft. Lbs. @ RPM	Normal Oil Pressure, psi
1.6L	SFI	3.11 x 3.00	9.5:1	103 @ 6000	107 @ 3600	35①

SFI — Sequential Fuel Injection ① — At idle speed. ② — Ratings are as installed in vehicle.

TUNE UP SPECIFICATIONS

| Engine | Spark Plug Gap, Inch | Ignition Timing, ° BTDC① | | | | Curb Idle Speed, RPM | | Fast Idle Speed, RPM | | Fuel Pump Pressure, psi | Valve Lash |
		Firing Order	Man. Trans.	Auto. Trans.	Mark	Man. Trans.	Auto. Trans.	Man. Trans.	Auto Trans.		
1.6L	.041	1-3-4-2	4	4	③	④	④	④	④	55–62	②

BTDC — Before Top Dead Center

① — Ignition timing is controlled by Powertrain Control Module (PCM).

② — Vehicle is equipped w/hydraulic valve lifters. No adjustment is required.

③ — Equipped with crankshaft position sensor.

④ — Idle speed is controlled by an idle air control (IAC) valve or an idle speed control (ISC) motor.

FRONT WHEEL ALIGNMENT SPECIFICATIONS

| Year | Caster Angle° | | Camber Angle° | | Total Toe° | Ball Joint Wear |
	Limits	Desired	Limits	Desired		
2004–08	+1.75 to +3.25	+2.50	-1.15 to +.35	-.75	-.10 to +.24	①

① — Refer to "Front Suspension & Steering" section for ball joint inspection procedure.

REAR WHEEL ALIGNMENT SPECIFICATIONS

| Year | Camber Angle° | | Total Toe° | Thrust Angle° |
	Limits	Desired		
2004–08	-2.00 to -1.00	-1.50	-.08 to +.58	—

FLUID CAPACITIES & COOLING SYSTEM DATA

| Year | Engine | Coolant Capacity, Qts. | Coolant Type | Surge Tank Cap Relief Pressure, psi | Thermo. Opening Temp., Deg. F | Fuel Tank Gals. | Engine Oil Refill, Qts. | Transaxle Oil | |
								5 Speed Manual Transaxle, Pts.	Auto. Transaxle, Qts.①
2004–08	1.6L	6.4	Ethylene Glycol	15	195	16.3	4	4	6.2

① — Approximate. Make final inspection w/dipstick.

LUBRICANT DATA

Year	Model	Lubricant Type				
		Transaxle		Clutch Hydraulic System	Power Steering System	Brake System
		Automatic	Manual			
2004–08	All	①	②	DOT 3 Or DOT 4	Dexron III	DOT 3 Or DOT 4

① — ESSO JWS 3309 or T-IV automatic transmission fluid (GM Part No. 88900925).

② — Manual transaxle fluid Part No. B0400075, or equivalent.

Electrical

NOTE: On Air Bag Equipped Models, Refer To "Air Bag System Precautions" Located In The Front Of This Manual For System Disarming & Arming Procedures.

NOTE: Refer To "Computer Relearn Procedures" Located In The Front Of This Manual When Battery Power To The Computer Has Been Interrupted.

INDEX

	Page No.
Air Bag System (Volume 2)	4-1
Air Conditioning	16-1
Alternator, Replace	15-3
Alternators	19-1
Blower Motor, Replace	15-4
Coil Pack, Replace	15-3
Cooling Fans	17-1
Cruise Control (Volume 2)	2-1
Dash Gauges (Volume 2)	1-1
Dash Panel Service (Volume 2)	5-1
Evaporator Core, Replace	15-5
Fuel Pump Relay Location	15-3
Fuse Panel & Flasher Location	15-3

	Page No.
Headlamp Switch, Replace	15-4
Heater Core, Replace	15-4
Ignition Lock, Replace	15-4
Ignition Switch, Replace	15-4
Instrument Cluster, Replace	15-4
Multi-Function Switch, Replace	15-4
Neutral Safety Switch, Replace	15-4
Installation	15-4
Removal	15-4
Passive Restraint Systems (Volume 2)	4-1
Precautions	15-3
Air Bag Systems	15-3
Battery Ground Cable	15-3

	Page No.
Relay Center Location	15-3
Speed Controls (Volume 2)	2-1
Starter Motors	18-1
Starter, Replace	15-3
Steering Columns	20-1
Steering Wheel, Replace	15-4
Stop Light Switch, Replace	15-4
Turn Signal Switch, Replace	15-4
Wiper Motor, Replace	15-4
Front	15-4
Rear	15-4
Wiper Switch, Replace	15-4
Wiper Systems (Volume 2)	3-1

PRECAUTIONS

Air Bag Systems

Refer to "Air Bag System Precautions" in the front of this manual for system disarming and arming procedures.

Battery Ground Cable

Prior to service, disconnect battery ground cable and isolate as required.

FUSE PANEL & FLASHER LOCATION

The instrument panel fuse block is located behind the lefthand side of the instrument panel, left of the steering column. The underhood fuse block is located on the front lefthand side of the engine compartment. The turn signal/hazard flasher is located behind the lefthand side of the instrument panel, next to the instrument panel fuse block.

FUEL PUMP RELAY LOCATION

The fuel pump relay is located on the front lefthand side of the engine compartment, in the underhood fuse block.

RELAY CENTER LOCATION

Relays are located in the instrument panel and underhood fuse blocks.

STARTER

REPLACE

1. Raise and support vehicle.
2. Disconnect electrical connectors from starter solenoid.
3. Remove starter motor mounting bolts, then the starter.
4. Reverse procedure to install.

ALTERNATOR

REPLACE

1. Disconnect intake air temperature (IAT) sensor electrical connector from air intake tube.
2. Remove breather tube clamp and all other clamps, then the air intake tube.
3. Disconnect battery harness connector from alternator.
4. Remove alternator shackle bracket bolt.
5. Loosen alternator adjustment bolt and remove drive belt.
6. Remove alternator lower mounting bolts, then the alternator.
7. Reverse procedure to install.

COIL PACK

REPLACE

1. Disconnect electronic ignition (EI) system ignition coil connector.
2. Remove ignition wire. Note position of wire for installation reference.

3. Remove ignition coil retaining nuts, then the ignition coil.
4. Reverse procedure to install.

IGNITION LOCK

REPLACE

1. Remove lower and upper steering column covers.
2. Turn switch to ACC position.
3. Press down on detent spring with a suitable allen wrench, then pull lock cylinder out of switch.
4. Reverse procedure to install.

IGNITION SWITCH

REPLACE

1. Remove lower and upper steering column covers.
2. Remove ignition switch retaining screw.
3. Disconnect switch electrical connector, then remove switch from steering column.
4. Reverse procedure to install.

NEUTRAL SAFETY SWITCH

REPLACE

Removal

1. Disconnect Park/Neutral Position (PNP) switch electrical connector.
2. Remove E-ring and disconnect shift control cable from PNP switch lever.
3. Remove retaining nut, then the washer and control lever.
4. Unstake lock washer and remove nut.

Installation

1. Install PNP switch onto manual valve lever shaft.
2. Temporarily install two adjusting bolts.
3. Install new lock washer and nuts, **torque** nuts to 106 inch lbs.
4. Temporarily install control lever.
5. Turn lever counterclockwise until it stops, then turn it clockwise two notches.
6. Remove control lever and align groove with neutral basic line.
7. Install two bolts and **torque** to 48 inch lbs.
8. Install control lever, washer and nut. **Torque** nut to 106 inch lbs.

HEADLAMP SWITCH

REPLACE

Refer to "Multi-Function Switch, Replace" for switch replacement procedure.

STOP LIGHT SWITCH

REPLACE

1. Remove lefthand trim panel attaching screws, then the trim panel from under lefthand side of instrument panel.
2. Turn stop lamp switch and connector

assembly, then pull switch from brake pedal bracket.
3. Disconnect stop lamp switch connector and remove switch.
4. Reverse procedure to install.

MULTI-FUNCTION SWITCH

REPLACE

1. Remove lower and upper steering column covers.
2. Remove switch by pushing in on tabs on either side of switch housing.
3. Disconnect switch electrical connectors, then remove switch from steering column.
4. Reverse procedure to install.

TURN SIGNAL SWITCH

REPLACE

Refer to "Multi-Function Switch, Replace" for switch replacement procedure.

STEERING WHEEL

REPLACE

1. Remove air bag module.
2. Remove steering wheel retaining nut and clip.
3. Remove steering wheel using steering wheel puller tool KM-210-A or J 1859-A with J 36541-A. Unclip contact ring from steering wheel.
4. Reverse procedure to install.

INSTRUMENT CLUSTER

REPLACE

1. Remove instrument cluster trim panel retaining screws, then the trim panel.
2. Remove instrument cluster retaining screws.
3. Disconnect cluster electrical connectors, then remove cluster.
4. Reverse procedure to install.

WIPER MOTOR

REPLACE

Front

1. Place wiper arms in upright position.
2. Remove nuts and wiper arms.
3. Remove lefthand side air inlet grille retaining screws, then the grille.
4. Remove wiper arm linkage to motor drive shaft retaining nut.
5. Pry wiper arm linkage off motor drive shaft.
6. Disconnect wiper motor electrical connectors.
7. Remove wiper motor attaching bolts, then the motor.
8. Reverse procedure to install.

Rear

1. Remove rear window wiper arm, then open hatchback door.

2. Remove lower garnish molding retaining clips, then the lower garnish molding.
3. Remove rear wiper motor retaining bolts.
4. Disconnect wiper motor electrical connector, then remove motor from hatchback door.
5. Reverse procedure to install.

WIPER SWITCH

REPLACE

1. Remove lower and upper steering column covers.
2. Remove switch by pushing in on tabs on either side of switch housing.
3. Disconnect switch electrical connectors, then remove switch from steering column.
4. Reverse procedure to install.

BLOWER MOTOR

REPLACE

The blower motor is located behind the righthand side of the instrument panel, in the heater/air distribution case.
1. Disconnect blower motor electrical connector.
2. Remove blower cooling hose.
3. Remove motor to heater/air distribution case attaching screws.
4. Remove motor and seal from heater/air distribution case by gently pulling the motor straight down and out.
5. Reverse procedure to install.

HEATER CORE

REPLACE

1. Remove instrument panel as outlined in "Dash Panel Service."
2. Drain cooling system.
3. Recover A/C refrigerant as outlined in "Air Conditioning" chapter.
4. Remove two heater hoses from core lines at cowl.
5. Turn condensation drain hose and pull hose off.
6. Remove A/C suction hose and liquid evaporator pipe connector block retaining nuts at cowl.
7. From engine side of cowl, remove heater/air distribution case assembly to cowl attaching screws.
8. Remove heater/air distribution case assembly from vehicle.
9. Remove linkage screw from lower heater core cover post.
10. Remove linkage lever. Note position of all levers for installation reference.
11. Remove heater core cover attaching screws.
12. Slowly separate lower heater core cover from assembly. Retain sealant.
13. Remove screw and bracket clamp that secure heater core lines to case.
14. Remove heater core body to case spring clamp, then the heater core from case.
15. Reverse procedure to install.

EVAPORATOR CORE
REPLACE

1. Remove instrument panel as outlined in "Dash Panel Service."
2. Drain cooling system.
3. Recover A/C refrigerant as outlined in "Air Conditioning" chapter.

4. Remove two heater hoses from core lines at cowl.
5. Turn condensation drain hose and pull hose off.
6. Remove A/C suction hose and liquid evaporator pipe connector block retaining nuts at cowl.
7. From engine side of cowl, remove heater/air distribution case assembly

to cowl attaching screws.
8. Remove heater/air distribution case assembly from vehicle.
9. Remove evaporator case cover attaching screws, then the cover.
10. Slide evaporator flange support plate upward, then remove evaporator core from case.
11. Reverse procedure to install.

1.6L Engine

NOTE: On Air Bag Equipped Models, Refer To "Air Bag System Precautions" Located In The Front Of This Manual For System Disarming & Arming Procedures.

NOTE: Refer To "Computer Relearn Procedures" Located In The Front Of This Manual When Battery Power To The Computer Has Been Interrupted.

INDEX

	Page No.		Page No.		Page No.
Camshaft, Replace	15-7	Fuel Pump, Replace	15-8	Radiator, Replace	15-8
Compression Pressure	15-5	Intake Manifold, Replace	15-6	Thermostat, Replace	15-8
Cooling System Bleed	15-8	Main & Rod Bearings	15-8	Tightening Specifications	15-9
Cylinder Head, Replace	15-6	Oil Pan, Replace	15-8	Timing Belt, Replace	15-7
Engine Rebuilding	29-1	Oil Pump, Replace	15-8	Installation	15-7
Engine, Replace	15-5	Precautions	15-5	Removal	15-7
Engine Mount, Replace	15-5	Air Bag Systems	15-5	Valve Cover, Replace	15-7
Exhaust Manifold, Replace	15-6	Battery Ground Cable	15-5	Water Pump, Replace	15-8
Fuel Filter, Replace	15-8	Fuel System Pressure Relief	15-5		

PRECAUTIONS
Air Bag Systems

Refer to "Air Bag System Precautions" in the front of this manual for system disarming and arming procedures.

Battery Ground Cable

Prior to service, disconnect battery ground cable and isolate as required.

Fuel System Pressure Relief

1. Remove fuel cap.
2. Remove fuel pump fuse EF10 from underhood fuse box.
3. Start engine and allow engine to stall.
4. Crank engine for an additional 10 seconds.

COMPRESSION PRESSURE

1. Start and run engine until it reaches normal operating temperature.
2. Turn engine off and remove spark plugs.
3. Ensure battery is fully charged and place approximately 3 squirts of oil

from a plunger-type oiler into each spark plug port.
4. Insert engine compression gage into each spark plug port.
5. With throttle wide open crank test each cylinder with 4-5 compression strokes.
6. Lowest reading should not be less than 70 percent of highest reading.
7. Compression gage reading should not be less than 100 psi for any cylinder.

ENGINE MOUNT
REPLACE

1. Remove upper radiator cover.
2. Raise and support vehicle, then remove right front splash shield.
3. Support engine assembly using the Universal Engine Support Fixture J 28467-B, or equivalent.
4. Remove engine mount bracket retaining bolts.
5. Remove engine mount retaining nuts.
6. Lower engine and remove engine mount.
7. Reverse procedure to install.

ENGINE
REPLACE

1. Drain engine oil, then remove battery and battery tray.
2. Recover A/C refrigerant as outlined in "Air Conditioning" chapter.

3. Relieve fuel system pressure as outlined under "Precautions."
4. Drain engine coolant.
5. Remove radiator and engine cooling fans as outlined under "Radiator, Replace."
6. Disconnect upper radiator hose from thermostat housing.
7. Disconnect power steering return hose from the power steering pump.
8. Remove union nut from power steering pressure hose, then disconnect power steering pressure hose from power steering pump.
9. Disconnect Intake Air Temperature (IAT) sensor connector.
10. Disconnect breather tube from valve cover and air intake tube from throttle body.
11. Remove air cleaner assembly.
12. Remove spark plug cover attaching bolts, then the cover.
13. Disconnect Idle Air Control (IAC) valve and Throttle Position Sensor (TPS) connectors.
14. **On models equipped with air conditioning,** disconnect A/C pressure transducer connector.
15. **On all models,** disconnect Camshaft Position (CMP) sensor connector.
16. Disconnect throttle cable from throttle body and from intake manifold bracket.
17. Disconnect Manifold Absolute Pressure (MAP) sensor connector.

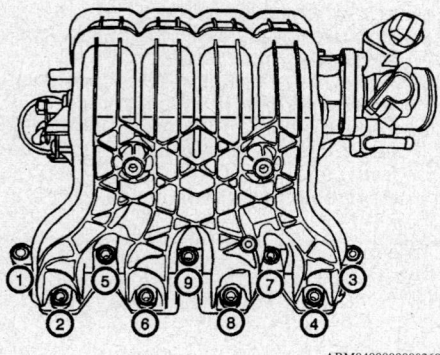

ARM0400000000268

Fig. 1   Intake manifold bolt removal sequence

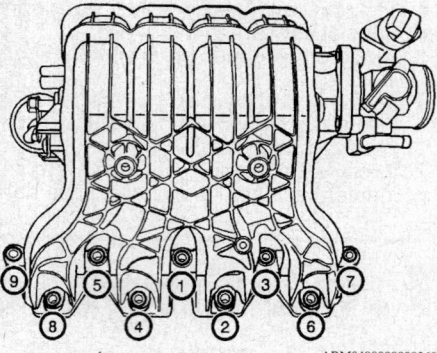

ARM0400000000269

Fig. 2   Intake manifold bolt tightening sequence

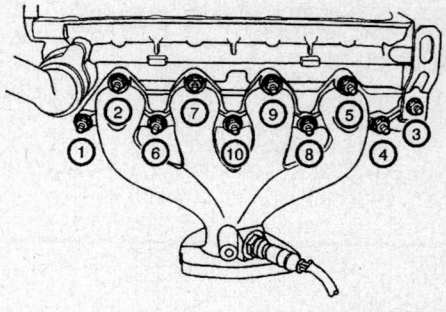

ARM0400000000270

Fig. 3   Exhaust manifold bolt removal sequence

18. Disconnect ignition wires from the spark plugs.
19. Disconnect surge tank coolant hose at throttle body.
20. Disconnect fuel injector connectors.
21. Disconnect EGR valve, ignition coil, oxygen sensor and Crankshaft Position Sensor (CPS) connectors.
22. Disconnect all required vacuum lines.
23. Disconnect brake booster vacuum hose at intake manifold.
24. Disconnect fuel feed line from fuel rail.
25. Remove battery tray support.
26. Disconnect lower radiator hose from coolant pipe.
27. **On models equipped with air conditioning,** remove bolt from A/C compressor pipe and hose assembly, then the pipe and hose assembly from compressor.
28. **On all models,** raise and support vehicle, then remove front tire and wheel assemblies.
29. Remove front splash shield and engine undercover.
30. **On models equipped with automatic transaxle,** disconnect automatic A/T oil cooler inlet/outlet pipe, shift cable and all electrical connectors from transaxle.
31. **On models equipped with air conditioning,** disconnect A/C compressor coil connector.
32. **On all models,** disconnect rear heated oxygen sensor connector.
33. Remove lower flange nuts from exhaust manifold studs. Retain gasket.
34. Remove front muffler pipe retaining nuts, then the front exhaust pipe as a unit. Retain gasket.
35. Remove damping block connection attaching bolt and nut.
36. Remove rear mounting bracket attaching bolts, then the bracket.
37. **On models equipped with automatic transaxle,** remove drive axles as outlined "Front Wheel Drive Axles" chapter.
38. **On all models,** disconnect oil pressure switch electrical connector.
39. Remove battery harness connector nut from alternator, then the connector from alternator voltage regulator.
40. Disconnect EVAP emission canister purge solenoid electrical connector.
41. Remove intake manifold support

bracket attaching bolts, then the support bracket.
42. Disconnect Engine Coolant Temperature (ECT) sensor connector.
43. Remove lower starter mounting bolt, then the solenoid nuts to disconnect electrical cable.
44. Remove lower engine wire harness.
45. Remove rubber from oil pan, torque converter service cover and bolts.
46. Install suitable engine lifting device.
47. Remove retaining bolts from engine mount bracket, then the bracket from engine block.
48. Remove upper transaxle mounting bracket attaching bolts.
49. Lift up vehicle slowly to separate engine and transaxle assembly from vehicle.
50. Separate engine block from transaxle.
51. Reverse procedure to install.

INTAKE MANIFOLD
REPLACE

1. Drain engine coolant.
2. Relieve fuel system pressure as outlined under "Precautions."
3. Disconnect Intake Air Temperature (IAT) sensor connector, then the air intake tube from throttle body.
4. Disconnect Idle Air Control (IAC) valve and Throttle Position Sensor (TPS) connectors.
5. Remove alternator adjusting bolt and alternator drive belt.
6. Disconnect Engine Coolant Temperature (ECT) sensor connector.
7. Disconnect heater inlet hose from cylinder head and surge tank coolant hose from throttle body.
8. Disconnect all required vacuum hoses, including the vacuum hose at fuel pressure regulator and brake booster.
9. Disconnect throttle body cable from throttle body and intake manifold.
10. Remove fuel injector rail and fuel injectors as an assembly.
11. Remove alternator adjusting bracket bolt, then the adjusting bracket from intake manifold.
12. Remove intake manifold support bracket attaching bolts, then the support bracket.

13. Remove intake manifold retaining nuts/bolts in sequence, **Fig. 1.**
14. Remove intake manifold and gasket.
15. Reverse procedure to install, noting the following:
    a. Clean sealing surfaces of intake manifold and cylinder head.
    b. **Torque** intake manifold retaining bolts to 18 ft. lbs., using sequence, **Fig. 2.**

EXHAUST MANIFOLD
REPLACE

1. Disconnect pre-converter oxygen sensor connector.
2. Remove exhaust manifold heat shield attaching bolts, then the heat shield.
3. Remove auxiliary catalytic converter nuts from exhaust manifold.
4. Remove exhaust manifold retaining nuts in sequence, **Fig. 3.**
5. Remove exhaust manifold and gasket.
6. Reverse procedure to install. Using sequence, **Fig. 4, torque** manifold retaining nuts to 18 ft. lbs.

CYLINDER HEAD
REPLACE

1. Drain engine coolant.
2. Relieve fuel system pressure as outlined under "Precautions."
3. Remove valve cover as outlined under "Valve Cover, Replace."
4. Disconnect the intake air temperature (IAT) sensor connector. Disconnect the air intake tube from the throttle body.
5. Remove the air filter housing bolts. Remove the air filter housing.
6. Disconnect A/C Pressure Transducer (ACP), idle air control (IAC) valve and Throttle Position (TP) sensor connectors.
7. Disconnect throttle cable from throttle body and intake manifold.
8. Disconnect engine coolant inlet/outlet hose from throttle body.
9. Disconnect Manifold Absolute Pressure (MAP) sensor connector.
10. Disconnect brake booster vacuum hose.
11. Disconnect Variable Geometry Induction Solenoid (VGIS) connector, then the VGIS vacuum tank hose.
12. Remove engine cover bolts and cover.
13. Disconnect Camshaft Position (CMP)

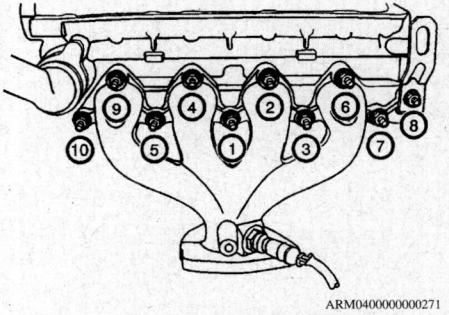

Fig. 4 Exhaust manifold bolt tightening sequence

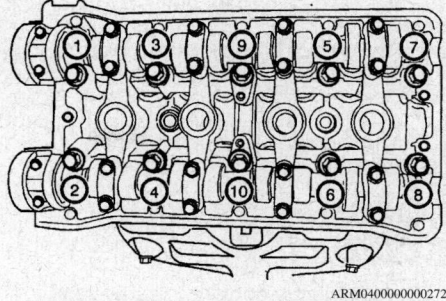

Fig. 5 Cylinder head bolt removal sequence

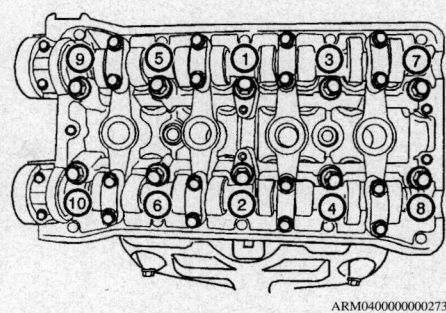

Fig. 6 Cylinder head bolt tightening sequence

sensor connector, then the ignition wires from spark plugs.
14. Disconnect fuel injector harness connectors.
15. Disconnect fuel line.
16. Remove bracket nut from power steering pressure pipe, then the power steering pressure pipe.
17. Remove alternator adjusting nut and the accessory drive belt.
18. Disconnect EGR valve and the ignition coil connector.
19. Disconnect front Heated Oxygen Sensor (HO2S) connector.
20. Raise and support vehicle, then remove right front wheel.
21. Remove engine undercover bolt and nuts, then the engine undercover.
22. Remove canister purge solenoid valve at intake manifold support bracket.
23. Remove bracket bolts from upper intake manifold support and lower intake manifold support.
24. Disconnect Engine Coolant Temperature (ECT) sensor connector.
25. Remove exhaust manifold heat shield bolts and the heat shield.
26. Remove catalytic converter.
27. Disconnect upper radiator hose from thermostat housing.
28. Remove timing belt as outlined under "Timing Belt, Replace."
29. While holding intake camshaft firmly in place, remove intake camshaft gear bolt and intake camshaft gear.
30. While holding exhaust camshaft firmly in place, remove exhaust camshaft gear bolt and exhaust camshaft gear.
31. Remove timing belt automatic tensioner mounting bolts, then the tensioner.
32. Remove Camshaft Position (CMP) sensor and timing belt idler pulley.
33. Remove rear timing belt cover.
34. Disconnect heater outlet hose from coolant pipe.
35. Loosen cylinder head bolts gradually and in sequence, **Fig. 5.**
36. Remove cylinder head with intake manifold and exhaust manifold attached.
37. Reverse procedure to install, tighten cylinder head bolts as follows:
    a. Refer to sequence, **Fig. 6,** then tighten cylinder head bolts in five steps.
    b. **First step, torque** bolts to 18 ft. lbs.
    c. **Second step,** tighten bolts an additional 60.°

d. **Third step,** tighten bolts an additional 60.°
e. **Fourth step,** tighten bolts an additional 60.°
f. **Fifth step,** tighten bolts an additional 10.°

VALVE COVER
REPLACE

1. Remove engine cover bolts and cover.
2. Disconnect breather tube and crankcase ventilation tube from valve cover.
3. Disconnect all required vacuum lines.
4. Disconnect ignition wires from spark plugs.
5. Remove valve cover attaching bolts and the valve cover.
6. Reverse procedure to install.

TIMING BELT
REPLACE
Removal

1. Disconnect Intake Air Temperature (IAT) sensor connector.
2. Disconnect air intake tube from throttle body and breather tube from valve cover.
3. Remove air filter housing.
4. Raise and support vehicle, then remove right front wheel and splash shield.
5. Remove accessory drive belt.
6. Remove crankshaft pulley bolt and crankshaft pulley.
7. Remove upper front timing belt cover attaching bolts and the cover.
8. Remove lower front timing belt cover attaching bolts and the cover.
9. Remove power steering pump mounting bolts.
10. Install crankshaft pulley bolt, then use crankshaft pulley bolt to rotate crankshaft clockwise until timing mark on crankshaft gear is aligned with notch at bottom of rear timing belt cover, **Fig. 7.**
11. Slightly loosen coolant pump retaining bolts, then rotate coolant pump counterclockwise to release timing belt tension.
12. Remove timing belt.

Installation

1. Align timing mark on crankshaft gear to

notch on bottom of rear timing belt cover, **Fig. 7.**
2. Align timing marks on camshaft gears and install timing belt.
3. Rotate coolant pump clockwise using until adjust arm pointer of timing belt automatic tensioner is aligned to notch in timing belt automatic tensioner bracket.
4. Tighten coolant pump retaining bolts.
5. Rotate crankshaft two full turns clockwise using crankshaft pulley bolt.
6. Loosen coolant pump retaining bolts and rotate coolant pump until adjust arm pointer of timing belt automatic tensioner is aligned with pointer on timing belt automatic tensioner bracket.
7. Tighten coolant pump retaining bolts.
8. Install upper and lower front timing belt covers.
9. Install crankshaft pulley, then tighten crankshaft pulley bolt in three steps. First step, **torque** bolt to 70 ft. lbs.; second step, tighten bolt an additional 30°; third step, tighten an additional 15.°
10. Install accessory drive belt, then the right front splash shield and right front wheel.
11. Install air filter housing.
12. Connect air intake tube to throttle body and breather tube to throttle body.
13. Connect IAT sensor connector.

CAMSHAFT
REPLACE

1. Remove the valve cover and gasket.
2. While holding intake camshaft firmly in place, remove intake camshaft gear retaining bolt, then the gear.
3. While holding exhaust camshaft firmly in place, remove exhaust camshaft gear retaining bolt, then the gear.
4. Remove camshaft cap bolts gradually and in sequence, **Fig. 8.**
5. Remove intake camshaft caps, then the intake camshaft. Note position of caps for installation reference.
6. Remove exhaust camshaft caps, then the exhaust camshaft. Note position of caps for installation reference.
7. Reverse procedure to install, noting the following:
    a. Lubricate camshaft journals and caps with clean engine oil.
    b. Reverse loosening sequence, **Fig. 8, torque** camshaft cap bolts to 12 ft. lbs.

Fig. 7 Crankshaft gear alignment

MAIN & ROD BEARINGS

Tighten crankshaft bearing cap bolts in two steps: First step, **torque** bolts to 37 ft. lbs.; second step, tighten bolts an atonal 45.°

Tighten connecting rod bearing cap bolts in two steps: First step, **torque** bolts to 18 ft. lbs.; second step, tighten bolts an additional 30°; third step, tighten bolts an additional 15.°

OIL PAN
REPLACE

1. Raise and support vehicle, then remove right front wheel.
2. Remove right front splash shield and drain engine oil.
3. Disconnect Heated Oxygen Sensor (HO2S) connector.
4. Remove catalytic lower flange nuts from exhaust manifold.
5. Remove front pipe to manifold retaining nuts, then the catalytic converter and exhaust pipe as a unit.
6. Remove oil pan to transaxle housing attaching bolts.
7. Remove oil pan retaining bolts, then the oil pan and gasket from engine block.
8. Reverse procedure to install.

OIL PUMP
REPLACE

1. Remove timing belt as outlined under "Timing Belt, Replace."
2. Remove Crankshaft Position (CKP) sensor bolt, then the CKP sensor.

3. Remove oil pan as outlined under "Oil Pan, Replace."
4. Remove oil pump pickup tube and support bracket.
5. Remove pump retaining bolts, then carefully separate oil pump and gasket from engine block and oil pan.
6. Reverse procedure to install.

COOLING SYSTEM BLEED

1. Add suitable coolant to surge tank.
2. Fill tank slowly so upper reservoir hose remains above water line, this will allow air inside cooling system to escape.
3. Start and run engine until thermostat opens.
4. Turn engine off and inspect coolant level.

THERMOSTAT
REPLACE

1. Drain engine coolant.
2. Disconnect upper radiator hose from thermostat housing.
3. Disconnect throttle body coolant inlet hose from thermostat housing.
4. Remove thermostat housing attaching bolts, then the housing, thermostat and gasket.
5. Reverse procedure to install.

WATER PUMP
REPLACE

1. Drain engine coolant.
2. Remove timing belt as outlined under "Timing Belt, Replace."
3. While holding intake camshaft firmly in place, remove intake camshaft gear bolt and intake camshaft gear.
4. While holding exhaust camshaft firmly in place, remove exhaust camshaft gear bolt and exhaust camshaft gear.
5. Remove timing belt automatic tensioner mounting bolts, then the tensioner.
6. Remove Camshaft Position (CMP) sensor and timing belt idler pulley.
7. Remove rear timing belt cover.
8. Remove water pump mounting bolts, then the water pump.
9. Remove seal ring from pump.
10. Reverse procedure to install.

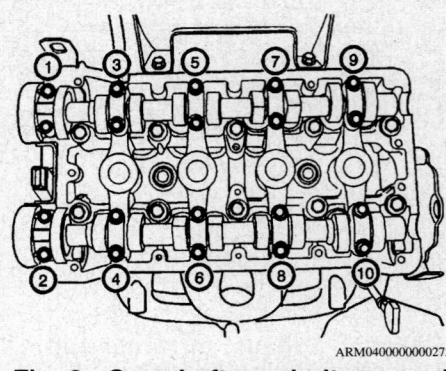

Fig. 8 Camshaft cap bolt removal sequence

RADIATOR
REPLACE

1. Drain engine coolant.
2. Remove electric cooling fans.
3. Remove upper radiator hose clamp.
4. Disconnect upper and lower radiator hoses from radiator.
5. Disconnect surge tank hose from radiator.
6. Remove left and right upper radiator retaining brackets.
7. Remove radiator from vehicle.
8. Reverse procedure to install.

FUEL PUMP
REPLACE

1. Relieve fuel system pressure as outlined under "Precautions."
2. Remove rear seat.
3. Remove fuel pump access cover.
4. Disconnect electrical connector at fuel pump assembly.
5. Disconnect fuel line.
6. Remove fuel pump assembly clip, then the fuel pump assembly from tank.
7. Remove and discard gasket.
8. Reverse procedure to install.

FUEL FILTER
REPLACE

The fuel filter is located in the fuel sender assembly. Refer to "Fuel Pump, Replace" for replacement procedure.

TIGHTENING SPECIFICATIONS

Year	Component	Torque Ft. Lbs
2004–08	A/C Compressor	20
	A/C Compressor Bracket	37
	Alternator Adjusting	15
	Auxiliary Catalytic Converter	30
	Camshaft Cap	12
	Camshaft Gear	49
	Camshaft Pressure Plate	89①
	Connecting Rod Bearing Caps	②
	Coolant Temperature Sensor	15
	Crankshaft Bearing Cap	②
	Crankshaft Position Sensor	89①
	Crankshaft Pulley	③
	Cylinder Head	④
	EGR Valve Adapter	18
	Engine Mounting Bracket	48
	Engine Mount Bracket To Engine Mount	44
	Exhaust Manifold	18
	Flywheel	⑤
	Fuel Rail	18
	Intake Manifold	18
	Intake Manifold Support Bracket	30
	Oil Pan	89①
	Oil Pressure Switch	30
	Oil Pump Rear Cover	53①
	Power Steering Pump	18
	Spark Plugs	18
	Thermostat Housing	15
	Throttle Cable Bracket	71①
	Timing Belt Automatic Tensioner	18
	Timing Belt Idler Pulley	30①
	Timing Belt Cover (Lower)	89①
	Timing Belt Cover (Rear)	89①
	Timing Belt Cover (Upper)	89①
	Torque Converter	48
	Transaxle Bell Housing	55
	Transaxle Brace	30
	Valve Cover	89①

① — Inch lbs.
② — Refer to "Main & Rod Bearings" for tightening procedure.
③ — Tighten in three steps: 1st step, torque to 70 ft. lbs; 2nd step, an additional 30°; 3rd step, an additional 15°.
④ — Refer to "Cylinder Head, Replace" for tightening procedure.
⑤ — Tighten in three steps: 1st step, torque to 26 ft. lbs; 2nd step, an additional 30°; 3rd step, an additional 15°.

Rear Axle & Suspension

INDEX

	Page No.		Page No.		Page No.
Coil Spring, Replace	15-10	Rear Axle, Replace	15-10	Tightening Specifications	15-11
Hub & Bearing, Replace	15-10	Shock Absorber, Replace	15-10		

REAR AXLE

REPLACE

1. Raise and support vehicle, then re-move rear wheel and tire assemblies.
2. Disconnect parking brake and anti-lock brake sensor line.
3. Disconnect brake pipes from brake hoses at rear axle brackets. Cap brake hose openings to prevent contamination.
4. Remove brake hose from rear axle brackets.
5. Place suitable jack stands under arms of rear axle, then raise rear axle arms slightly.
6. Remove shock absorbers as outlined under "Shock Absorber, Replace."
7. Lower support jacks and remove rear springs, **Fig. 1.**
8. Remove left and right rear axle mounting bolts, then the right rear axle mounting bracket bolts.
9. Remove rear axle.
10. Reverse procedure to install.

HUB & BEARING

REPLACE

The hub and bearing assembly are part of the brake drum assembly.
1. Release parking brake, then apply brake pedal at least 10 times.
2. Raise and support vehicle, then re-move wheel and tire assembly.
3. Remove lock ring and caulking nut from spindle, **Fig. 1.**
4. Pull drum straight off of spindle.
5. Reverse procedure to install.

SHOCK ABSORBER

REPLACE

1. Remove shock absorber upper mounting bolts, **Fig. 1.**
2. Raise and support vehicle, then place suitable jack stands under vehicle.
3. Remove shock absorber to axle bolt, then the shock absorber.
4. Reverse procedure to install.

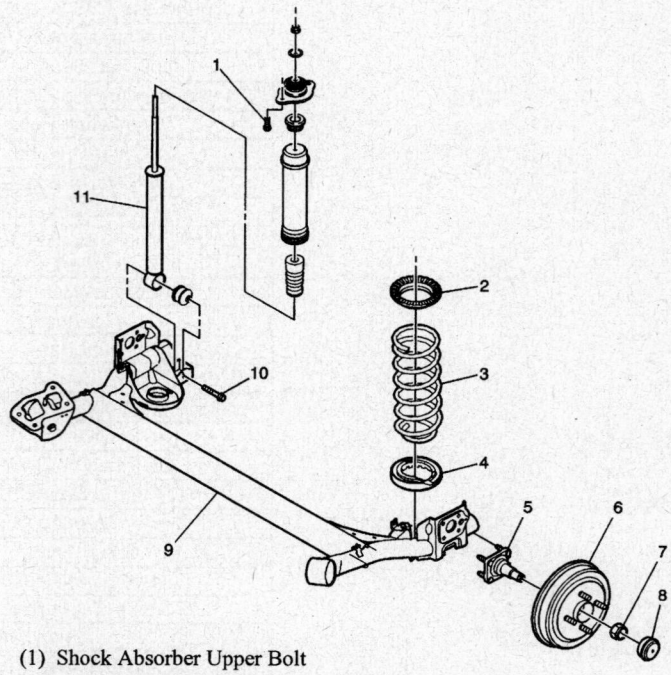

(1) Shock Absorber Upper Bolt
(2) Spring Upper Insulator
(3) Coil Spring
(4) Spring Lower Insulator
(5) Wheel Bearing Spindle
(6) Brake Drum
(7) Caulking Nut
(8) Spindle Cap
(9) Rear Axle
(10) Shock Absorber Lower Bolt
(11) Shock Absorber

ARM0400000000276

Fig. 1 Exploded view of rear suspension

COIL SPRING

REPLACE

1. Raise and support vehicle, then place suitable jack stands under rear axle.
2. Remove tire and wheel assembly.
3. Remove left and right shock absorber to axle mounting bolts.
4. Lower rear axle and remove coil springs.
5. Reverse procedure to install.

TIGHTENING SPECIFICATIONS

Year	Component	Torque Ft. Lbs.
2004–08	Rear Axle Mounting Bracket Bolts	52
	Rear Axle To Body Bracket Bolt	85
	Shock Absorber Bolt (Lower)	53
	Shock Absorber Bolt (Upper)	37
	Wheel Hub & Bearing	30
	Wheel Lug Nut	88

Front Suspension & Steering

INDEX

	Page No.
Ball Joint, Replace	15-11
Ball Joint Inspection	15-11
Coil Spring, Replace	15-11
Control Arm, Replace	15-12
Description	15-11
Power Steering	21-1
Power Steering Gear, Replace	15-12
Power Steering Pump, Replace	15-13

	Page No.
Precautions	15-11
Air Bag Systems	15-11
Battery Ground Cable	15-11
Steering Columns	20-1
Steering Knuckle, Replace	15-12
Strut, Replace	15-11
Strut Service	15-11
Assemble	15-12

	Page No.
Disassemble	15-11
Tie Rod End, Replace	15-12
Inner	15-12
Outer	15-12
Tightening Specifications	15-13
Wheel Bearing, Replace	15-11

PRECAUTIONS

Air Bag Systems

Refer to "Air Bag System Precautions" in the front of this manual for system disarming and arming procedures.

Battery Ground Cable

Prior to service, disconnect battery ground cable and isolate as required.

DESCRIPTION

The front suspension on this vehicle is a combination knuckle/strut and spring design. The control arms pivot from the body and the lower control arm pivots use rubber bushings. The upper end of the strut is isolated by a rubber mount and contains a bearing to allow the wheel to turn. The lower end of the steering knuckle pivots on a ball joint bolted to the control arm. The ball joint is fastened to the steering knuckle with a nut, and to the lower control arm with rivets.

WHEEL BEARING

REPLACE

1. Remove drive axle from wheel hub as outlined in "Front Drive Axle" section.
2. Remove inner retaining ring from hub, **Fig. 1.**
3. Remove wheel hub from steering knuckle using bearing puller tool No. J 36661-2, or equivalent.
4. Remove disc brake splash shield, then the outer snap ring from knuckle.
5. Remove wheel bearing from steering knuckle using puller tool No. J 36661-2, or equivalent.
6. Reverse procedure to install.

BALL JOINT INSPECTION

1. Raise front of vehicle and allow front suspension to hang free.
2. Grasp tire at top and bottom, then move top of tire in an in-and-out motion.
3. Inspect for any horizontal movement of knuckle relative to control arm.
4. Ball joints must be replaced under any of the following conditions:
   a. Joint is loose or ball seal is cut.
   b. Ball stud is disconnected from knuckle. ball stud is loose at the knuckle. The ball stud can be twisted in its socket with finger pressure.

BALL JOINT

REPLACE

1. Raise and support vehicle.
2. Place suitable jackstands under frame of vehicle, then lower vehicle slightly so weight of vehicle rests on jackstands and not on control arms.
3. Remove tire and wheel assembly.
4. Remove control arm as outlined under "Control Arm, Replace."
5. Remove ball joint to control arm mounting nuts, then the ball joint from control arm.
6. Reverse procedure to install.

COIL SPRING

REPLACE

Refer to "Strut Service" for coil spring replacement.

STRUT

REPLACE

1. Loosen top strut to body retaining nut, **Fig. 1.**
2. Raise and support vehicle.
3. Place jackstands under frame of vehicle.
4. Lower vehicle slightly so weight of vehicle rests on jackstands. **Control arms should not rest on jackstands.**
5. Remove tire and wheel assemblies.
6. Remove brake caliper from knuckle/strut assembly and support caliper. **Do not hang caliper from hydraulic brake hose.**
7. Disconnect ABS speed sensor electrical connector.
8. Remove ball joint to knuckle strut nut.
9. Separate steering knuckle assembly from ball joint using ball joint remover tool No. KM-507-C, or equivalent.
10. Remove outer tie rod from the steering knuckle assembly.
11. Push drive axle shaft from front wheel hub and support drive axle.
12. Lower vehicle to gain access to strut to body nuts and washers, then remove strut assembly to body nuts.
13. Remove strut assembly from vehicle.
14. Reverse procedure to install.

STRUT SERVICE

Disassemble

1. Position strut assembly to spring compressor tool No. KM-329-A, or equivalent.
2. Compress front spring, then while holding threaded piston rod with a suitable open end wrench, remove piston rod nut, **Fig. 1.**

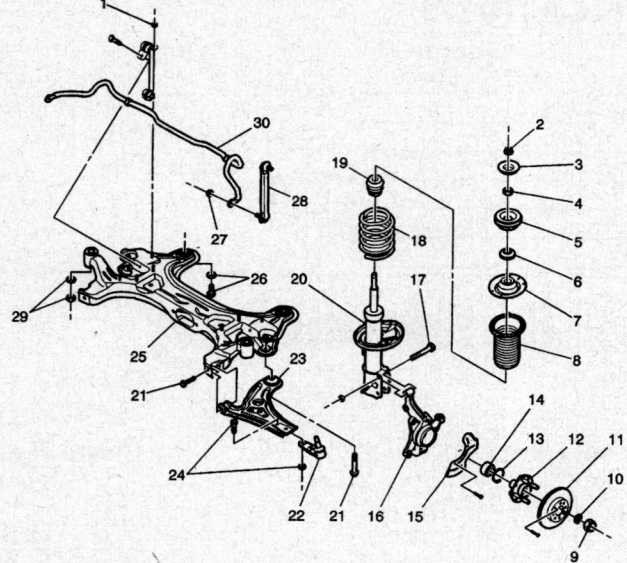

(1) Stabilizer Bar Nut
(2) Strut Upper Nut
(3) Washer
(4) Piston Rod Nut
(5) Strut Mount
(6) Bearing
(7) Spring Upper Seat
(8) Spring Upper Insulator
(9) Caulking Nut
(10) Washer
(11) Brake Disc
(12) Wheel Hub
(13) Retaining Ring
(14) Wheel Bearing
(15) Cover Seat
(16) Steering Knuckle
(17) Thrust Bracket Bolt
(18) Coil Spring
(19) Hallow Bumper
(20) Thrust
(21) Control Arm Connecting Bolt
(22) Ball Joint
(23) Control Arm
(24) Ball Joint Connecting Bolt
(25) Crossmember
(26) Crossmember Bolt - Front Direction
(27) Stabilizer Link Nut
(28) Stabilizer Link
(29) Crossmember Nut
(30) Stabilizer Bar

ARM0400000000278

Fig. 1   Exploded view of front suspension assembly

(1) Bulk Head Retaining Ring
(2) Tie Rod End
(3) Tie Rod End Lock Nut
(4) Rack and Pinion Boot
(5) Tie Rod
(6) Bearing
(7) Pinion Valve
(8) Pinion Shaft Seal
(9) Bushing
(10) Rack Bearing
(11) Adjust Spring
(12) Adjust Plug
(13) Retaining Ring
(14) Pinion Bearing
(15) Grommet
(16) Rack Inner Seal
(17) Cylinder Liner Cut
(18) Cylinder Liner Cut
(19) Steering Rack Gear
(20) Bush and Cylinder Bulk Head

ARM0400000000279

Fig. 2   Exploded view of steering gear

3. Mark position of front spring seat to strut assembly to knuckle bracket for assembly reference.
4. Remove strut mount, strut bearing, spring upper seat, spring upper insulator, hallow bumper, coil spring and strut.

Assemble

1. Install lower spring insulator and spring.
2. Compress spring using spring compressor tool No. KM-329-A, or equivalent.
3. Install strut mount, strut bearing spring upper seat, spring upper insulator, hallow bumper, coil spring and strut.
4. Use an open end wrench to hold threaded piston rod, then install rod nut.

CONTROL ARM
REPLACE

1. Raise and support vehicle.
2. Place jackstands under frame of vehicle.

3. Lower vehicle slightly so weight of vehicle rests on jackstands and not on control arms.
4. Remove wheel and tire assembly.
5. Disconnect stabilizer shaft from control arm by removing control arm-link bolt assembly.
6. Remove retaining clip and ball joint to knuckle/strut nut from ball joint.
7. Disconnect ball joint from steering knuckle using joint remover tool No. KM-507-C, or equivalent.
8. Remove control arm front mounting bolt.
9. Remove control arm rear mounting bolts and bracket.
10. Remove control arm from vehicle.
11. Reverse procedure to install.

STEERING KNUCKLE
REPLACE

1. Remove front wheels.
2. Remove caulking nut, then the tie rod end from knuckle.
3. Remove control arm ball joint and the brake caliper.
4. Remove brake disk and ABS wheel speed sensor.

5. Remove backing plate, then the front strut bolts.
6. Remove knuckle assembly.
7. Reverse procedure to install.

TIE ROD END
REPLACE

Inner

Refer to "Power Steering" chapter from inner tie rod replacement.

Outer

1. Raise and support vehicle.
2. Loosen tie rod end jam nut, **Fig. 2.**
3. Remove tie rod end to steering knuckle nut, then separate tie rod end ball joint from steering knuckle.
4. Remove tie rod end from steering gear. For installation reference, count number of times tie rod end has to be turned to remove from steering gear.
5. Reverse procedure to install.

POWER STEERING GEAR
REPLACE

1. Position tires straight ahead.
2. Raise and support vehicle.

3. Remove intermediate shaft, then the front tires.
4. Drain power steering fluid from rack and pinion.
5. Disconnect steering gear inlet and outlet pipe fittings.
6. Remove outer tie rod hex nuts.
7. Remove ball joint hex nuts and disconnect stabilizer shaft from knuckle.
8. Remove cross member to underbody

attaching nuts and bolts.
9. Remove steering gear bracket assembly retaining nuts, then steering gear.
10. Reverse procedure to install.

POWER STEERING PUMP
REPLACE

1. Remove air cleaner housing.

2. Rotate drive belt auto-tensioner and remove pump drive belt from pulley.
3. Remove power steering pump pulley bolt and the pulley.
4. Drain power steering fluid by disconnecting pressure and supply lines from pump.
5. Remove pump assembly retaining bolts and the pump.
6. Reverse procedure to install.

TIGHTENING SPECIFICATIONS

Year	Component	Torque Ft. Lbs.
2004–08	Adjuster Plug	108①
	Adjuster Plug Locknut	52
	Backing Plate Screws	35①
	Ball Joint Hex Nut	33
	Ball Joint To Control Arm Nuts	47
	Ball Joint To Knuckle Nut	41
	Control Arm Front Mounting Bolt	81
	Control Arm Rear Mounting Bolts	81
	Crossmember Assembly To Body Nut	111
	Drive Axle To Hub Caulking Nut	221
	Engine Mounting Reaction Rod Bolts	44
	Knuckle Assembly To Front Strut Bolts	74
	Outer Tie Rod Hex Nut	33
	Outer Tie Rod Nuts	40
	Pinion Locknut	22
	Piston Rod Nut	44
	Power Steering Pipe Fittings	16
	Power Steering Pump Pulley Bolts	18
	Power Steering Pump Retaining Bolts	18
	Stabilizer Shaft To Knuckle Bolts	33
	Stabilizer Shaft To Link Nut	37
	Steering Gear Inlet & Outlet Fittings	21
	Steering Gear Retaining Bracket Nuts	37
	Strut Assembly To Body	44
	Tie Rod End Ball Joint Nut	33
	U-Clamp Bolt	18
	Wheel Lug Nut	88

① — Inch lbs.

Wheel Alignment

INDEX

	Page No.
Front Wheel Alignment	15-14
Camber	15-14
Caster	15-14
Toe	15-14

	Page No.
Preliminary Inspection	15-14
Rear Wheel Alignment	15-14
Camber	15-14
Toe	15-14

	Page No.
Wheel Alignment Specifications	15-2

PRELIMINARY INSPECTION

1. Inspect tires for proper inflation pressures and normal tread wear.
2. Inspect wheel bearings for looseness.
3. Inspect for loose ball joints and tie rod ends.
4. Inspect runout of wheels and tires.
5. Inspect vehicle trim heights.
6. Inspect for loose rack and pinion mounting.
7. Inspect for loose control arms.

FRONT WHEEL ALIGNMENT

Caster

Front caster is not adjustable. If the front caster measurements are not within specifications, locate and replace or repair any damaged, loose, bent, dented, or worn suspension part.

Camber

Front camber is not adjustable. If the front camber measurements are not within specifications, locate and replace or repair any damaged, loose, bent, dented, or worn suspension part.

Toe

1. Raise and support vehicle.
2. Loosen right and left rod lock bolts. In this adjustment, the right and left tie rods must be equal in length.
3. Turn right and left tie rod adjusters to align toe to specifications.
4. **Torque** tie rod lock bolts 47 ft. lbs.

REAR WHEEL ALIGNMENT

Camber

Rear camber is not adjustable. If the rear front camber measurements are not within specifications, locate and replace or repair any damaged, loose, bent, dented, or worn suspension part.

Toe

Rear toe is not adjustable. If the toe measurement is not within specification, inspect the rear axle assembly and the hub and bearing assembly for possible damage.

AIR CONDITIONING

TABLE OF CONTENTS

	Page No.		Page No.
SPECIFICATIONS	16-9	SYSTEM TESTING	16-1
SYSTEM SERVICE	16-7		

System Testing

NOTE: On Air Bag Equipped Models, Refer To "Air Bag System Precautions" Located In The Front Of This Manual For System Disarming & Arming Procedures.

NOTE: Refer To "Computer Relearn Procedures" Located In The Front Of This Manual When Battery Power To The Computer Has Been Interrupted.

INDEX

	Page No.		Page No.		Page No.
Charging System	16-4	Leak Test	16-2	Air Bag Systems	16-1
Charging Station	16-4	Electronic Leak Detectors	16-2	Battery Ground Cable	16-1
Disposable Cans Or Refrigerant		Flame-Type (Halide) Leak		Hybrid Battery Service	16-1
Drum	16-5	Detectors	16-2	Connect	16-2
Charging System	16-5	Fluid Leak Detectors	16-3	Disconnect	16-1
Discharging System	16-3	Fluorescent Leak Detectors	16-3	System	16-2
Refrigerant Recovery &		Performance Test	16-2	System Evacuation	16-4
Recycling Operating Hints	16-4	Relative Temperature Of High &		Charging Station	16-4
Refrigerant Recovery	16-3	Low Sides	16-2	Vacuum Pump	16-4
Refrigerant Recycling	16-3	Precautions	16-1	Troubleshooting	16-2

PRECAUTIONS

Air Bag Systems

Refer to "Air Bag System Precautions" in the front of this manual for system disarming and arming procedures.

Battery Ground Cable

Prior to service, disconnect battery ground cable and isolate as required.

Hybrid Battery Service

DISCONNECT

To help avoid personal injury, always ensure the ignition switch is in the OFF position and the ignition key has been removed prior to working on any 36V components. After the key has been removed, disconnect the negative battery cable and then open the generator battery disconnect control module cover. After waiting for at least 5 minutes, measure the voltage potential using a DMM between the following: 36V positive and negative battery cables; 36V positive battery cable and vehicle ground; 36V negative battery cable and vehicle ground. All measured voltage levels must be below 3 volts.

1. Remove ignition key from ignition switch.
2. Secure ignition key to ensure that key CANNOT be installed without your knowledge.
3. Disconnect 12 volt negative battery cable.
4. Fold down both rear seat backs, then carefully lift up on load floor rear compartment cover at retaining clip locations, **Fig. 1.**
5. Tilt load floor rear compartment cover towards rear of vehicle slightly, disengage tabs and remove load floor rear compartment cover. **To avoid personal injury, be careful when working in vicinity of generator battery disconnect control module. Internal components will still be live, 36V potential, even when cover has been opened or removed.**
6. Remove generator battery disconnect control module cover bolt, **Fig. 2.**
7. Open and slide generator battery disconnect control module cover to right, removing cover. **Wait at least 5 minutes in order to allow generator control module capacitors to discharge.**
8. **Never assume battery pack is disabled when generator battery disconnect control module cover is opened. Generator battery will have to be checked for voltage potential using a voltmeter first**
9. Set voltmeter to DC voltage and measure vehicle 12-volt battery voltage, at 12-volt positive jumper location and negative battery cable.
10. Meter should read greater than 12 volts DC.
11. To ensure generator battery has been disabled, check generator battery for voltage potential as follows:
    a. Refer to **Fig. 3** for voltage measurement locations.
    b. Measure from positive stud to negative stud, voltage should be less than 3 volts.
    c. Measure from positive stud to vehicle chassis ground, voltage should be less than 3 volts.
    d. Measure from negative stud to vehicle chassis ground, voltage should be less than 3 volts.
12. After verifying there is no voltage present, vehicle is now safe to work on.

AIR CONDITIONING

CONNECT

1. Install and close generator battery disconnect control module cover.
2. Install generator battery cover bolt and **torque** to 89 inch lbs.
3. Tilt load floor rear compartment cover towards rear of vehicle slightly in order to insert tabs into battery tray rear support.
4. Set load floor rear compartment cover down, ensure retaining clips align to proper locations, carefully push down to secure cover.
5. Place rear seats backs to their proper positions.
6. Connect 12 volt negative battery cable.

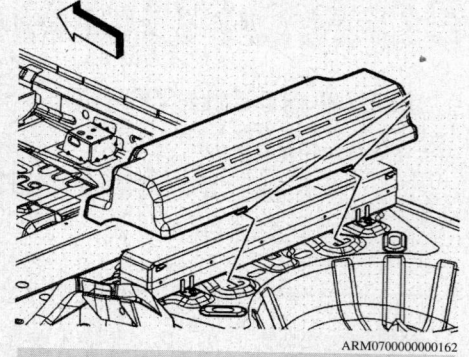

Fig. 1   Rear hybrid battery compartment. Aura

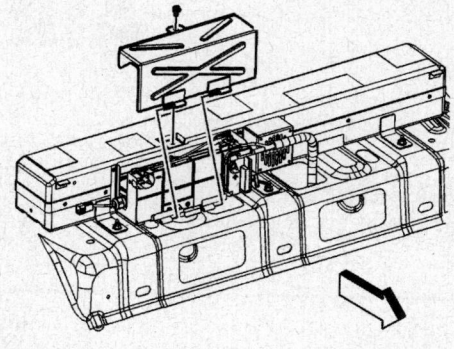

Fig. 2   Disconnect control module cover. Aura Hybrid

System

R-134a refrigerant is a non toxic, non-flammable, clear and odorless liquefied gas.

R-134a refrigerant is not compatible with R-12 refrigerant. Even small amounts of R-12 in a R-134a system will cause lubricant contamination, compressor failure or improper A/C performance. Never add R-12 to a R-134a system.

Avoid breathing R-134a refrigerant and lubricant vapor or mist. Exposure may irritate eyes, nose and throat. Use only approved service equipment to discharge R-134a systems. Do not heat refrigerant containers with open flame, if container warming is required, place bottom of container in a pail of warm water. R-134a refrigerant will displace oxygen, work only in a well ventilated area to prevent suffocation.

Always wear goggles and wrap clean cloth around fittings, valves and connections when performing work that involves opening the refrigerant system. Keep work area well ventilated and do not steam clean or weld on or near any of the air conditioning lines or components. If liquid coolant does touch the eyes, bathe eyes quickly in cold water, then apply a bland disinfectant oil. See an eye doctor.

Before removing and replacing any of the air conditioning refrigeration lines or components, the refrigerant must be completely removed. The refrigerant system may be evacuated and charged using an air conditioning service charging station or a manifold and gauge set with a 30 lb., drum of R-134a. **Never charge the air conditioning system through the high pressure side of the system.**

For efficient operation of the air conditioning system, be careful not to contaminate the system with foreign materials, such as dirt, air or moisture. Contamination of the air conditioning system will change the chemical stability of the R-134a refrigerant, in turn changing the viscosity of the refrigerant oil. They will also effect pressure, temperature and create corrosion and abnormal wear of moving components.

TROUBLESHOOTING

Refer to **Figs. 4 through 7** for symptom troubleshooting charts.

PERFORMANCE TEST

Remove leaves and debris from front of the condenser core, mounted at the front of the radiator. All obstructions must be removed, as they will reduce heat transfer and impair the efficiency of the system. Ensure space between the condenser and the radiator is free of foreign matter.

Ensure the evaporator drain is open. The evaporator cools and dehumidifies the air before it enters the passenger compartment. As the core cools the air, moisture condenses on it and is drained through the evaporator water drain tube.

The system should be operated for at least 15 minutes to allow sufficient time for all components to become completely stabilized. Determine if the system is fully charged by the use of test gauges and sight glass if one is installed on system. Head pressure will read from 180–220 psi or higher, depending upon ambient temperature and the type of unit being tested. The sight glass should be free of bubbles. Low side pressures should read approximately 15–30 psi, depending on the ambient temperature and the unit being tested. The type of control and component installation used on a particular system will directly influence the pressure readings on the high and low sides, **Fig. 8.**

The high side pressure will be affected by the ambient or outside air temperature. Refer to **Fig. 9** for approximate high side pressure readings at various ambient temperatures.

Relative Temperature Of High & Low Sides

The high side of the system should be uniformly hot to the touch throughout. A difference in temperature will indicate a partial blockage of liquid or gas at this point.

The low side of the system should be uniformly cool to the touch with no excessive sweating of the suction line or low side service valve. Excessive sweating or frosting of the low side service valve usually indicates an expansion valve is allowing an excessive amount of refrigerant into the evaporator.

LEAK TEST

Before beginning any leak test, attach a manifold gauge set and note pressure. If little or no pressure is indicated, a partial charge must be installed. Inspect all connections, compressor head gasket, oil filler plug and compressor shaft seal for leaks.

Electronic Leak Detectors

Current versions of electronic leak detectors have three settings, one for R-12, one for R-134a and one for gross. The gross setting is for isolating very large leaks already found in one of the other two settings. Refer to operating instructions for the unit being used and observe these general procedures.

1. Move detector probe one inch per second in areas of suspected leaks.
2. Position probe below test point, as refrigerant gas is heavier than air.
3. Inspect service access gauge port valve fittings, particularly when valve caps are missing, as dirt accumulations can destroy sealing area of valve core when manifold gauge set is attached. Replace missing valve caps after cleaning valve core area. **Valve caps should only be finger tightened. Using pliers to tighten valve caps may distort sealing surface of valve.**
4. Inspect for leaks in manifold gauge set and hoses, as well as rest of system.

Flame-Type (Halide) Leak Detectors

1. Adjust detector flame as low as possible to obtain maximum sensitivity. Ensure copper element is cherry red and not burned away, flame will be almost colorless.

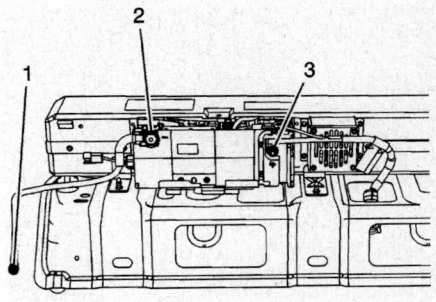

1-Chassis ground
2-Negative stud
3-Positive stud

ARM0700000000164

Fig. 3 Battery disconnect control module voltage measurement locations. Aura Hybrid

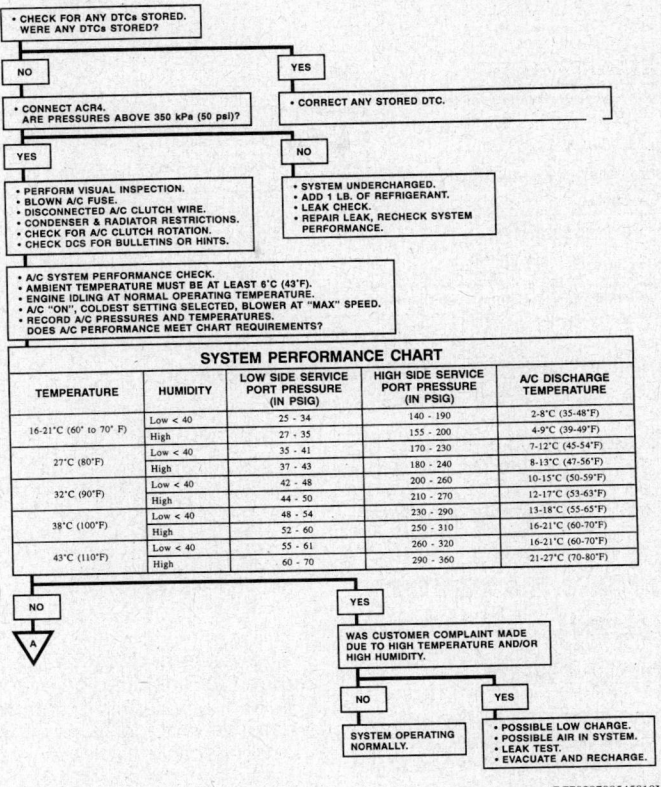

		LOW SIDE SERVICE PORT PRESSURE (IN PSIG)	HIGH SIDE SERVICE PORT PRESSURE (IN PSIG)	A/C DISCHARGE TEMPERATURE
TEMPERATURE	HUMIDITY			
16-21°C (60° to 70° F)	Low < 40	25 - 34	140 - 190	2-8°C (35-48°F)
	High	27 - 35	155 - 200	4-9°C (39-49°F)
27°C (80°F)	Low < 40	35 - 41	170 - 230	7-12°C (45-54°F)
	High	37 - 43	180 - 240	8-13°C (47-56°F)
32°C (90°F)	Low < 40	42 - 48	200 - 260	10-15°C (50-59°F)
	High	44 - 50	210 - 270	12-17°C (53-63°F)
38°C (100°F)	Low < 40	48 - 54	230 - 290	13-18°C (55-65°F)
	High	52 - 60	250 - 310	16-21°C (60-70°F)
43°C (110°F)	Low < 40	55 - 61	260 - 320	16-21°C (60-70°F)
	High	60 - 70	290 - 360	21-27°C (70-80°F)

GC7029700545010X

Fig. 4 Insufficient A/C cooling troubleshooting (Part 1 of 2)

2. Slowly move detector along areas of suspected leaks. A slight leak will cause flame to change to a bright yellow-green color. A significant leak will be indicated by a brilliant blue flame. Position flame under areas being tested as refrigerant gas is heavier than air. **Presence of dust in pickup hose may cause a change in color of flame. If not recognized, a false diagnosis could be made. Store leak detector in a clean place and ensure hose is free of dust before leak testing.**
3. Inspect manifold gauge set and hoses for leaks, as well as rest of system.
4. Use a small fan to ventilate areas where leak detector indicates refrigerant constantly. These areas are contaminated with refrigerant and must be ventilated before leak can be pinpointed.

Fluid Leak Detectors

Apply leak detector solution around joints to be tested. A cluster of bubbles will form immediately if there is a leak. A white foam that forms after a short while will indicate an extremely small leak. In some confined areas such as sections of the evaporator and condenser, use of an electronic leak detector is recommended.

Fluorescent Leak Detectors

The high density black light tool No. J2848-E, tracer dye injector tool No. J41436 and tracer dye tool No. J41447, or equivalents, were developed to detect refrigerant leaks on R-134a systems. **Do not use any other tracer dye in these systems. Another type dye may cause premature compressor failure. Use only a ¼ ounce charge of dye, larger amounts may effect system performance.** After adding tracer dye, clean service valves and all affected surfaces of the dye with GM en-gine degreaser part No. 1050436, or equivalent, to prevent any false leak diagnosis.

DISCHARGING SYSTEM
Refrigerant Recovery

The refrigerant system must be discharged using an air conditioning refrigerant recovery and recycling system. After completing any required repairs the refrigerant system can be evacuated and charged using an air conditioning service charging station. Service fitting caps are color coded for easy reference. Red cap indicates high side port. Blue cap indicates low side port.

Failure to inspect for residual oil from previous recovery can result in adding extra oil to the current vehicle being serviced. This will result in reduced performance and possible compressor damage.
1. Start vehicle and run with A/C On for two minutes, then attach manifold gauge set to A/C system, **Fig. 10.** Attach recovery station inlet hose to center fitting of manifold gauge set.
2. Open both valves of manifold gauge set. Ensure refrigerant tank vapor valve and liquid valve are open.
3. Turn main power switch On.
4. Depress compressor start switch. Amber Compressor On light will come on and compressor will start. Compressor will shutoff automatically when recovery is complete.
5. Wait two minutes and inspect for pressure rise. If pressure rise occurs, depress compressor start switch to repeat recovery procedure.
6. To drain receiver dehydrator of A/C system oil, open receiver dehydrator pressurizing valve for 15 seconds to allow compressor discharge pressure back into receiver dehydrator.
7. Open oil drain valve slowly and drain receiver dehydrator. When oil stops draining, close oil drain valve.
8. **Do not allow receiver dehydrator to completely depressurize.**

Refrigerant Recycling

1. Turn main power switch On.
2. Open both valves on recovery tank.
3. Turn Recycle Start switch On. Amber Recycle On light will come on and refrigerant pump will start.
4. Refrigerant will be seen going through Moisture Indicator at start up. If there is a sufficient supply of refrigerant, bubbles will clear after a few seconds. When bubbles clear from Moisture Indicator, refrigerant pump is operating at maximum efficiency.
5. Allow station to operate until dot in center of Moisture Indicator turns green. Moisture Indicator Dot should change to a shade indicated on reference decal. Always run recycling system a minimum of 30 minutes. If Moisture Indicator starts out yellow, it could take

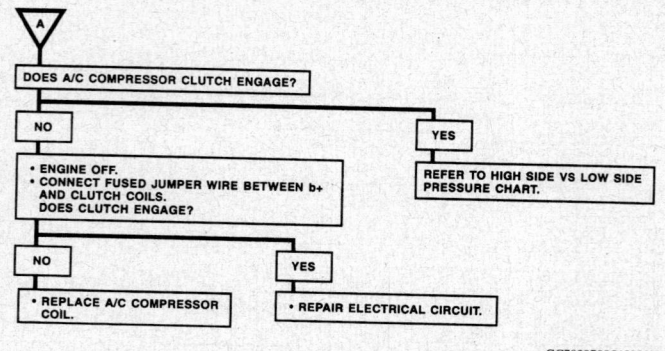

Fig. 4   Insufficient A/C cooling troubleshooting (Part 2 of 2)

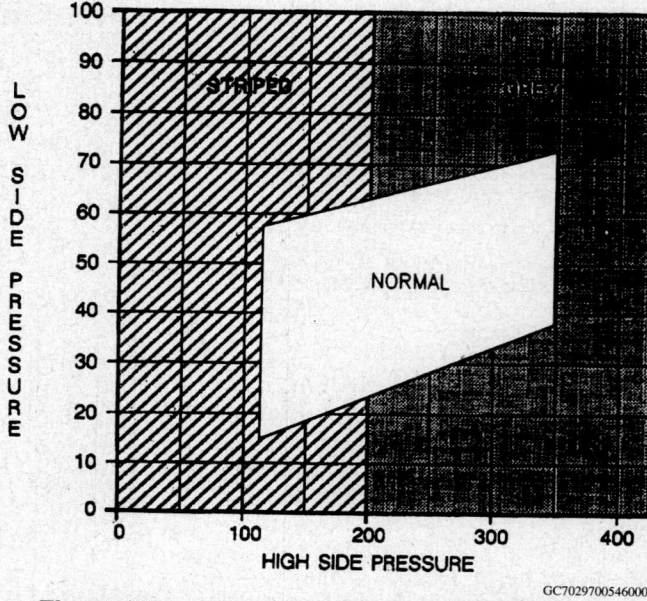

Fig. 5   High side vs. low side pressure chart

as long as two hours to turn green, depending on moisture content of refrigerant.

6. Turn Off station when recycling is complete.

Refrigerant Recovery & Recycling Operating Hints

1. When using recovery station in conjunction with a charging station, attach center port hose of manifold gauge set to inlet port of recovery station, then follow normal operating procedures for recovery/recycling station.
2. When using recovery station in conjunction with an automatic charging station, attach exhaust hose to inlet of recovery station.
3. **On automatic A/C service stations,** a hole has been added at rear of cabinet for access to exhaust hose.
4. **On older type stations,** open front doors of cabinet to reach exhaust hose.
5. **On all stations,** after attaching exhaust hose to recovery station, depress main power switch on automatic charging station. Depress exhaust switch. Then follow normal operating procedures for recovery station.
6. Air is automatically vented from recovery tank during recycling. This feature eliminates need to purge hoses before recovering refrigerant.
7. Operating engine with A/C Off during recovery may reduce recovery time.
8. To help prevent escape of refrigerant to atmosphere, recovery station can be attached to a Dial A Charge cylinder top vent port when filling cylinder.
9. Always inspect recovery station for residual oil from previous recovery.

SYSTEM EVACUATION

Charging Station

A vacuum pump is built into the charging station. Complete moisture removal from the system is possible only with a vacuum pump constructed for the purpose.

The system must be completely discharged before it can be evacuated. Damage to the vacuum pump may result if pressurized refrigerant is allowed to enter.

1. Connect hose to vacuum pump, if system was discharged through charging station.
2. Open low side gauge hand valve of charging station.
3. Turn vacuum pump on according to instructions for specific station being used.
4. Evacuate system with vacuum pump until low pressure gauge reads at least 28 inches of vacuum. Continue evacuating system for an additional 15 minutes for routine system servicing or 20–30 minutes, if any components have been replaced.
5. Close low side gauge hand valve, then turn vacuum pump off.
6. Verify ability of system to hold vacuum. Watch low side gauge to see that gauge does not rise at a rate faster than 1 inch vacuum every 4–5 minutes. If low side gauge rises at too rapid a rate, install partial charge and leak test.
7. If system holds vacuum, charge system with refrigerant.

Vacuum Pump

The specification for A/C system pump-down is 28–29 ½ inches vacuum. This reading can be attained at or near sea level only. For each 1000 feet of altitude, the reading will be 1 inch vacuum lower. As an example, at 5000 feet elevation, only 23–24 ½ inch of vacuum can be obtained. **The system must be completely discharged before it can be evacuated. Damage to vacuum pump may result if pressurized refrigerant is allowed to enter pump.**

1. With manifold gauge set connected to system, remove cap from vacuum hose connector. Install manifold gauge set center hose to vacuum pump connector. Open low side gauge manifold hand valve only.
2. Ensure low side gauge is calibrated correctly. It should be reading zero. If not, adjust calibration.
3. Evacuate system with vacuum pump until low pressure gauge reads at least 28 inches of vacuum.
4. Continue evacuating system for an additional 15 minutes for routine system servicing or 20–30 minutes, if components have been replaced.
5. When system evacuation is complete, close low side gauge manifold hand valve, then turn vacuum pump off.
6. Verify ability of system to hold vacuum. Watch low side gauge to see that gauge does not rise at a rate faster than 1 inch vacuum every 4–5 minutes. If low side gauge rises at too rapid a rate, install partial charge and leak test.
7. Correct leaks as required and evacuate system.
8. If system holds vacuum, charge system with refrigerant.

CHARGING SYSTEM

Charging Station

Use of the following procedures will prevent charging station from being accidentally exposed to high-side vehicle system pressure.

Use instructions provided with charging station noting the following:
1. Do not connect high pressure line to A/C system.
2. Always keep high pressure valve closed on charging station.
3. Perform all evacuation and charging through low-side pressure service fitting.

Gray Area Diagnosis and Service	
Check the following if pressures intersect in the gray area:	
NOTE V5 clutch cycling can occur when discharge pressure exceeds 400 psi.	
1. Improper condenser operation. This can result from :	• Extremely high ambient humidity. • Insufficient air flow across condenser. • Damaged or dirty condenser fins. • Faulty fan relay.
2. High side refrigerant restriction.	• Feel liquid line before expansion tube (orifice). If line feels cold, it indicates restriction in high side. • Visually check for frost spot to locate restriction and repair as necessary.
3. Refrigerant system overcharged (High discharge and high suction pressures).	• The clutch may cycle on/off and cause the compressor to be noisy.
4. Expansion tube (orifice) blocked (Low suction pressures).	
5. Air in system (High discharge and high suction pressures). Items 4, 5 and 6 in the striped area can be corrected by the same procedure.	• Discharge refrigerant system slowly using the low pressure fitting to prevent oil loss. • Check expansion (orifice) tube for blockage. Clean or replace as required. • Evacuate system to a vacuum. Improper evacuation of system prior to recharge will cause air to remain in system. • Recharge system with proper amount of refrigerant. • Leak check system.

GC7029700547000X

Fig. 6 Gray area diagnosis & service

Disposable Cans Or Refrigerant Drum

CHARGING SYSTEM

Never use disposable cans to charge into the high pressure side of the system (compressor discharge port) or into a system that is at high temperature, high system pressures could be transferred into the charging can causing it to explode.

1. Start and run engine until normal operating temperature is reached and allow to warm up (choke off, normal idle). Set A/C control lever to OFF.
2. **On all models except Cadillac equipped with display diagnosis,** when 1 lb., of refrigerant has entered system, engage compressor by setting A/C lever to NORM and blower switch to HI to draw in remainder of charge.
3. **On Cadillac models equipped with display diagnosis,** when 1 lb., of refrigerant has entered system, engage compressor by setting climate control panel to AUTO and blower switch to HI to draw in remainder of charge. If system switches to ECON when AUTO is pressed, low refrigerant is indicated, and compressor will not operate. To obtain compressor operation, clear diagnostic trouble codes and select AUTO again.
4. **On all models,** cooling condenser with a large fan will speed up charging procedure by maintaining condenser temperature below charging cylinder temperature.
5. Close refrigerant supply valve and run engine for 30 seconds to clear lines and gauges.
6. With engine running, remove charging low side hose adapter from accumulator service fitting. Unscrew rapidly to avoid excessive refrigerant loss. **Do not remove a gauge line from its adapter when line is connected to A/C system. To disconnect line, always remove line adapter from service fitting. Do not remove charging hose at gauge set while attached to accumulator, as system will be discharged due to depressed Schraeder valve.**
7. Replace protective cap on accumulator fitting and turn engine off.
8. Inspect system for leaks.
9. Start engine and inspect for proper system pressures.

Striped Area Diagnosis and Service	
Check the following if pressures intersect in the striped area:	
1. Compressor may be internally damaged.	• If suction and discharge pressure are equal and do not change when the A/C mode is turned on and off, the compressor may be internally damaged. • Excess heat at the clutch surfaces or a free wheeling clutch driver are signs of internal compressor damage. • When replacing the compressor, follow component replacement procedures to maintain correct oil charge in the system.
2. Missing expansion tube (orifice).	• Feel liquid line after expansion tube. If line is warm, discharge system and inspect for proper installation of expansion tube. If expansion tube or o-ring is missing replace expansion tube. • If expansion tube is present, remove, clean, or replace tube as necessary and install in system. • Evacuate and charge system.
3. Compressor at minimum stroke.	• If compressor discharge pressures remains only 10-30 psi above suction pressure, compressor may be at minimum stroke. • Run engine at approximately 3000 RPM for three minutes until pressures become normal. During this period, cycle mode lever from vent to A/C every 20 seconds. If no change, perform control valve low load test (step 4).

4. Compressor control valve set improperly. Run low load test to verify. Perform low load test as follows. This procedure is designed to create a low cooling load causing the V5 compressor to go toward minimum stroke which is absolutely necessary for evaluation of control valve set point.	• Start engine and run at fast idle speed.
	• Open hood, close windows and doors.
	• Set A/C controls to LOW blower and MAX cooling.
	• Record and evaluate test results:
	  1. If suction pressure is 25-35 psi, control valve is functioning properly.
	  2. If suction pressure is outside limits of 25-35 psi, replace control valve.

5. Refrigerant system undercharged.	• This condition may exist when the suction pressure is below 35 psi during the high load test (step 3). • The suction line before the accumulator will be warm if charge is low. • Add 1 lb. of refrigerant and recheck. Pressures should come into the white area. If so, find source of refrigerant leak and repair. • Evacuate and charge system with correct amount of refrigerant.
6. Expansion tube (orifice) blocked.	• Refer to step 5 in the gray area for diagnosis.

GC7029700548000X

Fig. 7 Striped area diagnosis & service

Evaporator Pressure Gauge Reading	Evaporator Temperature F°	High Pressure Gauge Reading	Ambient Temperature
0	-21°	45	20°
0.6	-20°	55	30°
2.4	-15°	72	40°
4.5	-10°	86	50°
6.8	-5°	105	60°
9.2	0°	126	70°
11.8	5°	140	75°
14.7	10°	160	80°
17.1	15°	185	90°
21.1	20°	195	95°
22.5	22°	220	100°
23.9	24°	240	105°
25.4	26°	260	110°
26.9	28°	275	115°
28.5	30°	290	120°
37.0	40°	305	125°
46.7	50°	325	130°
57.7	60°		
70.1	70°		
84.1	80°		
99.6	90°		
116.9	100°		
136.0	110°		
157.1	120°		
179.0	130°		

GC7029100025000X

Fig. 8   Pressure-temperature relationship. Conditions equivalent to 30 mph or 1750 engine RPM

Ambient Temp., °F	High Side Pressure
80	150–170
90	175–195
95	185–205
100	210–230
105	230–250
110	250–270

Fig. 9   High side pressure specifications

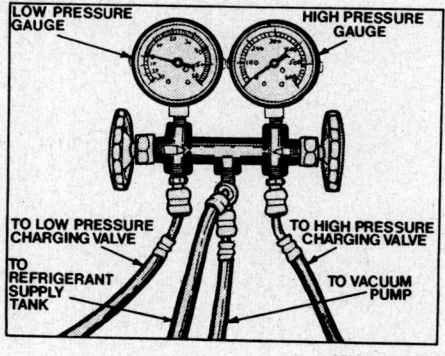

GC7029100026000X

Fig. 10   Manifold gauge set hose connections

System Service

NOTE: On Air Bag Equipped Models, Refer To "Air Bag System Precautions" Located In The Front Of This Manual For System Disarming & Arming Procedures.

NOTE: Refer To "Computer Relearn Procedures" Located In The Front Of This Manual When Battery Power To The Computer Has Been Interrupted.

NOTE: Prior To Performing Any Service Operations Listed In This Section, Consult The "Technical Service Bulletins" Section For Related Information.

INDEX

	Page No.		Page No.		Page No.
Oil Charge Data Table	16-7	Oil Charge	16-7	Oil Level Check	16-8

OIL CHARGE

When replacing certain components of an air conditioning system, an oil charge must be added to the system. Refer to "Oil Charge Data Table" for oil charge specifications.

If the refrigerant charge is abruptly lost due to a large refrigerant leak, approximately three ounces of refrigerant oil will be carried out of the system with the refrigerant. Upon replacement of a component which caused a large refrigerant leak, add three ounces of oil to the system plus the amount required for any component replaced as outlined in "Oil Charge Data Table." If possible, add oil directly to the replacement component.

OIL CHARGE DATA TABLE

Model	Year	Compressor Model	Oil Charge (Fl. Oz.) When Replacing Component				
			Compressor	Evaporator	Condenser	Accumulator	Receiver & Dehydrator
BUICK							
Century	2004–05	V-5	2.00④	3.00④	1.00④	⑩	—
LaCrosse	2005	7CVC	2.00④	3.00④	2.00④	⑩	—
	2006–08	7CVC	2.00④	3.00④	1.00④	⑩	—
LeSabre	2004–05	V-5	2.00④	3.00④	1.00④	2.00⑩	—
Lucerne	2007–08	Denso	2.50	1.40	1.40	—	—
Park Avenue	2004–05	V-5	2.00④	3.00④	1.00④	⑩	—
Regal	2004	V-5	2.00④	3.00④	1.00④	⑩	—
CADILLAC							
CTS	2004–07	Denso	1.18④	1.35④	1.35④	—	—
	2008	Denso	2.50④	1.35④	1.35④	—	—
DeVille	2004–05	Mitsubishi ASTT	2.70	1.00	1.00	4.00⑩	—
DTS	2006–08	Denso	2.50	1.40	1.40	—	—
Seville	2004	Mitsubishi ASTT	2.70	1.00	1.00	4.00⑩	—
STS	2005–08	Denso 7SBU16	4.73④	1.35④	1.35④	—	—
XLR	2004–08	Delphi CVC	5.00④	1.50④	2.00④	—	2.00
CHEVROLET							
Aveo	2005–08	V-5	③	—	—	⑤	—
Cavalier	2004–05	CVC6	2.50④	1.00④	1.00④	1.50⑤	—
Cobalt	2006–08	CVC6	2.50④	.75④	.75④	—	—
Corvette	2004	V-7	2.00④	2.00④	2.00④	2.00⑩	—
	2005–08	CVC	5.00④	1.50④	2.00④	—	2.00⑦
Impala	2005	CVC7	2.50④	3.00	2.00	—	1.00⑦
	2006–08	CVC7	2.00④	3.00④	1.00④	—	—

Continued

OIL CHARGE DATA TABLE—Continued

Model	Year	Compressor Model	Oil Charge (Fl. Oz.) When Replacing Component				
			Compressor	Evaporator	Condenser	Accumulator	Receiver & Dehydrator
CHEVROLET							
Malibu	2004–08	CVC6	2.50④	1.50④	1.00④	—	—
Monte Carlo	2004–05	CVC7	2.50④	3.00	2.00	—	1.00⑦
	2006–07	CVC7	2.00④	3.00④	1.00④	—	—
OLDSMOBILE							
Alero	2004⑧	V-5	2.00④	3.00④	1.00④	2.00⑩	—
PONTIAC							
Bonneville	2004–05①	V-5	2.00④	3.00④	1.00④	2.00⑩	—
	2005②	Mitsubishi	2.70④	1.00④	1.00④	4.00④	—
Grand Am	2004–05⑨	CVC7	2.50④	2.00④	1.00④	1.50⑥	—
	2004–05⑧	V-5	2.00④	3.00④	1.00④	2.00⑩	—
Grand Prix	2004–05	CVC7	2.50④	3.00	2.00	—	1.00⑦
	2006–08	7CVC	2.00④	3.00④	1.00④	—	—
GTO	2004–06	V-7	2.00④	2.00④	2.00④	2.00	—
G5	2007–08	CVC6	2.50④	.75④	.75④	—	—
G6	2005–08	CVC6 & CVC7	2.50④	1.50④	1.00④	—	—
Solstice	2006–08	Sanden PXV16	2.50④	1.00④	1.00④	—	—
Sunfire	2004–05⑨	CVC6	2.50④	1.00④	1.00④	1.50⑦	—
Vibe	2004–08	CVC6	2.50④	2.00④	2.00④	—	2.00④
SATURN							
AURA	2007–08	CVC7	2.5④	1.50④	1.00④	—	—
ION	2004–07	CVC6	2.50④	.75④	.75④	—	—
L-Series	2004–05	Zexcel	.37	2.43	1.28	—	.37
SKY	2007–08	Sanden PXV16	2.50④	1.00④	1.00④	—	—

① — 3.8L engine.
② — 4.6L engine.
③ — Drain oil from old compressor and measure, then drain new compressor. If more than 1 ounce is drained from old compressor, add equal amount to new compressor. If less than 1 ounce is drained from compressor, add 2 ounces.
④ — If more than specified amount of PAG oil was drained from component, add equal amount of new oil to component.
⑤ — Drain oil from accumulator and measure. Add equal amount of oil to new accumulator, plus specified amount.
⑥ — Drain oil from accumulator and measure. Add equal amount of oil to new accumulator, plus 1.5 ounces. If no oil is drained, add 1.5 ounces to new accumulator.
⑦ — Add PAG oil equal to amount drained from old accumulator or receiver dehydrator, plus specified amount.
⑧ — 3.4L engine.
⑨ — 2.2L DOHC engine.
⑩ — Drain oil from accumulator and measure. Add equal amount of oil to new accumulator, plus 2 ounces. If no oil is drained, add 2 ounces to new accumulator.

OIL LEVEL CHECK

Air conditioning oil levels can only be inspected with system discharged and compressor removed from vehicle. Replacement compressor may be shipped with new refrigerant oil. Drain the new oil into a suitable container and retain for later use.

1. Operate system for several minutes to stabilize system. Turn engine Off.
2. Discharge A/C system using a suitable refrigerant recovery/recycling station.
3. Remove compressor from vehicle.
4. Drain and measure refrigerant oil from old compressor through suction and discharge ports, and drain plug.
5. If no compressor oil leaks were noted and more than one ounce of oil is drained, add drained amount using new refrigerant oil.
6. If less than one ounce of oil is drained from compressor, add two ounces of new refrigerant oil.
7. When replacing other A/C components, add specified amount of new refrigerant oil to component as detailed in "Oil Charge Data Table."
8. Install compressor.
9. Evacuate and recharge system, perform leak test.
10. Ensure A/C system is operating properly.

Specifications

INDEX

	Page No.		Page No.		Page No.
A/C Specifications	16-9	Belt Tension	16-10	Charging Valve Location	16-10

A/C SPECIFICATIONS

Model	Year	Refrigerant Capacity, Lbs.	Refrigerant Type	Compressor Oil Viscosity	Total System Oil Capacity, Oz.	Compressor Clutch Air Gap, Inch
BUICK						
Century	2004–05	2.20	R-134a	②	9.00	⑤
LaCrosse	2005	2.30	R-134a	②	⑥	.012–.024
	2006–08	1.35	R-134a	②	5.0	.012–.024
LeSabre	2004–05	2.20	R-134a	②	9.00	.015–.020
Lucerne	2007–08	1.43	R-134a	②	4.7	—
Park Avenue	2004–05	2.20	R-134a	②	9.00	.015–.020
Regal	2004	2.20	R-134a	②	9.00	⑤
CADILLAC						
CTS	2004–07	1.30	R-134a	②	4.75	—
	2008	1.20	R-134a	②	3.72	—
DeVille	2004–05	2.20	R-134a	②	8.70	—
DTS	2006–08	1.43	R-134a	②	4.70	—
Seville	2004	2.20	R-134a	②	8.70	—
STS	2005–08	1.38	R-134a	②	4.73	—
XLR	2004–08	1.10	R-134a	②	5.00	—
CHEVROLET						
Aveo	2004–05	1.32	R-134a	⑨	7.40	.015–.025
	2006	1.32	R-134a	⑨	6.80	.015–.025
	2007–08	1.13	R-134a	⑨	6.80	.015–.025
Cavalier	2004–05	1.50	R-134a	②	5.00	.012–.024
Cobalt	2005–08	.90	R-134a	②	5.00	.012–.024
Corvette	2004	1.75	R-134a	②	9.00	.015
	2005–08	1.10	R-134a	②	5.00	.011–.024
Impala	2004	2.20	R-134a	②	9.00	⑤
	2005	2.30	R-134a	②	8.00	.012–.024
	2006–08	④	R-134a	②	5.00	.012–.024
Malibu	2004–08	1.10	R-134a	②	5.00	.012–.024
Monte Carlo	2004–05	2.30	R-134a	②	8.00	.012–.024
	2006–07	④	R-134a	②	5.00	.012–.024
OLDSMOBILE						
Alero	2004	1.35	R-134a	②	⑦	.015
PONTIAC						
Bonneville	2004–05	2.20	R-134a	②	⑧	.015–.020
Grand Am	2004–05	1.35	R-134a	②	⑦	.015
Grand Prix	2004–05	2.30	R-134a	②	5.00	.012–.024
	2006–08	④	R-134a	②	5.00	.012–.024
GTO	2004–06	1.75	R-134a	②	9.00	.015
G5	2007–08	.90	R-134a	②	5.00	.012–.024
G6	2005–08	1.10	R-134a	②	5.00	.012–.024
Solstice	2006–08	⑩	R-134a	②	4.00	—
Sunfire	2004–05	1.50	R-134a	②	5.00	.012–.024
Vibe	2004–08	1.48	R-134a	②	8.00	.012–.024

Continued

AIR CONDITIONING

A/C SPECIFICATIONS—Continued

Model	Year	Refrigerant Capacity, Lbs.	Refrigerant Type	Compressor Oil Viscosity	Total System Oil Capacity, Oz.	Compressor Clutch Air Gap, Inch
SATURN						
AURA	2007–08	1.10	R-134a	②	5.00	.012–.024
ION	2004–06	.90	R-134a	①	5.00	.012–.024
L-Series	2004–06	2.09	R-134a	③	7.43	.012–.024
SKY	2007–08	⑩	R-134a	②	4.00	—

① — PAG (Polyalkaline Glycol) synthetic refrigerant oil (Saturn part number 22695048), or equivalent.

② — PAG (Polyalkaline Glycol) synthetic refrigerant oil (GM part number 12378526), or equivalent.

③ — PAG oil Saturn part number 21030821, or equivalent.

④ — 3.5L engine, 1.35 lbs.; 5.3L engine, 1.2 lbs.

⑤ — Conventional mount compressor, .015–.020 inch; direct mount compressor, .015 inch.

⑥ — 3.6L engine, 6.60 oz.; 3.8L engine, 8.00 oz.

⑦ — 2.2L engine, 5.00 oz.; 3.4L engine, 9.00 oz.

⑧ — 3.8L engine, 9.00 oz.; 4.6L engine, 8.70 oz.

⑨ — Synthetic Polyalkaline Glycol (PAG) Union Carbide 488, or equivalent.

⑩ — 1st design condenser, 1.63 lbs; 2nd design condenser, 1.03 lbs., 2007 model year.

CHARGING VALVE LOCATION

The high pressure charging valve is located on the high pressure line and the low pressure charging valve is located either on the accumulator or low pressure line.

BELT TENSION

Belt tension is controlled automatically by the belt tensioner.

COOLING FANS

TABLE OF CONTENTS

Page No.

ELECTRIC COOLING FANS, GENERAL MOTORS 17-1

Page No.

SATURN 17-61

Electric Cooling Fans, General Motors

NOTE: On Air Bag Equipped Models, Refer To Air Bag System Precautions Located In The Front Of This Manual For System Disarming & Arming Procedures.

NOTE: "Wire Color Code & Electrical Symbol Identification" Located In The Front Of This Manual Can Be Used As An Aid When Using Wiring Circuits Found In This Section.

NOTE: Refer To "Computer Relearn Procedures" Located In The Front Of This Manual When Battery Power To The Computer Has Been Interrupted.

INDEX

Page No.

Component Replacement 17-7
  Cooling Fan Assembly 17-7
    Alero & Grand Am 17-7
    Aveo. 17-7
    Bonneville 17-7
    Cavalier & Sunfire 17-8
    Century, Grand Prix, Impala,
      Monte Carlo & Regal 17-8
    Cobalt & G5 17-8
    Corvette 17-8
    CTS 17-9
    DeVille. 17-9
    DTS 17-10
    GTO 17-10
    G6. 17-10
    LaCrosse 17-11
    LeSabre & Park Avenue 17-11
    Lucerne 17-11
    Malibu & Malibu Classic 17-12
    Seville 17-12
    Solstice 17-13
    STS 17-13
    Vibe 17-13
    XLR 17-13
Description 17-2
  Alero & Grand Am 17-2
  Aveo. 17-2
  Bonneville & LeSabre 17-2
  Cavalier & Sunfire 17-2
  Century & Regal 17-2
  Cobalt & G5 17-2
  Corvette 17-2
    2004. 17-2
    2005–08 17-2
  CTS 17-3

Page No.

  DeVille & Seville 17-3
  DTS & STS 17-3
  GTO 17-3
  G6. 17-4
  Grand Prix 17-3
  Impala & Monte Carlo. 17-4
    2004–05 17-4
    2006–08 17-4
  LaCrosse 17-4
  Lucerne 17-4
  Malibu & Malibu Classic 17-5
    2004–08 17-5
  Park Avenue 17-5
  Solstice 17-5
    2.0L Engine. 17-5
    2.4L Engine. 17-5
  Vibe 17-5
  XLR 17-5
Precautions. 17-2
  Air Bag Systems. 17-2
  Battery Ground Cable. 17-2
System Diagnosis & Testing 17-6
  Diagnostic Aids 17-6
  Diagnostic Tests 17-6
    Alero & Grand Am 17-6
    Aveo. 17-6
    Bonneville & LeSabre. 17-6
    Cavalier & Sunfire 17-6
    Century & Regal 17-6
    Cobalt & G5 17-6
    Corvette 17-6
    CTS 17-6
    DeVille & Seville 17-6
    DTS 17-6
    GTO 17-6

Page No.

    Grand Prix. 17-6
    G6. 17-6
    Impala & Monte Carlo. 17-6
    LaCrosse 17-6
    Lucerne 17-6
    Malibu & Malibu Classic 17-7
    Park Avenue 17-7
    Solstice 17-7
    STS 17-7
    Vibe 17-7
    XLR 17-7
Wiring Diagrams 17-6
  Alero & Grand Am 17-6
  Aveo. 17-6
  Bonneville & LeSabre 17-6
  Cavalier & Sunfire 17-6
  Century & Regal 17-6
  Cobalt & G5 17-6
  Corvette 17-6
  CTS 17-6
  DeVille & Seville 17-6
  DTS 17-6
  Grand Prix 17-6
  GTO 17-6
  G6. 17-6
  Impala & Monte Carlo. 17-6
  LaCrosse 17-6
  Lucerne 17-6
  Malibu & Malibu Classic 17-6
  Park Avenue 17-6
  Solstice 17-6
  STS 17-6
  Vibe 17-6
  XLR 17-6
Troubleshooting 17-6

PRECAUTIONS

Air Bag Systems

Refer to "Air Bag System Precautions" in the front of this manual for system disarming and arming procedures.

Battery Ground Cable

Prior to service, disconnect battery ground cable and isolate as required.

DESCRIPTION

Alero & Grand Am

The electric cooling fans are controlled by the Body Control Module (BCM) which enables the fans through the PCM. The PCM enables the ground path for the three cooling fan relays. The relays are used to control the high current flow to power the cooling fan motors.

When minimum cooling is required, the BCM will command the PCM to energize the No. 1 cooling fan relay and since both fans are connected in series through the Mode Control relay, both fans will run at low speed. When maximum cooling is required, the BCM will command the PCM to energize all three cooling fan relays. Power is supplied to the lefthand fan through the No. 1 cooling fan relay and is grounded through the Mode Control relay. The righthand fan is powered directly through the No. 2 cooling fan relay, causing both fans to run at high speed.

Aveo

The cooling fans are actuated by the engine control module (ECM) using a low speed cooling fan relay and a high speed cooling fan relay. On A/C equipped vehicles a series/parallel cooling fan relay is used. The ECM will turn the cooling fans ON at low speed when coolant temperature reaches (109°F) and high speed at (207°F). The ECM will change the cooling fan from high speed to low speed at (201°F) and turn the cooling fans OFF at (194°F).

The ECM will turn the cooling fans ON at low speed when the A/C system is ON. The ECM will change to high speed when the coolant temperature reaches (207°F) or high side A/C pressure reaches (273 psi). The cooling fans will return to low speed when the coolant temperature reaches (210°F) or high side A/C pressure reaches (210 psi).

Bonneville & LeSabre

The PCM controls the operation of the cooling fans. This is accomplished by providing a ground path for the cooling fan relay coils within the PCM. The relay contacts will close and complete the circuit between the fusible link at the battery junction block and the fan motors. Whenever the fans are commanded on both fans will be running.

Power for the fan motors is supplied through the Cooling Fan fuse in the righthand Maxi fuse block. The cooling fan relays are energized when current from the Cooling Fan fuse flows through the relay coils to ground through the PCM.

Low speed fan operation will be commanded on anytime engine coolant temperature exceeds 221°F, A/C is requested and ambient temperature is more than 48°F, or A/C pressure is greater than 190 psi.

Before the PCM operates the fans at high speed, it will delay control of the series/parallel and high speed fan relays for six seconds. This six second delay ensures the cooling fan electrical load will not exceed the capacity of the system.

Cavalier & Sunfire

Cooling fan operation is controlled by the PCM through the fan relay. The PCM uses signals from the engine coolant temperature sensor, intake air temperature sensor, A/C refrigerant pressure sensor and vehicle speed sensor to determine when and how long the fan should operate. The PCM turns the cooling fan on by providing a ground path for the cooling fan control circuit which activates the coolant fan relay.

The relay will be commanded on anytime engine coolant temperature exceeds 223°F, A/C clutch is requested, vehicle speed is less than 38 mph or any Diagnostic Trouble Code (DTC) that causes the MIL lamp to illuminate.

Century & Regal

The engine coolant fan motors receive power from maxifuses located in the underhood electrical center.

During low speed fan operation, the PCM supplies a ground path for the No. 1 Cool Fan relay. This energizes the relay coil, closes the fan relay contacts and supplies current to the primary cooling fan. The ground path for the primary is through the No. 2 Cool Fan relay and secondary fan motor. This results in a series circuit with both fans running at low speed.

To operate the fans at high speed, the PCM first supplies a ground path for the No. 1 Cool Fan relay, then after a three second delay the PCM supplies a ground circuit for the No. 2 and No. 3 Cool Fan relays. This results in a parallel circuit with both fan running at high speed.

Cobalt & G5

The engine cooling fan system consists of one cooling fan and two relays. Voltage is supplied to the relays through the 30 A cooling fan 1 and 30 A cooling fan 2 fuses. The engine control module (ECM) controls the low speed fan operation by grounding the cooling fan 1 relay control circuit. When the cooling fan 1 relay is energized, voltage is delivered to the cooling fan low speed winding. The ECM controls the high speed fan operation by grounding the cool fan 2 relay control circuit. When the cooling fan 2 relay is energized, voltage is delivered to the

cooling fan high speed winding. The cooling fan motor is grounded through its own ground circuit.

The ECM commands Low Speed Fans ON under the following conditions: Engine coolant temperature exceeds approximately 223°F. A/C refrigerant pressure exceeds 190 psi. After the vehicle is shut off, the ECT at key-off is greater than 284°F and system voltage is more than 12 volts. The fans will stay on for approximately 3 minutes.

The ECM commands High Speed Fans ON under the following conditions: ECT reaches 230°F. A/C refrigerant pressure exceeds 240 psi and when certain DTCs are set.

Corvette

2004

The PCM controls low speed operation by providing a ground path for the Cool Fan 1 relay. This closes the relay switch and allows current to flow from the battery, through the switch to the lefthand cooling fan. The ground circuit for the lefthand fan motor runs through the Cool Fan 3 relay to the righthand cooling fan. This creates a series circuit with both fans running at low speed.

The PCM controls high speed fan operation by providing a ground path for Cool Fan 1, Cool Fan 2 and Cool Fan 3 relays. Providing separate ground paths for the relays creates a parallel circuit, which allows both fans to run at high speed.

2005-08

The engine cooling fan is a variable speed fan. The ECM controls the fan speed by sending a pulse width modulated signal to the cooling fan control module. The cooling fan control module varies the voltage drop across the engine cooling fan motor in relation to the pulse width modulated signal.

Cooling fan speed is effected by many different conditions and can be adjusted from 10% to 90% duty cycle (PWM), 90% is considered high speed fan. When multiple cooling fan speed requests are received the ECM uses the highest cooling fan speed of all the requests.

The ECM commands the cooling fan ON under the following conditions: Cooling fan duty cycle starts when engine coolant temperature reaches approximately (204°F) and reaches high speed at temperatures above (235°F). Cooling fan duty cycle starts when A/C pressure reaches approximately (160 psi) and reaches high speed at A/C pressures of above (360 psi). At engine oil temperature above approximately (302°F) the cooling fan duty cycle will be commanded to high speed. At transmission oil temperature above approximately (270°F) the cooling fan duty cycle will be commanded to high speed. After the vehicle is shut OFF if the engine coolant temperature at key-off is greater then (235°F) or the A/C pressure above is greater than (249 psi) the cooling fan duty cycle is set to 50%, low speed. If the coolant temperature drops below (230°F) and the A/C PRES-SURE DROPS BELOW (241 psi) then fan will shut OFF. The fans will automatically shut OFF after 2 minutes regardless of coolant temperature.

CTS

The engine cooling fan system consists of, two electrical cooling fans and three fan relays. The relays are arranged in a series/parallel that allows the Engine Control Module (ECM) to operate both fans together at low or high speeds. The fans and relays receive battery positive power from the underhood fuse block. The ground path is provided at ground circuit G104.

During low speed operation, the ECM supplies the ground path to the low speed fan cooling relay control circuit. This energizes the low speed fan relay coil, closes the relay contacts, and supplies positive battery voltage to the lefthand or (low) speed cooling fan motor. The ground path for the lefthand cooling fan is through the cooling fan S/P relay and the righthand cooling fan. The result is a series circuit with both fans running at low speed.

During high speed operation the ECM supplies the ground path for the high speed fan relay control circuit. After a three second delay, the ECM supplies a ground path to the high speed fan relay control circuit. This energizes the cooling fan S/P relay coil, closes the relay contacts and provides a ground path for the lefthand cooling fan. At the same time the high speed fan relay coil is energized closing the relay contacts and provides positive voltage from the high fan fuse in the cooling fan voltage supply circuit to the righthand cooling fan. During this high speed fan operation both engine cooling fan have there own ground path. the results is a parallel circuit with both fans running at high speed.

The ECM commands the low speed fans On under the following conditions: Engine coolant temperature exceeds approximately (202°F). A/C refrigerant pressure exceeds (210 psi). After the vehicle is shut Off and the ignition key is in the Off position, and coolant temperature is (214°F), the low speed fans will run for a minimum of 60 seconds. After coolant temperature drops below 214°F the fans will shut Off. The fan will automatically shut Off after three minutes regardless of coolant temperature. If engine coolant temperature exceeds approximately (220°F) or the A/C refrigerant pressure exceeds 265 psi. The ECM will record a DTC and the engine MIL light will come on and a code will be recorded into the ECM memory.

DeVille & Seville

The PCM will command low speed fan operation when engine temperature is in excess of 229°F, transaxle fluid temperature is greater than 302°F, when A/C is requested, or after the vehicle is shutoff and coolant temperature is more than 304°F and system voltage is more than 12 volts the fans will stay on for approximately three minutes.

The PCM will command high fan speed operation when engine coolant temperature is in excess of 234°F, transaxle fluid temperature is greater than 304°F, or when certain DTCs are set.

To operate the fans at low speed the PCM provides a ground path for the Cooling Fan No. 1 relay. This allows current to flow through both cooling fans in a series circuit to ground.

To operate the fans at high speed the PCM provides a ground path for all three cooling fan relays. This changes the circuit to parallel and operates both fans at high speed.

DTS & STS

The engine cooling fan system consists of two puller type electrical cooling fans and three fan relays. The relays are arranged in a series parallel (S/P) configuration that allows the engine control module (ECM) to operate both fans together at low or high speeds. The cooling fans and fan relays receive battery positive voltage from the underhood fuse block. The ground path is provided at G104.

During low speed operation, the ECM supplies the ground path for the low speed fan relay through the low speed cooling fan relay control circuit. This energizes the low speed fan relay, closes the relay contacts, and supplies battery positive voltage from the low fan fuse through the cooling fan motor supply voltage circuit to the lefthand cooling fan. The ground path for the lefthand cooling fan is through the cooling fan S/P relay and the righthand cooling fan. The result is a series circuit with both fans running at low speed.

During high speed operation the ECM supplies the ground path for the low speed fan relay through the low speed cooling fan relay control circuit After a three second delay, the ECM supplies a ground path for the high speed fan relay and the cooling fan S/P relay through the high speed cooling fan relay control circuit. This energizes the cooling fan S/P relay coil, closes the relay contacts, and provides a ground path for lefthand cooling fan. At the same time , the high speed fan relay is energized closing the relay contacts, and provides battery positive voltage from the high fan fuse on the cooling fan motor supply voltage circuit, to the righthand cooling fan. During high speed fan operation, both engine cooling fans have their own ground path. The result is a parallel circuit with both fans running at high speed.

The ECM commands the low speed cooling fans ON under the following conditions: Engine coolant temperature exceeds approximately (202°F). A/C refrigerant pressure exceeds (210 psi). After the vehicle is shut OFF, if the engine coolant temperature at key-off is greater then (214°F), the fans will shut OFF. The fans will automatically shut OFF after three minutes, regardless of coolant temperature.

The ECM commands the fans ON under the following conditions: Engine coolant temperature exceeds approximately (202°F). A/C refrigerant pressure exceeds approximately (265 psi). When certain

DTCs set. At idle and very low vehicle speeds the cooling fans are only allowed to increase in speed, if required. This ensures isle stability by preventing the fans from cycling between high and low speed.

Grand Prix

The cooling fan motors receive power from maxifuses located in the underhood accessory wiring junction block.

During low speed fan operation, the PCM supplies a ground path for the Cool Fan 1 relay. This energizes the relay coil, closes the relay contacts and supplies current to the lefthand cooling fan motor. The ground path for the lefthand cooling fan motor is through the Cool Fan relay and righthand coolant fan motor. This results in a series circuit with both fans running at low speed.

To operate the fans at high speed, the PCM first supplies a ground path for the Cool Fan 1 relay. After a 3–5 second delay, the PCM supplies a ground path for the Cool Fan and Cool Fan 2 relays. The result is a parallel circuit with both fans running at high speed.

GTO

The cooling system includes two dual speed engine cooling fans motors, both of which drive fans with five asymmetrical blades to reduce air noise. The fans remove heat from both engine coolant flowing through the radiator and the refrigerant flowing through the air conditioning condenser. The fan and motor assemblies are mounted on a common shroud, which in turn is mounted onto the engine side of the radiator. The A/C condenser is mounted to the front of the radiator.

There are two relays used to control fan operation. The engine cooling fan relay one for low speed operation and the engine cooling fan relay two for high speed operation. The engine cooling fan relay one is energized by the body control module (BCM) in response to a request from the powertrain control module (PCM). The engine cooling fan relay two is energized by the PCM. After the PCM requests a change in the state of engine cooling fan one, the BCM will send a serial data response message back to the PCM confirming it received the message. Serial data communication between the PCM and BCM is via the powertrain interface module (PIM). The PCM determines when to enable and disable both engine cooling fan relays based on inputs from the A/C request signal, the engine coolant temperature (ECT) sensor and the vehicle speed sensor (VSS).

The engine cooling fan relay one will be turned ON and both fans driven at low speed when the A/C request indicates yes and either: Vehicle speed is less than (19 mph). A/C refrigerant pressure is greater than (218 psi). ECT is greater than (227°F). If an ECT fault is detected and a DTC is set. When and ECT sensor failure in conjunction with an intake air temperature (IAT) sensor failure is detected by the PCM.

COOLING FANS

When the ignition switch is turned from ON and OFF and the ECT is above (235°F), the BCM continues to energize the engine cooling fan relay for 4 minutes. The low speed cooling fan run-on time has a minimum default value of 30 seconds.

The engine cooling fan relay two is controlled by the PCM. The PCM will turn on the engine cooling high speed relay fan if the engine cooling fan relay one has been on for two seconds and the following conditions are satisfied: There is a BCM to PIM message response fault which will cause a PIM DTC to set. An ECT sensor fault is detected and a DTC is set. The ECT is greater than (235°F). The A/C refrigerant pressure is greater than (348 psi). The engine cooling fan relay two will be turned off when any of the following conditions have been met: The ECT is less than (227.3°F). An A/C request is not indicated. An A/C request is indicated and the A/C refrigerant pressure is less than (276 psi).

G6

The engine cooling fan consists of two electrical cooling fans and three relays. The relays are arranged in a series/parallel configuration that allows the powertrain control module (PCM) to operate both fan together at low or high speeds. The cooling fans and fan relays receive battery positive voltage from the underhood fuse block. The ground path is provided at G106.

During low speed operating the PCM supplies the ground path for the cooling fan one relay through the low speed cooling fan relay control circuit. After a three second delay, the PCM supplies a ground path for the cooling fan two relay and the cooling fan S/P relay through the high speed cooling fan relay control circuit. This energizes the cooling fan two relay coil, closes the relay contacts, and provides a ground path for the lefthand cooling fan. At the same time the cooling fan S/P relay coil is energized closing the relay contact and provides batter positive voltage from the cooling fan two fuse on the cooling fan motor supply voltage circuit to the righthand cooling fan. During high speed fan operation, both engine cooling fans have their own ground path. The result is a parallel circuit with both fans running at high speed.

The PCM commands Low Speed Fans on under the following conditions: Engine coolant temperature exceeds approximately (223°F). When A/C is requested and the ambient temperature is more than (122°F). A/C refrigerant pressure exceeds (190 psi). After the vehicle is shut off if the engine coolant temperature at key-off is more than (284°F) and system voltage is more than 12 volts. The fans will stay on for approximately three minutes.

The PCM commands High Speed Fans on under the following conditions: Engine coolant temperature exceeds approximately (233°F). A/C refrigerant pressure exceeds (240 psi). When certain DTCs set.

Impala & Monte Carlo

2004-05

This coolant fan system is equipped with two electric cooling fans and three fan relays which are controlled by the PCM. The relays are wired in a series/parallel arrangement that allows the PCM to operate both fans together at low or high speed.

The PCM controls low fan speed operation by grounding the control circuit for Cool Fan No. 1 relay. The relay supplies current to the No. 1 fan motor. The ground path for the No. 1 fan motor is through the Cool Fan No. 2 relay and the No. 2 fan motor. This results in a series circuit which operates both fans at low speed. The PCM operates the cooling fans at low speed whenever engine coolant temperature exceeds 223°F, A/C operation is requested and ambient temperature is greater than 50°F, A/C refrigerant pressure is greater than 190 psi, or the engine is shutoff and coolant temperature is more than 284.°

To control high speed fan operation, the PCM grounds the control circuit for the Cool Fan No. 1 relay. Then after a three second delay, the PCM grounds the control circuit for Cool Fan No. 2 and No. 3 relays. When the Cool Fan No. 2 relay is energized, both the fans have their own ground path creating a parallel circuit. This parallel circuit causes both fans to operate at high speed. The PCM operates the cooling fans at high speed whenever engine coolant temperature exceeds 230°F, A/C refrigerant pressure exceeds 240 psi.

2006-08

The engine cooling fan system consists of 2 electrical cooling fans and 3 fan relays. The relays are arranged in a series/parallel configuration that allows the engine control module (ECM) to operate both fans together at low or high speeds. The cooling fans receive positive voltage from the cooling fan relays which receive battery positive voltage from the underhood fuse block.

During low speed operation, the ECM supplies the ground path for the low speed fan relay through the low speed cooling fan relay control circuit. This energizes the low speed fan relay coil, closes the relay contacts, and supplies battery positive voltage from the low fan fuse through the cooling fan motor supply voltage circuit to the left cooling fan. The ground path for the left cooling fan is through the cooling fan S/P relay and the right cooling fan. The result is a series circuit with both fans running at low speed.

During high speed operation the ECM supplies the ground path for the low speed fan relay through the low speed cooling fan relay control circuit. The ECM grounds the high speed fan relay and the cooling fan control relay through the high speed cooling fan relay control circuit. This energizes the cooling fan S/P relay coil, closes the relay contacts, and provides a ground path for the left cooling fan. At the same time the

high speed fan relay coil is energized closing the relay contacts and provides battery positive voltage from the high fan fuse on the cooling fan motor supply voltage circuit to the right cooling fan. During high speed fan operation, both engine cooling fans have their own ground path. The result is a parallel circuit with both fans running at high speed.

LaCrosse

The engine cooling fan system consists of two electrical cooling fans and three fan relays. The relays are arranged in a series/parallel configuration that allows the powertrain control module (PCM) to operate both fans together at low or high speeds. The cooling fans and fan relays receive battery positive voltage from the underhood fuse block. The ground path is provided at G100.

During low speed operation, the PCM supplies the ground path for the low speed fan relay through the low speed cooling fan relay control circuit. This energizes the fan 1 relay coil, closes the relay contacts, and supplies battery positive voltage from the fan 1 fuse through the cooling fan motor supply voltage circuit to the lefthand cooling fan. The ground path for the lefthand cooling fan is through the fan 2 relay and the righthand cooling fan. The result is a series circuit with both fans running at low speed.

During high speed operation the PCM supplies the ground path for the fan 1 relay through the low speed cooling fan relay control circuit. After a 3-second delay, the PCM supplies a ground path for the fan 2 relay and the fan 3 relay through the high speed cooling fan relay control circuit. This energizes the fan 2 relay coil, closes the relay contacts, and provides a ground path for the lefthand cooling fan. At the same time the fan 3 relay coil is energized closing the relay contacts and provides battery positive voltage from the fan 2 fuse on the cooling fan motor supply voltage circuit to the righthand cooling fan. During high speed fan operation, both engine cooling fans have there own ground path. The result is a parallel circuit with both fans running at high speed.

Lucerne

The engine cooling fan system consists of 2 puller type electrical cooling fans and 3 fan relays. The relays are arranged in a series parallel (S/P) configuration that allows the engine control module (ECM) to operate both fans together at low or high speeds. The cooling fans and fan relays receive battery positive voltage from the underhood fuse block. The ground path is provided at G104.

During low speed operation, the ECM supplies the ground path for the low speed fan relay through the low speed cooling fan relay control circuit. This energizes the low speed fan relay coil, closes the relay contacts, and supplies battery positive voltage from the low fan fuse through the cooling fan motor supply voltage circuit to the left cooling fan. The ground path for the left cooling fan is through the cooling fan S/P relay and the right cooling fan. The result is a series circuit with both fans running at low speed.

During high speed operation the ECM supplies the ground path for the low speed fan relay through the low speed cooling fan relay control circuit. After a 3 second delay, the ECM supplies a ground path for the high speed fan relay and the cooling fan S/P relay through the high speed cooling fan relay control circuit. This energizes the cooling fan S/P relay coil, closes the relay contacts, and provides a ground path for the left cooling fan. At the same time, the high speed fan relay coil is energized closing the relay contacts, and provides battery positive voltage from the high fan fuse on the cooling fan motor supply voltage circuit, to the right cooling fan. During high speed fan operation, both engine cooling fans have their own ground path. The result is a parallel circuit with both fans running at high speed.

Malibu & Malibu Classic

2004–08

The engine cooling fan system consists of two electrical cooling fans and three fan relays. The relays are arranged in a series/parallel configuration that allows the Engine Control Module (ECM) to operate both fans together at low or high speeds. The cooling fans and fan relays receive battery positive voltage from the underhood fuse block.

During low speed operation, the ECM supplies the ground path for the low speed fan relay through the low speed cooling fan relay control circuit. This energizes the cooling fan No. 1 relay coil, closes the relay contacts and supplies battery positive voltage from the cool fan No. 1 fuse through the cooling fan motor supply voltage circuit to the lefthand cooling fan. The ground path for the lefthand cooling fan is through the cooling fan s/p relay and the righthand cooling fan. The result is a series circuit with both fans running at low speed.

During high speed operation the ECM supplies the ground path for the cooling fan No. 1 relay through the low speed cooling fan relay control circuit. After a 3-second delay, the ECM supplies a ground path for the cooling fan No. 2 relay and the cooling fan s/p relay through the high speed cooling fan relay control circuit. This energizes the cooling fan No. 2 relay coil, closes the relay contacts and provides a ground path for the lefthand cooling fan. At the same time the cooling fan s/p relay coil is energized closing the relay contacts and provides battery positive voltage from the cool fan No. 2 fuse on the cooling fan motor supply voltage circuit to the righthand cooling fan. During high speed fan operation, both engine cooling fans have there own ground path. The result is a parallel circuit with both fans running at high speed.

Park Avenue

Power for the cooling fan motors is supplied by the Cool Fan No. 1 and Cool Fan No. 2 Maxi fuses.

During low speed fan operation, the PCM supplies a ground path for the No. 1 Cool Fan relay through the low speed fan control circuit. This energizes the relay coil, closes the relay contacts and supplies current to the primary cooling fan. The ground path for the primary cooling fan is through the No. 2 Cool Fan (series/parallel) relay and secondary cooling fan motor. This results in a series circuit with both fans running at low speed.

To operate the cooling fans at high speed, the PCM first supplies a ground path for No. 1 Cool Fan relay. After a three second delay the PCM supplies a ground path for the No. 2 and No. 3 Cool Fan relays. During high speed operation, both the primary and secondary cooling fans are supplied current through their respective maxifuse and each fan has its own ground.

Solstice

2.0L ENGINE

The engine cooling fan is a variable speed fan. The engine control module (ECM) controls the fan speed by sending a pulse width modulated (PWM) signal to the cooling fan control module. The cooling fan control module varies the voltage drop across the engine cooling fan motor in relation to the PWM signal. The cooling fan speed can be adjusted from 10 percent to 94 percent duty cycle. 94 percent is considered high speed fan.

2.4L ENGINE

The engine cooling fan system consists of one cooling fan and two relays. Voltage is supplied to the relays through the 30 A cooling fan 1 and 30 A cooling fan 2 fuses. The engine control module (ECM) controls the low speed fan operation by grounding the cooling fan 1 relay control circuit. When the cooling fan 1 relay is energized, voltage is delivered to the cooling fan low speed winding. The ECM controls the high speed fan operation by grounding the cool fan 2 relay control circuit. When the cooling fan 2 relay is energized, voltage is delivered to the cooling fan high speed winding. The cooling fan motor is grounded through its own ground circuit.

The ECM commands Low Speed Fans ON under the following conditions: Engine coolant temperature exceeds approximately 223°F. A/C refrigerant pressure exceeds 190 psi. After the vehicle is shut off, the ECT at key-off is greater than 284°F and system voltage is more than 12 volts. The fans will stay on for approximately 3 minutes.

The ECM commands High Speed Fans ON under the following conditions: ECT reaches 230°F. A/C refrigerant pressure exceeds 240 psi and when certain DTCs are set.

Vibe

The engine cooling fan system of one electrical cooling fan, two fan relays and a fan resistor. The No. 1 relay controls power to the fan motor. The No. 2 relay control the ground path to the fan motor. The gauge fuse supplies ignition voltage to the coils of both the fan motor and the No. 1 fan relay. The Powertrain Control Module (PCM) controls the ground for the coils of both relays. The PCM controls low and high speed fan operation by energizing and de-energizing the No. 2 fan relay which changes the ground path of the fan motor.

During low sped operation when the A/C is operating and engine coolant temperature is below (181°F), The PCM supplies the ground path for the No. 1 fan relay through the fan 1 relay control circuit. This energizes the relay, closes the fan 1 relay contacts, and supplies battery voltage from the RDI fuse through the cooling fan motor supply voltage circuit to the fan motor. The fan motor ground path is through the closed contacts of the de-energized No. 2 fan relay, and the fan resistor to ground circuit No. G103.

During high speed fan operation when the engine coolant temperature reaches (199°F) or the A/C system pressure exceeds (220 psi), the PCM supplies the ground path for fan relay No. 1 through cooling fan 1 relay control circuit. this energizes the relay, closes the No. 1 fan relay contacts, and supplies battery voltage from the RDI fuse through the cooling fan motor supply voltage circuit to the fan motor. The PCM also supplies the ground path for fan relay No. 2. This energizes the relay, switches the fan 2 relay contacts and supplies a ground for the fan motor directly to ground circuit No. G103. The result is a series circuit with the fan running at high speed.

The A/C refrigerant pressure switch is in parallel with the PCM controlled ground for the coil of the No. 2 fan relay. If the A/C system pressure exceeds (220 psi), the pressure switch closes the ground circuit to the coil of the No. 1 fan relay, initiating high speed fan operation. The PCM commands low speed fan operation when all of the following conditions occur: The A/C system is operating. The A/C pressure is below (178 psi). The engine coolant temperature is below (181° F). The PCM commands high speed fan operation when all of the following conditions occur: The engine coolant temperature reaches (199° F). The A/C system pressure exceeds (220 psi).

XLR

The engine cooling fan is a variable speed fan. The ECM controls the fan speed by sending a pulse width modulated signal to the cooling fan control module. The cooling fan control module varies the voltage drop across the engine cooling fan motor in relation to the pulse width modulated signal. Cooling fan speed is effected by many different conditions and can be adjusted from 10% to 90% duty cycle (PWM), 90% is considered high speed fan. When multiple cooling fan speed requests are received the ECM uses the highest cooling fan speed of all the requests.

TROUBLESHOOTING

1. Inspect for open fuses.
2. Inspect for open fusible links.
3. Inspect for corrosion on cooling fan and cooling fan relay connectors.
4. Inspect for clean and tight grounds.

SYSTEM DIAGNOSIS & TESTING

Wiring Diagrams

ALERO & GRAND AM

Refer to **Fig. 1** for wiring diagram.

AVEO

Refer to **Figs. 2 and 3** for wiring diagram.

BONNEVILLE & LESABRE

Refer to **Fig. 4** for wiring diagram.

CAVALIER & SUNFIRE

Refer to **Fig. 5** for wiring diagram.

CENTURY & REGAL

Refer to **Fig. 6** for wiring diagram.

COBALT & G5

Refer to **Figs. 7 through 9** for wiring diagrams.

CORVETTE

Refer to **Figs. 10 and 11** for wiring diagrams.

CTS

Refer to **Fig. 12** for wiring diagram.

DEVILLE & SEVILLE

Refer to **Fig. 13** for wiring diagrams.

DTS

Refer to **Fig. 14** for wiring diagram.

GRAND PRIX

Refer to **Fig. 15** for wiring diagrams.

GTO

Refer to **Fig. 16** for wiring diagram.

G6

Refer to **Fig. 17** for wiring diagram.

IMPALA & MONTE CARLO

Refer to **Figs. 18 and 19** for wiring diagrams.

LACROSSE

Refer to **Fig. 20** for wiring diagram.

LUCERNE

Refer to **Fig. 21** for wiring diagram.

MALIBU & MALIBU CLASSIC

Refer to **Fig. 22** for wiring diagram.

PARK AVENUE

Refer to **Fig. 23** for wiring diagram.

SOLSTICE

Refer to **Fig. 24** for wiring diagram.

STS

Refer to **Fig. 25** for wiring diagram.

VIBE

Refer to **Fig. 26** for wiring diagram.

XLR

Refer to **Fig. 27** for wiring diagram.

Diagnostic Aids

If the temperature light or gauge indicated overheating, but no boil over is detected, the gauge or light should be inspected. The gauge accuracy can also be inspected using a scan tool to compare the coolant temperature reading with the gauge reading.

If the engine is actually overheating, and the gauge indicates overheating, but the cooling fan is not operating, the Engine Coolant Temperature (ETC) sensor may have shifted out of calibration and should be replaced.

If the engine is overheating and the cooling fan is operating, the cooling system should be inspected.

Diagnostic Tests

ALERO & GRAND AM

Refer to **Figs. 28 through 30** for diagnostic procedure. Refer to "Diagnostic Aids" as outlined when referenced by diagnostic tests.

AVEO

2004-05

Refer to **Figs. 31 and 32** for diagnostic procedures.

2006-08

Refer to **Figs. 33 through 35** for diagnostic procedures.

BONNEVILLE & LESABRE

Refer to **Figs. 36 through 38** when performing diagnostic procedures. Refer to "Diagnostic Aids" as previously outlined when referenced by diagnostic tests.

CAVALIER & SUNFIRE

Refer to **Figs. 39 and 40** for diagnostic procedures. Refer to "Diagnostic Aids" when referenced by diagnostic tests.

CENTURY & REGAL

Refer to **Figs. 41 through 43** when performing diagnostic procedures on these systems. Refer to "Diagnostic Aids" when referenced by diagnostic tests.

COBALT & G5

Refer to **Figs. 44 through 46** for diagnostic procedures. Refer to "Diagnostic Aids" as previously outlined when referenced by diagnostic tests.

CORVETTE

2004

Refer to **Figs. 47 through 49** for diagnostic procedures. Refer to "Diagnostic Aids" as previously outlined when referenced by diagnostic tests.

2005-08

Refer to **Figs. 50 through 52** for diagnostic procedures.

CTS

Refer to **Figs. 53 through 56** when performing diagnostic procedures on these systems.

DEVILLE & SEVILLE

Refer to **Figs. 57 through 59** when performing diagnostic procedures. Refer to "Diagnostic Aids" when referenced by diagnostic tests.

DTS

Refer to **Figs. 60 through 62** when performing diagnostic procedures. Refer to "Diagnostic Aids" when referenced by diagnostic tests.

GRAND PRIX

Refer to **Figs. 63 through 65** when performing diagnostic procedures on these systems. Refer to "Diagnostic Aids" as previously outlined when referenced by diagnostic tests.

GTO

Refer to **Figs. 66 and 67** for diagnostic procedures.

G6

Refer to **Figs. 68 through 70** for diagnostic procedures.

IMPALA & MONTE CARLO

Refer to **Figs. 71 through 73** when performing diagnostic procedures on these systems. Refer to "Diagnostic Aids" as previously outlined when referenced by diagnostic tests.

LACROSSE

Refer to **Figs. 74 through 76** when performing diagnostic procedures on these systems. Refer to "Diagnostic Aids" as previously outlined when referenced by diagnostic tests.

LUCERNE

Refer to **Figs. 77 through 79** for diagnostic procedures.

MALIBU & MALIBU CLASSIC

2004-08

Refer to **Figs. 80 through 82** when performing diagnostic procedures on these systems. Refer to "Diagnostic Aids" when referenced by diagnostic tests.

PARK AVENUE

Refer to **Figs. 83 through 85** when performing diagnostic procedures.

SOLSTICE

Refer to **Figs. 86 through 88** for diagnostic procedures.

STS

Refer to **Figs. 89 through 91** for diagnostic procedures.

VIBE

Refer to **Figs. 92 through 97** for diagnostic procedures.

XLR

Refer to **Figs. 98 through 100** for diagnostic procedures.

COMPONENT REPLACEMENT

Cooling Fan Assembly

ALERO & GRAND AM

1. Remove battery and battery tray.
2. Recover A/C refrigerant as outlined in "Air Conditioning" chapter.
3. Drain cooling system into suitable container.
4. Remove radiator inlet hose from radiator.
5. Remove surge tank/radiator outlet hose from surge tank.
6. Remove radiator vent hose from radiator.
7. Remove upper transaxle cooler line.
8. Disconnect refrigerant pressure sensor electrical connector.
9. Remove condenser inlet fitting from discharge hose. Discard sealing washer.
10. Disconnect cooling fan electrical connectors.
11. Remove surge tank/radiator outlet hose retaining bolt from intake manifold.
12. Raise and support vehicle.
13. Remove lower closeout panel.
14. Remove surge tank/radiator outlet hose from radiator.
15. Remove transaxle lower cooler line.
16. Disconnect evaporator hose from condenser. Discard sealing washer.
17. Remove lower radiator support mounting panel.
18. Remove radiator, fan and condenser from vehicle as an assembly.
19. Remove cooling fan shroud from radiator.
20. Reverse procedure to install.

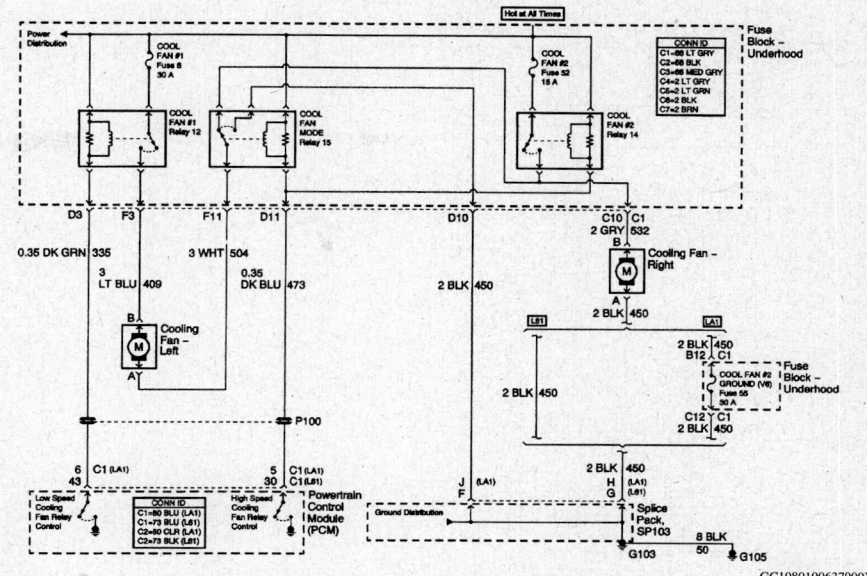

Fig. 1   Wiring diagram. Alero & Grand Am

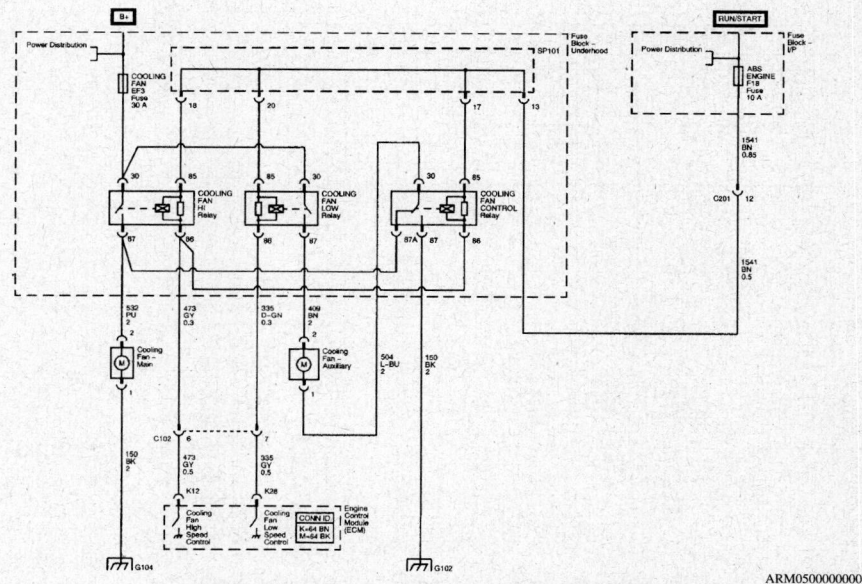

Fig. 2   Wiring diagram. 2004–05 Aveo

AVEO

1. Disconnect cooling fan electrical connector.
2. Remove cooling fan mounting bolts, then the cooling fan.
3. Reverse procedure to install.

BONNEVILLE

3.8L ENGINE

1. Remove headlamp/fascia panel support brackets and bolts.
2. Remove upper tie bar bolts, then the upper tie bar from vehicle.
3. Disconnect wiring harness electrical connector from motor and fan bracket.
4. Remove transaxle oil cooler pipe bracket bolt from fan shroud.
5. Remove two fan mounting bolts, then

lift fan assembly off lower holding tabs and remove from vehicle.
6. Reverse procedure to install.

4.6L ENGINE

1. Remove headlamp/fascia support bracket mounting bolts, then the support bracket.
2. Remove radiator support bracket.
3. Remove air cleaner assembly.
4. Drain coolant into suitable container.
5. Remove engine oil cooler bracket from fan shroud.
6. Remove transaxle oil cooler bracket from fan shroud.
7. Remove upper transaxle oil cooler pipe from radiator.
8. Disconnect cooling fan motor wiring harness electrical connectors.

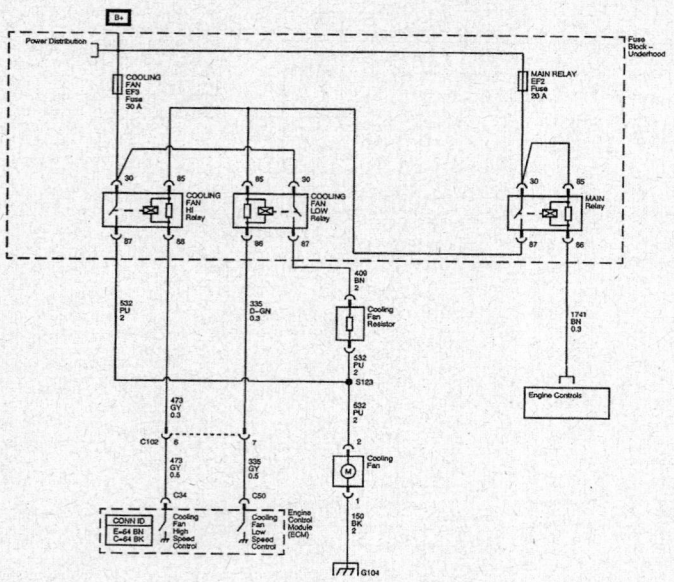

Fig. 3 Wiring diagram. 2006–08 Aveo

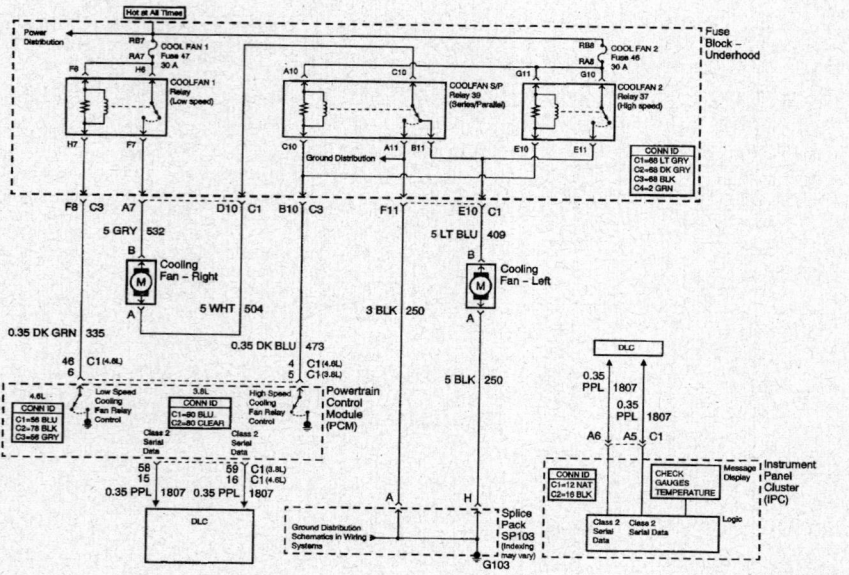

Fig. 4 Wiring diagram. Bonneville & LeSabre

9. Remove radiator outlet hose from radiator.
10. Remove two cooling fan mounting bolts.
11. Remove lower transaxle oil cooler line from radiator.
12. Remove fan assembly from vehicle.
13. Reverse procedure to install.

CAVALIER & SUNFIRE

1. Remove hood close out filler retainers, then the hood close out filler panel.
2. Remove upper radiator mount bolts.
3. Remove hood latch support bolts, then the hood latch support.
4. Raise and support vehicle.
5. Remove cooling fan mounting bolt, then disconnect fan electrical connector.

6. Remove cooling fan assembly.
7. Reverse procedure to install.

CENTURY, GRAND PRIX, IMPALA, MONTE CARLO & REGAL

1. Disconnect cooling fan electrical connector, then partially drain cooling system.
2. Remove engine mount strut to engine strut bracket attaching bolt and nut.
3. Remove engine mount strut to upper radiator support bracket attaching bolt and nut, then the engine mount strut from vehicle.
4. Remove front fender upper diagonal brace to inner fender attaching bolt.
5. Remove front fender upper diagonal brace to radiator support bolts, then

the diagonal brace from engine compartment.
6. Remove air cleaner and duct assembly.
7. Remove radiator inlet hose from radiator.
8. Remove PCM harness from fan shroud clip.
9. Remove cooling fan shroud bolts.
10. Raise and support vehicle.
11. Remove push pin retainer from lower lefthand side of fan shroud.
12. Remove transmission oil cooler lines from retainer clip at bottom of cooling fan shroud.
13. Lower vehicle and remove cooling fan shroud clip from top of radiator.
14. Remove fan shroud upper support brackets.
15. Remove fan motor heat shields, then the cooling fan shroud and fan assembly.
16. Reverse procedure to install.

COBALT & G5

1. Disconnect cooling fan electrical connector, then remove cooling fan wire from fan shroud.
2. Raise and support vehicle, then remove cooling fan assembly from radiator by pushing up on fan shroud to unsnap retaining features. Position cooling fan assembly away from radiator.
3. Remove air dam push-in retainers and air dam.
4. Remove righthand and lefthand engine splash shield to radiator mount push-in retainer
5. Remove lower radiator mount brackets and bolts, then support radiator and condenser.
6. Tilt radiator and condenser forward in vehicle. Remove cooling fan assembly from vehicle.
7. Reverse procedure to install.

CORVETTE

2004

1. Disconnect Mass Air Flow (MAF) sensor electrical connector.
2. Remove engine wiring harness from clip on radiator support.
3. Remove air cleaner intake duct.
4. Remove radiator support attaching bolts, then the radiator support.
5. Remove radiator inlet hose from radiator.
6. Raise and support vehicle.
7. Disconnect cooling fan electrical connectors, then remove forward lamp harness from retaining clips on fan shroud.
8. Remove radiator outlet hose from the radiator, then lower vehicle.
9. Remove fan shroud and fan assembly.
10. Remove cooling fan blade nut, then the cooling fan.
11. Reverse procedure to install.

2005–08

1. Remove radiator support mounting bolts, then the support.
2. Disconnect engine wiring harness from cooling fan shroud.

3. Disconnect surge tank outlet hose from retaining clips and position aside.
4. Raise and support vehicle.
5. Remove stabilizer from vehicle.
6. Disconnect cooling fan electrical connectors.
7. **On vehicles equipped with transmission fluid cooler,** disconnect lower oil cooler line from radiator.
8. **On vehicles equipped with engine oil cooler,** disconnect upper and lower oil cooler pipes.
9. **On all models,** remove cooling fan shroud mounting bolts, then the cooling fan.
10. Reverse procedure to install.

CTS

AUXILIARY

1. Raise and support vehicle.
2. Remove air deflector push-in retainers, then the air deflector, **Fig. 101.**
3. Disconnect auxiliary fan electrical connector.
4. Place a suitable container under transmission fluid cooler lines, then remove transmission fluid cooler lines using fitting disconnect tool No. J44827, or equivalent, position cooler lines aside.
5. Remove auxiliary cooling fan assembly mounting bolts, then the fan assembly.
6. Reverse procedure to install.

PRIMARY

1. Drain coolant into a suitable container.
2. Disconnect radiator to surge tank hose.
3. Remove radiator to fan shroud, then the fan shroud to air plenum attaching bolts.
4. Remove remaining fan shroud to radiator attaching bolts.
5. Remove upper radiator hose from radiator.
6. Remove coolant bypass valve retaining bolt, then position bypass valve aside.
7. Remove coolant bypass valve solenoid from fan shroud, **Fig. 102.**
8. Disconnect Mass Air Flow (MAF) sensor and Intake Air Temperature (IAT) sensor electrical connectors.
9. Disconnect air intake hose from MAF/IAT sensors.
10. Remove MAF/IAT sensor retaining screws from air cleaner assembly, then MAF/IAT sensors. **Handle MAF sensor carefully to prevent damage to sensor and screen located on air inlet end.**
11. Remove air cleaner assembly to shock tower and upper tie bar mounting bolts, then the air cleaner assembly.
12. Remove electrical connector from fan motor, then the harness clip and harness from shroud.
13. Remove coolant bypass hose from radiator.
14. Remove fan shroud attaching bolts.
15. Carefully lift fan and shroud assembly upward. **Do not damage radiator when removing fan shroud assembly.**
16. Remove fan blade retaining nut from

fan motor, then the fan blade from motor.
17. Remove cooling fan motor retaining bolts, then the fan motor, **Fig. 103.**
18. Reverse procedure to install, noting the following:
    a. **Torque** cooling fan motor to shroud bolts to 44 inch lbs.
    b. **Torque** cooling fan blade to motor nut to 62 inch lbs.
    c. **Torque** fan shroud to plenum mounting bolts to 58 inch lbs.
    d. **Torque** A/C retaining clip mounting bolt to 9 inch lbs.
    e. Install MAF/IAT sensors using a small amount of a suitable soap based solution to aid in installation.
    f. **Torque** sensor screws to 20 inch lbs.
    g. **Torque** air cleaner mounting bolts

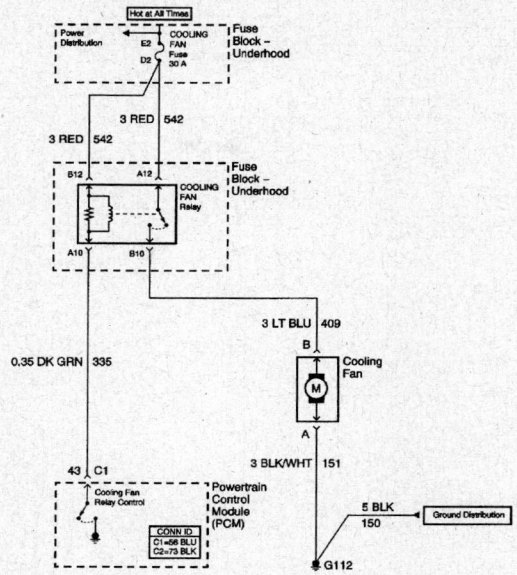

Fig. 5 Wiring diagram Cavalier & Sunfire

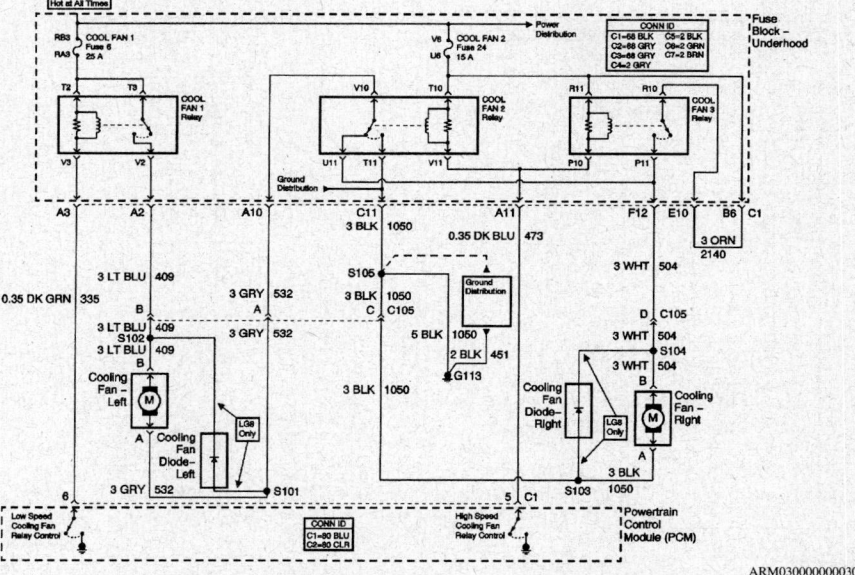

Fig. 6 Wiring diagram. Century & Regal

to 80 inch lbs.

DEVILLE

1. Remove upper filler panel push-in retainers, then the upper filler panel from engine compartment.
2. Raise and support vehicle.
3. Remove front air deflector push-in retainers, then the front air deflector from engine compartment.
4. Lower vehicle.
5. Remove hood latch support fasteners, then place a suitable fender cover on front bumper fascia and rest hood latch support on front bumper.
6. Pull upper radiator hose away from upper tie bar and temporarily position hose away from tie bar.
7. Remove upper radiator hose support to upper tie bar fastener, then the

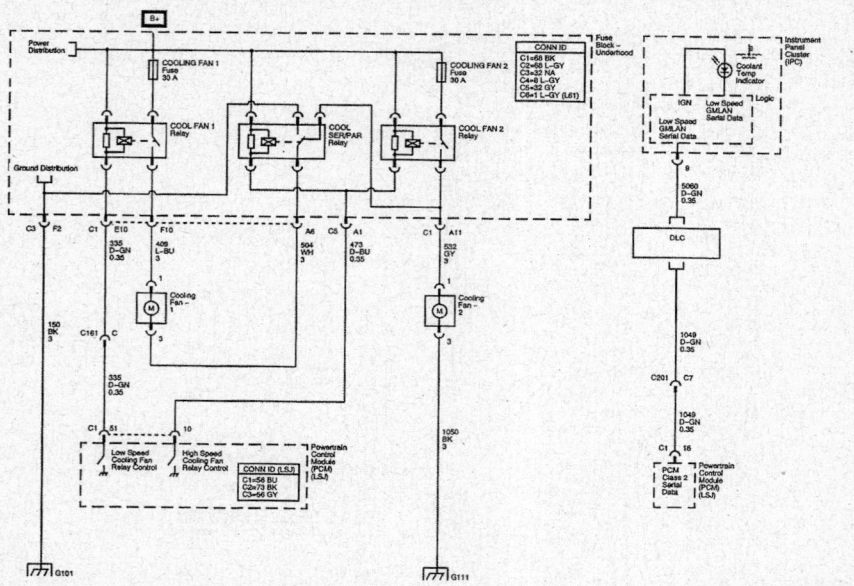

Fig. 7 Wiring diagram. Cobalt & G5 w/2.0L engine

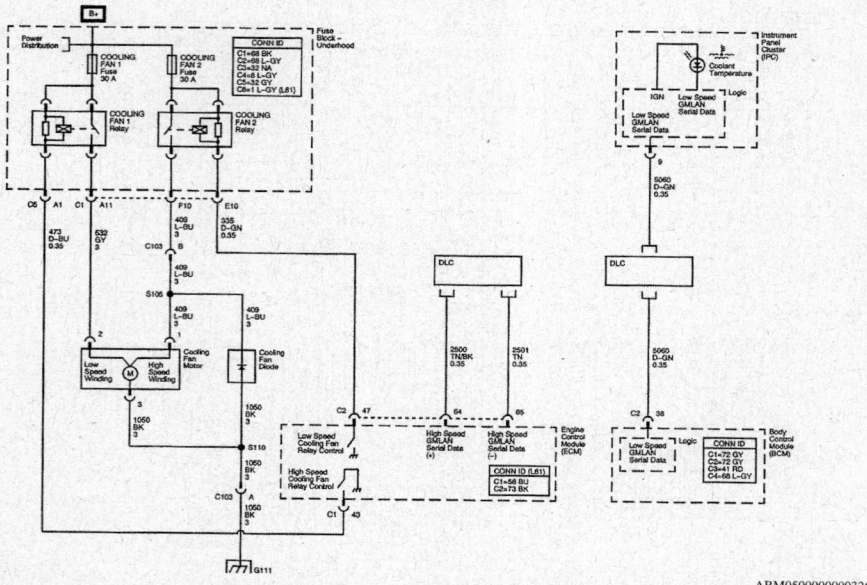

Fig. 8 Wiring diagram. Cobalt & G5 w/2.2L engine

upper radiator hose support from upper tie bar.

8. Remove upper radiator brackets to upper tie bar fasteners, then the brackets from upper tie bar.
9. Hold windshield solvent filler tube to side and remove righthand upper tie bar fasteners.
10. Remove lefthand upper tie bar fasteners, then the upper tie bar from vehicle.
11. Remove engine oil cooler pipe retaining clip and bolt from fan shroud.
12. Raise and support vehicle.
13. Drain cooling system.
14. Disconnect fan electrical connectors.
15. Remove fan to lower cradle attaching screws.
16. Lower vehicle.
17. Disconnect radiator hose.
18. Disconnect upper engine oil cooler

pipe from radiator.
19. Remove upper transaxle oil cooler pipe retaining bolt from fan shroud.
20. Slide plastic cap off upper transaxle oil cooler pipe quick connect fitting, then disconnect upper transaxle oil cooler pipe from radiator.
21. Disconnect wiring harness electrical connectors from cooling fan motors.
22. Remove clips attaching harness to fan shroud, then disconnect A/C discharge hose retainers.
23. Remove cooling fan mounting bolts.
24. Position cooling fan assembly towards lefthand side of vehicle, then pull upward on righthand side of fan assembly.
25. Position fan assembly towards righthand side of vehicle.
26. Pull upward on fan assembly and re-

move from vehicle.
27. Reverse procedure to install.

DTS

1. Remove battery and battery tray.
2. Recover A/C system refrigerant as outlined in "Air Conditioning" chapter.
3. Remove front compartment sight shield, then the upper tie bar.
4. Remove hood latch support, then the front air deflector and drain cooling system.
5. Raise and support vehicle, then remove engine oil cooler pipe retaining bolts from fan shroud.
6. Lower vehicle, then disconnect radiator inlet hose from radiator.
7. Remove transmission oil cooler pipe retaining bolts from fan shroud, the transmission lines from radiator.
8. Disconnect electrical connectors from cooling fan motors, then remove clips attaching harness to fan shroud.
9. Remove electric cooling fan mounting bolts. **Care should be taken when removing cooling fan assembly not to damage lower attachment points of both cooling fan assembly and radiator.**
10. Position cooling fan assembly towards lefthand side of vehicle, then pull upward on righthand side of fan assembly.
11. Position fan assembly towards righthand side of vehicle, then pull upward on fan assembly removing fan assembly from vehicle.
12. Remove cooling fan motor retaining bolts, then the cooling fan motor from fan shroud.
13. Reverse procedure to install.

GTO

1. Release locking lever on MAF sensor, then disconnect MAF electrical connector.
2. Release locking lever on IAT sensor, then disconnect IAT electrical connector.
3. Remove intake duct.
4. Drain cooling system into suitable container.
5. Disconnect vapor hose from retaining clips on fan shroud and radiator, then position aside.
6. Disconnect vapor hose retaining clip to surge tank at radiator and position aside.
7. Remove upper shroud retainers, then remove shroud by lifting up on righthand side then release locating tab on the lefthand side.
8. Remove radiator outlet hose.
9. Disconnect lefthand and righthand fan motor electrical connectors.
10. Depress fan shroud locking tab, then lift assembly upwards.
11. Disconnect intermediate fan motor electrical connector.
12. Reverse procedure to install.

G6

1. Drain coolant into suitable container.
2. Remove lefthand and righthand headlamp assemblies.
3. Remove upper transmission oil cooler

pipe from radiator.
4. Secure condenser to upper tie bar.
5. Remove upper radiator support bracket mounting bolts, then the support bracket.
6. Raise and support vehicle.
7. Remove lower radiator air deflector.
8. Remove front righthand inner fender shield.
9. Remove righthand and lefthand radiator air deflectors.
10. Remove radiator outlet hose from radiator.
11. Remove fan wire harness retainers.
12. Remove lower radiator support bracket mounting bolts, then the support bracket.
13. Place suitable drain pan under transmission oil cooler pipes, then remove cooler pipes from transmission.
14. Remove transmission oil cooler pipe retaining clip from fan shroud.
15. Remove lower transmission oil cooler pipe from radiator.
16. Remove transmission oil cooler pipes.
17. Remove cooling fan assembly.
18. Reverse procedure to install.

LACROSSE

3.6L ENGINE

1. Remove cooling fan attaching nut, then the cooling fan.
2. Remove cooling fan motor rivets.
3. Remove cooling fan motor assembly.
4. Reverse procedure to install.

3.8L ENGINE

1. Disconnect battery ground cable and isolate as required.
2. Remove lefthand and righthand engine mounts as outlined in "3.8L Engine" section of "Century, Grand Prix, Impala, Intrigue, LaCrosse, Monte Carlo & Regal" chapter.
3. Remove air cleaner assembly.
4. Remove PCM harness retainer from shroud.
5. Remove transmission oil cooler lines from lower fan shroud clip and reposition coil outside cooler lines.
6. Remove fan shroud clip from condenser tubes.
7. Remove radiator upper bracket bolts and brackets.
8. Remove cooling fan shroud bolts.
9. Remove bolt that connects fan shroud to the condenser hold down bracket.
10. Disconnect engine cooling fan motors electrical connectors.
11. Remove cooling fan electrical harness from fan shroud clips.
12. Remove cooling fan shroud.
13. Remove engine cooling fan blade nut, then the blade.
14. Remove engine cooling fan motor bolts, then the fan motor assembly.
15. Reverse procedure to install.

LESABRE & PARK AVENUE

1. Drain cooling system.
2. Remove air cleaner assembly.
3. Remove lefthand and righthand headlamp assembly to bracket retaining screws, then pull headlamp assem-

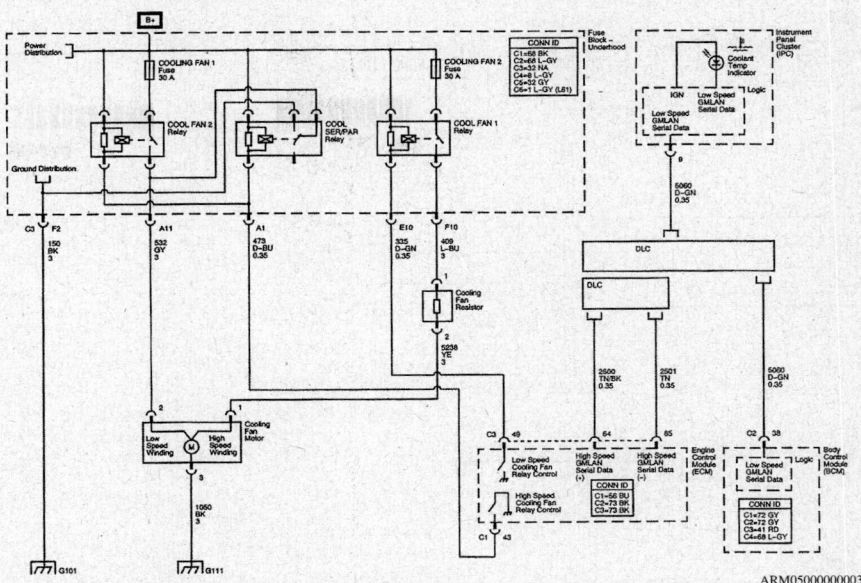

Fig. 9 Wiring diagram. Cobalt & G5 w/2.4L engine

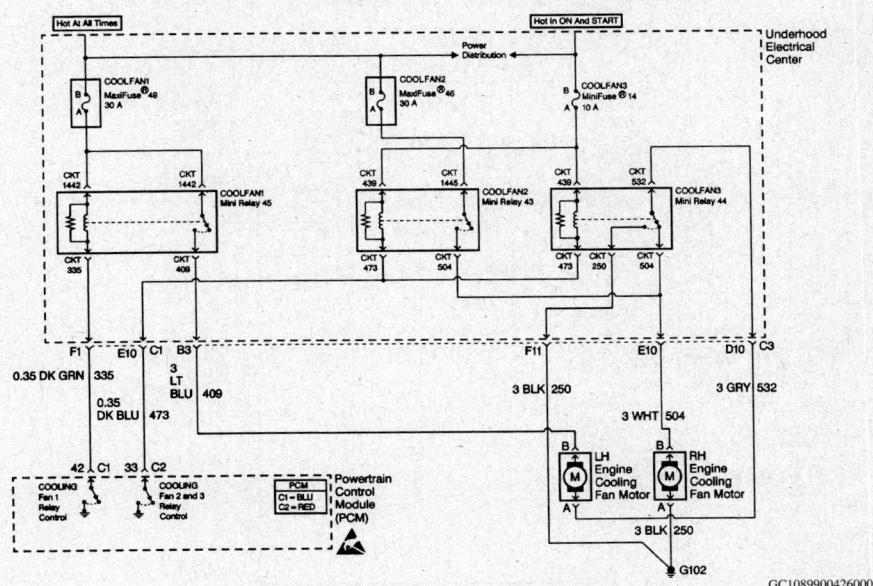

Fig. 10 Wiring diagram. 2004 Corvette

blies forward to disengage rear retaining pins.
4. Remove headlamp assemblies from vehicle and disconnect electrical connectors.
5. Remove upper radiator seal.
6. Remove battery ground to transmission oil cooler line clip and position cable aside.
7. Remove oil fill cap from sight shield, then the engine oil dipstick.
8. Disconnect upper transmission oil cooler line.
9. Disconnect upper radiator hose from radiator.
10. Disconnect cooling fan motor wiring harness connectors.
11. Remove cooling fan to radiator mounting bolts.
12. Remove coolant overflow hose from

fan assembly.
13. Release cooling fan lower mounting tabs, then raise lefthand side of fans and remove fans from vehicle.
14. Reverse procedure to install.

LUCERNE

1. Remove battery and battery tray.
2. Recover A/C system refrigerant as outlined in "Air Conditioning" chapter.
3. Remove front compartment sight shield, then the upper tie bar and front air deflector.
4. Remove hood latch support, then the front air deflector and drain cooling system.
5. Remove discharge hose nut from condenser, then the liquid line from condenser.
6. Remove suction hose from condenser

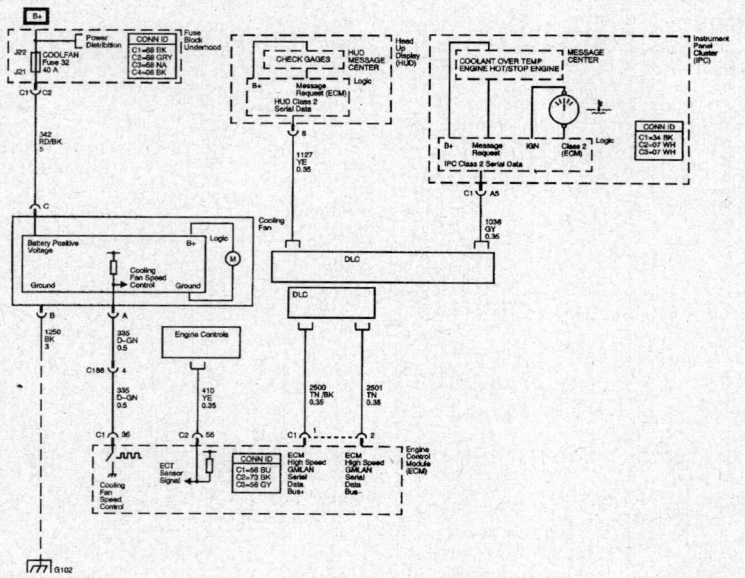

Fig. 11   Wiring diagram. 2005–08 Corvette

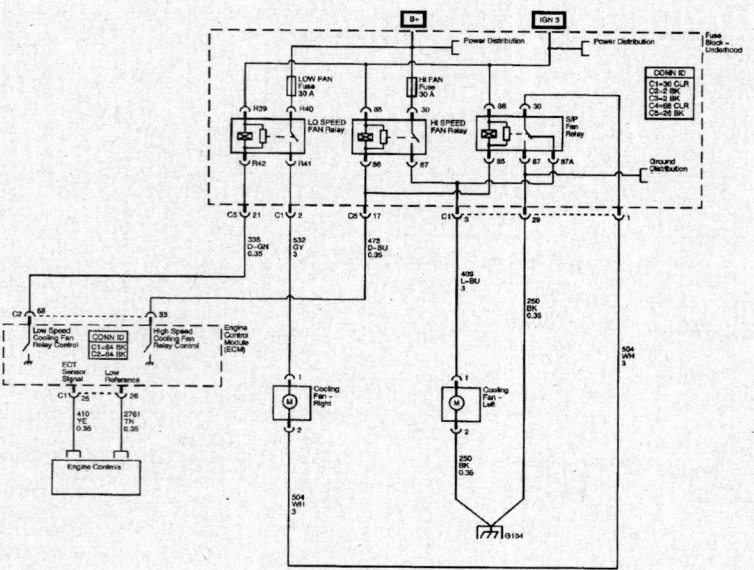

Fig. 12   Wiring diagram. CTS

discard washers.

7. Remove condenser lines to radiator mounting bolt, then condenser mounting bolts.
8. Remove condenser from radiator retainer and vehicle.
9. Remove transmission oil cooler pipe retaining bolts from fan shroud, then the hoses from radiator.
10. Slide transmission oil cooler line caps rearward to access lines to radiator.
11. Remove transmission oil cooler lines from radiator.
12. Disconnect electrical connectors from cooling fan motors.
13. Remove fan shroud clips and mounting bolts. **Care should be taken when removing cooling fan assembly not to damage lower attachment points**

of both cooling fan assembly and radiator.

14. Position fan shroud assembly towards left side of vehicle, then pull upward on right and left sides of fan shroud assembly.
15. Pull upward on fan shroud assembly removing fan shroud assembly from vehicle.
16. Remove retaining nut and cooling fan blade.
17. Reverse procedure to install.

MALIBU & MALIBU CLASSIC

2004–08

1. Remove righthand and lefthand headlamp assembly mounting bolts, then lift

headlamp assembly to unseat tabs on bottom edge of fender.
2. Disconnect headlamp assembly electrical connectors.
3. Remove headlamp assemblies from vehicle.
4. Unclip upper transmission oil cooler pipe from fan shroud. **Do not disconnect transmission oil cooler pipe from transmission or radiator.**
5. Loop a rope around each of upper two tabs on condenser and tie rope around upper tie bar.
6. Remove upper radiator support bracket bolts, then the brackets from vehicle.
7. Pry upward on fan shroud tabs at radiator clips.
8. Raise and support vehicle.
9. Remove lower radiator air deflector retainers, then the air deflector.
10. Remove front fender liner push-in retainers, then the front fender liner from vehicle.
11. Remove righthand radiator air deflector retainers, then the air deflector.
12. Remove lefthand radiator air deflector retainers, then the air deflector.
13. Remove lower radiator support bracket bolts and the support brackets.
14. Remove fan wire harness connectors.
15. Remove fan and fan shroud assembly.
16. Reverse procedure to install.

SEVILLE

1. Raise and support vehicle.
2. Drain cooling system.
3. Remove front air deflector push-in retainers, then the front air deflector.
4. Remove engine oil cooler pipe retaining bolt and retainer from fan shroud.
5. Lower vehicle, then remove fasteners securing hood latch to hood latch support.
6. Remove hood latch from hood latch support, then disconnect hood release cable from hood latch.
7. Disconnect lower engine oil cooler pipe from radiator and position aside.
8. Lower vehicle.
9. Remove push-in retainers securing upper filler panel, then disconnect ambient outside air temperature sensor electrical connector.
10. Remove upper filler panel from vehicle.
11. Remove righthand and lefthand headlamp assembly to headlamp mounting bracket fasteners.
12. Pull headlamp assemblies straight forward to disengage locator pin at outboard edge of headlamp.
13. Disconnect headlamp electrical connectors, then remove headlamp assemblies from vehicle.
14. Disconnect lower and upper engine oil cooler pipe from radiator and position aside.
15. Remove inlet radiator hose from radiator and place aside over engine.
16. Remove air cleaner assembly.
17. Remove upper transaxle oil cooler pipe retaining bolt from fan shroud.
18. Slide plastic cap off upper transaxle oil cooler pipe quick connect fitting, then

disconnect upper transaxle oil cooler pipe from radiator.

19. Remove outlet radiator hose from radiator.
20. Disconnect lower transaxle oil cooler pipe from radiator.
21. Remove radiator bracket mounting bolts and brackets.
22. Remove fan shroud, then lift radiator/condenser assembly from lower radiator support pads and tilt top of assembly forward.
23. Disconnect wiring harness electrical connectors from cooling fan motors.
24. Remove clips attaching harness to fan shroud.
25. Disconnect A/C discharge hose to fan shroud retaining clip.
26. Remove electric cooling fan mounting bolts.
27. Position cooling fan assembly towards righthand side of vehicle.
28. Pull upward on righthand side of fan assembly, then position fan assembly towards lefthand side of vehicle.
29. Pull upward on fan assembly and remove from vehicle.
30. Reverse procedure to install.

SOLSTICE

1. Remove clamp, then the air cleaner outlet duct resonator.
2. Remove clamp, then the positive crankcase ventilation hose.
3. Pull up on outlet duct assembly to disengage assembly from studs and remove air cleaner outlet resonator.
4. Disconnect MAF/IAT sensor electrical connector, then firmly tug on air cleaner to disengage air cleaner from studs and remove.
5. Disconnect cooling fan motor electrical connector.
6. Remove retaining bolt, then the radiator assembly.
7. Remove shroud assembly, then the cooling fan and motor.
8. Reverse procedure to install.

STS

1. Remove air cleaner assembly.
2. Disconnect surge tank inlet hose retainers from cooling fan shroud and position aside.
3. Remove cooling fan shroud to upper radiator mounting bolts.
4. Remove cooling fan shroud to lefthand lower radiator mounting bolts.
5. Disconnect cooling fan electrical connectors.

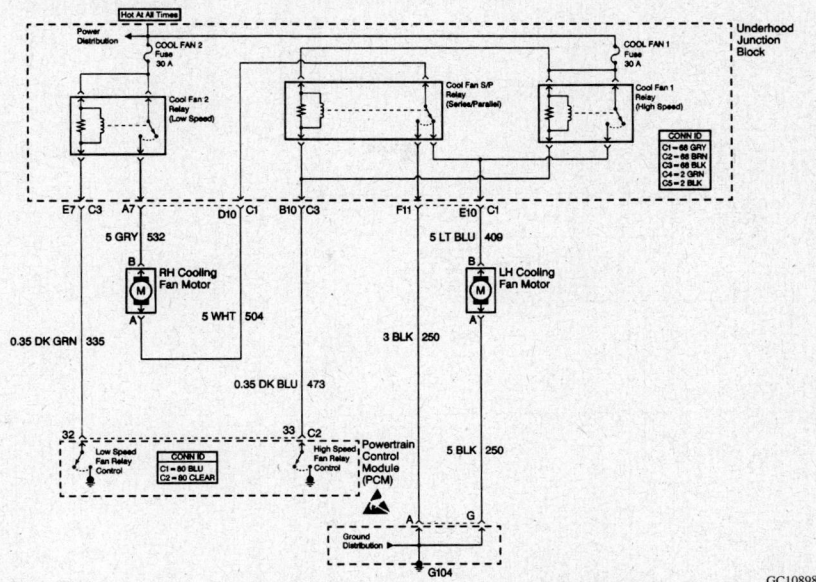

Fig. 13 Wiring diagram. DeVille & Seville

6. Raise and support vehicle.
7. Remove air deflector mounting bolts, then the air deflector.
8. Remove cooling fan shroud to righthand lower radiator mounting bolts.
9. Disconnect engine wiring harness from engine frame and position aside.
10. Remove power steering line to cooling fan shroud retainers.
11. Remove transmission oil cooler lines to fan shroud retainers.
12. Lower vehicle.
13. Remove cooling fan assembly.
14. Reverse procedure to install.

VIBE

1. Disconnect coolant reservoir hose from radiator.
2. Disconnect electrical connector from cooling fan motor.
3. Disconnect two electrical harness retaining clips from fan shroud.
4. Remove two fan shroud to radiator mounting bolts, then the cooling fan and shroud assembly from vehicle, **Fig. 104.**
5. Remove fan blade retaining nut, then the fan blade from motor shaft.
6. Remove two fan motor to shroud mounting bolts, then the fan motor from shroud.
7. Reverse procedure to install.

XLR

1. Remove air cleaner assembly.
2. Disconnect MAF sensor wire from radiator support retainer clip.
3. Disconnect surge tank inlet hose from radiator support tabs.
4. Remove radiator support bolts, then the radiator support.
5. Disconnect engine wiring harness from cooling fan shroud.
6. Disconnect surge tank outlet hose from retaining clips on cooling fan shroud.
7. Raise and support vehicle.
8. Remove tire and wheel assemblies.
9. Remove stabilizer shaft link nuts from stabilizer shaft.
10. Remove stabilizer shaft insulator clamps from front crossmember, then the stabilizer shaft from vehicle.
11. Disconnect cooling fan electrical connector.
12. Disconnect lower transmission oil cooler line from radiator.
13. Lift up on cooling fan and shroud to disengage retaining tabs from radiator.
14. Remove cooling fan and shroud.
15. Reverse procedure to install.

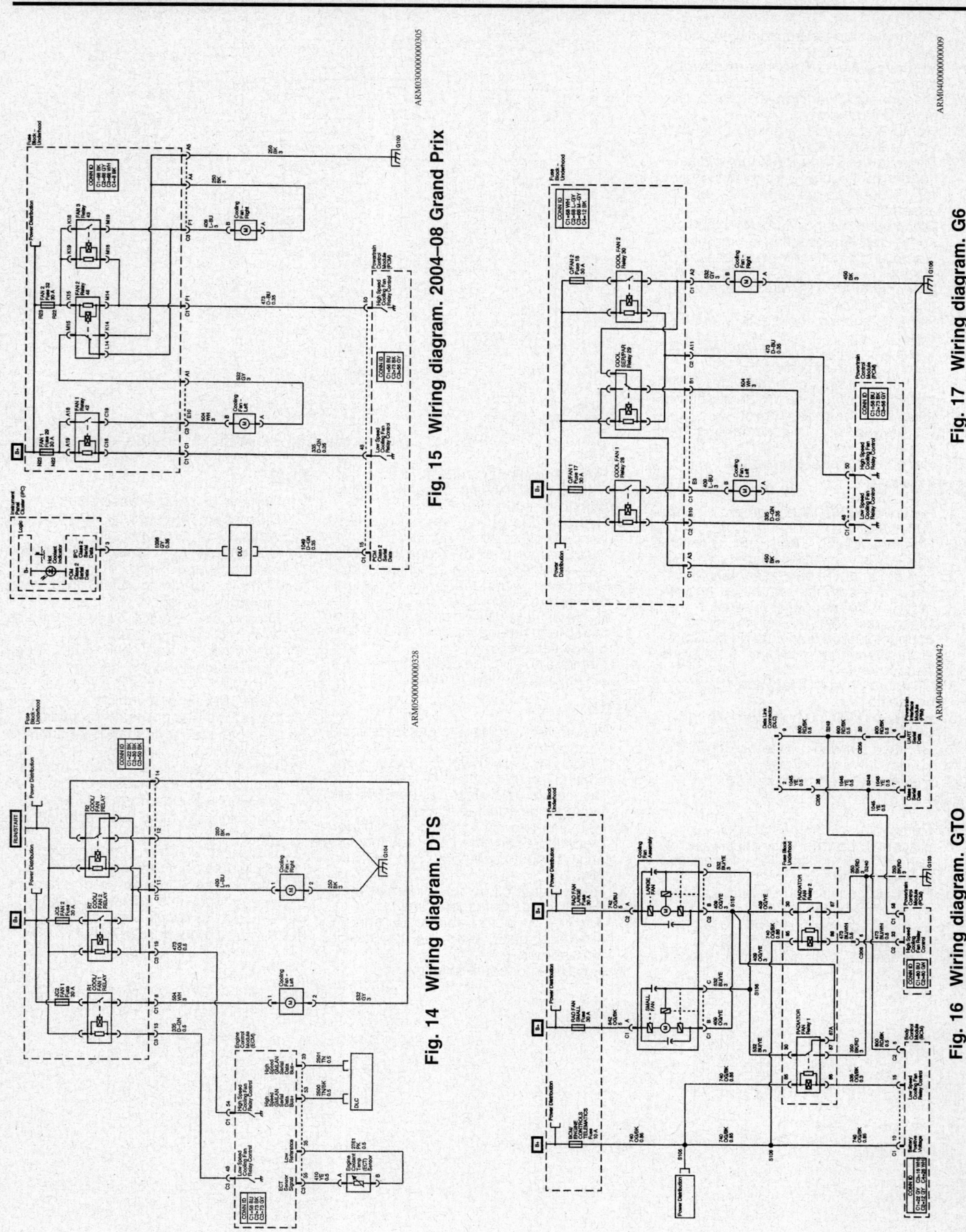

Fig. 15 Wiring diagram. 2004–08 Grand Prix

Fig. 17 Wiring diagram. G6

Fig. 14 Wiring diagram. DTS

Fig. 16 Wiring diagram. GTO

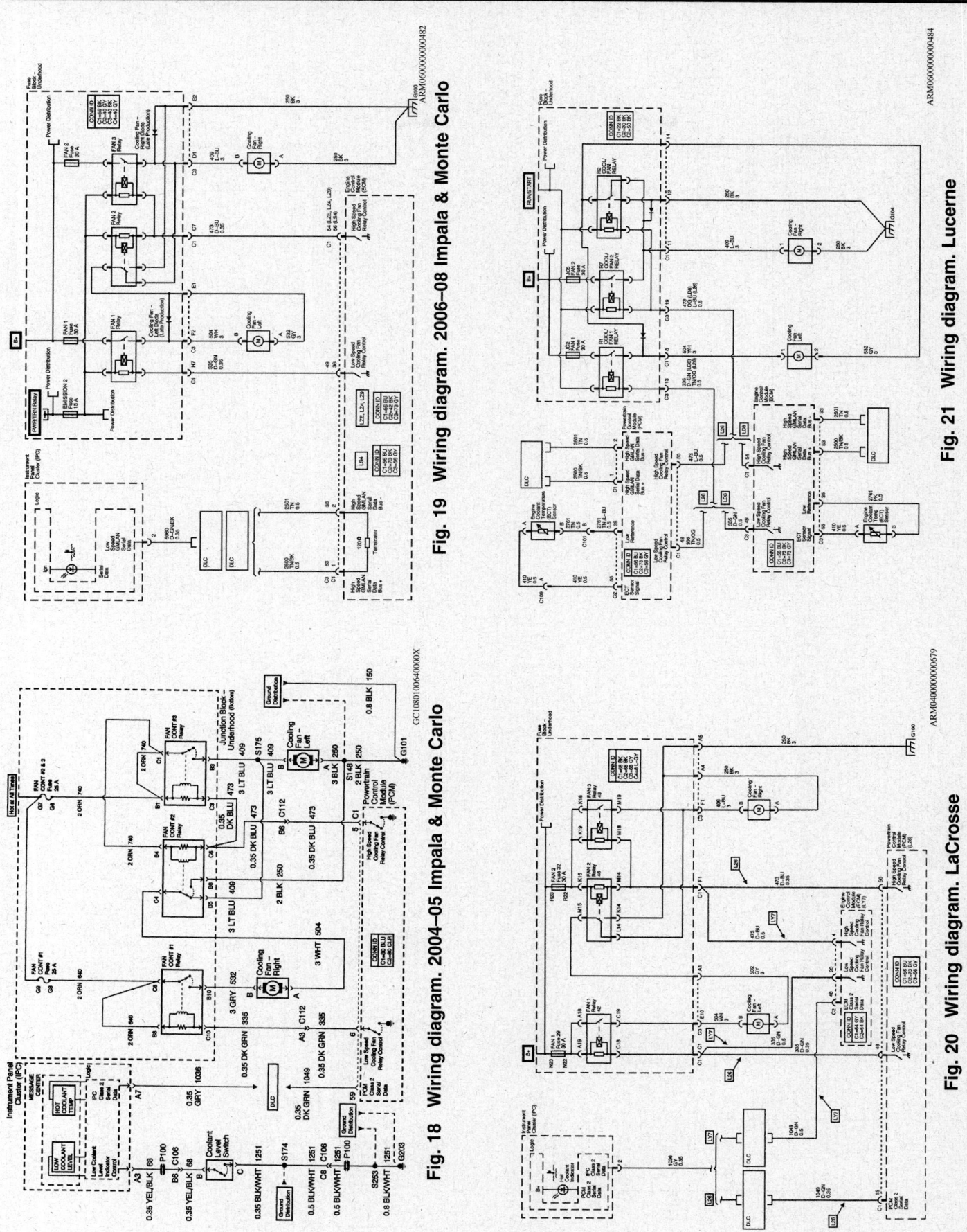

Fig. 19   Wiring diagram. 2006–08 Impala & Monte Carlo

Fig. 21   Wiring diagram. Lucerne

Fig. 18   Wiring diagram. 2004–05 Impala & Monte Carlo

Fig. 20   Wiring diagram. LaCrosse

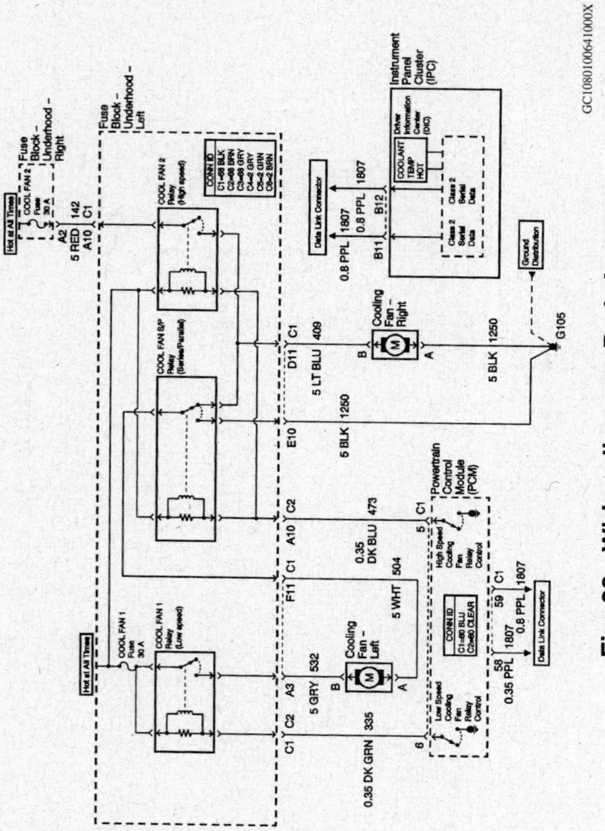

Fig. 23 Wiring diagram. Park Avenue

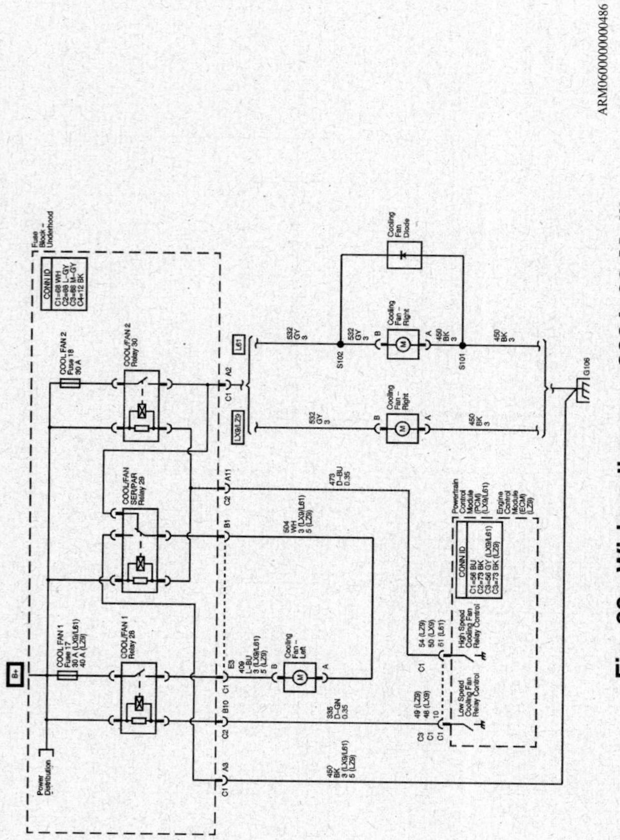

Fig. 22 Wiring diagram. 2004–08 Malibu

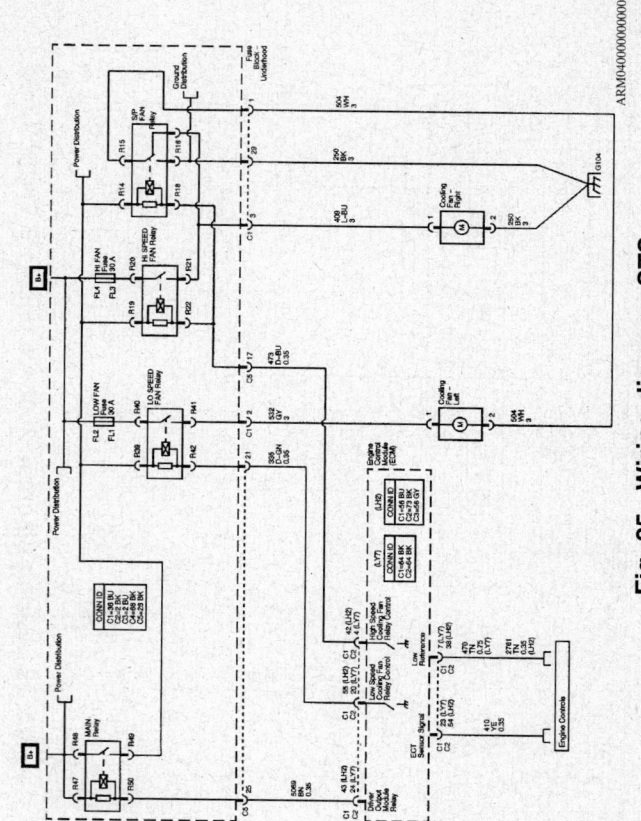

Fig. 25 Wiring diagram. STS

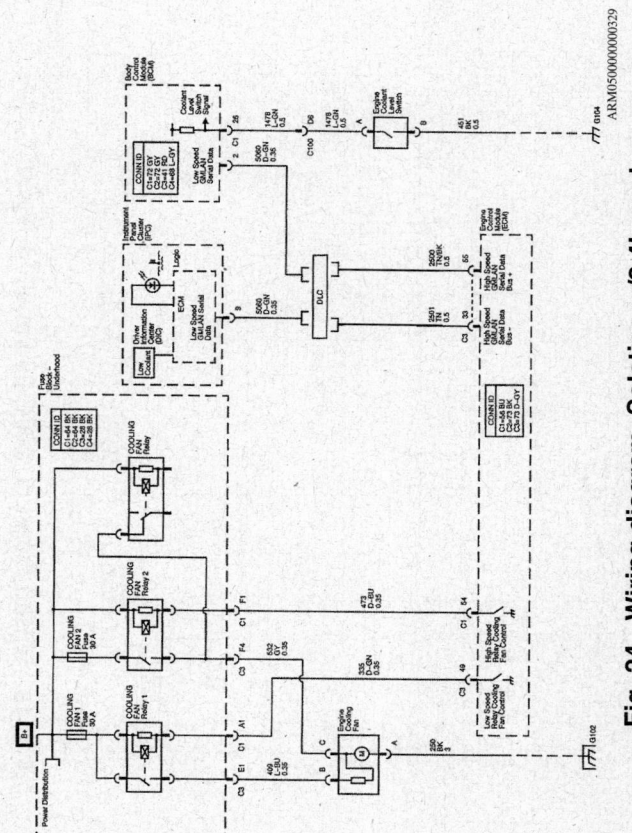

Fig. 24 Wiring diagram. Solstice w/2.4L engine

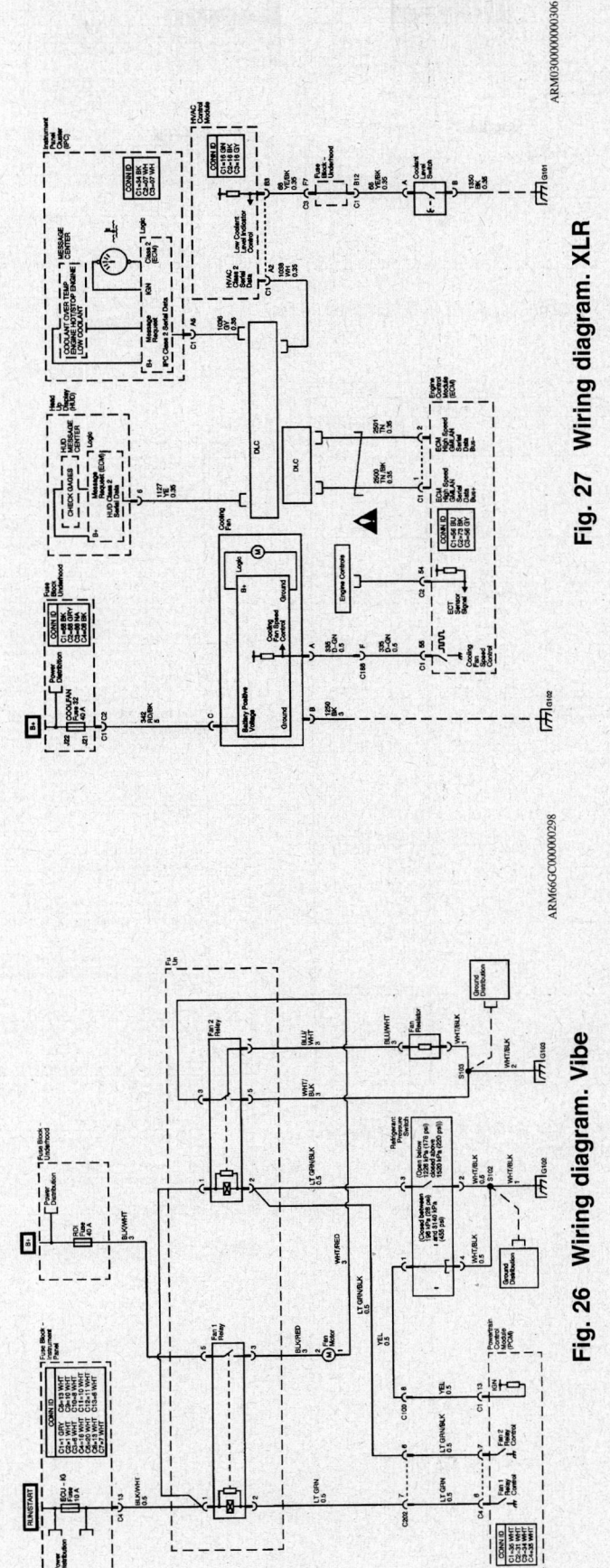

Fig. 27 Wiring diagram. XLR

Fig. 26 Wiring diagram. Vibe

Fig. 28 — Diagnostic system check table

Step	Action	Yes	No
1	Install a scan tool. Does the scan tool power up?	Go to Step 2	Diagnose Data Link Communications
2	1. Turn ON the ignition, with the engine OFF. 2. Attempt to establish communication with the following control modules: • Instrument Cluster • Powertrain Control Module Does the scan tool communicate with the control modules?	Go to Step 3	Diagnose Data Link Communications
3	Select the powertrain control module display DTCs function on the scan tool. Does the scan tool display any DTCs?	Go to Step 4	Diagnose Engine Cooling
4	Does the scan tool display any DTCs which begin with a "U"?	Diagnose Data Link Communications	Diagnose Trouble Code (DTC)

GC1080100643000X

Fig. 28 Diagnostic system check. Alero & Grand Am

Fig. 29 — Cooling fan always on

DEFINITION: One or both engine cooling fan motors run continuously in high or low speed modes.

Step	Action	Yes	No
1	Did you perform the Engine Cooling Diagnostic System Check?	Go to Step 2	Go To Diagnostic System Check -
2	Turn ON the ignition, with the engine OFF. Are one or both cooling fans running all the time?	Go to Step 3	Test for Intermittent and Poor Connections
3	Are both cooling fans running continuously?	Go to Step 5	Go to Step 4
4	Remove the cooling fan S/P relay. Did the eng cool RH fan turn OFF?	Go to Step 6	Go to Step 7
5	Repair the short in the eng cool LH fan supply voltage circuit. Did you complete the repair?	Go to Step 8	—
6	Repair the short in the eng cool LH fan low circuit. Did you complete the repair?	Go to Step 8	—
7	Repair the short in the eng cool RH fan supply voltage circuit. Did you complete the repair?	Go to Step 8	—
8	Operate the system in order to verify the repair. Did you correct the condition?	System OK	Go to Step 2

GC1080100644000X

Fig. 29 Cooling fan always on. Alero & Grand Am

Fig. 30 — Cooling fan inoperative (Part 1 of 3)

DEFINITION: One or both engine cooling fan motors do not operate properly in high or low speed modes.

Step	Action	Yes	No
1	Did you perform the Engine Cooling Diagnostic System Check?	Go to Step 2	Go to Diagnostic System Check -
2	1. Install a scan tool. 2. Turn ON the ignition, with the engine OFF. 3. With a scan tool, command the Fans Low Speed ON and OFF. Do the low speed engine cooling fans turn ON and OFF with each command?	Go to Step 3	Go to Step 4
3	Important: Before the PCM changes the speed of the cooling fans, a 3-second delay will occur. With a scan tool, command the Fans High Speed ON and OFF. Do the high speed engine cooling fans turn ON and OFF with each command?	Test Intermittent and Poor Connections	Go to Step 13
4	1. Turn the ignition OFF. 2. Disconnect the cooling fan 1 relay. 3. Turn the ignition ON, with the engine OFF. 4. Probe the battery positive voltage circuit of the cooling fan 1 relay switch side with a test lamp connected to a good ground. Does the test lamp illuminate?	Go to Step 5	Go to Step 20
5	Connect a 20 A fused jumper between the battery positive voltage circuit of the cooling fan 1 relay and the cooling fan motor supply voltage circuit of the cooling fan 1 relay. Do both cooling fans operate in low speed?	Go to Step 15	Go to Step 6
6	1. Leave the fused jumper wire in place of the cooling fan 1 relay. 2. Remove the cooling fan S/P relay. 3. Connect a 20 A fused jumper between the eng cool LH fan low circuit of the cooling fan S/P relay and the eng cool RH fan supply voltage circuit of the cooling fan S/P relay. Do both cooling fans operate in low speed?	Go to Step 16	Go to Step 7
7	1. Leave the fused jumper wire in place of the cooling fan 1 relay. 2. Connect a 20 A fused jumper between the battery positive voltage circuit of the cooling fan S/P relay and the cooling fan motor supply voltage circuit of the cooling fan S/P relay. Does the eng cool RH fan operate in high speed?	Go to Step 11	Go to Step 8
8	1. Leave the fused jumper wire in place of the cooling fan 1 relay. 2. Install the cooling fan S/P relay. 3. Disconnect the eng cool RH fan electrical connector. Does the eng cool LH fan operate in high speed?	Go to Step 24	Go to Step 9
9	1. Leave the fused jumper wire in place of the cooling fan 1 relay. 2. Connect a 20 Amp fused jumper wire from the cooling fan motor supply voltage circuit of the eng cool RH fan electrical connector to the cooling fan motor ground circuit of the eng cool RH fan electrical connector. Does the eng cool LH fan operate in high speed?	Go to Step 18	Go to Step 10

GC1080100645010X

Fig. 30 Cooling fan inoperative (Part 1 of 3). Alero & Grand Am

---

Fig. 30 — Cooling fan inoperative (Part 2 of 3)

Step	Action	Yes	No
10	1. Leave the fused jumper wire in place of the cooling fan 1 relay. 2. Connect a 20 Amp fused jumper wire from the cooling fan motor supply voltage circuit of the eng cool RH fan electrical connector to a good ground. Does the eng cool LH fan operate in high speed?	Go to Step 23	Go to Step 24
11	1. Leave the fused jumper wire in place of the cooling fan 1 relay. 2. Install the cooling fan S/P relay. 3. Disconnect the eng cool LH fan electrical connector. 4. Connect a 20 Amp fused jumper wire from battery positive voltage circuit of the eng cool LH fan electrical connector to the cooling fan motor ground circuit of the eng cool LH fan electrical connector. Does the eng cool RH fan operate in high speed?	Go to Step 19	Go to Step 12
12	1. Leave the fused jumper wire in place of the cooling fan 1 relay. 2. Connect a 20 Amp fused jumper wire from battery positive voltage to the eng cool LH fan low circuit of the of the eng cool LH fan electrical connector. Does the eng cool RH fan operate in high speed?	Go to Step 21	Go to Step 25
13	Is the eng cool RH fan operating properly in high speed?	Go to Step 14	Go to Step 17
14	1. Remove the cooling fan S/P relay 2. Connect a 20 A fused jumper between the eng cool LH fan low circuit of the cooling fan S/P relay and the ground circuit of the cooling fan S/P relay. Does the eng cool LH fan operate properly in high speed?	Go to Step 16	Go to Step 22
15	Inspect for poor connections at the cooling fan 1 relay. Did you find and correct the condition?	Go to Step 31	Go to Step 26
16	Inspect for poor connections at the cooling fan S/P relay. Did you find and correct the condition?	Go to Step 31	Go to Step 27
17	Inspect for poor connections at the cooling fan 2 relay. Did you find and correct the condition?	Go to Step 31	Go to Step 28
18	Inspect for poor connections at the harness connector of the eng cool RH fan. Did you find and correct the condition?	Go to Step 31	Go to Step 29
19	Inspect for poor connections at the harness connector of the eng cool LH fan. Did you find and correct the condition?	Go to Step 31	Go to Step 30
20	Repair the battery positive voltage circuit of the cooling fan 1 relay switch side. Did you complete the repair?	Go to Step 31	—
21	Repair the eng cool LH fan supply voltage circuit. Did you complete the repair?	Go to Step 31	—
22	Repair the eng cool LH fan ground circuit. Did you complete the repair?	Go to Step 31	—

GC1080100645020X

Fig. 30 Cooling fan inoperative (Part 2 of 3). Alero & Grand Am

Step	Action	Yes	No
23	Repair the eng cool RH fan ground circuit. Did you complete the repair?	Go to Step 31	—
24	Repair the eng cool RH fan supply voltage circuit. Did you complete the repair?	Go to Step 31	—
25	Repair the eng cool LH fan low circuit. Did you complete the repair?	Go to Step 31	—
26	Replace the cooling fan 1 relay. Did you complete the repair?	Go to Step 31	—
27	Replace the cooling fan S/P relay. Did you complete the repair?	Go to Step 31	—
28	Replace the cooling fan 2 relay. Did you complete the repair?	Go to Step 31	—
29	Replace the eng cool RH fan. Did you complete the repair?	Go to Step 31	—
30	Replace the eng cool LH fan. Did you complete the repair?	Go to Step 31	—
31	Operate the system in order to verify the repair. Did you correct the condition?	System OK	Go to Step 2

GC1080100645030X

Fig. 30 Cooling fan inoperative (Part 3 of 3). Alero & Grand Am

Step	Action	Yes	No
1	Install a scan tool. Does the scan tool power up?	Go to Step 2	Diagnose Data Link Communications
2	1. Turn On the ignition, with the engine OFF. 2. Attempt to establish communication with the engine control module (ECM). Does the scan tool communicate with ECM?	Go to Step 3	Diagnose Data Link Communications
3	Select the ECM. Display DTCs function on the scan tool. Does the scan tool display any DTCs?	Go to Diagnostic Trouble Code (DTC) List	Go to Symptoms

ARM0400000000034

Fig. 31 Diagnostic system check. 2004–05 Aveo

Step	Action	Yes	No
1	Did you perform the Diagnostic Starting Point - Engine Cooling?	Go to Step 2	Go to Diagnostic Starting Point
2	1. Inspect the I/P fuse block fuse F18 for the 1.4L/1.5L application, or underhood fuse EF2 for the 1.2L. 2. Replace the fuse as needed. Is the fuse OK?	Go to Step 3	Go to Diagnostic Aids
3	1. Inspect the engine fuse block fuse EF3. 2. Replace the fuse as needed. Is the fuse OK?	Go to Step 4	Go to Diagnostic Aids
4	1. Turn the ignition OFF. 2. Connect the scan tool to the data link connector (DLC). 3. Start the engine. 4. The cooling fan should run at low speed when the coolant temperature reaches 93°C (199°F). Does the cooling fan run at low speed?	Go to Step 5	Go to Step 6
5	1. Turn the ignition OFF. 2. Connect a scan tool to the DLC. 3. Start the engine. 4. The cooling fan should run at high speed when the coolant temperature reaches 97°C (207°F). Does the cooling fan run at high speed?	System OK	Go to Step 22

ARM0400000000035

Fig. 32 Cooling fan circuit diagnosis (Part 1 of 5). 2004–05 Aveo

Step	Action	Yes	No
6	1. Turn the ignition OFF. 2. Disconnect the engine control module (ECM) connector. 3. Connect a fused jumper between the ECM low cooling fan relay control circuit and ground. 4. Turn the ignition ON. Does the cooling fan run at low speed?	Go to Step 21	Go to Step 7
7	1. Turn the ignition OFF. 2. Connect a fused jumper between the ECM low cooling fan relay control circuit and ground. 3. Disconnect the cooling fan connector. 4. Connect a test light between the cooling fan connector terminal 2 and ground. 5. Turn the ignition ON. Is the test light ON?	Go to Step 8	Go to Step 9
8	1. Turn the ignition OFF. 2. Connect a test light between the cooling fan connector terminal 1 and battery positive. Is the test light ON?	Go to Step 18	Go to Step 17
9	1. Turn the ignition OFF. 2. Remove the jumper from the ECM low cooling fan control circuit. 3. Using a test light, connect to ground, probe the low speed relay connector terminal 86. 4. Turn the ignition ON. Is the test light ON?	Go to Step 10	Go to Step 13

ARM0400000000036

Fig. 32 Cooling fan circuit diagnosis (Part 2 of 5). 2004–05 Aveo

Step	Action	Yes	No
10	1. Turn the ignition OFF. 2. Connect a test light between the cooling fan relay LOW connector terminal 30 and ground. Is the test light ON?	Go to Step 11	Go to Step 14
11	Connect a test light between the cooling fan relay LOW connector terminal 87 and battery positive. Is the test light ON?	Go to Step 12	Go to Step 16
12	1. Connect a fused jumper between the ECM low cooling fan relay control circuit and ground. 2. Connect a test light between the cooling fan relay LOW connector terminal 85 and battery positive. Is the test light ON?	Go to Step 19	Go to Step 15
13	Repair the open wire between the cooling fan relay LOW connector terminal 85 and the ignition voltage supply. Is the repair complete?	System OK	--
14	Repair the open wire between the cooling fan relay LOW connector terminal 30 and the fuse EF3. Is the repair complete?	System OK	--
15	Repair the open wire between the cooling fan relay LOW connector terminal 86 and the ECM low cooling fan relay control circuit. Is the repair complete?	System OK	--
16	Inspect for an open wire between the cooling fan relay LOW connector terminal 87 and the cooling fan connector terminal 2. Is the problem found?	Go to Step 20	Go to Step 17

ARM0400000000037

Fig. 32 Cooling fan circuit diagnosis (Part 3 of 5). 2004–05 Aveo

Step	Action	Yes	No
17	Inspect for an open wire between the cooling fan connector terminal 1 and ground. Is the problem found?	Go to Step 20	Go to Step 18
18	Replace the cooling fan. Is the repair complete?	System OK	--
19	Replace the cooling fan relay LOW. Is the repair complete?	System OK	--
20	Repair the wire as needed. Is the repair complete?	System OK	--
21	Replace the ECM. Is the repair complete	System OK	--
22	1. Turn the ignition OFF. 2. Disconnect the ECM connector. 3. Connect a fused jumper between the ECM low cooling fan relay control circuit and ground. 4. Connect a fused jumper between the ECM high cooling fan relay control circuit and ground. 5. Turn the ignition ON. Does the cooling fan run at high speed?	Go to Step 21	Go to Step 23
23	1. Turn the ignition OFF. 2. Disconnect the cooling fan relay HI. 3. Connect a test light between the cooling fan relay high connector terminal 85 and ground. 4. Turn the ignition ON. Is the test light ON?	Go to Step 24	Go to Step 28

ARM0400000000038

Fig. 32 Cooling fan circuit diagnosis (Part 4 of 5). 2004–05 Aveo

			Go to Step 25	Go to Step 29
24	1. Turn the ignition OFF. 2. Connect a test light between the cooling fan relay HI connector terminal 30 and ground. Is the test light ON?			
25	Connect a test light between the cooling fan relay HI connector terminal 87 and ground. Is the test light ON?		Go to Step 26	Go to Step 30
26	1. Connect a fused jumper between the ECM high cooling fan control circuit and ground. 2. Connect a test light between the cooling fan relay HI connector terminal 86 and battery positive. Is the test light ON?		Go to Step 27	Go to Step 31
27	Replace the cooling fan relay HI. Is the repair complete?		System OK	--
28	Repair the open wire between the cooling fan relay HI connector terminal 85 and the ignition switch voltage supply. Is the repair complete?		System OK	--
29	Repair the open wire between the cooling fan relay HI connector terminal 30 and the fuse EF3. Is the repair complete?		System OK	--
30	Repair the open wire between the cooling fan relay HI connector terminal 87 and the cooling fan connector terminal 2. Is the repair complete?		System OK	--
31	Repair the open wire between the cooling fan relay HI connector terminal 86 and the ECM relay control circuit. Is the repair complete?		System OK	--

ARM0500000000932

Fig. 32 Cooling fan circuit diagnosis (Part 5 of 5). 2004–05 Aveo

2	Install a scan tool. Does the scan tool power up?	Go to Step 3	Go to Scan Tool Does Not Power Up
3	1. Turn ON the ignition, with the engine OFF. 2. Attempt to establish communication with all of the control modules on the vehicle. Does the scan tool communicate with all of the expected vehicle control modules?	Go to Step 4	Go to Control Module References
4	**Important:** • To ensure that retained accessory power (RAP) mode is inactive (if equipped), open the driver door during the following step. • The engine may start during the following step. Turn OFF the engine as soon as you have observed the crank power mode. 1. Access the ignition switch parameter on the scan tool. 2. Rotate the ignition switch, operate the ignition mode switch, through all positions while observing the switch parameter. Does the parameter reading on the scan tool match the ignition switch position for all switch positions?	Go to Step 5	Go to Symptoms
5	Attempt to start the engine. Does the engine crank?	Go to Step 6	Go to Symptoms
6	Attempt to start the engine. Does the engine start and idle?	Go to Step 7	Go to Symptoms

ARM0600000000488

Fig. 33 Diagnostic system check (Part 2 of 3). 2006–08 Aveo

Test Description

The numbers below refer to the step numbers on the diagnostic table.

1. This step insures that the battery, and the vehicle primary power and ground systems are functioning correctly.

3. Lack of communication may be due to a particular malfunction of a serial data circuit. The link to Scan Tool does not Communicate with Class 2 Device will provide a list of modules and the associated data network no communication diagnostic link.

4. A module that is operating in the incorrect power mode based on key position may cause other vehicle symptoms and/or DTCs to set. The link to Power Mode Mismatch will correct the condition before checking for module DTCs or symptoms.

8. This step insures that all data link communication DTCs are diagnosed before system level DTCs.

9. This step insures that all electronic control unit (ECU) internal DTCs are diagnosed before other system level DTCs.

10. This step insures that all device voltage DTCs are diagnosed before other system level DTCs.

Step	Action	Yes	No
1	Perform the following preliminary inspections: • Ensure that the battery is fully charged. • Ensure that the battery cables are clean and tight. • Inspect for any open fuses. • Inspect for the easily accessible systems or the visible system components for obvious damage or conditions that could cause the symptom. • Ensure that the grounds are clean, tight, and in the correct location. • Inspect for aftermarket devices that could affect the operation of the system. • Search for applicable service bulletins. Did you find and correct the condition?	System OK	Go to Step 2

ARM0600000000487

Fig. 33 Diagnostic system check (Part 1 of 3). 2006–08 Aveo

7	**Important:** Do not clear any DTCs unless instructed by a diagnostic procedure. Use the appropriate scan tool selections to obtain DTCs for each of the control modules. Does the scan tool display any DTCs?	Go to Step 8	Go to Step 12
8	Does the scan tool display any DTCs that begin with a "U"?	Go to Diagnostic Trouble Code (DTC)	Go to Step 9
9	**Important:** If any of these DTCs are displayed, diagnose them before diagnosing any other DTCs or symptoms. Does the scan tool display DTC B1000, B1001, B1004, B1007, B1009, B1013, C0550, P0601, P0602, P0603, P0604, P0605, P0606, P0607, P060D, P060E, P1600, P1621, P2107, P2108, or P2610?	Go to Diagnostic Trouble Code (DTC)	Go to Step 10
10	**Important:** If any of these DTCs are displayed, diagnose them before diagnosing any other DTCs or symptoms. Does the scan tool display DTC B1370, B1390, 1385, B1420, C0896, P0560, P0562, or P0563?	Go to Diagnostic Trouble Code (DTC)	Go to Step 11
11	**Important:** If any of the remaining DTCs are powertrain DTCs, select Capture Info in order to store the powertrain DTC information with a scan tool. If multiple DTCs are stored, diagnose the DTCs in the following order 1. Component level DTCs, such as sensor DTCs, solenoid DTCs, and relay DTCs. 2. System level DTCs, such as misfire DTCs, evaporative emission (EVAP) system DTCs, and fuel trim DTCs. Diagnose the remaining DTCs.	Go to Diagnostic Trouble Code (DTC)	--
12	Is the customers concern with inspection/maintenance (I/M) testing?	Go to Explanation of Scheduled	Go to Symptoms

ARM0600000000489

Fig. 33 Diagnostic system check (Part 3 of 3). 2006–08 Aveo

Circuit Description

The engine cooling fan circuit operates the cooling fan. The cooling fan is controlled by engine control module (ECM) based on input from the engine coolant temperature (ECT) sensor. The ECM controls the low speed cooling fan operation by providing a ground signal to the low speed fan relay. This energizes the low speed cooling fan relay and operates the cooling fan at low speed. The low speed cooling fan operation is achieved by the cooling fan resistor causing a drop in the voltage supplied to the cooling fan. The ECM controls the high speed cooling fan operation by providing a ground signal to the high speed fan relay. This energizes the high speed cooling fan relay, bypassing the radiator fan resistor. This results in high speed cooling fan operation.

Diagnostic Aids

- If the owner complained of an overheating problem, it must be determined if the complaint was due to an actual boil over, or the engine coolant temperature gage indicated overheating. If the engine is overheating and the cooling fans are ON, the cooling system should be inspected.
- If the I/P fuse block fuse F18 or the engine fuse block fuse EF3 or main relay fuse EF2 (1.2L only), become open, blown, immediately after installation, inspect for a short to ground in the wiring of the appropriate circuit. If the fuses become open, blown, when the cooling fan is to be turned ON by the ECM, suspect a faulty cooling fan motor.
- The ECM will turn the cooling fans ON at low speed when the coolant temperature is 93°C (199°F). The ECM will turn the cooling fans OFF when the coolant temperature is 90°C (194°F).
- The ECM will turn the cooling fans ON at high speed when the coolant temperature is 97°C (207°F). The ECM will change the cooling fans from high speed to low speed when the coolant temperature is 94°C (201°F).
- The cooling fan circuit can be inspected quickly by disconnecting the ECM connector and grounding the low cooling fan control circuit. This should create low speed cooling fan operation with the ignition ON. By grounding the ECM low cooling fan relay and high cooling fan relay control circuits and turning the ignition ON, high speed cooling fan operation should be achieved.

ARM0600000000490

Fig. 34   Cooling fan circuit diagnosis (Part 1 of 6). 2006–08 Aveo w/single fan

6	1. Turn the ignition OFF. 2. Disconnect the engine control module (ECM) connector. 3. Connect a fused jumper between the ECM low cooling fan relay control circuit and ground. 4. Turn the ignition ON. Does the cooling fan run at low speed?	Go to Step 21	Go to Step 7
7	1. Turn the ignition OFF. 2. Connect a fused jumper between the ECM low cooling fan relay control circuit and ground. 3. Disconnect the cooling fan connector. 4. Connect a test light between the cooling fan connector terminal 2 and ground. 5. Turn the ignition ON. Is the test light ON?	Go to Step 8	Go to Step 9
8	1. Turn the ignition OFF. 2. Connect a test light between the cooling fan connector terminal 1 and battery positive. Is the test light ON?	Go to Step 18	Go to Step 17
9	1. Turn the ignition OFF. 2. Remove the jumper from the ECM low cooling fan control circuit. 3. Using a test light, connect to ground, probe the low speed relay connector terminal 86. 4. Turn the ignition ON. Is the test light ON?	Go to Step 10	Go to Step 13
10	1. Turn the ignition OFF. 2. Connect a test light between the cooling fan relay LOW connector terminal 30 and ground. Is the test light ON?	Go to Step 11	Go to Step 14
11	Connect a test light between the cooling fan relay LOW connector terminal 87 and battery positive. Is the test light ON?	Go to Step 16 / Go to Step 12	

ARM0600000000492

Fig. 34   Cooling fan circuit diagnosis (Part 3 of 6). 2006–08 Aveo w/single fan

Test Description

The numbers below refer to the step numbers on the diagnostic table.

4. This step, along with step 5, checks for the ability of the ECM to operate the cooling fans.

22. By directly grounding the ECM low cooling fan relay and high cooling fan relay control circuits, the cooling fan should run at high speed.

Step	Action	Yes	No
1	Did you perform the Diagnostic System Check-Vehicle?	Go to Step 2	Go to Diagnostic System Check
2	1. Inspect the I/P fuse block fuse F18 for the 1.4L/1.5L application, or underhood fuse EF2 for the 1.2L. 2. Replace the fuse as needed. Is the fuse OK?	Go to Step 3	Go to Diagnostic Aids
3	1. Inspect the engine fuse block fuse EF3. 2. Replace the fuse as needed. Is the fuse OK?	Go to Step 4	Go to Diagnostic Aids
4	1. Turn the ignition OFF. 2. Connect the scan tool to the data link connector (DLC). 3. Start the engine. 4. The cooling fan should run at low speed when the coolant temperature reaches 93°C (199°F). Does the cooling fan run at low speed?	Go to Step 5	Go to Step 6
5	1. Turn the ignition OFF. 2. Connect a scan tool to the DLC. 3. Start the engine. 4. The cooling fan should run at high speed when the coolant temperature reaches 97°C (207°F). Does the cooling fan run at high speed?	System OK	Go to Step 22

ARM0600000000491

Fig. 34   Cooling fan circuit diagnosis (Part 2 of 6). 2006–08 Aveo w/single fan

12	1. Connect a fused jumper between the ECM low cooling fan relay control circuit and ground. 2. Connect a test light between the cooling fan relay LOW connector terminal 85 and battery positive. Is the test light ON?	Go to Step 19	Go to Step 15
13	Repair the open wire between the cooling fan relay LOW connector terminal 85 and the ignition voltage supply. Is the repair complete?	System OK	--
14	Repair the open wire between the cooling fan relay LOW connector terminal 30 and the fuse EF3. Is the repair complete?	System OK	--
15	Repair the open wire between the cooling fan relay LOW connector terminal 86 and the ECM low cooling fan relay control circuit. Is the repair complete?	System OK	--
16	Inspect for an open wire between the cooling fan relay LOW connector terminal 87 and the cooling fan connector terminal 2. Is the problem found?	Go to Step 20	Go to Step 17
17	Inspect for an open wire between the cooling fan connector terminal 1 and ground. Is the problem found?	Go to Step 20	Go to Step 18
18	Replace the cooling fan. Refer to Cooling Fan Replacement - Electric. Is the repair complete?	System OK	--

ARM0600000000493

Fig. 34   Cooling fan circuit diagnosis (Part 4 of 6). 2006–08 Aveo w/single fan

19	Replace the cooling fan relay LOW. Is the repair complete?	System OK	--
20	Repair the wire as needed. Is the repair complete?	System OK	--
21	Replace the ECM. Is the repair complete	System OK	--
22	1. Turn the ignition OFF. 2. Disconnect the ECM connector. 3. Connect a fused jumper between the ECM low cooling fan relay control circuit and ground. 4. Connect a fused jumper between the ECM high cooling fan relay control circuit and ground. 5. Turn the ignition ON. Does the cooling fan run at high speed?	Go to Step 21	Go to Step 23
23	1. Turn the ignition OFF. 2. Disconnect the cooling fan relay HI. 3. Connect a test light between the cooling fan relay high connector terminal 85 and ground. 4. Turn the ignition ON. Is the test light ON?	Go to Step 24	Go to Step 28
24	1. Turn the ignition OFF. 2. Connect a test light between the cooling fan relay HI connector terminal 30 and ground. Is the test light ON?	Go to Step 25	Go to Step 29
25	Connect a test light between the cooling fan relay HI connector terminal 87 and ground. Is the test light ON?	Go to Step 26	Go to Step 30
26	1. Connect a fused jumper between the ECM high cooling fan control circuit and ground. 2. Connect a test light between the cooling fan relay HI connector terminal 86 and battery positive. Is the test light ON?	Go to Step 27	Go to Step 31

ARM0600000000494

**Fig. 34   Cooling fan circuit diagnosis (Part 5 of 6).
2006–08 Aveo w/single fan**

Circuit Description

The engine cooling fan circuit operates the main cooling fan and the auxiliary cooling fan. The cooling fans are controlled by the engine control module (ECM) based on inputs from the engine coolant temperature (ECT) sensor and the air conditioning pressure (ACP) sensor. The ECM controls the low speed cooling fan operation by providing a ground signal to the low speed fan relay. This energizes the low speed cooling fan relay and operates the main cooling fan and the auxiliary cooling fan at low speed as the cooling fans are connected in a series circuit. The ECM controls the high speed cooling fan operation by providing a ground signal to the high speed cooling fan relay and the series/parallel relay a the same time. This energizes the low speed cooling fan relay, the high speed cooling fan relay, and the series/parallel cooling fan relay resulting in high speed fan operation as the cooling fans are now connected in a parallel circuit.

Diagnostic Aids

- If the owner complained of an overheating problem, it must be determined if the complaint was due to an actual boil over, or the engine coolant temperature gage indicated overheating. If the engine is overheating and the cooling fans are ON, the cooling system should be inspected.
- If the engine fuse block fuses EF3 become open, blown, immediately after installation, inspect for a short to ground in the wiring of the appropriate circuit. If the fuses become open, blown, when the cooling fans are to be turned ON by the ECM, suspect a faulty cooling fan motor.
- The ECM will turn the cooling fans ON at low speed when the coolant temperature is 97°C (207°F). The ECM will turn the cooling fans OFF when the coolant temperature is 94°C (201°F).
- The ECM will turn the cooling fans ON at high speed when the coolant temperature is 101°C (214°F). The ECM will change the cooling fans from high speed to low speed when the coolant temperature is 98°C (208°F).
- The ECM will turn the cooling fans ON at low speed when the A/C system is ON. The ECM will change the cooling fans from low speed to high speed when the high side A/C pressure is 1882 kPa (273 psi), then return to low speed when the high side A/C pressure is 1448 kPa (210 psi). When the A/C system is ON, the ECM will change the cooling fans from low to high speed when the coolant temperature reaches 117°C (244°F), then return to low speed when the coolant temperature reaches 114°C (237°F).
- The cooling fan circuit can be inspected quickly by disconnecting the ECM and ground the low speed relay control circuit. This should create low speed cooling fan operation with the ignition ON. By grounding the ECM low speed relay control circuit and the high speed relay control circuit and turning the ignition ON, high speed cooling fan operation should be achieved.

ARM0600000000496

**Fig. 35   Cooling fan circuit diagnosis (Part 1 of 9).
2006–08 Aveo w/dual fans**

27	Replace the cooling fan relay HI. Is the repair complete?	System OK	--
28	Repair the open wire between the cooling fan relay HI connector terminal 85 and the ignition switch voltage supply. Is the repair complete?	System OK	--
29	Repair the open wire between the cooling fan relay HI connector terminal 30 and the fuse EF3. Is the repair complete?	System OK	--
30	Repair the open wire between the cooling fan relay HI connector terminal 87 and the cooling fan connector terminal 2. Is the repair complete?	System OK	--
31	Repair the open wire between the cooling fan relay HI connector terminal 86 and the ECM relay control circuit. Is the repair complete?	System OK	--

ARM0600000000495

**Fig. 34   Cooling fan circuit diagnosis (Part 6 of 6).
2006–08 Aveo w/single fan**

Test Description

The numbers below refer to the step numbers on the diagnostic table.

4. This step, along with step 5, checks for the ability of the ECM to operate the cooling fans.

8. This step, along with step 9, checks for the ability of the ECM to operate the cooling fans in response to A/C pressure readings.

16. After confirming battery voltage and the ECM supplying a ground to the coil side of the cooling fan relay A, by jumpering connector terminals 30 and 87, it will be determined if the relay is at fault or a wiring problem is present.

31. This step checks for the presence of battery voltage to the main cooling fan when the A/C is ON. If battery voltage is present and the cooling fans are not operating, the problem is in the ground side of the cooling fan circuit.

37. By directly grounding the ECM low relay and high relay control circuits, the main and auxiliary cooling fans should run at high speed.

Step	Action	Yes	No
1	Did you perform the Diagnostic System Check - Vehicle?	Go to Step 2	Go to Diagnostic System Check
2	1. Inspect the I/P engine block fuse EF3. 2. Replace the fuse as needed. Is the fuse OK?	Go to Step 3	Go to Diagnostic Aids
3	1. Inspect the I/P fuse block fuse F18. 2. Replace the fuse as needed. Is the fuse OK?	Go to Step 4	Go to Diagnostic Aids
4	1. Turn the ignition OFF. 2. Turn the A/C switch OFF. 3. Connect a scan tool to the data link connector (DLC). 4. The cooling fans should run at low speed when the coolant temperature reaches 97°C (207°F). Do the cooling fans run at low speed?	Go to Step 5	Go to Step 10

ARM0600000000497

**Fig. 35   Cooling fan circuit diagnosis (Part 2 of 9).
2006–08 Aveo w/dual fans**

Step	Procedure	Yes	No
5	1. Turn the ignition OFF. 2. Turn the A/C switch OFF. 3. Connect a scan tool to the DLC. 4. Start the engine. 5. The cooling fans should run at high speed when the coolant temperature reaches 101°C (214°F). Do the cooling fans run at high speed?	Go to Step 6	Go to Step 33
6	1. Turn the ignition OFF. 2. Start the engine. 3. Turn the A/C switch ON. Does the A/C compressor clutch engage?	Go to Step 8	Go to Step 7
7	1. Diagnose the A/C compressor clutch circuit. 2. Repair the A/C compressor clutch circuit as needed. 3. Start the engine. 4. Turn the A/C switch ON. Does the A/C compressor clutch engage?	Go to Step 8	--
8	Do the cooling fans run at low speed?	Go to Step 9	Go to Step 31
9	1. Turn the ignition OFF. 2. Connect the A/C pressure gages. 3. Start the engine. 4. Turn the A/C switch ON. 5. The cooling fans should run at high speed when the high side A/C pressure reaches 1 882 kPa (273 psi). Do the cooling fans run at high speed?	Go to Step 10	Go to DTC P0532 or P0533
10	1. Turn the ignition OFF. 2. Connect a scan tool to the DLC. 3. The coolant temperature should be above 97°C (207°C). 4. Disconnect the main cooling fan connector. 5. Turn the ignition ON. 6. Connect a test light between the main cooling fan connector terminal 2 and ground. Is the test light ON?	Go to Step 11	Go to Step 12

ARM0600000000498

Fig. 35　Cooling fan circuit diagnosis (Part 3 of 9). 2006–08 Aveo w/dual fans

Step	Procedure	Yes	No
11	1. Turn the ignition OFF. 2. Connect a scan tool to the DLC. 3. The coolant temperature should be above 97°C (207°C). 4. Disconnect the main cooling fan connector. 5. Connect a test light between the main cooling fan connector terminal 1 and B+. Is the test light ON?	Go to Step 28	Go to Step 17
12	1. Turn the ignition OFF. 2. Disconnect the cooling fan relay LOW. 3. Connect a test light between the cooling fan relay LOW connector terminal 86 and ground. 4. Turn the ignition ON. Is the test light ON?	Go to Step 13	Go to Step 24
13	1. Turn the ignition OFF. 2. Connect the cooling fan relay LOW. 3. Disconnect engine control module (ECM) white connector. 4. Connect a fused jumper between the ECM low cooling fan relay control circuit and ground. 5. Turn the ignition ON. Do the cooling fans run at low speed?	Go to Step 30	Go to Step 14
14	Inspect for an open wire between the low speed cooling fan relay connector terminal 86 and the ECM low cooling fan relay control circuit. Is the problem found?	Go to Step 25	Go to Step 15
15	1. Turn the ignition OFF. 2. Disconnect the cooling fan relay LOW. 3. Connect a test light between the cooling fan relay LOW connector terminal 30 and ground. Is the test light ON?	Go to Step 16	Go to Step 23
16	Connect a fused jumper between the cooling fan relay LOW connector terminals 30 and 87. Do the cooling fans run at low speed?	Go to Step 26	Go to Step 17

ARM0600000000499

Fig. 35　Cooling fan circuit diagnosis (Part 4 of 9). 2006–08 Aveo w/dual fans

Step	Procedure	Yes	No
17	1. Disconnect the series/parallel fan series/parallel relay. 2. Connect a fused jumper between the cooling fan relay LOW connector terminals 30 and 87. 3. Connect a fused jumper between the cooling fan series/parallel relay connector terminals 30 and 87. Do the cooling fans run at low speed?	Go to Step 27	Go to Step 18
18	Inspect the wire between the cooling fan relay LOW connector terminal 87 to the main cooling fan connector terminal 2 for an open. Is the problem found?	Go to Step 22	Go to Step 19
19	Inspect the wire between the main cooling fan connector terminal 1 and the cooling fan control relay connector terminal 30 for an open. Is the problem found?	Go to Step 22	Go to Step 20
20	Inspect the wire between the cooling fan series/parallel relay connector terminal 87A and the auxiliary cooling fan connector terminal 2 for an open. Is the problem found?	Go to Step 22	Go to Step 21
21	Inspect for an open wire between the auxiliary cooling fan connector terminal 1 and ground. Is the problem found?	Go to Step 22	Go to Step 29
22	Repair the open wire as needed. Is the repair complete?	System OK	--
23	Repair the open between the cooling fan relay LOW connector terminal 30 and the fuse EF3. Is the repair complete?	System OK	--
24	Repair the open between the cooling fan relay LOW connector terminal 85 and the ignition switch. Is the repair complete?	System OK	--

ARM0600000000500

Fig. 35　Cooling fan circuit diagnosis (Part 5 of 9). 2006–08 Aveo w/dual fans

Step	Procedure	Yes	No
25	Repair the open wire between the cooling fan relay LOW connector terminal 86 and the ECM low cooling fan relay control circuit. Is the repair complete?	System OK	--
26	Replace the cooling fan relay LOW. Is the repair complete?	System OK	--
27	Replace the cooling fan series/parallel relay. Is the repair complete?	System OK	--
28	Replace the main cooling fan. Is the repair complete?	System OK	--
29	Replace the auxiliary cooling fan. Is the repair complete?	System OK	--
30	Replace the ECM. Is the repair complete?	System OK	--
31	1. Turn the ignition OFF. 2. Disconnect the main cooling fan connector. 3. Connect a test light between the main cooling fan connector terminal 2 and ground. 4. Turn the A/C switch ON. 5. Start the engine. Is the test light ON?	Go to Step 32	Go to Step 12
32	1. Turn the ignition OFF. 2. Connect a test light between the main cooling fan connector terminal 1 and battery positive. 3. Turn the A/C switch ON. 4. Start the engine. Is the test light ON?	Go to Step 28	Go to Step 17
33	1. Turn the ignition OFF. 2. Disconnect the cooling fan relay HI. 3. Connect a test light between the cooling fan relay HI connector terminal 85 and ground. 4. Turn the ignition ON. Is the test light ON?	Go to Step 34	Go to Step 44

ARM0600000000501

Fig. 35　Cooling fan circuit diagnosis (Part 6 of 9). 2006–08 Aveo w/dual fans

Step	Action	Yes	No
34	1. Turn the ignition OFF. 2. Connect a test light between the cooling fan relay HI connector terminal 30 and ground. Is the test light ON?	Go to Step 35	Go to Step 45
35	1. Disconnect the cooling fan series/parallel relay. 2. Connect a test light between the cooling fan series/parallel relay connector terminal 85 and ground. 3. Turn the ignition ON. Is the test light ON?	Go to Step 36	Go to Step 46
36	1. Turn the ignition OFF. 2. Connect a test light between the cooling fan series/parallel relay connector terminal 87 and battery positive. Is the test light ON?	Go to Step 37	Go to Step 47
37	1. Connect the main cooling fan connector. 2. Connect the cooling fan relay HI. 3. Connect the cooling fan series/parallel relay. 4. Disconnect the ECM connector. 5. Connect a fused jumper between the ECM low cooling fan relay control circuit and ground. 6. Connect a fused jumper between the ECM high cooling fan relay control circuit and ground. 7. Turn the ignition ON. Do the cooling fans run at high speed?	Go to Step 30	Go to Step 38 Go to Step 39
38	1. Turn the ignition OFF. 2. Inspect for an open wire between the cooling fan relay HI connector terminal 86 and the ECM high cooling fan relay control circuit and ground. Is the problem found?	Go to Step 22	--

ARM0600000000502

Fig. 35   Cooling fan circuit diagnosis (Part 7 of 9). 2006–08 Aveo w/dual fans

Step	Action	Yes	No
39	1. Disconnect the cooling fan relay HI. 2. Connect a test light between the cooling fan relay HI connector terminal 87 and battery positive. Is the test light ON?	Go to Step 40	Go to Step 48
40	1. Disconnect the ECM connector. 2. Connect a fused jumper between the ECM high cooling fan relay control circuit and ground. 3. Disconnect the cooling fan relay HI. 4. Connect a test light between the cooling fan control relay connector terminal 86 and battery positive. Is the test light ON?	Go to Step 41	Go to Step 49
41	1. Connect the cooling fan control relay. 2. Connect a fused jumper between the ECM high cooling fan relay control circuit and ground. 3. Disconnect the cooling fan relay HI. 4. Connect a fused jumper between the cooling fan relay HI connector terminals 30 and 87. 5. Disconnect the low speed cooling fan relay. 6. Connect a fused jumper between the low speed cooling fan relay connector terminals 30 and 87. 7. Turn the ignition ON. Do the cooling fans run at high speed?	Go to Step 43	Go to Step 42
42	1. Turn the ignition OFF. 2. Connect a fused jumper between the ECM high cooling fan relay control circuit and ground. 3. Disconnect the cooling fan series/parallel relay. 4. Connect a fused jumper between the cooling fan series/parallel relay connector terminals 30 and 87. 5. Connect a fused jumper between the low speed cooling fan relay connector terminals 30 and 87. 6. Turn the ignition ON. Do the cooling fans run at high speed?	Go to Step 27	--

ARM0600000000503

Fig. 35   Cooling fan circuit diagnosis (Part 8 of 9). 2006–08 Aveo w/dual fans

Step	Action	Yes	No
43	Replace the cooling fan relay HI. Is the repair complete?	System OK	--
44	Repair the open wire between the cooling fan relay HI connector terminal 85 and the ignition switch. Is the repair complete?	System OK	--
45	Repair the open wire between the cooling fan relay HI connector terminal 30 and the battery. Is the repair complete?	System OK	--
46	Repair the open wire between the cooling fan series/parallel relay connector terminal 85 and the ignition switch. Is the repair complete?	System OK	--
47	Repair the open wire between the cooling fan series/parallel relay connector terminal 87 and ground. Is the repair complete?	System OK	--
48	Repair the open wire between the cooling fan relay HI connector terminal 87 and the auxiliary cooling fan connector terminal 2. Is the repair complete?	System OK	--
49	Repair the open wire between the cooling fan series/parallel relay connector terminal 85 and the ECM connector terminal K12. Is the repair complete?	System OK	--

ARM0600000000504

Fig. 35   Cooling fan circuit diagnosis (Part 9 of 9). 2006–08 Aveo w/dual fans

Step	Action	Yes	No
1	Install a scan tool. Does the scan tool power up?	Go to Step 2	Diagnose Data Link Communications

2	1. Turn ON the ignition, with the engine OFF.
	2. Attempt to establish communication with the following control modules:
	  • Instrument Cluster
	  • Powertrain Control Module
	Does the scan tool communicate with the control modules?
		Go to Step 3	Diagnose Data Link Communications

3	Select the powertrain control module display DTCs function on the scan tool. Does the scan tool display any DTCs?	Go to Step 4	Diagnose Symptoms - Engine Cooling
4	Does the scan tool display any DTCs which begin with a "U"?	Diagnose Data Link Communications	Diagnose Trouble Code

GC1080100646000X

Fig. 36   Diagnostic system check. Bonneville & LeSabre

Step	Action	Yes	No
	DEFINITION: One or both engine cooling fan motors run continuously in high or low speed.		
1	Did you perform the Engine Cooling Diagnostic System Check?	Go to *Step 2*	Go To *Diagnostic System Check -*
2	**Important:** The cooling fan 1 relay and cooling fan 2 relay are improperly identified in the underhood fuse block. Turn ON the ignition, with the engine OFF. Are one or both cooling fans ON?	Go to *Step 3*	*Test Intermittent and Poor Connections*
3	Are both cooling fans running continuously?	Go to *Step 5*	Go to *Step 4*
4	Remove the cooling fan S/P relay. Did the left cooling fan turn OFF?	Go to *Step 6*	Go to *Step 7*
5	Repair the short to voltage in the right cooling fan motor supply voltage circuit. Did you complete the repair?	Go to *Step 8*	—
6	Repair the short to voltage in the cooling fan low reference circuit. Did you complete the repair?	Go to *Step 8*	—
7	Repair the short to voltage in the left cooling fan motor supply voltage circuit. Did you complete the repair?	Go to *Step 8*	—
8	Operate the system in order to verify the repair. Did you correct the condition?	System OK	Go to *Step 2*

GC1080100647000X

Fig. 37 Cooling fan always on. Bonneville & LeSabre

Step	Action	Yes	No
5	1. Disconnect the cooling fan S/P relay. 2. Connect the second 20-A fused jumper between the right cooling fan ground circuit of the cooling fan S/P relay and the left cooling fan motor supply voltage circuit of the cooling fan S/P relay. Do both cooling fans operate in low speed?	Go to *Step 14*	Go to *Step 6*
6	Connect a 20-A fused jumper between the battery positive voltage circuit of the cooling fan S/P relay and the cooling fan motor supply voltage circuit of the cooling fan S/P relay. Does the left cooling fan operate in high speed?	Go to *Step 9*	Go to *Step 7*
7	1. Install the cooling fan S/P relay. 2. Disconnect the left cooling fan electrical connector. 3. Connect the second 20-Amp fused jumper wire from the cooling fan motor supply voltage circuit of the left cooling fan electrical connector to the ground circuit of the left cooling fan electrical connector. Does the right cooling fan operate in high speed?	Go to *Step 16*	Go to *Step 8*
8	Connect a 20-Amp fused jumper wire from the cooling fan motor supply voltage circuit of the left cooling fan electrical connector to a good ground. Does the right cooling fan operate in high speed?	Go to *Step 20*	Go to *Step 21*
9	1. Install the cooling fan S/P relay. 2. Disconnect the right cooling fan electrical connector. 3. Connect the second 20-Amp fused jumper wire from the cooling fan motor supply voltage circuit of the right cooling fan electrical connector to the cooling fan low reference circuit of the right cooling fan electrical connector. Does the left cooling fan operate in high speed?	Go to *Step 17*	Go to *Step 10*
10	Connect the second 20-Amp fused jumper wire from battery positive voltage to the cooling fan low reference circuit of the of the right cooling fan electrical connector. Does the left cooling fan operate in high speed?	Go to *Step 18*	Go to *Step 22*
11	Is the left cooling fan operating properly in high speed?	Go to *Step 12*	Go to *Step 15*
12	1. Disconnect the cooling fan S/P relay. 2. Connect the second 20-A fused jumper between the cooling fan low reference circuit of the cooling fan S/P relay and the ground circuit of the cooling fan S/P relay. Does the right cooling fan operate properly in high speed?	Go to *Step 14*	Go to *Step 19*
13	Inspect for poor connections at the cooling fan 1 relay. Did you find and correct the condition?	Go to *Step 28*	Go to *Step 23*
14	Inspect for poor connections at the cooling fan S/P relay. Did you find and correct the condition?	Go to *Step 28*	Go to *Step 24*
15	Inspect for poor connections at the cooling fan 2 relay. Did you find and correct the condition?	Go to *Step 28*	Go to *Step 25*
16	Inspect for poor connections at the harness connector of the left cooling fan. Did you find and correct the condition?	Go to *Step 28*	Go to *Step 26*

GC1080100648020X

Fig. 38 Cooling fan inoperative (Part 2 of 3). Bonneville & LeSabre

Step	Action	Yes	No
	Schematic Reference: *Engine Cooling Schematics*		
1	Did you perform the Engine Cooling Diagnostic System Check?	Go to *Step 2*	Go to Diagnostic System Check -
2	**Important:** The cooling fan 1 relay and cooling fan 2 relay are improperly identified in the underhood fuse block. 1. Install a scan tool. 2. Turn ON the ignition, with the engine OFF. 3. With a scan tool, command the Fans Low Speed ON and OFF. Do the low speed engine cooling fans turn ON and OFF with each command?	Go to *Step 3*	Go to *Step 4*
3	**Important:** Before the PCM changes the speed of the cooling fans, a 3-second delay will occur. With a scan tool, command the Fans High Speed ON and OFF. Do the high speed engine cooling fans turn ON and OFF with each command?	*Test Intermittent and Poor Connections*	Go to *Step 11*
4	**Important:** Following this step, do NOT remove the 20-A fused jumper wire that is connected during this step. While performing the following steps, use a second 20-A fused jumper wire. 1. Disconnect the cooling fan 1 relay. 2. Connect a 20-A fused jumper between the battery positive voltage circuit of the cooling fan 1 relay and the cooling fan motor supply voltage circuit of the cooling fan 1 relay. Do both cooling fans operate in low speed?	Go to *Step 13*	Go to *Step 5*

GC1080100648010X

Fig. 38 Cooling fan inoperative (Part 1 of 3). Bonneville & LeSabre

Step	Action	Yes	No
17	Inspect for poor connections at the harness connector of the right cooling fan. Did you find and correct the condition?	Go to *Step 28*	Go to *Step 27*
18	Repair the right cooling fan motor supply voltage circuit. Did you complete the repair?	Go to *Step 28*	—
19	Repair the left cooling fan ground circuit. Did you complete the repair?	Go to *Step 28*	—
20	Repair the right cooling fan ground circuit. Did you complete the repair?	Go to *Step 28*	—
21	Repair the left cooling fan motor supply voltage circuit. Did you complete the repair?	Go to *Step 28*	—
22	Repair the cooling fan low reference circuit. Did you complete the repair?	Go to *Step 28*	—
23	Replace the cooling fan 1 relay. Did you complete the repair?	Go to *Step 28*	—
24	Replace the cooling fan S/P relay. Did you complete the repair?	Go to *Step 28*	—
25	Replace the cooling fan 2 relay. Did you complete the repair?	Go to *Step 28*	—
26	Replace the left cooling fan. Did you complete the repair?	Go to *Step 28*	—
27	Replace the right cooling fan. Did you complete the repair?	Go to *Step 28*	—
28	Operate the system in order to verify the repair. Did you correct the condition?	System OK	Go to *Step 3*

GC1080100648030X

Fig. 38 Cooling fan inoperative (Part 3 of 3). Bonneville & LeSabre

DEFINITION: The engine cooling fan motor runs continuously.

Step	Action	Yes	No
1	Did you perform the Engine Cooling Diagnostic System Check?	Go to Step 2	Go To Diagnostic System Check
2	Turn ON the ignition, with the engine OFF. Is the engine cooling fan running all the time?	Go to Step 3	Test for Intermittent and Poor Connections
3	Remove the cooling fan relay. Did the cooling fan turn OFF?	Go to Step 5	Go to Step 4
4	Repair the short to power in the cooling fan motor supply voltage circuit. Did you complete the repair?	Go to Step 7	--
5	Inspect for poor connections at the cooling fan relay. Did you find and correct the condition?	Go to Step 7	Go to Step 6
6	Replace the cooling fan relay. Did you complete the repair?	Go to Step 7	--
7	Operate the system in order to verify the repair. Did you correct the condition?	System OK	Go to Step 2

ARM0300000000307

Fig. 39 Cooling fan always on diagnosis. Cavalier & Sunfire

Step	Action	Yes	No
6	Probe the harness connector of the cooling fan motor with a test lamp connected between the cooling fan motor supply voltage circuit and the ground circuit of the cooling fan motor. Does the test lamp illuminate?	Go to Step 11	Go to Step 9
7	Repair the battery positive circuit of the cooling fan relay. Did you complete the repair?	Go to Step 14	--
8	Repair the supply voltage circuit of the cooling fan motor. Did you complete the repair?	Go to Step 14	--
9	Repair the ground circuit of the cooling fan motor. Did you complete the repair?	Go to Step 14	--
10	Inspect for poor connections at the cooling fan relay. Did you find and correct the condition?	Go to Step 14	Go to Step 12
11	Inspect for poor connections at the harness connector of the cooling fan motor. Did you find and correct the condition?	Go to Step 14	Go to Step 13
12	Replace the cooling fan relay. Did you complete the repair?	Go to Step 14	--
13	Replace the cooling fan motor. Did you complete the repair?	Go to Step 14	--
14	Operate the system in order to verify the repair. Did you correct the condition?	System OK	Go to Step 2

ARM0300000000309

Fig. 40 Cooling fan inoperative (Part 2 of 2). Cavalier & Sunfire

DEFINITION: The engine cooling fan motor does not operate.

Step	Action	Yes	No
1	Did you perform A Diagnostic System Check-Engine Cooling?	Go to Step 2	Go to Diagnostic System Check
2	1. Install a scan tool. 2. Turn ON the ignition, with the engine OFF. 3. With a scan tool, command the cooling fan ON and OFF. Does the engine cooling fan turn ON and OFF with each command?	Test for Intermittent and Poor Connections	Go to Step 3
3	1. Turn OFF the ignition. 2. Remove the cooling fan relay. 3. Probe the battery positive voltage circuit of the cooling fan relay switch side with a test lamp that is connected to a good ground. Does the test lamp illuminate?	Go to Step 4	Go to Step 7
4	Connect a 20 A fused jumper wire between the battery positive voltage circuit of the cooling fan relay and the cooling fan motor supply voltage circuit of the cooling fan relay. Does the cooling fan operate?	Go to Step 10	Go to Step 5
5	1. Disconnect the cooling fan connector. 2. Probe the cooling fan motor supply voltage circuit at the harness connector with a test lamp that is connected to a good ground. Does the test lamp illuminate?	Go to Step 6	Go to Step 8

ARM0300000000308

Fig. 40 Cooling fan inoperative (Part 1 of 2). Cavalier & Sunfire

Step	Action	Yes	No
1	Install a scan tool. Does the scan tool power up?	Go to Step 2	Diagnose Data Link Communications
2	1. Turn ON the ignition, with the engine OFF. 2. Attempt to establish communication with the following control modules: • Instrument Cluster • Powertrain Control Module Does the scan tool communicate with the control modules?	Go to Step 3	Diagnose Data Link Communications
3	Select the powertrain control module display DTCs function on the scan tool. Does the scan tool display any DTCs?	Go to Step 4	Diagnose engine cooling
4	Does the scan tool display any DTCs which begin with a "U"?	Diagnose Data Link Communications	Diagnose Diagnostic Trouble Code (DTC)

ARM0300000000318

Fig. 41 Diagnostic system check. Century & Regal

Step	Action	Yes	No
	DEFINITION: One or both engine cooling fan motors run continuously in high or low speed modes.		
1	Did you perform the Engine Cooling Diagnostic System Check?	Go to Step 2	Go to Diagnostic System Check
2	Turn ON the ignition, with the engine OFF. Are one or both cooling fans ON?	Go to Step 3	Test for Intermittent and Poor Connections
3	Are both cooling fans running continuously?	Go to Step 5	Go to Step 4
4	Remove the cooling fan 2 relay. Did the right cooling fan turn OFF?	Go to Step 8	Go to Step 6
5	Remove the cooling fan 1 relay. Did the cooling fans turn OFF?	Go to Step 10	Go to Step 7
6	Remove the cooling fan 3 relay. Did the right cooling fan turn OFF?	Go to Step 11	Go to Step 9

ARM0300000000310

Fig. 42   Cooling fan always on (Part 1 of 2). Century & Regal

7	Repair the short to voltage in the left cooling fan motor supply voltage circuit. Did you complete the repair?	Go to Step 14	--
8	Repair the short to voltage in the left cooling fan low reference circuit. Did you complete the repair?	Go to Step 14	--
9	Repair the short to voltage in the right cooling fan motor supply voltage circuit. Did you complete the repair?	Go to Step 14	--
10	Inspect for poor connections at the cooling fan 1 relay. Did you find and correct the condition?	Go to Step 14	Go to Step 12
11	Inspect for poor connections at the cooling fan 3 relay. Did you find and correct the condition?	Go to Step 14	Go to Step 13
12	Replace the cooling fan 1 relay. Did you complete the replacement?	Go to Step 14	--
13	Replace the cooling fan 3 relay. Did you complete the replacement?	Go to Step 14	--
14	Operate the system in order to verify the repair. Did you correct the condition?	System OK	Go to Step 2

ARM0300000000311

Fig. 42   Cooling fan always on (Part 2 of 2). Century & Regal

1	Did you perform the Engine Cooling Diagnostic System Check?	Go to Step 2	Go to Diagnostic System Check
2	1. Install a scan tool. 2. Turn ON the ignition, with the engine OFF. 3. With a scan tool, command the Fans Low Speed ON and OFF. Do the low speed engine cooling fans turn ON and OFF with each command?	Go to Step 3	Go to Step 4
3	**Important:** A 3-second delay occurs before the PCM changes the cooling fan speed. With a scan tool, command the Fans High Speed ON and OFF. Do the high speed engine cooling fans turn ON and OFF with each command?	Test for Intermittent and Poor Connections	Go to Step 12
4	**Important** Do NOT remove the 20-A fused jumper wire connected during this step. Use a second 20-A fused jumper wire while performing the following steps. 1. Remove the cooling fan 1 relay. 2. Connect a 20-A fused jumper between the battery positive switch side voltage circuit and the cooling fan motor supply voltage circuit of the cooling fan 1 relay. Do both cooling fans operate in low speed?	Go to Step 22	Go to Step 5

ARM0300000000312

Fig. 43   Cooling fan inoperative (Part 1 of 6). Century & Regal

5	1. Disconnect the cooling fan 2 relay 2. Connect the second 20-A fused jumper between the cooling fan low reference circuit and the cooling fan motor supply voltage circuit of the cooling fan 2 relay. Do both cooling fans operate in low speed?	Go to Step 23	Go to Step 6
6	Connect the second 20-A fused jumper between the battery positive voltage circuit and the cooling fan motor supply voltage circuit of the cooling fan 2 relay. Does the right cooling fan operate in high speed?	Go to Step 9	Go to Step 7
7	1. Install the cooling fan 2 relay. 2. Disconnect the right cooling fan electrical connector. 3. Connect the second 20-Amp fused jumper wire from the cooling fan motor supply voltage circuit to the ground circuit of the right cooling fan electrical connector. Does the left cooling fan operate in high speed?	Go to Step 25	Go to Step 8
8	Connect the second 20-Amp fused jumper wire from the cooling fan motor supply voltage circuit of the right cooling fan electrical connector to a good ground. Does the left cooling fan operate in high speed?	Go to Step 29	Go to Step 30
9	1. Install the cooling fan 2 relay. 2. Disconnect the left cooling fan electrical connector. 3. Connect the second 20-Amp fused jumper wire from the cooling fan motor supply voltage circuit to the cooling fan low reference circuit of the left cooling fan electrical connector. Does the right cooling fan operate in high speed?	Go to Step 26	Go to Step 10
10	Connect the second 20-Amp fused jumper wire from the coil side battery positive voltage circuit to the cooling fan low reference circuit of the of the left cooling fan electrical connector. Does the right cooling fan operate in high speed?	Go to Step 11	Go to Step 31

ARM0300000000313

Fig. 43   Cooling fan inoperative (Part 2 of 6). Century & Regal

		Go to	Go to
11	Probe the battery positive voltage circuit on the switch side of the cooling fan 1 relay with a test lamp that is connected to a good ground. Does the test lamp illuminate?	Go to Step 27	Go to Step 32
12	Is the right cooling fan operating properly in high speed?	Go to Step 19	Go to Step 13
13	1. Turn off the ignition. 2. Disconnect the cooling fan 3 relay. 3. Turn ON the ignition, with the engine OFF. 4. Connect a test lamp between the high speed cooling fan relay control circuit and the battery positive voltage circuit on the coil side of the cooling fan 3 relay. 5. With a scan tool command the High Speed Fans ON and OFF. Does the test lamp turn ON and OFF with each command?	Go to Step 15	Go to Step 14
14	Probe the battery positive voltage circuit on the coil side of the cooling fan 3 relay with a test lamp that is connected to a good ground. Does the test lamp illuminate?	Go to Step 34	Go to Step 33
15	Install a 20 amp fused jumper between the battery positive voltage circuit on the switch side of the cooling fan 3 relay and the cooling fan motor supply voltage circuit. Does the right cooling fan operate in high speed?	Go to Step 24	Go to Step 16
16	Probe the battery positive voltage circuit on the switch side of the cooling fan 3 relay with a test lamp connected to a good ground. Does the test lamp illuminate?	Go to Step 17	Go to Step 33
17	With the 20 amp fused jumper still installed. 1. Disconnect the right cooling fan electrical connector. 2. Connect a test lamp from the cooling fan motor supply voltage circuit to the ground circuit of the right cooling fan electrical connector. Does the test lamp illuminate?	Go to Step 25	Go to Step 18

ARM0300000000314

**Fig. 43 Cooling fan inoperative (Part 3 of 6).
Century & Regal**

		Go to	Go to
18	Probe the cooling fan motor supply voltage circuit of the right cooling fan electrical connector with a test lamp that is connected to a good ground. Does the test lamp illuminate?	Go to Step 29	Go to Step 30
19	1. Turn OFF the ignition. 2. Disconnect the cooling fan 2 relay 3. Turn ON the ignition, with the engine OFF. 4. Connect a 20-A fused jumper between the cooling fan low reference circuit and the ground circuit of the cooling fan 2 relay. 5. With a scan tool command the Fans High Speed ON and OFF. Does the left cooling fan operate in high speed?	Go to Step 20	Go to Step 28
20	1. Connect a test lamp between the high speed cooling fan relay control circuit of the cooling fan 2 relay and the battery positive voltage circuit of the cooling fan 2 relay. 2. With a scan tool command the Fans High Speed ON and OFF. Does the test lamp turn ON and OFF with each command?	Go to Step 23	Go to Step 21
21	Probe the battery positive voltage circuit of the cooling fan 2 relay with a test lamp that is connected to a good ground. Does the test lamp illuminate?	Go to Step 34	Go to Step 33
22	Inspect for poor connections at the cooling fan 1 relay. Did you find and correct the condition?	Go to Step 40	Go to Step 35
23	Inspect for poor connections at the cooling fan 2 relay. Did you find and correct the condition?	Go to Step 40	Go to Step 36
24	Inspect for poor connections at the cooling fan 3 relay. Did you find and correct the condition?	Go to Step 40	Go to Step 37

ARM0300000000315

**Fig. 43 Cooling fan inoperative (Part 4 of 6).
Century & Regal**

		Go to	Go to
25	Inspect for poor connections at the harness connector of the right cooling fan. Did you find and correct the condition?	Go to Step 40	Go to Step 38
26	Inspect for poor connections at the harness connector of the left cooling fan. Did you find and correct the condition?	Go to Step 40	Go to Step 39
27	Repair the left cooling fan motor supply voltage circuit for an open. Is the repair complete?	Go to Step 40	--
28	Repair the left cooling fan ground circuit for an open. Is the repair complete?	Go to Step 40	--
29	Repair the right cooling fan ground circuit for an open. Is the repair complete?	Go to Step 40	--
30	Repair the right cooling fan motor supply voltage circuit for an open. Is the repair complete?	Go to Step 40	--
31	Repair the left cooling fan low reference circuit for a short to ground or an open. Is the repair complete?	Go to Step 40	--
32	Repair the cooling fan 1 relay battery positive voltage circuit for an open. Is the repair complete?	Go to Step 40	--

ARM0300000000316

**Fig. 43 Cooling fan inoperative (Part 5 of 6).
Century & Regal**

33	Repair the battery positive voltage circuit for the cooling fan 2 and 3 relay for an open. Is the repair complete?	Go to Step 40	--
34	Repair the high speed cooling fan relay control circuit for an open. Is the repair complete?	Go to Step 40	--
35	Replace the cooling fan 1 relay. Is the repair complete?	Go to Step 40	--
36	Replace the cooling fan 2 relay. Is the repair complete?	Go to Step 40	--
37	Replace the cooling fan 3 relay. Is the repair complete?	Go to Step 40	--
38	Replace the right cooling fan. Is the repair complete?	Go to Step 40	--
39	Replace the left cooling fan. Is the repair complete?	Go to Step 40	--
40	Operate the system in order to verify the repair. Did you correct the condition?	System OK	Go to Step 3

ARM0300000000317

**Fig. 43 Cooling fan inoperative (Part 6 of 6).
Century & Regal**

Step	Action	Yes	No
1	Perform the following preliminary inspections: • Ensure that the battery is fully charged. • Ensure that the battery cables are clean and tight. • Inspect for any open fuses. • Inspect the easily accessible systems or the visible system components for obvious damage or conditions that could cause the symptom. • Ensure that the grounds are clean, tight, and in the correct location. • Inspect for aftermarket devices that could affect the operation of the system. • Search for applicable service bulletins. Did you find and correct the condition?	System OK	Go to Step 2
2	Install a scan tool. Does the scan tool power up?	Go to Step 3	Go to Scan Tool Does Not Power Up
3	1. Turn ON the ignition, with the engine OFF. 2. Attempt to establish communication with all of the control modules on the vehicle. Does the scan tool communicate with all of the expected vehicle control modules?	Go to Step 4	Go to Data Link References
4	**Important:** 1. To ensure that retained accessory power (RAP) mode is inactive (if equipped), open the drivers door during the following step. 2. The engine may start during the following step. Turn OFF the engine as soon as you have observed the crank power mode. 1. Access the Power Mode parameter on the scan tool. 2. Rotate the ignition switch (operate the ignition mode switch) through all positions while observing the Power Mode parameter. Does the Power Mode parameter reading on the scan tool match the ignition switch position for all switch positions?	Go to Step 5	Go to Power Mode Mismatch

ARM0500000000339

Fig. 44   Diagnostic system check (Part 1 of 3). Cobalt & G5

Step	Action	Yes	No
8	Is the customers concern with inspection/maintenance (I/M) testing?	Go to: • Inspection/Maintenance (I/M) System Check	Go to Symptoms - Vehicle

ARM0500000000341

Fig. 44   Diagnostic system check (Part 3 of 3). Cobalt & G5

Step	Action	Yes	No
5	Attempt to start the engine. Does the engine crank?	Go to Step 6	Go to Symptoms - Engine Electrical
6	Attempt to start the engine. Does the engine start and idle? Go to Step 7		Go to: • Engine Cranks but Does Not Run

7	**Important:** Do NOT clear any DTCs unless instructed by a diagnostic procedure.
	
	1. Diagnose the DTCs in the order that the DTCs appear on the scan tool or mis-diagnosis may occur.
	2. If multiple powertrain DTCs are stored, diagnose the DTCs in the following order:
	  A. Component level DTCs, such as sensor DTCs, solenoid DTCs, and relay DTCs.
	  B. System level DTCs, such as misfire DTCs, EVAP system DTCs, and fuel trim DTCs.
	
	Advance to the List All DTCs screen on the scan tool.
	
	Does the scan tool display any DTCs?
		Go to Diagnostic Trouble Code (DTC) List	Go to Step

ARM0500000000340

Fig. 44   Diagnostic system check (Part 2 of 3). Cobalt & G5

Step	Action	Yes	No
	DEFINITION: The dual speed cooling fan motor runs continuously in high or low speed.		
1	Did you perform the Diagnostic System Check - Vehicle?	Go to Step 2	Go to Diagnostic System Check - Vehicle
2	Turn ON the ignition, with the engine OFF. Is the cooling fan ON?	Go to Step 3	Test for Intermittent Conditions and Poor Connections
3	Is the cooling fan running continuously?	Go to Step 4	Go to Step 6
4	Is the cooling fan running continuously in high speed?	Go to Step 5	Go to Step 7
5	Test the low reference circuit of the A/C refrigerant pressure sensor for an open. Did you find and correct the condition?	Go to Step 15	Go to Step 12
6	Remove the cool fan 2 relay. Did the high speed cooling fan turn OFF?	Go to Step 10	Go to Step 8
7	Remove the cool fan 1 relay. Did the low speed cooling fan turn OFF?	Go to Step 11	Go to Step 8
8	Repair the short to ground on the low speed cooling fan motor supply voltage circuit prior to the resistor assembly. Did you complete the repair?	Go to Step 15	--

ARM0500000000342

Fig. 45   Cooling fan always on (Part 1 of 2). Cobalt & G5

Step	Action	Yes	No
9	Repair the short to ground on the low speed cooling fan supply voltage circuit between the resistor assembly and the two speed cooling fan motor. / Did you complete the repair?	Go to Step 15	--
10	Repair the short to voltage in the high speed cooling fan supply voltage circuit. / Did you complete the repair?	Go to Step 15	--
11	Inspect for poor connections at the cool fan 1 relay. / Did you find and correct the condition?	Go to Step 15	Go to Step 13
12	Inspect for poor connections at the A/C refrigerant pressure sensor. / Did you find and correct the condition?	Go to Step 15	Go to Step 14
13	Replace the cool fan 1 relay. / Did you complete the replacement?	Go to Step 15	--
14	Replace the A/C refrigerant pressure sensor. / Did you complete the replacement?	Go to Step 15	--
15	Operate the system in order to verify the repair. / Did you correct the condition?	System OK	Go to Step 2

ARM0500000000343

Fig. 45 Cooling fan always on (Part 2 of 2). Cobalt & G5

Step	Action	Yes	No
	DEFINITION: One or both cooling fan motors are inoperative in either high, low, or both speeds.		
1	Did you perform the Diagnostic System Check - Vehicle?	Go to Step 2	Go to Diagnostic System Check - Vehicle
2	1. Install a scan tool. 2. Turn ON the engine. 3. With a scan tool, monitor the engine coolant temperature (ECT) in the Inputs/Outputs scan tool data. 4. Bring the vehicle up to normal operating temperature. 5. At 106°C (223°F) the low speed engine cooling fans should engage. / Do the low speed engine cooling fans engage?	Go to Step 3	Go to Step 4
3	**Important::** A 3 second delay occurs before the powertrain control module (ECM) changes the cooling fan speed. 1. With a scan tool, monitor the ECT in the Inputs/Outputs scan tool data. 2. At 110°C (230°F) the high speed engine cooling fans should engage. / Do the high speed engine cooling fans engage?	Test for Intermittent Conditions and Poor Connections	Go to Step 6
4	**Important:** Do NOT remove the jumper wire that you will be connecting until your testing is completed. If the cool fan 1 fuse opens when you connect the jumper wire, repair the cooling fan motor supply voltage circuit of the left cooling fan motor for a short to ground. 1. Disconnect the cool fan 1 relay. 2. Connect a jumper wire between the battery positive voltage circuit and the cooling fan motor supply voltage circuit of the cool fan 1 relay. / Do both cooling fans operate in low speed?	Go to Step 12	Go to Step 5
5	With a test lamp connected to good ground, probe the cooling fan low reference or ground circuit at the dual speed cooling fan motor. / Does the test lamp illuminate?	Go to Step 9	Go to Step 8

ARM0500000000344

Fig. 46 Cooling fan inoperative (Part 1 of 3). Cobalt & G5

Step	Action	Yes	No
6	Does the dual speed cooling fan operate at high speed?	Go to Step 13	Go to Step 7
7	1. Disconnect the low speed circuit of the dual speed cooling fan motor connector. 2. With a test lamp connected to a good ground, probe the cooling fan motor supply voltage circuit at the low speed cooling fan connector. / Does the test lamp illuminate?	Go to Step 10	Go to Step 9
8	1. Disconnect the high speed circuit of the dual speed cooling fan motor connector. 2. With a test lamp connected to a good ground, probe the cooling fan motor supply voltage circuit at the high speed cooling fan connector. / Does the test lamp illuminate?	Go to Step 10	Go to Step 9
9	Inspect the appropriate cooling fan motor supply voltage circuit for an open or high resistance. / Did you find and correct the condition?	Go to Step 19	Go to Step 15
10	Inspect the dual speed cooling fan low reference or ground circuit for an open or high resistance / Did you find and correct the condition?	Go to Step 19	Go to Step 16
12	Inspect for poor connections at the cool fan 1 relay. / Did you find and correct the condition?	Go to Step 19	Go to Step 16
13	Inspect for poor connections at the cool fan 2 relay. / Did you find and correct the condition?	Go to Step 19	Go to Step 17
14	Inspect for poor connections at the harness connector of the low speed cooling fan circuit at the cooling fan motor. / Did you find and correct the condition?	Go to Step 19	Go to Step 18

ARM0500000000345

Fig. 46 Cooling fan inoperative (Part 2 of 3). Cobalt & G5

Step	Action	Yes	No
15	Inspect for poor connections at the harness connector of the high speed cooling fan circuit of the cooling fan motor. / Did you find and correct the condition?	Go to Step 19	Go to Step 18
16	Replace the cool fan 1 relay. / Did you complete the replacement?	Go to Step 19	--
17	Replace the cool fan 2 relay. / Did you complete the replacement?	Go to Step 19	--
18	Replace the dual speed cooling fan motor. / Did you complete the replacement?	Go to Step 19	--
19	Operate the system in order to verify the repair. / Did you correct the condition?	System OK	Go to Step 3

ARM0500000000346

Fig. 46 Cooling fan inoperative (Part 3 of 3). Cobalt & G5

Test Description

The number(s) below refer to the step number(s) on the diagnostic table.

2. Lack of communication may be due to a partial malfunction of the class 2 serial data circuit or due to a total malfunction of the class 2 serial data circuit. The specified procedure will determine the particular condition.

3. Determine if the Instrument Cluster or Powertrain Control Modules have set DTC's which may affect Engine Cooling operation are present.

4. The presence of DTCs which begin with "U" indicate some other module is not communicating. The specified procedure will compile all the available information before tests are performed.

Step	Action	Yes	No
1	Install a scan tool. Does the scan tool power up?	Go to Step 2	Diagnose Data Link Communications

2	1. Turn ON the ignition, with the engine OFF.
	2. Attempt to establish communication with the following control modules:
	  ○ Instrument Cluster
	  ○ Powertrain Control Module
	
	Does the scan tool communicate with the control modules?
		Go to Step 3	Diagnose Data Link Communications

3	Select the powertrain control module display DTCs function on the scan tool. Does the scan tool display any DTCs?	Go to Step 4	Diagnose Engine Cooling
4	Does the scan tool display any DTCs which begin with a "U"?	Diagnose Data Link Communications	Go to Diagnostic Trouble Code (DTC) List

GC1080100656000X

Fig. 47   Diagnostic system check. 2004 Corvette

Step	Action	Yes	No
	DEFINITION: One or both engine cooling fan motors do not operate properly in high or low speed modes.		
1	Did you perform the Engine Cooling Diagnostic System Check?	Go to Step 2	Go to Diagnostic System Check
2	1. Install a scan tool. 2. Turn ON the ignition, with the engine OFF. 3. With a scan tool, command the Fan Relay 1 ON and OFF. Do the low speed engine cooling fans turn ON and OFF with each command?	Go to Step 3	Go to Step 4
3	With a scan tool, command the Fan Relays 1, 2 & 3 ON and OFF. Do the high speed engine cooling fans turn ON and OFF with each command?	Test Intermittent and Poor Connections	Go to Step 11
4	**Important** Do NOT remove the 20-A fused jumper wire connected during this step. Use a second 20-A fused jumper wire while performing the following steps: 1. Disconnect the cool fan 1 relay. 2. Connect the first 20-A fused jumper between the battery positive voltage circuit of the cool fan 1 relay and the cooling fan motor supply voltage circuit of the cool fan 1 relay. Do both cooling fans operate in low speed?	Go to Step 13	Go to Step 5
5	1. Disconnect the cool fan 3 relay. 2. Connect the second 20-A fused jumper between the left cooling fan circuit of the cool fan 3 relay and the right cooling fan motor supply voltage circuit of the cool fan 3 relay. Do both cooling fans operate in low speed?	Go to Step 14	Go to Step 6

GC1080100658010X

Fig. 49   Cooling fan inoperative (Part 1 of 4). 2004 Corvette

Step	Action	Yes	No
	DEFINITION: One or both engine cooling fan motors run continuously in high or low speed.		
1	Did you perform the Engine Cooling Diagnostic System Check?	Go to Step 2	Go To Diagnostic System Check
2	Turn ON the ignition, with the engine OFF. Are one or both cooling fans ON?	Go to Step 3	Test for Intermittent and Poor Connections
3	Are both cooling fans running continuously?	Go to Step 5	Go to Step 4
4	Remove the cool fan 3 relay. Did the right cooling fan turn OFF?	Go to Step 6	Go to Step 7
5	Repair the short to voltage in the left cooling fan motor supply voltage circuit. Did you complete the repair?	Go to Step 8	--
6	Repair the short to voltage in the left cooling fan low reference circuit. Did you complete the repair?	Go to Step 8	--
7	Repair the short to voltage in the right cooling fan motor supply voltage circuit. Did you complete the repair?	Go to Step 8	--
8	Operate the system in order to verify the repair. Did you correct the condition?	System OK	Go to Step 2

GC1080100657000X

Fig. 48   Cooling fan always on. 2004 Corvette

Step	Action	Yes	No
6	Connect the second 20-A fused jumper from the battery positive voltage to the cooling fan motor supply voltage circuit of the cool fan 3 relay. Does the right cooling fan operate in high speed?	Go to Step 9	Go to Step 7
7	1. Install the cool fan 3 relay. 2. Disconnect the right cooling fan electrical connector. 3. Connect the second 20-Amp fused jumper wire from the cooling fan motor supply voltage circuit of the right electrical connector to the cooling fan ground circuit of the right electrical connector. Does the left cooling fan operate in high speed?	Go to Step 16	Go to Step 8
8	Connect the second 20-Amp fused jumper wire from the cooling fan supply voltage circuit of the right cooling fan electrical connector to a good ground. Does the left cooling fan motor operate in high speed?	Go to Step 20	Go to Step 21
9	1. Install the cool fan 3 relay. 2. Disconnect the left cooling fan electrical connector. 3. Connect the second 20-Amp fused jumper from the cooling fan motor supply voltage circuit of the left cooling fan electrical connector to the low reference circuit of the left cooling fan electrical connector. Does the right cooling fan motor operate in high speed?	Go to Step 17	Go to Step 10
10	Connect the second 20-Amp fused jumper wire from battery positive voltage to the left cooling fan low reference circuit of the left cooling fan electrical connector. Does the right cooling fan operate in high speed?	Go to Step 18	Go to Step 22
11	Does the right cooling fan operate in high speed?	Go to Step 12	Go to Step 15
12	1. Disconnect the cool fan 3 relay. 2. Connect a 20-A fused jumper between the left cooling fan low reference circuit of the cool fan 3 relay and the ground circuit of the cool fan 3 relay. Does the left cooling fan operate properly in high speed?	Go to Step 14	Go to Step 19
13	Inspect for poor connections at the cool fan 1 relay. Did you find and correct the condition?	Go to Step 28	Go to Step 23
14	Inspect for poor connections at the cool fan 3 relay. Did you find and correct the condition?	Go to Step 28	Go to Step 24
15	Inspect for poor connections at the cool fan 2 relay. Did you find and correct the condition?	Go to Step 28	Go to Step 25

GC1080100658020X

Fig. 49   Cooling fan inoperative (Part 2 of 4). 2004 Corvette

16	Inspect for poor connections at the harness connector of the right cooling fan.		
	Did you find and correct the condition?	Go to Step 28	Go to Step 26
17	Inspect for poor connections at the harness connector of the left cooling fan.		
	Did you find and correct the condition?	Go to Step 28	Go to Step 27
18	Repair the left cooling fan motor supply voltage circuit.		
	Did you complete the repair?	Go to Step 28	--
19	Repair the left cooling fan ground circuit.		
	Did you complete the repair?	Go to Step 28	--
20	Repair the right cooling fan ground circuit.		
	Did you complete the repair?	Go to Step 28	--
21	Repair the right cooling fan motor supply voltage circuit.		
	Did you complete the repair?	Go to Step 28	--
22	Repair the left cooling fan low reference circuit.		
	Did you complete the repair?	Go to Step 28	--
23	Replace the cool fan 1 relay.		
	Is the repair complete?	Go to Step 28	--
24	Replace the cool fan 3 relay.		
	Is the repair complete?	Go to Step 28	--

GC108010658030X

Fig. 49   Cooling fan inoperative (Part 3 of 4). 2004 Corvette

Step	Action	Yes	No
1	Perform the following preliminary inspections: • Ensure that the battery is fully charged. • Ensure that the battery cables are clean and tight. • Inspect for any open fuses. • Inspect the easily accessible systems or the visible system components for obvious damage or conditions that could cause the symptom. • Ensure that the grounds are clean, tight, and in the correct location. • Inspect for aftermarket devices that could affect the operation of the system. • Search for applicable service bulletins. Did you find and correct the condition?	System OK	Go to Step 2

ARM0400000000010

Fig. 50   Diagnostic system check (Part 1 of 3). 2005–08 Corvette

7	Important: Do NOT clear any DTCs unless instructed by a diagnostic procedure. • Diagnose the DTCs in the order that the DTCs appear on the scan tool or mis-diagnosis may occur. • If multiple powertrain DTCs are stored, diagnose the DTCs in the following order: 1. Component level DTCs, such as sensor DTCs, solenoid DTCs, and relay DTCs. 2. System level DTCs, such as misfire DTCs, evaporative emission (EVAP) system DTCs, and fuel trim DTCs. Advance to the List All DTCs screen on the scan tool. Does the scan tool display any DTCs?	Go to Diagnostic Trouble Code (DTC) List - Vehicle	Go to Step 8
8	Is the customers concern with inspection/maintenance (I/M) testing?	Go to Inspection/Maintenance (I/M) System Check	Go to Symptoms

ARM0500000000933

Fig. 50   Diagnostic system check (Part 3 of 3). 2005–08 Corvette

25	Replace the cool fan 2 relay.		
	Is the repair complete?	Go to Step 28	--
26	Replace the right cooling fan.		
	Is the repair complete?	Go to Step 28	--
27	Replace the left cooling fan.		
	Is the repair complete?	Go to Step 28	--
28	Operate the system in order to verify the repair.		
	Did you correct the condition?	System OK	Go to Step 3

GC1080100658040X

Fig. 49   Cooling fan inoperative (Part 4 of 4). 2004 Corvette

Step	Action	Yes	No
2	Install a scan tool. Does the scan tool power up?	Go to Step 3	Diagnose Scan Tool Does Not Power Up
3	Turn ON the ignition, with the engine OFF. Is the NO FOB DETECTED message displayed on the driver information center (DIC)?	Go to Key Fob Not Detected in Keyless Entry	Go to Step 4
4	1. Turn ON the ignition, with the engine OFF. 2. Attempt to establish communication with all of the control modules on the vehicle. Does the scan tool communicate with all of the expected vehicle control modules?	Go to Step 5	Diagnose Data Link References
5	Attempt to start the engine. Does the engine crank?	Go to Step 6	Go to Symptoms
6	Attempt to start the engine. Does the engine start and idle?	Go to Step 7	Go to Engine Cranks but Does Not Run

ARM0400000000011

Fig. 50   Diagnostic system check (Part 2 of 3). 2005–08 Corvette

Step	Action	Values	Yes	No
	DEFINITION: Engine cooling fan operates all the time when the vehicle is started or not started.			
1	Did you perform the Diagnostic System Check - Vehicle?	--	Go to Step 2	Go to Diagnostic System Check
2	**Important** The vehicle must be allowed to cool down. The HVAC control system must be in the OFF position and the coolant temperature must stay below 91° (195°F) for this diagnostic. 1. Start the vehicle. 2. Turn OFF the HVAC system. Is the cooling fan ON?	--	Go to Step 3	Go to Diagnostic Aids
3	1. Turn OFF the ignition. 2. Disconnect the fan control module connector. 3. Probe the cooling fan speed control circuit of the fan control module with a test lamp that is connected to voltage. Does the test lamp illuminate?	--	Go to Step 7	Go to Step 4

ARM0400000000012

Fig. 51   Cooling fan always on (Part 1 of 2). 2005–08 Corvette

Step	Action	Values	Yes	No
4	Inspect the battery positive voltage circuit of the cooling fan motor for a short to voltage. Did you find and correct the condition?	--	Go to Step 9	Go to Step 5
5	Inspect for poor connections at the fan control module. Did you find and correct the condition?	--	Go to Step 9	Go to Step 6
6	Replace the fan control module. Did you complete the replacement?	--	Go to Step 9	--
7	Inspect for poor connections at the engine control module (ECM). Did you find and correct the condition?	--	Go to Step 9	Go to Step 8
8	Replace the ECM. Did you complete the replacement?	--	Go to Step 9	--
9	Operate the system in order to verify the repair. Did you correct the condition?	--	System OK	Go to Step 2

ARM0400000000013

Fig. 51 Cooling fan always on (Part 2 of 2). 2005–08 Corvette

Step	Action	Values	Yes	No
3	1. Turn OFF the ignition. 2. Disconnect the fan control module connector. 3. Probe the battery positive voltage circuit of the fan control module with a test lamp that is connected to a good ground. Does the test lamp illuminate?	--	Go to Step 4	Go to Step 10
4	Inspect the ground circuit of the fan control module for an open. Did you complete the repair	--	Go to Step 16	Go to Step 5
5	1. Install a scan tool. 2. Turn ON the ignition, with the engine OFF. 3. Command the cooling fan ON to 90 percent. 4. Measure the voltage on the cooling fan speed control circuit at the fan control module. Is the voltage near the specified value?	0.45 V	Go to Step 6	Go to Step 9
6	**Important** When using jumpers in this step, if the wire gage of the jumpers you use is smaller than the production wire gage supplied to the cooling fan, the wires may get hot. Connect the jumper wires long enough to verify that the cooling fan motor operates, then remove the jumpers. 1. Jumper the fan control module ground circuit and the cooling fan motor ground circuit together at the fan control module connector. 2. Jumper the fan control module battery voltage circuit and the cooling fan motor battery voltage circuit together at the fan control module connector. Does the cooling fan operate?		Go to Step 7	Go to Step 11

ARM0400000000015

Fig. 52 Cooling fan inoperative (Part 2 of 4). 2005–08 Corvette

Step	Action	Values	Yes	No
1	Did you perform the Diagnostic System Check - Vehicle?	--	Go to Step 2	Go to Diagnostic System Check
2	1. Install a scan tool. 2. Turn ON the ignition, with the engine OFF. 3. With a scan tool, command the cooling fan ON and OFF. Does the cooling fan turn ON and OFF with each command?	--	Go to Diagnostic Aids	Go to Step 3

ARM0400000000014

Fig. 52 Cooling fan inoperative (Part 1 of 4). 2005–08 Corvette

Step	Action	Values	Yes	No
7	Inspect for poor connections at the fan control module. Did you find and correct the condition?	--	Go to Step 16	Go to Step 8
8	Replace the fan control module. Did you complete the replacement?	--	Go to Step 16	--
9	Inspect the cooling fan speed control circuit for the following: • An open • A short to ground • A short to voltage Did you find and correct the condition?	--	Go to Step 16	Go to Step 14
10	Repair the battery positive voltage circuit of the fan control module for an open or short to ground. Did you complete the repair?	--	Go to Step 16	--

ARM0400000000016

Fig. 52 Cooling fan inoperative (Part 3 of 4). 2005–08 Corvette

Step	Action	Values	Yes	No
11	Inspect the ground and battery positive voltage circuits of the cooling fan motor for the following: • An open • A short to ground • A short to voltage Did you find and correct the condition?	--	Go to Step 16	Go to Step 12
12	Inspect for poor connections at the cooling fan control module connector. Did you find and correct the condition?	--	Go to Step 16	Go to Step 13
13	Replace the cooling fan. Did you complete the replacement?	--	Go to Step 16	--
14	Inspect for poor connections at the engine control module (ECM). Did you find and correct the condition?	--	Go to Step 16	Go to Step 15
15	Replace the ECM. Did you complete the replacement?	--	Go to Step 16	--
16	Operate the system in order to verify the repair. Did you correct the condition?	--	System OK	Go to Step 2

ARM0500000000934

Fig. 52 Cooling fan inoperative (Part 4 of 4). 2005–08 Corvette

COOLING FANS

Step	Action	Yes	No
1	Did you perform the Engine Cooling System Check?	Go to Step 2	Check Engine Cooling
2	Turn ON the ignition, with the engine OFF. Are one or both cooling fans ON?	Go to Step 3	Test for Intermittent and Poor Connections
3	Are both cooling fans running continuously?	Go to Step 5	Go to Step 4
4	Remove the s/p fan relay. Did the right cooling fan turn OFF?	Go to Step 6	Go to Step 7
5	Repair the short to voltage in the left cooling fan motor supply voltage circuit. Did you complete the repair?	Go to Step 8	--
6	Repair the short to voltage in the left cooling fan low reference circuit. Did you complete the repair?	Go to Step 8	--
7	Repair the short to voltage in the right cooling fan motor supply voltage circuit. Did you complete the repair?	Go to Step 8	--
8	Operate the system in order to verify the repair. Did you correct the condition?	System OK	Go to Step 2

ARM66GC000000275

Fig. 53 Primary cooling fan always on. CTS

Step	Action	Yes	No
7	1. Install the s/p fan relay. 2. Disconnect the right cooling fan electrical connector. 3. Reconnect the second 20-Amp fused jumper wire from the cooling fan motor supply voltage circuit of the right cooling fan electrical connector to the cooling fan motor ground circuit of the right cooling fan electrical connector. Does the left cooling fan operate in high speed?	Go to Step 16	Go to Step 8
8	Reconnect the second 20-Amp fused jumper wire from the cooling fan motor supply voltage circuit of the right cooling fan electrical connector to a good ground. Does the left cooling fan operate in high speed?	Go to Step 20	Go to Step 21
9	1. Install the s/p fan relay. 2. Disconnect the left cooling fan electrical connector. 3. Reconnect the second 20-Amp fused jumper wire from cooling fan motor supply voltage circuit of cooling fan electrical connector to the cooling fan low reference circuit of the left cooling fan electrical connector. Does the right cooling fan operate in high speed?	Go to Step 17	Go to Step 10
10	Reconnect the second 20-Amp fused jumper wire from battery positive voltage to the left cooling fan low reference circuit of the of the left cooling fan electrical connector. Does the right cooling fan operate in high speed?	Go to Step 18	Go to Step 22
11	Does the right cooling fan operate in high speed?	Go to Step 12	Go to Step 15
12	1. Disconnect the s/p fan relay. 2. Connect a 20-A fused jumper between the left cooling fan low reference circuit of the s/p fan relay and the ground circuit of the s/p fan relay. Does the left cooling fan operate properly in high speed?	Go to Step 14	Go to Step 19
13	Inspect for poor connections at the low speed fan relay. Did you find and correct the condition?	Go to Step 28	Go to Step 23
14	Inspect for poor connections at the s/p fan relay. Did you find and correct the condition?	Go to Step 28	Go to Step 24

ARM66GC000000277

Fig. 54 Primary cooling fan inoperative (Part 2 of 3). CTS

Step	Action	Yes	No
1	Did you perform the Engine Cooling System Check?	Go to Step 2	Check - Engine Cooling
2	1. Install a scan tool. 2. Turn ON the ignition, with the engine OFF. 3. With a scan tool, command the Fans Low Speed ON and OFF. Do the low speed engine cooling fans turn ON and OFF with each command?	Go to Step 3	Go to Step 4
3	**Important:** A 3-second delay occurs before the PCM changes the cooling fan speed. With a scan tool, command the Fans High Speed ON and OFF. Do the high speed engine cooling fans turn ON and OFF with each command?	Test for Intermittent and Poor Connections	Go to Step 11
4	**Important** Do NOT remove the 20-A fused jumper wire connected during this step. Use a second 20-A fused jumper wire while performing the following steps. 1. Disconnect the low speed fan relay. 2. Connect the first 20-A fused jumper between the battery positive voltage circuit of the low speed fan relay and the cooling fan motor supply voltage circuit of the low speed fan relay. Do both cooling fans operate in low speed?	Go to Step 13	Go to Step 5
5	1. Disconnect the s/p fan relay. 2. Connect the second 20-A fused jumper between the left cooling fan motor low reference circuit of the s/p fan relay and the right cooling fan motor supply voltage circuit of the s/p fan relay. Do both cooling fans operate in low speed?	Go to Step 14	Go to Step 6
6	Reconnect the second 20-A fused jumper between the battery positive voltage circuit of the s/p fan relay and the cooling fan motor supply voltage circuit of the s/p fan relay. Does the right cooling fan operate in high speed?	Go to Step 9	Go to Step 7

ARM66GC000000276

Fig. 54 Primary cooling fan inoperative (Part 1 of 3). CTS

Step	Action	Yes	No
15	Inspect for poor connections at the high speed fan relay Did you find and correct the condition?	Go to Step 28	Go to Step 25
16	Inspect for poor connections at the harness connector of the right cooling fan. Did you find and correct the condition?	Go to Step 28	Go to Step 26
17	Inspect for poor connections at the harness connector of the left cooling fan Did you find and correct the condition?	Go to Step 28	Go to Step 27
18	Repair the left cooling fan motor supply voltage circuit. Did you complete the repair?	Go to Step 28	--
19	Repair the left cooling fan motor ground circuit. Did you complete the repair?	Go to Step 28	--
20	Repair the right cooling fan motor ground circuit. Did you complete the repair?	Go to Step 28	--
21	Repair the right cooling fan motor supply voltage circuit. Systems. Did you complete the repair?	Go to Step 28	--
22	Repair the left cooling fan low reference circuit. Did you complete the repair?	Go to Step 28	--
23	Replace the low speed fan relay. Did you complete the replacement?	Go to Step 28	--
24	Replace the s/p fan relay. Did you complete the replacement?	Go to Step 28	--
25	Replace the high speed fan relay. Did you complete the replacement?	Go to Step 28	--
26	Replace the right cooling fan. Did you complete the replacement?	Go to Step 28	--
27	Replace the left cooling fan. Did you complete the replacement?	Go to Step 28	--
28	Operate the system in order to verify the repair. Did you correct the condition?	System OK	Go to Step 3

ARM66GC000000278

Fig. 54 Primary cooling fan inoperative (Part 3 of 3). CTS

Step	Action	Yes	No
1	Did you perform the Engine Cooling System Check?	Go to Step 2	Check Engine Cooling
2	Is the auxiliary cooling fan always ON?	Go to Step 3	Test for Intermittent and Poor Connections
3	Disconnect the auxiliary cooling fan relay Does the auxiliary cooling fan turn OFF?	Go to Step 5	Go to Step 4
4	Repair the short to voltage in the auxiliary cooling fan motor supply voltage circuit. Did you complete the repair?	Go to Step 10	--
5	Probe the control circuit of the auxiliary fan relay with a test lamp connected to battery positive voltage. Does the test lamp illuminate?	Go to Step 7	Go to Step 6
6	Inspect for poor connections at the auxiliary cooling fan relay Did you find and correct the condition?	Go to Step 10	Go to Step 8
7	Inspect for poor connections at the harness connector of the Engine Control Module (ECM). Did you find and correct the condition?	Go to Step 10	Go to Step 9
8	Replace the auxiliary cooling fan relay. Did you complete the replacement?	Go to Step 10	--
9	**Important:** Perform the programming procedure for the ECM. Replace the ECM. Did you complete the repair?	Go to Step 10	--
10	Operate the system in order to verify the repair. Did you correct the condition?	System OK	Go to Step 3

ARM66GC000000279

Fig. 55   Auxiliary cooling fan always on. CTS

Step	Action	Yes	No
10	Repair the auxiliary cooling fan motor supply voltage circuit for a short to ground. Did you complete the repair?	Go to Step 17	--
11	Inspect for poor connections Engine Control module (ECM). Did you find and correct the condition?	Go to Step 17	Go to Step 14
12	Inspect for poor connections at the auxiliary fan relay. Did you find and correct the condition?	Go to Step 17	Go to Step 15
13	Inspect for poor connections at the harness connector of the auxiliary cooling fan. Did you find and correct the condition?	Go to Step 17	Go to Step 16
14	**Important:** Perform the programming procedure for the ECM. Replace the ECM. Did you complete the repair?	Go to Step 17	--
15	Replace the auxiliary fan relay. Did you complete the replacement?	Go to Step 17	--
16	Replace the auxiliary cooling fan. Did you complete the replacement?	Go to Step 17	--
17	Operate the system in order to verify the repair. Did you correct the condition?	System OK	Go to Step 2

ARM66GC000000281

Fig. 56   Auxiliary cooling fan inoperative (Part 2 of 2). CTS

Step	Action	Yes	No
1	Did you perform the Engine Cooling System Check?	Go to Step 2	Check - Engine Cooling
2	1. Install a scan tool. 2. Turn ON the ignition, with the engine OFF. 3. With a scan tool, command the auxiliary cooling fan ON and OFF. Does the auxiliary cooling fan turn ON and OFF with each command?	Test for Intermittent and Poor Connections	Go to Step 3
3	1. Disconnect the auxiliary fan relay. 2. Probe the control circuit of the auxiliary fan relay with a test lamp connected to battery positive voltage. Does the test lamp illuminate?	Go to Step 4	Go to Step 6
4	Probe the battery positive voltage circuit of the auxiliary fan relay with a test lamp that is connected to a good ground. Does the test lamp illuminate?	Go to Step 5	Go to Step 7
5	Connect a 20-A fused jumper between the battery positive voltage circuit of the auxiliary fan relay and the auxiliary cooling fan motor supply voltage circuit of the auxiliary fan relay. Does the auxiliary cooling fan operate?	Go to Step 12	Go to Step 8
6	Test the control circuit of the auxiliary fan relay for an open or high resistance. Did you find and correct the condition?	Go to Step 17	Go to Step 11
7	Test the battery positive voltage circuit of the auxiliary fan relay for a short to ground or an open. Did you find and correct the condition?	Go to Step 17	Go to Step 10
8	Test the auxiliary cooling fan motor supply voltage circuit of the auxiliary cooling fan for an open or high resistance. Did you find and correct the condition?	Go to Step 17	Go to Step 9
9	Test the auxiliary cooling fan motor ground circuit for an open or high resistance. Did you find and correct the condition?	Go to Step 17	Go to Step

ARM66GC000000280

Fig. 56   Auxiliary cooling fan inoperative (Part 1 of 2). CTS

Step	Action	Yes	No
1	Install a scan tool. Does the scan tool power up?	Go to Step 2	Diagnose Data Link Communications
2	1. Turn ON the ignition, with the engine OFF. 2. Attempt to establish communication with the following control modules: ○ Instrument Cluster ○ Powertrain Control Module Does the scan tool communicate with the control modules?	Go to Step 3	Diagnose Data Link Communications
3	Select the powertrain control module display DTCs function on the scan tool. Does the scan tool display any DTCs?	Go to Step 4	Diagnose engine cooling
4	Does the scan tool display any DTCs which begin with a "U"?	Diagnose Data Link Communications	Diagnose Diagnostic Trouble Code (DTC)

ARM0300000000319

Fig. 57   Diagnostic system check. DeVille & Seville

Step	Action	Yes	No
	DEFINITION: One or both engine cooling fan motors run continuously in high or low speed modes.		
1	Did you perform the Engine Cooling Diagnostic System Check?	Go to Step 2	Go To Diagnostic System Check
2	**Important** The cooling fan fuses and cooling fan relays 1 and 2 are labeled incorrectly on the underhood sticker. Turn ON the ignition, with the engine OFF. Are one or both cooling fans ON?	Go to Step 3	Test for Intermittent and Poor Connections
3	Are both cooling fans running continuously?	Go to Step 5	Go to Step 4
4	Remove the cooling fan S/P relay. Did the left cooling fan turn OFF?	Go to Step 8	Go to Step 6
5	Remove the cooling fan 1 relay. Did the cooling fans turn OFF?	Go to Step 10	Go to Step 7
6	Remove the cooling fan 2 relay. Did the left cooling fan turn OFF?	Go to Step 11	Go to Step 9

ARM0300000000320

Fig. 58   Cooling fan always on (Part 1 of 2). DeVille & Seville

7	Repair the short to voltage in the right cooling fan motor supply voltage circuit. Did you complete the repair?	Go to Step 14	--
8	Repair the short to voltage in the right cooling fan low reference circuit. Did you complete the repair?	Go to Step 14	--
9	Repair the short to voltage in the left cooling fan motor supply voltage circuit. Did you complete the repair?	Go to Step 14	--
10	Inspect for poor connections at the cooling fan 1 relay. Did you find and correct the condition?	Go to Step 14	Go to Step 12
11	Inspect for poor connections at the cooling fan 2 relay. Did you find and correct the condition?	Go to Step 14	Go to Step 13
12	Replace the cooling fan 1 relay. Did you complete the replacement?	Go to Step 14	--
13	Replace the cooling fan 2 relay. Did you complete the replacement?	Go to Step 14	--
14	Operate the system in order to verify the repair. Did you correct the condition?	System OK	Go to Step 2

ARM0300000000321

Fig. 58   Cooling fan always on (Part 2 of 2). DeVille & Seville

1	Did you perform the Engine Cooling Diagnostic System Check?	Go to Step 2	Go to Diagnostic System Check
2	**Important** The cooling fan fuses and cooling fan relays 1 and 2 are labeled incorrectly on the underhood sticker. 1. Install a scan tool. 2. Turn ON the ignition, with the engine OFF. 3. With a scan tool, command the Fans Low Speed ON and OFF. Do the low speed engine cooling fans turn ON and OFF with each command?	Go to Step 3	Go to Step 4
3	**Important:** A 3-second delay occurs before the PCM changes the cooling fan speed. With a scan tool, command the Fans High Speed ON and OFF. Do the high speed engine cooling fans turn ON and OFF with each command?	Test for Intermittent and Poor Connections	Go to Step 12
4	**Important** Do NOT remove the 20-A fused jumper wire connected during this step. Use a second 20-A fused jumper wire while performing the following steps. 1. Remove the cooling fan 1 relay. 2. Connect a 20-A fused jumper between the battery positive switch side voltage circuit and the cooling fan motor supply voltage circuit of the cooling fan 1 relay. Do both cooling fans operate in low speed?	Go to Step 22	Go to Step 5

ARM0300000000642

Fig. 59   Cooling fan inoperative (Part 1 of 6). DeVille & Seville

5	1. Disconnect the cooling fan S/P relay 2. Connect the second 20-A fused jumper between the cooling fan low reference circuit and the cooling fan motor supply voltage circuit of the cooling fan S/P relay. Do both cooling fans operate in low speed?	Go to Step 23	Go to Step 6
6	Connect the second 20-A fused jumper between the battery positive voltage circuit and the cooling fan motor supply voltage circuit of the cooling fan S/P relay. Does the left cooling fan operate in high speed?	Go to Step 9	Go to Step 7
7	1. Install the cooling fan S/P relay. 2. Disconnect the left cooling fan electrical connector. 3. Connect the second 20-A fused jumper wire from the cooling fan motor supply voltage circuit to the ground circuit of the left cooling fan electrical connector. Does the right cooling fan operate in high speed?	Go to Step 25	Go to Step 8
8	Connect the second 20-Amp fused jumper wire from the cooling fan motor supply voltage circuit of the left cooling fan electrical connector to a good ground. Does the right cooling fan operate in high speed?	Go to Step 29	Go to Step 30
9	1. Install the cooling fan S/P relay. 2. Disconnect the right cooling fan electrical connector. 3. Connect the second 20-Amp fused jumper wire from the cooling fan motor supply voltage circuit to the cooling fan low reference circuit of the right cooling fan electrical connector. Does the left cooling fan operate in high speed?	Go to Step 26	Go to Step 10
10	Connect the second 20-Amp fused jumper wire from the coil side battery positive voltage circuit to the cooling fan low reference circuit of the of the right cooling fan electrical connector. Does the left cooling fan operate in high speed?	Go to Step 11	Go to Step 31

ARM0300000000643

Fig. 59   Cooling fan inoperative (Part 2 of 6). DeVille & Seville

#	Action		
11	Probe the battery positive voltage circuit on the switch side of the cooling fan 1 relay with a test lamp that is connected to a good ground. Does the test lamp illuminate?	Go to Step 27	Go to Step 32
12	Is the left cooling fan operating properly in high speed?	Go to Step 19	Go to Step 13
13	1. Turn off the ignition. 2. Disconnect the cooling fan 2 relay. 3. Turn ON the ignition, with the engine OFF. 4. Connect a test lamp between the high speed cooling fan relay control circuit and the battery positive voltage circuit on the coil side of the cooling fan 2 relay. 5. With a scan tool command the High Speed Fans ON and OFF. Does the test lamp turn ON and OFF with each command?	Go to Step 15	Go to Step 14
14	Probe the battery positive voltage circuit on the coil side of the cooling fan 2 relay with a test lamp that is connected to a good ground. Does the test lamp illuminate?	Go to Step 34	Go to Step 33
15	Install a 20 amp fused jumper between the battery positive voltage circuit on the switch side of the cooling fan 2 relay and the cooling fan motor supply voltage circuit. Does the left cooling fan operate in high speed?	Go to Step 24	Go to Step 16
16	Probe the battery positive voltage circuit on the switch side of the cooling fan 2 relay with a test lamp connected to a good ground. Does the test lamp illuminate?	Go to Step 17	Go to Step 33
17	1. With the 20 amp fused jumper still installed. 2. Disconnect the left cooling fan electrical connector. 3. Connect a test lamp from the cooling fan motor supply voltage circuit to the ground circuit of the left cooling fan electrical connector. Does the test lamp illuminate	Go to Step 25	Go to Step 18

ARM0300000000644

Fig. 59 Cooling fan inoperative (Part 3 of 6). DeVille & Seville

#	Action		
18	Probe the cooling fan motor supply voltage circuit of the left cooling fan electrical connector with a test lamp that is connected to a good ground. Does the test lamp illuminate?	Go to Step 29	Go to Step 30
19	1. Turn OFF the ignition. 2. Disconnect the cooling fan S/P relay 3. Turn ON the ignition, with the engine OFF. 4. Connect a 20-A fused jumper between the cooling fan low reference circuit and the ground circuit of the cooling fan S/P relay. 5. With a scan tool command the Fans High Speed ON and OFF. Does the right cooling fan operate in high speed?	Go to Step 20	Go to Step 28
20	1. Connect a test lamp between the high speed cooling fan relay control circuit of the cooling fan S/P relay and the battery positive voltage circuit of the cooling fan S/P relay. 2. With a scan tool command the Fans High Speed ON and OFF. Does the test lamp turn ON and OFF with each command?	Go to Step 23	Go to Step 21
21	Probe the battery positive voltage circuit of the cooling fan S/P relay with a test lamp that is connected to a good ground. Does the test lamp illuminate?	Go to Step 34	Go to Step 33
22	Inspect for poor connections at the cooling fan 1 relay. Did you find and correct the condition?	Go to Step 40	Go to Step 35
23	Inspect for poor connections at the cooling fan S/P relay. Did you find and correct the condition?	Go to Step 40	Go to Step 36
24	Inspect for poor connections at the cooling fan 2 relay. Did you find and correct the condition?	Go to Step 40	Go to Step 37

ARM0300000000645

Fig. 59 Cooling fan inoperative (Part 4 of 6). DeVille & Seville

#	Action		
25	Inspect for poor connections at the harness connector of the left cooling fan. Did you find and correct the condition?	Go to Step 40	Go to Step 38
26	Inspect for poor connections at the harness connector of the right cooling fan. Did you find and correct the condition?	Go to Step 40	Go to Step 39
27	Repair the right cooling fan motor supply voltage circuit for an open. Is the repair complete?	Go to Step 40	--
28	Repair the right cooling fan ground circuit for an open. Is the repair complete?	Go to Step 40	--
29	Repair the left cooling fan ground circuit for an open. Is the repair complete?	Go to Step 40	--
30	Repair the left cooling fan motor supply voltage circuit for an open. Is the repair complete?	Go to Step 40	--
31	Repair the right cooling fan low reference circuit for a short to ground or an open. Is the repair complete?	Go to Step 40	--
32	Repair the cooling fan 1 relay battery positive voltage circuit for an open. Is the repair complete?	Go to Step 40	--

ARM0300000000646

Fig. 59 Cooling fan inoperative (Part 5 of 6). DeVille & Seville

#	Action		
33	Repair the battery positive voltage circuit for the cooling fan S/P and 2 relay for an open. Is the repair complete?	Go to Step 40	--
34	Repair the high speed cooling fan relay control circuit for an open. Is the repair complete?	Go to Step 40	--
35	Replace the cooling fan 1 relay. Is the repair complete?	Go to Step 40	--
36	Replace the cooling fan S/P relay. Is the repair complete?	Go to Step 40	--
37	Replace the cooling fan 2 relay. Is the repair complete?	Go to Step 40	--
38	Replace the left cooling fan. Is the repair complete?	Go to Step 40	--
39	Replace the right cooling fan. Is the repair complete?	Go to Step 40	--
40	Operate the system in order to verify the repair. Did you correct the condition?	System OK	Go to Step 3

ARM0300000000647

Fig. 59 Cooling fan inoperative (Part 6 of 6). DeVille & Seville

Step	Action	Yes	No
1	Perform the following preliminary inspections: • Ensure that the battery is fully charged. • Ensure that the battery cables are clean and tight. • Inspect for any open fuses. • Inspect the easily accessible systems or the visible system components for obvious damage or conditions that could cause the symptom. • Ensure that the grounds are clean, tight, and in the correct location. • Inspect for aftermarket devices that could affect the operation of the system. • Search for applicable service bulletins. Did you find and correct the condition?	System OK	Go to Step 2
2	Install a scan tool. Does the scan tool power up?	Go to Step 3	Go to Scan Tool Does Not Power Up
3	1. Turn ON the ignition, with the engine OFF. 2. Attempt to establish communication with all of the control modules on the vehicle. Does the scan tool communicate with all of the expected vehicle control modules?	Go to Step 4	Go to Data Link References

ARM0500000000330

Fig. 60   Diagnostic system check (Part 1 of 3). DTS

Step	Action	Yes	No
4	**Important:** 1. To ensure that retained accessory power (RAP) mode is inactive (if equipped), open the drivers door during the following step. 2. The engine may start during the following step. Turn OFF the engine as soon as you have observed the crank power mode. 1. Access the Power Mode parameter on the scan tool. 2. Rotate the ignition switch (operate the ignition mode switch) through all positions while observing the Power Mode parameter. Does the Power Mode parameter reading on the scan tool match the ignition switch position for all switch positions?	Go to Step 5	Go to Power Mode Mismatch
5	Attempt to start the engine. Does the engine crank?	Go to Step 6	Go to Symptoms -
6	Attempt to start the engine. Does the engine start and idle?	Go to Step 7	Go to Engine Cranks but Does Not Run
7	**Important:** Do not clear any DTCs unless instructed by a diagnostic procedure. Use the appropriate scan tool selections to obtain DTCs for each of the control modules. Does the scan tool display any DTCs?	Go to Step 8	Go to Step 12
8	Does the scan tool display any DTCs that begin with a "U"?	Go to Diagnostic Trouble Code (DTC) List - Vehicle	Go to Step 9

ARM0500000000331

Fig. 60   Diagnostic system check (Part 2 of 3). DTS

Step	Action	Yes	No
9	**Important:** If any of these DTCs are displayed, diagnose them before diagnosing any other DTCs or symptoms. Does the scan tool display DTC B1000, B1001, C0550, P0601, P0602, P0603, P0604, P0606, P0607, P062F, P1680, or P2610?	Go to Diagnostic Trouble Code (DTC) List - Vehicle	Go to Step 10
10	**Important:** If any of these DTCs are displayed, diagnose them before diagnosing any other DTCs or symptoms. Does the scan tool display DTC B1325, B1335, B1340, B1424, B1517, C0800, C0895, C0899, C0900, P0560, P0562, or P0563?	Go to Diagnostic Trouble Code (DTC) List - Vehicle	Go to Step 11
11	**Important:** If any of the remaining DTCs are powertrain DTCs, select Capture Info in order to store the powertrain DTC information with a scan tool. If multiple DTCs are stored, diagnose the DTCs in the following order: 1. Component level DTCs, such as sensor DTCs, solenoid DTCs, and relay DTCs. 2. System level DTCs, such as misfire DTCs, EVAP system DTCs, and fuel trim DTCs. Diagnose the remaining DTCs.	Go to Diagnostic Trouble Code (DTC) List - Vehicle	--
12	Is the customers concern with inspection/maintenance (I/M) testing?	Go to Inspection/Maintenance (I/M) System Check	Go to Symptoms

ARM0500000000332

Fig. 60   Diagnostic system check (Part 3 of 3). DTS

Step	Action	Yes	No
	DEFINITION: One or both fan motors run continuously in high or low speed.		
1	Did you perform the Diagnostic System Check - Vehicle?	Go to Step 2	Go to Diagnostic System Check - Vehicle
2	Turn ON the ignition, with the engine OFF. Are both cooling fans operating at low speed?	Go to Step 4	Go to Step 3
3	Is the left cooling fan operating at high speed?	Go to Step 5	Test for Intermittent Conditions and Poor Connections
4	Remove the low speed fan relay. Did the fans turn OFF?	Go to Step 8	Go to Step 6
5	Remove the high speed fan relay. Did the left cooling fan turn OFF?	Go to Step 9	Go to Step 7
6	Repair the cooling fan motor supply voltage circuit of the right cooling fan for a short to voltage. Did you complete the repair?	Go to Step 12	--
7	Repair the cooling fan motor supply voltage circuit of the left cooling fan for a short to voltage. Did you complete the repair?	Go to Step 12	--

ARM0500000000333

Fig. 61   Cooling fan always on (Part 1 of 2). DTS

Step	Action	Yes	No
8	Inspect for poor connections at the low speed fan relay. Did you find and correct the condition?	Go to Step 12	Go to Step 10
9	Inspect for poor connections at the high speed fan relay. Did you find and correct the condition?	Go to Step 12	Go to Step 11
10	Replace the low speed fan relay. Did you complete the replacement?	Go to Step 12	--
11	Replace the high speed fan relay. Did you complete the replacement?	Go to Step 12	--
12	Operate the system in order to verify the repair. Did you correct the condition?	System OK	Go to Step 2

ARM0500000000334

Fig. 61   Cooling fan always on (Part 2 of 2). DTS

Step	Action	Yes	No
	DEFINITION: One or both fan motors are inoperative in either high, low, or both speeds.		
1	Did you perform the Diagnostic System Check - Vehicle?	Go to Step 2	Go to Diagnostic System Check
2	1. Install a scan tool. 2. Turn ON the ignition, with the engine OFF. 3. With a scan tool, command the Fans Low Speed ON and OFF. Do the low speed engine cooling fans turn ON and OFF with each command?	Go to Step 3	Go to Step 4
3	**Important:** A 3 second delay occurs before the powertrain control module (PCM) changes the cooling fan speed. With a scan tool, command the Fans High Speed ON and OFF. Do the high speed engine cooling fans turn ON and OFF with each command?	Test for Intermittent Conditions and Poor Connections	Go to Step 6
4	**Important:** Do NOT remove the jumper wire that you will be connecting until your testing is completed. If the low speed fan fuse opens when you connect the jumper wire, repair the cooling fan motor supply voltage circuit of the right cooling fan motor for a short to ground. 1. Disconnect the low speed fan relay. 2. Connect a jumper wire between the battery positive voltage circuit and the cooling fan motor supply voltage circuit of the low speed fan relay. Do both cooling fans operate in low speed?	Go to Step 14	Go to Step 5

ARM0500000000335

Fig. 62   Cooling fan Inoperative (Part 1 of 4). DTS

Step	Action	Yes	No
5	1. Disconnect the S/P fan relay. 2. With a test lamp connected to a good ground, probe the cooling fan low reference circuit at the S/P fan relay. Does the test lamp illuminate?	Go to Step 9	Go to Step 8
6	Does the right cooling fan operate at high speed?	Go to Step 16	Go to Step 7
7	Inspect the ground circuit of the S/P fan relay for an open or high resistance. Did you find and correct the condition?	Go to Step 25	Go to Step 15
8	1. Install the S/P fan relay. 2. Disconnect the right cooling fan electrical connector. 3. With a test lamp connected to a good ground, probe the cooling fan motor supply voltage circuit at the right cooling fan motor connector. Does the test lamp illuminate?	Go to Step 12	Go to Step 13
9	1. Install the S/P fan relay. 2. Disconnect the left cooling fan motor connector. 3. With a test lamp connected to a good ground, probe the cooling fan motor supply voltage circuit at the left cooling fan connector. Does the test lamp illuminate?	Go to Step 11	Go to Step 10
10	Inspect the cooling fan motor supply voltage circuit for an open or high resistance. Did you find and correct the condition?	Go to Step 25	Go to Step 15
11	Inspect the ground circuit of the left cooling fan for an open or high resistance. Did you find and correct the condition?	Go to Step 25	Go to Step 18
12	Inspect the cooling fan low reference circuit for an open or high resistance. Did you find and correct the condition?	Go to Step 25	Go to Step 17
13	Inspect the cooling fan motor supply voltage circuit of the right cooling fan for an open or high resistance. Did you find and correct the condition?	Go to Step 25	Go to Step 19

ARM0500000000336

Fig. 62   Cooling fan Inoperative (Part 2 of 4). DTS

Step	Action	Yes	No
14	Inspect for poor connections at the low speed fan relay. Did you find and correct the condition?	Go to Step 25	Go to Step 20
15	Inspect for poor connections at the S/P fan relay. Did you find and correct the condition?	Go to Step 25	Go to Step 21
16	Inspect for poor connections at the high speed fan relay. Did you find and correct the condition?	Go to Step 25	Go to Step 22
17	Inspect for poor connections at the harness connector of the right cooling fan. Did you find and correct the condition?	Go to Step 25	Go to Step 23
18	Inspect for poor connections at the harness connector of the left cooling fan. Did you find and correct the condition?	Go to Step 25	Go to Step 24
19	Repair the battery positive voltage circuit for an open or high resistance. Did you complete the repair?	Go to Step 25	--
20	Replace the low speed fan relay. Did you complete the replacement?	Go to Step 25	--

ARM0500000000337

Fig. 62   Cooling fan Inoperative (Part 3 of 4). DTS

Step	Action	Yes	No
21	Replace the S/P fan relay. Did you complete the replacement?	Go to Step 25	--
22	Replace the high speed fan relay. Did you complete the replacement?	Go to Step 25	--
23	Replace the right cooling fan. Did you complete the replacement?	Go to Step 25	--
24	Replace the left cooling fan. Did you complete the replacement?	Go to Step 25	--
25	Operate the system in order to verify the repair. Did you correct the condition?	System OK	Go to Step 3

ARM0500000000338

Fig. 62   Cooling fan Inoperative (Part 4 of 4). DTS

Test Description

The number(s) below refer to the step number(s) on the diagnostic table.

2. Lack of communication may be due to a partial malfunction of the class 2 serial data circuit or due to a total malfunction of the class 2 serial data circuit. The specified procedure will determine the particular condition.

3. Determine if the Instrument Cluster or Powertrain Control Modules have set DTCs which may affect Engine Cooling operation are present.

4. The presence of DTCs which begin with "U" indicate some other module is not communicating. The specified procedure will compile all the available information before tests are performed.

Step	Action	Yes	No
1	Install a scan tool. Does the scan tool power up?	Go to Step 2	Diagnose Data Link Communications
2	1. Turn ON the ignition, with the engine OFF. 2. Attempt to establish communication with the powertrain control module. Does the scan tool communicate with the powertrain control module?	Go to Step 3	Data Link Communications
3	Select the powertrain control module display DTCs function on the scan tool. Does the scan tool display any DTCs?	Go to Step 4	Engine Cooling
4	Does the scan tool display any DTCs which begin with a "U"?	Data Link Communications	Diagnostic Trouble Code

GC1080100662000X

Fig. 63   Diagnostic system check. Grand Prix

DEFINITION: One or both engine cooling fan motors run continuously in high or low speed.

Step	Action	Yes	No
1	Did you perform the Engine Cooling Diagnostic System Check?	Go to Step 2	Diagnose System Check - Engine Cooling
2	Turn ON the ignition, with the engine OFF. Are one or both cooling fans ON?	Go to Step 3	Test for Intermittent and Poor Connections
3	Are both cooling fans running continuously?	Go to Step 5	Go to Step 4
4	Remove the cool fan relay. Did the left cooling fan turn OFF?	Go to Step 6	Go to Step 7
5	Repair the short to voltage in the right cooling fan supply voltage circuit. Did you complete the repair?	Go to Step 8	—
6	Repair the short to voltage in the right cooling fan low reference circuit. Did you complete the repair?	Go to Step 8	—
7	Repair the short to voltage in the left cooling fan supply voltage circuit. Did you complete the repair?	Go to Step 8	—
8	Operate the system in order to verify the repair. Did you correct the condition?	System OK	Go to Step 2

GC1080100663000X

Fig. 64　Cooling fan always on. Grand Prix

Step	Action	Yes	No
12	1. Disconnect the cool fan relay. 2. Connect the second 20-A fused jumper between the right cooling fan low reference circuit of the cool fan relay and the ground circuit of the cool fan relay. Does the right cooling fan operate properly in high speed?	Go to Step 14	Go to Step 19
13	Inspect for poor connections at the cool fan 1 relay. Did you find and correct the condition?	Go to Step 28	Go to Step 23
14	Inspect for poor connections at the cool fan relay. Did you find and correct the condition?	Go to Step 28	Go to Step 24
15	Inspect for poor connections at the cool fan 2 relay. Did you find and correct the condition?	Go to Step 28	Go to Step 25
16	Inspect for poor connections at the harness connector of the left cooling fan. Did you find and correct the condition?	Go to Step 28	Go to Step 26
17	Inspect for poor connections at the harness connector of the right cooling fan. Did you find and correct the condition?	Go to Step 28	Go to Step 27
18	Repair the right cooling fan supply voltage circuit. Did you complete the repair?	Go to Step 28	—
19	Repair the right cooling fan ground circuit. Did you complete the repair?	Go to Step 28	—
20	Repair the left cooling fan ground circuit. Did you complete the repair?	Go to Step 28	—
21	Repair the left cooling fan supply voltage circuit. Did you complete the repair?	Go to Step 28	—
22	Repair the right cooling fan low reference circuit. Did you complete the repair?	Go to Step 28	—
23	Replace the cool fan 1 relay. Is the repair complete?	Go to Step 28	—
24	Replace the cool fan relay. Is the repair complete?	Go to Step 28	—
25	Replace the cool fan 2 relay. Is the repair complete?	Go to Step 28	—
26	Replace the left cooling fan. Is the repair complete?	Go to Step 28	—
27	Replace the right cooling fan. Is the repair complete?	Go to Step 28	—
28	Operate the system in order to verify the repair. Did you correct the condition?	System OK	Go to Step 3

GC1080100664020X

Fig. 65　Cooling fan inoperative (Part 2 of 2). Grand Prix

Step	Action	Yes	No
1	Install a scan tool. Does the scan tool power up?	Go to Step 2	Diagnose Data Link Communications
2	1. Turn ON the ignition, with the engine OFF. 2. Attempt to establish communication with the following modules: o Powertrain control module (PCM) o Powertrain interface module (PIM) o Body control module (BCM) o Instrument panel cluster (IPC) Does the scan tool communicate with all of the modules?	Go to Step 3	Diagnose Data Link Communications

ARM0400000000039

Fig. 66　Diagnostic system check. GTO

DEFINITION: One or both engine cooling fan motors do not operate properly in high or low speed modes.

Step	Action	Yes	No
1	Did you perform the Engine Cooling Diagnostic System Check?	Go to Step 2	Diagnose Engine Cooling
2	1. Install a scan tool. 2. Turn ON the ignition, with the engine OFF. 3. With a scan tool, command the Fans Low Speed ON and OFF. Do the low speed engine cooling fans turn ON and OFF with each command?	Go to Step 3	Go to Step 4
3	Important: Before the PCM changes the speed of the cooling fans, a 3-second delay occurs. With a scan tool, command the Fans High Speed ON and OFF. Do the high speed engine cooling fans turn ON and OFF with each command?	Test for Intermittent and Poor Connections	Go to Step 11
4	Important: Following this step, do not remove the 20-A fused jumper wire that is connected during this step. While performing the following steps, use a second 20-A fused jumper wire. 1. Disconnect the cool fan 1 relay. 2. Connect a 20-A fused jumper between the battery positive voltage circuit of the cool fan 1 relay and the cooling fan motor supply voltage circuit of the cool fan 1 relay. Do both cooling fans operate in low speed?	Go to Step 13	Go to Step 5
5	1. Disconnect the cool fan relay. 2. Connect the second 20-A fused jumper between the right cooling fan low reference circuit of the cool fan relay and the left cooling fan motor supply voltage circuit of the cool fan relay. Do both cooling fans operate in low speed?	Go to Step 14	Go to Step 6
6	Connect the second 20-A fused jumper between the battery positive voltage circuit of the cool fan relay and the cooling fan motor supply voltage circuit of the cool fan relay. Does the left cooling fan operate in high speed?	Go to Step 9	Go to Step 7
7	1. Install the cool fan relay. 2. Disconnect the left cooling fan electrical connector. 3. Connect the second 20-Amp fused jumper wire from the cooling fan motor supply voltage circuit of the left cooling fan electrical connector to the cooling fan ground circuit of the left cooling fan electrical connector. Does the right cooling fan operate in high speed?	Go to Step 16	Go to Step 8
8	Connect the second 20-Amp fused jumper wire from the cooling fan motor supply voltage circuit of the left cooling fan electrical connector to a good ground. Does the right cooling fan operate in high speed?	Go to Step 20	Go to Step 21
9	1. Install the cool fan relay. 2. Disconnect the right cooling fan electrical connector. 3. Connect the second 20-Amp fused jumper wire from the motor supply voltage circuit of the right cooling fan electrical connector to the low reference circuit of the right cooling fan electrical connector. Does the left cooling fan operate in high speed?	Go to Step 17	Go to Step 10
10	Connect the second 20-Amp fused jumper wire from battery positive voltage to the right cooling fan low reference circuit of the of the right cooling fan electrical connector. Does the left cooling fan operate in high speed?	Go to Step 18	Go to Step 22
11	Is the left cooling fan operating properly in high speed?	Go to Step 12	Go to Step 15

GC1080100664010X

Fig. 65　Cooling fan inoperative (Part 1 of 2). Grand Prix

Step	Action	Yes	No
1	Did you review the Cooling System Description and Operation and perform the necessary inspections?	Go to Step 2	Go to Symptoms
2	1. Connect a scan tool. 2. Use the scan tool to command the low speed fan ON. Do the cooling fans operate at low speed?	Test for Intermittent Conditions and Poor Connections	Go to Step 3
3	1. Disconnect the low speed fan motor. 2. Connect a test lamp from the fan motor supply voltage circuit to the fan motor low speed ground circuit. 3. Use the scan tool to command the low speed fan ON. Does the test lamp illuminate?	Go to Step 10	Go to Step 4
4	1. Remove the fan 1 relay. 2. Install a 30-amp fused jumper between the low speed fan motor ground circuit and the fan 1 relay ground circuit, between cavities 30 and 87, of the cooling fan 1 relay connector. Do the cooling fans operate at low speed?	Go to Step 5	Go to Step 7

ARM0400000000040

Fig. 67　Cooling fan inoperative (Part 1 of 3). GTO

Step	Action	Yes	No
5	Test the fan 1 relay coil supply voltage circuit for an open.		
	Did you find and correct the condition?	Go to Step 13	Go to Step 6
6	Test the fan 1 relay coil control circuit for an open.		
	Did you find and correct the condition?	Go to Step 13	Go to Step 9
7	Test the fan motor low speed ground circuit for an open between the fan motors and the fan 1 relay.		
	Did you find and correct the condition?	Go to Step 13	Go to Step 8
8	Repair the open in the fan motor low speed ground circuit between the fan 1 relay and S240.		
	Did you find and correct the condition?	Go to Step 13	--
9	Inspect for a poor connection at the harness connector of the fan 1 relay.		
	Did you find and correct the condition?	Go to Step 13	Go to Step 11

ARM0400000000041

Fig. 67 Cooling fan inoperative (Part 2 of 3). GTO

Step	Action	Yes	No
10	Inspect for a poor connection at the harness connector of the fan motor.		
	Did you find and correct the condition?	Go to Step 13	Go to Step 12
11	Replace the fan 2 relay.		
	Did you complete the replacement?	Go to Step 13	--
12	Replace the fan motor.		
	Did you complete the replacement?	Go to Step 13	--
13	Operate the system in order to verify the repair.		
	Did you correct the condition?	System OK	Go to Step 2

ARM0500000000935

Fig. 67 Cooling fan inoperative (Part 3 of 3). GTO

Step	Action	Yes	No
1	Perform the following preliminary inspections: • Ensure that the battery is fully charged. • Ensure that the battery cables are clean and tight. • Inspect for any open fuses. • Inspect the easily accessible systems or the visible system components for obvious damage or conditions that could cause the symptom. • Ensure that the grounds are clean, tight, and in the correct location. • Inspect for aftermarket devices that could affect the operation of the system. • Search for applicable service bulletins. Did you find and correct the condition?	System OK	Go to Step 2

ARM0400000000025

Fig. 68 Diagnostic system check (Part 1 of 3). G6

Step	Action	Yes	No
2	Install a scan tool.		Diagnose Scan Tool Does Not Power Up
	Does the scan tool power up?	Go to Step 3	
3	1. Turn ON the ignition, with the engine OFF. 2. Attempt to establish communication with all of the control modules on the vehicle.		
	Does the scan tool communicate with all of the expected vehicle control modules?	Go to Step 4	Diagnose Data Link References
4	**Important** • To ensure that retained accessory power (RAP) mode is inactive, if equipped, open the driver door during the following step. • The engine may start during the following step. Turn OFF the engine as soon as you have observed the crank power mode. 1. Access the Power Mode parameter on the scan tool. 2. Rotate the ignition switch, operate the ignition mode switch, through all positions while observing the Power Mode parameter.		Go to Power Mode Mismatch
	Does the Power Mode parameter reading on the scan tool match the ignition switch position for all switch positions?	Go to Step 5	
5	Attempt to start the engine.		Go to Symptoms
	Does the engine crank?	Go to Step 6	

ARM0400000000026

Fig. 68 Diagnostic system check (Part 2 of 3). G6

Step	Action	Yes	No
6	Attempt to start the engine.		Go to Engine Cranks but Does Not Run
	Does the engine start and idle?	Go to Step 7	

7	**Important**
	
	Do NOT clear any DTCs unless instructed by a diagnostic procedure.
	
	1. Diagnose the DTCs in the order that the DTCs appear on the scan tool or mis-diagnosis may occur.
	2. If multiple powertrain DTCs are stored, diagnose the DTCs in the following order:
	  A. Component level DTCs, such as sensor DTCs, solenoid DTCs, and relay DTCs.
	  B. System level DTCs, such as misfire DTCs, evaporative emission (EVAP) system DTCs, and fuel trim DTCs.
	
	Advance to the List All DTCs screen on the scan tool.
	
	Does the scan tool display any DTCs?
		Go to Diagnostic Trouble Code (DTC) List	Go to Step 8

8	Is the customers concern with inspection/maintenance (I/M) testing?	Perform Inspection/Maintenance (I/M) System Check	Go to Symptoms

ARM0400000000027

Fig. 68 Diagnostic system check (Part 3 of 3). G6

Step	Action	Yes	No
1	Did you perform the Diagnostic System Check - Vehicle?	Go to Step 2	Go to Diagnostic System Check
2	Turn ON the ignition, with the engine OFF.		Test for Intermittent Conditions and Poor Connections
	Are one or both cooling fans ON?	Go to Step 3	
3	Are both cooling fans running continuously?	Go to Step 4	Go to Step 6
4	Are both fans running continuously in high speed?	Go to Step 5	Go to Step 7
5	Test the low reference circuit of the A/C refrigerant pressure sensor for an open.	Go to Step 18	Go to Step 14
6	Remove the cooling fan s/p relay.		
	Did the right cooling fan turn OFF?	Go to Step 10	Go to Step 8
7	Remove the cooling fan 1 relay.		
	Did the cooling fans turn OFF?	Go to Step 12	Go to Step 9
8	Remove the cooling fan 2 relay.		
	Did the right cooling fan turn OFF?	Go to Step 13	Go to Step 11
9	Repair the short to voltage in the left cooling fan motor supply voltage circuit.		
	Did you complete the repair?	Go to Step 18	--
10	Repair the short to voltage in the left cooling fan motor low reference circuit.		
	Did you complete the repair?	Go to Step 18	--

ARM0400000000028

Fig. 69 Cooling fan always on (Part 1 of 2). G6

#	Step	Yes	No
11	Repair the short to voltage in the right cooling fan motor supply voltage circuit. Did you complete the repair?	Go to Step 18	--
12	Inspect for poor connections at the cool fan 1 relay. Did you find and correct the condition?	Go to Step 18	Go to Step 15
13	Inspect for poor connections at the cool fan 2 relay. Did you find and correct the condition?	Go to Step 18	Go to Step 16
14	Inspect for poor connections at the A/C refrigerant pressure sensor. Did you find and correct the condition?	Go to Step 18	Go to Step 17
15	Replace the cool fan 1 relay. Did you complete the replacement?	Go to Step 18	--
16	Replace the cool fan 2 relay. Did you complete the replacement?	Go to Step 18	--
17	Replace the A/C refrigerant pressure sensor. Did you complete the replacement?	Go to Step 18	--
18	Operate the system in order to verify the repair. Did you correct the condition?	System OK	Go to Step 2

ARM0400000000029

Fig. 69   Cooling fan always on (Part 2 of 2). G6

#	Step	Yes	No
4	**Important** Do NOT remove the jumper wire that you will be connecting until your testing is completed. If the cool fan 1 fuse opens when you connect the jumper wire, repair the cooling fan motor supply voltage circuit of the left cooling fan motor for a short to ground. 1. Disconnect the cool fan 1 relay. 2. Connect a jumper wire between the battery positive voltage circuit and the cooling fan motor supply voltage circuit of the cool fan 1 relay. Do both cooling fans operate in low speed?	Go to Step 14	Go to Step 5
5	1. Disconnect the S/P fan relay. 2. With a test lamp connected to a good ground, probe the cooling fan low reference circuit at the S/P fan relay. Does the test lamp illuminate?	Go to Step 9	Go to Step 8
6	Does the left cooling fan operate at high speed?	Go to Step 16	Go to Step 7
7	Inspect the ground circuit of the S/P fan relay for an open or high resistance. Did you find and correct the condition?	Go to Step 25	Go to Step 15

ARM0400000000031

Fig. 70   Cooling fan inoperative (Part 2 of 5). G6

#	Step	Yes	No
13	Inspect the cooling fan motor supply voltage circuit of the left cooling fan for an open or high resistance. Did you find and correct the condition?	Go to Step 25	Go to Step 19
14	Inspect for poor connections at the cool fan 1 relay. Did you find and correct the condition?	Go to Step 25	Go to Step 20
15	Inspect for poor connections at the S/P fan relay. Did you find and correct the condition?	Go to Step 25	Go to Step 21
16	Inspect for poor connections at the cool fan 2 relay. Did you find and correct the condition?	Go to Step 25	Go to Step 22
17	Inspect for poor connections at the harness connector of the left cooling fan. Did you find and correct the condition?	Go to Step 25	Go to Step 23
18	Inspect for poor connections at the harness connector of the right cooling fan. Did you find and correct the condition?	Go to Step 25	Go to Step 24

ARM0400000000033

Fig. 70   Cooling fan inoperative (Part 4 of 5). G6

#	Step		
1	Did you perform the Diagnostic System Check - Vehicle?	Go to Step 2	Go to Diagnostic System Check
2	1. Install a scan tool. 2. Turn ON the ignition, with the engine OFF. 3. With a scan tool, command the Fan Control Relay 1 ON and OFF. Do the low speed engine cooling fans turn ON and OFF with each command?	Go to Step 3	Go to Step 4
3	**Important:** A 3 second delay occurs before the powertrain control module (PCM) changes the cooling fan speed. With a scan tool, command the Fan Control Relay 2 and 3 ON and OFF. Do the high speed engine cooling fans turn ON and OFF with each command?	Test for Intermittent Conditions and Poor Connections	Go to Step 6

ARM0400000000030

Fig. 70   Cooling fan inoperative (Part 1 of 5). G6

#	Step	Yes	No
8	1. Install the S/P fan relay. 2. Disconnect the left cooling fan electrical connector. 3. With a test lamp connected to a good ground, probe the cooling fan motor supply voltage circuit at the left cooling fan motor connector. Does the test lamp illuminate?	Go to Step 12	Go to Step 13
9	1. Install the S/P fan relay. 2. Disconnect the right cooling fan motor connector. 3. With a test lamp connected to a good ground, probe the cooling fan motor supply voltage circuit at the right cooling fan connector. Does the test lamp illuminate?	Go to Step 11	Go to Step 10
10	Inspect the cooling fan motor supply voltage circuit for an open or high resistance. Did you find and correct the condition?	Go to Step 25	Go to Step 15
11	Inspect the ground circuit of the right cooling fan for an open or high resistance. Did you find and correct the condition?	Go to Step 25	Go to Step 18
12	Inspect the cooling fan low reference circuit for an open or high resistance. Did you find and correct the condition?	Go to Step 25	Go to Step 17

ARM0400000000032

Fig. 70   Cooling fan inoperative (Part 3 of 5). G6

#	Step	Yes	No
19	Repair the battery positive voltage circuit for an open or high resistance. Did you complete the repair?	Go to Step 25	--
20	Replace the cool fan 1 relay. Did you complete the replacement?	Go to Step 25	--
21	Replace the S/P fan relay. Did you complete the replacement?	Go to Step 25	--
22	Replace the cool fan 2 relay. Did you complete the replacement?	Go to Step 25	--
23	Replace the left cooling fan. Did you complete the replacement?	Go to Step 25	--
24	Replace the right cooling fan. Did you complete the replacement?	Go to Step 25	--
25	Operate the system in order to verify the repair. Did you correct the condition?	System OK	Go to Step 3

ARM0500000000347

Fig. 70   Cooling fan inoperative (Part 5 of 5). G6

Step	Action	Yes	No
1	Install a scan tool. Does the scan tool power up?	Go to Step 2	Diagnose Data Link Communications
2	1. Turn ON the ignition, with the engine OFF. 2. Attempt to establish communication with the following control modules: ○ Instrument Cluster ○ Powertrain Control Module Does the scan tool communicate with the control modules?	Go to Step 3	Diagnose Data Link Communications
3	Select the powertrain control module display DTCs function on the scan tool. Does the scan tool display any DTCs?	Go to Step 4	Diagnose engine cooling
4	Does the scan tool display any DTCs which begin with a "U"?	Diagnose Data Link Communications	Diagnose Diagnostic Trouble Code (DTC)

ARM0300000000648

Fig. 71 Diagnostic system check. Impala & Monte Carlo

Step	Action	Yes	No
8	Repair the short to voltage in the right cooling fan low reference circuit. Did you complete the repair?	Go to Step 14	--
9	Repair the short to voltage in the left cooling fan motor supply voltage circuit. Did you complete the repair?	Go to Step 14	--
10	Inspect for poor connections at the FAN CONT #1 relay. Did you find and correct the condition?	Go to Step 14	Go to Step 12
11	Inspect for poor connections at the FAN CONT #3 relay. Did you find and correct the condition?	Go to Step 14	Go to Step 13
12	Replace the FAN CONT #1 relay. Did you complete the replacement?	Go to Step 14	--
13	Replace the FAN CONT #3 relay. Did you complete the replacement?	Go to Step 14	--
14	Operate the system in order to verify the repair. Did you correct the condition?	System OK	Go to Step 2

ARM0300000000650

Fig. 72 Cooling fan always on (Part 2 of 2). Impala & Monte Carlo

Step	Action	Yes	No
	DEFINITION: One or both engine cooling fan motors run continuously in high or low speed modes.		
1	Did you perform the Engine Cooling Diagnostic System Check?	Go to Step 2	Go To Diagnostic System Check
2	Turn ON the ignition, with the engine OFF. Are one or both cooling fans ON?	Go to Step 3	Test for Intermittent and Poor Connections
3	Are both cooling fans running continuously?	Go to Step 5	Go to Step 4
4	Remove the FAN CONT #2 relay. Did the left cooling fan turn OFF?	Go to Step 8	Go to Step 6
5	Remove the FAN CONT #1 relay. Did the cooling fans turn OFF?	Go to Step 10	Go to Step 7
6	Remove the FAN CONT #3 relay. Did the left cooling fan turn OFF?	Go to Step 11	Go to Step 9
7	Repair the short to voltage in the right cooling fan motor supply voltage circuit. Did you complete the repair?	Go to Step 14	--

ARM0300000000649

Fig. 72 Cooling fan always on (Part 1 of 2). Impala & Monte Carlo

Step	Action	Yes	No
1	Did you perform the Engine Cooling Diagnostic System Check?	Go to Step 2	Go to Diagnostic System Check
2	1. Install a scan tool. 2. Turn ON the ignition, with the engine OFF. 3. With a scan tool, command the Fans Low Speed ON and OFF. Do the low speed engine cooling fans turn ON and OFF with each command?	Go to Step 3	Go to Step 4
3	**Important:** A 3-second delay occurs before the PCM changes the cooling fan speed. With a scan tool, command the Fans High Speed ON and OFF. Do the high speed engine cooling fans turn ON and OFF with each command?	Test for Intermittent and Poor Connections	Go to Step 12
4	**Important** Do NOT remove the 20-A fused jumper wire connected during this step. Use a second 20-A fused jumper wire while performing the following steps. 1. Remove the FAN CONT #1 relay. 2. Connect a 20-A fused jumper between the battery positive switch side voltage circuit and the cooling fan motor supply voltage circuit of the FAN CONT #1 relay. Do both cooling fans operate in low speed?	Go to Step 22	Go to Step 5
5	1. Disconnect the FAN CONT #2 relay 2. Connect the second 20-A fused jumper between the cooling fan low reference circuit and the cooling fan motor supply voltage circuit of the FAN CONT #2 relay. Do both cooling fans operate in low speed?	Go to Step 23	Go to Step 6

ARM0300000000651

Fig. 73 Cooling fan inoperative (Part 1 of 7). Impala & Monte Carlo

6	Connect the second 20-ampere fused jumper between the battery positive voltage circuit and the cooling fan motor supply voltage circuit of the FAN CONT #2 relay. Does the left cooling fan operate in high speed?	Go to Step 9	Go to Step 7
7	1. Install the FAN CONT #2 relay. 2. Disconnect the left cooling fan electrical connector. 3. Connect the second 20-ampere fused jumper wire from the cooling fan motor supply voltage circuit to the ground circuit of the left cooling fan electrical connector. Does the right cooling fan operate in high speed?	Go to Step 25	Go to Step 8
8	Connect the second 20-ampere fused jumper wire from the cooling fan motor supply voltage circuit of the left cooling fan electrical connector to a good ground. Does the right cooling fan operate in high speed?	Go to Step 29	Go to Step 30
9	1. Install the FAN CONT #2 relay. 2. Disconnect the right cooling fan electrical connector. 3. Connect the second 20-ampere fused jumper wire from the cooling fan motor supply voltage circuit to the cooling fan low reference circuit of the right cooling fan electrical connector. Does the left cooling fan operate in high speed?	Go to Step 26	Go to Step 10
10	Connect the second 20-ampere fused jumper wire from the coil side battery positive voltage circuit to the cooling fan low reference circuit of the of the right cooling fan electrical connector. Does the left cooling fan operate in high speed?	Go to Step 11	Go to Step 31

ARM0300000000652

Fig. 73   Cooling fan inoperative (Part 2 of 7). Impala & Monte Carlo

11	Probe the battery positive voltage circuit on the switch side of the FAN CONT #1 relay with a test lamp that is connected to a good ground. Does the test lamp illuminate?	Go to Step 27	Go to Step 32
12	Is the left cooling fan operating properly in high speed?	Go to Step 19	Go to Step 13
13	1. Turn off the ignition. 2. Disconnect the FAN CONT #3 relay. 3. Turn ON the ignition, with the engine OFF. 4. Connect a test lamp between the high speed cooling fan relay control circuit and the battery positive voltage circuit on the coil side of the FAN CONT #3 relay. 5. With a scan tool command the High Speed Fans ON and OFF. Does the test lamp turn ON and OFF with each command?	Go to Step 15	Go to Step 14
14	Probe the battery positive voltage circuit on the coil side of the FAN CONT #3 relay with a test lamp that is connected to a good ground. Does the test lamp illuminate?	Go to Step 34	Go to Step 33
15	Install a 20 amp fused jumper between the battery positive voltage circuit on the switch side of the FAN CONT #3 relay and the cooling fan motor supply voltage circuit. Does the left cooling fan operate in high speed?	Go to Step 24	Go to Step 16
16	Probe the battery positive voltage circuit on the switch side of the FAN CONT #3 relay with a test lamp connected to a good ground. Does the test lamp illuminate?	Go to Step 17	Go to Step 33

ARM0300000000653

Fig. 73   Cooling fan inoperative (Part 3 of 7). Impala & Monte Carlo

17	1. With the 20 amp fused jumper still installed. 2. Disconnect the left cooling fan electrical connector. 3. Connect a test lamp from the cooling fan motor supply voltage circuit to the ground circuit of the left cooling fan electrical connector. Does the test lamp illuminate?	Go to Step 25	Go to Step 18
18	Probe the cooling fan motor supply voltage circuit of the left cooling fan electrical connector with a test lamp that is connected to a good ground. Does the test lamp illuminate?	Go to Step 29	Go to Step 30
19	1. Turn OFF the ignition. 2. Disconnect the FAN CONT #2 relay 3. Turn ON the ignition, with the engine OFF. 4. Connect a 20-A fused jumper between the cooling fan low reference circuit and the ground circuit of the FAN CONT #2 relay. 5. With a scan tool command the Fans High Speed ON and OFF. Does the right cooling fan operate in high speed?	Go to Step 20	Go to Step 28
20	1. Connect a test lamp between the high speed cooling fan relay control circuit of the FAN CONT #2 relay and the battery positive voltage circuit of the FAN CONT #2 relay. 2. With a scan tool command the Fans High Speed ON and OFF. Does the test lamp turn ON and OFF with each command?	Go to Step 23	Go to Step 21
21	Probe the battery positive voltage circuit of the FAN CONT #2 relay with a test lamp that is connected to a good ground. Does the test lamp illuminate?	Go to Step 34	Go to Step 33
22	Inspect for poor connections at the FAN CONT #1 relay. Did you find and correct the condition?	Go to Step 40	Go to Step 35

ARM0300000000654

Fig. 73   Cooling fan inoperative (Part 4 of 7). Impala & Monte Carlo

23	Inspect for poor connections at the FAN CONT #2 relay. Did you find and correct the condition?	Go to Step 40	Go to Step 36
24	Inspect for poor connections at the FAN CONT #3 relay. Did you find and correct the condition?	Go to Step 40	Go to Step 37
25	Inspect for poor connections at the harness connector of the left cooling fan. Did you find and correct the condition?	Go to Step 40	Go to Step 38
26	Inspect for poor connections at the harness connector of the right cooling fan. Did you find and correct the condition?	Go to Step 40	Go to Step 39
27	Repair the right cooling fan motor supply voltage circuit for an open. Is the repair complete?	Go to Step 40	--
28	Repair the right cooling fan ground circuit for an open. Is the repair complete?	Go to Step 40	--

ARM0300000000655

Fig. 73   Cooling fan inoperative (Part 5 of 7). Impala & Monte Carlo

	Action		
29	Repair the left cooling fan ground circuit for an open.		
	Is the repair complete?	Go to Step 40	--
30	Repair the left cooling fan motor supply voltage circuit for an open.		
	Is the repair complete?	Go to Step 40	--
31	Repair the right cooling fan low reference circuit for a short to ground or an open.		
	Is the repair complete?	Go to Step 40	--
32	Repair the FAN CONT #1 relay battery positive voltage circuit for an open.		
	Is the repair complete?	Go to Step 40	--
33	Repair the battery positive voltage circuit for the FAN CONT #2 and #3 relay for an open.		
	Is the repair complete?	Go to Step 40	--

ARM0300000000656

Fig. 73 Cooling fan inoperative (Part 6 of 7). Impala & Monte Carlo

	Action		
34	Repair the high speed cooling fan relay control circuit for an open.		
	Is the repair complete?	Go to Step 40	--
35	Replace the FAN CONT #1 relay.		
	Is the repair complete?	Go to Step 40	--
36	Replace the FAN CONT #2 relay.		
	Is the repair complete?	Go to Step 40	--
37	Replace the FAN CONT #3 relay.		
	Is the repair complete?	Go to Step 40	--
38	Replace the left cooling fan.		
	Is the repair complete?	Go to Step 40	--
39	Replace the right cooling fan.		
	Is the repair complete?	Go to Step 40	--
40	Operate the system in order to verify the repair.		
	Did you correct the condition?	System OK	Go to Step 3

ARM0300000000657

Fig. 73 Cooling fan inoperative (Part 7 of 7). Impala & Monte Carlo

Step	Action	Yes	No
1	Did you perform the Diagnostic System Check - Vehicle?	Go to Step 2	Go to Diagnostic System Check
2	Start the engine. Does the hot coolant indicator illuminate?	Go to Step 3	Test for Intermittent Conditions and Poor Connections
3	1. Install a scan tool. 2. With a scan tool, observe the engine coolant temperature (ECT) sensor parameter in the Powertrain Control Module data list. Does the scan tool indicate that the coolant temperature is within the temperature range shown on the temperature gauge?		Go to Step 4
4	Replace the IPC. Did you complete the replacement?	Go to Step 5	--
5	Operate the system in order to verify the repair. Did you correct the condition?	System OK	Go to Step 2

ARM0400000000680

Fig. 74 Engine coolant temperature indicator always on. LaCrosse

Step	Action	Yes	No
1	Did you perform the Diagnostic System Check - Vehicle?	Go to Step 2	Go to Diagnostic System Check
2	Turn ON the ignition, with the engine OFF. Are one or both cooling fans ON?	Go to Step 3	Test for Intermittent Conditions and Poor Connections
3	Are both cooling fans running continuously?	Go to Step 5	Go to Step 4
4	Remove the fan 2 relay. Did the right cooling fan turn OFF?	Go to Step 8	Go to Step 6
5	Remove the fan 1 relay. Did the cooling fans turn OFF?	Go to Step 10	Go to Step 7
6	Remove the fan 3 relay. Did the right cooling fan turn OFF?	Go to Step 11	Go to Step 9
7	Repair the short to voltage in the left cooling fan motor supply voltage circuit. Did you complete the repair?	Go to Step 14	--
8	Repair the short to voltage in the left cooling fan low reference circuit. Did you complete the repair?	Go to Step 14	--
9	Repair the short to voltage in the right cooling fan motor supply voltage circuit. Did you complete the repair?	Go to Step 14	--

ARM0400000000681

Fig. 75 Cooling fan always on (Part 1 of 2). LaCrosse

	Action		
10	Inspect for poor connections at the fan 1 relay.		
	Did you find and correct the condition?	Go to Step 14	Go to Step 12
11	Inspect for poor connections at the fan 3 relay.		
	Did you find and correct the condition?	Go to Step 14	Go to Step 13
12	Replace the fan 1 relay.		
	Did you complete the replacement?	Go to Step 14	--
13	Replace the fan 3 relay.		
	Did you complete the replacement?	Go to Step 14	--
14	Operate the system in order to verify the repair.		
	Did you correct the condition?	System OK	Go to Step 2

ARM0400000000682

Fig. 75 Cooling fan always on (Part 2 of 2). LaCrosse

Step	Action	Yes	No
	DEFINITION: One or both engine cooling fan motors do not operate properly in high or low speed modes.		
1	Did you perform the Diagnostic System Check - Vehicle?	Go to Step 2	Go to Diagnostic System Check
2	1. Install a scan tool. 2. Turn ON the ignition, with the engine OFF. 3. With a scan tool, command the Fans Low Speed ON and OFF. Do the low speed engine cooling fans turn ON and OFF with each command?	Go to Step 3	Go to Step 4
3	Important: A 3-second delay occurs before the powertrain control module (PCM) changes the cooling fan speed. With a scan tool, command the Fans High Speed ON and OFF. Do the high speed engine cooling fans turn ON and OFF with each command?	Test for Intermittent Conditions and Poor Connections	Go to Step 12
4	Important Do NOT remove the 20-amp fused jumper wire connected during this step. Use a second 20-amp fused jumper wire while performing the following steps. 1. Remove the fan 1 relay. 2. Connect a 20-amp fused jumper between the battery positive switch side voltage circuit and the fan motor supply voltage circuit of the cooling fan 1 relay. Do both cooling fans operate in low speed?	Go to Step 22	Go to Step 5

ARM0400000000683

Fig. 76 Cooling fan inoperative (Part 1 of 6). LaCrosse

Step	Action	Yes	No
5	1. Disconnect the fan 2 relay. 2. Connect the second 20-amp fused jumper between the cooling fan low reference circuit and the cooling fan motor supply voltage circuit of the fan 2 relay. Do both cooling fans operate in low speed?	Go to Step 23	Go to Step 6
6	Connect the second 20-amp fused jumper between the battery positive voltage circuit and the cooling fan motor supply voltage circuit of the fan 2 relay. Does the right cooling fan operate in high speed?	Go to Step 9	Go to Step 7
7	1. Install the fan 2 relay. 2. Disconnect the right cooling fan electrical connector. 3. Connect the second 20-amp fused jumper wire from the cooling fan motor supply voltage circuit to the ground circuit of the right cooling fan electrical connector. Does the left cooling fan operate in high speed?	Go to Step 25	Go to Step 8
8	Connect the second 20-amp fused jumper wire from the cooling fan motor supply voltage circuit of the right cooling fan electrical connector to a good ground. Does the left cooling fan operate in high speed?	Go to Step 29	Go to Step 30
9	1. Install the fan 2 relay. 2. Disconnect the left cooling fan electrical connector. 3. Connect the second 20-amp fused jumper wire from the cooling fan motor supply voltage circuit to the cooling fan low reference circuit of the left cooling fan electrical connector. Does the right cooling fan operate in high speed?	Go to Step 26	Go to Step 10
10	Connect the second 20-amp fused jumper wire from the coil side battery positive voltage circuit to the cooling fan low reference circuit of the cooling fan electrical connector. Does the right cooling fan operate in high speed?	Go to Step 11	Go to Step 31

ARM0400000000684

Fig. 76 Cooling fan inoperative (Part 2 of 6). LaCrosse

Step	Action	Yes	No
11	Probe the battery positive voltage circuit on the switch side of the fan 1 relay with a test lamp that is connected to a good ground. Does the test lamp illuminate?	Go to Step 27	Go to Step 32
12	Is the right cooling fan operating properly in high speed?	Go to Step 19	Go to Step 13
13	1. Turn OFF the ignition. 2. Disconnect the fan 3 relay. 3. Turn ON the ignition, with the engine OFF. 4. Connect a test lamp between the high speed cooling fan relay control circuit and the battery positive voltage circuit on the coil side of the fan 3 relay. 5. With a scan tool command the High Speed Fans ON and OFF. Does the test lamp turn ON and OFF with each command?	Go to Step 15	Go to Step 14
14	Probe the battery positive voltage circuit on the coil side of the fan 3 relay with a test lamp that is connected to a good ground. Does the test lamp illuminate?	Go to Step 34	Go to Step 33
15	Install a 20-amp fused jumper between the battery positive voltage circuit on the switch side of the fan 3 relay and the cooling fan motor supply voltage circuit. Does the right cooling fan operate in high speed?	Go to Step 24	Go to Step 16
16	Probe the battery positive voltage circuit on the switch side of the fan 3 relay with a test lamp connected to a good ground. Does the test lamp illuminate?	Go to Step 17	Go to Step 33
17	1. With the 20-amp fused jumper still installed. 2. Disconnect the right cooling fan electrical connector. 3. Connect a test lamp from the cooling fan motor supply voltage circuit to the ground circuit of the right cooling fan electrical connector. Does the test lamp illuminate?	Go to Step 25	Go to Step 18

ARM0400000000685

Fig. 76 Cooling fan inoperative (Part 3 of 6). LaCrosse

Step	Action	Yes	No
18	Probe the cooling fan motor supply voltage circuit of the right cooling fan electrical connector with a test lamp that is connected to a good ground. Does the test lamp illuminate?	Go to Step 29	Go to Step 30
19	1. Turn OFF the ignition. 2. Disconnect the fan 2 relay. 3. Turn ON the ignition, with the engine OFF. 4. Connect a 20-amp fused jumper between the cooling fan low reference circuit and the ground circuit of the fan 2 relay. 5. With a scan tool command the Fans High Speed ON and OFF. Does the left cooling fan operate in high speed?	Go to Step 20	Go to Step 28
20	1. Connect a test lamp between the high speed cooling fan relay control circuit of the fan 2 relay and the battery positive voltage circuit of the fan 2 relay. 2. With a scan tool command the Fans High Speed ON and OFF. Does the test lamp turn ON and OFF with each command?	Go to Step 23	Go to Step 21
21	Probe the battery positive voltage circuit of the fan 2 relay with a test lamp that is connected to a good ground. Does the test lamp illuminate?	Go to Step 34	Go to Step 33
22	Inspect for poor connections at the fan 1 relay. Did you find and correct the condition?	Go to Step 40	Go to Step 35
23	Inspect for poor connections at the fan 2 relay. Did you find and correct the condition?	Go to Step 40	Go to Step 36
24	Inspect for poor connections at the fan 3 relay. Wiring Systems. Did you find and correct the condition?	Go to Step 40	Go to Step 37

ARM0400000000686

Fig. 76 Cooling fan inoperative (Part 4 of 6). LaCrosse

25	Inspect for poor connections at the harness connector of the right cooling fan.		
	Did you find and correct the condition?	Go to Step 40	Go to Step 38
26	Inspect for poor connections at the harness connector of the left cooling fan.		
	Did you find and correct the condition?	Go to Step 40	Go to Step 39
27	Repair the left cooling fan motor supply voltage circuit for an open.		
	Is the repair complete?	Go to Step 40	--
28	Repair the left cooling fan ground circuit for an open.		
	Is the repair complete?	Go to Step 40	--
29	Repair the right cooling fan ground circuit for an open.		
	Is the repair complete?	Go to Step 40	--
30	Repair the right cooling fan motor supply voltage circuit for an open.		
	Is the repair complete?	Go to Step 40	--
31	Repair the left cooling fan low reference circuit for a short to ground or an open.		
	Is the repair complete?	Go to Step 40	--
32	Repair the fan 1 relay battery positive voltage circuit for an open.		
	Is the repair complete?	Go to Step 40	--
33	Repair the battery positive voltage circuit for the fan 2 relay and fan 3 relay for an open.		
	Is the repair complete?	Go to Step 40	--

ARM0400000000687

Fig. 76   Cooling fan inoperative (Part 5 of 6). LaCrosse

1. Verify that none of the following preliminary inspections/tests reveal the cause of the vehicle concern before beginning diagnosis:

    • Ensure that the battery is fully charged.

    • Ensure that the battery cables are clean and tight.

    • Inspect for any open fuses.

    • Ensure that the grounds are clean, tight, and in the correct location.

    • Inspect the easily accessible systems or the visible system components for obvious damage or conditions that could cause the concern.

    • Inspect for aftermarket devices that could affect the operation of the system.

    • Search for applicable service bulletins.

    ☐ If the preceding inspections/tests resolve the concern, go to Diagnostic Repair Verification .

2. Install a scan tool. Verify that the scan tool powers up.

    ☐ If the scan tool does not power up, refer to Scan Tool Does Not Power Up .

3. Ignition ON, Engine OFF, verify communication with all of the control modules on the vehicle.

    ☐ If the scan tool does not communicate with one or more of the expected control modules, refer to Data Link .

4. Verify that the following DTCs are not set: U1814, B1428.

    ☐ If either of the DTCs are set, refer to DTC U1814 or DTC B1428 .

ARM0600000000505

Fig. 77   Diagnostic system check (Part 1 of 3). Lucerne

34	Repair the high speed cooling fan relay control circuit for an open.		
	Is the repair complete?	Go to Step 40	--
35	Replace the fan 1 relay.		
	Is the repair complete?	Go to Step 40	
36	Replace the fan 2 relay.		
	Is the repair complete?	Go to Step 40	
37	Replace the fan 3 relay.		
	Is the repair complete?	Go to Step 40	
38	Replace the right cooling fan.		
	Is the repair complete?	Go to Step 40	
39	Replace the left cooling fan.		
	Is the repair complete?	Go to Step 40	--
40	Operate the system in order to verify the repair.		
	Did you correct the condition?	System OK	Go to Step 3

ARM0400000000688

Fig. 76   Cooling fan inoperative (Part 6 of 6). LaCrosse

Important: Open the drivers door to ensure retained accessory power mode (RAP) is inactive during this test. The engine may start during this test. Turn the engine OFF as soon as the crank power mode has been observed.

5   With a scan tool, access the Body Control Module Power Mode data display list.

    Verify that all the parameters listed in the following table correspond to the ignition key position. The PMM Power Mode parameters table below illustrates the correct state of these parameters (circuits) with the corresponding ignition switch positions. The circuits related to the parameters are in parenthesis.

    ☐ If any of the power mode parameters do not match in any ignition switch position, refer to Power Mode Mismatch .

6   Ignition ON, view the security indicator. The security indicator should not remain illuminated after the vehicle bulb check has completed.

    ☐ If the security indicator remains illuminated after the bulb check, refer to Diagnostic Trouble Code (DTC) and diagnose any of the following theft deterrent DTCs set as current: B1000, B302A, B3031, B3055, B3060, B3935, B3976, P0513, P0633, P1629, P1631, or P1632.

7   Attempt to start the engine. Verify that the engine cranks.

    ☐ If the engine does not crank, refer to Symptoms .

8   Attempt to start the engine. Verify the engine starts and runs.

    ☐ If the engine does not start and run, refer to one of the following:
    • Engine Cranks but Does Not Run

Important: Do not clear any DTCs unless instructed to do so by a diagnostic procedure.

Important: If any DTCs are Powertrain related DTCs, select Capture Info in order to store the DTC information with the scan tool.

ARM0600000000506

Fig. 77   Diagnostic system check (Part 2 of 3). Lucerne

9 Use the appropriate scan tool selections to obtain DTCs from each of the vehicle modules. Verify there are no DTCs reported from any module.

☐ If any DTCs are present, refer to Diagnostic Trouble Code (DTC) and diagnose any current DTCs in the following order:

9.1. DTCs that begin with a U.

9.2. Any of the following: B1000, B1001, B1008, B1016, C0550, C0558, C0569, P0601, P0602, P0603, P0604, P0606, P0607, P060D, P062F, P2107, P2108, or P2610.

9.3. Any of the following: B1325, B1335, B1424, B1517, C0895, C0899, C0900, P0560, P0562, or P0563.

9.4. Component level DTCs.

9.5. System level DTCs.

9.6. Any remaining DTCs.

10 If the customer concern is related to inspection/maintenance (I/M) testing, refer to one of the following:

• Inspection/Maintenance (I/M) System Check

☐ If none of the previous tests or inspections addresses the concern, refer to Symptoms

ARM0600000000507

Fig. 77   Diagnostic system check (Part 3 of 3). Lucerne

Circuit/System Testing

Important: You must perform the Circuit/System Verification before proceeding with Circuit/System Testing.

1. Ignition OFF, disconnect the relays.
2. Ignition ON, observe that the fan is not activated.

☐ If the fan is not activated, then replace the faulty relay.

☐ If the fan is activated, then test the fan voltage supply circuits for a short to voltage.

Repair Verification

1. Ignition ON, verify with a scan tool that the ECM is not commanding fan activation.
2. Ignition ON, observe that the fan is not activated.

ARM0600000000509

Fig. 78   Cooling fan always on (Part 2 of 2). Lucerne

Diagnostic Instructions

• Perform the Diagnostic System Check

• Review Strategy Based Diagnosis for an overview of the diagnostic approach.

• Diagnostic Procedure Instructions provides an overview of the diagnostic category.

Circuit/System Description

The engine control module (ECM) grounds the cooling fan relay control circuits through an internal solid state device called a driver. The primary function of the driver is to supply the ground for the component being controlled. Each driver has a fault line that is monitored by the ECM. When the ECM is commanding a component ON, the voltage potential of the control circuit should be low, near 0 volts. When the ECM is commanding the control circuit to a component OFF, the voltage potential of the circuit should be high, near battery voltage. If the ECM detects that the actual state of the control circuit does not match the expected state, a DTC will set.

Circuit/System Verification

1. If DTCs P0480 or P0481 are set, then perform those diagnostics first.
2. Ignition ON, verify with a scan tool that the ECM is not commanding fan activation.
3. Ignition ON, observe that the fan is not activated.

ARM0600000000508

Fig. 78   Cooling fan always on (Part 1 of 2). Lucerne

Diagnostic Instructions

• Perform the Diagnostic System Check - Vehicle prior to using this diagnostic procedure.

• Review Strategy Based Diagnosis for an overview of the diagnostic approach.

• Diagnostic Procedure Instructions provides an overview of the diagnostic category.

Circuit/System Description

The engine control module (ECM) grounds the low speed relay, which is relay 1, and the high speed relay, which is relay 2, control circuits through an internal solid state device called a driver. The primary function of the driver is to supply the ground for the component being controlled. Each driver has a fault line that is monitored by the ECM. When the ECM is commanding a component ON, the voltage potential of the control circuit should be low, near 0 volts. When the ECM is commanding the control circuit to a component OFF, the voltage potential of the circuit should be high, near battery voltage. If the ECM detects that the actual state of the control circuit does not match the expected state, a DTC will set.

Circuit/System Verification

1. If DTCs P0480 or P0481 are set, then perform those diagnostics first.
2. Ignition ON, command each relay ON and OFF with a scan tool. Observe to verify that the fan turns ON and OFF with each command.

ARM0600000000510

Fig. 79   Cooling fan inoperative (Part 1 of 2). Lucerne

Circuit/System Testing

Important: You must perform the Circuit/System Verification before proceeding with Circuit/System Testing.

1. Ignition OFF, disconnect fan high, fan low, and fan control relays.
2. Connect a 30A fused jumper between the normally-open switch contact terminals at the fan control relay connector in order to complete the left fan ground circuit. Leave this jumper in place for the remainder of this procedure.
3. One at a time, connect a 30A fused jumper between the positive terminal at the battery and the fan voltage supply circuit terminal at each relay connection and verify the appropriate fan activation.

   ☐ If the appropriate fan does not activate, test the fan voltage supply circuit for a short to ground or open/high resistance.

   ☐ If the circuit tests normal, test the fan ground circuit for an open/high resistance.

   ☐ If the circuits test normal, replace the fan.

6. Ignition ON, connect a 30A fused jumper between the relay switch voltage supply circuit terminal and the fan voltage supply circuit terminal at the low speed and then the high speed relay connections and verify the appropriate fan activation.

   ☐ If the appropriate fan does not activate, test the relay switch voltage supply circuit for a short to ground or high resistance.

7. If the circuits and fans test normal, replace the relay.

Repair Verification

Ignition ON, command the relay ON and OFF with a scan tool. Observe to verify that the fan turns ON and OFF with each command.

ARM0600000000511

Fig. 79   Cooling fan inoperative (Part 2 of 2). Lucerne

Important		
2 CANdi module J-45289 must be used with the Tech2. Install a scan tool. Does the scan tool power up?	Go to Step 3	**Diagnose** Scan Tool Does Not Power Up
3 1. Turn ON the ignition, with the engine OFF. 2. Select the Vehicle DTC Information on the scan tool. Does the scan tool display No Comm. for any control module?	**Diagnose Data Link Communications**	Go to Step 4
4 Attempt to start the engine. Does the engine crank over?	Go to Step 5	**Diagnose Engine Electrical**
5 Attempt to start the engine. Does the engine start and idle?	Go to Step 6	**Diagnose** Engine Cranks but Does Not Run

ARM0300000000675

Fig. 80   Diagnostic system check (Part 2 of 3). 2004–08 Malibu & Malibu Classic

Step	Action	Yes	No
1	Perform the following preliminary inspections: 1. Ensure that the battery is fully charged. 2. Ensure that the battery cables are clean and tight. 3. Inspect for any open fuses. 4. Inspect the easily accessible systems or the visible system components for obvious damage or conditions that could cause the symptom. 5. Ensure that the grounds are clean, tight, and in the correct location. 6. Inspect for aftermarket devices that could affect the operation of the system. 7. Search for applicable service bulletins. Did you find and correct the condition?	System OK	Go to Step 2

ARM0300000000674

Fig. 80   Diagnostic system check (Part 1 of 3). 2004–08 Malibu & Malibu Classic

Important		
Do NOT clear the DTCs unless instructed by a diagnostic procedure.		
6 1. Diagnose the DTCs in the order that the DTCs appear on the scan tool or mis-diagnosis may occur. 2. If multiple powertrain DTCs are stored, diagnose the DTCs in the following order: A. Component level DTCs, such as sensor DTCs, solenoid DTCs, and relay DTCs. B. System level DTCs, for example, misfire DTCs, EVAP system DTCs, and fuel trim DTCs. Advance to the List All DTCs screen on the scan tool. Does the scan tool display any DTCs?	Go to Step 7	System OK
7 If there are any powertrain DTCs, select Captured Info in order to store the powertrain DTC information with a scan tool. Did you complete the action?	Diagnose Trouble Code (DTC)	--

ARM0300000000676

Fig. 80   Diagnostic system check (Part 3 of 3). 2004–08 Malibu & Malibu Classic

Step	Action	Yes	No
	DEFINITION: The engine cooling fan motor runs continuously in high or low speed.		
1	Did you perform the Vehicle Diagnostic System Check?	Go to Step 2	Go to Diagnostic System Check
2	Turn the ignition ON, with the engine OFF. Are one or both cooling fans ON?	Go to Step 3	Test for Intermittent and Poor Connections
3	Are both cooling fans running continuously?	Go to Step 4	Go to Step 6
4	Are both fans running continuously in high speed?	Go to Step 5	Go to Step 7
5	Test the low reference circuit of the A/C refrigerant pressure sensor for an open.	Go to Step 18	Go to Step 14
6	Remove the cooling fan s/p relay. Did the right cooling fan turn OFF?	Go to Step 10	Go to Step 8
7	Remove the cooling fan 1 relay. Did the cooling fans turn OFF?	Go to Step 12	Go to Step 9
8	Remove the cooling fan 2 relay. Did the right cooling fan turn OFF?	Go to Step 13	Go to Step 11
9	Repair the short to voltage in the left cooling fan motor supply voltage circuit. Did you complete the repair?	Go to Step 18	--

Fig. 81   Coolant fan always on (Part 1 of 2). 2004–08 Malibu & Malibu Classic

ARM0300000000677

Step	Action	Yes	No
10	Repair the short to voltage in the left cooling fan motor low reference circuit. Did you complete the repair?	Go to Step 18	--
11	Repair the short to voltage in the right cooling fan motor supply voltage circuit. Did you complete the repair?	Go to Step 18	--
12	Inspect for poor connections at the cool fan 1 relay. Did you find and correct the condition?	Go to Step 18	Go to Step 15
13	Inspect for poor connections at the cool fan 2 relay. Did you find and correct the condition?	Go to Step 18	Go to Step 16
14	Inspect for poor connections at the A/C refrigerant pressure sensor. Did you find and correct the condition?	Go to Step 18	Go to Step 17
15	Replace the cool fan 1 relay. Did you complete the replacement?	Go to Step 18	--
16	Replace the cool fan 2 relay. Did you complete the replacement?	Go to Step 18	--
17	Replace the A/C refrigerant pressure sensor. Did you complete the replacement?	Go to Step 18	--
18	Operate the system in order to verify the repair. Did you correct the condition?	System OK	Go to Step 2

ARM0300000000678

Fig. 81   Coolant fan always on (Part 2 of 2). 2004–08 Malibu & Malibu Classic

Step	Action	Yes	No
1	Did you perform the Diagnostic System Check-Vehicle?	Go to Step 2	Go to Diagnostic System Check
2	1. Install a scan tool. 2. Turn ON the ignition, with the engine OFF. 3. With a scan tool, command the Fan Control Relay 1 ON and OFF. Do the low speed engine cooling fans turn ON and OFF with each command?	Go to Step 3	Go to Step 4
3	Important: A 3-second delay occurs before the PCM changes the cooling fan speed. With a scan tool, command the Fan Control Relay 2 and 3 ON and OFF. Do the high speed engine cooling fans turn ON and OFF with each command?	Test for Intermittent and Poor Connections	Go to Step 6
4	Important: Do NOT remove the jumper wire that you will be connecting until your testing is completed. If the cool fan 1 fuse opens when you connect the jumper wire, repair the cooling fan motor supply voltage circuit of the left cooling fan motor for a short to ground. 1. Disconnect the cool fan 1 relay. 2. Connect a jumper wire between the battery positive voltage circuit and the cooling fan motor supply voltage circuit of the cool fan 1 relay. Do both cooling fans operate in low speed?	Go to Step 14	Go to Step 5

ARM0300000000679

Fig. 82   Coolant fan inoperative (Part 1 of 4). 2004–08 Malibu & Malibu Classic

Step	Action	Yes	No
5	1. Disconnect the S/P fan relay. 2. With a test lamp connected to a good ground, probe the cooling fan low reference circuit at the S/P fan relay. Does the test lamp illuminate?	Go to Step 9	Go to Step 8
6	Does the left cooling fan operate at high speed?	Go to Step 16	Go to Step 7
7	Inspect the ground circuit of the S/P fan relay for an open or high resistance. Did you find and correct the condition?	Go to Step 25	Go to Step 15
8	1. Install the S/P fan relay. 2. Disconnect the left cooling fan electrical connector. 3. With a test lamp connected to a good ground, probe the cooling fan motor supply voltage circuit at the left cooling fan motor connector. Does the test lamp illuminate?	Go to Step 12	Go to Step 13
9	1. Install the S/P fan relay. 2. Disconnect the right cooling fan motor connector. 3. With a test lamp connected to a good ground, probe the cooling fan motor supply voltage circuit at the right cooling fan connector. Does the test lamp illuminate?	Go to Step 11	Go to Step 10
10	Inspect the cooling fan motor supply voltage circuit for an open or high resistance. Did you find and correct the condition?	Go to Step 25	Go to Step 15

ARM0300000000680

Fig. 82   Coolant fan inoperative (Part 2 of 4). 2004–08 Malibu & Malibu Classic

11	Inspect the ground circuit of the right cooling fan for an open or high resistance. Did you find and correct the condition?	Go to Step 25	Go to Step 18
12	Inspect the cooling fan low reference circuit for an open or high resistance. Did you find and correct the condition?	Go to Step 25	Go to Step 17
13	Inspect the cooling fan motor supply voltage circuit of the left cooling fan for an open or high resistance. Did you find and correct the condition?	Go to Step 25	Go to Step 19
14	Inspect for poor connections at the cool fan 1 relay. Did you find and correct the condition?	Go to Step 25	Go to Step 20
15	Inspect for poor connections at the S/P fan relay. Did you find and correct the condition?	Go to Step 25	Go to Step 21
16	Inspect for poor connections at the cool fan 2 relay. Did you find and correct the condition?	Go to Step 25	Go to Step 22

ARM0300000000681

Fig. 82 Coolant fan inoperative (Part 3 of 4). 2004–08 Malibu & Malibu Classic

17	Inspect for poor connections at the harness connector of the left cooling fan. Did you find and correct the condition?	Go to Step 25	Go to Step 23
18	Inspect for poor connections at the harness connector of the right cooling fan. Did you find and correct the condition?	Go to Step 25	Go to Step 24
19	Repair the battery positive voltage circuit for an open or high resistance. Did you complete the repair?	Go to Step 25	--
20	Replace the cool fan 1 relay. Did you complete the replacement?	Go to Step 25	--
21	Replace the S/P fan relay. Did you complete the replacement?	Go to Step 25	--
22	Replace the cool fan 2 relay. Did you complete the replacement?	Go to Step 25	--
23	Replace the left cooling fan. Did you complete the replacement?	Go to Step 25	--
24	Replace the right cooling fan. Did you complete the replacement?	Go to Step 25	--
25	Operate the system in order to verify the repair. Did you correct the condition?	System OK	Go to Step 3

ARM0300000000682

Fig. 82 Coolant fan inoperative (Part 4 of 4). 2004–08 Malibu & Malibu Classic

Step	Action	Yes	No
1	Install a scan tool. Does the scan tool power up?	Go to Step 2	Diagnose Data Link Communications
2	1. Turn ON the ignition, with the engine OFF. 2. Attempt to establish communication with the following control modules: • Instrument Cluster • Powertrain Control Module Does the scan tool communicate with the control modules?	Go to Step 3	Diagnose Data Link Communications
3	Select the powertrain control module display DTCs function on the scan tool. Does the scan tool display any DTCs?	Go to Step 4	Diagnose engine cooling
4	Does the scan tool display any DTCs which begin with a "U"?	Diagnose Data Link Communications	Diagnose Diagnostic Trouble Code (DTC)

ARM0300000000658

Fig. 83 Diagnostic system check. Park Avenue

Step	Action	Yes	No
	DEFINITION: One or both engine cooling fan motors run continuously in high or low speed.		
1	Did you perform the Engine Cooling Diagnostic System Check?	Go to Step 2	Go To Diagnostic System Check
2	**Important** The cooling fan fuses and cooling fan relays 1 and 2 are labeled incorrectly on the underhood sticker. Turn ON the ignition, with the engine OFF. Are one or both cooling fans ON?	Go to Step 3	Test for Intermittent and Poor Connections
3	Are both cooling fans running continuously?	Go to Step 5	Go to Step 4
4	Remove the cool fan S/P relay. Did the right cooling fan turn OFF?	Go to Step 8	Go to Step 6
5	Remove the cool fan 1 relay. Did the cooling fans turn OFF?	Go to Step 10	Go to Step 7
6	Remove the cool fan 2 relay. Did the right cooling fan turn OFF?	Go to Step 11	Go to Step 9
7	Repair the short to voltage in the left cooling fan motor supply voltage circuit. Did you complete the repair?	Go to Step 14	--

ARM0300000000659

Fig. 84 Cooling fan always on (Part 1 of 2). Park Avenue

		Go to	
8	Repair the short to voltage in the left cooling fan low reference circuit. Did you complete the repair?	Go to Step 14	--
9	Repair the short to voltage in the right cooling fan motor supply voltage circuit. Did you complete the repair?	Go to Step 14	--
10	Inspect for poor connections at the cool fan 1 relay. Did you find and correct the condition?	Go to Step 14	Go to Step 12
11	Inspect for poor connections at the cool fan 2 relay. Did you find and correct the condition?	Go to Step 14	Go to Step 13
12	Replace the cool fan 1 relay. Did you complete the replacement?	Go to Step 14	--
13	Replace the cool fan 2 relay. Did you complete the replacement?	Go to Step 14	--
14	Operate the system in order to verify the repair. Did you correct the condition?	System OK	Go to Step 2

ARM0300000000660

Fig. 84   Cooling fan always on (Part 2 of 2). Park Avenue

5	1. Disconnect the cooling fan S/P relay 2. Connect the second 20-A fused jumper between the cooling fan low reference circuit and the cooling fan motor supply voltage circuit of the cooling fan S/P relay. Do both cooling fans operate in low speed?	Go to Step 23	Go to Step 6
6	Connect the second 20-A fused jumper between the battery positive voltage circuit and the cooling fan motor supply voltage circuit of the cooling fan S/P relay. Does the right cooling fan operate in high speed?	Go to Step 9	Go to Step 7
7	1. Install the cooling fan S/P relay. 2. Disconnect the right cooling fan electrical connector. 3. Connect the second 20-Amp fused jumper wire from the cooling fan motor supply voltage circuit to the ground circuit of the right cooling fan electrical connector. Does the left cooling fan operate in high speed?	Go to Step 25	Go to Step 8
8	Connect the second 20-Amp fused jumper wire from the cooling fan motor supply voltage circuit of the right cooling fan electrical connector to a good ground. Does the left cooling fan operate in high speed?	Go to Step 29	Go to Step 30
9	1. Install the cooling fan S/P relay. 2. Disconnect the left cooling fan electrical connector. 3. Connect the second 20-Amp fused jumper wire from the cooling fan motor supply voltage circuit to the cooling fan low reference circuit of the left cooling fan electrical connector. Does the right cooling fan operate in high speed?	Go to Step 26	Go to Step 10
10	Connect the second 20-Amp fused jumper wire from the coil side battery positive voltage circuit to the cooling fan low reference circuit of the of the left cooling fan electrical connector. Does the right cooling fan operate in high speed?	Go to Step 11	Go to Step 31

ARM0300000000662

Fig. 85   Cooling fan inoperative (Part 2 of 6). Park Avenue

1	Did you perform the Engine Cooling Diagnostic System Check?	Go to Step 2	Go to Diagnostic System Check
2	**Important** The cooling fan fuses and cooling fan relays 1 and 2 are labeled incorrectly on the underhood sticker. 1. Install a scan tool. 2. Turn ON the ignition, with the engine OFF. 3. With a scan tool, command the Fans Low Speed ON and OFF. Do the low speed engine cooling fans turn ON and OFF with each command?	Go to Step 3	Go to Step 4
3	**Important:** A 3-second delay occurs before the PCM changes the cooling fan speed. With a scan tool, command the Fans High Speed ON and OFF. Do the high speed engine cooling fans turn ON and OFF with each command?	Test for Intermittent and Poor Connections	Go to Step 12
4	**Important** Do NOT remove the 20-A fused jumper wire connected during this step. Use a second 20-A fused jumper wire while performing the following steps. 1. Remove the cooling fan 1 relay. 2. Connect a 20-A fused jumper between the battery positive switch side voltage circuit and the cooling fan motor supply voltage circuit of the cooling fan 1 relay. Do both cooling fans operate in low speed?	Go to Step 22	Go to Step 5

ARM0300000000661

Fig. 85   Cooling fan inoperative (Part 1 of 6). Park Avenue

11	Probe the battery positive voltage circuit on the switch side of the cooling fan 1 relay with a test lamp that is connected to a good ground. Does the test lamp illuminate?	Go to Step 27	Go to Step 32
12	Is the right cooling fan operating properly in high speed?	Go to Step 19	Go to Step 13
13	1. Turn off the ignition. 2. Disconnect the cooling fan 2 relay. 3. Turn ON the ignition, with the engine OFF. 4. Connect a test lamp between the high speed cooling fan relay control circuit and the battery positive voltage circuit on the coil side of the cooling fan 2 relay. 5. With a scan tool command the High Speed Fans ON and OFF. Does the test lamp turn ON and OFF with each command?	Go to Step 15	Go to Step 14
14	Probe the battery positive voltage circuit on the coil side of the cooling fan 2 relay with a test lamp that is connected to a good ground. Does the test lamp illuminate?	Go to Step 34	Go to Step 33
15	Install a 20 amp fused jumper between the battery positive voltage circuit on the switch side of the cooling fan 2 relay and the cooling fan motor supply voltage circuit. Does the right cooling fan operate in high speed?	Go to Step 24	Go to Step 16
16	Probe the battery positive voltage circuit on the switch side of the cooling fan 2 relay with a test lamp connected to a good ground. Does the test lamp illuminate?	Go to Step 17	Go to Step 33
17	1. With the 20 amp fused jumper still installed. 2. Disconnect the right cooling fan electrical connector. 3. Connect a test lamp from the cooling fan motor supply voltage circuit to the ground circuit of the right cooling fan electrical connector. Does the test lamp illuminate?	Go to Step 25	Go to Step 18

ARM0300000000663

Fig. 85   Cooling fan inoperative (Part 3 of 6). Park Avenue

18	Probe the cooling fan motor supply voltage circuit of the right cooling fan electrical connector with a test lamp that is connected to a good ground. Does the test lamp illuminate?	Go to Step 29	Go to Step 30
19	1. Turn OFF the ignition. 2. Disconnect the cooling fan S/P relay 3. Turn ON the ignition, with the engine OFF. 4. Connect a 20-A fused jumper between the cooling fan low reference circuit and the ground circuit of the cooling fan S/P relay. 5. With a scan tool command the Fans High Speed ON and OFF. Does the left cooling fan operate in high speed?	Go to Step 20	Go to Step 28
20	1. Connect a test lamp between the high speed cooling fan relay control circuit of the cooling fan S/P relay and the battery positive voltage circuit of the cooling fan S/P relay. 2. With a scan tool command the Fans High Speed ON and OFF. Does the test lamp turn ON and OFF with each command?	Go to Step 23	Go to Step 21
21	Probe the battery positive voltage circuit of the cooling fan S/P relay with a test lamp that is connected to a good ground. Does the test lamp illuminate?	Go to Step 34	Go to Step 33
22	Inspect for poor connections at the cooling fan 1 relay. Did you find and correct the condition?	Go to Step 40	Go to Step 35

Fig. 85   Cooling fan inoperative (Part 4 of 6). Park Avenue

ARM0300000000664

23	Inspect for poor connections at the cooling fan S/P relay. Did you find and correct the condition?	Go to Step 40	Go to Step 36
24	Inspect for poor connections at the cooling fan S/P relay. Did you find and correct the condition?	Go to Step 40	Go to Step 37
25	Inspect for poor connections at the harness connector of the right cooling fan. Did you find and correct the condition?	Go to Step 40	Go to Step 38
26	Inspect for poor connections at the harness connector of the left cooling fan. Did you find and correct the condition?	Go to Step 40	Go to Step 39
27	Repair the left cooling fan motor supply voltage circuit for an open. Is the repair complete?	Go to Step 40	--
28	Repair the left cooling fan ground circuit for an open. Is the repair complete?	Go to Step 40	--
29	Repair the right cooling fan ground circuit for an open. Is the repair complete?	Go to Step 40	--
30	Repair the right cooling fan motor supply voltage circuit for an open. Is the repair complete?	Go to Step 40	--

ARM0300000000665

Fig. 85   Cooling fan inoperative (Part 5 of 6). Park Avenue

31	Repair the left cooling fan low reference circuit for a short to ground or an open. Is the repair complete?	Go to Step 40	--
32	Repair the cooling fan 1 relay battery positive voltage circuit for an open. Is the repair complete?	Go to Step 40	--
33	Repair the battery positive voltage circuit for the cooling fan S/P and 2 relay for an open. Is the repair complete?	Go to Step 40	--
34	Repair the high speed cooling fan relay control circuit for an open. Is the repair complete?	Go to Step 40	--
35	Replace the cooling fan 1 relay. Is the repair complete?	Go to Step 40	--
36	Replace the cooling fan S/P relay. Is the repair complete?	Go to Step 40	--
37	Replace the cooling fan 2 relay. Is the repair complete?	Go to Step 40	--
38	Replace the right cooling fan. Is the repair complete?	Go to Step 40	--
39	Replace the left cooling fan. Is the repair complete?	Go to Step 40	--
40	Operate the system in order to verify the repair. Did you correct the condition?	System OK	Go to Step 3

ARM0300000000666

Fig. 85   Cooling fan inoperative (Part 6 of 6). Park Avenue

Step	Action	Yes	No
1	Perform the following preliminary inspections: • Ensure that the battery is fully charged. • Ensure that the battery cables are clean and tight. • Inspect for any open fuses. • Inspect the easily accessible systems or the visible system components for obvious damage or conditions that could cause the symptom. • Ensure that the grounds are clean, tight, and in the correct location. • Inspect for aftermarket devices that could affect the operation of the system. • Search for applicable service bulletins. Did you find and correct the condition?	System OK	Go to Step 2
2	Install a scan tool. Does the scan tool power up?	Go to Step 3	Go to Scan Tool Does Not Power Up
3	1. Turn ON the ignition, with the engine OFF. 2. Attempt to establish communication with all of the control modules on the vehicle. Does the scan tool communicate with all of the expected vehicle control modules?	Go to Step 4	Go to Data Link References

ARM0500000000348

Fig. 86   Diagnostic system check (Part 1 of 3). Solstice

Step	Action	Yes	No
4	**Important:** • To ensure that retained accessory power (RAP) mode is inactive, if equipped, open the driver door during the following step. • The engine may start during the following step. Turn OFF the engine as soon as you have observed the crank power mode. 1. Access the Power Mode parameter on the scan tool. 2. Rotate the ignition switch (operate the ignition mode switch) through all positions while observing the Power Mode parameter. Does the Power Mode parameter reading on the scan tool match the ignition switch position for all switch positions?	Go to Step 5	Go to Power Mode Mismatch
5	Attempt to start the engine. Does the engine crank?	Go to Step 6	Go to Symptoms
6	Attempt to start the engine. Does the engine start and idle?	Go to Step 7	Go to Engine Cranks but Does Not Run
7	**Important:** Do not clear any DTCs unless instructed by a diagnostic procedure. Use the appropriate scan tool selections to obtain DTCs for each of the control modules. Does the scan tool display any DTCs?	Go to Step 8	Go to Step 12

ARM0500000000349

Fig. 86 Diagnostic system check (Part 2 of 3). Solstice

Step	Action	Yes	No
8	Does the scan tool display any DTCs that begin with a "U"?	Go to Diagnostic Trouble Code (DTC) List - Vehicle	Go to Step 9
9	**Important:** If any of the following DTCs are displayed, diagnose them before diagnosing any other DTCs or symptoms. Does the scan tool display DTC B1000, B1001, B1004, B1009, B1019, C0550, C0551, C0561, C0569, P0601, P0602, P0603, P0604, P0605, P0606, P0607, P062F, P1600, P1621, P1627, P1683, or P2610?	Go to Diagnostic Trouble Code (DTC) List - Vehicle	Go to Step 10
10	**Important:** If any of the following DTCs are displayed, diagnose them before diagnosing any other DTCs or symptoms. Does the scan tool display DTC B1325, B1370, C0899, C0900, P0560, P0561, P0562, or P0563?	Go to Diagnostic Trouble Code (DTC) List - Vehicle	Go to Step 11
11	**Important:** If any of the remaining DTCs are powertrain DTCs, select Captured Info in order to store the powertrain DTC information with a scan tool. If multiple DTCs are stored, diagnose the DTCs in the following order: 1. Component level DTCs, such as sensor DTCs, solenoid DTCs, and relay DTCs. 2. System level DTCs, such as misfire DTCs, evaporative emission (EVAP) system DTCs, and fuel trim DTCs. Diagnose the remaining DTCs.	Go to Diagnostic Trouble Code (DTC) List - Vehicle	--
12	Is the customers concern with inspection/maintenance (I/M) testing?	Go to Inspection/Maintenance (I/M) System Check	Go to Symptoms - Vehicle

ARM0500000000350

Fig. 86 Diagnostic system check (Part 3 of 3). Solstice

Step	Action	Yes	No
	DEFINITION: The engine cooling fan motor runs continuously in high or low speed.		
1	Did you perform the Diagnostic System Check - Vehicle?	Go to Step 2	Go to Diagnostic System Check - Vehicle
2	Turn ON the ignition, with the engine OFF. Is the engine cooling fan ON?	Go to Step 3	Test for Intermittent Conditions and Poor Connections
3	Disconnect the cooling fan 1 relay. Is the engine cooling fan ON?	Go to Step 4	Go to Step 8
4	Disconnect the cooling fan 2 relay. Is the engine cooling fan ON?	Go to Step 5	Go to Step 9
5	1. Turn OFF the ignition. 2. Disconnect the cooling fan connector. 3. Turn ON the ignition, with the engine OFF. 4. Probe the low speed cooling fan supply voltage circuit of the cooling fan 1 relay with a test lamp connected to a good ground. Does the test lamp illuminate?	Go to Step 6	Go to Step 7
6	Repair the short to voltage in the low speed cooling fan motor supply voltage circuit. Refer to Wiring Repairs . Did you complete the repair?	Go to Step 12	--

ARM0500000000351

Fig. 87 Cooling fan always on (Part 1 of 2). Solstice

Step	Action	Yes	No
7	Repair the short to voltage in the high speed cooling fan motor supply voltage circuit. Did you complete the repair?	Go to Step 12	--
8	Inspect for poor connections at the cooling fan 1 relay. Did you find and correct the condition?	Go to Step 12	Go to Step 10
9	Inspect for poor connections at the cooling fan 2 relay. Did you find and correct the condition?	Go to Step 12	Go to Step 11
10	Replace the cooling fan 1 relay. Did you complete the replacement?	Go to Step 12	--
11	Replace the cooling fan 2 relay. Did you complete the replacement?	Go to Step 12	--
12	Operate the system in order to verify the repair. Did you correct the condition?	System OK	Go to Step 2

ARM0500000000352

Fig. 87 Cooling fan always on (Part 2 of 2). Solstice

Step	Action	Yes	No
	DEFINITION: The engine cooling fan motor is inoperative in either high, low, or both speeds.		
1	Did you perform the Diagnostic System Check - Vehicle?	Go to Step 2	Go to Diagnostic System Check - Vehicle
2	1. Install a scan tool. 2. Turn ON the ignition, with the engine OFF. 3. With a scan tool, command the low speed fan relay ON and OFF. Does the cooling fan turn ON and OFF with each command?	Go to Step 3	Go to Step 4
3	With a scan tool, command the high speed fan relay ON and OFF. Does the cooling fan turn ON and OFF with each command?	Test for Intermittent Conditions and Poor Connections	Go to Step 7
4	1. Disconnect the cooling fan 1 relay. 2. Turn ON the ignition, with the engine OFF. 3. Probe the battery positive voltage circuit of the cooling fan 1 relay with a test lamp connected to a good ground. Does the test lamp illuminate?	Go to Step 5	Go to Step 11

ARM0500000000353

Fig. 88 Cooling fan inoperative (Part 1 of 3). Solstice

Step	Action	Yes	No
5	1. Connect the cooling fan 1 relay. 2. Disconnect the cooling fan. 3. Probe the low speed cooling fan supply voltage circuit with a test lamp connected to a good ground. 4. With a scan tool, command the low speed fan relay ON and OFF. Does the test lamp turn ON and OFF with each command?	Go to Step 6	Go to Step 9
6	Probe the ground circuit of the cooling fan with a test lamp connected to battery positive voltage. Does the test lamp illuminate?	Go to Step 13	Go to Step 12
7	1. Disconnect the cooling fan 2 relay. 2. Turn ON the ignition, with the engine OFF. 3. Probe the battery positive voltage circuit of the cooling fan 2 relay with a test lamp connected to a good ground. Does the test lamp illuminate?	Go to Step 8	Go to Step 11
8	1. Connect the cooling fan 2 relay. 2. Disconnect the cooling fan. 3. Probe the high speed cooling fan supply voltage circuit with a test lamp connected to a good ground. 4. With a scan tool, command the high speed fan relay ON and OFF. Does the test lamp turn ON and OFF with each command?	Go to Step 13	Go to Step 10
9	Test the low speed cooling fan supply voltage circuit for a high resistance and an open. Did you find and correct the condition?	Go to Step 21	Go to Step 15
10	Test the high speed cooling fan supply voltage circuit for a high resistance and an open. Did you find and correct the condition?	Go to Step 21	Go to Step 16

ARM0500000000354

Fig. 88 Cooling fan inoperative (Part 2 of 3). Solstice

Step	Action	Yes	No
11	Repair the battery positive voltage circuit of the cooling fans. Did you complete the repair?	Go to Step 21	--
12	Repair the ground circuit of the cooling fan. Did you complete the repair?	Go to Step 21	--
13	Inspect for poor connections at the harness connector of the cooling fan. Did you find and correct the condition?	Go to Step 21	Go to Step 17
14	Inspect for poor connections at the harness connector of the engine control module (ECM). Did you find and correct the condition?	Go to Step 21	Go to Step 18
15	Inspect for poor connections at the harness connector of the cool fan 1 relay. Did you find and correct the condition?	Go to Step 21	Go to Step 19
16	Inspect for poor connections at the harness connector of the cool fan 2 relay. Did you find and correct the condition?	Go to Step 21	Go to Step 20
17	Replace the cooling fan. Did you complete the replacement?	Go to Step 21	--
18	Replace the ECM. Did you complete the replacement?	Go to Step 21	--
19	Replace the cool fan 1 relay. Did you complete the replacement?	Go to Step 21	--
20	Replace the cool fan 2 relay. Did you complete the replacement?	Go to Step 21	--
21	Operate the system in order to verify the repair. Did you correct the condition?	System OK	Go to Step 3

ARM0500000000355

Fig. 88 Cooling fan inoperative (Part 3 of 3). Solstice

Step	Action	Yes	No
7	**Important:** Do NOT clear any DTCs unless instructed by a diagnostic procedure. • Diagnose the DTCs in the order that the DTCs appear on the scan tool or mis-diagnosis may occur. • If multiple powertrain DTCs are stored, diagnose the DTCs in the following order: 1. Component level DTCs, such as sensor DTCs, solenoid DTCs, and relay DTCs. 2. System level DTCs, such as misfire DTCs, EVAP system DTCs, and fuel trim DTCs. Advance to the List All DTCs screen on the scan tool. Does the scan tool display any DTCs?	Go to Diagnostic Trouble Code (DTC)	Go to Step 8
8	Is the customers concern with inspection/maintenance (I/M) testing?	Go to Inspection/Maintenance (I/M) System Check	Go to Symptoms

ARM0500000000936

Fig. 89 Diagnostic system check (Part 3 of 3). STS

Step	Action	Yes	No
1	Perform the following preliminary inspections: • Ensure that the battery is fully charged. • Ensure that the battery cables are clean and tight. • Inspect for any open fuses. • Inspect the easily accessible systems or the visible system components for obvious damage or conditions that could cause the symptom. • Ensure that the grounds are clean, tight, and in the correct location. • Inspect for aftermarket devices that could affect the operation of the system. • Search for applicable service bulletins. Did you find and correct the condition?	System OK	Go to Step 2

ARM0400000000017

Fig. 89 Diagnostic system check (Part 1 of 3). STS

Step	Action	Yes	No
2	Install a scan tool. Does the scan tool power up?	Go to Step 3	Diagnose Scan Tool Does Not Power Up
3	Turn ON the ignition, with the engine OFF. Is the NO FOB DETECTED message displayed on the driver information center (DIC)?	Go to Key Fob Not Detected in Keyless Entry	Go to Step 4
4	1. Turn ON the ignition, with the engine OFF. 2. Attempt to establish communication with all of the control modules on the vehicle. Does the scan tool communicate with all of the expected vehicle control modules?	Go to Step 5	Go to Data Link References
5	Attempt to start the engine. Does the engine crank?	Go to Step 6	Go to Symptoms
6	Attempt to start the engine. Does the engine start and idle?	Go to Step 7	Go to Engine Cranks but Does Not Run

ARM0400000000018

Fig. 89 Diagnostic system check (Part 2 of 3). STS

Step	Action	Yes	No
	DEFINITION: One or both engine cooling fan motors run continuously in high or low speed.		
1	Did you perform the Diagnostic System Check - Vehicle?	Go to Step 2	Go to Diagnostic System Check
2	Turn ON the ignition, with the engine OFF. Are both cooling fans operating at low speed?	Go to Step 4	Go to Step 3
3	Is the left cooling fan operating at high speed?	Go to Step 5	Test for Intermittent Conditions and Poor Connections
4	Remove the low speed fan relay. Did the fans turn OFF?	Go to Step 8	Go to Step 6
5	Remove the high speed fan relay. Did the left cooling fan turn OFF?	Go to Step 9	Go to Step 7
6	Repair the cooling fan motor supply voltage circuit of the right cooling fan for a short to voltage. Did you complete the repair?	Go to Step 12	--
7	Repair the cooling fan motor supply voltage circuit of the left cooling fan for a short to voltage. Did you complete the repair?	Go to Step 12	--

ARM0400000000019

Fig. 90 Cooling fan always on (Part 1 of 2). STS

Step	Action	Yes	No
8	Inspect for poor connections at the low speed fan relay. Did you find and correct the condition?	Go to Step 12	Go to Step 10
9	Inspect for poor connections at the high speed fan relay. Did you find and correct the condition?	Go to Step 12	Go to Step 11
10	Replace the low speed fan relay. Did you complete the replacement?	Go to Step 12	--
11	Replace the high speed fan relay. Did you complete the replacement?	Go to Step 12	--
12	Operate the system in order to verify the repair. Did you correct the condition?	System OK	Go to Step 2

ARM0400000000020

Fig. 90 Cooling fan always on (Part 2 of 2). STS

Step	Action	Yes	No
1	Did you perform the Diagnostic System Check - Vehicle?	Go to Step 2	Go to Diagnostic System Check
2	1. Install a scan tool. 2. Turn ON the ignition, with the engine OFF. 3. With a scan tool, command the Fans Low Speed ON and OFF. Do the low speed engine cooling fans turn ON and OFF with each command?	Go to Step 3	Go to Step 4
3	**Important** A 3-second delay occurs before the powertrain control module (PCM) changes the cooling fan speed. With a scan tool, command the Fans High Speed ON and OFF. Do the high speed engine cooling fans turn ON and OFF with each command?	Test for Intermittent Conditions and Poor Connections	Go to Step 6

ARM0400000000021

Fig. 91 Cooling fan inoperative (Part 1 of 5). STS

Step	Action	Yes	No
4	**Important** Do NOT remove the jumper wire that you will be connecting until your testing is completed. If the low speed fan fuse opens when you connect the jumper wire, repair the cooling fan motor supply voltage circuit of the right cooling fan motor for a short to ground. 1. Disconnect the low speed fan relay. 2. Connect a jumper wire between the battery positive voltage circuit and the cooling fan motor supply voltage circuit of the low speed fan relay. Do both cooling fans operate in low speed?	Go to Step 14	Go to Step 5
5	1. Disconnect the S/P fan relay. 2. With a test lamp connected to a good ground, probe the cooling fan low reference circuit at the S/P fan relay. Does the test lamp illuminate?	Go to Step 9	Go to Step 8
6	Does the right cooling fan operate at high speed?	Go to Step 16	Go to Step 7
7	Inspect the ground circuit of the S/P fan relay for an open or high resistance. Did you find and correct the condition?	Go to Step 25	Go to Step 15

ARM0400000000022

Fig. 91 Cooling fan inoperative (Part 2 of 5). STS

Step	Action	Yes	No
8	1. Install the S/P fan relay. 2. Disconnect the right cooling fan electrical connector. 3. With a test lamp connected to a good ground, probe the cooling fan motor supply voltage circuit at the right cooling fan motor connector. Does the test lamp illuminate?	Go to Step 12	Go to Step 13
9	1. Install the S/P fan relay. 2. Disconnect the left cooling fan motor connector. 3. With a test lamp connected to a good ground, probe the cooling fan motor supply voltage circuit at the left cooling fan connector. Does the test lamp illuminate?	Go to Step 11	Go to Step 10
10	Inspect the cooling fan motor supply voltage circuit for an open or high resistance. Did you find and correct the condition?	Go to Step 25	Go to Step 15
11	Inspect the ground circuit of the left cooling fan for an open or high resistance. Did you find and correct the condition?	Go to Step 25	Go to Step 18
12	Inspect the cooling fan low reference circuit for an open or high resistance. Did you find and correct the condition?	Go to Step 25	Go to Step 17

ARM0400000000023

Fig. 91 Cooling fan inoperative (Part 3 of 5). STS

Step	Action	Yes	No
13	Inspect the cooling fan motor supply voltage circuit of the right cooling fan for an open or high resistance. Did you find and correct the condition?	Go to Step 25	Go to Step 19
14	Inspect for poor connections at the low speed fan relay. Did you find and correct the condition?	Go to Step 25	Go to Step 20
15	Inspect for poor connections at the S/P fan relay. Did you find and correct the condition?	Go to Step 25	Go to Step 21
16	Inspect for poor connections at the high speed fan relay. Did you find and correct the condition?	Go to Step 25	Go to Step 22
17	Inspect for poor connections at the harness connector of the right cooling fan. Did you find and correct the condition?	Go to Step 25	Go to Step 23
18	Inspect for poor connections at the harness connector of the left cooling fan. Did you find and correct the condition?	Go to Step 25	Go to Step 24

ARM0400000000024

Fig. 91 Cooling fan inoperative (Part 4 of 5). STS

Step	Action	Yes	No
19	Repair the battery positive voltage circuit for an open or high resistance. Did you complete the repair?	Go to Step 25	--
20	Replace the low speed fan relay. Did you complete the replacement?	Go to Step 25	--
21	Replace the S/P fan relay. Did you complete the replacement?	Go to Step 25	--
22	Replace the high speed fan relay. Did you complete the replacement?	Go to Step 25	--
23	Replace the right cooling fan. Did you complete the replacement?	Go to Step 25	--
24	Replace the left cooling fan. Did you complete the replacement?	Go to Step 25	--
25	Operate the system in order to verify the repair. Did you correct the condition?	System OK	Go to Step 3

ARM0500000000937

Fig. 91 Cooling fan inoperative (Part 5 of 5). STS

Step	Action	Yes	No
1	Did you review the Cooling System Description and Operation and perform the necessary inspections?	Go to Step 2	Check Engine Cooling
2	1. Ensure that the ECT is below 93°C (199°F). 2. Depress the A/C switch to the OFF position. 3. Turn the blower switch to the OFF position. 4. Turn the ignition switch to the RUN position. Is the fan motor running continuously?	Go to Step 3	Test for Intermittent and Poor Connections
3	Remove the fan 1 relay from the underhood fuse block. Is the fan motor running continuously?	Go to Step 4	Go to Step 5
4	Repair the short to voltage in the fan motor supply voltage circuit. Did you find and correct the condition?	Go to Step 6	--
5	Replace the fan 1 relay. Did you complete the replacement?	Go to Step 6	--
6	Operate the system in order to verify the repair. Did you correct the condition?	System OK	Go to Step 3

ARM66GC000000289

Fig. 92   Cooling fan always On. Vibe

Step	Action	Yes	No
7	Inspect for a poor connection at the harness connector of the Powertrain Control Module (PCM). Did you find and correct the condition?	Go to Step 12	Go to Step 11
8	Repair the short to ground in the fan motor ground circuit. Did you complete the repair?	Go to Step 12	--
9	Replace the fan 2 relay. Did you complete the replacement?	Go to Step 12	--
10	Replace the refrigerant pressure switch Did you complete the replacement?	Go to Step 12	--
11	Replace the PCM. Did you complete the replacement?	Go to Step 12	--
12	Operate the system in order to verify the repair. Did you correct the condition?	System OK	Go to Step 3

ARM66GC000000291

Fig. 93   Cooling fan inoperative low speed operates in high speed (Part 2 of 2). Vibe

Step	Action	Yes	No
1	Did you review the Cooling System Description and Operation and perform the necessary inspections?	Go to Step 2	Check Engine Cooling
2	1. Connect a scan tool. The engine must be below operating temperature. 2. Use the scan tool to command the A/C compressor clutch relay ON. When the relay is energized the cooling fan will also run at low speed. Does the cooling fan operate at high speed?	Test for Intermittent and Poor Connections	Go to Step 3
3	1. Remove the fan 2 relay. 2. Use the scan tool to command the cooling fan ON. Does the cooling fan operate at high speed?	Go to Step 8	Go to Step 4
4	Test the fan 2 relay. The relay should be normally open between terminals 3 and 5 and normally closed between terminals 3 and 4. Did the relay test OK?	Go to Step 5	Go to Step 9
5	Test the fan 2 relay coil control circuits for a short to ground. Did you find and correct the condition?	Go to Step 12	Go to Step 6
6	Test the refrigerant pressure switch for a closed condition. The switch should be normally open between terminals 2 and 3. Did the switch test OK?	Go to Step 7	Go to Step 10

ARM66GC000000290

Fig. 93   Cooling fan inoperative low speed operates in high speed (Part 1 of 2). Vibe

Step	Action	Yes	No
1	Did you review the Cooling System Description and Operation and perform the necessary inspections?	Go to Step 2	Check Engine Cooling
2	Run the engine until operating temperature is reached and the thermostat opens. Does the cooling fan operate at high speed?	Test for Intermittent and Poor Connections	Go to Step 3
3	Test the fan 2 relay coil supply voltage circuit for an open. Did you find and correct the condition?	Go to Step 11	Go to Step 4
4	Test the fan 2 relay coil control circuits for an open or for a short to B+. Did you find and correct the condition?	Go to Step 11	Go to Step 5
5	1. Remove the fan 2 relay. 2. Install a 30 amp fused jumper between the fan motor control circuit and the high speed fan circuit (between cavities 3 and 5) of the fan 2 relay connector. Does the cooling fan operate at high speed?	Go to Step 7	Go to Step 6
6	Test for an open in the fan 2 relay high speed ground circuit. Did you find and correct the condition?	Go to Step 11	Go to Step 8

ARM66GC000000292

Fig. 94   Cooling fan inoperative in high speed (Part 1 of 2). Vibe

Step	Action	Yes	No
7	Inspect for a poor connection at the harness connector of the fan 2 relay. Did you find and correct the condition?	Go to Step 11	Go to Step 9
8	Inspect for a poor connection at the harness connector of the Powertrain Control Module (PCM). Did you find and correct the condition?	Go to Step 11	Go to Step 10
9	Replace the fan 2 relay. Did you complete the replacement?	Go to Step 11	--
10	Replace the PCM. Did you complete the replacement?	Go to Step 11	--
11	Operate the system in order to verify the repair. Did you correct the condition?	System OK	Go to Step 3

ARM66GC000000293

Fig. 94   Cooling fan inoperative in high speed (Part 2 of 2). Vibe

Step	Action	Yes	No
1	Did you review the Cooling System Description and Operation	Go to Step 2	Check Engine Cooling
2	1. Connect a scan tool. The engine must be below operating temperature. 2. Use the scan tool to command the A/C compressor clutch relay ON. When the relay is energized the cooling fan will also run at low speed. Does the cooling fan operate at low speed?	Test for Intermittent and Poor Connections	Go to Step 3
3	1. Remove the fan 2 relay. 2. Install a 30 amp fused jumper between the fan motor control circuit and the low speed fan circuit (between cavities 3 and 4) of the cooling fan 2 relay connector. 3. Use the scan tool to command the A/C compressor clutch relay ON. When the relay is energized the cooling fan will also run at low speed. Does the cooling fan operate at low speed?	Go to Step 6	Go to Step 4
4	Test the low speed fan motor ground circuit for an open, or for a short to B+, between the fan 2 relay terminal 4 and S103. Did you find and correct the condition?	Go to Step 9	Go to Step 5
5	Inspect for a poor connection at the harness connector of the fan resistor. Did you find and correct the condition?	Go to Step 9	Go to Step 8
6	Inspect for a poor connection at the harness connector of the fan 2 relay. Did you find and correct the condition?	Go to Step 9	Go to Step 7
7	Replace the fan 2 relay. Did you complete the replacement?	Go to Step 9	--
8	Replace the fan resistor. Did you complete the replacement?	Go to Step 9	--
9	Operate the system in order to verify the repair. Did you correct the condition?	System OK	Go to Step

ARM66GC000000294

Fig. 95 Cooling fan inoperative in low speed. Vibe

Step	Action	Yes	No
9	Test the fan motor ground circuit for an open or a short to ground Did you find and correct the condition?	Go to Step 16	Go to Step 12
10	Inspect for a poor connection at the harness connector of the fan 1 relay. Did you find and correct the condition?	Go to Step 16	Go to Step 13
11	Inspect for a poor connection at the harness connector of the fan motor. Did you find and correct the condition?	Go to Step 16	Go to Step 14
12	Inspect for a poor connection at the harness connector of the powertrain control module (PCM). Did you find and correct the condition?	Go to Step 16	Go to Step 15
13	Replace the fan 1 relay. Did you complete the replacement?	Go to Step 16	--
14	Replace the fan motor. Did you complete the replacement?	Go to Step 16	--
15	Replace the PCM. Did you complete the replacement?	Go to Step 16	--
16	Operate the system in order to verify the repair. Did you correct the condition?	System OK	Go to Step

ARM66GC000000296

Fig. 96 Cooling fan inoperative (Part 2 of 2). Vibe

Symptom	Causes
Fan motor inoperative in both speeds	• Open or short to ground in the fan 1 relay supply voltage circuits. • Open or short to B+ in the fan 1 relay coil control circuit. • Open or short to ground in the fan motor supply voltage circuit. • Short to ground in the fan 2 coil supply voltage circuit. • Open or short to B+ in the fan motor ground circuit. • Short to B+ in the fan 2 coil control circuit.
Fan motor inoperative in high speed only	• Open in the fan 2 relay supply voltage circuit. • Open in the fan 2 relay coil control circuit. • Open in the fan 2 relay high speed ground circuit.
Fan motor low speed operates at high speed	• Short to ground in the fan motor ground circuit. • Short to ground in the fan resistor circuit.
Fan motor inoperative in low speed only	Open or short to B+ in the fan resistor circuit.

ARM66GC000000297

Fig. 97 Cooling fan symptom table. Vibe

Step	Action	Yes	No
1	Did you review the Cooling System Description and Operation	Go to Step 2	Check Engine Cooling
2	Run the engine until operating temperature is reached and the thermostat opens. Does the cooling fan operate?	Test for Intermittent and Poor Connections	Go to Step 3
3	1. Stop the engine. 2. Disconnect the fan motor connector. 3. Connect a test lamp across the fan motor connector. 4. Start the engine. Does the test lamp illuminate?	Go to Step 11	Go to Step 4
4	1. Connect the fan motor. 2. Exchange the fan 1 relay with a known good relay (the horn relay). Does the cooling fan operate?	Go to Step 10	Go to Step 5
5	Test the fan 1 relay and the fan 2 relay supply voltage circuits for an open or a short to ground: Did you find and correct the condition?	Go to Step 16	Go to Step 6
6	Test the fan 1 relay coil control circuit for an open or a short to B+. Did you find and correct the condition?	Go to Step 16	Go to Step 7
7	Test the fan 2 relay coil control circuit for a short to B+. Did you find and correct the condition?	Go to Step 16	Go to Step 8
8	Test the fan motor supply voltage circuit for an open or a short to ground. Did you find and correct the condition?	Go to Step 16	Go to Step

ARM66GC000000295

Fig. 96 Cooling fan inoperative (Part 1 of 2). Vibe

Step	Action	Yes	No
1	Perform the following preliminary inspections: 1. Ensure that the battery is fully charged. 2. Ensure that the battery cables are clean and tight. 3. Inspect for any open fuses. 4. Inspect the easily accessible systems or the visible system components for obvious damage or conditions that could cause the symptom. 5. Ensure that the grounds are clean, tight, and in the correct location. 6. Inspect for aftermarket devices that could affect the operation of the system. 7. Search for applicable service bulletins. Did you find and correct the condition?	System OK	Go to Step 2

ARM0300000000683

Fig. 98 Diagnostic system check (Part 1 of 3). XLR

Step	Action	Yes	No
2	Install a scan tool. Does the scan tool power up?	Go to Step 3	Diagnose Scan Tool Does Not Power Up
3	1. Turn ON the ignition, with the engine OFF. 2. Select Vehicle Control Systems, Computer/Integrating Systems and then Vehicle DTC Information on the scan tool. Does the scan tool display No Comm. for any control module?	Diagnose Data Link Communications	Go to Step 4
4	Attempt to start the engine. Does the engine crank over?	Go to Step 5	Diagnose Engine Electrical
5	Attempt to start the engine. Does the engine start and idle?	Go to Step 6	Diagnose Engine Cranks but Does Not Run

ARM0300000000684

Fig. 98 Diagnostic system check (Part 2 of 3). XLR

Step	Action	Yes	No

6	**Important**
	
	Do NOT clear the DTCs unless instructed by a diagnostic procedure.
	
	1. Diagnose the DTCs in the order that the DTCs appear on the scan tool or mis-diagnosis may occur.
	2. If multiple powertrain DTCs are stored, diagnose the DTCs in the following order:
	  A. Component level DTCs, such as sensor DTCs, solenoid DTCs, and relay DTCs.
	  B. System level DTCs, for example, misfire DTCs, EVAP system DTCs, and fuel trim DTCs.
	
	Advance to the List All DTCs screen on the scan tool.
	
	Does the scan tool display any DTCs?
		Go to Step 7	System OK

7	If there are any powertrain DTCs, select Captured Info in order to store the powertrain DTC information with a scan tool. Did you complete the action?	Diagnose Trouble Code (DTC)	--

ARM0300000000685

Fig. 98   Diagnostic system check (Part 3 of 3). XLR

Step	Action	Yes	No
	Connector End View Reference: Cooling System Connector End Views		
1	Did you perform the Vehicle Diagnostic System Check?	Go to Step 2	Go to Diagnostic System Check
2	Turn ON the ignition with the engine OFF. Turn OFF the HVAC controls. Does the engine cooling fan operate?	Go to Step 3	Go to Diagnostic Aids
3	Turn OFF the ignition. Does the cooling fan still operate?	Go to Step 4	Go to Step 5
4	Replace the cooling fan speed control processor. Did you complete the replacement?	Go to Step 6	--
5	**Important** Perform the set up procedure for the ECM. Replace the ECM. Did you complete the replacement?	Go to Step 6	--
6	Operate the system in order to verify the repair. Did you correct the condition?	System OK	Go to Step 2

ARM0300000000686

Fig. 99   Cooling fan always on. XLR

Step	Action	Value	Yes	No
1	Did you perform the Vehicle Diagnostic System Check?	--	Go to Step 2	Go to Diagnostic System Check
2	1. Install a scan tool. 2. Turn ON the ignition, with the engine OFF. 3. With a scan tool, command the cooling fan ON and OFF. Does the cooling fan turn ON and OFF with each command?	--	Go to Diagnostic Aids	Go to Step 3
3	1. Turn OFF the ignition. 2. Disconnect the cooling fan. 3. Probe the battery positive voltage circuit of the cooling fan assembly with a test lamp that is connected to a good ground. Does the test lamp illuminate?	--	Go to Step 4	Go to Step 7
4	Inspect the ground circuit of the cooling fan assembly for an open. Did you complete the repair	--	Go to Step 12	Go to Step 5
5	1. Install a scan tool. 2. Turn ON the ignition, with the engine OFF. 3. Command the cooling fan ON to 90%. 4. Measure the voltage on the cooling fan speed control circuit. Is the specified voltage present?	4-5 V	Go to Step 8	Go to Step 6
6	Inspect the cooling fan speed control circuit for an open short to ground or short to voltage. Did you find and correct the condition?	--	Go to Step 12	Go to Step 10

ARM0300000000687

Fig. 100   Cooling fan inoperative (Part 1 of 2). XLR

Step	Action	Value	Yes	No
7	Repair the battery positive voltage circuit of the cooling fan assembly for an open or short to ground. Did you complete the repair	--	Go to Step 12	--
8	Inspect for poor connections at the cooling fan assembly. Did you find and correct the condition?	--	Go to Step 12	Go to Step 9
9	Replace the cooling fan assembly. Did you complete the replacement?	--	Go to Step 12	
10	Inspect for poor connections at the ECM. Did you find and correct the condition?	--	Go to Step 12	Go to Step 11
11	**Important** Perform the setup procedure for the ECM. Replace the ECM. Did you complete the replacement?	--	Go to Step 12	--
12	Operate the system in order to verify the repair. Did you correct the condition?	--	System OK	Go to Step 2

ARM0300000000688

Fig. 100   Cooling fan inoperative (Part 2 of 2). XLR

COOLING FANS

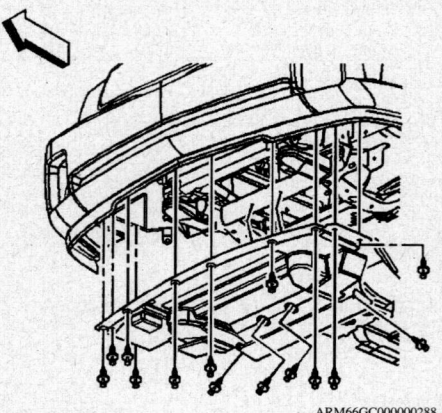

Fig. 101 Air deflector removal. CTS

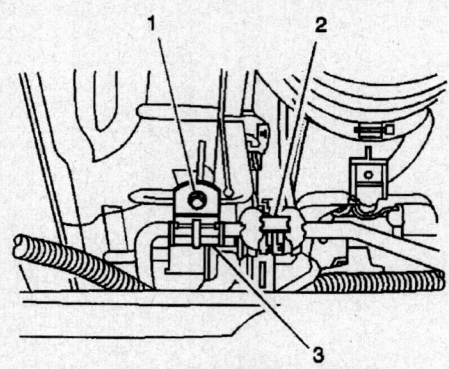

1- A/C CLIP RETAINING SCREW
2- COOLANT BYPASS VALVE
3- A/C LINE RETAINING CLIP

Fig. 102 Coolant bypass valve removal. CTS

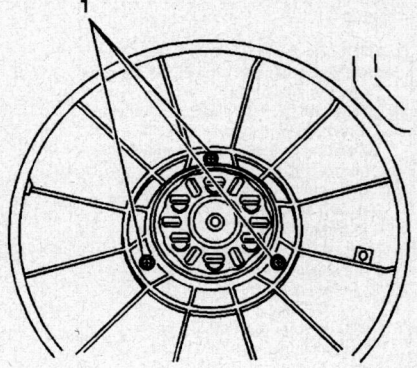

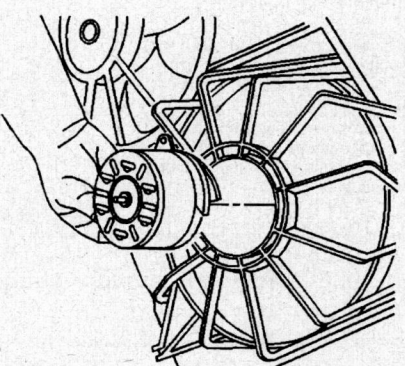

1- FAN MOTOR RETAINING BOLTS

Fig. 103 Cooling fan motor removal. CTS

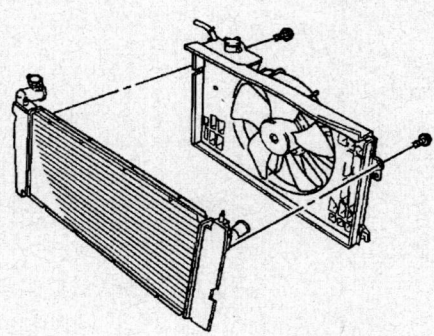

1. Disconnect the reservoir hose from the radiator.
2. Disconnect the fan motor electrical connector.
3. Disconnect two fan motor electrical harness clamps from the fan shroud.
4. Remove two fan shroud bolts.
5. Remove the fan shroud and motor assembly.
6. Remove the fan retaining nut.
7. Remove two radiator fan mount bolts.
8. Remove the radiator fan motor.

Fig. 104 Cooling fan assembly removal. Vibe

Saturn

NOTE: On Air Bag Equipped Models, Refer To "Air Bag System Precautions" Located In The Front Of This Manual For System Disarming & Arming Procedures.

NOTE: "Electrical Symbol & Wire Color Code Identification" Located In The Front Of This Manual Can Be Used As An Aid When Using Wiring Circuits Found In This Section.

NOTE: Refer To "Computer Relearn Procedures" Located In The Front Of This Manual When Battery Power To The Computer Has Been Interrupted.

INDEX

	Page No.		Page No.		Page No.
Component Replacement	17-62	Aura	17-61	Connect	17-61
Cooling Fan Assembly	17-62	ION	17-62	Disconnect	17-61
Aura	17-62	L Series	17-62	**System Diagnosis & Testing**	17-62
ION	17-63	SKY	17-62	Diagnostic Tests	17-62
SKY	17-63	2.0L Engine	17-62	Aura	17-62
Puller Fan Assembly	17-63	2.4L Engine	17-62	ION	17-62
L Series	17-63	**Precautions**	17-61	L Series	17-62
Pusher Fan Assembly	17-63	Air Bag Systems	17-61	SKY	17-62
L Series	17-63	Battery Ground Cable	17-61	Wiring Diagrams	17-62
Description	17-61	Hybrid Battery Service	17-61		

PRECAUTIONS

Air Bag Systems

Refer to "Air Bag System Precautions" in the front of this manual for system disarming and arming procedures.

Battery Ground Cable

Prior to service, disconnect battery ground cable and isolate as required.

Hybrid Battery Service

DISCONNECT

To help avoid personal injury, always ensure the ignition switch is in the OFF position and the ignition key has been removed prior to working on any 36V components. After the key has been removed, disconnect the negative battery cable and then open the generator battery disconnect control module cover. After waiting for at least 5 minutes, measure the voltage potential using a DMM between the following: 36V positive and negative battery cables; 36V positive battery cable and vehicle ground; 36V negative battery cable and vehicle ground. All measured voltage levels must be below 3 volts.

1. Remove ignition key from ignition switch.
2. Secure ignition key to ensure that key CANNOT be installed without your knowledge.
3. Disconnect 12 volt negative battery cable.
4. Fold down both rear seat backs, then carefully lift up on load floor rear compartment cover at retaining clip locations, **Fig. 1.**
5. Tilt load floor rear compartment cover towards rear of vehicle slightly, disengage tabs and remove load floor rear compartment cover. **To avoid personal injury, be careful when working in vicinity of generator battery disconnect control module. Internal components will still be live, 36V potential, even when cover has been opened or removed.**
6. Remove generator battery disconnect control module cover bolt, **Fig. 2.**
7. Open and slide generator battery disconnect control module cover to right, removing cover. **Wait at least 5 minutes in order to allow generator control module capacitors to discharge.**
8. **Never assume battery pack is disabled when generator battery disconnect control module cover is opened. Generator battery will have to be checked for voltage potential using a voltmeter first**
9. Set voltmeter to DC voltage and measure vehicle 12-volt battery voltage (at 12-volt positive jumper location and negative battery cable).
10. Meter should read greater than 12 volts DC.
11. To ensure generator battery has been disabled, check generator battery for voltage potential as follows:
    a. Refer to **Fig. 3** for voltage measurement locations.
    b. Measure from positive stud to negative stud, voltage should be less than 3 volts.
    c. Measure from positive stud to vehicle chassis ground, voltage should be less than 3 volts.
    d. Measure from negative stud to vehicle chassis ground, voltage should be less than 3 volts.
12. After verifying there is no voltage present, vehicle is now safe to work on.

CONNECT

1. Install and close generator battery disconnect control module cover.
2. Install generator battery cover bolt and **torque** to 89 inch lbs.
3. Tilt load floor rear compartment cover towards rear of vehicle slightly in order to insert tabs into battery tray rear support.
4. Set load floor rear compartment cover down, ensure retaining clips align to proper locations, carefully push down to secure cover.
5. Place rear seats backs to their proper positions.
6. Connect 12 volt negative battery cable.

DESCRIPTION

Aura

The engine cooling fan system consists of two electrical cooling fans and three fan relays. The relays are arranged in a series/parallel configuration that allows the Engine Control Module (ECM) to operate both

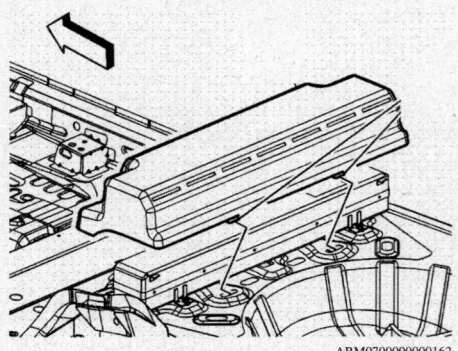

Fig. 1   Rear hybrid battery compartment. Aura

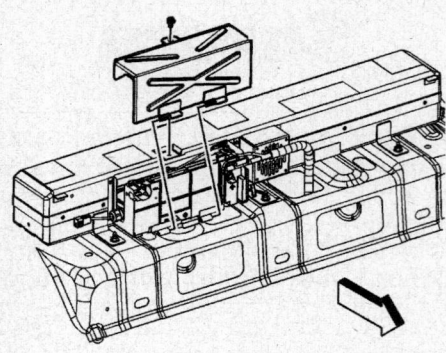

Fig. 2   Disconnect control module cover. Aura Hybrid

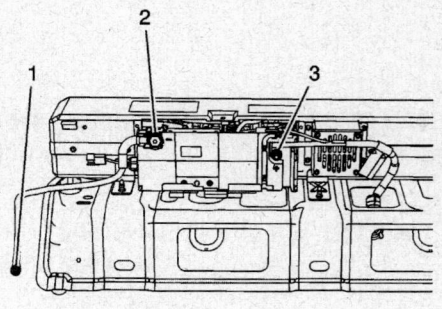

1-Chassis ground
2-Negative stud
3-Positive stud

Fig. 3   Battery disconnect control module voltage measurement locations. Aura Hybrid

fans together at low or high speeds. The cooling fans and fan relays receive battery positive voltage from the underhood fuse block.

During low speed operation, the ECM supplies the ground path for the low speed fan relay through the low speed cooling fan relay control circuit. This energizes the cooling fan No. 1 relay coil, closes the relay contacts and supplies battery positive voltage from the cool fan No. 1 fuse through the cooling fan motor supply voltage circuit to the lefthand cooling fan. The ground path for the lefthand cooling fan is through the cooling fan s/p relay and the righthand cooling fan. The result is a series circuit with both fans running at low speed.

During high speed operation the ECM supplies the ground path for the cooling fan No. 1 relay through the low speed cooling fan relay control circuit. After a 3-second delay, the ECM supplies a ground path for the cooling fan No. 2 relay and the cooling fan s/p relay through the high speed cooling fan relay control circuit. This energizes the cooling fan No. 2 relay coil, closes the relay contacts and provides a ground path for the lefthand cooling fan. At the same time the cooling fan s/p relay coil is energized closing the relay contacts and provides battery positive voltage from the cool fan No. 2 fuse on the cooling fan motor supply voltage circuit to the righthand cooling fan. During high speed fan operation, both engine cooling fans have there own ground path. The result is a parallel circuit with both fans running at high speed.

ION

On these models a cooling fan control module is used by the Powertrain Control Module (PCM) to control engine cooling fan operation. The engine cooling fan is turned On or Off by the Engine Control Module (ECM) dependent upon engine coolant temperature or A/C pressure. Under high ambient conditions, the cooling fan and heater water pump may run for several minutes after the ignition is turn to the Off position.

L Series

On these models a cooling fan control module is used by the Powertrain Control Module (PCM) to control engine cooling fan operation. These models have two cooling fan motors, the pusher fan mounted on the A/C or front side of the condenser/radiator assembly, pushes air through the front of the radiator/condenser assembly aiding in refrigerant and coolant heat disbursement, while the puller fan mounted to the radiator side of the condenser/radiator assembly further assist in engine coolant and ambient heat disbursement, these fans are turned On or Off by the Engine Control Module (ECM) dependent upon engine coolant temperature or A/C pressure. Under high ambient conditions, the cooling fans and heater water pump may run for several minutes after the ignition is turn to the Off position.

SKY

2.0L ENGINE

The engine cooling fan is a variable speed fan. The engine control module (ECM) controls the fan speed by sending a pulse width modulated (PWM) signal to the cooling fan control module. The cooling fan control module varies the voltage drop across the engine cooling fan motor in relation to the PWM signal. The cooling fan speed can be adjusted from 10 percent to 94 percent duty cycle. 94 percent is considered high speed fan.

2.4L ENGINE

The ECM commands Low Speed Fans ON under the following conditions: Engine coolant temperature exceeds approximately 223°F. A/C refrigerant pressure exceeds 190 psi. After the vehicle is shut off, the ECT at key-off is greater than 284°F and system voltage is more than 12 volts. The fans will stay on for approximately 3 minutes.

The ECM commands High Speed Fans ON under the following conditions: ECT reaches 230°F. A/C refrigerant pressure exceeds 240 psi and when certain DTCs are set.

SYSTEM DIAGNOSIS & TESTING

Wiring Diagrams

Refer to **Figs. 4 through 9** for electric cooling fan wiring diagrams.

Diagnostic Tests

AURA

Refer to **Figs. 10 through 12** for diagnostic procedures.

ION

Refer to **Figs. 13 through 19** for diagnostic procedures.

L SERIES

Refer to **Figs. 20 through 22** for diagnostic procedures.

SKY

Refer to **Figs. 23 through 27** for diagnostic procedures.

COMPONENT REPLACEMENT

Cooling Fan Assembly

AURA

1. Remove righthand and lefthand headlamp assembly mounting bolts, then lift headlamp assembly to unseat tabs on bottom edge of fender.
2. Disconnect headlamp assembly electrical connectors.

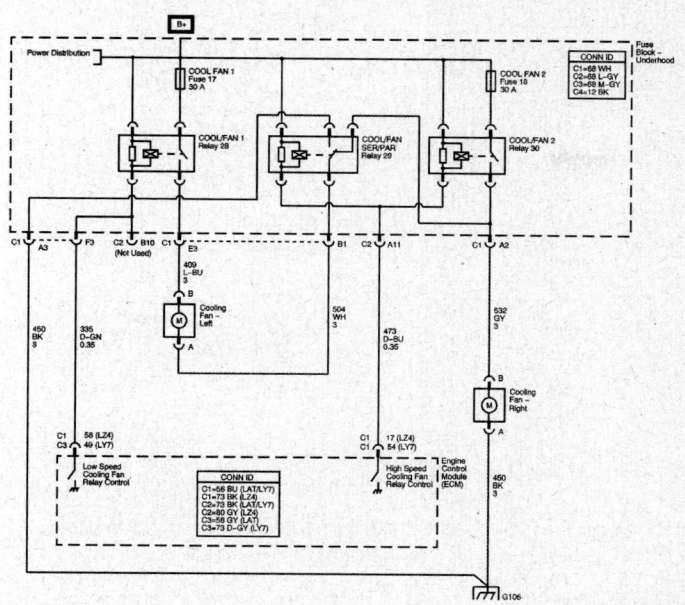

Fig. 4 Wiring diagram. Aura

ARM0600000000483

Fig. 5 Cooling fan wiring diagram. ION w/2.0L engine

ARM0500000000356

3. Remove headlamp assemblies from vehicle.
4. Unclip upper transmission oil cooler pipe from fan shroud. **Do not disconnect transmission oil cooler pipe from transmission or radiator.**
5. Loop a rope around each of upper two tabs on condenser and tie rope around upper tie bar.
6. Remove upper radiator support bracket bolts, then the brackets from vehicle.
7. Pry upward on fan shroud tabs at radiator clips.
8. Raise and support vehicle.
9. Remove lower radiator air deflector retainers, then the air deflector.
10. Remove front fender liner push-in retainers, then the front fender liner from vehicle.
11. Remove righthand radiator air deflector retainers, then the air deflector.
12. Remove lefthand radiator air deflector retainers, then the air deflector.
13. Remove lower radiator support bracket bolts and the support brackets.
14. Remove fan wire harness connectors.
15. Remove fan and fan shroud assembly.
16. Reverse procedure to install.

ION

1. Raise and support vehicle.
2. Disconnect cooling fan electrical connector.
3. Release wire harness retaining clips, then remove wire harness from shroud and position aside.
4. From under vehicle, push upward on fan shroud to unsnap cooling fan shroud assembly from radiator.
5. Position cooling fan shroud assembly away from radiator.
6. Remove air dam push-in retainers, then the righthand and lefthand splash shield to radiator push-in retainers, **Fig. 28.**
7. Remove air dam and splash shield.
8. Remove lower radiator mounting bolts and mount, then support radiator and condenser assemblies, **Fig. 29.**
9. Tilt radiator/condenser assemblies forward, then lower cooling fan and shroud assembly out of vehicle, **Fig. 30.**
10. Scribe an index mark on cooling fan blade and fan motor end shaft for installation reference.
11. Remove cooling fan blade retaining clip, then the fan blade, **Fig. 31.**
12. Remove cooling fan motor mounting bolts, then the fan motor from shroud, **Fig. 32.**
    a. **Torque** fan motor to shroud mounting bolts to 70 inch lbs.
    b. Align index scribe marks on fan blade and motor end shaft, then install fan blade and retaining clip.
    c. **Torque** lower radiator mount bolts to 18 ft. lbs.

SKY

1. Remove clamp, then the air cleaner outlet duct resonator.
2. Remove clamp, then the positive crankcase ventilation hose.
3. Pull up on outlet duct assembly to disengage assembly from studs and remove air cleaner outlet resonator.
4. Disconnect MAF/IAT sensor electrical connector, then firmly tug on air cleaner to disengage air cleaner from studs and remove.
5. Disconnect cooling fan motor electrical connector.
6. Remove retaining bolt, then the radiator assembly.

7. Remove shroud assembly, then the cooling fan and motor.
8. Reverse procedure to install.

Pusher Fan Assembly

L SERIES

1. Disconnect pusher fan electrical connector.
2. Release tabs, then remove pusher fan harness from puller fan shroud retainers and move harness clear of radiator end tank.
3. Raise and support vehicle, then remove pusher fan to condenser retaining bolts, **Fig. 33.**
4. Pull lower fan shroud forward, then downward to remove fan.
5. If fan is being replaced, release four finger guard to fan retaining clips, then remove finger guard, **Fig. 34.**
6. Reverse procedure to install. **Torque** lower fan to shroud bolts to 35 inch lbs.

Puller Fan Assembly

L SERIES

2.2L ENGINE

1. Disconnect battery ground and positive cables. **It is not required to disconnect fan control module electrical connector.**
2. Disconnect both cooling fan electrical connectors, then slide connectors out of retainers.
3. Remove pusher fan electrical harness from fan shroud retainer tabs, then wiring harness from clamp on fan shroud.
4. Remove battery hold-down and fan control module bracket, **Fig. 35.**
5. Remove battery insulating cover, then battery.
6. Remove fan shroud to radiator bolts, then fan and shroud assembly, **Fig. 36.**

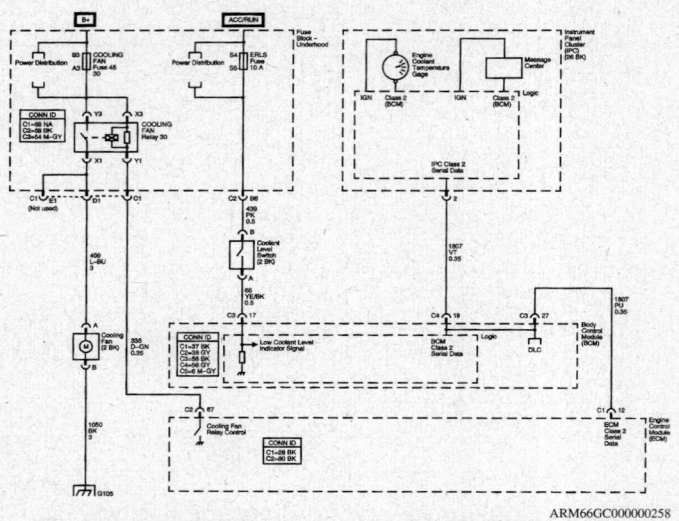

Fig. 6   Cooling fan wiring diagram. ION w/2.2L engine

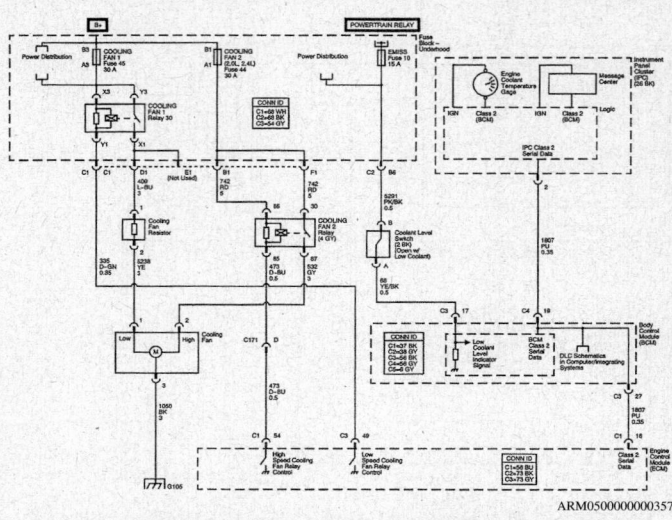

Fig. 7   Cooling fan wiring diagram. ION w/2.4L engine

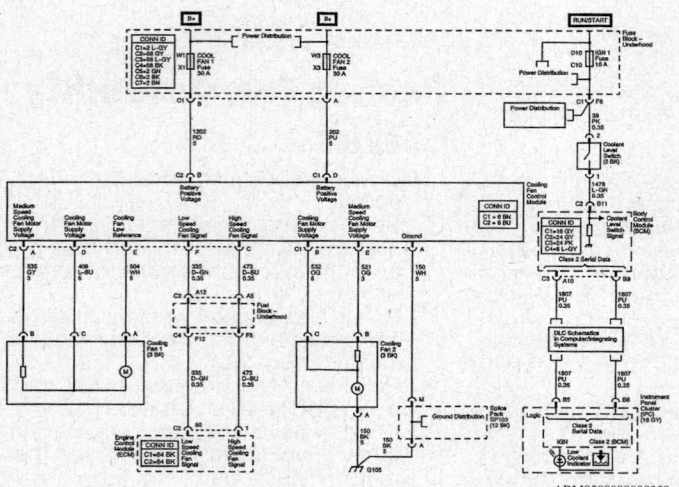

Fig. 8   Cooling fan wiring diagram. L Series

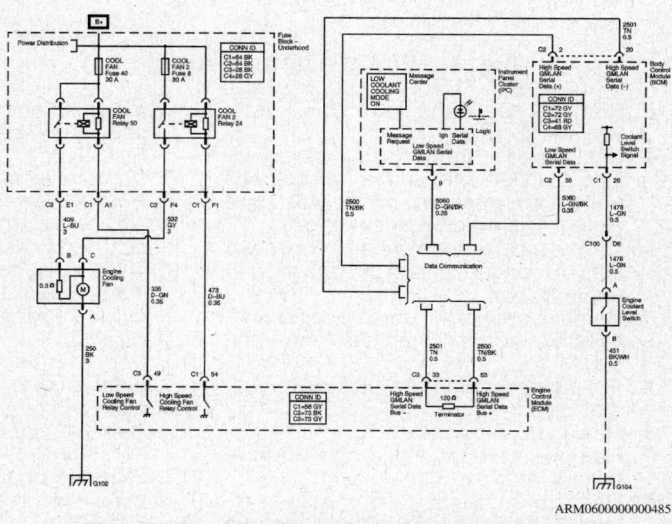

Fig. 9   Cooling fan wiring diagram. SKY

7. Reverse procedure to install. **Torque** lower fan to shroud bolts to 35 inch lbs.

3.0L ENGINE

1. Disconnect battery ground. **It is not required to disconnect fan control module electrical connector.**
2. Remove fan control module by sliding up and off bracket. Lay module and wiring aside.
3. Remove battery insulator cover, then battery hold-down and fan control module bracket.
4. Remove battery, then drain engine coolant into a suitable container.
5. Remove power steering fluid reservoir to fan shroud bolts, position reservoir rearward in vehicle.
6. Disconnect both cooling fan electrical connectors, then slide connectors out of retainers.
7. Remove pusher fan electrical harness from fan shroud retainer tabs.
8. Disconnect auxiliary water pump electrical connector, then remove harness from clip.
9. Remove upper transaxle cooler line from radiator, then unsnap from retainer at radiator end.
10. Remove auxiliary water pump outlet hose from radiator, then remove upper radiator hose.
11. Raise and support vehicle, then remove auxiliary water pump inlet hose from radiator.
12. Lower vehicle, then remove fan shroud to radiator bolts.
13. Remove fan and shroud assembly from vehicle.
14. Reverse procedure to install.

1. Before beginning vehicle diagnosis, the following preliminary inspections/tests must be performed:

   - Ensure that the battery is fully charged.
   - Ensure that the battery cables are clean and tight.
   - Inspect for any open fuses.
   - Ensure that the grounds are clean, tight, and in the correct location.
   - Inspect the easily accessible systems or the visible system components for obvious damage or conditions that could cause the concern.
   - Inspect for aftermarket devices that could affect the operation of the system.
   - Search for applicable service bulletins.
   - ☐ If the preceding inspections/tests resolve the concern, go to Repair Verification

2. Install a scan tool. Verify that the scan tool powers up.

   ☐ If the scan tool does not power up, diagnose scan tool.

3. Ignition ON, Engine OFF, verify communication with all of the control modules on the vehicle.

   ☐ If the scan tool does not communicate with all of the expected control modules, diagnose scan tool. .

Important: Open the drivers door to ensure retained accessory power mode (RAP) is inactive during this test. The engine may start during this test. Turn the engine OFF as soon as the crank power mode has been observed.

4. Access the Power Mode parameter on the scan tool. Verify the power mode parameter matches all the ignition switch positions.

   ☐ If the power mode parameter does not match the ignition switch position for all ignition switch positions, diagnose scan tool.

ARM0600000000522

Fig. 10 Diagnostic system check (Part 1 of 2). Aura

Diagnostic Instructions

- Perform the <u>Diagnostic System Check - Vehicle</u> prior to using this diagnostic procedure.
- Review <u>Strategy Based Diagnosis</u> for an overview of the diagnostic approach.
- <u>Diagnostic Procedure Instructions</u> provides an overview of each diagnostic category.

Circuit/System Description

The engine control module (ECM) grounds the low speed relay, which is relay 1, and the high speed relay, which is relay 2, control circuits through an internal solid state device called a driver. The primary function of the driver is to supply the ground for the component being controlled. Each driver has a fault line that is monitored by the ECM. When the ECM is commanding a component ON, the voltage potential of the control circuit should be low, near 0 volts. When the ECM is commanding the control circuit to a component OFF, the voltage potential of the circuit should be high, near battery voltage. If the ECM detects that the actual state of the control circuit does not match the expected state, a DTC will set.

Circuit/System Verification

1. If DTCs P0480 or P0481 are set, then perform those diagnostics first.
2. Ignition ON, verify with a scan tool that the ECM is not commanding fan activation.
3. Ignition ON, observe that the fan is not activated.

ARM0600000000524

Fig. 11 Cooling fan always on (Part 1 of 2). Aura

5. Attempt to start the engine. Verify that the engine cranks.

   ☐ If the engine does not crank, diagnose Symptoms

6. Attempt to start the engine. Verify the engine starts and idles.

   ☐ If the engine does not start and idle, diagnose engine.

Important: Do not clear any DTCs unless instructed to do so by a diagnostic procedure.

Important: If any DTCs are Powertrain related DTCs, select Capture Info in order to store the DTC information with the scan tool. If multiple Powertrain DTCs are stored, diagnose them in the following order:

1. Component level DTCs; such as sensor DTCs, solenoid DTCs, and relay DTCs.

2. System level DTCs; such as misfire DTCs, EVAP system DTCs, and fuel trim DTCs.

7. Advance to the List All DTCs screen on the scan tool selections to obtain DTCs from each of the vehicle modules. Verify there are no DTCs reported from any module.

   ☐ If any DTCs are present, refer to Diagnostic Trouble Code (DTC) and diagnose any current DTCs in the order the DTCs are displayed on the scan tool.

8. If the customer concern is related to inspection/maintenance (I/M) testing, check maintainance

   ☐ If none of the previous tests or inspections addresses the concern, diagnose Symptoms

ARM0600000000523

Fig. 10 Diagnostic system check (Part 2 of 2). Aura

Circuit/System Testing

Important: You must perform the Circuit/System Verification before proceeding with Circuit/System Testing.

1. Ignition OFF, leave the series/parallel relay in place while disconnecting the other relays.
2. Ignition ON, observe that the fan is not activated.

   ☐ If the fan is not activated, then replace the faulty relay.
   ☐ If the fan is activated, then test the fan voltage supply circuits for a short to voltage.

Repair Instructions

Perform the <u>Diagnostic Repair Verification</u> after completing the diagnostic procedure.

Repair Verification

1. Ignition ON, verify with a scan tool that the ECM is not commanding fan activation.
2. Ignition ON, observe that the fan is not activated.

ARM0600000000525

Fig. 11 Cooling fan always on (Part 2 of 2). Aura

Diagnostic Instructions

- Perform the Diagnostic System Check - Vehicle prior to using this diagnostic procedure.
- Review Strategy Based Diagnosis for an overview of the diagnostic approach.
- Diagnostic Procedure Instructions provides an overview of each diagnostic category.

Circuit/System Description

The engine control module (ECM) grounds the low speed relay, which is relay 1, and the high speed relay, which is relay 2, control circuits through an internal solid state device called a driver. The primary function of the driver is to supply the ground for the component being controlled. Each driver has a fault line that is monitored by the ECM. When the ECM is commanding a component ON, the voltage potential of the control circuit should be low, near 0 volts. When the ECM is commanding the control circuit to a component OFF, the voltage potential of the circuit should be high, near battery voltage. If the ECM detects that the actual state of the control circuit does not match the expected state, a DTC will set.

Circuit/System Verification

1. If DTCs P0480 or P0481 are set, then perform those diagnostics first.
2. Ignition ON, command each relay ON and OFF with a scan tool. Observe to verify that the fan turns ON and OFF with each command.

ARM0600000000526

Fig. 12   Cooling fan inoperative (Part 1 of 3). Aura

Repair Instructions

Perform the Diagnostic Repair Verification after completing the diagnostic procedure.

Repair Verification

Ignition ON, command the relay ON and OFF with a scan tool. Observe to verify that the fan turns ON and OFF with each command.

ARM0600000000528

Fig. 12   Cooling fan inoperative (Part 3 of 3). Aura

Circuit/System Testing

Important: You must perform the Circuit/System Verification before proceeding with Circuit/System Testing.

1. Ignition OFF, disconnect the fan relays.
2. Install a 30A fused jumper between the normally-open switch contact terminals at the series/parallel relay connector in order to complete the fan ground circuit. Leave this jumper in place for the remainder of this procedure.
3. One at a time, connect a 30A fused jumper between the positive terminal at the battery and the fan voltage supply circuit terminal at the cool/fan 1 and the cool/fan 2 relay connections and verify fan activation.

   ☐ If the appropriate fan does not activate, test the fan voltage supply circuit for a short to ground or open/high resistance. If the circuit tests normal, test the fan ground circuit for an open/high resistance. If the circuits test normal, replace the fan.

4. Ignition ON, connect a 30A fused jumper between the relay switch voltage supply circuit terminal and the fan voltage supply circuit terminal at the cool/fan 1 and the cool/fan 2 relay connections and verify fan activation.

   ☐ If the fan does not activate, test the relay switch voltage supply circuit for a short to ground or an open/high resistance. If the circuit tests normal and its fuse is open, test all connected components and replace as necessary.

5. If the circuits and fans test normal, replace the relay.

ARM0600000000527

Fig. 12   Cooling fan inoperative (Part 2 of 3). Aura

Step	Action	Yes	No
1	Perform the following preliminary inspections: • Ensure that the battery is fully charged. • Ensure that the battery cables are clean and tight. • Inspect for any open fuses. • Inspect the easily accessible systems or the visible system components for obvious damage or conditions that could cause the symptom. • Ensure that the grounds are clean, tight, and in the correct location. • Inspect for aftermarket devices that could affect the operation of the system. • Search for applicable service bulletins. Did you find and correct the condition?	System OK	Go to Step 2
2	Install a scan tool. Does the scan tool power up?	Go to Step 3	Go to Scan Tool Does Not Power Up
3	1. Turn ON the ignition, with the engine OFF. 2. Attempt to establish communication with all of the control modules on the vehicle. Does the scan tool communicate with all of the expected vehicle control modules?	Go to Step 4	Go to Data Link References

ARM0500000000359

Fig. 13   Diagnostic system check (Part 1 of 3). ION

4	**Important:** • To ensure that retained accessory power (RAP) mode is inactive, if equipped, open the driver door during the following step. • The engine may start during the following step. Turn OFF the engine as soon as you have observed the crank power mode. 1. Access the Power Mode parameter on the scan tool. 2. Rotate the ignition switch, operate the ignition mode switch, through all positions while observing the Power Mode parameter. Does the Power Mode parameter reading on the scan tool match the ignition switch position for all switch positions?	Go to Step 5	Go to Power Mode Mismatch
5	Attempt to start the engine. Does the engine crank?	Go to Step 6	Go to Symptoms
6	Attempt to start the engine. Does the engine start and idle?		Go to • Engine Cranks but Does Not Go to Step 7
7	**Important:** Do not clear any DTCs unless instructed by a diagnostic procedure. Use the appropriate scan tool selections to obtain DTCs for each of the control modules. Does the scan tool display any DTCs?	Go to Step 8	Go to Step 12

ARM0500000000360

Fig. 13   Diagnostic system check (Part 2 of 3). ION

Step	Action	Yes	No
8	Does the scan tool display any DTCs that begin with a "U"?	Go to Diagnostic Trouble Code (DTC) List - Vehicle	Go to Step 9
9	**Important:** If any of these DTCs are displayed, diagnose them before diagnosing any other DTCs or symptoms. Does the scan tool display DTC B1000, B1001, B1004, B1009, B1015, C0550, P0601, P0602, P0603, P0604, P0606, P0607, P1516, P1621, P1680, P1681, P1683, or P2610?	Go to Diagnostic Trouble Code (DTC) List - Vehicle	Go to Step 10
10	**Important:** If any of these DTCs are displayed, diagnose them before diagnosing any other DTCs or symptoms. Does the scan tool display DTC B1325, B1327, B1328, C0847, C0848, C0896, C0899, C0900, P0562, or P0563?	Go to Diagnostic Trouble Code (DTC) List - Vehicle	Go to Step 11
11	**Important:** If any of the remaining DTCs are powertrain DTCs, select Capture Info in order to store the powertrain DTC information with a scan tool. If multiple DTCs are stored, diagnose the DTCs in the following order 1. Component level DTCs, such as sensor DTCs, solenoid DTCs, and relay DTCs. 2. System level DTCs, such as misfire DTCs, evaporative emission (EVAP) system DTCs, and fuel trim DTCs. Diagnose the remaining DTCs.	Go to Diagnostic Trouble Code (DTC) List - Vehicle	--
12	Is the customers concern with inspection/maintenance (I/M) testing?	Go to • Inspection/Maintenance (I/M) System Check	Go to Symptoms - Vehicle

ARM0500000000361

Fig. 13   Diagnostic system check (Part 3 of 3). ION

Step	Action	Yes	No
	DEFINITION: One or both engine cooling fan motors run continuously in high or low speed.		
1	Did you perform the Diagnostic System Check - Vehicle?	Go to Step 2	Go to Diagnostic System Check -
2	Turn ON the ignition, with the engine OFF. Are one or both cooling fans ON?	Go to Step 3	Test for Intermittent Conditions and Poor Connections
3	Are both cooling fans running continuously?	Go to Step 4	Go to Step 6
4	Are both cooling fans running continuously in high speed?	Go to Step 5	Go to Step 7
5	Test the low reference circuit of the A/C refrigerant pressure sensor for an open. Did you find and correct the condition?	Go to Step 18	Go to Step 14
6	Remove the cool fan 3 relay. Did the right cooling fan turn OFF?	Go to Step 10	Go to Step 8
7	Remove the cool fan 1 relay. Did the cooling fans turn OFF?	Go to Step 12	Go to Step 9
8	Remove the cool fan S/P relay. Did the right cooling fan turn OFF?	Go to Step 13	Go to Step 11
9	Repair the short to voltage in the left cooling fan motor supply voltage circuit. Did you complete the repair?	Go to Step 18	--
10	Repair the short to voltage in the left cooling fan low reference circuit. Did you complete the repair?	Go to Step 18	--

ARM0500000000362

Fig. 14   Cooling fan always on (Part 1 of 2). ION w/2.0L engine

Step	Action	Yes	No
11	Repair the short to voltage in the right cooling fan motor supply voltage circuit. Did you complete the repair?	Go to Step 18	--
12	Inspect for poor connections at the cool fan 1 relay. Did you find and correct the condition?	Go to Step 18	Go to Step 15
13	Inspect for poor connections at the cool fan S/P relay. Did you find and correct the condition?	Go to Step 18	Go to Step 16
14	Inspect for poor connections at the A/C refrigerant pressure sensor. Did you find and correct the condition?	Go to Step 18	Go to Step 17
15	Replace the cool fan 1 relay. Did you complete the replacement?	Go to Step 18	--
16	Replace the cool fan S/P relay. Did you complete the replacement?	Go to Step 18	--
17	Replace the A/C refrigerant pressure sensor. Did you complete the replacement?	Go to Step 18	--
18	Operate the system in order to verify the repair. Did you correct the condition?	System OK	Go to Step 2

ARM0500000000363

Fig. 14   Cooling fan always on (Part 2 of 2). ION w/2.0L engine

Step	Action	Yes	No
1	Did you perform the Engine Cooling System Check?	Go to *Step 2*	*Check Engine Cooling*
2	Turn ON the ignition, with the engine OFF. Is the engine cooling fan running all the time?	Go to *Step 3*	*Test for Intermittent Conditions and Poor Connections*
3	Remove the cooling fan relay. Did the cooling fan turn OFF?	Go to *Step 5*	Go to *Step 4*
4	Repair the short to B+ in the cooling fan motor supply voltage circuit. Did you complete the repair?	Go to *Step 7*	
5	Inspect for poor connections at the cooling fan relay. Did you find and correct the condition?	Go to *Step 7*	Go to *Step 6*
6	Replace the cooling fan relay. Did you complete the repair?	Go to *Step 7*	—
7	Operate the system in order to verify the repair. Did you correct the condition?	System OK	Go to *Step 2*

ARM66GC000000261

Fig. 15   Cooling fan always on. ION w/2.2L engine

Step	Action	Yes	No
	DEFINITION: The dual speed cooling fan motor runs continuously in high or low speed.		
1	Did you perform the Diagnostic System Check - Vehicle?	Go to Step 2	Go to Diagnostic System Check - Vehicle
2	Turn ON the ignition, with the engine OFF. Is the cooling fan ON?	Go to Step 3	Test for Intermittent Conditions and Poor Connections
3	Is the cooling fan running continuously?	Go to Step 4	Go to Step 6
4	Is the cooling fan running continuously in high speed?	Go to Step 5	Go to Step 7
5	Test the low reference circuit of the A/C refrigerant pressure sensor for an open. Did you find and correct the condition?	Go to Step 15	Go to Step 12
6	Remove the cool fan 2 relay. Did the high speed cooling fan turn OFF?	Go to Step 10	Go to Step 8
7	Remove the cool fan 1 relay. Did the low speed cooling fan turn OFF?	Go to Step 11	Go to Step 8
8	Repair the short to ground on the low speed cooling fan motor supply voltage circuit prior to the resistor assembly. Did you complete the repair?	Go to Step 15	--
9	Repair the short to ground on the low speed cooling fan supply voltage circuit between the resistor assembly and the two speed cooling fan motor. Did you complete the repair?	Go to Step 15	--
10	Repair the short to voltage in the high speed cooling fan supply voltage circuit. Did you complete the repair?	Go to Step 15	--

ARM0500000000364

Fig. 16   Cooling fan always on (Part 1 of 2). ION w/2.4L engine

		Yes	No
11	Inspect for poor connections at the cool fan 1 relay. Did you find and correct the condition?	Go to Step 15	Go to Step 13
12	Inspect for poor connections at the A/C refrigerant pressure sensor. Did you find and correct the condition?	Go to Step 15	Go to Step 14
13	Replace the cool fan 1 relay. Did you complete the replacement?	Go to Step 15	--
14	Replace the A/C refrigerant pressure sensor Did you complete the replacement?	Go to Step 15	--
15	Operate the system in order to verify the repair. Did you correct the condition?	System OK	Go to Step 2

ARM0500000000365

Fig. 16   Cooling fan always on (Part 2 of 2). ION w/2.4L engine

Step	Action	Yes	No
	DEFINITION: One or both cooling fan motors are inoperative in either high, low, or both speeds.		
1	Did you perform the Diagnostic System Check - Vehicle?	Go to Step 2	Go to Diagnostic System Check - Vehicle
2	1. Install a scan tool. 2. Turn ON the engine. 3. With a scan tool, monitor the engine coolant temperature (ECT) in the Inputs/Outputs scan tool data. 4. Bring the vehicle up to normal operating temperature. 5. At 106°C (223°F) the low speed engine cooling fans should engage. Do the low speed engine cooling fans engage?	Go to Step 3	Go to Step 4
3	Important:: A 3 second delay occurs before the powertrain control module (PCM) changes the cooling fan speed. 1. With a scan tool, monitor the ECT in the Inputs/Outputs scan tool data. 2. At 110°C (230°F) the high speed engine cooling fans should engage. Do the high speed engine cooling fans engage?	Test for Intermittent Conditions and Poor Connections	Go to Step 6
4	Important: Do NOT remove the jumper wire that you will be connecting until your testing is completed. If the cool fan 1 fuse opens when you connect the jumper wire, repair the cooling fan motor supply voltage circuit of the left cooling fan motor for a short to ground. 1. Disconnect the cool fan 1 relay. 2. Connect a jumper wire between the battery positive voltage circuit and the cooling fan motor supply voltage circuit of the cool fan 1 relay. Do both cooling fans operate in low speed?	Go to Step 14	Go to Step 5
5	1. Disconnect the S/P fan relay. 2. With a test lamp connected to a good ground, probe the cooling fan low reference circuit at the S/P fan relay. Does the test lamp illuminate?	Go to Step 9	Go to Step 8

ARM0500000000366

Fig. 17   Cooling fan inoperative (Part 1 of 3). ION w/2.0L engine

		Yes	No
6	Does the left cooling fan operate at high speed?	Go to Step 16	Go to Step 7
7	Inspect the ground circuit of the S/P fan relay for an open or high resistance. Did you find and correct the condition?	Go to Step 25	Go to Step 15
8	1. Install the S/P fan relay. 2. Disconnect the left cooling fan electrical connector. 3. With a test lamp connected to a good ground, probe the cooling fan motor supply voltage circuit at the left cooling fan motor connector. Does the test lamp illuminate?	Go to Step 12	Go to Step 13
9	1. Install the S/P fan relay. 2. Disconnect the right cooling fan motor connector. 3. With a test lamp connected to a good ground, probe the cooling fan motor supply voltage circuit at the right cooling fan connector. Does the test lamp illuminate?	Go to Step 11	Go to Step 10
10	Inspect the cooling fan motor supply voltage circuit for an open or high resistance. Did you find and correct the condition?	Go to Step 25	Go to Step 15
11	Inspect the ground circuit of the right cooling fan for an open or high resistance. Did you find and correct the condition?	Go to Step 25	Go to Step 18
12	Inspect the cooling fan low reference circuit for an open or high resistance. Did you find and correct the condition?	Go to Step 25	Go to Step 17
13	Inspect the cooling fan motor supply voltage circuit of the left cooling fan for an open or high resistance. Did you find and correct the condition?	Go to Step 25	Go to Step 19
14	Inspect for poor connections at the cool fan 1 relay. Did you find and correct the condition?	Go to Step 25	Go to Step 20
15	Inspect for poor connections at the S/P fan relay. Did you find and correct the condition?	Go to Step 25	Go to Step 21

ARM0500000000367

Fig. 17   Cooling fan inoperative (Part 2 of 3). ION w/2.0L engine

Step	Action	Yes	No
16	Inspect for poor connections at the cool fan 2 relay. Did you find and correct the condition?	Go to Step 25	Go to Step 22
17	Inspect for poor connections at the harness connector of the left cooling fan. Did you find and correct the condition?	Go to Step 25	Go to Step 23
18	Inspect for poor connections at the harness connector of the right cooling fan. Did you find and correct the condition?	Go to Step 25	Go to Step 24
19	Repair the battery positive voltage circuit for an open or high resistance. Did you complete the repair?	Go to Step 25	--
20	Replace the cool fan 1 relay. Did you complete the replacement?	Go to Step 25	--
21	Replace the S/P fan relay. Did you complete the replacement?	Go to Step 25	--
22	Replace the cool fan 2 relay. Did you complete the replacement?	Go to Step 25	--
23	Replace the left cooling fan. Did you complete the replacement?	Go to Step 25	--
24	Replace the right cooling fan. Did you complete the replacement?	Go to Step 25	--
25	Operate the system in order to verify the repair. Did you correct the condition?	System OK	Go to Step 3

ARM0500000000368

Fig. 17 Cooling fan inoperative (Part 3 of 3). ION w/2.0L engine

Step	Action	Yes	No
1	Did you perform System Check-Engine Cooling?	Go to Step 2	Check Engine Cooling
2	1. Install a scan tool. 2. Turn ON the ignition, with the engine OFF. 3. With a scan tool, command the cooling fan ON and OFF. Does the engine cooling fan turn ON and OFF with each command?	Test for Intermittent and Poor Connections	Go to Step 3
3	1. Turn OFF the ignition. 2. Remove the cooling fan relay. 3. Probe the battery positive voltage circuit of the cooling fan relay switch side with a test lamp that is connected to a good ground. Does the test lamp illuminate?	Go to Step 4	Go to Step 7
4	Connect a 20 A fused jumper wire between the battery positive voltage circuit of the cooling fan relay and the cooling fan motor supply voltage circuit of the cooling fan relay. Does the cooling fan operate?	Go to Step 10	Go to Step 5
5	1. Disconnect the cooling fan connector. 2. Probe the cooling fan motor supply voltage circuit at the harness connector with a test lamp that is connected to a good ground. Does the test lamp illuminate?	Go to Step 6	Go to Step 8

ARM66GC000000262

Fig. 18 Cooling fan inoperative (Part 1 of 2). ION w/2.2L engine

Step	Action	Yes	No
6	Probe the harness connector of the cooling fan motor with a test lamp connected between the cooling fan motor supply voltage circuit and the ground circuit of the cooling fan motor. Does the test lamp illuminate?	Go to Step 11	Go to Step 9
7	Repair the battery positive circuit of the cooling fan relay. Did you complete the repair?	Go to Step 14	—
8	Repair the supply voltage circuit of the cooling fan motor. Did you complete the repair?	Go to Step 14	—
9	Repair the ground circuit of the cooling fan motor. Did you complete the repair?	Go to Step 14	—
10	Inspect for poor connections at the cooling fan relay. Did you find and correct the condition?	Go to Step 14	Go to Step 12
11	Inspect for poor connections at the harness connector of the cooling fan motor. Did you find and correct the condition?	Go to Step 14	Go to Step 13
12	Replace the cooling fan relay. Did you complete the repair?	Go to Step 14	—
13	Replace the cooling fan motor. Did you complete the repair?	Go to Step 14	—
14	Operate the system in order to verify the repair. Did you correct the condition?	System OK	Go to Step 2

ARM66GC000000263

Fig. 18 Cooling fan inoperative (Part 2 of 2). ION w/2.2L engine

Step	Action	Yes	No
	DEFINITION: One or both cooling fan motors are inoperative in either high, low, or both speeds.		
1	Did you perform the Diagnostic System Check - Vehicle?	Go to Step 2	Go to Diagnostic System Check - Vehicle
2	1. Install a scan tool. 2. Turn ON the engine. 3. With a scan tool, monitor the engine coolant temperature (ECT) in the Inputs/Outputs scan tool data. 4. Bring the vehicle up to normal operating temperature. 5. At 106°C (223°F) the low speed engine cooling fans should engage. Do the low speed engine cooling fans engage?	Go to Step 3	Go to Step 4
3	Important:: A 3 second delay occurs before the powertrain control module (ECM) changes the cooling fan speed. 1. With a scan tool, monitor the ECT in the Inputs/Outputs scan tool data. 2. At 110°C (230°F) the high speed engine cooling fans should engage. Do the high speed engine cooling fans engage?	Test for Intermittent Conditions and Poor Connections	Go to Step 6
4	Important: Do NOT remove the jumper wire that you will be connecting until your testing is completed. If the cool fan 1 fuse opens when you connect the jumper wire, repair the cooling fan motor supply voltage circuit of the left cooling fan motor for a short to ground. 1. Disconnect the cool fan 1 relay. 2. Connect a jumper wire between the battery positive voltage circuit and the cooling fan motor supply voltage circuit of the cool fan 1 relay. Do both cooling fans operate in low speed?	Go to Step 12	Go to Step 5

ARM0500000000369

Fig. 19 Cooling fan inoperative (Part 1 of 3). ION w/2.4L engine

		Yes	No
5	With a test lamp connected to good ground, probe the cooling fan low reference or ground circuit at the dual speed cooling fan motor. Does the test lamp illuminate?	Go to Step 9	Go to Step 8
6	Does the dual speed cooling fan operate at high speed?	Go to Step 13	Go to Step 7
7	1. Disconnect the low speed circuit of the dual speed cooling fan motor connector. 2. With a test lamp connected to a good ground, probe the cooling fan motor supply voltage circuit at the low speed cooling fan connector. Does the test lamp illuminate?	Go to Step 10	Go to Step 9
8	1. Disconnect the high speed circuit of the dual speed cooling fan motor connector. 2. With a test lamp connected to a good ground, probe the cooling fan motor supply voltage circuit at the high speed cooling fan connector. Does the test lamp illuminate?	Go to Step 10	Go to Step 9
9	Inspect the appropriate cooling fan motor supply voltage circuit for an open or high resistance. Did you find and correct the condition?	Go to Step 19	Go to Step 15
10	Inspect the dual speed cooling fan low reference or ground circuit for an open or high resistance. Did you find and correct the condition?	Go to Step 19	Go to Step 16
12	Inspect for poor connections at the cool fan 1 relay. Did you find and correct the condition?	Go to Step 19	Go to Step 16

ARM0500000000370

Fig. 19 Cooling fan inoperative (Part 2 of 3). ION w/2.4L engine

		Yes	No
13	Inspect for poor connections at the cool fan 2 relay. Did you find and correct the condition?	Go to Step 19	Go to Step 17
14	Inspect for poor connections at the harness connector of the low speed cooling fan circuit at the cooling fan motor. Did you find and correct the condition?	Go to Step 19	Go to Step 18
15	Inspect for poor connections at the harness connector of the high speed cooling fan circuit of the cooling fan motor. Did you find and correct the condition?	Go to Step 19	Go to Step 18
16	Replace the cool fan 1 relay. Did you complete the replacement?	Go to Step 19	--
17	Replace the cool fan 2 relay. Did you complete the replacement?	Go to Step 19	--
18	Replace the dual speed cooling fan motor. Did you complete the replacement?	Go to Step 19	--
19	Operate the system in order to verify the repair. Did you correct the condition?	System OK	Go to Step 3

ARM0500000000371

Fig. 19 Cooling fan inoperative (Part 3 of 3). ION w/2.4L engine

Step	Action	Yes	No
1	Perform the following preliminary inspections: • Ensure that the battery is fully charged. • Ensure that the battery cables are clean and tight. • Inspect for any open fuses. • Inspect the easily accessible systems or the visible system components for obvious damage or conditions that could cause the symptom. • Ensure that the grounds are clean, tight, and in the correct location. • Inspect for aftermarket devices that could affect the operation of the system. • Search for applicable service bulletins. Did you find and correct the condition?	System OK	Go to Step 2
2	Install a scan tool. Does the scan tool power up?	Go to Step 3	Go to Scan Tool Does Not Power Up
3	1. Turn ON the ignition, with the engine OFF. 2. Attempt to establish communication with all of the control modules on the vehicle. Device in Computer/Integrating Systems for the modules you should expect to observe. Does the scan tool communicate with all of the expected vehicle control modules?	Go to Step 4	Go to Scan Tool Does Not Communicate with Class 2 Device

ARM0500000000372

Fig. 20 Diagnostic system check (Part 1 of 3). L Series

4	**Important:** • To ensure that retained accessory power (RAP) mode is inactive, if equipped, open the driver door during the following step. • The engine may start during the following step. Turn OFF the engine as soon as you have observed the crank power mode. 1. Access the Power Mode parameter on the scan tool. 2. Rotate the ignition switch (operate the ignition mode switch) through all positions while observing the Power Mode parameter. Does the Power Mode parameter reading on the scan tool match the ignition switch position for all switch positions?	Go to Step 5	Go to Power Mode Mismatch
5	Attempt to start the engine. Does the engine crank?	Go to Step 6	Go to Symptoms
6	Attempt to start the engine. Does the engine start and idle?	Go to Step 7	Go to Engine Cranks but Does Not Run
7	**Important:** Do not clear any DTCs unless instructed by a diagnostic procedure. Use the appropriate scan tool selections to obtain DTCs for each of the control modules. Does the scan tool display any DTCs?	Go to Step 8	Go to Step 12
8	Does the scan tool display any DTCs that begin with a "U"?	Go to Diagnostic Trouble Code (DTC) List -	Go to Step 9

ARM0500000000373

Fig. 20 Diagnostic system check (Part 2 of 3). L Series

Step	Action	Yes	No
9	**Important:** If any of these DTCs are displayed, diagnose them before diagnosing any other DTCs or symptoms. Does the scan tool display DTC B1000, B1001, C0550, C0551, P0601, P0602, P0603, P0604, P0606, P2107, or P2610?	Go to Diagnostic Trouble Code (DTC) List - Vehicle	Go to Step 10
10	**Important:** If any of these DTCs are displayed, diagnose them before diagnosing any other DTCs or symptoms. Does the scan tool display DTC B1327, B1328, B1372, C0896, P0560, P0562, or P0563?	Go to Diagnostic Trouble Code (DTC) List - Vehicle	Go to Step 11
11	**Important:** If any of the remaining DTCs are powertrain DTCs, select Capture Info in order to store the powertrain DTC information with a scan tool. If multiple DTCs are stored, diagnose the DTCs in the following order 1. Component level DTCs, such as sensor DTCs, solenoid DTCs, and relay DTCs. 2. System level DTCs, such as misfire DTCs, evaporative emission (EVAP) system DTCs, and fuel trim DTCs. Diagnose the remaining DTCs.	Go to Diagnostic Trouble Code (DTC) List - Vehicle	--
12	Is the customers concern with inspection/maintenance (I/M) testing?	Go to Inspection/Maintenance (I/M) System Check	Go to Symptoms - Vehicle

ARM0500000000374

Fig. 20 Diagnostic system check (Part 3 of 3). L Series

Step	Action	Yes	No
7	Replace the ECM. Did you complete the replacement?	Go to Step 8	--
8	1. Use the scan tool in order to clear the DTCs. 2. Operate the vehicle within the Conditions for Running the DTC as specified in the supporting text. Does the DTC reset?	Go to Step 2	System OK

ARM0500000000376

Fig. 21 Cooling fan always on (Part 2 of 2). L Series

Step	Action	Yes	No
	DEFINITION: One or both engine cooling fan motors run continuously in high or low speed.		
1	Did you perform the Diagnostic System Check - Vehicle?	Go to Step 2	Go to Diagnostic System Check
2	1. Turn OFF the ignition. 2. Disconnect the cooling fan control module. 3. Disconnect the engine control module (ECM). 4. Turn ON the ignition, with the engine OFF. Test the control circuits of the cooling fan control module for a short to ground. Did you find and correct the condition?	Go to Step 8	Go to Step 3
3	1. Turn OFF the ignition. 2. Connect the ECM. 3. Turn ON the ignition, with the engine OFF. 4. Probe the control circuits of the cooling fan control module with a test lamp that is connected to voltage. Does the test lamp illuminate on any control circuit?	Go to Step 5	Go to Step 4
4	Inspect for poor connections at the cooling fan control module. Did you find and correct the condition?	Go to Step 8	Go to Step 6
5	Inspect for poor connections at the harness connector of the ECM. Did you find and correct the condition?	Go to Step 8	Go to Step 7
6	Replace the cooling fan control module. Did you complete the replacement?	Go to Step 8	--

ARM0500000000375

Fig. 21 Cooling fan always on (Part 1 of 2). L Series

Step	Action	Yes	No
	DEFINITION: One or both cooling fan motors are inoperative in either high, low, or both speeds.		
1	Did you perform the Diagnostic System Check - Vehicle?	Go to Step 2	Go to Diagnostic System Check - Vehicle
2	1. Install a scan tool. 2. Turn ON the ignition, with the engine OFF. 3. With a scan tool, increase and decrease the 3 speed fan through LOW, MEDIUM and HIGH. Do both fans operate at the proper speeds?	Test for Intermittent Conditions and Poor Connections	Go to Step 3
3	1. Turn OFF the ignition. 2. Disconnect the cooling fan control module. 3. Disconnect the engine control module (ECM). 4. Turn ON the ignition, with the engine OFF. Test the control circuits of the cooling fan control module for a short to ground, short to voltage, high resistance or an open. Did you find and correct the condition?	Go to Step 18	Go to Step 4
4	1. Turn OFF the ignition. 2. Connect the ECM. 3. Install a scan tool. 4. Turn ON the ignition, with the engine OFF. 5. Probe the control circuits of the cooling fan control module with a test lamp that is connected to voltage. 6. With a scan tool, command the appropriate fan control circuit ON and OFF. Does the test lamp turn ON and OFF with each command?	Go to Step 5	Go to Step 15

ARM0500000000377

Fig. 22 Cooling fan inoperative (Part 1 of 3). L Series

Step	Action	Yes	No
5	Test the medium speed voltage supply circuit of the cooling fan 1 for short to ground, short to voltage, high resistance or an open. Did you find and correct the condition?	Go to Step 18	Go to Step 6
6	Test the high/low speed voltage supply circuit of the cooling fan 1 for short to ground, short to voltage, high resistance or an open. Did you find and correct the condition?	Go to Step 18	Go to Step 7
7	Test the series/parallel circuit of the cooling fan 1 for short to ground, short to voltage, high resistance or an open. Did you find and correct the condition?	Go to Step 18	Go to Step 8
8	Test the low/high speed voltage supply circuit of the cooling fan 2 for short to ground, short to voltage, high resistance or an open. Did you find and correct the condition?	Go to Step 18	Go to Step 9
9	Test the medium speed voltage supply circuit of the cooling fan 2 for short to ground, short to voltage, high resistance or an open. Did you find and correct the condition?	Go to Step 18	Go to Step 10
10	Test the ground circuit of the cooling fan 2 for high resistance or an open. Did you find and correct the condition?	Go to Step 18	Go to Step 11
11	Test the ground circuit of the cooling fan control module for high resistance or an open. Did you find and correct the condition?	Go to Step 18	Go to Step 12
12	Test the battery positive voltage circuits of the cooling fan control module for a short to ground, high resistance or an open. Did you find and correct the condition?	Go to Step 18	Go to Step 13

ARM0500000000378

Fig. 22 Cooling fan inoperative (Part 2 of 3). L Series

13	Test the ignition 3 voltage supply circuit of the cooling fan control module for a short to ground, high resistance or an open.		
	Did you find and correct the condition?	Go to Step 18	Go to Step 14
14	Inspect for poor connections at the cooling fan control module		
	Did you find and correct the condition?	Go to Step 18	Go to Step 16
15	Inspect for poor connections at the harness connector of the powertrain control module (PCM)/ECM.		
	Did you find and correct the condition?	Go to Step 18	Go to Step 17
16	Replace the cooling fan control module.		
	Did you complete the replacement?	Go to Step 18	--
17	Replace the ECM.		
	Did you complete the replacement?	Go to Step 18	--
18	1. Use the scan tool in order to clear the DTCs. 2. Operate the vehicle within the Conditions for Running the DTC as specified in the supporting text.		
	Does the DTC reset?	Go to Step 2	System OK

ARM0500000000379

Fig. 22   Cooling fan inoperative (Part 3 of 3). L Series

5. Ignition ON, view the security indicator. The security indicator should not remain illuminated after the vehicle bulb check has completed.

   ☐ If the security indicator remains illuminated after the bulb check, refer to DTC and diagnose any of the following theft deterrent DTCs set as current:

   ☐ B1000, B302A, B3031, B3055, B3060, B3935, B3976, P0513, P0633, P1629, P1631, or P1632.

6. Attempt to start the engine. Verify that the engine cranks.

   ☐ If the engine does not crank, diagnose Engine Electrical.

7. Attempt to start the engine. Verify the engine starts and runs.

   ☐ If the engine does not start and run, diagnose engine.

Important: Do not clear any DTCs unless instructed to do so by a diagnostic procedure.

Important: If any DTCs are Powertrain related DTCs, select Capture Info in order to store the DTC information with the scan tool.

8. Use the appropriate scan tool selections to obtain DTCs from each of the vehicle modules. Verify there are no DTCs reported from any module.

   ☐ If any DTCs are present, refer to Diagnostic Trouble Code (DTC) List - Vehicle and diagnose any current DTCs in the following order:

   8.1. DTCs that begin with a U.
   8.2. Any of the following: B1000, B1001, B1004, B1009, B1019, C0550, C0551, C0561, C0569, P0601, P0602, P0603, P0604, P0606, P0607, P060D, P062B, P062F, P167A, P167D, P2105, P2107, or P2610.
   8.3. Any of the following: B1325, B1370, B1441, C0899, C0900, P0560, P0562, or P0563.
   8.4. Component level DTCs.
   8.5. System level DTCs.
   8.6. Any remaining DTCs.

15. If the customer concern is related to inspection/maintenance (I/M) testing, check maintenance.

   ☐ If none of the previous tests or inspections addresses the concern, check symptoms.

ARM0600000000513

Fig. 23   Diagnostic system check (Part 2 of 2). SKY

1. Verify that none of the following preliminary inspections/tests reveal the cause of the vehicle concern before beginning diagnosis:

   • Ensure that the battery is fully charged.
   • Ensure that the battery cables are clean and tight.
   • Inspect for any open fuses.
   • Ensure that the grounds are clean, tight, and in the correct location.
   • Inspect the easily accessible systems or the visible system components for obvious damage or conditions that could cause the concern.
   • Inspect for aftermarket devices that could affect the operation of the system.
   • Search for applicable service bulletins.

   ☐ If the preceding inspections/tests resolve the concern, go to Repair Verification.

2. Install a scan tool. Verify that the scan tool powers up.

   ☐ If the scan tool does not power up, diagnose Scan Tool.

3. Ignition ON, Engine OFF, verify communication with all of the control modules on the vehicle.

   ☐ If the scan tool does not communicate with one or more of the expected control modules, diagnose Scan Tool.

Important: Open the drivers door to ensure retained accessory power mode (RAP) is inactive during this test. The engine may start during this test. Turn the engine OFF as soon as the crank power mode has been observed.

4. With a scan tool, access the body control module power mode data display list. Operate the ignition switch through all positions while observing the power mode data parameters.

   Verify that all the power mode parameters displayed correspond to the ignition key positions.

ARM0600000000512

Fig. 23   Diagnostic system check (Part 1 of 2). SKY

Diagnostic Instructions

   • Perform the Diagnostic System Check - Vehicle prior to using this diagnostic procedure.
   • Review Strategy Based Diagnosis for an overview of the diagnostic approach.
   • Diagnostic Procedure Instructions provides an overview of each diagnostic category.

Circuit/System Description

The engine cooling fan is a variable speed fan. The engine control module (ECM) controls the fan speed by sending a pulse width modulated (PWM) signal to the cooling fan control module. The cooling fan control module varies the voltage drop across the engine cooling fan motor in relation to the pulse width modulated signal. The cooling fan speed can be adjusted from 10 percent to 90 percent duty cycle. 90-94 percent is considered high speed fan.

The ECM monitors the voltage on the cooling fan speed control circuit driver output. Voltage is near B+ when the driver is OFF, and near ground when the driver is ON. If the difference between the actual and expected voltage exceeds a calibrated value, a DTC will set.

ARM0600000000514

Fig. 24   Cooling fan always on (Part 1 of 2). SKY w/2.0L engine

Circuit/System Verification

1. If DTCs P0480, P0691, or P0692 are set, perform that diagnostic first.
2. Ignition ON, verify with a scan tool that the ECM is not commanding fan activation.
3. Ignition ON, observe that the fan is not activated.

☐ If the fan is activated, replace the cooling fan assembly.

Repair Instructions

Perform the Cooling Fan and Shroud Replacement after completing the diagnostic procedure.

Repair Verification

1. Ignition ON, verify with a scan tool that the ECM is not commanding fan activation.
2. Ignition ON, observe that the fan is not activated.

ARM0600000000515

Fig. 24   Cooling fan always on (Part 2 of 2). SKY w/2.0L engine

Circuit/System Testing

Important: You must perform the Circuit/System Verification before proceeding with Circuit/System Testing.

1. Ignition OFF, disconnect the relays.
2. Ignition ON, observe that the fan is not activated.

☐ If the fan is not activated, replace the faulty relay.
☐ If the fan is activated, test the fan voltage supply circuits for a short to voltage.

Repair Instructions

Cooling Fan and Shroud Replacement

Repair Verification

1. Ignition ON, verify with a scan tool that the ECM is not commanding fan activation.
2. Ignition ON, observe that the fan is not activated.

ARM0600000000517

Fig. 25   Cooling fan always on (Part 2 of 2). SKY w/2.4L engine

Diagnostic Instructions

- Perform the Diagnostic System Check - Vehicle prior to using this diagnostic procedure.
- Review Strategy Based Diagnosis for an overview of the diagnostic approach.
- Diagnostic Procedure Instructions provides an overview of each diagnostic category.

Circuit/System Description

The engine control module (ECM) grounds the low speed relay, which is relay 1, and the high speed relay, which is relay 2, control circuits through an internal solid state device called a driver. The primary function of the driver is to supply the ground for the component being controlled. Each driver has a fault line that is monitored by the ECM. When the ECM is commanding a component ON, the voltage potential of the control circuit should be low, near 0 volts. When the ECM is commanding the control circuit to a component OFF, the voltage potential of the circuit should be high, near battery voltage. If the ECM detects that the actual state of the control circuit does not match the expected state, a DTC will set.

Circuit/System Verification

1. If DTCs P0480 or P0481 are set, then perform those diagnostics first.
2. Ignition ON, verify with a scan tool that the ECM is not commanding fan activation.
3. Ignition ON, observe that the fan is not activated.

ARM0600000000516

Fig. 25   Cooling fan always on (Part 1 of 2). SKY w/2.4L engine

Diagnostic Instructions

- Perform the Diagnostic System Check - Vehicle prior to using this diagnostic procedure.
- Review Strategy Based Diagnosis for an overview of the diagnostic approach.
- Diagnostic Procedure Instructions provides an overview of each diagnostic category.

Circuit/System Description

The engine cooling fan is a variable speed fan. The engine control module (ECM) controls the fan speed by sending a pulse width modulated (PWM) signal to the cooling fan control module. The cooling fan control module varies the voltage drop across the engine cooling fan motor in relation to the pulse width modulated signal. The cooling fan speed can be adjusted from 10 percent to 90 percent duty cycle. 90-94 percent is considered high speed fan.

The ECM monitors the voltage on the cooling fan speed control circuit driver output. Voltage is near B+ when the driver is OFF, and near ground when the driver is ON. If the difference between the actual and expected voltage exceeds a calibrated value, a DTC will set.

Circuit/System Verification

1. If DTCs P0480, P0691, or P0692 are set, perform that diagnostic first.
2. Ignition ON, verify with a scan tool that the ECM is not commanding fan activation.
3. Ignition ON, command the cooling fan speed from 10-90 percent with a scan tool. The fan speed should transition with the commanded states.

ARM0600000000518

Fig. 26   Cooling fan inoperative (Part 1 of 2). SKY w/2.0L Engine

Circuit/System Testing

Important: The Circuit/System Verification must be performed first or misdiagnosis may result.

1. Ignition OFF, disconnect the cooling fan speed control module.
2. Ignition OFF, measure between ground and the cooling fan speed control module ground circuit terminal 2 at the engine harness connector for less than 1 ohm of resistance.

   ☐ If more than 1 ohm, test the ground circuit for an open/high resistance.

3. Connect a test lamp between the cooling fan control module voltage supply circuit terminal 1 and ground. The lamp should illuminate.

   ☐ If the lamp does not illuminate, test the voltage supply circuit for a short to ground or an open/high resistance. If the circuit tests normal and its fuse is open, replace the cooling fan assembly.

4. If all circuits test normal, replace the cooling fan assembly.

Repair Instructions

- Cooling Fan and Shroud Replacement
- Control Module References for replacement, setup, and programming

Repair Verification

1. Ignition ON, verify with a scan tool that the ECM is not commanding fan activation.
2. Ignition ON, command the cooling fan speed from 10-90 percent with a scan tool. The fan speed should transition with the commanded states.

ARM0600000000519

Fig. 26 Cooling fan inoperative (Part 2 of 2). SKY w/2.0L Engine

Circuit/System Testing

Important: You must perform the Circuit/System Verification before proceeding with Circuit/System Testing.

1. Ignition OFF, disconnect the relay.
2. Ignition OFF, connect a 30A fused jumper between the positive terminal at the battery and the fan voltage supply circuit terminal and verify fan activation.

   ☐ If the fan does not activate, test the fan voltage supply circuit for a short to ground or an open/high resistance. If the circuit tests normal, test the fan ground circuit for an open/high resistance. If the fan does not activate and the circuits test normal, replace the fan.

3. Ignition ON, connect a 30A fused jumper from the relay switch voltage supply circuit terminal to the fan voltage supply circuit terminal and verify fan activation.

   ☐ If the fan does not activate, test the relay switch voltage supply circuit for a short to ground or an open/high resistance.

   ☐ If the circuit tests normal and its fuse is open, test all connected components and replace as necessary.

5. If the fan and all circuits test normal, replace the faulty relay.

Repair Instructions

Cooling Fan and Shroud Replacement

Repair Verification

Ignition ON, command the relay ON and OFF with a scan tool. Observe to verify that the fan turns ON and OFF with each command.

ARM0600000000521

Fig. 27 Cooling fan inoperative (Part 2 of 2). SKY w/2.4L engine

Diagnostic Instructions

- Perform the Diagnostic System Check - Vehicle prior to using this diagnostic procedure.
- Review Strategy Based Diagnosis for an overview of the diagnostic approach.
- Diagnostic Procedure Instructions provides an overview of each diagnostic category.

Circuit/System Description

The engine control module (ECM) grounds the low speed relay, which is relay 1, and the high speed relay, which is relay 2, control circuits through an internal solid state device called a driver. The primary function of the driver is to supply the ground for the component being controlled. Each driver has a fault line that is monitored by the ECM. When the ECM is commanding a component ON, the voltage potential of the control circuit should be low, near 0 volts. When the ECM is commanding the control circuit to a component OFF, the voltage potential of the circuit should be high, near battery voltage. If the ECM detects that the actual state of the control circuit does not match the expected state, a DTC will set.

Circuit/System Verification

1. If DTCs P0480 or P0481 are set, perform those diagnostics first.
2. Ignition ON, command each relay ON and OFF with a scan tool. Observe to verify that the fan turns ON and OFF with each command.

ARM0600000000520

Fig. 27 Cooling fan inoperative (Part 1 of 2). SKY w/2.4L engine

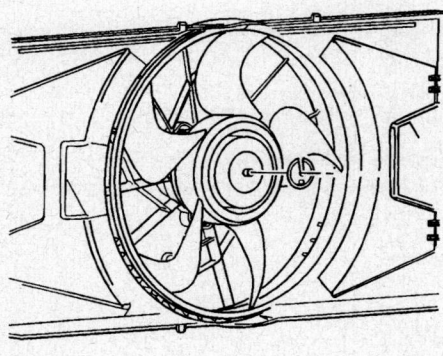

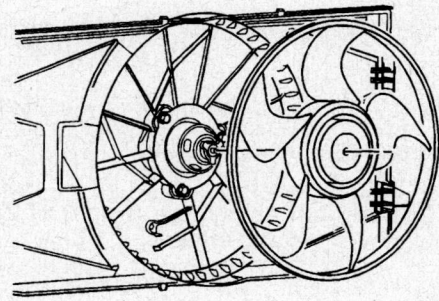

ARM66GC000000264

Fig. 28 Air dam & splash shield removal. ION

Fig. 29 Lower radiator mount
assembly removal. ION

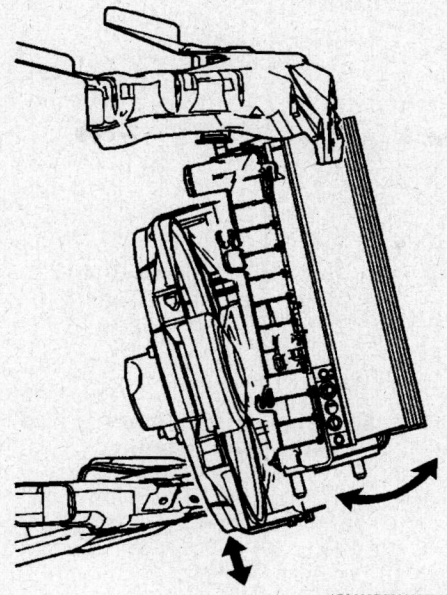

Fig. 30 Cooling fan & shroud
assembly removal. ION

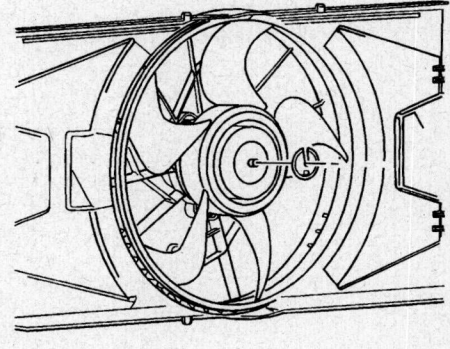

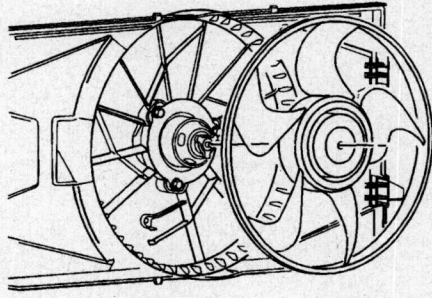

Fig. 31 Cooling fan blade
removal. ION

Fig. 32 Cooling fan motor
removal. ION

Fig. 33 Pusher fan removal.
L Series

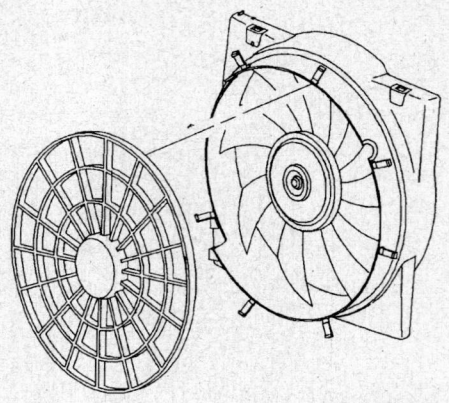

ARM66GC000000254

**Fig. 34   Pusher fan finger guard
removal. L Series**

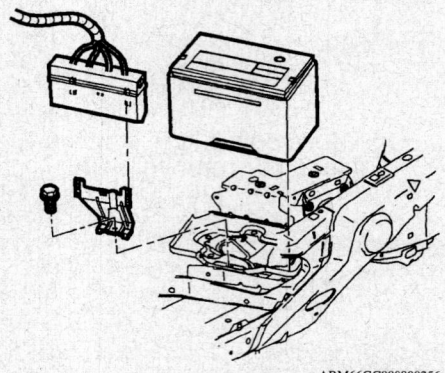

ARM66GC000000256

**Fig. 35   Battery hold-down & fan
control module bracket removal.
L Series w/2.2L engine**

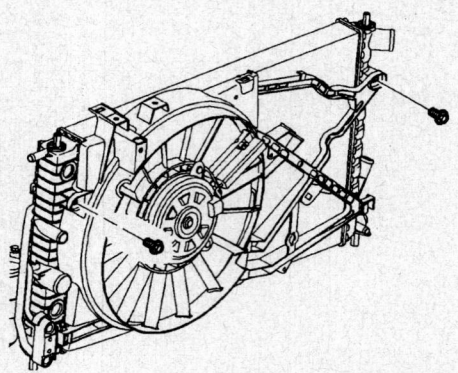

ARM66GC000000257

**Fig. 36   Fan & shroud assembly
removal. L Series w/2.2L engine**

STARTER MOTORS

TABLE OF CONTENTS

	Page No.		Page No.
APPLICATION CHART	18-1	MITSUBISHI STARTERS	18-13
AC-DELCO, BOSCH & DENSO STARTERS	18-4		

Application Chart

Model	Year	Engine	VIN①	Manufacturer	Model
BUICK					
Century	2004–05	3.1L	J	AC-Delco	PG-260D
Lacrosse	2005–08	3.6L	7	AC-Delco	PG
		3.8L	2	AC-Delco	PG
LeSabre	2004–05	3.8L	K	AC-Delco	PG-260L
			1	AC-Delco	PG-260L
Lucerne	2007–08	3.8L	2	AC-Delco	PG
		4.6L	Y	—	—
Park Avenue	2004–05	3.8L	1	AC-Delco	PG-260L
Regal	2004	3.8L	K	AC-Delco	PG-260G
			1	AC-Delco	PG-260L
CADILLAC					
CTS	2004	3.2L	N	Bosch	—
		3.6L	7	AC-Delco	PG-260G
		5.7L	S	AC-Delco	PG-260L
	2005	2.8L	T	Bosch	—
		3.6L	7	AC-Delco	PG-260G
		5.7L	S	AC-Delco	PG-260L
	2006–07	2.8L	T	Bosch	—
		3.6L	7	AC-Delco	PG-260G
		6.0L	U	AC-Delco	PG
	2008	3.6L	—	AC-Delco	PG-260G
Deville	2004–05	4.6L	9	AC-Delco	PG-260L
			Y	AC-Delco	PG-260L
DTS	2006–08	4.6L	9	AC-Delco	PG-260L
			Y	AC-Delco	PG-260L
Seville	2004	4.6L	9	AC-Delco	PG-260L
			Y	AC-Delco	PG-260L
STS	2005	3.6L	7	—	PG
		4.6L	A	—	PG
	2005–08	3.6L	7	—	PG
		4.4L	D	—	PG
		4.6L	A	—	PG
XLR	2004–05	4.6L	A	AC-Delco	PG-260L
	2004–08	4.4L	D	AC-Delco	PG-260L
		4.6L	A	AC-Delco	PG-260L
CHEVROLET					
Aveo & Aveo 5	2005–08	1.6L	6	—	—
Cavalier	2004	2.2L	F	AC-Delco	PG-260D
			6	AC-Delco	PG-260D
	2005	2.2L	F	AC-Delco	PG-260D

Continued

STARTER MOTORS

Model	Year	Engine	VIN①	Manufacturer	Model
CHEVROLET					
Cobalt	2005	2.0L	P	AC-Delco	PG
		2.2L	F	AC-Delco	PG
	2006–08	2.0L	P	AC-Delco	PG
		2.2L	F	AC-Delco	PG
		2.4L	B	AC-Delco	PG
Corvette	2004	5.7L	G	AC-Delco	PG-260L
			S	AC-Delco	PG
	2005–08	6.0L	U	AC-Delco	PG
		7.0L	E	AC-Delco	PG
	2008	6.2L	—	AC-Delco	PG
Impala	2004–05	3.4L	E	AC-Delco	PG-260D
		3.8L	K	AC-Delco	PG-260G
			1	AC-Delco	PG-260G
	2006	3.5L	K	—	—
		3.9L	1	AC-Delco	PG
		5.3L	C	—	—
	2007–08	3.5L	K	—	—
			N	AC-Delco	PG
		3.9L	R	AC-Delco	PG
		5.3L	C	—	—
	2008	3.9L	3	—	—
Malibu & Malibu Maxx	2004–05	2.2L	F	AC-Delco	PG-260D
		3.5L	8	AC-Delco	PG-260D
	2006	2.2L	F	AC-Delco	PG-260D
		3.5L	8	AC-Delco	PG-260D
		3.9L	1	AC-Delco	PG
	2007	2.2L	F	AC-Delco	PG-260D
		3.5L	N	AC-Delco	PG
			8	AC-Delco	PG-260D
		3.9L	1	AC-Delco	PG
Malibu Classic	2008	2.2L	F	AC-Delco	PG-260D
		3.5L	—	AC-Delco	PG
Monte Carlo	2004–05	3.4L	E	AC-Delco	PG-260D
		3.8L	K	AC-Delco	PG-260G
			1	AC-Delco	PG-260G
	2006–07	3.5L	K	—	—
		3.9L	1	AC-Delco	PG
		5.3L	C	—	—
OLDSMOBILE					
Alero	2004	2.2L	F	AC-Delco	PG-260D
		3.4L	E	AC-Delco	PG-260D
PONTIAC					
Bonneville	2004–05	3.8L	K	AC-Delco	PG-260L
		4.6L	Y	AC-Delco	PG-260G
Grand Am	2004–05	2.2L	F	AC-Delco	PG-260D
		3.4L	E	AC-Delco	PG-260D
Grand Prix	2004	3.8L	2	AC-Delco	PG
			4	AC-Delco	PG
	2005–08	3.8L	2	AC-Delco	PG
			4	AC-Delco	PG
		5.3L	C	AC-Delco	PG
GTO	2004	5.7L	G	Mitsubishi	—
	2005–06	6.0L	U	Mitsubishi	—
G5	2007–08	2.2L	F	AC-Delco	PG
		2.4L	B	AC-Delco	PG

Continued

APPLICATION CHART

Model	Year	Engine	VIN①	Manufacturer	Model
PONTIAC					
G6	2005	3.5L	8	AC-Delco	PG-260D
	2006	2.4L	B	AC-Delco	PG
		3.5L	8	AC-Delco	PG-260D
		3.9L	1	AC-Delco	PG
	2007–08	2.4L	B	AC-Delco	PG
		3.5L	N	AC-Delco	PG-260D
			8	AC-Delco	PG-260D
		3.6L	7	—	PG
		3.9L	1	AC-Delco	PG
Solstice	2006	2.4L	B	AC-Delco	PG
	2007–08	2.0L	X	AC-Delco	PG
		2.4L	B	AC-Delco	PG
Sunfire	2004–05	2.2L	F	AC-Delco	PG-260D
Vibe	2004–06	1.8L	L	Denso	LV6/LNK
			8	Denso	LV6/LNK
	2007–08	1.8L	8	Denso	LV6/LNK
SATURN					
Aura	2007–08	3.5L	N	AC-Delco	PG
		3.6L	7	AC-Delco	PG
Aura Hybrid	2008	2.4L	5	—	—
Ion	2004–05	2.0L	P	AC-Delco	PG-260D
		2.2L	F	AC-Delco	PG-260D
	2006–07	2.0L	P	AC-Delco	PG-260D
		2.2L	F	AC-Delco	PG-260D
		2.4L	B	AC-Delco	PG-260D
L-Series	2004–05	2.2L	F	AC-Delco	PG-260D
		3.0L	R	Mitsubishi	—
Sky	2007–08	2.0L	X	AC-Delco	PG
		2.4L	B	AC-Delco	PG

① — The eighth digit of VIN denotes engine code.

AC-Delco, Bosch & Denso Starters

NOTE: On Air Bag Equipped Models, Refer To "Air Bag System Precautions" Located In The Front Of This Manual For System Disarming & Arming Procedures.

NOTE: Refer To "Computer Relearn Procedures" Located In The Front Of This Manual When Battery Power To The Computer Has Been Interrupted.

INDEX

	Page No.		Page No.		Page No.
Description	18-5	Hybrid Battery Service	18-4	AC-Delco	18-5
Diagnosis & Testing	18-5	Connect	18-5	Bosch	18-5
Precautions	18-4	Disconnect	18-4	Denso	18-5
Air Bag Systems	18-4	**Starter Specifications**	18-13		
Battery Ground Cable	18-4	**Troubleshooting**	18-5		

PRECAUTIONS

Air Bag Systems

Refer to "Air Bag System Precautions" in the front of this manual for system disarming and arming procedures.

Battery Ground Cable

Prior to service, disconnect battery ground cable and isolate as required.

Hybrid Battery Service

DISCONNECT

To help avoid personal injury, always ensure the ignition switch is in the OFF position and the ignition key has been removed prior to working on any 36V components. After the key has been removed, disconnect the negative battery cable and then open the generator battery disconnect control module cover. After waiting for at least 5 minutes, measure the voltage potential using a DMM between the following: 36V positive and negative battery cables; 36V positive battery cable and vehicle ground; 36V negative battery cable and vehicle ground. All measured voltage levels must be below 3 volts.

1. Remove ignition key from ignition switch.
2. Secure ignition key to ensure that key CANNOT be installed without your knowledge.
3. Disconnect 12 volt negative battery cable.
4. Fold down both rear seat backs, then carefully lift up on load floor rear compartment cover at retaining clip locations, **Fig. 1.**

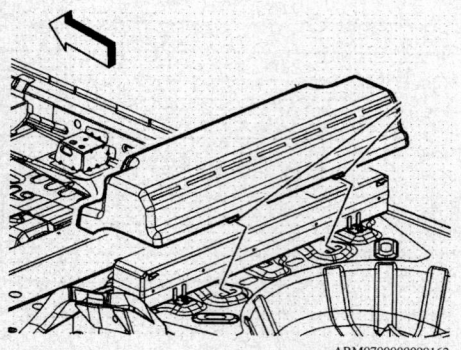

Fig. 1   Rear hybrid battery compartment. Aura

ARM0700000000162

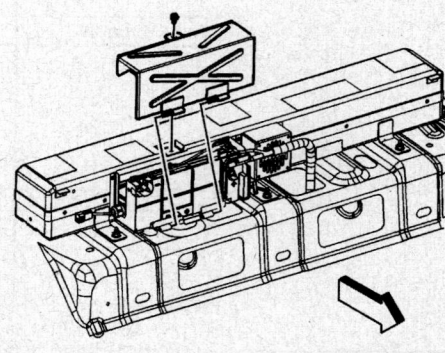

Fig. 2   Disconnect control module cover. Aura Hybrid

ARM0700000000163

5. Tilt load floor rear compartment cover towards rear of vehicle slightly, disengage tabs and remove load floor rear compartment cover. **To avoid personal injury, be careful when working in vicinity of generator battery disconnect control module. Internal components will still be live, 36V potential, even when cover has been opened or removed.**
6. Remove generator battery disconnect control module cover bolt, **Fig. 2.**
7. Open and slide generator battery disconnect control module cover to right, removing cover. **Wait at least 5 minutes in order to allow generator control module capacitors to discharge.**
8. **Never assume battery pack is disabled when generator battery disconnect control module cover is opened. Generator battery will have to be checked for voltage potential using a voltmeter first.**
9. Set voltmeter to DC voltage and measure vehicle 12-volt battery voltage (at 12-volt positive jumper location and negative battery cable).
10. Meter should read greater than 12 volts DC.
11. To ensure generator battery has been disabled, check generator battery for voltage potential as follows:
    a. Refer to **Fig. 3** for voltage measurement locations.
    b. Measure from positive stud to negative stud, voltage should be less than 3 volts.
    c. Measure from positive stud to vehicle chassis ground, voltage should be less than 3 volts.
    d. Measure from negative stud to vehicle chassis ground, voltage should be less than 3 volts.
12. After verifying there is no voltage present, vehicle is now safe to work on.

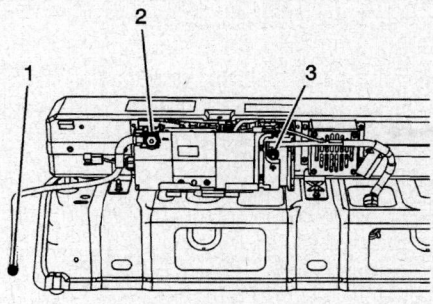

1-Chassis ground
2-Negative stud
3-Positive stud

ARM0700000000164

Fig. 3   Battery disconnect control module voltage measurement locations. Aura Hybrid

CONNECT

1. Install and close generator battery disconnect control module cover.
2. Install generator battery cover bolt and **torque** to 89 inch lbs.
3. Tilt load floor rear compartment cover towards rear of vehicle slightly in order to insert tabs into battery tray rear support.
4. Set load floor rear compartment cover down, ensure retaining clips align to proper locations, carefully push down to secure cover.
5. Place rear seats backs to their proper positions.
6. Connect 12 volt negative battery cable.

DESCRIPTION

These starter motors are a non-repairable starter motor. They have pole pieces that are arranged around the armature. Both solenoid windings are energized. The pull-in winding circuit is completed to the ground through the starter motor. The windings work together magnetically to pull and hold in the plunger moves the shift lever. This action causes the starter drive assembly to rotate on the armature shaft spline as it engages with the flywheel ring gear on the engine. Moving at the same time, the plunger also closes the solenoid switch contacts in the starter solenoid. Full battery voltage is applied directly to the starter motor and it cranks the engine.

Step	Action	Yes	No
1	Did you perform the Battery Inspection/Test?	Go to *Step 2*	*Battery Inspection/Test*
2	1. Install a scan tool 2. Turn ON the ignition, with the engine OFF. Does the scan tool power up?	Go to *Step 3*	Go to *Scan Tool Does Not Power Up*
3	Attempt to establish communication with the following components: • Body Control Module (BCM) • Instrument Panel Cluster (IPC) • Powertrain Control Module (PCM) • Vehicle Theft Deterrent Module (VTD) Does the scan tool communicate with the BCM, IPC, PCM and VTD?	Go to *Step 4*	*Scan Tool Does Not Communicate with Class 2 Device*
4	Select the BCM, IPC, PCM and VTD display DTC function on the scan tool. Does the scan tool display any DTCs?	Go to *Step 5*	Go to *Symptoms*
5	Does the scan tool display any DTCs which begin with a U?	*Scan Tool Does Not Communicate with Class 2 Device* Go to *Step 6*	
6	Does the scan tool display any DTCs in the PCM which begin with a P?	*Diagnostic Trouble Code (DTC) List/Type* Go to *Step 7*	
7	Does the scan tool display any DTCs in the VTD which begin with B?	*Diagnostic Trouble Code (DTC) List/Type* Go to *Step 8*	
8	Does the scan tool display any DTCs in the BCM which begin with B?	*Diagnostic Trouble Code (DTC) List/Type* Go to *Step 9*	
9	Does the scan tool display any DTCs in the IPC which begin with B?	*Diagnostic Trouble Code (DTC) List/Type* System OK	

GC1120100173000X

Fig. 4   System check. AC-Delco

Step	Action	Yes	No
1	Did you perform the Diagnostic System Check for starting and charging?	Go to *Step 2*	*System Check*
2	Turn the ignition to the START position. Does the engine crank?	Go to *Intermittent and Poor Connections*	Go to *Step 3*
3	1. Install a scan tool. 2. With a scan tool, observe the Crank Request parameter in the PCM data list. 3. Turn the ignition switch to the START position. Does the scan tool display Yes?	Go to *Step 5*	Go to *Step 4*
4	1. With a scan tool, observe the Crank parameter in the IPC data list. 2. Turn the ignition switch to the START position. Does the scan tool display Yes?	Go to *Step 12*	Go to *Step 13*
5	Turn the ignition to the START position. Does the CRANK relay click?	Go to *Step 8*	Go to *Step 6*

GC1120100170010X

Fig. 5   Starter solenoid does not click (Part 1 of 3). AC-Delco

TROUBLESHOOTING

AC-Delco

Refer to **Figs 4 through 7** for troubleshooting procedures.

Bosch

Refer to **Figs. 8 through 12** for troubleshooting procedures.

Denso

Refer to **Figs. 13 through 15** for troubleshooting procedures.

DIAGNOSIS & TESTING

Refer to **MOTOR's "Domestic Engine Performance & Driveability Manual"** or **"Engine Performance & Driveability 1994–2005 v6.0"** for diagnosis and testing procedures.

Step	Action	Yes	No
6	1. Turn OFF the ignition. 2. Disconnect the CRANK relay. 3. Turn ON the ignition, with the Engine OFF. 4. Connect a test lamp between the battery positive voltage circuit of the CRANK relay coil and a good ground. Does the test lamp illuminate?	Go to *Step 7*	Go to *Step 14*
7	1. Connect a test lamp between the battery positive voltage circuit of the CRANK relay coil and the control circuit of the CRANK relay. 2. Turn the ignition to the START position. Does the test lamp illuminate?	Go to *Step 18*	Go to *Step 15*
8	1. Turn OFF the ignition. 2. Disconnect the CRANK relay. 3. Connect a test lamp between the battery positive voltage circuit of the CRANK relay switch circuit and a good ground. Does the test lamp illuminate?	Go to *Step 9*	Go to *Step 22*
9	Connect a 30 amp fused jumper between the battery positive voltage circuit of the START relay switch circuit and the supply voltage circuit of the starter solenoid. Does the engine crank?	Go to *Step 18*	Go to *Step 10*
10	1. Disconnect the park neutral position (PNP) switch. 2. Connect a 30 amp fused jumper between the starter solenoid supply voltage circuits of the PNP switch harness connector. Does the engine crank?	Go to *Step 17*	Go to *Step 11*
11	Does the fuse in either jumper open?	Go to *Step 23*	Go to *Step 16*
12	Test the crank request signal circuit of the PCM for an open or high resistance. Did you find and correct the condition?	Go to *Step 29*	Go to *Step 19*
13	Test the crank signal circuit of the IPC for an open or high resistance. Did you find and correct the condition?	Go to *Step 29*	Go to *Step 20*
14	Test the battery positive voltage circuit of the CRANK relay coil for an open or high resistance. Did you find and correct the condition?	Go to *Step 29*	Go to *Step 20*
15	Test the control circuit of the CRANK relay for an open, high resistance or short to battery voltage. Did you find and correct the condition?	Go to *Step 29*	Go to *Step 19*
16	Test the supply voltage circuit of the starter solenoid for an open or high resistance. Did you find and correct the condition?	Go to *Step 29*	Go to *Step 21*
17	1. Inspect the PNP switch for proper operation. 2. Inspect for poor connection at the PNP switch harness connector. Did you find and correct the condition?	Go to *Step 29*	Go to *Step 24*
18	Inspect for poor connections at the CRANK relay. Did you find and correct the condition?	Go to *Step 29*	Go to *Step 25*

GC1120100170020X

Fig. 5 Starter solenoid does not click (Part 2 of 3). AC-Delco

Step	Action	Yes	No
19	Inspect for poor connection at the PCM harness connector. Did you find and correct the condition?	Go to *Step 29*	Go to *Step 26*
20	Inspect for poor connections at the ignition switch harness connector. Did you find and correct the condition?	Go to *Step 29*	Go to *Step 27*
21	Inspect for poor connections at the starter solenoid. Did you find and correct the condition?	Go to *Step 29*	Go to *Step 28*
22	Repair the open or high resistance in the battery positive voltage circuit of the CRANK relay switch. Did you complete the repair?	Go to *Step 29*	
23	Repair the high resistance or short to ground in the supply voltage circuit of the starter solenoid. Did you complete the repair?	Go to *Step 29*	
24	Replace the PNP switch. Did you complete the replacement?	Go to *Step 29*	
25	Replace the crank relay. Did you complete the replacement?	Go to *Step 29*	
26	**Important:** Perform the set up procedures for the PCM. Replace the PCM. Did you complete the replacement?	Go to *Step 29*	—
27	Replace the Ignition Switch. Did you complete the replacement?	Go to *Step 29*	—
28	Replace the Starter Motor. Did you complete the replacement?	Go to *Step 29*	—
29	Operate the system for which the symptom occurred. Did you correct the condition?	System OK	Go to *Step 2*

GC1120100170030X

Fig. 5 Starter solenoid does not click (Part 3 of 3). AC-Delco

Step	Action	Yes	No
1	Did you perform the Diagnostic System Check for starting and charging?	Go to *Step 2*	System Check
2	Turn the ignition to the START position. Did the starter solenoid click?	Go to *Step 3*	Go to *Starter Solenoid Does Not Click*
3	Inspect the engine and belt drive system for mechanical binding (seized engine, seized generator). Does the engine move freely?	Go to *Step 4*	Go to *Engine Overhaul*
4	Test the battery positive cable between the battery and the starter solenoid for high resistance. Did you find and correct the condition?	Go to *Step 8*	Go to *Step 5*
5	Test the ground circuit between the battery and the starter motor for a high resistance. Did you find and correct the condition?	Go to *Step 8*	Go to *Step 6*
6	Inspect for poor connections at the starter. Did you find and correct the condition?	Go to *Step 8*	Go to *Step 7*
7	Replace the Starter. Did you complete the replacement?	Go to *Step 8*	—
8	Operate the system for which the symptom occurred. Did you correct the condition?	System OK	Go to *Step 2*

GC1120100171000X

Fig. 6 Starter solenoid clicks, engine does not crank. AC-Delco

Step	Action	Yes	No
1	Did you review the engine electrical operation and perform the necessary inspections?	Go to *Step 2*	Go to *Symptoms*
2	Start the engine. Does the starter operate normally?	Test Intermittent and Poor Connections	Go to *Step 3*
3	Start the engine while listening to the starter motor turn. Is there a loud "whoop" (it may sound like a siren if the engine is revved while the starter is engaged) after the engine starts, but while the starter is still held in the engaged position?	Go to *Step 6*	Go to *Step 4*
4	Do you hear a "rumble", a "growl", or, in some cases, a "knock" as the starter is coasting down to a stop after starting the engine?	Go to *Step 7*	Go to *Step 5*
5	When the engine is cranked, do you hear a high-pitched whine after the engine cranks and starts normally? (This is often diagnosed as a starter drive gear hang-in or a weak solenoid.)	Go to *Step 8*	Go to *Step 7*
6	Inspect the flywheel ring gear for the following: • Chipped gear teeth • Missing gear teeth • milled teeth Does the flywheel have damaged teeth or is bent?	Go to *Step 9*	Go to *Step 10*
7	1. Remove the starter motor. 2. Inspect the starter motor bushings and clutch gear. Does the clutch gear have chipped or milled teeth or worn bushings?	Go to *Step 10*	Go to *Step 9*
8	Shim the starter motor away from the flywheel by adding shims one at a time, between the starter motor and the engine block. Flywheel runout may make this noise appear to be intermittent. Did you complete the repair?	Go to *Step 11*	—
9	Replace the flywheel. Did you complete the replacement?	Go to *Step 11*	—
10	Replace the starter motor. Has the noise stopped?	Go to *Step 11*	—
11	Operate the system in order to verify the repair. Did you correct the condition?	System OK	Go to *Step 2*

GC1120100172000X

Fig. 7 Starter motor noise. AC-Delco

Step	Action	Yes	No
1	Did you perform the Battery Inspection/Test?	Go to Step 2	Battery Inspection
2	1. Install a scan tool. 2. Turn ON the ignition, with the engine OFF. Does the scan tool power up?	Go to Step 3	Scan Tool Does Not Power Up
3	**Important** The engine may start during the following step. Turn OFF the engine as soon as you have observed the Crank power mode. 1. Access the Class 2 Power Mode in the Diagnostic Circuit Check on the scan tool. 2. Rotate the ignition switch through all positions while observing the Class 2 Power Mode parameter. Does the ignition switch parameter reading match the ignition switch position for all switch positions?	Go to Step 4	Power Mode Mismatch
4	1. Turn ON the ignition, with the engine OFF. 2. Attempt to communicate with each of the following modules on the class 2 serial data circuit: o Amplifier (AMP) o Climate Control Panel (CCP) o Dash Integration Module (DIM) o Instrument Panel Cluster (IPC) o Onstar (ONS) o Radio (IRC) o Rear Integration Module (RIM) o Remote Function Actuator (RFA) o Powertrain Control Module (PCM) o Supplemental Inflatable Restraint (SIR) Does the scan tool communicate with all modules on the class 2 serial data circuit?	Go to Step 5	Scan Tool Does Not Power Up

ARM66GC000000670

Fig. 8   System check (Part 1 of 2). Bosch

Step	Action	Yes	No
5	1. Select the Display DTCs function for each module. If using a Tech 2, use the Class 2 DTC Check feature in order to determine which modules have DTCs set. 2. Record all of the displayed DTCs, the DTC status, and the module which set the DTC. Does the scan tool display any DTCs?	Go to Step 6	Symptoms
6	Does the scan tool display any DTCs which begin with a "U"?	Scan Tool Does Not Communicate with Class 2 Device	Go to Step 7
7	Does the scan tool display DTC B1000, B1004, B1007, B1009, B1013 or B1014?	Diagnostic Trouble Code (DTC)	Diagnostic Trouble Code

ARM66GC000000671

Fig. 8   System check (Part 2 of 2). Bosch

Step	Action	Yes	No
1	Did you perform the Diagnostic System Check for Engine Electrical?	Go to Step 2	Diagnostic System Check
2	Turn the ignition to the START position. Does the starter solenoid click?	Test for Intermittent and Poor Connections	Go to Step 3
3	1. Install a scan tool. 2. With a scan tool, observe the Starter Relay Command parameter in the ECM data list. 3. Turn the ignition switch to the START position. Does the scan tool display On?	Go to Step 4	Go to Step 5
4	Turn the ignition back and forth from the OFF to ON position a few times. Does the Starter Relay click each time the ignition is turned to the ON position?	Go to Step 15	Go to Step 9
5	1. Turn ON the ignition, with the engine OFF. 2. With a scan tool, observe the Crank Request parameter in the ECM data list. 3. Turn the ignition switch to the START position. Does the scan tool display Yes?	Go to Step 6	Go to Step 8
6	1. Turn ON the ignition, with the engine OFF. 2. With a scan tool, observe the Start Disabled parameter in the VTD data list. Does the scan tool display Yes?	Diagnostic System Check	Go to Step 7

ARM66GC000000672

Fig. 9   Starter solenoid does not click (Part 1 of 5). Bosch w/automatic transmission

Step	Action	Yes	No
7	1. Turn ON the ignition, with the engine OFF. 2. Verify that the transmission is in Park or Neutral. 3. With a scan tool, observe the IMS Range parameter in the Transmission data list. Does the scan tool display Park or Neutral?	Go to Step 24	Diagnostic System Check
8	1. Turn OFF the ignition. 2. Disconnect the ECM. 3. Connect a test lamp between the Start Command circuit of the EMC and a good ground. 4. Turn the ignition to the Start position. Does the test lamp illuminate?	Go to Step 24	Go to Step 17
9	1. Turn OFF the ignition. 2. Disconnect the Run/Crank Relay. 3. Connect a test lamp between the battery positive voltage circuit of the Run/Crank Relay coil circuit and a good ground. 4. Turn On the ignition, with the engine OFF. Does the test lamp illuminate?	Go to Step 10	Go to Step 25
10	1. Turn OFF the ignition. 2. Connect a test lamp between the ignition 1 voltage circuit of the Run/Crank Relay coil and the ground circuit of the Run/Crank Relay coil. 3. Turn On the ignition, with the engine OFF. Does the test lamp illuminate?	Go to Step 11	Go to Step 26
11	1. Connect a 10 amp fused jumper between the battery positive voltage circuit of the Run/Crank Relay switch and the Starter Relay Ignition 1 circuit of the Run Crank Relay switch. 2. Turn the ignition switch to the START position. Does the starter solenoid click?	Go to Step 20	Go to Step 12

ARM66GC000000673

Fig. 9   Starter solenoid does not click (Part 2 of 5). Bosch w/automatic transmission

Step	Action	Yes	No
12	**Important** Leave the fused jumper in place. 1. Disconnect the Starter Relay. 2. Connect a test lamp between the ignition 1 voltage circuit of the Starter Relay coil and a good ground. Does the test lamp illuminate?	Go to Step 13	Go to Step 27
13	1. Connect a test lamp between the ignition 1 voltage circuit of the Starter Relay coil and the control circuit of the Starter Relay coil. 2. Turn the ignition to the Start position. Does the test lamp illuminate?	Go to Step 21	Go to Step 14
14	1. Turn OFF the ignition. 2. Disconnect the ECM. 3. Install the Starter Relay. 4. Connect a test lamp between the control circuit of the Starter Relay and a good ground. Does the test lamp illuminate?	Go to Step 24	Go to Step 28
15	**Important** The engine may crank when the fused jumper is put into place. Connect a 30 amp fused jumper between the battery positive voltage circuit of the Starter relay switch circuit and the supply voltage circuit of the starter solenoid. Does the engine crank?	Go to Step 21	Go to Step 16
16	Does the fuse in the jumper open?	Go to Step 18	Go to Step 19
17	Test the Start Command circuit of the ECM for a high resistance or open. Did you find and correct the condition?	Go to Step 34	Go to Step 23
18	Test the supply voltage circuit of the starter solenoid for a short to ground. Did you find and correct the condition?	Go to Step 34	Go to Step 22

ARM66GC000000674

Fig. 9   Starter solenoid does not click (Part 3 of 5). Bosch w/automatic transmission

Step	Action	Yes	No
19	Test the supply voltage circuit of the starter solenoid for a high resistance or open. Did you find and correct the condition?	Go to Step 34	Go to Step 22
20	Inspect for poor connection at the Run/Crank Relay. Did you find and correct the condition?	Go to Step 34	Go to Step 29
21	Inspect for poor connection at the Starter Relay. Did you find and correct the condition?	Go to Step 34	Go to Step 30
22	Inspect for poor connection at the starter solenoid. Did you find and correct the condition?	Go to Step 34	Go to Step 31
23	Inspect for poor connection at the ignition switch. Did you find and correct the condition?	Go to Step 34	Go to Step 32
24	Inspect for poor connection at the ECM. Did you find and correct the condition?	Go to Step 34	Go to Step 33
25	Repair the high resistance or open in the ignition 1 voltage circuit of the Run/Crank Relay coil. Did you complete the repair?	Go to Step 34	--
26	Repair the high resistance or open in the ground circuit of the Run/Crank Relay coil. Did you complete the repair?	Go to Step 34	--

ARM66GC000000675

Fig. 9   Starter solenoid does not click (Part 4 of 5). Bosch w/automatic transmission

Step	Action	Yes	No
27	Repair the high resistance or open in the ignition 1 voltage circuit of the Starter relay coil. Did you complete the repair?	Go to Step 34	--
28	Repair the high resistance or open in the control circuit of the Starter relay. Did you complete the repair?	Go to Step 34	--
29	Replace the Run/Crank relay. Did you complete the replacement?	Go to Step 34	--
30	Replace the Starter relay. Did you complete the replacement?	Go to Step 34	--
31	Replace the starter. Did you complete the replacement?	Go to Step 34	--
32	Replace the ignition switch. Did you complete the replacement?	Go to Step 34	--
33	**Important:** Perform the set up procedures for the ECM. Replace the ECM. Did you complete the replacement?	Go to Step 34	--
34	Operate the system for which the symptom occurred. Did you correct the condition?	System OK	Go to Step 2

ARM66GC000000676

Fig. 9   Starter solenoid does not click (Part 5 of 5). Bosch w/automatic transmission

Step	Action	Yes	No
1	Did you perform the Diagnostic System Check for Engine Electrical?	Go to Step 2	Diagnostic System Check
2	1. Depress the clutch pedal. 2. Turn the ignition to the START position. Does the starter solenoid click?	Test for Intermittent and Poor Connections	Go to Step 3
3	1. Install a scan tool. 2. Depress the clutch pedal. 3. With a scan tool, observe the Starter Relay Command parameter in the ECM data list. 4. Turn the ignition switch to the START position. Does the scan tool display On?	Go to Step 4	Go to Step 5
4	1. Depress the clutch pedal. 2. Turn the ignition back and forth from the OFF to ON position a few times. Does the Starter Relay click each time the ignition is turned to the ON position?	Go to Step 17	Go to Step 9
5	1. With a scan tool, observe the Crank Request parameter in the ECM data list. 2. Turn the ignition switch to the START position. Does the scan tool display Yes?	Go to Step 6	Go to Step 8
6	1. Turn ON the ignition, with the engine OFF. 2. With a scan tool, observe the Start Disabled parameter in the VTD data list. Does the scan tool display Yes?	Diagnostic System Check	Go to Step 7

ARM66GC000000677

Fig. 10   Starter solenoid does not click (Part 1 of 6). Bosch w/manual transmission

7	1. Turn ON the ignition, with the engine OFF. 2. Depress the clutch pedal. 3. With a scan tool, observe the Clutch Start Switch parameter in the ECM data list. Does the scan tool display On?	Go to Step 31	Go to Step 16
8	1. Turn OFF the ignition. 2. Disconnect the ECM. 3. Connect a test lamp between the Start Command circuit of the ECM and a good ground. 4. Turn the ignition to the Start position. Does the test lamp illuminate?	Go to Step 31	Go to Step 21
9	1. Turn OFF the ignition. 2. Disconnect the Run/Crank Relay. 3. Connect a test lamp between the battery positive voltage circuit of the Run/Crank Relay coil circuit and a good ground. 4. Turn On the ignition, with the engine OFF. Does the test lamp illuminate?	Go to Step 10	Go to Step 33
10	1. Turn OFF the ignition. 2. Connect a test lamp between the ignition 1 voltage circuit of the Run/Crank Relay coil and the ground circuit of the Run/Crank Relay coil. 3. Turn On the ignition, with the engine OFF. Does the test lamp illuminate?	Go to Step 11	Go to Step 34
11	1. Connect a 10 amp fused jumper between the battery positive voltage circuit of the Run/Crank Relay switch and the Ignition 1 voltage circuit of the clutch switch. 2. Depress the clutch pedal. 3. Turn the ignition switch to the START position. Does the starter solenoid click?	Go to Step 26	Go to Step 12
12	**Important** Leave the fused jumper in place. 1. Disconnect the Starter Relay. 2. Connect a test lamp between the ignition 1 voltage circuit of the Starter Relay coil and a good ground. 3. Depress the clutch pedal. Does the test lamp illuminate?	Go to Step 13	Go to Step 15

ARM66GC000000678

Fig. 10   Starter solenoid does not click (Part 2 of 6).
Bosch w/manual transmission

13	1. Connect a test lamp between the ignition 1 voltage circuit of the Starter Relay coil and the control circuit of the Starter Relay coil. 2. Depress the clutch pedal. 3. Turn the ignition to the Start position. Does the test lamp illuminate?	Go to Step 27	Go to Step 14
14	1. Turn OFF the ignition. 2. Disconnect the ECM. 3. Install the Starter Relay. 4. Connect a test lamp between the control circuit of the Starter Relay and a good ground. 5. Depress the clutch pedal. Does the test lamp illuminate?	Go to Step 31	Go to Step 35
15	1. Turn OFF the ignition. 2. Disconnect the clutch switch. 3. Connect a test lamp between the ignition 1 voltage of the clutch switch and a good ground. Does the test lamp illuminate?	Go to Step 22	Go to Step 32
16	1. Turn OFF the ignition. 2. Disconnect the clutch switch. 3. With a scan tool, observe the Clutch Start Switch parameter in the ECM data list. 4. Turn ON the ignition, with the engine OFF. Does the scan tool display On?	Go to Step 28	Go to Step 23
17	1. Place the transmission in neutral. 2. Apply the parking brake. **Important** The engine may crank when the fused jumper is put into place. 3. Connect a 30 amp fused jumper between the battery positive voltage circuit of the Starter relay switch circuit and the supply voltage circuit of the starter solenoid. Does the engine crank?	Go to Step 27	Go to Step 20
20	Does the fuse in the jumper open?	Go to Step 24	Go to Step 25
21	Test the Start Command circuit of the ECM for a high resistance or open. Did you find and correct the condition?	Go to Step 42	Go to Step 30

ARM66GC000000679

Fig. 10   Starter solenoid does not click (Part 3 of 6).
Bosch w/manual transmission

22	Test the Starter Relay coil supply voltage circuit for a high resistance or open. Did you find and correct the condition?	Go to Step 42	Go to Step 28
23	Test the clutch pedal position switch signal for a short to battery voltage. Did you find and correct the condition?	Go to Step 42	Go to Step 31
24	Test the supply voltage circuit of the starter solenoid for a short to ground. Did you find and correct the condition?	Go to Step 42	Go to Step 29
25	Test the supply voltage circuit of the starter solenoid for a high resistance or open. Did you find and correct the condition?	Go to Step 42	Go to Step 29
26	Inspect for poor connection at the Run/Crank Relay. Did you find and correct the condition?	Go to Step 42	Go to Step 36
27	Inspect for poor connection at the Starter Relay. Did you find and correct the condition?	Go to Step 42	Go to Step 37
28	Inspect for poor connection at the clutch switch. Did you find and correct the condition?	Go to Step 42	Go to Step 38
29	Inspect for poor connection at the starter solenoid. Did you find and correct the condition?	Go to Step 42	Go to Step 39

ARM66GC000000680

Fig. 10   Starter solenoid does not click (Part 4 of 6).
Bosch w/manual transmission

30	Inspect for poor connection at the ignition switch. Did you find and correct the condition?	Go to Step 42	Go to Step 40
31	Inspect for poor connection at the ECM. Did you find and correct the condition?	Go to Step 42	Go to Step 41
32	Repair the high resistance or open in the ignition 1 voltage circuit of the clutch switch. Did you complete the repair?	Go to Step 42	--
33	Repair the high resistance or open in the ignition 1 voltage circuit of the Run/Crank Relay coil. Did you complete the repair?	Go to Step 42	--
34	Repair the high resistance or open in the ground circuit of the Run/Crank Relay coil. Did you complete the repair?	Go to Step 42	--
35	Repair the high resistance or open in the control circuit of the Starter relay. Did you complete the repair?	Go to Step 42	--
36	Replace the Run/Crank relay. Did you complete the replacement?	Go to Step 42	--
37	Replace the Starter relay. Did you complete the replacement?	Go to Step 42	--
38	Replace the clutch switch. Did you complete the replacement?	Go to Step 42	--
39	Replace the starter. Did you complete the replacement?	Go to Step 42	--

ARM66GC000000681

Fig. 10   Starter solenoid does not click (Part 5 of 6).
Bosch w/manual transmission

Step	Action	Yes	No
40	Replace the ignition switch. / Did you complete the replacement?	Go to Step 42	--
41	Important: / Perform the set up procedures for the ECM. / Replace the ECM. / Did you complete the replacement?	Go to Step 42	--
42	Operate the system for which the symptom occurred. / Did you correct the condition?	System OK	Go to Step 2

ARM66GC000000682

Fig. 10   Starter solenoid does not click (Part 6 of 6). Bosch w/manual transmission

Step	Action	Yes	No
1	Did you perform the Diagnostic System Check for Engine Electrical?	Go to Step 2	Diagnostic System Check
2	Start the engine. / Does the starter operate normally?	Test for Intermittent and Poor Connections	Go to Step 3
3	Start the engine while listening to the starter motor turn. / Is there a loud "whoop", it may sound like a siren if the engine is revved while the starter is engaged, after the engine starts, but while the starter is still held in the engaged position?	Go to Step 6	Go to Step 4
4	Do you hear a "rumble", a "growl", or, in some cases, a "knock" as the starter is coasting down to a stop after starting the engine?	Go to Step 7	Go to Step 5
5	Important / This is often diagnosed as a starter drive gear hang-in or a weak solenoid. / When the engine is cranked, do you hear a high-pitched whine after the engine cranks and starts normally?	Go to Step 8	Go to Step 7

ARM66GC000000684

Fig. 12   Starter motor noise diagnosis (Part 1 of 2). Bosch

Step	Action	Yes	No
6	Inspect the flywheel ring gear for the following: • Chipped gear teeth • Missing gear teeth • Milled teeth / Is the flywheel bent, or does it have damaged teeth?	Go to Step 9	Go to Step 10
7	1. Remove the starter motor. / 2. Inspect the starter motor bushings and clutch gear. / Does the clutch gear have chipped or milled teeth or worn bushings?	Go to Step 10	Go to Step 9
8	Shim the starter motor away from the flywheel by adding shims between the starter motor and the engine block one at a time. / Flywheel runout may make this noise appear to be intermittent. / Did you complete the repair?	Go to Step 11	
9	Replace the flywheel. / Did you complete the replacement?	Go to Step 11	--
10	Replace the starter motor. / Did you complete the replacement?	Go to Step 11	--
11	Operate the system in order to verify the repair. / Did you correct the condition?	System OK	Go to Step 3

ARM66GC000000685

Fig. 12   Starter motor noise diagnosis (Part 2 of 2). Bosch

Step	Action	Yes	No
1	Did you perform the Diagnostic System Check for Engine Electrical?	Go to Step 2	Diagnostic System Check -
2	Turn the ignition to the START position. / Did the starter solenoid click?	Go to Step 3	Go to Starter Solenoid Does Not Click
3	Inspect the engine and belt drive system for mechanical binding, seized engine, seized generator. / Does the engine move freely?	Go to Step 4	Engine Will Not Crank - Crankshaft Will Not Rotate
4	Test the battery positive cable between the battery and the starter solenoid for high resistance. / Did you find and correct the condition?	Go to Step 8	Go to Step 5
5	Test the ground circuit between the battery and the starter motor for a high resistance. / Did you find and correct the condition?	Go to Step 8	Go to Step 6
6	Inspect for poor connections at the starter. / Did you find and correct the condition?	Go to Step 8	Go to Step 7
7	Replace the starter. / Did you complete the replacement?	Go to Step 8	--
8	Operate the system for which the symptom occurred. / Did you correct the condition?	System OK	Go to Step 2

ARM66GC000000683

Fig. 11   Starter solenoid clicks, engine does not crank. Bosch

Step	Action	Yes	No
1	Did you review following description and operations and perform the necessary inspections? / • Starting System Description and Operation	Go to Step 2	Symptoms
2	Turn the ignition to the START position. / Does the starter solenoid click?	Test for Intermittent and Poor Connections	Go to Step 3
3	Is the security indicator flashing?	Diagnostic Starting Point	Go to Step 4
4	1. Install a scan tool. / 2. With a scan tool, observe the Starter Switch parameter in the Engine Data list. / 3. Turn the ignition switch to the START position. / Does the scan tool display Cranking?	Go to Step 5	Go to Step 17
5	Does the vehicle have Theft Deterrent?	Go to Step 6	Go to Step 8
6	Turn the ignition to the START position. / Does the Starter Cut Relay click?	Go to Step 7	Go to Step 9
7	Turn the ignition to the START position. / Does the ST Relay click?	Go to Step 15	Go to Step 11
8	Turn the ignition to the START position. / Does the ST Relay click?	Go to Step 15	Go to Step 12
9	1. Turn OFF the ignition. / 2. Disconnect the Starter Cut Relay. / 3. Connect a test lamp between the crank voltage circuit of the Starter Cut Relay coil and ground. / 4. Turn the ignition to the START position. / Does the test lamp illuminate?	Go to Step 10	Go to Step 32

ARM66GC000000686

Fig. 13   Starter solenoid does not click (Part 1 of 6). Denso

			Yes	No
10	1. Connect a test lamp between the Starter Cut Relay coil and the control circuit of the Starter Cut Relay coil. 2. Turn the ignition to the START position. Does the test lamp illuminate?		Go to Step 25	Go to Step 22
11	1. Turn OFF the ignition. 2. Disconnect the ST Relay. 3. Connect a test lamp between the crank voltage circuit of the ST Relay coil and ground. 4. Turn the ignition to the START position. Does the test lamp illuminate?		Go to Step 13	Go to Step 14
12	1. Turn OFF the ignition. 2. Disconnect the ST Relay. 3. Connect a test lamp between the crank voltage circuit of the ST Relay coil and a good ground. 4. Turn the ignition to the START position. Does the test lamp illuminate?		Go to Step 13	Go to Step 33
13	1. Connect a test lamp between the crank voltage circuit of the ST Relay coil and the ground circuit of the ST Relay coil. 2. Turn the ignition to the START position. Does the test lamp illuminate?		Go to Step 26	Go to Step 34
14	1. Leaving the test lamp in place. 2. Turn OFF the ignition. 3. Disconnect the Starter Cut Relay. 4. Connect a 3 Amp fused jumper between the ignition voltage circuits of the Starter Cut Relay switch. 5. Turn the ignition to the START position. Does the test lamp illuminate?		Go to Step 25	Go to Step 35
15	1. Turn OFF the ignition. 2. Disconnect the ST Relay. 3. Connect a test lamp between the battery positive voltage circuit of the ST Relay switch and a good ground. Does the test lamp illuminate?		Go to Step 16	Go to Step 36
16	**Important** The engine may crank during this procedure. Connect a 30 amp fused jumper between the battery positive voltage circuit of the ST Relay switch and the starter solenoid crank voltage circuit. Does the engine crank?		Go to Step 26	Go to Step 23

ARM66GC000000687

Fig. 13 Starter solenoid does not click (Part 2 of 6). Denso

			Yes	No
17	Does the vehicle have an automatic transmission?		Go to Step 18	Go to Step 20
18	1. Turn OFF the ignition. 2. Disconnect the Park/Neutral Position (PNP) switch. 3. Connect a 10 Amp fused jumper between the crank voltage circuit and the starter solenoid crank voltage circuit of the PNP switch. 4. Turn the ignition to the START position. Does the engine crank?		Go to Step 27	Go to Step 19
19	1. Connect a test lamp between the crank voltage circuit of the PNP switch and ground. 2. Turn the ignition to the START position. Does the test lamp illuminate?		Go to Step 37	Go to Step 24
20	1. Turn OFF the ignition. 2. Disconnect the Clutch Pedal Position (CPP) switch. 3. Connect a 10 Amp fused jumper between the crank voltage circuit and the starter solenoid crank voltage circuit of the CPP switch. 4. Turn the ignition to the START position. Does the engine crank?		Go to Step 28	Go to Step 21
21	1. Connect a test lamp between the crank voltage circuit of the CPP switch and a good ground. 2. Turn the ignition to the START position. Does the test lamp illuminate?		Go to Step 38	Go to Step 24
22	Test the control circuit of the Starter Cut Relay coil for a high resistance or an open. Did you find and correct the condition?		Go to Step 46	Go to Step 31
23	Test the starter solenoid crank voltage circuit for a high resistance or an open. Did you find and correct the condition?		Go to Step 46	Go to Step 30
24	Test the crank voltage circuit of the PNP or CPP switch a high resistance or an open. Did you find and correct the condition?		Go to Step 46	Go to Step 29

ARM66GC000000688

Fig. 13 Starter solenoid does not click (Part 3 of 6). Denso

			Yes	No
25	Inspect for a poor connection at the Starter Cut Relay. Did you find and correct the condition?		Go to Step 46	Go to Step 39
26	Inspect for a poor connection at the ST Relay. Did you find and correct the condition?		Go to Step 46	Go to Step 40
27	Inspect for a poor connection at the PNP switch. Did you find and correct the condition?		Go to Step 46	Go to Step 41
28	Inspect for a poor connection at the CPP switch. Did you find and correct the condition?		Go to Step 46	Go to Step 42
29	Inspect for a poor connection at the ignition switch. Did you find and correct the condition?		Go to Step 46	Go to Step 43
30	Inspect for a poor connection at the starter solenoid. Did you find and correct the condition?		Go to Step 46	Go to Step 44
31	Inspect for a poor connection at the Theft Deterrent Module. Did you find and correct the condition?		Go to Step 46	Go to Step 45
32	Repair the high resistance or open in the crank voltage circuit of the Start Cut Relay between the Start Cut Relay and S111 for manual transmissions or SP108 for automatic transmissions. Did you complete the repair?		Go to Step 46	--
33	Repair the high resistance or open in the crank voltage circuit of the ST relay between the ST relay and S111 for manual transmissions or SP108 for automatic transmissions. Did you complete the repair?		Go to Step 46	

ARM66GC000000689

Fig. 13 Starter solenoid does not click (Part 4 of 6). Denso

			Yes	No
34	Repair the high resistance or open in the ground circuit of the ST Relay coil. Did you complete the repair?		Go to Step 46	--
35	Repair the high resistance or open in the crank voltage circuit of the ST Relay coil between the ST Relay and Starter Cut Relay. Did you complete the repair?		Go to Step 46	--
36	Repair the high resistance or open in the battery positive voltage circuit of the ST Relay switch. Did you complete the repair?		Go to Step 46	
37	Repair the high resistance or open in the starter solenoid crank voltage circuit between the PNP switch and S111. Did you complete the repair?		Go to Step 46	
38	Repair the high resistance or open in the starter solenoid crank voltage circuit between the CPP switch and SP108. Did you complete the repair?		Go to Step 46	
39	Replace the Starter Cut Relay. Did you complete the replacement?		Go to Step 46	
40	Replace the ST Relay. Did you complete the replacement?		Go to Step 46	
41	Replace the PNP switch. Did you complete the replacement?		Go to Step 46	
42	Replace the CPP switch. Did you complete the replacement?		Go to Step 46	--

ARM66GC000000690

Fig. 13 Starter solenoid does not click (Part 5 of 6). Denso

Step	Action	Yes	No
43	Replace the ignition switch. Did you complete the replacement?	Go to Step 46	--
44	Replace the starter. Did you complete the replacement?	Go to Step 46	--
45	Replace the Theft Deterrent Module. Did you complete the replacement?	Go to Step 46	--
46	Operate the system for which the symptom occurred. Did you correct the condition?	System OK	Go to Step 4

ARM66GC000000691

Fig. 13   Starter solenoid does not click (Part 6 of 6). Denso

Step	Action	Yes	No
1	Did you review the Diagnostic Starting Point for Engine Electrical and perform the necessary inspections?	Go to Step 2	Diagnostic Starting Point -
2	Start the engine. Does the starter operate normally?	Test for Intermittent and Poor Connections	Go to Step 3
3	Start the engine while listening to the starter motor turn. Is there a loud "whoop?" It may sound like a siren if the engine is revved while the starter is engaged, after the engine starts, but while the starter is still held in the engaged position.	Go to Step 6	Go to Step 4
4	Do you hear a "rumble", a "growl", or, in some cases, a "knock" as the starter is coasting down to a stop after starting the engine?	Go to Step 7	Go to Step 5
5	When the engine is cranked, do you hear a high-pitched whine after the engine cranks and starts normally? This is often diagnosed as a starter drive gear hang-in or a weak solenoid.	Go to Step 8	Go to Step 7
6	Inspect the flywheel ring gear for the following: • Chipped gear teeth • Missing gear teeth • Milled teeth Is the flywheel bent, or does it have damaged teeth?	Go to Step 9	Go to Step 10

ARM66GC000000693

Fig. 15   Starter motor diagnosis (Part 1 of 2). Denso

Step	Action	Yes	No
1	Did you review the following description and operations and perform the necessary inspections? • Starting System Description and Operation	Go to Step 2	Symptoms
2	Turn the ignition to the START position. Did the starter solenoid click?	Go to Step 3	Starter Solenoid Does Not Click
3	Inspect the engine and belt drive system for mechanical binding, seized engine, seized generator. Does the engine move freely?	Go to Step 4	Symptoms
4	Test the battery positive cable between the battery and the starter solenoid for high resistance. Did you find and correct the condition?	Go to Step 8	Go to Step 5
5	Test the ground circuit between the battery and the starter motor for a high resistance. Did you find and correct the condition?	Go to Step 8	Go to Step 6
6	Inspect for poor connections at the starter. Did you find and correct the condition?	Go to Step 8	Go to Step 7
7	Replace the Starter. Did you complete the replacement?	Go to Step 8	--
8	Operate the system for which the symptom occurred. Did you correct the condition?	System OK	Go to Step 3

ARM66GC000000692

Fig. 14   Starter solenoid clicks, engine does not crank. Denso

Step	Action	Yes	No
7	1. Remove the starter motor. 2. Inspect the starter motor bushings and clutch gear. Does the clutch gear have chipped or milled teeth or worn bushings?	Go to Step 10	Go to Step 9
8	Shim the starter motor away from the flywheel by adding shims between the starter motor and the engine block one at a time. Flywheel runout may make this noise appear to be intermittent. Did you complete the repair?	Go to Step 11	--
9	Replace the flywheel. Did you complete the replacement?	Go to Step 11	--
10	Replace the starter motor. Did you complete the replacement?	Go to Step 11	--
11	Operate the system in order to verify the repair. Did you correct the condition?	System OK	Go to Step 3

ARM66GC000000694

Fig. 15   Starter motor diagnosis (Part 2 of 2). Denso

STARTER SPECIFICATIONS

Starter Identifica-tion No.	Free Speed Test			Solenoid	
	Amps	Volts	RPM	Hold-In Windings, Amps	Pull-In Windings, Amps
Bosch	—	—	—	—	—
Denso	90	11.5	—	—	—
PG-260D	60–120	10.0	2900–3400	—	—
PG-260 F1	40–90	12.0	3200–4800	6–12	30–45
PG-260 F2	35–85	12.0	2550–4150	6–12	30–45
PG-260G	60–96	11.5	2925–3375	6–12	30–45
PG-260M	60–96	11.5	2925–3375	6–12	30–45

Mitsubishi Starters

NOTE: On Air Bag Equipped Models, Refer To "Air Bag System Precautions" Located In The Front Of This Manual For System Disarming & Arming Procedures.

NOTE: Refer To "Computer Relearn Procedures" Located In The Front Of This Manual When Battery Power To The Computer Has Been Interrupted.

INDEX

	Page No.
Description	18-13
Diagnosis & Testing	18-14
Precautions	18-13
Air Bag Systems	18-13
Battery Ground Cable	18-13
Starter Specifications	18-16

	Page No.
Troubleshooting	18-13
Slow Or Not Cranking	18-13
Lamps Dim	18-13
Lamps Go Out	18-13
Lamps Stay Bright, No Cranking Action	18-13

	Page No.
Solenoid Switches	18-14
Starter Drive Problems	18-14
Drive Clutch Failure	18-14
Drive Failure	18-14

PRECAUTIONS

Air Bag Systems

Refer to "Air Bag System Precautions" in the front of this manual for system disarming and arming procedures.

Battery Ground Cable

Prior to service, disconnect battery ground cable and isolate as required.

DESCRIPTION

Mitsubishi starters, **Figs. 1 and 2,** are either conventional or reduction gear types. The conventional type used on manual transmissions consists of a frame and field assembly, an armature assembly, an overrunning clutch assembly, a starter solenoid assembly, a commutator end housing, a brush holder and a shift lever. The reduction gear type starters used on automatic transmissions use all of the above components along with a reduction gear and shock absorber assembly.

TROUBLESHOOTING

Slow Or Not Cranking

1. Turn headlamps On.
2. Ensure headlamps are burning with normal intensity.
3. If headlamps are burning dim, inspect battery charge condition, then charge as required.
4. If battery is fully charged, operate starter motor.
5. Note whether headlamps go out, dim considerably, or stay bright without starter activating.
6. Refer to the following diagnostic procedures as applicable.

LAMPS GO OUT

If the lamps go out as the starter switch is closed, it indicates a poor connection between the battery and starter motor.
1. Inspect battery terminals.
2. If corroded, remove, clean and reinstall.
3. Apply corrosion inhibitor to terminals to retard formation of corrosion.

LAMPS DIM

If the lamps dim considerably as the starter switch is closed and the starter operates slowly or not at all, perform the following:
1. Inspect for a discharged battery, recharge or replace as required.
2. If battery is fully charged, inspect engine or starter motor.
3. Inspect engine for tight bearings, pistons, or other components.
4. Inspect engine timing, adjust as required.
5. Inspect for heavy engine oil. Low temperatures thicken engine oil and add considerable load to starting system.
6. Inspect starter motor for bent armature, loose pole screws, or worn bearings.
7. Inspect for thrown armature windings or commutator bars.

LAMPS STAY BRIGHT, NO CRANKING ACTION

Inspect for an open circuit in the starter, the starter switch or control circuit.
1. Place a heavy jumper lead across solenoid main terminals.

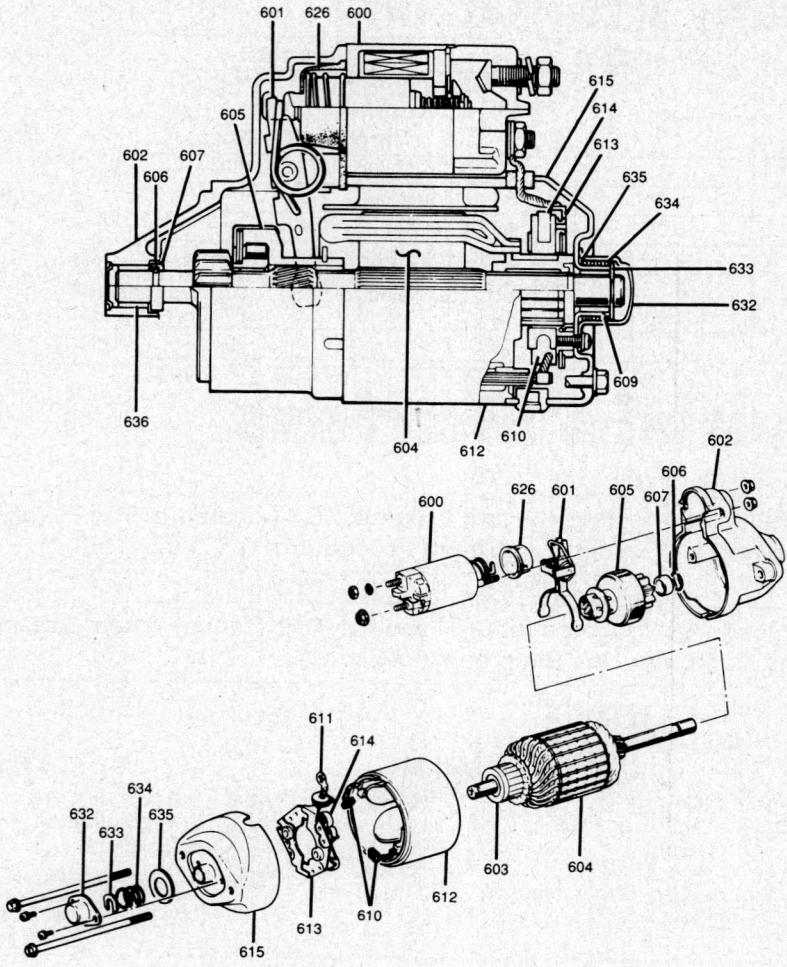

600	SOLENOID	607	ARMATURE STOP RING	615	COMMUTATOR END COVER
601	PINION DRIVE LEVER	609	COMMUTATOR END BUSHING	626	BOOT
602	DRIVE HOUSING	610	BRUSHES	632	COMMUTATOR END CAP
603	COMMUTATOR END	611	FIELD COIL LEAD WIRE	633	ARMATURE PLATE
604	ARMATURE	612	YOKE	634	ARMATURE BRAKE SPRING
605	OVERRUNNING CLUTCH ASSEMBLY	613	BRUSH HOLDER	635	END CAP GASKET
606	ARMATURE RETAINING RING	614	BRUSH SPRINGS	636	DRIVE HOUSING BUSHING

GC1129100033000X

Fig. 1 Exploded view of starter motor. Conventional w/manual transaxle

2. Starter should engage and operate.
3. If starter fails to perform as indicated, remove and inspect starter.

Starter Drive Problems

If the starter does not turn over or if it drags, inspect the starter or electrical supply system. If the starter is noisy, if it turns but does not engage the engine, or if the starter will not disengage after the engine is started, inspect for the following:
1. Worn or chipped ring gear or starter pinion.
2. Improper pinion clearance.
3. Bent starter armature shaft. Maximum radial runout is .003 inch.

DRIVE CLUTCH FAILURE

The overrunning clutch is directly activated by a fork and lever. If the overrunning clutch will not turn engine over, inspect for worn out overrunning clutch. Proper meshing of the pinion is controlled by the end clearance between the pinion gear and the starter housing or pinion stop, if used.
1. Inspect and adjust pinion clearance (if applicable).
2. If pinion clearance is not adjustable, remove starter and inspect for excessive wear of solenoid linkage, shift lever mechanism, or improper assembly of components.
3. Inspect overrunning clutch for signs of overheating.
4. If clutch shows signs of overheating

(bluish color), inspect for rust or gum buildup between armature shaft and drive or for burred splines.
5. Clean or deburr splines as required.
6. Overrunning clutches are not serviceable. Replace as required.

DRIVE FAILURE

If a Bendix type drive does not engage, inspect the following:
1. Inspect for a broken drive spring, or for sheared drive spring bolts.
2. If spring is broken, or spring bolts are sheared off, remove drive and replace damaged components.
3. Inspect for screw shaft.
4. If screw shaft threads are gummed or rusty, clean with kerosene or steel wool.
5. Ensure flywheel has adequate ventilation. Inspect breather hole in bottom of flywheel housing and clean if required.
6. If screw shaft threads are clean and rust free, look for mechanical failure within the drive itself.

Solenoid Switches

The solenoid switch on a cranking motor closes the circuit between the battery and the cranking motor and also shifts the drive pinion into mesh with the engine flywheel ring gear. This is done by means of a linkage between the solenoid switch plunger and the shift lever on the cranking motor.

There are two windings in the solenoid: a pull-in and a hold-in. Both windings are energized when the external control switch is closed. They produce a magnetic field which pulls the plunger in so that the drive pinion is shifted into mesh, and the main contacts in the solenoid switch are closed to connect the battery directly to the cranking motor. Closing the main switch contacts shorts out the pull-in winding since this winding is connected across the main contacts. The magnetism produced by the hold-in winding is sufficient to hold the plunger in, and shorting out the pull-in winding reduces battery drain. When the control switch is opened, it disconnects the hold-in winding from the battery. When the hold-in winding is disconnected from the battery, the shift lever spring withdraws the plunger from the solenoid, opening the solenoid switch contacts and at the same time withdrawing the drive pinion from mesh. Proper operation of the switch depends on maintaining a definite balance between the magnetic strength of the pull-in and hold-in windings.

This balance is determined by the size of the wire and the number of turns specified. An open circuit in the hold-in winding or attempts to crank with a discharged battery will cause the switch to chatter.

DIAGNOSIS & TESTING

Refer to **Figs. 3 and 4** when performing diagnostic testing procedures on these starter motors.

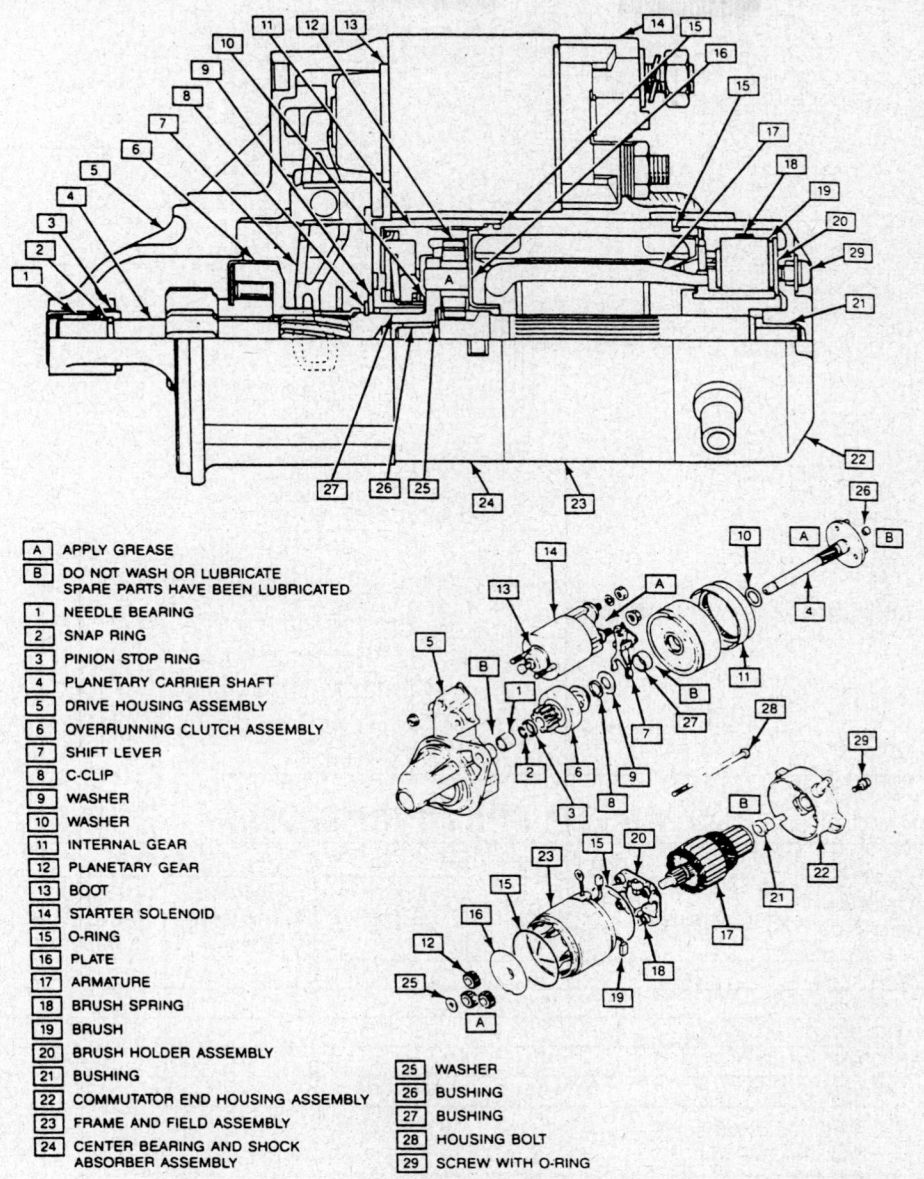

A	APPLY GREASE
B	DO NOT WASH OR LUBRICATE SPARE PARTS HAVE BEEN LUBRICATED
1	NEEDLE BEARING
2	SNAP RING
3	PINION STOP RING
4	PLANETARY CARRIER SHAFT
5	DRIVE HOUSING ASSEMBLY
6	OVERRUNNING CLUTCH ASSEMBLY
7	SHIFT LEVER
8	C-CLIP
9	WASHER
10	WASHER
11	INTERNAL GEAR
12	PLANETARY GEAR
13	BOOT
14	STARTER SOLENOID
15	O-RING
16	PLATE
17	ARMATURE
18	BRUSH SPRING
19	BRUSH
20	BRUSH HOLDER ASSEMBLY
21	BUSHING
22	COMMUTATOR END HOUSING ASSEMBLY
23	FRAME AND FIELD ASSEMBLY
24	CENTER BEARING AND SHOCK ABSORBER ASSEMBLY
25	WASHER
26	BUSHING
27	BUSHING
28	HOUSING BOLT
29	SCREW WITH O-RING

GC1129100034000X

Fig. 2 Exploded view of starter motor. Reduction w/automatic transaxle

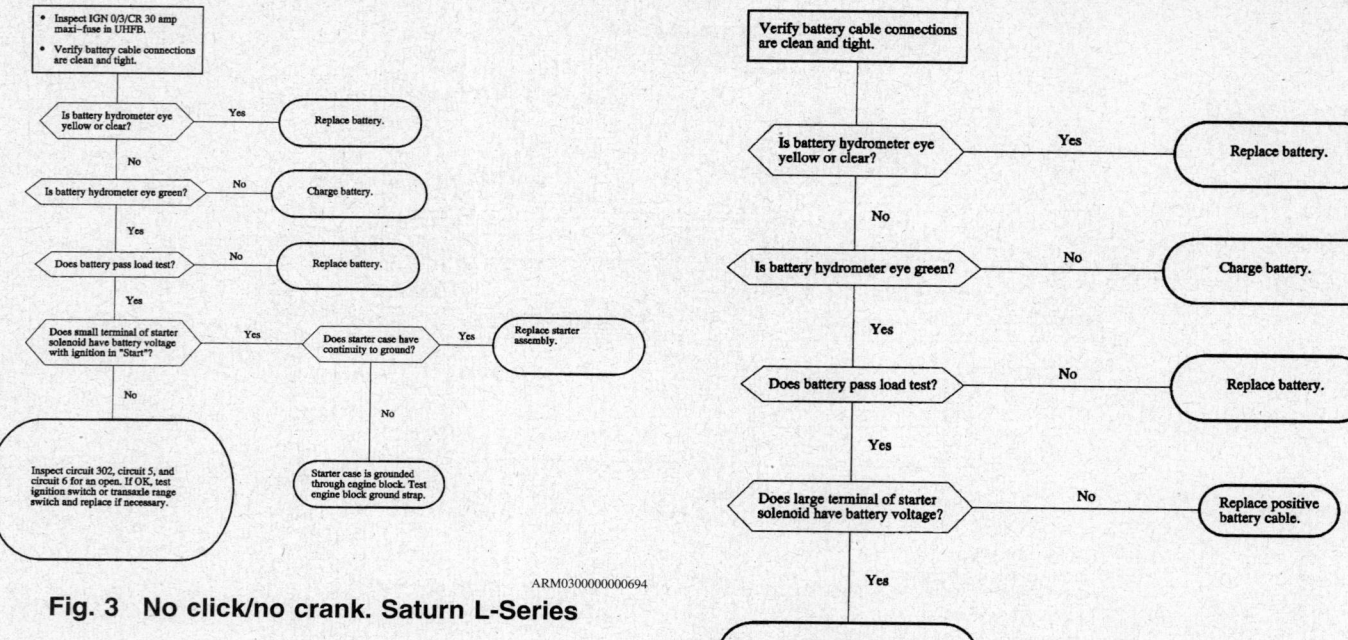

Fig. 3   No click/no crank. Saturn L-Series

ARM0300000000694

Fig. 4   Click/no crank. Saturn L-Series

ARM0300000000695

STARTER SPECIFICATIONS

Starter Identification No.	Free Speed Test			Solenoid	
	Amps	Volts	RPM	Hold-In Windings, Amps	Pull-In Windings, Amps
30005925①	75	11.0	—	—	—
30005226②	60	11.0	—	—	—
30005563②	60	11.0	—	—	—
90542967	—	—	—	—	—
94857220	90	11.5	3000	—	—

① — Automatic transaxle.
② — Manual transaxle.

ALTERNATORS

TABLE OF CONTENTS

Page No.

APPLICATION CHART 19-1
BOSCH ALTERNATORS 19-6
DELPHI ALTERNATORS 19-2

Page No.

DENSO & MITSUBISHI
ALTERNATORS 19-9
HITACHI ALTERNATORS 19-21
VALEO ALTERNATORS 19-15

Application Chart

Model	Year	Manufacturer
BUICK		
Century	2004–05	Delphi
LaCrosse	2005–07	Bosch
	2008	Bosch/Denso
LeSabre	2004–05	Delphi
Lucerne	2006–08	Denso
Park Avenue	2004–05	Delphi
Regal	2004	Delphi
CADILLAC		
CTS	2004–08	Denso
DeVille	2004–05	Denso
DTS	2006–08	Denso
Seville	2004	Denso
STS	2005–08	Denso
XLR	2004–08	Hitachi
CHEVROLET		
Aveo	2005–08	Delphi
Cavalier	2004–05	Valeo
Cobalt	2006–08	Denso
Corvette	2004–08	Valeo
Impala	2004–05	Bosch/Delphi
	2006–08	Bosch/Denso
Malibu	2004–07	Valeo
Malibu Classic	2008	Valeo
Malibu Maxx	2004–07	Valeo
Monte Carlo	2004–05	Bosch/Delphi
	2006–07	Bosch/Denso
OLDSMOBILE		
Alero	2004	Valeo
PONTIAC		
Bonneville	2004–05	Delphi
Grand Am	2004–05	Valeo
Grand Prix	2004	Delphi
	2005–08	Bosch/Denso
GTO	2004–06	Mitsubishi
G5	2007–08	Denso
G6	2005–08	Valeo/Denso
Solstice	2006–08	Valeo
Sunfire	2004–05	Valeo
Vibe	2004–08	Denso
SATURN		
AURA	2007–08	Denso/Valeo

Continued

Model	Year	Manufacturer
SATURN		
ION	2004–07	Denso/Valeo
L-Series	2004–05	Valeo
SKY	2007–08	Valeo

Delphi Alternators

NOTE: On Air Bag Equipped Models, Refer To "Air Bag System Precautions" Located In The Front Of This Manual For System Disarming & Arming Procedures.

NOTE: Refer To "Computer Relearn Procedure" Located In The Front Of This Manual When Battery Power To The Computer Has Been Interrupted.

INDEX

	Page No.		Page No.		Page No.
Alternator Specifications	19-5	Diagnosis & Testing	19-4	Precautions	19-2
Application Chart	19-2	Bench Testing	19-4	Air Bag Systems	19-2
Description	19-3	In-Vehicle Test	19-4	Battery Ground Cable	19-2
AD Alternators	19-3	General Information	19-3	Charging System	19-2
CS Alternators	19-3	Diode Rectifiers	19-3	System Operation	19-3

APPLICATION CHART

Model	Year	Model
BUICK		
Century	2004–05	AD230
LeSabre	2004–05	AD230
Park Avenue	2004–05	①
Regal	2004	AD230
CHEVROLET		
Aveo	2005–08	CS-121D
Impala	2004–05	AD230
Monte Carlo	2004–05	AD230
PONTIAC		
Bonneville	2004–05	①
Grand Am	2004–05	CS130D
Grand Prix	2004	CS130D

① — VIN K engine AD230; VIN 1 engine AD237.

PRECAUTIONS

Air Bag Systems

Refer to "Air Bag System Precautions" in the front of this manual for system disarming and arming procedures.

Battery Ground Cable

Prior to service, disconnect battery ground cable and isolate as required.

Charging System

1. Ensure battery polarity is proper when servicing units. Reversed battery polarity will damage rectifiers and regulators.
2. If booster battery is used for starting, use proper polarity in hookup.
3. When a fast charger is used to charge a vehicle battery, vehicle battery cables should be disconnected unless fast charger is equipped with a special Alternator Protector, in which case vehicle battery cables need not be disconnected. **Fast chargers should never be used to start a vehicle as rectifier damage will result.**
4. Unless this system includes a load relay or field relay, grounding alternator output terminal will damage alternator and/or circuits. This is true even when system is not in operation since no circuit breaker is used and battery is applied to alternator output terminal at all times. Field or load relay acts as a circuit breaker in that it is controlled by ignition switch.
5. Before making any on vehicle tests of alternator or regulator, battery should be inspected and circuit inspected for faulty wiring or insulation. loose or corroded connections and poor ground circuits.
6. Inspect alternator belt tension and condition.
7. Ignition should be Off and battery ground cable disconnected before making any test connections to prevent system damage.
8. Do not reverse connections to alternator.
9. Do not short across or ground any of

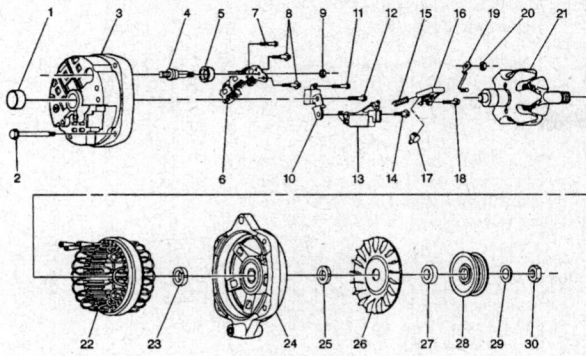

(1) Generator Rotor Slip Ring End Frame Bearing
(2) Generator Through Bolt
(3) Generator Slip Ring End Frame
(4) Generator Battery Terminal Stud
(5) Generator Battery Terminal Sleeve
(6) Generator Rectifier Bridge
(7) Generator Rectifier Bridge Bolt
(8) Generator Rectifier Bridge Bolt (Insulated)
(9) Generator Battery Terminal Nut
(10) Generator Capacitor
(11) Generator Rectifier Bridge Bolt
(12) Generator Capacitor/Rectifier Bolt (Insulated)
(13) Generator Voltage Regulator
(14) Generator Voltage Regulator Attaching Bolt (Insulated)
(15) Generator Brush Spring
(16) Generator Brush Holder
(17) Dust Shield
(18) Generator Brush Holder Bolt
(19) Generator Voltage Regulator Connector Strap
(20) Generator Stator Lead Attaching Nut
(21) Generator Rotor
(22) Generator Stator
(23) Generator Rotor Drive End Bearing Inside Collar
(24) Generator Rotor Drive End Bearing Frame
(25) Generator Rotor Drive End Bearing Outside Collar
(26) Generator Fan
(27) Generator Rotor Drive End Fan Collar
(28) Generator Pulley
(29) Generator Rotor Shaft Drive End Washer
(30) Generator Rotor Shaft Drive End Nut

GC1129700090000X

Fig. 1   Exploded view of CS type alternator

Step	Action	Value (s)	Yes	No
1	Did you perform the Diagnostic System Check for Engine Electrical?	--	Go to Step 2	Go to Diagnostic System Check -
2	Start the engine, observe the charge indicator on the instrument cluster (IPC) or message in the driver information center (DIC). Does the charge indicator illuminate or the DIC display a charging system message?	--	Go to Step 3	Test for Intermittent and Poor Connections
3	**Important** The green POWER lamp of the tester should remain illuminated while the tester is being used. 1. Turn OFF the ignition. 2. Connect the red lead of the J 41450-B Generator Electronic Tester to the generator output terminal. 3. Connect the black lead of the J 41450-B Generator Electronic Tester to the metal generator housing. Does the green POWER lamp on the tester illuminate?	--	Go to Step 6	Go to Step 4
4	Measure the voltage from the output terminal of the generator to the generator metal housing. Does the voltage measure equal to the specified value?	B +	Go to Step 14	Go to Step 5

ARM66GC000000730

Fig. 2   Charging system test (Part 1 of 4)

terminals in charging system.

10. Never disconnect output terminal while alternator is running.
11. Vehicle battery must be fully charged when testing charging system.

GENERAL INFORMATION

Alternators are composed of the same functional components as the conventional DC alternator but they operate differently. The field is called a rotor and is the turning portion of the unit. The generating part, called a stator, is the stationary member, comparable to the armature in a DC alternator. The regulator, similar to those used in a DC system, regulates the alternator-rectifier system output.

The power source of the system is the alternator. Current is transmitted from the field terminal of the regulator through a slip ring to the field coil and back to ground through another slip ring. The strength of the field regulates the output of the alternating current. This alternating current is then transmitted from the alternator to the rectifier where it is converted to direct current.

These alternators employ a three-phase stator winding in which the phase windings are electrically 120° apart. The rotor consists of a field coil encased between interleaved sections producing. When the rotor is energized, a magnetic field with alternate north and south poles is created. By rotating the rotor inside the stator the alternating current is induced in the stator windings. This alternating current is rectified (changed to DC) by silicon diodes and brought out to the output terminal of the alternator.

Diode Rectifiers

Six silicon diode rectifiers are used and act as electrical one-way valves. Three of the diodes have ground polarity and are pressed or screwed into a heat sink which is grounded. The other three diodes (ungrounded) are pressed or screwed into and insulated from the end head; these diodes are connected to the alternator output terminal.

Since the diodes have a high resistance to the flow of current in one direction and a low resistance in the opposite direction, they may be connected in a manner which allows current to flow from the alternator to the battery in the low resistance direction. The high resistance in the opposite direction prevents the flow of current from the battery to the alternator. Because of this feature no circuit breaker is required between the alternator and battery.

DESCRIPTION
CS Alternators

The CS alternator is available in two sizes: CS130 and CS144, **Fig. 1**. The numerals denote the outer diameter of the stator laminations in millimeters and the letters CS stand for charging system.

These alternators use a conventional fan mounted next to the pulley to pull air through the assembly for cooling. An internal fan mounted on the rotor pulls air through the slip ring end frame to cool the rectifier, bridge and regulator. Air is expelled through openings in the frame. No periodic maintenance is required.

AD Alternators

The AD alternators are similar to CS type alternators except for their dual cooling fans. The "AD" stands for Air-Cooled Dual internal fan. The "2" is an electric design designator. The "30" or "37" denotes the outside diameter of the stator laminations in millimeters.

SYSTEM OPERATION

The AD and CS alternators may be used with only two connections. The battery positive BAT terminal must be connected to a battery during operation. The second required connection is through the Powertrain Control Module (PCM) to the indicator lamp. Three other regulator terminals are available for optional use in vehicle systems. The P terminal is connected to the stator and may be connected to a tachometer or other device. The F terminal is connected internally to field positive and may be used as a fault indicator. The S terminal may be connected externally to a voltage, such as battery voltage, to sense voltage to be controlled.

The regulator voltage setting varies with temperature, and limits system voltage by controlling rotor field current. Unlike others regulators, this regulator switches field current on and off at a fixed frequency of about 400 cycles per second. By varying on–off time, proper average field current is obtained to provide proper system voltage. At high speeds, the on time may be 10% and off time 90%. At low speeds with high electrical loads, on–off time may be 90% and 10% respectively.

5	Measure the voltage from the output terminal of the generator to the battery negative terminal. Does the voltage measure equal to the specified value?	B +	Go to Step 12	Go to Step 11
6	**Caution** **Make sure that the load is completely turned off before connecting or disconnecting a carbon pile load tester to the battery. Otherwise, sparking could ignite battery gasses which are extremely flammable and may explode violently.** 1. Connect a carbon pile tester to the vehicle. **Important** **Be sure all of generator output circuit wires pass through the inductive probe.** 2. Connect an inductive ammeter to the output circuit of the generator. 3. Disconnect the generator harness connector. 4. Locate the matching harness connector on the J 41450-B and connect it to the generator. Does the red DIAGNOSTIC lamp on the tester illuminate?	--	Go to Step 7	Go to Step 13
7	1. Start the engine and allow it to idle for 30 seconds. 2. Increase the engine speed to 2500 RPM. Does the red DIAGNOSTIC lamp on the tester illuminate?	--	Go to Step 15	Go to Step 8

ARM66GC000000731

Fig. 2   Charging system test (Part 2 of 4)

DIAGNOSIS & TESTING

In-Vehicle Test

Refer to **Fig. 2** for in-vehicle charging system test on these alternators.

Bench Testing

1. Make connections as illustrated, **Fig. 3**, but leave carbon pile disconnected. Ground polarity of alternator and battery must be same. Battery must be fully charged. Use a 30-500 ohm resistor between battery and L terminal.
2. Slowly increase alternator speed and observe voltage.
3. If voltage is uncontrolled and increases above 16 volts, rotor field is shorted, regulator is faulty or both. A shorted rotor field can cause regulator to become faulty. **Battery must be fully charged when making this test.**
4. If voltage is below 16 volts, increase speed and adjust carbon pile obtain maximum amperage output, maintain voltage above 13 volts.
5. If output is within 15 amps of rated output, alternator is satisfactory.
6. If output is not within 15 amps of rated output, alternator is faulty and requires repair.

8	1. Maintain the engine speed at 2500 RPM. **Important** If the generator is not capable of producing the Load Test amps, operate the generator at it's maximum possible output. 2. Turn ON the load of the carbon pile tester and increase the load until the generator output is greater than or equal to the load test value given in Generator Usage . Does the red DIAGNOSTIC lamp on the tester illuminate?	--	Go to Step 15	Go to Step 9
9	1. Maintain the engine speed at 2500 RPM and continue to operate the generator at the load test value. 2. Measure the voltage drop from the output terminal of the generator to the positive terminal on the battery. Does the voltage measure greater than the specified value?	0.5 V	Go to Step 11	Go to Step 10
10	1. Maintain the engine speed at 2500 RPM and continue to operate the generator at the load test value. 2. Measure the voltage drop from the battery negative terminal to the metal housing of the generator. Does the voltage measure greater than the specified value?	0.5 V	Go to Step 12	Go to Step 16
11	Repair the high resistance or an open in the output circuit of the generator. Did you complete the repair?	--	Go to Step 16	--

ARM66GC000000732

Fig. 2   Charging system test (Part 3 of 4)

12	Repair the high resistance or open in the ground circuit of the generator. Did you complete the repair?	--	Go to Step 16	--
13	1. Disconnect the J 41450-B tester harness connector from the generator, but leave the alligator clips connected so that the green POWER lamp remains illuminated. 2. Connect a jumper lead, with an in-line 100-ohm resistor between the J 41450-B tester harness connector terminal B and a good ground. Does the red DIAGNOSTIC lamp illuminate?	--	Go to Step 15	Go to Step 14
14	There is a problem with the J 41450-B . Refer to the manufacturers instructions, how to test the J 41450-B for proper operation. Has the J 41450-B tester been replaced?	--	Go to Step 3	--
15	Replace the generator. Did you complete the replacement?	--	Go to Step 16	--
16	Operate the vehicle in order to verify the repair. Did you correct the condition?	--	System OK	Go to Step 2

ARM66GC000000733

Fig. 2   Charging system test (Part 4 of 4)

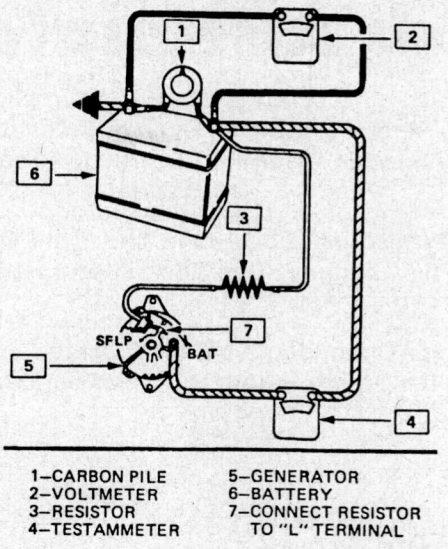

1—CARBON PILE   5—GENERATOR
2—VOLTMETER   6—BATTERY
3—RESISTOR   7—CONNECT RESISTOR
4—TESTAMMETER   TO "L" TERMINAL

GC1129100038000X

**Fig. 3   Alternator bench
inspection**

ALTERNATOR SPECIFICATIONS

Alternator Model	Rated Hot Output Amps
AD230	105
AD237	125
CS121D	75/85
CS130	105
CS130D	105
CS130 DIF	105
CS130DP	107
CS144①	124
CS144②	150

① — Except service part identification code KG9.

② — Service part identification code KG9.

Bosch Alternators

NOTE: On Air Bag Equipped Models, Refer To "Air Bag System Precautions" Located In The Front Of This Manual For System Disarming & Arming Procedures.

NOTE: Refer To "Computer Relearn Procedure" Located In The Front Of This Manual When Battery Power To The Computer Has Been Interrupted.

NOTE: "Electrical Symbol & Wire Color Code Identification" Located In The Front Of This Manual May Be Used As An Aid When Using Wiring Circuits Found In This Section.

INDEX

	Page No.		Page No.		Page No.
Alternator Specifications	19-8	Diagnosis & Testing	19-6	Battery Ground Cable	19-6
Application Chart	19-6	General Information	19-6	Charging System	19-6
Description	19-6	Precautions	19-6		
System Operation	19-6	Air Bag Systems	19-6		

APPLICATION CHART

Model	Year	Rated Hot Output Amps
Grand Prix	2005–08	125
Impala	2004–08	125
LaCrosse	2005–08	125
Monte Carlo	2004–07	125

GENERAL INFORMATION

Refer to "Delphi Alternators" for general information.

PRECAUTIONS

Air Bag Systems

Refer to "Air Bag System Precautions" in the front of this manual for system disarming and arming procedures.

Battery Ground Cable

Prior to service, disconnect battery ground cable and isolate as required.

Charging System

1. Ensure battery polarity is proper when servicing units. Reversed battery polarity will damage rectifiers and regulators.
2. If booster battery is used for starting, use proper polarity in hookup.
3. When a fast charger is used to charge a vehicle battery, vehicle battery cables should be disconnected unless fast charger is equipped with a special Alternator Protector, in which case vehicle battery cables need not be disconnected. **Fast chargers should never be used to start a vehicle as rectifier damage will result.**
4. Unless system includes a load relay or field relay, grounding alternator output terminal will damage alternator and/or circuits. This is true even when system is not in operation since no circuit breaker is used and battery is applied to alternator output terminal at all times. Field or load relay acts as a circuit breaker in that it is controlled by ignition switch.
5. Before making any on vehicle tests of alternator or regulator, battery should be inspected and circuit inspected for faulty wiring or insulation. loose or corroded connections and poor ground circuits.
6. Inspect alternator belt tension and condition.
7. Ignition should be Off and battery ground cable disconnected before making any test connections to prevent damage to system.
8. Do not reverse connections to alternator.
9. Do not short across or ground any of terminals in charging system.
10. Never disconnect output terminal while alternator is running.
11. Vehicle battery must be fully charged when testing charging system.

DESCRIPTION

The Bosch alternator is a 125 amp output alternator. The main components are the rotor, field coil, rectifier bridge and a digital regulator.

System Operation

A regulator supplies current to the field coil of the rotor. When the field coil is supplied with voltage, a magnetic field is created. As the rotor turns, this magnetic field creates AC voltage and current in the stator windings. The AC voltage and current is converted to DC by a rectifier bridge which is available to the vehicle's electrical system.

DIAGNOSIS & TESTING

Refer to wiring diagram **Figs. 1 through 3** and diagnosis charts, **Fig. 4** for charging system diagnosis.

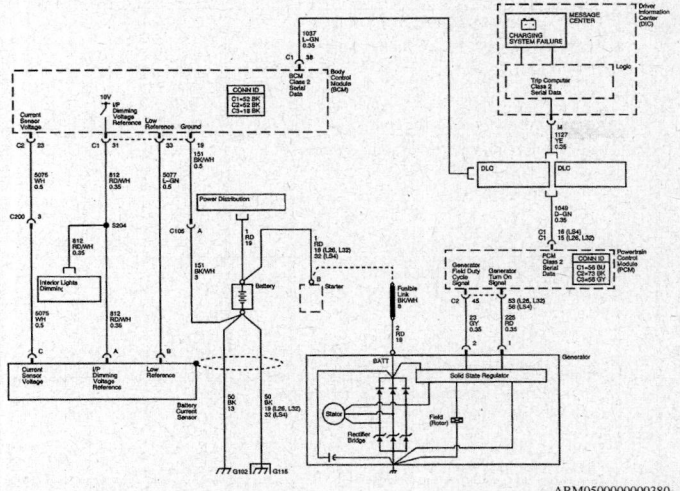

Fig. 1   Charging system wiring diagram. Grand Prix

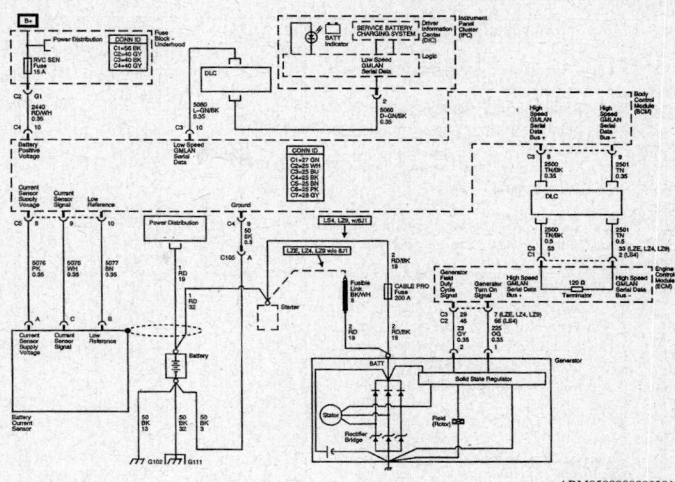

Fig. 2   Charging system wiring diagram. Impala & Monte Carlo

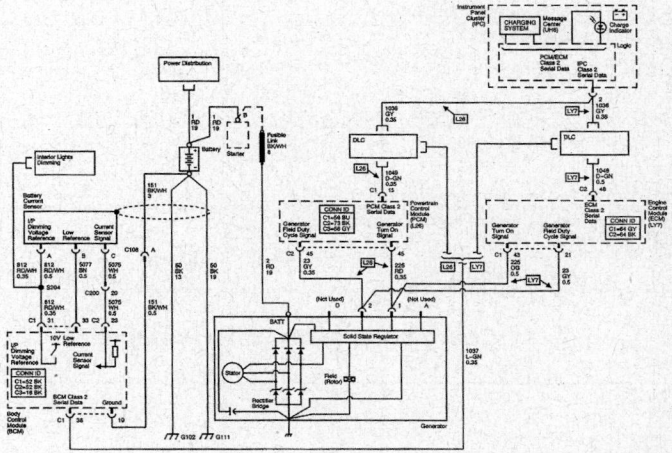

Fig. 3   Charging system wiring diagram. LaCrosse

Step	Action	Value (s)	Yes	No
1	Did you perform the Diagnostic System Check for Engine Electrical?	--	Go to Step 2	Go to Diagnostic System Check - Step 2
2	**Important** The battery must be above a 70 percent state of charge. Did you perform the Battery Inspection Test?	--	Go to Step 3	Battery Inspection/Test
3	1. Install a scan tool. 2. Start the engine. 3. With a scan tool, command the GEN-L Terminal OFF and ON. 4. Observe the Ignition 1 Signal parameter. Does the voltage change with each command?	--	Go to Step 4	Go to Step 8
4	1. Turn ON the following accessories: ○ Headlights (high beams) ○ A/C on Max ○ Blower fan (on high) ○ Heated seats (if equipped) 2. With a scan tool, observe the ignition 1 signal parameter in the engine data list. 3. Increase engine speed to 2,500 RPM. Is the voltage within the specified value?	12.0-15.5 V	Go to Step 5	Go to Step 6

Fig. 4   Charging system test, (Part 1 of 4)

	1. Turn OFF all accessories. 2. Turn OFF the Ignition. **Caution** Make sure that the load is completely turned off before connecting or disconnecting a carbon pile load tester to the battery. Otherwise, sparking could ignite battery gasses which are extremely flammable and may explode violently. 3. Connect a carbon pile tester to the vehicle. **Important**		
5	When measuring generator output current, be sure the inductive probe encircles the generator output wire. 4. Connect an inductive ammeter probe to the output circuit of the generator. 5. Start the engine. 6. With a scan tool, command the GEN-L Terminal ON. 7. Increase engine speed to 2,500 RPM. 8. Adjust the carbon pile as necessary in order to obtain the maximum current output. Is the generator output greater than or equal to the load test value as specified in Generator Usage ?	Generator OK	Go to Step 7
6	Is the voltage measured greater than 15.5 volts?	--	Go to Step 12	Go to Step 7
7	1. Leave the vehicle accessories ON or maintain load test value. 2. Maintain engine speed at 2,500 RPM. 3. Measure the voltage between the generator output terminal and the generator metal housing. Is the voltage measured equal to the specified value?	battery voltage	Go to Step 14	Go to Step 9

Fig. 4   Charging system test, (Part 2 of 4)

Step	Action	Value	Yes	No
8	1. Turn ON the ignition, with the engine OFF. 2. Disconnect the generator harness connector. 3. Measure the voltage between the generator turn on signal circuit and ground. 4. With a scan tool, command the GEN-L Terminal ON and OFF. Does the voltage measure greater than the first value ON and near the second value OFF?	4.7 V 0 V	Go to Step 14	Go to Step 11
9	1. Maintain the engine speed at 2500 RPM and continue to operate the generator at the load test value. 2. Measure the voltage drop from the battery negative terminal to the metal housing of the generator. Is the voltage measured less than the specified value?	0.5 V	Go to Step 10	Go to Step 15
10	1. Maintain the engine speed at 2500 RPM and continue to operate the generator at the load test value. 2. Measure the voltage drop from the output terminal of the generator to the positive terminal on the battery. Is the voltage measured less than the specified value?	0.5 V	Go to Step 14	Go to Step 16
11	Test the generator turn on signal circuit for a short, or open. Did you find and correct the condition?	--	Go to Step 19	Go to Step 13

ARM66GC000000726

Fig. 4   Charging system test, (Part 3 of 4)

Step	Action	Value	Yes	No
12	Test the generator battery voltage sense circuit, if equipped, for an open or high resistance. Did you find and correct the condition?	--	Go to Step 19	Go to Step 14
13	Inspect for poor connections at the harness connector of the PCM. Did you find and correct the condition?	--	Go to Step 19	Go to Step 17
14	Inspect for poor connections at the generator. Did you find and correct the condition?	--	Go to Step 19	Go to Step 18
15	Repair the high resistance or open in the ground circuit of the generator. Did you complete the repair?	--	Go to Step 19	--
16	Repair the high resistance or open in the generator output circuit. Did you complete the repair?	--	Go to Step 19	--
17	Replace the PCM. Did you complete the replacement?	--	Go to Step 19	--
18	Replace the generator. Did you complete the replacement?	--	Go to Step 19	--
19	Operate the vehicle in order to verify the repair. Did you correct the condition?	--	Generator OK	Go to Step 2

ARM66GC000000727

Fig. 4   Charging system test, (Part 4 of 4)

ALTERNATOR SPECIFICATIONS

Model	Year	Rated Hot Output Amps	Regulated Voltage	Brush Length Minimum, Inch	Commutator Diameter Minimum, Inch
All	2004–08	125	—	—	—

Denso & Mitsubishi Alternators

NOTE: On Air Bag Equipped Models, Refer To "Air Bag System Precautions" Located In The Front Of This Manual For System Disarming & Arming Procedures.

NOTE: Refer To "Computer Relearn Procedure" Located In The Front Of This Manual When Battery Power To The Computer Has Been Interrupted.

INDEX

	Page No.		Page No.		Page No.
Alternator Specifications	19-14	Charging System Test	19-10	Air Bag Systems	19-9
Application Chart	19-9	Wiring Diagrams	19-10	Battery Ground Cable	19-9
Description	19-10	General Information	19-9	Charging System	19-9
Diagnosis & Testing	19-10	Precautions	19-9		

APPLICATION CHART

Model	Year	Manufacturer	Rated Hot Output Amps
AURA	2007–08	Denso	③
Cobalt	2006–08	Denso	①
CTS	2004–08	Denso	135/155
DeVille	2004–05	Denso	140
DTS	2006–08	Denso	150
Grand Prix	2005–08	Denso	135
GTO	2004–06	Mitsubishi	140
G5	2007–08	Denso	①
G6	2007–08	Denso	③
Impala	2006–08	Denso	135
ION	2005–07	Denso	④
Lucerne	2006–08	Denso	②
Monte Carlo	2006–07	Denso	135
Seville	2004	Denso	140
STS	2005–08	Denso	155
Vibe	2004–08	Denso	80

① — 2.2L & 2.4L engine, 115 amps; 2.0L engine, 135 amps.
② — 3.8L engine, 135 amps; 4.6L engine, 150 amps.
③ — 3.6L engine, 155 amps.
④ — 2.0L engine, 135 amps.

GENERAL INFORMATION

Refer to "Delphi Alternators" for general information.

PRECAUTIONS

Air Bag Systems

Refer to "Air Bag System Precautions" in the front of this manual for system disarming and arming procedures.

Battery Ground Cable

Prior to service, disconnect battery ground cable and isolate as required.

Charging System

1. Ensure battery polarity is proper when servicing units. Reversed battery polarity will damage rectifiers and regulators.
2. If booster battery is used for starting, use proper polarity in hookup.
3. When a fast charger is used to charge a vehicle battery, vehicle battery cables should be disconnected unless fast charger is equipped with a special Alternator Protector, in which case vehicle battery cables need not be disconnected. **Fast chargers should never be used to start a vehicle as rectifier damage will result.**
4. Unless system includes a load relay or field relay, grounding alternator output terminal will damage alternator and/or circuits. This is true even when system is not in operation since no circuit breaker is used and battery is applied to alternator output terminal at all times. Field or load relay acts as a circuit breaker in that it is controlled by ignition switch.
5. Before making any on vehicle tests of alternator or regulator, battery should

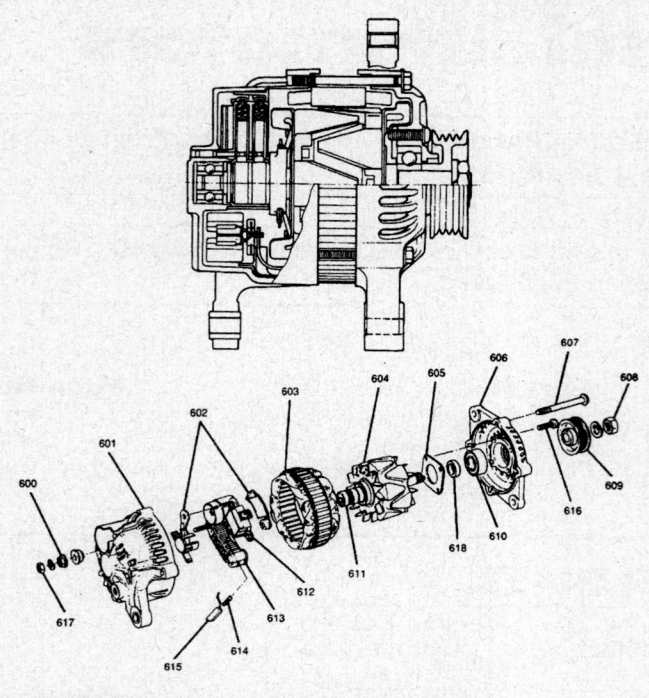

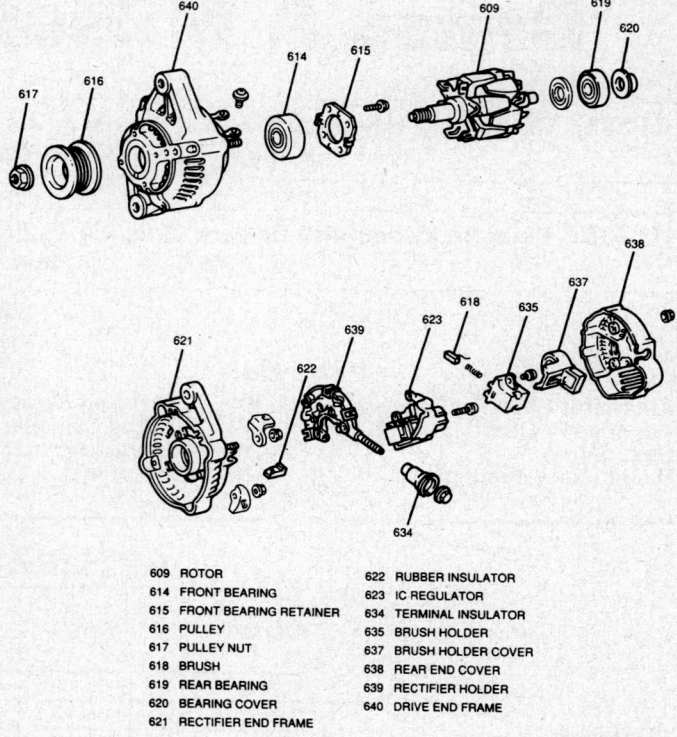

600	BATTERY TERMINAL RETAINING NUT
601	REAR HOUSING
602	BRUSH HOLDER
603	STATOR
604	ROTOR
605	FRONT BEARING RETAINER
606	FRONT HOUSING
607	GENERATOR HOUSING BOLT (4)
608	DRIVE PULLEY RETAINING NUT
609	DRIVE PULLEY

610	FRONT BEARING
611	REAR BEARING
612	REGULATOR
613	RECTIFIER
614	BRUSH SPRING (2)
615	BRUSH (2)
616	FRONT BEARING RETAINING SCREW (4)
617	"BAT" TERMINAL RETAINING NUT
618	FRONT BEARING SPACER

GC1129500063000X

Fig. 1 Exploded view of Mitsubishi alternator

609	ROTOR	622	RUBBER INSULATOR
614	FRONT BEARING	623	IC REGULATOR
615	FRONT BEARING RETAINER	634	TERMINAL INSULATOR
616	PULLEY	635	BRUSH HOLDER
617	PULLEY NUT	637	BRUSH HOLDER COVER
618	BRUSH	638	REAR END COVER
619	REAR BEARING	639	RECTIFIER HOLDER
620	BEARING COVER	640	DRIVE END FRAME
621	RECTIFIER END FRAME		

GC1129100036000X

Fig. 2 Exploded view of Denso alternator

be inspected and circuit inspected for faulty wiring or insulation. loose or corroded connections and poor ground circuits.

6. Inspect alternator belt tension and condition.
7. Ignition should be Off and battery ground cable disconnected before making any test connections to prevent system damage.
8. Do not reverse connections to alternator.
9. Do not short across or ground any of terminals in charging system.
10. Never disconnect output terminal while alternator is running.
11. Vehicle battery must be fully charged when testing charging system.

DESCRIPTION

These alternators have IC integral solid state regulators, **Figs. 1 and 2.** All regulator components are enclosed into a solid mold and are attached to the slip ring end frame along with the brush holder assembly. The alternator voltage setting cannot be adjusted.

The alternator rotor bearings contain enough grease to eliminate the need for periodic lubrication. Two brushes carry current through the two slip rings to the field coil mounted on the rotor.

The stator windings are assembled on the inside of a laminated core that form part of the alternator frame. The rectifier bridge contains six diodes which electrically change stator AC voltage into DC voltage. The neutral diodes serve to convert the voltage fluctuation at the neutral point to direct current for increasing alternator output.

DIAGNOSIS & TESTING

Wiring Diagrams

Refer to wiring diagrams **Figs. 3 through 16.**

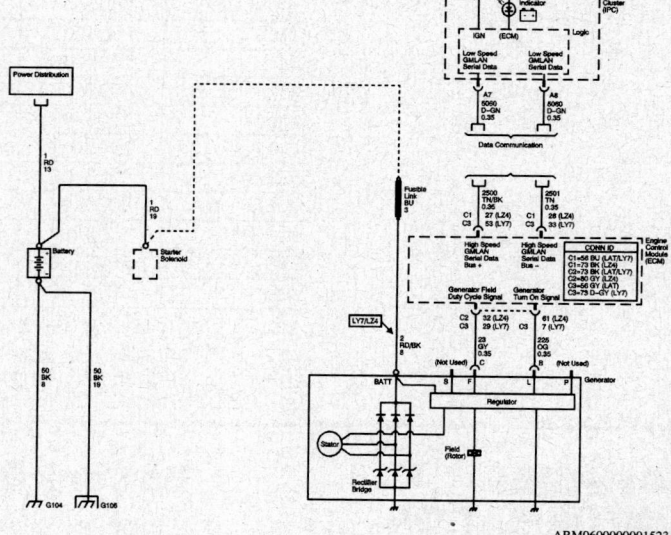

ARM0600000001523

Fig. 3 Wiring diagram. AURA w/3.6L engine

Charging System Test

Refer to **Fig. 17** for charging system test procedures.

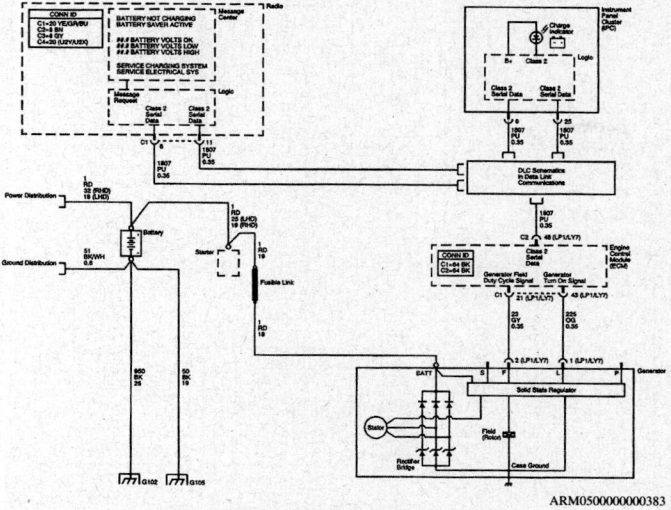

Fig. 4   Wiring diagram. CTS

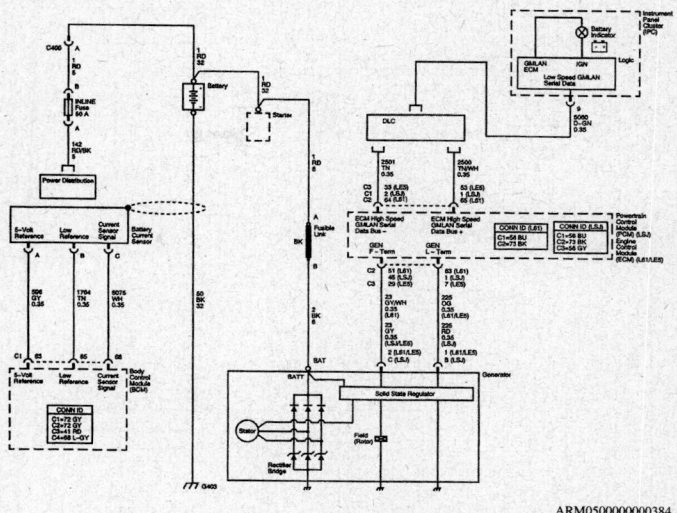

Fig. 5   Wiring diagram. Cobalt & G5

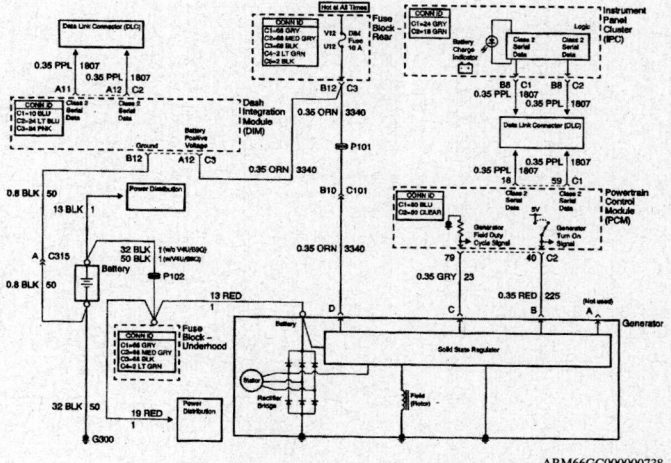

Fig. 6   Wiring diagram. DeVille

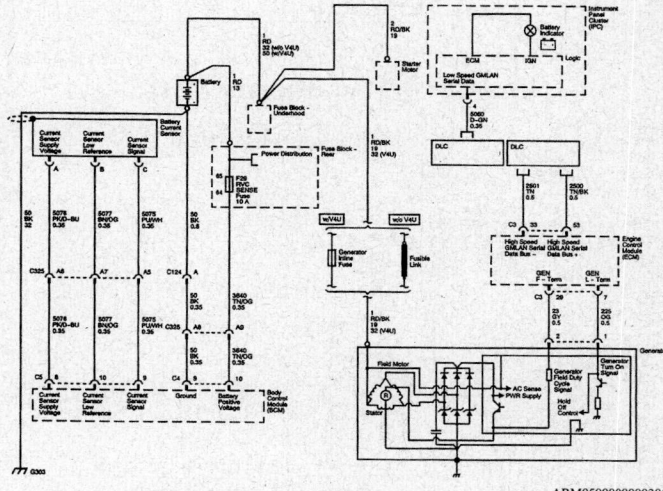

Fig. 7   Wiring diagram. DTS

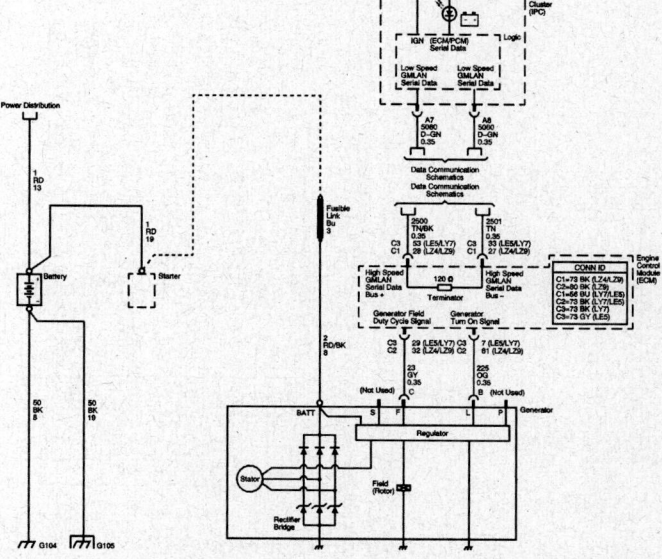

Fig. 8   Wiring diagram. G6 w/3.6L engine

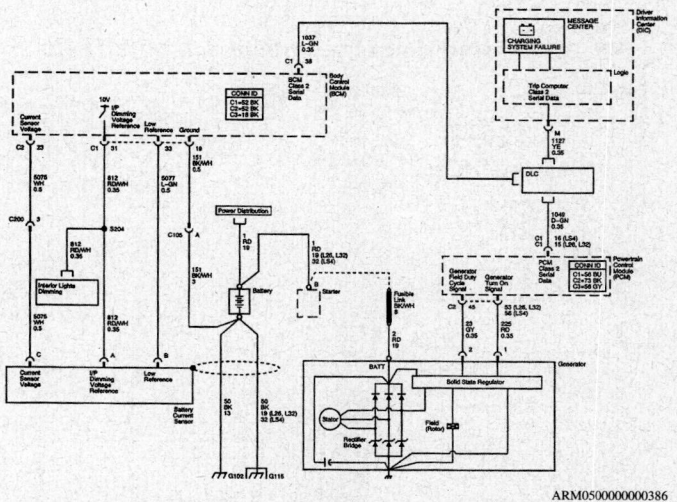

Fig. 9   Wiring diagram. Grand Prix

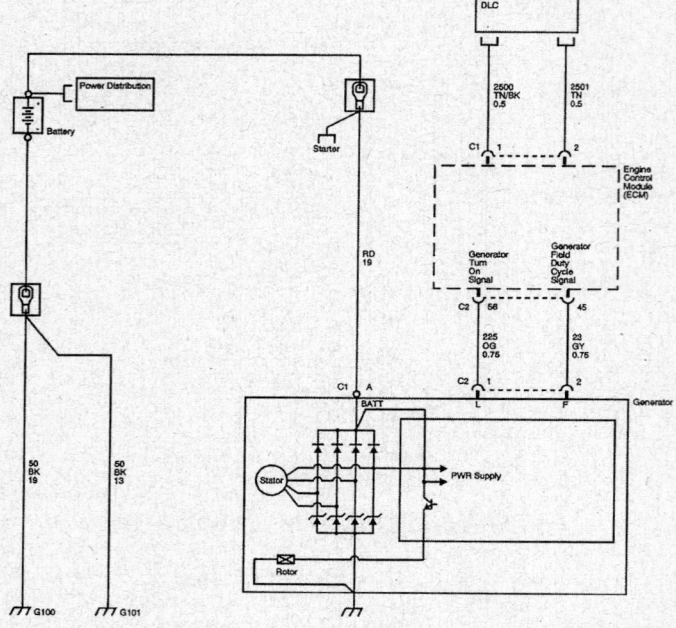

Fig. 10 Wiring diagram. GTO

ARM0500000000387

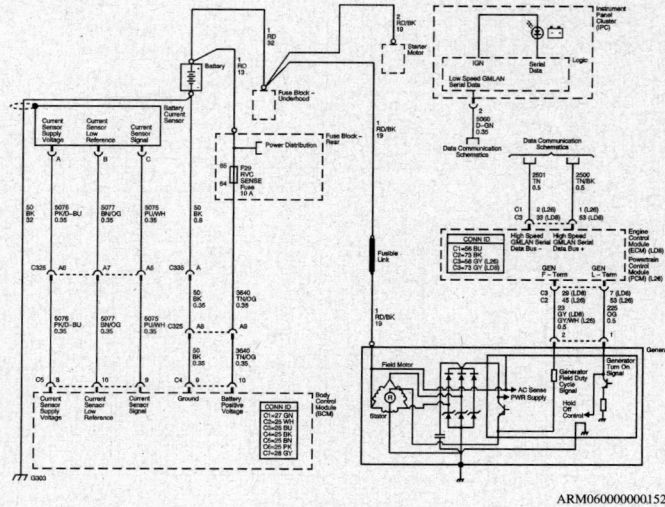

Fig. 11 Wiring diagram. Lucerne

ARM0600000001522

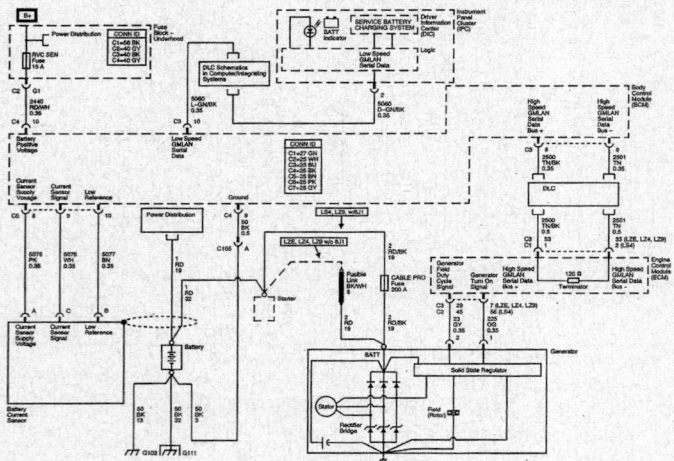

Fig. 12 Wiring diagram. Impala & Monte Carlo

ARM0500000000388

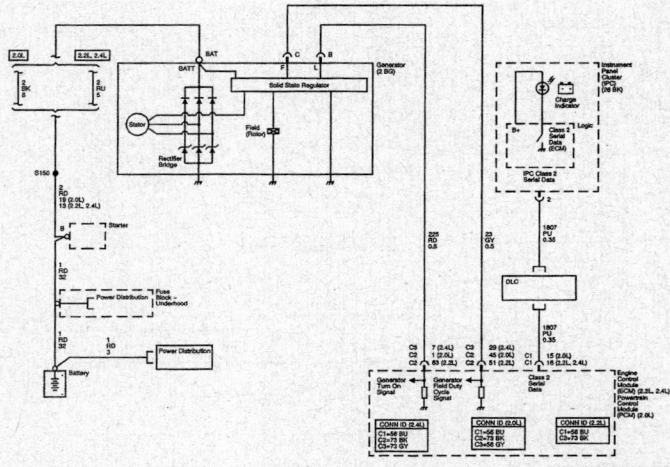

Fig. 13 Wiring diagram. ION

ARM0500000000389

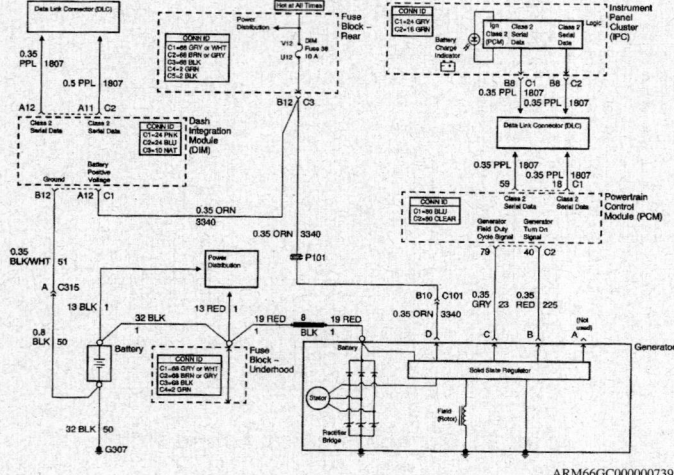

Fig. 14 Wiring diagram. Seville

ARM66GC000000739

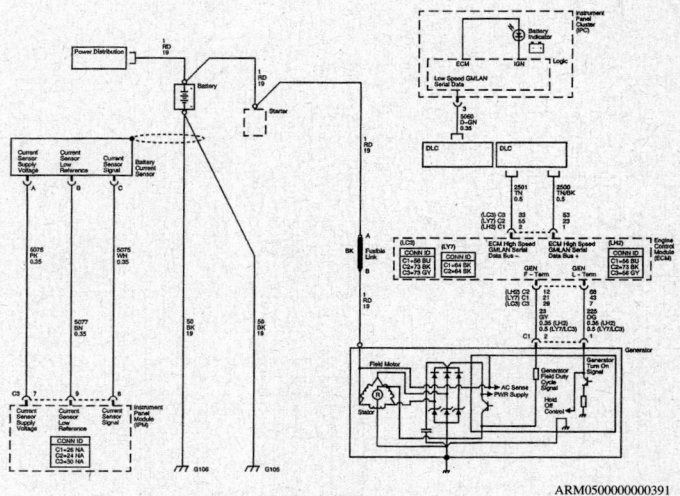

Fig. 15 Wiring diagram. STS

ARM0500000000391

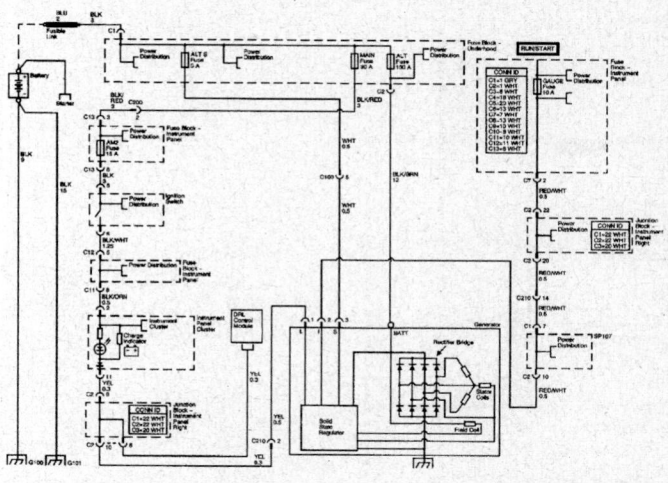

Fig. 16   Wiring diagram. Vibe

ARM66GC000000744

1	**Important** The battery must be above a 70 percent state of charge. Did you perform the Battery Inspection Test?	--	Go to Step 2	Go to Battery Inspection/Test
2	1. Install a scan tool. 2. Start the engine. 3. With a scan tool, command the GEN-L Terminal OFF and ON. 4. Observe the Ignition 1 Signal parameter. Does the voltage change with each command?	--	Go to Step 3	Go to Step 7

3	1. Turn ON the following accessories:
	   o Headlights -- high beams
	   o A/C on Max
	   o Blower fan -- ON high
	   o Heated seats -- if equipped
	2. With a scan tool, observe the ignition 1 signal parameter in the engine data list.
	3. Increase engine speed to 2,500 RPM.
	
	Is the voltage within the specified value?
		12.0-15.5 V	Go to Step 4	Go to Step 5

ARM0300000000696

Fig. 17   Charging system test (Part 1 of 4)

4	1. Turn OFF all accessories. 2. Turn OFF the ignition. **Caution** **Make sure that the load is completely turned off before connecting or disconnecting a carbon pile load tester to the battery. Otherwise, sparking could ignite battery gasses which are extremely flammable and may explode violently.** 3. Connect a carbon pile tester to the vehicle. **Important** When measuring generator output current, be sure the inductive probe encircles the generator output wire. 4. Connect an inductive ammeter probe to the output circuit of the generator. 5. Start the engine. 6. With a scan tool, command the GEN-L Terminal ON. 7. Increase engine speed to 2,500 RPM. 8. Adjust the carbon pile as necessary in order to obtain the maximum current output. Is the generator output greater than or equal to **98 amps**?	--	System OK	Go to Step 8
5	Is the voltage measured greater than 15.5 volts?	--	Go to Step 11	Go to Step 6
6	1. Leave the vehicle accessories ON or maintain load test value. 2. Maintain engine speed at 2,500 RPM. 3. Measure the voltage between the generator output terminal and the generator metal housing. Is the voltage measured equal to the specified value?	B+	Go to Step 13	Go to Step 8

ARM0300000000697

Fig. 17   Charging system test (Part 2 of 4)

7	1. Turn ON the ignition, with the engine OFF. 2. Disconnect the generator harness connector. 3. Measure the voltage between the generator turn ON signal circuit and ground. 4. With a scan tool, command the GEN-L Terminal ON and OFF. Does the voltage measure greater than the first value ON and near the second value OFF?	4.7 V 0 V	Go to Step 13	Go to Step 10
8	1. Maintain the engine speed at 2,500 RPM and continue to operate the generator at the load test value. 2. Measure the voltage drop from the battery negative terminal to the metal housing of the generator. Is the voltage measured less than the specified value?	0.5 V	Go to Step 9	Go to Step 14
9	1. Maintain the engine speed at 2,500 RPM and continue to operate the generator at the load test value. 2. Measure the voltage drop from the output terminal of the generator to the positive terminal on the battery. Is the voltage measured less than the specified value?	0.5 V	Go to Step 13	Go to Step 15
10	Test the generator turn on signal circuit for a short, or open. Did you find and correct the condition?	--	Go to Step 18	Go to Step 12
11	Test the generator battery voltage sense circuit, if equipped, for an open or high resistance. Did you find and correct the condition?	--	Go to Step 18	Go to Step 13

ARM0300000000698

Fig. 17   Charging system test (Part 3 of 4)

		Go to Step	Go to Step
12	Inspect for poor connections at the harness connector of the powertrain control module (PCM). Did you find and correct the condition?	Go to Step 18	Go to Step 16
13	Inspect for poor connections at the generator. Did you find and correct the condition?	Go to Step 18	Go to Step 17
14	Repair the high resistance or open in the ground circuit of the generator. Did you complete the repair?	Go to Step 18	--
15	Repair the high resistance or open in the generator output circuit. Did you complete the repair?	Go to Step 18	--
16	Replace the PCM. Did you complete the replacement?	Go to Step 18	--
17	Replace the generator. Did you complete the replacement?	Go to Step 18	--
18	Operate the vehicle in order to verify the repair. Did you correct the condition?	System OK	Go to Step 1

ARM030000000699

Fig. 17 Charging system test (Part 4 of 4)

ALTERNATOR SPECIFICATIONS

Model	Year	Alternator Manufacturer	Rated Hot Output Amps	Regulated Voltage
AURA	2007–08	Denso	③	13.5–15
CTS	2004–08	Denso	135/155	13.5–15
Cobalt	2006–08	Denso	①	13.5–15
DeVille	2004–05	Denso	140	13.5–15
DTS	2006–08	Denso	150	13.5–15
Grand Prix	2005–08	Denso	135	13.5–15
G5	2007–08	Denso	①	13.5–15
G6	2007–08	Denso	③	13.5–15
GTO	2004–06	Denso	140	13.5–15
Impala	2006–08	Denso	135	13.5–15
ION	2005–07	Denso	135	13.5–15
Lucerne	2006–08	Denso	②	13.9–15
Monte Carlo	2006–07	Denso	135	13.5–15
Seville	2004	Denso	140	13.5–15
STS	2005–08	Denso	155	13.5–15
Vibe	2004–08	Denso	80	13.5–15

① — 2.2L & 2.4L engine, 115 amps; 2.0L engine, 135 amps.
② — 3.8L engine, 135 amps; 4.6L engine, 150 amps.
③ — 3.6L engine, 155 amps.

Valeo Alternators

NOTE: On Air Bag Equipped Models, Refer To "Air Bag System Precautions" Located In The Front Of This Manual For System Disarming & Arming Procedures.

NOTE: Refer To "Computer Relearn Procedure" Located In The Front Of This Manual When Battery Power To The Computer Has Been Interrupted.

NOTE: "Electrical Symbol & Wire Color Code Identification" Located In The Front Of This Manual May Be Used As An Aid When Using Wiring Circuits Found In This Section.

INDEX

	Page No.		Page No.		Page No.
Alternator Specifications	19-21	Wiring Diagrams	19-16	Charging System	19-16
Application Chart	19-15	General Information	19-15	Hybrid Battery Service	19-15
Description	19-16	Precautions	19-15	Connect	19-16
Diagnosis & Testing	19-16	Air Bag Systems	19-15	Disconnect	19-15
Diagnostic Tests	19-16	Battery Ground Cable	19-15		

APPLICATION CHART

Model	Year	Rated Output Amps
Alero	2004	105
AURA	2007–08	125①
Cavalier	2004–05	105
Corvette	2004–08	140
Grand Am	2004–05	105
G6	2005–08	②
ION	2004–05	105
	2006	④
ION	2004–07	105/115
Malibu	2004–07	115
Malibu Classic	2008	125
Malibu Maxx	2004–07	125
Solstice	2006	115
	2007–08	③
Sunfire	2004–05	105
SKY	2007–08	③

① — 2.4L & 3.5L engines, 125 amps.
② — 2.4L, 3.5L& 3.9L engines, 125 amps.
③ — 2.0L engine, 140 amps; 2.4L engine, 125 amps
④ — 2.2L engine, 105 amps; 2.4L engine, 115 amps

GENERAL INFORMATION

Refer to "Delphi Alternators" for general information.

PRECAUTIONS

Air Bag Systems

Refer to "Air Bag System Precautions" in the front of this manual for system disarming and arming procedures.

Battery Ground Cable

Prior to service, disconnect battery ground cable and isolate as required.

Hybrid Battery Service

DISCONNECT

To help avoid personal injury, always ensure the ignition switch is in the OFF position and the ignition key has been removed prior to working on any 36V components. After the key has been removed, disconnect the negative battery cable and then open the generator battery disconnect control module cover. After waiting for at least 5 minutes, measure the voltage potential using a DMM between the following: 36V positive and negative battery cables; 36V positive battery cable and vehicle ground; 36V negative battery cable and vehicle ground. All measured voltage levels must be below 3 volts.

1. Remove ignition key from ignition switch.
2. Secure ignition key to ensure that key

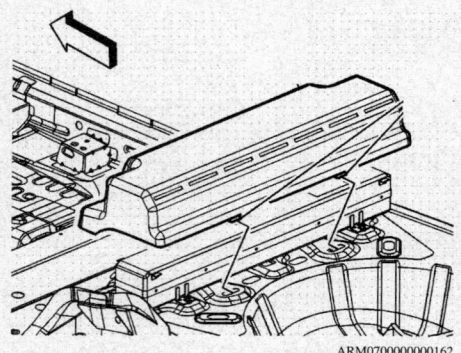

ARM0700000000162

Fig. 1   Rear hybrid battery compartment. Aura

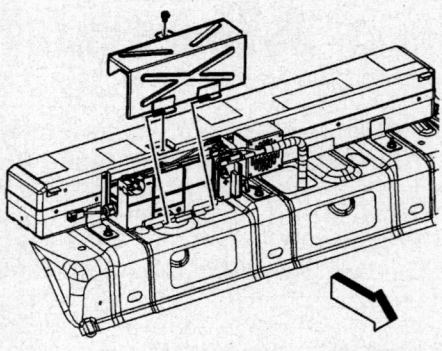

ARM0700000000163

Fig. 2   Disconnect control module cover. Aura Hybrid

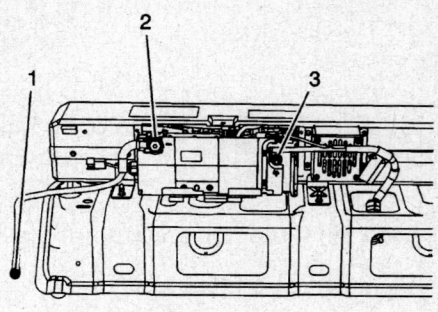

1-Chassis ground
2-Negative stud
3-Positive stud

ARM0700000000164

Fig. 3   Battery disconnect control module & voltage measurement locations. Aura Hybrid

CANNOT be installed without your knowledge.

3. Disconnect 12 volt negative battery cable.
4. Fold down both rear seat backs, then carefully lift up on load floor rear compartment cover at retaining clip locations, **Fig. 1.**
5. Tilt load floor rear compartment cover towards rear of vehicle slightly, disengage tabs and remove load floor rear compartment cover. **To avoid personal injury, be careful when working in vicinity of generator battery disconnect control module. Internal components will still be live, 36V potential, even when cover has been opened or removed.**
6. Remove generator battery disconnect control module cover bolt, **Fig. 2.**
7. Open and slide generator battery disconnect control module cover to right, removing cover. **Wait at least 5 minutes in order to allow generator control module capacitors to discharge.**
8. **Never assume battery pack is disabled when generator battery disconnect control module cover is opened. Generator battery will have to be checked for voltage potential using a voltmeter first**
9. Set voltmeter to DC voltage and measure vehicle 12-volt battery voltage (at 12-volt positive jumper location and negative battery cable).
10. Meter should read greater than 12 volts DC.
11. To ensure generator battery has been disabled, check generator battery for voltage potential as follows:
    a. Refer to **Fig. 3** for voltage measurement locations.
    b. Measure from positive stud to negative stud, voltage should be less than 3 volts.
    c. Measure from positive stud to vehicle chassis ground, voltage should

be less than 3 volts.
    d. Measure from negative stud to vehicle chassis ground, voltage should be less than 3 volts.
12. After verifying there is no voltage present, vehicle is now safe to work on.

CONNECT

1. Install and close generator battery disconnect control module cover.
2. Install generator battery cover bolt and **torque** to 89 inch lbs.
3. Tilt load floor rear compartment cover towards rear of vehicle slightly in order to insert tabs into battery tray rear support.
4. Set load floor rear compartment cover down, ensure retaining clips align to proper locations, carefully push down to secure cover.
5. Place rear seats backs to their proper positions.
6. Connect 12 volt negative battery cable.

Charging System

1. Ensure battery polarity is proper when servicing units. Reversed battery polarity will damage rectifiers and regulators.
2. If booster battery is used for starting, use proper polarity in hookup.
3. When a fast charger is used to charge a vehicle battery, vehicle battery cables should be disconnected unless fast charger is equipped with a special Alternator Protector, in which case vehicle battery cables need not be disconnected. **Fast chargers should never be used to start a vehicle as rectifier damage will result.**
4. Unless system includes a load relay or field relay, grounding alternator output terminal will damage alternator and/or circuits. This is true even when system is not in operation since no circuit breaker is used and battery is applied

to alternator output terminal at all times. Field or load relay acts as a circuit breaker in that it is controlled by ignition switch.
5. Before making any on vehicle tests of alternator or regulator, battery should be inspected and circuit inspected for faulty wiring or insulation. loose or corroded connections and poor ground circuits.
6. Inspect alternator belt tension and condition.
7. The ignition should be Off and battery ground cable disconnected before making any test connections to prevent damage to system.
8. Do not reverse connections to alternator.
9. Do not short across or ground any terminals in charging system.
10. Never disconnect output terminal while alternator is running.
11. Vehicle battery must be fully charged when testing charging system.

DESCRIPTION

The Valeo alternator is available in one size with a maximum output of 110 amps. The main components are the rotor, regulator and rectifier bridge. No periodic maintenance is required.

DIAGNOSIS & TESTING
Wiring Diagrams

Refer to **Figs. 4 through 13** for wiring diagrams.

Diagnostic Tests

Refer to **Figs. 14 through 16** for charging system diagnosis.

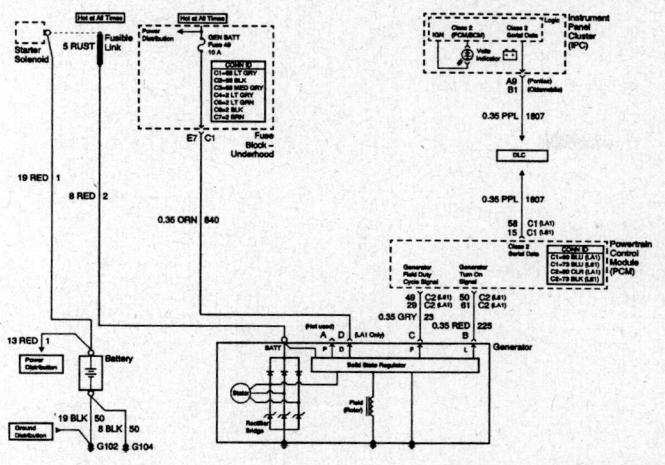

Fig. 4   Wiring diagram. Alero & Grand Am

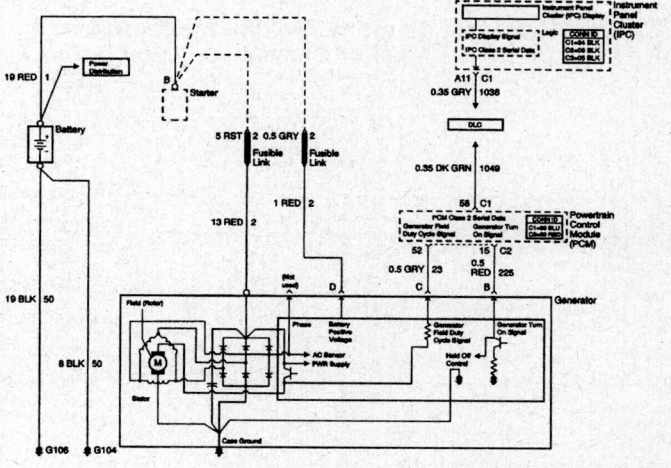

Fig. 6   Wiring diagram. 2004 Corvette

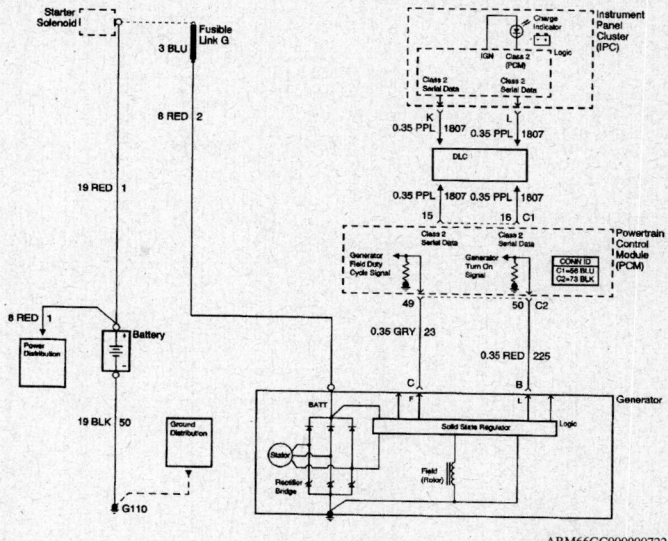

Fig. 5   Wiring diagram. Cavalier & Sunfire

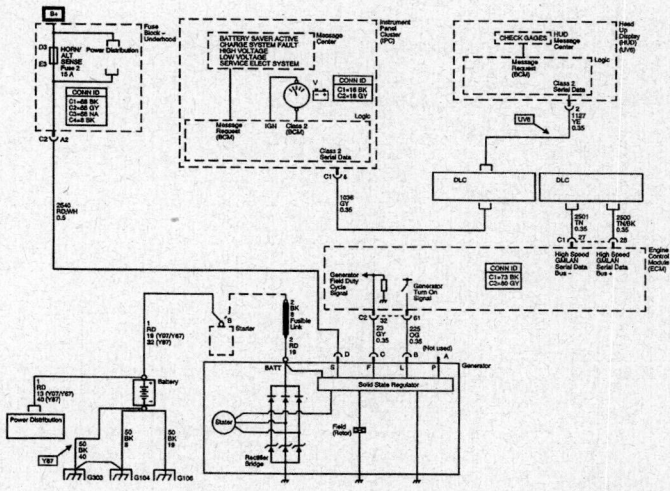

Fig. 7   Wiring diagram. 2005–06 Corvette

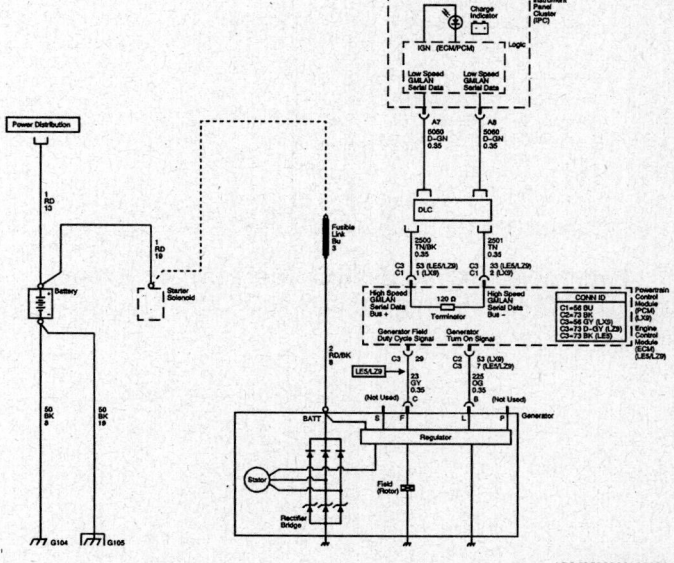

Fig. 8   Wiring diagram. G6 w/2.4L, 3.5L & 3.9L engines

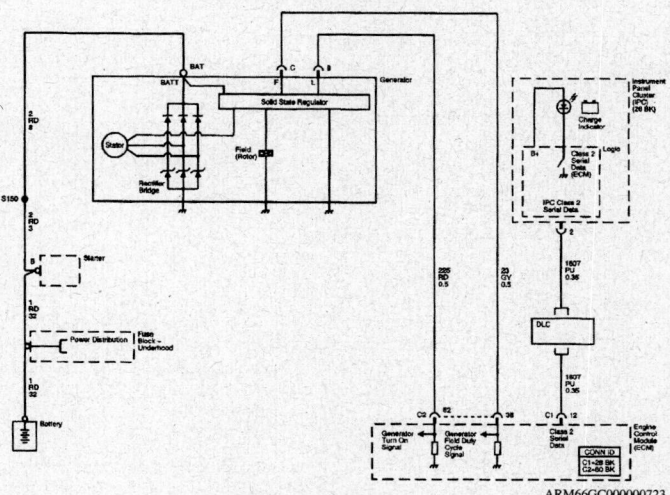

Fig. 9   Wiring diagram. ION

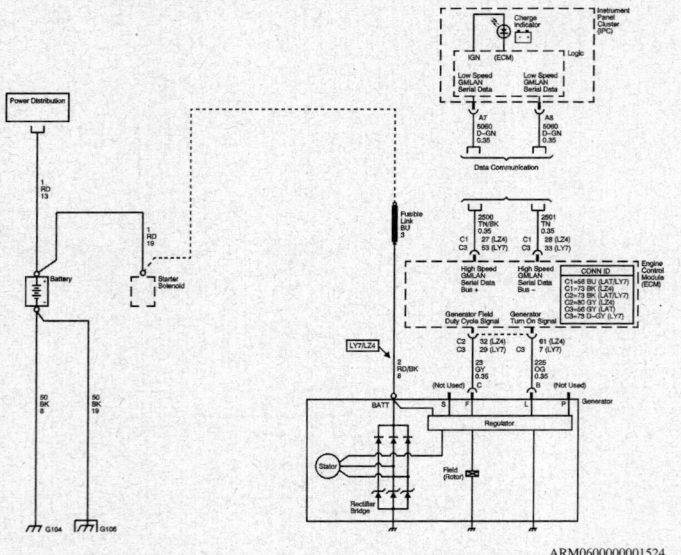

Fig. 10   Wiring diagram. AURA w/3.5L engine

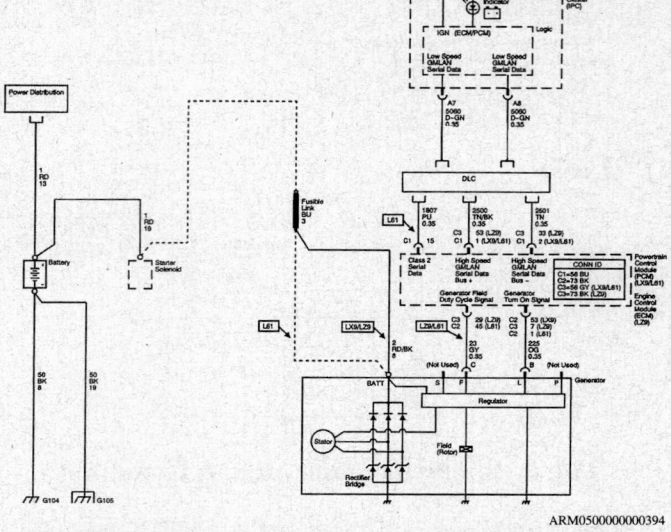

**Fig. 11   Wiring diagram. Malibu, Malibu Maxx &
Malibu Classic**

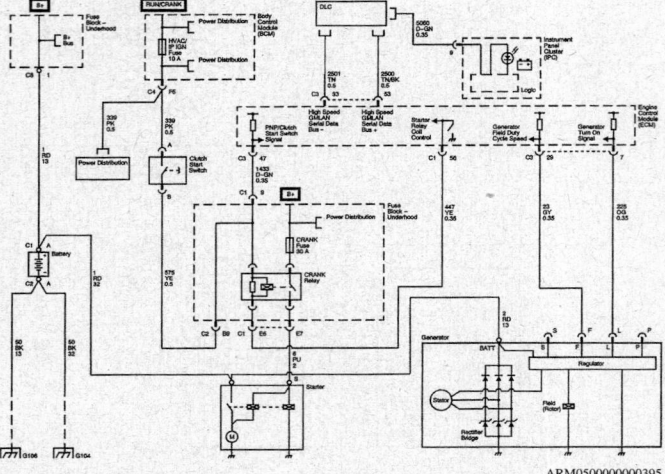

Fig. 12   Wiring diagram. Solstice

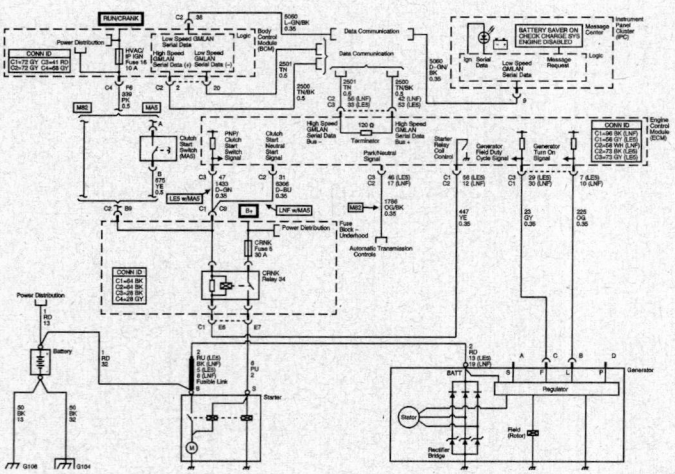

Fig. 13   Wiring diagram. SKY

Step	Action	Value (s)	Yes	No
1	Did you perform the Diagnostic System Check - Vehicle?	--	Go to Step 2	Go to Diagnostic System Check -
2	**Important:** The battery must be above a 70 percent state of charge. Did you perform the battery inspection test?	--	Go to Step 3	Go to Battery Inspection/Test
3	1. Install a scan tool. 2. Start the engine. 3. With a scan tool, command the GEN-L Terminal OFF and ON. 4. Observe the Ignition 1 Signal parameter. Does the voltage change with each command?	--	Go to Step 4	Go to Step 8
4	1. Turn ON the following accessories: - Headlight high beams ON - A/C on MAX - Blower fan on high - Heated seats, if equipped 2. With a scan tool, observe the ignition 1 signal parameter in the engine data list. 3. Increase engine speed to 2,500 RPM. Is the voltage within the specified value?	12-15.5 V	Go to Step 5	Go to Step 6

**Fig. 14   Charging system (Part 1 of 4). Except
Corvette, ION & SKY**

Step	Action	Value(s)	Yes	No
5	1. Turn OFF all accessories. 2. Turn OFF the ignition. **Caution: Make sure that the load is completely turned off before connecting or disconnecting a carbon pile load tester to the battery. Otherwise, sparking could ignite battery gasses which are extremely flammable and may explode violently.** 3. Connect a carbon pile tester to the vehicle. **Important:** When measuring generator output current, be sure the inductive probe encircles the generator output wire. 4. Connect an inductive ammeter probe to the output circuit of the generator. 5. Start the engine. 6. With a scan tool, command the GEN-L Terminal ON. 7. Increase engine speed to 2,500 RPM. 8. Adjust the carbon pile as necessary in order to obtain the maximum current output. Is the generator output greater than or equal to the load test value as specified in Generator Usage?	--	System OK	Go to Step 7
6	Is the voltage measured greater than 15.5 volts?	--	Go to Step 12	Go to Step 7
7	1. Leave the vehicle accessories ON or maintain load test value. 2. Maintain engine speed at 2,500 RPM. 3. Measure the voltage between the generator output terminal and the generator metal housing. Is the voltage measured equal to the specified value?	B+	Go to Step 14	Go to Step 9
8	1. Turn ON the ignition, with the engine OFF. 2. Disconnect the generator harness connector. 3. Measure the voltage between the generator turn ON signal circuit and ground. 4. With a scan tool, command the GEN-L Terminal ON and OFF. Does the voltage measure greater than the first value ON and near the second value OFF?	4.7 V 0 V	Go to Step 14	Go to Step 11

ARM0500000000397

Fig. 14   Charging system (Part 2 of 4). Except Corvette, ION & SKY

Step	Action	Value(s)	Yes	No
14	Inspect for poor connections at the generator. Did you find and correct the condition?	-	Go to Step 19	Go to Step 18
15	Repair the high resistance or open in the ground circuit of the generator. Did you complete the repair?	-	Go to Step 19	--
16	Repair the high resistance or open in the generator output circuit. Did you complete the repair?	-	Go to Step 19	--
17	Replace the PCM. Did you complete the replacement?	-	Go to Step 19	--
18	Replace the generator. Did you complete the replacement?	-	Go to Step 19	--
19	Operate the vehicle in order to verify the repair. Did you correct the condition?	-	System OK	Go to Step 2

ARM0500000000399

Fig. 14   Charging system (Part 4 of 4). Except Corvette, ION & SKY

Step	Action	Value(s)	Yes	No
9	1. Maintain the engine speed at 2,500 RPM and continue to operate the generator at the load test value. 2. Measure the voltage drop from the battery negative terminal to the metal housing of the generator. Is the voltage measured less than the specified value?	0.5 V	Go to Step 10	Go to Step 15
10	1. Maintain the engine speed at 2,500 RPM and continue to operate the generator at the load test value. 2. Measure the voltage drop from the output terminal of the generator to the positive terminal on the battery. Is the voltage measured less than the specified value?	0.5 V	Go to Step 14	Go to Step 16
11	Test the generator turn ON signal circuit for a short or open. Did you find and correct the condition?	--	Go to Step 19	Go to Step 13
12	Test the generator battery voltage sense circuit, if equipped, for an open or high resistance. Did you find and correct the condition?	--	Go to Step 19	Go to Step 14
13	Inspect for poor connections at the harness connector of the powertrain control module (PCM). Did you find and correct the condition?	--	Go to Step 19	Go to Step 17

ARM0500000000398

Fig. 14   Charging system (Part 3 of 4). Except Corvette, ION & SKY

Step	Action	Value(s)	Yes	No
1	Did you perform the Diagnostic System Check - Vehicle?	--	Go to Step 2	Go to Diagnostic System Check -
2	With ignition OFF, install the Midtronics Digital Battery Analyzer and verify the condition of the battery. Is the battery sufficiently charged for testing?	--	Go to Step 3	Go to Battery Inspection/Test
3	1. Disconnect the Midtronics Digital Battery Analyzer. 2. Connect the Sun Vat 40 tester or equivalent to the battery. 3. Turn the ignition to the OFF/LOCK position. 4. Observe and record the battery voltage reading at the battery terminals on the Sun Vat 40 tester. 5. Start the engine and observe the system voltage reading on the tester. Does the voltage increase from the first specified (engine OFF) to the second (engine ON specified range)?	Engine Off = B+ Engine On = 13.9 - 15.5 V	Go to Step 4	Go to Step 6
4	1. Turn ON the following accessories: - Headlights - Hi beams - A/C on Max - Blower Fan - ON high - Rear window defogger - Heated seats (If equipped) 2. Maintain engine speed at 2500 RPM. Is voltage still within the specified value?	13.9 - 15.5 V	Go to Step 5	Go to Step 6

ARM0500000000400

Fig. 15   Charging system (Part 1 of 3). Corvette

Step	Action	Value(s)	Yes	No
5	1. Turn OFF all accessories. 2. Turn OFF the ignition. 3. Connect a carbon pile tester to the vehicle. **Important:** When measuring generator output current, be sure the inductive probe encircles the generator output wire. 4. Connect an inductive ammeter probe to the output circuit of the generator. 5. Start the engine. 6. Increase engine speed to 2,500 RPM. 7. Adjust the carbon pile as necessary in order to obtain the maximum current output. Is the generator output greater than or equal to the load test value as specified in Generator Usage ?		System OK	Go to Step 10
6	1. Turn the generator OFF. 2. Disconnect the generator harness connector. 3. Turn the ignition to the ON position. 4. Using a DMM, measure the voltage on the L-terminal circuit. Is the voltage greater than the specified value	0V	Go to Step 11	Go to Step 7
7	1. Turn the engine OFF. 2. Start the engine and check the voltage on the L-terminal. Is the voltage within the specified value?	5V	Go to Step 8	Go to Step 12
8	1. Turn engine OFF. 2. Turn ignition switch to ON position. 3. Using the scan tool, observe the duty cycle in the F-terminal signal parameter. Does the scan tool display the indicated value?	0 %	Go to Step 9	Go to Step 13
9	Connect a test lamp to B+ and repeatedly touch the F-terminal at the generator harness connector while monitoring the GEN-F terminal signal parameter on the scan tool. Does the scan tool indicate that the generator pulse width modulation (PWM) is above the specified range?	90 %	Go to Step 10	Go to Step 14
10	1. Turn the engine OFF. 2. Inspect the generator B+ output terminal at the generator for an open or high resistance. Did you find and correct the condition?	--	Go to Step 19	Go to Step 15
11	Test the L-terminal circuit for a short to voltage. Did you find and correct the condition?	--	Go to Step 19	Go to Step 16

ARM0500000000401

Fig. 15   Charging system (Part 2 of 3). Corvette

Step	Action	Value(s)	Yes	No
12	Test the L-terminal circuit for open or short to ground. Did you find and correct the condition?	-	Go to Step 19	Go to Step 16
13	Test the GEN-F terminal for a short to voltage. Did you find and correct the condition?	-	Go to Step 19	Go to Step 16
14	Test the GEN-F terminal circuit for an open or short to ground. Did you find and correct the condition?	-	Go to Step 19	Go to Step 16
15	Inspect for poor connections at the generator. Did you find and correct the condition?		Go to Step 19	Go to Step 18
16	Inspect for poor connections at the harness connector of the engine control module (ECM). Did you find and correct the condition?		Go to Step 19	Go to Step 17
17	**Important:** The replacement ECM must be programmed. Replace the ECM. Did you complete the replacement?	-	Go to Step 19	--
18	Replace the generator. Did you complete the replacement?		Go to Step 19	--
19	Operate the vehicle in order to verify the repair. Did you correct the condition?		System OK	Go to Step 2

ARM0500000000802

Fig. 15   Charging system (Part 3 of 3). Corvette

Step	Action	Value(s)	Yes	No
4	Is the generator output current greater than or equal to the load test value given in Generator Usage ?	--	Go to Step 6	Go to Step 5
5	Replace the generator. Did you complete the replacement?	--	Go to Step 6	--
6	Operate the vehicle in order to verify the repair. Did you correct the condition?	--	Generator OK	Go to Step 2

ARM66GC000000743

Fig. 16   Charging system test (Part 2 of 2). ION & SKY

Step	Action	Value(s)	Yes	No
1	Did you perform the Diagnostic System Check for Engine Electrical?	--	Go to Step 2	Go to Diagnostic System Check
2	Start the engine, observe the charge indicator on the instrument panel cluster (IPC) or message in the driver information center (DIC). Does the charge indicator illuminate or the DIC display a charging system message?	--	Go to Step 3	Test for Intermittent and Poor Connections
3	1. Turn OFF the ignition. 2. Connect the red lead of the SA9154Z-A to the battery positive terminal 3. Connect the grey lead of the SA9154Z-A to the output circuit of the generator. 4. Start the engine. 5. Turn On the SA9154Z-A . 6. Turn Off all vehicle accessories Off. 7. Follow the SA9154Z-A prompts. 8. Press CHARGING SYSTEM TEST. Is the voltage displayed within the specified value?	13.0 V - 15.5 V	Go to Step 4	Go to Step 5

ARM66GC000000742

Fig. 16   Charging system test (Part 1 of 2). ION & SKY

ALTERNATOR SPECIFICATIONS

Model	Year	Rated Hot Output Amps
Alero & Grand Am	2004–05	105
AURA	2007–08	②
Cavalier & Sunfire	2004–05	105
Corvette	2004–08	140
G6	2005–08	③
ION	2004–05	105
	2006–07	①
Malibu	2004–07	115
Malibu Classic	2008	125
Malibu Maxx	2004–07	125
Solstice	2006	115
	2007–08	④
Sunfire	2004–05	105

① — 2.2L engine, 105 amps; 2.4L engine, 115 amps.
② — 2.4L & 3.5L engines, 125 amps.
③ — 2.4L, 3.5L & 3.9L engines, 125 amps.
④ — 2.0L engine, 140 amps, 2.4L engine, 125 amps

Hitachi Alternators

NOTE: On Air Bag Equipped Models, Refer To "Air Bag System Precautions" Located In The Front Of This Manual For System Disarming & Arming Procedures.

NOTE: Refer To "Computer Relearn Procedure" Located In The Front Of This Manual When Battery Power To The Computer Has Been Interrupted.

NOTE: "Electrical Symbol & Wire Color Code Identification" Located In The Front Of This Manual May Be Used As An Aid When Using Wiring Circuits Found In This Section.

INDEX

	Page No.		Page No.		Page No.
Alternator Specifications	19-24	Diagnostic Tests	19-22	Air Bag Systems	19-21
Application Chart	19-21	Wiring Diagrams	19-22	Battery Ground Cable	19-21
Diagnosis & Testing	19-22	Precautions	19-21	Charging System	19-21

APPLICATION CHART

Model	Year	Rated Output Amps
XLR	2004–08	150

PRECAUTIONS

Air Bag Systems

Refer to "Air Bag System Precautions" in the front of this manual for system disarming and arming procedures.

Battery Ground Cable

Prior to service, disconnect battery ground cable and isolate as required.

Charging System

1. Ensure battery polarity is proper when servicing units. Reversed battery polarity will damage rectifiers and regulators.
2. If booster battery is used for starting, use proper polarity in hookup.
3. When a fast charger is used to charge a vehicle battery, vehicle battery cables should be disconnected unless fast charger is equipped with a special Alternator Protector, in which case vehicle battery cables need not be disconnected. **Fast chargers should never be used to start a vehicle as rectifier damage will result.**
4. Unless system includes a load relay or field relay, grounding alternator output terminal will damage alternator and/or circuits. This is true even when system is not in operation since no circuit breaker is used and battery is applied to alternator output terminal at all times. Field or load relay acts as a circuit breaker in that it is controlled by ignition switch.
5. Before making any on vehicle tests of

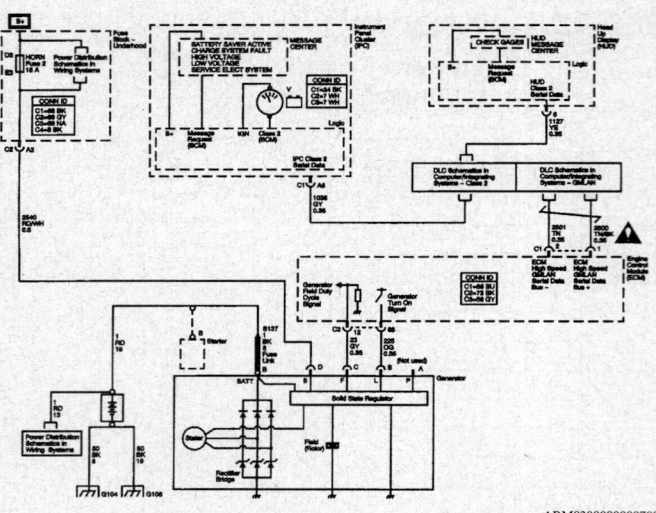

Fig. 1 Wiring diagram. XLR

alternator or regulator, battery should be inspected and circuit inspected for faulty wiring or insulation. loose or corroded connections and poor ground circuits.

6. Inspect alternator belt tension and condition.
7. The ignition should be Off and battery ground cable disconnected before making any test connections to prevent damage to system.
8. Do not reverse connections to alternator.
9. Do not short across or ground any terminals in charging system.
10. Never disconnect output terminal while alternator is running.
11. Vehicle battery must be fully charged when testing charging system.

DIAGNOSIS & TESTING

Wiring Diagrams

Refer to **Fig. 1** for wiring diagram.

Diagnostic Tests

Refer to **Fig. 2** for diagnostic test procedures.

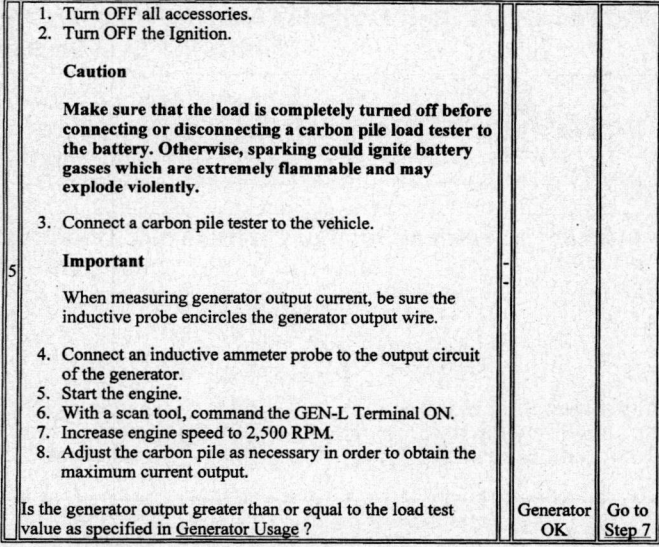

	Action	Value	Yes	No
1	Did you perform Diagnostic System Check?	--	Go to Step 2	Go to Diagnostic System Check
2	**Important** The battery must be above a 70 percent state of charge. Did you perform the Battery Inspection Test?	--	Go to Step 3	Inspect/Test Battery
3	1. Install a scan tool. 2. Start the engine. 3. With a scan tool, command the GEN-L Terminal OFF and ON. 4. Observe the Ignition 1 Signal parameter. Does the voltage change with each command?	--	Go to Step 4	Go to Step 8
4	1. Turn ON the following accessories: o Headlights (high beams) o A/C on Max o Blower fan (on high) o Heated seats (if equipped) 2. With a scan tool, observe the Ignition 1 Signal parameter in the engine data list. 3. Increase engine speed to 2,500 RPM. Is the voltage within the specified value?	12.0- 15.5 V	Go to Step 5	Go to Step 6

Fig. 2 Charging system test (Part 1 of 4). XLR

	Action			
5	1. Turn OFF all accessories. 2. Turn OFF the Ignition. **Caution** Make sure that the load is completely turned off before connecting or disconnecting a carbon pile load tester to the battery. Otherwise, sparking could ignite battery gasses which are extremely flammable and may explode violently. 3. Connect a carbon pile tester to the vehicle. **Important** When measuring generator output current, be sure the inductive probe encircles the generator output wire. 4. Connect an inductive ammeter probe to the output circuit of the generator. 5. Start the engine. 6. With a scan tool, command the GEN-L Terminal ON. 7. Increase engine speed to 2,500 RPM. 8. Adjust the carbon pile as necessary in order to obtain the maximum current output. Is the generator output greater than or equal to the load test value as specified in Generator Usage ?			Generator OK	Go to Step 7

Fig. 2 Charging system test (Part 2 of 4). XLR

6	Is the voltage measured greater than 15.5 volts?	--	Go to Step 12	Go to Step 7
7	1. Leave the vehicle accessories ON or maintain load test value. 2. Maintain engine speed at 2,500 RPM. 3. Measure the voltage of the battery. 4. Measure the voltage between the generator output terminal and the generator metal housing Is the voltage measured of the generator within 0.2 volts of the battery voltage?	--	Go to Step 14	Go to Step 9
8	1. Turn ON the ignition, with the engine OFF. 2. Disconnect the generator harness connector. 3. Measure the voltage between the generator turn on signal circuit and ground. 4. With a scan tool, command the GEN-L Terminal ON and OFF. Does the voltage measure greater than the first value ON and near the second value OFF?	4.7 V 0 V	Go to Step 14	Go to Step 11
9	1. Maintain the engine speed at 2,500 RPM and continue to operate the generator at the load test value. 2. Measure the voltage drop from the battery negative terminal to the metal housing of the generator. Is the voltage measured less than the specified value?	0.5 V	Go to Step 10	Go to Step 15
10	1. Maintain the engine speed at 2,500 RPM and continue to operate the generator at the load test value. 2. Measure the voltage drop from the output terminal of the generator to the positive terminal on the battery. Is the voltage measured less than the specified value?	0.2 V	Go to Step 14	Go to Step 16

ARM0300000000711

Fig. 2   Charging system test (Part 3 of 4). XLR

11	Test the generator turn on signal circuit for a short or an open. Did you find and correct the condition?	-	Go to Step 19	Go to Step 13
12	Test the generator battery voltage sense circuit, if equipped, for an open or high resistance. Did you find and correct the condition?	-	Go to Step 19	Go to Step 14
13	Inspect for poor connections at the harness connector of the powertrain control module (PCM). Did you find and correct the condition?	-	Go to Step 19	Go to Step 17
14	Inspect for poor connections at the generator. Did you find and correct the condition?	-	Go to Step 19	Go to Step 18
15	Repair the high resistance or open in the ground circuit of the generator. Did you complete the repair?	-	Go to Step 19	--
16	Repair the high resistance or open in the generator output circuit. Did you complete the repair?	-	Go to Step 19	--
17	Replace the PCM. Did you complete the replacement?	-	Go to Step 19	--
18	Replace the generator. Did you complete the replacement?	-	Go to Step 19	--
19	Operate the vehicle in order to verify the repair. Did you correct the condition?	-	Generator OK	Go to Step 2

ARM0300000000712

Fig. 2   Charging system test (Part 4 of 4). XLR

ALTERNATOR SPECIFICATIONS

Model	Year	Rated Hot Output Amps
XLR	2004–08	150

STEERING COLUMNS

NOTE: On Air Bag Equipped Models, Refer To "Air Bag System Precautions" Located In The Front Of This Manual For System Disarming & Arming Procedures.

NOTE: Refer To "Computer Relearn Procedures" Located In The Front Of This Manual When Battery Power To The Computer Has Been Interrupted.

NOTE: Prior To Performing Any Service Operations Listed In This Section, Consult The "Technical Service Bulletins" Section For Related Information.

INDEX

Page No.

Precautions...................... 20-3
  Air Bag Systems............... 20-3
  Battery Ground Cable........... 20-3
  Hybrid Battery Service.......... 20-3
    Connect..................... 20-3
    Disconnect.................. 20-3
  SIR Coil Damage.............. 20-3
  Service...................... 20-3
  Steering Column Collision
    Damage..................... 20-4
  Steering Column Damage....... 20-3
Steering Column, Replace....... 20-4
  AURA...................... 20-4
  Alero & Grand Am.............. 20-4
  Aveo........................ 20-4
  Bonneville & LeSabre........... 20-4
  Cavalier & Sunfire.............. 20-5
  Century, Grand Prix, Monte
    Carlo & Regal................ 20-5
  Cobalt & G5.................... 20-5
  Corvette...................... 20-6
  CTS......................... 20-6
    2004–07..................... 20-6
    2008........................ 20-6
  DeVille & Seville............... 20-6
  DTS & STS.................... 20-6
  GTO......................... 20-6
  G6.......................... 20-7
  Impala....................... 20-8
  ION......................... 20-7
  L-Series...................... 20-8
  LaCrosse..................... 20-7
  Lucerne...................... 20-7
  Malibu, Malibu Classic & Malibu
    Maxx....................... 20-8
  Park Avenue.................. 20-9
  Solstice & SKY................ 20-9
  Vibe........................ 20-9
  XLR........................ 20-9
**Steering Column Exploded
Views**...................... 20-2
Steering Column Service........ 20-10
  AURA...................... 20-11
    Intermediate Steering Shaft
      Replacement............... 20-11
    Steering Column Trim Covers
      Replacement............... 20-11
  Alero & Grand Am.............. 20-10
    Lower Bearing, Lower
      Steering Shaft & Column
      Jacket..................... 20-10
    SIR Coil Centering............ 20-11
    Steering Column Tilt Head.... 20-10
    Tilt Spring................... 20-10

Page No.

Bonneville & LeSabre........... 20-12
  Linear Shift.................. 20-12
  Lock Module................. 20-13
  Lower Bearing & Steering
    Shaft...................... 20-13
  SIR Coil, Centering........... 20-12
  SIR Coil..................... 20-12
  Steering Column Tilt Head
    Housing.................... 20-13
  Tilt Spring.................... 20-12
Cavalier & Sunfire.............. 20-13
  Column Housing, Ignition
    Switch Actuator, Pivot
    Switch, Steering Shaft,
    Steering Wheel Lock Shoe,
    Tilt Spring & Turn Signal
    Switch..................... 20-14
  Column Lock Cylinder Set,
    Shaft Lock, Turn Signal
    Cancel Cam & Upper
    Bearing.................... 20-13
  Lock Housing Cover & Tilt
    Spring..................... 20-15
Century, Grand Prix & Regal.... 20-16
  Electric Park Lock............ 20-17
  Linear Shift.................. 20-17
  Lock Module................. 20-17
  Lower Column................ 20-16
  Mid Column................. 20-16
  Shaft Lock Shield, Turn Signal
    Cam, Upper Bearing Spring,
    Upper Bearing Inner Race
    Seat & Inner Race........... 20-16
  Tilt Spring................... 20-17
  Upper Column................ 20-16
Cobalt & G5.................... 20-17
  Ignition Lock Cylinder Case... 20-18
  Ignition Lock................. 20-18
  Ignition Switch............... 20-18
  Intermediate Steering Shaft... 20-18
  Multi-Function Switch......... 20-18
  Steering Column Jacket....... 20-18
  Steering Column Trim Covers. 20-18
Corvette...................... 20-11
  Lock Cylinder Set, Shaft Lock,
    SIR Coil, Turn Signal Switch
    & Upper Bearing Spring..... 20-11
  Actuator Sector, Bearings,
    Column Housing, Lock Bolt,
    Lock Shoes & Switch
    Actuator Rack.............. 20-12
  Column Housing Support &
    Shift Tube.................. 20-12
  Dimmer Switch Actuator Rod,

Page No.

Lock Housing Cover, Pivot
  Switch & Tilt Spring......... 20-11
CTS........................... 20-18
  Ignition Lock Cylinder Case... 20-19
  Ignition Lock................. 20-19
  Ignition Switch............... 20-19
  Intermediate Steering Shaft... 20-18
  Multi-Function Switch......... 20-19
  Steering Column Tilt Head.... 20-19
  Steering Column Trim Covers. 20-19
  Steering Column Wiring
    Harness.................... 20-19
  Steering Wheel Position
    Sensor..................... 20-20
  Tilt Lever.................... 20-19
  Tilt Spring................... 20-19
  Turn Signal Cancel Cam &
    Upper Bearing.............. 20-19
DeVille & Seville................ 20-20
  Pass Key Lock Cylinder Set,
    Shaft Lock, Turn Signal
    Switch & Upper Bearing..... 20-20
  Bearing, Lock Bolt, Shift
    Tube, Steering Column
    Housing, Steering Shaft &
    Steering Wheel Lock Shoe .. 20-21
  Column Housing Cover End
    Cap, Lock Housing Cover,
    Pivot Switch, & Tilt Spring... 20-20
DTS & STS.................... 20-22
  Intermediate Steering Shaft... 20-22
  Steering Column Tilt Head.... 20-22
  Steering Column Trim Covers. 20-22
  Steering Column Wire
    Harness Assembly.......... 20-22
  Steering Wheel Position
    Sensor..................... 20-22
GTO......................... 20-22
G6.......................... 20-22
  Intermediate Steering Shaft... 20-22
  Steering Column Trim Covers. 20-22
ION......................... 20-23
Impala & Monte Carlo.......... 20-24
  Intermediate Steering Shaft... 20-24
  Steering Column Cover....... 20-24
  Steering Wheel Control
    Switch..................... 20-24
L Series...................... 20-24
LaCrosse..................... 20-23
  Intermediate Steering Shaft... 20-23
Lucerne...................... 20-23
  Intermediate Steering Shaft
    Replacement............... 20-23

STEERING COLUMNS

	Page No.
Steering Column Trim Covers Replacement	20-23
Malibu, Malibu Classic & Malibu Maxx	20-24
SIR Coil, Centering	20-24
SIR Coil	20-24
Park Avenue	20-24
Shaft Lock, SIR Coil, Turn Signal Cancel Cam & Upper Bearing	20-25
Linear Shift, Park Lock Cable, Shift Gate Lever & Shift Lever Clevis	20-25
Steering Column Covers	20-25
Solstice & SKY	20-25
Ignition Lock Cylinder Case	20-26
Ignition Lock	20-26
Ignition Switch	20-26
Intermediate Steering Shaft	20-25

	Page No.
Multi-Function Switch	20-26
Steering Column Trim Covers	20-25
Vibe	20-26
Ignition Lock Cylinder	20-26
Ignition Switch	20-26
Intermediate Steering Shaft w/FWD	20-26
Steering Column Trim Covers	20-26
Steering Shaft Coupling	20-26
XLR	20-26
Inflatable Restraint Steering Wheel Module Coil Centering	20-28
Lower Bearing & Steering Column Jacket	20-28
Steering Column Lock Control Module	20-26
Steering Wheel Control Switch Assembly	20-28

	Page No.
Telescope Actuator Assembly	20-28
Telescope Actuator Switch	20-28
Tilt Actuator Assembly	20-28
Tilt Spring	20-28
Turn Signal Cancel Cam & Steering Shaft Upper Bearing Spring	20-27
Technical Service Bulletins	20-29
Clunk Noise From Front Of Vehicle During Turning Maneuver/Steering Wheel Rotation	20-29
Bonneville, Cavalier, Grand Prix, Impala, Monte Carlo, Regal, Seville & Sunfire	20-29
Tightening Specifications	20-42
Troubleshooting	20-4

STEERING COLUMN EXPLODED VIEWS

Model	Year	Type		Shifter Position		Page No.	Fig. No.
		Standard	Tilt	Column	Floor		
Alero	2004	—	X	—	X	20-13	25
AURA	2007–08	—	X	—	X	20-14	26
		—	X	—	X	20-14	27
Aveo	2005–08	—	X	—	X	—	—
Bonneville & LeSabre	2004–05	—	X	X	—	20-18	33
Cavalier & Sunfire	2004–05	X	—	—	X	20-19	34
		—	X	—	X	20-20	35
Century	2004–05	—	X	X	—	20-23	37
Cobalt	2006–08	—	—	—	X	20-24	38
Corvette	2004–08	—	X	—	X	20-15	28①
		—	X	—	X	20-16	29②
		—	X	—	X	20-17	30③
CTS	2004–08	—	X	—	X	20-25	39
DeVille & Seville	2004–05	—	X	X	—	20-29	52
		—	X	—	X	20-30	53
DTS	2006–08	—	X	X	—	20-31	58
		—	X	—	X	20-31	59
		—	X	X	—	20-32	60
		—	X	—	X	20-33	61
Grand Am	2004–05	—	X	—	X	20-13	25
Grand Prix & Regal	2004–08	—	X	—	X	20-21	36
		—	X	X	—	20-23	37
GTO	2004–06	—	X	—	X	—	—
G5	2007–08	—	—	—	X	20-24	38
G6	2005–08	—	X	—	X	20-34	63
Impala	2004–08	—	X	X	—	20-36	67
		—	X	—	X	20-36	67
LaCrosse	2005–08	—	X	—	X	20-34	64
		—	X	X	—	20-34	65
Lucerne	2006–08	—	X	X	X	20-35	66
Malibu, Malibu Classic & Malibu Maxx	2004–08	—	X	—	—	20-37	71
Monte Carlo	2004–07	—	X	—	X	20-36	67
Park Avenue	2004–05	—	X	X	—	20-37	74
Solstice	2006–08	—	—	—	X	20-38	75
SKY	2007–08	—	—	—	X	20-38	75
STS	2005–08	—	X	—	X	20-33	62
Vibe	2004–08	—	X	—	X	20-39	76

Continued

STEERING COLUMN EXPLODED VIEWS—Continued

Model	Year	Type		Shifter Position		Page No.	Fig. No.
		Standard	Tilt	Column	Floor		
XLR	2004–08	—	X	—	X	20-41	77

① — Non-telescoping less sensor. ② — Non-telescoping w/sensor. ③ — Telescoping.

PRECAUTIONS

Air Bag Systems

Refer to "Air Bag System Precautions" in the front of this manual for system disarming and arming procedures.

Battery Ground Cable

Prior to service, disconnect battery ground cable and isolate as required.

Hybrid Battery Service

DISCONNECT

To help avoid personal injury, always ensure the ignition switch is in the OFF position and the ignition key has been removed prior to working on any 36V components. After the key has been removed, disconnect the negative battery cable and then open the generator battery disconnect control module cover. After waiting for at least 5 minutes, measure the voltage potential using a DMM between the following: 36V positive and negative battery cables; 36V positive battery cable and vehicle ground; 36V negative battery cable and vehicle ground. All measured voltage levels must be below 3 volts.

1. Remove ignition key from ignition switch.
2. Secure ignition key to ensure that key CANNOT be installed without your knowledge.
3. Disconnect 12 volt negative battery cable.
4. Fold down both rear seat backs, then carefully lift up on load floor rear compartment cover at retaining clip locations, **Fig. 1.**
5. Tilt load floor rear compartment cover towards rear of vehicle slightly, disengage tabs and remove load floor rear compartment cover. **To avoid personal injury, be careful when working in vicinity of generator battery disconnect control module. Internal components will still be live, 36V potential, even when cover has been opened or removed.**
6. Remove generator battery disconnect control module cover bolt, **Fig. 2.**
7. Open and slide generator battery disconnect control module cover to right, removing cover. **Wait at least 5 minutes in order to allow generator con-**

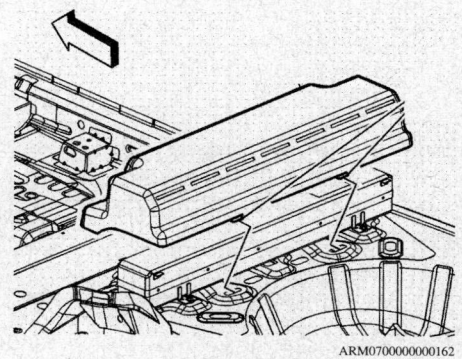

Fig. 1   Rear hybrid battery compartment & clip locations. Aura Hybrid

trol module capacitors to discharge.
8. **Never assume battery pack is disabled when generator battery disconnect control module cover is opened. Generator battery will have to be checked for voltage potential using a voltmeter.**
9. Set voltmeter to DC voltage and measure vehicle 12-volt battery voltage at 12-volt positive jumper location and negative battery cable.
10. Meter should read greater than 12 volts DC.
11. To ensure generator battery has been disabled, check generator battery for voltage potential as follows:
    a. Refer to **Fig. 3** for voltage measurement locations.
    b. Measure from positive stud to negative stud, voltage should be less than 3 volts.
    c. Measure from positive stud to vehicle chassis ground, voltage should be less than 3 volts.
    d. Measure from negative stud to vehicle chassis ground, voltage should be less than 3 volts.
12. After verifying there is no voltage present, vehicle is now safe to work on.

CONNECT

1. Install and close generator battery disconnect control module cover.
2. Install generator battery cover bolt and **torque** to 89 inch lbs.
3. Tilt load floor rear compartment cover towards rear of vehicle slightly in order to insert tabs into battery tray rear support.
4. Set load floor rear compartment cover down, ensure retaining clips align to proper locations, carefully push down

to secure cover.
5. Place rear seats backs to their proper positions.
6. Connect 12 volt negative battery cable.

Service

Use only the specified screws, bolts and nuts during the mandatory assembling sequence to ensure proper breakaway action of column under impact. Avoid using excessively long bolts as they may prevent a portion of the steering column from collapsing under impact.

When removing or installing, steering wheel, ignition switch or lock, turn signal switch, adjusting transmission linkage, or installing and adjusting neutral-start or back-up light switch, refer to appropriate chapter.

If a shift tube shows a sheared plastic injection, a new shift tube must be installed. If a steering shaft shows a sheared plastic, but it is not bent, it can be repaired by using a service steering shaft repair kit P/N 7810077. The kit contains instructions and dimensions for all steering columns. On some models, the attaching brackets will shear under impact and must also be replaced.

Steering Column Damage

When the steering column is removed, it is extremely susceptible to damage. Dropping the steering column on its end could collapse the steering shaft or loosen plastic injections that keep the steering column rigid. Leaning on the steering column could cause the jacket to bend or deform. Any of these conditions could impair the steering column's collapsible design. If the steering wheel must be removed, use only the specified steering wheel puller and steering wheel puller bolts. Never hammer on the end of the shaft.

SIR Coil Damage

The front wheels of the vehicle must be in a straight ahead position and the steering column must be in the locked position before disconnecting the steering column or intermediate shaft. Failure to follow these procedures will cause improper alignment of some components during installation and result in damage to the SIR coil.

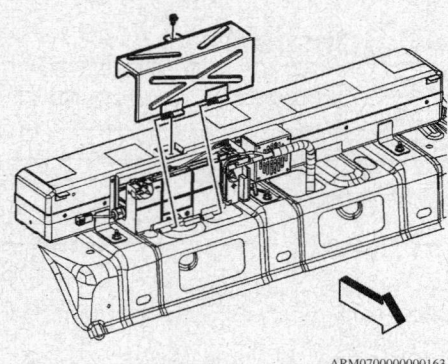

ARM0700000000163

Fig. 2 Disconnect control module cover. Aura Hybrid

Steering Column Collision Damage

Vehicles involved in accidents resulting in frame damage, major body or sheet metal damage, or where steering column has been impacted, or where supplemental inflatable restraints systems deployed, may also have a damaged or misaligned steering column. When performing service operations on steering columns, inspect the following components:

1. Ensure steering column bracket capsules are securely seated in bracket slots.
2. Inspected for steering column bracket capsules any looseness when pushed or pulled by hand, **Fig. 4.**
3. Replace bracket or jacket, as required.
4. Inspect for jacket assembly collapse by measuring distance from lower edge of upper jacket, **Fig. 5.** If measured dimensions are not as specified, replace jacket assembly.
5. Visually inspect steering column for sheared plastic, **Fig. 6.**
6. If steering shaft shows sheared plastic, replace steering shaft.
7. Remove inflatable restraint coil and allow to hang freely.
8. Rotate steering wheel and measure steering shaft lower end runout using suitable dial indicator.
9. If runout is more than .063 inch, replace steering shaft.

TROUBLESHOOTING

Refer to **Fig. 7** for steering column troubleshooting.

STEERING COLUMN

REPLACE

Alero & Grand Am

1. Ensure wheels are in straight ahead position and ignition switch is in LOCK position.
2. Remove steering wheel as outlined in "Electrical" section of "Alero, Grand Am & Malibu" chassis chapter.
3. Remove tilt lever, as required.

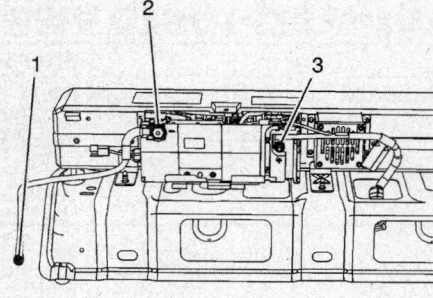

1-Chassis ground
2-Negative stud
3-Positive stud

ARM0700000000164

Fig. 3 Battery disconnect control module & voltage measurement locations. Aura Hybrid

4. Remove upper mounting screws and steering column cover.
5. Remove lower mounting screws and steering column cover.
6. Disconnect headlamp switch and windshield wiper switch.
7. Disconnect cruise control electrical connector.
8. Remove instrument cluster as outlined in "Electrical" section of "Alero, Grand Am & Malibu" chassis chapter.
9. Cut plastic wire wrap and route SIR coil wiring out of way.
10. Remove lefthand lower sound insulator retaining screws, then the cluster.
11. Position upper intermediate shaft boot out of way and remove upper shaft pinch bolt.
12. Remove lower steering column bracket support bolts.
13. Loosen upper column bolts.
14. Spread lower steering column intermediate shaft joint apart with suitable screwdriver.
15. Remove upper column bolts.
16. Rotate steering column 45° counterclockwise and remove steering column.
17. Reverse procedure to install.

AURA

1. Disarm air bags as outlined under "Precautions."
2. Remove steering wheel as outlined in "Electrical" section of "Saturn" chassis chapter.
3. Remove SIR coil assembly.
4. Remove Multi-Function switch as outlined in "Electrical" section of "Saturn" chassis chapter.
5. Remove steering column knee bolster.
6. Remove intermediate steering shaft from steering column shaft pinch bolt. Install a tie strap between rake bracket and base of steering column to prevent assembly from pulling apart, **Fig. 8.**
7. Disconnect steering column electrical connectors.
8. Remove adjustable pedal bracket assembly, if equipped. Place it aside with motor and brake pedal cable attached.

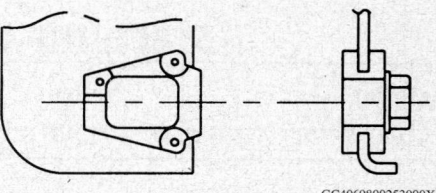

GC4069800253000X

Fig. 4 Inspecting for looseness on steering column bracket assembly

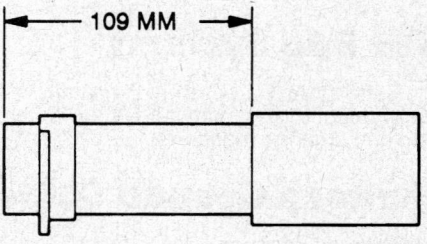

|← 109 MM →|

GC4069800255000X

Fig. 5 Jacket assembly collapse measurement

9. Remove upper and lower steering column attaching bolts.
10. Remove steering column.
11. Reverse procedure to install.

Aveo

1. Remove upper and lower steering column trim covers.
2. Ensure wheels are in straight ahead position and ignition switch is in lock position.
3. Remove turn signal switch by depressing tabs on both sides of switch housing.
4. Remove wiper/washer switch by depressing tabs on both sides of switch housing.
5. Remove lower instrument panel trim cover.
6. Disconnect air bag electrical connections.
7. Remove key interlock solenoid, do not drop key interlock solenoid spring.
8. Remove key reminder switch.
9. Disconnect ignition switch electrical connector.
10. Remove upper steering column shaft pinch bolt.
11. Remove steering column jacket assembly rear bracket retaining nut.
12. Remove steering column jacket assembly front bracket retaining nuts.
13. Remove steering column.
14. Reverse procedure to install.

Bonneville & LeSabre

1. Ensure wheels are in straight ahead position and ignition switch is in LOCK position.
2. Remove steering wheel as outlined in "Electrical" section of "Bonneville, LeSabre & Park Avenue" chassis chapter.
3. Remove deflector retaining screws.
4. **On models equipped with column**

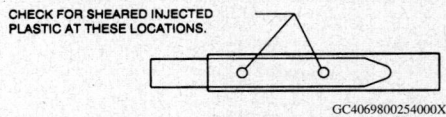

CHECK FOR SHEARED INJECTED PLASTIC AT THESE LOCATIONS.

GC4069800254000X

Fig. 6 Inspecting for sheared plastic

shift, disconnect shift indicator cable.

5. **On all models,** loosen column support bracket bolts.
6. Remove mounting bolt and steering column support brace, **Fig. 9.**
7. Disconnect steering column wiring harness, then support column and remove support bracket bolts, **Fig. 10.**
8. **On models equipped with column shift,** disconnect shift control cable from actuator and slot in lower column bracket.
9. **On models equipped with console shift,** disconnect park lock cable from ignition switch inhibitor.
10. **On all models,** remove upper intermediate steering shaft pinch bolt.
11. Disconnect steering column shaft from intermediate steering shaft.
12. Remove steering column.
13. Reverse procedure to install.

Cavalier & Sunfire

1. Ensure wheels are in straight ahead position and ignition switch is in LOCK position.
2. Remove steering wheel as outlined in "Electrical" section of "Cavalier, Cobalt, G5 & Sunfire" chassis chapter.
3. Remove lefthand lower sound insulator and side instrument panel covers.
4. Remove instrument panel pad by removing retaining screws located in righthand and lefthand A/C vents, two screws in glove compartment toward lefthand rear and three screws along glove compartment top.
5. Remove tilt lever, then the upper and lower column covers as outlined in "Steering Column Cover."
6. Disconnect cruise control, headlamp switch and windshield wiper switch connectors.
7. Remove ignition switch as outlined in "Electrical" section of "Cavalier, Cobalt, G5 & Sunfire" chassis chapter.
8. Disconnect Passlock cylinder connector.
9. **On models equipped with automatic transaxle,** disconnect shift interlock cable from lock cylinder housing.
10. **On all models,** remove upper flexible joint pinch bolt and lefthand side wire harness retaining clip, **Fig. 11.**
11. Remove lower column bracket support bolts.
12. Remove upper column support bolts.
13. Spread lower steering column flexible joint apart using suitable screwdriver and remove steering column.
14. Reverse procedure to install.

Condition	Cause
The lock system does not lock.	• A broken lock bolt spring • A worn lock bolt spring • A damaged sector • A damaged lock cylinder • A burr on the lock bolt • A damaged housing • A damaged rack • Interference between the bowl and the rack coupling • A binding ignition switch • A restricted actuator rod • The sector is installed incorrectly. • The shift lever is not in the PARK position. • The park lock cable is incorrectly adjusted. • The park lock components are damaged.

Condition	Cause
The lock system sticks in START.	• A deformed actuator rod • *High Lock Effort Between the Off Lock Positions*

Condition	Cause
The key cannot be removed in the OFF-LOCK position.	• The ignition switch is not set correctly. • A damaged lock cylinder • An improperly adjusted linkage • The shift lever is not in the PARK position.

Condition	Cause
The lock cylinder can be removed without depressing the retainer.	A missing lock cylinder retaining screw

Condition	Cause
The lock cylinder effort between OFF and OFF-LOCK is high.	A distorted rack

Condition	Cause
The lock bolt hits the shift lock in the OFF position and the PARK position.	The ignition switch is set incorrectly.

GC6049900276010X

Fig. 7 Steering column troubleshooting chart (Part 1 of 5)

Century, Grand Prix, Monte Carlo & Regal

1. Ensure wheels are in straight ahead position and ignition switch is in LOCK position.
2. Remove steering wheel as outlined in "Electrical" section of "Century, Grand Prix, Impala, LaCrosse, Monte Carlo & Regal" chassis chapter.
3. Remove lefthand instrument panel insulator.
4. **On Century and Regal models,** remove knee bolster bracket.
5. **On all models,** remove trim panel below steering column.
6. Push top of intermediate shaft seal down, then remove upper intermediate steering shaft pinch bolt, **Fig. 12.**
7. **On models equipped with console shift,** disconnect shift indicator cable and park lock cable from shift cam and automatic transmission control indicator.
8. **On models equipped with column shift,** disconnect transaxle shift cable from ball stud on steering column and transaxle shift cable casing from steering column bracket.
9. **On all models,** remove upper and lower steering column retaining bolts.
10. Disconnect electrical connector and remove steering column.
11. Reverse procedure to install.

Cobalt & G5

1. Place steering wheel in straight forward position.
2. Remove steering wheel as outlined in "Electrical" section of "Cavalier, Cobalt, G5 & Sunfire" chassis chapter.
3. Unsnap and remove upper steering column cover.
4. Remove lower steering column cover screws and trim cover.
5. Disconnect head lamp/turn signal harness connector, then the wiper/washer harness connector from SIR coil module assembly.
6. Disconnect SIR coil harness connector from SIR coil module assembly.
7. Pry retaining tabs away at base of SIR coil assembly using a small flat-bladed tool, then slide SIR coil assembly off of steering column.
8. Disconnect ignition lock cylinder, ignition switch theft deterrent control module electrical connectors.
9. Place match marks on intermediate shaft to steering column, then remove intermediate shaft pinch bolt at steering column and discard.
10. Slide intermediate shaft off steering column, then disconnect electronic power steering control module connectors.
11. Remove steering column pivot bolt, then the steering column mounting bolts.
12. Remove column from vehicle.
13. Reverse procedure to install.

Condition	Causes

A high lock effort exists.	• The lock cylinder is damaged.
	• The ignition switch is damaged.
	• A rack preload spring is broken.
	• A rack preload spring is broken.
	• Burrs exist on the following items:
	  – The sector
	  – The rack
	  – The housing
	  – The support
	  – The actuator rod coupling
	• The sector shaft is bent.
	• A rack is damaged.
	• The housing is extreme misaligned to the cover.
	• A coupling slot in the rack is distorted.
	• An actuator rod is damaged.
	• The ignition switch mounting bracket is bent.
	• An actuator rod is restricted.
	• The key cut is damaged.
	• The key cut is incorrect.
	• The park lock cable is incorrectly adjusted.
	• The park lock components are damaged.

Condition	Causes
Noise is present in the steering column.	• The pinch bolts are loose in the intermediate shaft coupling. • The column is misaligned • The contact ring is not lubricated. • The bearing lacks lubrication. • The column components are loose. • The steering shaft bearings are worn. • The steering shaft bearings are broken. • The shaft lock snap ring is not seated. • The spherical joint is not lubricated. • The dust seal is rubbing the column shaft coupling. • The contact ring is worn. • The contact ring is damaged. • The brushes are worn. • The brushes are damaged. • The lock bolt is bolt. • The lock bolt is improperly lubricated.

GC6049900276020X

Fig. 7 Steering column troubleshooting chart (Part 2 of 5)

Condition	Causes
High steering shaft effort exists.	• The column is misaligned. • The dust sel is improperly installed. • The dust seal is deformed. • The upper bearing is damaged. • The lower bearing is damaged. • The intermediate steering shaft universal joint is tight. • The shroud is rubbing on the column cover.

Condition	Causes
Lash exists in the steering column.	• The IP-to-column mounting bolts for the upper bracket are loose. • The IP-to-column mounting bolts for the lower bracket are loose. • The weld nuts on the jacket are broken. • The IP upper bracket capsule is sheared. • The shoes in the housing are loose. • The tilt head pivot pins are loose. • The shoe lock pin in the support is loose. • The support screws are loose. • The upper bracket-to-jacket bolts in the column are loose. • The lower bracket-to-jacket bolts in the column are loose. • The lower bracket-to-adapter screws are loose. • The bearing assembly mounting screws are loose. • The IP-to-jacket mounting bolts are loose.

Condition	Causes
The steering wheel is loose.	• Excessive clearance exists between the pivot pin diameters and the holes in the support or in the housing. • The anti-lash spring in the spheres is damaged. • The anti-lash spring in the spheres is missing. • The upper bearing is not seated in the housing. • The inner race seal is missing from the upper bearing. • The support screws are loose. • The bearing preload spring is missing. • The bearing preload spring is broken.

Condition	Causes
The steering wheel is loose in every other tilt position.	• A loose fit exists between the shoe and the shoe pivot pin. • The shoe is not free in the slot.

GC6049900276030X

Fig. 7 Steering column troubleshooting chart (Part 3 of 5)

Corvette

1. Ensure wheels are in straight ahead position and ignition switch is in LOCK position.
2. Remove driver's air bag module as outlined in "Passive Restraint Systems" chapter.
3. Remove upper intermediate steering shaft pinch bolt.
4. Remove steering wheel and tilt lever.
5. Remove lefthand knee bolster trim panel and knee bolster.
6. Disconnect electrical connectors from column.
7. Remove lower steering column support plate nuts, **Fig. 13.**
8. Remove upper steering column bracket nuts, then the steering column.
9. Reverse procedure to install.

CTS

2004–07

1. Ensure wheels are in straight ahead position.
2. Lock steering column using tool No. J42640, or equivalent.
3. Raise and support vehicle.
4. Remove upper to lower intermediate shaft retaining bolt, then lower vehicle.
5. Remove driver side lower instrument panel pad.
6. Remove steering column trim covers.
7. Disconnect steering column electrical connectors.
8. Supporting steering column, then remove column to support bracket nuts steering column, **Fig. 14.**
9. Reverse procedure to install.

2008

1. Ensure wheels are in straight ahead position.
2. Remove driver knee bolster bracket.
3. Disconnect all electrical connectors as needed.
4. Secure steering wheel utilizing a strap to prevent rotation.
5. Remove upper intermediate steering shaft bolt.
6. Separate upper intermediate steering shaft from steering column. **Do not pull intermediate steering shaft lower seal from its place.**
7. Remove steering column nuts and steering column bolts.
8. Remove steering column from vehicle.
9. Reverse procedure to install.

DeVille & Seville

1. Ensure wheels are in straight ahead position and ignition switch is in LOCK position.
2. Remove steering wheel as outlined in "Electrical" section of "DeVille, DTS, Seville & STS" chassis chapter.
3. Remove knee bolster and steering column reinforcement plate.
4. Disconnect electrical connectors from column.
5. Remove pinch bolt from intermediate shaft, **Fig. 15.**
6. Remove lower support bracket, **Fig. 16.**
7. Remove upper support and column.
8. Reverse procedure to install.

DTS & STS

1. Ensure wheels are in straight ahead

position and ignition switch is in LOCK position.
2. Lock steering column by inserting steering column lock pin tool No. J42640, or equivalent, into steering column access hole.
3. Raise and support vehicle.
4. Remove upper intermediate shaft to lower intermediate shaft retaining bolt, then lower vehicle.
5. Remove knee bolster.
6. Remove steering wheel as outlined in "Electrical" section of "DeVille, DTS, Seville & STS" chassis chapter.
7. Disconnect steering column electrical connectors.
8. Support steering column, then remove steering column mounting bolts.
9. Remove steering column.
10. Remove upper intermediate shaft to steering column attaching bolt, then disconnect upper intermediate shaft from steering column.
11. Reverse procedure to install.

GTO

1. Ensure wheels are in straight ahead position and ignition switch is in LOCK position.
2. Remove lefthand lower instrument panel trim panel and outer trim panel cover.
3. Remove lefthand side ventilation ducts.
4. Remove steering wheel as outlined in "Electrical" section of "GTO" chassis chapter.
5. Remove SIR coil.
6. Remove ignition switch, wiper/washer switch and multifunction switch as outlined in "Electrical" section of "GTO" chassis chapter.

• TPMS indicator FLASHES for 70 seconds and then remains ON solid when the ignition key is turned to the ON position, the message center (if equipped) displays TIRE PRESSURE MONITOR FAULT and DTC B287A is present	• All TPMS sensors not trained to the SJB or all TPMS sensors are not installed	• NOTE: If the vehicle has been stationary for more than 30 minutes, the sensors will go into a "sleep mode" to conserve battery power. It will be necessary to wake them up so they will transmit the latest tire pressure information to the SJB. ACTIVATE the TPMS sensors. REFER to _Tire Pressure Monitoring System (TPMS) Sensor Activation_ . Go To Pinpoint Test F .
• TPMS indicator FLASHES for 70 seconds and then remains ON solid when the ignition key is turned to the ON position, the message center (if equipped) displays TIRE PRESSURE MONITOR FAULT and there are no DTCs present	• Vehicle communication issue between the SJB and the instrument cluster	• Diagnose the no communication concern.
	• SJB	• Diagnose the SJB.
• One or more sensors will not train	• Tire pressure sensor(s) • Vehicle communication issue • SJB	• RETRIEVE and RECORD DTCs. REFER to Tire Pressure Monitor System (TPMS) DTC Chart.

ARM0700000000047

Fig. 7 Symptom Test (Part 2 of 3). Sable, Taurus & Taurus X

• One or more sensor will not train and no DTCs are present	• TPMS sensor(s)	• TRAIN all 4 tire pressure sensors. REFER to _Tire Pressure Monitoring System (TPMS) Sensor Training_ . • For any sensor(s) that did not train, ATTEMPT to activate the same sensor with the activation tool. If the sensor still does not respond, MOVE the vehicle to rotate the wheels at least 1/4 of a turn and ATTEMPT to activate the same sensor again. • If the sensor(s) fail to train a second time, INSTALL a new sensor(s).

ARM0700000000048

Fig. 7 Symptom Test (Part 3 of 3). Sable, Taurus & Taurus X

DIAGNOSTIC CHART INDEX

Test	Code	Description	Page No.	Fig. No.
CROWN VICTORIA & GRAND MARQUIS				
E	—	Low Tire Pressure Displayed	20-7	8
F	—	Driver Door Module (DDM) Will Not Enter Training Mode	20-7	9
G	B2872	Tire Pressure Sensor Or Monitor Fault	20-8	10
G	B287A	Tire Pressure Sensor Or Monitor Fault	20-8	10
H	B106A	Pressure Sensor Range Bit Incorrect State	20-8	11
I	B106B	Tire Pressure Sensor Low Battery	20-9	12
MUSTANG				
D	—	Low Tire Pressure Indicated	20-9	13
E	—	Smart Junction Box (SJB) Will Not Enter Sensor Training Mode	20-9	14
F	B287A or B2872	TPMS On Solid When Ignition Key is Turned to ON Position	20-10	15
G	B106A	Pressure Sensor Range Bit Incorrect State	20-11	16
H	B106B	Tire Pressure Sensor Low Battery	20-11	17
SABLE, TAURUS & TAURUS X				
D	—	Low Tire Pressure Indicated	20-11	18
E	—	Will Not Enter Sensor Training Mode When Using Training Procedure	20-12	19
F	B2872 or B287A	Tire Pressure Sensor Or Monitor Fault	20-12	20
G	B106A	Pressure Sensor Range Bit Incorrect State	20-13	21

Condition	Possible Sources	Action
• TPMS indicator FLASHES for 70 seconds and then remains ON solid when the ignition key is turned to the ON position, the message center (if equipped) displays TIRE MONITOR FAULT and there are no DTCs present in the DDM	• Vehicle communication bus DDM • Vehicle communication issue between DDM and instrument cluster	• Diagnose the standard corporate protocol (SCP) communication bus and high-speed controller area network (HS-CAN) bus.
• TPMS indicator FLASHES for 70 seconds and then remains ON solid when the ignition key is turned to the ON position, the message center (if equipped) displays TIRE PRESSURE MONITOR FAULT and DTC B287A is present	• All TPMS sensors not trained to the DDM or all TPMS sensors are not installed • DDM antenna • DDM	• NOTE: If the vehicle has been stationary for more than 30 minutes, the sensor will go into a "sleep mode" to conserve battery power. It will be necessary to wake them up so they will transmit the latest tire pressure information to the DDM. ACTIVATE the TPMS sensors. REFER to Tire Pressure Monitoring System (TPMS) Sensor Activation . Go To Pinpoint Test G .
• One or more sensors will not train	• Tire pressure sensor(s) • SCP communication bus • HS-CAN bus • DDM antenna • DDM	• RETRIEVE and RECORD DTCs. REFER to the Tire Pressure Monitor System (TPMS) DTC Chart.

ARM0700000000052

Fig. 5   Symptom Test (Part 2 of 2). Crown Victoria & Grand Marquis

Condition	Possible Sources	Action
• TPMS indicator ON continuously and message center (if equipped) displays LOW TIRE PRESSURE	• Spare tire currently in use • Air pressure not set to specifications listed on the vehicle certification label	• INSTALL the repaired road wheel/tire in place of the spare tire. • Go To Pinpoint Test D .
• Smart junction box (SJB) will not enter sensor training mode	• Brake on/off (BOO) switch • Ignition switch • Vehicle communication bus • ABS module • SJB	• Go To Pinpoint Test E .
• TPMS indicator FLASHES for 70 seconds and then remains ON solid when the ignition key is turned to the ON position and DTC B287A or DTC B2872 is present	• TPMS sensor(s) • TPMS sensor(s) not trained to the SJB • SJB	• NOTE: If the vehicle has been stationary for more than 30 minutes, the sensors will go into a "sleep mode" to conserve battery power. It will be necessary to wake them up so they will transmit the latest tire pressure information to the SJB. ACTIVATE the TPMS sensors. REFER to Tire Pressure Monitoring System (TPMS) Sensor Activation iGo To Pinpoint Test F .

ARM0700000000049

Fig. 6   Symptom Test (Part 1 of 2). Mustang

Condition	Possible Sources	Action
• TPMS indicator FLASHES for 70 seconds and then remains ON solid when the ignition key is turned to the ON position, the message center (if equipped) displays TIRE MONITOR FAULT and DTC B1342 is present	• SJB	• INSTALL a new SJB. REFER
• TPMS indicator FLASHES for 70 seconds and then remains ON solid when the ignition key is turned to the ON position, the message center (if equipped) displays TIRE MONITOR FAULT and there are no DTCs present in the SJB	• Vehicle communication bus • SJB • Vehicle communication issue between SJB and instrument cluster	• Diagnose the high-speed controller area network (HS-CAN) bus.
• One or more sensors will not train	• Tire pressure sensor(s) • Vehicle communication bus • SJB	• RETRIEVE and RECORD DTCs. REFER to the Tire Pressure Monitor System (TPMS) DTC Chart.

ARM0700000000050

Fig. 6   Symptom Test (Part 2 of 2). Mustang

Condition	Possible Sources	Action
• Tire pressure monitoring system (TPMS) indicator ON solid and message center (if equipped) displays LOW TIRE PRESSURE	• Spare tire currently in use • Air pressure not set to specifications listed on the vehicle certification label	• INSTALL the repaired road wheel/tire in place of the spare tire. • Go To Pinpoint Test D .
	• Sensors not trained following tire rotation.	• ADVISE customer that on vehicles with different front and rear tire pressure, the sensors must be trained as directed in their Owner's Literature.
• Smart junction box (SJB) will not enter sensor training mode when using the TPMS sensor training procedure	• Brake on/off (BOO) switch • Ignition switch • Vehicle communication bus • SJB	• Go To Pinpoint Test E .
• TPMS indicator FLASHES for 70 seconds and then remains ON solid when the ignition key is turned to the ON position, the message center (if equipped) displays TIRE PRESSURE SENSOR FAULT and DTC B2872 is present	• TPMS sensor(s) • TPMS sensor(s) not trained to the SJB • SJB	• NOTE: If the vehicle has been stationary for more than 30 minutes, the sensors will go into a "sleep mode" to conserve battery power. It will be necessary to wake them up so they will transmit the latest tire pressure information to the SJB. ACTIVATE the TPMS sensors. REFER to Tire Pressure Monitoring System (TPMS) Sensor Activation . Go To Pinpoint Test F .

ARM0700000000046

Fig. 7   Symptom Test (Part 1 of 3). Sable, Taurus & Taurus X

Condition	Causes
The steering wheel does not lock in any tilt position.	• The shoe seized on the pivot pin. • Burrs are present in the shoe grooves. • Dirt is present in the shoe grooves. • The shoe lock spring is weak. • The shoe lock spring is broken.

Condition	Causes
The steering wheel does not return to the top tilt position.	• The pivot pins are binding. • The wheel tilt spring is broken. • The wheel tilt spring is weak. • The turn signal switch wires are too tight.

Condition	Causes
Noise is present when tilting the column.	• The upper tilt bumpers are worn. • The tilt spring rubs in the housing.

Condition	Causes
The turn signal will not indicate lane change.	• The lane change pressure pad is broken. • The spring hanger is broken. • The lane change spring is broken. • The lane change spring is missing. • The lane change spring is misproportioned. • The base is jammed. • The wires are jammed.

Condition	Causes
The turn signal will not stay in the turn position.	• Foreign material is impeding movement of the yoke. • Loose parts are impeding movement of the yoke. • A detent is broken. • A detent is missing. • A canceling spring is broken. • A canceling spring is missing.

GC6049900276040X

Fig. 7 Steering column troubleshooting chart (Part 4 of 5)

Condition	Causes
The turn signal will not cancel.	• The switch mounting screws are loose. • A switch is broken. • The anchor bosses are broken. • A detent is broken. • A return is broken. • A canceling spring is broken. • A detent is missing. • A return is missing. • A canceling spring is missing. • A detent is out-of-position. • A return is out-of-position. • A canceling spring is out-of-position. • A cancelling cam is worn.

Condition	Causes
The turn signal is difficult to operate.	• A turn signal lever screw is loose. • A yoke is broken. Replace the switch. • A yoke is distorted. Replace the switch. • The springs are loose. • The springs are mispositioned. • Interference caused by foreign material exists. • The turn signal switch mounting screws are loose.

Condition	Causes
The electrical system will not function.	• The ignition switch is damaged. • The ignition switch is improperly adjusted. • A loose connection at the ignition switch exists. • A loose connection at the column connectors exists.

Condition	Causes
The switch cannot be set correctly.	• The switch actuator rod is deformed. • The sector is engaged in the wrong rack tooth.

GC6049900276050X

Fig. 7 Steering column troubleshooting chart (Part 5 of 5)

7. Loosen steering column to instrument panel mounting bolts. Do not remove at this time.
8. Raise and support vehicle.
9. Remove steering shaft coupling to steering gear pinion retaining nut. Do not reuse nut.
10. Remove mount bolt from coupling, then separate coupling from pinion.
11. Lower vehicle.
12. Remove lower column retaining nuts.
13. Support column, then remove upper column mounting bolts.
14. Remove steering column.
15. Reverse procedure to install.

G6

1. Ensure wheels are in straight ahead position and ignition switch is in LOCK position.
2. Remove steering wheel as outlined in "Electrical" section of "G6 & Malibu Maxx" chassis chapter.
3. Remove SIR coil assembly.
4. Remove multifunction switch as outlined in "Electrical" section of "G6 & Malibu Maxx" chassis chapter.
5. Remove steering column knee bolster.
6. Remove steering column shaft to intermediate shaft pinch bolt.
7. Disconnect steering column electrical connectors.
8. Remove adjustable pedal bracket and position aside, leaving brake cable and motor attached.
9. Remove upper steering column mounting bolt.
10. Remove lower steering column mounting bolt.
11. Remove steering column from vehicle.
12. Reverse procedure to install.

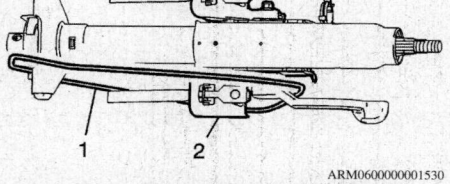

ARM0600000001530

Fig. 8 Rake bracket assembly

ION

1. Ensure steering wheel is in straight ahead position.
2. Remove steering wheel as outlined in "Electrical" section of "Saturn" chassis chapter.
3. Remove instrument panel lower panel.
4. Remove steering column trim covers, **Fig. 17.**
5. Disconnect head lamp, wiper washer and SIR electrical harness from SIR coil module, **Fig. 18.**
6. Remove SIR coil module as outlined in "Passive Restraint Systems" chapter.
7. Disconnect ignition lock cylinder and switch electrical connector.
8. Place matching marks on intermediate shaft to steering column, then remove intermediate shaft pinch bolt, **Fig. 19.**
9. Disconnect Electric Power Steering (EPS) control module electrical harness connectors.
10. Remove steering column pivot bolt, mounting bolts, then the steering column, **Fig. 20.**
11. Remove ignition lock cylinder case, **Fig. 21.**
12. Reverse procedure to install.

LaCrosse

1. Ensure wheels are in straight ahead position, then LOCK steering column by inserting steering column lock pin tool No. J42640, or equivalent, into steering column access hole.
2. Remove steering wheel air bag module.
3. Remove steering wheel as outlined in "Electrical" section of "Century, Grand Prix, Impala, LaCrosse, Monte Carlo & Regal" chassis chapter.
4. Remove lefthand instrument panel closeout panel.
5. Remove lefthand knee bolster.
6. Remove intermediate shaft from steering column.
7. Remove shift indicator cable, casing from shift cam and the automatic control indicator adjuster or park lock cable.
8. Disconnect A/T range selector cable from ball stud on steering column.
9. Remove transaxle shift cable casing from steering column bracket.
10. Remove lower and upper steering column mounting bolts.
11. Disconnect steering column electrical connectors.
12. Loosen steering column electrical connector bolt.
13. Separate electrical connector halves.
14. Remove steering column.
15. Reverse procedure to install.

Lucerne

1. Ensure wheels are in straight ahead position, then LOCK steering column by inserting steering column lock pin tool No. J42640, or equivalent, into steering column access hole.

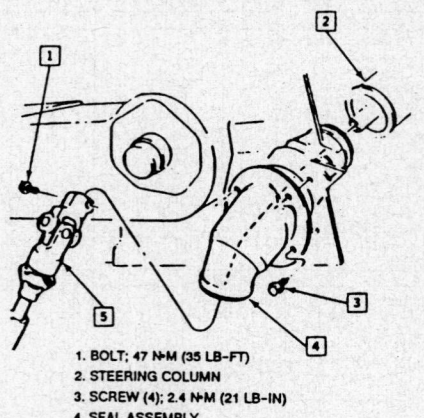

1. BOLT; 47 N·M (35 LB-FT)
2. STEERING COLUMN
3. SCREW (4); 2.4 N·M (21 LB-IN)
4. SEAL ASSEMBLY
5. INTERMEDIATE SHAFT ASSEMBLY

GC6049100044000X

Fig. 9 Intermediate shaft & boot installation. Bonneville & LeSabre

2. Raise and support vehicle.
3. Remove intermediate shaft lower pinch bolt, then remove shaft from steering gear.
4. Lower vehicle.
5. Remove lefthand knee bolster.
6. Disconnect steering column wiring harness, then the shift lever cable from linear shift assembly.
7. Remove the shift cable retaining clip.
8. Press shift cable tabs together, then remove shift cable from steering column, **Fig. 22.**
9. Support column, then remove upper and lower column retaining nuts.
10. Remove steering column from vehicle.
11. Reverse procedure to install.

L-Series

1. Ensure steering wheel is in straight ahead position.
2. Remove steering wheel as outlined in "Electrical" section of "Saturn" chassis chapter.
3. Remove HVAC duct and knee bolster.
4. Disconnect the following electrical connectors:
   a. Wiper/washer and headlamp/turn signal switches.
   b. Ignition switch from lefthand side of steering column.
   c. Interlock solenoid to righthand side of steering column.
   d. Ignition switch to righthand side of steering wheel.
5. Remove wiper/washer and headlamp/turn signal switches.
6. Remove signal switch housing and upper intermediate shaft bolt, then disconnect shaft from steering column.
7. Remove lower and upper steering column support bolts and nuts.
8. Remove steering column.
9. If new column is to be installed, ignition module must be removed as follows:
   a. Place steering column in suitable soft-jawed vise.
   b. Mark ignition module shear bolts center using suitable center punch.
   c. Drill ⅛ inch hole in bolts at each center mark.
   d. Remove bolts using suitable screw extractor and separate ignition module from column.
10. Reverse procedure to install.

Malibu, Malibu Classic & Malibu Maxx

Do not bend the steering column energy absorbing straps located on the upper steering column mounting bracket.

1. Ensure wheels are in straight ahead position and ignition switch is in LOCK position.
2. Remove steering wheel and multifunction switch as outlined in "Electrical" section of "Alero, Grand Am & Malibu" chassis chapter.
3. Remove steering column knee bolster retaining screws, then the bolster.
4. Remove clockspring as outlined in "Passive Restraint Systems" chapter.
5. Remove steering column shaft pinch bolt from intermediate steering shaft.
6. Secure rake lever to full up (LOCK) position using suitable tie straps, **Fig. 23. Rack lever must remain in LOCK position during removal and installation.**
7. Disconnect electrical connectors and

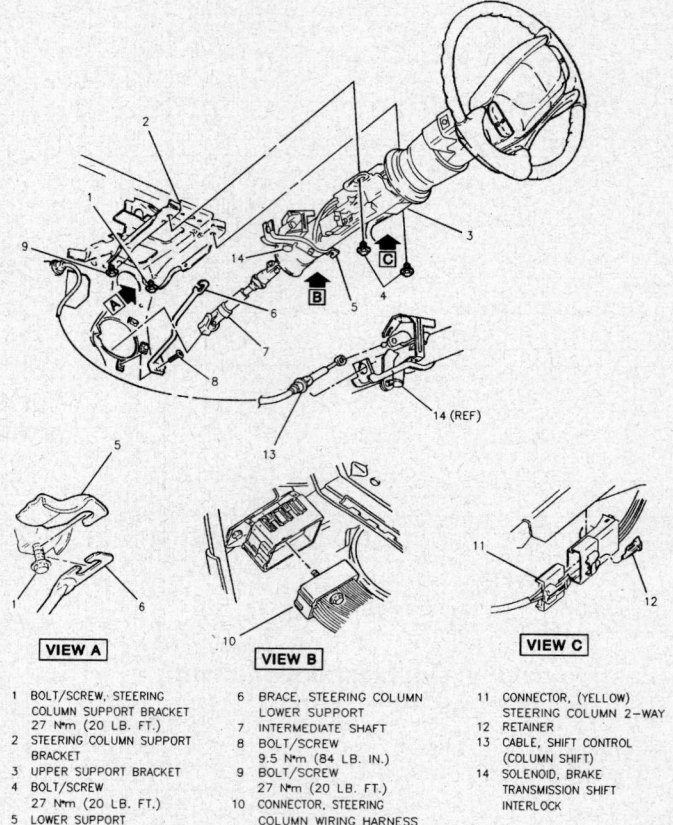

VIEW A

1	BOLT/SCREW, STEERING COLUMN SUPPORT BRACKET 27 N·m (20 LB. FT.)
2	STEERING COLUMN SUPPORT BRACKET
3	UPPER SUPPORT BRACKET
4	BOLT/SCREW 27 N·m (20 LB. FT.)
5	LOWER SUPPORT

VIEW B

6	BRACE, STEERING COLUMN LOWER SUPPORT
7	INTERMEDIATE SHAFT
8	BOLT/SCREW 9.5 N·m (84 LB. IN.)
9	BOLT/SCREW 27 N·m (20 LB. FT.)
10	CONNECTOR, STEERING COLUMN WIRING HARNESS

VIEW C

11	CONNECTOR, (YELLOW) STEERING COLUMN 2-WAY
12	RETAINER
13	CABLE, SHIFT CONTROL (COLUMN SHIFT)
14	SOLENOID, BRAKE TRANSMISSION SHIFT INTERLOCK

GC6049100045000A

Fig. 10 Steering column replacement. Bonneville & LeSabre

harness from steering column.
8. Remove accelerator pedal position sensor electrical connector.
9. Remove accelerator pedal mounting nuts from bracket, then the pedal assembly.
10. Remove upper and lower steering column mounting bolt.
11. Remove steering column.
12. Reverse procedure to install.

Impala

1. Ensure wheels are in straight ahead position and ignition switch is in LOCK position.
2. Remove steering wheel as outlined in "Electrical" section of "Century, Grand Prix, Impala, LaCrosse, Monte Carlo & Regal" chassis chapter.
3. Remove lefthand instrument panel insulator.
4. Remove trim panel below steering column.
5. Remove steering column knee bolster.
6. Remove steering column intermediate shaft pinch bolt from coupler.
7. Remove shift indicator cable, casing from shift cam and automatic control indicator adjuster and park lock cable.
8. Disconnect transaxle range selector cable from ball stud on steering column.
9. Remove transaxle shift cable casing

NOTE: A full-sized, matching spare wheel and tire, that is identical to the road wheel and tire, is available as an optional accessory. This spare wheel and tire is equipped with a tire pressure sensor but the sensor is not initially programmed to the driver door module (DDM).

If this spare wheel and tire is in use on the vehicle, the sensor must be trained to the DDM and the remaining 3 sensors must be retrained to the DDM as well. If all 4 sensors are not trained to the DDM, the tire pressure monitor system (TPMS) warning indicator will illuminate.

Make sure that all the wheels and tires installed on the vehicle are inflated to the correct pressure and trained to the DDM before attempting to diagnose a TPMS concern. Refer to Tire Pressure Monitoring System (TPMS) Sensor Training .

Normal Operation

If there is a fault in the TPMS, such as a damaged or missing sensor(s), damaged module or a communication issue within the vehicle, DTCs are set in the driver door module (DDM), the TPMS warning indicator will flash for 70 seconds and then remain ON solid when the ignition switch is turned to the ON position and the message center (if equipped) will display TIRE PRESSURE SENSOR FAULT. When any of the tire pressure sensors are faulted or not responding, the DDM will set DTC B2872 and the message center (if equipped) will display TIRE PRESSURE SENSOR FAULT. When the DDM does not get a response from any of the tire pressure sensors, DTC B287A will be set and the message center (if equipped) will display TIRE PRESSURE MONITOR FAULT.

- DTC B2872 Tire Pressure Sensor Fault — When 1, 2 or 3 of the tire pressure sensors are faulted or not responding, the smart junction box (SJB) will set DTC B2872.
- DTC B287A Tire Pressure Monitor Fault — When all 4 of the tire pressure sensors are faulted, not responding or not heard by the SJB, the SJB will set DTC B287A.

    This pinpoint test is intended to diagnose the following:

- TPMS sensor(s) missing
- TPMS sensor(s) not trained to the vehicle
- TPMS sensor(s) swapped due to wheel swap
- TPMS sensor(s) damaged
- Vehicle communication issue
- DDM antenna
- DDM

NOTE: If a warranty case is opened for an actual TPMS fault, document and include the actual tire pressure data in all warranty communications.

Test Step	Result / Action to Take
G1 CHECK FOR DTCs	
• Connect the scan tool. • Retrieve and record any DDM DTCs. • **Is DTC B287A present?**	**Yes** GO to G3 . **No** If DTC B2872 is present, GO to G2 . For all other DDM DTCs.

ARM0700000000057

Fig. 10   Pinpoint Test G: Codes B2872 Or B287A, Tire Pressure Sensor Or Monitor Fault (Part 1 of 3). Crown Victoria & Grand Marquis

Test Step	Result / Action to Take
G3 CHECK FOR CORRECT TPMS OPERATION	
• Train all 4 tire pressure sensors. Refer to Tire Pressure Monitoring System (TPMS) Sensor Training . • **Did all of the tire pressure sensors transmit correctly and did the horn sound when each tire pressure sensor transmitted to the DDM?**	**Yes** Using the scan tool, locate the updated TPMS sensor IDs trained to the DDM module. COMPARE these values to those recorded prior to the TPMS sensor training procedure. Disregarding sensor position (the system is not affected by tire rotation), any sensor IDs that do not match those retrieved from the module were changed but not retrained. The sensors are now trained to the vehicle, diagnosis is complete. DOCUMENT all TPMS sensor IDs on the applicable warranty claim. VERIFY system operation. **No** **Before diagnosing the DDM** : If the sensors do not respond to the special tool, ATTEMPT to activate the same sensor(s) with the special tool. If the sensor(s) still does not respond, MOVE the vehicle to rotate the wheels at least 1/4 of a turn and ATTEMPT to activate the same sensor(s) again. NOTE: The sensors may not be present. Dismount the wheel and tire. VERIFY that the sensors are present and mounted to the wheels, INSTALL sensor(s) as necessary. TRAIN the sensors. REFER to Tire Pressure Monitoring System (TPMS) Sensor Training . If the sensors are present but all of them failed to train the second time, GO to G4.
G4 CHECK FOR CORRECT DDM OPERATION	

• Disconnect all the DDM electrical connectors.
• Check the connectors for:
  ▪ corrosion.
  ▪ pushed-out pins.
  ▪ spread terminals.
• Connect all the DDM connectors and make sure that they are seated correctly.
• Operate the system and verify the concern is still present.
• **Is the concern still present?**
	Yes
	INSTALL a new DDM. CLEAR the DTCs. REPEAT the self-test.
	
	No
	The system is operating correctly at this time. The concern may have been caused by a loose or corroded connector. CLEAR the DTCs. REPEAT the self-test.

ARM0700000000059

Fig. 10   Pinpoint Test G: Codes B2872 Or B287A, Tire Pressure Sensor Or Monitor Fault (Part 3 of 3). Crown Victoria & Grand Marquis

Test Step	Result / Action to Take
G2 CARRY OUT THE SENSOR TRAINING PROCEDURE	
• Train all 4 tire pressure sensors. Refer to Tire Pressure Monitoring System (TPMS) Sensor Training . • **Did all of the tire pressure sensors transmit correctly and did the horn sound when each tire pressure sensor transmitted to the DDM?**	**Yes** Using the scan tool, locate the updated TPMS sensor IDs trained to the DDM module. COMPARE these values to those recorded prior to the TPMS sensor training procedure. Disregarding sensor position (the system is not affected by tire rotation), any sensor IDs that do not match those retrieved from the module were changed but not retrained. The sensors are now trained to the vehicle, diagnosis is complete. DOCUMENT all TPMS sensor IDs on the applicable warranty claim. VERIFY system operation. **No** **Before installing a new sensor(s)** : If a sensor(s) does not respond to the special tool, ATTEMPT to activate the same sensor(s) with the special tool. If the sensor(s) still does not respond, MOVE the vehicle to rotate the wheels at least 1/4 of a turn and ATTEMPT to activate the same sensor(s) again. If the sensor(s) fail to train a second time, INSTALL a new tire pressure sensor(s)..

ARM0700000000058

Fig. 10   Pinpoint Test G: Codes B2872 Or B287A, Tire Pressure Sensor Or Monitor Fault (Part 2 of 3). Crown Victoria & Grand Marquis

Normal Operation

If there is a fault in the tire pressure monitoring system (TPMS), such as a damaged or missing sensor(s), damaged module or a communication issue within the vehicle, DTCs are set in the driver door module (DDM), the TPMS warning indicator will flash for 70 seconds and then remain ON solid when the ignition switch is turned to the ON position and the message center (if equipped) will display TIRE PRESSURE SENSOR FAULT.

This DTC may be encountered if a high-pressure sensor (designed for trucks with much higher tire pressures and molded in green plastic) was installed. The DDM will only allow a low-pressure sensor to be trained using the TPMS sensor training procedure. Make sure the correct sensors are used to avoid compatibility issues.

- DTC B106A Pressure Sensor Range Bit Incorrect State — When an attempt has been made to train a non-compatible sensor, the smart junction box (SJB) will set DTC B106A.

    This pinpoint test is intended to diagnose the following:

- Tire pressure sensor(s)
- Incorrect tire pressure sensor(s) installed
- DDM

Test Step	Result / Action to Take
H1 DETERMINE IF THE VEHICLE IS EQUIPPED WITH AN INCORRECT SENSOR	
• Train all 4 tire pressure sensors. Refer to Tire Pressure Monitoring System (TPMS) Sensor Training . • **Did all of the tire pressure sensors transmit correctly and did the horn sound when each tire pressure sensor transmitted to the DDM?**	**Yes** CLEAR the DTCs. REPEAT the self-test. VERIFY system operation. **No** **Before installing a new sensor(s)** : If a sensor(s) does not respond to the special tool, ATTEMPT to activate the same sensor(s) with the special tool. If the sensor(s) still does not respond, MOVE the vehicle to rotate the wheels at least 1/4 of a turn and ATTEMPT to activate the same sensor(s) again. If the sensor(s) fails to train a second time, INSTALL a new tire pressure sensor(s)..

ARM0700000000060

Fig. 11   Pinpoint Test H: Code B106A —Pressure Sensor Range Bit Incorrect State. Crown Victoria & Grand Marquis

Normal Operation

The tire pressure monitoring system (TPMS) monitors the air pressure of all 4 road tires. The wheel-mounted tire pressure sensors transmit via radio frequency signals, to the driver door module (DDM). TPMS functionality is integral to the DDM. These transmissions are sent approximately every 60 seconds when the vehicle speed exceeds 20 mph. The TPMS function (integral to the DDM) compares each tire pressure sensor transmission against a low-pressure limit. If it has been determined that the tire pressure has fallen below this limit, the DDM communicates this on the vehicle communication bus to the instrument cluster. The instrument cluster then illuminates the TPMS indicator and displays the appropriate message(s) in the message center (if equipped).

This pinpoint test is intended to diagnose the following:

- Low air pressure in tire(s)
- Tire pressure sensor(s)

⚠ **CAUTION: Use only special tool 204-354 any time tire pressures are measured to be sure that accurate values are obtained.**

NOTE: If a warranty case is opened for an actual TPMS fault, document and include the actual tire pressure data in all warranty communications.

NOTE: A full-sized, matching spare wheel and tire, that is identical to the road wheel and tire, is available as an optional accessory. This spare wheel and tire is equipped with a tire pressure sensor but the sensor is not initially programmed to the driver door module (DDM). If this spare wheel and tire is in use on the vehicle, the sensor must be trained to the DDM and the remaining 3 sensors must be retrained to the DDM as well. If all 4 sensors are not trained to the DDM, the tire pressure monitor system (TPMS) warning indicator will illuminate. Make sure that all the wheels and tires installed on the vehicle are inflated to the correct pressure and trained to the DDM before attempting to diagnose a TPMS concern. Refer to Tire Pressure Monitoring System (TPMS) Sensor Training .

ARM0700000000053

Fig. 8   Pinpoint Test E: Low Tire Pressure Displayed (Part 1 of 2). Crown Victoria & Grand Marquis

Normal Operation

For the driver door module (DDM) to enter tire pressure monitoring system (TPMS) sensor training mode, it must receive valid inputs from the following:

- Brake pedal position switch — OFF-ON-OFF
- Ignition switch — both OFF and RUN
- Vehicle speed sensor — 0 km/h (0 mph)

Refer to Tire Pressure Monitoring System (TPMS) Sensor Training for the complete sensor training procedure.

The brake pedal position (BPP) switch input is supplied to central junction box (CJB) fuse 28 (7.5A) along circuit 511 (LG) and then to the lighting control module (LCM) along circuit 1651 (WH/RD). The LCM then provides the BPP information to the DDM along the standard corporate protocol (SCP) communication bus.

The ignition switch input is supplied to the LCM from CJB fuse 26 (10A) along circuit 640 (RD/YE and CJB fuse 5 (7.5A) along circuit 297 (BK/LG). The LCM then provides the ignition switch information to the DDM along the SCP communication bus. The vehicle speed input is supplied by the PCM to the instrument cluster along the high-speed controller area network (HS-CAN) bus then from the instrument cluster to the DDM along the SCP communication bus.

This pinpoint test is intended to diagnose the following:

- Fuse
- Wiring, terminals or connectors
- Ignition switch
- Vehicle speed sensor (VSS)
- BPP switch
- PCM
- DDM

⚠ **CAUTION: Use the Flex Probe Kit for all test connections to prevent damage to the wiring terminals. Do not use standard multi-meter probes.**

Test Step	Result / Action to Take
F1 CHECK FOR MODULE DTCs	
• Key in OFF position. • Connect the diagnostic tool. • Key in ON position. • Retrieve and record any LCM, PCM, DDM, HS-CAN bus or SCP bus DTCs. • **Are there any DTCs present?**	**Yes** Diagnose as appropriate **No** GO to F2 .
F2 CHECK THE VSS	
• Drive the vehicle and observe the speedometer.	**Yes**

ARM0700000000055

Fig. 9   Pinpoint Test F: Driver Door Module (DDM) Will Not Enter Training Mode (Part 1 of 2). Crown Victoria & Grand Marquis

Test Step	Result / Action to Take
E1 CHECK THE TIRE PRESSURE	
• Measure and record the air pressure in all 4 road tires. • Adjust the air pressure for those found to be below the specification listed on the vehicle certification label. • **NOTE:** If the vehicle has been stationary for more than 30 minutes, activate the TPMS sensors. Refer to Tire Pressure Monitoring System (TPMS) Sensor Activation . TPMS sensors do not transmit when the vehicle is stationary. • Verify system operation. • **Have the TPMS indicator and the message center (if equipped) warnings gone out?**	**Yes** The system is functioning normally, diagnosis is complete. INFORM the customer of correct tire pressure maintenance as instructed in the scheduled maintenance guide and the Owner's Literature. **No** GO to E2 .
E2 CHECK THE SYSTEM COMPONENTS	

• Train all 4 tire pressure sensors. Refer to Tire Pressure Monitoring System (TPMS) Sensor Training i.
• Connect the diagnostic tool.
• Key in ON position.
• Enter the following diagnostic mode on the diagnostic tool: DataLogger DDM.
• Read and record the following PIDs:
  ▪ Left front tire pressure (LF_PSI)
  ▪ Right front tire pressure (RF_PSI)
  ▪ Left rear tire pressure (LR_PSI)
  ▪ Right rear tire pressure (RR_PSI)
• Compare the air pressure readings recorded from the function test to those recorded in E1.
• **Do the compared tire pressure values match within ±5 psi, and have the TPMS indicator and the message center (if equipped) warnings gone out?**
	Yes
	The system is functioning normally, diagnosis complete.
	
	No
	Before installing a new sensor(s): If a sensor(s) does not respond to the special tool, ATTEMPT to activate the same sensor(s) with the special tool. If the sensor(s) still does not respond, MOVE the vehicle to rotate the wheels at least 1/4 of a turn and ATTEMPT to activate the same sensor(s) again. INSTALL new tire pressure sensors for those with discrepancies or those that fail to activate.

ARM0700000000054

Fig. 8   Pinpoint Test E: Low Tire Pressure Displayed (Part 2 of 2). Crown Victoria & Grand Marquis

Test Step	Result / Action to Take
• **Is the speedometer working and displaying the correct speed?**	**Yes** GO to F3 . **No** Diagnose the instrument cluster.
F3 CHECK THE LCM BRAKE PEDAL SWITCH (LCM_BOO) PID	
• Enter the following diagnostic mode on the diagnostic tool: DataLogger LCM. • Observe the LCM_BOO PID while pressing and releasing the brake pedal. • **Does the PID match the brake pedal position?**	**Yes** GO to F4 . **No** Diagnose the BPP switch.
F4 CHECK THE LCM IGNITION SWITCH (IGN_SW) PID	
• Observe the IGN_SW PID while turning the ignition switch from RUN to OFF and back to RUN again. • **Does the PID match the ignition switch position?**	**Yes** GO to F5 . **No** Diagnose the LCM.
F5 CHECK THE DDM CONNECTORS	

• Disconnect all the DDM connectors.
• Check for:
  ▪ corrosion.
  ▪ pushed-out pins.
  ▪ spread terminals.
• Connect all the DDM connectors and make sure that they are seated correctly.
• Operate the system and verify the concern is still present.
• **Is the concern still present?**
	Yes
	INSTALL a new DDM
	No
	The system is operating correctly at this time. The concern may have been caused by a loose or corroded connector. TEST the system for normal operation.

ARM0700000000056

Fig. 9   Pinpoint Test F: Driver Door Module (DDM) Will Not Enter Training Mode (Part 2 of 2). Crown Victoria & Grand Marquis

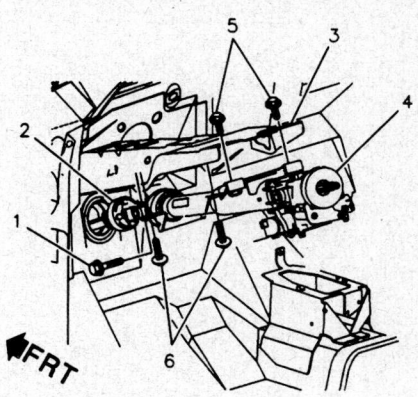

1 UPPER PINCH BOLT
2 FLANGE AND STEERING
   COUPLING
3 UPPER COLUMN
   SUPPORT
4 STEERING COLUMN
5 UPPER COLUMN BOLT
6 LOWER COLUMN BOLT

GC6049700227000X

Fig. 11 Steering column replacement. Cavalier & Sunfire

from steering column bracket by depressing two tabs.
10. Disconnect steering column electrical connectors.
11. Remove steering column electrical connector retaining bolt, then Separate electrical connectors.
12. Remove lower steering column mounting bolts.
13. Remove upper mounting bolts, then the steering column.
14. Reverse procedure to install.

Park Avenue

1. Ensure wheels are in straight ahead position and ignition switch is in LOCK position.
2. Remove steering wheel as outlined in "Electrical" section of "Bonneville, LeSabre & Park Avenue" chassis chapter.
3. Depress hazard button, then remove knee bolster and bracket.
4. **On models equipped with column shift,** remove shift lever cable.
5. **On models equipped with console shift,** unlock ignition and remove park lock cable, then lock ignition.
6. **On all models,** disconnect steering column electrical connectors.
7. Remove upper intermediate shaft pinch bolt, **Fig. 24.**
8. Remove steering column shaft from intermediate shaft, loosen do not remove lower steering column support mounting nuts.
9. Support steering column and remove upper steering column support mounting nuts. **Discard upper steering column support clips.**
10. Remove lower support nuts, then the steering column.
11. Reverse procedure to install.

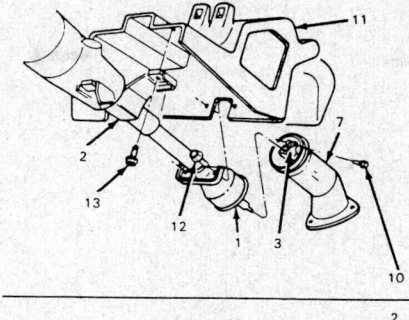

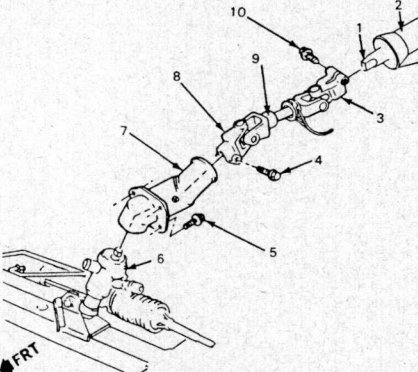

1 STEERING SHAFT-LOWER END
2 STEERING COLUMN ASSEMBLY
3 INTERMEDIATE SHAFT COUPLING-UPPER
4 PINCH BOLT-LOWER COUPLING
5 SCREW
6 STEERING GEAR
7 SEAL-INTERMEDIATE SHAFT
8 INTERMEDIATE SHAFT COUPLING-LOWER
9 INTERMEDIATE SHAFT
10 PINCH BOLT-UPPER COUPLING
11 BRACKET-BRAKE PEDAL
12 BOLT-LOWER STEERING COLUMN
13 BOLT-UPPER STEERING COLUMN

GC6049100057000X

Fig. 12 Steering column replacement. Century, Grand Prix, Monte Carlo & Regal

Solstice & SKY

1. Remove left instrument panel insulator, then the knee bolster panel and bracket.
2. Lower steering as required, then remove trim covers.
3. **On Solstice models,** remove steering wheel as outlined in "Electrical" section of "Solstice" chassis chapter.
4. **On SKY models,** remove steering wheel as outlined in "Electrical" section of "Saturn" chassis chapter.
5. **On all models,** disconnect ignition switch electrical connectors.
6. Remove steering column pinch bolt and nut, discard bolt.
7. Separate intermediate shaft from steering column.
8. Remove steering column support bolt and nut, then the column.
9. Reverse procedure to install.

Vibe

1. Ensure wheels are in straight ahead position and ignition switch is in LOCK position.

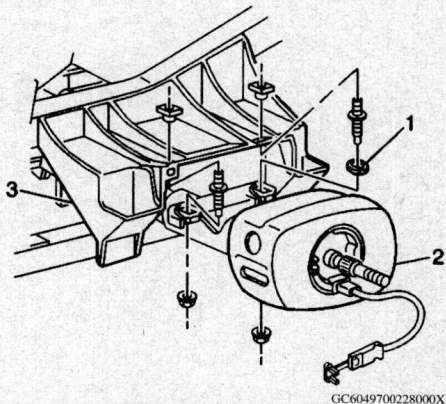

GC6049700228000X

Fig. 13 Steering column replacement. Corvette

2. Remove steering wheel and multifunction switch as outlined in "Electrical" section of "Vibe" chassis chapter.
3. Remove steering column trim covers.
4. Remove SIR coil as outlined in "Passive Restraint Systems" chapter.
5. **On models equipped with automatic transmission,** install key into cylinder, turn key to ACC position, release button, then disconnect park lock cable.
6. Lock steering column in original position, then remove ignition key.
7. **On all models,** remove lower pad from steering column.
8. Loosen upper bolt, then remove lower bolt from steering column intermediate shaft coupling.
9. Disconnect coupling at steering column.
10. Disconnect steering column electrical connectors.
11. Remove steering column retaining bolts, then the steering column.
12. Reverse procedure to install.

XLR

If steering column connectors are disconnected with the ignition in the ON position, the BCM will enter a fail enable mode and prevent steering column lock operation. The PCM will also inhibit vehicle motion by disabling fuel. To clear the BCM fail enable mode, disconnect BCM fuse No. 25 for no less than 15 seconds.

1. Turn steering wheel far enough to lefthand side to gain access to upper coupling bolt, then remove upper coupling bolt.
2. Turn steering wheel back to righthand side until wheels are in a straight ahead position, then lock steering column and install steering column lock pin tool No. J 42640, or equivalent, into steering column.
3. Remove trim panel from driver knee bolster.
4. Remove driver knee bolster bracket.
5. Disconnect electrical connectors from instrument panel wiring harness.
6. Disconnect steering column lock module harness from steering column lock module.

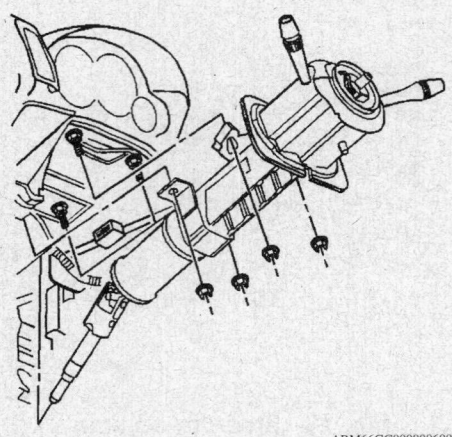

Fig. 14 Steering column removal. 2004–07 CTS

7. Remove lower steering column support plate mounting nuts.
8. Remove upper steering column bracket nuts from upper reinforcement assembly.
9. Slide steering column off of intermediate shaft.
10. Remove steering column from vehicle. Rotate steering column clockwise as bottom of steering column reaches reinforcement assembly. This will allow telescoping steering column motor and steering wheel position sensor room to clear instrument panel brace.
11. Reverse procedure to install.

STEERING COLUMN SERVICE

Alero & Grand Am

Refer to **Fig. 25** for exploded view of steering column.

TILT SPRING

1. Move tilt column into up position.
2. Pry spring upward until bulge occurs and most of spring tension is removed.
3. Secure spring with locking pliers.
4. Continue prying on spring until tilt spring disengages from post on steering column support and steering column housing.
5. Remove tilt spring guide from tilt spring.
6. Reverse procedure to install.

STEERING COLUMN TILT HEAD

1. Remove steering column as outlined in "Steering Column, Replace."
2. Remove SIR coil.
3. Compress cam orientation plate using lock plate compressor tool No. J23653-SIR and cam orientation plate adapter No. J42137, or equivalents.
4. Remove and dispose of bearing retainer.
5. Remove cam orientation plate.
6. Remove turn signal cam.

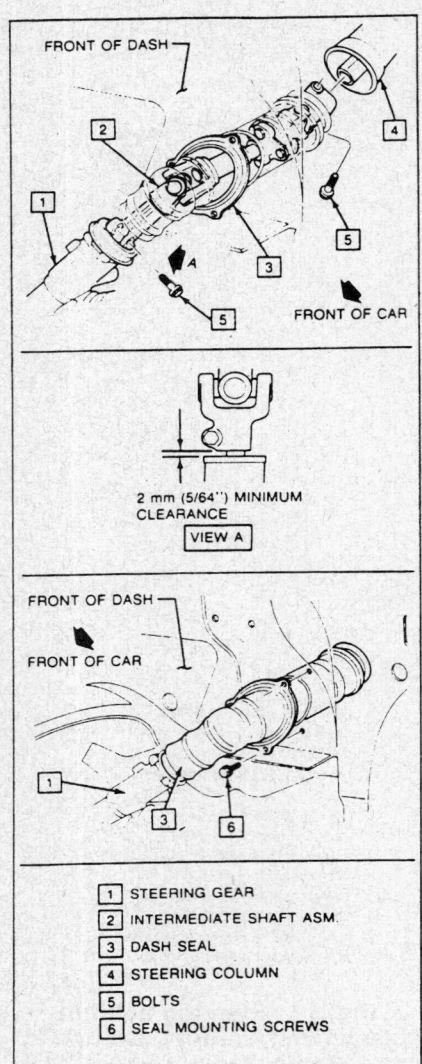

Fig. 15 Intermediate shaft & boot. DeVille & Seville

7. Remove upper bearing spring, inner race seat and inner race.
8. Remove pivot pins using pivot pin remover tool No. J21854-1, or equivalent.
9. Pull tilt arm to disengage steering wheel lock shoes from dowel pins in steering column support.
10. Remove bearing and housing.
11. Reverse procedure to assemble, noting the following:
    a. Lubricate pivot pins with grease.
    b. Press pivot pins until seated and stake at three locations.

LOWER BEARING, LOWER STEERING SHAFT & COLUMN JACKET

1. Remove steering column as outlined in "Steering Column, Replace."
2. Remove steering shaft seal from sensor retainer.
3. Remove sensor retainer from end of steering shaft.

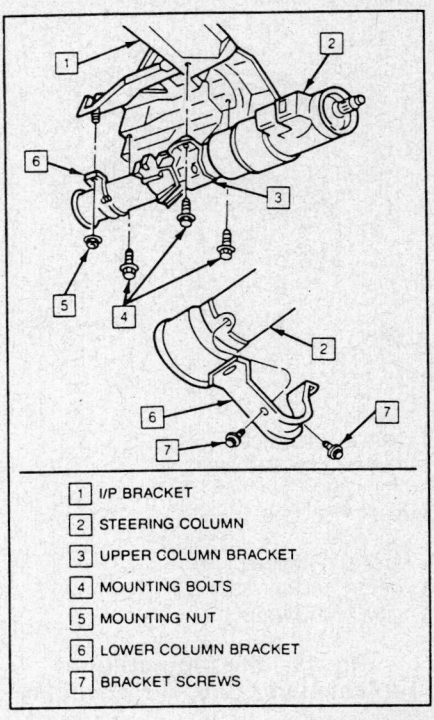

Fig. 16 Steering column replacement. DeVille & Seville

4. Remove lower spring retainer and steering wheel speed sensor, then the lower bearing spring and seat from steering shaft.
5. Remove adapter and bearing from steering column jacket.
6. Remove upper tilt head components.
7. Remove mounting screws from steering column support.
8. Remove steering shaft from steering column support.
9. Remove steering column support from steering column jacket.
10. Index mark, upper and lower steering shaft and race to ensure proper assembly.
11. Tilt race and upper shaft 90° toward each other.
12. Disengage, then remove race and upper shaft.
13. Remove centering sphere from race and upper shaft by rotating centering sphere 90°.
14. Lift centering sphere out of race and upper shaft.
15. Remove joint preload spring from centering sphere.
16. Inspect centering sphere and joint preload spring. Replace components, as required.
17. Reverse procedure to install, noting the following:
    a. Grease centering sphere with lithium grease.
    b. Assemble centering sphere and joint preload spring using centering sphere installer tool No. J41688, or equivalent.
    c. Apply lithium grease to exposed shaft engagement areas.

E4 CHECK FOR CORRECT SJB OPERATION	

• Disconnect all the SJB connectors.
• Check the connectors for:
   ▪ corrosion.
   ▪ pushed-out pins.
   ▪ spread terminals.
• Connect all the SJB connectors and make sure that they are seated correctly.
• Operate the system and verify the concern is still present.
• **Is the concern still present?**
	Yes
	INSTALL a new SJB. REPEAT the self-test.
	
	No
	The system is operating correctly at this time. The concern may have been caused by a loose or corroded connector. CLEAR the DTCs. REPEAT the self-test

ARM0700000000065

Fig. 14 Pinpoint Test E: Smart Junction Box (SJB) Will Not Enter Sensor Training Mode (Part 2 of 2). Mustang

Normal Operation

If there is a fault in the tire pressure monitor system (TPMS), such as a damaged or missing sensor(s), damaged module or a communication issue within the vehicle, DTCs are set in the smart junction box (SJB), the TPMS warning indicator will flash for 70 seconds and then remain ON solid when the ignition switch is turned to the ON position and the message center (if equipped) will display TIRE PRESSURE SENSOR FAULT.

• B2872 Tire Pressure Sensor Fault — When 1, 2 or 3 of the tire pressure sensors are faulted or not responding, the SJB will set DTC B2872.
• B287A Tire Pressure Monitor Fault — When **all 4** of the tire pressure sensors are faulted, not responding or not heard by the SJB, the SJB will set DTC B287A.

This pinpoint test is intended to diagnose the following:

• TPMS sensor(s) missing
• TPMS sensor(s) not trained to the vehicle
• TPMS sensor(s) swapped due to wheel swap
• TPMS sensor(s) damaged
• Vehicle communication issue
• SJB

NOTE: If a warranty case is opened for an actual TPMS fault, document and include the actual tire pressure data in all warranty communications.

Test Step	Result / Action to Take
F1 CHECK THE TPMS SENSOR ID PIDs AND TIRE PRESSURE SYSTEM STATE PID	

• Connect the scan tool.
• Key in ON position.
• Enter the following diagnostic mode on the diagnostic tool: DataLogger SJB.
• Read and record the following PIDs:
   ▪ Left Front Sensor Identifier (LF_ID).
   ▪ Right Front Sensor Identifier (RF_ID).
   ▪ Left Rear Sensor Identifier (LF_ID).
   ▪ Right Rear Sensor Identifier (RR_ID).
• Monitor the tire pressure state (TP_STAT) PID.
• **Is the TP_STAT PID equal to SENSOR FAULT?**
	Yes
	GO to F2 .
	
	No
	If the TP_STAT PID is equal to SYSTEM FAULT, GO to F3 .

ARM0700000000066

Fig. 15 Pinpoint Test F: Codes B287A or B2872 — TPMS On Solid When Ignition Key is Turned to ON Position (Part 1 of 3). Mustang

F2 CARRY OUT THE SENSOR TRAINING PROCEDURE	
• Train all 4 tire pressure sensors. Refer to Tire Pressure Monitoring System (TPMS) Sensor Training . • **Did all of the tire pressure sensors transmit correctly and did the horn sound when each tire pressure sensor transmitted to the SJB?**	**Yes** Using the scan tool, LOCATE the updated TPMS sensor IDs trained to the SJB module. COMPARE these values to those recorded prior to the TPMS sensor training procedure. Disregarding sensor position, any sensor IDs that do not match those retrieved from the module were changed but not retrained. The sensors are now trained to the vehicle, diagnosis is complete. DOCUMENT all TPMS sensor IDs on the applicable warranty claim. VERIFY system operation. **No** Before installing a new sensor(s) : If a sensor(s) does not respond to the special tool, ATTEMPT to activate the same sensor(s) with the special tool. If the sensor(s) still does not respond, MOVE the vehicle to rotate the wheels at least 1/4 of a turn and ATTEMPT to activate the same sensor(s) again. If the sensor(s) fail to train a second time, INSTALL a new tire pressure sensor(s). REFER to Tire Pressure Monitoring System (TPMS) Sensor .

ARM0700000000067

Fig. 15 Pinpoint Test F: Codes B287A or B2872 — TPMS On Solid When Ignition Key is Turned to ON Position (Part 2 of 3). Mustang

F3 TP_STAT PID EQUALS SYSTEM FAULT AND DTC B287A IS SET	
• Train all 4 tire pressure sensors. Refer to Tire Pressure Monitoring System (TPMS) Sensor Training . • **Did all of the tire pressure sensors transmit correctly and did the horn sound when each tire pressure sensor transmitted to the SJB?**	**Yes** Using the scan tool, LOCATE the updated TPMS sensor IDs trained to the SJB module. COMPARE these values to those recorded prior to the TPMS sensor training procedure. Disregarding sensor position, any sensor IDs that do not match those retrieved from the module were changed but not retrained. The sensors are now trained to the vehicle, diagnosis is complete. DOCUMENT all TPMS sensor IDs on the applicable warranty claim. VERIFY system operation. **No** Before diagnosing the SJB : If the sensors do not respond to the special tool, ATTEMPT to activate the same sensors with the special tool a second time. If the sensors still do not respond, MOVE the vehicle to rotate the wheels at least 1/4 of a turn and ATTEMPT to activate the same sensors again. NOTE: The sensors may not be present. DISMOUNT the tire. VERIFY that the sensors are present and mounted to the wheels. If missing, INSTALL new sensors. If the sensors are present but all 4 sensors failed to train a second time, GO to F4 .
F4 CHECK FOR CORRECT SJB OPERATION	

• Disconnect all the SJB electrical connectors.
• Check the connectors for:
   ▪ corrosion.
   ▪ pushed-out pins.
   ▪ spread terminals.
• Connect all the SJB connectors and make sure that they are seated correctly.
• Operate the system and verify the concern is still present.
• **Is the concern still present?**
	Yes
	INSTALL a new SJB module CLEAR the DTCs. REPEAT the self-test.
	
	No
	The system is operating correctly at this time. The concern may have been caused by a loose or corroded connector. CLEAR the DTCs. REPEAT the self-test.

ARM0700000000068

Fig. 15 Pinpoint Test F: Codes B287A or B2872 — TPMS On Solid When Ignition Key is Turned to ON Position (Part 3 of 3). Mustang

Normal Operation

If there is a fault in the tire pressure monitoring system (TPMS), such as a damaged or missing sensor(s), damaged module or a communication issue within the vehicle, DTCs are set in the driver door module (DDM), the TPMS warning indicator will flash for 70 seconds and then remain ON solid when the ignition switch is turned to the ON position and the message center (if equipped) will display TIRE PRESSURE SENSOR FAULT.

The tire pressure sensor is battery powered.

This DTC may be set when attempting to train a tire pressure sensor(s) with a low battery.

- DTC B106B Tire Pressure Sensor Low Battery — The pressure sensors are battery powered. If the battery is low and the sensors are trained, DTC B106B may be set. Also, if a new smart junction box (SJB) is installed and one or more sensors have low batteries, DTC B106B may be set.

This pinpoint test is intended to diagnose the following:

- Tire pressure sensor battery (part of the sensor)
- Tire pressure sensor(s)
- DDM

Test Step	Result / Action to Take
I1 DETERMINE WHICH SENSOR HAS A LOW BATTERY	
• Train all 4 tire pressure sensors. Refer to Tire Pressure Monitoring System (TPMS) Sensor Training. • **Did all of the tire pressure sensors transmit correctly and did the horn sound when each tire pressure sensor transmitted to the DDM?**	**Yes** CLEAR the DTCs. REPEAT the self-test. VERIFY system operation. **No** **Before installing a new sensor(s):** If a sensor(s) does not respond to the special tool, ATTEMPT to activate the same sensor(s) with the special tool. If the sensor(s) still does not respond, MOVE the vehicle to rotate the wheels at least 1/4 of a turn and ATTEMPT to activate the same sensor(s) again. If the sensor(s) fail to train a second time, INSTALL a new tire pressure sensor(s).

ARM0700000000061

Fig. 12   Pinpoint Test I: Code B106B — Tire Pressure Sensor Low Battery. Crown Victoria & Grand Marquis

D2 CHECK THE SYSTEM COMPONENTS	
• Train all 4 tire pressure sensors. Refer to Tire Pressure Monitoring System (TPMS) Sensor Training. • Connect the diagnostic tool. • Key in ON position. • Enter the following diagnostic mode on the diagnostic tool: DataLogger SJB. • Using the scan tool, read and record the following tire pressure PIDs: ▪ Left Front Tire Pressure (LF_PSI) ▪ Right Front Tire Pressure (RF_PSI) ▪ Left Rear Tire Pressure (LR_PSI) ▪ Right Rear Tire Pressure (RR_PSI) • Compare the air pressure readings recorded from the function test to those recorded in D1. • **Do the compared tire pressure values match within ±5 psi, and have the TPMS indicator and the message center (if equipped) warnings gone out?**	**Yes** The system is functioning normally, diagnosis complete. **No** **Before installing a new sensor(s):** If a sensor(s) does not respond to the special tool, ATTEMPT to activate the same sensor(s) with the special tool. If the sensor(s) still does not respond, MOVE the vehicle to rotate the wheels at least 1/4 of a turn and ATTEMPT to activate the same sensor(s) again. INSTALL new tire pressure sensors for those with discrepancies or those that fail to activate.

ARM0700000000063

Fig. 13   Pinpoint Test D: Low Tire Pressure Indicated (Part 2 of 2). Mustang

Normal Operation

The tire pressure monitoring system (TPMS) monitors the air pressure of all 4 road tires. The wheel-mounted tire pressure sensors transmit via radio frequency signals, to the smart junction box (SJB). TPMS functionality is integral to the SJB. These transmissions are sent approximately every 60 seconds when the vehicle speed exceeds 32 km/h (20 mph). The TPMS function (integral to the SJB) compares each tire pressure sensor transmission against a low-pressure limit. If it has been determined that the tire pressure has fallen below this limit, the SJB communicates this on the vehicle communication bus to the instrument cluster. The instrument cluster then illuminates the TPMS indicator and displays the appropriate message(s) in the message center (if equipped).

This pinpoint test is intended to diagnose the following:

- Low air pressure in tire(s)
- Tire pressure sensor(s)

NOTE: Use only special tool 204-354 any time tire pressures are measured to be sure that accurate values are obtained.

NOTE: If a warranty case is opened for an actual TPMS fault, document and include the actual tire pressure data in all warranty communications.

Test Step	Result / Action to Take
D1 CHECK THE TIRE PRESSURE	
• Measure and record the air pressure in all 4 road tires. • Adjust the air pressure for those found to be below the specification listed on the vehicle certification label. • NOTE: If the vehicle has been stationary for more than 30 minutes, activate each TPMS sensor. Refer to Tire Pressure Monitoring System (TPMS) Sensor Activation. The TPMS sensor does not transmit when the vehicle is stationary. • Verify system operation. • **Have the TPMS indicator and the message center (if equipped) warnings gone out?**	**Yes** The system is functioning normally, diagnosis is complete. INFORM the customer of correct tire pressure maintenance as instructed in the scheduled maintenance guide and the Owner's Literature. **No** GO to D2.

ARM0700000000062

Fig. 13   Pinpoint Test D: Low Tire Pressure Indicated (Part 1 of 2). Mustang

Normal Operation

For the smart junction box (SJB) to enter tire pressure monitoring system (TPMS) sensor training mode, the SJB must receive valid input from the brake pedal position switch (OFF-ON-OFF) and ignition switch (both OFF and RUN), and it must receive valid vehicle speed sensor input (0 km/h [0 mph]). Refer to Tire Pressure Monitoring System (TPMS) Sensor Training.

This pinpoint test is intended to diagnose the following:

- Wiring, terminals or connectors
- Brake on/off (BOO) switch
- Ignition switch

Test Step	Result / Action to Take
E1 CHECK THE SJB BRAKE ON/OFF (GEM_BOO) PID	
• Connect the diagnostic tool. • Key in ON position. • Enter the following diagnostic mode on the diagnostic tool: DataLogger SJB. • Press and release the brake pedal while monitoring the GEM_BOO PID (SJB reads the brake switch directly). • **Do the brake pedal PID values match the brake pedal positions?**	**Yes** GO to E2. **No** Diagnosis of the brake pedal switch.
E2 CHECK THE SJB IGNITION SWITCH (IGN_SW) PID	
• Cycle the ignition switch to the ON and OFF position while monitoring the IGN_SW PID (SJB reads the ignition switch directly). • **Do the ignition switch status PID values match the ignition switch positions?**	**Yes** GO to E3. **No** Diagnosis of the ignition switch.
E3 CHECK THE SJB VEHICLE SPEED (VSS_GEM) PID	
• Monitor the VSS_GEM PID. • **Does the vehicle speed PID value match the speed of the vehicle?**	**Yes** GO to E4. **No** Diagnose the vehicle speed concern.

ARM0700000000064

Fig. 14   Pinpoint Test E: Smart Junction Box (SJB) Will Not Enter Sensor Training Mode (Part 1 of 2). Mustang

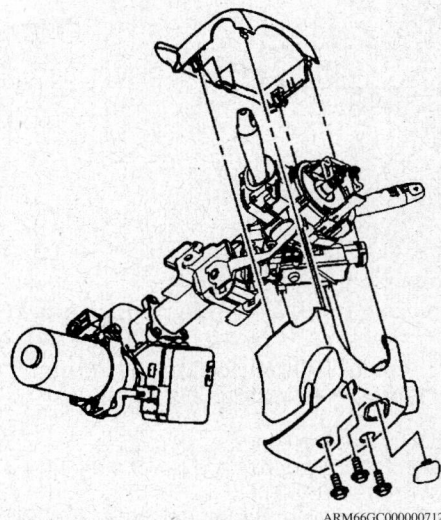

Fig. 17 Steering column trim cover removal. ION

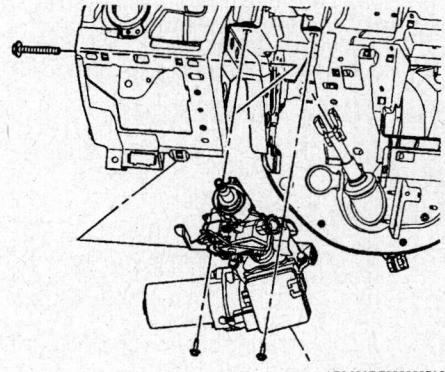

Fig. 20 Steering column removal. ION

SIR COIL CENTERING

The SIR coil will become uncentered if the steering column is separated from the steering gear and rotates, or if the centering spring is pushed down and the hub rotates while the coil is removed from the steering column. To center the coil, proceed as follows:

1. Remove clockspring coil as outlined in "Passive Restraint Systems" chapter.
2. Remove coil from steering column.
3. Hold coil with bottom facing upward.
4. Depress spring lock and rotate hub counterclockwise until it stops.
5. Ensure coil ribbon is wound against center hub.
6. Rotate coil hub clockwise approximately 2½ turns.
7. Release spring lock between locking tabs.

AURA

Refer to **Figs. 26 and 27** for exploded view of this steering column.

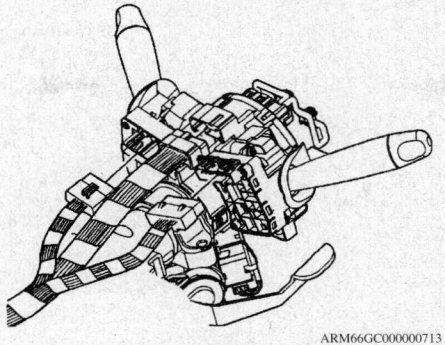

Fig. 18 Electrical harness removal. ION

STEERING COLUMN TRIM COVERS REPLACEMENT

1. Disarm air bags as outlined under "Precautions."
2. Lift up the upper trim cover, release lock rings from instrument panel seal, then remove upper trim panel.
3. Remove lower trim panel attaching screws.
4. Lower steering column rake lever, then remove lower trim cover.
5. Reverse procedure to install.

INTERMEDIATE STEERING SHAFT REPLACEMENT

1. Ensure wheels are in straight ahead position and ignition switch is in LOCK position.
2. Secure steering wheel to prevent it from rotating.
3. Raise and support vehicle, then remove left front tire.
4. Remove intermediate shaft to steering gear pinch bolt, then shaft from steering gear. Discard pinch bolt.
5. Lower vehicle.
6. Remove the intermediate shaft pinch bolt at the steering column shaft. Discard pinch bolt.
7. Slide intermediate shaft off steering column shaft.
8. Unseat intermediate shaft seal from dash by squeezing 4 tabs on the seal individually. Remove shaft from vehicle.
9. Reverse procedure to install.

Corvette

Refer to **Figs. 28 through 30,** for exploded view of these steering columns.

LOCK CYLINDER SET, SHAFT LOCK, SIR COIL, TURN SIGNAL SWITCH & UPPER BEARING SPRING

1. Remove steering wheel as outlined in "Electrical" section of "Corvette" chassis chapter.
2. Remove SIR coil and let hang freely. Remove wave washer.
3. Remove shaft lock retaining ring lock

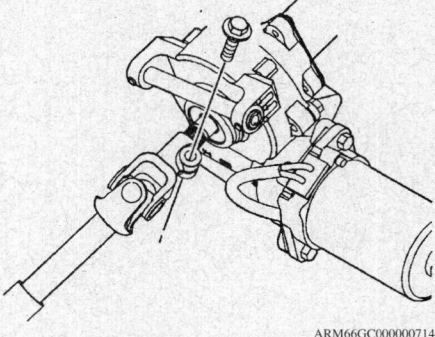

Fig. 19 Pinch bolt removal. ION

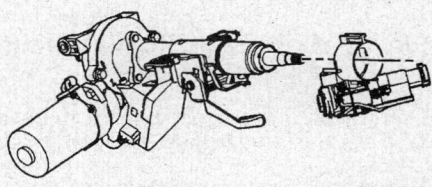

Fig. 21 Ignition lock cylinder case removal. ION

plate using compressor tool No. J23653-SIR, or equivalent.
4. Remove shaft lock assembly.
5. Remove turn signal cancel cam and upper bearing spring.
6. Remove upper bearing race seat and inner race.
7. Remove turn signal switch.
8. Remove wire protector and wire harness strap.
9. Attach suitable length of mechanics wire to both coil terminal connectors and gently pull wires through column.
10. Remove key from pass key lock cylinder set, then the buzzer switch.
11. Insert key in pass key lock cylinder and remove lock mounting screw.
12. Disconnect pass key lock cylinder terminal connector from bulkhead connector and remove wire protector.
13. Remove retaining clip from housing cover and gently pull wire harness through column.
14. Reverse procedure to install.

DIMMER SWITCH ACTUATOR ROD, LOCK HOUSING COVER, PIVOT SWITCH & TILT SPRING

1. Remove lock cylinder set, shaft lock, SIR coil, turn signal switch & upper bearing spring as outlined in "Lock Cylinder Set, Shaft Lock, SIR Coil, Turn Signal Switch & Upper Bearing Spring."
2. Remove lock cover housing end cap.
3. Remove mounting screws, lock housing cover and tilt lever.
4. Remove base plate and dimmer switch actuator rod, then gently pull pivot switch wiring harness through column housing and gear shift lever bowl.
5. **On models equipped with cruise**

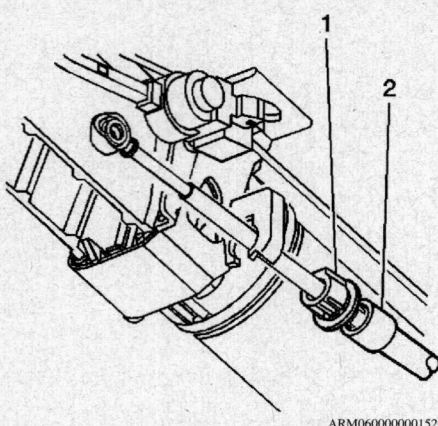

ARM0600000001529

Fig. 22 Shift cable from steering column removal

control, unplug connector from base plate and remove multi-function switch lever.
6. Pry tilt spring up until bulge occurs and most of tilt spring tension is removed.
7. Secure tilt spring with suitable locking pliers, continue prying until it disengages from steering column support post and tilt head.
8. Remove spring retainer, then the spring guide from tilt spring.
9. **On all models,** remove pin and pivot switch.
10. Reverse procedure to install, noting the following:
   a. Coat spring guide and spring with lithium grease.
   b. Tighten lock housing cover screw in three steps:
   c. First step, tighten to 12 o'clock position.
   d. Second step, tighten to 8 o'clock position.
   e. Third step, tighten to 3 o'clock position.

ACTUATOR SECTOR, BEARINGS, COLUMN HOUSING, LOCK BOLT, LOCK SHOES & SWITCH ACTUATOR RACK

1. Remove lock cylinder set, shaft lock, SIR coil, turn signal switch & upper bearing spring as outlined in "Lock Cylinder Set, Shaft Lock, SIR Coil, Turn Signal Switch & Upper Bearing Spring."
2. Remove dimmer switch actuator rod, lock housing cover, pivot switch & tilt spring as outlined in "Dimmer Switch Actuator Rod, Lock Housing Cover, Pivot Switch & Tilt Spring."
3. Remove lock housing cover retaining and tilt lever.
4. **On models equipped with cruise control,** unplug connector from base plate and remove multi-function lever.

5. **On all models,** remove retainer, spring and guide.
6. Remove tilt head pivot pins using pivot pin removal tool No. J21854-01, or equivalent, **Fig. 31,** then install tilt lever.
7. Remove column housing by pulling back on tilt lever and pulling housing down and away from column.
8. Remove bearing and mounting screw.
9. Remove lock bolt spring and lock bolt, then the switch actuator rack and rack preload spring.
10. Remove driveshaft and switch actuator sector.
11. Remove release lever pin and shoe release lever.
12. Remove release lever spring and dowel pin.
13. Remove steering wheel lock shoes and lock shoe springs.
14. Reverse procedure to install.

COLUMN HOUSING SUPPORT & SHIFT TUBE

1. Remove driver's side air bag module as outlined in "Passive Restraint Systems" chapter.
2. Remove ignition switch electrical connector.
3. Remove ignition switch mounting bolts, then the switch, **Fig. 32.**
4. Remove dimmer switch from actuator rod and wiring harness strap.
5. Disconnect positive assurance terminal, and dimmer switch connector from bulkhead connector.
6. Reverse procedure to install.

Bonneville & LeSabre

Refer to **Fig. 33** for exploded view of these steering columns.

SIR COIL

1. Remove steering wheel as outlined in "Electrical" section of "Bonneville, LeSabre & Park Avenue" chassis chapter.
2. Remove steering column as outlined in

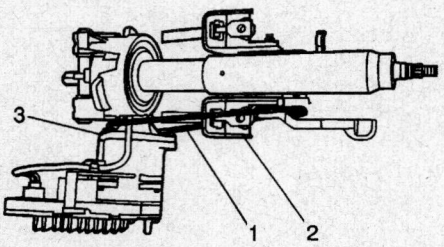

1 Tie straps
2 Rake lever bracket assemby
3 Electria Power Steering (EPS) assist mechanism bracket

ARM0300000000587

Fig. 23 Rake lever in LOCK position. Malibu, Malibu Classic & Malibu Maxx

"Steering Column, Replace."
3. Remove upper and lower steering column shrouds.
4. Remove wire harness straps and wire harness from wire restraint clip.
5. Remove black SIR connector from fused jumper connector.
6. Remove retaining ring using suitable snap ring pliers, then the SIR coil.
7. Remove wave washer.
8. Reverse procedure to assemble.

SIR COIL, CENTERING

Refer to "Passive Restraint Systems" chapter.

LINEAR SHIFT

1. Remove steering wheel as outlined in "Electrical" section of "Bonneville, LeSabre & Park Avenue" chassis chapter.
2. Remove steering column as outlined in "Steering Column, Replace."
3. Remove upper and lower steering column shrouds.
4. Remove wire harness straps and wire harness from wire restraint clip.
5. Disconnect shift lever electrical connector, slide shift lever seal up shift lever and remove lever mounting screw.
6. Remove shift lever and electric BTSI actuator from steering column.
7. Lock cylinder should be in Off-Lock position.
8. Remove mounting screws and linear shift from steering column.
9. Reverse procedure to assemble. Tighten to specification.

TILT SPRING

The tilt spring and guide are under pressure and could become projectiles. During disassembly and assembly procedures, secure the tilt spring.
1. Remove upper and lower steering column shrouds.
2. Move steering column to Up position.
3. Pry tilt spring until bulge occurs and most of tilt spring tension is removed.

Normal Operation

For the smart junction box (SJB) to enter tire pressure monitoring system (TPMS) sensor training mode, the SJB must receive valid inputs from the brake pedal position switch (OFF-ON-OFF) and ignition switch (both OFF and RUN), and it must receive valid vehicle speed sensor input (0 km/h [0 mph]. Refer to Tire Pressure Monitoring System (TPMS) Sensor Training in this section for the complete sensor training procedure.

This pinpoint test is intended to diagnose the following:

- Wiring, terminals or connectors
- Brake on/off (BOO) switch
- Ignition switch
- SJB

Test Step	Result / Action to Take
E1 CHECK THE SJB BRAKE ON/OFF (GEM — BOO) PID • Connect the scan tool. • Key in ON position. • Enter the following diagnostic mode on the diagnostic tool: DataLogger SJB. • Monitor the GEM_BOO PID (SJB reads the brake switch directly). • Press and release the brake pedal while monitoring the PID. • **Do the brake pedal PID values match the brake pedal positions?**	Yes GO to E2 . No Diagnosis of the stoplamp switch.
E2 CHECK THE SJB IGNITION SWITCH (IGN_SW) PID • Monitor the IGN_SW PID. • Cycle the ignition switch to the ON and OFF position while monitoring the PID (SJB reads the ignition switch directly). • **Do the ignition switch status PID values match the ignition switch positions?**	Yes GO to E3 . No Diagnosis of the ignition switch.
E3 CHECK THE SJB VEHICLE SPEED (GEM_VSS) PID • Monitor the GEM_VSS PID (SJB receives vehicle speed from the instrument cluster). • **Does the vehicle speed PID value match the speed of the vehicle?**	Yes GO to E4 . No Diagnosis of the instrument cluster/vehicle speed concern.

ARM0700000000073

Fig. 19 Pinpoint Test E: Will Not Enter Sensor Training Mode When Using Training Procedure (Part 1 of 2). Sable, Taurus & Taurus X

Normal Operation

If there is a fault with 1, 2 or 3 of the tire pressure monitoring system (TPMS) sensors, DTC B2872 will be set, the TPMS warning indicator will flash for 70 seconds and then remain ON solid when the ignition switch is turned to the ON position and the message center (if equipped) will display TIRE PRESSURE SENSOR FAULT.

If the smart junction box (SJB) does not get a response from all 4 of the TPMS sensors, DTC B287A will be set and the message center (if equipped) will display TIRE PRESSURE MONITOR FAULT.

- B2872 Tire Pressure Sensor Fault — When 1, 2 or 3 of the tire pressure sensors are faulted or not responding, the SJB will set DTC B2872.
- B287A Tire Pressure Monitor Fault — When all 4 of the tire pressure sensors are faulted, not responding or not heard by the SJB, the SJB will set DTC B287A.

This pinpoint test is intended to diagnose the following:

- TPMS sensor(s) missing
- TPMS sensor(s) not trained to the vehicle
- TPMS sensor(s) swapped due to wheel swap
- TPMS sensor(s) damaged
- Vehicle communication issue
- SJB

NOTE: If a warranty case is opened for an actual TPMS fault, document and include the actual tire pressure data in all warranty communications.

Test Step	Result / Action to Take
F1 CHECK THE SENSOR IDs AND SYSTEM STATUS PIDs • Connect the scan tool. • Key in ON position. • Enter the following diagnostic mode on the diagnostic tool: DataLogger SJB. • Read and record the following PIDs: ▪ Left Front Pressure Sensor Identifier (LF_ID) ▪ Right Front Pressure Sensor Identifier (RF_ID) ▪ Left Rear Pressure Sensor Identifier (LR_ID) ▪ Right Rear Pressure Sensor Identifier (RR_ID) • Monitor the TPMS system status (TP_STAT) PID.	Yes GO to F2 . No If the TP_STAT PID is equal to SYSTEM FAULT, GO to F3 .

ARM0700000000075

Fig. 20 Pinpoint Test F: Codes B2872 or B287A — Tire Pressure Sensor Or Monitor Fault (Part 1 of 3). Sable, Taurus & Taurus X

E4 CHECK FOR CORRECT SJB OPERATION	
• Disconnect all the SJB connectors. • Check the connectors for: ▪ corrosion. ▪ pushed-out pins. ▪ spread terminals. • Connect all the SJB connectors and make sure that they are seated correctly. • Operate the system and verify the concern is still present. • **Is the concern still present?**	Yes INSTALL a new SJB. CLEAR the DTCs. REPEAT the self-test. No The system is operating correctly at this time. The concern may have been caused by a loose or corroded connector. CLEAR the DTCs. REPEAT the self-test.

ARM0700000000074

Fig. 19 Pinpoint Test E: Will Not Enter Sensor Training Mode When Using Training Procedure (Part 2 of 2). Sable, Taurus & Taurus X

• Is the TP_STAT PID equal to SENSOR FAULT?	
F2 CARRY OUT THE SENSOR TRAINING PROCEDURE	
• Train all 4 tire pressure sensors. Refer to Tire Pressure Monitoring System (TPMS) Sensor Training . • **Did all of the tire pressure sensors transmit correctly and did the horn sound when each tire pressure sensor transmitted to the SJB?**	Yes Using the scan tool, LOCATE the updated TPMS sensor IDs trained to the SJB module. COMPARE these values to those recorded prior to the TPMS sensor training procedure. Disregarding sensor position, any sensor IDs that do not match those retrieved from the module were changed but not retrained. The sensors are now trained to the vehicle, diagnosis is complete. DOCUMENT all TPMS sensor IDs on the applicable warranty claim. VERIFY system operation. No **Before installing a new sensor(s)** : If a sensor(s) does not respond to the special tool, ATTEMPT to activate the same sensor(s) with the special tool. If the sensor(s) still does not respond, MOVE the vehicle to rotate the wheels at least 1/4 of a turn and ATTEMPT to activate the same sensor(s) again. If the sensor(s) fail to train a second time, INSTALL a new tire pressure sensor(s). REFER to Tire Pressure Monitoring System (TPMS) Sensor .

ARM0700000000076

Fig. 20 Pinpoint Test F: Codes B2872 or B287A — Tire Pressure Sensor Or Monitor Fault (Part 2 of 3). Sable, Taurus & Taurus X

Normal Operation

If there is a fault in the tire pressure monitoring system (TPMS), such as a damaged or missing sensor(s), damaged module or a communication issue within the vehicle, DTCs are set in the smart junction box (SJB), the TPMS warning indicator will flash for 70 seconds and then remain ON solid when the ignition switch is turned to the ON position and the message center (if equipped) will display TIRE PRESSURE SENSOR FAULT.

This DTC may be encountered if a high-pressure sensor (designed for trucks with much higher tire pressures and molded in green plastic) was installed. The SJB will only allow a low-pressure sensor to be trained using the TPMS sensor training procedure. Make sure the correct sensors are used to avoid compatibility issues.

- B106A Pressure Sensor Range Bit Incorrect State — When an attempt has been made to train a non-compatible sensor, the SJB will set DTC B106A.

This pinpoint test is intended to diagnose the following:

- Tire pressure sensor(s)
- Incorrect tire pressure sensor(s) installed
- SJB

Test Step	Result / Action to Take
G1 DETERMINE IF THE VEHICLE IS EQUIPPED WITH AN INCORRECT SENSOR	
• Train all 4 tire pressure sensors. Refer to Tire Pressure Monitoring System (TPMS) Sensor Training . • **Did all of the tire pressure sensors transmit correctly and did the horn sound when each tire pressure sensor transmitted to the SJB?**	**Yes** CLEAR the DTCs. REPEAT the self-test. VERIFY system operation. **No** **Before installing a new sensor(s)**: If a sensor(s) does not respond to the special tool, ATTEMPT to activate the same sensor(s) with the special tool. If the sensor(s) still does not respond, MOVE the vehicle to rotate the wheels at least 1/4 of a turn and ATTEMPT to activate the same sensor(s) again. If the sensor(s) fail to train a second time, INSTALL a new tire pressure sensor(s). REFER to Tire Pressure Monitoring System (TPMS) Sensor .

ARM0700000000069

Fig. 16   Pinpoint Test G: DTC B106A — Pressure Sensor Range Bit Incorrect State. Mustang

Normal Operation

The tire pressure monitoring system (TPMS) monitors the air pressure of all 4 road tires. The wheel-mounted tire pressure sensors transmit via radio frequency signals, to the smart junction box (SJB). TPMS functionality is integral to the SJB. These transmissions are sent approximately every 60 seconds when the vehicle speed exceeds 32 km/h (20 mph). The TPMS function (integral to the SJB) compares each tire pressure sensor transmission against a low-pressure limit. If it has been determined that the tire pressure has fallen below this limit, the SJB communicates this on the vehicle communication bus to the instrument cluster. The instrument cluster then illuminates the TPMS indicator and displays the appropriate message(s) in the message center (if equipped).

This symptom can also be caused by a spare tire currently being used in place of a road tire. Make sure that the spare tire is not currently in use. On vehicles with different front and rear tire pressures, if the sensors are not trained following a tire rotation, this symptom will also be present. Advise the customer that on vehicles with different front and rear tire pressures, the sensors must be trained as directed in the Owner's Literature.

This pinpoint test is intended to diagnose the following:

- Low air pressure in tire(s)
- Tire pressure sensor(s)

⚠ **CAUTION: Use only special tool 204-354 any time tire pressures are measured to be sure that accurate values are obtained.**

NOTE: If a warranty case is opened for an actual TPMS fault, document and include the actual tire pressure data in all warranty communications.

Test Step	Result / Action to Take
D1 CHECK THE TIRE PRESSURE	
• Measure and record the air pressure in all 4 road tires. • Adjust the air pressure for those found to be below the specification listed on the vehicle certification label. • **NOTE:** If the vehicle has been stationary for more than 30 minutes, activate each TPMS sensor. Refer to Tire Pressure Monitoring System (TPMS) Sensor Activation . The TPMS sensor does not transmit when the vehicle is stationary. • Verify system operation. • **Have the TPMS indicator and the message center (if equipped) warnings gone out?**	**Yes** The system is functioning normally, diagnosis is complete. INFORM the customer of correct tire pressure maintenance as instructed in the scheduled maintenance guide and the Owner's Literature. **No** GO to D2 .

ARM0700000000071

Fig. 18   Pinpoint Test D: Low Tire Pressure Indicated (Part 1 of 2). Sable, Taurus & Taurus X

Normal Operation

If there is a fault in the tire pressure monitoring system (TPMS), such as a damaged or missing sensor(s), damaged module or a communication issue within the vehicle, DTCs are set in the smart junction box (SJB), the TPMS warning indicator will flash for 70 seconds and then remain ON solid when the ignition switch is turned to the ON position and the message center (if equipped) will display TIRE PRESSURE SENSOR FAULT.

The tire pressure sensor is battery powered.

This DTC may be set when attempting to train a tire pressure sensor(s) with a low battery.

- B106B Tire Pressure Sensor Low Battery — The pressure sensors are battery powered. If the battery is low and the sensors are trained, DTC B106B may be set. Also, if a new SJB is installed and one or more sensors have low batteries, DTC B106B may be set.

This pinpoint test is intended to diagnose the following:

- Tire pressure sensor battery
- Tire pressure sensor(s)
- SJB

Test Step	Result / Action to Take
H1 DETERMINE WHICH SENSOR HAS A LOW BATTERY	
• Train all 4 tire pressure sensors. Refer to Tire Pressure Monitoring System (TPMS) Sensor Training . • **Did all of the tire pressure sensors transmit correctly and did the horn sound when each tire pressure sensor transmitted to the SJB?**	**Yes** CLEAR the DTCs. REPEAT the self-test. VERIFY system operation. **No** **Before installing a new sensor(s)** : If a sensor(s) does not respond to the special tool, ATTEMPT to activate the same sensor(s) with the special tool. If the sensor(s) still does not respond, MOVE the vehicle to rotate the wheels at least 1/4 of a turn and ATTEMPT to activate the same sensor(s) again. If the sensor(s) fail to train a second time, INSTALL a new tire pressure sensor(s). REFER to Tire Pressure Monitoring System (TPMS) Sensor .

ARM0700000000070

Fig. 17   Pinpoint Test H: DTC B106B — Tire Pressure Sensor Low Battery. Mustang

Test Step	Result / Action to Take
D2 CHECK THE SYSTEM COMPONENTS	

• Train all 4 tire pressure sensors. Refer to Tire Pressure Monitoring System (TPMS) Sensor Training
 • Connect the scan tool.
 • Key in ON position.
 • Enter the following diagnostic mode on the diagnostic tool: DataLogger SJB.
 • Read and record the following PIDs:
   ▪ Left Front Tire Pressure (LF_PSI)
   ▪ Right Front Tire Pressure (RF_PSI)
   ▪ Left Rear Tire Pressure (LR_PSI)
   ▪ Right Rear Tire Pressure (RR_PSI)
 • Compare the air pressure readings recorded from the function test to those recorded in D1.
 • **Do the compared tire pressure values match within ±5 psi, and have the TPMS indicator and the message center (if equipped) warnings gone out?**
	Yes
	 The system is functioning normally, diagnosis complete.
	
	 No
	 Before installing a new sensor(s): If a sensor(s) does not respond to the special tool, ATTEMPT to activate the same sensor(s) with the special tool. If the sensor(s) still does not respond, MOVE the vehicle to rotate the wheels at least 1/4 of a turn and ATTEMPT to activate the same sensor(s) again.
	
	 INSTALL new tire pressure sensors for those with discrepancies or those that fail to activate

ARM0700000000072

Fig. 18   Pinpoint Test D: Low Tire Pressure Indicated (Part 2 of 2). Sable, Taurus & Taurus X

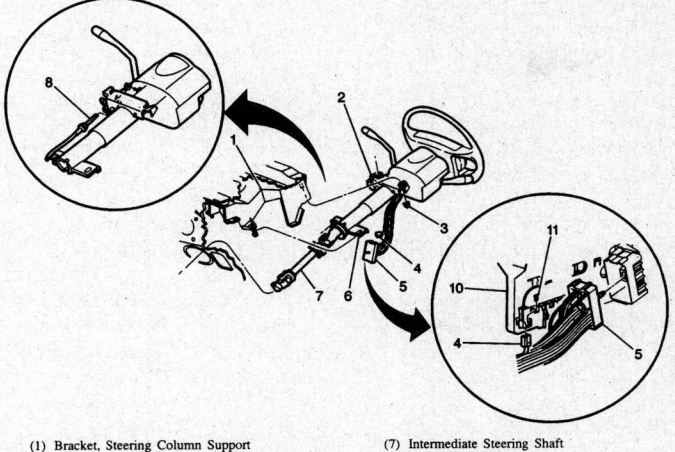

(1) Bracket, Steering Column Support
(2) Support, Steering Column Upper
(3) Nut
(4) Connector, SIR
(5) Connector, Steering Column Wiring Harness
(6) Support, Steering Column Lower
(7) Intermediate Steering Shaft
(8) Shift Lever Cable
(9) Park Lock Cable
(10) Bracket, Multiuse Module
(11) Connector, Position Assurance (CPA)

GC6049700226000X

Fig. 24 Steering column replacement. Park Avenue

4. Secure tilt spring and continue to pry until tilt spring disengages from post on steering wheel column and column tilt head.
5. Remove tilt spring guide from tilt spring.
6. Reverse procedure to assemble.

LOCK MODULE

1. Remove steering wheel as outlined in "Electrical" section of "Bonneville, Le-Sabre & Park Avenue" chassis chapter.
2. Remove coded key controller, ignition and key alarm switch.
3. Remove upper tilt head components.
4. Lock cylinder should be in Off-Lock position.
5. Insert suitable small screwdriver into slot on lock module, push against locking tab to remove.
6. Disconnect park lock cable.
7. Remove lock module mounting screws, then the module.
8. Reverse procedure to install noting the following:
   a. Ensure gear shift lever is in park position.
   b. Put ignition switch in Off-Lock position.
   c. Unlock adjuster ring on park lock cable with park lock cable pliers tool No. J41396, or equivalent.
   d. Pull on cable until park lock latch contacts gear shift lever. Release cable.
   e. Lock adjuster ring securely in place on park lock cable with suitable cable pliers.

STEERING COLUMN TILT HEAD HOUSING

1. Remove steering wheel as outlined in "Electrical" section of "Bonneville, Le-Sabre & Park Avenue" chassis chapter.
2. Remove bearing retainer using bearing removal tool No. J23653-SIR, or equivalent.

3. Remove shaft lock shield and turn signal cancel cam.
4. Remove upper bearing spring and inner race seat.
5. Remove inner race.
6. Reverse procedure to assemble.

LOWER BEARING & STEERING SHAFT

1. Remove steering wheel as outlined in "Electrical" section of "Bonneville, Le-Sabre & Park Avenue" chassis chapter.
2. Remove upper tilt head components.
3. Disconnect electrical connector from pivot and pulse switch.
4. Press on locking tabs of pivot and pulse switch, then pull out pivot and pulse switch from mounting bracket.
5. Remove screws and mounting bracket.
6. Remove turn signal and multi-function switch.
7. Remove tilt spring, linear shift, shift lever and BTSI actuator.
8. Remove steering column support pivot pins using pivot pin removal tool No. J21854-1, or equivalent.
9. Remove dual triangle sensor retainer, then the sensor.
10. Remove boot and steering shaft seals.
11. Remove mounting screws and cable support bracket.
12. Remove tilt head from steering column

(1) Tilt Lever
(2) Anti-Rotation Pin
(3) Tilt Spring and Guide
(4) Bearing and Housing Assembly
(5) Switch Adapter Plate
(6) Upper Bearing Spring
(7) Upper Bearing Inner Race Seat
(8) Upper Bearing Spring
(9) Turn Signal Cancel Cam Assembly
(10) Cam Orientation Plate
(11) Bearing Retainer
(12) Wave Washer
(13) SIR Coil Assembly
(14) Snap Ring
(15) Flanged Prevailing Torque Nut
(16) Race and Upper Shaft Assembly
(17) Centering Sphere
(18) Joint Preload Spring
(19) Centering Sphere
(20) Lower Shaft Assembly

GC6049900252000X

Fig. 25 Exploded view of tilt steering column. Alero & Grand Am

support with lower steering shaft still attached.
13. Remove tilt head from steering shaft.
14. Index mark race, upper shaft and lower steering shaft to ensure proper alignment.
15. Reverse procedure to assemble.

Cavalier & Sunfire

Refer to **Figs. 34 and 35** for exploded views of these steering columns.

COLUMN LOCK CYLINDER SET, SHAFT LOCK, TURN SIGNAL CANCEL CAM & UPPER BEARING

STANDARD COLUMN

1. Remove driver's air bag module as outlined in "Passive Restraint Systems" chapter.
2. Remove steering wheel as outlined in "Electrical" section of "Cavalier, Cobalt, G5 & Sunfire" chassis chapter.
3. Remove shaft lock cover and shaft lock retaining ring using plate compressor tool No. J23653-SIR, or equivalent, to depress shaft lock.
4. Remove shaft lock, turn signal canceling cam, upper bearing spring and thrust washer.
5. Move turn signal to righthand turn position.

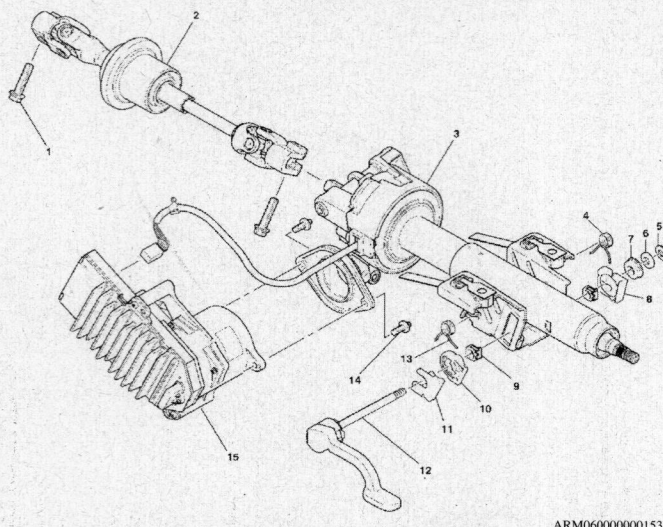

(1) Pinch Bolt
(2) Intermediate Steering Shaft
(3) Column and Assist Mechanism
(4) R/H Tilt Spring
(5) Nylon Insert Nut
(6) Thrust Bearing Assembly
(7) Bolt Spacer
(8) Bolt Retainer

(9) Tilt and Tele Teeth
(10) Tilt and Tele Adj Cam
(11) Follower Release
(12) Tilt Lever Assembly
(13) L/H Tilt Spring
(14) TORX® Bolt
(15) Motor and Controller Assembly

ARM0600000001532

Fig. 26 Exploded view of steering column (Part 2 of 2). AURA Electronic Power Steering

(1) Intermediate Steering Shaft
(2) Bolt and Retainer Assembly
(3) Steering Wheel Position Sensor
(4) Steering Column Assembly
(5) R/H Tilt Spring
(6) Nylon Insert Nut
(7) Thrust Bearing Assembly
(8) Bolt Spacer

(9) Bolt Retainer
(10) Rake and Tele Teeth
(11) Rake and Tele Adj Cam
(12) Follower Release
(13) Tilt Lever Assembly
(14) L/H Tilt Spring
(15) Pinch Bolt Nut

ARM0600000001534

Fig. 27 Exploded view of steering column (Part 2 of 2). AURA Hydraulic Power Steering

ARM0600000001531

Fig. 26 Exploded view of steering column (Part 1 of 2). AURA Electronic Power Steering

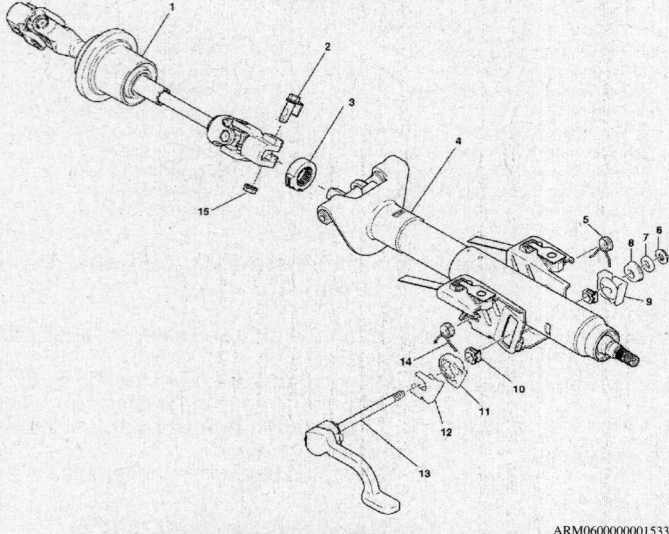

ARM0600000001533

Fig. 27 Exploded view of steering column (Part 1 of 2). AURA Hydraulic Power Steering

10. Remove mounting screw and lock cylinder.
11. Reverse procedure to install.

COLUMN HOUSING, IGNITION SWITCH ACTUATOR, PIVOT SWITCH, STEERING SHAFT, STEERING WHEEL LOCK SHOE, TILT SPRING & TURN SIGNAL SWITCH

STANDARD COLUMN

1. Remove steering wheel as outlined in "Electrical" section of "Cavalier, Cobalt, G5 & Sunfire" chassis chapter.
2. Remove steering column as outlined in "Steering Column, Replace."
3. Inspect steering column for damage.
4. Remove steering shaft retaining ring, then the shaft.
5. Remove steering column support bracket from housing.
6. Remove turn signal switch, mounting screw and nut, then the switch.
7. Remove dimmer switch, dimmer switch rod and switch mounting stud.
8. Remove ignition switch, mounting screws and inhibitor housing.
9. Remove cover screws and lock housing cover with floor shift lever bowl and shift bowl shroud. Pull housing cover from jacket and remove upper bearing retainer.
10. Remove mounting screws, floor shift lever bowl with shift bowl shroud and shroud from bowl.
11. If required, disassemble steering column housing as follows:
    a. Remove switch actuator rack with spring and bolt.
    b. Remove spring and bolt from switch actuator rack.

6. Remove multi-function lever and hazard knob.
7. Remove screw and signal switch arm, then the turn signal switch screws.
8. Remove turn signal switch and allow switch to hang freely.
9. Remove key from lock cylinder set, then the buzzer switch.
10. Install key in lock cylinder and turn to Lock position.
11. Remove mounting screw and lock cylinder set.
12. Reverse procedure to install.

TILT COLUMN

1. Remove steering wheel as outlined in "Electrical" section of "Cavalier, Cobalt, G5 & Sunfire" chassis chapter.

2. Remove shaft lock cover and retaining ring using plate compressor J23653-C, or equivalent, to depress shaft lock.
3. Remove shaft lock, turn signal canceling cam, upper bearing spring, upper bearing inner race seat and inner race.
4. Move turn signal to righthand turn position.
5. Remove multi-function lever and hazard knob.
6. Remove screw and signal switch arm, then the turn signal switch screws.
7. Remove turn signal switch and allow switch to hang freely.
8. Remove key from lock cylinder set, then the buzzer switch.
9. Install key in lock cylinder and turn to Lock position.

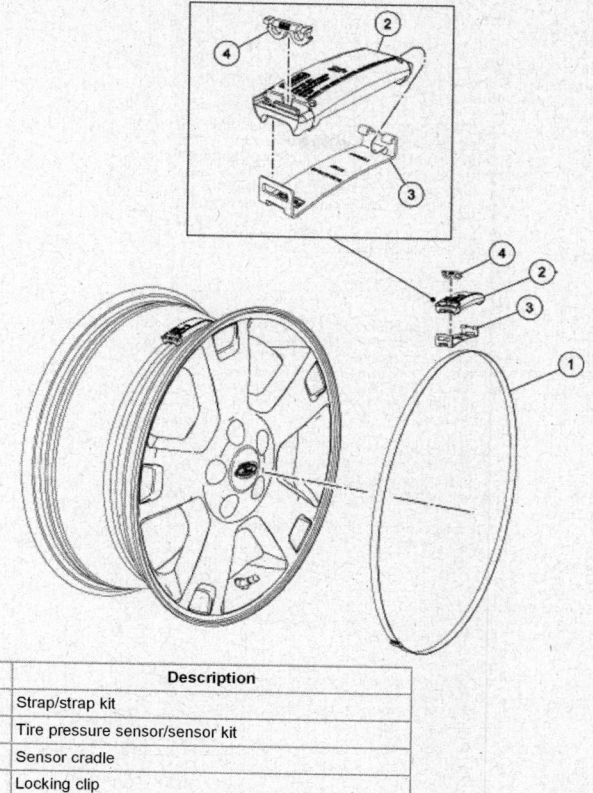

Item	Description
1	Strap/strap kit
2	Tire pressure sensor/sensor kit
3	Sensor cradle
4	Locking clip

ARM0600000000250

Fig. 22   Exploded view of strap & cradle type sensor

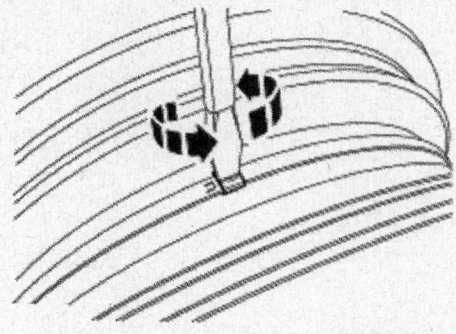

ARM0600000000249

Fig. 23   Unbuckling hold-down strap

COMPONENT SERVICE

Tire Pressure Monitoring System (TPMS) Sensor Activation

The tire pressure sensors will go into a sleep mode after 30 minutes of inactivity to conserve battery power. The sensors do not transmit information while in sleep mode, it will be necessary to wake them up so they will transmit the latest tire pressure information.

1. Turn ignition switch to ON position.
2. Position tire pressure monitor activation tool No. 204-363, or equivalent, against lefthand front tire sidewall 180° from tire valve stem.
3. Activate sensor at least twice by pressing activation tool test button. Activation tool will provide feedback in form of flashing green light and beep sound for each successful response from tire pressure sensor.
4. If sensor does not respond to activation tool, attempt activate same sensor with activation tool. If the sensor still does not respond, move vehicle to rotate wheels at least ¼ turn and attempt to activate same sensor, again.

5. Repeat procedure for each tire with sensor.

Tire Pressure Monitoring System (TPMS) Sensor Training

If the vehicle has been stationary for more than 30 minutes, the sensors will go into a sleep mode to conserve battery power. It will be necessary to wake them up so they will transmit the latest tire pressure information to the Smart Junction Box (SJB) or Driver Door Module (DDM). Refer to "Tire Pressure Monitoring System (TPMS) Sensor Activation."

The tire pressure sensor training procedure must be done on a single vehicle, in an area without radio frequency noise and at least three feet away from other vehicles equipped with TPMS. Radio frequency noise is generated by electrical motors and appliance operation, cellular telephones, remote transmitters, power inverters and portable entertainment equipment.

1. Turn ignition switch to OFF position, then press and release brake pedal.
2. Cycle ignition switch from OFF to RUN position three times, ending in RUN position.
3. Press and release brake pedal, then turn ignition switch to OFF position.
4. Cycle ignition switch from OFF to RUN position three times, ending in RUN position.
5. Horn will sound once and TPMS indicator will flash if training mode has been entered successfully. If equipped, message center will display TRAIN LF TIRE.
6. Place activation tool No. 204-363, or equivalent, on lefthand front tire sidewall opposite (180°) from valve stem.
7. Press and release test button on special tool. Horn will sound briefly to indicate that tire pressure sensor has been recognized by SJB or DDM..
8. It may take up to six seconds to activate a tire pressure sensor. During this time, activation tool must remain in place 180° from valve stem.
9. Within two minutes of the horn sounding, place activation tool on righthand front tire sidewall opposite (180°) from valve stem, then press and release test button to train righthand front tire pressure sensor.
10. Do not wait more than two minutes between training each sensor or SJB or DDM will time out and entire procedure must be repeated.
11. SJB or DDM has two-minute time limit between sensor responses. If SJB or DDM does not recognize any one of tire pressure sensors during this time limit, horn will sound twice and message center (if equipped) will display TIRE NOT TRAINED REPEAT. Entire procedure must be repeated.
12. Repeat procedure for right and lefthand rear tires.
13. When training procedure is complete, message center (if equipped) will display TIRE TRAINING COMPLETE. For vehicles not equipped with message center, successful completion of training procedure will be verified by turning ignition switch to OFF position without horn sounding. If the horn sounds twice when switch is turned to OFF position, training procedure was not successful.

F3 TP_STAT PID EQUALS SYSTEM FAULT WITH DTC B287A PRESENT	
• Train all 4 tire pressure sensors. Refer to Tire Pressure Monitoring System (TPMS) Sensor Training. • **Did all of the tire pressure sensors transmit correctly and did the horn sound when each tire pressure sensor transmitted to the SJB?**	**Yes** Using the scan tool, LOCATE the updated TPMS sensor IDs trained to the SJB module. COMPARE these values to those recorded prior to the TPMS sensor training procedure. Disregarding sensor position, any sensor IDs that do not match those retrieved from the module were changed, but not retrained. The sensors are now trained to the vehicle, diagnosis is complete. DOCUMENT all TPMS sensor IDs on the applicable warranty claim. VERIFY system operation. **No** **Before diagnosing the SJB** : If the sensors do not respond to the special tool, ATTEMPT to activate the same sensors with the special tool a second time. If the sensors still do not respond, MOVE the vehicle to rotate the wheels at least 1/4 of a turn and ATTEMPT to activate the same sensors again. **NOTE:** The sensors may not be present. DISMOUNT the tire, VERIFY that the sensors are present and mounted to the wheels. If missing, INSTALL new sensors. If the sensors are present but all 4 sensors failed to train the second time, GO to F4 .
F4 CHECK FOR CORRECT SJB OPERATION	
• Disconnect all the SJB electrical connectors. • Check the connectors for: ▪ corrosion. ▪ pushed-out pins. ▪ spread terminals. • Connect all the SJB connectors and make sure that they are seated correctly. • Operate the system and verify the concern is still present. • **Is the concern still present?**	**Yes** INSTALL a new SJB module. CLEAR the DTCs. REPEAT the self-test. **No** The system is operating correctly at this time. The concern may have been caused by a loose or corroded connector. CLEAR the DTCs. REPEAT the self-test.

ARM0700000000077

Fig. 20 Pinpoint Test F: Codes B2872 or B287A — Tire Pressure Sensor Or Monitor Fault (Part 3 of 3). Sable, Taurus & Taurus X

Normal Operation

This DTC may be encountered if a sensor designed for a different application is installed. Low pressure applications utilize a black- or blue-colored sensor, while heavy duty applications utilize a green-colored sensor. The smart junction box (SJB) will only allow one type of sensor to be trained using the tire pressure monitoring system (TPMS) sensor training procedure. Make sure the correct sensors are used to avoid compatibility issues.

- • B106A Pressure Sensor Range Bit Incorrect State — When an attempt has been made to train a non-compatible sensor, the SJB will set DTC B106A.

  This pinpoint test is intended to diagnose the following:

- • Incorrect tire pressure sensor(s) installed

Test Step	Result / Action to Take
G1 DETERMINE IF THE VEHICLE IS EQUIPPED WITH AN INCORRECT SENSOR	
• Train all 4 tire pressure sensors. Refer to Tire Pressure Monitoring System (TPMS) Sensor Training . • **Did all of the tire pressure sensors transmit correctly and did the horn sound when each tire pressure sensor transmitted to the SJB?**	**Yes** CLEAR the DTCs. REPEAT the self-test. VERIFY system operation. **No** **Before installing a new sensor(s)** : If a sensor(s) does not respond to the special tool, ATTEMPT to activate the same sensor(s) with the special tool. If the sensor(s) still does not respond, MOVE the vehicle to rotate the wheels at least 1/4 of a turn and ATTEMPT to activate the same sensor(s) again. If the sensor(s) fail to train a second time, INSTALL a new tire pressure sensor(s). REFER to Tire Pressure Monitoring System (TPMS) Sensor .

ARM0700000000078

Fig. 21   Pinpoint Test G: DTC B106A — Pressure Sensor Range Bit Incorrect State. Sable, Taurus & Taurus X

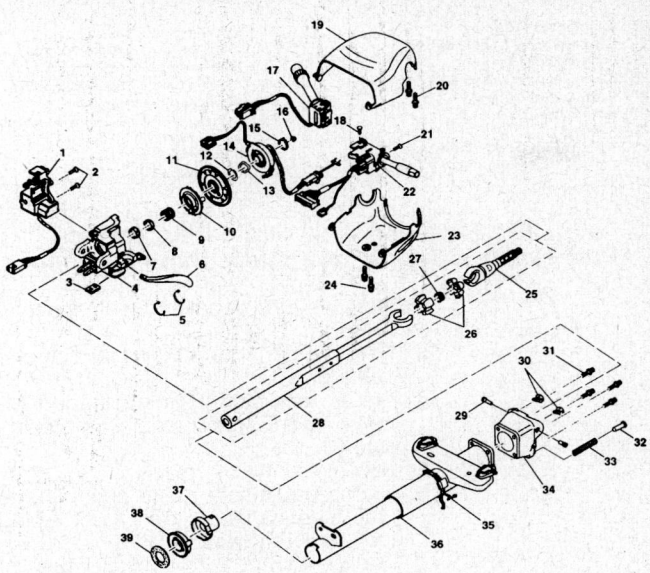

(1) Electric Column Lock
(2) Pan Head Tapping Screws
(3) Wire Harness Spacer
(4) Steering Column Tilt Head Assembly
(5) Wire Harness Straps
(6) Tilt Lever
(7) Inner Race
(8) Upper Bearing Inner Race Seat
(9) Upper Bearing Spring
(10) Turn Signal Cancel Cam Assembly
(11) Shaft Lock Shield Assembly
(12) Bearing Retainer
(13) Wave Washer

(14) SIR Coil Assembly
(15) Retaining Ring
(16) Flanged Prevailing Torque Nut
(17) Pivot and Pulse Switch Assembly
(18) Pan Head Tapping Screws
(19) Upper Shroud
(20) TORX® Head Screw
(21) Pan Head Tapping Screws
(22) Turn Signal and Multifunction Switch Assembly
(23) Lower Shroud
(24) Torx Head Screw
(25) Race and Upper Shaft Assembly

GC6049900278010X

**Fig. 28 Exploded view of steering column
(Part 1 of 2). Corvette non telescoping less sensor**

(26) Centering Sphere
(27) Joint Preload Spring
(28) Lower Steering Shaft Assembly
(29) Pivot Pin
(30) Tilt Bumper
(31) TORX® Head Screw
(32) Spring Guide

(33) Tilt Spring
(34) Steering Column Support Assembly
(35) Wire Harness Strap
(36) Steering Column Jacket Assembly
(37) Adapter and Bearing Assembly
(38) Sensor Retainer
(39) Steering Shaft Seal

GC6049900278020X

**Fig. 28 Exploded view of steering column
(Part 2 of 2). Corvette non telescoping less sensor**

c. Remove switch actuator rod from rack.
d. Remove spring thrust washer from spring and bolt.
e. Remove switch actuator sector, rack preload spring, switch actuator pivot pin and switch actuator pivot.
f. Remove bearing retaining bushing using suitable punch.
g. Remove bearing using suitable punch.
12. Reverse procedure to install. Assemble spring and bolt with switch actuator rack to housing. **First tooth of rack must interact with first and second tooth of sector. With rack fully inserted, block tooth of sector will rest in block tooth of rack.**

TILT COLUMN

1. Remove steering wheel as outlined in "Electrical" section of "Cavalier, Cobalt, G5 & Sunfire" chassis chapter.
2. Remove steering column as outlined in "Steering Column, Replace."
3. Inspect steering column for damage.
4. Disassemble lock housing cover, column housing cover end cap, pivot and pulse switch, dimmer switch rod actuator and tilt spring.
5. Remove turn signal switch with lock housing cover from steering column.
6. Remove mounting bolts and support bracket from steering column.
7. Remove wiring protectors and gently pull wire harness through column.
8. Remove pivot pins using pivot pin removal tool No. J21854-01, or equivalent, and install tilt lever.
9. Remove steering column housing and pull back on tilt lever, then pull steering column housing down and away from column.
10. Disassemble steering column housing as follows:
   a. Remove bearing , mounting screw, lock bolt spring, lock bolt, switch actuator rack and rack preload spring.
   b. Remove driveshaft and switch actuator sector.
   c. Remove release lever pin using lock shoe and release lever pin remover/installer tool No. J22635, or equivalent.
   d. Remove shoe release lever, release lever spring and dowel pin using lock shoe and release lever pin remover/installer tool No. J22635, or equivalent.
   e. Remove lock shoes and shoe springs.
11. Assemble steering column housing as follows:
   a. Install shoe springs and lock shoes.
   b. Install dowel pin using lock shoe and release lever remover/installer tool No. J22635, or equivalent.
   c. Install release lever spring and shoe release lever.

d. Install release lever pin using lock shoe and release lever pin remover/installer tool No. J22635, or equivalent.
e. Install switch actuator sector, driveshaft and rack preload spring.
f. Install switch actuator rack to actuator sector.
g. Assemble bearing lubricated with lithium grease to column housing using steering column housing bearing installer tool No. J38639 and driver handle tool No. J8092, or equivalents.
h. Install lock bolt, lock bolt spring and mounting screw.
12. Remove steering column jacket bushing and shaft.
13. Index mark upper and lower steering shaft to ensure proper alignment.
14. Disassemble steering column shaft as follows:
   a. Disassemble upper shaft from lower steering shaft. Tilt 90° to each other and disengage.
   b. Disassemble centering sphere from upper shaft. Rotate sphere 90° and slip out.
   c. Remove joint preload spring from centering sphere.
15. Assemble steering column shaft as follows:
   a. Install joint preload spring to centering sphere.
   b. Lubricate centering sphere with lithium grease.
   c. Slip into upper shaft and rotate sphere 90°.
   d. Install upper shaft to lower steering shaft.
   e. Align marks and tilt assemblies 90° to each other.
16. Remove mounting screws and column housing support with dimmer switch rod from steering column jacket. Remove rod from support.
17. Remove lock plate from steering column jacket and housing shroud.
18. Remove dimmer switch mounting nut & screw, then the switch.
19. Remove mounting stud and ignition switch with switch actuator.
20. Remove switch actuator.
21. Remove mounting screws and ignition switch inhibitor housing.
22. Remove ignition switch inhibitor from ignition switch.
23. Reverse procedure to install.

LOCK HOUSING COVER & TILT SPRING

1. Remove steering wheel as outlined in "Electrical" section of "Cavalier, Cobalt, G5 & Sunfire" chassis chapter.
2. Remove tilt lever, cover screws and

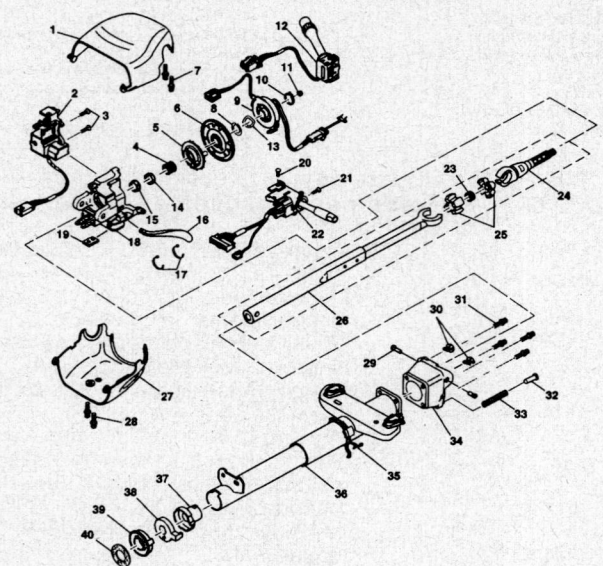

(23) Joint Preload Spring
(24) Race and Upper Shaft Assembly
(25) Centering Sphere
(26) Lower Steering Shaft Assembly
(27) Lower Shroud
(28) TORX® Head Screw
(29) Pivot Pin
(30) Tilt Bumper
(31) TORX® Head Screw
(32) Spring Guide

(33) Tilt Spring
(34) Steering Column Support Assembly
(35) Wire Harness Strap
(36) Steering Column Jacket Assembly
(37) Adapter and Bearing Assembly
(38) High Resolution Steering Wheel Position Sensor Assembly
(39) Sensor Retainer
(40) Steering Shaft Seal

GC6049900277020X

Fig. 29 Exploded view of steering column (Part 2 of 2). Corvette non telescoping w/sensor

2. Remove turn signal and multi-function switch.
3. Remove cam mounting bolt, ball and actuator.
4. Disconnect park lock cable and remove park lock cable mounting screws.
5. Remove shift lever clevis.
6. Pry up on tilt spring and spring guide until bulge appears and most spring tension is removed.
7. Secure spring with suitable pair of locking pliers and continue to pry until spring disengages from post.
8. Remove spring guide from spring.
9. Remove steering shaft seal and sensor retainer from adapter and bearing.
10. Remove lower spring retainer, bearing spring and seat.
11. Remove adapter and bearing from steering column jacket.
12. Remove pivot pins using pivot pin removal tool No J21854-01, or equivalent.
13. Remove steering column tilt head with steering shaft by installing and pulling tilt arm to disengage steering wheel lock shoes from dowel pins in steering column support.
14. Disconnect upper and lower steering shaft by tilting upper steering shaft 90° from lower steering shaft.
15. Rotate centering sphere 90° and lift centering sphere away from upper steering shaft.
16. Remove shaft preload spring from centering sphere.
17. Reverse procedure to install, noting the following:
   a. Install new centering sphere.
   b. Preload spring, using centering sphere installer tool No. J41688, or equivalent, and suitable vise.

SHAFT LOCK SHIELD, TURN SIGNAL CAM, UPPER BEARING SPRING, UPPER BEARING INNER RACE SEAT & INNER RACE

1. Remove steering wheel as outlined in "Electrical" section of "Century, Grand Prix, Impala, LaCrosse, Monte Carlo & Regal" chassis chapter.
2. Remove SIR coil and let hang freely.
3. Remove shaft lock by push down using lock plate compressor tool No. J23653-SIR, or equivalent.
4. Remove shaft lock shield.
5. Remove turn signal cancel cam.
6. Remove upper bearing spring, inner race seat, and inner race.
7. Reverse procedure to install.

(1) Upper Shroud
(2) Electric Column Lock
(3) Pan Head Tapping Screw
(4) Upper Bearing Spring
(5) Turn Signal Cancel Cam Assembly
(6) Shaft Lock Shield Assembly
(7) Torx Head Screw
(8) Bearing Retainer
(9) SIR Coil Assembly
(10) Retaining Ring
(11) Flanged Prevailing Torque Nut

(12) Pivot and Pulse Switch Assembly
(13) Wave Washer
(14) Upper Bearing Inner Race Seat
(15) Inner Race
(16) Tilt Lever
(17) Wire Harness Straps
(18) Steering Column Tilt Head Assembly
(19) Wire Harness Spacer
(20) Pan Head Tapping Screws
(21) Pan Head Tapping Screws
(22) Turn Signal and Multifunction Switch Assembly

GC6049900277010X

Fig. 29 Exploded view of steering column (Part 1 of 2). Corvette non telescoping w/sensor

lock housing cover. Let cover hang freely.
3. Remove column housing cover end cap with dimmer switch rod actuator and actuator from end cap.
4. Remove pivot, pivot and pulse switch actuator.
5. Remove spring retainer using suitable cross recess head screwdriver to push retainer down and turn clockwise to release.
6. Remove spring and spring guide.
7. Reverse procedure to install, noting the following:
   a. Coat spring guide and spring with lithium grease.
   b. Tighten lock housing cover screw in three steps:
   c. First step, tighten to 12 o'clock position.
   d. Second step, tighten to 8 o'clock position.
   e. Third step, tighten to 3 o'clock position.

Century, Grand Prix & Regal

Refer to **Figs. 36 and 37** for exploded view of steering columns.

UPPER COLUMN

1. Remove steering column as outlined in "Steering Column, Replace."
2. Remove retaining ring and SIR coil.

3. Remove shaft lock retaining ring using lock plate compressor tool No. J23653-SIR, or equivalent, and shaft lock plate.
4. Remove turn signal cancel cam, then the upper bearing spring, race seat and inner race.
5. Reverse procedure to install.

MID COLUMN

1. Remove steering column cover as outlined in "Steering Column, Replace."
2. Remove mounting bolt, ball and actuator.
3. Disconnect park lock cable and remove park lock cable mounting screws.
4. Remove shift lever clevis and park lock cable from support bracket.
5. Disconnect BTSI actuator arm from outer shift cable ball stud and transaxle shift cable from inner ball stud.
6. Remove mounting bolt and cable shift cam.
7. Remove cam bushing and cam mounting screws.
8. Remove gearshift lever support bracket.
9. Reverse procedure to install.

LOWER COLUMN

1. Remove steering guide from steering column jacket and steering column covers as outlined in "Steering Column, Replace."

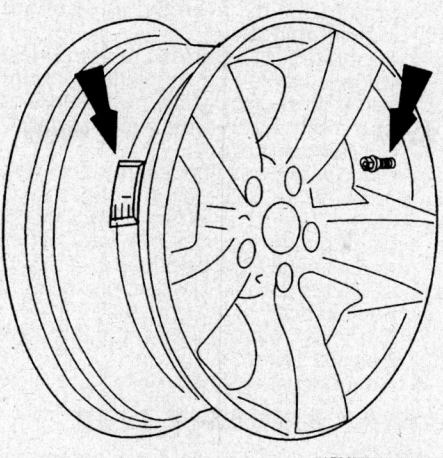

ARM0600000000251

Fig. 24   Sensor positioning

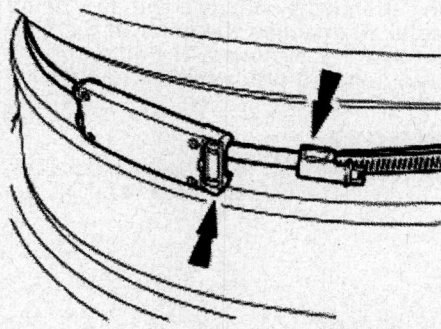

ARM0600000000252

Fig. 25   Strap positioning through sensor cradle

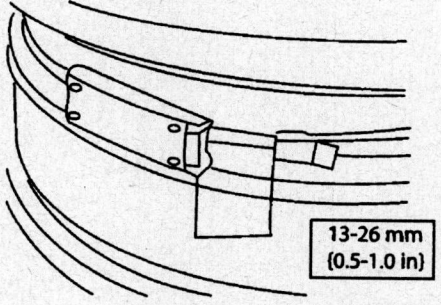

13-26 mm
(0.5-1.0 in)

ARM0600000000253

Fig. 26   Worm gear positioning

14. Program Vehicle Communication Module (VCM) and Integrated Diagnostic System (IDS) using suitable scan tool updating TPMS sensor IDs trained to SJB or DDM.
15. Clear Diagnostic Trouble code (DTC) C2780, exit SJB or DDM from manufacturing mode and ensure there are no other concerns with newly programmed SJB or DDM.
16. If new SJB or DDM was installed, clear all DTCs and perform SJB or DDM on-demand self test.

Pressure Monitor Sensor, Replace

VALVE STEM TYPE

1. Remove wheel and tire.
2. With valve stem at 6 o'clock position, remove sensor mounting nut and push sensor by hand into tire (with the cap on). **If valve stem core has been removed from valve stem, install original valve stem core. If original valve stem core is damaged, nickel-plated core must be installed.**
3. **Do not remove valve stem core to relieve tire pressure. Release tire pressure by removing sensor mounting nut.**
4. Separate both beads of tire from wheel using suitable tire machine. **Ensure valve stem mounting hole remains in 6 o'clock position while separating beads of tire.**
5. Place wheel and tire on turntable of tire machine so valve stem hole is positioned 270° from mounting/dismounting fixture. Mark valve stem and wheel weight positions.
6. Lubricate bead of tire and dismount outside bead of tire from rim.
7. Remove tire pressure sensor from tire. Discard grommet.
8. Reverse procedure to install.

STRAP & CRADLE TYPE

Tire pressure sensors are manufactured in multiple colors based on their application. When installing a new sensor, ensure the color of the sensor being installed matches the color of the sensor that was removed. The different colored sensors are not interchangeable, Fig. 22.

REMOVAL

1. Secure strap to wheel using suitable duct tape on both sides of buckle approximately .98 inch from buckle.
2. Unbuckle strap using suitable, large screwdriver and twisting motion, **Fig. 23.**
3. Turn worm gear screw until strap is fully released from worm gear. Discard the strap.
4. Mark cradle location for installation alignment.
5. Remove cradle by inserting suitable screwdriver under cradle and prying up.

INSTALLATION

1. Ensure sensor is fully seated into new cradle. Sensor will make click noise when fully seated.
2. Position sensor into new cradle by inserting hinge end of sensor into hook end of cradle and pushing opposite end of sensor down onto cradle.
3. Sensor and cradle must be installed in drop well of wheel, 180° from valve stem, **Fig. 24.**
4. Install tapered end of strap through opening of cradle on hinge side of sensor, **Fig. 25.** This will position worm gear on locking clip side of sensor.
5. Position worm gear .5–1.0 inch away from sensor and tighten worm gear, **Fig. 26.**

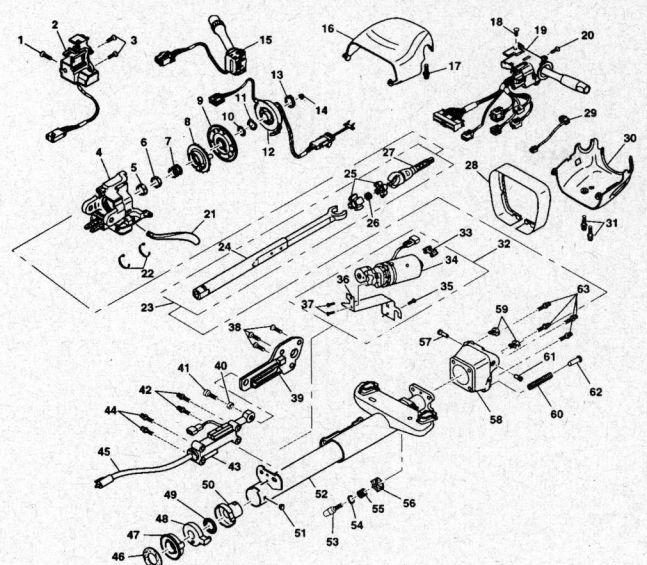

(1) Pan Head Tapping Screws
(2) Electric Column Lock
(3) Pan Head Tapping Screws
(4) Steering Column Tilt Head Assembly
(5) Inner Race
(6) Upper Bearing Inner Race Seat
(7) Upper Bearing Spring
(8) Turn Signal Cancel Cam Assembly
(9) Shaft Lock Shield Assembly
(10) Bearing Retainer
(11) Wave Washer
(12) SIR Coil Assembly
(13) Retaining Ring

(14) Flanged Prevailing Torque Nut
(15) Pivot and Pulse Switch Assembly
(16) Upper Shroud
(17) TORX® Head Screw
(18) Pan Head Tapping Screws
(19) Turn Signal and Multifunction Switch Assembly
(20) Pan Head Tapping Screws
(21) Tilt Lever
(22) Wire Harness Strap
(23) Steering Shaft Assembly
(24) Lower Steering Yoke Assembly
(25) Centering Sphere

GC6049900279010X

Fig. 30 Exploded view of steering column (Part 1 of 2). Corvette telescoping

(26) Joint Preload Spring
(27) Race and Upper Shaft Assembly
(28) Steering Column Close Out Shroud
(29) Telescoping Switch Assembly
(30) Lower Shroud
(31) Pan Head Tapping Screw
(32) Telescope Motor and Bracket Assembly
(33) Connector Clip
(34) Telescope Drive Motor Assembly
(35) Pan Head Tapping Screws
(36) Telescope Drive Bracket
(37) Pan Head Tapping Screws
(38) Flat Head 6–Lobed Soc Tap Screw
(39) Telescope Adapter Assembly
(40) Telescope Drive Ball
(41) Telescope Drive Bolt
(42) TORX® Head Screw
(43) Telescope Actuator Assembly
(44) TORX® Head Screw
(45) Cable Assembly

(46) Steering Shaft Seal
(47) Sensor Retainer
(48) Hi Resolution Steering Wheel Position Sensor Assembly
(49) Lower Spring Retainer
(50) Adapter and Bearing Assembly
(51) Switch Housing Blocking Plug
(52) Telebearing and Jacket Assembly
(53) Shoulder Bolt
(54) Retaining Ring
(55) Compression Spring
(56) Anti Rotation Ball
(57) Pivot Pin
(58) Steering Column Support Assembly
(59) Tilt Bumper
(60) Tilt Spring
(61) Pivot Pin
(62) Spring Guide
(63) Support Screw

GC6049900279020X

Fig. 30 Exploded view of steering column (Part 2 of 2). Corvette telescoping

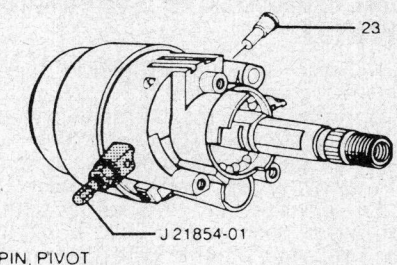

23 PIN, PIVOT

GC6049100092000X

Fig. 31 Pivot pin removal. Corvette, DeVille & Park Avenue

LOCK MODULE

1. Remove steering wheel as outlined in "Electrical" section of "Century, Grand Prix, Impala, LaCrosse, Monte Carlo & Regal" chassis chapter.
2. Remove shaft lock shield, turn signal cam, upper bearing spring, upper bearing inner race seat, and inner race.
3. Put lock cylinder in Off-Lock position and gear shift into Park position.
4. Insert small blade screwdriver into slot in lock module.
5. Push against locking tab on end of cable and remove.
6. Pry retaining clip on alarm switch with suitable small blade screwdriver.
7. Rotate alarm switch ¼ turn and remove.
8. Remove from ignition and key alarm switch mounting screws. Let switch hang freely.
9. **Lock bolt is under slight spring pressure from lock bolt spring. Hold lock bolt in place while removing lock module.**
10. Remove mounting screws and lock module.
11. Remove lock bolt with spring.
12. Remove spring from lock bolt.
13. Remove lock cylinder.
14. Reverse procedure to install.

ELECTRIC PARK LOCK

1. Remove transmission fuse No. 24 in instrument panel fuse panel.
2. Remove filler plug on bottom of lower shroud.
3. Insert suitable small screwdriver into hole and push up on manual override of electric park lock.
4. Turn key to Lock position, and remove.
5. Remove upper and lower steering column covers.
6. Remove mounting screw and black connector.
7. Remove electronic park lock from lock module with suitable small screwdriver.
8. Reverse procedure to install.

TILT SPRING

Tilt spring and spring guide are under pressure. During removal and installation secure spring with suitable locking pliers.
1. Remove lower shroud mounting screws.
2. Tilt shroud down, slide back to disengage locking tabs and remove.
3. Tilt column to up position.
4. Pry spring up until bulge occurs and most of spring tension is removed.
5. Secure spring with locking pliers and continue prying until spring disengag-

es from post on steering column.
6. Remove spring guide from tilt spring.
7. Reverse procedure to install.

LINEAR SHIFT

Linear shift may be removed as an assembly or certain components may be disassembled as required to do repairs. Remove or disassemble only those components required to do repairs.
1. Remove upper and lower covers as outlined in "Steering Column, Replace."
2. Place lock cylinder in Off-Lock position and gear shift in Park position.
3. Insert suitable small blade screwdriver into slot in lock module.
4. Push against locking tab on end of cable to release and remove park lock cable.
5. Pry actuator arm of electrical actuator from outer shift cable ball stud on cable shift cam and mounting pin on jacket.
6. Remove transaxle cable from inner shift cable ball stud on cable shift cam.
7. Shift column to Neutral position to gain access to lower mounting screw.
8. Remove mounting screws and linear shift.
9. Reverse procedure to install.

Cobalt & G5

Refer to **Fig. 38** for exploded view of steering column.

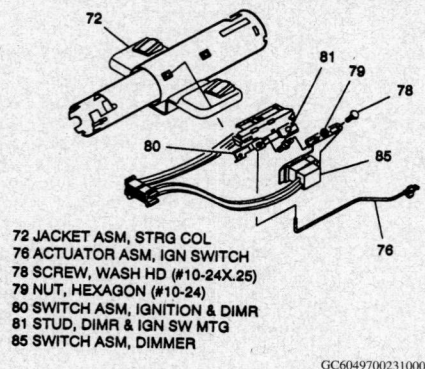

72 JACKET ASM, STRG COL
76 ACTUATOR ASM, IGN SWITCH
78 SCREW, WASH HD (#10-24X.25)
79 NUT, HEXAGON (#10-24)
80 SWITCH ASM, IGNITION & DIMR
81 STUD, DIMR & IGN SW MTG
85 SWITCH ASM, DIMMER

GC6049700231000X

Fig. 32 Ignition & dimmer switch replacement. Corvette

INTERMEDIATE STEERING SHAFT

1. Raise and support vehicle, then remove left front tire.
2. Remove intermediate shaft to steering gear pinch bolt. Discard bolt.
3. Disconnect intermediate shaft from steering gear, then lower vehicle.
4. Align steering wheel into straight forward position and lock. **Locking of steering column will prevent damage and a possible fault of SIR system.**
5. Place scribe marks on intermediate shaft to steering column connection prior to removal.
6. Remove intermediate shaft pinch bolt at steering column. Discard pinch bolt.
7. Slide intermediate shaft off steering column jacket.
8. Use a pulling, squeezing and twisting motion to unseat intermediate shaft seal from dash.
9. Remove intermediate shaft/seal from vehicle.
10. Reverse procedure to install.

STEERING COLUMN TRIM COVERS

1. Recover air conditioning refrigerant as outlined in "Air Conditioning" chapter.
2. Position steering column in full downward position, then unsnap and remove upper steering column cover.
3. Remove screws, then the lower steering column trim cover.
4. Reverse procedure to install.

IGNITION SWITCH

Refer to "Ignition Switch, Replace" in "Electrical" section of "Cavalier, Cobalt, G5 & Sunfire" chassis chapter for ignition switch replacement procedure.

IGNITION LOCK

Refer to "Ignition Lock, Replace" in "Electrical" section of "Cavalier, Cobalt, G5 & Sunfire" chassis chapter for ignition lock replacement procedure.

IGNITION LOCK CYLINDER CASE

Refer to "Ignition Switch, Replace" in "Electrical" section of "Cavalier, Cobalt, G5

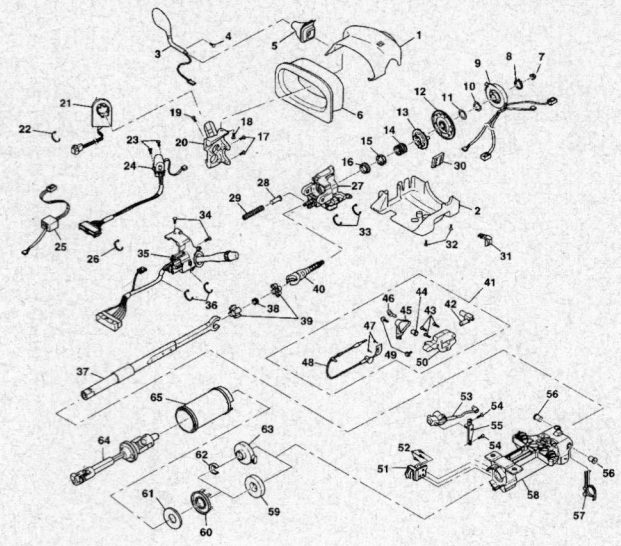

(1) Upper Shroud
(2) Lower Shroud
(3) Automatic Transmission Control Lever Assembly
(4) Shift Lever Screw
(5) Shift Lever Seal
(6) Steering Column Closeout Shroud
(7) Hexagon Locking Nut
(8) Retaining Ring
(9) SIR Coil Assembly
(10) Wave Washer
(11) Bearing Retainer

(12) Shaft Lock Shield Assembly
(13) Turn Signal Cancel Cam Assembly
(14) Upper Bearing Spring
(15) Upper Bearing Inner Race Seat
(16) Inner Race
(17) Pan Head Tapping Screw
(18) TORX® Head Screw
(19) Pan Head Tapping Screw
(20) Lock Module Assembly
(21) Coded Key Controller
(22) Wire Harness Strap
(23) Tapping Screw

GC6049900286010X

Fig. 33 Exploded view of steering column (Part 1 of 2). Bonneville & LeSabre

& Sunfire" chassis chapter for ignition switch replacement procedure.

MULTI-FUNCTION SWITCH

Refer to "Multi-Function Switch, Replace" in "Electrical" section of "Cavalier, Cobalt, G5 & Sunfire" chassis chapter for multi-function switch replacement procedure.

STEERING COLUMN JACKET

1. Place steering wheel in straight forward position.
2. Remove steering wheel as outlined in "Electrical" section of "Cavalier, Cobalt, G5 & Sunfire" chassis chapter.
3. Unsnap and remove upper steering column cover.
4. Remove lower steering column cover screws and trim cover.
5. Disconnect head lamp/turn signal harness connector, then the wiper/washer harness connector from SIR coil module assembly.
6. Disconnect SIR coil electrical connector from SIR coil module assembly.
7. Pry retaining tabs away at base of SIR coil assembly using a small flat-bladed tool, then slide SIR coil assembly off of steering column.
8. Remove multifunction/turn signal and wiper/washer switches.
9. Release left instrument panel trim plate assembly by pulling away from I/P retainer, then disconnect electrical connector for trunk release and re-

move steering column filler.
10. Remove ignition lock cylinder case as outlined under "Ignition Switch, Replace."
11. Remove steering column mounting bolts, then support lower column as required.
12. Remove jacket attaching bolts, then the upper jacket from steering column.
13. Reverse procedure to install.

CTS

Refer to **Fig. 39** for exploded view of steering column.

INTERMEDIATE STEERING SHAFT

UPPER

1. Ensure wheels are in straight ahead position and ignition in LOCK position with key removed.
2. Lock steering column using tool No. J42640, or equivalent.
3. Raise and support vehicle using suitable lift.
4. Remove upper to lower intermediate shaft attaching bolt, then lower vehicle, **Fig. 40.**
5. Remove steering column as outlined in "Steering Column, Replace."
6. Remove upper intermediate shaft to steering column attaching bolt, then the shaft from steering column.
7. Reverse procedure to install.

(24) Ignition & Key Alarm Switch Assembly
(25) Fused Jumper Assembly
(26) Wire Harness Strap
(27) Tilt Spring
(28) Spring Guide
(29) Steering Column Tilt Head Assembly
(30) Shroud Protector
(31) Tilt Lever Assembly
(32) Pan Head Tapping Screw
(33) Wire Harness Strap
(34) Pan Head Tapping Screw
(35) Turn Signal and Multifunction Switch
(36) Wire Harness Strap
(37) Lower Steering Shaft Assembly
(38) Joint Preload Spring
(39) Centering Sphere
(40) Race and Upper Shaft Assembly
(41) Linear Shift Assembly
(42) Shift Lever Clevis
(43) Flat Head 6-Lobed Socket Tapping Screw
(44) Cam Bushing

(45) Cable Shift Cam Assembly
(46) Ball and Actuator Assembly
(47) Oval Head 6-Lobed Socket Tapping Screw
(48) Park Lock Cable Assembly
(49) Hex Flanged Head Bolt
(50) Gear Shift Lever Assembly Support Bracket
(51) Cable Support Bracket
(52) Flat Head Screw
(53) Electrical BTSI Actuator
(54) Pan Head Tapping Screw
(55) BTSI Mounting Bracket Assembly
(56) Pivot Pin
(57) Wire Restraint Clip
(58) Steering Column Support Assembly
(59) Steering Shaft Seal
(60) Sensor Retainer
(61) Steering Shaft Seal
(62) Sensor Locator
(63) Sensor Steer Sensor Assembly
(64) Intermediate Steering Shaft Assembly
(65) Boot Seal

GC6049900286020X

Fig. 33 Exploded view of steering column (Part 2 of 2). Bonneville & LeSabre

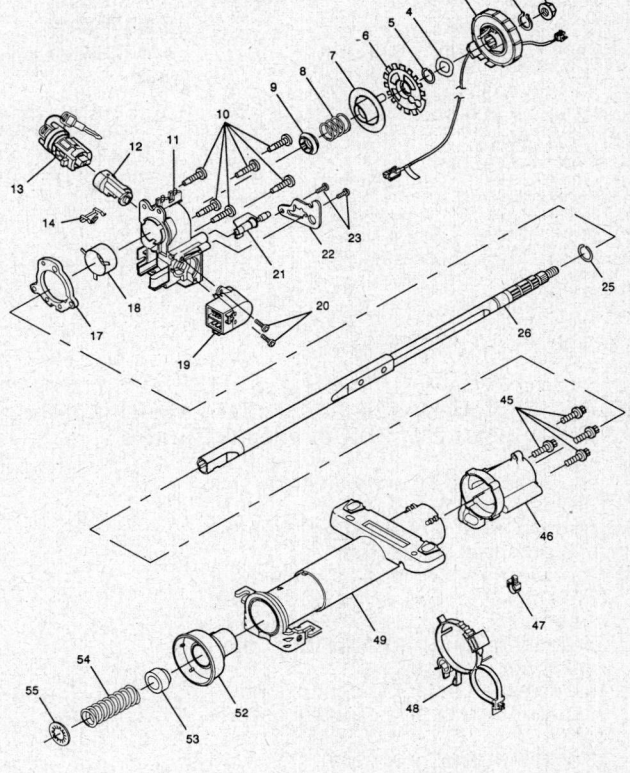

GC604950016600AX

Fig. 34 Exploded view of standard steering column (Part 1 of 2). Cavalier & Sunfire

LOWER

1. Ensure wheels are in straight ahead position and ignition in LOCK position with key removed.
2. Lock steering column using tool No. J42640, or equivalent.
3. Raise and support vehicle using suitable lift.
4. Remove upper to lower intermediate shaft attaching bolt, then lower vehicle, **Fig. 40.**
5. Remove lower intermediate shaft to power steering gear retaining bolt, then the shaft from steering gear.
6. Remove lower intermediate shaft from upper shaft.
7. Reverse procedure to install.

STEERING COLUMN TRIM COVERS

1. Remove steering wheel as outlined in "Electrical" section of "CTS" chassis chapter.
2. Remove tilt steering column lever.
3. Remove trim plug of lower trim cover.
4. Remove lower trim cover to steering column attaching screws, then the lower trim cover.
5. Remove upper trim cover screws, then the upper cover.
6. Reverse procedure to install.

IGNITION SWITCH

Refer to "Ignition Switch, Replace" in "Electrical" section of "CTS" chassis chapter for ignition switch replacement procedure.

IGNITION LOCK

Refer to "Ignition Lock, Replace" in "Electrical" section of "CTS" chassis chapter for ignition lock replacement procedure.

IGNITION LOCK CYLINDER CASE

Refer to "Ignition Switch, Replace" in "Electrical" section of "CTS" chassis chapter for ignition switch replacement procedure.

MULTI-FUNCTION SWITCH

Refer to "Multi-Function Switch, Replace" in "Electrical" section of "CTS" chas-

sis chapter for multi-function switch replacement procedure.

TILT LEVER

Pull tilt lever straight out from steering column to remove. Slide lever into position to install.

TILT SPRING

1. Remove steering column trim covers as outlined in "Steering Column Trim Covers."
2. Ensure tilt lever is in UP position, **Fig. 41.**
3. Remove tilt spring from steering column support using suitable locking pliers, **Fig. 42.**
4. Remove spring guide from tilt spring, **Fig. 43.**
5. Reverse procedure to install.

STEERING COLUMN TILT HEAD

1. Remove steering column as outlined in "Steering Column, Replace."
2. Remove lock cylinder as outlined in "Electrical" section of "CTS" chassis chapter.
3. Remove multi-function switch as outlined in "Electrical" section of "CTS" chassis chapter.
4. Remove tilt spring as outlined in "Tilt Spring."
5. Remove pivot pins from steering col-

umn tilt head using tool No. J21854-01, **Fig. 44.**
6. Install tilt lever to steering column tilt head assembly, then pull back lever at same time pull steering column tilt head assembly down and away from steering column.
7. Remove steering column tilt head, steering shaft and steering column jacket assembly, **Fig. 45,** then the tilt lever.
8. Remove lower bearing and sensor, then the steering shaft from steering column assembly, **Fig. 46.**
9. Reverse procedure to install.

TURN SIGNAL CANCEL CAM & UPPER BEARING

1. Remove steering wheel as outlined in "Electrical" section of "CTS" chassis chapter.
2. Remove SIR coil as outlined in "Passive Restraint Systems" chapter.
3. Remove bearing retainer using tool Nos. J23653 and J42137, or equivalents, **Fig. 47.**
4. Disassemble and remove cam and race in numbered sequence, **Fig. 48.**
5. Reverse procedure to install.

STEERING COLUMN WIRING HARNESS

1. Remove steering column trim covers

1-NUT, HEX LOCKING (M14x1.5)
2-RING, RETAINING
3-COIL ASM, SIR
4-WASHER, WAVE
5-RING, RETAINING
6-LOCK, SHAFT
7-CAM ASM, T/SIG CANCEL
8-SPRING, UPPER BEARING
9-SPACER, UPPER BEARING
10-SCREW, ADAPTER
11-HOUSING ASM, STRG COLUMN
12-ACTUATOR ASM, IGNITION LOCK
13-LOCK CYL SET, STRG COLUMN
14-SPRING, LOCK PRE-LOAD
17-PLATE, MOUNTING
18-RETAINER, BEARING
19-SWITCH ASM, IGNITION
20-SCREW, TAPPING
21-BOLT ASM, LOCK
22-BRACKET, LOCK BOLT SUPPORT
23-SCREW, TAPPING
25-RING, RETAINING
26-SHAFT ASM, STEERING
45-SCREW, SUPPORT
46-ADAPTER, SUPPORT MOUNTING
47- CLIP, WIRE RESTRAINT

48-STRAP, WIRE
49-JACKET ASM, STRG COL
52-BEARING ASM, ADAPTER &
53-SEAT, LOWER BEARING
54-SPRING, LOWER BEARING
55-RETAINER, LOWER SPRING

Service Kits

201-GREASE SERV KIT, (SYNTHETIC)

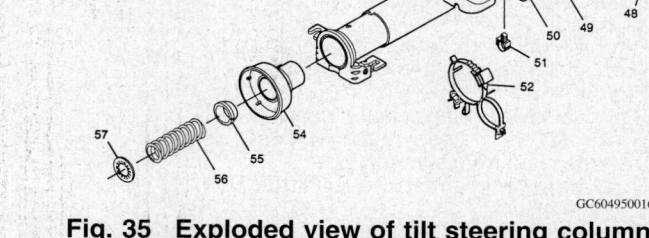

GC604950016600BX

Fig. 34 Exploded view of standard steering column (Part 2 of 2). Cavalier & Sunfire

as outlined in "Steering Column Trim Covers."

2. Remove wire harness strap, then the theft deterrent control module.
3. Remove lock cylinder as outlined in "Electrical" section of "CTS" chassis chapter.
4. Disconnect connector from theft deterrent control module.
5. Remove theft deterrent control module from ignition lock cylinder case assembly.
6. Rotate key alarm connector 90°, then pull connector from ignition lock cylinder case.
7. Disconnect ignition switch electrical connector, then remove wires in switch clip on side of ignition switch.
8. Disconnect all electrical connectors to wiring harness, **Fig. 49**.
9. Reverse procedure to install.

STEERING WHEEL POSITION SENSOR

1. Remove multi-function switch as outlined in "Electrical" section of "CTS" chassis chapter.
2. Remove tilt spring as outlined in "Tilt Spring."
3. Remove pivot pins using tool No. J21854, or equivalent, from steering column support, **Fig. 50**.
4. **On models equipped with sensor,** remove sensor locator, then the sensor, **Fig. 51**.
5. **On models less sensor,** remove steering shaft seal and sensor retainer, **Fig. 51**.
6. **On all models,** reverse procedure to install.

DeVille & Seville

Refer to **Figs. 52 and 53** for exploded view of these steering column.

PASS KEY LOCK CYLINDER SET, SHAFT LOCK, TURN SIGNAL SWITCH & UPPER BEARING

1. Remove steering wheel as outlined in

GC604950016700AX

Fig. 35 Exploded view of tilt steering column (Part 1 of 2). Cavalier & Sunfire

"Electrical" section of "DeVille, DTS, Seville & STS" chassis chapter.

2. Remove retaining ring and coil. Remove wave washer.
3. Remove shaft lock retaining ring using compressor tool No. J23653-C, or equivalent, to push down shaft lock.
4. Remove shaft lock and turn signal canceling cam.
5. Remove upper bearing spring and upper bearing inner race seat.
6. Remove inner race and move turn signal to righthand turn position.
7. Remove multi-function lever and hazard knob.
8. Remove signal switch arm and mounting screws.
9. Disconnect turn signal switch connector from bulkhead connector.
10. Remove wiring protector.
11. Gently pull wire harness through column.
12. **SIR coil will become uncentered if steering column is separated from steering gear and is allowed to rotate; or if centering spring is pushed down, letting hub rotate while coil is removed from steering column.**
13. Remove coil terminal from vehicle harness.
14. Remove yellow connector shroud from black terminal connector.
15. Remove wiring protector.
16. Attach suitable length of mechanics wire to coil terminal connector.
17. Gently pull wire through column.

18. Remove key from pass key lock cylinder set, **Fig. 54**.
19. Remove buzzer switch and insert key in pass key in lock cylinder. Ensure key is in Lock position.
20. Remove lock mounting screw.
21. Disconnect pivot switch connector from bulkhead connector and remove 13-way secondary lock.
22. Disconnect terminals of pass key wire harness from switch connector.
23. Remove retaining clip from housing cover and gently pull wire harness through column.
24. Reverse procedure to install, noting the following:
  a. Route wire from pass key lock cylinder, **Fig. 55,** and snap retaining clip into hole in housing.
  b. While holding SIR coil, depress spring lock to rotate hub clockwise until it stops, **Fig. 56**.
  c. Rotate coil hub counterclockwise approximately 2½ turns. Release spring lock between locking tabs in front of arrow, **Fig. 56**.
  d. Align opening in coil with horn tower and locating bump between two tabs on housing cover, **Fig. 57**.

COLUMN HOUSING COVER END CAP, LOCK HOUSING COVER, PIVOT SWITCH, & TILT SPRING

1. Remove upper column as outlined in

1- NUT, HEX LOCKING (M14x1.5)
2- RING, RETAINING
3- COIL ASM, SIR
4- WASHER, WAVE
5- RING, RETAINING
6- LOCK, SHAFT
7- CAM ASM, T/SIG CANCEL
8- SPRING, UPPER BEARING
9- SEAT, UPPER BEARING INNER RACE
10- RACE, INNER
11- HOUSING ASM, BRG &
12- ACTUATOR ASM, IGNITION LOCK
13- LOCK CYL SET, STRG COLUMN
14- SPRING, LOCK PRE-LOAD
19- SWITCH ASM, IGNITION
20- SCREW, TAPPING
21- BOLT ASM, LOCK
22- BRACKET, LOCK BOLT SUPPORT
23- SCREW, TAPPING
26- SHAFT ASM, RACE & UPPER
27- SPHERE, CENTERING
28- SPRING, JOINT PRELOAD
29- SHAFT ASM, LOWER
45- SCREW, SUPPORT
46- GUIDE, SPRING
47- SPRING, WHEEL TILT
48- PIN, PIVOT
49- SUPPORT ASM, STRG COL
50- RETAINER, SPRING
51- CLIP, WIRE RESTRAINT
52- STRAP, WIRE

53- JACKET ASM, STRG COL
54- BEARING ASM, ADAPTER &
55- SEAT, LOWER BEARING
56- SPRING, LOWER BEARING
57- RETAINER, LOWER SPRING

Service Kits

201- SPRING SERV KIT, TILT COLUMN
   -INCLUDES: 9,10,47
202- SPHERE SERV KIT, TILT COLUMN
   -INCLUDES: 27,28
203- GREASE SERV KIT, (SYNTHETIC)

GC604950016700BX

Fig. 35   Exploded view of tilt steering column (Part 2 of 2). Cavalier & Sunfire

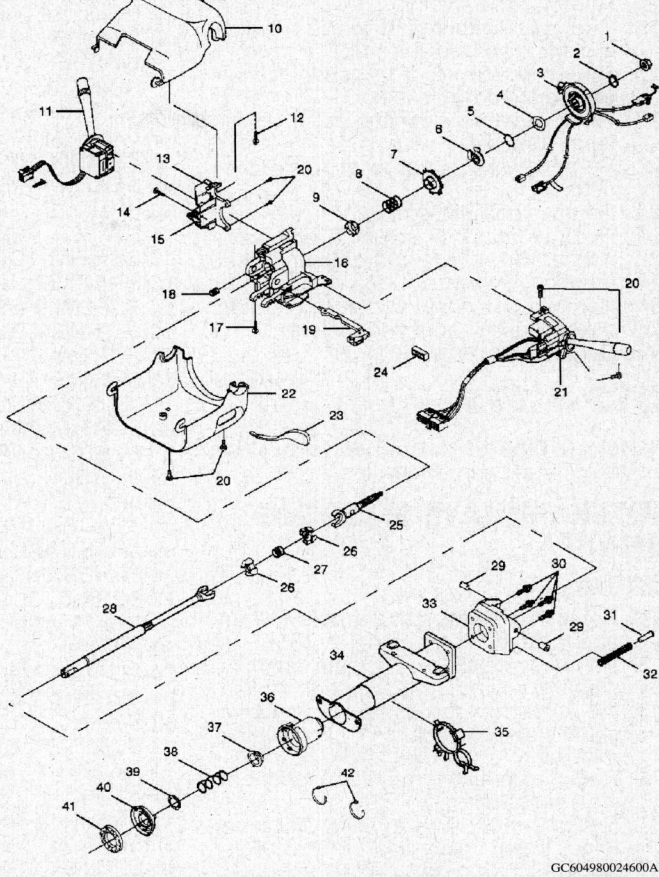

GC604980024600AX

Fig. 36   Exploded view of steering column (Part 1 of 2). Grand Prix w/floor shift

"Steering Column, Replace."
2. Remove housing end cap.
3. Remove cruise control and multi-function lever connectors from base plate and disconnect.
4. Remove multi-function lever.
5. Remove cover screws and tilt lever.
6. Remove lock housing cover.
7. Remove base plate and dimmer switch rod actuator.
8. Remove pin, pivot and pulse switch actuator, noting the following:
   a. Allow switch to hang freely if removal is not required.
   b. Disconnect pivot switch connector from bulkhead connector.
   c. Gently pull wire harness through column.
9. Remove spring retainer, spring and spring guide.
10. Reverse procedure to install, noting the following:
   a. Coat spring guide and spring with lithium grease.
   b. Tighten lock housing cover screw in three steps:
   c. First step, tighten to 12 o'clock position.
   d. Second step, tighten to 8 o'clock position.
   e. Third step, tighten to 3 o'clock position.

BEARING, LOCK BOLT, SHIFT TUBE, STEERING COLUMN HOUSING, STEERING SHAFT & STEERING WHEEL LOCK SHOE

1. Remove steering column as outlined in "Steering Column, Replace."
2. Perform all disassembling steps outlined in "Housing Cover."
3. Remove pivot pins using pivot pin removal tool No. J21854-01, or equivalent. Install tilt lever.
4. Remove steering column housing. Pull

back on tilt lever and pull steering column housing down and away from column.
5. Remove the following components to disassemble steering column housing assembly:
   a. Bearing.
   b. Wire abrasion shield.
   c. Mounting screw.
   d. Lock bolt spring.
   e. Lock bolt.
   f. Switch actuator rack and rack pre-load spring.
   g. Driveshaft.
   h. Switch actuator sector.
   i. Release lever pin using lock shoe and release lever pin tool No. J22635, or equivalent.
   j. Shoe release lever.
   k. Release lever spring.
   l. Dowel pin using lock shoe and release lever pin tool No. J22635, or equivalent.
   m. Lock shoes and shoe springs.
6. Remove lower spring retainer.
7. Remove bearing and seal retainer.
8. Remove lower spring retainer.
9. Remove lower bearing spring and lower bearing seat.
10. Remove mounting bolts, adapter and bearing.
11. Remove steering column shaft.
12. Mark upper shaft and lower steering

shaft to ensure proper alignment.
13. Disassemble steering column shaft as follows:
   a. Separate upper shaft from lower steering shaft. Tilt 90° to disengage.
   b. Separate centering sphere from upper shaft by rotating sphere 90° and sliding out.
   c. Remove joint preload spring from centering sphere.
14. Remove column housing support with dimmer switch rod from steering column jacket.
15. Remove mounting screws and shift lever gate from support.
16. Remove shift tube retaining ring, thrust washers and lock plate.
17. Remove wave washer and thrust washers, then the gearshift lever bowl with gearshift bowl shroud and shift tube.
18. Remove shroud from bowl.
19. Remove shift lever spring and shift tube from bowl. Use suitable press, as required.
20. Remove PRNDL adjuster mounting nut and screw.
21. Remove PRNDL adjuster bracket and dimmer switch.
22. Remove dimmer and ignition switch mounting stud.
23. Remove ignition switch from ignition

switch actuator.
24. Remove cam retainer.
25. Remove dimmer and ignition switch mounting screws and stud.
26. Remove cable clip from upper location of steering column jacket.
27. Remove cable mounting clip from solenoid bracket.
28. Remove ball joint socket from solenoid.
29. Remove ball joint spring.
30. Remove interlock solenoid and solenoid bracket to steering column jacket mounting screw.
31. Remove solenoid bracket to steering column jacket mounting screws.
32. Reverse procedure to install.

DTS & STS

Refer to **Figs. 58 through 62** for exploded views of steering columns.

INTERMEDIATE STEERING SHAFT

UPPER

1. Remove steering column as outlined under "Steering Column, Replace."
2. Remove upper intermediate shaft to steering column mounting bolt, noting the position of the upper intermediate shaft to steering column for installation reference.
3. Remove upper intermediate shaft from steering column.
4. Reverse procedure to install. **Torque** upper intermediate shaft bolt to 35 ft. lbs.

LOWER

1. Ensure wheels are in straight ahead position and ignition in LOCK position with key removed.
2. Lock steering column by inserting lock pin tool No. J42640, or equivalent.
3. Raise and support vehicle.
4. Remove center intermediate shaft to lower intermediate shaft mounting bolt.
5. Remove lower intermediate shaft to power steering gear mounting bolt.
6. Disconnect lower intermediate shaft from power steering gear.
7. Remove lower intermediate shaft from center intermediate shaft.
8. Reverse procedure to install.

STEERING COLUMN TRIM COVERS

1. Remove steering wheel as outlined in "Electrical" section of "Deville, DTS, Seville & STS" chassis chapter.
2. Remove knee bolster.
3. Remove lower steering column trim cover, then disconnect closeout shroud from lower trim cover.
4. Disconnect electrical connectors for power tilt and telescopic switch.
5. Remove telescopic switch electrical connector from lower trim cover.
6. Remove upper steering column trim cover retaining screws.
7. Lift upper trim cover to access lock cylinder access hole.

1-NUT, FLANGED PREVAIL TORQUE
2-RING, RETAINING
3-SIR, COIL ASSEMBLY
4-WASHER, WAVE
5-RING, RETAINING
6-SHIELD, SHAFT LOCK
7-CAM, T/S CANCEL
8-SPRING, UPPER BEARING
9-SEAT, UPPER BEARING
10-SHROUD, UPPER
11-SWITCH ASM, PIVOT & PULSE
12-SCREW, TORX HEAD
13-BRACKET, SWITCH MOUNTING
14-SCREW, TORX HEAD
16-TILT HEAD ASM, STRG COLUMN
17-SCREW, TORX HEAD
18-SPRING, TILT LEVER
19-LEVER ASM, SHOE RELEASE
20-SCREW, PAN HEAD TAPPING
21-SWITCH ASM, T/S MULTIFUNCTION
22-SHROUD, LOWER
23-LEVER ASM, TILT
24-SPACER, WIRE HARNESS
25-SHAFT ASM, RACE & UPPER
26-SPHERE, CENTERING
27-SPRING, JOINT PRELOAD
28-SHAFT ASM, LOWER STRG
29-PIN, PIVOT
30-SCREW, TORX HEAD
31-SPRING, GUIDE
32-SPRING, TILT
33-SUPPORT ASM, STRG COLUMN
34-JACKET ASM, STRG COLUMN
35-STRAP, WIRE HARNESS
36-BEARING ASM, ADAPTER &
37-SEAT, LOWER BEARING
38-SPRING, LOWER BEARING
39-RETAINER, LOWER SPRING
40-RETAINER, SENSOR
41-SEAL, STRG SHAFT
42-STRAP, WIRE HARNESS

GC604980024600BX

Fig. 36   Exploded view of steering column (Part 2 of 2). Grand Prix w/floor shift

8. Insert bent tip awl or equivalent, into access hole.
9. Turn ignition lock cylinder to start position.
10. Press down on ignition lock cylinder retaining pin using bent tip awl, or equivalent.
11. Release ignition lock cylinder to run position, then remove lock cylinder.
12. Remove upper trim cover.
13. Remove closeout shroud from upper trim cover.
14. Reverse procedure to install.

STEERING COLUMN TILT HEAD

1. Ensure wheels are in straight ahead position and ignition switch is in LOCK position.
2. Remove steering wheel as outlined in "Electrical" section of "Deville, DTS, Seville & STS" chassis chapter.
3. Remove SIR coil.
4. Remove bearing retainer using tool No. J23653–SIR, or equivalent.
5. Remove shaft lock shield assembly.

6. Remove turn signal cancel cam assembly.
7. Remove upper bearing spring.
8. Reverse procedure to install.

STEERING COLUMN WIRE HARNESS ASSEMBLY

1. Remove steering column as outlined under "Steering Column, Replace."
2. Remove upper and lower steering column trim covers.
3. Disconnect all electrical connectors attached to wire harness assembly.
4. Remove bulkhead connector from column shift and tilt motor bracket.
5. Reverse procedure to install.

STEERING WHEEL POSITION SENSOR

1. Remove steering column as outline under "Steering Column, Replace."
2. Remove from steering shaft: Boot seal, steering shaft seal, sensor retainer and sensor locator.
3. Remove steering wheel position sensor.
4. Reverse procedure to install.

G6

Refer to **Fig. 63,** for exploded view of steering column.

INTERMEDIATE STEERING SHAFT

1. Ensure steering column is in full up and LOCK position.
2. Raise and support vehicle.
3. Remove lefthand front wheel.
4. Remove intermediate to steering gear pinch mounting bolt.
5. Disconnect intermediate shaft from steering gear.
6. Lower vehicle.
7. Remove intermediate shaft to steering column pinch bolt. Discard pinch bolt.
8. Remove intermediate shaft from steering column shaft.
9. Remove intermediate shaft seal by pressing tabs on seal, then pull inwards.
10. Remove intermediate shaft from vehicle.
11. Reverse procedure to install.

STEERING COLUMN TRIM COVERS

1. Lift upper steering column trim cover, then remove retaining nuts from instrument panel seal.
2. Remove upper trim cover.
3. Remove lower column trim cover retaining screws, then remove cover.
4. Lower steering column and fully telescope toward driver, then remove lower trim cover.
5. Reverse procedure to install.

GTO

1. Tilt column to the lowest position.
2. Remove lower trim cover retaining screws, then press on back of lower cover to release tabs from upper cover.

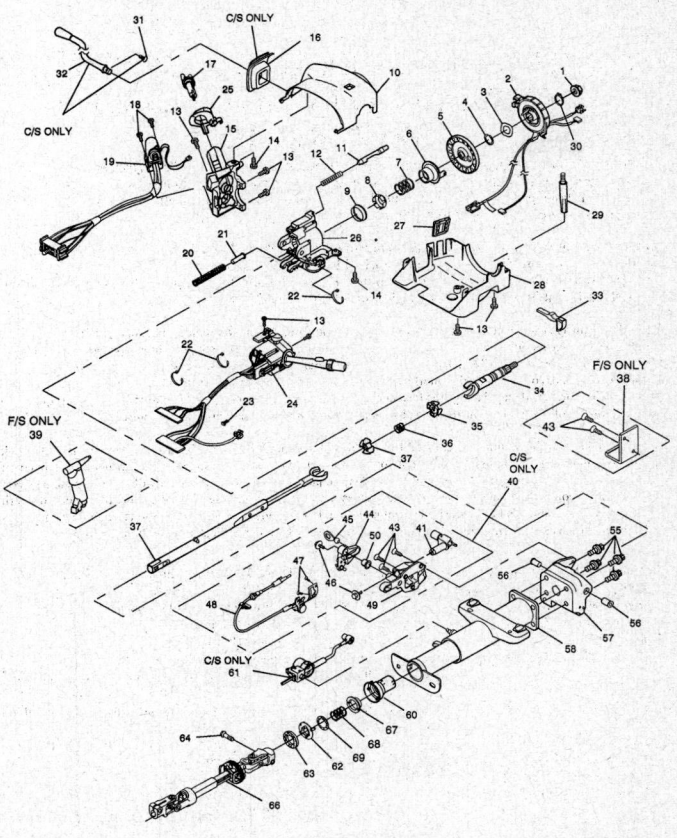

1-NUT, HEXAGON LOCKING (M14x1.5)
2-COIL ASM, SIR
3-WASHER, WAVE
4-RING, RETAINING
5-SHIELD ASM, SHAFT LOCK
6-CAM ASM, T/SIG CANCEL
7-SPRING, UPPER BEARING
8-SEAT, UPPER BEARING INNER RACE
9-RACE, INNER
10-SHROUD, UPPER
11-BOLT ASM, LOCK
12-SPRING, LOCK BOLT
13-SCREW, PAN HD TAPPING
14-SCREW, TORX HEAD
15-ASM, LOCK MODULE
16-SEAL, SHIFT LEVER
17-LOCK CYL SET, STRG COLUMN
18-SCREW, TAPPING
19-SWITCH ASM, IGN & KEY ALARM
20-SPRING, TILT
21-GUIDE, SPRING
22-STRAP, WIRE HARNESS
23-CONNECTOR, AXIAL POSN ASSUR
24-SWITCH ASM, T/S & MULTIFUNCTION
25-RING, TRIM
26- TILT HEAD ASM, STRG COL
27-PROTECTOR, SHROUD
28-SHROUD, LOWER
29-STUD, SHROUD MOUNTING
30-RING, RETAINING
31- SCREW, SHIFT LEVER
32-LEVER ASM, A/TRNS CONTROL
33-LEVER ASM, TILT
34-SHAFT ASM, RACE & UPPER
35-SPHERE, CENTERING
36-SPRING, JOINT PRELOAD
37-SHAFT ASM, LOWER STRG
38-STRAP REINFORCEMENT, STRG
39-ELEC PARK LOCK, STRG COL
40-SHIFT ASM, LINEAR
41-CLEVIS, SHIFT LEVER
43-SCREW, FLAT HD 6-LOBED SOC TAP
44-CAM ASM, CABLE SHIFT
45-ACTUATOR ASM, BALL &
46-BOLT, HEX FLANGE HEAD
47-SCREW, OVAL HD 6-LOBED SOC TAP
48-CABLE ASM, PARK LOCK
49-BRACKET, G/S LEVER ASM SUPPORT
50-BUSHING, CAM
55-SCREW, TORX HEAD
56-PIN, PIVOT

57-SUPPORT ASM, STRG COL
58-JACKET ASM, STRG COL
60-BEARING ASM, ADAPTER &
61-ACTUATOR, ELECTRICAL (BTSI)
62-RETAINER, SENSOR
63-SEAL, STEERING SHAFT
64-BOLT, PINCH
65-SHAFT ASM, INTER STRG
66-SHAFT ASM, INTER STRG
67-SEAT, LOWER BEARING
68-SPRING, LOWER BEARING
69-RETAINER, LOWER SPRING

GC604970024500AX

Fig. 37 Exploded view of steering column (Part 1 of 2). Century, Grand Prix & Regal w/column shift

GC604970024500BX

Fig. 37 Exploded view of steering column (Part 2 of 2). Century, Grand Prix & Regal w/column shift

3. Raise upper cover, release tab, then remove cover.
4. Push outer ring of theft deterrent reader into lower trim cover.
5. Remove ignition lock illumination socket and electrical connector from theft deterrent reader.
6. Slide lower trim cover rearward, disengage tab, then remover cover.
7. Reverse procedure to install.

LaCrosse

Refer to **Figs. 64 and 65** for exploded view of this steering column.

INTERMEDIATE STEERING SHAFT

1. Ensure wheels are in straight ahead position and ignition switch in LOCK position.
2. Raise and support vehicle.
3. Move seal to access lower pinch bolt on intermediate shaft.
4. Remove lower pinch bolt from power steering gear stub shaft.
5. Disconnect intermediate shaft from power steering gear stub shaft, noting shaft to gear alignment for installation reference.
6. Lower vehicle.
7. Reposition seal for access to upper in-

termediate shaft pinch bolt. then remove pinch bolt.
8. Disconnect intermediate steering shaft from steering column, noting intermediate shaft to steering column alignment for installation reference.
9. Remove intermediate shaft from vehicle.
10. Reverse procedure to install.

Lucerne

Refer to **Fig. 66** for exploded view of steering column.

INTERMEDIATE STEERING SHAFT REPLACEMENT

1. Disarm air bags as outlined under "Precautions."
2. Remove steering column as outlined under "Steering Column Replace."
3. Remove steering column boot seal.
4. Remove intermediate shaft bolt, then intermediate shaft.
5. Reverse procedure to install.

STEERING COLUMN TRIM COVERS REPLACEMENT

1. Disarm air bags as outlined under

"Precautions."
2. Disconnect battery ground cable.
3. Remove steering wheel as outlined in "Electrical" section of "Lucerne" chassis chapter.
4. Remove knee bolster and gap hider.
5. Place steering column in center position, then remove tilt lever.
6. Remove retaining screw from lower column trim cover, then disconnect closeout trim cover from lower trim cover.
7. Remove upper steering column trim cover retaining screws.
8. Lift upper trim cover, using a suitable awl insert tip into access hole in ignition lock cylinder.
9. Place ignition switch in START position.
10. Push down on retaining pin of ignition lock cylinder, release switch to RUN, then remove lock cylinder.
11. Remove upper trim cover.
12. Reverse procedure to install.

ION

The steering column is serviced only as an assembly. If a steering column fault or defect is found, replacement is required.

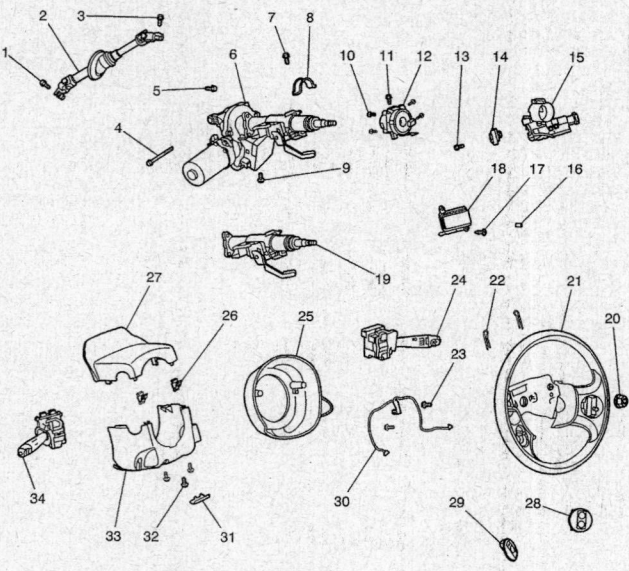

(1) Lower Intermediate Steering Shaft Bold
(2) Intermediate Steering Shaft Assembly
(3) Upper Intermediate Steering Shaft Bolt
(4) Lower Steering Column Support Bracket Bolt
(5) Lower Steering Column Jacket Bolt
(6) Steering Column Assembly
(7) Ignition / Start Switch Clamp Bolt
(8) Ignition / Start Switch Clamp

ARM0500000000803

**Fig. 38   Exploded view of steering wheel column
(Part 1 of 2). Cobalt & G5**

(9) Upper Steering Column Support Bracket Bolt
(10) Turn Signal Switch Bracket Screw
(11) Turn Signal Switch Bracket Screw
(12) Inflatable Restraint Steering Wheel Module Coil Assembly
(13) Ignition / Start Switch Screw
(14) Ignition / Start Switch Assembly
(15) Ignition / Start Switch Housing
(16) Spring
(17) Ignition Lock Cylinder Control Solenoid Screw
(18) Ignition Lock Cylinder Control Solenoid Assembly
(19) Steering Column Jacket Assembly
(20) Steering Wheel Nut
(21) Steering Wheel Assembly
(22) Inflatable Restraint Steering Wheel Module Retainer
(23) Steering Wheel Shroud Screw
(24) Wiper / Washer Switch Assembly
(25) Steering Wheel Shroud
(26) Lower Trim Cover Clip
(27) Upper Trim Cover
(28) Cruise Control Resume Switch Assembly
(29) Cruise Control Switch Assembly
(30) Harness Assembly
(31) Lower Trim Cover Plug
(32) Lower Trim Cover Screw
(33) Lower Trim Cover
(34) Headlamp / Dimmer / Park / Turn Signal Switch Assembly

ARM0500000000804

**Fig. 38   Exploded view of steering wheel column
(Part 2 of 2). Cobalt & G5**

Impala & Monte Carlo

Refer to **Fig. 67** for exploded view of this steering column.

INTERMEDIATE STEERING SHAFT

1. Raise and support vehicle.
2. Position intermediate steering shaft seal in order to provide access to lower pinch bolt.
3. Remove intermediate steering shaft lower pinch bolt from power steering gear stub shaft, **Fig. 68. Front wheels must be maintained in straight ahead position and ignition must be in Lock position before disconnecting steering column or intermediate shaft.**
4. Remove intermediate steering shaft from power steering gear stub shaft.
5. Lower vehicle.
6. Remove lefthand instrument panel insulator.
7. Position intermediate steering shaft seal to gain access to upper pinch bolt.
8. Remove intermediate steering shaft from steering column.
9. Disconnect intermediate steering shaft from steering column.
10. Remove intermediate shaft.
11. Reverse procedure to install.

STEERING COLUMN COVER

1. Remove tilt lever.
2. Remove ignition lock cylinder as outlined in "Electrical" section of "Century, Grand Prix, Impala, LaCrosse, Monte Carlo & Regal" chassis chapter.
3. Remove mounting screws and steering column trim covers, **Figs. 69 and 70.**
4. Reverse procedure to install.

STEERING WHEEL CONTROL SWITCH

1. Remove driver's air bag module as outlined in "Passive Restraint Systems" chapter.
2. Remove steering wheel controls, wire harness from retainers in steering wheel aluminum insert and plastic back shroud.
3. Remove cruise control switch bezel to steering wheel insert mounting screw.
4. Disconnect electrical connector from back of cruise control switch.
5. Remove steering wheel controls switch and bezel from steering wheel.
6. Reverse procedure to install.

L Series

The steering column is serviced only as an assembly. If a steering column fault or defect is found, replacement is required.

Malibu, Malibu Classic & Malibu Maxx

Refer to **Fig. 71** for exploded view of this steering column.

SIR COIL

1. Remove steering wheel as outlined in "Electrical" section of "Alero, Grand Am & Malibu" chassis chapter.
2. Remove nut, retaining ring and coil.
3. Remove wave washer.
4. Reverse procedure to install. Center SIR coil as outlined in "SIR Coil, Centering."

SIR COIL, CENTERING

1. Remove steering wheel as outlined in "Electrical" section of "Alero, Grand Am & Malibu" chassis chapter.
2. Ensure wheels are in straight ahead position and ignition switch is in LOCK position.
3. Ensure block tooth and centering mark of steering shaft assembly is in 12 o'clock position, **Fig. 72.**
4. Hold SIR coil by casing with face of coil pointing upward.
5. Rotate coil hub clockwise 2½ turns, then rotate coil hub 2½ turns counterclockwise.
6. Ensure ribbon cable is present in centering window, **Fig. 73.**
7. Ensure sub stator and rotator arrows are aligned, **Fig. 73.**
8. Slide SIR coil onto steering shaft.

Park Avenue

Refer to **Fig. 74** for exploded view of steering column.

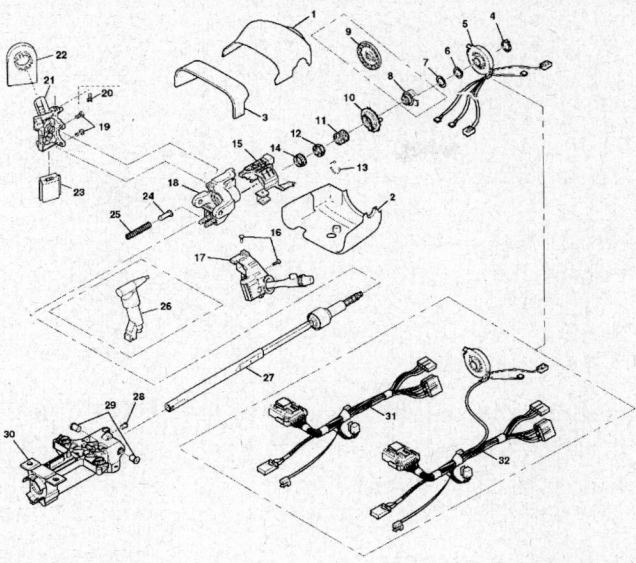

(1) Upper Trim Cover
(2) Lower Trim Cover
(3) Steering Column Closeout Trim Cover
(4) Retaining Ring
(5) Inflatable Restraint Steering Wheel Module Coil

ARM66GC000000697

Fig. 39 Exploded view of steering column (Part 1 of 2). CTS

(6) Wave Washer
(7) Bearing Retainer
(8) Cam Orientation Plate
(9) Shaft Lock Shield Assembly
(10) Turn Signal Cancel Cam Assembly
(11) Upper Bearing Spring
(12) Upper Bearing Inner Race Seat
(13) Wire Harness Strap
(14) Inner Race
(15) Signal Switch Housing
(16) Pan Head Tapping Screws
(17) Turn Signal and Multifunction Switch Assembly
(18) Steering Column Tilt Head Assembly
(19) Pan Head Tapping Screws
(20) TORX® Head Screw
(21) Ignition Lock Cylinder Case
(22) Coded Key Controller
(23) Ignition and Key Alarm Switch Assembly
(24) Spring Guide
(25) Tilt Spring
(26) Theft Deterrent Control Module Electric Park Lock
(27) Steering Shaft Assembly
(28) Tilt Bumper
(29) Pivot Pins
(30) Steering Column Support Assembly
(31) Coil Wire Harness Assembly
(32) Coil Wire Harness Assembly (Export)

ARM66GC000000698

Fig. 39 Exploded view of steering column (Part 2 of 2). CTS

STEERING COLUMN COVERS

1. Remove steering wheel as outlined in "Electrical" section of "Bonneville, Le-Sabre & Park Avenue" chassis chapter.
2. Remove tilt lever and lower column cover mounting screws.
3. Tilt lower column cover downward, slide back cover to disengage from locking tabs and remove column cover protector.
4. Remove mounting screws and upper column cover.
5. Reverse procedure to install.

SHAFT LOCK, SIR COIL, TURN SIGNAL CANCEL CAM & UPPER BEARING

1. Remove column covers as outlined in ."Steering Column Covers."
2. Remove steering column wiring harness straps and coil retaining ring.
3. Remove coil and wave washer.
4. Remove retaining ring using lock plate compressor tool No. J23653-SIR, or equivalent, and shaft lock.
5. Remove turn signal cancel cam and upper bearing spring.
6. Remove upper bearing inner race seat and race.
7. Reverse procedure to install.

LINEAR SHIFT, PARK LOCK CABLE, SHIFT GATE LEVER & SHIFT LEVER CLEVIS

1. Remove steering column as outlined in "Steering Column, Replace."
2. Tilt column to center position and re-move lower column cover mounting screws.
3. Remove lower and upper column cover mounting screws.
4. Remove upper column cover and shift lever.
5. Remove shift lever seal and park lock cable from lock module.
6. Pry actuator arm of electrical actuator from outer shift cable ball stud on cable shift cam and mounting pin on jacket.
7. Remove mounting bolt, ball and actuator.
8. Lifting up on shift gate, rotate shift lever clevis and remove clevis from gearshift lever support bracket.
9. Pry locking ring off of park lock cable and move park lock latch to gain access to lower mounting screw.
10. Remove shift gate mounting screws and park lock cable.
11. Pry transaxle shift cable from inner ball stud on cable shift cam and remove mounting bolt.
12. Remove cam bushing from cable shift cam and mounting screws.
13. Remove gearshift lever support bracket.
14. Reverse procedure to install.

Solstice & SKY

Refer to **Fig. 75** for exploded view of steering column.

INTERMEDIATE STEERING SHAFT

1. Remove bolts, then the hood latch.
2. Release hood latch release cable from hood latch assembly.
3. Attach a length of mechanic's wire to exterior end of cable, and note routing of cable for later installation.
4. Release retainers securing cable to inner fender, then push cable grommet through cowl panel and into interior of vehicle.
5. Remove screws attaching hood release handle to knee bolster, then the cable from release handle.
6. Pull cable rest of way through cowl panel and out from behind sound insulation.
7. Detach mechanic's wire from cable, leaving wire in position for aid in installation of cable and remove cable from vehicle.
8. Remove screw and bolts, then instrument panel driver knee bolster and bracket.
9. Remove intermediate shaft to steering column bolt, then discard bolt.
10. Remove intermediate shaft to steering gear bolt, then discard bolt.
11. Remove intermediate shaft to modular plate seal, ensure primary and secondary seals are properly seated in modular plate.
12. Remove intermediate shaft.
13. Reverse procedure to install.

STEERING COLUMN TRIM COVERS

1. Remove screw and bolts, then instrument panel driver knee bolster and bracket.
2. Remove steering column trim cover retainer, then bolts, screws and upper trim cover.
3. Remove steering column trim cover bolts, screws and lower trim cover and hole plug.
4. Reverse procedure to install.

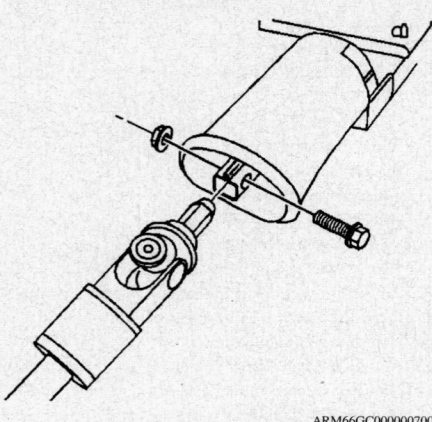

Fig. 40 Upper to lower intermediate bolt removal. CTS

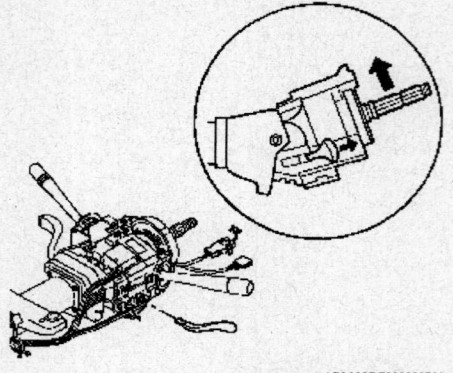

Fig. 41 Tilt column placement. CTS

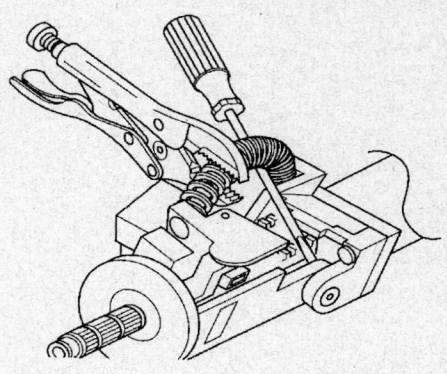

Fig. 42 Tilt spring removal

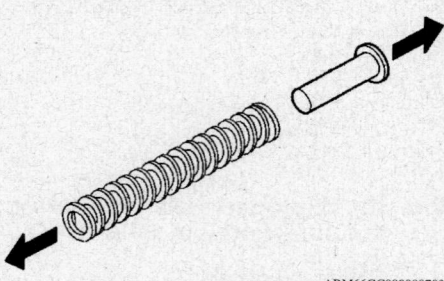

Fig. 43 Tilt guide spring removal

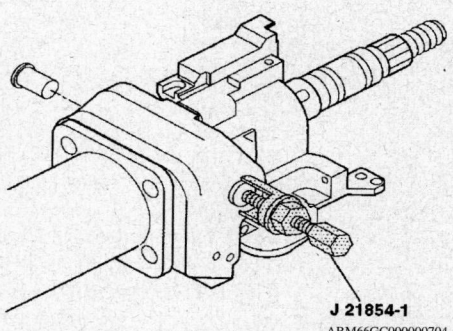

Fig. 44 Pivot pin removal. CTS

IGNITION SWITCH

SOLSTICE

Refer to "Ignition Switch, Replace" in "Electrical" section of "Solstice" chassis chapter for ignition switch replacement procedure.

SKY

Refer to "Ignition Switch, Replace" in "Electrical" section of "Saturn" chassis chapter for ignition switch replacement procedure.

IGNITION LOCK

SOLSTICE

Refer to "Ignition Lock, Replace" in "Electrical" section of "Solstice" chassis chapter for ignition lock replacement procedure.

SKY

Refer to "Ignition Lock, Replace" in "Electrical" section of "Saturn" chassis chapter for ignition lock replacement procedure.

IGNITION LOCK CYLINDER CASE

SOLSTICE

Refer to "Ignition Switch, Replace" in "Electrical" section of "Solstice" chassis chapter for ignition switch replacement procedure.

SKY

Refer to "Ignition Switch, Replace" in

"Electrical" section of "Saturn" chassis chapter for ignition switch replacement procedure.

MULTI-FUNCTION SWITCH

SOLSTICE

Refer to "Multi-Function Switch, Replace" in "Electrical" section of "Solstice" chassis chapter for multi-function switch replacement procedure.

SKY

Refer to "Multi-Function Switch, Replace" in "Electrical" section of "Saturn" chassis chapter for multi-function switch replacement procedure.

Vibe

Refer to **Fig. 76** for exploded views of these steering columns.

STEERING SHAFT COUPLING

1. Ensure front wheels are in straight ahead position and ignition switch is in LOCK position.
2. Remove steering column silencer pad.
3. Place matching marks on steering shaft coupling and shaft assemblies.
4. Remove upper and lower bolts from coupling.
5. Raise coupling onto steering column shaft, then remove from steering shaft.
6. Reverse procedure to install.

INTERMEDIATE STEERING SHAFT w/FWD

1. Ensure front wheels are in straight ahead position and ignition switch is in LOCK position.
2. Place matching marks on intermediate steering shaft and steering gear pinion shaft assemblies.
3. Remove intermediate shaft attaching bolt, then the intermediate shaft.
4. Remove steering column silencer pad.
5. Place matching marks on steering shaft coupling and intermediate steering shaft assemblies.
6. Loosen upper and lower bolts from coupling.
7. Raise coupling to steering column shaft, then separate coupling from in-

termediate shaft.
8. Remove intermediate steering shaft from steering gear pinion shaft.
9. Reverse procedure to install.

STEERING COLUMN TRIM COVERS

1. Remove lower trim cover retaining screws, then the lower and upper trim covers.
2. Reverse procedure to install.

IGNITION SWITCH

Refer to "Electrical" section of "Vibe" chassis chapter for ignition switch replacement.

IGNITION LOCK CYLINDER

Refer to "Electrical" section of "Vibe" chassis chapter for ignition lock replacement.

XLR

STEERING COLUMN LOCK CONTROL MODULE

1. Remove shifter knob, then open center console door.
2. Remove hinge cover from console bin, then pull at rear of cover to disengage retainer.
3. Remove console cupholder, ashtray and trim plate.
4. Remove console retaining nuts.
5. Remove front of console to instrument panel carrier retaining bolts.
6. Lift rear of console slightly and pull rearward to release front of console

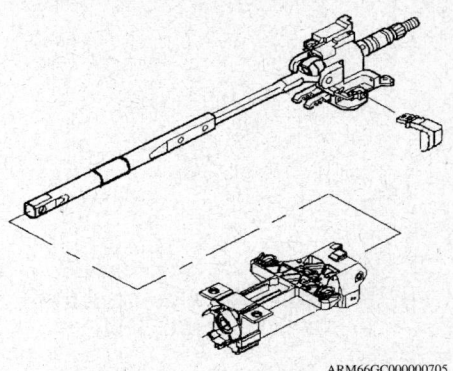

Fig. 45 Steering column disassembly. CTS

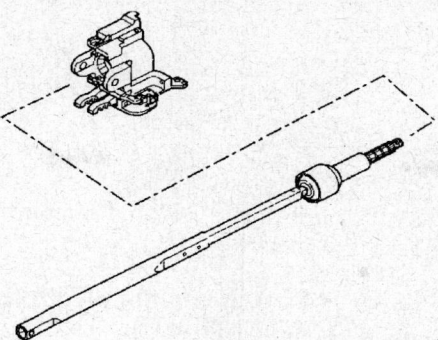

Fig. 46 Steering shaft removal. CTS

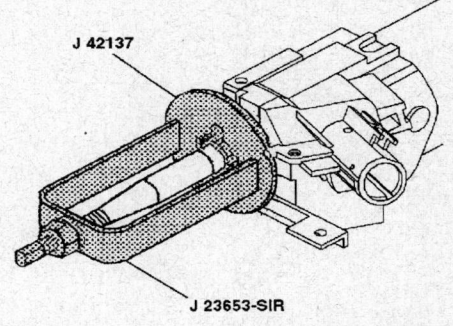

Fig. 47 Bearing retainer removal. CTS

from under instrument panel carrier.

7. Disconnect accessory plug electrical connector.
8. Remove accessory plug retainer from housing, then the housing from console.
9. Disengage lamp from retainer using a suitable flat-bladed tool.
10. Push lamp through hole in console bin, then remove console from vehicle.
11. Remove radio, then carefully pry instrument panel courtesy lamp assembly from righthand side lower closeout panel.
12. Remove righthand side lower closeout panel to instrument panel lower support beam push-in retainers.
13. Lower righthand side lower closeout panel slightly, then carefully maneuver lefthand side of closeout panel from above driveline tunnel.
14. Insert courtesy lamp assembly up through closeout panel opening.
15. Remove righthand closeout panel from instrument panel.
16. Pry fuel door and rear compartment lid release switch from knee bolster, then disconnect switch electrical connectors.
17. Remove driver knee bolster trim panel lower retaining screws.
18. Grasp knee bolster trim panel at side edges, then remove trim panel by pulling firmly to release locking tabs.
19. Carefully pry instrument panel courtesy lamp assembly from lefthand side lower closeout panel using a suitable flat-bladed tool.
20. Insert instrument panel courtesy lamp assembly up through opening in closeout panel.
21. Release notch in righthand side forward edge of closeout panel from tab on accelerator pedal bracket, then remove lefthand closeout panel.
22. Open door on instrument panel compartment, then disconnect door dampener.
23. Disconnect instrument panel compartment lamp switch electrical connector.
24. With compartment open, depress both rear corners of compartment and swing compartment down towards floor.

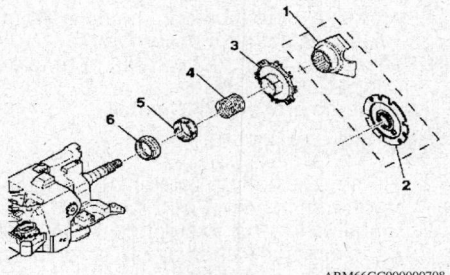

Fig. 48 Turn signal cancel cam & upper bearing inner race removal. CTS

25. Starting at outboard side, release compartment hinge from pin at bottom of door.
26. Slowly pull compartment far enough out of instrument panel to disconnect wiring harness connector from inflatable restraint module switch.
27. Remove instrument panel compartment.
28. Mark location of driver knee bolster bracket for installation reference.
29. Remove driver knee bolster bracket to steering column bracket retaining screws, then the driver knee bolster bracket from instrument panel.
30. Remove retaining screw from bottom of lefthand side trim panel.
31. Pull lefthand side trim panel outward to disengage retaining clips, then disconnect electrical connectors.
32. Remove fastener attaching top of upper trim panel and windshield side garnish molding to hinge pillar.
33. Unsnap hinge pillar upper trim from hinge pillar.
34. Remove lower hinge pillar trim.
35. Manually open folding top.
36. Pull windshield side garnish molding with its retainers from windshield frame.
37. Remove instrument panel trim pad retaining screws. Screws are located at each end of instrument panel, in center of instrument panel and behind DIC switch.
38. Pull up carefully on instrument panel trim pad to disengage retaining clips.

39. Disconnect sunload/twilight sensor from trim pad, then remove trim pad from vehicle.
40. Carefully lift HUD electrical harness from between instrument panel cluster and HUD.
41. Disconnect HUD electrical connector from cluster.
42. Remove cluster to steering column bracket retaining screws.
43. Raise rear of cluster slightly, then disconnect cluster electrical connector.
44. Remove cluster from vehicle.
45. Remove speaker retaining screws from speakers, then lift the speaker out from instrument panel carrier.
46. Disconnect speaker wire harness.
47. Remove GPS antenna to instrument panel carrier plastic rivet retainers, then the GPS antenna with antenna lead from carrier.
48. Remove remote control door lock receiver retaining screws, then the receiver from carrier.
49. Remove steering wheel.
50. Remove instrument panel carrier retaining bolts and nuts.
51. Remove carrier retaining bolts from lower beam behind compartment door.
52. Remove compartment striker from carrier.
53. Remove instrument panel carrier from mounting, then slowly route all wiring from carrier.
54. Remove instrument panel carrier from vehicle.
55. Disconnect lock module electrical connectors at lock module.
56. Pull module outward to release retaining clips, then remove module by sliding upward.
57. Reverse procedure to install.

TURN SIGNAL CANCEL CAM & STEERING SHAFT UPPER BEARING SPRING

1. Remove steering wheel and SIR coil assembly as outlined in "Electrical" section of "XLR" chassis chapter.
2. Remove bearing retainer using steering column lock plate tool No. J23653, or equivalent, **Fig. 77**.
3. Remove shaft lock shield assembly.

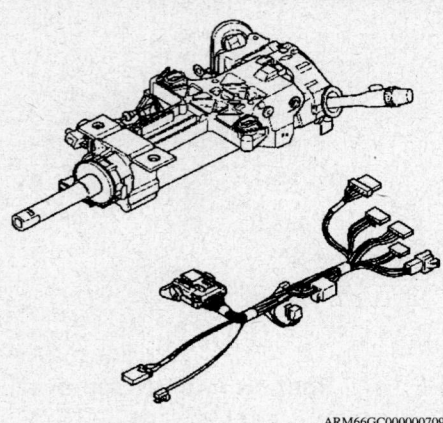

ARM66GC000000709

Fig. 49 Electrical connector removal. CTS

4. Remove turn signal cancel cam assembly, then the upper bearing spring.
5. Reverse procedure to install.

STEERING WHEEL CONTROL SWITCH ASSEMBLY

1. Remove steering wheel inflatable restraint module.
2. Disconnect steering wheel control switch electrical connectors.
3. Remove steering wheel control switch retaining screws.
4. Remove steering wheel control harness retainer and screw, **Fig. 77**.
5. Carefully pull steering wheel control switch assembly away from steering wheel, then remove wire harness from control switch assembly.
6. Reverse procedure to install.

TILT ACTUATOR ASSEMBLY

1. Remove driver knee bolster, then the lower trim cover from steering column.
2. Disconnect tilt actuator assembly electrical connector, **Fig. 77**.
3. Remove tilt actuator assembly fasteners, then the tilt actuator assembly from steering column.
4. Remove potentiometer housing from tilt actuator assembly.
5. Disconnect tilt cable from tilt actuator assembly.
6. Reverse procedure to install.

TELESCOPE ACTUATOR SWITCH

1. Remove driver knee bolster.
2. Remove lower steering column trim cover retaining screws.
3. Disconnect lower trim cover from closeout shroud.
4. Disconnect telescope actuator switch electrical connector.
5. Remove telescope actuator switch from lower trim cover.
6. Reverse procedure to install.

TELESCOPE ACTUATOR ASSEMBLY

1. Remove driver knee bolster.
2. Disconnect telescope actuator assembly electrical connector.

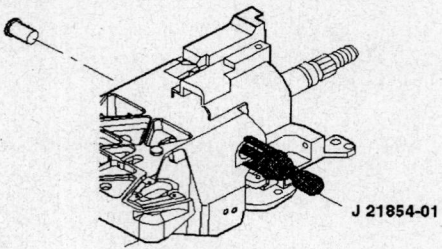

ARM66GC000000710

Fig. 50 Steering column pivot pin removal. CTS

3. Remove telescope actuator assembly fasteners.
4. Remove telescope actuator assembly from steering column, **Fig. 77**.
5. Remove potentiometer housing from telescope actuator assembly.
6. Disconnect telescope cable from telescope actuator assembly.
7. Reverse procedure to install.

TILT SPRING

1. Remove steering column upper and lower trim covers, **Fig. 77**.
2. Install tilt lever onto steering column tilt head assembly, then use tilt lever to tilt column to UP position.
3. Pry tilt spring upward until a bulge occurs and most tilt spring tension is removed.
4. Secure tilt spring with suitable locking pliers.
5. Continue prying up on tilt spring until tilt spring disengages from post on steering column support assembly and tilt head assembly.
6. Remove tilt spring from steering column support assembly and tilt head assembly.
7. Remove spring guide from tilt spring.
8. Reverse procedure to install.

LOWER BEARING & STEERING COLUMN JACKET

1. Remove steering wheel as outlined in "Electrical" section of "XLR" chassis chapter.
2. Remove steering column as outlined in "Steering Column, Replace."
3. Remove turn signal and multifunction switch assembly, **Fig. 77**.
4. Remove wire harness assembly from steering column.
5. Remove telescope drive motor assembly and cable.
6. Remove tilt drive motor assembly and cable.
7. Remove control module Torx head screw from control module.
8. Slide control module from steering column.
9. Remove boot seal, steering shaft seal, sensor retainer, sensor locator and steering shaft position sensor.
10. Remove Torx screw from bottom of gearshift and tilt motor bracket, then the bracket.
11. Gently pry lower shield assembly off of steering column.
12. Remove steering column support assembly pivot pins using pivot pin re-

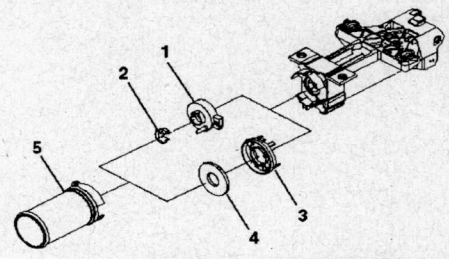

ARM66GC000000711

Fig. 51 Steering wheel position sensor removal. CTS

mover tool No. J21854-01, or equivalent.
13. Remove lead screw, then the tilt head assembly from steering column support assembly with steering shaft still attached.
14. Remove tilt head assembly from steering shaft assembly.
15. Mark race, upper shaft and lower steering shaft for assembly reference. Failure to assemble properly will cause steering wheel to be turned 180°.
16. Tilt upper shaft assembly 90° to steering shaft assembly and disengage.
17. Remove Torx screws from dampener.
18. Remove and discard support screws from steering column support.
19. Remove steering column support.
20. Reverse procedure to install.

INFLATABLE RESTRAINT STEERING WHEEL MODULE COIL CENTERING

1. Ensure wheels on vehicle are straight ahead, block tooth of steering shaft assembly is in 12 o'clock position and ignition switch assembly is in the LOCK position, **Figs. 78 through 81**.
2. If front of SIR coil has a centering window and back side has a spring service lock, **Fig. 78**, proceed as follows:
   a. Hold coil with face up.
   b. While depressing spring service lock, rotate coil hub clockwise until coil ribbon stops.
   c. Rotate coil hub slowly counterclockwise, until centering window appears yellow and both arrows line up.
   d. Release spring service lock between locking tab.
   e. SIR coil is now centered.
   f. Align centered SIR coil with horn tower and slide onto steering shaft assembly.
3. If front of SIR coil has a centering window and the back side does not have spring service lock, **Fig. 79**, proceed as follows:
   a. Hold coil with face up.
   b. Rotate coil hub clockwise until coil ribbon stops.
   c. Rotate coil hub slowly counterclockwise until centering window appears yellow and both arrows line up.
   d. This is Center position.
   e. While holding coil hub in Center position, align coil with horn tower and

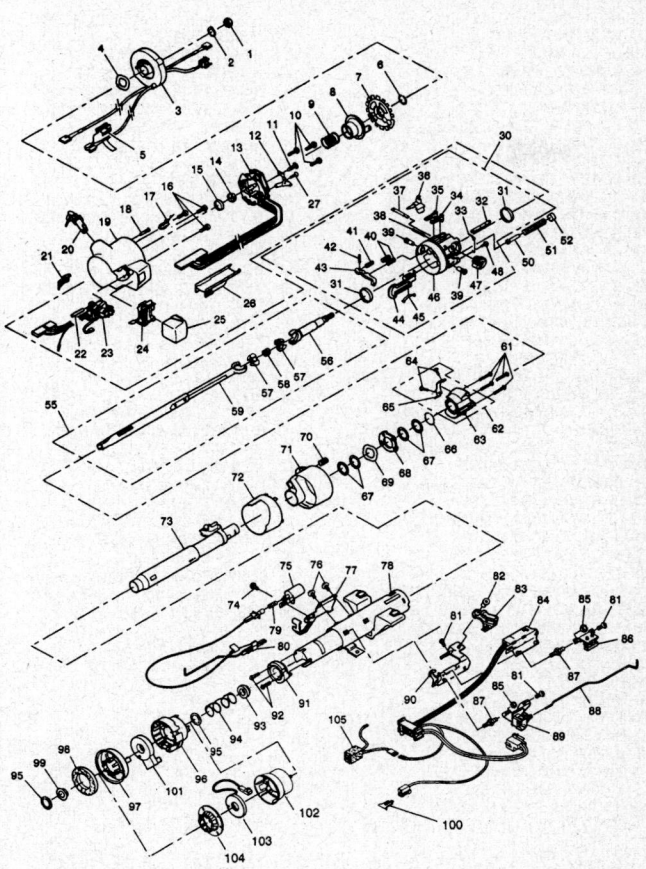

1 - NUT, HEXAGON LOCKING (M14x1.5)
2 - RING, RETAINING
3 - COIL ASM, SIR
4 - WASHER, WAVE
5 - SHROUD, CONNECTOR
6 - RING, RETAINING
7 - LOCK, SHAFT
8 - CAM ASM, T/SIG CANCEL
9 - SPRING, UPPER BEARING
10 - SCREW, BNDG HD CR RECESS
11 - SCREW, RD WASH HD (M4.2x1.41)
12 - ARM ASM, SIGNAL SWITCH
13 - SWITCH ASM, TURN SIGNAL
14 - SEAT, UPPER BRG INNER RACE
15 - RACE, INNER
16 - SCREW, PAN HD 6 LOBED SOC TAP
17 - SWITCH ASM, BUZZER
18 - SCREW, LOCK RETAINING
19 - COVER ASM, LOCK HOUSING
20 - LOCK CYLINDER SET, STRG COL
21 - ACTUATOR, DIMMER SW ROD
22 - PIN, SWITCH ACTUATOR PIVOT
23 - SWITCH ASM, PIVOT & (PULSE)
24 - BASE PLATE, COL HSG CVR END
25 - CAP, COL HSG COVER END
26 - PROTECTOR, WIRING
27 - SCREW, FLAT HEAD TAPPING
30 - HOUSING ASM, STRG COLUMN
31 - BEARING ASM
32 - BOLT, LOCK
33 - SPRING, LOCK BOLT
34 - SHOE, STEERING WHEEL LOCK
35 - SHOE, STEERING WHEEL LOCK
36 - SHIELD, WIRE PROTECTOR
37 - SHAFT, DRIVE
38 - PIN, DOWEL
39 - PIN, PIVOT
40 - SPRING, SHOE
41 - SPRING, RELEASE LEVER
42 - PIN, RELEASE LEVER
43 - LEVER, SHOE RELEASE
44 - RACK, SWITCH ACTUATOR
45 - SPRING, RACK PRELOAD
46 - HOUSING, STRG COLUMN
47 - SECTOR, SWITCH ACTUATOR
48 - SCREW, HEX WASHER HEAD
50 - GUIDE, SPRING
51 - SPRING, WHEEL TILT
52 - RETAINER, SPRING
55 - SHAFT ASM, STEERING
56 - SHAFT ASM, RACE & UPPER
57 - SPHERE, CENTERING
58 - SPRING, JOINT PRELOAD
59 - SHAFT ASM, LOWER STEERING
61 - SCREW, SUPPORT

62 - SUPPORT ASM, STRG COL HSG
63 - SUPPORT, STRG COL HSG
64 - SCREW, OVL HD CROSS RECESS
65 - GATE, SHIFT LEVER
66 - RING, SHIFT TUBE RETAINING
67 - WASHER, THRUST
68 - PLATE, LOCK
69 - WASHER, WAVE
70 - SPRING, SHIFT LEVER
71 - BOWL ASM, GEARSHIFT LEVER
72 - SHROUD, GEARSHIFT BOWL
73 - TUBE ASM, SHIFT
74 - SCREW, HEX WASH HD (#10-24X.25)
75 - SOLENOID ASM, INTERLOCK
76 - SCREW, WASH HD (#10-24X.25)
77 - BRACKET, SOLENOID
78 - JACKET ASM, STRG COL
79 - SPRING, BALL JOINT
80 - ACTUATOR ASM, IGNITION SWITCH
81 - SCREW, TORX WASHER HEAD
82 - RETAINER, CAM
83 - CAM ASM, CABLE SHIFT
84 - SWITCH ASM, IGNITION
85 - NUT, HEXAGON (#10-24)
86 - ADJUSTER ASM, PRNDL
87 - STUD, DIMR SW MTG
88 - ROD, DIMMER SWITCH
89 - SWITCH ASM, DIMMER
90 - BRACKET ASM, STUD &
91 - BEARING ASM, ADAPTER &
92 - SCREW, HEX WASHER HD TAP
93 - SEAT, LOWER BEARING
94 - SPRING, LOWER BEARING
95 - RETAINER, LOWER SPRING
96 - ADAPTER, STRG SENSOR
97 - RETAINER, SENSOR
98 - SEAL, STEERING SHAFT
99 - BUSHING, SEAL RETAINING
100 - CONNECTOR, AXIAL POSN ASSURANCE
101 - SENSOR ASM, HI RES STRG WHL POSN
102 - RETAINER, BEARING
103 - SENSOR ASM, STRG WHL POSN
104 - DAMPENER ASM, ROTATIONAL
105 - HARNESS ASM, JUMPER

GC604970023500BX

GC604970023500AX

Fig. 52 Exploded view of steering column (Part 1 of 2). DeVille & Seville w/column shift

Fig. 52 Exploded view of steering column (Part 2 of 2). DeVille & Seville w/column shift

slide coil onto steering shaft assembly.

4. If no centering window is present on front side of SIR coil, but a spring service lock is on back side, **Fig. 80**, proceed as follows:

a. Hold coil with back side up.
b. While depressing spring service lock, rotate coil hub in direction of arrow until coil ribbon stops.
c. Still pressing spring service lock, rotate coil hub in opposite direction 2½ revolutions.
d. Release spring service lock between locking tabs.
e. SIR coil is now centered.
f. Align centered coil with horn tower and slide coil onto steering shaft assembly.

5. If no centering window appears on front side of SIR coil and no spring service lock exists on back side, **Fig. 81**, proceed as follows:

a. Hold coil with face up.
b. Rotate coil hub in direction of arrow until coil ribbon stops.
c. Rotate coil hub, slowly, counterclockwise, for 2½ revolutions.
d. This is Center position.
e. While maintaining coil hub in Center position, align coil with horn tower and slide coil onto steering shaft assembly.

TECHNICAL SERVICE BULLETINS

Clunk Noise From Front Of Vehicle During Turning Maneuver/Steering Wheel Rotation

BONNEVILLE, CAVALIER, GRAND PRIX, IMPALA, MONTE CARLO, REGAL, SEVILLE & SUNFIRE

On some of these models there may be a clunk type noise coming from the front of the vehicle during a turning maneuver. This condition may also be felt through the steering wheel when the vehicle is stationary and the wheel is rotated from steering stop to steering stop. Typically, the clunk noise will be heard once for every 180° of steering wheel rotation in either direction for on Cavalier and Sunfire models. However, some vehicles may exhibit the noise once for every 360° of wheel rotation. On all other vehicles, this clunk noise will be noticed during low speed acceleration or deceleration, typically in light turns of the steering wheel.

This condition may be caused by inadequate lubrication of the steering intermediate shaft which results in a slip stick condition possibly resulting in the clunk noise.

This condition is commonly misdiagnosed as originating in the steering gear.

Do not replace following steering gear part Nos: 26063582, 26056808, 26031078, 26079915, 26055468, 26079917, 26079929, 26081813, 26080057, 26088612, 26086001, 26088334, 26088539, 26068964, 26058681, 26068967, 26088606, 26067451, 26087241, or 26087416.

Do not replace following intermediate shafts Nos: 10327501, 10327502, 10327553, 22680754, 22704392, 26050292, 26055042, 26073020, 26078302, 26079240, 26079787, or 26100571.

To correct this condition remove the intermediate steering shaft from the vehicle and lubricate the shaft with a steering column shaft lubrication kit (P/N 26098237). as follows:

1. Remove steering intermediate shaft.
2. Fully extend intermediate shaft by pulling two shafts apart.
3. Apply grease supplied in lubrication kit in aluminum end of yoke opening. Direct syringe tip as deep as possible

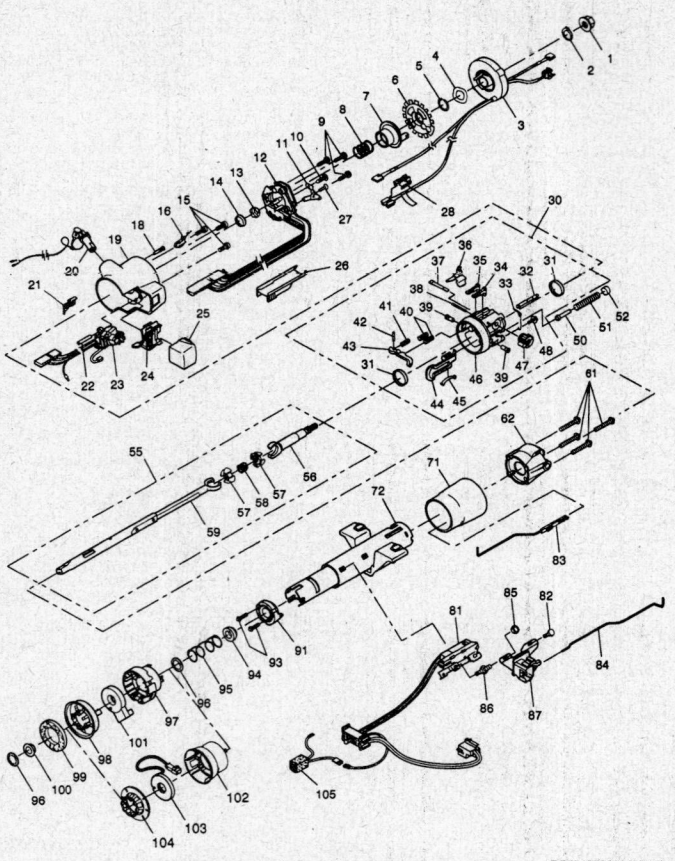

Fig. 53 Exploded view of steering column (Part 1 of 2). DeVille & Seville w/console shift

1- NUT, HEX LOCKING (M14x1.5)
2- RING, RETAINING
3- COIL ASM, SIR
4- WASHER, WAVE
5- RING, RETAINING
6- LOCK, SHAFT
7- CAM ASM, T/SIG CANCEL
8- SPRING, UPPER BEARING
9- SCREW, BNDG HD CR RECESS
10- SCREW, RD WASH HD (M4.2x1.41)
11- ARM ASM, SIGNAL SWITCH
12- SWITCH ASM, TURN SIGNAL
13- SEAT, UPPER BRG INNER RACE
14- RACE, INNER
15- SCREW, PAN HD 6 LOBED SOC TAP
16- SWITCH ASM, BUZZER
18- SCREW, LOCK RETAINING
19- COVER ASM, LOCK HOUSING
20- LOCK CYLINDER SET, STRG COL PASS KEY
21- ACTUATOR, DIMMER SWITCH ROD
22- PIN, SWITCH ACTUATOR PIVOT
23- SWITCH ASM, PIVOT & (PULSE)
24- BASE PLATE, COL HSG CVR END
25- CAP, COL HSG COVER END
26- PROTECTOR, WIRING
27- SCREW, FLT HD TAPPING
28- SHROUD, CONNECTOR
30- HOUSING ASM, STRG COLUMN
31- BEARING ASM
32- BOLT, LOCK
33- SPRING, LOCK BOLT
34- SHOE, STEERING WHEEL LOCK
35- SHOE, STEERING WHEEL LOCK
36- SHIELD, WIRE PROTECTOR
37- SHAFT, DRIVE
38- PIN, DOWEL
39- PIN, PIVOT
40- SPRING, SHOE
41- SPRING, RELEASE LEVER
42- PIN, RELEASE LEVER
43- LEVER, SHOE RELEASE
44- RACK, SWITCH ACTUATOR
45- SPRING, RACK PRELOAD
46- HOUSING, STRG COLUMN
47- SECTOR, SWITCH ACTUATOR

48- SCREW, HEX WASHER HEAD
50- GUIDE, SPRING
51- SPRING, WHEEL TILT
52- RETAINER, SPRING
55- SHAFT ASM, STEERING
56- SHAFT ASM, RACE & UPPER
57- SPHERE, CENTERING
58- SPRING, JOINT PRELOAD
59- SHAFT ASM, LOWER STEERING
61- SCREW, HEX WASHER HD TAPPING
62- SUPPORT ASM, STRG COL HSG
71- SHROUD, STRG COLUMN HSG
72- JACKET ASM, STRG COL
81- SWITCH ASM, COL LOCK & IGN
82- SCREW, WASH HD (#10-24X.25)
83- ACTUATOR ASM, IGNITION SWITCH
84- ROD, DIMMER SWITCH
85- NUT, HEXAGON (#10-24)
86- STUD, DIMR & IGN SW MTG
87- SWITCH ASM, DIMMER
91- BEARING ASM, ADAPTER &
93- SCREW, HEX WASHER HD TAP
94- SEAT, LOWER BEARING
95- SPRING, LOWER BEARING
96- RETAINER, LOWER SPRING
97- ADAPTER, STRG SENSOR
98- RETAINER, SENSOR
99- SEAL, STEERING SHAFT
100- BUSHING, SEAL RETAINING
101- SENSOR ASM, HI RES STRG WHL POSN
102- RETAINER, BEARING
103- SENSOR ASM, STRG WHL POSN
104- DAMPENER ASM, ROTATIONAL
105- HARNESS ASM, JUMPER

Fig. 53 Exploded view of steering column (Part 2 of 2). DeVille & Seville w/console shift

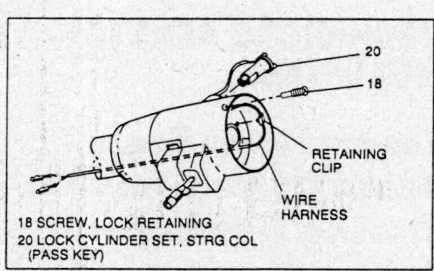

Fig. 54 Pass key wire connection locations. DeVille & Seville

into yoke and dispense full content of syringe.

4. Install rubber stop plug from kit into yoke opening.

5. Secure rubber plug by swinging upper yoke 90°. One ear of yoke should press rubber plug in.

6. Collapse of intermediate shaft on suitable hard surface. Use pumping action when collapsing shaft. Collapse shaft as far as possible. **Ensure intermediate shaft is being pressed over ears of solid shaft.**

7. Remove rubber stopper plug from yoke end of shaft.

Fig. 55 Pass key wire installation. DeVille & Seville

8. Slowly extend intermediate shaft apart.

9. Inspect intermediate shaft for minimum of .2 inch of grease on shaft splines. Repeat previous steps if less than .2 inch of grease is on shaft splines.

10. Stroke and extend intermediate shaft at least 15 times to completely lubricate internal surface of slip joint.

11. Install the intermediate shaft into vehicle.

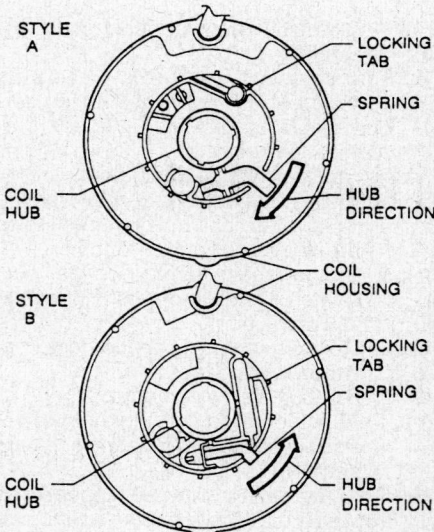

Fig. 56 Coil centering. DeVille & Seville

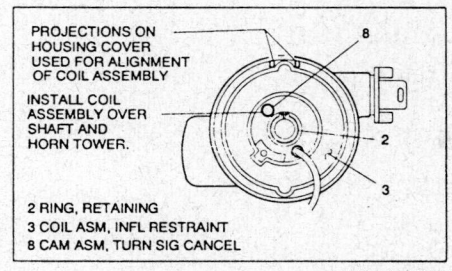

Fig. 57 Coil installation. DeVille & Seville

(5) Shift Lever Screw
(6) Shift Lever Seal
(7) Flanged Prevailing Torque Nut
(8) Retaining Ring
(9) SIR Coil
(10) Wave Washer
(11) Bearing Retainer
(12) Shaft Lock
(13) Turn Signal Cancel Cam
(14) Upper Bearing Spring
(15) Upper Bearing Inner Race Seat
(16) Inner Race
(17) Pan Head Tapping Screws
(18) TORX® Head Screw
(19) Pan Head Tapping Screw
(20) Ignition Lock Cylinder Case
(21) Theft Deterrent Control Module
(22) Tapping Screws
(23) Ignition Switch Assembly
(24) Wire Harness Strap
(25) Bearing and Housing Assembly

(26) Lock Bolt Spring
(27) Lock Bolt Assembly
(28) Spring Guide
(29) Tilt Spring
(30) Release Lever Spring
(31) Release Lever Pin
(32) Trim Cover Protector
(33) Tilt Lever
(34) Pan Head Tapping Screws
(35) Solenoid Opening Button
(36) Wire Harness Straps
(37) Pan Head Tapping Screws
(38) Turn Signal and Multifunction Switch Assembly
(39) Bearing Assembly
(40) Race and Upper Shaft Assembly
(41) Centering Sphere
(42) Joint Preload Spring
(43) Lower Shaft Assembly
(44) Flat Head 6-Lobed Soc Tap Screws
(45) Linear Shift Assembly

Fig. 58 Exploded view of steering column (Part 2 of 3). DTS w/manual tilt Column shift

(46) Electrical (BTSI) Actuator
(47) Pan Head Tapping Screws
(48) BTSI Mounting Bracket Assembly
(49) Cable Support Bracket
(50) Flat Head Screws
(51) Pivot Pins
(52) Steering Column Support Assembly
(53) Steering Wheel Position Sensor
(54) Steering Wheel Position Sensor (Optional)
(55) Retaining Ring
(56) Sensor Locator
(57) Sensor Retainer
(58) Steering Shaft Seal
(59) Boot Seal
(60) Bolt and Retainer Assembly
(61) Intermediate Steering Shaft Assembly
(62) Pinch Bolt Nut
(63) Main Wiring Harness

Fig. 58 Exploded view of steering column (Part 3 of 3). DTS w/manual tilt Column shift

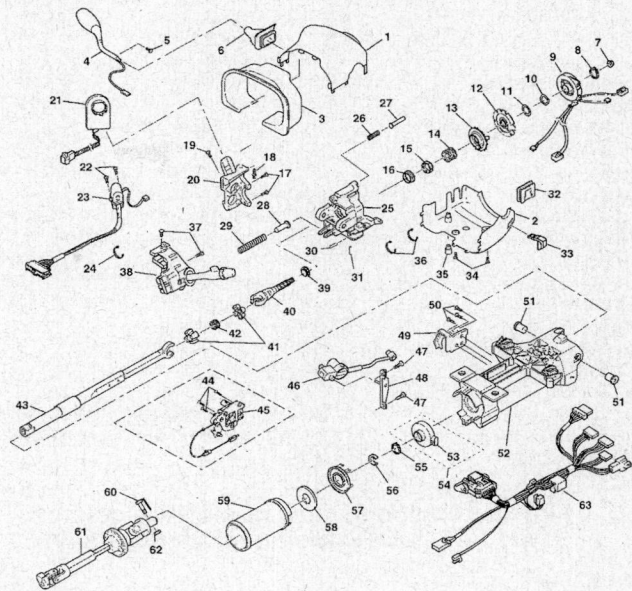

(1) Upper Trim Cover
(2) Lower Trim Cover
(3) Steering Column Closeout Trim Cover
(4) Shift Lever

Fig. 58 Exploded view of steering column (Part 1 of 3). DTS w/manual tilt Column shift

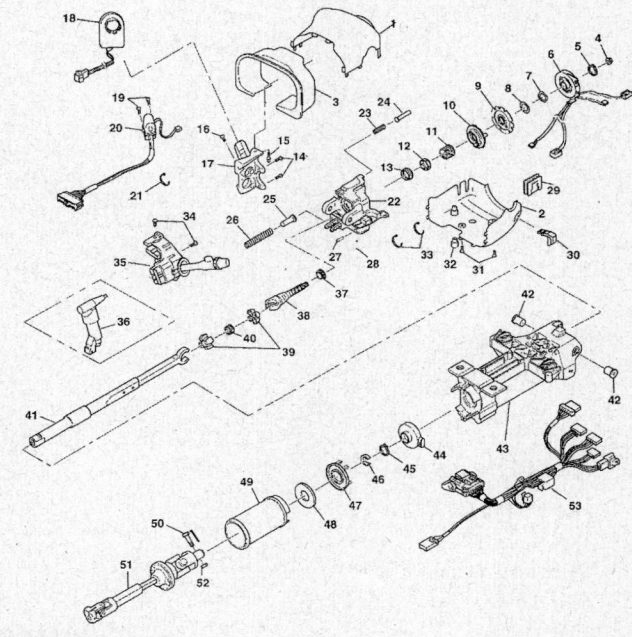

(1) Upper Trim Cover
(2) Lower Trim Cover
(3) Steering Column Closeout Trim Cover
(4) Flanged Prevailing Torque Nut

Fig. 59 Exploded view of steering column (Part 1 of 3). DTS w/manual tilt floor shift

(5) Retaining Ring
(6) SIR Coil
(7) Wave Washer
(8) Bearing Retainer
(9) Shaft Lock
(10) Turn Signal Cancel Cam
(11) Upper Bearing Spring
(12) Upper Bearing Inner Race Seat
(13) Inner Race
(14) Pan Head Tapping Screws
(15) TORX® Head Screw
(16) Pan Head Tapping Screw
(17) Ignition Lock Cylinder Case
(18) Theft Deterrent Control Module
(19) Tapping Screws
(20) Ignition Switch Assembly
(21) Wire Harness Strap
(22) Bearing and Housing Assembly
(23) Lock Bolt Spring
(24) Lock Bolt Assembly
(25) Spring Guide

(26) Tilt Spring
(27) Release Lever Spring
(28) Release Lever Pin
(29) Trim Cover Protector
(30) Tilt Knob
(31) Pan Head Tapping Screws
(32) Solenoid Opening Button
(33) Wire Harness Straps
(34) Pan Head Tapping Screws
(35) Turn Signal and Multifunction Switch Assembly
(36) Steering Column Electric Park Lock
(37) Bearing Assembly
(38) Race and Upper Shaft Assembly
(39) Centering Sphere
(40) Joint Preload Spring
(41) Lower Shaft Assembly
(42) Pivot Pins
(42) Pivot Pin
(43) Steering Column Support Assembly
(44) Steering Wheel Position Sensor Assembly

ARM0500000000809

Fig. 59 Exploded view of steering column (Part 2 of 3). DTS w/manual tilt floor shift

(45) Retaining Ring
(46) Sensor Locator
(47) Sensor Retainer
(48) Steering Shaft Seal
(49) Boot Seal
(50) Bolt and Retainer Assembly
(51) Intermediate Steering Shaft Assembly
(52) Pinch Bolt Nut
(53) Main Wiring Harness

ARM0500000000810

Fig. 59 Exploded view of steering column (Part 3 of 3). DTS w/manual tilt floor shift

(5) Shift Lever Screw
(6) Shift Lever Seal
(7) Flange Prevailing Torque Nut
(8) Retaining Ring
(9) SIR Coil
(10) Wave Washer
(11) Bearing Retainer
(12) Shaft Lock
(13) Turn Signal Cancel Cam
(14) Pan Head Tapping Screw
(15) Switch Mounting Bracket
(16) Lock Bolt
(17) Lock Bolt Spring
(18) Upper Bearing Spring
(19) Upper Bearing Inner Race Seat
(20) Inner Race
(21) Pan Head Tapping Screws
(22) TORX® Head Screw
(23) Pan Head Tapping Screw
(24) Ignition Lock Cylinder Case
(25) Pan Head Tapping Screws

(26) Ignition Switch Assembly
(27) Theft Deterrent Control Module
(28) Wire Harness Strap
(29) Wire Harness Strap
(30) Steering Column Tilt Head Assembly
(31) Bearing Holder
(31) Bearing Holder
(32) Trim Cover Protector
(33) Power Tilt and Telescope Toggle Switch Assembly
(34) Pan Head Tapping Screws
(35) Wire Harness Straps
(36) Pan Head Tapping Screws
(37) Turn Signal Multifunction Switch Assembly
(38) Wire Harness Strap
(39) Bearing Assembly
(40) Race and Upper Shaft Assembly
(41) Centering Sphere
(42) Joint Preload Spring
(43) Steering Shaft Assembly
(44) Flat Head Tapping Screws

ARM0500000000812

Fig. 60 Exploded view of steering column (Part 2 of 3). DTS w/power tilt & telescope column shift

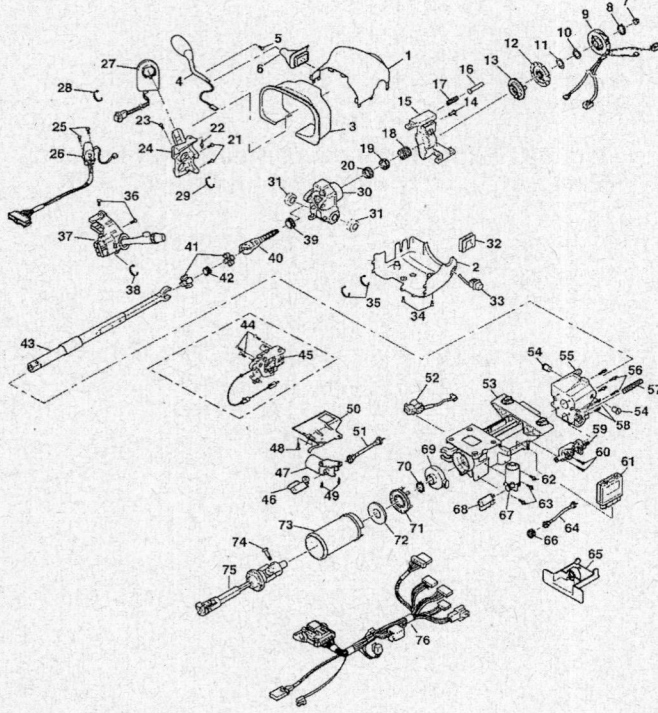

(1) Upper Trim Cover
(2) Lower Trim Cover
(3) Steering Column Closeout Trim Cover
(4) Shift Lever

ARM0500000000811

Fig. 60 Exploded view of steering column (Part 1 of 3). DTS w/power tilt & telescope column shift

(45) Linear Shift Assembly
(46) Potentiometer Housing
(47) Tilt and Telescope Drive Motor Assembly
(48) TORX® Head Screw
(49) Pan Head Tapping Screws
(50) Gear Shift and Tilt Motor Bracket
(51) Tilt and Cable Assembly
(52) Automatic Transmission Shift Lock Control
(53) Telescoping Jacket Assembly
(54) Pivot Pins
(54) Pivot Pin
(55) Steering Column Housing Support
(56) Pan Head Tapping Screws
(57) Lead Screw
(58) TORX® Head Screws
(59) Jackscrew Right Hand Telescoping Nut
(60) Pan Head Tapping Screws

(61) Tilt and Telescope Module
(62) TORX® Head Screw
(63) TORX® Head Screws
(64) Telescope Cable Assembly
(65) Lower Shield Assembly
(66) Cable Spring
(67) Tilt and Telescope Drive Motor Assembly
(68) Potentiometer Housing
(69) Steering Shaft Position Sensor
(70) Retaining Ring
(71) Sensor Retainer
(72) Steering Shaft Seal
(73) Boot Seal
(74) Pinch Bolt
(75) Intermediate Steering Shaft Assembly
(76) Main Harness

ARM0500000000813

Fig. 60 Exploded view of steering column (Part 3 of 3). DTS w/power tilt & telescope column shift

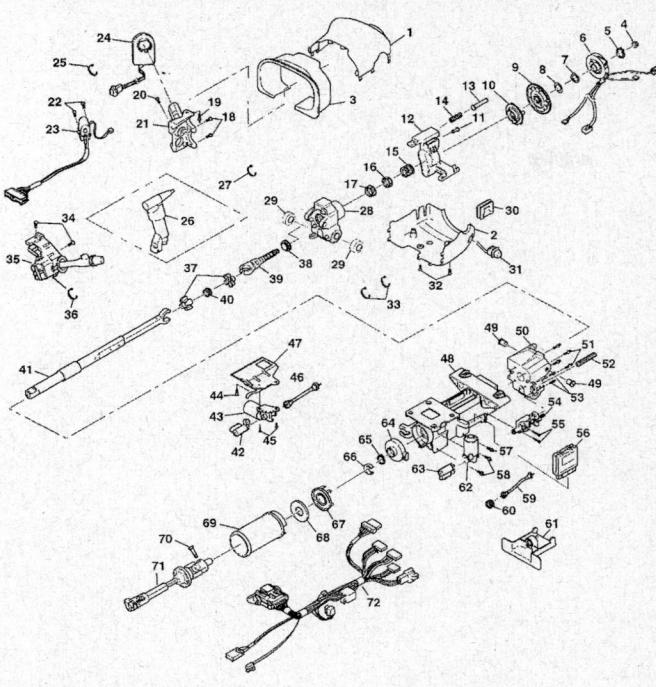

(1) Upper Trim Cover
(2) Lower Trim Cover
(3) Steering Column Closeout Trim Cover
(4) Flange Prevailing Torque Nut

ARM0500000000814

Fig. 61 Exploded view of steering column (Part 1 of 3). DTS w/power tilt & telescope floor shift

(45) Pan Head Tapping Screws	(59) Telescope Cable Assembly
(46) Tilt and Cable Assembly	(60) Cable Spring
(47) Gear Shift and Tilt Motor Bracket	(61) Lower Shield Assembly
(48) Telescoping Jacket Assembly	(62) Tilt and Telescope Drive Motor Assembly
(49) Pivot Pins	(63) Potentiometer Housing
(50) Steering Column Housing Support	(64) Steering Shaft Position Sensor
(51) TORX® Head Screws	(65) Retaining Ring
(52) Lead Screw	(66) Sensor Locator
(53) TORX® Head Screws	(67) Sensor Retainer
(54) Jackscrew Right Hand Telescoping Nut	(68) Steering Shaft Seal
(55) Pan Head Tapping Screws	(69) Boot Seal
(56) Tilt and Telescope Module	(70) Pinch Bolt
(57) TORX® Head Screw	(71) Intermediate Steering Shaft Assembly
(58) TORX® Head Screws	(72) Main Harness

ARM0500000000816

Fig. 61 Exploded view of steering column (Part 3 of 3). DTS w/power tilt & telescope floor shift

(5) Retaining Ring	(26) Electric Park Lock Assembly
(6) SIR Coil	(27) Wire Harness Strap
(7) Wave Washer	(28) Steering Column Tilt Head Assembly
(8) Bearing Retainer	(29) Bearing Holder
(9) Shaft Lock	(29) Bearing Holder
(10) Turn Signal Cancel Cam	(30) Trim Cover Protector
(11) Pan Head Tapping Screw	(31) Power Tilt and Telescope Toggle Switch Assembly
(12) Switch Mounting Bracket	(32) Pan Head Tapping Screws
(13) Lock Bolt	(33) Wire Harness Straps
(14) Lock Bolt Spring	(34) Pan Head Tapping Screws
(15) Upper Bearing Spring	(35) Turn Signal Multifunction Switch Assembly
(16) Upper Bearing Inner Race Seat	(36) Wire Harness Strap
(17) Inner Race	(37) Centering Sphere
(18) Pan Head Tapping Screws	(38) Bearing Assembly
(19) TORX® Head Screw	(39) Race and Upper Shaft Assembly
(20) Pan Head Tapping Screw	(40) Joint Preload Spring
(21) Ignition Lock Cylinder Case	(41) Steering Shaft Assembly
(22) Pan Head Tapping Screws	(42) Potentiometer Housing
(23) Ignition Switch Assembly	(43) Tilt and Telescope Drive Motor Assembly
(24) Theft Deterrent Control Module	(44) TORX® Head Screw
(25) Wire Harness Strap	

ARM0500000000815

Fig. 61 Exploded view of steering column (Part 2 of 3). DTS w/power tilt & telescope floor shift

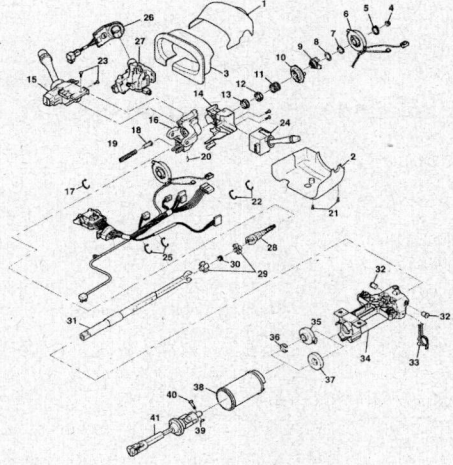

(1) Upper Trim Cover	(22) Wire Straps
(2) Lower Trim Cover	(23) Pan Head Tapping Screws
(3) Steering Column Closeout Trim	(24) Window Washer and Wiper Switch Assembly
(4) Flanged Prevailing Torque Nut	(25) Wire Straps
(5) Retaining Ring	(26) Theft Deterrent
(6) SIR Coil	(27) Ignition Lock Cylinder Case
(7) Wave Washer	(28) Race and Upper Shaft
(8) Bearing Retainer	(29) Centering Sphere
(9) Cam Orientation Plate	(30) Joint Preload Spring
(10) Turn Signal Cancel Cam	(31) Lower Steering Shaft
(11) Upper Bearing Spring	(32) Pivot Pins
(12) Upper Bearing Inner Race Seat	(33) Wire Strap
(13) Inner Race	(34) Steering Column Jacket Assembly
(14) Switch Mounting Bracket	(35) Steering Column Position Sensor
(15) Turn Signal and Multifunction Switch	(36) Sensor Clip
(16) Steering Column Tilt Head Assembly	(37) Sensor Seal
(17) Wire Strap	(38) Boot
(18) Spring Guide	(39) Bolt Retainer
(19) Tilt Spring	(40) Pinch Bolt
(20) Pin	(41) Intermediate Shaft Assembly
(21) Pan Head Tapping Screws	

ARM0400000000043

Fig. 62 Exploded view of steering column. STS

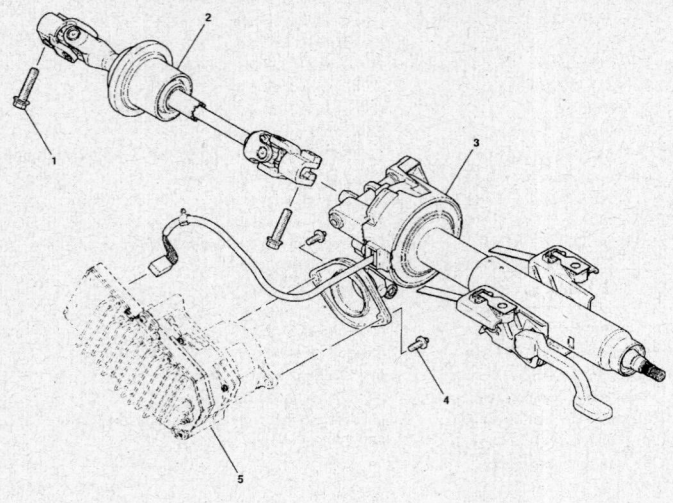

(1) Pinch Bolt
(2) Intermediate Steering Shaft
(3) Steering Column
(4) TORX® Bolts
(5) Motor/ Module Assembly

ARM0400000000044

Fig. 63   Exploded view of steering column. G6

(5) SIR Coil
(6) Wave Washer
(7) Bearing Retainer
(8) Shaft Lock Shield Assembly
(9) Turn Signal Cancel Cam Assembly
(10) Upper Bearing Spring
(11) Upper Bearing Inner Race Seat
(12) Inner Race
(13) Pan Head Tapping Screws
(14) TORX® Head Screw
(15) Ignition Lock Cylinder Case Assembly
(16) Steering Column Lock Cylinder Set
(17) Pan Head Tapping Screw
(18) Tapping Screws
(19) Ignition Switch Assembly
(20) Steering Column Tilt Head Assembly
(21) Lock Bolt Spring
(22) Lock Bolt Assembly
(23) Spring Guide
(24) Tilt Spring
(25) TORX® Head Screw

(26) Wire Harness Strap
(27) Trim Cover Protector
(28) Tilt Knob
(29) Pan Head Tapping Screws
(30) Pan Head Tapping Screws
(31) Turn Signal and Multifunction Switch Assembly
(32) Position Assurance Connector
(33) Wire Harness Straps
(34) Steering Wheel Theft Deterrent Park Lock
(35) Race and Upper Shaft Assembly
(36) Joint Preload Spring
(37) Centering Sphere
(38) Lower Shaft Assembly
(39) TORX® Head Screws
(40) Pivot Pins
(41) Steering Column Support Assembly
(42) Steering Column Jacket Assembly
(43) Adapter and Bearing Assembly
(44) Lower Bearing Seat
(45) Lower Bearing Spring

ARM0500000000820

Fig. 64   Exploded view of steering column (Part 2 of 3). LaCrosse w/floor shift

(46) Lower Spring Retainer
(47) Retainer
(48) Steering Shaft Seal
(49) Intermediate Steering Shaft Assembly
(50) Pinch Bolt

ARM0500000000821

Fig. 64   Exploded view of steering column (Part 3 of 3). LaCrosse w/floor shift

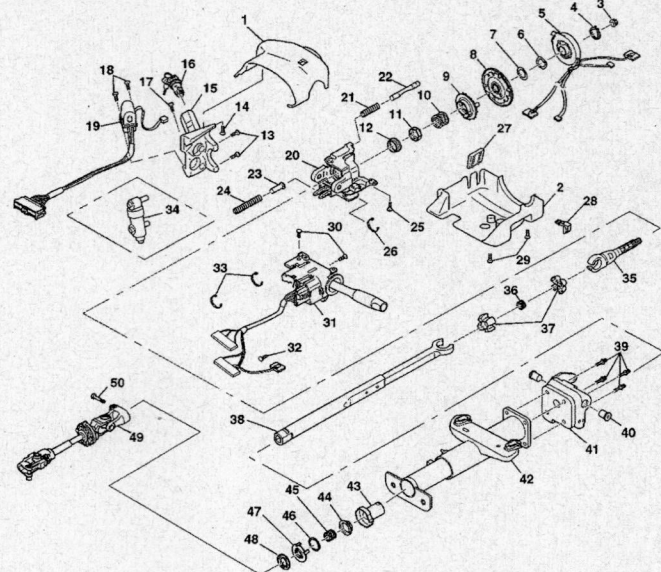

(1) Upper Trim Cover
(2) Lower Trim Cover
(3) Flanged Prevailing Torque Nut
(4) Retaining Ring

ARM0500000000819

Fig. 64   Exploded view of steering column (Part 1 of 3). LaCrosse w/floor shift

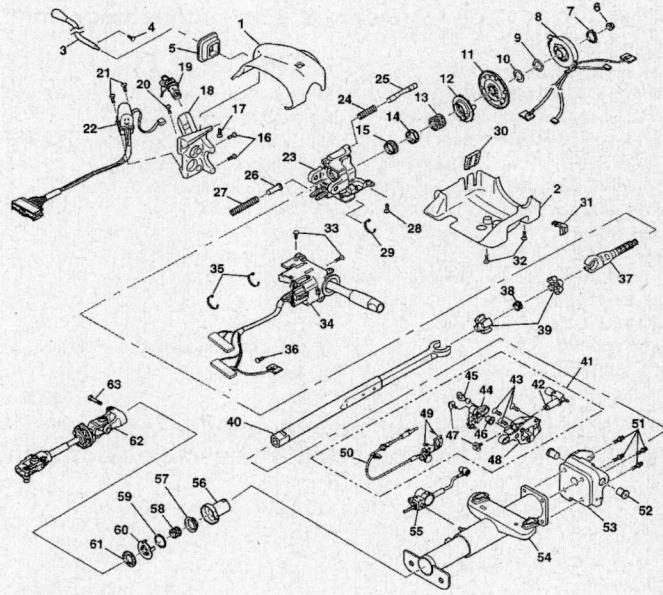

(1) Upper Trim Cover
(2) Lower Trim Cover
(3) Shift Lever Assembly
(4) Shift Lever Screw

ARM0500000000822

Fig. 65   Exploded view of steering column (Part 1 of 3). LaCrosse w/column shift

(5) Shift Lever Seal
(6) Flanged Prevailing Torque Nut
(7) Retaining Ring
(8) SIR Coil
(9) Wave Washer
(10) Bearing Retainer
(11) Shaft Lock Shield Assembly
(12) Turn Signal Cancel Cam Assembly
(13) Upper Bearing Spring
(14) Upper Bearing Inner Race Seat
(15) Inner Race
(16) Pan Head Tapping Screws
(17) TORX® Head Screw
(18) Ignition Lock Cylinder Case Assembly
(19) Steering Column Lock Cylinder Set
(20) Pan Head Tapping Screw
(21) Tapping Screws
(22) Ignition Switch Assembly
(23) Steering Column Tilt Head Housing Assembly
(24) Lock Bolt Spring
(25) Lock Bolt Assembly

(26) Spring Guide
(27) Tilt Spring
(28) TORX® Head Screw
(29) Wire Harness Strap
(30) Trim Cover Protector
(31) Tilt Knob
(32) TORX® Head Screws
(33) Pan Head Tapping Screws
(34) Turn Signal and Multifunction Switch Assembly
(35) Wire Harness Straps
(36) Position Assurance Connector
(37) Race and Upper Shaft Assembly
(38) Joint Preload Spring
(39) Centering Sphere
(40) Lower Steering Shaft Assembly
(41) Linear Shift Assembly
(42) Shift Lever Clevis
(43) Flat Head 6-Lobed Soc Tap Screws
(44) Cable Shift Cam Assembly
(45) Ball and Actuator Assembly

ARM0500000000823

**Fig. 65   Exploded view of steering column
(Part 2 of 3). LaCrosse w/column shift**

(46) Cam Bushing
(47) Hexagon Flange Head Bolts
(48) Gear Shift Lever Assembly Support Bracket
(49) Oval Head 6-Lobed Soc Tap Screws
(50) Park Lock Cable System
(51) TORX® Head Screws
(52) Pivot Pins
(53) Steering Column Support Assembly
(54) Steering Column Jacket Assembly
(55) Automatic Transmission Shift Lock Control
(56) Adapter and Bearing Assembly
(57) Lower Bearing Seat
(58) Lower Bearing Spring
(59) Lower Spring Retainer
(60) Retainer
(61) Steering Shaft Seal
(62) Intermediate Steering Shaft Assembly
(63) Pinch Bolt

ARM0500000000824

**Fig. 65   Exploded view of steering
column (Part 3 of 3). LaCrosse
w/column shift**

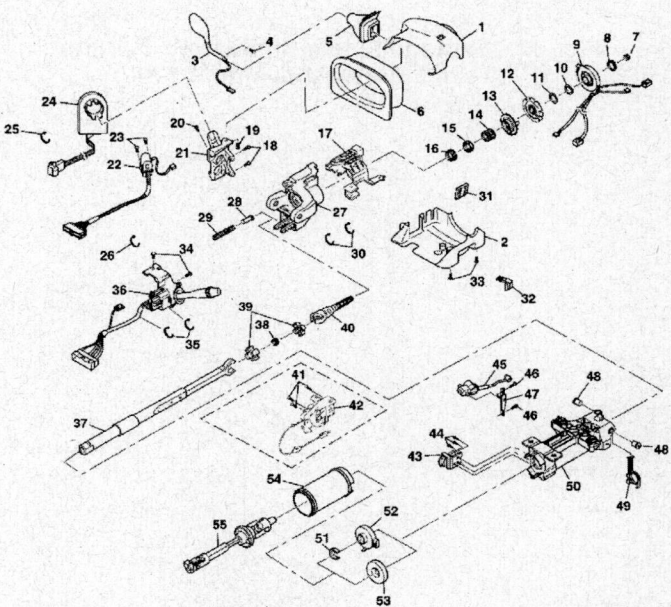

ARM0600000001527

**Fig. 66   Exploded view of steering column
(Part 1 of 2). Lucerne**

(1) Upper Trim Cover
(2) Lower Trim Cover
(3) Shift Lever Assembly
(4) Shift Lever Screw
(5) Shift Lever Seal
(6) Steering Column Closeout Trim Cover
(7) Hexagon Locking Nut
(8) Retaining Ring
(9) SIR Coil
(10) Wave Washer
(11) Bearing Retainer
(12) Shaft Lock Shield Assembly
(13) Turn Signal Cancel Cam Assembly
(14) Upper Bearing Spring
(15) Upper Bearing Inner Race Seat
(16) Inner Race
(17) Signal Switch Housing Assembly
(18) Pan Head Tapping Screws
(19) TORX® Head Screw
(20) Pan Head Tapping Screw
(21) Ignition Lock Cylinder Case
(22) Ignition Switch Assembly
(23) Tapping Screws
(24) Theft Deterrent Control Module
(25) Wire Harness Strap
(26) Wire Harness Strap
(27) Steering Column Tilt Head Assembly
(28) Spring Guide
(29) Tilt Spring
(30) Wire Harness Straps
(31) Trim Cover Protector
(32) Tilt Knob
(33) Pan Head Tapping Screws
(34) Pan Head Tapping Screws
(35) Wire Harness Straps
(36) Turn Signal and Multifunction Switch Assembly
(37) Lower Steering Shaft Assembly

(38) Joint Preload Spring
(39) Centering Sphere
(40) Race and Upper Shaft Assembly
(41) Flat Head 6-Lobed Socket Tapping Screws
(42) Linear Shift Shaft Assembly
(43) Cable Support Bracket
(44) Flat Head Screws
(45) Automatic Transmission Shift Lock Control
(46) Pan Head Tapping Screws
(47) Automatic Transmission Shift Lock Control Mounting Bracket Assembly
(48) Pivot Pins
(49) Wire Restraint Clip
(50) Steering Column Support Assembly
(51) Sensor Locator
(52) Steering Shaft Position Sensor
(53) Steering Shaft Seal
(54) Boot Seal
(55) Intermediate Steering Shaft Assembly

ARM0600000001528

**Fig. 66   Exploded view of steering column
(Part 2 of 2). Lucerne**

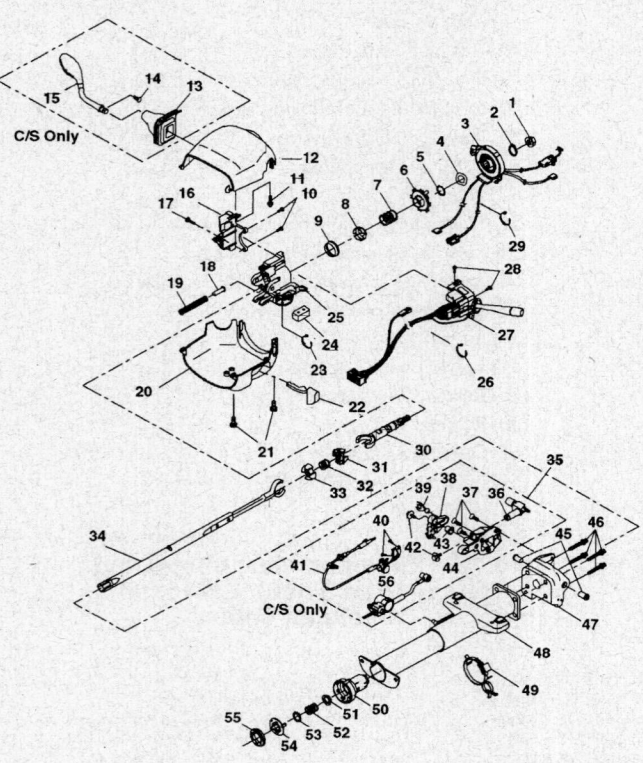

1. Hexagon Nut
2. Retaining Ring
3. SIR Coil Assembly
4. Wave Washer
5. Bearing Retainer
6. Turn Signal Cancel Cam Assembly
7. Upper Bearing Spring
8. Upper Bearing Inner Race Seat
9. Inner Race
10. Flat Head Screw
11. Pan Head Tapping Screw
12. Upper Shroud
13. Shift Lever Seal
14. Shift Lever Screw
15. Automatic Transmission Control Lever Assembly
16. Switch Mounting Bracket
17. Flat Head Screw
18. Spring Guide
19. Tilt Spring
20. Lower Shroud
21. TORX® Head Screw
22. Tilt Lever Assembly
23. Wire Harness Strap
24. Spacer
25. Steering Column Tilt Head
26. Wire Harness Strap
27. Turn Signal And Multifunction Switch Assembly
28. Pan Head Tapping Screw
29. Wire Harness Strap
30. Race And Upper Shaft Assembly
31. Centering Sphere
32. Joint Preload Spring

33. Centering Sphere
34. Lower Steering Shaft Assembly
35. Linear Shift Assembly
36. Shift Lever Clevis
37. Flat Head 6-Lobed Socket Tapping Screw
38. Cable Shift Cam Assembly
39. Ball and Actuator
40. Oval Head 6-Lobed Socket Tapping Screw
41. Park Lock Cable Assembly
42. Hex Flange Head Bolt
43. Cam Bushing
44. Gear Shift Lever Assembly Support Bracket
45. Pivot Pin
46. TORX® Head Screw
47. Steering Column Support Assembly
48. Steering Column Jacket Assembly
49. Wire Harness Strap
50. Adapter and Bearing Assembly
51. Lower Bearing Seat
52. Lower Bearing Spring
53. Lower Spring Retainer
54. Sensor Retainer
55. Steering Shaft Seal
56. Electrical (BTSI) Actuator

GC6040000291020X

Fig. 67   Exploded view of steering column (Part 2 of 2). Impala & Monte Carlo

GC6040000291010X

Fig. 67   Exploded view of steering column (Part 1 of 2). Impala & Monte Carlo

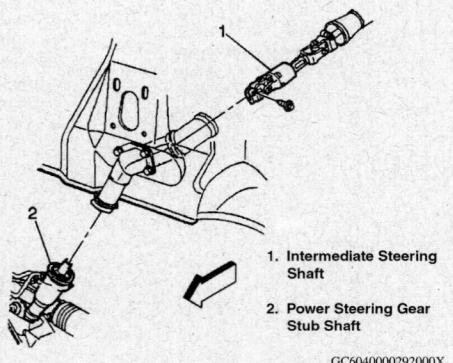

1. Intermediate Steering Shaft
2. Power Steering Gear Stub Shaft

GC6040000292000X

Fig. 68   Intermediate steering shaft replacement. Impala & Monte Carlo

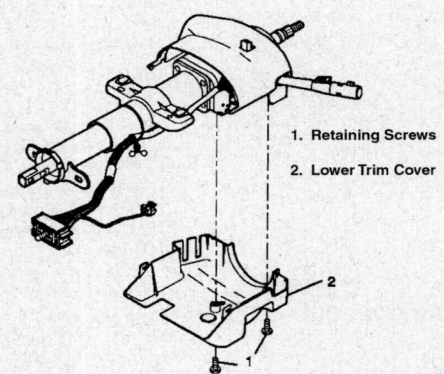

1. Retaining Screws
2. Lower Trim Cover

GC6040000293000X

Fig. 69   Steering column trim cover replacement (Lower). Impala & Monte Carlo

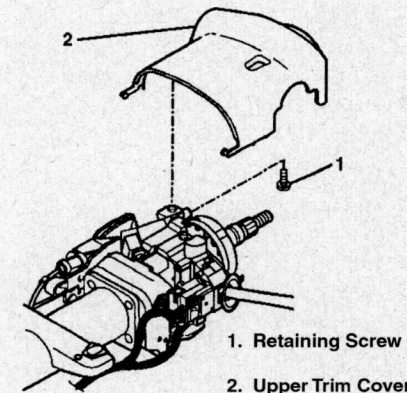

1. Retaining Screw
2. Upper Trim Cover

GC6040000294000X

Fig. 70   Steering column trim cover replacement (Upper). Impala & Monte Carlo

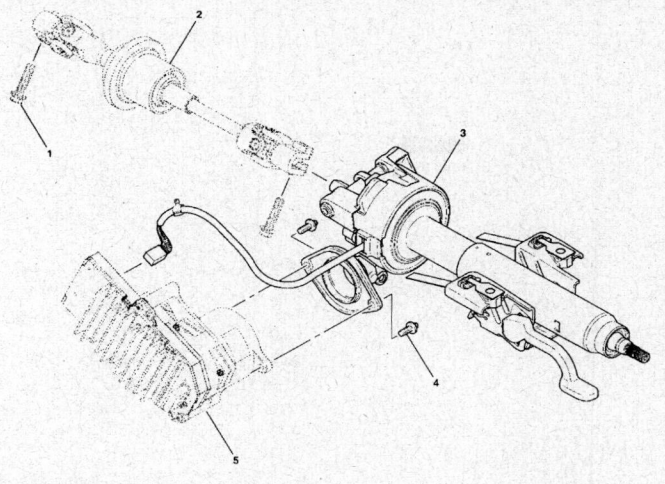

(1) Pinch Bolt
(2) Intermediate Steering Shaft
(3) Steering Column
(4) TORX® Bolts
(5) Motor/ Module Assembly

ARM0300000000586

Fig. 71 Exploded view of steering column. Malibu

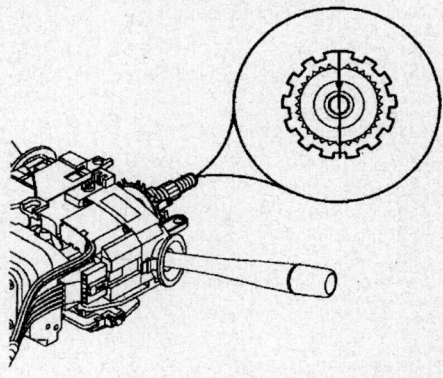

ARM0300000000589

Fig. 72 Steering shaft alignment. Malibu, Malibu Classic & Malibu Maxx

1 SIR coil face
2 Casing
3 Sub-stator alignment arrow
4 Cebtering window
5 Ribbon cable

ARM0300000000590

Fig. 73 SIR coil centering. Malibu, Malibu Classic & Malibu Maxx

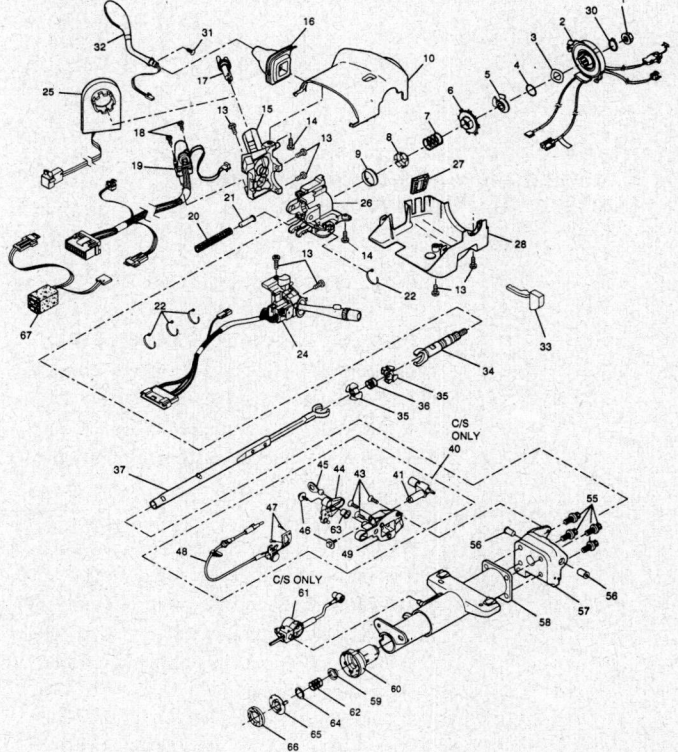

GC604970023800AX

Fig. 74 Exploded view of steering column (Part 1 of 2). Park Avenue

1-NUT,FLANGED PREVAIL TORQUE
2-COIL ASM, SIR
3-WASHER, WAVE
4-RING, RETAINER
5-SHIELD ASM, SHAFT LOCK
6-CAM ASM, T/SIG CANCEL
7-SPRING, UPPER BEARING
8-SEAT, UPPER BEARING INNER RACE
9-RACE, INNER
10-SHROUD, UPPER
11-BOLT ASM, LOCK
12-SPRING, LOCK BOLT
13-SCREW, PAN HD TAPPING
14-SCREW, TORX HEAD
15-ASM, LOCK MODULE
16-SEAL, SHIFT LEVER
17-LOCK CYL SET, STRG COLUMN
18-SCREW, TAPPING
19-SWITCH ASM, IGN & KEY ALARM
20-SPRING, TILT
21-GUIDE, SPRING
22-STRAP, WIRE HARNESS
24-SWITCH ASM, T/S & MULTIFUNCTION
25-CONTROL CODED KEY
26-TILT HEAD ASM, STRG COL
27-PROTECTOR, SHROUD
28-SHROUD, LOWER
29-STUD, SHROUD MOUNTING
30-RING, RETAINING
31-SCREW, SHIFT LEVER
32-LEVER ASM, A/TRNS CONTROL
33-LEVER ASM, TILT
34-SHAFT ASM, RACE & UPPER
35-SPHERE, CENTERING
36-SPRING, JOINT PRELOAD
37-SHAFT ASM, LOWER STRG
40-SHIFT ASM, LINEAR
41-CLEVIS, SHIFT LEVER
43-SCREW, FLAT HD 6-LOBED SOC TAP
44-CAM ASM, CABLE SHIFT
45-ACTUATOR ASM, BALL &
46-BOLT, HEX FLANGE HEAD
47-SCREW, OVAL HD 6-LOBED SOC TAP
48-CABLE ASM, PARK LOCK
49-BRACKET, G/S LEVER ASM SUPPORT
55-SCREW, TORX HEAD
56-PIN, PIVOT
57-SUPPORT ASM, STRG COL
58-JACKET ASM, STRG COL

59-SEAT, LOWER BEARING
60-BEARING ASM, ADAPTER &
61-ACTUATOR, ELECTRICAL (BTSI)
62-SPRING, LOWER BEARING
63-BUSHING, CAM
64-RETAINER, LOWER SPRING
65-RETAINER, SENSOR
66-SEAL, STEERING SHAFT
67-HARNESS ASM, JUMPER

GC604970023800BX

Fig. 74   Exploded view of steering column (Part 2 of 2). Park Avenue

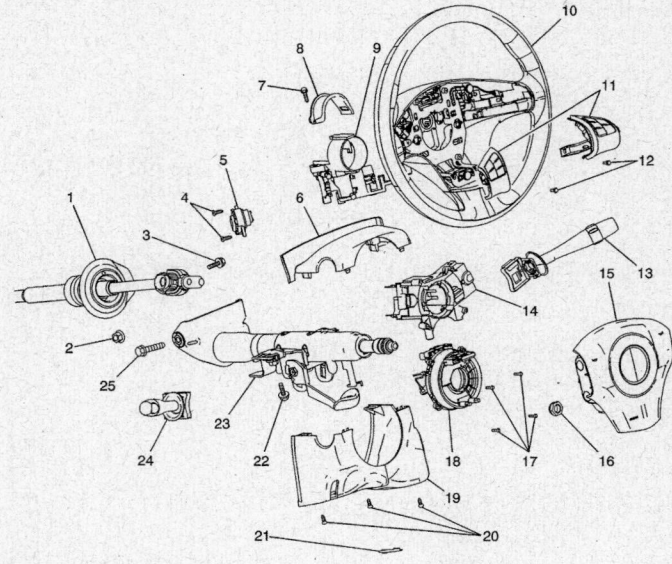

(1) Intermediate Steering Shaft
(2) Intermediate Steering Shaft Nut
(3) Intermediate Steering Shaft Bolt
(4) Ignition Switch Screws
(5) Ignition Switch
(6) Steering Column Upper Trim Cover
(7) Ignition Lock Cylinder Case Shear Bolt
(8) Ignition Lock Cylinder Case Clamp

ARM0500000000817

Fig. 75   Exploded view of steering column (Part 1 of 2). Solstice & SKY

(9) Ignition Lock Cylinder Case
(10) Steering Wheel
(11) Steering Wheel Control Switches
(12) Steering Wheel Control Switch Screws
(13) Windshield Wiper/Washer Switch
(14) Multi-Function Switch Housing
(15) Steering Wheel Inflatable Restraint Module
(16) Steering Wheel Nut
(17) SIR Coil Screws
(18) SIR Coil
(19) Steering Column Lower Trim Cover
(20) Steering Column Lower Trim Cover Screws
(21) Steering Column Lower Trim Cover Plug
(22) Steering Column Upper Mounting Bolt
(23) Steering Column
(24) Turn Signal Switch
(25) Steering Column Lower Mounting Bolt

ARM0500000000818

Fig. 75   Exploded view of steering column (Part 2 of 2). Solstice & SKY

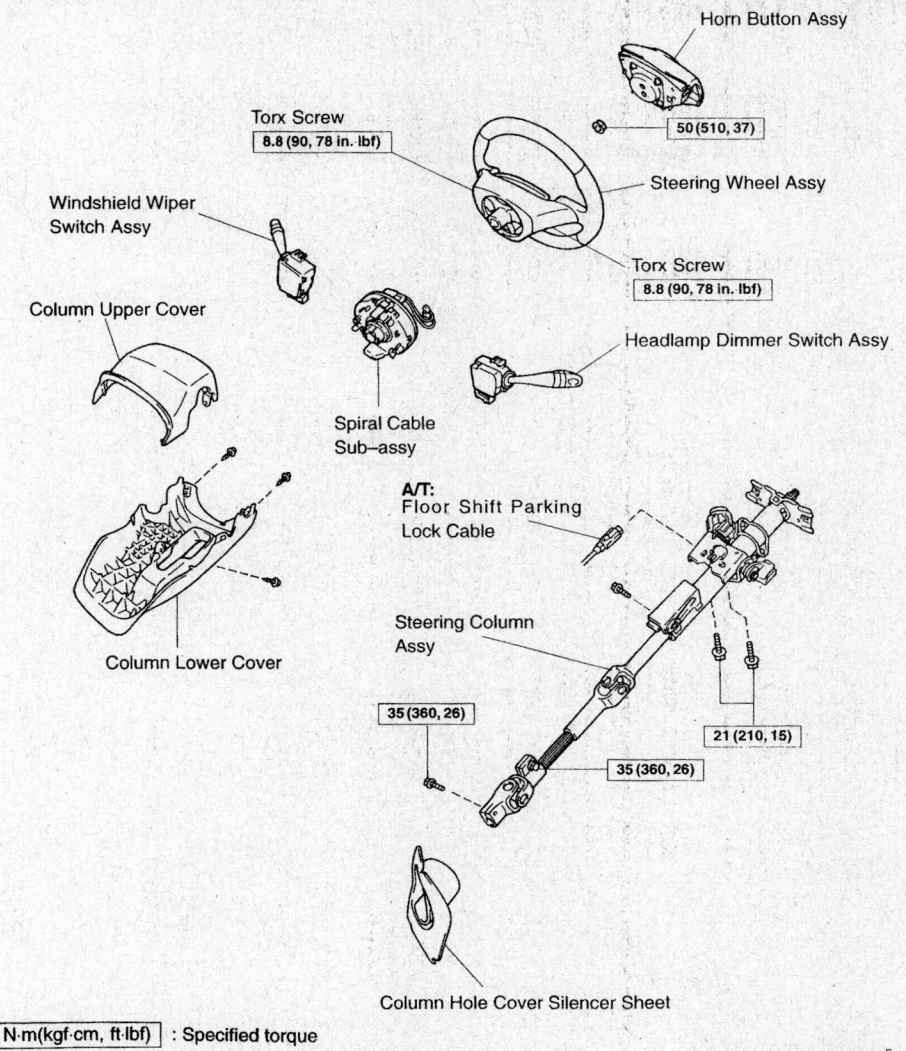

Horn Button Assy

Torx Screw
8.8 (90, 78 in. lbf)

50 (510, 37)

Windshield Wiper
Switch Assy

Steering Wheel Assy

Column Upper Cover

Torx Screw
8.8 (90, 78 in. lbf)

Headlamp Dimmer Switch Assy

Spiral Cable
Sub–assy

A/T:
Floor Shift Parking
Lock Cable

Steering Column
Assy

Column Lower Cover

35 (360, 26)

21 (210, 15)

35 (360, 26)

Column Hole Cover Silencer Sheet

N·m(kgf·cm, ft·lbf) : Specified torque

ARM66GC000000695

Fig. 76   Exploded view of steering column (Part 1 of 2). Vibe

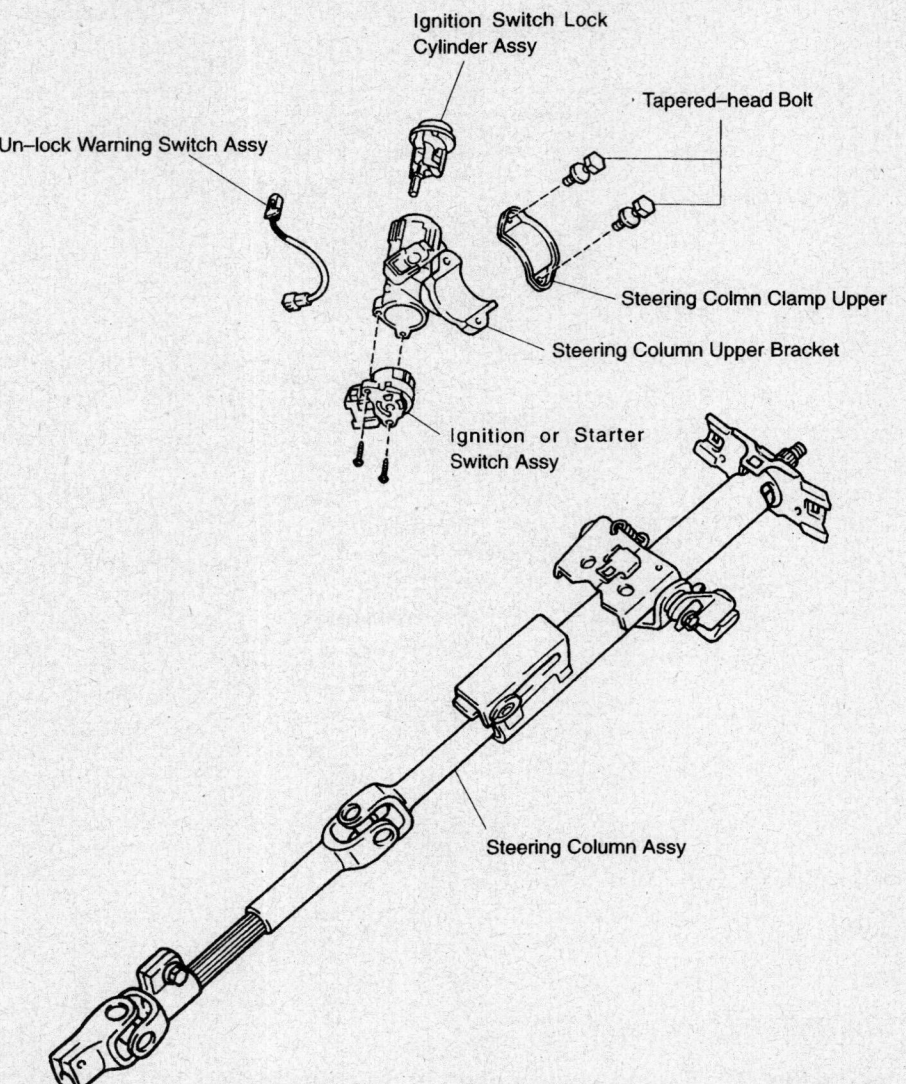

Ignition Switch Lock
Cylinder Assy

Tapered–head Bolt

Un–lock Warning Switch Assy

Steering Colmn Clamp Upper

Steering Column Upper Bracket

Ignition or Starter
Switch Assy

Steering Column Assy

ARM66GC000000696

Fig. 76 Exploded view of steering column (Part 2 of 2). Vibe

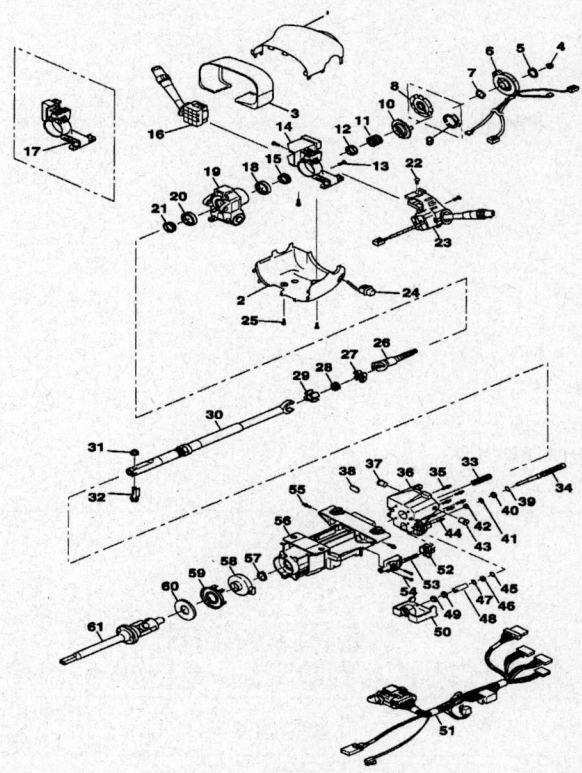

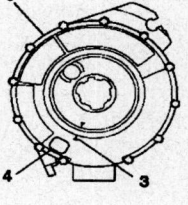 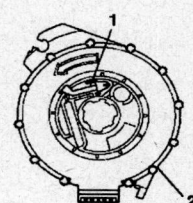

1-Spring service lock
2-Back side
3-Arrows
4-Centering window
5-Front side

ARM0300000000714

Fig. 78 SIR coil assembly. With centering window & spring service lock

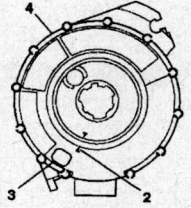 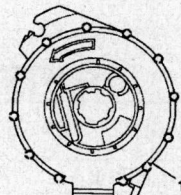

1-Back side
2-Arrows
3-Centering window
4-Front side

ARM0300000000715

Fig. 79 SIR coil assembly. With centering window & less spring service lock

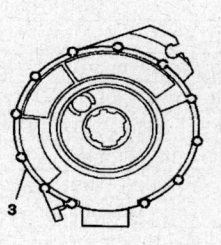 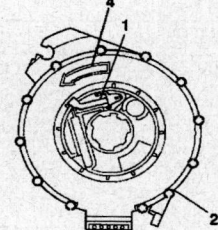

1-Spring service lock
2-Back side
3-Front side
4-Arrow

ARM0300000000716

Fig. 80 SIR coil assembly. Less centering window & w/spring service lock

(1) Upper Trim Cover (Kit)
(2) Lower Trim Cover (Kit)
(3) Steering Column Closeout Shroud
(4) Flanged Prevailing Torque Nut
(5) Retaing Ring
(6) Inflatable Restraint Steering Wheel Module Coil
(7) Wave Washer
(8) Shaft Lock Shield Assembly (Export)
(9) Cam Orientation Plate
(10) Turn Signal Cancel Cam Assembly
(11) Upper Bearing Spring
(12) Upper Bearing Inner Race Seat
(13) Pan Head Tapping Screw
(14) Switch Mounting Bracket
(15) Inner Race
(16) Washer Wiper Switch Assembly
(17) Switch Mounting Bracket
(18) Bearing Assembly
(19) Steering Column Tilt Head Assembly
(20) Bearing Assembly
(21) Inner Race
(22) Pan Head Tapping Screw
(23) Turn Signal and Multifunction Switch Assembly
(24) Power TNT Toggle Switch Assembly
(25) Pan Head Tapping Screw
(26) Race and Upper Shaft Assembly
(27) Centering Sphere (Kit)
(28) Joint Preload Spring (Kit)
(29) Centering Sphere (Kit)
(30) Lower Steering Shaft Assembly
(31) Bolt and Retainer Assembly

(32) Pinch Bolt
(33) Tilt Spring
(34) Lead Screw
(35) TORX Head Screw
(36) Tilt Support Assembly
(37) Pivot Pin
(38) Tilt Bumper
(39) Thrust Washer
(40) Thrust Bearing
(41) Thrust Washer
(42) Bearing Roller
(43) Pivot Pin
(44) TORX Head Screw
(45) Thrust Washer
(46) Thrust Bearing
(47) Thrust Washer
(48) Tilt Dampener Spacer
(49) Tilt Dampener Seal
(50) Lower Shield Assembly
(51) Steering Column Wiring Assembly
(52) Jacket Screw LH Telescoping Nut
(53) Jacket Screw Telescoping Actuator Assembly
(54) Pan Head Tapping Screw
(55) Pan Head Tapping Screw
(56) Telescoping Jacket Assembly
(57) Retaining Ring
(58) Steering Wheel Position Sensor
(59) Sensor Retainer
(60) Steering Shaft Seal
(61) Intermediate Steering Shaft Assembly

ARM0300000000713

Fig. 77 Exploded view of steering column. XLR

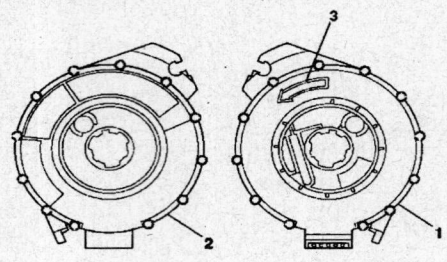

1-Back side
2-Front side
3-Arrow

ARM0300000000717

Fig. 81 SIR coil assembly. Less centering window & spring service lock

TIGHTENING SPECIFICATIONS

Year	Component	Torque Ft. Lbs.
ALERO		
2004	Column Bracket Support	19
	Intermediate Shaft Pinch Bolt	16
	Steering Wheel	30
AURA		
2007–08	Electronic Power Steering (EPS) Motor to Steering Column Bolts	80①
	Intermediate Steering Shaft to Steering Gear Pinch Bolt	36
	Steering Column Mounting Bolt Lower	20
	Steering Column Mounting Bolt Lower	20
	Steering Column Tilt Lever Nut	49①
	Steering Column Trim Cover Screw	13①
	Steering Wheel Nut	24
AVEO		
2005–08	Coupling Flange Pinch Bolt	16
	Ignition Switch Housing Sheer Bolts	97①
	Ignition Switch Retaining Screws	18①
	Lower Instrument Panel Trim Screws	27①
	Steering Wheel Nut	28
	Support Housing Screws	12
	Turn Signal Switch Housing Screws	27①
	Upper/Lower Steering Column Cover Screws	27①
BONNEVILLE & LESABRE		
2004–05	Cable Support Bracket Screws	26①
	Column Support Bolts	20
	Intermediate Shaft Pinch Bolt	35
	Intermediate Shaft Seal Screw	21①
	Multi-Function Switch Screws	62①
	Steering Column Trim Cover, Lower	31①
	Steering Column Trim Cover, Upper	13①
	Steering Column Wiring Harness Connector	71①
	Steering Wheel Nut	30

TIGHTENING SPECIFICATIONS—Continued

Year	Component	Torque Ft. Lbs.
BONNEVILLE & LESABRE		
2004–05	Steering Wheel Rear Bezel	26①
CAVALIER & SUNFIRE		
2004–05	Ignition Switch Screws	36①
	Lock Module Assembly Screws	61①
	Lower Pinch Bolt	30
	Multi-Function Switch Mounting Screws	36
	Steering Column Mounting Bolts	20
	Steering Column Trim Cover Screws	36①
	Steering Wheel Nut	27
	Upper Pinch Bolt	30
	Windshield Washer & Wiper Switch	36①
CENTURY, GRAND PRIX & REGAL		
2004–08	Column Cover, Lower	31①
	Column Cover, Upper	12①
	Mounting	18
	Park Lock Cable	58①
	Pinch Bolt	35
	Turn Signal Cam, Bolt	13
	Turn Signal Cam, Screws	84①
	Steering Wheel Cover Bolt	18
	Steering Wheel Nut	30
COBALT & G5		
2006–08	Column Mid Pivot Bolt	18
	Column Mounting Bolt	18
	Column Trim Cover Screws	18①
	Column Upper Jacket Bolt	97①
	Intermediate Shaft Pinch Bolt	25
	Steering Wheel Nut	30

Continued

TIGHTENING SPECIFICATIONS—Continued

Year	Component	Torque Ft. Lbs.
CORVETTE		
2004–08	Bracket	18
	Dimmer Switch	35①
	Lock Housing Cover	96①
	Pass Key Lock Cylinder	22①
	Pinch Bolt	35
	Support Plate	13
	Turn Signal Switch	30①
	Turn Signal Switch Arm	20①
	Steering Wheel Nut	30
CTS		
2004–07	Intermediate Shaft Bolt, Lower	37
	Intermediate Shaft Bolt, Upper	23
	Lock Cylinder Case Screws	62①
	Multi-Function Switch Front Screw	62①
	Multi-Function Switch Top Screw	27①
	Steering Column Mounting Nuts	18
	Steering Column Trim Cover Lower Screws	31①
	Steering Column Trim Cover Upper Screw	14①
	Steering Wheel Control Switch Upper Screws	20①
	Steering Wheel Nut	30
2008	Intermediate Steering Shaft Bolt, Upper	23
	Intermediate Steering Shaft Bolt, Lower	37
	Steering Column Bolt	20
	Steering Column Nut	20
	Steering Column Shroud Bolt	22①
	Steering Wheel Bolt	37
	Turn Signal Switch Bracket Bolt	80①
DEVILLE & SEVILLE		
2004–06	Cable Shift Cam	35①
	Gate	33①
	Interlock Solenoid Bracket	35①
	Lock	22①
	Lock Housing	80①
	Lower Bracket	12
	Pinch Bolt	35
	Support	20
	Turn Signal Switch	30①
	Turn Signal Switch Arm	20①
DTS & STS		
2005–08	Ignition Lock Cylinder Case Screws	62①
	Intermediate Shaft Bolts	22
	Intermediate Shaft to Steering Column Pinch Bolt	35
	Intermediate Shaft to Steering Gear Pinch Bolt	37
	Steering Column Mounting Nuts	18

TIGHTENING SPECIFICATIONS—Continued

Year	Component	Torque Ft. Lbs.
DTS & STS		
2005–08	Steering Column Lower Cover Trim Screws	31①
	Steering Column Upper Cover Trim Screws	13①
	Steering Wheel Nut	30
	Turn Signal Multifunction Switch Screw Side	62①
	Turn Signal Multifunction Switch Screw Top	27①
	Upper Intermediate Shaft to Lower Intermediate Shaft Pinch Bolt	22
GRAND AM		
2004–05	Column Bracket Support	19
	Intermediate Shaft Pinch Bolt	16
	Steering Wheel	30
GTO		
2004–06	Ignition Switch Bolt	11①
	Steering Column Bolts	17
	Steering Column Nuts	17
	Steering Coupling to Steering Gear Pinion Nut and Bolt	20
	Steering Wheel Retaining Bolt	13
G5		
2007–08	Intermediate Steering Shaft Bolt	25
	Steering Column Pivot Bolt	18
	Steering Column Mounting Bolt	18
	Steering Column Trim Cover Screw	18①
	Steering Column Jacket Bolt	97①
	Steering Wheel Nut	30
G6		
2005–08	EPS Motor to Steering Column Bolts	80①
	Intermediate Steering Shaft to Steering Column Pinch Bolt	36
	Intermediate Steering Shaft to Steering Gear Pinch Bolt	36
	Steering Column Mounting Bolt Lower	20
	Steering Column Mounting Bolts Upper	20
	Steering Column Trim Cover Screw	13①
	Steering Wheel Nut	24
	Steering Wheel Trim Cover Bolt	18①
IMPALA		
2004–08	Cover, Lower Trim	31①
	Cover, Upper Trim	13①
	Intermediate Shaft to the Steering Column Pinch Bolt	46
	Intermediate Shaft to the Steering Gear Pinch Bolt	35
	Steering Column Mounting Bolts	18
	Turn Signal Multifunction Switch Screws	9①

Continued

STEERING COLUMNS

TIGHTENING SPECIFICATIONS—Continued

Year	Component	Torque Ft. Lbs.
ION		
2004–07	Ignition Lock Cylinder Case Shear Bolt	15
	Ignition Lock Cylinder Solenoid Screw	17①
	Ignition Switch Screws	17①
	Intermediate Shaft Pinch Bolt	25
	Multi-Function Switch Screw	17①
	Steering Column Mid Pivot Bolt	18
	Steering Column Mounting Bolt	18
	Steering Column Trim Cover Screws	17①
	Steering Column Upper Jacket Bolts	97①
	Steering Wheel Nut	31
L-SERIES		
2004–05	Intermediate Shaft Pinch Bolt	22
	Signal Switch Housing To Steering Column	14①
	Steering Column To I/P Support Beam	22
LUCERNE		
2006–08	Cable Support Bracket Screw	31①
	Ignition Switch Assembly Screws	13①
	Intermediate Shaft To Steering Column Pinch Bolt	35
	Intermediate Shaft To Steering Gear Pinch Bolt	35
	Shift Lever Bolt	15
	Steering Column Mounting Bolts, Lower	20
	Steering Column Trim Cover Bolt, Lower	27①
	Steering Column Trim Cover Bolt, Upper	13①
	Steering Wheel Nut	30
	Turn Signal Multifunction Switch Bolt	62①
MALIBU, MALIBU CLASSIC & MALIBU MAXX		
2004–08	Intermediate Shaft Pinch Bolt	②
	Steering Column Mounting Bolts	18
	Steering Wheel Nut	24
	Support Bracket	18
MONTE CARLO		
2004–07	Cover, Lower Trim	31①
	Cover, Upper Trim	13①
	Mount	18
	Pinch Bolt	35
PARK AVENUE		
2004–05	Cover, Lower	60①
	Cover, Upper	13①
	Pinch Bolt	35
	Shift Lever, Bolt	14
	Shift Lever, Flat Head Tap Screw	84①
	Shift Lever, Oval Head Tap Screw	58①
	Support	20
	Wiring Harness Connector	72①

TIGHTENING SPECIFICATIONS—Continued

Year	Component	Torque Ft. Lbs.
SOLSTICE		
2006–08	Column Mid Pivot Bolt	18
	Column Mounting Bolt	18
	Column Trim Cover Screws	17①
	Column Upper Jacket Bolt	97①
	Cylinder Solenoid Screw	17①
	Ignition Switch Screws	17①
	Intermediate Shaft Pinch Bolt	43
	Steering Wheel Nut	31
SKY		
2007–08	Column Mid Pivot Bolt	18
	Column Mounting Bolt	18
	Column Trim Cover Screws	17①
	Column Upper Jacket Bolt	97①
	Cylinder Solenoid Screw	17①
	Ignition Switch Screws	17①
	Intermediate Shaft Pinch Bolt	43
	Steering Wheel Nut	31
VIBE		
2004–08	Intermediate Steering Shaft Bolt	26
	Steering Column Bolts	16
	Steering Shaft Coupling Bolts	26
	Steering Wheel Nut	37
XLR		
2004–08	Column Support Bracket Nuts	17
	Dampener Screws	13①
	Intermediate Shaft to the Steering Column Pinch Bolt	35
	Steering Column Bottom Bracket Screw	26①
	Steering Column Support Screws	13
	Steering Wheel & Column Lower To Upper Intermediate Shaft Retaining Bolts	35
	Steering Wheel Nut	30
	Telescope Actuator Assembly Screws	44①

① — Inch lbs.

② — EPS; 36 ft. lbs., HPS; 46 ft. lbs.

POWER STEERING

TABLE OF CONTENTS

	Page No.		Page No.
APPLICATION CHART	21-1	SAGINAW RACK & PINION POWER STEERING GEAR w/SPEED SENSITIVE STEERING	21-12
POWER STEERING PUMPS	21-3		
SAGINAW RACK & PINION POWER STEERING GEAR LESS SPEED SENSITIVE STEERING	21-7	SAGINAW ROTARY VALVE POWER STEERING GEAR	21-18
SAGINAW RACK & PINION POWER STEERING GEAR w/ELECTRONIC POWER STEERING	21-16	TOYOTA RACK & PINION POWER STEERING GEAR	21-21

Application Chart

Model	Year	Power Steering Type
BUICK		
Century	2004–05	Saginaw Rack & Pinion
LaCrosse	2005–08	Saginaw Rack & Pinion
LeSabre	2004–05	Saginaw Rack & Pinion
Lucerne	2006–08	Saginaw Rack & Pinion
Park Avenue	2004–05	Saginaw Rack & Pinion
Regal	2004	Saginaw Rack & Pinion
CADILLAC		
CTS	2004–08	Saginaw Rack & Pinion
DeVille	2004–05	Saginaw Rack & Pinion
DTS	2006–08	Saginaw Rack & Pinion
Seville	2004	Saginaw Rack & Pinion
STS	2005–08	Saginaw Rack & Pinion
XLR	2004–08	Saginaw Rack & Pinion
CHEVROLET		
Aveo	2005–08	Saginaw Rack & Pinion
Cavalier	2004–05	Saginaw Rack & Pinion
Cobalt	2005–08	Saginaw Rack & Pinion
Corvette	2004–08	Saginaw Rack & Pinion
Impala	2004–08	Saginaw Rack & Pinion
Malibu	2004–07	Saginaw Rack & Pinion
Malibu Classic	2008	Saginaw Rack & Pinion
Malibu Maxx	2004–07	Saginaw Rack & Pinion
Monte Carlo	2004–07	Saginaw Rack & Pinion
OLDSMOBILE		
Alero	2004	Saginaw Rack & Pinion
PONTIAC		
Bonneville	2004–05	Saginaw Rack & Pinion
Grand Am	2004–05	Saginaw Rack & Pinion
Grand Prix	2004–08	Saginaw Rack & Pinion
GTO	2004–06	Saginaw Rack & Pinion
G5	2007–08	Saginaw Rack & Pinion
G6	2005–08	Saginaw Rack & Pinion
Sunfire	2004–05	Saginaw Rack & Pinion
Solstice	2006–08	Saginaw Rack & Pinion
Vibe	2004–08	Toyota Rack & Pinion

Continued

Model	Year	Power Steering Type
SATURN		
AURA	2007–08	Saginaw Rack & Pinion
L-Series	2004–05	Saginaw Rack & Pinion
ION	2004–07	Saginaw Rack & Pinion
SKY	2007–08	Saginaw Rack & Pinion

POWER STEERING PRESSURE SPECIFICATIONS

Model	Engine	High Flow Rate, GPM	Pressure Relief, psi
Alero & Grand Am	2.2L & 2.4L	1.95–2.35	1300–1400
	3.4L	1.95–2.35	1400–1500
AURA	3.5L & 3.6L	1.95–2.35	1350–1500
Aveo	1.6L	—	—
Bonneville, LeSabre, Lucerne & Park Avenue	3.8L	1.90–2.40	1350–1450
Cavalier & Sunfire	2.2L	1.95–2.35	1300–1400
	2.4L	1.95–2.35	1400–1500
Century, Grand Prix, Impala, Monte Carlo & Regal	3.1L	2.40–2.80	1200–1350
	3.4L	2.40–2.80	1200–1350
	3.5L	2.40–2.80	1400–1500
	3.8L	2.40–2.80	1200–1350①
	3.9L	2.40–2.80	1400–1500
	5.3L	2.40–2.80	1428–1500
Cobalt	2.0L	—	—
	2.2L	—	—
	2.4L	—	—
Corvette	5.7L	2.40–2.80	1250–1350
	6.0L	2.40–2.80	1250–1350
	6.2L	—	—
	7.0L	2.40–2.80	1250–1350
CTS	2.8L	2.00	1640–1740
	3.2L	2.00	1640–1740
	3.6L	2.00	1640–1740
	5.7L	2.00	1640–1740
DeVille & Seville	4.6L	1.80–2.40	1700–1800
DTS	4.6L	1.80–2.40	1700–1800
GTO	5.7L	1.95–2.35	1100–1200
	6.0L	1.95–2.35	1100–1200
G5	2.0L	—	—
	2.2L	—	—
	2.4L	—	—
G6	3.5L	1.95–2.35	1350–1500
	3.9L	1.95–2.35	1350–1500
ION	2.2L	1.70–2.10	1300–1400
LaCrosse	3.6L	4.20	1400
	3.8L	2.40–2.80	1400
L-Series	2.2L	1.70–2.10	1300–1400
	3.0L	1.70–2.10	1400–1500
Malibu, Malibu Classic & Malibu Maxx	3.1L	1.95–2.35	1400–1500
	3.5L	1.95–2.35	1350–1500
	3.9L	1.95–2.35	1350–1500
Solstice	2.0L & 2.4L	2.00–2.20	1650
SKY	2.0L & 2.4L	2.00–2.20	1650
STS	3.6L	2.84–3.24	1668–1770
	4.6L	2.84–3.24	1668–1770
Vibe	1.8L	1.27–1.64②	1059–1204
XLR	4.6L	2.40–2.80	1250–1350

VALVE SPRINGS

All Measurements Given In Inches, Unless Otherwise Specified.

Engine Liter (VIN①)	Year	Free Length	Installed Height	Installed Pressure Lbs. @ Inches		Comp. Pressure Lbs. @ Inches		Out Of Square Limit
				Intake	Exhaust	Intake	Exhaust	
2.0L DOHC (N, P, 3 & 5)	2004–07	1.7010	1.3460	32.5 @ 1.3460	40.5 @ 1.3460	82.1 @ .9880	94.9 @ 1.0275	—
2.3L DOHC (Z)	2004–08	1.7680	1.4920	38.6670	38.6670	⑤	⑨	—
3.0L DOHC (S)③	2004–05	1.7400	1.3150	37.1–41.6 @ 1.3150	37.1–41.6 @ 1.3150	85.0–94.9 @ .9650	85.0–94.9 @ .9650	—
3.0L DOHC (S)②	2004–05	1.8430	1.5740	51.3 @ 1.5740	51.3 @ 1.5740	152.9 @ 1.1890	152.9 @ 1.1890	⑦
3.0L DOHC (1)	2005–08	1.8400	1.6528–1.7389	53.95 @ 2.6900	53.95 @ 2.6900	156 @ 1.1800	156 @ 1.1800	⑦
3.0L OHV (U & 2)	2004–07	1.8268	1.6528–1.7389	64.1–72.6 @ 1.5953	64.1–72.6 @ 1.5953	192.6–217.4 @ 1.1709	192.6–217.4 @ 1.1709	⑦
3.5L (C, T, Y)	2007–08	1.90	1.45	53 @ 1.45	53 @ 1.45	115 @ 1.08	115 @ 1.08	—
3.8L OHV (4)	2004	—	1.6024	78.7 @ 1.6024	78.7 @ 1.6024	224.8 @ 1.1496	224.8 @ 1.1496	—
3.9L DOHC (A & 6)	2004–06	—	—	—	—	—	—	—
4.0L SOHC (N)	2005–08	1.7000	1.5690–1.6090	72.0 @ 1.5690	72.0 @ 1.5690	202.8–224.9 @ 1.413–1.445	202.8–224.9 @ 1.413–1.445	1.5°
4.6L DOHC (R, V, X & Y)	2004–08	1.6598	1.4228	65.0 @ 1.4228	65.0 @ 1.4228	159.9 @ 1.0311	159.9 @ 1.0311	⑧
4.6L SOHC (H)	2005–08	2.0380–2.1642	1.6650–1.6890	63.6–72.1 @ 1.6756	63.6–72.1 @ 1.6756	161.9–179.8 @ 1.1339	161.9–179.8 @ 1.1339	⑦
4.6L SOHC (W & 9)	2004–08	1.9764	1.5984–1.7165	61.2–68.8 @ 1.5748	61.2–68.8 @ 1.5748	142.3–157.7 @ 1.1102	142.3–157.7 @ 1.1102	2.5°
5.4L DOHC (S)	2007–08	⑥	④	70 @ 1.6929	72 @ 1.555	183 @ 1.2528	171 @ 1.0827	—

DOHC — Dual Overhead Cam
OHV — Overhead Valve
SOHC — Single Overhead Cam
① — Eighth digit Vehicle Identification Number (VIN) denotes engine code.
② — Sable & Taurus.

③ — LS.
④ — Intake, 1.692 inches; exhaust, 1.555 inches.
⑤ — Intake, 97.032 ft. lbs, @ .35 inch of cam lift.
⑥ — Intake, 2.1417 inches; exhaust, 2.0039 inches.

⑦ — Service limit, 10% force loss @ specified height.
⑧ — 2004–05, 2%.
⑨ — Exhaust, 93.338 ft. lbs, @ .29 inch of cam lift.

VALVES

All Measurements Given In Inches, Unless Otherwise Specified.

Engine Liter (VIN①)	Year	Valves					
		Stem Diameter		Run Out	Face Angle, Degrees	Clearance	
		Intake	Exhaust			Intake	Exhaust
2.0L (N, 3 & 5)	2004–07	—	—	—	—	.0043–.0071⑦	.0106–.0134⑦
2.0L SOHC (P)	2004	.3159–.3167	.3152–.3156	—	45.50	⑥	⑥
2.3L DOHC (Z)	2004–08	.2153–.2159	.2151–.2157	.00100	45.00	.029	.031
3.0L DOHC (S)④	2004–05	.2156–.2162	.2151–.2157	.00160	45.50	.0069–.0089	.0128–.0148
3.0L DOHC (1)	2005–08	.2350–.2358	.2343–.2350	.00100	45.25–45.75	⑥	⑥
3.0L DOHC (S)⑤	2004–05	.2352–.2360	.2343–.2350	.00200	45.50	.0197–.0437②	.0197–.0437②
3.0L OHV (U & 2)	2004–07	.2744–.2752	.2740–.2748	.00200	45.00	.0878–.1878②	.0878–.1878②
3.5L (C, T, Y)	2007–08	.2157–.2164	.2151–.2159	.00100	—	.001–.006	.0118–.0157
3.8L OHV (4)	2004	.2738–.2751	.2728–.2741	.00197	45.67	.0890–.1890②	.0890–.1890②
3.9L DOHC (A & 6)	2004–06	.1959–.1960	.1951–.1957	.00160	45.00	—	—
4.0L DOHC (N)	2005–08	.2740–.2750	.2730–.2740	.00100	45.00	⑥	⑥

Continued

ENGINE REBUILDING SPECIFICATIONS

NOTE: Refer To The Engine Section In The Appropriate Chassis Chapter Of This Manual For Engine Tightening Specifications.

INDEX

	Page No.		Page No.		Page No.
Balance Shaft	21-4	Cylinder Head, Valve Guide & Valve Seats	21-1	Valve Springs	21-2
Camshaft	21-3			Valves	21-2
Crankshaft, Bearings & Rods	21-4	Oil Pump	21-6		
Cylinder Block	21-6	Pistons, Pins & Rings	21-5		

CYLINDER HEAD, VALVE GUIDE & VALVE SEATS

All Measurements Given In Inches, Unless Otherwise Specified.

Engine Liter (VIN①)	Year	Cylinder Head Warpage Limit	Valve Guides			Valve Seats			
			Bore Diameter	Stem to Guide Clearance		Seat Angle °	Seat Width		Run-Out
				Intake	Exhaust		Intake	Exhaust	
2.0L DOHC (N, P, 3 & 5)	2004–07	.0039	—	.0007–.0025	.0007–.0025	—	—	—	—
2.3L DOHC (Z)	2004–08	—		.0009	.0011	45.00	.0380–.0720	0380–.0720	.0029
3.0L DOHC (S)③	2004–05	.0047	—	.0009–.0026	.0014–.0031	44.50–45.00	.0433–.0551	.0551–.0669	.0008
3.0L DOHC (S)④	2004–05	②	—	.0007–.0027	.0018–.0037	44.75	.0433–.0551	.0551–.0669	.0020
3.0L DOHC (1)	2005–08	—	.2360–.2370	.0007–.0027	.0018–.0037	44.50–45.00	.0430–.0550	.0550–.0660	.001
3.0L OHV (U & 2)	2004–07	.0031	.2763–.2772	.0010–.0028	.0015–.0033	45.00	.0591–.0787	.0787–.0984	.0031–.0039
3.5L (C, T, Y)	2007–08	—	3.641	.0008–.0027	.0013–.0032	—	.051–.059	.055–.062	.001
3.8L OHV (4)	2004	.0071	.2763–.2773	.0008–.0027	.0015–.0033	44.75	.0591–.0787	.0591–.0787	.0030
3.9L DOHC (A & 6)	2004–06	.0031	—	.0009	.0012	⑥	.0394	.0787	.0016
4.0L SOHC (N)	2005–08	.0030	.2760–.2762	.0001–.0002	.0001–.0003	45.00	.0500–.0830	.0610–.0950	.0020
4.6L DOHC (R, V, X & Y)	2004–08	⑤	.2762–.2773	.0008–.0027	.0018–.0037	45.00	.0709–.0866	.0709–.0866	.0020
4.6L SOHC (H)	2005–08	.0039	—	.0008–.0027	.0018–.0037	45.00	.0512–0591	.0512–0591	.0020
4.6L SOHC (W & 9)	2004–08	.0039	—	.0008–.0027	.0018–.0037	45.00	.0709–.0866	.0709–.0866	.0020
5.4L DOHC (S)	2007–08	.0010	—	0022–.0009	0028–.0015	45	0551–.0472	0630–.0551	.0019

DOHC — Dual Overhead Cam

OHV — Overhead Valve

SOHC — Single Overhead Cam

① — Eighth digit Vehicle Identification Number (VIN) denotes engine code.

② — .0020 inch for each 5.91 inches of length.

③ — LS.

④ — Sable & Taurus.

⑤ — VIN R, .0059 inch; VIN Y, .0039 inch.

⑥ — Intake, 14°; Exhaust, 13°.

GPM — Gallons Per Minute   ① — 2004–08 Grand Prix, 1400–1500 RPM.   ② — At 1500 RPM.

Power Steering Pumps

NOTE: On Air Bag Equipped Models, Refer To "Air Bag System Precautions" Located In The Front Of This Manual For System Disarming & Arming Procedures.

NOTE: Refer To "Computer Relearn Procedures" Located In The Front Of This Manual When Battery Power To The Computer Has Been Interrupted.

NOTE: Prior To Performing Any Service Operations Listed In This Section, Consult The "Technical Service Bulletins" Section For Related Information.

INDEX

	Page No.		Page No.		Page No.
Diagnosis & Testing	21-3	TC Series Pump	21-4	2004–05 L-Series	21-5
System Pressure Test	21-3	**Technical Service Bulletins**	21-5	Momentary Reduction of Power	
Power Steering System Bleed	21-4	Cold Power Steering System		Steering Assist On Initial Start	
Bleeding w/Vacuum Pump	21-4	Squeal, Squawk Noise on		Up With Low Ambient	
Special Bleeding	21-5	Startup	21-6	Temperatures	21-6
Standard Bleeding	21-4	2004 CTS & CTS-V	21-6	2004–05 Alero, Cavalier,	
Power Steering System Service	21-3	Moan or Groan Noise While		Grand Am & Sunfire	21-6
Component Service	21-3	Turning Steering Wheel at			
CB Series Pump	21-3	Low Speeds	21-5		

DIAGNOSIS & TESTING

System Pressure Test

When performing system test procedures, power steering pressures can easily exceed 1000 psi. Extreme caution must be exercised when performing these tests to prevent personal injury.

Refer to "Power Steering Pressure Specifications" for the proper specifications.

1. Disconnect pressure hose at pump. Use suitable container to catch any fluid leakage.
2. Connect spare pressure hose to pump.
3. Connect pressure gauge tool kit No. J-44721, or equivalent.
4. Open gauge valve.
5. Start engine and allow system to reach normal operating temperature.
6. Inspect and adjust fluid level.
7. When engine is at operating temperature, pressure reading should be as specified. If pressure is more than maximum specification, inspect hoses for restrictions.
8. **Do not leave valve fully closed for more than five seconds.**
9. Fully close valve three times, noting the following:
   a. Three readings should be within 50 psi., of each other.
   b. If pressure readings are at least minimum specified under and are within 50 psi., of each other, pump

is functioning properly.
   c. If pressure readings are at least minimum specified, but not within 50 psi., of each other, flow control valve is sticking and requires removal and cleaning. Burrs can be removed using crocus cloth.
10. If pressure readings are within specifications, leave valve open and turn steering wheel to both stops. If pressure at stops is not same as maximum pressure specified, steering gear is leaking internally.
11. Turn engine off and remove testing gauge and hoses.
12. Connect pressure hose and inspect fluid level.

POWER STEERING SYSTEM SERVICE

Component Service

CB SERIES PUMP

DISASSEMBLE

1. Remove power steering pump from vehicle and outlined in "Front Suspension & Steering" section in appropriate chassis chapter.
2. Remove union fitting with O-ring and seal, **Fig. 1.**
3. Remove control valve and flow control spring.
4. Protect driveshaft with shim stock and

remove driveshaft seal by cutting with small chisel. Discard seal.
5. Remove end cover retaining ring by inserting punch in access hole.
6. Push on driveshaft to assist in removing end cover, O-ring, pressure plate spring, pump ring, pump vanes and driveshaft subassembly.
7. Remove O-ring from housing.
8. Record orientation of pump ring holes and dowel pins for assembly alignment.
9. Remove dowel pins and driveshaft seal.
10. Remove pressure plate, pressure plate spring and O-ring from end cover.
11. Remove shaft retaining ring from driveshaft, pump rotor and thrust plate.

INSPECTION

1. Clean all components in clean power steering fluid, then dry thoroughly.
2. Inspect pump ring, vanes, thrust plate, pressure plate and driveshaft for scoring, pitting or chatter marks.

ASSEMBLE

1. Lubricate new driveshaft seal with power steering fluid and press seal into pump housing using seal installer tool No. J-7728, or equivalent.
2. Install pump ring dowel pins into housing.
3. Install thrust plate and pump rotor onto driveshaft, **Fig. 2.**
4. Install new shaft retaining ring onto driveshaft.

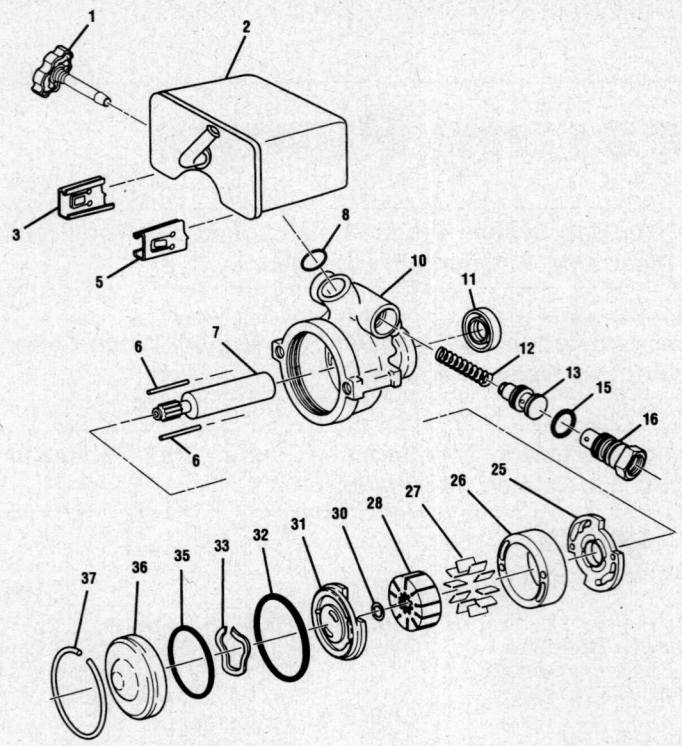

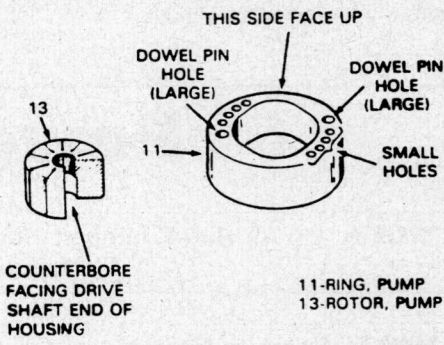

Fig. 2 Rotor and/or pump ring installation. CB series power steering pump

Fig. 1 Exploded view of CB series power steering pump

1 - CAPSTICK ASM, RESERVOIR
2 - RESERVOIR ASM, HYD PUMP (TYPICAL)
3 - CLIP, RESERVOIR RETAINING (LH)
5 - CLIP, RESERVOIR RETAINING (RH)
6 - PIN, PUMP RING DOWEL
7 - SHAFT, DRIVE
8 - SEAL, O-RING
10 - HOUSING ASM, HYD PUMP
11 - SEAL, DRIVE SHAFT
12 - SPRING, FLOW CONTROL
13 - VALVE ASM, CONTROL
15 - SEAL, O-RING

16 - FITTING, O-RING UNION
25 - PLATE, THRUST
26 - RING, PUMP
27 - VANE
28 - ROTOR, PUMP
30 - RING, SHAFT RETAINING
31 - PLATE, PRESSURE
32 - SEAL, O-RING
33 - SPRING, PRESSURE PLATE
35 - SEAL, O-RING
36 - COVER, END
37 - RING, RETAINING

GC6029700405000X

5. Install driveshaft subassembly into housing.
6. Install pump ring with holes positioned properly onto dowel pins in housing, **Fig. 2.**
7. Install vanes into pump rotor.
8. Lubricate new large O-ring with power steering fluid and install it into end cover.
9. Install pressure plate and spring.
10. Lubricate new small O-ring and install it into end cover.
11. Lubricate outer edge of end cover with power steering fluid and press it into housing.
12. Insert retaining ring into groove in housing with ring opening near access hole opening.

TC SERIES PUMP

Refer to **Fig. 3** when servicing this power steering pump.

POWER STEERING SYSTEM BLEED
STANDARD BLEEDING

Bleed power steering system after any component replacement, fluid line disconnection or in case of steering system noise. Bleed system to prevent pump damage, stop steering noise and to ensure proper system operation.

Inspect steering system before bleeding, looking for power steering lines touching frame, body or engine. Also inspect all hose connections for looseness or leaks.

1. Remove power steering pump reservoir cap.
2. Fill pump reservoir with fluid to minimum system level, full cold level.
3. **On models equipped with Hydroboost,** fluid level will appear falsely high if hydro-boost accumulator is not

fully charged. Do not apply brake pedal with engine OFF. this will discharge hydro-boost accumulator.
4. **On models equipped with Hydroboost,** fully charge hydro-boost accumulator using following procedure:
   a. Start the engine.
   b. Firmly apply the brake pedal 10-15 times.
   c. Turn the engine OFF.
5. **On all models,** raise vehicle until front wheels are off the ground.
6. With key in ON position and engine OFF, turn steering wheel from stop to stop 12 times.
7. **On models equipped with Hydroboost or extended length power steering hoses,** turn steering wheel from stop to stop 15 to 20 times.
8. **On all models,** verify power steering fluid level.
9. Start engine, rotate steering wheel from left to right.
10. Inspect for sign of cavitation or fluid aeration (pump noise/whining).
11. Verify fluid level.
12. Repeat bleed procedure, if necessary.

BLEEDING w/VACUUM PUMP

This procedure should only be used, after the standard bleeding procedure efforts have not obtained the desired results.

1. Remove power steering pump reservoir cap.
2. Fill reservoir with proper fluid to full cold level.
3. Connect vacuum pump tool No. J-35555 and power steering bleeder adapter tool No. J-43485, or equivalents, to reservoir filler neck, **Fig. 4.**
4. Apply maximum vacuum of 20 inches and wait five minutes.
5. Inspect vacuum level after five minute. Vacuum typically will drop 2–3 inches. If vacuum does not remain steady, refer to "Special Bleeding."
6. Install reservoir cap, then start and idle engine.

CRANKSHAFT, BEARINGS & RODS

All Measurements Given In Inches, Unless Otherwise Specified.

Engine Liter (VIN①)	Year	Crankshaft					Bearing Clearance		Connecting Rods	
		Main Bearing Journal Diameter	Connecting Rod Journal Diameter	Crankshaft Endplay	Max. Out of Round All	Max. Taper	Main Bearings	Connecting Rod Bearings	Pin Bore Diameter	Side Clearance
2.0L DOHC (N, P, 3 & 5)	2004–07	2.2827–2.2835	1.8461–1.8468	.0035–.0102	—	—	.0004–.0022	.0006–.0028	.7855–.7867	.0036–.0126
2.3L DOHC (Z)	2004–08	2.0460–2.0470	1.9670–1.9680	.0080–.0160	—	—	.0007–.0013	.0010–.0020	.8250–.8260	.0076–.0120
3.0L DOHC (S)②	2004–05	2.4690–2.4800	1.9673–1.9681	.0043–.0091	—	—	—	.0011–.0018	—	.0039–.0138
3.0L DOHC (S) ④	2004–05	2.4790–2.4800	1.9673–1.9681	.0053–.0100	—	—	.—	.0011–.0026	.8274–.8280	.0039–.0118
3.0L DOHC (1)	2005–08	2.4790–2.4800	1.9673–1.9681	.0050–.0100	.0082	.0003	—	.001–.0025	.8273–.8275	.0039–.0118
3.0L OHV (U & 2)	2004–07	2.5190–2.5198	2.1253–2.1261	.0039–.0079	.0003	.0024	.0009–.0027	.0009–.0027	.9096–.9112	.0059–.0142
3.5L (C, T, Y)	2007–08	2.657	2.204–2.205	.0012–.066	.00023	.00015	—	—	.9055–.9057	—
3.8L OHV (4)	2004	2.5190–2.5198	2.3103–2.3111	.0039–.0079	.0006	.0003	.0005–.0023	.0009–.0027	.9031–.9047	.0047–.0193
3.9L DOHC (A & 6)	2004–06	—	—	—	—	—	—	—	—	—
4.0L SOHC (N)	2005–08	2.243–2.244	2.125–2.126	.0020–.0126	.0003	.0003	.0003–.0024	.0003–.0024	.943–.944	.0036–.0106
4.6L DOHC (R)	2004	2.6567–2.6577	2.0859–2.2396	.0051–.0119	.0020	.0020	.0010–.0020	.0006–.0027	.8666–.8671	.0059–.0197
4.6L DOHC (V)	2004–08	③	2.0859–2.2396	.0051–.0119	.0020	.0020	.0010–.0020	.0011–.0027	.8666–.8671	.0059–.0197
4.6L DOHC (X & Y)	2004	2.6572	2.2396–2.2388	.0051–.0119	.0020	.0020	.0009–.0022	.0011–.0027	.8666–.8671	.0059–.0197
4.6L SOHC (H)	2005–08	2.6568–2.6576	2.0859–2.0867	.0030–.0148	.0020	—	.0010–.0020	.0011–.0027	.8666–.8671	.0049–.0197
4.6L SOHC (W & 9)	2004–08	2.6568–2.6576	2.0859–2.0867	.0119	.0020	.0002	.0009–.0026	.0008–.0023	.8666–.8671	.0059–.0177
5.4L DOHC (S)	2007–08	2.6567–2.6577	2.0867–2.0859	.0030–.0148	.0003	.0002	.0009–.0019	.0010–.0025	8665–0.8667	.0049–.0187

DOHC — Dual Overhead Cam
OHV — Overhead Valve
SOHC — Single Overhead Cam

① — Eighth digit Vehicle Identification Number (VIN) denotes engine code.
② — LS.

③ — Marauder & Mustang, 2.6567–2.6577 inches.
④ — Sable & Taurus.

BALANCE SHAFT

All Measurements Given In Inches, Unless Otherwise Specified.

Engine Liter (VIN①)	Year	Balance Shaft Bore		Balance Shaft		
		Inside Bore Diameter	End Play	Journal Diameter	End Play	Runout
3.8L OHV (4)	2004	2.1915–2.1924	.0030–.0060	2.0505–2.0515	.0030–.0079	.0010

OHV — Overhead Valve

① — Eighth digit Vehicle Identification Number (VIN) denotes engine code.

VALVES—Continued

All Measurements Given In Inches, Unless Otherwise Specified.

| Engine Liter (VIN①) | Year | Valves | | | | | |
| | | Stem Diameter | | Run Out | Face Angle, Degrees | Clearance | |
		Intake	Exhaust			Intake	Exhaust
4.6L DOHC (R, X & Y)	2004	.2746–.2754	.2736–.2744	.00200	45.50	.0315–.0472②	.0315–.0472②
4.6L DOHC (V)	2006–07	.2746–.2753	.2736–.2744	.00110	45.50	②③	②③
4.6L SOHC (H, W & 9)	2004–08	.2746–.2753	.2736–.2744	.00200	45.50	.0177–.0335②	.0177–.0335②
5.4L DOHC (S)	2007–08	2762–.2754	2762–.2754	.0019	45.00	.0177–.0335②	.0177–.0335②

DOHC — Dual Overhead Cam
OHV — Overhead Valve
SOHC — Single Overhead Cam
① — Eighth digit Vehicle Identification Number (VIN) denotes engine code.

② — With cylinder @ top dead center, hold steady pressure on lifter until fully collapsed to check clearance.
③ — Mustang, .1798–.2698 inch; Marauder, .0315–.0472 inch.
④ — LS.

⑤ — Sable & Taurus.
⑥ — Not adjustable, zero lash hydraulic lifters used.
⑦ — @ 59–77°F.

CAMSHAFT

All Measurements Given In Inches unless Otherwise Specified.

Engine Liter (VIN①)	Year	Camshaft Journal Diameter	Camshaft Bearing Inside Diameter	Camshaft Bearing Clearance	Camshaft Endplay	Lifter Diameter	Lifter To Bore Clearance
2.0L DOHC (N, P, 3 & 5)	2004–07	—	1.0220–1.0228	.0008–.0028	.0031–.0087	—	—
2.3L DOHC (Z)	2004–08	0.9820–0.9830	—	.0010–.0030	.0030–.0090	1.2192–2.2196	⑥
3.0L DOHC (S)③	2004–05	1.0603–1.604	—	.0010–.0059	.0028–.0109	—	—
3.0L DOHC (S)④	2004–05	1.0605–1.0615	1.0625–1.0635	.0010–.0048	.0075	.6294–.6299	.0007–.0027
3.0L DOHC (1)	2005–08	1.0610–1.0600	1.0625–1.0635	.0010–.0029	.0009–.0064	6290–.6294	.0007–.0027
3.0L OHV (U & 2)	2004–07	2.0074–2.0084	2.0094–2.0104	.0010–.0030	.0001	.8742	.0007–.0027
3.5L (C, T, Y)	2007–08	—	⑤	②	.0039–.0114	—	—
3.8L OHV (4)	2004	2.0525–2.0543	2.0670–2.0740	.0010–.0030	.0010–.0069	.8738–.8745	.0007–.0027
3.9L DOHC (A & 6)	2004–06	—	—	—	—	—	—
4.0L DOVC (N)	2005–08	1.0990–1.1010	1.1020–1.1040	.0020–.0040	.0030–.0070	—	—
4.6L DOHC (R, V, X & Y)	2004–08	1.0605–1.0615	1.0625–1.0635	.0010–.0030	.0011–.0075	.6294–.6299	.0006–.0027
4.6L SOHC (H, W & 9)	2004–08	1.0602–1.0615	1.0625–1.0634	.0010–.0030	.0012–.0075	.6294–.6299	.0007–.0027
5.4L DOHC (S)	2007–08	1.0615–1.0605	1.0635–1.0625	.0010–.0030	.0011–.0075	⑦	.0007–.0027

DOHC — Dual Overhead Cam
OHV — Overhead Valve
SOHC — Single Overhead Cam
① — Eighth digit Vehicle Identification Number (VIN) denotes engine code.

② — First journal, .0027 inch Max; Intermediate journals, .0029 inch Max.
③ — LS.
④ — Sable & Taurus.
⑤ — First journal, 1.221–1.222 inch; Intermediate journals, 1.023–1.024 inch

⑥ — Exhaust, .010–.013 inch; Intake, .008–.011 inch.
⑦ — Exhaust, 6299-0.6295 inch; Intake, 4724-0.4720 inch.

7. Stop engine and inspect power steering fluid level.
8. Wait five minutes, then repeat previous two steps until fluid level has stabilized.
9. Start and idle engine, then turn steering wheel 180–360°F in both directions five times. **Do not turn wheel all the way to stops.**
10. Stop engine and inspect power steering fluid level.
11. Connect vacuum pump and power steering bleeder adapter to reservoir filler neck, **Fig. 4.**
12. Apply maximum vacuum of 20 inches and wait five minutes.
13. Inspect vacuum level after five minute. Vacuum typically will drop 2–3 inches. If vacuum does not remain steady, refer to "Special Bleeding."

SPECIAL BLEEDING

1. If vacuum continued to drop during bleeding procedure, remove power steering pressure and return hoses from power steering pump.
2. Install plugs from power steering bleeder adapter tool No. J-43485, or equivalents, into power steering pump pressure and return ports.
3. Connect vacuum pump and power steering bleeder adapter to reservoir filler neck, **Fig. 4.**
4. Apply maximum vacuum of 20 inches.
5. If vacuum drops, repair or replace power steering pump.
6. If vacuum holds steady, proceed as follows:
   a. Inspect power steering fluid and ensure it is free of bubbles and is not discolored.
   b. Replace return hose clamps and O-rings.
   c. Replace pressure hose O-rings and reservoir to pump O-ring.
   d. Repeat bleeding procedure.
   e. Drive vehicle approximately 10 miles on smooth, flat surface to ensure power steering system reaches full operating temperature.

TECHNICAL SERVICE BULLETINS

Moan or Groan Noise While Turning Steering Wheel at Low Speeds

2004–05 L-SERIES

On some of these models equipped with 2.2L engine and automatic transaxle there may be moan or groan noise from the power steering system while turning the steering wheel at low vehicle speeds.

This condition may be caused by pressure pulses from the power steering pump

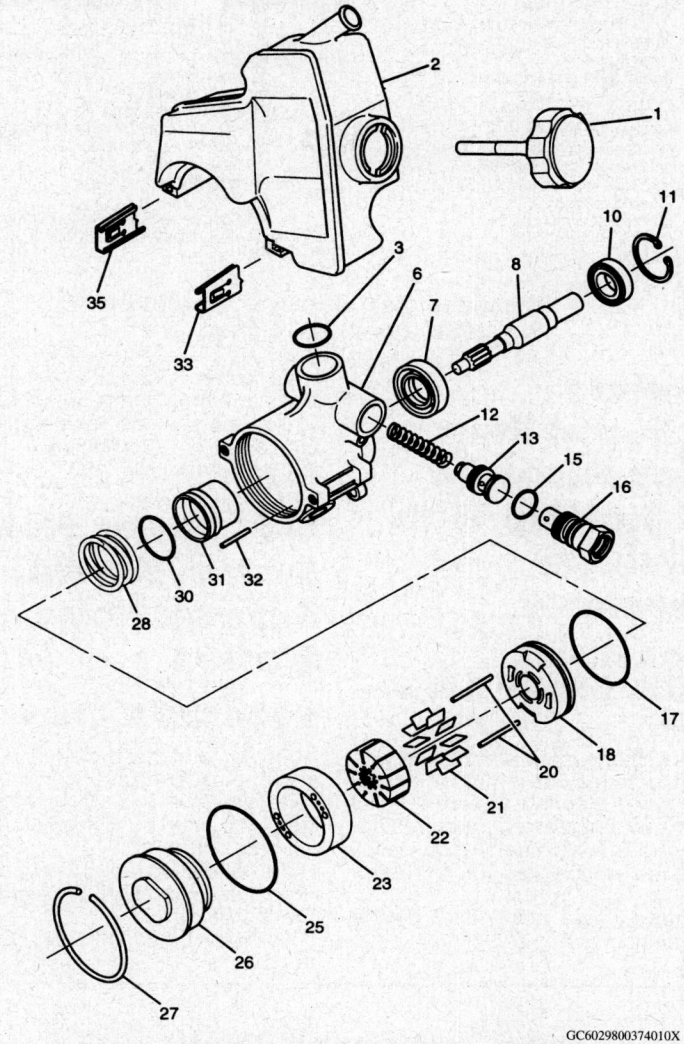

Fig. 3 Exploded view of power steering pump (Part 1 of 2). TC Series

GC6029800374010X

may create resonance throughout the steering system.

To correct this condition install new tuned power steering pressure hose GM P/N 22714174, flush fluid and vacuum bleed steering system as follows:

1. Remove power steering reservoir cap.
2. Drain power steering fluid from reservoir using vacuum tool No. SA9180NE/J35555, or equivalent, with siphon cup.
3. Place suitable drain container under power steering hoses at steering gear.
4. Remove power steering pressure hose from steering gear.
5. Disconnect clip between power steering pressure and return hoses.
6. Remove power steering pressure hose. Record hose routing for installation alignment.
7. Position new tuned power steering pressure hose following previously recorded route.
8. Hand start but do not tighten power

steering pressure hose to steering gear and pump connections.
9. Hold fitting at gear end of pressure hose so that it does not contact (ground out) any other part of vehicle.
10. **Torque** hose connections to 20 ft. lbs.
11. Twist power steering pressure hose at pump end so hose is centered between brake master cylinder and heater hoses.
12. While holding power steering pressure hose in centered position, **torque** power steering pressure hose fitting to pump to 20 ft. lbs.
13. Attach clip between power steering pressure and return hoses.
14. Inspect power steering pressure hose routing to ensure there are no ground outs.
15. Fill power steering pump fluid reservoir with suitable power steering fluid.
16. Bleed power steering system as outlined in "Power Steering System Service."

Key No.	Part Name
1 -	CAPSTICK ASM, RESERVOIR
2 -	RESERVOIR ASM, HYD PUMP
3 -	SEAL, O-RING
6 -	HOUSING ASM, HYD PUMP
7 -	SEAL, DRIVE SHAFT
8 -	SHAFT, DRIVE
10 -	BEARING ASM, BALL
11 -	RING, RETAINING
12 -	SPRING, FLOW CONTROL
13 -	VALVE ASM, CONTROL
15 -	SEAL, O-RING
16 -	FITTING, O-RING UNION
17 -	SEAL, O-RING
18 -	PLATE, PRESSURE

Key No.	Part Name
20 -	PIN, PUMP RING DOWEL (2)
21 -	VANE (10)
22 -	ROTOR, PUMP
23 -	RING, PUMP
25 -	SEAL, O-RING
26 -	PLATE ASM, THRUST
27 -	RING, THRUST PLATE RETAINING
28 -	SPRING, PRESSURE PLATE
30 -	SEAL, O-RING
31 -	SLEEVE ASM
32 -	PIN, DOWEL
33 -	CLIP, RESERVOIR RETAINING (RH)
35 -	CLIP, RESERVOIR RETAINING (LH)

GC6029800374020X

Fig. 3   Exploded view of power steering pump (Part 2 of 2). TC Series

J 43485   J 35555

GC6029800406000X

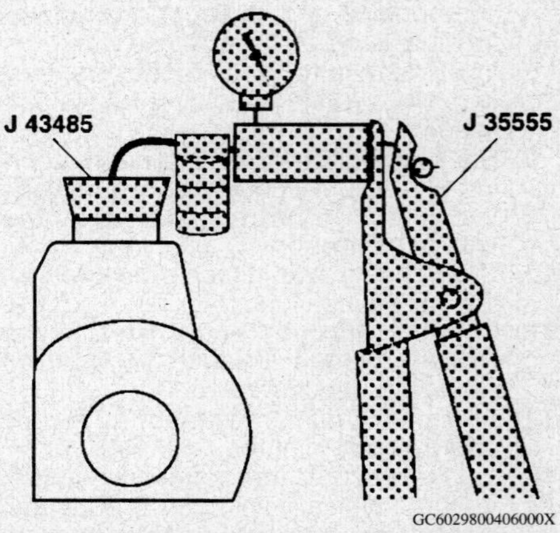

Fig. 4   Power steering bleeder tool installation in reservoir

Momentary Reduction of Power Steering Assist On Initial Start Up With Low Ambient Temperatures

2004–05 ALERO, CAVALIER, GRAND AM & SUNFIRE

On some of these models equipped with 2.2L engine there may be a momentary reduction of power steering assist on initial start up with low ambient temperatures approximately 10°F. The system returns to full assist after the vehicle has run for a few seconds.

This condition may be caused by the power steering pump.

To correct this condition, replace the power steering pump GM P/N 26047567.

Do not replace steering gears Nos. 26073992, 26086616, 26068967, 26068964 and 26074935.

Cold Power Steering System Squeal, Squawk Noise on Startup

2004 CTS & CTS-V

On some of these models equipped with a 3.6L or 5.7L engine, could experience a squeal/squawk noise from the power steering pump momentarily on start up after an extreme cold soak.

This condition may be caused by regions were outside temperatures could reach 12° F. or below.

To correct this condition, a cold climate power steering fluid has been approved for use in these vehicles in areas that regularly experience extreme cold weather.

1. Drain power steering fluid from reservoir using vacuum tool No. SA9180NE/J35555, or equivalent, with siphon cup.
2. Place suitable drain container under power steering hoses at steering gear.
3. Remove return hose and drain fluid in a suitable container.
4. Install return hose, fill with new fluid GM P/N 12345867.
5. Bleed power steering system as outlined in "Power Steering System Service."

㉙ — 2004–06, Top, .0003–.0009 inch;
bottom, .0118–.0031 inch

CYLINDER BLOCK

All Measurements Given In Inches, Unless Otherwise Specified.

Engine Liter (VIN①)	Year	Cylinder Bore Diameter (Std.)	Cylinder Bore Taper Max.	Cylinder Bore Out of Round Max.
2.0L DOHC (N, P, 3 & 5)	2004–07	②	—	—
2.3L DOHC (Z)	2004–08	3.4440–3.4450	—	.0003
3.0L DOHC (S)	2004–05	④	.0008	.0006
3.0L DOHC (1)	2005–08	③	.0008	.0007
3.0L OHV (U & 2)	2004–07	3.5039	.0020	.0010
3.5L (C, T, Y)	2007–08	3.641	—	—
3.8L OHV (4)	2004	3.8115	.0020	.0020
3.9L DOHC (A & 6)	2004–06	—	—	—
4.0L DOHC (N)	2005–08	3.9530	.0001	.0001
4.6L DOHC (R)	2004	—	.0002	.0006–.0008
4.6L DOHC (V)	2006–08	—	.0002	.0006
4.6L DOHC (Y)	2004	3.5511–3.5527	.0006	.0006
4.6L SOHC (H, W & 9)	2004–08	3.5516–3.5522	.0005	.0006
5.4L DOHC (S)	2007–08	3.5511–3.5515	.0002	.0008

DOHC — Dual Overhead Cam
OHV — Overhead Valve
SOHC — Single Overhead Cam
① — Eighth digit Vehicle Identification Number (VIN) denotes engine code.

② — Grade 1, 3.3386–3.3390 inches;
Grade 2, 3.3390–3.3394 inches;
Grade 3, 3.3394–3.3398 inches.
③ — Grade 1, 3.5043–3.5047 inch;
Grade 2, 3.5043–3.5047 inch;
Grade 3, 3.5047–3.5051 inch.

④ — Grade 1, 3.5039–3.5043 inches;
Grade 2, 3.5043–3.5047 inches;
Grade 3, 3.5047–3.5051 inches.

OIL PUMP

All Measurements Given In Inches, Unless Otherwise Specified.

Engine Liter (VIN①)	Year	Rotor Backlash	Rotor To Body Clearance	Rotor Endplay②	Driveshaft To Pump Body Clearance	Relief Valve To Body Clearance	Relief Spring Pressure Lbs./Inches
2.0L DOHC (N, P, 3 & 5)④	2004–07	—	—	—	—	—	—
2.3L DOHC (Z)	2004–08	—	—	—	—	—	—
3.0L DOHC (S)④	2004–05	—	—	—	—	—	—
3.0L DOHC (1)④	2005–08	—	—	—	—	—	—
3.0L OHV (U & 2)④	2004–07	—	—	—	—	—	—
3.5L (C, T, Y)	2007–08	—	—	—	—	—	—
3.8L OHV (4)	2004	.0080–.0012	.0020–.0055	.0005–.0055	③	.0017–.0029	15.2–17.1 @ 1.20
3.9L DOHC (A & 6)④	2004–06	—	—	—	—	—	—
4.0L DOHC (N)④	2005–08	—	—	—	—	—	—
4.6L DOHC (R, V & Y)④	2004–08	—	—	—	—	—	—
4.6L SOHC (H, W & 9)④	2004–08	—	—	—	—	—	—
5.4L DOHC (S)	2007–08	—	—	—	—	—	—

DOHC — Dual Overhead Cam
OHV — Overhead Valve
SOHC — Single Overhead Cam
① — Eighth digit Vehicle Identification Number (VIN) denotes engine code.

② — Measured between pump cover mounting surface & end of gear, using straightedge & feeler gauge.
③ — Driver shaft to body clearance,

.0015–.0030 inch; idler shaft to idler clearance, .0005–.0017 inch.
④ — Replace as an assembly. Not serviceable.

PISTONS, PINS & RINGS

All Measurements Given In Inches, Unless Otherwise Specified.

Engine Liter (VIN①)	Year	Piston Diameter (Std.)	Piston Clearance	Piston Pin Diameter	Pin To Piston Clearance	Piston End Ring Gap Comp.	Piston End Ring Gap Oil	Piston Ring Side Clearance Comp.	Piston Ring Side Clearance Oil
2.0L DOHC (N, P, 3 & 5)	2004–07	㉘	.0004–.0012	⑤	.0006–.0019	.01180–.01970	.01570–05510	—	—
2.3L DOHC (Z)	2004–08	3.4440–3.4450	.0009–.0019	.8266–.8268	.0003–.0006	⑥	.00070–00270	—	—
3.0L (S)⑨	2004–05	㉖	.0005–.0009	.8272–.8273	-.0002–.0001	⑯	.00590–.03540	—	—
3.0L DOHC (S) ⑫	2004–05	㉕㉖	.0005–.0009	.8272–.8273	-.0002–.0001	⑦	.00590–.03540	⑧	.0039
3.0L DOHC (1)	2005–08	⑱	.0007–.0016	.8271–.8273	—	⑬	.00590–.02550	—	—
3.0L OHV (U & 2)	2004–07	⑪	.0012–.0022	.9119–.9124	.0002–.0005	.00098–.01970	00098–.04920	.0016–.0037	—
3.5L (C, T, Y)	2007–08	3.6407–3.613	.0003–.0017	.9054–.9055	.0003.0007	.0059–.0098	.0059–.0177	.0015–.0031	—
3.8L OHV (4)	2004	⑮	.0007–.0017	.9031–.9047	.0004–.0007	.05750	⑭	.0012–.0031	—
3.9L DOHC (A & 6)	2004–06	—	—	—	—	—	—	—	—
4.0L DOHC (N)	2005–08	3.952–3.9528	.0012–.0020	⑩	.0004–.0006	.0008–.0018	.0016–.0024	—	—
4.6L DOHC (R)	2004	⑲	-.0004 to +.0010	.8662–.8663	-.0002 to .0001	㉒	.00590–.02560	⑰	⑭
4.6L DOHC (V)㉑	2004	⑲	-.0004 to +.0010	.8662–.8663	-.0002 to +.0001	㉒	.00590–.02600	㉙	⑭
4.6L DOHC (V)㉓	2004–08	㉗	-.0004 to +.0010	.8662–.8663	-.0002 to +.0001	㉒	.00590–.02560	.0012–.0027	⑭
4.6L DOHC (Y)	2004	3.5504–3.5507	-.0004 to +.0010	.8658–.8659	.0002–.0005	④	.02560	⑧	.0019–.0079
4.6L SOHC (H)	2005–08	②	-.0020 to +.0010	.8662–.8663	-.0002 to +.0005	㉔	.00590–.02560	③	⑭
4.6L SOHC (W)	2004–08	⑳	-.0002–.0010	.8659–.8660	.0004–.0006	.0598–.0606	.11930–.12030	.0008–.0024	.0012–.0028
4.6L SOHC (X)	2004	②	-.0020 to +.0010	.8662–.8663	-.0002 to +.0005	㉔	.00590–.02560	③	⑭
4.6L SOHC (9)	2004–05	⑳	—	.8662–.8663	.0002	.0059–.0118	.00590–.01180	—	—
5.4L DOHC (S)	2007–08	3.5502–3.5506	-.0002–.0010	8662–.8663	0002–.0005	0051–.0111	0059–.0256	.0008–.0024	.0012–.0028

DOHC — Dual Overhead Cam
OHV — Overhead Valve
SOHC — Single Overhead Cam

① — Eighth digit Vehicle Identification Number (VIN) denotes engine code.
② — Code red, 3.5506–3.5514 inches; Code blue, 3.5510–3.5518 inches; Code yellow, 3.5514–3.5522 inches.
③ — Top, .0020–.0035 inch; bottom, .0012–.0031 inch.
④ — Top, .0012 inch ; bottom, .0020 inch
⑤ — Code white, .7873–7874 inch; Code red, .8120–.8121 inch.
⑥ — Top, .0006–.0012 inch; Bottom, .0012–.0018 inch.
⑦ — Top, .0039–.0197 inch; bottom, .0106–.0256 inch.
⑧ — Top, .0016–.0031 inch; bottom, .0011–.0027 inch.
⑨ — LS.
⑩ — Code red, .9446–.9448 inch; Code blue, .9448–.9449 inch.

⑪ — Code red, 3.5024–3.5031 inch; Code blue, 3.5035–3.5041 inch; Code yellow, 3.5045–3.5051 inch.
⑫ — Sable & Taurus.
⑬ — Top, .0039–.0098 inch; Bottom, .0059–.0255 inch.
⑭ — Snug fit.
⑮ — Code red, 3.8103–3.8108 inch; Code blue, 3.8108–3.8113 inch; Code yellow, 3.8113–3.8118 inch.
⑯ — Top, .0039–.0197 inch; bottom, .0106–.0256 inch.
⑰ — Top, .0004–.0009 inch; bottom, .0012–.0031 inch
⑱ — Coated: Grade 1, 3.5035–3.5043 inch; Grade 2, 3.5039–3.5048 inch; Grade 3, 3.5043–3.5051 inch. Uncoated: Grade 1, 3.5027–3.5031 inch; Grade 2, 3.5030–3.5036 inch; Grade 3, 3.5035–3.5039 inch.
⑲ — Code red, 3.5499–3.5507 inch; Code blue, 3.5504–3.5510 inch; Code yellow, 3.5511–3.5515 inch.

⑳ — Code red, 3.5508–3.5514 inch; Code blue, 3.5513–3.5520 inch; Code yellow, 3.5518–3.5524 inch.
㉑ — Marauder
㉒ — Top, .0059–.0118 inch; bottom, .0118–.0217 inch.
㉓ — Crown Victoria & Grand Marquis.
㉔ — Top .0051–.0110 inch; bottom, .0118–.0217 inch.
㉕ — Uncoated: Grade 1, 3.5028–3.5031 inches; Grade 2, 3.5031–3.5036 inches; Grade 3, 3.5043–3.5051 inches.
㉖ — Coated: Grade 1, 3.5035–3.5043 inch; Grade 2, 3.5039–3.5048 inch; Grade 3, 3.5043–3.5051 inch.
㉗ — Code red, 3.5495–3.5505 inches; Code blue, 3.5504–3.5510 inches; Code yellow, 3.5509–3.5515 inches.
㉘ — Grade 1, 3.3374–3.3378 inch; Grade 2, 3.3378–3.3382 inch; Grade 3, 3.3382–3.3386 inch.

Saginaw Rack & Pinion Power Steering Gear Less Speed Sensitive Steering

---

NOTE: On Air Bag Equipped Models, Refer To "Air Bag System Precautions" Located In The Front Of This Manual For System Disarming & Arming Procedures.

NOTE: Refer To "Computer Relearn Procedures" Located In The Front Of This Manual When Battery Power To The Computer Has Been Interrupted.

INDEX

	Page No.
Description	21-7
Power Steering Gear	21-7
Diagnosis & Testing	21-7
External Leak Inspection	21-7
Power Steering System Bleed	21-9
Power Steering System Service	21-7
Component Service	21-7
Inner Tie Rod, Replace	21-7
Outer Tie Rod, Replace	21-7
Pinion Seal, Dust Seal & Bearing Annulus, Replace	21-8

	Page No.
Power Steering Gear, Replace	21-7
Rack & Pinion Boot & Breather Tube, Replace	21-8
Rack Bearing Preload	21-7
Technical Service Bulletins	21-9
Moan or Groan Noise While Turning Steering Wheel at Low Speeds	21-9
2004–05 L-Series	21-9
Power Steering Shudder or Vibration at Idle	21-9

	Page No.
2005-07 Chevrolet Corvette w/Automatic Transmission	21-9
Underhood Noise, Loose or Out of Position Power Steering Outlet Hose or (P/S) Fluid Leak from Power Steering Outlet Hose	21-9
2006 Lucerne	21-9
Tightening Specifications	21-11

DESCRIPTION
Power Steering Gear

This power steering gear assembly incorporates an integral tube and housing containing a pinion shaft and steering rack. The tube and housing are joined by a plastic injection-bonding process. The pinion shaft is supported in the housing by thrust bearings and bushings. A bushing and bulkhead assembly supports the steering in the tube.

A rotary-type valve body is used to control the hydraulic steering assist. Fluid under pressure is directed to the gear housing and into the valve body. The valve body then directs fluid to the power cylinder.

A spool valve, connected to the stub shaft by a locating pin, rotates within the valve body. Fluid directional passages, machined into the spool valve, are aligned with fluid passages in the valve body as the spool valve rotates. Fluid is directed through these passages, into either side of the power cylinder through the externally mounted oil lines.

DIAGNOSIS & TESTING
External Leak Inspection

1. With engine off, wipe entire power steering system clean and dry.

2. Ensure fluid level is at proper level.
3. Start engine and turn steering wheel from stop-to-stop a few times. **Do not hold at stop for long period.**
4. Find and repair exact area of leak and repair as required, **Fig. 1.**

POWER STEERING SYSTEM SERVICE
Component Service

POWER STEERING GEAR, REPLACE

Refer to **Fig. 2** for service procedures.

OUTER TIE ROD, REPLACE

1. Remove prevailing torque nut or cotter pin and hex slotted nut from outer tie rod, **Fig. 3.**
2. Loosen jam nut and remove outer tie rod from steering knuckle using steering linkage remover tool No. J-24319-01, or equivalent.
3. Remove outer from inner tie rod.
4. Reverse procedure to install, noting the following:
   a. **Torque** hex slotted nut to 35 ft. lbs., with maximum of 52 ft. lbs., to install cotter pin. **Do not back off nut when installing cotter pin.**
   b. Adjust toe by turning inner tie rod.
   c. **Torque** jam nut against outer tie rod to 50 ft. lbs.

INNER TIE ROD, REPLACE

Rack must be held during inner tie rod removal and installation.

REMOVAL

1. Remove rack and pinion.
2. Remove outer tie rod from inner tie rod, then rack and pinion boot.
3. Place wrench on flat of rack assembly and place wrench on flats of inner tie rod housing, **Fig. 4.**
4. Rotate housing counterclockwise until inner tie rod separates from rack.

INSTALLATION

1. Install inner tie rod on rack, **Fig. 5.**
2. Support rack and housing of inner tie rod and stake both sides of inner tie rod housing to flats on rack, **Fig. 6.**
3. Inspect both stakes by inserting .010 inch feeler gauge between rack and housing stake. **When properly staked, feeler gauge must not pass between rack and housing stakes.**
4. Slide shock damper over housing until it engages.
5. Install boot and rack outer tie rod, then the rack and pinion.

RACK BEARING PRELOAD

On all models except Century, Grand Prix and Regal, make adjustment with front wheels raised and steering wheel centered. Ensure steering wheel returns to center position after adjustment.

On Century, Grand Prix, Lucerne and

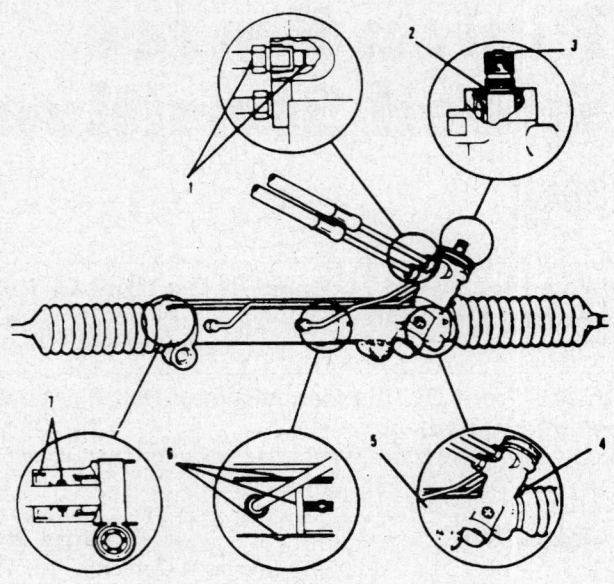

1. TIGHTEN FITTING TO 27 N·m (20 LB FT). IF LEAKAGE PERSISTS, REPLACE O-RING SEAL. IF LEAKAGE IS DUE TO DAMAGED THREADS, REPAIR FITTING NUT OR REPLACE LINE AS REQUIRED. IF HOUSING THREADS ARE BADLY DAMAGED, REPLACE HOUSING

2. REPLACE DUST AND STUB SHAFT SEALS

3. IF LEAKAGE IS OBSERVED BETWEEN TORSION BAR AND STUB SHAFT, PARTIAL GEAR REPLACEMENT WILL BE REQUIRED

4. IF LEAKAGE IS OBSERVED AT DRIVER SIDE AND IS NOT AFFECTED BY THE DIRECTION OF TURN, PARTIAL GEAR REPLACEMENT WILL BE REQUIRED

5. IF LEAKAGE IS OBSERVED AT THE HOUSING END AND SPURTS WHEN BOTTOMED IN LEFT TURN, PARTIAL GEAR REPLACEMENT WILL BE REQUIRED

6. PARTIAL GEAR REPLACEMENT MAY BE REQUIRED

7. IF LEAKAGE IS OBSERVED AT PASSENGER SIDE, IT IS NECESSARY TO REPLACE WITH A PARTIAL GEAR ASSEMBLY.

GC6029700407000X

Fig. 1 Power rack & pinion steering gear leak diagnosis

Regal models, make adjustment with the steering rack assembly removed.
1. Loosen locknut, turn adjuster plug clockwise until it bottoms in housing, then back off 50–70°.
2. Tighten locknut while holding adjuster plug.

RACK & PINION BOOT & BREATHER TUBE, REPLACE

REMOVAL
1. Remove outer tie rod.
2. Remove hex jam nut from inner tie rod.
3. Remove tie rod end clamp. then remove and discard boot clamp using suitable side cutters, **Fig. 7.**
4. Index mark breather tube to housing position for installation alignment.
5. Removing tube, boot and breather tube.

INSTALLATION
1. Install new boot clamp onto boot.
2. Apply grease to inner tie rod or housing, **Fig. 8.**
3. Align and install breather tube.
4. Install boot onto housing until seated in housing groove tang.
5. Position boot clamp on boot and crimp.
6. Position tie rod end clamp on boot and secure with pliers.

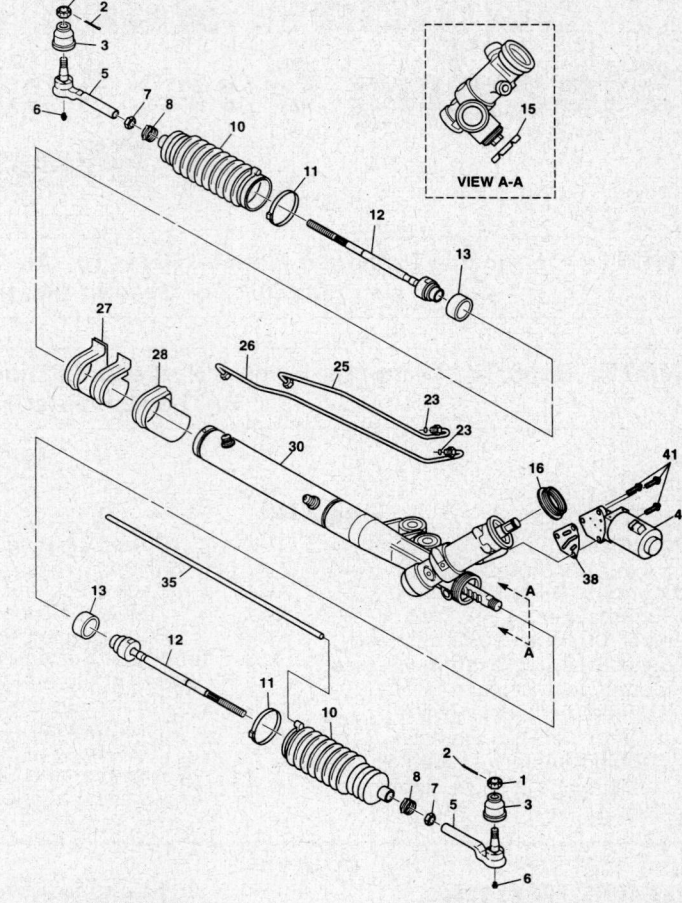

1 - NUT, HEXAGON SLOTTED	16 - ADAPTER, SEAL
2 - PIN, COTTER	23 - SEAL, O-RING
3 - SEAL, TIE ROD & END HSG	25 - LINE ASM, CYLINDER (RT)
5 - ROD ASM, OUTER TIE	26 - LINE ASM, CYLINDER (LT)
6 - FITTING, LUBRICATION	27 - BRACKET ASM, MOUNTING
7 - NUT, METRIC HEX (M14X1.5)	28 - GROMMET, MOUNTING
8 - CLAMP, TIE ROD END	30 - GEAR ASM, RACK & PINION (PARTIAL)
10 - BOOT, RACK & PINION	35 - TUBE, BREATHER
11 - CLAMP, SEAL RETAINING	38 - GASKET, MANIFOLD
12 - ROD ASM, INNER TIE	40 - MANIFOLD ASM, CONTROL VALVE &
13 - RING, SHOCK DAMPENER	41 - SCREW, PAN HD 6-LOBED SOC (M6X1)
15 - NUT, ADJUSTER PLUG LOCK	

GC6029600115000X

Fig. 2 Exploded view of power rack & pinion steering

PINION SEAL, DUST SEAL & BEARING ANNULUS, REPLACE

REMOVAL
1. Remove rack and pinion steering.
2. Remove adjuster plug locknut from adjuster plug, **Fig. 9.**
3. Remove adjuster plug, spring and rack bearing.
4. Remove retaining ring from valve bore of housing and dust cover, **Fig. 10.**
5. Holding stub shaft, remove hex locknut from pinion and valve. **Stub shaft must be held to prevent damage to pinion teeth.**
6. Press on threaded end of pinion using an arbor press until it is possible to remove stub shaft, dust seal, stub shaft seal and annulus bearing, **Fig. 11.**

INSTALLATION
1. While holding valve stub shaft, install hex locknut onto pinion. **Damage to pinion teeth will occur if stub shaft is not held.**
2. Install dust cover to gear.
3. Install stub shaft bearing annulus onto valve stub shaft.
4. Install seal protector tool No. J-29810, or equivalent, onto valve stub shaft.
5. Apply small amount of grease between seals, then install stub shaft seal and dust seal over protector and into gear.
6. Install retaining ring into groove in gear.
7. Lubricate stub shaft and dust seal area with grease.
8. Coat rack bearing, adjuster spring and adjuster plug with suitable lithium-base grease and install gear.
9. With rack centered in gear, turn adjuster plug clockwise until it bottoms in

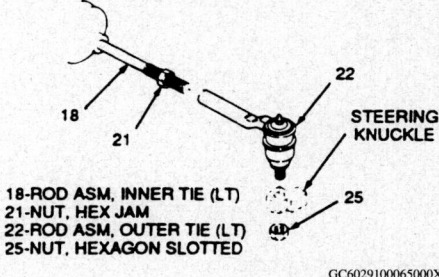

18-ROD ASM, INNER TIE (LT)
21-NUT, HEX JAM
22-ROD ASM, OUTER TIE (LT)
25-NUT, HEXAGON SLOTTED

GC6029100065000X

Fig. 3   Outer tie rod replacement

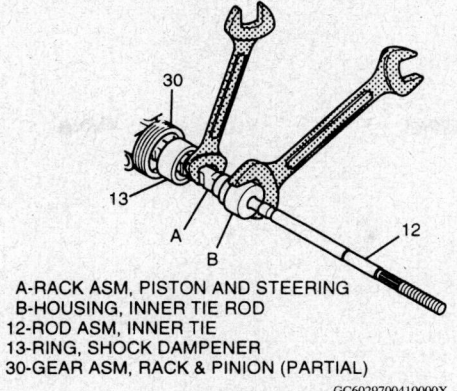

A-RACK ASM, PISTON AND STEERING
B-HOUSING, INNER TIE ROD
12-ROD ASM, INNER TIE
13-RING, SHOCK DAMPENER
30-GEAR ASM, RACK & PINION (PARTIAL)

GC6029700410000X

Fig. 4   Inner tie rod removal

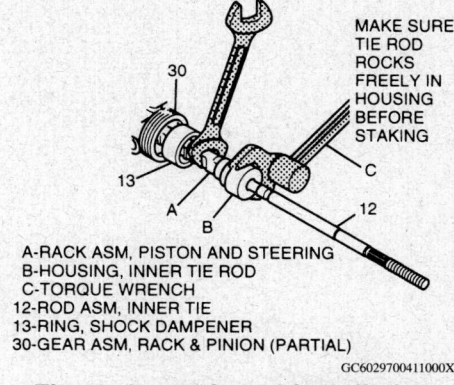

A-RACK ASM, PISTON AND STEERING
B-HOUSING, INNER TIE ROD
C-TORQUE WRENCH
12-ROD ASM, INNER TIE
13-RING, SHOCK DAMPENER
30-GEAR ASM, RACK & PINION (PARTIAL)

GC6029700411000X

Fig. 5   Inner tie rod installation

gear , then back off 50–70°.
10. Measure pinion rotational torque. Maximum preload torque should be 16 inch lbs.
11. Install adjuster plug locknut.
12. Tighten adjuster plug firmly against gear assembly while holding adjuster plug stationary.
13. Install rack and pinion.

POWER STEERING SYSTEM BLEED

Refer to "Power Steering System Bleed" section in "Power Steering Pumps" for power steering system bleed procedures.

TECHNICAL SERVICE BULLETINS

Moan or Groan Noise While Turning Steering Wheel at Low Speeds

2004–05 L-SERIES

On some of these models equipped with 2.2L engine and automatic transaxle there may be moan or groan noise from the power steering system while turning the steering wheel at low vehicle speeds.

This condition may be caused by pressure pulses from the power steering pump may create resonance throughout the steering system.

To correct this condition install new tuned power steering pressure hose GM P/N 22714174, flush fluid and vacuum bleed steering system as follows:
1. Remove power steering reservoir cap.
2. Drain power steering fluid from reservoir using vacuum tool No. SA9180NE/J35555, or equivalent, with siphon cup.
3. Place suitable drain container under power steering hoses at steering gear.
4. Remove power steering pressure hose from steering gear.
5. Disconnect clip between power steering pressure and return hoses.
6. Remove power steering pressure hose. Record hose routing for installation alignment.

7. Position new tuned power steering pressure hose following previously recorded route.
8. Hand start but do not tighten power steering pressure hose to steering gear and pump connections.
9. Hold fitting at gear end of pressure hose so that it does not contact (ground out) any other part of vehicle.
10. **Torque** hose connections to 20 ft. lbs.
11. Twist power steering pressure hose at pump end so hose is centered between brake master cylinder and heater hoses.
12. While holding power steering pressure hose in centered position, **torque** power steering pressure hose fitting to pump to 20 ft. lbs.
13. Attach clip between power steering pressure and return hoses.
14. Inspect power steering pressure hose routing to ensure there are no ground outs.
15. Fill power steering pump fluid reservoir with suitable power steering fluid.
16. Bleed power steering system as outlined in "Power Steering System Service."

Underhood Noise, Loose or Out of Position Power Steering Outlet Hose or (P/S) Fluid Leak from Power Steering Outlet Hose

2006 LUCERNE

On some of these models an underhood noise, an out of position or loose power steering outlet hose, or a power steering fluid leak.

This condition may be caused by power steering outlet hose retainer is loose, and the power steering outlet hose is out of position, it may cause the power steering outlet hose to rub against the steering gear boot.

To correct this condition proceed as follows:
1. Inspect power steering outlet hose and power steering outlet hose retainers.
   a. If power steering outlet hose is loose or out of position, but there is no power steering fluid leak or damage to power steering outlet hose, properly route, secure, and install power steering outlet hose and power steering outlet hose retainers.
   b. Ensure power steering outlet hose retainers are not out of position and seated firmly into frame.
   c. If power steering outlet hose is cut, scraped, or damaged, replace hose. Refer to step 2.
   d. If fluid is leaking from power steering outlet hose, replace hose. Refer to step 2.
2. Remove power steering outlet hose from vehicle.
3. Replace it with a new power steering outlet hose, GM P/N 25756516.
4. Inspect routing of the power steering outlet hose to ensure that hose will not rub against steering gear boot.
5. Ensure power steering outlet hose and power steering outlet hose retainers are not loose or out of position.
6. Fill power steering pump fluid reservoir with suitable power steering fluid.
7. Bleed power steering system as outlined in "Power Steering System Service."

Power Steering Shudder or Vibration at Idle

2005-07 CHEVROLET CORVETTE w/AUTOMATIC TRANSMISSION

On some of these models, a shudder/vibration may occur while rotating the steering wheel at idle. This vibration can be very minor to where it is only felt in the steering wheel or major enough to notice a slight shake in the interior components. Rougher road surfaces can increase the intensity as it increases the drag against the

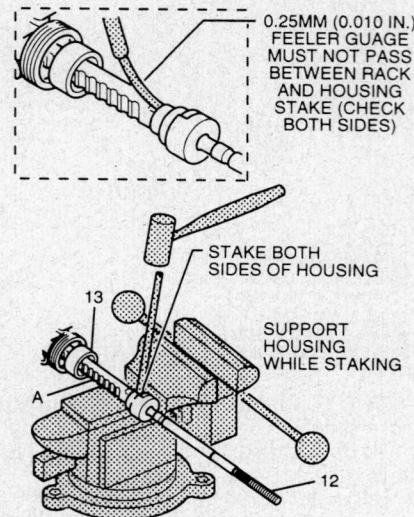

0.25MM (0.010 IN.) FEELER GUAGE MUST NOT PASS BETWEEN RACK AND HOUSING STAKE (CHECK BOTH SIDES)

STAKE BOTH SIDES OF HOUSING

SUPPORT HOUSING WHILE STAKING

A-RACK ASM, PISTON AND STEERING
12-ROD ASM, INNER TIE
13-RING, SHOCK DAMPENER

GC6029700412000X

Fig. 6   Inner tie rod staking procedure

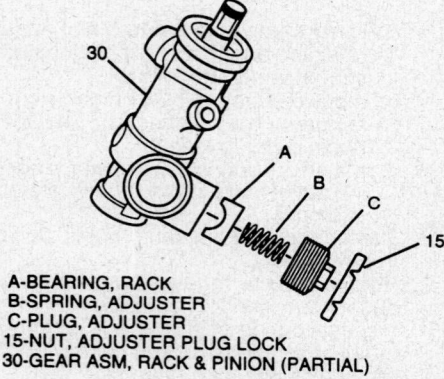

A-BEARING, RACK
B-SPRING, ADJUSTER
C-PLUG, ADJUSTER
15-NUT, ADJUSTER PLUG LOCK
30-GEAR ASM, RACK & PINION (PARTIAL)

GC6029700415000X

Fig. 9   Rack bearing removal

wheels as they attempt to turn. Slightly raising the engine idle should eliminate the vibration

This condition may be caused when at idle the wheels are turned causing the steering pressures to raise high enough to cause a load on the engine. The load is great enough to cause the idle to become rough and it can be felt in the vehicle.

To correct this condition, replace the

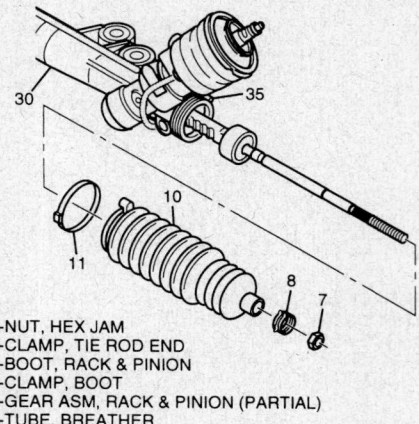

7-NUT, HEX JAM
8-CLAMP, TIE ROD END
10-BOOT, RACK & PINION
11-CLAMP, BOOT
30-GEAR ASM, RACK & PINION (PARTIAL)
35-TUBE, BREATHER

GC6029700413000X

Fig. 7   Boot replacement

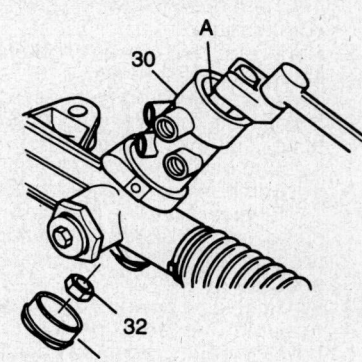

A-SHAFT, STUB
30-GEAR ASM, RACK & PINION (PARTIAL)
32-NUT, HEX LOCK
33-COVER, DUST

GC6029700416000X

Fig. 10   Retaining ring & locknut removal

power steering inlet (pressure) hose with a revised hose as follows:

1. Remove power steering reservoir cap.
2. Drain power steering fluid from reservoir using vacuum tool No. SA9180NE/J35555, or equivalent, with siphon cup.
3. Place suitable drain container under power steering hoses at steering gear.
4. Remove power steering inlet (pressure) hose.
5. **On models equipped w/FE1/FE2 suspension,** install new power steering inlet (pressure) hose GM P/N 15903239.
6. **On models equipped w/FE1/FE2**

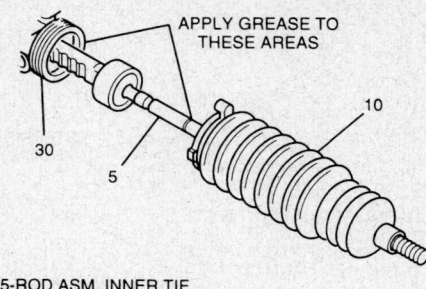

APPLY GREASE TO THESE AREAS

5-ROD ASM, INNER TIE
10-BOOT, RACK & PINION
30-GEAR ASM, RACK & PINION (PARTIAL)

GC6029700414000X

Fig. 8   Boot seal application

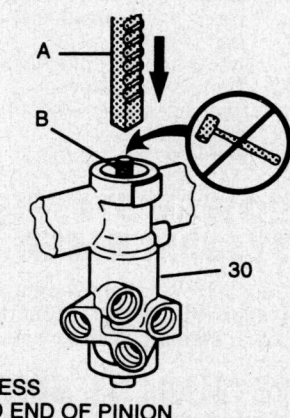

A-ARBOR PRESS
B-THREADED END OF PINION
30-GEAR ASM, RACK & PINION (PARTIAL)

GC6029700417000X

Fig. 11   Stub shaft, dust seal & stub shaft seal removal

suspension, a retaining clip GM P/N 88967174, is also required, attach clip to hose just before the crimp, secure other end of clip to existing power steering return line.

7. **On models equipped w/FE3/FE4 suspension,** install new power steering inlet (pressure) hose GM P/N 15903240.
8. **On models equipped w/FE3/FE4 suspension,** a screw GM P/N 11609268 is also required, secure clip to front crossmember with screw, **torque** to 20 ft. lbs.
9. **On all models,** Fill power steering pump fluid reservoir with suitable power steering fluid.
10. Bleed power steering system as outlined in "Power Steering System Service."

TIGHTENING SPECIFICATIONS

Year/Model	Component	Torque Ft. Lbs.
CENTURY, GRAND PRIX, MONTE CARLO & REGAL		
2004–08	Adjuster Plug Locknut	55
	Inner Tie Rod Housing To Rack	74
	Tie Rod End Nut	22②
	Tie Rod Jam Nut	50
CTS		
2004–08	Intermediate Steering Shaft Pinch Bolt	35
	Power Steering Cooler Screws	48①
	Power Steering Cooler to Frame	80①
	Power Steering Lines to Power Steering Gear	22
	Power Steering Pressure Hose to Frame	80①
	Power Steering Pressure Hose to Power Steering Gear	80①
	Power Steering Pressure Line to Power Steering Pump	30
	Power Steering Pump	26
	Power Steering Reservoir, Lower	18
	Power Steering Reservoir, Upper	80①
	Power Steering Return & Pressure Hoses to Steering Gear	71①
	Power Steering Gear	70
	Tie Rod to Knuckle	52
EXCEPT CENTURY, CTS, GRAND PRIX, IMPALA, MONTE CARLO & REGAL		
2004–08	Adjuster Plug Locknut	50
	Hex Locknut	22
	Hex Nut	50
	Hexagon Slotted Nut	35
	Inner Tie Rod Housing To Rack	70
	Tie Rod Jam Nut	50
IMPALA		
2004–08	Fluid Cooler Pipe	84①
	Inner Tie Rod	74
	Intermediate Shaft Pinch Bolt	35
	Steering Gear	59
	Steering Gear Cylinder Line Fitting	13
	Steering Gear Valve End Fitting	20
	Steering Pump	25
	Tie Rod End Nut	22②
	Tie Rod Jam Nut	50
LUCERNE		
2006–08	Inner Tie Rod to Gear	74
	Intermediate Steering Shaft Pinch Bolt	37
	Outer Tie Rod End to Knuckle Nut	22③
	Power Steering Hose Fittings	22
	Power Steering Pressure Hose Bracket Nut	80①
	Steering Gear Mounting Bolts	70

① — Inch lbs.
② — Tighten an additional 120°.
③ — Tighten an additional 180°.

Saginaw Rack & Pinion Power Steering Gear w/Speed Sensitive Steering

NOTE: On Air Bag Equipped Models, Refer To "Air Bag System Precautions" Located In The Front Of This Manual For System Disarming & Arming Procedures.

NOTE: Refer To "Computer Relearn Procedures" Located In The Front Of This Manual When Battery Power To The Computer Has Been Interrupted.

NOTE: "Electrical Symbol & Wire Color Code Identification" Located In The Front Of This Manual May Be Used As An Aid When Using Wiring Circuits Found In This Section.

NOTE: Prior To Performing Any Service Operations Listed In This Section, Consult The "Technical Service Bulletins" Section For Related Information.

INDEX

	Page No.		Page No.		Page No.
Description	21-12	Variable Effort Steering		Maxx	21-13
Power Steering System Bleed	21-12	Programming	21-12	Service Steering Message	21-12
Power Steering System Service	21-12	**Technical Service Bulletins**	21-12	2004–05 CTS	21-12
Component Service	21-12	Loss Of Power Steering Assist		**Troubleshooting**	21-12
EBCM	21-12	At High Engine RPM	21-13		
Power Steering Gear	21-12	2004–07 Malibu & Malibu			

DESCRIPTION

Speed sensitive steering (Variable Effort or Magnasteer) varies the driver effort required to steer as vehicle speed changes. At low speeds, the system provides maximum power assist. At higher speeds, steering effort is increased to provide firmer steering and directional stability. Variable steering effort is accomplished by reducing power steering fluid flow from the pump as vehicle speed increases. When the vehicle is stationary, the system provides maximum flow. The speed sensitive steering system is made up of an Electronic Brake Control Module (EBCM) or Electronic Brake Traction Control Module (EBTCM), power steering fluid flow actuating device, steering wheel speed sensor, power rack and pinion and power steering pump.

Except for differences in valve machining, the design of the speed sensitive power rack and pinion steering is the same as for the non-speed sensitive power rack and pinion.

TROUBLESHOOTING

Refer to **Figs. 1 through 4** for power steering system troubleshooting.

POWER STEERING SYSTEM SERVICE

Component Service

For procedures not covered in this section, refer to "Saginaw Rack & Pinion Power Steering Gear Less Speed Sensitive Steering."

POWER STEERING GEAR

Refer to **Figs. 5 through 7** for exploded views of power steering gears.

EBCM

1. Disconnect EBCM from bracket using pressure tabs.
2. Disconnect EBCM electrical connectors.
3. Remove EBCM.
4. Reverse procedure to install.

VARIABLE EFFORT STEERING PROGRAMMING

Refer to **Figs. 8 and 9** for variable effort steering programming procedures.

POWER STEERING SYSTEM BLEED

Refer to "Power Steering System Bleed" section in "Power Steering Pumps" for power steering system bleed procedures.

TECHNICAL SERVICE BULLETINS

Service Steering Message

2004–05 CTS

On some of these models there may be a Service Steering Message on the Driver's Information Center (DIC). Diagnostic Trouble Code (DTC) C0450 or C1241 may also be set.

This condition may be caused by an internal fault in the Variable Effort Steering (VES) solenoid.

To correct this condition, proceed as follows:
1. Raise and support vehicle, then remove lefthand front tire and wheel assembly.
2. Remove push-in retainers and front air deflector.
3. Clean dirt or debris from VES solenoid connector.
4. Disconnect VES solenoid harness retainers and electrical connector.

Step	Action	Yes	No
1	Did you review the Power Steering System General Description and perform the necessary inspections?	Go to Step 2	Go to Symptoms - Power Steering System
2	Verify that power steering fluid leaks are present. Is the power steering system leaking?	Go to Step 3	System OK
3	Inspect the power steering system fittings. Are the fittings leaking?	Go to Step 8	Go to Step 4
4	Inspect the power steering hoses. Are the hoses leaking?	Go to Step 9	Go to Step 5
5	Inspect the power steering sensors. Are the sensors leaking?	Go to Step 10	Go to Step 6
6	Inspect the power steering pump and the reservoir for leaks. Is the power steering pump or reservoir leaking?	Go to Step 11	Go to Step 7

ARM0500000000825

Fig. 1 Power steering fluid leaks (Part 1 of 2)

5. Measure resistance of VES actuator. noting the following:
   a. **On 2004–05 models,** if resistance is 5.7–7.2 ohms, continue with DTC C0450 diagnosis.
   b. **On all models,** if resistance not is 5.7–7.2 ohms, proceed to next step.
6. Remove VES solenoid from the steering gear. **Do not replace complete steering gear**
7. Install new VES solenoid, GM P/N 89047679 into steering gear.

Loss Of Power Steering Assist At High Engine RPM

2004–07 MALIBU & MALIBU MAXX

On some of these models there may be a loss of power steering assist at high engine RPM such as Wide Open Throttle (WOT). There may be some displays (radio/instrument panel) that are erratic. There is usually a code C0900 set and possibly a code B1325 set if the displays were erratic and or blanking.

This condition may be caused when the system voltage exceeds 16 volts for 1 second for code C0900 and the system shuts down to protect it from over voltage operation. If the voltage exceeds 18 volts for 5 seconds (B1325) then other electronic systems protect themselves and shut down.

To verify and correct this condition proceed as follows:
1. Verify that system voltage at high RPM does exceed 16 volts: use ECM voltage parameter to monitor system voltage.
2. If voltage parameter does exceed 16 volts check voltage drop on circuit from the generator to the starter. It should be less than 1 volt.
3. If it's greater than 1 volt check for resistance or poor connections at the generator or starter terminals. If the circuit does have excessive resistance and it has to be rewired the proper size fus-

Step	Action	Yes	No
7	Inspect the power steering gear for leaks. Is the power steering gear leaking?	Go to Step 12	Go to Step 8
8	Tighten the fittings. Did you complete the repair?	Go to Step 13	--
9	Replace the power steering hoses. Did you complete the repair?	Go to Step 13	--
10	Replace the power steering sensors. Did you complete the repair?	Go to Step 13	--
11	Replace the power steering pump or reservoir. Did you complete the repair?	Go to Step 13	--
12	Replace the power steering gear. Did you complete the repair?	Go to Step 13	--
13	Operate the system in order to verify the repair. Did you correct the condition?	System OK	Go to Step 3

ARM0500000000826

Fig. 1 Power steering fluid leaks (Part 2 of 2)

Step	Action	Yes	No
1	Did you review the Power Steering System General Description and perform the necessary inspections?	Go to Step 2	Go to Symptoms -
2	Verify that a rattle, clunk or shudder noise is present. Is a rattle, clunk or shudder noise present?	Go to Step 3	System OK
3	Inspect the power steering hoses for proper routing and clearance. Is the routing or clearance of the power steering hoses incorrect?	Go to Step 12	Go to Step 4
4	Inspect the engine drive belt for cracking or excessive wear. Is the drive belt cracked or excessively worn?	Go to Step 13	Go to Step 5
5	Inspect the power steering pump pulley for damage. Is the power steering pump pulley damaged?	Go to Step 14	Go to Step 6
6	Inspect the power steering pump and the power steering mounting bracket/brace for the proper installation. Is the power steering pump installation incorrect?	Go to Step 15	Go to Step 7
7	Inspect the power steering gear for the proper installation. Is the power steering gear installation incorrect?	Go to Step 16	Go to Step 8
8	Inspect the steering gear bearing preload for the proper adjustment. Is the steering gear bearing preload adjustment incorrect?	Go to Step 17	Go to Step 9
9	Inspect the steering linkage. Is the steering linkage worn?	Go to Step 18	Go to Step 10
10	Inspect the suspension. Is the suspension worn?	Go to Step 19	Go to Step 11
11	Inspect the intermediate shaft. Is the intermediate shaft worn?	Go to Step 20	Go to Step 3

ARM0500000000827

Fig. 2 Rattle, clunk or shudder noise from power steering system (Part 1 of 2)

ible link must also be installed.
4. If the voltage drop on circuit No. 2 is less than 1 volt and the system voltage parameter is above 16 volts proceed as follows:
   a. Replace the regulator.
   b. Install regulator GM P/N 25854910.
   c. Install pigtail connector GM P/N 89046837 for this regulator.
5. Install like wire colors of the pigtail to the harness.
6. Seal splice to avoid water intrusion.

Step	Action	Yes	No
12	Adjust or replace the hoses. Did you complete the repair?	Go to Step 21	--
13	Replace the engine drive belt. Did you complete the repair?	Go to Step 21	--
14	Replace the power steering pump pulley. Did you complete the repair?	Go to Step 21	--
15	Install the power steering pump correctly. Did you complete the repair?	Go to Step 21	--
16	Install the power steering gear correctly. Did you complete the repair?	Go to Step 21	--
17	Adjust the steering gear bearing preload. Did you complete the repair?	Go to Step 21	--
18	Replace the worn steering linkage. Did you complete the repair?	Go to Step 21	--
19	Replace the worn suspension components. Did you complete the repair?	Go to Step 21	--
20	Replace the intermediate shaft. Did you complete the repair?	Go to Step 21	--
21	Operate the system in order to verify the repair. Did you correct the condition?	System OK	Go to Step 3

ARM0500000000828

Fig. 2   Rattle, clunk or shudder noise from power steering system (Part 2 of 2)

Step	Action	Yes	No
1	Did you review the Power Steering System General Description and perform the necessary inspections?	Go to Step 2	Go to Symptoms
2	Verify that the steering effort is hard in one or both directions. Does the system operate normally?	System OK	Go to Step 3
3	Perform the power steering test procedure. Did you complete the procedure?	Go to Step 4	--
4	Operate the system in order to verify the repair. Did you correct the condition?	System OK	Go to Step 3

ARM0500000000830

Fig. 4   Steering effort hard or too easy in both directions

Step	Action	Yes	No
1	Did you review the Power Steering System Description and perform the necessary inspections?	Go to Step 2	Go to Symptoms -
2	Verify that a whine or growl noise is present. Is a whine or growl noise present?	Go to Step 3	System OK
3	Perform the power steering test procedure in order to diagnose a hydraulic condition and repair or replace a component. Did you repair or replace a power steering system component?	Go to Step 10	Go to Step 4
4	Using the J 39570 Chassis Ear, inspect the power steering gear for a whine or growl noise. Is the noise present at the power steering gear?	Go to Step 7	Go to Step 5
5	Using the J 39570 , inspect the power steering pump for a whine or growl noise. Is the noise present at the power steering pump?	Go to Step 8	Go to Step 6
6	Using the J 39570 , inspect the power steering hoses for a whine or growl noise. Is the noise present at the power steering hoses?	Go to Step 9	Go to Step 2
7	Replace the power steering gear. Did you complete the repair?	Go to Step 10	--
8	Replace the power steering pump. Did you complete the repair?	Go to Step 10	--
9	Adjust the routing of the power steering hoses. Did you complete the repair?	Go to Step 10	--
10	Operate the system in order to verify the repair. Did you correct the condition?	System OK	Go to Step 3

ARM0500000000829

Fig. 3   Whine or growl noise from power steering system

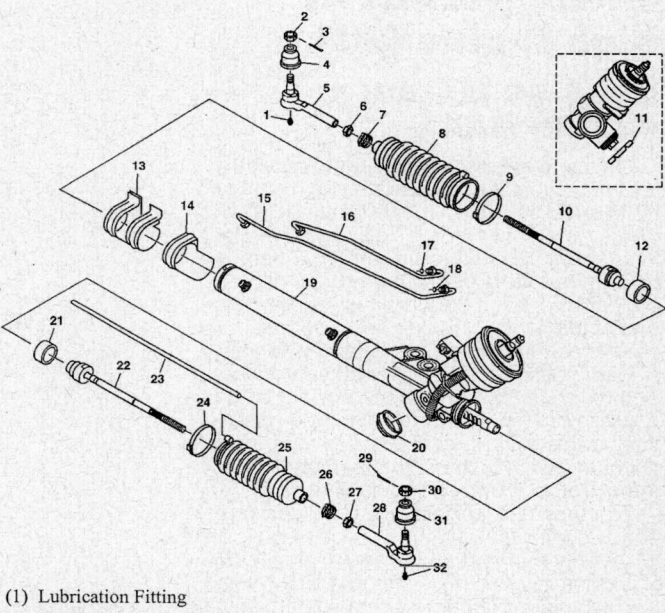

(1) Lubrication Fitting
(2) Hexagon Slotted Nut
(3) Cotter Pin
(4) Tie Rod Seal

ARM0500000000831

Fig. 5   Exploded view of power steering rack & pinion steering (Part 1 of 2). Corvette, DTS, Lucerne & STS

(5) Outer Tie Rod
(6) Hexagon Jam Nut
(7) Tie Rod End Clamp
(8) Rack and Pinion Boot
(9) Large Boot Retaining Clamp
(10) Inner Tie Rod
(11) Adjuster Plug Lock Nut
(12) Shock Dampener Ring
(13) Mounting Bracket Assembly
(14) Mounting Grommet
(15) Cylinder Line (LH)
(16) Cylinder Line (RH)
(17) O-ring Seal
(18) O-ring Seal

(19) Rack and Pinion Gear Assembly (Partial)
(20) Dust Cover
(21) Shock Dampener Ring
(22) Inner Tie Rod
(23) Breather Tube
(24) Large Boot Retaining Clamp
(25) Rack and Pinion Boot
(26) Tie Rod End Clamp
(27) Hexagon Jam Nut
(28) Outer Tie Rod
(29) Cotter Pin
(30) Hexagon Slotted Nut
(31) Tie Rod Seal
(32) Lubrication Fitting

ARM0500000000832

Fig. 5   Exploded view of power steering rack & pinion steering (Part 2 of 2). Corvette, DTS, Lucerne & STS

1 - NUT, HEXAGON SLOTTED
2 - PIN, COTTER
3 - SEAL, TIE ROD
5 - ROD ASM, OUTER TIE
7 - NUT, HEX JAM
8 - CLAMP, TIE ROD END
10 - BOOT, RACK & PINION
11 - CLAMP, BOOT
12 - ROD ASM, INNER TIE
13 - RING, SHOCK DAMPENER
15 - NUT, ADJUSTER PLUG LOCK
16 - ADAPTER, SEAL
17 - RING, RETAINING

20 - SEAL, STUB SHAFT
21 - ANNULUS ASM, BEARING
22 - PLUG ASM, O-RING
23 - SEAL, O-RING
25 - LINE ASM, CYLINDER (RH)
26 - LINE ASM, CYLINDER (LH)
27 - BRACKET ASM, MOUNTING
28 - GROMMET, MOUNTING
30 - GEAR ASM, RACK & PINION (PARTIAL)
32 - NUT, HEX LOCK
33 - COVER, DUST
35 - TUBE, BREATHER

GC6029800386020X

Fig. 6   Exploded view of power rack & pinion steering (Part 2 of 2). DeVille & Seville

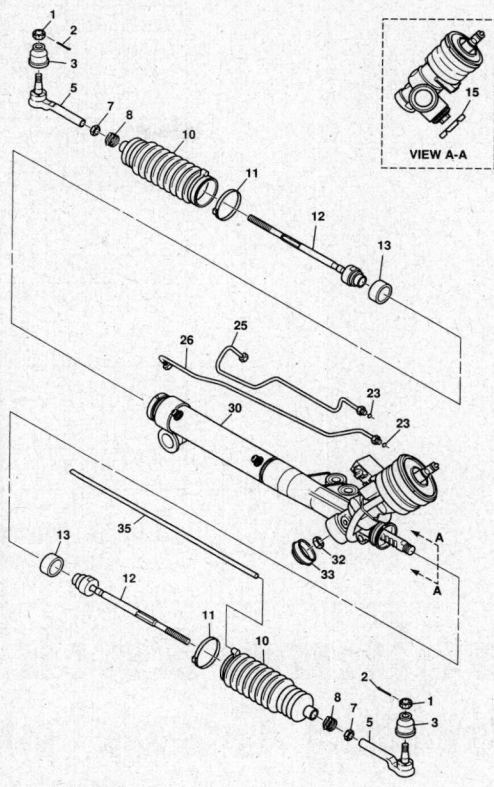

GC6029800386010X

Fig. 6   Exploded view of power rack & pinion steering (Part 1 of 2). DeVille & Seville

1 - NUT, HEX TORQUE PREVAILING
3 - SEAL, TIE ROD
5 - ROD ASM, OUTER TIE
7 - NUT, HEX JAM
8 - CLAMP, TIE ROD END
10 - BOOT, RACK & PINION
11 - CLAMP, BOOT
12 - ROD ASM, INNER TIE
13 - RING, SHOCK DAMPENER
15 - NUT, ADJUSTER PLUG LOCK
16 - ADAPTER, SEAL

17 - RING, RETAINING
20 - SEAL, STUB SHAFT
21 - ANNULUS BEARING ASM
23 - SEAL, O-RING
25 - LINE ASM, CYLINDER (RH)
26 - LINE ASM, CYLINDER (LH)
30 - GEAR ASM, RACK & PINION (PARTIAL)
32 - NUT, HEX LOCK
33 - COVER, DUST
35 - BREATHER TUBE

GC6029800385020X

Fig. 7   Exploded view of power rack & pinion steering (Part 2 of 2). Alero, Bonneville, Century, Grand Prix, LeSabre, Park Avenue, Regal & Grand Am

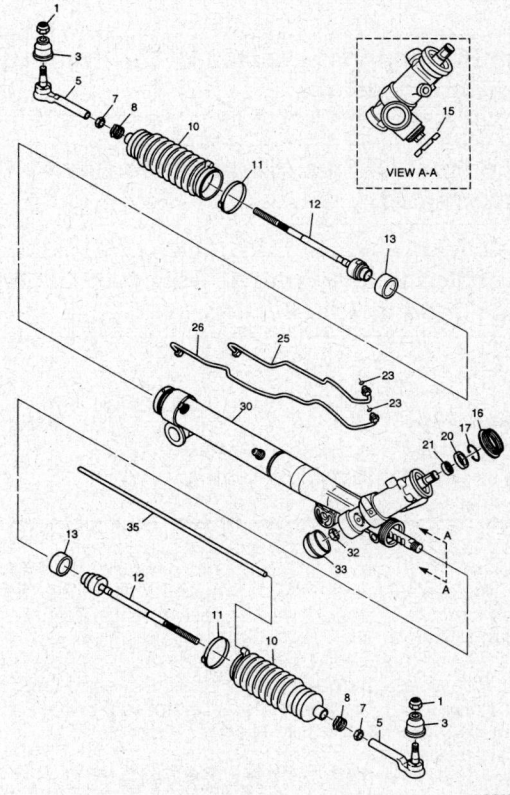

GC6029800385010X

Fig. 7   Exploded view of power rack & pinion steering (Part 1 of 2). Alero, Bonneville, Century, Grand Prix, LeSabre, Park Avenue, Regal & Grand Am

Step	Action	Scan Tool Display
1	1. Connect a scan tool to the data link connector (DLC). 2. Input the vehicle information and select Chassis.	• Delco Bosch ABS/TCS • Magna Steer
2	Select Magna Steer.	• Diagnostics • Recalibration
3	Select Recalibration.	• Magna Steer Recalibration Procedure - Ensure that the ignition is ON and the engine is OFF. • Press ENTER to Start.
4	Press ENTER.	Is the VIN correct?
5	Select YES.	Does the vehicle have Magna Steer RPO # <NV8 ?
6	Select YES.	Is the vehicle equipped with the Gran Touring Package RPO # <Y56 ?
7	Select YES.	Recal with the FACTORY STANDARD calibration
8	Select NO.	Select the calibration: • More firm • Factory calibration • Less firm
9	Select the desired response mode.	• Magna Steer Recalibration Procedure is complete. • Press EXIT in order to return to the menu.
10	Exit the scan tool.	Reprogramming is complete.

GC6029900427000X

Fig. 8   Variable effort steering programming. Bonneville, LeSabre & Park Avenue

Action	Result
1. Install a *Scan Tool*. 2. Input the vehicle information and select Chassis.	• ABS/TCS/ICCS • Magna Steer
Select Magna Steer.	• Diagnostics • Recalibration
Select Recalibration.	Magna Steer Recalibration Procedure - Be sure Ignition is ON Engine OFF Press [ENTER] to Start
Press [ENTER].	Is VIN Correct?
Select YES.	Factory Standard Calibration Will Be Used For This VIN. Press [ENTER] to Start
Press [ENTER].	Magna Steer Recalibration Procedure is complete Press [EXIT] to Return to Menu.
Exit the scan tool.	Reprogramming is complete.

GC6019800016000X

Fig. 9   Variable effort steering programming. Seville

Saginaw Rack & Pinion Power Steering Gear w/Electronic Power Steering

NOTE: On Air Bag Equipped Models, Refer To "Air Bag System Precautions" Located In The Front Of This Manual For System Disarming & Arming Procedures.

NOTE: Refer To "Computer Relearn Procedures" Located In The Front Of This Manual When Battery Power To The Computer Has Been Interrupted.

NOTE: "Electrical Symbol & Wire Color Code Identification" Located In The Front Of This Manual May Be Used As An Aid When Using Wiring Circuits Found In This Section.

INDEX

	Page No.
Description	21-16
Power Steering System Bleed	21-17

	Page No.
Power Steering System Service	21-17
Component Service	21-17

	Page No.
Power Steering Gear	21-17
Troubleshooting	21-16

DESCRIPTION

This Electric Power Steering (EPS) system reduces the effort needed to steer vehicle. This system uses the Body Control Module (BCM), Power Steering Control Module (PSCM), torque sensor, discrete battery voltage supply circuit, EPS motor, class 2 serial data circuit, and the Instrument Panel Cluster (IPC) message center to perform system functions. The PSCM, torque sensor, nor the EPS motor are serviced separately from each other or from steering column. All EPS components diagnosed as faulting requires the steering column assembly to be replaced, also known as EPS assembly.

The PSCM uses a combination of torque sensor inputs, vehicle speed, calculated system temperature and steering calibration to determine amount of steering assist. When steering wheel is turned, the PSCM uses signal voltage from the torque sensor to detect the amount of torque being applied to steering column shaft and amount of current to command to the EPS motor. The PSCM receives a class 2 vehicle speed message from the Engine Control Module (ECM) to determine speed of vehicle. At lower speeds more assist is provided to make parking maneuvers easier. At higher speeds less assist is provided for more improved road feel and stability.

TROUBLESHOOTING

Refer to **Figs. 1 through 4,** for power steering system troubleshooting.

Step	Action	Yes	No
1	Did you review the Power Steering System General Description and perform the necessary inspections?	Go to Step 2	Go to Symptoms
2	Verify that a rattle, clunk or shudder noise is present.		
	Is a rattle, clunk or shudder noise present?	Go to Step 3	System OK
3	Inspect the power steering gear for the proper installation.		
	Is the power steering gear installation incorrect?	Go to Step 6	Go to Step 4
4	Inspect the intermediate shaft.	Go to Step 8	
	Is the intermediate shaft worn?		Go to Step 5
5	Inspect the suspension.	Go to Step 7	Go to Noise Diagnosis - Front Suspension
	Is the suspension worn?		
6	Install the power steering gear correctly.		
	Did you complete the repair?	Go to Step 9	--
7	Replace the worn suspension components.		
	Did you complete the repair?	Go to Step 9	--
8	Replace the intermediate shaft.		
	Did you complete the repair?	Go to Step 9	--
9	Operate the system in order to verify the repair.		
	Did you correct the condition?	System OK	Go to Step 3

ARM0500000000833

Fig. 1   Rattle, clunk or shudder noise form power steering system

Step	Action	Yes	No
6	Check for a worn or binding steering gear.		
	Is the steering worn or binding?	Go to Step 9	System OK
7	Replace the outer tie rod end.		
	Did you complete the repair?	Go to Step 10	--
8	Replace the intermediate shaft.		
	Did you complete the repair?	Go to Step 10	--
9	Replace the steering gear.		
	Did you complete the repair?	Go to Step 10	--
10	Operate the system in order to verify the repair.		
	Did you correct the condition?	System OK	Go to Step 3

ARM0500000000835

Fig. 2   Increase in effort while turning steering wheel (Part 2 of 2)

POWER STEERING SYSTEM SERVICE

Component Service

POWER STEERING GEAR

The power steering gear on these models cannot be disassembled. Refer to the "Front Suspension & Steering" section of the appropriate chassis chapter for power steering gear replacement procedure.

POWER STEERING SYSTEM BLEED

Refer to "Power Steering System Bleed" section in "Power Steering Pumps" for power steering system bleed procedures.

Step	Action	Yes	No
1	Did you review the Power Steering System Description and Operation and perform the necessary inspections?	Go to Step 2	Go to Power Steering System Description and Operation
2	Verify that there is an increase in effort while turning is present.		
	Does the system operate normally?	System OK	Go to Step 3
3	Check for the following tire related conditions:		
	• Incorrect tire inflation		
	• Improper tire size		
	Did you find and correct the condition?	Go to Step 10	Go to Step 4
4	1. Raise and support the vehicle.		
	2. Check for a binding or worn tie rod end.		
	Is the tie rod binding or worn?	Go to Step 7	Go to Step 5
5	Check for a worn or binding intermediate shaft.		
	Is the intermediate shaft worn or binding?	Go to Step 8	Go to Step 6

ARM0500000000834

Fig. 2   Increase in effort while turning steering wheel (Part 1 of 2)

Step	Action	Yes	No
1	Did you review the Power Steering System Description and Operation and perform the necessary inspections?	Go to Step 2	Go to Power Steering System Description and Operation
2	Verify a poor return of the steering wheel is present.		
	Does the system operate normally?	System OK	Go to Step 3
3	Check for incorrect tire inflation.		
	Did you find and correct the condition?	Go to Step 11	Go to Step 4
4	1. Raise and support the vehicle.		
	2. Check for a binding or worn tie rod end.		
	Is the tie rod binding or worn?	Go to Step 8	Go to Step 5
5	Check for a worn or binding intermediate shaft.		
	Is the intermediate shaft worn or binding?	Go to Step 9	Go to Step 6

ARM0500000000836

Fig. 3   Poor return of steering wheel (Part 1 of 2)

Step	Action	Yes	No
6	Check for worn a or binding ball joint.		
	Are the ball joints worn or binding?	Go to Step 10	Go to Step 7
7	Check for proper alignment of the front suspension.		
	Did you complete the wheel alignment?	Go to Step 11	--
8	Replace the outer tie rod end.		
	Did you complete the repair?	Go to Step 11	--
9	Replace the intermediate Shaft.		
	Did you complete the repair?	Go to Step 11	--
10	Replace the ball joint.		
	Did you complete the repair?	Go to Step 11	--
11	Operate the system in order to verify the repair.		
	Did you correct the condition?	System OK	Go to Step 3

ARM0500000000837

Fig. 3   Poor return of steering wheel (Part 2 of 2)

Step	Action	Yes	No
1	Did you review the Power Steering System Description and Operation and perform the necessary inspections?	Go to Step 2	Go to Power Steering System Description and Operation
2	Verify that the steering wheel surges/jerks while turning. Does the system operate normally?	System OK	Go to Step 3
3	Check for worn or binding front suspension components. Did you find and correct the condition?	Go to Step 15	Go to Step 4
4	1. Raise and support the vehicle. 2. Check for a binding or worn tie rod end. Is the tie rod binding or worn?	Go to Step 11	Go to Step 5
5	Check for a worn or binding intermediate shaft. Is the intermediate shaft worn or binding?	Go to Step 12	Go to Step 6
6	Check for worn a binding steering gear. Is the steering gear worn or binding?	Go to Step 13	Go to Step 7

ARM0500000000838

Fig. 4   Steering wheel surges/jerks while turning (Part 1 of 2)

Step	Action	Yes	No
7	Check for a worn or binding steering column. Is the steering column worn or binding?	Go to Step 14	Go to Step 8
8	Check for excessive heat in the EPS motor. Does the EPS appear to be overheated?	Go to Step 09	Go to Step 10
9	**Important** • Do not perform excessive parking lot maneuvers during testing. • Excessive parking lot maneuvers can cause the EPS motor to heat up. Allow the EPS motor to cool and retest the system. Did you find and correct the condition?	Go to Step 15	Go to Step 10
10	Check for low battery voltage. Did you find and correct the condition?	Go to Step 15	System OK
11	Replace the outer tie rod end. Did you complete the repair?	Go to Step 15	--
12	Replace the intermediate Shaft. Did you complete the repair?	Go to Step 15	--
13	Replace the steering gear. Did you complete the repair?	Go to Step 15	--
14	Replace the steering column. Did you complete the repair?	Go to Step 15	--
15	Operate the system in order to verify the repair. Did you correct the condition?	System OK	Go to Step 3

ARM0500000000839

Fig. 4   Steering wheel surges/jerks while turning (Part 2 of 2)

Saginaw Rotary Valve Power Steering Gear

NOTE: On Air Bag Equipped Models, Refer To "Air Bag System Precautions" Located In The Front Of This Manual For System Disarming & Arming Procedures.

NOTE: Refer To "Computer Relearn Procedures" Located In The Front Of This Manual When Battery Power To The Computer Has Been Interrupted.

NOTE: "Electrical Symbol & Wire Color Code Identification" Located In The Front Of This Manual May Be Used As An Aid When Using Wiring Circuits Found In This Section.

INDEX

	Page No.		Page No.		Page No.
Description	21-19	Component Service	21-19	Module	21-19
Power Steering System Bleed	21-19	Power Steering Control		Tightening Specifications	21-20
Power Steering System Service	21-19				

DESCRIPTION

The Saginaw rotary valve steering gear incorporates a recirculating ball system in which steel balls act as a rolling thread between a steering worm shaft and the rack piston.

Variable Effort Steering (VES) or Speed Sensitive Steering (SSS) is a power steering system varies the steering effort required to steer the vehicle at different speeds. At low speeds, the system provides maximum power assist. At higher speeds, increased steering effort will provide firmer steering (road feel) and direction stability. The power steering control module uses speed input from the Electronic Braking Traction Control Module (EBTCM) to control the power steering fluid flow control valve actuator. The power steering fluid flow control valve actuator utilizes a pintle valve to control fluid flow to the steering gear.

GC6029800368000X

Fig. 1   Sound insulator self-locking screws location

POWER STEERING SYSTEM SERVICE

Component Service

POWER STEERING CONTROL MODULE

1. Twist self-locking screws to allow front of sound insulator to drop, **Fig. 1.**
2. Remove sound insulator.
3. Disconnect control module electrical connectors, **Fig. 2.**
4. Remove power steering control module.
5. Reverse procedure to install.

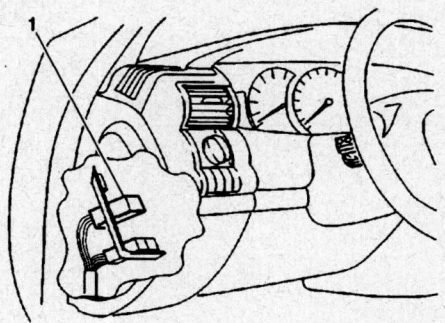

GC6029800369000X

Fig. 2   Power steering control module location

POWER STEERING SYSTEM BLEED

Refer to "Power Steering System Bleed" section in "Power Steering Pumps" for power steering system bleed procedures.

TIGHTENING SPECIFICATIONS

Year	Component	Torque Ft. Lbs.
2004–08	Ball Stud	44①
	Flow Control Valve Actuator	27②
	Idler Arm	44
	Steering Gear	30
	Steering Gear Coupler	16
	Tie Rod Adjuster Clamp	11

① — Tighten an additional 52°.
② — Inch lbs.

Toyota Rack & Pinion Power Steering Gear

NOTE: On Air Bag Equipped Models, Refer To "Air Bag System Precautions" Located In The Front Of This Manual For System Disarming & Arming Procedures.

NOTE: Refer To "Computer Relearn Procedures" Located In The Front Of This Manual When Battery Power To The Computer Has Been Interrupted.

INDEX

	Page No.		Page No.		Page No.
Description	21-21	Power Steering System Service	21-21	Steering Gear	21-21
Power Steering System Bleed	21-21	Component Service	21-21	Tightening Specifications	21-22
Standard Bleeding	21-21				

DESCRIPTION

This steering system converts rotary motion to linear motion as follows: when the steering wheel is turned, rotary motion is transferred to the steering shaft, the shaft joint and rack pinion. The pinion teeth mesh with teeth on the rack and the rotary motion is transferred to the rack and changed to linear motion. The linear force is then transmitted through the tie rods to the steering knuckles which steer the front wheels.

POWER STEERING SYSTEM SERVICE

Component Service

STEERING GEAR

DISASSEMBLE

The power steering gear on these models cannot be disassembled. Power steering rack cannot be disassembled. Refer to "Front Suspension & Steering" sections in the appropriate chassis chapter for power steering gear replacement.

POWER STEERING SYSTEM BLEED

STANDARD BLEEDING

Notice: If the power steering system has been serviced, an accurate fluid level reading cannot be obtained unless air is bled from the steering system. The air in the fluid may cause pump cavitation noise and may cause pump damage over a period of time.

1. Remove power steering pump reservoir cap.
2. Fill power steering fluid reservoir to "COLD MIN" mark.
3. Raise vehicle until front wheels are off the ground.
4. Turn ignition switch to ON position with engine OFF.
5. Rotate steering wheel from full left to full right 10 to 12 times.
6. Verify fluid level is correct, add fluid level if necessary.
7. Start engine, allow engine to idle.
8. Listen for power steering pump noise like whining or cavitation.
9. Inspect power steering fluid for aeration.
10. Verify fluid level is correct.
11. Repeat bleeding procedure if necessary.
12. Turn engine off, lower the vehicle.

TIGHTENING SPECIFICATIONS

Year	Component	Torque Ft. Lbs.
2004–08	Power Steering Gear Bolt, 2WD	48
	Power Steering Gear Bolt, AWD	61
	Power Steering Pipe Bracket Bolt	69①
	Power Steering Pressure Switch	16
	Power Steering Pump Housing Bolts	16
	Power Steering Pump Inlet Tube Bolt	106①
	Power Steering Pump Nuts and Bolts	27
	Power Steering Pump Fitting	51
	Power Steering Pump Fitting	30
	Power Steering Pump Rear Bracket Bolt	27
	Power Steering Return Pipe Nut	17
	Steering Column Intermediate Shaft Bolt	26
	Tie Rod End Nut, Outer	36
	Tie Rod Lock Nut	55

① — Inch lbs.

DISC BRAKES

NOTE: Refer To "Application Chart" To Determine Which Type Brakes Are Used On Vehicle Being Serviced.

TABLE OF CONTENTS

	Page No.		Page No.
AC-DELCO DUAL PISTON FRONT DISC BRAKE	22-3	**PBR DUAL PISTON FRONT DISC BRAKE**	22-12
AC-DELCO SINGLE PISTON FRONT DISC BRAKE	22-7	**PBR SINGLE PISTON REAR DISC BRAKE**	22-21
AC-DELCO SINGLE PISTON REAR DISC BRAKE	22-15	**SATURN/GM SINGLE PISTON**	22-25
APPLICATION CHART	22-1	**TOYOTA/GM SINGLE PISTON CALIPER**	22-32

Application Chart

Model	Year	Front/Rear Brakes	Application
BUICK			
Century	2004–05	Front	AC Delco Single Piston
		Rear	AC Delco Single Piston
LaCrosse	2005–08	Front	AC Delco Single Piston
		Rear	AC Delco Single Piston
LeSabre	2004–05	Front	AC Delco Single Piston
Lucerne	2006–08	Front	AC Delco Dual Piston
		Rear	AC Delco Single Piston
Park Avenue	2004–05	Front	AC Delco Single Piston
		Rear	AC Delco Single Piston
Regal	2004	Front	AC Delco Single Piston
		Rear	AC Delco Single Piston
CADILLAC			
CTS	2004–08	Front	AC Delco Dual Piston
		Rear	AC Delco Single Piston
DeVille	2004–05	Front	AC Delco Single Piston
		Rear	AC Delco Single Piston
DTS	2006–08	Front	A/C Delco Dual Piston
		Rear	A/C Delco Single Piston
Seville	2004	Front	AC Delco Single Piston
		Rear	AC Delco Single Piston
STS	2005–08	Front	A/C Delco Dual Piston
		Rear	A/C Delco Single Piston
XLR	2004–08	Front	PBR Dual Piston
		Rear	PBR Single Piston
CHEVROLET			
Aveo	2005–08	Front	A/C Delco Single Piston
Cavalier	2004–05	Front	AC Delco Single Piston
Cobalt	2005–08	Front	Saturn/GM Single Piston
		Rear	Saturn/GM Single Piston
Corvette	2004–08	Front	PBR Dual Piston
		Rear	PBR Single Piston
Impala	2004–08	Front	AC Delco Single Piston
		Rear	AC Delco Single Piston

Continued

DISC BRAKES

Model	Year	Front/Rear Brakes	Application
CHEVROLET			
Malibu	2004–07	Front	AC Delco Single Piston
	2004–07	Rear	AC Delco Single Piston
Malibu Classic	2008	Front	AC Delco Single Piston
	2008	Rear	AC Delco Single Piston
Malibu Maxx	2004–07	Front	AC Delco Single Piston
	2004–07	Rear	AC Delco Single Piston
Monte Carlo	2004–07	Front	AC Delco Single Piston
		Rear	AC Delco Single Piston
OLDSMOBILE			
Alero	2004	Front	AC Delco Single Piston
		Rear	AC Delco Single Piston
PONTIAC			
Bonneville	2004–05	Front	AC Delco Single Piston
Grand Am	2004–05	Front	AC Delco Single Piston
		Rear	AC Delco Single Piston
Grand Prix	2004–08	Front	AC Delco Single Piston
		Rear	AC Delco Single Piston
GTO	2004–06	Front	A/C Delco Dual Piston
		Rear	A/C Delco Single Piston
G5	2007–08	Front	Saturn/GM Single Piston
	2007–08	Rear	Saturn/GM Single Piston
G6	2005–08	Front	A/C Delco Single Piston
		Rear	A/C Delco Single Piston
Solstice	2006–08	Front	Saturn/GM Single Piston
		Rear	Saturn/GM Single Piston
Sunfire	2004–05	Front	AC Delco Single Piston
Vibe	2004–08	Front	Toyota/GM Single Piston
		Rear	Toyota/GM Single Piston
SATURN			
AURA	2007–08	Front	Saturn/GM Single Piston
	2007–08	Rear	Saturn/GM Single Piston
ION	2004–07	Front	Saturn/GM Single Piston
	2004–07	Rear	Saturn/GM Single Piston
L-Series	2004–05	Front	Saturn/GM Single Piston
		Rear	Saturn/GM Single Piston
SKY	2007–08	Front	Saturn/GM Single Piston
	2007–08	Rear	Saturn/GM Single Piston

AC-Delco Dual Piston Front Disc Brake

NOTE: On Air Bag Equipped Models, Refer To "Air Bag System Precautions" Located In The Front Of This Manual For System Disarming & Arming Procedures.

NOTE: Refer To "Computer Relearn Procedures" Located In The Front Of This Manual When Battery Power To The Computer Has Been Interrupted.

INDEX

	Page No.		Page No.		Page No.
Brake Pad Service	22-3	Mounting Bracket Service	22-4	Rotor Specifications	22-5
Brake System Bleed	22-3	Bushing & Boot Replacement	22-4	Precautions	22-3
Caliper Service	22-3	Installation	22-4	Rotor, Replace	22-4
Assemble	22-4	Removal	22-4	Tightening Specifications	22-6
Disassemble	22-3	Removal	22-3	Troubleshooting	22-3
Inspection	22-4	Description	22-3		
Installation	22-4	Disc Brake Specifications	22-5		

PRECAUTIONS

1. Keep grease and other foreign material off brake linings, caliper, surfaces of disc and external surfaces of hub.
2. Avoid deforming disc, and nicking or scratching brake linings.
3. Worn or damaged rubber piston seals should be replaced.
4. During removal and installation of a wheel assembly, ensure not to interfere with or damage caliper splash shield, or bleeder screw.
5. Front wheel bearings preload should be adjusted to specifications.
6. Ensure vehicle is centered on hoist before servicing any front end components to avoid bending or damaging disc splash shield on full left or right-hand wheel turns.
7. Before vehicle is moved after any brake service work, obtain a firm brake pedal.
8. Assembly bolts of two-piece caliper housings should not be disturbed unless caliper requires service.

DESCRIPTION

The dual piston sliding caliper is comprised of two interconnected bores and is attached to a mounting bracket with two mounting bolts, **Fig. 1.** Hydraulic pressure acting on the bottom of the caliper bores forces the pistons outward, enabling the caliper to slide inward, thereby clamping the brake shoes against the rotor.

TROUBLESHOOTING

The most common cause of brake chatter on disc brakes is a variation in disc thickness. If roughness or vibration is encountered during highway operation or if pedal pulsation is experienced at low speeds, the disc may have excessive thickness variation. To inspect for this condition, measure the disc at 12 points with a micrometer at a radius approximately one inch from edge of disc. If thickness measurements vary by more than .0005 inch, the disc should be replaced with a new one.

Excessive lateral runout of braking disc may cause a piston knocking back, possibly creating increased pedal travel and vibration when brakes are applied.

Before inspecting the runout, the wheel bearings should be adjusted. The adjustment is very important and will be required at the completion of the test to prevent bearing failure. Adjust the wheel bearings as outlined in "Front Suspension & Steering" section of appropriate chassis chapter.

BRAKE SYSTEM BLEED

Refer to "Hydraulic Brake Systems" for manual and pressure bleeding procedures.

BRAKE PAD SERVICE

1. Drain master cylinder fluid level to ⅓ full.
2. Raise and support vehicle, then remove front tire and wheel assemblies.
3. Mark wheel to hub and bearing relationship for installation alignment.
4. Push pistons back together into caliper bores using suitable C-clamp and block of wood.
5. **Do not disconnect brake line fitting from caliper.**
6. Remove two mounting bolts and caliper, then suspend caliper from chassis. **Do not allow caliper to hang by brake hose.**
7. Lift upward on outward retaining spring until it clears center lug and remove shoe.
8. Pull inboard shoe outward to disengage retainer springs from pistons and remove inboard shoe.
9. Reverse procedure to install, noting the following:
   a. Install inboard shoe into caliper. Ensure retainer spring tangs are fully positioned into pistons.
   b. Snap outboard shoe retaining spring over housing center lug and install outboard shoe into caliper.

CALIPER SERVICE

Removal

1. Drain master cylinder fluid level to ⅓ full.
2. Raise and support vehicle, then remove front tire and wheel assemblies.
3. Mark wheel to hub and bearing relationship for installation alignment.
4. Push pistons back together into caliper bores using suitable C-clamp and block of wood.
5. Remove mounting bolt, copper washer and inlet fitting. Plug opening in inlet fitting. **Do not crimp brake hose.**
6. Remove two mounting bolts and caliper.

Disassemble

1. Position shop towel in interior component of caliper, then slowly apply compressed air to inlet port and remove pistons. **One piston must be partially installed to facilitate removal of second piston. Pad or wooden spacer may be used to prevent complete removal of first piston.**

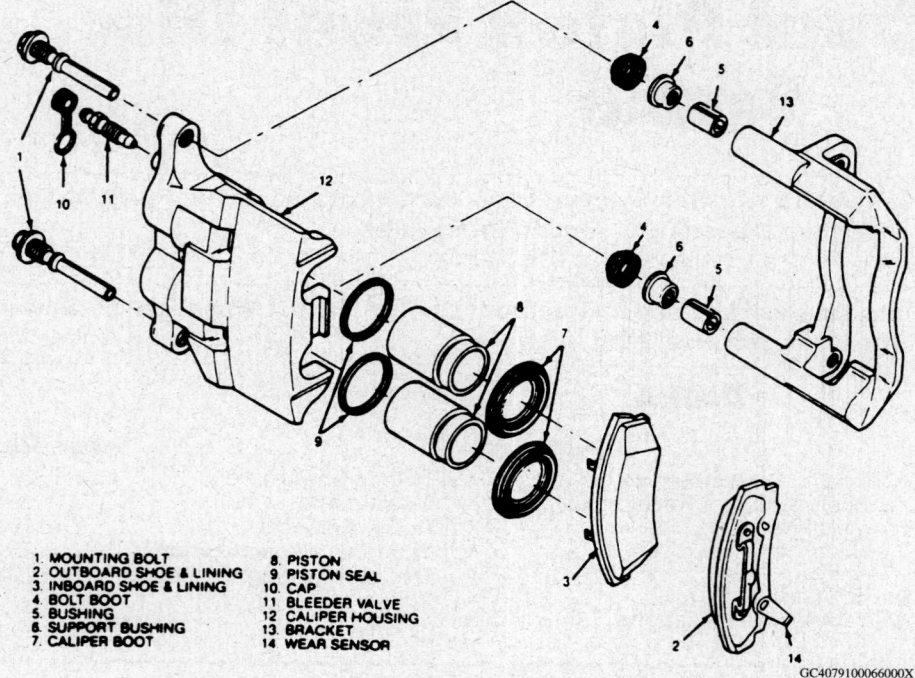

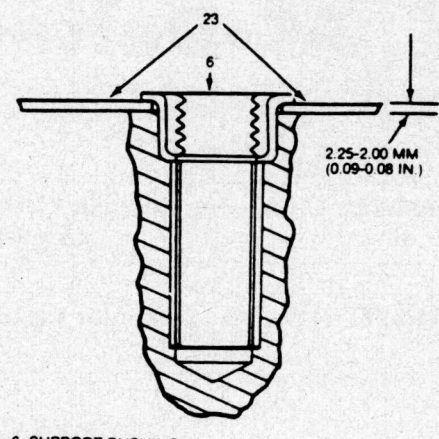

6. SUPPORT BUSHING
23. SHIM STOCK

GC4079100067000X

Fig. 2 Support bushing installation

1. MOUNTING BOLT
2. OUTBOARD SHOE & LINING
3. INBOARD SHOE & LINING
4. BOLT BOOT
5. BUSHING
6. SUPPORT BUSHING
7. CALIPER BOOT
8. PISTON
9. PISTON SEAL
10. CAP
11. BLEEDER VALVE
12. CALIPER HOUSING
13. BRACKET
14. WEAR SENSOR

GC4079100066000X

Fig. 1 Exploded view of dual piston caliper

2. Remove piston boots from caliper bores, then pry piston seals from caliper bore grooves using suitable wooden or plastic tool. **Do not use metal tool to remove seal.**
3. Remove bleeder valve from caliper.

Inspection

1. Inspect piston for scoring, nicks, corrosion, and wear.
2. Inspect caliper housing and seal grooves for corrosion, nicks, scoring and excessive wear. Use crocus cloth to polish away corrosion from housing bore.
3. Clean all components with denatured alcohol and dry with compressed air.
4. Blow out all passages in housing and bleeder valve.

Mounting Bracket Service

REMOVAL

1. Drain master cylinder fluid level to ⅓ full.
2. Raise and support vehicle, then remove front tire and wheel assemblies.
3. Mark wheel to hub and bearing relationship for installation alignment.
4. Push pistons back together into caliper bores using suitable C-clamp and block of wood.
5. Remove mounting bolt, copper washer and inlet fitting. Plug opening in inlet fit-

ting. **Do not crimp brake hose.**
6. Remove two mounting bolts and caliper.
7. Remove mounting bolts and mounting bracket.

BUSHING & BOOT REPLACEMENT

1. Remove bolt boots from support bushings.
2. Clamp bracket in suitable vise and pry support bushings from inner bushings in bracket ears with small screwdriver.
3. Pull inner bushings from mounting bracket ears using paper clip.
4. Lubricate inner bushings with silicone based grease and install bushings flush with bracket ears.
5. Position an .080–.090 inch thick shim stock on bracket ear face and drive support bushings into inner bushings, **Fig. 2.** Bushing should protrude .080–.090 inch above bracket ear face.
6. Snap new bolt boots over support bushing lip.

INSTALLATION

1. Coat mounting bracket mounting bolt threads with suitable Loctite sealant, or equivalent.
2. Align holes and install mounting bracket.

Assemble

1. Install bleeder valve.
2. Lubricate piston seals with clean brake

fluid, then carefully install seals into caliper bore grooves. **Ensure seals are not twisted.**
3. Lubricate boots and install onto pistons, then push pistons fully into caliper bores.
4. Seat boots into caliper bores using boot seal installer tool No. J-36349, or equivalent.

Installation

1. Position caliper over rotor and onto mounting bracket.
2. Lubricate entire length of with silicone based grease and install mounting bolts.
3. Install fitting using new copper washer.
4. Install front wheels, fill master cylinder to proper level, and bleed brake.
5. Pump brake pedal several times to ensure it is firm. **Do not move vehicle until firm pedal is obtained.**

ROTOR
REPLACE

1. Raise and support vehicle, then remove tire and wheel assembly.
2. Drain master cylinder fluid level to ⅓ full.
3. Raise and support vehicle, then remove front tire and wheel assemblies.
4. Mark wheel to hub and bearing relationship for installation alignment.
5. Push pistons back together into caliper bores using suitable C-clamp and block of wood.
6. Remove mounting bolt, copper washer and inlet fitting. Plug opening in inlet fitting. **Do not crimp brake hose.**
7. Remove two mounting bolts and caliper.
8. Remove rotor from hub and bearing.
9. Reverse procedure to install.

DISC BRAKE SPECIFICATIONS
Rotor Specifications

Model	Year	Brake Lining Wear Limit, Inch	Nominal Thickness, Inch	Minimum Refinish Thickness, Inch	Discard Limit, Inch①	Thickness Variation Parallelism, Inch	Lateral Run Out (T.I.R.), Inch	Maximum Scoring Depth, Inch
CTS	2004–07	.0390	1.2670	1.2090	1.2090	.0010	.0020	.0590
	2008	.0390	1.1810	1.1220	1.1220	.0010	.0020	.0059
DTS	2006–08	.0300	1.4960	1.4570	1.4170	.0010	.0020	.0590
GTO	2004	.0790	—	.9840	.9840	.0002	.0020	.0160
	2005–06	.0790	—	1.181	1.181	.0002	.0020	.0160
Lucerne	2006–08	.0300	1.1810	1.1260	1.1260	.0010	.0020	.0590
STS	2005–08	.0390	1.2670	1.2090	1.2090	.0010	.0020	.0590

① — Discard thickness is stamped on rotor.

DISC BRAKES

TIGHTENING SPECIFICATIONS

Year	Component	Torque Ft. Lbs.
CTS		
2004–07	Bleeder Valve	124①
	Caliper Bracket	96
	Caliper Pin	46
	Hose	37
	Pipe Fitting Tube	13
	Rotor	124①
2008	Caliper Bracket	166
	Caliper Pin (Less Heavy Duty)	20③
	Hose	36
	Rotor	89①
DTS		
2006–08	Bleeder Valve	115①
	Caliper Bracket	133④
	Caliper Pin	27⑤
	Hose	30
	Pipe Fitting Tube	13
	Rotor	106①
GTO		
2004–06	Brake Caliper Bolt	63②
	Caliper Pin	24
	Hose	26
	Pipe Fitting Tube	12

TIGHTENING SPECIFICATIONS—Continued

Year	Component	Torque Ft. Lbs.
LUCERNE		
2006–08	Brake Caliper Bracket Bolt	133
	Brake Caliper Pin Bolt	27
	Brake Hose to Caliper Bolt	30
	Brake Rotor Mounting Screw	106①
	Brake Caliper Bleeder Valve	115①
STS		
2006–08	Bleeder Valve	124①
	Caliper Bracket	96
	Caliper Pin	46
	Hose	37
	Pipe Fitting Tube	13
	Rotor	124①

① — Inch lbs.

② — Then an additional 45°.

③ — Heavy Duty, 48 ft. lbs.

④ — Heavy Duty, 181 ft. lbs.

⑤ — Heavy Duty, 83 ft. lbs.

AC-DELCO DUAL PISTON FRONT DISC BRAKE

AC-Delco Single Piston Front Disc Brake

NOTE: On Air Bag Equipped Models, Refer To "Air Bag System Precautions" Located In The Front Of This Manual For System Disarming & Arming Procedures.

NOTE: Refer To "Computer Relearn Procedures" Located In The Front Of This Manual When Battery Power To The Computer Has Been Interrupted.

INDEX

	Page No.		Page No.		Page No.
Brake Pad Service	22-7	Inspection	22-8	Rotor Specifications	22-10
Brake System Bleed	22-7	Replacement	22-7	Precautions	22-7
Caliper Service	22-7	**Description**	22-7	Rotor, Replace	22-8
Assemble	22-8	**Disc Brake Specifications**	22-10	Tightening Specifications	22-11
Disassemble	22-7	Caliper Specifications	22-10	Troubleshooting	22-7

PRECAUTIONS

1. Keep grease and other foreign material off brake linings, caliper, surfaces of disc and external surfaces of hub.
2. Avoid deforming disc, and nicking or scratching brake linings.
3. Worn or damaged rubber piston seals should be replaced.
4. During removal and installation of a wheel assembly, ensure not to interfere with or damage caliper splash shield, or bleeder screw.
5. Front wheel bearing preload should be adjusted to specifications.
6. Ensure vehicle is centered on hoist before servicing any front end components to avoid bending or damaging disc splash shield on full left or right-hand wheel turns.
7. Before vehicle is moved after any brake service work, ensure to obtain a firm brake pedal.
8. Assembly bolts of two-piece caliper housings should not be disturbed unless caliper requires service.

DESCRIPTION

The caliper has a single piston and is mounted to the support bracket by two mounting bolts, **Figs. 1 through 3.** The caliper assembly slides on the two mounting bolts. Upon brake application, fluid pressure against the piston forces the inboard shoe and lining assembly against the inboard side of the disc. This action causes the caliper assembly to slide until the outboard lining comes into contact with the disc. As pressure builds up the linings are pressed against the disc with increased force.

TROUBLESHOOTING

The most common cause of brake chatter on disc brakes is a variation in disc thickness. If roughness or vibration is encountered during highway operation or if pedal pulsation is experienced at low speeds, the disc may have excessive thickness variation. To inspect for this condition, measure the disc at 12 points with a micrometer at a radius approximately one inch from edge of disc. If thickness measurements vary by more than .0005 inch, the disc should be replaced with a new one.

Excessive lateral runout of braking disc may cause a piston knocking back, possibly creating increased pedal travel and vibration when brakes are applied.

Before inspecting the runout, the wheel bearings should be adjusted. The adjustment is very important and will be required at the completion of the test to prevent bearing failure. Adjust the wheel bearings as outlined in "Front Suspension & Steering" section of appropriate chassis chapter.

BRAKE SYSTEM BLEED

Refer to "Hydraulic Brake Systems" for manual and pressure bleeding procedures.

BRAKE PAD SERVICE

1. Remove approximately ⅔ of brake fluid from master cylinder.
2. Raise and support front of vehicle, then remove wheel and tire assembly.
3. Push piston back into caliper bore using suitable C-clamp, **Fig. 4.**
4. **Do not disconnect brake line fitting from caliper.**
5. Remove mounting bolts and caliper, then support aside, **Fig. 5. Do not allow caliper to hang from brake hose.** If there signs of corrosion, replace bolts when installing caliper.
6. Remove brake pads and pad retainers from caliper bracket.
7. Reverse procedure to install.

CALIPER SERVICE
Replacement

1. Remove approximately ⅔ of brake fluid from master cylinder.
2. Raise and support front of vehicle, then remove wheel and tire assembly.
3. Push piston back into caliper bore using suitable C-clamp, **Fig. 4.**
4. Remove inlet fitting mounting bolt, copper washer and inlet fitting from caliper housing. Plug opening in inlet fitting. **Do not crimp brake hose.**
5. Remove caliper mounting bolts and caliper, **Fig. 5.** If there are signs of corrosion, replace bolts when installing caliper assembly.
6. Reverse procedure to install.

Disassemble

1. Clean outside of caliper, then drain brake fluid from caliper into suitable container.
2. Place clean shop towels to pad caliper interior and remove piston by directing compressed air into caliper brake hose inlet hole, **Fig. 6.** Use just enough air pressure to ease piston out of bore. **Do not place fingers in front of piston.**
3. Remove dust boot from caliper bore using suitable screwdriver, **Fig. 7.**
4. Remove piston seal from bore using small piece of wood or plastic, **Do not use metal tool to remove seal.**
5. Remove bleeder valve.

Inspection

1. Inspect piston for scoring, nicks, corrosion, and wear and replace as needed.
2. Inspect caliper housing and seal groove for corrosion, nicks, scoring and excessive wear, then use crocus cloth to polish away corrosion from housing bore.
3. Clean all components with denatured alcohol and dry with compressed air.
4. Blow out all passages in housing and bleeder valve.

Assemble

1. Install bleeder valve.
2. Install piston seal and dust boot. Ensure to properly seat dust boot using installer tool No. J-36349, or equivalent, **Fig. 8.**
3. Install piston.

ROTOR

REPLACE

1. Remove approximately ⅔ of brake fluid from master cylinder.
2. Raise and support front of vehicle, then remove wheel and tire assembly.
3. Push piston back into caliper bore using suitable C-clamp, **Fig. 4.**
4. **Do not disconnect brake line fitting from caliper.**
5. Remove mounting bolts and caliper, then support caliper aside, **Fig. 5. Do not allow caliper to hang from brake hose.** If there signs of corrosion, replace bolts when installing caliper.
6. Remove mounting bolts and mounting bracket.
7. Remove rotor from hub and bearing.
8. Reverse procedure to install.

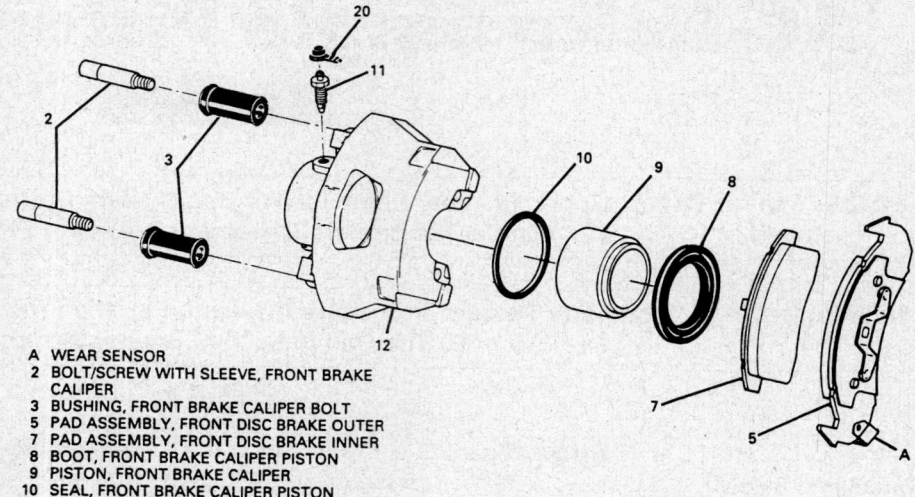

A WEAR SENSOR
2 BOLT/SCREW WITH SLEEVE, FRONT BRAKE CALIPER
3 BUSHING, FRONT BRAKE CALIPER BOLT
5 PAD ASSEMBLY, FRONT DISC BRAKE OUTER
7 PAD ASSEMBLY, FRONT DISC BRAKE INNER
8 BOOT, FRONT BRAKE CALIPER PISTON
9 PISTON, FRONT BRAKE CALIPER
10 SEAL, FRONT BRAKE CALIPER PISTON
11 VALVE, FRONT BRAKE CALIPER BLEEDER

12 HOUSING, FRONT BRAKE CALIPER
20 CAP, FRONT BRAKE CALIPER BLEEDER VALVE

GC4079100054000X

Fig. 1 Exploded view of caliper. Alero, Cavalier, Grand Am & Sunfire

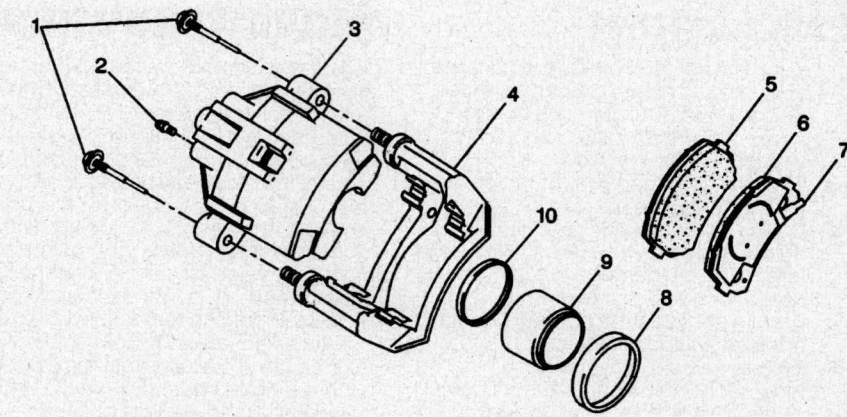

(1) Caliper Bolts
(2) Bleeder Valve
(3) Caliper Housing
(4) Caliper Bracket
(5) Inboard Pad

(6) Outboard Pad
(7) Wear Sensor
(8) Caliper Boot
(9) Piston
(10) Piston Seal

GC4079700137000X

Fig. 2 Exploded view of caliper. Century, DeVille, Grand Prix, LeSabre, Regal & Seville

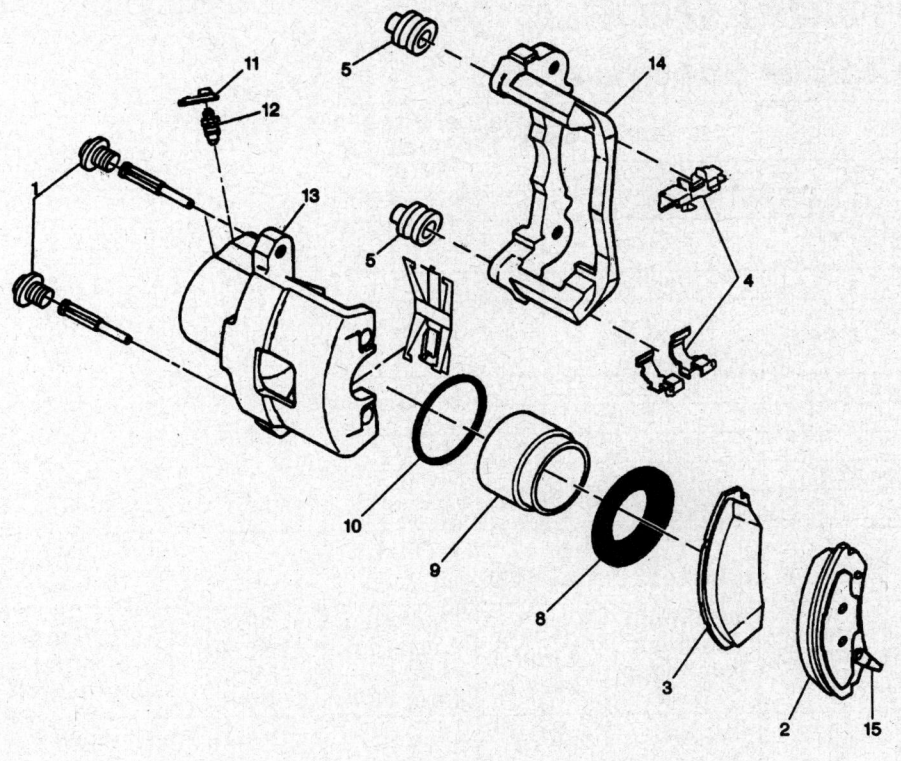

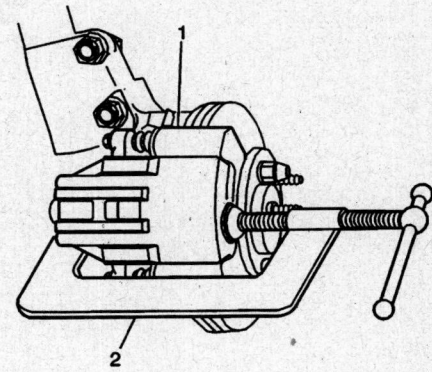

(1) Caliper
(2) C-Clamp

GC4079700136000X

Fig. 4   Piston compression

(1) Bolt and Slide Pin Assemblies
(2) Outboard Brake Pad
(3) Inboard Brake Pad
(4) Clips, Brake Pad
(5) Boot, Brake Pin Slide
(8) Seal, Brake Caliper Dust
(9) Piston, Brake Caliper

(10) Seal, Brake Caliper Piston
(11) Cap, Brake Bleeder Screw
(12) Screw, Brake Bleeder
(13) Caliper, Brake
(14) Bracket, Caliper to Knuckle
(15) Wear Sensor

GC4079700138000X

Fig. 3   Exploded view of caliper. Impala & Malibu

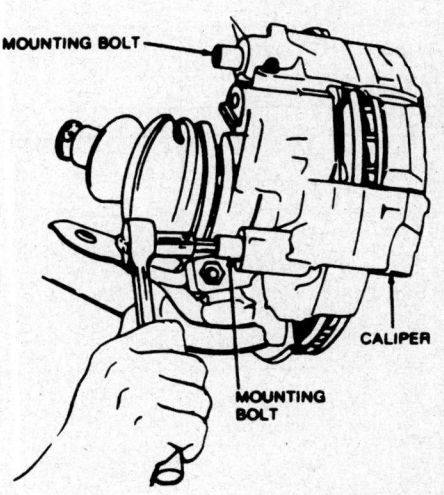

GC4079100059000X

Fig. 5   Caliper mounting bolts replacement

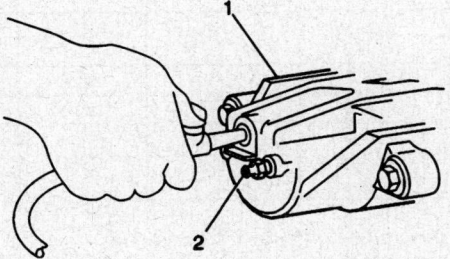

GC4079700147000X

Fig. 6   Caliper piston removal

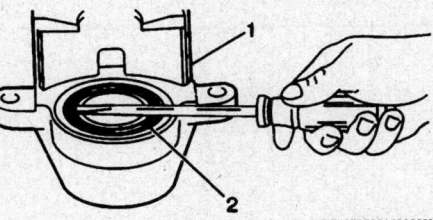

GC4079700148000X

Fig. 7   Dust boot removal

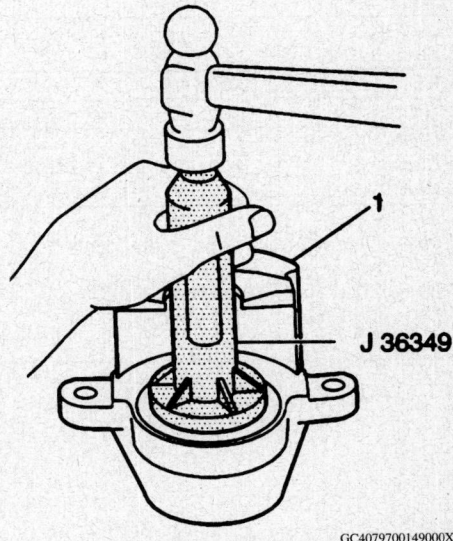

J 36349

GC4079700149000X

Fig. 8   Dust boot installation

DISC BRAKE SPECIFICATIONS
Caliper Specifications

Model	Year	Caliper Bore Dia. Inch
Alero & Grand Am	2004–05	2.36
Aveo	2005–08	2.12
Bonneville, LeSabre & Park Avenue	2004–05	2.52
Cavalier & Sunfire	2004–05	2.24
Century, Grand Prix, Impala, Monte Carlo & Regal	2004–08	2.50
DeVille & Seville	2004–05	2.52
G6	2005–08	2.36
LaCrosse	2005–08	—
Malibu & Malibu Maxx	2004–07	2.36
Malibu Classic	2008	2.36

Rotor Specifications

Model	Year	Brake Lining Wear Limit, Inch	Nominal Thickness, Inch	Minimum Refinish Thickness, Inch	Discard Limit, Inch①	Thickness Variation Parallelism, Inch	Lateral Run Out (T.I.R.), Inch	Maximum Scoring Depth, Inch
Alero & Grand Am	2004–05	.0300	1.0310	.9800	.9720	.0010	.0015	.0590
Aveo	2005–08	.0280	.9450	.8690	.8660	.0040	.0040	.0160
Bonneville, LeSabre & Park Avenue	2004–05	.0300	1.2670	1.2240	1.2090	.0010	.0020	.0590
Cavalier & Sunfire	2004–05	.0300	.7860	.7390	.7360	.0010	.0020	.0590
Century, Grand Prix, Impala, Monte Carlo & Regal	2004–08	.0300	1.2700	1.2500②	1.2100	.0010	.0020	.0590
DeVille & Seville	2004	.0300	1.2670⑦	1.2240⑥	1.2090③	.0010⑤	.0020④	.0590
G6	2005–08	.0300	1.0230	.9060	.8980	.0010	.0020	.0590
LaCrosse	2005–08	.0300	1.2700	1.2200	1.2100	.0010	.0020	.0590
Malibu, Malibu Classic & Malibu Maxx	2004–08	.0300	1.0230	.9060	.8980	.0010	.0020	.0590

① — Discard thickness is stamped on rotor.
② — 2004–08 Grand Prix, 1.2200 inches.
③ — Heavy Duty, 1.4370 inches.
④ — Heavy Duty, .0030 inch.
⑤ — Heavy Duty, .0004 inch.
⑥ — Heavy Duty, 1.4570 inches.
⑦ — Heavy Duty, 1.4960 inches.

TIGHTENING SPECIFICATIONS

Year	Component	Torque Ft. Lbs.
ALERO & GRAND AM		
2004–05	Bleeder Valve	115①
	Caliper	23
	Caliper Bracket	85
	Hose	37
AVEO		
2005–08	Bleeder Valve	53
	Caliper To Knuckle	70
	Hose	30
BONNEVILLE, LESABRE & PARK AVENUE		
2004–05	Bleeder Valve	115①
	Caliper	137
	Caliper Pin	63
	Hose	32
	Pipe Fitting Tube	11
CAVALIER & SUNFIRE		
2004–05	Bleeder Valve	115①
	Caliper	38
	Hose	37
	Inlet Fitting	34
CENTURY, IMPALA, GRAND PRIX, MONTE CARLO & REGAL		
2004–05	Bleeder Valve	115①
	Caliper	70
	Caliper Bracket	133
	Hose	40
DEVILLE & SEVILLE		
2004–05	Bleeder Valve	115①
	Caliper (Heavy Duty)	137
	Caliper (Less Heavy Duty)	181
	Caliper Pin (Heavy Duty)	83
	Caliper Pin (Less Heavy Duty)	63
	Hose	33
	Pipe Fitting	11

TIGHTENING SPECIFICATIONS—Continued

Year	Component	Torque Ft. Lbs.
GRAND PRIX		
2006–08	Caliper	70
	Caliper Bracket	133
	Hose	40
G6		
2005–06	Bleeder Valve	97①
	Caliper Bracket	85
	Caliper Pin	26
	Hose	37
2007–08	Bleeder Valve	97①
	Caliper Bracket	96
	Caliper Pin	26
	Hose	37
IMPALA & MONTE CARLO		
2006–08	Caliper	26
	Caliper Bracket	133
	Hose	40
LACROSSE		
2005–06	Bleeder Valve	97①
	Caliper Bracket	133
	Caliper Pin	70
	Hose	40
2007–08	Caliper Bracket	133
	Caliper Pin	70
	Hose	40
MALIBU, MALIBU CLASSIC & MALIBU MAXX		
2004–08	Bleeder Valve	97①
	Caliper Bracket	85
	Caliper Pin	26
	Hose	37

① — Inch lbs.

PBR Dual Piston Front Disc Brake

NOTE: On Air Bag Equipped Models, Refer To "Air Bag System Precautions" Located In The Front Of This Manual For System Disarming & Arming Procedures.

NOTE: Refer To "Computer Relearn Procedures" Located In The Front Of This Manual When Battery Power To The Computer Has Been Interrupted.

INDEX

	Page No.
Brake Pad Service	22-12
Corvette	22-12
Installation	22-12
Removal	22-12
XLR	22-13
Installation	22-13
Removal	22-13
Brake System Bleed	22-12
Caliper Service	22-13
Assemble	22-13
Disassemble	22-13

	Page No.
Inspection	22-13
Installation	22-13
Corvette	22-13
XLR	22-14
Removal	22-13
Corvette	22-13
XLR	22-13
Description	22-12
Disc Brake Specifications	22-14
Rotor Specifications	22-14
Precautions	22-12

	Page No.
Rotor, Replace	22-14
Corvette	22-14
Installation	22-14
Removal	22-14
XLR	22-14
Installation	22-14
Removal	22-14
Tightening Specifications	22-14
Troubleshooting	22-12

PRECAUTIONS

1. Keep grease and other foreign material off brake linings, caliper, surfaces of disc and external surfaces of hub.
2. Avoid deforming disc, and nicking or scratching brake linings.
3. Worn or damaged rubber piston seals should be replaced.
4. During removal and installation of a wheel assembly, ensure not to interfere with or damage caliper splash shield, or bleeder screw.
5. Front wheel bearings preload should be adjusted to specifications.
6. Ensure vehicle is centered on hoist before servicing any front end components to avoid bending or damaging disc splash shield on full left or right-hand wheel turns.
7. Before vehicle is moved after any brake service work, obtain a firm brake pedal.
8. Assembly bolts of two-piece caliper housings should not be disturbed unless caliper requires service.

DESCRIPTION

The front caliper consists of dual pistons and an aluminum housing which is suspended on the shoe and lining assemblies, **Fig. 1.** Hydraulic pressure, created by applying force to the brake pedal, acts equally against the pistons and the bottom of the caliper bores to move the pistons outward. This action slides the caliper inward, resulting in a clamping action on the brake rotor. This clamping action forces the linings against the rotor, creating the friction required to stop the vehicle.

TROUBLESHOOTING

The most common cause of brake chatter on disc brakes is a variation in disc thickness. If roughness or vibration is encountered during highway operation or if pedal pulsation is experienced at low speeds, the disc may have excessive thickness variation. To inspect for this condition, measure the disc at 12 points with a micrometer at a radius approximately one inch from edge of disc. If thickness measurements vary by more than .0005 inch, the disc should be replaced with a new one.

Excessive lateral runout of braking disc may cause a piston knocking back, possibly creating increased pedal travel and vibration when brakes are applied.

Before inspecting the runout, the wheel bearings should be adjusted. The adjustment is very important and will be required at the completion of the test to prevent bearing failure. Adjust the wheel bearings as outlined in "Front Suspension & Steering" section of appropriate chassis chapter.

BRAKE SYSTEM BLEED

Refer to "Hydraulic Brake Systems" for manual and pressure bleeding procedures.

BRAKE PAD SERVICE

Corvette

REMOVAL

1. Remove ⅔ of total brake fluid capacity from master cylinder reservoir.
2. Raise and support vehicle, then remove tire and wheel assembly.

3. If caliper requires overhaul, remove inlet fitting mounting bolt, then disconnect inlet fitting from caliper housing.
4. Discard both gaskets, then plug openings in inlet fitting and caliper. **Do not crimp brake hose.**
5. Remove caliper guide pin bolts, then the caliper from rotor and caliper mounting bracket. If only shoe and linings require replacement, suspend caliper from upper control arm.
6. Position suitable pliers over caliper and center of inboard shoe and lining, then squeeze pliers to bottom pistons in caliper bores, **Fig. 2.**
7. Remove shoe and lining assemblies.

INSTALLATION

1. Install inboard shoe and lining.
2. Ensure tangs on shoe fully engage pistons. Shoe should be flush with piston.
3. Install outboard shoe and lining into caliper housing. Ensure insulators are fully seated into holes in outboard side of housing.
4. Ensure guiding surfaces on shoe and lining assemblies and mounting bracket are seated properly, then position caliper over rotor and onto mounting bracket.
5. Press caliper housing downward to compress bias springs, then install new retainer pin and circlip.
6. If caliper was overhauled, connect inlet fitting using new gaskets, then bleed brake system.
7. Install wheel and tire assembly, then lower vehicle.
8. Fill master cylinder to proper level, then pump brake pedal to bring pads into contact with brake rotor.

XLR

REMOVAL

1. Remove brake master cylinder reservoir fluid to midway between maximum-full point and minimum allowable level.
2. Raise and support vehicle, then remove tire and wheel assembly.
3. Install large C-clamp over caliper with ends against rear of body and outboard brake pad.
4. Tighten C-clamp evenly until caliper pistons are compressed into caliper bores enough to allow caliper to slide past brake rotor. Remove C-clamp.
5. Remove upper brake caliper guide pin bolt.
6. Pivot brake caliper downward and secure caliper aside. Ensure there is no tension on hydraulic brake flexible hose. **Do not disconnect hydraulic brake flexible hose from caliper.**
7. Remove brake pads.
8. Remove and inspect retainers.

INSTALLATION

1. Install large C-clamp over caliper with ends against rear of body and old inboard brake pad or suitable wood block installed against pistons.
2. Tighten C-clamp evenly until pistons are compressed completely into bores. Remove C-clamp and old brake pad or wood block.
3. Install retainers and brake pad to bracket. Brake pad wear sensor, mounted on inboard brake pad, must be positioned so it is in trailing position during forward rotation of brake rotor.
4. Pivot brake caliper upward, over brake pads and into caliper bracket.
5. Install upper brake caliper guide pin bolt.
6. Install the tire and wheel assembly.
7. Lower vehicle.
8. With engine off, gradually apply brake pedal to approximately ⅔ of its travel distance. Slowly release brake pedal.
9. Wait 15 seconds, then repeat previous steps until firm brake pedal apply is obtained.
10. Fill brake master cylinder reservoir to proper level.

CALIPER SERVICE

Removal

CORVETTE

1. Remove ⅔ of total brake fluid capacity from master cylinder reservoir.
2. Raise and support vehicle, then remove tire and wheel assembly.
3. If caliper requires overhaul, remove inlet fitting mounting bolt, then disconnect inlet fitting from caliper housing.
4. Discard both gaskets, then plug openings in inlet fitting and caliper. **Do not crimp brake hose since this may damage hose's internal structure.**
5. Remove caliper guide pin bolts, then the caliper from rotor and caliper

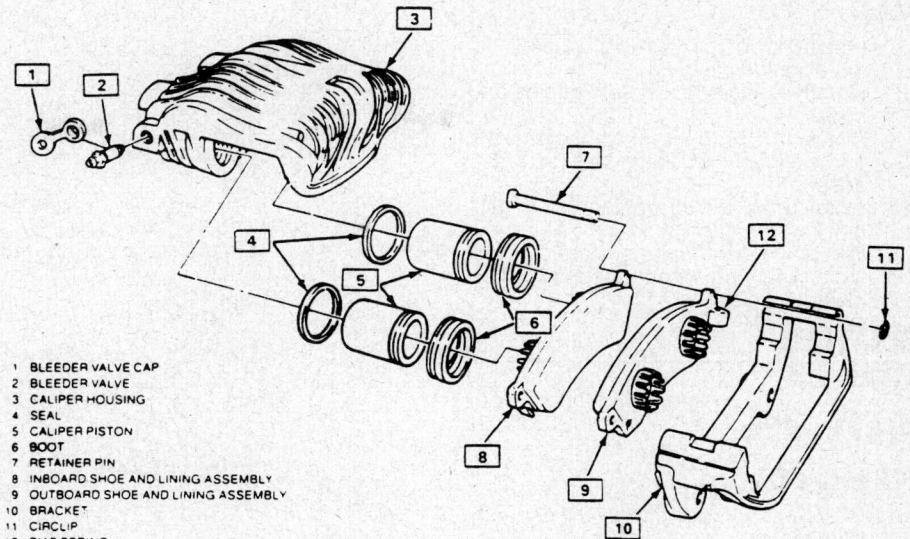

```
1  BLEEDER VALVE CAP
2  BLEEDER VALVE
3  CALIPER HOUSING
4  SEAL
5  CALIPER PISTON
6  BOOT
7  RETAINER PIN
8  INBOARD SHOE AND LINING ASSEMBLY
9  OUTBOARD SHOE AND LINING ASSEMBLY
10 BRACKET
11 CIRCLIP
12 BIAS SPRING
```
GC4079100068000X

Fig. 1 Exploded view of dual piston front caliper

mounting bracket. If only shoe and linings require replacement, suspend caliper from upper control arm to prevent damage to brake hose.

XLR

1. Remove brake master cylinder reservoir fluid to midway between maximum-full point and minimum allowable level.
2. Raise and support vehicle, then remove tire and wheel assembly.
3. Remove inlet fitting bolt and brake hose from caliper. Discard two copper brake hose gaskets.
4. Plug opening in caliper and brake hose.
5. Remove guide pin bolts and caliper from mounting bracket.

Disassemble

1. Pad caliper housing interior with suitable clean cloths.
2. Remove caliper pistons from bore by directing low pressure compressed air into bore through fluid inlet hole. Use just enough air to ease pistons out of bores. **Do not place finger in front of piston.**
3. Remove piston dust boot seals from caliper counterbores using suitable small wooden or plastic tool. Discard boot seals.
4. Remove bleeder valve and cap from caliper.

Inspection

1. Clean caliper piston bores, seal counterbores and pistons with denatured alcohol. **Do not use abrasives to clean pistons.**
2. Dry caliper piston bores, counterbores and pistons with non-lubricated, filtered compressed air.
3. Inspect caliper bores for cracks, scoring, pitting, excessive rust and/or ex-

cessive corrosion. If light rust or light corrosion are present , attempt to remove imperfection with fine emery paper.
4. Inspect pistons for cracks, scoring and/or damage to the chrome plating.

Assemble

1. Lubricate new piston seals with suitable DOT 3 brake fluid from clean, sealed brake fluid container.
2. Install lubricated, new piston seals into bores.
3. Install new piston dust boot seal over piston.
4. Install pistons into bores.
5. Install boots over pistons' ends so fold will face toward housing piston bore openings.
6. Seat boots into caliper bore grooves and slide pistons into bores.
7. Push pistons to bottom of caliper bores. Ensure boots are properly seated into piston and caliper bore grooves.
8. Install caliper bleed screw and cap.

Installation

CORVETTE

1. Ensure guiding surfaces on shoe and lining assemblies and mounting bracket are seated properly, then position caliper over rotor and onto mounting bracket.
2. Press caliper housing downward to compress bias springs, then install new retainer pin and circlip.
3. If caliper was overhauled, connect inlet fitting using new gaskets, then bleed brake system as required.
4. Install wheel and tire assembly, then lower vehicle.
5. Fill master cylinder to proper level, then pump brake pedal to bring pads into contact with brake rotor.

XLR

1. Install caliper to mounting bracket.
2. Install guide pin bolts.
3. Remove plug from caliper opening and hose.
4. Install new copper brake hose gaskets and caliper inlet fitting bolt to brake hose.
5. Install hose and inlet fitting bolt to caliper.
6. Bleed hydraulic brake system.
7. Install tire and wheel assembly, then lower vehicle.

ROTOR

REPLACE

Corvette

REMOVAL

1. Remove ⅔ of total brake fluid capacity from master cylinder reservoir.
2. Raise and support vehicle, then remove tire and wheel assembly.
3. Remove caliper guide pin bolts, then the caliper from rotor and caliper mounting bracket. Suspend caliper from upper control arm.
4. Remove mounting bolts and mounting bracket.
5. Remove rotor from hub assembly.

INSTALLATION

1. Ensure guiding surfaces on shoe and

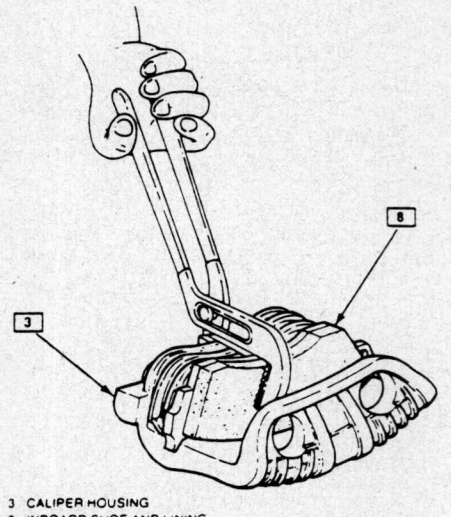

3 CALIPER HOUSING
8 INBOARD SHOE AND LINING

GC40791000069000X

Fig. 2 Piston retraction in caliper bores

lining assemblies and mounting bracket are seated properly, then position caliper over rotor and onto mounting bracket.
2. Press caliper housing downward to compress bias springs, then install new retainer pin and circlip.
3. Install wheel and tire assembly, then lower vehicle.

4. Fill master cylinder to proper level, then pump brake pedal to bring pads into contact with brake rotor.

XLR

REMOVAL

1. Raise and support vehicle, then remove tire and wheel assembly.
2. Install C-clamp over caliper of with ends against body rear and outboard disc brake pad.
3. Compress piston into bore just enough to allow caliper to slide away from rotor. Remove C-clamp.
4. Remove bracket bolts. **Do not disconnect brake flexible hose bolt.**
5. Remove caliper and mounting bracket, then support assembly aside. Ensure there is no tension on hydraulic brake flexible hose.
6. Mark brake rotor to wheel studs for installation alignment.
7. Remove brake rotor.

INSTALLATION

1. Install brake rotor to hub/axle flange.
2. Install caliper and bracket to suspension knuckle.
3. Install tire and wheel assembly, then lower vehicle.

DISC BRAKE SPECIFICATIONS

Rotor Specifications

Model	Year	Brake Lining Wear Limit, Inch	Nominal Thickness, Inch	Minimum Refinish Thickness, Inch	Discard Limit, Inch①	Thickness Variation Parallelism, Inch	Lateral Run Out (T.I.R.), Inch	Maximum Scoring Depth, Inch
Corvette	2004–08	.0300	1.260	1.205	1.190	.0010	.0020	.0590
XLR	2004–08	.0300	1.260	1.205	1.190	.0010	.0020	.0590

① — Discard thickness is stamped on rotor.

TIGHTENING SPECIFICATIONS

Year	Component	Torque Ft. Lbs.
2004–08	Bleeder Screw	106①
	Caliper Guide Pin	23
	Caliper Inlet Fitting	33
	Caliper Mounting Bracket	125
	Wheel Lug Nuts	100

① — Inch lbs.

AC-Delco Single Piston Rear Disc Brake

NOTE: On Air Bag Equipped Models, Refer To "Air Bag System Precautions" Located In The Front Of This Manual For System Disarming & Arming Procedures.

NOTE: Refer To "Computer Relearn Procedures" Located In The Front Of This Manual When Battery Power To The Computer Has Been Interrupted.

INDEX

	Page No.
Adjustments	22-18
Parking Brake	22-18
Brake Pad Service	22-16
All Models Except Century,	
Grand Prix & Regal	22-16
Installation	22-16
Removal	22-16
Century, Grand Prix & Regal	22-16
Brake System Bleed	22-16
Caliper Service	22-16
All Models Except Century,	

	Page No.
Grand Prix & Regal	22-16
Assemble	22-16
Disassemble	22-16
Inspection	22-16
Replacement	22-16
Century, Grand Prix & Regal	22-17
Assemble	22-17
Disassemble	22-17
Inspect	22-17
Replacement	22-17
Description	22-15

	Page No.
Disc Brake Specifications	22-19
Caliper Specifications	22-19
Rotor Specifications	22-19
Precautions	22-15
Rotor, Replace	22-17
All Models Except Century,	
Grand Prix & Regal	22-17
Century, Grand Prix & Regal	22-17
Tightening Specifications	22-20
Troubleshooting	22-15

PRECAUTIONS

1. Keep grease and other foreign material off brake linings, caliper, surfaces of disc and external surfaces of hub.
2. Avoid deforming disc, and nicking or scratching brake linings.
3. Worn or damaged rubber piston seals should be replaced.
4. During removal and installation of a wheel assembly, ensure not to interfere with or damage caliper splash shield, or bleeder screw.
5. Front wheel bearings preload should be adjusted to specifications.
6. Ensure vehicle is centered on hoist before servicing any front end components to avoid bending or damaging disc splash shield on full left or right-hand wheel turns.
7. Before vehicle is moved after any brake service work, ensure to obtain a firm brake pedal.
8. Assembly bolts of two-piece caliper housings should not be disturbed unless caliper requires service.

DESCRIPTION

On all models except Century, Grand Prix and Regal, the caliper assembly has a single bore and is mounted to the support bracket with two mounting bolt and sleeve assemblies, **Fig. 1.** Hydraulic pressure created by applying the brake pedal is converted by the caliper to a stopping force. This force acts equally against the piston and the bottom of the piston bore to move the piston outward and to slide the caliper inward resulting in a clamping action. This clamping action presses the linings against the rotor, creating friction to stop the vehicle.

On Century, Grand Prix and Regal models, the caliper has a single piston, and is mounted to the support bracket by two mounting bolts, **Fig. 2.** The caliper assembly slides on the two mounting bolts. Upon brake application, fluid pressure against the piston forces the inboard shoe and lining assembly against the inboard side of the disc. This action causes the caliper assembly to slide until the outboard lining comes into contact with the disc. As pressure builds up the linings are pressed against the disc with increased force.

On all models, when the parking brake is applied, the external caliper parking brake lever moves and rotates a spindle within the caliper housing. As the spindle rotates, a connecting rod is pushed against an internal adjusting screw which is threaded into a sleeve nut in the piston assembly. This causes the piston assembly to move outward bringing the inboard shoe and lining assembly against the rotor. As the inboard shoe and lining contacts the rotor, a reaction force causes the caliper housing to slide inward pressing the outboard shoe and lining against the rotor.

The piston assembly contains a self adjusting mechanism to keep the parking brake in proper adjustment. As the linings are worn, the piston moves through the seal to maintain proper lining to rotor clearance. The parking brake adjusts to proper clearances through an internal sleeve nut that rotates and moves as one unit with the piston.

TROUBLESHOOTING

The most common cause of brake chatter on disc brakes is a variation in disc thickness. If roughness or vibration is encountered during highway operation or if pedal pulsation is experienced at low speeds, the disc may have excessive thickness variation. To inspect for this condition, measure the disc at 12 points with a micrometer at a radius approximately one inch from edge of disc. If thickness measurements vary by more than .0005 inch, the disc should be replaced with a new one.

Excessive lateral runout of braking disc may cause a piston knocking back, possibly creating increased pedal travel and vibration when brakes are applied.

Before inspecting the runout, the wheel bearings should be adjusted. The adjustment is very important and will be required at the completion of the test to prevent bearing failure. Adjust the wheel bearings as outlined in "Front Suspension & Steering" section of appropriate chassis chapter.

BRAKE SYSTEM BLEED

Refer to "Hydraulic Brake Systems" for manual and pressure bleeding procedures.

BRAKE PAD SERVICE

All Models Except Century, Grand Prix & Regal

REMOVAL

1. Remove ⅔ of brake fluid from master cylinder reservoir.
2. Raise and support vehicle.
3. Mark wheel to axle flange relationship for installation alignment, then remove wheel and tire assembly.
4. Remove bolt and washer attaching cable support bracket to caliper, **Fig. 3.**
5. Remove sleeve bolt and pivot caliper, **Fig. 4. Do not completely remove caliper.**
6. Remove outboard and inboard shoe and linings, then two pad clips from caliper support.

INSTALLATION

1. Turn piston and thread it into caliper assembly using suitable spanner-type tool in piston slots.
2. After bottoming piston, lift inner edge of boot next to piston and press out trapped air.
3. Ensure slots in end of piston are positioned properly, **Fig. 5.**
4. Install pad clips, outboard and inboard shoe and linings in caliper support. **Ensure wear sensor is on outboard shoe positioned downward at leading edge of rotor during forward wheel rotation.**
5. Pivot caliper over shoe and lining assemblies. **Do not damage piston boot on inboard shoe.**
6. Inspect pad clips. Use small screwdriver to seat or center pad clips on support abutments.
7. Install sleeve bolt.
8. Install cable support bracket.
9. Install wheels and tires, then lower vehicle.
10. Apply approximately 175 lbs., of force to brake pedal three times to seat shoe and linings against rotor.

Century, Grand Prix & Regal

1. Remove ⅔ of brake fluid from master cylinder reservoir.
2. Raise and support vehicle.
3. Mark wheel to axle flange relationship for installation alignment, then remove wheel and tire assembly.
4. Compress caliper piston enough for clearance using suitable C-clamp and remove upper caliper bolt.
5. Pivot caliper down. **Do not remove caliper.**

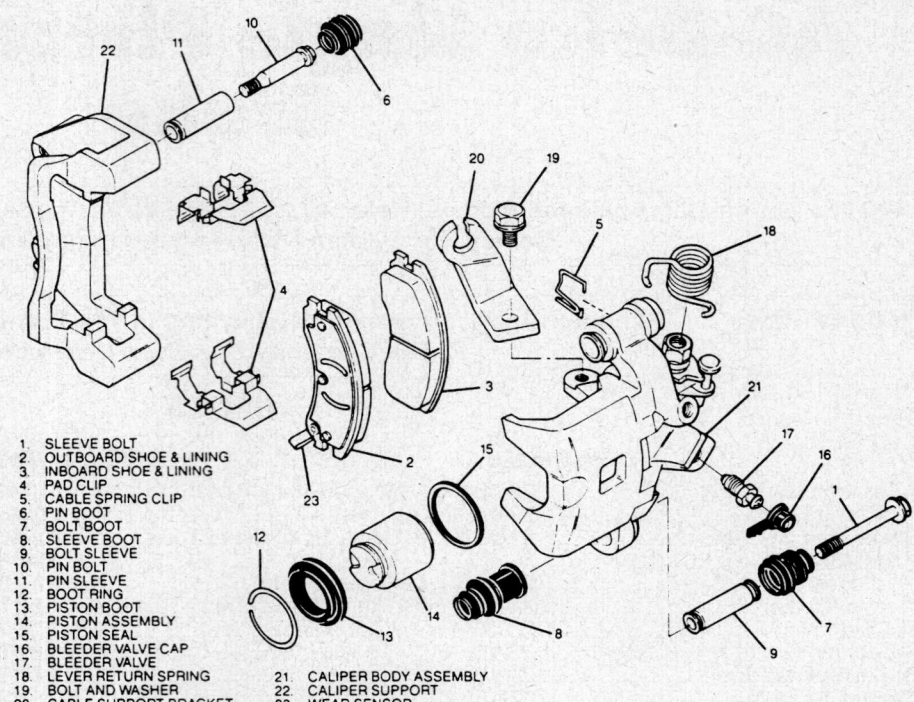

1. SLEEVE BOLT
2. OUTBOARD SHOE & LINING
3. INBOARD SHOE & LINING
4. PAD CLIP
5. CABLE SPRING CLIP
6. PIN BOOT
7. BOLT BOOT
8. SLEEVE BOOT
9. BOLT SLEEVE
10. PIN BOLT
11. PIN SLEEVE
12. BOOT RING
13. PISTON BOOT
14. PISTON ASSEMBLY
15. PISTON SEAL
16. BLEEDER VALVE CAP
17. BLEEDER VALVE
18. LEVER RETURN SPRING
19. BOLT AND WASHER
20. CABLE SUPPORT BRACKET
21. CALIPER BODY ASSEMBLY
22. CALIPER SUPPORT
23. WEAR SENSOR

GC4079100078000X

Fig. 1   Exploded view of rear disc brake caliper. Except Century, Grand Prix & Regal

6. Remove brake pads and pad clips from caliper bracket.
7. Reverse procedure to install.

CALIPER SERVICE

All Models Except Century, Grand Prix & Regal

REPLACEMENT

1. Raise and support vehicle.
2. Mark wheel to axle flange relationship for installation alignment, then remove wheel and tire assembly.
3. Remove brake hose from caliper. Plug openings in caliper and brake hose.
4. Lift able spring to free end of from lever, then disconnect parking brake cable from lever.
5. Remove cable support bracket mounting bolt and washer.
6. Remove sleeve bolt and caliper.
7. Reverse procedure to install, then bleed brakes.

DISASSEMBLE

1. Pad interior of caliper assembly with clean shop towel, then remove piston assembly using low pressure compressed air into caliper inlet hole, **Fig. 6. Do not place fingers in front of piston.**
2. Pry up one end of boot ring using small screwdriver, **Fig. 7.** Work boot ring out of caliper groove.

3. Remove piston seal from caliper bore groove using small wooden or plastic tool.
4. Remove bleeder valve and cap.
5. If lever return spring replacement is required, remove it using screwdriver to disengage return spring from parking brake lever, then unhook spring from stopper pin, **Fig. 8.**
6. Remove pin boot and bolt, then the bolt and sleeve bolt from caliper.
7. Remove pin bolt and pin sleeve from caliper support.

INSPECTION

1. Clean all components in clean denatured alcohol, then dry with low pressure compressed air.
2. Blow out passages in caliper and bleeder valve.
3. Inspect piston assembly for nicks, cracks, wear or corrosion.
4. Inspect piston bore for scoring, nicks, wear or corrosion. Use crocus cloth to polish out light corrosion. **Do not hone caliper bore.**
5. Inspect seal groove for nicks or burrs.
6. Inspect boots for cuts, tears or deterioration.
7. Inspect bolt sleeve and pin sleeve for corrosion or damage. **Do not polish away corrosion.**

ASSEMBLE

1. Lubricate pin sleeve with silicone grease, then install pin bolts and sleeve to caliper support.
2. Lubricate sleeve boot with silicone grease, then compress lip on sleeve boot and push it through caliper until lip

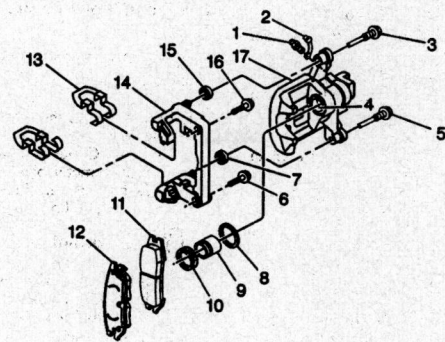

(1) Valve, Caliper Bleeder
(2) Cap, Bleeder Valve
(3) Bolt, Caliper
(4) Caliper Bore
(5) Bolt, Caliper
(6) Bolt, Caliper Bracket
(7) Boot, Caliper
(8) Seal, Caliper Piston
(9) Piston, Caliper

(10) Boot, Caliper Piston
(11) Pad, Inner
(12) Pad, Outer
(13) Clips, Retainer
(14) Bracket, Caliper
(15) Boot, Caliper
(16) Bolt, Caliper Bracket
(17) Housing, Caliper

GC4079700143000X

Fig. 2 Exploded view of rear caliper. Century, Grand Prix & Regal

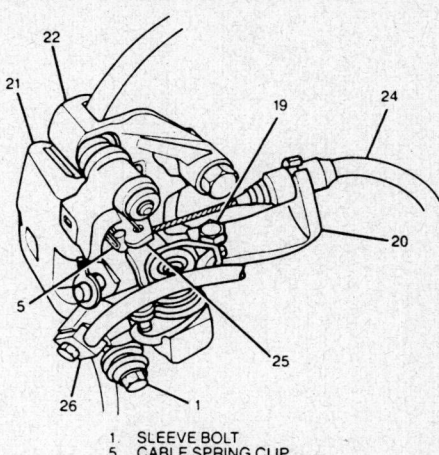

1. SLEEVE BOLT
5. CABLE SPRING CLIP
19. BOLT AND WASHER
20. CABLE SUPPORT BRACKET
21. CALIPER BODY ASSEMBLY
22. CALIPER SUPPORT
24. PARKING BRAKE CABLE
25. PARKING BRAKE LEVER
26. BRAKE HOSE

GC4079100079000X

Fig. 3 Caliper assembly. All models except Century, Grand Prix & Regal

emerges and seals on inboard face of caliper ear.
3. Lubricate push bolt sleeve with silicone grease, then push it in through lip end of boot until boot seats in sleeve groove at other end.
4. Install bolt boot onto caliper.
5. Install small end of pin boot over sleeve until boot seats in groove.
6. Position new lever return spring with hook end around stopper pin, then pry other end of spring over lever.
7. Install bleeder valve and cap.
8. Lubricate new piston seal with clean brake fluid and install in groove in caliper bore. Ensure seal is not twisted.
9. Install boot onto piston.
10. Lubricate piston with clean brake fluid.
11. Start piston assembly in by hand, then thread into bottom of caliper bore using spanner-type tool in slots in end of piston.
12. Ensure outside edge of piston boot is smoothly seated in counterbore.
13. Work boot ring into groove near open end of caliper bore. **Do not pinch piston boot between boot ring and caliper.**
14. Lift inner edge of boot next to piston and press out trapped air. Ensure boot lays flat.

Century, Grand Prix & Regal

REPLACEMENT

1. Remove ⅔ of brake fluid from master cylinder reservoir.
2. Raise and support vehicle.
3. Mark wheel to axle flange relationship for installation alignment, then remove wheel and tire assembly.
4. Compress caliper piston enough for

clearance using suitable C-clamp.
5. Remove brake hose from caliper. Plug openings in caliper and brake hose.
6. Remove mounting bolts and caliper.
7. Reverse procedure to install.

DISASSEMBLE

1. Pad interior of caliper assembly with clean shop towel, then remove piston using low pressure compressed air into caliper inlet hole. **Do not place fingers in front of piston.**
2. Pry up one end of boot ring and work boot ring out of caliper groove.
3. Remove piston seal from caliper bore groove.
4. Remove bleeder valve and cap.

INSPECT

1. Clean all components in clean denatured alcohol, then dry with low pressure compressed air.
2. Blow out passages in caliper and bleeder valve.
3. Inspect piston assembly for nicks, cracks, wear or corrosion.
4. Inspect piston bore for scoring, nicks, wear or corrosion. Use crocus cloth to polish out light corrosion. **Do not hone caliper bore.**
5. Inspect seal groove for nicks or burrs.
6. Inspect boots for cuts, tears or deterioration.

ASSEMBLE

1. Install bleeder valve and cap.
2. Install new lubricated piston seal into caliper bore grooves, then the piston boot onto piston.
3. Lubricate piston with clean brake fluid, then install piston and boot into bore of caliper.
4. Install piston ring. **Ensure outside edge of piston boot is seated smoothly in counterbore of caliper.**

ROTOR
REPLACE

All Models Except Century, Grand Prix & Regal

1. Raise and support vehicle.
2. Mark wheel to axle flange relationship for installation alignment, then remove wheel and tire assembly.
3. Remove brake hose from caliper. Plug openings in caliper and brake hose.
4. Lift able spring to free end of from lever, then disconnect parking brake cable from lever.
5. Remove cable support bracket mounting bolt and washer.
6. Remove sleeve bolt and caliper.
7. Remove mounting bolts and caliper mounting bracket.
8. Remove rotor from hub and bearing.
9. Reverse procedure to install. Adjust parking brake as outlined in "Adjustments."

Century, Grand Prix & Regal

1. Remove ⅔ of brake fluid from master cylinder reservoir.
2. Raise and support vehicle.
3. Mark wheel to axle flange relationship for installation alignment, then remove wheel and tire assembly.
4. Compress caliper piston enough for clearance using suitable C-clamp.
5. Remove brake hose from caliper. Plug openings in caliper and brake hose.

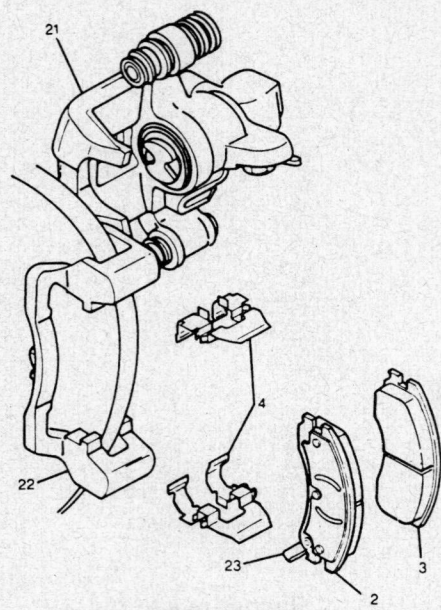

2. OUTBOARD SHOE & LINING
3. INBOARD SHOE & LINING
4. PAD CLIP
21. CALIPER BODY ASSEMBLY
22. CALIPER SUPPORT
23. WEAR SENSOR

GC4079100083000X

Fig. 4   Shoe & lining installation. All models except Century, Grand Prix & Regal

6. Remove mounting bolts and caliper.
7. Remove rotor from hub and bearing.
8. Reverse procedure to install. Adjust parking brake as outlined in "Adjustments."

ADJUSTMENTS
Parking Brake

1. Apply service brake with pedal force of 175 lbs., and release.
2. Fully apply parking brake using approximately 125 lbs., of force on final stroke and release.
3. Apply and release parking brake two additional times.
4. Inspect parking brake pedal assembly for full release by turning ignition On and observing brake warning lamp. Lamp should be off.
5. If brake warning lamp is on and parking brake appears to be fully released, operate manual pedal release lever and pull downward on front park brake cable to remove slack from pedal assembly.

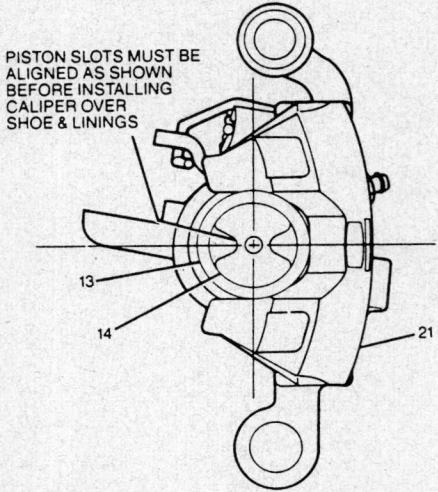

PISTON SLOTS MUST BE ALIGNED AS SHOWN BEFORE INSTALLING CALIPER OVER SHOE & LININGS

13. PISTON BOOT
14. PISTON ASSEMBLY
21. CALIPER BODY ASSEMBLY

GC4079100084000X

Fig. 5   Positioning piston slots. All models except Century, Grand Prix & Regal

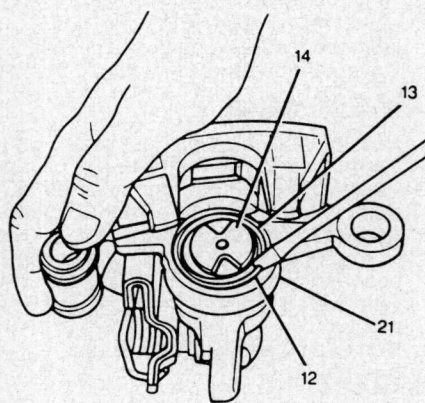

12. BOOT RING
13. PISTON BOOT
14. PISTON ASSEMBLY
21. CALIPER BODY ASSEMBLY

GC4079100081000X

Fig. 7   Boot ring removal. All models except Century, Grand Prix & Regal

6. Raise and support vehicle.
7. Inspect parking brake levers on rear calipers, noting the following:
   a. Levers should be against stops on caliper housing.
   b. If levers are not against stops, inspect for binding in rear brake ca-

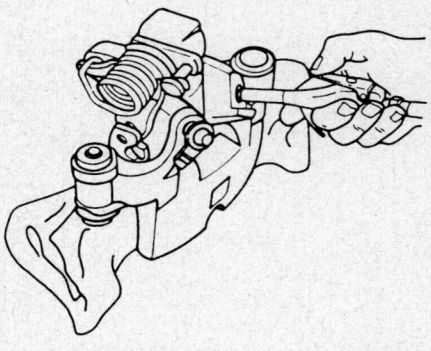

GC4079100080000X

Fig. 6   Piston removal. All models except Century, Grand Prix & Regal

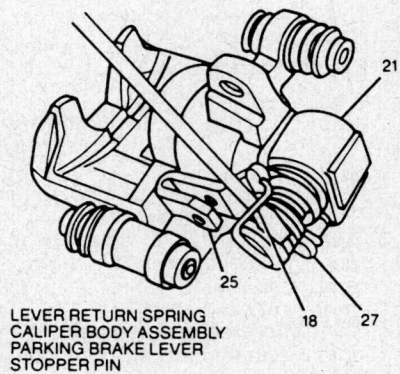

18. LEVER RETURN SPRING
21. CALIPER BODY ASSEMBLY
25. PARKING BRAKE LEVER
27. STOPPER PIN

GC4079100082000X

Fig. 8   Lever return spring removal. All models except Century, Grand Prix & Regal

bles and position levers against stops.
8. Tighten parking brake cable at adjuster until either left or righthand lever begins to move off of stop.
9. Loosen adjuster until lever which previously moved off the stop is again resting on the stop. **Both levers should be resting on caliper stops after completing this step.**
10. Operate parking brake several times to inspect adjustment.
11. Firm pedal feel should be obtained by pumping pedal less than one stroke.
12. Inspect left and righthand caliper levers. Both levers must be resting on stops after adjustment of parking brake.
13. Inspect operation of parking brake. If possible, place vehicle on grade and inspect parking brake holding ability.

DISC BRAKE SPECIFICATIONS
Caliper Specifications

Model	Year	Caliper Bore Dia. Inch
Alero, Grand Am, Malibu & Malibu Maxx	2004–08	1.50
Century, Grand Prix, Impala, Monte Carlo & Regal	2004–08	1.50
CTS	2004–08	1.50
DeVille & Seville	2004–05	1.50
DTS	2007–08	—
GTO	2004–06	—
G6	2005–08	1.50
LaCrosse	2005–08	—
Lucerne	2006–08	—
Park Avenue	2004–05	1.50
STS	2005–08	—

Rotor Specifications

Model	Year	Nominal Thickness, Inch	Minimum Refinish Thickness, Inch	Discard Thickness, Inch	Thickness Variation, Inch①	Lateral Runout (T.I.R.), Inch	Maximum Scoring Depth, Inch
Alero & Grand Am	2004–05	.4330	.4170	.3540	.0010	.0015	.0590
Century, Impala, Monte Carlo & Regal	2004–05	.4300	.4200	.3500	.0010	.0020	.0590
CTS	2004–07	1.023	.9440	.9440	.0010	.0020	.0590
	2008	.9060	.8460	.8460	.0010	.0020	.0590
DeVille & Seville	2004–05	.4330③	.4040②	.3540④	.0010	.0020	.0590
DTS	2006–08	1.1420	1.1020	1.0830	.0010	.0020	.0590
Grand Prix	2004–08	.5500	.5100	.4900	.0010	.0020	.0590
GTO	2004–06	.0790	.5470	.5470	.0050	.0030	.0160
G6	2005–08	.5510	.4720	.4650	.0010	.0020	.0590
Impala & Monte Carlo	2006–08	.4330	.3680	.3540	.0010	.0020	.0590
LaCrosse	2005–08	.5500	.5100	.4900	.0010	.0020	.0590
Lucerne	2006–08	.4720	.4130	.4130	.0010	.0020	.0590
Malibu, Malibu Classic & Malibu Maxx	2004–08	.5510	.4720	.4650	.0010	.0020	.0590
Park Avenue	2004–05	.4330	.4040	.3540	.0010	.0020	.0590
STS	2005–08	1.0230	.9440	.9440	.0010	.0020	.0590

① — Discard thickness is stamped on rotor.
② — Heavy Duty, 1.1020 inches.
③ — Heavy Duty, 1.1420 inches
④ — Heavy Duty, 1.0830 inches.

DISC BRAKES

TIGHTENING SPECIFICATIONS

Year	Component	Torque Ft. Lbs.
ALERO, GRAND AM, MALIBU, MALIBU CLASSIC & MALIBU MAXX		
2004–08	Bleeder Valve	98①
	Caliper	81
	Caliper Bracket	85
	Hose	37
CENTURY & REGAL		
2004–05	Caliper	32
	Caliper Bracket	85
	Rotor	25
	Hose	40
CTS		
2004–07	Caliper Bracket	88
	Caliper Pin	44
	Hose	37
2008	Caliper Bracket	96
	Caliper Pin	20
	Hose	36
DEVILLE & SEVILLE		
2004–05	Backing Plate	100
	Caliper Bracket (Heavy Duty)	181
	Caliper Bracket (Less Heavy Duty)	94
	Caliper Park Bake Cable Bracket	32
	Caliper Pin (Heavy Duty)	23
	Caliper Pin (Less Heavy Duty)	20
	Hose	33
	Park Brake Cable Guise	18
DTS		
2006–08	Bleeder Valve	115①
	Caliper Pin	25
	Caliper Bracket	94
	Hose	30
GRAND PRIX		
2004–08	Caliper	25
	Caliper Bracket	89
	Hose	40
GTO		
2004–06	Caliper Bracket	63
	Hose	26
	Caliper Pin	24

TIGHTENING SPECIFICATIONS—Continued

Year	Component	Torque Ft. Lbs.
G6		
2005–08	Bleeder Valve	97①
	Caliper Pin	26
	Hose	37
IMPALA & MONTE CARLO		
2004–05	Caliper	32
	Caliper Bracket	85
	Hose	40
2006–08	Caliper	32
	Caliper Bracket	88
	Hose	40
LACROSSE		
2005–07	Brake Hose Bolt	40
	Caliper Bolts	25
	Caliper Bracket Bolts	89
2008	Brake Hose Bolt	40
	Caliper Bolts	32
	Caliper Bracket Bolts	89
LUCERNE		
2006–08	Brake Caliper Bracket Bolt	94
	Brake Caliper Pin Bolt	25
	Brake Hose to Caliper Bolt	30
	Brake Rotor Mounting Screw	106①
	Brake Caliper Bleeder Valve	115①
PARK AVENUE		
2004–05	Caliper Bracket	94
	Caliper Pin	20
	Caliper Park Bake Cable Bracket	32
	Park Brake Cable Guide	18
STS		
2005–08	Bleeder Valve	124①
	Caliper Pin	44
	Hose	37

① — Inch lbs.

PBR Single Piston Rear Disc Brake

NOTE: On Air Bag Equipped Models, Refer To "Air Bag System Precautions" Located In The Front Of This Manual For System Disarming & Arming Procedures.

NOTE: Refer To "Computer Relearn Procedures" Located In The Front Of This Manual When Battery Power To The Computer Has Been Interrupted.

INDEX

	Page No.
Adjustments	22-23
Parking Brake	22-23
Corvette	22-23
XLR	22-24
Brake Pad Service	22-21
Corvette	22-21
Installation	22-21
Removal	22-21
XLR	22-22
Installation	22-22
Removal	22-22
Brake System Bleed	22-21

	Page No.
Caliper Service	22-22
Corvette	22-22
Assemble	22-22
Disassemble	22-22
Replacement	22-22
XLR	22-23
Assemble	22-23
Disassemble	22-23
Inspection	22-23
Installation	22-23
Removal	22-23
Description	22-21

	Page No.
Disc Brake Specifications	22-24
Rotor Specifications	22-24
Precautions	22-21
Rotor, Replace	22-23
Corvette	22-23
XLR	22-23
Installation	22-23
Removal	22-23
Tightening Specifications	22-24
Troubleshooting	22-21

PRECAUTIONS

1. Keep grease and other foreign material off brake linings, caliper, surfaces of disc and external surfaces of hub.
2. Avoid deforming disc, and nicking or scratching brake linings.
3. Worn or damaged rubber piston seals should be replaced.
4. During removal and installation of a wheel assembly, ensure not to interfere with or damage caliper splash shield, or bleeder screw.
5. Front wheel bearings preload should be adjusted to specifications.
6. Ensure vehicle is centered on hoist before servicing any front end components to avoid bending or damaging disc splash shield on full left or right-hand wheel turns.
7. Before vehicle is moved after any brake service work, obtain a firm brake pedal.
8. Assembly bolts of two-piece caliper housings should not be disturbed unless caliper requires service.

DESCRIPTION

The rear caliper consists of a single piston and an aluminum housing which is suspended in a mounting bracket through two slide pins, **Fig. 1.** Hydraulic pressure, created by applying force to the brake pedal, acts equally against the piston and the bottom of the caliper bore to move the piston outward. This action slides the caliper inward, resulting in a clamping action on the brake rotor. This clamping action forces the linings against the rotor, creating the friction required to stop the vehicle.

The parking brake mechanism on this caliper is completely independent of the hydraulic brake system. When the parking brake is applied, the lever on the caliper causes the pushrod, actuating collar and clamp rod assembly to move outward. This causes the caliper to move inward, mechanically forcing the linings against the rotor.

TROUBLESHOOTING

The most common cause of brake chatter on disc brakes is a variation in disc thickness. If roughness or vibration is encountered during highway operation or if pedal pulsation is experienced at low speeds, the disc may have excessive thickness variation. To inspect for this condition, measure the disc at 12 points with a micrometer at a radius approximately one inch from edge of disc. If thickness measurements vary by more than .0005 inch, the disc should be replaced with a new one.

Excessive lateral runout of braking disc may cause a piston knocking back, possibly creating increased pedal travel and vibration when brakes are applied.

Before inspecting the runout, the wheel bearings should be adjusted. The adjustment is very important and will be required at the completion of the test to prevent bearing failure. Adjust the wheel bearings as outlined in "Front Suspension & Steering" section of appropriate chassis chapter.

BRAKE SYSTEM BLEED

Refer to "Hydraulic Brake Systems" for manual and pressure bleeding procedures.

BRAKE PAD SERVICE

Corvette

REMOVAL

1. Remove ⅔ of total brake fluid capacity from master cylinder reservoir.
2. Raise and support vehicle, then remove tire and wheel assembly.
3. Install two wheel lug nuts to retain rotor in position.
4. Position one end of suitable C-clamp against inlet fitting bolt and other end against outboard shoe and lining.
5. Tighten clamp until piston fully bottoms in caliper bore, **Fig. 2.**
6. Remove upper guide pin bolt and discard.
7. Loosen lower guide pin bolt, then pivot caliper downward on lower guide pin bolt to expose shoe and lining assemblies.
8. Remove shoes and linings from mounting bracket.

INSTALLATION

1. Install outboard shoe and lining onto mounting bracket. Ensure insulator on shoe is positioned toward caliper housing.
2. Install inboard shoe and lining.
3. Ensure wear sensor is positioned nearest caliper piston. Sensor should be in trailing position when wheel is rotated in forward direction.
4. Pivot caliper into position over shoes and linings, noting the following:
   a. Ensure springs on outboard shoe do not protrude through inspection hole in housing.
   b. If protrusion is evident, lift caliper

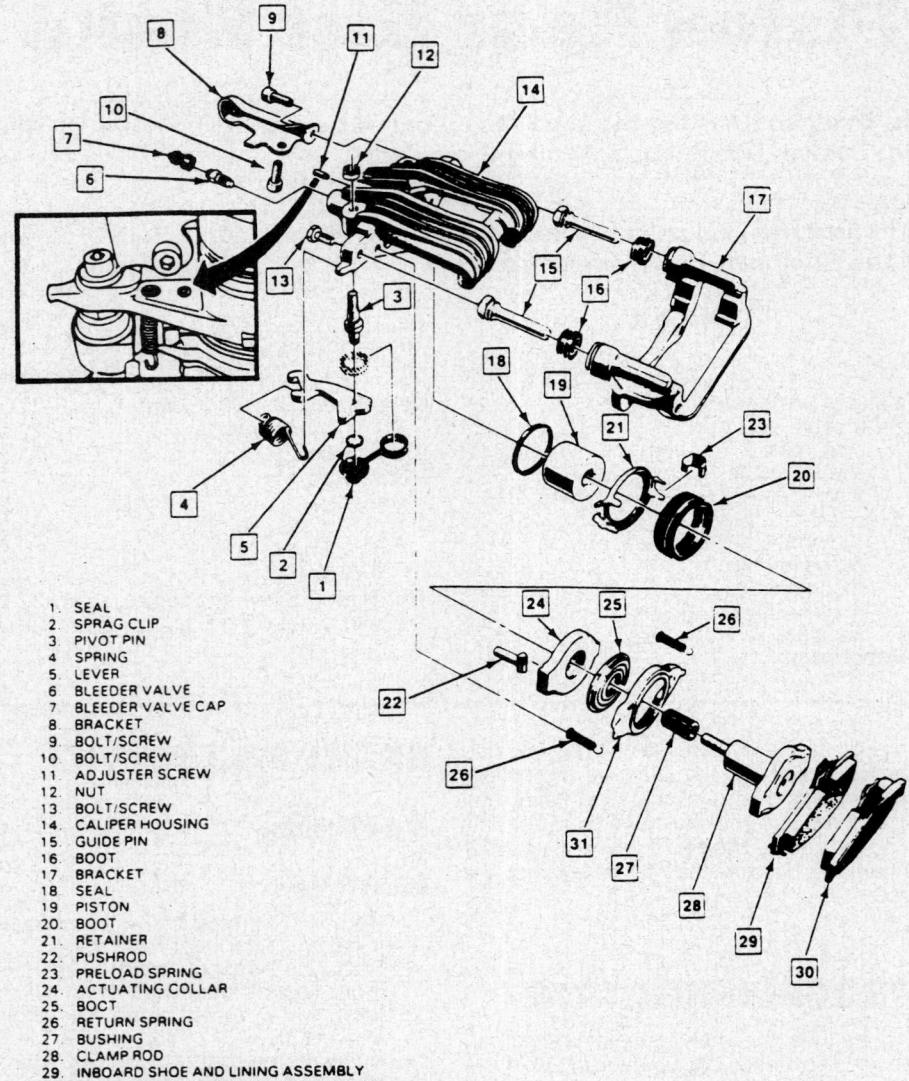

1. SEAL
2. SPRAG CLIP
3. PIVOT PIN
4. SPRING
5. LEVER
6. BLEEDER VALVE
7. BLEEDER VALVE CAP
8. BRACKET
9. BOLT/SCREW
10. BOLT/SCREW
11. ADJUSTER SCREW
12. NUT
13. BOLT/SCREW
14. CALIPER HOUSING
15. GUIDE PIN
16. BOOT
17. BRACKET
18. SEAL
19. PISTON
20. BOOT
21. RETAINER
22. PUSHROD
23. PRELOAD SPRING
24. ACTUATING COLLAR
25. BOOT
26. RETURN SPRING
27. BUSHING
28. CLAMP ROD
29. INBOARD SHOE AND LINING ASSEMBLY
30. OUTBOARD SHOE AND LINING ASSEMBLY
31. RETAINER

GC4079100094000X

Fig. 1 Typical exploded view of single piston rear caliper

housing and adjust position of outboard shoe and lining.
5. Install and tighten new upper guide pin bolt, then tighten lower bolt.
6. Fill master cylinder to proper level, then pump brake pedal to bring pads into contact with brake rotor.

XLR

REMOVAL

1. Remove brake master cylinder reservoir fluid to midway between maximum-full point and minimum allowable level.
2. Raise and support vehicle, then remove tire and wheel assembly.
3. Hand tighten wheel lug nut to stud to hold rotor to hub.
4. Install large C-clamp over caliper with ends against body rear and outboard brake pad.
5. Tighten C-clamp until caliper piston is

compressed into bore enough to allow caliper to slide past brake rotor. Remove C-clamp.
6. Remove caliper guide pin bolts.
7. Remove brake caliper from bracket and support aside. Ensure there is no tension on hydraulic brake flexible hose. **Do not disconnect hydraulic brake flexible hose from caliper.**
8. Remove brake pads and retainers.

INSTALLATION

1. Install large C-clamp over caliper with ends against body rear and old inboard brake pad or suitable wood block installed against caliper piston.
2. Tighten C-clamp until piston is compressed completely into bore. Remove C-clamp and old brake pad or wood block.
3. Install brake pad retainers and brake pads to bracket. Brake pad wear sensor, mounted on inboard brake pad, must be positioned so in trailing posi-

tion during forward rotation of brake rotor.
4. Install caliper to bracket.
5. Install brake caliper guide pin bolts.
6. Install tire and wheel assembly, then lower vehicle.
7. With engine off, gradually apply brake pedal to approximately ⅔ travel distance. Slowly release pedal.
8. Wait 15 seconds, then repeat previous steps until firm brake pedal apply is obtained.
9. Fill brake master cylinder reservoir to proper level.

CALIPER SERVICE

Corvette

REPLACEMENT

1. Raise and support vehicle, then remove tire and wheel assembly.
2. If caliper requires overhaul, remove inlet fitting mounting bolt, then disconnect inlet fitting from caliper housing.
3. Discard two gaskets, then plug openings in inlet fitting and caliper.
4. Remove brake caliper guide pin bolts, then the caliper from rotor and mounting bracket.
5. Reverse procedure to install.

DISASSEMBLE

1. Remove two return springs from actuating collar, pull collar out of caliper housing.
2. Remove clamp rod and bushing. Discard bushing.
3. Bend back boot retainer tabs, then remove retainers, boots and pushrod from actuating collar.
4. Remove preload spring from retainer. Discard retainers and boots.
5. Pad interior of caliper assembly with clean shop towels, then remove piston by directing compressed air into caliper brake hose inlet hole. Use just enough air pressure to ease piston out of bore. **Do not place fingers in front of piston.**
6. Remove piston seal from bore using small piece of wood or plastic. **Do not use metal tool to remove seal.**
7. Remove cap and bleeder valve.
8. Remove seal, sprag clip and lever from pivot pin. Discard sprag clip.
9. Clean all metal components with suitable solvent, then dry with compressed air.
10. Inspect parking brake lever components, piston, caliper bore and mounting bracket for scoring, excessive wear or corrosion.

ASSEMBLE

1. Lubricate piston sea with clean brake fluid, then install seal into caliper bore groove. Ensure seal is not twisted.
2. Lubricate caliper bore and piston with clean brake fluid.
3. Place piston into caliper bore, then push downward until fully bottomed in bore.

4. Lubricate actuating collar, then install pushrod, new boots and new retainers onto collar.
5. Clamp retainers firmly against collar, then bend tabs on retainer to hold assembly together.
6. Connect preload spring onto retainer.
7. Lubricate clamp rod, then slide rod through holes in boot and actuating collar. Ensure boot is firmly positioned against reaction plate at clamp rod.
8. Lubricate and install new compliance bushing onto clamp rod.
9. Lubricate grooved bead of inner boot, boot groove in caliper housing and actuating collar.
10. Push clamp rod to bottom of piston mating hole, then pull actuating collar and seat inner boot into boot groove in caliper housing.
11. Ensure pushrod is positioned in caliper housing hole, then install bleeder cap and valve.
12. If removed, install pivot pin and new nut onto caliper. Lubricate parking brake lever and pivot pin.
13. Install pivot pin seal, parking brake lever and new sprag clip.
14. Ensure teeth of sprag clip face away from lever and snap seal cap over pivot pin.
15. Install two collar return springs onto retainer. Ensure retainer enters springs at end of second coil.
16. Install adjustment screw into caliper housing until actuating collar is parallel to piston bore face of housing.
17. Lubricate guide pins with suitable grease and slide beads onto pins.
18. Fill boots with grease and install into mounting bracket. Ensure boots are properly positioned in grooves in pins and mounting bracket.
19. Install caliper and bleed brake system.

XLR

REMOVAL

1. Remove brake master cylinder reservoir fluid to midway between maximum-full point and minimum allowable level.
2. Raise and support vehicle, then remove tire and wheel assembly.
3. The brake caliper inlet fitting bolt and hose from caliper. Discard two copper brake hose gaskets.
4. Plug opening in brake caliper and brake hose.
5. Remove guide pin bolts and caliper from mounting bracket.

DISASSEMBLE

1. Pad caliper interior housing with suitable clean cloths.
2. Remove piston from caliper bore by directing low pressure compressed air into bore through fluid inlet hole. Use just enough air to ease pistons out of bores. **Do not place fingers in front of piston.**
3. Remove piston dust boot seal from seal counterbore using small wooden or plastic tool. Discard boot seal.

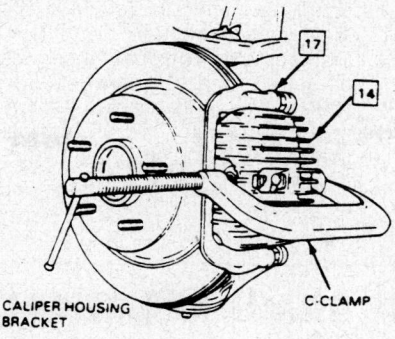

14 CALIPER HOUSING
17 BRACKET

GC4079100095000X

Fig. 2   Piston compression in caliper bore

4. Remove and discard piston seal from caliper bore.
5. Remove bleeder valve and cap from caliper.

INSPECTION

1. Clean caliper piston bore, seal counterbore and piston with denatured alcohol. **Do not use abrasives to clean caliper piston.**
2. Dry piston bore, counterbore and piston with non-lubricated, filtered compressed air.
3. Inspect caliper bore for cracks, scoring, pitting, excessive rust and/or excessive corrosion. If light rust or light corrosion are present in caliper bore, attempt to remove imperfection with fine emery paper.
4. Inspect caliper piston for cracks, scoring and/or damage to chrome plating.

ASSEMBLE

1. Lubricate new piston seal with suitable DOT 3 brake fluid from clean, sealed brake fluid container.
2. Install lubricated, new piston seal into caliper bore and new piston dust boot seal over piston.
3. Install piston into caliper bore and boot over end of piston so fold will face toward housing piston bore opening.
4. Seat boot into bore groove and slide piston into bore.
5. Push piston to bottom of bore. Ensure boot is properly seated into piston and caliper bore grooves.
6. Install caliper bleed screw and cap.

INSTALLATION

1. Install brake caliper to mounting bracket.
2. Install guide pin bolts.
3. Remove plug from caliper opening and brake hose.
4. Install new copper brake hose gaskets and brake caliper inlet fitting bolt to brake hose.
5. Install brake hose and caliper inlet fitting bolt to caliper.
6. Bleed hydraulic brake system.
7. Install tire and wheel assembly, then lower vehicle.

ROTOR

REPLACE

Whenever the brake rotor has been separated from the hub/axle flange, any rust or contaminants should be cleaned from the hub/axle flange and the brake rotor mating surfaces.

Corvette

1. Raise and support vehicle, then remove tire and wheel assembly.
2. Remove guide pin bolts, and caliper.
3. Remove mounting bolts and mounting bracket.
4. Remove rotor from hub and bearing.
5. Reverse procedure to install.

XLR

REMOVAL

1. Raise and support vehicle, then remove tire and wheel assembly.
2. Disconnect park brake cable from apply lever.
3. Install C-clamp over caliper with ends against body rear and outboard disc brake pad.
4. Compress piston into bore just enough to allow caliper to slide away from rotor. Remove C-clamp.
5. Remove caliper bracket bolts. **Do not disconnect brake flexible hose bolt.**
6. Remove caliper and mounting bracket, then support aside. Ensure there is no tension on hydraulic brake flexible hose.
7. Mark brake rotor to wheel studs position for installation alignment.
8. Remove brake rotor. **Do not force rotor off.** If rotor is difficult to remove, ease it off by gently rotating it while pulling outward.

INSTALLATION

1. Connect park brake cable to lever.
2. Adjust clearance of park brake shoe to drum-in-hat portion of brake rotor.
3. Install brake rotor to hub/axle flange.
4. Install brake caliper and bracket a to suspension knuckle.
5. Install tire and wheel assembly, then lower vehicle.

ADJUSTMENTS
Parking Brake

CORVETTE

1. Release parking brake lever, then raise and support vehicle.
2. Remove rear wheels, then install lug nuts on two opposite wheel studs to hold brake rotor in position.
3. Back caliper pistons into bores.
4. Loosen parking brake cable adjusting nut until there is no tension on parking brake shoes.
5. Turn each brake rotor until parking brake shoe star adjuster is visible through hole in rotor.

DISC BRAKES

6. Adjusting one side at a time, tighten adjuster until rotor cannot be turned by hand, then back star wheel off 5–7 notches. **Adjust parking brake shoes by inserting suitable tool through hole in rotor. On driver's side, tighten adjuster by moving tool handle upward. On passenger's side, tighten adjuster by moving tool handle downward.**

7. Install rear wheels and pull parking lever up two notches.
8. Tighten cable adjusting nut at equalizer until there is drag on wheels.
9. Release parking brake lever and inspect adjustment. No drag should be felt when rotating wheels.

XLR

The park brake cables are tensioned automatically by cycling the park brake pedal three times.

DISC BRAKE SPECIFICATIONS

Rotor Specifications

Model	Year	Nominal Thickness, Inch	Minimum Refinish Thickness, Inch	Discard Thickness, Inch①	Thickness Variation (Parallelism), Inch	Lateral Runout (T.I.R.), Inch	Maximum Scoring Depth, Inch
Corvette	2004–08	1.0200	.9800	.9650	.0010	.0020	.0590
XLR	2004–08	1.0200	.9800	.9650	.0010	.0020	.0590

① — Discard thickness is stamped on rotor.

TIGHTENING SPECIFICATIONS

Year	Component	Torque Ft. lbs.
2004–08	Bleed Screw	106①
	Caliper Guide Pin	23
	Caliper Inlet Fitting	33
	Caliper Mounting Bracket	129
	Wheel Lug Nut	100

① — Inch lbs

Saturn/GM Single Piston

NOTE: On Air Bag Equipped Models, Refer To "Air Bag System Precautions" Located In The Front Of This Manual For System Disarming & Arming Procedures.

NOTE: Refer To "Computer Relearn Procedures" Located In The Front Of This Manual When Battery Power To The Computer Has Been Interrupted.

INDEX

	Page No.
Adjustments	22-28
Parking Brake	22-28
AURA	22-28
Cobalt, G5 & ION	22-28
L-Series	22-28
Solstice & SKY	22-28
Brake Pad Service	22-25
AURA, Cobalt, G5, ION, Solstice & SKY	22-25
L-Series	22-25
Front	22-25
Rear	22-25
Brake System Bleed	22-25

	Page No.
Caliper Service	22-25
AURA, Cobalt, G5, ION, Solstice & SKY	22-25
Assemble	22-25
Disassemble	22-25
Replacement	22-25
L-Series	22-25
Front	22-25
Rear	22-26
Disc Brake Specifications	22-30
Caliper Specifications	22-30
Rotor Specifications	22-30
Parking Brake Service	22-26

	Page No.
Parking Brake Cable, Replace	22-26
AURA	22-26
Cobalt, G5 & ION	22-27
L-Series	22-27
Solstice & SKY	22-27
Parking Brake Equalizer Cable, Replace	22-26
Parking Brake Shoes, Replace	22-27
Rotor, Replace	22-26
AURA, Cobalt, G5 & ION	22-26
L-Series	22-26
Solstice & SKY	22-26
Tightening Specifications	22-31

BRAKE SYSTEM BLEED

Refer to "Hydraulic Brake Systems" for manual and pressure bleeding procedures.

BRAKE PAD SERVICE

AURA, Cobalt, G5, ION, Solstice & SKY

1. Raise and support vehicle, then remove tire and wheel assemblies.
2. Tighten suitable C-clamp until piston is compressed into caliper bore. Remove C-clamp.
3. Remove brake caliper lower guide pin bolt.
4. Pivot caliper upward and support aside using suitable wire.
5. Remove brake pads from caliper, **Fig. 1 and 2.**
6. Reverse procedure to install, noting the following:
   a. Inspect brake components.
   b. Bleed brake system as outlined in "Brake System Bleed."

L-Series

FRONT

1. Raise and support vehicle, then remove front tire and wheel assemblies.
2. Pry off locking plate and remove brake pressure hose from strut.
3. Remove pad retainer spring, guide pins and caliper.
4. Remove inboard, and outboard brake pads from caliper.
5. Reverse procedure to install.

REAR

1. Raise and support vehicle, then remove rear tire and wheel assemblies.
2. Drive out brake pad retaining pins from outside to inside.
3. Remove pins, retaining spring and pads.
4. Reverse procedure to install.

CALIPER SERVICE

AURA, Cobalt, G5, ION, Solstice & SKY

REPLACEMENT

1. Raise and support vehicle, then remove tire and wheel assemblies.
2. Install and tighten two wheel nuts opposite to retain rotor to hub.
3. Tighten suitable C-clamp to compress piston into caliper bore.
4. Remove mounting bolt and brake hose from caliper, **Fig. 3.**
5. Remove and discard copper brake hose gaskets.
6. Cap opening in brake caliper and brake hose.
7. Remove guide pin bolts, caliper and bracket.
8. Reverse procedure to install.

DISASSEMBLE

1. Remove caliper piston from bore using compressed air through fluid inlet hole.
2. Remove retaining ring to dust boot of caliper housing, **Fig. 4.**
3. Remove piston boot seal from counterbore in caliper, then the piston seal using suitable piece of wood, **Fig. 5.**

ASSEMBLE

1. Lubricate new piston seal using suitable DOT 3 brake fluid and install seal into caliper bore.
2. Apply suitable DOT 3 brake fluid to surface area of caliper piston.
3. Install bottom half of caliper piston into caliper bore and dust boot seal over caliper piston, **Fig. 6.**
4. Compress caliper piston to caliper bore and seat piston boot into counterbore.
5. Install retaining ring and bleeder valve.
6. Install bleeder valve cap and caliper.

L-Series

FRONT

REPLACEMENT

1. Raise and support vehicle, then remove tire and wheel assemblies.
2. Remove brake hose from caliper and plug opening.
3. Remove brake pad retaining spring from caliper and caliper-to-bracket guide pins.
4. Remove caliper from support bracket and pads from caliper.
5. Reverse procedure to install.

DISASSEMBLE

1. Inspect guide pin sleeves and covers for damage.
2. Inspect boot for deterioration. If damaged, overhaul caliper.
3. Remove piston boot ring and boot using small screwdriver.
4. Pad caliper interior with suitable cushion and apply non-lubricated compressed air to caliper inlet hole to remove piston.

5. Remove piston seal, bleeder valve and cap.

INSPECTION

1. Clean all components in clean denatured alcohol, and dry with non-lubricated compressed air.
2. Blow out all caliper and bleeder valve passages.
3. Inspect piston for damage.
4. Inspect caliper bore for damage, noting the following:
   a. Slight corrosion may be removed using suitable crocus cloth.
   b. If damage is excessive, replace caliper.
   c. **Do not hone caliper bore.**
5. Inspect seal groove for damage.

ASSEMBLE

1. Install bleeder valve.
2. Lubricate piston seal using clean brake fluid and install. Ensure seal is not twisted.
3. Install lubricated piston boot to piston.
4. Install lubricated piston to body. Push piston to bottom of bore.
5. Install boot ring, noting the following:
   a. Ensure piston boot outer edge is smoothly seated in counterbore.
   b. Work boot ring into groove near open end of caliper bore.
   c. **Do not pinch piston ring between boot ring and body.**
6. Lift piston boot inner edge to release trapped air, then install caliper and bleed brake system.

REAR

REPLACEMENT

1. Raise and support vehicle, then remove tire and wheel assemblies.
2. Drive out brake pad retaining pins from outside-to-inside, then remove pins, retaining spring and pads.
3. Remove brake pipe from caliper and plug opening.
4. Remove caliper to rear axle control arm fasteners and caliper.
5. Reverse procedure to install.

DISASSEMBLE

The rear caliper has a dual piston design. The caliper must not be completely disassembled. Disassemble only one piston at a time.

1. Carefully pry out piston boot clamp using small screwdriver and remove piston boot.
2. Pad caliper interior with suitable cushion and apply non-lubricated compressed air to caliper inlet hole to remove piston.
3. Remove piston seal, bleeder valve and cap.

INSPECTION

1. Clean all components in clean denatured alcohol and dry with non-lubricated compressed air.
2. Blow out all caliper and bleeder valve passages.
3. Inspect piston for damage.
4. Inspect caliper bore for damage, noting the following:

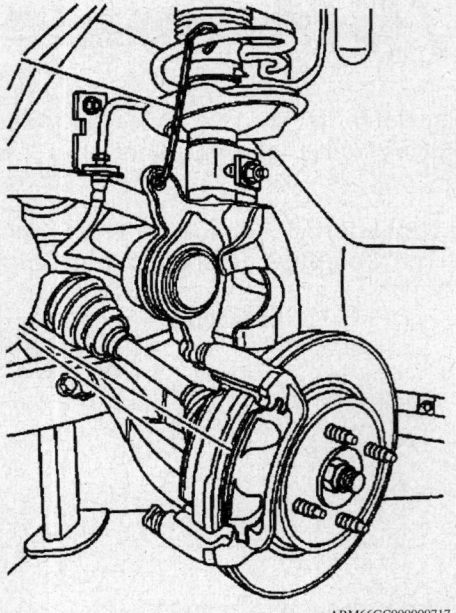

Fig. 1   Brake pad removal. AURA, Cobalt, G5 & ION

ARM66GC000000717

   a. Slight corrosion may be removed using suitable crocus cloth.
   b. If damage is excessive, replace caliper.
   c. **Do not hone caliper bore.**
5. Inspect seal groove for damage.

ASSEMBLE

1. Install bleeder valve and cap.
2. Lubricate piston seal using clean brake fluid and install. Ensure seal is not twisted.
3. Install lubricated piston boot to piston.
4. Insert lubricated piston into body, then install caliper and bleed brake system.

ROTOR
REPLACE

AURA, Cobalt, G5 & ION

1. Raise and support vehicle, then remove tire and wheel assembly.
2. Compress piston into caliper bore using suitable C-clamp to allow caliper pivot upward from brake pads.
3. Install and tighten two wheel nuts opposite to retain rotor to hub.
4. Remove guide pin bolts, caliper and bracket.
5. Mark rotor to wheel studs for installation alignment and remove rotor.
6. Reverse procedure to install.

Solstice & SKY

1. Raise and support vehicle, then remove tire and wheel assembly.
2. Compress piston into caliper bore using suitable C-clamp to allow caliper pivot upward from brake pads.

3. Remove caliper mounting bolts, then the caliper.
4. Remove caliper mounting bracket.
5. Remove screw holding rotor to hub, then rotor.
6. Reverse procedure to install.

L-Series

1. Raise and support vehicle, then remove tire and wheel assembly.
2. Pry off locking plate and remove brake pressure hose from strut.
3. Remove caliper bracket to steering knuckle mounting bolts and suspend caliper aside.
4. Remove mounting screw and rotor.
5. Reverse procedure to install.

PARKING BRAKE SERVICE

Parking Brake Equalizer Cable, Replace

1. Remove center console as outlined in "Dash Panel Service" chapter.
2. Remove adjuster nut and cables from equalizer, **Fig. 7.**
3. Place parking brake lever to highest position.
4. Lift equalizer cable over parking brake indicator switch and swing forward. Pull cable down and out of parking brake lever.
5. Reverse procedure to install. Adjust parking brake cable.

Parking Brake Cable, Replace

AURA

1. Ensure parking brake is fully released.
2. Remove console as follows:
   a. Remove console upper trim plate.
   b. Remove right and left side trim panels.
   c. Remove bolt covers using a suitable screwdriver.
   d. Remove console attaching bolts, then the console.
3. Remove rear carpet as follows:
   a. Remove front seats, then rear seat cushion.
   b. Remove front and rear carpet retainers, then the lower center pillar molding.
   c. Remove body lock pillar molding, then rear carpet.
4. Remove right or left rear park brake cable from console park bracket and front park brake cable equalizer, **Fig. 8.**
5. Raise and support vehicle.
6. Remove the plastic retainer clips from body, **Fig. 9.**
7. Remove the cable from the bracket.
8. Remove rear tires.
9. Remove rear parking brake cable retainer bolt.

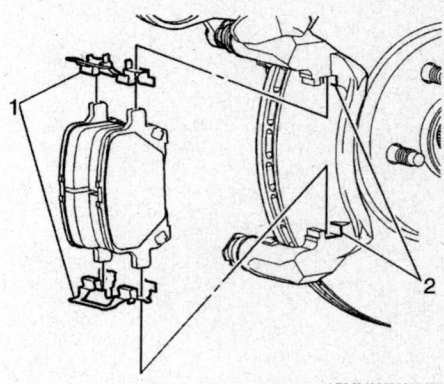

Fig. 2   Brake pad removal.
Solstice & SKY

10. Remove rear parking brake cable from caliper park brake lever
11. Lower vehicle, then remove plastic retainer clips from stud.
12. Remove parking brake cable and pass-through grommet from body, then the cable.
13. Reverse procedure to install noting the following:
    a. Reverse procedure to install. Adjust parking brake cable as outlined in "Adjustments."

COBALT, G5 & ION

FRONT

1. Raise park brake lever and unsnap park brake boot from console.
2. Lift up on rear of console compartment to release retaining fasteners.
3. Lift console compartment and push park brake boot through opening in compartment.
4. Slide console compartment over park brake lever.
5. Release park brake cable tension.
6. Remove park brake cable adjuster nut and washer, **Fig. 10.**
7. Disconnect rear park brake cables from front park brake cable equalizer, then remove front park brake cable by pulling rearward.
8. Reverse procedure to install. Adjust parking brake cable as outlined in "Adjustments."

REAR

1. Raise park brake lever and unsnap park brake boot from console.
2. Lift up on rear of console compartment to release retaining fasteners.
3. Lift console compartment and push park brake boot through opening in compartment.
4. Slide console compartment over park brake lever.
5. Release park brake cable tension.
6. Remove rear lower seat cushion.
7. Release rear edge of carpet from retainers.
8. Place carpeting forward to access rear park brake cables.

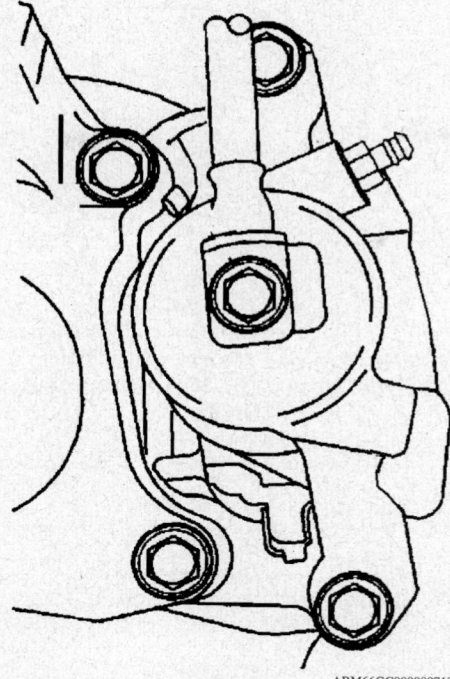

Fig. 3   Brake caliper hose removal. AURA, Cobalt, G5, ION, Solstice & SKY

9. With park brake lever released, remove rear brake cable from equalizer.
10. Release rear cable from retainer on park brake lever, then pass through grommet.
11. Raise and support vehicle.
12. Remove rear tire and wheel assembly.
13. Remove rear brake shoes as outlined in "Drum Brake" chapter.
14. Release park brake cable retainer from drum brake backing plate, **Fig. 11.**
15. Release rear cable to underbody retaining clip and park brake cable from clip, **Fig. 12.**
16. Release C-shaped retainer from park brake cable at bracket and remove cable, **Fig. 13.**
17. Reverse procedure to install. Adjust parking brake cable as outlined in "Adjustments."

L-SERIES

1. Release parking brake.
2. Remove parking brake boot by squeezing boot in sides while pulling upwards.
3. Loosen parking brake adjuster nut to provide ample slack in brake cable.
4. Raise and support vehicle, then disconnect exhaust resonator from exhaust manifold pipe.
5. Remove exhaust pipe to body insulator, then lower exhaust resonator pipe and muffler.
6. Remove exhaust heat shield and disconnect parking brake cable from rear parking brake cable. Discard clips.

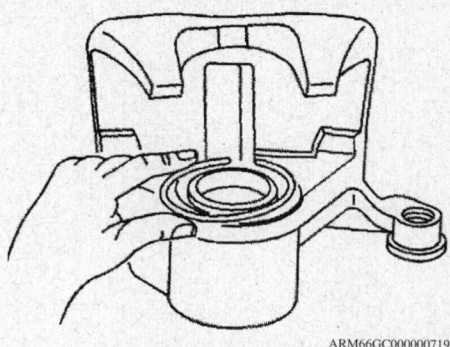

Fig. 4   Retaining ring removal.
AURA, Cobalt, G5, ION, Solstice & SKY

7. Disconnect front parking brake cable from equalizer.
8. Remove cable body attachment points.
9. Reverse procedure to install. Adjust parking brake cable as outlined in "Adjustments."

SOLSTICE & SKY

1. Remove front floor console by lifting upward. Console is held in place by three retaining clips.
2. Ensure park brake lever fully released, then completely back off adjustment nut.
3. Raise and support vehicle. Remove rear tires.
4. Carefully position driveline tunnel insulator downward just enough to access cable equalizer.
5. Rotate front cable end to release the cable from the equalizer.
6. Release wheel speed sensor harness clips from park brake cable.
7. Disconnect park brake cables from park brake actuator levers on brake calipers.
8. Remove park brake cable retainer.
9. Move cable conduit rearward to clear tunnel bracket, then lift cables to release cables from bracket.
10. Remove rear park brake cable as an assembly.
11. Reverse procedure to install

Parking Brake Shoes, Replace

1. Raise and support vehicle, then remove rear tire and wheel assemblies.
2. Remove rear caliper to rear axle control arm bolts and support caliper aside.
3. Remove mounting screw and rotor.
4. Remove return springs, parking brake shoes and hold-down retainers.
5. Remove parking brake shoes and adjuster.
6. Reverse procedure to install. Adjust parking brake as outlined in "Adjustments."

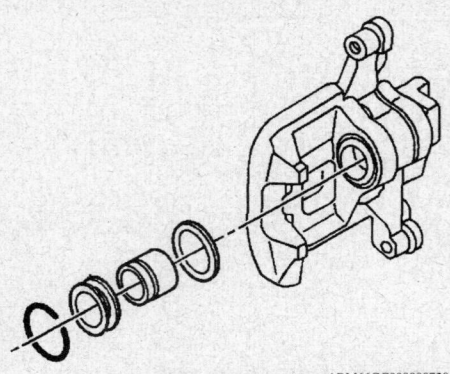

Fig. 5 Piston boot removal. AURA, Cobalt, G5, ION, Solstice & SKY

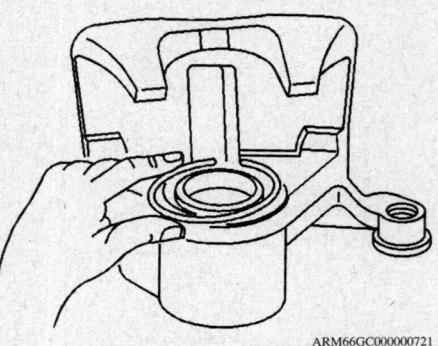

Fig. 6 Caliper piston installation. AURA, Cobalt, G5, ION, Solstice & SKY

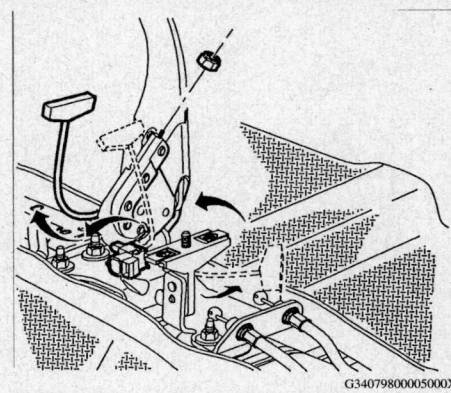

Fig. 7 Parking brake equalizer cable removal

ADJUSTMENTS

Parking Brake

AURA

1. Apply and release park brake several times. Ensure lever is released completely.
2. Turn ignition to On position and ensure red BRAKE lamp is not illuminated. If lamp is illuminated, verify following:
   a. Park brake lever is in released position and against stop.
   b. There is no slack in park brake cable.
3. Raise and support vehicle.
4. With parking brake pedal fully released, check parking brake levers on rear calipers. The levers should be against stops on caliper housings.
5. Apply and release parking three to five times, this will allow cable tensioner to take up slack in the parking brake cable.
6. Apply parking brake, a firm pedal should be felt by depressing pedal less than one full stroke.
7. Try to rotate rear wheel. They should not rotate in either direction.
8. Release parking brake. Tires should rotate freely with no drag.

COBALT, G5 & ION

1. Apply and release park brake several times. Ensure lever is released completely.
2. Turn ignition to On position and ensure red BRAKE lamp is not illuminated. If lamp is illuminated, verify following:
   a. Park brake lever is in released position and against stop.

   b. There is no slack in park brake cable.
3. Turn ignition to Off position.
4. Remove brake lever boot from console.
5. Pull boot away from console.
6. Loosen front park brake cable adjusting nut to end of front cable threaded rod.
7. Raise and support vehicle.
8. Adjust rear drum brakes as outlined in "Drum Brakes" chapter.
9. Ensure no brake shoe drag is present by rotating brake drums.
10. Install two wheel nuts to drums and lower vehicle.
11. Raise park brake lever six notched positions and install cable adjusting nut.
12. Tighten park brake cable adjusting nut.
13. Release park brake lever and ensure park brake is released.
14. If drums do not rotate freely, raise park brake lever three notched positions and rotate brake drum.
15. Righthand rear brake drum should not rotate forward or rearward and lefthand rear drum should not rotate in either direction.
16. Raise park brake lever one additional notched position and attempt to rotate brake drums.
17. Ensure left and righthand brake drums cannot be rotated. Raise vehicle.
18. Remove brake drum mounting bolts, then install tire and wheel assemblies.
19. Lower vehicle, position park brake lever boot to front console and release park brake lever.

L-SERIES

1. Remove parking brake boot by squeezing boot in sides while pulling upwards.
2. Raise and support vehicle, then remove rear tire and wheel assemblies.

3. Turn adjuster (through hole in front face of rotor) at rear rotor until brake disc locks. Turn back adjuster until disc just moves freely.
4. Pull parking brake lever to third click.
5. Tighten adjuster nut until heavy drag is felt at both rear wheels when turned by hand.
6. Apply and release parking brake several times. There should be no drag when lever is in rest position.
7. Pull lever to third click and ensure heavy drag exists at both rear wheels. Repeat procedure until proper adjustment is reached.

SOLSTICE & SKY

1. Remove front floor console by lifting upward. Console is held in place by three retaining clips.
2. Apply and release park brake several times. Ensure lever is released completely.
3. Loosen cable tension adjusting nut just enough to back nut away from lever cam.
4. Tighten adjusting nut until slack in front cable is removed and nut rests against lever cam.
5. Cycle park brake lever several times. Ensure lever is released completely.
6. Raise lever 1 detent position. Both sides should require high effort to rotate.
7. Raise lever 1 more detent. One side should be locked, other side should require high effort to rotate.
8. Raise the lever 1 more detent. Both sides should be locked.
9. Release park brake lever. Wheel should rotate without drag.
10. Inspect brake caliper park brake levers to ensure that they are resting against stops.

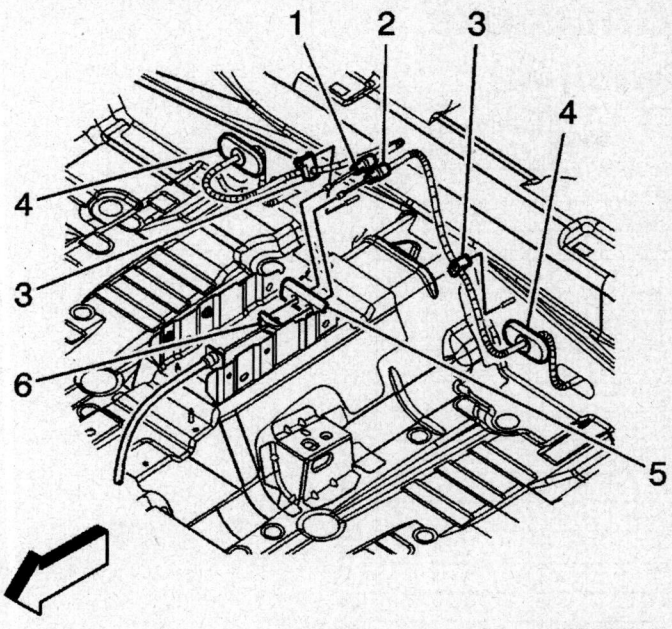

ARM0600000001536

Fig. 8 Parking brake assembly. AURA

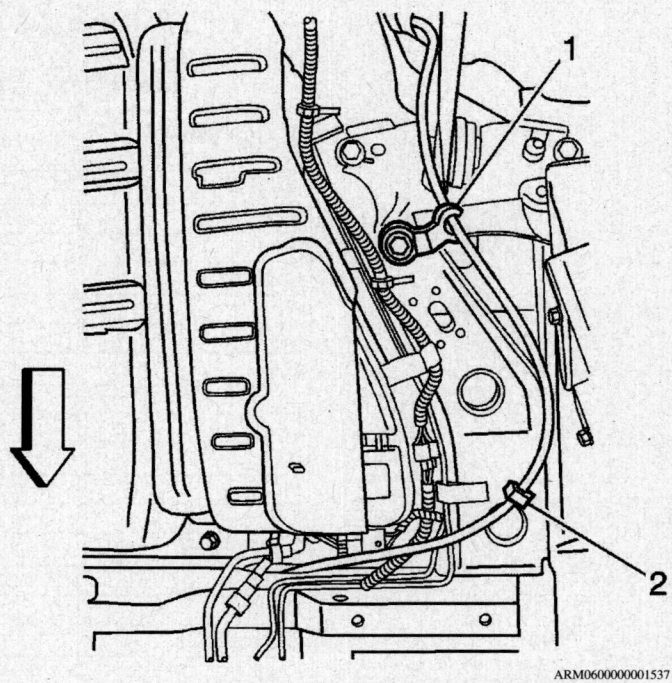

ARM0600000001537

Fig. 9 Retainer clip and bracket. AURA

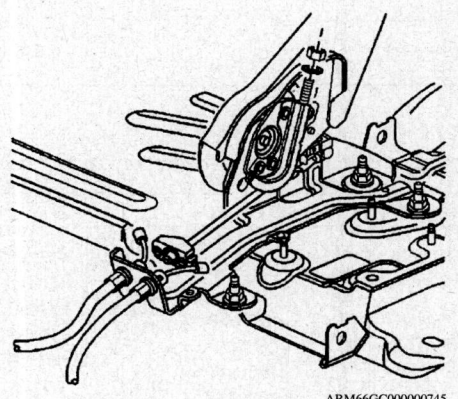

ARM66GC000000745

Fig. 10 Park brake cable removal. Cobalt, G5 & ION

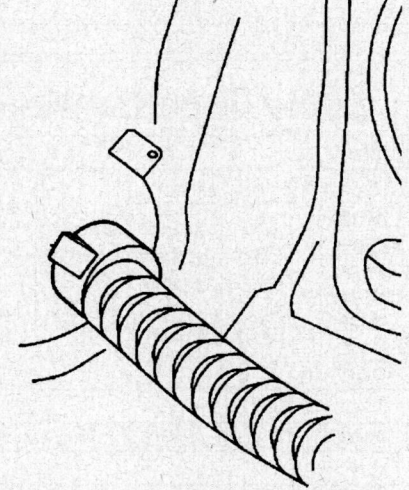

ARM66GC000000746

Fig. 11 Park brake cable retainer removal. Cobalt, G5 & ION

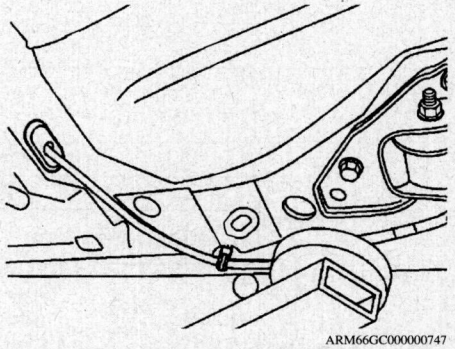

ARM66GC000000747

Fig. 12 Park brake cable removal. Cobalt, G5 & ION

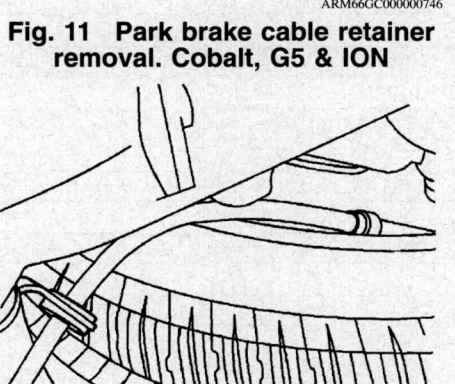

ARM66GC000000748

Fig. 13 Cable assembly removal. Cobalt, G5 & ION

DISC BRAKE SPECIFICATIONS
Caliper Specifications

Model	Year	Caliper Bore Dia. Inch
AURA		
Front	2007–08	2.36
Rear	2007–08	1.50
COBALT		
Front	2005–08	—
Rear	2005–08	—
G5		
Front	2007–08	—
Rear	2007–08	—
ION		
Front	2004–07	—
Rear	2004–07	—
L-SERIES		
Front	2004–05	2.24
Rear	2004–05	1.38
SOLSTICE		
Front	2006–08	—
Rear	2006–08	—
SKY		
Front	2006–08	—
Rear	2006–08	—

Rotor Specifications

Year	Brake Lining Wear Limit, Inch	Front Disc Brake Rotor Thickness, Inch Nominal	Min. Refinish	Discard Limit ①	Thickness Variation Parallelism, Inch	Lateral Run Out (T.I.R.), Inch	Maximum Scoring Depth, Inch	Brake Lining Wear Limit, Inch	Rear Disc Brake Rotor Thickness, Inch Nominal	Min. Refinish	Discard Limit ①	Thickness Variation Parallelism, Inch	Lateral Run Out (T.I.R.), Inch	Maximum Scoring Depth, Inch
AURA														
2007–08	.0300	1.0230	.9060	.8980	.0010	.0020	.0590	.0300	.5510	.4720	.4650	.0010	.0020	.0590
COBALT														
2005–08	.0390	.9330	.8960	.8700	.0010	.0020	.0590	.0390	.5510	.4720	.4650	.0010	.0020	.0590
G5														
2007–08	.0390	.9330	.8960	.8700	.0010	.0020	.0590	.0390	.5510	.4720	.4650	.0010	.0020	.0590
ION														
2004–07	.0390	.9330	.8960	.8700	.0010	.0020	.0590	.0390	.5510	.4720	.4650	.0010	.0020	.0590
L-SERIES														
2004–05	.0800	.9800	.9000	.8700	.0003	.0010	.0590	.0800	.3900	.3500	.3100	.0004	.0010	.0590
SOLSTICE														
2006–07	.0300	1.0230	.9250	.9060	.0010	.0020	.0590	.0300	.4650	.4130	.3940	.0010	.0020	.059
SKY														
2007–08	.0300	1.0230	.9250	.9060	.0010	.0020	.0590	.0300	.4650	.4130	.3940	.0010	.0020	.059

① — Discard thickness is stamped on rotor.

TIGHTENING SPECIFICATIONS

Year	Component	Torque Ft. Lbs.
AURA		
2007–08	Bleeder Valve	97①
	Caliper	26
	Caliper Bracket	96
	Hose	37
COBALT		
2005–08	Bleeder Valve	97①
	Caliper	25
	Caliper Bracket	85
	Hose	35
G5		
2007–08	Bleeder Valve	97①
	Caliper	25
	Caliper Bracket	85
	Hose	35
ION		
2004–07	Bleeder Valve	97①
	Brake Caliper Guide Pin	25
	Brake Caliper Mounting Bracket	85
	Brake Hose To Brake Caliper	35
	Park Brake Cable Adjusting Nut	35①
	Park Brake Lever	18
	Park Brake Warning Lamp Switch	27①
L-SERIES		
2004–05	Bleed Valve, Front	71①
	Bleed Valve, Rear	53①
	Brake Hose To Brake Pipe	12
	Brake Hose To Brake Caliper	30
	Brake Pipe To Caliper	12
	Brake Lever To Floor	89①
	Caliper To Bracket Guide Pins	22
	Caliper To Rear Axle Control Arm	59
	Caliper To Steering Knuckle	70
	Exhaust Heat Shield	35①
	Wheel Lug Nuts	92②
	Wheel Speed Sensor To Knuckle	72①
SOLSTICE		
2006–08	Bleeder Valve	97①
	Brake Rotor Screw	89①
	Caliper Guide Pin (Front)	25
	Caliper Guide Pin (Rear)	20
	Caliper Mounting Bracket	85
	Hose	30
SKY		
2007–08	Bleeder Valve	97①
	Brake Rotor Screw	89①
	Caliper Guide Pin (Front)	25
	Caliper Guide Pin (Rear)	20
	Caliper Mounting Bracket	85
	Hose	30

① — Inch lbs.
② — For steel wheel & optional aluminum wheel w/large center cap, install wheel cover or cap. With socket, hand tighten five cap nuts then, with wrench, tighten each cap an additional 90°.

Toyota/GM Single Piston Caliper

NOTE: On Air Bag Equipped Models, Refer To "Air Bag System Precautions" Located In The Front Of This Manual For System Disarming & Arming Procedures.

NOTE: Refer To "Computer Relearn Procedures" Located In The Front Of This Manual When Battery Power To The Computer Has Been Interrupted.

INDEX

	Page No.		Page No.		Page No.
Brake Pad Service	22-32	Inspection	22-33	**Rotor, Replace**	22-33
Installation	22-32	Installation	22-33	Installation	22-33
Removal	22-32	Removal	22-32	Removal	22-33
Brake System Bleed	22-32	**Description**	22-32	**Tightening Specifications**	22-34
Caliper Service	22-32	**Disc Brake Specifications**	22-34	**Troubleshooting**	22-32
Assemble	22-33	Rotor Specifications	22-34		
Disassemble	22-33	**Precautions**	22-32		

PRECAUTIONS

1. Keep grease and other foreign material off brake linings, caliper, surfaces of disc and external surfaces of hub.
2. Avoid deforming disc, and nicking or scratching brake linings.
3. Worn or damaged rubber piston seals should be replaced.
4. During removal and installation of a wheel assembly, ensure not to interfere with or damage caliper splash shield, or bleeder screw.
5. Front wheel bearing preload should be adjusted to specifications.
6. Ensure vehicle is centered on hoist before servicing any front end components to avoid bending or damaging disc splash shield on full left or right-hand wheel turns.
7. Before vehicle is moved after any brake service work, ensure to obtain a firm brake pedal.
8. Assembly bolts of two-piece caliper housings should not be disturbed unless caliper requires service.

DESCRIPTION

The caliper is a single bore design and is mounted to a carrier assembly, **Fig. 1.** Hydraulic pressure, created by applying the brake pedal, is converted by the caliper to a stopping force. This force acts equally against the piston and bottom of caliper bore to move the piston outward and to slide the caliper inward, resulting in a clamping action on the rotor. The clamping action forces the linings against the rotor, creating friction required to stop the vehicle.

TROUBLESHOOTING

The most common cause of brake chatter on disc brakes is a variation in disc thickness. If roughness or vibration is encountered during highway operation or if pedal pulsation is experienced at low speeds, the disc may have excessive thickness variation. To inspect for this condition, measure the disc at 12 points with a micrometer at a radius approximately one inch from edge of disc. If thickness measurements vary by more than .0005 inch, the disc should be replaced with a new one.

Excessive lateral runout of braking disc may cause a piston knocking back, possibly creating increased pedal travel and vibration when brakes are applied.

Before inspecting the runout, the wheel bearings should be adjusted. The adjustment is very important and will be required at the completion of the test to prevent bearing failure. Adjust the wheel bearings as outlined in "Front Suspension & Steering" section of appropriate chassis chapter.

BRAKE SYSTEM BLEED

Refer to "Hydraulic Brake Systems" for manual and pressure bleeding procedures.

BRAKE PAD SERVICE

Removal

Replace brake pads on one wheel at a time to prevent opposite side caliper piston from being forced out of bore.

1. Siphon ⅔ of brake fluid from master cylinder.
2. Raise and support vehicle, then remove tire and wheel assemblies.
3. Install two wheel lug nuts to retain rotor and remove caliper mounting bolts.
4. Remove union nut securing brake hose to caliper and drain fluid into suitable container. **If caliper is only being removed for brake pad replacement, do not disconnect brake hose.**
5. Compress piston and remove caliper. If brake hose remains connected, suspend caliper aside. **Do not support caliper with brake hose.**
6. Remove anti-rattle clips and brake pads, **Fig. 2.**
7. Remove pad wear indicator plates and anti-squeal shims.
8. Remove support plates.

Installation

1. Install new support plates on caliper mounting bracket.
2. Install new wear indicators and anti-squeal shims on each pad, then position pads in caliper mounting bracket. **Ensure a wear indicator arrow is pointing in rotating direction of rotor.**
3. Install anti-rattle springs.
4. Seat piston in caliper bore, then install caliper and mounting bolts.
5. Fill master cylinder and bleed brakes.
6. Seat piston in caliper bore. **Do not damage piston.**
7. Ensure support plates and anti-rattle springs are properly positioned, then mount caliper over rotor onto mounting bracket, **Fig. 3.**
8. Install caliper mounting bolts.
9. Install brake hose and mounting bolts using new copper gaskets.
10. Fill master cylinder and bleed brake system as outlined in "Hydraulic Brake Systems" chapter.

CALIPER SERVICE

Removal

1. Siphon ⅔ of brake fluid from master cylinder.
2. Raise and support vehicle, then remove tire and wheel assemblies.
3. Install two wheel lug nuts to retain rotor and remove caliper mounting bolts.
4. Remove union nut securing brake hose to caliper and drain fluid into suitable container. **If caliper is only being**

removed for brake pad replacement, do not disconnect brake hose.

5. Compress piston and remove caliper. If brake hose remains connected, suspend caliper aside. **Do not support caliper with brake hose.**

Disassemble

1. Remove two caliper slide bushings, four dust boots and spacer collars, **Fig. 1.**
2. Pry out caliper dust boot retaining ring and remove dust boot.
3. Place clean shop towels in caliper web and apply compressed air to caliper fluid inlet to force piston from bore. **Keep fingers clear of caliper web when removing piston. Use only enough air pressure to ease piston out of bore.**
4. Remove piston seal from caliper bore. **Do not mar machined surface of caliper.**
5. Remove bleeder valve.

Inspection

1. Clean components with alcohol and wipe dry with clean, lint free shop towels.
2. Blow out caliper and fluid passages with clean, filtered compressed air.
3. Inspect caliper and piston for damage, distortion, excessive wear and pitting.

Assemble

1. Apply lithium soap base glycol grease to components, **Fig. 4.**
2. Install piston seal in caliper. Ensure seal is squarely seated in groove.
3. Press piston into bore. Ensure piston enters bore straight.
4. Seat piston dust boot in caliper groove and install retaining ring.
5. Install two collars and four slide bushing dust boots, rotating boots as they are pressed in to ensure they are fully seated.
6. Install slide bushings through dust boots. Ensure boots remain seated in caliper grooves.

Installation

1. Seat piston in caliper bore. **Do not damage piston.**
2. Ensure support plates and anti-rattle springs are properly positioned, then mount caliper over rotor onto mounting bracket, **Fig. 3.**
3. Install caliper mounting bolts.
4. Install brake hose and mounting bolts using new copper gaskets.
5. Fill master cylinder and bleed brake system as outlined in "Hydraulic Brake Systems" chapter.

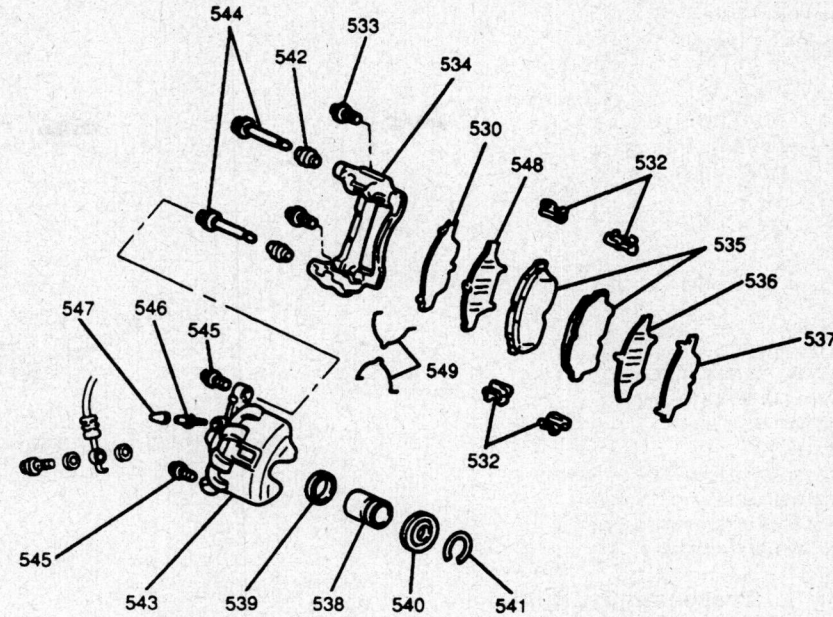

530	ANTI-SQUEAL SHIM (INBOARD)	540	PISTON BOOT
532	ANTI-RATTLE SPRINGS	541	CALIPER SET RING
533	CALIPER CARRIER BOLTS	542	DUST BOOTS
534	CALIPER CARRIER	543	CALIPER HOUSING
535	BRAKE PADS	544	SLIDE PINS
536	ANTI-SQUEAL SHIM (INNER OUTBOARD)	545	CALIPER MOUNTING BOLTS
537	ANTI-SQUEAL SHIM (OUTBOARD)	546	BLEEDER SCREW
538	PISTON	547	CAP
539	PISTON SEAL	548	ANTI-SQUEAL SHIM (INNER INBOARD)
		549	ANTI-SQUEAL SPRINGS

GC4079700151000X

Fig. 1 Exploded view of brake caliper

ROTOR
REPLACE
Removal

1. Siphon ⅔ of brake fluid from master cylinder.
2. Raise and support vehicle, then remove tire and wheel assemblies.
3. Install two wheel lug nuts to retain rotor and remove caliper mounting bolts.
4. Remove union nut securing brake hose to caliper and drain fluid into suitable container. **Do not disconnect brake hose.**
5. Compress piston and remove caliper. If brake hose remains connected, suspend caliper aside. **Do not support caliper with brake hose.**
6. Remove anti-rattle springs from caliper carrier.
7. Remove mounting bolts and caliper carrier.
8. Remove brake rotor from wheel hub. If

rotor cannot be removed by hand, install two 8 MM bolts into rotor. Tightening bolts will force rotor off wheel hub.
9. Reverse procedure to install.

Installation

1. Install brake rotor.
2. Install mounting bolts and caliper carrier.
3. Install anti-rattle springs from caliper carrier.
4. Seat piston in caliper bore. **Do not damage piston.**
5. Ensure support plates and anti-rattle springs are properly positioned, then mount caliper over rotor onto mounting bracket, **Fig. 3.**
6. Install caliper mounting bolts.
7. Install brake hose and mounting bolts using new copper gaskets.
8. Fill master cylinder and bleed brake system as outlined in "Hydraulic Brake Systems" chapter.

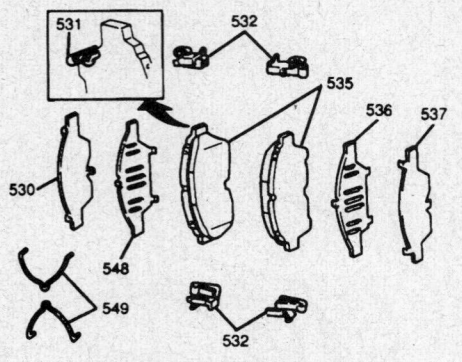

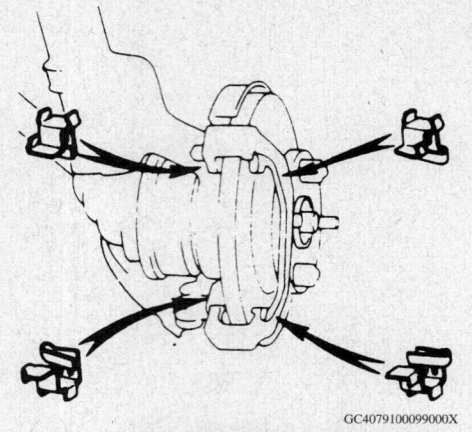

Fig. 3 Caliper support installation

GC4079100099000X

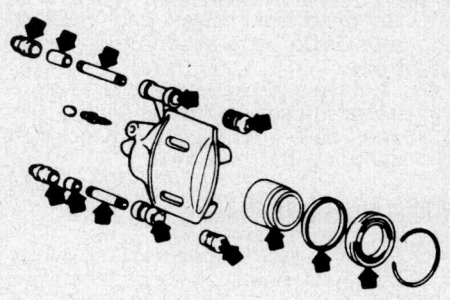

GC4079100103000X

Fig. 4 Caliper piston installation

530 ANTI-SQUEAL SHIM (INBOARD)
531 PAD WEAR INDICATOR PLATE
532 ANTI-RATTLE SPRINGS
535 BRAKE PADS
536 ANTI-SQUEAL SHIM (INNER OUTBOARD)
537 ANTI-SQUEAL SHIM (OUTBOARD)
548 ANTI-SQUEAL SHIM (INNER INBOARD)
549 ANTI-SQUEAL SPRINGS

GC4079700150000X

Fig. 2 Brake pad assembly

DISC BRAKE SPECIFICATIONS
Rotor Specifications

Year	Front Disc Brake							Rear Disc Brake						
	Brake Lining Wear Limit, Inch	Rotor						Brake Lining Wear Limit, Inch	Rotor					
		Thickness, Inch			Thickness Variation Parallelism, Inch	Lateral Run Out (T.I.R.), Inch	Maximum Scoring Depth, Inch		Thickness, Inch			Thickness Variation Parallelism, In, ch	Lateral Run Out (T.I.R.), Inch	Maximum Scoring Depth, Inch
		Nominal	Min. Refinish	Discard Limit ①					Nominal	Min. Refinish	Discard Limit ①			
VIBE														
2004–08	.0390	.9840	.9060	.9060	.0010	.0020	.0590	.0390	.3540	.2950	.2950	.0010	.0060	.0590

① — Discard thickness is stamped on rotor.

TIGHTENING SPECIFICATIONS

Year	Component	Torque Ft. Lbs.
VIBE		
2004–08	Bleeder Valve	73①
	Brake Hose To Caliper Fitting	21
	Caliper Bracket	79
	Caliper, Front	25
	Caliper, Rear	34
	Front Disc Brake Splash Shield	73①

① — Inch lbs.

DRUM BRAKES

TABLE OF CONTENTS

	Page No.		Page No.
ALERO, CENTURY, GRAND AM, MALIBU & VIBE	23-1	CAVALIER, COBALT, G5 & SUNFIRE	23-5
AVEO	23-8	SATURN	23-10

Alero, Century, Grand Am, Malibu & Vibe

NOTE: On Air Bag Equipped Models, Refer To "Air Bag System Precautions" Located In The Front Of This Manual For System Disarming & Arming Procedures.

NOTE: Refer To "Computer Relearn Procedures" Located In The Front Of This Manual When Battery Power To The Computer Has Been Interrupted.

INDEX

	Page No.		Page No.		Page No.
Adjustments	23-2	Description	23-1	Brake Linings & Springs	23-2
Parking Brake	23-2	Drum Brake Specifications	23-4	Parking Brake Cable	23-2
Service Brake	23-2	Inspection	23-1	Precautions	23-1
Brake Service	23-2	Adjuster Mechanism	23-2	Tightening Specifications	23-4
Installation	23-2	Backing Plate	23-2		
Removal	23-2	Brake Drums	23-1		

DESCRIPTION

A single spring holds both shoe and lining to the backing plate and acts as a retractor spring for the shoe and lining assemblies, **Fig. 1.**

PRECAUTIONS

When working on or around brake assemblies, care must be taken to prevent breathing asbestos dust, as many manufacturers incorporate asbestos fibers in the production of brake linings. During routine service operations the amount of asbestos dust from brake lining wear is at a low level because of a chemical breakdown during use and a few precautions will minimize exposure.

1. Do not sand or grind brake linings unless suitable local exhaust ventilation equipment is used to prevent excessive asbestos exposure.
2. Wear suitable respirator approved for asbestos dust use during repair procedures.
3. When cleaning brake dust from brake components, use vacuum cleaner with highly efficient filter system. If suitable vacuum cleaner is not available, use water soaked rag. **Do not use compressed air or dry brush to clean brake components.**
4. Keep work area clean.
5. Properly dispose of rags and vacuum cleaner bags by placing them in plastic bags.
6. Do not smoke or eat while working on brake systems. **Never use gasoline, kerosene, alcohol, motor oil, transmission fluid, or any fluid containing mineral oil to clean brake system components. These fluids will damage rubber caps and seals. If system contamination is suspected, inspect brake fluid in reservoir for dirt, discoloration, or separation (breakdown) of brake fluid into distinct layers. Drain fluid into suitable container and flush hydraulic system with clean brake fluid if contamination is suspected.**

INSPECTION

1. If any components are of doubtful strength or quality because of heat discoloration, or are worn, replace them.
2. Inspect wheel cylinder dust boots for signs of excessive wear or damage. If any leakage is apparent replace wheel cylinder.
3. Clean dirt and/or rust from brake drum, backing plate and other components. **Do not use compressed air or dry brush to clean brake components. Many brake components contain asbestos fibers which, if inhaled, can cause serious injury. Clean brake components with water soaked rag or suitable vacuum cleaner to minimize airborne dust.**

Brake Drums

Any time the brake drums are removed for brake service, the braking surface diameter should be inspected with suitable brake drum micrometer at several points to determine if they are within the safe oversize limit stamped on the brake drum outer surface. If the braking surface diameter exceeds specifications, the drum must be replaced. If the braking surface diameter is within specifications, drums should be cleaned and inspected for cracks, scores, deep grooves, taper, out-of-round and heat spotting. If drums are cracked or heat spotted, they must be replaced. Minor scores should be removed with sandpaper. Grooves and large scores can only be removed by machining with special equipment, as long as the braking surface is within specifications stamped on brake drum outer surface. Any brake drum sufficiently out-of-round to cause vehicle vibration or noise while braking or showing taper should also be machined, removing only enough stock to true up the brake drum.

After a brake drum is machined, wipe the braking surface diameter with a denatured alcohol soaked cloth. If one brake drum is machined, the other should also be machined to the same diameter to maintain equal braking forces.

Brake Linings & Springs

Inspect brake linings for excessive wear, damage, oil, grease or brake fluid contamination. If any of the these conditions exists, brake linings should be replaced. Do not attempt to replace only one set of brake shoes. they should be replaced as an axle set only to maintain equal braking forces. Examine brake shoe webbing, hold-down and return springs for signs of overheating indicated by a slight blue color. If any component exhibits overheating signs, replace hold-down and return springs with new ones. Overheated springs lose their pull and could cause brake linings to wear out prematurely. Inspect springs for sags, bends and external damage and replace as required.

Inspect hold-down retainers and pins for bends, rust and corrosion. If any of these are found, replace as required.

Backing Plate

Inspect backing plate shoe contact surface for grooves that may restrict shoe movement and cannot be removed by lightly sanding with emery cloth or other suitable abrasive. If backing plate exhibits these condition, it should be replaced. Also inspect for signs of cracks, warpage and excessive rust, indicating need for replacement.

Adjuster Mechanism

Inspect components for rust, corrosion, bends and fatigue. Replace as required. **On adjuster mechanism equipped with adjuster cable,** inspect cable for kinks, fraying or elongation of eyelet and replace as required.

Parking Brake Cable

Inspect parking brake cable end for kinks, fraying and elongation and replace as required. Use a small hose clamp to compress clamp where it enters backing plate to remove.

BRAKE SERVICE
Removal

1. Raise and support vehicle.
2. Mark relationship of wheel to axle, then remove wheel and tire assembly.
3. Remove brake drum. If drum is difficult to remove, proceed as follows:
   a. Ensure parking brake is released.
   b. Back off parking brake cable adjustment.
   c. Remove access hole plug from backing plate, insert screwdriver through hole and push parking brake lever off its stop.
   d. Insert punch through hole in splash shield, tap on punch to loosen drum and remove drum, **Fig. 2.**
4. Remove actuator spring using brake tool No. J-38400, or equivalent, to pry loop end of spring from adjuster actuator, **Fig. 3. Do not over stretch spring.**
5. Remove end of retractor spring from adjuster shoe and lining assembly, **Fig. 4. Keep finger away from retractor spring.**
6. Remove adjuster shoe, lining, actuator and screw.
7. Remove park brake lever from shoe assembly. Do not remove parking brake cable from lever unless parking brake lever is being replaced.
8. Remove retractor spring from park brake shoe and lining.
9. Pry end of retractor spring toward axle using suitable brake tool until it snaps off shoe web onto backing plate. Remove park brake shoe.

Installation

1. Lubricate raised shoe pads on backing plate, anchor surfaces on backing plate and adjuster screw threads using brake lubricant No. 1052196, or equivalent.
2. Install retractor spring by hooking center spring section under tab on anchor.
3. Place shoe on backing plate.
4. Pull end of retractor spring up to rest on web of brake shoe using brake tool No. J-38400, or equivalent, **Fig. 5.**
5. Pull end of retractor spring over until it locks into slot of brake shoe, **Fig. 6.**
6. Install park brake lever.
7. Place shoe on backing plate.
8. Pull end of retractor spring up to rest on web of brake shoe using suitable brake tool.
9. Pull end of retractor spring over until if locks into slot of brake shoe.
10. Install adjuster actuator by spreading shoes using suitable brake tool and move actuator into place, **Fig. 7.**
11. Install actuator spring.
12. Adjust brakes using suitable adjustment tool. Shoes' outer diameter should be .050 inch less than inside diameter of each drum.
13. Install drums, wheels and tires.

ADJUSTMENTS

Service Brake

1. Raise and support vehicle.
2. Mark relationship of wheel to axle, then remove wheel and tire assembly.
3. Remove brake drum. If drum is difficult to remove, proceed as follows:
   a. Ensure parking brake is released.
   b. Back off parking brake cable adjustment.
   c. Remove access hole plug from backing plate, insert screwdriver through hole and push parking brake lever off its stop.
   d. Insert punch through hole in splash shield, tap on punch to loosen drum and remove drum.
4. Measure inside diameter of drum using tool Nos. J-21177-A or J-22364-01, or equivalents.
5. Adjust by turning star wheel adjuster. Lining diameter should be .050 inch less than inside diameter of each drum.
6. Install drums, wheels and tires.
7. Lower vehicle and tighten wheel lug nuts.

Parking Brake

1. Adjust brakes as outlined in "Service Brake."
2. Apply and release parking brake five times to six clicks.
3. Ensure pedal is fully released by turning ignition On. Brake warning lamp should be off.
4. If brake warning lamp is lit, operate pedal release lever and pull downward on front parking brake cable.
5. Raise and support vehicle, then remove access hole plug.
6. Adjust cable until ⅛ inch drill bit can be inserted through access hole into space between shoe web and park lever, **Fig. 8.** Proper adjustment lets ⅛ inch drill bit fit in space but not ¼ inch bit.
7. Release brake and ensure wheels rotate freely.
8. Replace access hole plug and lower vehicle.

A ACCESS HOLE PLUG.
   NOT PART OF ASM.
   SERVICE ONLY ITEM.
1 ADJUSTER SOCKET
2 ADJUSTER SCREW
3 PIVOT NUT
4 RETRACTOR SPRING
5 ADJUSTER SHOE AND LINING
6 WHEEL CYLINDER
7 BLEEDER VALVE
8 BOLT
9 BACKING PLATE
10 PARK BRAKE SHOE AND LINING
11 PARK BRAKE LEVER
12 ACTUATOR SPRING
13 ADJUSTER ACTUATOR

10 BACKING PLATE ASSEMBLY
21 SPLASH SHIELD HOLE

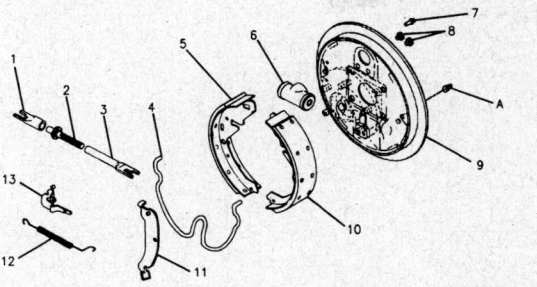

GC4089700048000X

Fig. 1 Brake drum assembly

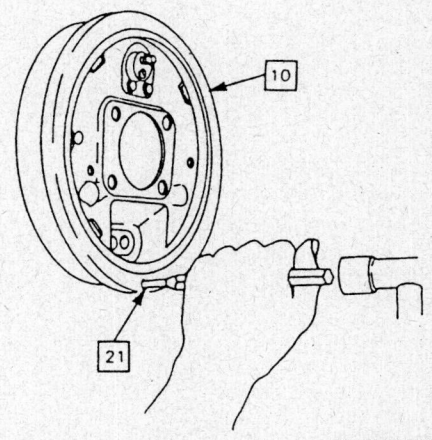

GC4089100035000X

Fig. 2 Loosening drum through splash shield

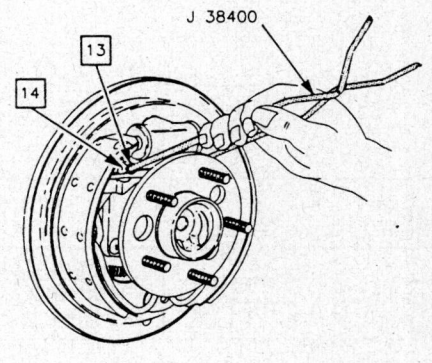

13 ACTUATOR SPRING
14 ADJUSTER ACTUATOR

GC4089100036000X

Fig. 3 Actuator spring removal

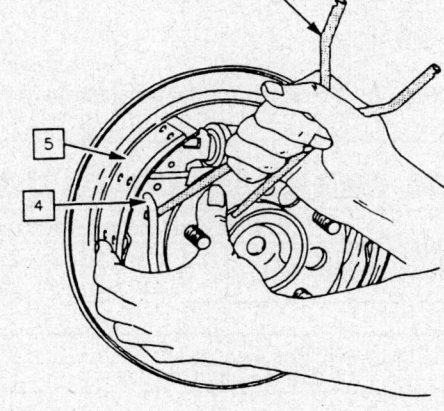

4 RETRACTOR SPRING
5 ADJUSTER SHOE LINING

GC4089100037000X

Fig. 4 Retractor spring disengagement

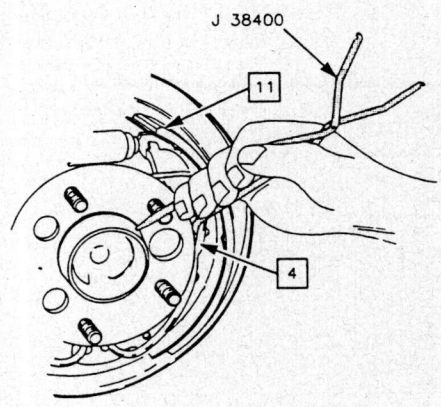

4 RETRACTOR SPRING
11 PARK BRAKE SHOE AND LINING

GC4089100038000X

Fig. 5 Spring end installation onto shoe web

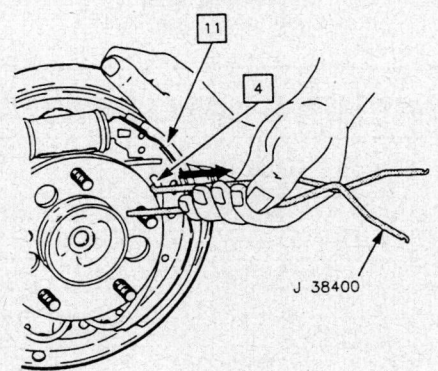

4 RETRACTOR SPRING
11 PARK BRAKE SHOE AND LINING

GC4089100039000X

Fig. 6 Spring end installation into shoe slot

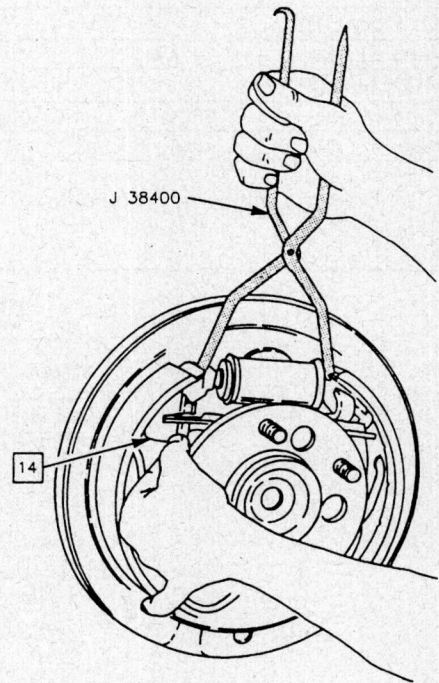

14 ADJUSTER ACTUATOR

GC4089100040000X

Fig. 7 Shoe spreading to install adjuster actuator

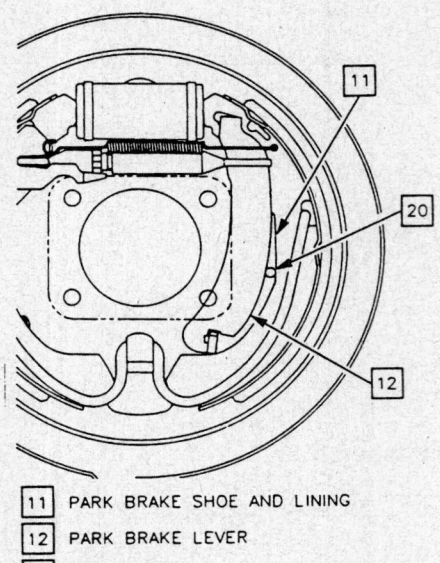

11	PARK BRAKE SHOE AND LINING
12	PARK BRAKE LEVER
20	1/8 INCH DRILL

GC4089100041000X

Fig. 8 Parking brake adjustment

DRUM BRAKE SPECIFICATIONS

| Model | Year | Lining Wear Limit, Inch② | Inside Diameter, Inches | | | Runout Limit, Inch | Allowable Scoring, Inch |
			Nominal	Maximum Refinish	Discard Limit①		
CHEVROLET							
Malibu	2004–05	.030	8.868	8.889	8.909	.004	.059
Malibu Maxx	2005–07	.030	9.060	9.075	9.094	.004	.060
OLDSMOBILE							
Alero	2004	.030	8.868	8.889	8.909	.004	.059
PONTIAC							
Grand Am	2004–05	.030	8.868	8.889	8.909	.004	.059
Vibe	2004–08	.039	9.000	9.039	9.039	.002	.039

① — Discard Limit is stamped on drum. ② — Above rivet head or shoe. Original equipment type brake linings.

TIGHTENING SPECIFICATIONS

Year	Component	Torque Ft. Lbs.
ALERO, GRAND AM, MALIBU & MALIBU MAXX		
2004–07	Bleeder Screw (Alero & Grand Am)	115①
	Bleeder Screw (Malibu)	62①
	Wheel Cylinder Line Fitting	11
	Wheel Cylinder To Backing Plate	108①
	Wheel Lug Nuts	100
VIBE		
2004–08	Bleeder Valve	73①
	Wheel Cylinder Line Fitting	11
	Wheel Cylinder To Backing Plate	86①

① — Inch lbs.

Cavalier, Cobalt, G5 & Sunfire

NOTE: On Air Bag Equipped Models, Refer To "Air Bag System Precautions" Located In The Front Of This Manual For System Disarming & Arming Procedures.

NOTE: Refer To "Computer Relearn Procedures" Located In The Front Of This Manual When Battery Power To The Computer Has Been Interrupted.

INDEX

	Page No.		Page No.		Page No.
Adjustments	23-6	Removal	23-6	Brake Drums	23-5
Parking Brake	23-7	**Drum Brake Specifications**	23-7	Brake Linings & Springs	23-5
Service Brake	23-7	**Inspection**	23-5	Parking Brake Cable	23-6
Brake Service	23-6	Adjuster Mechanism	23-5	**Precautions**	23-5
Installation	23-6	Backing Plate	23-5	**Tightening Specifications**	23-7

PRECAUTIONS

When working on or around brake assemblies, care must be taken to prevent breathing asbestos dust, as many manufacturers incorporate asbestos fibers in the production of brake linings. During routine service operations the amount of asbestos dust from brake lining wear is at a low level because of a chemical breakdown during use and a few precautions will minimize exposure.

1. Do not sand or grind brake linings unless suitable local exhaust ventilation equipment is used to prevent excessive asbestos exposure.
2. Wear suitable respirator approved for asbestos dust use during repair procedures.
3. When cleaning brake dust from brake components, use vacuum cleaner with highly efficient filter system. If suitable vacuum cleaner is not available, use water soaked rag. **Do not use compressed air or dry brush to clean brake components.**
4. Keep work area clean.
5. Properly dispose of rags and vacuum cleaner bags by placing them in plastic bags.
6. Do not smoke or eat while working on brake systems. **Never use gasoline, kerosene, alcohol, motor oil, transmission fluid, or any fluid containing mineral oil to clean brake system components.**
7. If system contamination is suspected, inspect brake fluid in reservoir for dirt, discoloration, or separation (breakdown). Drain fluid into suitable container and flush hydraulic system with clean brake fluid.

INSPECTION

1. Inspect components for damage or wear. Replace as required.
2. Inspect wheel cylinder boots for tears, cuts or heat damage. Replace as required.
3. Remove wheel cylinder links. If fluid spills from boot center hole, replace wheel cylinder.
4. Light fluid coatings on piston within cylinder is considered normal.
5. Inspect backing plate for evidence of axle seal leakage. If leakage exists, refer to individual vehicle chapters for axle seal replacement procedures.
6. Inspect backing plate mounting bolts and ensure they are tight.
7. Clean rust and dirt from shoe contact surface on backing plate using fine emery cloth or other suitable abrasive.

Brake Drums

Any time the brake drums are removed for brake service, the braking surface diameter should be inspected with suitable brake drum micrometer at several points to determine if they are within the safe oversize limit stamped on the brake drum outer surface. If the braking surface diameter exceeds specifications, the drum must be replaced. If the braking surface diameter is within specifications, drums should be cleaned and inspected for cracks, scores, deep grooves, taper, out-of-round and heat spotting. If drums are cracked or heat spotted, they must be replaced. Minor scores should be removed with sandpaper. Grooves and large scores can only be removed by machining with special equipment, as long as the braking surface is within specifications stamped on brake drum outer surface. Any brake drum sufficiently out-of-round to cause vehicle vibration or noise while braking or showing taper should also be machined, removing only enough stock to true up the brake drum.

After a brake drum is machined, wipe the braking surface diameter with a denatured alcohol soaked cloth. If one brake drum is machined, the other should also be machined to the same diameter to maintain equal braking forces.

Brake Linings & Springs

Inspect brake linings for excessive wear, damage, oil, grease or brake fluid contamination. If any of the these conditions exists, brake linings should be replaced. Do not attempt to replace only one set of brake shoes; they should be replaced as an axle set only to maintain equal braking forces. Examine brake shoe webbing, hold-down and return springs for signs of overheating indicated by a slight blue color. If any component exhibits overheating signs, replace hold-down and return springs with new ones. Overheated springs lose their pull and could cause brake linings to wear out prematurely. Inspect springs for sags, bends and external damage and replace as required.

Inspect hold-down retainers and pins for bends, rust and corrosion. If any of these are found, replace as required.

Backing Plate

Inspect backing plate shoe contact surface for grooves that may restrict shoe movement and cannot be removed by lightly sanding with emery cloth or other suitable abrasive. If backing plate exhibits these condition, it should be replaced. Also inspect for signs of cracks, warpage and excessive rust, indicating need for replacement.

Adjuster Mechanism

Inspect components for rust, corrosion, bends and fatigue. Replace as required. **On adjuster mechanism equipped with adjuster cable,** inspect cable for kinks, fraying or elongation of eyelet and replace as required.

DRUM BRAKES

Parking Brake Cable

Inspect parking brake cable end for kinks, fraying and elongation and replace as required. Use a small hose clamp to compress clamp where it enters backing plate to remove it.

BRAKE SERVICE

Removal

1. Raise and support rear of vehicle, then remove tire and wheel assembly.
2. Mark drum and axle hub, then remove brake drum. If brake lining is dragging on brake drum, back off brake adjustment by rotating adjustment screw. **If brake drum is rusted or corroded to axle flange and cannot be removed, lightly tap axle flange to drum mounting surface with suitable hammer.**
3. Unhook primary and secondary return springs using brake spring removal and installation tool Nos. J-8049 or J-29840, or equivalents, **Fig. 1.** Observe location of brake components being removed to aid during installation.
4. Remove brake hold-down springs with suitable tool.
5. Lift actuating lever, then unhook and remove actuating link from anchor pin.
6. Remove actuating lever(s) and return spring.
7. Spread shoes apart and remove parking brake strut and spring.
8. Disconnect parking brake cable from lever and remove brake shoes from backing plate.
9. Separate brake shoes by removing adjusting screw and spring, then unhook parking brake lever from shoe assembly.
10. Clean dirt from brake drum, backing plate and other components. **Do not use compressed air or dry brush to clean brake components. Clean brake components with water soaked rag or suitable vacuum cleaner to minimize airborne dust.**

Installation

1. Lubricate parking brake lever fulcrum with suitable brake lubricant and attach lever to brake shoe. Ensure lever operates smoothly.
2. Connect brake shoes with adjusting screw spring and position adjusting screw. **Ensure adjusting screw star wheel does not contact adjusting screw spring. Ensure righthand thread adjusting screw is installed on lefthand side of vehicle and lefthand thread adjusting screw is installed on righthand side of vehicle. Ensure star wheel lines up with adjusting hole in backing plate.**
3. Lubricate backing plate shoe contact surfaces with suitable brake lubricant and area where parking brake cable contacts backing plate.
4. Install brake shoes on backing plate

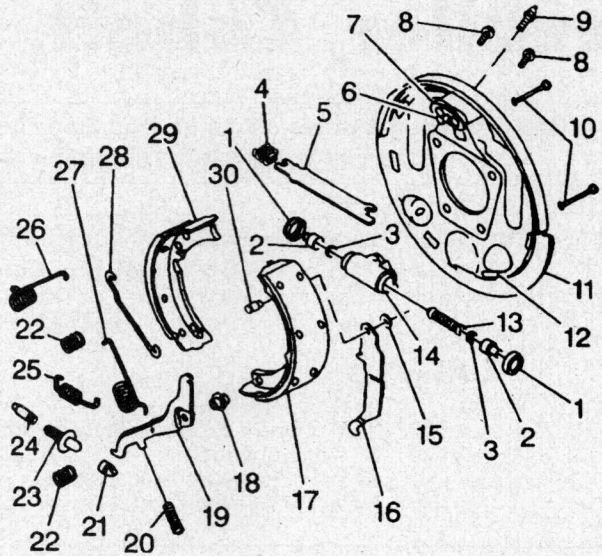

1. Boot
2. Piston
3. Seal
4. Strut Spring
5. Strut
6. Shoe Retainer
7. Anchor Pin
8. Bolt
9. Bleeder Screw
10. Hold down Pins
11. Backing Plate
12. Shoe Contact Points
13. Piston Spring
14. Cylinder
15. Reatainer Ring
16. Parking Brake Lever
17. Secondary Shoe
18. Sleeve
19. Actuator Lever
20. Return Spring
21. Socket
22. Hold Down Spring
23. Star Wheel
24. Pivot Nut
25. Adjuster Spring
26. Return Spring

GC4089700045000X

Fig. 1   Drum brake assembly

while engaging wheel cylinder links (if equipped) with shoe webbing. **Primary shoe (short lining) faces towards front of vehicle. End without strut spring should engage parking brake lever and secondary shoe. End with strut spring should engage primary shoe.**

5. Connect parking brake cable to parking brake lever.
6. Install actuating levers, actuating link and return spring.
7. Install hold-down springs with suitable tool.
8. Install primary and secondary shoe return springs using suitable brake spring pliers.
9. Measure inside diameter using suitable brake drum to shoe gauge.
10. Adjust brake shoes to dimension obtained on outside portion of gauge.
11. Install brake drum, wheel and tire assembly.
12. If any hydraulic connections have been opened, bleed brake system.
13. Adjust parking brake.
14. Inspect hydraulic lines and connections for leaks.
15. Inspect and adjust master cylinder fluid level.
16. Inspect brake pedal for proper feel and return.
17. Lower vehicle and road test. **Do not**

severely apply brakes immediately after installation of new brake linings or permanent damage may occur to linings, and/or brake drums may become scored. Brakes must be used moderately during first several hundred miles of operation to ensure proper burnishing of linings.

ADJUSTMENTS

These brakes have self-adjusting shoe mechanisms that ensure proper lining-to-drum clearances at all times. The automatic adjusters operate only when the brakes are applied as the vehicle is moving rearward.

An initial adjustment is required after the brake shoes have been relined or replaced, or when the length of the adjusting screw has been changed during service operations.

Frequent usage of an automatic transmission forward range to halt reverse vehicle motion may prevent the automatic adjusters from functioning, thereby inducing low pedal heights. Should low pedal heights be encountered, it is recommended that numerous forward and reverse stops be made until satisfactory pedal height is obtained. **If a low pedal condition cannot**

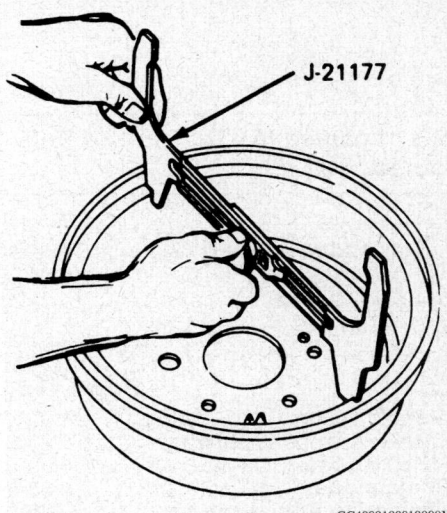

Fig. 2 Brake drum measurement

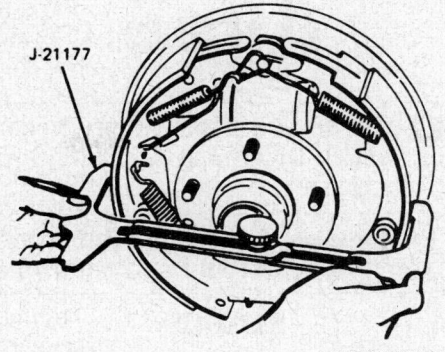

Fig. 3 Brake shoe measurement

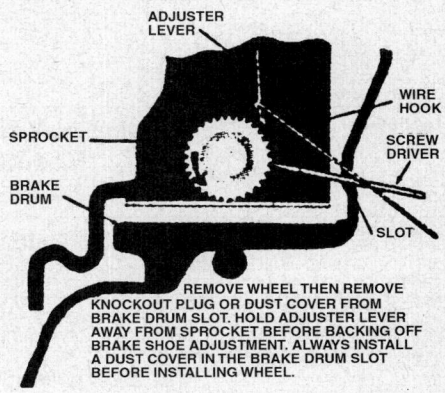

Fig. 4 Brake shoe adjustment

REMOVE WHEEL THEN REMOVE KNOCKOUT PLUG OR DUST COVER FROM BRAKE DRUM SLOT. HOLD ADJUSTER LEVER AWAY FROM SPROCKET BEFORE BACKING OFF BRAKE SHOE ADJUSTMENT. ALWAYS INSTALL A DUST COVER IN THE BRAKE DRUM SLOT BEFORE INSTALLING WHEEL.

be corrected by making numerous reverse stops (provided the hydraulic system is free of air) it indicates that the self-adjusting mechanism is not functioning. It will be required to remove the brake drum, clean, free up and lubricate the adjusting mechanism. Then adjust the brakes as follows, ensuring the parking brake is fully released.

Service Brake

Brake adjustment cannot be performed with the drums installed. The following procedure is mandatory after new linings are installed, or when the length of the brake shoe adjusting screw has been changed.

1. With brake drums removed, position caliper to inside diameter of drum and tighten clamp screw, **Fig. 2.**
2. Position brake shoe end of caliper tool over brake shoes, **Fig. 3.**
3. Rotate gauge slightly around shoes to ensure gauge contacts linings at largest diameter.
4. Adjust brake shoes until outside diameter is .030 inch less than drum's in-

side diameter. **If brake shoe must be backed off, hold adjuster lever away from adjuster screw, Fig. 4.**

Parking Brake

On these brake systems, no adjustment is required. These models have a self-adjusting parking brake system and it should not be adjusted or modified in any way.

Fully applying and releasing the parking brake 4–6 times the system will perform its self-adjustment procedure.

DRUM BRAKE SPECIFICATIONS

| Model | Year | Lining Wear Limit, Inch② | Inside Diameter, Inches | | | Runout Limit, Inch | Allowable Scoring, Inch |
			Nominal	Maximum Refinish	Discard Limit①		
Cavalier & Sunfire	2004–05	.030	9.055–9.065	9.075	9.094	.004	.059
Cobalt & G5	2005–08	.020	9.055–9.065	9.075	9.094	.004	.059

① — Discard Limit is stamped on drum.
② — Above rivet head or shoe. Original equipment type brake linings.

TIGHTENING SPECIFICATIONS

Year	Component	Torque Ft. Lbs.
CAVALIER & SUNFIRE		
2004–05	Wheel Cylinder Bleeder Screw	71①
	Wheel Cylinder Line Fitting	13
	Wheel Cylinder To Backing Plate	12
	Wheel Lug Nuts	100②
COBALT & G5		
2005–08	Wheel Cylinder Bleeder Screw	71①
	Wheel Cylinder Line Fitting	14
	Wheel Cylinder To Backing Plate	12
	Wheel Lug Nuts	100②

① — Inch lbs.
② — Tighten lug nuts in star sequence in increments of 20 ft. lbs. until final torque of 100 ft. lbs., is reached.

Aveo

NOTE: On Air Bag Equipped Models, Refer To "Air Bag System Precautions" Located In The Front Of This Manual For System Disarming & Arming Procedures.

NOTE: Refer To "Computer Relearn Procedures" Located In The Front Of This Manual When Battery Power To The Computer Has Been Interrupted.

INDEX

	Page No.		Page No.		Page No.
Adjustments	23-9	Removal	23-9	Brake Drums	23-8
Parking Brake	23-9	**Drum Brake Specifications**	23-9	Brake Linings & Springs	23-8
Service Brake	23-9	**Inspection**	23-8	Parking Brake Cable	23-9
Brake Service	23-9	Adjuster Mechanism	23-8	**Precautions**	23-8
Installation	23-9	Backing Plate	23-8	**Tightening Specifications**	23-9

PRECAUTIONS

When working on or around brake assemblies, care must be taken to prevent breathing asbestos dust, as many manufacturers incorporate asbestos fibers in the production of brake linings. During routine service operations the amount of asbestos dust from brake lining wear is at a low level because of a chemical breakdown during use and a few precautions will minimize exposure.

1. Do not sand or grind brake linings unless suitable local exhaust ventilation equipment is used to prevent excessive asbestos exposure.
2. Wear suitable respirator approved for asbestos dust use during repair procedures.
3. When cleaning brake dust from brake components, use vacuum cleaner with highly efficient filter system. If suitable vacuum cleaner is not available, use water soaked rag. **Do not use compressed air or dry brush to clean brake components.**
4. Keep work area clean.
5. Properly dispose of rags and vacuum cleaner bags by placing them in plastic bags.
6. Do not smoke or eat while working on brake systems. **Never use gasoline, kerosene, alcohol, motor oil, transmission fluid, or any fluid containing mineral oil to clean brake system components. These fluids will damage rubber caps and seals. If system contamination is suspected, inspect brake fluid in reservoir for dirt, discoloration, or separation (breakdown) of brake fluid into distinct layers. Drain fluid into suitable container and flush hydraulic system with clean brake fluid if contamination is suspected.**

INSPECTION

1. If any components are of doubtful strength or quality because of heat discoloration, or are worn, replace them.
2. Inspect wheel cylinder dust boots for signs of excessive wear or damage. If any leakage is apparent replace or rebuild wheel cylinder.
3. Clean dirt and/or rust from brake drum, backing plate and other components. **Do not use compressed air or dry brush to clean brake components. Many brake components contain asbestos fibers which, if inhaled, can cause serious injury. Clean brake components with water soaked rag or suitable vacuum cleaner to minimize airborne dust.**

Brake Drums

Any time the brake drums are removed for brake service, the braking surface diameter should be inspected with suitable brake drum micrometer at several points to determine if they are within the safe oversize limit stamped on the brake drum outer surface. If the braking surface diameter exceeds specifications, the drum must be replaced. If the braking surface diameter is within specifications, drums should be cleaned and inspected for cracks, scores, deep grooves, taper, out-of-round and heat spotting. If drums are cracked or heat spotted, they must be replaced. Minor scores should be removed with sandpaper. Grooves and large scores can only be removed by machining with special equipment, as long as the braking surface is within specifications stamped on brake drum outer surface. Any brake drum sufficiently out-of-round to cause vehicle vibration or noise while braking or showing taper should also be machined, removing only enough stock to true up the brake drum.

After a brake drum is machined, wipe the braking surface diameter with a denatured alcohol soaked cloth. If one brake drum is machined, the other should also be machined to the same diameter to maintain equal braking forces.

Brake Linings & Springs

Inspect brake linings for excessive wear, damage, oil, grease or brake fluid contamination. If any of the these conditions exists, brake linings should be replaced. Do not attempt to replace only one set of brake shoes. They should be replaced as an axle set only to maintain equal braking forces. Examine brake shoe webbing, hold-down and return springs for signs of overheating indicated by a slight blue color. If any component exhibits overheating signs, replace hold-down and return springs with new ones. Overheated springs lose their pull and could cause brake linings to wear out prematurely. Inspect springs for sags, bends and external damage and replace as required.

Inspect hold-down retainers and pins for bends, rust and corrosion. If any of these are found, replace as required.

Backing Plate

Inspect backing plate shoe contact surface for grooves that may restrict shoe movement and cannot be removed by lightly sanding with emery cloth or other suitable abrasive. If backing plate exhibits these condition, it should be replaced. Also inspect for signs of cracks, warpage and excessive rust, indicating need for replacement.

Adjuster Mechanism

Inspect components for rust, corrosion, bends and fatigue. Replace as required. **On adjuster mechanism equipped with adjuster cable,** inspect cable for kinks, fraying or elongation of eyelet and replace as required.

Parking Brake Cable

Inspect parking brake cable end for kinks, fraying and elongation and replace as required. Use a small hose clamp to compress clamp where it enters backing plate to remove.

BRAKE SERVICE

Removal

1. Raise and support vehicle, then remove tire and wheel assembly.
2. Remove lock ring and caulking nut from spindle, then remove brake drum. If drum is difficult to remove, proceed as follows:
   a. Ensure parking brake is released.
   b. Back off parking brake cable adjustment.
3. Loosen leading shoe hold down return spring.
4. Disconnect upper link of connecting link spring on leading shoe to release tension on upper return spring.
5. Remove upper return spring and adjuster.
6. Disconnect trailing shoe and lining assembly hold down return spring, then the trailing shoe and lining assembly.
7. Remove lower return spring.

Installation

1. Clean and grease adjuster assembly.
2. Install trailing shoe and lining assembly with hold down spring, washer and pin.
3. Verify parking brake cable routing and attach to shoe lever.
4. Install lower return spring on shoe. Do not overstretch spring.
5. Position leading shoe and adjuster assembly against backing plate, then attach lower return spring to leading shoe.
6. Install adjuster assembly, then turn adjuster in as far as possible.
7. Position spring clip toward the backing plate.
8. Install leading shoe with hold down spring.
9. Install leading shoe upper link spring connection.
10. Install upper return spring from spring connection link to brake shoe. Do not overstretch spring.
11. Ensure adjuster assembly nut is drawn to the stop, then adjust rear brakes.
12. Install brake drum, then adjust park brake.

ADJUSTMENTS

Service Brake

1. Raise and support vehicle, then remove tire and wheel assembly.
2. Remove brake drum.
3. Turn adjuster nut until sufficient amount of drag occurs on brake drum.
4. Place parking brake lever stops against edge of shoe web.
5. Install brake drum, then apply brake pedal at least 10 times. Ensure there is no clicking sound from either brake drum.
6. Adjust parking brake.

Parking Brake

1. Ensure parking brake is released, then raise and support vehicle.
2. Inspect parking brake cables for free movement.
3. Lower vehicle.
4. Remove plastic caps that cover parking brake hood to tunnel bracket screws access holes.
5. Remove parking brake console hood to tunnel bracket retaining screws.
6. Raise console hood to access parking brake lever assembly and adjustment nut.
7. Partially raise and support vehicle.
8. Turn adjustment nut on lever assembly until wheels are hard to turn.
9. Loosen nut until rear wheels are just free to turn.
10. Lower vehicle.
11. Install parking brake hood console and plastic caps on access holes.

DRUM BRAKE SPECIFICATIONS

| Model | Year | Lining Wear Limit, Inch | Inside Diameter, Inches | | | Runout Limit, Inch | Allowable Scoring, Inch |
			Nominal	Maximum Refinish	Discard Limit		
Aveo	2004–08	.020	7.870	—	7.91	.002	—

TIGHTENING SPECIFICATIONS

Year	Component	Torque Ft. Lbs.
2004–08	Brake Line	12
	Brake Wheel Hub/Backing Plate to Rear Axle Nuts	21
	Drum Caulking Nut	148
	Wheel Cylinder to Backing Plate Bolt	71①

① — Inch lbs.

Saturn

NOTE: On Air Bag Equipped Models, Refer To "Air Bag System Precautions" Located In The Front Of This Manual For System Disarming & Arming Procedures.

NOTE: Refer To "Computer Relearn Procedures" Located In The Front Of This Manual When Battery Power To The Computer Has Been Interrupted.

INDEX

	Page No.		Page No.		Page No.
Adjustments	23-10	Brake Service	23-10	Inspection	23-10
Parking Brake	23-10	Drum Brake Specifications	23-11	Tightening Specifications	23-12

INSPECTION

1. Release parking brake.
2. Raise and support vehicle.
3. Remove rear wheels and tires.
4. Remove brake drum. **Do not pry against brake backing plate.**
5. Inspect adjuster assembly, ensuring screw threads turn smoothly into nut over full threaded length.
6. Inspect wheel cylinder for damage, leakage or seizure.

BRAKE SERVICE

1. Release parking brake.
2. Raise and support vehicle.
3. Remove rear wheels.
4. Remove brake drum. **Do not pry against brake backing plate.**
5. Remove lower return spring, **Fig. 1.**
6. Remove adjuster spring.
7. Remove leading brake shoe hold-down, spring and pin.
8. Remove adjuster assembly and lever. If difficult, pull leading shoe toward

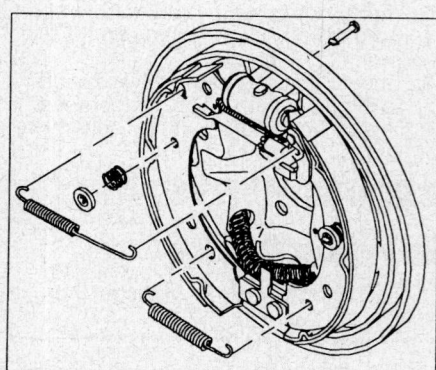

G34089100001000X

Fig. 1 Rear brake assembly

front of vehicle and or turn star wheel on adjuster to shorten length.
9. Twist shoe from upper return spring engagement to remove.
10. Remove parking brake shoe upper return spring.
11. Remove park brake shoe hold-down

cup, spring and pin.
12. Push park brake lever into cable spring to remove park brake cable from lever.
13. Remove park brake lever retainer and wave washer and separate from park brake shoe.
14. Reverse procedure to install, noting the following:
    a. Lubricate adjuster assembly, adjuster lever surface, backing plate at shoe contact pads and park brake lever pin and brake shoe web contact surface.
    b. Measure drum inner and brake shoe assembly outer diameters using brake drum clearance tool No. SA91109NE, or equivalent.
    c. Adjust brake adjuster to obtain measurement .050 inch less than drum inner diameter.

ADJUSTMENTS
Parking Brake

Refer to "Adjustments" in "Disc Brakes" chapter for parking brake adjustment.

DRUM BRAKE SPECIFICATIONS

Model	Year	Lining Wear Limit, Inch[2]	Inside Diameter, Inches			Runout Limit, Inch	Allowable Scoring, Inch
			Nominal	Maximum Refinish	Discard Limit[1]		
ION	2004–07	.020	9.055–9.065	9.075	9.094	.0040	.0590
L-Series	2004–05	.080	9.050	9.080	9.090	.0020	.0400

① — Discard Limit is stamped on drum.   ② — Above rivet head or shoe. Original equipment type brake linings.

DRUM BRAKES

TIGHTENING SPECIFICATIONS

Year	Component	Torque Ft. Lbs.
2004–07	Backing Plate To Knuckle	63
	Bleed Valve	66①
	Brake Line To Brake Hose	18
	Brake Line To Wheel Cylinder	36
	Brake Pipe To Union	14
	Wheel Cylinder To Backing Plate	84①
	Wheel Lug Nuts (ION)	100
	Wheel Lug Nuts (L-Series)	92②
	Wheel Lug Nuts (S-Series)	103

① — Inch lbs.
② — For steel wheel & optional aluminum wheel w/large center cap, install wheel cover or cap. With socket, hand tighten five cap nuts. With wrench, tighten each cap an additional 90°.

HYDRAULIC BRAKE SYSTEMS

NOTE: On Air Bag Equipped Models, Refer To "Air Bag System Precautions" Located In The Front Of This Manual For System Disarming & Arming Procedures.

NOTE: Refer To "Computer Relearn Procedures" Located In The Front Of This Manual When Battery Power To The Computer Has Been Interrupted.

INDEX

	Page No.
Brake System Bleed	24-6
Bleed Sequence	24-7
Manual	24-6
Pressure	24-6
Component Replacement	24-2
Master Cylinder	24-2
Except ION & L-Series	24-2
ION	24-2
L-Series	24-3
Component Service	24-3
Master Cylinder Overhaul	24-3
Aura, Bonneville, DTS, ION, LeSabre, Lucerne, Park Avenue, Solstice & SKY	24-3
Aveo	24-3
CTS	24-4
Corvette	24-4

	Page No.
Except Aura, Aveo, Bonneville, Cobalt, Corvette, CTS, DTS, G5, ION, L-Series, LaCrosse, LeSabre, Lucerne, Park Avenue, Solstice, SKY, STS, Vibe & XLR	24-3
L-Series	24-5
LaCrosse, STS & XLR	24-5
Vibe	24-5
Wheel Cylinder Overhaul	24-6
Assemble	24-6
Disassemble	24-6
Description	24-1
Components	24-1
Brake Distribution Valve & Switch	24-2

	Page No.
Brake Warning Lamp Switches	24-1
Combination Valve	24-1
Failure Warning Switch	24-2
Fluid Level Sensor	24-1
Metering Valve	24-1
Proportioning Or Pressure Control Valve	24-2
Warning Lamp	24-1
Diagonally Split System	24-1
Front & Rear Split System	24-1
Diagnosis & Testing	24-2
Hydraulic Brake System Flush	24-7
Tightening Specifications	24-10
Troubleshooting	24-2
Master Cylinder Internal Fluid Leakage Check	24-2
Road Test	24-2

DESCRIPTION

Front & Rear Split System

When the brake pedal is depressed, both the primary (front brake) and the secondary (rear brake) master cylinder pistons are moved simultaneously to exert hydraulic fluid pressure on their respective systems.

If the rear brake system fails, initial brake pedal movement will cause the unrestricted secondary piston to bottom in the master cylinder bore. Primary piston movement will displace hydraulic fluid in the primary section of the master cylinder to actuate the front brake system.

If the front brake system fails, initial brake pedal movement will cause the unrestricted primary piston to bottom out against the secondary piston. Continued downward movement of the brake pedal moves the secondary piston to displace hydraulic fluid in the rear brake system to actuate the rear brakes.

Diagonally Split System

This system operates on the same principle as conventional front and rear split systems, using primary and secondary master cylinders which move simultaneously to exert hydraulic pressure on their respective systems. The hydraulic brake lines on this system, however, have been diagonally split front to rear (lefthand front to righthand rear and righthand front to left-hand rear) in place of separate lines to the front and rear wheels.

In the event of a system failure, the remaining non-failed system will do all the braking on one front wheel and one rear wheel, maintaining 50% of the total braking force.

Components

WARNING LAMP

The warning lamp should illuminate when the ignition switch is in the start position and turn off when the switch returns to run. If the brake lamp remains on after the ignition returns to run, inspect fluid level in master cylinder reservoir and inspect parking brake. If the warning lamp does not turn on during cranking, inspect for faulty bulb or blown fuse.

FLUID LEVEL SENSOR

This sensor, mounted on the master cylinder, will activate the brake warning lamp if a low brake fluid level is detected. The lamp will turn off once the fluid level is corrected.

BRAKE WARNING LAMP SWITCHES

As pressure falls in one system, the other system's normal pressure forces the piston to the inoperative side, contacting the switch terminal, causing the warning lamp on the instrument panel to glow.

The switch is mounted directly in the master cylinder assembly. Whenever there is a specified differential pressure, the switch piston will activate the brake failure warning switch and cause the brake warning lamp to glow.

COMBINATION VALVE

The combination valve is a metering valve, failure warning switch, and a proportioning valve in one assembly and is used on disc brake applications. The metering valve delays front disc braking until the rear drum brake shoes contact the drum. The failure warning switch is actuated in event of front or rear brake system failure, in turn activating a dash warning lamp. The proportioning valve balances front to rear braking action during rapid deceleration.

METERING VALVE

When the brakes are not applied, the metering valve permits the brake fluid to flow through the valve allowing the fluid to expand and contract with temperature changes.

When the brakes are initially applied, the metering valve stem moves to the left, preventing fluid to flow through the valve to the front disc brakes. This is accomplished by the smooth end of the metering valve stem contacting the metering valve seal lip at 4–30 psi. The metering valve spring holds the retainer against the seal until a predetermined pressure is produced at the valve

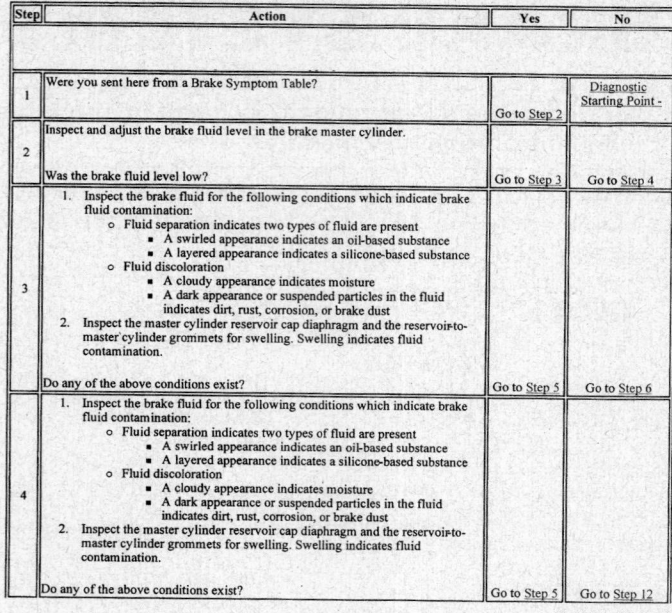

Fig. 1 Hydraulic brake system diagnosis chart (Part 1 of 4)

inlet port which overcomes the spring pressure and permits hydraulic pressure to actuate the front disc brakes. The increased pressure into the valve is metered through the valve seal, to the front disc brakes, producing an increased force on the diaphragm. The diaphragm then pulls the pin, in turn pulling the retainer, and reduces the spring pressure on the metering valve seal. Eventually, the pressure reaches a point at which the spring is pulled away by the diaphragm pin and retainer, leaving the metering valve unrestricted, permitting full pressure to pass through the metering valve.

FAILURE WARNING SWITCH

If the rear brake system fails, the front system pressure forces the switch piston to the right. The switch pin is then forced up into the switch, completing the electrical circuit and activates the dash warning lamp.

When repairs are made and pressure returns to the system, the piston moves to the left, resetting the switch. The detent on the piston requires approximately 100–450 psi to permit full reset of the piston. In event of front brake system failure, the piston moves to the left and the same sequence of events is followed as for rear system failure except the piston resets to the right.

PROPORTIONING OR PRESSURE CONTROL VALVE

During rapid deceleration, a portion of vehicle weight is transferred to the front wheels. This resultant loss of weight at rear wheels must be compensated for to avoid early rear wheel skid. The proportioning or pressure control valve reduces rear brake system pressure, delaying rear wheel skid.

When the proportioning or pressure control valve is incorporated in the combination valve assembly, pressure developed within the valve acts against the large end of the piston, overcoming the spring pressure, moving the piston left. The piston then contacts the stem seat and restricts line pressure through the valve.

During normal braking operation, the proportioning or pressure control valve is not functional. Brake fluid flows into the proportioning or pressure control valve between the piston center hole and the valve stem, through the stop plate and to the rear brakes. Spring pressure loads the piston during normal braking, causing it to rest against the stop plate.

On diagonally split brake systems, two proportioning or pressure control valves are used. One controls the lefthand rear brake, the other the righthand rear brake. The proportioning or pressure control valves are installed in the master cylinder rear brake outlet ports.

BRAKE DISTRIBUTION VALVE & SWITCH

This switch assembly is used on some diagonally split brake systems and Corvette four-wheel disc brake systems. It is connected to the outlet ports of the master cylinder and to the brake warning lamp and warns the driver if either the primary or secondary brake system has failed.

When hydraulic pressure is equal in both primary and secondary brake systems, the switch remains centered. If pressure fails in one of the systems, the piston moves toward the inoperative side. The shoulder of the piston contacts the switch terminal, providing a ground and lighting the warning lamp.

TROUBLESHOOTING

When troubleshooting the hydraulic brake system, perform the following inspections.

Master Cylinder Internal Fluid Leakage Check

Start engine and depress the brake pedal. If the pedal gradually falls under constant pressure, the hydraulic system may be leaking. Raise the vehicle on a lift and inspect all tubing lines and backing plates for signs of leakage. It may be required to lift or remove the carpeting or floor mats to inspect for booster or master cylinder leakage.

Road Test

When testing brakes, ensure the road is level and dry. Test brakes at both light and heavy pedal pressure. Do not lock up brakes or slide tires during a brake test.

Inspect the tires on the vehicle before performing a brake test. Tires should be equally inflated, identical in size and with equal tread pattern. Excessive camber and caster will cause the brakes to pull. An overloaded vehicle will also brake erratically.

DIAGNOSIS & TESTING

Refer to **Fig. 1** for diagnosis chart.

COMPONENT REPLACEMENT

Master Cylinder

EXCEPT ION & L-SERIES

1. **On Vibe models,** remove air filter hose clamp and hose from throttle body.
2. **On all models,** disconnect fluid level sensor retainer and electrical connector.
3. Drain master cylinder reservoir brake fluid into suitable container.
4. Plug hose.
5. Disconnect master cylinder brake pipes. Plug open pipes.
6. Remove mounting nuts and master cylinder.
7. Remove reservoir, as required.
8. Reverse procedure to install. Bleed hydraulic system as outlined in "Brake System Bleed."

ION

1. Remove underhood electrical center cover.
2. Remove Connector Position Assurance (CPA) connector from brake fluid level sensor, **Fig. 2.**
3. Remove underhood battery positive

terminal mounting bolt, then disconnect cables from electrical center and cable from underhood center, **Fig. 3.**

4. Remove engine wiring harness retainer at engine control module.
5. Disconnect electrical connector and remove ECM from bracket setting aside.
6. **On models equipped with automatic transmissions,** remove Transmission Control Module (TCM), **Fig. 4.**
7. **On all models,** remove cable retainer form underhood center and forward lamp harness retainer from ECM tray.
8. Remove surge tank clip from center bracket, then the underhood electrical center bracket and underhood electrical center from underhood.
9. Remove surge tank hose and electrical center bracket, **Fig. 5.**
10. Remove master cylinder reservoir assembly as outlined in "Fluid Reservoir."
11. Remove brake pipes from master cylinder. Cover pipe fittings to prevent contamination.
12. Remove mounting nuts and master cylinder, **Fig. 6.**
13. Reverse procedure to install. Bleed brake system as outlined in "Brake System Bleed."

L-SERIES

1. Remove brake fluid level sensor electrical connector.
2. Remove master cylinder brake line fitting nuts. **Plug open lines and fittings.**
3. Remove mounting nuts and master cylinder.
4. Reverse procedure to install.

COMPONENT SERVICE

Master Cylinder Overhaul

EXCEPT AURA, AVEO, BONNEVILLE, COBALT, CORVETTE, CTS, DTS, G5, ION, L-SERIES, LACROSSE, LESABRE, LUCERNE, PARK AVENUE, SOLSTICE, SKY, STS, VIBE & XLR

DISASSEMBLE

Refer to **Figs. 7 and 8** when performing the following procedures.
1. Disconnect and plug hydraulic lines.
2. Remove mounting nuts and master cylinder.
3. Remove reservoir cover and diaphragm. Discard old brake fluid.
4. Inspect cover and diaphragm.
5. Remove fluid level switch.
6. **On models equipped with compact master cylinder,** remove proportioning valve, **Fig. 8.**
7. **On all models,** depress primary piston and remove lock ring.
8. Plug primary fluid outlet (outlet nearest to cowl when master cylinder is installed), then remove primary and secondary pistons by applying compressed air into secondary fluid outlet.
9. Remove secondary piston spring retainer and seals.
10. Remove secondary piston spring retainer and seals.
11. Clamp the flange on the master cylinder body in a vise, then remove fluid reservoir, **Figs. 9 and 10.**
12. Remove reservoir grommets.
13. Inspect master cylinder bore for corrosion. **Do not use abrasive material on master cylinder bore.**

ASSEMBLE

Clean all components not included in repair kit with suitable brake fluid. **Do not dry with compressed air.** Lubricate all rubber components with clean brake fluid prior to installation.
1. Lubricate new reservoir grommets with suitable silicone brake lube.
2. Press grommets into master cylinder body. Ensure grommets are properly seated.
3. Lay reservoir upside down on flat, hard surface.
4. Press master cylinder body onto reservoir using rocking motion.
5. Install new seals on secondary piston and spring retainer.
6. Install spring and secondary piston into cylinder.
7. Install primary piston.
8. Depress primary piston into cylinder and install lock ring.
9. Install fluid level switch, if equipped.
10. **On models equipped with compact master cylinder,** install proportioning valve, **Fig. 8.**
11. **On all models,** install diaphragm into reservoir cover and cover onto reservoir.
12. Install master cylinder and bleed brake system.

AURA, BONNEVILLE, DTS, ION, LESABRE, LUCERNE, PARK AVENUE, SOLSTICE & SKY

These master cylinders are not serviceable. Master cylinder must be replaced as a complete unit. **Do not attempt to overhaul the master cylinder.**

AVEO

1. Disconnect electrical connector from reservoir.

5	1. Flush the hydraulic brake system. Refer to Hydraulic Brake System Flushing .
	 2. If the brake fluid WAS contaminated with an oil-based or a silicone-based fluid, complete the following steps and refer to the following procedures:
	   A. Remove ALL of the brake system components that utilize rubber seals or linings.
	   B. Clean out the hydraulic brake pipes and the reservoir using denatured alcohol, or equivalent.
	   C. Dry the brake pipes and the reservoir using non-lubricated, filtered air.
	
	 3. If the brake fluid was NOT contaminated with an oil-based fluid, but WAS contaminated with moisture, dirt, rust, corrosion, or brake dust, replace the brake master cylinder reservoir cap diaphragm. The diaphragm may have allowed moisture or dirt to enter the system.
	 4. Refill and bleed the hydraulic brake system. Refer to Hydraulic Brake System Bleeding .
	
	 Did you complete the operation and any required repairs and/or replacements?
		Go to Step 9	--

6	1. Inspect the following hydraulic brake system components for external fluid leaks. Repair or replace any of the components found to be leaking brake fluid.
	
	 2. If you repaired or replaced any of the brake system components listed, bleed the hydraulic brake system.
	   While bleeding the hydraulic brake system, observe for the following conditions:
	   ○ The presence of air in the system at a bleeder valve location other than at the repair location, except if the brake master cylinder was replaced
	   ○ An unrestricted and even flow of brake fluid per axle during the bleeding procedure
	
	 Did you find and correct a condition?
		Go to Step 7	Go to Step 12

7	Was air in the system at a bleeder valve location other than at the repair location, except if the brake master cylinder was replaced?	Go to Step 19	Go to Step 8
8	Was the flow of brake fluid unrestricted and even per axle during the bleeding procedure?	Go to Step 9	Go to Step 10

ARM66GC000000750

Fig. 1 Hydraulic brake system diagnosis chart (Part 2 of 4)

9	Inspect the hydraulic function of the brake calipers and wheel cylinders, if equipped, for proper operation. Do the brake calipers and wheel cylinders, if equipped, operate properly?	Go to Step 21	Go to Step 14
10	Was the flow of brake fluid restricted or uneven through front axle hydraulic components during the bleeding procedure?	Go to Step 13	Go to Step 11
11	Was the flow of brake fluid restricted or uneven through rear axle hydraulic components during the bleeding procedure?	Go to Step 17	--
12	Inspect the hydraulic function of the brake calipers and wheel cylinders, if equipped, for proper operation. Do the brake calipers and wheel cylinders, if equipped, operate properly?	Go to Step 15	Go to Step 13
13	Use the following procedure in order to determine if the brake caliper is restricting the flow of brake fluid and/or not operating properly: 1. Raise and support the vehicle. 2. Remove the tire and wheel assemblies. 3. Open the suspected caliper bleeder valve. 4. Using a large C-clamp, compress the caliper piston and observe for an unrestricted flow of brake fluid and for free movement of the caliper piston. 5. Close the caliper bleeder valve. Was the flow of brake fluid unrestricted and did the caliper piston move freely?	Go to Step 17	Go to Step 14
14	Repair or replace any brake caliper or wheel cylinder, if equipped, that was not operating properly. Did you complete the repair and/or replacement?	Go to Step 21	--
15	Bleed the hydraulic brake system. Observe the condition and the flow of the brake fluid. Was air in the system?	Go to Step 19	Go to Step 16
16	Was the flow of brake fluid unrestricted and even per axle during the bleeding procedure?	Go to Step 21	Go to Step 17
17	1. Inspect the brake pipes and flexible brake hoses for signs of a fluid restriction; such as being bent, kinked, pinched or damaged. 2. Replace any of the hydraulic brake pipes and/or flexible brake hoses found to be bent, kinked, pinched or damaged. 3. If none of the hydraulic brake pipes or flexible brake hoses were visibly bent, kinked, pinched or damaged, replace the hydraulic brake flex hose at the restricted location. Did you find and correct a condition?	Go to Step 21	Go to Step 18

ARM66GC000000751

Fig. 1 Hydraulic brake system diagnosis chart (Part 3 of 4)

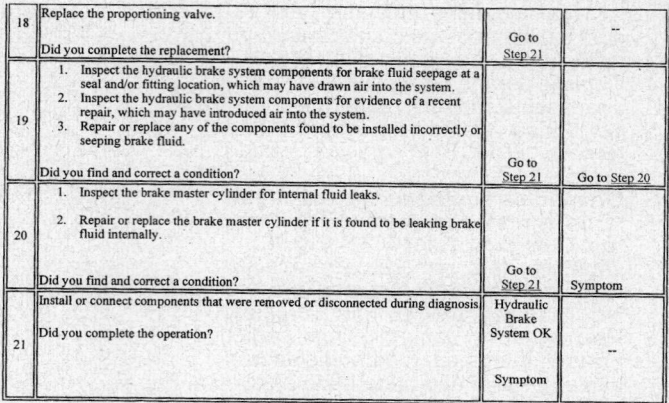

18	Replace the proportioning valve. Did you complete the replacement?	Go to Step 21	--
19	1. Inspect the hydraulic brake system components for brake fluid seepage at a seal and/or fitting location, which may have drawn air into the system. 2. Inspect the hydraulic brake system components for evidence of a recent repair, which may have introduced air into the system. 3. Repair or replace any of the components found to be installed incorrectly or seeping brake fluid. Did you find and correct a condition?	Go to Step 21	Go to Step 20
20	1. Inspect the brake master cylinder for internal fluid leaks. 2. Repair or replace the brake master cylinder if it is found to be leaking brake fluid internally. Did you find and correct a condition?	Go to Step 21	Symptom
21	Install or connect components that were removed or disconnected during diagnosis. Did you complete the operation?	Hydraulic Brake System OK Symptom	--

ARM66GC000000752

Fig. 1 Hydraulic brake system diagnosis chart (Part 4 of 4)

ing cup retaining ring, **Fig. 13.**
15. Remove recuperating guide.
16. Remove pistons' rubber seals, **Figs. 14 and 15. Do not damage any piston surfaces, particularly areas where seals seat.**
17. Remove pressure differential switch. **Do not disassemble spring or probe.**
18. Remove end plug and O-ring. **Do not lose small electrical bias spring located just inside end plug.**
19. Remove warning switch. **Keep warning switch and probe together as an assembly.**
20. Remove end plug, O-ring and electrical bias spring.
21. Gently tap cylinder body against suitable wood piece to dislodge proportioning valve spool.
22. Remove proportioning valve spool including O-ring and spacer. **Do not disassemble proportioning valve.**
23. Proportioning valve is lubricated with special grease. **Do not use cleaning solution to clean it or components included in repair kit.** Clean other components in suitable denatured alcohol. Dry components and passages within cylinder using filtered compressed air.
24. Reverse procedure to assemble. Ensure seals and components are lubricated with clean brake fluid.

CTS

1. Remove master cylinder as outlined in "Master Cylinder, Replace."
2. Place mounting flange into suitable vise so piston is accessible.
3. Ensure outside area of master cylinder is clean of dirt and debris.
4. Remove reservoir cap and diaphragm.
5. Remove fluid level sensor and drain master cylinder reservoir brake fluid into suitable container.
6. Remove retaining pins and reservoir from master cylinder.
7. Remove seals from master cylinder reservoir.
8. Remove piston retainer using suitable tool.
9. Remove piston from cylinder bore.
10. Plug cylinder inlet ports and rear outlet

2. Disconnect brake lines from master cylinder.
3. Plug brake line openings to prevent fluid loss and contamination.
4. Remove power booster mounting nuts.
5. Remove master cylinder assembly.
6. Remove brake fluid reservoir.
7. Remove seal ring from cylinder bore.
8. Remove retaining ring from cylinder body using suitable flat bladed tool. Discard ring.
9. Remove primary piston.
10. Carefully remove secondary piston assembly and spring from master cylinder bore.
11. Reverse procedure to install, noting the following:
    a. Clean all parts with clean brake fluid, then dry with compressed air.
    b. Replace all rubber parts and retaining rings.
    c. Lubricate master cylinder bore with clean brake fluid.

CORVETTE

1. Remove reservoir cap and diaphragm.
2. Drain fluid into suitable container.
3. Remove master cylinder prime pipe clamp and prime pipe.
4. Remove mounting screw and reservoir, **Fig. 11.**

5. Remove reservoir O-rings.
6. Slightly depress piston and remove retaining ring using suitable retaining ring pliers.
7. Invert cylinder so reservoir wells face downward.
8. Depress primary and secondary pistons until fully bottomed in bore using suitable brass rod or wooden dowel. Secondary stop pin should fall freely from cylinder.
9. Gently bump open end of cylinder body against suitable wood piece to dislodge primary piston. Remove primary piston.
10. Gently bump open end of cylinder body against suitable wood piece to dislodge secondary piston and center valve. Remove secondary piston. **Do not remove or disturb screw which retains primary spring to secondary piston.**
11. Remove secondary return spring.
12. Remove secondary piston spring retainer using suitable small screwdriver to lift crimp and allow retainer to slide off piston, **Fig. 12.**
13. Remove secondary piston center valve plunger and spring.
14. Remove primary piston seal retainer using suitable sharp knife or razor blade to cut and remove plastic retain-

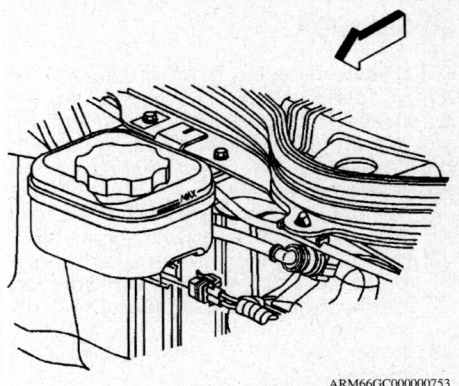

Fig. 2 CPA connector replacement. ION

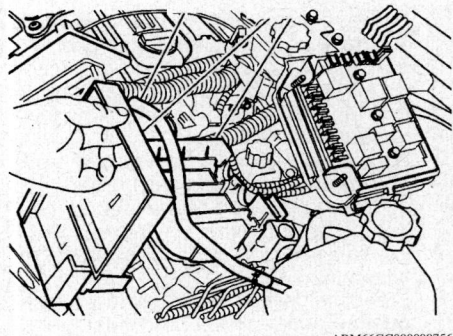

Fig. 5 Surge tank bracket replacement. ION

port, then apply low pressure compressed air into front outlet port to remove secondary piston assembly.

11. Reverse procedure to install.

L-SERIES

DISASSEMBLE

1. Remove master cylinder as outlined in "Component Replacement."
2. Wipe reservoir cap clean, remove cap and inspect reservoir cap and diaphragm for cuts, nicks or deformation.
3. Drain reservoir brake fluid into suitable container.
4. **On models equipped with anti-lock brakes,** remove modulator and motor pack.
5. **On all models,** remove brake fluid level sensor.
6. Remove reservoir as outlined in "Component Replacement."
7. While depressing master cylinder piston, remove retainer clip, **Fig. 16.**
8. Apply low pressure non-lubricated compressed air into upper brake fluid output port, **Fig. 17.**
9. Clean components with clean denatured alcohol. Dry with unlubricated, low pressure compressed air. Blow out cylinder body passages.
10. Inspect pistons and seals for nicks, cuts, cracks, wear or corrosion.
11. Inspect master cylinder bore for scoring or corrosion. If cylinder bore is damaged, replace master cylinder. **Do not hone master cylinder bore.**

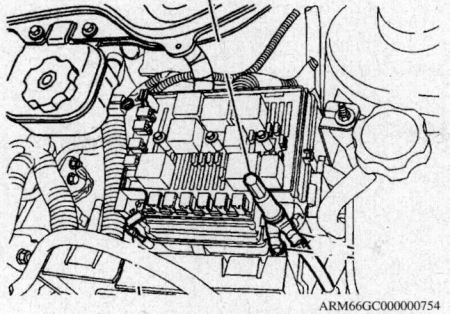

Fig. 3 Electrical connector replacement. ION

ASSEMBLE

1. Lubricate secondary seal and master cylinder bore with clean brake fluid.
2. Install spring and secondary piston into master cylinder bore, **Fig. 18.**
3. Lubricate primary seal and master cylinder bore with clean brake fluid.
4. Install primary piston into master cylinder bore.
5. While depressing master cylinder piston, install retainer clip.
6. Install reservoir as outlined in "Component Replacement."
7. Install brake fluid level sensor.
8. **On models equipped with anti-lock brakes,** install modulator and motor pack.
9. **On all models,** install master cylinder as outlined in "Component Replacement."

VIBE

1. Remove master cylinder from vehicle as outlined in "Master Cylinder, Replace."
2. Remove master cylinder bore O-ring and two attaching rubber grommets.
3. Secure master cylinder into suitable vise, then remove piston stopper bolt and gasket.
4. Remove snap ring pushing piston into master cylinder.
5. Remove plate, cylinder cup, O-ring, piston guide and primary piston assembly from master cylinder.
6. Remove secondary piston using suitable hammer to tap cylinder flange against blocks.
7. Inspect components for wear and damage, replace as required.
8. Reverse procedure to install. Bleed brake system as outlined in "Brake System Bleed."

LACROSSE, STS & XLR

DISASSEMBLE

1. Remove master cylinder as outlined in "Component Replacement."
2. Secure master cylinder mounting flange in suitable bench vise so primary piston rear is accessible.
3. Clean outside of master cylinder reservoir, then remove reservoir cap and diaphragm.
4. Replace cap and diaphragm if cut or cracked, nicked or deformed.
5. Secure master cylinder in suitable

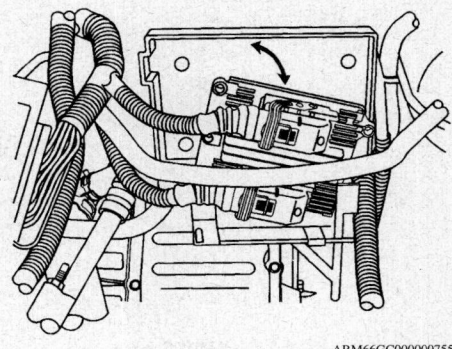

Fig. 4 TCM replacement. ION

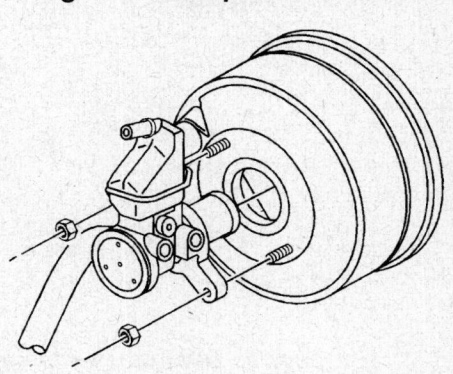

Fig. 6 Master cylinder replacement. ION

vise. **Do not clamp master cylinder body, secure only at flange.**

6. Remove brake fluid level sensor by depressing tab with suitable nose pliers and pressing sensor through reservoir.
7. Tap out reservoir retaining pins.
8. Remove reservoir and seals.
9. Depress primary piston using smooth, round-ended tool and remove piston retainer.
10. Remove primary piston from cylinder bore.
11. Plug cylinder inlet and rear outlet ports.
12. Apply low pressure, non-lubricated, filtered air into front outlet port and remove secondary piston with primary and secondary seals, and return spring.
13. Discard primary piston assembly, piston retainer, seals and retainer from secondary piston.

ASSEMBLE

1. Clean interior and exterior of master cylinder, secondary piston and return spring in denatured alcohol, or equivalent.
2. Inspect the master cylinder bore, inlet and outlet ports, secondary piston and return spring for cracks, scoring, pitting, and/or corrosion.
3. Dry master cylinder and components with non-lubricated, filtered air.
4. Lubricate master cylinder bore, secondary piston, return spring and components with suitable brake fluid.
5. Assemble lubricated, new primary seal, retainer and new secondary seal onto secondary piston.

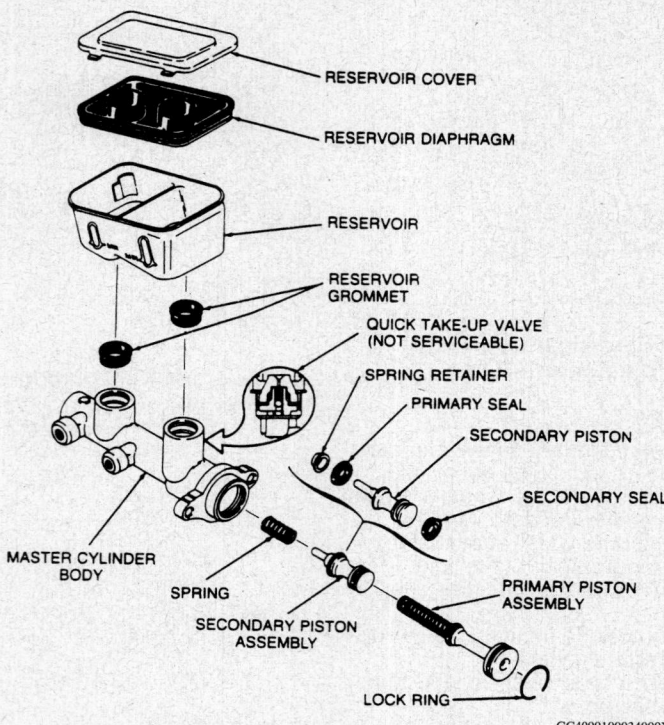

RESERVOIR COVER

RESERVOIR DIAPHRAGM

RESERVOIR

RESERVOIR GROMMET

QUICK TAKE-UP VALVE (NOT SERVICEABLE)

SPRING RETAINER

PRIMARY SEAL

SECONDARY PISTON

SECONDARY SEAL

MASTER CYLINDER BODY

SPRING

SECONDARY PISTON ASSEMBLY

PRIMARY PISTON ASSEMBLY

LOCK RING

GC4099100034000X

Fig. 7 Dual master cylinder assembly. Except Aura, Aveo, Bonneville, Cobalt, Corvette, CTS, DTS, G5, ION, L-Series, LaCrosse, LeSabre, Lucerne, Park Avenue, Solstice, SKY, STS, Vibe & XLR

6. Install lubricated return spring and secondary piston assembly into cylinder bore.
7. Install lubricated, new primary piston assembly into cylinder bore.
8. Depress primary piston using smooth, round-ended tool, and install new piston retainer.
9. Install lubricated reservoir seals. Ensure they are fully seated.
10. Install reservoir by pressing reservoir straight down on master cylinder until pin holes are aligned.
11. Tap reservoir retaining pins into place.
12. Place brake fluid level sensor into reservoir and press into place.
13. Install reservoir cap and diaphragm.

Wheel Cylinder Overhaul

DISASSEMBLE

1. Raise and support vehicle.
2. Remove wheel, drum and brake shoes.
3. Disconnect hydraulic line at wheel cylinder. **Do not pull metal line away from cylinder.** Line will separate from cylinder when cylinder is moved away from brake backing plate.
4. Remove mounting screws and wheel cylinder.
5. Remove boots, pistons, springs and cups, **Fig. 19.**

ASSEMBLE

1. Clean components with suitable brake fluid.
2. Inspect cylinder bore. Scored bore may be honed as long as diameter is not increased by more than .005 inch.
3. Ensure hands are clean before proceeding.
4. Lubricate cylinder wall and rubber cups with suitable brake fluid.
5. Install springs, cups, pistons and boots.
6. Wipe end of hydraulic line to remove any foreign matter and place wheel cylinder in position.
7. Enter tubing into cylinder and start threads on fitting.
8. Secure cylinder to backing plate and complete tightening of tubing fitting.
9. Install brake shoes, drum and wheel.
10. Bleed brake system and adjust brakes.

BRAKE SYSTEM BLEED

Brake fluid is corrosive to painted surfaces. Care must be taken not to allow brake fluid to come in contact with painted surfaces on vehicle.

When bleeding the brake system, always bleed righthand rear wheel circuit first, followed by the lefthand front, lefthand rear and, finally, righthand front.

Manual

Pressure bleeding is recommended for all hydraulic systems. However, if a pressure bleeder is unavailable, use the following procedure. **Brake fluid damages painted surfaces. Immediately clean any spilled fluid.**

1. Remove vacuum reserve by pumping brakes several times with engine off.
2. Fill master cylinder reservoir with clean brake fluid. **Do not let reservoir fall below half full during bleeding procedure.**
3. If required, bleed master cylinder as follows:
   a. Loosen master cylinder forward brake line connection until fluid flows from reservoir, then tighten brake line.
   b. Have assistant to slowly depress brake pedal one time and hold.
   c. Loosen front brake line connection and purge air from cylinder.
   d. Tighten connection and slowly release brake pedal.
   e. Wait 15 seconds, then repeat previous steps until all air is purged.
   f. Bleed rearward brake line connection by repeating previous steps.
4. Loosen and tighten bleeder valves at all four wheels.
5. Bleed calipers or wheel cylinders in sequence outlined in "Bleed Sequence."
6. Place one end of transparent tube over bleeder valve and submerge other end into transparent container filled with clean brake fluid.
7. Have assistant slowly depress brake pedal one time and hold.
8. Loosen bleeder valve and purge air from wheel cylinder or caliper. Tighten bleeder screw and slowly release pedal.
9. Wait 15 seconds and repeat previous steps until all air is bled from system.

Pressure

1. Loosen and tighten bleeder valves at all four wheels.
2. Install suitable bleeder adapter to master cylinder using diaphragm type pressure bleeder.
3. Charge bleeder ball to 20–25 psi.
4. Connect pressure bleeder line to adapter.
5. Open line valve on pressure bleeder and depress bleed-off valve on adapter until small amount of brake fluid is released.
6. Raise and support vehicle.
7. Bleed calipers or wheel cylinders in sequence as outlined in "Bleed Sequence."
8. Place one end of transparent tube over bleeder valve and submerge other end into transparent container filled with clean brake fluid.
9. Open bleeder valve approximately, ¾ turn and allow fluid to flow into container until all air is purged from line.

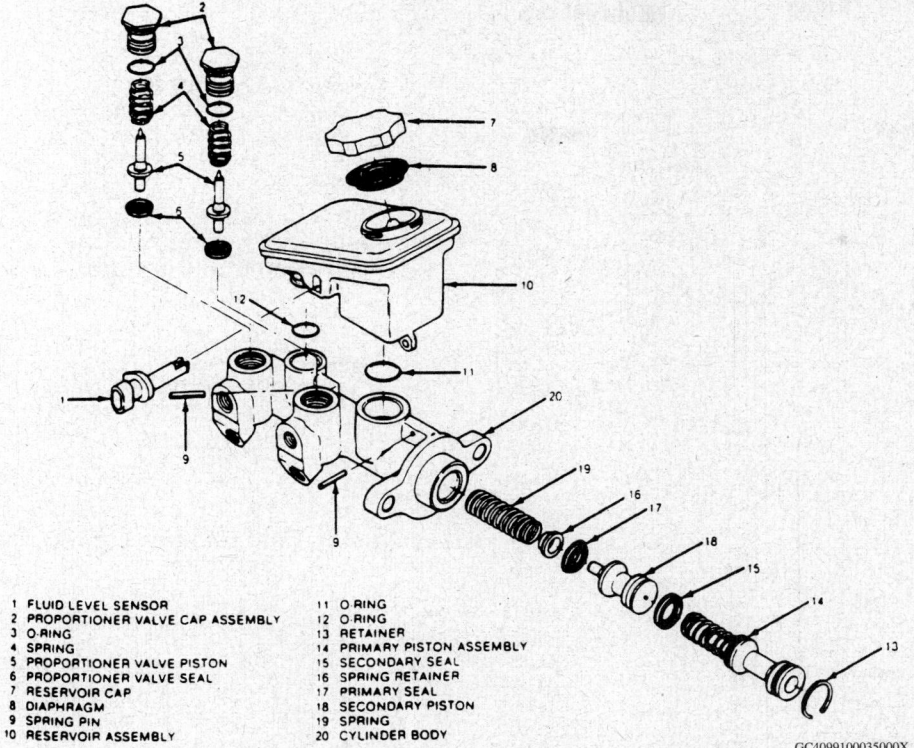

1 FLUID LEVEL SENSOR
2 PROPORTIONER VALVE CAP ASSEMBLY
3 O-RING
4 SPRING
5 PROPORTIONER VALVE PISTON
6 PROPORTIONER VALVE SEAL
7 RESERVOIR CAP
8 DIAPHRAGM
9 SPRING PIN
10 RESERVOIR ASSEMBLY
11 O-RING
12 O-RING
13 RETAINER
14 PRIMARY PISTON ASSEMBLY
15 SECONDARY SEAL
16 SPRING RETAINER
17 PRIMARY SEAL
18 SECONDARY PISTON
19 SPRING
20 CYLINDER BODY

GC4099100035000X

Fig. 8 Compact master cylinder assembly. Except Aura, Aveo, Bonneville, Cobalt, Corvette, CTS, DTS, G5, ION, L-Series, LaCrosse, LeSabre, Lucerne, Park Avenue, Solstice, SKY, STS, Vibe & XLR

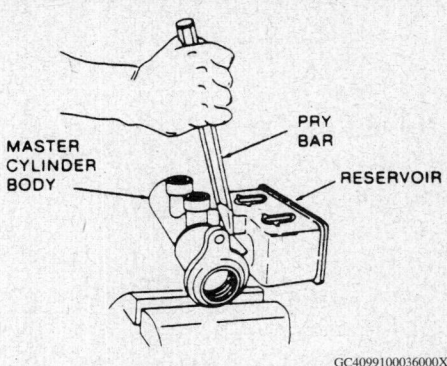

GC4099100036000X

Fig. 9 Master cylinder reservoir replacement. Composite type less retaining pins

Bleed Sequence

On models equipped with front & rear split system, righthand rear-lefthand rear-righthand front-lefthand front; if pressure bleeding, bleed front brakes together and rear brakes together.

On models equipped with diagonally split system, righthand rear-lefthand front-lefthand rear-righthand front.

HYDRAULIC BRAKE SYSTEM FLUSH

If brake fluid is old, rusty or contaminated or whenever new components are installed in hydraulic system, the system must be flushed. Bleed brakes, allowing at least one quart of clean brake fluid to pass through system. Any rubber components in hydraulic system which were exposed to contaminated fluid must be replaced.

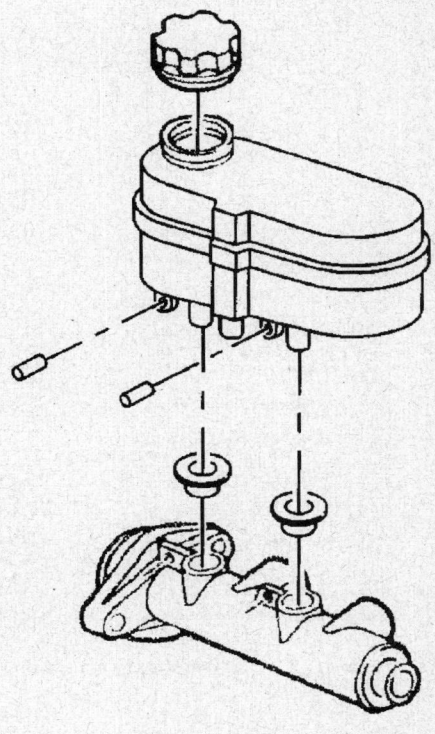

ARM66GC000000300

Fig. 10 Master cylinder reservoir replacement. Composite type w/retaining pins

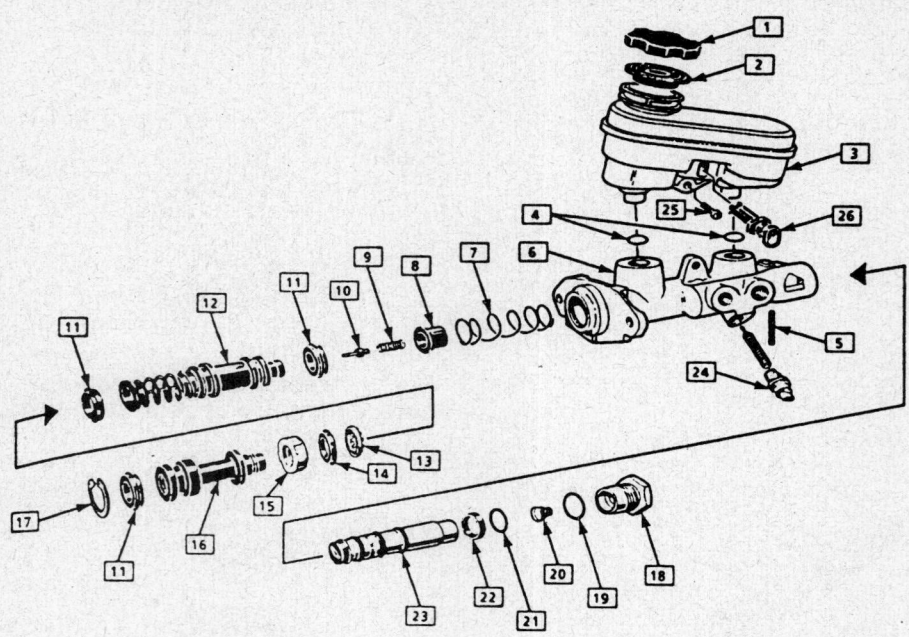

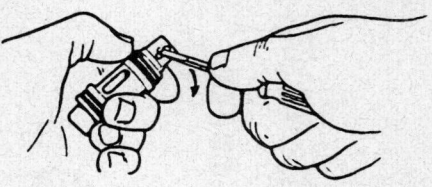

Fig. 12 Lifting crimp on secondary spring retainer replacement. Corvette

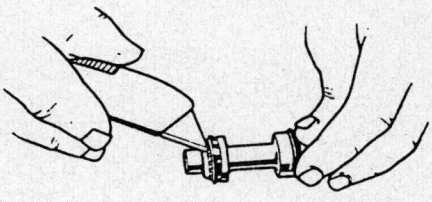

Fig. 13 Seal retainer cutting. Corvette

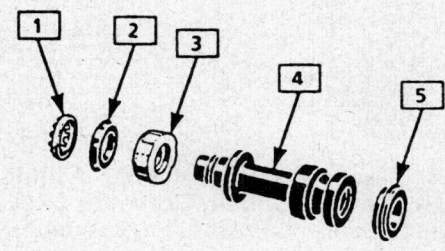

1	RESERVOIR CAP	14	RECUPERATING TYPE CUP SEAL
2	RESERVOIR CAP DIAPHRAGM	15	RECUPERATING GUIDE
3	RESERVOIR BODY	16	PRIMARY PISTON
4	RESERVOIR 'O' RING	17	RETAINING RING
5	SECONDARY PISTON STOP PIN	18	ENG PLUG
6	CYLINDER BODY	19	END PLUG 'O' RING
7	SECONDARY RETURN SPRING	20	ELECTRICAL BIAS SPRING
8	SECONDARY SPRING RETAINER	21	PROPORTIONING VALVE O-RING
9	CENTER VALVE SPRING	22	PROPORTIONING VALVE SPACER
10	CENTER VALVE PLUNGER	23	PROPORTIONING VALVE/PRESSURE DIFFERENTIAL ASSEMBLY
11	'L' TYPE CUP SEAL	24	PRESSURE DIFFERENTIAL WARNING SWITCH ASSEMBLY
12	SECONDARY PISTON ASSEMBLY	25	RESERVOIR RETAINER SCREW
13	PRIMARY CUP RETAINING RING	26	FLUID LEVEL SWITCH ASSEMBLY

1	PRIMARY CUP RETAINING RING
2	RECUPERATING TYPE CUP SEAL
3	RECUPERATING GUIDE
4	PRIMARY PISTON
5	'L' TYPE CUP SEAL

Fig. 11 Composite master cylinder replacement. Corvette

Fig. 14 Primary piston components. Corvette

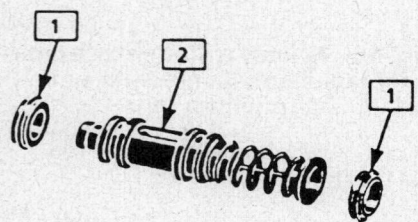

1	'L' TYPE CUP SEAL
2	SECONDARY PISTON ASSEMBLY

Fig. 15 Secondary piston components. Corvette

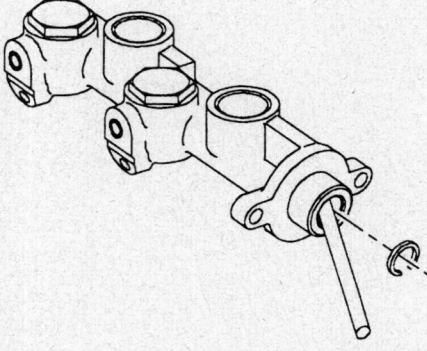

Fig. 16 Master cylinder retainer clip replacement. L-Series

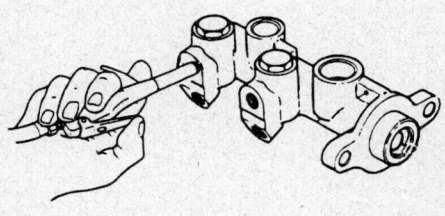

Fig. 17 Master cylinder piston replacement. L-Series

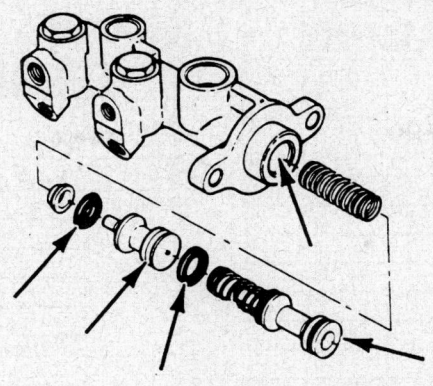

G34099100009000X

Fig. 18 Exploded view of master cylinder. L-Series

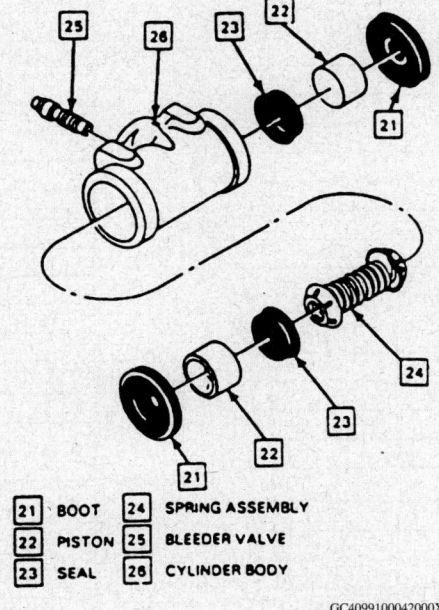

21	BOOT	24	SPRING ASSEMBLY
22	PISTON	25	BLEEDER VALVE
23	SEAL	26	CYLINDER BODY

GC4099100042000X

Fig. 19 Exploded view of wheel cylinder

HYDRAULIC BRAKE SYSTEMS

TIGHTENING SPECIFICATIONS

Year	Component	Torque Ft. Lbs.
ALERO, CENTURY, IMPALA, GRAND PRIX, LACROSSE, MONTE CARLO & REGAL		
2004–08	Brake Hose Caliper	40
	Brake Pedal	30
	Brake Pedal Bracket, Lower	16
	Brake Pedal Bracket, Upper	18
	Brake Pedal Reinforcement Bracket	37
	Brake Pipe Fitting To Hose Drum	20
	Brake Pipe Fitting To Tube (2004–05)	11
	Brake Pipe Fitting To Tube (2006–08)	13
	Front Brake Caliper Bleeder Screw	115①
	Master Cylinder (Less Alero)	24
	Master Cylinder (Alero)	20
	Proportioning Valve Caps	18
	Rear Wheel Cylinder Bleeder Screw	62①
AURA, CAVALIER, GRAND AM & SUNFIRE		
2004–05	ABS Modulator Bleeder Valve	80
	Booster To Pedal Bracket	20
	Brake Hose To Caliper	32
	Brake Pedal To Bracket	20
	Brake Pipe To Master Cylinder	17
	Brake Pipe Tube	17
	Caliper	38
	Caliper Bleeder Screw	115①
	Master Cylinder Booster	20
	Proportioning Valve Brake Line Fitting	20
	Proportioning Valve Caps	20
	Vacuum Brake Booster To Brake Pedal	20
	Wheel Cylinder Bleeder Screw	62①
	Wheel Cylinder To Backing Plate	15
AVEO		
2004–08	Bleeder Screw	80①
	Bleeder Valve	53①
	Booster & Support Bracket	18
	Booster Push Rod	12
	Booster To Support Bracket	106①
	Brake Hose To Caliper	30
	Brake Line	12
	Brake Pedal To Bracket	16
	Caliper	74
	Dust Cover	40①
	Hub To Disc	40①
	Master Cylinder	13
	Proportioning Valve	26–33
	Trim Panel	62①
	Wheel Hub	140

TIGHTENING SPECIFICATIONS—Continued

Year	Component	Torque Ft. Lbs.
BONNEVILLE, LESABRE & PARK AVENUE		
2004–05	Booster To Pedal Bracket	15
	Bracket To Rear Drum Plate	80①
	Brake Hose Bracket	13
	Brake Hose To Caliper	33
	Brake Pedal Bracket	18
	Brake Pipe Fittings To Master Cylinder Tube	24
	Brake Pipe Fitting To Tube	11
	Brake Pipe To Proportioning Valve	11
	Caliper Bleeder Valve	115①
	Master Cylinder	20
	Proportioning Valve To Brake Pipe Fitting	11
	Wheel Cylinder Bleeder Valve	88①
COBALT & G5		
2005–08	Accelerator Pedal & Sensor	80①
	Brake Hose Bracket	18
	Brake Hose Fitting	14
	Brake Hose To Caliper	35
	Brake Pedal Bracket	18
	Master Cylinder	18
	Master Cylinder Fitting	14
	Proportioning Valve Bracket	18
	Proportioning Valve Fitting	14
	Vacuum Brake Booster	14
CORVETTE		
2004–08	Battery Ground	11
	Brake Booster	20
	Brake Caliper Bleed Screw	106①
	Brake Caliper Inlet Fitting	30
	Brake Pedal Pivot	21
	Brake Pipe To Brake Valve	13
	Brake Pipe To Flexible Brake Hose Tube	13
	Brake Pipe To Master Cylinder Tube	18
	Master Cylinder	21
	Telescoping Column Motor Mounting Bracket	62①
	Vacuum Booster To Brake Bracket	15
CTS		
2004–08	Brake Hose To Caliper (CTS)	37
	Brake Hose To Caliper (CTS-V)	25
	Brake Master Cylinder	18
	Brake Pedal To Cowl (2004)	11
	Brake Pedal To Cowl (2005–08)	18
	Brake Pedal To Instrument Panel Carrier	18
	Brake Pipe Fitting	13
	Brake Pipe Fitting At Master Cylinder	24
	Intermediate Brake Hose (2004)	89①
	Intermediate Brake Hose (2005–08)	124①

TIGHTENING SPECIFICATIONS—Continued

Year	Component	Torque Ft. Lbs.
DEVILLE & SEVILLE		
2004–05	Brake Booster	20
	Brake Caliper Bleed Screw	110①
	Brake Caliper Inlet Fitting	33
	Brake Hose Bracket	10
	Brake Pipe Fittings At Master Cylinder Tube	24
	Brake Pipe Fittings To Tube	11
	Engine Oil Cooler Line Retaining Bracket	53①
	Hydraulic Brake Booster	21
	Hydraulic Pump	80①
	Master Cylinder	20
	Park Brake Cable Bracket To Caliper	32
	Pedal To Booster	22
	Pedal To Cowl	12
	Proportioning Valve To Brake Pipe Fittings	11
DTS & LUCERNE		
2006–08	Brake Hose Bracket To Frame	115①
	Brake Hose Bracket To Strut	13
	Brake Hose To Caliper	30
	Brake Pedal To Hydraulic Booster Stud	27
	Brake Pedal To Vacuum Booster Stud	22
	Brake Pipe Fitting	11
	Brake Pipe Fitting At Master Cylinder	21
	Brake Pipe Retainer	89①
	ETC Pedal	89①
	Master Cylinder	22
GTO		
2004–06	Bleeder Valve	106①
	Brake Hose To Caliper Fitting, Front	②
	Brake Hose To Caliper Fitting, Rear	26
	Brake Pedal Bracket	18
	Brake Pedal Shaft	41
	Brake Pipe To Hose	12
	Brake Pipe To Master Cylinder	10
	Master Cylinder	88①
	Master Cylinder Support Bracket	71①
G6 & MALIBU		
2005–08	Bleeder Valve	97①
	Brake Fluid Pressure Sensor	13
	Brake Hose-to-Brake Caliper Bolt	37
	Brake Pipe Fittings at ABS Modulator	15
	Brake Pipe Fittings at Master Cylinder	15
	Caliper Guide Pin Bolt	26
	Caliper Mounting Bracket Bolt	85
	Master Cylinder Mounting Nuts	18
	Proportioning Valve Bracket Bolts	89①
	Vacuum Brake Booster to Brake Pedal Retaining Nuts	11

TIGHTENING SPECIFICATIONS—Continued

Year	Component	Torque Ft. Lbs.
ION		
2004–07	Brake Hose To Caliper	35
	Brake Master Cylinder	15
	Brake Master Cylinder Auxiliary Reservoir	89①
	Brake Pedal Bracket To Steering Column Bracket	18
	Brake Pipe Fitting At Front Brake Hose	14
	Brake Pipe Fittings At Master Cylinder	14
	Brake Pipe Fitting At Proportioning Valve Assembly	14
	Brake Pipe Fitting At Rear Brake Hose	14
	Cooling System Surge Tank	89①
	Electric Power Steering Cable	89①
	Front Brake Hose Bracket	18
	Proportioning Valve Assembly	18
	Proportioning Valve Assembly Bracket	18
	Underhood Electrical Center Bracket	18
	Underhood Electrical Center Bracket	89①
	Underhood Positive Battery Lug	11
	Vacuum Brake Booster	18
L-SERIES		
2004–05	Brake Pipe To Master Cylinder	12
	Caliper Bleeder Valves	71①
	Cylinder To Brake Booster	25
	Proportioning Valve	12
	Rear Brake Hose	12
	Rear Crossover	12
SOLSTICE & SKY		
2006–08	Brake Hose Bracket	106①
	Brake Hose To Caliper	30
	Brake Pedal Bracket	80①
	Brake Pedal Pivot	37
	Brake Pipe Fitting	15
	Master Cylinder	11
	Master Cylinder Reservoir	71①
	Proportioning Valve	89①
	Vacuum Brake Booster	18
STS		
2005–08	Brake Hose to Caliper	37
	Brake Pedal Bracket Nut	18
	Brake Pipe Fittings at Master Cylinder	28
	Brake Pipe Tube Fitting	13
	Master Cylinder	18

Continued

TIGHTENING SPECIFICATIONS—Continued

Year	Component	Torque Ft. Lbs.
VIBE		
2004–08	Bleeder Valve	74①
	Brake Hose Bracket	21
	Bracket Hose To Bracket Pipe Fitting	11
	Brake Hose To Caliper Fitting	21
	Brake Pedal Bracket & Vacuum Booster	112①
	Brake Pedal Shaft	27
	Brake Pipe Flare	11
	Cruise Control Actuator Bracket	31
	Master Cylinder	110①
	Master Cylinder Piston Stopper	88①
	Proportioning Valve	48①
	Vacuum Booster Push Rod	19

TIGHTENING SPECIFICATIONS—Continued

Year	Component	Torque Ft. Lbs.
XLR		
2004–08	Brake Booster	15
	Brake Caliper Inlet Fitting	33
	Brake Pedal Pivot	21
	Brake Pipe To Flexible Brake Hose Tube	13
	Brake Pipe To Master Cylinder Tube	18
	Master Cylinder	21
	Telescoping Column Motor	62①

① — Inch lbs.

② — **Torque** to 115 inch lbs, then final tighten an additional 90°.

POWER BRAKE UNITS

NOTE: On Air Bag Equipped Models, Refer To "Air Bag System Precautions" Located In The Front Of This Manual For System Disarming & Arming Procedures.

NOTE: Refer To "Computer Relearn Procedures" Located In The Front Of This Manual When Battery Power To The Computer Has Been Interrupted.

INDEX

	Page No.		Page No.		Page No.
Adjustments	25-1	Application Chart	25-1	Power Brake Unit Service	25-2
Brake Pedal	25-1	Description	25-1	Precautions	25-1
GM/Toyota Single Diaphragm Type	25-1	AC-Delco Tandem Diaphragm Type	25-1	Troubleshooting	25-1
Pushrod	25-2	GM/Toyota Single Diaphragm Type	25-1	Brakes Grab	25-1
Air Method	25-2	General Service	25-2	Brakes Inefficient/Hard Pedal	25-1
Gauge Method	25-2			Slow Or No Release	25-1

APPLICATION CHART

Model	Power Brake Type
Except Vibe	AC-Delco Tandem Diaphragm
Vibe	GM/Toyota Single Diaphragm

PRECAUTIONS

1. After disassembling power brake unit, soak metal components in solvent.
2. Use only alcohol on components containing rubber. After components have been thoroughly cleaned and rinsed in solvent, they should be washed again in clean alcohol before assembly.
3. Use compressed air to blow dirt and cleaning fluid from recesses and internal passages.
4. Always use all components furnished in repair kit.
5. **Use extreme caution when disassembling power assist mechanisms. If internal spring tension is suddenly released it could cause damage or personal injury.**
6. **Brake boosters are not serviceable and should be replaced as an assembly.**

DESCRIPTION

AC-Delco Tandem Diaphragm Type

This unit utilizes a vacuum power chamber, consisting of a front and rear shell, housing divider, front and rear diaphragm, plate assemblies, hydraulic pushrod and a diaphragm return spring, **Fig. 1.**

In normal operating mode, with service brakes in released position, the booster operates with vacuum on both sides of its diaphragms. When brakes are applied, air at atmospheric pressure is admitted to one side of each diaphragm to provide power assist. When the service brake is released, atmospheric air is shut off from one side of each diaphragm. The air is then drawn from the booster through the vacuum check valve to the vacuum source.

GM/Toyota Single Diaphragm Type

The Toyota/GM single diaphragm type booster assembly is located between the master cylinder and brake pedal, **Fig. 2.** When the brake pedal is depressed, the force is transmitted to the master cylinder piston through the valve operating rod, booster air valve, reaction disc and piston rod. The force of the booster piston is developed because of the pressure difference between the front and rear chambers.

TROUBLESHOOTING

Brakes Grab

1. Contaminated, worn or faulty brake linings.
2. Drum or brake rotor out-of-round.
3. Faulty brake booster.

Brakes Inefficient/ Hard Pedal

1. Contaminated, glazed or faulty brake linings.
2. Frozen caliper piston.
3. Faulty vacuum pump, or leak in booster vacuum supply system.
4. Faulty brake booster.

Slow Or No Release

1. Faulty pushrod adjustment.
2. Bind in linkage.

ADJUSTMENTS

Brake Pedal

GM/TOYOTA SINGLE DIAPHRAGM TYPE

1. With engine running and brake pedal in rest position, measure distance between face of pedal and floor mat.
2. Distance should be 5.850–6.244 inches.
3. If distance is not as specified, adjust pedal height as follows:
   a. Remove lefthand lower instrument panel trim section and air duct.
   b. Loosen stop lamp switch sufficiently to access pedal adjustment.
   c. Loosen locknut and rotate pedal pushrod as required to obtain specified pedal height. Tighten locknut.
   d. Adjust brake lamp switch position so plunger lightly contacts pedal stopper and brake lamps are off when pedal is released.
   e. Inspect pedal free travel.
4. With engine stopped, depress brake pedal several times to ensure there is no vacuum pressure in booster.
5. Release pedal and press pedal down until beginning of resistance is felt. Measure pedal travel. **Pedal free travel is amount brake booster air valve is moved by pedal pushrod.**
6. If pedal travel is not .12–.24 inch, adjust pedal freeplay as follows:
   a. Adjust pedal free travel by loosening locknut and rotating pedal pushrod.
   b. Ensure brake lamp switch and pedal height are properly adjusted.
   c. Start engine and confirm free travel still exists.
   d. Inspect pedal reserve distance.
7. Release parking brake and start engine.
8. Depress brake pedal with applied

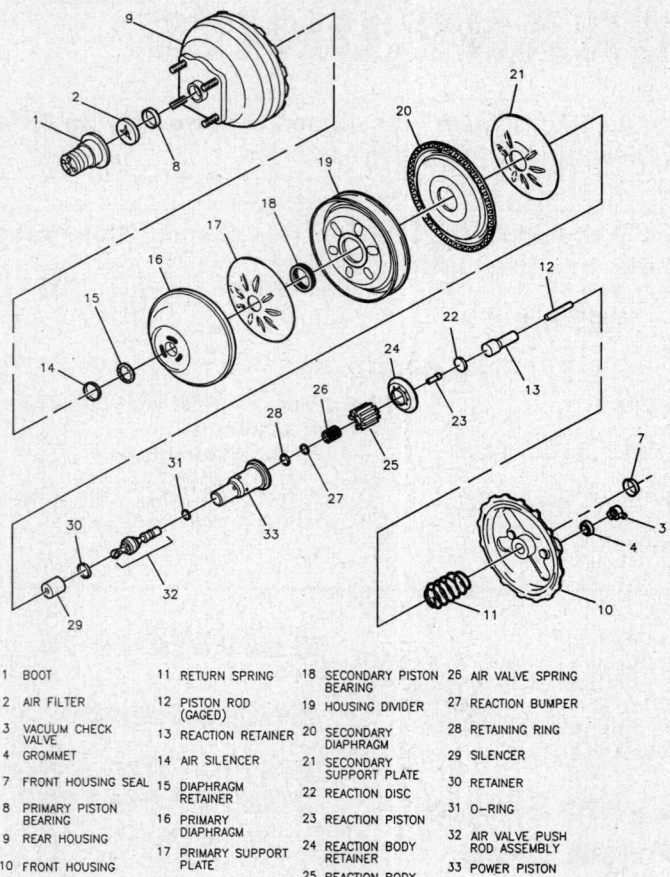

1	BOOT	11	RETURN SPRING	18	SECONDARY PISTON BEARING	26	AIR VALVE SPRING

1 BOOT
2 AIR FILTER
3 VACUUM CHECK VALVE
4 GROMMET
7 FRONT HOUSING SEAL
8 PRIMARY PISTON BEARING
9 REAR HOUSING
10 FRONT HOUSING

11 RETURN SPRING
12 PISTON ROD (GAGED)
13 REACTION RETAINER
14 AIR SILENCER
15 DIAPHRAGM RETAINER
16 PRIMARY DIAPHRAGM
17 PRIMARY SUPPORT PLATE

18 SECONDARY PISTON BEARING
19 HOUSING DIVIDER
20 SECONDARY DIAPHRAGM
21 SECONDARY SUPPORT PLATE
22 REACTION DISC
23 REACTION PISTON
24 REACTION BODY RETAINER
25 REACTION BODY

26 AIR VALVE SPRING
27 REACTION BUMPER
28 RETAINING RING
29 SILENCER
30 RETAINER
31 O-RING
32 AIR VALVE PUSH ROD ASSEMBLY
33 POWER PISTON

GC4099700059000X

Fig. 1   Exploded view of AC-Delco tandem diaphragm booster

force of 110 lbs., and measure distance from face of pedal to floor mat.

9. Pedal reserve distance should not be more than 3.35 inches.

10. If pedal reserve distance does not meet specifications, inspect and repair brake system.

Pushrod

Proper adjustment of the master cylinder pushrod is required to ensure proper operation of the power brake system. A pushrod that is too long will cause the master cylinder piston to close off the compensating port, preventing hydraulic pressure from being released and resulting in brake drag. A pushrod that is too short will cause excessive brake pedal travel and cause groaning noises to come from the booster when the brakes are applied. A properly adjusted pushrod that remains assembled to the booster with which it was matched during production should not require service adjustment. However, if the booster, master cylinder or pushrod are serviced, the pushrod may require adjustment.

There are two methods that can be used to inspect for proper pushrod length and installation. These are the gauge method and air method. Usually, if the power unit pushrod requires adjustment, use the power unit repair kit gauge. The gauge measures from the end of the pushrod to the power unit shell.

GAUGE METHOD
AC-DELCO TANDEM DIAPHRAGM TYPE

The master cylinder pushrod length is fixed and is usually only inspected after the unit has been overhauled. This procedure can be performed with the unit removed from the vehicle if a suitable vacuum source is available.

1. Assemble booster unit and install pushrod. Ensure pushrod is fully seated.
2. Apply 20 inches or maximum engine vacuum to booster.
3. Position gauge tool No. J-37839, or equivalent, over pushrod, **Fig. 3.**
4. Replace booster if output button length is not within gauge limits.
5. Install power unit and inspect adjustment.
6. Ensure master cylinder compensating port is open with engine running and brake pedal released.

AIR METHOD

1. Ensure master cylinder mounting nuts are tight.
2. Remove master cylinder filler cap.

3. With brake released, force compressed air into hydraulic outlet of master cylinder. **Regulate air pressure to value of approximately 5 psi to prevent spraying brake fluid from master cylinder.**
4. If air passes through compensating port, which is smaller of two holes in bottom of master cylinder reservoir, adjustment is satisfactory.
5. If air does not flow through compensating port, adjust pushrod as required, either by means of adjustment screw (if provided) or by adding shims between master cylinder and power unit shell until air flows freely.
6. Connect brake lines and bleed system.

GENERAL SERVICE

Two basic types of power assist mechanisms are used: vacuum assist diaphragm assemblies, which use engine vacuum or in some cases vacuum pressure developed by an external vacuum pump. The second type is a hydraulic pressure assist mechanism, which use pressure developed by an external pump (usually the power steering pump). Both systems act to increase the force exerted on the master cylinder piston by the operator. This in turn increases the hydraulic pressure delivered to the wheel cylinders while decreasing driver effort required to obtain acceptable stopping performance.

Vacuum assist units are similar in operation and get their energy by opposing engine vacuum to atmospheric pressure. A piston and cylinder, flexible diaphragm (bellows) utilize this energy to provide brake assistance. The fundamental difference between these types of vacuum assist systems lies simply in how the diaphragm within the power unit is suspended when the brakes are not applied.

In order to properly diagnose vacuum assist system faults it is important to know whether the diaphragm within a power unit is air suspended or vacuum suspended. Air-suspended units are under atmospheric pressure until the brakes are applied. Engine vacuum is then admitted, causing the piston or diaphragm to move (or the bellows to collapse). Vacuum-suspended types are balanced with engine vacuum until the brake pedal is depressed, allowing atmospheric pressure to unbalance the unit and apply force to the brake system.

Regardless of whether the brakes are vacuum or hydraulically assisted, certain general service procedures apply. Only specified, clean brake fluid should be used in brake systems. On hydro-boost systems, use of the specified hydraulic fluid in the boost circuit is essential to proper system operation. Care must be taken not to mix the fluids of the two separate operating circuits.

POWER BRAKE UNIT SERVICE

Hydro-boost brake boosters are not serviceable and should be replaced as an assembly.

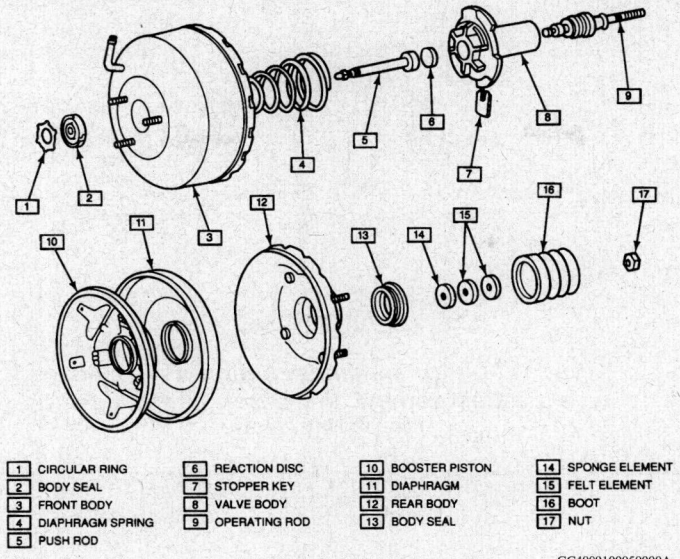

1 CIRCULAR RING	6 REACTION DISC	10 BOOSTER PISTON	14 SPONGE ELEMENT
2 BODY SEAL	7 STOPPER KEY	11 DIAPHRAGM	15 FELT ELEMENT
3 FRONT BODY	8 VALVE BODY	12 REAR BODY	16 BOOT
4 DIAPHRAGM SPRING	9 OPERATING ROD	13 BODY SEAL	17 NUT
5 PUSH ROD			

GC4099100050000A

Fig. 2   Exploded view of GM/Toyota brake booster

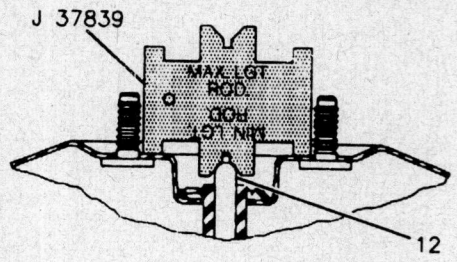

12 OUTPUT BUTTON / ROD

GC4099700063000X

Fig. 3 Master cylinder measurement. AC-Delco tandem diaphragm type

FRONT WHEEL DRIVE AXLES

NOTE: On Air Bag Equipped Models, Refer To "Air Bag System Precautions" Located In The Front Of This Manual For System Disarming & Arming Procedures.

NOTE: Refer To "Computer Relearn Procedures" Located In The Front Of This Manual When Battery Power To The Computer Has Been Interrupted.

INDEX

	Page No.
Description	26-1
Driveshaft, Replace	26-2
Alero, Grand Am & Malibu	26-2
Aura, G6 & Malibu MAXX	26-2
Aveo	26-2
Bonneville, DeVille, LeSabre, Park Avenue & Seville	26-2
Installation	26-2
Removal	26-2
Cavalier & Sunfire	26-3
Century, Grand Prix, Impala, Monte Carlo & Regal	26-3
Cobalt & G5	26-3
DTS & Lucerne	26-3
ION	26-4
L-Series	26-4
Installation	26-4
Removal	26-4
LaCrosse	26-4
Malibu	26-5
STS	26-5
Lefthand	26-5
Righthand	26-5
Vibe	26-5
Driveshaft Service	26-6

	Page No.
All Models Except Aveo, Cavalier, Cobalt, G5, ION, L-Series, STS, Sunfire & Vibe.	26-6
Inner Joint & Boot	26-6
Outer Joint & Boot	26-6
Aveo	26-7
Automatic	26-7
Manual	26-8
Cavalier & Sunfire	26-9
Inner Joint & Boot	26-9
Outer Joint & Boot	26-9
Cobalt & G5	26-11
Delphi	26-11
GKN	26-12
ION	26-13
Inner Joint & Seal	26-13
Outer Joint & Seal	26-13
L-Series	26-13
Assemble	26-14
Disassemble	26-13
Inspection	26-14
STS	26-14
Inner Joint & Seal	26-14
Outer Joint & Seal	26-15
Vibe	26-16

	Page No.
Inner Joint & Seal	26-16
Intermediate Shaft, Replace	26-16
All Models Except Cobalt, G5, ION & L-Series	26-16
Cobalt & G5	26-17
ION	26-17
L-Series	26-17
Installation	26-17
Removal	26-17
Intermediate Shaft Service	26-18
All Models Except ION, L-Series, STS & Vibe	26-18
Assemble	26-18
Disassemble	26-18
Precautions	26-1
Battery Ground Cable	26-1
Joint Protection	26-1
Tightening Specifications	26-21
Troubleshooting	26-1
Click Noise In Turns	26-1
Clunk Noise When Accelerating During Turns	26-2
Clunk When Accelerating from Coast	26-1

PRECAUTIONS

Battery Ground Cable

Prior to service, disconnect battery ground cable and isolate as required.

Joint Protection

On models equipped with tripod joints on inboard axles, care must be taken not to overextend joints.

On models equipped with ball type constant velocity inboard joints, install inner drive joint seal protector tool No. J34754 and axle boot protector tool No. J28712, or equivalents.

On models equipped with tripod inboard joints, install axle boot seal protector tool No. J28712 and tool No. J33162, or equivalents.

DESCRIPTION

Front wheel drive systems consist of an inner and outer constant velocity joint connected by an axle shaft, **Figs. 1 through 10.** The inner joint is completely flexible, and can move in and out. The outer joint is also flexible, but cannot move in and out.

TROUBLESHOOTING

Click Noise In Turns

A click noise occurring during turns may be caused by a worn or damaged wheel drive shaft outer joint. This click is caused by wear and/or damage to the constant velocity joint bearings and/or races. Commonly, this damage or wear is caused by the loss of lubricating grease from the constant velocity joint and the entry of foreign material or contaminates.
1. Carefully inspect wheel drive shaft seals for cuts, tears or other damage which may allow lubricating grease to escape.
2. If inspection reveals no visual evidence of wear or damage, it may be necessary to remove wheel drive shaft from vehicle and manipulate outer joint manually.

3. Any binding or impeded movement of joint may indicate damage which could contribute to concern.

Clunk When Accelerating from Coast

A clunk noise occurring when accelerating from coast or a standing start may be caused by a worn or damaged wheel drive shaft inner joint. The common cause of wheel drive shaft inner joint damage is the loss of lubricating grease and/or the presence of foreign material and contaminates in the joint. This usually occurs as a result of a torn or damaged inner joint seal.
1. Carefully inspect wheel drive shaft seal for cuts, tears or other damage that may allow loss of lubricating grease and/or entry of contaminates.
2. If inspection reveals no visual evidence of wear or damage, it may be necessary to remove wheel drive shaft from vehicle and manipulate inner joint manually.

3. Do not allow joint to separate from wheel drive shaft.
4. Any binding or impeded movement of joint may indicate damage which could contribute to concern.

Clunk Noise When Accelerating During Turns

A clunk noise that occurs while accelerating during turns may be caused by wear and/or damage to the inboard and the outboard joints in combination. The loss of lubricant and/or the presence of contaminates can cause damage to the internal components of the joints.

1. Carefully inspect joint seals for cuts, tears or other damage.
2. If inspection reveals no visual evidence of wear or damage, it may be necessary to remove wheel drive shaft from vehicle and manipulate joints manually.
3. **Do not allow joints to separate from wheel drive shaft.**
4. Any binding or impeded movement of joints may indicate damage which could contribute to concern.

DRIVESHAFT
REPLACE

Alero, Grand Am & Malibu

On Malibu models cover in under this head the fourth digit of the Vehicle Information Number (VIN) is the letter N.
On Malibu models with the fourth digit of the Vehicle Information Number (VIN) the letter Z, refer to "G6 & Malibu Maxx" head.

1. Raise and support vehicle, then remove tire and wheel assembly.
2. Disconnect tie rod from knuckle.
3. Prevent rotor from turning by inserting suitable drift into caliper and rotor, then remove axle shaft nut.
4. Disconnect stabilizer link and separate lower control arm ball joint from steering knuckle.
5. Remove hub and bearing using front hub spindle remover tool No. J28733-B, or equivalent.
6. Separate drive axle from transaxle using axle shaft remover tool No. J33008 and slide hammer tool J2619-01, or equivalents. **Do not overextend drive axle.**
7. Remove drive axle.
8. Reverse procedure to install. There two style axles nuts with different tightening specifications, **Figs. 11 and 12.**

Aura, G6 & Malibu MAXX

On Malibu models cover in under this head the fourth digit of the Vehicle Information Number (VIN) is the letter Z.
On Malibu models with the fourth digit of the Vehicle Information Number (VIN) the letter N, refer to "Alero, Grand Am & Malibu" Chapter .

1. Raise and support vehicle, then remove tire and wheel assembly.
2. Remove front wheel drive shaft nut.
3. Loosen outer tie rod inner tie rod jam nut.
4. Remove outer tie rod to steering knuckle prevailing nut. Discard nut.
5. Separate tie rod from steering knuckle using tie rod separator tool No. J24319-B, or equivalent. **Do not free ball stud by using pickle fork or wedge-type tool.**
6. Remove outer from inner tie rod.
7. **On models equipped with 3.5L engine,** proceed as follows:
   a. If removing lefthand drive shaft, remove side transmission mount as outlined under "Engine Mount, Replace" in "3.5L Engine" section of "G6 & Malibu Maxx" chapter.
   b. If removing righthand drive shaft, remove engine mount as outlined under "Engine Mount, Replace" in "3.5L Engine" section of "G6 & Malibu Maxx" chapter.
8. **On all models,** remove front and rear lower control arm bushing to frame bolts and nuts.
9. Mark orientation of lower control arm ball stud to steering knuckle pinch bolt for installation alignment.
10. Remove pinch bolt and discard.
11. Separate ball stud from steering knuckle.
12. Separate front wheel drive axle from shaft bearing using hub spindle remover tool No. J42129, or equivalent.
13. Partially installed to protect nut threads.
14. Remove wheel drive shaft from transaxle.
15. Separate axle from transaxle using axle shaft remover tool No. J33008-A , axle shaft remover extension tool No. J29794 and slide hammer tool No. J2619-01, or equivalents.
16. Reverse procedure to install, noting the following:
   a. Tighten lower control arm nuts with vehicle at proper Z trim height. Refer to "Vehicle Ride Height" in "Wheel Alignment" section of "G6 & Malibu Maxx" chapter.
   b. Install new ball stud to steering knuckle pinch bolt.
   c. **Torque** ball stud to steering knuckle pinch nut to 37 ft. lbs.
   d. Reverse nut ¾ turn.
   e. **Torque** nut to 37 ft. lbs.
   f. Final tighten an additional 40°.
   g. Tighten nuts and bolts with front suspension loaded using suitable jack stand.
   h. **Torque** front and rear bushing to frame bolts to 37 ft. lbs.
   i. Tighten bushing bolts an additional 90°.

Bonneville, DeVille, LeSabre, Park Avenue & Seville

REMOVAL

1. Raise and support vehicle, then remove tire and wheel assemblies.
2. Loosen or remove stabilizer shaft link.
3. Remove ball joint cotter pin and nut.
4. Loosen ball joint from steering knuckle using ball joint separator tool No. J43828, or equivalent.
5. Separate ball joint from steering knuckle using suitable pry bar between suspension support and lower control arm.
6. Prevent rotor from turning by inserting suitable drift or screwdriver into caliper and rotor, then remove hub nut.
7. Disconnect axle from hub using front hub spindle remover tool No. J28733-B, or equivalent.
8. Position strut and knuckle rearward.
9. Remove drive axle from transaxle using axle shaft remover tool No. J33008 and slide hammer tool No. J2619-01, or equivalents. **Do not overextend drive axle.**

INSTALLATION

1. Inspect tripot housing at transmission seal surface for corrosion. Remove corrosion by sanding sealing surface with 320 grit emery cloth.
2. Lubricate tripot housing surface with suitable transmission fluid.
3. Push axle into transaxle. Ensure drive axle is seated by grasping inner joint housing and pulling. **Do not pull on drive axle shaft.**
4. Install drive axle into transaxle by placing suitable screwdriver into groove on joint housing and tapping until axle is seated.
5. Insert drive axle into hub and bearing, then install new hub nut.
6. Prevent rotor from turning by inserting suitable drift or screwdriver into caliper and rotor, then tighten axle nut.
7. Attach ball joint to knuckle.
8. Install stabilizer shaft link.
9. Install wheels and lower vehicle.

Aveo

1. Raise and support vehicle, then remove tire and wheel assemblies.
2. Remove mounting nuts and bolts, then the engine under cover.
3. Remove and discard axle shaft caulking nut.
4. Remove lower ball joint nut and separate steering knuckle from lower ball joint using ball joint remover tool No. KM-507-C, or equivalent.
5. Remove tie rod nut and separate tie rod end using lower ball joint using ball joint remover tool.
6. Remove mounting bolts and rear mounting bracket.

7. Remove damping block connection mounting nut and bolt.
8. Push drive axle shaft from wheel hub.
9. Place suitable drain pan below transaxle to catch escaping fluid.
10. Remove drive axle from transaxle using axle shaft remover tool No. KM-460-B, or equivalent.
11. Cap transaxle drive opening.
12. Reverse procedure to install, noting the following:
    a. **Do not damage seals.**
    b. Loosely install new axle shaft caulking nut.
    c. Loosely install wheel lug nuts.
    d. Lower vehicle to floor.
    e. Tighten wheel lugs nuts.
    f. Install and tighten axle shaft caulking nut.
    g. Peen caulking nut with suitable punch and hammer until nut is locked into place on axle shaft hub.

Cavalier & Sunfire

1. Raise and support vehicle, then remove wheel and tire assembly.
2. Remove tie rod end to steering knuckle retaining nut, then disconnect tie rod end from steering knuckle.
3. Prevent rotor from turning by inserting suitable drift or punch into caliper and rotor, then remove drive axle nut and washer.
4. Remove ball joint cotter pin and nut, then separate joint from steering knuckle using ball joint separator tool No. J38892, or equivalent.
5. Disconnect ABS sensor wire.
6. Disconnect stabilizer link and separate joint using suitable ball joint separator.
7. Disconnect axle from hub and bearing using front hub spindle tool No. J28733-A, or equivalent.
8. Separate hub and bearing from axle.
9. Move strut and knuckle rearward.
10. Remove inner joint from transaxle using axle remover tool No. J33008, drive axle removal extension tool No. J29794 and slide hammer tool No. J2619-01, or equivalents.
11. Reverse procedure to install.

Century, Grand Prix, Impala, Monte Carlo & Regal

1. Raise and support vehicle, then remove tire and wheel assembly.
2. Remove stabilizer link.
3. Prevent rotor from turning by inserting suitable drift or flat-bladed tool into caliper and rotor, then remove drive axle nut.
4. Disconnect tie rod from steering knuckle.
5. Disconnect ball joint from steering knuckle using ball joint/stud separator tool No. J41820, or equivalent.
6. **On righthand drive axle,** separate drive axle from transaxle using axle shaft tool No. J3308, extension tool No. J29794 and puller tool No. J2619-01, or equivalents.

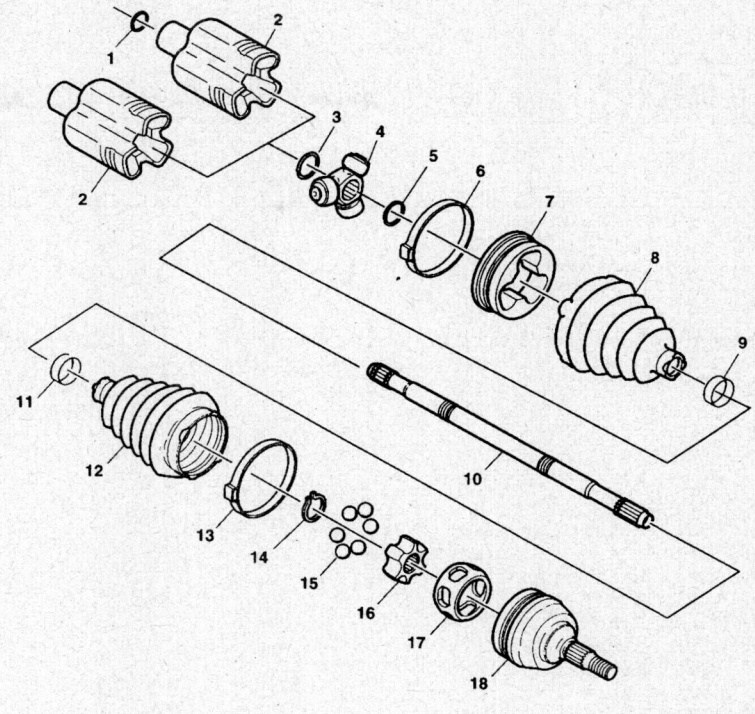

(1) Retaining Ring
(2) Retainer and Housing Assembly
(3) Shaft Retaining Ring
(4) Tripot Spider Assembly
(5) Spacer Ring
(6) Boot Retaining Clamp
(7) Tripot Trilobal Bushing
(8) Halfshaft Inboard Boot
(9) Swage Ring
(10) Halfshaft Bar
(11) Swage Ring
(12) Halfshaft Outboard Boot
(13) Boot Retaining Clamp
(14) Race Retaining Ring
(15) Chrome Alloy Ball
(16) CV Joint Inner Race
(17) CV Joint Cage
(18) CV Joint Outer Race

GC3039900339000X

Fig. 1   Exploded view of front drive axle. All models except Aveo, Cavalier, Cobalt, G5, ION, L-Series, STS, Sunfire & Vibe

7. **On lefthand drive axle,** use frame for leverage and separate drive axle from transaxle using suitable screwdriver or pry bar in inner joint groove.
8. **On all drive axles,** reverse procedure to install, noting the following:
    a. Install axle seal protector tool No. J37292-A, or equivalent, to righthand side of transaxle so it can be pulled out after drive axle is installed.
    b. Install new axle nut.

Cobalt & G5

1. Raise and support vehicle, then remove tire and wheel assembly.
2. Remove wheel drive shaft nut.
3. Loosen wheel drive shaft splines from wheel bearing/hub using suitable wood block and hammer.
4. Remove ball stud to steering knuckle pinch bolt and nut, then separate ball stud from steering knuckle.

5. Separate wheel drive shaft from wheel bearing/hub, then support shaft.
6. Separate wheel drive shaft from transaxle using rear wheel drive shaft removal tool No. J45341, and slide hammer tool No. J2619-A or equivalents.
7. Remove shaft.
8. Reverse procedure to install using axle seal protector tool No. J44394, or equivalent.

DTS & Lucerne

1. Raise and support vehicle, then remove tire and wheel assembly.
2. **On models equipped with road sensing suspension,** disconnect connector and height sensor link from ball stud.
3. **On all models,** remove outer tie rod nut and loosen inner tie rod jam nut. **Do not loosen tie rod end jam nut.**
4. Disconnect outer tie rod from steering

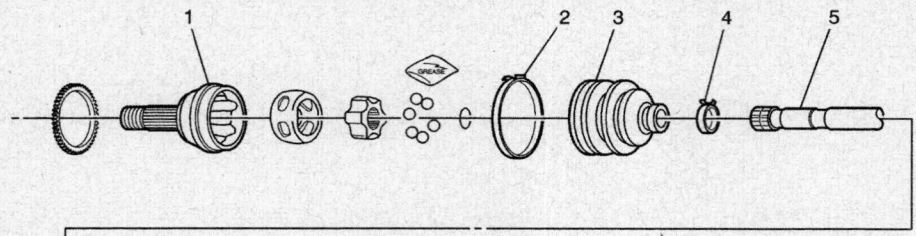

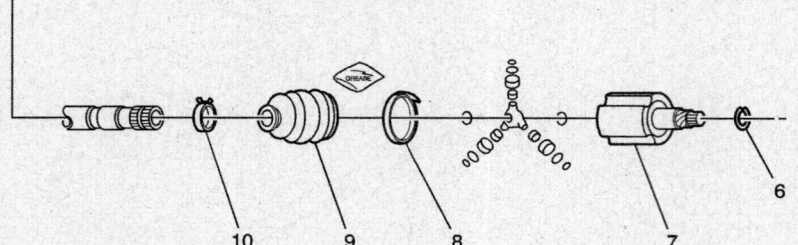

1. C/V Joint
2. Seal Retaining Clamp
3. Drive Axle Outboard Seal
4. Seal Retaining Clamp
5. Axle Shaft
6. Snap Ring
7. Tripot Housing
8. Seal Retaining Clamp
9. Drive Axle Inboard Seal
10. Seal Retaining Clamp

ARM0400000001364

Fig. 2 Exploded view of front drive axle. Aveo w/automatic transaxle

knuckle using steering linkage and tie rod puller tool No. J24319-B, or equivalent.

5. Prevent wheel hub and bearing from turning by inserting suitable drift or punch into brake rotor and against caliper.
6. Remove and discard drive shaft spindle nut.
7. Remove stabilizer link bolt and nut, then remove stabilizer link washers, insulators and spacer.
8. Disconnect electrical connector and position wheel speed sensor wiring harness away from ball joint.
9. Separate ball joint from control arm using ball joint separator tool No. J36226, or equivalent.
10. Install hub spindle remover tool No. J42129, or equivalent, onto wheel hub and secure with wheel nuts.
11. Disconnect shaft from wheel hub and bearing, then support drive shaft.
12. Disconnect shaft from transaxle using slide hammer with adapter tool No. J2619-O1, axle shaft remover extension tool No. J29794 and wheel drive shaft remover toll No. J33008-A, or equivalents.
13. Remove drive shaft.
14. Reverse procedure to install, noting the following:
   a. Ensure drive shaft is properly engaged to transaxle by grasping inner tripot housing and pulling outward. **Do not pull on drive shaft.**
   b. Install new drive shaft spindle nut.

ION

1. Raise and support vehicle, then remove tire and wheel assemblies.
2. Remove stabilizer link as outlined under "Front Suspension & Steering" in "Ion" chapter.
3. Remove driveshaft mounting nut and secure brake rotor using suitable flat bladed tool to prevent rotor from turning, **Fig. 13.**
4. Disconnect outer tie rod from knuckle as outlined under "Front Suspension & Steering" in "ION" chapter.
5. Remove wheel speed sensor electrical connector from sensor, then secure away from ball joint.
6. Remove ball joint as outlined under "Front Suspension & Steering" in "ION" chapter.
7. Remove driveshaft from transaxle using tool Nos. J45341 and SA9173G, or equivalents, **Fig. 14.**
8. Remove axle shaft from transaxle.
9. Reverse procedure to install.

L-Series

REMOVAL

1. Depress brake pedal, then remove cotter pin and drive axle nut. Discard cotter pin and nut.
2. Raise and support vehicle, then remove tire and wheel assembly.
3. Remove tie rod end torque prevailing nut. Discard nut.

4. Separate tie rod end from steering knuckle using removal tool No. SA91100-C, or equivalent. **Do not use wedge type tool to separate joint.**
5. Remove lower control arm to steering knuckle bolt and nut, then separate lower control arm from steering knuckle.
6. Pull outer end of drive axle out of wheel hub while pulling knuckle/strut away. If it is difficult to separate axle from hub, tap on end of drive axle shaft using suitable wood block and hammer.
7. Support or suspend drive axle using mechanics wire.
8. Place suitable container under transaxle to catch fluid spillage.
9. Remove drive axle by prying axle out of transaxle using suitable pry bar. **Do not contact transaxle oil seal.**
10. Remove and discard shaft retaining rings.

INSTALLATION

1. Install new retaining ring.
2. **On models equipped with automatic transaxle,** apply output shaft lubricant No. 7847638, or equivalent, to output shaft splines.
3. **On models equipped with manual transaxle,** install transaxle seal protector tool No. SA91112-T, or equivalent.
4. **On all models,** insert drive axle into transaxle.
5. After drive axle splines have passed transaxle oil seal, remove seal protector.
6. Fully seat drive axle into transaxle. **Do not tighten now.**
7. Insert drive axle outer end into wheel hub, then the hub washer and new nut.
8. Install lower control arm ball stud into steering knuckle.
9. Install tie rod end into steering knuckle.
10. Fully seat tie rod end using installer tool No. J44015, or equivalent, then install new nut.
11. **Torque** axle shaft nut to 85 ft. lbs.
12. Loosen nut until it turns freely by hand.
13. **Torque** shaft nut to 15 ft. lbs.
14. Tighten nut an additional 90° and align cotter pin slot.
15. Install new cotter pin.
16. Install wheels.
17. Lower vehicle from hoist.
18. **Torque** axle shaft to hub nut to 74–118 ft. lbs.
19. Release nut until it is free to turn by hand.
20. **Torque** axle shaft-to-hub nut 15 ft. lbs.
21. Final tighten nut an additional 90°.

LaCrosse

1. Raise and support vehicle, then remove tire and wheel assembly.
2. Remove mounting bolt and nut, then the stabilizer shaft link.
3. Prevent rotor from turning by Inserting suitable drift or flat-bladed tool into caliper and rotor, then remove front wheel drive shaft nut.

4. Remove prevailing torque nut from outer tie rod.
5. Loosen jam nut on inner tie rod.
6. Remove outer tie rod from steering knuckle using universal steering linkage puller tool No. J24319-B, or equivalent. **Do not attempt to disconnect steering linkage joint by driving wedge between joint and attached part.**
7. Remove outer from inner tie rod assembly.
8. Separate ball stud from steering knuckle by rotating nut counterclockwise and using ball joint/stud separator tool No. J41820, or equivalent.
9. Separate front wheel drive axle from shaft bearing using hub spindle remover tool No. J42129, or equivalent. Partially installed not to protect threads.
10. Remove drive axle from transaxle using axle shaft remover tools Nos. J33008-A, J29794, J29794 and J2619-01, or equivalents.
11. Reverse procedure to install.

Malibu

On Malibu models with the fourth digit of the Vehicle Information Number (VIN) the letter N, refer to "Alero, Grand Am & Malibu."

On Malibu models with the fourth digit of the Vehicle Information Number (VIN) the letter Z, refer to "G6 & Malibu MAXX."

STS

LEFTHAND

1. Raise and support vehicle, then remove tire and wheel assembly.
2. Remove outer tie rod mounting nut. **Do not loosen tie rod end jam nut.**
3. Disconnect outer tie rod from steering knuckle using steering linkage and tie rod puller tool No. J24319-B, or equivalent.
4. Prevent wheel hub and bearing from turning by inserting suitable drift or punch into brake rotor and against caliper.
5. Remove and discard drive shaft spindle nut.
6. Disconnect electrical connector and position wheel speed sensor wiring harness away from ball joint.
7. Remove upper control arm to steering knuckle nut.
8. Separate upper control arm from the steering knuckle using steering linkage and tie rod puller tool No. J24319-B, or equivalent.
9. Install wheel hub remover tool No. J45859, or equivalent, onto wheel hub and secure with wheel nuts.
10. Disconnect drive shaft from wheel hub and bearing, then support shaft.
11. Disconnect shaft from intermediate shaft using slide hammer with adapter tool No. J2619-O1, axle shaft remover extension tool No. J29794 and axle shaft puller tool No. J45341, or equivalents.
12. Remove drive shaft.

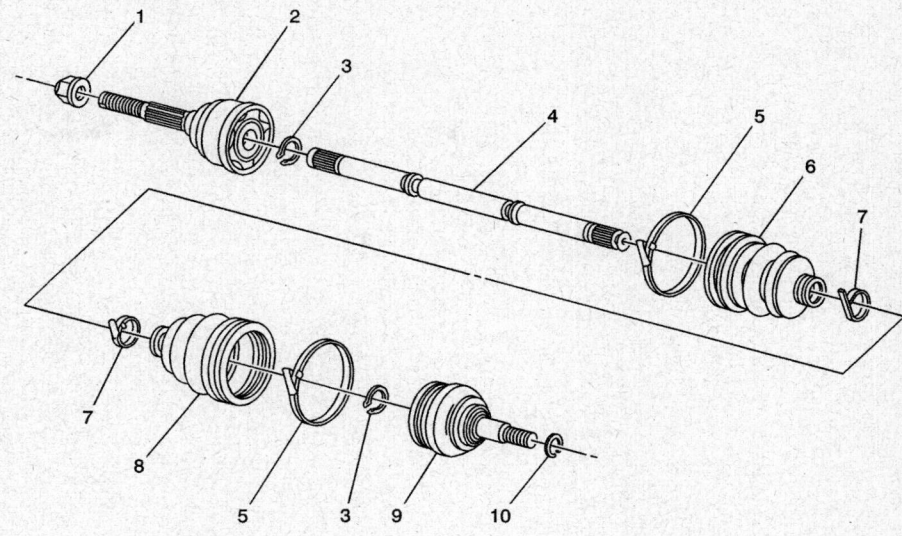

1. Caulking Nut
2. C/V Joint
3. Race Retaining Ring
4. Axle Shaft
5. Seal Retaining Clamp
6. Drive Axle Outboard Seal
7. Seal Retaining Clamp
8. Drive Axle Inboard Seal
9. Cross Groove Joint
10. Retaining Ring

ARM0400000001365

Fig. 3 Exploded view of front drive axle. Aveo w/manual transaxle

13. If using same intermediate shaft, remove and discard retaining ring and O-ring.
14. Reverse procedure to install, noting the following:
    a. Install new intermediate shaft retaining ring and O-ring.
    b. Apply small amount of suitable grease to intermediate wheel drive shaft splines.
    c. Ensure drive shaft is properly engaged to intermediate shaft by grasping inner tripot housing and pulling outward. **Do not pull on drive shaft.**
    d. Install new drive shaft spindle nut.

RIGHTHAND

1. Raise and support vehicle, then remove tire and wheel assembly.
2. Remove outer tie rod mounting nut. **Do not loosen tie rod end jam nut.**
3. Disconnect outer tie rod from steering knuckle using steering linkage and tie rod puller tool No. J24319-B, or equivalent.
4. Prevent wheel hub and bearing from turning by inserting suitable drift or punch into brake rotor and against caliper.
5. Remove and discard drive shaft spindle nut.
6. Disconnect electrical connector and position wheel speed sensor wiring harness away from ball joint.
7. Remove upper control arm to steering knuckle nut.
8. Separate upper control arm from the steering knuckle using steering link-

age and tie rod puller tool No. J24319-B, or equivalent.
9. Install wheel hub remover tool No. J45859, or equivalent, onto wheel hub and secure with wheel nuts.
10. Disconnect drive shaft from wheel hub and bearing, then support shaft.
11. **Seal protector tool No. J44394, or equivalent, must be installed into differential output shaft seal prior to removing and installing drive shaft.**
12. Disconnect shaft from differential using slide hammer with adapter tool No. J2619-O1, axle shaft remover extension tool No. J29794 and axle shaft puller tool No. J45341, or equivalents.
13. Install seal protector tool over drive shaft seal.
14. Remove drive shaft.
15. Reverse procedure to install, noting the following:
    a. **Seal protector tool No. J44394, or equivalent, must be installed into differential output shaft seal prior to installing drive shaft.**
    b. Install seal protector tool over drive shaft seal.
    c. **Do not damage oil seal.**
    d. Ensure drive shaft is properly engaged to differential by grasping inner tripot housing and pulling outward. **Do not pull on drive shaft.**
    e. Install new drive shaft spindle nut.

Vibe

1. Raise and support vehicle using suitable lift, then remove tire and wheel assemblies.

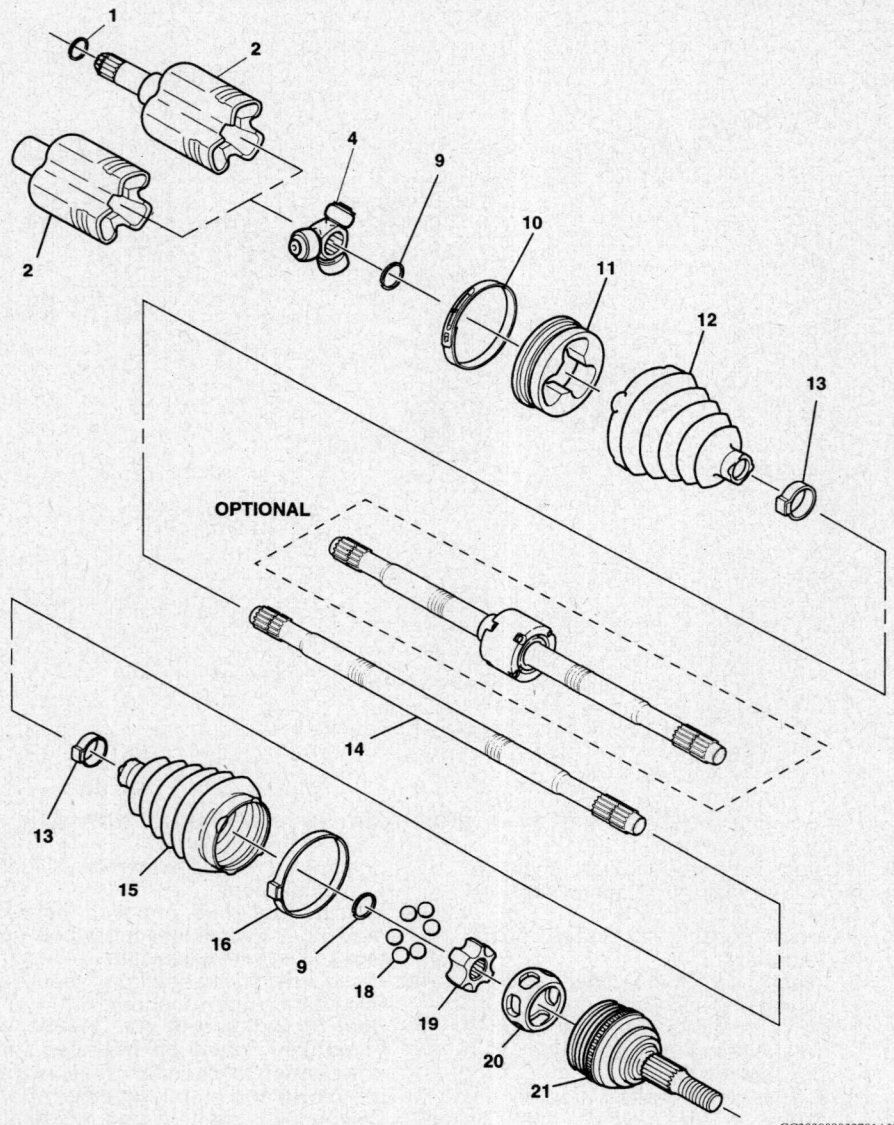

Fig. 4 Exploded view of front drive axle (Part 1 of 2). Cavalier & Sunfire

2. Remove engine splash shields.
3. Remove driveshaft locknut, then the wheel speed sensor wire and brake hose retainer from strut assembly.
4. Remove mounting bolt and wheel speed sensor from steering knuckle, **Fig. 15.**
5. Remove outer tie rod as outlined under "Front Suspension & Steering" in "Vibe" chapter.
6. Remove lower ball joint from steering knuckle as outlined under "Front Suspension & Steering" in "Vibe" chapter.
7. Remove wheel drive shaft from wheel hub and bearing using suitable hammer.
8. Remove axle shaft from transaxle.
9. **On models equipped with AWD,** proceed as follows:
   a. Drain transaxle and transfer case into suitable container.
   b. Remove bearing lock bolt and snap ring using suitable pliers, **Fig. 16.**

10. **On all models,** remove driveshaft and retaining ring.
11. Reverse procedure to install.

DRIVESHAFT SERVICE

All Models Except Aveo, Cavalier, Cobalt, G5, ION, L-Series, STS, Sunfire & Vibe

INNER JOINT & BOOT

DISASSEMBLE

When the halfshaft is removed for any reason, the transmission sealing surface (tripod male/female shank of CV) should be inspected for corrosion. If corrosion is present, surface should be cleaned using crocus cloth or suitable equivalent.

1. Cut through swage ring using suitable hand grinder. **Do not damage tripod housing.**
2. Remove large boot retaining clamp from tripod joint using suitable side cutter, discard clamp.
3. Separate inboard boot from tripot bushing at large diameter.
4. Slide boot away from joint along shaft.
5. Remove housing from tripod joint spider and shaft.
6. Remove tripot tripod bushing from housing.
7. Spread spacer ring using snap ring pliers No. J8059, or equivalent.
8. Slide spacer ring and tripod joint spider backward on shaft.
9. Remove retaining ring from shaft groove.
10. Slide tripod joint spider assembly off shaft.
11. Clean tripot balls and needle rollers with suitable solvent. Dry thoroughly.
12. Inspect tripod joint spider, housing, trilobal tripot bushing and needle rollers for damage or wear. Replace as required.

ASSEMBLE

1. Place new small clamp onto joint boot small end.
2. Slide boot and clamp onto shaft.
3. Position boot small end into groove.
4. Swage ring using swage tool No. J41048, or equivalent.
5. Install retaining ring using snap ring pliers tool No. J8059, or equivalent, **Fig. 17.**
6. Ensure counterbored face on joint spider faces toward end of shaft.
7. Slide tripot joint spider toward spacer ring as far as it will go. Ensure trilobal tripot bushing is flush with housing face.
8. Place half of kit provided grease in inboard boot. Use remaining grease to pack housing.
9. Install tripot bushing to housing.
10. Position larger new boot retaining clamp on inboard boot and slide housing over spider.
11. Slide inboard boot large diameter with clamp in place over outside of tripot tripod bushing and locate lip in groove.
12. Ensure shaft inboard boot is not dimpled, stretched out or out of shape. Correct using thin, flat, blunt tool between to equalize pressure and shape by hand.
13. Align inboard boot, tripot housing and large retaining clamp.
14. Ensure boot is positioned properly.
15. Tighten clamp using eared clamp tool No. J35910, or equivalent, suitable breaker bar and torque wrench, **Fig. 18.**

OUTER JOINT & BOOT

DISASSEMBLE

1. Remove large and small boot retaining clamps from CV joint using suitable side cutter. Discard clamps.

Key No.	Part Name	Key No.	Part Name
1 - RING, RETAINING		14 - SHAFT, AXLE (RH SHOWN, LH SIMILAR)	
2 - HOUSING ASM, RETAINER &		15 - SEAL, DRIVE AXLE OUTBOARD	
4 - SPIDER, TRIPOT JOINT		16 - CLAMP, SEAL RETAINING	
9 - RING, RETAINING		18 - BALL, CHROME ALLOY	
10 - CLAMP, SEAL RETAINING		19 - RACE, C/V JOINT INNER	
11 - BUSHING, TRILOBAL TRIPOT		20 - CAGE, C/V JOINT	
12 - SEAL, DRIVE AXLE INBOARD		21 - RACE, C/V JOINT OUTER	
13 - CLAMP, SEAL RETAINING			

GC303000033701BX

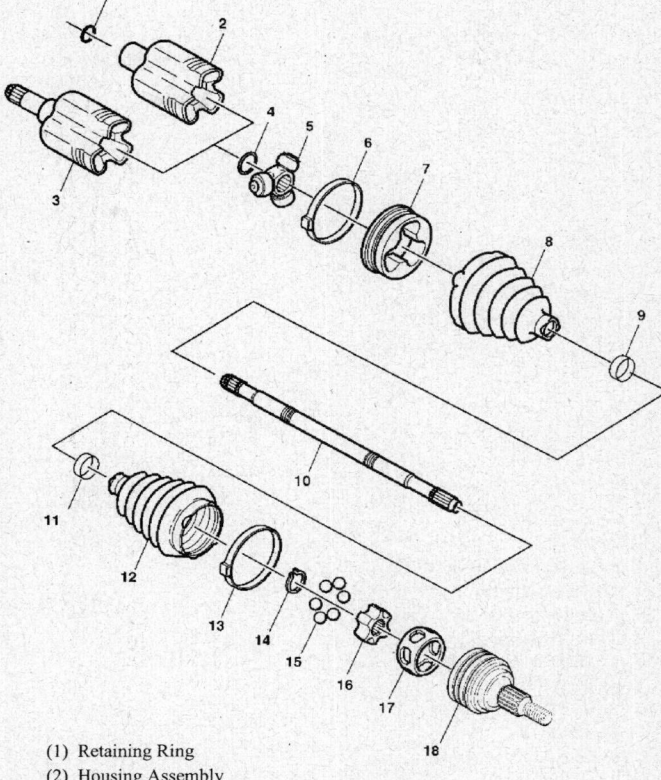

Fig. 4 Exploded view of front drive axle (Part 2 of 2). Cavalier & Sunfire

2. Separate outboard boot from CV joint outer race at large diameter and slide boot away form joint, **Fig. 19.**
3. Wipe grease from CV joint inner race face.
4. Spread retaining ring race ears using snap ring pliers No. J8059, or equivalent, and remove CV joint and boot.
5. Tap CV joint cage using suitable brass drift and hammer until it is tilted enough to remove first chrome alloy ball.
6. Tilt cage in opposite direction to remove opposing ball.
7. Repeat until six balls are removed.
8. Position CV joint cage and inner race 90° to outer race centerline, and align joint cage windows with outer race lands.
9. Remove CV joint cage and inner race from outer race.
10. Rotate CV joint inner race 90° to CV joint cage centerline with inner race lands aligned with CV joint cage windows.
11. Remove inner race by pivoting into cage window.
12. Clean inner and outer races, CV joint cage and balls using suitable solvent. Dry thoroughly.

ASSEMBLE

1. Install new boot swage ring onto neck.
2. Slide outboard boot onto shaft and position neck in groove.
3. Swage boot swage ring using swage tool No. J41048, or equivalent.
4. Lightly coat inner and outer race ball grooves with kit provided grease.
5. Hold inner race at a 90° angle to cage centerline, align inner race lands with cage windows, then install inner race into cage.
6. Hold cage and inner race at a 90° angle to outer race centerline, then align cage windows with outer race lands. Ensure inner race retaining ring side faces halfshaft.
7. Install cage and inner race into outer race.
8. Install first chrome ball, then tilt cage in opposite direction and install opposing ball. Repeat until all balls are in place.
9. Place approximately half of remaining kit provided grease inside outboard boot. Use remaining grease to pack CV joint.
10. Push CV joint onto shaft until retaining ring is seated in groove. Ensure boot is not dimpled, stretched out or out of shape. Correct by equalizing pressure and shaping by hand.
11. Slide large diameter of outboard boot with retaining clamp over outside CV joint outer race, locate lip in groove.

12. Crimp boot retaining clamp using seal clamp tool No. J35910, or equivalent, and suitable breaker bar. Ensure gap is .012 inch.

Aveo
AUTOMATIC
INNER JOINT & BOOT
Disassemble

1. Remove and discard large and small seal retaining clamps using seal retaining clamp tool No. J35566, or equivalent.
2. Separate joint housing from boot.
3. Degrease tripot.
4. Remove shaft retaining ring using

snap ring pliers tool No. J8059, or equivalent.
5. Remove retaining ring, then the tripot and tripot joint from axle shaft.
6. Remove tripot joint seal from axle shaft.

Assemble

1. Install new small seal retaining clamp onto seal.
2. Install seal onto axle shaft.
3. Install shaft retaining ring onto axle shaft using suitable snap ring pliers.
4. Fill tripot housing with 6.9–7.6 ounces of suitable grease.
5. Pack tripot with 6.9–7.6 ounces of suitable grease.
6. Install boot to joint housing.

(1) Retaining Ring
(2) Housing Assembly
(3) Retainer and Housing Assembly
(4) Spacer Ring
(5) Tripot Joint Spider Assembly
(6) Boot Retaining Clamp
(7) Trilobal Tripot Bushing
(8) Tripot Joint Boot
(9) Swage Ring
(10) Halfshaft Bar
(11) Swage Ring
(12) CV Joint Boot
(13) Boot Retaining Clamp
(14) Race Retaining Ring
(15) Chrome Alloy Ball
(16) CV Joint Inner Race
(17) CV Joint Cage
(18) CV Joint Outer Race

ARM0500000000185

Fig. 5 Exploded view of front drive axle. Cobalt & G5 w/Delphi axle

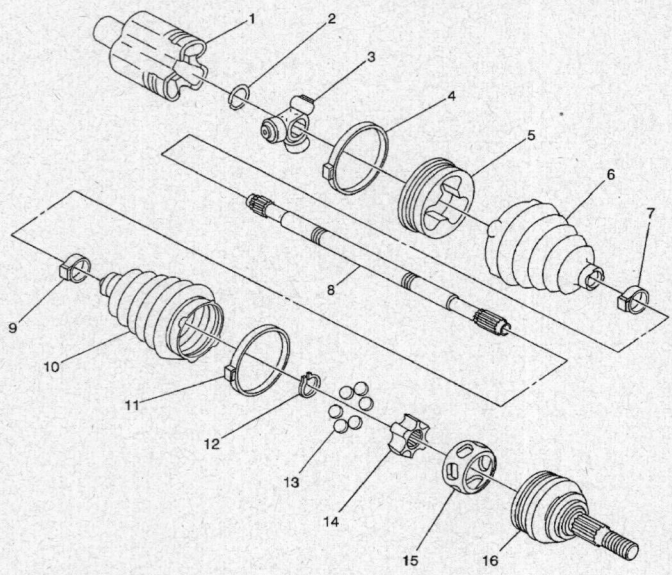

(1) Retainer and Housing Assembly
(2) Retaining Ring
(3) Tripot Joint Spider Assembly
(4) Boot Retaining Clamp
(5) Tripot Trilobal Bushing
(6) Inboard Boot
(7) Boot Retaining Clamp
(8) Axle Shaft
(9) Boot Retaining Clamp
(10) Outboard Boot
(11) Boot Retaining Clamp
(12) Race Retaining Ring
(13) Chrome Alloy Ball
(14) CV Joint Inner Race
(15) CV Joint Cage
(16) CV Joint Outer Race

ARM0500000000186

Fig. 6   Exploded view of front drive axle. Cobalt & G5 w/GKN axle

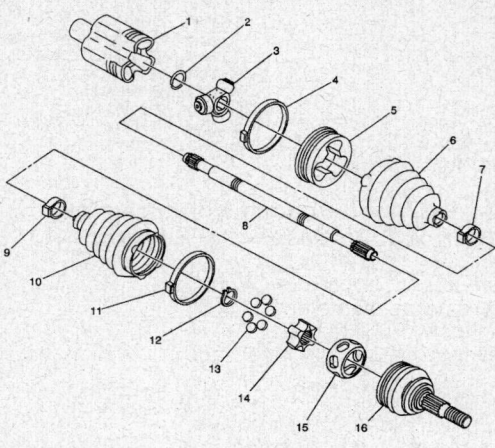

(1) Retainer and Housing Assembly	(6) Inboard Boot	(11) Boot Retaining Clamp
(2) Retaining Ring	(7) Boot Retaining Clamp	(12) Race Retaining Ring
(3) Tripot Joint Spider Assembly	(8) Axle Shaft	(13) Chrome Alloy Ball
(4) Boot Retaining Clamp	(9) Boot Retaining Clamp	(14) CV Joint Inner Race
(5) Tripot Trilobal Bushing	(10) Outboard Boot	(15) CV Joint Cage
		(16) CV Joint Outer Race

ARM66GC000000768

Fig. 7   Exploded view of front drive axle. ION

7. Install new large seal retaining clamp.
8. Crimp large and small seal retaining clamps using suitable seal retaining clamp tool.

OUTER JOINT & BOOT

The outer joint is designed to be replaced as a one piece unit. Do not attempt to disassemble or service the outer joint.

Disassemble

1. Remove and discard large and small seal retaining clamps using seal clamp pliers tool No. J35566, or equivalent.
2. Degrease joint.
3. Spread snap ring using snap ring pliers tool No. J8059, or equivalent, then remove outer joint and axle shaft.

Assemble

1. Install seal onto axle shaft.
2. Spread snap ring using suitable snap ring pliers , then remove outer joint and axle shaft.
3. Fill joint seal with 3.9–4.6 ounces of suitable grease.
4. Pack joint with 3.9–4.6 ounces of suitable grease.

5. Install new large and small seal retaining clamps.
6. Crimp clamps using suitable seal clamp pliers.

MANUAL

INNER JOINT & BOOT

The ball retainer is stacked in position and is not serviceable.

Disassemble

1. Remove and discard large and small seal retaining clamps using seal retaining clamp tool No. J35566, or equivalent.
2. Degrease joint.
3. Remove shaft retaining ring using snap ring pliers tool No. J8059 , or equivalent.
4. Remove axle shaft from joint.
5. Remove seal from joint.

Assemble

1. Install new small seal retaining clamp onto seal. Do not crimp.
2. Install seal and joint onto shaft.
3. Install shaft retaining ring using suitable snap ring pliers.

4. Fill joint with 4.2–4.9 ounces of suitable grease.
5. Pack tripot with 4.2–4.9 ounces of suitable grease.
6. Install new large seal retaining clamp.
7. Crimp new large and small seal retaining clamps using suitable seal clamp pliers.

OUTER JOINT & BOOT

The outer joint is designed to be replaced as a one piece unit. Do not attempt to disassemble or service the outer joint.
The ball retainer is stacked in position and is not serviceable.

Disassemble

1. Remove and discard large and small seal retaining clamps.
2. Degrease joint.
3. Remove shaft retaining ring using snap ring pliers tool No. J8059, or equivalent.
4. Remove axle shaft from joint.
5. Remove cross groove joint seal from joint.
6. Remove and discard large and small seal retaining clips.
7. Degrease joint.
8. Remove seal from joint.

Assemble

1. Install seal onto axle shaft.
2. Fill joint seal with 3.9–4.6 ounces of suitable grease.
3. Pack joint with 3.9–4.6 ounces of suitable grease.
4. Install new large and small seal retaining clamps.
5. Crimp new clamps with suitable seal clamp pliers.
6. Install new small seal retaining clamp onto cross groove joint seal. Do not crimp.
7. Install seal onto and joint onto axle shaft.

8. Install shaft retaining ring using suitable snap ring pliers.
9. Fill joint assembly with 4.2–4.9 ounces of suitable grease.
10. Pack tripot 4.2–4.9 ounces of suitable grease.
11. Install new large seal retaining clamp.
12. Crimp clamps suitable seal clamp pliers.

Cavalier & Sunfire

INNER JOINT & BOOT

DISASSEMBLE

1. **On models equipped with 2.4L engine,** if transaxle stub shaft disengages from transaxle during halfshaft tripot removal, separate shaft from tripod housing as follows:
   a. Remove and discard stub shaft snap ring.
   b. Remove shaft from tripot using stub shaft removal tool No. J38868 and impact slide hammer tool No. J6125-1B, or equivalents, **Fig. 20.**
   c. Install new snap rings onto stub shaft.
   d. Install stub axle into transaxle.
2. **On all models,** remove inboard boot retaining clamps. Discard clamps.
3. Separate large diameter of inboard boot from trilobal tripot bushing.
4. Slide boot away from joint along halfshaft.
5. Remove and discard spacer ring using snap ring pliers tool No. J8309-A, or equivalent, **Fig. 21.**
6. Remove tripod spider using suitable brass drift and hammer, **Fig. 22.**
7. Remove spacer ring from halfshaft shoulder using snap ring pliers tool No. J8309-A, or equivalent.
8. Remove trilobal tripot bushing.
9. Clean tripod balls, needle rollers and housing with suitable solvent. Dry thoroughly.
10. Remove axle shaft boot.
11. Inspect inboard boot, spider, housing, tripot tripod bushing, tripot balls, needle rollers and retaining ring for wear or damage.

ASSEMBLE

1. Install new small boot retaining clamp on boot neck. **Do not crimp now.**
2. Clean axle shaft using wire brush to remove rust from boot grooves.
3. Slide tripod boot onto halfshaft passing CV end boot grooves. Ensure spacer ring is next to halfshaft shoulder.
4. Install tripot spider.
5. Place axle assembly onto suitable arbor press with tripod spider on press plate and CV joint under press head, **Fig. 23.**
6. Lower arbor press head onto CV joint until tripod spider is next to spacer ring. **Do not exceed 4000 lbs. pressure.**
7. Remove axle assembly from arbor press.
8. Place new spacer ring in halfshaft end groove.
9. Slide tripod boot onto halfshaft groove.
10. Crimp small boot retaining clamp using

seal clamp tool No. J35910, or equivalent.
11. Place approximately one quarter of kit provided grease in boot. Use remaining grease to pack housing.
12. Install trilobal tripot bushing to housing. Ensure bushing is flush with housing face.
13. Slide housing over spider on halfshaft.
14. Position large boot retaining clamp around inboard boot.
15. Engage inboard boot.
16. Boot must not be dimpled, stretched or out of shape. Correct by equalizing pressure and shape using suitable thin, flat, blunt tool and hand.
17. Position joint properly, **Fig. 24.**
18. Ensure halfshaft inboard boot, housing and large clamp are aligned.
19. Latch boot retaining strap using seal clamp tool No. J35566, or equivalent.

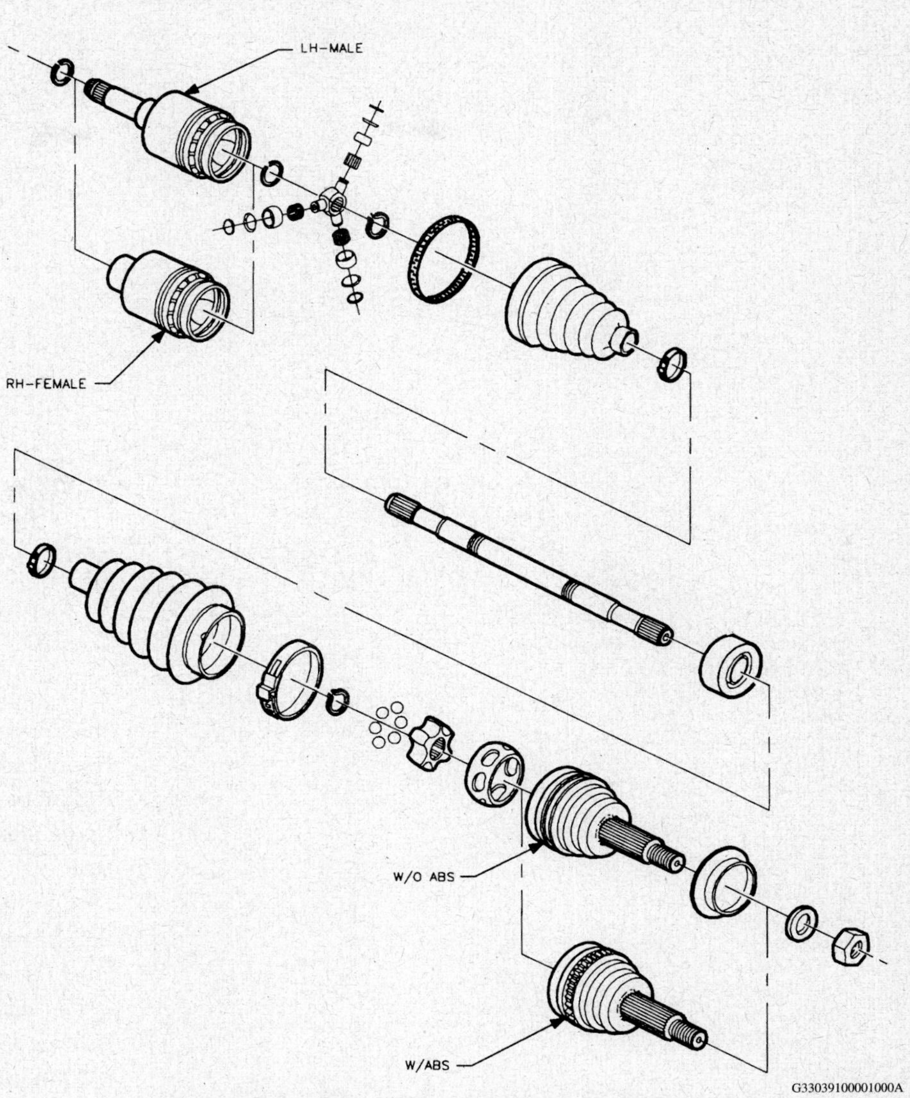

OUTER JOINT & BOOT

DISASSEMBLE

1. Remove large and small CV boot re-

taining clamps using suitable side cutters, discard clamps.
2. Separate large diameter of boot from CV joint and slide away from joint along axle shaft.
3. Wipe grease away from inner CV joint race face.
4. Place reference mark on halfshaft, then measure and record distance between reference mark and CV joint inner race face for assembly reference.
5. Clamp axle into suitable vise.
6. Remove CV joint using CV puller tool No. J41398 and slide hammer tool No. J2619-01, or equivalents, **Fig. 25.**
7. Remove and discard retaining ring.
8. Remove CV joint boot.
9. Gently tap CV joint cage using suitable brass drift and hammer until it is tilted enough to remove first chrome ball, then tilt in opposite direction and remove ball. Repeat until all six balls are removed.
10. Position cage and inner race at a 90° angle to outer race centerline, then

Fig. 8 Exploded view of front drive axle. L-Series

G33039100001000A

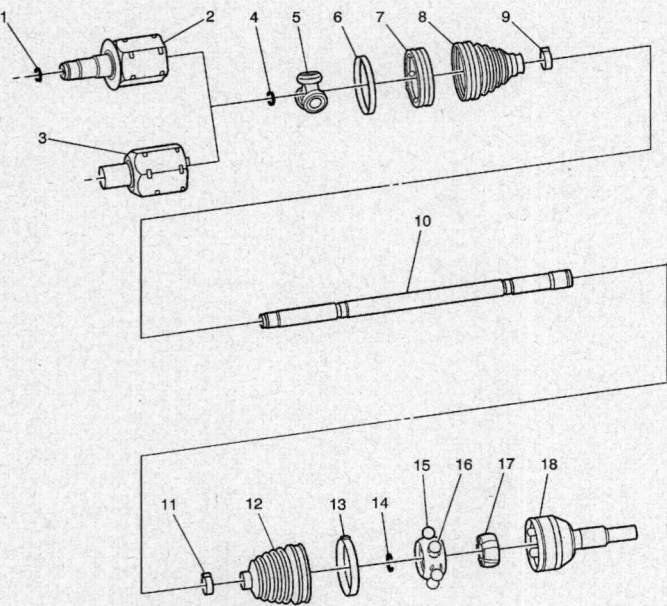

(1) Retaining Ring, Right Tripod Joint Race
(2) Tripod Joint Race, Right Inner AWD
(3) Tripod Joint Race, Left Inner AWD
(4) Spacer Retaining Ring
(5) Spider Assembly
(6) Joint Clamp
(7) Boot Trilobe Insert
(8) Inner Joint Seal
(9) Shaft Clamp
(10) Bar, Wheel Drive Shaft
(11) Shaft Clamp
(12) Outer Joint Seal
(13) Race Clamp
(14) Retaining Ring
(15) CV Joint Balls
(16) Fixed Cage
(17) Fixed Inner Race
(18) Fixed Outer Race

ARM0500000000189

Fig. 9 Exploded view of front drive axle. STS

(1) Outboard Joint Shaft	(12) Snap Ring
(2) Boot Clamp	(13) Tripod
(3) RH Inboard Shaft	(14) Boot
(4) Large Snap Ring	(15) Dynamic Damper
(5) Bearing	
(6) Straight Pin	
(7) Small Snap Ring	
(8) Dust Cover	
(9) Drive Shaft Dust Cover	
(10) Bearing Case	
(11) LH Inboard Shaft	

ARM66GC000000758

Fig. 10 Exploded view of front drive axle. Vibe

align cage windows with outer race lands.
11. Remove cage and inner race from outer race.
12. Remove inner race from cage by rotating inner race upward.
13. Clean inner and outer race assemblies, cage and balls with suitable solvent. Dry thoroughly.
14. Inspect for unusual war, cracks or damage.

ASSEMBLE

1. Lightly coat inner and outer race ball grooves with kit provided grease.
2. Hold inner race at a 90° angle to cage centerline and align inner race lands with cage windows, then insert race into cage.
3. Hold cage and inner race at a 90° angle to outer race centerline, then align cage windows with outer race lands. Ensure inner race retaining ring side faces outer race.
4. Install cage and inner race into outer race.

5. Tilt cage by gently tapping with suitable brass drift and hammer, then install first chrome ball. Repeat until all six balls are installed.
6. Pack CV joint with approximately half of kit provided grease.
7. Install new small retaining ring on CV boot neck. **Do not crimp now.**
8. Remove rust from CV boot mounting grooves with suitable wire brush.
9. Slide CV joint boot onto drive axle shaft far enough to expose reference mark made during disassembly.
10. Position large retaining clamp around CV joint boot.
11. Place new retaining ring in inner race.
12. While supporting tripot, place halfshaft assembly onto suitable arbor press with CV assembly under press head.
13. Lower arbor press head onto CV joint assembly until press cannot move any further, to ensure retaining ring engages into inner race. **Do not exceed 4000 lbs. of press load.**
14. Place neck of CV joint boot into seal

groove on drive axle shaft.
15. Measure distance between reference mark and CV joint inner race. If distance is not within .039 inch of distance recorded during disassembly, repeat previous steps 13 and 14.
16. Place CV joint boot neck into halfshaft boot groove. Ensure clamp is positioned correctly.
17. Crimp small retaining clamp using seal clamp tool No. J35910, or equivalent, suitable breaker bar and torque wrench.
18. Ensure gap dimension is .085 inch.
19. Place remaining kit provided grease inside boot.
20. Measure approximately $^{11}/_{16}$ inch up from CV outer joint bottom edge and slide large diameter of boot with clamp in place over outside of CV joint, **Fig. 26.**
21. Boot must not be dimpled, stretched or out of shape. Correct by equalizing pressure and shaping by hand.
22. Crimp large clamp using seal clamp

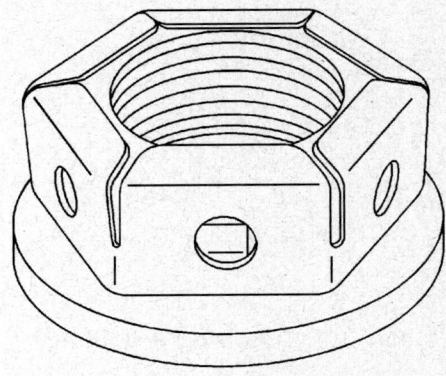

ARM0400000001362

Fig. 11 Type one drive axle nut. Alero, Grand Am & Malibu

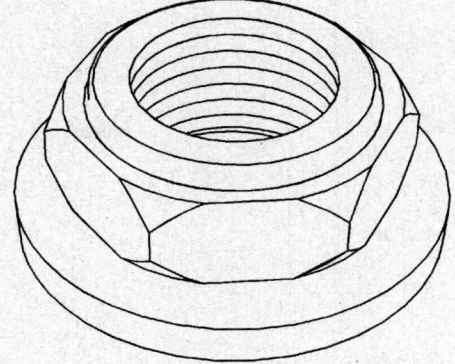

ARM0400000001363

Fig. 12 Type two drive axle nut. Alero, Grand Am & Malibu

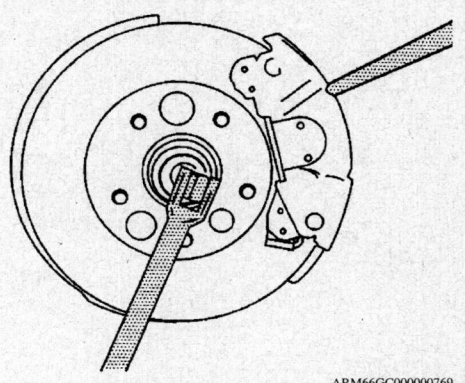

ARM66GC000000769

Fig. 13 Driveshaft nut removal. Ion

tool No. J35910, or equivalent, suitable breaker bar and torque wrench.
23. Ensure clamp gap is .102 inch.

Cobalt & G5

DELPHI

INNER JOINT & SEAL

Disassemble

1. Cut through swage ring using suitable hand grinder. **Do not damage tripot housing.**
2. Remove tripot joint large boot retaining clamp using suitable side cutter. Discard large boot retaining clamp.
3. **Do not cut through wheel drive shaft inboard seal.**
4. Separate wheel driveshaft inboard boot from trilobal tripot bushing at large diameter.
5. Slide boot away from joint along shaft.
6. Remove housing from tripot joint spider and shaft.
7. Remove and discard trilobal tripot bushing from housing.
8. Remove and discard lower spacer ring from shaft groove.
9. Slide tripot joint spider off shaft.
10. Remove and discard second spacer ring from shaft.

Assemble

1. Place new small boot clamp onto small end, then slide joint boot and small boot clamp onto shaft.
2. Position small end of joint boot into joint boot groove.
3. Mount drive axle swage ring clamp tool No. DT-47732, or equivalent, in suitable vice.
4. Position board end of wheel driveshaft in tool.
5. Align top of boot neck on bottom die using indicator.
6. Place top half of tool on lower half of tool.
7. Ensure there are no pinch points on wheel driveshaft inboard boot and install tool bolts. Tighten bolts by hand until snug.
8. Align inboard boot, shaft boot grooves and swage ring, then tighten tool bolts 180° at a time using suitable ratchet

wrench. Alternate between each bolt until both sides are bottomed.
9. Install spacer ring on shaft in groove using snap ring pliers tool No. J8059, or equivalent.
10. Slide tripot joint spider toward spacer ring as far as it will go on shaft.
11. Install haft retaining ring in groove.
12. Place approximately half of service kit grease in shaft inboard boot. Use remainder of grease to pack housing.
13. Ensure trilobal tripot bushing is flush with housing face.
14. Install trilobal tripot bushing to housing.
15. Position larger new boot retaining clamp on shaft inboard boot.
16. Slide housing over tripot joint spider.
17. Slide large diameter of inboard boot with larger clamp) in place, over outside of trilobal tripot bushing.
18. Locate boot lip in groove. Assembly dimension is 4.21 inches, **Fig. 27.**
19. Equalize pressure using thin flat blunt tool (no sharp edges) between large boot opening and trilobal tripot bushing.
20. Remove tool.
21. Align seal, tripot housing and large seal retaining clamp.
22. Crimp seal retaining clamp to 130 ft. lbs. using drive axle seal clamp pliers tool No. J35910, or equivalent.
23. Ensure crimp is .085 inches, **Fig. 28.**
24. Fully stroke joint several times to disperse grease.

OUTER JOINT & SEAL

Disassemble

1. Remove large seal retaining clamp from CV joint using suitable hand grinder. **Do not damage housing.** Discard clamp.
2. Remove small seal retaining clamp from shaft using suitable hand grinder. **Do not damage housing.** Discard clamp.
3. Separate CV joint seal from race at large diameter.
4. Slide seal away from joint along shaft.
5. Wipe grease from CV joint inner race face.
6. Reference mark shaft, then measure and record distance to CV joint inner

race face for assembly alignment.
7. Reference mark inboard side of CV joint inner race toward center of half shaft for assembly alignment.
8. Remove retaining ring using snap ring pliers tool No. J8039-A, or equivalent.
9. Clamp shaft into suitable vise.
10. Attach CV puller tool J41398, or equivalent, to threaded area of outer race. Attach slide hammer tool J2619-01 onto outer end of CV puller.
11. Remove CV joint.
12. Remove and discard shaft retaining ring.
13. Remove CV joint seal from shaft.
14. Tilt CV joint cage using suitable brass drift and hammer, then remove first chrome alloy ball.
15. Tilt CV joint cage in opposite direction to remove opposing chrome alloy ball.
16. Repeat procedure until all six balls are removed.
17. Pivot V joint cage and inner race 90° to outer race centerline and at same time, align cage windows with outer race lands.
18. Remove cage and inner race.
19. Rotate and remove inner race upward.

Assemble

1. Apply light coat of service kit grease on inner and outer races' ball grooves.
2. Hold inner race 90° to cage centerline with inner race lands aligned with cage windows.
3. Install inner race into cage.
4. Hold cage and inner race 90° to outer race centerline.
5. Align cage windows with outer race lands.
6. Ensure inner race is oriented as disassembled.
7. Install cage and inner race into outer race.
8. Tilt cage using suitable brass drift and hammer, then install first chrome alloy ball.
9. Repeat procedure to install all six balls.
10. Pack CV joint with half of service kit grease.
11. Install new swage ring on seal neck. **Do not crimp.**
12. Clean shaft using suitable wire brush to remove any rust in seal mounting area grooves.

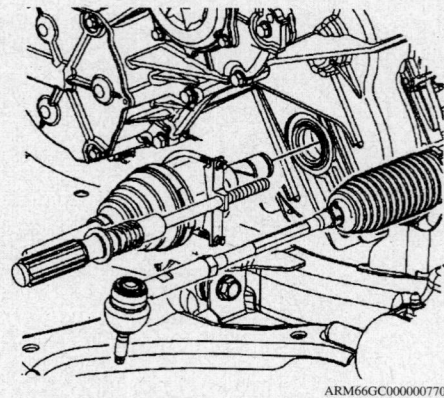

Fig. 14   Driveshaft & transaxle separation. ION

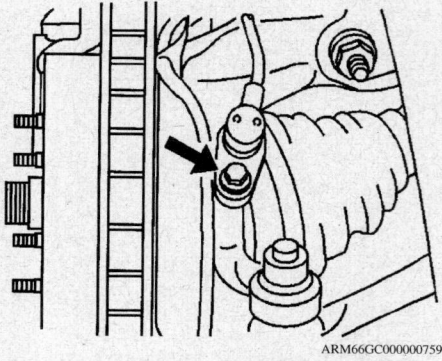

Fig. 15   Wheel speed sensor replacement. Vibe

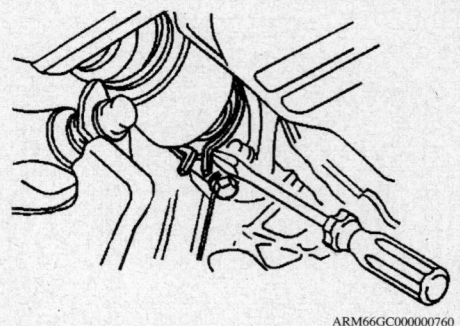

Fig. 16   Snap ring & lock bolt removal. Vibe

13. Slide CV joint seal onto shaft. Expose reference mark by sliding CV joint seal up shaft toward tripot end.
14. Position large seal retaining clamp around joint seal.
15. Place new retaining ring onto shaft.
16. Support tripot and place shaft onto arbor press with CV assembly under press head.
17. Lower press head onto CV joint until press cannot move further. **Do not exceed 4000 lbs.**
18. Remove shaft from press. Ensure reference mark to inner race is same as recorded during disassembly.
19. Place new swage ring onto small end of joint boot.
20. Slide boot and swage ring onto half shaft
21. Position small end of boot into boot groove on half shaft.
22. Mount drive axle swage ring clamp tool No. DT-47732, or equivalent, in suitable vise.
23. Position outboard end of shaft assembly in tool and align top of boot neck on bottom die using indicator.
24. Place top half of tool on lower half.
25. Ensure there are no pinch points on boot and install tool bolts hand snug.
26. Align shaft out board boot , grooves and swage ring.
27. Align inboard boot, shaft boot grooves and swage ring, then tighten tool bolts 180° at a time using suitable ratchet wrench. Alternate between each bolt until both sides are bottomed.
28. Place remaining kit grease inside seal.
29. Mount drive axle swage ring clamp tool No. DT-47732, or equivalent, in suitable vise.
30. Measure approximately $^{11}/_{16}$ inch up from bottom edge of CV outer joint.
31. Slide seal large diameter with large seal retaining clamp in place over outside of CV joint. CV joint seal must not be dimpled, stretched or out of shape.
32. Locate seal lip to ridge of CV outer joint.
33. Crimp seal retaining clamp using drive axle seal clamp pliers tool No. J35910, or equivalent, suitable breaker bar and torque wrench to 130 ft. lbs.
34. Ensure crimp dimension is .091 inch.

GKN

INNER JOINT & SEAL

Disassemble

1. Position shaft in suitable soft-jawed vise, the remove and discard small seal clamp using suitable side cutters.
2. Remove and discard large seal retaining clamp using suitable flat-bladed tool.
3. Separate seal from tripot housing at large diameter and slide seal away from joint along axle shaft.
4. Wipe excess grease from tripot spider face and tripot housing inside.
5. Remove tripot housing from spider and shaft, then the retaining ring from groove.
6. Remove spider and shaft seal.
7. Remove shaft seal.

Assemble

1. Install small seal clamp to seal. **Do not crimp clamp.**
2. Slide inner seal onto shaft and locate seal groove lip on shaft.
3. Crimp mall seal clamp using drive axle seal clamp pliers tool No. J35910, or equivalent. Clamp gap width should not exceed .85 inch.
4. Install tripot spider to shaft until seated against shoulder.
5. Install retaining ring in groove using suitable pliers.
6. Place approximately half of kit grease in seal and remainder in tripot housing.
7. Install large clamp over seal large diameter.
8. Install tripot housing to spider on shaft.
9. Slide seal large diameter over tripot housing outside and position seal lip in groove.
10. Place large seal retaining clamp around seal and close using drive axle seal clamp pliers tool No. J35910, or equivalent.
11. Continue tightening until clamp ear gap is $^5/_{64}$ inch.

OUTER JOINT & SEAL

Disassemble

1. Clamp shaft in suitable soft-jawed vice.
2. Disconnect large seal clamp tabs using suitable flat-bladed tool.

3. Remove and discard small seal clamp using suitable side cutters.
4. Separate Constant Velocity (CV) joint boot from race at large diameter.
5. Slide boot away from joint along shaft.
6. Wipe excess grease from CV inner race face.
7. Remove CV joint outer race using suitable wood block.
8. Remove shaft seal and CV joint retaining ring.
9. Tilt CV joint inner race using suitable brass drift and hammer, then remove first bearing roller.
10. Repeat previous step to remove all six bearing rollers.
11. Pivot CV joint cage and inner race 90° to outer race centerline, at same time align cage windows with outer race lands.
12. Remove cage and inner race.
13. Remove inner race from cage by rotating it upward.

Assemble

1. Install new small seal clamp on outboard seal neck. **Do not clamp.**
2. Slide outboard seal onto shaft and position seal neck in groove (largest groove below sight groove). Ensure seal clamp is positioned around entire circumference.
3. Crimp seal clamp using drive axle seal clamp pliers tool No. J35910, or equivalent. Clamp end gap should not exceed .85 inch.
4. Apply light coat of service kit grease on bearing roller grooves of inner and outer races.
5. Hold inner race 90° to cage centerline with inner race lands aligned with cage windows and insert inner race into cage.
6. Hold cage and inner race 90° to outer race center line and align cage windows with outer race lands.
7. Ensure inner race retaining ring side faces shaft.
8. Install cage and inner race into outer race.
9. Insert first bearing roller, then tilt cage to insert every other bearing roller. Repeat procedure until all six bearing rollers are in place.
10. Install CV joint retaining ring to shaft.
11. Place approximately half kit grease inside outboard seal and pack CV joint with remaining grease.

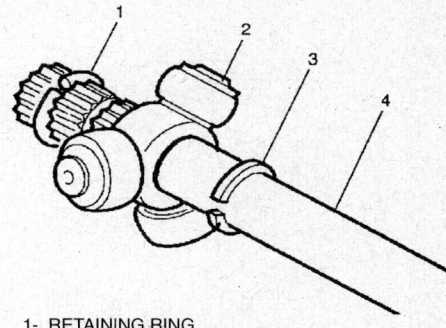

1- RETAINING RING
2- TRIPOT JOINT SPIDER
3- SPACER RING
4- HALFSHAFT BAR

GC3039900401000X

Fig. 17 Inner tripod joint assemble. Except Aveo, Cavalier, Cobalt, G5, ION, L-Series, STS, Sunfire & Vibe

12. Place wood block against CV joint spindle and tap block until CV joint inner race engages retaining ring.
13. Slide seal large diameter over CV race outside and locate seal lip in housing groove.
14. Install large seal retaining clamp over seal and close using drive axle seal clamp pliers. Continue tightening until gap is 5/64 inch.

ION

INNER JOINT & SEAL

DISASSEMBLE

1. Remove small boot retaining clamp from axle shaft using suitable side cutter, then the earless clamp. Discard components.
2. Remove larger boot retaining clamp from joint using suitable side cutters and separate inboard boot from bushing at larger diameter.
3. Remove boot sliding along axle shaft.
4. Remove housing from joint spider and retaining ring from axle shaft, then slide assembly from axle shaft.
5. Degrease entire assemble allowing to dry, then inspect components for wear and damage.

ASSEMBLE

1. Install small boot clamp to inboard boot, then slide boot onto axle shaft, and secure into position using suitable crimp pliers, **Fig. 29.**
2. Ensure end gap does not exceed .118 inch. Repeat procedure if not with specifications.
3. Install spider assembly until seated to shoulder, then the retaining ring into axle shaft groove, **Fig. 30.**
4. Install bushing to housing. Ensure bushing is seated flat against face of housing.
5. Install larger clamp on boot and slide onto axle shaft.
6. Install large diameter inboard boot with clamp in place over outside of bushing and clamp boot ring into place using suitable pliers, **Figs. 31 and 32.**

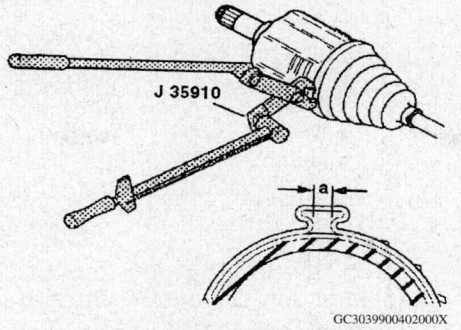

Fig. 18 Inner tripod joint alignment. Except Aveo, Cavalier, Cobalt, G5, ION, L-Series, STS, Sunfire & Vibe

GC3039900402000X

OUTER JOINT & SEAL

DISASSEMBLE

1. Remove retaining clamp and boot from CV joint using suitable side cutter.
2. Remove small clamp and boot from axle shaft using suitable hammer and flat bladed tool.
3. Separate boot from CV joint outer race, slide joint along bar and remove grease from CV joint inner race.
4. Remove CV joint using suitable hammer to tap on CV joint, then the boot from bar.
5. Tilt cage to remove first ball using suitable drift and hammer, **Fig. 33.** Tilt in opposite direction to remove remaining balls.
6. Secure CV joint cage and inner race at 90°, **Fig. 34.**
7. Remove CV joint cage and inner race from CV joint outer race.
8. Rotate CV joint 90° then pivot inner race into cage and remove inner race, **Fig. 35.**
9. Clean components thoroughly using suitable solvent and allow to dry.

ASSEMBLE

1. Install clamp to boot neck. **Do not crimp now.** Slide boot onto axle shaft and place both into groove on bar, **Fig. 36.**
2. Crimp boot clamp using tool no SA9203-C, or equivalent. Ensure end gap is not more than .118 inch.
3. Place grease on ball grooves of inner and outer race.
4. Install inner race into cage. Ensure retaining ring side of inner race faces axle shaft.
5. Install cage and inner race into outer race, then the first ball. Continue until all balls are installed.
6. Pack inside of boot and CV joint using suitable grease and push CV joint onto bar until seated into groove, **Fig. 37.**
7. Install boot with clamp over CV joint outer race and crimp clamp using suitable pliers.
8. Ensure end gap is not more than .118 inch.

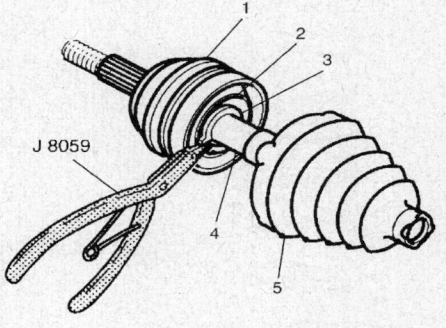

1- OUTER RACE
2- INNER RACE
3- RETAINING RING
4- HALFSHAFT
5- BOOT

GC3039900318000X

Fig. 19 Outer CV joint disassemble. Except Aveo, Cavalier, Cobalt, G5, ION, L-Series, STS, Sunfire & Vibe

L-Series

DISASSEMBLE

1. Clamp axle shaft in suitable soft metal or wood vise.
2. If deflector ring is damaged, remove from CV outer race using suitable brass drift and hammer, **Fig. 38.**
3. Disengage large and small boot clamps outer band from inner band at retainer peg using suitable hammer and chisel or flat-bladed screwdriver.
4. Separate large diameter of boot from CV joint race, then slide boot away from joint along axle shaft.
5. Wipe excess grease from CV inner race face.
6. Remove race retaining ring with suitable snap ring pliers, **Fig. 39.**
7. Remove CV joint from axle shaft, then the boot.
8. **On models equipped with dynamic damper,** if shaft or damper is being replaced, remove damper using suitable arbor press.
9. **On all models,** tap cage enough to remove first ball using suitable brass drift, **Fig. 40.** Remove remaining balls in similar manner.
10. Pivot cage and inner race at a 90° angle to outer race centerline, then align cage windows with outer race lands.
11. Remove cage and inner race.
12. Rotate inner race upward and out of cage.
13. Thoroughly clean and dry CV joint parts.
14. Cut tripot boot retaining clamp using suitable side cutters. Discard clamp.
15. Remove endless clamp using suitable small bladed screwdriver. Discard clamp.
16. Separate boot from large diameter of tripot housing, then slide boot along

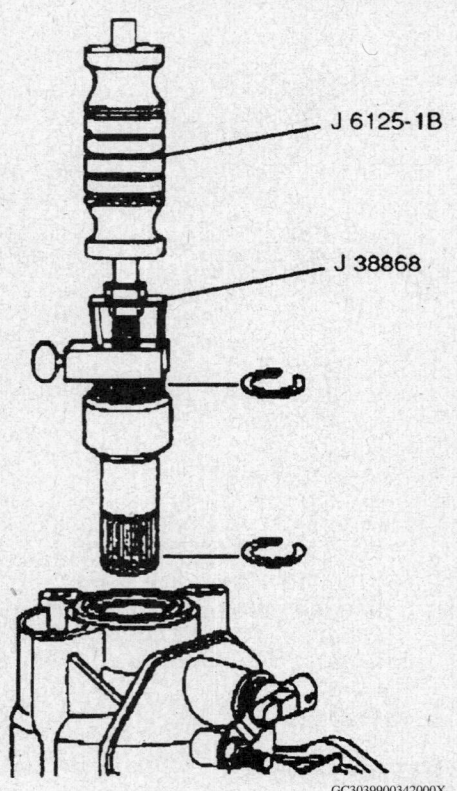

Fig. 20 Stub shaft removal. Cavalier & Sunfire

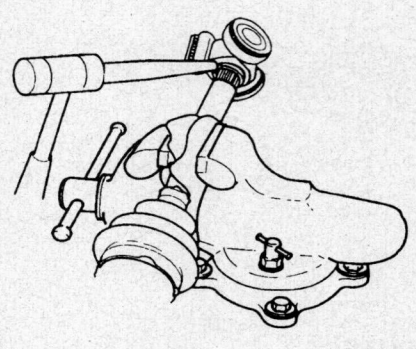

1- SPACER RING
2- TRIPOT BUSHING
3- TRILOBAL TRIPOT
4- HALFSHAFT

GC3039900404000X

Fig. 21 Inner tripod joint replacement. Cavalier & Sunfire

GC3039900348000X

Fig. 22 Tripod spider removal. Cavalier & Sunfire

axle shaft away from joint.
17. Wipe excess grease from tripot spider face and inside tripot housing.
18. Remove tripot housing from spider and shaft, **Fig. 41.**
19. Spread spacer ring using snap ring tool No. SA9198-C, or equivalent, then slide spacer ring and tripot spider back on axle, **Fig. 42.**
20. Remove spider retaining ring and slide spider off shaft. **Handle tripot spider with care. Tripot balls and needle rollers may separate from spider trunnions.**
21. Remove boot and thoroughly degrease housing. Allow to dry.

INSPECTION

1. Inspect tripot joint components for wear, cracks and damage.
2. Clean shaft.
3. Remove rust from shaft mounting groove with suitable wire brush.

ASSEMBLE

1. Install small retaining clamp on boot neck. **Do not crimp now.**
2. Slide boot onto shaft and position neck into groove.
3. Crimp boot retaining clamp using axle clamp installer tool No. SA9203-C, or equivalent, **Fig. 43.**
4. Ensure clamp is positioned correctly.
5. Measure clamp end gap and crimp, as required.
6. Install spacer ring beyond second groove.
7. Slide tripot spider past retaining

groove. Ensure tripot counterbored surface faces end of shaft.
8. Install retaining ring using C/V joint snap ring pliers tool No. SA9198-C, or equivalent.
9. Slide tripot spider toward shaft end and seat spacer ring into groove.
10. Pack approximately half of kit provided grease inside boot. Use remaining grease to pack tripot housing.
11. Install kit provided convolute retainer over boot.
12. Position retaining clamp around large diameter of boot, then slide housing over tripot spider.
13. Slide large diameter of boot over tripot housing and position lip into housing groove.
14. Ensure boot is not dimpled, stretched or out of shape. Adjust by hand with suitable thin, flat, blunt tool.
15. Ensure tripot is installed to proper length, **Fig. 44.**
16. Install large boot retaining clamp and crimp with boot clamp installer tool No. SA9161-C, or equivalent, **Fig. 45.**
17. **If replacing or installing damper,** proceed as follows:
   a. Clean shaft thoroughly.
   b. Mark damper installation point 7.95 inches from shaft outboard end with masking tape.
   c. Lubricate shaft with suitable liquid dishwashing detergent.
   d. Place shaft in suitable brass-jaw vice and start damper on by hand.
   e. Work damper onto shaft by twisting back and forth.
   f. Align damper inboard edge with tape.
   g. Remove tape.
   h. Secure damper by crimping clamp with axle boot clamp installer tool No. SA9164-C, or equivalent, to an .085 inch gap.
18. Lightly coat inner and outer race grooves with suitable grease.
19. Insert and rotate inner race into cage.
20. Install cage and inner race into outer race, align cage windows with outer race lines.
21. Install balls, use suitable brass drift to rotate and position cage and inner race.
22. Install inner race retaining ring.
23. Pack joint with service kit provided grease.
24. Install small retaining clamp on boot new. **Do not crimp now.**
25. Slide boot onto shaft, position neck into groove.

26. Crimp retaining clamp using axle clamp installer tool No. SA9203-C, or equivalent, **Fig. 46.**
27. Ensure clamp is positioned properly around entire circumference.
28. Pack approximately half of kit provided grease inside boot. Use remaining grease to pack CV.
29. Position large retaining clamp around boot. Ensure inner race retaining ring side faces axle shaft.
30. Push CV joint onto shaft until retaining ring seats into groove.
31. Slide large diameter of boot over outside of CV joint race, position lip into housing groove.
32. Ensure boot is not dimpled, stretched or out of shape. Adjust by hand with suitable thin, flat, blunt tool.
33. Crimp retaining clamp using axle clamp installer tool No. SA9203-C, or equivalent, **Fig. 47.**
34. Ensure clamp is positioned properly.
35. Position deflecting ring at CV joint outer race.
36. Tighten nut until deflector bottoms against CV outer race shoulder using M20 x 1.0 mm nut and axle deflector ring installer tool No. SA9160-C, or equivalent, **Fig. 48.**

STS

INNER JOINT & SEAL

DISASSEMBLE

1. Wrap suitable shop towel around drive shaft and place shaft horizontally in suitable bench vise.
2. Remove and discard drive shaft small seal clamp using suitable side cutters.
3. Disconnect and remove large seal retaining clamp from tripot joint using drive axle seal clamp pliers tool No. J35566, or equivalent.
4. Separate drive shaft inboard seal from trilobal tripot bushing.
5. Slide seal away from joint along drive shaft.
6. Remove housing from tripot joint spider and drive shaft.
7. Remove and discard retaining ring using snap ring pliers tool No. J8059 , or equivalent.
8. Reference mark tripot spider position on drive shaft for assembly alignment.

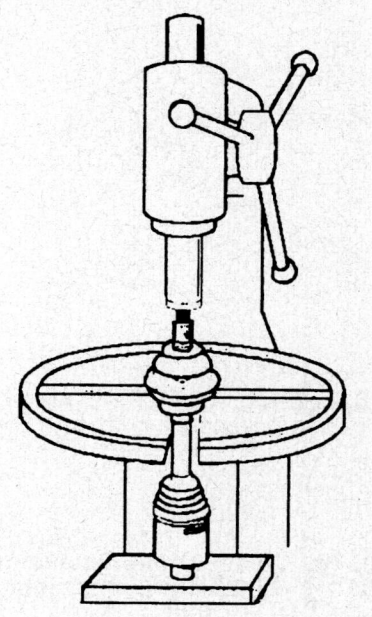

GC3039900349000X

Fig. 23 Driveshaft position in arbor press. Cavalier & Sunfire

9. Remove tripot spider from drive shaft by taping around face using suitable brass drift and hammer.
10. Remove joint seal from drive shaft.

ASSEMBLE

1. Install new small seal clamp onto small end of inner joint seal.
2. Slide inner joint seal and small seal clamp into drive shaft boot groove.
3. Position inner joint seal small end into drive shaft inner joint seal groove.
4. Crimp small seal retaining clamp until base of omega ohms shape has .039 inch gap using drive shaft seal clamp pliers tool No. J42572 , or equivalent. Hold clamping no less than two seconds. **Do not over- or under-tighten seal retaining clamp.**
5. Install tripot spider on drive shaft. If installing old tripot spider, align reference mark. Ensure beveled edge of tripot spider faces drive shaft.
6. install new retaining ring to drive shaft using snap ring pliers tool No. J8059, or equivalent.
7. Ensure positive engagement of tripot spider to drive shaft by grasping spider and attempting to pull it free from shaft.
8. Place approximately half of service kit grease in drive shaft inboard seal. Use remainder of grease to pack housing.
9. Install trilobal tripot bushing to housing.
10. Position larger new seal retaining clamp on drive shaft inboard seal.
11. Slide housing over tripot joint spider on drive shaft.
12. Slide large diameter of drive shaft inboard seal with larger clamp in place over outside of trilobal tripot bushing and locate seal lip in groove.
13. Ensure seal is not dimpled, stretched or deformed. If seal is not shaped cor-

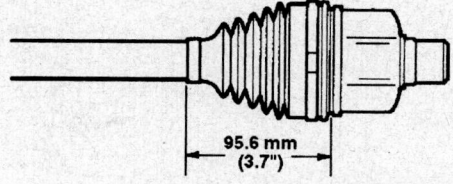

95.6 mm
(3.7")

GC3030000350020X

Fig. 24 Joint assembly dimension. Cavalier & Sunfire

rectly, equalize pressure in by lifting edge slightly and shape by hand.
14. Position joint assembly at 4.12 inches between seal edges, **Fig. 49.**
15. Burp air from inner joint seal.
16. Align drive shaft inboard seal, tripot housing and large seal retaining clamp while latching clamp using drive axle seal clamp pliers tool No. J35566, or equivalent.
17. Ensure latching tangs are fully engaged in large clamp band.

OUTER JOINT & SEAL
DISASSEMBLE

1. Wrap shop towel around axle shaft and place shaft horizontally in suitable bench vise.
2. Remove and discard large seal retaining clamp from outer joint seal using suitable side cutter.
3. Remove and discard small seal retaining clamp from joint seal using suitable side cutter.
4. Separate seal from joint outer race at large diameter end. Slide seal away from joint face.
5. Wipe grease from face of joint inner race, cage, balls, etc.
6. Hold outer joint housing horizontally to shaft, then place suitable wood block between seal and joint, on joint face.
7. Compress axle shaft retaining clip by striking wood block with suitable hammer. If joint refuses to move, use suitable brass drift against inner race face.
8. Remove outer joint from shaft by continuing to strike wood block.
9. Remove and discard axle shaft retaining ring and seal.
10. Remove drive shaft from vise. and wrap suitable shop towel around joint outer race splined shaft.
11. Place outer race vertically in suitable bench vise.
12. Tilt drive shaft joints inner cage by tapping using suitable brass drift and hammer enough to remove first ball.
13. Remove exposed ball using suitable small screwdriver.
14. Position cage and inner race level.
15. Repeat previous steps to remove all balls in sequence, **Fig. 50.**
16. Position cage and inner race 90° to outer race centerline.
17. Align cage windows with outer race lands.
18. Remove cage and inner race from outer race.
19. Position cage and inner race so windows' larger radius corners are up.
20. Rotate inner race 90° to cage centerline.

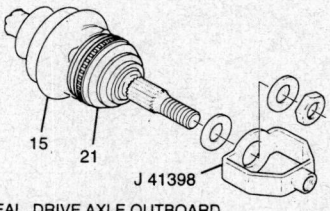

15   21

J 41398

15-SEAL, DRIVE AXLE OUTBOARD
21-RACE, C/V JOINT OUTER

GC3039900354000X

Fig. 25 Outer CV joint removal. Cavalier & Sunfire

21. Align inner race lands with cage windows.
22. Insert inner race land into a cage window, then pivot inner race down and remove it from cage.

ASSEMBLE

1. Position cage so windows' larger radius corners are up.
2. Position inner race 90° to cafe centerline.
3. Insert inner race up through cage bottom, then align and insert inner race land into cage window.
4. Rotate remainder of inner race into cage.
5. Rotate inner race within cage so race grooved surface is facing up.
6. Align inner race ball tracks with cage windows. Ensure inner race is fully assembled into cage.
7. Wrap suitable shop towel around joint outer race splined shaft.
8. Place outer race vertically in suitable bench vise.
9. Position cage and inner race 90° to outer race centerline.
10. Align two cage windows at 0 and 180° within outer race. Rotate inner race and cage downward in vertical plane.
11. Position cage and inner race level. Ensure inner race ring groove is positioned down.
12. Align cage windows and inner race ball tracks with outer race ball tracks.
13. Press cage down on one of outer race ball tracks. Opposing cage window and inner race ball track will be accessible for ball installation.
14. After installing first ball, use suitable brass drift and hammer to drive cage and inner race down completely.
15. Insert ball through cage window onto inner race ball track. Tap ball lightly with suitable plastic tipped hammer.
16. No gap should exist between ball and inner race ball track.
17. Position cage and inner race level.
18. Install all balls in sequence, **Fig. 50.**
19. Insert approximately 60% of service kit grease into ball tracks, balls, cage and inner race. Spread remainder of grease into bottom of outer race.
20. Remove outer joint from bench vise.
21. Wrap suitable shop towel around axle shaft.
22. Place drive shaft horizontally in suitable bench vise.
23. Install new small seal retaining clamp onto axle shaft.

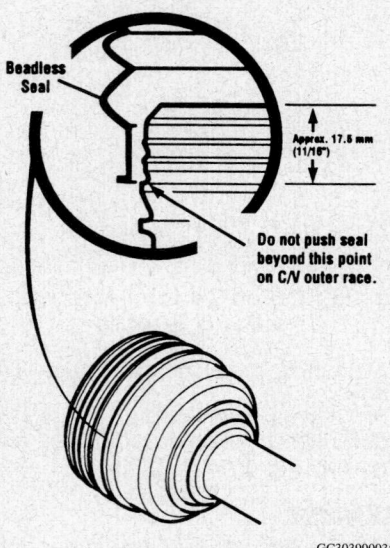

Fig. 26   CV outer joint installation measurement. Cavalier & Sunfire

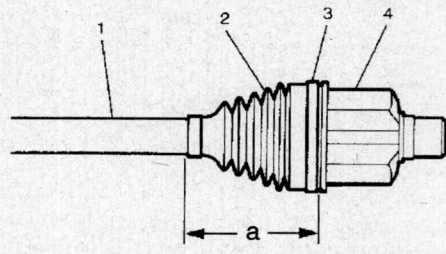

1- HALFSHAFT
2- BOOT
3- CLAMP
4- HOUSING

ARM0500000000187

Fig. 27   Boot assembly dimension. Cobalt & G5 w/Delphi inner joint & seal

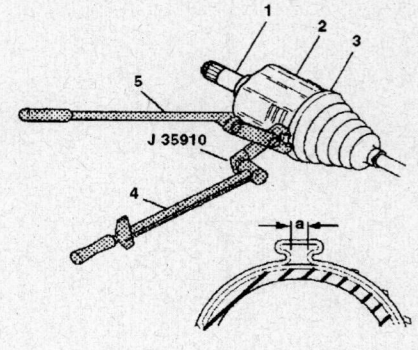

1- HALFSHAFT
2- TRIPOT HOUSING
3- SEAL
4- TORQUE WRENCH
5- BREAKER BAR

ARM0500000000188

Fig. 28   Clamp crimp dimension. Cobalt & G5 w/Delphi inner joint & seal

24. Install seal onto shaft and new retaining ring.
25. Position outer joint horizontally.
26. Engage inner race splines onto axle shaft splines.
27. Compress axle shaft retaining ring.
28. Press retaining ring end using suitable flat-bladed tool into groove while firmly pressing outer joint onto axle shaft.
29. Continue to work around retaining ring until it is compressed.
30. Install outer joint to axle shaft. Axle shaft and inner race must be fully seated to each other.
31. Position suitable wood block over outer joint threaded shaft end.
32. Drive outer joint onto shaft using suitable hammer. Drive outer joint until outer joint seats fully onto axle shaft.
33. Insert remaining service kit grease into seal.
34. Position small seal retaining clamp into seal boot groove.
35. Position seal and small retaining clamp to boot groove.
36. Crimp small seal retaining clamp until base of omega ohms shape has .039 inch gap using drive shaft seal clamp pliers tool No. J42572, or equivalent. Hold clamping no less than two seconds. **Do not over- or under-tighten seal retaining clamp.**
37. Position large seal retaining clamp onto seal.
38. Position seal and large retaining clamp to joint outer race.
39. Ensure seal is not dimpled, stretched or otherwise deformed. If seal is not shaped correctly, equalize pressure by lifting seal edge slightly and shape seal by hand.
40. Crimp large seal retaining clamp until base of omega ohms shape has .039 inch gap using drive shaft seal clamp pliers tool No. J42572 , or equivalent. Hold clamping no less than two seconds. **Do not over- or under-tighten seal retaining clamp.**

Vibe

INNER JOINT & SEAL

DISASSEMBLE

1. Remove small seal clamp from driveshaft using suitable side cutters, then the large seal clamp from tripod joint.
2. Separate driveshaft outboard seal from tripod bushing and slide seal from joint along driveshaft.
3. Remove housing from tripod joint and driveshaft.
4. Place matching marks on tripod spider and driveshaft, **Fig. 51.**
5. Remove snap ring and joint from driveshaft using suitable hammer, **Fig. 52.**
6. Remove inboard joint boot from driveshaft.
7. Remove dynamic damper from righthand driveshaft.
8. Remove joint seal from driveshaft.
9. Remove bearing from shaft using suitable press, **Fig. 53.**

ASSEMBLE

1. Install bearing using suitable press.
2. Install boots and clamps, placing vinyl tape over splined area.
3. Install dynamic damper to righthand side driveshaft.
4. Install outboard joint. Ensure alignment marks are referenced.
5. Install snap ring, then pack outboard and inboard joint and boot using 4.8–5.5 ounces of suitable grease.
6. Align matching marks on inboard and outboard joint shaft, then temporarily install boot to inboard joint and boots into grooves on driveshaft.
7. **On models equipped with FWD,** ensure that righthand driveshaft length is 33.201–33.595 inches and lefthand driveshaft length is 22.728–23.122 inches, **Fig. 54.**
8. **On models equipped with AWD,** ensure righthand driveshaft length is 33.661–34.055 inches and lefthand driveshaft length is 22.319–22.713

inches, **Fig. 55.**

9. **On all models,** ensure small seal is crimped using suitable shaft seal pliers.
10. Install retaining ring to driveshaft bar. Ensure 60° offset between inner and outer tripod spiders is maintained.
11. Install spider to driveshaft bar and compressing retaining ring using suitable flat bladed tool. Ensure component engagement attempting to pull free from each other.
12. Install driveshaft assembly in sequence, **Fig. 56.** Place half of grease to outboard seal and pack housing using remaining half of grease from service kit.
13. Install outboard seal over outside of tripod bushing and secure lip of seal in groove, **Fig. 57.**
14. Ensure driveshaft outboard seal, housing and large seal retaining clamp are aligned, then secure large retaining clamp.
15. Distribute grease throughout bearings.

INTERMEDIATE SHAFT
REPLACE

All Models Except Cobalt, G5, ION & L-Series

1. Raise and support vehicle, then remove righthand tire and wheel assembly.
2. Protect outer joint from sharp edges with suitable shop towels.
3. Remove stabilizer shaft from righthand control arm.
4. Remove righthand ball joint from knuckle.

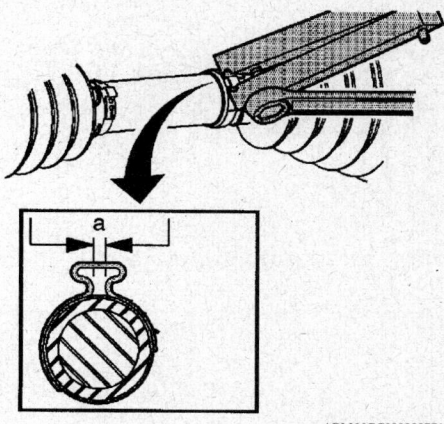

Fig. 29 Retaining clamp installation. ION

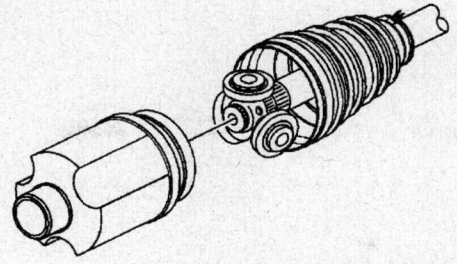

Fig. 30 Joint spider installation. ION

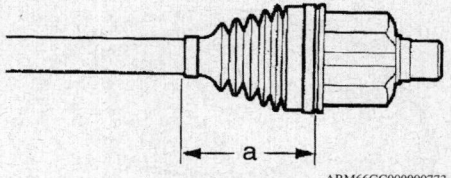

Fig. 31 Boot installation. ION

Fig. 33 CV joint ball removal. ION

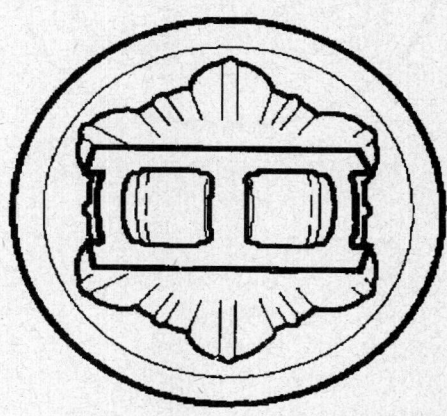

Fig. 34 CV joint cage & inner race alignment. ION

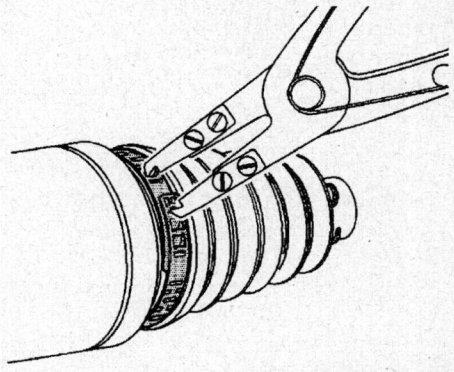

Fig. 32 Clamp crimp locations. ION

5. Remove drive axle from intermediate shaft as outlined under "Driveshaft, Replace."
6. Remove intermediate driveshaft support bracket to engine mounting bolts.
7. Remove intermediate shaft from transaxle.
8. Reverse procedure to install. Coat splines of intermediate shaft with suitable chassis grease.

Cobalt & G5

1. Raise and support vehicle, then remove righthand tire and wheel assembly.
2. Remove ball stud to steering knuckle pinch bolt and nut.
3. Turn steering knuckle aside.
4. Separate wheel drive shaft from intermediate drive shaft using rear wheel drive shaft removal tool No. J45341, and slide hammer tool No. J2619-A or equivalents.
5. Position and support drive shaft aside from intermediate drive shaft.
6. Remove intermediate drive shaft bracket-to-engine block mounting bolts.
7. Remove intermediate drive shaft. **Do not damage transaxle output shaft seal.**

8. Reverse procedure to install, noting the following:
   a. Protect seal using axle seal protector tool No. J44394, or equivalent.
   b. Apply very small amount of suitable grease to wheel drive shaft inner join splines.

ION

1. Raise and support vehicle, then remove righthand tire and wheel assembly.
2. Remove nut and disconnect stabilizer shaft link.
3. Remove mounting nut and disconnect outer tie rod from steering knuckle. **Do not loosen tie rod adjustment jamb nut.**
4. Rotate steering knuckle to access wheel drive shaft inner joint.
5. Separate wheel drive shaft from intermediate drive shaft using rear wheel drive shaft removal tool No. J45341 and slide hammer tool No. SA9173G, or equivalents.
6. Position and support wheel drive shaft from intermediate drive shaft.
7. Disconnect Vehicle Speed Sensor (VSS) electrical connector.
8. Remove rear or lefthand intermediate drive shaft bracket-to-engine block bolts and VSS with bracket.
9. Remove remaining intermediate shaft bracket-to-engine block bolt.
10. Remove intermediate drive shaft. **Do not damage transaxle output shaft seal.**
11. Reverse procedure to install, noting the following:
    a. Protect axle seal with axle seal protector tool No. SA91112T, or equivalent.
    b. **Do not tighten intermediate drive shaft bracket-to-engine block bolts** until VSS and bracket are installed.

c. Tighten bracket-to-engine block bolts, beginning with upper bolt. into transaxle output shaft seal.
d. Apply very small amount of grease No. 1051344, or equivalent, to wheel drive shaft inner joint splines.
e. **Torque** new outer tie rod nut to 15 ft. lbs.
f. Then tighten nut an additional 180°.

L-Series

REMOVAL

1. Remove righthand driveshaft as outlined under "Driveshaft, Replace."
2. **On models equipped with DOHC engine,** proceed as follows:
   a. Loosen intake manifold to intermediate axle shaft support bracket top mounting bolt. **Do not remove.**
   b. Remove intake manifold to intermediate axle shaft support bracket lower mounting bolt.
   c. Position intake manifold to intermediate axle shaft support bracket aside to provide clearance.
   d. Tighten intake manifold bracket mounting bolts to hold bracket in position.
3. **On all models,** remove support bracket to engine block mounting bolt and intermediate axle shaft.

INSTALLATION

A new inner tripot joint must be installed whenever a new intermediate axle shaft is installed.

1. Install transaxle seal protector tool No. SA91112-T, or equivalent.
2. Install intermediate driveshaft into transaxle. **Do not contact oil seal with shaft splines.**
3. After intermediate driveshaft splines

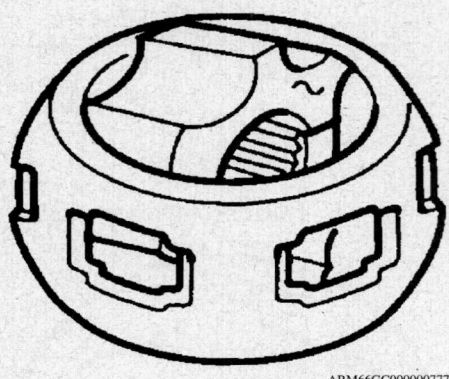

Fig. 35 CV joint inner race removal. ION

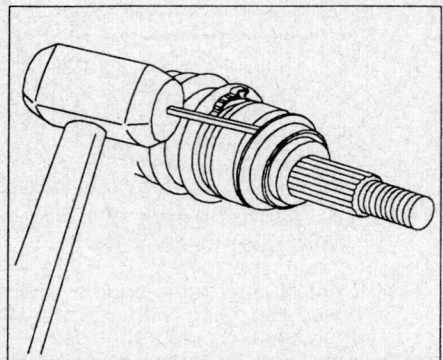

Fig. 38 Deflector ring removal. L-Series

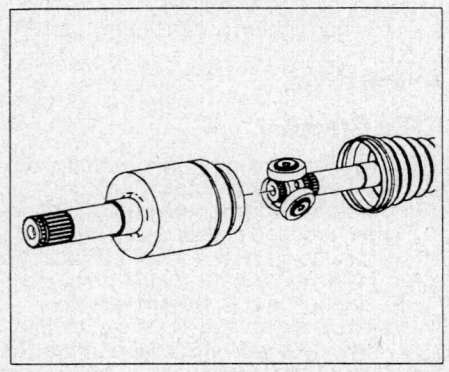

Fig. 41 Tripot housing removal. L-Series

have safely passed transaxle oil seal, remove seal protector.

4. Fully seat intermediate driveshaft into transaxle.
5. **On models equipped with DOHC engine,** proceed as follows:
   a. Install lower support bracket to engine block mounting bolts. **Do not tighten now.**
   b. Loosen support bracket to intake manifold mounting bolt and align holes.

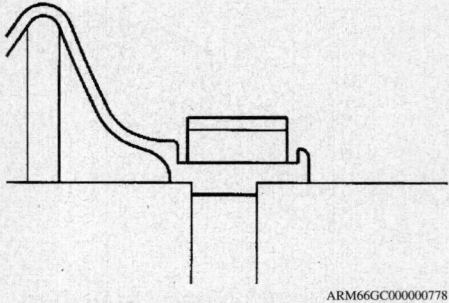

Fig. 36 Retaining boot & clamp installation. ION

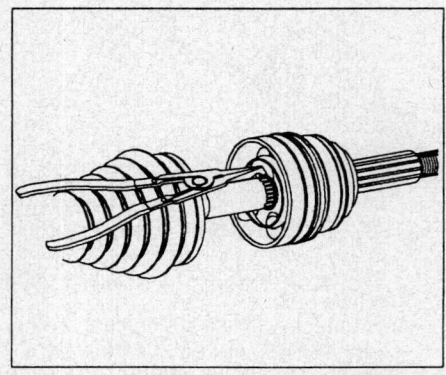

Fig. 39 Race retaining ring removal. L-Series

   c. Tighten support bracket to intake manifold mounting bolts.
6. **On models equipped with SOHC engine,** install shaft support to engine block mounting bolts. **Do not tighten now.**
7. **On all models,** tighten support bracket to engine block mounting bolts.

INTERMEDIATE SHAFT SERVICE

All Models Except ION, L-Series, STS & Vibe

DISASSEMBLE

1. Remove retaining ring and lip seal, **Fig. 58.**
2. Press shaft from bearing by positioning split plate tool No. J22912-1, or equivalent, behind inner slinger.
3. Remove retainer from support screws.
4. Press bearing from support using joint seal installer tool No. J23694, or equivalent.

ASSEMBLE

1. Press bearing into support using suitable press arbor plate across bearing.

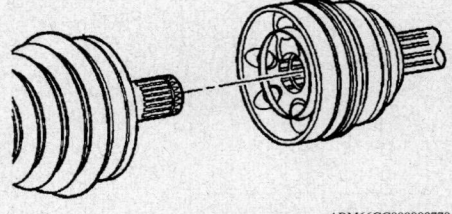

Fig. 37 CV joint installation. ION

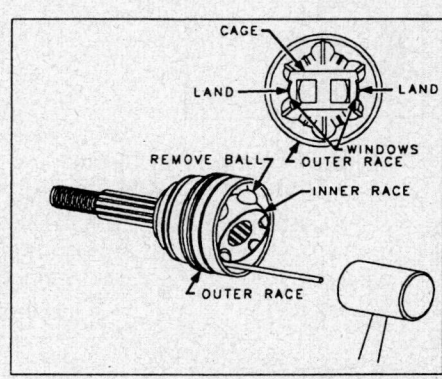

Fig. 40 CV joint ball removal. L-Series

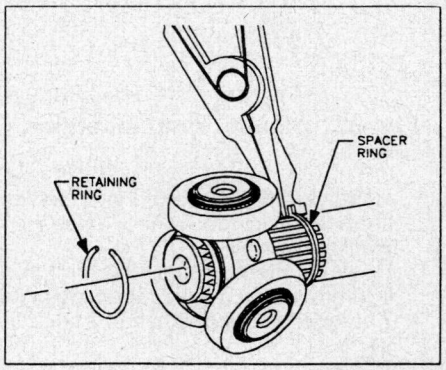

Fig. 42 Spider retaining ring removal. L-Series

2. Press inner slinger on shaft using split plate tool No. J22912-1, or equivalent.
3. Install retainer over shaft.
4. Place support with bearing on press arbor plate and press shaft into bearing until bearing inner race contacts shaft chamfer. **Do not press bearing beyond where chamfer begins on shaft.**
5. Press outer slinger on shaft using split plate.
6. Apply suitable RTV sealer to outer slinger and shaft joint.
7. Install lip seal using seal installer tool No. J34115, or equivalent.
8. Install retaining ring.
9. Install retainer to support.

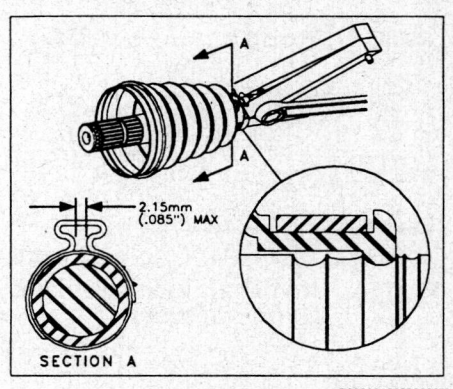

Fig. 43 Small tripot retaining ring crimp. L & S Series

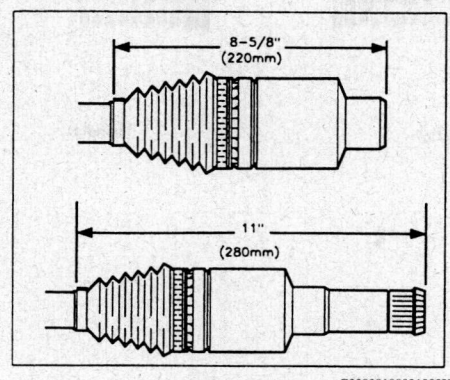

Fig. 44 Tripot assembly dimension. L-Series

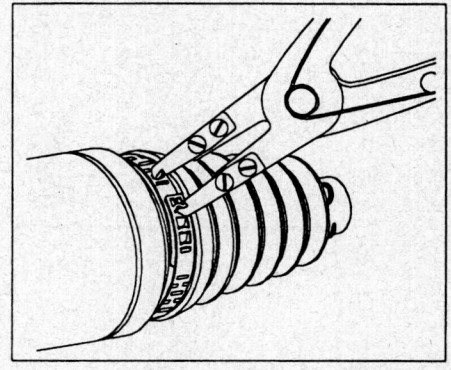

Fig. 45 Tripot large retaining clamp installation. L-Series

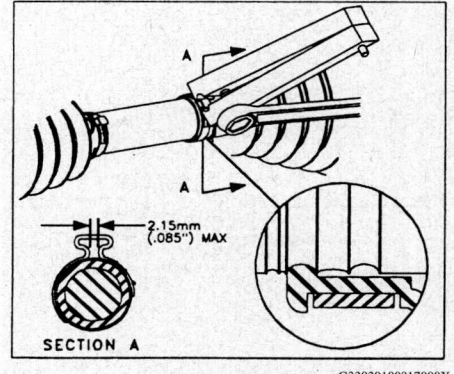

Fig. 46 Small CV joint retaining clamp installation. L-Series

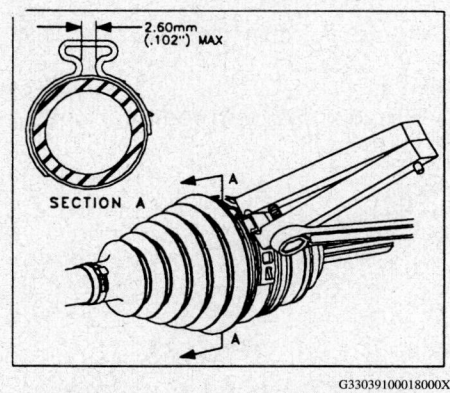

Fig. 47 Large CV joint retaining clamp crimp. L-Series

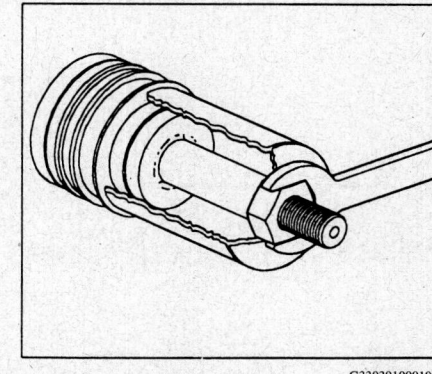

Fig. 48 Deflector ring installation. L-Series

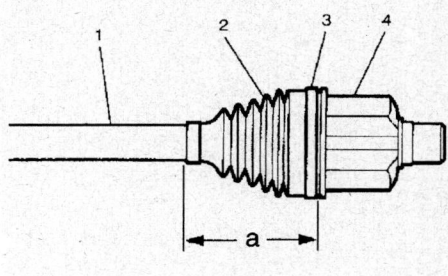

1- HALFSHAFT
2- BOOT
3- CLAMP
4- TRIPOT HOUSING

Fig. 49 Seal edge position. STS lefthand drive shaft

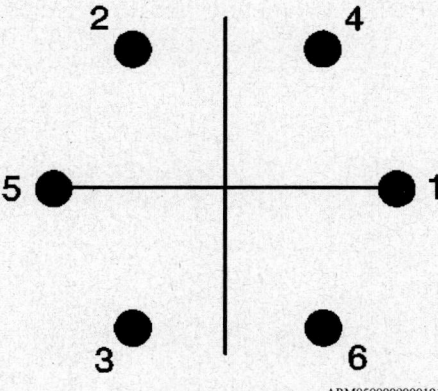

Fig. 50 Ball replacement sequence. STS outer joint

Fig. 51 Driveshaft & tripod reference locations. Vibe

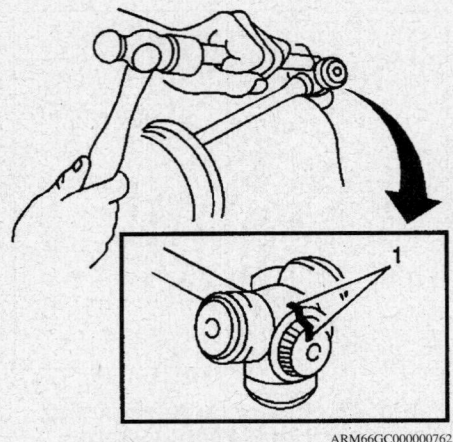

Fig. 52   Joint removal. Vibe

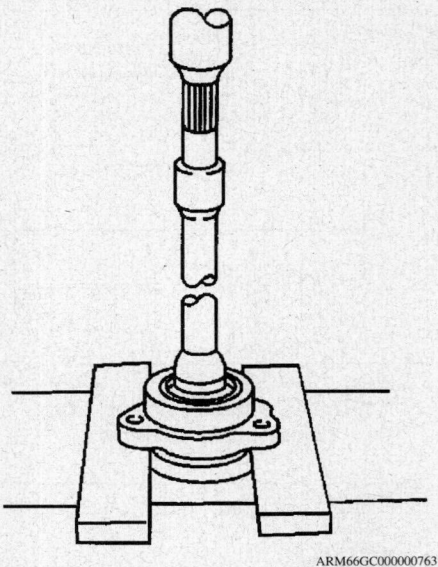

Fig. 53   Bearing removal. Vibe

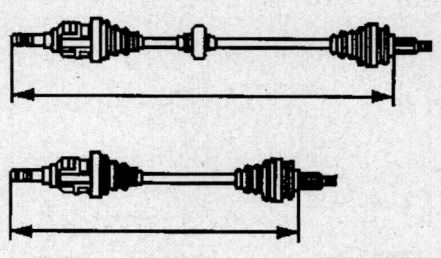

Fig. 54   Driveshaft measurement. Vibe w/FWD

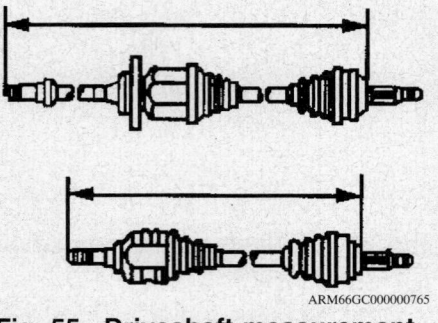

Fig. 55   Driveshaft measurement. Vibe w/AWD

Fig. 56   Driveshaft assembly. Vibe

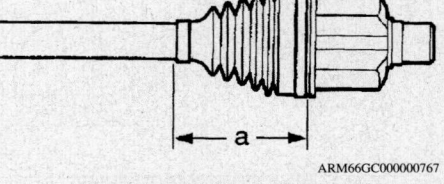

Fig. 57   Outboard seal installation. Vibe

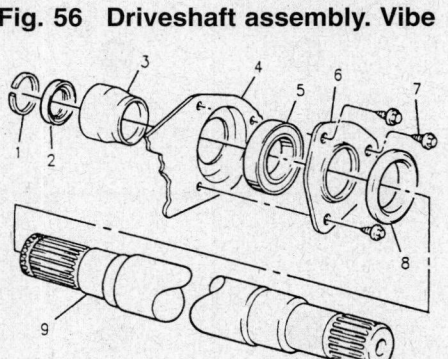

1   RETAINING RING
2   LIP SEAL
3   OUTER SLINGER
4   SUPPORT
5   BEARING
6   RETAINER
7   SCREW
8   INNER SLINGER
9   SHAFT

GC3039100203000X

Fig. 58   Exploded view of intermediate shaft. All models except ION, L-Series, STS & Vibe

TIGHTENING SPECIFICATIONS

Year	Component	Torque Ft. Lbs.
ALERO, GRAND AM & MALIBU		
2004–05	Axle Nut	284⑥
	Ball Joint To Steering Knuckle	41
	CV Joint Large Boot Clamp	130
	CV Joint Small Boot Clamp	100
	Stabilizer Link	22
	Tie Rod To Knuckle	③
	Wheel Lug Nuts	100
AURA, G6, MALIBU CLASSIC & MALIBU MAXX		
2004–08	Axle Nut	159
	Lower Control Arm Bushing	37②
	Steering Knuckle Ball Stud	37②
	Tie Rod Ball Stud	44
	Wheel Lug Nut	100
AVEO		
2004–08	Axle Shaft	221
	Damping Block Connection	59
	Engine Under Cover	31①
	Lower Ball Joint	37
	Rear Mounting Bracket	44
	Tie Rod	33
	Wheel Lug Nut	88
BONNEVILLE, LESABRE & PARK AVENUE		
2004–05	Axle Nut	118
	Ball Joint To Steering Knuckle	50
	CV Joint Boot Clamp	130
	Stabilizer Shaft Bracket	35
	Stabilizer Shaft Link	13
	Wheel Lug Nuts	100
CAVALIER & SUNFIRE		
2004–05	ABS Speed Sensor	107①
	Axle Nut	148
	Ball Joint To Knuckle	⑧
	CV Joint Large Boot Clamp	130
	CV Joint Small Boot Clamp	100
	Stabilizer Link	13
	Wheel Lug Nuts	100
CENTURY, GRAND PRIX, IMPALA, MONTE CARLO & REGAL		
2004–08	Axle Nut	118
	Ball Joint To Steering Knuckle	⑤
	CV Joint Large Boot Clamp	130
	CV Joint Small Boot Clamp	100
	Stabilizer Shaft Bracket	35
	Stabilizer Link	17
	Wheel Lug Nuts	100
COBALT & G5		
2005–08	Intermediate Drive Shaft Bracket	37
	Ball Joint To Steering Knuckle	⑩
	Wheel Drive Shaft Nut	155
	Wheel Lug Nuts	100

TIGHTENING SPECIFICATIONS—Continued

Year	Component	Torque Ft. Lbs.
DEVILLE		
2004–05	Axle Nut	⑦
	Ball Joint To Steering Knuckle Nut	37
	CV Joint Boot Clamp	130
	Stabilizer Bracket To Frame	33
	Stabilizer Link	41
	Wheel Lug Nuts	100
DTS & LUCERNE		
2006–08	Axle Nut	⑦
	Outer Tie Rod	⑪
	Seal Clamp	130
	Stabilizer Link Nuts	13
	Wheel Lugs Nuts	100
ION		
2004–07	Driveshaft Wheel Nut	81
	Intermediate Drive Shaft Bracket-to-Engine Block	37
	Outer Tie Rod	⑨
	Stabilizer Shaft Link.	63
	Vehicle Speed Sensor	89①
L-SERIES		
2004	Axle Nut	②
	Ball Joint Stud Castle Nut	55
	Lower Control Arm Ball Stud	75
	Tie Rod End To Steering Knuckle	44
	Wheel Lugs Nuts	92
LACROSSE		
2005–08	Control Arm Ball Stud	50
	Drive Axle Seal Clamp	128
	Front Wheel Drive Shaft Nut	118
	Outer Tie Rod	34
	Stabilizer Shaft Link	17
	Wheel Lugs Nuts	100
SEVILLE		
2004	Axle Nut	118
	Ball Joint To Steering Knuckle Nut	④
	CV Joint Boot Clamp	130
	Stabilizer Bracket To Frame	33
	Stabilizer Link	41
	Wheel Lug Nuts	100
STS		
2006–08	Intermediate Wheel Drive Shaft Bearing Housing-to-Oil Pan	44
	Outer Tie Rod	41
	Wheel Drive Shaft Spindle	118
	Wheel Lug Nuts	100
VIBE		
2004–08	ABS Speed Sensor Retaining Bolt	71①
	Ball Joint To Control Arm Bolts & Nuts	66
	Drive Axle Nut	159
	Splash Shield	71①
	Tie Rod End Nut	36
	Wheel Lug Nuts	76

① — Inch lbs.

② — Refer to for tightening specifications and sequence.

③ — **Torque** to 15 ft. lbs, then tighten an additional 180°.

④ — **Torque** to 88 inch lbs., then tighten an additional 150°.

⑤ — **Torque** to 15 ft. lbs, then tighten an additional 120°.

⑥ — Type one, 284 ft. lbs; Type two, 173 ft. lbs.

⑦ — Soft Ride & Sport Suspension Systems (RPO codes FE1 & FE3), 118 ft. lbs; Heavy Duty, VAR 3, Suspension System (RPO code FE7), 170 ft. lbs.

⑧ — **Torque** to 50 ft. lbs, then tighten an additional 180°.

⑨ — Refer to for tightening specifications and sequence.

⑩ — First pass; torque to 37 ft. lbs, then reverse nut ¾ turn. Second pass; torque to 37 ft. lbs., then tighten an additional 30°.

⑪ — **Torque** to 22 ft. lbs., then tighten an additional 180°.

DRIVE AXLES

NOTE: On Air Bag Equipped Models, Refer To "Air Bag System Precautions" Located In The Front Of This Manual For System Disarming & Arming Procedures.

NOTE: Refer To "Computer Relearn Procedures" Located In The Front Of This Manual When Battery Power To The Computer Has Been Interrupted.

INDEX

	Page No.		Page No.		Page No.
Adjustments	27-6	Cleaning & Inspection	27-6	GTO	27-4
Differential Side Bearing		Description	27-1	Solstice & SKY	27-4
Preload	27-6	CTS & STS	27-1	Drive Axle Specifications	27-12
Corvette & XLR	27-6	Corvette	27-1	Identification	27-1
Drive Pinion Depth	27-7	GTO	27-1	Subassembly Service	27-4
Corvette & XLR	27-7	Solstice & SKY	27-2	Limited Slip	27-5
Application Chart	27-1	XLR	27-2	Corvette & XLR	27-5
Assemble	27-7	Disassemble	27-3	Solstice & SKY	27-6
Differential	27-7	Differential	27-3	Standard Differential	27-4
Corvette & XLR	27-7	CTS & STS	27-3	Troubleshooting	27-2
Solstice & SKY	27-8	Corvette & XLR	27-3	Diagnosis	27-3
Drive Pinion	27-8	GTO	27-3	Corvette, CTS, STS & XLR	27-3
Corvette & XLR	27-8	Solstice & SKY	27-4	GTO	27-3
GTO	27-9	Drive Pinion	27-4	Solstice & SKY	27-3
Ring Gear & Differential		CTS & STS	27-4	Preliminary Inspections	27-2
Housing	27-12	Corvette & XLR	27-4		

APPLICATION CHART

Model	Gear Ratio	Ring Gear Diameter, Inch
Corvette	2.56	8.000
	2.73	①
	3.15	①
	3.42	①
CTS	3.23	7.625
	3.42	7.625
	3.73	7.625
	3.91	7.625
GTO	3.46	—
Solstice & SKY	3.23	7.625
	3.42	7.625
	3.73	7.625
	3.91	7.625
STS	3.23	7.625
	3.73	7.625
	3.91	7.625
XLR	2.56	8.000
	2.73	8.000
	2.93	8.000

① — 2004, 7.625–inch; 2005–08, 8–inch.

IDENTIFICATION

Axle identification numbers can be found on a tag, located on the side of the differential carrier, **Figs. 1 through 5.**

DESCRIPTION

Corvette

The splined output shaft of the transmission drives the pinion, which in turn, rotates the ring gear and differential case assembly. The limited slip differential distributes torque/power to the rear wheels via individual axle shaft assemblies. The limited-slip differential is of a conventional separator plate and friction disc type design. The differential housing, side covers, pinion housing, and differential case halves are constructed of cast aluminum. The internal components incorporate a hypoid gear set, ring and pinion, carrier assembly, and pinion housing assembly. The pinion is supported in a pinion housing by tapered roller bearings. The pinion is positioned rearward of the ring gear centerline. Pinion position, ring gear position, and carrier bearing preload are determined by shimming procedures.

Each ring gear has specific setup dimensions, A1 and A2 values, stamped onto the side area of the gear. The A1 and A2 values are unique to each ring gear/pinion and are determined during the manufacturers gear/pinion noise and vibration setup and testing. The vehicle speed sensor reluctor ring is incorporated into the outside area of the ring gear. The vehicle speed sensor detects the rotational pulses produced by the reluctor ring and send the signal to the Vehicle Control Module (VCM). The differential assembly is available in three gear ratios. The 3.42 ratio axle is used in all manual transmission applications. The 2.73 ratio axle is standard equipment for automatic transmission applications with an optional 2.56 & 3.15 ratio axles available.

Some 2005–08 models have a differential lubricant pump and cooler. Oil is pulled from the sump through an external oil pipe into the pump. Oil is pumped through an external oil pipe to the cooler. The oil is cooled by dissipating heat with transmission oil returning from radiator mounted cooler.

CTS & STS

The differential housing, side cover and pinion housing are constructed of cast aluminum. The internal components incorporate a hypoid gear set, ring and pinion, carrier assembly and pinion housing assembly. The pinion is supported in a pinion housing by tapered roller bearings. The pinion is positioned forward of the ring gear centerline. All models have a 7 ⅝-inch ring gear. Each ring gear has specific setup dimensions, A1 and A2 values, stamped onto the side area of the gear. The A1 and A2 values are unique to each ring gear/pinion and are determined during the manufacturers gear/pinion noise and vibration setup and testing. Pinion position, ring gear position and carrier bearing preload are determined by shimming procedures

GTO

The differential assembly, is a four pinion type limited slip differential final drive assembly mounted to an independent rear suspension. The differential is mounted directly to the crossmember which is rubber mounted to the underbody. The differential

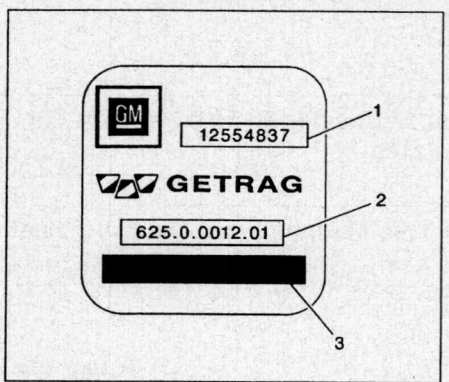

(1) GM Part Number
(2) Getrag Part Number
(3) Serial Number

Available Axle Ratios

GM P/N	Axle Ratio	Transmission
12551769	342	Manual
12554837	273 (Base)	Automatic
12556313	315 (Optional)	Automatic

GC3039700290000X

**Fig. 1   Axle identification.
Corvette**

case and drive pinion are mounted in opposed taper roller bearing in the carrier. Differential case side bearing preload adjustment is provided by screw adjusters in the sides of the case. Pinion bearing preload is provided by a collapsible spacer. Torque is transferred from the propeller shaft to the differential via the pinion flange which is splined to the hypoid pinion. The torque is then transferred from the pinion through the ring gear, differential case, differential pinion cross shafts, differential pinions, side gears, and then via splines to the inner axle shafts and the drive shafts.

The limited slip differential performs the same functions as the conventual type differential. However, should the opposite wheel begin to spin, it transfers driving force to the wheel with traction. The differential case houses a cone type clutch pack that is an integral part of the side gears. The four pinion type limited slip differential has three pre-load springs inclosed in the center pinion cross shaft. The limited slip differential directs the major driving force to the wheel with greater amount of traction, but will not interfere with steering characteristics of differential action. The partial locking action, due to the spring load on the cones, is automatically increased by the inherent separating forces between the side gears and pinion, which progressively increases the resistance in the differential as applied torque is increased.

When the rear wheels are under extremely unbalanced conditions, such as one wheel on dry road and the other in mud or snow, with a standard differential, wheel spin easily occurs if over acceleration is attempted. However, with a limited slip differential, when the tendency for wheel spin occurs friction generated inside the case transfers driving force to the non-spinning

(1) Ratio
(2) GM Part Number
(3) Getrag Part Number
(4) Serial Number

Available Axle Ratios

Axle Ratio	Drive/Engine	Flange Size
3:23	RWD/3.6L V6	105 mm
3:42	RWD/3.2L V6	96 mm
3:42	RWD/2.8L V6	105 mm
3:73	RWD/5.7L V8	86 mm
3:91	RWD/2.6L V6	96 mm

ARM0400000001025

Fig. 2   Axle identification. CTS

wheel. In the event of continued spinning, a whirring sound from the over-running cones is produced, but this condition/sound does not indicate a failure of the unit.

Solstice & SKY

The differential housing, side cover and pinion housing are constructed of cast aluminum. The internal components incorporate a hypoid gear set, ring and pinion, carrier assembly and pinion housing assembly. The pinion is supported in a pinion housing by tapered roller bearings. The pinion is positioned forward of the ring gear centerline. All models have a 7 5/8 inch ring gear. Each ring gear has specific setup dimensions, A1 and A2 values, stamped onto the side area of the gear. The A1 and A2 values are unique to each ring gear/pinion and are determined during the manufacturers gear/pinion noise and vibration setup and testing.

Pinion position, ring gear position and carrier bearing preload are determined by shimming procedures.

XLR

The limited slip differential distributes torque/power to the rear wheels via individual axle shaft assemblies. The limited-slip differential is of a conventional separator plate and friction disc type design.

The differential housing, side covers, pinion housing, and differential case halves are constructed of cast aluminum. The internal components incorporate a hypoid gear set, ring and pinion, carrier assembly, and pinion housing assembly. The pinion is supported in a pinion housing by tapered roller bearings.

The pinion is positioned rearward of the ring gear centerline. Pinion position, ring gear position, and carrier bearing preload are determined by shimming procedures.

All models have an 8-inch ring gear.

Each ring gear has specific setup dimensions, A1 and A2 values, stamped onto the side area of the gear. The A1 and A2 values are unique to each ring gear/pinion and are determined during the manufacturers gear/pinion noise and vibration setup and testing.

The 2.93 ratio axle is standard equipment for 2004–05 automatic transmissions. The 2.73 ratio axle is standard for 2006–08 automatic transmissions.

The 2.56 ratio axle is standard equipment for 2006–08 XLR-V automatic transmissions.

TROUBLESHOOTING
Preliminary Inspections

Before the rear axle is to be serviced, ensure the source of the problem is the rear axle itself and not originating in other sources such as noise from the tires, road surface, engine, transmission, wheel bearings, muffler or body components. Perform the following procedures to inspect for other sources that could be mistaken for axle noise:

1. Ensure rear axle lubricant is at proper level and type, then select level asphalt road to reduce tire and body noise.
2. After vehicle has been driven far enough to warm lubricant, record speed noise occurs.
3. Stop vehicle.
4. With vehicle in neutral run engine slowly through RPM range that noise occurred to determine if noise was caused by exhaust or powertrain.
5. Inspect for tire noise by temporarily inflating all tires to approximately 50 psi for test purposes only.
6. Drive vehicle on level asphalt road and

(1) Ratio
(2) GM Part Number
(3) Getrag Part Number
(4) Serial Number

ARM0600000001022

Fig. 3   Axle identification. Solstice & SKY

(1) Ratio
(2) GM Part Number
(3) Getrag Part Number
(4) Serial Number

Available Axle Ratios

Axle Ratio	Drive/Engine	Flange Size
3:23	RWD/4.6L V8	105 mm
3:23	AWD/4.6L V8	96 mm
3:73	RWD/3.6L V6	105 mm
3:91	AWD/3.6L V6	96 mm

ARM0400000001041

Fig. 4   Axle identification. STS

observe if change in noise occurs compared to noise while tires are inflated at normal pressure.

7. After test is completed ensure tires are inflated to manufacturer's specifications.

8. Inspect front and rear wheel bearings by lightly applying brakes while keeping vehicle speed steady. If the noise diminishes, inspect front and rear wheel bearings by jacking up front wheels, then spinning or shaking them to determine if bearings are loose.

9. With vehicle jacked up, inspect for metal to metal contact: between spring and opening in frame; upper and lower control arm bushings, and frame and axle housing brackets. Ensure there is no metal to metal contact between floor of body and frame.

Diagnosis

CORVETTE, CTS, STS & XLR

Refer to **Figs. 6 through 10** for differential noise diagnosis.

GTO

Refer to **Figs. 11 through 15** for differential noise diagnosis.

SOLSTICE & SKY

Refer to **Figs. 16 through 20** for differential noise diagnosis.

DISASSEMBLE

Differential

CORVETTE & XLR

1. Remove rear axle assembly as outlined under "Rear Axle & Suspension" in "Corvette" or "XLR" chapter.

2. **On models equipped with automat-**

ic transmission, remove differential carrier seal plate from front of differential carrier housing, then O-ring. Discard O-ring.

3. **On all models,** remove differential carrier mount.

4. Remove fill plug washer and fill tag.

5. Remove drain plug, allowing fluid to drain into suitable container.

6. Remove mounting bolt and vehicle speed sensor.

7. Remove mounting bolts, righthand side differential carrier cover and O-ring seal, **Fig. 21.** Discard O-ring.

8. Install two 10 mm nuts onto righthand side transmission mounting stud and remove stud from block.

9. Remove mounting bolts and righthand side transmission stud mount from differential carrier.

10. Remove righthand side output shaft snap ring.

11. Remove differential case assembly from differential carrier using differential housing lifting tool No. J-42155, or equivalent.

12. Remove differential carrier cover bolts, then rear cover and O-ring seal. Discard O-ring.

13. Remove pinion cartridge bolts.

14. Heat differential carrier around pinion cartridge using heat gun tool No. J-25070, or equivalent.

15. Remove pinion cartridge from differential carrier by threading two long bolts into pinion cartridge.

16. Remove pinion cartridge O-ring seal. Discard O-ring.

17. Remove pinion cartridge shim pack from differential carrier. **Tag shim pack to indicate its installation position.**

18. Remove lefthand side differential carrier cover bolts, then the cover and O-ring. Discard O-ring.

CTS & STS

1. Remove bearing carrier bolts from pinion housing, **Fig. 22.**

2. Heat around pinion housing to ease

pinion removal using suitable heat gun.

3. Place two bolts in jackscrew holes, then tighten bolts equally to push out pinion assembly.

4. Remove pinion housing assembly, shims and O-ring seal from differential housing. **Tag shims for reference during assembly.**

5. Remove nine housing side cover bolts.

6. Remove housing side cover from housing using pry tabs.

7. Remove O-ring seal from cover.

8. Remove differential carrier from housing.

9. Remove axle oil seal from housing side cover.

10. Install bearing race remover tool No. J-42194, or equivalent, into bearing race, **Fig. 23.**

11. Place side cover on suitable press, then using pinion bearing race installer tool No. J-5590, or equivalent, press out bearing race and shim. **Tag shim and race for reference during assembly.**

12. Remove axle oil seal from housing.

13. Install bearing race remover tool No. J-42194, or equivalent, behind bearing race, **Fig. 24.**

14. Place housing on suitable press, then using pinion bearing race installer tool No. J-5590, or equivalent, press out bearing and race. **Tag shim and race for reference during assembly.**

GTO

1. Raise and support vehicle.

2. Remove rear suspension support, **Fig. 25.**

3. Mark relationship of inner constant velocity joints to axle shafts.

4. Remove inner drive shaft constant velocity joint bolts and retainer plates. Support drive shafts so that they do not hang.

5. Remove rear differential mount bolts from differential cover.

6. Remove differential carrier attach bolts from crossmember.

7. Remove differential carrier.

DRIVE AXLES

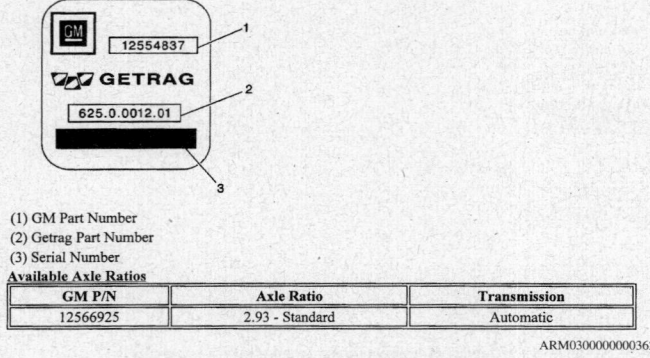

(1) GM Part Number
(2) Getrag Part Number
(3) Serial Number

Available Axle Ratios

GM P/N	Axle Ratio	Transmission
12566925	2.93 - Standard	Automatic

ARM0300000000362

Fig. 5   Axle identification. XLR

SOLSTICE & SKY

1. Open hood, then remove connector position assurance retainer.
2. Disconnect HO2S electrical connector from engine wiring harness electrical connector.
3. Raise and support vehicle, then remove HO2S and catalytic converter to muffler nuts.
4. Have an assistant support muffler assembly, then separate muffler insulators from hangers.
5. With aid of an assistant, remove muffler assembly.
6. Remove driveline tunnel closeout panel bolts and panel.
7. Support rear differential assembly with a suitable jack stand.
8. Remove left and right rear differential support bolts, then the front differential support bolt.
9. Remove propeller shaft bolts from transmission output flange, then the propeller shaft nut and bolts from differential drive flange.
10. Lower rear differential assembly enough to remove propeller shaft from vehicle.
11. Remove rear tire and wheel assemblies, then brake caliper bracket.
12. Without disconnecting brake hose from brake caliper, remove brake caliper and bracket as an assembly. Support with heavy mechanics wire or equivalent.
13. Remove and discard wheel drive shaft spindle nut.
14. Using tool No. J–42129 or equivalent, disengage wheel drive shaft from wheel bearing/hub.
15. Remove nut, and adjustment link.
16. Using tool No. J-42188-B or equivalent, separate rear adjustment link and ball joint from suspension knuckle. Do not loosen adjustment jamb nut.
17. Remove wheel drive shaft from vehicle using tool No. J-44394 or equivalent.
18. Position a transmission jack under differential, then secure differential to jack.
19. Remove front differential carrier bracket to frame bolt, then the left and right differential rear mounting bolts.
20. Lower jack slightly until mounting ear at front of differential clears support attachment point.
21. Remove differential from vehicle.

Cause	Correction
Important	
Inspect for the proper gear oil levels prior to performing system diagnosis.	
Transmission noise	Repair or replace as required.
Driveline assembly noise	Repair or replace as required.
Worn axle shaft constant velocity joints	Replace the constant velocity joints as required.
Worn, loose, or damaged axle mount and/or bracket	Repair or replace the axle mount and/or bracket as required.
Bearing noise within the differential assembly	A grinding or roar type noise will increase or decrease relative to the vehicle speed. 1. Inspect for the proper fluid level. Fill as required. 2. If the noise continues, repair or replace the unit as required.
Gear set whine noise within the differential assembly	A whine type noise will increase or decrease relative to the vehicle speed, approximately 31-37 km/h (50-60 mph). Typical causes of a gear set whine type noise may include incorrect backlash and/or pinion depth adjustment or worn or scored gear set teeth. 1. Inspect for the proper fluid level. Fill as required. 2. Repair or replace the unit as required.

ARM0400000001035

Fig. 6   Noisy In Drive. Corvette, CTS, STS & XLR

Drive Pinion

CORVETTE & XLR

1. Unstake drive pinion nut from drive pinion using suitable punch.
2. Remove drive pinion nut from drive pinion using spanner wrench tool No. J-42163 and pinion gear holder tool No. J-42164, or equivalents.
3. Remove drive pinion bearing using hydraulic press, V-blocks and side gear compressor tool No. J-42162, or equivalent. Discard bearing and spacer. **Drive pinion bearings and spacer must be replaced as a set.**
4. Remove front drive pinion bearing from drive pinion using hydraulic press, side gear compressor tool No. J-42162 and front pinion bearing remover tool No. J-42166, or equivalents. Discard bearing.
5. Remove front drive pinion bearing inner race from drive pinion housing using hydraulic press and bearing race remover tool No. J-42194, or equivalent. Discard bearing race.
6. Remove rear drive pinion bearing outer race from drive pinion housing using hydraulic press and bearing race remover tool No. J-42194, or equivalent. Discard bearing race.

CTS & STS

1. Remove pinion flange nut from pinion shaft using holding tool No. J-45012, or equivalent.
2. Remove pinion flange from shaft.

GTO

1. Drain rear axle lubricant into suitable container.
2. Center punch alignment marks on pinion flange, nut and end for assembly alignment.
3. Measure and record pinion shaft rotational torque.
4. Remove pinion flange nut and pinion flange using flange holding tool No. DT-47735, or equivalent.

5. Remove pinion seal using suitable seal puller.

SOLSTICE & SKY

1. Raise and support vehicle.
2. Remove driveline tunnel closeout panel.
3. Support rear drive module (RDM).
4. Remove bolt from differential case bracket assembly to body.
5. Remove propeller shaft coupler-to-differntial flange bolts, nuts, and washers. **Remove only propeller shaft coupler-to-differential flange bolts. Do not remove coupler from propeller shaft.**
6. Push rear propeller shaft toward front of vehicle in order to release propeller shaft coupler from differential pinion flange.
7. Lower propeller shaft and front of RDM until disconnected.
8. Carefully position propeller shaft out of way and support propeller shaft using a suitable jack.
9. Install holding fixture tool No. J 45012, or equivalent, onto flange.
10. While holding fixture tool No. J 45012, or equivalent, remove drive pinion nut, using tool hub nut socket tool No. J 34826, or equivalent.
11. Remove holding fixture tool No. J 45012, or equivalent.
12. Remove flange using flange and pinion cage remover tool No. J 45019, or equivalent.
13. Using a flat-bladed tool, remove drive pinion seal.

SUBASSEMBLY SERVICE

Standard Differential

1. If side carrier bearings are to be replaced, remove bearings using suitable bearing puller.
2. Remove differential pinion shaft lock bolt and pinion shaft.

Cause	Correction
Important	
Inspect for the proper gear oil levels prior to performing system diagnosis. Refer to Lubricant Level Inspection - Rear Drive Axle .	
Worn axle shaft constant velocity joints	Replace the constant velocity joints as required.
Worn, loose, or damaged axle mount and/or bracket	Repair or replace the axle mount and/or bracket as required.
Bearing noise within the differential assembly	A grinding or roar type noise will increase or decrease relative to the vehicle speed. 1. Inspect for the proper fluid level. Fill as required. 2. If the noise continues, repair or replace the unit as required.
Gear set whine noise within the differential assembly	A whine type noise will increase or decrease relative to the vehicle speed, approximately 31-37 km/h (50-60 mph). Typical causes of a gear set whine type noise may include incorrect backlash and/or pinion depth adjustment or worn or scored gear set teeth. 1. Inspect for the proper fluid level. Fill as required. 2. Repair or replace the unit as required.

ARM0400000001034

Fig. 7 Noisy When Coasting. Corvette, CTS, STS & XLR

Cause	Correction
Important	
Inspect for the proper gear oil levels prior to performing system diagnosis.	
Low gear oil levels	Faulty oil seals or other type leaks may contribute to lower than required fluid levels. Fill to the proper level with the correct gear oil and friction modifier additive.
Worn, loose, or damaged axle mount and/or bracket	Repair or replace the axle mount and/or bracket as required.
Bearing noise within the differential assembly	A grinding or roar type noise will increase or decrease relative to the vehicle speed. 1. Inspect for the proper fluid level. Fill as required. 2. If the noise continues, repair or replace the unit as required.
Gear set whine noise within the differential assembly	A whine type noise will increase or decrease relative to the vehicle speed, approximately 31-37 km/h (50-60 mph). Typical causes of a gear set whine type noise may include incorrect backlash and/or pinion depth adjustment or worn or scored gear set teeth. 1. Inspect for the proper fluid level. Fill as required. 2. Repair or replace the unit as required.

ARM0400000001032

Fig. 9 Constant Noise. Corvette, CTS, STS & XLR

Cause	Correction
Important	
Inspect for the proper gear oil levels prior to performing system diagnosis.	
Worn, loose, or damaged axle mount and/or bracket	Repair or replace the axle mount and/or bracket as required.
Incorrect gear oil	Replace with the correct gear oil and friction modifier additive.

ARM0400000001033

Fig. 8 Intermittent Noise. Corvette, CTS, STS & XLR

Cause	Correction
Important	
• Inspect for the proper gear oil levels prior to performing system diagnosis. • Operate the vehicle turning in tight circles in both left and right directions. A chatter type concern may indicate an incorrect type gear oil, lack of the friction modifier additive, or worn friction discs and/or plates.	
Worn or loose rear axle mount and/or bracket	Repair or replace as required.
Worn axle shaft constant velocity joints	Replace the constant velocity joints as required.
Worn wheel bearings	Replace the wheel bearings as required.
Incorrect gear oil	Drain and fill to the proper level with the correct gear oil and friction modifier additive. Adding friction modifier to the existing fluid without draining will not correct this condition.
Worn clutch plates	Replace the friction discs and plates as required.

ARM0400000001031

Fig. 10 Noisy On Turns. Corvette, CTS, STS & XLR

Inspect	Causes
Rear Axle Lubricant	Low lubricant level contamination

ARM0400000001036

Fig. 11 Noisy In Drive. GTO

3. Remove differential pinions and thrust washers, side gears and side gear thrust washers. Record installation position for assembly. Keep thrust washers with respective gears.
4. Remove bolts, ring gear and driving ring gear from case using drift and hammer. Ring gear bolts have lefthand hand threads. **Do not pry between ring gear and case.**
5. Inspect components as outlined in "Cleaning & Inspection."
6. Lubricate all components with specified gear lubricant prior to assembly.
7. Install thrust washers on side gears and mount side gears in case.
8. Position one differential pinion less thrust washer between side gears and rotate gears until pinion is directly opposite case loading opening.
9. Install other pinion with pinion shaft holes aligned, then rotate side gears and ensure pinions align with shaft openings in case.
10. When pinions are properly aligned, rotate pinions toward loading opening just enough and install thrust washer.
11. Align pinions with shaft opening in case, insert pinion shaft through case and install new lock bolt. **Do not tighten lock bolt now.**
12. Ensure ring gear and case mating surfaces are clean and free from burrs.
13. Mount gear on case, install two new mounting bolts at opposite sides of gear and alternately tighten bolts to draw gear on case.
14. Install remaining new ring gear bolts hand tight and ensure gear is squarely seated on case. **Do not use old bolts.**
15. Alternately **torque** ring gear bolts to 89 ft. lbs.
16. Press side bearings onto case. If using previously installed bearings, ensure they are installed in original positions.

Limited Slip
CORVETTE & XLR

1. Remove ring gear to differential case mounting bolts.
2. Separate ring gear from differential case using brass punch and hammer.
3. Remove righthand differential case side bearing from case using hydraulic press with righthand side differential bearing remover tool No. J-42159 and side gear compressor tool No. J-42162, or equivalents. Discard bearing.
4. Remove differential case bolts and separate righthand differential case from lefthand differential case.
5. Remove lefthand output shaft from differential case.
6. Remove lefthand clutch pack from differential case.
7. Keep plates and discs in specific order in which they were removed.
8. Inspect clutch plates and discs. If any plate or disc shows wear or scoring, replace complete pack.
9. Tag clutch pack to indicate installation position.
10. Remove lefthand differential case side bearing using hydraulic press with suitable V-blocks and side gear compressor tool No. J-42162, or equivalent.
11. Remove C-clip and lefthand output shaft from side gear.
12. Remove cross pin from righthand differential using hydraulic press and side gear compressor tool.
13. Record spider gears positions for installation alignment.
14. Remove spider gears from righthand differential case.
15. Remove righthand output shaft and side gear from differential case.
16. Remove righthand clutch pack from differential case, noting the following:
17. Keep plates and discs in specific order in which they were removed.

Inspect	Causes
Wheels or Tires	Imbalance or improper inflation
Front Wheel Bearings	Wear or damage
Propeller Shaft	Excessive drive line angle
Ring and Pinion Gears	• Incorrect backlash • Incorrect pinion depth • Wear or damage

ARM0400000001037

Fig. 12   Noisy When Coasting. GTO

Inspect	Causes
Wheels and Tires	Imbalance or improper inflation
Rear Axle Shafts	Excessive end play
Pinion Shaft or Pinion Bearing	Wear or damage
Differential Case Side Gear Hub	Worn, oversized or damage
Universal Joint	Wear or damage

ARM0400000001038

Fig. 13   Intermitten Noise. GTO

Inspect	Causes
Pinion Bearings	Wear or damage

ARM0400000001039

Fig. 14   Constant Noise. GTO

Inspect	Causes
Differential Side Gears and Pinion Gears	• Wear or damage • Excessive backlash

ARM0400000001040

Fig. 15   Noisy On Turns, GTO

18. Inspect clutch plates and discs. If any plate or disc shows wear or scoring, replace complete pack.
19. Tag clutch pack to indicate its installation position.

SOLSTICE & SKY

1. Remove ring gear bolts and ring gear from differential carrier using a punch and a hammer through bolt hole. Discard ring gear bolt.
2. Using tool No. J–22912-01 or equivalent and a press, remove side bearings. **It may be necessary to cut cage and remove rollers so tool will grip race.**
3. Pry halves apart using pry points. **Friction discs and separator plates develop specific wear patterns. During disc and plate removal, keep components in order in which they were removed.**
4. Remove axle side gear and clutch pack from right half.
5. Remove clutch pack and axle gear from right half. Note thick pressure plate side that has friction material faces away from gear teeth.
6. Remove beveled washer from axle side gear. Note that orientation of beveled washer faces out.
7. Tag clutch pack to indicate position of components.
8. Using tool No. J–42162 and a press, apply light pressure so differential shaft can be removed.
9. Remove differential shaft, release pressure from press.
10. Remove pinion gears and washers, then clutch pack and axle gear from left half. Note thick pressure plate side that has friction material faces away from gear teeth.
11. Remove beveled washer from axle side gear. Note that orientation of the beveled washer faces out.
12. Tag clutch pack to indicate position of components.

CLEANING & INSPECTION

1. Clean components in solvent and blow dry with compressed air.
2. Keep all components in order to ensure proper assembly.
3. Do not use brush when cleaning bearings.
4. Do not spin dry bearings.

5. Lightly lubricate components after cleaning.
6. Inspect gears for cracks, chipped teeth, wear and scoring and damaged bearing or mounting surfaces. Replace gears that are damaged or excessively worn. **Ring gear and pinion must be replaced as an assembly.**
7. Inspect differential case for cracks, damage, worn side gear bores and scored bearing surfaces.
8. Inspect housing for scored bearing mount surfaces, cracks and distortion.
9. Inspect bearing rollers and races for pitting, scoring, overheating and damage.
10. Mate bearing with race and inspect operation.
11. Replace bearings that are damaged, excessively worn or that fail to operate smoothly.
12. Mount differential case along with side bearings and ring gear in housing and measure runout with side bearings adjusted for zero preload and dial indicator positioned against machined edge of ring gear.
13. If runout exceeds .003 inch and gear cannot be positioned to eliminate runout, ring gear and/or case should be replaced.

ADJUSTMENTS

Differential Side Bearing Preload

CORVETTE & XLR

1. Place depth gauge tool No. J-42168-7, or equivalent, onto flat of gauge block tool No. J-42168-2, or equivalent, **Fig. 26.**
2. Place depth gauge tool plunger tip against bottom of differential carrier bearing bore. Tighten setscrew to lock plunger into place.
3. Install gauge block tool No. J-42168-6, or equivalent, onto gauge plate tool No. J-42168-5, or equivalent, with proper gear step closest to the outer edge.
4. Install gauge plate tool into suitable vise, **Fig. 27.**
5. Mount ring gear and case assembly onto gauge plate tool. Ensure lefthand side bearing seats in lefthand side bearing race.

6. Place depth gauge tool No. J-42168-7, or equivalent, onto back face of ring gear.
7. Measure distance between depth gauge tool and block.
8. Determine proper shim thickness, then tag lefthand side bearing shim pack for assembly as follows:
   a. Ring gear value stamping is in millimeters.
   b. If ring gear has a zero (0) stamping, measured value is shim thickness.
   c. If ring gear has plus (+) or minus (−) value stamped on it, add or subtract that value from feeler gauge reading to calculate shim thickness.
9. Remove gauge block tools from differential housing.
10. Install righthand side cover bearing race using suitable hydraulic press and race installer tool No. J-42172, or equivalent, **Fig. 28.**
11. Install lefthand side bearing race and shim pack into differential housing using suitable hydraulic press and race installer tool.
12. Place differential carrier onto ring gear holder tool No. J-42173, or equivalent.
13. Install ring gear and case into differential carrier using differential case lifting tool No. J-42155, or equivalent.
14. Install righthand side differential carrier cover and bolts. **Torque** mounting bolts to 18 ft. lbs.
15. Position suitable dial indicator onto end of righthand axle shaft, **Fig. 29.**
16. Grip output shaft, then move it up and down to measure total travel, **Fig. 30.**
17. Add .004 inch to measurement from previous step. This is righthand side outer bearing race shim pack size.
18. Remove righthand side differential carrier cover and bolts.
19. Remove righthand side outer bearing race using hydraulic press and bearing race remover tool No. J-42194, or equivalent.
20. Install righthand side outer bearing race and shim pack.
21. Install bearing race using hydraulic press and race installer tool No. J-42172, or equivalent.
22. Install lefthand side output shaft bearing into cover using hydraulic press and bearing installer tool No. J-42157, or equivalent.
23. Install lefthand side axle seal into cover using seal installer tool No. J-36797, or equivalent.

Cause	Correction
Inspect for the proper gear oil levels prior to performing system diagnosis.	
Worn clutch disc and/or pressure plate assembly	Repair or replace as required. Refer to Clutch Noisy in Clutch.
Transmission noise	Repair or replace as required.
Worn axle shaft constant velocity joints	Replace the constant velocity joints as required.
Worn, loose, or damaged axle mount and/or bracket	Repair or replace the axle mount and/or bracket as required.
Bearing noise within the differential assembly	A grinding or roar type noise will increase or decrease relative to the vehicle speed. 1. Check for the proper fluid level. Fill as required. 2. If the noise continues, repair or replace the unit as required.
Gear set whine noise within the differential assembly	A whine type noise will increase or decrease relative to the vehicle speed, approximately 80-96 km/h (50-60 mph). Typical causes of a gear set whine type noise may include incorrect backlash and/or pinion depth adjustment or worn or scored gear set teeth. 1. Check for the proper fluid level. Fill as required. 2. Repair or replace the unit as required.

ARM0500000000043

Fig. 16 Noisy In Drive. Solstice & SKY

Cause	Correction
Important	
Inspect for the proper gear oil levels prior to performing system diagnosis.	
Worn, loose, or damaged axle mount and/or bracket	Repair or replace the axle mount and/or bracket as required.
Incorrect gear oil	Replace with the correct gear oil and friction modifier additive.

ARM0500000000045

Fig. 18 Intermittent Noise. Solstice & SKY

24. Remove ring gear and case from differential housing using differential case lifting tool No. J-42155, or equivalent.

Drive Pinion Depth

CORVETTE & XLR

1. Install gauge cylinder tool No. J-42168-1 and gauge block tool No. J-42168-2, or equivalents, into differential housing in lefthand side bearing race location, **Fig. 31.**
2. Measure distance between tip of gauge cylinder tool No. J-42168-1 and gauge block tool No. J-42168-2, or equivalents. **If pinion gear has plus (+) or minus (–) number stamped on end, shim thickness must be adjusted by that amount.**
3. Subtract measured value from .10826 inch. Value of .10826 inch is shim thickness required if pinion has zero stamped on end.
4. Remove gauge cylinder and gauge block tools from carrier.

ASSEMBLE

Differential

CORVETTE & XLR

1. Install righthand clutch pack into differential case. Install steel plates and friction discs alternately, thicker friction washer, concave washer, then steel washer.
2. Install righthand output shaft and spider gears into differential case.
3. Install cross pin into differential case using hydraulic press and side gear compressor tool No. J-42162, or equivalent.
4. Install lefthand output shaft into side gear, and C-clip onto shaft.
5. Install lefthand differential case side bearing using bearing installer tool No. J-42160, or equivalent.
6. Install lefthand clutch pack into differential case. Install steel plates and friction discs alternately, thicker friction washer, concave washer, then steel washer.
7. Install lefthand output shaft and side gear into differential case.
8. Install lefthand differential case to righthand differential case.
9. **Torque** differential case bolts, to 41 ft. lbs.
10. Install ring gear onto differential case.
11. Install ring gear bolts using ring gear holder tool No. J-42173, or equivalent, to support differential case. **Torque** bolts to 144 ft. lbs.
12. Install righthand differential case side bearing using bearing installer tool No. J-42160, or equivalent.
13. Install gauge block tool No. J-42168-2 and plug tool No. J-42168-12, or equivalents, into drive pinion location of differential carrier.
14. Place depth gauge tool No. J-42168-7, or equivalent, onto flat end of gauge block tool No. J-42168-2, or equivalent, **Fig. 26.**
15. Place tip of plunger on depth gauge tool No. J-42168-7, or equivalent, against bottom of bearing bore in differential carrier. Tighten set screw to lock plunger in place.
16. Install gauge block tool No. J-42168-6,

Cause	Correction
Important	
Inspect for the proper gear oil levels prior to performing system diagnosis.	
Worn axle shaft constant velocity joints	Replace the constant velocity joints as required.
Worn, loose, or damaged axle mount and/or bracket	Repair or replace the axle mount and/or bracket as required.
Bearing noise within the differential assembly	A grinding or roar type noise will increase or decrease relative to the vehicle speed. 1. Check for the proper fluid level. Fill as required. 2. If the noise continues, repair or replace the unit as required.
Gear set whine noise within the differential assembly	A whine type noise will increase or decrease relative to the vehicle speed, approximately 31-37 km/h (50-60 mph). Typical causes of a gear set whine type noise may include incorrect backlash and/or pinion depth adjustment or worn or scored gear set teeth. 1. Check for the proper fluid level. Fill as required. 2. Repair or replace the unit as required.

ARM0500000000044

Fig. 17 Noisy When Coasting. Solstice & SKY

Cause	Correction
Important	
Inspect for the proper gear oil levels prior to performing system diagnosis.	
Low gear oil levels	Faulty oil seals or other type leaks may contribute to lower than required fluid levels. Fill to the proper level with the correct gear oil and friction modifier additive.
Worn, loose, or damaged axle mount and/or bracket	Repair or replace the axle mount and/or bracket as required.
Bearing noise within the differential assembly	A grinding or roar type noise will increase or decrease relative to the vehicle speed. 1. Check for the proper fluid level. Fill as required. 2. If the noise continues, repair or replace the unit as required.
Gear set whine noise within the differential assembly	A whine type noise will increase or decrease relative to the vehicle speed, approximately 31-37 km/h (50-60 mph). Typical causes of a gear set whine type noise may include incorrect backlash and/or pinion depth adjustment or worn or scored gear set teeth. 1. Check for the proper fluid level. Fill as required. 2. Repair or replace the unit as required.

ARM0500000000046

Fig. 19 Constant Noise. Solstice & SKY

Cause	Correction
Important	
• Inspect for the proper gear oil levels prior to performing system diagnosis. • Operate the vehicle turning in tight circles in both left and right directions. A chatter type concern may indicate an incorrect type gear oil, lack of the friction modifier additive, or worn friction discs and/or plates.	
Worn or loose rear axle mount and/or bracket	Repair or replace as required.
Worn axle shaft constant velocity joints	Replace the constant velocity joints as required.
Worn wheel bearings	Replace the wheel bearings as required.
Incorrect gear oil	Fill to the proper level with the correct gear oil and friction modifier additive.

ARM0500000000047

Fig. 20 Noisy On Turns. Solstice & SKY

or equivalent, onto gauge plate tool No. J-42168-5, or equivalent, with proper gear step closest to outer edge.
17. Place ring gear and case assembly onto gauge plate tool No. J-42168-5, or equivalent, **Fig. 27.**
18. Remove depth gauge tool No. J-42168-7, or equivalent. If ring gear has plus (+) or minus (–) stamped on the side the shim thickness must be adjusted by that amount.
19. Measure distance between plunger tip of depth gauge tool No. J-42168-7 and gauge block tool No. J-42168-6, or equivalents, **Fig. 27.** This distance is shim thickness required if ring gear has zero stamped on side.
20. Remove gauge block and plug tools.
21. Install lefthand side shim pack into housing.
22. Install lefthand side outer bearing race into carrier using bearing race installer tool No. J-42172, or equivalent.
23. Install output shaft bearing into lefthand differential carrier cover using hydraulic press and output shaft bearing installer tool No. J-42157, or equivalent.
24. Install new output shaft oil seal into lefthand differential carrier cover using seal installer tool No. J-36797, or equivalent.
25. Install new O-ring seal into lefthand

cover. **Torque** cover mounting bolts to 18 ft. lbs.

26. Place differential carrier on rear gear holder tool No. J-42173, or equivalent.
27. Install ring gear and case assembly into differential carrier using differential case lifting tool No. J-42155, or equivalent.
28. Install righthand side differential carrier cover and **torque** mounting bolts to 18 ft. lbs.
29. Position measuring tool No. J-8001, or equivalent, onto end of righthand axle shaft, **Fig. 29**.
30. Move output shaft up and down and measure total travel. To obtain proper size shim, add .004 inch to total travel measurement.
31. Remove righthand side outer bearing race using hydraulic press and bearing race remover tool No. J-42194, or equivalent.
32. Install righthand side shim pack into differential carrier cover.
33. Install righthand side outer bearing race using hydraulic press and bearing race installer tool No. J-42172, or equivalent.
34. Install righthand side output shaft bearing using hydraulic press and bearing installer tool No. J-42157, or equivalent.
35. Install righthand side output shaft oil seal into carrier cover using seal installer tool No. J-36797, or equivalent.
36. Remove ring gear and case assembly from differential carrier using differential case lifting tool No. J-42155, or equivalent.
37. Install lefthand side carrier cover with new O-ring. **Torque** cover mounting bolts to 18 ft. lbs.
38. Install drive pinion shim pack onto pinion cartridge.
39. Lubricate new pinion cartridge O-ring seal with clean engine oil, and install into groove on pinion cartridge.
40. Heat differential carrier around drive pinion cartridge opening using heat gun tool No. J-25070, or equivalent, and install drive pinion cartridge into differential carrier.
41. **Torque** drive pinion cartridge bolts to 41 ft. lbs.
42. Measure pinion rotating torque using torque wrench and pinion gear holder tool No. J-42164, or equivalent. Measurement should not be more than 22 inch lbs.
43. Install rear differential cover, magnet and O-ring . **Torque** rear cover mounting bolts to 89 inch lbs.
44. Install differential case assembly into carrier using differential case lifting tool No. J-42155, or equivalent.
45. Install C-clip onto righthand output shaft.
46. Install righthand side transmission stud mount and **torque** mounting bolts to 89 inch lbs.
47. **Torque** righthand side transmission mounting stud to 31 ft. lbs.
48. Install righthand side differential carrier cover and O-ring. **Torque** mounting bolts to 18 ft. lbs.
49. Install vehicle speed sensor and

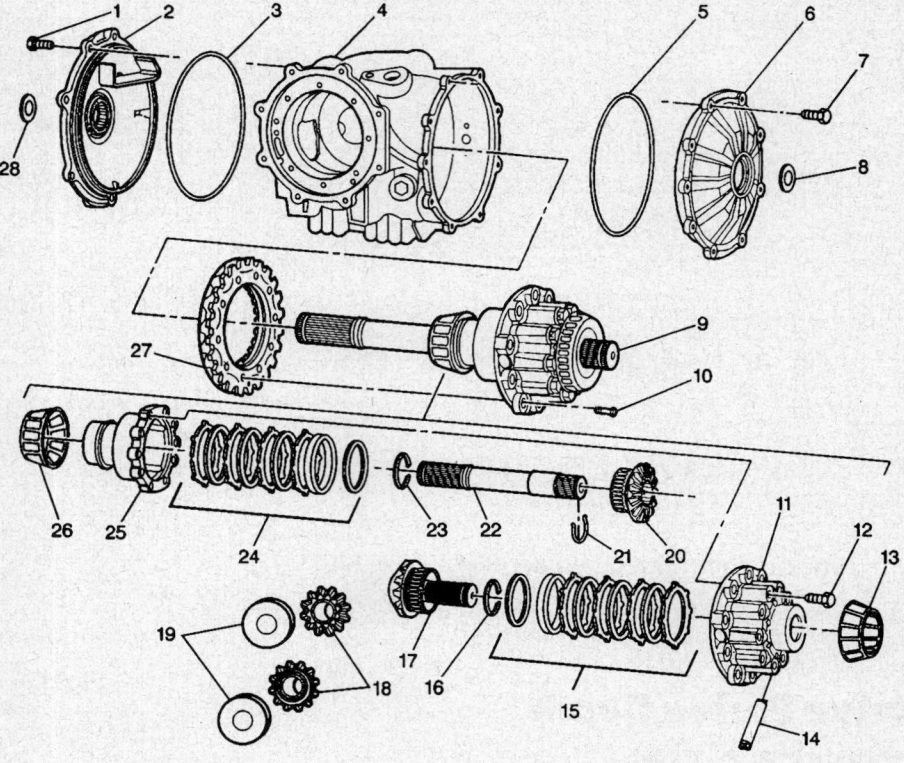

(1) Bolt
(2) Left Side Cover
(3) O-Ring Seal
(4) ifferential Carrier
(5) O-Ring Seal
(6) Right Side Cover
(7) Bolt
(8) Output Shaft Oil Seal
(9) Differential Case Assembly
(10) Bolt
(11) Right Side Differential Case
(12) Bolt
(13) Bearing
(14) Pin
(15) Clutch Pack
(16) C-Clip
(17) Right Output Gear and Shaft
(18) Side Gears
(19) Side Gear Washers
(20) Left Output Gear
(21) C-Clip
(22) Left Output Shaft
(23) C-Clip
(24) Clutch Pack

GC3039700363000X

Fig. 21   Exploded view of differential assembly. Corvette & XLR

torque mounting bolt to 89 inch lbs.
50. **Torque** axle lubricant drain plug to 26 ft. lbs.
51. Fill differential with synthetic axle lubricant part No. 12378261 and limited slip additive part No. 1052358, or equivalent.
52. Install axle lubricant fill tag and washer. **Torque** plug to 26 ft. lbs.

SOLSTICE & SKY

1. Install a beveled washer on axle side gear with bevel facing out.
2. Install a thick pressure plate with friction material facing away from gear teeth.
3. **Friction discs and separator plates develop specific wear patterns. During disc and plate installation, keep components in the order in which they were removed.**
4. Install steel plate against friction material of pressure plate. Alternate installation of steel plates and friction discs.
5. Ensure that last steel plate of clutch pack is against case half. Repeat procedure for other side.

6. Install assembled axle side gear into right case half, then align tabs on steel plates to fit grooves.
7. Install assembled axle side gear into left case half, then align tabs on steel plates to fit grooves.
8. Using tool No. J–42162 or equivalent and a press, apply light pressure on pinion gears and washers so they align with pinion differential shaft bores.
9. Install differential shaft ensuring that it moves through washers and gears properly.
10. Align bolt holes between halves and lightly press them together.

Drive Pinion

CORVETTE & XLR

Drive pinion bearings and spacer must be replaced as a set.

1. Install front drive pinion bearing inner race into drive pinion housing using hydraulic press and bearing race installer tool No. J-42172, or equivalent.
2. Install rear drive pinion bearing outer

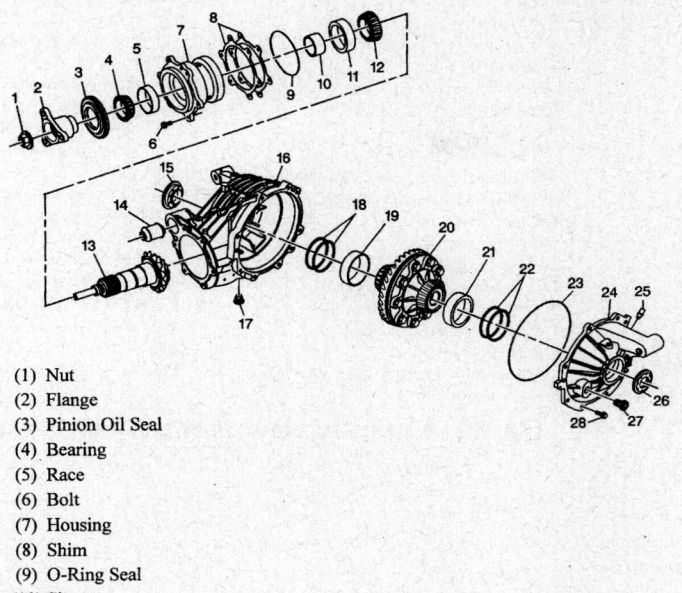

(1) Nut
(2) Flange
(3) Pinion Oil Seal
(4) Bearing
(5) Race
(6) Bolt
(7) Housing
(8) Shim
(9) O-Ring Seal
(10) Sleeve
(11) Race
(12) Bearing
(13) Pinion Gear
(14) Mount Bushing
(15) Axle Oil Seal
(16) Differential Housing

ARM66GC000000809

Fig. 22   Exploded view of differential assembly (Part 1 of 2). CTS & STS

(17) Drain Plug
(18) Shim
(19) Race
(20) Differential Assembly
(21) Race
(22) Shim
(23) O-Ring Seal
(24) Housing Cover
(25) Vent
(26) Axle Seal
(27) Fill Plug
(28) Bolt

ARM66GC000000810

Fig. 22   Exploded view of differential assembly (Part 2 of 2). CTS & STS

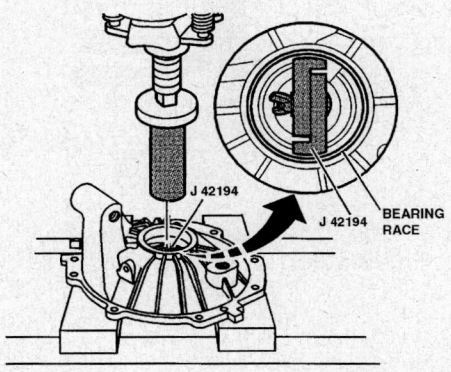

ARM66GC000000811

Fig. 23   Side cover bearing race removal. CTS & STS

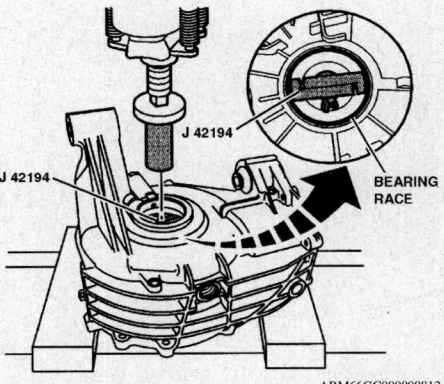

ARM66GC000000812

Fig. 24   Housing bearing race removal. CTS & STS

race into drive pinion housing using hydraulic press and bearing race installer tool No. J-42170, or equivalent.

3. Install front pinion bearing onto drive pinion using hydraulic press, pinion bearing installer tool No. J-42160 and pinion gear holder tool No. J-42164, or equivalents.
4. Install drive pinion and bearing into drive pinion housing.
5. Install drive pinion bearing spacer onto drive pinion.
6. Install rear drive pinion bearing onto drive pinion using hydraulic press, pinion bearing installer tool No. J-42160 and pinion gear holder tool No. J-42164, or equivalents.
7. Install drive pinion nut and **torque** to 392 ft. lbs., using a ¾ inch torque wrench, spanner wrench tool No. J-42163 and pinion gear holder tool No. J-42164, or equivalents.
8. Stake areas of drive pinion nut into two notches in end of drive pinion.

GTO

1. Coat pinion shaft splines with suitable gear oil.
2. Lubricate seal with suitable gear oil.
3. Install new pinion shaft seal until it is flush with differential housing, using pinion seal installer tool No. DT-46853, or equivalent.
4. Install pinion flange on to shaft aligning punch marks.
5. Install pinion flange holding tool No. DT-47735, or equivalent, on pinion flange.
6. Apply thread locking compound to pinion shaft threads.
7. Tighten pinion nut until three punch marks are aligned. **Do not overtighten pinion nut.**
8. Tighten nut to position no more than 5° past punch marks.

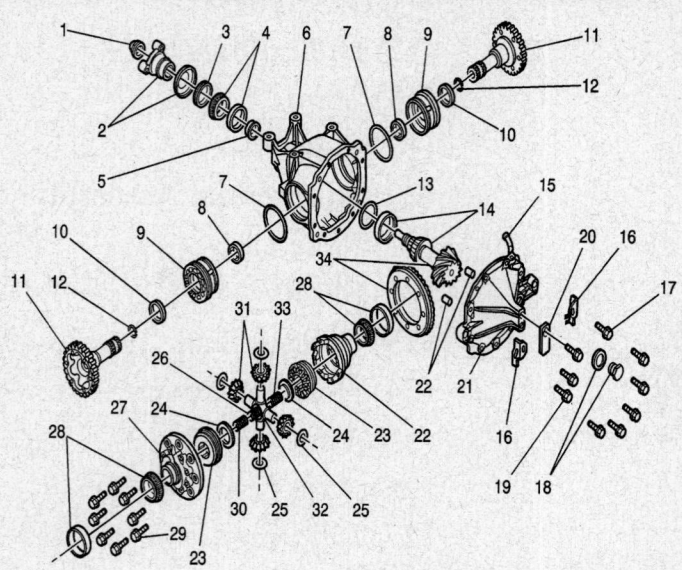

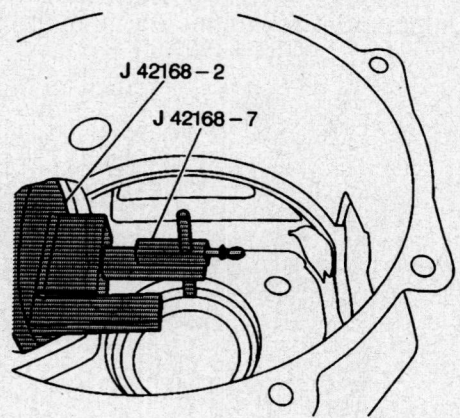
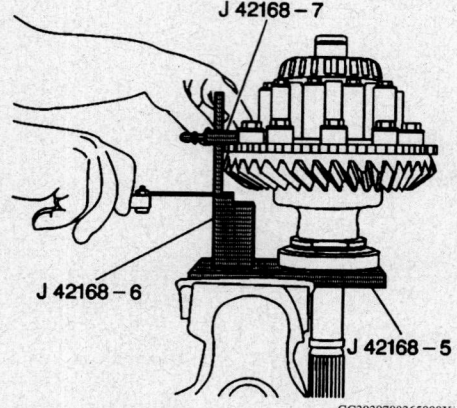
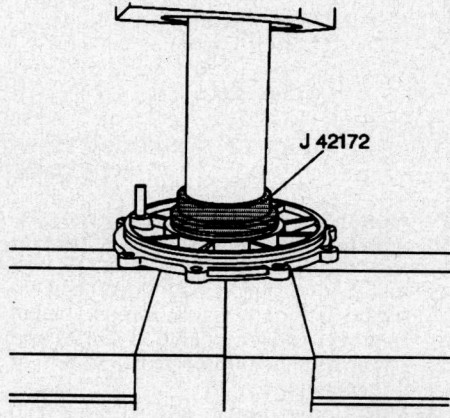

(1) Pinion Nut
(2) Pinion Flange Assembly
(3) Pinon Oil Seal
(4) Front Pinon Bearing
(5) Pinon Bearing Spacer
(6) Differential Carrier
(7) Screw Adjuster O-ring
(8) Inner Axle Shaft Bearing Assembly
(9) Side Bearing Adjusting Screw Bearing Assembly
(10) Inner Axle Shaft Seal
(11) Inner Axle Shaft
(12) Inner Axle Shaft Retainer Clip
(13) Pinion Position Adjusting Shims
(14) Rear Pinion Bearing Assembly
(15) Differential Breather Assembly
(16) Screw Adjuster Lock Plate
(17) Rear Cover Attaching Bolts

(18) Differential Filler Plug and Gasket
(19) Differential Drain Plug
(20) Lubrication Tag
(21) Differential Housing Cover
(22) Dowel Pins
(23) Side Gear Clutch Cone
(24) Thrust Spring Plate
(25) Differential Pinion Gear Thrust Washer
(26) Differential Pre-load Spring - Middle
(27) Differential Case
(28) Differential Side Bearing Assembly
(29) Differential Case Cover Bolts
(30) Differential Spring Pre-load - Inner
(31) Differential Pinon Gears
(32) Pinion Cross Shaft
(33) Differential Pre-load Spring - Outer
(34) Ring and Pinion Gear

ARM0500000000049

Fig. 25 Exploded view of differential. (Part 2 of 2) GTO

ARM0500000000048

Fig. 25 Exploded view of differential. (Part 1 of 2) GTO

Fig. 26 Depth gauge & block setup. Corvette & XLR

GC3039700364000X

Fig. 27 Gauge plate tool installation in vise. Corvette & XLR

GC3039700365000X

Fig. 28 Righthand side cover bearing race installation. Corvette & XLR

GC3039700366000X

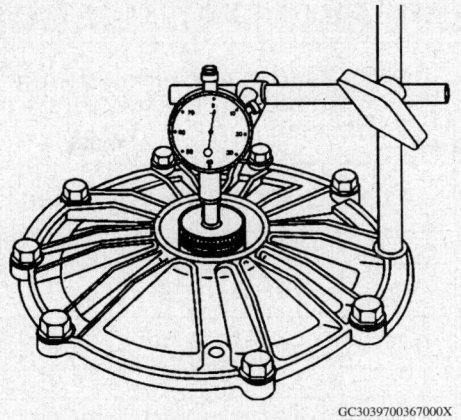

GC3039700367000X

Fig. 29 Dial indicator installation onto righthand axle shaft. Corvette & XLR

J 8001

GC3039700368000X

Fig. 30 Output shaft total travel measurement. Corvette & XLR

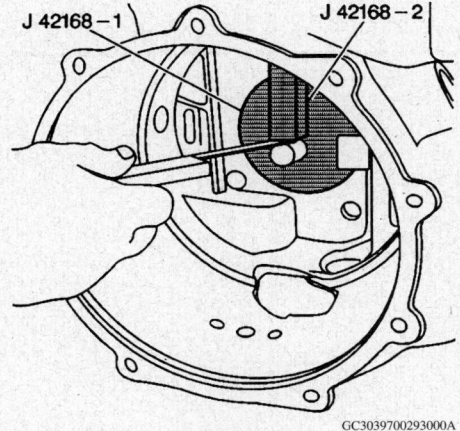

J 42168–1   J 42168–2

GC3039700293000A

Fig. 31 Pinion depth measurement. Corvette & XLR

DRIVE AXLE SPECIFICATIONS

Year	Ratio	Ring Gear Back-lash, Inch	Pinion Flange Rotational Torque, Inch Lbs.	Ring Gear/ Pinion Nominal Value, Inch		Pinion Bearing Preload, Inch Lbs.		Total Assembly Preload, Inch Lbs.		Differential Bearings, Inch Lbs.	
				A1	A2	New	Used	New	Used	Used	New
CORVETTE											
2004–05	2.73	.0067–.0082	12–25	4.055	2.93	②	②	②	②	②	②
	3.15–3.42	.0067–.0082	12–25	4.055	2.58	②	②	②	②	②	②
2006–08	2.56	.0063-.0102	12–25	③	2.93	②	②	②	②	②	②
	2.73	.0063-.0102	12–25	③	2.59	②	②	②	②	②	②
	3.42	.0063-.0102	12–25	③	2.58	②	②	②	②	②	②
CTS											
2004–08	3.23	.009–.014	22–35	4.37	2.50	②	②	②	②	②	②
	3.42	.009–.014	22–35	4.37	2.50	②	②	②	②	②	②
	3.73	.008–.013	22–35	4.37	2.50	②	②	②	②	②	②
GTO											
2004–06	3.46	—	2–4	—	—	—	—	—	—	—	—
SOLSTICE & SKY											
2006–08	3.91	.010–.016	22–35	4.37	2.50	②	②	②	②	②	②
STS											
2005–08	3.23	①	22–35	4.37	2.50	②	②	②	②	②	②
	3.73	.007–.012	22–35	4.37	2.50	②	②	②	②	②	②
	3.91	.010–.016	22–35	4.37	2.50	②	②	②	②	②	②
XLR & XLRV											
2004	2.93	.0067–.0082	12–25	4.055	2.93	②	②	②	②	②	②
2005–08	2.56	.0063–.0102	12–25	4.055	2.93	②	②	②	②	②	②
	2.93	.0063–.0102	12–25	4.055	2.93	②	②	②	②	②	②

① — 4.6L engine w/AWD, .008–.013 inch; 4.6L engine w/RWD, .009–.014 inch.

② — Adjustment is determined by markings on ring gear & pinion set.

③ — Base; 4.055 inch., Z06; 4.449 inch.

TIRE PRESSURE MONITORING SYSTEM

INDEX

Page No.

Component Service 28-66
Pressure Monitor Sensor
  Programming 28-67
  Alero & Grand Am 28-67
  Bonneville 28-67
  CTS 28-68
  Century & Regal 28-67
  Corvette 28-67
  DTS, Lucerne & STS 28-68
  Deville & Seville 28-68
  Grand Prix & LaCrosse 28-69
  Impala & Monte Carlo......... 28-69
  LeSabre & Park Avenue 28-69
  Vibe 28-70
  XLR 28-69
Pressure Monitor Sensor
  Replacement 28-70
Resetting Tire Pressure Monitor
  Lamp 28-66
  Alero & Grand Am 28-66
  Bonneville 28-66
  CTS, DTS, STS, Vibe & XLR . 28-66
  Century & Regal 28-66
  Corvette 28-66
  DeVille & Seville 28-66
  Grand Prix 28-66
  Impala & Monte Carlo......... 28-67

Page No.

  LeSabre & Park Avenue 28-67
  Lucerne 28-67
Description 28-2
Diagnosis & Testing 28-2
  Accessing Diagnostic Trouble
   Codes 28-2
  Clearing Diagnostic Trouble
   Codes 28-2
  Diagnostic Tests 28-2
   Alero & Grand Am 28-2
   Bonneville 28-2
   CTS 28-2
   Century & Regal 28-2
   Corvette 28-2
   DTS 28-2
   Deville & Seville 28-2
   Grand Prix 28-2
   Impala & Monte Carlo....... 28-2
   LaCrosse 28-2
   LeSabre & Park Avenue 28-2
   Lucerne 28-2
   STS 28-2
   Vibe 28-2
   XLR 28-2
  Intermittent & Poor
   Connections 28-2
   Intermittents 28-2

Page No.

  Poor Connections............. 28-2
Wiring Diagrams 28-2
  Alero & Grand Am 28-2
  Bonneville 28-2
  CTS 28-2
  Century & Regal 28-2
  Corvette 28-2
  DTS 28-2
  Deville & Seville 28-2
  Grand Prix 28-2
  Impala & Monte Carlo........ 28-2
  LaCrosse 28-2
  LeSabre & Park Avenue 28-2
  Lucerne 28-2
  STS 28-2
  Vibe 28-2
  XLR 28-2
Diagnostic Chart Index 28-10
Precautions.................... 28-1
  Air Bag Systems.............. 28-1
  Battery Ground Cable......... 28-1
  Hybrid Battery Service 28-1
   Connect 28-1
   Disconnect 28-1
Tightening Specifications 28-70

PRECAUTIONS

Air Bag Systems

Refer to "Air Bag System Precautions" in the front of this manual for system disarming and arming procedures.

Battery Ground Cable

Prior to service, disconnect battery ground cable and isolate as required.

Hybrid Battery Service

DISCONNECT

To help avoid personal injury, always ensure the ignition switch is in the OFF position and the ignition key has been removed prior to working on any 36V components. After the key has been removed, disconnect the negative battery cable and then open the generator battery disconnect control module cover. After waiting for at least 5 minutes, measure the voltage potential using a DMM between the following: 36V positive and negative battery cables; 36V positive battery cable and vehicle ground; 36V negative battery cable and vehicle ground. All measured voltage levels must be below 3 volts.

1. Remove ignition key from ignition switch.
2. Secure ignition key to ensure that key CANNOT be installed without your knowledge.
3. Disconnect 12 volt negative battery cable.
4. Fold down both rear seat backs, then carefully lift up on load floor rear compartment cover at retaining clip locations, **Fig. 1.**
5. Tilt load floor rear compartment cover towards rear of vehicle slightly, disengage tabs and remove load floor rear compartment cover. **To avoid personal injury, be careful when working in vicinity of generator battery disconnect control module. Internal components will still be live, 36V potential, even when cover has been opened or removed.**
6. Remove generator battery disconnect control module cover bolt, **Fig. 2.**
7. Open and slide generator battery disconnect control module cover to right, removing cover. **Wait at least 5 minutes in order to allow generator control module capacitors to discharge.**
8. **Never assume battery pack is disabled when generator battery disconnect control module cover is opened. Generator battery will have to be checked for voltage potential using a voltmeter first.**
9. Set voltmeter to DC voltage and measure vehicle 12-volt battery voltage (at 12-volt positive jumper location and negative battery cable).
10. Meter should read greater than 12 volts DC.
11. To ensure generator battery has been disabled, check generator battery for voltage potential as follows:
    a. Refer to **Fig. 3** for voltage measurement locations.
    b. Measure from positive stud to negative stud, voltage should be less than 3 volts.
    c. Measure from positive stud to vehicle chassis ground, voltage should be less than 3 volts.
    d. Measure from negative stud to vehicle chassis ground, voltage should be less than 3 volts.
12. After verifying there is no voltage present, vehicle is now safe to work on.

CONNECT

1. Install and close generator battery disconnect control module cover.
2. Install generator battery cover bolt and **torque** to 89 inch lbs.
3. Tilt load floor rear compartment cover towards rear of vehicle slightly in order to insert tabs into battery tray rear support.
4. Set load floor rear compartment cover down, ensure retaining clips align to proper locations, carefully push down to secure cover.

5. Place rear seats backs to their proper positions.
6. Connect 12 volt negative battery cable.

DESCRIPTION

The tire pressure monitor (TPM) system alerts the driver when a large change in the pressure of one tire exists. The system detects a tire pressure condition while the vehicle is in motion, once a tire pressure condition is detected, the system alerts the driver whenever the ignition is turned On.

The TPM system uses electronic brake control module, wheel speed sensors, pressure sensors, data messages and instrument cluster to perform system functions as required.

DIAGNOSIS & TESTING

Accessing Diagnostic Trouble Codes

Connect a suitably programmed scan tool to Data Link Connector (DLC) and follow manufacturer's instructions.

Wiring Diagrams

ALERO & GRAND AM

Refer to **Fig. 4** for wiring diagram.

BONNEVILLE

Refer to **Fig. 5** for wiring diagram.

CENTURY & REGAL

Refer to **Fig. 6** for wiring diagram.

CORVETTE

Refer to **Figs. 7 and 8** for wiring diagram.

CTS

Refer to **Figs. 9 and 10** for wiring diagram.

DEVILLE & SEVILLE

Refer to **Figs. 11 and 12** for wiring diagrams.

DTS

Refer to **Fig. 13** for wiring diagram.

GRAND PRIX

Refer to **Figs. 14 and 15** for wiring diagram.

IMPALA & MONTE CARLO

Refer to **Figs. 16 and 17** for wiring diagram.

LACROSSE

Refer to **Figs. 18 and 19** for wiring diagram.

LESABRE & PARK AVENUE

Refer to **Fig. 20** for wiring diagram.

LUCERNE

Refer to **Fig. 21** for wiring diagram.

STS

Refer to **Figs. 22 and 23** for wiring diagram.

XLR

Refer to **Fig. 24** for wiring diagram.

VIBE

Refer to **Figs. 25 and 26** for wiring diagram.

Diagnostic Tests

ALERO & GRAND AM

Refer to **Figs. 27 through 31** for diagnostic test procedures.

BONNEVILLE

Refer to **Figs. 32 through 37** for diagnostic test procedures.

CENTURY & REGAL

Refer to **Figs. 38 through 43** for diagnostic test procedures.

CORVETTE

Refer to **Figs. 44 through 49** for diagnostic test procedures.

CTS

Refer to **Figs. 50 through 57** for diagnostic test procedures.

DEVILLE & SEVILLE

Refer to **Figs. 58 and 59** for diagnostic test procedures.

DTS

Refer to **Figs. 60 through 68** for diagnostic test procedures.

GRAND PRIX

Refer to **Figs. 69 through 76** for diagnostic test procedures.

IMPALA & MONTE CARLO

Refer to **Figs. 77 through 91** for diagnostic test procedures.

LACROSSE

Refer to **Figs. 92 through 98** for diagnostic test procedures.

LESABRE & PARK AVENUE

Refer to **Figs. 99 and 100** for diagnostic test procedures.

LUCERNE

Refer to **Figs. 101 through 106** for diagnostic test procedures.

STS

Refer to **Figs. 107 through 114** for diagnostic test procedures.

XLR

Refer to **Figs. 115 through 120** for diagnostic test procedures.

VIBE

Refer to **Figs. 121 through 136** for diagnostic test procedures.

Clearing Diagnostic Trouble Codes

Connect a suitably programmed scan tool to Data Link Connector (DLC), and follow manufacturer's instructions.

Intermittent & Poor Connections

INTERMITTENTS

Most intermittents are caused by faulty electrical connections or wiring. Inspect for the following:
1. Wiring broken inside insulation.
2. Poor connection between male and female terminal at connector.
3. Poor terminal to wire connection. Some conditions which fall under this are:
   a. Poor crimps.
   b. Poor solder joints.
   c. Crimping over wire insulation rather than wire.
   d. Corrosion in wire to terminal contact.
4. Wire insulation which is rubbed through. This causes an intermittent short as bare area touches other wiring or components.

POOR CONNECTIONS

1. It is important to test terminal contact at component and any inline connectors before replacing suspect component.
2. Mating terminals must be inspected to ensure good terminal contact.
3. Poor connection between male and female terminal at a connector may be result of contamination or deformation.
4. Contamination may be caused by:
   a. Connector halves being improperly connected.
   b. Missing or damaged seal.
   c. Damaged connector.
   d. Exposing terminals to moisture and dirt.
5. Deformation is caused by:
   a. Probing connector terminal mating side without proper adapter.
   b. Improperly joining connector halves.
   c. Repeatedly separating and joining connector halves.

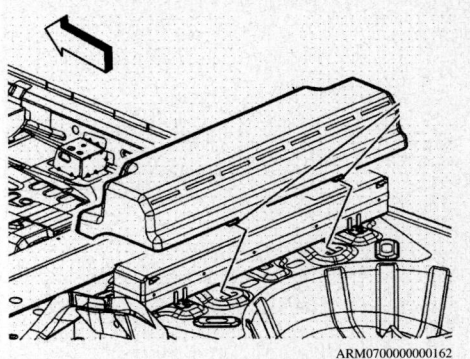

Fig. 1   Rear hybrid battery compartment. Aura

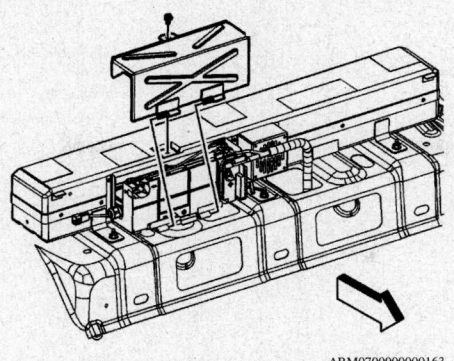

Fig. 2   Disconnect control module cover. Aura Hybrid

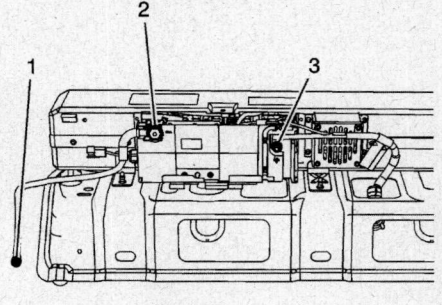

1-Chassis ground
2-Negative stud
3-Positive stud

Fig. 3   Battery disconnect control module voltage measurement locations. Aura Hybrid

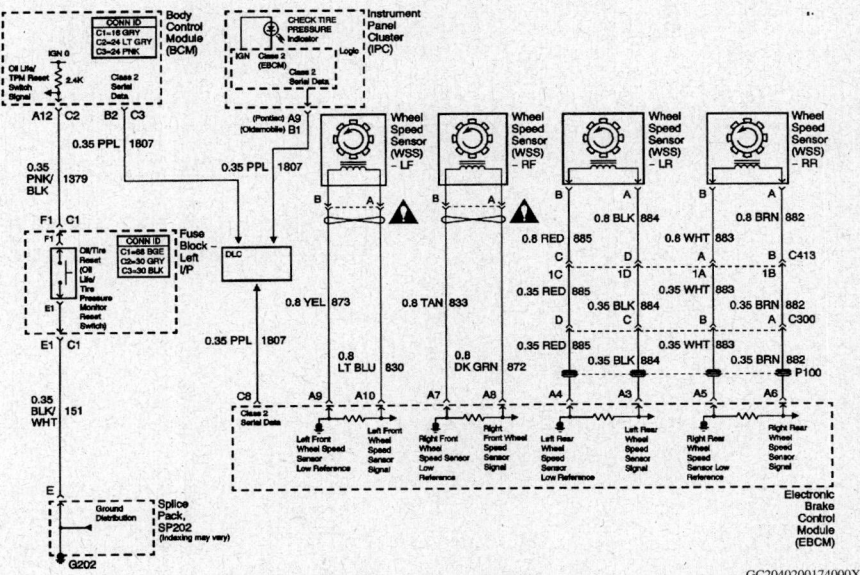

Fig. 4   Wiring diagram. Alero & Grand Am

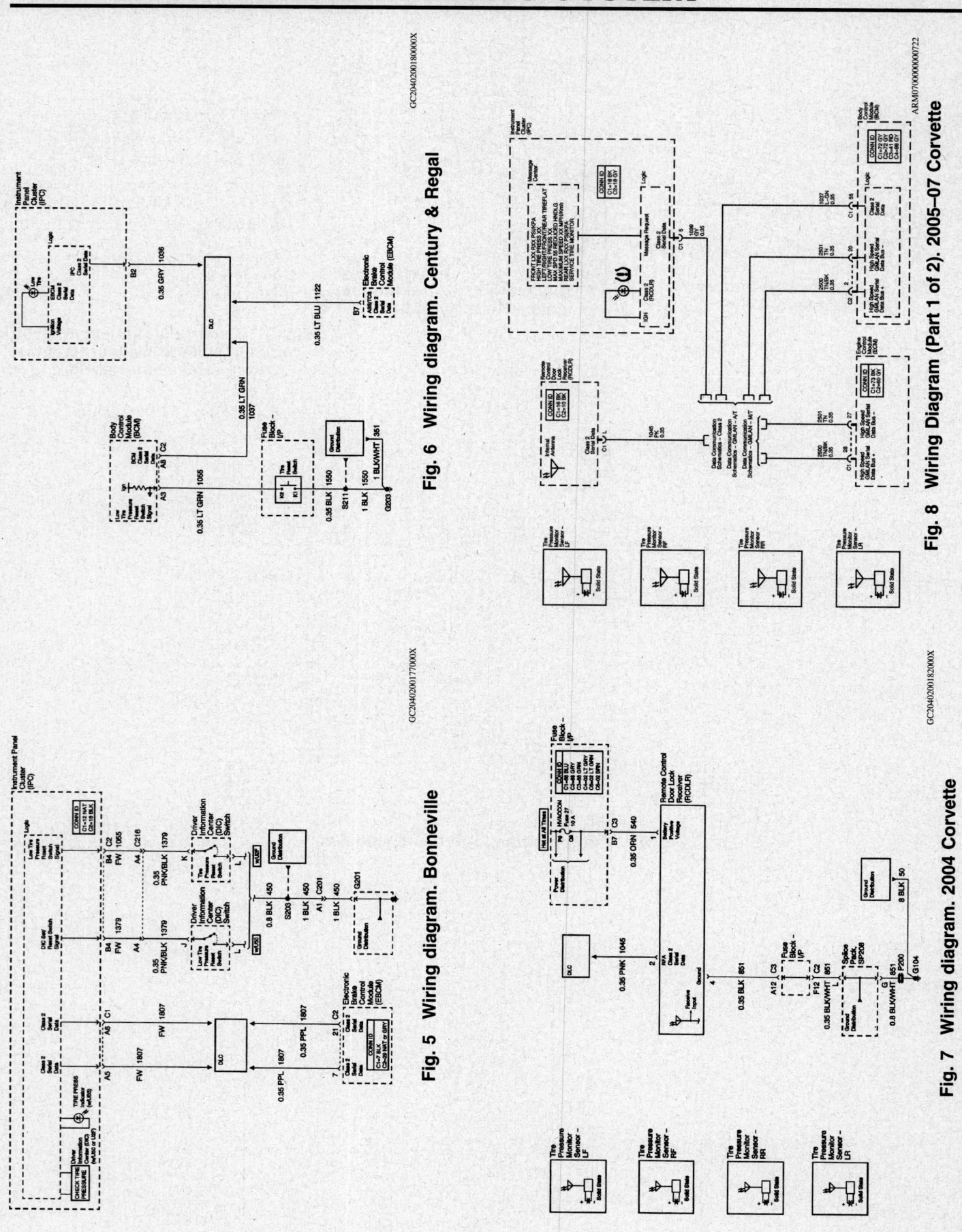

Fig. 6 Wiring diagram. Century & Regal

Fig. 8 Wiring Diagram (Part 1 of 2). 2005–07 Corvette

Fig. 5 Wiring diagram. Bonneville

Fig. 7 Wiring diagram. 2004 Corvette

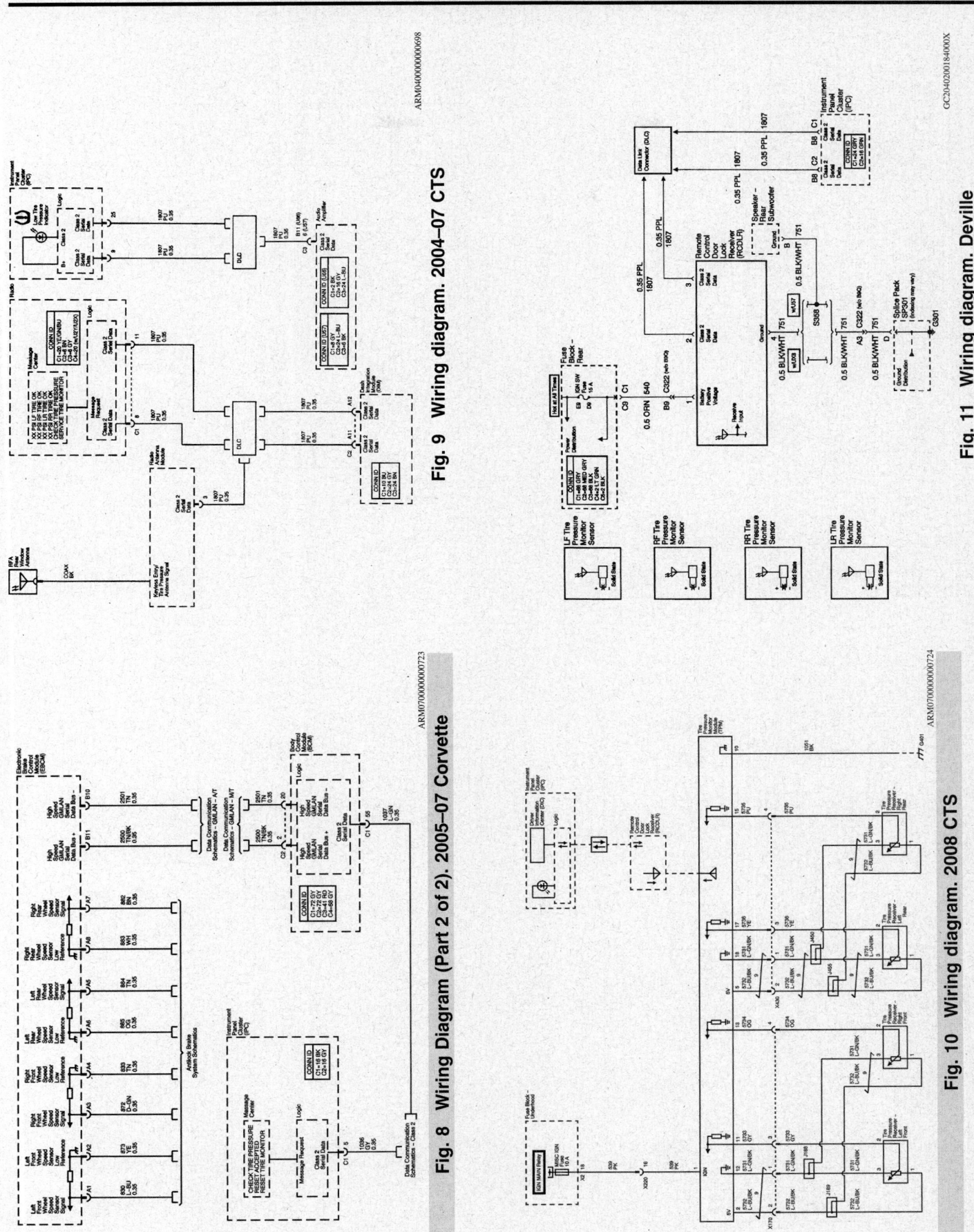

Fig. 9   Wiring diagram. 2004–07 CTS

Fig. 11   Wiring diagram. Deville

Fig. 8   Wiring Diagram (Part 2 of 2). 2005–07 Corvette

Fig. 10   Wiring diagram. 2008 CTS

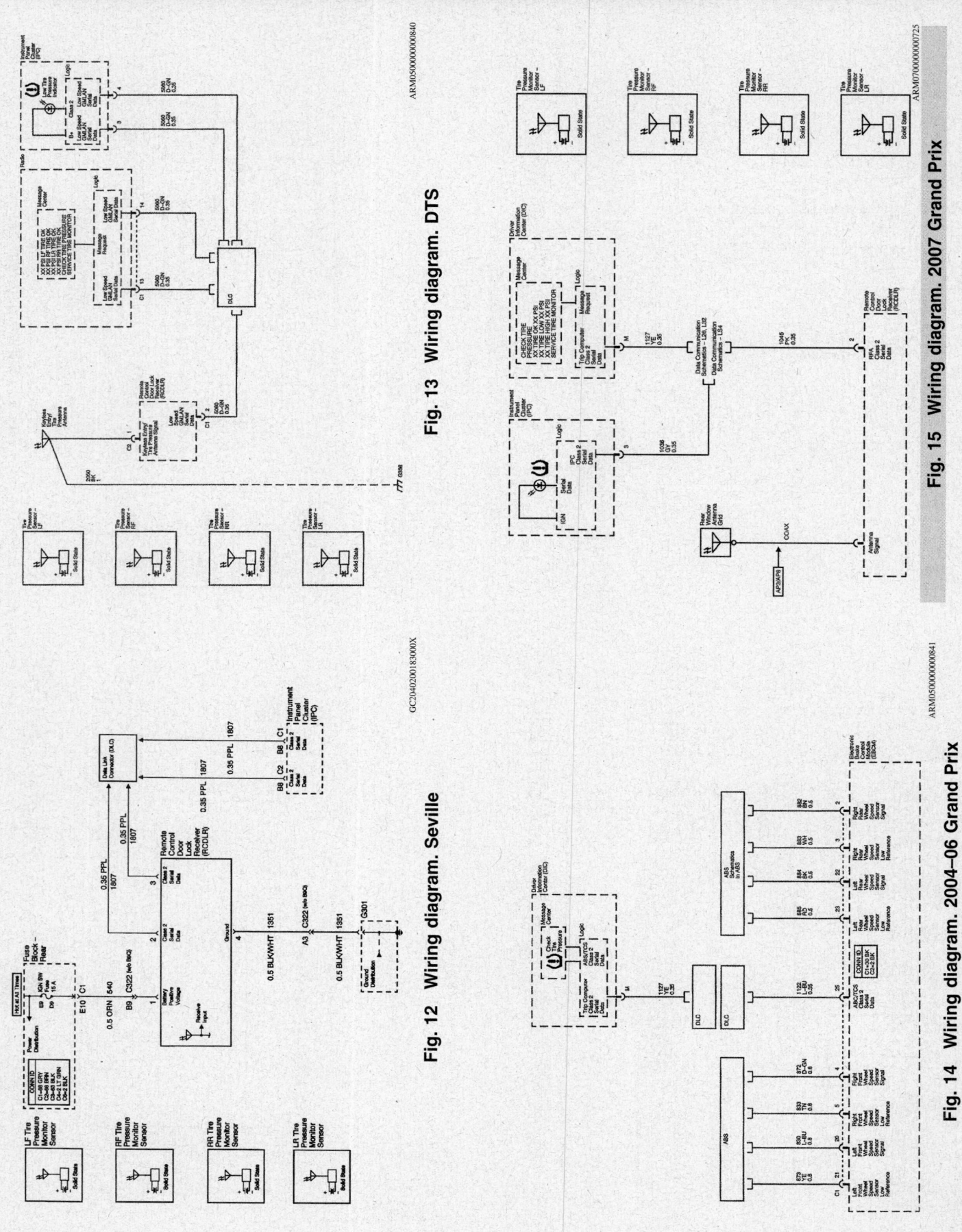

Fig. 13   Wiring diagram. DTS

Fig. 15   Wiring diagram. 2007 Grand Prix

Fig. 12   Wiring diagram. Seville

Fig. 14   Wiring diagram. 2004-06 Grand Prix

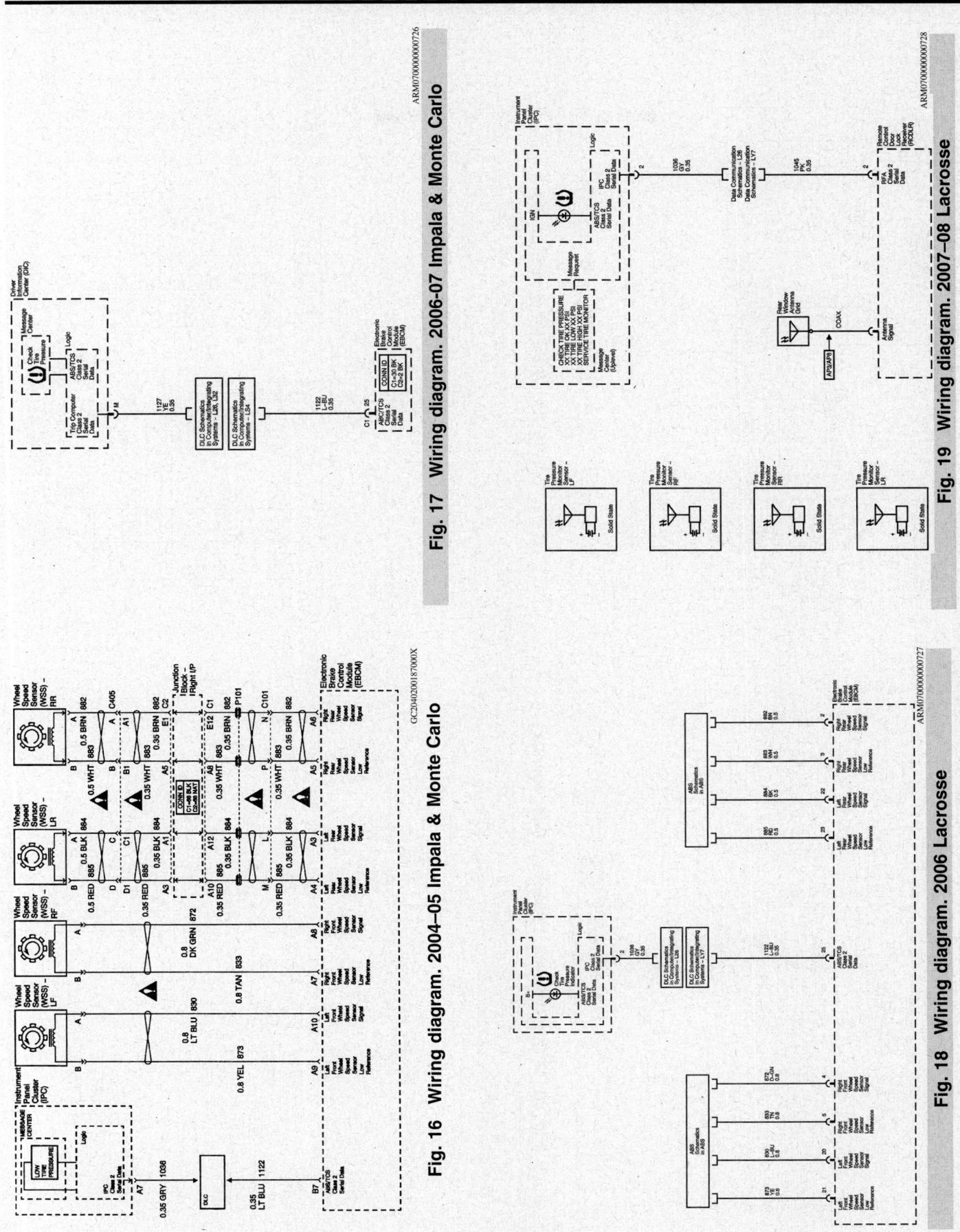

Fig. 17 Wiring diagram. 2006–07 Impala & Monte Carlo

Fig. 19 Wiring diagram. 2007–08 Lacrosse

Fig. 16 Wiring diagram. 2004–05 Impala & Monte Carlo

Fig. 18 Wiring diagram. 2006 Lacrosse

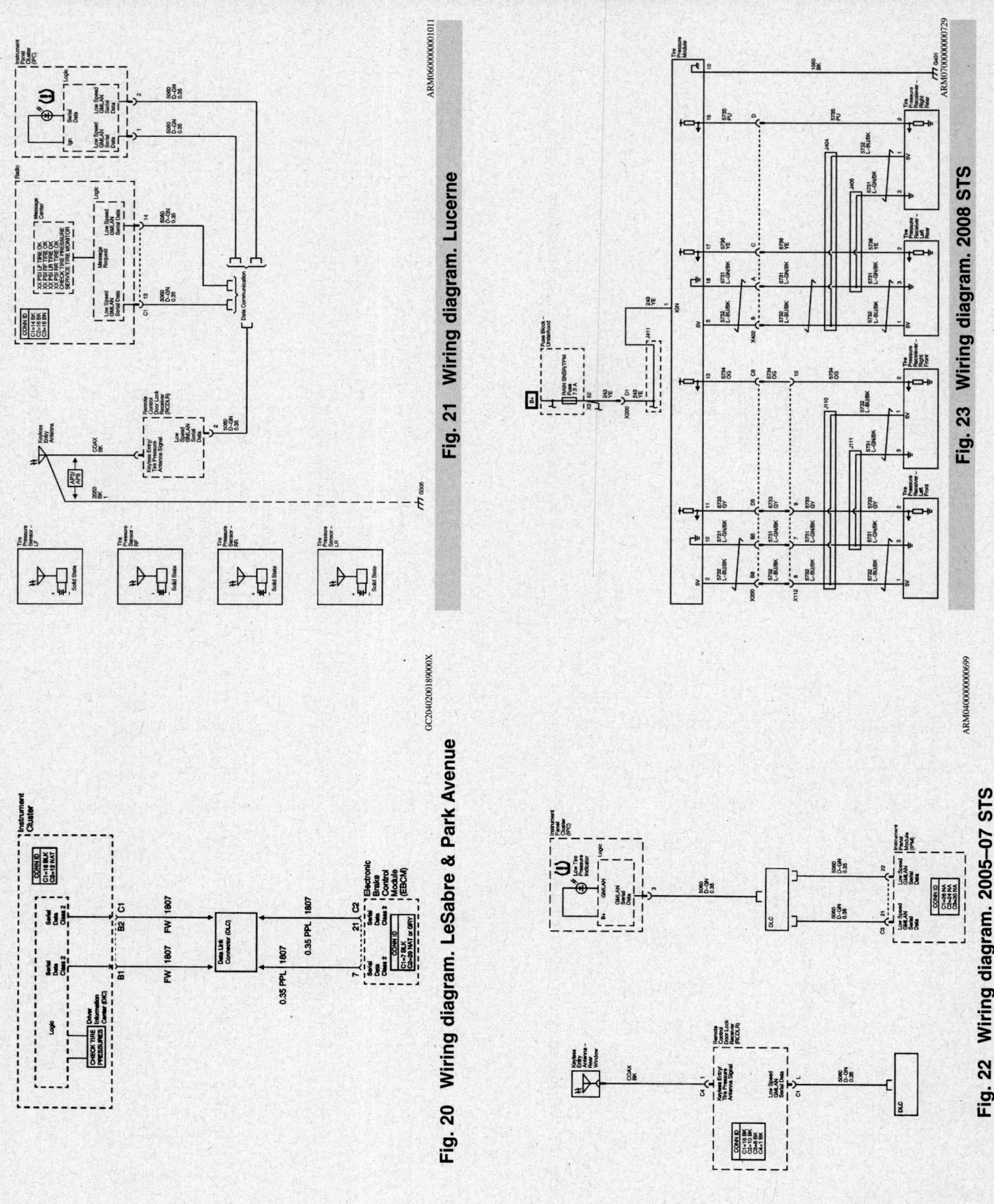

Fig. 21 Wiring diagram. Lucerne

Fig. 23 Wiring diagram. 2008 STS

Fig. 20 Wiring diagram. LeSabre & Park Avenue

Fig. 22 Wiring diagram. 2005-07 STS

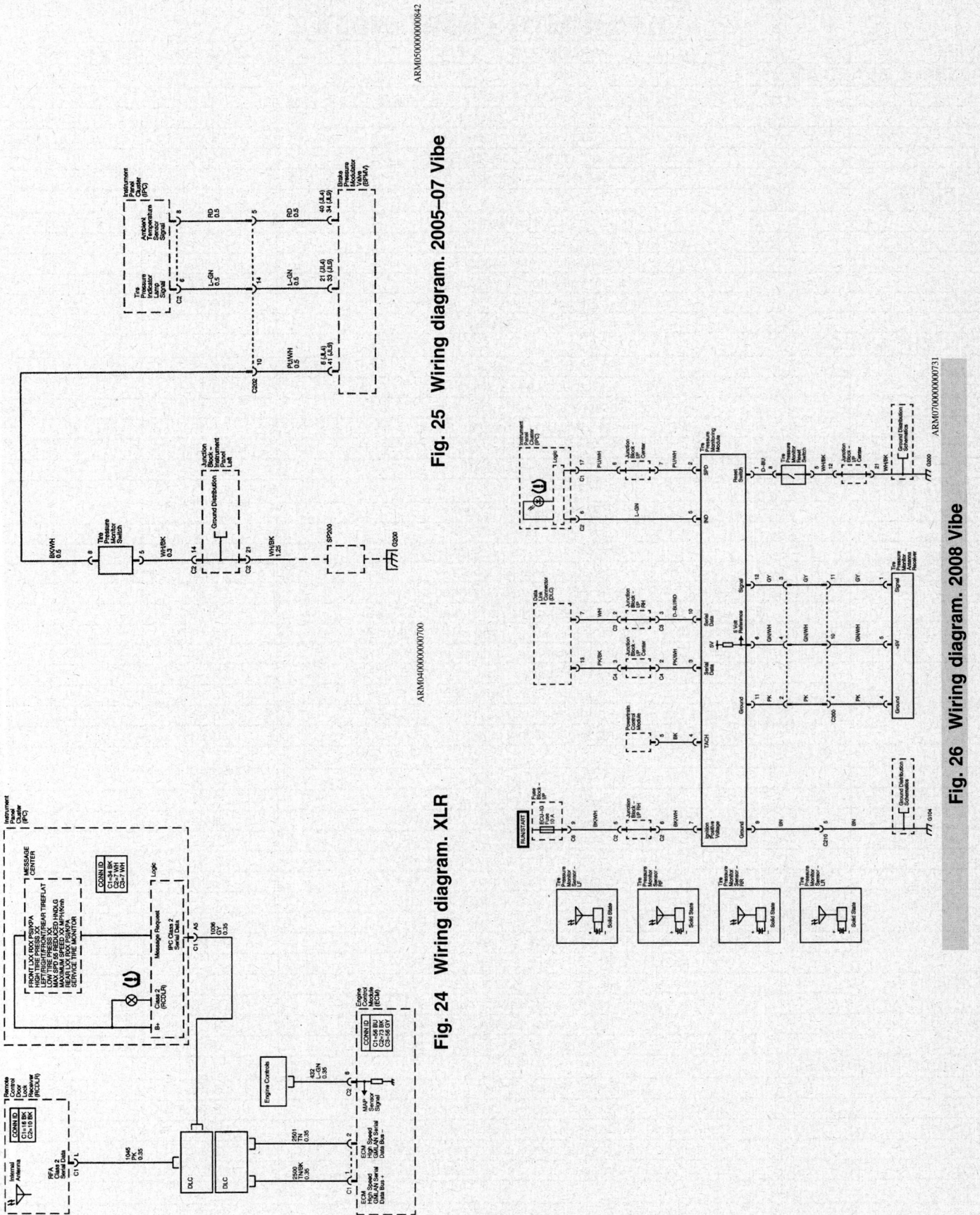

Fig. 25   Wiring diagram. 2005–07 Vibe

Fig. 26   Wiring diagram. 2008 Vibe

Fig. 24   Wiring diagram. XLR

DIAGNOSTIC CHART INDEX

Code	Description	Page No.	Fig. No.
ALERO & GRAND AM			
—	Diagnostic System Check	28-13	27
—	Low Tire Pressure Indicator Always On	28-14	29
—	Low Tire Pressure Indicator Inoperative	28-14	30
—	Low Tire Pressure Indicator Does Not Reset	28-14	31
C1245	Low Tire Pressure Detected	28-13	28
BONNEVILLE			
—	Diagnostic System Check	28-15	32
—	Low Tire Pressure Indicator Always On	28-15	35
—	Low Tire Pressure Indicator Inoperative	28-16	36
—	Low Tire Pressure Indicator Does Not Reset	28-16	37
B2818	Low Tire Pressure System Reset Circuit Low	28-15	33
C1245	Low Tire Pressure Detected	28-15	34
CENTURY & REGAL			
—	Diagnostic System Check	28-16	38
—	Low Tire Pressure Indicator Always On	28-17	41
—	Low Tire Pressure Indicator Inoperative	28-17	42
—	Low Tire Pressure Indicator Does Not Reset	28-18	43
B2818	Low Tire Pressure Detected	28-17	39
C1245	Low Tire Pressure Detected	28-17	40
CORVETTE			
—	Diagnostic System Check (2004)	28-18	44
—	Diagnostic System Check (2005–08)	28-19	45
—	Low Tire Pressure Indicator Always On	28-20	48
—	Low Tire Pressure Indicator Operative	28-20	49
C0750	No Current Tire Pressure Information Transmitted (2004–06)	28-19	46
	No Current Tire Pressure Information Transmitted (2007–08)	28-19	47
C0755	No Current Tire Pressure Information Transmitted (2004–06)	28-19	46
	No Current Tire Pressure Information Transmitted (2007–08)	28-19	47
C0760	No Current Tire Pressure Information Transmitted (2004–06)	28-19	46
	No Current Tire Pressure Information Transmitted (2007–08)	28-19	47
C0765	No Current Tire Pressure Information Transmitted (2004–06)	28-19	46
	No Current Tire Pressure Information Transmitted (2007–08)	28-19	47
CTS			
—	Diagnostic System Check (2004–06)	28-20	50
—	Diagnostic System Check (2007–08)	28-21	51
—	Low Tire Pressure Indicator Always On (2004–06)	28-22	54
—	Low Tire Pressure Indicator Always On (2007–08)	28-23	55
—	Low Tire Pressure Indicator Inoperative (2004–06)	28-23	56
—	Low Tire Pressure Indicator Inoperative (2007–08)	28-23	57
C0750	Lefthand Front Tire Pressure Sensor (2004–06)	28-21	52
	Lefthand Front Tire Pressure Sensor (2007–08)	28-22	53
C0755	Righthand Front Tire Pressure Sensor (2004–06)	28-21	52
	Righthand Front Tire Pressure Sensor (2007–08)	28-22	53
C0760	Lefthand Rear Tire Pressure Sensor (2004–06)	28-21	52
	Lefthand Rear Tire Pressure Sensor (2007–08)	28-22	53
C0765	Righthand Rear Tire Pressure Sensor (2004–06)	28-21	52
	Righthand Rear Tire Pressure Sensor (2007–08)	28-22	53
DEVILLE & SEVILLE			
—	Diagnostic System Check	28-24	58
C0750	No Current Tire Pressure Information Transmitted	28-24	59
C0755	No Current Tire Pressure Information Transmitted	28-24	59
C0760	No Current Tire Pressure Information Transmitted	28-24	59
C0765	No Current Tire Pressure Information Transmitted	28-24	59
DTS			
—	Diagnostic System Check (2006–07)	28-25	60

Continued

DIAGNOSTIC CHART INDEX—Continued

Code	Description	Page No.	Fig. No.
DTS			
—	Diagnostic System Check (2008)	28-25	61
—	Low Tire Pressure Indicator Always On (2006)	28-27	65
—	Low Tire Pressure Indicator Always On (2007–08)	28-27	66
—	Low Tire Pressure Indicator Inoperative (2006)	28-27	67
—	Low Tire Pressure Indicator Inoperative (2007–08)	28-28	68
C0569	System Configuration Error	28-25	62
C0750	No Current Tire Pressure Information Transmitted	28-26	63
C0755	No Current Tire Pressure Information Transmitted	28-26	63
C0760	No Current Tire Pressure Information Transmitted	28-26	63
C0765	No Current Tire Pressure Information Transmitted	28-26	63
C0775	Low Tire Pressure System Sensors Not Learned	28-26	64
GRAND PRIX			
—	Diagnostic System Check (2004)	28-28	69
—	Diagnostic System Check (2005–06)	28-28	70
—	Diagnostic System Check (2007–08)	28-29	71
—	Low Tire Pressure Indicator Always On	28-31	75
—	Low Tire Pressure Indicator Inoperative	28-31	76
C0569	System Configuration Error	28-30	72
C0750	No Current Tire Pressure Information Transmitted	28-30	73
C0755	No Current Tire Pressure Information Transmitted	28-30	73
C0760	No Current Tire Pressure Information Transmitted	28-30	73
C0765	No Current Tire Pressure Information Transmitted	28-30	73
C0775	Low Tire Pressure System Sensors Not Learned	28-30	74
IMPALA & MONTE CARLO			
—	Diagnostic System Check (2004)	28-32	77
—	Diagnostic System Check (2005)	28-32	78
—	Diagnostic System Check (2006–07)	28-33	79
—	Diagnostic System Check (2008)	28-33	80
—	Low Tire Pressure Indicator Always On (2006)	28-37	88
—	Low Tire Pressure Indicator Always On (2007–08)	28-37	89
—	Low Tire Pressure Indicator Inoperative (2006)	28-37	90
—	Low Tire Pressure Indicator Inoperative (2007–08)	28-38	91
C0569	System Configuration Error (2006–07)	28-34	81
	System Configuration Error (2008)	28-34	82
C0750	Left Front Low Tire Pressure Sensor (2006)	28-35	83
	Left Front Low Tire Pressure Sensor (2007–08)	28-35	84
C0755	Right Front Low Tire Pressure Sensor (2006)	28-35	83
	Right Front Low Tire Pressure Sensor (2007–08)	28-35	84
C0760	Left Rear Low Tire Pressure Sensor (2006)	28-35	83
	Left Rear Low Tire Pressure Sensor (2007–08)	28-35	84
C0765	Right Rear Low Tire Pressure Sensor (2006)	28-35	83
	Right Rear Low Tire Pressure Sensor (2007–08)	28-35	84
C0775	Low Tire Pressure System Sensors Not Learned (2006–07)	28-36	85
	Low Tire Pressure System Sensors Not Learned (2008)	28-36	86
C1245	Low Tire Pressure Detected	28-36	87
LACROSSE			
—	Diagnostic System Check (2005–06)	28-38	92
—	Diagnostic System Check (2007–08)	28-39	93
—	Low Tire Pressure Indicator Always On	28-41	97
—	Low Tire Pressure Indicator Inoperative	28-41	98
C0569	System Configuration Error	28-39	94
C0750	Left Front Low Tire Pressure Sensor	28-40	95
C0755	Right Front Low Tire Pressure Sensor	28-40	95
C0760	Left Rear Low Tire Pressure Sensor	28-40	95
C0765	Right Rear Low Tire Pressure Sensor	28-40	95
C0775	Low Tire Pressure System Sensors Not Learned	28-40	96

Continued

DIAGNOSTIC CHART INDEX—Continued

Code	Description	Page No.	Fig. No.
LESABRE & PARK AVENUE			
—	Diagnostic System Check	28-42	99
C1245	Low Tire Pressure Detected	28-42	100
LUCERNE			
—	Diagnostic System Check	28-42	101
—	Low Tire Pressure Indicator Always On	28-44	105
—	Low Tire Pressure Indicator Inoperative	28-44	106
C0569	System Configuration Error	28-43	102
C0750	Left Front Low Tire Pressure Sensor	28-43	103
C0755	Right Front Low Tire Pressure Sensor	28-43	103
C0760	Left Rear Low Tire Pressure Sensor	28-43	103
C0765	Right Rear Low Tire Pressure Sensor	28-43	103
C0775	Low Tire Pressure System Sensors Not Learned	28-44	104
STS			
—	Diagnostic System Check (2005–06)	28-44	107
—	Diagnostic System Check (2007–08)	28-45	108
—	Low Tire Pressure Indicator Always On	28-47	113
—	Low Tire Pressure Indicator Inoperative	28-48	114
C0750	Lefthand Front Tire Pressure Sensor Less UH3 (2005–06)	28-45	109
	Lefthand Front Tire Pressure Sensor w/UH3 (2005–06)	28-46	111
C0750	Lefthand Front Tire Pressure Sensor Less UH3 (2007–08)	28-46	110
	Lefthand Front Tire Pressure Sensor w/UH3 (2007–08)	28-46	112
C0755	Righthand Front Tire Pressure Sensor Less UH3 (2005–06)	28-45	109
	Righthand Front Tire Pressure Sensor w/UH3 (2005–06)	28-46	111
C0755	Righthand Front Tire Pressure Sensor Less UH3 (2007–08)	28-46	110
	Righthand Front Tire Pressure Sensor w/UH3 (2007–08)	28-46	112
C0760	Lefthand Rear Tire Pressure Sensor Less UH3 (2005–06)	28-45	109
	Lefthand Rear Tire Pressure Sensor w/UH3 (2005–06)	28-46	111
C0760	Lefthand Rear Tire Pressure Sensor Less UH3 (2007–08)	28-46	110
	Lefthand Rear Tire Pressure Sensor w/UH3 (2007–08)	28-46	112
C0765	Righthand Rear Tire Pressure Sensor Less UH3 (2005–06)	28-45	109
	Righthand Rear Tire Pressure Sensor w/UH3 (2005–06)	28-46	111
C0765	Righthand Rear Tire Pressure Sensor Less UH3 (2007–08)	28-46	110
	Righthand Rear Tire Pressure Sensor w/UH3 (2007–08)	28-46	112
XLR			
—	Diagnostic System Check (2004–06)	28-48	115
—	Diagnostic System Check (2007–08)	28-49	116
—	Low Tire Pressure Indicator Always On	28-50	119
—	Low Tire Pressure Indicator Inoperative	28-51	120
C0750	Lefthand Front Tire Pressure Sensor (2004–06)	28-49	119
	Lefthand Front Tire Pressure Sensor (2007–08)	28-49	118
C0755	Righthand Front Tire Pressure Sensor (2004–06)	28-49	117
	Righthand Front Tire Pressure Sensor (2007–08)	28-49	118
C0760	Lefthand Rear Tire Pressure Sensor (2004–06)	28-49	117
	Lefthand Rear Tire Pressure Sensor (2007–08)	28-49	118
C0765	Righthand Rear Tire Pressure Sensor (2004–06)	28-49	117
	Righthand Rear Tire Pressure Sensor (2007–08)	28-49	118
VIBE			
—	Diagnostic System Check	28-51	121
—	Low Tire Pressure Indicator Always On (2005–07)	28-61	131
—	Low Tire Pressure Indicator Always On (2008)	28-61	132
—	Low Tire Pressure Indicator Inoperative (2005–07)	28-62	133
—	Low Tire Pressure Indicator Inoperative (2008)	28-64	134
—	Low Tire Pressure Indicator Does Not Reset (2005–07)	28-64	135
—	Low Tire Pressure Indicator Does Not Reset (2008)	28-65	136
C2111	Tire Pressure Sensor 1 in Shipping Mode	28-52	122

Continued

DIAGNOSTIC CHART INDEX—Continued

Code	Description	Page No.	Fig. No.
VIBE			
C2112	Tire Pressure Sensor 2 in Shipping Mode	28-52	122
C2113	Tire Pressure Sensor 3 in Shipping Mode	28-52	122
C2114	Tire Pressure Sensor 4 in Shipping Mode	28-52	122
C2121	Tire Pressure Sensor 1 Signal Missing - Main Set	28-55	123
C2122	Tire Pressure Sensor 2 Signal Missing - Main Set	28-55	123
C2123	Tire Pressure Sensor 3 Signal Missing - Main Set	28-55	123
C2124	Tire Pressure Sensor 4 Signal Missing - Main Set	28-55	123
C2126	Tire Pressure Sensor ID Not Received	28-55	124
C2141	Tire Pressure Sensor 1 Performance	28-56	125
C2142	Tire Pressure Sensor 2 Performance	28-56	125
C2143	Tire Pressure Sensor 3 Performance	28-56	125
C2144	Tire Pressure Sensor 4 Performance	28-56	125
C2165	Tire Pressure Sensor 1 Tire Overtemperature	28-57	126
C2166	Tire Pressure Sensor 2 Tire Overtemperature	28-57	126
C2167	Tire Pressure Sensor 3 Tire Overtemperature	28-57	126
C2168	Tire Pressure Sensor 4 Tire Overtemperature	28-57	126
C2171	Low Tire Pressure Sensors Not Learned -- Main	28-57	127
C2176	Tire Pressure Sensors Antenna Performance	28-58	128
C2177	Initialization Not Complete	28-59	129
C2181	Tire Pressure Sensor 1 Transmitter Identification	28-60	130
C2182	Tire Pressure Sensor 2 Transmitter Identification	28-60	130
C2183	Tire Pressure Sensor 3 Transmitter Identification	28-60	130
C2184	Tire Pressure Sensor 4 Transmitter Identification	28-60	130

Step	Action	Yes	No
1	Install a scan tool. Does the scan tool power up?	Go to Step 2	Scan Tool Does Not Power Up
2	1. Turn ON the ignition, with the engine OFF. 2. Attempt to establish communications with the Electronic Brake Control Module (EBCM). Does the scan tool communicate with the EBCM?	Go to Step 3	Scan Tool Does Not Communicate with Class 2 Device
3	Select the ABS Diagnostic Trouble Codes DTC function on the scan tool. Does the scan tool display any DTCs that begin with a "U"?	Diagnostic Trouble Code (DTC) List	Go to Step 4
4	Does the scan tool display any ABS DTCs?	Go to Diagnostic System Check	Go to Step 5
5	Does the scan tool display DTC C1245?	Go to DTC C1245	System OK

GC2040200191000X

Fig. 27 Diagnostic System Check. Alero & Grand Am

Step	Action	Yes	No
1	Did you perform the Tire Pressure Monitor Diagnostic System Check?	Go to Step 2	Go to Diagnostic System Check -
2	1. Install a scan tool. 2. Turn ON the ignition, with the engine OFF. 3. With a scan tool, monitor the DTC Information for DTC C1245 in the TIM Diagnostic Trouble Codes (DTCs) selection. Does the scan tool indicate that DTC C1245 is current?	Go to Step 3	Go to Diagnostic Aids
3	Since some occurrences of this DTC are caused by driving conditions, or tire size differences, review the TPM system with the customer to verify the conditions under which the DTC set. Did driving conditions, or tire size cause the DTC to set?	Go to Step 5	Go to Step 4
4	1. Calibrate the TPM system. 2. Use the scan tool in order to clear the DTC. 3. Operate the vehicle within the Conditions for Running the DTC as specified in the supporting text. Does the DTC reset as a current DTC?	Go to Diagnostic Aids	System OK
5	Inspect the tire pressures and adjust to manufacturer's specification if needed. Calibrate the TPM system if tire pressures were adjusted. Did you complete the repair?	System OK	--

GC2040200192000X

Fig. 28 Code C1245: Low Tire Pressure Detected. Alero & Grand Am

Step	Action	Yes	No
1	Did you perform the TPM Diagnostic System Check?	Go to Step 2	Go to Diagnostic System Check -
2	1. Turn OFF the ignition. 2. Turn ON the ignition, with the engine OFF. 3. Observe the tire pressure indicator on the systems monitor, or the instrument Panel cluster (IPC) during the bulb check. Does the indicator illuminate during the bulb check and then turn OFF?	Go to Intermittent and Poor Connections	Go to Step 3
3	Replace the IPC. Did you complete the replacement?	Go to Step 4	--
4	Operate the system in order to verify the repair. Did you correct the condition?	System OK	Go to Step 2

GC2040200194000X

Fig. 29 Low Tire Pressure Indicator Always On. Alero & Grand Am

Step	Action	Yes	No
1	Did you perform the TPM Diagnostic System Check?	Go to Step 2	Go to Diagnostic System Check -
2	1. Turn OFF the ignition. 2. Turn ON the ignition, with the engine OFF. 3. Observe the tire pressure indicator on the systems monitor, or the Instrument Panel Cluster (IPC) during the bulb check. Does the warning indicator illuminate during the bulb check?	Go to Intermittent and Poor Connections	Go to Step 3
3	Replace the IPC. Did you complete the replacement?	Go to Step 4	--
4	Operate the system in order to verify the repair. Did you correct the condition?	System OK	Go to Step 2

GC2040200196000X

Fig. 30 Low Tire Pressure Indicator Inoperative. Alero & Grand Am

Step	Action	Yes	No
1	Did you perform the TPM Diagnostic System Check?	Go to Step 2	Go to Diagnostic System Check -
2	1. Install a scan tool. 2. Turn ON the ignition, with the engine OFF. 3. With a scan tool, observe the TIM Reset Switch parameter in the Chassis data display list. 4. Press the tire pressure monitor reset switch. Does the scan tool display On when the switch is pressed?	Go to Intermittent and Poor Connections	Go to Step 3
3	1. Turn OFF the ignition. 2. Disconnect the oil life/TIM reset switch. 3. Connect a 3 amp fused jumper wire between the tire pressure monitor reset signal circuit of the reset switch and a good ground. 4. Turn ON the ignition, with the engine OFF. 5. With a scan tool, observe the TIM Reset Switch parameter. Does the scan tool display On?	Go to Step 6	Go to Step 4

GC2040200197010X

Fig. 31 Low Tire Pressure Indicator Does Not Reset (Part 1 of 2). Alero & Grand Am

Step	Action	Yes	No
4	Test the tire pressure monitor reset signal circuit of the reset switch for a high resistance or an open. Did you find and correct the condition?	Go to Step 10	Go to Step 5
5	Test the ground circuit of the TIM reset switch for a high resistance or an open. Did you find and correct the condition?	Go to Step 10	Go to Step 7
6	Inspect for poor connections at the harness connector of the TIM reset switch. Did you find and correct the condition?	Go to Step 10	Go to Step 8
7	Inspect for poor connections at the harness connector of the instrument cluster (IPC). Did you find and correct the condition?	Go to Step 10	Go to Step 9
8	Replace the TIM reset switch. Did you complete the replacement?	Go to Step 10	--
9	Replace the IPC. Did you complete the replacement?	Go to Step 10	--
10	Operate the system in order to verify the repair. Did you correct the condition?	System OK	Go to Step 2

GC2040200197020X

Fig. 31 Low Tire Pressure Indicator Does Not Reset (Part 2 of 2). Alero & Grand Am

Step	Action	Value (s)	Yes	No
1	Install a scan tool. Does the scan tool power up?	--	Go to Step 2	Scan Tool Does Not Power Up
2	1. Turn ON the ignition, with the engine OFF. 2. Attempt to establish communications with the following control modules: o Electronic brake control module (EBCM) o Instrument cluster (IPC) Does the scan tool communicate with the control modules listed above?	--	Go to Step 3	Scan Tool Does Not Communicate with Class 2 Device
3	Select the DRP/ABS/TCS/TIM/VSES display DTC function on the scan tool. Does the scan tool display any DRP/ABS/TCS/VSES DTCs?	--	Go to Diagnostic System Check -	Go to Step 4
4	Does the scan tool display DTC C1245?	--	Go to DTC C1245 Low Tire Pressure Detected	Go to Step 5
5	Select the instrument cluster (IPC) display DTC function on the scan tool. Does the scan tool display DTC B2818?	--	Go to DTC B2818 Low Tire Pressure System Reset Circuit Low	Go to Symptoms

GC2040200200000X

Fig. 32 Diagnostic System Check. Bonneville

Step	Action	Yes	No
1	Did you perform the Tire Pressure Monitor Diagnostic System Check?	Go to Step 2	Go to Diagnostic System Check -
2	1. Install a scan tool. 2. Turn ON the ignition, with the engine OFF. 3. With a scan tool, select the TIM Diagnostic Trouble Codes (DTCs) function. Does the scan tool indicate that DTC C1245 is current?	Go to Step 3	Go to Diagnostic Aids
3	Since some occurrences of this DTC are caused by driving conditions, or tire size difference, review the TPM system with the customer to verify the conditions under which the DTC set. Did driving conditions, or tire size cause this DTC to set?	Go to Step 4	Go to Step 5
4	1. Calibrate the TPM system. 2. Use the scan tool in order to clear the DTCs. 3. Operate the vehicle within the Conditions for Running the DTC as specified in the supporting text. Does the DTC reset as a current DTC?	Go to Step 5	System OK
5	Inspect the tire pressures and adjust to manufacturers specification if needed. Calibrate the TPM system if tire pressures were adjusted. Did you complete the repair?	System OK	--

GC2040200202000X

Fig. 34 Code C1245: Low Tire Pressure Detected. Bonneville

Step	Action	Value (s)	Yes	No
1	Did you perform the TPM Diagnostic System Check?	--	Go to Step 2	Go to Diagnostic System Check
2	1. Install a scan tool. 2. Turn ON the ignition, with the engine OFF. 3. With a scan tool, select the BCM Diagnostic Trouble Codes (DTC) function. Does the scan tool display DTC B2818 as current?	--	Go to Step 3	Intermittent and Poor Connections
3	1. Turn OFF the ignition. 2. Disconnect the reset switch. 3. Turn ON the ignition, with the engine OFF 4. With the scan tool, observe the Tire Reset Switch, w/Systems Monitor, or the DIC Reset Button, w/DIC, data parameter in the IPC Data list. Does the scan tool display OFF?	--	Go to Step 6	Go to Step 4
4	Test the signal circuit of the reset switch for a short to ground. Did you find and correct the condition?	--	Go to Step 7	Go to Step 5
5	Replace the IPC. Did you complete the replacement?	--	Go to Step 7	--
6	Replace the reset switch. Did you complete the replacement?	--	Go to Step 7	--
7	1. Use the scan tool in order to clear the DTC. 2. Operate the vehicle within the Conditions for Running the DTC as specified in the supporting text. Does the DTC reset?	--	Go to Step 2	System OK

GC2040200201000X

Fig. 33 Code B2818: Low Tire Pressure System Reset Circuit Low. Bonneville

Step	Action	Value (s)	Yes	No
1	Did you perform the TIM Diagnostic System Check?	--	Go to Step 2	Go to Diagnostic System Check -
2	1. Turn OFF the ignition. 2. Turn ON the ignition, with the engine OFF. 3. Observe the TIRE PRESS indicator on the systems monitor of the instrument cluster (IPC) during the bulb check. Does the TIRE PRESS indicator illuminate during the bulb check and then turn OFF?	--	Intermittent and Poor Connections	Go to Step 3
3	Replace the instrument cluster (IPC). Did you complete the replacement?	--	Go to Step 4	--
4	Operate the system in order to verify the repair. Did you correct the condition?	--	System OK	Go to Step 2

GC2040200203000X

Fig. 35 Low Tire Pressure Indicator Always On. Bonneville

TIRE PRESSURE MONITORING SYSTEM

Step	Action	Value(s)	Yes	No
1	Did you perform the TIM Diagnostic System Check?	--	Go to Step 2	Go to Diagnostic System Check -
2	1. Turn OFF the ignition. 2. Turn ON the ignition, with the engine OFF. 3. Observe the TIRE PRESS indicator on the systems monitor of the instrument cluster (IPC) during the bulb check. Does the TIRE PRESS indicator illuminate during the bulb check?	--	Intermittent and Poor Connections	Go to Step 3
3	Replace the instrument cluster (IPC). Did you complete the replacement?	--	Go to Step 4	--
4	Operate the system in order to verify the repair. Did you correct the condition?	--	System OK	Go to Step 2

GC2040200204000X

Fig. 36 Low Tire Pressure Indicator Inoperative. Bonneville

Step	Action	Value(s)	Yes	No
6	Inspect for poor connections at the harness connector of the reset switch. Did you find and correct the condition?	--	Go to Step 10	Go to Step 8
7	Inspect for poor connections at the harness connector of the instrument cluster (IPC). Did you find and correct the condition?	--	Go to Step 10	Go to Step 9
8	Replace the reset switch. Did you complete the replacement?	--	Go to Step 10	--
9	Replace the IPC. Did you complete the replacement?	--	Go to Step 10	--
10	Operate the system in order to verify the repair. Did you correct the condition?	--	System OK	Go to Step 2

GC2040200205020X

Fig. 37 Low Tire Pressure Indicator Does Not Reset (Part 2 of 2). Bonneville

Step	Action	Value(s)	Yes	No
1	Did you perform the TPM Diagnostic System Check?	--	Go to Step 2	Go to Diagnostic System Check -
2	1. Install a scan tool. 2. Turn ON the ignition, with the engine OFF. 3. With a scan tool, observe the Tire Reset Switch parameter in the IPC data list. 4. Press the TIRE PRESS RESET switch. Does the scan tool display On when the switch is pressed?	--	Intermittent and Poor Connections	Go to Step 3
3	1. Turn OFF the ignition. 2. Disconnect the reset switch. 3. Connect a 3 amp fused jumper wire between the harness connector of the reset switch signal circuit and a good ground. 4. Turn ON the ignition, with the engine OFF. 5. With a scan tool, observe the Tire Reset Switch parameter. Does the scan tool display On?	--	Go to Step 6	Go to Step 4
4	Test the reset switch signal circuit for a high resistance or an open. Did you find and correct the condition?	--	Go to Step 10	Go to Step 5
5	Test the ground circuit of the reset switch for a high resistance or an open. Did you find and correct the condition?	--	Go to Step 10	Go to Step 7

GC2040200205010X

Fig. 37 Low Tire Pressure Indicator Does Not Reset (Part 1 of 2). Bonneville

Step	Action	Yes	No
1	Install a scan tool. Does the scan tool power up?	Go to Step 2	Scan Tool Does Not Power Up
2	1. Turn ON the ignition, with the engine OFF. 2. Attempt to establish communications with the Electronic Brake Control Module (EBCM). Does the scan tool communicate with the EBCM?	Go to Step 3	Scan Tool Does Not Communicate with Class 2 Device
3	Select the ABS Diagnostic Trouble Codes DTC function on the scan tool. Does the scan tool display any DTCs that begin with a "U"?	Go to Diagnostic Trouble Code (DTC)	Go to Step 4
4	Does the scan tool display any ABS DTCs?	Go to Diagnostic System Check	Go to Step 5
5	Does the scan tool display DTC C1245?	Go to DTC C1245	System OK

GC2040200207000X

Fig. 38 Diagnostic System Check. Century & Regal

Step	Action	Yes	No
1	Did you perform the Tire Pressure Monitor Diagnostic System Check?	Go to Step 2	Go to Diagnostic System Check -
2	1. Install a scan tool. 2. Turn ON the ignition, with the engine OFF. 3. With a scan tool, observe the TIM Reset Switch data parameter in the TIM data list. Does the scan tool display Released?	Go to Step 3	Go to Step 4
3	1. Depress the RESET switch. 2. With the scan tool, observe the TIM Reset Switch data parameter. Does the TIM Reset Switch data parameter change states?	Test for Intermittent and Poor Connections	Go to Step 4
4	1. Turn OFF the ignition. 2. Disconnect the BCM harness connector. 3. disconnect the Low Tire Pressure Reset Switch Signal circuit from the BCM harness connector. 4. Reconnect the BCM harness connector to the BCM. 5. Turn ON the ignition, with the engine OFF. 6. With a scan tool, observe the TIM Reset Switch data parameter. Does the scan tool display Released?	Go to Step 5	Go to Step 6
5	Test the signal circuit of the RESET switch for a short to ground. Did you find and correct the condition?	Go to Step 8	Go to Step 7
6	Replace the BCM. Did you complete the replacement?	Go to Step 8	--

GC2040200209010X

Fig. 39 Code B2818: Low Tire Pressure Detected (Part 1 of 2). Century & Regal

Step	Action	Yes	No
7	Replace the RESET switch. Did you complete the replacement?	Go to Step 8	--
8	1. Use the scan tool in order to clear the DTCs. 2. Operate the vehicle within the Conditions for Running the DTC as specified in the supporting text. Does the DTC reset?	Go to Step 2	System OK

GC2040200209020X

Fig. 39 Code B2818: Low Tire Pressure Detected (Part 2 of 2). Century & Regal

Step	Action	Yes	No
1	Did you perform the TPM Diagnostic System Check?	Go to Step 2	Go to Diagnostic System Check
2	1. Turn OFF the ignition. 2. Turn ON the ignition, with the engine OFF. 3. Observe the tire pressure indicator on the systems monitor, or the instrument Panel cluster (IPC) during the bulb check. Does the indicator illuminate during the bulb check and then turn OFF?	Go to Testing for Intermittent and Poor Connections	Go to Step 3
3	Replace the IPC. Did you complete the replacement?	Go to Step 4	--
4	Operate the system in order to verify the repair. Did you correct the condition?	System OK	Go to Step 2

GC2040200215000X

Fig. 41 Low Tire Pressure Indicator Always On. Century & Regal

Step	Action	Yes	No
1	Did you perform the Tire Pressure Monitor Diagnostic System Check?	Go to Step 2	Go to Diagnostic System Check -
2	1. Install a scan tool. 2. Turn ON the ignition, with the engine OFF. 3. With a scan tool, select the Diagnostic Trouble Codes (DTCs) function. Does the scan tool indicate that DTC C1245 is current?	Go to Step 3	Go to Diagnostic Aids
3	Since some occurrences of this DTC are caused by driving conditions, or different tire size, review the TPM system with the customer to verify the conditions under which the DTC set. Did driving conditions, or tire size cause this DTC to set?	Go to Step 5	Go to Step 4
4	1. Calibrate the TPM system. 2. Use the scan tool in order to clear the DTCs. 3. Operate the vehicle within the Conditions for Running the DTC as specified in the supporting text. Does the DTC reset as a current DTC?	Go to Step 5	System OK
5	Inspect the tire pressures and set to manufacturers specification if needed. Calibrate the TPM system if tire pressures were adjusted. Did you complete the repair?	System OK	--

GC2040200212000X

Fig. 40 Code C1245: Low Tire Pressure Detected. Century & Regal

Step	Action	Yes	No
1	Did you perform the TPM Diagnostic System Check?	Go to Step 2	Go to Diagnostic System Check -
2	1. Turn OFF the ignition. 2. Turn ON the ignition, with the engine OFF. 3. Observe the tire pressure indicator on the systems monitor, or the Instrument Panel Cluster (IPC) during the bulb check. Does the warning indicator illuminate during the bulb check?	Testing for Intermittent and Poor Connections	Go to Step 3
3	Replace the IPC. Did you complete the replacement?	Go to Step 4	--
4	Operate the system in order to verify the repair. Did you correct the condition?	System OK	Go to Step 2

GC2040200217000X

Fig. 42 Low Tire Pressure Indicator Inoperative. Century & Regal

Step	Action	Yes	No
1	Did you perform the Tire Pressure Monitor Diagnostic System Check? Go to Step 2		Diagnostic System Check -
2	1. Install a scan tool. 2. Turn ON the ignition, with the engine OFF. 3. With a scan tool, observe the TIM Reset Switch parameter in the TIM data list. 4. Press the RESET switch. Does the scan tool display Pressed when the switch is pressed?	Testing for Intermittent and Poor Connections	Go to Step 3
3	1. Turn OFF the ignition. 2. Disconnect the reset switch signal circuit from the IP Fuse Block. 3. Connect a 3 amp fused jumper wire between the reset switch signal circuit and a good ground. 4. Turn ON the ignition, with the engine OFF. 5. With a scan tool, observe the TIM Reset Switch parameter. Does the scan tool display Pressed?	Go to Step 5	Go to Step 4
4	Test the reset switch signal circuit for a high resistance or an open. Did you find and correct the condition?	Go to Step 10	Go to Step 7

GC2040200218010X

Fig. 43 Low Tire Pressure Indicator Does Not Reset (Part 1 of 2). Century & Regal

Step	Action	Yes	No
1	Install a scan tool. Does the scan tool power up?	Go to Step 2	Scan Tool Does Not Power Up
2	1. Turn ON the ignition, with the engine OFF. 2. Attempt to establish communication with the RCDLR. Does the scan tool communicate with the RCDLR?	Go to Step 3	Go to Scan Tool Does Not Communicate with Class 2 Device
3	Select the RKE Diagnostic Trouble Codes (DTC) function on the scan tool. Does the scan tool display any DTCs that begin with a "U"?	Go to Diagnostic Trouble Code (DTC)	Go to Step 4
4	Does the scan tool display any RKE DTCs?	Go to Diagnostic Trouble Code (DTC)	Go to Step 5
5	Does the scan tool display any TPM DTCs?	Go to Diagnostic Trouble Code (DTC)	System OK

GC2040200222000X

Fig. 44 Diagnostic System Check. 2004 Corvette

Step	Action	Yes	No
5	Test the ground circuit of the TIM reset switch for a high resistance or an open. Did you find and correct the condition?	Go to Step 10	Go to Step 6
6	Inspect for poor connections at the harness connector of the TIM reset switch. Did you find and correct the condition?	Go to Step 10	Go to Step 8
7	Inspect for poor connections at the harness connector of the Body Control Module (BCM). Did you find and correct the condition?	Go to Step 10	Go to Step 9
8	Replace the TIM reset switch. Did you complete the replacement?	Go to Step 10	--
9	Replace the BCM. Did you complete the replacement?	Go to Step 10	--
10	Operate the system in order to verify the repair. Did you correct the condition?	System OK	Go to Step 2

GC2040200218020X

Fig. 43 Low Tire Pressure Indicator Does Not Reset (Part 2 of 2). Century & Regal

Circuit Description

The ignition mode switch has 2 contact buttons.

The upper button, with a circle indicator on it, that starts the engine if the brake pedal is applied for automatic transmissions, or the clutch pedal is depressed for manual transmissions.

The lower button has 2 indicators on it, O and ACC. This button cycles the ignition through the following modes:

- *OFF*
  This is the normal state upon entering the vehicle, and can also be reached from any other mode by depressing the button. The O indicator illuminates.
- *Accessory*
  This mode can be reached from the Off state by depressing the button. The ACC indicator illuminates.
- *ON with the engine OFF*
  This state can be reached from the Off or Accessory modes by depressing the button for about 5-6 seconds. The upper LED illuminates.

Circuit/System Testing

1. Before beginning vehicle diagnosis, the following preliminary inspections/tests must be performed:

   - Ensure that the battery is fully charged.
   - Ensure that the battery cables are clean and tight.
   - Inspect for any open fuses.
   - Ensure that the grounds are clean, tight, and in the correct location.
   - Inspect the easily accessible systems or the visible system components for obvious damage or conditions that could cause the concern. This would include checking to ensure that all connections/connectors are fully seated and secured.
   - Inspect for aftermarket devices that could affect the operation of the system.
   - Search for applicable service bulletins.
   ⇒ If the preceding inspections/tests resolve the concern, go to Diagnostic Repair Verification.

2. Ignition ON and engine OFF, verify that the NO FOB DETECTED message is not displayed on the driver information center (DIC).

   ⇒ If the NO FOB DETECTED message is displayed, refer to Key Fob Not Detected .

3. Install a scan tool. Verify that the scan tool powers up.

   ⇒ If the scan tool does not power up, refer to Scan Tool Does Not Power Up .

ARM0700000000772

Fig. 45 Diagnostic System Check (Part 1 of 2). 2005–08 Corvette

4. Ignition ON, Engine OFF, verify communication with all of the control modules on the vehicle.

⇒ If the scan tool does not communicate with one or more of the expected control modules, refer to Data Link References.

5. Attempt to start the engine. Verify that the engine cranks.

⇒ If the engine does not crank, refer to Symptoms - Engine Electrical .

6. Attempt to start the engine. Verify the engine starts and idles.

⇒ If the engine does not start and idle, refer to Engine Cranks but Does Not Run.

7. Important:

- Do not clear any DTCs unless instructed to do so by a diagnostic procedure.
- If any DTCs are Powertrain related DTCs, select Capture Info in order to store the DTC information with the scan tool.

8. Advance to the List All DTCs selection on the scan tool. Verify there are no DTCs reported from any module.

⇒ If any DTCs are present, refer to Diagnostic Trouble Code (DTC) List - Vehicle and diagnose any current DTCs in the order they are displayed on the scan tool.

9. If the customer concern is related to inspection/maintenance (I/M) testing, refer to Inspection/Maintenance (I/M) System Check.

⇒ If none of the previous tests or inspections addresses the concern, refer to Symptoms - Vehicle .

ARM0700000000773

Fig. 45   Diagnostic System Check (Part 2 of 2). 2005–08 Corvette

Step	Action	Yes	No
5	Replace the TPM sensor. Did you complete the replacement?	Go to Step 6	System OK
6	1. Use the scan tool in order to clear the DTCs. 2. Operate the vehicle within normal operating conditions. Does the DTC reset?	Go to Step 7	System OK
7	1. Replace the RCDLR. 2. Program the TPM sensors. Refer to Tire Pressure Monitoring Sensor Programming. 3. Operate the vehicle within normal operating conditions. Does the DTC reset?	Go to Diagnostic Aids	System OK

GC2040200231020X

Fig. 46   Codes C0750, C0755, C0760 & C0765: No Current Tire Pressure Information Transmitted (Part 2 of 2). 2004–06 Corvette

Step	Action	Yes	No
1	Did you perform the TPM Diagnostic System Check?	Go to Step 2	Go to Diagnostic System Check -
2	1. Install a scan tool. 2. Turn ON the ignition, with the engine OFF. 3. With a scan tool, select the Remote Function Actuation (RFA) system Diagnostic Trouble Codes (DTC) function. Does the scan tool indicate that DTC C0750, C0755, C0760 or C0765 is current?	Go to Step 3	Go to Diagnostic Aids
3	Since some occurrences of this DTC are caused by radio interference, or driving conditions, review the TPM system with the customer to verify the conditions under which the DTC set. Did radio interference, or driving conditions cause this DTC to set?	Go to Diagnostic Aids	Go to Step 4
4	1. Clear the DTCs. 2. Reprogram all the TPM sensors. 3. Operate the vehicle within normal operating conditions. Does the DTC reset?	Go to Step 5	System OK

GC2040200231010X

Fig. 46   Codes C0750, C0755, C0760 & C0765: No Current Tire Pressure Information Transmitted (Part 1 of 2). 2004–06 Corvette

Diagnostic Instructions

- Perform the Diagnostic System Check - Vehicle prior to using this diagnostic procedure.

Circuit/System Description

The tire pressure monitor (TPM) system has a radio frequency (RF) transmitting pressure sensor in each wheel/tire assembly. As vehicle speed increases, centrifugal force closes the sensors internal roll switch, which puts the sensor into drive mode. The remote control door lock receiver (RCDLR) receives and translates the data contained in the tire pressure sensor RF transmissions into sensor presence, sensor mode, and tire pressure. Once vehicle speed is greater than 40km/h (25 mph), the RCDLR waits for the sensors to go into rolling mode. If one or more sensors do not go into rolling mode, or do not transmit at all, the RCDLR will set DTC C0750, C0755, C0760, or C0765 respectively.

Conditions for Running the DTC

Vehicle speed is greater than 25 mph.

Conditions for Setting the DTC

- A sensor does not transmit for 18 minutes.
- A sensor low battery condition.

Action Taken When the DTC Sets

- The Tire Pressure Monitor Indicator icon on the instrument panel cluster (IPC) flashes for 1 minute and then remains illuminated.
- If equipped, the driver information center (DIC) displays the suspect tire pressure as dashes.
- If equipped, the DIC displays a service tire monitor type message.

Conditions for Clearing the DTC

- A current DTC will clear when the malfunction is no longer present.
- The RCDLR automatically clears the history DTC when a current DTC is not detected in 100 consecutive drive cycles.

ARM0700000000777

Fig. 47   Codes C0750, C0755, C0760 & C0765: No Current Tire Pressure Information Transmitted (Part 1 of 2). 2007–08 Corvette

Diagnostic Aids

- Some aftermarket wheel valve stem holes are located further from the wheel rim than original equipment wheels. When using the TPM special tool to activate a sensor, ensure the tool antenna is no further than 15 cm (6 in) from the sensor and is aiming upward.
- Aftermarket wheel valve stem locations can cause a sensor to not function correctly.
- A sensor may have been damaged due to a previous wheel/tire service or flat tire event.
- The use of tire sealants can obstruct the sensor pressure sensing port and cause inaccurate tire pressure readings. If this condition is verified, remove the sealer from the tire and replace the sensor. Refer to Tire Pressure Indicator Sensor Replacement.
- Occasionally sensor transmissions are not received by the RCDLR due to vehicle level RF interference from items such as but not limited to aftermarket ignition systems, DVD players, CB radios, or metallic type window tinting.
- The sensor activation procedure may have to be repeated up to 3 times before determining a sensor is malfunctioning. In the event a particular sensor's information is displayed on the special tool upon activation but the horn does not chirp, it may be necessary to rotate the wheel valve stem to a different position due to the RF signal is being blocked by another component.
- Occasionally sensors can become mislocated due to previous tire rotations where the sensor learn procedure was not performed or stray sensor transmissions have been received from other vehicles . Always learn the sensors to ensure the DTC set is for that actual physical corner of the vehicle.
- A sensor low battery condition will set a sensor DTC but will not illuminate the low tire pressure indicator or display a message on the DIC, if equipped. The sensor battery condition can be verified in the scan tool RCDLR data list. If a sensor low battery condition is indicated on the scan tool, the sensor will need to be replaced. Refer to Tire Pressure Indicator Sensor Replacement .

Circuit/System Verification

1. Using the J-46079 or equivalent, activate each tire pressure sensor and record each sensors transmission data and physical location. Verify J-46079 or equivalent displays the 8-digit ID number, accurate tire pressure within 4 psi, Learn Mode, and at least a 1/4 graph signal strength displayed.

   ⇒ If any of the parameters listed above are not displayed, replace the suspect tire pressure sensor.

2. With the scan tool, verify tire pressure sensors ID and locations displayed on the scan tool match the IDs and locations recorded from the special tool.

   ⇒ If the IDs and locations do not match, perform the Tire Pressure Sensor Learn .

3. Enable the TPM learn mode. Use the TPM special tool in simulate mode to learn 4 simulated sensor transmissions into the RCDLR. Verify all 4 sensor locations, IDs, and that the tire pressures are within 4 psi., as they are displayed on the TPM special tool match what the scan tool displays.

   ⇒ If the scan tool does not match, replace the RCDLR.

4. Test drive the vehicle above 25 mph for greater than 2 minutes. With the scan tool, observe the suspect Pressure Sensor Mode data parameter. Verify sensor mode changes to Rolling.

   ⇒ If the suspect Pressure Sensor Mode does not change, replace the suspect tire pressure sensor.

Repair Instructions

Perform the Diagnostic Repair Verification after completing the diagnostic procedure.

- Tire Pressure Indicator Sensor Replacement
- Tire Pressure Sensor Learn
- Control Module References for RCDLR replacement, setup, and programming

ARM0700000000778

Fig. 47 Codes C0750, C0755, C0760 & C0765: No Current Tire Pressure Information Transmitted (Part 2 of 2). 2007–08 Corvette

Circuit/System Verification

1. With the scan tool, select instrument panel special functions Lamp Test. Command the instrument panel lamps ON. Verify tire pressure monitor indicator icon turns ON.

   If the icon does not turn ON, replace the IPC.

2. Using the tire pressure monitor tool No. J-46079 or equivalent, to observe the tire pressure of the suspected faulty sensor. Check the air pressure with a known accurate tire pressure gage. Compare the pressure reading to the display on the TPM special tool. Verify the pressure readings from special tool do not differ 4 psi., or more than actual tire pressure.

   If not within the specified range, replace the suspect tire pressure sensor.

3. With the scan tool, observe tire pressures in the scan tool data display. Verify pressure readings from special tool do not differ 4 psi or more than scan tool data display.

   If not within the specified range, replace the RCDLR.

4. Replace the RCDLR.

ARM0700000000732

Fig. 49 Low Tire Pressure Indicator Inoperative. Corvette

Circuit/System Testing

1. Inflate all tires to the proper pressure and drive the vehicle over 25 MPH for over 2 minutes.

2. Using tool No. J-46079 or equivalent, activate each tire pressure sensor and record each sensors tire pressure reading. Check the tire pressures with a known accurate hand held tire pressure gauge. Verify that the pressure readings from the special tool do not differ more than 4 psi., from the actual tire pressure readings.

   If not within the specified range, replace the suspect tire pressure sensor.

3. Using a scan tool, enable the TPM learn mode. Use the J-46079 or equivalent, in simulate mode to learn 4 simulated sensor transmissions into the RCDLR. Observe tire pressures in the scan tool data display. Verify the simulated tire pressures do not differ more than 4 psi., of the scan tool reading.

   If not within the specified range, replace the RCDLR.

4. Using a scan tool, select instrument panel special functions Lamp Test. Command the instrument panel warning lamps OFF. Verify the tire pressure monitor indicator icon turns OFF.

   If the tire pressure monitor icon does not turn OFF, replace the IPC.

5. Replace the RCDLR.

ARM0700000000730

Fig. 48 Low Tire Pressure Indicator Always On. Corvette

Step	Action	Yes	No
1	Perform the following preliminary inspections: • Ensure that the battery is fully charged. Refer to Battery Inspection/Test in Engine Electrical. • Ensure that the battery cables are clean and tight. • Inspect for any open fuses. • Inspect the easily accessible systems or the visible system components for obvious damage or conditions that could cause the symptom. • Ensure that the grounds are clean, tight, and in the correct location. • Inspect for aftermarket devices that could affect the operation of the system. • Search for applicable service bulletins. Did you find and correct the condition?	System OK	Go to Step 2
2	Install a scan tool. Does the scan tool power up?	Go to Step 3	Check Scan Tool Does Not Power Up
3	1. Turn ON the ignition, with the engine OFF. 2. Attempt to establish communication with all of the control modules on the vehicle. Does the scan tool communicate with all of the expected vehicle control modules?	Go to Step 4	Check Data Link References
4	**Important** 1. To ensure that RAP mode is inactive (if equipped), open the drivers door during the following step. 2. The engine may start during the following step. Turn OFF the engine as soon as you have observed the crank power mode. 1. Access the Power Mode parameter on the scan tool. 2. Rotate the ignition switch (operate the ignition mode switch) through all positions while observing the Power Mode parameter. Does the Power Mode parameter reading on the scan tool match the ignition switch position for all switch positions?	Go to Step 5	Check Power Mode Mismatch
5	Attempt to start the engine. Does the engine crank?	Go to Step 6	Go to Symptoms

ARM0400000000701

Fig. 50 Diagnostic System Check (Part 1 of 2). 2004–06 CTS

				Go to Engine Cranks but Does Not Run
6	Attempt to start the engine. Does the engine start and idle?		Go to Step 7	
7	**Important** Do not clear any DTCs unless instructed by a diagnostic procedure. Use the appropriate scan tool selections to obtain DTCs for each of the control modules. Does the scan tool display any DTCs?		Go to Step 8	Go to Step 12
8	Does the scan tool display any DTCs that begin with a "U"?		Go to Diagnostic Trouble Code (DTC)	Go to Step 9
9	**Important** If any of these DTCs are displayed, diagnose them before diagnosing any other DTCs or symptoms. Does the scan tool display DTC B1000, B1004, B1007, B1009, C0550, C0551, C0565, P0601, P0602, P0603, P0604, P0605, P0606, P0607, P1600, P1621, or P2610?		Diagnostic Trouble Code (DTC)	Go to Step 10
10	**Important** If any of these DTCs are displayed, diagnose them before diagnosing any other DTCs or symptoms. Does the scan tool display DTC B1327, B1328, B1336, B1372, B1382, B1390, B1420, B1513, B1514, C0820, C0870, C0880, C0899, C0900, P0560, P0562, or P0563?		Go to Diagnostic Trouble Code (DTC)	Go to Step 11
11	**Important** If any of the remaining DTCs are powertrain DTCs, select Captured Info in order to store the powertrain DTC information with a scan tool. If multiple DTCs are stored, diagnose the DTCs in the following order: 1. Component level DTCs, such as sensor, solenoid DTCs, and relay DTCs. 2. System level DTCs, such as misfire DTCs, EVAP system DTCs, and fuel trim DTCs. Diagnose the remaining DTCs.		Go to Diagnostic Trouble Code (DTC) List - Vehicle	
12	Is the customers concern with inspection/maintenance (I/M) testing?		Go to Inspection/Maintenance (I/M) System Check / Go to Inspection/Maintenance (I/M) System Check / Go to Inspection/Maintenance (I/M) System Check	Go to Symptoms

ARM0400000000702

Fig. 50   Diagnostic System Check (Part 2 of 2). 2004–06 CTS

6. Ignition ON, view the security indicator. The security indicator should not remain illuminated after the vehicle bulb check has completed.

⇒ If the security indicator remains illuminated after the bulb check, refer to Diagnostic Trouble Code (DTC) List - Vehicle and diagnose any of the following theft deterrent DTCs set as current: B1000, B302A, B3031, B3055, B3060, B3935, B3976, P0513, P0633, P1629, P1631, or P1632.

7. Attempt to start the engine. Verify that the engine cranks.

⇒ If the engine does not crank, refer to Symptoms - Engine Electrical .

8. Attempt to start the engine. Verify the engine starts and runs.

⇒ If the engine does not start and run, refer to Engine Cranks but Does Not Run .

Important: Do not clear any DTCs unless instructed to do so by a diagnostic procedure.
Important: If any DTCs are Powertrain related DTCs, select Capture Info in order to store the DTC information with the scan tool.

9. Use the appropriate scan tool selections to obtain DTCs from each of the vehicle modules. Verify there are no DTCs reported from any module.

⇒ If any DTCs are present, refer to Diagnostic Trouble Code (DTC) List - Vehicle and diagnose any current DTCs in the following order:

9.1. DTCs that begin with a U
9.2. Any of the following: B1000, B1001, B1008, B1015, B1016, B1019, C0550, C0551, C0561, C0563, C0565, P0601, P0602, P0603, P0604, P0606, P0607, P060D, P062F, P2105, P2107, or P2610.
9.3. Any of the following: B1325, B1327, B1328, B1424, B1441, B1517, C0895, C0899, C0900, P0560, P0562, or P0563
9.4. Component level DTCs.
9.5. System level DTCs.
9.6. Any remaining DTCs.

10. If the customer concern is related to inspection/maintenance (I/M) testing, refer to Inspection/Maintenance (I/M) System Check.

⇒ If none of the previous tests or inspections addresses the concern, refer to Symptoms - Vehicle.

PMM Power Mode Parameters	Current Power Mode	Ignition Off/Run/Crank (Off/Run Crank Voltage Circuit)	Ignition Accessory/Run (Accessory Voltage Circuit)	Ignition Run/Crank (Ignition 1 Voltage Circuit)
Ignition Switch Position				
Off Key Out	Off	Key Out/ACC	Inactive	Inactive
Off Key IN	Off	Key In/Off	Inactive	Inactive
Accessory	Accessory	Key Out/ACC	Active	Inactive
Run	Run	Run	Active	Active
Start	Crank Request	Crank	Inactive	Active

ARM0700000000780

Fig. 51   Diagnostic System Check (Part 2 of 2). 2007–08 CTS

Diagnostic System Check - CTS

1. Verify that none of the following preliminary inspections/tests reveal the cause of the vehicle concern before beginning diagnosis:

- Ensure that the battery is fully charged.
- Ensure that the battery cables are clean and tight.
- Inspect for any open fuses.
- Ensure that the grounds are clean, tight, and in the correct location.
- Inspect the easily accessible systems or the visible system components for obvious damage or conditions that could cause the concern. This would include checking to ensure that all connections/connectors are fully seated and secured.
- Inspect for aftermarket devices that could affect the operation of the system.
- Search for applicable service bulletins.

2. Install a scan tool. Verify that the scan tool powers up.

⇒ If the scan tool does not power up, refer to Scan Tool Does Not Power Up.

3. Ignition ON, Engine OFF, verify communication with all of the control modules on the vehicle. Refer to Data Link References for information on the modules you should expect to communicate.

⇒ If the scan tool does not communicate with one or more of the expected control modules, refer to Data Link References.

4. Verify that the following DTCs are not set: U1814, B1428.

⇒ If either of the DTCs are set, refer to DTC U1814 or DTC B1428.

Important: Open the driver's door to ensure retained accessory power mode (RAP) is inactive during this test. The engine may start during this test. Turn the engine OFF as soon as the crank power mode has been observed.

5. With a scan tool, access the Body Control Module Power Mode data display list. Verify that all the parameters listed in the following table correspond to the ignition key position. The PMM Power Mode parameters table below illustrates the correct state of these parameters (circuits) with the corresponding ignition switch positions. The circuits related to the parameters are in parenthesis.

⇒ If any of the power mode parameters do not match in any ignition switch position, refer to Power Mode Mismatch.

ARM0700000000779

Fig. 51   Diagnostic System Check (Part 1 of 2). 2007–08 CTS

The numbers below refer to the step numbers on the diagnostic table.

2. Tests if the sensors can transmit valid data with good signal strength in response to a low frequency activation. During this step it is important to observe the signal strength graph on the TPM tool's display screen. Any more that 1/4 graph displayed can be considered good signal strength.

3. Tests if any sensors are mislocated.

4. Tests if the driver antenna module can receive, learn and translate the data contained in simulated sensor transmissions.

6. Tests if the sensor's internal roll switch is functioning properly.

Step	Action	Yes	No
1	Did you perform the Diagnostic System Check - Vehicle?	Go to Step 2	Go to Diagnostic System Check - Vehicle
2	Using the J-46079 TPM diagnostic tool, activate each tire pressure sensor and record each sensor's transmission data and physical location on the repair order. Does the TPM diagnostic tool display each sensor's transmission data as an 8-digit ID number, accurate tire pressure +/- 2 psi, Learn Mode, good signal strength?	Go to Step 3	Go to Step 7
3	1. Turn ON the ignition, with the engine OFF. 2. Observe all 4 sensor IDs and their locations with a scan tool. Do the IDs and their locations observed on the scan tool match the IDs and locations recorded on the repair order?	Go to Step 4	Go to Step 5
4	1. Enable The TPM learn mode. 2. Using the TPM diagnostic tool in simulate mode, learn 4 simulated sensor transmissions into the driver antenna module's memory. 3. With the scan tool, observe all 4 sensor location, Ids and tire pressures. Does the scan tool display all 4 sensor locations, IDs, and tire pressures as specified?	Go to Step 5	Go to Step 8
5	Learn the tire pressure sensors. Did you complete the procedure?	Go to Step 6	—
6	1. Test drive the vehicle above 32 km/h (20 mph) for 10 seconds. 2. Observe the suspect Pressure Sensor Mode data parameter with the scan tool. Does the suspect Pressure Sensor Mode data parameter change from Wake to Drive above 32 km/h (20 mph)?	System OK	Go to Step 7
7	Replace the suspect tire pressure sensor. Did a horn chirp sound when learning the suspect sensor?	Go to Step 9	—
8	Replace the driver side antenna module. Did you complete the replacement?	Go to Step 9	—
9	1. Clear the DTCs with a scan tool. 2. Operate the vehicle within the Conditions for Running the DTC. Does the DTC reset?	Go to Step 2	System OK

ARM0400000000703

Fig. 52   Codes C0750, C0755, C0760 & C0765: Tire Pressure Sensor Low. 2004–06 CTS

Diagnostic Instructions

- Perform the Diagnostic System Check - Vehicle prior to using this diagnostic procedure.

Circuit/System Description

The tire pressure monitor (TPM) system has a radio frequency (RF) transmitting pressure sensor in each wheel/tire assembly. As vehicle speed increases, centrifugal force closes the sensors internal roll switch, which puts the sensor into drive mode. The remote control door lock receiver (RCDLR) receives and translates the data contained in the tire pressure sensor RF transmissions into sensor presence, sensor mode, and tire pressure. Once vehicle speed is greater than 25 mph, the RCDLR waits for the sensors to go into rolling mode. If one or more sensors do not go into rolling mode, or do not transmit at all, the RCDLR will set DTC C0750, C0755, C0760, or C0765 respectively.

Conditions for Running the DTC

Vehicle speed is greater than 25 mph.

Conditions for Setting the DTC

- A sensor does not transmit for 18 minutes.
- A sensor low battery condition.

Action Taken When the DTC Sets

- The Tire Pressure Monitor Indicator icon on the instrument panel cluster (IPC) flashes for 1 minute and then remains illuminated.
- If equipped, the driver information center (DIC) displays the suspect tire pressure as dashes.
- If equipped, the DIC displays a service tire monitor type message.

Conditions for Clearing the DTC

- A current DTC will clear when the malfunction is no longer present.
- The RCDLR automatically clears the history DTC when a current DTC is not detected in 100 consecutive drive cycles.

ARM0700000000781

Fig. 53 Codes C0750, C0755, C760 & C0765: Tire Pressure Sensor Low (Part 1 of 3). 2007–08 CTS

Circuit/System Verification

1. Using the J-46079 or equivalent, activate each tire pressure sensor and record each sensors transmission data and physical location. Verify J-46079 displays the 8-digit ID number, accurate tire pressure within 4 psi, Learn Mode, and at least a 1/4 graph signal strength displayed.

   ⇒ If any of the parameters listed above are not displayed, replace the suspect tire pressure sensor.

2. With the scan tool, verify tire pressure sensors ID and locations displayed on the scan tool match the IDs and locations recorded from the special tool.

   ⇒ If the IDs and locations do not match, perform the Tire Pressure Sensor Learn.

3. Enable the TPM learn mode. Use the TPM special tool in simulate mode to learn 4 simulated sensor transmissions into the RCDLR. Verify all 4 sensor locations, IDs, and that the tire pressures are within 4 psi as they are displayed on the TPM special tool match what the scan tool displays.

   ⇒ If the scan tool does not match, replace the RCDLR.

4. Test drive the vehicle above 25 mph for greater than 2 minutes. With the scan tool, observe the suspect Pressure Sensor Mode data parameter. Verify sensor mode changes to Rolling.

   ⇒ If the suspect Pressure Sensor Mode does not change, replace the suspect tire pressure sensor.

Repair Instructions

Perform the Diagnostic Repair Verification after completing the diagnostic procedure.

- Tire Pressure Indicator Sensor Replacement
- Tire Pressure Sensor Learn
- Control Module References for RCDLR replacement, setup, and programming

ARM0700000000783

Fig. 53 Codes C0750, C0755, C760 & C0765: Tire Pressure Sensor Low (Part 3 of 3). 2007–08 CTS

Diagnostic Aids

- Some aftermarket wheel valve stem holes are located further from the wheel rim than original equipment wheels. When using the TPM special tool to activate a sensor, ensure the tool antenna is no further than 15 cm (6 in) from the sensor and is aiming upward.
- Aftermarket wheel valve stem locations can cause a sensor to not function correctly.
- A sensor may have been damaged due to a previous wheel/tire service or flat tire event.
- The use of tire sealants can obstruct the sensor pressure sensing port and cause inaccurate tire pressure readings. If this condition is verified, remove the sealer from the tire and replace the sensor. Refer to Tire Pressure Indicator Sensor Replacement.
- Occasionally sensor transmissions are not received by the RCDLR due to vehicle level RF interference from items such as but not limited to aftermarket ignition systems, DVD players, CB radios, or metallic type window tinting.
- The sensor activation procedure may have to be repeated up to 3 times before determining a sensor is malfunctioning. In the event a particular sensor's information is displayed on the special tool upon activation but the horn does not chirp, it may be necessary to rotate the wheel valve stem to a different position due to the RF signal is being blocked by another component.
- Occasionally sensors can become mislocated due to previous tire rotations where the sensor learn procedure was not performed or stray sensor transmissions have been received from other vehicles . Always learn the sensors to ensure the DTC set is for that actual physical corner of the vehicle. Refer to Tire Pressure Sensor Learn.
- A sensor low battery condition will set a sensor DTC but will not illuminate the low tire pressure indicator or display a message on the DIC, if equipped. The sensor battery condition can be verified in the scan tool RCDLR data list. If a sensor low battery condition is indicated on the scan tool, the sensor will need to be replaced.

ARM0700000000782

Fig. 53 Codes C0750, C0755, C760 & C0765: Tire Pressure Sensor Low (Part 2 of 3). 2007–08 CTS

Step	Action	Yes	No
1	Did you perform the Diagnostic System Check - Vehicle?	Go to Step 2	Go to Diagnostic System Check
2	1. Turn OFF the ignition. 2. Turn ON the ignition, with the engine OFF. 3. Observe the low tire pressure indicator on the instrument panel cluster (IPC) during bulb check. Does the indicator illuminate during bulb check and then turn OFF?	Test for Intermittent Conditions and Poor Connections	Go to Step 3
3	Inspect the tires for proper inflation pressure and inflate to the recommended kPa/psi, if needed. Did you find and correct the condition?	Go to Step 5	Go to Step 4
4	Replace the IPC. Did you complete the replacement?	Go to Step 5	--
5	Operate the system in order to verify the repair. Did you correct the condition?	System OK	Go to Step 2

ARM0400000000704

Fig. 54 Low Tire Pressure Indicator Always On. 2004–06 CTS

Diagnostic Instructions

- Perform the Diagnostic System Check - Vehicle prior to using this diagnostic procedure.

Circuit/System Description

The remote control door lock receiver (RCDLR) receives a radio frequency (RF) transmission from each tire pressure sensor. Each sensor RF transmission contains its own unique identification (ID) code that must be learned into the RCDLR memory. Once all 4 IDs have been learned and vehicle speed is greater than 25 mph, the RCDLR continuously compares IDs in received transmission to its learned IDs to determine if all 4 sensors are present. If the remote control door lock receiver (RCDLR) detects a low tire pressure condition or a malfunction in the system, it will send a serial data message to the instrument panel cluster (IPC) requesting tire pressure monitor indicator illumination and to display a data message on the driver information center (DIC,) if equipped.

Diagnostic Aids

- Some aftermarket wheel valve stem holes are located further from the wheel rim than original equipment wheels. When using the TPM special tool to activate a sensor, ensure the tool antenna is no further than 15 cm (6 in) from the sensor and is aiming upward.
- Aftermarket wheel value stem locations can cause a sensor to not function correctly.
- A sensor may have been damaged due to a previous wheel/tire service or flat tire event.
- The use of tire sealants can obstruct the sensor pressure sensing port and cause inaccurate tire pressure readings. If this condition is verified, remove the sealer from the tire and replace the sensor. Refer to Tire Pressure Indicator Sensor Replacement.
- Occasionally sensor transmissions are not received by the RCDLR due to vehicle level RF interference from items such as but not limited to aftermarket ignition systems, DVD players, CB radios, or metallic type window tinting.
- The sensor activation procedure may have to be repeated up to 3 times before determining a sensor is malfunctioning. In the event a particular sensor's information is displayed on the special tool upon activation but the horn does not chirp, it may be necessary to rotate the wheel valve stem to a different position due to the RF signal is being blocked by another component.
- Occasionally sensors can become mislocated due to previous tire rotations where the sensor learn procedure was not performed or stray sensor transmissions have been received from other vehicles. Always learn the sensors to ensure the DTC set is for that actual physical corner of the vehicle. Refer to Tire Pressure Sensor Learn .

Circuit/System Verification

Important: When a TPM DTC is set, the tire pressure monitor indicator icon will flash for 1 minute after the IPC bulb check is completed and then remains illuminated. If equipped with a DIC, a service tire monitor type message will also be displayed.

Low tire pressure in one or more tires is indicated by a continuously illuminated tire pressure monitor indicator icon after the IPC bulb check is completed. If equipped with a DIC, a check tire pressure type message will also be displayed.

Cycle the ignition from OFF to ON. After the instrument panel cluster (IPC) bulb check is complete, the tire pressure monitor indicator icon should not be illuminated.

ARM0700000000784

Fig. 55   Low Tire Pressure Indicator Always On (Part 1 of 2). 2007–08 CTS

Step	Action	Yes	No
1	Did you perform the Diagnostic System Check - Vehicle?	Go to Step 2	Go to Diagnostic System Check - Vehicle
2	1. Turn OFF the ignition. 2. Turn ON the ignition, with the engine OFF. 3. Observe the low tire pressure indicator on the instrument panel cluster (IPC) during bulb check. Does the indicator illuminate during bulb check and then turn OFF?		Go to Step 3
3	Replace the IPC. Did you complete the replacement?	Go to Step 4	--
4	Operate the system in order to verify the repair. Did you correct the condition?	System OK	Go to Step 2

ARM0400000000705

Fig. 56   Low Tire Pressure Indicator Inoperative. 2004–06 CTS

Circuit/System Testing

1. Inflate all tires to the proper pressure and drive the vehicle over 25 MPH for over 2 minutes.
2. Using the J-46079 or equivalent, activate each tire pressure sensor and record each sensors tire pressure reading. Check the tire pressures with a known accurate hand held tire pressure gauge. Verify that the pressure readings from the special tool do not differ more than 4 psi., from the actual tire pressure readings.

   ⇒ If not within the specified range, replace the suspect tire pressure sensor.

3. Using a scan tool, enable the TPM learn mode. Use the J-46079 in simulate mode to learn 4 simulated sensor transmissions into the RCDLR. Observe tire pressures in the scan tool data display. Verify the simulated tire pressures do not differ more than +/- 4 psi of the scan tool reading.

   ⇒ If not within the specified range, replace the RCDLR.

4. Using a scan tool, select instrument panel special functions Lamp Test. Command the instrument panel warning lamps OFF. Verify the tire pressure monitor indicator icon turns OFF.

   ⇒ If the tire pressure monitor icon does not turn OFF, replace the IPC.

5. Ignition ON, use the scan tool to setup the Tire Type/Pressure Selection in the RCDLR Module Setup menu. Verify the tire pressure monitor indicator icon turns OFF.

   ⇒ If the tire pressure monitor icon does not turn OFF, replace the RCDLR.

Repair Instructions

Perform the Diagnostic Repair Verification after completing the diagnostic procedure.

- Tire Pressure Indicator Sensor Replacement
- Tire Pressure Sensor Learn
- Control Module References for IPC or RCDLR replacement, setup, and programming

ARM0700000000785

Fig. 55   Low Tire Pressure Indicator Always On (Part 2 of 2). 2007–08 CTS

Diagnostic Fault Information

- Perform the Diagnostic System Check - Vehicle prior to using this diagnostic procedure.

Circuit/System Description

The remote control door lock receiver (RCDLR) receives a radio frequency (RF) transmission from each tire pressure sensor. Each sensor RF transmission contains its own unique identification (ID) code that must be learned into the RCDLR memory. Once all 4 IDs have been learned and vehicle speed is greater than 25 mph, the RCDLR continuously compares IDs in received transmission to its learned IDs to determine if all 4 sensors are present. If the remote control door lock receiver (RCDLR) detects a low tire pressure condition or a malfunction in the system, it will send a serial data message to the instrument panel cluster (IPC) requesting tire pressure monitor indicator icon illumination and to display a data message on the driver information center (DIC) if equipped.

Diagnostic Aids

- Some aftermarket wheel valve stem holes are located further from the wheel rim than original equipment wheels. When using the TPM special tool to activate a sensor, ensure the tool antenna is no further than 15 cm (6 in) from the sensor and is aiming upward.
- Aftermarket wheel value stem locations can cause a sensor to not function correctly.
- A sensor may have been damaged due to a previous wheel/tire service or flat tire event.
- The use of tire sealants can obstruct the sensor pressure sensing port and cause inaccurate tire pressure readings. If this condition is verified, remove the sealer from the tire and replace the sensor. Refer to Tire Pressure Indicator Sensor Replacement.
- Occasionally sensor transmissions are not received by the RCDLR due to vehicle level RF interference from items such as but not limited to aftermarket ignition systems, DVD players, CB radios, or metallic type window tinting.
- The sensor activation procedure may have to be repeated up to 3 times before determining a sensor is malfunctioning. In the event a particular sensor's information is displayed on the special tool upon activation but the horn does not chirp, it may be necessary to rotate the wheel valve stem to a different position due to the RF signal is being blocked by another component.
- Occasionally sensors can become mislocated due to previous tire rotations where the sensor learn procedure was not performed or stray sensor transmissions have been received from other vehicles . Always learn the sensors to ensure the DTC set is for that actual physical corner of the vehicle. Refer to Tire Pressure Sensor Learn .

ARM0700000000786

Fig. 57   Low Tire Pressure Indicator Inoperative (Part 1 of 2). 2007–08 CTS

Circuit/System Testing

1. With the scan tool, select instrument panel special functions Lamp Test. Command the instrument panel lamps ON. Verify tire pressure monitor indicator icon turns ON.

   ⇒ If the icon does not turn ON, replace the IPC.

2. Using the tire pressure monitor (TPM) special tool to observe the tire pressure of the suspected faulty sensor. Check the air pressure with a known accurate tire pressure gage. Compare the pressure reading to the display on the TPM special tool. Verify the pressure readings from special tool do not differ 4 psi or more than actual tire pressure.

   ⇒ If not within the specified range, replace the suspect tire pressure sensor.

3. With the scan tool, observe tire pressures in the scan tool data display. Verify pressure readings from special tool do not differ 4 psi or more than scan tool data display.

   ⇒ If not within the specified range, replace the RCDLR.

Repair Instructions

Perform the Diagnostic Repair Verification after completing the diagnostic procedure.

- Tire Pressure Indicator Sensor Replacement
- Tire Pressure Sensor Learn

ARM0700000000787

Fig. 57   Low Tire Pressure Indicator Inoperative (Part 2 of 2). 2007-08 CTS

Step	Action	Yes	No
1	Did you perform the TPM Diagnostic System Check?	Go to Step 2	Go to Diagnostic System Check -
2	1. Install a scan tool. 2. Turn ON the ignition, with the engine OFF. 3. With a scan tool, select the Diagnostic Trouble Code (DTC) function in Tire Pressure Monitor. Does the scan tool indicate that DTC C0750, C0755, C0760, or C0765 is current?	Go to Step 3	Go to Diagnostic Aids
3	Since some occurrences of this DTC are caused by radio frequency interference, or driving conditions, review the TPM system with the customer to verify the conditions under which the DTC set. Did vehicle operation cause this DTC to set?	Go to Diagnostic Aids	Go to Step 4
4	With the scan tool, observe the suspect sensor's Tire Pressure Sensor Battery Status data parameter in the Tire Pressure Monitor Data Display list. Does the scan tool indicate that the sensor battery status is OK?	Go to Step 5	Go to Step 6

GC2040200233010X

Fig. 59   Codes C0750, C0755, C0760 & C0765: No Current Tire Pressure Information Transmitted (Part 1 of 2). Deville & Seville

Step	Action	Yes	No
1	Install a scan tool. Does the scan tool power up?	Go to Step 2	Scan Tool Does Not Power Up
2	1. Turn ON the ignition, with the engine OFF. 2. Attempt to establish communication with the RCDLR. Does the scan tool communicate with the RCDLR?	Go to Step 3	Scan Tool Does Not Communicate with Class 2 Device
3	Select the RKE Diagnostic Trouble Codes (DTC) function on the scan tool. Does the scan tool display any DTCs that begin with a "U"?	Go to Diagnostic Trouble Code (DTC)	Go to Step 4
4	Does the scan tool display any RKE DTCs?	Go to Diagnostic Trouble Code (DTC)	Go to Step 5
5	Does the scan tool display any TPM DTCs?	Go to Diagnostic Trouble Code (DTC)	System OK

GC2040200232000X

Fig. 58   Diagnostic System Check. Deville & Seville

Step	Action	Yes	No
5	1. Use the scan tool in order to clear the DTCs. 2. Operate the vehicle within normal operating conditions. Does the DTC reset?	Go to Step 6	System OK
6	Replace the TPM sensor. Did you complete the replacement?	Go to Step 7	System OK
7	1. Use the scan tool in order to clear the DTCs. 2. Operate the vehicle within normal operating conditions. Does the DTC reset?	Go to Step 8	System OK
8	1. Replace the RCDLR. 2. Program the TPM sensors. 3. Operate the vehicle within normal operating conditions. Does the DTC reset?	Go to Diagnostic Aids	System OK

GC2040200233020X

Fig. 59   Codes C0750, C0755, C0760 & C0765: No Current Tire Pressure Information Transmitted (Part 2 of 2). Deville & Seville

Diagnostic System Check - Tire Pressure Monitoring

Perform the Diagnostic System Check - Vehicle prior to using this diagnostic procedure.

Review the systems description and operation in order to familiarize yourself with the system functions. Refer to Tire Pressure Monitor Description and Operation.

1. Inspect for aftermarket devices which could affect the operation of the Tire Pressure Monitoring (TPM) system to verify that none are installed. Refer to Checking Aftermarket Accessories.

   ⇒ If such devices are installed, remove/disable them and retest.

2. Inspect the easily accessible or visible system components for obvious damage or conditions which could cause the symptom.

   ⇒ If damage or such conditions are found, repair as required.

3. Verify that the scan tool Selected Front and Rear Tire Pressure parameters are correct compared to the tires actual pressure ratings.

   ⇒ If Tire Pressure parameters are not correct, use scan tool special functions to adjust setting.

4. Using J-46079 Tire Pressure Monitor Diagnostic Tool or equivalent, verify that the scan tool pressure sensor ID parameters match the actual on-vehicle locations.

   ⇒ If actual pressure sensor locations do not match scan tool readings, refer to Tire Pressure Sensor Learn .

5. Verify that the scan tool TPM System Enabled parameter is YES.

   ⇒ If the TPM System Enabled parameter is NO, use scan tool special functions to adjust setting.

6. Verify that tires are inflated to the correct pressure.

ARM0700000000734

Fig. 60 Diagnostic System Check. 2006–07 DTS

7. Attempt to start the engine. Verify that the engine cranks.

   ⇒ If the engine does not crank, refer to Symptoms - Engine Electrical .

8. Attempt to start the engine. Verify the engine starts and runs.

   ⇒ If the engine does not start and run, refer to Engine Cranks but Does Not Run .

   Important: Do not clear any DTCs unless instructed to do so by a diagnostic procedure.
   Important: If any DTCs are Powertrain related DTCs, select Capture Info in order to store the DTC information with the scan tool.

9. Use the appropriate scan tool selections to obtain DTCs from each of the vehicle modules. Verify there are no DTCs reported from any module.

   ⇒ If any DTCs are present, refer to Diagnostic Trouble Code (DTC) List - Vehicle and diagnose any current DTCs in the following order:

   9.1. DTCs that begin with a U

   9.2. Any of the following: B1000, B1001, B1008, B1015, B1016, B1019, C0550, C0558, C0569, C1002, P0601, P0602, P0603, P0604, P0606, P0607, P060D, P062F, or P2610

   9.3. Any of the following: B1325, B1335, B1340, B1370, B1424, B1441, B1517, C0800, C0895, C0899, C0900, P0562, or P0563

   9.4. Component level DTCs

   9.5. System level DTCs

   9.6. Any remaining DTCs

10. If the customer concern is related to inspection/maintenance (I/M) testing, refer to Inspection/Maintenance (I/M) System Check.

PMM Power Mode Parameters / Ignition Switch Position	Current Power Mode	Ign. Off/Run/Crank (Off/Run Crank voltage circuit)	Ignition Accessory/Run (Accessory voltage circuit)	Ignition Run/Crank (Ignition 1 Voltage circuit)
Off Key Out	Off	Key Out/ACC	Inactive	Inactive
Off Key IN	Off	Key In/Off	Inactive	Inactive
Accessory	Accessory	Key Out/ACC	Active	Inactive
Run	Run	Run	Active	Active
Start	Crank Request	Crank	Inactive	Active

ARM0700000000789

Fig. 61 Diagnostic System Check (Part 2 of 2). 2008 DTS

Diagnostic System Check - DTS

1. Verify that none of the following preliminary inspections/tests reveal the cause of the vehicle concern before beginning diagnosis:

   • Ensure that the battery is fully charged.
   • Ensure that the battery cables are clean and tight.
   • Inspect for any open fuses.
   • Ensure that the grounds are clean, tight, and in the correct location.
   • Inspect the easily accessible systems or the visible system components for obvious damage or conditions that could cause the concern. This would include checking to ensure that all connections/connectors are fully seated and secured.
   • Inspect for aftermarket devices that could affect the operation of the system.
   • Search for applicable service bulletins.

   ⇒ If the preceding inspections/tests resolve the concern, refer to Diagnostic Repair Verification.

2. Install a scan tool. Verify that the scan tool powers up.

   ⇒ If the scan tool does not power up, refer to Scan Tool Does Not Power Up.

3. Ignition ON, engine OFF, verify communication with all of the control modules on the vehicle. Refer to Data Link References for information on the modules you should expect to communicate.

   ⇒ If the scan tool does not communicate with one or more of the expected control modules, refer to Data Link References.

4. Verify that the following DTCs are not set: U1814, B1428.

   ⇒ If either of the DTCs are set, refer to DTC U1814 or DTC B1428.

   Important: Open the driver's door to ensure retained accessory power mode (RAP) is inactive during this test. The engine may start during this test. Turn the engine OFF as soon as the crank power mode has been observed. With a scan tool, access the Body Control Module Power Mode data display list.

5. Verify that all the parameters listed in the following table correspond to the ignition key position. The PMM Power Mode parameters table below illustrates the correct state of these parameters (circuits) with the corresponding ignition switch positions. The circuits related to the parameters are in parenthesis.

   ⇒ If any of the power mode parameters do not match in any ignition switch position, refer to Power Mode Mismatch.

6. Ignition ON, view the security indicator. The security indicator should not remain illuminated after the vehicle bulb check has completed.

   ⇒ If the security indicator remains illuminated after the bulb check, refer to Diagnostic Trouble Code (DTC) List - Vehicle and diagnose any of the following theft deterrent DTCs set as current: B1000, B302A, B3031, B3055, B3060, B3935, B3976, P0513, P0633, P1629, P1631, or P1632.

ARM0700000000788

Fig. 61 Diagnostic System Check (Part 1 of 2). 2008 DTS

Diagnostic Fault Information

Important: Always perform the Diagnostic System Check - Tire Pressure Monitoring prior to using this diagnostic procedure.

Circuit/System Description

The remote control door lock receiver (RCDLR) receives a radio frequency (RF) transmission from each tire pressure sensor. Each sensors RF transmission contains its own unique identification (ID) code that must be learned into the RCDLR memory. Once all 4 IDs have been learned and vehicle speed is 25 mph, or greater, the RCDLR continuously compares IDs in received transmission to its learned IDs to determine if all 4 sensors are present.

Conditions for Running the DTC

The ignition is ON.

Conditions for Setting the DTC

The RCDLR has not undergone the tire type and tire pressure selection setup procedure.

Action Taken When the DTC Sets

The driver information center (DIC) displays the SERVICE TIRE MONITOR warning message.

Conditions for Clearing the DTC

A current DTC will clear when the RCDLR has undergone the setup procedure.

ARM0500000000846

Fig. 62 Code C0569: System Configuration Error (Part 1 of 2). DTS

Diagnostic Aids

A newly replaced RCDLR will set DTC C0569 on its initial ignition ON cycle. Tire type and tire pressure selection setup must be performed.

Important: Always perform the Diagnostic Repair Verification after completing the diagnostic procedure.

Control Module References for RCDLR replacement, setup, and programming.

ARM0500000000847

Fig. 62   Code C0569: System Configuration Error (Part 2 of 2). DTS

Diagnostic Aids

- Some aftermarket wheel valve stem holes are located further from the wheel rim than original equipment wheels. When using the TPM special tool to activate a sensor, ensure the tools antenna is no further than 15 cm (6 in) from the sensor.
- The sensor activation procedure may have to be repeated up to 3 times before determining a sensor is malfunctioning.
- Occasionally sensors can become mislocated due to previous tire rotations where the sensor learn procedure was not performed. Always learn the sensors to ensure the DTC set is for that actual physical corner of the vehicle.
- Occasionally sensor transmissions are not received by the RCDLR due to vehicle level RF interference.

Test drive the vehicle at a speed of 25 mph or greater for 2 minutes. No tire pressure monitor DTCs should set.

Circuit/System Testing

Note: Tire pressure sensors should transmit valid data with good signal strength in response to low frequency activation from the TPM special tool. It is important to observe the signal strength graph on the TPM special tool display screen after the activate button has been pressed and released. Any more than 1/4 graph displayed can be considered good signal strength.

1. Using the special tool, activate each tire pressure sensor and record each sensors transmission data and physical location. Verify tool displays 8-digit ID number, accurate tire pressure +/- 2 psi, Learn Mode, and good signal strength.
   ⇒ If any of the parameters listed above are not displayed, replace the suspect tire pressure sensor.
2. With the scan tool, verify tire pressure sensors ID and locations displayed on the scan tool match the IDs and locations recorded from the special tool.
   ⇒ If the IDs and locations do not match, perform Sensor Learn procedure.
3. Enable the TPM learn mode. Use the TPM special tool in simulate mode to learn 4 simulated sensor transmissions into the RCDLR. Verify all 4 sensor locations, IDs, and tire pressures (+/- 2 psi) as they are displayed on the TPM special tool match what the scan tool displays.
   If the scan tool does not match, replace the RCDLR.

ARM0500000000849

Fig. 63   Codes C0750, C0755, C0760 & C0765: Tire Pressure Sensor Low (Part 2 of 3). DTS

Diagnostic Fault Information

Important: Always perform the Diagnostic System Check - Tire Pressure Monitoring prior to using this diagnostic procedure.

Circuit/System Description

The remote control door lock receiver (RCDLR) receives a radio frequency (RF) transmission from each tire pressure sensor. Each sensors RF transmission contains its own unique identification (ID) code that must be learned into the RCDLR memory. Once all 4 IDs have been learned and vehicle speed is 25 mph or greater, the RCDLR continuously compares IDs in received transmission to its learned IDs to determine if all 4 sensors are present.

Conditions for Running the DTC

The ignition is ON.

Conditions for Setting the DTC

The RCDLR has not undergone the tire pressure sensor learn procedure.

Action Taken When the DTC Sets

The driver information center (DIC) displays the SERVICE TIRE MONITOR warning message.

Conditions for Clearing the DTC

A current DTC will clear when the RCDLR has undergone the sensor learn procedure.

ARM0500000000851

Fig. 64   Code C0775: Low Tire Pressure System Sensors Not Learned (Part 1 of 2). DTS

Diagnostic Fault Information

Important: Always perform the Diagnostic System Check - Tire Pressure Monitoring prior to using this diagnostic procedure.

Circuit/System Description

The tire pressure monitor (TPM) system has a radio frequency (RF) transmitting pressure sensor in each wheel/tire assembly. As vehicle speed increases, centrifugal force closes the sensors internal roll switch, which puts the sensor into drive mode. The remote control door lock receiver (RCDLR) receives and translates the data contained in the tire pressure sensor RF transmissions into sensor presence, sensor mode, and tire pressure. Once vehicle speed is 20 mph or greater, the RCDLR waits for the first sensor to go into drive mode, then checks if all sensors have gone into drive mode. If one or more sensors do not go into drive mode, or do not transmit at all, the RCDLR will set DTC C0750, C0755, C0760, or C0765.

Conditions for Running the DTC

Vehicle speed is 25 mph or greater for 2 minutes.

Conditions for Setting the DTC

- Any given sensor does not go into drive mode.
- Any given sensor does not transmit for 5 minutes.

Action Taken When the DTC Sets

- The driver information center (DIC) displays the suspect tire pressure as dashes.
- The DIC displays the SERVICE TIRE MONITOR message.

Conditions for Clearing the DTC

- A current DTC will clear when the malfunction is no longer present.
- The electronic brake control module (EBCM) automatically clears the history DTC when a current DTC is not detected in 100 consecutive drive cycles.
- The DTC is cleared with a scan tool.

ARM0500000000848

Fig. 63   Codes C0750, C0755, C0760 & C0765: Tire Pressure Sensor Low (Part 1 of 3). DTS

4. Test drive the vehicle above 40 km/h (25 mph) for greater than 10 seconds. With the scan tool, observe the suspect Pressure Sensor Mode data parameter. Verify sensor mode changes from Wake to Drive.
   ⇒ If the suspect Pressure Sensor Mode does not change, replace the suspect tire pressure sensor.
5. If no faults are found, go to Diagnostic Aids.

Repair Instructions

Important: Always perform the Diagnostic Repair Verification after completing the diagnostic procedure.

- Tire Pressure Sensor Learn
- Tire Pressure Sensor Replacement
- Control Module References for RCDLR replacement, setup, and programming

ARM0500000000850

Fig. 63   Codes C0750, C0755, C0760 & C0765: Tire Pressure Sensor Low (Part 3 of 3). DTS

Diagnostic Aids

A newly replaced RCDLR will set DTC C0775 on its initial ignition ON cycle. Tire pressure sensor learn procedure must be performed.

Repair Instructions

Important: Always perform the Diagnostic Repair Verification after completing the diagnostic procedure.

- Tire Pressure Sensor Learn
- Control Module References for IPC or RCDLR replacement, setup, and programming

ARM0500000000852

Fig. 64   Code C0775: Low Tire Pressure System Sensors Not Learned (Part 2 of 2). DTS

Diagnostic Fault Information

Important: Always perform the <u>Diagnostic System Check - Tire Pressure Monitoring</u> prior to using this diagnostic procedure.

Circuit/System Description

The remote control door lock receiver (RCDLR) sends a serial data message to the instrument panel cluster (IPC) requesting low tire pressure indicator illumination.

Circuit/System Testing

1. Inflate tires to the proper pressure.

2. Using the tire pressure monitor (TPM) special tool, activate each tire pressure sensor and record each sensors tire pressure reading in psi. Check tire pressures with a known accurate hand held tire pressure gauge. Verify pressure readings from special tool do not differ 4 psi or more lower than actual tire pressure.
   ⇒ If 4 psi or more lower than actual tire pressure, replace the suspect tire pressure sensor.

3. With the scan tool, select instrument panel special functions Lamp Test. Command the instrument panel warning lamps OFF. Verify low tire pressure indicator lamp turns OFF.
   ⇒ If the lamp does not turn OFF, replace the IPC.

4. Enable the TPM learn mode. Use the TPM special tool in simulate mode to learn 4 simulated sensor transmissions into the RCDLR. Observe tire pressures in the scan tool data display. Verify simulated tire pressures do not differ more than +/- 4 psi of the scan tool reading.
   ⇒ If the tire pressures differ more than +/- 4 psi, replace the RCDLR.

Repair Instructions

Important: Always perform the <u>Diagnostic Repair Verification</u> after completing the diagnostic procedure.

- <u>Tire Pressure Sensor Learn</u>
- <u>Control Module References</u> for IPC or RCDLR replacement, setup, and programming

ARM0500000000853

Fig. 65 Low Tire Pressure Indicator Always On. 2006 DTS

Circuit/System Verification

Important: When a TPM DTC is set, the tire pressure monitor indicator icon will flash for 1 minute after the IPC bulb check is completed and then remains illuminated. If equipped with a DIC, a service tire monitor type message will also be displayed.

Low tire pressure in one or more tires is indicated by a continuously illuminated tire pressure monitor indicator icon after the IPC bulb check is completed. If equipped with a DIC, a check tire pressure type message will also be displayed.

1. Inflate all tires to the proper pressure and drive the vehicle over 25 mph for greater than 2 minutes.

2. Using the J-46079 or equivalent, activate each tire pressure sensor and record each sensors tire pressure reading. Check the tire pressures with a known accurate hand held tire pressure gauge. Verify that the pressure readings from the special tool do not differ more than 4 psi from the actual tire pressure readings.

   ⇒ If not within the specified range, replace the suspect tire pressure sensor.

3. Using a scan tool, enable the TPM learn mode. Use the J-46079 in simulate mode to learn 4 simulated sensor transmissions into the RCDLR. Observe tire pressures in the scan tool data display. Verify the simulated tire pressures do not differ more than +/- 4 psi of the scan tool reading.

   ⇒ If not within the specified range, replace the RCDLR.

4. Using a scan tool, select instrument panel special functions Lamp Test. Command the instrument panel warning lamps OFF. Verify the tire pressure monitor indicator icon turns OFF.

   ⇒ If the tire pressure monitor icon does not turn OFF, replace the IPC.

5. Ignition ON, use the scan tool to setup the Tire Type/Pressure Selection in the RCDLR Module Setup menu. Verify the tire pressure monitor indicator icon turns OFF.

   ⇒ If the tire pressure monitor icon does not turn OFF, replace the RCDLR.

Repair Instructions

Perform the Diagnostic Repair Verification after completing the diagnostic procedure.

- Tire Pressure Indicator Sensor Replacement
- Tire Pressure Sensor Learn
- Control Module References for IPC or RCDLR replacement, setup, and programming

ARM0700000000791

Fig. 66 Low Tire Pressure Indicator Always On (Part 2 of 2). 2007–08 DTS

Diagnostic Instructions

- Perform the Diagnostic System Check - Vehicle prior to using this diagnostic procedure.

Circuit/System Description

The remote control door lock receiver (RCDLR) receives a radio frequency (RF) transmission from each tire pressure sensor. Each sensor RF transmission contains its own unique identification (ID) code that must be learned into the RCDLR memory. Once all 4 IDs have been learned and vehicle speed is greater than 25 mph, the RCDLR continuously compares IDs in received transmission to its learned IDs to determine if all 4 sensors are present. If the RCDLR detects a low tire pressure condition or a malfunction in the system, it will send a serial data message to the instrument panel cluster (IPC) requesting tire pressure monitor indicator illumination and to display a data message on the driver information center (DIC), if equipped.

Diagnostic Aids

- Some aftermarket wheel valve stem holes are located further from the wheel rim than original equipment wheels. When using the TPM special tool to activate a sensor, ensure the tool antenna is no further than 15 cm (6 in) from the sensor and is aiming upward.

- Aftermarket wheel value stem locations can cause a sensor to not function correctly.

- A sensor may have been damaged due to a previous wheel/tire service or flat tire event.

- The use of tire sealants can obstruct the sensor pressure sensing port and cause inaccurate tire pressure readings. If this condition is verified, remove the sealer from the tire and replace the sensor. Refer to Tire Pressure Indicator Sensor Replacement.

- Occasionally sensor transmissions are not received by the RCDLR due to vehicle level RF interference from items such as but not limited to aftermarket ignition systems, DVD players, CB radios, or metallic type window tinting.

- The sensor activation procedure may have to be repeated up to 3 times before determining a sensor is malfunctioning. In the event a particular sensor's information is displayed on the special tool upon activation but the horn does not chirp, it may be necessary to rotate the wheel valve stem to a different position due to the RF signal is being blocked by another component.

- Occasionally sensors can become mislocated due to previous tire rotations where the sensor learn procedure was not performed or stray sensor transmissions have been received from other vehicles. Always learn the sensors to ensure the DTC set is for that actual physical corner of the vehicle. Refer to Tire Pressure Sensor Learn.

ARM0700000000790

Fig. 66 Low Tire Pressure Indicator Always On (Part 1 of 2). 2007–08 DTS

Diagnostic Fault Information

Important: Always perform the <u>Diagnostic System Check - Tire Pressure Monitoring</u> prior to using this diagnostic procedure.

Circuit/System Description

The remote control door lock receiver (RCDLR) sends a serial data message to the instrument panel cluster (IPC) requesting low tire pressure indicator illumination.

Circuit/System Testing

1. With the scan tool, select instrument panel special functions Lamp Test. Command the instrument panel lamps ON. Verify low tire pressure indicator lamp turns ON.
   ⇒ If the lamp does not turn ON, replace the IPC.

2. Using the tire pressure monitor (TPM) special tool to observe the tire pressure of the suspected faulty sensor. Check air pressure with a known accurate hand held tire pressure gage. Compare the psi reading to the display on the TPM special tool. Verify pressure readings from special tool do not differ 2 psi or more than actual tire pressure.
   ⇒ If the difference is 2 psi more, replace the suspect tire pressure sensor.

3. With the scan tool, observe tire pressures in the scan tool data display. Verify pressure readings from special tool do not differ 2 psi or more than scan tool data display.
   ⇒ If the difference is 2 psi more, replace the RCDLR.

Repair Instructions

Important: Always perform the <u>Diagnostic Repair Verification</u> after completing the diagnostic procedure.

- <u>Tire Pressure Sensor Learn</u>
- <u>Control Module References</u> for RCDLR replacement, setup, and programming.

ARM0500000000854

Fig. 67 Low Tire Pressure Indicator Inoperative. 2006 DTS

TIRE PRESSURE MONITORING SYSTEM

Diagnostic Instructions

- Perform the Diagnostic System Check - Vehicle prior to using this diagnostic procedure.

Circuit/System Description

The remote control door lock receiver (RCDLR) receives a radio frequency (RF) transmission from each tire pressure sensor. Each sensor RF transmission contains its own unique identification (ID) code that must be learned into the RCDLR memory. Once all 4 IDs have been learned and vehicle speed is greater than 25 mph, the RCDLR continuously compares IDs in received transmission to its learned IDs to determine if all 4 sensors are present. If the RCDLR detects a low tire pressure condition or a malfunction in the system, it will send a serial data message to the instrument panel cluster (IPC) requesting tire pressure monitor indicator icon illumination and to display a data message on the driver information center (DIC), if equipped.

Diagnostic Aids

- Some aftermarket wheel valve stem holes are located further from the wheel rim than original equipment wheels. When using the TPM special tool to activate a sensor, ensure the tool antenna is no further than 15 cm (6 in) from the sensor and is aiming upward.
- Aftermarket wheel value stem locations can cause a sensor to not function correctly.
- A sensor may have been damaged due to a previous wheel/tire service or flat tire event.
- The use of tire sealants can obstruct the sensor pressure sensing port and cause inaccurate tire pressure readings. If this condition is verified, remove the sealer from the tire and replace the sensor. Refer to Tire Pressure Indicator Sensor Replacement.
- Occasionally sensor transmissions are not received by the RCDLR due to vehicle level RF interference from items such as but not limited to aftermarket ignition systems, DVD players, CB radios, or metallic type window tinting.
- The sensor activation procedure may have to be repeated up to 3 times before determining a sensor is malfunctioning. In the event a particular sensor's information is displayed on the special tool upon activation but the horn does not chirp, it may be necessary to rotate the wheel valve stem to a different position due to the RF signal is being blocked by another component.
- Occasionally sensors can become mislocated due to previous tire rotations where the sensor learn procedure was not performed or stray sensor transmissions have been received from other vehicles . Always learn the sensors to ensure the DTC set is for that actual physical corner of the vehicle. Refer to Tire Pressure Sensor Learn.

ARM0700000000792

Fig. 68 Low Tire Pressure Indicator Inoperative (Part 1 of 2). 2007–08 DTS

Circuit/System Verification

1. Ignition ON, with the scan tool, setup the Tire Type and Pressure Selection information in the RCDLR.
2. With the scan tool, select instrument panel special functions Lamp Test. Command the instrument panel lamps ON. Verify tire pressure monitor indicator icon turns ON.

   ⇒ If the icon does not turn ON, replace the IPC.

3. Using the tire pressure monitor (TPM) special tool to observe the tire pressure of the suspected faulty sensor. Check the air pressure with a known accurate tire pressure gage. Compare the pressure reading to the display on the TPM special tool. Verify the pressure readings from special tool do not differ 4 psi or more than actual tire pressure.

   ⇒ If not within the specified range, replace the suspect tire pressure sensor.

4. With the scan tool, observe tire pressures in the scan tool data display. Verify pressure readings from special tool do not differ 4 psi or more than scan tool data display.

   ⇒ If not within the specified range, replace the RCDLR.

Repair Instructions

Perform the Diagnostic Repair Verification after completing the diagnostic procedure.

- Tire Pressure Indicator Sensor Replacement
- Tire Pressure Sensor Learn
- Control Module References for IPC and RCDLR replacement, setup, and programming

ARM0700000000793

Fig. 68 Low Tire Pressure Indicator Inoperative (Part 2 of 2). 2007–08 DTS

Step	Action	Yes	No
1	Perform the following preliminary inspections: • Ensure that the battery is fully charged. • Ensure that the battery cables are clean and tight. • Inspect for any open fuses. • Inspect the easily accessible systems or the visible system components for obvious damage or conditions that could cause the symptom. • Ensure that the grounds are clean, tight, and in the correct location. • Inspect for aftermarket devices that could affect the operation of the system. • Search for applicable service bulletins. Did you find and correct the condition?	System OK	Go to Step 2
2	Install a scan tool. Does the scan tool power up?	Go to Step 3	Go to Scan Tool Does Not Power Up
3	1. Turn ON the ignition, with the engine OFF. 2. Attempt to establish communication with all of the control modules on the vehicle. Does the scan tool communicate with all of the expected vehicle control modules?	Go to Step 4	Go to Data Link References

ARM0500000000855

Fig. 70 Diagnostic System Check (Part 1 of 3). 2005–06 Grand Prix

Step	Action	Yes	No
1	Install a scan tool. Does the scan tool turn on?	Go to Step 2	Go to Scan Tool Does Not Power Up in Data Link Communications
2	1. Turn ON the ignition, with the engine OFF. 2. Attempt to establish communication with the EBCM. Does the scan tool communicate with the EBCM?	Go to Step 3	Go to Scan Tool Does Not Communicate with Class 2 Device in Data Link Communications
3	Does the scan tool display any DTCs which begin with a "U"?	Go to Diagnostic Trouble Code (DTC) List in Data Link Communications	Go to Step 4
4	Select the Diagnostic Trouble Codes (DTC) function on the scan tool Does the scan tool display any ABS DTCs?	Go to Diagnostic System Check - ABS in Antilock Brake System	System OK

ARM0700000000737

Fig. 69 Diagnostic System Check. 2004 Grand Prix

4	**Important:** • To ensure that retained accessory power (RAP) mode is inactive (if equipped), open the driver door during the following step. • The engine may start during the following step. Turn OFF the engine as soon as you have observed the crank power mode. 1. Access the Power Mode parameter on the scan tool. 2. Rotate the ignition switch, operate the ignition mode switch, through all positions while observing the Power Mode parameter. Does the Power Mode parameter reading on the scan tool match the ignition switch position for all switch positions?	Go to Step 5	Go to Power Mode Mismatch
5	Attempt to start the engine. Does the engine crank?	Go to Step 6	Go to Symptoms - Engine Electrical
6	Attempt to start the engine. Does the engine start and idle?	Go to Step 7	Go to Engine Cranks but Does Not Run for the 3.8L engine or Engine Cranks but Does Not Run for the 5.3L engine
7	**Important:** Do not clear any DTCs unless instructed by a diagnostic procedure. Use the appropriate scan tool selections to obtain DTCs for each of the control modules. Does the scan tool display any DTCs?	Go to Step 8	Go to Step 12
8	Does the scan tool display any DTCs that begin with a "U"?	Go to Diagnostic Trouble Code (DTC) List - Vehicle	Go to Step 9

ARM0500000000856

Fig. 70 Diagnostic System Check (Part 2 of 3). 2005–06 Grand Prix

Diagnostic System Check – Grand Prix

1. Before beginning vehicle diagnosis, the following preliminary inspections/tests must be performed:

   • Ensure that the battery is fully charged.
   • Ensure that the battery cables are clean and tight.
   • Inspect for any open fuses.
   • Ensure that the grounds are clean, tight, and in the correct location.
   • Inspect the easily accessible systems or the visible system components for obvious damage or conditions that could cause the concern. This would include checking to ensure that all connections/connectors are fully seated and secured.
   • Inspect for aftermarket devices that could affect the operation of the system.
   • Search for applicable service bulletins.
   ⇒ If the preceding inspections/tests resolve the concern, go to Diagnostic Repair Verification .

2. Install a scan tool. Verify that the scan tool powers up.

   ⇒ If the scan tool does not power up, refer to Scan Tool Does Not Power Up.

3. Ignition ON, Engine OFF, verify communication with all of the control modules on the vehicle. Refer to Data Link References for information on the modules you should expect to communicate.

   ⇒ If the scan tool does not communicate with one or more of the expected control modules, refer to Data Link References.

   Important: Open the driver's door to ensure retained accessory power mode (RAP) is inactive during this test. The engine may start during this test. Turn the engine OFF as soon as the crank power mode has been observed.
   Access the Power Mode parameter on the scan tool. Verify the power mode parameter matches all the ignition switch positions. Refer to Power Mode

4. Description and Operation for information on the power mode states that correspond to each ignition switch position.

   ⇒ If the power mode parameter does not match the ignition switch position for all ignition switch positions, refer to Power Mode Mismatch.

ARM0700000000794

Fig. 71 Diagnostic System Check (Part 1 of 2). 2007–08 Grand Prix

9	**Important:** If any of these DTCs are displayed, diagnose them before diagnosing any other DTCs or symptoms. Does the scan tool display DTC B1000, B1001, B1004, B1007, B1009, B1013, B1014, C0550, P0601, P0602, P0603, P0604, P0606, P0607, P060D, P060E, P062F, P1621, P2107, P2108, or P2610?	Go to Diagnostic Trouble Code (DTC) List - Vehicle	Go to Step 10
10	**Important:** If any of these DTCs are displayed, diagnose them before diagnosing any other DTCs or symptoms. Does the scan tool display DTC B1327, B1328, B1370, B1390, C0875, P0560, P0562, or P0563?	Go to Diagnostic Trouble Code (DTC) List - Vehicle	Go to Step 11
11	**Important:** If any of the remaining DTCs are powertrain DTCs, select Capture Info in order to store the powertrain DTC information with a scan tool. If multiple DTCs are stored, diagnose the DTCs in the following order 1. Component level DTCs, such as sensor DTCs, solenoid DTCs, and relay DTCs. 2. System level DTCs, such as misfire DTCs, evaporative emission (EVAP) system DTCs, and fuel trim DTCs. Diagnose the remaining DTCs.	Go to Diagnostic Trouble Code (DTC) List - Vehicle	--
12	Is the customers concern with inspection/maintenance (I/M) testing?	Go to Inspection/Maintenance (I/M) System Check for the 3.8L engine or Inspection/Maintenance (I/M) System Check for the 5.3L engine	Go to Symptoms - Vehicle

ARM0500000000857

Fig. 70 Diagnostic System Check (Part 3 of 3). 2005–06 Grand Prix

5. Attempt to start the engine. Verify that the engine cranks.

   ⇒ If the engine does not crank, refer to Symptoms - Engine Electrical.

6. Attempt to start the engine. Verify the engine starts and idles.

   ⇒ If the engine does not start and idle, refer to Engine Cranks but Does Not Run for the 3.8L engine or Engine Cranks but Does Not Run for the 5.3L engine.

   Important: Do not clear any DTCs unless instructed to do so by a diagnostic procedure.
   Important: If any DTCs are Powertrain related DTCs, select Capture Info in order to store the DTC information with the scan tool.

7. Use the appropriate scan tool selections to obtain DTCs from each of the vehicle modules. Verify there are no DTCs reported from any module.

   ⇒ If any DTCs are present, refer to Diagnostic Trouble Code (DTC) List - Vehicle and diagnose any current DTCs in the following order:

   7.1. DTCs that begin with a U.

   7.2. Any of the following: B1000, B1001, B1004, B1007, B1009, B1013, B1014, C0550, P0601, P0602, P0603, P0604, P0606, P0607, P060D, P062F, P2107, P2108, or P2610.

   7.3. Any of the following: B1327, B1328, B1370, C0875, P0560, P0562, or P0563.

   7.4. Component level DTCs.

   7.5. System level DTCs.

   7.6. Any remaining DTCs.

8. If the customer concern is related to inspection/maintenance (I/M) testing, refer to Inspection/Maintenance (I/M) System Check for the 3.8L engine or Inspection/Maintenance (I/M) System Check for the 5.3L engine.

ARM0700000000795

Fig. 71 Diagnostic System Check (Part 2 of 2). 2007–08 Grand Prix

Diagnostic Fault Information

Always perform the Diagnostic System Check - Vehicle prior to using this diagnostic procedure.

Circuit/System Description

If the tire type and pressure selection information is not entered with the scan tool during the RCDLR setup, the tire pressure monitor indicator icon on the instrument panel cluster (IPC) will flash for 1 minute and then remain illuminated after the ignition switch is cycled ON and the IPC bulb check is complete. If equipped, the driver information center (DIC) will also display a service tire monitor type message. Under these circumstances, DTC C0569 will be set and the tire type and pressure information will need to be entered for the system to function correctly.

Conditions for Running the DTC

The ignition is ON.

Conditions for Setting the DTC

The RCDLR has not undergone the tire type and pressure selection setup procedure.

Action Taken When the DTC Sets

- The tire pressure monitor indicator icon on the instrument panel cluster (IPC) will flash for 1 minute and then remain illuminated after the ignition switch is cycled ON and the IPC bulb check is complete.
- If equipped, the driver information center (DIC) displays a service tire monitor type warning message.

Conditions for Clearing the DTC

A current DTC will clear when the RCDLR has undergone the tire type and pressure selection setup procedure and 1 ignition cycle has occurred.

Diagnostic Aids

A newly replaced RCDLR will set DTC C0569 on its initial ignition ON cycle if the module setup information has not been entered. The Tire Type and Tire Pressure Selection setup must be performed with the scan tool.

Circuit/System Verification

Verify that the DTC C0569 is not set.

⇒ If the DTC is set, perform the RCDLR tire type and pressure selection setup with the scan tool and cycle the ignition. If the DTC resets, replace the RCDLR.

ARM0700000000733

Fig. 72   Code C0569: System Configuration Error. Grand Prix

Diagnostic Aids

- Some aftermarket wheel valve stem holes are located further from the wheel rim than original equipment wheels. When using the TPM special tool to activate a sensor, ensure the tool antenna is no further than 6 inches from the sensor and is aiming upward.
- Aftermarket wheel valve stem locations can cause a sensor to not function correctly.
- A sensor may have been damaged due to a previous wheel/tire service or flat tire event.
- The use of tire sealants can obstruct the sensor pressure sensing port and cause inaccurate tire pressure readings. If this condition is verified, remove the sealer from the tire and replace the sensor.
- Occasionally sensor transmissions are not received by the RCDLR due to vehicle level RF interference from items such as but not limited to aftermarket ignition systems, DVD players, CB radios, or metallic type window tinting.
- The sensor activation procedure may have to be repeated up to 3 times before determining a sensor is malfunctioning. In the event a particular sensor information is displayed on the special tool upon activation but the horn does not chirp, it may be necessary to rotate the wheel valve stem to a different position due to the RF signal is being blocked by another component.
- Occasionally sensors can become mislocated due to previous tire rotations where the sensor learn procedure was not performed or stray sensor transmissions have been received from other vehicles . Always learn the sensors to ensure the DTC set is for that actual physical corner of the vehicle. Perform Sensor Learn Procedure.
- A sensor low battery condition will set a sensor DTC but will not illuminate the low tire pressure indicator or display a message on the DIC, if equipped. The sensor battery condition can be verified in the scan tool RCDLR data list. If a sensor low battery condition is indicated on the scan tool, the sensor will need to be replaced. Refer to Tire Pressure Indicator Sensor Replacement.

Circuit/System Verification

1. Using the J-46079, activate each tire pressure sensor and record each sensors transmission data and physical location. Verify J-46079 displays the 8-digit ID number, accurate tire pressure +/- 4 psi., Learn Mode, and at least a 1/4 graph signal strength displayed.

   ⇒ If any of the parameters listed above are not displayed, replace the suspect tire pressure sensor.

2. With the scan tool, verify tire pressure sensors ID and locations displayed on the scan tool match the IDs and locations recorded from the special tool.

   ⇒ If the IDs and locations do not match, perform the Tire Pressure Sensor Learn .

3. Enable the TPM learn mode. Use the J-46079 in simulate mode to learn 4 simulated sensor transmissions into the RCDLR. Verify that all 4 simulated sensor locations, IDs, and tire pressures displayed on the TPM special tool match the corresponding scan tool parameters displayed.

   ⇒ If the scan tool does not match, replace the RCDLR.

4. Test drive the vehicle above 25 mph for greater than 2 minutes. With the scan tool, observe the suspect Pressure Sensor Mode data parameter. Verify the sensor mode changes to Rolling.

   ⇒ If the Pressure Sensor Mode does not change, replace the suspect tire pressure sensor.

ARM0700000000736

Fig. 73   Codes C0750, C0755, C0760, C0765: Tire Pressure Low (Part 2 of 2). Grand Prix

Diagnostic Fault Information

Always perform the Diagnostic System Check - Vehicle prior to using this diagnostic procedure.

Circuit/System Description

The tire pressure monitor (TPM) system has a radio frequency (RF) transmitting pressure sensor in each wheel/tire assembly. As vehicle speed increases, centrifugal force closes the sensors internal roll switch, which puts the sensor into Rolling mode. The remote control door lock receiver (RCDLR) receives and translates the data contained in the tire pressure sensor RF transmissions into sensor presence, sensor mode, and tire pressure. Once vehicle speed is greater than 25 mph, the RCDLR waits for the first sensor to go into Rolling mode, then checks if all sensors have gone into Rolling mode. If one or more sensors do not go into these modes, or do not transmit at all, the RCDLR will set DTC C0750, C0755, C0760, or C0765 respectively.

Conditions for Running the DTC

Vehicle speed is greater than 25 mph.

Conditions for Setting the DTC

- A sensor does not transmit for 18 minutes.
- A sensor low battery condition.

Action Taken When the DTC Sets

- The tire pressure monitor indicator icon on the instrument panel cluster (IPC) flashes for 1 minute and then remains illuminated after the ignition switch is cycled ON and the IPC bulb check is complete.
- If equipped, the driver information center (DIC) displays the suspect tire pressure as dashes.
- If equipped, the DIC displays a service tire monitor type message.

Conditions for Clearing the DTC

- A current DTC will clear when the malfunction is no longer present and 1 ignition cycle occurs.
- The RCDLR automatically clears the history DTC when a current DTC is not detected in 100 consecutive drive cycles.

ARM0700000000735

Fig. 73   Codes C0750, C0755, C0760, C0765: Tire Pressure Low (Part 1 of 2). Grand Prix

Diagnostic Fault Information.

- Always perform the Diagnostic System Check - Vehicle prior to using this diagnostic procedure.

Circuit/System Description

If the tire pressure sensor learn procedure has not been performed, the tire pressure monitor indicator icon on the instrument panel cluster (IPC) will flash for 1 minute and then remain illuminated after the ignition switch is cycled ON and the IPC bulb check is complete. If equipped, the driver information center (DIC) will also display a service tire monitor type message. Under these circumstances, DTC C0775 will be set and the tire pressure sensor learn procedure will need to be performed for the system to function correctly.

Conditions for Running the DTC

The ignition is ON.

Conditions for Setting the DTC

The RCDLR has not undergone the tire pressure sensor learn procedure.

Action Taken When the DTC Sets

- The tire pressure monitor indicator icon on the instrument panel cluster (IPC) will flash for 1 minute and then remain illuminated after the ignition switch is cycled ON and the IPC bulb check is complete.
- If equipped, the driver information center (DIC) displays a service tire monitor type warning message.

Conditions for Clearing the DTC

A current DTC will clear when the RCDLR has undergone the tire pressure sensor learn procedure and 1 ignition cycle has occurred.

Diagnostic Aids

A newly replaced RCDLR will set DTC C0569 on its initial ignition ON cycle if the module setup information has not been entered. The Tire Type and Tire Pressure Selection setup must be performed with the scan tool.

Circuit/System Verification

Verify that the DTC C0775 is not set.
⇒ If the DTC is set, perform the tire pressure sensor learn procedure. Cycle the ignition. If the DTC resets, replace the RCDLR.

Repair Instructions

Perform the Diagnostic Repair Verification after completing the diagnostic procedure.

Control Module References for RCDLR replacement and setup.

ARM0700000000738

Fig. 74   Code C0775: Low Tire Pressure System Sensors Not Learned. Grand Prix

Diagnostic Fault Information

• Perform the Diagnostic System Check - Vehicle prior to using this diagnostic procedure.

Circuit/System Description

The remote control door lock receiver (RCDLR) receives a radio frequency (RF) transmission from each tire pressure sensor. Each sensor RF transmission contains its own unique identification (ID) code that must be learned into the RCDLR memory. Once all 4 IDs have been learned and vehicle speed is greater than 25 mph, the RCDLR continuously compares IDs in received transmission to its learned IDs to determine if all 4 sensors are present. If the RCDLR detects a low tire pressure condition or a malfunction in the system, it will send a serial data message to the instrument panel cluster (IPC) requesting tire pressure monitor indicator illumination and to display a data message on the driver information center (DIC), if equipped.

Diagnostic Aids

• Some aftermarket wheel valve stem holes are located further from the wheel rim than original equipment wheels. When using the TPM special tool to activate a sensor, ensure the tool antenna is no further than 6 inches from the sensor and is aiming upward.

• Aftermarket wheel value stem locations can cause a sensor to not function correctly.

• A sensor may have been damaged due to a previous wheel/tire service or flat tire event.

• The use of tire sealants can obstruct the sensor pressure sensing port and cause inaccurate tire pressure readings. If this condition is verified, remove the sealer from the tire and replace the sensor. Refer to Tire Pressure Indicator Sensor Replacement.

• Occasionally sensor transmissions are not received by the RCDLR due to vehicle level RF interference from items such as but not limited to aftermarket ignition systems, DVD players, CB radios, or metallic type window tinting.

• The sensor activation procedure may have to be repeated up to 3 times before determining a sensor is malfunctioning. In the event a particular sensor's information is displayed on the special tool upon activation but the horn does not chirp, it may be necessary to rotate the wheel valve stem to a different position due to the RF signal is being blocked by another component.

• Occasionally sensors can become mislocated due to previous tire rotations where the sensor learn procedure was not performed or stray sensor transmissions have been received from other vehicles. Always learn the sensors to ensure the DTC set is for that actual physical corner of the vehicle. Refer to Tire Pressure Sensor Learn.

ARM0700000000739

Fig. 75   Low Tire Pressure Indicator Always On (Part 1 of 2). Grand Prix

Diagnostic Fault Information

• Perform the Diagnostic System Check - Vehicle prior to using this diagnostic procedure.

Circuit/System Description

The remote control door lock receiver (RCDLR) receives a radio frequency (RF) transmission from each tire pressure sensor. Each sensor RF transmission contains its own unique identification (ID) code that must be learned into the RCDLR memory. Once all 4 IDs have been learned and vehicle speed is greater than 25 mph, the RCDLR continuously compares IDs in received transmission to its learned IDs to determine if all 4 sensors are present. If the RCDLR detects a low tire pressure condition or a malfunction in the system, it will send a serial data message to the instrument panel cluster (IPC) requesting tire pressure monitor indicator icon illumination and to display a data message on the driver information center (DIC), if equipped.

Diagnostic Aids

• Some aftermarket wheel valve stem holes are located further from the wheel rim than original equipment wheels. When using the TPM special tool to activate a sensor, ensure the tool antenna is no further than 6 inches from the sensor and is aiming upward.

• Aftermarket wheel value stem locations can cause a sensor to not function correctly.

• A sensor may have been damaged due to a previous wheel/tire service or flat tire event.

• The use of tire sealants can obstruct the sensor pressure sensing port and cause inaccurate tire pressure readings. If this condition is verified, remove the sealer from the tire and replace the sensor. Refer to Tire Pressure Indicator Sensor Replacement.

• Occasionally sensor transmissions are not received by the RCDLR due to vehicle level RF interference from items such as but not limited to aftermarket ignition systems, DVD players, CB radios, or metallic type window tinting.

• The sensor activation procedure may have to be repeated up to 3 times before determining a sensor is malfunctioning. In the event a particular sensor's information is displayed on the special tool upon activation but the horn does not chirp, it may be necessary to rotate the wheel valve stem to a different position due to the RF signal is being blocked by another component.

• Occasionally sensors can become mislocated due to previous tire rotations where the sensor learn procedure was not performed or stray sensor transmissions have been received from other vehicles. Always learn the sensors to ensure the DTC set is for that actual physical corner of the vehicle. Refer to Tire Pressure Sensor Learn.

ARM0700000000741

Fig. 76   Low Tire Pressure Indicator Inoperative (Part 1 of 2). Grand Prix

Circuit/System Verification

Important: When a TPM DTC is set, the tire pressure monitor indicator icon will flash for 1 minute after the IPC bulb check is completed and then remains illuminated. If equipped with a DIC, a service tire monitor type message will also be displayed.

Low tire pressure in one or more tires is indicated by a continuously illuminated tire pressure monitor indicator icon after the IPC bulb check is completed. If equipped with a DIC, a check tire pressure type message will also be displayed.

1. Inflate all tires to the proper pressure and drive the vehicle over 25 mph for greater than 2 minutes.

2. Using the J-46079 or equivalent, activate each tire pressure sensor and record each sensors tire pressure reading. Check the tire pressures with a known accurate hand held tire pressure gauge. Verify that the pressure readings from the special tool do not differ more than 4 psi., from the actual tire pressure readings.

⇒ If not within the specified range, replace the suspect tire pressure sensor.

3. Using a scan tool, enable the TPM learn mode. Use the J-46079 or equivalent, in simulate mode to learn 4 simulated sensor transmissions into the RCDLR. Observe tire pressures in the scan tool data display. Verify the simulated tire pressures do not differ more than +/- 4 psi., of the scan tool reading.

⇒ If not within the specified range, replace the RCDLR.

4. Using a scan tool, select instrument panel special functions Lamp Test. Command the instrument panel warning lamps OFF. Verify the tire pressure monitor indicator icon turns OFF.

⇒ If the tire pressure monitor icon does not turn OFF, replace the IPC.

5. Ignition ON, use the scan tool to setup the Tire Type/Pressure Selection in the RCDLR Module Setup menu. Verify the tire pressure monitor indicator icon turns OFF.

⇒ If the tire pressure monitor icon does not turn OFF, replace the RCDLR.

ARM0700000000740

Fig. 75   Low Tire Pressure Indicator Always On (Part 2 of 2). Grand Prix

Circuit/System Verification

1. Ignition ON, with the scan tool, setup the Tire Type and Pressure Selection information in the RCDLR.

2. With the scan tool, select instrument panel special functions Lamp Test. Command the instrument panel lamps ON. Verify tire pressure monitor indicator icon turns ON.

⇒ If the icon does not turn ON, replace the IPC.

3. Using the tire pressure monitor (TPM) special tool to observe the tire pressure of the suspected faulty sensor. Check the air pressure with a known accurate tire pressure gage. Compare the pressure reading to the display on the TPM special tool. Verify the pressure readings from special tool do not differ 4 psi., or more than actual tire pressure.

⇒ If not within the specified range, replace the suspect tire pressure sensor.

4. With the scan tool, observe tire pressures in the scan tool data display. Verify pressure readings from special tool do not differ 4 psi., or more than scan tool data display.

⇒ If not within the specified range, replace the RCDLR.

ARM0700000000742

Fig. 76   Low Tire Pressure Indicator Inoperative (Part 2 of 2). Grand Prix

Step	Action	Yes	No
1	Install a scan tool. Does the scan tool power up?	Go to Step 2	Go to Scan Tool Does Not Power Up in Data Link Communications
2	1. Turn ON the ignition, with the engine OFF. 2. Attempt to establish communications with the Electronic Brake Control Module (EBCM). Does the scan tool communicate with the EBCM?	Go to Step 3	Go to Scan Tool Does Not Communicate with Class 2 Device in Data Link Communications
3	Select the ABS Diagnostic Trouble Codes DTC function on the scan tool. Does the scan tool display any DTCs that begin with a "U"?	Go to Diagnostic Trouble Code (DTC) List in Data Link Communications	Go to Step 4
4	Does the scan tool display any ABS DTCs?	Go to Diagnostic System Check - ABS in Antilock Brake System	Go to Step 5
5	Does the scan tool display DTC C1245?	Go to DTC C1245	System OK

ARM0700000000746

Fig. 77 Diagnostic System Check. 2004 Impala & Monte Carlo

Step	Action	Yes	No
2	Install a scan tool. Does the scan tool power up?	Go to Step 3	Go to Scan Tool Does Not Power Up in Computer/Integrating Systems
3	1. Turn ON the ignition, with the engine OFF. 2. Attempt to establish communication with all of the control modules on the vehicle. Refer to Scan Tool Does Not Communicate with Class 2 Device in Computer/Integrating Systems for the modules you should expect to observe. Does the scan tool communicate with all of the expected vehicle control modules?	Go to Step 4	Go to Scan Tool Does Not Communicate with Class 2 Device in Computer/Integrating Systems

ARM0700000000748

Fig. 78 Diagnostic System Check (Part 2 of 5). 2005 Impala & Monte Carlo

Step	Action	Yes	No
1	Perform the following preliminary inspections: • Ensure that the battery is fully charged. • Ensure that the battery cables are clean and tight. • Inspect for any open fuses. • Inspect the easily accessible systems or the visible system components for obvious damage or conditions that could cause the symptom. • Ensure that the grounds are clean, tight, and in the correct location. • Inspect for aftermarket devices that could affect the operation of the system. • Search for applicable service bulletins. Did you find and correct the condition?	System OK	Go to Step 2

ARM0700000000747

Fig. 78 Diagnostic System Check (Part 1 of 5). 2005 Impala & Monte Carlo

Step	Action	Yes	No
4	**Important:** • To ensure that retained accessory power (RAP) mode is inactive (if equipped), open the driver door during the following step. • The engine may start during the following step. Turn OFF the engine as soon as you have observed the crank power mode. 1. Access the Power Mode parameter on the scan tool. 2. Rotate the ignition switch (operate the ignition mode switch) through all positions while observing the Power Mode parameter. Refer to Body Control System Description and Operation in Computer/Integrating Systems for a list of the power mode states that correspond with each switch position. Does the Power Mode parameter reading on the scan tool match the ignition switch position for all switch positions?	Go to Step 5	Go to Power Mode Mismatch in Computer/Integrating Systems
5	Attempt to start the engine. Does the engine crank?	Go to Step 6	Go to Symptoms - Engine Electrical in Engine Electrical

ARM0700000000749

Fig. 78 Diagnostic System Check (Part 3 of 5). 2005 Impala & Monte Carlo

6	Attempt to start the engine. Does the engine start and idle?		Go to Engine Cranks but Does Not Run in Engine Controls - 3.4L or Engine Cranks but Does Not Run in Engine Controls - 3.8L (L36 and L67) Go to Step 7
7	**Important:** Do not clear any DTCs unless instructed by a diagnostic procedure. Use the appropriate scan tool selections to obtain DTCs for each of the control modules. Does the scan tool display any DTCs?	Go to Step 8	Go to Step 12
8	Does the scan tool display any DTCs that begin with a "U"?	Go to Diagnostic Trouble Code (DTC) List - Vehicle	Go to Step 9
9	**Important:** If any of these DTCs are displayed, diagnose them before diagnosing any other DTCs or symptoms. Does the scan tool display DTC B1000, B1001, B1007, B1009, C0550, C1255, C1256, P0601, P0602, or P2610?	Go to Diagnostic Trouble Code (DTC) List - Vehicle	Go to Step 10
10	**Important:** If any of these DTCs are displayed, diagnose them before diagnosing any other DTCs or symptoms. Does the scan tool display DTC B1327, B1507, B1508, C1236, C1237, or P0560?	Go to Diagnostic Trouble Code (DTC) List - Vehicle	Go to Step 11

ARM0700000000750

Fig. 78 Diagnostic System Check (Part 4 of 5). 2005 Impala & Monte Carlo

Diagnostic System Check - Tire Pressure Monitoring

Always perform the Diagnostic System Check - Vehicle prior to using this diagnostic procedure.

Review the systems description and operation in order to familiarize yourself with the system functions. Refer to Tire Pressure Monitor Description and Operation.

1. Inspect for aftermarket devices which could affect the operation of the Tire Pressure Monitoring (TPM) system to verify that none are installed. Refer to Checking Aftermarket Accessories.

   ⇒ If such devices are installed, remove/disable them and retest.

2. Inspect the easily accessible or visible system components for obvious damage or conditions which could cause the symptom.

   ⇒ If damage or such conditions are found, repair as required.

3. Verify that the scan tool Selected Front and Rear Tire Pressure parameters are correct compared to the tires actual pressure ratings.

   ⇒ If Tire Pressure parameters are not correct, use scan tool special functions to adjust setting.

4. Using J-46079 Tire Pressure Monitor Diagnostic Tool or equivalent, verify that the scan tool pressure sensor ID parameters match the actual on-vehicle locations.

   ⇒ If actual pressure sensor locations do not match scan tool readings, refer to Tire Pressure Sensor Learn.

5. Verify that the scan tool TPM System Enabled parameter is YES.

   ⇒ If the TPM System Enabled parameter is NO, use scan tool special functions to adjust setting.

6. Verify that tires are inflated to the correct pressure.

ARM0700000000752

Fig. 79 Diagnostic System Check. 2006–07 Impala & Monte Carlo

11	**Important:** If any of the remaining DTCs are powertrain DTCs, select Capture Info in order to store the powertrain DTC information with a scan tool. If multiple DTCs are stored, diagnose the DTCs in the following order 1. Component level DTCs, such as sensor DTCs, solenoid DTCs, and relay DTCs. 2. System level DTCs, such as misfire DTCs, evaporative emission (EVAP) system DTCs, and fuel trim DTCs. Diagnose the remaining DTCs.	Go to Diagnostic Trouble Code (DTC) List - Vehicle	--
12	Is the customers concern with inspection/maintenance (I/M) testing?	Go to Inspection/Maintenance (I/M) System Check in Engine Controls - 3.4L or Inspection/Maintenance (I/M) System Check in Engine Controls - 3.8L (L36 and L67)	Go to Symptoms - Vehicle

ARM0700000000751

Fig. 78 Diagnostic System Check (Part 5 of 5). 2005 Impala & Monte Carlo

Diagnostic System Check - Impala

1. Verify that none of the following preliminary inspections/tests reveal the cause of the vehicle concern before beginning diagnosis:

   • Ensure that the battery is fully charged. Refer to Battery Inspection/Test.

   • Ensure that the battery cables are clean and tight.

   • Inspect for any open fuses.

   • Ensure that the grounds are clean, tight, and in the correct location.

   • Inspect the easily accessible systems or the visible system components for obvious damage or conditions that could cause the concern. This would include checking to ensure that all connections/connectors are fully seated and secured.

   • Inspect for aftermarket devices that could affect the operation of the system.

   • Search for applicable service bulletins.

   ⇒ If the preceding inspections/tests resolve the concern, go to Diagnostic Repair Verification.

2. Install a scan tool. Verify that the scan tool powers up.

   ⇒ If the scan tool does not power up, refer to Scan Tool Does Not Power Up.

3. Ignition ON, Engine OFF, verify communication with all of the control modules on the vehicle.

   ⇒ If the scan tool does not communicate with one or more of the expected control modules, refer to Data Link References.

4. Verify that the following DTCs are not set: U1814, B1428.

   ⇒ If either of the DTCs are set, refer to DTC U1814 or DTC B1428.

5. **Important:** Open the driver's door to ensure retained accessory power mode (RAP) is inactive during this test. The engine may start during this test. Turn the engine OFF as soon as the crank power mode has been observed.

ARM0700000000753

Fig. 80 Diagnostic System Check (Part 1 of 3). 2008 Impala

6. With a scan tool, access the Body Control Module Power Mode data display list.

Verify that all the parameters listed in the following table correspond to the ignition key position. The PMM Power Mode parameters table below illustrates the correct state of these parameters (circuits) with the corresponding ignition switch positions. The circuits related to the parameters are in parenthesis.

⇒ If any of the power mode parameters do not match in any ignition switch position, refer to Power Mode Mismatch.

7. Ignition ON, view the security indicator. The security indicator should not remain illuminated after the vehicle bulb check has completed.

⇒ If the security indicator remains illuminated after the bulb check, refer to Diagnostic Trouble Code (DTC) List - Vehicle and diagnose any of the following theft deterrent DTCs set as current:
⇒ B1000, B302A, B3031, B3055, B3060, B3935, B3976, P0513, P0633, P1629, P1631, or P1632.

8. Attempt to start the engine. Verify that the engine cranks.

⇒ If the engine does not crank, refer to Symptoms - Engine Electrical .

9. Attempt to start the engine. Verify the engine starts and runs.

⇒ If the engine does not start and run, refer to one of the following:
• Engine Cranks but Does Not Run for the 3.5L engine
• Engine Cranks but Does Not Run for the 3.9L engine
• Engine Cranks but Does Not Run for the 5.3L engine

10. **Important:** Do not clear any DTCs unless instructed to do so by a diagnostic procedure.
11. **Important:** If any DTCs are Powertrain related DTCs, select Capture Info in order to store the DTC information with the scan tool.

ARM0700000000754

Fig. 80 Diagnostic System Check (Part 2 of 3). 2008 Impala

Diagnostic Fault Information

• Always perform the Diagnostic System Check - Vehicle prior to using this diagnostic procedure.

Circuit/System Description

The remote control door lock receiver (RCDLR) receives a radio frequency (RF) transmission from each tire pressure sensor. Each sensors RF transmission contains its own unique identification (ID) code that must be learned into the RCDLR memory. Once all 4 IDs have been learned and vehicle speed is 25 mph, or greater, the RCDLR continuously compares IDs in received transmission to its learned IDs to determine if all 4 sensors are present.

Conditions for Running the DTC

The ignition is ON.

Conditions for Setting the DTC

The RCDLR has not undergone the tire type and tire pressure selection setup procedure.

Action Taken When the DTC Sets

The driver information center (DIC) displays the SERVICE TIRE MONITOR warning message.

Conditions for Clearing the DTC

A current DTC will clear when the RCDLR has undergone the setup procedure.

Diagnostic Aids

A newly replaced RCDLR will set DTC C0569 on its initial ignition ON cycle. Tire type and tire pressure selection setup must be performed. Refer to Repair Instructions.

Diagnostic Instructions

• Always perform the Diagnostic System Check - Vehicle prior to using this diagnostic procedure.

ARM0700000000743

Fig. 81 Code C0569: System Configuration Error. 2006–07 Impala & Monte Carlo

12. Use the appropriate scan tool selections to obtain DTCs from each of the vehicle modules. Verify there are no DTCs reported from any module.

⇒ If any DTCs are present, refer to Diagnostic Trouble Code (DTC) List - Vehicle and diagnose any current DTCs in the following order:
9.1. DTCs that begin with a U.
9.2. Any of the following: B1000, B1001, B1016, B1019, C0550, C0558, C0569, P0601, P0602, P0603, P0604, P0606, P0607, P060D, P062F, or P2610.
9.3. Any of the following: B1325, B1370, B1424, B1441, B1517, C0899, C0900, P0562, or P0563.
9.4. Component level DTCs.
9.5. System level DTCs.
9.6. Any remaining DTCs.

13. If the customer concern is related to inspection/maintenance (I/M) testing, refer to one of the following:

• Inspection/Maintenance (I/M) System Check for the 3.5L engine
• Inspection/Maintenance (I/M) System Check for the 3.9L engine
• Inspection/Maintenance (I/M) System Check for the 5.3L engine

⇒ If none of the previous tests or inspections addresses the concern, refer to Symptoms - Vehicle .

PMM Power Mode Parameters Ignition Switch Position	Current Power Mode	Ignition Off/Run/Crank (Off/Run Crank Voltage Circuit)	Ignition Accessory/Run (Accessory Voltage Circuit)	Ignition Run/Crank (Ignition 1 Voltage Circuit)
Off Key Out	Off	Key Out/ACC	Inactive	Inactive
Off Key IN	Off	Key In/Off	Inactive	Inactive
Accessory	Accessory	Key Out/ACC	Active	Inactive
Run	Run	Run	Active	Active
Start	Crank Request	Crank	Inactive	Active

ARM0700000000755

Fig. 80 Diagnostic System Check (Part 3 of 3). 2008 Impala

Circuit/System Description

If the tire type and pressure selection information is not entered with the scan tool during the remote control door lock receiver (RCDLR) setup, the tire pressure monitor indicator icon on the instrument panel cluster (IPC) will flash for 1 minute and then remain illuminated after the ignition switch is cycled ON and the IPC bulb check is complete. If equipped, the driver information center (DIC) will also display a service tire monitor type message. Under these circumstances, DTC C0569 will be set and the tire type and pressure information will need to be entered for the system to function correctly.

Conditions for Running the DTC

The ignition is ON.

Conditions for Setting the DTC

The RCDLR has not undergone the programming procedure.

Action Taken When the DTC Sets

• The tire pressure monitor indicator icon on the instrument panel cluster (IPC) flashes for 1 minute and then remains illuminated after the ignition switch is cycled ON and the IPC bulb check is complete.
• If equipped, the driver information center (DIC) displays the suspect tire pressure as dashes.
• If equipped, the DIC displays a service tire monitor type message.

Conditions for Clearing the DTC

A current DTC will clear when the RCDLR has undergone the tire type and pressure selection setup procedure and 1 ignition cycle has occurred.

Diagnostic Aids

A newly replaced RCDLR will set DTC C0569 after programming on its initial ignition ON cycle if the module setup information has not been entered. The Tire Type and Tire Pressure Selection setup must be performed with the scan tool.

Circuit/System Verification

Verify that the DTC C0569 is not set.
⇒ If the DTC is set, perform the RCDLR tire type and pressure selection setup with the scan tool and cycle the ignition. If the DTC resets, replace the RCDLR.

Repair Instructions

Perform the Diagnostic Repair Verification after completing the diagnostic procedure.

Control Module References for RCDLR replacement, setup, and programming

ARM0700000000744

Fig. 82 Code C0569: System Configuration Error. 2008 Impala

Diagnostic Fault information

- Always perform the Diagnostic System Check - Vehicle prior to using this diagnostic procedure.

Circuit/System Description

The tire pressure monitor (TPM) system has a radio frequency (RF) transmitting pressure sensor in each wheel/tire assembly. As vehicle speed increases, centrifugal force closes the sensors internal roll switch, which puts the sensor into drive mode. The remote control door lock receiver (RCDLR) receives and translates the data contained in the tire pressure sensor RF transmissions into sensor presence, sensor mode, and tire pressure. Once vehicle speed is 20 mph or greater, the RCDLR waits for the first sensor to go into drive mode, then checks if all sensors have gone into drive mode. If one or more sensors do not go into drive mode, or do not transmit at all, the RCDLR will set DTC C0750, C0755, C0760, or C0765.

Conditions for Running the DTC

Vehicle speed is 25 mph or greater for 2 minutes.

Conditions for Setting the DTC

- Any given sensor does not go into drive mode.
- Any given sensor does not transmit for 5 minutes.

Action Taken When the DTC Sets

- The driver information center (DIC) displays the suspect tire pressure as dashes.
- The DIC displays the SERVICE TIRE MONITOR message.

Conditions for Clearing the DTC

- A current DTC will clear when the malfunction is no longer present.
- The electronic brake control module (EBCM) automatically clears the history DTC when a current DTC is not detected in 100 consecutive drive cycles.

ARM0700000000756

Fig. 83   Codes C0750, C0755, C0760 & C0765: Low Tire Pressure (Part 1 of 2). 2006 Impala & Monte Carlo

Diagnostic Fault Information

- Always perform the Diagnostic System Check - Vehicle prior to using this diagnostic procedure.

Circuit/System Description

The tire pressure monitor (TPM) system has a radio frequency (RF) transmitting pressure sensor in each wheel/tire assembly. As vehicle speed increases, centrifugal force closes the sensors internal roll switch, which puts the sensor into Rolling mode. The remote control door lock receiver (RCDLR) receives and translates the data contained in the tire pressure sensor RF transmissions into sensor presence, sensor mode, and tire pressure. Once vehicle speed is greater than 25 mph, the RCDLR waits for the sensors to go into rolling mode. If one or more sensors do not go into rolling mode, or do not transmit at all, the RCDLR will set DTC C0750, C0755, C0760, or C0765 respectively.

Conditions for Running the DTC

Vehicle speed is greater than 25 mph.

Conditions for Setting the DTC

- A sensor does not transmit for 18 minutes.
- A sensor low battery condition.

Action Taken When the DTC Sets

- The tire pressure monitor indicator icon on the instrument panel cluster (IPC) flashes for 1 minute and then remains illuminated after the ignition switch is cycled ON and the IPC bulb check is complete.
- If equipped, the driver information center (DIC) displays the suspect tire pressure as dashes.
- If equipped, the DIC displays a service tire monitor type message.

Conditions for Clearing the DTC

- A current DTC will clear when the malfunction is no longer present and 1 ignition cycle occurs.
- The RCDLR automatically clears the history DTC when a current DTC is not detected in 100 consecutive drive cycles.

ARM0700000000759

Fig. 84   Codes C0750, C0755, C0760, C0765: Low Tire Pressure (Part 1 of 3). 2007–08 Impala & Monte Carlo

Diagnostic Aids

- Some aftermarket wheel valve stem holes are located further from the wheel rim than original equipment wheels. When using the TPM special tool to activate a sensor, ensure the tools antenna is no further than 15 cm (6 in) from the sensor.
- The sensor activation procedure may have to be repeated up to 3 times before determining a sensor is malfunctioning.
- Occasionally sensors can become mislocated due to previous tire rotations where the sensor learn procedure was not performed. Always learn the sensors to ensure the DTC set is for that actual physical corner of the vehicle.
- Occasionally sensor transmissions are not received by the RCDLR due to vehicle level RF interference.

Circuit/System Verification

Test drive the vehicle at a speed of 25 mph or greater for 2 minutes. No tire pressure monitor DTCs should set.

Circuit/System Testing

Important: Tire pressure sensors should transmit valid data with good signal strength in response to low frequency activation from the TPM special tool. It is important to observe the signal strength graph on the TPM special tool display screen after the activate button has been pressed and released. Any more than 1/4 graph displayed can be considered good signal strength.

1. Using the special tool, activate each tire pressure sensor and record each sensors transmission data and physical location. Verify tool displays 8-digit ID number, accurate tire pressure +/- 2 psi., Learn Mode, and good signal strength.

   ⇒ If any of the parameters listed above are not displayed, replace the suspect tire pressure sensor.

2. With the scan tool, verify tire pressure sensors ID and locations displayed on the scan tool match the IDs and locations recorded from the special tool.

   ⇒ If the IDs and locations do not match, perform Sensor Learn procedure.

3. IDs, and tire pressures +/- 2 psi., as they Enable the TPM learn mode. Use the TPM special tool in simulate mode to learn 4 simulated sensor transmissions into the RCDLR. Verify all 4 sensor locations, are displayed on the TPM special tool match what the scan tool displays.

   ⇒ If the scan tool does not match, replace the RCDLR.

4. Test drive the vehicle above 25 mph for greater than 10 seconds. With the scan tool, observe the suspect Pressure Sensor Mode data parameter. Verify sensor mode changes from Wake to Drive.

   ⇒ If the suspect Pressure Sensor Mode does not change, replace the suspect tire pressure sensor.

5. If no faults are found, go to Diagnostic Aids.

ARM0700000000757

Fig. 83   Codes C0750, C0755, C0760 & C0765: Low Tire Pressure (Part 2 of 2). 2006 Impala & Monte Carlo

Diagnostic Aids

- Some aftermarket wheel valve stem holes are located further from the wheel rim than original equipment wheels. When using the TPM special tool to activate a sensor, ensure the tool antenna is no further than 6 inches from the sensor and is aiming upward.
- Aftermarket wheel valve stem locations can cause a sensor to not function correctly.
- A sensor may have been damaged due to a previous wheel/tire service or flat tire event.
- The use of tire sealants can obstruct the sensor pressure sensing port and cause inaccurate tire pressure readings. If this condition is verified, remove the sealer from the tire and replace the sensor. Refer to Tire Pressure Indicator Sensor Replacement.
- Occasionally sensor transmissions are not received by the RCDLR due to vehicle level RF interference from items such as but not limited to aftermarket ignition systems, DVD players, CB radios, or metallic type window tinting.
- The sensor activation procedure may have to be repeated up to 3 times before determining a sensor is malfunctioning. In the event a particular sensor's information is displayed on the special tool upon activation but the horn does not chirp, it may be necessary to rotate the wheel valve stem to a different position due to the RF signal is being blocked by another component.
- Occasionally sensors can become mislocated due to previous tire rotations where the sensor learn procedure was not performed or stray sensor transmissions have been received from other vehicles . Always learn the sensors to ensure the DTC set is for that actual physical corner of the vehicle. Refer to Tire Pressure Sensor Learn .
- A sensor low battery condition will set a sensor DTC but will not illuminate the low tire pressure indicator or display a message on the DIC, if equipped. The sensor battery condition can be verified in the scan tool RCDLR data list. If a sensor low battery condition is indicated on the scan tool, the sensor will need to be replaced. Refer to Tire Pressure Indicator Sensor Replacement .

ARM0700000000760

Fig. 84   Codes C0750, C0755, C0760, C0765: Low Tire Pressure (Part 2 of 3). 2007-08 Impala & Monte Carlo

Circuit/System Verification

1. Using the J-46079 or equivalent, activate each tire pressure sensor and record each sensors transmission data and physical location. Verify J-46079 or equivalent, displays the 8-digit ID number, accurate tire pressure ±4 psi., Learn Mode, and at least a 1/4 graph signal strength displayed.

   ⇒ If any of the parameters listed above are not displayed, replace the suspect tire pressure sensor.

2. With the scan tool, verify tire pressure sensors ID and locations displayed on the scan tool match the IDs and locations recorded from the special tool.

   ⇒ If the IDs and locations do not match, perform the Tire Pressure Sensor Learn.

3. Enable the TPM learn mode. Use the J-46079 or equivalent, in simulate mode to learn 4 simulated sensor transmissions into the RCDLR. Verify that all 4 simulated sensor locations, IDs, and tire pressures displayed on the TPM special tool match the corresponding scan tool parameters displayed.

   ⇒ If the scan tool does not match, replace the RCDLR.

4. Test drive the vehicle above 25 mph for greater than 2 minutes. With the scan tool, observe the suspect Pressure Sensor Mode data parameter. Verify the sensor mode changes to Rolling.

   ⇒ If the Pressure Sensor Mode does not change, replace the suspect tire pressure sensor.

Repair Instructions

Perform the Diagnostic Repair Verification after completing the diagnostic procedure.

- Tire Pressure Indicator Sensor Replacement
- Tire Pressure Sensor Learn
- Control Module References for RCDLR replacement, programming, and setup.

ARM0700000000761

Fig. 84   Codes C0750, C0755, C0760, C0765: Low Tire Pressure (Part 3 of 3). 2007-08 Impala & Monte Carlo

Diagnostic Fault Information

- Always perform the Diagnostic System Check - Vehicle prior to using this diagnostic procedure.

Circuit/System Description

If the tire pressure sensor learn procedure has not been performed, the tire pressure monitor indicator icon on the instrument panel cluster (IPC) will flash for 1 minute and then remain illuminated after the ignition switch is cycled ON and the IPC bulb check is complete. If equipped, the driver information center (DIC) will also display a service tire monitor type message. Under these circumstances, DTC C0775 will be set and the tire pressure sensor learn procedure will need to be performed for the system to function correctly.

Conditions for Running the DTC

The ignition is ON.

Conditions for Setting the DTC

The remote control door lock receiver (RCDLR) has not undergone the tire pressure sensor learn procedure.

Action Taken When the DTC Sets

- The tire pressure monitor indicator icon on the instrument panel cluster (IPC) will flash for 1 minute and then remain illuminated after the ignition switch is cycled ON and the IPC bulb check is complete.
- If equipped, the driver information center (DIC) displays a service tire monitor type warning message.

Conditions for Clearing the DTC

A current DTC will clear when the RCDLR has undergone the tire pressure sensor learn procedure and 1 ignition cycle has occurred.

Diagnostic Aids

A newly replaced RCDLR will set DTC C0775 on its initial ignition ON cycle. The tire pressure sensor learn procedure must be performed.

Circuit/System Verification

Verify that the DTC C0775 is not set.
⇒ If the DTC is set, perform the tire pressure sensor learn procedure. Cycle the ignition. If the DTC resets, replace the RCDLR.

Repair Instructions

Perform the Diagnostic Repair Verification after completing the diagnostic procedure.

- Tire Pressure Sensor Learn

ARM0700000000764

Fig. 86   Code C0775: Low Tire Pressure System Sensors Not Learned. 2008 Impala

Diagnostic Fault Information

- Always perform the Diagnostic System Check - Vehicle prior to using this diagnostic procedure.

Circuit/System Description

The remote control door lock receiver (RCDLR) receives a radio frequency (RF) transmission from each tire pressure sensor. Each sensor RF transmission contains its own unique identification (ID) code that must be learned into the RCDLR memory. Once all 4 IDs have been learned and vehicle speed is 25 mph or greater, the RCDLR continuously compares IDs in received transmission to its learned IDs to determine if all 4 sensors are present.

Conditions for Running the DTC

The ignition is ON.

Conditions for Setting the DTC

The RCDLR has not undergone the tire pressure sensor learn procedure.

Action Taken When the DTC Sets

The driver information center (DIC) displays the SERVICE TIRE MONITOR warning message.

Conditions for Clearing the DTC

A current DTC will clear when the RCDLR has undergone the sensor learn procedure.

Diagnostic Aids

A newly replaced RCDLR will set DTC C0775 on its initial ignition ON cycle. Tire pressure sensor learn procedure must be performed.

Circuit/System Verification

Verify that the DTC C0775 is not set.
⇒ If the DTC is set, program/setup the RCDLR. If the DTC resets, replace the RCDLR.

Repair Instructions

Perform the Diagnostic Repair Verification after completing the diagnostic procedure.
- Tire Pressure Sensor Learn
- Control Module References for RCDLR replacement, setup, and programming

ARM0700000000762

Fig. 85   Code C0775: Low Tire Pressure System Sensors Not Learned. 2006–07 Impala & Monte Carlo

Step	Action	Value(s)	Yes	No
1	Did you perform the TPM Diagnostic System Check?	--	Go to Step 2	Go to Diagnostic System Check -
2	1. Install a scan tool. 2. Turn ON the ignition, with the engine OFF. 3. With a scan tool, monitor the DTC Information for DTC C1245 in the ABS/TCS/TPM (if equipped) Diagnostic Trouble Codes (DTCs). Does the scan tool indicate that DTC C1245 is current?	--	Go to Step 3	Go to Diagnostic Aids
3	Since most occurrences of this DTC are caused by low tire pressure, review the TPM system with the customer to verify the conditions under which the DTC set. Did vehicle operation cause this DTC to set?	--	Go to Step 5	Go to Step 4
4	1. Perform the tire inflation monitoring reset if tire pressures were adjusted. 2. Use the scan tool in order to clear the DTCs. 3. Operate the vehicle within the Conditions for Running the DTC as specified in the supporting text. Does the DTC reset as a current DTC?	--	Go to Diagnostic Aids	System OK
5	Inspect the tire pressures and adjust if needed. Perform the tire inflation monitoring reset if tire pressures were adjusted. Did you complete the repair?	--	System OK	--

GC2040200235000X

Fig. 87   Code C1245: Low Tire Pressure Detected. Impala & Monte Carlo

Diagnostic Fault Information

- Perform the Diagnostic System Check - Vehicle prior to using this diagnostic procedure.

Circuit/System Description

The remote control door lock receiver (RCDLR) sends a serial data message to the instrument panel cluster (IPC) requesting low tire pressure indicator illumination.

Circuit/System Testing

1. Inflate tires to the proper pressure.
2. Using the tire pressure monitor (TPM) special tool, activate each tire pressure sensor and record each sensors tire pressure reading in psi. Check tire pressures with a known accurate hand held tire pressure gauge. Verify pressure readings from special tool do not differ 4 psi or more lower than actual tire pressure.

   ⇒ If 4 psi or more lower than actual tire pressure, replace the suspect tire pressure sensor.

3. With the scan tool, select instrument panel special functions Lamp Test. Command the instrument panel warning lamps OFF. Verify low tire pressure indicator lamp turns OFF.

   ⇒ If the lamp does not turn OFF, replace the IPC.

4. Enable the TPM learn mode. Use the TPM special tool in simulate mode to learn 4 simulated sensor transmissions into the RCDLR. Observe tire pressures in the scan tool data display. Verify simulated tire pressures do not differ more than +/- 4 psi of the scan tool reading.

   ⇒ If the tire pressures differ more than +/- 4 psi, replace the RCDLR.

Repair Instructions

Perform the Diagnostic Repair Verification after completing the diagnostic procedure.

- Tire Pressure Sensor Learn
- Control Module References for IPC or RCDLR replacement, setup, and programming

ARM0700000000766

Fig. 88 Low Tire Pressure Indicator Always On. 2006 Impala & Monte Carlo

Circuit/System Verification

Important: When a TPM DTC is set, the tire pressure monitor indicator icon will flash for 1 minute after the IPC bulb check is completed and then remains illuminated. If equipped with a DIC, a service tire monitor type message will also be displayed.

Cycle the ignition from OFF to ON. After the instrument panel cluster (IPC) bulb check is complete, the tire pressure monitor indicator icon should not be illuminated.

Circuit/System Testing

1. Inflate all tires to the proper pressure and drive the vehicle over 25 MPH for over 2 minutes.
2. Using the J-46079 , activate each tire pressure sensor and record each sensors tire pressure reading. Check the tire pressures with a known accurate hand held tire pressure gauge. Verify that the pressure readings from the special tool do not differ more than 4 psi from the actual tire pressure readings.

   ⇒ If not within the specified range, replace the suspect tire pressure sensor.

3. Using a scan tool, enable the TPM learn mode. Use the J-46079 in simulate mode to learn 4 simulated sensor transmissions into the RCDLR. Observe tire pressures in the scan tool data display. Verify the simulated tire pressures do not differ more than +/- 4 psi of the scan tool reading.

   ⇒ If not within the specified range, replace the RCDLR.

4. Using a scan tool, select instrument panel special functions Lamp Test. Command the instrument panel warning lamps OFF. Verify the tire pressure monitor indicator icon turns OFF.

   ⇒ If the tire pressure monitor icon does not turn OFF, replace the IPC.

5. Ignition ON, use the scan tool to setup the Tire Type/Pressure Selection in the RCDLR Module Setup menu. Verify the tire pressure monitor indicator icon turns OFF.

   ⇒ If the tire pressure monitor icon does not turn OFF, replace the RCDLR.

Repair Instructions
Perform the Diagnostic Repair Verification after completing the diagnostic procedure.
- Tire Pressure Indicator Sensor Replacement
- Tire Pressure Sensor Learn
- Control Module References for IPC or RCDLR replacement, setup, and programming

ARM0700000000768

Fig. 89 Low Tire Pressure Indicator Always On (Part 2 of 2). 2007-08 Impala & Monte Carlo

Diagnostic Fault Information

- Perform the Diagnostic System Check - Vehicle prior to using this diagnostic procedure.

Circuit/System Description
The remote control door lock receiver (RCDLR) receives a radio frequency (RF) transmission from each tire pressure sensor. Each sensor RF transmission contains its own unique identification (ID) code that must be learned into the RCDLR memory. Once all 4 IDs have been learned and vehicle speed is greater than 40 km/h (25 mph), the RCDLR continuously compares IDs in received transmission to its learned IDs to determine if all 4 sensors are present. If the remote control door lock receiver (RCDLR) detects a low tire pressure condition or a malfunction in the system, it will send a serial data message to the instrument panel cluster (IPC) requesting tire pressure monitor indicator illumination and to display a data message on the driver information center (DIC,) if equipped.

Diagnostic Aids

- Some aftermarket wheel valve stem holes are located further from the wheel rim than original equipment wheels. When using the TPM special tool to activate a sensor, ensure the tool antenna is no further than 6 inches the sensor and is aiming upward.
- Aftermarket wheel value stem locations can cause a sensor to not function correctly.
- A sensor may have been damaged due to a previous wheel/tire service or flat tire event.
- The use of tire sealants can obstruct the sensor pressure sensing port and cause inaccurate tire pressure readings. If this condition is verified, remove the sealer from the tire and replace the sensor.
- Occasionally sensor transmissions are not received by the RCDLR due to vehicle level RF interference from items such as but not limited to aftermarket ignition systems, DVD players, CB radios, or metallic type window tinting.
- The sensor activation procedure may have to be repeated up to 3 times before determining a sensor is malfunctioning. In the event a particular sensor's information is displayed on the special tool upon activation but the horn does not chirp, it may be necessary to rotate the wheel valve stem to a different position due to the RF signal is being blocked by another component.
- Occasionally sensors can become mislocated due to previous tire rotations where the sensor learn procedure was not performed or stray sensor transmissions have been received from other vehicles. Always learn the sensors to ensure the DTC set is for that actual physical corner of the vehicle. Refer to Tire Pressure Sensor Learn.

ARM0700000000767

Fig. 89 Low Tire Pressure Indicator Always On (Part 1 of 2). 2007-08 Impala & Monte Carlo

Diagnostic Fault Information

- Always perform the Diagnostic System Check - Vehicle prior to using this diagnostic procedure.

Circuit/System Description

The remote control door lock receiver (RCDLR) sends a serial data message to the instrument panel cluster (IPC) requesting low tire pressure indicator illumination.

Circuit/System Testing

1. With the scan tool, select instrument panel special functions Lamp Test. Command the instrument panel lamps ON. Verify low tire pressure indicator lamp turns ON.

   ⇒ If the lamp does not turn ON, replace the IPC.

2. Using the tire pressure monitor (TPM) special tool to observe the tire pressure of the suspected faulty sensor. Check air pressure with a known accurate hand held tire pressure gage. Compare the psi reading to the display on the TPM special tool. Verify pressure readings from special tool do not differ 2 psi or more than actual tire pressure.

   ⇒ If the difference is 2 psi more, replace the suspect tire pressure sensor.

3. With the scan tool, observe tire pressures in the scan tool data display. Verify pressure readings from special tool do not differ 2 psi or more than scan tool data display.

   ⇒ If the difference is 2 psi more, replace the RCDLR.

Repair Instructions

Perform the Diagnostic Repair Verification after completing the diagnostic procedure.

- Tire Pressure Sensor Learn
- Control Module References for RCDLR replacement, setup, and programming

ARM0700000000769

Fig. 90 Low Tire Pressure Indicator Inoperative. 2006 Impala & Monte Carlo

Diagnostic Fault Information

- Always perform the Diagnostic System Check - Vehicle prior to using this diagnostic procedure.

Circuit/System Description

The remote control door lock receiver (RCDLR) receives a radio frequency (RF) transmission from each tire pressure sensor. Each sensor RF transmission contains its own unique identification (ID) code that must be learned into the RCDLR memory. Once all 4 IDs have been learned and vehicle speed is greater than 25 mph, the RCDLR continuously compares IDs in received transmission to its learned IDs to determine if all 4 sensors are present. If the remote control door lock receiver (RCDLR) detects a low tire pressure condition or a malfunction in the system, it will send a serial data message to the instrument panel cluster (IPC) requesting tire pressure monitor indicator icon illumination and to display a data message on the driver information center (DIC) if equipped.

Diagnostic Aids

- Some aftermarket wheel valve stem holes are located further from the wheel rim than original equipment wheels. When using the TPM special tool to activate a sensor, ensure the tool antenna is no further than 6 inches from the sensor and is aiming upward.
- Aftermarket wheel value stem locations can cause a sensor to not function correctly.
- A sensor may have been damaged due to a previous wheel/tire service or flat tire event.
- The use of tire sealants can obstruct the sensor pressure sensing port and cause inaccurate tire pressure readings. If this condition is verified, remove the sealer from the tire and replace the sensor. Refer to Tire Pressure Indicator Sensor Replacement .
- Occasionally sensor transmissions are not received by the RCDLR due to vehicle level RF interference from items such as but not limited to aftermarket ignition systems, DVD players, CB radios, or metallic type window tinting.
- The sensor activation procedure may have to be repeated up to 3 times before determining a sensor is malfunctioning. In the event a particular sensor's information is displayed on the special tool upon activation but the horn does not chirp, it may be necessary to rotate the wheel valve stem to a different position due to the RF signal is being blocked by another component.
- Occasionally sensors can become mislocated due to previous tire rotations where the sensor learn procedure was not performed or stray sensor transmissions have been received from other vehicles . Always learn the sensors to ensure the DTC set is for that actual physical corner of the vehicle. Refer to Tire Pressure Sensor Learn .

ARM0700000000770

Fig. 91 Low Tire Pressure Indicator Inoperative (Part 1 of 2). 2007–08 Impala & Monte Carlo

Circuit/System Testing

1. With the scan tool, select instrument panel special functions Lamp Test. Command the instrument panel lamps ON. Verify tire pressure monitor indicator icon turns ON.

   ⇒ If the icon does not turn ON, replace the IPC.

2. Using the tire pressure monitor (TPM) special tool to observe the tire pressure of the suspected faulty sensor. Check the air pressure with a known accurate tire pressure gage. Compare the pressure reading to the display on the TPM special tool. Verify the pressure readings from special tool do not differ 4 psi or more than actual tire pressure.

   ⇒ If not within the specified range, replace the suspect tire pressure sensor.

3. With the scan tool, observe tire pressures in the scan tool data display. Verify pressure readings from special tool do not differ 4 psi or more than scan tool data display.

   ⇒ If not within the specified range, replace the RCDLR.

Repair Instructions

Perform the Diagnostic Repair Verification after completing the diagnostic procedure.

- Tire Pressure Indicator Sensor Replacement
- Tire Pressure Sensor Learn
- Control Module References for IPC and RCDLR replacement, setup, and programming

ARM0700000000771

Fig. 91 Low Tire Pressure Indicator Inoperative (Part 2 of 2). 2007–08 Impala & Monte Carlo

Step	Action		Yes	No
5	Attempt to start the engine. Does the engine crank?		Go to Step 6	Go to Symptoms.
6	Attempt to start the engine. Does the engine start and idle?		Go to Step 7	Go to Engine Cranks but Does Not Run
7	**Important** Do not clear any DTCs unless instructed by a diagnostic procedure. Use the appropriate scan tool selections to obtain DTCs for each of the control modules. Does the scan tool display any DTCs?		Go to Step 8	Go to Step 12
8	Does the scan tool display any DTCs that begin with a "U"?		Go to Diagnostic Trouble Code List (DTC)	Go to Step 9
9	**Important** If any of these DTCs are displayed, diagnose them before diagnosing any other DTCs or symptoms. Does the scan tool display DTC B1000, B1001, B1004, B1007, B1009, C0550, P0601, P0602, P0604, P0606, or P2610?		Go to Diagnostic Trouble Code List (DTC)	Go to Step 10
10	**Important** If any of these DTCs are displayed, diagnose them before diagnosing any other DTCs or symptoms. Does the scan tool display DTC B1370, B1390, B1420, C0896, or P0560?		Go to Diagnostic Trouble Code List (DTC)	Go to Step 11

ARM0400000000713

Fig. 92 Diagnostic System Check (Part 2 of 3). 2005–06 LaCrosse

Step	Action	Yes	No
1	Perform the following preliminary inspections: • Ensure that the battery is fully charged. • Ensure that the battery cables are clean and tight. • Inspect for any open fuses. • Inspect the easily accessible systems or the visible system components for obvious damage or conditions that could cause the symptom. • Ensure that the grounds are clean, tight, and in the correct location. • Inspect for aftermarket devices that could affect the operation of the system. • Search for applicable service bulletins. Did you find and correct the condition?	System OK	Go to Step 2
2	Install a scan tool. Does the scan tool power up?	Go to Step 3	Go to Scan Tool Does Not Power Up
3	1. Turn ON the ignition, with the engine OFF. 2. Attempt to establish communication with all of the control modules on the vehicle. Does the scan tool communicate with all of the expected vehicle control modules?	Go to Step 4	Go to Data Link References
4	**Important** • To ensure that retained accessory power (RAP) mode is inactive (if equipped), open the drivers door during the following step. • The engine may start during the following step. Turn OFF the engine as soon as you have observed the crank power mode. 1. Access the Power Mode parameter on the scan tool. 2. Rotate the ignition switch (operate the ignition mode switch) through all positions while observing the Power Mode parameter. Does the Power Mode parameter reading on the scan tool match the ignition switch position for all switch positions?	Go to Step 5	Go to Power Mode Mismatch

ARM0400000000712

Fig. 92 Diagnostic System Check (Part 1 of 3). 2005–06 LaCrosse

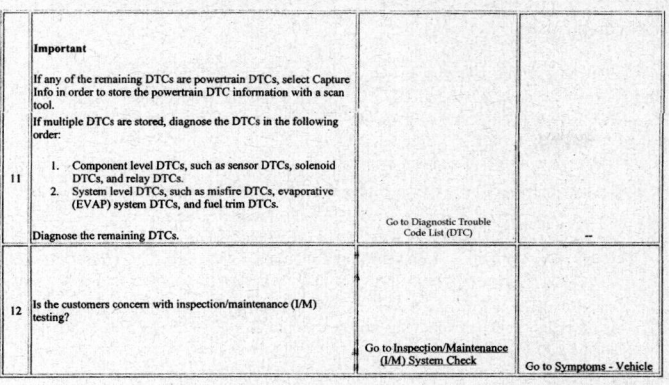

	Important		
11	If any of the remaining DTCs are powertrain DTCs, select Capture Info in order to store the powertrain DTC information with a scan tool.		
	If multiple DTCs are stored, diagnose the DTCs in the following order:		
	1. Component level DTCs, such as sensor DTCs, solenoid DTCs, and relay DTCs.		
	2. System level DTCs, such as misfire DTCs, evaporative (EVAP) system DTCs, and fuel trim DTCs.		
		Go to Diagnostic Trouble Code List (DTC)	—
	Diagnose the remaining DTCs.		
12	Is the customers concern with inspection/maintenance (I/M) testing?		
		Go to Inspection/Maintenance (I/M) System Check	Go to Symptoms - Vehicle

ARM0400000000714

Fig. 92   Diagnostic System Check (Part 3 of 3). 2005–06 LaCrosse

5. Attempt to start the engine. Verify that the engine cranks.

⇒ If the engine does not crank, refer to Symptoms - Engine Electrical .

6. Attempt to start the engine. Verify the engine starts and idles.

⇒ If the engine does not start and idle, refer to Engine Cranks but Does Not Run for the 3.6L (LY7) engine or Engine Cranks but Does Not Run for the 3.8L engine.

Important: Do not clear any DTCs unless instructed to do so by a diagnostic procedure.

Important: If any DTCs are Powertrain related DTCs, select Capture Info in order to store the DTC information with the scan tool.

7. Use the appropriate scan tool selections to obtain DTCs from each of the vehicle modules. Verify there are no DTCs reported from any module.

⇒ If any DTCs are present, refer to Diagnostic Trouble Code (DTC) List - Vehicle and diagnose any current DTCs in the following order:

7.1. DTCs that begin with a U.

7.2. Any of the following: B1000, B1004, B1007, B1009, B1013, B1014, C0550, C0569, P0601, P0602, P0603, P0604, P0606, P2107, P2108,, or P2610.

7.3. Any of the following: B1327, B1328, B1370, B1390, P0560, P0562, or P0563.

7.4. Component level DTCs.

7.5. System level DTCs.

7.6. Any remaining DTCs.

8. If the customer concern is related to inspection/maintenance (I/M) testing, refer to Inspection/Maintenance (I/M) System Check for the 3.6L (LY7) engine or Inspection/Maintenance (I/M) System Check for the 3.8L engine.

ARM0700000000797

Fig. 93   Diagnostic System Check (Part 2 of 2). 2007–08 LaCrosse

Diagnostic System Check - LaCrosse

1. Before beginning vehicle diagnosis, the following preliminary inspections/tests must be performed:

- Ensure that the battery is fully charged.
- Ensure that the battery cables are clean and tight.
- Inspect for any open fuses.
- Ensure that the grounds are clean, tight, and in the correct location.
- Inspect the easily accessible systems or the visible system components for obvious damage or conditions that could cause the concern. This would include checking to ensure that all connections/connectors are fully seated and secured.
- Inspect for aftermarket devices that could affect the operation of the system.
- Search for applicable service bulletins.

⇒ If the preceding inspections/tests resolve the concern, go to Diagnostic Repair Verification .

2. Install a scan tool. Verify that the scan tool powers up.

⇒ If the scan tool does not power up, refer to Scan Tool Does Not Power Up.

3. Ignition ON, Engine OFF, verify communication with all of the control modules on the vehicle. Refer to Data Link References for information on the modules you should expect to communicate.

⇒ If the scan tool does not communicate with one or more of the expected control modules, refer to Data Link References.

Important: Open the driver's door to ensure retained accessory power mode (RAP) is inactive during this test. The engine may start during this test. Turn the engine OFF as soon as the crank power mode has been observed.

4. Access the Power Mode parameter on the scan tool. Verify the power mode parameter matches all the ignition switch positions. Refer to Power Mode Description and Operation for information on the power mode states that correspond to each ignition switch position.

⇒ If the power mode parameter does not match the ignition switch position for all ignition switch positions, refer to Power Mode Mismatch.

ARM0700000000796

Fig. 93   Diagnostic System Check (Part 1 of 2). 2007–08 LaCrosse

Diagnostic Fault Information

- Perform the Diagnostic System Check - Vehicle prior to using this diagnostic procedure.

Circuit/System Description

The remote control door lock receiver (RCDLR) receives a radio frequency (RF) transmission from each tire pressure sensor. Each sensors RF transmission contains its own unique identification (ID) code that must be learned into the RCDLR memory. Once all 4 IDs have been learned and vehicle speed is 25 mph, or greater, the RCDLR continuously compares IDs in received transmission to its learned IDs to determine if all 4 sensors are present.

Conditions for Running the DTC

The ignition is ON.

Conditions for Letting the DTC

The RCDLR has not undergone the programming procedure.

Action Taken When the DTC Sets

The driver information center (DIC) displays the SERVICE TIRE MONITOR warning message.

Conditions for Clearing the DTC

A current DTC will clear when the RCDLR has undergone the setup procedure.

Diagnostic Aids

A newly replaced RCDLR will set DTC C0569 on its initial ignition ON cycle. Tire type and tire pressure selection setup must be performed.

Circuit/System Verification

Verify that the DTC C0569 is not set.

⇒ If the DTC is set, program/setup the RCDLR. If the DTC resets, replace the RCDLR

Repair Instructions

Perform the Diagnostic Repair Verification after completing the diagnostic procedure.

Control Module References for RCDLR replacement, setup, and programming

ARM0700000000745

Fig. 94   Code C0569: System Configuration Error. LaCrosse

Diagnostic Instructions

- Perform the <u>Diagnostic System Check - Vehicle</u> prior to using this diagnostic procedure.

Circuit/System Description

The tire pressure monitor (TPM) system has a radio frequency (RF) transmitting pressure sensor in each wheel/tire assembly. As vehicle speed increases, centrifugal force closes the sensors internal roll switch, which puts the sensor into drive mode. The remote control door lock receiver (RCDLR) receives and translates the data contained in the tire pressure sensor RF transmissions into sensor presence, sensor mode, and tire pressure. Once vehicle speed is greater than 25 mph, the RCDLR waits for the sensors to go into rolling mode. If one or more sensors do not go into rolling mode, or do not transmit at all, the RCDLR will set DTC C0750, C0755, C0760, or C0765 respectively.

Conditions for Running the DTC

Vehicle speed is greater than 25 mph.

Conditions for Setting the DTC

- A sensor does not transmit for 18 minutes.
- A sensor low battery condition.

Action Taken When the DTC Sets

- The Tire Pressure Monitor Indicator icon on the instrument panel cluster (IPC) flashes for 1 minute and then remains illuminated.
- If equipped, the driver information center (DIC) displays the suspect tire pressure as dashes.
- If equipped, the DIC displays a service tire monitor type message.

Conditions for Clearing the DTC

- A current DTC will clear when the malfunction is no longer present.
- The RCDLR automatically clears the history DTC when a current DTC is not detected in 100 consecutive drive cycles.

ARM0700000000798

Fig. 95   Codes C0750, C0755, C0760 & C0765: Low Tire Pressure (Part 1 of 3). LaCrosse

Circuit/System Verification

1. Using the J-46079 or equivalent, activate each tire pressure sensor and record each sensors transmission data and physical location. Verify J-46079 displays the 8-digit ID number, accurate tire pressure within 4 psi, Learn Mode, and at least a 1/4 graph signal strength displayed.

   ⇒ If any of the parameters listed above are not displayed, replace the suspect tire pressure sensor.

2. With the scan tool, verify tire pressure sensors ID and locations displayed on the scan tool match the IDs and locations recorded from the special tool.

   ⇒ If the IDs and locations do not match, perform the Tire Pressure Sensor Learn.

3. Enable the TPM learn mode. Use the TPM special tool in simulate mode to learn 4 simulated sensor transmissions into the RCDLR. Verify all 4 sensor locations, IDs, and that the tire pressures are within 4 psi, as they are displayed on the TPM special tool match what the scan tool displays.

   ⇒ If the scan tool does not match, replace the RCDLR.

4. Test drive the vehicle above 25 mph for greater than 2 minutes. With the scan tool, observe the suspect Pressure Sensor Mode data parameter. Verify sensor mode changes to Rolling.

   ⇒ If the suspect Pressure Sensor Mode does not change, replace the suspect tire pressure sensor.

Repair Instructions

Perform the Diagnostic Repair Verification after completing the diagnostic procedure.

- Tire Pressure Indicator Sensor Replacement
- Tire Pressure Sensor Learn
- Control Module References for RCDLR replacement, setup, and programming

ARM0700000000800

Fig. 95   Codes C0750, C0755, C0760 & C0765: Low Tire Pressure (Part 3 of 3). LaCrosse

Diagnostic Aids

- Some aftermarket wheel valve stem holes are located further from the wheel rim than original equipment wheels. When using the TPM special tool to activate a sensor, ensure the tool antenna is no further than 15 cm (6 in) from the sensor and is aiming upward.
- Aftermarket wheel valve stem locations can cause a sensor to not function correctly.
- A sensor may have been damaged due to a previous wheel/tire service or flat tire event.
- The use of tire sealants can obstruct the sensor pressure sensing port and cause inaccurate tire pressure readings. If this condition is verified, remove the sealer from the tire and replace the sensor. Refer to Tire Pressure Indicator Sensor Replacement.
- Occasionally sensor transmissions are not received by the RCDLR due to vehicle level RF interference from items such as but not limited to aftermarket ignition systems, DVD players, CB radios, or metallic type window tinting.
- The sensor activation procedure may have to be repeated up to 3 times before determining a sensor is malfunctioning. In the event a particular sensor's information is displayed on the special tool upon activation but the horn does not chirp, it may be necessary to rotate the wheel valve stem to a different position due to the RF signal is being blocked by another component.
- Occasionally sensors can become mislocated due to previous tire rotations where the sensor learn procedure was not performed or stray sensor transmissions have been received from other vehicles. Always learn the sensors to ensure the DTC set is for that actual physical corner of the vehicle. Refer to Tire Pressure Sensor Learn.
- A sensor low battery condition will set a sensor DTC but will not illuminate the low tire pressure indicator or display a message on the DIC, if equipped. The sensor battery condition can be verified in the scan tool RCDLR data list. If a sensor low battery condition is indicated on the scan tool, the sensor will need to be replaced. Refer to Tire Pressure Indicator Sensor Replacement.

ARM0700000000799

Fig. 95   Codes C0750, C0755, C0760 & C0765: Low Tire Pressure (Part 2 of 3). LaCrosse

Diagnostic Instructions

Circuit/System Description

The remote control door lock receiver (RCDLR) receives a radio frequency (RF) transmission from each tire pressure sensor. Each sensor RF transmission contains its own unique identification (ID) code that must be learned into the RCDLR memory. Once all 4 IDs have been learned and vehicle speed is 25 mph or greater, the RCDLR continuously compares IDs in received transmission to its learned IDs to determine if all 4 sensors are present.

Conditions for Running the DTC

The ignition is ON.

Conditions for Setting the DTC

The RCDLR has not undergone the tire pressure sensor learn procedure.

Action Taken When the DTC Sets

The driver information center (DIC) displays the SERVICE TIRE MONITOR warning message.

Conditions for Clearing the DTC

A current DTC will clear when the RCDLR has undergone the sensor learn procedure.

Diagnostic Aids

A newly replaced RCDLR will set DTC C0775 on its initial ignition ON cycle. Tire pressure sensor learn procedure must be performed.

Circuit/System Verification

Verify that the DTC C0775 is not set.

⇒ If the DTC is set, program/setup the RCDLR. If the DTC resets, replace the RCDLR.

Repair Instructions

Perform the Diagnostic Repair Verification after completing the diagnostic procedure.

- Tire Pressure Sensor Learn
- Control Module References for RCDLR replacement, setup, and programming

ARM0700000000758

Fig. 96   Code C0775: Low Tire Pressure Not Learned. LaCrosse

Diagnostic Instructions

- Perform the Diagnostic System Check - Vehicle prior to using this diagnostic procedure.

Circuit/System Description

The remote control door lock receiver (RCDLR) receives a radio frequency (RF) transmission from each tire pressure sensor. Each sensor RF transmission contains its own unique identification (ID) code that must be learned into the RCDLR memory. Once all 4 IDs have been learned and vehicle speed is greater than 25 mph, the RCDLR continuously compares IDs in received transmission to its learned IDs to determine if all 4 sensors are present. If the remote control door lock receiver (RCDLR) detects a low tire pressure condition or a malfunction in the system, it will send a serial data message to the instrument panel cluster (IPC) requesting tire pressure monitor indicator illumination and to display a data message on the driver information center (DIC,) if equipped.

Diagnostic Aids

- Some aftermarket wheel valve stem holes are located further from the wheel rim than original equipment wheels. When using the TPM special tool to activate a sensor, ensure the tool antenna is no further than 15 cm (6 in) from the sensor and is aiming upward.
- Aftermarket wheel value stem locations can cause a sensor to not function correctly.
- A sensor may have been damaged due to a previous wheel/tire service or flat tire event.
- The use of tire sealants can obstruct the sensor pressure sensing port and cause inaccurate tire pressure readings. If this condition is verified, remove the sealer from the tire and replace the sensor.
- Occasionally sensor transmissions are not received by the RCDLR due to vehicle level RF interference from items such as but not limited to aftermarket ignition systems, DVD players, CB radios, or metallic type window tinting.
- The sensor activation procedure may have to be repeated up to 3 times before determining a sensor is malfunctioning. In the event a particular sensor's information is displayed on the special tool upon activation but the horn does not chirp, it may be necessary to rotate the wheel valve stem to a different position due to the RF signal is being blocked by another component.
- Occasionally sensors can become mislocated due to previous tire rotations where the sensor learn procedure was not performed or stray sensor transmissions have been received from other vehicles. Always learn the sensors to ensure the DTC set is for that actual physical corner of the vehicle.

Circuit/System Verification

Important: When a TPM DTC is set, the tire pressure monitor indicator icon will flash for 1 minute after the IPC bulb check is completed and then remains illuminated. If equipped with a DIC, a service tire monitor type message will also be displayed.

Low tire pressure in one or more tires is indicated by a continuously illuminated tire pressure monitor indicator icon after the IPC bulb check is completed. If equipped with a DIC, a check tire pressure type message will also be displayed.

Cycle the ignition from OFF to ON. After the instrument panel cluster (IPC) bulb check is complete, the tire pressure monitor indicator icon should not be illuminated.

ARM0700000000801

Fig. 97   Low Tire Pressure Indicator Always On (Part 1 of 2). LaCrosse

Diagnostic Instructions

- Perform the Diagnostic System Check - Vehicle prior to using this diagnostic procedure.

Circuit/System Description

The remote control door lock receiver (RCDLR) receives a radio frequency (RF) transmission from each tire pressure sensor. Each sensor RF transmission contains its own unique identification (ID) code that must be learned into the RCDLR memory. Once all 4 IDs have been learned and vehicle speed is greater than 25 mph, the RCDLR continuously compares IDs in received transmission to its learned IDs to determine if all 4 sensors are present. If the remote control door lock receiver (RCDLR) detects a low tire pressure condition or a malfunction in the system, it will send a serial data message to the instrument panel cluster (IPC) requesting tire pressure monitor indicator icon illumination and to display a data message on the driver information center (DIC) if equipped.

Diagnostic Aids

- Some aftermarket wheel valve stem holes are located further from the wheel rim than original equipment wheels. When using the TPM special tool to activate a sensor, ensure the tool antenna is no further than 15 cm (6 in) from the sensor and is aiming upward.
- Aftermarket wheel value stem locations can cause a sensor to not function correctly.
- A sensor may have been damaged due to a previous wheel/tire service or flat tire event.
- The use of tire sealants can obstruct the sensor pressure sensing port and cause inaccurate tire pressure readings. If this condition is verified, remove the sealer from the tire and replace the sensor. Refer to Tire Pressure Indicator Sensor Replacement .
- Occasionally sensor transmissions are not received by the RCDLR due to vehicle level RF interference from items such as but not limited to aftermarket ignition systems, DVD players, CB radios, or metallic type window tinting.
- The sensor activation procedure may have to be repeated up to 3 times before determining a sensor is malfunctioning. In the event a particular sensor's information is displayed on the special tool upon activation but the horn does not chirp, it may be necessary to rotate the wheel valve stem to a different position due to the RF signal is being blocked by another component.
- Occasionally sensors can become mislocated due to previous tire rotations where the sensor learn procedure was not performed or stray sensor transmissions have been received from other vehicles . Always learn the sensors to ensure the DTC set is for that actual physical corner of the vehicle. Refer to Tire Pressure Sensor Learn .

ARM0700000000803

Fig. 98   Low Tire Pressure Indicator Inoperative (Part 1 of 2). LaCrosse

Circuit/System Testing

1. Inflate all tires to the proper pressure and drive the vehicle over 25 MPH for over 2 minutes.
2. Using the J-46079 or equivalent, activate each tire pressure sensor and record each sensors tire pressure reading. Check the tire pressures with a known accurate hand held tire pressure gauge. Verify that the pressure readings from the special tool do not differ more than 4 psi from the actual tire pressure readings.

   ⇒ If not within the specified range, replace the suspect tire pressure sensor.

3. Using a scan tool, enable the TPM learn mode. Use the J-46079 in simulate mode to learn 4 simulated sensor transmissions into the RCDLR. Observe tire pressures in the scan tool data display. Verify the simulated tire pressures do not differ more than +/- 4 psi of the scan tool reading.

   ⇒ If not within the specified range, replace the RCDLR.

4. Using a scan tool, select instrument panel special functions Lamp Test. Command the instrument panel warning lamps OFF. Verify the tire pressure monitor indicator icon turns OFF.

   ⇒ If the tire pressure monitor icon does not turn OFF, replace the IPC.

5. Ignition ON, use the scan tool to setup the Tire Type/Pressure Selection in the RCDLR Module Setup menu. Verify the tire pressure monitor indicator icon turns OFF.

   ⇒ If the tire pressure monitor icon does not turn OFF, replace the RCDLR.

Repair Instructions

Perform the Diagnostic Repair Verification after completing the diagnostic procedure.

- Tire Pressure Indicator Sensor Replacement
- Tire Pressure Sensor Learn
- Control Module References for IPC or RCDLR replacement, setup, and programming

ARM0700000000802

Fig. 97   Low Tire Pressure Indicator Always On (Part 2 of 2). LaCrosse

Circuit/System Testing

1. With the scan tool, select instrument panel special functions Lamp Test. Command the instrument panel lamps ON. Verify tire pressure monitor indicator icon turns ON.

   ⇒ If the icon does not turn ON, replace the IPC.

2. Using the tire pressure monitor (TPM) special tool to observe the tire pressure of the suspected faulty sensor. Check the air pressure with a known accurate tire pressure gage. Compare the pressure reading to the display on the TPM special tool. Verify the pressure readings from special tool do not differ 4 psi or more than actual tire pressure.

   ⇒ If not within the specified range, replace the suspect tire pressure sensor.

3. With the scan tool, observe tire pressures in the scan tool data display. Verify pressure readings from special tool do not differ 4 psi or more than scan tool data display.

   ⇒ If not within the specified range, replace the RCDLR.

Repair Instructions

Perform the Diagnostic Repair Verification after completing the diagnostic procedure.

- Tire Pressure Indicator Sensor Replacement
- Tire Pressure Sensor Learn
- Control Module References for IPC and RCDLR replacement, setup, and programming

ARM0700000000804

Fig. 98   Low Tire Pressure Indicator Inoperative (Part 2 of 2). LaCrosse

Step	Action	Yes	No
1	Install a scan tool. Does the scan tool power up?	Go to Step 2	Scan Tool Does Not Power Up
2	1. Turn ON the ignition, with the engine OFF. 2. Attempt to establish communications with the Electronic Brake Control Module (EBCM). Does the scan tool communicate with the EBCM?	Go to Step 3	Scan Tool Does Not Communicate with Class 2 Device
3	Select the ABS Diagnostic Trouble Code DTC function on the scan tool. Does the scan tool display any DTCs that begin with a "U"?	Go to Diagnostic Trouble Code (DTC)	Go to Step 4
4	Does the scan tool display any ABS DTCs?	Go to Diagnostic System Check	Go to Step 5
5	Does the scan tool display DTC C1245?	Go to DTC C1245	System OK

GC2040200239000X

Fig. 99 Diagnostic System Check. LeSabre & Park Avenue

Diagnostic System Check - Lucerne

1. Verify that none of the following preliminary inspections/tests reveal the cause of the vehicle concern before beginning diagnosis:
   - Ensure that the battery is fully charged.
   - Ensure that the battery cables are clean and tight.
   - Inspect for any open fuses.
   - Ensure that the grounds are clean, tight, and in the correct location.
   - Inspect the easily accessible systems or the visible system components for obvious damage or conditions that could cause the concern. This would include checking to ensure that all connections/connectors are fully seated and secured.
   - Inspect for aftermarket devices that could affect the operation of the system.

2. Install a scan tool. Verify that the scan tool powers up.

3. Ignition ON, Engine OFF, verify communication with all of the control modules on the vehicle.

4. Verify that the following DTCs are not set: U1814, B1428.
   ⇒ If either of the DTCs are set, refer to DTC U1814 or DTC B1428.

   Important: Open the driver's door to ensure retained accessory power mode (RAP) is inactive during this test. The engine may start during this test. Turn the engine OFF as soon as the crank power mode has been observed.

5. With a scan tool, access the Body Control Module Power Mode data display list.

   Verify that all the parameters listed in the following table correspond to the ignition key position. The PMM Power Mode parameters table below illustrates the correct state of these parameters (circuits) with the corresponding ignition switch positions. The circuits related to the parameters are in parenthesis.

ARM0700000000805

Fig. 101 Diagnostic System Check (Part 1 of 2). Lucerne

Step	Action	Yes	No
1	Did you perform the Tire Pressure Monitor Diagnostic System Check?	Go to Step 2	Go to Diagnostic System Check -
2	1. Install a scan tool. 2. Turn ON the ignition, with the engine OFF. 3. With a scan tool, select the ABS Diagnostic Trouble Codes (DTCs) function. Does the scan tool indicate that DTC C1245 is current?	Go to Step 3	Go to Diagnostic Aids
3	Since some occurrences of this DTC are caused by driving condition, or tire size difference, review the TPM system with the customer to verify the conditions under which the DTC set. Did driving conditions, or tire size cause this DTC to set?	Go to Step 4	Go to Step 5
4	1. Calibrate the TPM system. 2. Use the scan tool in order to clear the DTCs. 3. Operate the vehicle within the Conditions for Running the DTC as specified in the supporting text. Does the DTC reset as a current DTC?	Go to Diagnostic Aids	System OK
5	Inspect the tire pressures and adjust to manufacturers specification if needed. Calibrate the TPM system if tire pressures were adjusted. Did you complete the repair?	System OK	--

GC2040200242000X

Fig. 100 Code C1245: Low Tire Pressure Detected. LeSabre & Park Avenue

6. Ignition ON, view the security indicator. The security indicator should not remain illuminated after the vehicle bulb check has completed.

   ⇒ If the security indicator remains illuminated after the bulb check, refer to Diagnostic Trouble Code (DTC) List - Vehicle and diagnose any of the following theft deterrent DTCs set as current: B1000, B302A, B3031, B3055, B3060, B3935, B3976, P0513, P0633, P1629, P1631, or P1632.

7. Attempt to start the engine. Verify that the engine cranks.

   ⇒ If the engine does not crank, refer to Symptoms - Engine Electrical.

8. Attempt to start the engine. Verify the engine starts and runs.

   ⇒ If the engine does not start and run, refer to one of the following:
   - Engine Cranks but Does Not Run for the 3.8L engine
   - Engine Cranks but Does Not Run for the 4.6L engine

   Important: Do not clear any DTCs unless instructed to do so by a diagnostic procedure.
   Important: If any DTCs are Powertrain related DTCs, select Capture Info in order to store the DTC information with the scan tool.

9. Use the appropriate scan tool selections to obtain DTCs from each of the vehicle modules. Verify there are no DTCs reported from any module.

   ⇒ If any DTCs are present, refer to Diagnostic Trouble Code (DTC) List - Vehicle and diagnose any current DTCs in the following order:
   9.1. DTCs that begin with a U.
   9.2. Any of the following: B1000, B1001, B1008, B1016, C0550, C0558, C0569, P0601, P0602, P0603, P0604, P0606, P0607, P060D, P062F, P2107, P2108, or P2610.
   9.3. Any of the following: B1325, B1335, B1424, B1517, C0895, C0899, C0900, P0560, P0562, or P0563.
   9.4. Component level DTCs.
   9.5. System level DTCs.
   9.6. Any remaining DTCs.

10. If the customer concern is related to inspection/maintenance (I/M) testing, refer to one of the following:
    - Inspection/Maintenance (I/M) System Check for the 3.8L engine
    - Inspection/Maintenance (I/M) System Check for the 4.6L engine
    ⇒ If none of the previous tests or inspections addresses the concern, refer to Symptoms - Vehicle.

PMM Power Mode Parameters Ignition Switch Position	Current Power Mode	Ign. Off/Run/Crank (Off/Run Crank voltage circuit)	Ignition Accessory/Run (Accessory voltage circuit)	Ignition Run/Crank (Ignition 1 Voltage circuit)
Off Key Out	Off	Key Out/ACC	Inactive	Inactive
Off Key IN	Off	Key In/Off	Inactive	Inactive
Accessory	Accessory	Key Out/ACC	Active	Inactive
Run	Run	Run	Active	Active
Start	Crank Request	Crank	Inactive	Active

ARM0700000000806

Fig. 101 Diagnostic System Check (Part 2 of 2). Lucerne

Diagnostic Instructions

- Perform the Diagnostic System Check - Vehicle prior to using this diagnostic procedure.
- Review Strategy Based Diagnosis for an overview of the diagnostic approach.
- Diagnostic Procedure Instructions provides an overview of each diagnostic category.

DTC Descriptor
DTC C0569 00: System Configuration Error

Circuit/System Description
The remote control door lock receiver (RCDLR) receives a radio frequency (RF) transmission from each tire pressure sensor. Each sensors RF transmission contains its own unique identification (ID) code that must be learned into the RCDLR memory. Once all 4 IDs have been learned and vehicle speed is 25 mph, or greater, the RCDLR continuously compares IDs in received transmission to its learned IDs to determine if all 4 sensors are present.

Conditions for Running the DTC
The ignition is ON.

Conditions for Setting the DTC
The RCDLR has not undergone the tire type and tire pressure selection setup procedure.

Action Taken When the DTC Sets
The driver information center (DIC) displays the SERVICE TIRE MONITOR warning message.

Conditions for Clearing the DTC
A current DTC will clear when the RCDLR has undergone the setup procedure.

Diagnostic Aids
A newly replaced RCDLR will set DTC C0569 on its initial ignition ON cycle. Tire type and tire pressure selection setup must be performed. Refer to Repair Instructions.

ARM0600000001015

Fig. 102   Code C0569: System Configuration Error. Lucerne

Action Taken When the DTC Sets

- The driver information center (DIC) displays the suspect tire pressure as dashes.
- The DIC displays the SERVICE TIRE MONITOR message.

Conditions for Clearing the DTC

- A current DTC will clear when the malfunction is no longer present.
- The electronic brake control module (EBCM) automatically clears the history DTC when a current DTC is not detected in 100 consecutive drive cycles.

Diagnostic Aids

- Some aftermarket wheel valve stem holes are located further from the wheel rim than original equipment wheels. When using the TPM special tool to activate a sensor, ensure the tools antenna is no further than 15 cm (6 in) from the sensor.
- The sensor activation procedure may have to be repeated up to 3 times before determining a sensor is malfunctioning.
- Occasionally sensors can become mislocated due to previous tire rotations where the sensor learn procedure was not performed. Always learn the sensors to ensure the DTC set is for that actual physical corner of the vehicle. Refer to Tire Pressure Sensor Learn .
- Occasionally sensor transmissions are not received by the RCDLR due to vehicle level RF interference.

Circuit/System Verification

Test drive the vehicle at a speed of 25 mph or greater for 2 minutes. No tire pressure monitor DTCs should set.

ARM0600000001017

Fig. 103   Codes C0750, C0755, C0760, Or C0765: Low Tire Pressure Sensor (Part 2 of 3). Lucerne

Diagnostic Instructions

- Perform the Diagnostic System Check - Vehicle prior to using this diagnostic procedure.
- Review Strategy Based Diagnosis for an overview of the diagnostic approach.
- Diagnostic Procedure Instructions provides an overview of each diagnostic category.

DTC Descriptors
DTC C0750: Left Front Low Tire Pressure Sensor

DTC C0755: Right Front Low Tire Pressure Sensor

DTC C0760: Left Rear Low Tire Pressure Sensor

DTC C0765: Right Rear Low Tire Pressure Sensor

Circuit/System Description

The Tire Pressure Monitor (TPM) System has a radio frequency (RF) transmitting pressure sensor in each wheel/tire assembly. As vehicle speed increases, centrifugal force closes the sensors internal roll switch, which puts the sensor into drive mode. The remote control door lock receiver (RCDLR) receives and translates the data contained in the tire pressure sensor RF transmissions into sensor presence, sensor mode, and tire pressure. Once vehicle speed is 20 mph or greater, the RCDLR waits for the first sensor to go into drive mode, then checks if all sensors have gone into drive mode. If one or more sensors do not go into drive mode, or do not transmit at all, the RCDLR will set DTC C0750, C0755, C0760, or C0765.

Conditions for Running the DTC

Vehicle speed is 25 mph or greater for 2 minutes.

Conditions for Setting the DTC

- Any given sensor does not go into drive mode.
- Any given sensor does not transmit for 5 minutes.

ARM0600000001016

Fig. 103   Codes C0750, C0755, C0760, Or C0765: Low Tire Pressure Sensor (Part 1 of 3). Lucerne

Circuit/System Testing

Important: Tire pressure sensors should transmit valid data with good signal strength in response to low frequency activation from the TPM special tool. It is important to observe the signal strength graph on the TPM special tool display screen after the activate button has been pressed and released. Any more than 1/4 graph displayed can be considered good signal strength.

1. Using the special tool, activate each tire pressure sensor and record each sensors transmission data and physical location. Verify tool displays 8-digit ID number, accurate tire pressure +/- 2 psi, Learn Mode, and good signal strength.

   ☐ If any of the parameters listed above are not displayed, replace the suspect tire pressure sensor.

2. With the scan tool, verify tire pressure sensors ID and locations displayed on the scan tool match the IDs and locations recorded from the special tool.

   ☐ If the IDs and locations do not match, perform Sensor Learn procedure.

3. Enable the TPM learn mode. Use the TPM special tool in simulate mode to learn 4 simulated sensor transmissions into the RCDLR. Verify all 4 sensor locations, IDs, and tire pressures (+/- 2 psi) as they are displayed on the TPM special tool match what the scan tool displays.

   ☐ If the scan tool does not match, replace the RCDLR.

4. Test drive the vehicle above 40 km/h (25 mph) for greater than 10 seconds. With the scan tool, observe the suspect Pressure Sensor Mode data parameter. Verify sensor mode changes from Wake to Drive.

   ☐ If the suspect Pressure Sensor Mode does not change, replace the suspect tire pressure sensor.

5. If no faults are found, go to Diagnostic Aids.

Repair Instructions
Perform the Diagnostic Repair Verification after completing the diagnostic procedure.
- Tire Pressure Sensor Learn
- Tire Pressure Sensor Replacement
- Control Module References for RCDLR replacement, setup, and programming

ARM0600000001018

Fig. 103   Codes C0750, C0755, C0760, Or C0765: Low Tire Pressure Sensor (Part 3 of 3). Lucerne

Diagnostic Instructions

- Perform the Diagnostic System Check - Vehicle prior to using this diagnostic procedure.
- Review Strategy Based Diagnosis for an overview of the diagnostic approach.
- Diagnostic Procedure Instructions provides an overview of each diagnostic category.

DTC Descriptor

DTC C0775: Low Tire Pressure System Sensors Not Learned

Circuit/System Description

The remote control door lock receiver (RCDLR) receives a radio frequency (RF) transmission from each tire pressure sensor. Each sensors RF transmission contains its own unique identification (ID) code that must be learned into the RCDLR memory. Once all 4 IDs have been learned and vehicle speed is 25 mph or greater, the RCDLR continuously compares IDs in received transmission to its learned IDs to determine if all 4 sensors are present.

Conditions for Running the DTC

The ignition is ON.

Conditions for Setting the DTC

The RCDLR has not undergone the tire pressure sensor learn procedure.

Action Taken When the DTC Sets

The driver information center (DIC) displays the SERVICE TIRE MONITOR warning message.

Conditions for Clearing the DTC

A current DTC will clear when the RCDLR has undergone the sensor learn procedure.

Diagnostic Aids

A newly replaced RCDLR will set DTC C0775 on its initial ignition ON cycle. Tire pressure sensor learn procedure must be performed.

ARM0600000001019

Fig. 104   Code C0775: Low Tire Pressure System Sensors Not Learned. Lucerne

Diagnostic Instructions

- Perform the Diagnostic System Check - Vehicle prior to using this diagnostic procedure.
- Review Strategy Based Diagnosis for an overview of the diagnostic approach.
- Diagnostic Procedure Instructions provides an overview of each diagnostic category.

Circuit/System Description

The remote control door lock receiver (RCDLR) sends a serial data message to the instrument panel cluster (IPC) requesting low tire pressure indicator illumination.

Circuit/System Testing

1. With the scan tool, select instrument panel special functions Lamp Test. Command the instrument panel lamps ON. Verify low tire pressure indicator lamp turns ON.

   □ If the lamp does not turn ON, replace the IPC.

2. Using the tire pressure monitor (TPM) special tool to observe the tire pressure of the suspected faulty sensor. Check air pressure with a known accurate hand held tire pressure gage. Compare the psi reading to the display on the TPM special tool. Verify pressure readings from special tool do not differ 2 psi or more than actual tire pressure.

   □ If the difference is 2 psi more, replace the suspect tire pressure sensor.

3. With the scan tool, observe tire pressures in the scan tool data display. Verify pressure readings from special tool do not differ 2 psi or more than scan tool data display.

   □ If the difference is 2 psi more, replace the RCDLR.

Repair Instructions

Perform the Diagnostic Repair Verification after completing the diagnostic procedure.

- Tire Pressure Sensor Learn
- Control Module References for RCDLR replacement, setup, and programming

ARM0600000001021

Fig. 106   Low Tire Pressure Indicator Inoperative. Lucerne

Diagnostic Instructions

- Perform the Diagnostic System Check prior to using this diagnostic procedure.
- Review Strategy Based Diagnosis for an overview of the diagnostic approach.
- Diagnostic Procedure Instructions provides an overview of each diagnostic category.

Circuit/System Description

The remote control door lock receiver (RCDLR) sends a serial data message to the instrument panel cluster (IPC) requesting low tire pressure indicator illumination.

Circuit/System Testing

1. Inflate tires to the proper pressure.
2. Using the tire pressure monitor (TPM) special tool, activate each tire pressure sensor and record each sensors tire pressure reading in psi. Check tire pressures with a known accurate hand held tire pressure gage. Verify pressure readings from special tool do not differ 4 psi or more lower than actual tire pressure.

   □ If 4 psi or more lower than actual tire pressure, replace the suspect tire pressure sensor.

3. With the scan tool, select instrument panel special functions Lamp Test. Command the instrument panel warning lamps OFF. Verify low tire pressure indicator lamp turns OFF.

   □ If the lamp does not turn OFF, replace the IPC.

4. Enable the TPM learn mode. Use the TPM special tool in simulate mode to learn 4 simulated sensor transmissions into the RCDLR. Observe tire pressures in the scan tool data display. Verify simulated tire pressures do not differ more than +/- 4 psi of the scan tool reading.

   □ If the tire pressures differ more than +/- 4 psi, replace the RCDLR.

Repair Instructions

Perform the Diagnostic Repair Verification after completing the diagnostic procedure.

- Tire Pressure Sensor Learn
- Control Module References for IPC or RCDLR replacement, setup, and programming

ARM0600000001020

Fig. 105   Low Tire Pressure Indicator Always On. Lucerne

Step	Action	Yes	No
1	Perform the following preliminary inspections: • Ensure that the battery is fully charged. • Ensure that the battery cables are clean and tight. • Inspect for any open fuses. • Inspect the easily accessible systems or the visible system components for obvious damage or conditions that could cause the symptom. • Ensure that the grounds are clean, tight, and in the correct location. • Inspect for aftermarket devices that could affect the operation of the system. • Search for applicable service bulletins. Did you find and correct the condition?	System OK	Go to Step 2
2	Install a scan tool. Does the scan tool power up?	Go to Step 3	Check Scan Tool Does Not Power Up
3	Turn ON the ignition, with the engine OFF. Is the NO FOB DETECTED message displayed on the driver information center (DIC)?	Go to Key Fob Not Detected	Go to Step 4
4	1. Turn ON the ignition, with the engine OFF. 2. Attempt to establish communication with all of the control modules on the vehicle. Does the scan tool communicate with all of the expected vehicle control modules?	Go to Step 5	Check Data Link References in Computer/Integrating Systems
5	Attempt to start the engine. Does the engine crank?	Go to Step 6	Go to Engine Electrical
6	Attempt to start the engine. Does the engine start and idle?	Go to Step 7	Check Engine Cranks but Does Not Run

ARM0400000000706

Fig. 107   Diagnostic System Check (Part 1 of 2). 2005–06 STS

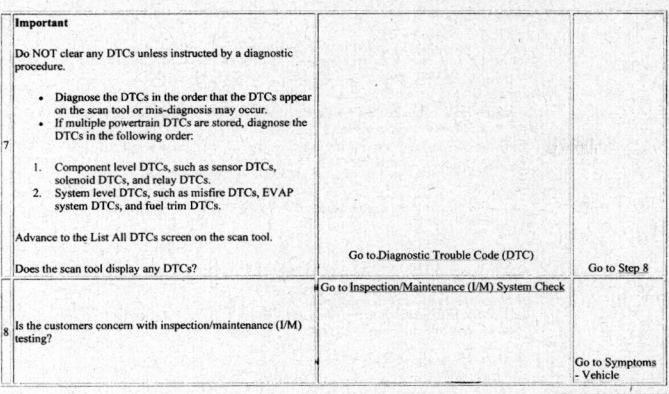

Important		
Do NOT clear any DTCs unless instructed by a diagnostic procedure. • Diagnose the DTCs in the order that the DTCs appear on the scan tool or mis-diagnosis may occur. • If multiple powertrain DTCs are stored, diagnose the DTCs in the following order: 1. Component level DTCs, such as sensor DTCs, solenoid DTCs, and relay DTCs. 2. System level DTCs, such as misfire DTCs, EVAP system DTCs, and fuel trim DTCs. Advance to the List All DTCs screen on the scan tool. Does the scan tool display any DTCs?	Go to Diagnostic Trouble Code (DTC)	Go to Step 8
Is the customers concern with inspection/maintenance (I/M) testing?	Go to Inspection/Maintenance (I/M) System Check	Go to Symptoms - Vehicle

ARM0400000000707

Fig. 107   Diagnostic System Check (Part 2 of 2). 2005–06 STS

4. Ignition ON, Engine OFF, verify communication with all of the control modules on the vehicle. Refer to Data Link References for information on the modules you should expect to communicate.

⇒ If the scan tool does not communicate with one or more of the expected control modules, refer to Data Link References .

5. Attempt to start the engine. Verify that the engine cranks.

⇒ If the engine does not crank, refer to Symptoms - Engine Electrical .

6. Attempt to start the engine. Verify the engine starts and idles.

⇒ If the engine does not start and idle, refer to one of the following:
• Engine Cranks but Does Not Run for the 3.6L (LLY) engine
• Engine Cranks but Does Not Run for the 4.4L engine
• Engine Cranks but Does Not Run for the 4.6L (LH2) engine

Important: Do not clear any DTCs unless instructed to do so by a diagnostic procedure.
Important: If any DTCs are Powertrain related DTCs, select Capture Info in order to store the DTC information with the scan tool.

7. Advance to the List All DTCs selection on the scan tool. Verify there are no DTCs reported from any module.

⇒ If any DTCs are present, refer to Diagnostic Trouble Code (DTC) List - Vehicle and diagnose any current DTCs in the order they are displayed on the scan tool.

8. If the customer concern is related to inspection/maintenance (I/M) testing, refer to one of the following:

• Inspection/Maintenance (I/M) System Check for the 3.6L (LLY) engine
• Inspection/Maintenance (I/M) System Check for the 4.4L engine
• Inspection/Maintenance (I/M) System Check for the 4.6L (LH2) engine

ARM0700000000808

Fig. 108   Diagnostic System Check (Part 2 of 2). 2007–08 STS

Diagnostic System Check - STS

Circuit Description

The ignition mode switch has 2 contact buttons.

The upper button, with a circle indicator on it, that starts the engine if the brake pedal is applied for automatic transmissions, or the clutch pedal is depressed for manual transmissions.

The lower button has 2 indicators on it, O and ACC. This button cycles the ignition through the following modes:

• *OFF*

This is the normal state upon entering the vehicle, and can also be reached from any other mode by depressing the button. The O indicator illuminates.

• *Accessory*

This mode can be reached from the Off state by depressing the button. The ACC indicator illuminates.

• *ON with the engine OFF*

This state can be reached from the Off or Accessory modes by depressing the button for about 5-6 seconds. The upper LED illuminates.

Circuit/System Testing

1. Before beginning vehicle diagnosis, the following preliminary inspections/tests must be performed:

• Ensure that the battery is fully charged.
• Ensure that the battery cables are clean and tight.
• Inspect for any open fuses.
• Ensure that the grounds are clean, tight, and in the correct location.
• Inspect the easily accessible systems or the visible system components for obvious damage or conditions that could cause the concern. This would include checking to ensure that all connections/connectors are fully seated and secured.
• Inspect for aftermarket devices that could affect the operation of the system.
• Search for applicable service bulletins.

⇒ If the preceding inspections/tests resolve the concern, go to Diagnostic Repair Verification.

2. Ignition ON and engine OFF, verify that the NO FOB DETECTED message is not displayed on the driver information center (DIC)

⇒ If the NO FOB DETECTED message is displayed, refer to Key Fob Not Detected.

3. Install a scan tool. Verify that the scan tool powers up.

⇒ If the scan tool does not power up, refer to Scan Tool Does Not Power Up .

ARM0700000000807

Fig. 108   Diagnostic System Check (Part 1 of 2). 2007–08 STS

Step	Action	Yes	No
1	Did you perform the Diagnostic System Check - Vehicle?	Go to Step 2	Go to Diagnostic System Check - Vehicle
2	1. Turn ON the ignition, with the engine OFF. 2. Observe the suspect Pressure Sensor Mode data parameter with a scan tool. Does the scan tool display the suspect Pressure Sensor Mode as Low Bat?	Go to Step 6	Go to Step 3
3	Review the Tire Pressure Monitor (TPM) System with the customer to verify the conditions under which the DTC set. Certain vehicle conditions may cause this DTC to set. Did vehicle conditions cause this DTC to set?	Go to Step 8	Go to Step 4
4	Learn the tire pressure sensors. Did a horn chirp sound when learning the suspect sensor?	Go to Step 5	Go to Step 6
5	1. Test drive the vehicle above 32 km/h (20 mph). 2. Observe the suspect Pressure Sensor Mode data parameter with the scan tool. Does the suspect Pressure Sensor Mode data parameter change from Wake to Drive above 32 km/h (20 mph)?	System OK	Go to Step 6
6	Replace the suspect tire pressure sensor. Did a horn chirp sound when learning the suspect sensor?	Go to Step 8	Go to Step 7
7	Replace the RCDLR. Did you complete the replacement?	Go to Step 8	—
8	1. Clear the DTCs with the scan tool. 2. Operate the vehicle within the Conditions for Running the DTC. Does the DTC reset?	Go to Step 2	System OK

ARM0400000000708

Fig. 109   Codes C0750, C0755, C0760 & C0765: Low Tire Pressure Sensor Less UH3. 2005–06 STS

Diagnostic Instructions

- Perform the Diagnostic System Check - Vehicle prior to using this diagnostic procedure.

DTC Descriptors

DTC C0750: Left Front Low Tire Pressure Sensor

DTC C0755: Right Front Low Tire Pressure Sensor

DTC C0760: Left Rear Low Tire Pressure Sensor

DTC C0765: Right Rear Low Tire Pressure Sensor

Circuit/System Description

The tire pressure monitor (TPM) system has a radio frequency (RF) transmitting pressure sensor in each wheel/tire assembly. As vehicle speed increases, centrifugal force closes the sensors internal roll switch, which puts the sensor into drive mode. The remote control door lock receiver (RCDLR) receives and translates the data contained in the tire pressure sensor RF transmissions into sensor presence, sensor mode, and tire pressure. Once vehicle speed is 25 mph or greater, the RCDLR waits for the sensors to go into Rolling mode. If one or more sensors do not go into Rolling mode, or do not transmit at all, the RCDLR will set DTC C0750, C0755, C0760, or C0765 respectively.

Conditions for Running the DTC

Vehicle speed is 25 mph or greater for 2 minutes.

Conditions for Setting the DTC

A sensor does not transmit for 18 minutes.

Action Taken When the DTC Sets

- The driver information center (DIC) displays the suspect tire pressure as dashes.
- The DIC displays the service tire monitor type message.

Conditions for Clearing the DTC

- A current DTC will clear when the malfunction is no longer present and 1 ignition cycle occurs.
- The RCDLR automatically clears the history DTC when a current DTC is not detected in 100 consecutive drive cycles.

ARM0700000000809

Fig. 110 Codes C0750, C0755, C0760 & C0765: Low Tire Pressure Sensor Less UH3 (Part 1 of 2). 2007–08 STS

Step	Action	Yes	No
1	Did you perform the Diagnostic System Check - Vehicle?	Go to Step 2	Go to Diagnostic System Check - Vehicle
2	1. Turn ON the ignition, with the engine OFF. 2. Observe the suspect Pressure Sensor Mode data parameter with a scan tool. Does the scan tool display the suspect Pressure Sensor Mode as Low Bat?	Go to Step 10	Go to Step 3
3	Learn the tire pressure sensors. Did a horn chirp sound when learning the suspect sensor?	Go to Step 5	Go to Step 4
4	1. Remove the suspect wheel/tire assembly and exchange it with the opposite side wheel/tire assembly. 2. Perform the learn procedure. Did a horn chirp sound when learning the suspect sensor?	Go to Step 10	Go to Step 6
5	1. Test drive the vehicle above 32 km/h (20 mph). 2. Observe the suspect Pressure Sensor Mode data parameter with the scan tool. Does the suspect Pressure Sensor Mode data parameter change from Wake to Drive above 32 km/h (20 mph)?	System OK	Go to Step 10
6	1. Remove the suspect tire pressure receiver and exchange it with the opposite side tire pressure receiver. 2. Perform the learn procedure. Did a horn chirp sound when learning the suspect sensor?	Go to Step 11	Go to Step 7
7	Test the suspect tire pressure receiver's power, ground and signal circuits for a short to voltage, short to ground, or an open. Did you find and correct the condition?	Go to Step 14	Go to Step 8
8	Inspect for poor connections at the suspect tire pressure receiver harness connector. Did you find and correct the condition?	Go to Step 14	Go to Step 9
9	Inspect for poor connections at the tire pressure module harness connector. Did you find and correct the condition?	Go to Step 14	Go to Step 12
10	Replace the suspect tire pressure sensor. Did you complete the replacement?	Go to Step 14	--
11	Replace the suspect tire pressure receiver. Did you complete the replacement?	Go to Step 14	--
12	Replace the tire pressure module. Did a horn chirp sound when learning the suspect sensor?	Go to Step 14	Go to Step 13
13	Replace the RCDLR. Did you complete the replacement?	Go to Step 14	--
14	1. Clear the DTCs with a scan tool. 2. Operate the vehicle within the Conditions for Running the DTC. Does the DTC reset?	Go to Step 2	System OK

ARM0400000000709

Fig. 111 Codes C0750, C0755, C0760 & C0765: Low Tire Pressure Sensor w/UH3. 2005–06 STS

Diagnostic Aids

- Some aftermarket wheel valve stem holes are located further from the wheel rim than original equipment wheels. When using the TPM special tool to activate a sensor, ensure the tools antenna is no further than 15 cm (6 in) from the sensor.
- Aftermarket wheel valve stem locations can cause a sensor to not function correctly.
- The sensor activation procedure may have to be repeated up to 3 times before determining a sensor is malfunctioning.
- Occasionally sensors can become mislocated due to previous tire rotations where the sensor learn procedure was not performed. Always learn the sensors to ensure the DTC set is for that actual physical corner of the vehicle. Refer to Tire Pressure Sensor Learn.
- Occasionally sensor transmissions are not received by the RCDLR due to vehicle level RF interference.

Circuit/System Testing

1. Using the J-46079 or equivalent, activate each tire pressure sensor and record each sensors transmission data and physical location. Verify J-46079 displays the 8-digit ID number, accurate tire pressure within 4 psi, Learn Mode, and at least a 1/4 graph signal strength displayed.

   ⇒ If any of the parameters listed above are not displayed, replace the suspect tire pressure sensor.

2. With the scan tool, verify tire pressure sensors ID and locations displayed on the scan tool match the IDs and locations recorded from the special tool.

   ⇒ If the IDs and locations do not match, perform the Tire Pressure Sensor Learn.

3. Enable the TPM learn mode. Use the TPM special tool in simulate mode to learn 4 simulated sensor transmissions into the RCDLR. Verify all 4 sensor locations, IDs, and tire pressures are within 4 psi as they are displayed on the TPM special tool match what the scan tool displays.

   ⇒ If the scan tool does not match, replace the RCDLR.

4. Test drive the vehicle above 40 km/h (25 mph) for greater than 10 seconds. With the scan tool, observe the suspect Pressure Sensor Mode data parameter. Verify sensor mode changes to Rolling.

   ⇒ If the suspect Pressure Sensor Mode does not change, replace the suspect tire pressure sensor.

Repair Instructions

Perform the Diagnostic Repair Verification after completing the diagnostic procedure.

- Tire Pressure Indicator Sensor Replacement
- Tire Pressure Sensor Learn
- Control Module References for RCDLR replacement, setup, and programming

ARM0700000000810

Fig. 110 Codes C0750, C0755, C0760 & C0765: Low Tire Pressure Sensor Less UH3 (Part 2 of 2). 2007–08 STS

Diagnostic Instructions

- Perform the Diagnostic System Check - Vehicle prior to using this diagnostic procedure.

Diagnostic Fault Information

Circuit	Short to Ground	Open/High Resistance	Short to Voltage	Signal Performance
Left Front Tire Pressure Receiver Voltage Reference	C0750	C0750	C0750	--
Right Front Tire Pressure Receiver Voltage Reference	C0755	C0755	C0755	--
Left Rear Tire Pressure Receiver Voltage Reference	C0760	C0760	C0760	--
Right Rear Tire Pressure Receiver Voltage Reference	C0765	C0765	C0765	--
Left Front Tire Pressure Receiver Low Reference	--	C0750	--	--
Right Front Tire Pressure Receiver Low Reference	--	C0755	--	--
Left Rear Tire Pressure Receiver Low Reference	--	C0760	--	--
Right Rear Tire Pressure Receiver Low Reference	--	C0765	--	--
Left Front Tire Pressure Receiver Signal	C0750	C0750	C0750	--
Right Front Tire Pressure Receiver Signal	C0755	C0755	C0755	--
Left Rear Tire Pressure Receiver Signal	C0760	C0760	C0760	--
Right Rear Tire Pressure Receiver Signal	C0765	C0765	C0765	--

Circuit/System Description

The tire pressure monitor (TPM) system has a radio frequency (RF) transmitting pressure sensor in each wheel/tire assembly. As vehicle speed increases, centrifugal force closes the sensor internal roll switch, which puts the sensor into drive mode. The sensor signals are received by the tire pressure receivers mounted near each wheel. Each receiver has a 5 volt reference circuit, a low reference circuit, and signal circuit connected to the tire pressure module. The tire pressure module transmits the individual sensor signals to the remote control door lock receiver (RCDLR) which translates the data contained in the tire pressure sensor RF transmissions into sensor presence, sensor mode, and tire pressure. Once vehicle speed is 25 mph or greater, the RCDLR waits for the sensors to go into Rolling mode. If one or more sensors do not go into Rolling mode, or do not transmit at all, the RCDLR will set DTC C0750, C0755, C0760, or C0765 respectively.

ARM0700000000811

Fig. 112 Codes C0750, C0755, C0760 & C0765: Low Tire Pressure Sensor w/UH3 (Part 1 of 4). 2007–08 STS

Conditions for Running the DTC

Vehicle speed is 25 mph or greater for 2 minutes.

Conditions for Setting the DTC

- A sensor does not transmit for 18 minutes.
- A receiver does not receive a sensor signal after 18 minutes.
- A malfunctioning tire pressure receiver.
- An open/high resistance, short to voltage, or short to ground in the tire pressure module power or ground circuit.
- An open, short to voltage, short to ground, or high resistance in a tire pressure receiver 5 volt reference, low reference, or signal circuit.

Action Taken When the DTC Sets

- The driver information center (DIC) displays the suspect tire pressure as dashes.
- The DIC displays the service tire monitor type message.

Conditions for Clearing the DTC

- A current DTC will clear when the malfunction is no longer present and 1 ignition cycle occurs.
- The RCDLR automatically clears the history DTC when a current DTC is not detected in 100 consecutive drive cycles.

Diagnostic Aids

- Some aftermarket wheel valve stem holes are located further from the wheel rim than original equipment wheels. When using the TPM special tool to activate a sensor, ensure the tools antenna is no further than 15 cm (6 in) from the sensor.
- Aftermarket wheel valve stem locations can cause a sensor to not function correctly.
- The sensor activation procedure may have to be repeated up to 3 times before determining a sensor is malfunctioning.
- Occasionally sensors can become mislocated due to previous tire rotations where the sensor learn procedure was not performed. Always learn the sensors to ensure the DTC set is for that actual physical corner of the vehicle. Refer to Tire Pressure Sensor Learn .
- Occasionally sensor transmissions are not received by the RCDLR due to vehicle level RF interference.

ARM0700000000812

Fig. 112   Codes C0750, C0755, C0760 & C0765: Low Tire Pressure Sensor w/UH3 (Part 2 of 4). 2007–08 STS

10. Verify that the tire pressure sensors ID and locations displayed on the scan tool match the ID and location recorded from the special tool.

⇒ If the ID and location do not match, perform the Tire Pressure Sensor Learn procedure.

11. Test drive the vehicle above 25 mph for greater than 2 minutes. With the scan tool, observe the suspect Pressure Sensor Mode data parameter. Verify sensor mode changes to Rolling.

⇒ If the suspect Pressure Sensor Mode does not change, replace the suspect tire pressure sensor.

Repair Instructions

Perform the Diagnostic Repair Verification after completing the diagnostic procedure.

- Tire Pressure Indicator Sensor Replacement
- Tire Pressure Monitoring Receiver Replacement
- Low Tire Pressure Indicator Module Replacement
- Tire Pressure Sensor Learn
- Control Module References for RCDLR replacement, setup, and programming

ARM0700000000814

Fig. 112   Codes C0750, C0755, C0760 & C0765: Low Tire Pressure Sensor w/UH3 (Part 4 of 4). 2007–08 STS

Circuit/System Testing

1. Ignition OFF, test for less than 2.0 ohms of resistance between the tire pressure module ground circuit terminal 10 and ground.

⇒ If greater than the specified range, test the ground circuit for an open/high resistance.

2. Ignition ON, verify that a test lamp illuminates between the tire pressure module terminal 1 and ground.

⇒ If the test lamp does not illuminate, test for an open/high resistance or short to ground in the B+ circuit. If the circuit tests normal, replace the tire pressure module.

3. Ignition OFF, disconnect the harness connector at the affected tire pressure receiver.

4. Ignition OFF, test for less than 2 ohms of resistance between the low reference circuit terminal 3 and ground.

⇒ If greater than the specified range, test the low reference circuit for an open/high resistance. If circuit tests normal, replace the tire pressure module.

5. Ignition ON, test for 4.75-5.25 volts between the 5 volt reference circuit terminal 1 and ground.

⇒ If less than the specified range, test the 5 volt reference circuit for a short to ground or an open/high resistance. If the circuit tests normal, replace the tire pressure module.

⇒ If greater than the specified range, test the 5 volt reference circuit for a short to voltage. If the circuit tests normal, replace the tire pressure module.

7. Ignition OFF, replace the affected tire pressure receiver with a known good part from one of the other locations.

8. Ignition ON, use the special tool to simulate the tire pressure sensor. Verify the scan tool displays an accurate tire pressure that matches within 4 psi of the special tool simulation display parameters.

⇒ If the parameters do not match, test the signal circuit for a short to ground, open/high resistance, or short to voltage. If the circuit tests normal, replace the tire pressure module.

9. Using the J-46079 or equivalent, activate each tire pressure sensor and record each sensors transmission data and physical location. Verify the J-46079 displays an 8-digit ID number, accurate tire pressure within 4 psi, Learn Mode, and at least a 1/4 graph signal strength displayed.

⇒ If any of the parameters listed above are not displayed, replace the suspect tire pressure sensor.

ARM0700000000813

Fig. 112   Codes C0750, C0755, C0760 & C0765: Low Tire Pressure Sensor w/UH3 (Part 3 of 4). 2007–08 STS

Diagnostic Instructions

- Perform the Diagnostic System Check - Vehicle prior to using this diagnostic procedure.

Circuit/System Description

The remote control door lock receiver (RCDLR) receives a radio frequency (RF) transmission from each tire pressure sensor. Each sensor RF transmission contains its own unique identification (ID) code that must be learned into the RCDLR memory. Once all 4 IDs have been learned and vehicle speed is greater than 25 mph, the RCDLR continuously compares IDs in received transmission to its learned IDs to determine if all 4 sensors are present. If the remote control door lock receiver (RCDLR) detects a low tire pressure condition or a malfunction in the system, it will send a serial data message to the instrument panel cluster (IPC) requesting tire pressure monitor indicator illumination and to display a data message on the driver information center (DIC), if equipped.

Diagnostic Aids

- Some aftermarket wheel valve stem holes are located further from the wheel rim than original equipment wheels. When using the TPM special tool to activate a sensor, ensure the tool antenna is no further than 15 cm (6 in) from the sensor and is aiming upward.
- Aftermarket wheel value stem locations can cause a sensor to not function correctly.
- A sensor may have been damaged due to a previous wheel/tire service or flat tire event.
- The use of tire sealants can obstruct the sensor pressure sensing port and cause inaccurate tire pressure readings. If this condition is verified, remove the sealer from the tire and replace the sensor.
- Occasionally sensor transmissions are not received by the RCDLR due to vehicle level RF interference from items such as but not limited to aftermarket ignition systems, DVD players, CB radios, or metallic type window tinting.
- The sensor activation procedure may have to be repeated up to 3 times before determining a sensor is malfunctioning. In the event a particular sensor's information is displayed on the special tool upon activation but the horn does not chirp, it may be necessary to rotate the wheel valve stem to a different position due to the RF signal is being blocked by another component.
- Occasionally sensors can become mislocated due to previous tire rotations where the sensor learn procedure was not performed or stray sensor transmissions have been received from other vehicles. Always learn the sensors to ensure the DTC set is for that actual physical corner of the vehicle.

Circuit/System Verification

Important:

- When a TPM DTC is set, the tire pressure monitor indicator icon will flash for 1 minute after the IPC bulb check is completed and then remains illuminated. If equipped with a DIC, a SERVICE TIRE MONITOR SYSTEM message will also be displayed.
- Low tire pressure in one or more tires is indicated by a continuously illuminated tire pressure monitor indicator icon after the IPC bulb check is completed. If equipped with a DIC, a CHECK TIRE PRESSURE message will also be displayed.

Cycle the ignition from OFF to ON. After the instrument panel cluster (IPC) bulb check is complete, the tire pressure monitor indicator icon should not be illuminated.

ARM0700000000815

Fig. 113   Low Tire Pressure Indicator Always On (Part 1 of 2). STS

Circuit/System Testing

1. Inflate all tires to the proper pressure and drive the vehicle over 25 MPH for over 2 minutes.
2. Using the J-46079 or equivalent, activate each tire pressure sensor and record each sensors tire pressure reading. Check the tire pressures with a known accurate hand held tire pressure gauge. Verify that the pressure readings from the special tool do not differ more than 4 psi from the actual tire pressure readings.

   ⇒ If not within the specified range, replace the suspect tire pressure sensor.

3. Using a scan tool, enable the TPM learn mode. Use the J-46079 in simulate mode to learn 4 simulated sensor transmissions into the RCDLR. Observe tire pressures in the scan tool data display. Verify the simulated tire pressures do not differ more than 27.6 kPa (4 psi) of the scan tool reading.

   ⇒ If not within the specified range, replace the RCDLR.

4. Using a scan tool, select instrument panel special functions Lamp Test. Command the instrument panel warning lamps OFF. Verify the tire pressure monitor indicator icon turns OFF.

   ⇒ If the tire pressure monitor icon does not turn OFF, replace the IPC.

5. Replace the RCDLR.

Repair Instructions

Perform the Diagnostic Repair Verification after completing the diagnostic procedure.

- Tire Pressure Indicator Sensor Replacement
- Tire Pressure Sensor Learn
- Control Module References for IPC or RCDLR replacement, setup, and programming

ARM0700000000816

Fig. 113 Low Tire Pressure Indicator Always On (Part 2 of 2). STS

Circuit/System Verification

1. With the scan tool, select instrument panel special functions Lamp Test. Command the instrument panel lamps ON. Verify tire pressure monitor indicator icon turns ON.

   ⇒ If the icon does not turn ON, replace the IPC.

2. Using the tire pressure monitor (TPM) special tool to observe the tire pressure of the suspected faulty sensor. Check the air pressure with a known accurate tire pressure gage. Compare the pressure reading to the display on the TPM special tool. Verify the pressure readings from special tool do not differ 4 psi or more than actual tire pressure.

   ⇒ If not within the specified range, replace the suspect tire pressure sensor.

3. With the scan tool, observe tire pressures in the scan tool data display. Verify pressure readings from special tool do not differ 4 psi or more than scan tool data display.

   ⇒ If not within the specified range, replace the RCDLR.

4. Replace the RCDLR.

Repair Instructions

Perform the Diagnostic Repair Verification after completing the diagnostic procedure.

- Tire Pressure Indicator Sensor Replacement
- Tire Pressure Sensor Learn
- Control Module References for IPC and RCDLR replacement, setup, and programming

ARM0700000000818

Fig. 114 Low Tire Pressure Indicator Inoperative (Part 2 of 2). STS

Diagnostic Instructions

- Perform the Diagnostic System Check - Vehicle prior to using this diagnostic procedure.

Circuit/System Description

The remote control door lock receiver (RCDLR) receives a radio frequency (RF) transmission from each tire pressure sensor. Each sensor RF transmission contains its own unique identification (ID) code that must be learned into the RCDLR memory. Once all 4 IDs have been learned and vehicle speed is greater than 25 mph, the RCDLR continuously compares IDs in received transmission to its learned IDs to determine if all 4 sensors are present. If the remote control door lock receiver (RCDLR) detects a low tire pressure condition or a malfunction in the system, it will send a serial data message to the instrument panel cluster (IPC) requesting tire pressure monitor indicator icon illumination and to display a data message on the driver information center (DIC) if equipped.

Diagnostic Aids

- Some aftermarket wheel valve stem holes are located further from the wheel rim than original equipment wheels. When using the TPM special tool to activate a sensor, ensure the tool antenna is no further than 15 cm (6 in) from the sensor and is aiming upward.
- Aftermarket wheel value stem locations can cause a sensor to not function correctly.
- A sensor may have been damaged due to a previous wheel/tire service or flat tire event.
- The use of tire sealants can obstruct the sensor pressure sensing port and cause inaccurate tire pressure readings. If this condition is verified, remove the sealer from the tire and replace the sensor. Refer to Tire Pressure Indicator Sensor Replacement.
- Occasionally sensor transmissions are not received by the RCDLR due to vehicle level RF interference from items such as but not limited to aftermarket ignition systems, DVD players, CB radios, or metallic type window tinting.
- The sensor activation procedure may have to be repeated up to 3 times before determining a sensor is malfunctioning. In the event a particular sensors information is displayed on the special tool upon activation but the horn does not chirp, it may be necessary to rotate the wheel valve stem to a different position due to the RF signal is being blocked by another component.
- Occasionally sensors can become mislocated due to previous tire rotations where the sensor learn procedure was not performed or stray sensor transmissions have been received from other vehicles . Always learn the sensors to ensure the DTC set is for that actual physical corner of the vehicle. Refer to Tire Pressure Sensor Learn .

ARM0700000000817

Fig. 114 Low Tire Pressure Indicator Inoperative (Part 1 of 2). STS

Step	Action	Yes	No
1	Did you perform the Diagnostic System Check - Vehicle?	Go to Step 2	Go to Diagnostic System Check
2	1. Turn ON the ignition, with the engine OFF. 2. With a scan tool, select the Remote Function Actuation (RFA) system Diagnostic Trouble Codes (DTC) function. Does the scan tool indicate that DTC C0750, C0755, C0760 or C0765 is current?	Go to Step 3	Go to Diagnostic Aids
3	Since some occurrences of this DTC are caused by certain vehicle conditions, review the tire pressure monitor (TPM) System with the customer to verify the conditions under which the DTC set. Did vehicle conditions cause the DTC to set?	Go to Diagnostic Aids	Go to Step 4
4	Learn the tire pressure sensors. Did a horn chirp sound when learning the suspect sensor?	Go to Step 5	Go to Step 6
5	1. Clear the DTCs with the scan tool. 2. Operate the vehicle within the condition for running and setting the DTC. Does the DTC reset?	Go to Step 6	System OK
6	Replace the suspect tire pressure sensor. Did a horn chirp sound when learning the suspect sensor?	Go to Step 8	Go to Step 7
7	Replace the remote control door lock receiver (RCDLR). Did you complete the replacement?	Go to Step 8	--
8	1. Clear the DTCs with the scan tool. 2. Operate the vehicle within the conditions for running and setting the DTC. Does the DTC reset?	Go to Step 2	System OK

ARM0400000000710

Fig. 115 Diagnostic System Check. 2004–06 XLR

Diagnostic System Check - XLR

Circuit Description

The ignition mode switch has 2 contact buttons.

The upper button, with a circle indicator on it, that starts the engine if the brake pedal is applied for automatic transmissions, or the clutch pedal is depressed for manual transmissions.

The lower button has 2 indicators on it, O and ACC. This button cycles the ignition through the following modes:

- *OFF*
  This is the normal state upon entering the vehicle, and can also be reached from any other mode by depressing the button. The O indicator illuminates.
- *Accessory*
  This mode can be reached from the Off state by depressing the button. The ACC indicator illuminates.
- *ON with the engine OFF*
  This state can be reached from the Off or Accessory modes by depressing the button for about 5-6 seconds. The upper LED illuminates.

Circuit/System Testing

1. Before beginning vehicle diagnosis, the following preliminary inspections/tests must be performed:
   - Ensure that the battery is fully charged.
   - Ensure that the battery cables are clean and tight.
   - Inspect for any open fuses.
   - Ensure that the grounds are clean, tight, and in the correct location.
   - Inspect the easily accessible systems or the visible system components for obvious damage or conditions that could cause the concern. This would include checking to ensure that all connections/connectors are fully seated and secured.
   - Inspect for aftermarket devices that could affect the operation of the system.

2. Ignition ON and engine OFF, verify that the NO FOB DETECTED message is not displayed on the driver information center (DIC)
   ⇒ If the NO FOB DETECTED message is displayed, refer to Key Fob Not Detected .

3. Install a scan tool. Verify that the scan tool powers up.

ARM0700000000819

ARM0400000000711

Fig. 117   Codes C0750, C0755, C0760 & C0765: Low Tire Pressure Sensor. 2004–06 XLR

4. Ignition ON, Engine OFF, verify communication with all of the control modules on the vehicle. Refer to Data Link References for information on the modules you should expect to communicate.

   ⇒ If the scan tool does not communicate with one or more of the expected control modules, refer to Data Link References.

5. Attempt to start the engine. Verify that the engine cranks.

   ⇒ If the engine does not crank, refer to Symptoms - Engine Electrical .

6. Attempt to start the engine. Verify the engine starts and idles.

   ⇒ If the engine does not start and idle, refer to Engine Cranks but Does Not Run for the 4.4L engine or Engine Cranks but Does Not Run for the 4.6L (LH2) engine.

   Important: Do not clear any DTCs unless instructed to do so by a diagnostic procedure.
   Important: If any DTCs are Powertrain related DTCs, select Capture Info in order to store the DTC information with the scan tool.

7. Advance to the List All DTCs selection on the scan tool. Verify there are no DTCs reported from any module.

   ⇒ If any DTCs are present, refer to Diagnostic Trouble Code (DTC) List - Vehicle and diagnose any current DTCs in the order they are displayed on the scan tool.

8. If the customer concern is related to inspection/maintenance (I/M) testing, refer to Inspection/Maintenance (I/M) System Check for the 4.4L engine or Inspection/Maintenance (I/M) System Check for the 4.6L (LH2) engine.

ARM0700000000820

Diagnostic Instructions

- Perform the Diagnostic System Check - Vehicle prior to using this diagnostic procedure.

Circuit/System Description

The tire pressure monitor (TPM) system has a radio frequency (RF) transmitting pressure sensor in each wheel/tire assembly. As vehicle speed increases, centrifugal force closes the sensors internal roll switch, which puts the sensor into drive mode. The remote control door lock receiver (RCDLR) receives and translates the data contained in the tire pressure sensor RF transmissions into sensor presence, sensor mode, and tire pressure. Once vehicle speed is greater than 25 mph, the RCDLR waits for the sensors to go into rolling mode. If one or more sensors do not go into rolling mode, or do not transmit at all, the RCDLR will set DTC C0750, C0755, C0760, or C0765 respectively.

Conditions for Running the DTC

Vehicle speed is greater than 25 mph.

Conditions for Setting the DTC

- A sensor does not transmit for 18 minutes.
- A sensor low battery condition.

Action Taken When the DTC Sets

- The Tire Pressure Monitor Indicator icon on the instrument panel cluster (IPC) flashes for 1 minute and then remains illuminated.
- If equipped, the driver information center (DIC) displays the suspect tire pressure as dashes.
- If equipped, the DIC displays a service tire monitor type message.

Conditions for Clearing the DTC

- A current DTC will clear when the malfunction is no longer present.
- The RCDLR automatically clears the history DTC when a current DTC is not detected in 100 consecutive drive cycles.

ARM0700000000821

Diagnostic Aids

- Some aftermarket wheel valve stem holes are located further from the wheel rim than original equipment wheels. When using the TPM special tool to activate a sensor, ensure the tool antenna is no further than 15 cm (6 in) from the sensor and is aiming upward.

- Aftermarket wheel valve stem locations can cause a sensor to not function correctly.

- A sensor may have been damaged due to a previous wheel/tire service or flat tire event.

- The use of tire sealants can obstruct the sensor pressure sensing port and cause inaccurate tire pressure readings. If this condition is verified, remove the sealer from the tire and replace the sensor. Refer to Tire Pressure Indicator Sensor Replacement.

- Occasionally sensor transmissions are not received by the RCDLR due to vehicle level RF interference from items such as but not limited to aftermarket ignition systems, DVD players, CB radios, or metallic type window tinting.

- The sensor activation procedure may have to be repeated up to 3 times before determining a sensor is malfunctioning. In the event a particular sensor's information is displayed on the special tool upon activation but the horn does not chirp, it may be necessary to rotate the wheel valve stem to a different position due to the RF signal is being blocked by another component.

- Occasionally sensors can become mislocated due to previous tire rotations where the sensor learn procedure was not performed or stray sensor transmissions have been received from other vehicles . Always learn the sensors to ensure the DTC set is for that actual physical corner of the vehicle. Refer to Tire Pressure Sensor Learn.

- A sensor low battery condition will set a sensor DTC but will not illuminate the low tire pressure indicator or display a message on the DIC, if equipped. The sensor battery condition can be verified in the scan tool RCDLR data list. If a sensor low battery condition is indicated on the scan tool, the sensor will need to be replaced. Refer to Tire Pressure Indicator Sensor Replacement.

ARM0700000000822

Fig. 118   Codes C0750, C7055, C0760 & C0765: Low Tire Pressure (Part 2 of 3). 2007–08 XLR

Diagnostic Instructions

- Perform the <u>Diagnostic System Check - Vehicle</u> prior to using this diagnostic procedure.

Circuit/System Description

The remote control door lock receiver (RCDLR) receives a radio frequency (RF) transmission from each tire pressure sensor. Each sensor RF transmission contains its own unique identification (ID) code that must be learned into the RCDLR memory. Once all 4 IDs have been learned and vehicle speed is greater than 25 mph, the RCDLR continuously compares IDs in received transmission to its learned IDs to determine if all 4 sensors are present. If the remote control door lock receiver (RCDLR) detects a low tire pressure condition or a malfunction in the system, it will send a serial data message to the instrument panel cluster (IPC) requesting tire pressure monitor indicator illumination and to display a data message on the driver information center (DIC), if equipped.

Diagnostic Aids

- Some aftermarket wheel valve stem holes are located further from the wheel rim than original equipment wheels. When using the TPM special tool to activate a sensor, ensure the tool antenna is no further than 15 cm (6 in) from the sensor and is aiming upward.

- Aftermarket wheel value stem locations can cause a sensor to not function correctly.

- A sensor may have been damaged due to a previous wheel/tire service or flat tire event.

- The use of tire sealants can obstruct the sensor pressure sensing port and cause inaccurate tire pressure readings. If this condition is verified, remove the sealer from the tire and replace the sensor. Refer to Tire Pressure Indicator Sensor Replacement.

- Occasionally sensor transmissions are not received by the RCDLR due to vehicle level RF interference from items such as but not limited to aftermarket ignition systems, DVD players, CB radios, or metallic type window tinting.

- The sensor activation procedure may have to be repeated up to 3 times before determining a sensor is malfunctioning. In the event a particular sensor's information is displayed on the special tool upon activation but the horn does not chirp, it may be necessary to rotate the wheel valve stem to a different position due to the RF signal is being blocked by another component.

- Occasionally sensors can become mislocated due to previous tire rotations where the sensor learn procedure was not performed or stray sensor transmissions have been received from other vehicles. Always learn the sensors to ensure the DTC set is for that actual physical corner of the vehicle. Refer to Tire Pressure Sensor Learn.

ARM0700000000824

Fig. 119   Low Tire Pressure Indicator Always On (Part 1 of 2). XLR

Circuit/System Verification

1. Using the J-46079 or equivalent, activate each tire pressure sensor and record each sensors transmission data and physical location. Verify J-46079 displays the 8-digit ID number, accurate tire pressure within 4 psi, Learn Mode, and at least a 1/4 graph signal strength displayed.

   ⇒ If any of the parameters listed above are not displayed, replace the suspect tire pressure sensor.

2. With the scan tool, verify tire pressure sensors ID and locations displayed on the scan tool match the IDs and locations recorded from the special tool.

   ⇒ If the IDs and locations do not match, perform the Tire Pressure Sensor Learn.

3. Enable the TPM learn mode. Use the TPM special tool in simulate mode to learn 4 simulated sensor transmissions into the RCDLR. Verify all 4 sensor locations, IDs, and that the tire pressures are within 4 psi as they are displayed on the TPM special tool match what the scan tool displays.

   ⇒ If the scan tool does not match, replace the RCDLR.

4. Test drive the vehicle above 25 mph for greater than 2 minutes. With the scan tool, observe the suspect Pressure Sensor Mode data parameter. Verify sensor mode changes to Rolling.

   ⇒ If the suspect Pressure Sensor Mode does not change, replace the suspect tire pressure sensor.

Repair Instructions

Perform the Diagnostic Repair Verification after completing the diagnostic procedure.

- Tire Pressure Indicator Sensor Replacement
- Tire Pressure Sensor Learn
- Control Module References for RCDLR replacement, setup, and programming

ARM0700000000823

Fig. 118   Codes C0750, C7055, C0760 & C0765: Low Tire Pressure (Part 3 of 3). 2007–08 XLR

Circuit/System Verification
Important:

- When a TPM DTC is set, the tire pressure monitor indicator icon will flash for 1 minute after the IPC bulb check is completed and then remains illuminated. If equipped with a DIC, a SERVICE TIRE MONITOR SYSTEM message will also be displayed.

- Low tire pressure in one or more tires is indicated by a continuously illuminated tire pressure monitor indicator icon after the IPC bulb check is completed. If equipped with a DIC, a CHECK TIRE PRESSURE message will also be displayed.

Cycle the ignition from OFF to ON. After the instrument panel cluster (IPC) bulb check is complete, the tire pressure monitor indicator icon should not be illuminated.

Circuit/System Testing

1. Inflate all tires to the proper pressure and drive the vehicle over 25 MPH for over 2 minutes.

2. Using the J-46079 or equivalent, activate each tire pressure sensor and record each sensors tire pressure reading. Check the tire pressures with a known accurate hand held tire pressure gauge. Verify that the pressure readings from the special tool do not differ more than 4 psi from the actual tire pressure readings.

   ⇒ If not within the specified range, replace the suspect tire pressure sensor.

3. Using a scan tool, enable the TPM learn mode. Use the J-46079 in simulate mode to learn 4 simulated sensor transmissions into the RCDLR. Observe tire pressures in the scan tool data display. Verify the simulated tire pressures do not differ more than 4 psi of the scan tool reading.

   ⇒ If not within the specified range, replace the RCDLR.

4. Using a scan tool, select instrument panel special functions Lamp Test. Command the instrument panel warning lamps OFF. Verify the tire pressure monitor indicator icon turns OFF.

   ⇒ If the tire pressure monitor icon does not turn OFF, replace the IPC.

5. Replace the RCDLR.

Repair Instructions

Perform the Diagnostic Repair Verification after completing the diagnostic procedure.

- Tire Pressure Indicator Sensor Replacement
- Tire Pressure Sensor Learn
- Control Module References for IPC or RCDLR replacement, setup, and programming

ARM0700000000825

Fig. 119   Low Tire Pressure Indicator Always On (Part 2 of 2). XLR

Diagnostic Instructions

- Perform the <u>Diagnostic System Check - Vehicle</u> prior to using this diagnostic procedure.

Circuit/System Description

The remote control door lock receiver (RCDLR) receives a radio frequency (RF) transmission from each tire pressure sensor. Each sensor RF transmission contains its own unique identification (ID) code that must be learned into the RCDLR memory. Once all 4 IDs have been learned and vehicle speed is greater than 25 mph, the RCDLR continuously compares IDs in received transmission to its learned IDs to determine if all 4 sensors are present. If the remote control door lock receiver (RCDLR) detects a low tire pressure condition or a malfunction in the system, it will send a serial data message to the instrument panel cluster (IPC) requesting tire pressure monitor indicator icon illumination and to display a data message on the driver information center (DIC) if equipped.

Diagnostic Aids

- Some aftermarket wheel valve stem holes are located further from the wheel rim than original equipment wheels. When using the TPM special tool to activate a sensor, ensure the tool antenna is no further than 15 cm (6 in) from the sensor and is aiming upward.
- Aftermarket wheel value stem locations can cause a sensor to not function correctly.
- A sensor may have been damaged due to a previous wheel/tire service or flat tire event.
- The use of tire sealants can obstruct the sensor pressure sensing port and cause inaccurate tire pressure readings. If this condition is verified, remove the sealer from the tire and replace the sensor. Refer to Tire Pressure Indicator Sensor Replacement.
- Occasionally sensor transmissions are not received by the RCDLR due to vehicle level RF interference from items such as but not limited to aftermarket ignition systems, DVD players, CB radios, or metallic type window tinting.
- The sensor activation procedure may have to be repeated up to 3 times before determining a sensor is malfunctioning. In the event a particular sensors information is displayed on the special tool upon activation but the horn does not chirp, it may be necessary to rotate the wheel valve stem to a different position due to the RF signal is being blocked by another component.
- Occasionally sensors can become mislocated due to previous tire rotations where the sensor learn procedure was not performed or stray sensor transmissions have been received from other vehicles . Always learn the sensors to ensure the DTC set is for that actual physical corner of the vehicle. Refer to Tire Pressure Sensor Learn.

ARM0700000000826

Fig. 120   Low Tire Pressure Indicator Inoperative (Part 1 of 2). XLR

Circuit/System Verification

1. With the scan tool, select instrument panel special functions Lamp Test. Command the instrument panel lamps ON. Verify tire pressure monitor indicator icon turns ON.

    ⇒ If the icon does not turn ON, replace the IPC.

2. Using the tire pressure monitor (TPM) special tool to observe the tire pressure of the suspected faulty sensor. Check the air pressure with a known accurate tire pressure gage. Compare the pressure reading to the display on the TPM special tool. Verify the pressure readings from special tool do not differ 4 psi or more than actual tire pressure.

    ⇒ If not within the specified range, replace the suspect tire pressure sensor.

3. With the scan tool, observe tire pressures in the scan tool data display. Verify pressure readings from special tool do not differ 4 psi or more than scan tool data display.

    ⇒ If not within the specified range, replace the RCDLR.

4. Replace the RCDLR.

Repair Instructions

Perform the Diagnostic Repair Verification after completing the diagnostic procedure.

- Tire Pressure Indicator Sensor Replacement
- Tire Pressure Sensor Learn
- Control Module References for IPC and RCDLR replacement, setup, and programming

ARM0700000000827

Fig. 120   Low Tire Pressure Indicator Inoperative (Part 2 of 2). XLR

Step	Action	Yes	No
1	Perform the following preliminary inspections: • Ensure that the battery is fully charged. • Ensure that the battery cables are clean and tight. • Inspect for any open fuses. • Inspect the easily accessible systems or the visible system components for obvious damage or conditions that could cause the symptom. • Ensure that the grounds are clean, tight, and in the correct location. • Inspect for aftermarket devices that could affect the operation of the system. • Search for applicable service bulletins. Did you find and correct the condition?	System OK	Go to Step 2
2	Install a scan tool. Does the scan tool power up?	Go to Step 3	Check Scan Tool Does Not Power Up
3	1. Turn ON the ignition, with the engine OFF. 2. Attempt to establish communication with all of the control modules on the vehicle. Does the scan tool communicate with all of the expected vehicle control modules?	Go to Step 4	Check Data Link References
4	Attempt to start the engine. Does the engine crank?	Go to Step 5	Go to Symptoms
5	Attempt to start the engine. Does the engine start and idle?	Go to Step 6	Check Engine Cranks but Does Not Run in Engine Controls

ARM0500000000858

Fig. 121   Diagnostic System Check (Part 1 of 3). Vibe

6	**Important** Do not clear the DTCs unless instructed by a diagnostic procedure. Use the appropriate scan tool selections to obtain DTCs for each of the control modules. Does the scan tool display any DTCs?	Go to Step 7	Go to Step 11
7	Does the scan tool display and DTCs that begin with a "U"?	Go to Diagnostic Trouble Code (DTC) List - Vehicle	Go to Step 8
8	**Important** If any of these DTCs are displayed, diagnose them before diagnosing any other DTCs or symptoms. Does the scan tool display DTC B1000, B1004, B1008, C0550, P0601, P0602, P0604?	Go to Diagnostic Trouble Code (DTC) List - Vehicle	Go to Step 9
9	**Important** If any of these DTCs are displayed, diagnose them before diagnosing any other DTCs or symptoms. Does the scan tool display DTC B1372, B1377, B1378, or B1382?	Go to Diagnostic Trouble Code (DTC) List - Vehicle	Go to Step 10
10	**Important** If any of the remaining DTCs are powertrain DTCs, select Captured Info in order to store the powertrain DTC information with a scan tool. If multiple DTCs are stored, diagnose the DTCs in the following order: 1. Component level DTCs, such as sensor DTCs, solenoid DTCs, and relay DTCs 2. System level DTCs, for example, misfire DTCs, evaporative emission (EVAP) system DTCs, and fuel trim DTCs 3. Diagnose the remaining DTCs.	Go to Diagnostic Trouble Code (DTC) List - Vehicle	--

ARM0500000000859

Fig. 121   Diagnostic System Check (Part 2 of 3). Vibe

| 11 | Is the customers concern with inspection/maintenance (I/M) testing? | Go to Inspection/Maintenance (I/M) System Check in Engine Controls - 1.8L (LNK) or Go to Engine Cranks but Does Not Run in Engine Controls - 1.8L (LV6) | Go to Symptoms - Vehicle |

ARM0500000000860

Fig. 121   Diagnostic System Check (Part 3 of 3). Vibe

Diagnostic Instructions

- Perform the Diagnostic System Check - Vehicle prior to using this diagnostic procedure.

Circuit/System Description

The tire pressure monitor (TPM) system has a radio frequency (RF) transmitting pressure sensor in each wheel/tire assembly. The module receives and translates the data contained in the tire pressure sensor RF transmissions into sensor presence, sensor mode, and tire pressure.

The receiver module receives a radio frequency (RF) transmission from each tire pressure sensor. Each sensor RF transmission contains its own unique identification (ID) code that must be learned into the module memory. Once all 4 IDs have been learned, the module continuously compares IDs received in transmission to its learned IDs to determine if all 4 sensors are present.

Conditions for Running the DTC

The ignition is ON.

Conditions for Setting the DTC

The tire pressure sensors stop transmitting signals.

Action Taken When the DTC Sets

The Tire Pressure Warning Light is illuminated.

Conditions for Clearing the DTC

A current DTC will clear when the signal transmission is resumed.

Diagnostic Aids

If the displayed tire pressure data did not change within 3 minutes, refer to DTC C2121-C2124.

Circuit/System Verification

With the scan tool, record tire pressure sensors ID and locations:

1. Rapidly reduce the tire pressure for each wheel at least 6 psi within 30 seconds. It may take up to 3 minutes for the display to change.
2. Check that each tire pressure data displayed has changed.

⇒ If the tire pressure data did not change for each wheel, refer to DTC C2141-C2144.

ARM0700000000765

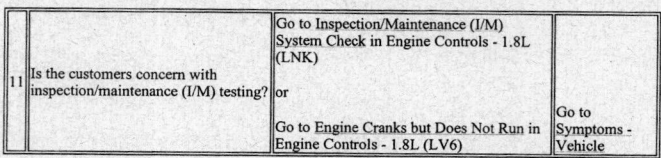

Fig. 122   Codes C2111, C2112, C2113 & C2114: Tire Pressure Sensor In Shipping Mode. Vibe

Diagnostic Instructions

- Perform the Diagnostic System Check - Vehicle prior to using this diagnostic procedure.

Circuit/System Description

The tire pressure monitor (TPM) system has a radio frequency (RF) transmitting pressure sensor in each wheel/tire assembly. The module receives and translates the data contained in the tire pressure sensor RF transmissions into sensor presence, sensor mode, and tire pressure.

The receiver module receives a radio frequency (RF) transmission from each tire pressure sensor. Each sensor RF transmission contains its own unique identification (ID) code that must be learned into the module memory. Once all 4 IDs have been learned, the module continuously compares IDs received in transmission to its learned IDs to determine if all 4 sensors are present.

Conditions for Running the DTC

Vehicle speed is 5 mph or greater for 20 minutes.

Conditions for Setting the DTC

No signals are received after the vehicle is driven 20 minutes or more.

Action Taken When the DTC Sets

The Tire Pressure Warning Light is illuminated.

Conditions for Clearing the DTC

The condition responsible for setting the DTC no longer exists and the scan tool Clear DTCs function is used.

Diagnostic Aids

- The sensor activation procedure may have to be repeated up to 3 times before determining a sensor is malfunctioning.
- Occasionally sensor transmissions are not received by the tire pressure receiver module due to vehicle level RF interference.

ARM0700000000832

Fig. 123 Codes C2121, C2122, C2123 & C2124: Tire Pressure Sensor Signal Missing (Part 1 of 2). Vibe

Circuit/System Testing

1. With the scan tool, verify that DTC C2173 is not set.

    ⇒ If DTC C2173 is set, refer to DTC C2173.

2. With the scan tool, locate and record tire pressure sensors ID and locations:

    2.1. Rapidly reduce the tire pressure for each wheel at least 6 psi within 30 seconds. It may take up to 3 minutes for the display to change.

    2.2. Record the sensor ID and location.

    ⇒ If any of the parameters listed above do not change or are not displayed for on sensor, replace the suspect tire pressure sensor.

5. Disconnect the harness connector at the Tire Pressure Control Module.
6. Disconnect the harness connector at the Tire Pressure Receiver Module.
7. Test for less than 1 ohm between the 5-volt reference circuit terminal 6 and terminal 5.

    ⇒ If greater than the specified value, test the 5-volt reference circuit for an open/high resistance.

8. Test for less than 1 ohm between the signal circuit terminal 12 and terminal 1.

    ⇒ If greater than the specified value, test the signal circuit for an open/high resistance.

9. Test for less than 1 ohm between the ground circuit terminal 11 and terminal 4.

    ⇒ If greater than the specified value, test the ground circuit for an open/high resistance.

10. Test for infinite resistance between the 5-volt reference circuit terminal 6 and ground.

    ⇒ If not the specified value, test the 5-volt reference circuit for a short to ground.

11. Test for infinite resistance between the signal circuit terminal 12 and ground.

    ⇒ If not the specified value, test the signal circuit for a short to ground.

12. Enable the TPM learn mode. Verify all 4 sensor locations, IDs, and tire pressures match what the scan tool displays.

    ⇒ If the scan tool data does not display, replace the Tire Pressure Receiver Module. If DTC sets again, replace the Tire Pressure Control Module

Repair Instructions

Perform the Diagnostic Repair Verification after completing the diagnostic procedure.

- Tire Pressure Indicator Sensor Replacement
- Tire Pressure Sensor Learn
- Control Module References for module replacement, setup, and programming

ARM0700000000833

Fig. 123 Codes C2121, C2122, C2123 & C2124: Tire Pressure Sensor Signal Missing (Part 2 of 2). Vibe

Diagnostic Instructions

- Perform the Diagnostic System Check - Vehicle prior to using this diagnostic procedure.

Circuit/System Description

After all IDs are learned, DTC C2126 is set in the tire pressure control module and the tire pressure indicator blinks for 1 minute then comes on.

Conditions for Running the DTC

The ignition is ON.

Conditions for Setting the DTC

Tire pressure control module does not receive radio waves for sensors whose IDs are stored in the module.

Action Taken When the DTC Sets

The Tire Pressure Warning Light is illuminated.

Conditions for Clearing the DTC

The tire pressure control module successfully receives radio waves from the sensors whose IDs are stored in the tire pressure control module.

Circuit/System Testing

1. With the scan tool, verify tire pressure sensors ID and locations:

   1.1. Rapidly reduce the tire pressure for each wheel at least 6 psi within 30 seconds. It may take up to 3 minutes for the display to change.

   1.2. Record the sensor ID and location.

   ⇒ If any of the parameters listed above are not displayed for one sensor, verify the sensor ID and correct it as necessary. If sensor ID matches, replace the tire pressure sensor.

4. Enable the TPM learn mode. Verify all 4 sensor locations, IDs, and tire pressures match what the scan tool displays.

   ⇒ If the scan tool data does not display, replace the Tire Pressure Receiver Module. If scan tool data still does not display, replace the Tire Pressure Control Module

Repair Instructions

Perform the Diagnostic Repair Verification after completing the diagnostic procedure.

- Tire Pressure Sensor Learn
- Control Module References for replacement, setup, and programming

ARM0700000000834

Fig. 124   Code C2126: Tire Pressure Sensor ID Not Received. Vibe

Diagnostic Instructions

- Perform the Diagnostic System Check - Vehicle prior to using this diagnostic procedure.

Circuit/System Description

The tire pressure monitor (TPM) system has a radio frequency (RF) transmitting pressure sensor in each wheel/tire assembly. The module receives and translates the data contained in the tire pressure sensor RF transmissions into sensor presence, sensor mode, and tire pressure.

The receiver module receives a radio frequency (RF) transmission from each tire pressure sensor. Each sensor RF transmission contains its own unique identification (ID) code that must be learned into the module memory. Once all 4 IDs have been learned, the module continuously compares IDs received in transmission to its learned IDs to determine if all 4 sensors are present.

Conditions for Running the DTC

The ignition is ON.

Conditions for Setting the DTC

The tire pressure sensor battery is depleted.

Action Taken When the DTC Sets

The Tire Pressure Warning Light is illuminated.

Conditions for Clearing the DTC

A current DTC will clear when the signal transmission is resumed.

Diagnostic Aids

If the displayed tire pressure data did not change within 3 minutes, refer to DTC C2121-C2124.

Circuit/System Testing

1. With the scan tool, verify tire pressure sensors ID and locations:

   1.1. Rapidly reduce the tire pressure for each wheel at least 6 psi within 30 seconds. It may take up to 3 minutes for the display to change.

   1.2. Record the sensor ID and location.

   ⇒ If any of the parameters listed above did not change or are not displayed, replace the suspect tire pressure sensor.

4. Perform the tire pressure sensor learn procedure.
5. Perform the tire pressure system configuration procedure. Verify all 4 sensor locations, IDs, and tire pressures match what the scan tool displays.

   ⇒ If the scan tool data does not match, replace the Tire Pressure Control Module.

Repair Instructions

Perform the Diagnostic Repair Verification after completing the diagnostic procedure.

- Tire Pressure Sensor Learn
- Control Module References for module replacement, setup, and programming

ARM0700000000835

Fig. 125   Code C2141, C2142, C2143 & C2144: Tire Pressure Sensor Performance. Vibe

Diagnostic Fault Information

- Perform the Diagnostic System Check - Vehicle prior to using this diagnostic procedure.

Circuit/System Description

The tire pressure sensor measures the internal tire temperature as well as tire pressure, this information is transmitted to the tire pressure control module.

Conditions for Running the DTC

The ignition is ON.

Conditions for Setting the DTC

Temperature inside the tire exceeds 246.2°F.

Action Taken When the DTC Sets

The Tire Pressure Warning Light is illuminated after blinking for 1 minute.

Conditions for Clearing the DTC

The condition responsible for setting the DTC no longer exists.

Circuit/System Testing

1. With the scan tool, verify tire pressure sensors ID and locations:

   1.1. Rapidly reduce the tire pressure for each wheel at least 6 psi within 30 seconds. It may take up to 3 minutes for the display to change.

   1.2. Record the sensor ID and location.

   ⇒ If any of the parameters listed above do not change or are not displayed, replace the suspect tire pressure sensor.

2. Perform the tire pressure sensor learn procedure.
3. Perform the tire pressure system configuration procedure. Verify all 4 sensor locations, IDs, and tire pressures match what the scan tool displays.

   ⇒ If the scan tool data does not match, replace the Tire Pressure Control Module.

Repair Instructions

Perform the Diagnostic Repair Verification after completing the diagnostic procedure.

- Tire Pressure Sensor Learn
- Control Module References for replacement, setup, and programming

ARM0700000000836

Fig. 126 Codes C2165, C2166, C2167 & C2168: Tire Pressure Sensor Tire Overtemperature. Vibe

Diagnostic Fault Information

- Perform the Diagnostic System Check - Vehicle prior to using this diagnostic procedure.

Circuit/System Description

The tire pressure monitor (TPM) system has a radio frequency (RF) transmitting pressure sensor in each wheel/tire assembly. The module receives and translates the data contained in the tire pressure sensor RF transmissions into sensor presence, sensor mode, and tire pressure.

The receiver module receives a radio frequency (RF) transmission from each tire pressure sensor. Each sensor RF transmission contains its own unique identification (ID) code that must be learned into the module memory. Once all 4 IDs have been learned, the module continuously compares IDs received in transmission to its learned IDs to determine if all 4 sensors are present.

Conditions for Running the DTC

The ignition is ON.

Conditions for Setting the DTC

Tire Pressure Sensor ID code is not learned.

Action Taken When the DTC Sets

The Tire Pressure Warning Light is illuminated.

Conditions for Clearing the DTC

A current DTC will clear when the Tire Pressure Control Module has undergone the sensor learn procedure.

Circuit/System Verification

Verify that the Sensor ID's are learned.

⇒ If the ID's are not learned, program/setup the Tire Pressure Control Module. If the DTC resets, replace the Tire Pressure Control Module.

Repair Instructions

Perform the Diagnostic Repair Verification after completing the diagnostic procedure.

- Tire Pressure Sensor Learn
- Control Module References for Module replacement, setup, and programming

ARM0700000000837

Fig. 127 Code C2171: Low Tire Pressure Sensors Not Learned. Vibe

Diagnostic Instructions

- Perform the Diagnostic System Check - Vehicle prior to using this diagnostic procedure.

Circuit/System Description

The tire pressure monitor (TPM) system has a radio frequency (RF) transmitting pressure sensor in each wheel/tire assembly. The module receives and translates the data contained in the tire pressure sensor RF transmissions into sensor presence, sensor mode, and tire pressure.

The receiver module receives a radio frequency (RF) transmission from each tire pressure sensor. Each sensor RF transmission contains its own unique identification (ID) code that must be learned into the module memory. Once all 4 IDs have been learned, the module continuously compares IDs received in transmission to its learned IDs to determine if all 4 sensors are present.

Conditions for Running the DTC

The ignition is ON.

Conditions for Setting the DTC

- Tire Pressure Control Module malfunction.
- Short to ground in 5 V reference circuit.
- Tire Pressure Receiver Module malfunction.

Action Taken When the DTC Sets

The Tire Pressure Warning Light is illuminated.

Conditions for Clearing the DTC

The condition responsible for setting the DTC no longer exists.

ARM0700000000838

Fig. 128   Code C2176: Tire Pressure Sensors Antenna Performance (Part 1 of 2). Vibe

Circuit/System Testing

1. Ignition OFF, disconnect the harness connector at the Tire Pressure Control Module.
2. Disconnect the harness connector at the Tire Pressure Receiver Module.
3. Test for less than 1 ohm between the 5-volt reference circuit terminal 6 and terminal 5.

   ⇒ If greater than the specified value, test the 5-volt reference circuit for an open/high resistance.

4. Test for less than 1 ohm between the signal circuit terminal 12 and terminal 1.

   ⇒ If greater than the specified value, test the signal circuit for an open/high resistance.

5. Test for less than 1 ohm between the ground circuit terminal 11 and terminal 4.

   ⇒ If greater than the specified value, test the ground circuit for an open/high resistance.

6. Test for infinite resistance between the 5-volt reference circuit terminal 6 and ground.

   ⇒ If not the specified value, test the 5-volt reference circuit for a short to ground.

7. Test for infinite resistance between the signal circuit terminal 12 and ground.

   ⇒ If not the specified value, test the signal circuit for a short to ground.

8. Connect the Tire Pressure Control Module connector.
9. Ignition ON, test for 4.5-5.5 volts between the 5-volt reference circuit terminal 5 and ground circuit terminal 4.

   ⇒ If not within the specified range, replace the Tire Pressure Control Module.

   ⇒ If within the specified range, replace the Tire Pressure Receiver Module.

Repair Instructions

Perform the Diagnostic Repair Verification after completing the diagnostic procedure.

- Tire Pressure Sensor Learn
- Control Module References for LGM replacement, setup, and programming

ARM0700000000839

Fig. 128   Code C2176: Tire Pressure Sensors Antenna Performance (Part 2 of 2). Vibe

Diagnostic Instructions

• Perform the <u>Diagnostic System Check - Vehicle</u> prior to using this diagnostic procedure.

Circuit/System Description

Initialization is required after replacing the tire pressure control module, tire pressure sensors, tire pressure, or rotating the tires.

Conditions for Running the DTC

The ignition is ON.

Conditions for Setting the DTC

All of the following are met:

• Tire Pressure Sensor is not in stop mode.
• Tire Pressure Sensor signal is not received for 20 minutes or more.
• Vehicle Speed is more than 5 mph for 20 minutes or more.

Action Taken When the DTC Sets

The Tire Pressure Warning Light is illuminated.

Conditions for Clearing the DTC

Vehicle speed is greater than 12 mph for 3 seconds.

ARM0700000000840

Fig. 129   Code C2177: Initialization Not Complete (Part 1 of 2). Vibe

Circuit/System Testing

1. With the scan tool, verify tire pressure sensors ID and locations:
   1.1. Rapidly reduce the tire pressure for each wheel at least 6 psi within 30 seconds. It may take up to 3 minutes for the display to change.
   1.2. Record the sensor ID and location.
   ⇒ If any of the parameters listed above do not change or are not displayed for one sensor, replace the suspect tire pressure sensor.
2. Disconnect the harness connector at the Tire Pressure Control Module.
3. Disconnect the harness connector at the Tire Pressure Receiver Module.
4. Test for less than 1 ohm between the 5-volt reference circuit terminal 6 and terminal 5.
   ⇒ If greater than the specified value, test the 5-volt reference circuit for an open/high resistance.
5. Test for less than 1 ohm between the signal circuit terminal 12 and terminal 1.
   ⇒ If greater than the specified value, test the signal circuit for an open/high resistance.
6. Test for less than 1 ohm between the ground circuit terminal 11 and terminal 4.
   ⇒ If greater than the specified value, test the ground circuit for an open/high resistance.
7. Test for infinite resistance between the 5-volt reference circuit terminal 6 and ground.
   ⇒ If not the specified value, test the 5-volt reference circuit for a short to ground.
8. Test for infinite resistance between the signal circuit terminal 12 and ground.
   ⇒ If not the specified value, test the signal circuit for a short to ground.
9. Enable the TPM learn mode. Verify all 4 sensor locations, IDs, and tire pressures match what the scan tool displays.
   ⇒ If the scan tool data does not display, replace the Tire Pressure Receiver Module. If DTC sets again, replace the Tire Pressure Control Module

ARM0700000000841

Fig. 129   Code C2177: Initialization Not Complete (Part 2 of 2). Vibe

Diagnostic Instructions

- Perform the Diagnostic System Check - Vehicle prior to using this diagnostic procedure.

Circuit/System Description

The tire pressure monitor (TPM) system has a radio frequency (RF) transmitting pressure sensor in each wheel/tire assembly. The module receives and translates the data contained in the tire pressure sensor RF transmissions into sensor presence, sensor mode, and tire pressure.

The receiver module receives a radio frequency (RF) transmission from each tire pressure sensor. Each sensor RF transmission contains its own unique identification (ID) code that must be learned into the module memory. Once all 4 IDs have been learned, the module continuously compares IDs received in transmission to its learned IDs to determine if all 4 sensors are present.

Conditions for Running the DTC

Vehicle speed is 5 mph or greater for 20 minutes.

Conditions for Setting the DTC

Malfunction in the transmitting/receiving circuit.

Action Taken When the DTC Sets

The Tire Pressure Warning Light is illuminated.

Conditions for Clearing the DTC

The condition responsible for setting the DTC no longer exists and the scan tool Clear DTCs function is used.

Diagnostic Aids

- The sensor activation procedure may have to be repeated up to 3 times before determining a sensor is malfunctioning.
- Occasionally sensor transmissions are not received by the tire pressure receiver module due to vehicle level RF interference.

ARM0700000000842

Fig. 130   Codes C2181, C2182, C2183 & C2184: Tire Pressure Sensor Transmitter Identification (Part 1 of 2). Vibe

Circuit/System Testing

1. With the scan tool, verify that DTC C2173 is not set.
   ⇒ If DTC C2173 is set, refer to DTC C2173.
2. With the scan tool, locate and record tire pressure sensors ID and locations:
   2.1. Rapidly reduce the tire pressure for each wheel at least 6 psi within 30 seconds. It may take up to 3 minutes for the display to change.
   2.2. Record the sensor ID and location.
   ⇒ If any of the parameters listed above do not change or are not displayed for one sensor, replace the suspect tire pressure sensor.
3. Disconnect the harness connector at the Tire Pressure Control Module.
4. Disconnect the harness connector at the Tire Pressure Receiver Module.
5. Test for less than 1 ohm between the 5-volt reference circuit terminal 6 and terminal 5.
   ⇒ If greater than the specified value, test the 5-volt reference circuit for an open/high resistance.
6. Test for less than 1 ohm between the signal circuit terminal 12 and terminal 1.
   ⇒ If greater than the specified value, test the signal circuit for an open/high resistance.
7. Test for less than 1 ohm between the ground circuit terminal 11 and terminal 4.
   ⇒ If greater than the specified value, test the ground circuit for an open/high resistance.
8. Test for infinite resistance between the 5-volt reference circuit terminal 6 and ground.
   ⇒ If not the specified value, test the 5-volt reference circuit for a short to ground.
9. Test for infinite resistance between the signal circuit terminal 12 and ground.
   ⇒ If not the specified value, test the signal circuit for a short to ground.
10. Perform the tire pressure sensor learn procedure.
11. Perform the tire pressure system configuration procedure. Verify all 4 sensor locations, IDs, and tire pressures match what the scan tool displays.
    ⇒ If the scan tool data does not display, replace the Tire Pressure Receiver Module. If DTC sets again, replace the Tire Pressure Control Module

ARM0700000000843

Fig. 130   Codes C2181, C2182, C2183 & C2184: Tire Pressure Sensor Transmitter Identification (Part 2 of 2). Vibe

Step	Action	Yes	No
1	Did you perform a Diagnostic System Check - Vehicle?	Go to Step 2	Go to Diagnostic System Check
2	Check the tires for incorrect pressure. Did you find and correct the condition?	Go to Step 10	Go to Step 3
3	Check if the vehicle has the appropriate size tires? Did you find and correct the condition?	Go to Step 10	Go to Step 4
4	Is the instrument panel cluster outside temperature reading equal to the actual outside temperature?	Go to Step 5	Check Outside Air Temperature Display Inaccurate or Inoperative
5	Test the ambient temperature sensor circuit for an open or short to ground. Did you find and correct the condition?	Go to Step 10	Go to Step 6
6	Test the tire pressure warning indicator control circuit for a open or high resistance. Did you find and correct the condition?	Go to Step 10	Go to Step 7
7	Apply a ground to the tire pressure warning indicator control circuit. Is the tire pressure warning indicator ON?	Go to Step 8	Go to Step 9
8	Replace the instrument panel cluster assembly. Is the repair complete?	Go to Step 10	--
9	Replace the brake pressure modulator valve (BPMV). Is the repair complete?	Go to Step 10	--
10	Operate the system in order to verify the repair. Did you correct the condition?	System OK	Go to Step 2

ARM0500000000861

Fig. 131   Low Tire Pressure Indicator Always On. 2005–07 Vibe

Diagnostic Instructions

- Perform the Diagnostic System Check - Vehicle prior to using this diagnostic procedure.

Circuit/System Description

The tire pressure monitor (TPM) system has a radio frequency (RF) transmitting pressure sensor in each wheel/tire assembly. The module receives and translates the data contained in the tire pressure sensor RF transmissions into sensor presence, sensor mode, and tire pressure.

The receiver module receives a radio frequency (RF) transmission from each tire pressure sensor. Each sensor RF transmission contains its own unique identification (ID) code that must be learned into the module memory. Once all 4 IDs have been learned, the module continuously compares IDs received in transmission to its learned IDs to determine if all 4 sensors are present.

If the control module detects a low tire pressure condition or a malfunction in the system, it will illuminate the tire pressure monitor indicator.

Diagnostic Aids

- A sensor may have been damaged due to a previous wheel/tire service or flat tire event.
- The use of tire sealants can obstruct the sensor pressure sensing port and cause inaccurate tire pressure readings. If this condition is verified, remove the sealer from the tire and replace the sensor. Refer to Tire Pressure Indicator Sensor Replacement.
- Occasionally sensor transmissions are not received by the control module due to vehicle level RF interference from items such as but not limited to aftermarket ignition systems, DVD players, CB radios, or metallic type window tinting.
- The sensor activation procedure may have to be repeated before determining a sensor is malfunctioning. In the event a particular sensor information is displayed on the special tool, it may be necessary to rotate the wheel valve stem to a different position due to the RF signal is being blocked by another component.

Important: When a TPM DTC is set, the tire pressure monitor indicator icon will flash for 1 minute after the IPC bulb check is completed and then remains illuminated.

Low tire pressure in one or more tires is indicated by a continuously illuminated tire pressure monitor indicator icon after the IPC bulb check is completed.

ARM0700000000828

Fig. 132   Low Tire Pressure Indicator Always On (Part 1 of 2). 2008 Vibe

Circuit/System Verification

1. Inflate all tires to the proper pressure and drive the vehicle over 25 mph for over 2 minutes.
2. Using a scan tool, select instrument panel special functions Lamp Test. Command the instrument panel warning lamps OFF. Verify the tire pressure monitor indicator icon turns OFF.

   ⇒ If the tire pressure monitor icon does not turn OFF, replace the IPC.

3. Disconnect the harness connector at the Tire Pressure Control Module.
4. Disconnect the harness connector at the IPC.
5. Test for less than 1 ohm between the warning light control circuit terminal 6 and terminal 1.

   ⇒ If greater than the specified value, test the warning light control circuit for an open/high resistance.

6. Test for infinite resistance between the warning light control circuit terminal 6 and ground.

   ⇒ If less than the specified value, test the warning light control circuit for a short to ground. If circuit tests normal, replace the tire pressure control module.

Repair Instructions

Perform the Diagnostic Repair Verification after completing the diagnostic procedure.

- Tire Pressure Indicator Sensor Replacement
- Tire Pressure Sensor Learn
- Control Module References for IPC or module replacement, programming, and setup

ARM0700000000829

Fig. 132   Low Tire Pressure Indicator Always On (Part 2 of 2). 2008 Vibe

Step	Action	Yes	No
1	Did you perform a Diagnostic System Check - Vehicle?	Go to Step 2	Go to Diagnostic System Check
2	Turn ON the ignition, with the engine OFF. Does the tire pressure warning indicator turn ON for 3-4 seconds and go OFF?	Go to Step 4	Go to Step 3
3	Do any of the other instrument cluster indicators or gages function?	Go to Step 3	Check Gages Inoperative
4	Check if the vehicle has the appropriate size tires. Did you find and correct the condition?	Go to Step 11	Go to Step 5
5	Is the instrument panel cluster (IPC) outside temperature reading equal to the actual outside temperature?	Go to Step 6	Check Outside Air Temperature Display Inaccurate or Inoperative

ARM0500000000862

Fig. 133   Low Tire Pressure Indicator Inoperative (Part 1 of 2). 2005–07 Vibe

6	Test the ambient temperature sensor circuit for an open or short to ground. Did you find and correct the condition?	Go to Step 11	Go to Step 7
7	1. Turn OFF the ignition. 2. Disconnect the electronic brake control module (EBCM) electrical connector. 3. Turn ON the ignition, with the engine OFF. Does the tire pressure warning indicator turn ON?	Go to Step 10	Go to Step 8
8	Test the tire pressure warning indicator control circuit for a short to ground. Did you find and correct the condition?	Go to Step 11	Go to Step 9
9	Replace the instrument panel cluster assembly. Did you complete the replacement?	Go to Step 11	--
10	Replace the brake pressure modulator valve (BPMV). Is the repair complete?	Go to Step 11	--
11	Operate the system in order to verify the repair. Did you correct the condition?	System OK	Go to Step 2

ARM0500000000863

Fig. 133   Low Tire Pressure Indicator Inoperative
(Part 2 of 2). 2005–07 Vibe

Diagnostic Instructions

- Perform the <u>Diagnostic System Check - Vehicle</u> prior to using this diagnostic procedure.

Circuit/System Description

The tire pressure monitor (TPM) system has a radio frequency (RF) transmitting pressure sensor in each wheel/tire assembly. The module receives and translates the data contained in the tire pressure sensor RF transmissions into sensor presence, sensor mode, and tire pressure.

The receiver module receives a radio frequency (RF) transmission from each tire pressure sensor. Each sensor RF transmission contains its own unique identification (ID) code that must be learned into the module memory. Once all 4 IDs have been learned, the module continuously compares IDs received in transmission to its learned IDs to determine if all 4 sensors are present.

If the control module detects a low tire pressure condition or a malfunction in the system, it will illuminate the tire pressure monitor indicator.

Diagnostic Aids

- Some aftermarket wheel valve stem holes are located further from the wheel rim than original equipment wheels. When using the TPM special tool to activate a sensor, ensure the tool antenna is no further than 15 cm (6 in) from the sensor and is aiming upward.
- Aftermarket wheel value stem locations can cause a sensor to not function correctly.
- A sensor may have been damaged due to a previous wheel/tire service or flat tire event.
- The use of tire sealants can obstruct the sensor pressure sensing port and cause inaccurate tire pressure readings. If this condition is verified, remove the sealer from the tire and replace the sensor. Refer to Tire Pressure Indicator Sensor Replacement.
- Occasionally sensor transmissions are not received by the module due to vehicle level RF interference from items such as but not limited to aftermarket ignition systems, DVD players, CB radios, or metallic type window tinting.
- The sensor activation procedure may have to be repeated up to 3 times before determining a sensor is malfunctioning. In the event a particular sensor's information is displayed on the special tool upon activation but the horn does not chirp, it may be necessary to rotate the wheel valve stem to a different position due to the RF signal is being blocked by another component.
- Occasionally sensors can become mislocated due to previous tire rotations where the sensor learn procedure was not performed or stray sensor transmissions have been received from other vehicles. Always learn the sensors to ensure the DTC set is for that actual physical corner of the vehicle. Refer to Tire Pressure Sensor Learn.

ARM0700000000830

Fig. 134   Low Tire Pressure Indicator Inoperative
(Part 1 of 2). 2008 Vibe

Circuit/System Verification

1. With the scan tool, select instrument panel special functions Lamp Test. Command the instrument panel lamps ON. Verify tire pressure monitor indicator icon turns ON.

   ⇒ If the icon does not turn ON, replace the IPC.

2. Disconnect the harness connector at the Tire Pressure Control Module.
3. Disconnect the harness connector at the IPC.
4. Test for less than 1 ohm of resistance between the warning light control circuit terminal 6 and terminal 1.

   ⇒ If greater than the specified value, test the warning light control circuit for an open/high resistance.

5. Test for infinite resistance between the warning light control circuit terminal 6 and ground.

   ⇒ If less than the specified value, test the warning light control circuit for a short to ground. If circuit tests normal, replace the tire pressure control module.

Repair Instructions

Perform the Diagnostic Repair Verification after completing the diagnostic procedure.

- Tire Pressure Indicator Sensor Replacement
- Tire Pressure Sensor Learn
- Control Module References for IPC and module replacement, programming, and setup.

ARM0700000000831

Fig. 134 Low Tire Pressure Indicator Inoperative (Part 2 of 2). 2008 Vibe

Step	Action	Values	Yes	No
1	Did you perform a Diagnostic System Check - Vehicle?	--	Go to Step 2	Go to Diagnostic System Check - Vehicle in Vehicle DTC Information
2	1. Turn OFF the ignition. 2. Using a service wire, connect terminals 4 and 12 of the diagnostic link connector (DLC). 3. Turn ON the ignition. 4. Press the Tire Pressure Warning System reset switch. Did the tire pressure warning indicator illuminate?	--	Go to Step 3	Go to Step 4
3	Check the tires for incorrect pressure. Did you find and correct the condition?	--	Go to Step 7	--
4	1. Turn OFF the ignition. 2. Disconnect the tire pressure warning system reset switch connector. 3. Measure the resistance of the tire pressure warning system reset switch in the OFF position. Is resistance as specified?	Above 10K ohms	Go to Step 5	Go to Step 8
5	1. Turn OFF the ignition. 2. Disconnect the tire pressure warning system reset switch connector. 3. Measure the resistance of the tire pressure warning system reset switch in the ON position. Is resistance as specified?	Below 1 ohms	Go to Step 6	Go to Step 8

ARM0500000000864

Fig. 135 Low Tire Pressure Indicator Does Not Reset (Part 1 of 2). 2005–07 Vibe

6	Test the tire pressure warning system reset circuit for the following conditions: • An open or high resistance • A short to ground Did you find and correct the condition?	Go to Step 9	Go to Low Tire Pressure Indicator Always On
7	Reset and initialize the tire pressure warning system. Did you complete the procedure?	Go to Step 9	--
8	Replace the tire pressure warning system reset switch. Is the repair complete?	Go to Step 9	--
9	Operate the system in order to verify the repair. Did you correct the condition?	System OK	Go to Step 2

ARM0500000000865

Fig. 135   Low Tire Pressure Indicator Does Not Reset (Part 2 of 2). 2005–07 Vibe

Diagnostic Instructions
• Perform the Diagnostic System Check - Vehicle prior to using this diagnostic procedure.

Circuit/System Description
The tire pressure control module enters initialization mode and performs initialization automatically when the tire pressure control module receives a signal from the reset switch. If the control module receives a signal, the tire pressure warning light will blink 3 times.

Circuit/System Verification
1. Ignition ON, with the scan tool, enter tire pressure monitor test mode.
2. Press the tire pressure warning reset switch. Tire pressure warning indicator should illuminate.
3. Disconnect the harness connector at the tire pressure warning reset switch.
4. Test for less than 1 ohm between terminal 5 and terminal 8 of the reset switch with the switch in the On position.
   ⇒ If not within the specified range, replace the tire pressure reset switch.
5. Test for infinite resistance between terminal 5 and terminal 8 of the reset switch with the switch in the Off position.
   ⇒ If not within the specified range, replace the tire pressure reset switch.
6. Disconnect the harness connector at the Tire Pressure Control Module.
7. Test for less than 1 ohm between the reset switch signal circuit terminal 1 and terminal 8.
   ⇒ If greater than the specified value, test the reset switch signal circuit for an open/high resistance.
8. Test for infinite resistance between the reset switch signal circuit terminal 1 and ground.
   ⇒ If less than the specified value, test the reset switch signal circuit for a short to ground.
9. Test for less than 1 ohm between the reset switch ground circuit terminal 5 and ground.
   ⇒ If greater than the specified value, test the reset switch ground circuit for an open/high resistance. If circuit tests normal, replace the tire pressure control module.

ARM0700000000763

Fig. 136   Low Tire Pressure Indicator Does Not Reset. 2008 Vibe

COMPONENT SERVICE

Resetting Tire Pressure Monitor Lamp

ALERO & GRAND AM

The Tire Low Tire Pressure indicator will turn On when the pressure in one of the tires becomes 12 psi. lower or higher then the other three. The low tire pressure monitor system uses the ABS wheel speed sensors to determine if a tire is low by a variation in wheel speed.

1. Inflate all tires to vehicle manufacturer's specifications.
2. Place the ignition switch in the On position.
3. Press the RESET button located on driver side instrument panel fuse box.
4. The OIL CHANGE indicator should begin to flash.
5. Press the RESET button again, the CHANGE OIL indicator should go Off and the LOW TIRE PRESSURE indicator should begin to flash.
6. Press RESET button until a chime sounds and the LOW TIRE PRESSURE indicator turns Off.
7. To calibrate system, operate vehicle for 30 minutes in each of the following three speed ranges:
   a. 15–40 mph.
   b. 40–70 mph.
   c. 70–90 mph.

BONNEVILLE

USING SYSTEM MONITOR

The Low Tire Pressure indicator will turn On when the pressure in one of the tires becomes 10 psi. lower or higher then the other three. The low tire pressure monitor system uses the ABS wheel speed sensors to determine if a tire is low by a variation in wheel speed.

1. Inflate all tires to vehicle manufacturer's specifications.
2. Place the ignition switch in the On position.
3. Press and hold the TIRE PRESS RESET button until TIRE PRESS indicator begins to flash.
4. Release TIRE PRESS RESET button. Tire pressure indicator will turn Off.
5. To calibrate system, operate vehicle for 30 minutes in each of the following three speed ranges:
   a. 15–40 mph.
   b. 40–70 mph.
   c. 70–90 mph.

USING DIC (DRIVER INFORMATION CENTER)

The Low Tire Pressure indicator will turn On when the pressure in one of the tires becomes 12 psi. lower or higher then the other three. The low tire pressure monitor system uses the ABS wheel speed sensors to determine if a tire is low by a variation in wheel speed.

1. Inflate all tires to vehicle manufacturer's specifications.
2. Place the ignition switch in the On position.
3. Press the DIC MODE button until TIRE PRESSURE is displayed.
4. Press and hold the RESET button until TIRE PRESSURE RESET is displayed.
5. Release the RESET button, TIRE PRESSURE NORMAL should be displayed.
6. To calibrate system, operate vehicle for 30 minutes in each of the following three speed ranges:
   a. 15–40 mph.
   b. 40–70 mph.
   c. 70–90 mph.

CENTURY & REGAL

The Low Tire Pressure indicator will turn On when the pressure in one of the tires becomes 12 psi. lower or higher then the other three. The low tire pressure monitor system uses the ABS wheel speed sensors to determine if a tire is low by a variation in wheel speed.

1. Inflate all tires to vehicle manufacturer's specifications.
2. Place the ignition switch in the On position.
3. Press the RESET button located on passenger side instrument panel fuse box.
4. The LOW TIRE indicator should flash 3 times and turn Off.
5. To calibrate system, operate vehicle for 30 minutes in each of the following three speed ranges:
   a. 15–40 mph.
   b. 40–70 mph.
   c. 70–90 mph.

CORVETTE

The tire pressure monitor will display the 4 tire pressure on the DIC (Driver Information Center) while the vehicle is being driven. If the system detects a tire pressure above 42 psi., the HIGH TIRE PRESSURE message will be displayed on the DIC. If the system detects a tire pressure between 5 and 25 psi., LOW TIRE PRESSURE will be displayed. If a tire pressure below 5 psi. is detected, FLAT TIRE will be displayed followed by two chime sounds and the message MAX. SPEED 55 mph and REDUCED HANDLING. After servicing or inflating tire to recommended pressure, press DIC RESET button to clear DIC warning messages.

CTS, DTS, STS, VIBE & XLR

The Tire Pressure Monitor system warns the driver when a significant loss, or gain of tire pressure occurs in any of the 4 tires. Adjusting tire to recommended pressure will clear the tire message.

DEVILLE & SEVILLE

If system detects proper tire pressure, TIRE OK will be displayed on the DIC (Driver Information Center). If the system detects a tire pressure above 38 psi., the TIRE HIGH message will be displayed, if the system detects a tire pressure below 25 psi., TIRE LOW will be displayed followed by CHECK TIRE PRESSURE. Inflating tire to recommended pressure will clear the tire message.

GRAND PRIX

2004–05

The Low Tire Pressure indicator will turn On when the pressure in one of the tires becomes 12 psi. lower or higher then the other three. The low tire pressure monitor system uses the ABS wheel speed sensors to determine if a tire is low by a variation in wheel speed.

1. Turn the ignition On with the engine Off.
2. Press vehicle information button until Tire Inflation Monitor System Press (down/left arrow) Switch to Reset is displayed.
3. Press and hold down/left arrow button until Tire Inflation Monitor System Has Been Reset is displayed.
4. Release down/left arrow button and Tire Pressure Normal is displayed.
5. To calibrate system, operate vehicle for a distance of 5 miles on a flat smooth surface in each of the following four speed ranges:
   a. 19–40 mph.
   b. 40–59 mph.
   c. 59–75 mph.
   d. 75–90 mph.

2006

1. Inflate all tires to vehicle manufacturer's specifications.
2. Place the ignition switch in the On position.
3. Press information button until TIRE INFLATION MONITOR SYSTEM PRESS SWITCH TO RESET is displayed.
4. If the system is being reset due to a low tire pressure, press and hold the down/left arrow button until TIRE INFLATION MONITOR SYSTEM HAS BEEN RESET is displayed.
5. If the system is being reset due to a tire rotation, press and hold the down/left arrow button for 5 seconds.
6. Release the down/left arrow button and TIRE PRESSURE NORMAL is displayed.
7. To calibrate system, operate vehicle for a distance of 5 miles on a flat smooth surface in each of the following four speed ranges:
   a. 19–40 mph.
   b. 40–59 mph.
   c. 59–75 mph.
   d. 75–90 mph.

2007–08 LESS KEYLESS ENTRY

1. Place ignition switch in RUN position.
2. Press and release driver information center (DIC) INFO button until RELEARN TIRE POSITIONS message appears on DIC display.
3. Press and hold SET/RESET button until a double horn chirp sounds and DIC displays a TIRE LEARNING ACTIVE message indicating Learn Mode has been enabled, left front turn signal will also be illuminated.
4. Starting with left front tire, learn tire

pressure, using the following method:

5. Increase/decrease tire pressure for 8-10 seconds then wait for a horn chirp. Note: Horn chirp may occur before or up to 30 seconds after the 8-10 second pressure increase/decrease time period has been reached.
6. After horn chirp has sounded and right front turn signal is illuminated, repeat above step for remaining 3 sensors in following order: Right front, right rear & left rear.
7. After Left rear sensor has been learned, a double horn chirp will sound indicating all sensors have been learned.
8. Turn OFF ignition to exit learn mode.
9. After learn mode has been exited, adjust all tires to recommended pressures.

2007-08 WITH KEYLESS ENTRY

1. Place ignition switch in ACCY position.
2. Simultaneously press keyless entry transmitters lock and unlock buttons until a double horn chirp sounds indicating Learn Mode has been enabled, left front turn signal will also be illuminated.
3. Starting with left front tire, learn tire pressure, using the following method:
4. Increase/decrease tire pressure for 8-10 seconds then wait for a horn chirp. Note: Horn chirp may occur before or up to 30 seconds after the 8-10 second pressure increase/decrease time period has been reached.
5. After horn chirp has sounded and right front turn signal is illuminated, repeat above step for remaining 3 sensors in following order: Right front, right rear & left rear.
6. After Left rear sensor has been learned, a double horn chirp will sound indicating all sensors have been learned.
7. Turn OFF ignition to exit learn mode.
8. After learn mode has been exited, adjust all tires to recommended pressures.

IMPALA & MONTE CARLO

2004-05

Using RDS Radio

The Low Tire Pressure indicator will turn On when the pressure in one of the tires becomes 12 psi. lower or higher then the other three. The low tire pressure monitor system uses the ABS wheel speed sensors to determine if a tire is low by a variation in wheel speed.

1. Inflate all tires to vehicle manufacturer's specifications.
2. Place the ignition switch in the On position.
3. Place radio in Off position.
4. Press and hold DISP button until SETTINGS is displayed.
5. Press the SEEK up or down buttons until TIRE MON is displayed.
6. Press the PREV or NEXT buttons until RESET is displayed.
7. Press the DISP button, a chime will

sound and DONE will be displayed.

8. Scroll menu until EXIT is displayed, then press DISP button. A chime will sound to indicate system exit from TIRE MON.
9. To calibrate system, operate vehicle for 30 minutes in each of the following three speed ranges:
   a. 15–40 mph.
   b. 40–70 mph.
   c. 70–90 mph.

Using Light Switch

The Low Tire Pressure indicator will turn On when the pressure in one of the tires becomes 12 psi. lower or higher then the other three. The low tire pressure monitor system uses the ABS wheel speed sensors to determine if a tire is low by a variation in wheel speed.

1. Inflate all tires to vehicle manufacturer's specifications.
2. Place the ignition switch in the On position.
3. Cycle the light switch from Off to Parking Lamps 3 times within 5 seconds.
4. To calibrate system, operate vehicle for 30 minutes in each of the following three speed ranges:
   a. 15–40 mph.
   b. 40–70 mph.
   c. 70–90 mph.

2006-08

When the Tire Pressure Monitor system detects a significant loss, or gain of tire pressure, the CHECK TIRE PRESSURE message is displayed on the DIC. Adjusting tire to recommended pressure will clear the tire message.

LESABRE & PARK AVENUE

The Low Tire Pressure indicator will turn On when the pressure in one of the tires becomes 12 psi. lower or higher then the other three. The low tire pressure monitor system uses the ABS wheel speed sensors to determine if a tire is low by a variation in wheel speed.

1. Inflate all tires to vehicle manufacturer's specifications.
2. Place the ignition switch in the On position.
3. Press the GAUGE INFO button until TIRE PRESSURE is displayed.
4. Press the RESET button until TIRE PRESSURE RESET is displayed.
5. Release the RESET button, TIRE PRESSURE NORMAL is displayed.
6. To calibrate system, operate vehicle for 30 minutes in each of the following three speed ranges:
   a. 15–40 mph.
   b. 40–70 mph.
   c. 70–90 mph.

LUCERNE

1. Inflate all tires to vehicle manufacturer's specifications.
2. Place the ignition switch in the Run position with the engine.
3. Press the vehicle information button until Press To Reset Tire Pressure displays.
4. Press and hold Set/Reset button until

TIRE PRESSURE RESET is displayed.

5. Release RESET button.
6. The system will complete the calibration process as the vehicle is driven.
7. If the system does not reset, repeat procedure.

Pressure Monitor Sensor Programming

ALERO & GRAND AM

The "Tire Low Tire Pressure" indicator will be turn On when the pressure in one of the tires is 12 psi. lower or higher then the other three tires.

1. Inflate all tires to specifications.
2. Place ignition switch in On position.
3. Depress RESET button located on driver side instrument panel fuse box.
4. The OIL CHANGE indicator should begin to flash.
5. Press RESET button again, CHANGE OIL indicator should go Off and LOW TIRE PRESSURE indicator should begin to flash.
6. Depress RESET button until a chime sounds and LOW TIRE PRESSURE indicator turns Off.

BONNEVILLE

Tire Driver Information Center (DIC) will display Normal when tire pressure is normal. When low tire pressure is detected the DIC will display Low Tire Pressure.

1. Inflate all tires to specifications.
2. Place ignition switch in On position.
3. Depress DIC SET button for 3 seconds.
4. DIC will display TIRE PRESSURE RESET for 3 seconds indicating monitor has been reset.

CENTURY & REGAL

The "Tire Low Tire Pressure" indicator will be turn On when the pressure in one of the tires is 12 psi. lower or higher then the other three tires.

1. Inflate all tires to vehicle manufacturers specifications.
2. Place ignition switch in On position.
3. Depress RESET button located on passenger side instrument panel fuse box.
4. LOW TIRE indicator should flash 3 times and turn Off.

CORVETTE

USING KEYLESS ENTRY TRANSMITTER

Before proceeding with the steps below, ensure that no other sensor learn procedure is being performed simultaneously, or that no tire pressures are being adjusted on another TPM equipped vehicle within close proximity.

The learn mode will cancel if the ignition is cycled to OFF or if more than 2 minutes has elapsed for any sensor that has not been learned. If the learn mode is cancelled, the original sensor IDs will be maintained.

If the learn mode is cancelled after any

TIRE PRESSURE MONITORING SYSTEM

sensor is learned, the DIC will display dashes instead of tire pressures for the remaining unlearned sensors and the learn procedure will need to be repeated for the system to function properly.

1. Place electronic keyless ignition in ACCY position.
2. Simultaneously press keyless entry transmitters lock and unlock buttons until a horn chirp sounds indicating the Learn Mode has been enabled.
3. Starting with left front tire, hold antenna of tool No. J-46079 or equivalent, against tire sidewall close to wheel rim at valve stem location then press and release activate button and wait for a horn chirp.
4. After horn chirp has sounded, proceed to next 3 sensors in following order, righthand front, righthand rear and lefthand rear.
5. After lefthand rear sensor has been learned, a double horn chirp will sound indicating all sensors have been learned.
6. Place electronic keyless ignition in OFF position to exit learn mode.
7. After learn mode has been exited, adjust all tires to recommended pressures.

USING SCAN TOOL

Before proceeding with the steps below, ensure that no other sensor learn procedure is being performed simultaneously, or that no tire pressures are being adjusted on another TPM equipped vehicle within close proximity.

1. Place electronic keyless ignition in ACCY position.
2. Install suitably programmed scan tool.
3. With scan tool, initiate TPM Learn Mode, a horn chirp will sound indicating Learn Mode has been enabled.
4. Starting with left front tire, hold antenna of tool No. J-46079 or equivalent, against tire sidewall close to wheel rim at valve stem location then press and release activate button and wait for a horn chirp.
5. After horn chirp has sounded, proceed to next 3 sensors in following order, righthand front, righthand rear and lefthand rear.
6. After lefthand rear sensor has been learned, a double horn chirp will sound indicating all sensors have been learned.
7. Place electronic keyless ignition in OFF position to exit learn mode.
8. After learn mode has been exited, adjust all tires to recommended pressures.

CTS

USING KEYLESS ENTRY TRANSMITTER

Before proceeding with the steps below, ensure that no other sensor learn procedure is being performed simultaneously, or that no tire pressures are being adjusted on another TPM equipped vehicle within close proximity.

1. Place ignition in ON position, with engine OFF.

2. Lock and unlock vehicle doors 3 times in order to synchronize transmitter with antenna module using keyless entry transmitter.
3. Simultaneously, press keyless entry transmitter's lock and unlock buttons until a single horn chirp sounds indicating learn mode has been enabled.
4. Starting with lefthand side front tire, increase or decrease pressure for 5-8 seconds, or until a horn chirp sounds.
5. Horn chirp may occur before 5-8 second pressure increase/decrease time period has been reached, or up to 30 seconds after 5-8 second pressure increase/decrease time period has been reached.
6. After horn chirp has sounded, proceed to next 3 sensors in following order, righthand front, righthand rear and lefthand rear.
7. After all sensors have been learned, exit learn mode by turning OFF ignition.
8. After learn mode has been exited, adjust all tire pressures to recommended psi.

USING SCAN TOOL

Before proceeding with the steps below, ensure that no other sensor learn procedure is being performed simultaneously, or that no tire pressures are being adjusted on another TPM equipped vehicle within close proximity.

1. Install suitably programmed scan tool.
2. Place ignition in ON position, with engine OFF.
3. With scan tool, select "Special Functions."
4. Select "Sensor Learn Mode Enable" and press ENTER key.
5. Press ON soft key. A single horn chirp will sound indicating learn mode has been enabled.
6. Starting with lefthand side front tire, increase or decrease the pressure for 5-8 seconds, or until a horn chirp sounds.
7. Horn chirp may occur before 5-8 second pressure increase/decrease time period has been reached, or up to 30 seconds after 5-8 second pressure increase/decrease time period has been reached.
8. After horn chirp has sounded, proceed to next 3 sensors in following order, righthand front, righthand rear and lefthand rear.
9. After all sensor ID's have been learned, exit learn mode by turning OFF ignition.
10. After learn mode has been exited, adjust all tire pressures to recommended psi.

DEVILLE & SEVILLE

The Remote Control Door Lock Receiver (RCDLR) will cancel the learn mode if more than one minute has passed and no sensor IDs have been learned, more than five minutes has passed for the entire procedure, all four sensor IDs have been learned, vehicle battery voltage is less than eight volts, or ignition is turned OFF. If the learn mode is cancelled before any sensor IDs are

learned, the RCDLR will remember all previously stored sensor IDs and their locations. As soon as the RCDLR learns the first sensor ID, all previously stored IDs are erased from the RCDLRs memory.

1. Turn ON ignition, with engine OFF.
2. Simultaneously press keyless entry transmitter's lock and unlock buttons until a horn chirp sounds indicating Tire Pressure Monitor (TPM) mode has been enabled. If sensor learn mode cannot be enabled, ensure TPM option is enabled in RCDLR. If the horn chirp does not sound after 15 seconds, remove and then replace sensor activating tool No. J 41760, or equivalent, over valve stem.
3. Beginning with left front tire, hold sensor activating tool No. J 41760, or equivalent, over left front valve stem until a horn chirp sounds.
4. After horn chirp sounds, proceed to right front, right rear and left rear in that order.
5. After left rear sensor ID is learned, a double horn chirp will sound indicating all four sensor IDs have been learned.
6. Turn OFF the ignition.

DTS, LUCERNE & STS

If using pressure increase/decrease method, following procedure must be completed within 15 minutes from when vehicle is stationary after being driven at 20 mph, or greater for 10 seconds.

Before proceeding with steps below, ensure that no other learn procedure is being performed simultaneously, or that no tire pressures are being adjusted on another TPM equipped vehicle within close proximity.

1. Place ignition switch in ACC mode.
2. Simultaneously press keyless entry transmitter's lock and unlock buttons until a horn chirp sounds, or use scan tool and select "Special Functions/Sensor Learn Mode Enable/Enable" soft key. A horn chirp will sound indicating mode has been enabled. When increasing tire pressure do not exceed maximum inflation pressure as noted on tire sidewall.
3. Starting with lefthand side front tire, hold antenna of tool No. J-46079 or equivalent, against tire sidewall close to wheel rim at valve stem location then press and release activate button and wait for a horn chirp, or increase/decrease tire pressure for 5-8 seconds then wait for a horn chirp.
4. Horn chirp may occur before 5-8 second pressure increase/decrease time period has been reached, or up to 30 seconds after 5-8 second pressure increase/decrease time period has been reached.
5. After a horn chirp has sounded, proceed to next 3 sensors in following order, righthand front, righthand rear and lefthand rear.
6. After lefthand rear sensor has been learned a double horn chirp will sound indicating all sensors have been learned.
7. With ignition switch, select OFF mode to exit learn mode.

8. After learn mode has been exited, adjust all tire pressures to recommended pressure.

GRAND PRIX & LACROSSE

2004-06

After resetting, the tire pressure monitoring (TPM) system requires vehicle to be driven up to 5 miles on a flat, smooth road straight line driving in each of the 4 speed ranges to complete the calibration process.

1. Set all tire pressures to recommended psi.
2. Turn ON ignition, with engine OFF.
3. Press vehicle information button until TIRE INFLATION MONITOR SYSTEM PRESS (down/left arrow) SWITCH TO RESET is displayed.
4. If system is being reset due to a low tire pressure condition, press and hold down/left arrow button until TIRE INFLATION MONITOR SYSTEM HAS BEEN RESET is displayed. If system is being reset due to a tire rotation, press and hold down/left arrow button for 5 seconds.
5. Release down/left arrow button and TIRE PRESSURE NORMAL is displayed.

2007-08

Less Scan Tool

1. Place ignition switch in RUN mode.
2. Simultaneously press keyless entry transmitters LOCK and UNLOCK buttons until a horn chirp sounds.
3. When increasing tire pressure, do not exceed the maximum inflation pressure as noted on tire sidewall.
4. Beginning with left front tire, hold antenna of Tire Pressure Monitor Diagnostic Tool No. J-46079, or equivalent, against tire sidewall close to wheel rim at valve stem location.
5. Press and release activate button and wait for a horn chirp, or increase/decrease tire pressure for 5-8 seconds then wait for a horn chirp. Horn chirp may occur before 5-8 second pressure increase/decrease time period has been reached, or up to 30 seconds after 5-8 second pressure increase/decrease time period has been reached.
6. After a horn chirp has sounded, proceed right front tire, right rear tire, then the left rear tire.
7. After left rear sensor has been learned, a double horn chirp will sound indicating all sensors have been learned.
8. Place ignition switch in OFF mode to exit learn mode.
9. After learn mode has been exited, adjust all tire pressures to recommended pressure.

With Scan Tool

1. Place ignition switch in RUN mode.
2. Connect a suitably programmed scan tool to Data Link Connector (DLC) and select "Special Functions/Sensor Learn Mode Enable/Enable" soft key. A horn chirp will sound indicating the mode has been enabled.

3. Beginning with left front tire, hold antenna of Tire Pressure Monitor Diagnostic Tool No. J-46079, or equivalent, against tire sidewall close to wheel rim at valve stem location.
4. Press and release activate button and wait for a horn chirp, or increase/decrease tire pressure for 5-8 seconds then wait for a horn chirp. Horn chirp may occur before 5-8 second pressure increase/decrease time period has been reached, or up to 30 seconds after 5-8 second pressure increase/decrease time period has been reached.
5. After a horn chirp has sounded, proceed right front tire, right rear tire, then the left rear tire.
6. After left rear sensor has been learned, a double horn chirp will sound indicating all sensors have been learned.
7. Place ignition switch in OFF mode to exit learn mode.
8. After learn mode has been exited, adjust all tire pressures to recommended pressure.

IMPALA & MONTE CARLO

2004-05 USING RDS RADIO

The "Tire Low Tire Pressure" indicator will be turn On when the pressure in one of the tires is 12 psi. lower or higher then the other three tires.

1. Inflate all tires to specifications.
2. Place ignition switch in On position.
3. Place radio in Off position.
4. Depress and hold DISP button until SETTINGS is displayed.
5. Press SEEK up or down buttons until TIRE MON is displayed.
6. Press PREV or NEXT buttons until RESET is displayed.
7. Press DISP button, a chime will sound and DONE will be displayed.
8. Scroll menu until EXIT is displayed, then press DISP button. A chime will sound to indicate system exit from TIRE MON.

2004-05 USING LIGHT SWITCH

The "Tire Low Tire Pressure" indicator will be turn On when the pressure in one of the tires is 12 psi. lower or higher then the other three tires.

1. Inflate all tires to specifications.
2. Place ignition switch in On position.
3. Cycle light switch from Off to Parking Lamps 3 times within 5 seconds.

2006-08 LESS KEYLESS ENTRY

1. Place ignition switch in RUN position.
2. Press and release driver information center (DIC) INFO button until RELEARN TIRE POSITIONS message appears on DIC display.
3. Press and hold SET/RESET button until a double horn chirp sounds and DIC displays a TIRE LEARNING ACTIVE message indicating Learn Mode has been enabled, left front turn signal will also be illuminated.
4. Starting with left front tire, learn tire pressure, using the following method:
5. Increase/decrease tire pressure for

8-10 seconds then wait for a horn chirp. Note: Horn chirp may occur before or up to 30 seconds after the 8-10 second pressure increase/decrease time period has been reached.
6. After horn chirp has sounded and right front turn signal is illuminated, repeat above step for remaining 3 sensors in following order: Right front, right rear & left rear.
7. After Left rear sensor has been learned, a double horn chirp will sound indicating all sensors have been learned.
8. Turn OFF ignition to exit learn mode.
9. After learn mode has been exited, adjust all tires to recommended pressures.

2006-08 WITH KEYLESS ENTRY

1. Place ignition switch in ACCY position.
2. Simultaneously press keyless entry transmitters lock and unlock buttons until a double horn chirp sounds indicating Learn Mode has been enabled, left front turn signal will also be illuminated.
3. Starting with left front tire, learn tire pressure, using the following method:
4. Increase/decrease tire pressure for 8-10 seconds then wait for a horn chirp. Note: Horn chirp may occur before or up to 30 seconds after the 8-10 second pressure increase/decrease time period has been reached.
5. After horn chirp has sounded and right front turn signal is illuminated, repeat above step for remaining 3 sensors in following order: Right front, right rear & left rear.
6. After Left rear sensor has been learned, a double horn chirp will sound indicating all sensors have been learned.
7. Turn OFF ignition to exit learn mode.
8. After learn mode has been exited, adjust all tires to recommended pressures.

LESABRE & PARK AVENUE

The "Tire Low Tire Pressure" indicator will be turn On when the pressure in one of the tires is 12 psi. lower or higher then the other three tires.

1. Inflate all tires to specifications.
2. Place ignition switch in On position.
3. Press GAUGE INFO button until TIRE PRESSURE is displayed.
4. Depress and hold RESET button until TIRE PRESSURE RESET is displayed.
5. Release RESET button, TIRE PRESSURE NORMAL should be displayed.

XLR

The RCDLR will cancel the TPM learn mode if more than 1 minute passes and no sensors have been learned, or if more than 5 minutes pass for the entire procedure. If the learn mode is cancelled before any sensor ID's are learned, the RCDLR will remember all previously stored ID's and their locations. As soon as the RCDLR learns the first sensor ID, all previously stored ID's are erased from the RCDLR's memory.

1. Place ignition switch in ACC position.
2. Simultaneously press keyless entry transmitter lock and unlock buttons until a double horn chirp sounds, indicating TPM learn mode has been enabled. **If a horn chirp does not sound after 15 seconds using J-41760 or J-46079 tool, repeat step 1.**
3. Starting with lefthand side front tire, hold antenna of J-46079 TPM tool against tire sidewall close to wheel rim at valve stem location then press and release the "Activate" button and wait for a horn chirp, or hold J 41760 sensor activating tool over lefthand side front valve stem until a horn chirp sounds.
4. After horn chirp sounds, proceed to next 3 sensors in following order, righthand front, righthand rear and lefthand rear.
5. After lefthand rear sensor is learned, a double horn chirp will sound indicating all sensor ID's have been learned.
6. Select OFF position on ignition switch to exit TPM learn mode.

VIBE
2004–07

After resetting, the tire pressure monitoring (TPM) system requires 60 minutes or more of driving at a speed 19 mph or above to complete the calibration process to have full capability for detecting a tire pressure condition.

1. Inflate all tires to specifications.
2. Place ignition switch in On position.
3. Press and hold tire pressure warning reset switch for three seconds until tire pressure warning indicator blinks three times.
4. Ensure tire pressure warning indicator goes out.
5. If tire pressure warning indicator does not blink, repeat procedure starting at step 2.
6. Drive vehicle for 60 minutes or more at a speed of 19 mph.
7. Verify system has initialized, turn ON ignition with engine OFF and observe tire pressure warning indicator.

2008

It is necessary to register the sensor IDs in the tire pressure control module, when replacing any of the sensors and/or the control module. Prepare all sensor ID data before starting registration procedure.

1. Read and record sensor IDs that are stored in control module.
2. If sensor IDs cannot be read due to component malfunctions, remove tires from wheels and record IDs located on sensors. Important: When replacing a sensor, record the 7-digit ID number on the sensor.
3. With scan tool, input sensor IDs and transmit them to control module.
4. Confirm that tire pressure data is displayed for all tires.
5. Confirm that tire pressure warning light is Off.

Pressure Monitor Sensor Replacement

Ensure cap and valve are placed in a dry and clean location after removal. The cap is aluminum and valve is nickel plated to prevent corrosion and are not to be substituted with any other material.

When using a machine to separate tire and bead from wheel, position bead breaking tool 90° from valve stem to ensure sensor is not damaged.

1. Raise and support vehicle using suitable lift.
2. Remove tire and wheel assembly, then the tire from wheel.
3. Remove TPM sensor nut, then the sensor.
4. Reverse procedure to install.

TIGHTENING SPECIFICATIONS

Year	Component	Torque Ft. Lbs.
CTS, DTS, STS & XLR		
2004–06	Tire Pressure Sensor	62①
	Wheel Lug Nuts	100
EXCEPT CTS, DTS, STS & XLR		
2004–06	Tire Pressure Sensor	46①
	Wheel Lug Nuts	100
EXCEPT VIBE		
2007–08	Tire Pressure Sensor	62①
	Wheel Lug Nuts	100
VIBE		
2007–08	Tire Pressure Sensor	36①
	Wheel Lug Nuts	76

① — Inch lbs.

ENGINE REBUILDING SPECIFICATIONS

NOTE: For Engine Tightening Specifications, Refer To The Engine Section In The Appropriate Chassis Chapter Of This Manual.

INDEX

	Page No.		Page No.		Page No.
Balance Shaft	29-5	Cylinder Head, Valve Guide &		Valve Springs	29-2
Camshaft	29-3	Valve Seats	29-1	Valves	29-3
Crankshaft, Bearings & Rods	29-4	Oil Pump	29-7		
Cylinder Block	29-6	Pistons, Pins & Rings	29-5		

CYLINDER HEAD, VALVE GUIDE & VALVE SEATS

All Measurements Given In Inches Unless Otherwise Specified

Engine (VIN①)	Year	Cylinder Head Warpage Limit	Cylinder Head Height/ Thickness	Valve Guides Inside Diameter	Stem To Guide Clearance Intake	Stem To Guide Clearance Exhaust	Seat Angle, Deg.	Seat Width Intake	Seat Width Exhaust	Runout
1.6L (6)	2004–08	.0020	5.2790–5.2850	.2360–.2370	—	—	44.50–45.00	.0461–.0618	.0550–.0710	.0197
1.8L (L)	2004–07	.0080	—	.2169–.2177	.0010–.0039	.0011–.0039	45.00	.1300	.1300	—
1.8L (8)	2004–08	.0080	—	.2169–.2177	.0010–.0039	.0011–.0039	45.00	.1300	.1300	—
2.0L (P)	2005–08	.0040	—	.2362–.2367	.0012–.0022	.0020–.0026	—	—	—	—
2.2L DOHC (F)	2004–08	.0040	—	.2362–.2367	.0012–.0022	.0020–.0026	45.00	—	—	.0020
2.4L (B)	2006–08	.0040	—	.2362–.2367	.0012–.0022	.0020–.0026	—	—	—	.0020
2.6L (M)	2004	④	5.2800	—	.0012–.0024	.0016–.0028	89.50	.0394–.0551	.0051–.0708	.0020
2.8L (T)	2005–08	.0020	—	.2362–.2370	.0010–.0026	.0014–.0030	45.00	.0394–.0551	.0551–.0709	.0020
3.0L (R)	2004–05	⑤	5.2720–5.2800	.2362–.2367	.0012–.0022	.0016–.0026	45.00	.0394–.0551	.0551–.0709	—
3.1L (J)	2004–06	②	—	.3150	.0010–.0027	.0010–.0027	46.00	.0610–.0710	.0670–.0790	.0015
3.2L (N)	2004	④	5.2800	—	.0012–.0024	.0016–.0028	89.50	.0394–.0551	.0051–.0708	.0020
3.4L (E)	2004–05	②	—	.3150	.0010–.0027	.0010–.0027	46.00	.0610–.0710	.0670–0790	.0015
3.5L (8)	2004–08	③	—	.3150	.0010–.0027	.0010–.0027	46.00	.0610–.0710	.0607–.0790	—
3.6L (7)	2004–08	.0020	—	.2362–.2370	.0010–.0026	.0014–.0030	45.00	.0394–.5510	.0551–.0709	.0020
3.8L (K, 1, 2 & 4)	2004–08	.0040	4.0745–4.1015	.3150–.3158	.0012–.0028	.0014–.0029	45.00	.0600–.0800	.0900–.1100	.0020
3.9L (1)	2006–08	②	—	—	.0010–.0027	.0010–.0027	46.00	.0610–.0710	.0670–.0790	.0020
4.4L (D)	2006–08	.0039	5.3543	.2331–.2339	.0011–.0043	.0020–.0047	45.75	.0165–.0323	.0512–.0669	.0003
4.6L (A, Y & 9)	2004–08	.0039	5.3540	.2350–.2358	.0011–.0043	.0020–.0047	45.75	.0165–.0323	.0512–.0669	.0020
5.3L (C)	2006–08	0040	4.7320	.3130	.0037	.0037	46.00	.0400	.0700	.0020
5.7L (G & S)	2004–05	.0030	4.7320	—	.0010–.0037	.0010–.0037	46.00	.0400	.0700	.0020

Continued

CYLINDER HEAD, VALVE GUIDE & VALVE SEATS—Continued

All Measurements Given In Inches Unless Otherwise Specified

Engine (VIN①)	Year	Cylinder Head Warpage Limit	Cylinder Head Height/ Thickness	Valve Guides				Valve Seats			
				Inside Diameter	Stem To Guide Clearance		Seat Angle, Deg.	Seat Width			Runout
					Intake	Exhaust		Intake	Exhaust	
6.0L (U)	2005–08	.0080	—	—	.0010–.0037	.0010–.0037	46.00	.0400	.0700	.0020
7.0L (Y/E)	2006–08	.0080	5.0350	.3130–.3140	.0037	.0037	45.00	.0490–.0610	.0670–.0790	.0020

① — The eighth digit of Vehicle Identification Number (VIN) denotes engine code.

② — .003 inch per 6.000 inches.
③ — .0019 inch per 6 inches.

④ — .001 inch per 3.917 inches.
⑤ — .002 inch per 3.937 inches.

VALVE SPRINGS

All Measurements Given In Inches Unless Otherwise Specified

Engine (VIN①)	Year	Free Length	Installed Height	Seated Pressure, Lbs. @ Inches	Comp. Pressure, Lbs. @ Inches	Out Of Square Limit
1.6L (6)	2004–08	—	—	—	—	—
1.8L (L)	2004–07	②	—	—	—	.063
1.8L (8)	2004–08	②	—	—	—	.063
2.0L (P)	2005–08	—	—	55.1–60.9 @ 1.275	118.0–129.3 @ 1.279	—
2.2L DOHC (F)	2004–08	1.5430	1.2795	55.1–60.9 @ 1.2795	118.0–129.3 @ 1.2795	—
2.4L (B)	2006–08	—	—	—	—	—
2.6L (M)	2004	1.6500	1.3400	61.0 @ 1.3400	147.0 @ .9450	—
2.8L (T)	2005–08	1.6555–1.7657	1.3779	—	—	—
3.0L (R)	2004–05	—	1.3380	56.6 @ 1.3380	—	—
3.1L (J)	2004–06	1.8900	1.7010	75.0 @ 1.7010	230.0 @ 1.2600	—
3.2L (N)	2004	1.6500	1.3400	61.0 @ 1.3400	147.0 @ .9450	—
3.4L (E)	2004–05	1.8900	1.7010	75.0 @ 1.7010	230.0 @ 1.2600	—
3.5L (8)	2004–08	1.9100	1.7400	77.0 @ 1.7400	234 @ 1.299	—
3.6L (7)	2004–08	1.6555–1.7657	1.3779	56.0–61.0 @ 1.3779	136.0–147.0 @ .9449	—
3.8L (K, 1, 2 & 4)	2004–08	1.9600	1.6900–1.7500	75.0 @ 1.7200	228.0 @ 1.2770	—
3.9L (1)	2006–08	1.8900	1.7010	75.5 @ 1.7010	230.0 @ 1.2600	—
4.4L (D)	2006–08	1.6059–1.7201	1.3780	47.5–52.5 @ 1.3780	130.2–141.9 @ .9650	—
4.6L (A, Y & 9)	2004–08	1.6059–1.7201	1.3780	47.5–52.5 @ 1.3780	130.2–141.9 @ .9650	—
5.3L (C)	2006–08	2.0800	1.8000	76.0 @ 1.8000	220.0 @ 1.3200	—
5.7L (G & S)	2004–05	2.0800	1.8000	76.0 @ 1.8000	220.0 @ 1.3200	—
6.0L (U)	2005–08	2.0800	1.8000	76.0 @ 1.8000	220.0 @ 1.3200	—
7.0L (Y/E)	2006–08	2.3130	1.9590	76.0 @ 1.8000	220.0 @ 1.3200	—

① — The eighth digit of Vehicle Identification Number (VIN) denotes engine code.

② — Intake, 1.830 inches; exhaust, 1.831 inches.

VALVES

All Measurements Given In Inches Unless Otherwise Specified

Engine (VIN①)	Year	Stem Diameter		Valve Lash, Cold		Face Angle	Margin
		Intake	Exhaust	Intake	Exhaust		
1.6L (6)	2004–08	.2340–.2350	.2336–.2342	—	—	45.00	—
1.8L (L)	2004–07	.2150–.2155	.2143–.2153	.0031–.0071	.0087–.0126	45.00	—
1.8L (8)	2004–08	.2150–.2155	.2143–.2153	.0060–.0100	.0100–.0140	45.00	—
2.0L (P)	2005–08	.2344–.2355	.2337–.2343	②	②.	—	—
2.2L DOHC (F)	2004–08	.2344–.2355	.2337–.2343	②	②	45.00	—
2.4L (B)	2006–08	.2344–.2355	.2337–.2343	.0012–.0022	.0020–.0026	—	—
2.6L (M)	2004	.2345–.2350	.2341–.2346	—	—	89.50	—
2.8L (T)	2005–08	.2344–.2352	.2341–.2348	—	—	44.25	—
3.0L (R)	2004–05	.2344–.2350	.2341–.2346	—	—	45.00	—
3.1L (J)	2004–06	.3137–.3142	.3128–.3136	—	—	46.00	③
3.2L (N)	2004	.2345–.2350	.2341–.2346	—	—	89.50	—
3.4L (E)	2004–05	—	—	②	②	45.00	③
3.5L (8)	2004–08	—	—	②	②	45.00	—
3.6L (7)	2004–08	.2344–.2352	.2341–.2348	②	②	44.25	—
3.8L (K, 1, 2 & 4)	2004–08	.3129–.3136	.3129–.3136	②	②	46.00	.0250
3.9L (1)	2006–08	—	—	②	②	46.00	—
4.4L (D)	2006–08	.2331–.2339	.2331–.2339	②	②	45.00	—
4.6L (A, Y & 9)	2004–08	.2331–.2339	.2331–.2339	②	②	45.00	—
5.3L (C)	2006–08	.3130–.3144	.3130–.3144	②	②	46.00	—
5.7L (G & S)	2004–05	.3130–.3144	.3130–.3144	②	②	45.00	.0500
6.0L (U)	2005–08	.3130–.3144	.3130–.3144	②	②	45.00	—
7.0L (Y/E)	2006–08	.3130–.3140	3130–.3140	②	②	45.00	—

① — The eighth digit of Vehicle Identification Number (VIN) denotes engine code.

② — Hydraulic lifters, zero lash.

③ — Intake, .083 inch; exhaust, .106 inch.

CAMSHAFT

All Measurements Given In Inches Unless Otherwise Specified

Engine (VIN①)	Year	Camshaft Journal Diameter	Maximum Journal Runout	Camshaft Bearing Clearance	Camshaft Endplay	Lifter Bore Diameter	Lifter Diameter	Lifter To Bore Clearance
1.6L (6)	2004–08	④	—	—	.0039–.0079	—	—	—
1.8L (L)	2004–07	②	.0012	.0014–.0039	.0016–.0059	—	—	—
1.8L (8)	2004–08	②	.0012	.0014–.0039	.0016–.0059	—	—	—
2.0L (P)	2005–08	1.0604–1.0614	—	—	.0016–.0057	.4730–.4739	—	—
2.2L DOHC (F)	2004–08	1.0604–1.0614	.0010	.0016–.0034	.0016–.0057	.4730–.4739	.4719–.4724	.0005–.0020
2.4L (B)	2006–08	1.0604–1.0614	—	—	.0016–.0057	.4730–.4739	.4719–.4724	.0005–.0020
2.6L (M)	2004	1.1000–1.1008	.0015	.0035	.0016–.0057	—	—	—
2.8L (T)	2005–08	③	.0002	.0016–.0033	.0018–.0085	.4728–.4736	.4523–.4724	.0015–.0016
3.0L (R)	2004–05	1.0990–1.1010	.0023	.0015–.0020	.0016–.0057	—	1.2976–1.282	.0010–.0030
3.1L (J)	2004–06	1.8680–1.8690	.0012	.0020–.0040	.0020	—	.8420–.8427	.0005–.0027
3.2L (N)	2004	1.1000–1.1008	.0015	.0035	.0016–.0057	—	—	—
3.4L (E)	2004–05	1.8680–1.8690	.0010	.0010–.0039	—	.8430–.8440	—	—
3.5L (8)	2004–08	1.8680–1.8690	.0010	—	—	—	—	—
3.6L (7)	2004–08	③	.0002	.0016–.0033	.0018–.0085	.4728–.4736	.4719–.4724	.0015–.0016
3.8L (K, 1, 2 & 4)	2004–08	1.8478–1.8492	.00025	.0016–.0047	—	.8435–.8445	.8420–.8430	—
3.9L (1)	2006–08	2.024–2.025	.0010	—	—	.8430–.8440	—	—
4.4L (D)	2006–08	1.0610–1.0619	.0020	.0016–.0035	.0050–.0087	.4730–.4739	.4719–.4724	.0015–.0016
4.6L (A, Y & 9)	2004–08	1.0610–1.0619	.0020	.0016–.0035	.0050–.0087	.4730–.4739	.4719–.4724	.0015–.0016
5.3L (C)	2006–08	2.1640–2.1660	.0020	—	.0010–.0120	.8430–.8440	—	—
5.7L (G & S)	2004–05	2.1640–2.1660	.0010	—	.0010–.0120	.8430–.8440	—	—
6.0L (U)	2005–08	2.164–2.166	.0010	—	.0020	.8430–.8440	—	—
7.0L (Y/E)	2006–08	2.164–2.166	.0020	—	0010–.0120	.8430–.8440	—	—

ENGINE REBUILDING SPECIFICATIONS

① — The eighth digit of Vehicle Identification Number (VIN) denotes engine code.

② — Journal No. 1, 1.3563–1.3569 inches; journals Nos. 2–5, 1.1003–1.1010 inches.

③ — Journal No. 1, 1.3754–1.3764 inches; journals Nos. 2–4, 1.0605–1.0614 inches.

④ — Journal No. 1, 1.185–1.1791 inches; journal Nos. 2–5, 1.0604–1.0610 inches.

CRANKSHAFT, BEARINGS & RODS

All Measurements Given In Inches Unless Otherwise Specified

| Engine (VIN①) | Year | Crankshaft | | | | | Bearing Clearance | | Connecting Rod Side Clearance |
		Main Bearing Journal Diameter	Connecting Rod Journal Diameter	Max. Out of Round	Max. Taper	Crankshaft Endplay	Main Bearings	Connecting Rod Bearings	
1.6L (6)	2004–08	2.164–2.165	1.6900	.00015	.00019	.0020–.0110	.00100–.00165	.0007–.0027	.0027–.0090
1.8L (L)	2004–07	1.8892–1.8898	1.7713–1.7717	.00080	.00080	.0016–.0118	.0008–.0118	.0011–.0031	.0063–.0138
1.8L (8)	2004–08	1.8893–1.8898	1.73197–1.73228	.00040	.00040	.0016–.0118	.0008–.0118	.0011–.0031	.0063–.0138
2.0L (P)	2005–08	2.2045–2.2050	1.9291–1.9297	—	—	.0012–.0150	.0012–.0026	.0011–.0027	.0028–.0146
2.2L DOHC (F)	2004–08	2.2045–2.2050	1.92910–1.9297	—	—	.0012–.0150	.0012–.0026	.0011–.0029	.0028–.0146
2.4L (B)	2006–07	2.2045–2.2050	1.9291–1.9297	—	—	0012–.0150	.0012–.0026	.0011–.0027	.0028–.0146
2.6L (M)	2004	2.676–2.667	1.929–1.928	.00119	.00119	.0039–.00795	.0006–.0017	.0004–.0024	.0027–.0110
2.8L (T)	2005–08	2.6768–2.6775	2.2044–2.2050	.00020	.00020	.0039–.0130	0004–.0024	.0004–.0028	.0374–.0140
3.0L (R)	2004–05	2.6763–2.6770	1.92700–1.92800	.00120	—	.0004–.0300	.0006–.0017	.0005–.0024	.0027–.0110
3.1L (J)	2004–06	2.6473–2.6483	1.99870–1.99940	.00020	.00020	.0024–.0083	②	.0007–.0170	.0100–.0150
3.2L (N)	2004	2.676–2.667	2.6764–2.6770	.00119	.00119	.0039–.00795	.0006–.0017	.0008–.0024	.0027–.0110
3.4L (E)	2004–05	2.6473–2.6483	1.99870–1.9994	.00020	.00020	.0024–.0083	②	.0007–.0024	.0070–.0170
3.5L (8)	2004–08	2.6473–2.6483	2.2480–2.2490	.00020	.00030	.0024–.0083	.0008–.0025	.0007–.0170	.0080–.0090
3.6L (7)	2004–08	2.6768–2.6775	2.2044–2.2050	.00020	.00020	.0039–.0130	.0004–.0024	.0013	.01590
3.8L (K, 1, 2 & 4)	2004–08	2.4988–2.4998	2.24870–2.2499	.00025	.00035	.0030–.0110	③	.0005–.0026	.0040–.0200
3.9L (1)	2006–08	2.6473–2.6483	2.2480–2.2490	.00020	.00020	.0024–.0083	.0008–.0025	.0007–.0170	.0080–.0090
4.4L (D)	2006–08	2.5335–2.5341	2.21390–2.1245	.00020	.00020	.0020–.0197	.0006–.0025	.0010–.0030	.0079–.0197
4.6L (A, Y & 9)	2004–08	2.5335–2.5341	2.12390–2.1245	.00020	.00020	.0020–.0197	.0006–.0025	.0010–.0030	.0079–.0197
5.3L (C)	2006–08	2.5580–2.559	2.0991–2.0999	.000118–.00031	.00040–.00780	.0015–.0078	.0008–.0025	.0009–.0030	.00433–.0200
5.7L (G & S)	2004–05	2.5580–2.559	2.0987–2.0999	.000118–.00031	.00039–.00780	.0015–.0078	.0008–.0025	.0009–.0030	.0043–.0200
6.0L (U)	2005–08	2.5580–2.5590	2.0987–2.0999	2.0987–2.0999	.00040–.000780	.0010	.0080–.0025	.0009–.0030	.00433–.0200
7.0L (Y/E)	2006–08	2.5580–2.5590	2.0987–2.0999	2.0987–2.0999	.00040–.000780	.0015–.0078	.0080–.0025	.0009–.0030	.00433–.0200

① — The eighth digit of Vehicle Identification Number (VIN) denotes engine code.

② — Except No. 3, .0008–.0025 inch; No. 3, .0012–.0030 inch.

③ — No 1. , .0070–.0016 inch; Nos. 2–4, .0009–.0018 inch.

BALANCE SHAFT

All Measurements Given In Inches, Unless Otherwise Specified.

Engine Liter (VIN①)	Year	Bearing			Bushing		End Play
		Bore Diameter	Journal Diameter	Clearance	Journal Diameter	Clearance	
2.0L (P)	2005–08	④	.7474–.7882	.0013–.0040	1.4458–1.4466	.0013–.0040	.0020–.0118
2.2L DOHC (F)	2004–08	1.6535–1.6542	.7874–.7882	.0012–.0025	1.4458–1.4466	.0013–.0040	.0020–.0118
2.4L (B)	2006–08	1.6526–1.6534	.7874–.7882	.0012–.0025	1.4458–1.4466	.0013–.0040	—
3.8L (K, 1, 2 & 4)	2004–08	②	1.4994–1.5002	③	—	—	0–.0067

DOHC — Dual Overhead Cams.
① — Eighth digit of Vehicle Identification Number (Vehicle Identification Number (VIN) denotes engine code.

② — Front, 2.0462–2.0472 inches; rear, 1.8735–1.8745 inches.

③ — Front, 0–.001 inch; rear, .0005–.0048 inch.

④ — Inside carrier, .7894–.7899 inch; outside carrier, 1.6562–1.6534 inches.

PISTONS, PINS & RINGS

All Measurements Given In Inches Unless Otherwise Specified

Engine (VIN①)	Year	Piston Diameter	Piston Clearance	Piston Pin Diameter⑨	Piston Pin To Piston Clearance	Piston Ring End Gap			Piston Ring Side Clearance		
						Comp.		Oil	Comp.		Oil
						Top	2nd		Top	2nd	
1.6L (6)	2004–08	3.1090	.0008–.0016	.7080	—	0060–.0120	0120–.0190	—	0019–.0031	.0020–.0030	—
1.8L (L)	2004–08	3.2274–3.2281	.0003–.0039	—	—	.0098–.0413	.0138–.0472	.0059–.0413	.0009–.0028	.0012–.0028	—
1.8L (8)	2004–08	3.2274–3.2281	.0003–.0039	—	—	.0098–.0413	.0138–.0472	.0059–..0413	.0009–.0028	.0012–.0028	—
2.0L (P)	2005–08	3.3845–3.3851⑪	.0004–.0016	.7872–.7874	.0001–.0005	.0080–.0160	.0140–.0220	.010–.030	.0015–.0031	.0012–.0027	.0035–.0042
2.2L DOHC (F)	2004–08	3.3845–3.3851⑪	.0004–.0016	.7872–.7874	.0001–.0005	.0080–.0160	.0140–.0220	.0100–.0300	.0461–.0469	.0579–,0587	.0035–.0042
2.4L (B)	2006–08	3.3845–3.3851⑪	.0004–.0016	.7872–.7874	.0001–.0005	.0080–.0160	.0140–.0220	.0100–.0300	.0461–.0469	.0579–,0587	.0035–.0042
2.6L (M)	2004	3.2732–3.2752	.0010–.0018	.8263–.8267	.0004–.0006	.0118–.0196	.0118–.0196	.0158–.0551	.00079–.0024	.00079–.0024	.00079–.0024
2.8L (T)	2005–08	3.6990–3.6998	.0010–.0021	.9448–.9449	.0002–.0005	.0059–.0118	.0110–.0189	.0059–.0236	.0012–.0026	.0006–.0024	.0012–.0067
3.0L (R)	2004–05	3.3834–3.3854	.0010–.0018	.8267	.0001–.0003	.0118–.0196	—	.0157–.0551	.0008–.0015	—	.0004–.0012
3.1L (J)	2004–06	3.503–3.504	.0003–.0018	—	—	.0060–.0140	.0197–.0280	.0090–.0400	.002–.0033	.002–.0035	.0028–.0037
3.2L (N)	2004	3.4425–3.4445	.0010–.0018	.8264–.8268	.0004–.0006	.0118–.0196	.0118–.0196	.0158–.0551	.00079–.0024	.00079–.0024	.00079–.0024
3.4L (E)	2004–05	⑩	⑦	.9053–.9054	.0001–.0006	.0060–.0140	.0188–.0291	.0098–.0303	.0020–.033	.0020–.0031	.0028–.0037
3.5L (8)	2004–08	3.699–3.701	–.00101–.0030	.9447–.9448	.0003–.0006	.0070–.0150	.0190–.0290	.0100–.0290	.001–.003	.002–.003	.0040
3.6L (7)	2004–08	3.6990–3.6998	.0010–.0021	.9448–.9449	.0002–.0005	.0059–.0118	.0110–.0189	.0098–.0295	.0012–.0026	.0002–.0013	.0083–.0155
3.8L (K & 2)	2004–08	3.7969–3.7991	.0004–.0036	.8659–.8661	.00008–.00051	.0100–.0180	.0230–.0330	.0100–.0300	.0013–.0031	.0013–.0031	.0009–.0079
3.8L (1 & 4)	2004–08	3.7966–3.8003	.0008–.0039	②	.00061–.00026	.0100–.0180	.0230–.0330	.0100–.0300	.0013–.0031	.0013–.0031	.0009–.0079
3.9L (1)	2006–08	3.896–3.897	.0003–.0018	.9420–.9430	.00008–.0004	.006–.0110	.0090–00.0170	.0600–0.0250	.0010–.0020	.0007–.0020	.0040
4.4L (D)	2006–08	3.5814–3.5823⑬	.0006–.0012	.9448–.9449	.0001–.0005	.0059–.0118	.0118–.0177	.0098–.0197	.0016–.0037	.0016–.0037	⑫
4.6L (A, Y & 9)	2004–08	3.6597–3.6603⑬	.0008–.0020	.9056–.9058	.0001–.0005	.0098–.0157	.0138–.0196	.0098–.0299	.0016–.0037	.0016–.0037	⑫

Continued

PISTONS, PINS & RINGS—Continued
All Measurements Given In Inches Unless Otherwise Specified

Engine (VIN①)	Year	Piston Diameter	Piston Clearance	Piston Pin Diameter⑨	Piston Pin To Piston Clearance	Piston Ring End Gap			Piston Ring Side Clearance		
						Comp.		Oil	Comp.		Oil
						Top	2nd		Top	2nd	
5.3L (C)	2006–08	3.7790–3.780	.0028	.9447–.9448	.00008–.00004	.009–.0196	0173–.0300	.0070–.0320	00157–.00335	00157–.0031	.0005–.0078
5.7L (G & S)	2004–05	④	③	⑤	⑥	.0090–.0196	.0173–.0300	.0070–.0320	.00157–.00330	.0020–.0034	−.0003–.0069
6.0L (U)	2005–08	4.0000–4.0010⑭	⑧	.9430	.00027–.00086	.0080–.0160	.0150–.0270	.0090–.0310	.0012–.0040	.0014–.0031	.0005–.0079
7.0L (Y/E)	2006–08	4.1240–4.1260⑭	.0010	0.9250–.9250	.0003–.0009	.0087–.0185	.0157–.0259	.0098–.0299	.0012–.0040	.0014–.0031	.0005–.0079

① — The eighth digit of Vehicle Identification Number (VIN) denotes engine code.

② — VIN 1, .90531–.90551 inch; VIN 4, .8659–.8661 inch.

③ — Non–coated, .0005–.0019 inch; coated, .0005–.0029 inch.

④ — Non–coated, 3.8964–3.897 inches; coated (measure over coating), 3.897–3.899 inches.

⑤ — 2004, first design, .9447–.9448 inch; 2004, second design & 2005–08, .943 inch

⑥ — 2004, first design, .0004–.0008 inch; 2004, second design & 2005–08, .00008–.00040 inch.

⑦ — Cylinders Nos. 1–4, .0006–.0036 inch; Cylinders Nos. 5 & 6, −.0003–.0036 inch.

⑧ — Production, .0009–.0012 inch; Service limit w/skirt coating worn off, .00094–.0031 inch.

⑨ — Pistons & pins are matched set & should be replaced as an assembly.

⑩ — Cylinders Nos. 1–4, 3.619–3.622 inches; Cylinders Nos. 5 & 6, 3.619–3.623 inches.

⑪ — Measured .5708 inch from bottom of piston.

⑫ — Zero clearance; side sealing ring.

⑬ — Measured 1.6353 inches from top of piston.

⑭ — Measured over skirt coating.

CYLINDER BLOCK
All Measurements Given In Inches Unless Otherwise Specified

Engine (VIN①)	Year	Cylinder Bore Diameter	Cylinder Bore Taper Max.	Cylinder Bore Out of Round Max.
1.6L (6)	2004–08	3.1102	.00025	.00025
1.8L (L)	2004–07	3.1102–3.1107	—	—
1.8L (8)	2004–08	3.1102–3.1107	—	—
2.0L (P)	2005–08	3.3855–3.3861	.0004	.0004
2.2L DOHC (F)	2004–08	3.3855–3.3861	.0004	.0004
2.4L	2006–08	3.4668–3.4675	.0004	.0004
2.6L (M)	2004	3.2745–3.2766	.0003	.0026
2.8L (T)	2005–08	3.7005–3.7011	.0005	.0005
3.0L (R)	2004–05	3.3848–3.3868	.0003	.0026
3.1L (J)	2004–06	3.5046–3.5056	.0010	.0010
3.2L (N)	2004	3.4439–3.4459	.0003	.0026
3.4L (E)	2004–05	3.6220–3.6230	.0010	.0010
3.5L (8)	2004–08	3.700–3.701	.0010	.0010
3.6L (7)	2004–08	3.7005–3.7011	—	.0005
3.8L (K, 1, 2 & 4)	2004–08	3.8000	.0010	.0010
3.9L (1)	2006–08	3.8970–3.8980	.0011	.0011
4.4L (D)	2006–08	3.5824–3.5830	.0039	.0039
4.6L (A, Y & 9)	2004–08	3.6611–3.6617②	.0039	.0039
5.3L (C)	2006–08	3.7790–3.7800	—	.0002
5.7L (G & S)	2004–05	3.8970–3.8980	.0007	.0002
6.0L (U)	2005–08	4.0007–4.0017	—	.0002
7.0L (Y/E)	2006–08	4.1250–4.1250	—	.0002

① — The eighth digit of Vehicle Identification Number (VIN) denotes engine code.

② — Measure 1.610 inch below deck surface.

OIL PUMP

All Measurements Given In Inches Unless Otherwise Specified

Engine (VIN①)	Year	Gear Backlash	Gear To Body Clearance	Gear Endplay	Gear Pocket		Pump Gear Thickness	Pump Gear Diameter	Relief Valve To Body Clearance
					Depth	Diameter			
1.6L (6)	2004–07	—	.0157–.0191	.0018–.0039	—	—	—	—	—
1.8L (L)	2004–07	.0024–.0138	.0012–.0062	.0049–.0128	—	—	—	—	—
1.8L (8)	2004–08	.0024–.0138	.0012–.0062	.0049–.0128	—	—	—	—	—
2.2L DOHC (F)	2004	.0120	.0030	.0060	.5510	—	—	—	—
2.6L (M)	2004	—	—	.0026	—	—	—	—	—
2.8L (T)	2005–08	—	.0012–.0033	—	.6128–.6142	3.4360–3.4380	.6107–.6117	2.0988–2.0998	0018–.0043
3.0L (R)②	2004–05	.0110	③	.0060	—	—	—	—	—
3.1L (J)	2004–06	.0037–.0077	—	—	1.2020–1.2040	1.5030–1.5050	—	1.498–1.5000	.0015–.0035
3.2L (N)	2004	—	—	.0026	—	—	—	—	—
3.4L (E)	2004–05	.0037–.0077	.0010–.0030	.0020–.0050	1.2020–1.2040	1.5030–1.5050	1.1990–1.2000	1.4980–1.5000	.0015–.0035
3.5L (8)	2004–08	.0037–.0077	—	—	1.2020–1.2040	1.5030–1.5050	—	1.4980–1.5000	.0015–.0035
3.6L (7)	2004–07	.0030–.0071	.0039–.0091	.0016–.0051	.6128–.6142	3.4360–3.4380	.6107–.6117	3.4289–3.4321	.0018–.0043
3.8L (K, 1,2 & 4)	2004–08	.0060	.0080–.0150	.0010–.0035	.4610–.4625	3.5080–3.5120	—	—	.0015–.0030
3.9L (1)	2006–08	.0037–.0077	—	—	1.2020–1.2040	1.5030–1.5050	—	1.498–1.500	.0015–.0035

① — The eighth digit of Vehicle Identification Number (VIN) denotes engine code.

② — Pump components are not serviced separately. If any component is damaged or worn, pump should be replaced.

③ — Inner gear to housing, .003 inch; outer gear to housing, .004 inch.

MANUAL INFORMATION LOCATOR

Front Wheel Drive Models

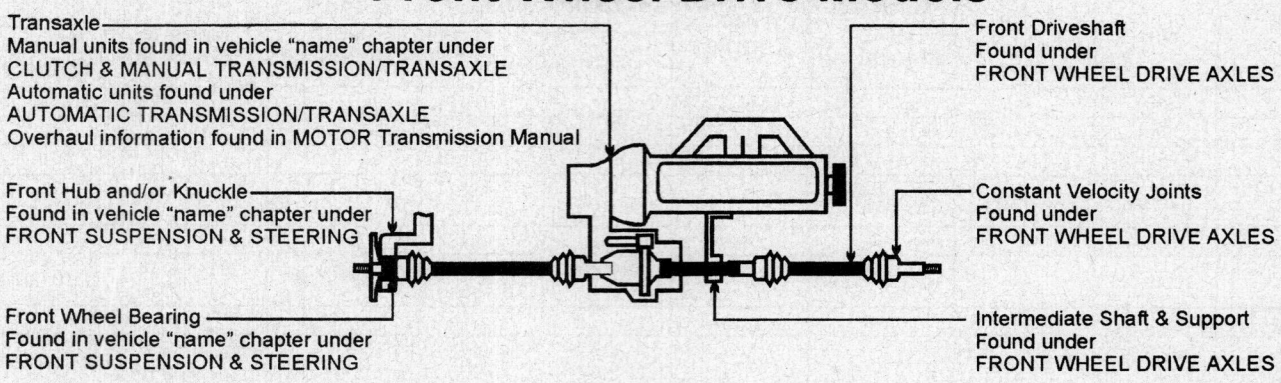

Transaxle
Manual units found in vehicle "name" chapter under
CLUTCH & MANUAL TRANSMISSION/TRANSAXLE
Automatic units found under
AUTOMATIC TRANSMISSION/TRANSAXLE
Overhaul information found in MOTOR Transmission Manual

Front Hub and/or Knuckle
Found in vehicle "name" chapter under
FRONT SUSPENSION & STEERING

Front Wheel Bearing
Found in vehicle "name" chapter under
FRONT SUSPENSION & STEERING

Front Driveshaft
Found under
FRONT WHEEL DRIVE AXLES

Constant Velocity Joints
Found under
FRONT WHEEL DRIVE AXLES

Intermediate Shaft & Support
Found under
FRONT WHEEL DRIVE AXLES

All Wheel Drive Models

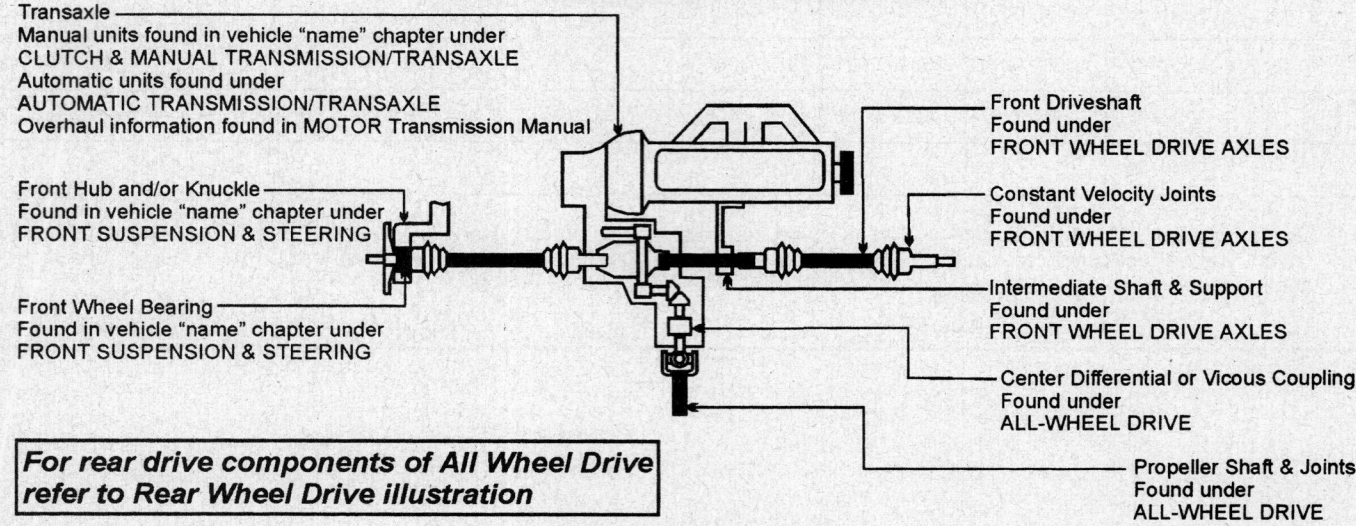

Transaxle
Manual units found in vehicle "name" chapter under
CLUTCH & MANUAL TRANSMISSION/TRANSAXLE
Automatic units found under
AUTOMATIC TRANSMISSION/TRANSAXLE
Overhaul information found in MOTOR Transmission Manual

Front Hub and/or Knuckle
Found in vehicle "name" chapter under
FRONT SUSPENSION & STEERING

Front Wheel Bearing
Found in vehicle "name" chapter under
FRONT SUSPENSION & STEERING

Front Driveshaft
Found under
FRONT WHEEL DRIVE AXLES

Constant Velocity Joints
Found under
FRONT WHEEL DRIVE AXLES

Intermediate Shaft & Support
Found under
FRONT WHEEL DRIVE AXLES

Center Differential or Vicous Coupling
Found under
ALL-WHEEL DRIVE

Propeller Shaft & Joints
Found under
ALL-WHEEL DRIVE

*For rear drive components of All Wheel Drive
refer to Rear Wheel Drive illustration*

Rear Wheel Drive Models

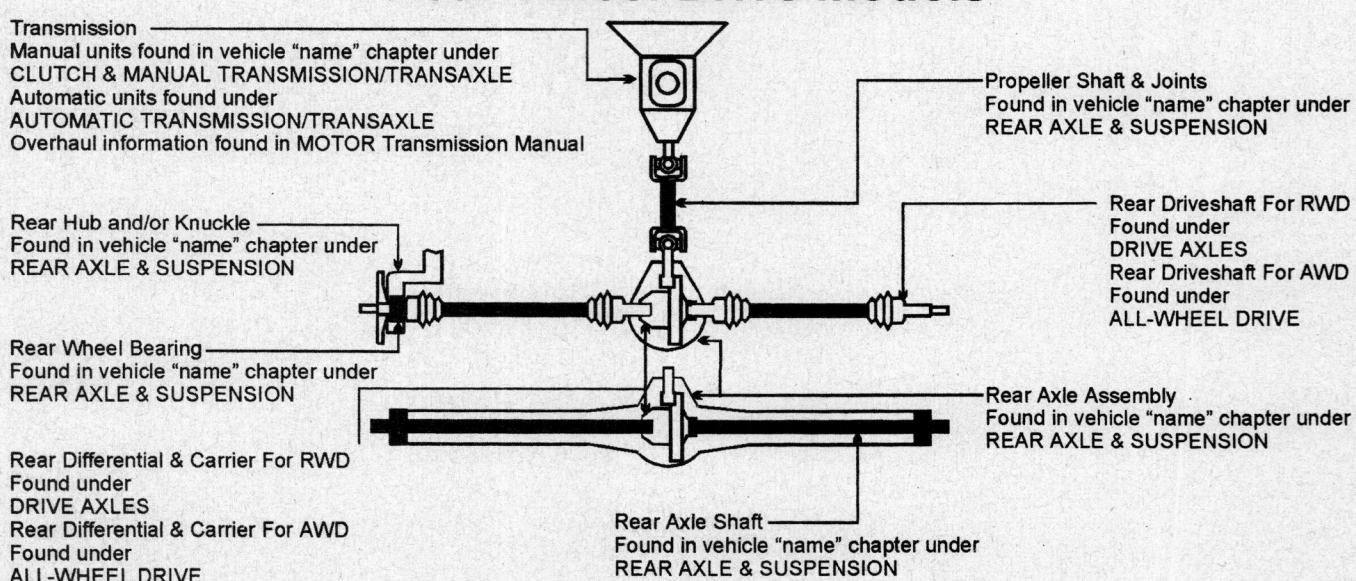

Transmission
Manual units found in vehicle "name" chapter under
CLUTCH & MANUAL TRANSMISSION/TRANSAXLE
Automatic units found under
AUTOMATIC TRANSMISSION/TRANSAXLE
Overhaul information found in MOTOR Transmission Manual

Rear Hub and/or Knuckle
Found in vehicle "name" chapter under
REAR AXLE & SUSPENSION

Rear Wheel Bearing
Found in vehicle "name" chapter under
REAR AXLE & SUSPENSION

Rear Differential & Carrier For RWD
Found under
DRIVE AXLES
Rear Differential & Carrier For AWD
Found under
ALL-WHEEL DRIVE

Propeller Shaft & Joints
Found in vehicle "name" chapter under
REAR AXLE & SUSPENSION

Rear Driveshaft For RWD
Found under
DRIVE AXLES
Rear Driveshaft For AWD
Found under
ALL-WHEEL DRIVE

Rear Axle Assembly
Found in vehicle "name" chapter under
REAR AXLE & SUSPENSION

Rear Axle Shaft
Found in vehicle "name" chapter under
REAR AXLE & SUSPENSION

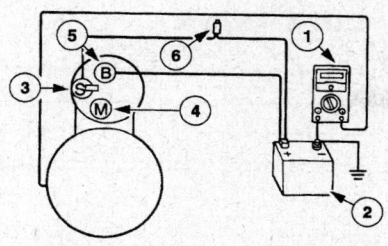

Item	Part Number	Description
1	—	Rotunda 73 Digital Multimeter
2	10653	Battery
3	—	S-Terminal
4	—	M-Terminal
5	—	B-Terminal
6	—	Remote Starter Switch

FM1120100599000X

Fig. 11 Starter motor ground circuit voltage drop test

Condition	Possible Sources	Action
• Normal current and speed	• Battery. • Switches. • Wiring.	• RECHECK battery, switches and wiring, including voltage drop tests, if cranking starter motor operation on engine is slow or sluggish.
• Current flow with test circuit switch open	• Solenoid contacts.	• TEST and, if necessary, INSTALL a new solenoid assembly.
• Failure to operate with very little or no current	• Solenoid winding.	• INSPECT and TEST solenoid assembly.
	• Field circuit.	• INSPECT and TEST frame and field coil assembly.
	• Armature coil or commutator bars.	• INSPECT armature.
	• Brush springs or brushes.	• INSPECT brushes and brush springs.
• Failure to operate with high current	• Bearing or drivetrain.	• INSPECT bearing, armature, driveshaft and related drive parts.

FM1120100604010X

Fig. 12 Starter motor no load test results (Part 1 of 2)

Condition	Possible Sources	Action
• Low speed with high current	• Terminals or fields.	• INSPECT and TEST frame and field coil assembly, solenoid assembly and brush installations for shorts.
	• Bushings, gear reduction unit, armature shaft, pole shoe or driveshaft.	• INSPECT bearing, armature, driveshaft and gear reduction gears.
	• Armature.	• INSPECT and TEST armature.
	• Armature or fields.	• INSPECT and TEST frame and field coil assembly and armature.
• Low speed with normal or low current	• Connections, leads or commutator.	• INSPECT internal wiring, electrical connections and armature commutator.
	• Solenoid winding.	• INSPECT and TEST solenoid assembly.
	• Field circuit.	• INSPECT and TEST frame and field coil assembly.
	• Armature coils or commutator bars.	• INSPECT armature.
	• Brush springs or brushes.	• INSPECT brushes and brush springs.
• High speed with high current	• Fields.	• INSPECT and TEST field and frame assembly.

FM1120100604020X

Fig. 12 Starter motor no load test results (Part 2 of 2)

DIAGNOSTIC CHART INDEX

Test	Description	Page No.	Fig. No.
CROWN VICTORIA, GRAND MARQUIS & MARAUDER			
Test A	Engine Does Not Crank	10-6	13
Test B	Unusual Starter Noise	10-9	14
FIVE HUNDRED, FREESTYLE, MONTEGO, 2004–07 SABLE & TAURUS			
Test A	Engine Does Not Crank	10-21	24
Test B	Unusual Starter Noise	10-23	25
2004–07 FOCUS			
Test A	Engine Does Not Crank & Relay Clicks	10-9	15
Test B	Engine Does Not Crank & Relay Does Not Click	10-10	16
Test C	Engine Cranks Slowly	10-11	17
FUSION, MILAN, MKZ & ZEPHYR			
Test A	Engine Does Not Crank	10-19	22
Test B	Unusual Starter Noise	10-21	23
LS & THUNDERBIRD			
Test A	Engine Does Not Crank	10-12	18
Test B	Unusual Starter Noise	10-16	19
MUSTANG			
Test A	Engine Does Not Crank	10-16	20
Test B	Unusual Starter Noise	10-18	21
2008 SABLE, TAURUS & TAURUS X			
Test A	Engine Does Not Crank	10-23	26
Test B	One-Touch Integrated Start (OTIS) Does Not Operate Correctly	10-25	27
Test C	Unusual Starter Noise	10-26	28

DIAGNOSTIC CHART INDEX—Continued

Test	Description	Page No.	Fig. No.
TOWN CAR			
Test A	Engine Does Not Crank	10-26	29
Test B	Unusual Starter Noise	10-29	30

TEST CONDITIONS	TESTDETAILS/RESULTS/ACTIONS

A1 CHECK THE BATTERY	1 Check the battery condition and charge.
	
	• Is the battery OK?
	
	→ **Yes**
	   GO to **A2**.
	
	→ **No**
	   CHARGE or REPLACE the battery as required. TEST the system for normal operation.

A2 CHECK THE BATTERY GROUND CABLE	1 Measure the voltage between the positive battery post and the battery ground cable connection at the cylinder block (6010).
	
	• Is the voltage reading greater than 10 volts?
	
	→ **Yes**
	   GO to **A3**.
	
	→ **No**
	   REPLACE the battery ground cable (14301). TEST the system for normal operation.

FM1120100613010X

Fig. 13   Test A: Engine Does Not Crank (Part 1 of 13). Crown Victoria, Grand Marquis & Marauder

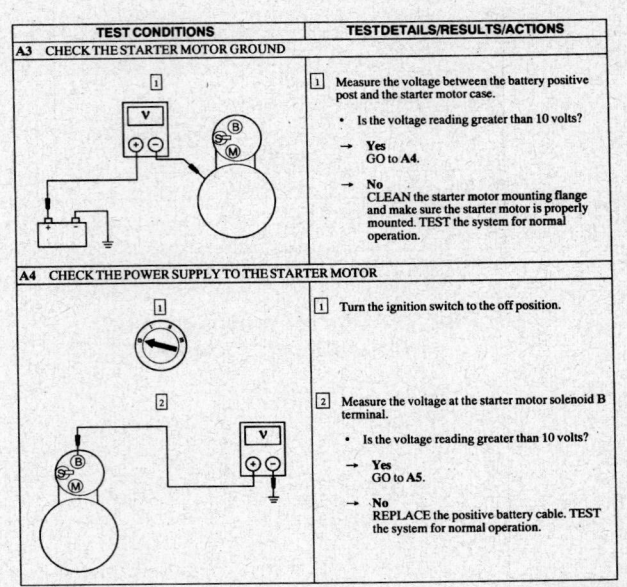

TEST CONDITIONS	TESTDETAILS/RESULTS/ACTIONS

A3 CHECK THE STARTER MOTOR GROUND	1 Measure the voltage between the battery positive post and the starter motor case.
	
	• Is the voltage reading greater than 10 volts?
	
	→ **Yes**
	   GO to **A4**.
	
	→ **No**
	   CLEAN the starter motor mounting flange and make sure the starter motor is properly mounted. TEST the system for normal operation.

A4 CHECK THE POWER SUPPLY TO THE STARTER MOTOR	1 Turn the ignition switch to the off position.
	
	2 Measure the voltage at the starter motor solenoid B terminal.
	
	• Is the voltage reading greater than 10 volts?
	
	→ **Yes**
	   GO to **A5**.
	
	→ **No**
	   REPLACE the positive battery cable. TEST the system for normal operation.

FM1120100613020X

Fig. 13   Test A: Engine Does Not Crank (Part 2 of 13). Crown Victoria, Grand Marquis & Marauder

TEST CONDITIONS	TESTDETAILS/RESULTS/ACTIONS

A5 CHECK THE STARTER MOTOR	1 Connect one end of a jumper wire to the starter motor solenoid B terminal of the starter motor and momentarily connect the other end to the starter motor solenoid S-terminal.
	
	• Does the starter motor engage and the engine crank?
	
	→ **Yes**
	   GO to **A6**.
	
	→ **No**
	   REPLACE the starter motor. TEST the system for normal operation.

A6   CHECK START INPUT TO THE STARTER MOTOR
 	
Starter S Connector
	1 Disconnect the starter motor solenoid S-terminal.
	
	2 Hold the ignition switch to the START position.
	
	3 Measure the voltage at the starter motor solenoid S connector.
	
	• Is the voltage reading greater than 10 volts?
	
	→ **Yes**
	   CLEAN the starter motor solenoid S-terminal stud and connector. CHECK the wiring and the starter motor for a loose or intermittent connection. TEST the system for normal operation.
	
	→ **No**
	   GO to **A7**.

FM1120100613030X

Fig. 13   Test A: Engine Does Not Crank (Part 3 of 13). Crown Victoria, Grand Marquis & Marauder

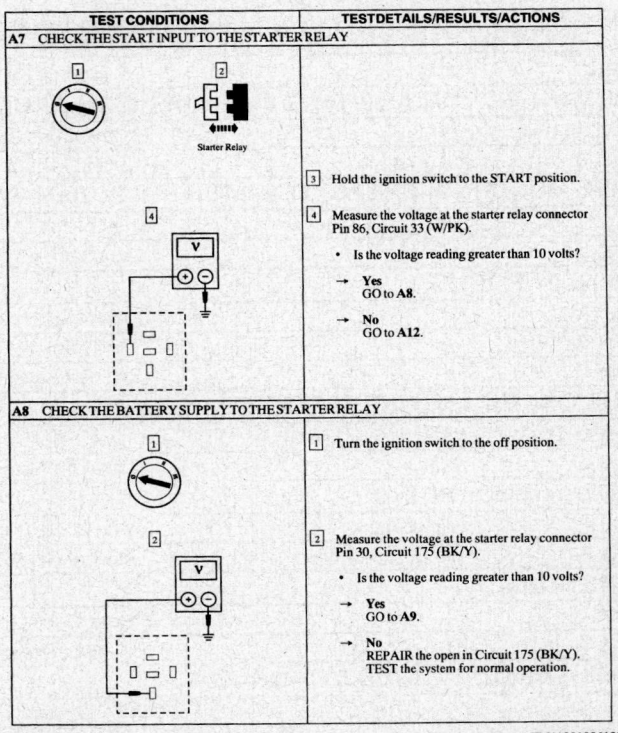

TEST CONDITIONS	TESTDETAILS/RESULTS/ACTIONS

A7   CHECK THE START INPUT TO THE STARTER RELAY
 	
Starter Relay
	3 Hold the ignition switch to the START position.
	
	4 Measure the voltage at the starter relay connector Pin 86, Circuit 33 (W/PK).
	
	• Is the voltage reading greater than 10 volts?
	
	→ **Yes**
	   GO to **A8**.
	
	→ **No**
	   GO to **A12**.

A8 CHECK THE BATTERY SUPPLY TO THE STARTER RELAY	1 Turn the ignition switch to the off position.
	
	2 Measure the voltage at the starter relay connector Pin 30, Circuit 175 (BK/Y).
	
	• Is the voltage reading greater than 10 volts?
	
	→ **Yes**
	   GO to **A9**.
	
	→ **No**
	   REPAIR the open in Circuit 175 (BK/Y). TEST the system for normal operation.

FM1120100613040X

Fig. 13   Test A: Engine Does Not Crank (Part 4 of 13). Crown Victoria, Grand Marquis & Marauder

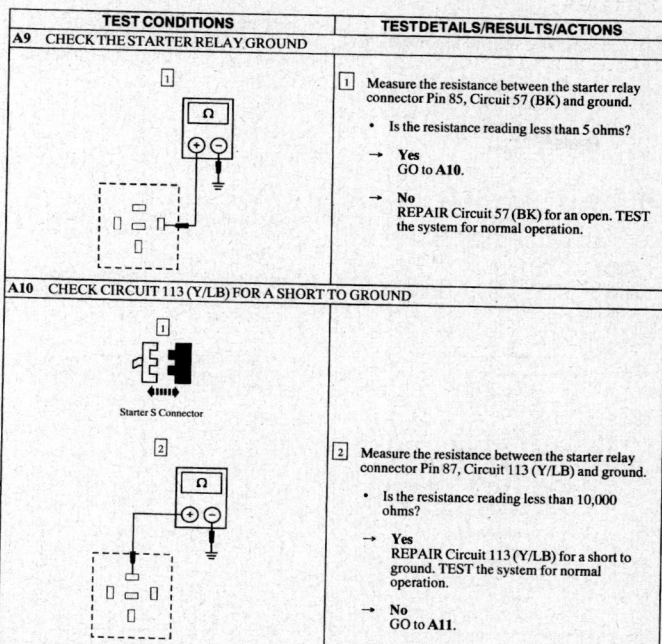

TEST CONDITIONS	TESTDETAILS/RESULTS/ACTIONS
A9 CHECK THE STARTER RELAY GROUND	1 Measure the resistance between the starter relay connector Pin 85, Circuit 57 (BK) and ground. • Is the resistance reading less than 5 ohms? → **Yes** GO to **A10**. → **No** REPAIR Circuit 57 (BK) for an open. TEST the system for normal operation.
A10 CHECK CIRCUIT 113 (Y/LB) FOR A SHORT TO GROUND	2 Measure the resistance between the starter relay connector Pin 87, Circuit 113 (Y/LB) and ground. • Is the resistance reading less than 10,000 ohms? → **Yes** REPAIR Circuit 113 (Y/LB) for a short to ground. TEST the system for normal operation. → **No** GO to **A11**.

FM1120100613050X

Fig. 13 Test A: Engine Does Not Crank (Part 5 of 13). Crown Victoria, Grand Marquis & Marauder

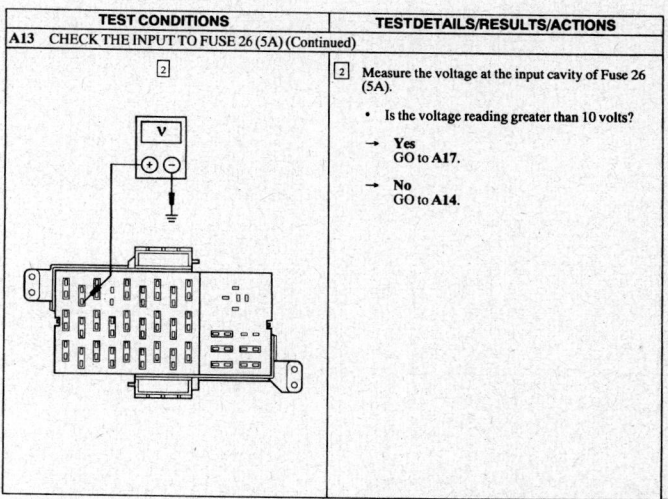

TEST CONDITIONS	TESTDETAILS/RESULTS/ACTIONS
A13 CHECK THE INPUT TO FUSE 26 (5A) (Continued)	2 Measure the voltage at the input cavity of Fuse 26 (5A). • Is the voltage reading greater than 10 volts? → **Yes** GO to **A17**. → **No** GO to **A14**.

FM1120100613070X

Fig. 13 Test A: Engine Does Not Crank (Part 7 of 13). Crown Victoria, Grand Marquis & Marauder

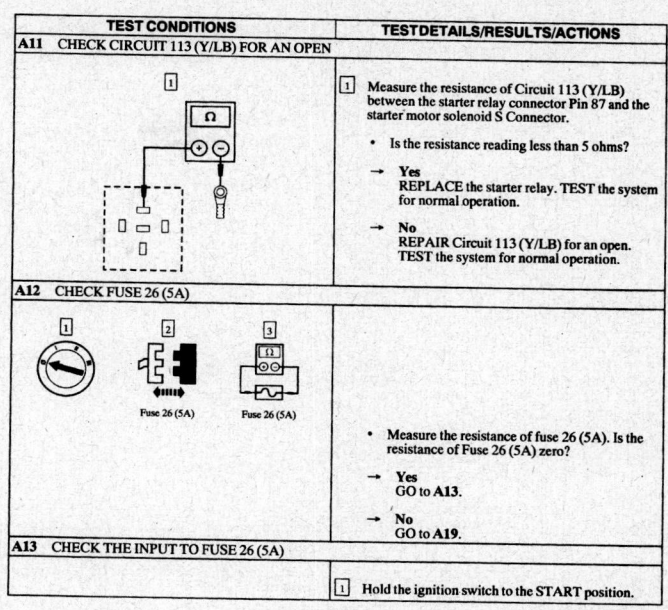

TEST CONDITIONS	TESTDETAILS/RESULTS/ACTIONS
A11 CHECK CIRCUIT 113 (Y/LB) FOR AN OPEN	1 Measure the resistance of Circuit 113 (Y/LB) between the starter relay connector Pin 87 and the starter motor solenoid S Connector. • Is the resistance reading less than 5 ohms? → **Yes** REPLACE the starter relay. TEST the system for normal operation. → **No** REPAIR Circuit 113 (Y/LB) for an open. TEST the system for normal operation.
A12 CHECK FUSE 26 (5A)	• Measure the resistance of fuse 26 (5A). Is the resistance of Fuse 26 (5A) zero? → **Yes** GO to **A13**. → **No** GO to **A19**.
A13 CHECK THE INPUT TO FUSE 26 (5A)	1 Hold the ignition switch to the START position.

FM1120100613060X

Fig. 13 Test A: Engine Does Not Crank (Part 6 of 13). Crown Victoria, Grand Marquis & Marauder

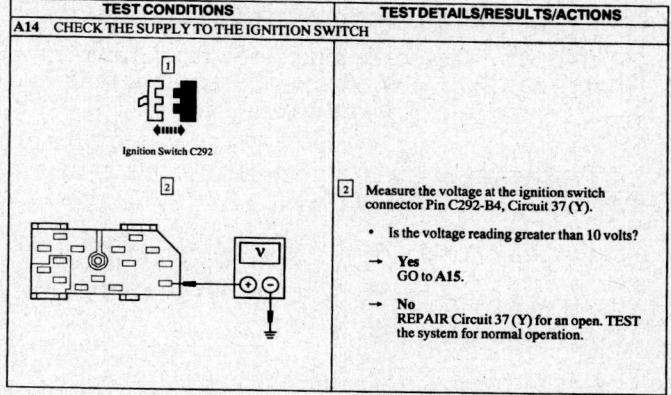

TEST CONDITIONS	TESTDETAILS/RESULTS/ACTIONS
A14 CHECK THE SUPPLY TO THE IGNITION SWITCH	2 Measure the voltage at the ignition switch connector Pin C292-B4, Circuit 37 (Y). • Is the voltage reading greater than 10 volts? → **Yes** GO to **A15**. → **No** REPAIR Circuit 37 (Y) for an open. TEST the system for normal operation.

FM1120100613080X

Fig. 13 Test A: Engine Does Not Crank (Part 8 of 13). Crown Victoria, Grand Marquis & Marauder

TEST CONDITIONS	TESTDETAILS/RESULTS/ACTIONS
A15 CHECK CIRCUIT 32 (R/LB) FOR AN OPEN	

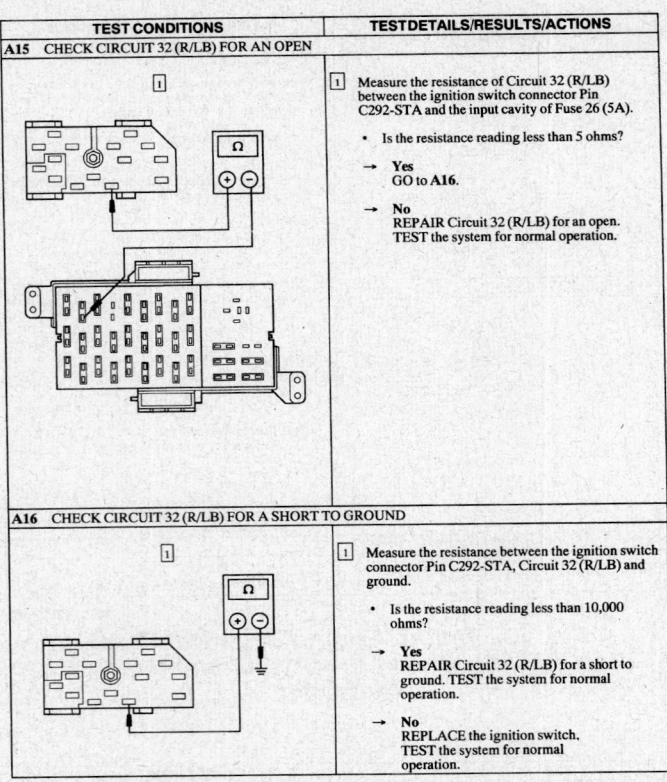

1. Measure the resistance of Circuit 32 (R/LB) between the ignition switch connector Pin C292-STA and the input cavity of Fuse 26 (5A).

- Is the resistance reading less than 5 ohms?

→ **Yes**
  GO to **A16**.

→ **No**
  REPAIR Circuit 32 (R/LB) for an open. TEST the system for normal operation.

TEST CONDITIONS	TESTDETAILS/RESULTS/ACTIONS
A16 CHECK CIRCUIT 32 (R/LB) FOR A SHORT TO GROUND	

1. Measure the resistance between the ignition switch connector Pin C292-STA, Circuit 32 (R/LB) and ground.

- Is the resistance reading less than 10,000 ohms?

→ **Yes**
  REPAIR Circuit 32 (R/LB) for a short to ground. TEST the system for normal operation.

→ **No**
  REPLACE the ignition switch. TEST the system for normal operation.

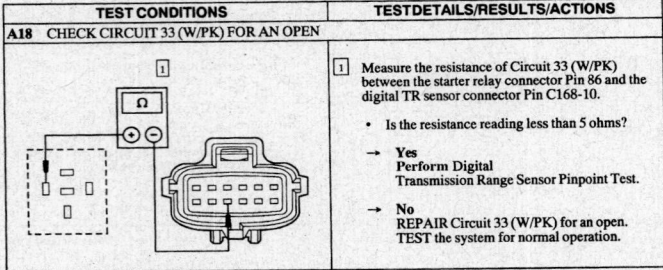

FM1120100613090X

Fig. 13   Test A: Engine Does Not Crank (Part 9 of 13). Crown Victoria, Grand Marquis & Marauder

TEST CONDITIONS	TESTDETAILS/RESULTS/ACTIONS
A18 CHECK CIRCUIT 33 (W/PK) FOR AN OPEN	

1. Measure the resistance of Circuit 33 (W/PK) between the starter relay connector Pin 86 and the digital TR sensor connector Pin C168-10.

- Is the resistance reading less than 5 ohms?

→ **Yes**
  Perform Digital Transmission Range Sensor Pinpoint Test.

→ **No**
  REPAIR Circuit 33 (W/PK) for an open. TEST the system for normal operation.

FM1120100613110X

Fig. 13   Test A: Engine Does Not Crank (Part 11 of 13). Crown Victoria, Grand Marquis & Marauder

TEST CONDITIONS	TESTDETAILS/RESULTS/ACTIONS
A17 CHECK CIRCUIT 262 (BR/PK) FOR AN OPEN	

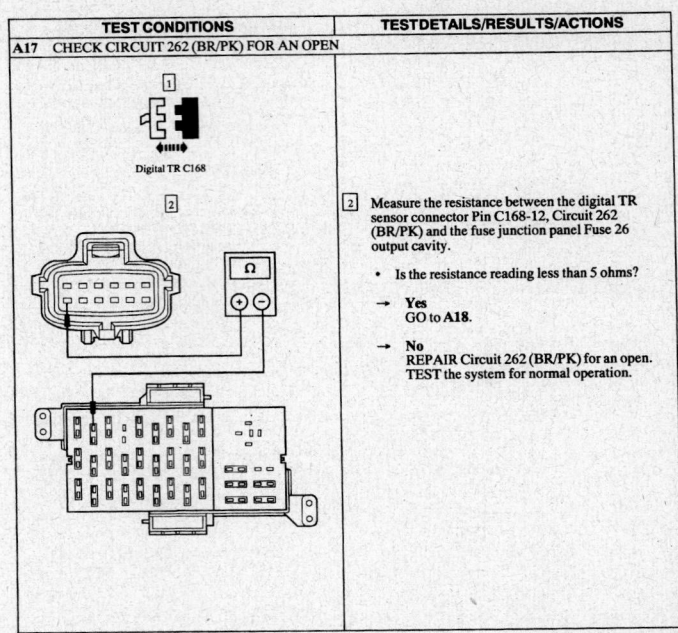

Digital TR C168

2. Measure the resistance between the digital TR sensor connector Pin C168-12, Circuit 262 (BR/PK) and the fuse junction panel Fuse 26 output cavity.

- Is the resistance reading less than 5 ohms?

→ **Yes**
  GO to **A18**.

→ **No**
  REPAIR Circuit 262 (BR/PK) for an open. TEST the system for normal operation.

FM1120100613100X

Fig. 13   Test A: Engine Does Not Crank (Part 10 of 13). Crown Victoria, Grand Marquis & Marauder

TEST CONDITIONS	TESTDETAILS/RESULTS/ACTIONS
A19 CHECK FOR A SHORTED SYSTEM	

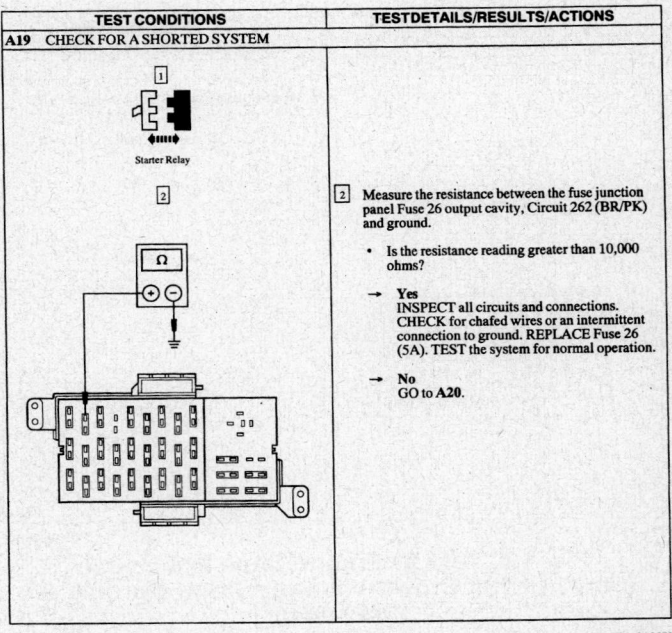

Starter Relay

2. Measure the resistance between the fuse junction panel Fuse 26 output cavity, Circuit 262 (BR/PK) and ground.

- Is the resistance reading greater than 10,000 ohms?

→ **Yes**
  INSPECT all circuits and connections. CHECK for chafed wires or an intermittent connection to ground. REPLACE Fuse 26 (5A). TEST the system for normal operation.

→ **No**
  GO to **A20**.

FM1120100613120X

Fig. 13   Test A: Engine Does Not Crank (Part 12 of 13). Crown Victoria, Grand Marquis & Marauder

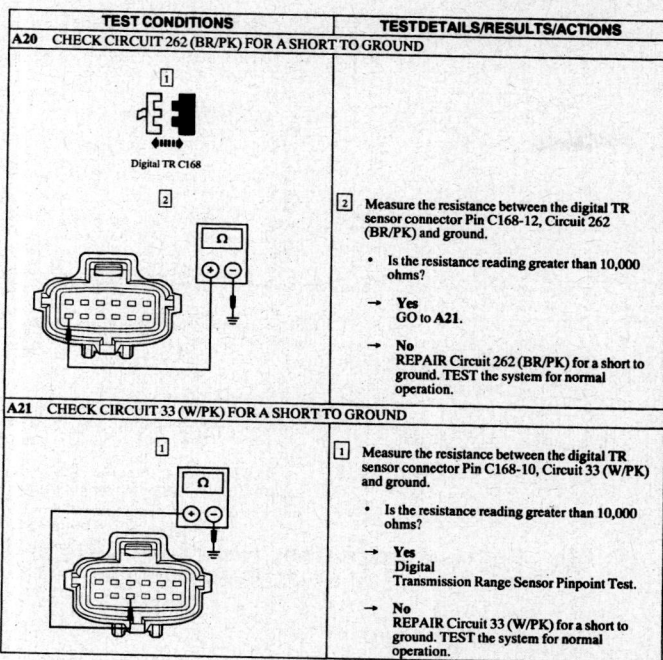

TEST CONDITIONS	TEST DETAILS/RESULTS/ACTIONS
A20 CHECK CIRCUIT 262 (BR/PK) FOR A SHORT TO GROUND	
① Digital TR C168 ②	② Measure the resistance between the digital TR sensor connector Pin C168-12, Circuit 262 (BR/PK) and ground. • Is the resistance reading greater than 10,000 ohms? → **Yes** GO to **A21**. → **No** REPAIR Circuit 262 (BR/PK) for a short to ground. TEST the system for normal operation.
A21 CHECK CIRCUIT 33 (W/PK) FOR A SHORT TO GROUND	
①	① Measure the resistance between the digital TR sensor connector Pin C168-10, Circuit 33 (W/PK) and ground. • Is the resistance reading greater than 10,000 ohms? → **Yes** Digital Transmission Range Sensor Pinpoint Test. → **No** REPAIR Circuit 33 (W/PK) for a short to ground. TEST the system for normal operation.

FM1120100613130X

Fig. 13   Test A: Engine Does Not Crank (Part 13 of 13). Crown Victoria, Grand Marquis & Marauder

TEST CONDITIONS	TEST DETAILS/RESULTS/ACTIONS
B3 CHECK FOR UNUSUAL WEAR	
	① Remove the starter motor. ② Inspect the ring gear for damaged or worn teeth. • Is the noise due to flywheel ring gear (6384) tooth damage? → **Yes** REPLACE the flywheel ring gear. EXAMINE the starter pinion teeth. If damaged, REPLACE the starter motor. TEST the system for normal operation. → **No** REPLACE the starter motor. TEST the system for normal operation.

FM1120100614020X

Fig. 14   Test B: Unusual Starter Noise (Part 2 of 2). Crown Victoria, Grand Marquis & Marauder

TEST CONDITIONS	TEST DETAILS/RESULTS/ACTIONS
B1 CHECK THE STARTER MOUNTING	
	① Inspect the starter motor mounting bolts and brackets for looseness. • Is the starter motor mounted properly? → **Yes** GO to **B2**. → **No** INSTALL the starter motor properly; TEST the system for normal operation.
B2 CHECK FOR ENGINE NOISE	
① ② ③	② Connect a remote starter switch between the starter motor solenoid B and S terminals. ③ Engage the starter motor and verify the noise is due to the starter operation. • Is the noise due to the starter motor engagement? → **Yes** GO to **B3**. → **No** Diagnose engine mechanical components.

FM1120100614010X

Fig. 14   Test B: Unusual Starter Noise (Part 1 of 2). Crown Victoria, Grand Marquis & Marauder

CONDITIONS	DETAILS/RESULTS/ACTIONS
A1: CHECK THE BATTERY	
	① Check the battery. Carry out the battery capacity test using a scan tool. • Is the battery OK? → Yes GO TO A2 → No INSTALL a new battery. TEST the system for normal operation.
A2: CHECK THE STARTER RELAY	
① Starter Relay	② Carry out the ISO mini relay component test. For additional information refer to the wiring diagrams. • Is the relay OK? → Yes GO TO A3 → No INSTALL a new starter relay. TEST the system for normal operation.
A3: CHECK VOLTAGE TO STARTER RELAY CIRCUIT 50-BB17 (GY/OG)	
①	

FM1120100686010X

Fig. 15   Test A: Engine Does Not Crank & Relay Clicks (Part 1 of 3). 2004–07 Focus

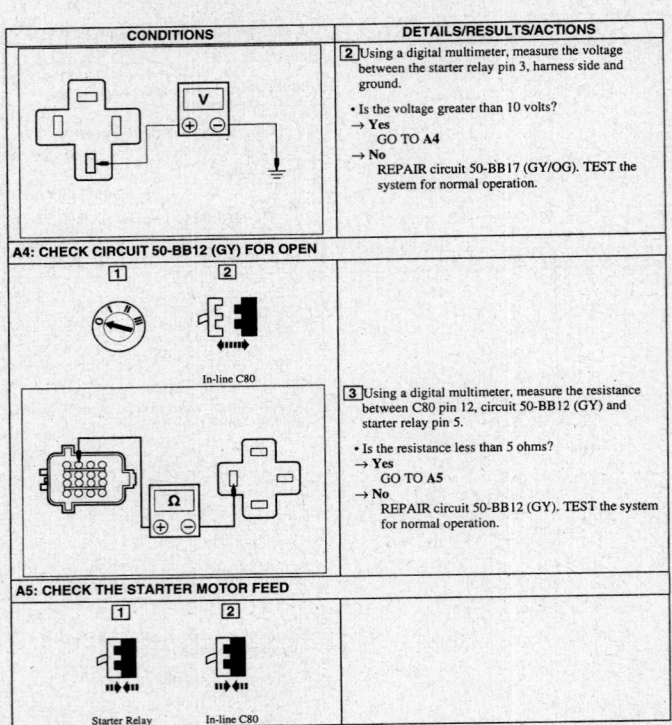

CONDITIONS	DETAILS/RESULTS/ACTIONS

	2 Using a digital multimeter, measure the voltage between the starter relay pin 3, harness side and ground.
	
	 • Is the voltage greater than 10 volts?
	 → Yes
	     GO TO **A4**
	 → No
	     REPAIR circuit 50-BB17 (GY/OG). TEST the system for normal operation.

A4: CHECK CIRCUIT 50-BB12 (GY) FOR OPEN	

	3 Using a digital multimeter, measure the resistance between C80 pin 12, circuit 50-BB12 (GY) and starter relay pin 5.
	
	 • Is the resistance less than 5 ohms?
	 → Yes
	     GO TO **A5**
	 → No
	     REPAIR circuit 50-BB12 (GY). TEST the system for normal operation.

A5: CHECK THE STARTER MOTOR FEED	

FM1120100686020X

Fig. 15   Test A: Engine Does Not Crank & Relay Clicks (Part 2 of 3). 2004–07 Focus

CONDITIONS	DETAILS/RESULTS/ACTIONS
B1: CHECK CONDITION OF PATS SYSTEM	

	1 Observe the PATS warning indicator.
	
	 • Does the indicator flash when attempting to start the vehicle?
	 → Yes
	     Fault within the PATS system.
	 → No
	     GO TO **B2**

FM1120100687010X

Fig. 16   Test B: Engine Does Not Crank & Relay Does Not Click (Part 1 of 5). 2004–07 Focus

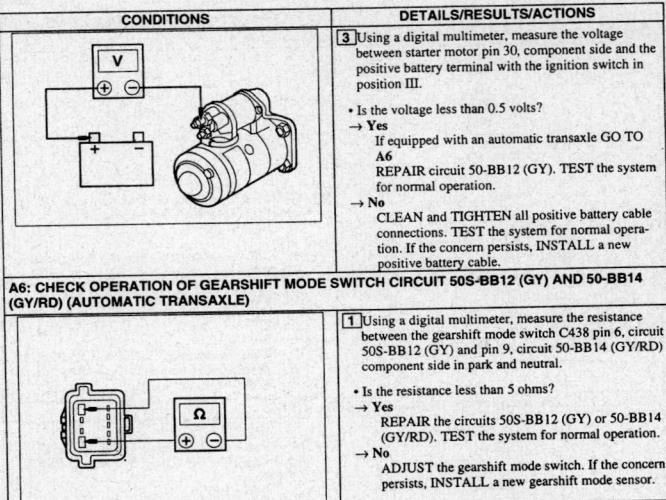

CONDITIONS	DETAILS/RESULTS/ACTIONS

	3 Using a digital multimeter, measure the voltage between starter motor pin 30, component side and the positive battery terminal with the ignition switch in position III.
	
	 • Is the voltage less than 0.5 volts?
	 → Yes
	     If equipped with an automatic transaxle GO TO **A6**
	     REPAIR circuit 50-BB12 (GY). TEST the system for normal operation.
	 → No
	     CLEAN and TIGHTEN all positive battery cable connections. TEST the system for normal operation. If the concern persists, INSTALL a new positive battery cable.

A6: CHECK OPERATION OF GEARSHIFT MODE SWITCH CIRCUIT 50S-BB12 (GY) AND 50-BB14 (GY/RD) (AUTOMATIC TRANSAXLE)	

	1 Using a digital multimeter, measure the resistance between the gearshift mode switch C438 pin 6, circuit 50S-BB12 (GY) and pin 9, circuit 50-BB14 (GY/RD) component side in park and neutral.
	
	 • Is the resistance less than 5 ohms?
	 → Yes
	     REPAIR the circuits 50S-BB12 (GY) or 50-BB14 (GY/RD). TEST the system for normal operation.
	 → No
	     ADJUST the gearshift mode switch. If the concern persists, INSTALL a new gearshift mode sensor.

FM1120100686030X

Fig. 15   Test A: Engine Does Not Crank & Relay Clicks (Part 3 of 3). 2004–07 Focus

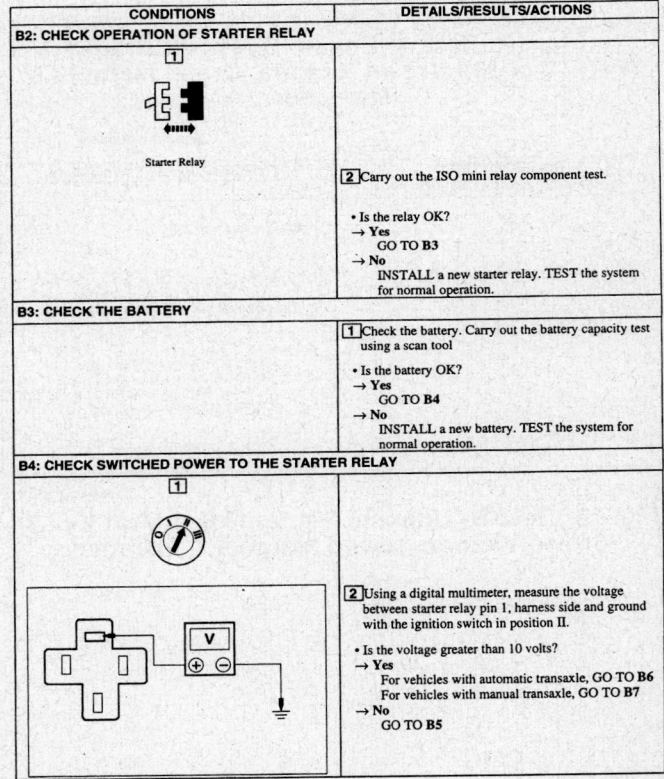

CONDITIONS	DETAILS/RESULTS/ACTIONS
B2: CHECK OPERATION OF STARTER RELAY	

	2 Carry out the ISO mini relay component test.
	
	 • Is the relay OK?
	 → Yes
	     GO TO **B3**
	 → No
	     INSTALL a new starter relay. TEST the system for normal operation.

B3: CHECK THE BATTERY	

	1 Check the battery. Carry out the battery capacity test using a scan tool.
	
	 • Is the battery OK?
	 → Yes
	     GO TO **B4**
	 → No
	     INSTALL a new battery. TEST the system for normal operation.

B4: CHECK SWITCHED POWER TO THE STARTER RELAY	

	2 Using a digital multimeter, measure the voltage between starter relay pin 1, harness side and ground with the ignition switch in position II.
	
	 • Is the voltage greater than 10 volts?
	 → Yes
	     For vehicles with automatic transaxle, GO TO **B6**
	     For vehicles with manual transaxle, GO TO **B7**
	 → No
	     GO TO **B5**

FM1120100687020X

Fig. 16   Test B: Engine Does Not Crank & Relay Does Not Click (Part 2 of 5). 2004–07 Focus

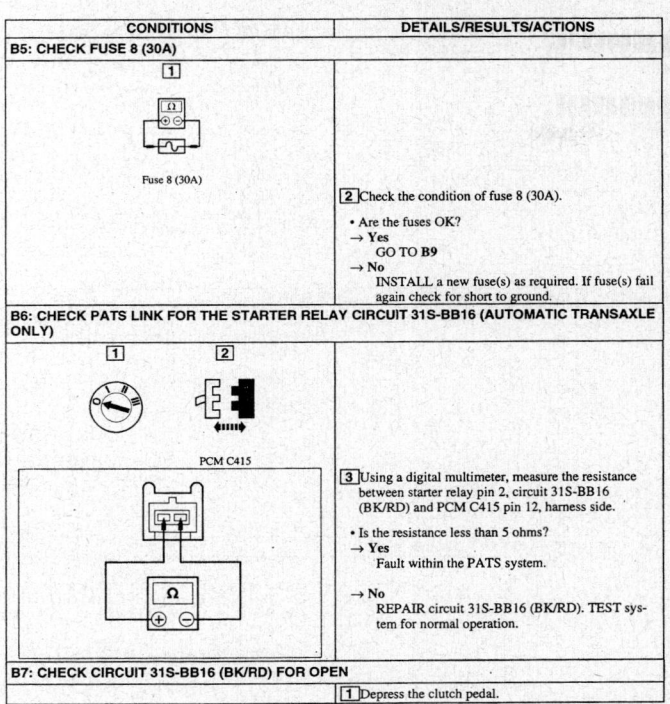

CONDITIONS	DETAILS/RESULTS/ACTIONS
B5: CHECK FUSE 8 (30A)	
①	

Fuse 8 (30A)	② Check the condition of fuse 8 (30A).
	
	• Are the fuses OK?
	→ **Yes**
	   GO TO **B9**
	→ **No**
	   INSTALL a new fuse(s) as required. If fuse(s) fail again check for short to ground.

B6: CHECK PATS LINK FOR THE STARTER RELAY CIRCUIT 31S-BB16 (AUTOMATIC TRANSAXLE ONLY)	
① ②	

PCM C415	③ Using a digital multimeter, measure the resistance between starter relay pin 2, circuit 31S-BB16 (BK/RD) and PCM C415 pin 12, harness side.
	
	• Is the resistance less than 5 ohms?
	→ **Yes**
	   Fault within the PATS system.
	→ **No**
	   REPAIR circuit 31S-BB16 (BK/RD). TEST system for normal operation.

B7: CHECK CIRCUIT 31S-BB16 (BK/RD) FOR OPEN	
	① Depress the clutch pedal.

FM1120100687030X

Fig. 16 Test B: Engine Does Not Crank & Relay Does Not Click (Part 3 of 5). 2004–07 Focus

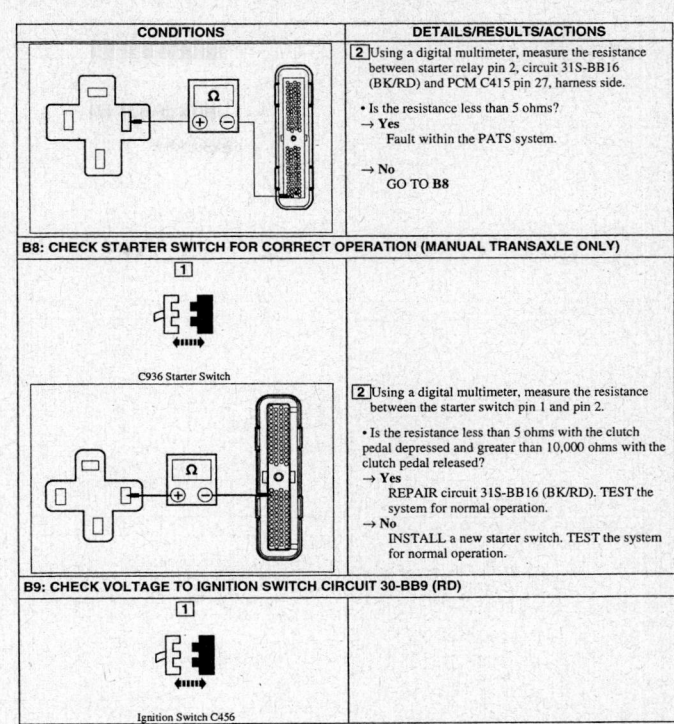

CONDITIONS	DETAILS/RESULTS/ACTIONS

	② Using a digital multimeter, measure the resistance between starter relay pin 2, circuit 31S-BB16 (BK/RD) and PCM C415 pin 27, harness side.
	
	• Is the resistance less than 5 ohms?
	→ **Yes**
	   Fault within the PATS system.
	→ **No**
	   GO TO **B8**

B8: CHECK STARTER SWITCH FOR CORRECT OPERATION (MANUAL TRANSAXLE ONLY)	

①
 	
C936 Starter Switch
	② Using a digital multimeter, measure the resistance between the starter switch pin 1 and pin 2.
	
	• Is the resistance less than 5 ohms with the clutch pedal depressed and greater than 10,000 ohms with the clutch pedal released?
	→ **Yes**
	   REPAIR circuit 31S-BB16 (BK/RD). TEST the system for normal operation.
	→ **No**
	   INSTALL a new starter switch. TEST the system for normal operation.

B9: CHECK VOLTAGE TO IGNITION SWITCH CIRCUIT 30-BB9 (RD)	
① Ignition Switch C456	

FM1120100687040X

Fig. 16 Test B: Engine Does Not Crank & Relay Does Not Click (Part 4 of 5). 2004–07 Focus

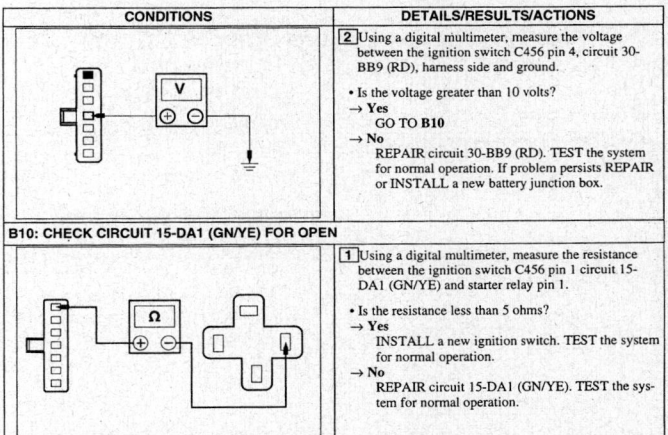

CONDITIONS	DETAILS/RESULTS/ACTIONS

	② Using a digital multimeter, measure the voltage between the ignition switch C456 pin 4, circuit 30-BB9 (RD), harness side and ground.
	
	• Is the voltage greater than 10 volts?
	→ **Yes**
	   GO TO **B10**
	→ **No**
	   REPAIR circuit 30-BB9 (RD). TEST the system for normal operation. If problem persists REPAIR or INSTALL a new battery junction box.

B10: CHECK CIRCUIT 15-DA1 (GN/YE) FOR OPEN	

①	① Using a digital multimeter, measure the resistance between the ignition switch C456 pin 1 circuit 15-DA1 (GN/YE) and starter relay pin 1.
	
	• Is the resistance less than 5 ohms?
	→ **Yes**
	   INSTALL a new ignition switch. TEST the system for normal operation.
	→ **No**
	   REPAIR circuit 15-DA1 (GN/YE). TEST the system for normal operation.

FM1120100687050X

Fig. 16 Test B: Engine Does Not Crank & Relay Does Not Click (Part 5 of 5). 2004–07 Focus

CONDITIONS	DETAILS/RESULTS/ACTIONS
C1: CHECK THE STARTER MOTOR LOAD	

	① Carry out the starter motor load test on the starter motor.
	
	• Is the starter motor OK?
	→ **Yes**
	   GO TO **C2**
	→ **No**
	   INSTALL a new starter motor. TEST the system for normal operation

FM1120100688010X

Fig. 17 Test C: Engine Cranks Slowly (Part 1 of 2). 2004–07 Focus

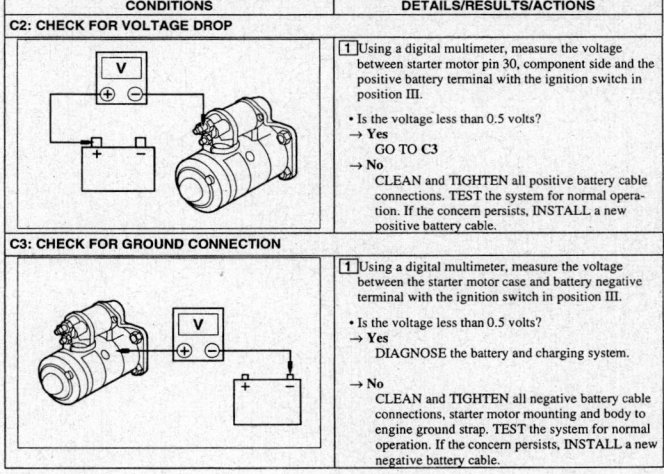

CONDITIONS	DETAILS/RESULTS/ACTIONS
C2: CHECK FOR VOLTAGE DROP	

	① Using a digital multimeter, measure the voltage between starter motor pin 30, component side and the positive battery terminal with the ignition switch in position III.
	
	• Is the voltage less than 0.5 volts?
	→ **Yes**
	   GO TO **C3**
	→ **No**
	   CLEAN and TIGHTEN all positive battery cable connections. TEST the system for normal operation. If the concern persists, INSTALL a new positive battery cable.

C3: CHECK FOR GROUND CONNECTION	

	① Using a digital multimeter, measure the voltage between the starter motor case and battery negative terminal with the ignition switch in position III.
	
	• Is the voltage less than 0.5 volts?
	→ **Yes**
	   DIAGNOSE the battery and charging system.
	→ **No**
	   CLEAN and TIGHTEN all negative battery cable connections, starter motor mounting and body to engine ground strap. TEST the system for normal operation. If the concern persists, INSTALL a new negative battery cable.

FM1120100688020X

Fig. 17 Test C: Engine Cranks Slowly (Part 2 of 2). 2004–07 Focus

TEST CONDITIONS	TESTDETAILS/RESULTS/ACTIONS
A1 CHECK FOR INSTRUMENT CLUSTER DIAGNOSTIC TEST CODES	
	1 **Note:** The instrument cluster PATS DTCs are the only DTCs of concern in this step. Only repair retrieved non-PATS DTCs if a customer concern is reported. Carry out the instrument cluster self-test. • Were any PATS DTCs retrieved from the instrument cluster? → **Yes** Diagnose the PATS DTCs. → **No** GO to A2.
A2 CHECK THE BATTERY	
	1 Check the battery condition and charge. • Is the battery OK? → **Yes** GO to A3. → **No** CHARGE or INSTALL a new battery as necessary. TEST the system for normal operation.
A3 CHECK THE BATTERY GROUND CABLE	
1	1 Measure the voltage between the positive battery post and the battery ground cable connection on the engine. • Is the voltage greater than 10 volts? → **Yes** GO to A4. → **No** INSTALL a new battery ground cable. TEST the system for normal operation.

FM1120100653010X

Fig. 18   Test A: Engine Does Not Crank (Part 1 of 17). LS & Thunderbird

TEST CONDITIONS	TESTDETAILS/RESULTS/ACTIONS
A7 CHECK THE START INPUT TO THE STARTER MOTOR	
1 Starter motor C197 2 3	2 Measure the voltage between starter motor C197, circuit 50-BB12 (GY/BK), harness side and ground while holding the ignition switch in the START position. • Is the voltage greater than 10 volts in START? → **Yes** CLEAN the starter motor S-terminal and connector. CHECK the wiring and the starter motor for a loose or intermittent connection. TEST the system for normal operation. → **No** GO to A8.
A8 CHECK THE START INPUT TO THE STARTER RELAY	
1 Starter relay	2 For manual transmissions, depress the clutch pedal position (CPP) switch.

FM1120100653030X

Fig. 18   Test A: Engine Does Not Crank (Part 3 of 17). LS & Thunderbird

TEST CONDITIONS	TESTDETAILS/RESULTS/ACTIONS
A4 CHECK THE STARTER MOTOR GROUND	
1	1 Measure the voltage between the battery positive post and the starter motor case. • Is the voltage greater than 10 volts? → **Yes** GO to A5. → **No** CLEAN the starter motor mounting flange and make sure the starter motor is correctly mounted. TEST the system for normal operation.
A5 CHECK THE POWER SUPPLY TO THE STARTER MOTOR	
1	1 Measure the voltage between starter motor B-terminal and ground. • Is the voltage greater than 10 volts? → **Yes** GO to A6. → **No** REPAIR circuit 30-BB10 (RD). TEST the system for normal operation.
A6 CHECK THE STARTER MOTOR B-TERMINAL	
1	1 Connect a fused jumper wire to the B-terminal of the starter motor. Momentarily connect the other lead of the jumper wire to the starter motor S-terminal. • Did the starter motor engage and the engine crank? → **Yes** GO to A7. → **No** INSTALL a new starter motor; TEST the system for normal operation.

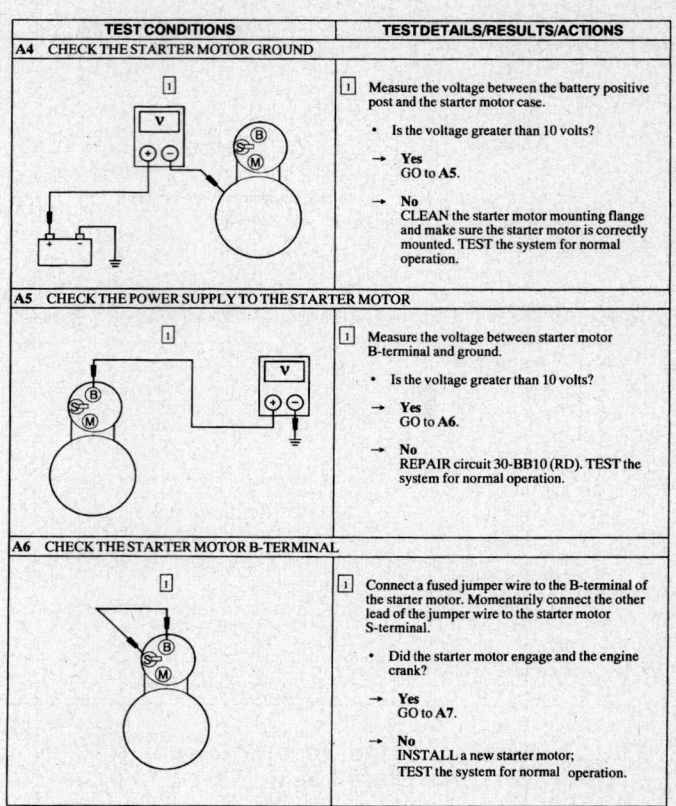

FM1120100653020X

Fig. 18   Test A: Engine Does Not Crank (Part 2 of 17). LS & Thunderbird

TEST CONDITIONS	TESTDETAILS/RESULTS/ACTIONS
A8 CHECK THE START INPUT TO THE STARTER RELAY (Continued)	
	3 Make sure the vehicle is in PARK or NEUTRAL.
	4 Turn the ignition switch to START and hold.
5	5 Measure the voltage between starter relay pin 86, circuit 50-SBB12 (GY), harness side and ground. • Is the voltage greater than 10 volts? → **Yes** GO to A9. → **No** GO to A17.
A9 CHECK THE GROUND SUPPLY TO THE STARTER RELAY	
	1 For manual transmissions, depress the clutch pedal position (CPP) switch.
	2 Make sure the vehicle is in PARK or NEUTRAL.
	3 Turn the ignition switch to START and hold.

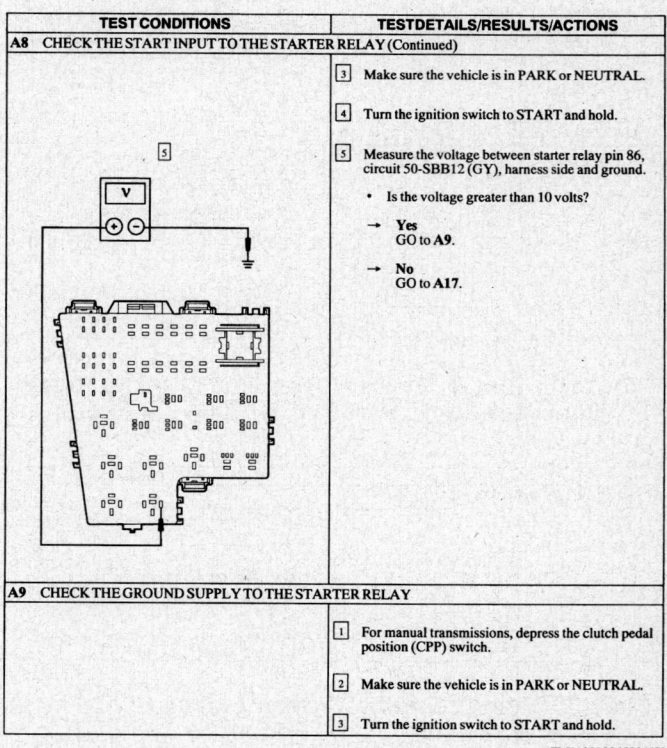

FM1120100653040X

Fig. 18   Test A: Engine Does Not Crank (Part 4 of 17). LS & Thunderbird

TEST CONDITIONS	TESTDETAILS/RESULTS/ACTIONS
A9 CHECK THE GROUND SUPPLY TO THE STARTER RELAY (Continued)	

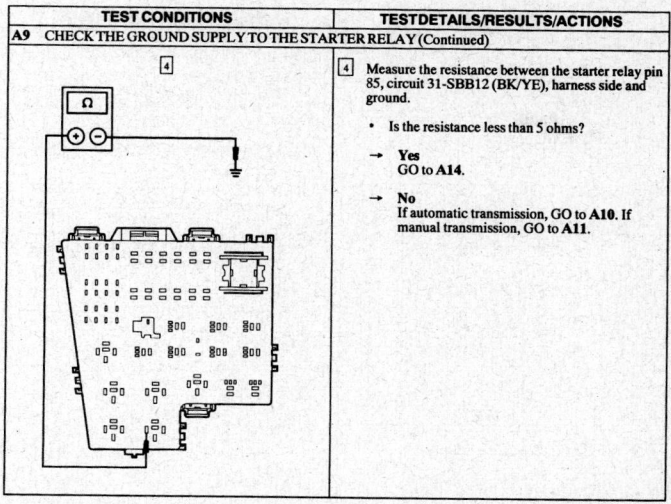

⁴ Measure the resistance between the starter relay pin 85, circuit 31-SBB12 (BK/YE), harness side and ground.

- Is the resistance less than 5 ohms?

→ **Yes**
  GO to **A14**.

→ **No**
  If automatic transmission, GO to **A10**. If manual transmission, GO to **A11**.

FM1120100653050X

Fig. 18   Test A: Engine Does Not Crank (Part 5 of 17). LS & Thunderbird

TEST CONDITIONS	TESTDETAILS/RESULTS/ACTIONS
A11 CHECK THE GROUND SUPPLY TO THE CLUTCH PEDAL POSITION (CPP) SWITCH (Continued)	

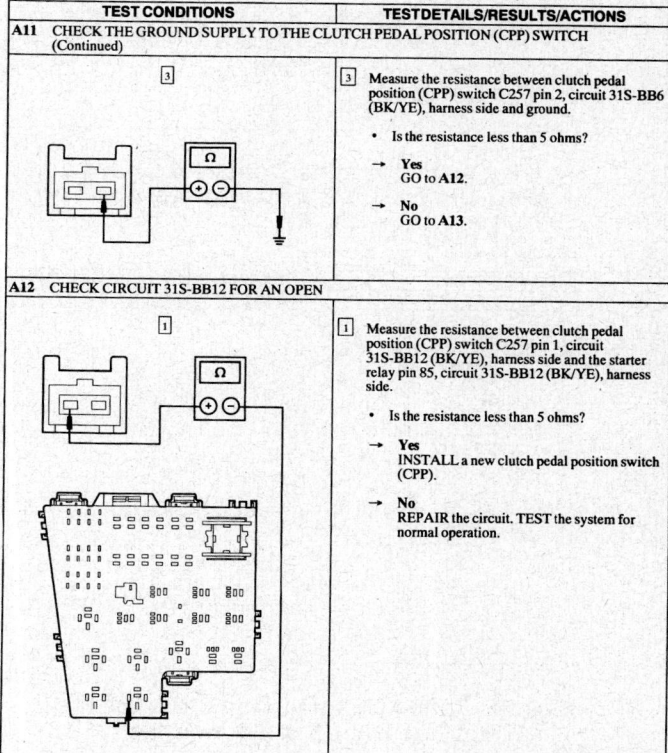

³ Measure the resistance between clutch pedal position (CPP) switch C257 pin 2, circuit 31S-BB6 (BK/YE), harness side and ground.

- Is the resistance less than 5 ohms?

→ **Yes**
  GO to **A12**.

→ **No**
  GO to **A13**.

| A12   CHECK CIRCUIT 31S-BB12 FOR AN OPEN | |

¹ Measure the resistance between clutch pedal position (CPP) switch C257 pin 1, circuit 31S-BB12 (BK/YE), harness side and the starter relay pin 85, circuit 31S-BB12 (BK/YE), harness side.

- Is the resistance less than 5 ohms?

→ **Yes**
  INSTALL a new clutch pedal position switch (CPP).

→ **No**
  REPAIR the circuit. TEST the system for normal operation.

FM1120100653070X

Fig. 18   Test A: Engine Does Not Crank (Part 7 of 17). LS & Thunderbird

TEST CONDITIONS	TESTDETAILS/RESULTS/ACTIONS
A10 CHECK THE CIRCUIT 31S-BB12 FOR AN OPEN	

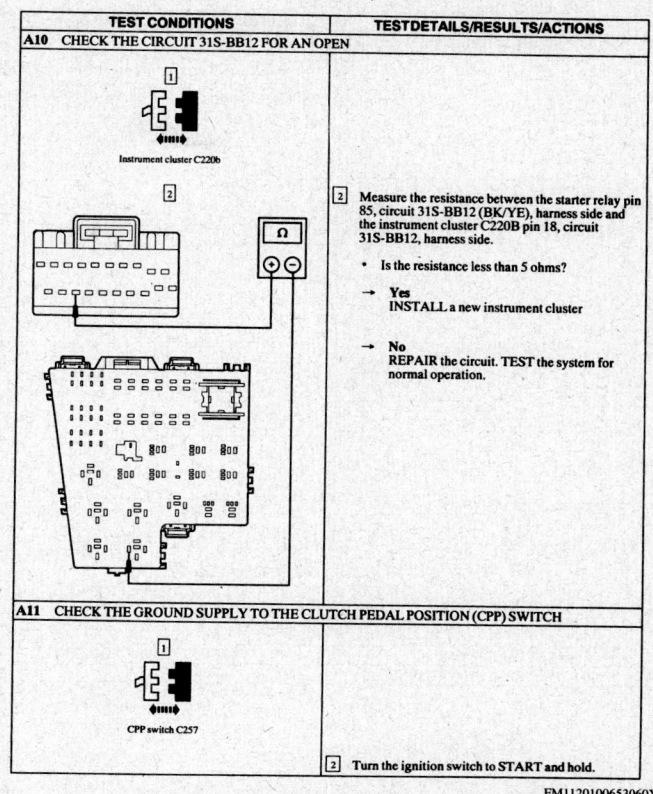

Instrument cluster C220b

² Measure the resistance between the starter relay pin 85, circuit 31S-BB12 (BK/YE), harness side and the instrument cluster C220B pin 18, circuit 31S-BB12, harness side.

- Is the resistance less than 5 ohms?

→ **Yes**
  INSTALL a new instrument cluster

→ **No**
  REPAIR the circuit. TEST the system for normal operation.

| A11   CHECK THE GROUND SUPPLY TO THE CLUTCH PEDAL POSITION (CPP) SWITCH | |

CPP switch C257

² Turn the ignition switch to START and hold.

FM1120100653060X

Fig. 18   Test A: Engine Does Not Crank (Part 6 of 17). LS & Thunderbird

TEST CONDITIONS	TESTDETAILS/RESULTS/ACTIONS
A13 CHECK CIRCUIT(S) 31S-BB12 AND 31S-BB6 FOR AN OPEN	

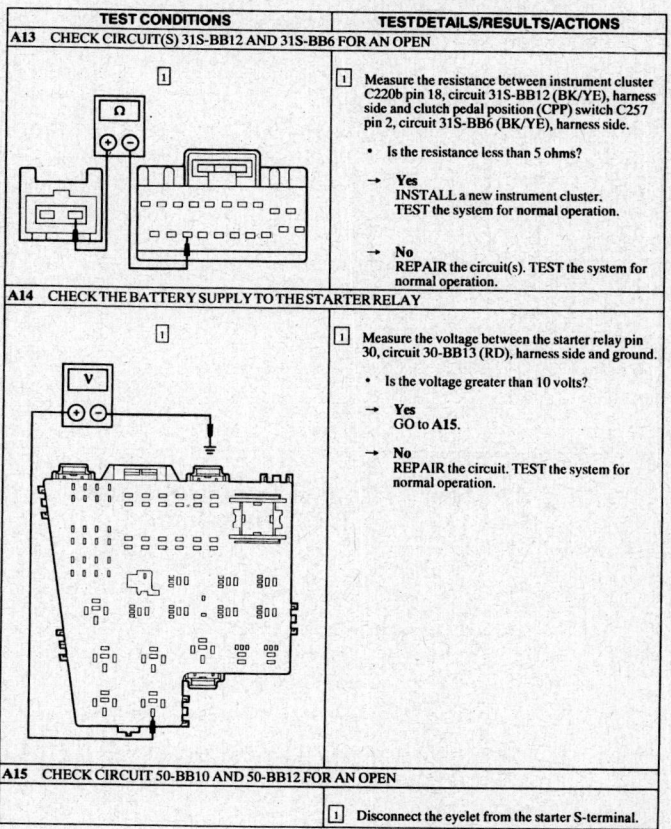

¹ Measure the resistance between instrument cluster C220b pin 18, circuit 31S-BB12 (BK/YE), harness side and clutch pedal position (CPP) switch C257 pin 2, circuit 31S-BB6 (BK/YE), harness side.

- Is the resistance less than 5 ohms?

→ **Yes**
  INSTALL a new instrument cluster. TEST the system for normal operation.

→ **No**
  REPAIR the circuit(s). TEST the system for normal operation.

| A14   CHECK THE BATTERY SUPPLY TO THE STARTER RELAY | |

¹ Measure the voltage between the starter relay pin 30, circuit 30-BB13 (RD), harness side and ground.

- Is the voltage greater than 10 volts?

→ **Yes**
  GO to **A15**.

→ **No**
  REPAIR the circuit. TEST the system for normal operation.

| A15   CHECK CIRCUIT 50-BB10 AND 50-BB12 FOR AN OPEN | |

¹ Disconnect the eyelet from the starter S-terminal.

FM1120100653080X

Fig. 18   Test A: Engine Does Not Crank (Part 8 of 17). LS & Thunderbird

TEST CONDITIONS		TESTDETAILS/RESULTS/ACTIONS
A15	CHECK CIRCUIT 50-BB10 AND 50-BB12 FOR AN OPEN (Continued)	
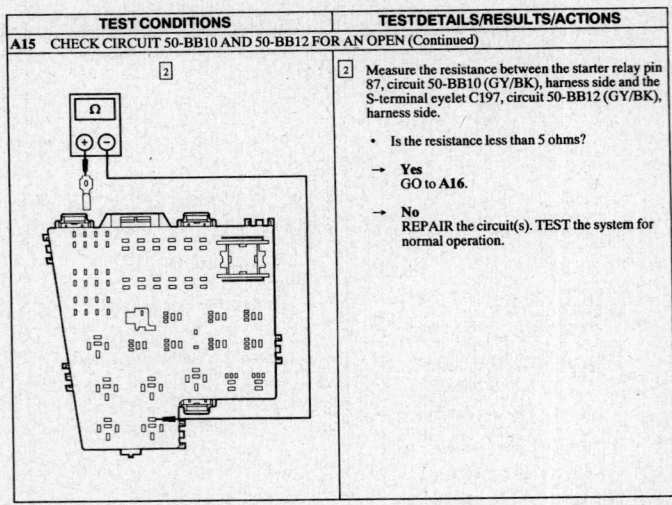		② Measure the resistance between the starter relay pin 87, circuit 50-BB10 (GY/BK), harness side and the S-terminal eyelet C197, circuit 50-BB12 (GY/BK), harness side. • Is the resistance less than 5 ohms? → **Yes** GO to A16. → **No** REPAIR the circuit(s). TEST the system for normal operation.

FM1120100653090X

Fig. 18 Test A: Engine Does Not Crank (Part 9 of 17). LS & Thunderbird

TEST CONDITIONS		TESTDETAILS/RESULTS/ACTIONS
A16	CHECK CIRCUIT 50-BB10 AND 50-BB12 FOR A SHORT TO GROUND	
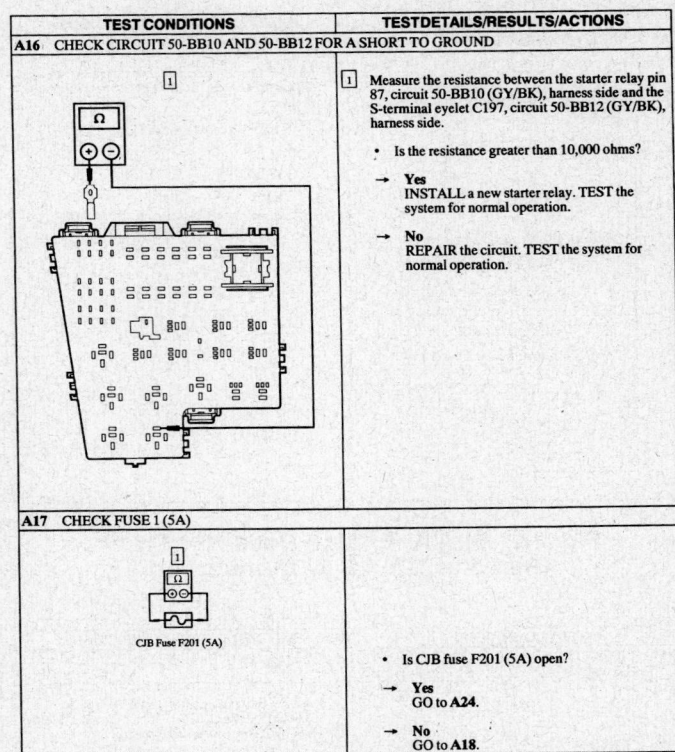		① Measure the resistance between the starter relay pin 87, circuit 50-BB10 (GY/BK), harness side and the S-terminal eyelet C197, circuit 50-BB12 (GY/BK), harness side. • Is the resistance greater than 10,000 ohms? → **Yes** INSTALL a new starter relay. TEST the system for normal operation. → **No** REPAIR the circuit. TEST the system for normal operation.
A17	CHECK FUSE 1 (5A)	
CJB Fuse F201 (5A)		• Is CJB fuse F201 (5A) open? → **Yes** GO to A24. → **No** GO to A18.

FM1120100653100X

Fig. 18 Test A: Engine Does Not Crank (Part 10 of 17). LS & Thunderbird

TEST CONDITIONS		TESTDETAILS/RESULTS/ACTIONS
A18	CHECK THE START INPUT TO FUSE 1	
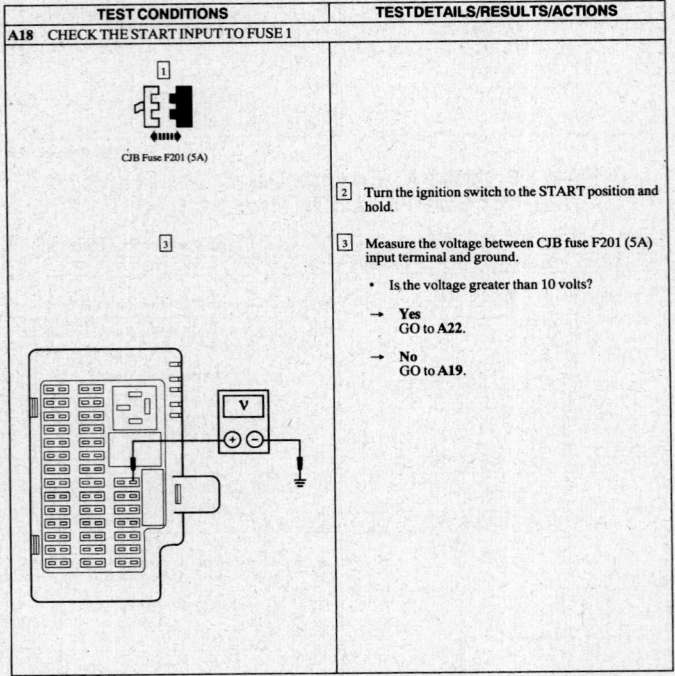 CJB Fuse F201 (5A)		② Turn the ignition switch to the START position and hold. ③ Measure the voltage between CJB fuse F201 (5A) input terminal and ground. • Is the voltage greater than 10 volts? → **Yes** GO to A22. → **No** GO to A19.

FM1120100653110X

Fig. 18 Test A: Engine Does Not Crank (Part 11 of 17). LS & Thunderbird

TEST CONDITIONS		TESTDETAILS/RESULTS/ACTIONS
A19	CHECK THE BATTERY INPUT TO THE IGNITION SWITCH	
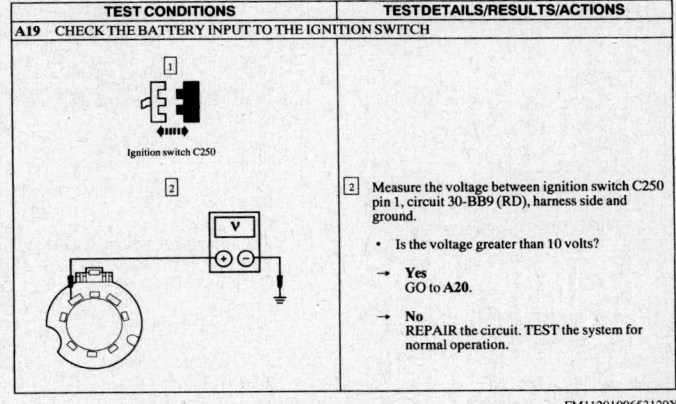 Ignition switch C250		② Measure the voltage between ignition switch C250 pin 1, circuit 30-BB9 (RD), harness side and ground. • Is the voltage greater than 10 volts? → **Yes** GO to A20. → **No** REPAIR the circuit. TEST the system for normal operation.

FM1120100653120X

Fig. 18 Test A: Engine Does Not Crank (Part 12 of 17). LS & Thunderbird

TEST CONDITIONS	TESTDETAILS/RESULTS/ACTIONS
A20 CHECK CIRCUIT 50-DD5 FOR AN OPEN	

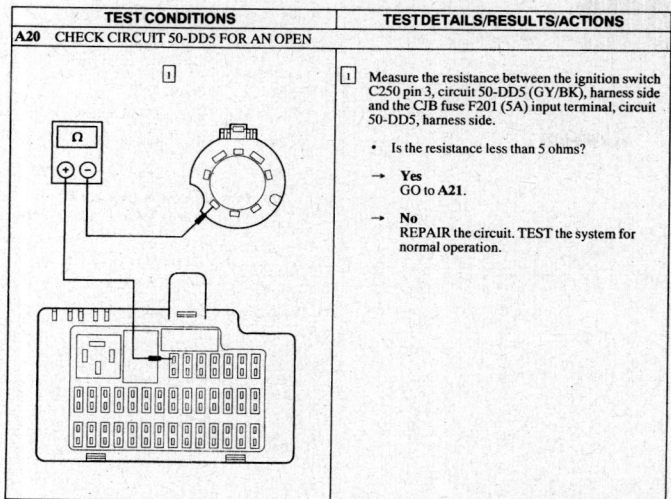

1 Measure the resistance between the ignition switch C250 pin 3, circuit 50-DD5 (GY/BK), harness side and the CJB fuse F201 (5A) input terminal, circuit 50-DD5, harness side.

• Is the resistance less than 5 ohms?

→ **Yes**
GO to **A21**.

→ **No**
REPAIR the circuit. TEST the system for normal operation.

FM1120100653130X

Fig. 18   Test A: Engine Does Not Crank (Part 13 of 17). LS & Thunderbird

TEST CONDITIONS	TESTDETAILS/RESULTS/ACTIONS
A22 CHECK CIRCUIT 50-BB15 FOR AN OPEN (Continued)	

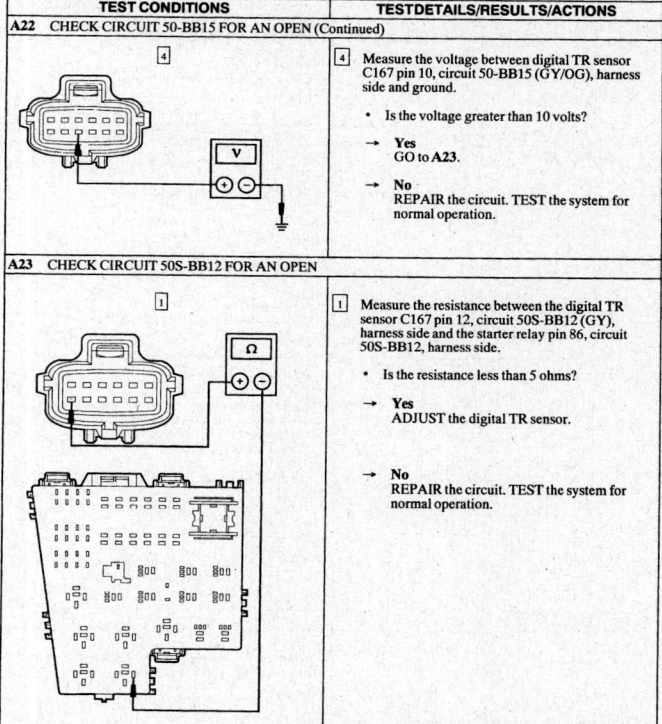

4 Measure the voltage between digital TR sensor C167 pin 10, circuit 50-BB15 (GY/OG), harness side and ground.

• Is the voltage greater than 10 volts?

→ **Yes**
GO to **A23**.

→ **No**
REPAIR the circuit. TEST the system for normal operation.

| **A23** CHECK CIRCUIT 50S-BB12 FOR AN OPEN | |

1 Measure the resistance between the digital TR sensor C167 pin 12, circuit 50S-BB12 (GY), harness side and the starter relay pin 86, circuit 50S-BB12, harness side.

• Is the resistance less than 5 ohms?

→ **Yes**
ADJUST the digital TR sensor.

→ **No**
REPAIR the circuit. TEST the system for normal operation.

FM1120100653150X

Fig. 18   Test A: Engine Does Not Crank (Part 15 of 17). LS & Thunderbird

TEST CONDITIONS	TESTDETAILS/RESULTS/ACTIONS
A21 CHECK CIRCUIT 50-DD5 FOR A SHORT TO GROUND	

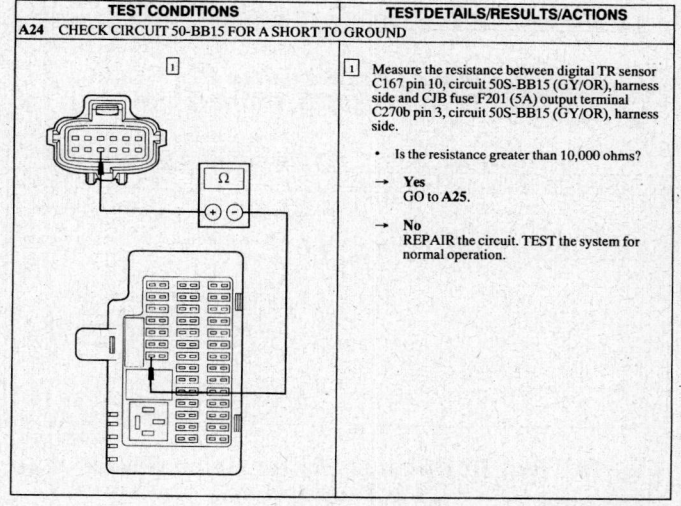

1 Measure the resistance between ignition switch C250 pin 3, circuit 50-DD5 (GY/BK), harness side and the CJB fuse F201 (5A) input terminal, circuit 50-DD5, harness side.

• Is the resistance greater than 10,000 ohms?

→ **Yes**
INSTALL a new ignition switch
TEST the system for normal operation.

→ **No**
REPAIR the circuit. TEST the system for normal operation.

| **A22** CHECK CIRCUIT 50-BB15 FOR AN OPEN | |

CJB Fuse F201 (5A)   Digital TR sensor C167

3 Turn the ignition switch to the START position and hold.

FM1120100653140X

Fig. 18   Test A: Engine Does Not Crank (Part 14 of 17). LS & Thunderbird

TEST CONDITIONS	TESTDETAILS/RESULTS/ACTIONS
A24 CHECK CIRCUIT 50-BB15 FOR A SHORT TO GROUND	

1 Measure the resistance between digital TR sensor C167 pin 10, circuit 50S-BB15 (GY/OR), harness side and CJB fuse F201 (5A) output terminal C270b pin 3, circuit 50S-BB15 (GY/OR), harness side.

• Is the resistance greater than 10,000 ohms?

→ **Yes**
GO to **A25**.

→ **No**
REPAIR the circuit. TEST the system for normal operation.

FM1120100653160X

Fig. 18   Test A: Engine Does Not Crank (Part 16 of 17). LS & Thunderbird

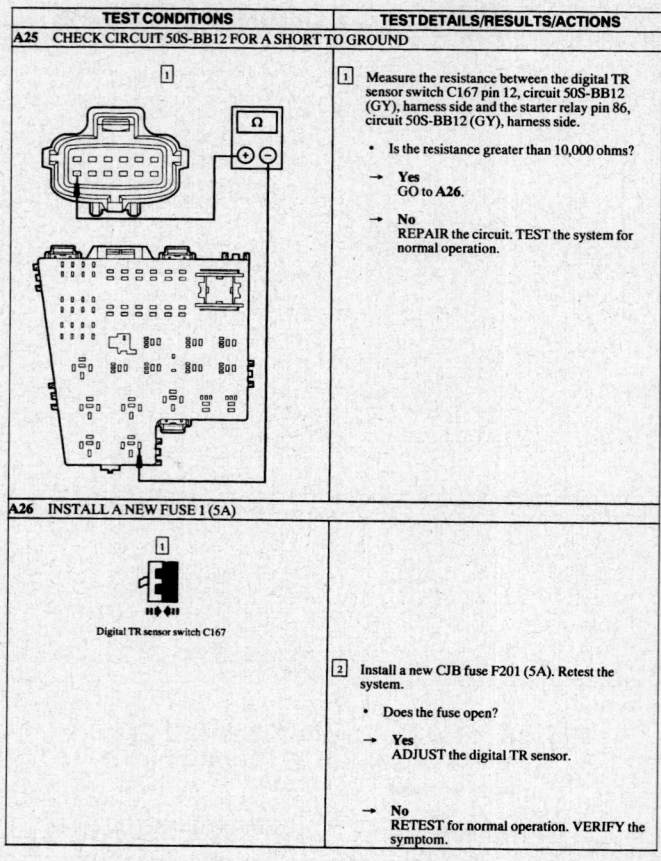

TEST CONDITIONS	TESTDETAILS/RESULTS/ACTIONS
A25 CHECK CIRCUIT 50S-BB12 FOR A SHORT TO GROUND	1 Measure the resistance between the digital TR sensor switch C167 pin 12, circuit 50S-BB12 (GY), harness side and the starter relay pin 86, circuit 50S-BB12 (GY), harness side. • Is the resistance greater than 10,000 ohms? → **Yes** GO to **A26**. → **No** REPAIR the circuit. TEST the system for normal operation.
A26 INSTALL A NEW FUSE 1 (5A)	2 Install a new CJB fuse F201 (5A). Retest the system. • Does the fuse open? → **Yes** ADJUST the digital TR sensor. → **No** RETEST for normal operation. VERIFY the symptom.

FM1120100653170X

Fig. 18   Test A: Engine Does Not Crank (Part 17 of 17). LS & Thunderbird

TEST CONDITIONS	TESTDETAILS/RESULTS/ACTIONS
B3 CHECK FOR UNUSUAL WEAR (Continued)	2 Inspect the ring gear for damaged or worn teeth. • Is the noise due to flywheel ring gear tooth damage? → **Yes** INSTALL a new flywheel ring gear. EXAMINE the starter pinion teeth. If damaged, INSTALL a new starter motor. TEST the system for normal operation. → **No** INSTALL a new starter motor. TEST the system for normal operation.

FM1120100654020X

Fig. 19   Test B: Unusual Starter Noise (Part 2 of 2). LS & Thunderbird

TEST CONDITIONS	TESTDETAILS/RESULTS/ACTIONS
B1 CHECK THE STARTER MOUNTING	1 Inspect the starter motor mounting bolts and brackets for looseness. • Is the starter motor mounted correctly? → **Yes** GO to **B2**. → **No** INSTALL the starter motor correctly. TEST the system for normal operation.
B2 CHECK FOR ENGINE NOISE	1 Turn the ignition switch to the OFF position. 2 Connect a fused jumper wire from the B-terminal to the S-terminal of the starter motor. Engage the starter motor and verify the noise is due to the starter operation. • Is the noise due to the starter motor engagement? → **Yes** GO to **B3**. → **No** Diagnose Engine Mechanical Components
B3 CHECK FOR UNUSUAL WEAR	1 Remove the starter motor.

FM1120100654010X

Fig. 19   Test B: Unusual Starter Noise (Part 1 of 2). LS & Thunderbird

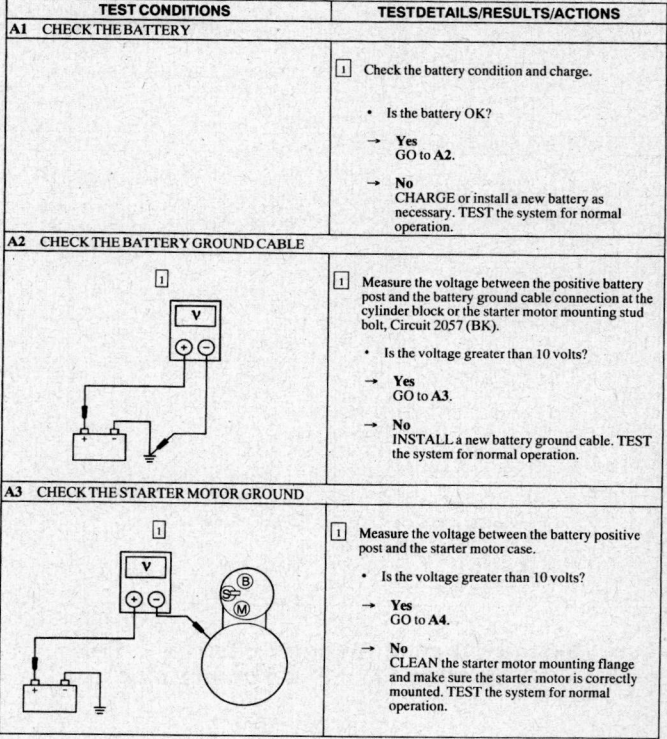

TEST CONDITIONS	TESTDETAILS/RESULTS/ACTIONS
A1 CHECK THE BATTERY	1 Check the battery condition and charge. • Is the battery OK? → **Yes** GO to **A2**. → **No** CHARGE or install a new battery as necessary. TEST the system for normal operation.
A2 CHECK THE BATTERY GROUND CABLE	1 Measure the voltage between the positive battery post and the battery ground cable connection at the cylinder block or the starter motor mounting stud bolt, Circuit 2057 (BK). • Is the voltage greater than 10 volts? → **Yes** GO to **A3**. → **No** INSTALL a new battery ground cable. TEST the system for normal operation.
A3 CHECK THE STARTER MOTOR GROUND	1 Measure the voltage between the battery positive post and the starter motor case. • Is the voltage greater than 10 volts? → **Yes** GO to **A4**. → **No** CLEAN the starter motor mounting flange and make sure the starter motor is correctly mounted. TEST the system for normal operation.

FM1120100660010X

Fig. 20   Test A: Engine Does Not Crank (Part 1 of 9). Mustang

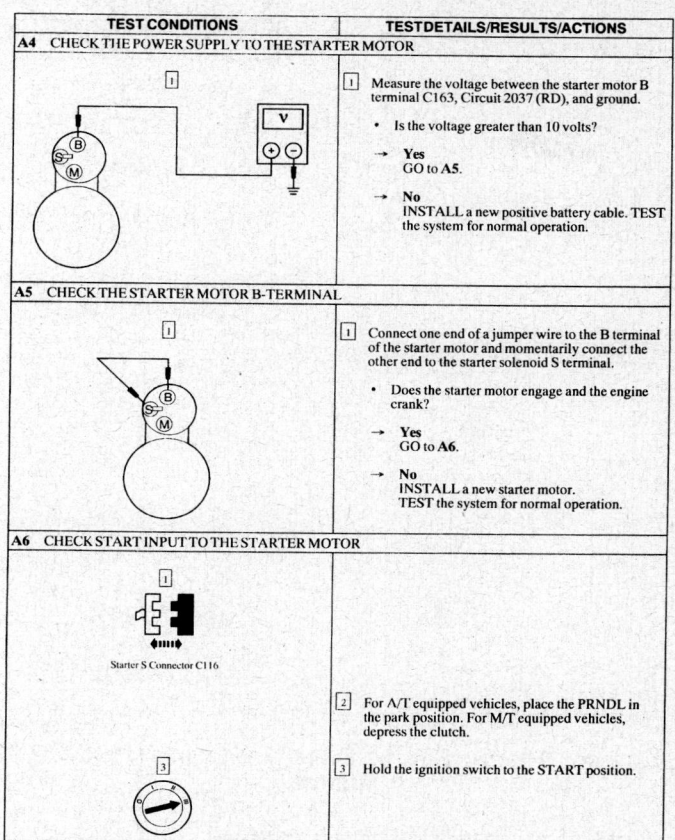

TEST CONDITIONS	TEST DETAILS/RESULTS/ACTIONS
A4 CHECK THE POWER SUPPLY TO THE STARTER MOTOR	
1	1 Measure the voltage between the starter motor B terminal C163, Circuit 2037 (RD), and ground. • Is the voltage greater than 10 volts? → **Yes** GO to **A5**. → **No** INSTALL a new positive battery cable. TEST the system for normal operation.
A5 CHECK THE STARTER MOTOR B-TERMINAL	
1	1 Connect one end of a jumper wire to the B terminal of the starter motor and momentarily connect the other end to the starter solenoid S terminal. • Does the starter motor engage and the engine crank? → **Yes** GO to **A6**. → **No** INSTALL a new starter motor. TEST the system for normal operation.
A6 CHECK START INPUT TO THE STARTER MOTOR	
Starter S Connector C116	2 For A/T equipped vehicles, place the PRNDL in the park position. For M/T equipped vehicles, depress the clutch. 3 Hold the ignition switch to the START position.

Fig. 20   Test A: Engine Does Not Crank (Part 2 of 9). Mustang

FM1120100660020X

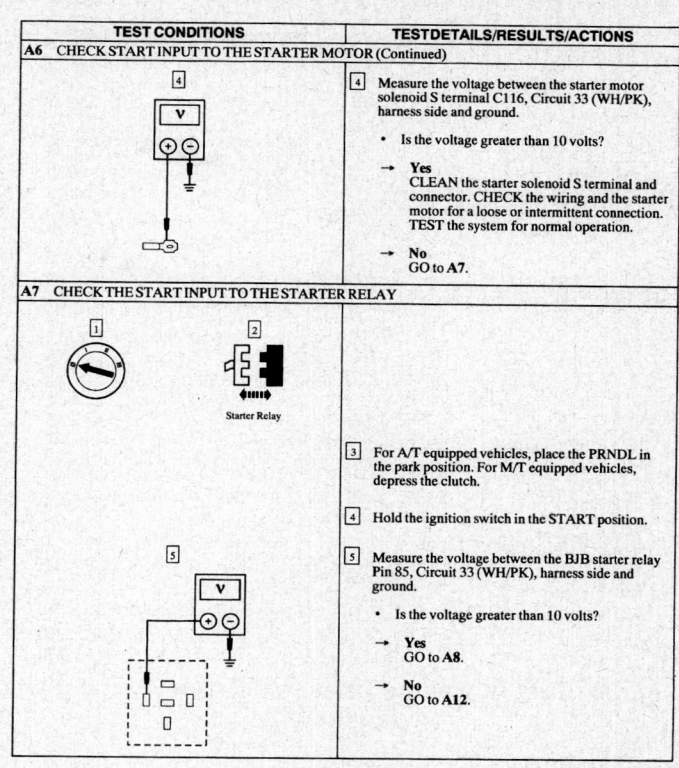

TEST CONDITIONS	TEST DETAILS/RESULTS/ACTIONS
A6 CHECK START INPUT TO THE STARTER MOTOR (Continued)	
4	4 Measure the voltage between the starter motor solenoid S terminal C116, Circuit 33 (WH/PK), harness side and ground. • Is the voltage greater than 10 volts? → **Yes** CLEAN the starter solenoid S terminal and connector. CHECK the wiring and the starter motor for a loose or intermittent connection. TEST the system for normal operation. → **No** GO to **A7**.
A7 CHECK THE START INPUT TO THE STARTER RELAY	
1 2 Starter Relay	3 For A/T equipped vehicles, place the PRNDL in the park position. For M/T equipped vehicles, depress the clutch. 4 Hold the ignition switch in the START position. 5 Measure the voltage between the BJB starter relay Pin 85, Circuit 33 (WH/PK), harness side and ground. • Is the voltage greater than 10 volts? → **Yes** GO to **A8**. → **No** GO to **A12**.

FM1120100660030X

Fig. 20   Test A: Engine Does Not Crank (Part 3 of 9). Mustang

TEST CONDITIONS	TEST DETAILS/RESULTS/ACTIONS
A8 CHECK THE BATTERY SUPPLY TO THE STARTER RELAY	
1 2	2 Measure the voltage between the BJB starter relay Pin 30, Circuit 1050 (LG/VT), harness side and ground. • Is the voltage greater than 10 volts? → **Yes** GO to **A9**. → **No** REPAIR the circuit. TEST the system for normal operation.
A9 CHECK THE STARTER RELAY GROUND	
1	1 Measure the resistance between the BJB starter relay Pin 86, Circuit 1205 (BK), harness side and ground. • Is the resistance less than 5 ohms? → **Yes** GO to **A10**. → **No** REPAIR the Circuit (BK). TEST the system for normal operation.

FM1120100660040X

Fig. 20   Test A: Engine Does Not Crank (Part 4 of 9). Mustang

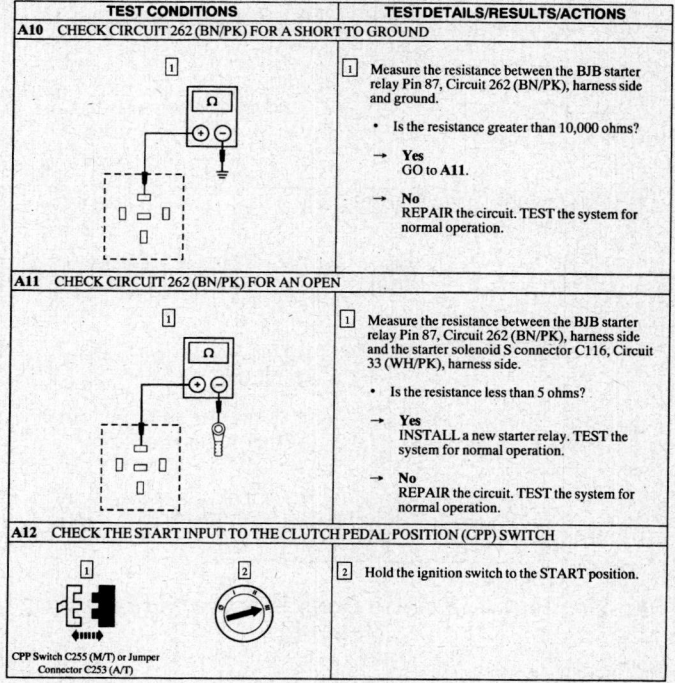

TEST CONDITIONS	TEST DETAILS/RESULTS/ACTIONS
A10 CHECK CIRCUIT 262 (BN/PK) FOR A SHORT TO GROUND	
1	1 Measure the resistance between the BJB starter relay Pin 87, Circuit 262 (BN/PK), harness side and ground. • Is the resistance greater than 10,000 ohms? → **Yes** GO to **A11**. → **No** REPAIR the circuit. TEST the system for normal operation.
A11 CHECK CIRCUIT 262 (BN/PK) FOR AN OPEN	
1	1 Measure the resistance between the BJB starter relay Pin 87, Circuit 262 (BN/PK), harness side and the starter solenoid S connector C116, Circuit 33 (WH/PK), harness side. • Is the resistance less than 5 ohms? → **Yes** INSTALL a new starter relay. TEST the system for normal operation. → **No** REPAIR the circuit. TEST the system for normal operation.
A12 CHECK THE START INPUT TO THE CLUTCH PEDAL POSITION (CPP) SWITCH	
1 2 CPP Switch C255 (M/T) or Jumper Connector C253 (A/T)	2 Hold the ignition switch to the START position.

FM1120100660050X

Fig. 20   Test A: Engine Does Not Crank (Part 5 of 9). Mustang

TEST CONDITIONS	TESTDETAILS/RESULTS/ACTIONS
A12 CHECK THE START INPUT TO THE CLUTCH PEDAL POSITION (CPP) SWITCH (Continued)	③ Measure the voltage between the CPP switch C255 (M/T), or jumper connector C253 (A/T), Circuit 32 (RD/LB), harness side and ground. • Is the voltage greater than 10 volts? → **Yes** GO to **A14**. → **No** GO to **A13**.
A13 CHECK THE INPUT TO CJB FUSE 6 (20A)	① Hold the ignition switch to the START position. ② Measure the voltage between CJB Fuse 6 (20A) Pin 1, Circuit 33 (WH/PK), harness side and ground. • Is the voltage greater than 10 volts? → **Yes** REPAIR circuit. TEST the system for normal operation. → **No** GO to **A17**.

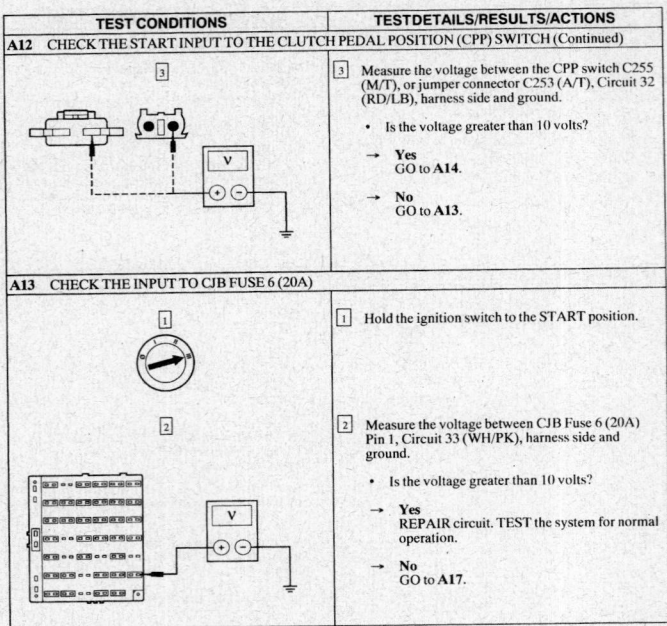

FM1120100660060X

Fig. 20   Test A: Engine Does Not Crank (Part 6 of 9). Mustang

TEST CONDITIONS	TESTDETAILS/RESULTS/ACTIONS
A14 CHECK CPP OUTPUT FOR AN OPEN	① Measure the resistance between the CPP switch connector C255 (M/T) or jumper connector C253 (A/T), Circuit 33 (WH/PK), harness side and the BJB starter relay Pin 85, Circuit 33 (WH/PK), harness side. • Is the resistance less than 5 ohms? → **Yes** INSTALL a new clutch pedal position switch or jumper. TEST the system for normal operation. → **No** For manual transmission, REPAIR Circuit 32 (RD/LB) or Circuit 33 (WH/PK). TEST the system for normal operation. For automatic transmission, GO to **A15**.
A15 CHECK CIRCUIT 33 (WH/PK) AND 32 (RD/LB) FOR AN OPEN	① Digital TR Sensor C110 ② Measure the resistance between the jumper connector C253, Circuit 33 (WH/PK), harness side and the digital TR sensor connector C110 Pin 10, Circuit 32 (RD/LB), harness side. • Is the resistance less than 5 ohms? → **Yes** GO to **A16**. → **No** REPAIR Circuit 32 (RD/LB) or Circuit 33 (WH/PK). TEST the system for normal operation.

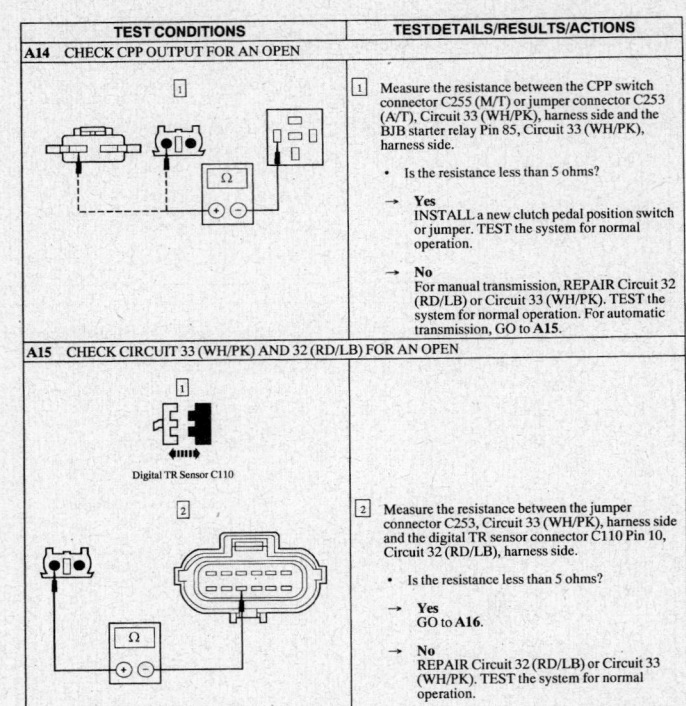

FM1120100660070X

Fig. 20   Test A: Engine Does Not Crank (Part 7 of 9). Mustang

TEST CONDITIONS	TESTDETAILS/RESULTS/ACTIONS
A16 CHECK CIRCUIT 33 (WH/PK) FOR AN OPEN	① Measure the resistance between the BJB starter relay Pin 85, Circuit 33 (WH/PK), harness side and the digital TR sensor connector C110 Pin 12, Circuit 33 (WH/PK), harness side. • Is the resistance less than 5 ohms? → **Yes** CHECK the digital TR sensor adjustment. If the digital TR sensor is adjusted correctly, INSTALL a new digital TR sensor. TEST the system for normal operation. → **No** REPAIR Circuit 33 (WH/PK). TEST the system for normal operation.
A17 CHECK THE SUPPLY TO THE IGNITION SWITCH	① ② Ignition Switch C209 ③ Measure the voltage between the ignition switch connector C209, Pin B4, Circuit 1050 (LG/VT), harness side and ground. • Is the voltage greater than 10 volts? → **Yes** GO to **A18**. → **No** REPAIR Circuit 1050 (LG/VT). TEST the system for normal operation.

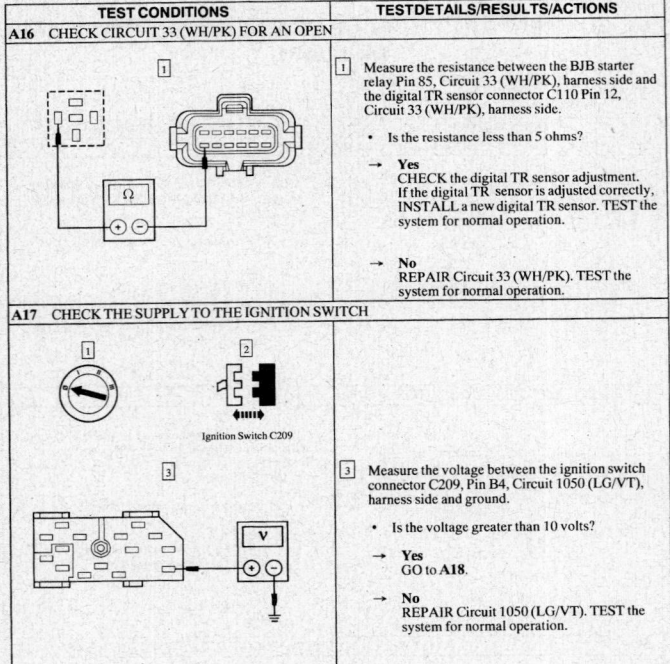

FM1120100660080X

Fig. 20   Test A: Engine Does Not Crank (Part 8 of 9). Mustang

TEST CONDITIONS	TESTDETAILS/RESULTS/ACTIONS
A18 CHECK CIRCUIT 33 (WH/PK) FOR AN OPEN	① Measure the resistance between the ignition switch connector C209 Pin STA, Circuit 33 (WH/PK), harness side and CJB Fuse 6 (20A) Pin 1, Circuit 33 (WH/PK) harness side. • Is the resistance less than 5 ohms? → **Yes** INSTALL a new ignition switch. TEST the system for normal operation. → **No** REPAIR the circuit. TEST the system for normal operation.

FM1120100660090X

Fig. 20   Test A: Engine Does Not Crank (Part 9 of 9). Mustang

TEST CONDITIONS	TESTDETAILS/RESULTS/ACTIONS
B1 CHECK STARTER MOUNTING	① Inspect the starter mounting bolts and brackets for looseness. • Is the starter motor mounted correctly? → **Yes** GO to **B2**. → **No** INSTALL the starter motor correctly. TEST the system for normal operation.

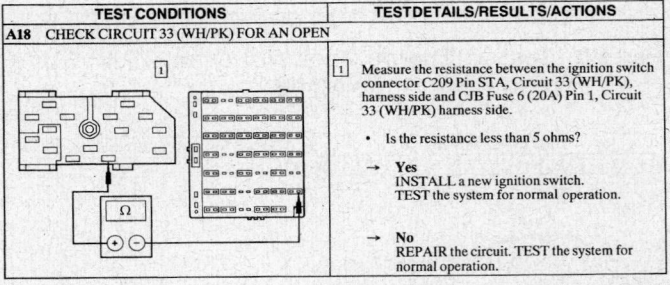

FM1120100661010X

Fig. 21   Test B: Unusual Starter Noise (Part 1 of 3). Mustang

TEST CONDITIONS	TEST DETAILS/RESULTS/ACTIONS
B2 CHECK FOR ENGINE NOISE	
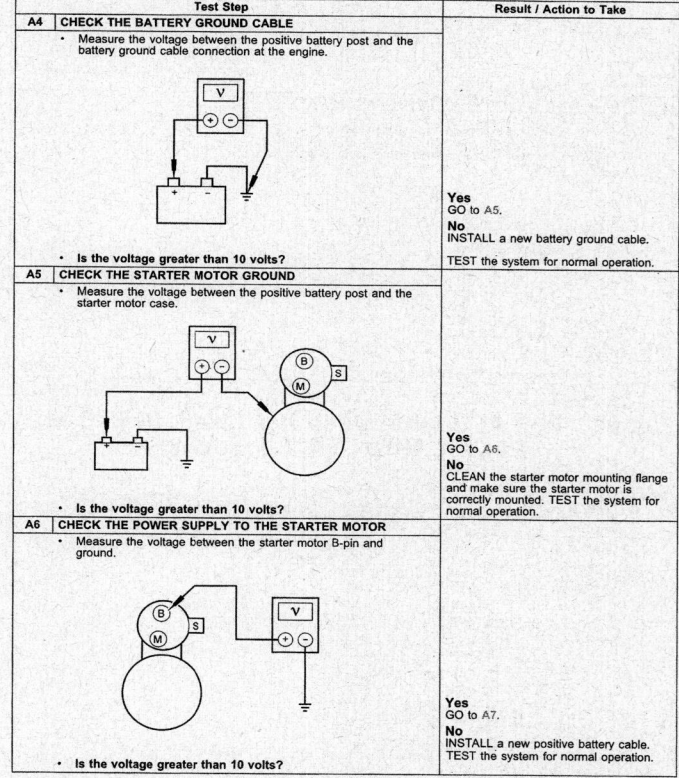	**2** Connect a remote starter switch between the starter solenoid B and S terminals.
	3 Engage the starter motor and verify the noise is due to the starter operation. • Is the noise due to the starter motor engagement? → **Yes** GO to **B3**. → **No** continue the diagnosis.
B3 CHECK FOR UNUSUAL WEAR	
	1 Remove the starter motor.

FM1120100661020X

Fig. 21   Test B: Unusual Starter Noise (Part 2 of 3). Mustang

Test Step	Result / Action to Take
A1 CHECK THE BATTERY	
• Check the battery condition and charge. ~~Refer to Section 414-01.~~ • **Is the battery OK?**	**Yes** GO to A2. **No** CHARGE or INSTALL a new battery as necessary. TEST the system for normal operation.
A2 CHECK THE CONDITION OF THE PATS	
• **NOTE:** The PATS diagnostic trouble codes (DTCs) are the only DTCs of concern in this step. Only repair retrieved non-PATS DTCs if a customer concern is reported. Check for PATS DTCs. • Were any PATS DTCs retrieved?	**Yes** Diagnose PATS DTC's. **No** GO to A3.
A3 CHECK THE AUTOMATIC TRANSMISSION RANGE (TR) SENSOR	
• Enter the following diagnostic mode on the diagnostic tool: PCM TR sensor PID • While observing the PCM TR sensor PID, place the vehicle in PARK and NEUTRAL. • **Does the PID match the gear selection?**	**Yes** GO to A4. **No** GO to the appropriate automatic transmission section to diagnose the TR sensor.

ARM0500000000509

Fig. 22   Test A: Engine Does Not Crank (Part 1 of 6). Fusion, Milan, MKZ & Zephyr

TEST CONDITIONS	TEST DETAILS/RESULTS/ACTIONS
B3 CHECK FOR UNUSUAL WEAR (Continued)	
	2 Inspect the ring gear. • Is the noise due to ring gear tooth damage? → **Yes** INSTALL a new ring gear. EXAMINE the starter pinion teeth. If damaged, INSTALL a new starter motor. normal operation. → **No** INSTALL a new starter motor. TEST the system for normal operation.

FM1120100661030X

Fig. 21   Test B: Unusual Starter Noise (Part 3 of 3). Mustang

Test Step	Result / Action to Take
A4 CHECK THE BATTERY GROUND CABLE	
• Measure the voltage between the positive battery post and the battery ground cable connection at the engine. • **Is the voltage greater than 10 volts?**	**Yes** GO to A5. **No** INSTALL a new battery ground cable. TEST the system for normal operation.
A5 CHECK THE STARTER MOTOR GROUND	
• Measure the voltage between the positive battery post and the starter motor case. • **Is the voltage greater than 10 volts?**	**Yes** GO to A6. **No** CLEAN the starter motor mounting flange and make sure the starter motor is correctly mounted. TEST the system for normal operation.
A6 CHECK THE POWER SUPPLY TO THE STARTER MOTOR	
• Measure the voltage between the starter motor B-pin and ground. • **Is the voltage greater than 10 volts?**	**Yes** GO to A7. **No** INSTALL a new positive battery cable. TEST the system for normal operation.

ARM0500000000510

Fig. 22   Test A: Engine Does Not Crank (Part 2 of 6). Fusion, Milan, MKZ & Zephyr

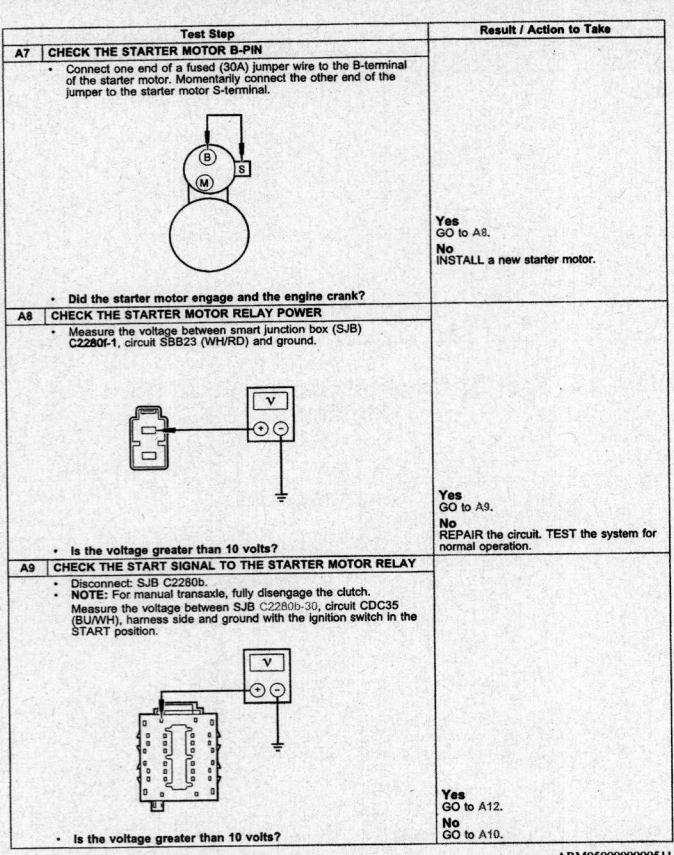

Test Step		Result / Action to Take
A7	CHECK THE STARTER MOTOR B-PIN	
	• Connect one end of a fused (30A) jumper wire to the B-terminal of the starter motor. Momentarily connect the other end of the jumper to the starter motor S-terminal.	**Yes** GO to A8. **No** INSTALL a new starter motor.
	• Did the starter motor engage and the engine crank?	
A8	CHECK THE STARTER MOTOR RELAY POWER	
	• Measure the voltage between smart junction box (SJB) C2280f-1, circuit SBB23 (WH/RD) and ground.	**Yes** GO to A9. **No** REPAIR the circuit. TEST the system for normal operation.
	• Is the voltage greater than 10 volts?	
A9	CHECK THE START SIGNAL TO THE STARTER MOTOR RELAY	
	• Disconnect: SJB C2280b. • NOTE: For manual transaxle, fully disengage the clutch. Measure the voltage between SJB C2280b-30, circuit CDC35 (BU/WH), harness side and ground with the ignition switch in the START position.	**Yes** GO to A12. **No** GO to A10.
	• Is the voltage greater than 10 volts?	

ARM0500000000511

Fig. 22 Test A: Engine Does Not Crank (Part 3 of 6). Fusion, Milan, MKZ & Zephyr

Test Step		Result / Action to Take
A12	CHECK THE GROUND SIGNAL TO THE STARTER RELAY (Continued)	
	• NOTE: For manual transaxle, fully disengage the clutch. Measure the voltage between SJB C2280b-30, circuit CDC35 (BU/WH) and SJB C2280a-18, circuit CDC12 (YE), while placing the ignition switch in the START position.	**Yes** GO to A15. **No** GO to A13.
	• Is the voltage greater than 10 volts?	
A13	CHECK CIRCUIT CDC12 (YE) FOR AN OPEN	
	• Key in OFF position. • Disconnect: PCM C175B. • Measure the resistance between SJB C2280a-18, circuit CDC12 (YE), harness side and PCM C175B-34, circuit CDC12 (YE), harness side.	**Yes** For 2.3L vehicles, INSTALL a new PCM. For 3.0L vehicles, GO to A14. **No** REPAIR the circuit. TEST the system for normal operation.
	• Is the resistance less than 5 ohms?	

ARM0500000000513

Fig. 22 Test A: Engine Does Not Crank (Part 5 of 6). Fusion, Milan, MKZ & Zephyr

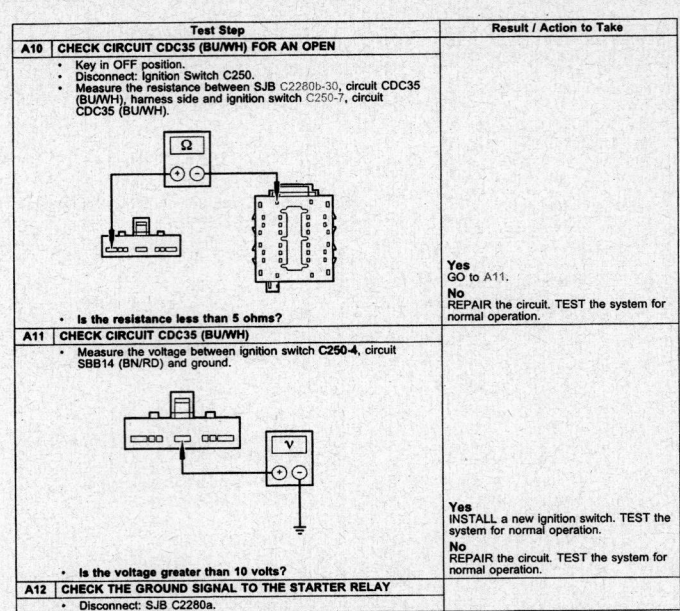

Test Step		Result / Action to Take
A10	CHECK CIRCUIT CDC35 (BU/WH) FOR AN OPEN	
	• Key in OFF position. • Disconnect: Ignition Switch C250. • Measure the resistance between SJB C2280b-30, circuit CDC35 (BU/WH), harness side and ignition switch C250-7, circuit CDC35 (BU/WH).	**Yes** GO to A11. **No** REPAIR the circuit. TEST the system for normal operation.
	• Is the resistance less than 5 ohms?	
A11	CHECK CIRCUIT CDC35 (BU/WH)	
	• Measure the voltage between ignition switch C250-4, circuit SBB14 (BN/RD) and ground.	**Yes** INSTALL a new ignition switch. TEST the system for normal operation. **No** REPAIR the circuit. TEST the system for normal operation.
	• Is the voltage greater than 10 volts?	
A12	CHECK THE GROUND SIGNAL TO THE STARTER RELAY	
	• Disconnect: SJB C2280a.	

ARM0500000000512

Fig. 22 Test A: Engine Does Not Crank (Part 4 of 6). Fusion, Milan, MKZ & Zephyr

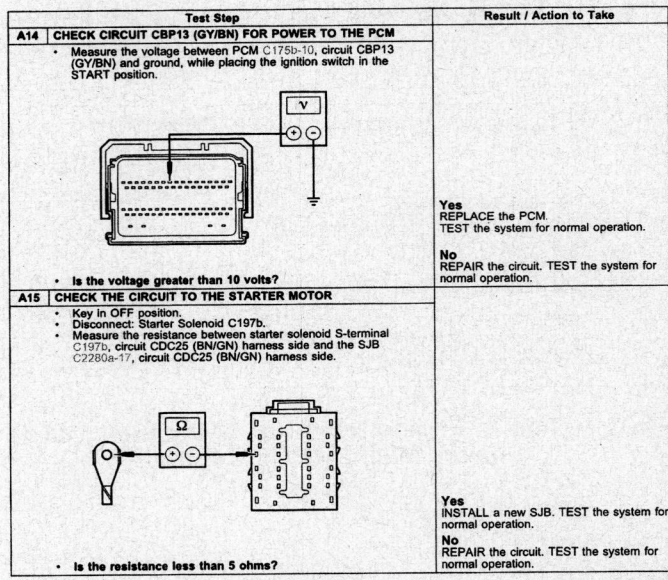

Test Step		Result / Action to Take
A14	CHECK CIRCUIT CBP13 (GY/BN) FOR POWER TO THE PCM	
	• Measure the voltage between PCM C175b-10, circuit CBP13 (GY/BN) and ground, while placing the ignition switch in the START position.	**Yes** REPLACE the PCM. TEST the system for normal operation. **No** REPAIR the circuit. TEST the system for normal operation.
	• Is the voltage greater than 10 volts?	
A15	CHECK THE CIRCUIT TO THE STARTER MOTOR	
	• Key in OFF position. • Disconnect: Starter Solenoid C197b. • Measure the resistance between starter solenoid S-terminal C197b, circuit CDC25 (BN/GN) harness side and the SJB C2280a-17, circuit CDC25 (BN/GN) harness side.	**Yes** INSTALL a new SJB. TEST the system for normal operation. **No** REPAIR the circuit. TEST the system for normal operation.
	• Is the resistance less than 5 ohms?	

ARM0500000000514

Fig. 22 Test A: Engine Does Not Crank (Part 6 of 6). Fusion, Fusion, Milan, MKZ & Zephyr

Test Step	Result / Action to Take
B1 CHECK THE STARTER MOUNTING	
• Inspect the starter motor mounting bolts and brackets for looseness. • **Is the starter motor mounted correctly?**	**Yes** GO to B2 . **No** INSTALL the starter motor correctly. REFER to Starter Motor. TEST the system for normal operation.
B2 CHECK FOR ENGINE NOISE	
• Turn the ignition switch to the OFF position. • Connect a fused jumper wire from the B-terminal to the S-terminal of the starter motor. Engage the starter motor and verify the noise is due to the starter operation. • **Is the noise due to the starter motor engagement?**	**Yes** GO to B3 . **No** REFER to Section 303-01 to continue the diagnosis.
B3 CHECK FOR UNUSUAL WEAR	
• Remove the starter motor. Refer to Starter Motor in this section. • Inspect the ring gear for damaged or worn teeth. • **Is the noise due to flywheel ring gear tooth damage?**	**Yes** INSTALL a new flywheel ring gear. EXAMINE the starter pinion teeth. If damaged, INSTALL a new starter motor. REFER to Starter Motor TEST the system for normal operation. **No** INSTALL a new starter motor. REFER to Starter Motor TEST the system for normal operation.

ARM050000000515

Fig. 23   Test B: Unusual Starter Noise. Fusion, Fusion, Milan, MKZ & Zephyr

TEST CONDITIONS	TESTDETAILS/RESULTS/ACTIONS
A4 CHECK THE STARTER MOTOR GROUND	
1	1 Measure the resistance between the starter motor case and ground. • Is the resistance greater than 5 ohms? → **No** GO to A5. → **Yes** CLEAN the starter motor mounting flange and make sure the starter motor is correctly mounted. TEST the system for normal operation.
A5 CHECK THE POWER SUPPLY TO THE STARTER MOTOR	
1	1 Measure the voltage between starter motor B-terminal and ground. • Is the voltage greater than 10 volts? → **Yes** GO to A6. → **No** INSTALL a new positive battery cable. TEST the system for normal operation.
A6 CHECK THE STARTER MOTOR SOLENOID OPERATION	
1	1 Connect a fused jumper wire to the B-terminal of the starter motor. Momentarily connect the other lead of the fused jumper wire to the starter motor S-terminal. • Did the starter motor engage and the engine crank? → **Yes** GO to A7. → **No** INSTALL a new starter motor. TEST the system for normal operation.

FM1120100673020X

Fig. 24   Test A: Engine Does Not Crank (Part 2 of 8). Five Hundred, Freestyle, Montego, 2004–07 Sable & Taurus

TEST CONDITIONS	TESTDETAILS/RESULTS/ACTIONS
A1 CHECK FOR POWERTRAIN CONTROL MODULE (PCM) DTCS	
	1 **Note:** The PATS system DTCs are the only DTCs of concern in this step. Only repair retrieved non-PATS DTCs if a customer concern is reported. Carry out the powertrain control module (PCM) self-test. • Were any PATS DTCs retrieved? → **Yes** GO to Section 419-01B to repair the PATS system DTCs before proceeding with this test. → **No** GO to A2.
A2 CHECK THE BATTERY	
	1 Check the battery condition and charge. • Is the battery OK? → **Yes** GO to A3. → **No** CHARGE or INSTALL a new battery. TEST the system for normal operation.
A3 CHECK THE BATTERY GROUND CABLE	
1	1 Measure the resistance between the negative battery post and the battery ground cable connection on the engine. • Is the resistance greater than five ohms? → **No** GO to A4. → **Yes** INSTALL a new battery ground cable. TEST the system for normal operation.

FM1120100673010X

Fig. 24   Test A: Engine Does Not Crank (Part 1 of 8). Five Hundred, Freestyle, Montego, 2004–07 Sable & Taurus

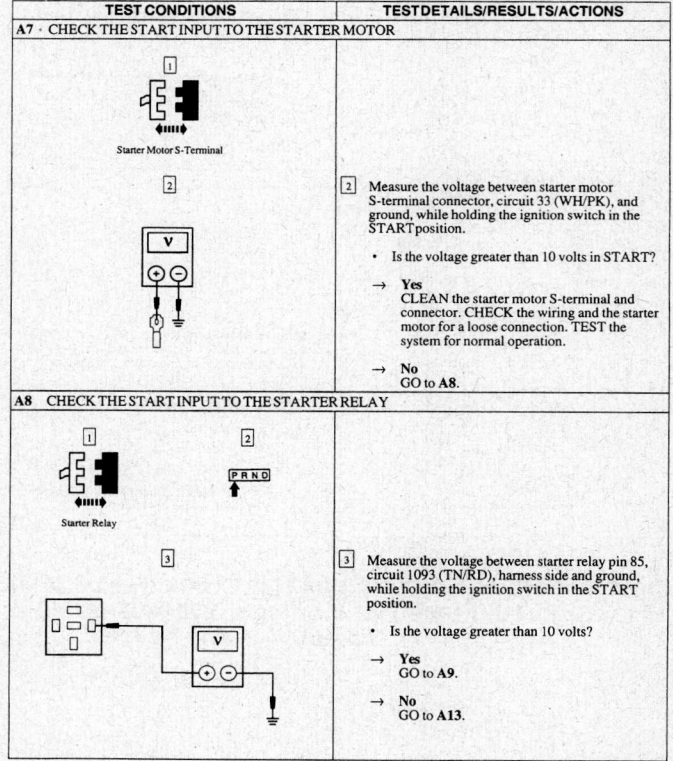

TEST CONDITIONS	TESTDETAILS/RESULTS/ACTIONS
A7 · CHECK THE START INPUT TO THE STARTER MOTOR	
1 Starter Motor S-Terminal 2	2 Measure the voltage between starter motor S-terminal connector, circuit 33 (WH/PK), and ground, while holding the ignition switch in the START position. • Is the voltage greater than 10 volts in START? → **Yes** CLEAN the starter motor S-terminal and connector. CHECK the wiring and the starter motor for a loose connection. TEST the system for normal operation. → **No** GO to A8.
A8 CHECK THE START INPUT TO THE STARTER RELAY	
1 2 Starter Relay 3	3 Measure the voltage between starter relay pin 85, circuit 1093 (TN/RD), harness side and ground, while holding the ignition switch in the START position. • Is the voltage greater than 10 volts? → **Yes** GO to A9. → **No** GO to A13.

FM1120100673030X

Fig. 24   Test A: Engine Does Not Crank (Part 3 of 8). Five Hundred, Freestyle, Montego, 2004–07 Sable & Taurus

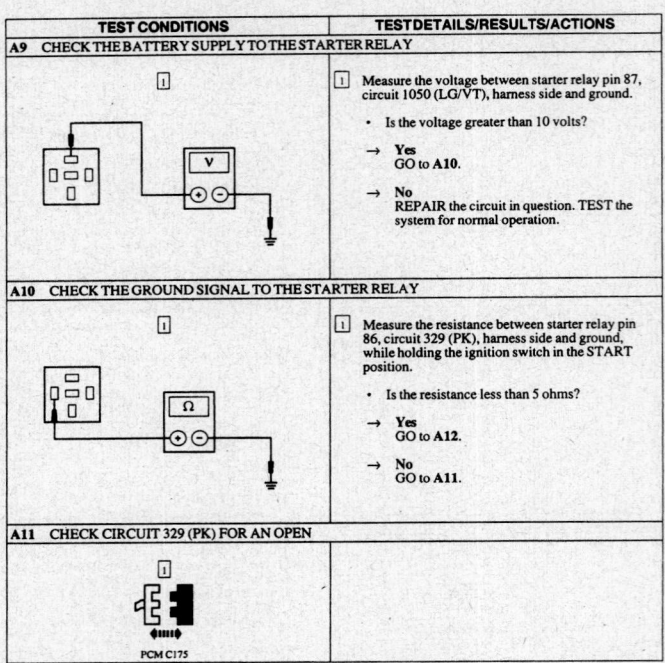

TEST CONDITIONS	TESTDETAILS/RESULTS/ACTIONS
A9 CHECK THE BATTERY SUPPLY TO THE STARTER RELAY	1 Measure the voltage between starter relay pin 87, circuit 1050 (LG/VT), harness side and ground. • Is the voltage greater than 10 volts? → **Yes** GO to **A10**. → **No** REPAIR the circuit in question. TEST the system for normal operation.
A10 CHECK THE GROUND SIGNAL TO THE STARTER RELAY	1 Measure the resistance between starter relay pin 86, circuit 329 (PK), harness side and ground, while holding the ignition switch in the START position. • Is the resistance less than 5 ohms? → **Yes** GO to **A12**. → **No** GO to **A11**.
A11 CHECK CIRCUIT 329 (PK) FOR AN OPEN	

Fig. 24   Test A: Engine Does Not Crank (Part 4 of 8). Five Hundred, Freestyle, Montego, 2004–07 Sable & Taurus

FM1120100673040X

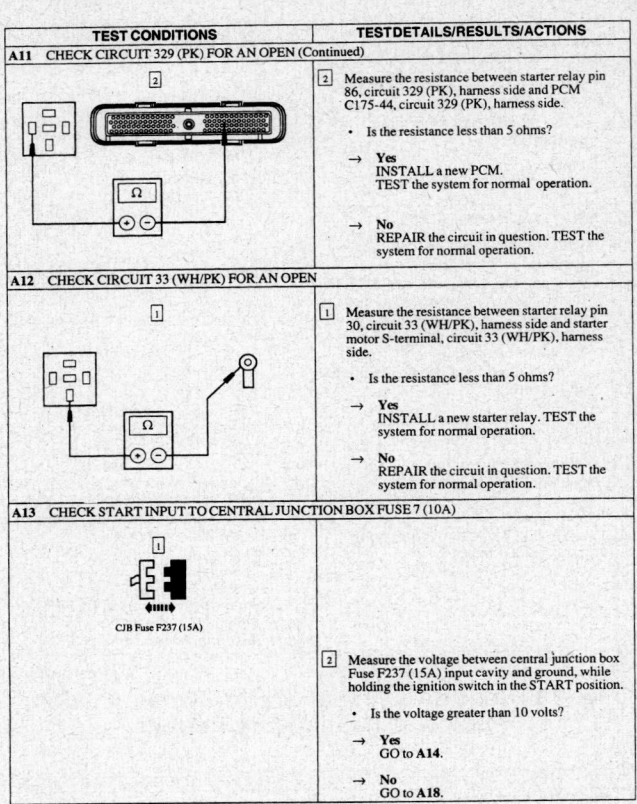

TEST CONDITIONS	TESTDETAILS/RESULTS/ACTIONS
A11 CHECK CIRCUIT 329 (PK) FOR AN OPEN (Continued)	2 Measure the resistance between starter relay pin 86, circuit 329 (PK), harness side and PCM C175-44, circuit 329 (PK), harness side. • Is the resistance less than 5 ohms? → **Yes** INSTALL a new PCM. TEST the system for normal operation. → **No** REPAIR the circuit in question. TEST the system for normal operation.
A12 CHECK CIRCUIT 33 (WH/PK) FOR AN OPEN	1 Measure the resistance between starter relay pin 30, circuit 33 (WH/PK), harness side and starter motor S-terminal, circuit 33 (WH/PK), harness side. • Is the resistance less than 5 ohms? → **Yes** INSTALL a new starter relay. TEST the system for normal operation. → **No** REPAIR the circuit in question. TEST the system for normal operation.
A13 CHECK START INPUT TO CENTRAL JUNCTION BOX FUSE 7 (10A)	2 Measure the voltage between central junction box Fuse F237 (15A) input cavity and ground, while holding the ignition switch in the START position. • Is the voltage greater than 10 volts? → **Yes** GO to **A14**. → **No** GO to **A18**.

FM1120100673050X

Fig. 24   Test A: Engine Does Not Crank (Part 5 of 8). Five Hundred, Freestyle, Montego, 2004–07 Sable & Taurus

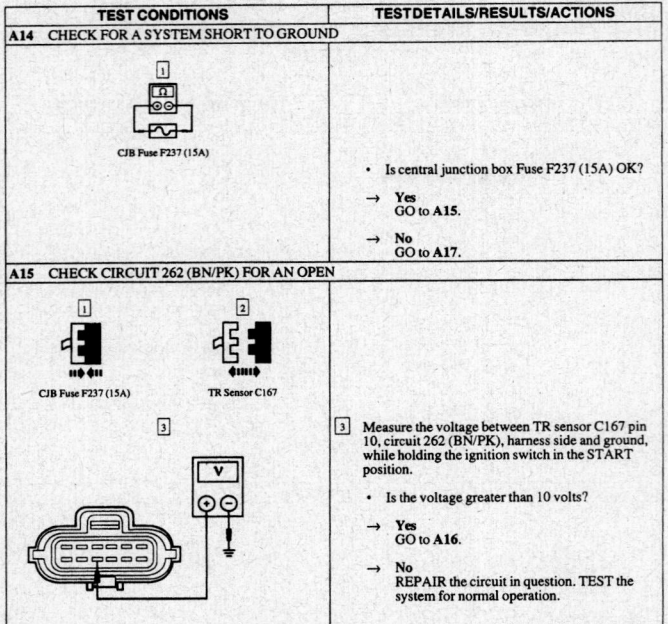

TEST CONDITIONS	TESTDETAILS/RESULTS/ACTIONS
A14 CHECK FOR A SYSTEM SHORT TO GROUND	• Is central junction box Fuse F237 (15A) OK? → **Yes** GO to **A15**. → **No** GO to **A17**.
A15 CHECK CIRCUIT 262 (BN/PK) FOR AN OPEN	3 Measure the voltage between TR sensor C167 pin 10, circuit 262 (BN/PK), harness side and ground, while holding the ignition switch in the START position. • Is the voltage greater than 10 volts? → **Yes** GO to **A16**. → **No** REPAIR the circuit in question. TEST the system for normal operation.

FM1120100673060X

Fig. 24   Test A: Engine Does Not Crank (Part 6 of 8). Five Hundred, Freestyle, Montego, 2004–07 Sable & Taurus

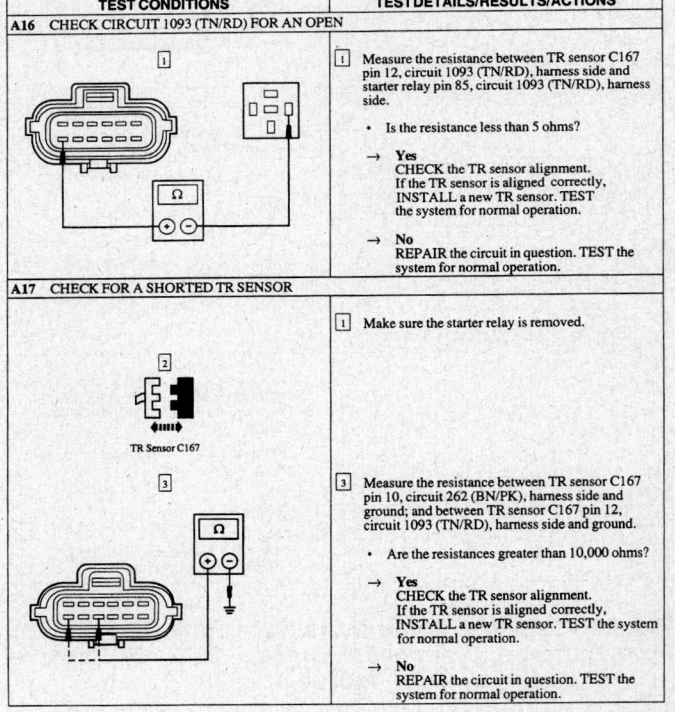

TEST CONDITIONS	TESTDETAILS/RESULTS/ACTIONS
A16 CHECK CIRCUIT 1093 (TN/RD) FOR AN OPEN	1 Measure the resistance between TR sensor C167 pin 12, circuit 1093 (TN/RD), harness side and starter relay pin 85, circuit 1093 (TN/RD), harness side. • Is the resistance less than 5 ohms? → **Yes** CHECK the TR sensor alignment. If the TR sensor is aligned correctly, INSTALL a new TR sensor. TEST the system for normal operation. → **No** REPAIR the circuit in question. TEST the system for normal operation.
A17 CHECK FOR A SHORTED TR SENSOR	1 Make sure the starter relay is removed. 3 Measure the resistance between TR sensor C167 pin 10, circuit 262 (BN/PK), harness side and ground; and between TR sensor C167 pin 12, circuit 1093 (TN/RD), harness side and ground. • Are the resistances greater than 10,000 ohms? → **Yes** CHECK the TR sensor alignment. If the TR sensor is aligned correctly, INSTALL a new TR sensor. TEST the system for normal operation. → **No** REPAIR the circuit in question. TEST the system for normal operation.

FM1120100673070X

Fig. 24   Test A: Engine Does Not Crank (Part 7 of 8). Five Hundred, Freestyle, Montego, 2004–07 Sable & Taurus

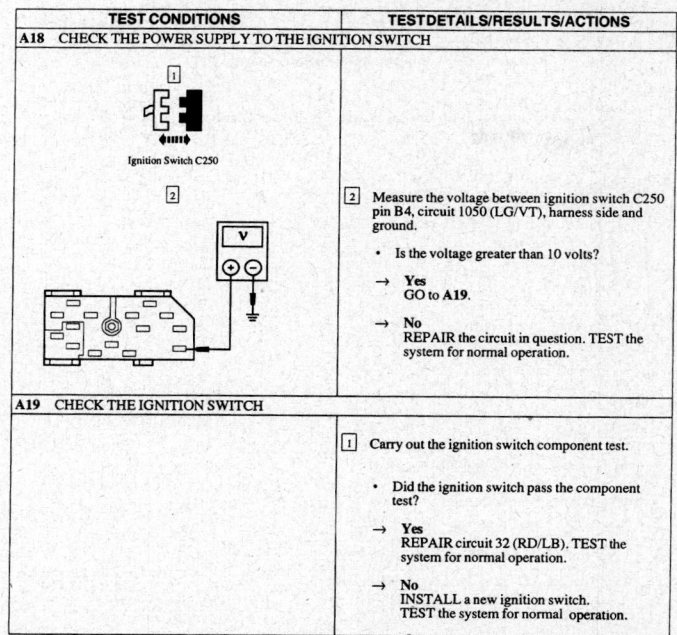

TEST CONDITIONS	TEST DETAILS/RESULTS/ACTIONS
A18 CHECK THE POWER SUPPLY TO THE IGNITION SWITCH	
Ignition Switch C250	[2] Measure the voltage between ignition switch C250 pin B4, circuit 1050 (LG/VT), harness side and ground. • Is the voltage greater than 10 volts? → **Yes** GO to **A19**. → **No** REPAIR the circuit in question. TEST the system for normal operation.
A19 CHECK THE IGNITION SWITCH	
	[1] Carry out the ignition switch component test. • Did the ignition switch pass the component test? → **Yes** REPAIR circuit 32 (RD/LB). TEST the system for normal operation. → **No** INSTALL a new ignition switch. TEST the system for normal operation.

FM1120100673080X

Fig. 24   Test A: Engine Does Not Crank (Part 8 of 8). Five Hundred, Freestyle, Montego, 2004–07 Sable & Taurus

TEST CONDITIONS	TEST DETAILS/RESULTS/ACTIONS
B3 CHECK FOR UNUSUAL WEAR	
	[1] Remove the starter motor. [2] Inspect the ring gear for damaged or worn teeth. • Is the noise due to ring gear tooth damage? → **Yes** INSTALL a new ring gear. EXAMINE the starter pinion teeth. If damaged, INSTALL a new starter motor. TEST the system for normal operation. → **No** INSTALL a new starter motor. system for normal operation.

FM1120100674020X

Fig. 25   Test B: Unusual Starter Noise (Part 2 of 2). Five Hundred, Freestyle, Montego, 2004–07 Sable & Taurus

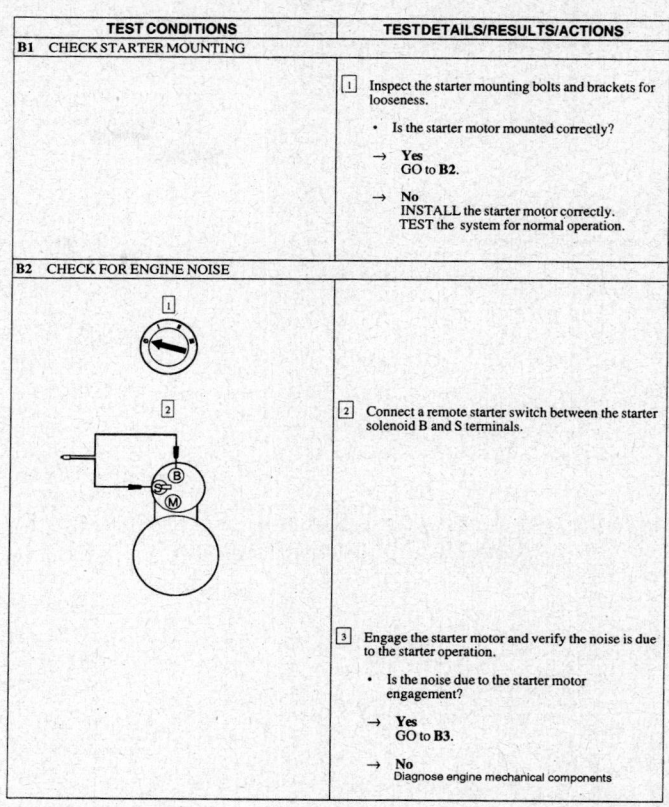

TEST CONDITIONS	TEST DETAILS/RESULTS/ACTIONS
B1 CHECK STARTER MOUNTING	
	[1] Inspect the starter mounting bolts and brackets for looseness. • Is the starter motor mounted correctly? → **Yes** GO to **B2**. → **No** INSTALL the starter motor correctly. TEST the system for normal operation.
B2 CHECK FOR ENGINE NOISE	
	[2] Connect a remote starter switch between the starter solenoid B and S terminals. [3] Engage the starter motor and verify the noise is due to the starter operation. • Is the noise due to the starter motor engagement? → **Yes** GO to **B3**. → **No** Diagnose engine mechanical components

FM1120100674010X

Fig. 25   Test B: Unusual Starter Noise (Part 1 of 2). Five Hundred, Freestyle, Montego, 2004–07 Sable & Taurus

Test Step	Result / Action to Take
A1 CHECK THE BATTERY	
• Check the battery condition and charge. • Is the battery OK?	**Yes** GO to A2. **No** CHARGE or INSTALL a new battery as necessary. TEST the system for normal operation.
A2 CHECK FOR PASSIVE ANTI-THEFT SYSTEM (PATS) DTCs	
• **NOTE:** PATS system DTCs are the only DTCs of concern in this step. Only repair retrieved non-PATS DTCs if a customer concern is reported. • Check for PATS DTCs. • Were any PATS DTCs retrieved?	**Yes** REFER to Anti-Theft to diagnose the PATS DTCs. **No** GO to A3.
A3 CHECK THE BATTERY GROUND CABLE	
• Measure the voltage between the positive battery post and the battery ground cable connection at the engine. • Is the voltage greater than 10 volts?	**Yes** GO to A4. **No** INSTALL a new battery ground cable. TEST the system for normal operation.
A4 CHECK THE STARTER MOTOR GROUND	
• Measure the voltage between the positive battery post and the starter motor case. • Is the voltage greater than 10 volts?	**Yes** GO to A5. **No** CLEAN the starter motor mounting flange and make sure the starter motor is correctly mounted. TEST the system for normal operation

ARM0700000000420

Fig. 26   Test A: Engine Does Not Crank (Part 1 of 7). 2008 Sable, Taurus & Taurus X

A5 CHECK THE POWER SUPPLY TO THE STARTER MOTOR

- Measure the voltage between starter motor C197a, circuit SDC02 (RD) and ground.

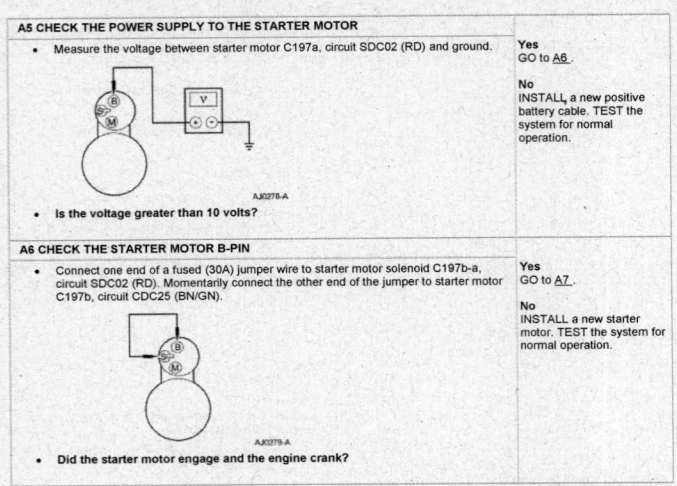

- Is the voltage greater than 10 volts?

Yes
GO to A6 .

No
INSTALL a new positive battery cable. TEST the system for normal operation.

A6 CHECK THE STARTER MOTOR B-PIN

- Connect one end of a fused (30A) jumper wire to starter motor solenoid C197b-a, circuit SDC02 (RD). Momentarily connect the other end of the jumper to starter motor C197b, circuit CDC25 (BN/GN).

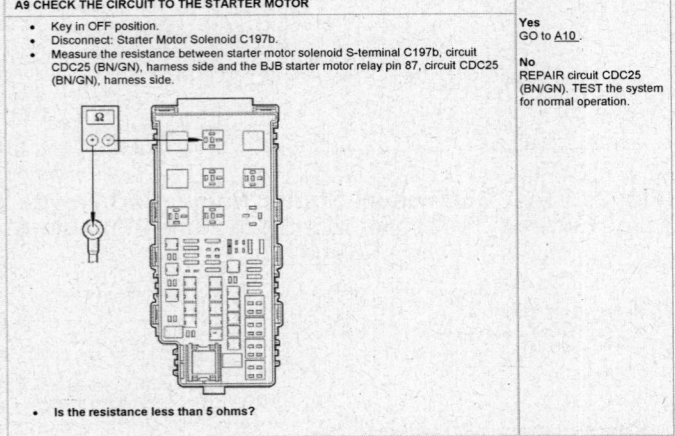

- Did the starter motor engage and the engine crank?

Yes
GO to A7 .

No
INSTALL a new starter motor. TEST the system for normal operation.

ARM0700000000421

Fig. 26   Test A: Engine Does Not Crank (Part 2 of 7). 2008 Sable, Taurus & Taurus X

A9 CHECK THE CIRCUIT TO THE STARTER MOTOR

- Key in OFF position.
- Disconnect: Starter Motor Solenoid C197b.
- Measure the resistance between starter motor solenoid S-terminal C197b, circuit CDC25 (BN/GN), harness side and the BJB starter motor relay pin 87, circuit CDC25 (BN/GN), harness side.

- Is the resistance less than 5 ohms?

Yes
GO to A10 .

No
REPAIR circuit CDC25 (BN/GN). TEST the system for normal operation.

ARM0700000000423

Fig. 26   Test A: Engine Does Not Crank (Part 4 of 7). 2008 Sable, Taurus & Taurus X

A7 CHECK STARTER MOTOR RELAY POWER

⚠ **CAUTION: Use the correct probe adapter(s) when making measurements. Failure to use the correct probe adapter(s) may damage the connector.**

- Disconnect: Starter Motor Relay.
- Measure the voltage between battery junction box (BJB) starter motor relay pin 30, circuit SBB10 (YE/RD), harness side and ground.

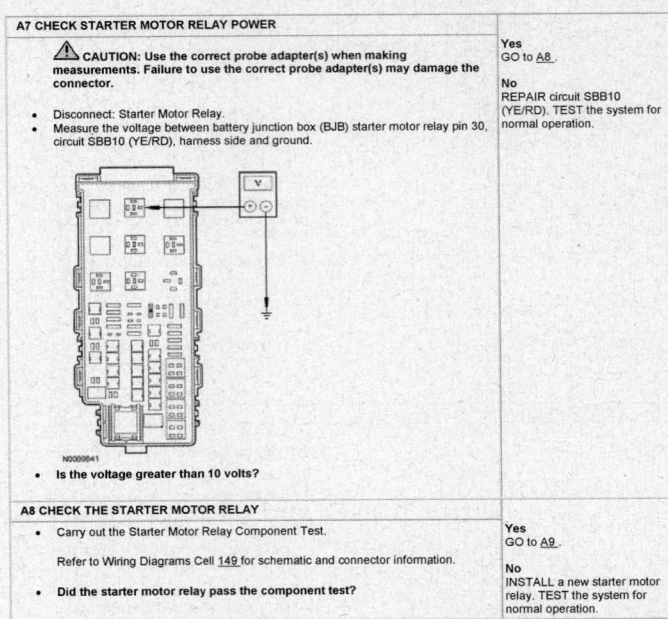

- Is the voltage greater than 10 volts?

Yes
GO to A8 .

No
REPAIR circuit SBB10 (YE/RD). TEST the system for normal operation.

A8 CHECK THE STARTER MOTOR RELAY

- Carry out the Starter Motor Relay Component Test.

  Refer to Wiring Diagrams Cell 149 for schematic and connector information.

- Did the starter motor relay pass the component test?

Yes
GO to A9 .

No
INSTALL a new starter motor relay. TEST the system for normal operation.

ARM0700000000422

Fig. 26   Test A: Engine Does Not Crank (Part 3 of 7). 2008 Sable, Taurus & Taurus X

Test Step	Result / Action to Take
A1 CHECK THE BATTERY CONDITION • Carry out the Battery — Condition Test to determine if the battery can hold a charge and is OK for use. • **Does the battery pass the condition test?**	**Yes** GO to A2 . **No** INSTALL a new battery. TEST the system for normal operation.
A2 CHECK THE GENERATOR OUTPUT • Carry out the Generator On-Vehicle Load Test and No Load Test. Refer to the Component Tests in this section. • **Does the generator pass the component tests?**	**Yes** GO to A3 . **No** Go To Pinpoint Test B .
A3 CHECK FOR CURRENT DRAINS • Carry out the Battery — Drain Testing. • **Are any circuits causing excessive current drains?**	**Yes** REPAIR as necessary. TEST the system for normal operation. **No** GO to A4 .
A4 CHECK THE VEHICLE GROUNDS • Key in START position. • Turn on accessory loads, such as high blower and high-beam headlamps. • With the engine running, measure the voltage drop between the generator housing and the negative battery terminal. • **Is the voltage drop less than 0.1 volt?**	**Yes** GO to A5 . **No** CHECK the engine ground, generator ground and the battery ground for corrosion. TEST the system for normal operation.
A5 CHECK THE VOLTAGE DROP IN THE B+ CIRCUIT SDC02 (RD) • With the engine running and accessory loads ON, measure the voltage drop between generator B+ C102b, circuit SDC02 (RD) and the positive battery terminal. • **Is the voltage drop less than 0.5 volt?**	**Yes** CHECK if the customer left any electrical system(s) on or if there is an intermittent excessive battery draw. TEST the system for normal operation. **No** CHECK for any corrosion in the B+ SDC02 (RD), positive battery cable and/or connections. REPAIR as necessary. TEST the system for normal operation.

ARM0700000000424

Fig. 26   Test A: Engine Does Not Crank (Part 5 of 7). 2008 Sable, Taurus & Taurus X

A13 CHECK THE STARTER DIODE

- Carry out a Starter Diode Test.

Yes
INSTALL a new starter diode. TEST the system for normal operation.
No
GO to A14.

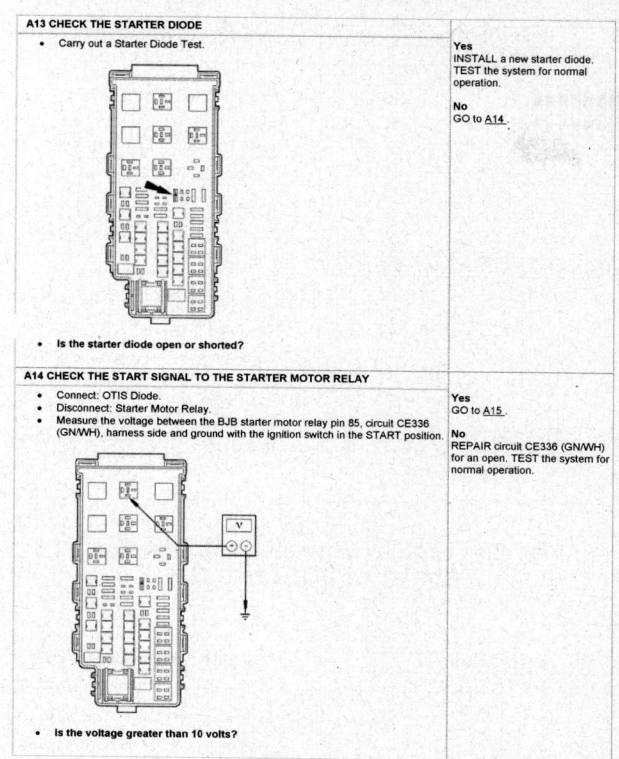

- Is the starter diode open or shorted?

A14 CHECK THE START SIGNAL TO THE STARTER MOTOR RELAY

- Connect: OTIS Diode.
- Disconnect: Starter Motor Relay.
- Measure the voltage between the BJB starter motor relay pin 85, circuit CE336 (GN/WH), harness side and ground with the ignition switch in the START position.

Yes
GO to A15.
No
REPAIR circuit CE336 (GN/WH) for an open. TEST the system for normal operation.

- Is the voltage greater than 10 volts?

ARM0700000000425

Fig. 26 Test A: Engine Does Not Crank (Part 6 of 7). 2008 Sable, Taurus & Taurus X

A15 CHECK CIRCUIT CDC12 (YE) FOR AN OPEN

- Disconnect: PCM C175b.
- Measure the resistance between the BJB starter relay pin 86, circuit CDC12 (YE), harness side and PCM C175b-34, circuit CDC12 (YE), harness side.

Yes
INSTALL a new PCM.
No
REPAIR circuit CDC12 (YE). TEST the system for normal operation.

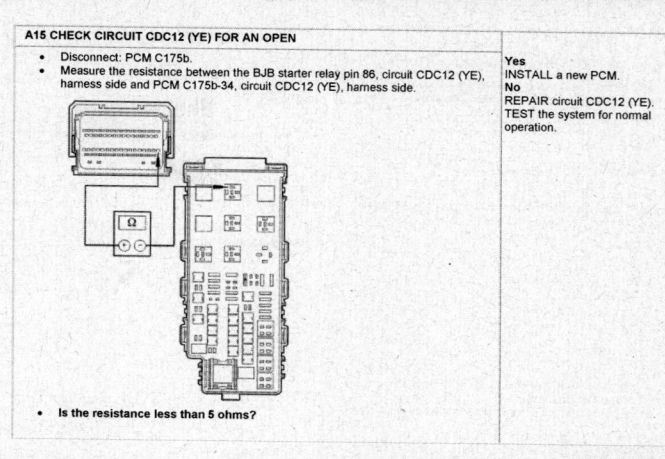

- Is the resistance less than 5 ohms?

ARM0700000000426

Fig. 26 Test A: Engine Does Not Crank (Part 7 of 7). 2008 Sable, Taurus & Taurus X

Test Step	Result / Action to Take
B1 CHECK THE STATUS OF ONE-TOUCH INTEGRATED START (OTIS) (OTS_STAT) PID • Enter the following diagnostic mode on the diagnostic tool: PCM DataLogger/PID. • NOTE: The vehicle must be in PARK for OTIS to operate. • Monitor the PCM PID OTS_STAT with the ignition switch in the RUN position. • Is the OTIS PID enabled?	**Yes** GO to B2. **No** Enable OTIS. TEST the system for normal operation. If OTIS will not enable, INSTALL a new PCM. TEST the system for normal operation.
B2 CHECK THE KEY POSITION FOR START INDICATED (START_KEY) PID • Enter the following diagnostic mode on the diagnostic tool: PCM DataLogger/PID. • Monitor the PCM PID START_KEY with the ignition switch in the START position. • Does the PID change from OFF to ON?	**Yes** GO to B4. **No** GO to B3.
B3 CHECK CIRCUIT CDC35 (BU/WH) • Disconnect: Start Diode. • Disconnect: PCM C175b. • Measure the resistance between the start diode cell, circuit CDC35 (BU/WH), harness side and PCM C175b-9, circuit CDC35 (BU/WH), harness side. • Is the resistance less than 5 ohms?	**Yes** INSTALL a new PCM. TEST the system for normal operation. **No** REPAIR circuit CDC35 (BU/WH). TEST the system for normal operation.
B4 CHECK THE STARTER MOTOR RELAY ENABLE (STRT_RLY) PID • Enter the following diagnostic mode on the diagnostic tool: PCM DataLogger/PID. • Monitor the PCM PID STRT_RLY with the ignition switch in the START position. • Does the PID change from DISABLED to ENABLED?	**Yes** GO to B6. **No** GO to B5.

ARM0700000000427

Fig. 27 Test B: One-Touch Integrated Start (OTIS) Does Not Operate Correctly (Part 1 of 2). 2008 Sable, Taurus & Taurus X

B5 CHECK THE CIRCUIT CE336 (GN/WH) BETWEEN THE BJB AND THE PCM

- Key in OFF position.
- Disconnect: PCM C175b.
- Measure the resistance between the BJB starter motor relay pin 85, circuit CE336 (GN/WH), harness side and PCM C175b-35, circuit CE336 (GN/WH), harness side.

Yes
INSTALL a new PCM. TEST the system for normal operation.
No
REPAIR circuit CE336 (GN/WH). TEST the system for normal operation.

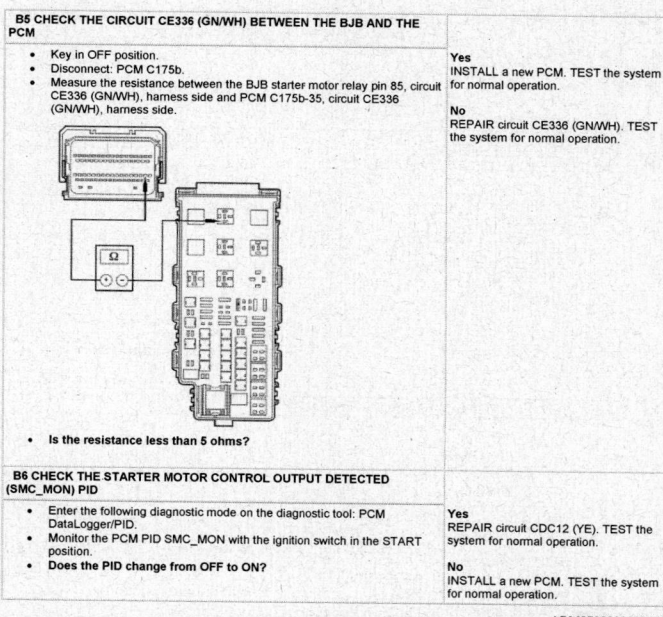

- Is the resistance less than 5 ohms?

B6 CHECK THE STARTER MOTOR CONTROL OUTPUT DETECTED (SMC_MON) PID

- Enter the following diagnostic mode on the diagnostic tool: PCM DataLogger/PID.
- Monitor the PCM PID SMC_MON with the ignition switch in the START position.
- Does the PID change from OFF to ON?

Yes
REPAIR circuit CDC12 (YE). TEST the system for normal operation.
No
INSTALL a new PCM. TEST the system for normal operation.

ARM0700000000428

Fig. 27 Test B: One-Touch Integrated Start (OTIS) Does Not Operate Correctly (Part 2 of 2). 2008 Sable, Taurus & Taurus X

Test Step	Result / Action to Take
C1 CHECK THE STARTER MOUNTING • Inspect the starter mounting bolts for looseness. • **Is the starter motor mounted correctly?**	**Yes** GO to C2. **No** INSTALL the starter motor correctly. TEST the system for normal operation.
C2 CHECK FOR ENGINE NOISE • Key in OFF position. • Connect a remote starter switch between the starter solenoid B- and S-terminals. • Engage the starter motor and verify the noise is due to the starter operation. • Is the noise due to the starter motor engagement?	**Yes** GO to C3. **No** Continue diagnosis.
C3 CHECK FOR UNUSUAL WEAR • Remove the starter motor. • Inspect the ring gear for damaged or worn teeth. • Is the noise due to ring gear tooth damage?	**Yes** INSTALL a new flexplate ring gear. EXAMINE the starter pinion teeth. If damaged, INSTALL a new starter motor. TEST the system for normal operation. **No** INSTALL a new starter motor. TEST the system for normal operation.

ARM0700000000429

Fig. 28   Test C: Unusual Starter Noise. 2008 Sable, Taurus & Taurus X

TEST CONDITIONS	TESTDETAILS/RESULTS/ACTIONS
A3 CHECK THE STARTER MOTOR GROUND	1 Measure the voltage between the battery positive post and the starter motor case. • Is the voltage reading greater than 10 volts? → **Yes** GO to A4. → **No** CLEAN the starter motor mounting flange and make sure the starter motor is properly mounted. TEST the system for normal operation.
A4 CHECK THE POWER SUPPLY TO THE STARTER MOTOR	1 Turn the ignition switch to the off position. 2 Measure the voltage at the starter motor solenoid B terminal. • Is the voltage reading greater than 10 volts? → **Yes** GO to A5. → **No** REPLACE the positive battery cable. TEST the system for normal operation.

FM1120100683020X

Fig. 29   Test A: Engine Does Not Crank (Part 2 of 12). Town Car

TEST CONDITIONS	TESTDETAILS/RESULTS/ACTIONS
A1 CHECK THE BATTERY	1 Check the battery condition and charge. • Is the battery OK? → **Yes** GO to A2. → **No** CHARGE or REPLACE the battery as required. TEST the system for normal operation.
A2 CHECK THE BATTERY GROUND CABLE	1 Measure the voltage between the positive battery post and the battery ground cable connection at the cylinder block (6010). • Is the voltage reading greater than 10 volts? → **Yes** GO to A3. → **No** REPLACE the battery ground cable (14301). TEST the system for normal operation.

FM1120100683010X

Fig. 29   Test A: Engine Does Not Crank (Part 1 of 12). Town Car

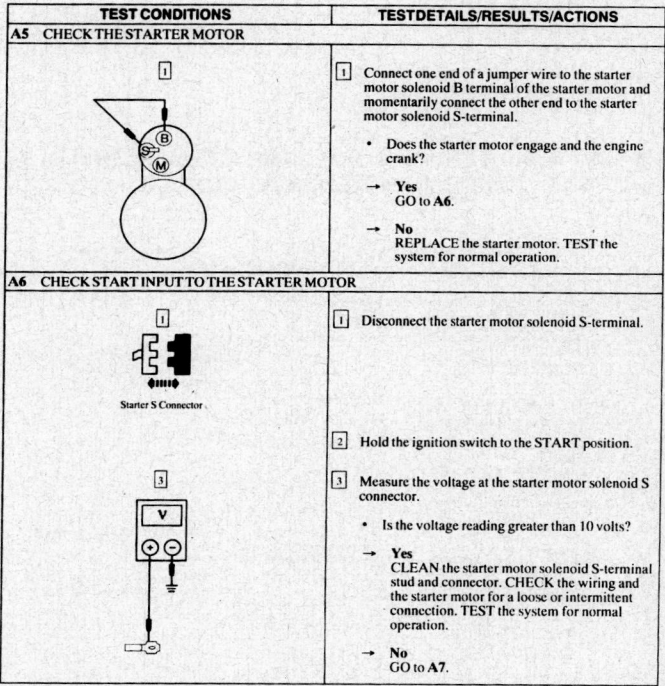

TEST CONDITIONS	TESTDETAILS/RESULTS/ACTIONS
A5 CHECK THE STARTER MOTOR	1 Connect one end of a jumper wire to the starter motor solenoid B terminal of the starter motor and momentarily connect the other end to the starter motor solenoid S-terminal. • Does the starter motor engage and the engine crank? → **Yes** GO to A6. → **No** REPLACE the starter motor. TEST the system for normal operation.
A6 CHECK START INPUT TO THE STARTER MOTOR Starter S Connector	1 Disconnect the starter motor solenoid S-terminal. 2 Hold the ignition switch to the START position. 3 Measure the voltage at the starter motor solenoid S connector. • Is the voltage reading greater than 10 volts? → **Yes** CLEAN the starter motor solenoid S-terminal stud and connector. CHECK the wiring and the starter motor for a loose or intermittent connection. TEST the system for normal operation. → **No** GO to A7.

FM1120100683030X

Fig. 29   Test A: Engine Does Not Crank (Part 3 of 12). Town Car

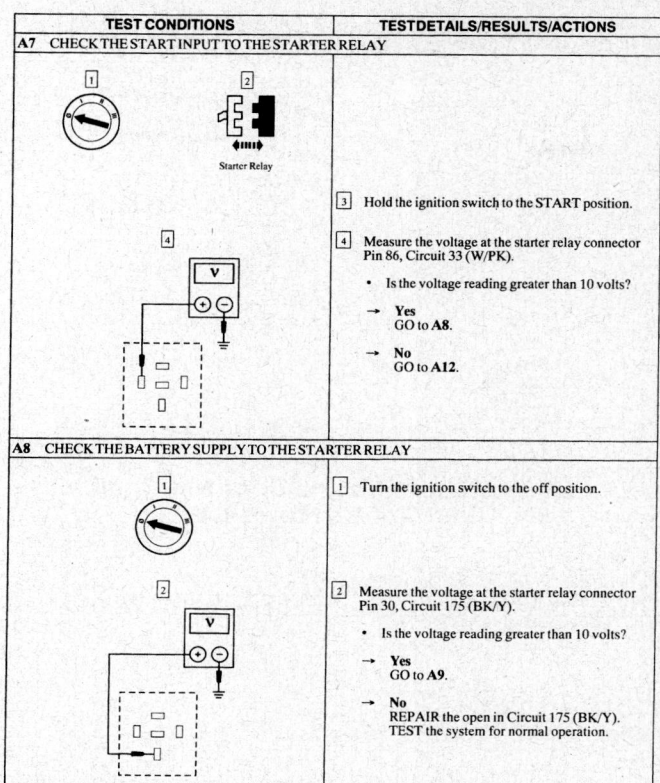

Fig. 29 Test A: Engine Does Not Crank
(Part 4 of 12). Town Car

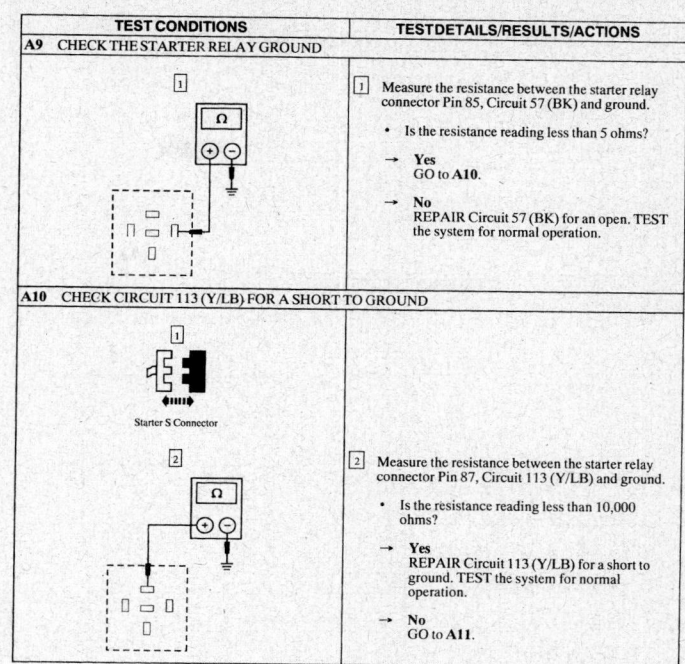

Fig. 29 Test A: Engine Does Not Crank
(Part 5 of 12). Town Car

TEST CONDITIONS	TESTDETAILS/RESULTS/ACTIONS
A11 CHECK CIRCUIT 113 (Y/LB) FOR AN OPEN	

1 Measure the resistance of Circuit 113 (Y/LB) between the starter relay connector Pin 87 and the starter motor solenoid S Connector.

• Is the resistance reading less than 5 ohms?

→ **Yes**
REPLACE the starter relay. TEST the system for normal operation.

→ **No**
REPAIR Circuit 113 (Y/LB) for an open. TEST the system for normal operation.

A12 CHECK FUSE 26 (5A)	

• Measure the resistance of fuse 26 (5A). Is the resistance of Fuse 26 (5A) zero?

→ **Yes**
GO to A13.

→ **No**
GO to A19.

A13 CHECK THE INPUT TO FUSE 26 (5A)	

1 Hold the ignition switch to the START position.

FM1120100683060X

Fig. 29 Test A: Engine Does Not Crank
(Part 6 of 12). Town Car

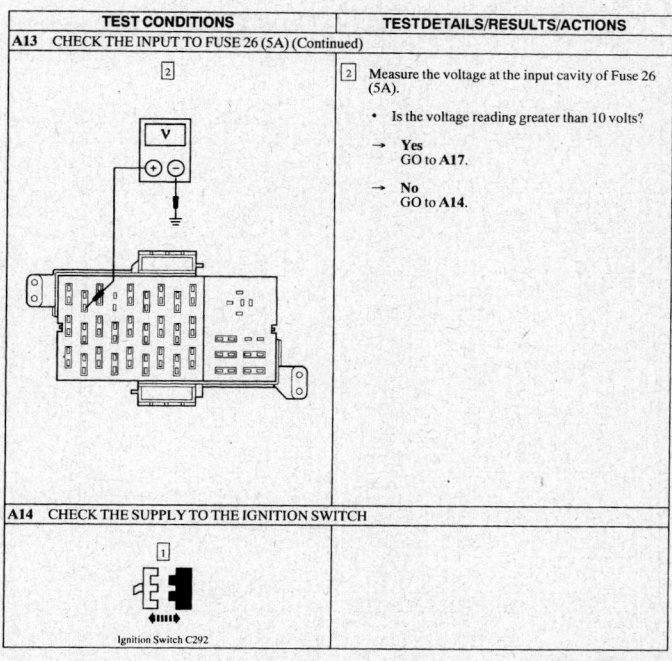

Fig. 29 Test A: Engine Does Not Crank
(Part 7 of 12). Town Car

TEST CONDITIONS	TESTDETAILS/RESULTS/ACTIONS
A14 CHECK THE SUPPLY TO THE IGNITION SWITCH (Continued)	

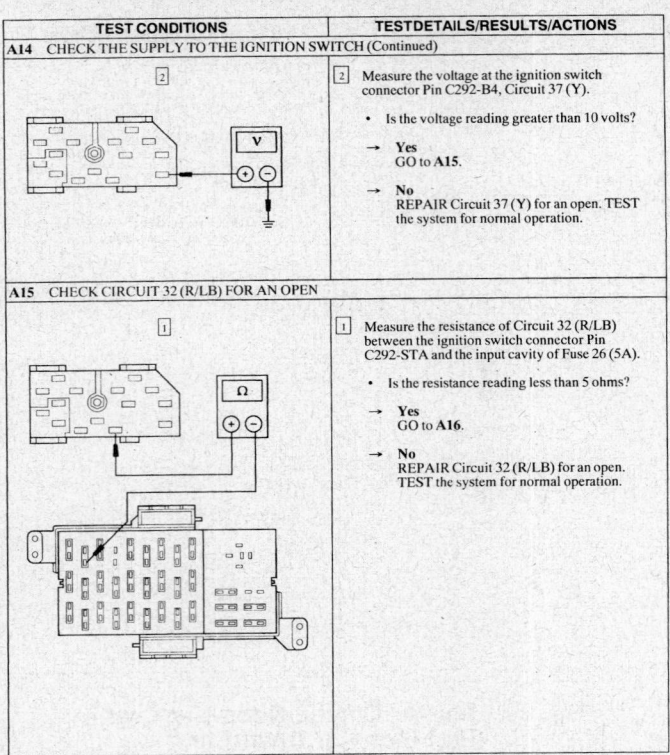

2	2 Measure the voltage at the ignition switch connector Pin C292-B4, Circuit 37 (Y). • Is the voltage reading greater than 10 volts? → **Yes** GO to **A15**. → **No** REPAIR Circuit 37 (Y) for an open. TEST the system for normal operation.

A15 CHECK CIRCUIT 32 (R/LB) FOR AN OPEN	
1	1 Measure the resistance of Circuit 32 (R/LB) between the ignition switch connector Pin C292-STA and the input cavity of Fuse 26 (5A). • Is the resistance reading less than 5 ohms? → **Yes** GO to **A16**. → **No** REPAIR Circuit 32 (R/LB) for an open. TEST the system for normal operation.

FM1120100683080X

Fig. 29 Test A: Engine Does Not Crank (Part 8 of 12). Town Car

TEST CONDITIONS	TESTDETAILS/RESULTS/ACTIONS
A17 CHECK CIRCUIT 262 (BR/PK) FOR AN OPEN (Continued)	

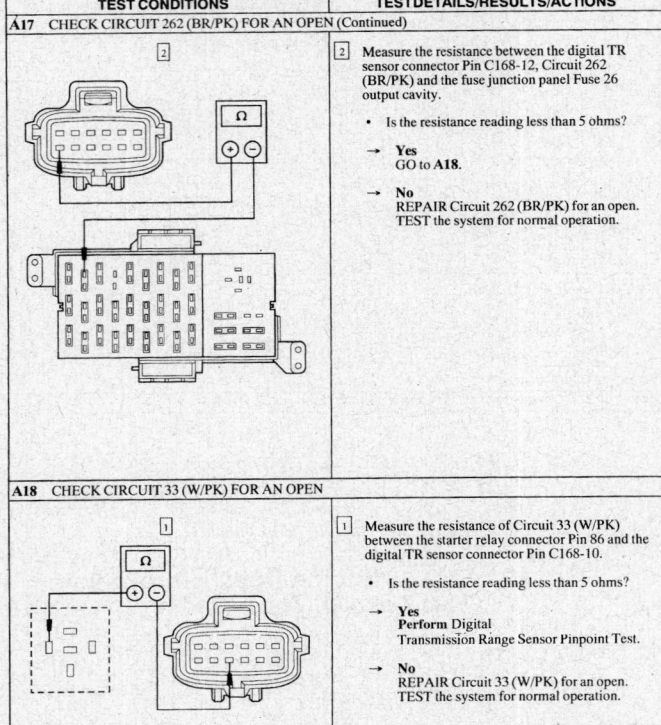

2	2 Measure the resistance between the digital TR sensor connector Pin C168-12, Circuit 262 (BR/PK) and the fuse junction panel Fuse 26 output cavity. • Is the resistance reading less than 5 ohms? → **Yes** GO to **A18**. → **No** REPAIR Circuit 262 (BR/PK) for an open. TEST the system for normal operation.

A18 CHECK CIRCUIT 33 (W/PK) FOR AN OPEN	
1	1 Measure the resistance of Circuit 33 (W/PK) between the starter relay connector Pin 86 and the digital TR sensor connector Pin C168-10. • Is the resistance reading less than 5 ohms? → **Yes** **Perform** Digital Transmission Range Sensor Pinpoint Test. → **No** REPAIR Circuit 33 (W/PK) for an open. TEST the system for normal operation.

FM1120100683100X

Fig. 29 Test A: Engine Does Not Crank (Part 10 of 12). Town Car

TEST CONDITIONS	TESTDETAILS/RESULTS/ACTIONS
A16 CHECK CIRCUIT 32 (R/LB) FOR A SHORT TO GROUND	

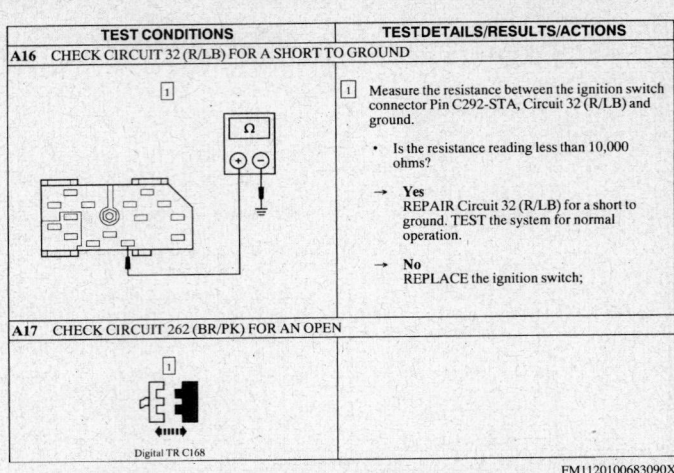

1	1 Measure the resistance between the ignition switch connector Pin C292-STA, Circuit 32 (R/LB) and ground. • Is the resistance reading less than 10,000 ohms? → **Yes** REPAIR Circuit 32 (R/LB) for a short to ground. TEST the system for normal operation. → **No** REPLACE the ignition switch;

A17 CHECK CIRCUIT 262 (BR/PK) FOR AN OPEN	
1 Digital TR C168	

FM1120100683090X

Fig. 29 Test A: Engine Does Not Crank (Part 9 of 12). Town Car

TEST CONDITIONS	TESTDETAILS/RESULTS/ACTIONS
A19 CHECK FOR A SHORTED SYSTEM	

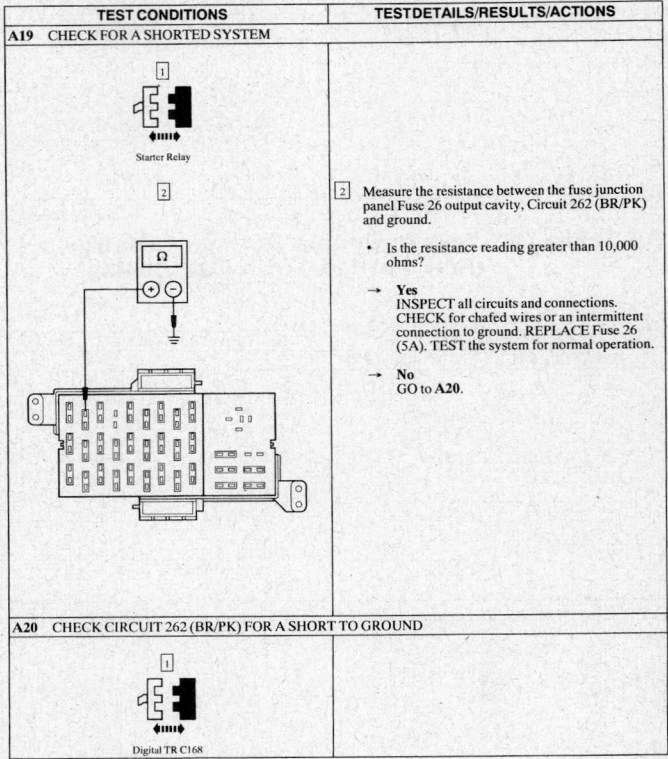

1 Starter Relay 2	2 Measure the resistance between the fuse junction panel Fuse 26 output cavity, Circuit 262 (BR/PK) and ground. • Is the resistance reading greater than 10,000 ohms? → **Yes** INSPECT all circuits and connections. CHECK for chafed wires or an intermittent connection to ground. REPLACE Fuse 26 (5A). TEST the system for normal operation. → **No** GO to **A20**.

A20 CHECK CIRCUIT 262 (BR/PK) FOR A SHORT TO GROUND	
1 Digital TR C168	

FM1120100683110X

Fig. 29 Test A: Engine Does Not Crank (Part 11 of 12). Town Car

TEST CONDITIONS	TESTDETAILS/RESULTS/ACTIONS
A20 CHECK CIRCUIT 262 (BR/PK) FOR A SHORT TO GROUND (Continued)	2 Measure the resistance between the digital TR sensor connector Pin C168-12, Circuit 262 (BR/PK) and ground. • Is the resistance reading greater than 10,000 ohms? → **Yes** GO to **A21**. → **No** REPAIR Circuit 262 (BR/PK) for a short to ground. TEST the system for normal operation.
A21 CHECK CIRCUIT 33 (W/PK) FOR A SHORT TO GROUND	1 Measure the resistance between the digital TR sensor connector Pin C168-10, Circuit 33 (W/PK) and ground. • Is the resistance reading greater than 10,000 ohms? → **Yes** REFER to Digital Transmission Range Sensor Pinpoint Test. → **No** REPAIR Circuit 33 (W/PK) for a short to ground. TEST the system for normal operation.

FM1120100683120X

Fig. 29 Test A: Engine Does Not Crank (Part 12 of 12). Town Car

TEST CONDITIONS	TESTDETAILS/RESULTS/ACTIONS
B1 CHECK THE STARTER MOUNTING	1 Inspect the starter motor mounting bolts and brackets for looseness. • Is the starter motor mounted properly? → **Yes** GO to **B2**. → **No** INSTALL the starter motor properly; TEST the system for normal operation.

FM1120100684010X

Fig. 30 Test B: Unusual Starter Noise (Part 1 of 2). Town Car

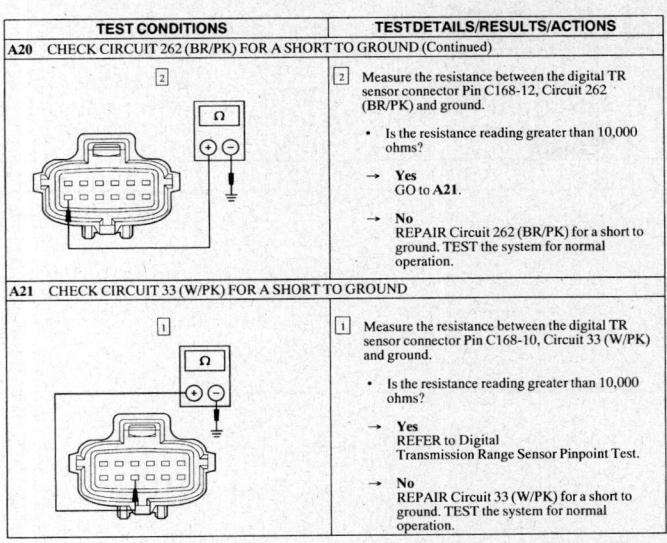

TEST CONDITIONS	TESTDETAILS/RESULTS/ACTIONS
B2 CHECK FOR ENGINE NOISE	2 Connect a remote starter switch between the starter motor solenoid B and S terminals. 3 Engage the starter motor and verify the noise is due to the starter operation. • Is the noise due to the starter motor engagement? → **Yes** GO to **B3**. → **No** **Diagnose engine mechanical components**
B3 CHECK FOR UNUSUAL WEAR	1 Remove the starter motor; 2 Inspect the ring gear for damaged or worn teeth. • Is the noise due to flywheel ring gear (6384) tooth damage? → **Yes** REPLACE the flywheel ring gear. EXAMINE the starter pinion teeth. If damaged, REPLACE the starter motor. TEST the system for normal operation. → **No** REPLACE the starter motor. TEST the system for normal operation.

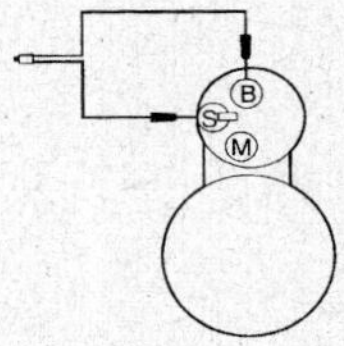

FM1120100684020X

Fig. 30 Test B: Unusual Starter Noise (Part 2 of 2). Town Car

STARTER MOTORS

STARTER SPECIFICATIONS

Starter Frame Dia., Inch	Brush Spring Tension, Ounces	No Load, Amps	Max Load, Amps	Normal Load Current Draw, Amps	Normal Engine Cranking, RPM	Minimum Stall, Ft. Lbs. @ 5 Volts
3.0	64	60–80	②	130–190	①	—

① — Five Hundred, Freestyle, Montego, Sable, Taurus & Taurus X; 200–250 RPM; Mustang, 100–140 RPM; Except Five Hundred, Freestyle, Montego, Sable, Taurus & Taurus X, 140–220 RPM.

② — Except Mustang, 800 amps; Mustang, 400 amps.

ALTERNATORS
Ford Motorcraft Alternator

NOTE: On Air Bag Equipped Models, Refer To "Air Bag System Precautions" Located In The Front Of This Manual For System Disarming & Arming Procedures.

NOTE: Refer To "Computer Relearn Procedures" Located In The Front Of This Manual When Battery Power To The Computer Has Been Interrupted.

NOTE: "Electrical Symbol & Wire Color Code Identification" Located In The Front Of This Manual May Be Used As An Aid When Using Wiring Circuits Found In This Section.

INDEX

	Page No.
Alternator Specifications	11-58
Application Chart	11-1
Description	11-1
2004	11-1
2005–08	11-1
Diagnosis & Testing	11-2
Drain Test	11-2
Battery Cable Disconnected Test	11-3
Clamp On DC Ammeter Test	11-3
Electronic Drains Which Shut Off w/Battery Cable Disconnected Test	11-3
Inline Multimeter Test	11-3
Load Test	11-2
Except Town Car	11-2

	Page No.
Town Car	11-2
No-Load Test	11-2
Crown Victoria, Focus, Fusion, Milan, MKZ, Grand Marquis, LS, Marauder, Mustang, Thunderbird & Zephyr	11-2
Five Hundred, Freestyle, Montego, Sable, Taurus, Taurus X & Town Car	11-2
Symptom Related Tests	11-4
2004–07 Sable & Taurus	11-4
2008 Sable, Taurus & Taurus X	11-4
Crown Victoria, Grand Marquis & Marauder	11-4

	Page No.
Five Hundred, Freestyle & Montego	11-4
Focus	11-4
Fusion, Milan, MKZ & Zephyr	11-4
LS & Thunderbird	11-4
Mustang	11-4
Town Car	11-4
Symptoms	11-3
Wiring Diagrams	11-2
Diagnostic Chart Index	11-7
Precautions	11-1
Air Bag Systems	11-1
Battery Ground Cable	11-1
General	11-1

PRECAUTIONS

Air Bag Systems

Refer to "Air Bag System Precautions" in the front of this manual for system disarming and arming procedures.

Battery Ground Cable

Prior to service, disconnect battery ground cable and isolate as required.

General

1. Ensure proper battery polarity when servicing units. Reversed polarity will damage rectifiers and regulators.
2. If booster battery is used for starting, ensure proper polarity.
3. When fast charger is used to charge battery, vehicle battery cables should be disconnected unless fast charger is equipped with special alternator protector, in which case vehicle battery cables need not be disconnected. A fast charger should never be used to start vehicle as damage to rectifiers will result.
4. Unless system includes load relay or field relay, grounding alternator output terminal will damage alternator and/or circuits. This is true even when system is not in operation since circuit breaker is not used and battery voltage is applied to alternator output terminal at all times. Field or load relay acts as circuit breaker in that it is controlled by ignition switch.
5. Before starting any on vehicle tests of alternator or regulator, battery should be inspected and circuit inspected for faulty wiring or insulation, loose or corroded connections and poor ground circuits.
6. Ensure alternator belt tension is tight enough to prevent slipping under load.
7. To prevent damage to system, ignition should be in Off position and battery ground cable disconnected before making any test connections.
8. Vehicle battery must be fully charged or fully charged battery may be installed for test purposes.

DESCRIPTION
2004

This vehicle is equipped with a power-train control module (PCM) controlled charging system whereby the PCM determines the optimal voltage set-point for the charging system and communicates this information to the voltage regulator. This system is unique in that it has two unidirectional communication lines between the PCM and the alternator/regulator. Both of these communication lines are pulse-width modulated. The alternator communication (GEN COM) line communicates the desired set-point from the PCM to the voltage regulator and the alternator monitor (GEN MON) line communicates the alternator load and error conditions to the PCM. The third pin on the voltage regulator, the A circuit pin, is a dedicated battery voltage sense line.

2005–08

This vehicle is equipped with a power-train control module (PCM) controlled charging system whereby the PCM determines the optimal voltage set-point for the charging system and communicates this information to the voltage regulator. This system is unique in that it has 2 unidirectional communication lines between the PCM and the alternator/regulator. Both of these

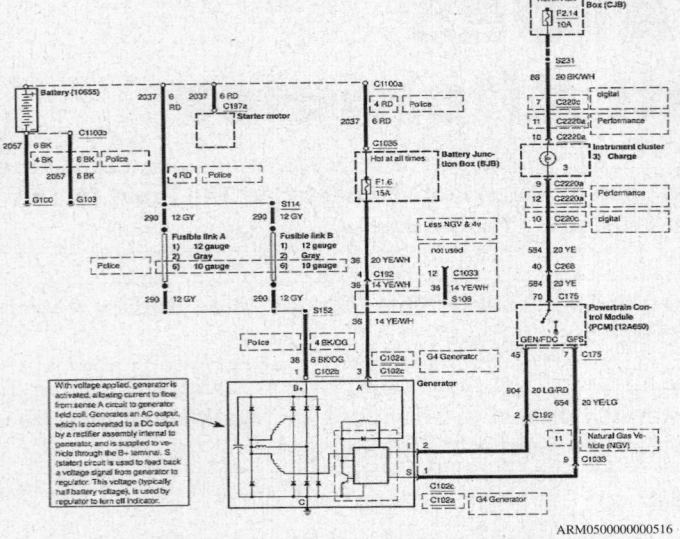

Fig. 1   Wiring diagram. Marauder, 2004 Crown Victoria & Grand Marquis

ARM0500000000516

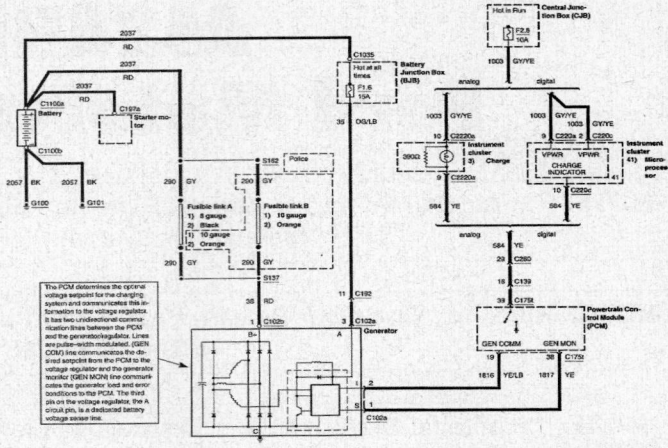

ARM0500000000517

Fig. 2   Wiring diagram. 2005 Crown Victoria & Grand Marquis

communication lines are pulse-width modulated (PWM). The alternator communication (GEN COM) line communicates the desired set-point from the PCM to the voltage regulator while the alternator monitor (GEN MON) line communicates the alternator load and error conditions to the PCM. The third pin on the voltage regulator, the A circuit pin, is a dedicated battery voltage sense line.

The charging system voltage is controlled by the PCM. The alternator charges the battery, and at the same time supplies power for all of the electrical loads that are required. The battery is more effectively charged with a higher voltage when the battery is cold and a lower voltage when the battery is warm. The PCM is able to adjust the charging voltage according to the battery temperature by using a signal from the intake air temperature (IAT) sensor. This means the voltage set-point is calculated by the PCM and communicated to the regulator by a communication link.

The PCM simultaneously controls and monitors the output of the alternator. When the current consumption is high or the battery is discharged, the system is able to increase the idle speed.

To minimize the engine drag when starting the engine, the PCM controls the alternator. The alternator does not produce any output until the engine has started. The PCM then progressively increases the output of the alternator.

The PCM controls the operation of the charging system warning indicator in the instrument cluster. The PCM is responsible for turning the charging system warning indicator off after the engine is started and illuminating it under fault conditions (when the alternator is not generating the correct amount of current with the engine running). The charging system warning indicator is also illuminated by the PCM at key ON engine OFF, and stall condition.

This is a System 4 charging system, which uses the GEN MON and GEN COM

lines to control and monitor the charging system through the PCM. System 4 charging systems are virtually identical in design and therefore, share the same diagnostics. The circuit numbers and colors may be different, but the functions are the same. System 4 charging systems may use any type of alternator, as the alternator type usually depends on the engine packaging and/or output requirements versus cost.

DIAGNOSIS & TESTING

Wiring Diagrams

Refer to **Fig. 1 through 20** for charging system wiring diagram.

No-Load Test

FIVE HUNDRED, FREESTYLE, MONTEGO, SABLE, TAURUS, TAURUS X & TOWN CAR

1. Switch Rotunda alternator tester tool No. 010-00725, or equivalent, to voltmeter function.
2. Connect voltmeter positive lead to alternator B+ terminal and negative lead to ground.
3. Turn all electrical accessories off.
4. With engine running at 2000 RPM, measure alternator output voltage.
5. Measurement should be 13–15 volts.
6. If voltage is not as specified, refer to "Symptom Related Tests."

CROWN VICTORIA, FOCUS, FUSION, GRAND MARQUIS, LS, MARAUDER, MILAN, MKZ, , MUSTANG, THUNDERBIRD & ZEPHYR

1. Connect voltmeter leads across battery terminals.

2. Measure base voltage.
3. Start and run engine at 1500 RPM with no electrical load.
4. Voltage should be 14.1–15.1 volts.
5. If voltage increase is less than 2.5 volts over base voltage, refer to "Load Test."
6. If there is no voltage increase or voltage increase is more than 2.5 volts, refer to "Symptom Related Tests."

Load Test

EXCEPT TOWN CAR

1. Connect leads of voltmeter across battery terminals.
2. Measure base voltage.
3. With engine running, turn on air conditioner, set blower motor to high speed and headlamps to high beam position.
4. Increase engine speed to approximately 2000 RPM.
5. Voltage should increase at least .5 volts above base voltage.
6. If voltage does not increase, refer to "Symptom Related Tests."
7. If voltage increases as specified, charging system is operating properly.

TOWN CAR

1. Turn off lamps and electrical components.
2. Apply parking brake and place transmission in Neutral position.
3. Switch Rotunda alternator tester tool No. 010-00725, or equivalent, to ammeter function.
4. Connect positive and negative leads to battery.
5. Connect current probe to alternator B+ output lead.
6. With engine running at 2000 RPM, adjust tester load bank to determine output of alternator.
7. Alternator output should be more than 87 amps at 2000 RPM.
8. If alternator output is not as specified, refer to "Symptom Related Tests."

Drain Test

A periodic pulsing of up to .080 amp is

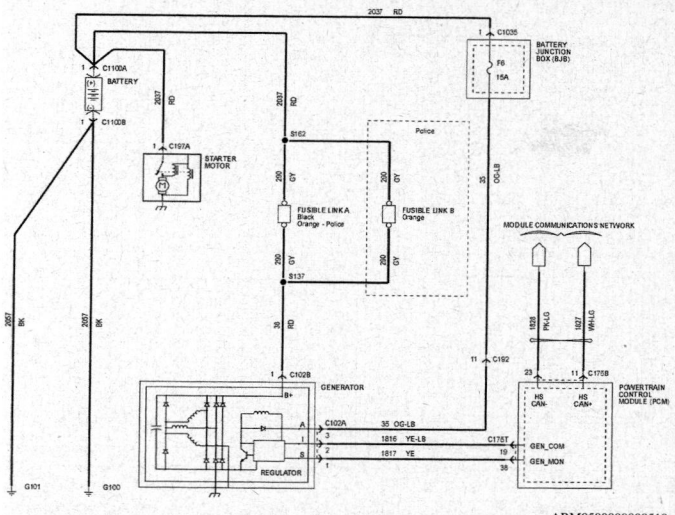

Fig. 3 Wiring diagram. 2006–08 Crown Victoria & Grand Marquis

ARM0500000000518

Fig. 4 Wiring diagram. 2004–06 Five Hundred, Freestyle & Montego

ARM0400000000746

caused by the Integrated Control Panel (ICP) and is considered normal. However, no production vehicle should have a continuous draw of more than .050 amp.

Inspect for current drains on battery in excess of 50 milliamperes with all the electrical accessories off and the vehicle at rest. **Do not perform these tests on a recently recharged lead-acid battery. Explosive gases can cause personal injury.**

CLAMP ON DC AMMETER TEST

1. Connect 12-volt test lamp in series with battery positive terminal. If test lamp glows, drain exists.
2. Use clamp-type current probe to battery positive or ground terminal. Ensure probe is properly calibrated to prevent false readings.
3. Connect inline ammeter between battery positive or ground post, and its respective cable.
4. Turn ignition switch to Off position.
5. Ensure electrical loads are off.
6. Ensure engine compartment lamp operates properly, then disconnect lamp.
7. Clamp meter clip securely around positive or battery ground. **Do not start vehicle with clip on cable.**
8. Measure current. Reading should be less than .05 amp.
9. If current reading is more .05 amps, there is constant drain.
10. Possible sources of current drain are vehicle lamps such as engine compartment, glove compartment or luggage compartment.
11. If drain is not caused by vehicle lamps, remove fuses one at a time until cause of drain is located.
12. If drain is still undetermined, disconnect leads at starter relay one at a time to find offending circuit.

INLINE MULTIMETER TEST

This test will require a digital volt amp ohmmeter with an appropriate ampere scale.

1. Drive vehicle at least five minutes at more than 30 mph to turn on and exercise vehicle systems.
2. Turn ignition switch to Off position.
3. Allow vehicle to sit with key off at least 40 minutes to allow modules to time out and power down.
4. Ensure electrical loads are turned off.
5. Connect suitable fused jumper wire between battery ground cable and negative battery post to prevent modules from resetting and to catch capacitive drains.
6. Disconnect battery ground cable without breaking jumper wire connection.
7. Ensure engine compartment lamp operates properly, then disconnect lamp.
8. Measure battery voltage. If measurement is less than 11.5 volts, charge battery to more than 11.5 volts.
9. Set ammeter to DC amperage scale **Do not crank engine with ammeter connected.**
10. Current reading should be less than .05 amp.
11. If reading is .2–.9 amp, drain may be present.
12. Possible sources of current drain are vehicle lamps such as engine compartment, glove compartment or luggage compartment.
13. If drain is not caused by vehicle lamps, remove fuses one at a time until cause is located.
14. If cause of drain is still undetermined, disconnect leads at starter relay one at a time to find offending circuit.

BATTERY CABLE DISCONNECTED TEST

1. Connect suitable 12-volt test lamp in series with battery positive terminal. If test lamp glows, drain exists.
2. Use clamp type current probe to battery positive or ground terminal. Ensure probe is properly calibrated to prevent false readings.
3. Connect inline ammeter between battery positive or ground post and its re-

spective cable.
4. Without starting engine, turn ignition switch to On position for a few seconds, then Off.
5. **On models equipped with illuminated entry lamps,** wait one minute for those lamps to turn off.
6. **On all models,** connect ammeter and read amperage.
7. Current reading should be less than .05 amp.
8. If reading is more than .05 amp after few minutes and drain did not show up in previous tests, drain is most likely caused by faulty electronic component.
9. Remove fuses and disconnect starter leads one at a time to locate offending circuit.

ELECTRONIC DRAINS WHICH SHUT OFF w/BATTERY CABLE DISCONNECTED TEST

1. Perform "Inline Multimeter Test."
2. Ensure doors are closed and accessories are turned off.
3. Turn ignition to Run position for a moment without starting engine, then turn ignition switch to Off position.
4. **On models equipped with illuminated entry lamps,** wait few minutes for those lamps to turn off.
5. **On all models,** connect ammeter and record amperage drain.
6. Current drain reading should not be more than .05 amp.
7. If drain exceeds specifications after few minutes and if this drain did not appear in previous tests, it is most likely caused by an inoperative electronic component. Remove fuses from battery/central junction box one at a time to locate offending circuit.

Symptoms

Refer to **Figs. 21 through 34** for symptoms.

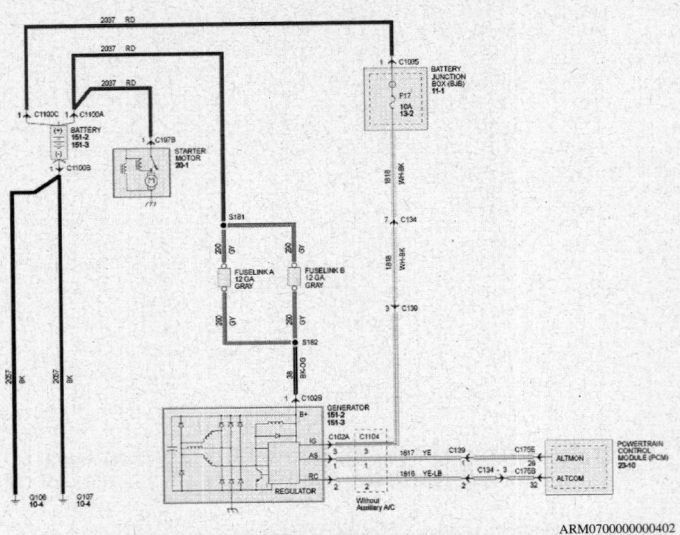

Fig. 5   Wiring diagram. 20007 Five Hundred, Freestyle & Montego

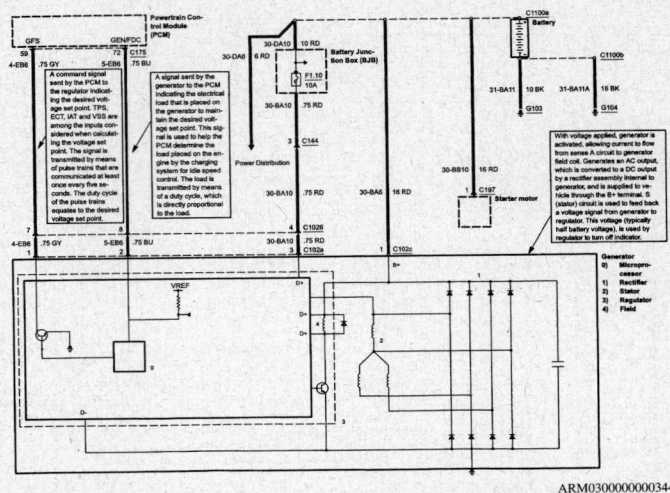

ARM0300000000344

Fig. 6   Wiring diagram. 2004 Focus w/2.0L DOHC engine

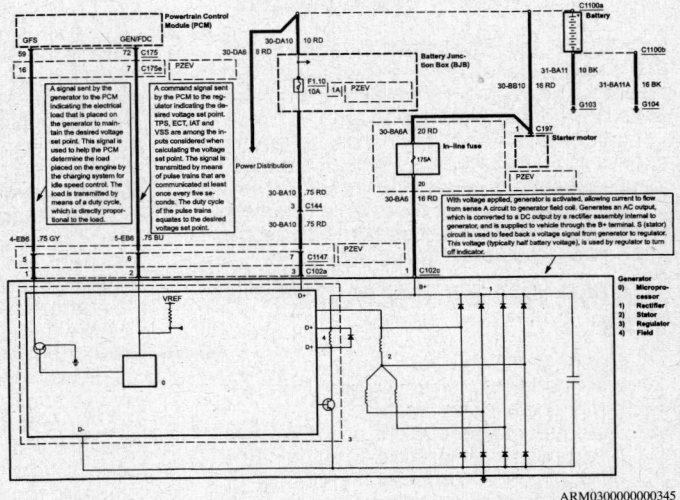

ARM0300000000345

Fig. 7   Wiring diagram. 2004 Focus w/2.0L SOHC engine

Symptom Related Tests

CROWN VICTORIA, GRAND MARQUIS & MARAUDER

Refer to **Figs. 35 through 49** for symptom related tests.

FIVE HUNDRED, FREESTYLE & MONTEGO

Refer to **Figs. 50 through 56** for symptom related tests.

FOCUS

Refer to **Figs. 57 through 65** for symptom related tests.

FUSION, MILAN, MKZ & ZEPHYR

Refer to **Figs. 66 through 72** for symptom related tests.

LS & THUNDERBIRD

Refer to **Figs. 73 through 88** for symptom related tests.

MUSTANG

Refer to **Figs. 89 through 103** for symptom related tests.

2004–07 SABLE & TAURUS

Refer to **Figs. 104 through 118** for symptom related tests.

2008 SABLE, TAURUS & TAURUS X

Refer to **Figs. 119 through 124** for symptom related tests.

TOWN CAR

Refer to **Figs. 125 through 139** for symptom related tests.

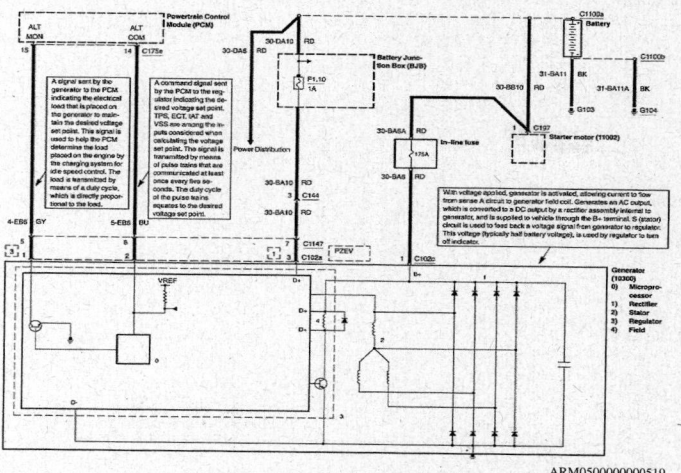

Fig. 8   Wiring diagram. 2005–07 Focus

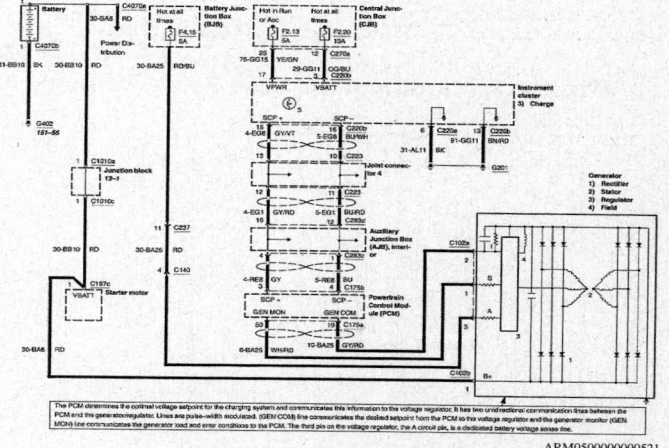

Fig. 10   Wiring diagram. 2004–06 LS

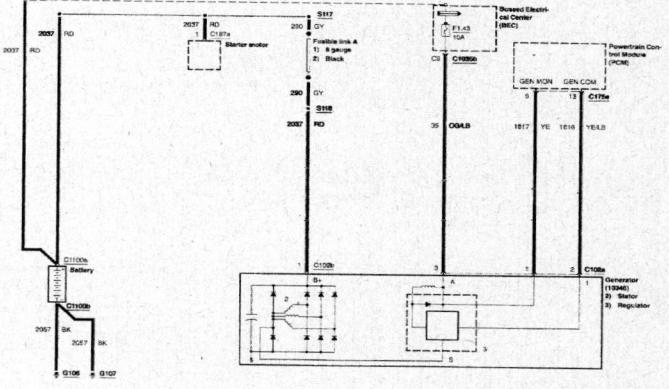

Fig. 12   Wiring diagram. 2005 Mustang

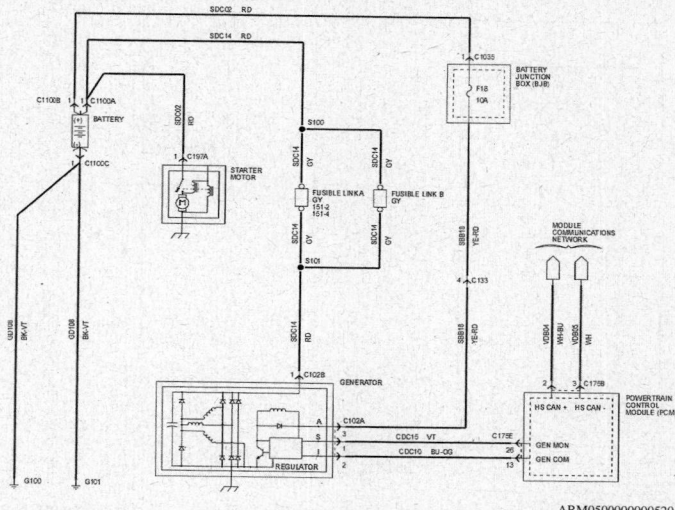

Fig. 9   Wiring diagram. Fusion, Milan, MKZ & Zephyr

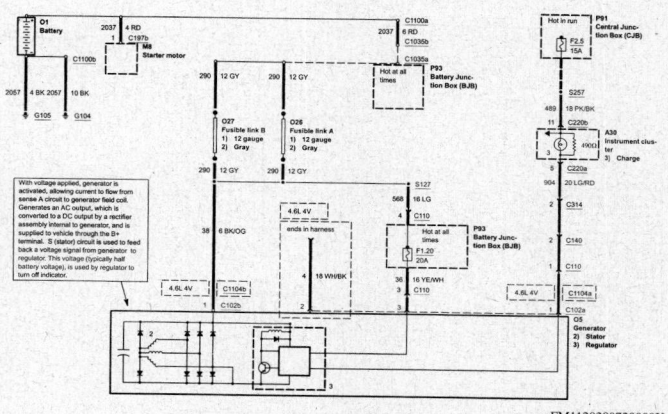

Fig. 11   Wiring diagram. 2004 Mustang

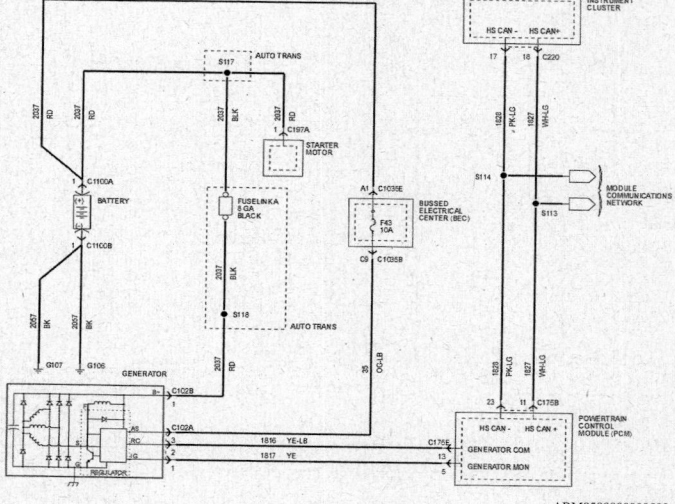

Fig. 13   Wiring diagram. 2006–08 Mustang w/4.0L engine

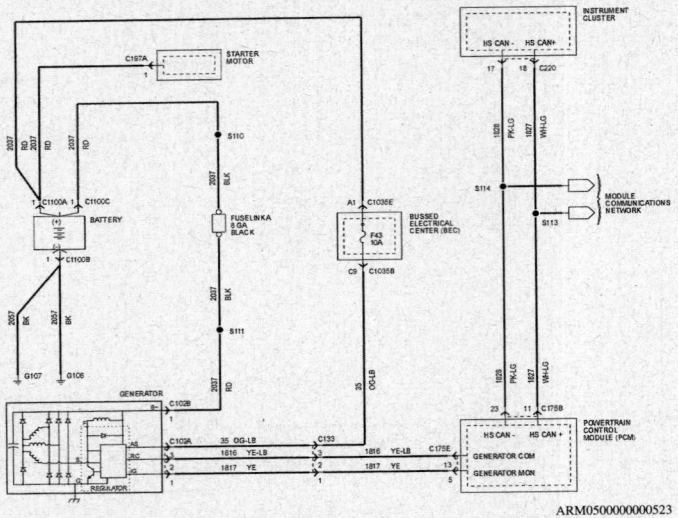

Fig. 14 Wiring diagram. 2006–08 Mustang w/4.6L engine

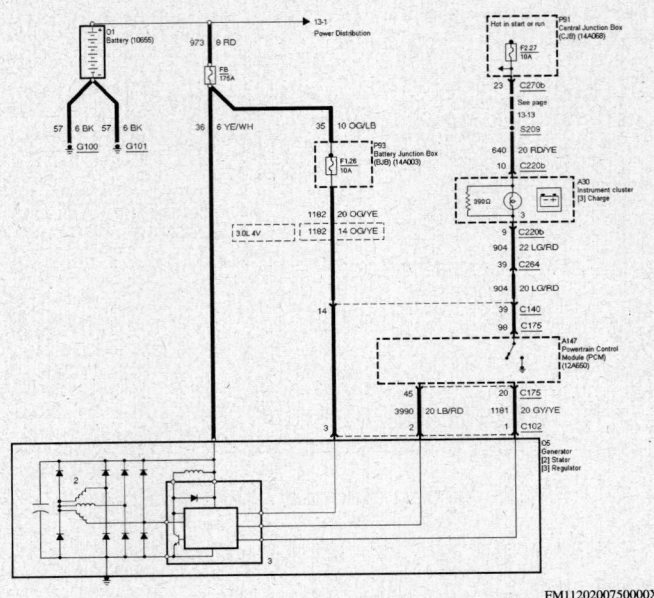

Fig. 15 Wiring Diagram. 2004 Sable, Taurus

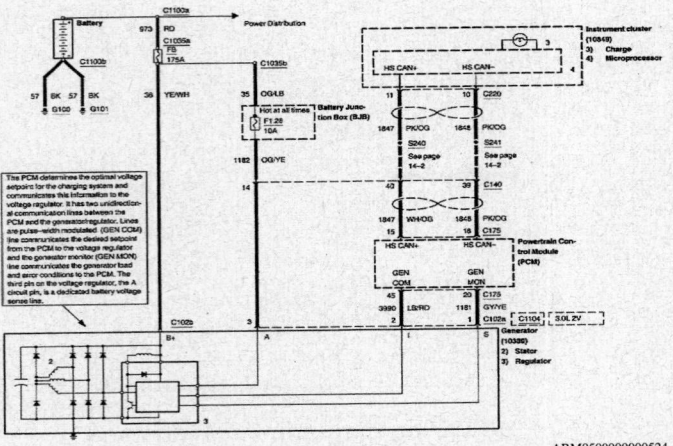

Fig. 16 Wiring diagram. 2005–07 Sable & Taurus

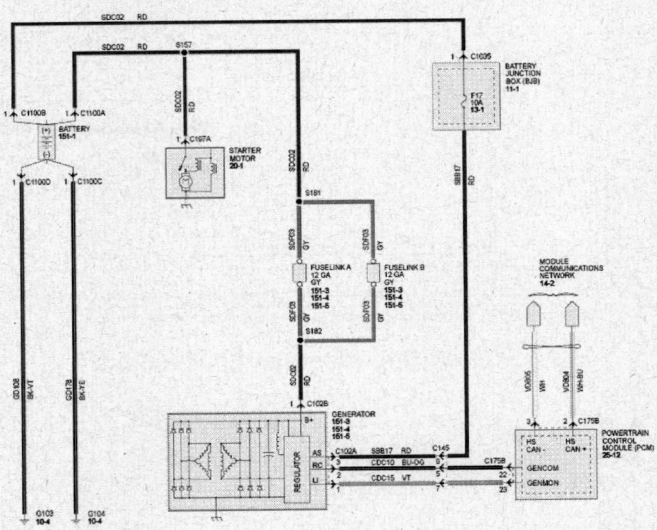

Fig. 17 Wiring diagram. 2008 Sable, Taurus & Taurus X

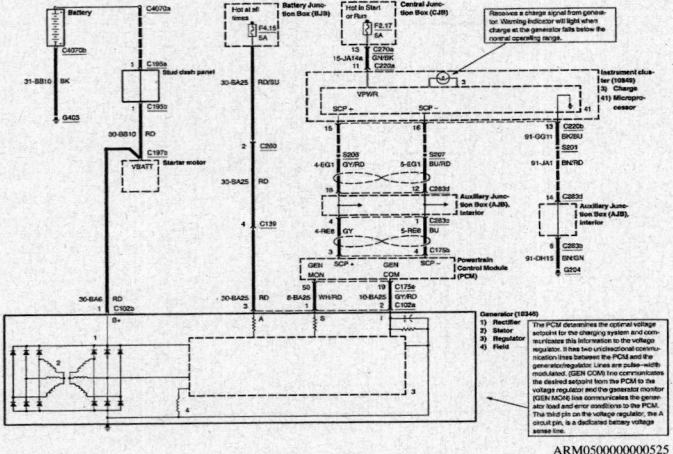

Fig. 18 Wiring diagram. 2004–05 Thunderbird

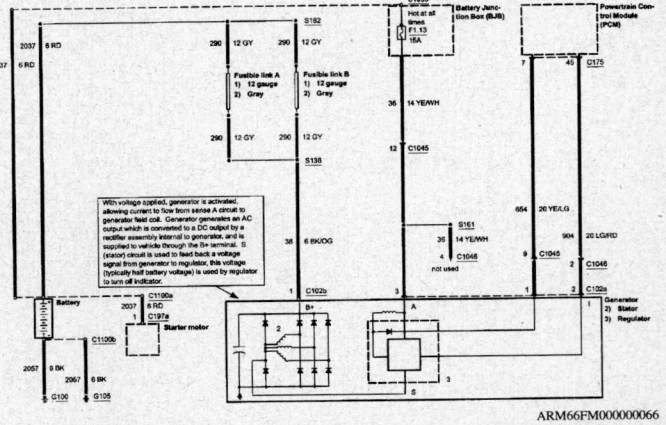

Fig. 19 Wiring diagram. 2004 Town Car

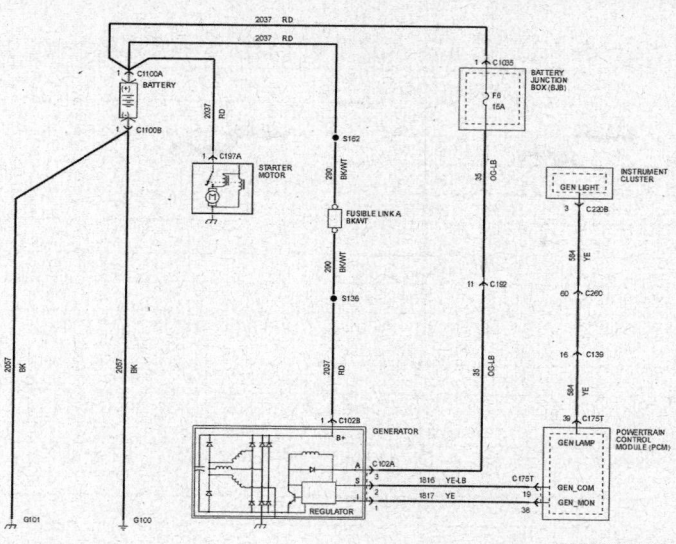

Fig. 20   Wiring diagram. 2005–07 Town Car

DIAGNOSTIC CHART INDEX

Test	Description	Page No.	Fig. No.
2004 CROWN VICTORIA & GRAND MARQUIS			
—	Symptoms	11-10	21
Test A	Battery Is Discharged Or Battery Voltage Is Low	11-14	35
Test B	Charging System Warning Indicator Is On w/Engine Running, Engine Voltage Does Not Increase	11-14	36
Test C	System Overcharges, Battery Voltage More Than 15	11-14	37
Test D	Charging System Warning Indicator Is On w/Engine Running, System Increases Voltage	11-15	38
Test E	Charging System Warning Indicator Is Off w/Ignition Switch In Run Position & Engine Off	11-15	39
Test F	Charging System Warning Indicator Lamp Flickers Or Is Intermittent	11-16	40
Test G	Alternator Is Noisy	11-16	41
Test H	Radio Interference	11-16	42
2005–07 CROWN VICTORIA & GRAND MARQUIS			
—	Symptoms	11-11	22
Test A	Battery Is Discharged Or Battery Voltage Is Low	11-17	43
Test B	Charging System Warning Indicator Is On w/Engine Running, Engine Voltage Does Not Increase	11-17	44
Test C	System Overcharges, Battery Voltage More Than 15.5 Volts	11-18	45
Test D	Charging System Warning Indicator Is On w/Engine Running, System Increases Voltage	11-18	46
Test E	Charging System Warning Indicator Is Off w/Ignition Switch In Run Position & Engine Off	11-19	47
Test F	Alternator Is Noisy	11-19	48
Test G	Radio Interference	11-19	49
FIVE HUNDRED, FREESTYLE & MONTEGO			
Test A	Battery Is Discharged Or Battery Voltage Is Low	11-19	50
Test B	Charging System Warning Indicator Is On w/Engine Running, Engine Voltage Does Not Increase	11-19	51
Test C	System Overcharges, Battery Voltage Is More Than 15.5 Volts	11-20	52
Test D	Charging System Warning Indicator Is On w/Engine Running, System Increases Voltage	11-21	53
Test E	Charging System Warning Indicator Is Off w/Ignition Switch In Run Position & Engine Off	11-21	54
Test F	Alternator Is Noisy	11-21	55
Test G	Radio Interference	11-21	56

Continued

DIAGNOSTIC CHART INDEX—Continued

Test	Description	Page No.	Fig. No.
2004 FOCUS			
—	Symptoms	11-0	23
Test A	Charging System Warning Indicator Is On w/Engine Running	11-0	57
Test B	Radio Interference	11-0	58
2005–07 FOCUS			
—	Symptoms	11-11	24
Test A	Battery Is Discharged Or Battery Voltage Is Low	11-22	59
Test B	Charging System Warning Indicator Is On w/Engine Running & Battery Voltage Does Not Increase	11-22	60
Test C	Charging System Overcharges, Voltage Is Greater Than 15.5 Volts	11-23	61
Test D	Charging System Warning Indicator Is On w/Engine Running & Battery Increases Voltage	11-23	62
Test E	Charging System Warning Indicator Is Off w/Ignition Switch In Run Position & Engine Off	11-24	63
Test F	Alternator Is Noisy	11-24	64
Test G	Radio Interference	11-24	65
FUSION, MILAN, MKZ & ZEPHYR			
—	Symptoms	11-11	25
Test A	Battery Is Discharged Or Battery Voltage Is Low.	11-24	66
Test B	Charging System Warning Indicator Is On w/Engine Running & Voltage Does Not Increase	11-25	67
Test C	Charging System Overcharge Battery Voltage Is Greater Than 15.5 Volts	11-26	68
Test D	Charging System Warning Indicator Is On w/Engine Running & Voltage Increases	11-26	69
Test E	Charging System Warning Indicator Is Off w/Ignition Switch In Run Position & Engine Is Off	11-27	70
Test F	Alternator Is Noisy	11-27	71
Test G	Radio Interference	11-27	72
2004 LS & THUNDERBIRD			
—	Symptoms	11-11	26
Test A	Battery Is Discharged Or Battery Voltage Is Low	11-27	73
Test B	Charging System Warning Indicator Is On w/Engine Running, Charging System Voltage Does Not Increase	11-27	74
Test C	Charging System Overcharges, Battery Voltage Is More Than 15	11-29	75
Test D	Charging System Warning Indicator Is On w/Engine Running & Battery Increases Voltage	11-29	76
Test E	Charging System Warning Indicator Is Off w/Ignition Switch In Run Position & Engine Is Off	11-31	77
Test F	Charging System Warning Indicator Flickers Or Is Intermittent	11-32	78
Test G	Alternator Is Noisy	11-33	79
Test H	Radio Interference	11-34	80
2005–07 LS & THUNDERBIRD			
—	Symptoms	11-12	27
Test A	Battery Is Discharged Or Battery Voltage Is Low.	11-34	81
Test B	Charging System Warning Indicator Is On w/Engine Running, Charging System Voltage Does Not Increase	11-34	82
Test C	Charging System Overcharges, Battery Voltage Is More Than 15.5 Volts	11-35	83
Test D	Charging System Warning Indicator Is On w/Engine Running & Battery Increases Voltage	11-35	84
Test E	Charging System Warning Indicator Is Off w/Ignition Switch In Run Position & Engine Is Off	11-35	85
Test F	Charging System Warning Indicator Flickers Or Is Intermittent	11-35	86
Test G	Alternator Is Noisy	11-36	87
Test H	Radio Interference	11-36	88
MARAUDER			
—	Symptoms	11-10	21
Test A	Battery Is Discharged Or Battery Voltage Is Low	11-14	35
Test B	Charging System Warning Indicator Is On w/Engine Running, Engine Voltage Does Not Increase	11-14	36
Test C	System Overcharges, Battery Voltage More Than 15	11-14	37

Continued

DIAGNOSTIC CHART INDEX—Continued

Test	Description	Page No.	Fig. No.
MARAUDER			
Test D	Charging System Warning Indicator Is On w/Engine Running, System Increases Voltage	11-15	38
Test E	Charging System Warning Indicator Is Off w/Ignition Switch In Run Position & Engine Off	11-15	39
Test F	Charging System Warning Indicator Lamp Flickers Or Is Intermittent	11-16	40
Test G	Alternator Is Noisy	11-16	41
Test H	Radio Interference	11-16	42
2004 MUSTANG			
—	Symptoms	11-12	28
Test A	Battery Is Charged Or Voltage Is Low	11-36	89
Test B	Charging System Warning Indicator Is On w/Engine Running, Battery Voltage Does Not Increase	11-36	90
Test C	System Overcharges, Battery Voltage Is More Than 15	11-37	91
Test D	Charging System Warning Indicator Is On w/Engine Running & Battery Increases Voltage	11-38	92
Test E	Charging System Warning Indicator Is Off w/Ignition Switch In Run Position & Engine Off	11-38	93
Test F	Charging System Warning Indicator Lamp Flickers Or Is Intermittent	11-38	94
Test G	Alternator Is Noisy	11-39	95
Test H	Radio Interference	11-39	96
2005–07 MUSTANG			
—	Symptoms	11-12	29
Test A	Battery Is Charged Or Voltage Is Low	11-40	97
Test B	Discharging System Warning Indicator Is On w/Engine Running, Battery Voltage Does Not Increase	11-40	98
Test C	System Overcharges, Battery Voltage Is More Than 15.5 Volts	11-41	99
Test D	Charging System Warning Indicator Is On w/Engine Running & Battery Increases Voltage	11-41	100
Test E	Charging System Warning Indicator Is Off w/Ignition Switch In Run Position & Engine Off	11-42	101
Test G	Alternator Is Noisy	11-42	102
Test H	Radio Interference	11-42	103
2004 SABLE & TAURUS			
—	Symptoms	11-12	30
Test A	Battery Is Discharged Or Voltage Is Low	11-42	104
Test B	Charging System Warning Indicator Is On w/Engine Running, System Voltage Does Not Increase	11-42	105
Test C	System Overcharges, Battery Voltage More Than 15 Volts	11-43	106
Test D	Charging System Warning Indicator Is On w/Engine Running, System Increases Voltage	11-44	107
Test E	Charging System Warning Indicator Is Off w/Ignition Switch In Run Position & Engine Off	11-44	108
Test F	Charging System Warning Indicator Lamp Flickers Or Is Intermittent	11-45	109
Test G	Alternator Is Noisy	11-46	110
Test H	Radio Interference	11-46	111
2005–07 SABLE & TAURUS			
—	Symptoms	11-13	31
Test A	Battery Is Discharged Or Voltage Is Low	11-46	112
Test B	Charging System Warning Indicator Is On w/Engine Running, System Voltage Does Not Increase	11-47	113
Test C	System Overcharges, Battery Voltage More Than 15.5 Volts	11-48	114
Test D	Charging System Warning Indicator Is On w/Engine Running, System Increases Voltage	11-48	115
Test E	Charging System Warning Indicator Is Off w/Ignition Switch In Run Position & Engine Off	11-49	116
Test F	Alternator Is Noisy	11-49	117
Test G	Radio Interference	11-49	118

Continued

DIAGNOSTIC CHART INDEX—Continued

Test	Description	Page No.	Fig. No.
2008 SABLE, TAURUS, TAURUS X			
—	Symptoms	11-13	32
Test A	Battery Is Discharged Or Battery Voltage Is Low	11-49	119
Test B	Charging System Warning Indicator Is On And Any Charging System DTC Is Stored	11-49	120
Test C	Charging System Warning Indicator Is On With Engine Running & No Charging System DTC's Present	11-51	121
Test D	Generator Is Noisy	11-52	122
Test E	Radio Interference	11-52	123
Test F	Battery Voltage Low Or Battery Voltage Out Of Range	11-52	124
2004 TOWN CAR			
—	Symptoms	11-13	33
Test A	Battery Is Discharged Or Battery Voltage Is Low	11-53	125
Test B	Charging System Warning Indicator Is On w/Engine Running, Charging System Voltage Does Not Increase	11-53	126
Test C	Charging System Overcharges, Battery Voltage More Than 15	11-53	127
Test D	Charging System Warning Indicator Is On w/Engine Running & Battery Increases Voltage	11-54	128
Test E	Charging System Warning Indicator Is Off w/Ignition Switch In Run Position & Engine Is Off	11-54	129
Test F	Charging System Warning Indicator Lamp Flickers Or Is Intermittent	11-55	130
Test G	Alternator Is Noisy	11-55	131
Test H	Radio Interference	11-55	132
2005–07 TOWN CAR			
—	Symptoms	11-13	34
Test A	Battery Is Discharged Or Battery Voltage Is Low	11-55	133
Test B	Charging System Warning Indicator Is On w/Engine Running, Charging System Voltage Does Not Increase	11-56	134
Test C	Charging System Overcharges, Battery Voltage More Than 15.5 Volts	11-56	135
Test D	Charging System Warning Indicator Is On w/Engine Running & Battery Increases Voltage	11-57	136
Test E	Charging System Warning Indicator Is Off w/Ignition Switch In Run Position & Engine Is Off	11-57	137
Test F	Alternator Is Noisy	11-57	138
Test G	Radio Interference	11-58	139

Condition	Possible Source	Action
• Battery is discharged or voltage is low	• Corroded terminal(s). • Loose connection(s). • High key-off current drain(s). • Battery. • Generator.	• GO to Pinpoint Test A.
• The charging system warning indicator is on with the engine running (the system voltage does not increase)	• Circuitry. • Voltage regulator. • Generator.	• GO to Pinpoint Test B.
• The system overcharges (battery voltage greater than 15.5 volts)	• Circuitry. • Voltage regulator. • Generator.	• GO to Pinpoint Test C.
• The charging system warning indicator is on with the engine running and the system increases voltage	• Circuitry. • Instrument cluster. • Voltage regulator. • Generator.	• GO to Pinpoint Test D.
• The charging system warning indicator is off with the ignition switch in the RUN position and the engine off	• Bulb. • Circuitry. • Instrument cluster. • Voltage regulator. • Generator.	• GO to Pinpoint Test E.
• The charging system warning indicator flickers or is intermittent	• Corroded terminal(s). • Fuse(s). • Circuitry. • Voltage regulator. • Generator.	• GO to Pinpoint Test F.
• The generator is noisy	• Bolts or brackets. • Drive belt. • Generator or pulley.	• GO to Pinpoint Test G.
• Radio interference	• Generator. • Circuitry. • In-vehicle entertainment system.	• GO to Pinpoint Test H.

FM1120000541000X

Fig. 21   Symptoms. 2004 Crown Victoria, Grand Marquis & Marauder

Condition	Possible Sources	Action
• The battery is discharged or battery voltage is low	• Circuitry • High key-off current drain(s) • Battery • Generator	• Go To Pinpoint Test A.
• The charging system warning indicator is on with the engine running (the charging system voltage does not increase)	• Generator • Fuse • Circuitry • Powertrain control module (PCM)	• Go To Pinpoint Test B.
• The charging system overcharges (battery voltage is greater than 15.5 volts)	• Fuse • Generator • Circuitry • Powertrain control module (PCM)	• Go To Pinpoint Test C.
• The charging system warning indicator is on with the engine running and the battery increases voltage	• Generator • Instrument cluster • Powertrain control module (PCM)	• Go To Pinpoint Test D.
• The charging system warning indicator is off with the ignition switch in the RUN position and the engine off	• Instrument cluster • Powertrain control module (PCM)	• Go To Pinpoint Test E.
• The charging system warning indicator flickers or is intermittent	• Instrument cluster	• INSTALL a new instrument cluster.
• The generator is noisy	• Loose bolts/brackets • Drive belt • Generator/pulley	• Go To Pinpoint Test F.
• Radio interference	• Generator • Wiring/routing • In-vehicle entertainment	• Go To Pinpoint Test G.

ARM0500000000542

Fig. 22 Symptoms. 2005–08 Crown Victoria & Grand Marquis

Condition	Possible Sources	Action
• The battery is discharged or battery voltage is low	• Circuitry • High key-off current drain(s) • Battery • Generator	• Go To Pinpoint Test A.
• The charging system warning indicator is on with the engine running (the charging system voltage does not increase)	• Generator • Fuse • Circuitry • Powertrain control module (PCM)	• Go To Pinpoint Test B.
• The charging system overcharges (battery voltage is greater than 15.5 volts)	• Fuse • Generator • Circuitry • Powertrain control module (PCM)	• Go To Pinpoint Test C.
• The charging system warning indicator is on with the engine running and the battery increases voltage	• Generator • Instrument cluster • Powertrain control module (PCM)	• Go To Pinpoint Test D.
• The charging system warning indicator is off with the ignition switch in the RUN position and the engine off	• Instrument cluster • Powertrain control module (PCM)	• Go To Pinpoint Test E.
• The charging system warning indicator flickers or is intermittent	• Instrument cluster	• INSTALL a new instrument cluster.
• The generator is noisy	• Loose bolts/brackets • Drive belt • Generator/pulley	• Go To Pinpoint Test F.
• Radio interference	• Generator • In-vehicle entertainment system	• Go To Pinpoint Test G.

ARM0500000000543

Fig. 24 Symptoms. 2004–07 Focus

Condition	Possible Sources	Action
Charging System Warning Indicator Is On w/Engine Running	Accessory Drive Belt	Refer To "Pinpoint test A"
	Battery Junction Box Fuse No. 10 (10A)	
	Wiring Circuit	
	Alternator	
Charging System Warning Indicator Is Off w/Ignition On & Engine Off	Bulb	—
	Circuit	
	Alternator	
Radio Interference	Circuit	Refer To "Pinpoint Test B"
	Alternator	
System Overcharges	Alternator	—

Fig. 23 Symptoms. 2004 Focus

Condition	Possible Sources	Action
• The battery is discharged or battery voltage is low	• Circuitry • High key-off current drain(s) • Battery • Generator	• GO to Pinpoint Test A.
• The charging system warning indicator is on with the engine running (the charging system voltage does not increase)	• Circuitry • Generator • Powertrain control module (PCM)	• GO to Pinpoint Test B.
• The charging system overcharges (battery voltage is greater than 15.5 volts)	• Fuse • Circuitry • Generator • Powertrain control module (PCM)	• GO to Pinpoint Test C.
• The charging system warning indicator is on with the engine running and the battery increases voltage	• Generator • Instrument cluster • Powertrain control module (PCM)	• GO to Pinpoint Test D.
• The charging system warning indicator is off with the ignition switch in the RUN position and the engine off	• Instrument cluster • Powertrain control module (PCM)	• GO to Pinpoint Test E.
• The charging system warning indicator flickers or is intermittent	• Instrument cluster	• INSTALL a new instrument cluster.
• The generator is noisy	• Loose bolts/brackets • Accessory drive belt • Generator/pulley	• GO to Pinpoint Test F.
• Radio interference	• Generator • In-vehicle entertainment system	• GO to Pinpoint Test G.

ARM0500000000527

Fig. 25 Symptoms. Fusion, Milan, MKZ & Zephyr

Condition	Possible Sources	Action
• The battery is discharged or battery voltage is low	• Circuitry. • High key-off current drain(s). • Battery. • Generator.	• GO to Pinpoint Test A.
• The charging system warning indicator is on with the engine running (the charging system voltage does not increase)	• Generator. • Rear battery junction box (BJB) fuse 20 (5A). • Circuitry.	• GO to Pinpoint Test B.
• The charging system overcharges (battery voltage is greater than 15.5 volts)	• Rear BJB fuse 20 (5A). • Circuitry. • Generator.	• GO to Pinpoint Test C.
• The charging system warning indicator is on with the engine running and the battery increases voltage	• Rear BJB fuse 20 (5A). • Generator. • Instrument cluster. • Powertrain control module(PCM). • Circuitry.	• GO to Pinpoint Test D.
• The charging system warning indicator is off with the ignition switch in the RUN position and the engine off	• Generator connector unplugged C102a. • Battery. • Circuitry. • Instrument cluster. • PCM.	• GO to Pinpoint Test E.
• The charging system warning indicator flickers or is intermittent	• Rear BJB fuse 20 (5A). • Generator connector unplugged (C102a). • Circuitry. • Generator.	• GO to Pinpoint Test F.
• The generator is noisy	• Loose bolts/brackets. • Drive belt. • Generator/pulley.	• GO to Pinpoint Test G.
• Radio interference	• Generator. • Wiring/routing. • In-vehicle entertainment system.	• GO to Pinpoint Test H.

FM1120200791000X

Fig. 26 Symptoms. 2004 LS & Thunderbird

Condition	Possible Sources	Action
• The battery is discharged or battery voltage is low	• Circuitry • High key-off current drain(s) • Battery • Generator	• Go To Pinpoint Test A.
• The charging system warning indicator is on with the engine running (the charging system voltage does not increase)	• Generator • Circuitry • Powertrain control module (PCM)	• Go To Pinpoint Test B.
• The charging system overcharges (battery voltage is greater than 15.5 volts)	• Circuitry • Battery ground connections • Generator	• Go To Pinpoint Test C.
• The charging system warning indicator is on with the engine running and the battery increases voltage	• Generator • Instrument cluster • Powertrain control module (PCM) • Circuitry	• Go To Pinpoint Test D.
• The charging system warning indicator is off with the ignition switch in the RUN position and the engine off	• Generator C102a unplugged • Generator • Instrument cluster • Powertrain control module (PCM)	• Go To Pinpoint Test E.
• The charging system warning indicator flickers or is intermittent	• Rear battery junction box (BJB) fuse 15 (5A) connections • Generator C102a unplugged • Circuitry • Instrument cluster • Generator	• Go To Pinpoint Test F.
• The generator is noisy	• Drive belt • Loose bolts or brackets • Generator or pulley	• Go To Pinpoint Test G.
• Radio interference	• Generator • In-vehicle entertainment system	• Go To Pinpoint Test H.

ARM0500000000544

Fig. 27   Symptoms. 2005–07 LS & Thunderbird

Condition	Possible Sources	Action
• The battery is discharged or battery voltage is low	• Circuitry • High key-off current drain(s) • Battery • Generator	Go To Pinpoint Test A.
• The charging system warning indicator is on with the engine running (the charging system voltage does not increase)	• Generator • Fusible links • Circuitry • Powertrain control module (PCM)	Go To Pinpoint Test B.
• The charging system overcharges (battery voltage is greater than 15.5 volts)	• Fuse • Generator • Circuitry • Powertrain control module (PCM)	Go To Pinpoint Test C.
• The charging system warning indicator is on with the engine running and the battery increases voltage	• Generator • Instrument cluster • Powertrain control module (PCM)	Go To Pinpoint Test D.
• The charging system warning indicator is off with the ignition switch in the RUN position and the engine off	• Instrument cluster • Powertrain control module (PCM)	Go To Pinpoint Test E.
• The charging system warning indicator flickers or is intermittent	• Instrument cluster	INSTALL a new instrument cluster.
• The generator is noisy	• Loose bolts/brackets • Drive belt • Generator or pulley (conventional) • One-way-clutch (OWC) pulley	Go To Pinpoint Test F.
• Radio interference	• Generator • Wiring/routing • In-vehicle entertainment	Go To Pinpoint Test G.

ARM0500000000541

Fig. 29   Symptoms. 2005–08 Mustang

Condition	Possible Sources	Action
• Battery is discharged or voltage is low	• Circuitry. • High key-off current drain(s). • Battery. • Generator.	• GO to Pinpoint Test A.
• The charging system warning indicator is on with the engine running (the system voltage does not increase)	• Circuitry. • Voltage regulator. • Generator.	• GO to Pinpoint Test B.
• The system overcharges (the battery voltage is greater than 15.5 volts)	• Circuitry. • Voltage regulator. • Generator.	• GO to Pinpoint Test C.
• The charging system warning indicator is on with the engine running and the battery increases voltage	• Circuitry. • Instrument cluster. • Voltage regulator. • Generator.	• GO to Pinpoint Test D.
• The charging system warning indicator is off with the ignition switch in the RUN position and the engine off	• Bulb. • Circuitry. • Instrument cluster. • Voltage regulator. • Generator.	• GO to Pinpoint Test E.
• The charging system warning indicator flickers or is intermittent	• Central junction box (CJB) fuse 5 (15A). • Generator connector unplugged (C102a). • Circuitry. • Generator.	• GO to Pinpoint Test F.
• The generator is noisy	• Bolts or brackets. • Drive belt. • Generator or pulley.	• GO to Pinpoint Test G.
• Radio interference	• Generator. • Circuitry. • In-vehicle entertainment system.	• GO to Pinpoint Test H.

FM1120200761000X

Fig. 28   Symptoms. 2004 Mustang

Condition	Possible Sources	Action
• Battery is discharged or voltage is low	• Circuitry. • High key-off current drain(s). • Battery. • Generator.	• GO to Pinpoint Test A.
• The charging system warning indicator is on with the engine running (the system voltage does not increase)	• Generator. • BJB fuse 2 (10A). • Circuitry.	• GO to Pinpoint Test B.
• The system overcharges (battery voltage greater than 15 volts)	• BJB fuse 2 (10A). • Circuitry. • Generator.	• GO to Pinpoint Test C.
• The charging system warning indicator is on with the engine running (the system increases voltage)	• BJB fuse 2 (10A). • Generator. • Instrument cluster. • PCM. • Circuitry.	• GO to Pinpoint Test D.
• The charging system warning indicator is off with the ignition switch in the RUN position and the engine off	• Generator connector unplugged (C102). • Battery. • Circuitry. • Instrument cluster. • PCM.	• GO to Pinpoint Test E.
• The charging system warning indicator flickers or is intermittent	• BJB fuse 2 (10A). • Generator connector unplugged (C102). • Circuitry. • Generator.	• GO to Pinpoint Test F.
• The generator is noisy	• Loose bolts/brackets. • Drive belt. • Generator/pulley.	• GO to Pinpoint Test G.
• Radio interference	• Generator. • Wiring/routing. • In-vehicle entertainment system.	• GO to Pinpoint Test H.

FM1120200770000X

Fig. 30   Symptoms. 2004 Sable & Taurus

Condition	Possible Sources	Action
• The battery is discharged or battery voltage is low	• Circuitry • High key-off current drain(s) • Battery • Generator	• Go To Pinpoint Test A.
• The charging system warning indicator is on with the engine running (the charging system voltage does not increase)	• Circuitry • Generator • Powertrain control module (PCM)	• Go To Pinpoint Test B.
• The charging system overcharges (battery voltage is greater than 15.5 volts)	• Fuse • Circuitry • Generator • Powertrain control module (PCM)	• Go To Pinpoint Test C.
• The charging system warning indicator is on with the engine running and the battery increases voltage	• Generator • Instrument cluster • Powertrain control module (PCM)	• Go To Pinpoint Test D.
• The charging system warning indicator is off with the ignition switch in the RUN position and the engine off	• Instrument cluster • Powertrain control module (PCM)	• Go To Pinpoint Test E.
• The charging system warning indicator flickers or is intermittent	• Instrument cluster	• INSTALL a new instrument cluster.
• The generator is noisy	• Loose bolts/brackets • Accessory drive belt • Generator/pulley	• Go To Pinpoint Test F.
• Radio interference	• Generator • Wiring/routing • In-vehicle entertainment system	• Go To Pinpoint Test G.

ARM0500000000539

Fig. 31 Symptoms. 2005–07 Sable & Taurus

Condition	Possible Sources	Action
• Battery is discharged or voltage is low	• Corroded terminal(s). • Loose connection(s). • High key-off current drain(s). • Battery. • Generator.	• GO to Pinpoint Test A.
• The charging system warning indicator is on with the engine running (the system voltage does not increase)	• Circuitry. • Voltage regulator. • Generator.	• GO to Pinpoint Test B.
• The system overcharges (battery voltage greater than 15.5 volts)	• Circuitry. • Voltage regulator. • Generator.	• GO to Pinpoint Test C.
• The charging system warning indicator is on with the engine running and the system increases voltage	• Circuitry. • Instrument cluster. • Voltage regulator. • Generator.	• GO to Pinpoint Test D.
• The charging system warning indicator is off with the ignition switch in the RUN position and the engine off	• Bulb. • Circuitry. • Instrument cluster. • Voltage regulator. • Generator.	• GO to Pinpoint Test E.
• The charging system warning indicator flickers or is intermittent	• Corroded terminal(s). • Fuse(s). • Circuitry. • Voltage regulator. • Generator.	• GO to Pinpoint Test F.
• The generator is noisy	• Bolts or brackets. • Drive belt. • Generator or pulley.	• GO to Pinpoint Test G.
• Radio interference	• Generator. • Circuitry. • In-vehicle entertainment system.	• GO to Pinpoint Test H.

FM1120200779000X

Fig. 33 Symptoms. 2004 Town Car

Condition	Possible Sources	Action
• The battery is discharged or battery voltage is low	• High key-off current drain(s) • Engine, generator and battery grounds • Positive battery cable • Circuitry • Battery • Generator	• Go To Pinpoint Test A.
• The charging system warning indicator is ON with the engine running and no charging system DTCs present	• Circuitry • PCM • Generator • Instrument cluster	• Go To Pinpoint Test C.
• The generator is noisy	• Accessory drive belt • Loose bolts/brackets • Generator/pulley	• Go To Pinpoint Test D.
• Radio interference	• Generator • Circuitry • In-vehicle entertainment system	• Go To Pinpoint Test E.

ARM0700000000404

Fig. 32 Symptoms. 2008 Sable, Taurus & Taurus X

Condition	Possible Sources	Action
• The battery is discharged or battery voltage is low	• Circuitry • High key-off current drain(s) • Battery • Generator	• Go To Pinpoint Test A.
• The charging system warning indicator is on with the engine running (the charging system voltage does not increase)	• Generator • Circuitry • Powertrain control module (PCM)	• Go To Pinpoint Test B.
• The charging system overcharges (battery voltage is greater than 15.5 volts)	• Circuitry • Fuse • Generator • Powertrain control module (PCM)	• Go To Pinpoint Test C.
• The charging system warning indicator is on with the engine running and the battery increases voltage	• Generator • Instrument cluster • Powertrain control module (PCM)	• Go To Pinpoint Test D.
• The charging system warning indicator is off with the ignition switch in the RUN position and the engine off	• Instrument cluster • Powertrain control module (PCM)	• Go To Pinpoint Test E.
• The charging system warning indicator flickers or is intermittent	• Instrument cluster	• INSTALL a new instrument cluster.
• The generator is noisy	• Loose bolts/brackets • Drive belt • Generator/pulley	• Go To Pinpoint Test F.
• Radio interference	• Generator • Wiring/routing • In-vehicle entertainment	• Go To Pinpoint Test G.

ARM0500000000540

Fig. 34 Symptoms. 2005–07 Town Car

Test Step	Result / Action to Take
A1 CHECK BATTERY CONDITION	**Yes** GO to A2 .
• Carry out the Battery — Condition Test to determine if the battery can hold a charge and is OK for use. • Is the battery OK?	**No** INSTALL a new battery. TEST the system for normal operation.
A2 CHECK THE GENERATOR OUTPUT	**Yes** GO to A3 .
• Carry out the Generator On-Vehicle Test—Load Test and No-Load Test. • Is the generator OK?	**No** Go To Pinpoint Test B .
A3 CHECK FOR CURRENT DRAINS	**Yes** REPAIR as necessary. TEST the system for normal operation.
• Carry out the Battery — Drain Testing. • Are there any excessive current drains?	**No** Go To Pinpoint Test B .

ARM66FM000000068

Fig. 35   Test A: Battery Is Discharged Or Battery Voltage Is Low. Marauder, 2004 Crown Victoria & Grand Marquis

Test Step	Result / Action to Take
B3 CHECK CIRCUIT 904 (LG/RD) FOR AN OPEN	**Yes** GO to B4 .
• Key in OFF position. • Disconnect: PCM C175. • Measure the resistance between the PCM C175 pin 45, circuit 904 (LG/RD), harness side and the generator C102a (4G) pin 2, C102c (6G) pin 2, circuit 904 (LG/RD), harness side. • Is the resistance less than 5 ohms?	**No** REPAIR the circuit. TEST the system for normal operation.
B4 CHECK THE GENERATOR OUTPUT	**Yes** GO to B5 .
• Connect: PCM C175. • Connect: C102a (4G), C102c (6G). • Carry out the generator load test. • Is the generator ok?	**No** INSTALL a new generator. TEST the system for normal operation.
B5 CHECK FOR CORRECT MODULE OPERATION	**Yes** INSTALL a new PCM. REPEAT the PCM self-test.

• Check for:
  ○ corrosion
  ○ pushed-out pins
• Connect any disconnected connectors.
• Make sure all other system connectors are fully seated.
• Operate the system and verify the concern is still present.
• Is the concern still present?
	No
	The system is operating correctly at this time. Concern may have been caused by a loose or corroded connector. CLEAR the DTCs. REPEAT the self-test.

ARM66FM000000070

Fig. 36   Test B: Charging System Warning Indicator Is On w/Engine Running, Engine Voltage Does Not Increase (Part 2 of 2). Marauder, 2004 Crown Victoria & Grand Marquis

Test Step	Result / Action to Take
B1 CHECK THE FAULT CODES IN THE PCM	**Yes** REFER to PCM Diagnostic Trouble Code (DTC) Index.
• Connect the diagnostic tool. • Key in ON position. • Use the recorded PCM DTCs from the continuous and on-demand self-test. • Are any DTCs recorded?	**No** GO to B2 .
B2 CHECK CIRCUIT 904 (LG/RD)	**Yes** GO to B3 .
• Key in OFF position. • Disconnect the diagnostic tool. • Disconnect: Generator C102a (4G), C102c (6G). • Key in ON position. • Measure the voltage between the generator C102a (4G), C102c (6G) pin 2, circuit 904 (LG/RD), harness side and ground. • Is the voltage 0 volts?	**No** GO to B4 .

ARM66FM000000069

Fig. 36   Test B: Charging System Warning Indicator Is On w/Engine Running, Engine Voltage Does Not Increase (Part 1 of 2). Marauder, 2004 Crown Victoria & Grand Marquis

Test Step	Result / Action to Take
C1 CHECK THE FAULT CODES IN THE PCM	**Yes** REFER to PCM Diagnostic Trouble Code (DTC) Index.
• Connect the diagnostic tool. • Key in ON position. • Use the recorded PCM DTCs from the continuous and on-demand self-test. • Are any DTCs recorded?	**No** GO to C2 .
C2 CHECK THE BATTERY VOLTAGE	**Yes** GO to C3 .
• Key in OFF position. • Disconnect the diagnostic tool. • Key in START position. • With the engine running and all accessories turned off, measure the voltage at the battery while varying the engine rpm. • Is the voltage greater than 15.5 volts?	**No** GO to C4 .

ARM66FM000000071

Fig. 37   Test C: System Overcharges, Battery Voltage More Than 15.5 Volts (Part 1 of 2). Marauder, 2004 Crown Victoria & Grand Marquis

C3 CHECK CIRCUIT 36 (YE/WH)	
• Measure the voltage between the generator C102a (4G) pin 3, C102c (6G) pin 3, circuit 36 (YE/WH), harness side and ground. 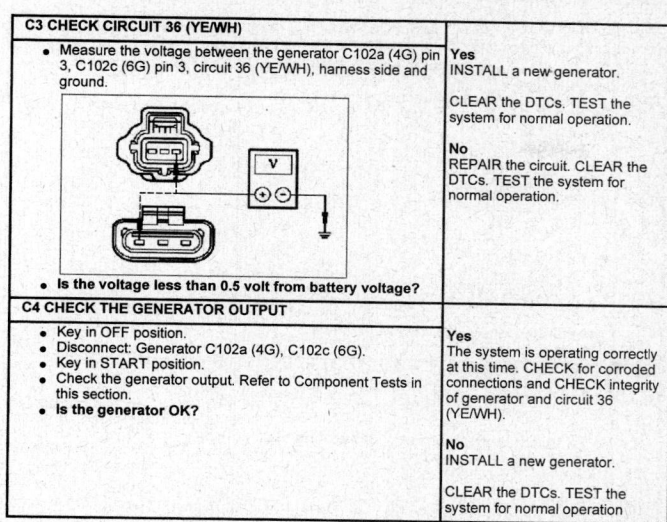 • **Is the voltage less than 0.5 volt from battery voltage?**	**Yes** INSTALL a new generator. CLEAR the DTCs. TEST the system for normal operation. **No** REPAIR the circuit. CLEAR the DTCs. TEST the system for normal operation.
C4 CHECK THE GENERATOR OUTPUT	
• Key in OFF position. • Disconnect: Generator C102a (4G), C102c (6G). • Key in START position. • Check the generator output. Refer to Component Tests in this section. • **Is the generator OK?**	**Yes** The system is operating correctly at this time. CHECK for corroded connections and CHECK integrity of generator and circuit 36 (YE/WH). **No** INSTALL a new generator. CLEAR the DTCs. TEST the system for normal operation

ARM66FM000000072

Fig. 37   Test C: System Overcharges, Battery Voltage More Than 15.5 Volts (Part 2 of 2). Marauder, 2004 Crown Victoria & Grand Marquis

Test Step	Result / Action to Take
D1 CHECK THE FAULT CODES IN THE PCM	
• Connect the diagnostic tool. • Key in ON position. • Use the recorded PCM DTCs from the continuous and on-demand self-test. • **Are any DTCs recorded?**	**Yes** REFER to PCM Diagnostic Trouble Code (DTC) Index. **No** GO to D2 .
D2 CHECK THE SYSTEM FOR OVERCHARGING	
• Key in OFF position. • Disconnect the diagnostic tool. • Key in START position. • With the engine running and all accessories off, measure the voltage at the battery terminals while varying the engine rpm. • **Is the voltage greater than 15.5 volts?**	**Yes** Go To Pinpoint Test C . **No** GO to D3 .

ARM66FM000000073

Fig. 38   Test D: Charging System Warning Indicator Is On w/Engine Running, System Increases Voltage (Part 1 of 2). Marauder, 2004 Crown Victoria & Grand Marquis

D3 CHECK CIRCUIT 36 (YE/WH)	
• Key in OFF position. • Disconnect: Generator C102a (4G), C102c (6G). • Key in ON position. • Measure the voltage between generator C102a (4G) pin 3, C102c (6G) pin 3, circuit 36 (YE/WH), harness side, and ground. 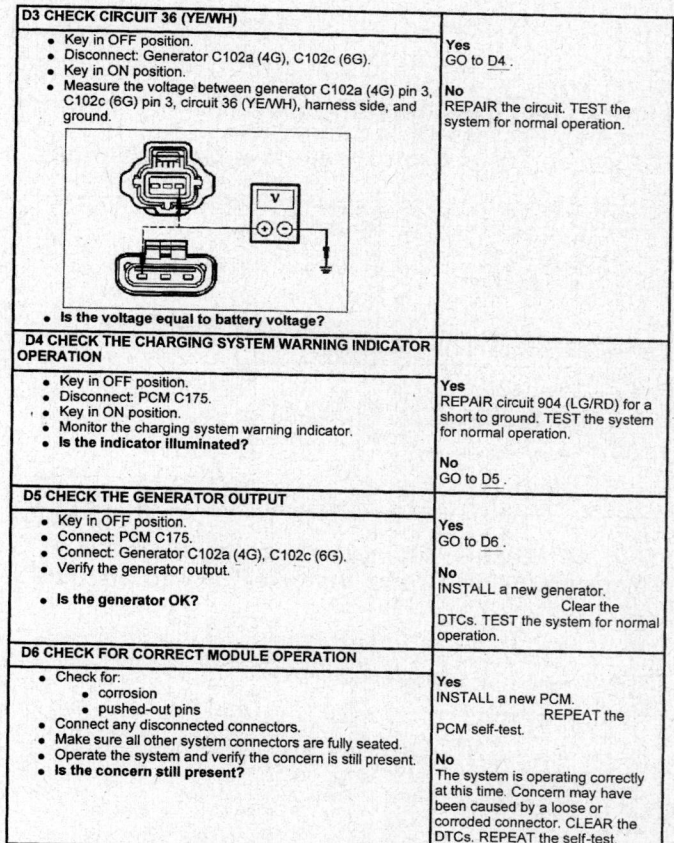 • **Is the voltage equal to battery voltage?**	**Yes** GO to D4 . **No** REPAIR the circuit. TEST the system for normal operation.
D4 CHECK THE CHARGING SYSTEM WARNING INDICATOR OPERATION	
• Key in OFF position. • Disconnect: PCM C175. • Key in ON position. • Monitor the charging system warning indicator. • **Is the indicator illuminated?**	**Yes** REPAIR circuit 904 (LG/RD) for a short to ground. TEST the system for normal operation. **No** GO to D5 .
D5 CHECK THE GENERATOR OUTPUT	
• Key in OFF position. • Connect: PCM C175. • Connect: Generator C102a (4G), C102c (6G). • Verify the generator output. • **Is the generator OK?**	**Yes** GO to D6 . **No** INSTALL a new generator. Clear the DTCs. TEST the system for normal operation.
D6 CHECK FOR CORRECT MODULE OPERATION	

• Check for:
  • corrosion
  • pushed-out pins
• Connect any disconnected connectors.
• Make sure all other system connectors are fully seated.
• Operate the system and verify the concern is still present.
• **Is the concern still present?**
	Yes
	INSTALL a new PCM. REPEAT the PCM self-test.
	
	No
	The system is operating correctly at this time. Concern may have been caused by a loose or corroded connector. CLEAR the DTCs. REPEAT the self-test.

ARM66FM000000074

Fig. 38   Test D: Charging System Warning Indicator Is On w/Engine Running, System Increases Voltage (Part 2 of 2). Marauder, 2004 Crown Victoria & Grand Marquis

Test Step	Result / Action to Take
E1 CHECK THE FAULT CODES IN THE PCM	
• Connect the diagnostic tool. • Key in ON position. • Use the recorded PCM DTCs from the continuous and on-demand self-test. • **Are any DTCs recorded?**	**Yes** REFER to PCM Diagnostic Trouble Code (DTC) Index. **No** GO to E2 .
E2 CHECK THE CHARGING SYSTEM WARNING INDICATOR OPERATION	
• Key in OFF position. • Disconnect the diagnostic tool. • Disconnect: Generator C102a (4G), C102c (6G). • Key in ON position. • With the engine off, connect a fused (15A) jumper wire between the generator C102a (4G) pin 2, C102c (6G) pin 2, circuit 904 (LG/RD), harness side and ground. • **Does the charging system warning indicator illuminate?**	**Yes** INSTALL a new generator. TEST the system for normal operation. **No** GO to E3 .
E3 CHECK FOR CORRECT MODULE OPERATION	

• Check for:
  • corrosion
  • pushed-out pins
• Connect any disconnected connectors.
• Make sure all other system connectors are fully seated.
• Operate the system and verify the concern is still present.
• **Is the concern still present?**
	Yes
	INSTALL a new PCM. REPEAT the PCM self-test.
	
	No
	The system is operating correctly at this time. Concern may have been caused by a loose or corroded connector. CLEAR the DTCs. REPEAT the self-test.

ARM66FM000000075

Fig. 39   Test E: Charging System Warning Indicator Is Off w/Ignition Switch In Run Position & Engine Off. Marauder, 2004 Crown Victoria & Grand Marquis

Test Step	Result / Action to Take
F1 CHECK THE FAULT CODES IN THE PCM	
• Connect the diagnostic tool. • Key in ON position. • Use the recorded PCM DTCs from the continuous and on-demand self-test. • **Are any DTCs recorded?**	**Yes** REFER to PCM Diagnostic Trouble Code (DTC) Index. **No** GO to F2 .
F2 CHECK FOR LOOSE CONNECTIONS	
• Disconnect: Generator C102a (4G), C102c (6G). • Check all generator, battery, and power distribution connections for looseness, corrosion, loose or bent terminals, or loose eyelets. • Connect: Generator C102a (4G), C102c (6G). • **Are all connections clean and tight?**	**Yes** GO to F3 . **No** REPAIR as necessary. TEST the system for normal operation.
F3 CHECK FUSE CONNECTIONS	
• Key in START position. • With the engine running, check BJB fuse 101 (30A) in circuit 37 (YE) for looseness by wiggling the fuse and noting the charging system warning indicator lamp operation. • **Does the charging system warning indicator flicker?**	**Yes** REPAIR loose fuse connection(s) as necessary. TEST the system for normal operation. **No** GO to F4 .
F4 CHECK THE BATTERY VOLTAGE	
• Key in START position. • With the engine running, and all accessories turned off, measure the voltage at the battery while varying the engine rpm.	**Yes** Go To Pinpoint Test C . **No** GO to F5 .
• **Is the voltage greater than 15.5 volts?**	

ARM66FM000000076

Fig. 40   Test F: Charging System Warning Indicator Lamp Flickers Or Is Intermittent (Part 1 of 2). Marauder, 2004 Crown Victoria & Grand Marquis

Test Step	Result / Action to Take
G1 CHECK FOR ACCESSORY DRIVE NOISE	
• Check the accessory drive belt for damage and correct installation. • Check the accessory mounting brackets and generator pulley for looseness or misalignment. • **Is the accessory drive OK?**	**Yes** If equipped with a one-way clutch (OWC) pulley, GO to G2 . If not equipped with a OWC pulley, GO to G3 . **No** REPAIR as necessary. TEST the system for normal operation.
G2 CHECK ONE-WAY CLUTCH (OWC) PULLEY	
• With the front-end accessory drive (FEAD) belt removed, spin the OWC pulley in a clockwise direction, then reverse the direction of the pulley by spinning it in a counterclockwise direction. • **Does the OWC pulley engage with the rotor when spun in a clockwise direction and free-wheel when spun in a counterclockwise direction with minimal noise as compared to a known good vehicle?**	**Yes** GO to G3 . **No** INSTALL a new generator assembly with OWC pulley. TEST the system for normal operation.
G3 CHECK GENERATOR MOUNTING	
• Check the generator mounting for loose bolts or misalignment. • **Is the generator mounted correctly?**	**Yes** GO to G4 . **No** REPAIR as necessary. TEST the system for normal operation.

ARM66FM000000078

Fig. 41   Test G: Alternator Is Noisy (Part 1 of 2). Marauder, 2004 Crown Victoria & Grand Marquis

Test Step	Result / Action to Take
F5 CHECK THE WARNING SYSTEM INDICATOR OPERATION	
• Key in OFF position. • Disconnect: Generator C102a (4G), C102c (6G). • Key in ON position. • Connect a fused jumper wire between generator C102a (4G) pin 2, C102c (6G) pin 2, circuit 904 (LG/RD), harness side and ground. 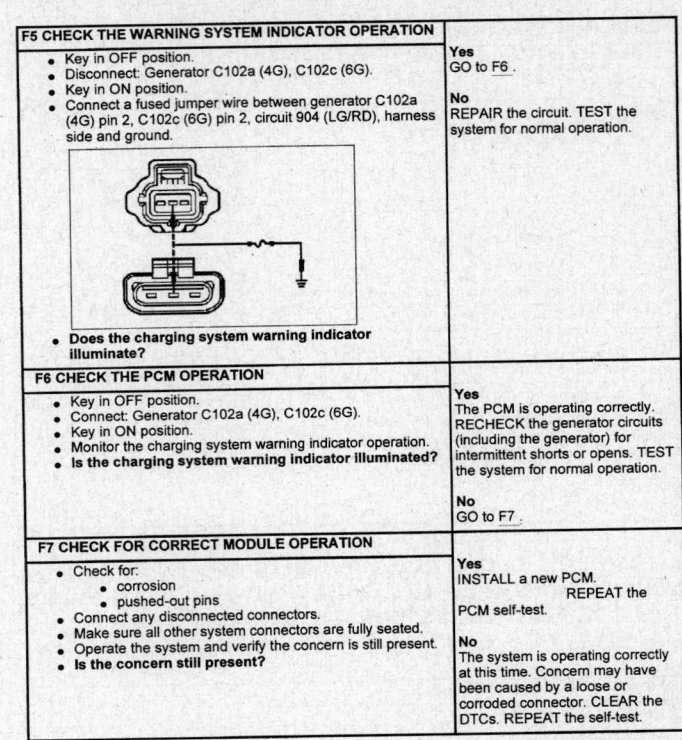 • **Does the charging system warning indicator illuminate?**	**Yes** GO to F6 . **No** REPAIR the circuit. TEST the system for normal operation.
F6 CHECK THE PCM OPERATION	
• Key in OFF position. • Connect: Generator C102a (4G), C102c (6G). • Key in ON position. • Monitor the charging system warning indicator operation. • **Is the charging system warning indicator illuminated?**	**Yes** The PCM is operating correctly. RECHECK the generator circuits (including the generator) for intermittent shorts or opens. TEST the system for normal operation. **No** GO to F7 .
F7 CHECK FOR CORRECT MODULE OPERATION	

• Check for:
  • corrosion
  • pushed-out pins
• Connect any disconnected connectors.
• Make sure all other system connectors are fully seated.
• Operate the system and verify the concern is still present.
• **Is the concern still present?**
	Yes
	INSTALL a new PCM. REPEAT the PCM self-test.
	
	No
	The system is operating correctly at this time. Concern may have been caused by a loose or corroded connector. CLEAR the DTCs. REPEAT the self-test.

ARM66FM000000077

Fig. 40   Test F: Charging System Warning Indicator Lamp Flickers Or Is Intermittent (Part 2 of 2). Marauder, 2004 Crown Victoria & Grand Marquis

Test Step	Result / Action to Take
G4 CHECK GENERATOR FOR ELECTRICAL NOISE	
• Disconnect: Generator C102a (4G), C102c (6G). • Key in START position. • With the engine running. • **Is the noise still present?**	**Yes** GO to G5 . **No** INSTALL a new generator. TEST the system for normal operation.
G5 CHECK GENERATOR FOR MECHANICAL NOISE	
• Key in OFF position. • Key in START position. • Turn all accessories OFF. With the engine running, use a stethoscope or equivalent listening device to probe the generator for unusual mechanical noise. • **Is the generator the noise source?**	**Yes** INSTALL a new generator. TEST the system for normal operation. **No** diagnose the source of the engine noise.

ARM66FM000000079

Fig. 41   Test G: Alternator Is Noisy (Part 2 of 2). Marauder, 2004 Crown Victoria & Grand Marquis

Test Step	Result / Action to Take
H1 VERIFY GENERATOR IS SOURCE OF RADIO INTERFERENCE	
• Key in START position. • Start and run the engine. • Tune the radio to a station where the interference is present. • Key in OFF position. • Disconnect: Generator C102a (4G), C102c (6G). • Key in START position. • **Is the interference present with the generator disconnected?**	**Yes** diagnose and test the in-vehicle entertainment system. **No** INSTALL a new generator. TEST the system for normal operation.

ARM66FM000000080

Fig. 42   Test H: Radio Interference. Marauder, 2004 Crown Victoria & Grand Marquis

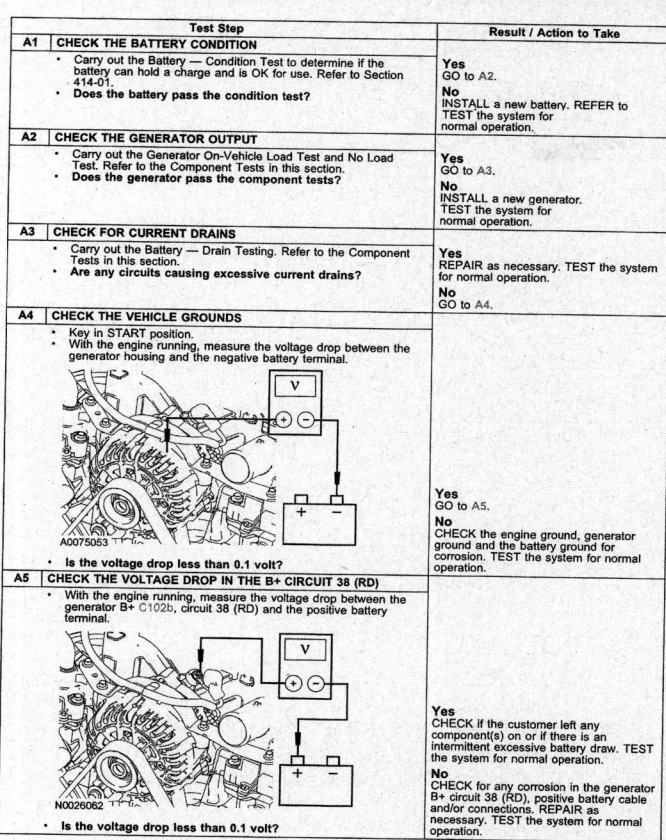

Test Step	Result / Action to Take
A1 CHECK THE BATTERY CONDITION	
• Carry out the Battery — Condition Test to determine if the battery can hold a charge and is OK for use. Refer to Section 414-01. • **Does the battery pass the condition test?**	**Yes** GO to A2. **No** INSTALL a new battery. REFER to TEST the system for normal operation.
A2 CHECK THE GENERATOR OUTPUT	
• Carry out the Generator On-Vehicle Load Test and No Load Test. Refer to the Component Tests in this section. • **Does the generator pass the component tests?**	**Yes** GO to A3. **No** INSTALL a new generator. TEST the system for normal operation.
A3 CHECK FOR CURRENT DRAINS	
• Carry out the Battery — Drain Testing. Refer to the Component Tests in this section. • **Are any circuits causing excessive current drains?**	**Yes** REPAIR as necessary. TEST the system for normal operation. **No** GO to A4.
A4 CHECK THE VEHICLE GROUNDS	
• Key in START position. • With the engine running, measure the voltage drop between the generator housing and the negative battery terminal.	
• **Is the voltage drop less than 0.1 volt?**	**Yes** GO to A5. **No** CHECK the engine ground, generator ground and the battery ground for corrosion. TEST the system for normal operation.
A5 CHECK THE VOLTAGE DROP IN THE B+ CIRCUIT 38 (RD)	
• With the engine running, measure the voltage drop between the generator B+ C102b, circuit 38 (RD) and the positive battery terminal.	
• **Is the voltage drop less than 0.1 volt?**	**Yes** CHECK if the customer left any component(s) on or if there is an intermittent excessive battery draw. TEST the system for normal operation. **No** CHECK for any corrosion in the generator B+ circuit 38 (RD), positive battery cable and/or connections. REPAIR as necessary. TEST the system for normal operation.

ARM0500000000545

Fig. 43 Test A: Battery Is Discharged Or Battery Voltage Is Low. 2005–08 Crown Victoria & Grand Marquis

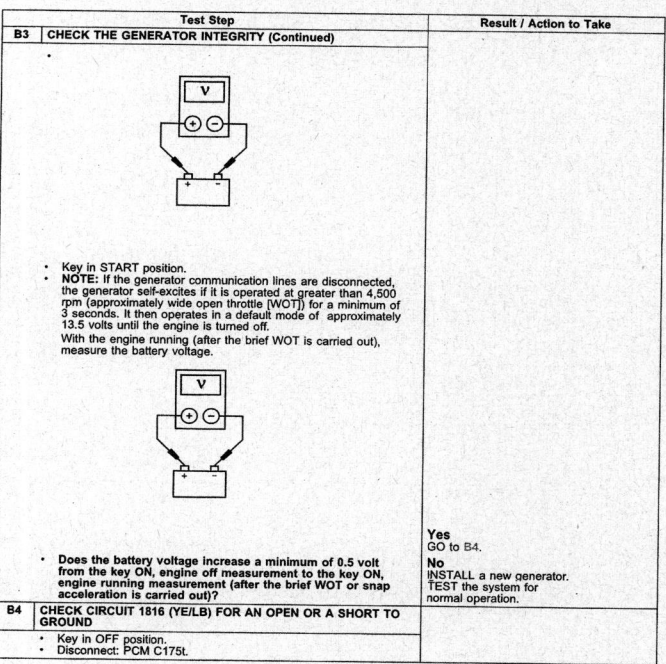

Test Step	Result / Action to Take
B3 CHECK THE GENERATOR INTEGRITY (Continued)	
• Key in START position. • **NOTE:** If the generator communication lines are disconnected, the generator self-excites if it is operated at greater than 4,500 rpm (approximately wide open throttle [WOT]) for a minimum of 3 seconds. It then operates in a default mode of approximately 13.5 volts until the engine is turned off. With the engine running (after the brief WOT is carried out), measure the battery voltage.	
• **Does the battery voltage increase a minimum of 0.5 volt from the key ON, engine off measurement to the key ON, engine running measurement (after the brief WOT or snap acceleration is carried out)?**	**Yes** GO to B4. **No** INSTALL a new generator. TEST the system for normal operation.
B4 CHECK CIRCUIT 1816 (YE/LB) FOR AN OPEN OR A SHORT TO GROUND	
• Key in OFF position. • Disconnect: PCM C175t.	

ARM0500000000547

Fig. 44 Test B: Charging System Warning Indicator Is On w/Engine Running, Engine Voltage Does Not Increase (Part 2 of 3). 2005–08 Crown Victoria & Grand Marquis

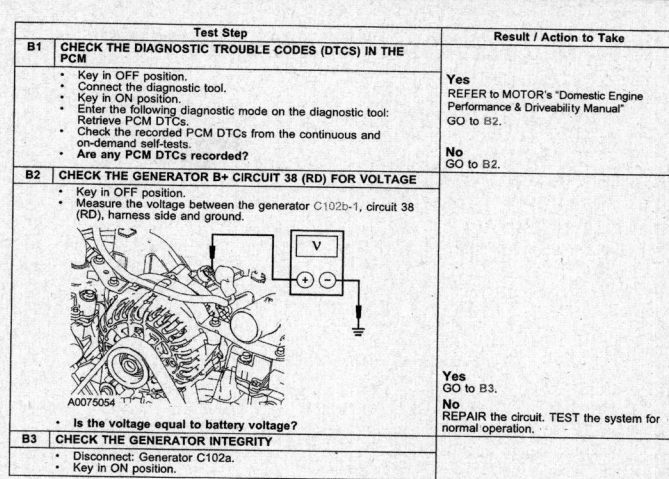

Test Step	Result / Action to Take
B1 CHECK THE DIAGNOSTIC TROUBLE CODES (DTCS) IN THE PCM	
• Key in OFF position. • Connect the diagnostic tool. • Key in ON position. • Enter the following diagnostic mode on the diagnostic tool: Retrieve PCM DTCs. • Check the recorded PCM DTCs from the continuous and on-demand self-tests. • **Are any PCM DTCs recorded?**	**Yes** REFER to MOTOR's "Domestic Engine Performance & Driveability Manual" GO to B2. **No** GO to B2.
B2 CHECK THE GENERATOR B+ CIRCUIT 38 (RD) FOR VOLTAGE	
• Key in OFF position. • Measure the voltage between the generator C102b-1, circuit 38 (RD), harness side and ground.	
• **Is the voltage equal to battery voltage?**	**Yes** GO to B3. **No** REPAIR the circuit. TEST the system for normal operation.
B3 CHECK THE GENERATOR INTEGRITY	
• Disconnect: Generator C102a. • Key in ON position.	

ARM0500000000546

Fig. 44 Test B: Charging System Warning Indicator Is On w/Engine Running, Engine Voltage Does Not Increase (Part 1 of 3). 2005–08 Crown Victoria & Grand Marquis

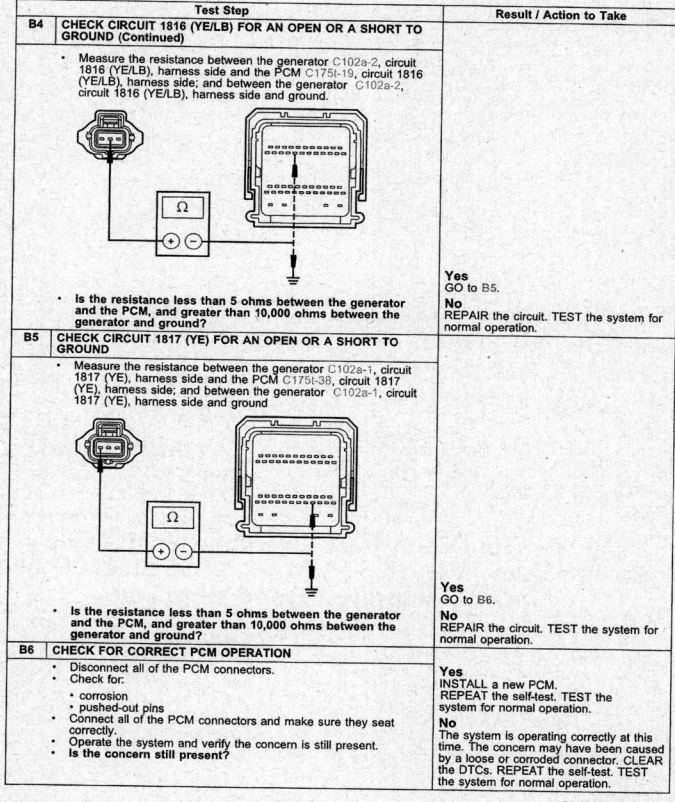

Test Step	Result / Action to Take
B4 CHECK CIRCUIT 1816 (YE/LB) FOR AN OPEN OR A SHORT TO GROUND (Continued)	
• Measure the resistance between the generator C102a-2, circuit 1816 (YE/LB), harness side and the PCM C175t-19, circuit 1816 (YE/LB), harness side; and between the generator C102a-2, circuit 1816 (YE/LB), harness side and ground.	
• **Is the resistance less than 5 ohms between the generator and the PCM, and greater than 10,000 ohms between the generator and ground?**	**Yes** GO to B5. **No** REPAIR the circuit. TEST the system for normal operation.
B5 CHECK CIRCUIT 1817 (YE) FOR AN OPEN OR A SHORT TO GROUND	
• Measure the resistance between the generator C102a-1, circuit 1817 (YE), harness side and the PCM C175t-38, circuit 1817 (YE), harness side; and between the generator C102a-1, circuit 1817 (YE), harness side and ground.	
• **Is the resistance less than 5 ohms between the generator and the PCM, and greater than 10,000 ohms between the generator and ground?**	**Yes** GO to B6. **No** REPAIR the circuit. TEST the system for normal operation.
B6 CHECK FOR CORRECT PCM OPERATION	

• Disconnect all of the PCM connectors.
• Check for:
  • corrosion
  • pushed-out pins
• Connect all of the PCM connectors and make sure they seat correctly.
• Operate the system and verify the concern is still present.
• **Is the concern still present?**
	Yes INSTALL a new PCM. REPEAT the self-test. TEST the system for normal operation.
	No The system is operating correctly at this time. The concern may have been caused by a loose or corroded connector. CLEAR the DTCs. REPEAT the self-test. TEST the system for normal operation.

ARM0500000000548

Fig. 44 Test B: Charging System Warning Indicator Is On w/Engine Running, Engine Voltage Does Not Increase (Part 3 of 3). 2005–08 Crown Victoria & Grand Marquis

Test Step	Result / Action to Take
C1	**CHECK THE DIAGNOSTIC TROUBLE CODES (DTCS) IN THE PCM**
• Key in OFF position. • Connect the diagnostic tool. • Key in ON position. • Enter the following diagnostic mode on the diagnostic tool: Retrieve PCM DTCs. • Check the recorded PCM DTCs from the continuous and on-demand self-tests. • **Are any PCM DTCs recorded?**	**Yes** REFER to MOTOR's "Domestic Engine Performance & Driveability Manual" GO to C2. **No** GO to C2.
C2	**CHECK THE BATTERY VOLTAGE**
• Key in OFF position. • Disconnect the diagnostic tool. • Key in START position. • With the engine running and all of the accessories turned off, measure the voltage at the battery while varying the engine rpm. • **Is the voltage greater than 15.5 volts?**	**Yes** GO to C3. **No** GO to C4.
C3	**CHECK FOR A VOLTAGE DROP IN CIRCUIT 35 (OG/LB)**
• Key in OFF position. • Disconnect: Generator C102a.	

ARM0500000000549

Fig. 45 Test C: System Overcharges, Battery Voltage More Than 15.5 Volts (Part 1 of 3). 2005–08 Crown Victoria & Grand Marquis

Test Step	Result / Action to Take
C5	**CHECK THE GENERATOR INTEGRITY (Continued)**
• **NOTE:** If the generator communication lines are disconnected, the generator self-excites if it is operated at greater than 4,500 rpm (approximately wide open throttle (WOT)) for a minimum of 3 seconds. It then operates in a default mode of approximately 13.5 volts until the engine is turned off. With the engine running (after the brief WOT is carried out), measure the battery voltage. • **Does the battery voltage increase a minimum of 0.5 volt from the key ON, engine off measurement to the key ON, engine running measurement (after the brief WOT or snap acceleration is carried out)?**	**Yes** GO to C6. **No** INSTALL a new generator. TEST the system for normal operation.
C6	**CHECK FOR CORRECT PCM OPERATION**

• Key in OFF position.
• Disconnect all of the PCM connectors.
• Check for:
  • corrosion
  • pushed-out pins
• Connect all of the PCM connectors and make sure they seat correctly.
• Operate the system and verify the concern is still present.
• **Is the concern still present?**
	Yes
	INSTALL a new PCM. REPEAT the self-test. TEST the system for normal operation.
	
	No
	The system is operating correctly at this time. The concern may have been caused by a loose or corroded connector. CLEAR the DTCs. REPEAT the self-test. TEST the system for normal operation.

ARM0500000000551

Fig. 45 Test C: System Overcharges, Battery Voltage More Than 15.5 Volts (Part 3 of 3). 2005–08 Crown Victoria & Grand Marquis

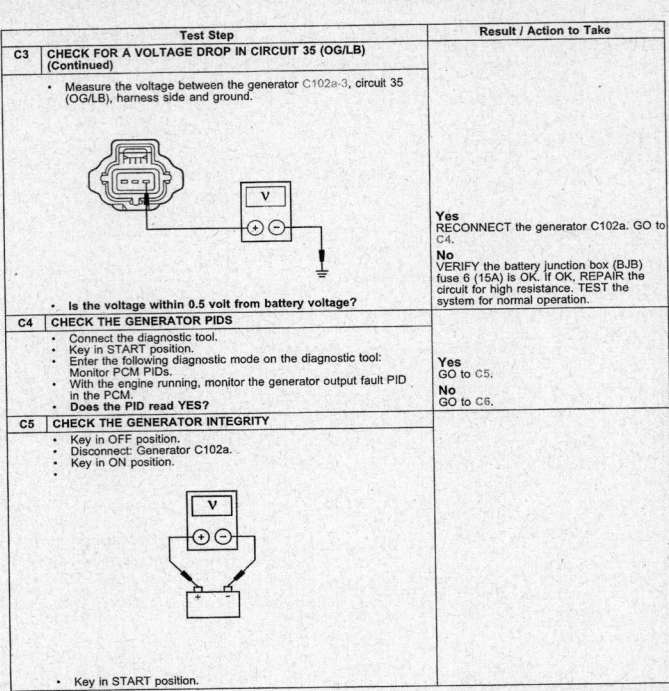

Test Step	Result / Action to Take
C3	**CHECK FOR A VOLTAGE DROP IN CIRCUIT 35 (OG/LB) (Continued)**
• Measure the voltage between the generator C102a-3, circuit 35 (OG/LB), harness side and ground. • **Is the voltage within 0.5 volt from battery voltage?**	**Yes** RECONNECT the generator C102a. GO to C4. **No** VERIFY the battery junction box (BJB) fuse 6 (15A) is OK. If OK, REPAIR the circuit for high resistance. TEST the system for normal operation.
C4	**CHECK THE GENERATOR PIDS**
• Connect the diagnostic tool. • Key in START position. • Enter following diagnostic mode on the diagnostic tool: Monitor PCM PIDs. • With the engine running, monitor the generator output fault PID in the PCM. • **Does the PID read YES?**	**Yes** GO to C5. **No** GO to C6.
C5	**CHECK THE GENERATOR INTEGRITY**
• Key in OFF position. • Disconnect: Generator C102a. • Key in ON position. • Key in START position.	

ARM0500000000550

Fig. 45 Test C: System Overcharges, Battery Voltage More Than 15.5 Volts (Part 2 of 3). 2005–08 Crown Victoria & Grand Marquis

Test Step	Result / Action to Take
D1	**CHECK THE DIAGNOSTIC TROUBLE CODES (DTCS) IN THE PCM**
• Key in OFF position. • Connect the diagnostic tool. • Key in ON position. • Enter the following diagnostic mode on the diagnostic tool: Retrieve PCM DTCs. • Check the recorded PCM DTCs from the continuous and on-demand self-tests. • **Are any PCM DTCs recorded?**	**Yes** REFER to MOTOR's "Domestic Engine Performance & Driveability Manual" GO to D2. **No** GO to D2.
D2	**CHECK THE SYSTEM FOR OVERCHARGING**
• Key in START position. • With the engine running and all of the accessories off, measure the voltage at the battery terminals while varying the engine rpm. • **Is the voltage greater than 15.5 volts?**	**Yes** GO to Pinpoint Test C. **No** GO to D3.
D3	**CHECK THE PCM PIDS**
• Enter the following diagnostic mode on the diagnostic tool: Monitor PCM PIDs. • With the engine running, monitor the generator output fault PID in the PCM. • **Does the PID read YES?**	**Yes** GO to D4. **No** Diagnose system charging system warning indicator.
D4	**CHECK THE GENERATOR OUTPUT**
• Verify the generator output. Refer to the Component Tests, Generator On-Vehicle Tests in this section. • **Does the generator pass the component tests?**	**Yes** GO to D5. **No** INSTALL a new generator. REPEAT the self-test. TEST the system for normal operation.
D5	**CHECK FOR CORRECT PCM OPERATION**

• Key in OFF position.
• Disconnect all of the PCM connectors.
• Check for:
  • corrosion
  • pushed-out pins
• Connect all of the PCM connectors and make sure they seat correctly.
• Operate the system and verify the concern is still present.
• **Is the concern still present?**
	Yes
	INSTALL a new PCM. REPEAT the self-test. TEST the system for normal operation.
	
	No
	The system is operating correctly at this time. The concern may have been caused by a loose or corroded connector. CLEAR the DTCs. REPEAT the self-test. TEST the system for normal operation.

ARM0500000000552

Fig. 46 Test D: Charging System Warning Indicator Is On w/Engine Running, System Increases Voltage. 2005–08 Crown Victoria & Grand Marquis

Test Step		Result / Action to Take
E1	CHECK THE CHARGING SYSTEM WARNING INDICATOR OPERATION	
	• Key in OFF position. • Connect the diagnostic tool. • Key in ON position. • Enter the following diagnostic mode on the diagnostic tool: Active Commands. • Using Active Commands, turn on the charging system warning indicator in the instrument cluster. • **Is the charging system warning indicator on?**	**Yes** GO to **E2**. **No** Diagnose charging system warning indicator.
E2	CHECK FOR CORRECT PCM OPERATION	

	• Key in OFF position.
	• Disconnect all of the PCM connectors.
	• Check for:
	  • corrosion
	  • pushed-out pins
	• Connect all of the PCM connectors and make sure they seat correctly.
	• Operate the system and verify the concern is still present.
	• **Is the concern still present?**
		Yes
		INSTALL a new PCM. REPEAT the self-test. TEST the system for normal operation.
		
		No
		The system is operating correctly at this time. The concern may have been caused by a loose or corroded connector. CLEAR the DTCs. REPEAT the self-test. TEST the system for normal operation.

ARM0500000000553

Fig. 47 Test E: Charging System Warning Indicator Is Off w/Ignition Switch In Run Position & Engine Off. 2005–08 Crown Victoria & Grand Marquis

Test Step		Result / Action to Take
G1	VERIFY THE GENERATOR IS THE SOURCE OF THE RADIO INTERFERENCE	
	NOTE: If the original equipment manufactured (OEM) audio unit has been replaced with an aftermarket unit, the vehicle may not pass this test. Return the vehicle to OEM condition before following this pinpoint test. • Key in START position. • Start and run the engine. • Tune the audio unit to a station where the interference is present. • Key in OFF position. • Disconnect: Generator C102b. • Key in START position. • With the engine running, determine if the interference is still present. • **Is the interference present with the generator disconnected?**	**Yes** Diagnose in-vehicle entertainment system. **No** INSTALL a new generator. TEST the system for normal operation.

ARM0500000000555

Fig. 49 Test G: Radio Interference. 2005–08 Crown Victoria & Grand Marquis

Test Step		Result / Action to Take
A1	CHECK THE BATTERY CONDITION	
	• Carry out the Battery — Condition Test to determine if the battery can hold a charge and is OK for use. • **Does the battery pass the condition test?**	**Yes** GO to **A2**. **No** INSTALL a new battery.
A2	CHECK THE GENERATOR OUTPUT	
	• Carry out the Generator On-Vehicle Load Test and No Load Test. Refer to Component Tests in this section. • **Does the generator pass the component tests?**	**Yes** GO to **A3**. **No** INSTALL a new generator
A3	CHECK FOR CURRENT DRAINS	
	• Carry out the Battery — Drain Test. • **Are any excessive current drains present?**	**Yes** REPAIR as necessary. TEST the system for normal operation. **No** GO to **A4**.
A4	CHECK THE VEHICLE GROUNDS	
	• Key in START position. • With the engine running, measure the voltage drop between the generator housing and the negative battery terminal. • **Is the voltage drop less than 0.1 volt?**	**Yes** GO to **A5**. **No** CHECK the engine ground, generator ground and the battery ground for corrosion, TEST the system for normal operation.
A5	CHECK THE VOLTAGE DROP IN THE B+ CIRCUIT	
	• With the engine running, measure the voltage drop between the generator B+ C102b, circuit 38 (BK/OG) and the positive battery terminal. • **Is the voltage drop less than 0.1 volt?**	**Yes** VERIFY if the customer left any component(s) on or if there is an intermittent excessive battery draw. TEST the system for normal operation. **No** CHECK for any corrosion in the positive battery cable and/or connections. REPAIR as necessary. TEST the system for normal operation.

ARM0400000000747

Fig. 50 Test A: Battery Or Battery Voltage Is Low. Five Hundred, Freestyle & Montego

Test Step		Result / Action to Take
F1	CHECK FOR ACCESSORY DRIVE NOISE AND MOUNTING BRACKETS	
	• Key in OFF position. • Check the accessory drive belt for damage and correct installation. • Check the accessory mounting brackets and the generator pulley for looseness or misalignment. • **Is the accessory drive OK?**	**Yes** If equipped with a one-way-clutch (OWC) pulley, GO to **F2**. If not equipped with a OWC pulley, GO to **F3**. **No** REPAIR as necessary. TEST the system for normal operation.
F2	CHECK THE OWC PULLEY	
	• With the accessory drive belt removed, spin the OWC pulley in a clockwise direction, then reverse the direction of the pulley by spinning it in a counterclockwise direction. • **Does the OWC pulley engage with the rotor when spun in a clockwise direction and free-wheel when spun in a counterclockwise direction with minimal noise as compared to a known good vehicle?**	**Yes** GO to **F3**. **No** INSTALL a new generator assembly with OWC pulley. TEST the system for normal operation.
F3	CHECK THE GENERATOR FOR EXCESSIVE ELECTRICAL NOISE	
	• Disconnect: Generator C102b. • Key in START position. • With the engine running, determine if the generator is still noisy. • **Is the noise still present?**	**Yes** GO to **F4**. **No** INSTALL a new generator. TEST the system for normal operation.
F4	CHECK THE GENERATOR FOR MECHANICAL NOISE	
	• Turn all of the accessories off. With the engine running, use a stethoscope or equivalent listening device to probe the generator for unusual mechanical noise. • **Is the generator the noise source?**	**Yes** INSTALL a new generator. TEST the system for normal operation. **No** diagnose the source of the engine noise.

ARM0500000000554

Fig. 48 Test F: Alternator Is Noisy. 2005–08 Crown Victoria & Grand Marquis

Test Step		Result / Action to Take
B1	CHECK THE DTCs IN THE PCM	
	• Check the recorded PCM DTCs from the continuous and on-demand self-tests. • **Are any PCM DTCs recorded?**	**Yes** REFER to MOTOR's Domestic Engine Performanc & Driveability manual. **No** GO to **B2**.
B2	CHECK THE GENERATOR B+ CIRCUIT FOR VOLTAGE	
	• Key in OFF position. • Measure the voltage between the generator C102b, circuit 38 (BK/OG) and ground. • **Is the voltage equal to positive battery voltage?**	**Yes** GO to **B3**. **No** REPAIR the circuit. TEST the system for normal operation.
B3	CHECK THE GENERATOR INTEGRITY	
	• Disconnect: Generator C102a. • Key in START position.	

ARM0400000000748

Fig. 51 Test B: Charging System Warning Indicator Is On w/Engine Running & Battery Voltage Does Not Increase (Part 1 of 3). Five Hundred, Freestyle & Montego

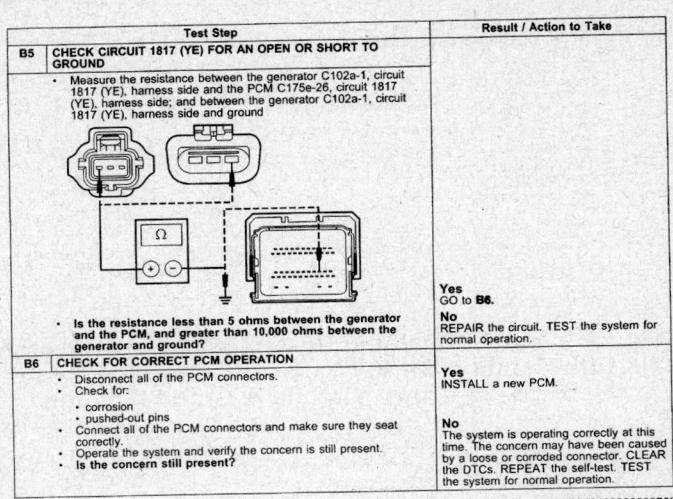

Test Step	Result / Action to Take
B5 CHECK CIRCUIT 1817 (YE) FOR AN OPEN OR SHORT TO GROUND	
• Measure the resistance between the generator C102a-1, circuit 1817 (YE), harness side and the PCM C175e-26, circuit 1817 (YE), harness side; and between the generator C102a-1, circuit 1817 (YE), harness side and ground.	
• Is the resistance less than 5 ohms between the generator and the PCM, and greater than 10,000 ohms between the generator and ground?	**Yes** GO to **B6**. **No** REPAIR the circuit. TEST the system for normal operation.
B6 CHECK FOR CORRECT PCM OPERATION	

• Disconnect all of the PCM connectors.
• Check for:
  • corrosion
  • pushed-out pins
• Connect all of the PCM connectors and make sure they seat correctly.
• Operate the system and verify the concern is still present.
• **Is the concern still present?**
	Yes
	INSTALL a new PCM.
	
	No
	The system is operating correctly at this time. The concern may have been caused by a loose or corroded connector. CLEAR the DTCs. REPEAT the self-test. TEST the system for normal operation.

ARM0400000000750

Fig. 51   Test B: Charging System Warning Indicator Is On w/Engine Running & Battery Voltage Does Not Increase (Part 3 of 3). Five Hundred, Freestyle & Montego

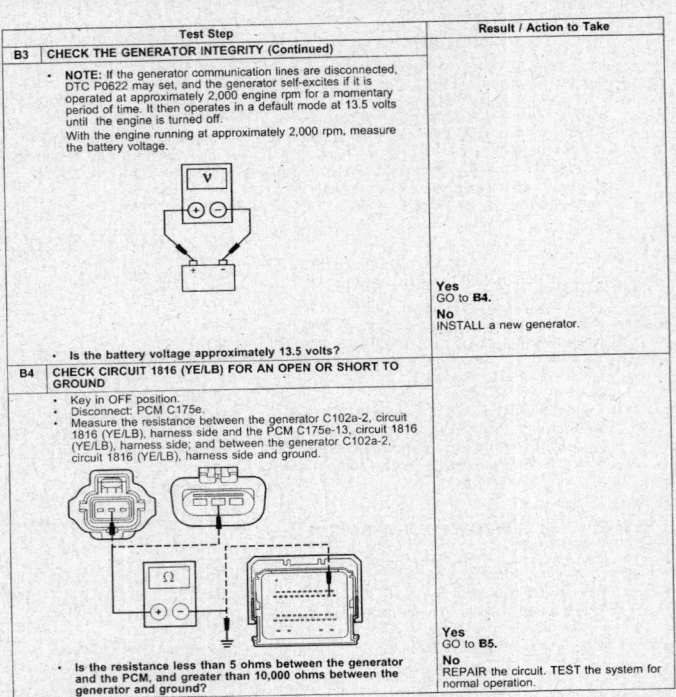

Test Step	Result / Action to Take
B3 CHECK THE GENERATOR INTEGRITY (Continued)	
• NOTE: If the generator communication lines are disconnected, DTC P0622 may set, and the generator self-excites if it is operated at approximately 2,000 engine rpm for a momentary period of time. It then operates in a default mode at 13.5 volts until the engine is turned off. With the engine running at approximately 2,000 rpm, measure the battery voltage.	
• Is the battery voltage approximately 13.5 volts?	**Yes** GO to **B4**. **No** INSTALL a new generator.
B4 CHECK CIRCUIT 1816 (YE/LB) FOR AN OPEN OR SHORT TO GROUND	
• Key in OFF position. • Disconnect: PCM C175e. • Measure the resistance between the generator C102a-2, circuit 1816 (YE/LB), harness side and the PCM C175e-13, circuit 1816 (YE/LB), harness side; and between the generator C102a-2, circuit 1816 (YE/LB), harness side and ground.	
• Is the resistance less than 5 ohms between the generator and the PCM, and greater than 10,000 ohms between the generator and ground?	**Yes** GO to **B5**. **No** REPAIR the circuit. TEST the system for normal operation.

ARM0400000000749

Fig. 51   Test B: Charging System Warning Indicator Is On w/Engine Running & Battery Voltage Does Not Increase (Part 2 of 3). Five Hundred, Freestyle & Montego

Test Step	Result / Action to Take
C1 CHECK THE DTCs IN THE PCM	
• Check the recorded PCM DTCs from the continuous and on-demand self-tests. • **Are any PCM DTCs recorded?**	**Yes** REFER to MOTOR's Domestic Engine Performanc & Driveability manual. **No** GO to **C2**.
C2 CHECK THE BATTERY VOLTAGE	
• Key in START position. • With the engine running and all the accessories turned off, measure the voltage at the battery while varying the engine RPM.	
• Is the voltage greater than 15.5 volts?	**Yes** GO to **C3**. **No** GO to **C4**.
C3 CHECK THE VOLTAGE IN CIRCUIT 1818 (WH/BK)	
• Key in OFF position. • Disconnect: Generator C102a. • Measure the voltage between the generator C102a-3, circuit 1818 (WH/BK), harness side and ground.	
• Is the voltage within 0.5 volt of battery voltage?	**Yes** CONNECT the generator C102a. GO to **C4**. **No** REPAIR the circuit for high resistance. TEST the system for normal operation.
C4 CHECK THE GENERATOR PIDs	
• Connect the diagnostic tool. • Key in START position. • Enter the following diagnostic mode on the diagnostic tool: Monitor PCM PIDs. • With the engine running, monitor the generator output fault PID in the PCM. • **Does the PID read YES?**	**Yes** GO to **C5**. **No** GO to **C6**.
C5 CHECK THE GENERATOR INTEGRITY	
• Key in OFF position. • Disconnect: Generator C102a. • Key in START position.	

ARM0400000000751

Fig. 52   Test C: Charging System Overcharges (Part 1 of 2). Five Hundred, Freestyle & Montego

Test Step	Result / Action to Take
C5 CHECK THE GENERATOR INTEGRITY (Continued)	
• NOTE: If the generator communication lines are disconnected, DTC P0622 may be set, and the generator self-excites if it is operated at approximately 2,000 engine rpm for a momentary period of time. It then operates in a default mode at 13.5 volts until the engine is turned off. With the engine running at approximately 2,000 rpm, measure the battery voltage.	
• Is the battery voltage approximately 13.5 volts?	**Yes** GO to **C6**. **No** INSTALL a new generator.
C6 CHECK FOR CORRECT PCM OPERATION	

• Disconnect all of the PCM connectors.
• Check for:
  • corrosion
  • pushed-out pins
• Connect all of the PCM connectors and make sure they seat correctly.
• Operate the system and verify the concern is still present.
• **Is the concern still present?**
	Yes
	INSTALL a new PCM.
	
	No
	The system is operating correctly at this time. The concern may have been caused by a loose or corroded connector. CLEAR the DTCs. REPEAT the self-test. TEST the system for normal operation.

ARM0400000000752

Fig. 52   Test C: Charging System Overcharges (Part 2 of 2). Five Hundred, Freestyle & Montego

Test Step		Result / Action to Take
D1	CHECK THE DTCs IN THE PCM • Check the recorded PCM DTCs from the continuous and on-demand self-tests. • **Are any PCM DTCs recorded?**	**Yes** REFER to MOTOR's Domestic Engine Performanc & Driveability manual. **No** GO to D2.
D2	CHECK THE SYSTEM FOR OVERCHARGING • Key in START position. • With the engine running and all accessories off, measure the voltage at the battery terminals while varying the engine RPM. • **Is the voltage greater than 15.5 volts?**	**Yes** GO to Pinpoint Test C. **No** GO to D3.
D3	CHECK THE CHARGING SYSTEM WARNING INDICATOR OPERATION • Enter the following diagnostic mode on the diagnostic tool: PCM PIDs. • With the engine running, monitor the generator output fault PID in the PCM. • **Does the PID read YES?**	**Yes** GO to D4. **No** Diagnose the charging system warning indicator.
D4	CHECK THE GENERATOR OUTPUT • Verify the generator output. • **Does the generator pass the component tests?**	**Yes** GO to D5. **No** INSTALL a new generator.

D5	CHECK FOR CORRECT PCM OPERATION
	• Disconnect all of the PCM connectors.
	• Check for:
	  • corrosion
	  • pushed-out pins
	• Connect all of the PCM connectors and make sure they seat correctly.
	• Operate the system and verify the concern is still present.
	• **Is the concern still present?**
		Yes
		INSTALL a new PCM.
		No
		The system is operating correctly at this time. The concern may have been caused by a loose or corroded connector. CLEAR the DTCs. REPEAT the self-test. TEST the system for normal operation.

ARM0400000000753

Fig. 53   Test D: Charging System Warning Indicator Is On w/Engine Running & Battery Increases Voltage. Five Hundred, Freestyle & Montego

Test Step		Result / Action to Take
F1	CHECK FOR ACCESSORY DRIVE NOISE AND MOUNTING BRACKETS • Key in OFF position. • Check the accessory drive belt for damage and correct installation. Refer to Section 303-05. • Check the accessory mounting brackets and generator pulley for looseness or misalignment. • **Is the accessory drive OK?**	**Yes** GO to F2. **No** REPAIR as necessary. TEST the system for normal operation.

ARM0400000000755

Fig. 55   Test F: Alternator Is Noisy (Part 1 of 2). Five Hundred, Freestyle & Montego

Test Step		Result / Action to Take
F2	CHECK THE GENERATOR FOR EXCESSIVE ELECTRICAL NOISE • Disconnect: Generator C102b. • Key in START position. • With the engine running, determine if the generator is still noisy. • **Is the noise still present?**	**Yes** GO to F3. **No** INSTALL a new generator.
F3	CHECK THE GENERATOR FOR MECHANICAL NOISE • Turn all the accessories off. With the engine running, use a stethoscope or equivalent listening device to probe the generator for unusual mechanical noise. • **Is the generator the noise source?**	**Yes** INSTALL a new generator. **No** Diagnose the source of the engine noise.

ARM0400000000756

Fig. 55   Test F: Alternator Is Noisy (Part 2 of 2). Five Hundred, Freestyle & Montego

Test Step		Result / Action to Take
G1	VERIFY THE GENERATOR IS THE SOURCE OF THE RADIO INTERFERENCE NOTE: If the original equipment manufactured (OEM) audio unit has been replaced with an aftermarket unit, the vehicle may not pass this test. Return the vehicle to OEM condition before following this pinpoint test. • Key in START position. • With the engine running, tune the radio to a station where the interference is present. • Key in OFF position. • Disconnect: Generator C102b. • Key in START position. • With the engine running, determine if the interference is still present. • **Is the interference present with the generator disconnected?**	**Yes** Diagnose netertainment system. **No** INSTALL a new generator.

ARM0400000000757

Fig. 56   Test G: Radio Interference. Five Hundred, Freestyle & Montego

Test Step		Result / Action to Take
E1	CHECK THE CHARGING SYSTEM WARNING INDICATOR OPERATION • Key in ON position. • Enter the following diagnostic mode on the diagnostic tool: Instrument Cluster Active Commands. • Using the instrument cluster Active Commands, turn on the charging system warning indicator. • **Is the charging system warning indicator on?**	**Yes** GO to E2. **No** Diagnose the charging system warning indicator.

E2	CHECK FOR CORRECT PCM OPERATION
	• Disconnect all of the PCM connectors.
	• Check for:
	  • corrosion
	  • pushed-out pins
	• Connect all of the PCM connectors and make sure they seat correctly.
	• Operate the system and verify the concern is still present.
	• **Is the concern still present?**
		Yes
		INSTALL a new PCM.
		No
		The system is operating correctly at this time. The concern may have been caused by a loose or corroded connector. CLEAR the DTCs. REPEAT the self-test. TEST the system for normal operation.

ARM0400000000754

Fig. 54   Test E: Charging System Warning Indicator Is Off w/Ignition Switch In Run Position & Engine Off. Five Hundred, Freestyle & Montego

Test Condition	Test Details/Results/Actions
TEST A1: INSPECT BATTERY	
Inspect battery capacity	If battery capacity is not at normal operating range, replace battery
Inspect system operation	—
TEST A2: INSPECT CHARGING SYSTEM	
Perform "Load Test"	If alternator output is not as specified, refer to "Test A3: Inspect For A Good Ground"
TEST A3: INSPECT FOR A GOOD GROUND	
Measure voltage between alternator case and battery ground terminal	If voltage is less than .5 volts, refer to "Test A4: Inspect Battery Cable"
	If voltage is more than .5 volts, clean and tighten alternator mounting bolts, engine to body ground strap and battery ground cable
Inspect system operation	—
TEST A4: INSPECT BATTERY CABLE	
Measure voltage between alternator B+ terminal and battery positive terminal	Voltage should be less than .5 volts
	If voltage is as specified, refer to "Test A5: Inspect Battery Feed To Alternator"
	If voltage is not as specified, clean and tighten battery positive cable connections
Inspect system operation	If voltage is still not as specified, replace battery positive cable
TEST A5: INSPECT BATTERY FEED TO ALTERNATOR	
Measure voltage between alternator B+ terminal and ground	Battery voltage should be present
	If voltage is as specified, refer to "Test A6: Inspect Power To Voltage Regulator"
	If voltage is not as specified, inspect fusible links and fuses and replace as required
Inspect system operation	If voltage is not as specified, repair battery positive cable
TEST A6: INSPECT POWER TO VOLTAGE REGULATOR	
Measure voltage between alternator connector pin No. 3 harness side and ground	Battery voltage should be present
	If voltage is as specified, replace alternator and inspect system once again
	If voltage is not as specified, inspect fuse No. F10 and repair circuit 30-BA10

Fig. 57   Test A: Charging System Warning Indicator Is On w/Engine Running. 2004 Focus

Test Condition	Test Details/Results/Actions
Test B1: ISOLATE THE ALTERNATOR	
Remove accessory drive belt	—
Run engine for a few seconds with radio turned on	If radio interference is still present, inspect audio entertainment system for faults
	If radio interference is not present, clean and tighten battery clamps and alternator mounting bolts
	If interference is still present, replace alternator

Fig. 58   Test B: Radio Interference. 2004 Focus

Test Step	Result / Action to Take
A5 CHECK THE VOLTAGE DROP IN THE B+ CIRCUIT 30-BA6 (RD)	
• With the engine running, measure the voltage drop between the generator C102c, circuit 30-BA6 (RD) and the positive battery terminal.	**Yes** CHECK if the customer left any component(s) on or if there is an intermittent excessive battery draw. TEST the system for normal operation. **No** CHECK for any corrosion in the circuit 30-BA6 (RD), positive battery cable and/or connections. REPAIR as necessary. TEST the system for normal operation.
• Is the voltage drop less than 0.1 volt?	

ARM0500000000557

Fig. 59   Test A: Battery Is Discharged Or Battery Voltage Is Low (Part 2 of 2). 2005–07 Focus

Test Step	Result / Action to Take
B1 CHECK THE DTCS IN THE POWERTRAIN CONTROL MODULE (PCM)	
• Key in OFF position. • Connect the diagnostic tool. • Key in ON position. • Enter the following diagnostic mode on the diagnostic tool: Retrieve PCM DTCs. • Check the recorded PCM DTCs from the continuous and on-demand self-tests. • Are any PCM DTCs recorded?	**Yes** REFER to MOTOR's "Domestic Engine Performance & Driveability Manual" GO to B2. **No** GO to B2.
B2 CHECK THE GENERATOR CIRCUIT 30-BA6 (RD) FOR VOLTAGE	
• Key in OFF position.	

ARM0500000000558

Fig. 60   Test B: Charging System Warning Indicator Is On w/Engine Running & Battery Voltage Does Not Increase (Part 1 of 3). 2005–07 Focus

Test Step	Result / Action to Take
A1 CHECK THE BATTERY CONDITION	
• Carry out the Battery — Condition Test to determine if the battery can hold a charge and is OK for use. • Does the battery pass the condition test?	**Yes** GO to A2. **No** INSTALL a new battery. TEST the system for normal operation.
A2 CHECK THE GENERATOR OUTPUT	
• Carry out the Generator On-Vehicle Load Test and No Load Test. Refer to the Component Tests in this section. • Does the generator pass the component tests?	**Yes** GO to A3. **No** INSTALL a new generator. TEST the system for normal operation.
A3 CHECK FOR CURRENT DRAINS	
• Carry out the Battery — Drain Testing. • Are any circuits causing excessive current drains?	**Yes** REPAIR as necessary. TEST the system for normal operation. **No** GO to A4.
A4 CHECK THE VEHICLE GROUNDS	
• Key in START position. • With the engine running, measure the voltage drop between the generator housing and the negative battery terminal.	
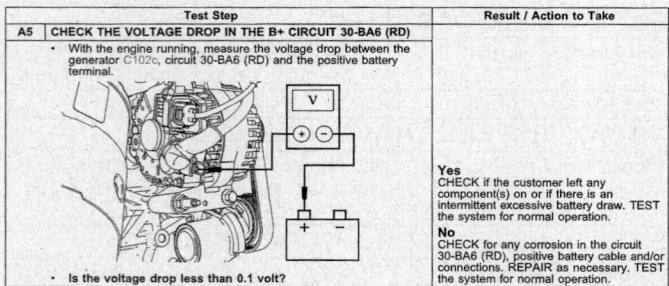	
• Is the voltage drop less than 0.1 volt?	**Yes** GO to A5. **No** CHECK the engine ground, generator ground and the battery ground for corrosion. TEST the system for normal operation.

ARM0500000000556

Fig. 59   Test A: Battery Is Discharged Or Battery Voltage Is Low (Part 1 of 2). 2005–07 Focus

Test Step	Result / Action to Take
B2 CHECK THE GENERATOR CIRCUIT 30-BA6 (RD) FOR VOLTAGE (Continued)	
• Measure the voltage between the generator C102c, circuit 30-BA6 (RD) and ground.	
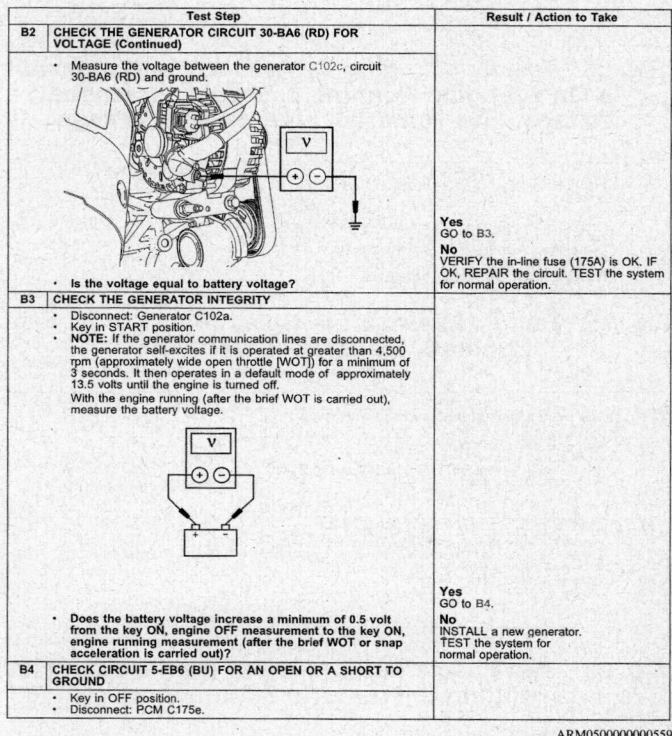	
• Is the voltage equal to battery voltage?	**Yes** GO to B3. **No** VERIFY the in-line fuse (175A) is OK. If OK, REPAIR the circuit. TEST the system for normal operation.
B3 CHECK THE GENERATOR INTEGRITY	
• Disconnect: Generator C102a. • Key in START position. • **NOTE:** If the generator communication lines are disconnected, the generator self-excites if it is operated at greater than 4,500 rpm (approximately wide open throttle [WOT]) for a minimum of 3 seconds. It then operates in a default mode of approximately 13.5 volts until the engine is turned off. With the engine running (after the brief WOT is carried out), measure the battery voltage.	
• Does the battery voltage increase a minimum of 0.5 volt from the key ON, engine OFF measurement to the key ON, engine running measurement (after the brief WOT or snap acceleration is carried out)?	**Yes** GO to B4. **No** INSTALL a new generator. TEST the system for normal operation.
B4 CHECK CIRCUIT 5-EB6 (BU) FOR AN OPEN OR A SHORT TO GROUND	
• Key in OFF position. • Disconnect: PCM C175e.	

ARM0500000000559

Fig. 60   Test B: Charging System Warning Indicator Is On w/Engine Running & Battery Voltage Does Not Increase (Part 2 of 3). 2005–07 Focus

Test Step	Result / Action to Take
B4 CHECK CIRCUIT 5-EB6 (BU) FOR AN OPEN OR A SHORT TO GROUND (Continued) • Measure the resistance between the generator C102a-2, circuit 5-EB6 (BU), harness side and the PCM C175e-14, circuit 5-EB6 (BU), harness side; and between the generator C102a-2, circuit 5-EB6 (BU), harness side and ground. 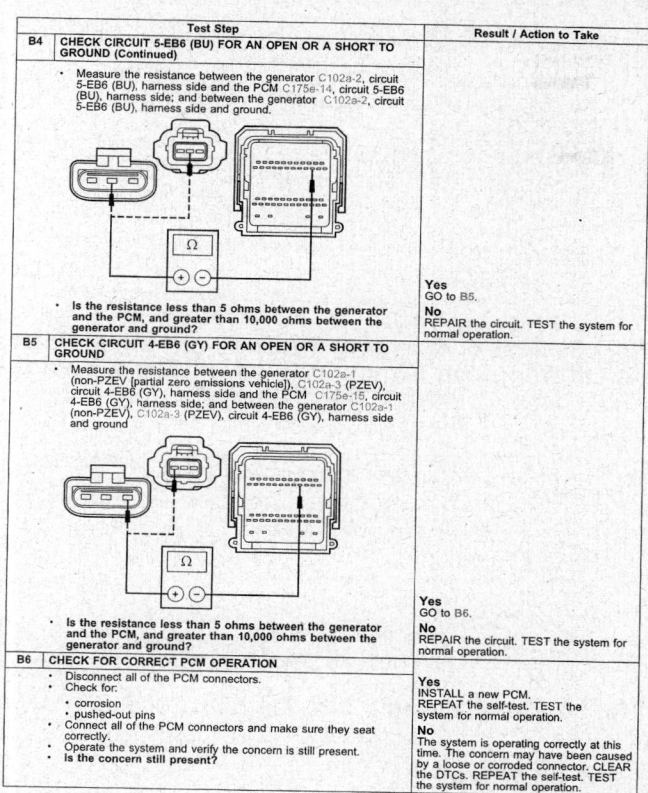 • Is the resistance less than 5 ohms between the generator and the PCM, and greater than 10,000 ohms between the generator and ground?	**Yes** GO to B5. **No** REPAIR the circuit. TEST the system for normal operation.
B5 CHECK CIRCUIT 4-EB6 (GY) FOR AN OPEN OR A SHORT TO GROUND • Measure the resistance between the generator C102a-1 (non-PZEV [partial zero emissions vehicle]), C102a-3 (PZEV), circuit 4-EB6 (GY), harness side and the PCM C175e-15, circuit 4-EB6 (GY), harness side; and between the generator C102a-1 (non-PZEV), C102a-3 (PZEV), circuit 4-EB6 (GY), harness side and ground • Is the resistance less than 5 ohms between the generator and the PCM, and greater than 10,000 ohms between the generator and ground?	**Yes** GO to B6. **No** REPAIR the circuit. TEST the system for normal operation.

B6 CHECK FOR CORRECT PCM OPERATION
• Disconnect all of the PCM connectors.
• Check for:
  • corrosion
  • pushed-out pins
• Connect all of the PCM connectors and make sure they seat correctly.
• Operate the system and verify the concern is still present.
• Is the concern still present?
	Yes
	INSTALL a new PCM. REPEAT the self-test. TEST the system for normal operation.
	No
	The system is operating correctly at this time. The concern may have been caused by a loose or corroded connector. CLEAR the DTCs. REPEAT the self-test. TEST the system for normal operation.

ARM0500000000560

Fig. 60   Test B: Charging System Warning Indicator Is On w/Engine Running & Battery Voltage Does Not Increase (Part 3 of 3). 2005–07 Focus

Test Step	Result / Action to Take
C3 CHECK FOR A VOLTAGE DROP IN CIRCUIT 30-BA10 (RD) (Continued) • Measure the voltage between the generator C102a-3 (non-PZEV [partial zero emissions vehicle]), C102a-1 (PZEV), circuit 30-BA10 (RD), harness side and ground. • Is the voltage within 0.5 volt from battery voltage?	**Yes** RECONNECT the generator C102a. GO to C4. **No** VERIFY the battery junction box (BJB) fuse 10 (1A) is OK. If OK, REPAIR the circuit. TEST the system for normal operation.
C4 CHECK THE GENERATOR PIDS • Connect the diagnostic tool. • Key in START position. • Enter the following diagnostic mode on the diagnostic tool: Monitor PCM PIDs. • With the engine running, monitor the generator output fault PID in the PCM. • Does the PID read YES?	**Yes** GO to C5. **No** GO to C6.
C5 CHECK THE GENERATOR INTEGRITY • Key in OFF position. • Disconnect: Generator C102a. • Key in START position. • NOTE: If the generator communication lines are disconnected, the generator self-excites if it is operated at greater than 4,500 rpm (approximately wide open throttle [WOT]) for a minimum of 3 seconds. It then operates in a default mode of approximately 13.5 volts until the engine is turned off. • With the engine running (after the brief WOT is carried out), measure the battery voltage. • Does the battery voltage increase a minimum of 0.5 volt from the key ON, engine OFF measurement to the key ON, engine running measurement (after the brief WOT or snap acceleration is carried out)?	**Yes** GO to C6. **No** INSTALL a new generator. TEST the system for normal operation.

ARM0500000000722

Fig. 61   Test C: Charging System Overcharges, Voltage Is Greater Than 15.5 Volts (Part 2 of 3). 2005–07 Focus

Test Step	Result / Action to Take
C1 CHECK THE DTCS IN THE POWERTRAIN CONTROL MODULE (PCM) • Key in OFF position. • Connect the diagnostic tool. • Key in ON position. • Enter the following diagnostic mode on the diagnostic tool: Retrieve PCM DTCs. • Check the recorded PCM DTCs from the continuous and on-demand self-tests. • Are any PCM DTCs recorded?	**Yes** REFER to MOTOR's "Domestic Engine Performance & Driveability Manual" GO to C2. **No** GO to C2.
C2 CHECK THE BATTERY VOLTAGE • Key in OFF position. • Disconnect the diagnostic tool. • Key in START position. • With the engine running and all of the accessories turned off, measure the voltage at the battery while varying the engine rpm. • Is the voltage greater than 15.5 volts?	**Yes** GO to C3. **No** GO to C4.
C3 CHECK FOR A VOLTAGE DROP IN CIRCUIT 30-BA10 (RD) • Key in OFF position. • Disconnect: Generator C102a.	

ARM0500000000561

Fig. 61   Test C: Charging System Overcharges, Voltage Is Greater Than 15.5 Volts (Part 1 of 3). 2005–07 Focus

Test Step	Result / Action to Take

C6 CHECK FOR CORRECT PCM OPERATION
• Key in OFF position.
• Disconnect all of the PCM connectors.
• Check for:
  • corrosion
  • pushed-out pins
• Connect all of the PCM connectors and make sure they seat correctly.
• Operate the system and verify the concern is still present.
• Is the concern still present?
	Yes
	INSTALL a new PCM. REPEAT the self-test. TEST the system for normal operation.
	No
	The system is operating correctly at this time. The concern may have been caused by a loose or corroded connector. CLEAR the DTCs. REPEAT the self-test. TEST the system for normal operation.

ARM0500000000723

Fig. 61   Test C: Charging System Overcharges, Voltage Is Greater Than 15.5 Volts (Part 3 of 3). 2005–07 Focus

Test Step	Result / Action to Take
D1 CHECK THE DTCS IN THE POWERTRAIN CONTROL MODULE (PCM) • Key in OFF position. • Connect the diagnostic tool. • Key in ON position. • Enter the following diagnostic mode on the diagnostic tool: Retrieve PCM DTCs. • Check the recorded PCM DTCs from the continuous and on-demand self-tests. • Are any PCM DTCs recorded?	**Yes** REFER to MOTOR's "Domestic Engine Performance & Driveability Manual" GO to D2. **No** GO to D2.
D2 CHECK THE SYSTEM FOR OVERCHARGING • Key in START position.	

ARM0500000000724

Fig. 62   Test D: Charging System Warning Indicator Is On w/Engine Running & Battery Increases Voltage (Part 1 of 2). 2005–07 Focus

Test Step	Result / Action to Take
D2 **CHECK THE SYSTEM FOR OVERCHARGING (Continued)**	
• With the engine running and all of the accessories off, measure the voltage at the battery terminals while varying the engine rpm.	
• Is the voltage greater than 15.5 volts?	**Yes** GO to Pinpoint Test C. **No** GO to D3.
D3 **CHECK THE PCM PIDS**	
• Enter the following diagnostic mode on the diagnostic tool: Monitor PCM PIDs. • With the engine running, monitor the generator output fault PID in the PCM. • Does the PID read YES?	**Yes** GO to D4. **No** Diagnose charging system warning indicator.
D4 **CHECK THE GENERATOR OUTPUT**	
• Verify the generator output. Refer to the Component Tests, Generator On-Vehicle Tests in this section. • Does the generator pass the component tests?	**Yes** GO to D5. **No** INSTALL a new generator. CLEAR the DTCs. REPEAT the self-test. TEST the system for normal operation.
D5 **CHECK FOR CORRECT PCM OPERATION**	
• Key in OFF position. • Disconnect all of the PCM connectors. • Check for: – corrosion – pushed-out pins • Connect all of the PCM connectors and make sure they seat correctly. • Operate the system and verify the concern is still present. • Is the concern still present?	**Yes** INSTALL a new PCM. REPEAT the self-test. TEST the system for normal operation. **No** The system is operating correctly at this time. The concern may have been caused by a loose or corroded connector. CLEAR the DTCs. REPEAT the self-test. TEST the system for normal operation.

ARM0500000000725

Fig. 62   Test D: Charging System Warning Indicator Is On w/Engine Running & Battery Increases Voltage (Part 2 of 2). 2005–07 Focus

Test Step	Result / Action to Take
E1 **CHECK THE CHARGING SYSTEM WARNING INDICATOR OPERATION**	
• Key in OFF position. • Connect the diagnostic tool. • Key in ON position. • Enter the following diagnostic mode on the diagnostic tool: Active Commands. • Using Active Commands, turn on the charging system warning indicator in the instrument cluster. • Is the charging system warning indicator on?	**Yes** GO to E2. **No** Diagnose charging system warning indicator.
E2 **CHECK FOR CORRECT PCM OPERATION**	
• Key in OFF position. • Disconnect all of the PCM connectors. • Check for: – corrosion – pushed-out pins • Connect all of the PCM connectors and make sure they seat correctly. • Operate the system and verify the concern is still present. • Is the concern still present?	**Yes** INSTALL a new PCM. REPEAT the self-test. TEST the system for normal operation. **No** The system is operating correctly at this time. The concern may have been caused by a loose or corroded connector. CLEAR the DTCs. REPEAT the self-test. TEST the system for normal operation.

ARM0500000000726

Fig. 63   Test E: Charging System Warning Indicator Is Off w/Ignition Switch In Run Position & Engine Off. 2005–07 Focus

Test Step	Result / Action to Take
G1 **VERIFY THE GENERATOR IS THE SOURCE OF THE RADIO INTERFERENCE**	
NOTE: If the original equipment manufactured (OEM) audio unit has been replaced with an aftermarket unit, the vehicle may not pass this test. Return the vehicle to OEM condition before following this pinpoint test. • Key in START position. • Start and run the engine. • Tune the audio unit to a station where the interference is present. • Key in OFF position. • Disconnect: Generator C102c. • Key in START position. • With the engine running, determine if the interference is still present. • Is the interference present with the generator disconnected?	**Yes** Diagnose in-vehicle entertainment system. **No** INSTALL a new generator. TEST the system for normal operation.

ARM0500000000728

Fig. 65   Test G: Radio Interference. 2005–07 Focus

Test Step	Result / Action to Take
F1 CHECK FOR ACCESSORY DRIVE NOISE AND MOUNTING BRACKETS	
• Key in OFF position. • Check the accessory drive belt for damage and correct installation. • Check the accessory mounting brackets and the generator pulley for looseness or misalignment. • Is the accessory drive OK?	**Yes** If equipped with a one-way-clutch (OWC) pulley, GO to F2 . If not equipped with a OWC pulley, GO to F3 . **No** REPAIR as necessary. TEST the system for normal operation.
F2 CHECK THE OWC PULLEY	
• With the accessory drive belt removed, spin the OWC pulley in a clockwise direction, then reverse the direction of the pulley by spinning it in a counterclockwise direction. • Does the OWC pulley engage with the rotor when spun in a clockwise direction and free-wheel when spun in a counterclockwise direction with minimal noise as compared to a known good vehicle?	**Yes** GO to F3 . **No** INSTALL a new generator. TEST the system for normal operation.
F3 CHECK THE GENERATOR FOR EXCESSIVE ELECTRICAL NOISE	
• Disconnect: Generator C102c. • Key in START position. • With the engine running, determine if the generator is still noisy. • Is the noise still present?	**Yes** GO to F4 . **No** INSTALL a new generator. TEST the system for normal operation.
F4 CHECK THE GENERATOR FOR MECHANICAL NOISE	
• Turn off all of the accessories. With the engine running, use a stethoscope or equivalent listening device to probe the generator for unusual mechanical noise. • Is the generator the noise source?	**Yes** INSTALL a new generator. TEST the system for normal operation. **No** diagnose the source of the engine noise.

ARM0500000000727

Fig. 64   Test F: Alternator Is Noisy. 2005–07 Focus

Test Step	Result / Action to Take
A1 **CHECK THE BATTERY CONDITION**	
• Carry out the Battery — Condition Test to determine if the battery can hold a charge and is OK for use. Refer to Section 414-01. • Does the battery pass the condition test?	**Yes** GO to A2. **No** INSTALL a new battery. TEST the system for normal operation.
A2 **CHECK THE GENERATOR OUTPUT**	
• Carry out the Generator On-Vehicle Load Test and No Load Test. Refer to the Component Tests in this section. • Does the generator pass the component tests?	**Yes** GO to A3. **No** INSTALL a new generator. TEST the system for normal operation.
A3 **CHECK FOR CURRENT DRAINS**	
• Carry out the Battery — Drain Testing. Refer to the Component Tests in this section. • Are any circuits causing excessive current drains?	**Yes** REPAIR as necessary. TEST the system for normal operation. **No** GO to A4.
A4 **CHECK THE VEHICLE GROUNDS**	
• Key in START position. • With the engine running, measure the voltage drop between the generator housing and the battery ground terminal. N0026342	
• Is the voltage drop less than 0.1 volt?	**Yes** GO to A5. **No** CHECK the engine ground, generator ground, and the battery ground for corrosion. TEST the system for normal operation.
A5 **CHECK THE VOLTAGE DROP IN CIRCUIT SDC14 (RD)**	
• With the engine running, measure the voltage drop between the generator C102b, circuit SDC14 (RD) and the positive battery terminal. N0026343	
• Is the voltage drop less than 0.1 volt?	**Yes** DETERMINE if the customer left any component(s) on or if there is an intermittent excessive battery draw. TEST the system for normal operation. **No** CHECK for any corrosion in the circuit SDC14 (RD) and/or connections. REPAIR as necessary. TEST the system for normal operation.

ARM0500000000528

Fig. 66   Test A: Battery Is Discharged Or Battery Voltage Is Low. Fusion, Milan, MKZ & Zephyr

Circuit Description

The PCM monitors various parameters and will not allow traction control operation if any parameter falls below a specified value.

DTC Descriptor

This diagnostic procedure supports the following DTC:

DTC C0240 Powertrain Control Module (PCM) Traction Control Not Allowed

Conditions for Running the DTC

The ignition is ON.

Conditions for Setting the DTC

The PCM detects a malfunction and then causes TCS shut down until the malfunction has been corrected.

Action Taken When the DTC Sets

If equipped, the following actions occur:

- The electronic brake control module (EBCM) disables the traction control system (TCS)/vehicle stability enhancement system (VSES) for the duration of the ignition cycle.
- A DTC C0240 is stored.
- The TCS is disabled.
- The Stability Off indicator is turned ON.
- If the TCS is again allowed to function, the indicator will be turned OFF, but the DTC will be stored.

ARM0500000000530

Fig. 67 Test B: Charging System Warning Indicator Is On w/Engine Running & Voltage Does Not Increase (Part 1 of 4). Fusion, Milan, MKZ & Zephyr

	Action	Yes	No
4	1. Using the scan tool, clear the DTC. 2. Remove the scan tool from the data link connector (DLC). 3. Carefully drive the vehicle above 12 km/h (8 mph) for several minutes. Did DTC C0240 set as a current DTC?	Go to Step 5	Go to Diagnostic System Check
5	Perform the Powertrain OBD System Check. Did the vehicle pass the OBD System Check?	Go to Step 6	Go to Diagnostic Trouble Code (DTC)
6	1. Use the scan tool in order to clear the DTCs. 2. Operate the vehicle within the Conditions for Running the DTC as specified in the supporting text. Does the DTC reset?	Go to Step 2	System OK

ARM0500000000532

Fig. 67 Test B: Charging System Warning Indicator Is On w/Engine Running & Voltage Does Not Increase (Part 3 of 4). Fusion, Milan, MKZ & Zephyr

Conditions for Clearing the DTC

- The condition for the DTC is no longer present and the DTC is cleared with a scan tool.
- The electronic brake control module (EBCM) automatically clears the history DTC when a current DTC is not detected in 100 consecutive drive cycles.

Test Description

The number below refers to the step number on the diagnostic table.

4. This step checks if DTC C0240 resets.

Step	Action	Yes	No
1	Did you perform the Diagnostic System Check - Vehicle?	Go to Step 2	Go to Diagnostic System Check
2	1. Turn the ignition switch to the RUN position, with the engine OFF. 2. Using a scan tool, read the antilock brake system (ABS)/traction control system (TCS) DTCs. Are any other DTCs set?	Go to Diagnostic Trouble Code (DTC)	Go to Step 3
3	Is DTC C0240 set as a current code? Go to Step 5	Go to Step 4	

ARM0500000000531

Fig. 67 Test B: Charging System Warning Indicator Is On w/Engine Running & Voltage Does Not Increase (Part 2 of 4). Fusion, Milan, MKZ & Zephyr

B6 CHECK FOR CORRECT PCM OPERATION	

- Disconnect all of the PCM connectors.
- Check for:
  - corrosion
  - pushed-out pins
- Connect all of the PCM connectors and make sure they seat correctly.
- Operate the system and verify the concern is still present.
- **Is the concern still present?**
	Yes
	INSTALL a new PCM. REPEAT the self-test. TEST the system for normal operation.
	
	No
	The system is operating correctly at this time. The concern may have been caused by a loose or corroded connector. CLEAR the DTCs. REPEAT the self-test. TEST the system for normal operation.

ARM0600000001832

Fig. 67 Test B: Charging System Warning Indicator Is On w/Engine Running & Voltage Does Not Increase (Part 4 of 4). Fusion, Milan, MKZ & Zephyr

Test Step	Result / Action to Take
C1 CHECK THE FAULT CODES IN THE PCM • Connect the diagnostic tool. • Key in ON position. • Enter the following diagnostic mode on the diagnostic tool: Retrieve PCM DTCs. • Check for recorded PCM DTCs from the continuous and on-demand self-tests. • **Are any PCM DTCs recorded?**	**Yes** GO to <u>C2</u>. **No** GO to <u>C2</u>.
C2 CHECK THE BATTERY VOLTAGE • Key in START position. • With the engine running and all the accessories turned off, measure the voltage at the battery while varying the engine rpm. • **Is the voltage greater than 15.5 volts?**	**Yes** GO to <u>C3</u>. **No** GO to <u>C4</u>.

ARM0600000002035

Fig. 68 Test C: Charging System Overcharge (Battery Voltage Is Greater Than 15.5 Volts) (Part 1 of 3). Fusion, Milan, MKZ & Zephyr

Test Step	Result / Action to Take
C3 CHECK FOR A VOLTAGE DROP IN CIRCUIT SBB18 (YE/RD) (Continued) • Measure the voltage between the generator C102a-3, circuit SBB18 (YE/RD), harness side and ground. 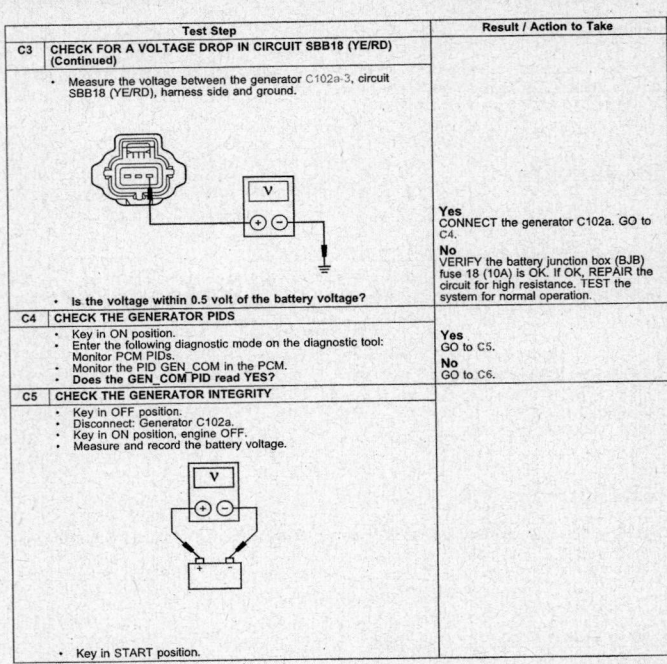 • **Is the voltage within 0.5 volt of the battery voltage?**	**Yes** CONNECT the generator C102a. GO to C4. **No** VERIFY the battery junction box (BJB) fuse 18 (10A) is OK. If OK, REPAIR the circuit for high resistance. TEST the system for normal operation.
C4 CHECK THE GENERATOR PIDS • Key in ON position. • Enter the following diagnostic mode on the diagnostic tool: Monitor PCM PIDs. • Monitor the PID GEN_COM in the PCM. • **Does the GEN_COM PID read YES?**	**Yes** GO to C5. **No** GO to C6.
C5 CHECK THE GENERATOR INTEGRITY • Key in OFF position. • Disconnect: Generator C102a. • Key in ON position, engine OFF. • Measure and record the battery voltage. • Key in START position.	

ARM0500000000533

Fig. 68 Test C: Charging System Overcharge (Battery Voltage Is Greater Than 15.5 Volts) (Part 2 of 3). Fusion, Milan, MKZ & Zephyr

Test Step	Result / Action to Take
C5 CHECK THE GENERATOR INTEGRITY (Continued) • NOTE: If the generator communication lines are disconnected (DTC P0626 may be set), the generator self-excites if it is operated at greater than 4,500 rpm (approximately wide open throttle [WOT]) for a minimum of 3 seconds. It then operates in a default mode at approximately 13.5 volts until the engine is turned off. With the engine running (after the brief WOT is carried out), measure the battery voltage. • **Does the battery voltage increase a minimum of 0.5 volt from the key ON, engine OFF measurement to the key ON, engine running measurement (after the brief WOT or snap acceleration is carried out)?**	 **Yes** GO to C6. **No** INSTALL a new generator. TEST for normal operation.

C6 CHECK FOR CORRECT PCM OPERATION
 	
• Disconnect all of the PCM connectors.
• Check for:
  • corrosion
  • pushed-out pins
• Connect all of the PCM connectors and make sure they seat correctly.
• Operate the system and verify the concern is still present.
• **Is the concern still present?**
	Yes
	INSTALL a new PCM. TEST the system for normal operation.
	
	No
	The system is operating correctly at this time. The concern may have been caused by a loose or corroded connector. CLEAR the DTCs. REPEAT the self-test. TEST the system for normal operation.

ARM0500000000534

Fig. 68 Test C: Charging System Overcharge (Battery Voltage Is Greater Than 15.5 Volts) (Part 3 of 3). Fusion, Milan, MKZ & Zephyr

Test Step	Result / Action to Take
D1 CHECK THE FAULT CODES IN THE PCM • Connect the diagnostic tool. • Key in ON position. • Enter the following diagnostic mode on the diagnostic tool: Retrieve PCM DTCs. • Check the recorded PCM DTCs from the continuous and on-demand self-tests. • **Are any PCM DTCs recorded?**	**Yes** REFER to MOTOR's "Domestic Engine Performance & Driveability Manual" GO to D2. **No** GO to D2.
D2 CHECK THE SYSTEM FOR OVERCHARGING • Key in START position. • With the engine running and all accessories off, measure the voltage at the battery terminals while varying the engine rpm. • **Is the voltage greater than 15.5 volts?**	 **Yes** GO to Pinpoint Test C. **No** GO to D3.
D3 CHECK THE PCM PIDS • Enter the following diagnostic mode on the diagnostic tool: Monitor PCM PIDs. • With the engine running, monitor the generator output fault PID in the PCM. • **Does the PID read YES?**	**Yes** GO to D4. **No** Diagnose charging system.
D4 CHECK THE GENERATOR OUTPUT • Verify the generator output. Refer to the Component Tests, Generator On-Vehicle Tests in this section. • **Does the generator pass the component tests?**	**Yes** GO to D5. **No** INSTALL a new generator. REPEAT the self-test. TEST the system for normal operation.

D5 CHECK FOR CORRECT PCM OPERATION
 	
• Key in OFF position.
• Disconnect all of the PCM connectors.
• Check for
  • corrosion
  • pushed-out pins
• Connect all of the PCM connectors and make sure they seat correctly.
• Operate the system and verify the concern is still present.
• **Is the concern still present?**
	Yes
	INSTALL a new PCM. REPEAT the self-test. TEST the system for normal operation.
	
	No
	The system is operating correctly at this time. The concern may have been caused by a loose or corroded connector. CLEAR the DTCs. REPEAT the self-test. TEST the system for normal operation.

ARM0500000000535

Fig. 69 Test D: Charging System Warning Indicator Is On w/Engine Running & Voltage Increases. Fusion, Milan, MKZ & Zephyr

Test Step		Result / Action to Take
E1	CHECK THE CHARGING SYSTEM WARNING INDICATOR OPERATION	
	• Connect the diagnostic tool. • Key in ON position. • Enter the following diagnostic mode on the diagnostic tool: Active Commands. • Using Active Commands, turn on the charging system warning indicator in the instrument cluster. • **Is the charging system warning indicator on?**	**Yes** GO to E2. **No** Diagnose charging system warning indicator.
E2	CHECK FOR CORRECT PCM OPERATION	

	• Key in OFF position.
	• Disconnect all of the PCM connectors.
	• Check for
	  • corrosion
	  • pushed-out pins
	• Connect all of the PCM connectors and make sure they seat correctly.
	• Operate the system and verify the concern is still present.
	• **Is the concern still present?**
		Yes
		INSTALL a new PCM. REPEAT the self-test. TEST the system for normal operation.
		No
		The system is operating correctly at this time. The concern may have been caused by a loose or corroded connector. CLEAR the DTCs. REPEAT the self-test. TEST the system for normal operation.

ARM0500000000536

Fig. 70   Test E: Charging System Warning Indicator Is Off w/Ignition Switch In Run Position & Engine Is Off. Fusion, Milan, MKZ & Zephyr

Test Step	Result / Action to Take
G1	VERIFY THE GENERATOR IS THE SOURCE OF THE RADIO INTERFERENCE	
NOTE: If the original equipment manufactured (OEM) audio unit has been replaced with an aftermarket unit, the system may not pass this test. Return the vehicle to OEM condition before following this pinpoint test. • Key in START position. • Start and run the engine. • Tune the radio to a station where the interference is present. • Key in OFF position. • Disconnect: Generator C102b. • Key in START position. • With the engine running, determine if the interference is still present. • **Is the interference present with the generator disconnected?**	**Yes** Diagnose in-vehicle entertainment system. **No** INSTALL a new generator. TEST the system for normal operation.

ARM0500000000538

Fig. 72   Test G: Radio Interference. Fusion, Milan, MKZ & Zephyr

CONDITIONS	DETAILS/RESULTS/ACTIONS
A1 CHECK THE GENERATOR OUTPUT	

	1 Carry out the On-Vehicle Generator Load/No Load Tests.
	
	  • **Is the generator OK?**
	
	→ **Yes**
	  GO to A2.
	
	→ **No**
	  GO to Pinpoint Test B.

A2 CHECK FOR CURRENT DRAINS	

	1 Carry out the Battery — Drain Test.
	
	  • **Are there any excessive current drains?**
	
	→ **Yes**
	  REPAIR as necessary. TEST the system for normal operation.
	
	→ **No**
	  GO to A3.

A3 CHECK FOR CURRENT DRAINS WHICH SHUT OFF WHEN THE BATTERY IS DISCONNECTED	

	1 Carry out the Battery — Electronic Drains Which Shut Off When the Battery Cable is Disconnected Test.
	
	  • **Are there any current drains which shut off when the battery is disconnected?**
	
	→ **Yes**
	  REPAIR as necessary. TEST the system for normal operation.
	
	→ **No**
	  GO to Pinpoint Test B.

FM1120200792000X

Fig. 73   Test A: Battery Is Discharged Or Battery Voltage Is Low. 2004 LS & Thunderbird

Test Step	Result / Action to Take
F1 CHECK FOR ACCESSORY DRIVE NOISE AND MOUNTING BRACKETS	
• Key in OFF position. • Check the accessory drive belt for damage and correct installation. • Check the accessory mounting brackets and the generator pulley for looseness or misalignment. • **Is the accessory drive OK?**	**Yes** If equipped with an OWC pulley, GO to F2. If not equipped with a OWC pulley, GO to F3. **No** REPAIR as necessary. TEST the system for normal operation.
F2 CHECK THE OWC PULLEY	
• With the accessory drive belt removed, spin the OWC pulley in a clockwise direction, then reverse the direction of the pulley by spinning it in a counterclockwise direction. • **Does the OWC pulley engage with the rotor when spun in a clockwise direction and free-wheel when spun in a counterclockwise direction with minimal noise as compared to a known good vehicle?**	**Yes** GO to F3. **No** INSTALL a new generator assembly with OWC pulley. TEST the system for normal operation.
F3 CHECK THE GENERATOR FOR EXCESSIVE ELECTRICAL NOISE	
• Disconnect: Generator C102b (4.0L), C1100a (4.6L) (generator B+ harness connector at the battery). • Key in START position. • With the engine running, determine if the generator is still noisy. • **Is the noise still present?**	**Yes** GO to F4. **No** INSTALL a new generator. TEST the system for normal operation.
F4 CHECK THE GENERATOR FOR MECHANICAL NOISE	
• Turn all of the accessories off. With the engine running, use a stethoscope or equivalent listening device to probe the generator for unusual mechanical noise. • **Is the generator the noise source?**	**Yes** INSTALL a new generator. TEST the system for normal operation. **No** diagnose the source of the engine noise.

ARM0500000000537

Fig. 71   Test F: Alternator Is Noisy. Fusion, Milan, MKZ & Zephyr

CONDITIONS	DETAILS/RESULTS/ACTIONS
B1 CHECK THE FAULT CODES IN THE PCM	

1
2
3
	3 Use the recorded PCM DTCs from the continuous and on-demand self-test.
	
	  • **Are any DTCs recorded?**
	
	→ **Yes**
	  REFER to PCM Diagnostic Trouble Code (DTC) Index.
	
	→ **No**
	  GO to B2.

FM1120200793010X

Fig. 74   Test B: Charging System Warning Indicator Is On w/Engine Running, Charging System Voltage Does Not Increase (Part 1 of 5). 2004 LS & Thunderbird

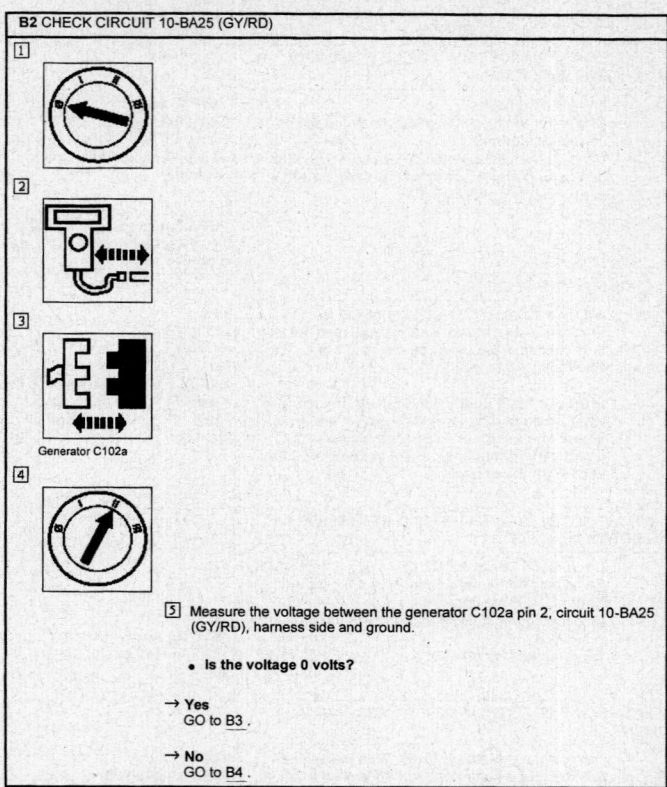

B2 CHECK CIRCUIT 10-BA25 (GY/RD)

Generator C102a

5 Measure the voltage between the generator C102a pin 2, circuit 10-BA25 (GY/RD), harness side and ground.

- **Is the voltage 0 volts?**

→ **Yes**
GO to B3 .

→ **No**
GO to B4 .

FM1120200793020X

Fig. 74   Test B: Charging System Warning Indicator Is On w/Engine Running, Charging System Voltage Does Not Increase (Part 2 of 5). 2004 LS & Thunderbird

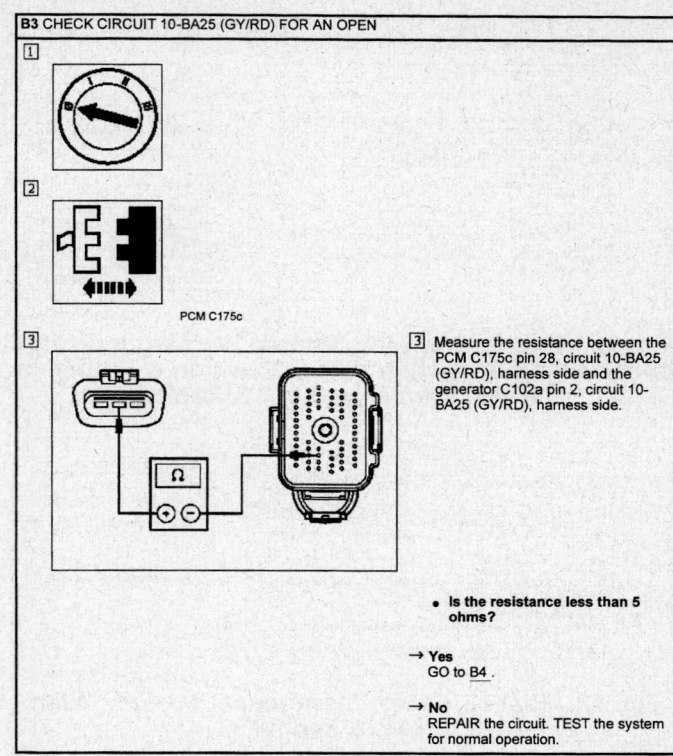

B3 CHECK CIRCUIT 10-BA25 (GY/RD) FOR AN OPEN

PCM C175c

3 Measure the resistance between the PCM C175c pin 28, circuit 10-BA25 (GY/RD), harness side and the generator C102a pin 2, circuit 10-BA25 (GY/RD), harness side.

- **Is the resistance less than 5 ohms?**

→ **Yes**
GO to B4 .

→ **No**
REPAIR the circuit. TEST the system for normal operation.

FM1120200793030X

Fig. 74   Test B: Charging System Warning Indicator Is On w/Engine Running, Charging System Voltage Does Not Increase (Part 3 of 5). 2004 LS & Thunderbird

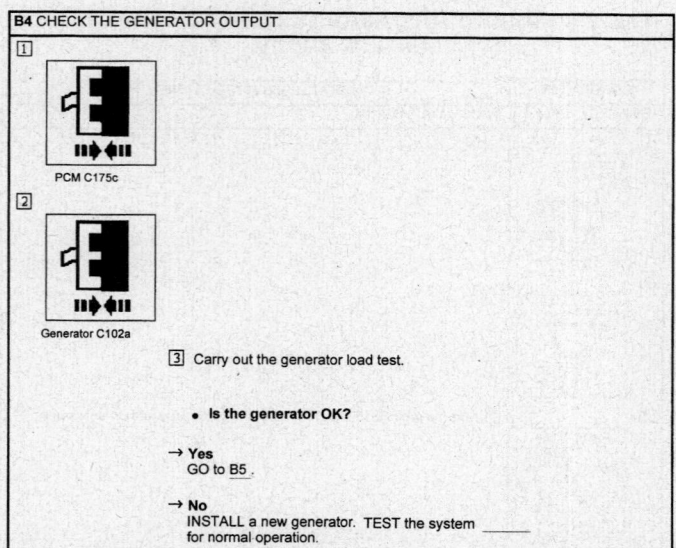

B4 CHECK THE GENERATOR OUTPUT

PCM C175c

Generator C102a

3 Carry out the generator load test.

- **Is the generator OK?**

→ **Yes**
GO to B5 .

→ **No**
INSTALL a new generator. TEST the system _____ for normal operation.

FM1120200793040X

Fig. 74   Test B: Charging System Warning Indicator Is On w/Engine Running, Charging System Voltage Does Not Increase (Part 4 of 5). 2004 LS & Thunderbird

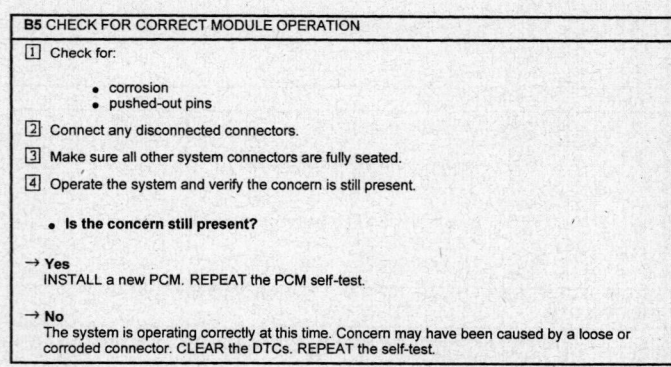

B5 CHECK FOR CORRECT MODULE OPERATION

1 Check for:

- corrosion
- pushed-out pins

2 Connect any disconnected connectors.

3 Make sure all other system connectors are fully seated.

4 Operate the system and verify the concern is still present.

- **Is the concern still present?**

→ **Yes**
INSTALL a new PCM. REPEAT the PCM self-test.

→ **No**
The system is operating correctly at this time. Concern may have been caused by a loose or corroded connector. CLEAR the DTCs. REPEAT the self-test.

FM1120200793050X

Fig. 74   Test B: Charging System Warning Indicator Is On w/Engine Running, Charging System Voltage Does Not Increase (Part 5 of 5). 2004 LS & Thunderbird

CONDITIONS	DETAILS/RESULTS/ACTIONS

C1 CHECK THE FAULT CODES IN THE PCM

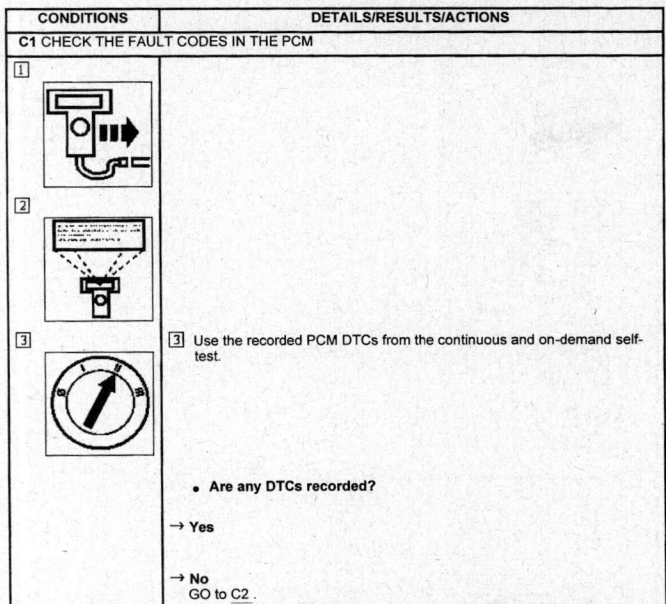

3 Use the recorded PCM DTCs from the continuous and on-demand self-test.

• Are any DTCs recorded?

→ Yes

→ No
GO to C2 .

FM1120200794010X

Fig. 75 Test C: Charging System Overcharges, Battery Voltage Is More Than 15.5 Volts (Part 1 of 3). LS & 2004 LS & Thunderbird

C3 CHECK CIRCUIT 30-BA25 (RD)

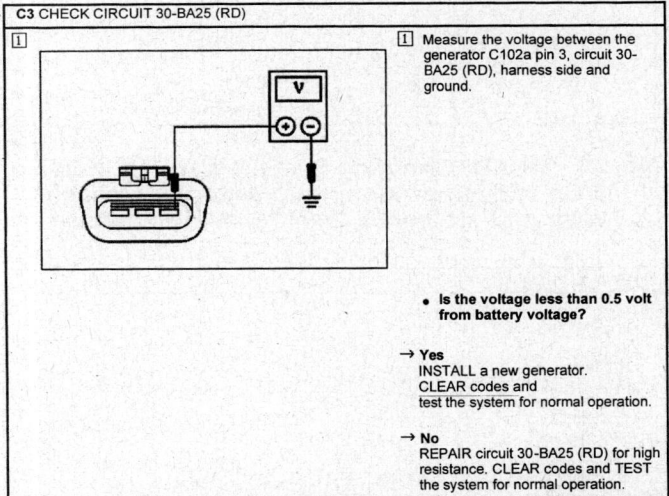

1 Measure the voltage between the generator C102a pin 3, circuit 30-BA25 (RD), harness side and ground.

• Is the voltage less than 0.5 volt from battery voltage?

→ Yes
INSTALL a new generator.
CLEAR codes and
test the system for normal operation.

→ No
REPAIR circuit 30-BA25 (RD) for high resistance. CLEAR codes and TEST the system for normal operation.

FM1120200794030X

Fig. 75 Test C: Charging System Overcharges, Battery Voltage Is More Than 15.5 Volts (Part 3 of 3). 2004 LS & Thunderbird

C2 CHECK THE GENERATOR OUTPUT

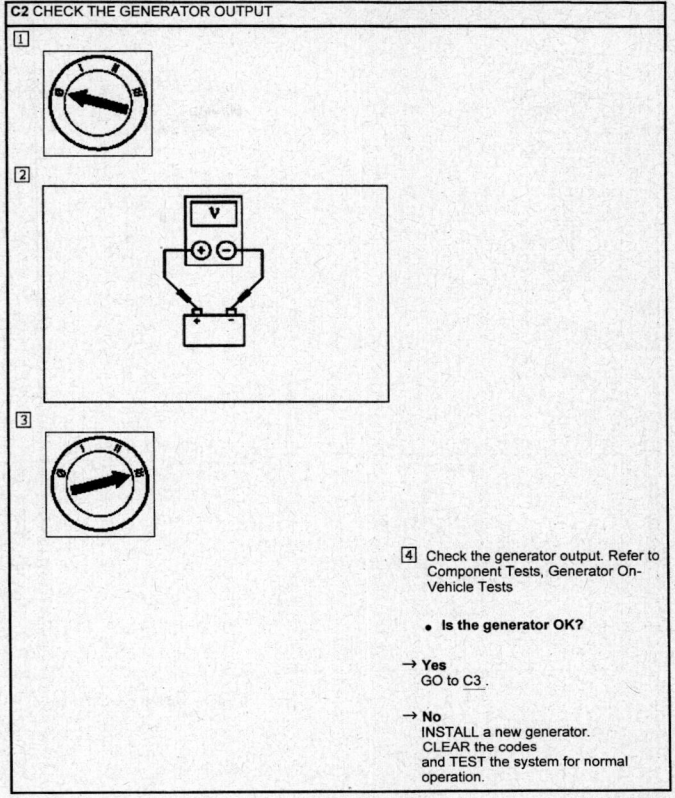

4 Check the generator output. Refer to Component Tests, Generator On-Vehicle Tests

• Is the generator OK?

→ Yes
GO to C3 .

→ No
INSTALL a new generator.
CLEAR the codes
and TEST the system for normal operation.

FM1120200794020X

Fig. 75 Test C: Charging System Overcharges, Battery Voltage Is More Than 15.5 Volts (Part 2 of 3). 2004 LS & Thunderbird

CONDITIONS	DETAILS/RESULTS/ACTIONS

D1 CHECK THE FAULT CODES IN THE PCM

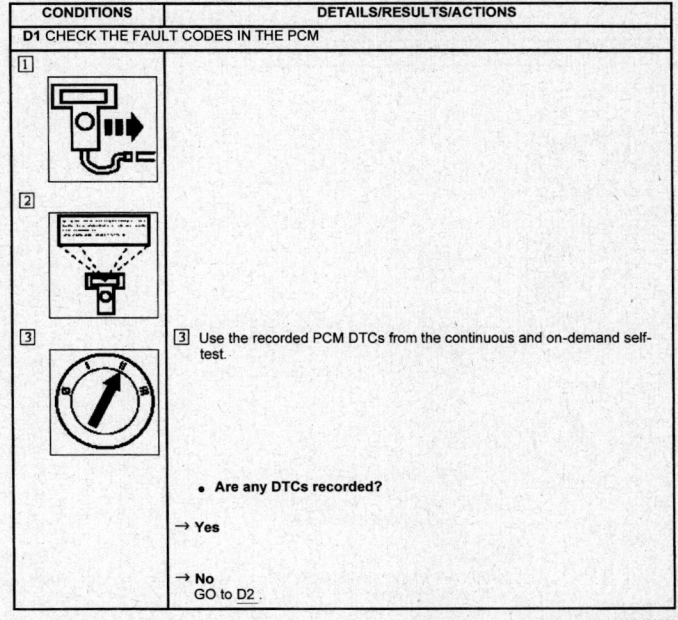

3 Use the recorded PCM DTCs from the continuous and on-demand self-test.

• Are any DTCs recorded?

→ Yes

→ No
GO to D2 .

FM1120200795010X

Fig. 76 Test D: Charging System Warning Indicator Is On w/Engine Running & Battery Increases Voltage (Part 1 of 6). 2004 LS & Thunderbird

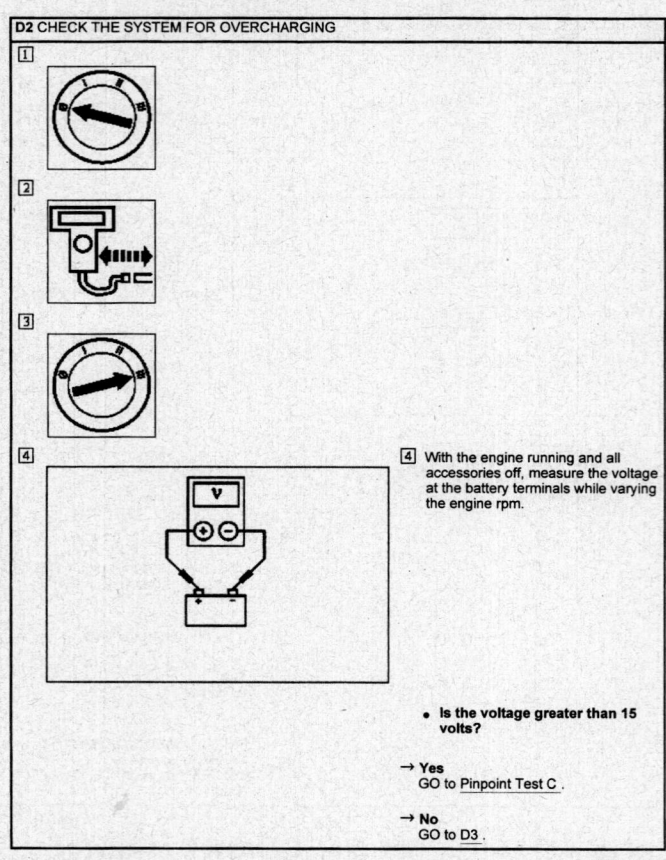

D2 CHECK THE SYSTEM FOR OVERCHARGING

4 With the engine running and all accessories off, measure the voltage at the battery terminals while varying the engine rpm.

● **Is the voltage greater than 15 volts?**

→ **Yes**
GO to Pinpoint Test C .

→ **No**
GO to D3 .

FM1120200795020X

Fig. 76   Test D: Charging System Warning Indicator Is On w/Engine Running & Battery Increases Voltage (Part 2 of 6). 2004 LS & Thunderbird

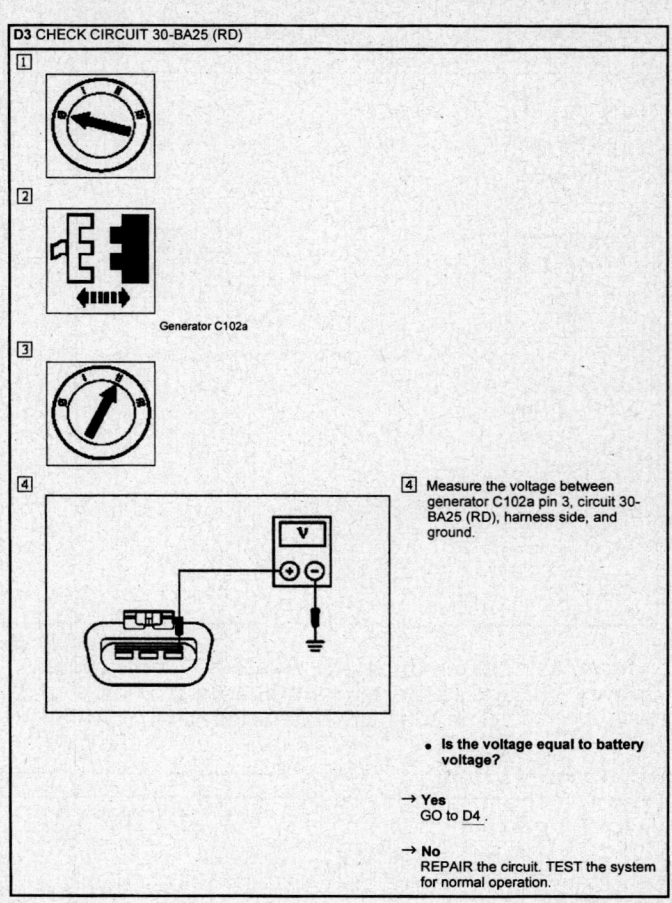

D3 CHECK CIRCUIT 30-BA25 (RD)

Generator C102a

4 Measure the voltage between generator C102a pin 3, circuit 30-BA25 (RD), harness side, and ground.

● **Is the voltage equal to battery voltage?**

→ **Yes**
GO to D4 .

→ **No**
REPAIR the circuit. TEST the system for normal operation.

FM1120200795030X

Fig. 76   Test D: Charging System Warning Indicator Is On w/Engine Running & Battery Increases Voltage (Part 3 of 6). 2004 LS & Thunderbird

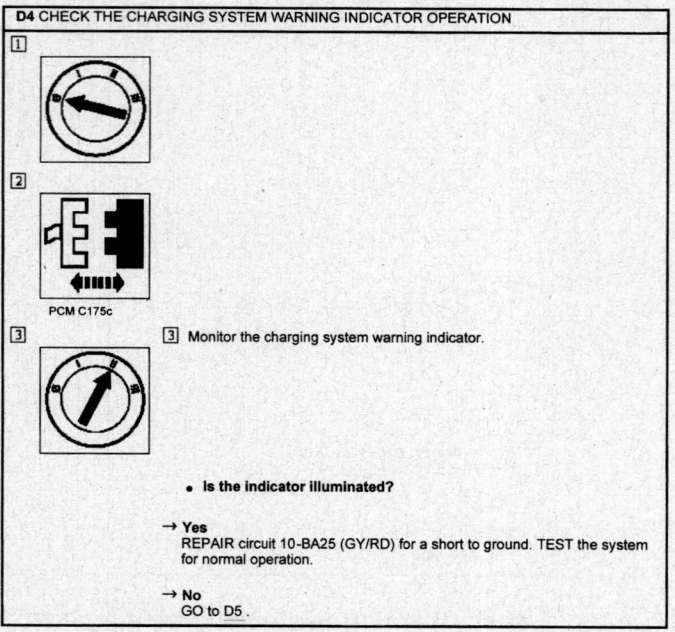

D4 CHECK THE CHARGING SYSTEM WARNING INDICATOR OPERATION

PCM C175c

3 Monitor the charging system warning indicator.

● **Is the indicator illuminated?**

→ **Yes**
REPAIR circuit 10-BA25 (GY/RD) for a short to ground. TEST the system for normal operation.

→ **No**
GO to D5 .

FM1120200795040X

Fig. 76   Test D: Charging System Warning Indicator Is On w/Engine Running & Battery Increases Voltage (Part 4 of 6). 2004 LS & Thunderbird

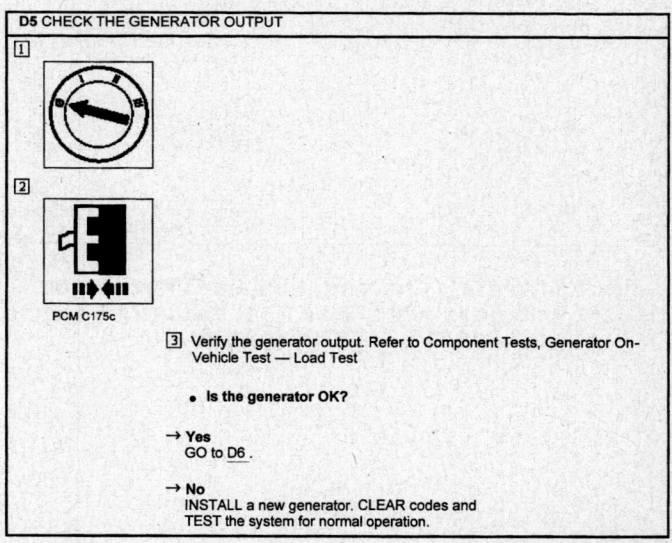

D5 CHECK THE GENERATOR OUTPUT

PCM C175c

3 Verify the generator output. Refer to Component Tests, Generator On-Vehicle Test — Load Test

● **Is the generator OK?**

→ **Yes**
GO to D6 .

→ **No**
INSTALL a new generator. CLEAR codes and TEST the system for normal operation.

FM1120200795050X

Fig. 76   Test D: Charging System Warning Indicator Is On w/Engine Running & Battery Increases Voltage (Part 5 of 6). 2004 LS & Thunderbird

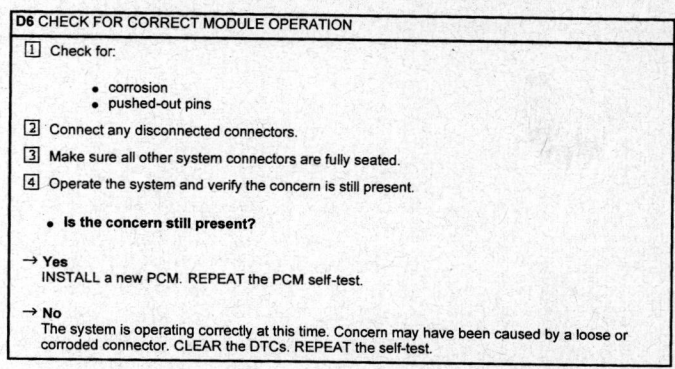

D6 CHECK FOR CORRECT MODULE OPERATION

1. Check for:

   - corrosion
   - pushed-out pins

2. Connect any disconnected connectors.

3. Make sure all other system connectors are fully seated.

4. Operate the system and verify the concern is still present.

   - **Is the concern still present?**

→ **Yes**
   INSTALL a new PCM. REPEAT the PCM self-test.

→ **No**
   The system is operating correctly at this time. Concern may have been caused by a loose or corroded connector. CLEAR the DTCs. REPEAT the self-test.

FM1120200795060X

Fig. 76   Test D: Charging System Warning Indicator Is On w/Engine Running & Battery Increases Voltage (Part 6 of 6). 2004 LS & Thunderbird

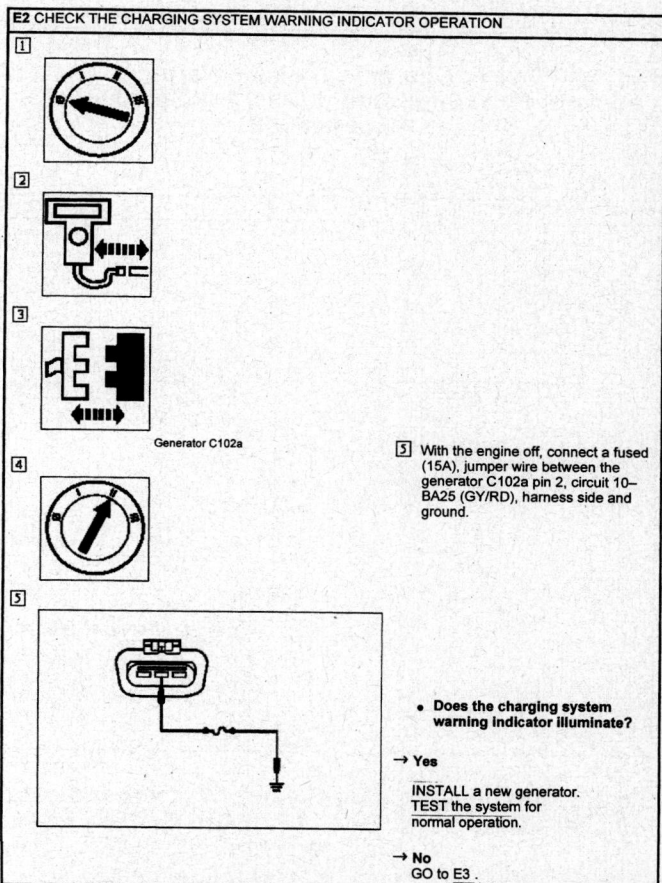

E2 CHECK THE CHARGING SYSTEM WARNING INDICATOR OPERATION

Generator C102a

5. With the engine off, connect a fused (15A), jumper wire between the generator C102a pin 2, circuit 10–BA25 (GY/RD), harness side and ground.

   - **Does the charging system warning indicator illuminate?**

→ **Yes**
   INSTALL a new generator. TEST the system for normal operation.

→ **No**
   GO to E3.

FM1120200796020X

Fig. 77   Test E: Charging System Warning Indicator Is Off w/Ignition Switch In Run Position & Engine Is Off (Part 2 of 3). 2004 LS & Thunderbird

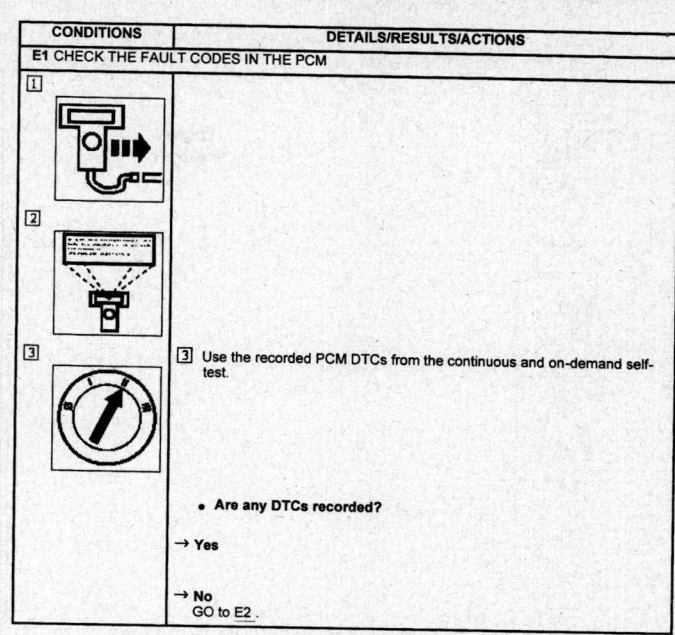

CONDITIONS	DETAILS/RESULTS/ACTIONS
E1 CHECK THE FAULT CODES IN THE PCM	

3. Use the recorded PCM DTCs from the continuous and on-demand self-test.

   - **Are any DTCs recorded?**

→ **Yes**

→ **No**
   GO to E2.

FM1120200796010X

Fig. 77   Test E: Charging System Warning Indicator Is Off w/Ignition Switch In Run Position & Engine Is Off (Part 1 of 3). 2004 LS & Thunderbird

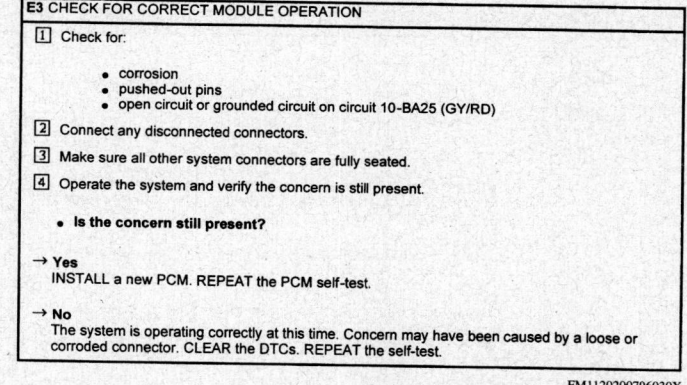

E3 CHECK FOR CORRECT MODULE OPERATION

1. Check for:

   - corrosion
   - pushed-out pins
   - open circuit or grounded circuit on circuit 10-BA25 (GY/RD)

2. Connect any disconnected connectors.

3. Make sure all other system connectors are fully seated.

4. Operate the system and verify the concern is still present.

   - **Is the concern still present?**

→ **Yes**
   INSTALL a new PCM. REPEAT the PCM self-test.

→ **No**
   The system is operating correctly at this time. Concern may have been caused by a loose or corroded connector. CLEAR the DTCs. REPEAT the self-test.

FM1120200796030X

Fig. 77   Test E: Charging System Warning Indicator Is Off w/Ignition Switch In Run Position & Engine Is Off (Part 3 of 3). 2004 LS & Thunderbird

CONDITIONS	DETAILS/RESULTS/ACTIONS

F1 CHECK THE FAULT CODES IN THE PCM

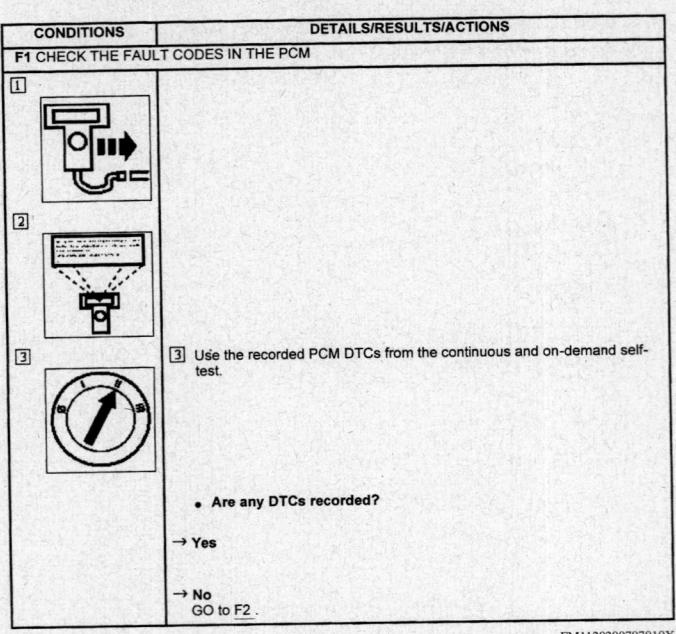

3 Use the recorded PCM DTCs from the continuous and on-demand self-test.

• Are any DTCs recorded?

→ Yes

→ No
GO to F2 .

FM1120200797010X

Fig. 78   Test F: Charging System Warning Indicator Flickers Or Is Intermittent (Part 1 of 6). 2004 LS & Thunderbird

F3 CHECK FUSE CONNECTION

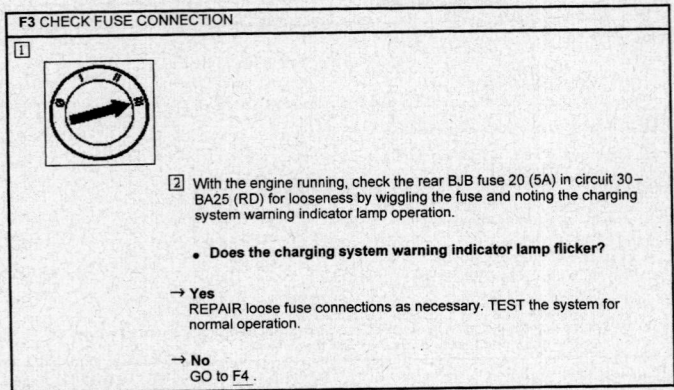

2 With the engine running, check the rear BJB fuse 20 (5A) in circuit 30−BA25 (RD) for looseness by wiggling the fuse and noting the charging system warning indicator lamp operation.

• Does the charging system warning indicator lamp flicker?

→ Yes
REPAIR loose fuse connections as necessary. TEST the system for normal operation.

→ No
GO to F4 .

FM1120200797030X

Fig. 78   Test F: Charging System Warning Indicator Flickers Or Is Intermittent (Part 3 of 6). 2004 LS & Thunderbird

F2 CHECK FOR LOOSE CONNECTIONS

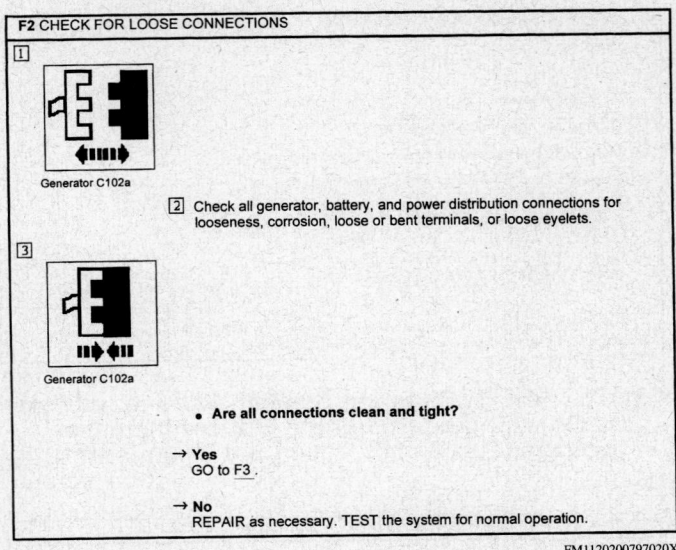

Generator C102a

2 Check all generator, battery, and power distribution connections for looseness, corrosion, loose or bent terminals, or loose eyelets.

Generator C102a

• Are all connections clean and tight?

→ Yes
GO to F3 .

→ No
REPAIR as necessary. TEST the system for normal operation.

FM1120200797020X

Fig. 78   Test F: Charging System Warning Indicator Flickers Or Is Intermittent (Part 2 of 6). 2004 LS & Thunderbird

F4 CHECK THE BATTERY VOLTAGE

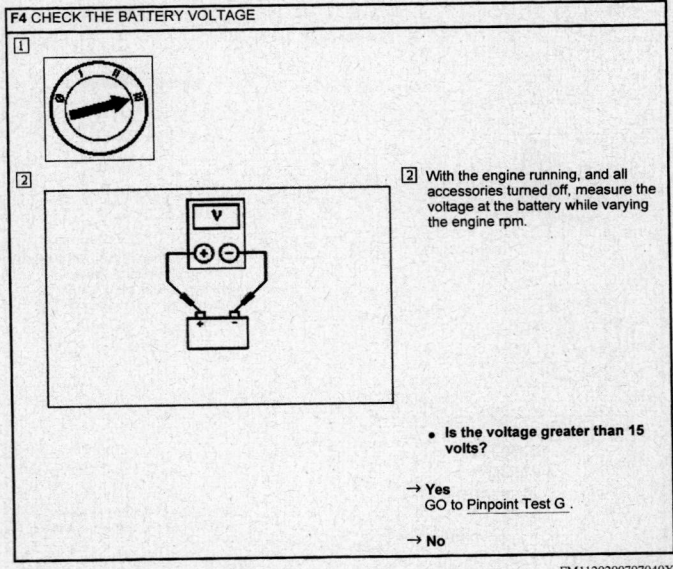

2 With the engine running, and all accessories turned off, measure the voltage at the battery while varying the engine rpm.

• Is the voltage greater than 15 volts?

→ Yes
GO to Pinpoint Test G .

→ No

FM1120200797040X

Fig. 78   Test F: Charging System Warning Indicator Flickers Or Is Intermittent (Part 4 of 6). 2004 LS & Thunderbird

F5 CHECK THE WARNING SYSTEM INDICATOR OPERATION

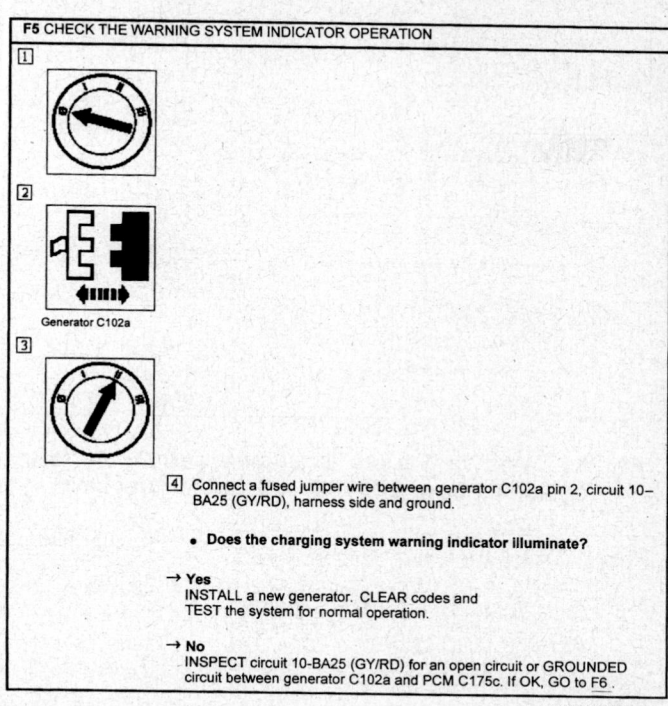

Generator C102a

④ Connect a fused jumper wire between generator C102a pin 2, circuit 10–BA25 (GY/RD), harness side and ground.

- **Does the charging system warning indicator illuminate?**

→ **Yes**
INSTALL a new generator. CLEAR codes and TEST the system for normal operation.

→ **No**
INSPECT circuit 10-BA25 (GY/RD) for an open circuit or GROUNDED circuit between generator C102a and PCM C175c. If OK, GO to F6 .

FM1120200797050X

Fig. 78   Test F: Charging System Warning Indicator Flickers Or Is Intermittent (Part 5 of 6). 2004 LS & Thunderbird

CONDITIONS	DETAILS/RESULTS/ACTIONS
G1 CHECK FOR ACCESSORY DRIVE NOISE AND MOUNTING BRACKETS	

① Check the accessory drive belt for damage and correct installation.

② Check the accessory mounting brackets and generator pulley for looseness or misalignment.

- **Is the accessory drive OK?**

→ **Yes**
GO to G2 .

→ **No**
REPAIR as necessary. TEST the system for normal operation.

G2 CHECK GENERATOR FOR ELECTRICAL NOISE

Generator C102a

③ With the engine running.

- **Is the noise still present?**

→ **Yes**
GO to G3 .

→ **No**
INSTALL a new generator. TEST the system for normal operation.

FM1120200798010X

Fig. 79   Test G: Alternator Is Noisy (Part 1 of 2). 2004 LS & Thunderbird

F6 CHECK FOR CORRECT MODULE OPERATION

① Check for:

- corrosion
- pushed-out pins

② Connect any disconnected connectors.

③ Make sure all other system connectors are fully seated.

④ Operate the system and verify the concern is still present.

- **Is the concern still present?**

→ **Yes**
INSTALL a new PCM. REPEAT the PCM self-test.

→ **No**
The system is operating correctly at this time. Concern may have been caused by a loose or corroded connector. CLEAR the DTCs. REPEAT the self-test.

FM1120200797060X

Fig. 78   Test F: Charging System Warning Indicator Flickers Or Is Intermittent (Part 6 of 6). 2004 LS & Thunderbird

G3 CHECK GENERATOR FOR MECHANICAL NOISE

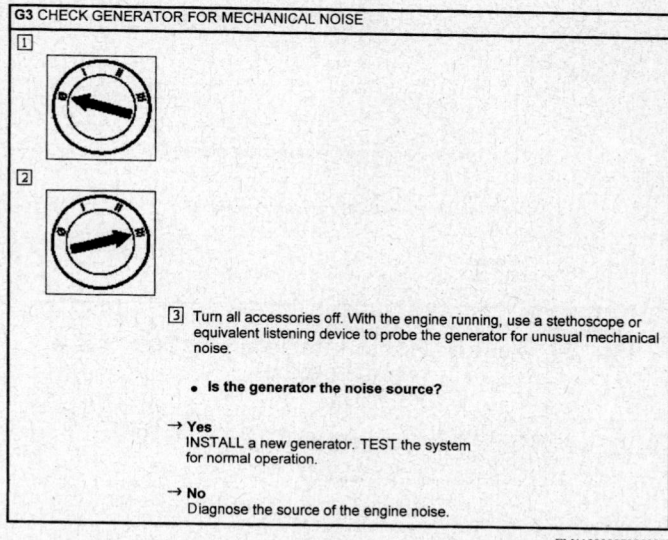

③ Turn all accessories off. With the engine running, use a stethoscope or equivalent listening device to probe the generator for unusual mechanical noise.

- **Is the generator the noise source?**

→ **Yes**
INSTALL a new generator. TEST the system for normal operation.

→ **No**
Diagnose the source of the engine noise.

FM1120200798020X

Fig. 79   Test G: Alternator Is Noisy (Part 2 of 2). 2004 LS & Thunderbird

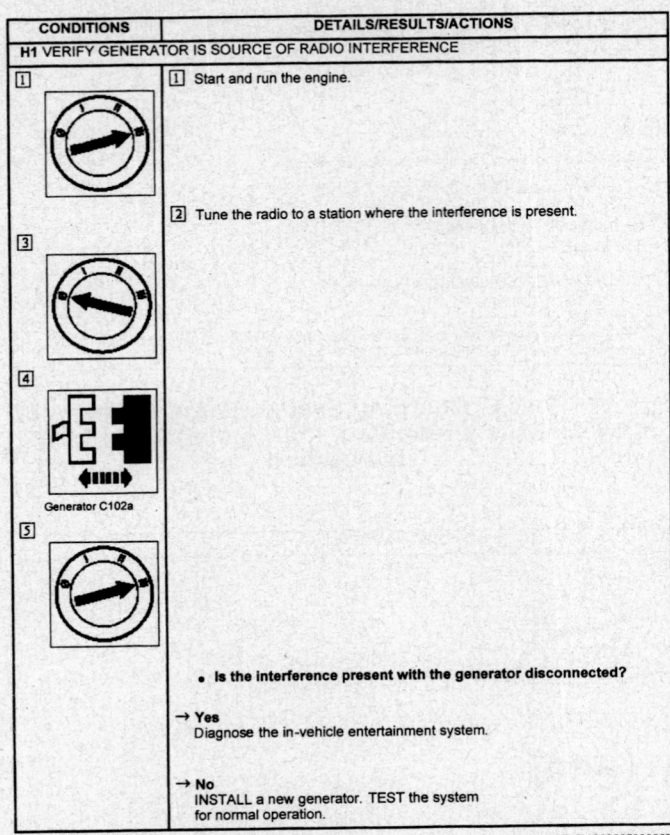

CONDITIONS | **DETAILS/RESULTS/ACTIONS**

H1 VERIFY GENERATOR IS SOURCE OF RADIO INTERFERENCE

1. Start and run the engine.

2. Tune the radio to a station where the interference is present.

Generator C102a

- Is the interference present with the generator disconnected?

→ **Yes**
Diagnose the in-vehicle entertainment system.

→ **No**
INSTALL a new generator. TEST the system for normal operation.

FM1120200799000X

Fig. 80 Test H: Radio Interference. 2004 LS & Thunderbird

Test Step	Result / Action to Take
B1 CHECK GENERATOR B+ OUTPUT CIRCUIT 30-BA6 (RD)	
• Key in OFF position. • Measure the voltage between the generator positive battery (B+) output terminal, circuit 30-BA6 (RD), component side and ground. A0006228 • Is the voltage within 0.5 volt of B+ voltage ?	**Yes** GO to B2. **No** REPAIR the circuit. TEST the system for normal operation.
B2 CHECK I CIRCUIT 10-BA25 (GY/RD) FOR AN OPEN	
• Key in START position.	

ARM0500000000730

Fig. 82 Test B: Charging System Warning Indicator Is On w/Engine Running, Charging System Voltage Does Not Increase (Part 1 of 2). 2005–07 LS & Thunderbird

Test Step	Result / Action to Take
A1 CHECK THE BATTERY CONDITION	
• Carry out the Battery—Condition Test to determine if the battery can hold a charge and is OK for use. • Does the battery pass the condition test?	**Yes** GO to A2. **No** INSTALL a new battery. TEST the system for normal operation.
A2 CHECK THE GENERATOR OUTPUT	
• Carry out the Generator On-Vehicle Tests—Load Test and No-Load Test. • Does the generator pass the component tests?	**Yes** GO to A3. **No** GO to Pinpoint Test B to continue the diagnosis.
A3 CHECK FOR CURRENT DRAINS	
• Carry out the Battery — Drain Test. • Are any circuits causing excessive current drains?	**Yes** REPAIR the faulty circuit as necessary. TEST the system for normal operation. **No** GO to A4.
A4 CHECK FOR CURRENT DRAINS THAT SHUT OFF WHEN THE BATTERY IS DISCONNECTED	
• Carry out the Battery — Electronic Drains Which Shut Off When the Battery Cable is Disconnected Test. • Are any components causing excessive current drains?	**Yes** REPAIR the faulty component as necessary. TEST the system for normal operation. **No** GO to Pinpoint Test B to diagnose the charging system.

ARM0500000000729

Fig. 81 Test A: Battery Is Discharged Or Battery Voltage Is Low. 2005–07 LS & Thunderbird

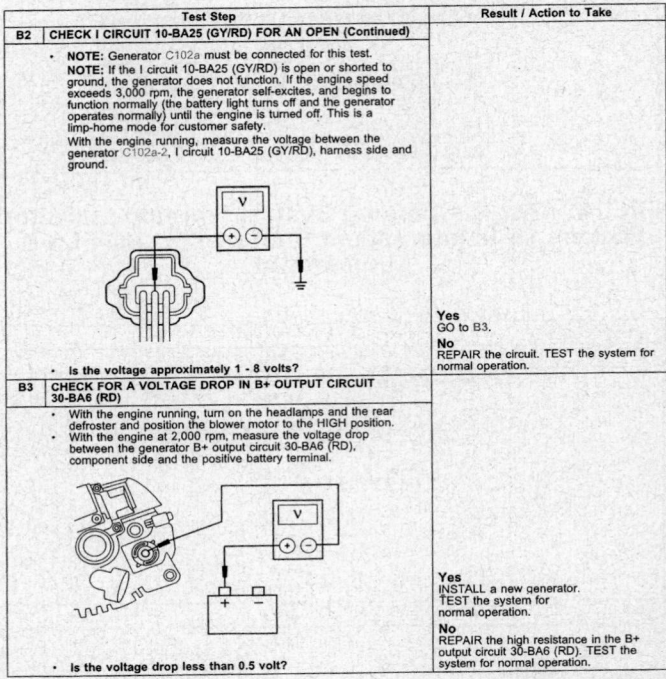

Test Step	Result / Action to Take
B2 CHECK I CIRCUIT 10-BA25 (GY/RD) FOR AN OPEN (Continued)	
• NOTE: Generator C102a must be connected for this test. NOTE: If the I circuit 10-BA25 (GY/RD) is open or shorted to ground, the generator does not function. If the engine speed exceeds 3,000 rpm, the generator self-excites, and begins to function normally (the battery light turns off and the generator operates normally) until the engine is turned off. This is a limp-home mode for customer safety. With the engine running, measure the voltage between generator C102a-2, I circuit 10-BA25 (GY/RD), harness side and ground. • Is the voltage approximately 1 - 8 volts?	**Yes** GO to B3. **No** REPAIR the circuit. TEST the system for normal operation.
B3 CHECK FOR A VOLTAGE DROP IN B+ OUTPUT CIRCUIT 30-BA6 (RD)	
• With the engine running, turn on the headlamps and the rear defroster and position the blower motor to the HIGH position. • With the engine at 2,000 rpm, measure the voltage drop between the generator B+ output circuit 30-BA6 (RD), component side and the positive battery terminal. • Is the voltage drop less than 0.5 volt?	**Yes** INSTALL a new generator. TEST the system for normal operation. **No** REPAIR the high resistance in the B+ output circuit 30-BA6 (RD). TEST the system for normal operation.

ARM0500000000739

Fig. 82 Test B: Charging System Warning Indicator Is On w/Engine Running, Charging System Voltage Does Not Increase (Part 2 of 2). 2005–07 LS & Thunderbird

Test Step	Result / Action to Take
C1 CHECK FOR A VOLTAGE DROP IN A CIRCUIT 30-BA25 (RD) • Key in OFF position. • Disconnect: Generator C102a. • Measure the voltage drop between the generator C102a-3, A circuit 30-BA25 (RD), harness side and the positive battery terminal. 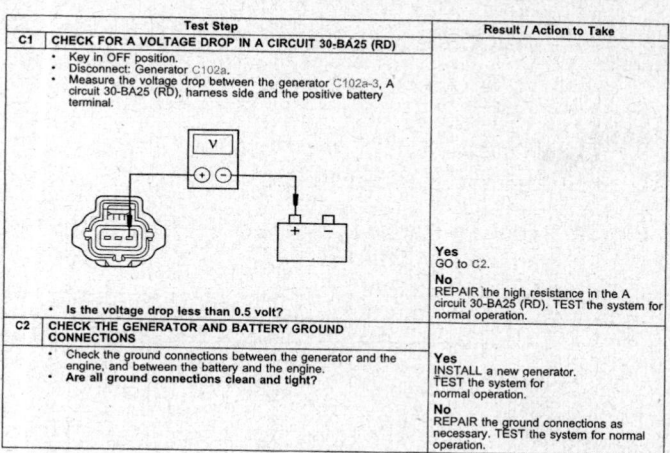 • Is the voltage drop less than 0.5 volt?	**Yes** GO to C2. **No** REPAIR the high resistance in the A circuit 30-BA25 (RD). TEST the system for normal operation.
C2 CHECK THE GENERATOR AND BATTERY GROUND CONNECTIONS • Check the ground connections between the generator and the engine, and between the battery and the engine. • Are all ground connections clean and tight?	**Yes** INSTALL a new generator. TEST the system for normal operation. **No** REPAIR the ground connections as necessary. TEST the system for normal operation.

ARM0500000000731

Fig. 83 Test C: Charging System Overcharges, Battery Voltage Is More Than 15.5 Volts. LS & 2005–07 LS & Thunderbird

Test Step	Result / Action to Take
D2 CHECK CIRCUIT 8-BA25 (WH/RD) FOR AN OPEN OR SHORT TO GROUND • Measure the resistance between the PCM C175c-50, circuit 8-BA25 (WH/RD), harness side and the generator C102a-1, circuit 8-BA25 (WH/RD), harness side; and between the PCM C175c-50, circuit 8-BA25 (WH/RD), harness side and ground. 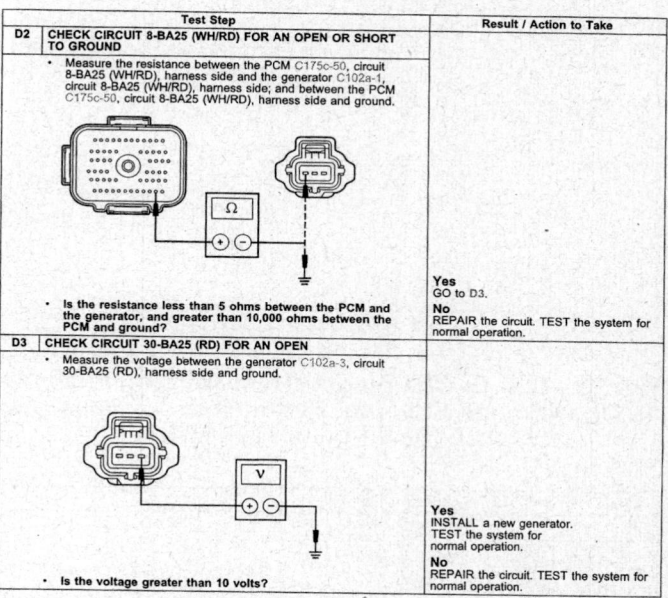 • Is the resistance less than 5 ohms between the PCM and the generator, and greater than 10,000 ohms between the PCM and ground?	**Yes** GO to D3. **No** REPAIR the circuit. TEST the system for normal operation.
D3 CHECK CIRCUIT 30-BA25 (RD) FOR AN OPEN • Measure the voltage between the generator C102a-3, circuit 30-BA25 (RD), harness side and ground. • Is the voltage greater than 10 volts?	**Yes** INSTALL a new generator. TEST the system for normal operation. **No** REPAIR the circuit. TEST the system for normal operation.

ARM0500000000733

Fig. 84 Test D: Charging System Warning Indicator Is On w/Engine Running & Battery Increases Voltage (Part 2 of 2). 2005–07 LS & Thunderbird

Test Step	Result / Action to Take
F1 CHECK FOR LOOSE CONNECTIONS • Key in OFF position. • NOTE: If the I circuit 10-BA25 (GY/RD) is open or short to ground, the generator does not function. If the engine speed exceeds 3,000 rpm, the generator self-excites, and begins to function normally (the battery light turns off and the generator operates normally) until the engine is turned off. This is a limp-home mode for customer safety. • Check all generator, battery, rear BJB connections for looseness, corrosion, loose or bent terminals, or loose eyelets. • Are all connections clean and tight?	**Yes** If the charging system warning indicator flickers, INSTALL a new instrument cluster. If the charging system warning indicator is intermittent, GO to F2. **No** REPAIR as necessary. TEST the system for normal operation.

ARM0500000000735

Fig. 86 Test F: Charging System Warning Indicator Flickers Or Is Intermittent (Part 1 of 2). 2005–07 LS & Thunderbird

Test Step	Result / Action to Take
D1 CHECK I CIRCUIT 10-BA25 (GY/RD) FOR AN OPEN OR SHORT TO GROUND • Key in OFF position. • Disconnect: Generator C102a. • Disconnect: PCM C175c. • Measure the resistance between the PCM C175c-19, circuit 10-BA25 (GY/RD), harness side and the generator C102a-2, circuit 10-BA25 (GY/RD), harness side; and between the PCM C175c-19, circuit 10-BA25 (GY/RD), harness side and ground. 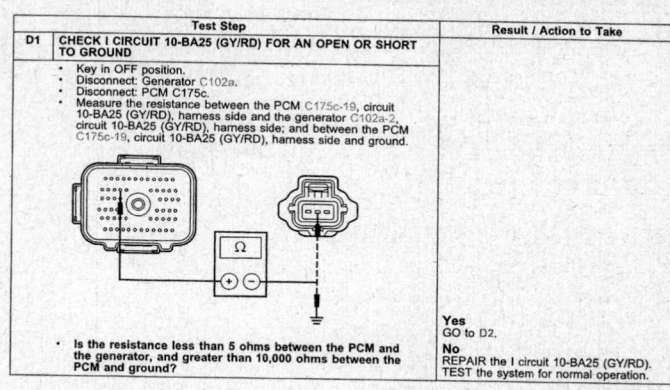 • Is the resistance less than 5 ohms between the PCM and the generator, and greater than 10,000 ohms between the PCM and ground?	**Yes** GO to D2. **No** REPAIR the I circuit 10-BA25 (GY/RD). TEST the system for normal operation.

ARM0500000000732

Fig. 84 Test D: Charging System Warning Indicator Is On w/Engine Running & Battery Increases Voltage (Part 1 of 2). 2005–07 LS & Thunderbird

Test Step	Result / Action to Take
E1 CHECK THE CHARGING SYSTEM WARNING INDICATOR • Key in OFF position. • Disconnect: Generator C102a. • With the engine off, connect a fused (15A) jumper wire between the generator C102a-1, GEN MON circuit 8-BA25 (WH/RD), harness side and ground. 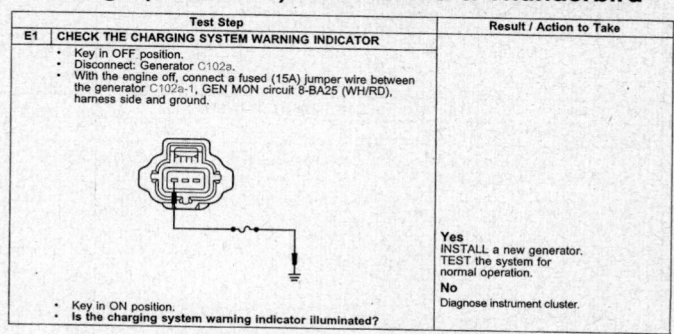 • Key in ON position. • Is the charging system warning indicator illuminated?	**Yes** INSTALL a new generator. TEST the system for normal operation. **No** Diagnose instrument cluster.

ARM0500000000734

Fig. 85 Test E: Charging System Warning Indicator Is Off w/Ignition Switch In Run Position & Engine Is Off. 2005–07 LS & Thunderbird

Test Step	Result / Action to Take
F2 CHECK FOR LOOSE FUSE CONNECTIONS • Key in START position. • Check the rear BJB fuse 15 (5A) in A circuit 30-BA25 (RD) for looseness by wiggling the fuse and noting the charging system warning indicator operation. • Does the charging system warning indicator flicker?	**Yes** REPAIR the loose fuse connection(s) as necessary. TEST system for normal operation. **No** GO to F3.
F3 CHECK A CIRCUIT 30-BA25 (RD) FOR LOOSE CONNECTIONS • Key in OFF position. • Connect a fused (15A) jumper wire between the generator C102a-3, A circuit 30-BA25 (RD) (backprobed) and the positive battery terminal. 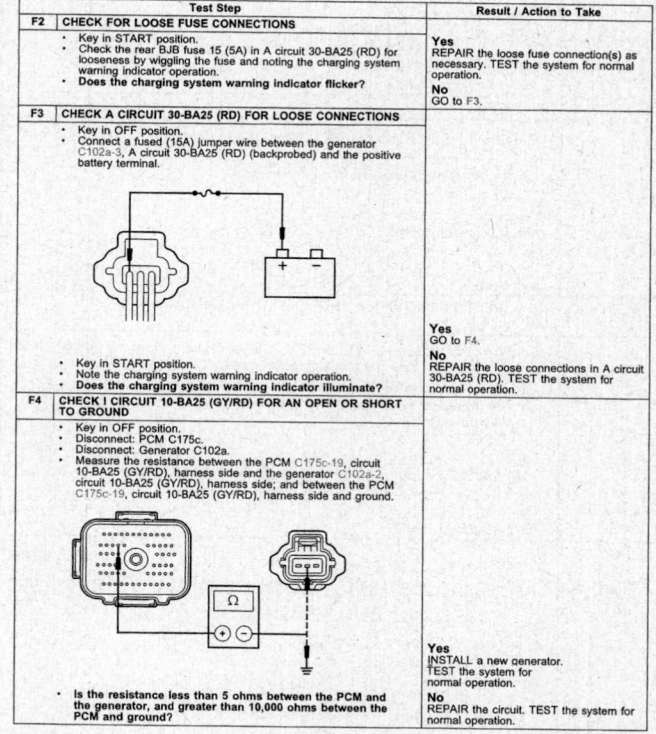 • Key in START position. • Note the charging system warning indicator operation. • Does the charging system warning indicator illuminate?	**Yes** GO to F4. **No** REPAIR the loose connections in A circuit 30-BA25 (RD). TEST the system for normal operation.
F4 CHECK I CIRCUIT 10-BA25 (GY/RD) FOR AN OPEN OR SHORT TO GROUND • Key in OFF position. • Disconnect: PCM C175c. • Disconnect: Generator C102a. • Measure the resistance between the PCM C175c-19, circuit 10-BA25 (GY/RD), harness side and the generator C102a-2, circuit 10-BA25 (GY/RD), harness side; and between the PCM C175c-19, circuit 10-BA25 (GY/RD), harness side and ground. • Is the resistance less than 5 ohms between the PCM and the generator, and greater than 10,000 ohms between the PCM and ground?	**Yes** INSTALL a new generator. TEST the system for normal operation. **No** REPAIR the circuit. TEST the system for normal operation.

ARM0500000000736

Fig. 86 Test F: Charging System Warning Indicator Flickers Or Is Intermittent (Part 2 of 2). 2005–07 LS & Thunderbird

Test Step		Result / Action to Take
G1	CHECK FOR ACCESSORY DRIVE NOISE	
	• Key in OFF position. • Check the accessory drive belt for damage and correct installation. Check the accessory mounting brackets and the generator pulley for looseness or misalignment. • Is the accessory drive OK?	**Yes** GO to G2. **No** REPAIR as necessary. TEST the system for normal operation.
G2	CHECK THE GENERATOR MOUNTING	
	• Check the generator mounting for loose bolts or misalignment. • Is the generator mounted correctly?	**Yes** GO to G3. **No** REPAIR as necessary. TEST the system for normal operation.
G3	CHECK THE GENERATOR FOR ELECTRICAL NOISE	
	• Disconnect: Generator C102a. • Key in START position. • NOTE: Do not exceed 3,000 engine rpm or the generator may become electrically functional. With the engine running, use a stethoscope or equivalent listening device to probe the generator. • Is the noise still present?	**Yes** GO to G4. **No** INSTALL a new generator. TEST the system for normal operation.
G4	CHECK THE GENERATOR FOR MECHANICAL NOISE	
	• With the engine running, use a stethoscope or equivalent listening device to probe the generator and the accessory drive area for unusual mechanical noise. • Is the generator the source of the noise ?	**Yes** INSTALL a new generator. TEST the system for normal operation. **No** diagnose the source of the noise.

ARM0500000000737

Fig. 87   Test G: Alternator Is Noisy. 2005–07 LS & Thunderbird

CONDITIONS	DETAILS/RESULTS/ACTIONS
A1 CHECK BATTERY CONDITION	
	1 Carry out the Battery—Condition Test to determine if the battery can hold a charge and is OK for use. • Is the battery OK? → **Yes** GO to A2. → **No** INSTALL a new battery. TEST the system for normal operation.
A2 CHECK THE GENERATOR OUTPUT	
	1 Carry out the On-Vehicle Generator Load/No Load Test. • Is the generator OK? → **Yes** GO to A3. → **No** GO to Pinpoint Test B.
A3 CHECK FOR CURRENT DRAINS	
	1 Carry out the Battery—Drain Test. • Are there any excessive current drains? → **Yes** REPAIR as necessary. TEST the system for normal operation. → **No** GO to A4.
A4 CHECK FOR CURRENT DRAINS WHICH SHUT OFF WHEN THE BATTERY IS DISCONNECTED	
	1 Carry out the Battery—Electronic Drains Which Shut Off When the Battery Cable is Disconnected Test. Refer or Component Tests • Are there any current drains which shut off when the battery is disconnected? → **Yes** REPAIR as necessary. TEST the system for normal operation. → **No** GO to Pinpoint Test B.

FM1120200762000X

Fig. 89   Test A: Battery Is Charged Or Voltage Is Low. 2004 Mustang

Test Step		Result / Action to Take
H1	VERIFY THE GENERATOR IS THE SOURCE OF THE RADIO INTERFERENCE	
	• Key in START position. • With the engine running, tune the audio unit to a station where the interference is present. • Key in OFF position. • Disconnect: Generator C102a. • Key in START position. • NOTE: Do not exceed 3,000 engine rpm or the generator may become electrically functional. With the engine running, note any audio unit interference. • Is the interference present with the generator disconnected?	**Yes** Diagnose entertainment system. **No** INSTALL a new generator. TEST the system for normal operation.

ARM0500000000738

Fig. 88   Test H: Radio Interference. 2005–07 LS & Thunderbird

CONDITIONS	DETAILS/RESULTS/ACTIONS
B1 CHECK GENERATOR B+ CIRCUIT 38 (BK/OG)	
1 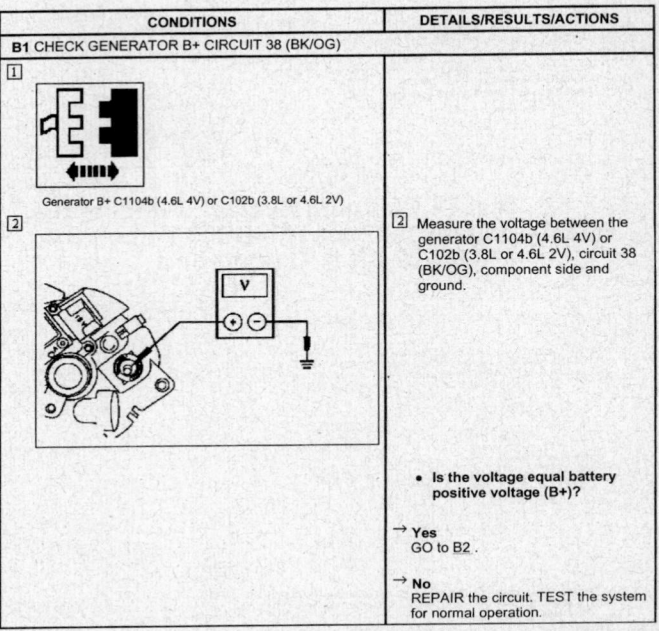 Generator B+ C1104b (4.6L 4V) or C102b (3.8L or 4.6L 2V)	2 Measure the voltage between the generator C1104b (4.6L 4V) or C102b (3.8L or 4.6L 2V), circuit 38 (BK/OG), component side and ground. • Is the voltage equal battery positive voltage (B+)? → **Yes** GO to B2. → **No** REPAIR the circuit. TEST the system for normal operation.

FM1120200763010X

Fig. 90   Test B: Charging System Warning Indicator Is On w/Engine Running, Battery Voltage Does Not Increase (Part 1 of 4). 2004 Mustang

CONDITIONS	DETAILS/RESULTS/ACTIONS
B2 CHECK GENERATOR A CIRCUIT 36 (YE/WH)	
1 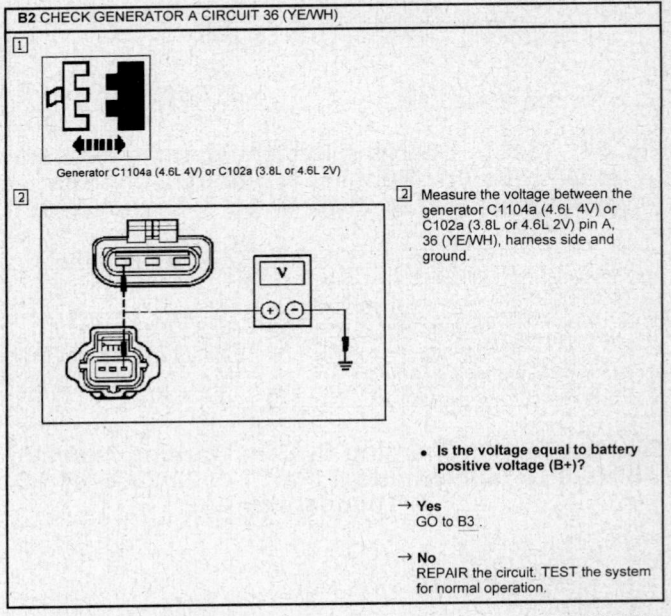 Generator C1104a (4.6L 4V) or C102a (3.8L or 4.6L 2V)	2 Measure the voltage between the generator C1104a (4.6L 4V) or C102a (3.8L or 4.6L 2V) pin A, 36 (YE/WH), harness side and ground. • Is the voltage equal to battery positive voltage (B+)? → **Yes** GO to B3. → **No** REPAIR the circuit. TEST the system for normal operation.

FM1120200763020X

Fig. 90   Test B: Charging System Warning Indicator Is On w/Engine Running, Battery Voltage Does Not Increase (Part 2 of 4). 2004 Mustang

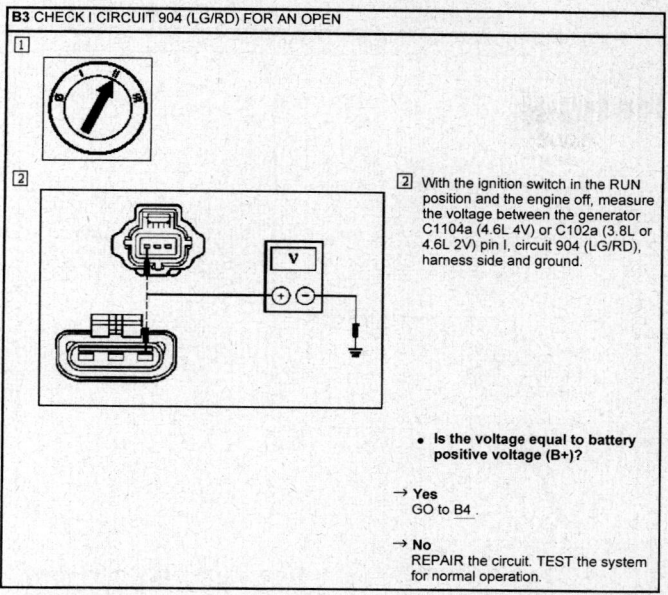

Fig. 90 Test B: Charging System Warning Indicator Is On w/Engine Running, Battery Voltage Does Not Increase (Part 3 of 4). 2004 Mustang

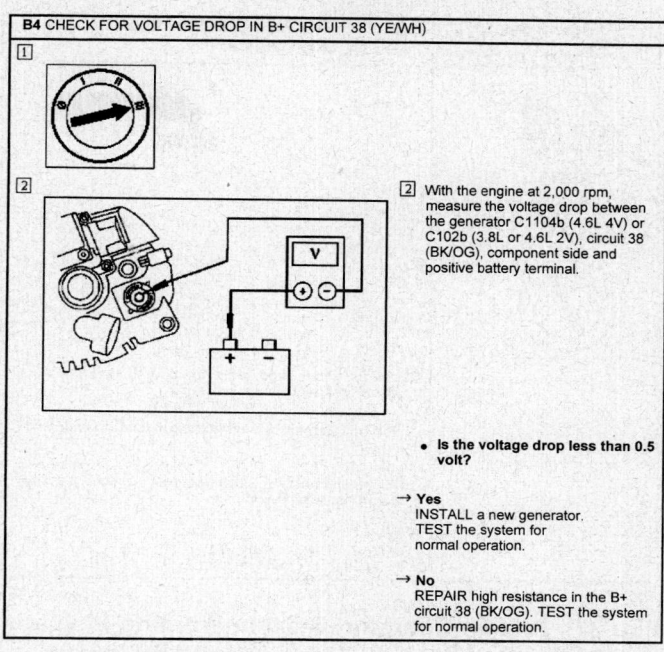

Fig. 90 Test B: Charging System Warning Indicator Is On w/Engine Running, Battery Voltage Does Not Increase (Part 4 of 4). 2004 Mustang

CONDITIONS	DETAILS/RESULTS/ACTIONS

C1 CHECK FOR VOLTAGE DROP IN A CIRCUIT 36 (YE/WH)

Fig. 91 Test C: System Overcharges, Battery Voltage Is More Than 15.5 Volts (Part 1 of 2). 2004 Mustang

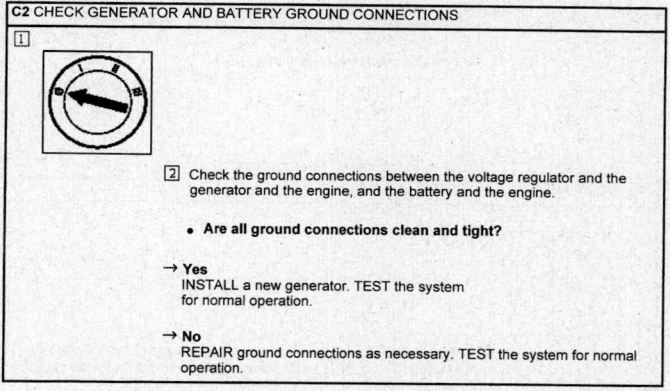

Fig. 91 Test C: System Overcharges, Battery Voltage Is More Than 15.5 Volts (Part 2 of 2). 2004 Mustang

CONDITIONS	DETAILS/RESULTS/ACTIONS
D1 CHECK I CIRCUIT 904 (LG/RD) FOR A SHORT TO GROUND	

[1]

Generator C1104a (4.6L 4V) or C102a
(3.8L or 4.6L 2V)

[2]

[3] With the ignition switch in the RUN position, check the charging system warning indicator.

• **Is the charging system warning indicator illuminated?**

→ **Yes**
REPAIR I circuit 904 (LG/RD) for a short to ground. TEST the system for normal operation.

→ **No**
INSTALL a new generator. TEST the system for normal operation.

FM1120200765000X

Fig. 92   Test D: Charging System Warning Indicator Is On w/Engine Running & Battery Increases Voltage. 2004 Mustang

CONDITIONS	DETAILS/RESULTS/ACTIONS
F1 CHECK FOR LOOSE CONNECTIONS	

[1] Check all generator, battery, and power distribution connections for looseness, corrosion, loose or bent terminals, or loose eyelets.

• **Are all connections clean and tight?**

→ **Yes**
GO to F2.

→ **No**
REPAIR as necessary. TEST the system for normal operation.

F2 CHECK FUSE	

[1]

[2] With the engine running, check battery junction box (BJB) fuse 20 (20A) in A circuit 36 (YE/WH) for looseness by wiggling the fuse and noting the charging system warning indicator lamp operation.

• **Does the charging system warning indicator lamp flicker?**

→ **Yes**
REPAIR loose fuse connections as necessary. TEST the system for normal operation.

→ **No**
GO to F3.

FM1120200767010X

Fig. 94   Test F: Charging System Warning Indicator Lamp Flickers Or Is Intermittent (Part 1 of 2). 2004 Mustang

CONDITIONS	DETAILS/RESULTS/ACTIONS
E1 CHECK THE CHARGING SYSTEM WARNING INDICATOR LAMP	

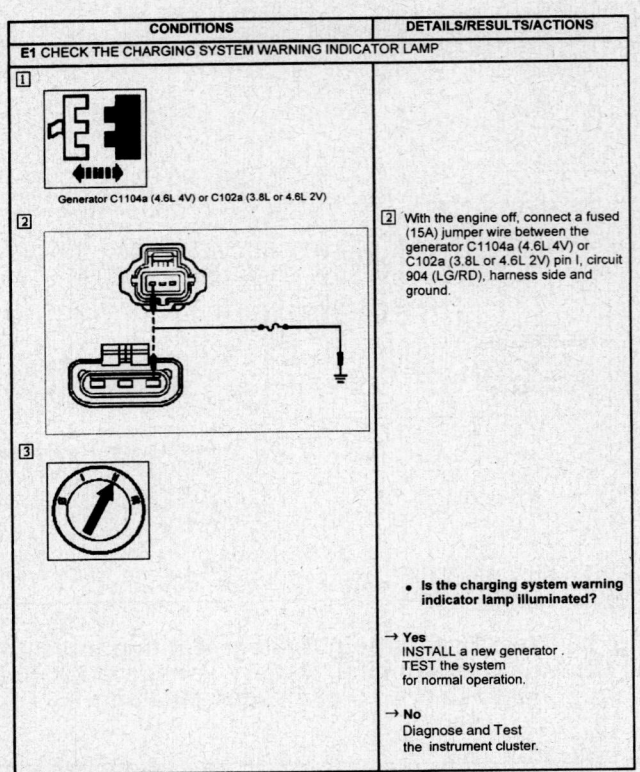

Generator C1104a (4.6L 4V) or C102a (3.8L or 4.6L 2V)

[2] With the engine off, connect a fused (15A) jumper wire between the generator C1104a (4.6L 4V) or C102a (3.8L or 4.6L 2V) pin I, circuit 904 (LG/RD), harness side and ground.

[3]

• **Is the charging system warning indicator lamp illuminated?**

→ **Yes**
INSTALL a new generator. TEST the system for normal operation.

→ **No**
Diagnose and Test the instrument cluster.

FM1120200766000X

Fig. 93   Test E: Charging System Warning Indicator Is Off w/Ignition Switch In Run Position & Engine Off. 2004 Mustang

F3 CHECK A CIRCUIT 36 (YE/WH) CONNECTIONS	

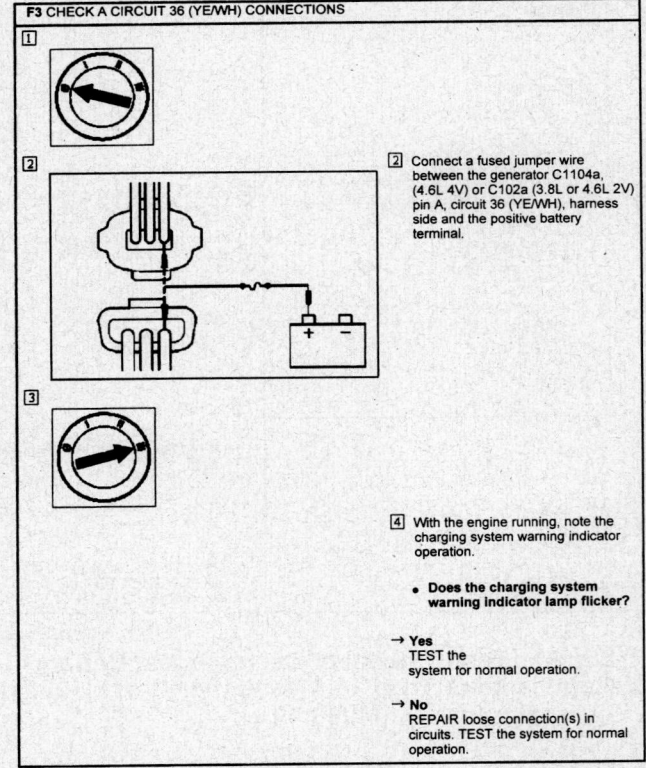

[1]

[2] Connect a fused jumper wire between the generator C1104a, (4.6L 4V) or C102a (3.8L or 4.6L 2V) pin A, circuit 36 (YE/WH), harness side and the positive battery terminal.

[3]

[4] With the engine running, note the charging system warning indicator operation.

• **Does the charging system warning indicator lamp flicker?**

→ **Yes**
TEST the system for normal operation.

→ **No**
REPAIR loose connection(s) in circuits. TEST the system for normal operation.

FM1120200767020X

Fig. 94   Test F: Charging System Warning Indicator Lamp Flickers Or Is Intermittent (Part 2 of 2). 2004 Mustang

CONDITIONS	DETAILS/RESULTS/ACTIONS
G1 CHECK FOR ACCESSORY DRIVE NOISE	
	① Check the accessory drive belt for damage and correct installation. Check the accessory mounting brackets and generator pulley for looseness or misalignment. • **Is the accessory drive OK?** → **Yes** GO to G2 . → **No** REPAIR as necessary. TEST the system for normal operation.
G2 CHECK GENERATOR MOUNTING	
	① Check the generator mounting for loose bolts or misalignment. • **Is the generator mounted correctly?** → **Yes** GO to G3 . → **No** REPAIR as necessary. TEST the system for normal operation.

FM1120200768010X

Fig. 95 Test G: Alternator Is Noisy (Part 1 of 3). 2004 Mustang

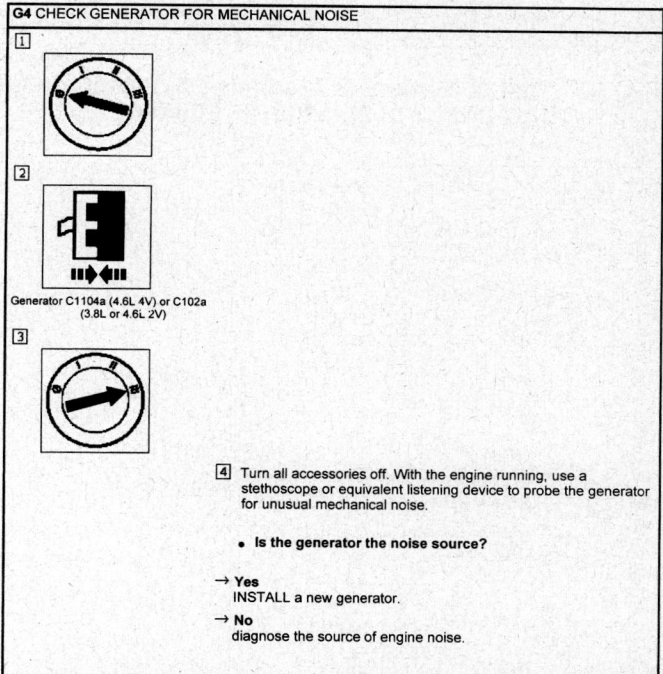

④ Turn all accessories off. With the engine running, use a stethoscope or equivalent listening device to probe the generator for unusual mechanical noise.

• **Is the generator the noise source?**

→ **Yes**
INSTALL a new generator.

→ **No**
diagnose the source of engine noise.

FM1120200768030X

Fig. 95 Test G: Alternator Is Noisy (Part 3 of 3). 2004 Mustang

G3 CHECK GENERATOR FOR ELECTRICAL NOISE

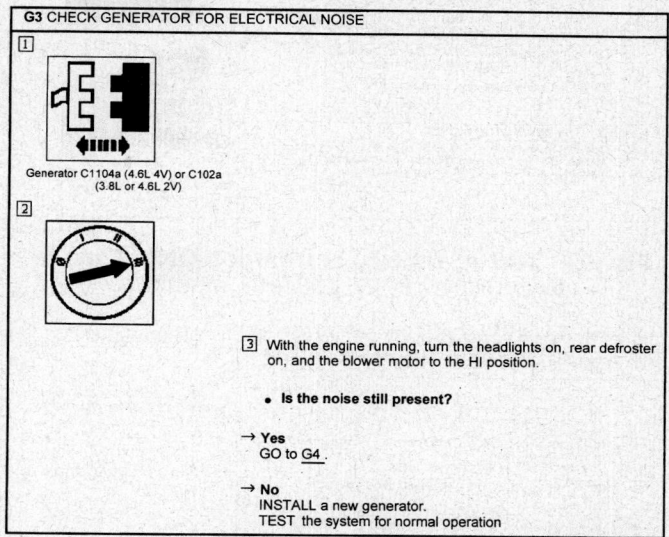

Generator C1104a (4.6L 4V) or C102a (3.8L or 4.6L 2V)

③ With the engine running, turn the headlights on, rear defroster on, and the blower motor to the HI position.

• **Is the noise still present?**

→ **Yes**
GO to G4 .

→ **No**
INSTALL a new generator.
TEST the system for normal operation

FM1120200768020X

Fig. 95 Test G: Alternator Is Noisy (Part 2 of 3). 2004 Mustang

CONDITIONS	DETAILS/RESULTS/ACTIONS
H1 VERIFY GENERATOR IS SOURCE OF RADIO INTERFERENCE	

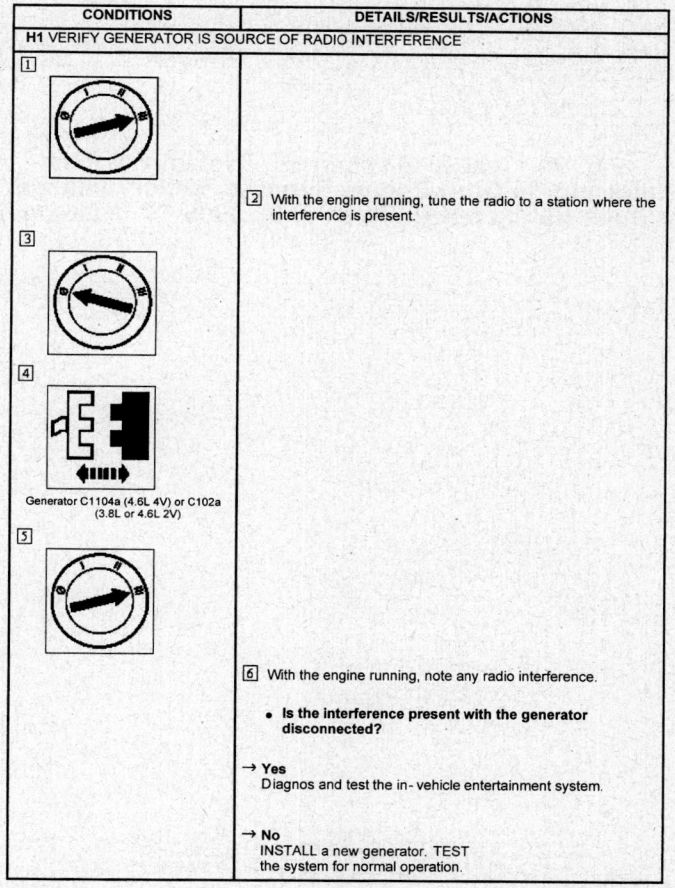

Generator C1104a (4.6L 4V) or C102a (3.8L or 4.6L 2V)

② With the engine running, tune the radio to a station where the interference is present.

⑥ With the engine running, note any radio interference.

• **Is the interference present with the generator disconnected?**

→ **Yes**
Diagnos and test the in-vehicle entertainment system.

→ **No**
INSTALL a new generator. TEST the system for normal operation.

FM1120200769000X

Fig. 96 Test H: Radio Interference. 2004 Mustang

Test Step		Result / Action to Take
A1	**CHECK THE BATTERY CONDITION**	**Yes** GO to A2. **No** INSTALL a new battery. TEST the system for normal operation.
	• Carry out the Battery — Condition Test to determine if the battery can hold a charge and is OK for use. • **Does the battery pass the condition test?**	
A2	**CHECK THE GENERATOR OUTPUT**	**Yes** GO to A3. **No** INSTALL a new generator. TEST the system for normal operation.
	• Carry out the Generator On-Vehicle Load Test and No Load Test. Refer to the Component Tests in this section. • **Does the generator pass the component tests?**	

ARM0500000000740

Fig. 97 Test A: Battery Is Charged Or Voltage Is Low (Part 1 of 2). 2005–07 Mustang

Test Step		Result / Action to Take
B1	**CHECK THE DTCS IN THE POWERTRAIN CONTROL MODULE (PCM)**	**Yes** REFER to MOTOR's "Domestic Engine Performance & Driveability Manual" GO to B2. **No** GO to B2.
	• Key in OFF position. • Connect the diagnostic tool. • Key in ON position. • Enter the following diagnostic mode on the diagnostic tool: Retrieve PCM DTCs. • Check the recorded PCM DTCs from the continuous and on-demand self-tests. • **Are any PCM DTCs recorded?**	
B2	**CHECK THE GENERATOR B+ CIRCUIT 2037 (RD) FOR VOLTAGE**	
	• Key in OFF position. • Measure the voltage between the generator C102b, circuit 2037 (RD) and ground. 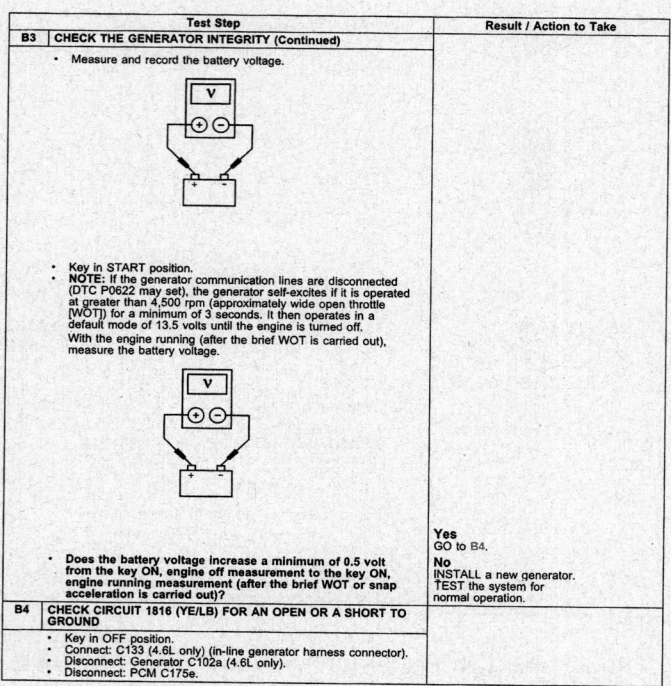	**Yes** GO to B3. **No** REPAIR the circuit. TEST the system for normal operation.
	• **Is the voltage equal to battery voltage?**	
B3	**CHECK THE GENERATOR INTEGRITY**	
	• Disconnect: Generator C102a (4.0L), C133 (4.6L) (in-line generator harness connector). • Key in ON position, engine OFF.	

ARM0500000000742

Fig. 98 Test B: Discharging System Warning Indicator Is On w/Engine Running, Battery Voltage Does Not Increase (Part 1 of 3). 2005–07 Mustang

Test Step		Result / Action to Take
B3	**CHECK THE GENERATOR INTEGRITY (Continued)**	
	• Measure and record the battery voltage. 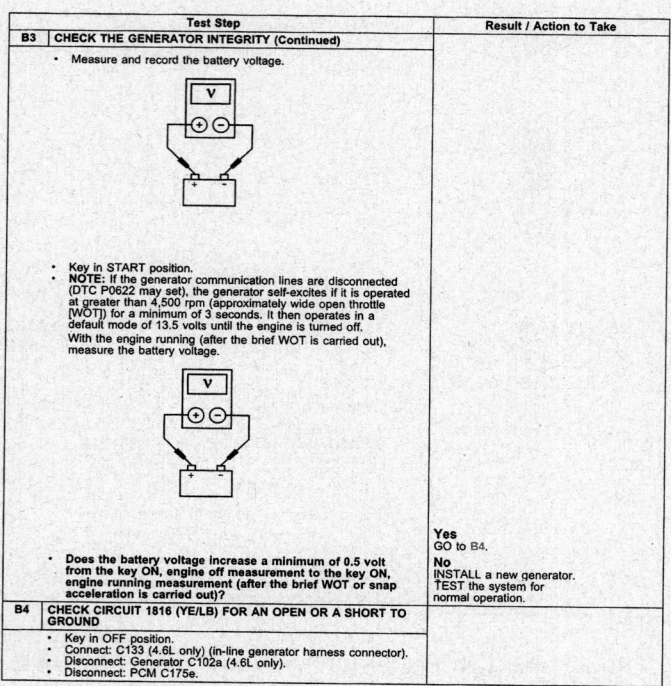• Key in START position. • **NOTE:** If the generator communication lines are disconnected (DTC P0622 may set), the generator self-excites if it is operated at greater than 4,500 rpm (approximately wide open throttle (WOT)) for a minimum of 3 seconds. It then operates in a default mode of 13.5 volts until the engine is turned off. With the engine running (after the brief WOT is carried out), measure the battery voltage.	
	• **Does the battery voltage increase a minimum of 0.5 volt from the key ON, engine off measurement to the key ON, engine running measurement (after the brief WOT or snap acceleration is carried out)?**	**Yes** GO to B4. **No** INSTALL a new generator. TEST the system for normal operation.
B4	**CHECK CIRCUIT 1816 (YE/LB) FOR AN OPEN OR A SHORT TO GROUND**	
	• Key in OFF position. • Connect: C133 (4.6L only) (in-line generator harness connector). • Disconnect: Generator C102a (4.6L only). • Disconnect: PCM C175e.	

ARM0500000000743

Fig. 98 Test B: Charging System Warning Indicator Is On w/Engine Running, Battery Voltage Does Not Increase (Part 2 of 3). 2005–07 Mustang

Test Step		Result / Action to Take
A3	**CHECK FOR CURRENT DRAINS**	**Yes** REPAIR as necessary. TEST the system for normal operation. **No** GO to A4.
	• Carry out the Battery — Drain Testing. • **Are any circuits causing excessive current drains?**	
A4	**CHECK THE VEHICLE GROUNDS**	
	• Key in START position. • With the engine running, measure the voltage drop between the generator housing and the negative battery terminal. 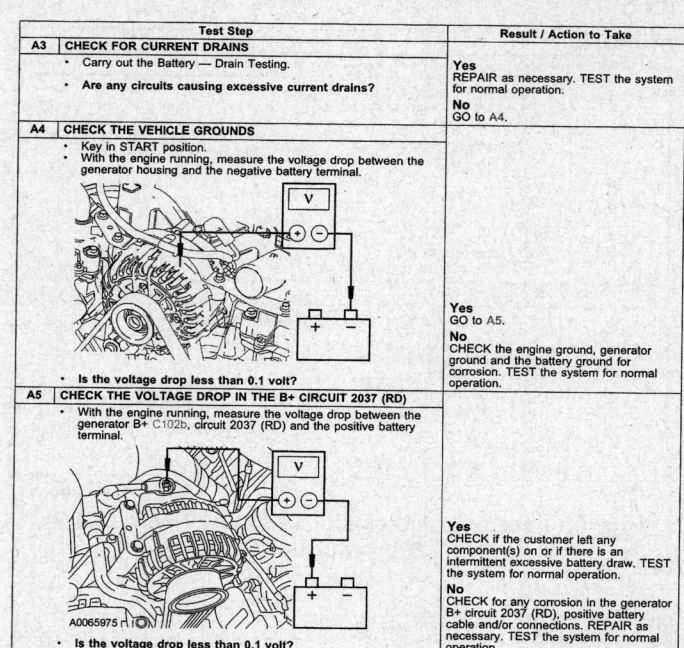	
	• **Is the voltage drop less than 0.1 volt?**	**Yes** GO to A5. **No** CHECK the engine ground, generator ground and the battery ground for corrosion. TEST the system for normal operation.
A5	**CHECK THE VOLTAGE DROP IN THE B+ CIRCUIT 2037 (RD)**	
	• With the engine running, measure the voltage drop between the generator B+ C102b, circuit 2037 (RD) and the positive battery terminal. 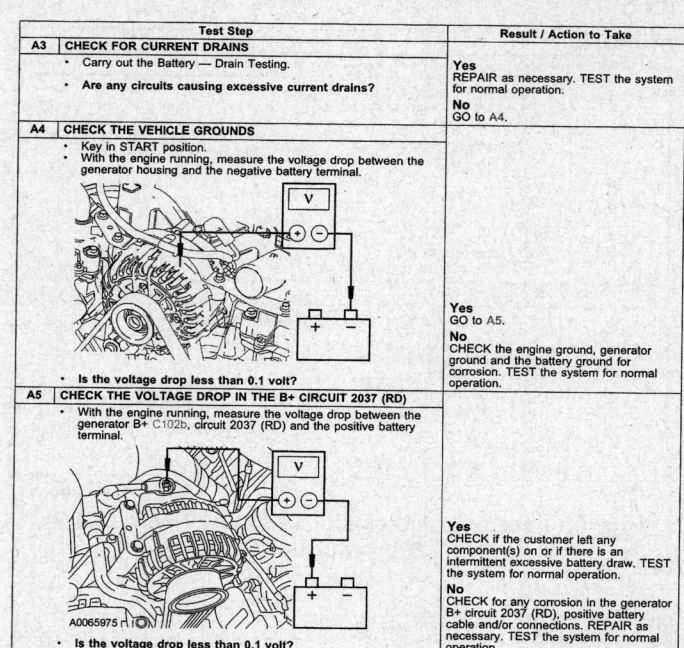 A0065975	
	• **Is the voltage drop less than 0.1 volt?**	**Yes** CHECK if the customer left any component(s) on or if there is an intermittent excessive battery draw. TEST the system for normal operation. **No** CHECK for any corrosion in the generator B+ circuit 2037 (RD), positive battery cable and/or connections. REPAIR as necessary. TEST the system for normal operation.

ARM0500000000741

Fig. 97 Test A: Battery Is Discharged Or Voltage Is Low (Part 2 of 2). 2005–07 Mustang

Test Step		Result / Action to Take
B4	**CHECK CIRCUIT 1816 (YE/LB) FOR AN OPEN OR A SHORT TO GROUND (Continued)**	
	• Measure the resistance between the generator C102a-2, circuit 1816 (YE/LB), harness side and the PCM C175e-13, circuit 1816 (YE/LB), harness side; and between the generator C102a-2, circuit 1816 (YE/LB), harness side and ground. 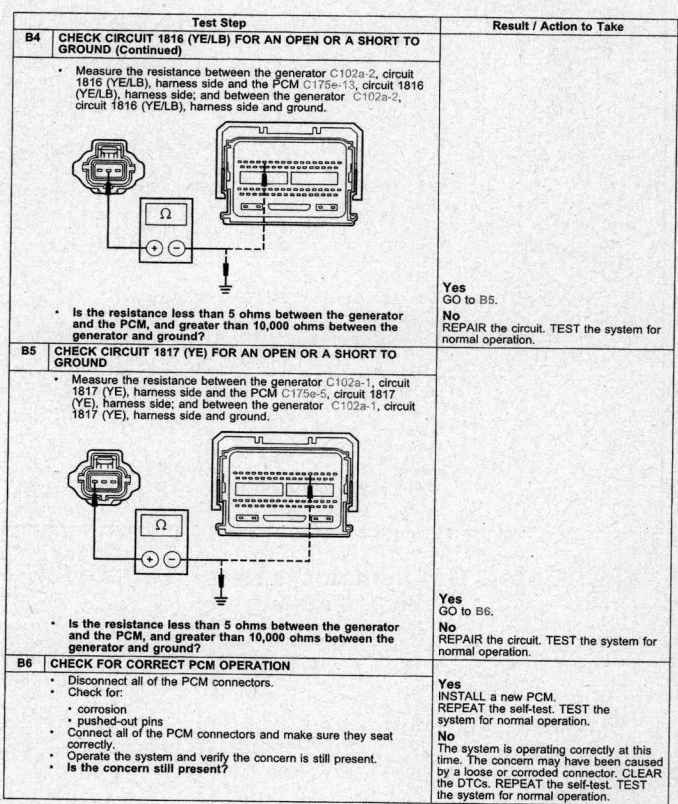	
	• **Is the resistance less than 5 ohms between the generator and the PCM, and greater than 10,000 ohms between the generator and ground?**	**Yes** GO to B5. **No** REPAIR the circuit. TEST the system for normal operation.
B5	**CHECK CIRCUIT 1817 (YE) FOR AN OPEN OR A SHORT TO GROUND**	
	• Measure the resistance between the generator C102a-1, circuit 1817 (YE), harness side and the PCM C175e-5, circuit 1817 (YE), harness side; and between the generator C102a-1, circuit 1817 (YE), harness side and ground. 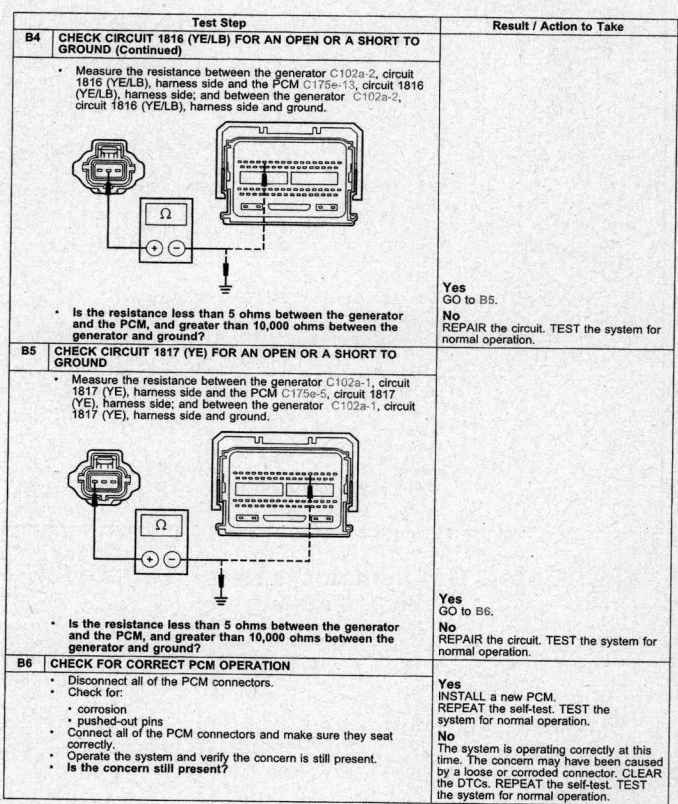	
	• **Is the resistance less than 5 ohms between the generator and the PCM, and greater than 10,000 ohms between the generator and ground?**	**Yes** GO to B6. **No** REPAIR the circuit. TEST the system for normal operation.
B6	**CHECK FOR CORRECT PCM OPERATION**	**Yes** INSTALL a new PCM. REPEAT the self-test. TEST the system for normal operation. **No** The system is operating correctly at this time. The concern may have been caused by a loose or corroded connector. CLEAR the DTCs. REPEAT the self-test. TEST the system for normal operation.

	• Disconnect all of the PCM connectors.
	• Check for:
	  • corrosion
	  • pushed-out pins
	• Connect all of the PCM connectors and make sure they seat correctly.
	• Operate the system and verify the concern is still present.
	• **Is the concern still present?**	

ARM0500000000744

Fig. 98 Test B: Charging System Warning Indicator Is On w/Engine Running, Battery Voltage Does Not Increase (Part 3 of 3). 2005–07 Mustang

Test Step		Result / Action to Take
C1	**CHECK THE DTCS IN THE PCM**	
	• Key in OFF position. • Connect the diagnostic tool. • Key in ON position. • Enter the following diagnostic mode on the diagnostic tool: Retrieve PCM DTCs. • Check the recorded PCM DTCs from the continuous and on-demand self-tests. • **Are any PCM DTCs recorded?**	**Yes** REFER to MOTOR's "Domestic Engine Performance & Driveability Manual" GO to C2. **No** GO to C2.
C2	**CHECK THE BATTERY VOLTAGE**	
	• Key in OFF position. • Disconnect the diagnostic tool. • Key in START position. • With the engine running and all of the accessories turned off, measure the voltage at the battery while varying the engine rpm. • **Is the voltage greater than 15.5 volts?**	**Yes** GO to C3. **No** GO to C4.
C3	**CHECK FOR A VOLTAGE DROP IN CIRCUIT 35 (OG/LB)**	
	• Key in OFF position. • Disconnect: Generator C102a.	

ARM0500000000745

Fig. 99   Test C: System Overcharges, Battery Voltage Is More Than 15.5 Volts (Part 1 of 3). 2005–07 Mustang

Test Step		Result / Action to Take
C5	**CHECK THE GENERATOR INTEGRITY (Continued)**	
	• **NOTE:** If the generator communication lines are disconnected (DTC P0622 may be set), the generator self-excites if it is operated at greater than 4,500 rpm (approximately wide open throttle [WOT]) for a minimum of 3 seconds. It then operates in a default mode at 13.5 volts until the engine is turned off. With the engine running (after the brief WOT is carried out) measure the battery voltage. • **Does the battery voltage increase a minimum of 0.5 volt from the key ON, engine off measurement to the key ON, engine running measurement (after the brief WOT or snap acceleration is carried out)?**	**Yes** GO to C6. **No** INSTALL a new generator. TEST the system for normal operation.
C6	**CHECK FOR CORRECT PCM OPERATION**	

	• Key in OFF position.
	• Disconnect all of the PCM connectors.
	• Check for:
	  • corrosion
	  • pushed-out pins
	• Connect all of the PCM connectors and make sure they seat correctly.
	• Operate the system and verify the concern is still present.
	• **Is the concern still present?**
		Yes
		INSTALL a new PCM. REPEAT the self-test. TEST the system for normal operation.
		
		No
		The system is operating correctly at this time. The concern may have been caused by a loose or corroded connector. CLEAR the DTCs. REPEAT the self-test. TEST the system for normal operation.

ARM0500000000747

Fig. 99   Test C: System Overcharges, Battery Voltage Is More Than 15.5 Volts (Part 3 of 3). 2005–07 Mustang

Test Step		Result / Action to Take
C3	**CHECK FOR A VOLTAGE DROP IN CIRCUIT 35 (OG/LB)** (Continued)	
	• Measure the voltage between the generator C102a-3, circuit 35 (OG/LB), harness side and ground. 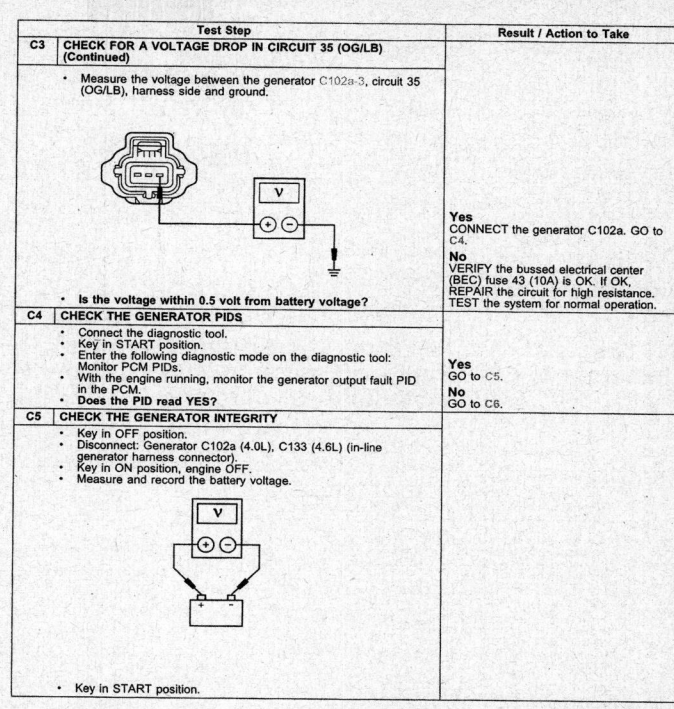 • **Is the voltage within 0.5 volt from battery voltage?**	**Yes** CONNECT the generator C102a. GO to C4. **No** VERIFY the bussed electrical center (BEC) fuse 43 (10A) is OK. If OK, REPAIR the circuit for high resistance. TEST the system for normal operation.
C4	**CHECK THE GENERATOR PIDS**	
	• Connect the diagnostic tool. • Key in START position. • Enter the following diagnostic mode on the diagnostic tool: Monitor PCM PIDs. • With the engine running, monitor the generator output fault PID in the PCM. • **Does the PID read YES?**	**Yes** GO to C5. **No** GO to C6.
C5	**CHECK THE GENERATOR INTEGRITY**	
	• Key in OFF position. • Disconnect: Generator C102a (4.0L), C133 (4.6L) (in-line generator harness connector). • Key in ON position, engine OFF. • Measure and record the battery voltage. • Key in START position.	

ARM0500000000746

Fig. 99   Test C: System Overcharges, Battery Voltage Is More Than 15.5 Volts (Part 2 of 3). 2005–07 Mustang

Test Step		Result / Action to Take
D1	**CHECK THE DTCS IN THE PCM**	
	• Key in OFF position. • Connect the diagnostic tool. • Key in ON position. • Enter the following diagnostic mode on the diagnostic tool: Retrieve PCM DTCs. • Check the recorded PCM DTCs from the continuous and on-demand self-tests. • **Are any PCM DTCs recorded?**	**Yes** REFER to MOTOR's "Domestic Engine Performance & Driveability Manual" GO to D2. **No** GO to D2.
D2	**CHECK THE SYSTEM FOR OVERCHARGING**	
	• Key in START position. • With the engine running and all of the accessories off, measure the voltage at the battery terminals while varying the engine rpm. • **Is the voltage greater than 15.5 volts?**	**Yes** GO to Pinpoint Test C. **No** GO to D3.
D3	**CHECK THE PCM PIDS**	
	• Enter the following diagnostic mode on the diagnostic tool: Monitor PCM PIDs. • With the engine running, monitor the generator output fault PID in the PCM. • **Does the PID read YES?**	**Yes** GO to D4. **No** Diagnose the charging system warning indicator.
D4	**CHECK THE GENERATOR OUTPUT**	
	• Verify the generator output. Generator On-Vehicle Tests in this section. • **Does the generator pass the component tests?**	**Yes** GO to D5. **No** INSTALL a new generator. CLEAR the DTCs. REPEAT the self-test. TEST the system for normal operation.
D5	**CHECK FOR CORRECT PCM OPERATION**	

	• Key in OFF position.
	• Disconnect all of the PCM connectors.
	• Check for:
	  • corrosion
	  • pushed-out pins
	• Connect all of the PCM connectors and make sure they seat correctly.
	• Operate the system and verify the concern is still present.
	• **Is the concern still present?**
		Yes
		INSTALL a new PCM. REPEAT the self-test. TEST the system for normal operation.
		
		No
		The system is operating correctly at this time. The concern may have been caused by a loose or corroded connector. CLEAR the DTCs. REPEAT the self-test. TEST the system for normal operation.

ARM0500000000748

Fig. 100   Test D: Charging System Warning Indicator Is On w/Engine Running & Battery Increases Voltage. 2005–07 Mustang

Test Step		Result / Action to Take
E1	CHECK THE CHARGING SYSTEM WARNING INDICATOR OPERATION • Key in OFF position. • Connect the diagnostic tool. • Key in ON position. • Enter the following diagnostic mode on the diagnostic tool: Active Commands. • Using Active Commands, turn on the charging system warning indicator in the instrument cluster. • **Is the charging system warning indicator on?**	**Yes** GO to E2. **No** Diagnose the charging system warning indicator.

E2	CHECK FOR CORRECT PCM OPERATION
	• Key in OFF position.
	• Disconnect all of the PCM connectors.
	• Check for:
	  – corrosion
	  – pushed-out pins
	• Connect all of the PCM connectors and make sure they seat correctly.
	• Operate the system and verify the concern is still present.
	• **Is the concern still present?**
		Yes
		INSTALL a new PCM. 303-14. REPEAT the self-test. TEST the system for normal operation.
		No
		The system is operating correctly at this time. The concern may have been caused by a loose or corroded connector. CLEAR the DTCs. REPEAT the self-test. TEST the system for normal operation.

ARM0500000000749

Fig. 101   Test E: Charging System Warning Indicator Is Off w/Ignition Switch In Run Position & Engine Off. 2005–07 Mustang

Test Step		Result / Action to Take
F2	CHECK THE OWC PULLEY • With the accessory drive belt removed, spin the OWC pulley in a clockwise direction, then reverse the direction of the pulley by spinning it in a counterclockwise direction. • **Does the OWC pulley engage with the rotor when spun in a clockwise direction and free-wheel when spun in a counterclockwise direction with minimal noise as compared to a known good vehicle?**	**Yes** GO to F3. **No** INSTALL a new generator assembly with OWC pulley. TEST the system for normal operation.
F3	CHECK THE GENERATOR FOR EXCESSIVE ELECTRICAL NOISE • Disconnect: Generator C102b (4.0L), C1100a (4.6L) (generator B+ harness connector at the battery). • Key in START position. • With the engine running, determine if the generator is still noisy. • **Is the noise still present?**	**Yes** GO to F4. **No** INSTALL a new generator. TEST the system for normal operation.
F4	CHECK THE GENERATOR FOR MECHANICAL NOISE • Turn all of the accessories off. With the engine running, use a stethoscope or equivalent listening device to probe the generator for unusual mechanical noise. • **Is the generator the noise source?**	**Yes** INSTALL a new generator. TEST the system for normal operation. **No** Diagnose the source of the engine noise.

ARM0500000000751

Fig. 102   Test F: Alternator Is Noisy (Part 2 of 2). 2005–07 Mustang

CONDITIONS	DETAILS/RESULTS/ACTIONS
A1 CHECK THE GENERATOR OUTPUT	1 Carry out the On-Vehicle Generator Load/No Load Tests. • Is the generator OK? → **Yes** GO to A2. → **No** GO to Pinpoint Test B.
A2 CHECK FOR CURRENT DRAINS	1 Carry out the Battery — Drain Test. • Are there any excessive current drains? → **Yes** REPAIR as necessary. TEST the system for normal operation. → **No** GO to A3.
A3 CHECK FOR CURRENT DRAINS WHICH SHUT OFF WHEN THE BATTERY IS DISCONNECTED	1 Carry out the Battery — Electronic Drains Which Shut Off When the Battery Cable is Disconnected Test. • Are there any current drains which shut off when the battery is disconnected? → **Yes** REPAIR as necessary. TEST the system for normal operation. → **No** GO to Pinpoint Test B.

FM1120200771000X

Fig. 104   Test A: Battery Is Discharged Or Voltage Is Low. 2004 Sable & Taurus

Test Step		Result / Action to Take
F1	CHECK FOR ACCESSORY DRIVE NOISE AND MOUNTING BRACKETS • Key in OFF position. • Check the accessory drive belt for damage and correct installation. • Check the accessory mounting brackets and the generator pulley for looseness or misalignment. • **Is the accessory drive OK?**	**Yes** If equipped with an OWC pulley, GO to F2. If not equipped with a OWC pulley, GO to F3. **No** REPAIR as necessary. TEST the system for normal operation.

ARM0500000000750

Fig. 102   Test F: Alternator Is Noisy (Part 1 of 2). 2005–07 Mustang

Test Step		Result / Action to Take
G1	VERIFY THE GENERATOR IS THE SOURCE OF THE RADIO INTERFERENCE NOTE: If the original equipment manufactured (OEM) audio unit has been replaced with an aftermarket unit, the vehicle may not pass this test. Return the vehicle to OEM condition before following this pinpoint test. • Key in START position. • Start and run the engine. • Tune the audio unit to a station where the interference is present. • Key in OFF position. • Disconnect: Generator C102a (4.0L), C1100a (4.6L) (generator B+ harness connector at the battery). • Key in START position. • With the engine running, determine if the interference is still present. • **Is the interference present with the generator disconnected?**	**Yes** Diagnosis and testing of the in-vehicle entertainment system. **No** INSTALL a new generator. TEST the system for normal operation.

ARM0500000000752

Fig. 103   Test G: Radio Interference. 2005–07 Mustang

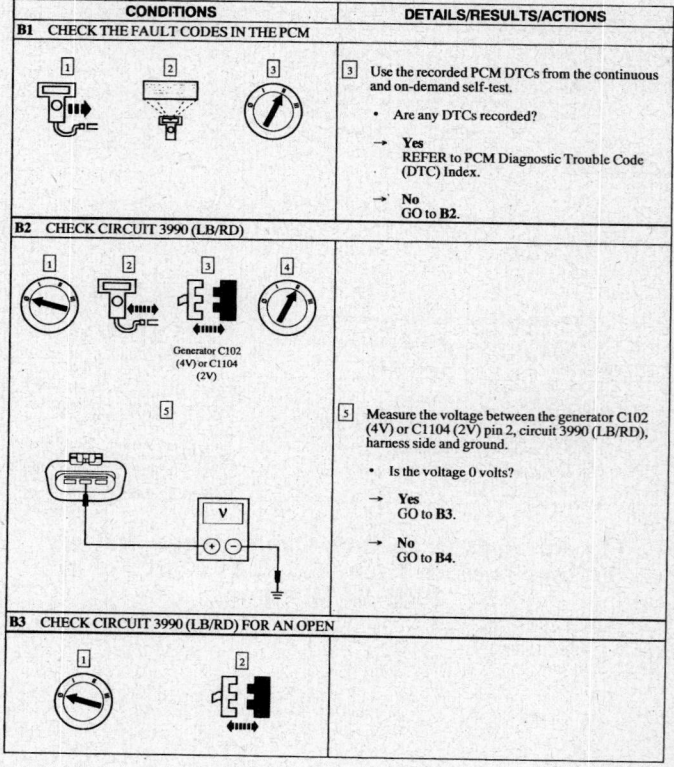

FM1120200772010X

Fig. 105   Test B: Charging System Warning Indicator Is On w/Engine Running, System Voltage Does Not Increase (Part 1 of 3). 2004 Sable & Taurus

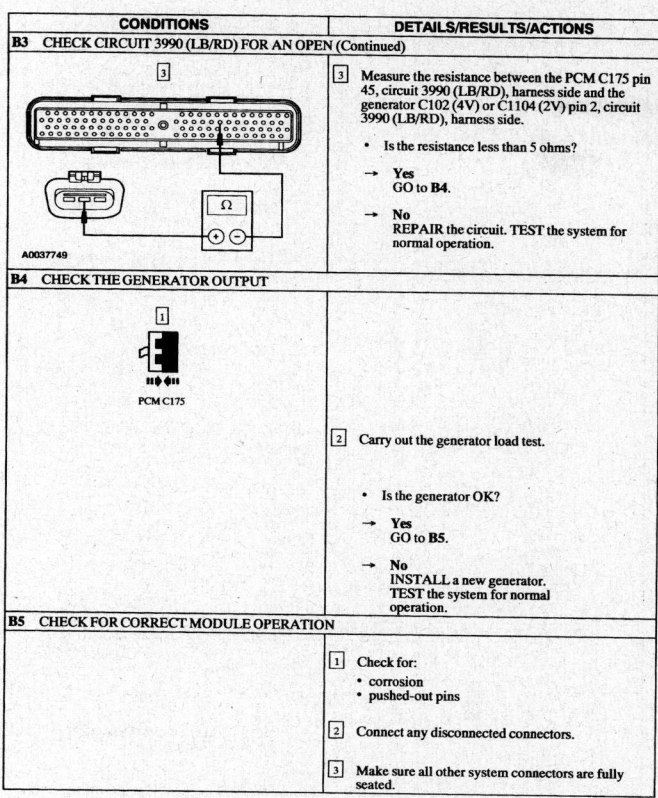

CONDITIONS	DETAILS/RESULTS/ACTIONS
B3 CHECK CIRCUIT 3990 (LB/RD) FOR AN OPEN (Continued)	3 Measure the resistance between the PCM C175 pin 45, circuit 3990 (LB/RD), harness side and the generator C102 (4V) or C1104 (2V) pin 2, circuit 3990 (LB/RD), harness side. • Is the resistance less than 5 ohms? → **Yes** GO to **B4**. → **No** REPAIR the circuit. TEST the system for normal operation.
B4 CHECK THE GENERATOR OUTPUT	
	2 Carry out the generator load test. • Is the generator OK? → **Yes** GO to **B5**. → **No** INSTALL a new generator. TEST the system for normal operation.
B5 CHECK FOR CORRECT MODULE OPERATION	
	1 Check for: • corrosion • pushed-out pins 2 Connect any disconnected connectors. 3 Make sure all other system connectors are fully seated.

FM1120200772020X

Fig. 105   Test B: Charging System Warning Indicator Is On w/Engine Running, System Voltage Does Not Increase (Part 2 of 3). 2004 Sable & Taurus

CONDITIONS	DETAILS/RESULTS/ACTIONS
C1 CHECK THE FAULT CODES IN THE PCM	
	3 Use the recorded PCM DTCs from the continuous and on-demand self-test. • Are any DTCs recorded? → **Yes** REFER to PCM Diagnostic Trouble Code (DTC) Index. → **No** GO to **C2**.
C2 CHECK THE BATTERY VOLTAGE	

FM1120200773010X

Fig. 106   Test C: System Overcharges, Battery Voltage More Than 15 Volts (Part 1 of 3). 2004 Sable & Taurus

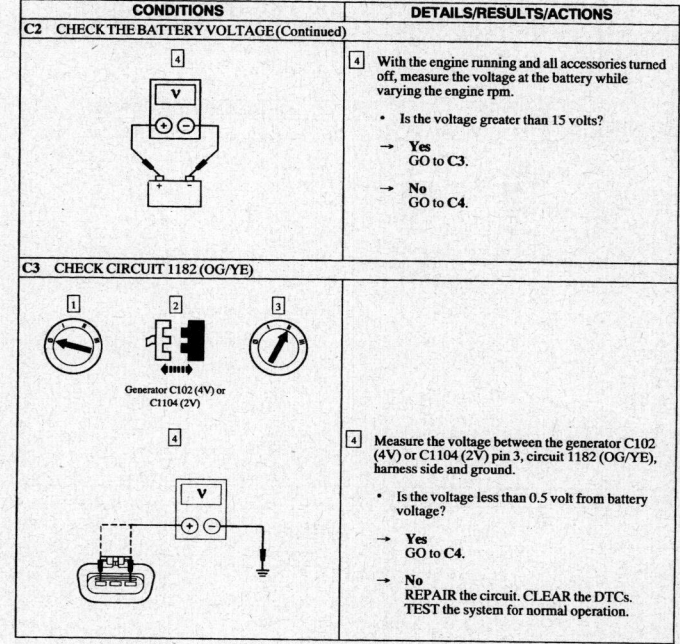

CONDITIONS	DETAILS/RESULTS/ACTIONS
B5 CHECK FOR CORRECT MODULE OPERATION (Continued)	4 Operate the system and verify the concern is still present. • Is the concern still present? → **Yes** INSTALL a new PCM. CLEAR the DTCs. REPEAT the PCM self-test. → **No** The system is operating correctly at this time. Concern may have been caused by a loose or corroded connector. CLEAR the DTCs. REPEAT the self-test.

FM1120200772030X

Fig. 105   Test B: Charging System Warning Indicator Is On w/Engine Running, System Voltage Does Not Increase (Part 3 of 3). 2004 Sable & Taurus

CONDITIONS	DETAILS/RESULTS/ACTIONS
C2 CHECK THE BATTERY VOLTAGE (Continued)	4 With the engine running and all accessories turned off, measure the voltage at the battery while varying the engine rpm. • Is the voltage greater than 15 volts? → **Yes** GO to **C3**. → **No** GO to **C4**.
C3 CHECK CIRCUIT 1182 (OG/YE)	4 Measure the voltage between the generator C102 (4V) or C1104 (2V) pin 3, circuit 1182 (OG/YE), harness side and ground. • Is the voltage less than 0.5 volt from battery voltage? → **Yes** GO to **C4**. → **No** REPAIR the circuit. CLEAR the DTCs. TEST the system for normal operation.

FM1120200773020X

Fig. 106   Test C: System Overcharges, Battery Voltage More Than 15 Volts (Part 2 of 3). 2004 Sable & Taurus

CONDITIONS	DETAILS/RESULTS/ACTIONS
C4 CHECK THE GENERATOR OUTPUT	
	4 Check the generator output. • Is the generator OK? → **Yes** The system is operating correctly at this time. CHECK for corroded connections and CHECK integrity of generator and circuit 1182 (OG/YE). → **No** INSTALL a new generator. CLEAR the DTCs. TEST the system for normal operation.

FM1120200773030X

Fig. 106   Test C: System Overcharges, Battery Voltage More Than 15 Volts (Part 3 of 3). 2004 Sable & Taurus

CONDITIONS	DETAILS/RESULTS/ACTIONS
D1 CHECK THE FAULT CODES IN THE PCM	[3] Use the recorded PCM DTCs from the continuous and on-demand self-test. • Are any DTCs recorded? → **Yes** REFER to PCM Diagnostic Trouble Code (DTC) Index. → **No** GO to **D2**.
D2 CHECK THE SYSTEM FOR OVERCHARGING	

FM1120200774010X

Fig. 107 Test D: Charging System Warning Indicator Is On w/Engine Running, System Increases Voltage (Part 1 of 3). 2004 Sable & Taurus

CONDITIONS	DETAILS/RESULTS/ACTIONS
D5 CHECK THE GENERATOR OUTPUT [2] PCM C175 [3] Generator C102 (4V) or C1104 (2V)	[4] Verify the generator output. • Is the generator OK? → **Yes** GO to **D6**. → **No** INSTALL a new generator. Clear the DTCs. TEST the system for normal operation.
D6 CHECK FOR CORRECT MODULE OPERATION	[1] Check for: • corrosion • pushed-out pins [2] Connect any disconnected connectors. [3] Make sure all other system connectors are fully seated. [4] Operate the system and verify the concern is still present. • Is the concern still present? → **Yes** INSTALL a new PCM. REPEAT the PCM self-test. → **No** The system is operating correctly at this time. Concern may have been caused by a loose or corroded connector. CLEAR the DTCs. REPEAT the self-test.

FM1120200774030X

Fig. 107 Test D: Charging System Warning Indicator Is On w/Engine Running (System Increases Voltage, (Part 3 of 3). 2004 Sable & Taurus

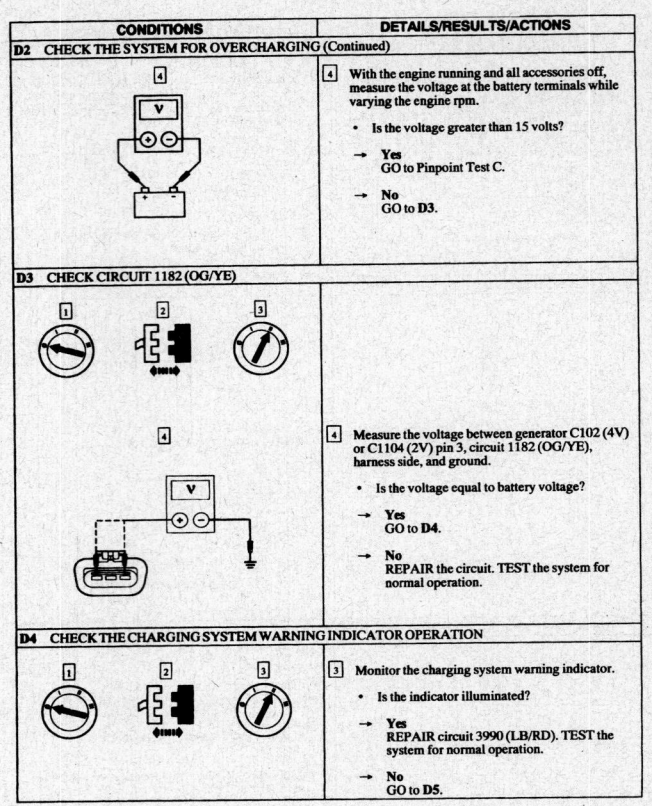

CONDITIONS	DETAILS/RESULTS/ACTIONS
D2 CHECK THE SYSTEM FOR OVERCHARGING (Continued)	[4] With the engine running and all accessories off, measure the voltage at the battery terminals while varying the engine rpm. • Is the voltage greater than 15 volts? → **Yes** GO to Pinpoint Test C. → **No** GO to **D3**.
D3 CHECK CIRCUIT 1182 (OG/YE)	[4] Measure the voltage between generator C102 (4V) or C1104 (2V) pin 3, circuit 1182 (OG/YE), harness side, and ground. • Is the voltage equal to battery voltage? → **Yes** GO to **D4**. → **No** REPAIR the circuit. TEST the system for normal operation.
D4 CHECK THE CHARGING SYSTEM WARNING INDICATOR OPERATION	[3] Monitor the charging system warning indicator. • Is the indicator illuminated? → **Yes** REPAIR circuit 3990 (LB/RD). TEST the system for normal operation. → **No** GO to **D5**.

FM1120200774020X

Fig. 107 Test D: Charging System Warning Indicator Is On w/Engine Running, System Increases Voltage (Part 2 of 3). 2004 Sable & Taurus

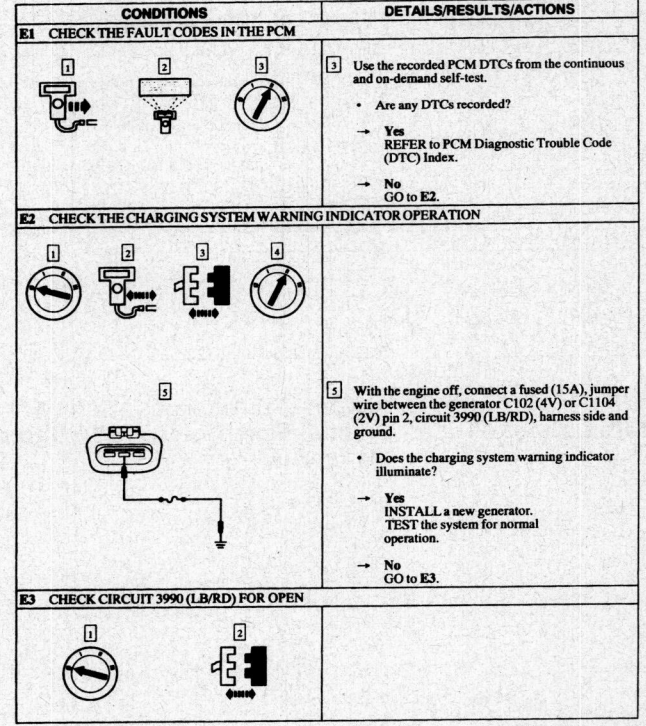

CONDITIONS	DETAILS/RESULTS/ACTIONS
E1 CHECK THE FAULT CODES IN THE PCM	[3] Use the recorded PCM DTCs from the continuous and on-demand self-test. • Are any DTCs recorded? → **Yes** REFER to PCM Diagnostic Trouble Code (DTC) Index. → **No** GO to **E2**.
E2 CHECK THE CHARGING SYSTEM WARNING INDICATOR OPERATION	[5] With the engine off, connect a fused (15A), jumper wire between the generator C102 (4V) or C1104 (2V) pin 2, circuit 3990 (LB/RD), harness side and ground. • Does the charging system warning indicator illuminate? → **Yes** INSTALL a new generator. TEST the system for normal operation. → **No** GO to **E3**.
E3 CHECK CIRCUIT 3990 (LB/RD) FOR OPEN	

FM1120200775010X

Fig. 108 Test E: Charging System Warning Indicator Is Off w/Ignition Switch In Run Position & Engine Off (Part 1 of 2). 2004 Sable & Taurus

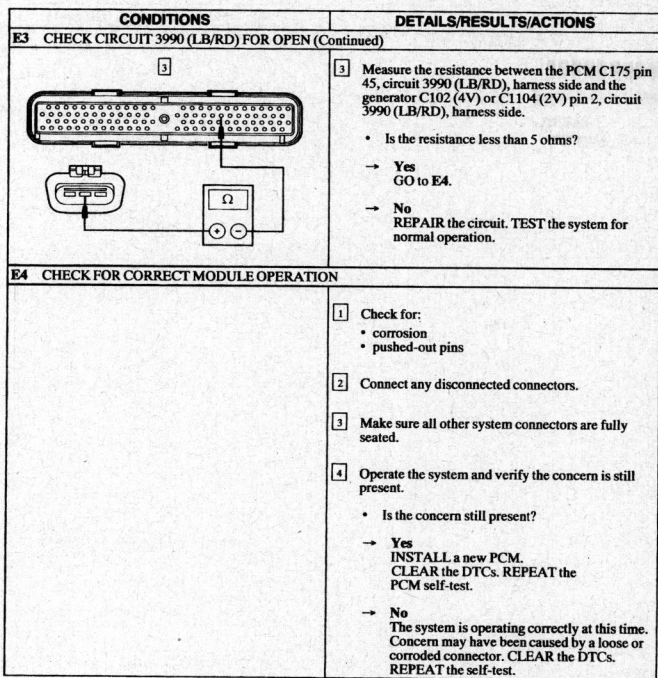

CONDITIONS	DETAILS/RESULTS/ACTIONS
E3 CHECK CIRCUIT 3990 (LB/RD) FOR OPEN (Continued)	
③	③ Measure the resistance between the PCM C175 pin 45, circuit 3990 (LB/RD), harness side and the generator C102 (4V) or C1104 (2V) pin 2, circuit 3990 (LB/RD), harness side. • Is the resistance less than 5 ohms? → **Yes** GO to E4. → **No** REPAIR the circuit. TEST the system for normal operation.
E4 CHECK FOR CORRECT MODULE OPERATION	
	① Check for: • corrosion • pushed-out pins ② Connect any disconnected connectors. ③ Make sure all other system connectors are fully seated. ④ Operate the system and verify the concern is still present. • Is the concern still present? → **Yes** INSTALL a new PCM. CLEAR the DTCs. REPEAT the PCM self-test. → **No** The system is operating correctly at this time. Concern may have been caused by a loose or corroded connector. CLEAR the DTCs. REPEAT the self-test.

FM1120200775020X

Fig. 108 Test E: Charging System Warning Indicator Is Off w/Ignition Switch In Run Position & Engine Off (Part 2 of 2). 2004 Sable & Taurus

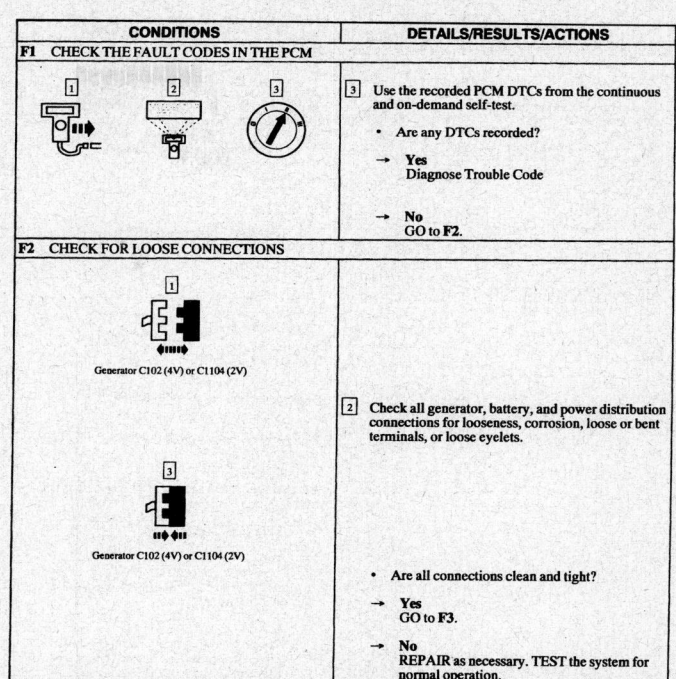

CONDITIONS	DETAILS/RESULTS/ACTIONS
F1 CHECK THE FAULT CODES IN THE PCM	
① ② ③	③ Use the recorded PCM DTCs from the continuous and on-demand self-test. • Are any DTCs recorded? → **Yes** Diagnose Trouble Code → **No** GO to F2.
F2 CHECK FOR LOOSE CONNECTIONS	
① Generator C102 (4V) or C1104 (2V) ③ Generator C102 (4V) or C1104 (2V)	② Check all generator, battery, and power distribution connections for looseness, corrosion, loose or bent terminals, or loose eyelets. • Are all connections clean and tight? → **Yes** GO to F3. → **No** REPAIR as necessary. TEST the system for normal operation.

FM1120200776010X

Fig. 109 Test F: Charging System Warning Indicator Lamp Flickers Or Is Intermittent (Part 1 of 4). 2004 Sable & Taurus

CONDITIONS	DETAILS/RESULTS/ACTIONS
F3 CHECK FUSE CONNECTION	
①	② With the engine running, check BJB fuse 2 (10A) in circuit 1182 (OG/YE) for looseness by wiggling the fuse and noting the charging system warning indicator lamp operation. • Does the charging system warning indicator lamp flicker? → **Yes** REPAIR loose fuse connections as necessary. TEST the system for normal operation. → **No** GO to F4.
F4 CHECK THE BATTERY VOLTAGE	
① ②	② With the engine running, and all accessories turned off, measure the voltage at the battery while varying the engine rpm. • Is the voltage greater than 15 volts? → **Yes** GO to Pinpoint Test C. → **No** GO to F5.

FM1120200776020X

Fig. 109 Test F: Charging System Warning Indicator Lamp Flickers Or Is Intermittent (Part 2 of 4). 2004 Sable & Taurus

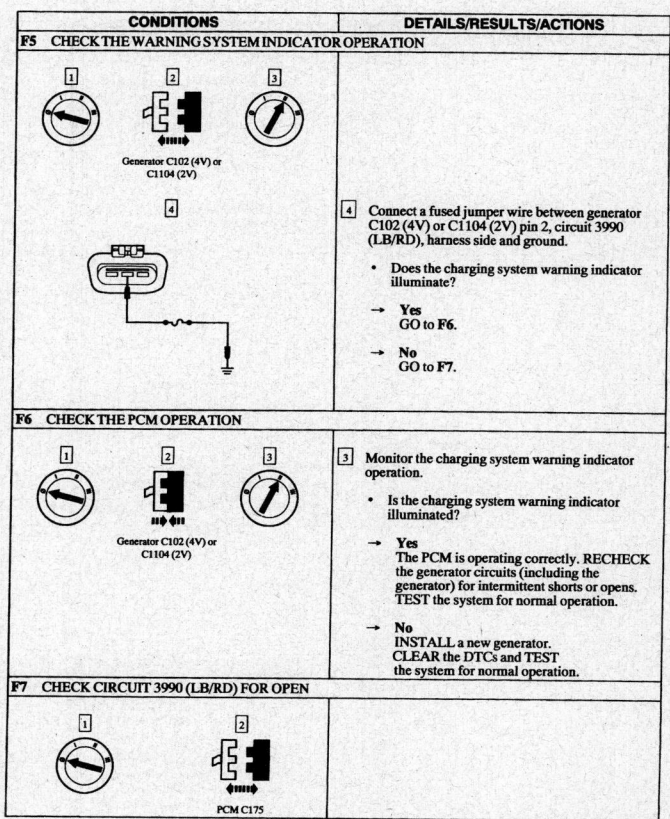

CONDITIONS	DETAILS/RESULTS/ACTIONS
F5 CHECK THE WARNING SYSTEM INDICATOR OPERATION	
① ② ③ Generator C102 (4V) or C1104 (2V) ④	④ Connect a fused jumper wire between generator C102 (4V) or C1104 (2V) pin 2, circuit 3990 (LB/RD), harness side and ground. • Does the charging system warning indicator illuminate? → **Yes** GO to F6. → **No** GO to F7.
F6 CHECK THE PCM OPERATION	
① ② ③ Generator C102 (4V) or C1104 (2V)	③ Monitor the charging system warning indicator operation. • Is the charging system warning indicator illuminated? → **Yes** The PCM is operating correctly. RECHECK the generator circuits (including the generator) for intermittent shorts or opens. TEST the system for normal operation. → **No** INSTALL a new generator. CLEAR the DTCs and TEST the system for normal operation.
F7 CHECK CIRCUIT 3990 (LB/RD) FOR OPEN	
① ② PCM C175	

FM1120200776030X

Fig. 109 Test F: Charging System Warning Indicator Lamp Flickers Or Is Intermittent (Part 3 of 4). 2004 Sable & Taurus

CONDITIONS	DETAILS/RESULTS/ACTIONS
F7 CHECK CIRCUIT 3990 (LB/RD) FOR OPEN (Continued)	

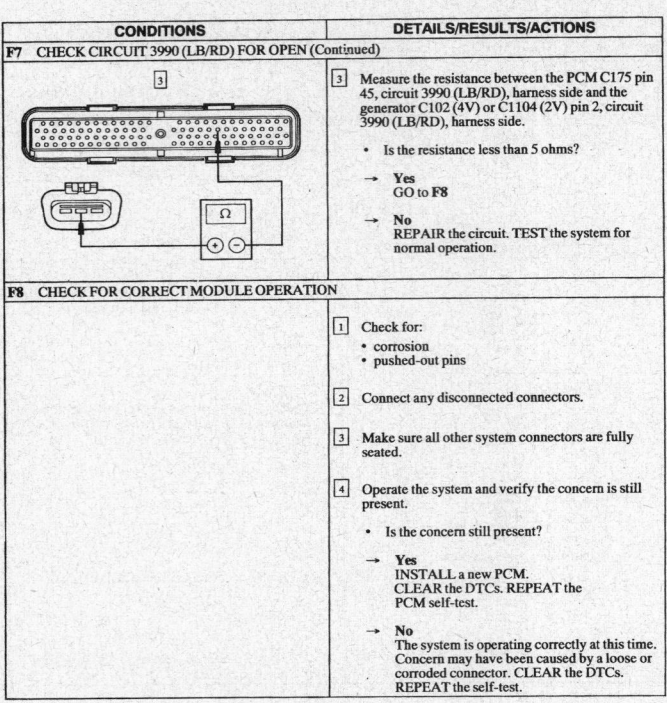

	[3] Measure the resistance between the PCM C175 pin 45, circuit 3990 (LB/RD), harness side and the generator C102 (4V) or C1104 (2V) pin 2, circuit 3990 (LB/RD), harness side. • Is the resistance less than 5 ohms? → **Yes** GO to **F8** → **No** REPAIR the circuit. TEST the system for normal operation.

CONDITIONS	DETAILS/RESULTS/ACTIONS
F8 CHECK FOR CORRECT MODULE OPERATION	
	[1] Check for: • corrosion • pushed-out pins [2] Connect any disconnected connectors. [3] Make sure all other system connectors are fully seated. [4] Operate the system and verify the concern is still present. • Is the concern still present? → **Yes** INSTALL a new PCM. CLEAR the DTCs. REPEAT the PCM self-test. → **No** The system is operating correctly at this time. Concern may have been caused by a loose or corroded connector. CLEAR the DTCs. REPEAT the self-test.

FM1120200776040X

Fig. 109   Test F: Charging System Warning Indicator Lamp Flickers Or Is Intermittent (Part 4 of 4). 2004 Sable & Taurus

CONDITIONS	DETAILS/RESULTS/ACTIONS
G1 CHECK FOR ACCESSORY DRIVE NOISE AND MOUNTING BRACKETS (Continued)	
	[2] Check the accessory mounting brackets and generator pulley for looseness or misalignment. • Is the accessory drive OK? → **Yes** GO to **G2**. → **No** REPAIR as necessary. TEST the system for normal operation.
G2 CHECK GENERATOR FOR ELECTRICAL NOISE	
Generator C102 (4V) or C1104 (2V)	• Is the noise still present? → **Yes** GO to **G3**. → **No** INSTALL a new generator. TEST the system for normal operation.
G3 CHECK GENERATOR FOR MECHANICAL NOISE	
	[3] Turn all accessories off. With the engine running, use a stethoscope or equivalent listening device to probe the generator for unusual mechanical noise. • Is the generator the noise source? → **Yes** INSTALL a new generator. TEST the system for normal operation. → **No** Diagnose source of engine noise.

FM1120200777020X

Fig. 110   Test G: Alternator Is Noisy (Part 2 of 2). 2004 Sable & Taurus

CONDITIONS	DETAILS/RESULTS/ACTIONS
G1 CHECK FOR ACCESSORY DRIVE NOISE AND MOUNTING BRACKETS	
	[1] Check the accessory drive belt for damage and correct installation

FM1120200777010X

Fig. 110   Test G: Alternator Is Noisy (Part 1 of 2). 2004 Sable & Taurus

CONDITIONS	DETAILS/RESULTS/ACTIONS
H1 VERIFY GENERATOR IS SOURCE OF RADIO INTERFERENCE	
Generator C102 (4V) or C1104 (2V)	[1] Start and run the engine. [2] Tune the radio to a station where the interference is present. • Is the interference present with the generator disconnected? → **Yes** Diagnosis and test the in-vehicle entertainment system. → **No** INSTALL a new generator. TEST the system for normal operation.

FM1120200778000X

Fig. 111   Test H: Radio Interference. 2004 Sable & Taurus

Test Step		Result / Action to Take
A1	CHECK THE BATTERY CONDITION	
	• Carry out the Battery — Condition Test to determine if the battery can hold a charge and is OK for use. • Did the battery pass the condition test?	**Yes** GO to A2. **No** INSTALL a new battery. TEST the system for normal operation.
A2	CHECK THE GENERATOR OUTPUT	
	• Carry out the Generator On-Vehicle Load Test and No Load Test. Refer to the Component Tests in this section. • Did the generator pass the component tests?	**Yes** GO to A3. **No** INSTALL a new generator. TEST the system for normal operation.

ARM0500000000753

Fig. 112   Test A: Battery Is Discharged Or Voltage Is Low (Part 1 of 3). 2005–07 Sable & Taurus

Test Step		Result / Action to Take
A3	CHECK FOR CURRENT DRAINS	
	• Carry out the Battery — Drain Testing. • Are any circuits causing excessive current drains?	**Yes** REPAIR as necessary. TEST the system for normal operation. **No** GO to A4.
A4	CHECK THE VEHICLE GROUNDS	
	• Key in START position. • Measure the voltage drop between the generator housing and the negative battery terminal. • Is the voltage drop less than 0.1 volt?	**Yes** GO to A5. **No** CHECK the engine ground, generator ground, and the battery ground for corrosion. TEST the system for normal operation.

ARM0500000000754

Fig. 112   Test A: Battery Is Discharged Or Voltage Is Low (Part 2 of 3). 2005–07 Sable & Taurus

Test Step	Result / Action to Take
A5 CHECK THE VOLTAGE DROP IN B+ CIRCUIT 36 (YE/WH) • Measure the voltage drop between the generator B+ C1104b, circuit 36 (YE/WH) and the positive battery terminal. 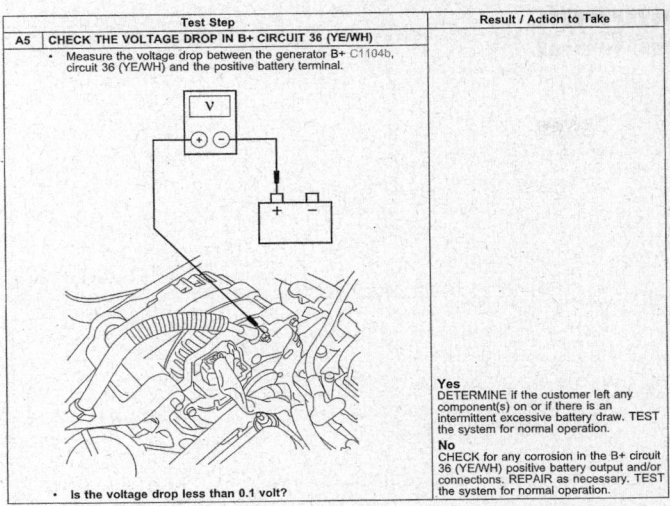 • Is the voltage drop less than 0.1 volt?	**Yes** DETERMINE if the customer left any component(s) on or if there is an intermittent excessive battery draw. TEST the system for normal operation. **No** CHECK for any corrosion in the B+ circuit 36 (YE/WH) positive battery output and/or connections. REPAIR as necessary. TEST the system for normal operation.

ARM0500000000755

Fig. 112 Test A: Battery Is Discharged Or Voltage Is Low (Part 3 of 3). 2005–07 Sable & Taurus

Test Step	Result / Action to Take
B3 CHECK THE GENERATOR INTEGRITY (Continued) • Measure and record the battery voltage. 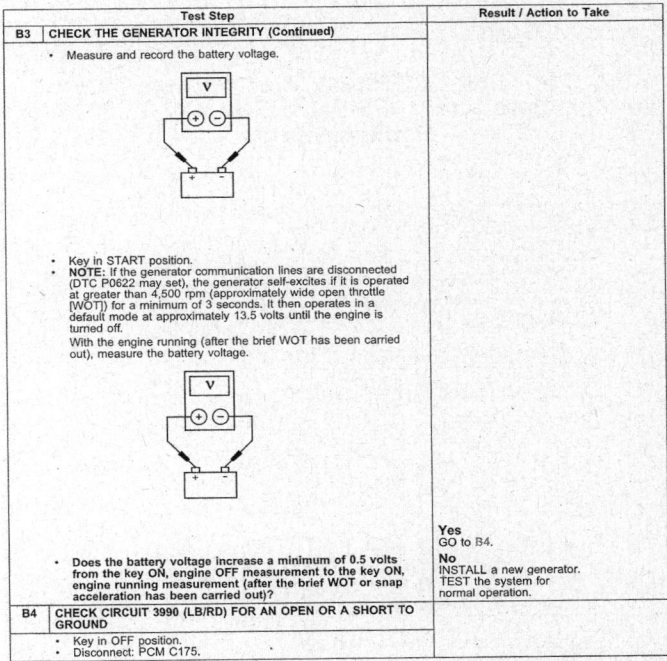 • Key in START position. • **NOTE:** If the generator communication lines are disconnected (DTC P0622 may set), the generator self-excites if it is operated at greater than 4,500 rpm (approximately wide open throttle (WOT)) for a minimum of 3 seconds. It then operates in a default mode at approximately 13.5 volts until the engine is turned off. With the engine running (after the brief WOT has been carried out), measure the battery voltage. • Does the battery voltage increase a minimum of 0.5 volts from the key ON, engine OFF measurement to the key ON, engine running measurement (after the brief WOT or snap acceleration has been carried out)?	**Yes** GO to B4. **No** INSTALL a new generator. TEST the system for normal operation.
B4 CHECK CIRCUIT 3990 (LB/RD) FOR AN OPEN OR A SHORT TO GROUND • Key in OFF position. • Disconnect: PCM C175.	

ARM0500000000757

Fig. 113 Test B: Charging System Warning Indicator Is On w/Engine Running, System Voltage Does Not Increase (Part 2 of 3). 2005–07 Sable & Taurus

Test Step	Result / Action to Take
B1 CHECK THE FAULT CODES IN THE POWERTRAIN CONTROL MODULE (PCM) • Connect the diagnostic tool. • Key in ON position. • Enter the following diagnostic mode on the diagnostic tool: Retrieve PCM DTCs. • Check the recorded PCM DTCs from the continuous and on-demand self-tests. • **Are any PCM DTCs recorded?**	**Yes** REFER to MOTOR's "Domestic Engine Performance & Driveability Manual" GO to B2. **No** GO to B2.
B2 CHECK THE GENERATOR B+ CIRCUIT 36 (YE/WH) FOR VOLTAGE • Key in OFF position. • Measure the voltage between the generator C1104b, circuit 36 (YE/WH), and ground. 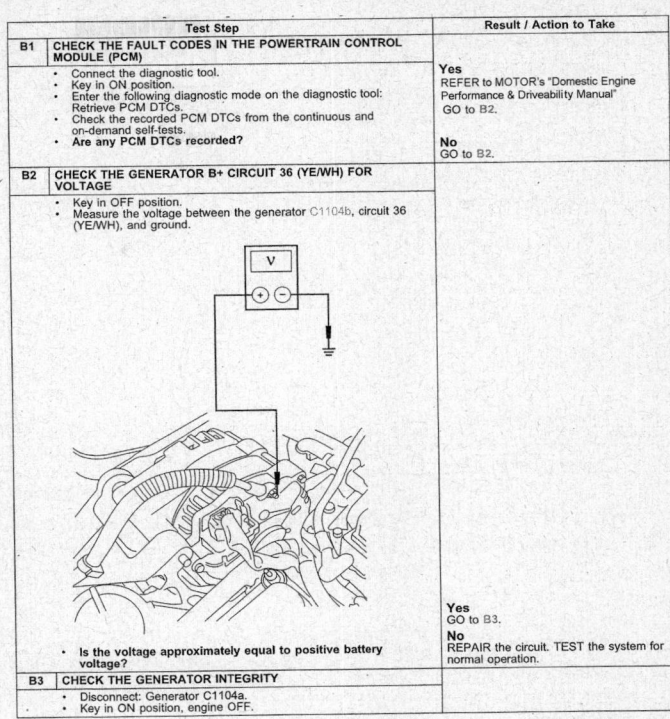 • Is the voltage approximately equal to positive battery voltage?	**Yes** GO to B3. **No** REPAIR the circuit. TEST the system for normal operation.
B3 CHECK THE GENERATOR INTEGRITY • Disconnect: Generator C1104a. • Key in ON position, engine OFF.	

ARM0500000000756

Fig. 113 Test B: Charging System Warning Indicator Is On w/Engine Running, System Voltage Does Not Increase (Part 1 of 3). 2005–07 Sable & Taurus

Test Step	Result / Action to Take
B4 CHECK CIRCUIT 3990 (LB/RD) FOR AN OPEN OR A SHORT TO GROUND (Continued) • Measure the resistance between the generator C1104a-2, circuit 3990 (LB/RD), harness side and the PCM C175-45, circuit 3990 (LB/RD), harness side; and between the generator C1104a-2, circuit 3990 (LB/RD), harness side and ground. 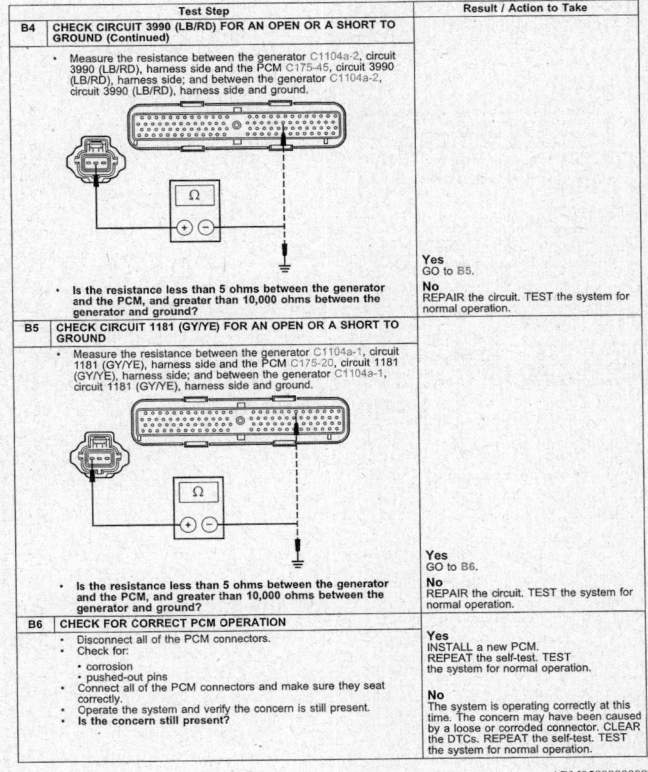 • Is the resistance less than 5 ohms between the generator and the PCM, and greater than 10,000 ohms between the generator and ground?	**Yes** GO to B5. **No** REPAIR the circuit. TEST the system for normal operation.
B5 CHECK CIRCUIT 1181 (GY/YE) FOR AN OPEN OR A SHORT TO GROUND • Measure the resistance between the generator C1104a-1, circuit 1181 (GY/YE), harness side and the PCM C175-20, circuit 1181 (GY/YE), harness side; and between the generator C1104a-1, circuit 1181 (GY/YE), harness side and ground. • Is the resistance less than 5 ohms between the generator and the PCM, and greater than 10,000 ohms between the generator and ground?	**Yes** GO to B6. **No** REPAIR the circuit. TEST the system for normal operation.

B6 CHECK FOR CORRECT PCM OPERATION
• Disconnect all of the PCM connectors.
• Check for:
  • corrosion
  • pushed-out pins
• Connect all of the PCM connectors and make sure they seat correctly.
• Operate the system and verify the concern is still present.
• Is the concern still present?
	Yes
	INSTALL a new PCM. REPEAT the self-test. TEST the system for normal operation.
	No
	The system is operating correctly at this time. The concern may have been caused by a loose or corroded connector. CLEAR the DTCs. REPEAT the self-test. TEST the system for normal operation.

ARM0500000000758

Fig. 113 Test B: Charging System Warning Indicator Is On w/Engine Running, System Voltage Does Not Increase (Part 3 of 3). 2005–07 Sable & Taurus

Test Step		Result / Action to Take
C1	CHECK THE FAULT CODES IN THE POWERTRAIN CONTROL MODULE (PCM) • Connect the diagnostic tool. • Key in ON position. • Enter the following diagnostic mode on the diagnostic tool: Retrieve PCM DTCs. • Check for recorded PCM DTCs from the continuous and on-demand self-tests. • **Are any PCM DTCs recorded?**	**Yes** REFER to MOTOR's "Domestic Engine Performance & Driveability Manual" GO to C2. **No** GO to C2.
C2	CHECK THE BATTERY VOLTAGE • Key in START position. • With the engine running and all the accessories turned off, measure the voltage at the battery while varying the engine rpm. • **Is the voltage greater than 15.5 volts?**	**Yes** GO to C3. **No** GO to C4.
C3	CHECK FOR A VOLTAGE DROP IN CIRCUIT 1182 (OG/YE) • Key in OFF position. • Disconnect: Generator C1104a.	

ARM0500000000759

Fig. 114   Test C: System Overcharges, Battery Voltage More Than 15.5 Volts (Part 1 of 3). 2005–07 Sable & Taurus

Test Step		Result / Action to Take
C5	CHECK THE GENERATOR INTEGRITY (Continued) • NOTE: If the generator communication lines are disconnected (DTC P0622 may be set), the generator self-excites if it is operated at greater than 4,500 rpm (approximately wide open throttle [WOT]) for a minimum of 3 seconds. It then operates in a default mode at approximately 13.5 volts until the engine is turned off. With the engine running (after the brief WOT has been carried out), measure the battery voltage. • **Does the battery voltage increase a minimum of 0.5 volts from the key ON, engine OFF measurement to the key ON, engine running measurement (after the brief WOT or snap acceleration has been carried out)?**	**Yes** GO to C6. **No** INSTALL a new generator. TEST for normal operation.

C6	CHECK FOR CORRECT PCM OPERATION
	• Disconnect all of the PCM connectors.
	• Check for:
	  • corrosion
	  • pushed-out pins
	• Connect all of the PCM connectors and make sure they seat correctly.
	• Operate the system and verify the concern is still present.
	• **Is the concern still present?**
		Yes
		INSTALL a new PCM. TEST the system for normal operation.
		
		No
		The system is operating correctly at this time. The concern may have been caused by a loose or corroded connector. CLEAR the DTCs. REPEAT the self-test. TEST the system for normal operation.

ARM0500000000761

Fig. 114   Test C: System Overcharges, Battery Voltage More Than 15.5 Volts (Part 3 of 3). 2005–07 Sable & Taurus

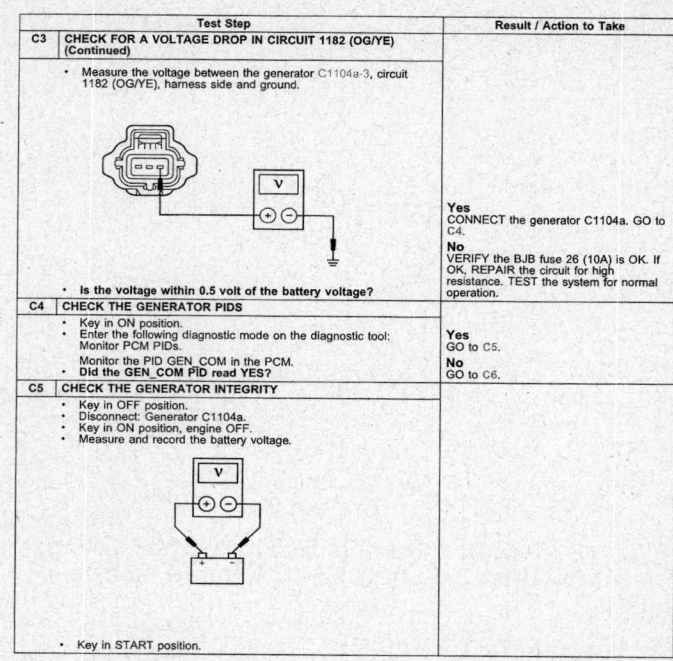

Test Step		Result / Action to Take
C3	CHECK FOR A VOLTAGE DROP IN CIRCUIT 1182 (OG/YE) (Continued) • Measure the voltage between the generator C1104a-3, circuit 1182 (OG/YE), harness side and ground. • **Is the voltage within 0.5 volt of the battery voltage?**	**Yes** CONNECT the generator C1104a. GO to C4. **No** VERIFY the BJB fuse 26 (10A) is OK. If OK, REPAIR the circuit for high resistance. TEST the system for normal operation.
C4	CHECK THE GENERATOR PIDS • Key in ON position. • Enter the following diagnostic mode on the diagnostic tool: Monitor PCM PIDs. Monitor the PID GEN_COM in the PCM. • **Did the GEN_COM PID read YES?**	**Yes** GO to C5. **No** GO to C6.
C5	CHECK THE GENERATOR INTEGRITY • Key in OFF position. • Disconnect: Generator C1104a. • Key in ON position, engine OFF. • Measure and record the battery voltage. • Key in START position.	

ARM0500000000760

Fig. 114   Test C: System Overcharges, Battery Voltage More Than 15.5 Volts (Part 2 of 3). 2005–07 Sable & Taurus

Test Step		Result / Action to Take
D1	CHECK THE FAULT CODES IN THE POWERTRAIN CONTROL MODULE (PCM) • Connect the diagnostic tool. • Key in ON position. • Enter the following diagnostic mode on the diagnostic tool: Retrieve PCM DTCs. • Check the recorded PCM DTCs from the continuous and on-demand self-tests. • **Are any PCM DTCs recorded?**	**Yes** REFER to MOTOR's "Domestic Engine Performance & Driveability Manual" GO to D2. **No** GO to D2.
D2	CHECK THE SYSTEM FOR OVERCHARGING • Key in START position. • With the engine running and all accessories off, measure the voltage at the battery terminals while varying the engine rpm. • **Is the voltage greater than 15.5 volts?**	**Yes** GO to Pinpoint Test C. **No** GO to D3.
D3	CHECK THE PCM PIDS • Enter the following diagnostic mode on the diagnostic tool: Monitor PCM PIDs. • With the engine running, monitor the generator output fault PID in the PCM. • **Does the PID read YES?**	**Yes** GO to D4. **No** Diagnose the charging system warning indicator.
D4	CHECK THE GENERATOR OUTPUT • Verify the generator output. Refer to the Component Tests, Generator On-Vehicle Tests in this section. • **Did the generator pass the component tests?**	**Yes** GO to D5. **No** INSTALL a new generator. CLEAR the DTCs. REPEAT the self-test. TEST the system for normal operation.

D5	CHECK FOR CORRECT PCM OPERATION
	• Key in OFF position.
	• Disconnect all of the PCM connectors.
	• Check for
	  • corrosion
	  • pushed-out pins
	• Connect all of the PCM connectors and make sure they seat correctly.
	• Operate the system and verify the concern is still present.
	• **Is the concern still present?**
		Yes
		INSTALL a new PCM. REPEAT the self-test. TEST the system for normal operation.
		
		No
		The system is operating correctly at this time. The concern may have been caused by a loose or corroded connector. CLEAR the DTCs. REPEAT the self-test. TEST the system for normal operation.

ARM0500000000762

Fig. 115   Test D: Charging System Warning Indicator Is On w/Engine Running, System Increases Voltage. 2005–07 Sable & Taurus

Test Step	Result / Action to Take
E1 CHECK THE CHARGING SYSTEM WARNING INDICATOR OPERATION • Connect the diagnostic tool. • Key in ON position. • Enter the following diagnostic mode on the diagnostic tool: Instrument Cluster Active Commands. • Using Instrument Cluster Active Commands, turn on the charging system warning indicator in the instrument cluster. • **Is the charging system warning indicator on?**	**Yes** GO to E2. **No** Diagnose the charging system warning indicator.

E2 CHECK FOR CORRECT PCM OPERATION
• Key in OFF position.
• Disconnect all of the PCM connectors.
• Check for
  • corrosion
  • pushed-out pins
• Connect all of the PCM connectors and make sure they seat correctly.
• Operate the system and verify the concern is still present.
• **Is the concern still present?**
	Yes
	INSTALL a new PCM. REPEAT the self-test. TEST the system for normal operation.
	
	No
	The system is operating correctly at this time. The concern may have been caused by a loose or corroded connector. CLEAR the DTCs. REPEAT the self-test. TEST the system for normal operation.

ARM0500000000763

Fig. 116 Test E: Charging System Warning Indicator Is Off w/Ignition Switch In Run Position & Engine Off. 2005–07 Sable & Taurus

Test Step	Result / Action to Take
G1 VERIFY THE GENERATOR IS THE SOURCE OF THE RADIO INTERFERENCE **NOTE:** If the original equipment manufactured (OEM) audio unit has been replaced with an aftermarket unit, the vehicle may not pass this test. Return the vehicle to OEM condition before following this pinpoint test. • Key in START position. • Start and run the engine. • Tune the radio to a station where the interference is present. • Key in OFF position. • Disconnect: Generator C1104b. • Key in START position. • With the engine running, determine if the interference is still present. • **Is the interference present with the generator disconnected?**	**Yes** Diagnosis and testing of the in-vehicle entertainment system. **No** INSTALL a new generator. TEST the system for normal operation.

ARM0500000000765

Fig. 118 Test G: Radio Interference. 2005–07 Sable & Taurus

Test Step	Result / Action to Take
F1 CHECK FOR ACCESSORY DRIVE NOISE AND MOUNTING BRACKETS • Key in OFF position. • Check the accessory drive belt for damage and correct installation. • Check the accessory mounting brackets and generator pulley for looseness or misalignment. • **Is the accessory drive OK?**	**Yes** GO to F2. **No** REPAIR as necessary. TEST the system for normal operation.
F2 CHECK THE GENERATOR FOR EXCESSIVE ELECTRICAL NOISE • Disconnect: Generator C1104b. • Key in START position. • With the engine running, determine if the generator is still noisy. • **Is the noise still present?**	**Yes** GO to F3. **No** INSTALL a new generator. TEST the system for normal operation.
F3 CHECK THE GENERATOR FOR MECHANICAL NOISE • Turn all of the electrical accessories off. With the engine running, use a stethoscope or equivalent listening device to probe the generator for unusual mechanical noise. • **Is the generator the noise source?**	**Yes** INSTALL a new generator. TEST the system for normal operation. **No** diagnose the source of the engine noise.

ARM0500000000764

Fig. 117 Test F: Alternator Is Noisy. 2005–07 Sable & Taurus

Test Step	Result / Action to Take
A1 CHECK THE BATTERY CONDITION • Carry out the Battery — Condition Test to determine if the battery can hold a charge and is OK for use. • **Does the battery pass the condition test?**	**Yes** GO to A2. **No** INSTALL a new battery. TEST the system for normal operation.
A2 CHECK THE GENERATOR OUTPUT • Carry out the Generator On-Vehicle Load Test and No Load Test. Refer to the Component Tests in this section. • **Does the generator pass the component tests?**	**Yes** GO to A3. **No** Go To Pinpoint Test B.
A3 CHECK FOR CURRENT DRAINS • Carry out the Battery — Drain Testing. Refer to the Component Tests in this section. • **Are any circuits causing excessive current drains?**	**Yes** REPAIR as necessary. TEST the system for normal operation. **No** GO to A4.
A4 CHECK THE VEHICLE GROUNDS • Key in START position. • Turn on accessory loads, such as high blower and high-beam headlamps. • With the engine running, measure the voltage drop between the generator housing and the negative battery terminal. • **Is the voltage drop less than 0.1 volt?**	**Yes** GO to A5. **No** CHECK the engine ground, generator ground and the battery ground for corrosion. TEST the system for normal operation.
A5 CHECK THE VOLTAGE DROP IN THE B+ CIRCUIT SDC02 (RD) • With the engine running and accessory loads ON, measure the voltage drop between generator B+ C102b, circuit SDC02 (RD) and the positive battery terminal. • **Is the voltage drop less than 0.5 volt?**	**Yes** CHECK if the customer left any electrical system(s) on or if there is an intermittent excessive battery draw. TEST the system for normal operation. **No** CHECK for any corrosion in the B+ SDC02 (RD), positive battery cable and/or connections. REPAIR as necessary. TEST the system for normal operation.

ARM0700000000405

Fig. 119 Test A: Battery Is Discharged Or Battery Voltage Is Low. 2008 Sable, Taurus & Taurus X

Test Step	Result / Action to Take
B1 CONFIRM THE BATTERY CONDITION • Carry out the Battery Condition Test. • **Is the battery OK?**	**Yes** GO to B2. **No** CORRECT the battery condition and GO to B2.
B2 CHECK BATTERY JUNCTION BOX (BJB) FUSE F17 (10A) • Check fuse: BJB F17 (10A). • **Is BJB fuse F17 (10A) OK?**	**Yes** GO to B3. **No** REPAIR circuit SBB17 (RD) and INSTALL a new fuse. INSPECT PCM and engine ground circuits and make sure they are securely attached. CLEAR the DTCs. REPEAT the self-test. TEST the system for normal operation.
B3 CHECK THE GENERATOR B+ CONNECTION • Key in OFF position. • Inspect generator C102b, B+ circuit SDC02 (RD) connection. Connection should be tight. • Measure the voltage between generator C102b, B+ circuit SDC02 (RD) and ground. • Is generator C102b connection tight and does the generator B+ measure battery voltage?	**Yes** GO to B4. **No** TIGHTEN the generator B+ connection or REPAIR the circuit. CLEAR the DTCs. REPEAT the self-test. TEST the system for normal operation.

B4 MONITOR THE PCM PID GENERATOR MONITOR WITH THE KEY ON/ENGINE OFF (KOEO)
• Key in ON position.
• Enter the following diagnostic mode on the diagnostic tool: Clear the PCM DTCs.
• Enter the following diagnostic mode on the diagnostic tool: Select PCM PIDs.
• **NOTE:** Many of the PCM PIDs selected will be monitored later in this pinpoint test.
• Select and monitor the following PCM PIDs:
  • Generator Monitor (GENMON).
  • Generator Command Duty Cycle GENCMD.
  • Generator Voltage Desired (GENVDSD).
  • Generator Fault Indicator Lamp (GEN_FL).
  • Engine Revolutions Per Minute (RPM).
  • Module Supply Voltage (VPWR).
• Monitor the GENMON PID.
• **Does the GENMON PID read 0%?**
	Yes
	GO to B5.
	
	No
	GO to B8.

ARM0700000000406

Fig. 120 Test B: Charging System Warning Indicator Is On And Any Charging System DTC Is Stored (Part 1 of 7). 2008 Sable, Taurus & Taurus X

B5 MONITOR THE PCM PID GENERATOR MONITOR WITH THE KEY ON/ENGINE RUNNING (KOER)

- Key in START position.
- With the engine at idle, wait 15 seconds for the GENVDSD PID to increase to greater than 13 volts.
- Monitor PID GENMON at idle and 3,000 rpm.
- **Does the GENMON PID read between 3% and 98% at engine idle speed and at 3,000 rpm?**

Yes
GO to B6.

No
GO to B8.

B6 MONITOR THE PCM PIDs GENERATOR MONITOR, MODULE SUPPLY VOLTAGE AND GENERATOR DESIRED VOLTAGE WITH THE ENGINE AT 3,000 RPM

- Turn all electrical accessories (lights, blower motor) off.
- NOTE: If GENMON PID does not remain below 85%, make sure that the battery is at an acceptable state of charge and that all electrical accessories are off.
- Increase the engine speed to 3,000 rpm (or road test).
- **Does the VPWR PID remain within ± 0.5 volt of the GENVDSD PID when the GENMON PID is less than 85%?**

Yes
GO to B7.

No
GO to B17.

B7 MONITOR THE PCM PIDs GENERATOR MONITOR, MODULE SUPPLY VOLTAGE AND GENERATOR DESIRED VOLTAGE WITH THE ENGINE AT IDLE

- Return the engine speed to idle.
- ⚠ CAUTION: On vehicles with low electrical loads, it may be necessary to add external loads (devices connected to power points) to determine the maximum GENMON value. GENMON value will not read between 95%-98% on a vehicle with minimal electrical accessories. As long as there is a significant increase in the GENMON PID following the procedure below, answer YES to the question.
- Determine the maximum GENMON PID value by lowering engine idle rpm to 500 rpm or less using output state control (OSC) and turn on all electrical accessories until the VPWR PID is less than the GENVDSD PID by at least 0.7 volt. Under this condition the GENMON PID should read between 95% and 98%.
- **Does the GENMON PID read between 95% and 98%?**

Yes
GO to B19.

No
GO to B17.

B8 CHECK THE VOLTAGE OUTPUTS FROM THE PCM

- Key in OFF position.
- Disconnect: Generator C102a.
- Key in ON position.
- Measure the voltage of the following circuits:

Expected Voltages

Generator Connector	Circuit	Expected Voltage (Approximate)
C102a-1	CDC15 (VT)	8-11 volts (should be less than battery voltage)
C102a-2	CDC10 (BU/OG)	0 volt
C102a-3	SBB17 (RD)	Battery voltage

- •
- **Are the voltages as indicated for each circuit?**

Yes
GO to B13.

If a fault is detected in the GENCOM circuit CDC10 (BU/OG) or GENMON circuit CDC15 (VT), GO to B9.

If a fault is detected in the A sense SBB17 (RD) circuit, GO to B12.

B9 CHECK CIRCUITS CDC10 (BU/OG) AND CDC15 (VT) FOR DAMAGE OR AN OPEN

- Key in OFF position.
- Disconnect: Generator C102a.

Yes
GO to B10.

ARM0700000000407

Fig. 120   Test B: Charging System Warning Indicator Is On And Any Charging System DTC Is Stored (Part 2 of 7). 2008 Sable, Taurus & Taurus X

- Disconnect: PCM C175b.
- Inspect the following for damaged or pushed-out pins:
  - PCM C175b-22, circuit CDC10 (BU/OG)
  - PCM C175b-23, circuit CDC15 (VT)
  - Generator C102a-2, circuit CDC10 (BU/OG)
  - Generator C102a-1, circuit CDC15 (VT)
- Measure the resistance between circuit C175b-22 and C102a-2.
- Measure the resistance between circuit C175b-23 and C102a-1.
- **Are the connectors and pins free of damage and are the resistances less than 5 ohms?**

No
REPAIR the affected circuit. CLEAR the DTCs. REPEAT the self-test. TEST the system for normal operation.

B10 CHECK CIRCUITS CDC10 (BU/OG) AND CDC15 (VT) FOR A SHORT TO VOLTAGE

- Key in ON position.
- Measure the voltage of the following circuits:
  - C102a-1, CDC15 (VT)
  - C102a-2, CDC10 (BU/OG)
- **Are the voltages approximately 0 volt?**

Yes
GO to B11.

No
REPAIR the affected circuits. CLEAR the DTCs. REPEAT the self-test. TEST the system for normal operation.

B11 CHECK CIRCUITS CDC10 (BU/OG) AND CDC15 (VT) FOR A SHORT TO GROUND

- Key in OFF position.
- Measure the resistance between the following circuits and ground and between each other:
  - C102a-1, CDC15 (VT)
  - C102a-2, CDC10 (BU/OG).
- **Are the resistances less than 5 ohms?**

Yes
GO to B24.

No
REPAIR the affected circuits. CLEAR the self-test. TEST the system for normal operation.

B12 CHECK CIRCUIT SBB17 (RD) FOR DAMAGE OR AN OPEN

- Key in OFF position.
- Disconnect: Generator C102a.
- Inspect C102a-3 for damaged or pushed-out pins.
- Measure the resistance of the circuit A sense SBB17 (RD) between the battery and C102a-3 generator connector.
- **Are the connectors and pins free of damage and are the resistances less than 5 ohms?**

Yes
GO to B24.

No
REPAIR the affected circuit. CLEAR the DTCs. REPEAT the self-test. TEST the system for normal operation.

B13 CHECK FOR SHORTED CIRCUITS

- Key in OFF position.
- Disconnect: Generator C102a.
- Verify that PID GENMON reads 100%.
- Carry out the wiggle test of wiring to determine if PID GENMON changes from 100%.
- **Does PID GENMON change from 100%?**

Yes
REPAIR short circuit on CDC15 (VT) C102a-1.

No
GO to B14.

ARM0700000000408

Fig. 120   Test B: Charging System Warning Indicator Is On And Any Charging System DTC Is Stored (Part 3 of 7). 2008 Sable, Taurus & Taurus X

B14 CHECK THE PCM PID GENERATOR MONITOR INPUT TO THE PCM

- Connect a fused (10A) jumper wire between generator C102a-1, circuit CDC15 (VT), harness side and ground.

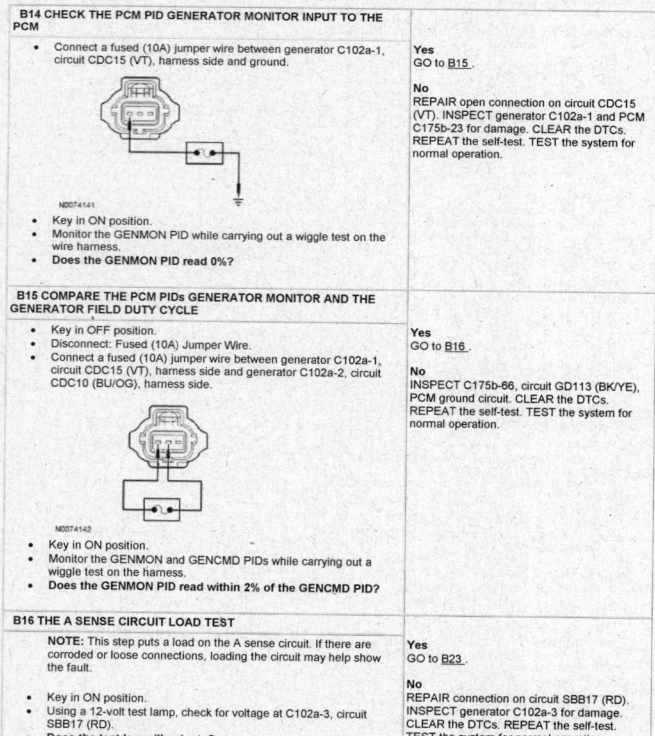

N0074141

- Key in ON position.
- Monitor the GENMON PID while carrying out a wiggle test on the wire harness.
- **Does the GENMON PID read 0%?**

Yes
GO to B15.

No
REPAIR open connection on circuit CDC15 (VT). INSPECT generator C102a-1 and PCM C175b-23 for damage. CLEAR the DTCs. REPEAT the self-test. TEST the system for normal operation.

B15 COMPARE THE PCM PIDs GENERATOR MONITOR AND THE GENERATOR FIELD DUTY CYCLE

- Key in OFF position.
- Disconnect: Fused (10A) Jumper Wire.
- Connect a fused (10A) jumper wire between generator C102a-1, circuit CDC15 (VT), harness side and generator C102a-2, circuit CDC10 (BU/OG), harness side.

N0074142

- Key in ON position.
- Monitor the GENMON and GENCMD PIDs while carrying out a wiggle test on the harness.
- **Does the GENMON PID read within 2% of the GENCMD PID?**

Yes
GO to B16.

No
INSPECT C175b-66, circuit GD113 (BK/YE), PCM ground circuit. CLEAR the DTCs. REPEAT the self-test. TEST the system for normal operation.

B16 THE A SENSE CIRCUIT LOAD TEST

- NOTE: This step puts a load on the A sense circuit. If there are corroded or loose connections, loading the circuit may help show the fault.
- Key in ON position.
- Using a 12-volt test lamp, check for voltage at C102a-3, circuit SBB17 (RD).
- **Does the test lamp illuminate?**

Yes
GO to B23.

No
REPAIR connection on circuit SBB17 (RD). INSPECT generator C102a-3 for damage. CLEAR the DTCs. REPEAT the self-test. TEST the system for normal operation.

ARM0700000000409

Fig. 120   Test B: Charging System Warning Indicator Is On And Any Charging System DTC Is Stored (Part 4 of 7). 2008 Sable, Taurus & Taurus X

B17 CHECK THE PCM VPWR PID

- With the engine running, measure the battery voltage.

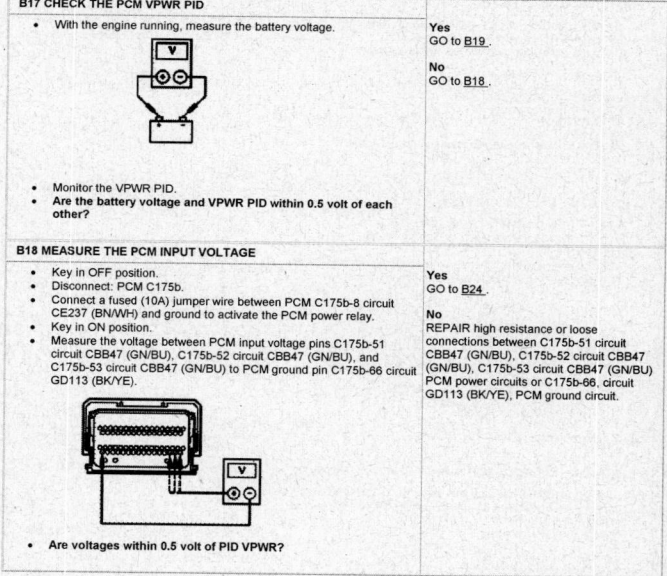

- Monitor the VPWR PID.
- **Are the battery voltage and VPWR PID within 0.5 volt of each other?**

Yes
GO to B19.

No
GO to B18.

B18 MEASURE THE PCM INPUT VOLTAGE

- Key in OFF position.
- Disconnect: PCM C175b.
- Connect a fused (10A) jumper wire between PCM C175b-8 circuit CE237 (BN/WH) and ground to activate the PCM power relay.
- Key in ON position.
- Measure the voltage between PCM input voltage pins C175b-51 circuit CBB47 (GN/BU), C175b-52 circuit CBB47 (GN/BU), and C175b-53 circuit CBB47 (GN/BU) to PCM ground pin C175b-66 circuit GD113 (BK/YE).

- **Are voltages within 0.5 volt of PID VPWR?**

Yes
GO to B24.

No
REPAIR high resistance or loose connections between C175b-51 circuit CBB47 (GN/BU), C175b-52 circuit CBB47 (GN/BU), C175b-53 circuit CBB47 (GN/BU) PCM power circuits or C175b-66, circuit GD113 (BK/YE), PCM ground circuit.

ARM0700000000410

Fig. 120   Test B: Charging System Warning Indicator Is On And Any Charging System DTC Is Stored (Part 5 of 7). 2008 Sable, Taurus & Taurus X

B19 CHECK THE GENERATOR B+ RESISTANCE

- Key in OFF position.
- Disconnect: Battery.
- Disconnect: Generator C102b.
- Measure the resistance between generator C102b circuit SDC02 (RD), component side and the generator housing.

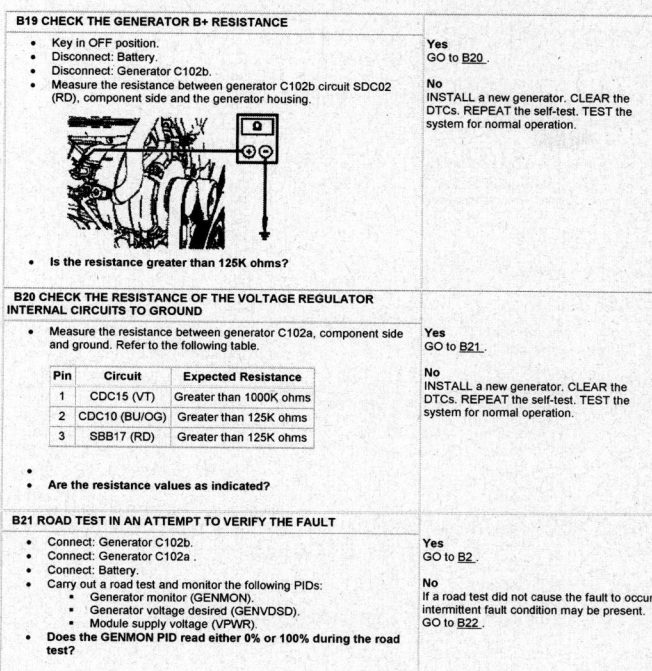

- Is the resistance greater than 125K ohms?

Yes
GO to B20 .

No
INSTALL a new generator. CLEAR the DTCs. REPEAT the self-test. TEST the system for normal operation.

B20 CHECK THE RESISTANCE OF THE VOLTAGE REGULATOR INTERNAL CIRCUITS TO GROUND

- Measure the resistance between generator C102a, component side and ground. Refer to the following table.

Pin	Circuit	Expected Resistance
1	CDC15 (VT)	Greater than 1000K ohms
2	CDC10 (BU/OG)	Greater than 125K ohms
3	SBB17 (RD)	Greater than 125K ohms

- Are the resistance values as indicated?

Yes
GO to B21 .

No
INSTALL a new generator. CLEAR the DTCs. REPEAT the self-test. TEST the system for normal operation.

B21 ROAD TEST IN AN ATTEMPT TO VERIFY THE FAULT

- Connect: Generator C102b.
- Connect: Generator C102a .
- Connect: Battery.
- Carry out a road test and monitor the following PIDs:
  - Generator monitor (GENMON).
  - Generator voltage desired (GENVDSD).
  - Module supply voltage (VPWR).
- Does the GENMON PID read either 0% or 100% during the road test?

Yes
GO to B2 .

No
If a road test did not cause the fault to occur, intermittent fault condition may be present. GO to B22 .

ARM0700000000411

Fig. 120   Test B: Charging System Warning Indicator Is On And Any Charging System DTC Is Stored (Part 6 of 7). 2008 Sable, Taurus & Taurus X

B22 USE THE VEHICLE DATA RECORDER (VDR) TO CAPTURE INTERMITTENT FAULT CONDITION

- Connect a VDR to the vehicle and set up to capture the following PIDs:
  - Generator monitor GENMON.
  - Generator command duty cycle GENCMD.
  - Generator voltage desired (GENVDSD).
  - Generator fault indicator lamp (GEN_FL).
  - Engine revolutions per minute (RPM).
  - Module supply voltage (VPWR).
- Set the VDR to trigger if any of the following events occur during vehicle operation (waiting 15 seconds after start):
  - VPWR PID reads greater than 15.2 volts.
  - GENMON PID reads 0% or 100%.
- Road test the vehicle.
- Was a fault captured by the VDR?

Yes
RECORD any values from the VDR that may have been captured. If no charging system DTCs (see PCM DTC Chart) are present, Go To Pinpoint Test C . If any charging system DTCs (see PCM DTC Chart) are present, GO to B3 .

No
No problem found at this time. CLEAR the DTCs. REPEAT the self-test. TEST the system for normal operation.

B23 CHECK THE CHARGING SYSTEM CIRCUITS FOR INTERMITTENT FAULTS

- Key in OFF position.
- Connect: Generator C102b.
- Connect: Generator C102a .
- Connect: PCM C175b.
- Connect the diagnostic tool.
- Key in START position.
- With the engine running, monitor the charging system warning indicator lamp and the scan tool for DTCs.
- Does the charging system warning indicator lamp illuminate and does any charging system DTC (see PCM DTC Chart) get stored into memory?

Yes
INSTALL a new generator. CLEAR the DTCs. REPEAT the self-test. TEST the system for normal operation.

No
The fault is not present and cannot be recreated at this time. This may indicate an intermittent fault. GO to B19 .

B24 CHECK THE CHARGING SYSTEM CIRCUITS FOR INTERMITTENT FAULTS

- Key in OFF position.
- Connect: Generator C102b.
- Connect: Generator C102a.
- Connect: PCM C175b.
- Connect the diagnostic tool.
- Key in START position.
- With the engine running, monitor the charging system warning indicator lamp and the scan tool for DTCs.
- Does the charging system warning indicator lamp illuminate and does any charging system DTC (see PCM DTC Chart) get stored into memory?

Yes
INSTALL a new PCM. REFLASH the PCM.

No
The fault is not present and cannot be recreated at this time. This may indicate an intermittent fault. GO to B19 .

ARM0700000000412

Fig. 120   Test B: Charging System Warning Indicator Is On And Any Charging System DTC Is Stored (Part 7 of 7). 2008 Sable, Taurus & Taurus X

Test Step	Result / Action to Take

C1 CHECK THE BATTERY CONDITION

- Carry out the Battery — Condition Test to determine if the battery can hold a charge and is OK for use.
- Does the battery pass the condition test?

Yes
GO to C2 .

No
INSTALL a new battery. TEST the system for normal operation.

C2 CHECK THE GENERATOR B+ CONNECTION

- Key in OFF position.
- Inspect generator C102b connection. Connection should be tight.
- Measure the voltage between generator C102b, circuit SDC02 (RD) and ground.
- Is generator C102b connection tight and does the generator B+ measure battery voltage?

Yes
GO to C3 .

No
TIGHTEN the generator B+ connection or REPAIR the circuit. CLEAR the DTCs. REPEAT the self-test. TEST the system for normal operation.

C3 CHECK THE VOLTAGE DROP IN THE B+ CIRCUIT SDC02 (RD)

- With the engine running, measure the voltage drop between generator B+ C102b, circuit SDC02 (RD) and the positive battery terminal.
- Is the voltage drop less than 0.5 volt?

Yes
GO to C4 .

No
CHECK for any corrosion in the B+ C102b, circuit SDC02 (RD), positive battery cable and/or connections. REPAIR as necessary. TEST the system for normal operation.

C4 CHECK THE DTCs IN THE PCM

- Key in OFF position.
- Connect the diagnostic tool.
- Key in START position.
- Enter the following diagnostic mode on the diagnostic tool: Retrieve PCM DTCs.
- Use the recorded PCM DTCs from the continuous and on-demand self tests.
- Are any PCM DTCs recorded?

Yes
For all DTCs REFER to the DTC Chart. If any charging system DTCs (see DTC Chart) are present, Go To Pinpoint Test B . If referred here by the PC/ED, GO to C5 .

No
GO to C5 .

ARM0700000000413

Fig. 121   Test B: Charging System Warning Indicator Is On And Any Charging System DTC Is Stored (Part 1 of 3). 2008 Sable, Taurus & Taurus X

C5 MONITOR PID GEN_FL

- With the engine running, monitor PID GEN_FL.
- Does PID GEN_FL show fault?

Yes
GO to C6 .

No
REPAIR/INSTALL a new instrument cluster, instrument cluster-to-PCM connection or the PCM. TEST the system for normal operation.

C6 MONITOR PID VPWR

- With the engine running, monitor PID VPWR, GEN_FL, GENVDSD.
- Is PIDs VPWR greater than 15.6 volts?

Yes
GO to C7 .

No
GO to C8 .

C7 CHECK THE PCM VPWR PID

- With the engine running, measure the battery voltage.

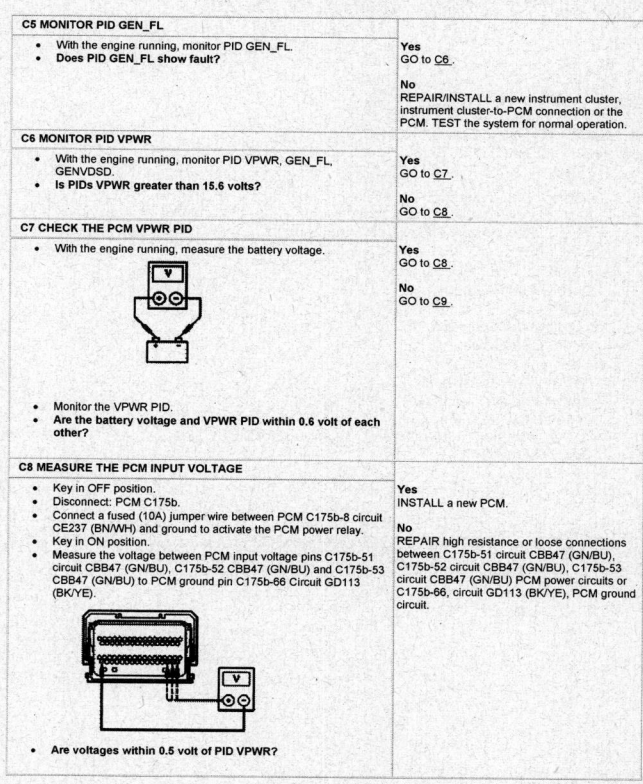

- Monitor the VPWR PID.
- Are the battery voltage and VPWR PID within 0.6 volt of each other?

Yes
GO to C8 .

No
GO to C9 .

C8 MEASURE THE PCM INPUT VOLTAGE

- Key in OFF position.
- Disconnect: PCM C175b.
- Connect a fused (10A) jumper wire between PCM C175b-8 circuit CE237 (BN/WH) and ground to activate the PCM power relay.
- Key in ON position.
- Measure the voltage between PCM input voltage pins C175b-51 circuit CBB47 (GN/BU), C175b-52 circuit CBB47 (GN/BU) and C175b-53 CBB47 (GN/BU) to PCM ground pin C175b-66 Circuit GD113 (BK/YE).

- Are voltages within 0.5 volt of PID VPWR?

Yes
INSTALL a new PCM.

No
REPAIR high resistance or loose connections between C175b-51 circuit CBB47 (GN/BU), C175b-52 circuit CBB47 (GN/BU), C175b-53 circuit CBB47 (GN/BU) PCM power circuits or C175b-66, circuit GD113 (BK/YE), PCM ground circuit.

ARM0700000000414

Fig. 121   Test C: Charging System Warning Indicator Is On With Engine Running And No Charging System DTCs Present (Part 2 of 3). 2008 Sable, Taurus & Taurus X

Test Step	Result / Action to Take
C9 MONITOR THE PCM PID GENERATOR MONITOR WITH THE KEY ON/ENGINE RUNNING	
• Key in START position. • With the engine at idle, wait 15 seconds for the GENVDSD PID to increase to greater than 13 volts. • Monitor PID GENMON at idle and 3000 rpm. • **Does the GENMON PID read between 3% and 98% at engine idle speed and at 3,000 rpm?**	**Yes** GO to C10. **No** GO to C11.
C10 MONITOR PID GENVDSD	
• With the engine running, monitor PID GENVDSD. • **Is PID GENVDSD greater than 15.2 volts?**	**Yes** REPAIR connection on circuit SBB17 (RD). INSPECT generator C102a-3 for damage. CLEAR the DTCs. REPEAT the self-test. TEST the system for normal operation. If no problems are found, INSTALL a new generator. TEST the system for normal operation. **No** INSTALL a new PCM.
C11 CHECK FOR SHORTED CIRCUITS	
• Key in OFF position. • Disconnect: Generator C102a. • Key in ON position. • Verify that PID GENMON reads 100%. • Carry out the wiggle test of wiring to determine if PID GENMON changes from 100%. • **Does PID GENMON change from 100%?**	**Yes** REPAIR short circuit on C102a-1 CDC15 (VT). **No** GO to C12.
C12 CHECK THE PCM PID GENERATOR MONITOR INPUT TO THE PCM	
• Connect a fused (10A) jumper wire between generator C102a-1, circuit CDC15 (VT), harness side and ground. *(connector diagram)* • Key in ON position. • Monitor the GENMON PID while carrying out a wiggle test on the wire harness. • **Does the GENMON PID read 0%?**	**Yes** REPAIR open connection on circuit CDC15 (VT) C102a-1, and PCM C175b-23. CLEAR the DTCs. REPEAT the self-test. TEST the system for normal operation. **No** INSTALL a new generator. CLEAR the DTCs. REPEAT the self-test. TEST the system for normal operation.

ARM0700000000415

Fig. 121 Test C: Charging System Warning Indicator Is On With Engine Running And No Charging System DTCs Present (Part 3 of 3). 2008 Sable, Taurus & Taurus X

Test Step	Result / Action to Take
E1 VERIFY THE GENERATOR IS THE SOURCE OF THE RADIO INTERFERENCE	
NOTE: If the OEM audio unit has been replaced with an aftermarket unit, the vehicle may not pass this test. Return the vehicle to OEM condition before following this pinpoint test. • Key in START position. • Start and run the engine. • Tune the audio unit to a station where the interference is present. • Key in OFF position. • Disconnect: Generator C102b. • Key in START position. • With the engine running, determine if the interference is still present. • **Is the interference present with the generator disconnected?**	**Yes** REFER to Audio Systems for diagnosis and testing of the in-vehicle entertainment system. **No** INSTALL a new generator.

ARM0700000000417

Fig. 123 Test E: Radio Interference. 2008 Sable, Taurus & Taurus X

Test Step	Result / Action to Take
D1 CHECK FOR ACCESSORY DRIVE BELT NOISE AND LOOSE MOUNTING BRACKETS	
• Key in OFF position. • Check the accessory drive belt for damage and correct installation. • Check the accessory mounting brackets and generator pulley for looseness or misalignment. • **Is the accessory drive OK?**	**Yes** GO to D2. **No** REPAIR as necessary. TEST the accessory drive system. TEST the system for normal operation.
D2 CHECK THE GENERATOR MOUNTING	
• Check the generator mounting for loose bolts or misalignment. • **Is the generator mounted correctly?**	**Yes** GO to D3. **No** REPAIR as necessary. TEST the system for normal operation.
D3 CHECK THE GENERATOR FOR ELECTRICAL NOISE	
• Disconnect: Generator C102b. • Key in START position. • With the engine running, use a stethoscope or equivalent listening device to probe the generator. • **Is the noise still present?**	**Yes** GO to D4. **No** INSTALL a new generator. TEST the system for normal operation.
D4 CHECK THE GENERATOR FOR MECHANICAL NOISE	
• With the engine running, use a stethoscope or equivalent listening device to probe the generator and the accessory drive area for unusual mechanical noise. • **Is the generator the noise source?**	**Yes** INSTALL a new generator. TEST the system for normal operation. **No** Diagnose the source of the engine noise.

ARM0700000000416

Fig. 122 Test D: Generator Is Noisy. 2008 Sable, Taurus & Taurus X

Test Step	Result / Action to Take
F1 CHECK FOR DTCs	
• Key in OFF position. • Connect the diagnostic tool. • Enter the following diagnostic mode on the diagnostic tool. Retrieve All Continuous DTCs. • **Is DTC B1318 or B1676 present in only one module?**	**Yes** If DTC B1317 or B1676 are recorded in only one module, GO to F2. **No** If DTC B1318 or B1676 are recorded in more than one module, Go To Pinpoint Test B.
F2 CHECK THE BATTERY VOLTAGE	
• Measure the battery voltage between the positive and negative battery posts with the key ON engine OFF (KOEO), and with the engine running, all accessory loads OFF. • **Is the battery voltage between 10 and 13 volts with KOEO, and between 11 and 17 volts with the engine running?**	**Yes** GO to F3. **No** CHECK and/or REPAIR the charging system as necessary. TEST the system for normal operation. CLEAR the DTCs. REPEAT the self-test.
F3 CHECK THE VOLTAGE TO THE MODULE	
• Key in OFF position. • Disconnect: Affected module which recorded the DTC B1317 or B1676. • Key in ON position. • Measure all of the affected module's power circuits, harness side to ground. Refer to affected module Wiring Diagrams Cell for schematic and connector information. • **Is the voltage greater than 10 volts?**	**Yes** GO to F4. **No** REPAIR the module power circuit(s). CLEAR the DTCs. REPEAT the self-test.
F4 CHECK THE MODULE GROUNDS	
• Key in OFF position. • Measure the resistance between all of the affected module's ground circuits, harness side to ground. Refer to affected module Wiring Diagrams Cell for schematic and connector information. • **Is the resistance less than 5 ohms?**	**Yes** GO to F5. **No** REPAIR the module ground circuit(s). CLEAR the DTCs. REPEAT the self-test.
F5 CHECK THE MODULE FOR CORRECT OPERATION	

• Key in OFF position.
• Disconnect: All of the affected module connectors.
• Check the connector and module for:
  ▪ corrosion.
  ▪ pushed-out or damaged pins.
  ▪ connector or module damage.
• Connect: All of the affected module connectors.
• Clear all DTCs.
• Operate the system and verify the concern is still present.
• **Is the concern still present?**
	Yes
	INSTALL a new module. REFER to the removal and installation procedure in the affected module's section. CLEAR the DTCs. REPEAT the self-test.
	
	No
	The system is operating correctly at this time. The concern may have been the result of a loose connection, may recently have had a discharged battery or may have been jump started. CLEAR the DTCs. REPEAT the self-test.

ARM0700000000418

Fig. 124 Test F: DTC B1318 Or B1676, Battery Voltage Low Or Battery Voltage Out Of Range. 2008 Sable, Taurus & Taurus X

Test Step	Result / Action to Take
A1 CHECK BATTERY CONDITION	
• Carry out the Battery — Condition Test to determine if the battery can hold a charge and is OK for use. • **Is the battery OK?**	**Yes** GO to A2 . **No** INSTALL a new battery. TEST the system for normal operation.
A2 CHECK THE GENERATOR OUTPUT	
• Carry out the Generator On-Vehicle Tests—Load Test and No Load Test. • **Is the generator OK?**	**Yes** GO to A3 . **No** Go To Pinpoint Test B .
A3 CHECK FOR CURRENT DRAINS	
• Carry out the Battery — Drain Testing. • **Are there any excessive current drains?**	**Yes** REPAIR as necessary. TEST the system for normal operation. **No** Go To Pinpoint Test B .

ARM66FM000000162

Fig. 125   Test A: Battery Is Discharged Or Battery Voltage Is Low. 2004 Town Car

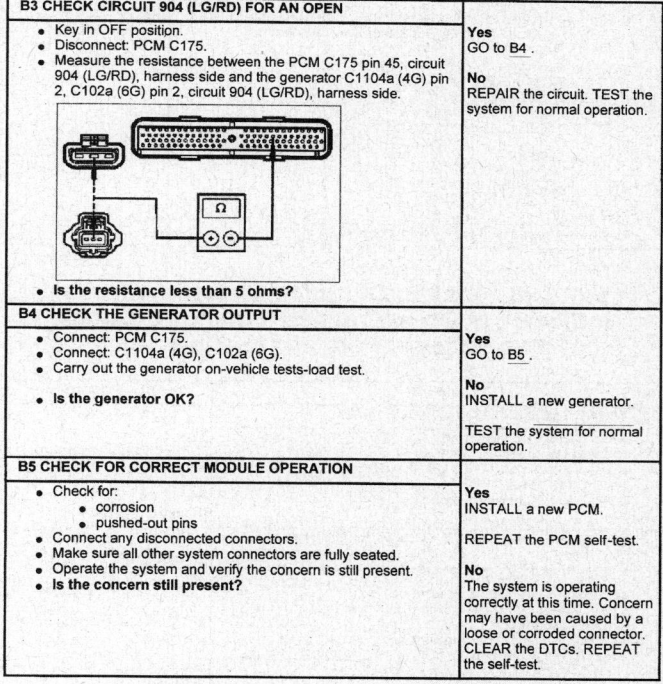

Test Step	Result / Action to Take
B3 CHECK CIRCUIT 904 (LG/RD) FOR AN OPEN	
• Key in OFF position. • Disconnect: PCM C175. • Measure the resistance between the PCM C175 pin 45, circuit 904 (LG/RD), harness side and the generator C1104a (4G) pin 2, C102a (6G) pin 2, circuit 904 (LG/RD), harness side. • **Is the resistance less than 5 ohms?**	**Yes** GO to B4 . **No** REPAIR the circuit. TEST the system for normal operation.
B4 CHECK THE GENERATOR OUTPUT	
• Connect: PCM C175. • Connect: C1104a (4G), C102a (6G). • Carry out the generator on-vehicle tests-load test. • **Is the generator OK?**	**Yes** GO to B5 . **No** INSTALL a new generator. TEST the system for normal operation.
B5 CHECK FOR CORRECT MODULE OPERATION	

• Check for:
   • corrosion
   • pushed-out pins
 • Connect any disconnected connectors.
 • Make sure all other system connectors are fully seated.
 • Operate the system and verify the concern is still present.
 • **Is the concern still present?**
	Yes
	 INSTALL a new PCM.
	
	 REPEAT the PCM self-test.
	
	 No
	 The system is operating correctly at this time. Concern may have been caused by a loose or corroded connector. CLEAR the DTCs. REPEAT the self-test.

ARM66FM000000164

Fig. 126   Test B: Charging System Warning Indicator Is On w/Engine Running, Charging System Voltage Does Not Increase (Part 2 of 2). 2004 Town Car

Test Step	Result / Action to Take
B1 CHECK THE FAULT CODES IN THE PCM	
• Connect the diagnostic tool. • Key in ON position. • Use the recorded PCM DTCs from the continuous and on-demand self-test. • **Are any DTCs recorded?**	**Yes** REFER to PCM Diagnostic Trouble Code (DTC) Index. **No** GO to B2 .
B2 CHECK CIRCUIT 904 (LG/RD)	
• Key in OFF position. • Disconnect the diagnostic tool. • Disconnect: Generator C1104a (4G), C102a (6G). • Key in ON position. • Measure the voltage between the generator C1104a (4G) pin 2, C102a (6G) pin 2, circuit 904 (LG/RD), harness side and ground. • **Is the voltage 0 volts?**	**Yes** GO to B3 . **No** GO to B4 .

ARM66FM000000163

Fig. 126   Test B: Charging System Warning Indicator Is On w/Engine Running, Charging System Voltage Does Not Increase (Part 1 of 2). 2004 Town Car

Test Step	Result / Action to Take
C1 CHECK THE FAULT CODES IN THE PCM	
• Connect the diagnostic tool. • Key in ON position. • Use the recorded PCM DTCs from the continuous and on-demand self-test. • **Are any DTCs recorded?**	**Yes** REFER to PCM Diagnostic Trouble Code (DTC) Index. **No** GO to C2 .
C2 CHECK THE BATTERY VOLTAGE	
• Key in OFF position. • Disconnect the diagnostic tool. • Key in START position. • With the engine running and all accessories turned off, measure the voltage at the battery while varying the engine rpm. • **Is the voltage greater than 15.5 volts?**	**Yes** GO to C3 . **No** GO to C4 .

ARM66FM000000165

Fig. 127   Test C: Charging System Overcharges, Battery Voltage More Than 15.5 Volts (Part 1 of 2). 2004 Town Car

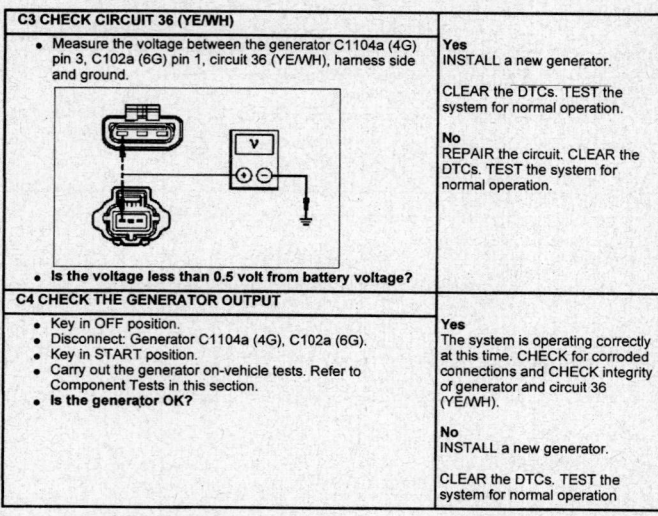

C3 CHECK CIRCUIT 36 (YE/WH)	
• Measure the voltage between the generator C1104a (4G) pin 3, C102a (6G) pin 1, circuit 36 (YE/WH), harness side and ground. • Is the voltage less than 0.5 volt from battery voltage?	**Yes** INSTALL a new generator. CLEAR the DTCs. TEST the system for normal operation. **No** REPAIR the circuit. CLEAR the DTCs. TEST the system for normal operation.
C4 CHECK THE GENERATOR OUTPUT	
• Key in OFF position. • Disconnect: Generator C1104a (4G), C102a (6G). • Key in START position. • Carry out the generator on-vehicle tests. Refer to Component Tests in this section. • Is the generator OK?	**Yes** The system is operating correctly at this time. CHECK for corroded connections and CHECK integrity of generator and circuit 36 (YE/WH). **No** INSTALL a new generator. CLEAR the DTCs. TEST the system for normal operation

ARM66FM000000166

Fig. 127 Test C: Charging System Overcharges, Battery Voltage More Than 15.5 Volts (Part 2 of 2). 2004 Town Car

D4 CHECK THE CHARGING SYSTEM WARNING INDICATOR OPERATION	
• Key in OFF position. • Disconnect: PCM C175. • Key in ON position. • Monitor the charging system warning indicator. • Is the indicator illuminated?	**Yes** REPAIR circuit 904 (LG/RD) for a short to ground. TEST the system for normal operation. **No** GO to D5 .
D5 CHECK THE GENERATOR OUTPUT	
• Key in OFF position. • Connect: PCM C175. • Connect: Generator C1104a (4G), C102a (6G). • Carry out generator on-vehicle tests. • Is the generator OK?	**Yes** GO to D6 . **No** INSTALL a new generator. Clear the DTCs. TEST the system for normal operation.
D6 CHECK FOR CORRECT MODULE OPERATION	

• Check for:
  • corrosion
  • pushed-out pins
• Connect any disconnected connectors.
• Make sure all other system connectors are fully seated.
• Operate the system and verify the concern is still present.
• Is the concern still present?
	Yes
	INSTALL a new PCM. REPEAT the PCM self-test.
	
	No
	The system is operating correctly at this time. Concern may have been caused by a loose or corroded connector. CLEAR the DTCs. REPEAT the self-test.

ARM66FM000000168

Fig. 128 Test D: Charging System Warning Indicator Is On w/Engine Running & Battery Increases Voltage (Part 2 of 2). 2004 Town Car

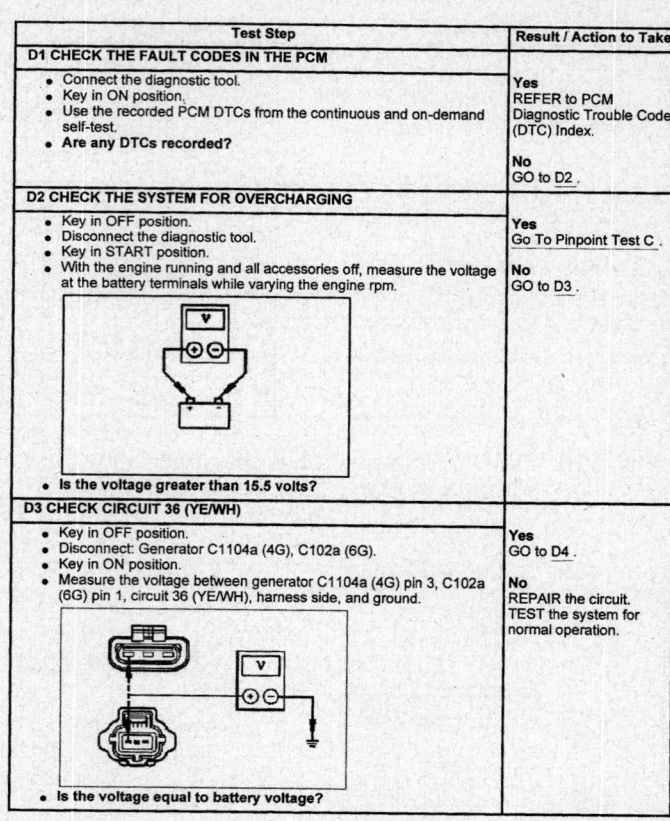

Test Step	Result / Action to Take
D1 CHECK THE FAULT CODES IN THE PCM	
• Connect the diagnostic tool. • Key in ON position. • Use the recorded PCM DTCs from the continuous and on-demand self-test. • **Are any DTCs recorded?**	**Yes** REFER to PCM Diagnostic Trouble Code (DTC) Index. **No** GO to D2 .
D2 CHECK THE SYSTEM FOR OVERCHARGING	
• Key in OFF position. • Disconnect the diagnostic tool. • Key in START position. • With the engine running and all accessories off, measure the voltage at the battery terminals while varying the engine rpm. • Is the voltage greater than 15.5 volts?	**Yes** Go To Pinpoint Test C . **No** GO to D3 .
D3 CHECK CIRCUIT 36 (YE/WH)	
• Key in OFF position. • Disconnect: Generator C1104a (4G), C102a (6G). • Key in ON position. • Measure the voltage between generator C1104a (4G) pin 3, C102a (6G) pin 1, circuit 36 (YE/WH), harness side, and ground. • Is the voltage equal to battery voltage?	**Yes** GO to D4 . **No** REPAIR the circuit. TEST the system for normal operation.

ARM66FM000000167

Fig. 128 Test D: Charging System Warning Indicator Is On w/Engine Running & Battery Increases Voltage (Part 1 of 2). 2004 Town Car

Test Step	Result / Action to Take
E1 CHECK THE FAULT CODES IN THE PCM	
• Connect the diagnostic tool. • Key in ON position. • Use the recorded PCM DTCs from the continuous and on-demand self-test. • **Are any DTCs recorded?**	**Yes** REFER to PCM Diagnostic Trouble Code (DTC) Index. **No** GO to E2 .
E2 CHECK THE CHARGING SYSTEM WARNING INDICATOR OPERATION	
• Key in OFF position. • Disconnect the diagnostic tool. • Disconnect: Generator C1104a (4G), C102a (6G). • Key in ON position. • With the engine off, connect a fused (15A) jumper wire between the generator C1104a (4G) pin 2, C102a (6G) pin 2, circuit 904 (LG/RD), harness side and ground. • Does the charging system warning indicator illuminate?	**Yes** INSTALL a new generator. TEST the system for normal operation. **No** GO to E3 .
E3 CHECK FOR CORRECT MODULE OPERATION	

• Check for:
  • corrosion
  • pushed-out pins
• Connect any disconnected connectors.
• Make sure all other system connectors are fully seated.
• Operate the system and verify the concern is still present.
• Is the concern still present?
	Yes
	INSTALL a new PCM. REPEAT the PCM self-test.
	
	No
	The system is operating correctly at this time. Concern may have been caused by a loose or corroded connector. CLEAR the DTCs. REPEAT the self-test.

ARM66FM000000169

Fig. 129 Test E: Charging System Warning Indicator Is Off w/Ignition Switch In Run Position & Engine Is Off. 2004 Town Car

Test Step	Result / Action to Take
F1 CHECK THE FAULT CODES IN THE PCM	
• Connect the diagnostic tool. • Key in ON position. • Use the recorded PCM DTCs from the continuous and on-demand self-test. • **Are any DTCs recorded?**	**Yes** REFER to PCM Diagnostic Trouble Code (DTC) Index. **No** GO to F2 .
F2 CHECK FOR LOOSE CONNECTIONS	
• Disconnect: Generator C1104a (4G), C102a (6G). • Check all generator, battery, and power distribution connections for looseness, corrosion, loose or bent terminals, or loose eyelets. • Connect: Generator C1104a (4G), C102a (6G). • **Are all connections clean and tight?**	**Yes** GO to F3 . **No** REPAIR as necessary. TEST the system for normal operation.
F3 CHECK FUSE CONNECTION	
• Key in START position. • With the engine running, check BJB fuse 13 (15A) in circuit 36 (YE/WH) for looseness by wiggling the fuse and noting the charging system warning indicator lamp operation. • **Does the charging system warning indicator lamp flicker?**	**Yes** REPAIR loose fuse connections as necessary. TEST the system for normal operation. **No** GO to F4 .
F4 CHECK THE BATTERY VOLTAGE	
• Key in START position. • With the engine running, and all accessories turned off, measure the voltage at the battery while varying the engine rpm. 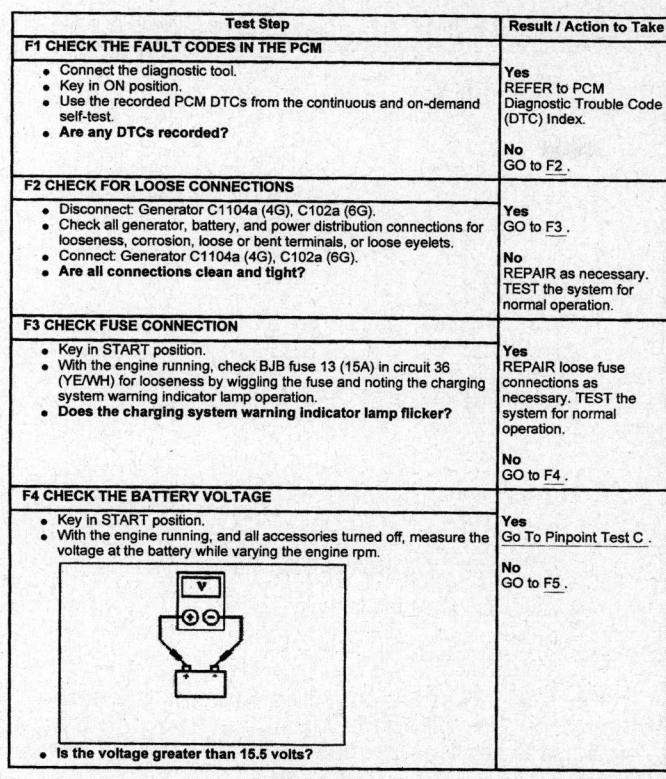 • **Is the voltage greater than 15.5 volts?**	**Yes** Go To Pinpoint Test C . **No** GO to F5 .

ARM66FM000000170

Fig. 130   Test F: Charging System Warning Indicator Lamp Flickers Or Is Intermittent (Part 1 of 2). 2004 Town Car

Test Step	Result / Action to Take
F5 CHECK THE WARNING SYSTEM INDICATOR OPERATION	
• Key in OFF position. • Disconnect: Generator C1104a (4G), C102a (6G). • Key in ON position. • Connect a fused jumper wire between generator C1104a (4G) pin 2, C102a (6G) pin 2, circuit 904 (LG/RD), harness side and ground. 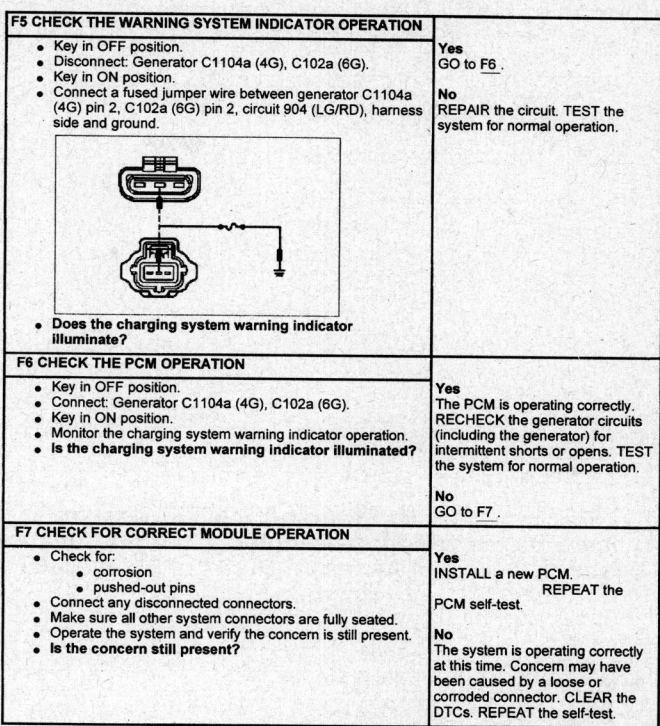 • **Does the charging system warning indicator illuminate?**	**Yes** GO to F6 . **No** REPAIR the circuit. TEST the system for normal operation.
F6 CHECK THE PCM OPERATION	
• Key in OFF position. • Connect: Generator C1104a (4G), C102a (6G). • Key in ON position. • Monitor the charging system warning indicator operation. • **Is the charging system warning indicator illuminated?**	**Yes** The PCM is operating correctly. RECHECK the generator circuits (including the generator) for intermittent shorts or opens. TEST the system for normal operation. **No** GO to F7 .
F7 CHECK FOR CORRECT MODULE OPERATION	

• Check for:
  • corrosion
  • pushed-out pins
• Connect any disconnected connectors.
• Make sure all other system connectors are fully seated.
• Operate the system and verify the concern is still present.
• **Is the concern still present?**
	Yes
	INSTALL a new PCM. REPEAT the PCM self-test.
	
	No
	The system is operating correctly at this time. Concern may have been caused by a loose or corroded connector. CLEAR the DTCs. REPEAT the self-test.

ARM66FM000000171

Fig. 130   Test F: Charging System Warning Indicator Lamp Flickers Or Is Intermittent (Part 2 of 2). 2004 Town Car

Test Step	Result / Action to Take
G1 CHECK FOR ACCESSORY DRIVE NOISE AND MOUNTING BRACKETS	
• Check the accessory drive belt for damage and correct installation. • Check the accessory mounting brackets and generator pulley for looseness or misalignment. • **Is the accessory drive OK?**	**Yes** GO to G2 . **No** REPAIR as necessary. TEST the system for normal operation.
G2 CHECK GENERATOR FOR ELECTRICAL NOISE	
• Disconnect: Generator C1104a (4G), C102a (6G). • Key in START position. • With the engine running, • **Is the noise still present?**	**Yes** GO to G3 . **No** INSTALL a new generator. TEST the system for normal operation.
G3 CHECK GENERATOR FOR MECHANICAL NOISE	
• Key in OFF position. • Key in START position. • With the engine running, use a stethoscope or equivalent listening device to probe the generator for unusual mechanical noise. • **Is the generator the noise source?**	**Yes** INSTALL a new generator. TEST the system for normal operation. **No** diagnose the source of the engine noise.

ARM66FM000000172

Fig. 131   Test G: Alternator Is Noisy. 2004 Town Car

Test Step	Result / Action to Take
H1 VERIFY GENERATOR IS SOURCE OF RADIO INTERFERENCE	
• Key in START position. • Start and run the engine. • Tune the radio to a station where the interference is present. • Key in OFF position. • Disconnect: Generator C1104 (4G), C102a (6G). • Key in START position. • **Is the interference present with the generator disconnected?**	**Yes** diagnose and test the in-vehicle entertainment system. **No** INSTALL a new generator. TEST the system for normal operation.

ARM66FM000000173

Fig. 132   Test H: Radio Interference. 2004 Town Car

	Test Step	Result / Action to Take
A1	**CHECK THE BATTERY CONDITION**	
	• Carry out the Battery — Condition Test to determine if the battery can hold a charge and is OK for use. • **Does the battery pass the condition test?**	**Yes** GO to A2. **No** INSTALL a new battery. TEST the system for normal operation.
A2	**CHECK THE GENERATOR OUTPUT**	
	• Carry out the Generator On-Vehicle Load Test and No Load Test. Refer to the Component Tests in this section. • **Does the generator pass the component tests?**	**Yes** GO to A3. **No** INSTALL a new generator. TEST the system for normal operation.
A3	**CHECK FOR CURRENT DRAINS**	
	• Carry out the Battery — Drain Testing • **Are any circuits causing excessive current drains?**	**Yes** REPAIR as necessary. TEST the system for normal operation. **No** GO to A4.
A4	**CHECK THE VEHICLE GROUNDS**	
	• Key in START position. • With the engine running, measure the voltage drop between the generator housing and the negative battery terminal. • **Is the voltage drop less than 0.1 volt?**	**Yes** GO to A5. **No** CHECK the engine ground, generator ground and the battery ground for corrosion. TEST the system for normal operation.
A5	**CHECK THE VOLTAGE DROP IN THE B+ CIRCUIT 2037 (RD)**	
	• With the engine running, measure the voltage drop between the generator B+ C102b, circuit 2037 (RD) and the positive battery terminal. • **Is the voltage drop less than 0.1 volt?**	**Yes** CHECK if the customer left any component(s) on or if there is an intermittent excessive battery draw. TEST the system for normal operation. **No** CHECK for any corrosion in the generator B+ circuit 2037 (RD), positive battery cable and/or connections. REPAIR or REPLACE the battery cables. TEST the system for normal operation.

ARM0500000000766

Fig. 133   Test A: Battery Is Discharged Or Battery Voltage Is Low. 2005–07 Town Car

Test Step	Result / Action to Take
B1 **CHECK THE DIAGNOSTIC TROUBLE CODES (DTCS) IN THE PCM** • Key in OFF position. • Connect the diagnostic tool. • Key in ON position. • Enter the following diagnostic mode on the diagnostic tool: Retrieve PCM DTCs. • Check for recorded PCM DTCs from the continuous and on-demand self-tests. • **Are any PCM DTCs recorded?**	**Yes** REFER to MOTOR's "Domestic Engine Performance & Driveability Manual" GO to B2. **No** GO to B2.
B2 **CHECK THE GENERATOR B+ CIRCUIT 2037 (RD) FOR VOLTAGE** • Key in OFF position. • Measure the voltage between the generator C102b-, circuit 2037 (RD) and ground. 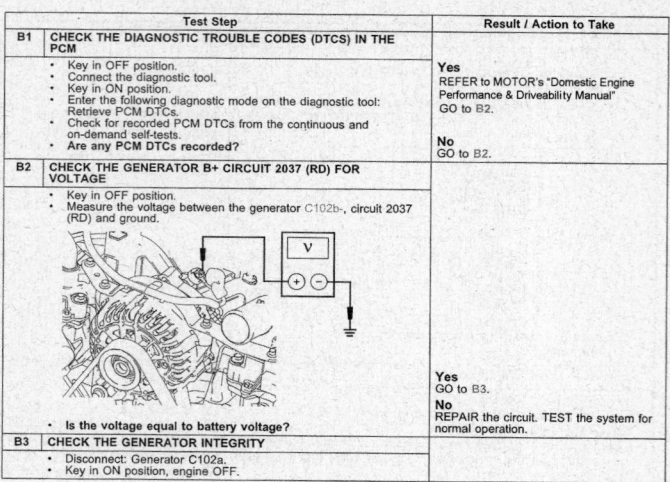 • **Is the voltage equal to battery voltage?**	**Yes** GO to B3. **No** REPAIR the circuit. TEST the system for normal operation.
B3 **CHECK THE GENERATOR INTEGRITY** • Disconnect: Generator C102a. • Key in ON position, engine OFF.	

ARM0500000000767

Fig. 134   Test B: Charging System Warning Indicator Is On w/Engine Running, Charging System Voltage Does Not Increase (Part 1 of 3). 2005–07 Town Car

Test Step	Result / Action to Take
B4 **CHECK CIRCUIT 1816 (YE/LB) FOR AN OPEN OR A SHORT TO GROUND (Continued)** • Measure the resistance between the generator C102a-2, circuit 1816 (YE/LB), harness side and the PCM C175t-19, circuit 1816 (YE/LB), harness side; and between the generator C102a-2, circuit 1816 (YE/LB), harness side and ground. 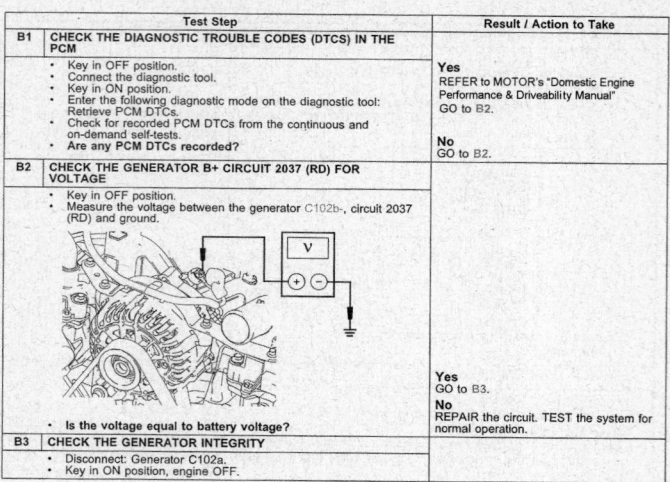 • **Is the resistance less than 5 ohms between the generator and the PCM, and greater than 10,000 ohms between the generator and ground?**	**Yes** GO to B5. **No** REPAIR the circuit. TEST the system for normal operation.
B5 **CHECK CIRCUIT 1817 (YE) FOR AN OPEN OR A SHORT TO GROUND** • Measure the resistance between the generator C102a-1, circuit 1817 (YE), harness side and the PCM C175t-38, circuit 1817 (YE), harness side; and between the generator C102a-1, circuit 1817 (YE), harness side and ground 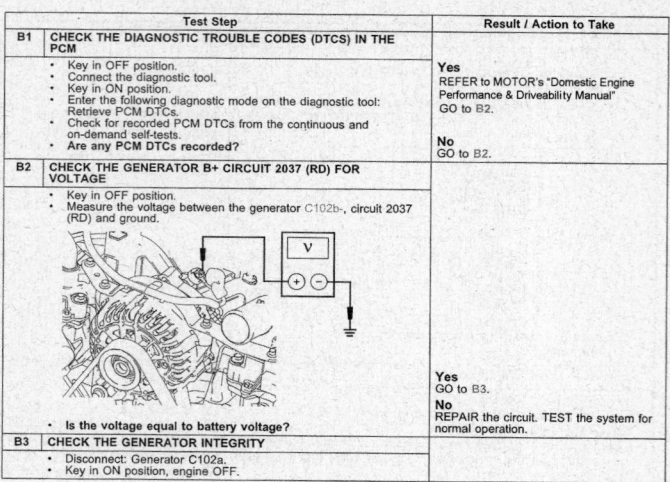 • **Is the resistance less than 5 ohms between the generator and the PCM, and greater than 10,000 ohms between the generator and ground?**	**Yes** GO to B6. **No** REPAIR the circuit. TEST the system for normal operation.

B6 **CHECK FOR CORRECT PCM OPERATION**
• Disconnect all of the PCM connectors.
• Check for:
  • corrosion
  • pushed-out pins
• Connect all of the PCM connectors and make sure they seat correctly.
• Operate the system and verify the concern is still present.
• **Is the concern still present?**
	Yes
	INSTALL a new PCM. REPEAT the self-test. TEST the system for normal operation.
	No
	The system is operating correctly at this time. The concern may have been caused by a loose or corroded connector. CLEAR the DTCs. REPEAT the self-test. TEST the system for normal operation.

ARM0500000000769

Fig. 134   Test B: Charging System Warning Indicator Is On w/Engine Running, Charging System Voltage Does Not Increase (Part 3 of 3). 2005–07 Town Car

Test Step	Result / Action to Take
B3 **CHECK THE GENERATOR INTEGRITY (Continued)** • Measure and record the battery voltage. 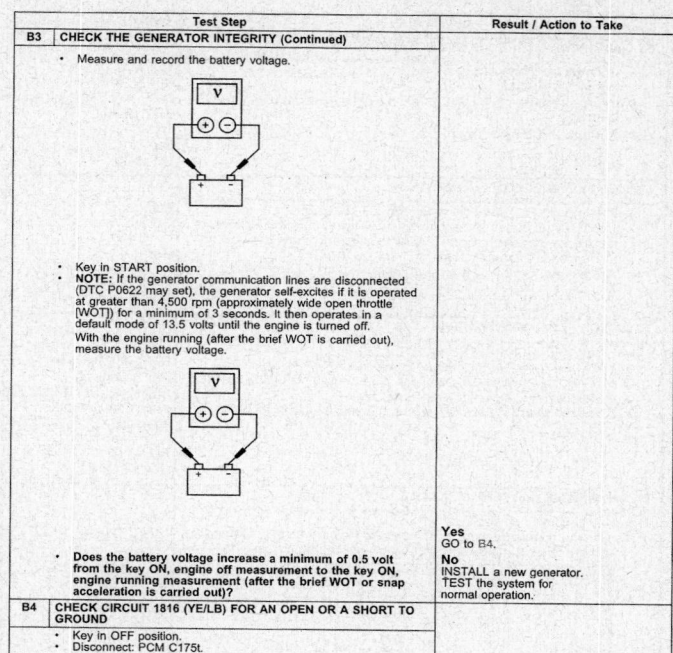 • Key in START position. • **NOTE:** If the generator communication lines are disconnected (DTC P0622 may set), the generator self-excites if it is operated at greater than 4,500 rpm (approximately wide open throttle [WOT]) for a minimum of 3 seconds. It then operates in a default mode of 13.5 volts until the engine is turned off. With the engine running (after the brief WOT is carried out), measure the battery voltage. • **Does the battery voltage increase a minimum of 0.5 volt from the key ON, engine off measurement to the key ON, engine running measurement (after the brief WOT or snap acceleration is carried out)?**	**Yes** GO to B4. **No** INSTALL a new generator. TEST the system for normal operation.
B4 **CHECK CIRCUIT 1816 (YE/LB) FOR AN OPEN OR A SHORT TO GROUND** • Key in OFF position. • Disconnect: PCM C175t.	

ARM0500000000768

Fig. 134   Test B: Charging System Warning Indicator Is On w/Engine Running, Charging System Voltage Does Not Increase (Part 2 of 3). 2005–07 Town Car

Test Step	Result / Action to Take
C1 **CHECK THE DIAGNOSTIC TROUBLE CODES (DTCS) IN THE PCM** • Key in OFF position. • Connect the diagnostic tool. • Key in ON position. • Enter the following diagnostic mode on the diagnostic tool: Retrieve PCM DTCs. • Check for recorded PCM DTCs from the continuous and on-demand self-tests. • **Are any PCM DTCs recorded?**	**Yes** REFER to MOTOR's "Domestic Engine Performance & Driveability Manual" GO to C2. **No** GO to C2.
C2 **CHECK THE BATTERY VOLTAGE** • Key in OFF position. • Disconnect the diagnostic tool. • Key in START position. • With the engine running and all of the accessories turned off, measure the voltage at the battery while varying the engine rpm. 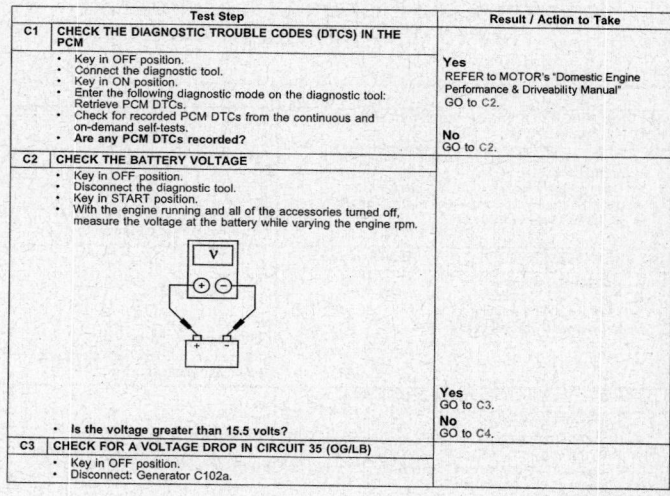 • **Is the voltage greater than 15.5 volts?**	**Yes** GO to C3. **No** GO to C4.
C3 **CHECK FOR A VOLTAGE DROP IN CIRCUIT 35 (OG/LB)** • Key in OFF position. • Disconnect: Generator C102a.	

ARM0500000000770

Fig. 135   Test C: Charging System Overcharges, Battery Voltage More Than 15.5 Volts (Part 1 of 3). 2005–07 Town Car

FORD MOTORCRAFT

Fig. 135 Test C (Part 2 of 3)

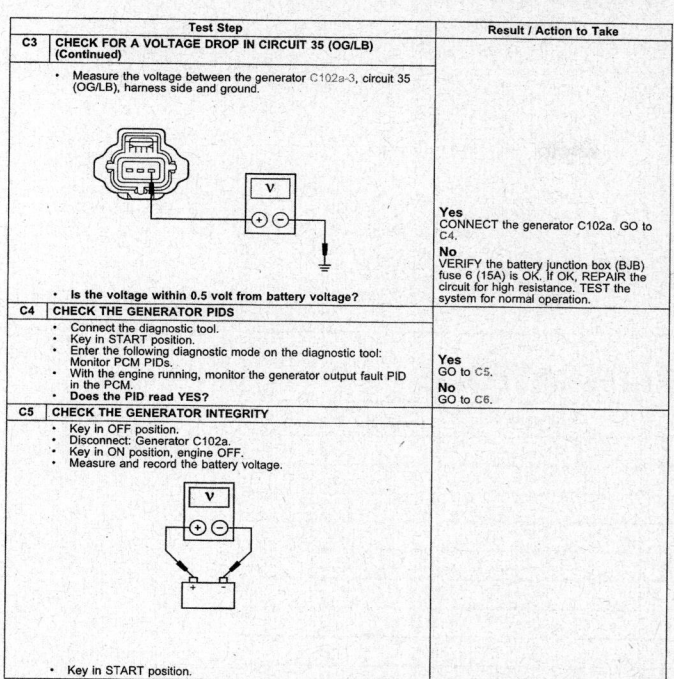

Test Step	Result / Action to Take
C3 CHECK FOR A VOLTAGE DROP IN CIRCUIT 35 (OG/LB) (Continued) • Measure the voltage between the generator C102a-3, circuit 35 (OG/LB), harness side and ground. • **Is the voltage within 0.5 volt from battery voltage?**	**Yes** CONNECT the generator C102a. GO to C4. **No** VERIFY the battery junction box (BJB) fuse 6 (15A) is OK. If OK, REPAIR the circuit for high resistance. TEST the system for normal operation.
C4 CHECK THE GENERATOR PIDS • Connect the diagnostic tool. • Key in START position. • Enter the following diagnostic mode on the diagnostic tool: Monitor PCM PIDs. • With the engine running, monitor the generator output fault PID in the PCM. • **Does the PID read YES?**	**Yes** GO to C5. **No** GO to C6.
C5 CHECK THE GENERATOR INTEGRITY • Key in OFF position. • Disconnect: Generator C102a. • Key in ON position, engine OFF. • Measure and record the battery voltage. • Key in START position.	

Fig. 135 Test C: Charging System Overcharges, Battery Voltage More Than 15.5 Volts (Part 2 of 3). 2005-07 Town Car

ARM0500000000771

Fig. 136 Test D

Test Step	Result / Action to Take
D1 CHECK THE DIAGNOSTIC TROUBLE CODES (DTCS) IN THE PCM • Key in OFF position. • Connect the diagnostic tool. • Key in ON position. • Enter the following diagnostic mode on the diagnostic tool: Retrieve PCM DTCs. • Check for recorded PCM DTCs from the continuous and on-demand self-tests. • **Are any PCM DTCs recorded?**	**Yes** REFER to MOTOR's "Domestic Engine Performance & Driveability Manual" GO to D2. **No** GO to D2.
D2 CHECK THE SYSTEM FOR OVERCHARGING • Key in START position. • With the engine running and all of the accessories off, measure the voltage at the battery terminals while varying the engine rpm. • **Is the voltage greater than 15.5 volts?**	**Yes** GO to Pinpoint Test C. **No** GO to D3.
D3 CHECK THE PCM PIDS • Enter the following diagnostic mode on the diagnostic tool: Monitor PCM PIDs. • With the engine running, monitor the generator output fault PID in the PCM. • **Does the PID read YES?**	**Yes** GO to D4. **No** Diagnose the charging system warning indicator.
D4 CHECK THE GENERATOR OUTPUT • Verify the generator output. Refer to the Component Tests, Generator On-Vehicle Tests in this section. • **Does the generator pass the component tests?**	**Yes** GO to D5. **No** INSTALL a new generator. CLEAR the DTCs. REPEAT the self-test. TEST the system for normal operation.

D5 CHECK FOR CORRECT PCM OPERATION
• Key in OFF position.
• Disconnect all of the PCM connectors.
• Check for:
  • corrosion
  • pushed-out pins
• Connect all of the PCM connectors and make sure they seat correctly.
• Operate the system and verify the concern is still present.
• **Is the concern still present?**
	Yes
	INSTALL a new PCM. REPEAT the self-test. TEST the system for normal operation.
	No
	The system is operating correctly at this time. The concern may have been caused by a loose or corroded connector. CLEAR the DTCs. REPEAT the self-test. TEST the system for normal operation.

Fig. 136 Test D: Charging System Warning Indicator Is On w/Engine Running & Battery Increases Voltage. 2005-07 Town Car

ARM0500000000773

Fig. 135 Test C (Part 3 of 3)

Test Step	Result / Action to Take
C5 CHECK THE GENERATOR INTEGRITY (Continued) • NOTE: If the generator communication lines are disconnected (DTC P0622 may be set), the generator self-excites if it is operated at greater than 4,500 rpm (approximately wide open throttle [WOT]) for a minimum of 3 seconds. It then operates in a default mode at 13.5 volts until the engine is turned off. With the engine running (after the brief WOT is carried out), measure the battery voltage. • **Does the battery voltage increase a minimum of 0.5 volt from the key ON, engine off measurement to the key ON, engine running measurement (after the brief WOT or snap acceleration is carried out)?**	**Yes** GO to C6. **No** INSTALL a new generator. TEST the system for normal operation.

C6 CHECK FOR CORRECT PCM OPERATION
• Key in OFF position.
• Disconnect all of the PCM connectors.
• Check for:
  • corrosion
  • pushed-out pins
• Connect all of the PCM connectors and make sure they seat correctly.
• Operate the system and verify the concern is still present.
• **Is the concern still present?**
	Yes
	INSTALL a new PCM. REPEAT the self-test. TEST the system for normal operation.
	No
	The system is operating correctly at this time. The concern may have been caused by a loose or corroded connector. CLEAR the DTCs. REPEAT the self-test. TEST the system for normal operation.

ARM0500000000772

Fig. 135 Test C: Charging System Overcharges, Battery Voltage More Than 15.5 Volts (Part 3 of 3). 2005-07 Town Car

Fig. 137 Test E

Test Step	Result / Action to Take
E1 CHECK THE CHARGING SYSTEM WARNING INDICATOR OPERATION • Key in OFF position. • Connect the diagnostic tool. • Key in ON position. • Enter the following diagnostic mode on the diagnostic tool: Active Commands. • Using Active Commands, turn on the charging system warning indicator in the instrument cluster. • **Is the charging system warning indicator on?**	**Yes** GO to E2. **No** Diagnose the charging system warning indicator.

E2 CHECK FOR CORRECT PCM OPERATION
• Key in OFF position.
• Disconnect all of the PCM connectors.
• Check for:
  • corrosion
  • pushed-out pins
• Connect all of the PCM connectors and make sure they seat correctly.
• Operate the system and verify the concern is still present.
• **Is the concern still present?**
	Yes
	INSTALL a new PCM. REPEAT the self-test. TEST the system for normal operation.
	No
	The system is operating correctly at this time. The concern may have been caused by a loose or corroded connector. CLEAR the DTCs. REPEAT the self-test. TEST the system for normal operation.

ARM0500000000774

Fig. 137 Test E: Charging System Warning Indicator Is Off w/Ignition Switch In Run Position & Engine Is Off. 2005-07 Town Car

Fig. 138 Test F

Test Step	Result / Action to Take
F1 CHECK FOR ACCESSORY DRIVE NOISE AND MOUNTING BRACKETS • Key in OFF position. • Check the accessory drive belt for damage and correct installation. • Check the accessory mounting brackets and generator pulley for looseness or misalignment. • **Is the accessory drive OK?**	**Yes** GO to F2. **No** REPAIR as necessary. TEST the system for normal operation.
F2 CHECK THE GENERATOR FOR EXCESSIVE ELECTRICAL NOISE • Disconnect: Generator C1104b. • Key in START position. • With the engine running, determine if the generator is still noisy. • **Is the noise still present?**	**Yes** GO to F3. **No** INSTALL a new generator. TEST the system for normal operation.
F3 CHECK THE GENERATOR FOR MECHANICAL NOISE • Turn all of the electrical accessories off. With the engine running, use a stethoscope or equivalent listening device to probe the generator for unusual mechanical noise. • **Is the generator the noise source?**	**Yes** INSTALL a new generator. TEST the system for normal operation. **No** diagnose the source of the engine noise.

ARM0500000000775

Fig. 138 Test F: Alternator Is Noisy. 2005-07 Town Car

Test Step		Result / Action to Take
G1	VERIFY THE GENERATOR IS THE SOURCE OF THE RADIO INTERFERENCE	
	NOTE: If the original equipment manufactured (OEM) audio unit has been replaced with an aftermarket unit, the vehicle may not pass this test. Return the vehicle to OEM condition before following this pinpoint test. • Start and run the engine. • Tune the audio unit to a station where the interference is present. • Key in OFF position. • Disconnect: Generator C102b. • Key in START position. • With the engine running, determine if the interference is still present. • Is the interference present with the generator disconnected?	**Yes** Diagnosis and testing of the in-vehicle entertainment system. **No** INSTALL a new generator. TEST the system for normal operation.

ARM0500000000776

Fig. 139   Test G: Radio Interference. 2005–07 Town Car

ALTERNATOR SPECIFICATIONS

Model	Year	Engine	Model	Amp Rating
Crown Victoria	2004	4.6L	F6LU-CA	130
	2005–08	4.6L	—	135
Five Hundred	2005–07	3.0L	—	120
Focus	2004	2.0L	—	—
	2005–07	2.0L	—	110
		2.0L (PZEV)	—	120
		2.3L	—	110
Freestyle	2005–07	3.0L	—	120
Fusion	2006–08	2.3L	—	150
		3.0L	—	150
Grand Marquis	2004	4.6L	F6LU-CA	130
	2005–08	4.6L	—	135
LS	2004	3.0L	XR8U-AC	105
		3.9L	XR8U-CD	105
	2005–07	3.9L	—	135
Marauder	2004	4.6L	F6LU-CA	130
Milan	2006–08	2.3L	—	150
		3.0L	—	150
		3.5L	—	150
MKZ	2007–08	2.3L	—	150
		3.0L	—	150
		3.5L	—	150
Montego	2005–07	3.0L	—	120
Mustang	2004–08	3.8L	1R3U-BA	110
		4.0L	—	135
		4.6L DOHC	F6ZU-BE	120
		4.6L SOHC	XR3U-AB	110
Sable	2004–05	3.0L DOHC	XF2V-BC	125
		3.0L OHV	XF2V-AB	110
	2008	3.5L	—	①
Taurus	2004–07	3.0L DOHC	XF2V-BC	125
		3.0L OHV	XF2V-AB	110
	2008	3.5L	—	①
Taurus X	2008	3.5L	—	①
Thunderbird	2004–05	3.9L	XR8U-CD	105
Town Car	2004–04	4.6L	F6LU-CA	130
	2005–07	4.6L	—	135
Zephyr	2006	2.3L	—	150
		3.0L	—	150
		3.5L	—	150

① — Standard alternator, 78–143 Amp's ; Optional alternator, 102–170 Amp's.

STEERING COLUMNS

NOTE: On Air Bag Equipped Models, Refer To "Air Bag System Precautions" Located In The Front Of This Manual For System Disarming & Arming Procedures.

NOTE: Refer To "Computer Relearn Procedures" Located In The Front Of This Manual When Battery Power To The Computer Has Been Interrupted.

NOTE: Models Equipped With "Automatic Ride Control System" Utilize A Steering Sensor Located On The Steering Column Assembly. For Sensor Replacement, Refer To "Automatic Ride Control System" In The "Active Suspension" Section.

INDEX

	Page No.
Description	12-1
Precautions	12-1
Air Bag Systems	12-1
Battery Ground Cable	12-1
Steering Column, Replace	12-1
2004–05 Sable & 2004–07 Taurus	12-3
Crown Victoria, Grand Marquis, Marauder & Town Car	12-1
Five Hundred, Freestyle, Montego, 2008 Sable, Taurus & Taurus X	12-1
Focus	12-2

	Page No.
Fusion, Milan, MKZ & Zephyr	12-2
LS & Thunderbird	12-2
Mustang	12-2
Steering Column Service	12-3
Crown Victoria, Grand Marquis, Marauder & Town Car	12-3
Five Hundred, Freestyle, Montego, 2008 Sable, Taurus & Taurus X	12-4
Focus	12-4
Fusion, Milan, MKZ & Zephyr	12-4

	Page No.
LS & Thunderbird	12-4
Assemble	12-5
Disassemble	12-4
Mustang	12-5
Assemble	12-6
Disassemble	12-5
2004–05 Sable & 2004–07 Taurus	12-7
Column Shift	12-8
Console Shift	12-7
Tightening Specifications	12-11

PRECAUTIONS

Air Bag Systems

Refer to "Air Bag System Precautions" in the front of this manual for system disarming and arming procedures.

Battery Ground Cable

Prior to service, disconnect battery ground cable and isolate as required. Allow one minute for back-up power supply to be depleted.

DESCRIPTION

The steering column used on models equipped with air bags is of a modular construction and features easy to service electrical switches. The washer/wiper switch and the combination turn signal/hazard/horn/flash-to-pass/dimmer switch are attached with self-tapping screws.

These models are equipped with either a brush type or a clockspring type slip ring. Removal and installation procedures for the two types are the same except where noted.

Fasteners used on steering column components must be replaced after removal. The fasteners are coated with an epoxy adhesive and cannot be used again.

Whenever the steering column is removed or is separated from the steering gear, the steering column must be in locked position to prevent the steering wheel from being rotated accidentally and damaging the air bag slip ring.

The LS and Thunderbird models are equipped with a power tilt/telescopic steering column of modular construction. It has easy-to-service electrical switches. This column is equipped with an electric tilt and telescopic mechanism that allows the steering wheel angle and length to be adjusted to suit the driver.

On models equipped with the memory package, the steering wheel position is stored in memory the same way as driver seat position and retrieved as a personality feature. The steering column is controlled by the instrument cluster module.

STEERING COLUMN

REPLACE

Crown Victoria, Grand Marquis, Marauder & Town Car

1. Ensure wheels are in straight-ahead position.
2. Remove air bag sliding contact.
3. Disconnect multi-function switch electrical connectors.
4. Remove mounting screws and multi-function switch.
5. Remove instrument panel reinforcement brace.
6. Disconnect ignition switch electrical connector.
7. Disconnect brake shift interlock solenoid connector.
8. Remove Passive Anti-Theft System (PATS) sensor ring.
9. Remove shift cable and bracket from steering column.
10. Remove and discard lower steering column shaft pinch bolt.
11. Disconnect lower steering column shaft from steering column lower yoke.
12. Remove and discard steering column mounting nuts, then lower steering column to floor.
13. Disconnect parking brake release vacuum hose extension from parking brake release switch.
14. Disconnect, then position shift cable and bracket aside.
15. Remove steering column.
16. Reverse procedure to install.

Five Hundred, Freestyle, Montego, 2008 Sable, Taurus & Taurus X

Do not allow the steering column to rotate while the intermediate shaft is disconnected, damage to the clockspring may result.

1. Ensure wheels are in straight-ahead position, then remove ignition key.

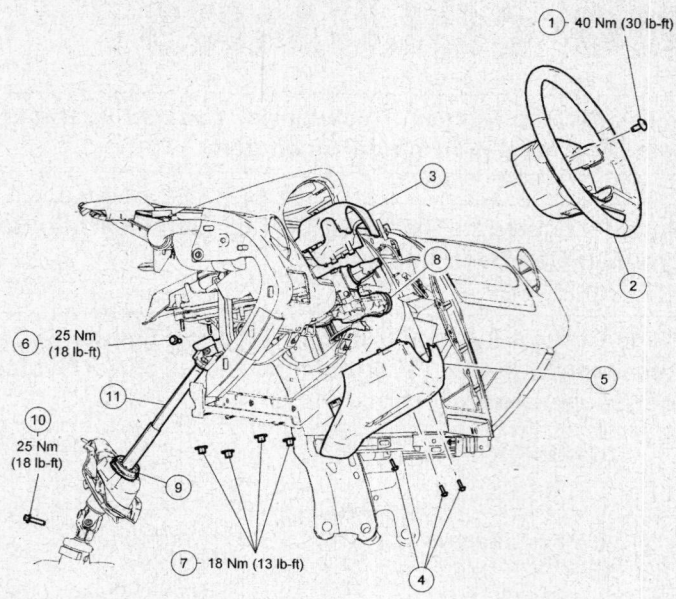

1. Steering wheel bolt
2. Steering wheel
3. Upper steering column shroud
4. Lower steering column shroud screws
5. Lower steering column shroud
6. Intermediate shaft to steering column bolt
7. Steering column nuts
8. Steering column
9. Intermediate shaft boot bearing clamp
10. Intermediate shaft to steering gear bolt
11. Intermediate shaft

ARM0400000000758

Fig. 1 Exploded view of steering column. Five Hundred, Freestyle, Montego, 2008 Sable, Taurus & Taurus X

2. Remove instrument panel lower trim cover.
3. Remove upper and lower steering column shrouds, **Fig. 1.**
4. Disconnect intermediate shaft to steering column retaining bolt, then disconnect shaft from column.
5. Disconnect ignition switch, multi-function switch and anti-theft system transceiver electrical connectors.
6. Disconnect wire harness to steering column 2-pin type retainers, then position harness aside.
7. Remove four steering column to instrument panel mounting bolts.
8. Remove steering column.
9. Reverse procedure to install. Ensure intermediate shaft boot bearing clamp does not contact boot after installation, **Fig. 2.**

Focus

1. Ensure wheels are in straight-ahead position.
2. Remove ignition key.
3. Remove mounting screws, release fastener and disconnect instrument panel lower panel.
4. Disconnect hood release cable and data link electrical connector, then remove instrument panel lower panel.

5. Remove steering column upper shroud using suitable thin bladed screwdriver to release clips on each side.
6. Release steering column locking lever, then remove mounting screws and steering column lower shroud.
7. Disconnect Passive Anti-Theft System (PATS) transceiver, wiper/washer switch and air bag sliding contact/speed control on righthand side of steering column.
8. Disconnect ignition switch and turn signal/flash-to-pass switch electrical connectors on lefthand side of steering column.
9. Disconnect steering column wiring harness by releasing locating pin.
10. Remove mounting bolt and disconnect steering column shaft from steering gear pinion extension.
11. Remove mounting bolts and steering column.
12. Reverse procedure to install.

Fusion, Milan, MKZ & Zephyr

Do not allow the steering column to ro-

tate while the intermediate shaft is disconnected, damage to the clockspring may result.
1. Ensure wheels are in straight-ahead position, then remove ignition key.
2. Remove the instrument panel steering column cover by pulling straight outward. Note instrument panel steering column cover is held in by tabs that clip into instrument panel.
3. Remove four bolts, then the instrument panel reinforcement, **Fig. 3.**
4. Release upper steering column shroud by pressing inward on both sides, then lift upward to remove shroud.
5. Release tilt lever, remove three screws, then the lower steering column shroud.
6. Disconnect multi-function switch, ignition switch and clockspring electrical connectors.
7. Disconnect Passive Anti-Theft System (PATS) electrical and Key in connector.
8. Disconnect wiring harness retainer, then position wiring harness aside.
9. Remove lower steering column shaft joint cover bolts, then the cover.
10. Index mark steering column shaft position to steering gear, **Fig. 4,** for reference during installation.
11. Remove steering column shaft bolt and disconnect shaft from steering gear.
12. Remove four steering column support bracket nuts, then the steering column.
13. Reverse procedure to install.

LS & Thunderbird

1. Ensure wheels are in straight-ahead position.
2. Remove driver's air bag module and air bag sliding contact as outlined in "Passive Restraint Systems" chapter.
3. Remove steering wheel as outlined in "Electrical" section of "LS & Thunderbird" chassis chapter.
4. Remove steering column shaft pinch bolt and separate intermediate shaft from steering column yoke. Discard pinch bolt.
5. Disconnect electronic steering sensor and steering column release motor electrical connectors.
6. **On models equipped with automatic transmission,** remove and discard locknuts while supporting steering column.
7. **On models equipped with manual transmission,** remove and discard locknuts while supporting steering column. Lower steering column and disconnect lock actuator electrical connector.
8. **On all models,** remove steering column.
9. Reverse procedure to install.

Mustang

1. Remove steering wheel as outlined in "Electrical" section of "Mustang" chassis chapter.
2. Remove steering column lower yoke to lower steering column shaft mounting bolt.

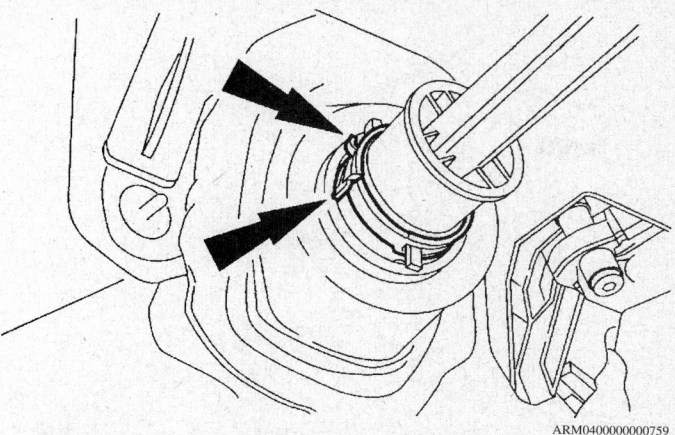

Fig. 2 Intermediate shaft bearing boot clamp position. Five Hundred, Freestyle, Montego, 2008 Sable, Taurus & Taurus X

3. Remove ignition switch lock cylinder as outlined in "Electrical" section of "Mustang" chassis chapter.
4. Remove steering column opening cover, reinforcement and instrument panel cross brace.
5. Remove upper and lower steering column shrouds.
6. Disconnect ignition switch and key warning buzzer electrical connectors.
7. Remove mounting screws and position multi-function switch aside.
8. Remove nuts mounting steering shaft tube boot to dash panel.
9. Remove mounting nuts and lower steering column to clear mounting bolts.
10. **On models equipped with automatic transmission,** remove ignition/shifter interlock cable.
11. **On all models,** remove steering column.
12. Reverse procedure to install.

2004–05 Sable & 2004–07 Taurus

Do not remove steering wheel or air bag module as an assembly unless the column is locked or the steering column gear input shaft coupling is secured to keep it from turning.

1. Ensure wheels are in straight-ahead position.
2. Remove steering wheel as outlined in "Electrical" section of "Sable & Taurus" chassis chapter.
3. Remove steering column intermediate shaft coupling to steering column lower yoke mounting bolt.
4. Remove lower instrument panel steering column cover.
5. Push in on release pin by inserting suitable tool into access hole located in bottom of lower steering column shroud, then rotate ignition cylinder clockwise to Run position and remove cylinder.
6. Remove lower and upper steering column shrouds.
7. Remove mounting screws and position Passive Anti-Theft System (PATS)

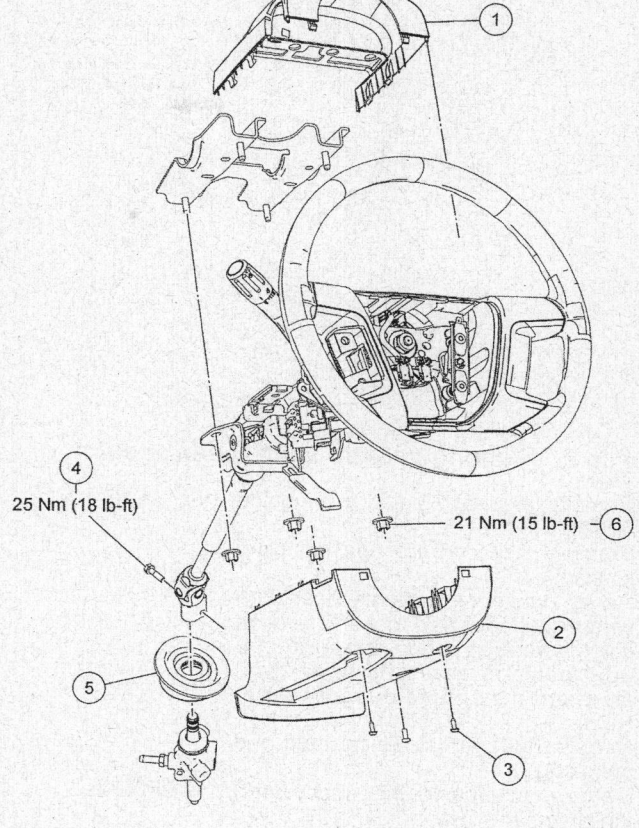

25 Nm (18 lb-ft)

21 Nm (15 lb-ft)

Item	Description
1	Upper steering column shroud
2	Lower steering column shroud

Item	Description
3	Lower steering column shroud screw (3 required)
4	Steering column shaft bolt
5	Steering column dust seal

ARM0500000000777

Fig. 3 Exploded view of steering column. Fusion, Milan, MKZ & Zephyr

transceiver aside.
8. **On models equipped with column shift,** disconnect and slide shift control selector lever boot toward end of control lever. Remove control lever by removing retaining pin.
9. **On models equipped with overdrive lock-out switch on column lever,** disconnect wiring connector at bottom of steering column and remove wiring from column with control lever.
10. **On all models,** disconnect wiring connectors for ignition switch, horn, speed control, interlock switch and air bag module.
11. Remove mounting screws and position multi-function switch aside.
12. Remove shift indicator cable from shifter tube.
13. Remove shifter indicator retainer mounting screw from column adjustment cable.
14. Remove mounting nuts and lower steering column.
15. **On models equipped with console shift,** disconnect BTSI electrical connector.

16. **On all models,** remove steering column.
17. Reverse procedure to install. Adjust shift indicator cable.

STEERING COLUMN SERVICE

Crown Victoria, Grand Marquis, Marauder & Town Car

1. **Record positions of steering column lock gear, bearing and retainer for assembly alignment.**
2. Remove bearing retainer, lock housing bearing and lock gear, **Fig. 5.**
3. Disconnect electrical connector, then remove screws and shock absorber electronic steering sensor.
4. Remove steering column lower bearing spring and sensor ring.
5. Remove steering column bearing tolerance ring from column shaft.

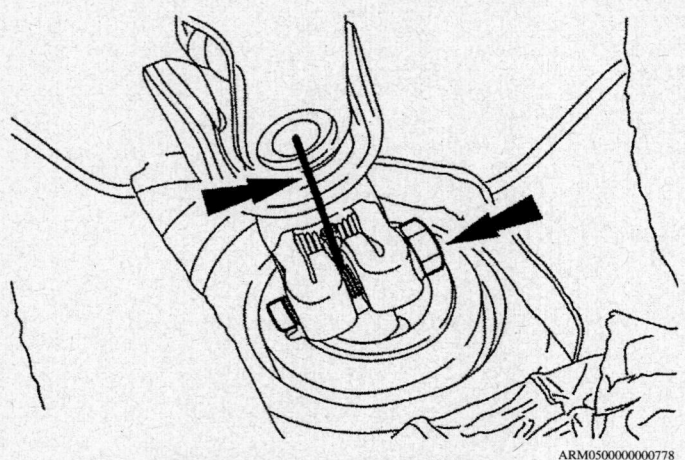

Fig. 4 Steering column shaft index position

ARM05000000000778

6. Remove mounting bolts and ignition switch.
7. Remove lock cylinder housing pivot screws.
8. Pry up on steering column locking levers using fabricated tool and remove column position spring. **Steering column position spring is under tension and may come out with great force.**
9. Remove turn signal cancel cam and snap ring.
10. Remove steering column upper bearing spring and sleeve.
11. Slide steering column shaft in toward steering column lock cylinder housing and out.
12. Slide steering column bearing tolerance ring off steering column shaft.
13. Remove column bearing from steering column lock cylinder housing using suitable punch.
14. Remove mounting screws and parking brake release switch.
15. Remove mounting bolts and brake shift interlock solenoid.
16. Remove mounting bolts, clamps and shift tube.
17. Remove mounting bolts, transaxle selector lever arm and support.
18. Remove gearshift selector tube spring and drive out shift tube gearshift lever pin.
19. Remove gearshift lever and column shift selector lever plunger. Replace lever plunger if it is bent.
20. Remove gearshift lever socket bushings and transaxle control selector lever spring clip.
21. Drive out steering column lock lever pin and remove steering column lock pawl.
22. Remove lower steering column bearing and sleeve.
23. Remove mounting bolts and steering column lower bearing retainer.
24. Remove upper and lower steering column actuators.
25. Reverse procedure to assemble.

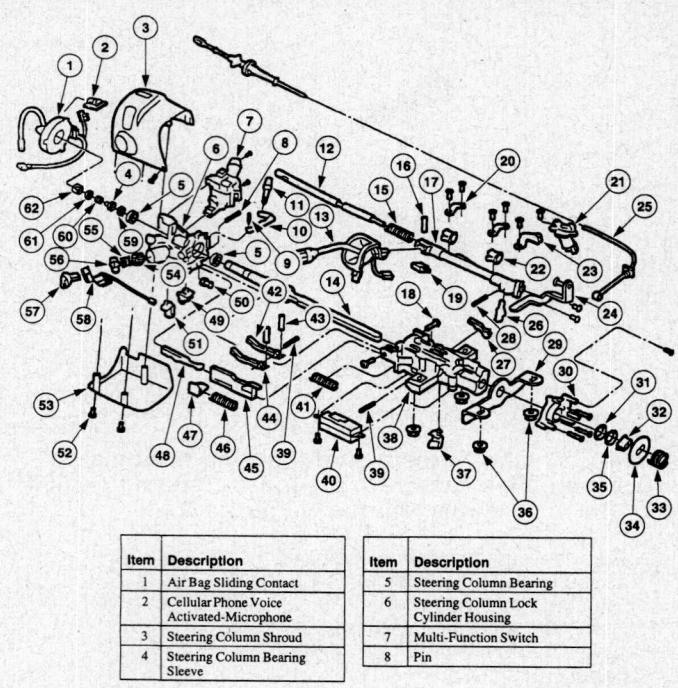

Item	Description
1	Air Bag Sliding Contact
2	Cellular Phone Voice Activated-Microphone
3	Steering Column Shroud
4	Steering Column Bearing Sleeve
5	Steering Column Bearing
6	Steering Column Lock Cylinder Housing
7	Multi-Function Switch
8	Pin

FM6049900124010X

Fig. 5 Exploded view of steering column (Part 1 of 2). Crown Victoria, Grand Marquis, Marauder & Town Car

Focus

The steering column is serviced as an assembly. If service other than the air bag clockspring, combination switch or ignition switch assembly is required, the steering column must be replaced, **Fig. 6**.

Five Hundred, Freestyle, Montego, 2008 Sable, Taurus & Taurus X

The steering column is serviced as an assembly. If service other than the air bag clockspring, combination switch or ignition switch assembly is required, the steering column must be replaced, **Fig. 1**.

Fusion, Milan, MKZ & Zephyr

The steering column is serviced as an assembly. If service other than the air bag clockspring, combination switch or ignition switch assembly is required, the steering column must be replaced.

LS & Thunderbird

DISASSEMBLE

1. Place steering column in suitable vise.
2. **On models equipped with manual transmission,** proceed as follows:
   a. Remove shear bolts' heads using suitable drill motor with ⅜ inch drill bit.
   b. Remove steering wheel lock actuator. **Do not damage actuator.**
   c. Remove steering column upper shaft assembly shear bolts using suitable locking pliers.
3. **On all models,** remove electronic steering sensor, **Fig. 7**.
4. Disconnect steering column release motor (telescopic) electrical connector.
5. Connect telescopic release motor electrical terminals using suitable 1 amp 12 volt battery charger and telescope column out until it is fully extended. **Do not telescope steering column manually.**
6. Connect steering column release motor (telescopic) electrical connector.
7. Replace steering column release motor if it is damaged or inoperable before installing telescoping steering column.
8. Remove mounting screws and steering column release motors. **Do not disconnect steering column release motors' harness electrical connectors.**
9. Remove mounting bolts, steering column outer housing cover plate, outer housing and column track.
10. Remove steering column connector link.
11. Install spring compressor tool No. 211-201, or equivalent, on steering column position spring and tighten by hand.
12. Remove spring mounting bolts.
13. Release spring tension using spring

Item	Description
9	Steering Column Release Lever Pin
10	Steering Column Release Lever
11	Tilt Wheel Handle and Shank
12	Column Shift Selector Lever Plunger
13	Gearshift Lever
14	Steering Column Shaft
15	Transmission Control Selector Lever Plunger Spring
16	Gearshift Lever Pin
17	Transmission Column Shift Selector Tube
18	Tilt Column Pivot Screw
19	Transmission Control Selector Lever Spring Clip
20	Gearshift Tube Bushing Clamp
21	Brake Shift Interlock Solenoid
22	Gearshift Lever Socket Bushing
23	Transmission Shift Selector Position Insert
24	Transmission Selector Lever Arm and Support
25	Shift Cable and Bracket
26	Gearshift Lever
27	Steering Column Lock Pawl
28	Gearshift Lever Pin
29	Steering Column Instrument Panel Bracket
30	Steering Column Lower Bearing Retainer
31	Steering Column Bearing Sleeve
32	Steering Column Bearing Tolerance Ring
33	Steering Column Bearing Spring
34	Suspension Height Sensor Control Ring

Item	Description
35	Steering Column Bearing
36	Steering Column Retaining Nuts
37	Wiring Harness Retainer
38	Steering Actuator Housing
39	Steering Column Lock Lever Pin
40	Ignition Switch
41	Steering Column Position Spring
42	Steering Column Lock Lever
43	Steering Column Position Lock Spring
44	Steering Column Locking Lever
45	Steering Column Lock Lever Actuator
46	Steering Column Lock Spring
47	Steering Column Lock Pawl
48	Steering Column Lock Actuator
49	Steering Column Lock Cam
50	Steering Column Tilt Flange Bumper
51	Wiring Harness Retainer
52	Shroud Screws
53	Steering Column Shroud
54	Steering Column Lock Gear
55	Steering Column Lock Housing Bearing
56	Bearing Retainer
57	Ignition Switch Lock Cylinder
58	Passive Anti-Theft System (PATS) Sensor Ring
59	Steering Column Bearing Tolerance Ring
60	Steering Column Upper Bearing Spring
61	Bearing Retainer
62	Turn Indicator Cancel Cam

FM6049900124020X

Fig. 5   Exploded view of steering column (Part 2 of 2). Crown Victoria, Grand Marquis, Marauder & Town Car

compressor tool, then remove spring and tool.

14. Separate front and rear halves of steering column upper shaft and column inner housing. Upper shaft sensor ring and coupler are serviced as an assembly.
15. Remove rear half of steering column upper shaft from support.
16. Remove steering column telescopic actuator. **Curl strap on steering column actuator must not be bent or altered.** Replace steering column telescopic actuator if curl strap is damaged.
17. Remove column track from support and potentiometer.
18. Remove steering column release pin and place inner housing in suitable vise.
19. Remove steering column tilt actuator, inner track bearing retainers and column tracks.
20. Remove steering column tube flange and upper bearing retainer.
21. Remove column upper bearing spring and sleeve.
22. Spread steering column upper bearing tolerance ring using suitable flat blade screwdriver and slide it out of column upper shaft.
23. Remove front half of steering column upper shaft.
24. Drive out small and large steering column tube bearing assemblies using suitable brass drifts.

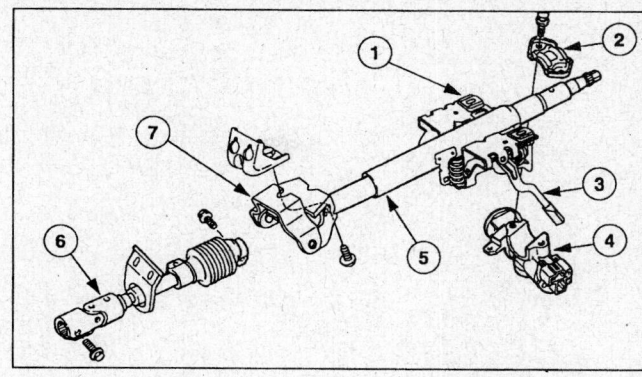

FM6049700096000X

Fig. 6   Exploded view of steering column. Focus

Item	Description
1	Steering Column Upper Mounting Bracket
2	Ignition Switch Lock Cylinder Bracket
3	Tilt Lever (If Equipped)
4	Lock Cylinder

Item	Description
5	Steering Column
6	Steering Column Intermediate Shaft Coupling
7	Steering Column Support Bracket

ASSEMBLE

1. Install large and small steering column tube bearings using suitable bearing installer tools.
2. Slide steering shaft into tilt housing and install steering column upper bearing tolerance ring.
3. Install column bearing sleeve and upper bearing spring.
4. Install steering column upper bearing retainer, tube flange and mounting bolts.
5. Position steering column tilt actuator and install mounting bolts.
6. Install steering column release pin, potentiometer and mounting screws.
7. Install steering column telescopic actuator and mounting nuts.
8. Install steering column track on support. Apply Premium Long-Life Grease part No. XG-1-C, or equivalent, to steering column track bearing surface.
9. Attach steering column tracks and inner track bearings to steering column inner housing.
10. Apply Premium Long-Life Grease to column track bearings and steering column tracks' bearing surface.
11. Install rear half of steering column upper shaft into steering column support and mounting bolts.
12. Join front and rear halves of steering column upper shaft and steering column inner housing in column support housing.
13. Position steering column spring.
14. Compress spring until actuator telescopic assembly bolt until holes align using compressor tool No. 211-201, or equivalent, Install mounting bolts and remove tool.
15. Install steering column connector link and column track on outer housing. Apply grease to bearing surface of steering column track.
16. Ensure steering column inner track

bearing retainers are properly staged.

17. Install steering column outer housing and housing cover plate. Hand tighten loosely.
18. Ensure steering column inner track bearings are properly staged. **Steering column inner track bearings must be installed against rear column inner housing track bearing retaining end. Inner housing must be installed in fully extended (out) position.**
19. Apply Threadlock 262 part No. E2FZ-19554-B, or equivalent, to threads and tighten mounting bolts.
20. Install steering column release motors and mounting screws.
21. Disconnect steering column telescopic release motor electrical connector.
22. Connect motor electrical connector terminals to suitable 1 amp 12-volt battery charger and test column for normal operation.
23. Connect steering column telescopic release motor electrical connector.
24. Disconnect steering column tilt release motor electrical connector.
25. Connect motor electrical connector terminals to battery charger and test column for normal operation.
26. Connect steering column tilt release motor electrical connector.
27. Install electronic steering sensor with screws.
28. **On models equipped with manual transmission,** install steering wheel lock actuator and new shear bolts.

Mustang

DISASSEMBLE

1. Remove steering column lower yoke and upper bearing spring, then the suspension height sensor control ring and upper bearing tolerance ring, **Fig. 8.**

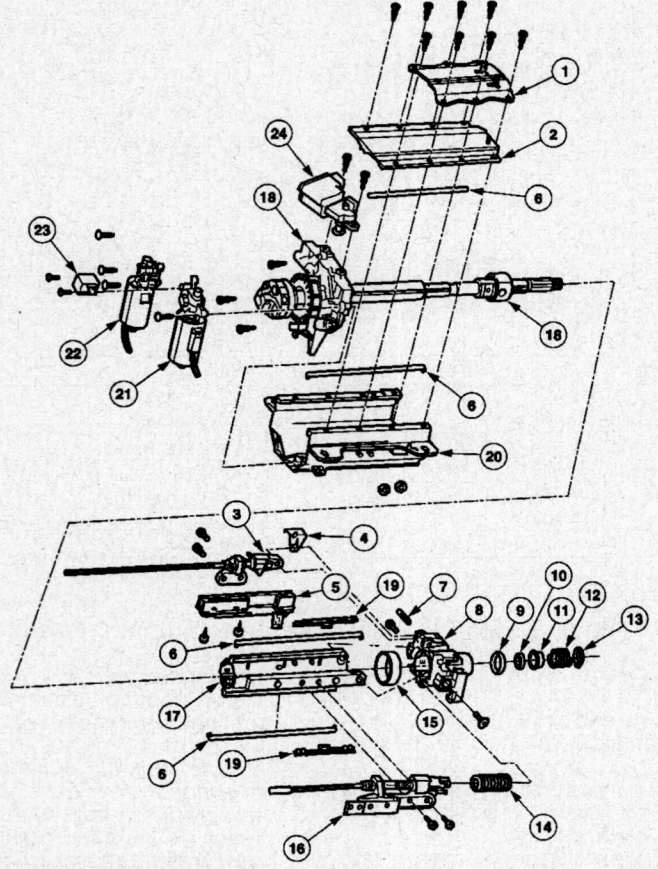

4	3A517	Steering column connector link
5	14A605	Steering column potentiometer assembly
6	3B628	Steering column track
7	3D545	Steering column release pin
8	3511	Steering column tube flange
9	3517	Steering column tube bearing assembly
10	3L539	Steering column upper bearing tolerance ring
11	3518	Steering column bearing sleeve
12	3520	Steering column upper bearing spring
13	97663	Steering column upper bearing retainer
14	3D655	Steering column position spring
15	3517	Steering column tube bearing assembly
16	3F797	Steering column actuator assembly (telescopic)
17	3F791	Steering column inner housing
18	3524	Steering column upper shaft assembly
19	3F795	Steering column inner track bearing retainer assembly
20	3B718	Steering column support assembly
21	3D538	Steering column release motor assembly (telescopic)
22	3D538	Steering column release motor assembly (tilt)
23	18B015	Steering wheel absorber electronic steering sensor
24	3K772	Steering wheel lock actuator (manual transmission only)

FM6049900122020X

Fig. 7   Exploded view of steering column (Part 2 of 2). LS & Thunderbird

Item	Part Number	Description
1	3F790	Steering column outer housing plate
2	3F789	Steering column outer housing
3	3F797	Steering column actuator assembly (tilt)

FM6049900122010X

Fig. 7   Exploded view of steering column (Part 1 of 2). LS & Thunderbird

2. Remove turn indicator cancel cam by pushing up with suitable flat-bladed screwdriver. **Record flush surface direction.**
3. Remove ignition switch, steering column bearing retainer and spring.
4. Remove steel steering column upper bearing tolerance ring and bearing sleeve.
5. Remove ignition switch bore plastic steering column upper bearing retainer.
6. Remove metal steering column lock housing bearing from ignition switch bore and steering column lock gear.
7. Remove pivot bolts and lock cylinder housing. **Steering column position spring will release when bolts are removed.**
8. Remove steering gear input worm gear and rack from steering column tube.
9. Remove steering column lock lever actuator and steering actuator housing.
10. Remove lower steering column tube bearing and steering column lower bearing retainer.
11. Remove tilt position lever using suitable drift.
12. Remove steering column lock lefthand lever and steering column locking lever springs.

ASSEMBLE

1. Install steering gear input worm gear and rack into steering actuator housing.
2. Install lower steering column tube bearing and steering column instrument panel clamp.
3. Install suspension height sensor control and upper bearing tolerance rings.
4. Install steering column upper bearing spring and lower yoke to steering gear input worm gear and rack.
5. Position steering column lock lever actuator and steering actuator housing in lock cylinder housing.
6. Spray actuators with multi-purpose grease part No. DOAZ-19584-AA, or equivalent.
7. Position actuator cam in lock cylinder housing and install cam pivot pin with small hammer. Tap pin in until flush with lock cylinder housing.
8. Install one steering column locking lever spring and righthand steering column locking lever with steering column lock actuator lever pin.
9. Tap steering column lock actuator lever pin into place while driving out drift.
10. Support steering actuator housing in suitable vise and drive steering column lock actuator lever pin flush with steering actuator housing.
11. Place two nuts or spacers to hold steering column lock lefthand lever/

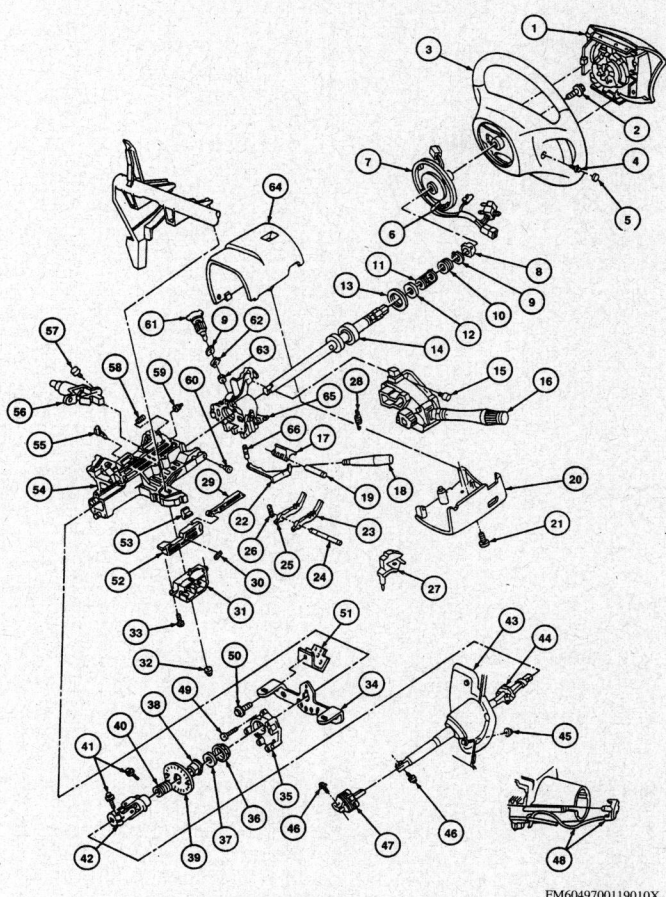

Fig. 8 Exploded view of steering column (Part 1 of 2). Mustang

FM6049700119010X

Item	Description	Item	Description
1	Driver Air Bag Module	35	Steering Column Lower Bearing Retainer
2	Steering Wheel Bolt	36	Steering Column Bearing Sleeve
3	Steering Wheel	37	Steering Column Bearing (Lower)
4	Air Bag Module Retaining Screws (2 Req'd)	38	Steering Column Bearing Tolerance Ring (Lower)
5	Steering Wheel Spoke Cover (2 Req'd)	39	Suspension Height Sensor Control Ring
6	Locking Tabs	40	Steering Column Upper Bearing Spring
7	Air Bag Sliding Contact	41	Bolt - Flange Yoke
8	Turn Indicator Cancel Cam	42	Steering Column Lower Yoke
9	Snap Ring	43	Steering Column Tube Boot
10	Steering Column Upper Bearing Spring	44	Lower Steering Column Shaft
11	Steering Column Bearing Sleeve (Upper)	45	Nut
12	Steering Column Bearing (Upper)(Small)	46	Bolt
13	Steering Column Bearing (Large)	47	Steering Column Intermediate Shaft Coupling
14	Steering Shaft Assy	48	Ignition Key Warning Switch Terminal and Wire
15	Screw	49	Lower Bearing Housing Retaining Screw
16	Multi-Function Switch	50	Screw
17	Steering Column Lock Cam	51	Wire Connector Bracket
18	Tilt Wheel Handle and Shank	52	Steering Column Lock Lever Actuator (Lower)
19	Pin - Lock Cam Pivot	53	Steering Column Lock Pawl
20	Steering Column Shroud (Lower)	54	Steering Actuator Housing
21	Shroud Retaining Screws	55	Steering Column Lock Actuator Cover
22	Steering Column Release Lever	56	Ignition / Shifter Interlock Cable
23	Steering Column Lock RH Lever	57	Screw
24	Steering Column Lock Actuator Lever Pin	58	Steering Column Position Spring
25	Steering Column Lock Left Hand Lever	59	Steering Column Tilt Flange Bumper
26	Steering Column Locking Lever Spring	60	Tilt Pivot Screws
27	Wiring Shield	61	Ignition Switch Lock Cylinder
28	Steering Column Position Spring	62	Steering Column Lock Housing Bearing
29	Steering Column Lock Lever Actuator	63	Steering Column Lock Gear
30	Steering Column Lock Spring (Shaft)	64	Steering Column Shroud (Upper)
31	Ignition Switch	65	Steering Column Lock Cylinder Housing
32	Lower Column Mounting Nuts	66	Steering Column Lock Actuator Lever Pin
33	Screw		
34	Steering Column Mounting Bracket		

FM6049700119020X

Fig. 8 Exploded view of steering column (Part 2 of 2). Mustang

righthand steering column locking lever away from steering actuator housing.

12. Lubricate pivot bolts with multi-purpose grease part No. DOAZ-19584-AA, or equivalent.

13. Position steering column position spring on lock cylinder housing, then install lock cylinder housing and pivot bolts.

14. Install steel steering column upper bearing tolerance ring and tube bearing sleeve over steering column.

15. Install steering column upper bearing spring and new steering retainer on top side of spring using ¾ inch by ⅔ inch PVC pipe.

16. Install turn indicator cancel cam flush with surface facing up.

17. Install ignition switch.

18. Align pin from ignition switch with slot in lock/column and position slot in lock/column with index mark on casting.

19. Install steering column and coat lock gear with multi-purpose grease part No. DOAZ-19584-AA, or equivalent.

20. Install metal steering column lock housing bearing and coat lock gear with multi-purpose grease.

21. Install steering column upper bearing retainer.

2004–05 Sable & 2004–07 Taurus

CONSOLE SHIFT

1. Remove mounting screws and ignition switch.
2. Record steering column lock gear, bearing and retainer positions for installation alignment, **Fig. 9.**
3. Remove bearing retainer, lock housing bearing and lock gear.
4. Remove lower bearing spring and sensor ring.
5. Remove lower bearing tolerance ring from shaft.
6. Remove tilt pivot mounting screws.
7. Remove lock cylinder housing and shaft assembly from actuator housing by prying up on lock actuator lever using suitable fabricated tool, **Fig. 10.**
8. Remove position spring. **Steering column position spring is under tension and can come out with great force.**
9. Remove turn indicator cancel cam.
10. Remove snap ring, upper bearing spring and sleeve.
11. Slide steering column shaft in toward lock cylinder housing and steering column bearing tolerance ring from steering column shaft, then remove shaft.

12. Remove lower bearing from lock cylinder housing using suitable punch.
13. Remove lock cylinder housing bearing using suitable punch.
14. Remove lower bearing and sleeve.
15. Remove mounting bolts and lower bearing retainer.
16. Remove upper and lower lock lever actuators.
17. Remove ignition lock cylinder lockout lever and lock actuator lever return spring.
18. Remove pin and lock actuator lever, then the pin and locking lever cam using suitable pin punch.
19. Remove pin, tilt locking levers and springs using suitable pin punch. **Do not remove tilt lock levers if not required.**
20. Reverse procedure to install, noting the following:
   a. Lock lever with two teeth is installed on lefthand side.
   b. Lubricate lock lever actuator with ignition lock grease part No. F0AZ-19584-A, or equivalent.
   c. Lower bearing UP position must face forward.
   d. Install steering column bearing so inner race is visible using suitable bearing installer tool or socket.
   e. Lubricate tilt pivot bushings and mounting screws with ignition lock grease.

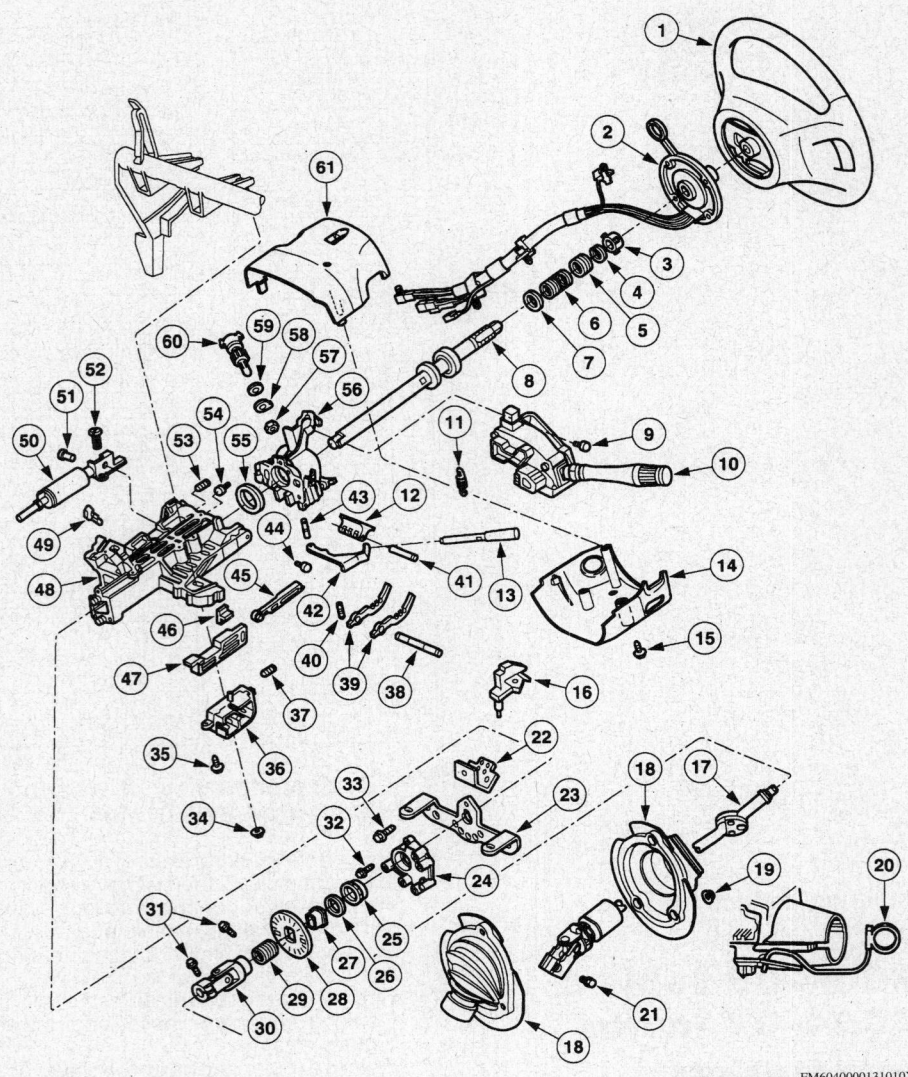

Item	Description		Item	Description
1	Steering wheel		32	Bearing housing retaining screw
2	Air bag sliding contact		33	Screw
3	Turn indicator cancel cam		34	Steering column mounting lower nuts
4	Snap ring		35	Screw
5	Bearing spring		36	Ignition switch
6	Upper bearing sleeve		37	Lock spring (shaft)
7	Upper bearing (small)		38	Lock actuator lever pin
8	Shaft assembly		39	Lock actuator lever
9	Screw		40	Lock lever spring (2 req'd)
10	Multi-function switch		41	Lock cam pivot pin
11	Lock lever spring return		42	Release lever
12	Lock cam		43	Lock actuator lever pin
13	Tilt wheel handle		44	Tilt pivot screws
14	Lower shroud		45	Lock lever upper actuator
15	Shroud retaining screws		46	Lock pawl
16	Wiring shield		47	Lock lever lower actuator
17	Intermediate shaft		48	Actuator housing
18	Tube boot		49	Lock actuator cover
19	Nut		50	Ignition/shifter interlock cable
20	Perimeter anti-theft system (PATS) sensor		51	Screw
21	Bolt		52	Screw
22	Wire connector bracket		53	Position spring
23	Mounting bracket		54	Tilt flange bumper
24	Bearing retaining		55	Lower bearing (large)
25	Bearing sleeve		56	Lock cylinder housing
26	Lower bearing		57	Lock gear
27	Lower bearing tolerance ring		58	Lock housing bearing
28	Sensor ring		59	Bearing retainer
29	Bearing spring		60	Ignition switch lock cylinder
30	Coupling		61	Upper shroud
31	Bolt — flange yoke			

FM6040000131020X

Fig. 9 Exploded view of steering column (Part 2 of 2). 2004–05 Sable & 2004–07 Taurus w/console shift

FM6040000131010X

Fig. 9 Exploded view of steering column (Part 1 of 2). 2004–05 Sable & 2004–07 Taurus w/console shift

f. Ensure upper and lower lock actuators are aligned.

g. Align ignition switch with actuator housing slot and index mark.

h. Ensure narrow section of lock gear keyhole is in 1 o'clock position with tab inboard at 3 o'clock position.

i. Coat lock gear with ignition lock grease.

j. Lubricate lock housing bearing with ignition lock grease and rotate counterclockwise.

k. Ensure upper bearing retainer firmly engages lock housing retention tabs.

COLUMN SHIFT

1. Disconnect steering column opening gearshift lever seal, then remove retaining pin and gearshift lever.

2. Record steering column lock gear, bearing and retainer prior positions for assembly alignment, **Fig. 11.**

3. Remove steering column lock housing bearing and gear.

4. **On models equipped with fixed steering column,** remove steering column shaft bottom snap ring.

5. **On models equipped with tilt steering column,** remove steering column lower bearing spring and sensor ring.

6. **On all models,** remove steering column bearing tolerance ring.

7. Remove lock cylinder housing pivot mounting screws.

8. Pry steering column locking levers up using suitable fabricated tool, **Fig. 10.**

9. Remove lock cylinder housing and steering column shaft from steering actuator housing.

10. **On models equipped with tilt steering column,** remove steering column position spring. **Steering column position spring is under tension and can come out with great force.**

11. **On all models,** remove turn indicator cancel cam by prying up flush surface using suitable flat-blade screwdriver.

12. Remove snap ring, upper bearing spring and sleeve.

13. Slide steering column shaft in toward steering column lock cylinder housing, then remove bearing tolerance ring and shaft.

14. Remove steering column upper bearing from lock cylinder housing using suitable punch.

15. **On models equipped with tilt steering column,** remove steering column lower bearing from lock cylinder housing using suitable punch.

16. **On all models,** remove mounting screws and plastic harness retainer.

17. Remove mounting bolts, brake shift interlock solenoid and transaxle shift position insert.

18. Remove mounting bolts, clamps and shift tube.

19. Remove mounting bolts and transaxle shift arm assembly.

20. Remove gearshift lever spring from shift tube.

21. Drive pin out and remove gearshift lever from shift tube.

22. Remove column shift selector lever plunger. Replace lever plunger if it is bent.

23. Remove gearshift lever socket bushings and transaxle control selector lever spring clip.

24. Drive out steering column lock lever pin and remove steering column lock pawl.

25. Remove mounting screws and ignition switch.

26. Remove steering column lower bearing and sleeve.

27. Remove mounting bolts and steering column lower bearing retainer.

28. Remove steering column upper and

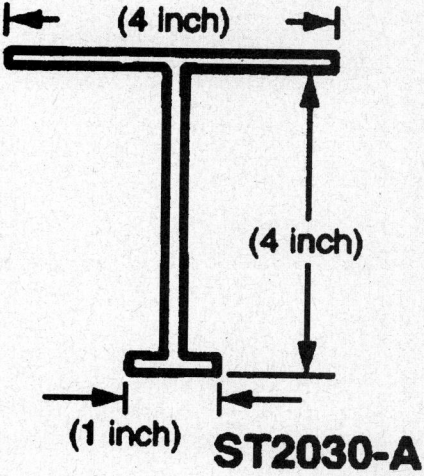

ST2030-A

FM6040000133000X

Fig. 10 Steering column locking lever fabricated tool dimensions. 2004–05 Sable & 2004–07 Taurus

lower lock actuator.

29. Reverse procedure to install, noting the following:
   a. Lubricate steering column lock actuators, and coat lock pawl and pin surfaces with ignition lock grease part No. F0AZ-19584-A, or equivalent.
   b. Steering column lower bearing UP position must face engine.
   c. Install steering column lower bearing and sleeve so inner race is visible.
   d. Align ignition switch with steering column slot and index mark.
   e. Coat gearshift lever socket bushings and column shift selector plunger with steering gear grease part No. C3AZ-19578-A, or equivalent.
   f. Coat gearshift selector tube spring with steering gear grease.
   g. Install upper and large steering column bearings so inner race is visible with suitable bearing installer tool or socket.
   h. Lubricate lock cylinder housing bushings and mounting screws with rust penetrant and inhibitor part No. F2AZ-19A501-A, or equivalent.
   i. Ensure upper and lower steering column lock actuators are aligned.

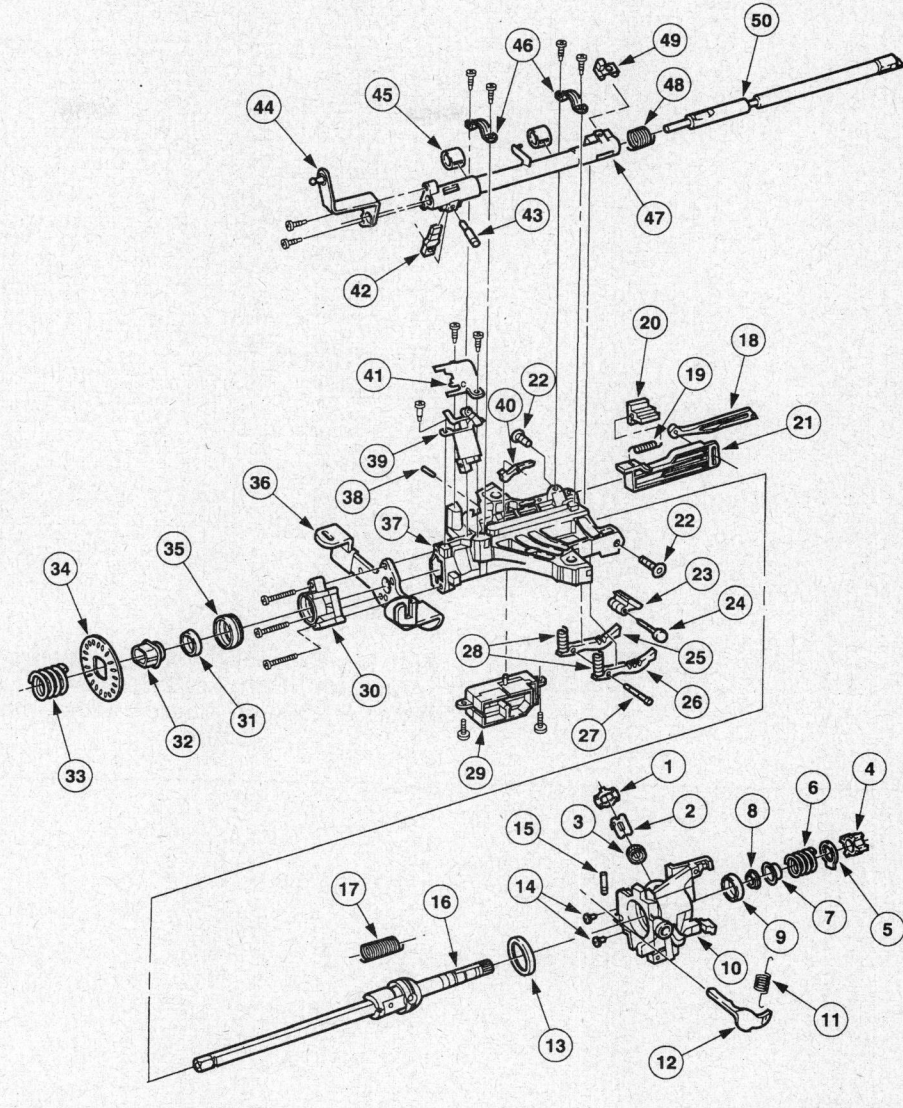

FM6040000132010X

Fig. 11 Exploded view of steering column (Part 1 of 2). 2004–05 Sable & 2004–07 Taurus w/column shift

   j. Narrow section of lock gear keyhole must be in 1 o'clock position with tab inboard at 3 o'clock position.
   k. Coat steering column lock gear with ignition lock grease.
   l. Rotate lock gear counterclockwise.
   m. Lubricate steering column lock housing bearing with ignition lock grease.
   n. Ensure steering column lock housing bearing engages housing retention tabs.

Item	Description	Item	Description
1	Steering column upper bearing retainer	27	Steering column lock lever actuator pin
2	Steering column lock housing bearing	28	Steering column locking lever spring
3	Steering column lock gear	29	Ignition switch
4	Turn indicator cancel cam	30	Steering column lower bearing retainer
5	Snap ring	31	Steering column bearing
6	Steering column upper bearing spring	32	Lower steering column bearing tolerance ring
7	Steering column bearing sleeve	33	Steering column bearing spring
8	Steering column upper bearing tolerance ring	34	Suspension height sensor control ring
9	Upper steering column bearing (small)	35	Steering column bearing sleeve
10	Lock cylinder housing	36	Steering column lower mounting bracket
11	Steering column release lever spring	37	Steering actuator housing
12	Steering column release lever	38	Steering column lock lever pin (shifter)
13	Upper steering column bearing (large)	39	Brake shift interlock solenoid
14	Lock cylinder housing bumper	40	Steering column lock pawl (shifter)
15	Tilt release lever pivot pin	41	Transmission shift selector position insert
16	Steering shaft assy	42	Transmission gearshift lever
17	Steering column position spring	43	Transmission gearshift lever pin
18	Upper lock actuator assy	44	Shift arm assy
19	Steering column lock spring	45	Gearshift lever socket bushing
20	Steering column lock pawl	46	Gearshift tube bushing clamp
21	Lower lock actuator assy	47	Transmission column shift selector tube
22	Tilt pivot screws	48	Gearshift selector tube spring
23	Steering column lock cam	49	Transmission control selector lever spring clip
24	Steering column lock cam pivot pin	50	Column shift selector lever plunger
25	Steering column locking lever (RH)		
26	Steering column locking lever (LH)		

FM6040000132020X

Fig. 11 Exploded view of steering column (Part 2 of 2). 2004–05 Sable & 2004–07 Taurus w/column shift

TIGHTENING SPECIFICATIONS

Year	Component	Torque/Ft. Lbs.
CROWN VICTORIA & GRAND MARQUIS		
2004–08	Brake Shift Interlock Solenoid	80①
	Driver's Air Bag Module	108①
	Ignition Switch	53①
	Lock Cylinder Housing	16
	Lower Steering Column Shaft, Lower	35
	Lower Steering Column Shaft, Upper	22
	Parking Brake Release Switch	27①
	Shift Tube	80①
	Shock Absorber Electronic Steering Sensor	9①
	Steering Column Lower Bearing	80①
	Steering Column Support	11
	Steering Wheel	30
	Transmission Range Indicator	27①
	Transmission Selector Lever Arm & Support	11
FIVE HUNDRED, FREESTYLE, MONTEGO, 2008 SABLE, TAURUS & TAURUS X		
2005–08	Column Shroud Screws	62①
	Multi-Function Switch Screws	18①
	Shift Tube Bolts	80①
	Steering Column Coupler Bolts	18
	Steering Column Nuts	11
	Steering Column Shaft Bolts	18
	Steering Wheel Bolt	30
FOCUS		
2004–07	Air Bag Module	44①
	Hood Release Cable	15
	Steering Column	10
	Steering Column Shaft	21
	Steering Wheel	37
FUSION, MILAN, MKZ & ZEPHYR		
2006–08	Instrument Panel Reinforcement	18①
	Steering Column Shaft	18
	Steering Column Support Bracket	15
	Steering Wheel Nut	10
LS		
2004–06	Driver's Air Bag Module	108①
	Electronic Steering Sensor	27①
	Steering Column	13
	Steering Column Actuator Telescopic Bolt	11
	Steering Column Actuator Telescopic Nut	13
	Steering Column Actuator Tilt, Bolt	11
	Steering Column Actuator Tilt, Nut	13
	Steering Column Outer Housing Cover Plate	10
	Steering Column Release Motor	27①
	Steering Column Tube Flange Pivot Bolts	17
	Steering Column Upper Shaft	10
	Steering Shaft Pinch Bolt	22
	Steering Wheel	38
	Steering Wheel Lock Actuator Mounting	108①

TIGHTENING SPECIFICATIONS—Continued

Year	Component	Torque/Ft. Lbs.
MARAUDER		
2004	Brake Shift Interlock Solenoid	80①
	Driver's Air Bag Module	108①
	Ignition Switch	53①
	Lock Cylinder Housing	16
	Lower Steering Column Shaft, Lower	35
	Lower Steering Column Shaft, Upper	22
	Parking Brake Release Switch	27①
	Shift Tube	80①
	Shock Absorber Electronic Steering Sensor	9①
	Steering Column Lower Bearing	80①
	Steering Column Support	11
	Steering Wheel	30
	Transmission Range Indicator	27①
	Transmission Selector Lever Arm & Support	11
MUSTANG		
2004–08	Air Bag Sliding Contact	18–26
	Driver's Air Bag Module	36–53①
	Ignition Switch	45–61①
	Interlock Cable	14–17①
	Intermediate Shaft Coupler	19
	Lock Cylinder	17
	Steering Column Gear Input Shaft Coupling To Column Shaft	30–40
	Steering Column Gear Input Shaft Coupling To Gear Pinch	19–25
	Steering Column Lower Bearing	80①
	Steering Column Lower Mount	62–97①
	Steering Column Mount	10–12
	Steering Column Pivot	14–19
	Steering Column Tube Boot	71–88①
	Steering Wheel	23–32
2004–05 SABLE & 2004–07 TAURUS		
2004–07	Brake Shift Interlock Solenoid	80①
	Ignition Switch	54①
	Instrument Panel Opening Cover Support	11
	Lock Cylinder Housing	17
	Shift Tube	80①
	Steering Column	11
	Steering Column Coupler	18
	Steering Column Finish Panel	62①
	Steering Column Lower Bearing	80①
	Steering Column Shaft	36
	Steering Wheel Pinion Shaft	13
	Transaxle Selector Lever Arm & Support	11

TIGHTENING SPECIFICATIONS—Continued

Year	Component	Torque/Ft. Lbs.
THUNDERBIRD		
2004–05	Driver's Air Bag Module	108①
	Electronic Steering Sensor	27①
	Steering Column	13
	Steering Column Actuator Telescopic Bolt	11
	Steering Column Actuator Telescopic Nut	13
	Steering Column Actuator Tilt, Bolt	11
	Steering Column Actuator Tilt, Nut	13
	Steering Column Outer Housing Cover Plate	10
	Steering Column Release Motor	27①
	Steering Column Tube Flange Pivot Bolts	17
	Steering Column Upper Shaft	10
	Steering Shaft Pinch Bolt	22
	Steering Wheel	38
	Steering Wheel Lock Actuator Mounting	108①

TIGHTENING SPECIFICATIONS—Continued

Year	Component	Torque/Ft. Lbs.
TOWN CAR		
2004–08	Brake Shift Interlock Solenoid	80①
	Ignition Switch	62①
	Lock Cylinder Housing	16
	Parking Brake Release Switch	27①
	Shift Tube	80①
	Shock Absorber Electronic Steering Sensor	13①
	Steering Column Lower Bearing	80①
	Steering Column Support	11
	Steering Wheel	30
	Transmission Range Indicator	80①
	Transmission Selector Arm & Support	11
	Upper Intermediate Shaft To Lower Intermediate Shaft	22
	Upper Intermediate Steering Shaft To Steering Column Shaft	22

① — Inch lbs.

POWER STEERING

TABLE OF CONTENTS

	Page No.		Page No.
APPLICATION CHART	13-2	FORD TORSION BAR POWER STEERING GEAR	13-14
ATSUGI VANE-TYPE PUMP	13-3	FORD VARIABLE ASSIST ELECTRONIC VARIABLE ORIFICE (EVO) SYSTEM	13-18
FOCUS POWER STEERING PUMP	13-3	FORD VARIABLE ASSIST POWER STEERING (VAPS) SYSTEM	13-31
FOCUS RACK & PINION STEERING GEAR	13-7	POWER STEERING PRESSURE SPECIFICATIONS	13-1
FORD CIII VANE-TYPE PUMP	13-7	ZUA VANE-TYPE PUMP	13-7
FORD INTEGRAL RACK & PINION STEERING GEAR	13-8		
FORD MODEL CII SLIPPER-TYPE PUMP	13-3		

Power Steering Pressure Specifications

Vehicle	Engine	Minimum Flow, GPM①	Minimum Relief Pressure, psi	Maximum Relief Pressure, psi	Pump Model②	Maximum Free Flow, GPM @ RPM
Crown Victoria	4.6L	1.40	1200	1380	CII	3.2 @ 2500
Five Hundred	3.0L	1.15	1450	1580	CIII	③
Focus	2.0L DOHC	1.15	1117	1247	CIII	2.4 @ 1500
	2.0L SOHC	1.15	1117	1247	CIII	2.4 @ 1500
Freestyle	3.0L	1.15	1450	1580	CIII	③
Fusion	2.3L	1.84	1409	1475	CIII	2.5 @ 2100
	3.0L	1.95	1284	1318	CIII	2.5 @ 2000
	3.5L	1.95	1284	1318	CIII	2.5 @ 2000
Grand Marquis	4.6L	1.40	1200	1380	CII	3.2 @ 2500
LS	3.0L	1.40	1400	1530	CII	2.4 @ 1500
	3.9L	1.40	1400	1530	CII	2.4 @ 1500
Marauder	4.6L	1.40	1400	1530	CII	3.2 @ 2500
Milan	2.3L	1.84	1409	1475	CIII	2.5 @ 2100
	3.0L	1.95	1284	1318	CIII	2.5 @ 2000
	3.5L	1.95	1284	1318	CIII	2.5 @ 2000
MKZ	2.3L	1.84	1409	1475	CIII	2.5 @ 2100
	3.0L	1.95	1284	1318	CIII	2.5 @ 2000
	3.5L	1.95	1284	1318	CIII	2.5 @ 2000
Montego	3.0L	1.15	1450	1580	CIII	③
Mustang	3.8L	.90	1050	1230	CII	2.6 @ 1500
	4.0L	1.30	1400	1530	CIII	2.2 @ 2150
	4.6L	1.25	1200	1380	CIII	2.6 @ 1500
Sable & Taurus	3.0L OHV	1.15	1400	1530	CII	2.8 @ 1500
	3.0L DOHC	1.15	1400	1530	CIII	2.8 @ 1500
	3.5L	1.95	1284	1318	CIII	2.5 @ 2000
Thunderbird	3.9L	1.40	1400	1530	CII	2.6 @ 1500
Town Car	4.6L	1.40	1200	1380	CII	3.2 @ 2500
Zephyr	2.3L	1.84	1409	1475	CIII	2.5 @ 2100
	3.0L	1.95	1284	1318	CIII	2.5 @ 2000

POWER STEERING

GPM — Gallons per minute

① — Flow is dependent on pump model, engine RPM & pulley ratio. Engine idle speed must be within specifications when measuring minimum flow.

② — Power steering pump identification tag is located on the reservoir body.

③ — Maximum flow @ curb idle 2.8 GPM.

Application Chart

Model	Year	Power Steering Pump Type	Power Steering Pump Page No.	Power Steering Gear Type	Power Steering Gear Page No.	Power Steering Assist Type	Power Steering Assist Page No.
Crown Victoria	2004–08	Ford Model CII Slipper-Type Pump	13-3	Ford Integral Rack & Pinion Steering Gear	13-8	Ford Variable Assist Power Steering (VAPS) System	13-18
Five Hundred	2005–07	Ford CIII Vane-Type Pump	13-7	Ford Integral Rack & Pinion Steering Gear	13-8	—	—
Focus	2004–07	①	13-7	Focus Rack & Pinion Steering Gear	13-7	—	—
Freestyle	2005–07	Ford CIII Vane-Type Pump	13-7	Ford Integral Rack & Pinion Steering Gear	13-8	—	—
Fusion	2006–08	Ford CIII Vane-Type Pump	13-7	Ford Integral Rack & Pinion Steering Gear	13-8	—	—
Grand Marquis	2004–08	Ford Model CII Slipper-Type Pump	13-3	Ford Integral Rack & Pinion Steering Gear	13-8	Ford Variable Assist Power Steering (VAPS) System	13-18
LS	2004–06	Ford Model CII Slipper-Type Pump	13-3	Ford Integral Rack & Pinion Steering Gear	13-8	Ford Variable Assist Power Steering (VAPS) System	13-18
Marauder	2004	Ford Model CII Slipper-Type Pump	13-3	Ford Integral Rack & Pinion Steering Gear	13-8	Ford Variable Assist Power Steering (VAPS) System	13-18
Milan	2006–08	Ford CIII Vane-Type Pump	13-7	Ford Integral Rack & Pinion Steering Gear	13-8	—	—
MKZ	2007	Ford CIII Vane-Type Pump	13-7	Ford Integral Rack & Pinion Steering Gear	13-8	—	—
Montego	2005–07	Ford CIII Vane-Type Pump	13-7	Ford Integral Rack & Pinion Steering Gear	13-8	—	—
Mustang	2004–08	②	④	Ford Integral Rack & Pinion Steering Gear	13-8	—	—
Sable	2004–05	③	④	Ford Integral Rack & Pinion Steering Gear	13-8	—	—
	2008	Ford CIII Vane-Type Pump	13-7	Ford Integral Rack & Pinion Steering Gear	13-8	—	—
Taurus	2004–07	③	④	Ford Integral Rack & Pinion Steering Gear	13-8	—	—
	2008	Ford CIII Vane-Type Pump	13-7	Ford Integral Rack & Pinion Steering Gear	13-8	—	—
Taurus X	2008	Ford CIII Vane-Type Pump	13-7	Ford Integral Rack & Pinion Steering Gear	13-8	—	—
Town Car	2004–07	Ford Model CII Slipper-Type Pump	13-3	Ford Integral Rack & Pinion Steering Gear	13-8	Ford Variable Assist Power Steering (VAPS) System	13-18
Thunderbird	2004–05	Ford Model CII Slipper-Type Pump	13-3	Ford Integral Rack & Pinion Steering Gear	13-8	Ford Variable Assist Power Steering (VAPS) System	13-18
Zephyr	2006	Ford CIII Vane-Type Pump	13-7	Ford Integral Rack & Pinion Steering Gear	13-8	—	—

① — 2.0L DOHC engine, Ford CIII Vane-Type Pump; 2.0L SOHC engine, Focus Power Steering Pump.

② — 3.8L engine, Ford Model CII Slipper-Type Pump; 4.6L engine, Ford CIII Vane-Type Pump.

③ — 3.0L DOHC engine, Atsugi Vane-Type Pump; 3.0L OHV engine, Ford Model CII Slipper-Type Pump.

④ — See Table of Contents for specific type.

Atsugi Vane-Type Pump

NOTE: These Pumps Are Not Serviceable. If Service Is Required, Pump Must Be Replaced.

Focus Power Steering Pump

NOTE: These Pumps Are Not Serviceable. If Service Is Required, Pump Must Be Replaced.

Ford Model CII Slipper-Type Pump

NOTE: On Air Bag Equipped Models, Refer To "Air Bag System Precautions" Located In The Front Of This Manual For System Disarming & Arming Procedures.

NOTE: Refer To "Computer Relearn Procedures" Located In The Front Of This Manual When Battery Power To The Computer Has Been Interrupted.

INDEX

	Page No.			Page No.			Page No.
Description	13-3		Precautions	13-3		Troubleshooting	13-3
Power Steering Pump	13-3		Air Bag Systems	13-3		Power Steering Pump Leaks	13-3
Assemble	13-4		Battery Ground Cable	13-3		Power Steering Pump Noise,	
Disassemble	13-3		Tightening Specifications	13-6		Moan Or Whine	13-3

PRECAUTIONS

Air Bag Systems

Refer to "Air Bag System Precautions" in the front of this manual for system disarming and arming procedures.

Battery Ground Cable

Prior to service, disconnect battery ground cable and isolate as required.

DESCRIPTION

The Ford model CII power steering pump is a belt driven 10-slipper type pump incorporating a fiberglass filled nylon reservoir. The reservoir is attached to the rear side of the aluminum pump housing assembly. The pump body is encased within the housing and reservoir assembly. The pump design incorporates a pump pressure fitting which allows the pump pressure line to swivel. A pressure sensitive identification tag is attached to the reservoir body. This tag indicates the basic model number and the suffix.

TROUBLESHOOTING

Power Steering Pump Leaks

1. Excessive fluid fill.
2. Dipstick missing, loose, damaged or missing O-ring.
3. Broken or cracked fluid reservoir.
4. Loose or damaged hose fittings.
5. Shaft seal not pressed flush with housing surface.
6. Shaft seal damage.
7. Rotor shaft damage, helical grooving or OD has an axial scratch.
8. Shaft bushing worn.
9. Plugged drain back hole.
10. Damaged or missing reservoir O-ring.
11. Damaged or missing outlet fitting O-rings.
12. Excessive pump assembly bracket vibration.
13. Plate and bushing reservoir seal groove damage, metal chips or foreign material in seal groove.
14. Faulty outlet fitting.

Power Steering Pump Noise, Moan Or Whine

1. Fluid aeration.
2. Low fluid.
3. Hose grounded.
4. Steering column grounded.
5. Valve cover O-ring or baffle missing or damaged.
6. Interference between components in pumping elements.
7. Loose or poor bracket alignment.
8. Cam contour damaged.

POWER STEERING PUMP

Disassemble

1. Remove pulley, **Fig. 1.**
2. Remove outlet fitting, flow control valve and flow control valve spring from pump, then the reservoir.
3. Place suitable C-clamp in vise.
4. Position lower support plate tool No. T78P-3733-A2, or equivalent, over pump rotor shaft.
5. Install upper compressor plate tool No. T78P-3733-A1, or equivalent, into upper portion of C-clamp.
6. While holding compressor tool, place pump assembly into C-clamp with rotor shaft facing downward, **Fig. 2.**
7. Tighten C-clamp until slight bottoming of valve cover is observed.
8. Through small hole located on side of pump housing, insert suitable drift and push inward on valve cover snap ring.

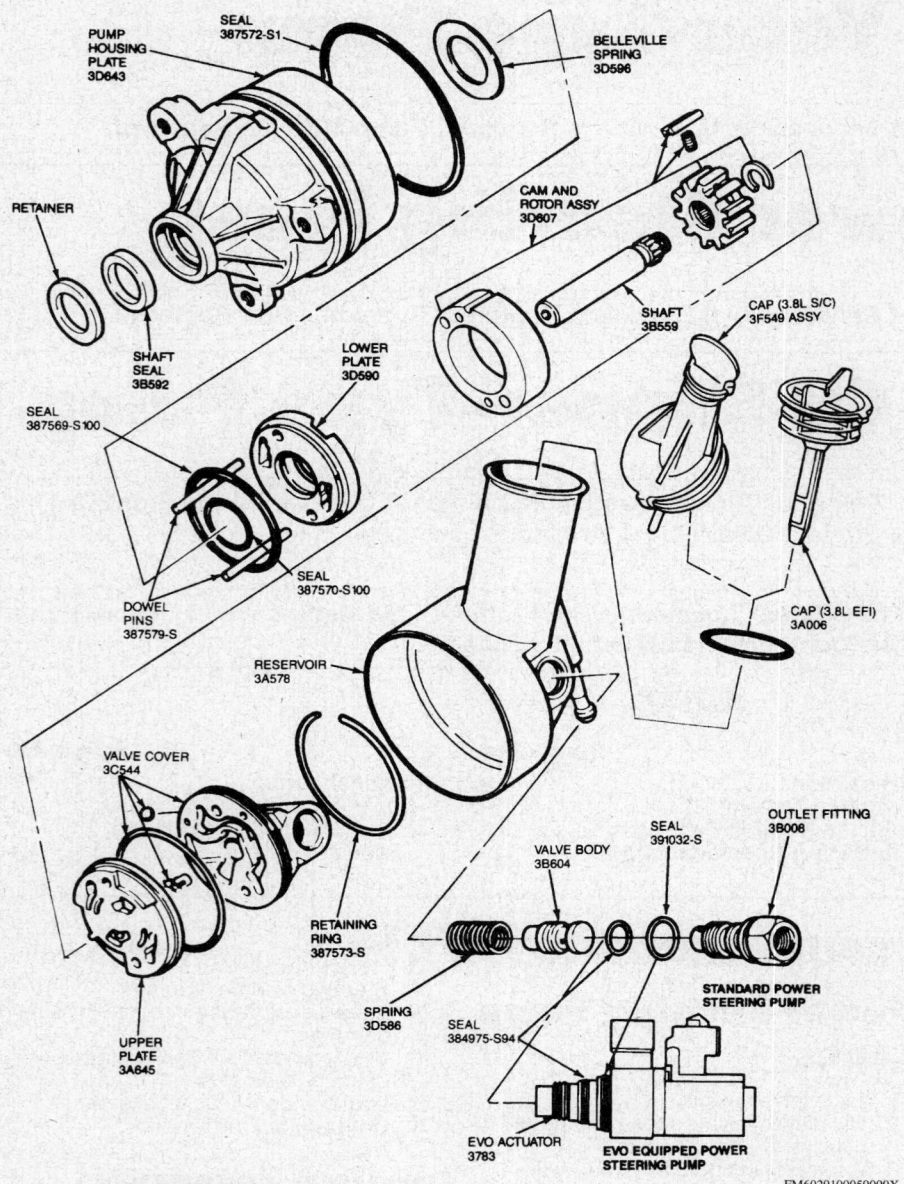

Fig. 1 Exploded view of Ford Model CII power steering pump

or equivalent, to outside diameter of seal and Locquic NF or T primer, or equivalent to seal bore in housing.

9. Install rotor shaft seal using seal driver tool No. T78P-3733-A3, or equivalent.
10. Drive seal into bore until properly seated using suitable plastic mallet.
11. Position pump plate on flat surface with pulley side facing downward.
12. Install two dowel pins and spring into housing. **Spring must be inserted with dished surface facing upward.**
13. Lubricate inner and outer O-ring seals with suitable power steering fluid, then install seals on lower pressure plate.
14. Install lower pressure plate into housing and over dowel pin with O-ring seals facing toward front of pump.
15. Position assembly on C-clamp.
16. Seat outer O-ring seal by placing seal driver tool No. T78P-3733-A3, or equivalent, into rotor shaft hole and press on lower plate lightly until it bottoms in pump housing. This will seat outer O-ring seal.
17. Install cam, rotor and slippers and rotor shaft assembly into pump housing over dowel pins.
18. When installing assembly into pump housing, stepped holes must be used for dowel pins and notch in cam insert must be toward reservoir and approximately 180° opposite square mounting lug on housing, **Fig. 6.**
19. Position upper pressure plate over dowel pins with recess directly over recessed notch on cam insert and approximately 180° opposite square mounting lug, **Fig. 7.**
20. Lubricate O-ring seal with suitable power steering fluid, then position O-ring on valve cover. Ensure plastic baffle is securely in position on valve cover. Coat of petroleum jelly may be used to hold baffle in position.
21. Insert valve cover over dowel pins. Ensure outlet fitting hole in valve cover is aligned with square mounting lug on housing, **Fig. 8.**
22. Place assembly in C-clamp and compress valve cover into pump housing until snap ring groove on housing is exposed.
23. Install valve cover snap ring in pump housing. Ensure snap ring ends are near access hole in pump housing.
24. Remove pump from C-clamp.
25. Lubricate O-ring seal with suitable power steering fluid and place it on pump housing.
26. Install reservoir on pump housing.
27. Install flow control valve and spring into valve cover.
28. Lubricate O-ring seals with suitable power steering fluid and lace them on outlet fitting.
29. Install outlet fitting on valve cover.
30. Tighten outlet fitting.
31. **Do not cock flow control valve when installing.**
32. **Do not force valve forward.**

9. While pushing inward on snap ring, place screwdriver under snap ring edge and remove ring from housing, **Fig. 3.**
10. Loosen C-clamp, then remove lower support plate tool and pump.
11. Remove pump valve cover and O-ring.
12. Remove rotor shaft, upper plate, cam and rotor, then the two dowel pins.
13. Remove lower plate and spring by tapping housing on flat surface.
14. Remove rotor shaft seal using suitable screwdriver.

Assemble

1. Position rotor on rotor shaft splines with triangle detent on rotor counterbore facing upward.

2. Install snap ring into groove on end of rotor shaft.
3. Position insert cam over rotor. Ensure recessed notch on insert cam is facing upward.
4. With rotor extended upward approximately half out of cam, insert spring into rotor pocket, **Fig. 4.**
5. Install slipper to compress spring and slipper with groove facing cam, **Fig. 5.**
6. Repeat pervious steps on slipper cavity beneath opposite inlet recess.
7. While holding cam stationary, index rotor left or right one space, then install another spring and slipper until all 10 rotor cavities have been filled. Ensure when turning rotor that springs and slippers remain in position.
8. Apply Loctite No. 242 or 271 adhesive,

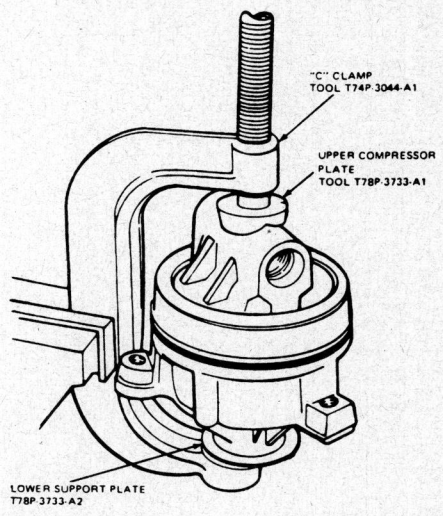

"C" CLAMP TOOL T74P-3044-A1

UPPER COMPRESSOR PLATE TOOL T78P-3733-A1

LOWER SUPPORT PLATE T78P-3733-A2

FM6029100060000X

Fig. 2   Positioning pump in C-clamp

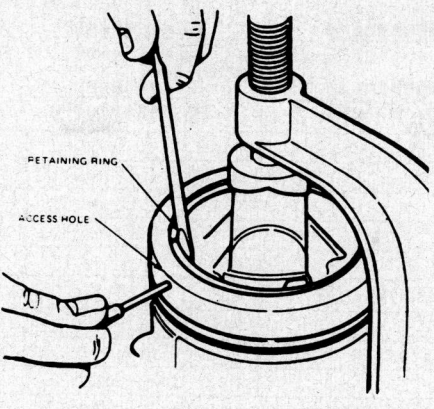

RETAINING RING

ACCESS HOLE

FM6029100061000X

Fig. 3   Valve cover retaining ring removal

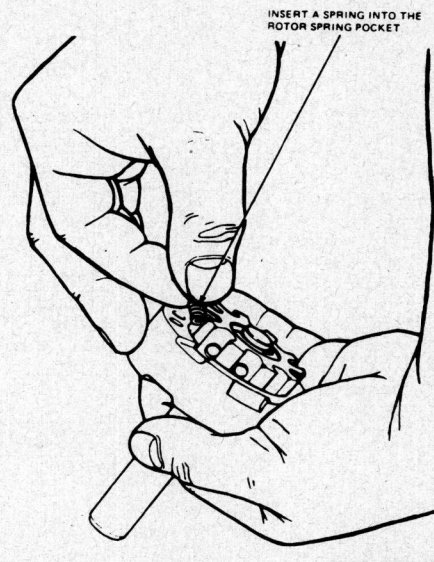

INSERT A SPRING INTO THE ROTOR SPRING POCKET

FM6029100062000X

Fig. 4   Slipper springs installation

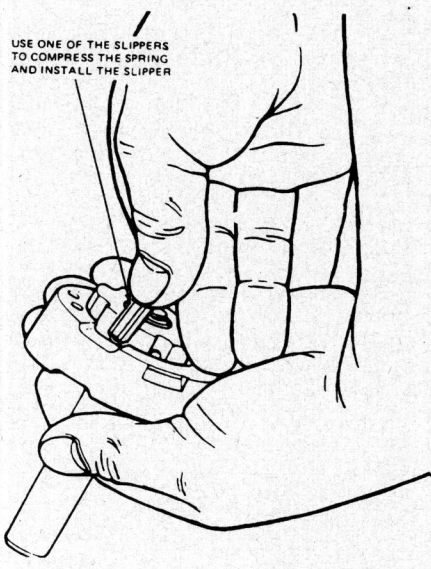

USE ONE OF THE SLIPPERS TO COMPRESS THE SPRING AND INSTALL THE SLIPPER

FM6029100063000X

Fig. 5   Slipper installation

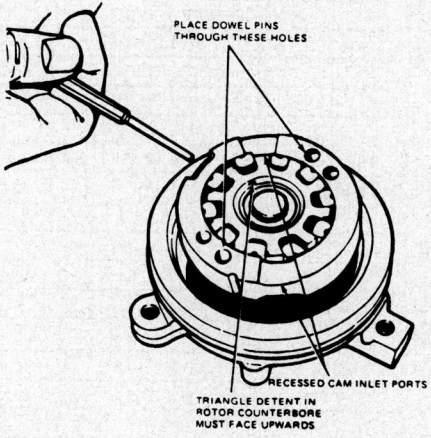

RECESSED NOTCH IN CAM INSERT APPROXIMATELY 180 DEGREES OPPOSITE THE SQUARE MOUNTING LUG ON THE ALUMINUM HOUSING

PLACE DOWEL PINS THROUGH THESE HOLES

RECESSED CAM INLET PORTS

TRIANGLE DETENT IN ROTOR COUNTERBORE MUST FACE UPWARDS

FM6029100064000X

Fig. 6   Assembling cam, slippers & rotor

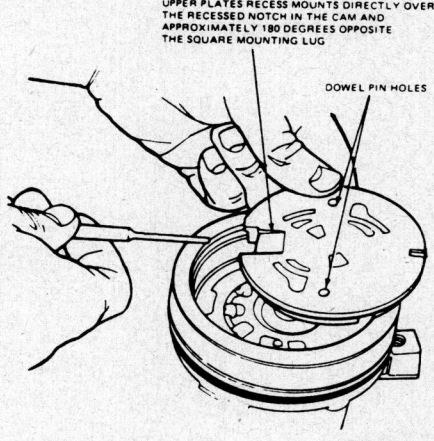

UPPER PLATES RECESS MOUNTS DIRECTLY OVER THE RECESSED NOTCH IN THE CAM AND APPROXIMATELY 180 DEGREES OPPOSITE THE SQUARE MOUNTING LUG

DOWEL PIN HOLES

FM6029100065000X

Fig. 7   Upper pressure plate installation

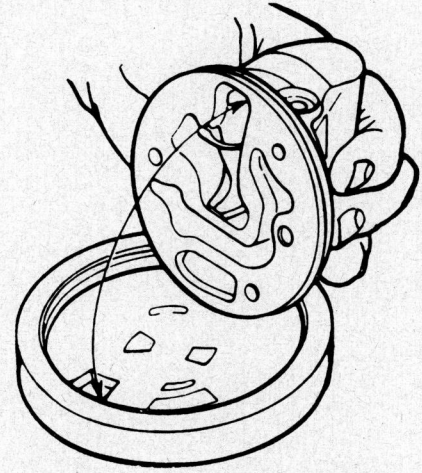

PRESSURE CHANNEL IN THE VALVE COVER FITS DIRECTLY OVER THE RECESS IN THE UPPER PLATE

FM6029100066000X

Fig. 8   Valve cover installation

TIGHTENING SPECIFICATIONS

Year	Component	Torque Ft. Lbs.
CROWN VICTORIA & GRAND MARQUIS		
2004–08	Pressure Line Bracket To Engine	62①
	Pressure Line Fitting To Pump	48
	Reservoir Isolator Bolt Lower	108①
	Steering Line Clamp Plate	13
	Steering Pump	18
LS & THUNDERBIRD		
2004–06	Pump Bolts	18
	Pressure Line Fitting	24
	Reservoir Isolator Bolt (Lower)	89①
	Reservoir Isolator Bolt (Upper)	35①
MARAUDER		
2004	Power Steering Pump	18
	Pressure Line Fitting	48
	Reservoir	96①
MUSTANG		
2004	Power Steering Pump	38
	Pressure Line Fitting	30
2005–08	Power Steering Pump	18
	Pressure Line Fitting	48
	Steering Pump Pulley 4.0L	18
	Steering Pump Pulley Shield 4.6L	89①
SABLE & TAURUS		
2004–07	Hose Bracket	89①
	Pressure Hose Fitting	27
	Return Line	27
	Support Bracket	35
TOWN CAR		
2004–07	Power Steering Pump	18
	Pressure Line Fitting	48
	Reservoir	96①

① — Inch lbs.

Ford CIII Vane-Type Pump

NOTE: These Pumps Are Not Serviceable. If Service Is Required, Pump Must Be Replaced.

ZUA Vane-Type Pump

NOTE: These Pumps Are Not Serviceable. If Service Is Required, Pump Must Be Replaced.

Focus Rack & Pinion Steering Gear

NOTE: On Air Bag Equipped Models, Refer To "Air Bag System Precautions" Located In The Front Of This Manual For System Disarming & Arming Procedures.

NOTE: Refer To "Computer Relearn Procedures" Located In The Front Of This Manual When Battery Power To The Computer Has Been Interrupted.

INDEX

	Page No.		Page No.		Page No.
Description	13-7	Air Bag Systems	13-7	Steering Gear Bushing,	
Power Steering System Bleed	13-7	Battery Ground Cable	13-7	Replace	13-7
Precautions	13-7			Tightening Specifications	13-8

PRECAUTIONS

Air Bag Systems

Refer to "Air Bag System Precautions" in the front of this manual for system disarming and arming procedures.

Battery Ground Cable

Prior to service, disconnect battery ground cable and isolate as required.

DESCRIPTION

The steering gear is operated and controlled by the hydraulic fluid supplied by the power steering pump.

The rack and pinion is held in position by two mounting brackets and rubber bushings. The gear uses an integral piston and rack design to provide power assisted steering control.

STEERING GEAR BUSHING

REPLACE

1. Remove steering gear as outlined in "Front Suspension & Steering" section of "Focus" chassis chapter.
2. Remove insulator bushings using bushing remover and installer tool No.

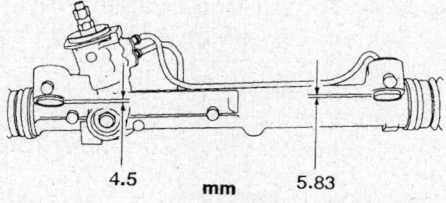

4.5   mm   5.83

FM6020000438000X

Fig. 1   Steering gear bushing installation depths

205-297 and wheel hub installer tool No. 204-148, or equivalents.
3. If housing is damaged, replace steering gear.
4. Reverse procedure to install, noting the following:
   a. Lubricate new bushings with suitable rubber lubricant.
   b. Install new bushings to proper depth using bushing and hub installer tools, **Fig. 1**.

POWER STEERING SYSTEM BLEED

1. Fill reservoir to MAX mark with proper power steering fluid. Inspect level when fluid is cold.
2. Ensure fluid in reservoir does not drop below MIN mark.
3. Start engine and slowly turn steering wheel once from lock to lock.
4. Stop engine and examine all hose connections, steering gear boots, valve body and steering pump for external leaks.
5. Inspect power steering fluid reservoir fluid level and adjust fluid level.
6. Apply 15 inches of vacuum using hand vacuum pump tool No. D95L-7559-A, or equivalent.
7. Observe vacuum gauge reading. If it decreases by more than two inches in five minutes inspect power steering system for leaks.
8. Start engine and slowly turn steering wheel from lock to lock once, then turn to right, but just off lock stop.
9. Stop engine and apply 15 inches of vacuum for at least minutes until air is evacuated from system.
10. Release vacuum at pump tool.
11. Repeat bleed procedure, but this time turn steering wheel to left, just off lock stop.
12. Remove vacuum pump and adjust reservoir level.
13. Start engine and turn steering wheel from lock to lock.
14. Repeat bleed procedure if there is excessive noise.
15. If noise level is still excessive, allow vehicle to sit overnight, then repeat bleed procedure next day.

TIGHTENING SPECIFICATIONS

Year	Component	Torque Ft. Lbs.
2004–08	Crossmember, Front	85
	Crossmember, Rear	148
	Fluid Cooler	44①
	Power Steering Gear Hose Clamps	17
	Power Steering Pressure (PSP) Switch	15
	Power Steering Pump	17
	Pressure Line Support Bracket (DOHC Engine)	18
	Pressure Line Support Bracket (SOHC Engine)	44①
	Pressure Line To Pump Union	48
	Stabilizer Bar Link	37
	Steering Column Shaft Coupling	18
	Steering Column Shaft To Pinion	26
	Steering Gear	59
	Steering Gear Heat Shield	53①
	Support Insulator	37
	Tie Rod End	35
	Wheel Lug Nuts	63

① — Inch lbs.

Ford Integral Rack & Pinion Steering Gear

NOTE: On Air Bag Equipped Models, Refer To "Air Bag System Precautions" Located In The Front Of This Manual For System Disarming & Arming Procedures.

NOTE: Refer To "Computer Relearn Procedures" Located In The Front Of This Manual When Battery Power To The Computer Has Been Interrupted.

INDEX

	Page No.		Page No.		Page No.
Description	13-8	**Power Steering System Bleed**	13-10	**Precautions**	13-8
Operation	13-8	**Power Steering System Service**	13-10	Air Bag Systems	13-8
Diagnosis & Testing	13-9	Adjustments	13-10	Battery Ground Cable	13-8
Pinpoint Tests	13-9	Component Service	13-10	**Tightening Specifications**	13-13
Power Steering Pump Flow & Pressure Test	13-9	Steering Gear	13-10	**Troubleshooting**	13-9
Steering Gear Valve Test	13-9	Tie Rod Ends, Bellows & Ball Joint Sockets	13-10		
Turning Effort Test	13-9				

PRECAUTIONS

Air Bag Systems

Refer to "Air Bag System Precautions" in the front of this manual for system disarming and arming procedures.

Battery Ground Cable

Prior to service, disconnect battery ground cable and isolate as required.

DESCRIPTION

These power rack and pinion steering gears are hydraulic-mechanical units, using an integral piston and rack to provide power assisted steering control. Internal valve controls pump flow and pressure as required during operation, **Figs. 1 and 2.** The unit consists of a rotary hydraulic control valve connected to the input shaft and a boost cylinder integral with the rack.

Operation

The rotary control valve utilizes the relative rotational position of the input shaft and valve sleeve to control fluid flow. As the steering wheel is turned, the resistance of the wheels and weight of the vehicle cause a torsion bar to deflect. This deflection changes position of rotary valve and sleeve ports, thereby directing fluid under pressure to the proper end of the power cylinder. The pressure differential acting on the piston attached to the rack provides the power assist.

The control valve is forced back to a centered position by the torsion bar when steering effort is removed. Pressure is then equalized on each side of the piston and the front wheels tend to return to a straight ahead position.

TROUBLESHOOTING

Refer to **Fig. 3** for troubleshooting procedure.

DIAGNOSIS & TESTING

Pinpoint Tests

Refer to **Figs. 4 through 7** for system diagnosis and testing.

Turning Effort Test

Ensure that the front wheels are correctly aligned and the tire pressure is correct before inspecting the steering effort.
1. Park vehicle on dry concrete and set parking brake.
2. Insert suitable thermometer into power steering fluid reservoir.
3. Idle engine for two to three minutes. Turn steering wheel from stop to stop several times to warm fluid to 122-140° F.
4. With engine running, attach spring scale to rim of steering wheel.
5. Measure pull required to turn steering wheel one complete revolution in each direction, turning pressure effort should not exceed 96 inch lbs.

Power Steering Pump Flow & Pressure Test

During the following procedure, power steering system pressure may exceed 1200 psi. Confirm proper tool fit prior to performing test. Exercise extreme.

Ensure that the connection point will not interfere with any of the engine accessory drive components or drive belts.

Do not touch the flow meter during the test procedure, or severe burns and serious injury can occur.
1. Install power steering analyzer Tool No. 014–00207, or equivalent, at high pressure port of power steering pump. Ensure power steering analyzer gate valve is fully OPEN.
2. Place a suitable dial thermometer in power steering pump reservoir.
3. Inspect power steering fluid level. If required, add specified power steering fluid.
4. Install suitable digital tachometer following manufacturer's instructions.
5. Start engine, then place transmission in NEUTRAL and set parking brake.
6. Raise power steering fluid temperature to 165-175° F by rotating steering wheel fully to the left and right several times. **Do not hold steering wheel against stops for more than three to five seconds at a time. Damage to power steering pump can occur.**
7. With steering wheel in straight ahead position, set engine speed to 2,100 RPM. Record flow rate and pressure readings.
8. If flow rate is below flow rate specification, refer to "Power Steering Pressure Specifications" in this section, then continue with the test procedure.
9. If pressure reading is above maximum pressure specification, inspect power steering hoses for kinks and restrictions.
10. Partially close gate valve to obtain 750 psi, set engine speed at idle. Record flow rate.
11. If flow rate is less than specification, refer to "Power Steering Pressure Specifications" in this section, install a new power steering pump.
12. Completely CLOSE and partially OPEN gate valve three times. Record pressure relief valve actuation pressure reading. **Do not allow gate valve to remain closed for more than five seconds. Damage to power steering pump can occur.**
13. If pressure does not meet relief pressure specification refer to "Power Steering Pressure Specifications" in this section, then install a new power steering pump.
14. Set engine speed to 2,100 RPM. Record flow rate.
15. If flow rate varies more than 1 gallon per minute (GPM) from initial flow rate reading, install a new power steering pump.
16. Set engine speed at idle. Turn steering wheel to left and right stops. Record

flow rate and pressure readings at stops:
 a. Pressure reading at both stops should be nearly the same as maximum pump relief pressure.
 b. Flow rate should drop below .5 gallons per minute (GPM).
 c. If pressure does not reach maximum pump relief pressure or flow rate does not drop below specified value, an excessive internal leakage is occurring. Install a new steering gear.
17. Turn steering wheel slightly in both directions and release quickly while watching pressure gauge:
18. Pressure reading should move from normal back pressure reading and snap back as steering wheel is released.
19. If pressure returns slowly or sticks, rotary valve in steering gear is sticking or steering column is binding. Inspect steering column and linkages before replacing steering gear.

Steering Gear Valve Test

1. With vehicle in motion, place transmission in NEUTRAL, then turn engine Off.
2. If vehicle does not pull with engine Off, replace steering gear.
3. If vehicle pulls with engine Off, switch righthand front wheel to lefthand side of vehicle and lefthand front wheel to righthand side of vehicle.
4. If vehicle pulls to opposite side, switch front wheels with rear wheels keeping them on same side of vehicle.
5. If vehicle pull direction does not change, inspect front suspension components, wheel alignment and frame alignment.

Fig. 1 Exploded view of steering gear. Mustang

ITEM	DESCRIPTION
1	GEAR HOUSING
2	PINION SEAL
3	VALVE ASSY
4	PLASTIC RINGS
5	INPUT SHAFT BEARING
6	INPUT SHAFT SEAL
7	SNAP RING-SEAL RETAINER
8	INPUT SHAFT DUST SEAL
9	PINION BEARING
10	PINION BEARING LOCKNUT
11	PINION BEARING PLUG
12	BACKUP O-RING-RUBBER
13	PISTON SEAL-PLASTIC
14	INNER RACK SEAL
15	RACK BUSHING O-RING
16	RACK BUSHING
17	OUTER RACK SEAL
18	HOUSING END PLATE
19	SNAP RING
20	TRAVEL RESTRICTORS
21	INNER BELLOWS CLAMP
22	BELLOWS
23	OUTER BELLOWS CLAMP
24	SPIRAL PIN
25	TIE ROD ASSY
26	JAM NUT
27	TIE ROD END ASSY
28	CASTELLATED NUT
29	RACK YOKE
30	YOKE SPRING
31	YOKE PLUG
32	YOKE PLUG LOCKNUT
33	BREATHER TUBE
34	RIGHT TURN TRANSFER TUBE
34	LEFT TURN TRANSFER TUBE

FM6029100082000X

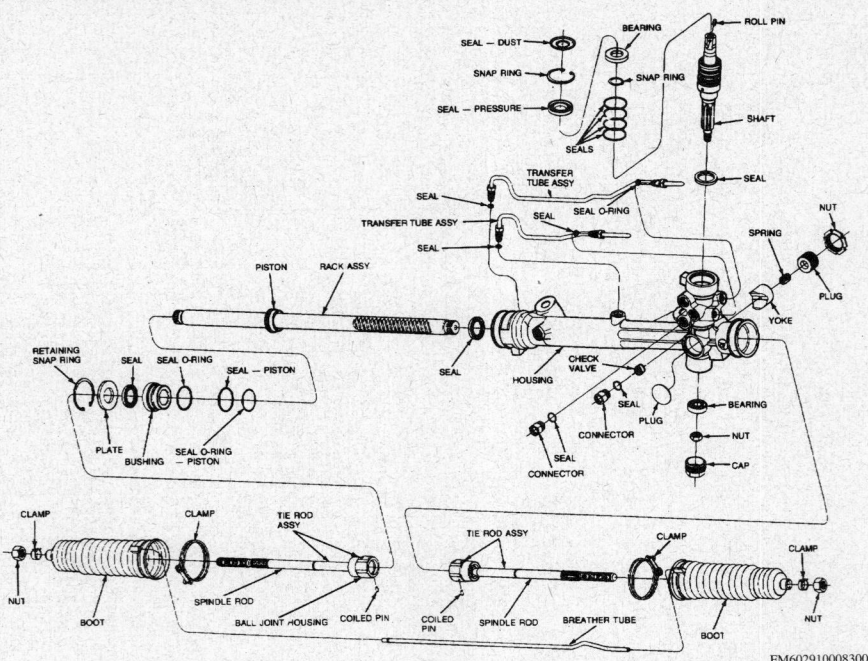

Fig. 2 Exploded view of steering gear. Sable & Taurus

POWER STEERING SYSTEM SERVICE

Adjustments

The steering gear on these models are not serviceable and no adjustments are required.

Component Service

STEERING GEAR

The steering gear on these models are not serviceable and must be replaced as an assembly.

TIE ROD ENDS, BELLOWS & BALL JOINT SOCKETS

FIVE HUNDRED, FREESTYLE, FUSION, MILAN, MKZ, MONTEGO, MUSTANG, SABLE, TAURUS, TAURUS X & ZEPHYR

Disassemble

1. Install two long bolts and washers through bushings and attach gear to holding fixture tool No. T57L-500-B, or equivalent.
2. Loosen jam nuts, then remove tie rod ends and jam nuts.
3. Remove four clamps attaching bellows to tie rods and gear housing.
4. Drain power steering fluid into suitable container.
5. Remove bellows with breather tube. **Do not damage bellows.**
6. If pinion is to be removed, remove pinion.
7. Thread point of roll pin remover tool No. T78P-3504-N, or equivalent, into roll pin on ball socket and hand tighten.
8. Remove roll pins, **Fig. 8.**
9. If pinion was not removed, remove gear housing from holding fixture and place it on bench.
10. Position rack so several teeth are exposed. Hold rack using suitable adjustable wrench on end teeth while loosening ball sockets with nut wrench tool No. T74P-3504-U, or equivalent, **Fig. 9.**

Assemble

This procedure has been revised by a Technical Service Bulletin.
1. **On models equipped with tie rods retained by rivet or pin,** proceed as follows:
   a. **If pinion was not removed from housing, these steps must be performed with steering gear removed from holding fixture and positioned on bench.**
   b. Install tie rod and ball socket assemblies onto rack.
   c. Hold one ball socket with 1 $\frac{5}{16}$ inch wrench while tightening other ball socket, using nut wrench tool No. T74P-3504-U, or equivalent.
   d. Both ball socket assemblies will be torqued simultaneously.
   e. Support ball housing using suitable wooden block and install roll pins by tapping lightly with suitable plastic mallet.
   f. If pinion was removed, install pinion.
   g. Thoroughly clean rack and housing bore.
   h. Apply suitable lubricant to bellows clamp under cut on tie rod, then install bellows and breather tube.
   i. Install clamps retaining bellows to steering gear securing clamp using tool No. T63P-9171-A, or equivalent.
   j. Install clamps retaining bellows to tie rods, jam nuts and tie rod ends.
2. **On models equipped with tie rods not retained by rivet or pin,** proceed as follows:
   a. Turn rack to lefthand stop, then place suitable adjustable wrench on rack to prevent turning during tightening procedures.
   b. Install tie rod to rack.
   c. Install rack boots, then secure to rack body and tie rod using suitable clamps.
   d. Install tie rod end jam nuts and tie rod ends to tie rods.

LS & THUNDERBIRD

1. Secure steering gear in holding fixture tool No. T57L-500-B, or equivalent.
2. Loosen tie rod end jam nuts, then remove tie rod ends and jam nuts from tie rods. Record turns required to remove tie rod ends.
3. Remove clamps and rack boots.
4. Place suitable adjustable wrench only on rack end teeth, then, loosen and remove tie rods using suitable pipe wrench. **Do not allow rack to turn in gear.**
5. Reverse procedure to install.

POWER STEERING SYSTEM BLEED

Air trapped in power steering system may be removed with power steering pump air evacuator assembly vacuum tester tool No. 021-00014, or equivalent. **Do not use engine vacuum to purge power steering system.**
1. Remove reservoir cap.
2. Inspect and adjust fluid level to cold fill mark.
3. Disconnect ignition coil wire, then raise and support front wheels.
4. Crank engine with starter motor and inspect fluid level. **Do not turn steering wheel.**
5. If fluid level has dropped, fill reservoir to cold fill mark, crank engine with starter motor while turning steering wheel lock to lock. Inspect fluid level.
6. Install air evacuator rubber stopper tightly to pump reservoir and connect coil wire.
7. With engine at idle, apply 15 inches maximum vacuum to pump reservoir for at least three minutes.
8. As air purges from system, vacuum will decrease. Maintain adequate vacuum.
9. Release vacuum and remove source. If fluid level has dropped, fill to cold fill mark.
10. With engine at idle, apply 15 inches maximum vacuum to pump reservoir, then turn steering wheel from lock to lock every 30 seconds for approximately five minutes. **Do not hold steering wheel on stops when turning.** Maintain adequate vacuum.
11. Release vacuum and remove equipment.
12. Adjust power steering fluid and install cap.

Condition	Possible Sources	Action
• Steering system noise	• Low fluid level • Fluid aeration • Steering gear • Power steering pump • Loose or damaged steering linkage • Loose or damaged suspension component(s) • Steering column • Steering column boot bushing • Steering column shaft • Loose dash boot seal • Drive belt • Drive belt tensioner	• Go To Pinpoint Test A .
• Steering is very difficult/very easy	• Seized steering column shaft U-joints • Damaged, fractured steering column bearing(s) • Steering gear • Power steering pump • Power steering hoses • Ball joints • Strut bearing plate (if applicable) • Binding dash boot seal	• Go To Pinpoint Test B .
• Excessive steering wheel play	• Steering gear • Steering column • Steering column bearings • Steering column shaft U-joints • Steering linkage • Ball joints • Strut bearing plate (if applicable)	• Go To Pinpoint Test C .
• Steering system drift/pull/wander	• Tire pressure • Wheel alignment • Steering gear	• Go To Pinpoint Test D .
	• Unevenly loaded vehicle • Steering column shaft • Strut bearing plate (if applicable) • Frame alignment	• CORRECT the vehicle loading as necessary.
• Feedback	• Loose, worn or damaged tie-rod(s)	• GO to Component Test, Steering Linkage

ARM0500000000779

Fig. 3 Troubleshooting (Part 1 of 2)

	Possible Sources	Action
	• Loose or damaged steering gear insulators or bolts	• INSTALL new steering gear insulators or bolts if necessary, or TIGHTEN the bolts as needed.
	• Loose steering column shaft U-joint or pinch bolts	• INSTALL a new steering column and pinch bolts or TIGHTEN the pinch bolts as needed.
	• Loose suspension bushings, fasteners, ball joints or strut bearing plate (if applicable)	• INSTALL new components as necessary.
	• Worn or damaged steering column bearing(s)	• INSTALL a new steering column.
• Poor returnability/sticky steering	• Binding steering column shaft U-joints	• INSTALL a new steering column.
	• Loose, worn or damaged tie rod(s)	• GO to Component Test, Steering Linkage
	• Suspension components	• REFER to suspension diagnosis and testing.
	• Binding steering column bearing(s) • Binding dash boot seal	• INSTALL a new steering column. • INSTALL a new dash boot seal.
• Shimmy	• Loose, worn or damaged tie rod(s)	• GO to Component Test, Steering Linkage
	• Suspension components	• REFER to suspension diagnosis and testing.

ARM0500000000780

Fig. 3 Troubleshooting (Part 2 of 2)

Test Step	Result / Action to Take
A1 **CHECK FOR MECHANICAL NOISE** • Test drive the vehicle to verify the steering system noise. • **Does the steering system make a clunk noise?**	**Yes** CHECK for loose, worn or damaged tie-rod ends. If the noise is from the steering column, CHECK the steering column intermediate shaft for grounding through the body and REPAIR as necessary. If the noise is from the steering column boot bushing, INSTALL a new steering column boot bushing. If the noise is from the suspension components, INSTALL new suspension components as necessary. If the noise is from loose, worn or damaged steering column shaft U-joint(s), INSTALL a new steering column. **No** If a squeak is present in the steering column, REPAIR the steering column as necessary. For all other concerns, GO to A2.
A2 **VERIFY THE CONCERN** NOTE: Make sure that the vehicle is on a flat dry surface, the transmission is in PARK, and that the windows are rolled up. NOTE: Some power steering noise is expected. If in doubt of the acceptability of the noise level, evaluate another vehicle of the same model and powertrain. • Key in START position. • Turn the steering wheel one-half turn off-center to the right then one-half turn off-center to the left. • **Is the power steering noisy?**	**Yes** If a grunt noise is present, VERIFY the steering column boot is OK and the exhaust system is not grounding out. If a moan is present, VERIFY that the tie-rod ends and ball joints are OK. GO to A3. **No** If a squeal is present, INSPECT and INSTALL a new engine drive belt or belt tensioner as necessary. If the steering system noise is a hiss or whistle, INSPECT the steering column boot at the dash panel. REPAIR or INSTALL a new boot as necessary. INSPECT the steering gear input shaft and valve for wear or damage and REPAIR as necessary. INSPECT the power steering gear, intermediate shaft and power steering lines and hoses for grounding to the body and REPAIR as necessary. INSPECT for openings or missing plugs in the instrument panel cowl and REPAIR as necessary. If there are no missing plugs or openings in the cowl, grounded power steering gear, intermediate shaft or power steering lines or hoses, GO to A6.

ARM0500000000781

Fig. 4 Test A: Steering System Noise (Part 1 of 2)

Test Step	Result / Action to Take
A3 **CHECK FOR COLD START NOISE** NOTE: Some noise during an extremely cold start -25.5°C (-14°F) is normal and should improve as the steering system warms up (usually within 60 seconds). • Key in START position. • Verify the noise condition. • **Is the noise present only during cold start up?**	**Yes** CHECK for contamination in the power steering reservoir screen. FLUSH the power steering system as necessary. TEST the system for normal operation. **No** GO to A4.
A4 **INSPECT THE POWER STEERING FLUID** • Key in OFF position. • With the engine OFF, inspect the power steering fluid for aeration. • **Is the power steering fluid foamy or aerated?**	**Yes** PURGE the power steering system. If a whine or moan is still present, INSTALL a new power steering pump. If the power steering noise is a grunt, INSTALL a new power steering gear. **No** GO to A5.
A5 **CHECK THE POWER STEERING FLUID LEVEL WITH THE ENGINE ON AND OFF** NOTE: Record the vacuum level when the pump noise occurs with no steering input. Vacuum level should be greater than 10 inches of mercury on the CII pump and 15 inches of mercury on the CIII pump. • Key in START position. • With the engine running, inspect the power steering fluid level. • Key in OFF position. • With the engine OFF, inspect the power steering fluid level. • **Does the power steering fluid level change with the engine off?**	**Yes** PURGE the power steering system. **No** GO to A6.
A6 **CHECK THE POWER STEERING PUMP** NOTE: Do not turn the steering wheel to either the right or left stop. Power steering relief noise will occur and is normal at the stop positions. • Key in START position. • With the engine running, rotate the steering wheel 90 degrees to the left then to the right. • **Does the frequency of the hiss change between the left and right positions?**	**Yes** INSTALL a new power steering gear. **No** INSTALL a new power steering pump.

ARM0500000000782

Fig. 4 Test A: Steering System Noise (Part 2 of 2)

Test Step	Result / Action to Take
B1 CHECK THE STEERING COLUMN BEARINGS AND THE STEERING COLUMN SHAFT	
NOTE: Be sure to keep the clockspring centered when disconnecting the steering column shaft. • Check the steering column and shaft for grounding. • Disconnect the steering column shaft at the steering gear. • Verify that the steering column shaft U-joints do not bind and move freely and that the steering column bearing rotates freely. • **Are the steering column bearing and steering column shaft U-joints OK?**	**Yes** GO to B2. **No** If the steering column or the steering column shaft are grounding, REPAIR as necessary. If the steering column bearings or the steering column shaft are binding, INSTALL a new steering column.
B2 CHECK THE FRONT BALL JOINTS AND UPPER STRUT BEARINGS	
• Check that the front ball joints and upper strut bearings move freely and are not binding or sticking. • **Are the front ball joints and upper strut bearings OK?**	**Yes** GO to B3. **No** INSTALL new ball joints or upper strut bearings as necessary.
B3 MONITOR ENGINE RPM CHANGES	
NOTE: Make sure that the vehicle is on a flat, dry surface. • Key in START position. ⚠ CAUTION: Do not hold the steering wheel at the stops for an extended amount of time. Damage to the power steering pump can occur. • Turn the steering wheel once to the left stop position and then to the right stop position. • Note the engine rpm during the turns. • **Does the engine rpm change when turning the steering wheel?**	**Yes** If no power steering assist is present and the engine rpm changes, INSTALL a new steering gear. If left-to-right variation is present, INSTALL a new steering gear. If no power steering assist is present and the engine rpm does not change, INSTALL a new power steering pump. If excessive effort is required in one or both directions, INSTALL a new power steering pump. **No** CARRY OUT the Power Steering Pump Flow and Pressure Test.

ARM0500000000783

Fig. 5   Test B: Steering Is Very Difficult Or Easy

Test Step	Result / Action to Take
D1 CHECK FOR TIRE PULL	
• Rotate the front wheel and tire assemblies side-to-side • Carry out a road test on a smooth, flat, dry road. • **Does the vehicle drift/pull?**	**Yes** If vehicle pulls in the opposite direction, GO to D2. If vehicle pulls in the original direction, GO to D3. **No** Concern has been corrected.
D2 ROTATE THE WHEEL AND TIRE ASSEMBLIES FRONT TO REAR	
• Rotate the wheel and tire assemblies front to rear • Carry out a road test on a smooth, flat, dry road. • **Does the vehicle drift/pull?**	**Yes** GO to D3. **No** Concern has been corrected.
D3 CHECK THE STEERING COLUMN SHAFT	
NOTE: Be sure to keep the clockspring centered when disconnecting the steering column shaft.. • Check the steering column and shaft for grounding. • Disconnect the steering column shaft at the steering column. • Inspect the steering column intermediate shaft U-joints for looseness or wear. • **Are the steering column shaft U-joints OK?**	**Yes** GO to D4. **No** INSTALL a new steering column.
D4 CHECK THE STEERING GEAR MOUNTING	
• Check the steering gear mounts for looseness or wear. • **Are the steering gear mounts OK?**	**Yes** GO to D5. **No** INSTALL new steering gear mounts.
D5 CHECK THE STEERING GEAR	
• Carry out the Steering Gear Valve component test. Refer to Component Tests in this section. • **Is the steering gear valve OK?**	**Yes** GO to D6. **No** REPAIR or INSTALL a new steering gear.
D6 CHECK THE SUSPENSION COMPONENTS	
• Check for loose or worn suspension components. • **Are the suspension components OK?**	**Yes** GO to D7. **No** INSTALL new suspension components
D7 CHECK THE WHEEL ALIGNMENT	
NOTE: The vehicle will tend to pull toward the side with the least positive caster and the most positive camber. • Using a suitable alignment system, measure the wheel alignment settings • **Are the alignment settings within specifications?**	**Yes** CHECK for correct frame alignments **No** ADJUST the alignment angles to specifications. DO NOT exceed specifications. TEST the system for normal operation.

ARM0500000000785

Fig. 7   Test D: Steering System Drift, Pull Or Wander

Test Step	Result / Action to Take
C1 CHECK THE STEERING COLUMN BEARINGS	
• Inspect the steering column mounting fasteners and bearings for looseness. • **Are the fasteners and bearings OK?**	**Yes** GO to C2. **No** TIGHTEN the steering column mounting fasteners or INSTALL a new steering column.
C2 CHECK THE STEERING LINKAGE FOR LOOSENESS	
• Carry out the Steering Linkage component test. • **Is the steering linkage OK?**	**Yes** Diagnose the suspension components. **No** INSTALL new steering linkage as necessary.

ARM0500000000784

Fig. 6   Test C: Excessive Steering Wheel Play

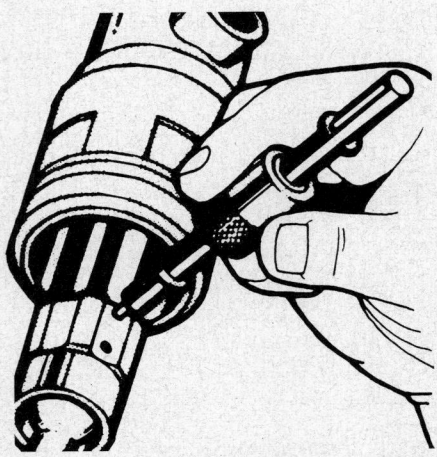

FM6029100093000X

Fig. 8   Roll pin removal from ball socket. Five Hundred, Freestyle, Montego, Mustang, Sable, Taurus & Taurus X

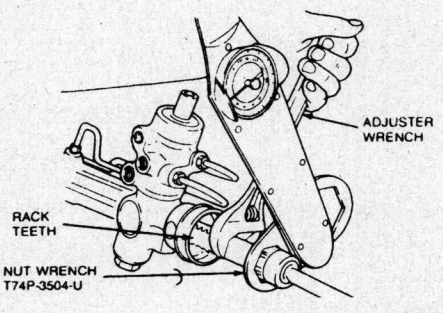

FM6029100094000X

Fig. 9   Tie rod & ball socket removal. Five Hundred, Freestyle, Montego, Mustang, Sable, Taurus & Taurus X

TIGHTENING SPECIFICATIONS

Year	Component	Torque Ft. Lbs.
FIVE HUNDRED, FREESTYLE, MONTEGO, 2008 SABLE, TAURUS & TAURUS X		
2005–08	Power Steering Line Clamp Plate Bolt	15
	Pressure Line Bracket To Engine	89①
	Pressure Line Fitting	48
	Pressure Line Fitting To Pump Adapter	48
	Return Line Bracket To Frame Bolts	89①
	Steering Gear Mounting Nuts	86
	Steering Pump Mounting Nuts	18
	Tie Rod End Jam Nuts	59
	Tie Rod End Nuts	66
FUSION, MILAN, MKZ & ZEPHYR		
2006–08	Inner Tie Rod	70
	Outer Tie Rod	35
	Power Steering Pressure Line Banjo Bolts	26
	Steering Column Shaft To Gear	18
	Steering Gear To Subframe	79
	Tie Rod End Jam Nuts	55
LS & THUNDERBIRD		
2004	Hose Bracket To Steering Gear	89①
	Steering Gear To Crossmember	46②
	Steering Gear Fluid Lines	24
	Steering Shaft To Gear Pinch Bolt	26
	Tie Rod To Steering Knuckle	74
	Tie Rod To Rack	88
2005–06	Hose Bracket To Steering Gear	89①
	Steering Gear To Crossmember	66②
	Steering Gear Fluid Lines	24
	Steering Shaft To Gear Pinch Bolt	26
	Tie Rod Jam Nut	41
	Tie Rod To Steering Knuckle	59
MUSTANG		
2004	Front Wheel Spindle Tie Rod	74
	Pressure Line Fitting	48
	Steering Gear	35
	Steering Intermediate Shaft Coupling Pinch Bolt	25
	Tie Rod End Castellated Nut	11
	Tie Rod End Jam Nut	41

TIGHTENING SPECIFICATIONS—Continued

Year	Component	Torque Ft. Lbs.
MUSTANG		
2005–08	Front Wheel Spindle Tie Rod	59
	Pressure Line Fitting	48
	Steering Gear	85
	Steering Intermediate Shaft Coupling Pinch Bolt	18
	Tie Rod End Jam Nut	41
2004–05 SABLE & 2004–07 TAURUS		
2004	Bellows Clamp	20–30①
	Gear Hose Fittings	15–25
	Gear Housing Return Line	24–30
	Gear To Crossmember	85–100
	Intermediate Shaft To Steering Column	15–25
	Intermediate Shaft To Steering Gear	30–38
	Pressure Line Fitting To Actuator Banjo Bolt	22–28
	Pump Pressure Line Fitting	42–54
	Tie Rod Ball Socket To Rack	66–81
	Tie Rod End Jam Nut	35–50
	Tie Rod End To Spindle Arm	35–47
2005–07	Gear Hose Fittings	27
	Gear Housing Return Line	27
	Gear To Crossmember	85
	Intermediate Shaft To Steering Gear	35
	Pressure Line Fitting To Actuator Banjo Bolt	28
	Pump Pressure Line Fitting	48
	Tie Rod Ball Socket To Rack	81
	Tie Rod End Jam Nut	50
	Tie Rod End To Spindle Arm	47

① — Inch lbs.

② — Discard and replace nuts.

Ford Torsion Bar Power Steering Gear

NOTE: On Air Bag Equipped Models, Refer To "Air Bag System Precautions" Located In The Front Of This Manual For System Disarming & Arming Procedures.

NOTE: Refer To "Computer Relearn Procedures" Located In The Front Of This Manual When Battery Power To The Computer Has Been Interrupted.

NOTE: Also Refer To "Ford Variable Assist Electronic Variable Orifice (EVO) System," For Models Equipped With EVO System.

INDEX

	Page No.		Page No.		Page No.
Description	13-14	Air Bag Systems	13-14	Clicking Type Noise	13-15
Operation	13-14	Battery Ground Cable	13-14	Moan or Whine Type Noise	13-15
Power Steering System Service	13-15	Tightening Specifications	13-17	Swish Type Noise	13-15
Adjustments	13-15	Troubleshooting	13-14	Poor Returnability, Sticky Feel	13-15
Mesh Load	13-15	Feedback (Rattle, Chuckle or		Power Steering Pump Leaks At	
Component Service	13-15	Knocking Noises From		EVO Control Valve Actuator	13-15
Inspection	13-16	Steering Gear)	13-15	Pulls To One Side	13-14
Overhaul	13-15	Heavy Steering Effort, Poor		Steering Drift/Wander	13-14
Replacement	13-16	Assist or Loss Of Assist	13-15		
Precautions	13-14	Noisy Pump	13-15		

PRECAUTIONS

Air Bag Systems

Refer to "Air Bag System Precautions" in the front of this manual for system disarming and arming procedures.

Battery Ground Cable

Prior to service, disconnect battery ground cable and isolate as required.

DESCRIPTION

The power steering unit is a torsion bar type of hydraulic-assisted system, **Fig. 1.** This system furnishes power to reduce the amount of turning effort required at the steering wheel. It also reduces road shock and vibrations.

The unit includes a worm and one piece rack-piston which is meshed to the gear teeth on the steering sector shaft. The unit also includes a hydraulic valve, valve actuator, input shaft and torsion bar assembly which are mounted on the end of the worm shaft and operated by a twisting action of the torsion bar.

The gear unit is designed with the one piece rack-piston, worm and sector shaft in the one housing and the valve spool in an attaching housing. This makes internal fluid passages possible between valve and cylinder, thus eliminating all external lines and hoses except the pressure and return hoses between pump and gear.

The power cylinder is an integral part of the gear housing. The piston is double acting in that fluid pressure may be applied to either of its sides.

Operation

The operation of the hydraulic control valve spool is governed by the twisting of a torsion bar. All effort applied to the steering wheel is transmitted directly through the input shaft and torsion bar to the worm and piston. Any resistance to the turning of the front wheels results in twisting of the bar. The twisting of the bar increases as the front wheel turning effort increases. The control valve spool, actuated by the twisting of the torsion bar, directs fluid to the side of the piston where hydraulic assistance is required.

As the torsion bar twists, its radial motion is transferred into axial motion by three helical threads. Thus, the valve is moved off center, and fluid is directed to one side of the piston or the other.

TROUBLESHOOTING

Steering Drift/Wander

1. Tire size and pressure.
2. Loose or worn tie rod ends or ball joints.
3. Steering gear mounting insulators or retaining bolts loose or damaged.
4. Loose front suspension lower arm struts.
5. Steering column gear input shaft coupling connecting bolts loose.
6. Steering gear input shaft coupling joints lose or worn.
7. Improper wheel alignment.
8. Excessive toe-in.
9. Excessive friction between components.

Pulls To One Side

1. Improper tire pressure.
2. Improper tire size or type.
3. Vehicle is unevenly loaded.
4. Improper wheel alignment.
5. Damaged front or rear suspension components.
6. Steering gear valve effort out of adjustment.
7. Front or rear brakes operating improperly.
8. Bent rear axle housing, damaged or

sagging front coil springs or damaged or worn rear suspension component.
9. loose or damaged rear suspension retaining fasteners.

Feedback (Rattle, Chuckle or Knocking Noises From Steering Gear)

1. Steering column gear input shaft coupling joints loose or worn.
2. Loose tie rod ends.
3. Steering gear retaining bolts loose or damaged.
4. Loose suspension bushings, fasteners or ball joints.
5. Improper steering gear adjustment.

Poor Returnability, Sticky Feel

1. Improper tire pressure, tire size or tire type.
2. Misaligned steering column or column flange.
3. Steering column gear input shaft universal joints binding.
4. Steering column tube boot tears.
5. Binding or damaged tie rod ends.
6. Damaged or worn front suspension components.
7. Improper wheel alignment.
8. Column bearing binding.
9. Contamination in system.
10. Improper steering gear adjustment.

Heavy Steering Effort, Poor Assist or Loss Of Assist

1. Contamination of system by foreign objects in power steering oil reservoir or metallic particles in fluid being generated by cam pack discrepancies.
2. Low power steering fluid.
3. Steering gear assembly internal or external leak.
4. Improper drive belt tension.
5. Hose or cooler external leak or internal restriction.
6. Improper engine idle speed.
7. Power steering pump pulley loose or warped.
8. Power steering pump flow or pressure not to specifications.
9. Improper steering gear adjustments.
10. System contamination.
11. EVO power steering control valve actuator sticking.

Power Steering Pump Leaks At EVO Control Valve Actuator

1. Damaged power steering control valve actuator ring.
2. EVO power steering control valve ac-

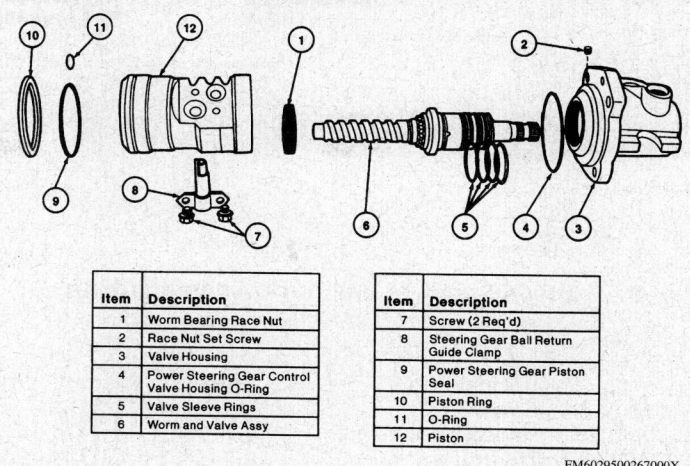

Fig. 1 Exploded view of Ford power steering gear

Item	Description
1	Worm Bearing Race Nut
2	Race Nut Set Screw
3	Valve Housing
4	Power Steering Gear Control Valve Housing O-Ring
5	Valve Sleeve Rings
6	Worm and Valve Assy

Item	Description
7	Screw (2 Req'd)
8	Steering Gear Ball Return Guide Clamp
9	Power Steering Gear Piston Seal
10	Piston Ring
11	O-Ring
12	Piston

FM6029500267000X

tuator electrical connector damaged.
3. EVO power steering control valve actuator damaged.

Noisy Pump

SWISH TYPE NOISE

A swish type noise may be created by the flow of excessive fluid into the bypass port of the pump valve housing with temperatures below 130°. This is a normal condition and will diminish when fluid temperature increases.
1. Low fluid level and possible leak.

CLICKING TYPE NOISE

1. Excessive power steering pump wear.

MOAN OR WHINE TYPE NOISE

1. Fluid aeration.
2. Power steering pump loose or misaligned with engine.
3. Low fluid.
4. Hose or steering column grounded.
5. Damaged internal components.

POWER STEERING SYSTEM SERVICE

Adjustments

MESH LOAD

Perform the following adjustment with the steering gear and fluid lines disconnected from the vehicles steering system components.
1. Rotate input shaft either right or left to stop.
2. Rotate shaft in opposite direction and count number of turns.
3. Rotate shaft back one half number of turns counted.
4. Measure torque required to rotate input shaft 45° either side of center using suitable inch pounds torque wrench. If torque reading is not 12–16 inch lbs., turn sector shaft adjusting screw to adjust mesh load.

Component Service

OVERHAUL

GEAR

Disassemble

1. Hold steering gear over drain pan in inverted position and cycle input shaft six times to drain remaining fluid.
2. Install gear in bench mounting fixture tool No. T57L-500-B, or equivalent, using suitable mounting pads for support.
3. Remove locknut from adjusting screw.
4. Turn input shaft to either stop and back approximately 1 5/8 turns to center gear. **Input shaft spline indexing flat should be facing downward.**
5. Remove sector shaft cover bolts.
6. Tap lower end of sector shaft with suitable soft-faced hammer to loosen it, then lift cover and shaft from housing as a unit. Discard O-ring.
7. Turn sector shaft cover counterclockwise off adjuster screw.
8. Remove valve housing mounting bolts.
9. Lift valve housing from gear housing while holding piston to prevent it from rotating off worm shaft.
10. Remove valve housing and lube passage O-rings.
11. Remove valve housing mounting bolts and ID tag, while holding piston separate valve housing from housing. Remove and discard O-rings.
12. With piston held, remove ball clamp screws and guide clamp, **Fig. 2.**
13. With finger over ball guide opening, turn piston so ball guide faces downward over clean container. Allow guide tubes to drop into container.
14. Rotate input shaft from stop to stop, until all balls fall from piston, then remove valve assembly from piston. **Ensure all balls have been removed. Worm may no longer be removed from piston.**
15. Install valve body to bench mounting fixture tool No. T57L-500-B, or equivalent, then loosen valve housing race nut lockscrew.

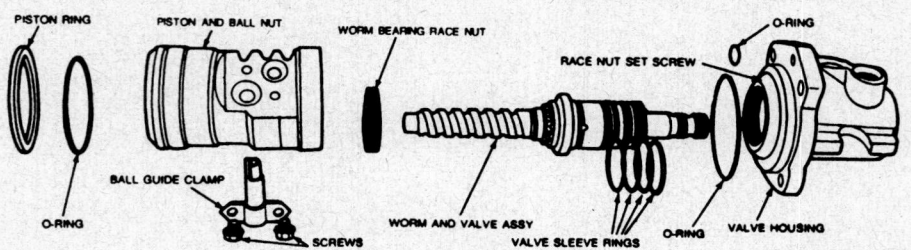

Fig. 2   Exploded view of ball nut & valve housing

FM6029100126000X

16. Remove worm bearing race using adjuster locknut wrench tool No. T66P-3553-B and spacer valve housing tool No. T66P-3553-C, or equivalents.
17. Slide input shaft, worm and valve assembly from valve housing, **Fig. 3.**

Assemble

1. Install worm and valve in housing.
2. Install retaining nut in housing, then tighten nut using adjuster and locknut wrench tool No. T66P-3553, or equivalent. Because length of tool required to tighten nut will affect torque wrench reading, the following formula for determining torque must be used: torque (using tool T66P-3553-B, or equivalent) equals (length of torque wrench X 72 ft. lbs., length of torque wrench + 5.5 inches).
3. Install race nut screw and tighten.
4. Place piston on bench with ball guide holes facing up.
5. Insert worm shaft into piston so first groove is in alignment with hole nearest to center of piston, **Fig. 4.**
6. Place ball guide into piston. Place balls in guide (27 minimum), turning worm clockwise (viewed from input end of shaft). If all balls have not been fed into guide upon reaching righthand stop, rotate input shaft in one direction and then in the other while installing balls. After balls have been installed, do not rotate input shaft or piston more than 3½ turns off righthand stop.
7. Secure guides to ball nut with clamp and tighten.
8. Apply petroleum jelly to piston seal.
9. Place new O-ring on valve housing.
10. Slide piston and valve into gear housing. **Do not damage seal.**
11. Align lube passage in valve housing with one in gear housing, place O-ring in gear housing oil passage hole, then identification tag and install. **Do not tighten mounting bolts at this time.**
12. Rotate ball nut so teeth are in same plane as sector teeth. Tighten valve housing mounting bolts.
13. Position sector shaft cover O-ring in gear housing. Turn input shaft to center piston.
14. Apply petroleum jelly to sector shaft journal, then position sector shaft and cover into gear housing.
15. Install air conditioner line mounting bracket and two sector shaft cover bolts.
16. Attach an inch pound torque wrench to input shaft and adjust mesh load as outlined in "Adjustments."

FM6029100130000X

Fig. 4   Piston assembly on worm shaft

GEAR HOUSING

1. Remove lower end housing snap ring, **Fig. 5.**
2. Remove and discard dust and pressure seals using puller attachment tool No. T58L-101-B, or equivalent. **Bearing is not serviceable and must be replaced as an assembly.**
3. Lubricate new pressure, dust seal and sector shaft seal bore.
4. Install dust seal on sector shaft using seal replacer tool No. T77L-3576-A, or equivalent, with seal raised lip toward tool.
5. Install pressure seal with lip away from tool. Pressure seal flat side should be against flat side of dust deal.
6. Install tool to sector shaft bore, then drive tool until seals clear snap ring grooves. **Do not bottom seal against bearing.**
7. Install snap ring in housing groove.

REPLACEMENT

VALVE HOUSING

Disassemble

1. Remove and discard dust seal using puller attachment tool No. T58L-101-B, or equivalent, **Fig. 6.**
2. Remove snap ring from valve housing and turn fixture so valve housing is upside down.
3. Install bearing remover tool No. T65P-3524-A2 and installer tool No. T65P-3524-A3, or equivalents, to valve body opposite oil seal.
4. Gently tap bearing and seal from housing. Discard seal. **Do not damage housing valve bore.**
5. If damaged, remove oil inlet and outlet tube seats with rack bushing holding tool No. T74P-3504-L, or equivalent.

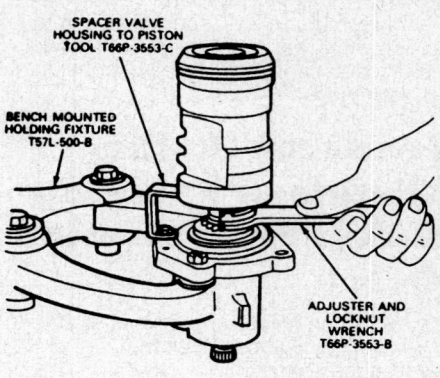

FM6029100127000X

Fig. 3   Input shaft removal

Assemble

1. Coat tube seats with petroleum jelly and position them in housing.
2. Install and tighten tube nuts to press seats to proper location using brass tube seat replacer tool No. T74P-3504-M, or equivalent.
3. Coat bearing and seal surface in housing with film of petroleum jelly.
4. Install bearing with metal side that covers rollers facing downward, then seat bearing using bearing installer tool No. T65P-3524-A, or equivalent. Inspect for smooth bearing operation.
5. Dip new oil seal in suitable premium power steering fluid and place it in housing with metal side of seal facing outward.
6. Drive seal into housing until outer edge of seal does not quite clear snap ring.
7. Place snap ring in housing, then drive on ring until snap ring seats in its groove to properly locate seal.
8. Apply coating of suitable multipurpose grease between seals.
9. Place dust seal in housing with dished side (rubber side) facing outward.
10. Drive dust seal in place so that it is located behind undercut in input shaft when it is installed.

WORM & VALVE SLEEVES

1. Cut valve sleeve rings from valve sleeve, then position worm end in suitable soft jawed vice.
2. Install four valve sleeve rings using tool kit No. T75L-3517-A1, or equivalent.
3. Ensure sleeve ring turn freely in grooves after installation.

PISTON & BALL NUT

1. Remove plastic ring and O-ring from piston and ball nut.
2. Dip new O-ring in suitable premium power steering fluid, then lubricate and install on piston and ball nut.
3. Install new Teflon ring on piston and ball nut. **Do not stretch ring more than needed.**

INSPECTION

VALVE SPOOL CENTERING INSPECTION

The out of and in-vehicle valve centering inspection are same except the torque and

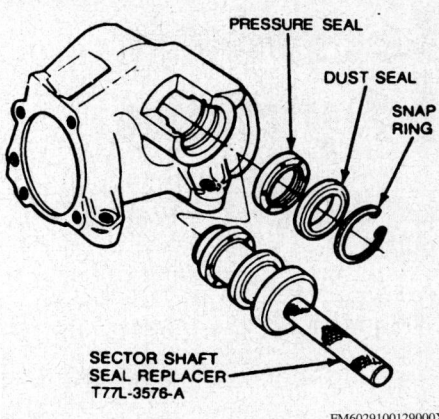

PRESSURE SEAL

DUST SEAL

SNAP RING

SECTOR SHAFT
SEAL REPLACER
T77L-3576-A

FM6029100129000X

Fig. 5 Exploded view of steering gear housing

simultaneous pressure reading must be made at the left and righthand stops instead of either side of center.

1. Install satiable 2000 psi pressure gauge in pressure line between pump outlet port and steering gear inlet port. Ensure valve on gauge is in fully open position.
2. Inspect and adjust fluid level in reservoir.
3. Start engine and cycle steering wheel from stop to stop to bring steering lubricant up to normal operating temperature.
4. Stop engine and inspect reservoir. Adjust fluid level.
5. With engine running at fast idle speed (1000 RPM) and steering wheel centered, attach an inch pound torque wrench to steering wheel nut.
6. Apply sufficient torque to wrench in

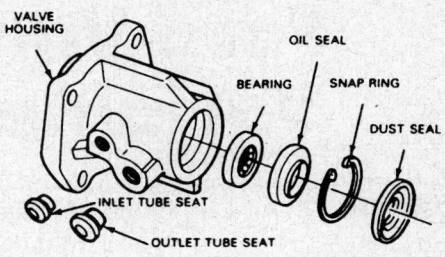

VALVE HOUSING

OIL SEAL

BEARING

SNAP RING

DUST SEAL

INLET TUBE SEAT

OUTLET TUBE SEAT

FM6029100128000X

Fig. 6 Exploded view of valve housing

each direction (either side of center) to get gauge reading of 250 psi.

7. Torque reading should be same in both directions. If difference exceed 4 inch lbs., replace shaft and control assemblies.

TIGHTENING SPECIFICATIONS

Year	Component	Torque Ft. Lbs.
2004–08	Ball Return Guide Clamp	42–70①
	Flex Coupling To Gear Input Shaft	20–30
	Gear To Side Rail	50–65
	Hose Clamps	12–24①
	Mesh Load Adjusting Screw Locknut	35–45
	Piston End Cap	70–110
	Pitman Arm To Sector Shaft	200–250
	Pressure Hose To Gear	16–25
	Race Nut Setscrew	15–25①
	Return Hose To Gear	16–25
	Sector Shaft Cover	55–70
	Valve Housing To Gear Housing	30–45

① — Inch lbs.

Ford Variable Assist Electronic Variable Orifice (EVO) System

NOTE: On Air Bag Equipped Models, Refer To "Air Bag System Precautions" Located In The Front Of This Manual For System Disarming & Arming Procedures.

NOTE: Refer To "Computer Relearn Procedures" Located In The Front Of This Manual When Battery Power To The Computer Has Been Interrupted.

NOTE: "Electrical Symbol & Wire Color Code Identification" Located In The Front Of This Manual May Be Used As An Aid When Using Wiring Circuits Found In This Section.

INDEX

	Page No.		Page No.		Page No.
Control Module, Replace	13-31	Town Car	13-18	Steering Sensor Ring, Replace	13-31
Control Valve Actuator, Replace	13-31	Diagnostic Chart Index	13-20	Troubleshooting	13-18
Description	13-18	Power Steering System Service	13-31	Crown Victoria, Grand Marquis,	
Diagnosis & Testing	13-18	Precautions	13-18	Marauder & Town Car	13-18
Pinpoint Tests	13-18	Air Bag Systems	13-18		
Crown Victoria, Grand Marquis & Marauder	13-18	Battery Ground Cable	13-18		
		Speed Sensor, Replace	13-31		
		Steering Sensor, Replace	13-31		

PRECAUTIONS

Air Bag Systems

Refer to "Air Bag System Precautions" in the front of this manual for system disarming and arming procedures.

Battery Ground Cable

Prior to service, disconnect battery ground cable and isolate as required.

DESCRIPTION

The electronic variable orifice system is designed to vary the flow from the power steering pump based on vehicle speed and the rate of steering wheel rotation, **Fig. 1.** The system provides full assist at low speed for light parking effort and minimum assist at high speed for good road feel and directional stability. In the event of system failure, full assist is provided.

TROUBLESHOOTING

Crown Victoria, Grand Marquis, Marauder & Town Car

Refer to **Figs. 2 and 3** for troubleshooting procedures.

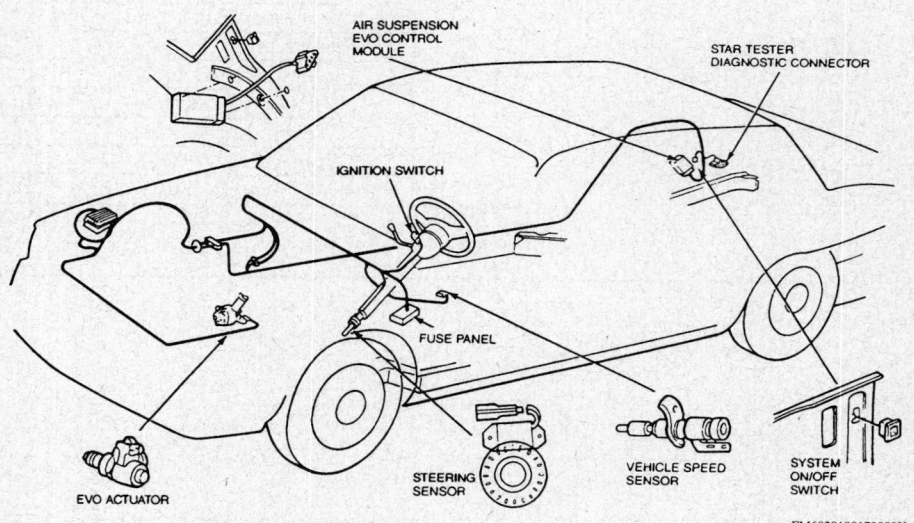

Fig. 1   Electronic variable orifice system component locations

DIAGNOSIS & TESTING

Pinpoint Tests

CROWN VICTORIA, GRAND MARQUIS & MARAUDER

Diagnosis and testing requires the use of Worldwide diagnostic tester, Rotunda model No. 418-F224 or New Generation Star, Rotunda model No. 418-F052, or equivalent.

Refer to **MOTOR's "Engine Performance & Driveability 1994–2005 v6.0 DVD"** for trouble code index.

If vehicle is equipped with air suspension, perform the "Auto Test" procedure.

Refer to **Fig. 4** for symptom chart and **Figs. 5 through 17** for system diagnosis and testing.

TOWN CAR

Refer to **Fig. 18** for symptom chart and **Figs. 19 through 24** for pinpoint tests.

Condition	Possible Sources	Action
• No communication with the front electronics module	• Circuit. • Module.	• REFER to MOTOR's "Domestic Engine Performance & Driveability Manual"
• Hard steering or lack of assist	• Seized lower steering column shaft U-joints.	• INSTALL a new lower steering column shaft.
	• Damaged, fractured steering column bearing(s).	• REPAIR the steering column.
	• Power steering pump.	• Check Pump Flow.
	• Suspension components.	• Inspect for suspension system
	• Steering gear internal leakage.	• Check Pump Flow.
• Excessive steering pump noise	• Power steering pump.	• Check Pump Flow.
• Excessive steering wheel play	• Damaged, loose, or worn tie-rod end (3290). • Loose, worn or damaged tie-rod (3280).	• Inspect Steering Linkage Component
	• Damaged/worn steering gear.	• INSTALL a new steering gear.
	• Loose, worn or damaged steering column bearing(s).	• INSTALL new steering column bearing(s).
	• Loose, worn or damaged lower steering column shaft U-joint(s).	• INSTALL a new lower steering column shaft.
• Wander	• Unevenly loaded or overloaded vehicle. • Loose, worn or damaged tie-rod.	• INFORM the customer of incorrect vehicle loading. •
	• Loose, worn or damaged tie-rod ends. • Loose or damaged steering gear mounting bolts.	• INSTALL new bolts or TIGHTEN the bolts.
	• Loose lower steering column shaft U-joint bolts. • Loose, worn or damaged lower steering column shaft U-joints. • Loose, worn or damaged steering column bearing(s).	• TIGHTEN the bolts. • INSTALL a new lower steering column shaft. • INSTALL new steering column bearings.

ARM66FM000000242

Fig. 2   Steering systems symptom chart (Part 1 of 2). Crown Victoria, Grand Marquis, Marauder & Town Car

Condition	Possible Sources	Action
• Drift/pull	• Unevenly loaded or overloaded vehicle. • Wheel alignment.	• INFORM the customer of incorrect vehicle loading. • ADJUST as required.
	• Loose, worn or damaged tie-rod.	• INSPECT steering components
	• Loose, worn or damaged tie-rod ends.	• INSPECT
	• The steering gear valve effort out of balance.	• CHECK valve operation.
	• Check the brake system for correct operation. • Incorrect frame/underbody alignment.	• CORRECT as required.
• Feedback	• Loose, worn or damaged tie-rod.	• INSPECT
	• Loose, worn or damaged tie-rod ends.	• INSPECT
	• Loose or damaged steering gear insulators or bolts.	• INSTALL new bolts or TIGHTEN the retaining bolts.
	• Loose lower steering column shaft U-joint bolts. • Loose suspension bushings, fasteners or ball joints. • Worn or damaged steering column bearing(s).	• TIGHTEN the bolts. • INSTALL new as necessary. • INSTALL new steering column bearing(s).
• Poor returnability/sticky steering	• Binding lower steering column shaft U-joints.	• INSTALL a new lower steering column shaft.
	• Loose, worn or damaged front wheel spindle tie-rod.	• INSPECT
	• Loose, worn or damaged tie-rod ends. • Suspension components.	• INSPECT
	• Binding steering column bearing(s).	• INSTALL new steering column bearing(s).
• Shimmy	• Loose, worn or damaged tie-rod end. • Loose, worn or damaged tie-rod.	• INSPECT • INSPECT
	• Suspension components.	• INSPECT

ARM66FM000000243

Fig. 2   Steering systems symptom chart (Part 2 of 2). Crown Victoria, Grand Marquis, Marauder & Town Car

Condition	Possible Sources	Action
• Power steering pump noisy	• Low fluid level and possible leakage.	• FILL reservoir to specified level. CHECK for leaks. REPAIR as necessary.
	• Plugged reservoir filter.	• INSTALL a new reservoir;
	• Power steering pump.	• INSTALL a new power steering pump;

ARM66FM000000244

Fig. 3   Power steering pump noise symptom chart. Crown Victoria, Grand Marquis, Marauder & Town Car

DIAGNOSTIC CHART INDEX

Test/Code	Description	Page No.	Fig. No.
CROWN VICTORIA, GRAND MARQUIS & MARAUDER			
—	Symptom Chart	13-20	4
Test A	No Communication w/EVO Control Module	13-20	5
Test B	No Communication w/Air Suspension Control Module	13-21	6
Test C	Unable To Enter Auto Test — EVO Control Module	13-21	7
Test D	Unable To Enter Auto Test– Air Suspension Control Module	13-21	8
Test E	EVO Actuator	13-22	9
Code 16	EVO Actuator Shorted	13-22	9
Code 17	EVO Actuator Shorted or Open	13-22	9
Code 18	EVO Actuator Resistance Out Of Range	13-22	9
Code 27	EVO Actuator Circuit Open	13-23	10
Code 28	EVO Actuator Circuit Shorted	13-23	11
Code 29	EVO Actuator Circuit High Side Shorted To Ground	13-24	12
Code 30	EVO Actuator Circuit Shorted To Battery	13-24	13
Code 31	EVO Actuator Circuit Low Side Shorted To Ground	13-24	14
Code 33	Steering Rotation Not Detected	13-25	15
Code 35	Vehicle Speed Above 15 mph Not Detected	13-25	16
Code 74	Steering Rotation Not Detected	13-26	17
TOWN CAR			
—	Symptom Chart	13-27	18
Test A	Steering Sensor Circuit Failure	13-27	19
Test B	Steering VAPS II Circuit Loop Failure	13-28	20
Test C	Steering Is Very Difficult/Very Easy	13-29	21
Test D	Steering Does Not Vary w/Increased Wheel Rotation	13-30	22
Test E	Steering Does Not Vary w/Vehicle Speed	13-30	23
Test F	No Communication w/Rear Air Suspension Control Module	13-30	24
C1441	Steering Sensor Circuit Failure	13-27	19
C1442	Steering Sensor Circuit Failure	13-27	19
C1897	Steering VAPS II Circuit Loop Failure	13-29	20

Condition	Possible Source	Action
• No communication with the EVO control module	• CJB Fuse: — 5 (15A). • Battery junction box (BJB) Fuse: — 8 (30A). • Circuitry. • EVO control module.	• GO to Pinpoint Test A.
• No communication with the air suspension control module	• CJB Fuse: — 5 (15A). • BJB Fuse: — 8 (30A). • Circuitry. • Air suspension control module.	• GO to Pinpoint Test B.
• Unable to enter auto test — EVO control module	• CJB Fuse: — 5 (15A). • BJB Fuse: — 8 (30A). • Circuitry. • EVO control module.	• GO to Pinpoint Test C.
• Unable to enter auto test — air suspension control module	• CJB Fuse: — 5 (15A). • BJB Fuse: — 8 (30A). • Circuitry. • Air suspension control module.	• GO to Pinpoint Test D.
• Steering very difficult/very easy	• Power steering pump actuator valve. • Circuitry open/shorted. • EVO control module. • Air suspension module.	• PERFORM actuator output test and steering wheel sensor test. PERFORM Pinpoint Test E (with air suspension).
• Steering does not vary with increased wheel rotation	• Steering wheel rotation sensor inoperative. • Open/shorted circuitry.	• PERFORM Steering Wheel Sensor Test. PERFORM Pinpoint Test E (with air suspension).

FM6029900334000X

Fig. 4   Symptom chart. Crown Victoria, Grand Marquis & Marauder

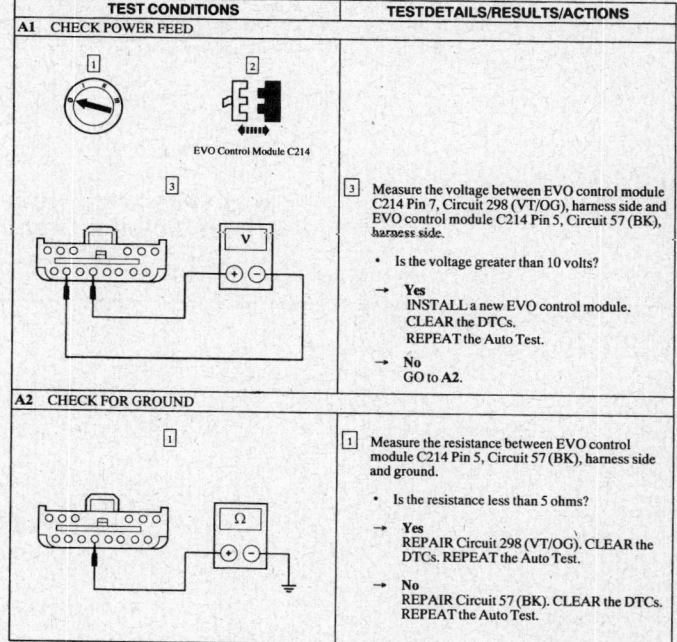

FM6029900335000X

Fig. 5   Test A: No Communication w/EVO Control Module. Crown Victoria, Grand Marquis & Marauder

TEST CONDITIONS	TESTDETAILS/RESULTS/ACTIONS
B1 CHECK CIRCUIT 1053 (LB/PK) AND CIRCUIT 298 (VT/OG) FOR AN OPEN	

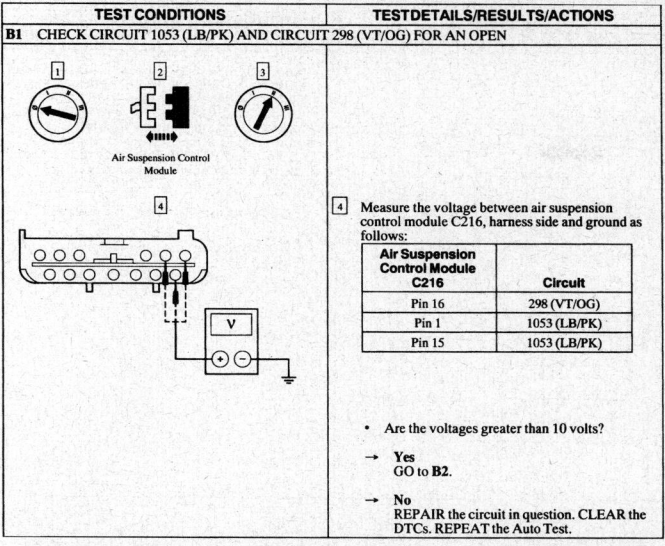

[4] Measure the voltage between air suspension control module C216, harness side and ground as follows:

Air Suspension Control Module C216	Circuit
Pin 16	298 (VT/OG)
Pin 1	1053 (LB/PK)
Pin 15	1053 (LB/PK)

• Are the voltages greater than 10 volts?

→ Yes
GO to B2.

→ No
REPAIR the circuit in question. CLEAR the DTCs. REPEAT the Auto Test.

FM6029900336010X

Fig. 6 Test B: No Communication w/Air Suspension Control Module. (Part 1 of 4). Crown Victoria, Grand Marquis & Marauder

TEST CONDITIONS	TESTDETAILS/RESULTS/ACTIONS
B4 CHECK CIRCUIT 419 (DG/LG) FOR VOLTAGE AT THE AIR SUSPENSION TEST CONNECTOR	

[1] Measure the voltage between air suspension test connector C459 Pin 4, Circuit 419 (DG/LG), harness side and ground.

• Is the voltage greater than 10 volts?

→ Yes
GO to B5.

→ No
REPAIR the circuit. CLEAR the DTCs. REPEAT the Auto Test.

| B5 CHECK CIRCUIT 844 (GY/RD) | |

[1] Measure the resistance between air suspension control module C215 Pin 9, Circuit 844 (GY/RD), harness side and air suspension test connector C459 Pin 5, Circuit 844 (GY/RD), harness side; and between air suspension control module C215 Pin 9, Circuit 844 (GY/RD), harness side and ground.

• Is the resistance less than 5 ohms between air suspension control module and air suspension test connector; and greater than 10,000 ohms between air suspension control module and ground?

→ Yes
GO to B6.

→ No
REPAIR the circuit. CLEAR the DTCs. REPEAT the Auto Test.

FM6029900336030X

Fig. 6 Test B: No Communication w/Air Suspension Control Module. (Part 3 of 4). Crown Victoria, Grand Marquis & Marauder

TEST CONDITIONS	TESTDETAILS/RESULTS/ACTIONS
C1 CHECK COMMUNICATION TO THE EVO CONTROL MODULE	

[1] Check communication between the Super Star II Tester and the EVO control module.

• Does the Super Star II Tester communicate?

→ Yes
INSTALL a new EVO control module. REPEAT the Auto Test.

→ No
GO to Pinpoint Test A.

FM6029900337000X

Fig. 7 Test C: Unable To Enter Auto Test — EVO Control Module. Crown Victoria, Grand Marquis & Marauder

TEST CONDITIONS	TESTDETAILS/RESULTS/ACTIONS
B2 CHECK CIRCUIT 57 (BK) AND CIRCUIT 676 (PK/OG) FOR AN OPEN	

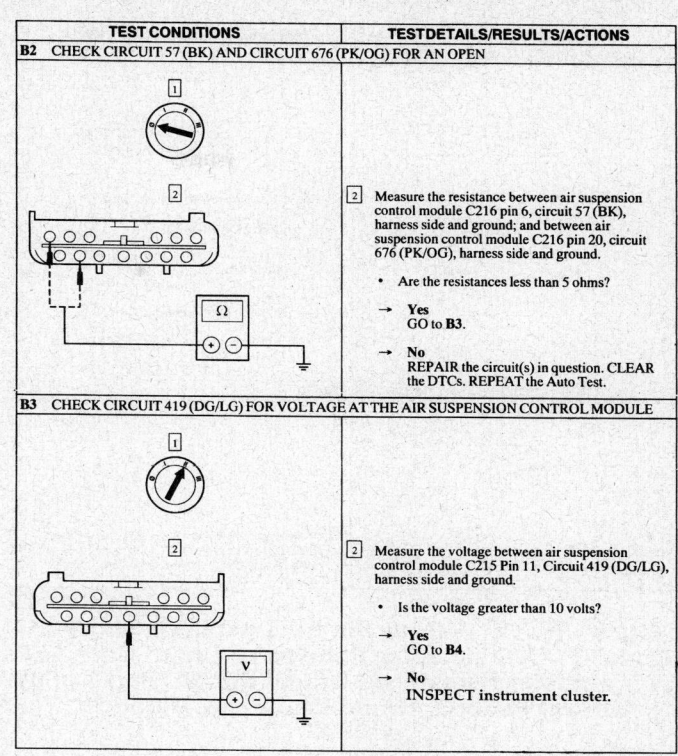

[2] Measure the resistance between air suspension control module C216 pin 6, circuit 57 (BK), harness side and ground; and between air suspension control module C216 pin 20, circuit 676 (PK/OG), harness side and ground.

• Are the resistances less than 5 ohms?

→ Yes
GO to B3.

→ No
REPAIR the circuit(s) in question. CLEAR the DTCs. REPEAT the Auto Test.

| B3 CHECK CIRCUIT 419 (DG/LG) FOR VOLTAGE AT THE AIR SUSPENSION CONTROL MODULE | |

[2] Measure the voltage between air suspension control module C215 Pin 11, Circuit 419 (DG/LG), harness side and ground.

• Is the voltage greater than 10 volts?

→ Yes
GO to B4.

→ No
INSPECT instrument cluster.

FM6029900336020X

Fig. 6 Test B: No Communication w/Air Suspension Control Module. (Part 2 of 4). Crown Victoria, Grand Marquis & Marauder

TEST CONDITIONS	TESTDETAILS/RESULTS/ACTIONS
B6 CHECK CIRCUIT 432 (BK/PK)	

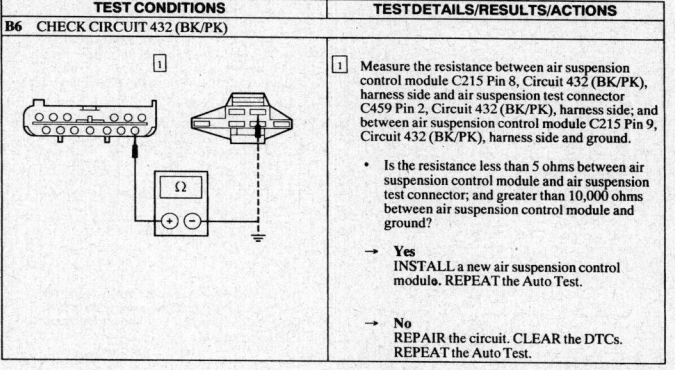

[1] Measure the resistance between air suspension control module C215 Pin 8, Circuit 432 (BK/PK), harness side and air suspension test connector C459 Pin 2, Circuit 432 (BK/PK), harness side; and between air suspension control module C215 Pin 9, Circuit 432 (BK/PK), harness side and ground.

• Is the resistance less than 5 ohms between air suspension control module and air suspension test connector; and greater than 10,000 ohms between air suspension control module and ground?

→ Yes
INSTALL a new air suspension control module. REPEAT the Auto Test.

→ No
REPAIR the circuit. CLEAR the DTCs. REPEAT the Auto Test.

FM6029900336040X

Fig. 6 Test B: No Communication w/Air Suspension Control Module. (Part 4 of 4). Crown Victoria, Grand Marquis & Marauder

TEST CONDITIONS	TESTDETAILS/RESULTS/ACTIONS
D1 CHECK COMMUNICATION TO THE AIR SUSPENSION CONTROL MODULE	

[1] Check communication between the Super Star II Tester and the air suspension control module.

• Does the Super Star II Tester communicate?

→ Yes
INSTALL a new air suspension control module. REPEAT the Auto Test.

→ No
GO to Pinpoint Test B.

FM6029900338000X

Fig. 8 Test D: Unable To Enter Auto Test — Air Suspension Control Module. Crown Victoria & Grand Marquis

TEST CONDITIONS	TEST DETAILS/RESULTS/ACTIONS
E1 EVO ACTUATOR VALVE CHECK (DTC 16)	

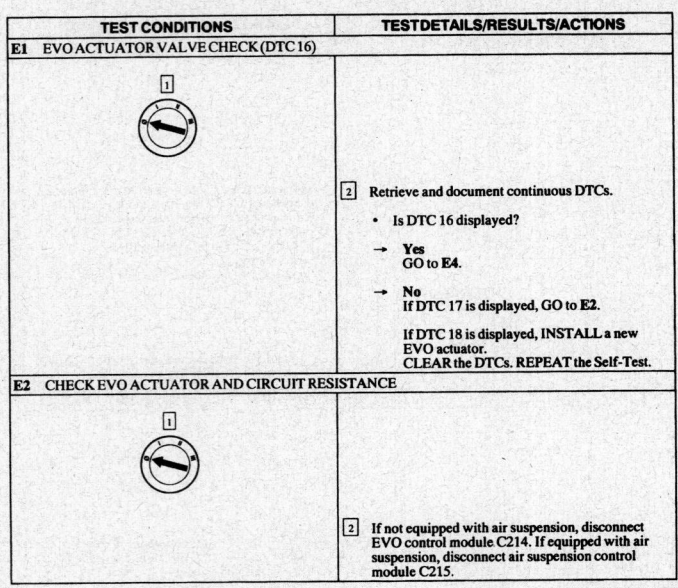

E1 EVO ACTUATOR VALVE CHECK (DTC 16)	**2** Retrieve and document continuous DTCs. • Is DTC 16 displayed? → **Yes** GO to E4. → **No** If DTC 17 is displayed, GO to E2. If DTC 18 is displayed, INSTALL a new EVO actuator. CLEAR the DTCs. REPEAT the Self-Test.
E2 CHECK EVO ACTUATOR AND CIRCUIT RESISTANCE	**2** If not equipped with air suspension, disconnect EVO control module C214. If equipped with air suspension, disconnect air suspension control module C215.

FM6029900339010X

Fig. 9 Test E — Code 16: EVO Actuator Shorted; Code 17: EVO Actuator Shorted or Open; Code 18: EVO Actuator Resistance Out Of Range (Part 1 of 6). Crown Victoria, Grand Marquis & Marauder

TEST CONDITIONS	TEST DETAILS/RESULTS/ACTIONS
E2 CHECK EVO ACTUATOR AND CIRCUIT RESISTANCE	

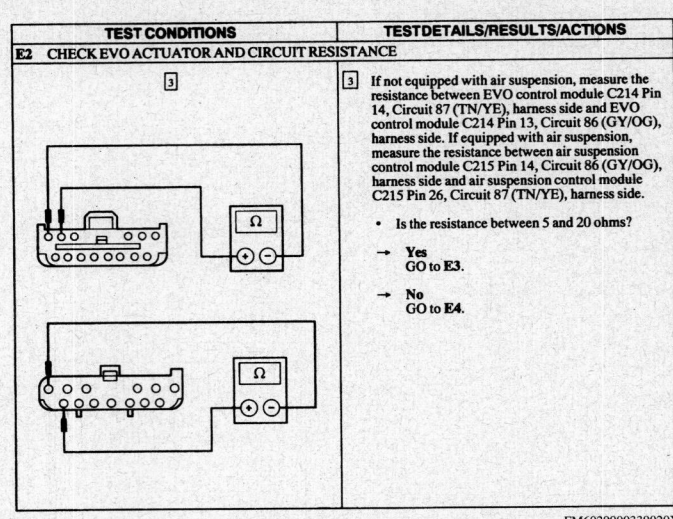

	3 If not equipped with air suspension, measure the resistance between EVO control module C214 Pin 14, Circuit 87 (TN/YE), harness side and EVO control module C214 Pin 13, Circuit 86 (GY/OG), harness side. If equipped with air suspension, measure the resistance between air suspension control module C215 Pin 14, Circuit 86 (GY/OG), harness side and air suspension control module C215 Pin 26, Circuit 87 (TN/YE), harness side. • Is the resistance between 5 and 20 ohms? → **Yes** GO to E3. → **No** GO to E4.

FM6029900339020X

Fig. 9 Test E — Code 16: EVO Actuator Shorted; Code 17: EVO Actuator Shorted or Open; Code 18: EVO Actuator Resistance Out Of Range (Part 2 of 6). Crown Victoria, Grand Marquis & Marauder

TEST CONDITIONS	TEST DETAILS/RESULTS/ACTIONS
E3 CHECK CIRCUITS 86 (GY/OG) AND 87 (TN/YE)	

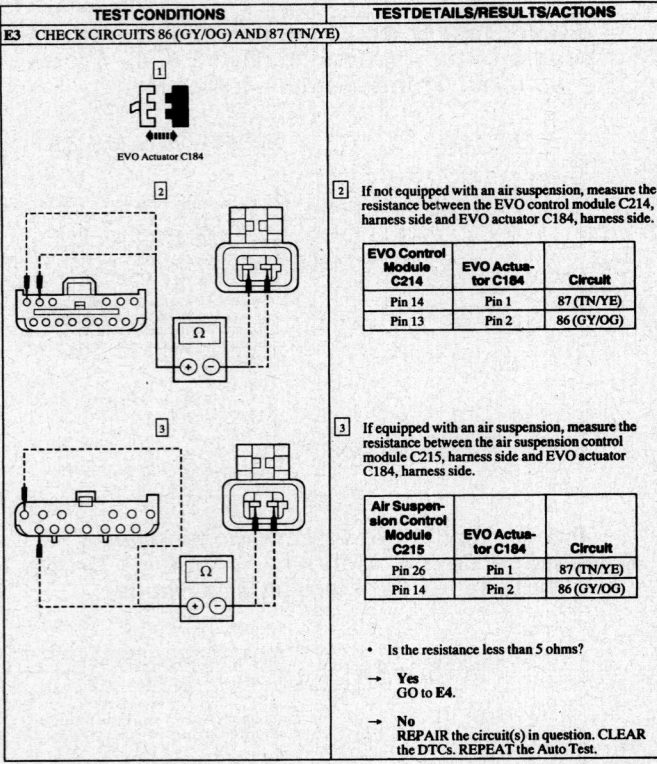

EVO Actuator C184

2 If not equipped with an air suspension, measure the resistance between the EVO control module C214, harness side and EVO actuator C184, harness side.

EVO Control Module C214	EVO Actuator C184	Circuit
Pin 14	Pin 1	87 (TN/YE)
Pin 13	Pin 2	86 (GY/OG)

3 If equipped with an air suspension, measure the resistance between the air suspension control module C215, harness side and EVO actuator C184, harness side.

Air Suspension Control Module C215	EVO Actuator C184	Circuit
Pin 26	Pin 1	87 (TN/YE)
Pin 14	Pin 2	86 (GY/OG)

• Is the resistance less than 5 ohms?

→ **Yes**
 GO to E4.

→ **No**
 REPAIR the circuit(s) in question. CLEAR the DTCs. REPEAT the Auto Test.

FM6029900339030X

Fig. 9 Test E — Code 16: EVO Actuator Shorted; Code 17: EVO Actuator Shorted or Open; Code 18: EVO Actuator Resistance Out Of Range (Part 3 of 6). Crown Victoria, Grand Marquis & Marauder

TEST CONDITIONS	TEST DETAILS/RESULTS/ACTIONS
E4 CHECK EVO ACTUATOR RESISTANCE	

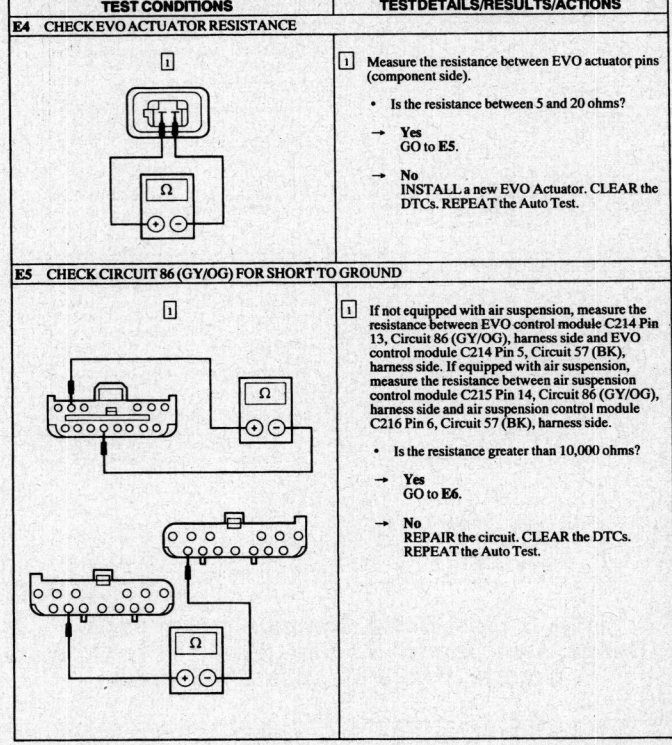

E4 CHECK EVO ACTUATOR RESISTANCE	**1** Measure the resistance between EVO actuator pins (component side). • Is the resistance between 5 and 20 ohms? → **Yes** GO to E5. → **No** INSTALL a new EVO Actuator. CLEAR the DTCs. REPEAT the Auto Test.
E5 CHECK CIRCUIT 86 (GY/OG) FOR SHORT TO GROUND	**1** If not equipped with air suspension, measure the resistance between EVO control module C214 Pin 13, Circuit 86 (GY/OG), harness side and EVO control module C214 Pin 5, Circuit 57 (BK), harness side. If equipped with air suspension, measure the resistance between air suspension control module C215 Pin 14, Circuit 86 (GY/OG), harness side and air suspension control module C216 Pin 6, Circuit 57 (BK), harness side. • Is the resistance greater than 10,000 ohms? → **Yes** GO to E6. → **No** REPAIR the circuit. CLEAR the DTCs. REPEAT the Auto Test.

FM6029900339040X

Fig. 9 Test E — Code 16: EVO Actuator Shorted; Code 17: EVO Actuator Shorted or Open; Code 18: EVO Actuator Resistance Out Of Range (Part 4 of 6). Crown Victoria, Grand Marquis & Marauder

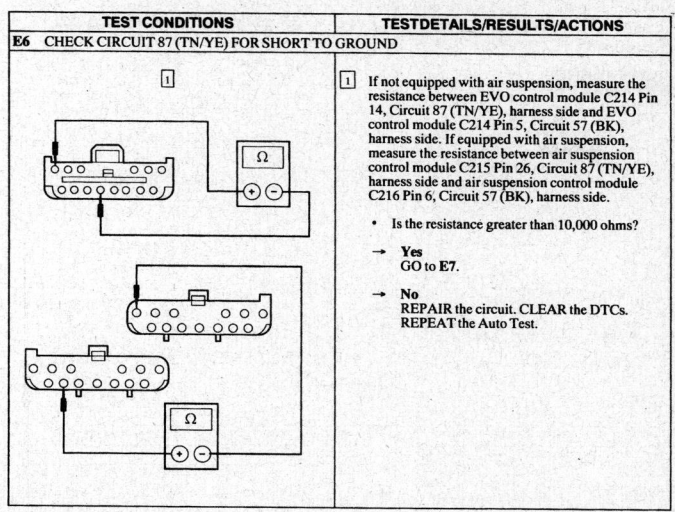

TEST CONDITIONS	TESTDETAILS/RESULTS/ACTIONS
E6 CHECK CIRCUIT 87 (TN/YE) FOR SHORT TO GROUND	

1   If not equipped with air suspension, measure the resistance between EVO control module C214 Pin 14, Circuit 87 (TN/YE), harness side and EVO control module C214 Pin 5, Circuit 57 (BK), harness side. If equipped with air suspension, measure the resistance between air suspension control module C215 Pin 26, Circuit 87 (TN/YE), harness side and air suspension control module C216 Pin 6, Circuit 57 (BK), harness side.

- Is the resistance greater than 10,000 ohms?

→ **Yes**
GO to E7.

→ **No**
REPAIR the circuit. CLEAR the DTCs. REPEAT the Auto Test.

FM6029900339050X

Fig. 9   Test E — Code 16: EVO Actuator Shorted; Code 17: EVO Actuator Shorted or Open; Code 18: EVO Actuator Resistance Out Of Range (Part 5 of 6). Crown Victoria, Grand Marquis & Marauder

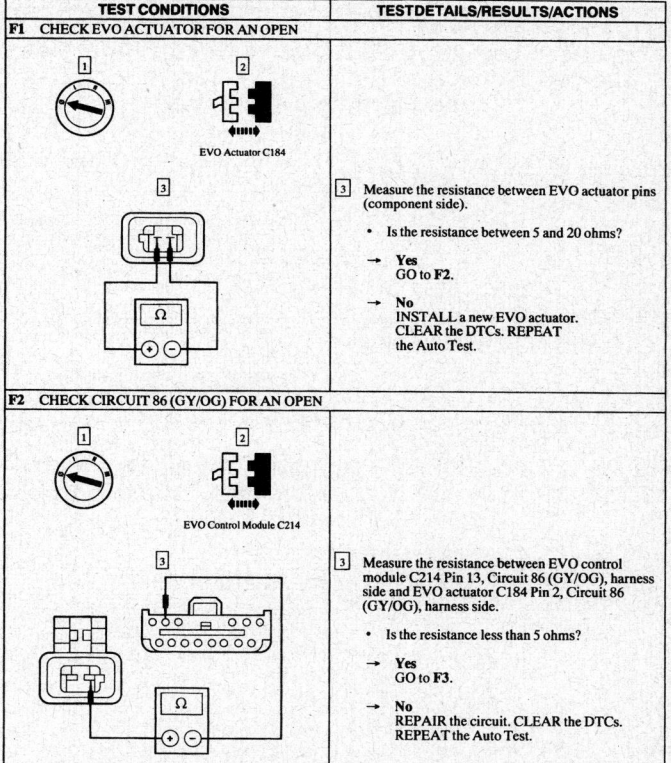

TEST CONDITIONS	TESTDETAILS/RESULTS/ACTIONS
F1 CHECK EVO ACTUATOR FOR AN OPEN	

EVO Actuator C184

3   Measure the resistance between EVO actuator pins (component side).

- Is the resistance between 5 and 20 ohms?

→ **Yes**
GO to F2.

→ **No**
INSTALL a new EVO actuator. CLEAR the DTCs. REPEAT the Auto Test.

F2 CHECK CIRCUIT 86 (GY/OG) FOR AN OPEN	

EVO Control Module C214

3   Measure the resistance between EVO control module C214 Pin 13, Circuit 86 (GY/OG), harness side and EVO actuator C184 Pin 2, Circuit 86 (GY/OG), harness side.

- Is the resistance less than 5 ohms?

→ **Yes**
GO to F3.

→ **No**
REPAIR the circuit. CLEAR the DTCs. REPEAT the Auto Test.

FM6029900340010X

Fig. 10   Code 27: EVO Actuator Circuit Open (Part 1 of 2). Crown Victoria, Grand Marquis & Marauder

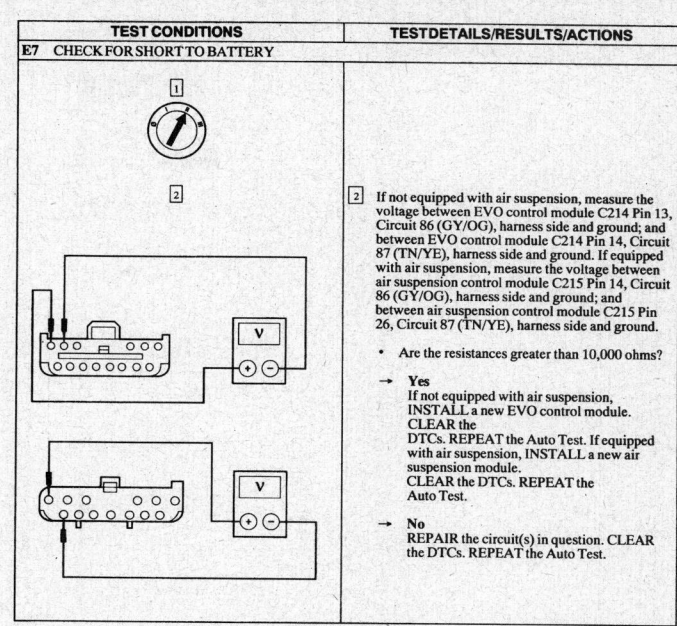

TEST CONDITIONS	TESTDETAILS/RESULTS/ACTIONS
E7 CHECK FOR SHORT TO BATTERY	

2   If not equipped with air suspension, measure the voltage between EVO control module C214 Pin 13, Circuit 86 (GY/OG), harness side and ground; and between EVO control module C214 Pin 14, Circuit 87 (TN/YE), harness side and ground. If equipped with air suspension, measure the voltage between air suspension control module C215 Pin 14, Circuit 86 (GY/OG), harness side and ground; and between air suspension control module C215 Pin 26, Circuit 87 (TN/YE), harness side and ground.

- Are the resistances greater than 10,000 ohms?

→ **Yes**
If not equipped with air suspension, INSTALL a new EVO control module. CLEAR the DTCs. REPEAT the Auto Test. If equipped with air suspension, INSTALL a new air suspension module. CLEAR the DTCs. REPEAT the Auto Test.

→ **No**
REPAIR the circuit(s) in question. CLEAR the DTCs. REPEAT the Auto Test.

FM6029900339060X

Fig. 9   Test E — Code 16: EVO Actuator Shorted; Code 17: EVO Actuator Shorted or Open; Code 18: EVO Actuator Resistance Out Of Range (Part 6 of 6). Crown Victoria, Grand Marquis & Marauder

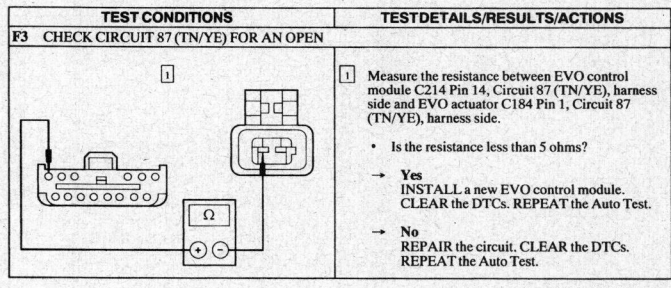

TEST CONDITIONS	TESTDETAILS/RESULTS/ACTIONS
F3 CHECK CIRCUIT 87 (TN/YE) FOR AN OPEN	

1   Measure the resistance between EVO control module C214 Pin 14, Circuit 87 (TN/YE), harness side and EVO actuator C184 Pin 1, Circuit 87 (TN/YE), harness side.

- Is the resistance less than 5 ohms?

→ **Yes**
INSTALL a new EVO control module. CLEAR the DTCs. REPEAT the Auto Test.

→ **No**
REPAIR the circuit. CLEAR the DTCs. REPEAT the Auto Test.

FM6029900340020X

Fig. 10   Code 27: EVO Actuator Circuit Open (Part 2 of 2). Crown Victoria, Grand Marquis & Marauder

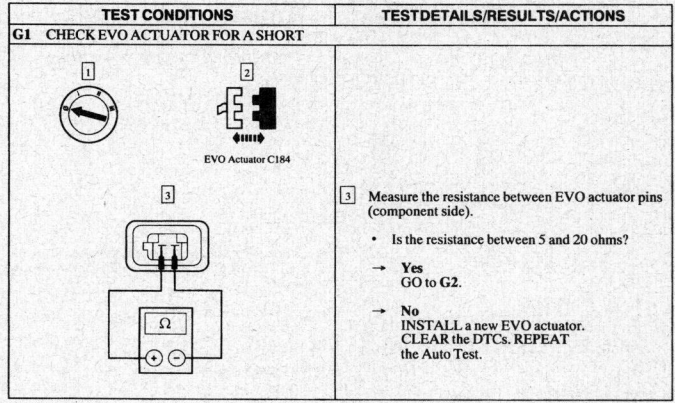

TEST CONDITIONS	TESTDETAILS/RESULTS/ACTIONS
G1 CHECK EVO ACTUATOR FOR A SHORT	

EVO Actuator C184

3   Measure the resistance between EVO actuator pins (component side).

- Is the resistance between 5 and 20 ohms?

→ **Yes**
GO to G2.

→ **No**
INSTALL a new EVO actuator. CLEAR the DTCs. REPEAT the Auto Test.

FM6029900341010X

Fig. 11   Code 28: EVO Actuator Circuit Shorted (Part 1 of 3). Crown Victoria, Grand Marquis & Marauder

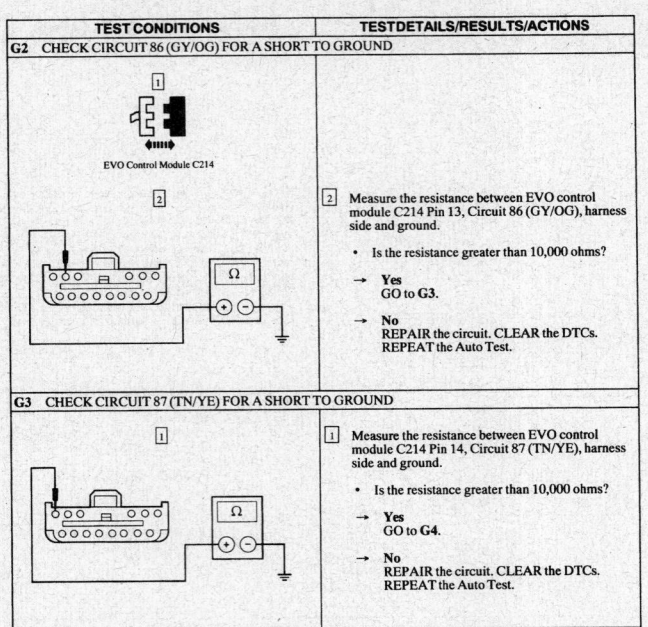

TEST CONDITIONS	TEST DETAILS/RESULTS/ACTIONS
G2 CHECK CIRCUIT 86 (GY/OG) FOR A SHORT TO GROUND	

EVO Control Module C214

2 Measure the resistance between EVO control module C214 Pin 13, Circuit 86 (GY/OG), harness side and ground.

- Is the resistance greater than 10,000 ohms?

→ **Yes**
GO to G3.

→ **No**
REPAIR the circuit. CLEAR the DTCs. REPEAT the Auto Test.

TEST CONDITIONS	TEST DETAILS/RESULTS/ACTIONS
G3 CHECK CIRCUIT 87 (TN/YE) FOR A SHORT TO GROUND	

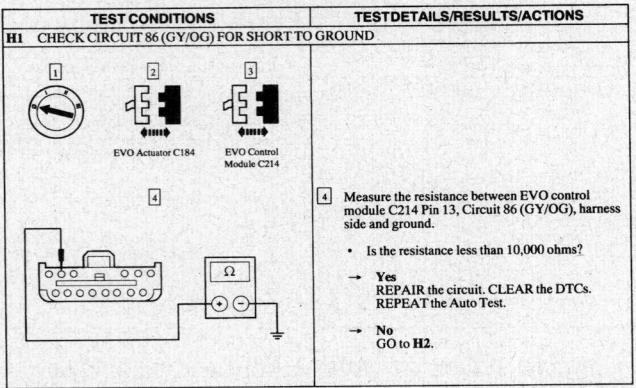

1 Measure the resistance between EVO control module C214 Pin 14, Circuit 87 (TN/YE), harness side and ground.

- Is the resistance greater than 10,000 ohms?

→ **Yes**
GO to G4.

→ **No**
REPAIR the circuit. CLEAR the DTCs. REPEAT the Auto Test.

FM6029900341020X

Fig. 11   Code 28: EVO Actuator Circuit Shorted (Part 2 of 3). Crown Victoria, Grand Marquis & Marauder

TEST CONDITIONS	TEST DETAILS/RESULTS/ACTIONS
H1 CHECK CIRCUIT 86 (GY/OG) FOR SHORT TO GROUND	

EVO Actuator C184   EVO Control Module C214

4 Measure the resistance between EVO control module C214 Pin 13, Circuit 86 (GY/OG), harness side and ground.

- Is the resistance less than 10,000 ohms?

→ **Yes**
REPAIR the circuit. CLEAR the DTCs. REPEAT the Auto Test.

→ **No**
GO to H2.

FM6029900342010X

Fig. 12   Code 29: EVO Actuator Circuit High Side Shorted To Ground (Part 1 of 2). Crown Victoria, Grand Marquis & Marauder

TEST CONDITIONS	TEST DETAILS/RESULTS/ACTIONS
I1 CHECK CIRCUIT 86 (GY/OG) FOR SHORT TO BATTERY	

EVO Actuator C184   EVO Control Module C214

4 Measure the voltage between EVO control module C214 Pin 13, Circuit 86 (GY/OG), harness side and ground.

- Is voltage present?

→ **Yes**
REPAIR the circuit. CLEAR the DTCs. REPEAT the Auto Test.

→ **No**
GO to I2.

FM6029900343010X

Fig. 13   Code 30: EVO Actuator Circuit Shorted To Battery (Part 1 of 2). Crown Victoria, Grand Marquis & Marauder

TEST CONDITIONS	TEST DETAILS/RESULTS/ACTIONS
G4 CHECK CIRCUIT RESISTANCE	

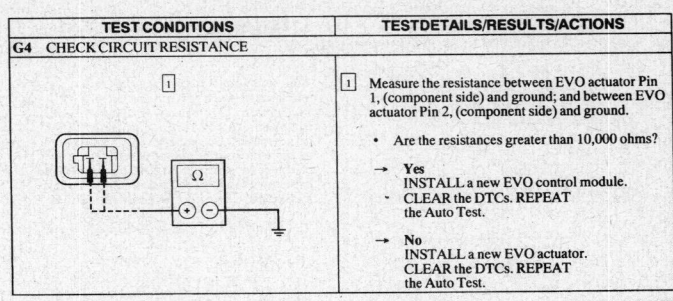

1 Measure the resistance between EVO actuator Pin 1, (component side) and ground; and between EVO actuator Pin 2, (component side) and ground.

- Are the resistances greater than 10,000 ohms?

→ **Yes**
INSTALL a new EVO control module.
CLEAR the DTCs. REPEAT the Auto Test.

→ **No**
INSTALL a new EVO actuator.
CLEAR the DTCs. REPEAT the Auto Test.

FM6029900341030X

Fig. 11   Code 28: EVO Actuator Circuit Shorted (Part 3 of 3). Crown Victoria, Grand Marquis & Marauder

TEST CONDITIONS	TEST DETAILS/RESULTS/ACTIONS
H2 CHECK EVO ACTUATOR FOR SHORT TO GROUND	

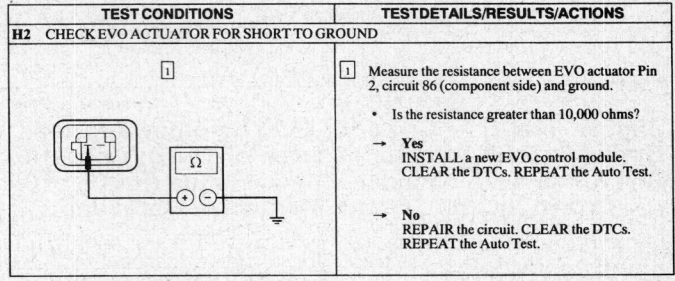

1 Measure the resistance between EVO actuator Pin 2, circuit 86 (component side) and ground.

- Is the resistance greater than 10,000 ohms?

→ **Yes**
INSTALL a new EVO control module.
CLEAR the DTCs. REPEAT the Auto Test.

→ **No**
REPAIR the circuit. CLEAR the DTCs. REPEAT the Auto Test.

FM6029900342020X

Fig. 12   Code 29: EVO Actuator Circuit High Side Shorted To Ground (Part 2 of 2). Crown Victoria, Grand Marquis & Marauder

TEST CONDITIONS	TEST DETAILS/RESULTS/ACTIONS
I2 CHECK CIRCUIT 87 (TN/YE) FOR SHORT TO BATTERY	

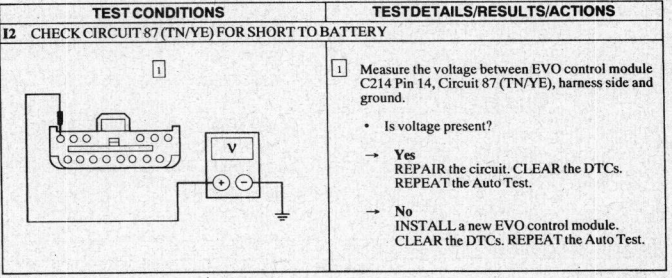

1 Measure the voltage between EVO control module C214 Pin 14, Circuit 87 (TN/YE), harness side and ground.

- Is voltage present?

→ **Yes**
REPAIR the circuit. CLEAR the DTCs. REPEAT the Auto Test.

→ **No**
INSTALL a new EVO control module. CLEAR the DTCs. REPEAT the Auto Test.

FM6029900343020X

Fig. 13   Code 30: EVO Actuator Circuit Shorted To Battery (Part 2 of 2). Crown Victoria, Grand Marquis & Marauder

TEST CONDITIONS	TEST DETAILS/RESULTS/ACTIONS
J1 CHECK CIRCUIT 87 (TN/YE) FOR SHORT TO GROUND	

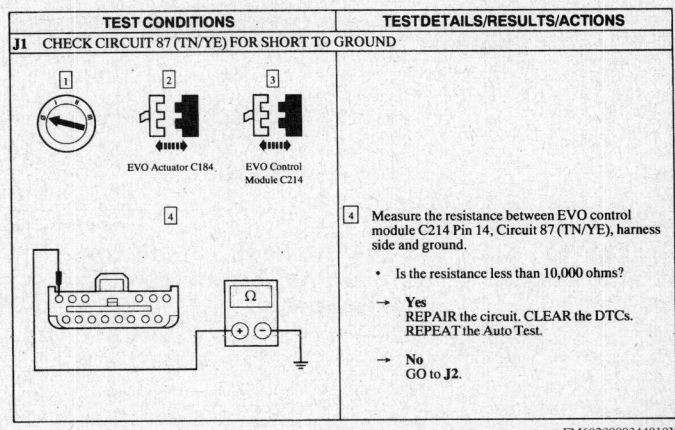

EVO Actuator C184   EVO Control Module C214

4 Measure the resistance between EVO control module C214 Pin 14, Circuit 87 (TN/YE), harness side and ground.

- Is the resistance less than 10,000 ohms?

→ **Yes**
REPAIR the circuit. CLEAR the DTCs. REPEAT the Auto Test.

→ **No**
GO to J2.

FM6029900344010X

Fig. 14   Code 31: EVO Actuator Circuit Low Side Shorted To Ground (Part 1 of 2). Crown Victoria, Grand Marquis & Marauder

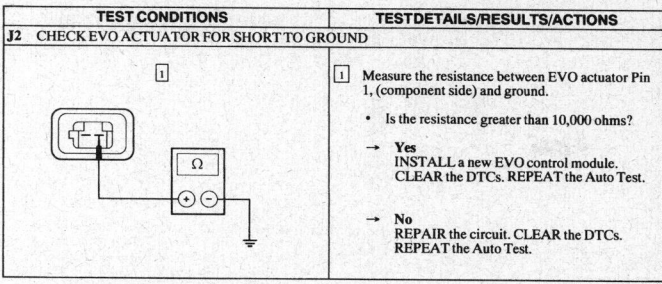

TEST CONDITIONS	TEST DETAILS/RESULTS/ACTIONS
J2 CHECK EVO ACTUATOR FOR SHORT TO GROUND	

1 Measure the resistance between EVO actuator Pin 1, (component side) and ground.

- Is the resistance greater than 10,000 ohms?

→ **Yes**
INSTALL a new EVO control module. CLEAR the DTCs. REPEAT the Auto Test.

→ **No**
REPAIR the circuit. CLEAR the DTCs. REPEAT the Auto Test.

FM6029900344020X

Fig. 14 Code 31: EVO Actuator Circuit Low Side Shorted To Ground (Part 2 of 2). Crown Victoria, Grand Marquis & Marauder

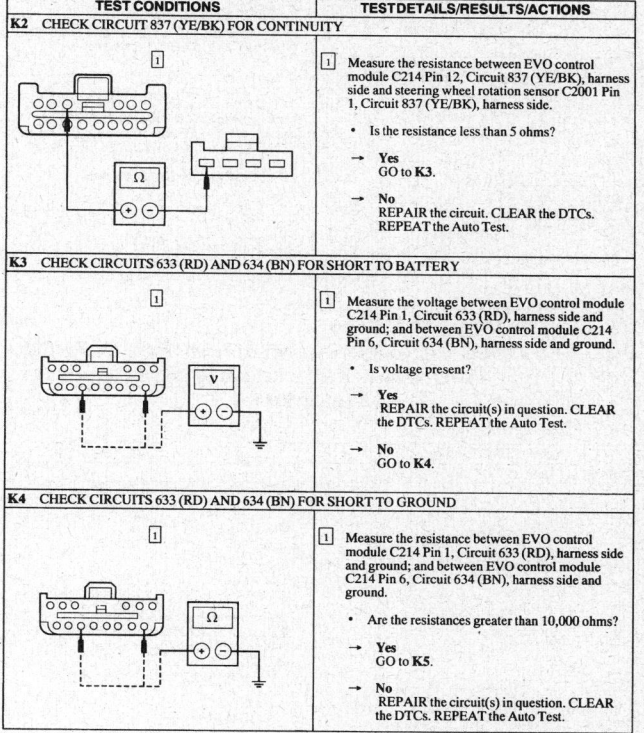

TEST CONDITIONS	TEST DETAILS/RESULTS/ACTIONS
K2 CHECK CIRCUIT 837 (YE/BK) FOR CONTINUITY	

1 Measure the resistance between EVO control module C214 Pin 12, Circuit 837 (YE/BK), harness side and steering wheel rotation sensor C2001 Pin 1, Circuit 837 (YE/BK), harness side.

- Is the resistance less than 5 ohms?

→ **Yes**
GO to **K3**.

→ **No**
REPAIR the circuit. CLEAR the DTCs. REPEAT the Auto Test.

| **K3** CHECK CIRCUITS 633 (RD) AND 634 (BN) FOR SHORT TO BATTERY | |

1 Measure the voltage between EVO control module C214 Pin 1, Circuit 633 (RD), harness side and ground; and between EVO control module C214 Pin 6, Circuit 634 (BN), harness side and ground.

- Is voltage present?

→ **Yes**
REPAIR the circuit(s) in question. CLEAR the DTCs. REPEAT the Auto Test.

→ **No**
GO to **K4**.

| **K4** CHECK CIRCUITS 633 (RD) AND 634 (BN) FOR SHORT TO GROUND | |

1 Measure the resistance between EVO control module C214 Pin 1, Circuit 633 (RD), harness side and ground; and between EVO control module C214 Pin 6, Circuit 634 (BN), harness side and ground.

- Are the resistances greater than 10,000 ohms?

→ **Yes**
GO to **K5**.

→ **No**
REPAIR the circuit(s) in question. CLEAR the DTCs. REPEAT the Auto Test.

FM6029900345020X

Fig. 15 Code 33: Steering Rotation Not Detected (Part 2 of 4). Crown Victoria, Grand Marquis & Marauder

TEST CONDITIONS	TEST DETAILS/RESULTS/ACTIONS
K6 CHECK STEERING WHEEL ROTATION SENSOR	

5 **Note:** Touch 73 Digital Multimeter leads together to be sure the audio (beep) function is operational.

Note: The 73 Digital Multimeter should beep several times while rotating the steering wheel.

Connect 73 Digital Multimeter leads between EVO control module C214 Pin 1, Circuit 633 (RD), harness side and ground; and between EVO control module C214 Pin 6, Circuit 634 (BN), harness side and ground. Listen for an audible beep while turning the steering wheel one quarter turn in each direction.

- Does 73 Digital Multimeter beep multiple times in each direction?

→ **Yes**
INSTALL a new EVO control module. CLEAR the DTCs. REPEAT the Auto Test.

→ **No**
INSTALL a new steering wheel rotation sensor. CLEAR the DTCs. REPEAT the Auto Test.

FM6029900345040X

Fig. 15 Code 33: Steering Rotation Not Detected (Part 4 of 4). Crown Victoria, Grand Marquis & Marauder

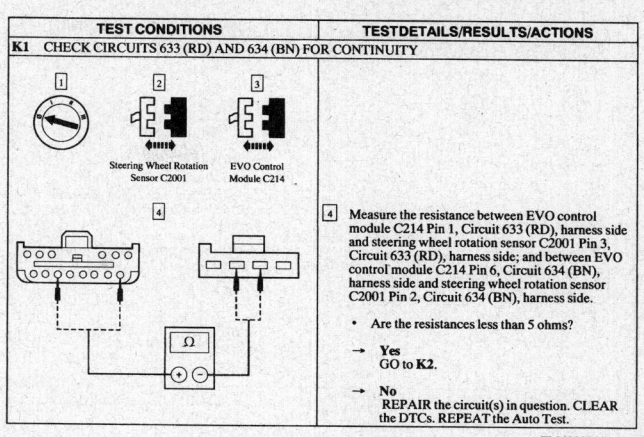

TEST CONDITIONS	TEST DETAILS/RESULTS/ACTIONS
K1 CHECK CIRCUITS 633 (RD) AND 634 (BN) FOR CONTINUITY	

4 Measure the resistance between EVO control module C214 Pin 1, Circuit 633 (RD), harness side and steering wheel rotation sensor C2001 Pin 3, Circuit 633 (RD), harness side; and between EVO control module C214 Pin 6, Circuit 634 (BN), harness side and steering wheel rotation sensor C2001 Pin 2, Circuit 634 (BN), harness side.

- Are the resistances less than 5 ohms?

→ **Yes**
GO to **K2**.

→ **No**
REPAIR the circuit(s) in question. CLEAR the DTCs. REPEAT the Auto Test.

FM6029900345010X

Fig. 15 Code 33: Steering Rotation Not Detected (Part 1 of 4). Crown Victoria, Grand Marquis & Marauder

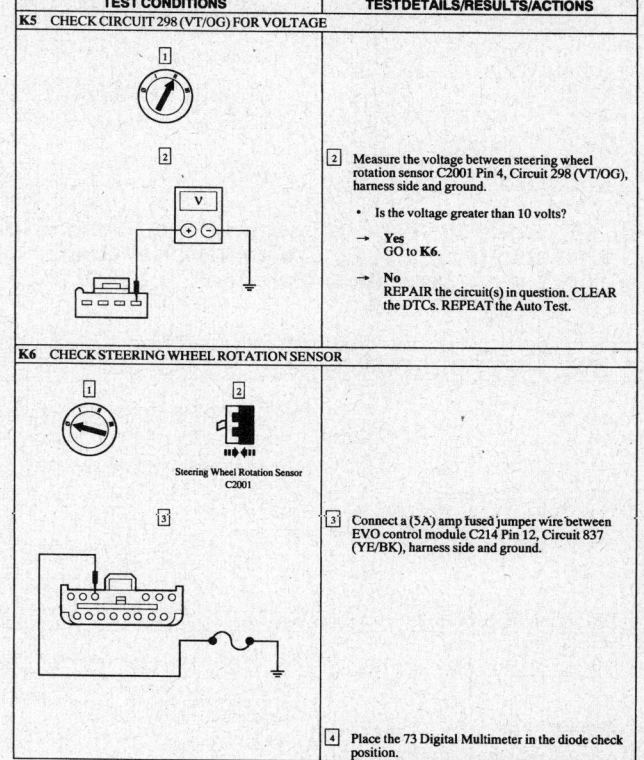

TEST CONDITIONS	TEST DETAILS/RESULTS/ACTIONS
K5 CHECK CIRCUIT 298 (VT/OG) FOR VOLTAGE	

2 Measure the voltage between steering wheel rotation sensor C2001 Pin 4, Circuit 298 (VT/OG), harness side and ground.

- Is the voltage greater than 10 volts?

→ **Yes**
GO to **K6**.

→ **No**
REPAIR the circuit(s) in question. CLEAR the DTCs. REPEAT the Auto Test.

| **K6** CHECK STEERING WHEEL ROTATION SENSOR | |

3 Connect a (5A) amp fused jumper wire between EVO control module C214 Pin 12, Circuit 837 (YE/BK), harness side and ground.

4 Place the 73 Digital Multimeter in the diode check position.

FM6029900345030X

Fig. 15 Code 33: Steering Rotation Not Detected (Part 3 of 4). Crown Victoria, Grand Marquis & Marauder

TEST CONDITIONS	TEST DETAILS/RESULTS/ACTIONS
L1 CHECK SPEEDOMETER OPERATION	

1 Drive the vehicle and check for correct speedometer operation.

- Does the speedometer indicate vehicle speeds above 24 km/h (15 mph)?

→ **Yes**
GO to **L2**.

→ **No**
INSPECT instrument cluster. CLEAR the DTCs. REPEAT the Auto Test.

FM6029900346010X

Fig. 16 Code 35: Vehicle Speed Above 15 mph Not Detected (Part 1 of 2). Crown Victoria, Grand Marquis & Marauder

TEST CONDITIONS	TESTDETAILS/RESULTS/ACTIONS
L2 CHECK CIRCUIT 676 (PK/OG) FOR AN OPEN	

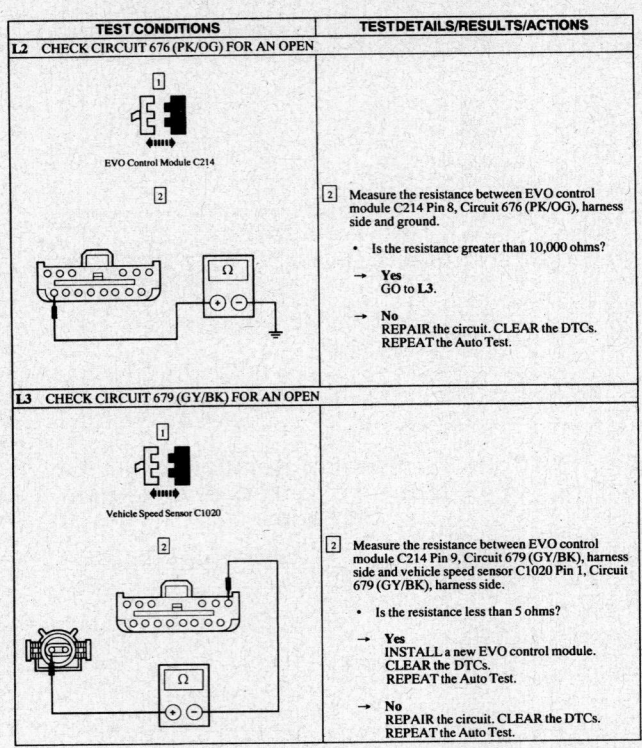

2 Measure the resistance between EVO control module C214 Pin 8, Circuit 676 (PK/OG), harness side and ground.

- Is the resistance greater than 10,000 ohms?

→ **Yes**
GO to L3.

→ **No**
REPAIR the circuit. CLEAR the DTCs. REPEAT the Auto Test.

| **L3** CHECK CIRCUIT 679 (GY/BK) FOR AN OPEN | |

2 Measure the resistance between EVO control module C214 Pin 9, Circuit 679 (GY/BK), harness side and vehicle speed sensor C1020 Pin 1, Circuit 679 (GY/BK), harness side.

- Is the resistance less than 5 ohms?

→ **Yes**
INSTALL a new EVO control module. CLEAR the DTCs. REPEAT the Auto Test.

→ **No**
REPAIR the circuit. CLEAR the DTCs. REPEAT the Auto Test.

FM6029900346020X

Fig. 16   Code 35: Vehicle Speed Above 15 mph Not Detected (Part 2 of 2). Crown Victoria, Grand Marquis & Marauder

TEST CONDITIONS	TESTDETAILS/RESULTS/ACTIONS
M3 CHECK CIRCUIT 837 (YE/BK) FOR GROUND	

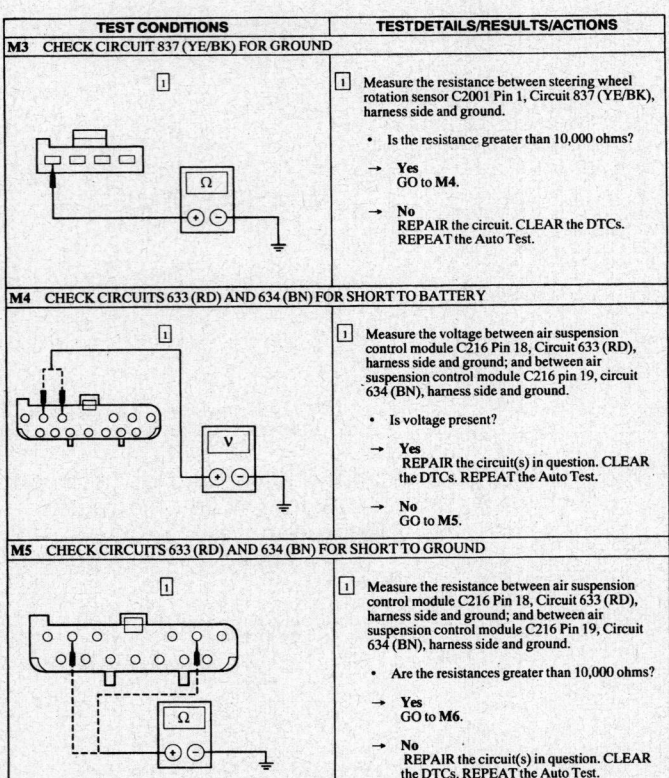

1 Measure the resistance between steering wheel rotation sensor C2001 Pin 1, Circuit 837 (YE/BK), harness side and ground.

- Is the resistance greater than 10,000 ohms?

→ **Yes**
GO to M4.

→ **No**
REPAIR the circuit. CLEAR the DTCs. REPEAT the Auto Test.

| **M4** CHECK CIRCUITS 633 (RD) AND 634 (BN) FOR SHORT TO BATTERY | |

1 Measure the voltage between air suspension control module C216 Pin 18, Circuit 633 (RD), harness side and ground; and between air suspension control module C216 pin 19, circuit 634 (BN), harness side and ground.

- Is voltage present?

→ **Yes**
REPAIR the circuit(s) in question. CLEAR the DTCs. REPEAT the Auto Test.

→ **No**
GO to M5.

| **M5** CHECK CIRCUITS 633 (RD) AND 634 (BN) FOR SHORT TO GROUND | |

1 Measure the resistance between air suspension control module C216 Pin 18, Circuit 633 (RD), harness side and ground; and between air suspension control module C216 Pin 19, Circuit 634 (BN), harness side and ground.

- Are the resistances greater than 10,000 ohms?

→ **Yes**
GO to M6.

→ **No**
REPAIR the circuit(s) in question. CLEAR the DTCs. REPEAT the Auto Test.

FM6029900347020X

Fig. 17   Code 74: Steering Rotation Not Detected (Part 2 of 4). Crown Victoria, Grand Marquis & Marauder

TEST CONDITIONS	TESTDETAILS/RESULTS/ACTIONS
M1 CHECK CIRCUITS 633 (RD) AND 634 (BN) FOR CONTINUITY	

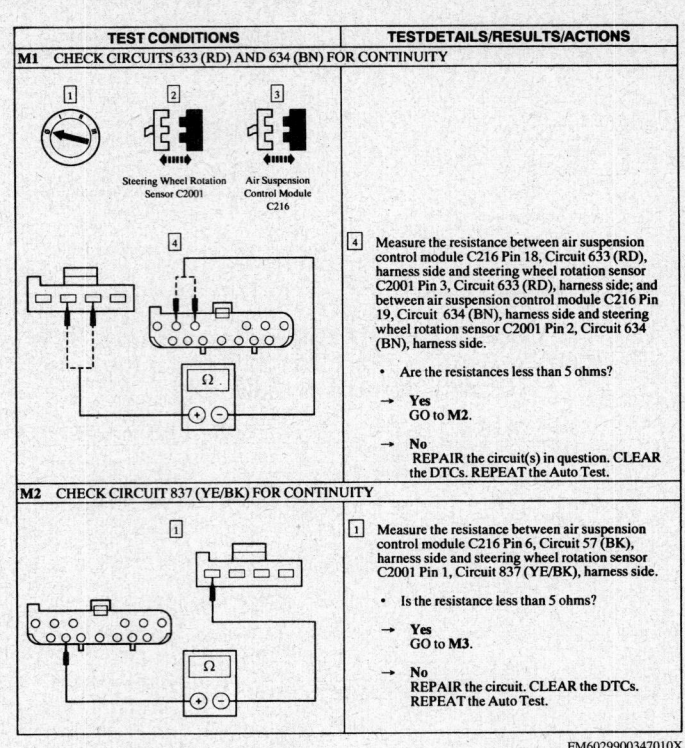

4 Measure the resistance between air suspension control module C216 Pin 18, Circuit 633 (RD), harness side and steering wheel rotation sensor C2001 Pin 3, Circuit 633 (RD), harness side; and between air suspension control module C216 Pin 19, Circuit 634 (BN), harness side and steering wheel rotation sensor C2001 Pin 2, Circuit 634 (BN), harness side.

- Are the resistances less than 5 ohms?

→ **Yes**
GO to M2.

→ **No**
REPAIR the circuit(s) in question. CLEAR the DTCs. REPEAT the Auto Test.

| **M2** CHECK CIRCUIT 837 (YE/BK) FOR CONTINUITY | |

1 Measure the resistance between air suspension control module C216 Pin 6, Circuit 57 (BK), harness side and steering wheel rotation sensor C2001 Pin 1, Circuit 837 (YE/BK), harness side.

- Is the resistance less than 5 ohms?

→ **Yes**
GO to M3.

→ **No**
REPAIR the circuit. CLEAR the DTCs. REPEAT the Auto Test.

FM6029900347010X

Fig. 17   Code 74: Steering Rotation Not Detected (Part 1 of 4). Crown Victoria, Grand Marquis & Marauder

TEST CONDITIONS	TESTDETAILS/RESULTS/ACTIONS
M6 CHECK CIRCUIT 298 (VT/OG) FOR VOLTAGE	

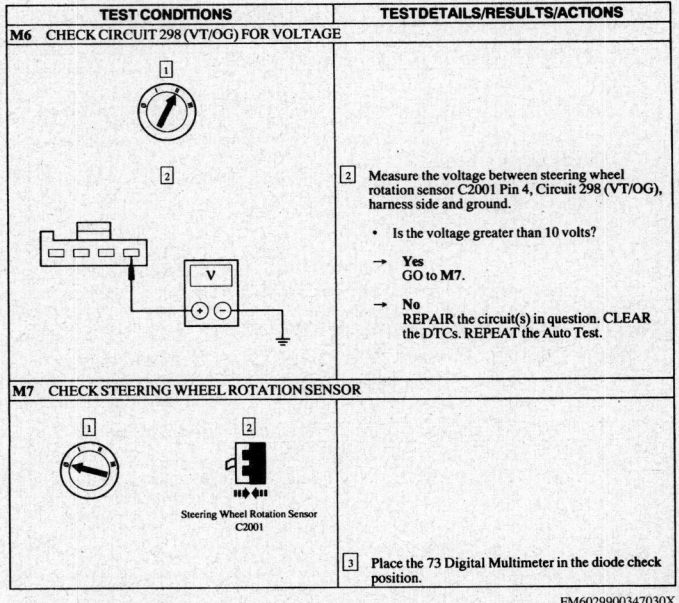

2 Measure the voltage between steering wheel rotation sensor C2001 Pin 4, Circuit 298 (VT/OG), harness side and ground.

- Is the voltage greater than 10 volts?

→ **Yes**
GO to M7.

→ **No**
REPAIR the circuit(s) in question. CLEAR the DTCs. REPEAT the Auto Test.

| **M7** CHECK STEERING WHEEL ROTATION SENSOR | |

3 Place the 73 Digital Multimeter in the diode check position.

FM6029900347030X

Fig. 17   Code 74: Steering Rotation Not Detected (Part 3 of 4). Crown Victoria, Grand Marquis & Marauder

TEST CONDITIONS	TEST DETAILS/RESULTS/ACTIONS
M7 CHECK STEERING WHEEL ROTATION SENSOR	
④	④ **Note:** Touch 73 Digital Multimeter leads together to be sure the audio (beep) function is operational. **Note:** The 73 Digital Multimeter should beep several times while rotating the steering wheel. Connect 73 Digital Multimeter leads between air suspension control module C216 Pin 18, Circuit 633 (RD), harness side and ground; and between air suspension control module C216 Pin 19, Circuit 634 (BN), harness side and ground. Listen for an audible beep while turning the steering wheel one quarter turn in each direction. • Does 73 Digital Multimeter beep multiple times in each direction? → **Yes** INSTALL a new EVO control module. CLEAR the DTCs. REPEAT the Auto Test. → **No** INSTALL a new steering wheel rotation sensor. CLEAR the DTCs. REPEAT the Auto Test.

FM6029900347040X

Fig. 17 Code 74: Steering Rotation Not Detected (Part 4 of 4). Crown Victoria, Grand Marquis & Marauder

Condition	Possible Source	Action
• Steering Is Very Difficult/Very Easy	• Power steering pump. • Power steering linkage. • Steering gear.	• GO to Pinpoint Test C.
• Steering Does Not Vary With Increased Wheel Rotation	• Power steering pump. • Power steering hose(s).	• GO to Pinpoint Test D.
• Steering Does Not Vary With Vehicle Speed	• Circuitry. • Rear Air suspension control module.	• GO to Pinpoint Test E.
• No Communication With The Module — Rear Air Suspension Control Module	• Fuse. • Circuitry. • Rear Air suspension control module.	• GO to Pinpoint Test F.
• Power Steering Pump Noisy	• Low fluid level and possible leakage. • Plugged reservoir filter. • Power steering pump.	• REFILL to specified level. Refer to Final Fill. CHECK for leaks. REPAIR and/or REPLACE as necessary. • REPLACE the reservoir • REPLACE the power steering pump
• System Back Pressure	• Power steering pump. • Power steering gear. • Hoses or fittings. • Power steering pump.	• REFER to Pump Flow And Pressure Test.

FM6029800289000X

Fig. 18 Symptom chart. Town Car

TEST CONDITIONS	TEST DETAILS/RESULTS/ACTIONS
A1 CHECK FUSE JUNCTION PANEL FUSE 8 (10A)	
① ② Fuse Junction Panel Fuse 8 (10A)	• Is the fuse OK? → **Yes** GO to A2. → **No** REPLACE the fuse. TEST the system for normal operation. If the fuse fails again, CHECK for short to ground. REPAIR as necessary. TEST the system for normal operation.
A2 CHECK STEERING WHEEL ROTATION SENSOR SIGNAL CIRCUIT 633 (R) AT THE REAR AIR SUSPENSION CONTROL MODULE	
① ② Rear Air Suspension Control Module	③ Place the 73 Digital Multimeter in the diode check position.

FM6029800290010X

Fig. 19 Test A, Codes C1441 & C1442: Steering Sensor Circuit Failure (Part 1 of 5). Town Car

TEST CONDITIONS	TEST DETAILS/RESULTS/ACTIONS
A2 CHECK STEERING WHEEL ROTATION SENSOR SIGNAL CIRCUIT 633 (R) AT THE REAR AIR SUSPENSION CONTROL MODULE (Continued)	
④	④ **NOTE:** Touch 73 Digital Multimeter leads together to be sure the audio (beep) function is operational. **NOTE:** The 73 Digital Multimeter should beep several times while rotating the steering wheel. Connect 73 Digital Multimeter leads between rear air suspension control module C250-18, circuit 633 (R), and ground, and listen for an audible beep while turning the steering wheel one quarter turn in each direction. • Does 73 Digital Multimeter beep multiple times in both directions? → **Yes** GO to A3. → **No** GO to A4.
A3 CHECK STEERING WHEEL ROTATION SENSOR SIGNAL CIRCUIT 644 (BR) AT THE REAR AIR SUSPENSION CONTROL MODULE	
①	① With 73 Digital Multimeter in the diode check position, connect 73 Digital Multimeter leads between rear air suspension control module C250-19, circuit 634 (BR), and ground, and listen for an audible beep while turning the steering wheel one quarter turn in each direction. • Does 73 Digital Multimeter beep multiple times in both directions? → **Yes** REPLACE the rear air suspension control module. TEST the system for normal operation. → **No** GO to A9.

FM6029800290020X

Fig. 19 Test A, Codes C1441 & C14422: Steering Sensor Circuit Failure (Part 2 of 5). Town Car

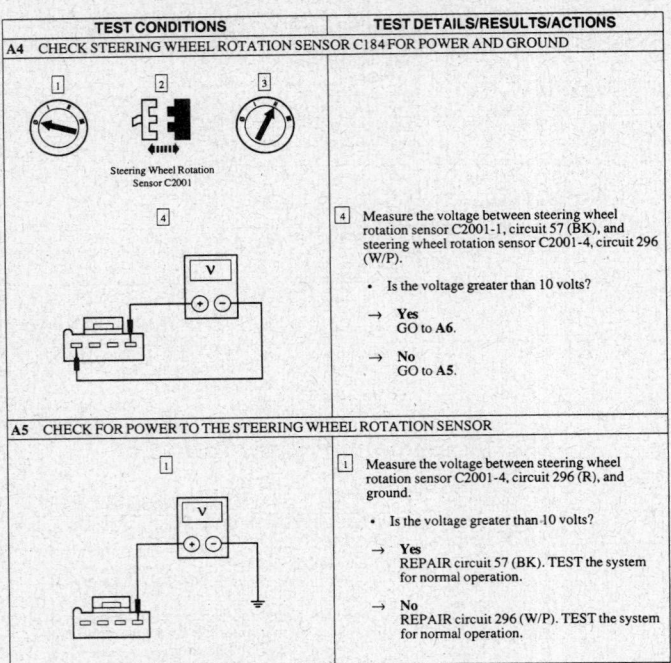

TEST CONDITIONS	TEST DETAILS/RESULTS/ACTIONS
A4 CHECK STEERING WHEEL ROTATION SENSOR C184 FOR POWER AND GROUND	
	4 Measure the voltage between steering wheel rotation sensor C2001-1, circuit 57 (BK), and steering wheel rotation sensor C2001-4, circuit 296 (W/P). • Is the voltage greater than 10 volts? → **Yes** GO to **A6**. → **No** GO to **A5**.
A5 CHECK FOR POWER TO THE STEERING WHEEL ROTATION SENSOR	
	1 Measure the voltage between steering wheel rotation sensor C2001-4, circuit 296 (R), and ground. • Is the voltage greater than 10 volts? → **Yes** REPAIR circuit 57 (BK). TEST the system for normal operation. → **No** REPAIR circuit 296 (W/P). TEST the system for normal operation.

FM6029800290030X

Fig. 19   Test A, Codes C1441 & C1442: Steering Sensor Circuit Failure (Part 3 of 5). Town Car

TEST CONDITIONS	TEST DETAILS/RESULTS/ACTIONS
A6 CHECK CIRCUIT 633 (R) FOR SHORT TO POWER	
	1 Measure the voltage between steering wheel rotation sensor C2001-3, circuit 633 (R), and ground. • Is voltage present? → **Yes** REPAIR circuit 633 (R). TEST the system for normal operation. → **No** GO to **A7**.
A7 CHECK CIRCUIT 633 (R) FOR SHORT TO GROUND	
	1 Measure the resistance between steering wheel rotation sensor C2001-3, circuit 633 (R), and ground. • Is the resistance greater than 10,000 ohms? → **Yes** GO to **A8**. → **No** REPAIR circuit 633 (R). TEST the system for normal operation.
A8 CHECK CIRCUIT 633 (R) FOR OPEN	
	1 Measure the resistance between rear air suspension control module C250-18, circuit 633 (R), and steering wheel rotation sensor C2001-3, circuit 633 (R). • Is the resistance less than 5 ohms? → **Yes** REPLACE the steering wheel rotation sensor. TEST the system for normal operation. → **No** REPAIR circuit 633 (R). TEST the system for normal operation.

FM6029800290040X

Fig. 19   Test A, Codes C1441 & C1442: Steering Sensor Circuit failure (Part 4 of 5). Town Car

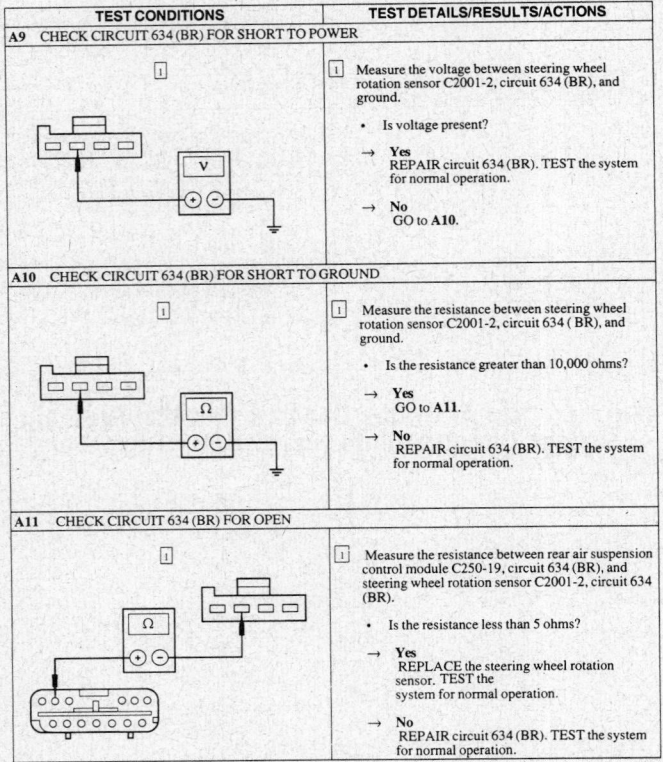

TEST CONDITIONS	TEST DETAILS/RESULTS/ACTIONS
A9 CHECK CIRCUIT 634 (BR) FOR SHORT TO POWER	
	1 Measure the voltage between steering wheel rotation sensor C2001-2, circuit 634 (BR), and ground. • Is voltage present? → **Yes** REPAIR circuit 634 (BR). TEST the system for normal operation. → **No** GO to **A10**.
A10 CHECK CIRCUIT 634 (BR) FOR SHORT TO GROUND	
	1 Measure the resistance between steering wheel rotation sensor C2001-2, circuit 634 (BR), and ground. • Is the resistance greater than 10,000 ohms? → **Yes** GO to **A11**. → **No** REPAIR circuit 634 (BR). TEST the system for normal operation.
A11 CHECK CIRCUIT 634 (BR) FOR OPEN	
	1 Measure the resistance between rear air suspension control module C250-19, circuit 634 (BR), and steering wheel rotation sensor C2001-2, circuit 634 (BR). • Is the resistance less than 5 ohms? → **Yes** REPLACE the steering wheel rotation sensor. TEST the system for normal operation. → **No** REPAIR circuit 634 (BR). TEST the system for normal operation.

FM6029800290050X

Fig. 19   Test A, Codes C1441 & C1442: Steering Sensor Circuit Failure (Part 5 of 5). Town Car

TEST CONDITIONS	TEST DETAILS/RESULTS/ACTIONS
B1 CHECK THE POWER STEERING CONTROL VALVE ACTUATOR	
	3 Check the power steering control valve actuator C184 for damaged pigtail, bent pins, dirt, or corrosion. • Are the connector and pigtail OK? → **Yes** GO to **B2**. → **No** REPAIR as necessary. TEST the system for normal operation.
B2 CHECK THE POWER STEERING CONTROL VALVE ACTUATOR FOR SHORT TO GROUND	
	1 Measure the resistance between power steering control valve actuator terminal (component side), and ground. • Is the resistance greater than 10,000 ohms? → **Yes** GO to **B3**. → **No** REPLACE the power steering control valve actuator. TEST the system for normal operation.

FM6029800291010X

Fig. 20   Test A, Codes C1441 & C1442: Steering VAPS II Circuit Loop Failure (Part 1 of 4). Town Car

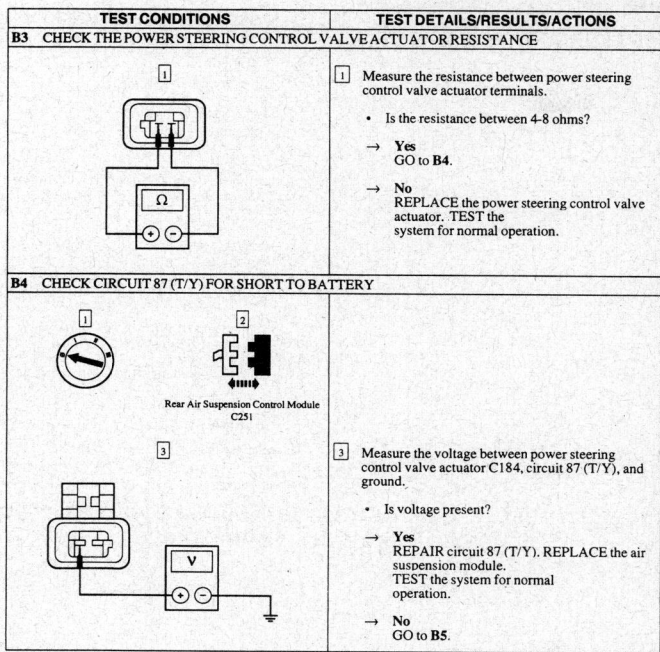

TEST CONDITIONS	TEST DETAILS/RESULTS/ACTIONS
B3 CHECK THE POWER STEERING CONTROL VALVE ACTUATOR RESISTANCE	
[1]	[1] Measure the resistance between power steering control valve actuator terminals. • Is the resistance between 4-8 ohms? → **Yes** GO to **B4**. → **No** REPLACE the power steering control valve actuator. TEST the system for normal operation.
B4 CHECK CIRCUIT 87 (T/Y) FOR SHORT TO BATTERY	
[1] [2] Rear Air Suspension Control Module C251 [3]	[3] Measure the voltage between power steering control valve actuator C184, circuit 87 (T/Y), and ground. • Is voltage present? → **Yes** REPAIR circuit 87 (T/Y). REPLACE the air suspension module. TEST the system for normal operation. → **No** GO to **B5**.

FM6029800291020X

Fig. 20   Test B, Code C1897: Steering VAPS II Circuit Loop Failure (Part 2 of 4). Town Car

TEST CONDITIONS	TEST DETAILS/RESULTS/ACTIONS
B8 CHECK CIRCUIT 87 (T/Y) FOR AN OPEN	
[1]	[1] Measure the resistance between power steering control valve actuator C184, circuit 87 (T/Y), and rear air suspension control module C251-26, circuit 87 (T/Y). • Is the resistance less than 5 ohms? → **Yes** GO to **B9**. → **No** REPAIR circuit 87 (T/Y). TEST the system for normal operation.
B9 CHECK CIRCUIT 86 (GY/O) FOR AN OPEN	
[1]	[1] Measure the resistance between power steering control valve actuator C184, circuit 86 (GY/O), and rear air suspension control module C251-14, circuit 86 (GY/O). • Is the resistance less than 5 ohms? → **Yes** REPLACE the rear air suspension control module. TEST the system for normal operation. → **No** REPAIR circuit 86 (GY/O). TEST the system for normal operation.

FM6029800291040X

Fig. 20   Test B, Code C1897: Steering VAPS II Circuit Loop Failure (Part 4 of 4). Town Car

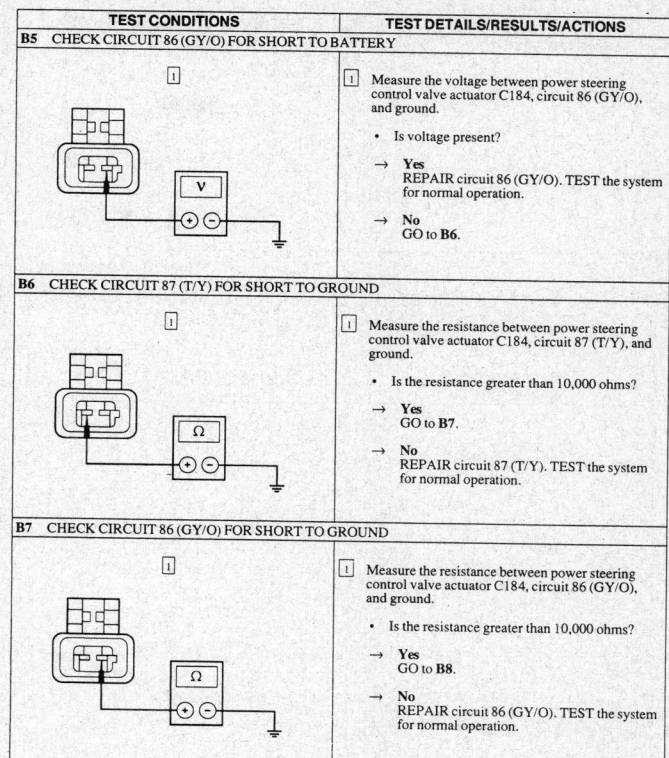

TEST CONDITIONS	TEST DETAILS/RESULTS/ACTIONS
B5 CHECK CIRCUIT 86 (GY/O) FOR SHORT TO BATTERY	
[1]	[1] Measure the voltage between power steering control valve actuator C184, circuit 86 (GY/O), and ground. • Is voltage present? → **Yes** REPAIR circuit 86 (GY/O). TEST the system for normal operation. → **No** GO to **B6**.
B6 CHECK CIRCUIT 87 (T/Y) FOR SHORT TO GROUND	
[1]	[1] Measure the resistance between power steering control valve actuator C184, circuit 87 (T/Y), and ground. • Is the resistance greater than 10,000 ohms? → **Yes** GO to **B7**. → **No** REPAIR circuit 87 (T/Y). TEST the system for normal operation.
B7 CHECK CIRCUIT 86 (GY/O) FOR SHORT TO GROUND	
[1]	[1] Measure the resistance between power steering control valve actuator C184, circuit 86 (GY/O), and ground. • Is the resistance greater than 10,000 ohms? → **Yes** GO to **B8**. → **No** REPAIR circuit 86 (GY/O). TEST the system for normal operation.

FM6029800291030X

Fig. 20   Test B, Code C1897: Steering VAPS II Circuit Loop Failure (Part 3 of 4). Town Car

TEST CONDITIONS	TEST DETAILS/RESULTS/ACTIONS
C1 CHECK THE POWER STEERING PUMP (Continued)	
[1] Ignition ON, Engine Running [2] Check power steering pump for leaks by turning steering Wheel and observing pump	[3] Perform the Pump Flow and Pressure Test; go to Component Tests. • Is the power steering pump OK? → **Yes** GO to **C2**. → **No** REPLACE the power steering pump TEST the system for normal operation.
C2 CHECK THE STEERING LINKAGE	
	[1] Visually check the steering linkage while an assistant rotates the steering wheel from stop to stop. • Does the steering linkage move smoothly from stop to stop? → **Yes** GO to **C3**. → **No** REPLACE the damaged steering linkage component(s) TEST the system for normal operation.
C3 CHECK THE STEERING ASSEMBLY	
	[1] Check the ball joints for worn surfaces. • Are the ball joints OK ? → **Yes** GO to **C4**. → **No** REPLACE worn ball joints. TEST the system for normal operation.
C4 CHECK THE STEERING GEAR	
	[1] Visually check the steering gear operation while an assistant rotates the steering wheel from stop to stop.

FM6029800292010X

Fig. 21   Test C: Steering Is Very Difficult/Very Easy (Part 1 of 2). Town Car

TEST CONDITIONS	TEST DETAILS/RESULTS/ACTIONS
C4 CHECK THE STEERING GEAR (Continued)	
	2 Check the steering gear mounting fasteners for loose bolts.
	• Is the steering gear OK?
	→ **Yes** If condition still exists, GO to the Symptom Chart.
	→ **No** TIGHTEN and/or REPLACE the steering gear; TEST the system for normal operation.

FM6029800292020X

Fig. 21 Test C: Steering Is Very Difficult/Very Easy (Part 2 of 2). Town Car

TEST CONDITIONS	TEST DETAILS/RESULTS/ACTIONS
E1 CHECK THE SPEEDOMETER	
	2 Check the speedometer by driving the vehicle and observing the speedometer operation.
	• Does the speedometer operate properly?
	→ **Yes** GO to **E2**.
	→ **No**
E2 CHECK FOR DTC U1041	
NGS	4 Retrieve and document DTCs.
	• Is DTC U1041 retrieved?
	→ **Yes**
	→ **No** If any DTCs are retrieved. **GO TO** (DTC) Index. If no DTCs are retrieved, REPLACE the rear air suspension control module. TEST the system for normal operation.

FM6029800294000X

Fig. 23 Test E: Steering Does Not Vary w/Vehicle Speed. Town Car

TEST CONDITIONS	TEST DETAILS/RESULTS/ACTIONS
F1 CHECK THE FUSES	
Fuse Junction Panel Fuse 8 (10A) Power Distribution Box Fuse 17 (10A)	• Are fuse junction panel fuse 8 (10A) and power distribution box fuse 17 (10A) OK?
	→ **Yes** GO to **F2**.
	→ **No** REPLACE the fuse in question. TEST the system for normal operation. If the fuse fails again, CHECK for short to ground. REPAIR as necessary. TEST the system for normal operation.
F2 CHECK CIRCUIT 296 (W/P) FOR AN OPEN	
Rear Air Suspension Control Module C250	4 Measure the voltage between rear air suspension control module C250-16, circuit 296 (W/P), and ground.
	• Is the voltage greater than 10 volts?
	→ **Yes** GO to **F3**.
	→ **No** REPAIR circuit 296 (W/P). TEST the system for normal operation.

FM6029800295010X

Fig. 24 Test F: No Communication w/Rear Air Suspension Control Module (Part 1 of 2). Town Car

TEST CONDITIONS	TEST DETAILS/RESULTS/ACTIONS
D1 CHECK THE POWER STEERING PUMP	

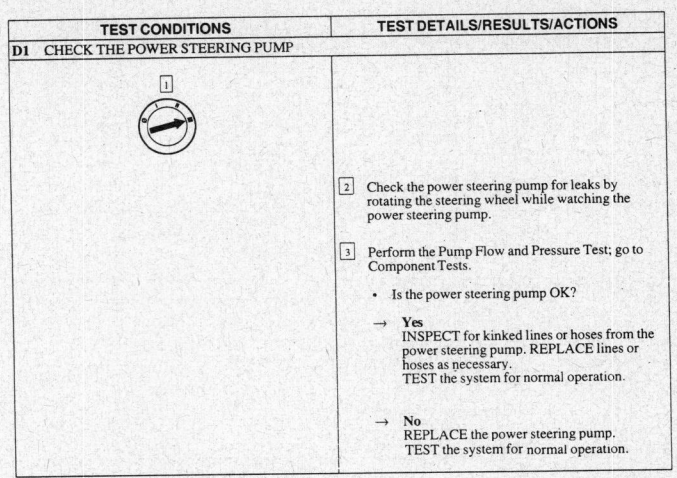

	2 Check the power steering pump for leaks by rotating the steering wheel while watching the power steering pump.
	3 Perform the Pump Flow and Pressure Test; go to Component Tests.
	• Is the power steering pump OK?
	→ **Yes** INSPECT for kinked lines or hoses from the power steering pump. REPLACE lines or hoses as necessary. TEST the system for normal operation.
	→ **No** REPLACE the power steering pump. TEST the system for normal operation.

FM6029800293000X

Fig. 22 Test D: Steering Does Not Vary w/Increased Wheel Rotation. Town Car

TEST CONDITIONS	TEST DETAILS/RESULTS/ACTIONS
F3 CHECK CIRCUIT 418 (DG/Y) FOR AN OPEN	
	1 Measure the voltage between rear air suspension control module C250-1, circuit 418 (DG/Y), and ground.
	• Is the voltage greater than 10 volts?
	→ **Yes** GO to **F4**.
	→ **No** REPAIR circuit 418 (DG/Y). TEST the system for normal operation.
F4 CHECK CIRCUIT 57 (BK) FOR AN OPEN	
	2 Measure the resistance between rear air suspension control module C250-6, circuit 57 (BK), and ground.
	• Is the resistance less than 5 ohms?
	→ **Yes**
	→ **No** REPAIR circuit 57 (BK). TEST the system for normal operation.

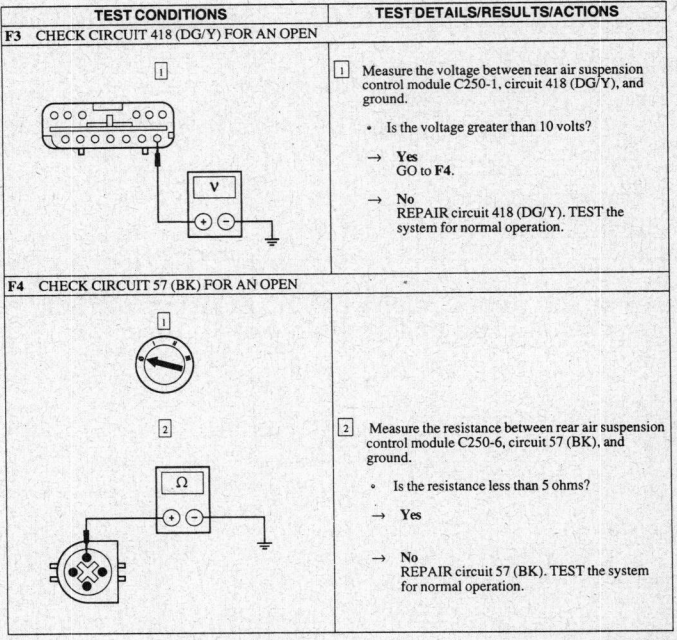

FM6029800295020X

Fig. 24 Test F: No Communication w/Rear Air Suspension Control Module (Part 2 of 2). Town Car

POWER STEERING SYSTEM SERVICE

CONTROL MODULE

REPLACE

The EVO control module and air suspension modules are one unit.
1. Turn air suspension switch to Off position.
2. Pull module out to access connectors.
3. Disconnect each electrical connectors.
4. Reverse procedure to install. **Torque** mounting nuts to 60–84 inch lbs.

CONTROL VALVE ACTUATOR

REPLACE

1. Raise and support vehicle.
2. Remove engine oil filter.
3. Disconnect power steering auxiliary actuator electrical connector.

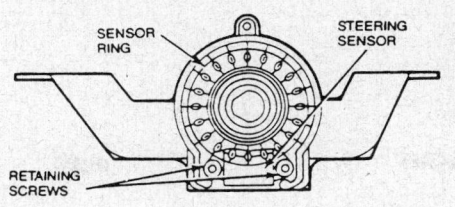

Fig. 25   Steering sensor replacement

FM6029100190000X

4. Remove mounting screw and power steering auxiliary actuator.
5. Reverse procedure to install.

STEERING SENSOR

REPLACE

1. Disconnect sensor electrical connector.
2. Remove sensor electrical connector from bracket under instrument panel.
3. Remove two mounting screws and sensor, **Fig. 25.**
4. Reverse procedure to install.

STEERING SENSOR RING

REPLACE

1. Remove steering column as outlined in "Steering Columns" chapter.
2. Remove steering shaft and sensor ring.
3. Reverse procedure to install.

SPEED SENSOR

REPLACE

1. Raise and support vehicle.
2. Remove clip mounting bolt, speed sensor and driven gear.
3. Disconnect sensor electrical connector.
4. Remove retainer and driven gear.
5. Reverse procedure to install. Ensure internal O-ring is seated in sensor housing.

Ford Variable Assist Power Steering (VAPS) System

NOTE: On Air Bag Equipped Models, Refer To "Air Bag System Precautions" Located In The Front Of This Manual For System Disarming & Arming Procedures.

NOTE: Refer To "Computer Relearn Procedures" Located In The Front Of This Manual When Battery Power To The Computer Has Been Interrupted.

NOTE: "Electrical Symbol & Wire Color Code Identification" Located In The Front Of This Manual May Be Used As An Aid When Using Wiring Circuits Found In This Section.

INDEX

	Page No.
Description	13-31
Diagnosis & Testing	13-32
Accessing Diagnostic Trouble Codes	13-32
Pinpoint Tests	13-32
Wiring Diagrams	13-32
Precautions	13-31
Air Bag Systems	13-31
Battery Ground Cable	13-31

	Page No.
Troubleshooting	13-32
Drift/Pull	13-32
Excessive Steering Pump Noise	13-32
Excessive Steering Wheel Play	13-32
Feedback	13-32
Hard Steering Or Lack Of Assist	13-32

	Page No.
Poor Returnability/Sticky Steering	13-32
Power Steering Pump Noisy	13-32
Shimmy	13-32
Steering Wander	13-32

PRECAUTIONS

Air Bag Systems

Refer to "Air Bag System Precautions" in the front of this manual for system disarming and arming procedures.

Battery Ground Cable

Prior to service, disconnect battery ground cable and isolate as required.

DESCRIPTION

The Variable Assist Power Steering (VAPS) System uses the Front Electronics Module (FEM) to improve steering characteristics. The VAPS system begins operation when engine speed exceeds 100 RPM.

The level of assist provided by the VAPS system depends on vehicle speed. The faster the vehicle speed, the less assist provided by the VAPS system. Vehicle

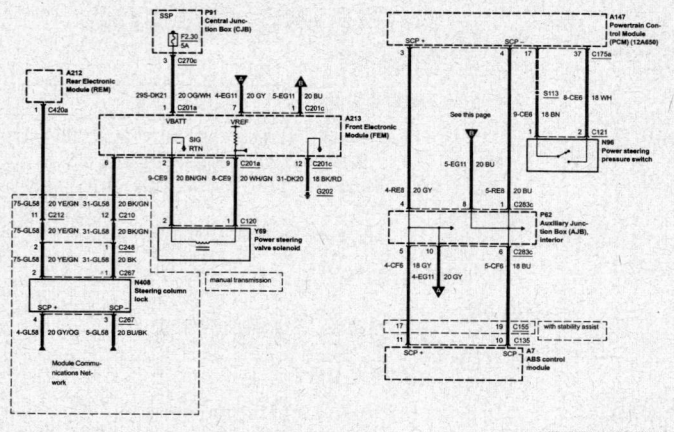

Fig. 1 VAPS wiring diagram. LS & Thunderbird

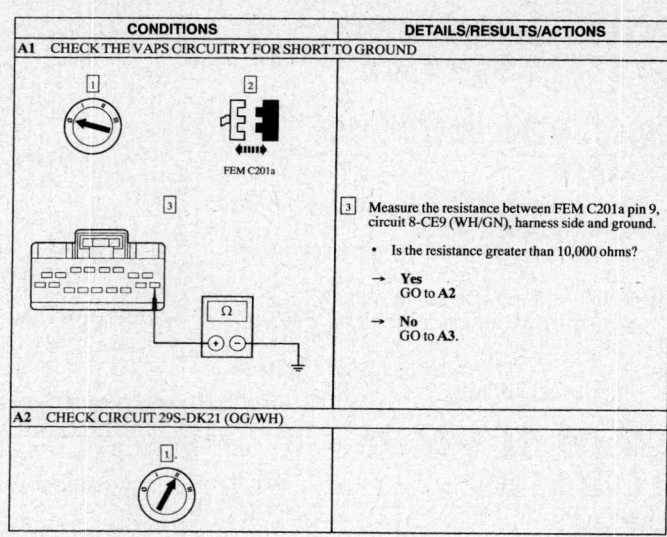

CONDITIONS	DETAILS/RESULTS/ACTIONS
A1 CHECK THE VAPS CIRCUITRY FOR SHORT TO GROUND	

Fig. 2 Test A, Code C1924: VAPS Solenoid Actuator Output Circuit Short To Ground (Part 1 of 2)

speed is determined by the FEM and is based on Pulse Width Modulated (PWM) current sent to the control valve actuator.

Engine RPM is provided to the FEM by the Powertrain Control Module (PCM) through the Standard Corporate Protocol (SCP). Vehicle speed is provided through the ABS system.

TROUBLESHOOTING

Hard Steering Or Lack Of Assist

1. Seized lower steering column shaft U-joint.
2. Damaged or fractured steering column bearings.
3. Power steering pump.
4. Suspension components.
5. Steering gear internal leakage.

Excessive Steering Pump Noise

Power steering pump failure.

Excessive Steering Wheel Play

1. Damaged, loose or worn tie-rod.
2. Damaged or worn steering gear.
3. Loose, worn or damaged steering column bearings.
4. Loose, worn or damaged lower steering column shaft U-joint.

Steering Wander

1. Unevenly loaded or overloaded vehicle.
2. Loose, worn or damaged tie-rod.
3. Loose or damaged steering gear mounting bolts.

4. Loose lower steering column shaft U-joint bolts or joints.
5. Loose, worn or damaged steering column bearings.
6. Suspension components.

Drift/Pull

1. Unevenly loaded or overloaded vehicle.
2. Loose, worn or damaged tie-rod.
3. Wheel alignment.
4. Suspension components.
5. Steering gear valve effort out of balance.
6. Inspect brake system for correct operation.
7. Incorrect frame or underbody alignment.

Feedback

1. Loose, worn or damaged tie-rod.
2. Loose, worn or damaged steering gear insulators or bolts.
3. Loose lower steering column shaft U-joint bolts.
4. Loose suspension bushings, fasteners or ball joints.
5. Worn or damaged steering column bearings.

Poor Returnability/ Sticky Steering

1. Binding lower steering column shaft U-joints.
2. Loose, worn or damaged tie-rod ends.
3. Suspension components.
4. Binding steering column bearings.

Shimmy

1. Loose, worn or damaged tie-rod.
2. Suspension components.

Power Steering Pump Noisy

1. Low fluid level and possible leakage.
2. Plugged reservoir.
3. Power steering pump.

DIAGNOSIS & TESTING

Accessing Diagnostic Trouble Codes

Diagnosing and testing requires the use of a New Generation Star (NGS) scan tool No. 418-F052, or equivalent and suitable digital volt/ohm meter. The Data Link Connector (DLC) is located under the instrument panel, between the steering column and radio.

Wiring Diagrams

Refer to **Fig. 1** for wiring diagram.

Pinpoint Tests

Refer to **Figs. 2 through 4** for pinpoint tests.

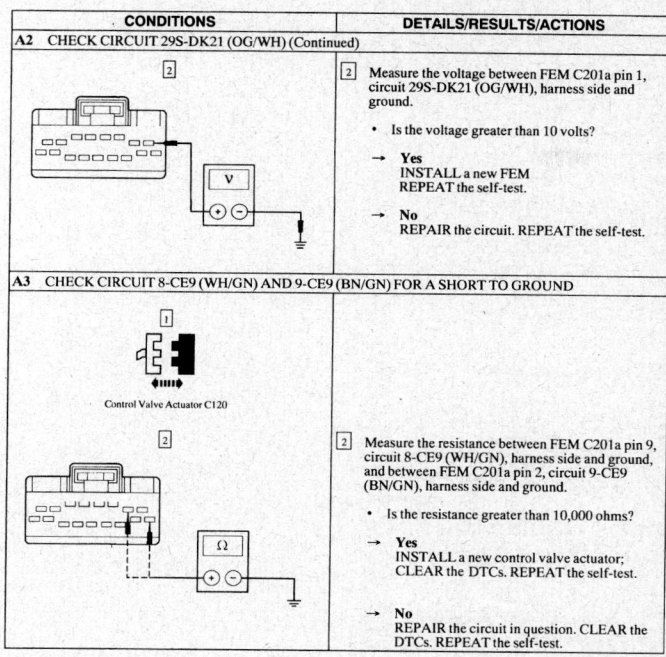

CONDITIONS	DETAILS/RESULTS/ACTIONS
A2 CHECK CIRCUIT 29S-DK21 (OG/WH) (Continued)	2 Measure the voltage between FEM C201a pin 1, circuit 29S-DK21 (OG/WH), harness side and ground. • Is the voltage greater than 10 volts? → **Yes** INSTALL a new FEM REPEAT the self-test. → **No** REPAIR the circuit. REPEAT the self-test.
A3 CHECK CIRCUIT 8-CE9 (WH/GN) AND 9-CE9 (BN/GN) FOR A SHORT TO GROUND Control Valve Actuator C120	2 Measure the resistance between FEM C201a pin 9, circuit 8-CE9 (WH/GN), harness side and ground, and between FEM C201a pin 2, circuit 9-CE9 (BN/GN), harness side and ground. • Is the resistance greater than 10,000 ohms? → **Yes** INSTALL a new control valve actuator; CLEAR the DTCs. REPEAT the self-test. → **No** REPAIR the circuit in question. CLEAR the DTCs. REPEAT the self-test.

FM6020100446020X

Fig. 2 Test A, Code C1924: VAPS Solenoid Actuator Output Circuit Short To Ground (Part 2 of 2)

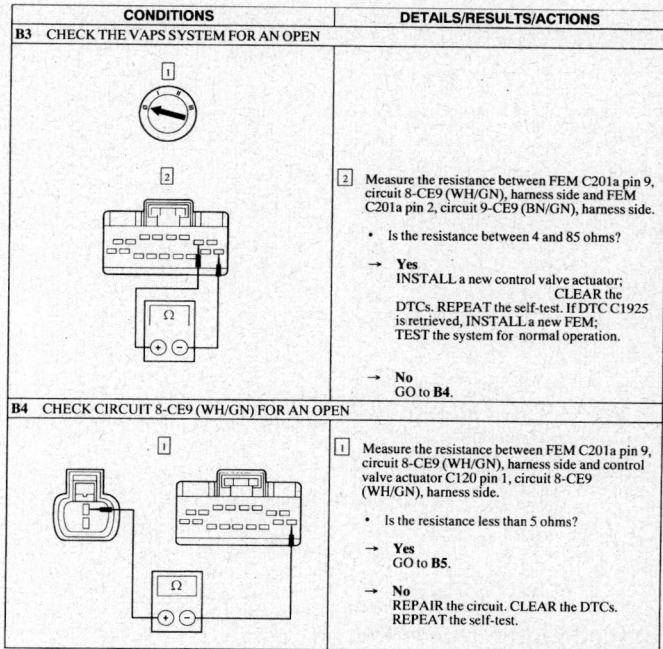

CONDITIONS	DETAILS/RESULTS/ACTIONS
B3 CHECK THE VAPS SYSTEM FOR AN OPEN	2 Measure the resistance between FEM C201a pin 9, circuit 8-CE9 (WH/GN), harness side and FEM C201a pin 2, circuit 9-CE9 (BN/GN), harness side. • Is the resistance between 4 and 85 ohms? → **Yes** INSTALL a new control valve actuator; CLEAR the DTCs. REPEAT the self-test. If DTC C1925 is retrieved, INSTALL a new FEM; TEST the system for normal operation. → **No** GO to **B4**.
B4 CHECK CIRCUIT 8-CE9 (WH/GN) FOR AN OPEN	1 Measure the resistance between FEM C201a pin 9, circuit 8-CE9 (WH/GN), harness side and control valve actuator C120 pin 1, circuit 8-CE9 (WH/GN), harness side. • Is the resistance less than 5 ohms? → **Yes** GO to **B5**. → **No** REPAIR the circuit. CLEAR the DTCs. REPEAT the self-test.

FM6020100447020X

Fig. 3 Test B, Code C1925: VAPS Solenoid Actuator Return Circuit Failure (Part 2 of 3)

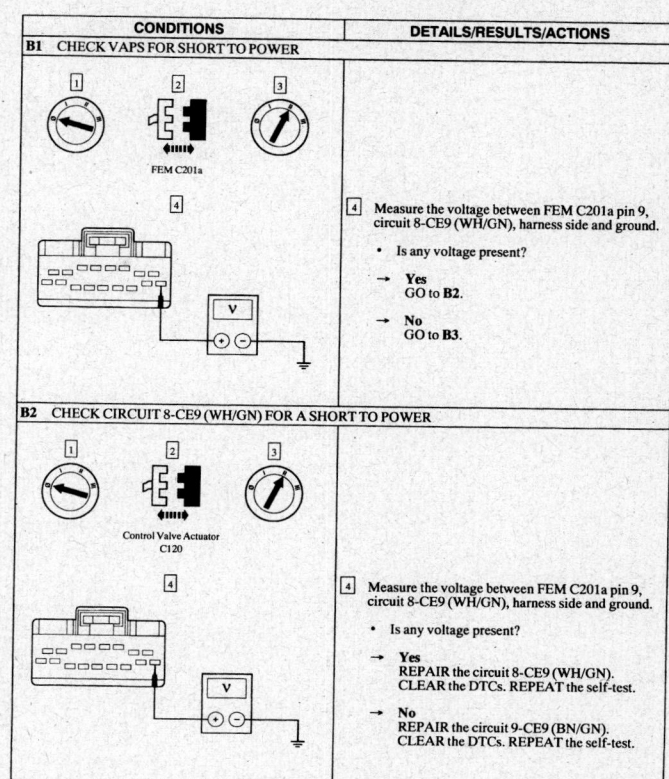

CONDITIONS	DETAILS/RESULTS/ACTIONS
B1 CHECK VAPS FOR SHORT TO POWER FEM C201a	4 Measure the voltage between FEM C201a pin 9, circuit 8-CE9 (WH/GN), harness side and ground. • Is any voltage present? → **Yes** GO to **B2**. → **No** GO to **B3**.
B2 CHECK CIRCUIT 8-CE9 (WH/GN) FOR A SHORT TO POWER Control Valve Actuator C120	4 Measure the voltage between FEM C201a pin 9, circuit 8-CE9 (WH/GN), harness side and ground. • Is any voltage present? → **Yes** REPAIR the circuit 8-CE9 (WH/GN). CLEAR the DTCs. REPEAT the self-test. → **No** REPAIR the circuit 9-CE9 (BN/GN). CLEAR the DTCs. REPEAT the self-test.

FM6020100447010X

Fig. 3 Test B, Code C1925: VAPS Solenoid Actuator Return Circuit Failure (Part 1 of 3)

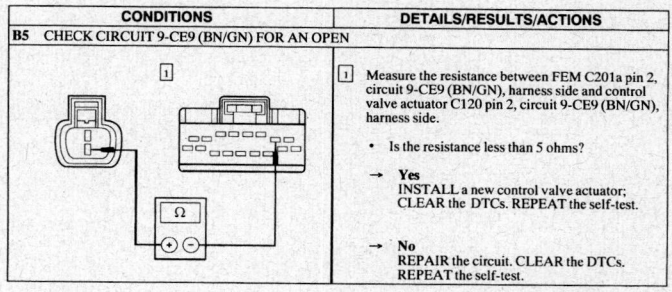

CONDITIONS	DETAILS/RESULTS/ACTIONS
B5 CHECK CIRCUIT 9-CE9 (BN/GN) FOR AN OPEN	1 Measure the resistance between FEM C201a pin 2, circuit 9-CE9 (BN/GN), harness side and control valve actuator C120 pin 2, circuit 9-CE9 (BN/GN), harness side. • Is the resistance less than 5 ohms? → **Yes** INSTALL a new control valve actuator; CLEAR the DTCs. REPEAT the self-test. → **No** REPAIR the circuit. CLEAR the DTCs. REPEAT the self-test.

FM6020100447030X

Fig. 3 Test B, Code C1925: VAPS Solenoid Actuator Return Circuit Failure (Part 3 of 3))

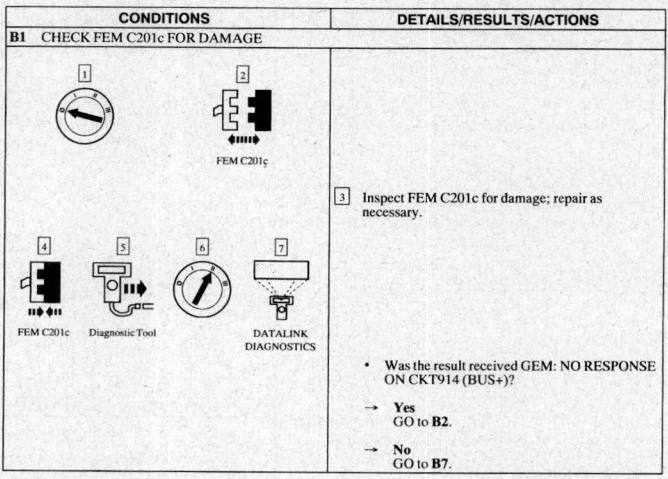

Fig. 4   Test C: Front Electronics Module Does Not Respond To Diagnostic Tool (Part 1 of 6)

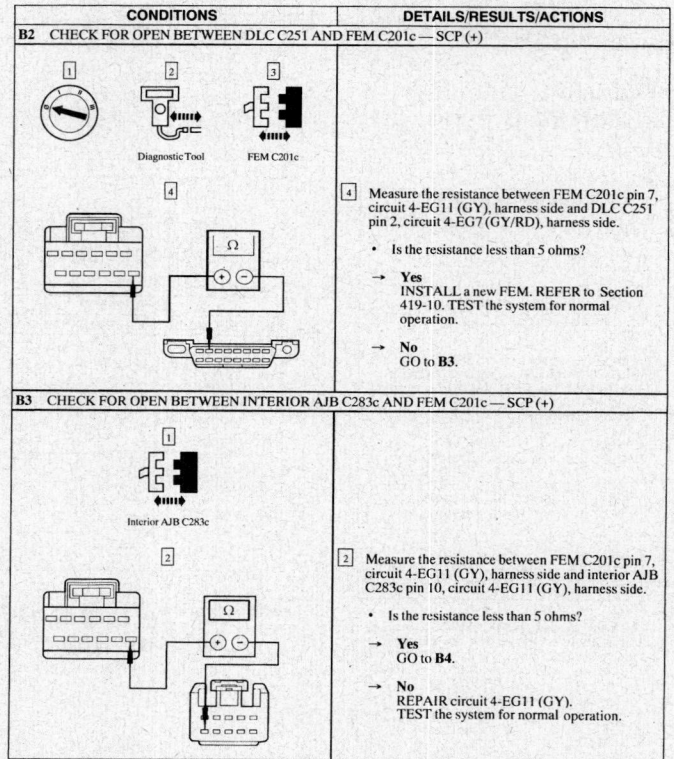

Fig. 4   Test C: Front Electronics Module Does Not Respond To Diagnostic Tool (Part 2 of 6)

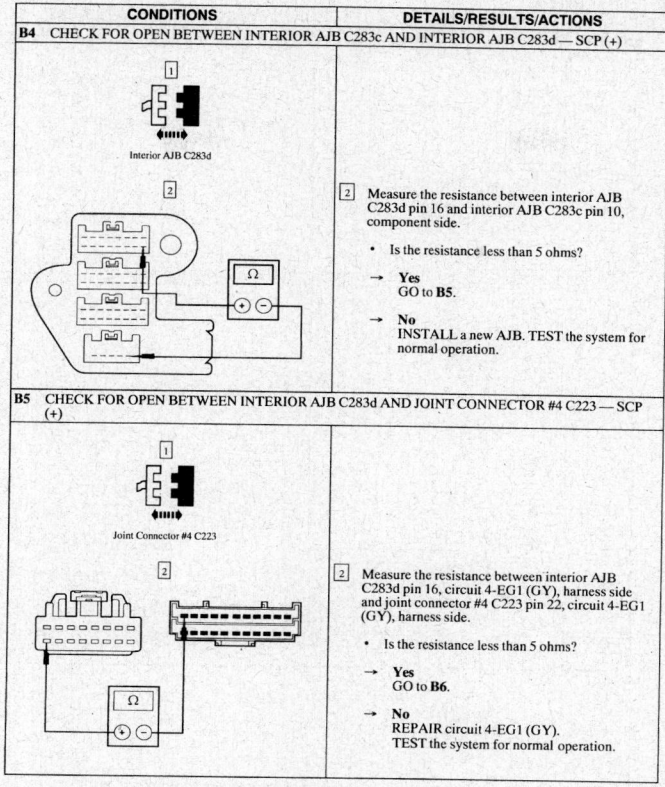

CONDITIONS	DETAILS/RESULTS/ACTIONS
B4 CHECK FOR OPEN BETWEEN INTERIOR AJB C283c AND INTERIOR AJB C283d — SCP (+)	
Interior AJB C283d	☐2 Measure the resistance between interior AJB C283d pin 16 and interior AJB C283c pin 10, component side. • Is the resistance less than 5 ohms? → **Yes** GO to **B5**. → **No** INSTALL a new AJB. TEST the system for normal operation.
B5 CHECK FOR OPEN BETWEEN INTERIOR AJB C283d AND JOINT CONNECTOR #4 C223 — SCP (+)	
Joint Connector #4 C223	☐2 Measure the resistance between interior AJB C283d pin 16, circuit 4-EG1 (GY), harness side and joint connector #4 C223 pin 22, circuit 4-EG1 (GY), harness side. • Is the resistance less than 5 ohms? → **Yes** GO to **B6**. → **No** REPAIR circuit 4-EG1 (GY). TEST the system for normal operation.

FM6020100448030X

Fig. 4   Test C: Front Electronics Module Does Not Respond To Diagnostic Tool (Part 3 of 6)

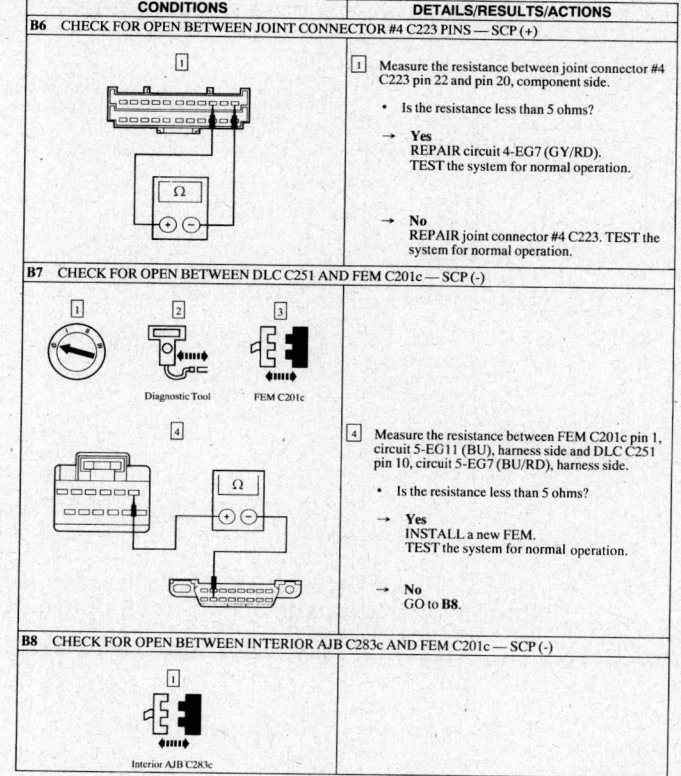

CONDITIONS	DETAILS/RESULTS/ACTIONS
B6 CHECK FOR OPEN BETWEEN JOINT CONNECTOR #4 C223 PINS — SCP (+)	
	☐1 Measure the resistance between joint connector #4 C223 pin 22 and pin 20, component side. • Is the resistance less than 5 ohms? → **Yes** REPAIR circuit 4-EG7 (GY/RD). TEST the system for normal operation. → **No** REPAIR joint connector #4 C223. TEST the system for normal operation.
B7 CHECK FOR OPEN BETWEEN DLC C251 AND FEM C201c — SCP (-)	
Diagnostic Tool FEM C201c	☐4 Measure the resistance between FEM C201c pin 1, circuit 5-EG11 (BU), harness side and DLC C251 pin 10, circuit 5-EG7 (BU/RD), harness side. • Is the resistance less than 5 ohms? → **Yes** INSTALL a new FEM. TEST the system for normal operation. → **No** GO to **B8**.
B8 CHECK FOR OPEN BETWEEN INTERIOR AJB C283c AND FEM C201c — SCP (-)	
Interior AJB C283c	

FM6020100448040X

Fig. 4   Test C: Front Electronics Module Does Not Respond To Diagnostic Tool (Part 4 of 6)

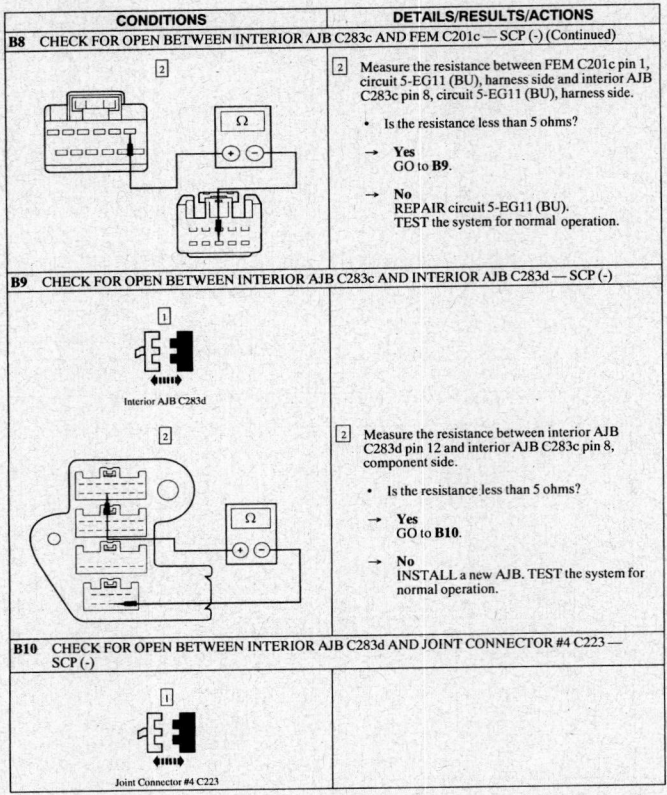

CONDITIONS	DETAILS/RESULTS/ACTIONS
B8 CHECK FOR OPEN BETWEEN INTERIOR AJB C283c AND FEM C201c — SCP (-) (Continued)	
[2]	[2] Measure the resistance between FEM C201c pin 1, circuit 5-EG11 (BU), harness side and interior AJB C283c pin 8, circuit 5-EG11 (BU), harness side. • Is the resistance less than 5 ohms? → **Yes** GO to **B9**. → **No** REPAIR circuit 5-EG11 (BU). TEST the system for normal operation.
B9 CHECK FOR OPEN BETWEEN INTERIOR AJB C283c AND INTERIOR AJB C283d — SCP (-)	
[1] Interior AJB C283d [2]	[2] Measure the resistance between interior AJB C283d pin 12 and interior AJB C283c pin 8, component side. • Is the resistance less than 5 ohms? → **Yes** GO to **B10**. → **No** INSTALL a new AJB. TEST the system for normal operation.
B10 CHECK FOR OPEN BETWEEN INTERIOR AJB C283d AND JOINT CONNECTOR #4 C223 — SCP (-)	
[1] Joint Connector #4 C223	

FM6020100448050X

Fig. 4   Test C: Front Electronics Module Does Not Respond To Diagnostic Tool (Part 5 of 6)

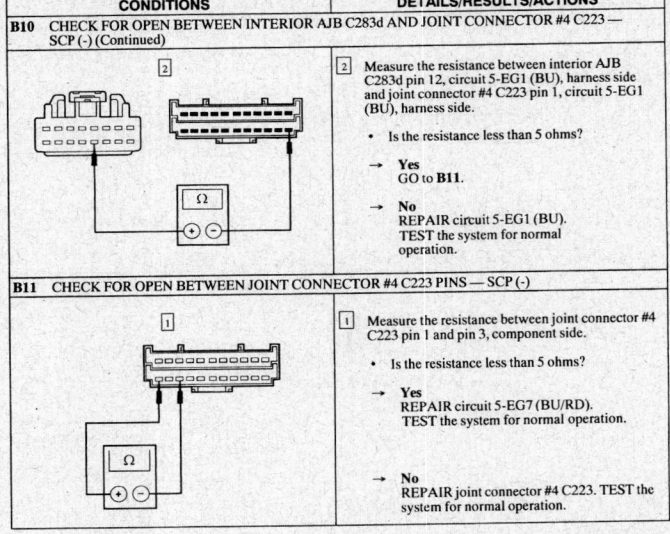

CONDITIONS	DETAILS/RESULTS/ACTIONS
B10 CHECK FOR OPEN BETWEEN INTERIOR AJB C283d AND JOINT CONNECTOR #4 C223 — SCP (-) (Continued)	
[2]	[2] Measure the resistance between interior AJB C283d pin 12, circuit 5-EG1 (BU), harness side and joint connector #4 C223 pin 1, circuit 5-EG1 (BU), harness side. • Is the resistance less than 5 ohms? → **Yes** GO to **B11**. → **No** REPAIR circuit 5-EG1 (BU). TEST the system for normal operation.
B11 CHECK FOR OPEN BETWEEN JOINT CONNECTOR #4 C223 PINS — SCP (-)	
[1]	[1] Measure the resistance between joint connector #4 C223 pin 1 and pin 3, component side. • Is the resistance less than 5 ohms? → **Yes** REPAIR circuit 5-EG7 (BU/RD). TEST the system for normal operation. → **No** REPAIR joint connector #4 C223. TEST the system for normal operation.

FM6020100448060X

Fig. 4   Test C: Front Electronics Module Does Not Respond To Diagnostic Tool (Part 6 of 6)

DISC BRAKES

TABLE OF CONTENTS

Page No.

FRONT DISC BRAKES............ 14-1

Page No.

REAR DISC & PARKING BRAKES........................ 14-9

Front Disc Brakes

NOTE: On Air Bag Equipped Models, Refer To "Air Bag System Precautions" Located In The Front Of This Manual For System Disarming & Arming Procedures.

NOTE: Refer To "Computer Relearn Procedures" Located In The Front Of This Manual When Battery Power To The Computer Has Been Interrupted.

INDEX

Page No.

Brake Disc Service 14-3
Brake Pad Service 14-4
  Crown Victoria, Five Hundred,
    Freestyle, Fusion, Grand
    Marquis, LS, Marauder, Milan,
    MKZ, Montego, Sable, Taurus,
    Taurus X, Thunderbird, Town
    Car & Zephyr 14-4
    Installation 14-4
    Removal....................... 14-4
  Focus 14-4
    Installation 14-4
    Removal....................... 14-4
  Mustang 14-4
    Cobra.......................... 14-4
    Except Cobra 14-4
Brake System Bleed 14-3
  System Priming................. 14-3
  Wheel Bleeding Sequence 14-3
Caliper Service 14-5
  Overhaul 14-5

Page No.

Crown Victoria, Five Hundred,
  Freestyle, Fusion, Grand
  Marquis, LS, Marauder,
  Milan, MKZ, Montego,
  Sable, Taurus, Taurus X,
  Thunderbird, Town Car &
  Zephyr 14-5
  Focus 14-6
  Mustang 14-6
  Replacement 14-5
  Crown Victoria, Five Hundred,
    Freestyle, Fusion, Grand
    Marquis, LS, Marauder,
    Milan, MKZ, Montego,
    Sable, Taurus, Taurus X,
    Thunderbird, Town Car &
    Zephyr 14-5
    Focus 14-5
    Mustang 14-5
Description 14-1
  Dual Piston Calipers 14-1
  Single Piston Calipers 14-1

Page No.

Disc Brake Specifications 14-7
Inspection 14-3
Precautions...................... 14-1
  Air Bag Systems................ 14-1
  Battery Ground Cable........... 14-1
  System Depressurizing 14-1
Rotor, Replace 14-6
  Installation 14-6
  Removal....................... 14-6
Tightening Specifications 14-8
Troubleshooting 14-2
  Brake Booster Operation Test... 14-2
  Brake Master Cylinder 14-2
    Abnormal Conditions......... 14-2
    Bypass Condition Inspection .. 14-2
    Non-Pressure Leaks 14-3
    Normal Conditions 14-2
  Brake Roughness............... 14-2
    Lateral Runout............... 14-2
    Thickness Variation 14-2
    Wheel Bearing Looseness 14-2

PRECAUTIONS

Air Bag Systems

Refer to "Air Bag System Precautions" in the front of this manual for system disarming and arming procedures.

Battery Ground Cable

Prior to service, disconnect battery ground cable and isolate as required.

System Depressurizing

On models equipped with anti-lock brakes, hydraulic system must be depressurized prior to disconnecting any hydraulic lines or fittings, by pumping the brake pedal at least 25 times with ignition in Off position.

DESCRIPTION

Dual Piston Calipers

The caliper consists of a sliding bridge type caliper housing with dual pistons, caliper mounting frame and inner and outer friction pad assemblies, **Figs. 1 and 2.** The caliper is located into and slides on the anchor frame by its thrust face and a locating pin and clip. The friction pads are retained into the anchor frame by the caliper sliding bridge assembly and use an anti-rattle spring clip to reduce brake noise. The fric-

tion pads are retained into the sliding bridge assembly by clips located on the back of the friction pad.

Lefthand and righthand caliper and inner and outer lefthand and righthand friction pads are unique and cannot be interchanged. When servicing this system, mark all components with location marks for later reference and assembly.

Single Piston Calipers

The caliper consists of a pin sliding caliper housing, inner and outer shoe and lining assemblies and a single piston, **Fig. 3** . The caliper slides on two pins which also act as mounting bolts between caliper and the combination anchor plate and spindle. The outer brake shoe and lining assembly

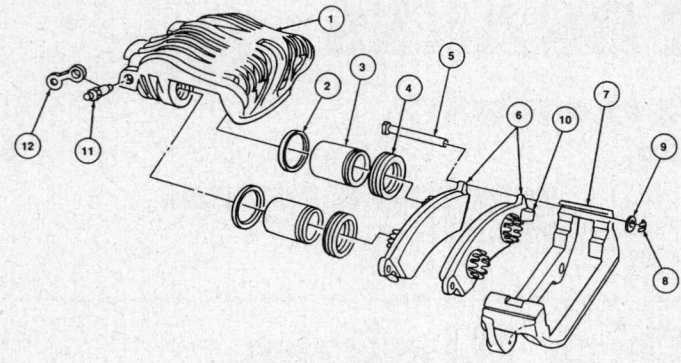

Item	Description
1	Caliper Housing (Part of 2B119)
2	Piston Seal (2 Req'd)
3	Caliper Piston (2 Req'd)
4	Dust Boot (2 Req'd)
5	Front Brake Locating Pin
6	Brake Shoe and Lining

Item	Description
7	Front Disc Brake Caliper Anchor Plate
8	Clip
9	Washer
10	Anti-Rattle Clip and Insulator
11	Wheel Cylinder Bleeder Screw
12	Cover

FM4079500073000X

Fig. 1 Exploded view of dual piston disc brake caliper. Mustang Cobra

is longer than the inner brake shoe and lining assembly. Inner and outer shoe and lining assemblies are attached to the caliper by spring clips riveted to the shoe surfaces. The inner shoe is attached to the caliper by installing the spring clip to the inside of the caliper piston. The outer shoe clips directly to the caliper housing. A wear indicator is incorporated, which emits a noise when the lining is worn to a point for required replacement. Lefthand and righthand inner and outer shoes are not interchangeable.

TROUBLESHOOTING
Brake Roughness
THICKNESS VARIATION

If roughness or vibration is encountered during highway operation or if pedal pumping is experienced at low speeds, the disc may have excessive thickness variation. Measure the disc at 12 points with a micrometer at a radius approximately one inch from edge of disc. If thickness measurements vary by more than .0005 inch, replace the disc.

LATERAL RUNOUT

Excessive lateral runout of braking disc may cause a knocking back of the pistons, possibly creating increased pedal travel and vibration when brakes are applied.

WHEEL BEARING LOOSENESS

Adjust the wheel bearings as outlined in "Front Steering & Suspension" in appropriate chassis chapter before measuring lateral runout. The adjustment is important and will be required at the completion of the test to prevent bearing failure.

Brake Booster Operation Test

1. Inspect hydraulic system for leaks or insufficient fluid.
2. With transmission in park, stop engine.
3. Apply brakes several times to release system vacuum.
4. Depress brake pedal and hold in applied position.
5. Start engine and note whether brake pedal moves downward under constant foot pressure.
6. If no pedal movement is felt, brake booster system is inoperative.
7. Remove vacuum hose from power brake booster valve.
8. Inspect for vacuum at valve end of hose with engine at idle speed and transmission in neutral.
9. Ensure unused vacuum ports are properly capped and vacuum hoses are not cracked or deteriorated.
10. If manifold vacuum is present and no pedal movement is noted during testing, replace power brake booster.
11. Operate engine at least 10 seconds at fast idle. Stop engine and let vehicle stand for 10 minutes.
12. Apply brake pedal with approximately 20 ft. lbs., force.
13. Pedal feel should be same as that noted with engine operating.
14. If bake pedal feels hard (no power assist), replace check valve and repeat test.
15. If brake pedal still feels hard after check valve replacement, replace power brake booster.
16. If pedal movement feels spongy, bleed hydraulic system to remove air.

Brake Master Cylinder
NORMAL CONDITIONS

The following conditions are considered normal and are not indications the brake master cylinder is faulting:
1. Slight turbulence in brake master cylinder reservoir fluid occurring when brake pedal is released. Turbulence occurs as brake fluid returns to master cylinder after releasing brakes.
2. Trace of brake fluid on booster shell below master cylinder mounting flange. This condition results from lubricating action of master cylinder wiping seal.

ABNORMAL CONDITIONS

Prior to performing any diagnosis, ensure brake system warning indicator is functional.

Diagnostic procedures use brake pedal feel, warning indicator illumination and brake fluid level indicators in diagnosing brake system problems. The following conditions are considered abnormal:
1. **Brake pedal goes down fast.** Inspect for external or internal leak.
2. **Brake pedal eases down slowly.** Inspect for internal or external leak.
3. **Brake pedal is low or feels spongy.** Proceed as follows:
   a. Inspect fluid level in brake master cylinder reservoir.
   b. Inspect brake master cylinder reservoir cap vent holes for clogging.
   c. Inspect rear brake adjustment.
   d. Inspect for air in hydraulic system.
4. **Brake pedal effort is excessive.** Inspect for binding or obstructed brake pedal linkage or insufficient power brake booster vacuum.
5. **Rear brakes lock up during light brake pedal application.** Inspect for wrong tire pressure, worn tires, grease or fluid on brake linings, damaged linings, improperly adjusted parking brakes or damaged brake pressure control valve.
6. **Brake pedal effort is erratic.** Inspect for power brake booster fault, extreme caliper piston knock back or improperly installed disc brake shoe or lining.
7. **Brake warning indicator is on.** Inspect for low fluid level, ignition wire routing too close to fluid level indicator or float assembly damage.

BYPASS CONDITION INSPECTION

1. Inspect fluid level in brake master cylinder reservoir.
2. Observe fluid level in brake master cylinder. If, after several brake applications fluid level remains same, measure wheel turning torque required to rotate wheels with brakes applied as follows:
   a. Place transmission in neutral.
   b. Raise vehicle on hoist.
   c. Apply brakes slowly to at least of

100 ft. lbs., and hold for approximately 15 seconds.

d. With brakes still applied, exert 75 ft. lbs., of torque on one front wheel and one rear wheel.

e. If either wheel rotates, inspect internal components of brake master cylinder.

NON-PRESSURE LEAKS

An empty brake master cylinder reservoir condition may be caused by either of the following non-pressure external leaks:

1. Inspect for an external leak that may occur at the brake master cylinder reservoir cap because of improper positioning of gasket and cap.
2. Inspect for a leak at the brake master cylinder reservoir mounting grommets. Install new grommets if required.

BRAKE SYSTEM BLEED

Pressure bleeding is recommended for all hydraulic disc brake systems.

Do not reuse brake fluid drained from the hydraulic system when bleeding the brakes. Ensure disc brake pistons are returned to their normal positions and the shoe and lining assemblies are properly seated.

Do not shake the pressure bleeder tank while air is being added or after it has been pressurized. This will prevent air from the tank getting into the lines. Do not move the tank during the bleeding operation. The tank should be kept at least one third full.

On models equipped with power brakes, exhaust the vacuum in the power unit by pumping the brake pedal several times with the engine Off.

On vehicles equipped with disc brakes and master cylinders without proportioners or pressure control valves located in the master cylinder outlet port, the brake metering valve or combination valve must be held in position using suitable tool.

On vehicles equipped with plastic reservoirs, do not exceed 25 psi bleeding pressure.

When bleeding without pressure, open the bleed valve three quarters of a turn, depress the pedal a full stroke, close the bleeder and allow the pedal to return slowly to its released position. Repeat until no more air is visible in fluid.

Discard drained or bled brake fluid. Do not spill fluid on vehicle surfaces, brake fluid will damage painted finishes.

Flushing is essential if there is water, mineral oil or other contaminants in the lines, and whenever new components are installed in the hydraulic system. Fluid contamination is usually indicated by swollen and deteriorated cups and other rubber components.

If air has entered system because of low fluid levels, or removal of master cylinder brake lines, all four wheels will require bleeding. If a line is disconnected at only one cylinder, then only that cylinder needs to be bled.

Master cylinders equipped with bleeder valves should be bled first before the wheel cylinders are bled. In all cases where a

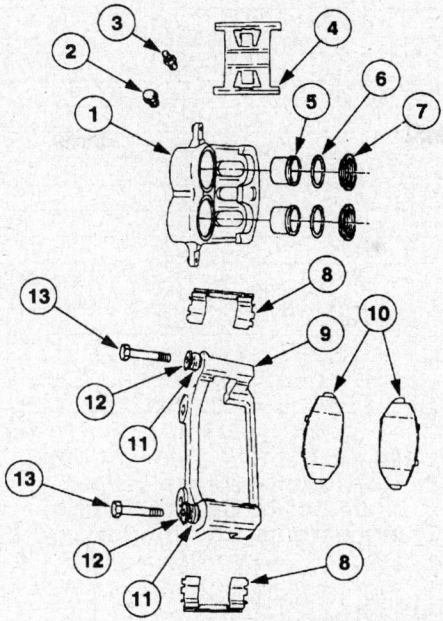

FM4079800099010X

Fig. 2 Exploded view of dual piston disc brake caliper (Part 1 of 2). Crown Victoria, Grand Marquis, LS, Thunderbird & Town Car

master cylinder has been overhauled, it must be bled. Where there is no bleeder valve, leave the lines loose, then actuate the brake pedal to expel the air. Tighten lines and repeat until no air is visible in expelled fluid.

System Priming

When a new master cylinder is installed or if the brake system has been partially or completely emptied, fluid may not flow from the bleeder screws during normal bleeding. It may be required to prime the system using the following procedure:

1. Remove brake lines from master cylinder.
2. Install short brake lines in master cylinder and position them back into the reservoir. Ensure short brake line ends are submerged in reservoir brake fluid.
3. Fill reservoir with recommended brake fluid, then cover master cylinder fluid reservoir with shop towel.
4. Pump brakes until clear, bubble-free fluid comes out of both brake lines. If any brake fluid spills on paint, wash it off immediately with water.
5. Remove short brake lines, then install original brake lines.
6. Bleed each brake line at master cylinder using the following procedure:
   a. Have assistant pump brake pedal 10 times, then hold firm pressure on pedal.
   b. Open rearmost brake line fittings until stream of brake fluid comes out. Have assistant maintain pressure on brake pedal until brake line fitting is tightened.
   c. Repeat this operation until clear,

bubble-free fluid comes out from around tube fitting.
   d. Repeat bleeding operation at front brake line fitting.
7. If any of brake lines or calipers have been removed, it may be required to prime system by gravity bleeding. Gravity bleed system after master cylinder is primed and bled. To prime system using gravity method, proceed as follows:
   a. Fill master cylinder with manufacturer recommended brake fluid or equivalent.
   b. Loosen both rear bleeder screws and leave open until clear brake fluid flows out. **Inspect reservoir fluid level frequently. Do not allow fluid level to drop below halfway.**
   c. Tighten rear bleeder screws.
   d. Loosen bleeder screw on front caliper and leave open until clear fluid flows out. **Bleed front calipers one side at a time.**
8. After master cylinder has been primed, lines bled at master cylinder and brake system primed, resume normal brake system bleeding at each wheel.

Wheel Bleeding Sequence

Rear Wheel Drive	RR-LR-RF-LF
Front Wheel Drive	RR-LF-LR-RF

INSPECTION

Remove wheels and inspect brake disc, caliper and linings. Inspect wheel bearings and repack if required.

If the caliper is cracked or fluid leakage through the casting is evident, it must be replaced as a unit.

If caliper is removed when installing new components, clean all components in alcohol, then wipe dry using lint-free cloths. Blow out drilled passages and bores with compressed air. Inspect dust boots for punctures or tears, replace as required.

Inspect piston bores in both housings for scoring or pitting. Bores showing light scratches or corrosion can be cleaned with crocus cloth. Bores with deep scratches or scoring may be honed, provided the diameter of the bore is not increased more than .002 inch. If the bore does not clean up within this specification, replace the caliper. **Black stains on the bore walls are caused by piston seals and do not adversely affect caliper performance.**

When using a hone, install the hone baffle before honing the bore. The baffle is used to protect the hone stones from damage. Use extreme care in cleaning the caliper after honing. Remove all dust and grit by flushing the caliper with alcohol. Wipe the caliper dry with a clean lint-free cloth, then repeat cleaning procedure.

BRAKE DISC SERVICE

Disc brake service is critical because of the close tolerances required in machining the brake disc to ensure proper brake operation.

DISC BRAKES

Maintaining close control of the shape of the rubbing surfaces is required to prevent brake roughness. In addition, the surface finish must be non-directional and maintained at a micro-inch finish. This is required to avoid pulls and erratic performance, and to promote long lining life and equal lining wear of both the lefthand and righthand brakes.

Do not attempt to refinish the rubbing surfaces unless precision equipment, capable of measuring in micro inches (millionths of an inch), is available.

To inspect the disc lateral runout, mount a dial indicator, so the indicator's plunger contacts the disc one inch from the outer edge, **Fig. 4.** If the total indicated runout exceeds specifications, install a new disc.

To inspect parallelism (thickness variation), mount dial indicators so the plunger contacts the rotor approximately one inch from the outer edge, **Fig. 5.** If parallelism exceeds specifications, replace the rotor.

BRAKE PAD SERVICE

On models with anti-lock brakes, the brake hydraulic system must be depressurized before disconnecting any hydraulic lines or fittings. Depressurize the system by pumping the brake pedal at least 25 times with the ignition in the Off position.

Crown Victoria, Five Hundred, Freestyle, Fusion, Grand Marquis, LS, Marauder, Milan, MKZ, Montego, Sable, Taurus, Taurus X, Thunderbird, Town Car & Zephyr

REMOVAL

1. Remove brake fluid until reservoir is half full.
2. **On models equipped with air suspension,** turn air suspension service switch to Off position.
3. **On all models,** raise and support front of vehicle, then remove tire and wheel assembly.
4. Remove two caliper anchor bracket mounting bolts and discard.
5. Lift front disc brake caliper anchor plate away from rotor using rotating motion.
6. Remove outer brake shoe from disc brake caliper by sliding brake shoe away from outer leg to disconnect it from anchor plate.
7. Remove inner brake shoe and lining assembly by sliding brake shoe away from piston disconnecting it from caliper anchor plate.
8. Suspend caliper from inner fender housing with suitable wire.

Item	Part Number	Description
1	2B120	Disc brake caliper
2	2L126	Bleeder screw cap
3	2208	Bleeder screw
4	2B164	Anti-rattle spring
5	2196	Caliper piston
6	2B115	Piston seal
7	2207	Piston dust boot
8	2L200	Shoe slipper
9	2B292	Front disc brake caliper anchor plate
10	2001	Brake pads
11	2A492	Guide pin boot
12	2B296	Guide pin
13	2N386	Caliper bolt

FM4079800099020X

Fig. 2 Exploded view of dual piston disc brake caliper (Part 2 of 2). Crown Victoria, Grand Marquis, LS, Thunderbird & Town Car

INSTALLATION

Some models have pistons made of phenolic material. **Do not seat these pistons in bore by applying C-clamp directly to piston.** Use extra care during to prevent damage to the piston. Metal or sharp objects should not come into direct contact with the piston.

1. Seat caliper piston in bore using suitable C-clamp and block of 2¾ x 1 inch and approximately ¾ inch thick wood. Remove C-clamp and wooden block.
2. Install caliper anchor plate with caliper guide pin bolts. Tighten lower bolt first, then the upper bolt.
3. Ensure anti-rattle spring and clip are seated in caliper lining inspection opening. Anti-rattle clips must be installed from lining side.
4. Engage brake shoe and lining in anchor plate by first engaging the side opposite anti-rattle clip.
5. Press other end of brake shoe and lining to compress disc brake pad anti-rattle clip, then engage brake shoe lining in front anchor plate.
6. Inspect caliper and anchor plate to ensure brake shoes and linings are properly installed.
7. Position caliper and anchor plate over rotor. Install two new caliper anchor bracket bolts.
8. Inspect caliper locating pin and pin boots. If caliper locating pin is binding, remove and clean.
9. Install tire and wheel assembly, then lower vehicle.
10. **On models equipped with air suspension,** turn air suspension service switch to On position.
11. **On all models,** fill master cylinder, then pump brake pedal several times to position brake linings before moving vehicle.

Focus

REMOVAL

1. Raise and support vehicle, then remove tire and wheel assembly.
2. Disconnect brake hose from front strut support bracket.
3. Remove outer brake pad retaining clip.
4. Remove covers and bolts, then pull caliper outwards to release piston.
5. Support brake caliper from wire hook. **Do not allow caliper to hang from brake hose.**
6. Lift outer pad retaining clip over spring retaining lugs, then remove outer and inner brake pads.

INSTALLATION

1. Fully retract caliper piston into caliper.
2. Install inner, then outer brake pads.
3. Push outer retaining clip over spring retaining lugs.
4. Install caliper, bolts and covers.
5. Install brake hose onto support bracket.
6. Install outer pad retaining clip.
7. Install tire and wheel assemblies, then inspect brake fluid level.

Mustang

EXCEPT COBRA

Refer to "Crown Victoria, Five Hundred, Freestyle, Fusion, Grand Marquis, LS, Marauder, Milan, MKZ, Montego, Sable, Taurus, Taurus X, Thunderbird, Town Car & Zephyr" for brake pad service procedure.

COBRA

Brake components are not interchangeable. Ensure each component is installed in it's original location.

REMOVAL

1. Remove approximately ½ of brake fluid from master cylinder reservoir.
2. Raise and support vehicle, then remove tire and wheel assemblies. **Do not damage disc brake shields or bleeder screws.**
3. Remove clip and washer, then the caliper locating pin.
4. Lift caliper with pads from anchor frame.
5. Secure assembly aside with suitable wire or tie wrap.
6. Mark inner and outer friction pads for installation alignment. Remove pads.

INSPECTION

Inspect caliper piston and caliper pin boots for damage.

Inspect rotor for wear and runout. Minor glazing of surfaces can be removed by hand sanding with medium grit sandpaper.

INSTALLATION

1. Clean sliding and contact surfaces of brake components.
2. Remove protective paper from adhesive insulator material on friction pads. **Do not to contaminate adhesive surface.**

3. Install pads into caliper. Ensure correct pad is fully seated into proper caliper position.
4. Compress pistons into caliper using suitable C-clamp. Ensure sufficient clearance exists to allow pads to fit over rotor.
5. Place caliper into position on anchor frame, then install locating pin, washer and clip.
6. Install tire and wheel assemblies. **Do not damage brake shields or bleeder screws.**
7. Lower vehicle. Pump brake pedal until firm pedal is achieved.

CALIPER SERVICE

Replacement

On models with anti-lock brakes, the brake booster system must be depressurized before disconnecting any hydraulic lines or fittings. Depressurize the system by pumping the brake pedal at least 25 times with the ignition in the Off position.

CROWN VICTORIA, FIVE HUNDRED, FREESTYLE, FUSION, GRAND MARQUIS, LS, MARAUDER, MILAN, MKZ, MONTEGO, SABLE, TAURUS, TAURUS X, THUNDERBIRD, TOWN CAR & ZEPHYR

Before removing calipers, mark lefthand and righthand calipers so they can be installed in their original position.
1. **On models equipped with air suspension,** turn air suspension service switch to Off position.
2. **On all models,** raise and support front of vehicle, then remove tire and wheel assembly.
3. Loosen brake tube fitting connecting brake tube to fitting on frame. Plug brake tube.
4. Remove retaining clip from brake hose and bracket, then disconnect brake hose from caliper.
5. Remove caliper locating pins.
6. Lift caliper from rotor and spindle anchor plate assembly.
7. **On models equipped with phenolic caliper piston,** do not pry directly against piston.
8. **On all models,** reverse procedure to install, noting the following:
   a. Install caliper over rotor with outer shoe against rotor braking surface to prevent pinching piston boot between inner brake shoe and piston. **Ensure calipers are installed in proper position.**
   b. Bleed brake system as outlined in "Brake System Bleed."
   c. Pump brake pedal several times to position brake shoes before moving vehicle.
   d. Turn air suspension switch to ON position.

FOCUS
1. Raise and support vehicle, then remove front tire and wheel assemblies.
2. Disconnect brake hose from support bracket on front strut.
3. Loosen brake hose fitting on caliper.
4. Remove front brake pads as outlined in "Brake Pad Service."
5. Disconnect front caliper from brake hose. Cap brake hose.
6. Reverse procedure to install. Bleed brakes as outlined in "Brake System Bleed."

MUSTANG

EXCEPT COBRA
Refer to "Crown Victoria, Five Hundred, Freestyle, Fusion, Grand Marquis, LS, Marauder, Milan, MKZ, Montego, Sable, Taurus, Taurus X, Thunderbird, Town Car & Zephyr" for caliper replacement procedure.

COBRA
Brake components are unique and are not interchangeable. Ensure each component is installed in its original location.
1. Remove brake pads as outlined in "Brake Pad Service."
2. Remove brake flex hose from caliper and discard copper sealing washers.
3. Remove two mounting bolts and lift caliper/anchor frame assembly off rotor.
4. Reverse procedure to install, noting the following:
   a. Use new copper sealing washers.
   b. Bleed brakes as outlined in "Brake System Bleed."

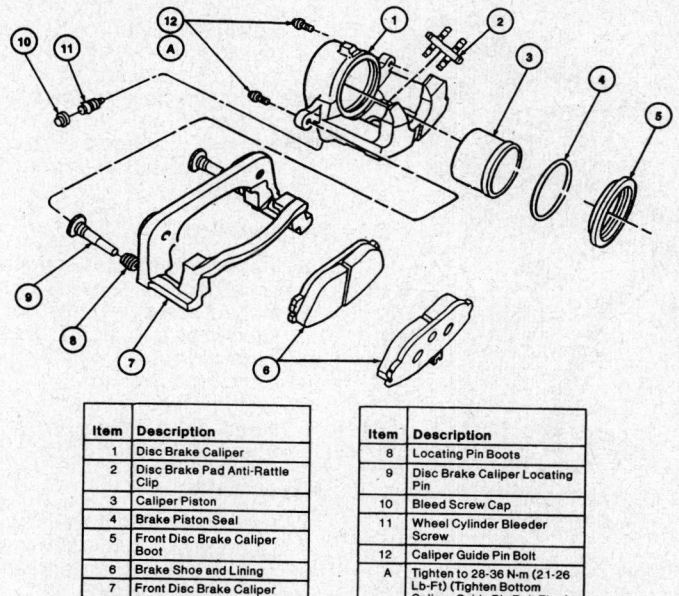

Item	Description		Item	Description
1	Disc Brake Caliper		8	Locating Pin Boots
2	Disc Brake Pad Anti-Rattle Clip		9	Disc Brake Caliper Locating Pin
3	Caliper Piston		10	Bleed Screw Cap
4	Brake Piston Seal		11	Wheel Cylinder Bleeder Screw
5	Front Disc Brake Caliper Boot		12	Caliper Guide Pin Bolt
6	Brake Shoe and Lining		A	Tighten to 28-36 N·m (21-26 Lb-Ft) (Tighten Bottom Caliper Guide Pin Bolt First)
7	Front Disc Brake Caliper Anchor Plate			

FM4079500072000X

Fig. 3   Exploded view of single piston disc brake caliper. Five Hundred, Freestyle, Fusion, Montego, Milan, MKZ, Mustang (except Cobra), Sable, Taurus, Taurus X & Zephyr

Overhaul

CROWN VICTORIA, FIVE HUNDRED, FREESTYLE, FUSION, GRAND MARQUIS, LS, MARAUDER, MILAN, MKZ, MONTEGO, SABLE, TAURUS, TAURUS X, THUNDERBIRD, TOWN CAR & ZEPHYR

DISASSEMBLE
1. Position fiber block and shop towels between caliper piston and caliper housing, then apply compressed air to caliper brake line fitting bore to force piston from caliper.
2. Remove dust boot, **Fig. 3.**
3. Remove piston seal from cylinder and discard.

INSPECTION
1. Inspect piston for scratches, scoring or damage.
2. Inspect caliper bore for scratches, scoring or corrosion. Light scratches or slight corrosion can be polished out using crocus cloth.
3. Ensure bleeder screw and bleeder screw bore hole in caliper are fully open.
4. Inspect caliper bushings for corrosion and dust boot retaining ring for damage or tension loss. Replace components as required.

ASSEMBLE
1. Lubricate piston seal with suitable, clean brake fluid, then install seal in caliper bore. **Ensure seal is firmly**

Fig. 4 Rotor lateral runout inspection

seated in groove.
2. Install new dust boot in outer groove of caliper bore.
3. Coat clean brake fluid and install piston in caliper bore.
4. Spread dust boot over piston as it is installed, then seat dust boot in piston groove.

FOCUS

DISASSEMBLE

1. Place block of wood or some shop towels between brake caliper piston and housing.
2. Remove caliper piston using compressed air applied to caliper.
3. Remove and discard caliper dust seal and piston seal.
4. Inspect caliper piston and piston bore for pitting or scoring.
5. Replace damaged or scored components.

ASSEMBLE

1. Lubricate piston bore, piston seal and caliper piston with DOT 3 brake fluid.
2. Install new caliper seal into machined groove in piston bore.
3. Install new dust seal onto caliper piston.
4. Install caliper piston into caliper bore.
5. Seat dust seal and install caliper.

MUSTANG

EXCEPT COBRA

Refer to "Crown Victoria, Five Hundred, Freestyle, Fusion, Grand Marquis, LS, Marauder, Milan, MKZ, Montego, Sable, Taurus, Taurus X, Thunderbird, Town Car & Zephyr" for caliper overhaul procedure.

COBRA

Disassemble

1. Drain remaining brake fluid from caliper into suitable container.

---

2. Position fiber block and shop towels between caliper pistons and caliper housing.
3. Apply compressed air to caliper brake line fitting bore to force pistons from caliper.
4. Remove dust boots from caliper.
5. Remove piston seals from cylinder and discard.

Inspection

1. Inspect pistons for scratches, scoring or damage.
2. Inspect caliper bores for scratches, scoring or corrosion. Light scratches or slight corrosion can be polished out using crocus cloth.
3. Ensure bleeder screw and bleeder screw bore hole in caliper are fully open.

Assemble

1. Lubricate piston seals with suitable, clean brake fluid, then install seals in caliper bore. **Ensure seals are firmly seated in groove.**
2. Install new dust boots in outer groove of caliper bore.
3. Coat pistons with clean brake fluid and install pistons in caliper bore.
4. Install dust boots over piston as they are installed, then seat dust boots in piston groove.

ROTOR

REPLACE

This procedure has been revised by a Technical Service Bulletin.

On 2004–05 Sable and 2004–07 Taurus models, the disc rotor is a hat section-type of composite steel and cast iron. A Rotunda Rotor Mounting Adapter tool No. 054-00032, or equivalent, is required for use on the brake lathe for refinishing. **Failure to use the adapter will result in gouging the brake disc, making it unfit for use.**

On 2004–05 Sable and 2004–07 Taurus models, if service is required, install the new full cast front disc rotors, part No. F10Y-1125-B, in pairs only. **Never install a full cast rotor on one side of the vehicle with a composite rotor on the other side.**

On all models if caliper does not require servicing, do not disconnect brake hose or remove caliper. Position caliper aside with wire or tie straps.

If excessive force must be used to remove the rotor, then it should be inspected for lateral runout before installation.

Removal

1. **On models equipped with air suspension,** turn service switch to Off position.
2. **On all models,** raise and support vehicle, then remove tire and wheel assembly. **Do not damage or**

Fig. 5 Rotor parallelism (thickness variation) inspection

interference with caliper bleeder screw fitting and brake rotor shield.
3. Remove caliper anchor bracket bolts.
4. Position caliper aside with suitable wire or tie straps. **Prevent deformation of rotor and nicking, scratching or contaminating brake lining and rotor surfaces.**
5. Remove front rotor from hub assembly by pulling it off hub studs, noting the following:
   a. If excessive force is required to remove rotor, inspect rotor for lateral runout prior to installation.
   b. If additional force is required to remove front disc brake rotor, apply suitable rust penetrant and inhibitor on front and rear rotor/hub mating surfaces.
   c. Strike rotor between studs with suitable plastic hammer.
   d. If rotor still will not come off, install three-jaw puller tool No. D80L-1013-A, or equivalent, and remove rotor.

Installation

1. If front disc brake rotor is being replaced, remove protective coating from new rotor with suitable carburetor cleaner.
2. If original rotor is being installed, ensure rotor braking and mounting surfaces are clean.
3. Apply suitable lubricant to pilot diameter of front disc brake rotor, then install rotor on wheel hub assembly.
4. Install caliper and caliper anchor bracket bolts on rotor.
5. Install tire and wheel assembly. **Tighten wheel hub bolt nuts with torque wrench in star pattern.**
6. Lower vehicle, then pump brake pedal to position brake linings prior to moving vehicle.
7. Turn air suspension service switch to On position.
8. Road test vehicle.

DISC BRAKE SPECIFICATIONS

Model	Year	Front Disc Brake - Brake Lining Wear Limit, Inch [1]	Rotor Thickness, Inch - Normal	Rotor - Min. Refinish	Rotor - Discard Limit [3]	Thickness Variation Parallelism, Inch	Lateral Run Out (T.I.R.), Inch	Rear Disc Brake - Brake Lining Wear Limit, Inch [2]	Rotor Thickness, Inch - Nominal	Rotor - Min. Refinish	Rotor - Discard Limit [3]	Thickness Variation Parallelism, Inch	Lateral Run Out (T.I.R.), Inch
Crown Victoria	2004	.039	1.063	—	1.010	.00035	.002	.039	.550	—	.510	.0004	.002
	2004–08	.039	1.063	—	1.037	—	—	.039	—	—	.790	—	.003
Five Hundred	2005–07	.039	1.024	—	.974	.00040	.002	.039	.550	—	.502	.0004	.004
Focus	2004–07	.059	[4]	—	.870	.00080	.002	.059	.390	—	.350	.0008	—
Freestyle	2005–07	.039	1.024	—	.974	.00040	.002	.039	.550	—	.502	.0004	.004
Fusion	2006–08	.039	.980	—	.910	—	.002	.118	.390	—	.310	—	—
Grand Marquis	2004–08	.039	1.063	—	1.037	—	—	.039	—	—	.790	—	.003
LS	2004–06	.080	1.181	—	1.120	.00040	.004	.040	.787	—	.740	.0004	.004
Marauder	2004	.039	1.063	—	1.037	—	—	.039	—	—	.790	—	.003
Milan	2006–08	.039	.980	—	.910	—	.002	.118	.390	—	.310	—	—
MKZ	2007–08	.039	.980	—	.910	—	.002	.118	.390	—	.310	—	—
Montego	2005–07	.039	1.024	—	.974	.00040	.002	.039	.550	—	.502	.0004	.004
Mustang	2004–08	.080	[5]	—	[6]	.00035	.002	.039	.550	—	0.50	.0004	.004
Sable	2004–05	.039	1.024	—	.974	.00040	.002	.039	.550	—	.502	.0004	.004
	2008	.039	1.024	—	.974	.00040	.002	.039	.550	—	.502	.0004	.004
Taurus	2004–07	.039	1.024	—	.974	.00040	.002	.039	.550	—	.502	.0004	.004
	2008	.039	1.024	—	.974	.00040	.002	.039	.550	—	.502	.0004	.004
Taurus X	2008	.039	1.024	—	.974	.00040	.002	.039	.550	—	.502	.0004	.004
Thunderbird	2004–05	.079	—	—	1.120	.00040	.004	.039	—	—	.740	.0004	.004
Town Car	2004–08	.039	1.063	—	1.037	—	—	.039	—	—	.790	—	.003
Zephyr	2006	.039	.980	—	.910	—	.002	.118	.390	—	.310	—	—

[1] — With 16 inch wheels.

[2] — Above rivet head or backing plate. Original equipment type brake lining.

[3] — Discard thickness is stamped on rotor.

[4] — Models w/2.0L DOHC engine .95 inch; w/2.0L SOHC engine, .870 inch.

[5] — Except Cobra, 1.02 inch; Cobra, 1.10 inch.

[6] — Except Cobra .97 inch; Cobra, 1.04 inch.

TIGHTENING SPECIFICATIONS

Year/ Model	Component	Torque Ft. Lbs.
CROWN VICTORIA, GRAND MARQUIS, MARAUDER & TOWN CAR		
2004–08	Brake Hose	41
	Caliper	32
	Caliper Bleeder Screw	15
	Wheel Lug Nut	95
FIVE HUNDRED, FREESTYLE, MONTEGO, 2008 SABLE, TAURUS & TAURUS X		
2005–08	Brake Hose	108①
	Caliper Bolts	44
	Wheel Lug Nuts	85–104
FOCUS		
2004–07	Brake Hose To Caliper Union	11
	Caliper To Knuckle	21
	Wheel Lug Nut	94
FUSION, MILAN, MKZ & ZEPHYR		
2006–08	Bleeder Screw	71①
	Brake Line Banjo Bolt	18
	Caliper Anchor Plate	66
	Caliper Bolts	20
	Rotor To Hub	15
LS		
2004–06	Brake Hose	16–44
	Wheel Lug Nut	100
MUSTANG		
2004–08	Brake Hose	30
	Caliper	23
	Caliper Bleeder Screw	7
	Wheel Lug Nuts	95
SABLE & TAURUS		
2004–07	Brake Hoses	16–44
	Locating Pin	18–25
	Wheel Lug Nuts	85–104

① — Inch lbs.

Rear Disc & Parking Brakes

NOTE: On Air Bag Equipped Models, Refer To "Air Bag System Precautions" Located In The Front Of This Manual For System Disarming & Arming Procedures.

NOTE: Refer To "Computer Relearn Procedures" Located In The Front Of This Manual When Battery Power To The Computer Has Been Interrupted.

INDEX

	Page No.
Adjustments	14-14
Parking Brake	14-14
Crown Victoria, Grand Marquis, Marauder & Town Car	14-14
Five Hundred, Freestyle, Montego, Sable, Taurus & Taurus X	14-14
Fusion, Milan, MKZ & Zephyr	14-14
Mustang	14-14
Brake Disc Service	14-11
Brake Pad Service	14-11
Crown Victoria, Grand Marquis, Marauder & Town Car	14-11
Installation	14-11
Removal	14-11
Five Hundred, Freestyle, Fusion Milan, MKZ, Montego, Mustang, Sable, Taurus, Taurus X & Zephyr	14-11
Installation	14-11
Removal	14-11
LS & Thunderbird	14-11
Brake System Bleed	14-10
System Priming	14-10
Wheel Bleeding Sequence	14-10
Caliper Service	14-12

	Page No.
Overhaul	14-12
Crown Victoria, Grand Marquis, Marauder & Town Car	14-12
Five Hundred, Freestyle, Fusion, Milan, MKZ, Montego, Mustang, Sable, Taurus, Taurus X & Zephyr	14-12
LS & Thunderbird	14-13
Replacement	14-12
Crown Victoria, Grand Marquis, Marauder & Town Car	14-12
Five Hundred, Freestyle, Fusion, Milan, MKZ, Montego, Mustang, Sable, Taurus, Taurus X & Zephyr	14-12
LS & Thunderbird	14-12
Description	14-9
Crown Victoria, Grand Marquis, Marauder & Town Car	14-9
Five Hundred, Freestyle, Fusion, LS, Milan, MKZ, Montego, Mustang, Sable, Taurus, Taurus X & Zephyr	14-9
Disc Brake Specifications	14-14
Caliper Specifications	14-15

	Page No.
Rotor Specifications	14-14
Inspection	14-10
Parking Brake Service	14-13
Parking Brake Linings, Replace	14-13
Crown Victoria, Grand Marquis, Marauder & Town Car	14-13
Precautions	14-9
Air Bag Systems	14-9
Battery Ground Cable	14-9
System Depressurizing	14-9
Rotor, Replace	14-13
Crown Victoria, Grand Marquis, Marauder & Town Car	14-13
Installation	14-13
Removal	14-13
Five Hundred, Freestyle, Fusion, Milan, MKZ, Montego, Mustang, Sable, Taurus, Taurus X & Zephyr	14-13
Installation	14-13
Removal	14-13
LS & Thunderbird	14-13
Tightening Specifications	14-16
Troubleshooting	14-10

PRECAUTIONS

Air Bag Systems

Refer to "Air Bag System Precautions" in the front of this manual for system disarming and arming procedures.

Battery Ground Cable

Prior to service, disconnect battery ground cable and isolate as required.

System Depressurizing

On models equipped with anti-lock brakes, hydraulic system must be depressurized prior to disconnecting any hydraulic lines or fittings, by pumping the brake pedal at least 25 times with ignition in Off position.

DESCRIPTION

Five Hundred, Freestyle, Fusion, LS, Milan, MKZ, Montego, Mustang, Sable, Taurus, Taurus X & Zephyr

Sliding caliper rear disc brakes are used on these models. The caliper is basically the same as the larger front wheel caliper. However, a parking brake mechanism and a larger inner brake shoe anti-rattle spring have been added.

The parking brake lever, located at the rear of the caliper, is actuated by a cable system similar to rear drum brake applications. When the parking brake is applied, the cable rotates the lever and operating shaft, driving the caliper piston and brake shoe assembly against the rotor. An automatic adjuster in the assembly compensates for lining wear and maintains proper clearance in the parking brake mechanism.

The cast iron rotors are ventilated by curved fins located between the braking surfaces and are designed to cause the rotor to act as an air pump when the vehicle is traveling forward. The rotors are not interchangeable and are identified by a Right or Left marking cast inside the hat section of the rotor. The rotor is secured to the axle flange in the same manner as a rear brake drum. A splash shield is bolted to a forged axle adapter to protect the inboard rotor surface.

Crown Victoria, Grand Marquis, Marauder & Town Car

The rear disc brake system uses a pin slider-type caliper, and a cast iron rotor bolted to the rear axle shaft flange. The caliper has a phenolic piston with a seal and a press-in type dust boot.

The inner pads are interchangeable left to right and use a three-finger clip fit inside the caliper piston. The outer pads are interchangeable left to right and use a dual-purpose clip which holds the brake pads on the caliper housing and also prevents caliper rattle.

The flanges on both inner and outer pads slide on a machined surfaces of the brake adapter.

TROUBLESHOOTING

If roughness or vibration is encountered during highway operation or if pedal pumping is experienced at low speeds, the disc may have excessive thickness variation. Measure the disc at 12 points with a micrometer at a radius approximately one inch from the edge of the disc. If thickness measurements vary by more than .0005 inch, replace the rotor.

Excessive lateral runout of braking disc may cause a knocking back of the pistons, possibly creating increased pedal travel and vibration when brakes are applied.

Adjust the wheel bearings before inspecting the runout. The readjustment is very important and will be required at the completion of the test to prevent bearing failure. Adjust the wheel bearings as outlined in "Front Suspension & Steering" in appropriate chassis chapter.

BRAKE SYSTEM BLEED

Pressure bleeding is recommended for all hydraulic disc brake systems.

Do not use brake fluid drained from the hydraulic system when bleeding the brakes. Ensure disc brake pistons are returned to their normal positions and the shoe and lining assemblies are properly seated. Before driving the vehicle, inspect the brake operation.

Do not shake the pressure bleeder tank while air is being added or after it has been pressurized. This will prevent air from the tank getting into the lines. Set the tank in the required location, then bring the air hose to the tank. Do not move the tank during the bleeding operation. The tank should be kept at least one third full.

On models equipped with power brakes, exhaust the vacuum in the power unit by pumping the brake pedal several times with the engine Off before starting to bleed the system.

On vehicles equipped with disc brakes and master cylinders without proportioners or pressure control valves located in the master cylinder outlet port, the brake metering valve or combination valve must be held in position using suitable tool.

On vehicles equipped with plastic reservoirs, do not exceed 25 psi bleeding pressure.

When bleeding without pressure, open the bleed valve three quarters of a turn, depress the brake pedal a full stroke, then close the bleeder valve and allow the pedal to return slowly to its released position. Repeat as required until fluid is free of air bubbles.

Discard drained or bled brake fluid. Brake fluid will damage painted finishes. Do not spill fluid on vehicle surfaces.

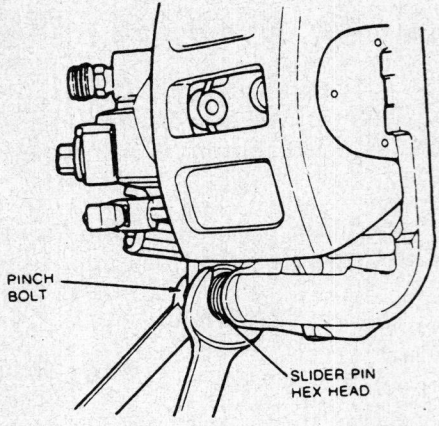

PINCH BOLT

SLIDER PIN HEX HEAD

FM4079100033000X

Fig. 1 Slider pin removal. Five Hundred, Freestyle, Fusion Milan, MKZ, Montego, Mustang, Sable, Taurus, Taurus X & Zephyr

Flushing is essential if there is water, mineral oil or other contaminants in the lines, and whenever new components are installed in the hydraulic system. Fluid contamination is usually indicated by swollen and deteriorated cups and other rubber components.

Bleeding is required on all four wheels if air has entered the system because of low fluid level or the line or lines have been disconnected. If a line is disconnected at any one wheel cylinder, only that cylinder needs to be bled.

Master cylinders equipped with bleeder valves should be bled first before the wheel cylinders are bled. In all cases where a master cylinder has been overhauled, it must be bled. Where there is no bleeder valve, this can be done by leaving the lines loose, actuating the brake pedal to expel the air then tightening the lines.

After overhauling a dual master cylinder used in conjunction with disc brakes, air may be trapped between the master cylinder pistons. Bleed the cylinder before installing it on the vehicle.

System Priming

When a new master cylinder is installed or the brake system is partially or completely emptied, fluid may not flow from the bleeder screws during normal bleeding. If required, prime the system using the following procedure:

1. Remove brake lines from master cylinder.
2. Install short brake lines in master cylinder and position them back into the reservoir. Ensure short brake line ends are submerged in reservoir brake fluid.
3. Fill reservoir with recommended brake fluid, then cover master cylinder fluid reservoir with shop towel.
4. Pump brakes until clear, bubble-free fluid comes out of both brake lines. **If any brake fluid spills on paint, wash it off immediately with water.**
5. Remove short brake lines, then reinstall original brake lines.

6. Bleed each brake line at master cylinder as follows:
   a. Have assistant pump brake pedal 10 times, then hold firm pressure on pedal.
   b. Open rearmost brake line fittings with tubing wrench until stream of brake fluid comes out. Have assistant maintain pressure on brake pedal until brake line fitting is tightened.
   c. Repeat until clear, bubble-free fluid comes out from around tube fitting.
   d. Repeat bleeding operation at front brake line fitting.
7. If any of brake lines or calipers have been removed, it may be helpful to prime system by gravity bleeding. This should be done after master cylinder is primed and bled. To prime system using gravity method, use following procedure:
   a. Fill master cylinder with manufacturer's recommended brake fluid, or equivalent.
   b. Loosen both rear bleeder screws and leave open until clear brake fluid flows out. **Inspect reservoir fluid level frequently. Do not allow fluid level to drop below halfway.**
   c. Tighten rear bleeder screws.
   d. Loosen bleeder screw on front caliper and leave open until clear fluid flows out. **Bleed front calipers one side at a time.**
8. After master cylinder has been primed, lines bled at master cylinder and brake system primed, resume normal brake system bleeding at each wheel.

Wheel Bleeding Sequence

Rear Wheel Drive...............RR-LR-RF-LF
Front Wheel Drive ....RR-LF-LR-RF

INSPECTION

Remove wheels and inspect brake disc, calipers and linings.

If the caliper is cracked or fluid leakage through the casting is evident, it must be replaced as a unit.

If caliper was removed when installing new components, clean all components in alcohol, then wipe dry using lint-free cloths. Using an air hose, blow out drilled passages and bores. Inspect dust boots for punctures or tears. If punctures or tears are evident, install new boots during assembly.

Inspect piston bores in both housings for scoring or pitting. Bores showing light scratches or corrosion can usually be cleaned with crocus cloth. Bores with deep scratches or scoring may be honed, provided the diameter of the bore is not increased more than .002 inch. If the bore does not clean up within this specification, a new caliper housing should be installed. Black stains on the bore walls are caused by piston seals and will not adversely affect caliper performance.

When using a hone, install the hone baffle before honing the bore. The baffle is used to protect the hone stones from damage. Use extreme care in cleaning the caliper after honing. Remove all dust and grit by flushing the caliper with alcohol. Wipe the caliper dry with a clean lint-free cloth, then repeat cleaning procedure.

BRAKE DISC SERVICE

Disc brake service is critical because of the close tolerances required in machining the brake disc to ensure proper brake operation.

Maintaining close control of the shape of the rubbing surfaces is required to prevent brake roughness. In addition, the surface finish must be non-directional and maintained at a micro-inch finish. This is required to avoid pulls and erratic performance and promote long lining life and equal lining wear of both the lefthand and righthand brakes.

Do not attempt to refinish the rubbing surfaces unless precision equipment, capable of measuring in micro inches (millionths of an inch) is available.

To inspect the disc lateral runout, mount a dial indicator on a convenient part, such as a steering knuckle, tie rod, or caliper housing, so the indicator's plunger contacts the disc one inch from the outer edge. If the total indicated runout exceeds specifications, install a new disc.

To inspect parallelism (thickness variation), mount dial indicators so the plunger contacts the rotor approximately one inch from the outer edge. If parallelism exceeds specifications, replace the rotor.

BRAKE PAD SERVICE

On models with anti-lock brakes, the brake system power booster must be depressurized before disconnecting any hydraulic lines or fittings. Depressurize the system by pumping the brake pedal at least 25 times with the ignition in the Off position.

After performing any service work, obtain a firm brake pedal before moving the vehicle.

Five Hundred, Freestyle, Fusion Milan, MKZ, Montego, Mustang, Sable, Taurus, Taurus X & Zephyr

REMOVAL

1. **On models equipped with air suspension,** turn service switch Off position.
2. **On all models,** raise and support rear of vehicle, then remove tire and wheel assembly.
3. Remove brake hose bracket to shock unit bracket screw.

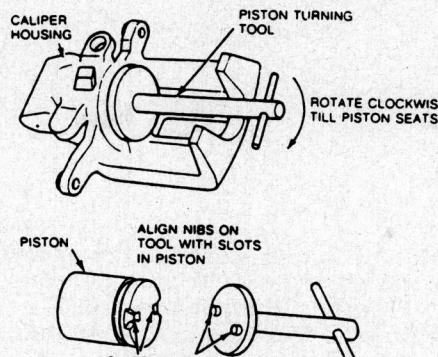

Fig. 2 Caliper piston seating. Five Hundred, Freestyle, Fusion Milan, MKZ, Montego, Mustang, Sable, Taurus, Taurus X & Zephyr

4. Remove retaining clip, then disconnect parking brake cable from lever.
5. Remove upper pinch bolt using open end wrench to hold slider pin in position, **Fig. 1.** Loosen, but do not lower, slider pin pinch bolt.
6. Rotate caliper away from rotor, then remover inner and outer brake pads and anti-rattle springs from anchor plate.

INSTALLATION

1. Rotate caliper piston clockwise until fully seated using rear caliper piston adjuster tool No. T87P-2588-A, or equivalent, **Fig. 2.**
2. Position one of two piston slots so it will engage nib on rear of brake pad, **Fig. 3.**
3. Position inner and outer brake pads on anchor plate, then install anti-rattle springs.
4. Rotate caliper over brake rotor. Ensure brake pads and anti-rattle springs are properly positioned, **Fig. 4.**
5. Apply suitable thread sealer and locking compound to pinch bolt threads. Install pinch bolts, while holding slider pin in position with suitable open end wrench.
6. Position parking brake cable to lever and install retaining clip.
7. Position brake hose and bracket to shock unit bracket and install mounting bolt.
8. Install tire and wheel assembly, then lower vehicle.
9. **On models equipped with air suspension,** turn service switch to On position.
10. **On all models,** cycle brake pedal several times to position brake pads and caliper piston.

Crown Victoria, Grand Marquis, Marauder & Town Car

REMOVAL

1. **On models equipped with air sus-**

pension, turn service switch to Off position.
2. **On all models,** remove master cylinder cap and inspect fluid level in reservoir. Remove brake fluid until reservoir is half full.
3. Raise and support vehicle, then remove tire and wheel assembly.
4. Remove caliper as outlined in "Caliper Service."
5. Remove inner and outer brake linings.

INSTALLATION

1. Inspect both rotor braking surfaces. Minor scoring or buildup of lining material does not require machining or replacement of the rotor assembly. Hand sand glaze from both rotor braking surfaces using garnet paper 100-A (medium grit) or aluminum oxide 150-J (medium).
2. Suspend caliper inside fender housing with suitable wire or tie straps. **Do not damage caliper or stretch brake hose.**
3. **Prevent damaging plastic piston. Metal or sharp objects should not come in direct contact with piston surface or damage will result.**
4. Seat caliper piston in piston bore using suitable C-clamp and wood block approximately 2¾ inch x 1 inch and at least ¾ inch thick.
5. Remove all rust buildup from inside of caliper legs (outer shoe contact area).
6. Install inner shoe and lining assembly in caliper piston(s). **Do not bend shoe clips during installation.**
7. Install outer pad in caliper. Ensure clips are properly seated.
8. Install caliper as outlined in "Caliper Service."
9. Install tire and wheel assemblies, and lower vehicle.
10. **On models equipped with air suspension,** turn service switch to On position.

LS & Thunderbird

1. Raise and support vehicle, then remove tire and wheel assembly.
2. Remove mounting bolts and caliper. **Do not allow caliper to hang from brake hose.**
3. Remove brake pads.
4. Measure brake disc and resurface as required. **Use hub-mount brake lathe if required to machine brake disc.**
5. Compress disc brake piston and adjuster into disc brake caliper using rear caliper piston adjuster tool No. T87P-2588-A, or equivalent.
6. Reverse procedure to install.

DISC BRAKES

CALIPER SERVICE

Replacement

FIVE HUNDRED, FREESTYLE, FUSION, MILAN, MKZ, MONTEGO, MUSTANG, SABLE, TAURUS, TAURUS X & ZEPHYR

REMOVAL

1. Raise and support rear of vehicle, then remove tire and wheel assembly.
2. Disconnect brake hose from caliper.
3. Remove retaining clip and disconnect parking brake cable from lever arm.
4. Remove pinch bolts using open end wrench to hold slider pin in position.
5. Lift caliper from anchor plate, then remove slider pins and boots.

INSTALLATION

1. Apply suitable silicone dielectric compound to slider pins and inside of boots.
2. Place slider pins and boots on anchor plate, then position caliper on anchor plate. Ensure brake pads and anti-rattle springs are properly positioned.
3. Apply suitable sealer and thread locking compound to threads, then install pinch bolts.
4. Tighten pinch bolts using open end wrench to hold slider pin in position.
5. Attach parking brake cable to lever arm and install retaining clip.
6. Connect brake hose to caliper using replacement washers.
7. Bleed brake system as outlined in "Brake System Bleed."
8. Install tire and wheel assembly.
9. Cycle brake pedal several times to position brake pads and caliper piston.

CROWN VICTORIA, GRAND MARQUIS, MARAUDER & TOWN CAR

Visually inspect caliper. If the caliper housing is leaking, it should be replaced. If a seal is leaking, the caliper must be disassembled and new seals and dust boot installed. If a piston is seized in the bore, replace caliper. Care must be taken when removing plastic piston.

REMOVAL

1. **On models equipped with air suspension,** turn service switch to Off position.
2. **On all models,** raise and support vehicle, then remove tire and wheel assembly.
3. Remove flexible brake hose mounting bolt from caliper. Plug hose and caliper fitting.
4. Remove caliper locating pins using Torx drive bit tool No. D79P-2100-T40, or equivalent.
5. Lift caliper off rotor and anchor plate using rotating motion. **Do not pry directly against plastic piston.**

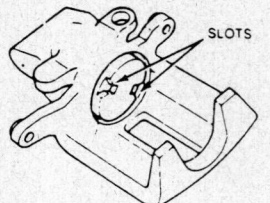
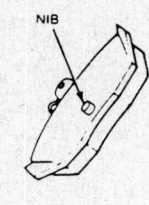

Fig. 3   Caliper piston to brake pad nib positioning. Five Hundred, Freestyle, Fusion Milan, MKZ, Montego, Mustang, Sable, Taurus, Taurus X & Zephyr

INSTALLATION

1. Retract piston fully into piston bore and position caliper above rotor with anti-rattle spring located on lower adapter support arm.
2. Install caliper over rotor with rotating motion. Ensure inner shoe is properly positioned.
3. Install caliper locating pins. **Caliper locating pins must be inserted and started by hand.**
4. Tighten locating pins.
5. Remove plugs from caliper fittings, then install flexible brake hose on caliper with new gasket on each side of fitting outlet.
6. Insert mounting bolt through washers and fittings.
7. Bleed brake system as outlined in "Brake System Bleed."
8. Pump brake pedal to position brake linings before moving vehicle.
9. **On models equipped with air suspension,** turn service switch to On position.

LS & THUNDERBIRD

1. Raise and support vehicle, then remove tire and wheel assembly.
2. Disconnect parking brake cable end from parking brake lever arm.
3. Remove parking brake cable and conduit.
4. Remove mounting bolts, flow bolt and caliper.
5. Discard copper washers.
6. Reverse procedure to install using new copper washers.
7. Bleed brake system.

Overhaul

FIVE HUNDRED, FREESTYLE, FUSION, MILAN, MKZ, MONTEGO, MUSTANG, SABLE, TAURUS, TAURUS X & ZEPHYR

DISASSEMBLE

1. Remove caliper as outlined in "Caliper Service."
2. Position caliper in suitable soft-jawed vise.
3. Remove from caliper bore using tool No. T75P-2588-B, or equivalent, to ro-

tate caliper piston counterclockwise.
4. Remove piston dust boot and seal from caliper piston bore.
5. Remove snap ring retaining pushrod to caliper. Use care when removing, snap ring and spring cover are under spring load.
6. Remove spring cover, spring, washer, key plate and pushrod and strut pin from caliper.
7. Remove O-ring from pushrod.
8. Remove parking brake lever return spring, then the brake lever stop bolt and pull lever from caliper.

CLEANING & INSPECTION

1. Clean all metal components with Isopropyl alcohol.
2. Use compressed air to clean out passages and grooves.
3. Inspect caliper bore for damage and excessive wear.
4. Inspect caliper piston for pitting, scoring or worn plating.

ASSEMBLE

1. Apply light coating of suitable silicone dielectric compound to parking brake lever bore and parking brake lever seal. Position seal into caliper bore.
2. Apply suitable silicone dielectric compound to parking brake lever shaft. Install shaft into caliper housing bore.
3. Install O-ring into groove on pushrod, then apply suitable silicone dielectric compound to recesses in pushrod.
4. Place strut pin into caliper housing and recess of parking brake lever shaft.
5. Position pushrod into caliper housing bore. Ensure strut pin is properly located between shaft recesses and recess at end of pushrod.
6. Position key plate over pushrod, so washer nib is located in hole in caliper housing.
7. Install flat washer, spring and spring cage into caliper bore.
8. Install snap ring using rear caliper spring compressor set No. T87P-2588-P, or equivalent. Ensure snap ring is properly seated in recess.
9. Lubricate replacement piston seal with suitable, clean brake fluid. Install seal into caliper bore groove.
10. Lubricate piston and dust boot with clean brake fluid, then install dust boot into caliper bore.
11. Position piston into dust boot, seating dust boot in piston groove.
12. Turn piston in clockwise direction until piston is fully seated in caliper bore using rear caliper spring compressor set No. T75P-2588-B, or equivalent, **Fig. 2.**
13. Position one of two slots on piston so it will engage nib on rear of disc pad when caliper is installed, **Fig. 3.**
14. Install caliper as outlined in "Caliper Service."

CROWN VICTORIA, GRAND MARQUIS, MARAUDER & TOWN CAR

Visually inspect caliper. If the caliper housing is leaking, it should be replaced. If a seal is leaking, the caliper must be disassembled and new seals and dust boot installed. If a piston is seized in the bore, replace the caliper. Care must be taken when removing the plastic piston.

DISASSEMBLE

1. **On models equipped with air suspension,** turn service switch to Off position.
2. **On all models,** remove caliper from mounting bracket.
3. Remove outer pad by slipping down caliper leg until clip is disconnected, then inner pad by pulling it straight out of piston.
4. Place shop towels between caliper piston and caliper bridge. **Do not place fingers between these areas.**
5. If air pressure is not available, slowly apply brake pedal until caliper piston is forced from bore. This method can only be done one caliper at a time.
6. If air pressure is to be used, use following procedure:
   a. Disconnect flexible hose from caliper and remove caliper.
   b. Apply light air pressure to brake hose inlet until piston is free from caliper. **Do not use shop pressure if it cannot be adjusted down 15–30 psi.**
7. Remove seal and dust boot from caliper.

CLEANING & INSPECTION

Clean all metal components with Isopropyl alcohol. Dry grooves and passageways with compressed air. Ensure caliper bore and component components are cleaned thoroughly. Inspect cylinder bore and piston for damage or excessive wear.

Examine piston for surface irregularities or small chips and cracks. Minor surface imperfections are allowable, provided they do not enter the dust boot groove area. Replace piston if damaged.

ASSEMBLE

1. Coat new seal and dust boot with suitable, clean brake fluid, then install in caliper.
2. Coat piston with suitable, clean brake fluid, then place piston in caliper and push firmly into bore.
3. With piston seated, completely seat piston using suitable C-clamp and block of wood approximately 2¾ inch x 1 inch x ¾ inch thick.
4. Ensure dust boot is tight in boot groove on piston and in caliper.
5. Install brake pads as outlined in "Brake Pad Service," then the caliper.

LS & THUNDERBIRD

1. Remove brake caliper as outlined in "Caliper Service."
2. Drain brake fluid from caliper into suitable container.
3. Secure brake caliper in suitable vise.
4. Turn brake piston counterclockwise with rear caliper piston adjuster tool No. T87P-2588-A, or equivalent.
5. Remove brake piston from caliper bore.
6. Remove and discard piston dust boot

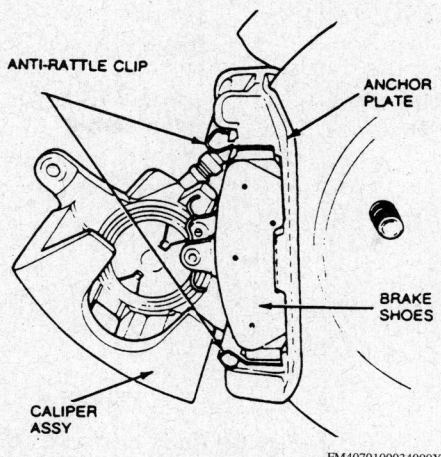

Fig. 4   Anti-rattle clip positioning. Five Hundred, Freestyle, Fusion Milan, MKZ, Montego, Mustang, Sable, Taurus, Taurus X & Zephyr

and piston seal from caliper bore.
7. Reverse procedure to assemble, noting the following:
   a. Install new seals and dust boots.
   b. Use new brake fluid when assembling and bleeding brake system.

ROTOR
REPLACE

Five Hundred, Freestyle, Fusion, Milan, MKZ, Montego, Mustang, Sable, Taurus, Taurus X & Zephyr

REMOVAL

1. Remove rear disc brake caliper as outlined in "Caliper Service." **Do not disconnect flexible hose unless caliper requires service.**
2. Support caliper with suitable wire or tie strap so flexible hose is not stretched or twisted.
3. Remove rear disc support bracket to wheel knuckle bolts.
4. Remove rear disc support bracket and brake shoes and linings.
5. Remove two nuts and rotor.

INSTALLATION

1. If installing new rotor, remove protective coating from rotor with suitable carburetor cleaner.
2. Lubricate rear hub pilot diameter with suitable grease.
3. Install rotors on axle shaft flange, then the two mounting nuts.
4. Install inner and outer brake shoes and linings in rear disc support bracket.
5. Clean rear disc support bracket and bolt threads, then add one drop of suitable sealer to each bolt.

6. Install caliper/rear support bracket to rear wheel knuckle.
7. Install bolts and tighten.
8. Install inner and outer brake shoes and linings as outlined in "Brake Pad Service."
9. Install rear disc brake caliper as outlined in "Caliper Service."

Crown Victoria, Grand Marquis, Marauder & Town Car

REMOVAL

1. Raise and support vehicle, then remove tire and wheel assembly.
2. Remove rear disc brake caliper as outlined in "Caliper Service." **Do not disconnect flexible hose unless caliper requires service.**
3. Position caliper aside and support with suitable wire or tie strap.
4. Remove rotor push nuts, then the disc brake rotor. If additional force is required, use following procedure:
   a. Apply rust penetrant and inhibitor part No. D7AZ-19A501-AA, or equivalent, to rotor/flange mating surface.
   b. Install three-jaw puller tool No. D80L-1013-A, or equivalent.
   c. Remove rear disc brake rotor. **If excessive force is required to remove rotor, it should be inspected for lateral runout prior to installation.**

INSTALLATION

1. If installing new rotor, remove protective coating with suitable carburetor cleaner.
2. If installing original rotor, ensure rotor braking and mounting surfaces are clean.
3. Install rotor and push nuts.
4. Install caliper as outlined in "Caliper Service."
5. Install tire and wheel assembly, then lower vehicle.
6. Pump brake pedal to position brake shoes and linings before moving vehicle and road testing.

LS & Thunderbird

1. Remove support bracket.
2. Remove and discard pushups.
3. Remove brake disc.
4. Reverse procedure to install.

PARKING BRAKE SERVICE

Parking Brake Linings, Replace

CROWN VICTORIA, GRAND MARQUIS, MARAUDER & TOWN CAR

1. Remove tire and wheel assembly.

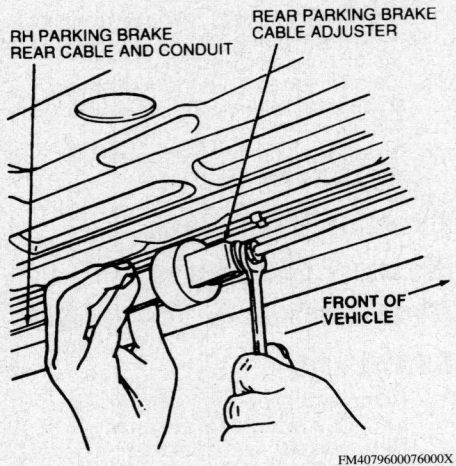

RH PARKING BRAKE
REAR CABLE AND CONDUIT

REAR PARKING BRAKE
CABLE ADJUSTER

FRONT OF
VEHICLE

FM4079600076000X

Fig. 5 Park brake adjustment.
Five Hundred, Freestyle, Montego,
Sable, Taurus & Taurus X

2. Remove brake rotor.
3. Remove spring and brake shoe adjusting screw.
4. Remove brake shoe hold down springs.
5. Remove parking bake shoe and linings.
6. Reverse procedure to install noting the following:
   a. Lubricate brake shoe contact point before installation with silicone brake caliper grease and dielectric compound part No. D7AZ-19A331-A, or equivalent.
   b. Adjust rear brake shoe and lining diameter to .020 inch less than inside diameter of drum portion of rear brake using suitable brake adjusting gauge.
   c. Adjust parking brake cable tension.

ADJUSTMENTS

Parking Brake

CROWN VICTORIA, GRAND MARQUIS, MARAUDER & TOWN CAR

1. Apply parking brake control fully with 100 lbs., foot pedal effort, then release brake control.
2. Place transmission in Neutral position, then raise and support vehicle.
3. With parking brake control in Off position, grasp pensioner around housing.
4. Unlock clip by pulling downward with

suitable hook tool place into rounded end of clip and support pensioner.
5. Tensioner spring will take up cable slack and load cables, while holding pensioner, lock clip by pushing up on bottom of clip. If clip does not slide up move assembly slightly to align closest groove on adjuster rod to clip.
6. Examine pensioner for remaining cable take up capability. If none is present, inspect all cables, parking brake control and brackets for possible damage or deflection.

FIVE HUNDRED, FREESTYLE, MONTEGO, SABLE, TAURUS & TAURUS X

1. Ensure parking brake control is fully released, then raise and support vehicle.
2. **Torque** adjusting nut against rear parking brake cable adjuster until cable tension is 34–46 lbs., using Rotunda cable tension gauge tool No. 014-R1056, or equivalent, **Fig. 5.**
3. Apply parking brake control fully, then release.
4. Ensure cable tension is still within specification and there is no drag on rear brakes.
5. Lower vehicle and ensure operation of parking brake.

FUSION, MILAN, MKZ & ZEPHYR

1. Remove floor console rear access panel, **Fig. 6.**
2. With vehicle in Neutral, position it on a hoist.
3. Adjust parking brake adjustment nut, **Fig. 7.** Dimension from tip of adjust-

ment rod and adjustment nut should be .55–.62 inches. Dimension will vary depending on amount of cable stretch. New cables require cycling parking brake control 5-10 times to remove cable slack.
4. Verify correct operation of the parking brake system as follows:
   a. At 2 clicks of parking brake control, slight drag at rear wheels should be present.
   b. At 5 clicks of parking brake control, no movement at rear wheels should be present.

MUSTANG

1. Place parking brake control in released position.
2. Remove console top panel by pry finish panel up from retaining clips and disconnect electrical connectors.
3. Raise and support vehicle with assistant inside.
4. Have another assistant pull parking brake cable and equalizer rearward approximately 1–2 ½ inches to rotate self-adjuster reel backward, **Fig. 8.**
5. Insert steel locking through holes in lever and parking brake control assembly to lock ratchet wheel in cable-released position. **Do not remove steel locking until rear cable and conduit are connected to parking brake cable and equalizer.**

DISC BRAKE SPECIFICATIONS

Rotor Specifications

Refer to "Front Disc Brakes" for disc specifications.

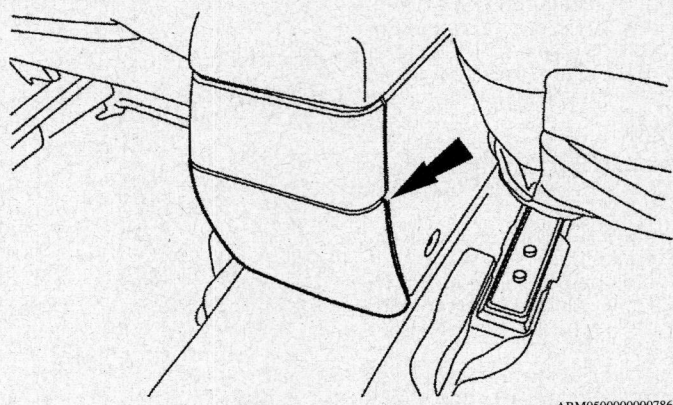

ARM0500000000786

Fig. 6 floor console rear access panel removal.
Fusion, Milan, MKZ & Zephyr

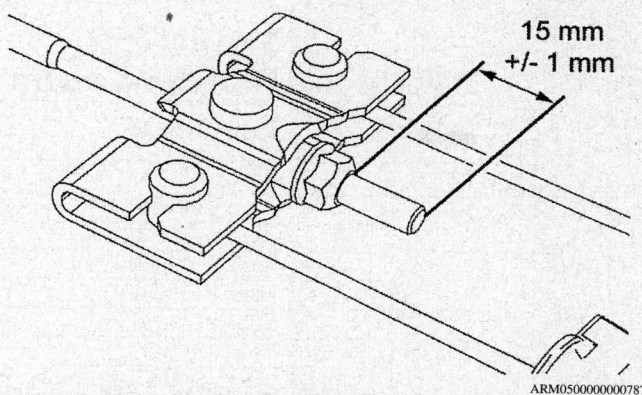

Fig. 7   Parking brake adjustment & dimension. Fusion, Milan, MKZ & Zephyr

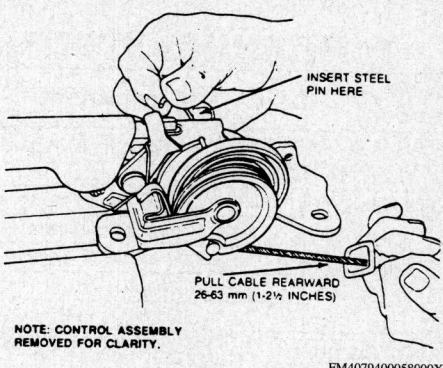

Fig. 8   Self-adjuster reel rotation. Mustang

Caliper Specifications

Model	Year	Caliper Bore Diameter Inch
FRONT		
Crown Victoria	2004–08	①
Five Hundred	2005–07	①
Focus	2004–07	①
Freestyle	2005–08	①
Fusion	2006–08	①
Grand Marquis	2004–08	①
LS	2004–06	①
Marauder	2004	①
Milan	2006–08	①
MKZ	2007–08	①
Montego	2005–08	①
Mustang	2004–06	①
Sable & Taurus	2004–07	①
Taurus X	2008	①
Thunderbird	2004–05	①
Town Car	2004–08	①
Zephyr	2006	①
REAR		
Crown Victoria	2004–08	①
Five Hundred	2005–07	①
Freestyle	2005–08	①
Fusion	2006–08	①
Grand Marquis	2004–08	①
LS	2004–06	①
Marauder	2004–05	①
Milan	2006–08	①
MKZ	2007–08	①
Montego	2005–08	①
Mustang	2004–08	①
Sable & Taurus	2004–07	①
Taurus X	2008	①
Thunderbird	2004–05	①
Town Car	2004–08	①
Zephyr	2006	①

① — Replace brake caliper if there is scoring or damage to caliper cylinder. Do not hone cylinder.

DISC BRAKES

TIGHTENING SPECIFICATIONS

Year/Model	Component	Torque Ft. Lbs.
CROWN VICTORIA, GRAND MARQUIS, MARAUDER & TOWN CAR		
2004–08	Anchor Plate To Spindle	118
	Brake Hose To Caliper, Banjo	41
	Caliper Bleed Screw	15
	Rear Caliper Anchor Plate	50
	Wheel Lug	95
FIVE HUNDRED, FREESTYLE, MONTEGO & TAURUS X		
2005–08	Anchor Plate, Front	74
	Anchor Plate, Rear	81
	Bleeder Screw, Front	96①
	Bleeder Screw, Rear	89①
	Brake Disc Shield, Front	96①
	Brake Disc Shield, Rear	10
	Caliper Bolts, Front	44
	Caliper Bolts, Rear	23
	Flex Hose, Front	108①
	Flex Hose, Rear	18
	Line Fitting	13
	Parking Brake Cable Bracket Bolt	108①
	Upper Control Arm Parking Brake Cable Bracket Nut	27
FUSION, MILAN, MKZ & ZEPHYR		
2006–08	Bleeder Crew	71①
	Caliper Anchor Plate	52
	Caliper To Mount Bracket	19
	Disc Shield	17
	Fluid Line Banjo Bolt	18
	Rotor To Hub	15
LS & THUNDERBIRD		
2004–06	Anchor Plate	76
	Axle Shaft	221
	Caliper	26
	Caliper Bleeder Screw	60–120①
	Caliper Flow Bolt	35
	Master Cylinder Tube Fitting	11–15
	Support Bracket	36
	Wheel Lug	100

TIGHTENING SPECIFICATIONS—Continued

Year/Model	Component	Torque Ft. Lbs.
MUSTANG		
2004–08	Anchor Plate	85
	Brake Hose To Axle	24
	Brake Hose To Caliper, Banjo	30
	Caliper, Front	23
	Caliper, Rear	25
	Limiting Bolt	84①
	Parking Brake Cable To Axle Bracket	25
	Rear Disc Shield	89①
	Rear Disc Shield Support Bracket	76
	Wheel Lug	95
SABLE & TAURUS		
2004–07	Anchor Plate	64–88
	Axle Nut	188–254
	Brake Adapter	44–60
	Brake Hose Bracket To Shock	8–11
	Brake Hose To Caliper, Banjo	30–40
	Brake Pin Mounting Bolt	23–26
	Disc Brake Shield	72–108①
	Hub Nut	188–254
	Park Brake Lever Limit Bolt	60–84①
	Rear Anti-Lock Sensor	36–60①

① — Inch lbs.

DRUM BRAKES

TABLE OF CONTENTS

	Page No.		Page No.
FOCUS	15-3	**2004–05 SABLE & 2004–07 TAURUS**	15-1

2004–05 Sable & 2004–07 Taurus

NOTE: On Air Bag Equipped Models, Refer To "Air Bag System Precautions" Located In The Front Of This Manual For System Disarming & Arming Procedures.

NOTE: Refer To "Computer Relearn Procedures" Located In The Front Of This Manual When Battery Power To The Computer Has Been Interrupted.

INDEX

	Page No.		Page No.		Page No.
Adjustments	15-2	Removal	15-1	Battery Ground Cable	15-1
Parking Brake	15-2	**Drum Brake Specifications**	15-3	Safety Precautions	15-1
Service Brakes	15-2	**Inspection**	15-1	**Tightening Specifications**	15-3
Brake Service	15-1	**Precautions**	15-1	
Installation	15-2	Air Bag Systems	15-1	

PRECAUTIONS

Air Bag Systems

Refer to "Air Bag System Precautions" in the front of this manual for system disarming and arming procedures.

Battery Ground Cable

Prior to service, disconnect battery ground cable and isolate as required.

Safety Precautions

When working on or around brake assemblies, care must be taken to prevent breathing asbestos dust, as many manufacturers incorporate asbestos fibers in the production of brake linings. During routine service operations the amount of asbestos dust from brake lining wear is at a low level, due to a chemical breakdown during use. A few precautions will minimize exposure. **Do not sand or grind brake linings unless suitable local exhaust ventilation equipment is used to prevent excessive asbestos exposure.**

1. Wear suitable respirator approved for asbestos dust use during all repair procedures.
2. When cleaning brake dust from brake components, use vacuum cleaner with highly efficient filter system. If suitable vacuum cleaner is not available, use water-soaked rag. **Do not use compressed air or dry brush to clean brake components.**
3. Keep work area clean, using same equipment as for cleaning brake components.
4. Properly dispose of rags and vacuum cleaner bags by placing them in plastic bags.
5. **Never use gasoline, kerosene, alcohol, motor oil, transmission fluid, or any fluid containing mineral oil to clean brake system components. These fluids will damage rubber caps and seals. If system contamination is suspected, inspect brake fluid in reservoir for dirt, discoloration, or separation (breakdown) of brake fluid into distinct layers. Drain and flush hydraulic system with clean brake fluid if contamination is suspected.**

INSPECTION

1. Inspect components for damage and unusual wear.
2. Inspect wheel cylinders. Boots which are torn, cut, or heat damaged indicate need for wheel cylinder replacement. Fluid spilling from boot center hole, or wetness around wheel cylinder ends indicates cup leakage and need for wheel cylinder replacement. **A small amount of fluid is always present and is considered normal, acting as lubricant for cylinder pistons.**
3. Inspect backing plate for evidence of seal leakage. If leakage exists, refer to appropriate chassis chapter for axle seal replacement procedure.
4. Inspect backing plate bolts and ensure they are tight.
5. Inspect adjuster screw operation. If satisfactory, lightly lubricate adjusting screw and washer with suitable brake lubricant. If operation is unsatisfactory, replace.
6. Clean rust and dirt from shoe contact surfaces on backing plate using fine emery cloth or other suitable abrasive.

BRAKE SERVICE

Removal

1. Raise and support rear of vehicle, then remove tire and wheel assembly.
2. Remove retainer push nuts and slide drum off hub, **Fig. 1.**
3. If drum is stuck to hub, use suitable hammer to lightly tap on face of drum in flange mounting area to release.
4. If brake lining is dragging on brake drum, back off brake adjustment by holding adjustment lever off and loosen star wheel, **Fig. 2.**
5. Remove hub nut cover and discard.
6. Remove hub nut and discard. Slide hub and one-piece bearing off spindle.
7. Install suitable wheel cylinder piston retainer tool.

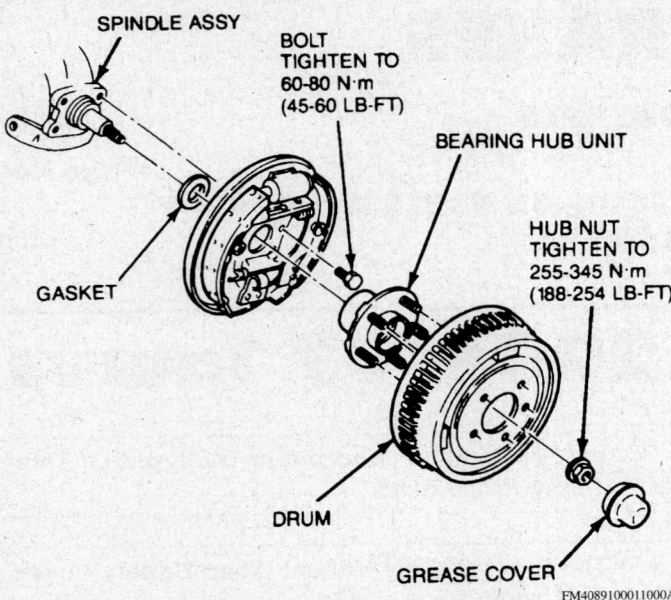

Fig. 1 Drum & hub assembly

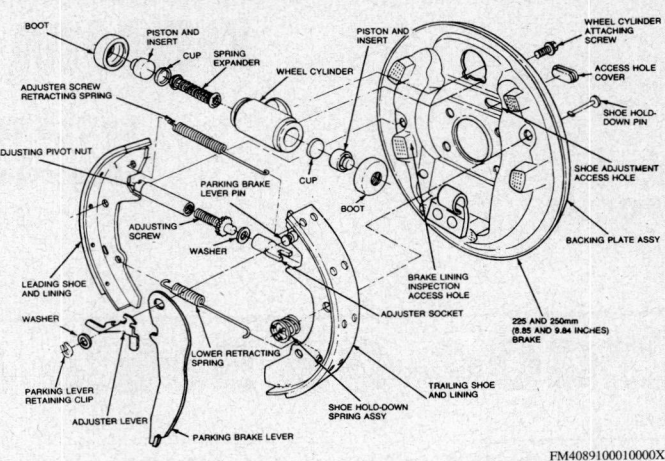

Fig. 2 Drum brake assembly

8. Remove shoe hold-down springs and pins.
9. Lift shoes, springs and adjuster off backing plate and wheel cylinder. **Do not bend adjusting lever.**
10. Remove parking brake cable from parking brake lever.
11. Remove retracting springs from lower shoe attachments and upper shoe to adjusting lever attachment points.
12. Disconnect shoes and adjuster mechanism.
13. Clean dirt from drum, backing plate and other components. **Do not use compressed air or dry brush to clean brake components. Clean brake components with water-soaked rag or suitable vacuum cleaner to minimize airborne dust.**

Installation

1. Lightly lubricate backing plate shoe contact surfaces with suitable brake lubrication.
2. Apply thin uniform coat of suitable brake lubricant to adjuster screw threads and socket end of adjusting screw.
3. Install stainless steel washer over socket end of adjusting screw.
4. Install socket, turn adjusting screw fully into adjusting pivot nut and back off ½ turn.
5. Assemble parking brake lever to trailing shoe and lining by installing spring washer and new horseshoe retaining clip. Crimp clip until it securely retains lever to shoe.
6. Attach parking brake cable to lever.

7. Attach lower shoe retracting spring to leading and trailing shoe assemblies, then install on backing plate. Stretch retracting spring as shoes are installed downward over anchor plate to inside of retaining plate.
8. Install adjuster screw assembly between leading shoe slot and slot in trailing shoe and parking brake lever. Adjuster socket end slot must fit into trailing shoe and parking brake lever. **Adjuster socket blade is marked R or L for righthand and lefthand brake assemblies. The adjuster blade must be installed with letter R or L in upright position (facing wheel cylinder) on proper side to ensure deeper of two slots in adjuster sockets fits into parking brake lever.**
9. Assemble adjuster lever in groove located in parking brake lever pin and into slot of adjuster socket that fits into trailing shoe web.
10. Attach upper retracting spring to leading shoe slot and stretch other end of spring into notch on adjuster lever using suitable tool. **If adjuster lever does not contact star wheel after installing spring, adjuster socket may be improperly installed.**
11. Install hub to spindle and tighten new hub nut. Install new hub nut cover.
12. Install brake drum to hub, then the drum retainer push nuts.
13. Install tire and wheel assembly.
14. If any hydraulic connections have been opened, bleed system as outlined in "Hydraulic Brake System" chapter.
15. Adjust parking brake as outlined in "Adjustments."

16. Inspect hydraulic lines and connections for leakage.
17. Adjust master cylinder fluid level.
18. Inspect brake pedal for proper feel and return.
19. Lower vehicle and road test. **Do not severely apply brakes immediately after installation of new linings. Brakes must be used moderately during first several hundred miles of operation to ensure proper burnishing of linings.**

ADJUSTMENTS

Service Brakes

Although the brakes are self-adjusting, an initial adjustment is required after a brake repair.
1. Determine inside diameter of brake drum surface using brake shoe gauge tool No. D81L-1103-A, or equivalent.
2. Adjust brake shoe diameter to fit gauge.
3. Hold automatic adjusting lever out of engagement while rotating adjusting screw.
4. Ensure screw rotates freely.
5. Install brake drum, then the tire and wheel assembly.

Parking Brake

1. Ensure parking brake lever is released.
2. With transmission in Neutral, raise and support vehicle.
3. Tighten parking brake nut against brake equalizer until rear brakes drag.
4. Loosen nut until rear brakes are fully released.
5. Lower vehicle and inspect parking brake operation.

DRUM BRAKE SPECIFICATIONS

Model	Year	Brake Lining Wear Limit, Inch③	Brake Drum Inside Diameter, Inches			Drum Runout Limit, Inch	Drum Maximum Out Of Roundness, Inch
			Nominal	Maximum Refinish	Maximum Inside Diameter (Discard Limit)①		
Sable	2004–05	②	8.86	—	8.92	.005	—
Taurus	2004–07	②	8.86	—	8.92	.005	—

① — Maximum brake drum inside diameter (discard limit) is stamped on drum.

② — Wear limit, riveted lining, 1/32 inch above rivet head; bonded lining, 1/16 inch lining thickness.

③ — Above rivet head or shoe. Original equipment type brake linings.

TIGHTENING SPECIFICATIONS

Year	Component	Torque Ft. Lbs.
SABLE & TAURUS		
2004–07	ABS Sensor	72–96①
	Axle Nut	188–254
	Brake Backing Plate To Spindle	45–59
	Brake Hose	12–14
	Hub Nut	188–254
	Parking Brake Stop Bolt	96–108①
	Wheel Cylinder	9–13
	Wheel Lug Nuts	85–104

① — Inch lbs.

Focus

NOTE: On Air Bag Equipped Models, Refer To "Air Bag System Precautions" Located In The Front Of This Manual For System Disarming & Arming Procedures.

NOTE: Refer To "Computer Relearn Procedures" Located In The Front Of This Manual When Battery Power To The Computer Has Been Interrupted.

INDEX

	Page No.
Adjustments	15-5
Parking Brake	15-5
Service Brakes	15-5
Brake Service	15-4
Installation	15-4
Removal	15-4
Drum Brake Specifications	15-6
Inspection	15-4
Precautions	15-3
Air Bag Systems	15-3
Battery Ground Cable	15-3
Safety Precautions	15-3
Tightening Specifications	15-6

PRECAUTIONS

Air Bag Systems

Refer to "Air Bag System Precautions" in the front of this manual for system disarming and arming procedures.

Battery Ground Cable

Prior to service, disconnect battery ground cable and isolate as required.

Safety Precautions

When working on or around brake assemblies, care must be taken to prevent breathing asbestos dust. Many manufacturers incorporate asbestos fibers in the production of brake linings. During routine service operations, the amount of asbestos dust from brake lining wear is at a low level due to a chemical breakdown during use. **Do not sand or grind brake linings unless suitable local exhaust ventilation equipment is used to prevent excessive asbestos exposure.**

1. Wear suitable respirator approved for asbestos dust use during all repair procedures.
2. When cleaning brake dust from brake components, use vacuum cleaner with

DRUM BRAKES

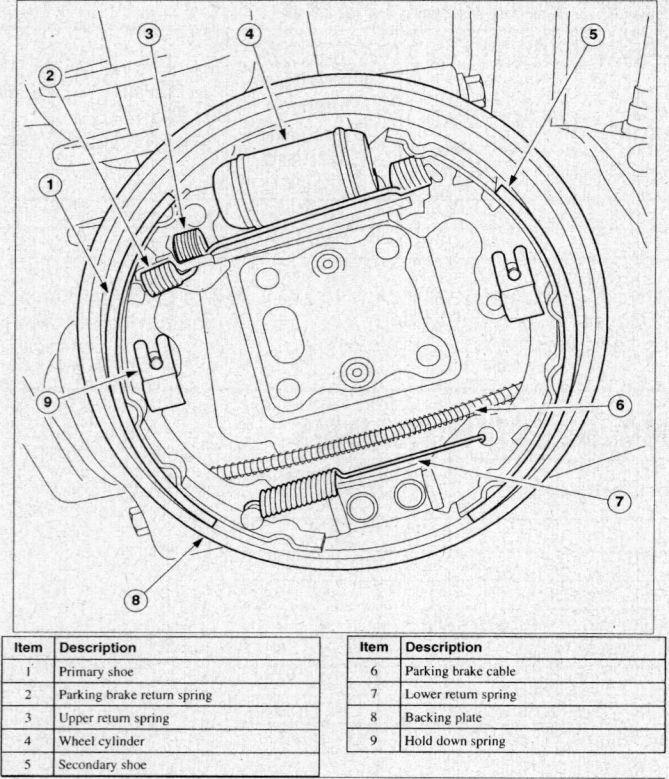

Item	Description	Item	Description
1	Primary shoe	6	Parking brake cable
2	Parking brake return spring	7	Lower return spring
3	Upper return spring	8	Backing plate
4	Wheel cylinder	9	Hold down spring
5	Secondary shoe		

FM4080100043000X

Fig. 1 Rear brake spring locations

highly efficient filter system. If suitable vacuum cleaner is not available, use water-soaked rag. **Do not use compressed air or dry brush to clean brake components.**
3. Keep work area clean, using same equipment as for cleaning brake components.
4. Properly dispose of rags and vacuum cleaner bags by placing them in plastic bags.
5. **Never use gasoline, kerosene, alcohol, motor oil, transmission fluid, or any fluid containing mineral oil to clean brake system components. These fluids will damage rubber caps and seals. If system contamination is suspected, inspect brake fluid in reservoir for dirt, discoloration, or separation (breakdown) of brake fluid into distinct layers. Drain and flush hydraulic system with clean brake fluid if contamination is suspected.**

INSPECTION

1. Inspect components for damage and unusual wear.
2. Inspect wheel cylinders. Boots which are torn, cut, or heat damaged indicate need for wheel cylinder replacement. Fluid spilling from boot center hole or wetness around wheel cylinder ends indicates cup leakage and need for

wheel cylinder replacement. **A small amount of fluid is always present and is considered normal, acting as lubricant for cylinder pistons.**
3. Inspect backing plate for evidence of seal leakage. If leakage exists, refer to "Focus" chassis chapter for axle seal replacement procedure.
4. Inspect backing plate bolts and ensure they are tight.
5. Inspect adjuster screw operation. If satisfactory, lightly lubricate adjusting screw and washer with suitable brake lubricant. If operation is unsatisfactory, replace.
6. Clean rust and dirt from shoe contact surfaces on backing plate using fine emery cloth or other suitable abrasive.

BRAKE SERVICE
Removal

1. Release parking brake.
2. Raise and support vehicle, then remove tire and wheel assemblies.
3. **On models equipped with anti-lock brakes,** remove wheel speed sensor.
4. **On all models,** remove brake drum and wheel hub.
5. Remove brake shoe hold down springs and pins, **Fig. 1.**
6. Disconnect brake shoes from wheel

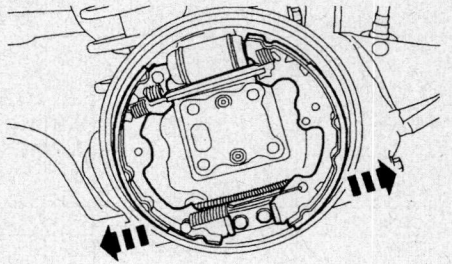

FM4080100044000X

Fig. 2 Brake shoe removal

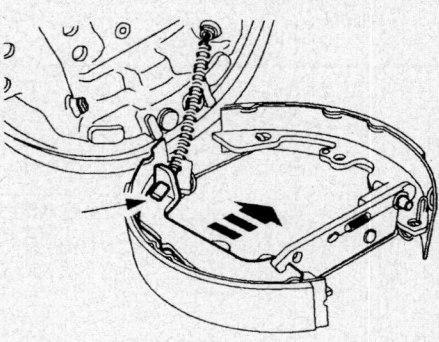

FM4080100045000X

Fig. 3 Parking brake cable removal

cylinders. Hold wheel cylinder pistons in place with suitable rubber bands.
7. Remove shoes from anchor block, **Fig. 2.**
8. Push parking brake lever inward and remove cable, **Fig. 3.**
9. Remove lower and upper return springs.
10. Remove primary shoe from strut and brake shoe adjuster, **Fig. 4.**
11. Remove secondary shoe from support, **Fig. 5. Support spring is under pressure.**
12. Remove parking brake return spring.

Installation

1. Clean, inspect and apply Silicone dielectric compound to backing plate contact points.
2. Install parking brake return spring, then the strut support and move upward.
3. Install strut to primary brake shoe, push shoe inwards and rotate adjuster fully clockwise, **Fig. 6.**
4. Install upper and lower return springs.
5. Push parking brake lever inward and connect parking brake cable.
6. Remove rubber band holding wheel cylinders in place.
7. Install brake shoes to wheel cylinder to anchor block.
8. Install hold down springs, then the brake drum and wheel hub assembly.
9. **On models equipped with anti-lock brake system,** install wheel speed sensor.

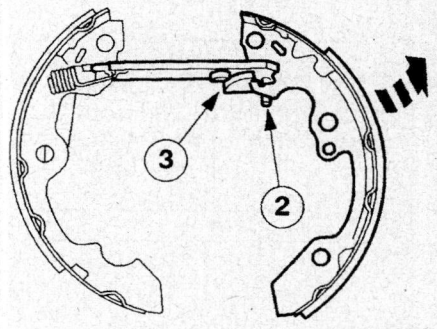

Fig. 4   Primary brake shoe removal

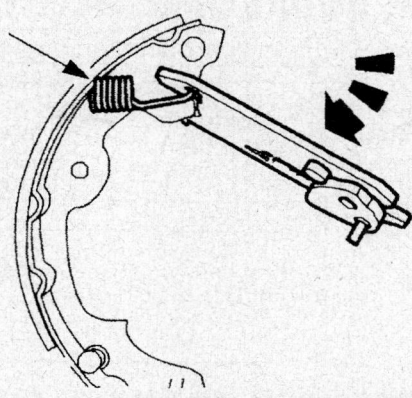

Fig. 5   Secondary brake shoe removal

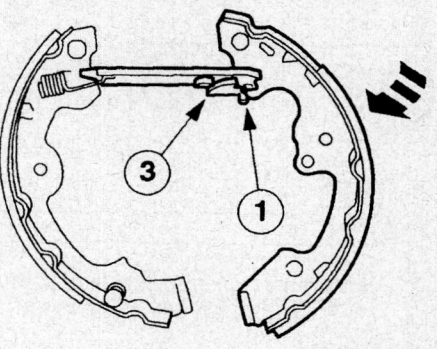

Fig. 6   Primary brake shoe to strut assembly

10. **On all models,** install tire and wheel assemblies.
11. Operate brake pedal to achieve automatic brake adjustment.

ADJUSTMENTS
Service Brakes

These models are equipped with self adjusting brake mechanisms and require no adjustment. The brakes are adjusted as required whenever the service brakes are applied.

Parking Brake

1. Remove clip and parking brake boot.
2. Ensure rear brakes are not hot when adjusting.
3. Release parking brake to its lowest position.
4. Remove clip and loosen parking brake

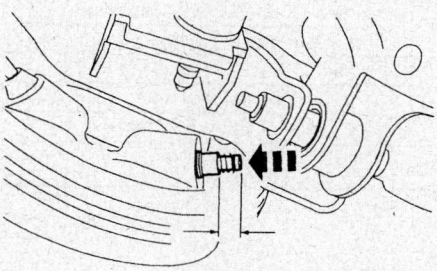

Fig. 7   Parking brake cable plunger inspection

cable adjustment nut until there is no tension in cable.
5. Apply and release brake pedal to ensure brakes are adjusted correctly.
6. Raise and support vehicle.

7. Ensure parking brake cable is correctly routed in its clips.
8. Lower vehicle.
9. Raise parking brake control lever up four notches.
10. Tighten parking brake cable adjustment nut until increased torque is felt.
11. Apply and release hand-brake lever several times with sufficient force to settle parking brake system.
12. Release parking brake lever to its lowest position.
13. Inspect movement of plunger in righthand and lefthand backing plates while moving lever up and down, **Fig. 7.**
14. Total movement of both righthand and lefthand plungers added together should be .039–.315 inch.
15. If further adjustment is required, adjust cable using parking brake cable adjustment nut.
16. Install parking brake adjustment nut clip and control lever boot.

DRUM BRAKES

DRUM BRAKE SPECIFICATIONS

Year	Brake Lining Wear Limit, Inch[2]	Brake Drum Inside Diameter, Inches			Drum Runout Limit, Inch	Drum Maximum Out Of Roundness, Inch
		Nominal	Maximum Refinish	Maximum Inside Diameter (Discard Limit)[1]		
2004–08	.039	7.99	—	8.03	—	—

① — Maximum brake drum inside diameter (discard limit) is stamped on drum.

② — Above rivet head or shoe. Original equipment type brake linings.

TIGHTENING SPECIFICATIONS

Year	Component	Torque Ft. Lbs.
2004–07	Brake Drum & Wheel Hub Nuts	49
	Brake Pipe To Wheel Cylinder	71①
	Wheel Cylinder To Backing Plate	108①
	Wheel Lug Nuts	94
	Wheel Speed Sensor	80①

① — Inch lbs.

HYDRAULIC BRAKE SYSTEMS

NOTE: On Air Bag Equipped Models, Refer To "Air Bag System Precautions" Located In The Front Of This Manual For System Disarming & Arming Procedures.

NOTE: Refer To "Computer Relearn Procedures" Located In The Front Of This Manual When Battery Power To The Computer Has Been Interrupted.

INDEX

	Page No.
Brake System Bleed	16-3
System Priming	16-4
Wheel Bleeding Sequence	16-4
Clutch System Bleeding	16-4
Component Replacement	16-2
Master Cylinder	16-2
Crown Victoria, Grand Marquis, Marauder, Mustang & Town Car	16-2
Five Hundred, Freestyle, Montego, Sable, Taurus & Taurus X	16-3
Focus	16-2
Fusion, Milan, MKZ & Zephyr	16-3

	Page No.
LS & Thunderbird	16-3
Wheel Cylinders	16-3
Installation	16-3
Removal	16-3
Component Service	16-3
Master Cylinder	16-3
Assemble	16-3
Disassemble	16-3
Inspection	16-3
Wheel Cylinders	16-3
Description	16-1
Brake Distribution Valve & Switch	16-2
Brake Warning Light Systems	16-1

	Page No.
Testing Warning Light Systems	16-1
Combination Valve	16-1
Failure Warning Switch	16-2
Metering Valve	16-1
Proportioner Or Pressure Control Valve	16-2
Proportioning Valve & Switch	16-2
Description	16-2
Testing	16-2
Hydraulic Brake System Flush	16-4
Precautions	16-1
Air Bag Systems	16-1
Battery Ground Cable	16-1

PRECAUTIONS

Air Bag Systems

Refer to "Air Bag System Precautions" in the front of this manual for system disarming and arming procedures.

Battery Ground Cable

Prior to service, disconnect battery ground cable and isolate as required.

DESCRIPTION

This system operates on the same principles as conventional front and rear split systems using primary and secondary master cylinders moving simultaneously to exert hydraulic pressure on their respective systems, **Fig. 1.**

The hydraulic brake lines on this system, however, have been diagonally split front to rear (left front to right rear and right front to left rear) in place of separate lines to the front and rear wheels.

In the event of a system failure this would cause the remaining good system to do all the braking on one front wheel and the opposite rear wheel, thus maintaining 50% of the total braking force. The hydraulic pressure loss would result in a pressure differential in the system and cause a warning light on the dashboard to glow as in front and rear split systems.

Brake Warning Light Systems

When a pressure differential occurs between the front and rear brake systems, the valves will shuttle toward the side with the low pressure. Movement of the differential valve forces the switch plunger upward over the tapered shoulder of the valve to close the switch contacts and light the dual brake warning lamp, signaling a brake system failure.

The valve assembly consists of two valves in a common bore that are spring loaded toward the centered position. The spring-loaded switch contact plunger rests on top of the valves in the centered position. When a pressure differential occurs between the front and rear brake systems, the valves will shuttle toward the side with the low pressure. The spring-loaded switch plunger is triggered and the ground circuit for the warning light is completed, lighting the lamp.

As pressure falls in one system, the other system's normal pressure forces the piston to the inoperative side, contacting the switch terminal, causing the warning light on the instrument panel to glow.

On front wheel drive models, a fluid level indicator replaces the pressure differential valve used in previous brake systems. It is contained inside the body of the master cylinder plastic reservoir and activates the brake warning light when fluid level is low.

TESTING WARNING LIGHT SYSTEMS

If the parking brake light is connected into the service brake warning light system, the brake warning light will flash only when the parking brake is applied with the ignition turned ON. The same light will also glow should one of the two service brake systems fail when the brake pedal is applied.

To test the system, turn the ignition on and apply the parking brake. If the lamp fails to light, inspect for a burned out bulb, disconnected socket, a broken or disconnected wire at the switch.

To test the brake warning system, raise the vehicle and open a wheel bleeder valve while a helper depresses the brake pedal and observes the warning light on the instrument panel. If the bulb fails to light, inspect for a burned out bulb, disconnected socket, or a broken or disconnected wire at the switch. If the bulb is not burned out, and wire continuity is proven, replace the brake warning switch.

Combination Valve

The combination valve is a metering valve, failure warning switch, and a proportioned in one assembly and is used on disc brake applications. The metering valve delays front disc braking until the rear drum brake shoes contact the drum. The failure warning switch is actuated in event of front or rear brake system failure, in turn activating a dash warning lamp. The proportioned balances front to rear braking action during rapid deceleration.

Combination valves used on diagonally split brake systems do not use metering valves instead two proportioning valves are used.

METERING VALVE

When the brakes are not applied, the metering valve permits the brake fluid to flow through the valve, thus allowing the fluid to expand and contract with temperature changes.

When the brakes are initially applied, the metering valve, stem moves to the left, preventing fluid to flow through the valve to the

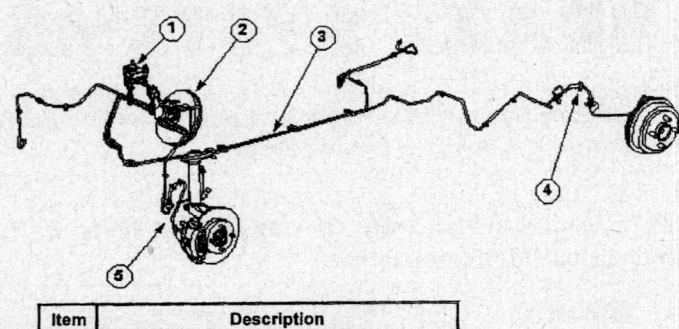

Item	Description
1	Brake fluid reservoir
2	Brake booster and master cylinder
3	Brake hydraulic tubes
4	Rear brake hose
5	Front brake hose

ARM66FM000000402

Fig. 1 Diagonally split brake system

front disc brakes. This is accomplished by the smooth end of the metering valve stem contacting the metering valve seal lip at 4–30 psi. The metering valve spring holds the retainer against the seal until a predetermined pressure is produced at the valve inlet port which overcomes the spring pressure and permits hydraulic pressure to actuate the front disc brakes. The increased pressure into the valve is metered through the valve seal, to the front disc brakes, producing an increased force on the diaphragm. The diaphragm then pulls the pin, in turn pulling the retainer and reduces the spring pressure on the metering valve seal. Eventually, the pressure reaches a point at which the spring is pulled away by the diaphragm pin and retainer, leaving the metering valve unrestricted, permitting full pressure to pass through the metering valve.

On some applications, two- or three-way combination valves are used. The three-way combination valve consists of a metering valve, failure warning switch and a proportioned mounted in an aluminum body. The two-way combination valve consists of a failure warning switch and a proportioned. On models equipped with metering valves, the metering valve release rod must be pushed in during bleeding operations on the front wheels.

FAILURE WARNING SWITCH

If the rear brake system fails, the front system pressure forces the switch piston to one side. The switch pin is then forced up into the switch, completing the electrical circuit and activates the dash warning lamp.

When repairs are made and pressure returns to the system, the piston moves to the left, resetting the switch. The detent on the piston requires approximately 100–450 psi to permit full reset of the piston. In event of front brake system failure, the piston moves to the left and the same sequence of events is followed as for rear system failure except the piston resets to the right.

PROPORTIONER OR PRESSURE CONTROL VALVE

During rapid deceleration, a portion of vehicle weight is transferred to the front wheels. This resultant loss of weight at rear wheels must be compensated for to avoid early rear wheel skid. The proportioned or pressure control valve reduces rear brake system pressure, delaying rear wheel skid. When the proportioned or pressure control valve is incorporated in the combination valve assembly, pressure developed within the valve acts against the large end of the piston, overcoming the spring pressure, moving the piston. The piston then contacts the stem seat and restricts line pressure through the valve.

During normal braking operation, the proportioned or pressure control valve is not functional. Brake fluid flows into the proportioned or pressure control valve between the piston center hole and the valve stem, through the stop plate and to the rear brakes. Spring pressure loads the piston during normal braking, causing it to rest against the stop plate.

On diagonally split brake systems, two proportioners or pressure control valves are used. One controls the left rear brake, the other the right rear brake. On front wheel drive models less power brakes, the proportioners or pressure control valves are located in the combination valve. On front wheel drive models with power brakes, the proportioners or pressure control valves are installed in the master cylinder rear brake outlet ports.

Brake Distribution Valve & Switch

This switch assembly which is used on some diagonally split brake systems, is connected to the outlet ports of the master cylinder and also to the brake warning light that warns the driver if either the primary or secondary brake system has failed.

When hydraulic pressure is equal in both primary and secondary brake systems, the switch remains centered. If pressure fails in one of the systems, hydraulic pressure moves the piston toward the inoperative side. The shoulder of the piston contacts the switch terminal, providing a ground and lighting the warning lamp.

Proportioning Valve & Switch

DESCRIPTION

The proportioning valve provides balanced braking action between front and rear brakes under a wide range of braking conditions. The valve regulates the hydraulic pressure applied to the rear wheel cylinders, thus limiting rear braking action when high pressures are required at the front brakes. In this manner, premature rear wheel skid is prevented.

TESTING

When a premature rear wheel slide is obtained on a brake application, it usually is an indication that the fluid pressure to the rear wheels is above the 50% reduction ratio for the rear line pressure and that fault has occurred within the proportioning valve.

To test the valve, install gauge set in brake line between master cylinder and proportioning valve, and at output end of proportioning valve and brake line as outlined. Ensure all joints are fluid tight.

Have a helper exert pressure on brake pedal (holding pressure). Obtain a reading on master cylinder output of approximately 700 psi. While pressure is being held as above, reading on valve outlet should be 550–610 psi. If the pressure readings do not meet these specifications, the valve should be removed and a new valve installed.

COMPONENT REPLACEMENT

Master Cylinder

CROWN VICTORIA, GRAND MARQUIS, MARAUDER, MUSTANG & TOWN CAR

1. Depress brake pedal several times to exhaust system vacuum.
2. Disconnect master cylinder brake lines and electrical connectors.
3. Disconnect hydraulic control unit supply hose at master cylinder. Secure hose aside.
4. Remove two mounting bolts, then secure proportioning valve and tubes aside.
5. Remove mounting nuts and master cylinder.
6. Reverse procedure to install.

FOCUS

1. Disconnect electrical connector and remove filler cap.

2. Raise and support vehicle, remove front tire and wheel assemblies.
3. Drain brake fluid into suitable container.
4. Lower vehicle and install brake fluid cap.
5. Remove air cleaner and tube.
6. Disconnect electrical connector, then remove retaining screw and central box.
7. Disconnect brake fluid feed tube and remove remaining brake tubes.
8. Remove brake booster vacuum hose.
9. Remove master cylinder.
10. Reverse procedure to install.

LS & THUNDERBIRD

1. Disconnect fluid level sensor connector.
2. Remove mounting nuts and hose, then position Vapor Management Valve (VMV) aside.
3. Disconnect brake tubes.
4. Disconnect brake master cylinder IVD solenoid electrical connector.
5. Remove brake master cylinder mounting nuts.
6. Disconnect, then position fuel line and vapor management hose aside.
7. Remove brake master cylinder.
8. Reverse procedure to install. Bleed brake system.

FIVE HUNDRED, FREESTYLE, MONTEGO, SABLE, TAURUS & TAURUS X

1. Disconnect brake fluid level sensor electrical connector.
2. Loosen fittings and disconnect brake tubes from master cylinder.
3. Remove mounting bolts and master cylinder.
4. Reverse procedure to install. Bleed system.

FUSION, MILAN, MKZ & ZEPHYR

1. Disconnect brake fluid level warning switch electrical connector, **Fig. 2.**
2. Remove brake fluid from master cylinder reservoir using suitable suction device.
3. **On models equipped with manual transaxle,** disconnect clutch master cylinder feed hose. Plug clutch master cylinder feed hose openings.
4. **On all models,** disconnect brake tube fittings. Plug brake tubes and brake master cylinder openings.
5. Remove master cylinder mounting nuts, then the master cylinder.
6. Reverse procedure to install, noting the following:
   a. **On models equipped with manual transaxle,** bleed clutch master cylinder as outlined under "Clutch System Bleeding."
   b. **On all models,** bleed brake master cylinder as outlined under "Brake System Bleed."
   c. Inspect system for normal operation.

Wheel Cylinders

REMOVAL

1. Remove wheel, drum and brake shoes.
2. Disconnect hydraulic line at wheel cylinder. **Do not pull metal line away from cylinder.** Line will separate from cylinder when cylinder is moved away from brake backing plate.
3. Remove mounting screws and cylinder from brake plate.

INSTALLATION

1. Wipe end of hydraulic line to remove any foreign matter.
2. Place hydraulic cylinder in position. Enter tubing into cylinder and start connecting fitting.
3. Secure cylinder to backing plate and then complete tightening of tubing fitting.
4. Install brake shoes, drum and wheel.
5. Bleed system as outlined in "Brake System Bleed."

COMPONENT SERVICE

Master Cylinder

DISASSEMBLE

1. Clean outside of master cylinder thoroughly. Drain brake fluid from master cylinder into suitable container.
2. Remove stop bolt and pressure control valves.
3. Pry up and remove reservoir from master cylinder body.
4. Remove fluid control valve.
5. Depress primary piston and remove snap ring from retaining groove at open end of bore.
6. Remove primary and secondary piston assemblies from master cylinder. If secondary piston does not come out, apply air pressure to secondary outlet port to remove.

INSPECTION

1. Wash components in clean brake fluid only. Use an air hose to blow out all passages, orifices and valve holes.
2. Air dry and place components on clean paper or lint-free cloth.
3. Inspect master cylinder bore for scoring, rust, pitting or etching. Any of these conditions will require housing replacement.
4. Inspect master cylinder pistons for scoring, pitting or distortion. Replace piston if any of these conditions exist.
5. If either master cylinder housing or piston is replaced, clean new components with clean brake fluid and blow out all passages with air hose.
6. Examine reservoirs for foreign matter and inspect all passages for restrictions. If there is any suspicion of contamination or evidence of corrosion, completely flush hydraulic system.
7. When overhauling a master cylinder, use all components contained in repair kit.

8. Dip all cups, seals, pistons, springs, check valves and retainers in clean brake fluid and place in clean pan or on clean paper.
9. Wash hands with soap and water only to prevent contamination of rubber components from oil, kerosene or gasoline.
10. During assembly, dip all components in clean brake fluid.
11. Inspect through side outlet of dual master cylinder housing to ensure cup lips do not hang up on edge of hole or turn back, which would result in faulty operation. Piece of 3/16 inch rod with an end rounded off will help guide cups past hole.
12. Inspect aluminum master cylinder bore for corrosion. If corroded, replace master cylinder. **Do not hone or use abrasives on bore.**

ASSEMBLE

1. Coat replacement piston assemblies in clean heavy duty DOT 3 brake fluid.
2. Install secondary piston into bore, spring end first.
3. Install primary piston, spring end first.
4. Depress primary piston and install snap ring.
5. Install fluid control valve and **torque** to 96–120 inch lbs.
6. Install stop bolt and pressure control valves.
7. Lubricate new reservoir grommets with brake fluid and install in master cylinder body.
8. Install reservoir into new grommets.
9. Fill and bench bleed master cylinder.

Wheel Cylinders

1. Refer to **Fig. 3** when serving wheel cylinders.
2. Place all components, except cylinder casting in clean brake fluid. Wipe cylinder walls with clean brake fluid.
3. Examine cylinder bore. A scored bore may be honed providing diameter is not increased more than .005 inch. Replace worn or damaged components from repair kit.
4. Wash hands with soap and water only, as oil, kerosene or gasoline will contaminate rubber components.
5. Lubricate cylinder wall and rubber cups with brake fluid.
6. Install springs, cups, pistons and boots in housing.

BRAKE SYSTEM BLEED

Pressure bleeding is recommended for all hydraulic brake systems. Ensure all dirt and contaminants are removed from master cylinder area prior to removing reservoir cap.

To prevent air from the pressure tank getting into the lines, do not shake the tank while air is being added to the tank or after it has been pressurized. Set the tank in the required location, bring the air hose to the tank, and do not move it during the bleeding operation. The tank should be kept at least one-third full.

HYDRAULIC BRAKE SYSTEMS

On vehicles equipped with disc brakes and master cylinders without proportioners or pressure control valves located in the master cylinder outlet port, the brake metering valve or combination valve must be held in position using suitable tool.

If air does get into the fluid, releasing the pressure will cause the bubbles to increase in size, rise to the top of the fluid, and escape. Pressure should not be greater than about 35 psi.

On vehicles equipped with plastic reservoirs, do not exceed 25 psi during bleeding pressure.

When bleeding without pressure, open the bleed valve three-quarters of a turn, depress the pedal a full stroke, then allow the pedal to return slowly to its released position. It is suggested that after the pedal has been depressed to the end of its stroke, the bleeder valve should be closed before the start of the return stroke. On models with power brakes, first reduce the vacuum in the power unit to zero by pumping the brake pedal several times with the engine off before starting to bleed the system.

Pressure bleeding eliminates the need for pedal pumping.

Discard drained or bled brake fluid. Care should be taken not to spill brake fluid, since this can damage the finish of the car.

Flushing is essential if there is water, mineral oil or other contaminants in the lines, and whenever new components are installed in the hydraulic system. Fluid contamination is usually indicated by swollen and deteriorated cups and other rubber components.

Wheel cylinders on disc brakes are equipped with bleeder valves, and are bled in the same manner as wheel cylinders for drum brakes.

Bleeding is required on all four wheels if air has entered the system because of low fluid level, or the line or lines have been disconnected. If a line is disconnected at any one wheel cylinder, that cylinder only need be bled. On brake reline jobs, bleeding is advisable to remove any air or contaminants.

Master cylinders equipped with bleeder valves should be bled first before the wheel cylinders are bled. In all cases where a master cylinder has been overhauled, it must be bled. Where there is no bleeder valve, this can be done by leaving the lines loose, actuating the brake pedal to expel the air and then tightening the lines.

After overhauling a dual master cylinder used in conjunction with disc brakes, it is advisable to bleed the cylinder before installing it on the car. The reason for this recommendation is that air may be trapped between the master cylinder pistons because there is only one residual pressure valve (check valve) used in these units.

System Priming

When a new master cylinder has been installed or the brake system emptied or partially emptied, fluid may not flow from the bleeder screws during normal bleeding. It may be required to prime the system using the following procedure:

1. Remove brake lines from master cylinder.
2. Install short brake lines in master cylinder and position them back into reservoir, ensure short brake line ends are submerged in reservoir brake fluid.
3. Fill reservoir with recommended brake fluid, then cover master cylinder fluid reservoir with shop towel.
4. Pump brakes until clear, bubble free fluid comes out of both brake lines. **If any brake fluid spills on paint, wash it off immediately with water.**
5. Remove short brake lines, then reinstall original brake lines.
6. Bleed each brake line at master cylinder using the following procedure:
   a. Have assistant pump brake pedal ten times, then hold firm pressure on pedal.
   b. Open rearmost brake line fittings with a tubing wrench until a stream of brake fluid comes out. Have assistant maintain pressure on brake pedal until brake line fitting is tightened again.
   c. Repeat this operation until clear, bubble free fluid comes out from around tube fitting.
   d. Repeat this bleeding operation at front brake line fitting.
7. If any of brake lines or calipers have been removed, it may be helpful to prime system by gravity bleeding. this should be done after the master cylinder is primed and bled. To prime the system using the gravity method, proceed as follows:
   a. Fill master cylinder with recommended brake fluid.
   b. Loosen both rear bleeder screws and leave them open until clear brake fluid flows out. **Inspect reservoir fluid level frequently; do not allow fluid level to drop below half full.**
   c. Tighten rear bleeder screws.
   d. Loosen bleeder screw on front caliper, leave open until clear fluid flows out. **Bleed front calipers one side at a time.**
8. After master cylinder has been primed, lines bled at master cylinder and brake system primed, normal brake system bleeding can be resumed at each wheel.

Wheel Bleeding Sequence

Rear Wheel Drive...............RR-LR-RF-LF
Front Wheel Drive ....RR-LF-LR-RF

CLUTCH SYSTEM BLEEDING

1. Attach a rubber drain hose to bleeder screw of clutch master cylinder, then submerge free end of hose in a container partially filled with clean brake fluid.
2. Slowly pump clutch pedal to floor several times and hold it.
3. With clutch pedal held to floor, loosen bleeder screw until fluid and air are expelled from system.
4. With clutch pedal held to floor, tighten bleeder screw.
5. Repeat steps two through four until no air bubbles appear in fluid.
6. Add suitable brake fluid to reservoir. Fill to level in between MIN and MAX lines.

HYDRAULIC BRAKE SYSTEM FLUSH

Whenever new brake components are installed in the hydraulic system, it is recommended that the entire hydraulic system be thoroughly flushed with clean brake fluid.

It may sometime become required to flush out the system due to the presence of mineral oil, kerosene, gasoline, etc., which will cause swelling of rubber piston cups and valves and render them inoperative.

Flushing is performed at each wheel in the same manner as the bleeding operation except that the bleeder valve is opened 1½ turns and the fluid is forced through the lines and bleeder valve until it emerges clear in color, **Fig. 4.** Approximately one quart of clean brake fluid is required to flush the hydraulic system. After completing the flushing operation at all bleeder valves, inspect to ensure the master cylinder is filled to the proper level.

NOTE: Automatic transmission shown, manual transmission similar.

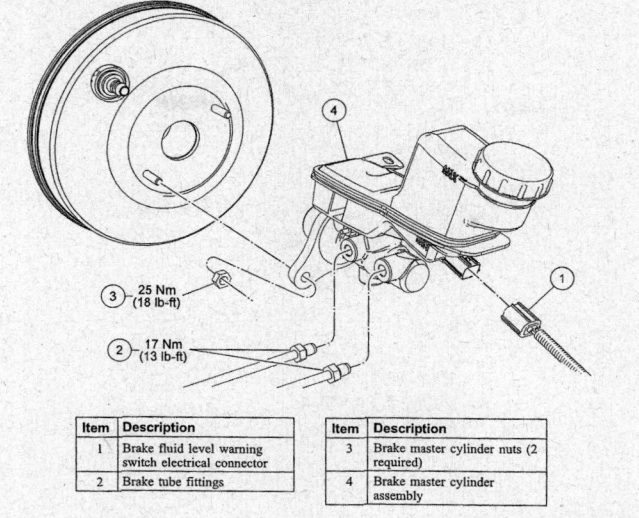

Item	Description		Item	Description
1	Brake fluid level warning switch electrical connector		3	Brake master cylinder nuts (2 required)
2	Brake tube fittings		4	Brake master cylinder assembly

ARM0500000000788

Fig. 2 Master cylinder replacement. Fusion, Milan, MKZ & Zephyr

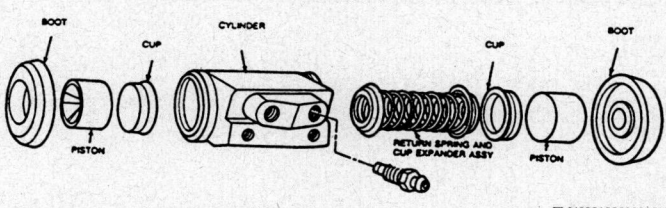

FM4099100008000X

Fig. 3 Exploded view of typical wheel cylinder

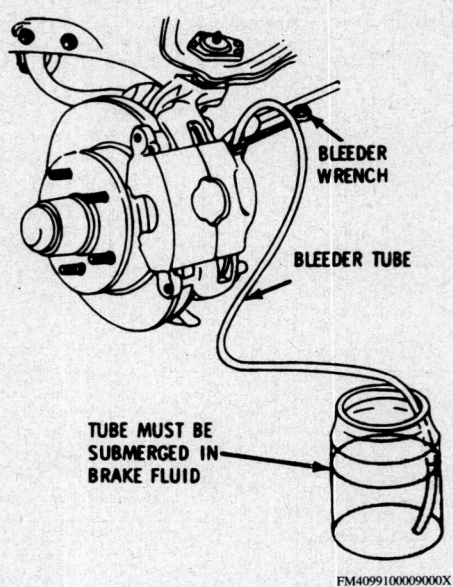

BLEEDER
WRENCH

BLEEDER TUBE

TUBE MUST BE
SUBMERGED IN
BRAKE FLUID

FM4099100009000X

**Fig. 4   Hydraulic brake system
flushing**

POWER BRAKE UNITS

NOTE: On Models Equipped With Anti-Lock Brakes, Refer To "Anti-Lock Brake" Section.

NOTE: On Air Bag Equipped Models, Refer To "Air Bag System Precautions" Located In The Front Of This Manual For System Disarming & Arming Procedures.

NOTE: Refer To "Computer Relearn Procedures" Located In The Front Of This Manual When Battery Power To The Computer Has Been Interrupted.

INDEX

	Page No.
Adjustments	17-3
Bendix System	17-3
Single Diaphragm Booster	17-3
Application Chart	17-1
Description	17-2
Bendix Diaphragm System	17-2
Bendix Hydro-Boost System	17-2
Vacuum Assist Diaphragm System	17-2
Power Brake Unit Service	17-3
Overhaul	17-4
Power Booster, Replace	17-3
Crown Victoria, Grand Marquis, Marauder & Town Car	17-3

	Page No.
Five Hundred, Freestyle, Montego, Sable, Taurus & Taurus X	17-4
Focus	17-4
Fusion, Milan, MKZ & Zephyr	17-4
LS & Thunderbird	17-4
Mustang	17-4
Precautions	17-2
Air Bag Systems	17-2
Battery Ground Cable	17-2
Troubleshooting	17-2
Bendix Diaphragm System	17-3
Brakes Grab	17-3
Hard Pedal Or No Assist	17-3
No Or Slow Release	17-3

	Page No.
Bendix Hydro-Boost System	17-3
Erratic Booster Operation, Binding, Grabbing Or Sticking	17-3
No Power Assist	17-3

APPLICATION CHART

Model	Year	Power Brake Booster System
Crown Victoria	2004–08	Bendix Tandem Diaphragm
Five Hundred	2005–07	Dual Diaphragm
Focus	2004–07	Single Diaphragm
Freestyle	2005–07	Dual Diaphragm
Fusion	2006–08	Single Diaphragm
Grand Marquis	2004–08	Bendix Tandem Diaphragm
LS	2004–06	Dual Diaphragm
Marauder	2004	Bendix Tandem Diaphragm
Milan	2006–08	Single Diaphragm
MKZ	2007–08	Single Diaphragm
Montego	2005–07	Dual Diaphragm
Mustang	2004	①
	2005–08	Dual Diaphragm
Sable	2004–05	Bendix Single Diaphragm
	2008	Bendix Single Diaphragm
Taurus	2004–07	Bendix Single Diaphragm
	2008	Bendix Single Diaphragm
Taurus X	2008	Dual Diaphragm
Thunderbird	2004–05	Dual Diaphragm
Town Car	2004–08	Bendix Tandem Diaphragm
Zephyr	2006	Single Diaphragm

① — 3.8L and 4.0L engines, Bendix Tandem Diaphragm. 4.6L engine, Bendix Hydro-Boost system.

PRECAUTIONS

Air Bag Systems

Refer to "Air Bag System Precautions" in the front of this manual for system disarming and arming procedures.

Battery Ground Cable

Prior to service, disconnect battery ground cable and isolate as required.

DESCRIPTION

Bendix Diaphragm System

These units are of the vacuum suspended system. Some units are of the single diaphragm system, while others are of the tandem diaphragm system. Both single piston and double piston or split system master cylinders are used.

The vacuum suspended diaphragm system units utilize engine manifold vacuum and atmospheric pressure for its power. It consists of three basic elements combined into a single power unit. The three basic elements of the single diaphragm system are:

1. Vacuum power section which includes front and rear shell, power diaphragm, return spring and pushrod.
2. Control valve, built integral with power diaphragm and connected through valve rod to brake pedal, controls degree of brake application or release in accordance with pressure applied to brake pedal.
3. Hydraulic master cylinder, attached to vacuum power section which contains all elements of conventional brake master cylinder except for pushrod, supplies fluid under pressure to wheel brakes in proportion to pressure applied to brake pedal.

Upon application of the brakes, the valve rod and plunger move to the lefthand in the power diaphragm to close the vacuum port and open the atmospheric port to admit air through the air cleaner and valve at the rear diaphragm chamber. With vacuum present in the rear chamber, a force is developed to move the power diaphragm, hydraulic pushrod and hydraulic piston or pistons to close the compensating port or ports and force fluid under pressure through the residual check valve or valves and lines into the front and rear wheel cylinders to actuate the brakes.

As pressure is developed within the master cylinder a counter force acting through the hydraulic pushrod and reaction disc against the vacuum power diaphragm and valve plunger sets up a reaction force opposing the force applied to the valve rod and plunger. This reaction force tends to close the atmospheric port and reopen the vacuum port. Since this force is in opposition to the force applied to the brake pedal by the driver it gives the driver a feel of the amount of brake applied. The proportion of

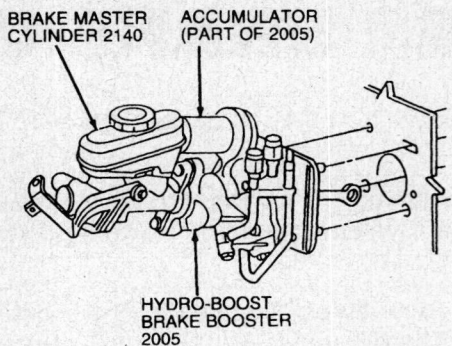

BRAKE MASTER CYLINDER 2140   ACCUMULATOR (PART OF 2005)

HYDRO-BOOST BRAKE BOOSTER 2005

FM4099600012000X

Fig. 1 Bendix Hydro-Boost

reactive force applied to the valve plunger through the reaction disc is designed into the Master-Vac to ensure maximum power consistent with maintaining pedal feel. The reaction force is in direct proportion to the hydraulic pressure developed within the brake system.

Bendix Hydro-Boost System

The Bendix Hydro-Boost System is a hydraulically operated booster with fluid provided by the power steering pump, **Fig. 1.** If power steering fluid flow is interrupted, a reserve accumulator system stores enough fluid under pressure to provide at least two power-assisted stops. Manual brake application is permitted if the reserve system is depleted.

The Hydro-Boost booster, power steering pump and hydraulic hoses are all serviced separately. If the booster becomes inoperative or is damaged, it must be replaced as an assembly.

Vacuum Assist Diaphragm System

The vacuum assist diaphragm assembly multiplies the force exerted on the master cylinder piston in order to increase the hydraulic pressure delivered to the wheel cylinders while decreasing the effort required to obtain acceptable stopping performance.

Vacuum assist units get their energy by opposing engine vacuum to atmospheric pressure. A piston, cylinder and flexible diaphragm utilize this energy to provide brake assistance. The diaphragm is balanced with engine vacuum until the brake pedal is depressed, allowing atmospheric pressure to unbalance the unit and apply force to the brake system.

Brakes will operate even if the power unit fails. This means the conventional brake system and the power assist system are completely separate. Troubleshooting conventional and power assist systems are exactly the same until the power unit is reached. As with conventional hydraulic brakes, a spongy pedal still means air is trapped in the hydraulic system. Power brakes give higher line pressure, making leaks more critical.

TROUBLESHOOTING

Power brake operation concerns should be handled as if two separate systems exist.

1. Inspect for faults in hydraulic system first.
2. If hydraulic system is satisfactory, inspect power brake circuit.
3. Press brake pedal firmly and then start engine.
4. Pedal should fall away slightly and less pressure should be needed to maintain pedal in any position.
5. Install of suitable pressure gauge in brake hydraulic system.
6. Record pressure with engine off and power unit not operating.
7. Maintain pedal height, start engine and record measurement.
8. There should be substantial pressure increase in second measurement.
9. Pedal travel should be kept strictly to specifications.
10. Measure manifold vacuum or inspect operation of external vacuum pump if power unit is not giving enough assistance. On emission controlled engines, manifold vacuum readings may be less than 15 inches Hg. at idle.
11. If manifold vacuum is abnormally low, tune engine and then inspect power brakes.
12. Loose vacuum lines and clogged air intake filters will cut down brake efficiency.
13. Most units have check valve that retains some vacuum in system when engine is off. Vacuum gauge inspection of this valve will tell when it is restricted, stuck open or closed.
14. Failure of brakes to release in most instances is caused by tight or misaligned connection between power unit and brake linkage.
15. If this connection is free, look for broken piston, diaphragm or bellows and return spring.
16. Loosen connection between master cylinder and brake booster.
17. If brakes release, trouble is in power unit; if brakes still will not release, look for restricted brake line or similar difficulties in regular hydraulic circuit.
18. Residual pressure check valve is usually located immediately under brake line connection on hydraulic assist power brakes.
19. This valve maintains slight hydraulic pressure within brake lines and wheel cylinders to give better pedal response. If it is sticking, brakes may not release.
20. Power brakes that have hard pedal are usually suffering from milder form of same ills that cause complete power unit failure. Collapsed or leaking vacuum lines or insufficient manifold vacuum, as well as punctured diaphragms or bellows and leaky piston seals, all lead to weak power unit operation.
21. Steady hiss when brake is held down means vacuum leak that will cause poor power unit operation.
22. Do not immediately condemn power unit if brakes grab. Proceed as follows:

a. Look for greasy linings, scored rotors or drums.
b. Investigate power unit.
c. Inspect for damaged reaction control. Reaction control is usually made up of diaphragm, spring and valves that tends to resist pedal action. It is put in system to give the pedal feel.

23. **On models equipped with Bendix Hydro-Boost system,** proceed as follows:
 a. Ensure engine is in off position.
 b. Press and release brake pedal several times to relieve all hydraulic pressure from booster.
 c. Depress and hold pedal with light pressure.
 d. Start engine and note pedal reaction.
 e. If it does not fall slightly and hold, press and release pedal several times, then depress and hold with medium foot pressure.
 f. If the pedal now moves toward floor, inspect for brake fluid leakage at master cylinder, brake hoses and all connections, **Fig. 2.**
 g. Idle engine, then depress and hold brake pedal for no more than five seconds with heavy foot pressure.
 h. If booster shows any signs of fluid leakage, it must be replaced.
24. **On all models,** operating engine at idle, then depress and hold brake pedal for not less than five seconds with heavy foot pressure or holding steering wheel at full stop.
25. Turn ignition switch to Off position and wait 8–12 hours.
26. Depress brake pedal and inspect for reserve.
27. If no reserve is present, booster is faulty.

Bendix Diaphragm System

HARD PEDAL OR NO ASSIST

1. Air cleaner element clogged.
2. Control valve faulty.
3. Faulty diaphragm.
4. Worn or distorted reaction plate or levers.
5. Cracked or broken power piston or levers.
6. Internal or external leaks.

BRAKES GRAB

1. Control valve faulty or sticking.
2. Bind in linkage.
3. Reaction diaphragm leaking.
4. Worn or distorted levers or plate.

NO OR SLOW RELEASE

1. Pushrod adjustment improper.
2. Linkage binding.
3. Return spring faulty.

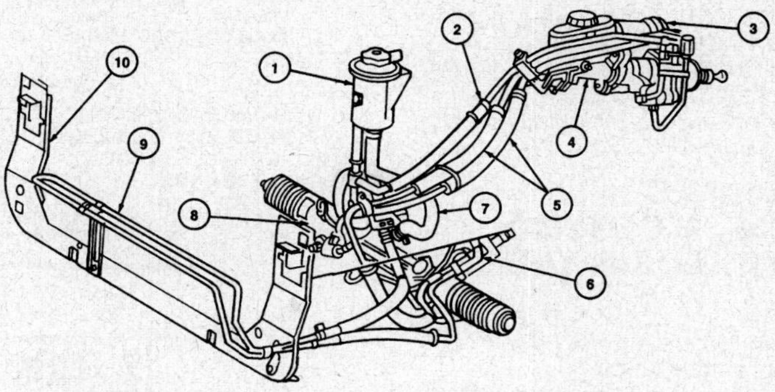

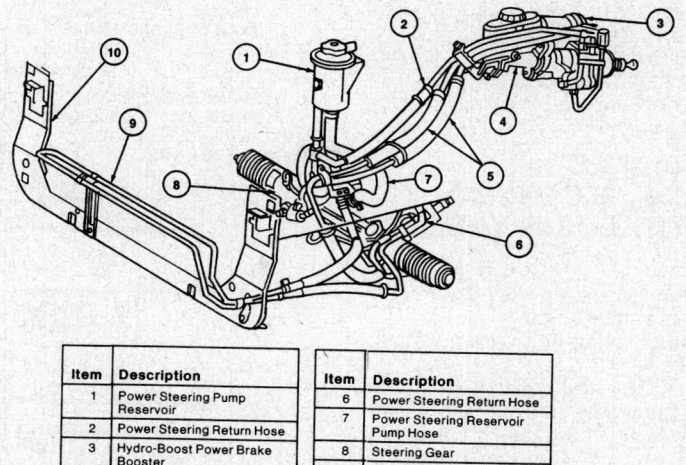

Item	Description
1	Power Steering Pump Reservoir
2	Power Steering Return Hose
3	Hydro-Boost Power Brake Booster
4	Brake Master Cylinder
5	Power Steering Pressure Hose
6	Power Steering Return Hose
7	Power Steering Reservoir Pump Hose
8	Steering Gear
9	Power Steering Fluid Cooler
10	Radiator Support

FM4099600013000X

Fig. 2 Hydro-Boost system fluid distribution. Mustang w/4.6L engine

Bendix Hydro-Boost System

NO POWER ASSIST

1. Power steering pump drive belt slipping or worn.
2. Power steering pump fluid level improper.
3. Linkage binding.
4. Hydro-Boost unit failure.

ERRATIC BOOSTER OPERATION, BINDING, GRABBING OR STICKING

1. Supply hose leakage or obstructions.
2. Hydro-Boost unit seal leakage.

ADJUSTMENTS

Bendix System

1. Disconnect master cylinder from booster leaving brake lines connected and secure cylinder aside.
2. Start engine and operate engine at idle speed.
3. With engine running, position gauge over pushrod. Gauge should bottom against booster housing with force of approximately five lbs. applied to pushrod, **Fig. 3. Ensure pushrod is properly seated in booster when performing gauge inspection.**
4. If force required to seat gauge is more than five lbs., shorten length of pushrod.
5. If force required to seat gauge is less than five lbs., lengthen pushrod.
6. Install master cylinder and remove reservoir cover.
7. With engine running, observe fluid surface in reservoir when brakes are applied and released rapidly. If no movement is observed on fluid surface, pushrod is adjusted too long.

Single Diaphragm Booster

1. Remove master cylinder.
2. Position master cylinder gauge T87C-2500-A, or equivalent, on end of master cylinder.
3. Loosen setscrew and push gauge plunger against bottom of primary piston.
4. While holding gauge in position, tighten setscrew.
5. Invert gauge and place over brake booster pushrod. Measurement should be zero.
6. If clearance is not zero, loosen pushrod locknut and adjust pushrod.
7. Reverse procedure to install.

POWER BRAKE UNIT SERVICE

Power Booster, Replace

CROWN VICTORIA, GRAND MARQUIS, MARAUDER & TOWN CAR

1. Disconnect fluid level sensor connector.
2. Position speed control cable aside.
3. Disconnect power brake booster check valve.
4. Remove brake master cylinder mounting nuts.
5. Remove wiring harness bracket and position aside.
6. Remove brake master cylinder and position aside.
7. Remove push-pins and instrument close-out panel.
8. Remove stoplight switch retaining pin.

9. Slide stoplight switch and booster push rod off brake pedal pin.
10. Remove mounting nuts and power brake booster.
11. Reverse procedure to install. **Torque** mounting nuts to 16–21 ft. lbs.

FIVE HUNDRED, FREESTYLE, MONTEGO, SABLE, TAURUS & TAURUS X

1. Disconnect Mass Air Flow (MAF) sensor and breather tubes.
2. Disconnect outlet tube from throttle body.
3. Remove cover and position engine air cleaner housing aside.
4. Remove wiper mounting arm and pivot shaft.
5. Remove brake master cylinder as outlined in "Hydraulic Brake Systems" chapter.
6. Disconnect electrical connector and remove mounting nuts, then position speed control module and bracket aside.
7. Disconnect manual control lever cable from transmission range sensor, then remove manual cable bracket and nut.
8. Remove mounting bolts and position manual cable bracket aside.
9. Remove vacuum outlet manifold.
10. Disconnect vacuum check valve from brake booster.
11. Remove retainer strap and position heater hose aside.
12. Remove wiring harnesses and connectors from brake booster.
13. Remove steering column opening cover.
14. Disconnect stoplight switch electrical connector, then remove retainer and push rod off pin.
15. Remove stoplight switch, washer and bushing.
16. Remove and discard brake booster mounting nuts.
17. Remove brake booster.
18. Reverse procedure to install, noting the following:
    a. Adjust pushrod as outlined in "Adjustments."
    b. Install new brake booster mounting nuts.

FOCUS

1. Remove master cylinder as outlined in "Hydraulic Brake Systems" chapter.
2. **On models equipped with speed control,** disconnect electrical connector and remove speed control unit.
3. **On all models,** remove brake tubes from bulkhead retainers.
4. Disconnect hydraulic control unit electrical connector.
5. Disconnect brake lines from hydraulic control unit. Cap all fittings.
6. Remove brake booster actuating rod from brake pedal.
7. Remove mounting nuts and brake booster.
8. Reverse procedure to install.

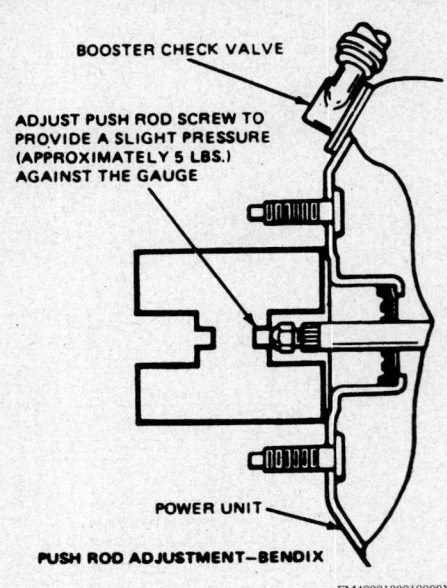

BOOSTER CHECK VALVE

ADJUST PUSH ROD SCREW TO PROVIDE A SLIGHT PRESSURE (APPROXIMATELY 5 LBS.) AGAINST THE GAUGE

POWER UNIT

PUSH ROD ADJUSTMENT–BENDIX

FM4099100010000X

Fig. 3 Master cylinder pushrod adjustment. Bendix system vacuum booster

FUSION, MILAN, MKZ & ZEPHYR

1. Remove brake master cylinder as outlined under "Component Replacement."
2. Remove Powertrain Control Module (PCM) mounting bolts, disconnect PCM ground, then position module and wire harness aside.
3. Remove battery and battery tray.
4. Disconnect brake tube clip, PCM mounting bracket bolts and bracket.
5. **On models equipped with automatic transaxle,** remove transmission fluid level indicator tube bolt, then position tube aside.
6. **On all models,** remove brake booster push rod pin and clip, **Fig. 4,** then disconnect push rod from brake pedal.
7. Remove four brake booster mounting nuts, then the booster.
8. Reverse procedure to install, noting the following:
    a. Prior to installation, ensure distance between booster mating surface to pushrod center point, **Fig. 5,** is approximately 5.12 inches (130 mm).
    b. **Torque** booster push rod jam nut to 13 ft. lbs.
    c. Torque power booster mounting nuts to 17 ft. lbs.

LS & THUNDERBIRD

1. Remove mounting nuts and wiper arms, then disconnect washer hose.
2. Remove push-pins, rubber trim and cowl cover.
3. Remove mounting nut and position vacuum hose bracket aside.
4. Remove cowl brace center and end bolts, then the bracket.

5. Disconnect coolant reservoir return hose.
6. Remove brake master cylinder.
7. Disconnect power brake booster check valve and electrical connector.
8. Remove coolant reservoir mounting bolts and disconnect hose.
9. Remove coolant reservoir.
10. Remove clip and brake pedal pin.
11. Remove mounting nuts and power brake booster.
12. Reverse procedure to install.

MUSTANG

3.8L ENGINE

1. Remove air cleaner housing.
2. Remove mounting nuts and position master cylinder aside.
3. Discharge accumulator by depress brake pedal several times with engine off.
4. Disconnect booster vacuum hose.
5. Remove stop lamp self-locking pin.
6. Remove stop lamp switch and brake booster push rod from brake pedal pin.
7. Remove mounting nuts and power brake booster.
8. Reverse procedure to install. **Torque** power brake booster and brake master cylinder mounting nuts to 19 ft. lbs.

4.6L ENGINE

Do not carry the booster by the accumulator. Do not drop booster on accumulator. Keep the accumulator away from excessive heat, fire or incineration. Before disposal, drill a 1/16 inch diameter hole in the accumulator can's end to relieve the high pressure nitrogen gas pressure. Wear safety glasses while performing this operation. Do not activate the booster when the master cylinder has been removed.

1. Apply brake pedal several times to discharge accumulator.
2. Disconnect brake fluid level sensor electrical connector.
3. Disconnect brake lines.
4. Disconnect power steering return and pressure lines.
5. Remove self-locking pin.
6. Remove stop lamp switch and brake booster push rod from brake pedal pin.
7. Remove mounting nuts and power brake booster.
8. Reverse procedure to install, noting the following:
    a. Install new Teflon seals on power steering pressure fittings.
    b. **Torque** booster nuts to 19 ft. lbs.
    c. **Torque** power steering pressure lines to 14 ft. lbs.
    d. **Torque** brake lines to 13 ft. lbs.

Overhaul

Overhaul is not required. Replace power brake unit as an assembly. In some instances, the only service required is replacement of the check valve, grommet and pushrod adjustment.

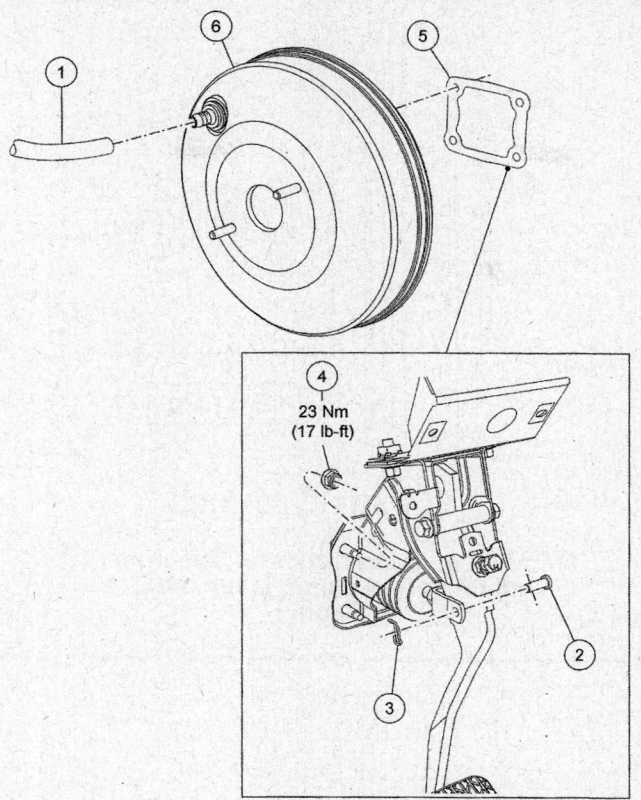

Item	Description	Item	Description
1	Vacuum hose/aspirator assembly	4	Brake booster nut (4 required)
2	Brake booster push rod pin	5	Brake booster-to-cowl gasket
3	Brake booster push rod clip	6	Brake booster with check valve

ARM0500000000789

Fig. 4   Power booster replacement. Fusion, Milan, MKZ & Zephyr

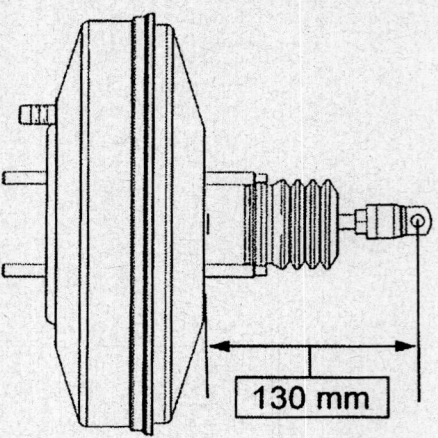

130mm= 5.12 inch

ARM0500000000790

Fig. 5   Power booster pushrod adjustment. Fusion, Milan, MKZ & Zephyr

FRONT WHEEL DRIVE AXLES

TABLE OF CONTENTS

Page No.

**FIVE HUNDRED, FREESTYLE,
MONTEGO, 2008 SABLE,
TAURUS & TAURUS X** 18-2
FOCUS 18-1

Page No.

**FUSION, MILAN, MKZ &
ZEPHYR** 18-4
**2004–05 SABLE & 2004–07
TAURUS** 18-6

Focus

NOTE: On Air Bag Equipped Models, Refer To "Air Bag System Precautions" Located In The Front Of This Manual For System Disarming & Arming Procedures.

NOTE: Refer To "Computer Relearn Procedures" Located In The Front Of This Manual When Battery Power To The Computer Has Been Interrupted.

INDEX

Page No.

Driveshaft, Replace 18-2
Driveshaft Service 18-2
Precautions 18-1
  Air Bag Systems 18-1
  Battery Ground Cable 18-1

Page No.

Tightening Specifications 18-2
Troubleshooting 18-1
  Clicking, Popping or Grinding
    Noises While Turning 18-1
  Halfshaft Joint Pullout 18-1

Page No.

Shudder Vibration During
  Acceleration 18-1
Vibration At Highway Speeds ... 18-1

PRECAUTIONS

Air Bag Systems

Refer to "Air Bag System Precautions" in the front of this manual for system disarming and arming procedures.

Battery Ground Cable

Prior to service, disconnect battery ground cable and isolate as required.

TROUBLESHOOTING

Clicking, Popping or Grinding Noises While Turning

1. Another component contacting halfshaft.
2. Inadequate or contaminated lube in outboard/inboard front wheel halfshaft joint.
3. Wheel bearings, brakes, suspension or steering components.

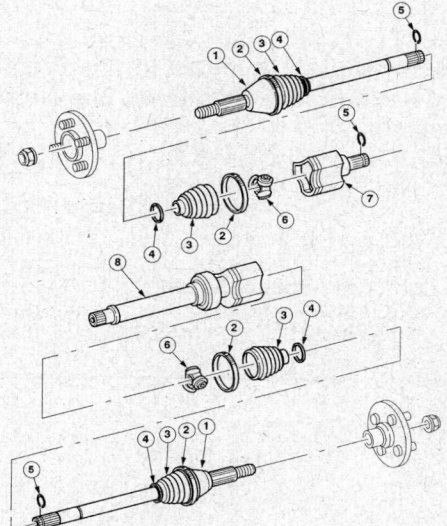

FM3030000338010X

Fig. 1 Exploded view of driveshaft (Part 1 of 2)

Vibration At Highway Speeds

1. Out of balance front wheels or tires.
2. Out of round tires.
3. Incorrectly seated outboard front wheel halfshaft joint in front wheel hub.

Shudder Vibration During Acceleration

1. Excessively high CV joint operating angles caused by incorrect ride height.
2. Excessively worn or damaged inboard front wheel halfshaft joint or outboard front wheel halfshaft joint.

Halfshaft Joint Pullout

1. Inboard halfshaft bearing retainer circlip missing or not correctly seated in differential side gear.
2. Engine/transaxle assembly misaligned.

3. Frame rail or strut tower out of position or damaged.
4. Front suspension components worn or damaged.

DRIVESHAFT
REPLACE

1. Loosen suspension strut locknut five turns.
2. Loosen driveshaft stub nut and front wheel nuts.
3. Raise and support vehicle, then remove front tire and wheel assembly.
4. Remove driveshaft stub nut.
5. Remove bolt and disconnect lower arm ball joint.
6. Remove hub nut and press halfshaft stub out from wheel hub using suitable

Item	Description
1	Fixed ball joint with front drive halfshaft
2	Clamping strap (large)
3	Boot
4	Clamping strap (small)
5	Snap-ring - CV joint, transmission end
6	Tripod star with constant velocity rollers
7	Tripode housing
8	Intermediate shaft with intermediate shaft bearing

FM3030000338020X

Fig. 1 Exploded view of driveshaft (Part 2 of 2)

puller. Mark nut usage. **Hub nut can be reused four times.**

7. Disconnect driveshaft from transaxle.
8. Remove driveshaft.
9. Reverse procedure to install.

DRIVESHAFT SERVICE

1. Hold intermediate shaft in suitable vise, then separate and discard clamping straps. Push back boot along shaft.
2. Pull apart tripod joint, then remove grease and tripod snap ring, **Fig. 1.**
3. Remove tripod using tool No. T81P-1104C, or equivalent, then the boot.
4. Separate and discard clamping straps. Remove boot over transaxle side and accessible grease.
5. Reverse procedure to assemble.

TIGHTENING SPECIFICATIONS

Year	Component	Torque Ft. Lbs.
2004–07	Ball Joint	63
	Driveshaft Nut	214
	Gaiter Clamps	15
	Hub Nut	214
	Suspension Strut Nut	35

Five Hundred, Freestyle, Montego, 2008 Sable, Taurus & Taurus X

NOTE: On Air Bag Equipped Models, Refer To "Air Bag System Precautions" Located In The Front Of This Manual For System Disarming & Arming Procedures.

NOTE: Refer To "Computer Relearn Procedures" Located In The Front Of This Manual When Battery Power To The Computer Has Been Interrupted.

INDEX

	Page No.
Driveshaft, Replace	18-3
Lefthand	18-3
Righthand	18-3
Driveshaft Service	18-3
Precautions	18-3

	Page No.
Air Bag Systems	18-3
Battery Ground Cable	18-3
Tightening Specifications	18-4
Troubleshooting	18-3
Driveshaft Or CV Joint Pull-Out	18-3

	Page No.
Noise & Vibration On Turns	18-3
Shudder Or Vibration On Acceleration	18-3
Vibration At Highway Speeds	18-3

PRECAUTIONS

Air Bag Systems

Refer to "Air Bag System Precautions" in the front of this manual for system disarming and arming procedures.

Battery Ground Cable

Prior to service, disconnect battery ground cable and isolate as required.

TROUBLESHOOTING

Noise & Vibration On Turns

1. Cut or damaged CV joint boots, resulting in contaminated lube in outboard or inboard CV joints.
2. Loose CV joint clamps.
3. Worn, damaged or improperly installed wheel bearings.
4. Foreign object contacting driveshaft assembly.

Shudder Or Vibration On Acceleration

1. Excessively worn or damaged inboard or outboard CV joint.
2. Excessively high CV joint operating angles caused by improper ride height.

Vibration At Highway Speeds

1. Front wheels or tires out of balance.
2. Improperly seated outboard CV joint in front wheel hub.
3. Bent intermediate driveshaft.
4. Front tires out of round.

Driveshaft Or CV Joint Pull-Out

1. Inboard CV joint circlip missing or improperly seated in transaxle side gear.
2. Engine or transaxle improperly positioned. Inspect engine mounts.
3. Frame rail or strut tower improperly positioned or damaged.
4. Front suspension components worn or damaged.

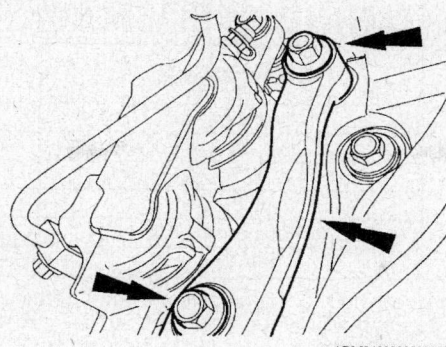

Fig. 1   Caliper anchor removal

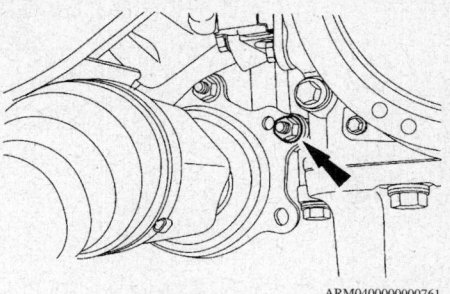

ARM0400000000761

Fig. 2   Righthand halfshaft removal

DRIVESHAFT

REPLACE

Lefthand

1. Remove and discard front axle retainer nut.
2. Raise and support vehicle.
3. Support suspension at steering stop using suitable jack stand.
4. Remove brake caliper anchor mounting bolts, **Fig. 1,** then position caliper and anchor assembly aside. Secure assembly to suspension using suitable wire.
5. Press halfshaft from wheel hub using wheel hub removal tool No. D93P-1175–B, or equivalent.
6. Remove and discard lower ball joint retaining nut, then disconnect ball joint from lower control arm.
7. Separate halfshaft from wheel hub.
8. **On models equipped with six speed transaxle,** remove halfshaft from transaxle using slide hammer tool No. T50T-100–A and halfshaft removal plate No. T89P–3415–B, or equivalents.
9. **On models equipped with CVT transaxle,** remove halfshaft from transaxle using slide hammer tool No. T50T-100–A and halfshaft removal plate No. T86P–3514–A, or equivalents.
10. **On all models,** inspect halfshaft seal replace if required.
11. Reverse procedure to install, noting the following:
    a. Install new driveshaft bearing retainer circlip.
    b. **Do not damage seal when installing driveshaft joints into transaxle.**
    c. Ensure bearing retainer circlip is properly seated in transaxle.
    d. Use old axle hub nut and washer to seat halfshaft into wheel hub.
    e. Install tighten new front axle retaining nut to specification in a continu-

ous rotation. **Stopping rotation during installation will cause nylon lock to seat incorrectly. Causing incorrect torque reading and lead to bearing failure.**
    f. Install new ball joint nut.

Righthand

1. Remove and discard front axle retainer nut.
2. Raise and support vehicle.
3. Support suspension at steering stop using suitable jack stand.
4. Remove brake caliper anchor mounting bolts, **Fig. 1,** then position caliper and anchor assembly aside. Secure assembly to suspension using suitable mechanic's wire.
5. Press halfshaft from wheel hub using wheel hub removal tool No. D93P-1175–B, or equivalent.
6. Remove and discard lower ball joint retaining nut, then disconnect ball joint from lower control arm.
7. Separate halfshaft from wheel hub.
8. Remove two halfshaft to transaxle bearing mounting nuts, **Fig. 2.**
9. Remove halfshaft assembly.
10. **On all models,** inspect halfshaft seal, replace if required.
11. Reverse procedure to install, noting the following:
    a. Install halfshaft to transaxle mounting bolts.
    b. Install new ball joint nut.
    c. Use old axle hub nut and washer to seat halfshaft into wheel hub.
    d. Install tighten new front axle retaining nut to specification in a continuous rotation. **Stopping rotation during installation will cause nylon lock to seat incorrectly. Causing incorrect torque reading and lead to bearing failure.**

DRIVESHAFT SERVICE

Driveshafts are not serviceable and should be replaced as an assembly.

TIGHTENING SPECIFICATIONS

Year	Component	Torque Ft. Lbs.
2005–08	Ball Joint Nut	59
	Caliper Anchor Bolts	74
	Halfshaft To Transaxle Nuts	20
	Hub Nut	184①
	Lower Suspension Arm Nut	59
	Wheel Lug Nut	85

① — Tighten new hub to specification in one continuous rotation. Stopping will cause nylon lock to set causing incorrect torque readings.

Fusion, Milan, MKZ & Zephyr

NOTE: On Air Bag Equipped Models, Refer To "Air Bag System Precautions" Located In The Front Of This Manual For System Disarming & Arming Procedures.

NOTE: Refer To "Computer Relearn Procedures" Located In The Front Of This Manual When Battery Power To The Computer Has Been Interrupted.

INDEX

	Page No.		Page No.		Page No.
Description	18-4	**Precautions**	18-4	Driveshaft Or CV Joint Pull-Out	18-4
Driveshaft, Replace	18-4	Air Bag Systems	18-4	Noise & Vibration On Turns	18-4
Lefthand	18-4	Battery Ground Cable	18-4	Shudder Or Vibration On	
Righthand	18-5	**Tightening Specifications**	18-6	Acceleration	18-4
Driveshaft Service	18-6	**Troubleshooting**	18-4	Vibration At Highway Speeds	18-4

PRECAUTIONS

Air Bag Systems

Refer to "Air Bag System Precautions" in the front of this manual for system disarming and arming procedures.

Battery Ground Cable

Prior to service, disconnect battery ground cable and isolate as required.

DESCRIPTION

Inboard and outboard constant velocity (CV) joints connect to a splined shaft. Driveshaft bearing retainer circlips retain the CV joints to the splined shaft. Inboard and outboard constant velocity (CV) joints connect to a splined shaft. Driveshaft bearing retainer circlips retain the CV joints to the splined shaft.

On the RH side, a driveshaft bearing retainer circlip retains the splined inboard CV joint to the link shaft. Install a new circlip every time you disconnect the intermediate shaft from the vehicle. A front axle wheel hub retainer secures the splined outboard CV joint to the wheel hub.

The lubed-for-life CV joints uses special CV joint grease. They require no periodic lubrication. The halfshafts are not serviceable. If worn or damaged, they must be replaced.

TROUBLESHOOTING

Noise & Vibration On Turns

1. Cut or damaged CV joint boots, resulting in contaminated lube in outboard or inboard CV joints.
2. Loose CV joint clamps.
3. Worn, damaged or improperly installed wheel bearings.
4. Foreign object contacting driveshaft assembly.

Shudder Or Vibration On Acceleration

1. Excessively worn or damaged inboard or outboard CV joint.
2. Excessively high CV joint operating angles caused by improper ride height.

Vibration At Highway Speeds

1. Front wheels or tires out of balance.

2. Improperly seated outboard CV joint in front wheel hub.
3. Bent intermediate driveshaft.
4. Front tires out of round.

Driveshaft Or CV Joint Pull-Out

1. Inboard CV joint circlip missing or improperly seated in transaxle side gear.
2. Engine or transaxle improperly positioned. Inspect engine mounts.
3. Frame rail or strut tower improperly positioned or damaged.
4. Front suspension components worn or damaged.

DRIVESHAFT

REPLACE

Lefthand

1. Raise and support vehicle.
2. Apply brake to keep halfshaft from rotating, then remove and discard front axle retainer nut, **Fig. 1.**
3. Support suspension at steering knuckle using suitable jack stand.
4. Remove front and rear lower control arm nuts.
5. Separate front and rear lower control arm ball joints from wheel knuckle

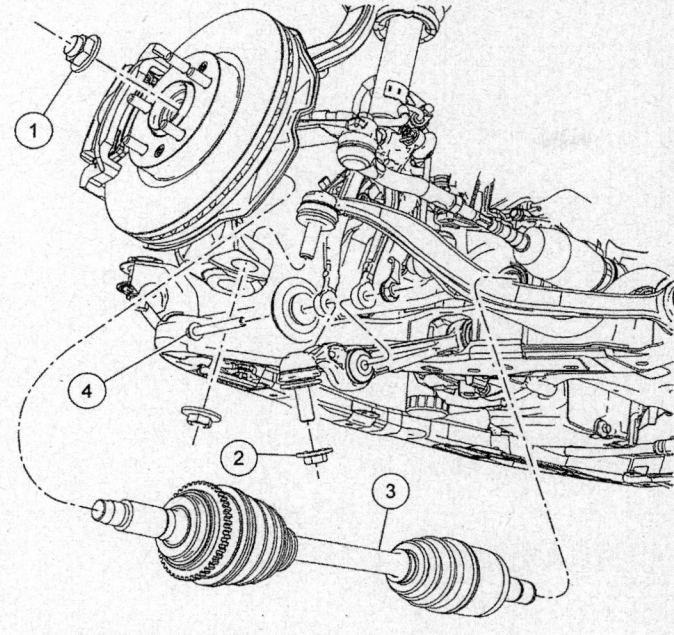

ARM0500000000792

Fig. 1 Lefthand driveshaft replacement. Fusion, Milan, MKZ & Zephyr

Item	Description
1	Axle hub nut
2	Ball joint nut
3	Left halfshaft
4	Damper yoke bolt

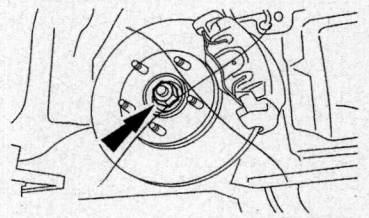

ARM0500000000791

Fig. 2 Righthand driveshaft replacement. Fusion, Milan, MKZ & Zephyr

Item	Description
1	Axle hub nut
2	Lower control arm nut
3	Intermediate shaft support
4	Intermediate shaft support bolt
5	Right halfshaft
6	Intermediate shaft
7	Damper yoke bolt

using ball joint removal tool No. 204–592, or equivalent. **Place a block of wood, or similar item, between lower arm and outer CV joint to prevent lower arm from striking outer CV joint.**

6. Press halfshaft from wheel hub using wheel hub removal tool No. D93P-1175–B, or equivalent.
7. Remove bolt connecting damper fork to lower control arm.
8. Remove brake caliper hose retaining bolt.
9. Pull steering knuckle outward and rotate toward rear of vehicle.
10. Remove lower control arm to subframe bolt and nut, then the lower arm.
11. Remove four pushpins and position inner fender splash shield aside.
12. Remove halfshaft from transmission slide hammer tool No. T50T-100–A and halfshaft removal tool No. 205–832, or equivalents.
13. Remove and discard circlip from stub shaft.
14. Reverse procedure to install, noting the following:
    a. Install new driveshaft bearing retainer circlip.
    b. **Do not damage seal when installing driveshaft joints into transaxle.**
    c. Ensure bearing retainer circlip is properly seated in transaxle.
    d. Install halfshaft into wheel hub using halfshaft installation tool No. T97P-1175–A, or equivalent.

e. Tighten new front axle retaining nut to specification in a continuous rotation. **Stopping rotation during installation will cause nylon lock to seat incorrectly, causing incorrect torque reading and lead to bearing failure.**
f. Install new ball joint nut.

Righthand

1. Raise and support vehicle.
2. Apply brake to keep halfshaft from rotating, then remove and discard front axle retainer nut, **Fig. 2.**
3. Support suspension at steering knuckle using suitable jack stand.
4. Remove front and rear lower control arm nuts.
5. Separate front and rear lower control arm ball joints from wheel knuckle using ball joint removal tool No. 204–592, or equivalent. **Place a block of wood, or similar item, between lower arm and outer CV joint to prevent lower arm from striking outer CV joint.**
6. Press halfshaft from wheel hub using wheel hub removal tool No. D93P-1175–B, or equivalent.
7. Remove bolt connecting damper fork to lower control arm.
8. Remove brake caliper hose retaining bolt.
9. Pull steering knuckle outward and rotate toward rear of vehicle.

10. Remove lower control arm to subframe bolt and nut, then the lower arm.
11. Remove four pushpins and position inner fender splash shield aside.
12. Remove two intermediate shaft support bracket bolts.
13. Remove ground wire eyelet bolt.
14. Disconnect oxygen sensor electrical connector.
15. Remove bolt for oxygen sensor harness bracket.
16. Remove halfshaft from transmission.
17. Pull strut forward, remove halfshaft from damper fork. Position halfshaft in front of damper fork towards front of vehicle, remove halfshaft.
18. Separate halfshaft from intermediate shaft as follows:
    a. Secure intermediate shaft using suitable soft-jawed vise.
    b. With intermediate shaft secured in vise, use a brass drift to strike halfshaft in indicated area, **Fig. 3.**
19. Remove and discard circlip from stub shaft.
20. Reverse procedure to install, noting the following:
    a. Install new driveshaft bearing retainer circlip.
    b. **Do not damage seal when installing driveshaft joints into transaxle.**
    c. Ensure bearing retainer circlip is properly seated in transaxle.
    d. Install halfshaft into wheel hub using halfshaft installation tool No. T97P-1175–A, or equivalent.
    e. Tighten new front axle retaining nut to specification in a continuous rotation. **Stopping rotation during**

installation will cause nylon lock to seat incorrectly, causing incorrect torque reading and lead to bearing failure.

f. Install new ball joint nut.

DRIVESHAFT SERVICE

Driveshafts are not serviceable and should be replaced as an assembly.

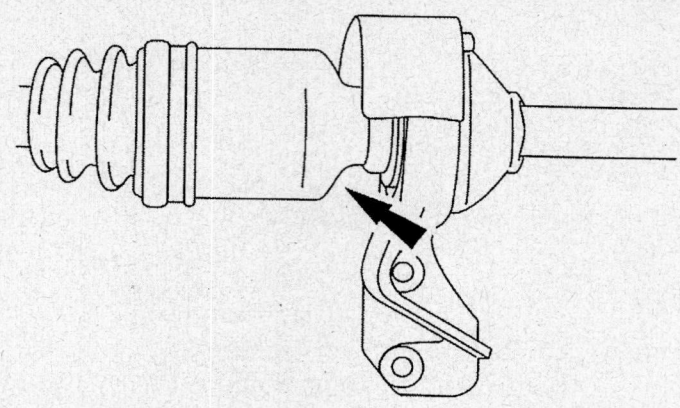

ARM0500000000793

Fig. 3 Intermediate shaft removal from righthand halfshaft. Fusion, Milan, MKZ & Zephyr

TIGHTENING SPECIFICATIONS

Year	Component	Torque Ft. Lbs.
2006–08	Ball Joint To Lower Arm	148
	Caliper Hose	16
	Damper Fork	80
	Halfshaft Support Bracket	41
	Hub Nut	185①
	Lower Control Arm Inner Bolt	81
	Lower Control Arm Outer Bolt & Nut	76

① — Tighten new hub to specification in one continuous rotation. Stopping will cause nylon lock to set causing incorrect torque readings.

2004–05 Sable & 2004–07 Taurus

NOTE: On Air Bag Equipped Models, Refer To "Air Bag System Precautions" Located In The Front Of This Manual For System Disarming & Arming Procedures.

NOTE: Refer To "Computer Relearn Procedures" Located In The Front Of This Manual When Battery Power To The Computer Has Been Interrupted.

INDEX

	Page No.
Driveshaft, Replace	18-7
Driveshaft Service	18-7
Anti-Lock Brake Sensor Wheel	18-8
Assemble	18-8
Disassemble	18-8
Inspection	18-8
Dust Seal	18-8
Inboard Joint & Boot	18-8
Assemble	18-8

	Page No.
Disassemble	18-8
Intermediate Shaft	18-8
Outboard Joint & Boot	18-7
Assemble	18-7
Disassemble	18-7
Inspection	18-7
Precautions	18-7
Air Bag Systems	18-7
Battery Ground Cable	18-7

	Page No.
Tightening Specifications	18-12
Troubleshooting	18-7
Driveshaft Or CV Joint Pull-Out	18-7
Noise & Vibration On Turns	18-7
Shudder Or Vibration On Acceleration	18-7
Vibration At Highway Speeds	18-7

PRECAUTIONS

Air Bag Systems

Refer to "Air Bag System Precautions" in the front of this manual for system disarming and arming procedures.

Battery Ground Cable

Prior to service, disconnect battery ground cable and isolate as required.

TROUBLESHOOTING

Noise & Vibration On Turns

1. Cut or damaged CV joint boots, resulting in contaminated lube in outboard or inboard CV joints.
2. Loose CV joint clamps.
3. Worn, damaged or improperly installed wheel bearings.
4. Foreign object contacting driveshaft assembly.

Shudder Or Vibration On Acceleration

1. Excessively worn or damaged inboard or outboard CV joint.
2. Excessively high CV joint operating angles caused by improper ride height.

Vibration At Highway Speeds

1. Front wheels or tires out of balance.
2. Improperly seated outboard CV joint in front wheel hub.
3. Bent intermediate driveshaft.
4. Front tires out of round.

Driveshaft Or CV Joint Pull-Out

1. Inboard CV joint circlip missing or improperly seated in transaxle side gear.
2. Engine or transaxle improperly positioned. Inspect engine mounts.
3. Frame rail or strut tower improperly positioned or damaged.
4. Front suspension components worn or damaged.

DRIVESHAFT

REPLACE

1. Raise and support vehicle, then remove front tire and wheel assemblies.
2. Remove and discard front axle retainer nut and washer.
3. Remove anti-lock brake sensor wiring harness retaining clip from bracket on lower end of strut assembly.
4. Remove sensor from mounting bracket. Discard nut and position sensor aside.
5. Remove lower strut to steering knuckle

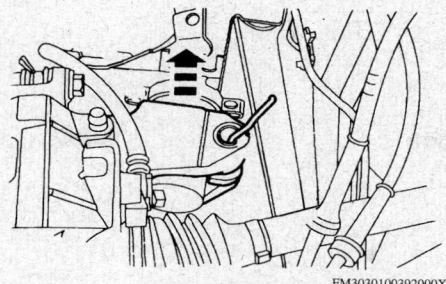

Fig. 1   Steering knuckle positioned on strut

FM3030100392000X

mounting bolt and nut, then separate steering knuckle from strut.
6. Position knuckle on strut body and secure it to strut using suitable wire, **Fig. 1.**
7. Pull upward on knuckle to raise it approximately ½ inch on strut body and secure it to strut with suitable wire.
8. Remove and discard nut from lower ball joint.
9. Loosen ball joint in lower control arm using suitable suspension arm puller.
10. Release lower ball joint by prying down on control arm using suitable pry bar through opening in lower control arm and under frame.
11. Separate outer CV joint from hub using suitable front wheel hub removal tool, **Fig. 2. Do not use hammer to drive joint from hub.**
12. **Do not allow driveshaft to hang from inner joint.**
13. Remove inner joint from transaxle.
14. Reverse procedure to install, noting the following:
    a. Install new front axle retainer nut.
    b. Install new driveshaft bearing retainer circlip.
    c. Instal new ball joint nut.
    d. **Do not damage seal when installing driveshaft joints into transaxle.**
    e. Ensure proper engagement of lefthand driveshaft inner joint spline into transaxle side gears.
    f. Ensure bearing retainer circlip is properly seated.
    g. Ensure proper engagement of transaxle shaft spline into righthand inner CV joint.
    h. Ensure bearing retainer circlip is properly seated.

DRIVESHAFT SERVICE

Outboard Joint & Boot

During manufacturing, CV joint components are matched. Components cannot be interchanged with another joint's components. If a joint component is faulty, entire joint should be replaced.

DISASSEMBLE

1. Position driveshaft in suitable soft jaw vise. **Do not allow vise to contact CV joint boot or clamps.**

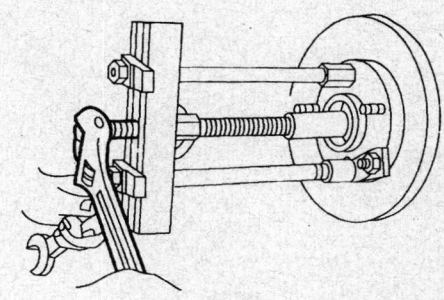

Fig. 2   Outer CV Joint removal from hub

FM3030100393000X

2. Cut large boot clamp using suitable side cutting pliers and peel away from boot.
3. Roll boot back over driveshaft, **Fig. 3.**
4. Turn driveshaft over in vise and angle CV joint so inner bearing race is exposed, **Fig. 4.**
5. Disconnect internal snap ring by rapping inner bearing race using suitable brass drift and hammer.
6. Separate CV joint from driveshaft and remove boot.
7. Inspect CV joint grease for contamination. If grease appears contaminated or has a gritty feeling, inspect for worn components. If grease is not contaminated and joint was operating satisfactorily, add grease and replace boot.
8. Remove and discard circlip from end of shaft. Inspect stop ring located below circlip.
9. Clamp CV joint stub axle in suitable soft jaw vise. **Do not damage dust seal.**
10. Push CV joint inner race down until it tilts enough to allow ball removal, **Fig. 5.** If inner race is tight, it can be tilted by tapping inner race with wooden dowel and hammer. **Do not hit cage.**
11. Remove balls from cage. If balls are tight, use blunt screwdriver to pry balls from cage.
12. Pivot cage and inner race assembly until it is straight up, **Fig. 6.**
13. Align cage windows with outer race lands while pivoting bearing cage, then lift out cage and inner race.
14. Rotate inner race up and out of cage, **Fig. 7.**

INSPECTION

If any components are cracked, broken, severely pitted, worn or otherwise unserviceable, replace CV joint.

If any components appear polished, do not replace joint as this is a normal condition.

If anti-lock brake sensor wheel's teeth are chipped or cracked, install replacement sensor wheel.

ASSEMBLE

1. Apply light coating of Ford CV joint grease No. E2FZ-19590-A, or equivalent, on inner and outer races.
2. Install inner race in bearing cage.
3. Install inner race and cage in outer race, **Fig. 8.**

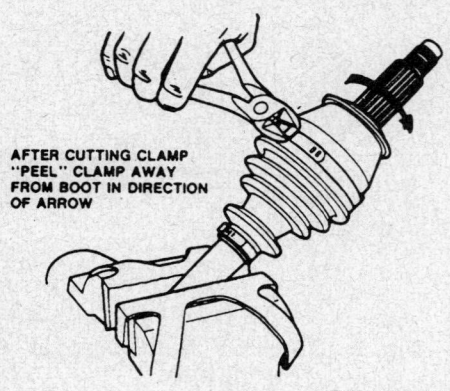

Fig. 3   Boot clamp removal

4. Install CV joint assembly into outer race and pivot 90° into position, **Fig. 9.**
5. Align bearing cage and inner race with outer race, then tilt inner race and install ball Install remaining five balls.
6. Determine which end of driveshaft is for outboard CV joint. The outboard joint side has a shorter end of boot groove to end of shaft dimension, **Fig. 10.**
7. Install CV joint boot and small boot clamp.
8. Install stop ring. If stop ring was not removed, ensure it is seated properly in groove.
9. Install new circlip.
10. Pack CV joint with Ford CV joint grease No. E2FZ-19590-A, or equivalent. Spread remaining grease evenly inside CV boot.
11. With boot peeled back, position CV joint on driveshaft and tap into position with suitable plastic hammer. Joint is properly seated when circlip locks into position. Inspect for proper retention by attempting to pull off joint.
12. Remove excess grease from external surfaces, then position boot over joint.
13. Ensure boot is seated in its groove and install clamp.

Anti-Lock Brake Sensor Wheel

DISASSEMBLE

1. Remove outer CV joint as outlined in "Outboard Joint & Boot."
2. Place CV joint into removal tool No. T88P-20202-A, or equivalent, **Fig. 11.**
3. Push CV joint out of sensor wheel using suitable press.
4. **Do not damage sensor wheel teeth.**

INSPECTION

If anti-lock brake sensor wheel's teeth are chipped or cracked, install replacement sensor wheel.

ASSEMBLE

1. Position sensor wheel onto remover tool.

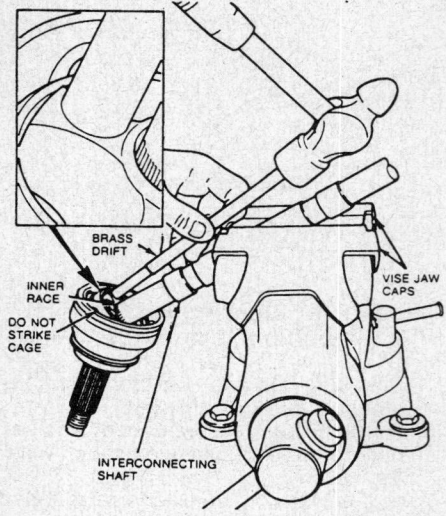

Fig. 4   Internal snap ring removal

2. Position CV joint into sensor wheel and tool.
3. Push joint into sensor wheel using replacer tool No. T88P-20202-A, or equivalent, until joint bottoms in tool. **Do not damage sensor wheel teeth.**

Dust Seal

1. Remove seal using suitable light duty hammer and screwdriver to tap evenly around seal, **Fig. 12.**
2. Install dust seal using spindle/axle seal tool No. T83T-3132-A1, and dust seal installer tool No. T83P-3425-AH, or equivalents.

Inboard Joint & Boot

The tripod is an integral part of the intermediate driveshaft and inboard CV joint housing and are not repairable and must be replace with new components if damaged. Only inner driveshaft boot can be replaced, **Figs. 13 and 14.**

Three types of boots and CV joints are used, **Fig. 15.** These components are not interchangeable. Always use matching type when replacing components.

DISASSEMBLE

1. Remove large and small boot clamp, then remove inner joint outer housing.
2. If boot replacement is required, remove outer CV joint as outlined in "Outboard Joint & Boot," then remove outer joint stop ring.
3. Remove old boot by sliding off outboard end of driveshaft.

ASSEMBLE

1. Slide new boot onto shaft and into position groove of shaft from outer end of driveshaft.
2. Position new small boot clamp onto boot from outer end of driveshaft and tighten clamp.
3. **On models equipped with Ford CV**

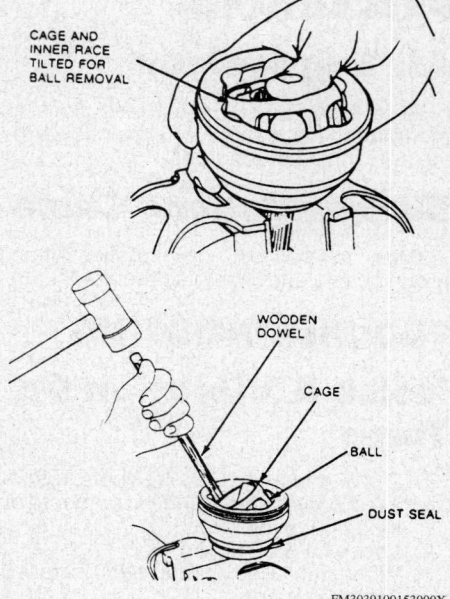

Fig. 5   CV joint ball removal

joints, fill inner CV joint and boot with 5.88 ounces of suitable CV joint grease.
4. **On models equipped with GKN CV joints,** fill inner CV joint and boot with 16.75 ounces of suitable CV joint grease.
5. **On all models,** install outer joint stop ring, then outer CV joint as outlined in "Outboard Joint & Boot."
6. Position inner joint outer housing onto tripod and install large end of boot onto joint outer housing.
7. Ensure boot is not stretched or collapsed. Allow air pressure to equalize using suitable blunt flat tool to pry up boot lip.
8. Ensure driveshaft length is proper, **Fig. 16.**
9. Clean excess grease from outside of boot.
10. Position new large boot clamp onto boot and tighten clamp.
11. Position clamp replacement tool No. T95P-3514-A, or equivalent, on clamp ear and tighten tool through bolt until tool is in closed position.

Intermediate Shaft

1. Clamp intermediate shaft in suitable vise with driveshaft supported.
2. Separate intermediate shaft from driveshaft using puller adapter tool No. T86P-3514-A and slide hammer tool No. D79P-100-A, or equivalents, **Fig. 17.**
3. Pry seal from link shaft with suitable screwdriver.
4. Position intermediate shaft in suitable arbor press and press off bearing.
5. Reverse procedure to install. Coat shaft splines with Ford CV joint grease No. E2FZ-19590-A, or equivalent.

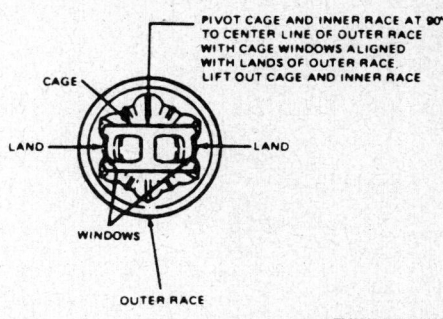

Fig. 6 Cage & inner race removal

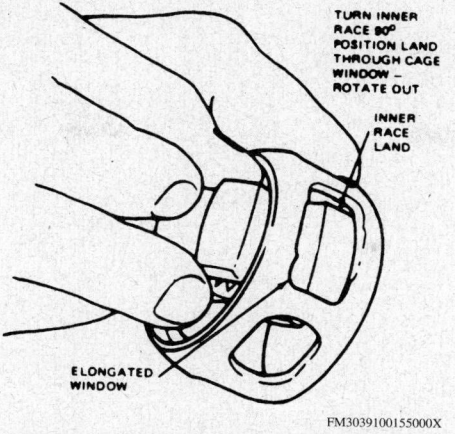

Fig. 7 Inner race replacement

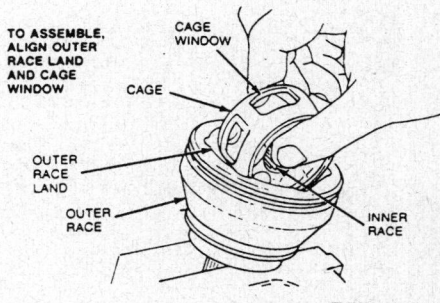

Fig. 9 CV joint assembly installation into outer race

Fig. 8 Inner race & cage assembly

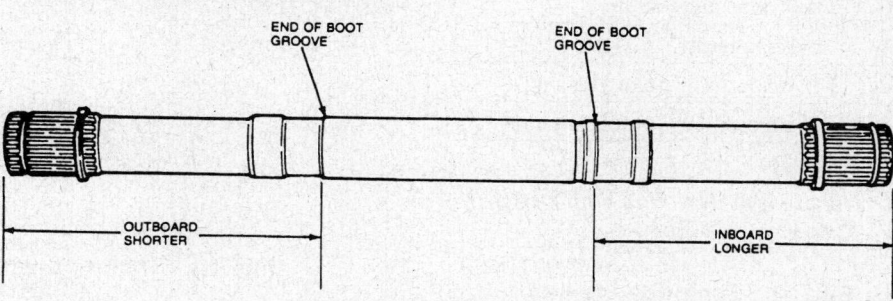

Fig. 10 Driveshaft end identification

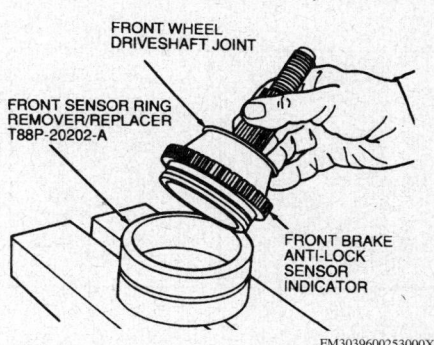

Fig. 11 Anti-Lock brake sensor wheel removal

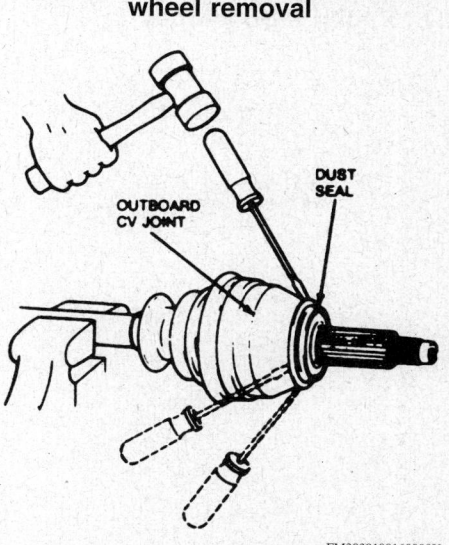

Fig. 12 Dust seal removal

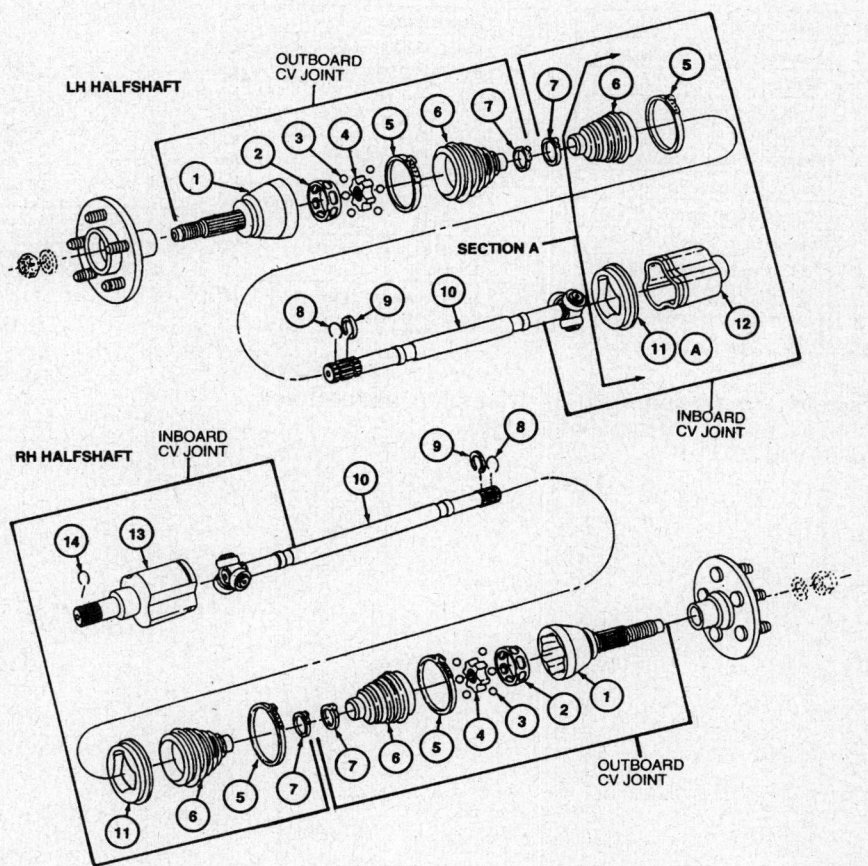

Fig. 13 Exploded view of driveshaft assemblies (Part 1 of 2). Ford

Item	Description
1	Front Wheel Driveshaft Joint
2	Ball Cage
3	Balls (6 required)
4	Inner Race
5	Front Wheel Driveshaft Joint Boot Clamp (Large)
6	Front Wheel Driveshaft Joint Boot
7	Front Wheel Driveshaft Joint Boot Clamp (Small)
8	Circlip
9	Stop Ring
10	Interconnecting Shaft
11	Tri-Lobe Insert
12	LH Inboard CV Joint Housing
13	RH Inboard CV Joint Housing
14	Circlip
A	Part Used Only With Ford Design Conventional Boot

FM3039600254020X

Fig. 13 Exploded view of driveshaft assemblies (Part 2 of 2). Ford

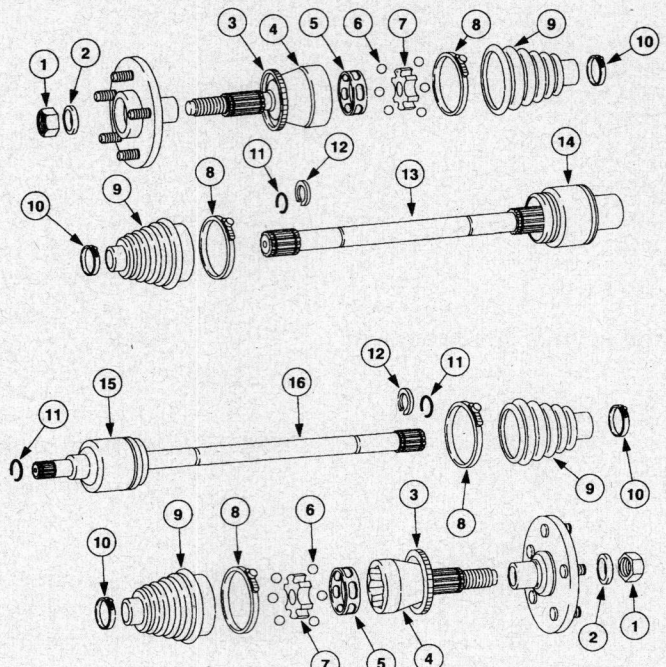

FM3030100394010X

Fig. 14 Exploded view of driveshaft assemblies (Part 1 of 2). GKN

Item	Description	Item	Description
1	Front axle wheel hub retainer	10	Front wheel driveshaft joint boot clamp (small)
2	Washer	11	Circlip
3	Front brake anti-lock sensor indicator	12	Stop ring
4	Front wheel driveshaft joint	13	Interconnecting shaft (part of 3B437)
5	Ball cage (part of 3B413)	14	Inboard CV joint housing assembly
6	Balls (6 req'd) (part of 3B413)	15	Inboard CV joint housing assembly
7	Race (part of 3B413)	16	Interconnecting shaft (part of 3B436)
8	Front wheel driveshaft joint boot clamp (large)		
9	Front wheel driveshaft joint boot		

FM3030100394020X

Fig. 14 Exploded view of driveshaft assemblies (Part 2 of 2). GKN

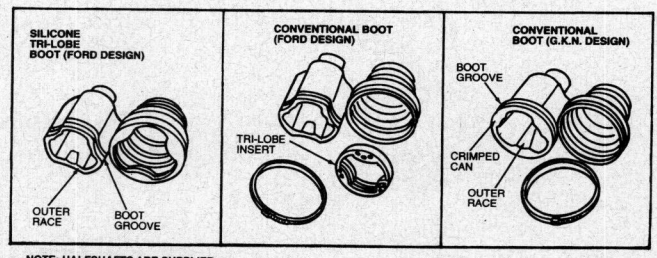

NOTE: HALFSHAFTS ARE SUPPLIED BY FORD AND G.K.N. CHECK LABEL ON SHAFT FOR MANUFACTURER. ALTHOUGH THE DESIGNS ARE SIMILAR, THERE IS NOT INTERCHANGEABILITY OF BOOTS BETWEEN THE THREE DESIGNS.

FM3039600255000X

Fig. 15 CV joint & boot types

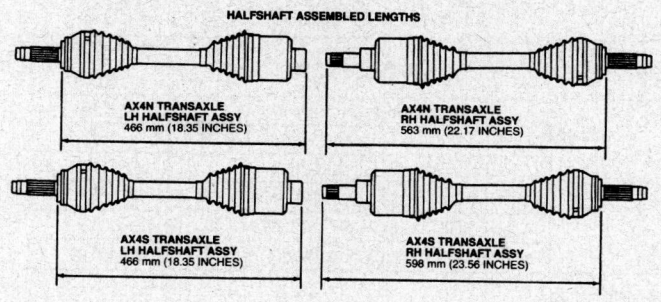

HALFSHAFT ASSEMBLED LENGTHS

AX4N TRANSAXLE
LH HALFSHAFT ASSY
466 mm (18.35 INCHES)

AX4N TRANSAXLE
RH HALFSHAFT ASSY
563 mm (22.17 INCHES)

AX4S TRANSAXLE
LH HALFSHAFT ASSY
466 mm (18.35 INCHES)

AX4S TRANSAXLE
RH HALFSHAFT ASSY
598 mm (23.56 INCHES)

FM3039600256000X

Fig. 16   Driveshaft assembled length

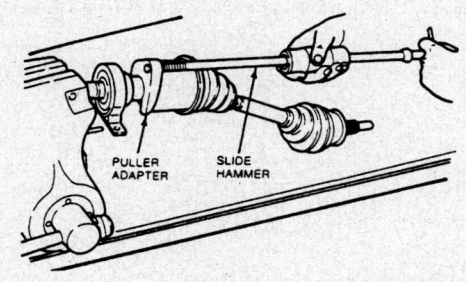

PULLER
ADAPTER

SLIDE
HAMMER

FM3039100165000X

Fig. 17   Link shaft removal

TIGHTENING SPECIFICATIONS

Year	Component	Torque Ft. Lbs.
2004–07	Ball Joint Nut	59
	Hub Nut	184②
	Knuckle To Strut Bolt & Nut	108①
	Lower Suspension Arm Nut	59
	Stabilizer Bar Joint Nut	65
	Wheel Lug Nut	85

① — Inch lbs.
② — Tighten new hub to specification in one continuous rotation. Stopping will cause nylon lock to set causing incorrect torque readings.

DRIVE AXLES

NOTE: On Air Bag Equipped Models, Refer To "Air Bag System Precautions" Located In The Front Of This Manual For System Disarming & Arming Procedures.

NOTE: Refer To "Computer Relearn Procedures" Located In The Front Of This Manual When Battery Power To The Computer Has Been Interrupted.

INDEX

	Page No.
Assemble	19-9
Crown Victoria, Grand Marquis, Marauder, Mustang & Town Car	19-9
LS & Thunderbird	19-10
Cleaning & Inspection	19-8
Conventional Differential	19-8
Traction-Lok Limited Slip Differential	19-9
Disassemble	19-3
Crown Victoria, Grand Marquis, Marauder, Mustang & Town Car	19-3
Differential Case	19-3
Drive Pinion	19-3
Five Hundred, Freestyle, Montego, 2008 Sable, Taurus & Taurus X	19-4
Active On-Demand Coupling Oil Pump	19-4
Active On-Demand Coupling	19-4
Differential Case	19-4
Differential Electronic Module (DEM)	19-4

	Page No.
Drive Pinion Flange & Outer Pinion Seal	19-4
Inner Drive Pinion Seal	19-4
LS & Thunderbird	19-5
Identification	19-1
Rear Axle Tag	19-1
Vehicle Certification Label	19-1
Subassembly Service	19-5
Conventional Differential	19-5
Crown Victoria, Grand Marquis, Marauder, Mustang & Town Car	19-5
LS & Thunderbird	19-6
Traction-Lok Limited Slip Differential	19-8
Except Five Hundred, Freestyle, Montego, 2008 Sable, Taurus & Taurus X	19-8
Five Hundred, Freestyle, Montego, 2008 Sable, Taurus & Taurus X	19-8
Troubleshooting	19-1
Axle Noise	19-1
Bearing Rumble	19-2

	Page No.
Bearing Whine	19-2
Chatter On Cornering	19-2
Chuckle	19-1
Click At Engagement	19-2
Clunk	19-2
Gear Noise	19-1
Knock	19-2
Noise Acceptability	19-1
Except Five Hundred, Freestyle, Montego, 2008 Sable, Taurus & Taurus X	19-1
Five Hundred, Freestyle, Montego, 2008 Sable, Taurus & Taurus X	19-1
Leakage Conditions	19-2
Axle Vent	19-2
Drive Pinion Seal	19-2
Pinion Nut	19-2
Porous Casting	19-2
Traction-Lok Differential Operation Inspection	19-3
Vibration Conditions	19-2
Driveline Angle	19-3
Tires	19-3

IDENTIFICATION

Rear Axle Tag

The plant code on the axle identification tag identifies the axle assembly, **Fig. 1.** The plant code will not change as long as that particular axle assembly never undergoes an external design change. If an internal design change is made to an axle during its production life and that internal change affects service components interchangeability, a dash and numerical suffix will be added to the plant code, **Fig. 2.**

Information on axle ratio, differential type and ring gear diameter may also be found on this tag.

Vehicle Certification Label

Information on axle ratio and differential type may be found on the vehicle certification label, which is affixed to the lefthand front door lock panel or door pillar. A code found in the AX or AXLE box on the label will identify the originally installed axle, **Figs. 3 through 6.**

TROUBLESHOOTING

Except Five Hundred, Freestyle, Montego, 2008 Sable & Taurus X

Refer to **Fig. 7** for rear axle troubleshooting symptoms.

Five Hundred, Freestyle, Montego, 2008 Sable, Taurus & Taurus X

To access Diagnostic Trouble Codes (DTC) connect a suitably programed scan tool to the Diagnostic Link Connector (DLC) located under the lefthand side of the instrument panel, then follow scan tool manufacturer's instructions.

Refer to **Fig. 8** for AWD rear axle DTC interpretations & troubleshooting. If scan tool returns the message, No communication with the Differential Electronic Module (DEM), refer to **Fig. 9.**

Axle Noise

NOISE ACCEPTABILITY

Drive axles produce a certain amount of noise. Some noise is acceptable and may be audible at certain speeds or under various driving conditions, such as a newly paved blacktop road. The slight noise is in no way detrimental to rear axle operation and may be considered normal.

With Traction-Lok limited slip differential axle, slight chatter noise on slow, tight turns after extended highway driving is considered acceptable and has no detrimental effect on the axle's locking function.

GEAR NOISE

Gear noise is the typical howling or whining of the ring gear and pinion because of an improper gear pattern, gear damage or improper bearing preload. It can occur at various speeds and driving conditions or it can be continuous.

CHUCKLE

Chuckle is a particular rattling noise that sounds like a stick against the spokes of a bicycle wheel. It occurs while decelerating from 40 mph and can be heard all the way to a stop. The frequency varies with the vehicle's speed.

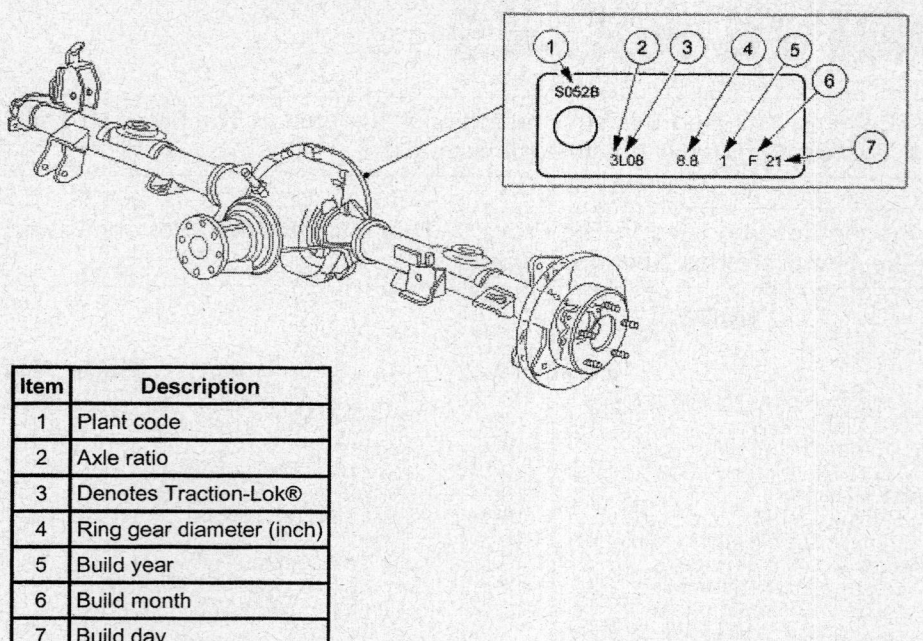

Item	Description
1	Plant code
2	Axle ratio
3	Denotes Traction-Lok®
4	Ring gear diameter (inch)
5	Build year
6	Build month
7	Build day

ARM0500000000794

Fig. 1   Rear axle identification tag

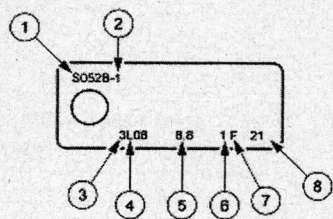

Item	Description
1	Plant code
2	Denotes interchangeability affected internally
3	Axle ratio
4	Denotes Traction-Lok®
5	Ring gear diameter (inch)
6	Build year
7	Build month
8	Build day

ARM0500000000795

Fig. 2   Internally modified rear axle identification tag

KNOCK

Knock is very similar to chuckle, though it may be louder and occurs on acceleration or deceleration.

CLUNK

Clunk may be a metallic noise heard when the automatic transmission is engaged in Reverse or Drive or it may occur when the throttle is applied or released. It is caused by backlash somewhere in the driveline or loose suspension components.

BEARING WHINE

Bearing whine is a high pitched sound similar to a whistle. It is usually caused by faulting pinion bearings, which are operating at driveshaft speed. Bearing noise occurs at all driving speeds. This distinguishes it from gear whine, which usually comes and goes as speed changes.

BEARING RUMBLE

Bearing rumble sounds like marbles being tumbled. This condition is usually caused by a faulting wheel bearing. The lower pitch is because the wheel bearing turns at only about one third of driveshaft speed. In addition, wheel bearing noise may be high pitched, similar to gear noise but will be evident in all four driving modes.

CHATTER ON CORNERING

Chattering noise when cornering is a condition where the whole rear end vibrates only when the vehicle is moving. The vibration is plainly felt as well as heard. In conventional axles, extra differential thrust washers cause a partial lockup condition which creates this chatter. Chatter noise on Traction-Lok axles can usually be traced to

erratic movement between adjacent clutch plates and can be corrected with a lubricant change.

CLICK AT ENGAGEMENT

Click at engagement is a condition on axles of a slight noise, distinct from a clunk that happens in Reverse or Drive engagement. It can be corrected by installing a slinger between the companion flange and front pinion bearing.

Leakage Conditions

Most rear axle leakage conditions can be corrected without a tear-down. However, it is important to clean the leaking area enough to identify the exact source of the leak.

A plugged or seized jiggle cap vent will cause excessive seal lip wear because of internal pressure buildup. When a leak occurs, inspect cap by pressing down on it with index finger. If the cap moves up and down freely, it is working properly. If it does not move freely, it must be replaced.

Inspect axle lubricant level, which should be 9/16 inch below bottom of filler hole.

DRIVE PINION SEAL

If the drive pinion seal leaks, it is usually because of improper installation or because of poor quality of the seal journal surface. Any damage to the seal bore, such as dings, dents and gouges, will distort the seal casing and allow leakage past the outer edge of the seal.

PINION NUT

Some models may experience oil leakage past the threads of the pinion nut. The condition can be corrected by removing the nut and applying pipe sealant with Teflon part No. D8AZ-19554-A, or equivalent, on

the pinion threads and nut face. **Ensure the proper procedure for setting the bearing preload is followed when the nut is installed.**

POROUS CASTING

The differential carrier may leak through small pockets in the metal. These pockets (casting leakage) are caused by gas bubbles in the casting process.

Because the axle's sound characteristics may be changed if torn down to replace the carrier, servicing the porosity is preferable. Below are two recommended procedures that may be employed to fix a porous axle:

1. Peen small amount of body lead into hole and seal pocket with suitable epoxy sealer metallic plastic.
2. In larger pockets, drill shallow hole and tap it for small setscrew.
3. Install setscrew and seal it over with suitable epoxy sealer metallic plastic.

AXLE VENT

There have been some occurrences of lubricant leaking through the axle vent. This may be caused by a clogged or sticking axle vent cap. If this is the case, the vent assembly should be replaced. Use Stud and Bearing Mount part No. EOAZ-19554-BA, or equivalent, on vent's threads to ensure retention.

Vibration Conditions

Few vibration conditions are caused by the axle. Most rear end vibration is caused by the tires or driveline angle.

Vehicles equipped with a Traction-Lok differential will always have both wheels driving. If only one wheel is raised off the floor and the rear axle is driven by the engine, the wheel on the floor could drive the vehicle off the safety stand. Ensure both rear wheels are raised off the floor.

Axle Code	Differential Type	Gear Ratio
AZ	Conventional	3.08
C	Limited Slip	3.27
C6	Conventional	3.55
C8	Conventional	2.73
F	Locker	3.55
X5	Locker	3.27
Z5	Conventional	3.27
1	Conventional	2.73
4	Conventional	3.27
5	Limited Slip	3.55
56	Locker	3.55
58	Conventional	2.73

Fig. 3 Drive axle identification. Crown Victoria & Grand Marquis

Axle Code	Differential Type	Gear Ratio
FIVE HUNDRED, MONTEGO, 2008 SABLE & TAURUS		
1	Traction-Lok	3.46
2	Traction-Lok	4.98
3	Traction-Lok	5.19
FREESTYLE & TAURUS X		
CD	Traction-Lok	5.54
3A	Traction-Lok	5.19

Fig. 4 Drive axle identification. Five Hundred, Freestyle, Montego, 2008 Sable, Taurus & Taurus X

Axle Code	Differential Type	Gear Ratio
1	Conventional	3.58
2	Conventional	3.31
3	Conventional	3.07

Fig. 5 Drive axle identification. LS & Thunderbird

Axle Code	Differential Type	Gear Ratio
BG	Conventional	3.31
CD	Traction-Lok	3.55
CG	Traction-Lok	3.31
LE	Locker	3.27
ME	Traction-Lok	3.55
TE	Locker	3.55
VM	Locker	2.73
X5	Conventional	3.27
Z5	Conventional	3.27

Fig. 6 Drive axle identification. Mustang

TIRES

Some vehicles are equipped with directional tires. See tire rotation arrows on tire sidewall. If a directional tire is removed for service, it must be mounted in its original location.

Do not balance the rear wheels and tires while they are mounted on the vehicle. Use only an off-vehicle wheel and tire balancer.

A vibration can sometimes be corrected by properly rotating or inflating the tires. The best tires should be placed on the rear to minimize vibration, especially on vehicles with rear coil springs.

DRIVELINE ANGLE

An improper driveline (pinion) angle can often be detected by the driving condition when vibration occurs.

1. Vibration during coasting from 35–45 mph is often caused by high pinion angle.
2. Vibration during acceleration from 35–45 mph may indicate lower than specified pinion angle.

Traction-Lok Differential Operation Inspection

A Traction-Lok differential can be inspected for proper operation without removing it from the axle housing using procedure outlined below:

1. Raise and support one rear wheel, then remove wheel cover.
2. Install adapter for Traction-Lok differential tool No. T59L-4204-A, or equivalent, and suitable torque wrench.
3. Rotate axle shaft. **Ensure transmis-** sion is in Neutral, one wheel is on floor and other rear wheel is raised off floor.
4. Breakaway torque required to start rotation should be at least 20 ft. lbs. Initial breakaway torque may be higher than continuous turning torque. This is normal.
5. Axle shaft should turn with even pressure throughout inspection without slipping or binding. If torque reading is less than specified, inspect differential for improper assembly.

DISASSEMBLE

Crown Victoria, Grand Marquis, Marauder, Mustang & Town Car

DIFFERENTIAL CASE

1. Raise and support rear of vehicle, then loosen axle housing cover bolts and drain lubricant into suitable container, **Figs. 10 and 11.**
2. Wipe excess lubricant from inside axle housing and visually inspect components for wear and/or damage.
3. Rotate gears and inspect for roughness, indicating damaged bearings or gears.
4. Inspect and record ring gear back face runout using suitable dial indicator mounted on axle housing cover flange. Maximum back face runout is .004 inch.
5. Remove rear axles and propeller shaft.

Refer to "Rear Axle & Suspension" section of appropriate chassis chapter for procedures.

6. Scribe reference marks on differential bearing caps for assembly alignment and loosen bearing cap bolts. **Observe and record direction arrows are facing on bearing caps. Arrows must installed facing in original direction.**
7. Pry differential case, bearing cups and shims out of housing until loose in bearing caps using suitable tool.
8. Remove bearing caps and differential assembly. Mark side cups and shims for assembly alignment.

DRIVE PINION

1. Scribe reference mark between drive pinion and companion flange.
2. Remove pinion nut and pinion flange using holding tool No. T78P-4851-A, or equivalent.
3. Drive pinion out of front bearing cone and remove from rear of axle housing using suitable soft faced hammer.
4. Remove oil seal, front bearing cone and roller from pinion housing.
5. Remove rear pinion bearing using suitable arbor press and adapters.
6. Measure and record thickness of shim which is found under rear bearing cone.
7. Remove pinion bearing cups from pinion housing with suitable brass drift.
8. Install cups using suitable bearing cup installer. Cups are not properly installed if .015 feeler gauge can be installed between cup and bottom of bore at any point around cup.

Condition	Possible Sources	Action
• Traction-Lok® does not work in snow, mud or on ice	• Differential.	• CARRY OUT the Traction-Lok® Differential Operation Check REPAIR as necessary.
• Lubricant leaking from the pinion seal or axle shaft oil seals	• Vent.	• CLEAN the axle housing vent.
	• Damage in the seal contact area or dust slinger on the pinion flange dust shield.	• INSTALL new pinion flange and the pinion seal if damage is found.
• Differential side gears/pinion gears are scored	• Insufficient lubrication.	• INSTALL new gears. FILL the axle to specification.
	• Incorrect or contaminated lubricant type.	• INSTALL new gears. CLEAN and REFILL the axle to specification.
• Axle overheating	• Lubricant level too low.	• CHECK the lubricant level. FILL the axle to specification.
	• Incorrect or contaminated lubricant type.	• INSPECT the axle for damage. REPAIR as necessary. CLEAN and REFILL the axle to specification.
	• Bearing preload adjusted too tight.	• CHECK the ring and pinion for damage. INSPECT the ring and pinion wear pattern. ADJUST the preload as necessary.
	• Excessive gear wear.	• INSPECT all the axle gears for wear or damage. INSTALL new components as necessary.
	• Incorrect ring gear backlash.	• INSPECT the ring gear for scoring. INSPECT the ring and pinion wear pattern. ADJUST the ring gear backlash as necessary.
• Broken gear teeth on the ring gear or pinion	• Overloading the vehicle.	• INSTALL a new ring and pinion.
• Axle shaft broken	• Overloading the vehicle.	• INSTALL a new axle shaft.
	• Misaligned axle shaft tube.	• INSPECT the axle for damage. CHECK axle shaft tube alignment. INSTALL a new axle shaft.

FM3030100370000X

Fig. 7 Troubleshooting chart. Except Five Hundred, Freestyle, Montego, 2008 Sable, Taurus & Taurus X

9. **If any bearing cups are replaced, respective cone and roller must also be replaced.**

Five Hundred, Freestyle, Montego, 2008 Sable, Taurus & Taurus X

DIFFERENTIAL CASE

The differential is not serviceable, should internal failure occur it will be required to replace the differential assembly.

DRIVE PINION FLANGE & OUTER PINION SEAL

REMOVAL

1. Place index marks on driveshaft to rear axle pinion flange, Power Take Off (PTO) flange and center bearing bracket for installation reference.
2. Remove and discard front and rear driveshaft flange bolts, **Fig. 12.**
3. Remove and discard drive pinion flange nut.
4. Remove drive pinion flange.
5. Remove outer drive pinion seal using suitable screwdriver or seal removal pry bar.

INSTALLATION

1. Install outer drive pinion seal using halfshaft seal installer tool No. 205–814, or equivalent, **Fig. 13.**
2. Install drive pinion flange and nut. **Torque** pinion flange nut to 74 ft. lbs.
3. Install drive shaft, **Fig. 12,** noting the following:
   a. Align center bearing bracket, front and rear flange index marks made during removal.
   b. **Torque** driveshaft to flange bolts to 18 ft. lbs.
   c. **Torque** center bearing bolts to 15 ft. lbs.
   d. **Torque** center bearing bracket bolts to 18 ft. lbs.
   e. **Torque** exhaust support brace bolts to 22 ft. lbs.

INNER DRIVE PINION SEAL

1. Remove active on-demand coupling as outlined under "Active On-Demand Coupling."

2. Drive pinion inner seal is a two piece design, remove and discard both pieces using suitable screwdriver or seal removal pry bar.
3. Reverse procedure to install, noting the following:
   a. Install both seals as an assembly using seal installation tool No. 205–812, or equivalent, **Fig. 14.**
   b. If seals become misaligned in there bore during installation, install new seals.

ACTIVE ON-DEMAND COUPLING

REMOVAL

1. Drain active on-demand coupling fluid into suitable container.
2. Disconnect Differential Electronic Module (DEM) electrical connector, **Fig. 15.**
3. Remove four active on-demand coupling mounting bolts, **Fig. 16. Record bolt locations before removal, bolt length varies and need to be install in the correct locations.**
4. Remove active on-demand coupling.

INSTALLATION

1. Clean and inspect axle assembly cavity for foreign material.
2. Install new coupling seal.
3. Install coupling and mounting bolts, torque mounting bolts to 35 ft. lbs. **Ensure mounting bolts are installed in correct positions, as marked during removal.**
4. Connect DEM electrical connector.
5. Fill active on-demand coupling with Volvo transmission oil part No. 116–1641, or equivalent, to bottom of fill hole, **Fig. 17.**

ACTIVE ON-DEMAND COUPLING OIL PUMP

1. Remove drive pinion flange as outlined under "Drive Pinion Flange & Outer Pinion Seal."
2. Disconnect active on-demand coupling oil pump electrical connector.
3. Remove oil pump to coupling mounting bolts, **Fig. 18.**
4. Remove active on-demand coupling oil pump.
5. Reverse procedure to install. **Torque** oil pump mounting bolts to 53 inch lbs.

DIFFERENTIAL ELECTRONIC MODULE (DEM)

REMOVAL

Differential electronic module, solenoid valve and oil temperature sensor are calibrated together and must be replaced as a set.

1. Remove active on-demand coupling as outlined under "Active On-Demand Coupling."
2. Remove two DEM mounting bolts, **Fig. 19,** then the DEM.
3. Remove and discard spacer plate, **Fig. 20.**
4. Remove solenoid valve and discard O-ring seals, **Fig. 21.**

5. Remove and discard solenoid valve seat seal, **Fig. 22.**
6. Remove and discard oil temperature sensor seal.

INSTALLATION

1. Lubricate all seals with Volvo transmission fluid part No. 116–1641, or equivalent, before installation.
2. Install new spacer plate, **Fig. 20.**
3. Install new temperature sensor seal.
4. Install new solenoid valve seal, **Fig. 22.**
5. Install new solenoid valve O-ring seals, **Fig. 21.**
6. Install solenoid valve and oil temperature sensor into DEM.
7. Install active on demand coupling spacer plate and DEM onto active on-demand coupling. **Torque** DEM mounting bolts to 53 inch lbs.
8. Flash DEM with most current software.

LS & Thunderbird

Do not damage aluminum rear axle housing.
1. Remove differential housing cover.
2. Install dial indicator with bracket tool No. 4201-G, or equivalent.
3. Measure and record ring gear runout, **Fig. 23.**
4. Attach housing spreader adapters tool No. T93P-4000-A, or equivalent, to rear axle housing with four cover bolts.
5. Attach housing spreader adapters to holding fixture tool No. T57L-500-B, or equivalent, with two ⅜ inch x 1-½ inch bolts.
6. Install differential carrier spreader tool No. T4000-E, or equivalent, onto housing spreader adapters with spreader pins aligned with housing spreader adapters holes.
7. **On models equipped with aluminum axle,** proceed as follows:
   a. Install dial indicator tool and attach clutch housing alignment adapter tool No. T75L-4201-A, or equivalent, to dial indicator with tip positioned in spreader adapter hole.
   b. Tighten and loosen housing spreader adapter screw to normalize housing spreader adapters prior to final dial indicator reading. **Overspreading can damage rear axle housing.**
   c. Adjust dial indicator to zero and tighten housing spreader screw until rear axle housing is spread to .030 inch. Remove dial indicator.
8. **On models equipped with nodular iron axle,** housing spreader adapters are used to give the rear axle housing stability. **Do not spread rear axle housing.**
9. **On all models,** mark position of bearing caps as arrows may not be visible. Bearing caps must be installed in original locations and positions.
10. Remove mounting bolts and bearing caps.
11. **On models equipped with aluminum axle,** proceed as follows:
    a. Position wood blocks on top and bottom of differential.
    b. Pry differential case and bearing shims out of rear axle housing, **Fig. 24.**
    c. Remove special tool.
12. **On models equipped with nodular iron axle,** remove differential case.
13. **On all models,** remove 10 ring gear bolts.
14. Drive ring gear off using suitable punch in bolt holes. **Do not damage bolt hole threads.**
15. Remove differential bearing using two-jaw puller tool No. D97L-4221-A and step plate tool No. D83T-4205-C2, or equivalents.
16. Repeat procedure on other side.
17. Remove differential lock bolt, pinion shaft, gears and side gears.
18. Install suitable torque wrench on pinion nut and record torque required to maintain rotation of drive pinion gear through several revolutions.
19. Install flange holding tool No. 205-478, or equivalent. **Ensure to install cotter key in special tool.**
20. Remove pinion nut using suitable breaker bar. **Discard pinion nut.**
21. Mark pinion flange in relation to drive pinion stem for assembly alignment .
22. Remove pinion flange using flange remover tool No. 307-408I, or equivalent.
23. Install pinion thread protector tool No. 205-460, or equivalent.
24. Drive pinion out of front bearing cone using suitable soft-faced hammer. Remove pinion through rear of housing.
25. Remove rear axle drive pinion shaft oil slinger, pinion seal and collapsible spacer.
26. Position pinion bearing cone remover tool No. T71P-4621-B, or equivalent, under pinion bearing.
27. Remove pinion bearing using suitable press.
28. Remove front pinion bearing.
29. Measure and record thickness of drive pinion bearing adjustment shim found under differential pinion bearing.
30. Remove drive pinion bearing adjustment shim.
31. Remove damaged rear axle pinion bearing cups from rear axle housing using pinion outer bearing cup remover tool No. 205-482 and pinion inner bearing cup remover tool No. 205-481, or equivalents.

SUBASSEMBLY SERVICE

Conventional Differential

CROWN VICTORIA, GRAND MARQUIS, MARAUDER, MUSTANG & TOWN CAR

DIFFERENTIAL CASE BEARINGS

1. If differential bearings are to be replaced, remove and replace with suitable puller.
2. If ring gear backlash measured during removal exceeded .015 inch, proceed as follows:
   a. Install differential bearing cups on cones, then the differential case in rear housing with drive pinion removed.
   b. Install .265 inch shim on lefthand side of case.
   c. Install bearing cap and hand tighten bolts.
   d. Install progressively larger shims on righthand side of case until largest shim selected can be installed with slight drag.
   e. Install bearing cap and **torque** bolts to 70–85 ft. lbs.

Code	Description	Action
P0562	System Voltage Low	Inspect Charging System
P0563	System Voltage High	Inspect Charging System
P0602	Powertrain Control Module PCM Programing Error	Install New Differential Electronic Module (DEM)
P0606	ECM/PCM Processor	Install New Differential Electronic Module (DEM)
P0610	Control Module Vehicle Option Error	Reconfigure Differential Electronic Module (DEM)
P0932	Hydraulic Pressure Sensor Circuit	Install New Axle Oil Temperature Sensor
P0937	Hydraulic Oil Temperature Sensor Circuit	Install New Rear Axle Oil Temperature Sensor
P0939	Hydraulic Oil Temperature Sensor Circuit, Low Input	Install New Rear Axle Oil Temperature Sensor
P0940	Hydraulic Oil Temperature Sensor Circuit, High Input	Install New Rear Axle Oil Temperature Sensor
P0960	Pressure Control Solenoid A Control Circuit Open	Install New Active On-Demand Coupling Oil Pump
P0961	Pressure Control Solenoid A Control Circuit Range Performance	Install New Active On-Demand Coupling Oil Pump
P1889	Oil Pressure Pump Performance	Install New Active On-Demand Coupling Oil Pump

Fig. 8 DTC interpretations & troubleshooting chart. Five Hundred, Freestyle, Montego, 2008 Sable, Taurus & Taurus X

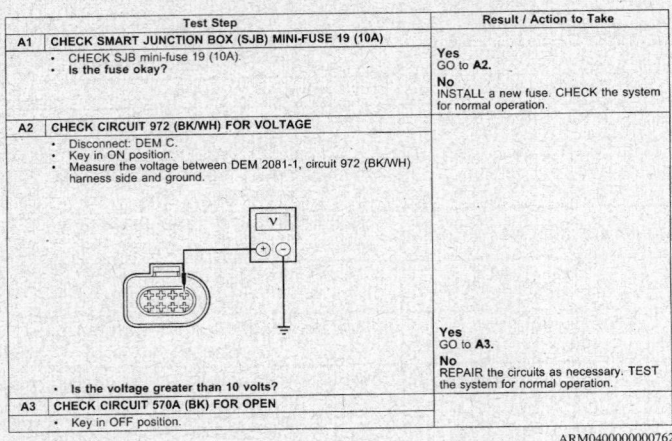

Test Step	Result / Action to Take
A1 CHECK SMART JUNCTION BOX (SJB) MINI-FUSE 19 (10A) • CHECK SJB mini-fuse 19 (10A). • Is the fuse okay?	**Yes** GO to **A2**. **No** INSTALL a new fuse. CHECK the system for normal operation.
A2 CHECK CIRCUIT 972 (BK/WH) FOR VOLTAGE • Disconnect: DEM C. • Key in ON position. • Measure the voltage between DEM 2081-1, circuit 972 (BK/WH) harness side and ground. • Is the voltage greater than 10 volts?	**Yes** GO to **A3**. **No** REPAIR the circuits as necessary. TEST the system for normal operation.
A3 CHECK CIRCUIT 570A (BK) FOR OPEN • Key in OFF position.	

ARM0400000000762

Fig. 9   Test A: No communication with DEM (Part 1 of 2). Five Hundred, Freestyle, Montego, 2008 Sable, Taurus & Taurus X

Test Step	Result / Action to Take
A3 CHECK CIRCUIT 570A (BK) FOR OPEN (Continued) • Measure the resistance between DEM 2081-2, circuit 570a (BK) harness side and ground. • Is the resistance less than 5 ohms?	**Yes** CHECK the module communication network. **No** REPAIR the circuit. TEST the system for normal operation.

ARM0400000000763

Fig. 9   Test A: No communication with DEM (Part 2 of 2). Five Hundred, Freestyle, Montego, 2008 Sable, Taurus & Taurus X

3. Rotate differential several turns in either direction to ensure free rotation and to seat bearings.
4. Inspect ring gear back face runout using suitable dial indicator mounted to axle housing.
5. Ring gear back face runout should be within .004 inch. If ring gear back face runout is within specifications, original reading was caused by insufficient differential bearing preload. If ring gear back face runout is still not within specifications, proceed as follows:
   a. Inspect differential case runout. It should be within .004 inch.
   b. If runout is within specifications, ring gear is out of specifications and should be replaced.
   c. If runout is not within specifications, differential case is damaged and should be replaced.
6. Remove differential case from axle housing, then the ring gear.
7. Install differential case less ring gear in housing.
8. Inspect differential case runout. Runout should be within .004 inch. If runout is within specifications, ring gear is out of specifications and should be replaced. If runout is not within specifications, differential case is damaged and should be replaced.

DRIVE PINION DEPTH DETERMINATION

Prior to determining drive pinion depth, clean pinion bearing cups and differential bearing pedestals thoroughly to ensure an accurate reading. Apply only light oil film to bearing assemblies to avoid false readings.

1. Assemble aligning adapter, gauge disc and gauge block to tool No. T79P-4020-A, or equivalent, **Fig. 25**.
2. Place rear pinion bearing over aligning adapter, then install tool and bearing in rear pinion bearing cup in pinion housing bore.
3. Place front pinion bearing over screw in front pinion bearing cup and assemble tool handle onto screw.
4. **Torque** handle to 20 inch lbs. Ensure tool is mounted securely between front

and rear bearings.
5. Rotate gauge block several half turns to ensure bearings are seated properly. Rotational torque should be 20 inch lbs., with new bearings. Set gauge block at an angle approximately 45° from horizontal, **Fig. 26**.
6. Install gauge tube in differential bearing mounts, then the bearing caps and bolts.
7. install pinion shims between gauge block and gauge tube. Proper shim will fit with slight drag. **Do not force shim between block and tube. Do not use shims that are bent, dirty, nicked or mutilated as gauge.**
8. Record proper shim size and remove tool from axle housing.
9. Remove rear pinion bearing using suitable arbor press and adapters.
10. Install previously determined shim on pinion shaft and bearing using arbor press. **Rear pinion bearing used to determine drive pinion depth must be used in final assembly.**

DRIVE PINION INSTALLATION

1. Lubricate pinion bearings with suitable axle lubricant, then install pinion shaft and rear bearing, collapsible spacer and front bearing.
2. Install slinger and pinion oil seal, then install pinion flange in seal and hold firmly in place against front bearing.
3. From rear of housing, install pinion shaft into flange.
4. Install pinion yoke nut. While holding pinion flange, tighten nut only enough to remove bearing endplay.
5. When there is an increase in pinion nut turning effort stop tightening pinion nut.
6. Rotate pinion several times in both directions to seat bearings.
7. Continue to tighten pinion nut in very small increments.
8. Measure pinion rotational torque occasionally. Rotating torque must not exceed 20 inch lbs. **Do not exceed specified preload torque. Do not loosen pinion nut if preload torque is exceeded. If preload torque is exceeded, remove pinion nut, yoke, oil**

seal, slinger and collapsible spacer. Replace collapsible spacer and oil seal and repeat procedure.

LS & THUNDERBIRD

Do not damage aluminum rear axle housing.

1. Lubricate differential side gear thrust washers with Premium Long-Life Grease XG-1-C, or equivalent.
2. Install differential side gears in differential case.
3. Lubricate differential pinion thrust washers with Premium Long-Life Grease XG-1-C, or equivalent.
4. Install differential pinion gears with differential pinion thrust washers in differential case.
5. If new pinion shaft lock bolt is unavailable, coat threads with Threadlock and Sealer EOAZ-19554-AA, or equivalent, prior to installation.
6. Install differential pinion shaft and new pinion shaft lock bolt.
7. Install differential bearing on differential case using differential side bearing replacer tool No. T57L-4221-A2, or equivalent. Repeat for other side.
8. Start two of ring gear bolts through differential case and into ring gear to ensure ring gear bolt holes align with differential case bolt holes correctly then press ring gear on differential case.
9. Install ring gear bolts. Apply Stud and Bearing Mount EOAZ-19554-BA, or equivalent, to bolts.
10. With pinion removed, place differential case/gear subassembly with differential bearing and rear axle pinion bearing cups in rear axle housing.
11. Install differential bearing shim of thickness outlined on lefthand side of differential case.
12. Install lefthand bearing cap hand tight.
13. Apply pressure toward lefthand side to fully seat differential bearing cup.
14. Install progressively larger differential bearing shims on righthand side until largest differential bearing shim selected can be assembled with slight drag feel.
15. Install righthand bearing cap and **torque** bearing caps to 77 ft. lbs.
16. Rotate differential assembly to ensure it rotates freely.
17. Install dial indicator with bracket tool No. T4201-C, or equivalent.

18. Measure and record ring gear runout, **Fig. 23.**
19. If runout is .003 inch, original out-of-specification runout was caused by insufficient bearing preload.
20. If runout is more than .003 inch, proceed as follows:
    a. Remove differential case.
    b. Remove ring gear.
    c. Install differential case without ring gear.
    d. Rotate differential case to correctly seat differential bearings.
    e. Measure differential case flange runout using dial indicator.
    f. If runout is .003 inch, install new ring gear and pinion.
    g. If runout is more than .003 inch, ring gear is true. Concern is because of either damaged differential case or differential bearings.
    h. Inspect differential bearings.
    i. If differential bearings are not damaged, install new differential case and differential bearings.
    j. Measure runout with new differential case and differential bearings.
21. Install new inner rear axle pinion bearing cup in rear axle housing using pinion inner bearing cup tool No. 205-480 and cup replacer tool No. T71P-4616-A, or equivalents.
22. Install new outer rear axle pinion bearing cup in rear axle housing using cup replacer tools.
23. Coat new rear axle pinion bearing cup with SAE 5W-30 Super Premium Motor Oil XO-5W30-QSP, or equivalent.
24. Position rear axle pinion bearing cup on handle tool No. T76P-4020-A11, screw tool No. T76P-4020-A9, pinion depth gauge aligner tool No. 205-477, pinion depth gauge disc tool No. 205-476, and gauge block tool No. T76P-4020-A10, or equivalent, **Fig. 25.**
25. Position bearing cup replacer in rear axle housing and tighten special tool to fully seat rear axle pinion bearing cup in bore.
26. Apply light film of SAE 75W140 Synthetic Rear Axle Lubricant F1TZ-19580-B, or equivalent, on front differential pinion bearing and rear differential pinion bearing assemblies.
27. Thread handle onto screw and **torque** to 20 inch lbs.
28. Rotate gauge block tool several half turns to correctly seat pinion bearings, **Fig. 26. Gauge block tool must be offset to obtain an accurate reading.**
29. Position gauge tube tool No. T93P-4020-A, or equivalent, on differential bearing seat of rear axle housing.
30. Install differential bearing caps and cap bolts. **Torque** cap bolts to 77 ft. lbs.
31. Slight drag should be felt for correct shim selection. Remove special tool.
32. Same pinion bearings and drive pinion bearing adjustment shim used in drive pinion shim selection procedure must be used in final axle assembly.
33. Position drive pinion bearing adjustment shim, pinion bearing, and

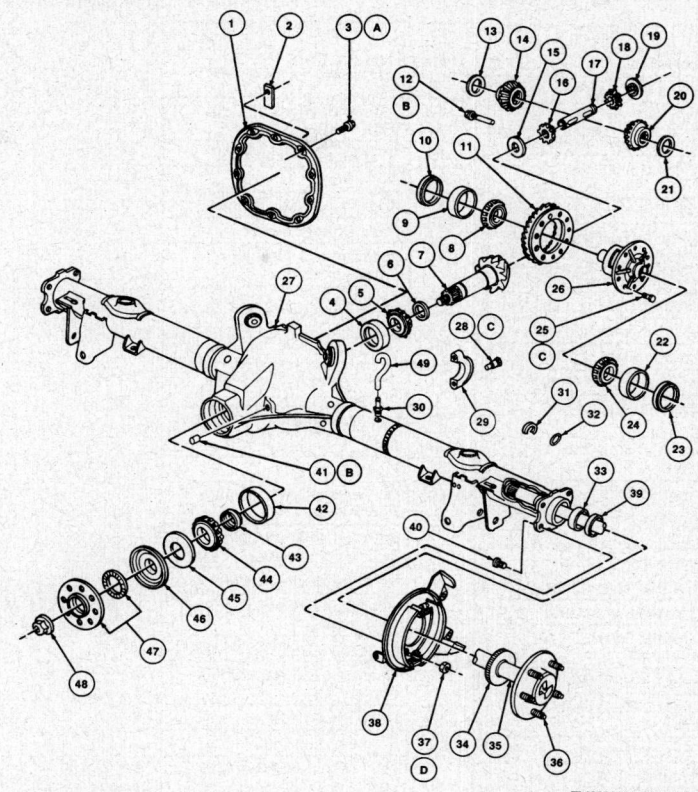

Fig. 10 Exploded view of 8.8 inch rear axles (Part 1 of 2). Crown Victoria, Grand Marquis, Marauder & Town Car

FM3039500279010X

bearing/seal service plate tool No. T75L-1165-B and universal bearing puller tool No. T53T-4621-C, or equivalents, on pinion stem.
34. Firmly seat drive pinion bearing adjustment shim and pinion bearing on pinion stem using suitable press.
35. Install front pinion bearing, rear axle drive pinion shaft oil slinger and rear axle drive pinion seal.
36. Ensure pinion stem splines are free of burrs. Remove burrs using fine crocus cloth working in rotational motion.
37. Install new drive pinion collapsible spacer on pinion stem against pinion stem shoulder.
38. Install drive pinion and drive pinion collapsible spacer into rear axle housing.
39. Master bearings are marked LH and RH.
40. Remove differential bearings and install righthand master bearing tool No. T93P-4222-B and lefthand master bearing tool No. T93P-4222-A, or equivalents, on differential case.
41. Lubricate rear axle pinion flange splines using SAE 75W140 Synthetic Rear Axle Lubricant F1TZ-19580-B, or equivalent.
42. Align rear axle pinion flange with drive pinion shaft and install rear axle pinion flange. Disregard scribe marks if new rear axle pinion flange is being installed.
43. With drive pinion in place in rear axle housing, install rear axle pinion flange

using pinion flange installer tool No. 205-479 and flange holding tool No. 205-478, or equivalents.
44. Tighten pinion nut using flange holding tool No. 205-478, or equivalent. **Ensure to install cotter key in special tool.**
45. Rotate pinion occasionally to ensure differential pinion bearings seat correctly.
46. Take frequent differential pinion bearing torque preload readings by rotating pinion with suitable torque wrench. Preload **torque** should be 8–10 inch lbs., with used bearings or 16–28 inch lbs., with new bearings.
47. **Do not loosen pinion nut to reduce preload. If it is required to reduce preload, install new collapsible spacer and pinion nut.**
48. **On models equipped with aluminum axle,** proceed as follows:
    a. Place differential case and dial indicator into rear axle housing. Position dial indicator on outside mounting hole.
    b. Attach dial indicator with indicator tip positioned on machined surface of differential case flange.
    c. Move differential case to lefthand and righthand as far as possible.
    d. Repeat procedure until consistent reading is obtained.
    e. Record reading.
    f. Remove special tool and differential case from rear axle housing.

Item	Description
1	Axle Housing Cover
2	I.D. Tag
3	Axle Housing Cover Bolt
4	Rear Axle Pinion Bearing Cup
5	Differential Pinion Bearing
6	Drive Pinion Bearing Adjustment Shim
7	Drive Pinion (Part of 4209)
8	Differential Bearing (RH)
9	Differential Bearing Cup
10	Differential Bearing Shim
11	Ring Gear (Part of 4209)
12	Differential Pinion Shaft Lock Pin
13	Differential Side Gear Thrust Washer
14	Differential Side Gear
15	Differential Pinion Thrust Washer
16	Differential Pinion Gear
17	Differential Pinion Shaft
18	Differential Pinion Gear
19	Differential Pinion Thrust Washer
20	Differential Side Gear
21	Differential Side Gear Thrust Washer
22	Differential Bearing
23	Differential Bearing Shim
24	Differential Bearing (LH)
25	Rear Axle Differential Gear Case Bolt
26	Differential Case
27	Rear Axle Housing

Item	Description
28	Bolt
29	Differential Bearing Cap (Part of 4010)
30	Rear Axle Housing Vent
31	U-Washer
32	Rear Axle Shaft O-Ring
33	Rear Wheel Bearing
34	Rear Brake Anti-Lock Sensor Indicator
35	Axle Shaft
36	Lug Bolt
37	Nut
38	Rear Wheel Disc Brake Adapter
39	Inner Wheel Bearing Oil Seal
40	Bolt
41	Fill Plug
42	Differential Drive Pinion Bearing Cup
43	Differential Drive Pinion Collapsible Spacer
44	Differential Pinion Bearing
45	Rear Axle Drive Pinion Shaft Oil Slinger
46	Rear Axle Drive Pinion Seal
47	Rear Axle Universal Joint Flange
48	Drive Pinion Nut
49	Formed Vent Hose
A	Tighten to 38-52 N·m (28-38 Lb-Ft)
B	Tighten to 20-41 N·m (15-30 Lb-Ft)
C	Tighten to 95-115 N·m (70-85 Lb-Ft)
D	Tighten to 27-40 N·m (20-30 Lb-Ft)

FM3039500279020X

Fig. 10 Exploded view of 8.8 inch rear axles (Part 2 of 2). Crown Victoria, Grand Marquis, Marauder & Town Car

FM3039800326010X

Fig. 11 Exploded view of 7½ & 8.8 inch rear axles (Part 1 of 2). Mustang

Traction-Lok Limited Slip Differential

EXCEPT FIVE HUNDRED, FREESTYLE, MONTEGO, 2008 SABLE, TAURUS & TAURUS X

For differential case and ring gear runout inspections and differential bearing replacement, refer to "Conventional Differential."

1. Remove and discard ring gear to differential case mounting bolts.
2. Tap on ring gear using a suitable mallet and remove ring gear from case.
3. Remove pinion shaft lock screw and pinion shaft.
4. Remove preloaded S shaped spring, **Fig. 27. S shaped spring is under tension.**
5. Rotate pinion gears and thrust washers using 12-inch socket extension installed into pinion gear rotator tool No. T80P-4205-A, or equivalent, until they can be removed through access hole.
6. Remove lefthand and righthand side gears, clutch packs and shims, **Fig. 28**. Record order and side removed from, then tag for assembly alignment.
7. Apply suitable lubricant to clutch plates, then install lefthand side gear, clutch pack and new shim into differential case. Repeat procedure for righthand hand side.
8. Install pinion gears and thrust washers 180° apart and in contact with side gears.
9. Align gears with pinion shaft bore using 12-inch socket extension installed in pinion shaft rotator, **Fig. 29**.
10. Install S shaped preload spring into differential using soft faced hammer.

FIVE HUNDRED, FREESTYLE, MONTEGO, 2008 SABLE, TAURUS & TAURUS X

These vehicles have no serviceable subassemblies, should internal failure occur it will be required to replace the differential assembly.

CLEANING & INSPECTION

Conventional Differential

Clean all components in suitable solvent. Dry all components except bearings with compressed air or shop towels. Allow bearings to air dry or use shop towels. **Do not use compressed air to dry bearings.**

Inspect differential bearings and cups for wear, pitting, galling, flat spots or cracks. Any bearing or cup showing any signs of wear or damage must be replaced. Bearings and respective cups must be replaced as an assembly only. Do not attempt to interchange bearings and cups as bearing life will be affected.

Inspect non-machined differential case surfaces for nicks and burrs which can be removed with an oil stone or fine tooth file. Inspect pinion shaft bore to ensure it is not elongated or worn. If damage is evident, differential case must be replaced. Inspect machined differential surfaces and counterbores. They must be smooth and free of nicks, gouges, cracks and other visible damage. If damage is evident, differential case must be replaced.

Item	Description
1	Axle Housing Cover Bolt
2	Rear Axle Brake Line Clip
3	Axle Housing Cover
4	Differential Pinion Thrust Washer
5	Differential Pinion Gear
6	Differential Side Gear
7	Differential Side Gear Thrust Washer
8	Differential Bearing
9	Differential Bearing Cup
10	Differential Bearing Shim
11	Rear Axle Housing
12	Filler Plug
13	Pinion Nut
14	Rear Axle Universal Joint Flange
15	Rear Axle Drive Pinion Seal
16	Rear Axle Drive Pinion Shaft Oil Slinger
17	Differential Pinion Bearing
18	Differential Drive Pinion Collapsible Spacer
19	Differential Drive Pinion Bearing Cup
20	Rear Disc Brake Rotor
21	Rear Disc Brake Caliper
22	Rear Brake Anti-Lock Sensor Indicator
23	Axle Shaft Flange
24	Bolt (3 Req'd)
25	Rear Wheel Disc Brake Shield
26	Caliper Anchor Bolt
27	Left Hand Rear Disc Brake Adapter
28	Rear Brake Anti-Lock Sensor

Item	Description
29	Bolt
30	Bolt
31	Clip
32	Rear Axle Pinion Bearing Cup
33	Differential Pinion Bearing
34	Drive Pinion Bearing Adjustment Shim
35	Drive Pinion
36	Bearing Cap
37	Ring Gear
38	Differential Pinion Shaft Lock Pin
39	U-Washer
40	Differential Pinion Shaft
41	Rear Axle Differential Gear Case Bolt
42	Bearing Cap Bolt
43	Differential Case
A	Tighten to 38-52 N·m (28-38 Lb-Ft)
B	Tighten to 95-115 N·m (70-84 Lb-Ft)
C	Tighten to 20-41 N·m (15-30 Lb-Ft)
D	Tighten to 190 N·m (140 Lb-Ft)
E	Tighten to 8-12 N·m (70-106 Lb-In)
F	Tighten to 87-119 N·m (65-87 Lb-Ft)
G	Tighten to 4.5-6.8 N·m (40-60 Lb-In)
H	Tighten to 10-14 N·m (89-123 Lb-In)
J	Tighten to 102-122 N·m (76-89 Lb-Ft)
K	Tighten to 20-41 N·m (15-30 Lb-Ft)

FM3039800326020X

Fig. 11 Exploded view of 7½ & 8.8 inch rear axles (Part 2 of 2). Mustang

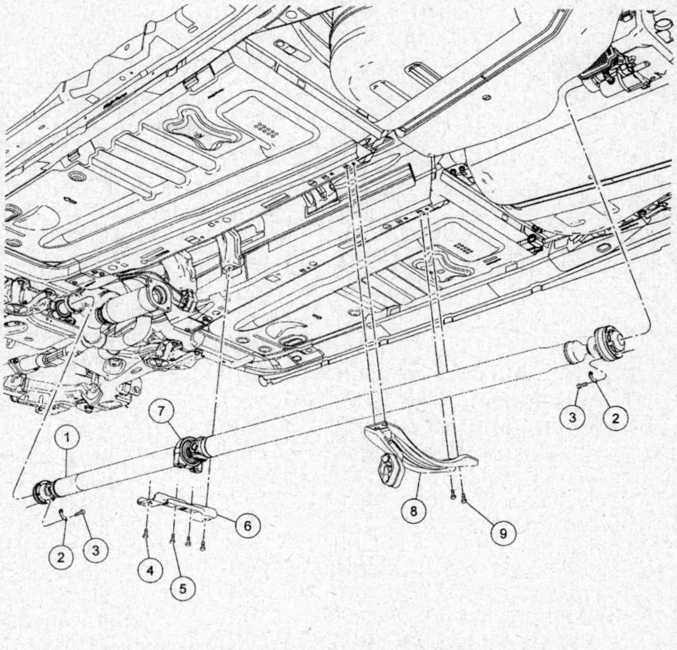

Item	Description
1	Driveshaft assembly
2	Driveshaft flange washer (6 required)
3	Driveshaft flange bolts (12 required)
4	Center bearing bracket bolts (2 required)

Item	Description
5	Center bearing bolts (2 required)
6	Center bearing bracket
7	Center bearing
8	Exhaust support brace
9	Exhaust support brace bolts (4 required) (part of

ARM0400000000764

Fig. 12 Driveshaft replacement. Five Hundred, Freestyle, Montego, 2008 Sable, Taurus & Taurus X

Inspect pinion shaft for excessive wear, scoring or galling. Ensure shaft is smooth and concentric. If any wear or damage is evident, replace the shaft. Inspect pinion shaft lockpin for damage and to ensure it has a snug fit in the differential case. Replace lockpin or case as required.

Inspect pinion and ring gears for worn or chipped teeth, cracks, damaged bearing journals or mounting bolt threads. If any of the above are evident, replace ring gear and pinion as a matched set.

Inspect pinion and side gears. Gears must exhibit a uniform contact pattern without any signs of cracks, wear, scoring or galling. If any of the above are evident, replace all the gears. Inspect thrust washers for wear and replace as required.

Inspect pinion and ring gears for worn or chipped teeth, cracks, damaged bearing journals or mounting bolt threads. If any of the above are evident, replace ring gear and pinion as a matched set.

Inspect axle shaft C-locks (if equipped) for signs of cracks or wear and replace as required.

Traction-Lok Limited Slip Differential

The cleaning and inspection of these units is the same as for conventional differentials except that cleaning solvent should not be allowed to contact the clutch plates. The clutch plates should be wiped clean only. In addition, the following steps should be performed which only apply to the Traction-Lok differential.

Visually inspect clutch packs, side gears, pinion gears and pinion shaft for damage or wear.

Place each clutch pack without shims into tool No. T80P-4946-A, or equivalent, **Fig. 30**. **Torque** nut to 60 inch lbs. Determine thickness of new shims by installing thickest feeler blade possible between clutch pack and too, then note size for use during assembly, **Fig. 31**.

ASSEMBLE

Crown Victoria, Grand Marquis, Marauder, Mustang & Town Car

1. Install replacement ring gear. Apply suitable locking compound to new bolts and **torque** to 70–85 ft. lbs.
2. Apply suitable axle lubricant to differential bearing bores.
3. Place differential bearing cups on bearings and set differential assembly in axle housing. **If ring gear and pinion gear have punch marks, assemble ring gear in carrier so marked tooth on pinion is indexed between marked teeth of ring gear.**
4. Mount suitable dial indicator on axle housing cover flange and measure ring gear backlash. Refer to **Fig. 32** for specifications.
5. If backlash is within specifications, increase both lefthand and righthand side shims by .006 inch to provide proper differential bearing preload. Ensure shims are fully seated and case assembly turns freely.
6. If backlash is not within specifications, correct by increasing thickness of one shim and decreasing thickness on other shim by same amount. Refer to **Fig. 33** for approximate shim change.
7. If backlash measured more than zero, add .020 inch to righthand side of case and subtract .020 inch from lefthand side of case, then inspect backlash again.
8. If backlash now ranges within specifications, install shims and bearing caps.
9. **Torque** bearing cap bolts to 70–85 ft.

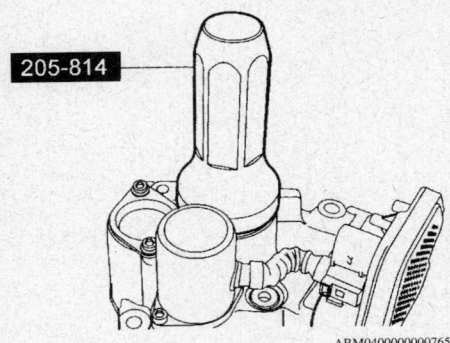

205-814

ARM0400000000765

Fig. 13 Outer drive pinion seal installation. Five Hundred, Freestyle, Montego, 2008 Sable, Taurus & Taurus X

lbs., then rotate differential case assembly several turns in both directions.

10. Inspect tooth mesh contacting pattern using suitable white marking compound applied to ring gear. **Tooth mesh contacting pattern can be improved by installing propeller shaft and axle assemblies and rotating both tires in drive and coast direction.**
11. Contacting pattern should be within primary area of ring gear tooth surface avoiding narrow contact with outer perimeter of tooth. Inspect pattern on drive (pull) side of ring gear. If serious error is determined, inspect pinion shim selection.
12. Install axle housing cover, driveshaft and axle assemblies.
13. Fill rear axle assembly with suitable axle lubricant .
14. **On models equipped with 7½ inch Traction-Lok differential,** subtract 3 ounces of axle lubricant and replace with 3 ounces of Friction Modifier part No. C8AZ-19546-A, or equivalent.

LS & Thunderbird

1. Draw-file differential ring gear mounting surface to remove any nicks or burrs.
2. Place ring gear onto differential case, then hand start three bolts to align ring gear holes and differential case.
3. Place differential case and ring gear onto press bed blocks with ring gear teeth facing down.
4. Press ring gear into place
5. Install remaining ring gear bolts and **torque** to 77 ft. lbs.
6. **On models equipped with aluminum axle,** proceed as follows:
   a. Place differential case, lefthand master bearing tool No. T93P-4222-A, righthand master bearing tool No. T93P-4222-B, or equivalents, and ring gear into rear axle housing.
   b. Ring gear bolt heads inside rear

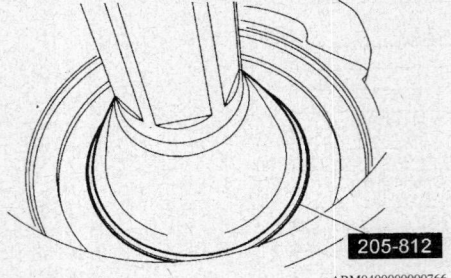

205-812

ARM0400000000766

Fig. 14 Inner drive pinion seal installation. Five Hundred, Freestyle, Montego, 2008 Sable, Taurus & Taurus X

axle housing may interfere. If so, remove 3–5 bolts to provide clearance.
   c. Attach dial indicator with indicator tip positioned on machined surface of case flange.
   d. Rock ring gear to allow full mesh with pinion gear.
   e. With gears in full mesh, set dial indicator to zero.
   f. Move differential case as far as possible and record reading.
   g. Record reading for differential bearing shim selection procedure.
   h. Remove dial indicator and differential case from rear axle housing.
   i. Stand height of both differential bearings must be measured prior to installation.
   j. Place bearing preload tool No. T93P-4220-AR, or equivalent, base in suitable soft-jawed vise with bearing mounting surface above vise jaws.
   k. Position differential bearing on bearing preload tool base.
   l. Attach bolt, spring, washers and spacer. Tighten bolt.
   m. Mark differential bearings, lefthand and righthand before measuring.
   n. Invert bearing preload tool No. T93P-4220-AR, or equivalent, and clamp bolt head in suitable vise.
   o. Position suitable depth micrometer flat on differential bearing.
   p. Measure stand height of both differential bearings and record for differential bearing shim selection.
   q. Press lefthand and righthand differential bearing on differential case.
   r. Install differential carrier spreader tool No. T4000-E, or equivalent, and dial indicator.
   s. **Overspreading may damage rear axle housing.**
   t. Tighten and loosen housing spreader adapter screw to normalize housing spreader adapters prior to final dial indicator reading.
   u. Adjust dial indicator to zero and tighten differential carrier spreader screw to spread rear axle housing to .030 inch.
   v. Remove dial indicator.

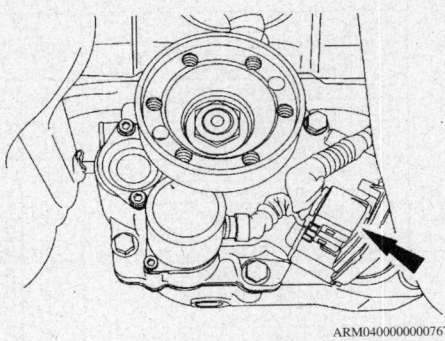

ARM0400000000767

Fig. 15 Differential Electronic Module (DEM) connector location. Five Hundred, Freestyle, Montego, 2008 Sable, Taurus & Taurus X

7. **On all models,** apply light coating of Premium Long-Life Grease XG-1-C, or equivalent, to differential bearing shim to help hold in place.
8. Select correct size lefthand side differential bearing shim as follows:
   a. Add end play and bearing height.
   b. Subtract backlash.
   c. Round off initial thickness to nearest shim thickness.
9. Add end play and bearing height.
10. Add backlash.
11. Round off initial thickness to nearest shim thickness.
12. Install differential bearing shims in rear axle housing.
13. Position differential bearing cups on differential bearings.
14. Lower differential case in place between differential bearing shims.
15. Install bearing caps in original positions and **torque** bolts to 77 ft. lbs.
16. Tighten bearing cap bolts prior to releasing housing spreader.
17. Remove differential carrier spreader and move dial indicator to 12 o'clock position.
18. Position indicator needle centrally on drive tooth and zero indicator.
19. Turn ring gear without turning pinion gear.
20. Record indicator reading.
21. Measure ring gear backlash at four places to obtain consistent reading.
22. If backlash is not .004 inch, correct by increasing thickness of one differential bearing shim and decreasing thickness of other differential bearing shim by the same amount.
23. Ensure machined surfaces on both rear axle housing and differential housing cover are clean and free of oil before installing new silicone sealant.
24. Inside of rear axle must be covered when cleaning machined surface to prevent contamination.
25. Apply new continuous bead of Silicone Rubber D6AZ-19562-AA, or equivalent, sealant to differential housing cover.
26. Install differential housing cover.
27. Install rear axle and refill.

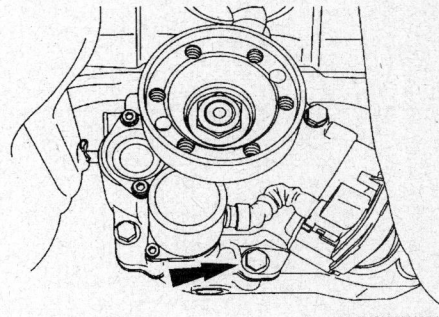

Fig. 16   Active on-demand coupling removal. Five Hundred, Freestyle, Montego, 2008 Sable, Taurus & Taurus X

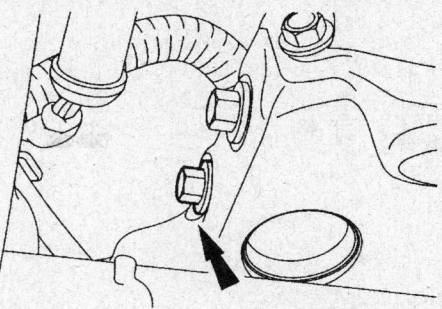

Fig. 17   Active on-demand coupling oil fill hole location. Five Hundred, Freestyle, Montego, 2008 Sable, Taurus & Taurus X

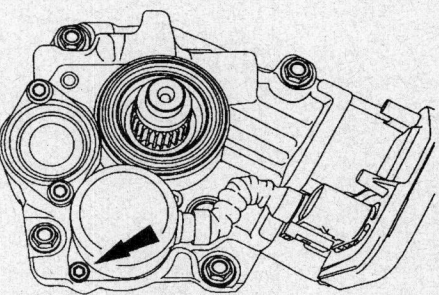

Fig. 18   Active on-demand coupling oil pump replacement. Five Hundred, Freestyle, Montego, 2008 Sable, Taurus & Taurus X

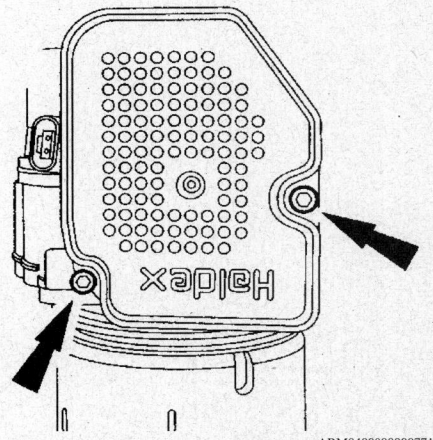

Fig. 19   Differential Electronic Module (DEM) mounting bolt locations. Five Hundred, Freestyle, Montego, 2008 Sable, Taurus & Taurus X

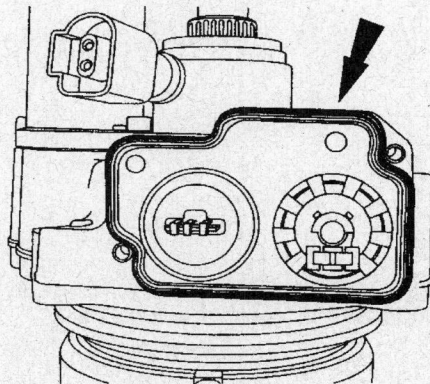

Fig. 20   Differential Electronic Module (DEM) spacer plate. Five Hundred, Freestyle, Montego, 2008 Sable, Taurus & Taurus X

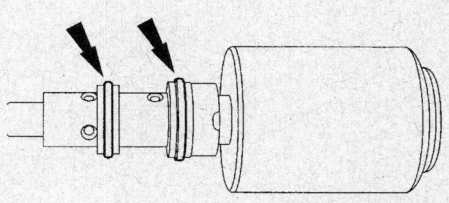

Fig. 21   Differential Electronic Module (DEM) solenoid valve & O-ring seals. Five Hundred, Freestyle, Montego, 2008 Sable, Taurus & Taurus X

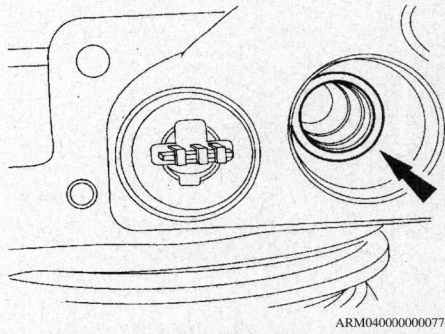

Fig. 22   Differential Electronic Module (DEM) solenoid valve seat seal. Five Hundred, Freestyle, Montego, 2008 Sable, Taurus & Taurus X

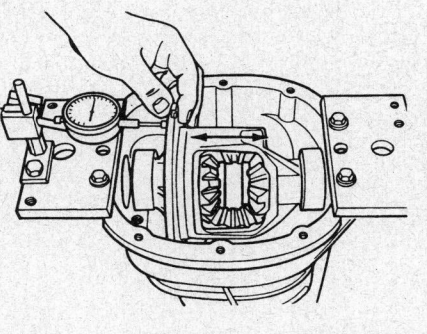

Fig. 23   Differential case end play measurement

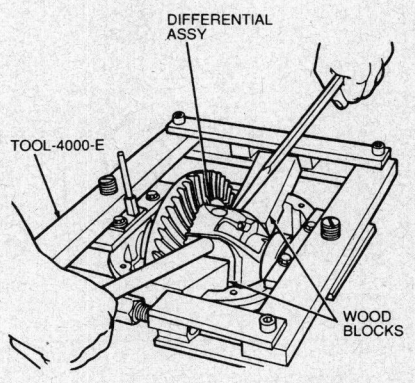

Fig. 24   Differential case removal

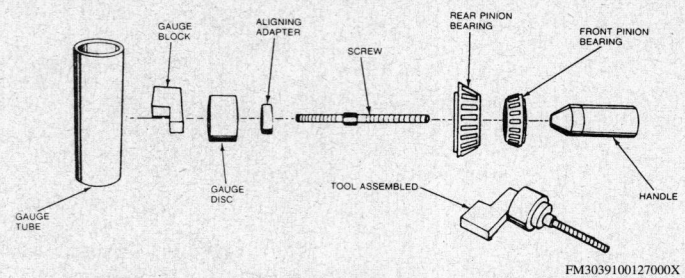

Fig. 25   Rear axle pinion depth gauge

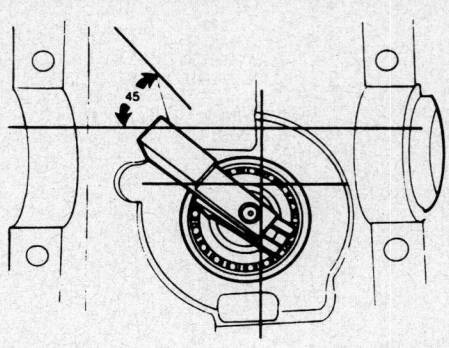

Fig. 26   Pinion depth gauge block installation

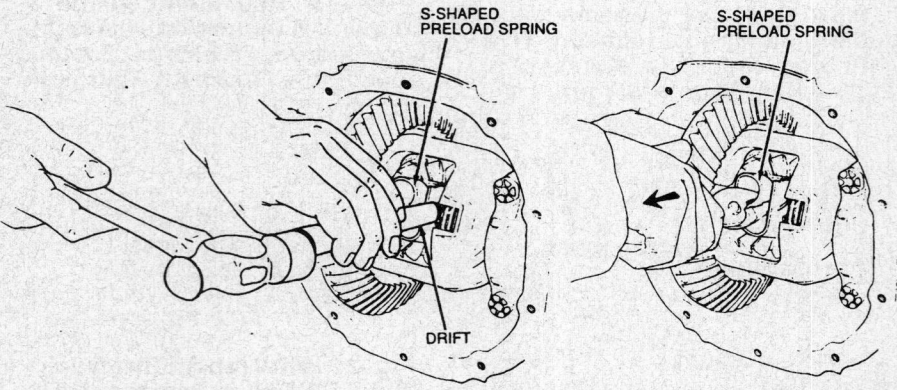

Fig. 27   C-clips S shaped preload spring removal. Traction-Lok. Except Five Hundred, Freestyle, Montego, 2008 Sable, Taurus & Taurus X

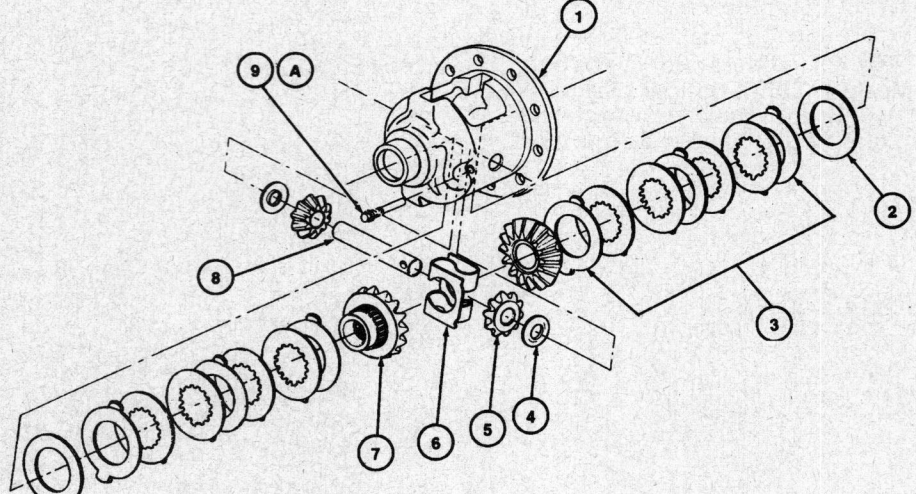

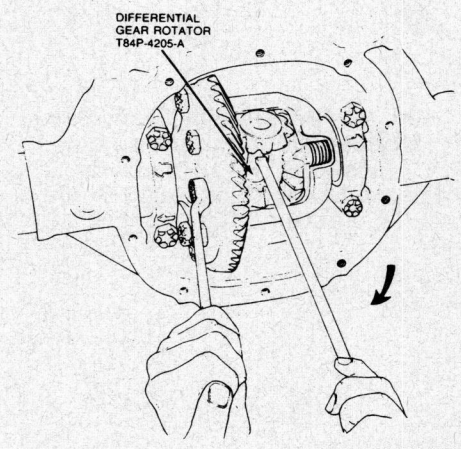

Fig. 29   Pinion gear removal & installation. Traction-Lok

Item	Description	Item	Description
1	Differential Case	6	Differential Clutch Spring
2	Rear Axle Differential Clutch Shim	7	Differential Side Gear
3	Differential Clutch Pack	8	Differential Pinion Shaft
4	Differential Pinion Thrust Washer	9	Differential Pinion Shaft Lock Pin
5	Differential Pinion Gear	A	Tighten to 20-41 N·m (15-30 Lb-Ft)

Fig. 28   Exploded view of Traction-Lok., Except Five Hundred, Freestyle, Montego, 2008 Sable, Taurus & Taurus X

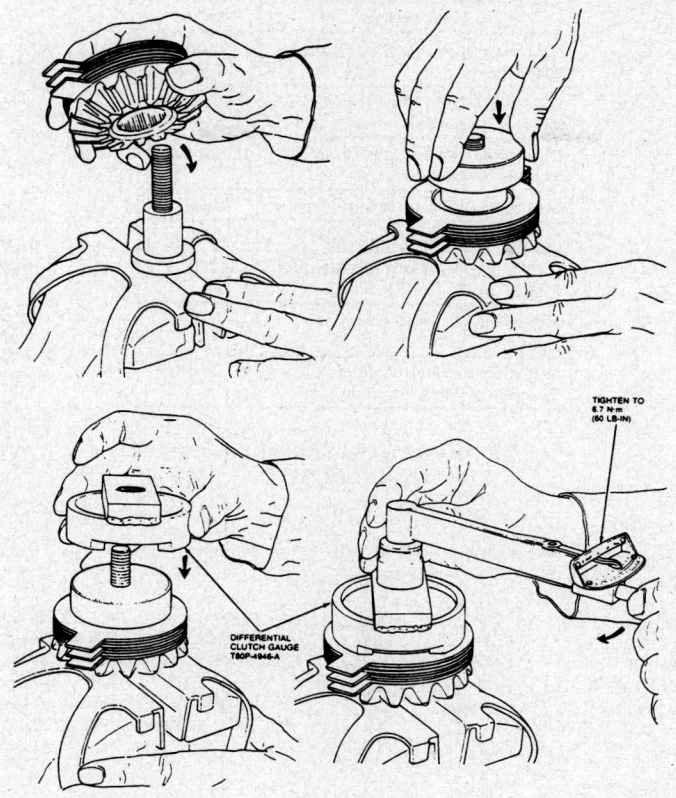

FM3039100124000X

Fig. 30 Shim thickness measuring. Traction-Lok

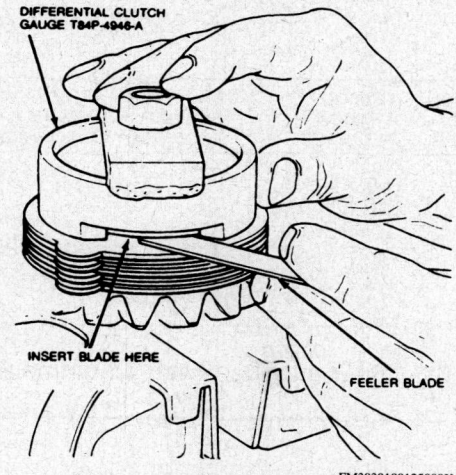

FM3039100125000X

Fig. 31 Shim thickness measurement using tool No. T80P-4946-A, or equivalent. Traction-Lok

Description	inches
Maximum Runout of Backface of Ring Gear	0.004
Differential Side Gear Thrust Washer Thickness	0.030-0.032
Differential Pinion Gear Thrust Washer Thickness	0.030-0.032
Maximum Differential Case Runout	0.003
Nominal Pinion Locating Shim	0.030
Backlash Between Ring Gear and Pinion Teeth	0.008-0.015
Maximum Backlash Variation Between Teeth	0.004
Maximum Radial Runout of Companion Flange in Assembly	0.010 TIR

FM3039400281000X

Fig. 32 Rear axle specifications & tolerances

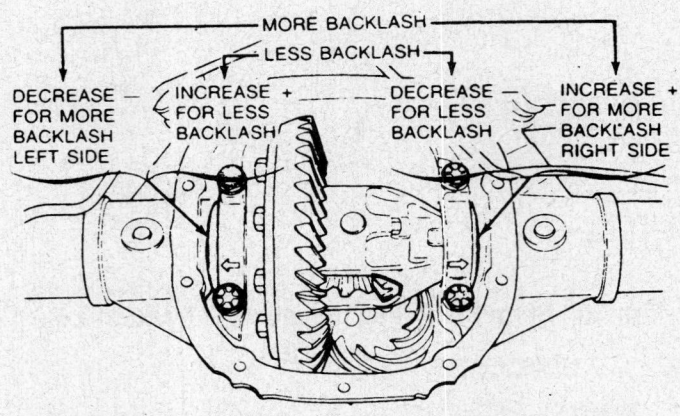

BACKLASH CHANGE REQUIRED	THICKNESS CHANGE REQUIRED	BACKLASH CHANGE REQUIRED	THICKNESS CHANGE REQUIRED
.001	.002	.009	.012
.002	.002	.010	.014
.003	.004	.011	.014
.004	.006	.012	.016
.005	.006	.013	.018
.006	.008	.014	.018
.007	.010	.015	.020
.008	.010		

FM3039100129000X

Fig. 33 Rear axle backlash adjustment

TIRE PRESSURE MONITORING SYSTEM

INDEX

	Page No.
Component Service	20-14
Pressure Monitor Sensor, Replace	20-15
Strap & Cradle Type	20-15
Valve Stem Type.............	20-15
Tire Pressure Monitoring System (TPMS) Sensor Activation.....................	20-14
Tire Pressure Monitoring System (TPMS) Sensor Training...............	20-14
Description	20-1
Diagnosis & Testing.............	20-2
Accessing Diagnostic Trouble Codes	20-2
Clearing Diagnostic Trouble Codes	20-3

	Page No.
Diagnostic (Pinpoint) Tests......	20-2
Crown Victoria & Grand Marquis	20-2
Mustang	20-2
Sable, Taurus & Taurus X.....	20-2
Diagnostic Trouble Code Interpretation	20-2
Intermittent & Poor Connections	20-2
Intermittents	20-2
Poor Connections.............	20-3
Symptom Tests	20-2
Diagnostic Chart Index........	20-6
Precautions......................	20-1
Air Bag Systems................	20-1
Ambient Temperature Change & Tire Pressure	20-1

	Page No.
Battery Ground Cable...........	20-1
TPMS Sensor Battery...........	20-1
Tire Inflation	20-1
Troubleshooting	20-1
Inspection & Verification	20-2
TPMS Indicator Flashes	20-2
No Communication w/SJB or DDM	20-2
Tire Pressure Monitor Fault ...	20-2
Tire Pressure Sensor Fault ...	20-2
TPMS Indicator Illuminates Continuously..................	20-2
Low Tire Pressure	20-2

PRECAUTIONS

Air Bag Systems

Refer to "Air Bag System Precautions" in the front of this manual for system disarming and arming procedures.

Battery Ground Cable

Prior to service, disconnect battery ground cable and isolate as required.

TPMS Sensor Battery

The Tire Pressure Monitoring System (TPMS) sensor battery may release hazardous chemicals if exposed to extreme mechanical damage. If these chemicals contact the skin or eyes, flush immediately with water for at least 15 minutes and get prompt medical attention. If any part of the battery is swallowed, contact a physician immediately. When disposing of TPMS sensors, follow the correct procedures for hazardous material disposal.

Tire Inflation

Measure tire pressures using digital tire gauge tool No. 204-354, or equivalent. Place air chuck straight on the valve stem to inflate tire. **Do not cock air chuck during inflation cycle.** Use a round head air chuck on tire pressure sensors. **Do not use air chucks with long shanks.**

Ambient Temperature Change & Tire Pressure

Tire pressures fluctuate with tempera-ture changes. Tire pressure must be set to specification when tires are at outdoor ambient temperatures. If the vehicle is allowed to warm up to shop temperatures and the outside temperature is less than shop temperature, the tire inflation pressure must be adjusted accordingly.

If the tires are inflated to specification at shop temperatures and the vehicle is moved outdoors when the outdoor ambient temperature is significantly lower, the tire pressure may drop enough to be detected by the TPMS and activate the TPMS warning lamp.

As the ambient temperature decreases by 10°F, tire pressure decreases 1 psi. Adjust the tire pressure by 1 psi for each 10°F ambient temperature drop required to keep the tire at the specified vehicle certification label pressure, **Fig. 1.**

DESCRIPTION

The Tire Pressure Monitoring System (TPMS) monitors the air pressure of all tires.

On Mustang, Sable, Taurus and Taurus X models, the wheel-mounted pressure sensors transmit signals via radio frequency signals to the Smart Junction Box (SJB).

On Crown Victoria and Grand Marquis models, the wheel-mounted pressure sensors transmit signals via radio frequency signals to the Drive Door Module (DDM).

On all models, the TPMS function is integral to the SJB or DDM. These transmissions are sent approximately every 60 seconds when the vehicle speed exceeds 20 mph. The TPMS compares each tire pressure sensor transmission against a low-pressure limit. If it has been determined that the tire pressure has fallen below this limit, the SJB or DDM communicates this on the vehicle communication bus to the instrument cluster. The instru-ment cluster then illuminates the TPMS indicator and displays the appropriate message(s) in the message center.

TROUBLESHOOTING

A full-sized, matching spare wheel and tire, that is identical to the road wheel and tire, is available as an optional accessory. This spare wheel and tire is equipped with a tire pressure sensor but the sensor is not initially programmed.

If this spare wheel and tire is in use on the vehicle, the sensor must be trained and the remaining three sensors must be re-trained as well. If all 4 sensors are not trained, the (TPMS) warning indicator will illuminate.

If the spare tire is in use (including the optional full-sized, matching spare wheel and tire), damaged road tire must be repaired and installed on vehicle to restore complete TPMS functionality before carrying out any diagnosis.

For vehicles with different front and rear tire pressures), the tire pressure sensors must be trained following a tire rotation. Failure to train the sensors will cause the TPMS indicator to illuminate. For vehicles with the same tire pressures for front and rear tires, tire rotation will not affect the system.

Ensure that all the wheels and tires installed on the vehicle are inflated to the correct pressure and trained before attempting to diagnose a TPMS concern. Refer to "Tire Pressure Monitoring System (TPMS) Sensor Training."

The TPMS sensors do not transmit when the vehicle is stationary. If the vehicle has been stationary for more than 30 minutes, it will be necessary to wake up the sensors so they will transmit the latest tire pressure information. Refer to "Tire Pressure Monitoring System (TPMS) Sensor Training."

Table is based on a Garage Temperature of 70°F. Max Pressure Adjustment is 7 psi.

Outside Temperature (°F)	Tire Placard Pressure (PSI)																	
	30	32	34	35	38	40	41	42	45	50	55	60	65	70	75	80	85	90
70	30	32	34	35	38	40	41	42	45	50	55	60	65	70	75	80	85	90
60	31	33	35	36	39	41	42	43	46	51	56	61	67	72	77	82	87	92
50	32	34	36	37	40	42	43	44	47	53	58	63	68	73	79	84	89	94
40	33	35	37	38	41	43	44	45	49	54	59	64	70	75	80	86	91	96
30	34	36	38	39	42	44	46	47	50	55	61	66	72	77	82	87	92	97
20	35	37	39	40	43	46	47	48	51	57	62	67	72	77	82	87	92	97
10	36	38	40	41	43	47	48	49	52	57	62	67	72	77	82	87	92	97
0	37	39	41	42	45	47	48	49	52	57	62	67	72	77	82	87	92	97
-10	37	39	41	42	45	47	48	49	52	57	62	67	72	77	82	87	92	97
-20	37	39	41	42	45	47	48	49	52	57	62	67	72	77	82	87	92	97
-30	37	39	41	42	45	47	48	49	52	57	62	67	72	77	82	87	92	97
-40	37	39	41	42	45	47	48	49	52	57	62	67	72	77	82	87	92	97

ARM0700000000039

Fig. 1 Tire pressure adjustment chart

TPMS Indicator Illuminates Continuously

LOW TIRE PRESSURE

The TPMS indicator remains on continuously for the following condition:
1. TPMS indicator is illuminated solid and message center displays LOW TIRE PRESSURE
2. This is displayed when any of tire pressures are low.
3. When this condition exists, tire pressure must be adjusted to recommended cold pressure as indicated on vehicle certification label.

TPMS Indicator Flashes

The TPMS indicator flashes for 70 seconds and then remains ON solid when the ignition key is turned to the ON position for the following conditions:

TIRE PRESSURE SENSOR FAULT

1. Message center displays TIRE SENSOR FAULT when tire pressure sensor is malfunctioning.
2. Refer "Symptom Tests."

NO COMMUNICATION w/SJB OR DDM

1. TPMS indicator is illuminated when instrument cluster has received no signals from the SJB or DDM for more than five seconds
2. Message center displays TIRE MONITOR FAULT
3. Refer "Symptom Tests."

TIRE PRESSURE MONITOR FAULT

1. Message center will display TIRE MONITOR FAULT when TPMS is malfunctioning or communication with instrument cluster has been lost.
2. Refer "Symptom Tests."

Inspection & Verification

1. Tire pressure sensors are not designed to be used with aftermarket wheels.
2. Use of run-flat tires (tires with steel body cord plies in tire sidewall) where not originally equipped, may cause TPMS system to malfunction.
3. Valve-mounted and strap-mounted TPMS sensors are not compatible. Swapping wheels from one vehicle to another with different systems will adversely affect TPMS operation.
4. Swapping wheels on vehicles with same TPMS will set TPMS fault if sensors are not trained. Refer to "Tire Pressure Monitoring System (TPMS) Sensor Training."
5. Non-OEM modifications made to vehicle may result in false TPMS warnings.
6. Inspect for following mechanical concerns:
   a. Low tire pressure.
   b. TPMS sensor damaged or missing.
   c. Spare tire installed as road wheel.
   d. Incorrect TPMS sensor installed.
   e. TPMS sensor installed incorrectly.
   f. Non-OEM wheels installed (aftermarket rims).
   g. Non-OEM equipped run-flat tires installed.
   h. Other non-OEM modifications (roll cages, service barriers, part racks, ladder racks).
7. Inspect for following electrical concerns:
   a. Wiring, terminals or connectors.
   b. Electrical connectors.
   c. SJB or DDM missing or damaged.
   d. Aftermarket electronic accessories.
   e. Battery Junction Box (BJB) fuse.
   f. Central JUNCTION BOX (CJB) fuses.
   g. DDM antenna disconnected.
8. If an obvious cause is found, correct cause before proceeding.
9. Ensure to use latest scan tool software release.
10. If cause is not visually evident, connect suitably programmed scan tool to Data Link Connector (DLC).
11. If scan tool does not communicate with Vehicle Communication Module (VCM), proceed as follows:
    a. Inspect VCM connection to vehicle.
    b. Inspect scan tool connection to VCM.
    c. Inspect for no power to scan tool.
12. If scan tool does not communicate with vehicle, proceed as follows:
    a. Ensure ignition key is in ON position.
    b. Ensure scan tool operation with known good vehicle.
    c. Inspect for no response from PCM,
13. Perform network test.
14. If scan tool responds with no communication for one or more modules, inspect appropriate network.
15. Clear continuous DTCs and carry out self-test diagnostics for TPMS module.

DIAGNOSIS & TESTING

Accessing Diagnostic Trouble Codes

Connect a suitably programmed scan tool to Data Link Connector (DLC) and follow manufacturer's instructions.

Diagnostic Trouble Code Interpretation

Refer to **Figs. 2 through 4** for Diagnostic Trouble Code (DTC) interpretation.

Symptom Tests

Refer to **Figs. 5 through 7** for symptom test procedures.

Diagnostic (Pinpoint) Tests

CROWN VICTORIA & GRAND MARQUIS

Refer to **Figs. 8 through 12** for diagnostic (pinpoint) test procedures.

MUSTANG

Refer to **Figs. 13 through 17** for diagnostic (pinpoint) test procedures.

SABLE, TAURUS & TAURUS X

Refer to **Figs. 18 through 21** for diagnostic (pinpoint) test procedures.

Intermittent & Poor Connections

INTERMITTENTS

Most intermittents are caused by faulty electrical connections or wiring. Inspect for the following:

DTC	Description	Source	Action
B106A	Pressure Sensor Range Bit Incorrect State	Driver door module (DDM)	Go To Pinpoint Test H .
B106B	Tire Pressure Sensor Low Battery (Could be set configuring new DDM)	DDM	Go To Pinpoint Test I .
B106D	Tire Pressure Monitor System (TPMS) Initiators Not Configured	DDM	DTC B106D is only present when a new DDM is installed, the DDM is incorrectly flashed or the DDM is incorrectly configured. Successfully configuring the DDM is the only way to clear this DTC. VERIFY the DDM is correctly configured. If DTC B106D is still present.
B2477	Module Configuration Failure/Mismatch	DDM	DTC B2477 is only present when a new DDM is installed, the DDM is incorrectly flashed or the DDM is incorrectly configured. Successfully configuring the DDM is the only way to clear this DTC. Make sure the DDM is configured correctly. If DTC B2477 is still present.
B2868	LF Tire Pressure Sensor Fault	DDM	DTC B2868 is only present when a new DDM is installed, the DDM is flashed or the DDM is reconfigured. TRAIN the tire pressure sensors. REFER to Tire Pressure Monitoring System (TPMS) Sensor Training .
B2869	RF Tire Pressure Sensor Fault	DDM	DTC B2869 is only present when a new DDM is installed, the DDM is flashed or the DDM is reconfigured. TRAIN the tire pressure sensors. REFER to Tire Pressure Monitoring System (TPMS) Sensor Training .
B287A	Tire Pressure System Fault	DDM	Go To Pinpoint Test G .
B2870	RR Tire Pressure Sensor Fault	DDM	DTC B2870 is only present when a new DDM is installed, the DDM is flashed or the DDM is reconfigured. TRAIN the tire pressure sensors. REFER to Tire Pressure Monitoring System (TPMS) Sensor Training .
B2871	LR Tire Pressure Sensor Fault	DDM	DTC B2871 is only present when a new DDM is installed, the DDM is flashed or the DDM is reconfigured. TRAIN the tire pressure sensors. REFER to Tire Pressure Monitoring System (TPMS) Sensor Training .

ARM0700000000040

Fig. 2   DTC interpretation (Part 1 of 2). Crown Victoria & Grand Marquis

1. Wiring broken inside insulation.
2. Poor connection between male and female terminal at connector.
3. Poor terminal to wire connection. Some conditions which fall under this are:
   a. Poor crimps.
   b. Poor solder joints.
   c. Crimping over wire insulation rather than wire.
   d. Corrosion in wire to terminal contact.
4. Wire insulation which is rubbed through. This causes an intermittent short as bare area touches other wiring or components.

POOR CONNECTIONS

1. It is important to test terminal contact at component and any inline connectors before replacing suspect component.
2. Mating terminals must be inspected to ensure good terminal contact.
3. Poor connection between male and female terminal at a connector may be result of contamination or deformation.
4. Contamination may be caused by:
   a. Connector halves being improperly connected.
   b. Missing or damaged seal.
   c. Damaged connector.
   d. Exposing terminals to moisture and dirt.
5. Deformation is caused by:
   a. Probing connector terminal mating side without proper adapter.
   b. Improperly joining connector halves.
   c. Repeatedly separating and joining connector halves.

DTC	Description	Source	Action
B2872	Tire Pressure Sensor Fault	DDM	NOTE: If the vehicle has been stationary for more than 30 minutes, the sensors will go into a "sleep mode" to conserve battery power. It will be necessary to wake them up so they will transmit the latest tire pressure information to the DDM. ACTIVATE the TPMS sensors. REFER to Tire Pressure Monitoring System (TPMS) Sensor Activation . Go To Pinpoint Test G .
C2780	Electrical Control Unit (ECU) in Manufacturing Mode	DDM	DTC C2780 is only present when a new DDM is installed, the DDM is flashed or the DDM is reconfigured. TRAIN the tire pressure sensors. REFER to Tire Pressure Monitoring System (TPMS) Sensor Training

ARM0700000000041

Fig. 2   DTC interpretation (Part 2 of 2). Crown Victoria & Grand Marquis

DTC	Description	Source	Action
B106A	Pressure Sensor Range Bit Incorrect State	Smart Junction Box (SJB)	Go To Pinpoint Test G .
B106B	Tire Pressure Sensor Low Battery (Could be set configuring new SJB)	SJB	Go To Pinpoint Test H .
B106D	Tire Pressure Monitor System (TPMS) Initiators Not Configured	SJB	DTC B106D is only present when a new SJB is installed, the SJB is flashed or the SJB is incorrectly configured. Successfully configuring the SJB is the only way to clear this DTC. VERIFY the SJB is correctly configured. If DTC B106D is still present.
B1342	ECU is Defective	SJB	INSTALL a new SJB.
B2477	Module Configuration Failure/Mismatch	SJB	DTC B2477 is only present when a new SJB is installed, the SJB is incorrectly flashed or the SJB is incorrectly configured. Successfully configuring the SJB is the only way to clear this DTC. Make sure the SJB is configured correctly. If the DTC B2477 is still present.
B2868	Left Front Tire Pressure Sensor Fault	SJB	DTC B2868 is only present when a new SJB is installed, the SJB is flashed or the SJB is reconfigured. TRAIN the tire pressure sensors. REFER to Tire Pressure Monitoring System (TPMS) Sensor Training .
B2869	Right Front Tire Pressure Sensor Fault	SJB	DTC B2869 is only present when a new SJB is installed, the SJB is flashed or the SJB is reconfigured. TRAIN the tire pressure sensors. REFER to Tire Pressure Monitoring System (TPMS) Sensor Training .
B278A	Tire Pressure System Fault	SJB	Go To Pinpoint Test F .
B2870	Right Rear Tire Pressure Sensor Fault	SJB	DTC B2870 is only present when a new SJB is installed, the SJB is flashed or the SJB is reconfigured. TRAIN the tire pressure sensors. REFER to Tire Pressure Monitoring System (TPMS) Sensor Training .
B2871	Left Rear Tire Pressure Sensor Fault	SJB	DTC B2871 is only present when a new SJB is installed, the SJB is flashed or the SJB is reconfigured. TRAIN the tire pressure sensors. REFER to Tire Pressure Monitoring System (TPMS) Sensor Training .

ARM0700000000042

Fig. 3   DTC interpretation (Part 1 of 2). Mustang

Clearing Diagnostic Trouble Codes

Connect a suitably programmed scan tool to Data Link Connector (DLC) and follow manufacturer's instructions.

DTC	Description	Source	Action
B106A	Pressure Sensor Range Bit Incorrect State	Smart Junction Box (SJB)	Go To Pinpoint Test G .
B106B	Tire Pressure Sensor Low Battery (Could be set configuring new SJB)	SJB	Go To Pinpoint Test H .
B106D	Tire Pressure Monitor System (TPMS) Initiators Not Configured	SJB	DTC B106D is only present when a new SJB is installed, the SJB is incorrectly flashed or the SJB is incorrectly configured. Successfully configuring the SJB is the only way to clear this DTC. VERIFY the SJB is correctly configured. If DTC B106D is still present.
B1342	ECU is Defective	SJB	INSTALL a new SJB.
B2477	Module Configuration Failure/Mismatch	SJB	DTC B2477 is only present when a new SJB is installed, the SJB is incorrectly flashed or the SJB is incorrectly configured. Successfully configuring the SJB is the only way to clear this DTC. Make sure the SJB is configured correctly. If the DTC B2477 is still present.
B2868	Left Front Tire Pressure Sensor Fault	SJB	DTC B2868 is only present when a new SJB is installed, the SJB is flashed or the SJB is reconfigured. TRAIN the tire pressure sensors. REFER to Tire Pressure Monitoring System (TPMS) Sensor Training .
B2869	Right Front Tire Pressure Sensor Fault	SJB	DTC B2869 is only present when a new SJB is installed, the SJB is flashed or the SJB is reconfigured. TRAIN the tire pressure sensors. REFER to Tire Pressure Monitoring System (TPMS) Sensor Training .
B278A	Tire Pressure System Fault	SJB	Go To Pinpoint Test F .
B2870	Right Rear Tire Pressure Sensor Fault	SJB	DTC B2870 is only present when a new SJB is installed, the SJB is flashed or the SJB is reconfigured. TRAIN the tire pressure sensors. REFER to Tire Pressure Monitoring System (TPMS) Sensor Training .
B2871	Left Rear Tire Pressure Sensor Fault	SJB	DTC B2871 is only present when a new SJB is installed, the SJB is flashed or the SJB is reconfigured. TRAIN the tire pressure sensors. REFER to Tire Pressure Monitoring System (TPMS) Sensor Training .

ARM0700000000043

Fig. 3 DTC interpretation (Part 2 of 2). Mustang

DTC	Description	Source	Action
C2780	ECU in Manufacturing Mode	SJB	DTC C2780 is only present when a new SJB is installed, the SJB is flashed or the SJB is reconfigured. TRAIN the tire pressure sensors. REFER to Tire Pressure Monitoring System (TPMS) Sensor Training .
U0155	Lost Communication with Instrument Cluster	SJB	Diagnose the no communication problem.

ARM0700000000045

Fig. 4 DTC interpretation (Part 2 of 2). Sable, Taurus & Taurus X

DTC	Description	Source	Action
B106A	Pressure Sensor Range Bit Incorrect State	Smart Junction Box (SJB)	Go To Pinpoint Test G .
B106D	Tire Pressure Monitor System (TPMS) Initiators Not Configured	SJB	DTC B106D is only present when a new SJB is installed, the SJB is incorrectly flashed or the SJB is incorrectly configured. Successfully configuring the SJB is the only way to clear this DTC. VERIFY the SJB is correctly configured. If DTC B106D is still present.
B2477	Module Configuration Failure/Mismatch	SJB	DTC B2477 is only present when a new SJB is installed, the SJB is incorrectly flashed or the SJB is incorrectly configured. Successfully configuring the SJB is the only way to clear this DTC. MAKE SURE the SJB is configured correctly. If DTC B2477 is still present.
B2868	LF Tire Pressure Sensor Fault	SJB	DTC B2868 is only present when a new SJB is installed, the SJB is flashed or the SJB is reconfigured. TRAIN the tire pressure sensors. REFER to Tire Pressure Monitoring System (TPMS) Sensor Training .
B2869	RF Tire Pressure Sensor Fault	SJB	DTC B2869 is only present when a new SJB is installed, the SJB is flashed or the SJB is reconfigured. TRAIN the tire pressure sensors. REFER to Tire Pressure Monitoring System (TPMS) Sensor Training .
B2870	RR Tire Pressure Sensor Fault	SJB	DTC B2870 is only present when a new SJB is installed, the SJB is flashed or the SJB is reconfigured. TRAIN the tire pressure sensors. REFER to Tire Pressure Monitoring System (TPMS) Sensor Training .
B2871	LR Tire Pressure Sensor Fault	SJB	DTC B2871 is only present when a new SJB is installed, the SJB is flashed or the SJB is reconfigured. TRAIN the tire pressure sensors. REFER to Tire Pressure Monitoring System (TPMS) Sensor Training .
B2872	Tire Pressure Sensor Fault	SJB	NOTE: If the vehicle has been stationary for more than 30 minutes, the sensors will go into a "sleep mode" to conserve battery power. It will be necessary to wake them up so they will transmit the latest tire pressure information to the SJB. ACTIVATE the TPMS sensors. REFER to Tire Pressure Monitoring System (TPMS) Sensor Activation in. Go To Pinpoint Test F .
B287A	Tire Pressure System Fault	SJB	Go To Pinpoint Test F .

ARM0700000000044

Fig. 4 DTC interpretation (Part 1 of 2). Sable, Taurus & Taurus X

Condition	Possible Sources	Action
• TPMS indicator ON solid when the ignition key is turned to the ON position and message center (if equipped) displays LOW TIRE PRESSURE	• Spare tire currently in use	• INSTALL the repaired road wheel/tire in place of the spare tire.
	• Air pressure not set to specifications listed on the vehicle certification label	Go To Pinpoint Test E .
• DDM will not enter sensor training mode	• Brake on/off (BOO) switch • Ignition switch • Vehicle communication bus • PCM • Driver door module (DDM)	Go To Pinpoint Test F .
• TPMS indicator FLASHES for 70 seconds and then remains ON solid when the ignition key is turned to the ON position, the message center (if equipped) displays TIRE PRESSURE SENSOR FAULT and DTC B2872 is present	• TPMS sensor(s) • TPMS sensor(s) not trained to the DDM • DDM antenna • DDM	• NOTE: If the vehicle has been stationary for more than 30 minutes, the sensors will go into a "sleep mode" to conserve battery power. It will be necessary to wake them up so they will transmit the latest tire pressure information to the DDM. ACTIVATE the TPMS sensors. REFER to Tire Pressure Monitoring System (TPMS) Sensor Activation . Go To Pinpoint Test G .

ARM0700000000051

Fig. 5 Symptom Test (Part 1 of 2). Crown Victoria & Grand Marquis

DECIMAL & MILLIMETER EQUIVALENTS

Inch	Inch	mm
1/64	.015625	.397
1/32	.03125	.794
3/64	.046875	1.191
1/16	.0625	1.587
5/64	.078125	1.984
3/32	.09375	2.381
7/64	.109375	2.778
1/8	.125	3.175
9/64	.140625	3.572
5/32	.15625	3.969
11/64	.17185	4.366
3/16	.1875	4.762
13/64	.203125	5.159
7/32	.21875	5.556
15/64	.234375	5.953
1/4	.25	6.350
17/64	.265626	6.747
9/32	.28125	7.144
19/64	.296875	7.541
5/16	.3125	7.937
21/64	.328125	8.334
11/32	.34375	8.731

Inch	Inch	mm
23/64	.359375	9.128
3/8	.375	9.525
25/64	.390625	9.922
13/32	.40625	10.319
27/64	.421875	10.716
7/16	.4375	11.113
29/64	.453125	11.509
15/32	.46875	11.906
31/64	.484375	12.303
1/2	.5	12.700
33/64	.515625	13.097
17/32	.53125	13.494
35/64	.546875	13.890
9/16	.5625	14.287
37/64	.578125	14.684
19/32	.59375	15.081
39/64	.609375	15.478
5/8	.625	15.875
41/64	.640625	16.272
21/32	.65625	16.669
43/64	.671875	17.065

Inch	Inch	mm
11/16	.6875	17.462
45/64	.703125	17.859
23/32	.71875	18.265
47/64	.734375	18.653
3/4	.75	19.505
49/64	.765625	19.447
25/32	.78125	19.884
51/64	.796875	20.240
13/16	.8125	20.637
53/64	.828125	21.034
27/32	.84375	21.431
55/64	.859375	21.828
7/8	.875	22.225
57/64	.890625	22.622
29/32	.90625	23.019
59/64	.921875	23.415
15/16	.9375	23.812
61/64	.953125	24.209
31/32	.96875	24.606
63/64	.984375	25.003
1	1	25.400

Special Service Tools

Throughout this manual references are made to and illustrations may depict the use of special tools required to perform certain jobs. These special tools can generally be ordered through the dealers of the make vehicle being serviced. It is also suggested that you check with local automotive supply firms as they also supply tools manufactured by other firms that will assist in the performance of these jobs. The vehicle manufacturers special tools are supplied by:

Chrysler LLC . . . . Miller Special Tools
OTC Division
28635 Mound Rd.
Warren, Michigan 48092-3499

Ford Motor Company . . . . SPX Corporation, OTC
Attn: Ford Rotunda
28635 Mound Rd.
Warren, Michigan 48092-3499

General Motors Corporation . . . . Kent-Moore
SPX Corporation
28635 Mound Rd.
Warren, Michigan 48092-3499

MANUAL INFORMATION LOCATOR

Operation/Subject/Topic	Auto Repair Manual, Vol. 1	Auto Repair Manual, Vol. 2	Engine Performance & Driveability DVD
Active Suspension System	—	X	—
Air Bags	—	X	—
Air Bag System Precautions	X	X	X
Air Conditioning	X	—	—
AIR Systems	—	—	X
All-Wheel Drive Systems	X	—	—
Alternator Specifications	X	—	—
Alternator Systems	X	—	—
Anti-Lock Brake Systems	—	X	—
Automatic Seat Belts	—	X	—
Axle Shaft Service	X	—	—
Back-Up Light Switch, Replace	X	—	—
Balance Shaft Service	X	—	—
Ball Joint Service	X	—	—
Belt Tension Data	X	—	—
Blower Motor, Replace	X	—	—
Brake Booster Service	X	—	—
Brake Service	X	—	—
Camber Adjustment	X	—	—
Camshaft Service	X	—	—
Capacity Data	X	—	—
Caster Adjustment	X	—	—
Catalytic Converters	—	—	X
Coil Pack, Replace	X	—	X
Coil Spring, Replace	X	—	—
Compression Check	X	—	X
Compression Pressures	X	—	X
Computer Relearn Procedures	X	X	X
Computerized Engine Control Systems	—	—	X
Control Arm Service	X	—	—
Cooling System Bleed	X	—	—
Cooling System Data	X	—	—
Crankshaft Pulley, Replace	X	—	—
Crankshaft Rear Oil Seal Service	X	—	—
Cruise Control Systems	—	X	—
Cylinder Block Specifications	X	—	—
Cylinder Head Service	X	—	—
Cylinder Head Specifications	X	—	—
Cylinder Head, Replace	X	—	—
Cylinder Liner, Replace	X	—	—
Dash Panel Service	—	X	—
Differential Service	X	—	—
Dimmer Switch, Replace	X	—	—
Disc Brake Service	X	—	—
Distributor Service	—	—	X
Distributor, Replace	X	—	X
Distributorless Ignition Systems	—	—	X
Drive Axle Service	X	—	—
Drive Belt Tension Data	X	—	—
Drive Cycles	—	—	X
Drum Brake Service	X	—	—
EGR System	—	—	X
Electric Engine Cooling Fans	X	—	—
Electric Fuel Pumps	X	—	X
Electrical Symbol Identification	X	X	X
Electronic Fuel Injection	—	—	X
Electronic Ignition	—	—	X
Electronic Instrumentation	—	—	X
Electronic Level Controls	—	X	—
Emission Control Application Charts	—	—	X
Emission Controls	—	—	X
Emission Vacuum Hose Routings	—	—	X
Engine Compartment Reference Diagrams	—	—	X
Engine Cooling Fans	X	—	—
Engine Control Module, Replace	—	—	X
Engine Control Unit, Replace	—	—	X
Engine Front Cover Service	X	—	—
Engine Mounts, Replace	X	—	—
Engine Oil Seal Service	X	—	—
Engine Rebuilding Specifications	X	—	—
Engine Repairs	X	—	—
Engine Sensor Location	—	—	X
Engine Sensor Replacement	—	—	X
Engine Sensor Specifications	—	—	X
Engine System Identification Charts	—	—	—
Engine Tightening Specifications	X	—	—
Engine, Replace	X	—	—
Evaporator Core, Replace	X	—	—
Exhaust Gas Recirculation (EGR) Systems	—	—	X
Exhaust Manifold, Replace	X	—	—
Fast Idle Speed Adjustment	—	—	X
Federal Air Quality Standards	—	—	—
Flasher Location	X	—	—
Front Drive Axle Service	X	—	—
Front Wheel Alignment	X	—	—
Fuel Control System Identification	—	—	X
Fuel Filter, Replace	X	—	—
Fuel Injection Systems	—	—	X
Fuel Injector Cleaning Procedures	—	—	X
Fuel Injector, Replace	—	—	X
Fuel Pump Pressure Specifications	X	—	X
Fuel Pump Pressure Test	—	—	X
Fuel Pump Relay Location	X	—	X
Fuel Pump Replacement	X	—	X
Fuse Panel Location	X	—	—
General Engine Specifications	X	—	—
Headlight Switch, Replace	X	—	—
Heated Air Cleaners	—	—	X
Heater Core, Replace	X	—	—
Hub & Bearing Assembly Service	X	—	—
Hydraulic Brake System Service	X	—	—
Hydraulic Engine Cooling Fans	X	—	—
Hydraulic Valve Lifter Service	X	—	—
Idle Mixture Adjustments	—	—	X
Idle Speed Adjustments	—	—	X
Ignition Lock, Replace	X	—	—
Ignition Switch, Replace	X	—	—
Ignition System Application	—	—	X
Ignition Timing Procedures	—	—	X
Instrument Cluster, Replace	X	—	—
Intake Manifold, Replace	X	—	—
Intermittent Malfunction Computer Diagnosis	—	—	X
Knock Sensor, Replace	—	—	X
Leaf Spring, Replace	X	—	—
Lift Point Illustrations	X	X	—
Locking Differential Service	X	—	—
Locking Hub Service	X	—	—
Lower Ball Joint, Replace	X	—	—
Lower Control Arm Service	X	—	—
Lubricant Data	X	—	—
MacPherson Strut Service	X	—	—
Main & Rod Bearing Specifications	X	—	—
Maintenance & Warning Lamp Reset Procedures	X	X	X
Maintenance Schedules	X	X	X